Births

_____

_____

_____

_____

_____

_____

_____

_____

_____

_____

_____

_____

Marriages

_____

_____

_____

_____

_____

_____

_____

_____

_____

_____

_____

Deaths

_____

_____

_____

_____

_____

_____

_____

_____

_____

_____

Family Record

_____

_____

_____

_____

_____

_____

_____

_____

_____

_____

Church Record

NEW INTERNATIONAL VERSION OF
The Holy Bible

The
HOLY
BIBLE

NEW INTERNATIONAL VERSION

*Containing The Old Testament
and The New Testament*

ZONDERVAN BIBLE PUBLISHERS
GRAND RAPIDS, MICHIGAN

You will be pleased to know that a portion of the purchase price of your
new NIV Bible has been provided to the International Bible Society to
help spread the Gospel of Jesus Christ around the world!

Contents

Alphabetical Order of
The Books of the Bible

Acts	1506	Isaiah	928	Obadiah	1275
Amos	1261				
		James	1669	1 Peter	1675
1 Chronicles	513	Jeremiah	1035	2 Peter	1681
2 Chronicles	562	Job	658	Philemon	1651
Colossians	1624	Joel	1253	Philippians	1618
1 Corinthians	1573	John	1468	Proverbs	855
2 Corinthians	1592	1 John	1685	Psalms	708
		2 John	1691		
Daniel	1215	3 John	1693	Revelation	1698
Deuteronomy	225	Jonah	1278	Romans	1552
		Joshua	274	Ruth	340
Ecclesiastes	902	Jude	1695		
Ephesians	1611	Judges	307	1 Samuel	346
Esther	647			2 Samuel	389
Exodus	73	1 Kings	428	Song of Songs	917
Ezekiel	1145	2 Kings	471		
Ezra	610			1 Thessalonians	1629
		Lamentations	1132	2 Thessalonians	1634
Galatians	1604	Leviticus	128	1 Timothy	1637
Genesis	1	Luke	1416	2 Timothy	1643
				Titus	1648
Habakkuk	1298	Malachi	1327		
Haggai	1310	Mark	1385	Zechariah	1313
Hebrews	1653	Matthew	1335	Zephaniah	1304
Hosea	1236	Micah	1282		
		Nahum	1293		
		Nehemiah	626		
		Numbers	167		

Preface

THE NEW INTERNATIONAL VERSION is a completely new translation of the Holy Bible made by over a hundred scholars working directly from the best available Hebrew, Aramaic and Greek texts. It had its beginning in 1965 when, after several years of exploratory study by committees from the Christian Reformed Church and the National Association of Evangelicals, a group of scholars met at Palos Heights, Illinois, and concurred in the need for a new translation of the Bible in contemporary English. This group, though not made up of official church representatives, was transdenominational. Its conclusion was endorsed by a large number of leaders from many denominations who met in Chicago in 1966.

Responsibility for the new version was delegated by the Palos Heights group to a self-governing body of fifteen, the Committee on Bible Translation, composed for the most part of biblical scholars from colleges, universities and seminaries. In 1967 the New York Bible Society (now the International Bible Society) generously undertook the financial sponsorship of the project—a sponsorship that made it possible to enlist the help of many distinguished scholars. The fact that participants from the United States, Great Britain, Canada, Australia and New Zealand worked together gave the project its international scope. That they were from many denominations —including Anglican, Assemblies of God, Baptist, Brethren, Christian Reformed, Church of Christ, Evangelical Free, Lutheran, Mennonite, Methodist, Nazarene, Presbyterian, Wesleyan and other churches—helped to safeguard the translation from sectarian bias.

How it was made helps to give the New International Version its distinctiveness. The translation of each book was assigned to a team of scholars. Next, one of the Intermediate Editorial Committees revised the initial translation, with constant reference to the Hebrew, Aramaic or Greek. Their work then went to one of the General Editorial Committees, which checked it in detail and made another thorough revision. This revision in turn was carefully reviewed by the Committee on Bible Translation, which made further changes and then released the final version for publication. In this way the entire Bible underwent three revisions, during each of which the translation was examined for its faithfulness to the original languages and for its English style.

All this involved many thousands of hours of research and discussion regarding the meaning of the texts and the precise way of putting them into English. It may well be that no other translation has been made by a more thorough process of review and revision from committee to committee than this one.

From the beginning of the project, the Committee on Bible Translation held to certain goals for the New International Version: that it would be an accurate translation and one that would have clarity and literary quality and so prove suitable for public and private reading, teaching, preaching, memorizing and liturgical use. The Committee also sought to preserve some measure of continuity with the long tradition of translating the Scriptures into English.

In working toward these goals, the translators were united in their commitment to the authority and infallibility of the Bible as God's Word in written form. They believe that it contains the divine answer to the deepest needs of humanity, that it sheds unique light on our path in a dark world, and that it sets forth the way to our eternal well-being.

The first concern of the translators has been the accuracy of the translation and its fidelity to the thought of the biblical writers. They have weighed the significance of the lexical and grammatical details of the Hebrew, Aramaic and Greek texts. At the same time, they have striven for more than a word-for-word translation. Because thought patterns and syntax differ from language to language, faithful communication of the meaning of the writers of the Bible demands frequent modifications in sentence structure and constant regard for the contextual meanings of words.

A sensitive feeling for style does not always accompany scholarship. Accordingly the Committee on Bible Translation submitted the developing version to a number of stylistic consultants. Two of them read every book of both Old and New Testaments twice—once before and once after the last major revision—and made invaluable suggestions. Samples of the translation were tested for clarity and ease of reading by various kinds of people—young and old, highly educated and less well educated, ministers and laymen.

Concern for clear and natural English—that the New International Version should be idiomatic but not idiosyncratic, contemporary but not dated—motivated the translators and consultants. At the same time, they tried to reflect the differing styles of the biblical writers. In view of the international use of English, the translators sought to avoid obvious Americanisms on the one hand and obvious Anglicisms on the other. A British edition reflects the comparatively few differences of significant idiom and of spelling.

As for the traditional pronouns "thou," "thee" and "thine" in reference to the Deity, the translators judged that to use these archaisms (along with the old verb forms such as "doest," "wouldest" and "hadst") would violate accuracy in translation. Neither Hebrew, Aramaic nor Greek uses special pronouns for the persons of the Godhead. A present-day translation is not enhanced by forms that in the time of the King James Version were used in everyday speech, whether referring to God or man.

For the Old Testament the standard Hebrew text, the Masoretic Text as published in the latest editions of *Biblia Hebraica*, was used throughout. The Dead Sea Scrolls contain material bearing on an earlier stage of the Hebrew text. They were consulted, as were the Samaritan Pentateuch and the ancient scribal traditions relating to textual changes. Sometimes a variant Hebrew reading in the margin of the Masoretic Text was followed instead of the text itself. Such instances, being variants within the Masoretic tradition, are not specified by footnotes. In rare cases, words in the consonantal text were divided differently from the way they appear in the Masoretic Text. Footnotes indicate this. The translators also consulted the more important early versions—the Septuagint; Aquila, Symmachus and Theodotion; the Vulgate; the Syriac Peshitta; the Targums; and for the Psalms the *Juxta Hebraica* of Jerome. Readings from these versions were occasionally followed where the Masoretic Text seemed doubtful and where accepted principles of textual criticism showed that one or more of these textual witnesses appeared to provide the correct reading. Such instances are footnoted. Sometimes vowel letters and vowel signs did not, in the judgment of the translators, represent the correct vowels for the original consonantal text. Accordingly some words were read with a different set of vowels. These instances are usually not indicated by footnotes.

The Greek text used in translating the New Testament was an eclectic one. No other piece of ancient literature has such an abundance of manuscript witnesses as does the New Testament. Where existing manuscripts differ, the translators made their choice of readings according to accepted principles of New Testament textual criticism. Footnotes call attention to places where there was uncertainty about what the original text was. The best current printed texts of the Greek New Testament were used.

There is a sense in which the work of translation is never wholly finished. This applies to all great literature and uniquely so to the Bible. In 1973 the New Testament in the New International Version was published. Since then, suggestions for corrections and revisions have been received from various sources. The Committee on Bible Translation carefully considered the suggestions and adopted a number of them. These were incorporated in the first printing of the entire Bible in 1978. Additional revisions were made by the Committee on Bible Translation in 1983 and appear in printings after that date.

As in other ancient documents, the precise meaning of the biblical texts is sometimes uncertain. This is more often the case with the Hebrew and Aramaic texts than with the Greek text. Although archaeological and linguistic discoveries in this century aid in understanding difficult passages, some uncertainties remain. The more significant of these have been called to the reader's attention in the footnotes.

In regard to the divine name YHWH, commonly referred to as the *Tetragrammaton*, the translators adopted the device used in most English versions of rendering that name as "Lord" in capital letters to distinguish it from *Adonai*, another Hebrew word rendered "Lord," for which small letters are used. Wherever the two names stand together in the Old Testament as a compound name of God, they are rendered "Sovereign Lord."

Because for most readers today the phrases "the Lord of hosts" and "God of hosts" have little meaning, this version renders them "the Lord Almighty" and "God Almighty." These renderings convey the sense of the Hebrew, namely, "he who is sovereign over all the 'hosts' (powers) in heaven and on earth, especially over the 'hosts' (armies) of Israel." For readers unacquainted with Hebrew this does not make clear the distinction between *Sabaoth* ("hosts" or "Almighty") and *Shaddai* (which can also be translated "Almighty"), but the latter occurs infrequently and is always footnoted. When *Adonai* and *YHWH Sabaoth* occur together, they are rendered "the Lord, the Lord Almighty."

As for other proper nouns, the familiar spellings of the King James Version are generally retained. Names traditionally spelled with "ch," except where it is final, are usually spelled in this translation with "k" or "c," since the biblical languages do not have the sound that "ch" frequently indicates in English—for example, in *chant*. For well-known names such as Zechariah, however, the traditional spelling has been retained. Variation in the spelling of names in the original languages has usually not been indicated. Where a person or place has two or more different names in the Hebrew, Aramaic or Greek texts, the more familiar one has generally been used, with footnotes where needed.

To achieve clarity the translators sometimes supplied words not in the original texts but required by the context. If there was uncertainty about such material, it is enclosed in brackets. Also for the sake of clarity or style, nouns, including some proper nouns, are sometimes substituted for pronouns, and vice versa. And though the Hebrew writers often shifted back and forth between first, second and third personal pronouns without change of antecedent, this translation often makes them uniform, in accordance with English style and without the use of footnotes.

Poetical passages are printed as poetry, that is, with indentation of lines and with separate stanzas. These are generally designed to reflect the structure of Hebrew poetry. This poetry is normally characterized by parallelism in balanced lines. Most of the poetry in the Bible is in the Old Testament, and scholars differ regarding the scansion of Hebrew lines. The translators determined the stanza divisions for the most part by analysis of the subject matter. The stanzas therefore serve as poetic paragraphs.

As an aid to the reader, italicized sectional headings are inserted in most of the books. They are not to be regarded as part of the NIV text, are not for oral reading, and are not intended to dictate the interpretation of the sections they head.

The footnotes in this version are of several kinds, most of which need no explanation. Those giving alternative translations begin with "Or" and generally introduce the alternative with the last word preceding it in the text, except when it is a single-word alternative; in poetry quoted in a footnote a slant mark indicates a line division. Footnotes introduced by "Or" do not have uniform significance. In some cases two possible translations were considered to have about equal validity. In other cases, though the translators were convinced that the translation in the text was correct, they judged that another interpretation was possible and of sufficient importance to be represented in a footnote.

In the New Testament, footnotes that refer to uncertainty regarding the original text are introduced by "Some manuscripts" or similar expressions. In the Old Testament, evidence for the reading chosen is given first and evidence for the alternative is added after a semicolon (for example: Septuagint; Hebrew *father*). In such notes the term "Hebrew" refers to the Masoretic Text.

It should be noted that minerals, flora and fauna, architectural details, articles of clothing and jewelry, musical instruments and other articles cannot always be identified with precision. Also measures of capacity in the biblical period are particularly uncertain (see the table of weights and measures following the text).

Like all translations of the Bible, made as they are by imperfect man, this one undoubtedly falls short of its goals. Yet we are grateful to God for the extent to which he has enabled us to realize these goals and for the strength he has given us and our colleagues to complete our task. We offer this version of the Bible to him in whose name and for whose glory it has been made. We pray that it will lead many into a better understanding of the Holy Scriptures and a fuller knowledge of Jesus Christ the incarnate Word, of whom the Scriptures so faithfully testify.

The Committee on Bible Translation

June 1978
(Revised August 1983)

Names of the translators and editors may be secured
from the International Bible Society,
translation sponsors of the New International Version,
144 Tices Lane, East Brunswick, New Jersey 08816 U.S.A.

Introduction to the Cross-Reference System

The New International Version has one of the most thorough, accurate and best organized cross-reference systems available. It began with the vision of one individual more than a decade ago and by the time it was completed involved more than forty people and a half-dozen computers.

The cross references link words or phrases in the NIV text with counterpart Biblical references listed in a side column on each page. The raised letters indicating these cross references are set in a bold typeface to distinguish them from the NIV text note letters, which use a light italic typeface. When a single word is addressed by both, the italic NIV text note comes first, as in Matthew 1:21, "Jesus ^c ^q."

The lists of references are in Biblical order with one exception: If reference is made to a verse within the same chapter, that verse (indicated by "ver") is listed first.

In the Old Testament some references are marked with an asterisk (*), which means that the Old Testament verse or phrase is quoted in the New Testament (see, for example, Genesis 1:3). The corresponding information is provided in the New Testament by the NIV text note (see 2 Corinthians 4:6).

An important feature of this cross-reference system is in its notation of parallel and reference passages. When two or more sections of Scripture are nearly identical or deal with the same event, the "parallel passage" ("pp") is noted at the sectional heading (see Matthew 21:33-46). These parallel passages are especially common in the Gospels and in Samuel, Kings, and Chronicles. When the passages are similar but do not deal with the same event, they are noted with "Ref" at the sectional headings (see Matthew 22:2-14).

To conserve space and avoid repetition, parallel passages or references that are noted at sectional headings are not repeated in the reference column.

Introduction to the Cross-Reference System

The
Old Testament

Genesis

Title and Background

The first phrase in the Hebrew text of Genesis 1:1 means "In the beginning." The book of Genesis is about many beginnings—the beginning of the universe, the beginning of man and woman, the beginning of human sin, and the beginning of God's promises and plans for salvation.

Author and Date of Writing

Jews and Christians alike hold that Moses was the author/compiler of Genesis, the first of the five books of the Old Testament known as the Pentateuch (meaning "five-volumned book").

The historical period during which Moses lived is most likely the one referred to in 1 Kings 6:1, which states that "the fourth year of Solomon's reign over Israel" was the same as "the four hundred and eightieth year after the Israelites had come out of Egypt." Since the former was about 966 B.C., the latter—and thus the date of the exodus—was about 1446 B.C. The forty-year period of Israel's wanderings in the desert, which lasted from about 1446 to about 1406 B.C., would have been the most likely time for Moses to write Genesis.

Theme and Message

The message of Genesis is rich and complex, but it is mainly a book of relationships, highlighting those between God and nature, God and man, and man and man. It stresses the fact that the one true God is sovereign over all that exists, whether good or evil. It introduces us to the way in which God initiates and enters into covenants with his chosen people, pledging his love and faithfulness to them.

Outline

I. Primeval History: Four Great Events (1:1-11:32)
   A. The Creation of the Universe, Adam and Eve (1:1-2:25)
   B. Man's Fall and the Results of Sin (3:1-5:32)
   C. The Flood (6:1-9:29)
   D. The Scattering of the Nations (10:1-11:32)

II. Patriarchal History: Four Great Characters (12:1-50:26)
   A. Abraham (12:1-20:18)
   B. Isaac (21:1-26:35)
   C. Jacob (27:1-37:1)
   D. Joseph (37:2-50:26)

The Beginning

1 In the beginning[a] God created the heavens and the earth.[b] 2Now the earth was[a] formless and empty,[c] darkness was over the surface of the deep, and the Spirit of God[d] was hovering over the waters.

[a]2 Or possibly *became*

1:1
aJn 1:1-2
bJob 38:4;
Ps 90:2;
Isa 42:5; 44:24;
45:12,18;
Ac 17:24;
Heb 11:3;
Rev 4:11
1:2
cJer 4:23
dPs 104:30

[3]And God said,[e] "Let there be light," and there was light.[f] [4]God saw that the light was good, and he separated the light from the darkness. [5]God called the light "day," and the darkness he called "night."[g] And there was evening, and there was morning—the first day.

[6]And God said, "Let there be an expanse[h] between the waters to separate water from water." [7]So God made the expanse and separated the water under the expanse from the water above it.[i] And it was so. [8]God called the expanse "sky." And there was evening, and there was morning—the second day.

[9]And God said, "Let the water under the sky be gathered to one place,[j] and let dry ground appear." And it was so. [10]God called the dry ground "land," and the gathered waters he called "seas." And God saw that it was good.

[11]Then God said, "Let the land produce vegetation:[k] seed-bearing plants and trees on the land that bear fruit with seed in it, according to their various kinds." And it was so. [12]The land produced vegetation: plants bearing seed according to their kinds and trees bearing fruit with seed in it according to their kinds. And God saw that it was good. [13]And there was evening, and there was morning—the third day.

[14]And God said, "Let there be lights[l] in the expanse of the sky to separate the day from the night, and let them serve as signs[m] to mark seasons[n] and days and years, [15]and let them be lights in the expanse of the sky to give light on the earth." And it was so. [16]God made two great lights—the greater light to govern[o] the day and the lesser light to govern[p] the night. He also made the stars.[q] [17]God set them in the expanse of the sky to give light on the earth, [18]to govern the day and the night,[r] and to separate light from darkness. And God saw that it was good. [19]And there was evening, and there was morning—the fourth day.

[20]And God said, "Let the water teem with living creatures, and let birds fly above the earth across the expanse of the sky." [21]So God created the great creatures of the sea and every living and moving thing with which the water teems,[s] according to their kinds, and every winged bird according to its kind. And God saw that it was good. [22]God blessed them and said, "Be fruitful and increase in number and fill the water in the seas, and let the birds increase on the earth."[t] [23]And there was evening, and there was morning—the fifth day.

[24]And God said, "Let the land produce living creatures according to their kinds: livestock, creatures that move along the ground, and wild animals, each according to its kind." And it was so. [25]God made the wild animals[u] according to their kinds, the livestock according to their kinds, and all the creatures that move along the ground according to their kinds. And God saw that it was good.

[26]Then God said, "Let us[v] make man in our image,[w] in our likeness, and let them rule[x] over the fish of the sea and the birds of the air, over the livestock, over all the earth,[a] and over all the creatures that move along the ground."

1:3 ePs 33:6,9; 148:5; Heb 11:3 f2Co 4:6*
1:5 gPs 74:16
1:6 hJer 10:12
1:7 iJob 38:8-11,16; Ps 148:4
1:9 jJob 38:8-11; Ps 104:6-9; Pr 8:29; Jer 5:22; 2Pe 3:5
1:11 kPs 65:9-13; 104:14
1:14 lPs 74:16 mJer 10:2 nPs 104:19
1:16 oPs 136:8 pPs 136:9 qJob 38:7, 31-32; Ps 8:3; Isa 40:26
1:18 rJer 33:20,25
1:21 sPs 104:25-26
1:22 tver 28; Ge 8:17
1:25 uPs 27:5
1:26 vPs 100:3 wGe 9:6; Jas 3:9 xPs 8:6-8

a26 Hebrew; Syriac *all the wild animals*

²⁷So God created man in his own image,ʸ
in the image of God he created him;
male and femaleᶻ he created them.

²⁸God blessed them and said to them, "Be fruitful and increase in number; fill the earthª and subdue it. Rule over the fish of the sea and the birds of the air and over every living creature that moves on the ground."

²⁹Then God said, "I give you every seed-bearing plant on the face of the whole earth and every tree that has fruit with seed in it. They will be yours for food. ᵇ ³⁰And to all the beasts of the earth and all the birds of the air and all the creatures that move on the ground—everything that has the breath of life in it—I give every green plant for food.ᶜ" And it was so.

³¹God saw all that he had made,ᵈ and it was very good.ᵉ And there was evening, and there was morning—the sixth day.

2 Thus the heavens and the earth were completed in all their vast array.

²By the seventh day God had finished the work he had been doing; so on the seventh day he restedª from all his work.ᶠ ³And God blessed the seventh day and made it holy,ᵍ because on it he rested from all the work of creating that he had done.

Adam and Eve

⁴This is the account of the heavens and the earth when they were created.

When the Lᴏʀᴅ God made the earth and the heavens— ⁵and no shrub of the field had yet appeared on the earthᵇ and no plant of the field had yet sprung up,ʰ for the Lᴏʀᴅ God had not sent rain on the earthᵇⁱ and there was no man to work the ground, ⁶but streamsᶜ came up from the earth and watered the whole surface of the ground— ⁷the Lᴏʀᴅ God formed the manᵈ from the dustʲ of the groundᵏ and breathed into his nostrils the breathˡ of life,ᵐ and the man became a living being.ⁿ

⁸Now the Lᴏʀᴅ God had planted a garden in the east, in Eden;ᵒ and there he put the man he had formed. ⁹And the Lᴏʀᴅ God made all kinds of trees grow out of the ground—trees that were pleasing to the eye and good for food. In the middle of the garden were the tree of lifeᵖ and the tree of the knowledge of good and evil.�q

¹⁰A river watering the garden flowed from Eden; from there it was separated into four headwaters. ¹¹The name of the first is the Pishon; it winds through the entire land of Havilah, where there is gold. ¹²(The gold of that land is good; aromatic resinᵉ and onyx are also there.) ¹³The name of the second river is the Gihon; it winds through the entire land of Cush.ᶠ ¹⁴The name of the third river is the Tigris;ʳ it runs along the east side of Asshur. And the fourth river is the Euphrates.

¹⁵The Lᴏʀᴅ God took the man and put him in the Garden of Eden to

1:27
y1Co 11:7
zGe 5:2;
Mt 19:4*;
Mk 10:6*
1:28
aGe 9:1,7;
Lev 26:9
1:29
bPs 104:14
1:30
cPs 104:14,27;
145:15
1:31
dPs 104:24
e1Ti 4:4
2:2
fEx 20:11;
31:17; Heb 4:4*
2:3
gLev 23:3;
Isa 58:13
2:5
hGe 1:11
iPs 65:9-10
2:7
jGe 3:19
kPs 103:14
lJob 33:4
mAc 17:25
n1Co 15:45*
2:8
oGe 3:23,24;
Isa 51:3
2:9
pGe 3:22,24;
Rev 2:7; 22:2,
14,19
qEze 47:12
2:14
rDa 10:4

ª2 Or *ceased*; also in verse 3   ᵇ5 Or *land*; also in verse 6   ᶜ6 Or *mist*   ᵈ7 The Hebrew for *man (adam)* sounds like and may be related to the Hebrew for *ground (adamah)*; it is also the name *Adam* (see Gen. 2:20).   ᵉ12 Or *good; pearls*   ᶠ13 Possibly southeast Mesopotamia work it and take care of it. [16]And the LORD God commanded the man, "You are free to eat from any tree in the garden; [17]but you must not eat from the tree of the knowledge of good and evil, for when you eat of it you will surely die."[s]

[18]The LORD God said, "It is not good for the man to be alone. I will make a helper suitable for him."[t]

[19]Now the LORD God had formed out of the ground all the beasts of the field[u] and all the birds of the air. He brought them to the man to see what he would name them; and whatever the man called each living creature,[v] that was its name. [20]So the man gave names to all the livestock, the birds of the air and all the beasts of the field.

But for Adam[a] no suitable helper was found. [21]So the LORD God caused the man to fall into a deep sleep; and while he was sleeping, he took one of the man's ribs[b] and closed up the place with flesh. [22]Then the LORD God made a woman from the rib[c][w] he had taken out of the man, and he brought her to the man.

[23]The man said,

> "This is now bone of my bones
>   and flesh of my flesh;[x]
> she shall be called 'woman,[d]'
>   for she was taken out of man."

[24]For this reason a man will leave his father and mother and be united[y] to his wife, and they will become one flesh.[z]

[25]The man and his wife were both naked,[a] and they felt no shame.

The Fall of Man

3 Now the serpent[b] was more crafty than any of the wild animals the LORD God had made. He said to the woman, "Did God really say, 'You must not eat from any tree in the garden'?"

[2]The woman said to the serpent, "We may eat fruit from the trees in the garden, [3]but God did say, 'You must not eat fruit from the tree that is in the middle of the garden, and you must not touch it, or you will die.'"

[4]"You will not surely die," the serpent said to the woman.[c] [5]"For God knows that when you eat of it your eyes will be opened, and you will be like God,[d] knowing good and evil."

[6]When the woman saw that the fruit of the tree was good for food and pleasing to the eye, and also desirable[e] for gaining wisdom, she took some and ate it. She also gave some to her husband, who was with her, and he ate it.[f] [7]Then the eyes of both of them were opened, and they realized they were naked; so they sewed fig leaves together and made coverings for themselves.

[8]Then the man and his wife heard the sound of the LORD God as he was walking[g] in the garden in the cool of the day, and they hid[h] from the LORD God among the trees of the garden. [9]But the LORD God called to the man, "Where are you?"

[10]He answered, "I heard you in the garden, and I was afraid because I was naked; so I hid."

2:17
sDt 30:15,19;
Ro 5:12; 6:23;
Jas 1:15
2:18
t1Co 11:9
2:19
uPs 8:7
vGe 1:24
2:22
w1Co 11:8,9,12
2:23
xGe 29:14;
Eph 5:28-30
2:24
yMal 2:15
zMt 19:5*;
Mk 10:7-8*;
1Co 6:16*;
Eph 5:31*
2:25
aGe 3:7,10-11
3:1
b2Co 11:3;
Rev 12:9; 20:2
3:4
cJn 8:44;
2Co 11:3
3:5
dIsa 14:14;
Eze 28:2
3:6
eJas 1:14-15;
1Jn 2:16
f1Ti 2:14
3:8
gDt 23:14
hJob 31:33;
Ps 139:7-12;
Jer 23:24

---

[a]20 Or *the man*   [b]21 Or *took part of the man's side*   [c]22 Or *part*   [d]23 The Hebrew for *woman* sounds like the Hebrew for *man*.

¹¹And he said, "Who told you that you were naked? Have you eaten from the tree that I commanded you not to eat from?"

¹²The man said, "The woman you put here with me—she gave me some fruit from the tree, and I ate it."

¹³Then the LORD God said to the woman, "What is this you have done?"

The woman said, "The serpent deceived me,ⁱ and I ate."

¹⁴So the LORD God said to the serpent, "Because you have done this,

> "Cursedʲ are you above all the livestock
>   and all the wild animals!
> You will crawl on your belly
>   and you will eat dustᵏ
>   all the days of your life.
> ¹⁵And I will put enmity
>   between you and the woman,
>   and between your offspring[a1] and hers;ᵐ
> he will crushᵇ your head,ⁿ
>   and you will strike his heel."

¹⁶To the woman he said,

> "I will greatly increase your pains in childbearing;
>   with pain you will give birth to children.
> Your desire will be for your husband,
>   and he will rule over you.ᵒ"

¹⁷To Adam he said, "Because you listened to your wife and ate from the tree about which I commanded you, 'You must not eat of it,'

> "Cursedᵖ is the ground because of you;
>   through painful toil you will eat of it
>   all the days of your life.�q
> ¹⁸It will produce thorns and thistles for you,
>   and you will eat the plants of the field.ʳ
> ¹⁹By the sweat of your brow
>   you will eat your foodˢ
> until you return to the ground,
>   since from it you were taken;
> for dust you are
>   and to dust you will return."ᵗ

²⁰Adamᶜ named his wife Eve,ᵈ because she would become the mother of all the living.

²¹The LORD God made garments of skin for Adam and his wife and clothed them. ²²And the LORD God said, "The man has now become like one of us, knowing good and evil. He must not be allowed to reach out his hand and take also from the tree of lifeᵘ and eat, and live forever." ²³So the LORD God banished him from the Garden of Edenᵛ to work the groundʷ from which he had been taken. ²⁴After he drove the man out, he placed on the east sideᵉ of the Garden of Eden cherubimˣ

3:13
i2Co 11:3;
1Ti 2:14
3:14
jDt 28:15-20
kIsa 65:25;
Mic 7:17
3:15
lJn 8:44;
Ac 13:10;
1Jn 3:8
mIsa 7:14;
Mt 1:23;
Rev 12:17
nRo 16:20;
Heb 2:14
3:16
o1Co 11:3;
Eph 5:22
3:17
pGe 5:29;
Ro 8:20-22
qJob 5:7; 14:1;
Ecc 2:23
3:18
rPs 104:14
3:19
s2Th 3:10
tGe 2:7;
Ps 90:3; 104:29;
Ecc 12:7
3:22
uRev 22:14
3:23
vGe 2:8
wGe 4:2
3:24
xEx 25:18-22

ᵃ15 Or *seed*   ᵇ15 Or *strike*   ᶜ20 Or *The man*   ᵈ20 *Eve* probably means *living.*   ᵉ24 Or *placed in front* and a flaming sword^y flashing back and forth to guard the way to the tree of life.^{z}

Cain and Abel

4 Adam^a lay with his wife Eve, and she became pregnant and gave birth to Cain.^{b} She said, "With the help of the LORD I have brought forth^c a man." ^{2}Later she gave birth to his brother Abel.^{a}

Now Abel kept flocks, and Cain worked the soil. ^{3}In the course of time Cain brought some of the fruits of the soil as an offering to the LORD.^{b} ^{4}But Abel brought fat portions^c from some of the firstborn of his flock.^{d} The LORD looked with favor on Abel and his offering,^{e} ^{5}but on Cain and his offering he did not look with favor. So Cain was very angry, and his face was downcast.

^{6}Then the LORD said to Cain, "Why are you angry? Why is your face downcast? ^{7}If you do what is right, will you not be accepted? But if you do not do what is right, sin is crouching at your door;^{f} it desires to have you, but you must master it.^{g}"

^{8}Now Cain said to his brother Abel, "Let's go out to the field."^{d} And while they were in the field, Cain attacked his brother Abel and killed him.^{h}

^{9}Then the LORD said to Cain, "Where is your brother Abel?"

"I don't know," he replied. "Am I my brother's keeper?"

^{10}The LORD said, "What have you done? Listen! Your brother's blood cries out to me from the ground.^{i} ^{11}Now you are under a curse and driven from the ground, which opened its mouth to receive your brother's blood from your hand. ^{12}When you work the ground, it will no longer yield its crops for you. You will be a restless wanderer on the earth."

^{13}Cain said to the LORD, "My punishment is more than I can bear. ^{14}Today you are driving me from the land, and I will be hidden from your presence;^{j} I will be a restless wanderer on the earth, and whoever finds me will kill me."^{k}

^{15}But the LORD said to him, "Not so^e; if anyone kills Cain^l, he will suffer vengeance seven times over.^{m}" Then the LORD put a mark on Cain so that no one who found him would kill him. ^{16}So Cain went out from the LORD's presence and lived in the land of Nod,^{f} east of Eden.^{n}

^{17}Cain lay with his wife, and she became pregnant and gave birth to Enoch. Cain was then building a city, and he named it after his son^o Enoch. ^{18}To Enoch was born Irad, and Irad was the father of Mehujael, and Mehujael was the father of Methushael, and Methushael was the father of Lamech.

^{19}Lamech married two women, one named Adah and the other Zillah. ^{20}Adah gave birth to Jabal; he was the father of those who live in tents and raise livestock. ^{21}His brother's name was Jubal; he was the father of all who play the harp and flute. ^{22}Zillah also had a son, Tubal-Cain, who forged all kinds of tools out of^g bronze and iron. Tubal-Cain's sister was Naamah.

^{23}Lamech said to his wives,

3:24
yPs 104:4
zGe 2:9
4:2
aLk 11:51
4:3
bNu 18:12
4:4
cLev 3:16
dEx 13:2,12
eHeb 11:4
4:7
fNu 32:23
gRo 6:16
4:8
hMt 23:35;
1Jn 3:12
4:10
iGe 9:5;
Nu 35:33;
Heb 12:24;
Rev 6:9-10
4:14
j2Ki 17:18;
Ps 51:11;
139:7-12;
Jer 7:15; 52:3
kGe 9:6;
Nu 35:19,21,
27,33
4:15
lEze 9:4,6
mver 24;
Ps 79:12
4:16
nGe 2:8
4:17
oPs 49:11

$^a1$ Or *The man* $^b1$ *Cain* sounds like the Hebrew for *brought forth* or *acquired*. $^c1$ Or *have acquired* $^d8$ Samaritan Pentateuch, Septuagint, Vulgate and Syriac; Masoretic Text does not have "*Let's go out to the field.*" $^e15$ Septuagint, Vulgate and Syriac; Hebrew *Very well* $^f16$ *Nod* means *wandering* (see verses 12 and 14). $^g22$ Or *who instructed all who work in*

"Adah and Zillah, listen to me;
    wives of Lamech, hear my words.
I have killed[a][p] a man for wounding me,
    a young man for injuring me.
[24]If Cain is avenged[q] seven times,[r]
    then Lamech seventy-seven times."

[25]Adam lay with his wife again, and she gave birth to a son and named him Seth,[b][s] saying, "God has granted me another child in place of Abel, since Cain killed him."[t] [26]Seth also had a son, and he named him Enosh.

At that time men began to call on[c] the name of the LORD.[u]

From Adam to Noah

5 This is the written account of Adam's line.

When God created man, he made him in the likeness of God.[v] [2]He created them male and female[w] and blessed them. And when they were created, he called them "man.[d]"

[3]When Adam had lived 130 years, he had a son in his own likeness, in his own image;[x] and he named him Seth. [4]After Seth was born, Adam lived 800 years and had other sons and daughters. [5]Altogether, Adam lived 930 years, and then he died.[y]

[6]When Seth had lived 105 years, he became the father[e] of Enosh. [7]And after he became the father of Enosh, Seth lived 807 years and had other sons and daughters. [8]Altogether, Seth lived 912 years, and then he died.

[9]When Enosh had lived 90 years, he became the father of Kenan. [10]And after he became the father of Kenan, Enosh lived 815 years and had other sons and daughters. [11]Altogether, Enosh lived 905 years, and then he died.

[12]When Kenan had lived 70 years, he became the father of Mahalalel. [13]And after he became the father of Mahalalel, Kenan lived 840 years and had other sons and daughters. [14]Altogether, Kenan lived 910 years, and then he died.

[15]When Mahalalel had lived 65 years, he became the father of Jared. [16]And after he became the father of Jared, Mahalalel lived 830 years and had other sons and daughters. [17]Altogether, Mahalalel lived 895 years, and then he died.

[18]When Jared had lived 162 years, he became the father of Enoch.[z] [19]And after he became the father of Enoch, Jared lived 800 years and had other sons and daughters. [20]Altogether, Jared lived 962 years, and then he died.

[21]When Enoch had lived 65 years, he became the father of Methuselah. [22]And after he became the father of Methuselah, Enoch walked with God[a] 300 years and had other sons and daughters. [23]Altogether, Enoch lived 365 years. [24]Enoch walked with God;[b] then he was no more, because God took him away.[c]

[25]When Methuselah had lived 187 years, he became the father of Lamech. [26]And after he became the father of Lamech, Methuselah lived

4:23
pEx 20:13;
Lev 19:18

4:24
qDt 32:35
rver 15

4:25
sGe 5:3 tver 8

4:26
uGe 12:8;
1Ki 18:24;
Ps 116:17;
Joel 2:32;
Zep 3:9;
Ac 2:21;
1Co 1:2

5:1
vGe 1:27;
Eph 4:24;
Col 3:10

5:2
wGe 1:27;
Mt 19:4;
Mk 10:6;
Gal 3:28

5:3
xGe 1:26;
1Co 15:49

5:5
yGe 3:19

5:18
zJude 1:14

5:22
aver 24;
Ge 6:9; 17:1;
48:15; Mic 6:8;
Mal 2:6

5:24
bver 22
c2Ki 2:1,11;
Heb 11:5

[a]23 Or *I will kill*   [b]25 *Seth* probably means *granted.*   [c]26 Or *to proclaim*   [d]2 Hebrew *adam*
[e]6 *Father* may mean *ancestor*; also in verses 7-26.

...ad other sons and daughters. ²⁷Altogether, Methuselah
...s, and then he died.

...mech had lived 182 years, he had a son. ²⁹He named him
...said, "He will comfort us in the labor and painful toil of our
...sed by the ground the LORD has cursed. ᵈ" ³⁰After Noah was
...mech lived 595 years and had other sons and daughters.
...ther, Lamech lived 777 years, and then he died.

...er Noah was 500 years old, he became the father of Shem, Ham
...apheth.

The Flood

6 When men began to increase in number on the earthᵉ and daughters were born to them, ²the sons of God saw that the daughters of men were beautiful, and they married any of them they chose. ³Then the LORD said, "My Spirit will not contend withᵇ man forever,ᶠ for he is mortalᶜ;ᵍ his days will be a hundred and twenty years."

⁴The Nephilimʰ were on the earth in those days—and also afterward—when the sons of God went to the daughters of men and had children by them. They were the heroes of old, men of renown.

⁵The LORD saw how great man's wickedness on the earth had become, and that every inclination of the thoughts of his heart was only evil all the time.ⁱ ⁶The LORD was grievedʲ that he had made man on the earth, and his heart was filled with pain. ⁷So the LORD said, "I will wipe mankind, whom I have created, from the face of the earth—men and animals, and creatures that move along the ground, and birds of the air—for I am grieved that I have made them." ⁸But Noah found favor in the eyes of the LORD.ᵏ

⁹This is the account of Noah.

Noah was a righteous man, blameless among the people of his time,ˡ and he walked with God.ᵐ ¹⁰Noah had three sons: Shem, Ham and Japheth.ⁿ

¹¹Now the earth was corrupt in God's sight and was full of violence.ᵒ ¹²God saw how corrupt the earth had become, for all the people on earth had corrupted their ways.ᵖ ¹³So God said to Noah, "I am going to put an end to all people, for the earth is filled with violence because of them. I am surely going to destroy both them and the earth.�q ¹⁴So make yourself an ark of cypressᵈ wood;ʳ make rooms in it and coat it with pitchˢ inside and out. ¹⁵This is how you are to build it: The ark is to be 450 feet long, 75 feet wide and 45 feet high.ᵉ ¹⁶Make a roof for it and finishᶠ the ark to within 18 inchesᵍ of the top. Put a door in the side of the ark and make lower, middle and upper decks. ¹⁷I am going to bring floodwaters on the earth to destroy all life under the heavens, every creature that has the breath of life in it. Everything on earth will perish.ᵗ ¹⁸But I will establish my covenant with you,ᵘ and you will enter the arkᵛ—you and your sons and your wife and your sons' wives

5:29
ᵈGe 3:17;
Ro 8:20
6:1
ᵉGe 1:28
6:3
ᶠIsa 57:16
ᵍPs 78:39
6:4
ʰNu 13:33
6:5
ⁱGe 8:21;
Ps 14:1-3
6:6
ʲ1Sa 15:11,35;
Isa 63:10
6:8
ᵏGe 19:19;
Ex 33:12,13,17;
Lk 1:30; Ac 7:46
6:9
ˡGe 7:1;
Eze 14:14,20;
Heb 11:7;
2Pe 2:5
ᵐGe 5:22
6:10
ⁿGe 5:32
6:11
ᵒEze 7:23; 8:17
6:12
ᵖPs 14:1-3
6:13
qver 17;
Eze 7:2-3
6:14
ʳHeb 11:7;
1Pe 3:20 ˢEx 2:3
6:17
ᵗGe 7:4,21-23;
2Pe 2:5
6:18
ᵘGe 9:9-16
ᵛGe 7:1,7,13

ᵃ29 *Noah* sounds like the Hebrew for *comfort.*   ᵇ3 Or *My spirit will not remain in*   ᶜ3 Or *corrupt*   ᵈ14 The meaning of the Hebrew for this word is uncertain.   ᵉ15 Hebrew *300 cubits long, 50 cubits wide and 30 cubits high* (about 140 meters long, 23 meters wide and 13.5 meters high)   ᶠ16 Or *Make an opening for light by finishing*   ᵍ16 Hebrew *a cubit* (about 0.5 meter) with you. [19]You are to bring into the ark two of all living creatures, male and female, to keep them alive with you. [20]Two[w] of every kind of bird, of every kind of animal and of every kind of creature that moves along the ground will come to you to be kept alive. [21]You are to take every kind of food that is to be eaten and store it away as food for you and for them."

[22]Noah did everything just as God commanded him.[x]

7 The LORD then said to Noah, "Go into the ark, you and your whole family,[y] because I have found you righteous[z] in this generation. [2]Take with you seven[a] of every kind of clean[a] animal, a male and its mate, and two of every kind of unclean animal, a male and its mate, [3]and also seven of every kind of bird, male and female, to keep their various kinds alive throughout the earth. [4]Seven days from now I will send rain on the earth for forty days and forty nights, and I will wipe from the face of the earth every living creature I have made."

[5]And Noah did all that the LORD commanded him.[b]

[6]Noah was six hundred years old when the floodwaters came on the earth. [7]And Noah and his sons and his wife and his sons' wives entered the ark to escape the waters of the flood. [8]Pairs of clean and unclean animals, of birds and of all creatures that move along the ground, [9]male and female, came to Noah and entered the ark, as God had commanded Noah. [10]And after the seven days the floodwaters came on the earth.

[11]In the six hundredth year of Noah's life, on the seventeenth day of the second month—on that day all the springs of the great deep[c] burst forth, and the floodgates of the heavens[d] were opened. [12]And rain fell on the earth forty days and forty nights.[e]

[13]On that very day Noah and his sons, Shem, Ham and Japheth, together with his wife and the wives of his three sons, entered the ark. [14]They had with them every wild animal according to its kind, all livestock according to their kinds, every creature that moves along the ground according to its kind and every bird according to its kind, everything with wings. [15]Pairs of all creatures that have the breath of life in them came to Noah and entered the ark.[f] [16]The animals going in were male and female of every living thing, as God had commanded Noah. Then the LORD shut him in.

[17]For forty days[g] the flood kept coming on the earth, and as the waters increased they lifted the ark high above the earth. [18]The waters rose and increased greatly on the earth, and the ark floated on the surface of the water. [19]They rose greatly on the earth, and all the high mountains under the entire heavens were covered.[h] [20]The waters rose and covered the mountains to a depth of more than twenty feet.[b,c] [21]Every living thing that moved on the earth perished—birds, livestock, wild animals, all the creatures that swarm over the earth, and all mankind.[i] [22]Everything on dry land that had the breath of life[j] in its nostrils died. [23]Every living thing on the face of the earth was wiped out; men and animals and the creatures that move along the ground and the birds of the air were wiped from the earth.[k] Only Noah was left, and those with him in the ark.[l]

6:20
w Ge 7:15
6:22
x Ge 7:5,9,16
7:1
y Mt 24:38;
Heb 11:7;
1Pe 3:20;
2Pe 2:5
z Ge 6:9;
Eze 14:14
7:2
a ver 8;
Ge 8:20;
Lev 10:10;
11:1-47
7:5
b Ge 6:22
7:11
c Eze 26:19
d Ge 8:2
7:12
e ver 4
7:15
f Ge 6:19
7:17
g ver 4
7:19
h Ps 104:6
7:21
i Ge 6:7,13
7:22
j Ge 1:30
7:23
k Mt 24:39;
Lk 17:27;
1Pe 3:20;
2Pe 2:5
l Heb 11:7

---

a2 Or *seven pairs*; also in verse 3   b20 Hebrew *fifteen cubits* (about 6.9 meters)   c20 Or *rose more than twenty feet, and the mountains were covered*

²⁴The waters flooded the earth for a hundred and fifty days.^m

8 But God rememberedⁿ Noah and all the wild animals and the livestock that were with him in the ark, and he sent a wind over the earth,^o and the waters receded. ²Now the springs of the deep and the floodgates of the heavens^p had been closed, and the rain had stopped falling from the sky. ³The water receded steadily from the earth. At the end of the hundred and fifty days the water had gone down, ⁴and on the seventeenth day of the seventh month the ark came to rest on the mountains of Ararat. ⁵The waters continued to recede until the tenth month, and on the first day of the tenth month the tops of the mountains became visible.

⁶After forty days Noah opened the window he had made in the ark ⁷and sent out a raven, and it kept flying back and forth until the water had dried up from the earth. ⁸Then he sent out a dove to see if the water had receded from the surface of the ground. ⁹But the dove could find no place to set its feet because there was water over all the surface of the earth; so it returned to Noah in the ark. He reached out his hand and took the dove and brought it back to himself in the ark. ¹⁰He waited seven more days and again sent out the dove from the ark. ¹¹When the dove returned to him in the evening, there in its beak was a freshly plucked olive leaf! Then Noah knew that the water had receded from the earth. ¹²He waited seven more days and sent the dove out again, but this time it did not return to him.

¹³By the first day of the first month of Noah's six hundred and first year, the water had dried up from the earth. Noah then removed the covering from the ark and saw that the surface of the ground was dry. ¹⁴By the twenty-seventh day of the second month the earth was completely dry.

¹⁵Then God said to Noah, ¹⁶"Come out of the ark, you and your wife and your sons and their wives.^q ¹⁷Bring out every kind of living creature that is with you—the birds, the animals, and all the creatures that move along the ground—so they can multiply on the earth and be fruitful and increase in number upon it."^r

¹⁸So Noah came out, together with his sons and his wife and his sons' wives. ¹⁹All the animals and all the creatures that move along the ground and all the birds—everything that moves on the earth—came out of the ark, one kind after another.

²⁰Then Noah built an altar to the LORD^s and, taking some of all the clean animals and clean^t birds, he sacrificed burnt offerings^u on it. ²¹The LORD smelled the pleasing aroma^v and said in his heart: "Never again will I curse the ground^w because of man, even though^a every inclination of his heart is evil from childhood.^x And never again will I destroy all living creatures,^y as I have done.

²²"As long as the earth endures,
    seedtime and harvest,
    cold and heat,
    summer and winter,
    day and night
    will never cease."^z

7:24
mGe 8:3
8:1
nGe 9:15;
19:29; Ex 2:24;
1Sa 1:11,19
oEx 14:21
8:2
pGe 7:11
8:16
qGe 7:13
8:17
rGe 1:22
8:20
sGe 12:7-8;
13:18; 22:9
tGe 7:8;
Lev 11:1-47
uGe 22:2,13;
Ex 10:25
8:21
vLev 1:9,13;
2Co 2:15
wGe 3:17
xGe 6:5;
Ps 51:5;
Jer 17:9
yGe 9:11,15;
Isa 54:9
8:22
zGe 1:14;
Jer 33:20,25

^a21 Or *man, for*

God's Covenant With Noah

9 Then God blessed Noah and his sons, saying to them, "Be fruitful and increase in number and fill the earth.ᵃ ²The fear and dread of you will fall upon all the beasts of the earth and all the birds of the air, upon every creature that moves along the ground, and upon all the fish of the sea; they are given into your hands. ³Everything that lives and moves will be food for you.ᵇ Just as I gave you the green plants, I now give you everything.

⁴"But you must not eat meat that has its lifeblood still in it.ᶜ ⁵And for your lifeblood I will surely demand an accounting. I will demand an accounting from every animal.ᵈ And from each man, too, I will demand an accounting for the life of his fellow man.ᵉ

6"Whoever sheds the blood of man,
    by man shall his blood be shed;ᶠ
for in the image of Godᵍ
    has God made man.

⁷As for you, be fruitful and increase in number; multiply on the earth and increase upon it."ʰ

⁸Then God said to Noah and to his sons with him: ⁹"I now establish my covenant with youⁱ and with your descendants after you ¹⁰and with every living creature that was with you—the birds, the livestock and all the wild animals, all those that came out of the ark with you —every living creature on earth. ¹¹I establish my covenantʲ with you: Never again will all life be cut off by the waters of a flood; never again will there be a flood to destroy the earth.ᵏ"

¹²And God said, "This is the sign of the covenantˡ I am making between me and you and every living creature with you, a covenant for all generations to come: ¹³I have set my rainbow in the clouds, and it will be the sign of the covenant between me and the earth. ¹⁴Whenever I bring clouds over the earth and the rainbow appears in the clouds, ¹⁵I will remember my covenantᵐ between me and you and all living creatures of every kind. Never again will the waters become a flood to destroy all life. ¹⁶Whenever the rainbow appears in the clouds, I will see it and remember the everlasting covenantⁿ between God and all living creatures of every kind on the earth."

¹⁷So God said to Noah, "This is the sign of the covenantᵒ I have established between me and all life on the earth."

The Sons of Noah

¹⁸The sons of Noah who came out of the ark were Shem, Ham and Japheth. (Ham was the father of Canaan.)ᵖ ¹⁹These were the three sons of Noah, and from them came the people who were scattered over the earth.�q

²⁰Noah, a man of the soil, proceededᵃ to plant a vineyard. ²¹When he drank some of its wine, he became drunk and lay uncovered inside his tent. ²²Ham, the father of Canaan, saw his father's nakedness and told his two brothers outside. ²³But Shem and Japheth took a garment and laid it across their shoulders; then they walked in backward and cov-

ᵃ20 Or *soil, was the first*

9:1
ᵃGe 1:22
9:3
ᵇGe 1:29
9:4
ᶜLev 3:17;
17:10-14;
Dt 12:16,23-25;
1Sa 14:33
9:5
ᵈEx 21:28-32
ᵉGe 4:10
9:6
ᶠGe 4:14;
Ex 21:12,14;
Lev 24:17;
Mt 26:52
ᵍGe 1:26
9:7
ʰGe 1:22
9:9
ⁱGe 6:18
9:11
ʲver 16; Isa 24:5
ᵏGe 8:21;
Isa 54:9
9:12
ˡver 17;
Ge 17:11
9:15
ᵐEx 2:24;
Lev 26:42,45;
Dt 7:9;
Eze 16:60
9:16
ⁿver 11;
Ge 17:7,13,19;
2Sa 7:13; 23:5
9:17
ᵒver 12;
Ge 17:11
9:18
ᵖver 25-27;
Ge 10:6,15
9:19
qGe 10:32

ered their father's nakedness. Their faces were turned the other way so that they would not see their father's nakedness.

²⁴When Noah awoke from his wine and found out what his youngest son had done to him, ²⁵he said,

> "Cursed be Canaan!ʳ
> The lowest of slaves
> will he be to his brothers. ˢ "

²⁶He also said,

> "Blessed be the Lord, the God of Shem!
> May Canaan be the slave of Shem. ᵃ
> ²⁷May God extend the territory of Japhethᵇ;
> may Japheth live in the tents of Shem,
> and may Canaan be hisᶜ slave."

²⁸After the flood Noah lived 350 years. ²⁹Altogether, Noah lived 950 years, and then he died.

The Table of Nations

10 This is the accountᵗ of Shem, Ham and Japheth, Noah's sons, who themselves had sons after the flood.

The Japhethites

10:2–5pp — 1Ch 1:5-7

²The sonsᵈ of Japheth:
Gomer, ᵘ Magog, ᵛ Madai, Javan, Tubal, ʷ Meshech and Tiras.
³The sons of Gomer:
Ashkenaz, ˣ Riphath and Togarmah. ʸ
⁴The sons of Javan:
Elishah, Tarshish, ᶻ the Kittim and the Rodanim. ᵉ ⁵(From these the maritime peoples spread out into their territories by their clans within their nations, each with its own language.)

The Hamites

10:6–20pp — 1Ch 1:8-16

⁶The sons of Ham:
Cush, Mizraim,ᶠ Put and Canaan. ᵃ
⁷The sons of Cush:
Seba, Havilah, Sabtah, Raamah and Sabteca.
The sons of Raamah:
Sheba and Dedan.

⁸Cush was the fatherᵍ of Nimrod, who grew to be a mighty warrior on the earth. ⁹He was a mighty hunter before the Lord; that is why it is said, "Like Nimrod, a mighty hunter before the Lord." ¹⁰The first centers of his kingdom were Babylon, ᵇ Erech, Akkad and Calneh, inʰ Shinar. ᶦᶜ ¹¹From that land he went to Assyria, ᵈ where he built Nine-

### Cross references (margin)

9:25
ʳver 18
ˢGe 25:23;
Jos 9:23
10:1
ᵗGe 2:4
10:2
ᵘEze 38:6
ᵛEze 38:2;
Rev 20:8
ʷIsa 66:19
10:3
ˣJer 51:27
ʸEze 27:14;
38:6
10:4
ᶻEze 27:12,25;
Jnh 1:3
10:6
ᵃver 15;
Ge 9:18
10:10
ᵇGe 11:9
ᶜGe 11:2
10:11
ᵈPs 83:8;
Mic 5:6

ᵃ26 Or *be his slave*   ᵇ27 *Japheth* sounds like the Hebrew for *extend.*   ᶜ27 Or *their*   ᵈ2 *Sons* may mean *descendants* or *successors* or *nations*; also in verses 3, 4, 6, 7, 20-23, 29 and 31.   ᵉ4 Some manuscripts of the Masoretic Text and Samaritan Pentateuch (see also Septuagint and 1 Chron. 1:7); most manuscripts of the Masoretic Text *Dodanim*   ᶠ6 That is, Egypt; also in verse 13   ᵍ8 *Father* may mean *ancestor* or *predecessor* or *founder;* also in verses 13, 15, 24 and 26.   ʰ10 Or *Erech and Akkad—all of them in*   ᶦ10 That is, Babylonia veh,[e] Rehoboth Ir,[a] Calah [12]and Resen, which is between Nineveh and Calah; that is the great city.

[13]Mizraim was the father of
the Ludites, Anamites, Lehabites, Naphtuhites, [14]Pathrusites, Casluhites (from whom the Philistines[f] came) and Caphtorites.
[15]Canaan[g] was the father of
Sidon[h] his firstborn,[b] and of the Hittites,[i] [16]Jebusites,[j] Amorites, Girgashites, [17]Hivites, Arkites, Sinites, [18]Arvadites, Zemarites and Hamathites.

Later the Canaanite[k] clans scattered [19]and the borders of Canaan[l] reached from Sidon[m] toward Gerar as far as Gaza, and then toward Sodom, Gomorrah, Admah and Zeboiim, as far as Lasha.
[20]These are the sons of Ham by their clans and languages, in their territories and nations.

The Semites

10:21-31pp — Ge 11:10-27; 1Ch 1:17-27

[21]Sons were also born to Shem, whose older brother was[c] Japheth; Shem was the ancestor of all the sons of Eber.[n]

[22]The sons of Shem:
Elam,[o] Asshur, Arphaxad,[p] Lud and Aram.
[23]The sons of Aram:
Uz,[q] Hul, Gether and Meshech.[d]
[24]Arphaxad was the father of[e] Shelah,
and Shelah the father of Eber.[r]
[25]Two sons were born to Eber:
One was named Peleg,[f] because in his time the earth was divided; his brother was named Joktan.
[26]Joktan was the father of
Almodad, Sheleph, Hazarmaveth, Jerah, [27]Hadoram, Uzal, Diklah, [28]Obal, Abimael, Sheba, [29]Ophir, Havilah and Jobab. All these were sons of Joktan.

[30]The region where they lived stretched from Mesha toward Sephar, in the eastern hill country.
[31]These are the sons of Shem by their clans and languages, in their territories and nations.

[32]These are the clans of Noah's sons,[s] according to their lines of descent, within their nations. From these the nations spread out over the earth[t] after the flood.

The Tower of Babel

11 Now the whole world had one language and a common speech. [2]As men moved eastward,[g] they found a plain in Shinar[h][u] and settled there.
[3]They said to each other, "Come, let's make bricks[v] and bake them

---

a11 Or *Nineveh with its city squares*   b15 Or *of the Sidonians, the foremost*   c21 Or *Shem, the older brother of*   d23 See Septuagint and 1 Chron. 1:17; Hebrew *Mash*   e24 Hebrew; Septuagint *father of Cainan, and Cainan was the father of*   f25 *Peleg* means *division*.   g2 Or *from the east; or in the east*   h2 That is, Babylonia

---

*Cross references (right column):*

10:11 eJnh 1:2; 4:11; Na 1:1
10:14 fGe 21:32,34; 26:1,8
10:15 gver 6; Ge 9:18; hEze 28:21; iGe 23:3,20
10:16 j1Ch 11:4
10:18 kGe 12:6; Ex 13:11
10:19 lGe 11:31; 13:12; 17:8; mver 15
10:21 nver 24; Nu 24:24
10:22 oJer 49:34; pLk 3:36
10:23 qJob 1:1
10:24 rver 21
10:32 sver 1 tGe 9:19
11:2 uGe 10:10
11:3 vEx 1:14

thoroughly." They used brick instead of stone, and tar[w] for mortar. [4]Then they said, "Come, let us build ourselves a city, with a tower that reaches to the heavens,[x] so that we may make a name[y] for ourselves and not be scattered over the face of the whole earth."[z]

[5]But the LORD came down[a] to see the city and the tower that the men were building. [6]The LORD said, "If as one people speaking the same language they have begun to do this, then nothing they plan to do will be impossible for them. [7]Come, let us[b] go down and confuse their language so they will not understand each other."[c]

[8]So the LORD scattered them from there over all the earth,[d] and they stopped building the city. [9]That is why it was called Babel[a] [e]—because there the LORD confused the language of the whole world. From there the LORD scattered them over the face of the whole earth.

From Shem to Abram

11:10–27pp — Ge 10:21–31; 1Ch 1:17–27

[10]This is the account of Shem.

Two years after the flood, when Shem was 100 years old, he became the father[b] of Arphaxad. [11]And after he became the father of Arphaxad, Shem lived 500 years and had other sons and daughters.

[12]When Arphaxad had lived 35 years, he became the father of Shelah.[f] [13]And after he became the father of Shelah, Arphaxad lived 403 years and had other sons and daughters.[c]

[14]When Shelah had lived 30 years, he became the father of Eber. [15]And after he became the father of Eber, Shelah lived 403 years and had other sons and daughters.

[16]When Eber had lived 34 years, he became the father of Peleg. [17]And after he became the father of Peleg, Eber lived 430 years and had other sons and daughters.

[18]When Peleg had lived 30 years, he became the father of Reu. [19]And after he became the father of Reu, Peleg lived 209 years and had other sons and daughters.

[20]When Reu had lived 32 years, he became the father of Serug. [g] [21]And after he became the father of Serug, Reu lived 207 years and had other sons and daughters.

[22]When Serug had lived 30 years, he became the father of Nahor. [23]And after he became the father of Nahor, Serug lived 200 years and had other sons and daughters.

[24]When Nahor had lived 29 years, he became the father of Terah. [h] [25]And after he became the father of Terah, Nahor lived 119 years and had other sons and daughters.

[26]After Terah had lived 70 years, he became the father of Abram,[i] Nahor[j] and Haran.

[27]This is the account of Terah.

Terah became the father of Abram, Nahor and Haran. And Haran

### Cross references (margin)

11:3
wGe 14:10
11:4
xDt 1:28; 9:1
yGe 6:4
zDt 4:27
11:5
aver 7;
Ge 18:21;
Ex 3:8; 19:11,
18,20
11:7
bGe 1:26
cGe 42:23
11:8
dGe 9:19;
Lk 1:51
11:9
eGe 10:10
11:12
fLk 3:35
11:20
gLk 3:35
11:24
hLk 3:34
11:26
iLk 3:34
jJos 24:2

---

[a]9 That is, Babylon; *Babel* sounds like the Hebrew for *confused.*   [b]10 *Father* may mean *ancestor;* also in verses 11-25.   [c]12,13 Hebrew; Septuagint (see also Luke 3:35, 36 and note at Gen. 10:24) *35 years, he became the father of Cainan. Arphaxad lived 430 years and had other sons and daughters, and then he died. When Cainan had lived 130 years, he became the father of Shelah. And after he became the father of Shelah, Cainan lived 330 years and had other sons and daughters*

became the father of Lot. ᵏ ²⁸While his father Terah was still alive, Haran died in Ur of the Chaldeans,ˡ in the land of his birth. ²⁹Abram and Nahor both married. The name of Abram's wife was Sarai, ᵐ and the name of Nahor's wife was Milcah;ⁿ she was the daughter of Haran, the father of both Milcah and Iscah. ³⁰Now Sarai was barren; she had no children.º

³¹Terah took his son Abram, his grandson Lot son of Haran, and his daughter-in-law Sarai, the wife of his son Abram, and together they set out from Ur of the Chaldeansᴾ to go to Canaan. �q But when they came to Haran, they settled there.

³²Terah lived 205 years, and he died in Haran.

The Call of Abram

12 The Lᴏʀᴅ had said to Abram, "Leave your country, your people and your father's household and go to the land I will show you. ʳ

2"I will make you into a great nationˢ
    and I will bless you;ᵗ
I will make your name great,
    and you will be a blessing.
³I will bless those who bless you,
    and whoever curses you I will curse;ᵘ
and all peoples on earth
    will be blessed through you. ᵛ"

⁴So Abram left, as the Lᴏʀᴅ had told him; and Lot went with him. Abram was seventy-five years old when he set out from Haran. ʷ ⁵He took his wife Sarai, his nephew Lot, all the possessions they had accumulated and the peopleˣ they had acquired in Haran, and they set out for the land of Canaan, and they arrived there.

⁶Abram traveled through the landʸ as far as the site of the great tree of Morehᶻ at Shechem. At that time the Canaanitesª were in the land. ⁷The Lᴏʀᴅ appeared to Abramᵇ and said, "To your offspringª I will give this land."ᶜ So he built an altar there to the Lᴏʀᴅ,ᵈ who had appeared to him.

⁸From there he went on toward the hills east of Bethelᵉ and pitched his tent, with Bethel on the west and Ai on the east. There he built an altar to the Lᴏʀᴅ and called on the name of the Lᴏʀᴅ. ⁹Then Abram set out and continued toward the Negev. ᶠ

Abram in Egypt

12:10–20Ref — Ge 20:1–18; 26:1–11

¹⁰Now there was a famine in the land, and Abram went down to Egypt to live there for a while because the famine was severe. ¹¹As he was about to enter Egypt, he said to his wife Sarai, "I know what a beautiful woman you are. ¹²When the Egyptians see you, they will say, 'This is his wife.' Then they will kill me but will let you live. ¹³Say you are my sister, g so that I will be treated well for your sake and my life will be spared because of you."

¹⁴When Abram came to Egypt, the Egyptians saw that she was a very beautiful woman. ¹⁵And when Pharaoh's officials saw her, they praised

11:27
kver 31;
Ge 12:4; 14:12;
19:1; 2Pe 2:7
11:28
lver 31; Ge 15:7
11:29
mGe 17:15
nGe 22:20
11:30
oGe 16:1; 18:11
11:31
pGe 15:7;
Ne 9:7; Ac 7:4
qGe 10:19
12:1
rAc 7:3*;
Heb 11:8
12:2
sGe 15:5; 17:2,
4; 18:18; 22:17;
Dt 26:5
tGe 24:1,35
12:3
uGe 27:29;
Ex 23:22;
Nu 24:9
vGe 18:18;
22:18; 26:4;
Ac 3:25;
Gal 3:8*
12:4
wGe 11:31
12:5
xGe 14:14;
17:23
12:6
yHeb 11:9
zGe 35:4;
Dt 11:30
aGe 10:18
12:7
bGe 17:1; 18:1;
Ex 6:3
cGe 13:15,17;
15:18; 17:8;
Ps 105:9-11
dGe 13:4
12:8
eGe 13:3
12:9
fGe 13:1,3
12:13
gGe 20:2; 26:7

a7 Or *seed*

her to Pharaoh, and she was taken into his palace. [16]He treated Abram well for her sake, and Abram acquired sheep and cattle, male and female donkeys, menservants and maidservants, and camels.

[17]But the LORD inflicted serious diseases on Pharaoh and his household[h] because of Abram's wife Sarai. [18]So Pharaoh summoned Abram. "What have you done to me?"[i] he said. "Why didn't you tell me she was your wife? [19]Why did you say, 'She is my sister,' so that I took her to be my wife? Now then, here is your wife. Take her and go!" [20]Then Pharaoh gave orders about Abram to his men, and they sent him on his way, with his wife and everything he had.

Abram and Lot Separate

13 So Abram went up from Egypt to the Negev,[j] with his wife and everything he had, and Lot went with him. [2]Abram had become very wealthy in livestock and in silver and gold.

[3]From the Negev he went from place to place until he came to Bethel,[k] to the place between Bethel and Ai where his tent had been earlier [4]and where he had first built an altar.[l] There Abram called on the name of the LORD.

[5]Now Lot, who was moving about with Abram, also had flocks and herds and tents. [6]But the land could not support them while they stayed together, for their possessions were so great that they were not able to stay together.[m] [7]And quarreling[n] arose between Abram's herdsmen and the herdsmen of Lot. The Canaanites and Perizzites were also living in the land[o] at that time.

[8]So Abram said to Lot, "Let's not have any quarreling between you and me,[p] or between your herdsmen and mine, for we are brothers.[q] [9]Is not the whole land before you? Let's part company. If you go to the left, I'll go to the right; if you go to the right, I'll go to the left."

[10]Lot looked up and saw that the whole plain of the Jordan was well watered, like the garden of the LORD,[r] like the land of Egypt, toward Zoar.[s] (This was before the LORD destroyed Sodom and Gomorrah.)[t] [11]So Lot chose for himself the whole plain of the Jordan and set out toward the east. The two men parted company: [12]Abram lived in the land of Canaan, while Lot lived among the cities of the plain[u] and pitched his tents near Sodom.[v] [13]Now the men of Sodom were wicked and were sinning greatly against the LORD.[w]

[14]The LORD said to Abram after Lot had parted from him, "Lift up your eyes from where you are and look north and south, east and west.[x] [15]All the land that you see I will give to you and your offspring[a] forever.[y] [16]I will make your offspring like the dust of the earth, so that if anyone could count the dust, then your offspring could be counted. [17]Go, walk through the length and breadth of the land,[z] for I am giving it to you."

[18]So Abram moved his tents and went to live near the great trees of Mamre[a] at Hebron,[b] where he built an altar to the LORD.[c]

Abram Rescues Lot

14 At this time Amraphel king of Shinar,[bd] Arioch king of Ellasar, Kedorlaomer king of Elam and Tidal king of Goiim [2]went to war

---

12:17
h1Ch 16:21
12:18
iGe 20:9; 26:10
13:1
jGe 12:9
13:3
kGe 12:8
13:4
lGe 12:7
13:6
mGe 36:7
13:7
nGe 26:20,21
oGe 12:6
13:8
pPr 15:18; 20:3
qPs 133:1
13:10
rGe 2:8-10;
Isa 51:3
sGe 19:22,30
tGe 14:8;
19:17-29
13:12
uGe 19:17,25,29
vGe 14:12
13:13
wGe 18:20;
Eze 16:49-50;
2Pe 2:8
13:14
xGe 28:14;
Dt 3:27
13:15
yGe 12:7;
Gal 3:16*
13:17
zver 15;
Nu 13:17-25
13:18
aGe 14:13,24;
18:1 bGe 35:27
cGe 8:20
14:1
dGe 10:10

---

[a]15 Or *seed*; also in verse 16   [b]1 That is, Babylonia; also in verse 9

against Bera king of Sodom, Birsha king of Gomorrah, Shinab king of Admah, Shemeber king of Zeboiim,ᵉ and the king of Bela (that is, Zoar).ᶠ ³All these latter kings joined forces in the Valley of Siddim (the Salt Seaᵈᵍ). ⁴For twelve years they had been subject to Kedorlaomer, but in the thirteenth year they rebelled.

⁵In the fourteenth year, Kedorlaomer and the kings allied with him went out and defeated the Rephaitesʰ in Ashteroth Karnaim, the Zuzites in Ham, the Emitesⁱ in Shaveh Kiriathaim ⁶and the Horitesʲ in the hill country of Seir,ᵏ as far as El Paranˡ near the desert. ⁷Then they turned back and went to En Mishpat (that is, Kadesh), and they conquered the whole territory of the Amalekites, as well as the Amorites who were living in Hazazon Tamar.ᵐ

⁸Then the king of Sodom, the king of Gomorrah,ⁿ the king of Admah, the king of Zeboiimᵒ and the king of Bela (that is, Zoar) marched out and drew up their battle lines in the Valley of Siddim ⁹against Kedorlaomer king of Elam, Tidal king of Goiim, Amraphel king of Shinar and Arioch king of Ellasar—four kings against five. ¹⁰Now the Valley of Siddim was full of tar pits, and when the kings of Sodom and Gomorrah fled, some of the men fell into them and the rest fled to the hills.ᵖ ¹¹The four kings seized all the goods of Sodom and Gomorrah and all their food; then they went away. ¹²They also carried off Abram's nephew Lot and his possessions, since he was living in Sodom.

¹³One who had escaped came and reported this to Abram the Hebrew. Now Abram was living near the great trees of Mamre�q the Amorite, a brotherᵇ of Eshcol and Aner, all of whom were allied with Abram. ¹⁴When Abram heard that his relative had been taken captive, he called out the 318 trained men born in his householdʳ and went in pursuit as far as Dan.ˢ ¹⁵During the night Abram divided his men to attack them and he routed them, pursuing them as far as Hobah, north of Damascus. ¹⁶He recovered all the goods and brought back his relative Lot and his possessions, together with the women and the other people.

¹⁷After Abram returned from defeating Kedorlaomer and the kings allied with him, the king of Sodom came out to meet him in the Valley of Shaveh (that is, the King's Valley).ᵗ

¹⁸Then Melchizedekᵘ king of Salemᶜᵛ brought out bread and wine. He was priest of God Most High, ¹⁹and he blessed Abram,ʷ saying,

> "Blessed be Abram by God Most High,
>   Creatorᵈ of heaven and earth.ˣ
> ²⁰And blessed beᵉ God Most High,ʸ
>   who delivered your enemies into your hand."

Then Abram gave him a tenth of everything.ᶻ

²¹The king of Sodom said to Abram, "Give me the people and keep the goods for yourself."

²²But Abram said to the king of Sodom, "I have raised my handᵃ to the LORD, God Most High, Creator of heaven and earth,ᵇ and have taken an oath ²³that I will accept nothing belonging to you,ᶜ not even a thread or the thong of a sandal, so that you will never be able to say, 'I

14:2
eGe 10:19
fGe 13:10
14:3
gNu 34:3,12;
Dt 3:17;
Jos 3:16; 15:2,5
14:5
hGe 15:20;
Dt 2:11,20
iDt 2:10
14:6
jDt 2:12,22
kDt 2:1,5,22
lGe 21:21;
Nu 10:12
14:7
m2Ch 20:2
14:8
nGe 13:10;
19:17-29
oDt 29:23
14:10
pGe 19:17,30
14:13
qver 24;
Ge 13:18
14:14
rGe 15:3
sDt 34:1;
Jdg 18:29
14:17
t2Sa 18:18
14:18
uPs 110:4;
Heb 5:6
vPs 76:2;
Heb 7:2
14:19
wHeb 7:6
xver 22
14:20
yGe 24:27
zGe 28:22;
Dt 26:12;
Heb 7:4
14:22
aEx 6:8;
Da 12:7;
Rev 10:5-6
bver 19
14:23
c2Ki 5:16

ᵃ3 That is, the Dead Sea   ᵇ13 Or *a relative; or an ally*   ᶜ18 That is, Jerusalem   ᵈ19 Or
Possessor; also in verse 22   ᵉ20 Or *And praise be to*

made Abram rich.' 24I will accept nothing but what my men have eaten and the share that belongs to the men who went with me—to Aner, Eshcol and Mamre. Let them have their share.''

God's Covenant With Abram

15 After this, the word of the LORD came to Abram[d] in a vision:

"Do not be afraid,[e] Abram.
    I am your shield,[a][f]
    your very great reward.[b]''

2But Abram said, "O Sovereign LORD, what can you give me since I remain childless[g] and the one who will inherit[c] my estate is Eliezer of Damascus?'' 3And Abram said, "You have given me no children; so a servant[h] in my household will be my heir.''

4Then the word of the LORD came to him: "This man will not be your heir, but a son coming from your own body will be your heir.[i]'' 5He took him outside and said, "Look up at the heavens and count the stars[j]—if indeed you can count them.'' Then he said to him, "So shall your offspring be.''[k]

6Abram believed the LORD, and he credited it to him as righteousness.[l]

7He also said to him, "I am the LORD, who brought you out of Ur of the Chaldeans to give you this land to take possession of it.''

8But Abram said, "O Sovereign LORD, how can I know[m] that I will gain possession of it?''

9So the LORD said to him, "Bring me a heifer, a goat and a ram, each three years old, along with a dove and a young pigeon.''

10Abram brought all these to him, cut them in two and arranged the halves opposite each other;[n] the birds, however, he did not cut in half.[o] 11Then birds of prey came down on the carcasses, but Abram drove them away.

12As the sun was setting, Abram fell into a deep sleep,[p] and a thick and dreadful darkness came over him. 13Then the LORD said to him, "Know for certain that your descendants will be strangers in a country not their own, and they will be enslaved[q] and mistreated four hundred years.[r] 14But I will punish the nation they serve as slaves, and afterward they will come out[s] with great possessions.[t] 15You, however, will go to your fathers in peace and be buried at a good old age.[u] 16In the fourth generation your descendants will come back here, for the sin of the Amorites[v] has not yet reached its full measure.''

17When the sun had set and darkness had fallen, a smoking firepot with a blazing torch appeared and passed between the pieces.[w] 18On that day the LORD made a covenant with Abram and said, "To your descendants I give this land,[x] from the river[d] of Egypt[y] to the great river, the Euphrates— 19the land of the Kenites, Kenizzites, Kadmonites, 20Hittites, Perizzites, Rephaites, 21Amorites, Canaanites, Girgashites and Jebusites.''

### Cross references (margin)

15:1
dDa 10:1
eGe 21:17;
26:24; 46:3;
2Ki 6:16;
Ps 27:1;
Isa 41:10,13-14
fDt 33:29;
2Sa 22:3,31;
Ps 3:3
15:2
gAc 7:5
15:3
hGe 24:2,34
15:4
iGal 4:28
15:5
jPs 147:4;
Jer 33:22
kGe 12:2;
22:17; Ex 32:13;
Ro 4:18*;
Heb 11:12
15:6
lPs 106:31;
Ro 4:3*,20-24*;
Gal 3:6*;
Jas 2:23*
15:8
mLk 1:18
15:10
nver 17;
Jer 34:18
oLev 1:17
15:12
pGe 2:21
15:13
qEx 1:11
rver 16;
Ex 12:40;
Ac 7:6,17
15:14
sAc 7:7*
tEx 12:32-38
15:15
uGe 25:8
15:16
v1Ki 21:26
15:17
wver 10
15:18
xGe 12:7
yNu 34:5

---

[a]1 Or *sovereign*   [b]1 Or *shield; / your reward will be very great*   [c]2 The meaning of the Hebrew for this phrase is uncertain.   [d]18 Or *Wadi*

Hagar and Ishmael

16 Now Sarai, Abram's wife, had borne him no children.[z] But she had an Egyptian maidservant[a] named Hagar; [2]so she said to Abram, "The LORD has kept me from having children. Go, sleep with my maidservant; perhaps I can build a family through her."[b]

Abram agreed to what Sarai said. [3]So after Abram had been living in Canaan[c] ten years, Sarai his wife took her Egyptian maidservant Hagar and gave her to her husband to be his wife. [4]He slept with Hagar, and she conceived.

When she knew she was pregnant, she began to despise her mistress. [5]Then Sarai said to Abram, "You are responsible for the wrong I am suffering. I put my servant in your arms, and now that she knows she is pregnant, she despises me. May the LORD judge between you and me."[d]

[6]"Your servant is in your hands," Abram said. "Do with her whatever you think best." Then Sarai mistreated Hagar; so she fled from her.

[7]The angel of the LORD[e] found Hagar near a spring in the desert; it was the spring that is beside the road to Shur.[f] [8]And he said, "Hagar, servant of Sarai, where have you come from, and where are you going?"

"I'm running away from my mistress Sarai," she answered.

[9]Then the angel of the LORD told her, "Go back to your mistress and submit to her." [10]The angel added, "I will so increase your descendants that they will be too numerous to count."[g]

[11]The angel of the LORD also said to her:

> "You are now with child
>   and you will have a son.
> You shall name him Ishmael,[a]
>   for the LORD has heard of your misery.[h]
> [12]He will be a wild donkey of a man;
>   his hand will be against everyone
>   and everyone's hand against him,
> and he will live in hostility
>   toward[b] all his brothers.[i]"

[13]She gave this name to the LORD who spoke to her: "You are the God who sees me,"[c] for she said, "I have now seen[c] the One who sees me."[j] [14]That is why the well was called Beer Lahai Roi[d]; it is still there, between Kadesh and Bered.

[15]So Hagar bore Abram a son,[k] and Abram gave the name Ishmael to the son she had borne. [16]Abram was eighty-six years old when Hagar bore him Ishmael.

The Covenant of Circumcision

17 When Abram was ninety-nine years old, the LORD appeared to him and said, "I am God Almighty[e];[l] walk before me and be blameless. [m] [2]I will confirm my covenant between me and you[n] and will greatly increase your numbers."

16:1
[z]Ge 11:30;
Gal 4:24-25
[a]Ge 21:9
16:2
[b]Ge 30:3-4,9-10
16:3
[c]Ge 12:5
16:5
[d]Ge 31:53
16:7
[e]Ge 21:17;
22:11,15; 31:11
[f]Ge 20:1
16:10
[g]Ge 13:16;
17:20
16:11
[h]Ex 2:24; 3:7,9
16:12
[i]Ge 25:18
16:13
[j]Ge 32:30
16:15
[k]Gal 4:22
17:1
[l]Ge 28:3; Ex 6:3
[m]Dt 18:13
17:2
[n]Ge 15:18

---

[a]11 *Ishmael* means *God hears.*   [b]12 Or *live to the east / of*   [c]13 Or *seen the back of*   [d]14 *Beer Lahai Roi* means *well of the Living One who sees me.*   [e]1 Hebrew *El-Shaddai*

³Abram fell facedown, and God said to him, ⁴"As for me, this is my covenant with you:° You will be the father of many nations.ᴾ ⁵No longer will you be called Abramᵃ; your name will be Abraham,ᵇ�q for I have made you a father of many nations.ʳ ⁶I will make you very fruitful;ˢ I will make nations of you, and kings will come from you.ᵗ ⁷I will establish my covenant as an everlasting covenant between me and you and your descendants after you for the generations to come, to be your Godᵘ and the God of your descendants after you.ᵛ ⁸The whole land of Canaan,ʷ where you are now an alien,ˣ I will give as an everlasting possession to you and your descendants after you;ʸ and I will be their God."

⁹Then God said to Abraham, "As for you, you must keep my covenant, you and your descendants after you for the generations to come. ¹⁰This is my covenant with you and your descendants after you, the covenant you are to keep: Every male among you shall be circumcised.ᶻ ¹¹You are to undergo circumcision,ᵃ and it will be the sign of the covenantᵇ between me and you. ¹²For the generations to come every male among you who is eight days old must be circumcised,ᶜ including those born in your household or bought with money from a foreigner —those who are not your offspring. ¹³Whether born in your household or bought with your money, they must be circumcised. My covenant in your flesh is to be an everlasting covenant. ¹⁴Any uncircumcised male, who has not been circumcised in the flesh, will be cut off from his people;ᵈ he has broken my covenant."

¹⁵God also said to Abraham, "As for Sarai your wife, you are no longer to call her Sarai; her name will be Sarah. ¹⁶I will bless her and will surely give you a son by her.ᵉ I will bless her so that she will be the mother of nations;ᶠ kings of peoples will come from her."

¹⁷Abraham fell facedown; he laughedᵍ and said to himself, "Will a son be born to a man a hundred years old? Will Sarah bear a child at the age of ninety?" ¹⁸And Abraham said to God, "If only Ishmael might live under your blessing!"

¹⁹Then God said, "Yes, but your wife Sarah will bear you a son,ʰ and you will call him Isaac.ᶜ I will establish my covenant with himⁱ as an everlasting covenant for his descendants after him. ²⁰And as for Ishmael, I have heard you: I will surely bless him; I will make him fruitful and will greatly increase his numbers.ʲ He will be the father of twelve rulers,ᵏ and I will make him into a great nation.ˡ ²¹But my covenant I will establish with Isaac, whom Sarah will bear to you by this time next year."ᵐ ²²When he had finished speaking with Abraham, God went up from him.

²³On that very day Abraham took his son Ishmael and all those born in his household or bought with his money, every male in his household, and circumcised them, as God told him. ²⁴Abraham was ninety-nine years old when he was circumcised,ⁿ ²⁵and his son Ishmael was thirteen; ²⁶Abraham and his son Ishmael were both circumcised on that same day. ²⁷And every male in Abraham's household, including those born in his household or bought from a foreigner, was circumcised with him.

17:4
oGe 15:18
pver 16;
Ge 12:2; 35:11;
48:19
17:5
qver 15; Ne 9:7
rRo 4:17*
17:6
sGe 35:11
tMt 1:6
17:7
uEx 29:45,46
vRo 9:8;
Gal 3:16
17:8
wPs 105:9,11
xGe 23:4; 28:4;
Ex 6:4 yGe 12:7
17:10
zver 23;
Ge 21:4;
Jn 7:22; Ac 7:8;
Ro 4:11
17:11
aEx 12:48;
Dt 10:16
bRo 4:11
17:12
cLev 12:3;
Lk 2:21
17:14
dEx 4:24-26
17:16
eGe 18:10
fGe 35:11;
Gal 4:31
17:17
gGe 18:12; 21:6
17:19
hGe 18:14; 21:2
iGe 26:3
17:20
jGe 16:10
kGe 25:12-16
lGe 21:18
17:21
mGe 21:2
17:24
nRo 4:11

ᵃ5 *Abram* means *exalted father*.   ᵇ5 *Abraham* means *father of many*.   ᶜ19 *Isaac* means *he laughs*.

The Three Visitors

18 The LORD appeared to Abraham near the great trees of Mamre[o] while he was sitting at the entrance to his tent in the heat of the day. [2]Abraham looked up and saw three men[p] standing nearby. When he saw them, he hurried from the entrance of his tent to meet them and bowed low to the ground.

[3]He said, "If I have found favor in your eyes, my lord,[a] do not pass your servant by. [4]Let a little water be brought, and then you may all wash your feet[q] and rest under this tree. [5]Let me get you something to eat,[r] so you can be refreshed and then go on your way—now that you have come to your servant."

"Very well," they answered, "do as you say."

[6]So Abraham hurried into the tent to Sarah. "Quick," he said, "get three seahs[b] of fine flour and knead it and bake some bread."

[7]Then he ran to the herd and selected a choice, tender calf and gave it to a servant, who hurried to prepare it. [8]He then brought some curds and milk and the calf that had been prepared, and set these before them.[s] While they ate, he stood near them under a tree.

[9]"Where is your wife Sarah?" they asked him.

"There, in the tent," he said.

[10]Then the LORD[c] said, "I will surely return to you about this time next year, and Sarah your wife will have a son."[t]

Now Sarah was listening at the entrance to the tent, which was behind him. [11]Abraham and Sarah were already old and well advanced in years,[u] and Sarah was past the age of childbearing.[v] [12]So Sarah laughed[w] to herself as she thought, "After I am worn out and my master[dx] is old, will I now have this pleasure?"

[13]Then the LORD said to Abraham, "Why did Sarah laugh and say, 'Will I really have a child, now that I am old?' [14]Is anything too hard for the LORD?[y] I will return to you at the appointed time next year and Sarah will have a son."

[15]Sarah was afraid, so she lied and said, "I did not laugh."

But he said, "Yes, you did laugh."

Abraham Pleads for Sodom

[16]When the men got up to leave, they looked down toward Sodom, and Abraham walked along with them to see them on their way. [17]Then the LORD said, "Shall I hide from Abraham[z] what I am about to do?[a] [18]Abraham will surely become a great and powerful nation,[b] and all nations on earth will be blessed through him. [19]For I have chosen him, so that he will direct his children[c] and his household after him to keep the way of the LORD[d] by doing what is right and just, so that the LORD will bring about for Abraham what he has promised him."

[20]Then the LORD said, "The outcry against Sodom and Gomorrah is so great and their sin so grievous [21]that I will go down[e] and see if what they have done is as bad as the outcry that has reached me. If not, I will know."

[22]The men turned away and went toward Sodom,[f] but Abraham

18:1
oGe 13:18;
14:13
18:2
pver 16,22;
Ge 32:24;
Jos 5:13;
Jdg 13:6-11;
Heb 13:2
18:4
qGe 19:2; 43:24
18:5
rJdg 13:15
18:8
sGe 19:3
18:10
tRo 9:9*
18:11
uGe 17:17
vRo 4:19
18:12
wGe 17:17;
21:6 x1Pe 3:6
18:14
yJer 32:17,27;
Zec 8:6;
Mt 19:26;
Lk 1:37;
Ro 4:21
18:17
zAm 3:7
aGe 19:24
18:18
bGal 3:8*
18:19
cDt 4:9-10; 6:7
dJos 24:15;
Eph 6:4
18:21
eGe 11:5
18:22
fGe 19:1

---

[a]3 Or *O Lord*   [b]6 That is, probably about 20 quarts (about 22 liters)   [c]10 Hebrew *Then he*
[d]12 Or *husband*

remained standing before the LORD. ª 23Then Abraham approached him and said: "Will you sweep away the righteous with the wicked?ᵍ 24What if there are fifty righteous people in the city? Will you really sweep it away and not spareᵇ the place for the sake of the fifty righteous people in it?ʰ 25Far be it from you to do such a thing—to kill the righteous with the wicked, treating the righteous and the wicked alike. Far be it from you! Will not the Judgeᶜ of all the earth do right?"ⁱ

26The LORD said, "If I find fifty righteous people in the city of Sodom, I will spare the whole place for their sake.ʲ "

27Then Abraham spoke up again: "Now that I have been so bold as to speak to the Lord, though I am nothing but dust and ashes,ᵏ 28what if the number of the righteous is five less than fifty? Will you destroy the whole city because of five people?"

"If I find forty-five there," he said, "I will not destroy it."

29Once again he spoke to him, "What if only forty are found there?"

He said, "For the sake of forty, I will not do it."

30Then he said, "May the Lord not be angry, but let me speak. What if only thirty can be found there?"

He answered, "I will not do it if I find thirty there."

31Abraham said, "Now that I have been so bold as to speak to the Lord, what if only twenty can be found there?"

He said, "For the sake of twenty, I will not destroy it."

32Then he said, "May the Lord not be angry, but let me speak just once more.ˡ What if only ten can be found there?"

He answered, "For the sake of ten,ᵐ I will not destroy it."

33When the LORD had finished speaking with Abraham, he left, and Abraham returned home.

Sodom and Gomorrah Destroyed

19 The two angels arrived at Sodomⁿ in the evening, and Lot was sitting in the gateway of the city. º When he saw them, he got up to meet them and bowed down with his face to the ground. 2"My lords," he said, "please turn aside to your servant's house. You can wash your feetᵖ and spend the night and then go on your way early in the morning."

"No," they answered, "we will spend the night in the square."

3But he insisted so strongly that they did go with him and entered his house. He prepared a meal for them, baking bread without yeast, and they ate. ۹ 4Before they had gone to bed, all the men from every part of the city of Sodom—both young and old—surrounded the house. 5They called to Lot, "Where are the men who came to you tonight? Bring them out to us so that we can have sex with them."ʳ

6Lot went outside to meet themˢ and shut the door behind him 7and said, "No, my friends. Don't do this wicked thing. 8Look, I have two daughters who have never slept with a man. Let me bring them out to you, and you can do what you like with them. But don't do anything to these men, for they have come under the protection of my roof."ᵗ

ª22 Masoretic Text; an ancient Hebrew scribal tradition *but the* LORD *remained standing before Abraham*
ᵇ24 Or *forgive;* also in verse 26   ᶜ25 Or *Ruler*

⁹"Get out of our way," they replied. And they said, "This fellow came here as an alien, and now he wants to play the judge!ᵘ We'll treat you worse than them." They kept bringing pressure on Lot and moved forward to break down the door.

¹⁰But the men inside reached out and pulled Lot back into the house and shut the door. ¹¹Then they struck the men who were at the door of the house, young and old, with blindnessᵛ so that they could not find the door.

¹²The two men said to Lot, "Do you have anyone else here—sons-in-law, sons or daughters, or anyone else in the city who belongs to you?ʷ Get them out of here, ¹³because we are going to destroy this place. The outcry to the LORD against its people is so great that he has sent us to destroy it."ˣ

¹⁴So Lot went out and spoke to his sons-in-law, who were pledged to marryᵃ his daughters. He said, "Hurry and get out of this place, because the LORD is about to destroy the city!ʸ" But his sons-in-law thought he was joking. ᶻ

¹⁵With the coming of dawn, the angels urged Lot, saying, "Hurry! Take your wife and your two daughters who are here, or you will be swept awayᵃ when the city is punished. ᵇ"

¹⁶When he hesitated, the men grasped his hand and the hands of his wife and of his two daughters and led them safely out of the city, for the LORD was merciful to them. ¹⁷As soon as they had brought them out, one of them said, "Flee for your lives!ᶜ Don't look back,ᵈ and don't stop anywhere in the plain! Flee to the mountains or you will be swept away!"

¹⁸But Lot said to them, "No, my lords,ᵇ please! ¹⁹Yourᶜ servant has found favor in yourᶜ eyes, and youᶜ have shown great kindness to me in sparing my life. But I can't flee to the mountains; this disaster will overtake me, and I'll die. ²⁰Look, here is a town near enough to run to, and it is small. Let me flee to it—it is very small, isn't it? Then my life will be spared."

²¹He said to him, "Very well, I will grant this request too; I will not overthrow the town you speak of. ²²But flee there quickly, because I cannot do anything until you reach it." (That is why the town was called Zoar.ᵈ)

²³By the time Lot reached Zoar, the sun had risen over the land. ²⁴Then the LORD rained down burning sulfur on Sodom and Gomorrahᵉ—from the LORD out of the heavens.ᶠ ²⁵Thus he overthrew those cities and the entire plain, including all those living in the cities—and also the vegetation in the land. ᵍ ²⁶But Lot's wife looked back,ʰ and she became a pillar of salt. ⁱ

²⁷Early the next morning Abraham got up and returned to the place where he had stood before the LORD. ʲ ²⁸He looked down toward Sodom and Gomorrah, toward all the land of the plain, and he saw dense smoke rising from the land, like smoke from a furnace. ᵏ

²⁹So when God destroyed the cities of the plain, he remembered Abraham, and he brought Lot out of the catastropheˡ that overthrew the cities where Lot had lived.

19:9
uEx 2:14;
Ac 7:27
19:11
vDt 28:28-29;
2Ki 6:18;
Ac 13:11
19:12
wGe 7:1
19:13
x1Ch 21:15
19:14
yNu 16:21
zEx 9:21;
Lk 17:28
19:15
aNu 16:26
bRev 18:4
19:17
cJer 48:6
dver 26
19:24
eDt 29:23;
Isa 1:9; 13:19
fLk 17:29;
2Pe 2:6; Jude 7
19:25
gPs 107:34;
Eze 16:48
19:26
hver 17
iLk 17:32
19:27
jGe 18:22
19:28
kRev 9:2; 18:9
19:29
l2Pe 2:7

ᵃ14 Or *were married to*   ᵇ18 Or *No, Lord; or No, my lord*   ᶜ19 The Hebrew is singular.
ᵈ22 *Zoar* means *small.*

Lot and His Daughters

³⁰Lot and his two daughters left Zoar and settled in the mountains, ᵐ for he was afraid to stay in Zoar. He and his two daughters lived in a cave. ³¹One day the older daughter said to the younger, "Our father is old, and there is no man around here to lie with us, as is the custom all over the earth. ³²Let's get our father to drink wine and then lie with him and preserve our family line through our father."

³³That night they got their father to drink wine, and the older daughter went in and lay with him. He was not aware of it when she lay down or when she got up.

³⁴The next day the older daughter said to the younger, "Last night I lay with my father. Let's get him to drink wine again tonight, and you go in and lie with him so we can preserve our family line through our father." ³⁵So they got their father to drink wine that night also, and the younger daughter went and lay with him. Again he was not aware of it when she lay down or when she got up.

³⁶So both of Lot's daughters became pregnant by their father. ³⁷The older daughter had a son, and she named him Moab[a]; he is the father of the Moabites[n] of today. ³⁸The younger daughter also had a son, and she named him Ben-Ammi[b]; he is the father of the Ammonites[o] of today.

Abraham and Abimelech

20:1–18Ref — Ge 12:10–20; 26:1–11

20 Now Abraham moved on from there[p] into the region of the Negev and lived between Kadesh and Shur. For a while he stayed in Gerar, [q] ²and there Abraham said of his wife Sarah, "She is my sister.[r]" Then Abimelech king of Gerar sent for Sarah and took her. [s]

³But God came to Abimelech in a dream[t] one night and said to him, "You are as good as dead because of the woman you have taken; she is a married woman."[u]

⁴Now Abimelech had not gone near her, so he said, "Lord, will you destroy an innocent nation?[v] ⁵Did he not say to me, 'She is my sister,' and didn't she also say, 'He is my brother'? I have done this with a clear conscience and clean hands."

⁶Then God said to him in the dream, "Yes, I know you did this with a clear conscience, and so I have kept[w] you from sinning against me. That is why I did not let you touch her. ⁷Now return the man's wife, for he is a prophet, and he will pray for you[x] and you will live. But if you do not return her, you may be sure that you and all yours will die."

⁸Early the next morning Abimelech summoned all his officials, and when he told them all that had happened, they were very much afraid. ⁹Then Abimelech called Abraham in and said, "What have you done to us? How have I wronged you that you have brought such great guilt upon me and my kingdom? You have done things to me that should not be done.[y]" ¹⁰And Abimelech asked Abraham, "What was your reason for doing this?"

¹¹Abraham replied, "I said to myself, 'There is surely no fear of God[z] in this place, and they will kill me because of my wife.'[a] ¹²Besides, she

---

19:30
mver 19
19:37
nDt 2:9
19:38
oDt 2:19
20:1
pGe 18:1
qGe 26:1,6,17
20:2
rver 12;
Ge 12:13; 26:7
sGe 12:15
20:3
tJob 33:15;
Mt 27:19
uPs 105:14
20:4
vGe 18:25
20:6
w1Sa 25:26,34
20:7
xver 17;
1Sa 7:5;
Job 42:8
20:9
yGe 12:18;
26:10; 34:7
20:11
zGe 42:18;
Ps 36:1
aGe 12:12; 26:7

---

a37 *Moab* sounds like the Hebrew for *from father.*   b38 *Ben-Ammi* means *son of my people.*

really is my sister, the daughter of my father though not of my mother; and she became my wife. [13]And when God had me wander from my father's household, I said to her, 'This is how you can show your love to me: Everywhere we go, say of me, "He is my brother." ' "

[14]Then Abimelech brought sheep and cattle and male and female slaves and gave them to Abraham, [b] and he returned Sarah his wife to him. [15]And Abimelech said, "My land is before you; live wherever you like." [c]

[16]To Sarah he said, "I am giving your brother a thousand shekels[a] of silver. This is to cover the offense against you before all who are with you; you are completely vindicated."

[17]Then Abraham prayed to God, [d] and God healed Abimelech, his wife and his slave girls so they could have children again, [18]for the LORD had closed up every womb in Abimelech's household because of Abraham's wife Sarah. [e]

The Birth of Isaac

21 Now the LORD was gracious to Sarah[f] as he had said, and the LORD did for Sarah what he had promised. [g] [2]Sarah became pregnant and bore a son[h] to Abraham in his old age, [i] at the very time God had promised him. [3]Abraham gave the name Isaac[bj] to the son Sarah bore him. [4]When his son Isaac was eight days old, Abraham circumcised him, [k] as God commanded him. [5]Abraham was a hundred years old when his son Isaac was born to him.

[6]Sarah said, "God has brought me laughter, [l] and everyone who hears about this will laugh with me." [7]And she added, "Who would have said to Abraham that Sarah would nurse children? Yet I have borne him a son in his old age."

Hagar and Ishmael Sent Away

[8]The child grew and was weaned, and on the day Isaac was weaned Abraham held a great feast. [9]But Sarah saw that the son whom Hagar the Egyptian had borne to Abraham[m] was mocking, [n] [10]and she said to Abraham, "Get rid of that slave woman and her son, for that slave woman's son will never share in the inheritance with my son Isaac." [o]

[11]The matter distressed Abraham greatly because it concerned his son. [p] [12]But God said to him, "Do not be so distressed about the boy and your maidservant. Listen to whatever Sarah tells you, because it is through Isaac that your offspring[c] will be reckoned. [q] [13]I will make the son of the maidservant into a nation[r] also, because he is your offspring."

[14]Early the next morning Abraham took some food and a skin of water and gave them to Hagar. He set them on her shoulders and then sent her off with the boy. She went on her way and wandered in the desert of Beersheba. [s]

[15]When the water in the skin was gone, she put the boy under one of the bushes. [16]Then she went off and sat down nearby, about a bowshot away, for she thought, "I cannot watch the boy die." And as she sat there nearby, she[d] began to sob.

20:14
b Ge 12:16
20:15
c Ge 13:9
20:17
d Job 42:9
20:18
e Ge 12:17
21:1
f 1Sa 2:21
g Ge 8:1; 17:16, 21; Gal 4:23
21:2
h Ge 17:19
i Gal 4:22; Heb 11:11
21:3
j Ge 17:19
21:4
k Ge 17:10,12; Ac 7:8
21:6
l Ge 17:17; Isa 54:1
21:9
m Ge 16:15
n Gal 4:29
21:10
o Gal 4:30*
21:11
p Ge 17:18
21:12
q Ro 9:7*; Heb 11:18*
21:13
r ver 18
21:14
s ver 31,32

---

a16 That is, about 25 pounds (about 11.5 kilograms)　　b3 *Isaac* means *he laughs*.　　c12 Or *seed*
d16 Hebrew; Septuagint *the child*

¹⁷God heard the boy crying,ᵗ and the angel of God called to Hagar from heaven and said to her, "What is the matter, Hagar? Do not be afraid; God has heard the boy crying as he lies there. ¹⁸Lift the boy up and take him by the hand, for I will make him into a great nation.ᵘ"

¹⁹Then God opened her eyesᵛ and she saw a well of water. So she went and filled the skin with water and gave the boy a drink.

²⁰God was with the boyʷ as he grew up. He lived in the desert and became an archer. ²¹While he was living in the Desert of Paran, his mother got a wife for himˣ from Egypt.

The Treaty at Beersheba

²²At that time Abimelech and Phicol the commander of his forces said to Abraham, "God is with you in everything you do. ²³Now swearʸ to me here before God that you will not deal falsely with me or my children or my descendants. Show to me and the country where you are living as an alien the same kindness I have shown to you."

²⁴Abraham said, "I swear it."

²⁵Then Abraham complained to Abimelech about a well of water that Abimelech's servants had seized.ᶻ ²⁶But Abimelech said, "I don't know who has done this. You did not tell me, and I heard about it only today."

²⁷So Abraham brought sheep and cattle and gave them to Abimelech, and the two men made a treaty.ᵃ ²⁸Abraham set apart seven ewe lambs from the flock, ²⁹and Abimelech asked Abraham, "What is the meaning of these seven ewe lambs you have set apart by themselves?"

³⁰He replied, "Accept these seven lambs from my hand as a witnessᵇ that I dug this well."

³¹So that place was called Beersheba,ᵃᶜ because the two men swore an oath there.

³²After the treaty had been made at Beersheba, Abimelech and Phicol the commander of his forces returned to the land of the Philistines. ³³Abraham planted a tamarisk tree in Beersheba, and there he called upon the name of the Lord,ᵈ the Eternal God.ᵉ ³⁴And Abraham stayed in the land of the Philistines for a long time.

Abraham Tested

22 Some time later God testedᶠ Abraham. He said to him, "Abraham!"

"Here I am," he replied.

²Then God said, "Take your son,ᵍ your only son, Isaac, whom you love, and go to the region of Moriah.ʰ Sacrifice him there as a burnt offering on one of the mountains I will tell you about."

³Early the next morning Abraham got up and saddled his donkey. He took with him two of his servants and his son Isaac. When he had cut enough wood for the burnt offering, he set out for the place God had told him about. ⁴On the third day Abraham looked up and saw the place in the distance. ⁵He said to his servants, "Stay here with the donkey while I and the boy go over there. We will worship and then we will come back to you."

⁶Abraham took the wood for the burnt offering and placed it on his

---

21:17
tEx 3:7
21:18
uver 13
21:19
vNu 22:31
21:20
wGe 26:3,24;
28:15;
39:2,21,23
21:21
xGe 24:4,38
21:23
yver 31;
Jos 2:12
21:25
zGe 26:15,18,
20-22
21:27
aGe 26:28,31
21:30
bGe 31:44,47,
48,50,52
21:31
cGe 26:33
21:33
dGe 4:26
eDt 33:27
22:1
fDt 8:2,16;
Heb 11:17;
Jas 1:12-13
22:2
gver 12,16;
Jn 3:16;
Heb 11:17;
1Jn 4:9
h2Ch 3:1

ᵃ31 *Beersheba* can mean *well of seven* or *well of the oath*.

son Isaac,[i] and he himself carried the fire and the knife. As the two of them went on together, [7]Isaac spoke up and said to his father Abraham, "Father?"

"Yes, my son?" Abraham replied.

"The fire and wood are here," Isaac said, "but where is the lamb[j] for the burnt offering?"

[8]Abraham answered, "God himself will provide the lamb for the burnt offering, my son." And the two of them went on together.

[9]When they reached the place God had told him about, Abraham built an altar there and arranged the wood on it. He bound his son Isaac and laid him on the altar,[k] on top of the wood. [10]Then he reached out his hand and took the knife to slay his son. [11]But the angel of the LORD called out to him from heaven, "Abraham! Abraham!"

"Here I am," he replied.

[12]"Do not lay a hand on the boy," he said. "Do not do anything to him. Now I know that you fear God,[l] because you have not withheld from me your son, your only son.[m]"

[13]Abraham looked up and there in a thicket he saw a ram[a] caught by its horns. He went over and took the ram and sacrificed it as a burnt offering instead of his son.[n] [14]So Abraham called that place The LORD Will Provide. And to this day it is said, "On the mountain of the LORD it will be provided.[o]"

[15]The angel of the LORD called to Abraham from heaven a second time [16]and said, "I swear by myself,[p] declares the LORD, that because you have done this and have not withheld your son, your only son, [17]I will surely bless you and make your descendants[q] as numerous as the stars in the sky[r] and as the sand on the seashore.[s] Your descendants will take possession of the cities of their enemies,[t] [18]and through your offspring[b] all nations on earth will be blessed,[u] because you have obeyed me."[v]

[19]Then Abraham returned to his servants, and they set off together for Beersheba. And Abraham stayed in Beersheba.

Nahor's Sons

[20]Some time later Abraham was told, "Milcah is also a mother; she has borne sons to your brother Nahor:[w] [21]Uz the firstborn, Buz his brother, Kemuel (the father of Aram), [22]Kesed, Hazo, Pildash, Jidlaph and Bethuel." [23]Bethuel became the father of Rebekah.[x] Milcah bore these eight sons to Abraham's brother Nahor. [24]His concubine, whose name was Reumah, also had sons: Tebah, Gaham, Tahash and Maacah.

The Death of Sarah

23 Sarah lived to be a hundred and twenty-seven years old. [2]She died at Kiriath Arba[y] (that is, Hebron)[z] in the land of Canaan, and Abraham went to mourn for Sarah and to weep over her.

[3]Then Abraham rose from beside his dead wife and spoke to the

---

22:6
iJn 19:17
22:7
jLev 1:10
22:9
kHeb 11:17-19;
Jas 2:21
22:12
lISa 15:22;
Jas 2:21-22
mver 2; Jn 3:16
22:13
nRo 8:32
22:14
over 8
22:16
pLk 1:73;
Heb 6:13
22:17
qHeb 6:14*
rGe 15:5
sGe 26:24;
32:12 tGe 24:60
22:18
uGe 12:2,3;
Ac 3:25*;
Gal 3:8* vver 10
22:20
wGe 11:29
22:23
xGe 24:15
23:2
yJos 14:15
zver 19;
Ge 13:18

---

[a]13 Many manuscripts of the Masoretic Text, Samaritan Pentateuch, Septuagint and Syriac; most manuscripts of the Masoretic Text *a ram behind him*   [b]18 Or *seed*

Hittites.ª He said, ⁴"I am an alien and a strangerª among you. Sell me some property for a burial site here so I can bury my dead."

⁵The Hittites replied to Abraham, ⁶"Sir, listen to us. You are a mighty princeᵇ among us. Bury your dead in the choicest of our tombs. None of us will refuse you his tomb for burying your dead."

⁷Then Abraham rose and bowed down before the people of the land, the Hittites. ⁸He said to them, "If you are willing to let me bury my dead, then listen to me and intercede with Ephron son of Zoharᶜ on my behalf ⁹so he will sell me the cave of Machpelah, which belongs to him and is at the end of his field. Ask him to sell it to me for the full price as a burial site among you."

¹⁰Ephron the Hittite was sitting among his people and he replied to Abraham in the hearing of all the Hittites who had come to the gateᵈ of his city. ¹¹"No, my lord," he said. "Listen to me; I giveᵇᵉ you the field, and I giveᵇ you the cave that is in it. I giveᵇ it to you in the presence of my people. Bury your dead."

¹²Again Abraham bowed down before the people of the land ¹³and he said to Ephron in their hearing, "Listen to me, if you will. I will pay the price of the field. Accept it from me so I can bury my dead there."

¹⁴Ephron answered Abraham, ¹⁵"Listen to me, my lord; the land is worth four hundred shekelsᶜ of silver,ᶠ but what is that between me and you? Bury your dead."

¹⁶Abraham agreed to Ephron's terms and weighed out for him the price he had named in the hearing of the Hittites: four hundred shekels of silver,ᵍ according to the weight current among the merchants.

¹⁷So Ephron's field in Machpelah near Mamreʰ—both the field and the cave in it, and all the trees within the borders of the field—was deeded ¹⁸to Abraham as his property in the presence of all the Hittites who had come to the gate of the city. ¹⁹Afterward Abraham buried his wife Sarah in the cave in the field of Machpelah near Mamre (which is at Hebron) in the land of Canaan. ²⁰So the field and the cave in it were deededⁱ to Abraham by the Hittites as a burial site.

Isaac and Rebekah

24 Abraham was now old and well advanced in years, and the LORD had blessed him in every way.ʲ ²He said to the chiefᵈ servant in his household, the one in charge of all that he had,ᵏ "Put your hand under my thigh.ˡ ³I want you to swear by the LORD, the God of heaven and the God of earth,ᵐ that you will not get a wife for my sonⁿ from the daughters of the Canaanites,ᵒ among whom I am living, ⁴but will go to my country and my own relativesᵖ and get a wife for my son Isaac."

⁵The servant asked him, "What if the woman is unwilling to come back with me to this land? Shall I then take your son back to the country you came from?"

⁶"Make sure that you do not take my son back there," Abraham said. ⁷"The LORD, the God of heaven, who brought me out of my father's household and my native land and who spoke to me and promised me on oath, saying, 'To your offspringᵉq I will give this land'ʳ—he will send his angel before youˢ so that you can get a wife for my son from

23:4
ªGe 17:8;
1Ch 29:15;
Ps 105:12;
Heb 11:9,13
23:6
ᵇGe 14:14-16;
24:35
23:8
ᶜGe 25:9
23:10
ᵈGe 34:20-24;
Ru 4:4
23:11
ᵉ2Sa 24:23
23:15
ᶠEze 45:12
23:16
ᵍJer 32:9;
Zec 11:12
23:17
ʰGe 25:9;
49:30-32;
50:13; Ac 7:16
23:20
ⁱJer 32:10
24:1
ʲver 35
24:2
ᵏGe 39:4-6
ˡver 9; Ge 47:29
24:3
ᵐGe 14:19
ⁿGe 28:1;
Dt 7:3
ᵒGe 10:15-19
24:4
ᵖGe 12:1; 28:2
24:7
qGal 3:16ª
ʳGe 12:7; 13:15
ˢEx 23:20,23

ª3 Or *the sons of Heth*; also in verses 5, 7, 10, 16, 18 and 20   ᵇ11 Or *sell*   ᶜ15 That is, about 10 pounds (about 4.5 kilograms)   ᵈ2 Or *oldest*   ᵉ7 Or *seed* there. [8]If the woman is unwilling to come back with you, then you will be released from this oath of mine. Only do not take my son back there." [9]So the servant put his hand under the thigh[t] of his master Abraham and swore an oath to him concerning this matter.

[10]Then the servant took ten of his master's camels and left, taking with him all kinds of good things from his master. He set out for Aram Naharaim[a] and made his way to the town of Nahor. [11]He had the camels kneel down near the well[u] outside the town; it was toward evening, the time the women go out to draw water.[v]

[12]Then he prayed, "O LORD, God of my master Abraham,[w] give me success today, and show kindness to my master Abraham. [13]See, I am standing beside this spring, and the daughters of the townspeople are coming out to draw water. [14]May it be that when I say to a girl, 'Please let down your jar that I may have a drink,' and she says, 'Drink, and I'll water your camels too'—let her be the one you have chosen for your servant Isaac. By this I will know[x] that you have shown kindness to my master."

[15]Before he had finished praying,[y] Rebekah[z] came out with her jar on her shoulder. She was the daughter of Bethuel son of Milcah,[a] who was the wife of Abraham's brother Nahor. [b] [16]The girl was very beautiful,[c] a virgin; no man had ever lain with her. She went down to the spring, filled her jar and came up again.

[17]The servant hurried to meet her and said, "Please give me a little water from your jar."

[18]"Drink,[d] my lord," she said, and quickly lowered the jar to her hands and gave him a drink.

[19]After she had given him a drink, she said, "I'll draw water for your camels too,[e] until they have finished drinking." [20]So she quickly emptied her jar into the trough, ran back to the well to draw more water, and drew enough for all his camels. [21]Without saying a word, the man watched her closely to learn whether or not the LORD had made his journey successful. [f]

[22]When the camels had finished drinking, the man took out a gold nose ring[g] weighing a beka[b] and two gold bracelets weighing ten shekels.[c] [23]Then he asked, "Whose daughter are you? Please tell me, is there room in your father's house for us to spend the night?"

[24]She answered him, "I am the daughter of Bethuel, the son that Milcah bore to Nahor.[h]" [25]And she added, "We have plenty of straw and fodder, as well as room for you to spend the night."

[26]Then the man bowed down and worshiped the LORD,[i] [27]saying, "Praise be to the LORD,[j] the God of my master Abraham, who has not abandoned his kindness and faithfulness[k] to my master. As for me, the LORD has led me on the journey[l] to the house of my master's relatives."[m]

[28]The girl ran and told her mother's household about these things. [29]Now Rebekah had a brother named Laban,[n] and he hurried out to the man at the spring. [30]As soon as he had seen the nose ring, and the bracelets on his sister's arms, and had heard Rebekah tell what the man said to her, he went out to the man and found him standing by the

24:9
t ver 2
24:11
u Ex 2:15
v ver 13;
1Sa 9:11
24:12
w ver 27,42,48;
Ge 26:24;
Ex 3:6,15,16
24:14
x Jdg 6:17,37
24:15
y ver 45
z Ge 22:23
a Ge 22:20
b Ge 11:29
24:16
c Ge 26:7
24:18
d ver 14
24:19
e ver 14
24:21
f ver 12
24:22
g ver 47
24:24
h ver 15
24:26
i ver 48,52;
Ex 4:31
24:27
j Ex 18:10;
Ru 4:14;
1Sa 25:32
k ver 49;
Ge 32:10;
Ps 98:3 l ver 21
m ver 12,48
24:29
n ver 4;
Ge 29:5,12,13

---

[a]10 That is, Northwest Mesopotamia   [b]22 That is, about 1/5 ounce (about 5.5 grams)
[c]22 That is, about 4 ounces (about 110 grams)

camels near the spring. [31]"Come, you who are blessed by the LORD,"[o] he said. "Why are you standing out here? I have prepared the house and a place for the camels."

[32]So the man went to the house, and the camels were unloaded. Straw and fodder were brought for the camels, and water for him and his men to wash their feet.[p] [33]Then food was set before him, but he said, "I will not eat until I have told you what I have to say."

"Then tell us," Laban said.

[34]So he said, "I am Abraham's servant. [35]The LORD has blessed my master abundantly,[q] and he has become wealthy. He has given him sheep and cattle, silver and gold, menservants and maidservants, and camels and donkeys.[r] [36]My master's wife Sarah has borne him a son in her[a] old age,[s] and he has given him everything he owns.[t] [37]And my master made me swear an oath, and said, 'You must not get a wife for my son from the daughters of the Canaanites, in whose land I live,[u] [38]but go to my father's family and to my own clan, and get a wife for my son.'[v]

[39]"Then I asked my master, 'What if the woman will not come back with me?'[w]

[40]"He replied, 'The LORD, before whom I have walked, will send his angel with you[x] and make your journey a success, so that you can get a wife for my son from my own clan and from my father's family. [41]Then, when you go to my clan, you will be released from my oath even if they refuse to give her to you—you will be released from my oath.'[y]

[42]"When I came to the spring today, I said, 'O LORD, God of my master Abraham, if you will, please grant success[z] to the journey on which I have come. [43]See, I am standing beside this spring;[a] if a maiden comes out to draw water and I say to her, "Please let me drink a little water from your jar,"[b] [44]and if she says to me, "Drink, and I'll draw water for your camels too," let her be the one the LORD has chosen for my master's son.'

[45]"Before I finished praying in my heart,[c] Rebekah came out, with her jar on her shoulder.[d] She went down to the spring and drew water, and I said to her, 'Please give me a drink.'[e]

[46]"She quickly lowered her jar from her shoulder and said, 'Drink, and I'll water your camels too.'[f] So I drank, and she watered the camels also.

[47]"I asked her, 'Whose daughter are you?'[g]

"She said, 'The daughter of Bethuel son of Nahor, whom Milcah bore to him.'[h]

"Then I put the ring in her nose and the bracelets on her arms,[i] [48]and I bowed down and worshiped the LORD.[j] I praised the LORD, the God of my master Abraham, who had led me on the right road to get the granddaughter of my master's brother for his son.[k] [49]Now if you will show kindness and faithfulness[l] to my master, tell me; and if not, tell me, so I may know which way to turn."

[50]Laban and Bethuel answered, "This is from the LORD;[m] we can say nothing to you one way or the other.[n] [51]Here is Rebekah; take her and

24:31
o Ge 26:29;
Ru 3:10;
Ps 115:15
24:32
p Ge 43:24;
Jdg 19:21
24:35
q ver 1 r Ge 13:2
24:36
s Ge 21:2,10
t Ge 25:5
24:37
u ver 3
24:38
v ver 4
24:39
w ver 5
24:40
x ver 7
24:41
y ver 8
24:42
z ver 12
24:43
a ver 13 b ver 14
24:45
c 1Sa 1:13
d ver 15 e ver 17
24:46
f ver 18-19
24:47
g ver 23 h ver 24
i Eze 16:11-12
24:48
j ver 26 k ver 27
24:49
l Ge 47:29;
Jos 2:14
24:50
m Ps 118:23
n Ge 31:7,24
29,42

go, and let her become the wife of your master's son, as the LORD has directed."

⁵²When Abraham's servant heard what they said, he bowed down to the ground before the LORD. ° ⁵³Then the servant brought out gold and silver jewelry and articles of clothing and gave them to Rebekah; he also gave costly giftsᴾ to her brother and to her mother. ⁵⁴Then he and the men who were with him ate and drank and spent the night there.

When they got up the next morning, he said, "Send me on my way�q to my master."

⁵⁵But her brother and her mother replied, "Let the girl remain with us ten days or so; then youª may go."

⁵⁶But he said to them, "Do not detain me, now that the LORD has granted success to my journey. Send me on my way so I may go to my master."

⁵⁷Then they said, "Let's call the girl and ask her about it." ⁵⁸So they called Rebekah and asked her, "Will you go with this man?"

"I will go," she said.

⁵⁹So they sent their sister Rebekah on her way, along with her nurseʳ and Abraham's servant and his men. ⁶⁰And they blessed Rebekah and said to her,

> "Our sister, may you increase
>   to thousands upon thousands;ˢ
> may your offspring possess
>   the gates of their enemies."ᵗ

⁶¹Then Rebekah and her maids got ready and mounted their camels and went back with the man. So the servant took Rebekah and left.

⁶²Now Isaac had come from Beer Lahai Roi, ᵘ for he was living in the Negev. ᵛ ⁶³He went out to the field one evening to meditate,ᵇʷ and as he looked up, he saw camels approaching. ⁶⁴Rebekah also looked up and saw Isaac. She got down from her camel ⁶⁵and asked the servant, "Who is that man in the field coming to meet us?"

"He is my master," the servant answered. So she took her veil and covered herself.

⁶⁶Then the servant told Isaac all he had done. ⁶⁷Isaac brought her into the tent of his mother Sarah, and he married Rebekah.ˣ So she became his wife, and he loved her;ʸ and Isaac was comforted after his mother's death.ᶻ

The Death of Abraham
25:1–4pp — 1Ch 1:32–33

25 Abraham tookᶜ another wife, whose name was Keturah. ²She bore him Zimran, Jokshan, Medan, Midian, Ishbak and Shuah. ª ³Jokshan was the father of Sheba and Dedan; the descendants of Dedan were the Asshurites, the Letushites and the Leummites. ⁴The sons of Midian were Ephah, Epher, Hanoch, Abida and Eldaah. All these were descendants of Keturah.

⁵Abraham left everything he owned to Isaac. ᵇ ⁶But while he was still living, he gave gifts to the sons of his concubinesᶜ and sent them away from his son Isaacᵈ to the land of the east.

ª55 Or *she*   ᵇ63 The meaning of the Hebrew for this word is uncertain.   ᶜ1 Or *had taken*

24:52
o ver 26
24:53
p ver 10,22
24:54
q ver 56,59
24:59
r Ge 35:8
24:60
s Ge 17:16
t Ge 22:17
24:62
u Ge 16:14;
25:11 v Ge 20:1
24:63
w Ps 1:2; 77:12;
119:15,27,48,97,
148; 143:5;
145:5
24:67
x Ge 25:20
y Ge 29:18,20
z Ge 23:1-2
25:2
a 1Ch 1:32,33
25:5
b Ge 24:36
25:6
c Ge 22:24
d Ge 21:10,14

[7]Altogether, Abraham lived a hundred and seventy-five years. [8]Then Abraham breathed his last and died at a good old age,[e] an old man and full of years; and he was gathered to his people.[f] [9]His sons Isaac and Ishmael buried him[g] in the cave of Machpelah near Mamre, in the field of Ephron son of Zohar the Hittite,[h] [10]the field Abraham had bought from the Hittites.[a][i] There Abraham was buried with his wife Sarah. [11]After Abraham's death, God blessed his son Isaac, who then lived near Beer Lahai Roi.[j]

Ishmael's Sons

25:12–16pp — 1Ch 1:29–31

[12]This is the account of Abraham's son Ishmael, whom Sarah's maidservant, Hagar[k] the Egyptian, bore to Abraham.[l]

[13]These are the names of the sons of Ishmael, listed in the order of their birth: Nebaioth the firstborn of Ishmael, Kedar, Adbeel, Mibsam, [14]Mishma, Dumah, Massa, [15]Hadad, Tema, Jetur, Naphish and Kedemah. [16]These were the sons of Ishmael, and these are the names of the twelve tribal rulers[m] according to their settlements and camps. [17]Altogether, Ishmael lived a hundred and thirty-seven years. He breathed his last and died, and he was gathered to his people.[n] [18]His descendants settled in the area from Havilah to Shur, near the border of Egypt, as you go toward Asshur. And they lived in hostility toward[b] all their brothers.[o]

Jacob and Esau

[19]This is the account of Abraham's son Isaac.

Abraham became the father of Isaac, [20]and Isaac was forty years old[p] when he married Rebekah[q] daughter of Bethuel the Aramean from Paddan Aram[c] and sister of Laban[r] the Aramean.

[21]Isaac prayed to the LORD on behalf of his wife, because she was barren. The LORD answered his prayer,[s] and his wife Rebekah became pregnant. [22]The babies jostled each other within her, and she said, "Why is this happening to me?" So she went to inquire of the LORD.[t]

[23]The LORD said to her,

"Two nations[u] are in your womb,
    and two peoples from within you will be separated;
one people will be stronger than the other,
    and the older will serve the younger.[v]"

[24]When the time came for her to give birth, there were twin boys in her womb. [25]The first to come out was red, and his whole body was like a hairy garment;[w] so they named him Esau.[d] [26]After this, his brother came out, with his hand grasping Esau's heel;[x] so he was named Jacob.[e][y] Isaac was sixty years old when Rebekah gave birth to them.

[27]The boys grew up, and Esau became a skillful hunter, a man of the open country,[z] while Jacob was a quiet man, staying among the tents.

25:8
[e]Ge 15:15
[f]ver 17;
Ge 35:29;
49:29,33
25:9
[g]Ge 35:29
[h]Ge 50:13
25:10
[i]Ge 23:16
25:11
[j]Ge 16:14
25:12
[k]Ge 16:1
[l]Ge 16:15
25:16
[m]Ge 17:20
25:17
[n]ver 8
25:18
[o]Ge 16:12
25:20
[p]ver 26;
Ge 26:34
[q]Ge 24:67
[r]Ge 24:29
25:21
[s]1Ch 5:20;
2Ch 33:13;
Ezr 8:23;
Ps 127:3;
Ro 9:10
25:22
[t]1Sa 9:9; 10:22
25:23
[u]Ge 17:4
[v]Ge 27:29,40;
Mal 1:3;
Ro 9:11-12*
25:25
[w]Ge 27:11
25:26
[x]Hos 12:3
[y]Ge 27:36
25:27
[z]Ge 27:3,5

---

[a]10 Or *the sons of Heth*   [b]18 Or *lived to the east of*   [c]20 That is, Northwest Mesopotamia   [d]25 *Esau* may mean *hairy*; he was also called Edom, which means *red.*   [e]26 *Jacob* means *he grasps the heel* (figuratively, *he deceives*).

²⁸Isaac, who had a taste for wild game,ᵃ loved Esau, but Rebekah loved Jacob.ᵇ

²⁹Once when Jacob was cooking some stew, Esau came in from the open country, famished. ³⁰He said to Jacob, "Quick, let me have some of that red stew! I'm famished!" (That is why he was also called Edom.ᵃ)

³¹Jacob replied, "First sell me your birthright."

³²"Look, I am about to die," Esau said. "What good is the birthright to me?"

³³But Jacob said, "Swear to me first." So he swore an oath to him, selling his birthrightᶜ to Jacob.

³⁴Then Jacob gave Esau some bread and some lentil stew. He ate and drank, and then got up and left.

So Esau despised his birthright.

Isaac and Abimelech

26:1–11Ref — Ge 12:10–20; 20:1–18

26 Now there was a famine in the landᵈ—besides the earlier famine of Abraham's time—and Isaac went to Abimelech king of the Philistines in Gerar.ᵉ ²The Lᴏʀᴅ appearedᶠ to Isaac and said, "Do not go down to Egypt; live in the land where I tell you to live.ᵍ ³Stay in this land for a while,ʰ and I will be with you and will bless you.ⁱ For to you and your descendants I will give all these landsʲ and will confirm the oath I swore to your father Abraham. ⁴I will make your descendants as numerous as the stars in the skyᵏ and will give them all these lands, and through your offspringᵇ all nations on earth will be blessed,ˡ ⁵because Abraham obeyed meᵐ and kept my requirements, my commands, my decrees and my laws." ⁶So Isaac stayed in Gerar.

⁷When the men of that place asked him about his wife, he said, "She is my sister,ⁿ" because he was afraid to say, "She is my wife." He thought, "The men of this place might kill me on account of Rebekah, because she is beautiful."

⁸When Isaac had been there a long time, Abimelech king of the Philistines looked down from a window and saw Isaac caressing his wife Rebekah. ⁹So Abimelech summoned Isaac and said, "She is really your wife! Why did you say, 'She is my sister'?"

Isaac answered him, "Because I thought I might lose my life on account of her."

¹⁰Then Abimelech said, "What is this you have done to us?ᵒ One of the men might well have slept with your wife, and you would have brought guilt upon us."

¹¹So Abimelech gave orders to all the people: "Anyone who molestsᵖ this man or his wife shall surely be put to death."

¹²Isaac planted crops in that land and the same year reaped a hundredfold, because the Lᴏʀᴅ blessed him.�q ¹³The man became rich, and his wealth continued to grow until he became very wealthy.ʳ ¹⁴He had so many flocks and herds and servantsˢ that the Philistines envied him.ᵗ ¹⁵So all the wellsᵘ that his father's servants had dug in the time of his father Abraham, the Philistines stopped up,ᵛ filling them with earth.

ᵃ30 *Edom* means *red.*   ᵇ4 Or *seed*

25:28
aGe 27:19
bGe 27:6
25:33
cGe 27:36;
Heb 12:16
26:1
dGe 12:10
eGe 20:1
26:2
fGe 12:7; 17:1;
18:1 gGe 12:1
26:3
hGe 20:1; 28:15
iGe 12:2;
22:16-18
jGe 12:7;
13:15; 15:18
26:4
kGe 15:5;
22:17; Ex 32:13
lGe 12:3;
22:18; Gal 3:8
26:5
mGe 22:16
26:7
nGe 12:13;
20:2,12;
Pr 29:25
26:10
oGe 20:9
26:11
pPs 105:15
26:12
qver 3;
Job 42:12
26:13
rPr 10:22
26:14
sGe 24:36
tGe 37:11
26:15
uGe 21:30
vGe 21:25

¹⁶Then Abimelech said to Isaac, "Move away from us; you have become too powerful for us. ^w"

¹⁷So Isaac moved away from there and encamped in the Valley of Gerar and settled there. ¹⁸Isaac reopened the wells^x that had been dug in the time of his father Abraham, which the Philistines had stopped up after Abraham died, and he gave them the same names his father had given them.

¹⁹Isaac's servants dug in the valley and discovered a well of fresh water there. ²⁰But the herdsmen of Gerar quarreled with Isaac's herdsmen and said, "The water is ours!"^y So he named the well Esek,^a because they disputed with him. ²¹Then they dug another well, but they quarreled over that one also; so he named it Sitnah.^b ²²He moved on from there and dug another well, and no one quarreled over it. He named it Rehoboth,^c saying, "Now the LORD has given us room and we will flourish^z in the land."

²³From there he went up to Beersheba. ²⁴That night the LORD appeared to him and said, "I am the God of your father Abraham.^a Do not be afraid,^b for I am with you; I will bless you and will increase the number of your descendants^c for the sake of my servant Abraham."^d

²⁵Isaac built an altar^e there and called on the name of the LORD. There he pitched his tent, and there his servants dug a well.

²⁶Meanwhile, Abimelech had come to him from Gerar, with Ahuzzath his personal adviser and Phicol the commander of his forces.^f ²⁷Isaac asked them, "Why have you come to me, since you were hostile to me and sent me away?^g"

²⁸They answered, "We saw clearly that the LORD was with you;^h so we said, 'There ought to be a sworn agreement between us'—between us and you. Let us make a treaty with you ²⁹that you will do us no harm, just as we did not molest you but always treated you well and sent you away in peace. And now you are blessed by the LORD."ⁱ

³⁰Isaac then made a feast^j for them, and they ate and drank. ³¹Early the next morning the men swore an oath^k to each other. Then Isaac sent them on their way, and they left him in peace.

³²That day Isaac's servants came and told him about the well they had dug. They said, "We've found water!" ³³He called it Shibah,^d and to this day the name of the town has been Beersheba.^e ^l

³⁴When Esau was forty years old,^m he married Judith daughter of Beeri the Hittite, and also Basemath daughter of Elon the Hittite.ⁿ ³⁵They were a source of grief to Isaac and Rebekah.^o

Jacob Gets Isaac's Blessing

27 When Isaac was old and his eyes were so weak that he could no longer see,^p he called for Esau his older son^q and said to him, "My son."

"Here I am," he answered.

²Isaac said, "I am now an old man and don't know the day of my death.^r ³Now then, get your weapons—your quiver and bow—and go out to the open country^s to hunt some wild game for me. ⁴Prepare me

26:16
wEx 1:9
26:18
xGe 21:30
26:20
yGe 21:25
26:22
zGe 17:6;
Ex 1:7
26:24
aGe 24:12;
Ex 3:6 bGe 15:1
cver 4 dGe 17:7
26:25
eGe 12:7,8;
13:4,18;
Ps 116:17
26:26
fGe 21:22
26:27
gver 16
26:28
hGe 21:22
26:29
iGe 24:31;
Ps 115:15
26:30
jGe 19:3
26:31
kGe 21:31
26:33
lGe 21:14
26:34
mGe 25:20
nGe 28:9; 36:2
26:35
oGe 27:46
27:1
pGe 48:10;
1Sa 3:2
qGe 25:25
27:2
rGe 47:29
27:3
sGe 25:27

---

^a20 *Esek* means *dispute.*   ^b21 *Sitnah* means *opposition.*   ^c22 *Rehoboth* means *room.*
^d33 *Shibah* can mean *oath* or *seven.*   ^e33 *Beersheba* can mean *well of the oath* or *well of seven.*

the kind of tasty food I like and bring it to me to eat, so that I may give you my blessing[t] before I die."

[5]Now Rebekah was listening as Isaac spoke to his son Esau. When Esau left for the open country to hunt game and bring it back, [6]Rebekah said to her son Jacob,[u] "Look, I overheard your father say to your brother Esau, [7]'Bring me some game and prepare me some tasty food to eat, so that I may give you my blessing in the presence of the LORD before I die.' [8]Now, my son, listen carefully and do what I tell you:[v] [9]Go out to the flock and bring me two choice young goats, so I can prepare some tasty food for your father, just the way he likes it. [10]Then take it to your father to eat, so that he may give you his blessing before he dies."

[11]Jacob said to Rebekah his mother, "But my brother Esau is a hairy man,[w] and I'm a man with smooth skin. [12]What if my father touches me?[x] I would appear to be tricking him and would bring down a curse on myself rather than a blessing."

[13]His mother said to him, "My son, let the curse fall on me.[y] Just do what I say;[z] go and get them for me."

[14]So he went and got them and brought them to his mother, and she prepared some tasty food, just the way his father liked it. [15]Then Rebekah took the best clothes[a] of Esau her older son, which she had in the house, and put them on her younger son Jacob. [16]She also covered his hands and the smooth part of his neck with the goatskins. [17]Then she handed to her son Jacob the tasty food and the bread she had made.

[18]He went to his father and said, "My father."

"Yes, my son," he answered. "Who is it?"

[19]Jacob said to his father, "I am Esau your firstborn. I have done as you told me. Please sit up and eat some of my game so that you may give me your blessing."[b]

[20]Isaac asked his son, "How did you find it so quickly, my son?"

"The LORD your God gave me success,[c]" he replied.

[21]Then Isaac said to Jacob, "Come near so I can touch you,[d] my son, to know whether you really are my son Esau or not."

[22]Jacob went close to his father Isaac, who touched him and said, "The voice is the voice of Jacob, but the hands are the hands of Esau." [23]He did not recognize him, for his hands were hairy like those of his brother Esau;[e] so he blessed him. [24]"Are you really my son Esau?" he asked.

"I am," he replied.

[25]Then he said, "My son, bring me some of your game to eat, so that I may give you my blessing."[f]

Jacob brought it to him and he ate; and he brought some wine and he drank. [26]Then his father Isaac said to him, "Come here, my son, and kiss me."

[27]So he went to him and kissed him[g]. When Isaac caught the smell of his clothes,[h] he blessed him and said,

> "Ah, the smell of my son
>   is like the smell of a field
>   that the LORD has blessed.[i]
> [28]May God give you of heaven's dew[j]
>   and of earth's richness[k]—
>   an abundance of grain and new wine.[l]

27:4
tver 10,25,31;
Ge 49:28;
Dt 33:1;
Heb 11:20
27:6
uGe 25:28
27:8
vver 13,43
27:11
wGe 25:25
27:12
xver 22
27:13
yMt 27:25
zver 8
27:15
aver 27
27:19
bver 4
27:20
cGe 24:12
27:21
dver 12
27:23
ever 16
27:25
fver 4
27:27
gHeb 11:20
hSS 4:11
iPs 65:9-13
27:28
jDt 33:13
kver 39
lGe 45:18;
Nu 18:12;
Dt 33:28

²⁹May nations serve you
    and peoples bow down to you. ^m
Be lord over your brothers,
    and may the sons of your mother bow down to you. ⁿ
May those who curse you be cursed
    and those who bless you be blessed. ^o"

³⁰After Isaac finished blessing him and Jacob had scarcely left his father's presence, his brother Esau came in from hunting. ³¹He too prepared some tasty food and brought it to his father. Then he said to him, "My father, sit up and eat some of my game, so that you may give me your blessing."^p

³²His father Isaac asked him, "Who are you?"^q

"I am your son," he answered, "your firstborn, Esau."

³³Isaac trembled violently and said, "Who was it, then, that hunted game and brought it to me? I ate it just before you came and I blessed him—and indeed he will be blessed!^r"

³⁴When Esau heard his father's words, he burst out with a loud and bitter cry^s and said to his father, "Bless me—me too, my father!"

³⁵But he said, "Your brother came deceitfully^t and took your blessing."

³⁶Esau said, "Isn't he rightly named Jacob^a?^u He has deceived me these two times: He took my birthright,^v and now he's taken my blessing!" Then he asked, "Haven't you reserved any blessing for me?"

³⁷Isaac answered Esau, "I have made him lord over you and have made all his relatives his servants, and I have sustained him with grain and new wine.^w So what can I possibly do for you, my son?"

³⁸Esau said to his father, "Do you have only one blessing, my father? Bless me too, my father!" Then Esau wept aloud.^x

³⁹His father Isaac answered him,

"Your dwelling will be
    away from the earth's richness,
    away from the dew^y of heaven above.
⁴⁰You will live by the sword
    and you will serve^z your brother.^a
But when you grow restless,
    you will throw his yoke
    from off your neck.^b"

Jacob Flees to Laban

⁴¹Esau held a grudge^c against Jacob^d because of the blessing his father had given him. He said to himself, "The days of mourning^e for my father are near; then I will kill my brother Jacob."^f

⁴²When Rebekah was told what her older son Esau had said, she sent for her younger son Jacob and said to him, "Your brother Esau is consoling himself with the thought of killing you. ⁴³Now then, my son, do what I say:^g Flee at once to my brother Laban^h in Haran.ⁱ ⁴⁴Stay with him for a while^j until your brother's fury subsides. ⁴⁵When your brother is no longer angry with you and forgets what you did to him,^k

---

^a36 *Jacob* means *he grasps the heel* (figuratively, *he deceives*).

27:29
m Isa 45:14,23;
49:7,23
n Ge 9:25;
25:23; 37:7
o Ge 12:3;
Nu 24:9;
Zep 2:8
27:31
p ver 4
27:32
q ver 18
27:33
r ver 29;
Ge 28:3,4;
Ro 11:29
27:34
s Heb 12:17
27:35
t Jer 9:4; 12:6
27:36
u Ge 25:26
v Ge 25:33
27:37
w ver 28
27:38
x Heb 12:17
27:39
y ver 28
27:40
z 2Sa 8:14
a Ge 25:23
b 2Ki 8:20-22
27:41
c Ge 37:4
d Ge 32:11
e Ge 50:4,10
f Ob 1:10
27:43
g ver 8
h Ge 24:29
i Ge 11:31
27:44
j Ge 31:38,41
27:45
k ver 35

I'll send word for you to come back from there. Why should I lose both of you in one day?"

46Then Rebekah said to Isaac, "I'm disgusted with living because of these Hittite women. If Jacob takes a wife from among the women of this land, from Hittite women like these, my life will not be worth living."[1]

28 So Isaac called for Jacob and blessed[a] him and commanded him: "Do not marry a Canaanite woman.[m] 2Go at once to Paddan Aram,[b] to the house of your mother's father Bethuel.[n] Take a wife for yourself there, from among the daughters of Laban, your mother's brother. 3May God Almighty[c][o] bless you and make you fruitful[p] and increase your numbers until you become a community of peoples. 4May he give you and your descendants the blessing given to Abraham,[q] so that you may take possession of the land where you now live as an alien,[r] the land God gave to Abraham." 5Then Isaac sent Jacob on his way, and he went to Paddan Aram,[s] to Laban son of Bethuel the Aramean, the brother of Rebekah,[t] who was the mother of Jacob and Esau.

6Now Esau learned that Isaac had blessed Jacob and had sent him to Paddan Aram to take a wife from there, and that when he blessed him he commanded him, "Do not marry a Canaanite woman,"[u] 7and that Jacob had obeyed his father and mother and had gone to Paddan Aram. 8Esau then realized how displeasing the Canaanite women[v] were to his father Isaac;[w] 9so he went to Ishmael and married Mahalath, the sister of Nebaioth[x] and daughter of Ishmael son of Abraham, in addition to the wives he already had.[y]

Jacob's Dream at Bethel

10Jacob left Beersheba and set out for Haran.[z] 11When he reached a certain place, he stopped for the night because the sun had set. Taking one of the stones there, he put it under his head and lay down to sleep. 12He had a dream[a] in which he saw a stairway[d] resting on the earth, with its top reaching to heaven, and the angels of God were ascending and descending on it.[b] 13There above it[e] stood the LORD,[c] and he said: "I am the LORD, the God of your father Abraham and the God of Isaac.[d] I will give you and your descendants the land[e] on which you are lying. 14Your descendants will be like the dust of the earth, and you[f] will spread out to the west and to the east, to the north and to the south.[g] All peoples on earth will be blessed through you and your offspring.[h] 15I am with you[i] and will watch over you[j] wherever you go, and I will bring you back to this land. I will not leave you[k] until I have done what I have promised you."[l]

16When Jacob awoke from his sleep, he thought, "Surely the LORD is in this place, and I was not aware of it." 17He was afraid and said, "How awesome is this place![m] This is none other than the house of God; this is the gate of heaven."

18Early the next morning Jacob took the stone he had placed under his head and set it up as a pillar[n] and poured oil on top of it.[o] 19He called that place Bethel,[f] though the city used to be called Luz.[p]

27:46
lGe 26:35
28:1
mGe 24:3
28:2
nGe 25:20
28:3
oGe 17:1
pGe 17:6
28:4
qGe 12:2,3
rGe 17:8
28:5
sHos 12:12
tGe 24:29
28:6
uver 1
28:8
vGe 24:3
wGe 26:35
28:9
xGe 25:13
yGe 26:34
28:10
zGe 11:31
28:12
aGe 20:3
bJn 1:51
28:13
cGe 12:7; 35:7, 9; 48:3
dGe 26:24
eGe 13:15; 35:12
28:14
fGe 26:4
gGe 13:14
hGe 12:3; 18:18; 22:18; Gal 3:8
28:15
iGe 26:3; 48:21
jNu 6:24; Ps 121:5,7-8
kDt 31:6,8
lNu 23:19
28:17
mEx 3:5; Jos 5:15
28:18
nGe 35:14
oLev 8:11
28:19
pJdg 1:23,26

---

[a]1 Or *greeted*   [b]2 That is, Northwest Mesopotamia; also in verses 5, 6 and 7   [c]3 Hebrew *El-Shaddai*   [d]12 Or *ladder*   [e]13 Or *There beside him*   [f]19 *Bethel* means *house of God.*

²⁰Then Jacob made a vow,^q saying, "If God will be with me and will watch over me^r on this journey I am taking and will give me food to eat and clothes to wear ²¹so that I return safely^s to my father's house, then the LORD^a will be my God^t ²²and^b this stone that I have set up as a pillar will be God's house,^u and of all that you give me I will give you a tenth.^v"

Jacob Arrives in Paddan Aram

29 Then Jacob continued on his journey and came to the land of the eastern peoples.^w ²There he saw a well in the field, with three flocks of sheep lying near it because the flocks were watered from that well. The stone over the mouth of the well was large. ³When all the flocks were gathered there, the shepherds would roll the stone away from the well's mouth and water the sheep. Then they would return the stone to its place over the mouth of the well.

⁴Jacob asked the shepherds, "My brothers, where are you from?" "We're from Haran,^x" they replied.

⁵He said to them, "Do you know Laban, Nahor's grandson?"

"Yes, we know him," they answered.

⁶Then Jacob asked them, "Is he well?"

"Yes, he is," they said, "and here comes his daughter Rachel with the sheep."

⁷"Look," he said, "the sun is still high; it is not time for the flocks to be gathered. Water the sheep and take them back to pasture."

⁸"We can't," they replied, "until all the flocks are gathered and the stone has been rolled away from the mouth of the well. Then we will water the sheep."

⁹While he was still talking with them, Rachel came with her father's sheep,^y for she was a shepherdess. ¹⁰When Jacob saw Rachel daughter of Laban, his mother's brother, and Laban's sheep, he went over and rolled the stone away from the mouth of the well and watered his uncle's sheep.^z ¹¹Then Jacob kissed Rachel and began to weep aloud.^a ¹²He had told Rachel that he was a relative^b of her father and a son of Rebekah. So she ran and told her father.^c

¹³As soon as Laban^d heard the news about Jacob, his sister's son, he hurried to meet him. He embraced him and kissed him and brought him to his home, and there Jacob told him all these things. ¹⁴Then Laban said to him, "You are my own flesh and blood."^e

Jacob Marries Leah and Rachel

After Jacob had stayed with him for a whole month, ¹⁵Laban said to him, "Just because you are a relative of mine, should you work for me for nothing? Tell me what your wages should be."

¹⁶Now Laban had two daughters; the name of the older was Leah, and the name of the younger was Rachel. ¹⁷Leah had weak^c eyes, but Rachel was lovely in form, and beautiful. ¹⁸Jacob was in love with Rachel and said, "I'll work for you seven years in return for your younger daughter Rachel."^f

¹⁹Laban said, "It's better that I give her to you than to some other

28:20
qGe 31:13;
Jdg 11:30;
2Sa 15:8 rver 15
28:21
sJdg 11:31
tDt 26:17
28:22
uGe 35:7,14
vGe 14:20;
Lev 27:30
29:1
wJdg 6:3,33
29:4
xGe 28:10
29:9
yEx 2:16
29:10
zEx 2:17
29:11
aGe 33:4
29:12
bGe 13:8;
14:14,16
cGe 24:28
29:13
dGe 24:29
29:14
eGe 2:23;
Jdg 9:2;
2Sa 19:12-13
29:18
fHos 12:12

---

^a20,21 Or *Since God . . . father's house, the* LORD   ^b21,22 Or *house, and the* LORD *will be my God,*
²²*then*   ^c17 Or *delicate*

man. Stay here with me." [20]So Jacob served seven years to get Rachel, but they seemed like only a few days to him because of his love for her.[g]

[21]Then Jacob said to Laban, "Give me my wife. My time is completed, and I want to lie with her.[h]"

[22]So Laban brought together all the people of the place and gave a feast.[i] [23]But when evening came, he took his daughter Leah and gave her to Jacob, and Jacob lay with her. [24]And Laban gave his servant girl Zilpah to his daughter as her maidservant.

[25]When morning came, there was Leah! So Jacob said to Laban, "What is this you have done to me?[j] I served you for Rachel, didn't I? Why have you deceived me?[k]"

[26]Laban replied, "It is not our custom here to give the younger daughter in marriage before the older one. [27]Finish this daughter's bridal week;[l] then we will give you the younger one also, in return for another seven years of work."

[28]And Jacob did so. He finished the week with Leah, and then Laban gave him his daughter Rachel to be his wife. [29]Laban gave his servant girl Bilhah[m] to his daughter Rachel as her maidservant.[n] [30]Jacob lay with Rachel also, and he loved Rachel more than Leah.[o] And he worked for Laban another seven years.[p]

Jacob's Children

[31]When the LORD saw that Leah was not loved,[q] he opened her womb,[r] but Rachel was barren. [32]Leah became pregnant and gave birth to a son. She named him Reuben,[a] for she said, "It is because the LORD has seen my misery.[s] Surely my husband will love me now."

[33]She conceived again, and when she gave birth to a son she said, "Because the LORD heard that I am not loved, he gave me this one too." So she named him Simeon.[b][t]

[34]Again she conceived, and when she gave birth to a son she said, "Now at last my husband will become attached to me,[u] because I have borne him three sons." So he was named Levi.[c][v]

[35]She conceived again, and when she gave birth to a son she said, "This time I will praise the LORD." So she named him Judah.[d][w] Then she stopped having children.

30 When Rachel saw that she was not bearing Jacob any children,[x] she became jealous of her sister.[y] So she said to Jacob, "Give me children, or I'll die!"

[2]Jacob became angry with her and said, "Am I in the place of God, who has kept you from having children?"[z]

[3]Then she said, "Here is Bilhah, my maidservant. Sleep with her so that she can bear children for me and that through her I too can build a family."[a]

[4]So she gave him her servant Bilhah as a wife.[b] Jacob slept with her,[c] [5]and she became pregnant and bore him a son. [6]Then Rachel said, "God has vindicated me;[d] he has listened to my plea and given me a son." Because of this she named him Dan.[e][e]

---

[a]32 *Reuben* sounds like the Hebrew for *he has seen my misery*; the name means *see, a son.*
[b]33 *Simeon* probably means *one who hears.*   [c]34 *Levi* sounds like and may be derived from the Hebrew for *attached.*   [d]35 *Judah* sounds like and may be derived from the Hebrew for *praise.*
[e]6 *Dan* here means *he has vindicated.*

29:20
gSS 8:7;
Hos 12:12
29:21
hJdg 15:1
29:22
iJdg 14:10;
Jn 2:1-2
29:25
jGe 12:18
kGe 27:36
29:27
lJdg 14:12
29:29
mGe 30:3
nGe 16:1
29:30
over 16
pGe 31:41
29:31
qDt 21:15-17
rGe 11:30;
30:1; Ps 127:3
29:32
sGe 16:11;
31:42; Ex 4:31;
Dt 26:7;
Ps 25:18
29:33
tGe 34:25; 49:5
29:34
uGe 30:20;
1Sa 1:2-4
vGe 49:5-7
29:35
wGe 49:8;
Mt 1:2-3
30:1
xGe 29:31;
1Sa 1:5-6
yLev 18:18
30:2
zGe 16:2;
20:18; 29:31
30:3
aGe 16:2
30:4
bver 9,18
cGe 16:3-4
30:6
dPs 35:24;
43:1; La 3:59
eGe 49:16-17

⁷Rachel's servant Bilhah conceived again and bore Jacob a second son. ⁸Then Rachel said, "I have had a great struggle with my sister, and I have won."ᶠ So she named him Naphtali.ᵃ ᵍ

⁹When Leah saw that she had stopped having children, she took her maidservant Zilpah and gave her to Jacob as a wife.ʰ ¹⁰Leah's servant Zilpah bore Jacob a son. ¹¹Then Leah said, "What good fortune!"ᵇ So she named him Gad.ᶜ ⁱ

¹²Leah's servant Zilpah bore Jacob a second son. ¹³Then Leah said, "How happy I am! The women will call meʲ happy."ᵏ So she named him Asher.ᵈ ˡ

¹⁴During wheat harvest, Reuben went out into the fields and found some mandrake plants,ᵐ which he brought to his mother Leah. Rachel said to Leah, "Please give me some of your son's mandrakes."

¹⁵But she said to her, "Wasn't it enoughⁿ that you took away my husband? Will you take my son's mandrakes too?"

"Very well," Rachel said, "he can sleep with you tonight in return for your son's mandrakes."

¹⁶So when Jacob came in from the fields that evening, Leah went out to meet him. "You must sleep with me," she said. "I have hired you with my son's mandrakes." So he slept with her that night.

¹⁷God listened to Leah,ᵒ and she became pregnant and bore Jacob a fifth son. ¹⁸Then Leah said, "God has rewarded me for giving my maidservant to my husband." So she named him Issachar.ᵉ ᵖ

¹⁹Leah conceived again and bore Jacob a sixth son. ²⁰Then Leah said, "God has presented me with a precious gift. This time my husband will treat me with honor, because I have borne him six sons." So she named him Zebulun.ᶠ ᵠ

²¹Some time later she gave birth to a daughter and named her Dinah.

²²Then God remembered Rachel;ʳ he listened to her and opened her womb.ˢ ²³She became pregnant and gave birth to a sonᵗ and said, "God has taken away my disgrace."ᵘ ²⁴She named him Joseph,ᵍ ᵛ and said, "May the LORD add to me another son."ʷ

Jacob's Flocks Increase

²⁵After Rachel gave birth to Joseph, Jacob said to Laban, "Send me on my wayˣ so I can go back to my own homeland. ²⁶Give me my wives and children, for whom I have served you,ʸ and I will be on my way. You know how much work I've done for you."

²⁷But Laban said to him, "If I have found favor in your eyes, please stay. I have learned by divination thatʰ the LORD has blessed me because of you."ᶻ ²⁸He added, "Name your wages,ᵃ and I will pay them."

²⁹Jacob said to him, "You know how I have worked for youᵇ and how your livestock has fared under my care.ᶜ ³⁰The little you had before I came has increased greatly, and the LORD has blessed you wherever I have been. But now, when may I do something for my own household?ᵈ"

### Cross references (margin)

30:8
fHos 12:3-4
gGe 49:21

30:9
hver 4

30:11
iGe 49:19

30:13
jPs 127:3
kPr 31:28;
Lk 1:48
lGe 49:20

30:14
mSS 7:13

30:15
nNu 16:9,13

30:17
oGe 25:21

30:18
pGe 49:14

30:20
qGe 35:23;
49:13; Mt 4:13

30:22
rGe 8:1;
1Sa 1:19-20
sGe 29:31

30:23
tver 6 uIsa 4:1;
Lk 1:25

30:24
vGe 35:24;
37:2; 39:1;
49:22-26
wGe 35:17

30:25
xGe 24:54

30:26
yGe 29:20,30;
Hos 12:12

30:27
zGe 26:24;
39:3,5

30:28
aGe 29:15

30:29
bGe 31:6
cGe 31:38-40

30:30
d1Ti 5:8

ᵃ8 *Naphtali* means *my struggle.*   ᵇ11 Or *"A troop is coming!"*   ᶜ11 *Gad* can mean *good fortune* or *a troop.*   ᵈ13 *Asher* means *happy.*   ᵉ18 *Issachar* sounds like the Hebrew for *reward.* ᶠ20 *Zebulun* probably means *honor.*   ᵍ24 *Joseph* means *may he add.*   ʰ27 Or possibly *have become rich and*

³¹"What shall I give you?" he asked.

"Don't give me anything," Jacob replied. "But if you will do this one thing for me, I will go on tending your flocks and watching over them: ³²Let me go through all your flocks today and remove from them every speckled or spotted sheep, every dark-colored lamb and every spotted or speckled goat. ᵉ They will be my wages. ³³And my honesty will testify for me in the future, whenever you check on the wages you have paid me. Any goat in my possession that is not speckled or spotted, or any lamb that is not dark-colored, will be considered stolen."

³⁴"Agreed," said Laban. "Let it be as you have said." ³⁵That same day he removed all the male goats that were streaked or spotted, and all the speckled or spotted female goats (all that had white on them) and all the dark-colored lambs, and he placed them in the care of his sons. ᶠ ³⁶Then he put a three-day journey between himself and Jacob, while Jacob continued to tend the rest of Laban's flocks.

³⁷Jacob, however, took fresh-cut branches from poplar, almond and plane trees and made white stripes on them by peeling the bark and exposing the white inner wood of the branches. ³⁸Then he placed the peeled branches in all the watering troughs, so that they would be directly in front of the flocks when they came to drink. When the flocks were in heat and came to drink, ³⁹they mated in front of the branches. And they bore young that were streaked or speckled or spotted. ⁴⁰Jacob set apart the young of the flock by themselves, but made the rest face the streaked and dark-colored animals that belonged to Laban. Thus he made separate flocks for himself and did not put them with Laban's animals. ⁴¹Whenever the stronger females were in heat, Jacob would place the branches in the troughs in front of the animals so they would mate near the branches, ⁴²but if the animals were weak, he would not place them there. So the weak animals went to Laban and the strong ones to Jacob. ⁴³In this way the man grew exceedingly prosperous and came to own large flocks, and maidservants and menservants, and camels and donkeys. ᵍ

Jacob Flees From Laban

31 Jacob heard that Laban's sons were saying, "Jacob has taken everything our father owned and has gained all this wealth from what belonged to our father." ²And Jacob noticed that Laban's attitude toward him was not what it had been.

³Then the LORD said to Jacob, "Go back ʰ to the land of your fathers and to your relatives, and I will be with you." ⁱ

⁴So Jacob sent word to Rachel and Leah to come out to the fields where his flocks were. ⁵He said to them, "I see that your father's attitude toward me is not what it was before, but the God of my father has been with me. ʲ ⁶You know that I've worked for your father with all my strength, ᵏ ⁷yet your father has cheated me by changing my wages ten times.ˡ However, God has not allowed him to harm me. ᵐ ⁸If he said, 'The speckled ones will be your wages,' then all the flocks gave birth to speckled young; and if he said, 'The streaked ones will be your wages,'ⁿ then all the flocks bore streaked young. ⁹So God has taken away your father's livestock and has given them to me. ᵒ

¹⁰"In breeding season I once had a dream in which I looked up and

---

30:32
ᵉGe 31:8,12
30:35
ᶠGe 31:1
30:43
ᵍver 30;
Ge 12:16; 13:2;
24:35; 26:13-14
31:3
ʰver 13;
Ge 32:9
ⁱGe 21:22;
26:3; 28:15
31:5
ʲGe 21:22; 26:3
31:6
ᵏGe 30:29
31:7
ˡver 41;
Job 19:3
ᵐver 52;
Ps 37:28;
105:14
31:8
ⁿGe 30:32
31:9
ᵒver 1,16;
Ge 30:42

saw that the male goats mating with the flock were streaked, speckled or spotted. ¹¹The angel of Godᴾ said to me in the dream, 'Jacob.' I answered, 'Here I am.' ¹²And he said, 'Look up and see that all the male goats mating with the flock are streaked, speckled or spotted, for I have seen all that Laban has been doing to you. �q ¹³I am the God of Bethel, ʳ where you anointed a pillar and where you made a vow to me. Now leave this land at once and go back to your native land. ˢ' "

¹⁴Then Rachel and Leah replied, "Do we still have any share in the inheritance of our father's estate? ¹⁵Does he not regard us as foreigners? Not only has he sold us, but he has used up what was paid for us. ᵗ ¹⁶Surely all the wealth that God took away from our father belongs to us and our children. So do whatever God has told you."

¹⁷Then Jacob put his children and his wives on camels, ¹⁸and he drove all his livestock ahead of him, along with all the goods he had accumulated in Paddan Aram, ᵃ to go to his father Isaacᵘ in the land of Canaan. ᵛ

¹⁹When Laban had gone to shear his sheep, Rachel stole her father's household gods. ʷ ²⁰Moreover, Jacob deceivedˣ Laban the Aramean by not telling him he was running away. ʸ ²¹So he fled with all he had, and crossing the River, ᵇ he headed for the hill country of Gilead. ᶻ

Laban Pursues Jacob

²²On the third day Laban was told that Jacob had fled. ²³Taking his relatives with him, he pursued Jacob for seven days and caught up with him in the hill country of Gilead. ²⁴Then God came to Laban the Aramean in a dream at night and said to him, ᵃ "Be careful not to say anything to Jacob, either good or bad."ᵇ

²⁵Jacob had pitched his tent in the hill country of Gilead when Laban overtook him, and Laban and his relatives camped there too. ²⁶Then Laban said to Jacob, "What have you done? You've deceived me, ᶜ and you've carried off my daughters like captives in war. ᵈ ²⁷Why did you run off secretly and deceive me? Why didn't you tell me, so I could send you away with joy and singing to the music of tambourinesᵉ and harps?ᶠ ²⁸You didn't even let me kiss my grandchildren and my daughters good-by. ᵍ You have done a foolish thing. ²⁹I have the power to harm you;ʰ but last night the God of your fatherⁱ said to me, 'Be careful not to say anything to Jacob, either good or bad.' ³⁰Now you have gone off because you longed to return to your father's house. But why did you steal my gods?ʲ "

³¹Jacob answered Laban, "I was afraid, because I thought you would take your daughters away from me by force. ³²But if you find anyone who has your gods, he shall not live. ᵏ In the presence of our relatives, see for yourself whether there is anything of yours here with me; and if so, take it." Now Jacob did not know that Rachel had stolen the gods.

³³So Laban went into Jacob's tent and into Leah's tent and into the tent of the two maidservants, but he found nothing. After he came out of Leah's tent, he entered Rachel's tent. ³⁴Now Rachel had taken the

31:11
ᵖGe 16:7; 48:16
31:12
qEx 3:7
31:13
rGe 28:10-22
sver 3; Ge 32:9
31:15
tGe 29:20
31:18
uGe 35:27
vGe 10:19
31:19
wver 30,32,
34-35; Ge 35:2;
Jdg 17:5;
1Sa 19:13;
Hos 3:4
31:20
xGe 27:36
yver 27
31:21
zGe 37:25
31:24
aGe 20:3;
Job 33:15
bGe 24:50
31:26
cGe 27:36
d1Sa 30:2-3
31:27
eEx 15:20
fGe 4:21
31:28
gver 55
31:29
hver 7 iver 53
31:30
jver 19;
Jdg 18:24
31:32
kGe 44:9

ᵃ18 That is, Northwest Mesopotamia   ᵇ21 That is, the Euphrates household gods and put them inside her camel's saddle and was sitting on them. Laban searched[1] through everything in the tent but found nothing.

[35]Rachel said to her father, "Don't be angry, my lord, that I cannot stand up in your presence;[m] I'm having my period." So he searched but could not find the household gods.

[36]Jacob was angry and took Laban to task. "What is my crime?" he asked Laban. "What sin have I committed that you hunt me down? [37]Now that you have searched through all my goods, what have you found that belongs to your household? Put it here in front of your relatives[n] and mine, and let them judge between the two of us.

[38]"I have been with you for twenty years now. Your sheep and goats have not miscarried, nor have I eaten rams from your flocks. [39]I did not bring you animals torn by wild beasts; I bore the loss myself. And you demanded payment from me for whatever was stolen by day or night.[o] [40]This was my situation: The heat consumed me in the daytime and the cold at night, and sleep fled from my eyes. [41]It was like this for the twenty years I was in your household. I worked for you fourteen years for your two daughters[p] and six years for your flocks, and you changed my wages ten times.[q] [42]If the God of my father,[r] the God of Abraham and the Fear of Isaac,[s] had not been with me,[t] you would surely have sent me away empty-handed. But God has seen my hardship and the toil of my hands,[u] and last night he rebuked you."

[43]Laban answered Jacob, "The women are my daughters, the children are my children, and the flocks are my flocks. All you see is mine. Yet what can I do today about these daughters of mine, or about the children they have borne? [44]Come now, let's make a covenant,[v] you and I, and let it serve as a witness between us."[w]

[45]So Jacob took a stone and set it up as a pillar.[x] [46]He said to his relatives, "Gather some stones." So they took stones and piled them in a heap, and they ate there by the heap. [47]Laban called it Jegar Sahadutha,[a] and Jacob called it Galeed.[b]

[48]Laban said, "This heap is a witness between you and me today." That is why it was called Galeed. [49]It was also called Mizpah,[c][y] because he said, "May the LORD keep watch between you and me when we are away from each other. [50]If you mistreat my daughters or if you take any wives besides my daughters, even though no one is with us, remember that God is a witness[z] between you and me."

[51]Laban also said to Jacob, "Here is this heap, and here is this pillar[a] I have set up between you and me. [52]This heap is a witness, and this pillar is a witness,[b] that I will not go past this heap to your side to harm you and that you will not go past this heap and pillar to my side to harm me.[c] [53]May the God of Abraham[d] and the God of Nahor, the God of their father, judge between us."[e]

So Jacob took an oath[f] in the name of the Fear of his father Isaac.[g] [54]He offered a sacrifice there in the hill country and invited his relatives to a meal. After they had eaten, they spent the night there.

[55]Early the next morning Laban kissed his grandchildren and his daughters[h] and blessed them. Then he left and returned home.[i]

31:34
lver 37;
Ge 44:12
31:35
mEx 20:12;
Lev 19:3,32
31:37
nver 23
31:39
oEx 22:13
31:41
pGe 29:30
qver 7
31:42
rver 5; Ex 3:15;
1Ch 12:17
sver 53; Isa 8:13
tPs 124:1-2
uGe 29:32
31:44
vGe 21:27;
26:28
wJos 24:27
31:45
xGe 28:18
31:49
yJdg 11:29;
1Sa 7:5-6
31:50
zJer 29:23; 42:5
31:51
aGe 28:18
31:52
bGe 21:30
cver 7;
Ge 26:29
31:53
dGe 28:13
eGe 16:5
fGe 21:23,27
gver 42
31:55
hver 28
iGe 18:33;
30:25

---

[a]47 The Aramaic *Jegar Sahadutha* means *witness heap.*   [b]47 The Hebrew *Galeed* means *witness heap.*   [c]49 *Mizpah* means *watchtower.*

Jacob Prepares to Meet Esau

32 Jacob also went on his way, and the angels of God[j] met him. [2]When Jacob saw them, he said, "This is the camp of God!"[k] So he named that place Mahanaim.[a] [l]

[3]Jacob sent messengers ahead of him to his brother Esau[m] in the land of Seir, the country of Edom.[n] [4]He instructed them: "This is what you are to say to my master Esau: 'Your servant Jacob says, I have been staying with Laban and have remained there till now. [5]I have cattle and donkeys, sheep and goats, menservants and maidservants.[o] Now I am sending this message to my lord, that I may find favor in your eyes.[p] '"

[6]When the messengers returned to Jacob, they said, "We went to your brother Esau, and now he is coming to meet you, and four hundred men are with him."[q]

[7]In great fear[r] and distress Jacob divided the people who were with him into two groups,[b] and the flocks and herds and camels as well. [8]He thought, "If Esau comes and attacks one group,[c] the group[c] that is left may escape."

[9]Then Jacob prayed, "O God of my father Abraham, God of my father Isaac,[s] O LORD, who said to me, 'Go back to your country and your relatives, and I will make you prosper,'[t] [10]I am unworthy of all the kindness and faithfulness[u] you have shown your servant. I had only my staff when I crossed this Jordan, but now I have become two groups. [11]Save me, I pray, from the hand of my brother Esau, for I am afraid he will come and attack me,[v] and also the mothers with their children.[w] [12]But you have said, 'I will surely make you prosper and will make your descendants like the sand[x] of the sea, which cannot be counted.'[y] "

[13]He spent the night there, and from what he had with him he selected a gift[z] for his brother Esau: [14]two hundred female goats and twenty male goats, two hundred ewes and twenty rams, [15]thirty female camels with their young, forty cows and ten bulls, and twenty female donkeys and ten male donkeys. [16]He put them in the care of his servants, each herd by itself, and said to his servants, "Go ahead of me, and keep some space between the herds."

[17]He instructed the one in the lead: "When my brother Esau meets you and asks, 'To whom do you belong, and where are you going, and who owns all these animals in front of you?' [18]then you are to say, 'They belong to your servant[a] Jacob. They are a gift sent to my lord Esau, and he is coming behind us.' "

[19]He also instructed the second, the third and all the others who followed the herds: "You are to say the same thing to Esau when you meet him. [20]And be sure to say, 'Your servant Jacob is coming behind us.' " For he thought, "I will pacify him with these gifts I am sending on ahead; later, when I see him, perhaps he will receive me."[b] [21]So Jacob's gifts went on ahead of him, but he himself spent the night in the camp.

Jacob Wrestles With God

[22]That night Jacob got up and took his two wives, his two maidservants and his eleven sons and crossed the ford of the Jabbok.[c] [23]After

32:1
jGe 16:11;
2Ki 6:16-17;
Ps 34:7; 91:11;
Heb 1:14
32:2
kGe 28:17
l2Sa 2:8,29
32:3
mGe 27:41-42
nGe 25:30;
36:8,9
32:5
oGe 12:16;
30:43 pGe 33:8,
10,15
32:6
qGe 33:1
32:7
rver 11
32:9
sGe 28:13;
31:42 tGe 31:13
32:10
uGe 24:27
32:11
vPs 59:2
wGe 27:41
32:12
xGe 22:17
yGe 28:13-15;
Hos 1:10;
Ro 9:27
32:13
zGe 43:11,15,
25,26; Pr 18:16
32:18
aGe 18:3
32:20
bGe 33:10;
Pr 21:14
32:22
cDt 2:37; 3:16;
Jos 12:2

---

[a]2 *Mahanaim* means *two camps.*　　[b]7 Or *camps;* also in verse 10　　[c]8 Or *camp*

he had sent them across the stream, he sent over all his possessions. [24]So Jacob was left alone, and a man[d] wrestled with him till daybreak. [25]When the man saw that he could not overpower him, he touched the socket of Jacob's hip[e] so that his hip was wrenched as he wrestled with the man. [26]Then the man said, "Let me go, for it is daybreak."

But Jacob replied, "I will not let you go unless you bless me."[f]

[27]The man asked him, "What is your name?"

"Jacob," he answered.

[28]Then the man said, "Your name will no longer be Jacob, but Israel,[a g] because you have struggled with God and with men and have overcome."

[29]Jacob said, "Please tell me your name."[h]

But he replied, "Why do you ask my name?"[i] Then he blessed[j] him there.

[30]So Jacob called the place Peniel,[b] saying, "It is because I saw God face to face,[k] and yet my life was spared."

[31]The sun rose above him as he passed Peniel,[c] and he was limping because of his hip. [32]Therefore to this day the Israelites do not eat the tendon attached to the socket of the hip, because the socket of Jacob's hip was touched near the tendon.

Jacob Meets Esau

33 Jacob looked up and there was Esau, coming with his four hundred men;[l] so he divided the children among Leah, Rachel and the two maidservants. [2]He put the maidservants and their children in front, Leah and her children next, and Rachel and Joseph in the rear. [3]He himself went on ahead and bowed down to the ground[m] seven times as he approached his brother.

[4]But Esau ran to meet Jacob and embraced him; he threw his arms around his neck and kissed him. And they wept.[n] [5]Then Esau looked up and saw the women and children. "Who are these with you?" he asked.

Jacob answered, "They are the children God has graciously given your servant.[o]"

[6]Then the maidservants and their children approached and bowed down. [7]Next, Leah and her children came and bowed down. Last of all came Joseph and Rachel, and they too bowed down.

[8]Esau asked, "What do you mean by all these droves I met?"[p]

"To find favor in your eyes, my lord,"[q] he said.

[9]But Esau said, "I already have plenty, my brother. Keep what you have for yourself."

[10]"No, please!" said Jacob. "If I have found favor in your eyes, accept this gift from me. For to see your face is like seeing the face of God,[r] now that you have received me favorably.[s] [11]Please accept the present[t] that was brought to you, for God has been gracious to me[u] and I have all I need." And because Jacob insisted, Esau accepted it.

[12]Then Esau said, "Let us be on our way; I'll accompany you."

[13]But Jacob said to him, "My lord knows that the children are tender and that I must care for the ewes and cows that are nursing their young.

32:24
d Ge 18:2
32:25
e ver 32
32:26
f Hos 12:4
32:28
g Ge 17:5;
35:10; 1Ki 18:31
32:29
h Jdg 13:17
i Jdg 13:18
j Ge 35:9
32:30
k Ge 16:13;
Ex 24:11;
Nu 12:8;
Jdg 6:22; 13:22
33:1
l Ge 32:6
33:3
m Ge 18:2; 42:6
33:4
n Ge 45:14-15
33:5
o Ge 48:9;
Ps 127:3;
Isa 8:18
33:8
p Ge 32:14-16
q Ge 24:9; 32:5
33:10
r Ge 16:13
s Ge 32:20
33:11
t 1Sa 25:27
u Ge 30:43

---

[a]28 *Israel* means *he struggles with God.*   [b]30 *Peniel* means *face of God.*   [c]31 Hebrew *Penuel,* a variant of *Peniel*

If they are driven hard just one day, all the animals will die. ¹⁴So let my lord go on ahead of his servant, while I move along slowly at the pace of the droves before me and that of the children, until I come to my lord in Seir. ᵛ"

¹⁵Esau said, "Then let me leave some of my men with you."

"But why do that?" Jacob asked. "Just let me find favor in the eyes of my lord." ᵂ

¹⁶So that day Esau started on his way back to Seir. ¹⁷Jacob, however, went to Succoth, ˣ where he built a place for himself and made shelters for his livestock. That is why the place is called Succoth. ᵃ

¹⁸After Jacob came from Paddan Aram, ᵇʸ he arrived safely at theᶜ city of Shechemᶻ in Canaan and camped within sight of the city. ¹⁹For a hundred pieces of silver, ᵈ he bought from the sons of Hamor, the father of Shechem, ᵃ the plot of groundᵇ where he pitched his tent. ²⁰There he set up an altar and called it El Elohe Israel. ᵉ

Dinah and the Shechemites

34 Now Dinah, ᶜ the daughter Leah had borne to Jacob, went out to visit the women of the land. ²When Shechem son of Hamor the Hivite, the ruler of that area, saw her, he took her and violated her. ³His heart was drawn to Dinah daughter of Jacob, and he loved the girl and spoke tenderly to her. ⁴And Shechem said to his father Hamor, "Get me this girl as my wife."

⁵When Jacob heard that his daughter Dinah had been defiled, his sons were in the fields with his livestock; so he kept quiet about it until they came home.

⁶Then Shechem's father Hamor went out to talk with Jacob. ᵈ ⁷Now Jacob's sons had come in from the fields as soon as they heard what had happened. They were filled with grief and fury, because Shechem had done a disgraceful thing inᶠ Israelᵉ by lying with Jacob's daughter—a thing that should not be done. ᶠ

⁸But Hamor said to them, "My son Shechem has his heart set on your daughter. Please give her to him as his wife. ⁹Intermarry with us; give us your daughters and take our daughters for yourselves. ¹⁰You can settle among us;ᵍ the land is open to you. ʰ Live in it, tradeᵍ in it, ⁱ and acquire property in it."

¹¹Then Shechem said to Dinah's father and brothers, "Let me find favor in your eyes, and I will give you whatever you ask. ¹²Make the price for the brideʲ and the gift I am to bring as great as you like, and I'll pay whatever you ask me. Only give me the girl as my wife."

¹³Because their sister Dinah had been defiled, Jacob's sons replied deceitfully as they spoke to Shechem and his father Hamor. ¹⁴They said to them, "We can't do such a thing; we can't give our sister to a man who is not circumcised. ᵏ That would be a disgrace to us. ¹⁵We will give our consent to you on one condition only: that you become like us by circumcising all your males.ˡ ¹⁶Then we will give you our daughters and take your daughters for ourselves. We'll settle among you and

---

33:14
vGe 32:3

33:15
wGe 34:11;
47:25; Ru 2:13

33:17
xJos 13:27;
Jdg 8:5,6,8,14,
14-16,15,16;
Ps 60:6

33:18
yGe 25:20; 28:2
zJos 24:1;
Jdg 9:1

33:19
aJos 24:32
bJn 4:5

34:1
cGe 30:21

34:6
dJdg 14:2-5

34:7
eDt 22:21;
Jdg 20:6;
2Sa 13:12
fJos 7:15

34:10
gGe 47:6,27
hGe 13:9; 20:15
iGe 42:34

34:12
jEx 22:16;
Dt 22:29;
1Sa 18:25

34:14
kGe 17:14;
Jdg 14:3

34:15
lEx 12:48

ᵃ17 *Succoth* means *shelters.*   ᵇ18 That is, Northwest Mesopotamia   ᶜ18 Or *arrived at Shalem,*
a   ᵈ19 Hebrew *hundred kesitahs;* a kesitah was a unit of money of unknown weight and value.
ᵉ20 *El Elohe Israel* can mean *God, the God of Israel* or *mighty is the God of Israel.*   f7 Or *against*
g10 Or *move about freely;* also in verse 21

become one people with you. ¹⁷But if you will not agree to be circumcised, we'll take our sister*ᵃ* and go."

¹⁸Their proposal seemed good to Hamor and his son Shechem. ¹⁹The young man, who was the most honored of all his father's household, lost no time in doing what they said, because he was delighted with Jacob's daughter.ᵐ ²⁰So Hamor and his son Shechem went to the gate of their cityⁿ to speak to their fellow townsmen. ²¹"These men are friendly toward us," they said. "Let them live in our land and trade in it; the land has plenty of room for them. We can marry their daughters and they can marry ours. ²²But the men will consent to live with us as one people only on the condition that our males be circumcised, as they themselves are. ²³Won't their livestock, their property and all their other animals become ours? So let us give our consent to them, and they will settle among us."

²⁴All the men who went out of the city gateᵒ agreed with Hamor and his son Shechem, and every male in the city was circumcised.

²⁵Three days later, while all of them were still in pain, two of Jacob's sons, Simeon and Levi, Dinah's brothers, took their swordsᵖ and attacked the unsuspecting city, killing every male.�q ²⁶They put Hamor and his son Shechem to the sword and took Dinah from Shechem's house and left. ²⁷The sons of Jacob came upon the dead bodies and looted the city whereᵇ their sister had been defiled. ²⁸They seized their flocks and herds and donkeys and everything else of theirs in the city and out in the fields. ²⁹They carried off all their wealth and all their women and children, taking as plunder everything in the houses.

³⁰Then Jacob said to Simeon and Levi, "You have brought trouble on me by making me a stenchʳ to the Canaanites and Perizzites, the people living in this land.ˢ We are few in number,ᵗ and if they join forces against me and attack me, I and my household will be destroyed."

³¹But they replied, "Should he have treated our sister like a prostitute?"

Jacob Returns to Bethel

35 Then God said to Jacob, "Go up to Bethelᵘ and settle there, and build an altar there to God, who appeared to you when you were fleeing from your brother Esau."ᵛ

²So Jacob said to his householdʷ and to all who were with him, "Get rid of the foreign godsˣ you have with you, and purify yourselves and change your clothes.ʸ ³Then come, let us go up to Bethel, where I will build an altar to God, who answered me in the day of my distressᶻ and who has been with me wherever I have gone.ᵃ" ⁴So they gave Jacob all the foreign gods they had and the rings in their ears, and Jacob buried them under the oak at Shechem.ᵇ ⁵Then they set out, and the terror of Godᶜ fell upon the towns all around them so that no one pursued them.

⁶Jacob and all the people with him came to Luzᵈ (that is, Bethel) in the land of Canaan. ⁷There he built an altar, and he called the place El Bethel,ᶜ because it was there that God revealed himself to himᵉ when he was fleeing from his brother.

34:19
ᵐver 3
34:20
ⁿRu 4:1;
2Sa 15:2
34:24
ᵒGe 23:10
34:25
ᵖGe 49:5
qGe 49:7
34:30
ʳEx 5:21;
1Sa 13:4
ˢGe 13:7
ᵗGe 46:27;
1Ch 16:19;
Ps 105:12
35:1
ᵘGe 28:19
ᵛGe 27:43
35:2
ʷGe 18:19;
Jos 24:15
ˣEx 31:19
ʸEx 19:10,14
35:3
ᶻGe 32:7
ᵃGe 28:15,
20-22; 31:3,42
35:4
ᵇJos 24:25-26
35:5
ᶜEx 15:16;
23:27; Jos 2:9
35:6
ᵈGe 28:19; 48:3
35:7
ᵉGe 28:13

ᵃ17 Hebrew *daughter*   *ᵇ27* Or *because*   *ᶜ7 El Bethel* means *God of Bethel.*

[8]Now Deborah, Rebekah's nurse,[f] died and was buried under the oak below Bethel. So it was named Allon Bacuth.[a]

[9]After Jacob returned from Paddan Aram,[b] God appeared to him again and blessed him.[g] [10]God said to him, "Your name is Jacob,[c] but you will no longer be called Jacob; your name will be Israel.[d]"[h] So he named him Israel.

[11]And God said to him, "I am God Almighty[e];[i] be fruitful and increase in number. A nation[j] and a community of nations will come from you, and kings will come from your body.[k] [12]The land I gave to Abraham and Isaac I also give to you, and I will give this land to your descendants after you."[m] [13]Then God went up from him[n] at the place where he had talked with him.

[14]Jacob set up a stone pillar at the place where God had talked with him, and he poured out a drink offering on it; he also poured oil on it.[o] [15]Jacob called the place where God had talked with him Bethel.[f][p]

The Deaths of Rachel and Isaac

35:23–26pp — 1Ch 2:1–2

[16]Then they moved on from Bethel. While they were still some distance from Ephrath, Rachel began to give birth and had great difficulty. [17]And as she was having great difficulty in childbirth, the midwife said to her, "Don't be afraid, for you have another son."[q] [18]As she breathed her last—for she was dying—she named her son Ben-Oni.[g] But his father named him Benjamin.[h]

[19]So Rachel died and was buried on the way to Ephrath (that is, Bethlehem[r]). [20]Over her tomb Jacob set up a pillar, and to this day that pillar marks Rachel's tomb.[s]

[21]Israel moved on again and pitched his tent beyond Migdal Eder. [22]While Israel was living in that region, Reuben went in and slept with his father's concubine[t] Bilhah,[u] and Israel heard of it.

Jacob had twelve sons:

[23]The sons of Leah:

    Reuben the firstborn[v] of Jacob,

    Simeon, Levi, Judah,[w] Issachar and Zebulun.[x]

[24]The sons of Rachel:

    Joseph[y] and Benjamin.[z]

[25]The sons of Rachel's maidservant Bilhah:

    Dan and Naphtali.[a]

[26]The sons of Leah's maidservant Zilpah:

    Gad[b] and Asher.[c]

These were the sons of Jacob, who were born to him in Paddan Aram.

[27]Jacob came home to his father Isaac in Mamre,[d] near Kiriath Arba[e] (that is, Hebron), where Abraham and Isaac had stayed. [28]Isaac lived a hundred and eighty years.[f] [29]Then he breathed his last and died and was gathered to his people,[g] old and full of years.[h] And his sons Esau and Jacob buried him.[i]

35:8
f Ge 24:59
35:9
g Ge 32:29
35:10
h Ge 17:5
35:11
i Ge 17:1; Ex 6:3
j Ge 28:3; 48:4
k Ge 17:6
35:12
l Ge 13:15;
28:13
m Ge 12:7; 26:3
35:13
n Ge 17:22
35:14
o Ge 28:18
35:15
p Ge 28:19
35:17
q Ge 30:24
35:19
r Ge 48:7;
Ru 1:1,19;
Mic 5:2;
Mt 2:16
35:20
s 1Sa 10:2
35:22
t Ge 49:4;
1Ch 5:1
u Ge 29:29;
Lev 18:8
35:23
v Ge 46:8
w Ge 29:35
x Ge 30:20
35:24
y Ge 30:24
z ver 18
35:25
a Ge 30:8
35:26
b Ge 30:11
c Ge 30:13
35:27
d Ge 13:18; 18:1
e Jos 14:15
35:28
f Ge 25:7,20
35:29
g Ge 25:8; 49:33
h Ge 15:15
i Ge 25:9

---

a8 Allon Bacuth means oak of weeping.   *b9 That is, Northwest Mesopotamia; also in verse 26*   *c10 Jacob means he grasps the heel (figuratively, he deceives).*   *d10 Israel means he struggles with God.*   *e11 Hebrew El-Shaddai*   *f15 Bethel means house of God.*   *g18 Ben-Oni means son of my trouble.*   *h18 Benjamin means son of my right hand.*

Esau's Descendants

36:10–14pp — 1Ch 1:35–37
36:20–28pp — 1Ch 1:38–42

36 This is the account of Esau (that is, Edom).[j]

[2]Esau took his wives from the women of Canaan:[k] Adah daughter of Elon the Hittite,[l] and Oholibamah daughter of Anah[m] and granddaughter of Zibeon the Hivite— [3]also Basemath daughter of Ishmael and sister of Nebaioth.

[4]Adah bore Eliphaz to Esau, Basemath bore Reuel,[n] [5]and Oholibamah bore Jeush, Jalam and Korah. These were the sons of Esau, who were born to him in Canaan.

[6]Esau took his wives and sons and daughters and all the members of his household, as well as his livestock and all his other animals and all the goods he had acquired in Canaan,[o] and moved to a land some distance from his brother Jacob. [7]Their possessions were too great for them to remain together; the land where they were staying could not support them both because of their livestock.[p] [8]So Esau[q] (that is, Edom) settled in the hill country of Seir.[r]

[9]This is the account of Esau the father of the Edomites in the hill country of Seir.

[10]These are the names of Esau's sons:

Eliphaz, the son of Esau's wife Adah, and Reuel, the son of Esau's wife Basemath.

[11]The sons of Eliphaz:[s]

Teman,[t] Omar, Zepho, Gatam and Kenaz.

[12]Esau's son Eliphaz also had a concubine named Timna, who bore him Amalek.[u] These were grandsons of Esau's wife Adah.[v]

[13]The sons of Reuel:

Nahath, Zerah, Shammah and Mizzah. These were grandsons of Esau's wife Basemath.

[14]The sons of Esau's wife Oholibamah daughter of Anah and granddaughter of Zibeon, whom she bore to Esau:

Jeush, Jalam and Korah.

[15]These were the chiefs[w] among Esau's descendants:

The sons of Eliphaz the firstborn of Esau:

Chiefs Teman,[x] Omar, Zepho, Kenaz, [16]Korah,[a] Gatam and Amalek. These were the chiefs descended from Eliphaz in Edom; they were grandsons of Adah.[y]

[17]The sons of Esau's son Reuel:[z]

Chiefs Nahath, Zerah, Shammah and Mizzah. These were the chiefs descended from Reuel in Edom; they were grandsons of Esau's wife Basemath.

[18]The sons of Esau's wife Oholibamah:

Chiefs Jeush, Jalam and Korah. These were the chiefs descended from Esau's wife Oholibamah daughter of Anah.

36:1
jGe 25:30
36:2
kGe 28:8-9
lGe 26:34
mver 25
36:4
n1Ch 1:35
36:6
oGe 12:5
36:7
pGe 13:6; 17:8;
28:4
36:8
qDt 2:4
rGe 32:3
36:11
sver 15-16;
Job 2:11
tAm 1:12;
Hab 3:3
36:12
uEx 17:8,16;
Nu 24:20;
1Sa 15:2 vver 16
36:15
wGe 15:15
xJob 2:11
36:16
yver 12
36:17
z1Ch 1:37

---

[a]16 Masoretic Text; Samaritan Pentateuch (see also Gen. 36:11 and 1 Chron. 1:36) does not have *Korah.*

¹⁹These were the sons of Esau (that is, Edom),ᵃ and these were their chiefs.

²⁰These were the sons of Seir the Horite,ᵇ who were living in the region:

> Lotan, Shobal, Zibeon, Anah, ²¹Dishon, Ezer and Dishan. These sons of Seir in Edom were Horite chiefs.

²²The sons of Lotan:

> Hori and Homam.ᵃ Timna was Lotan's sister.

²³The sons of Shobal:

> Alvan, Manahath, Ebal, Shepho and Onam.

²⁴The sons of Zibeon:

> Aiah and Anah. This is the Anah who discovered the hot springsᵇ in the desert while he was grazing the donkeys of his father Zibeon.

²⁵The children of Anah:

> Dishon and Oholibamah daughter of Anah.

²⁶The sons of Dishonᶜ:

> Hemdan, Eshban, Ithran and Keran.

²⁷The sons of Ezer:

> Bilhan, Zaavan and Akan.

²⁸The sons of Dishan:

> Uz and Aran.

²⁹These were the Horite chiefs:

> Lotan, Shobal, Zibeon, Anah, ³⁰Dishon, Ezer and Dishan. These were the Horite chiefs, according to their divisions, in the land of Seir.

The Rulers of Edom

36:31-43pp — 1Ch 1:43-54

³¹These were the kings who reigned in Edom before any Israelite kingᶜ reignedᵈ:

> ³²Bela son of Beor became king of Edom. His city was named Dinhabah.

³³When Bela died, Jobab son of Zerah from Bozrahᵈ succeeded him as king.

³⁴When Jobab died, Husham from the land of the Temanitesᵉ succeeded him as king.

³⁵When Husham died, Hadad son of Bedad, who defeated Midian in the country of Moab,ᶠ succeeded him as king. His city was named Avith.

³⁶When Hadad died, Samlah from Masrekah succeeded him as king.

³⁷When Samlah died, Shaul from Rehoboth on the riverᵉ succeeded him as king.

³⁸When Shaul died, Baal-Hanan son of Acbor succeeded him as king.

36:19
ᵃGe 25:30
36:20
ᵇGe 14:6;
Dt 2:12,22;
1Ch 1:38
36:31
ᶜGe 17:6;
1Ch 1:43
36:33
ᵈJer 49:13,22
36:34
ᵉEze 25:13
36:35
ᶠGe 19:37;
Nu 22:1;
Dt 1:5; Ru 1:1,6

ᵃ22 Hebrew *Hemam*, a variant of *Homam* (see 1 Chron. 1:39)   ᵇ24 Vulgate; Syriac *discovered water*; the meaning of the Hebrew for this word is uncertain.   ᶜ26 Hebrew *Dishan*, a variant of *Dishon*   ᵈ31 Or *before an Israelite king reigned over them*   ᵉ37 Possibly the Euphrates

39When Baal-Hanan son of Acbor died, Hadad*a* succeeded him as king. His city was named Pau, and his wife's name was Mehetabel daughter of Matred, the daughter of Me-Zahab.

40These were the chiefs descended from Esau, by name, according to their clans and regions:

Timna, Alvah, Jetheth, 41Oholibamah, Elah, Pinon, 42Kenaz, Teman, Mibzar, 43Magdiel and Iram. These were the chiefs of Edom, according to their settlements in the land they occupied.

This was Esau the father of the Edomites.

Joseph's Dreams

37 Jacob lived in the land where his father had stayed,*g* the land of Canaan.*h*

2This is the account of Jacob.

Joseph, a young man of seventeen, was tending the flocks*i* with his brothers, the sons of Bilhah*j* and the sons of Zilpah,*k* his father's wives, and he brought their father a bad report*l* about them. 3Now Israel loved Joseph more than any of his other sons,*m* because he had been born to him in his old age;*n* and he made a richly ornamented*b* robe*o* for him. 4When his brothers saw that their father loved him more than any of them, they hated him*p* and could not speak a kind word to him.

5Joseph had a dream,*q* and when he told it to his brothers, they hated him all the more. 6He said to them, "Listen to this dream I had: 7We were binding sheaves of grain out in the field when suddenly my sheaf rose and stood upright, while your sheaves gathered around mine and bowed down to it."*r*

8His brothers said to him, "Do you intend to reign over us? Will you actually rule us?"*s* And they hated him all the more because of his dream and what he had said.

9Then he had another dream, and he told it to his brothers. "Listen," he said, "I had another dream, and this time the sun and moon and eleven stars were bowing down to me."

10When he told his father as well as his brothers,*t* his father rebuked him and said, "What is this dream you had? Will your mother and I and your brothers actually come and bow down to the ground before you?"*u* 11His brothers were jealous of him,*v* but his father kept the matter in mind.*w*

Joseph Sold by His Brothers

12Now his brothers had gone to graze their father's flocks near Shechem, 13and Israel said to Joseph, "As you know, your brothers are grazing the flocks near Shechem. Come, I am going to send you to them."

"Very well," he replied.

14So he said to him, "Go and see if all is well with your brothers and

37:1
gGe 17:8
hGe 10:19
37:2
iPs 78:71
jGe 35:25
kGe 35:26
l1Sa 2:24
37:3
mGe 25:28
nGe 44:20
o2Sa 13:18-19
37:4
pGe 27:41;
49:22-23;
Ac 7:9
37:5
qGe 20:3; 28:12
37:7
rGe 42:6,9;
43:26,28;
44:14; 50:18
37:8
sGe 49:26
37:10
tver 5 uver 7;
Ge 27:29
37:11
vAc 7:9
wLk 2:19,51

---

*a*39 Many manuscripts of the Masoretic Text, Samaritan Pentateuch and Syriac (see also 1 Chron. 1:50); most manuscripts of the Masoretic Text *Hadar*   *b*3 The meaning of the Hebrew for *richly ornamented* is uncertain; also in verses 23 and 32.

with the flocks, and bring word back to me." Then he sent him off from the Valley of Hebron. ˣ

When Joseph arrived at Shechem, ¹⁵a man found him wandering around in the fields and asked him, "What are you looking for?"

¹⁶He replied, "I'm looking for my brothers. Can you tell me where they are grazing their flocks?"

¹⁷"They have moved on from here," the man answered. "I heard them say, 'Let's go to Dothan.ʸ'"

So Joseph went after his brothers and found them near Dothan. ¹⁸But they saw him in the distance, and before he reached them, they plotted to kill him. ᶻ

¹⁹"Here comes that dreamer!" they said to each other. ²⁰"Come now, let's kill him and throw him into one of these cisternsᵃ and say that a ferocious animal devoured him. Then we'll see what comes of his dreams."ᵇ

²¹When Reuben heard this, he tried to rescue him from their hands. "Let's not take his life," he said. ᶜ ²²"Don't shed any blood. Throw him into this cistern here in the desert, but don't lay a hand on him." Reuben said this to rescue him from them and take him back to his father.

²³So when Joseph came to his brothers, they stripped him of his robe—the richly ornamented robe he was wearing— ²⁴and they took him and threw him into the cistern. ᵈ Now the cistern was empty; there was no water in it.

²⁵As they sat down to eat their meal, they looked up and saw a caravan of Ishmaelites coming from Gilead. Their camels were loaded with spices, balm and myrrh, ᵉ and they were on their way to take them down to Egypt. ᶠ

²⁶Judah said to his brothers, "What will we gain if we kill our brother and cover up his blood?ᵍ ²⁷Come, let's sell him to the Ishmaelites and not lay our hands on him; after all, he is our brother,ʰ our own flesh and blood." His brothers agreed.

²⁸So when the Midianiteⁱ merchants came by, his brothers pulled Joseph up out of the cistern and sold him for twenty shekelsᵃ of silver to the Ishmaelites, who took him to Egypt. ʲ

²⁹When Reuben returned to the cistern and saw that Joseph was not there, he tore his clothes. ᵏ ³⁰He went back to his brothers and said, "The boy isn't there! Where can I turn now?"ˡ

³¹Then they got Joseph's robe, ᵐ slaughtered a goat and dipped the robe in the blood. ³²They took the ornamented robe back to their father and said, "We found this. Examine it to see whether it is your son's robe."

³³He recognized it and said, "It is my son's robe! Some ferocious animalⁿ has devoured him. Joseph has surely been torn to pieces."ᵒ

³⁴Then Jacob tore his clothes, ᵖ put on sackclothᑫ and mourned for his son many days. ʳ ³⁵All his sons and daughters came to comfort him, but he refused to be comforted. "No," he said, "in mourning will I go down to the graveᵇˢ to my son." So his father wept for him.

ᵃ28 That is, about 8 ounces (about 0.2 kilogram)   ᵇ35 Hebrew *Sheol*

37:14
ˣGe 13:18;
35:27

37:17
ʸ2Ki 6:13

37:18
ᶻ1Sa 19:1;
Mk 14:1;
Ac 23:12

37:20
ᵃJer 38:6,9
ᵇGe 50:20

37:21
ᶜGe 42:22

37:24
ᵈJer 41:7

37:25
ᵉGe 43:11
ᶠver 28

37:26
ᵍver 20;
Ge 4:10

37:27
ʰGe 42:21

37:28
ⁱGe 25:2;
Jdg 6:1-3
ʲGe 45:4-5;
Ps 105:17;
Ac 7:9

37:29
ᵏver 34;
Ge 44:13;
Job 1:20

37:30
ˡver 22;
Ge 42:13,36

37:31
ᵐver 3,23

37:33
ⁿver 20
ᵒGe 44:20,28

37:34
ᵖver 29
ᑫ2Sa 3:31
ʳGe 50:3,10,11

37:35
ˢGe 42:38;
44:22,29,31

³⁶Meanwhile, the Midianites*ᵃ* sold Joseph in Egypt to Potiphar, one of Pharaoh's officials, the captain of the guard.ᵗ

Judah and Tamar

38 At that time, Judah left his brothers and went down to stay with a man of Adullam named Hirah. ²There Judah met the daughter of a Canaanite man named Shua.ᵘ He married her and lay with her; ³she became pregnant and gave birth to a son, who was named Er.ᵛ ⁴She conceived again and gave birth to a son and named him Onan. ⁵She gave birth to still another son and named him Shelah.ʷ It was at Kezib that she gave birth to him.

⁶Judah got a wife for Er, his firstborn, and her name was Tamar. ⁷But Er, Judah's firstborn, was wicked in the LORD's sight; so the LORD put him to death.ˣ

⁸Then Judah said to Onan, "Lie with your brother's wife and fulfill your duty to her as a brother-in-law to produce offspring for your brother."ʸ ⁹But Onan knew that the offspring would not be his; so whenever he lay with his brother's wife, he spilled his semen on the ground to keep from producing offspring for his brother. ¹⁰What he did was wicked in the LORD's sight; so he put him to death also.ᶻ

¹¹Judah then said to his daughter-in-law Tamar, "Live as a widow in your father's house until my son Shelah grows up."ᵃ For he thought, "He may die too, just like his brothers." So Tamar went to live in her father's house.

¹²After a long time Judah's wife, the daughter of Shua, died. When Judah had recovered from his grief, he went up to Timnah,ᵇ to the men who were shearing his sheep, and his friend Hirah the Adullamite went with him.

¹³When Tamar was told, "Your father-in-law is on his way to Timnah to shear his sheep," ¹⁴she took off her widow's clothes, covered herself with a veil to disguise herself, and then sat down at the entrance to Enaim, which is on the road to Timnah. For she saw that, though Shelahᶜ had now grown up, she had not been given to him as his wife.

¹⁵When Judah saw her, he thought she was a prostitute, for she had covered her face. ¹⁶Not realizing that she was his daughter-in-law,ᵈ he went over to her by the roadside and said, "Come now, let me sleep with you."

"And what will you give me to sleep with you?" she asked.

¹⁷"I'll send you a young goatᵉ from my flock," he said.

"Will you give me something as a pledgeᶠ until you send it?" she asked.

¹⁸He said, "What pledge should I give you?"

"Your sealᵍ and its cord, and the staff in your hand," she answered. So he gave them to her and slept with her, and she became pregnant by him. ¹⁹After she left, she took off her veil and put on her widow's clothesʰ again.

²⁰Meanwhile Judah sent the young goat by his friend the Adullamite in order to get his pledge back from the woman, but he did not find her.

37:36
tGe 39:1
38:2
u1Ch 2:3
38:3
vver 6;
Ge 46:12;
Nu 26:19
38:5
wNu 26:20;
1Ch 2:3; 4:21
38:7
xver 10;
Ge 46:12;
1Ch 2:3
38:8
yDt 25:5-6;
Mt 22:24-28
38:10
zGe 46:12;
Dt 25:7-10
38:11
aRu 1:13
38:12
bver 14;
Jos 15:10,57
38:14
cver 11
38:16
dLev 18:15;
20:12
38:17
eEze 16:33
fver 20
38:18
gver 25
38:19
hver 14

---

*a*36 Samaritan Pentateuch, Septuagint, Vulgate and Syriac (see also verse 28); Masoretic Text *Medanites*

²¹He asked the men who lived there, "Where is the shrine prostitute[i] who was beside the road at Enaim?"

"There hasn't been any shrine prostitute here," they said.

²²So he went back to Judah and said, "I didn't find her. Besides, the men who lived there said, 'There hasn't been any shrine prostitute here.'"

²³Then Judah said, "Let her keep what she has, or we will become a laughingstock. After all, I did send her this young goat, but you didn't find her."

²⁴About three months later Judah was told, "Your daughter-in-law Tamar is guilty of prostitution, and as a result she is now pregnant."

Judah said, "Bring her out and have her burned to death!"[j]

²⁵As she was being brought out, she sent a message to her father-in-law. "I am pregnant by the man who owns these," she said. And she added, "See if you recognize whose seal and cord and staff these are."[k]

²⁶Judah recognized them and said, "She is more righteous than I,[l] since I wouldn't give her to my son Shelah.[m]" And he did not sleep with her again.

²⁷When the time came for her to give birth, there were twin boys in her womb.[n] ²⁸As she was giving birth, one of them put out his hand; so the midwife took a scarlet thread and tied it on his wrist and said, "This one came out first." ²⁹But when he drew back his hand, his brother came out, and she said, "So this is how you have broken out!" And he was named Perez.[a][o] ³⁰Then his brother, who had the scarlet thread on his wrist, came out and he was given the name Zerah.[b][p]

Joseph and Potiphar's Wife

39 Now Joseph had been taken down to Egypt. Potiphar, an Egyptian who was one of Pharaoh's officials, the captain of the guard,[q] bought him from the Ishmaelites who had taken him there.[r]

²The LORD was with Joseph[s] and he prospered, and he lived in the house of his Egyptian master. ³When his master saw that the LORD was with him[t] and that the LORD gave him success in everything he did,[u] ⁴Joseph found favor in his eyes and became his attendant. Potiphar put him in charge of his household, and he entrusted to his care everything he owned.[v] ⁵From the time he put him in charge of his household and of all that he owned, the LORD blessed the household of the Egyptian because of Joseph.[w] The blessing of the LORD was on everything Potiphar had, both in the house and in the field. ⁶So he left in Joseph's care everything he had; with Joseph in charge, he did not concern himself with anything except the food he ate.

Now Joseph was well-built and handsome,[x] ⁷and after a while his master's wife took notice of Joseph and said, "Come to bed with me!"[y]

⁸But he refused.[z] "With me in charge," he told her, "my master does not concern himself with anything in the house; everything he owns he has entrusted to my care. ⁹No one is greater in this house than I am.[a] My master has withheld nothing from me except you, because you are his wife. How then could I do such a wicked thing and sin against God?"[b] ¹⁰And though she spoke to Joseph day after day, he refused to go to bed with her or even be with her.

---

[a]29 *Perez* means *breaking out.*   [b]30 *Zerah* can mean *scarlet* or *brightness.*

38:21
iLev 19:29;
Hos 4:14
38:24
jLev 21:9;
Dt 22:21,22
38:25
kver 18
38:26
l1Sa 24:17
mver 11
38:27
nGe 25:24
38:29
oGe 46:12;
Nu 26:20,21;
Ru 4:12,18;
1Ch 2:4; Mt 1:3
38:30
p1Ch 2:4
39:1
qGe 37:36
rGe 37:25;
Ps 105:17
39:2
sGe 21:20,22;
Ac 7:9
39:3
tGe 21:22;
26:28 uPs 1:3
39:4
vver 8,22;
Ge 24:2
39:5
wGe 26:24;
30:27
39:6
x1Sa 16:12
39:7
y2Sa 13:11;
Pr 7:15-18
39:8
zPr 6:23-24
39:9
aGe 41:33,40
bGe 20:6;
42:18;
2Sa 12:13

[11]One day he went into the house to attend to his duties, and none of the household servants was inside. [12]She caught him by his cloak[c] and said, "Come to bed with me!" But he left his cloak in her hand and ran out of the house.

[13]When she saw that he had left his cloak in her hand and had run out of the house, [14]she called her household servants. "Look," she said to them, "this Hebrew has been brought to us to make sport of us! He came in here to sleep with me, but I screamed. [d] [15]When he heard me scream for help, he left his cloak beside me and ran out of the house."

[16]She kept his cloak beside her until his master came home. [17]Then she told him this story: [e] "That Hebrew slave you brought us came to me to make sport of me. [18]But as soon as I screamed for help, he left his cloak beside me and ran out of the house."

[19]When his master heard the story his wife told him, saying, "This is how your slave treated me," he burned with anger. [f] [20]Joseph's master took him and put him in prison, [g] the place where the king's prisoners were confined.

But while Joseph was there in the prison, [21]the LORD was with him; he showed him kindness and granted him favor in the eyes of the prison warden. [h] [22]So the warden put Joseph in charge of all those held in the prison, and he was made responsible for all that was done there. [i] [23]The warden paid no attention to anything under Joseph's care, because the LORD was with Joseph and gave him success in whatever he did. [j]

The Cupbearer and the Baker

40 Some time later, the cupbearer[k] and the baker of the king of Egypt offended their master, the king of Egypt. [2]Pharaoh was angry[l] with his two officials, the chief cupbearer and the chief baker, [3]and put them in custody in the house of the captain of the guard, [m] in the same prison where Joseph was confined. [4]The captain of the guard assigned them to Joseph, [n] and he attended them.

After they had been in custody for some time, [5]each of the two men—the cupbearer and the baker of the king of Egypt, who were being held in prison—had a dream the same night, and each dream had a meaning of its own. [o]

[6]When Joseph came to them the next morning, he saw that they were dejected. [7]So he asked Pharaoh's officials who were in custody with him in his master's house, "Why are your faces so sad today?" [p]

[8]"We both had dreams," they answered, "but there is no one to interpret them." [q]

Then Joseph said to them, "Do not interpretations belong to God? [r] Tell me your dreams."

[9]So the chief cupbearer told Joseph his dream. He said to him, "In my dream I saw a vine in front of me, [10]and on the vine were three branches. As soon as it budded, it blossomed, and its clusters ripened into grapes. [11]Pharaoh's cup was in my hand, and I took the grapes, squeezed them into Pharaoh's cup and put the cup in his hand."

[12]"This is what it means, [s]" Joseph said to him. "The three branches are three days. [13]Within three days Pharaoh will lift up your head and restore you to your position, and you will put Pharaoh's cup in his

39:12
c Pr 7:13
39:14
d Dt 22:24,27
39:17
e Ex 23:1,7;
Ps 101:5
39:19
f Pr 6:34
39:20
g Ge 40:3;
Ps 105:18
39:21
h Ex 3:21
39:22
i ver 4
39:23
j ver 3
40:1
k Ne 1:11
40:2
l Pr 16:14,15
40:3
m Ge 39:20
40:4
n Ge 39:4
40:5
o Ge 41:11
40:7
p Ne 2:2
40:8
q Ge 41:8,15
r Ge 41:16;
Da 2:22,28,47
40:12
s Ge 41:12,15,
25; Da 2:36;
4:19

hand, just as you used to do when you were his cupbearer. [14]But when all goes well with you, remember me[t] and show me kindness;[u] mention me to Pharaoh and get me out of this prison. [15]For I was forcibly carried off from the land of the Hebrews,[v] and even here I have done nothing to deserve being put in a dungeon."

[16]When the chief baker saw that Joseph had given a favorable interpretation, he said to Joseph, "I too had a dream: On my head were three baskets of bread.[a] [17]In the top basket were all kinds of baked goods for Pharaoh, but the birds were eating them out of the basket on my head."

[18]"This is what it means," Joseph said. "The three baskets are three days.[w] [19]Within three days Pharaoh will lift off your head[x] and hang you on a tree.[b] And the birds will eat away your flesh."

[20]Now the third day was Pharaoh's birthday,[y] and he gave a feast for all his officials.[z] He lifted up the heads of the chief cupbearer and the chief baker in the presence of his officials: [21]He restored the chief cupbearer to his position, so that he once again put the cup into Pharaoh's hand,[a] [22]but he hanged[c] the chief baker,[b] just as Joseph had said to them in his interpretation.[c]

[23]The chief cupbearer, however, did not remember Joseph; he forgot him.[d]

Pharaoh's Dreams

41 When two full years had passed, Pharaoh had a dream:[e] He was standing by the Nile, [2]when out of the river there came up seven cows, sleek and fat,[f] and they grazed among the reeds.[g] [3]After them, seven other cows, ugly and gaunt, came up out of the Nile and stood beside those on the riverbank. [4]And the cows that were ugly and gaunt ate up the seven sleek, fat cows. Then Pharaoh woke up.

[5]He fell asleep again and had a second dream: Seven heads of grain, healthy and good, were growing on a single stalk. [6]After them, seven other heads of grain sprouted—thin and scorched by the east wind. [7]The thin heads of grain swallowed up the seven healthy, full heads. Then Pharaoh woke up; it had been a dream.

[8]In the morning his mind was troubled,[h] so he sent for all the magicians[i] and wise men of Egypt. Pharaoh told them his dreams, but no one could interpret them for him.

[9]Then the chief cupbearer said to Pharaoh, "Today I am reminded of my shortcomings. [10]Pharaoh was once angry with his servants,[j] and he imprisoned me and the chief baker in the house of the captain of the guard.[k] [11]Each of us had a dream the same night, and each dream had a meaning of its own.[l] [12]Now a young Hebrew was there with us, a servant of the captain of the guard. We told him our dreams, and he interpreted them for us, giving each man the interpretation of his dream.[m] [13]And things turned out exactly as he interpreted them to us: I was restored to my position, and the other man was hanged.[c] [n]"

[14]So Pharaoh sent for Joseph, and he was quickly brought from the dungeon.[o] When he had shaved and changed his clothes, he came before Pharaoh.

40:14
tLk 23:42
uJos 2:12;
1Sa 20:14,42;
1Ki 2:7
40:15
vGe 37:26-28
40:18
wver 12
40:19
xver 13
40:20
yMt 14:6-10
zMk 6:21
40:21
aver 13
40:22
bver 19
cPs 105:19
40:23
dJob 19:14;
Ecc 9:15
41:1
eGe 20:3
41:2
fver 26
gIsa 19:6
41:8
hDa 2:1,3; 4:5,
19 iEx 7:11,22;
Da 1:20; 2:2,
27; 4:7
41:10
jGe 40:2
kGe 39:20
41:11
lGe 40:5
41:12
mGe 40:12
41:13
nGe 40:22
41:14
oPs 105:20;
Da 2:25

---

[a]16 Or *three wicker baskets*   [b]19 Or *and impale you on a pole*   [c]22,13 Or *impaled*

¹⁵Pharaoh said to Joseph, "I had a dream, and no one can interpret it. But I have heard it said of you that when you hear a dream you can interpret it." ᵖ

¹⁶"I cannot do it," Joseph replied to Pharaoh, "but God will give Pharaoh the answer he desires." �q

¹⁷Then Pharaoh said to Joseph, "In my dream I was standing on the bank of the Nile, ¹⁸when out of the river there came up seven cows, fat and sleek, and they grazed among the reeds. ¹⁹After them, seven other cows came up—scrawny and very ugly and lean. I had never seen such ugly cows in all the land of Egypt. ²⁰The lean, ugly cows ate up the seven fat cows that came up first. ²¹But even after they ate them, no one could tell that they had done so; they looked just as ugly as before. Then I woke up.

²²"In my dreams I also saw seven heads of grain, full and good, growing on a single stalk. ²³After them, seven other heads sprouted —withered and thin and scorched by the east wind. ²⁴The thin heads of grain swallowed up the seven good heads. I told this to the magicians, but none could explain it to me. ʳ "

²⁵Then Joseph said to Pharaoh, "The dreams of Pharaoh are one and the same. God has revealed to Pharaoh what he is about to do. ˢ ²⁶The seven good cows ᵗ are seven years, and the seven good heads of grain are seven years; it is one and the same dream. ²⁷The seven lean, ugly cows that came up afterward are seven years, and so are the seven worthless heads of grain scorched by the east wind: They are seven years of famine. ᵘ

²⁸"It is just as I said to Pharaoh: God has shown Pharaoh what he is about to do. ²⁹Seven years of great abundance ᵛ are coming throughout the land of Egypt, ³⁰but seven years of famine ʷ will follow them. Then all the abundance in Egypt will be forgotten, and the famine will ravage the land. ˣ ³¹The abundance in the land will not be remembered, because the famine that follows it will be so severe. ³²The reason the dream was given to Pharaoh in two forms is that the matter has been firmly decided ʸ by God, and God will do it soon.

³³"And now let Pharaoh look for a discerning and wise man ᶻ and put him in charge of the land of Egypt. ³⁴Let Pharaoh appoint commissioners over the land to take a fifth ᵃ of the harvest of Egypt during the seven years of abundance. ᵇ ³⁵They should collect all the food of these good years that are coming and store up the grain under the authority of Pharaoh, to be kept in the cities for food. ᶜ ³⁶This food should be held in reserve for the country, to be used during the seven years of famine that will come upon Egypt, ᵈ so that the country may not be ruined by the famine."

³⁷The plan seemed good to Pharaoh and to all his officials. ᵉ ³⁸So Pharaoh asked them, "Can we find anyone like this man, one in whom is the spirit of God ᵃ ?" ᶠ

³⁹Then Pharaoh said to Joseph, "Since God has made all this known to you, there is no one so discerning and wise as you. ⁴⁰You shall be in charge of my palace, and all my people are to submit to your orders. ᵍ Only with respect to the throne will I be greater than you."

ᵃ38 Or *of the gods*

41:15
ᵖDa 5:16
41:16
qGe 40:8;
Da 2:30;
Ac 3:12;
2Co 3:5
41:24
ʳver 8
41:25
ˢDa 2:45
41:26
ᵗver 2
41:27
ᵘGe 12:10;
2Ki 8:1
41:29
ᵛver 47
41:30
ʷver 54;
Ge 47:13
ˣver 56
41:32
ʸNu 23:19;
Isa 46:10-11
41:33
ᶻver 39
41:34
ᵃ1Sa 8:15
ᵇver 48
41:35
ᶜver 48
41:36
ᵈver 48
41:37
ᵉGe 45:16
41:38
ᶠNu 27:18;
Job 32:8;
Da 4:8,8-9,18;
5:11,14
41:40
ᵍPs 105:21-22;
Ac 7:10

Joseph in Charge of Egypt

⁴¹So Pharaoh said to Joseph, "I hereby put you in charge of the whole land of Egypt."ʰ ⁴²Then Pharaoh took his signet ringⁱ from his finger and put it on Joseph's finger. He dressed him in robes of fine linen and put a gold chain around his neck.ʲ ⁴³He had him ride in a chariot as his second-in-command,ᵃ and men shouted before him, "Make wayᵇ!"ᵏ Thus he put him in charge of the whole land of Egypt.

⁴⁴Then Pharaoh said to Joseph, "I am Pharaoh, but without your word no one will lift hand or foot in all Egypt."ˡ ⁴⁵Pharaoh gave Joseph the name Zaphenath-Paneah and gave him Asenath daughter of Potiphera, priest of On,ᶜ to be his wife.ᵐ And Joseph went throughout the land of Egypt.

⁴⁶Joseph was thirty years oldⁿ when he entered the serviceᵒ of Pharaoh king of Egypt. And Joseph went out from Pharaoh's presence and traveled throughout Egypt. ⁴⁷During the seven years of abundance the land produced plentifully. ⁴⁸Joseph collected all the food produced in those seven years of abundance in Egypt and stored it in the cities. In each city he put the food grown in the fields surrounding it. ⁴⁹Joseph stored up huge quantities of grain, like the sand of the sea; it was so much that he stopped keeping records because it was beyond measure.

⁵⁰Before the years of famine came, two sons were born to Joseph by Asenath daughter of Potiphera, priest of On.ᵖ ⁵¹Joseph named his firstbornᑫ Manassehᵈ and said, "It is because God has made me forget all my trouble and all my father's household." ⁵²The second son he named Ephraimᵉʳ and said, "It is because God has made me fruitfulˢ in the land of my suffering."

⁵³The seven years of abundance in Egypt came to an end, ⁵⁴and the seven years of famine began,ᵗ just as Joseph had said. There was famine in all the other lands, but in the whole land of Egypt there was food. ⁵⁵When all Egypt began to feel the famine,ᵘ the people cried to Pharaoh for food. Then Pharaoh told all the Egyptians, "Go to Joseph and do what he tells you."ᵛ

⁵⁶When the famine had spread over the whole country, Joseph opened the storehouses and sold grain to the Egyptians, for the famineʷ was severe throughout Egypt. ⁵⁷And all the countries came to Egypt to buy grain from Joseph,ˣ because the famine was severe in all the world.

Joseph's Brothers Go to Egypt

42 When Jacob learned that there was grain in Egypt,ʸ he said to his sons, "Why do you just keep looking at each other?" ²He continued, "I have heard that there is grain in Egypt. Go down there and buy some for us, so that we may live and not die."ᶻ

³Then ten of Joseph's brothers went down to buy grain from Egypt. ⁴But Jacob did not send Benjamin, Joseph's brother, with the others, because he was afraid that harm might come to him.ᵃ ⁵So Israel's sons were among those who went to buy grain,ᵇ for the famine was in the land of Canaan also.ᶜ

41:41
ʰGe 42:6;
Da 6:3
41:42
ⁱEst 3:10
ʲDa 5:7,16,29
41:43
ᵏEst 6:9
41:44
ˡPs 105:22
41:45
ᵐver 50;
Ge 46:20,27
41:46
ⁿGe 37:2
ᵒ1Sa 16:21;
Da 1:19
41:50
ᵖGe 46:20; 48:5
41:51
ᑫGe 48:14,18,20
41:52
ʳGe 48:1,5;
50:23 ˢGe 17:6;
28:3; 49:22
41:54
ᵗver 30;
Ps 105:11;
Ac 7:11
41:55
ᵘDt 32:24
ᵛver 41
41:56
ʷGe 12:10
41:57
ˣGe 42:5; 47:15
42:1
ʸAc 7:12
42:2
ᶻGe 43:8
42:4
ᵃver 38
42:5
ᵇGe 41:57
ᶜGe 12:10;
Ac 7:11

ᵃ43 Or *in the chariot of his second-in-command; or in his second chariot*   ᵇ43 Or *Bow down*
ᶜ45 That is, Heliopolis; also in verse 50   ᵈ51 *Manasseh* sounds like and may be derived from the Hebrew for *forget*.   ᵉ52 *Ephraim* sounds like the Hebrew for *twice fruitful*.

6Now Joseph was the governor of the land,[d] the one who sold grain to all its people. So when Joseph's brothers arrived, they bowed down to him with their faces to the ground.[e] 7As soon as Joseph saw his brothers, he recognized them, but he pretended to be a stranger and spoke harshly to them.[f] "Where do you come from?" he asked.

"From the land of Canaan," they replied, "to buy food."

8Although Joseph recognized his brothers, they did not recognize him.[g] 9Then he remembered his dreams[h] about them and said to them, "You are spies! You have come to see where our land is unprotected."

10"No, my lord," they answered. "Your servants have come to buy food. 11We are all the sons of one man. Your servants are honest men, not spies."

12"No!" he said to them. "You have come to see where our land is unprotected."

13But they replied, "Your servants were twelve brothers, the sons of one man, who lives in the land of Canaan. The youngest is now with our father, and one is no more."[i]

14Joseph said to them, "It is just as I told you: You are spies! 15And this is how you will be tested: As surely as Pharaoh lives,[j] you will not leave this place unless your youngest brother comes here. 16Send one of your number to get your brother; the rest of you will be kept in prison, so that your words may be tested to see if you are telling the truth.[k] If you are not, then as surely as Pharaoh lives, you are spies!" 17And he put them all in custody[l] for three days.

18On the third day, Joseph said to them, "Do this and you will live, for I fear God:[m] 19If you are honest men, let one of your brothers stay here in prison, while the rest of you go and take grain back for your starving households. 20But you must bring your youngest brother to me,[n] so that your words may be verified and that you may not die." This they proceeded to do.

21They said to one another, "Surely we are being punished because of our brother.[o] We saw how distressed he was when he pleaded with us for his life, but we would not listen; that's why this distress[p] has come upon us."

22Reuben replied, "Didn't I tell you not to sin against the boy?[q] But you wouldn't listen! Now we must give an accounting[r] for his blood."[s] 23They did not realize that Joseph could understand them, since he was using an interpreter.

24He turned away from them and began to weep, but then turned back and spoke to them again. He had Simeon taken from them and bound before their eyes.[t]

25Joseph gave orders to fill their bags with grain,[u] to put each man's silver back in his sack,[v] and to give them provisions for their journey.[w] After this was done for them, 26they loaded their grain on their donkeys and left.

27At the place where they stopped for the night one of them opened his sack to get feed for his donkey, and he saw his silver in the mouth of his sack.[x] 28"My silver has been returned," he said to his brothers. "Here it is in my sack."

Their hearts sank and they turned to each other trembling and said, "What is this that God has done to us?"[y]

29When they came to their father Jacob in the land of Canaan, they

42:6
d Ge 41:41
e Ge 37:7-10
42:7
f ver 30
42:8
g Ge 37:2
42:9
h Ge 37:7
42:13
i Ge 37:30,33;
44:20
42:15
j 1Sa 17:55
42:16
k ver 11
42:17
l Ge 40:4
42:18
m Ge 20:11;
Lev 25:43
42:20
n ver 15,34;
Ge 43:5; 44:23
42:21
o Ge 37:26-28
p Hos 5:15
42:22
q Ge 37:21-22
r Ge 9:5
s 1Ki 2:32;
2Ch 24:22;
Ps 9:12
42:24
t ver 13;
Ge 43:14,23;
45:14-15
42:25
u Ge 43:2
v Ge 44:1,8
w Ro 12:17,
20-21
42:27
x Ge 43:21-22
42:28
y Ge 43:23

told him all that had happened to them. They said, 30"The man who is lord over the land spoke harshly to us[z] and treated us as though we were spying on the land. 31But we said to him, 'We are honest men; we are not spies.[a] 32We were twelve brothers, sons of one father. One is no more, and the youngest is now with our father in Canaan.'

33"Then the man who is lord over the land said to us, 'This is how I will know whether you are honest men: Leave one of your brothers here with me, and take food for your starving households and go.[b] 34But bring your youngest brother to me so I will know that you are not spies but honest men. Then I will give your brother back to you, and you can trade[a] in the land.[c]'"

35As they were emptying their sacks, there in each man's sack was his pouch of silver! When they and their father saw the money pouches, they were frightened.[d] 36Their father Jacob said to them, "You have deprived me of my children. Joseph is no more and Simeon is no more, and now you want to take Benjamin.[e] Everything is against me!"

37Then Reuben said to his father, "You may put both of my sons to death if I do not bring him back to you. Entrust him to my care, and I will bring him back."

38But Jacob said, "My son will not go down there with you; his brother is dead[f] and he is the only one left. If harm comes to him[g] on the journey you are taking, you will bring my gray head down to the grave[b][h] in sorrow.[i]"

The Second Journey to Egypt

43 Now the famine was still severe in the land.[j] 2So when they had eaten all the grain they had brought from Egypt, their father said to them, "Go back and buy us a little more food."

3But Judah said to him, "The man warned us solemnly, 'You will not see my face again unless your brother is with you.'[k] 4If you will send our brother along with us, we will go down and buy food for you. 5But if you will not send him, we will not go down, because the man said to us, 'You will not see my face again unless your brother is with you.'[l]"

6Israel asked, "Why did you bring this trouble on me by telling the man you had another brother?"

7They replied, "The man questioned us closely about ourselves and our family. 'Is your father still living?'[m] he asked us. 'Do you have another brother?'[n] We simply answered his questions. How were we to know he would say, 'Bring your brother down here'?"

8Then Judah said to Israel his father, "Send the boy along with me and we will go at once, so that we and you and our children may live and not die.[o] 9I myself will guarantee his safety; you can hold me personally responsible for him. If I do not bring him back to you and set him here before you, I will bear the blame before you all my life.[p] 10As it is, if we had not delayed, we could have gone and returned twice."

11Then their father Israel said to them, "If it must be, then do this: Put some of the best products of the land in your bags and take them down to the man as a gift[q]—a little balm[r] and a little honey, some spices[s] and myrrh, some pistachio nuts and almonds. 12Take double the amount of silver with you, for you must return the silver that was put back into

42:30
z ver 7
42:31
a ver 11
42:33
b ver 19,20
42:34
c Ge 34:10
42:35
d Ge 43:12,15,18
42:36
e Ge 43:14
42:38
f Ge 37:33
g ver 4
h Ge 37:35
i Ge 44:29,34
43:1
j Ge 12:10;
41:56-57
43:3
k Ge 42:15;
44:23
43:5
l Ge 42:15;
2Sa 3:13
43:7
m ver 27
n Ge 42:13
43:8
o Ge 42:2;
Ps 33:18-19
43:9
p Ge 42:37;
44:32;
Phm 1:18-19
43:11
q Ge 32:20;
Pr 18:16
r Ge 37:25;
Jer 8:22
s 1Ki 10:2

a34 Or *move about freely*   b38 Hebrew *Sheol*

the mouths of your sacks.[t] Perhaps it was a mistake. [13]Take your brother also and go back to the man at once. [14]And may God Almighty[a][u] grant you mercy before the man so that he will let your other brother and Benjamin come back with you.[v] As for me, if I am bereaved, I am bereaved."[w]

[15]So the men took the gifts and double the amount of silver, and Benjamin also. They hurried[x] down to Egypt and presented themselves[y] to Joseph. [16]When Joseph saw Benjamin with them, he said to the steward of his house,[z] "Take these men to my house, slaughter an animal and prepare dinner;[a] they are to eat with me at noon."

[17]The man did as Joseph told him and took the men to Joseph's house. [18]Now the men were frightened[b] when they were taken to his house. They thought, "We were brought here because of the silver that was put back into our sacks the first time. He wants to attack us and overpower us and seize us as slaves and take our donkeys."

[19]So they went up to Joseph's steward and spoke to him at the entrance to the house. [20]"Please, sir," they said, "we came down here the first time to buy food.[c] [21]But at the place where we stopped for the night we opened our sacks and each of us found his silver—the exact weight—in the mouth of his sack. So we have brought it back with us.[d] [22]We have also brought additional silver with us to buy food. We don't know who put our silver in our sacks."

[23]"It's all right," he said. "Don't be afraid. Your God, the God of your father, has given you treasure in your sacks;[e] I received your silver." Then he brought Simeon out to them.[f]

[24]The steward took the men into Joseph's house,[g] gave them water to wash their feet[h] and provided fodder for their donkeys. [25]They prepared their gifts for Joseph's arrival at noon, because they had heard that they were to eat there.

[26]When Joseph came home, they presented to him the gifts[i] they had brought into the house, and they bowed down before him to the ground.[j] [27]He asked them how they were, and then he said, "How is your aged father you told me about? Is he still living?"[k]

[28]They replied, "Your servant our father is still alive and well." And they bowed low to pay him honor.[l]

[29]As he looked about and saw his brother Benjamin, his own mother's son, he asked, "Is this your youngest brother, the one you told me about?"[m] And he said, "God be gracious to you,[n] my son." [30]Deeply moved[o] at the sight of his brother, Joseph hurried out and looked for a place to weep. He went into his private room and wept[p] there.

[31]After he had washed his face, he came out and, controlling himself,[q] said, "Serve the food."

[32]They served him by himself, the brothers by themselves, and the Egyptians who ate with him by themselves, because Egyptians could not eat with Hebrews,[r] for that is detestable to Egyptians.[s] [33]The men had been seated before him in the order of their ages, from the firstborn to the youngest; and they looked at each other in astonishment. [34]When portions were served to them from Joseph's table, Benjamin's portion was five times as much as anyone else's.[t] So they feasted and drank freely with him.

[a]14 Hebrew *El-Shaddai*

43:12
tGe 42:25
43:14
uGe 17:1; 28:3;
35:11 vGe 42:24
wEst 4:16
43:15
xGe 45:9,13
yGe 47:2,7
43:16
zGe 44:1,4,12
aver 31;
Lk 15:23
43:18
bGe 42:35
43:20
cGe 42:3
43:21
dver 15;
Ge 42:27,35
43:23
eGe 42:28
fGe 42:24
43:24
gver 16
hGe 18:4; 24:32
43:26
iMt 2:11
jGe 37:7,10
43:27
kver 7
43:28
lGe 37:7
43:29
mGe 42:13
nNu 6:25;
Ps 67:1
43:30
oJn 11:33,38
pGe 42:24;
45:2,14,15;
46:29
43:31
qGe 45:1
43:32
rGal 2:12
sGe 46:34;
Ex 8:26
43:34
tGe 37:3; 45:22

A Silver Cup in a Sack

44 Now Joseph gave these instructions to the steward of his house: "Fill the men's sacks with as much food as they can carry, and put each man's silver in the mouth of his sack.ᵘ ²Then put my cup, the silver one, in the mouth of the youngest one's sack, along with the silver for his grain." And he did as Joseph said.

³As morning dawned, the men were sent on their way with their donkeys. ⁴They had not gone far from the city when Joseph said to his steward, "Go after those men at once, and when you catch up with them, say to them, 'Why have you repaid good with evil?ᵛ ⁵Isn't this the cup my master drinks from and also uses for divination?ʷ This is a wicked thing you have done.'"

⁶When he caught up with them, he repeated these words to them. ⁷But they said to him, "Why does my lord say such things? Far be it from your servants to do anything like that! ⁸We even brought back to you from the land of Canaan the silver we found inside the mouths of our sacks.ˣ So why would we steal silver or gold from your master's house? ⁹If any of your servants is found to have it, he will die;ʸ and the rest of us will become my lord's slaves."

¹⁰"Very well, then," he said, "let it be as you say. Whoever is found to have it will become my slave; the rest of you will be free from blame."

¹¹Each of them quickly lowered his sack to the ground and opened it. ¹²Then the steward proceeded to search, beginning with the oldest and ending with the youngest. And the cup was found in Benjamin's sack.ᶻ ¹³At this, they tore their clothes.ᵃ Then they all loaded their donkeys and returned to the city.

¹⁴Joseph was still in the house when Judah and his brothers came in, and they threw themselves to the ground before him.ᵇ ¹⁵Joseph said to them, "What is this you have done? Don't you know that a man like me can find things out by divination?ᶜ"

¹⁶"What can we say to my lord?" Judah replied. "What can we say? How can we prove our innocence? God has uncovered your servants' guilt. We are now my lord's slavesᵈ—we ourselves and the one who was found to have the cup.ᵉ"

¹⁷But Joseph said, "Far be it from me to do such a thing! Only the man who was found to have the cup will become my slave. The rest of you, go back to your father in peace."

¹⁸Then Judah went up to him and said: "Please, my lord, let your servant speak a word to my lord. Do not be angryᶠ with your servant, though you are equal to Pharaoh himself. ¹⁹My lord asked his servants, 'Do you have a father or a brother?'ᵍ ²⁰And we answered, 'We have an aged father, and there is a young son born to him in his old age.ʰ His brother is dead,ⁱ and he is the only one of his mother's sons left, and his father loves him.'ʲ

²¹"Then you said to your servants, 'Bring him down to me so I can see him for myself.'ᵏ ²²And we said to my lord, 'The boy cannot leave his father; if he leaves him, his father will die.'ˡ ²³But you told your servants, 'Unless your youngest brother comes down with you, you will not see my face again.'ᵐ ²⁴When we went back to your servant my father, we told him what my lord had said.

²⁵"Then our father said, 'Go back and buy a little more food.'ⁿ ²⁶But

---

44:1
ᵘGe 42:25

44:4
ᵛPs 35:12

44:5
ʷGe 30:27;
Dt 18:10-14

44:8
ˣGe 42:25;
43:21

44:9
ʸGe 31:32

44:12
ᶻver 2

44:13
ᵃGe 37:29;
Nu 14:6;
2Sa 1:11

44:14
ᵇGe 37:7,10

44:15
ᶜver 5;
Ge 30:27

44:16
ᵈver 9;
Ge 43:18 ᵉver 2

44:18
ᶠGe 18:30;
Ex 32:22

44:19
ᵍGe 43:7

44:20
ʰGe 37:3
ⁱGe 37:33
ʲGe 42:13

44:21
ᵏGe 42:15

44:22
ˡGe 37:35

44:23
ᵐGe 43:5

44:25
ⁿGe 43:2

we said, 'We cannot go down. Only if our youngest brother is with us will we go. We cannot see the man's face unless our youngest brother is with us.'

27"Your servant my father said to us, 'You know that my wife bore me two sons.° 28One of them went away from me, and I said, "He has surely been torn to pieces."ᴾ And I have not seen him since. 29If you take this one from me too and harm comes to him, you will bring my gray head down to the graveᵃ in misery.'�q

30"So now, if the boy is not with us when I go back to your servant my father and if my father, whose life is closely bound up with the boy's life,ʳ 31sees that the boy isn't there, he will die. Your servants will bring the gray head of our father down to the grave in sorrow. 32Your servant guaranteed the boy's safety to my father. I said, 'If I do not bring him back to you, I will bear the blame before you, my father, all my life!'ˢ

33"Now then, please let your servant remain here as my lord's slaveᵗ in place of the boy,ᵘ and let the boy return with his brothers. 34How can I go back to my father if the boy is not with me? No! Do not let me see the misery that would come upon my father."ᵛ

Joseph Makes Himself Known

45 Then Joseph could no longer control himselfʷ before all his attendants, and he cried out, "Have everyone leave my presence!" So there was no one with Joseph when he made himself known to his brothers. 2And he weptˣ so loudly that the Egyptians heard him, and Pharaoh's household heard about it.ʸ

3Joseph said to his brothers, "I am Joseph! Is my father still living?"ᶻ But his brothers were not able to answer him,ᵃ because they were terrified at his presence.

4Then Joseph said to his brothers, "Come close to me." When they had done so, he said, "I am your brother Joseph, the one you sold into Egypt!ᵇ 5And now, do not be distressedᶜ and do not be angry with yourselves for selling me here,ᵈ because it was to save lives that God sent me ahead of you.ᵉ 6For two years now there has been famine in the land, and for the next five years there will not be plowing and reaping. 7But God sent me ahead of you to preserve for you a remnantᶠ on earth and to save your lives by a great deliverance.ᵇ ᵍ

8"So then, it was not you who sent me here, but God. He made me fatherʰ to Pharaoh, lord of his entire household and ruler of all Egypt.ⁱ 9Now hurry back to my father and say to him, 'This is what your son Joseph says: God has made me lord of all Egypt. Come down to me; don't delay.ʲ 10You shall live in the region of Goshenᵏ and be near me—you, your children and grandchildren, your flocks and herds, and all you have. 11I will provide for you there,ˡ because five years of famine are still to come. Otherwise you and your household and all who belong to you will become destitute.'

12"You can see for yourselves, and so can my brother Benjamin, that it is really I who am speaking to you. 13Tell my father about all the honor accorded me in Egypt and about everything you have seen. And bring my father down here quickly.ᵐ"

14Then he threw his arms around his brother Benjamin and wept,

---

ᵃ29 Hebrew Sheol; also in verse 31   ᵇ7 Or save you as a great band of survivors

44:27
°Ge 46:19
44:28
pGe 37:33
44:29
qGe 42:38
44:30
r1Sa 18:1
44:32
sGe 43:9
44:33
tGe 43:18
uJn 15:13
44:34
vEst 8:6
45:1
wGe 43:31
45:2
xGe 29:11
yver 16;
Ge 46:29
45:3
zAc 7:13 aver 15
45:4
bGe 37:28
45:5
cGe 42:21
dGe 42:22
ever 7-8;
Ge 50:20;
Ps 105:17
45:7
f2Ki 19:4,30,31;
Isa 10:20,21;
Mic 4:7;
Zep 2:7
gEx 15:2;
Est 4:14;
Isa 25:9
45:8
hJdg 17:10
iGe 41:41
45:9
jGe 43:10
45:10
kGe 46:28,34;
47:1
45:11
lGe 47:12
45:13
mAc 7:14

and Benjamin embraced him, weeping. [15]And he kissed[n] all his brothers and wept over them. Afterward his brothers talked with him. [o]

[16]When the news reached Pharaoh's palace that Joseph's brothers had come, [p] Pharaoh and all his officials were pleased. [17]Pharaoh said to Joseph, "Tell your brothers, 'Do this: Load your animals and return to the land of Canaan, [18]and bring your father and your families back to me. I will give you the best of the land of Egypt[q] and you can enjoy the fat of the land.'[r]

[19]"You are also directed to tell them, 'Do this: Take some carts[s] from Egypt for your children and your wives, and get your father and come. [20]Never mind about your belongings, because the best of all Egypt will be yours.'"

[21]So the sons of Israel did this. Joseph gave them carts, as Pharaoh had commanded, and he also gave them provisions for their journey. [t] [22]To each of them he gave new clothing, but to Benjamin he gave three hundred shekels[a] of silver and five sets of clothes. [u] [23]And this is what he sent to his father: ten donkeys loaded with the best things of Egypt, and ten female donkeys loaded with grain and bread and other provisions for his journey. [24]Then he sent his brothers away, and as they were leaving he said to them, "Don't quarrel on the way!"[v]

[25]So they went up out of Egypt and came to their father Jacob in the land of Canaan. [26]They told him, "Joseph is still alive! In fact, he is ruler of all Egypt." Jacob was stunned; he did not believe them. [w] [27]But when they told him everything Joseph had said to them, and when he saw the carts[x] Joseph had sent to carry him back, the spirit of their father Jacob revived. [28]And Israel said, "I'm convinced! My son Joseph is still alive. I will go and see him before I die."

Jacob Goes to Egypt

46 So Israel set out with all that was his, and when he reached Beersheba, [y] he offered sacrifices to the God of his father Isaac. [z] [2]And God spoke to Israel in a vision at night[a] and said, "Jacob! Jacob!"

"Here I am," [b] he replied.

[3]"I am God, the God of your father," [c] he said. "Do not be afraid to go down to Egypt, for I will make you into a great nation[d] there. [e] [4]I will go down to Egypt with you, and I will surely bring you back again. [f] And Joseph's own hand will close your eyes. [g]"

[5]Then Jacob left Beersheba, and Israel's sons took their father Jacob and their children and their wives in the carts[h] that Pharaoh had sent to transport him. [6]They also took with them their livestock and the possessions they had acquired in Canaan, and Jacob and all his offspring went to Egypt. [i] [7]He took with him to Egypt his sons and grandsons and his daughters and granddaughters—all his offspring.[j]

[8]These are the names of the sons of Israel[k] (Jacob and his descendants) who went to Egypt:

Reuben the firstborn of Jacob.
[9]The sons of Reuben:[l]
Hanoch, Pallu, Hezron and Carmi.

45:15
n Lk 15:20
over 3
45:16
p Ac 7:13
45:18
q Ge 27:28;
46:34; 47:6,11,
27; Nu 18:12,29
r Ps 37:19
45:19
s Ge 46:5
45:21
t Ge 42:25
45:22
u Ge 37:3; 43:34
45:24
v Ge 42:21-22
45:26
w Ge 44:28
45:27
x ver 19
46:1
y Ge 21:14;
28:10
z Ge 26:24;
28:13; 31:42
46:2
a Ge 15:1;
Job 33:14-15
b Ge 22:1; 31:11
46:3
c Ge 28:13
d Ge 12:2;
Dt 26:5 e Ex 1:7
46:4
f Ge 28:15;
48:21; Ex 3:8
g Ge 50:1,24
46:5
h Ge 45:19
46:6
i Dt 26:5;
Jos 24:4;
Ps 105:23;
Isa 52:4;
Ac 7:15
46:7
j Ge 45:10
46:8
k Ex 1:1;
Nu 26:4
46:9
l 1Ch 5:3

---

[a]22 That is, about 7 1/2 pounds (about 3.5 kilograms)

¹⁰The sons of Simeon:[m]
Jemuel,[n] Jamin, Ohad, Jakin, Zohar and Shaul the son of a
Canaanite woman.
¹¹The sons of Levi:[o]
Gershon, Kohath and Merari.
¹²The sons of Judah:[p]
Er, Onan, Shelah, Perez and Zerah (but Er and Onan had died
in the land of Canaan).
The sons of Perez:[q]
Hezron and Hamul.
¹³The sons of Issachar:[r]
Tola, Puah,[a][s] Jashub[b] and Shimron.
¹⁴The sons of Zebulun:[t]
Sered, Elon and Jahleel.
¹⁵These were the sons Leah bore to Jacob in Paddan Aram,[c] besides
his daughter Dinah. These sons and daughters of his were thirty-three
in all.

¹⁶The sons of Gad:[u]
Zephon,[d][v] Haggi, Shuni, Ezbon, Eri, Arodi and Areli.
¹⁷The sons of Asher:[w]
Imnah, Ishvah, Ishvi and Beriah.
Their sister was Serah.
The sons of Beriah:
Heber and Malkiel.
¹⁸These were the children born to Jacob by Zilpah,[x] whom Laban had
given to his daughter Leah[y]—sixteen in all.

¹⁹The sons of Jacob's wife Rachel:
Joseph and Benjamin.[z] ²⁰In Egypt, Manasseh[a] and Ephraim[b]
were born to Joseph by Asenath daughter of Potiphera, priest
of On.[e]
²¹The sons of Benjamin:[c]
Bela, Beker, Ashbel, Gera, Naaman, Ehi, Rosh, Muppim, Hup-
pim and Ard.
²²These were the sons of Rachel who were born to Jacob—fourteen in
all.

²³The son of Dan:
Hushim.
²⁴The sons of Naphtali:
Jahziel, Guni, Jezer and Shillem.
²⁵These were the sons born to Jacob by Bilhah,[d] whom Laban had
given to his daughter Rachel[e]—seven in all.

²⁶All those who went to Egypt with Jacob—those who were his direct
descendants, not counting his sons' wives—numbered sixty-six persons.[f] ²⁷With the two sons[f] who had been born to Joseph in Egypt, the

46:10
mGe 29:33;
Nu 26:14
nEx 6:15
46:11
oGe 29:34;
Nu 3:17
46:12
pGe 29:35
q1Ch 2:5;
Mt 1:3
46:13
rGe 30:18
s1Ch 7:1
46:14
tGe 30:20
46:16
uGe 30:11
vNu 26:15
46:17
wGe 30:13;
1Ch 7:30-31
46:18
xGe 30:10
yGe 29:24
46:19
zGe 44:27
46:20
aGe 41:51
bGe 41:52
46:21
cNu 26:38-41;
1Ch 7:6-12; 8:1
46:25
dGe 30:8
eGe 29:29
46:26
fver 5-7; Ex 1:5;
Dt 10:22

[a]13 Samaritan Pentateuch and Syriac (see also 1 Chron. 7:1); Masoretic Text *Puvah*
[b]13 Samaritan Pentateuch and some Septuagint manuscripts (see also Num. 26:24 and 1 Chron.
7:1); Masoretic Text *Iob*   [c]15 That is, Northwest Mesopotamia   [d]16 Samaritan Pentateuch
and Septuagint (see also Num. 26:15); Masoretic Text *Ziphion*   [e]20 That is, Heliopolis
[f]27 Hebrew; Septuagint *the nine children*

members of Jacob's family, which went to Egypt, were seventy[a] in all. [g]

28Now Jacob sent Judah ahead of him to Joseph to get directions to Goshen. [h] When they arrived in the region of Goshen, 29Joseph had his chariot made ready and went to Goshen to meet his father Israel. As soon as Joseph appeared before him, he threw his arms around his father[b] and wept for a long time. [i]

30Israel said to Joseph, "Now I am ready to die, since I have seen for myself that you are still alive."

31Then Joseph said to his brothers and to his father's household, "I will go up and speak to Pharaoh and will say to him, 'My brothers and my father's household, who were living in the land of Canaan, have come to me. [j] 32The men are shepherds; they tend livestock, and they have brought along their flocks and herds and everything they own.' 33When Pharaoh calls you in and asks, 'What is your occupation?'[k] 34you should answer, 'Your servants have tended livestock from our boyhood on, just as our fathers did.' Then you will be allowed to settle in the region of Goshen, [l] for all shepherds are detestable to the Egyptians. [m]'"

47 Joseph went and told Pharaoh, "My father and brothers, with their flocks and herds and everything they own, have come from the land of Canaan and are now in Goshen."[n] 2He chose five of his brothers and presented them before Pharaoh.

3Pharaoh asked the brothers, "What is your occupation?"[o]

"Your servants are shepherds," they replied to Pharaoh, "just as our fathers were." 4They also said to him, "We have come to live here awhile,[p] because the famine is severe in Canaan[q] and your servants' flocks have no pasture. So now, please let your servants settle in Goshen."[r]

5Pharaoh said to Joseph, "Your father and your brothers have come to you, 6and the land of Egypt is before you; settle your father and your brothers in the best part of the land. [s] Let them live in Goshen. And if you know of any among them with special ability, [t] put them in charge of my own livestock."

7Then Joseph brought his father Jacob in and presented him before Pharaoh. After Jacob blessed[c] Pharaoh, [u] 8Pharaoh asked him, "How old are you?"

9And Jacob said to Pharaoh, "The years of my pilgrimage are a hundred and thirty. [v] My years have been few and difficult, [w] and they do not equal the years of the pilgrimage of my fathers. [x]" 10Then Jacob blessed[d] Pharaoh[y] and went out from his presence.

11So Joseph settled his father and his brothers in Egypt and gave them property in the best part of the land, the district of Rameses, [z] as Pharaoh directed. 12Joseph also provided his father and his brothers and all his father's household with food, according to the number of their children. [a]

Joseph and the Famine

13There was no food, however, in the whole region because the

---

**Cross references (left margin):**

46:27
[g]Ac 7:14
46:28
[h]Ge 45:10
46:29
[i]Ge 45:14-15;
Lk 15:20
46:31
[j]Ge 47:1
46:33
[k]Ge 47:3
46:34
[l]Ge 45:10
[m]Ge 43:32;
Ex 8:26
47:1
[n]Ge 46:31
47:3
[o]Ge 46:33
47:4
[p]Ge 15:13;
Dt 26:5
[q]Ge 43:1
[r]Ge 46:34
47:6
[s]Ge 45:18
[t]Ex 18:21,25
47:7
[u]ver 10;
2Sa 14:22
47:9
[v]Ge 25:7
[w]Heb 11:9,13
[x]Ge 35:28
47:10
[y]ver 7
47:11
[z]Ex 1:11; 12:37
47:12
[a]Ge 45:11

---

[a]27 Hebrew (see also Exodus 1:5 and footnote); Septuagint (see also Acts 7:14) *seventy-five*
[b]29 Hebrew *around him*   [c]7 Or *greeted*   [d]10 Or *said farewell to*

famine was severe; both Egypt and Canaan wasted away because of the famine.[b] 14Joseph collected all the money that was to be found in Egypt and Canaan in payment for the grain they were buying, and he brought it to Pharaoh's palace.[c] 15When the money of the people of Egypt and Canaan was gone, all Egypt came to Joseph and said, "Give us food. Why should we die before your eyes?[d] Our money is used up."

16"Then bring your livestock," said Joseph. "I will sell you food in exchange for your livestock, since your money is gone." 17So they brought their livestock to Joseph, and he gave them food in exchange for their horses,[e] their sheep and goats, their cattle and donkeys. And he brought them through that year with food in exchange for all their livestock.

18When that year was over, they came to him the following year and said, "We cannot hide from our lord the fact that since our money is gone and our livestock belongs to you, there is nothing left for our lord except our bodies and our land. 19Why should we perish before your eyes—we and our land as well? Buy us and our land in exchange for food, and we with our land will be in bondage to Pharaoh. Give us seed so that we may live and not die, and that the land may not become desolate."

20So Joseph bought all the land in Egypt for Pharaoh. The Egyptians, one and all, sold their fields, because the famine was too severe for them. The land became Pharaoh's, 21and Joseph reduced the people to servitude,[a] from one end of Egypt to the other. 22However, he did not buy the land of the priests, because they received a regular allotment from Pharaoh and had food enough from the allotment[f] Pharaoh gave them. That is why they did not sell their land.

23Joseph said to the people, "Now that I have bought you and your land today for Pharaoh, here is seed for you so you can plant the ground. 24But when the crop comes in, give a fifth[g] of it to Pharaoh. The other four-fifths you may keep as seed for the fields and as food for yourselves and your households and your children."

25"You have saved our lives," they said. "May we find favor in the eyes of our lord;[h] we will be in bondage to Pharaoh."

26So Joseph established it as a law concerning land in Egypt—still in force today—that a fifth of the produce belongs to Pharaoh. It was only the land of the priests that did not become Pharaoh's.[i]

27Now the Israelites settled in Egypt in the region of Goshen. They acquired property there and were fruitful and increased greatly in number.[j]

28Jacob lived in Egypt[k] seventeen years, and the years of his life were a hundred and forty-seven. 29When the time drew near for Israel to die,[l] he called for his son Joseph and said to him, "If I have found favor in your eyes, put your hand under my thigh[m] and promise that you will show me kindness and faithfulness.[n] Do not bury me in Egypt, 30but when I rest with my fathers, carry me out of Egypt and bury me where they are buried."[o]

"I will do as you say," he said.

47:13
b Ge 41:30;
Ac 7:11
47:14
c Ge 41:56
47:15
d ver 19; Ex 16:3
47:17
e Ex 14:9
47:22
f Dt 14:28-29;
Ezr 7:24
47:24
g Ge 41:34
47:25
h Ge 32:5
47:26
i ver 22
47:27
j Ge 17:6; 46:3;
Ex 1:7
47:28
k Ps 105:23
47:29
l Dt 31:14
m Ge 24:2
n Ge 24:49
47:30
o Ge 49:29-32;
50:5,13;
Ac 7:15-16

---

*a21 Samaritan Pentateuch and Septuagint (see also Vulgate); Masoretic Text *and he moved the people into the cities*

³¹"Swear to me," ᵖ he said. Then Joseph swore to him, ۹ and Israel worshiped as he leaned on the top of his staff. ᵃ ʳ

Manasseh and Ephraim

48 Some time later Joseph was told, "Your father is ill." So he took his two sons Manasseh and Ephraimˢ along with him. ²When Jacob was told, "Your son Joseph has come to you," Israel rallied his strength and sat up on the bed.

³Jacob said to Joseph, "God Almightyᵇ appeared to me at Luzᵗ in the land of Canaan, and there he blessed meᵘ ⁴and said to me, 'I am going to make you fruitful and will increase your numbers. ᵛ I will make you a community of peoples, and I will give this land as an everlasting possession to your descendants after you.'

⁵"Now then, your two sons born to you in Egyptʷ before I came to you here will be reckoned as mine; Ephraim and Manasseh will be mine, ˣ just as Reuben and Simeon are mine. ⁶Any children born to you after them will be yours; in the territory they inherit they will be reckoned under the names of their brothers. ⁷As I was returning from Paddan,ᶜ to my sorrow Rachel died in the land of Canaan while we were still on the way, a little distance from Ephrath. So I buried her there beside the road to Ephrath" (that is, Bethlehem). ʸ

⁸When Israel saw the sons of Joseph, he asked, "Who are these?"

⁹"They are the sons God has given me here,"ᶻ Joseph said to his father.

Then Israel said, "Bring them to me so I may blessᵃ them."

¹⁰Now Israel's eyes were failing because of old age, and he could hardly see. ᵇ So Joseph brought his sons close to him, and his father kissed themᶜ and embraced them.

¹¹Israel said to Joseph, "I never expected to see your face again, and now God has allowed me to see your children too."ᵈ

¹²Then Joseph removed them from Israel's knees and bowed down with his face to the ground. ¹³And Joseph took both of them, Ephraim on his right toward Israel's left hand and Manasseh on his left toward Israel's right hand,ᵉ and brought them close to him. ¹⁴But Israel reached out his right hand and put it on Ephraim's head, though he was the younger, and crossing his arms, he put his left hand on Manasseh's head, even though Manasseh was the firstborn. ᶠ

¹⁵Then he blessedᵍ Joseph and said,

> "May the God before whom my fathers
>   Abraham and Isaac walked,
>   the God who has been my shepherdʰ
>   all my life to this day,
> ¹⁶the Angel who has delivered me from all harm
>   —may he bless these boys. ⁱ
>   May they be called by my name
>   and the names of my fathers Abraham and Isaac, ʲ
>   and may they increase greatly
>   upon the earth."

47:31
pGe 21:23
qGe 24:3
rHeb 11:21 *fn*
1Ki 1:47
48:1
sGe 41:52
48:3
tGe 28:19
uGe 28:13;
35:9-12
48:4
vGe 17:6
48:5
wGe 41:50-52;
46:20 xGe 5:1;
Jos 14:4
48:7
yGe 35:19
48:9
zGe 33:5
aGe 27:4
48:10
bGe 27:1
cGe 27:27
48:11
dGe 50:23;
Ps 128:6
48:13
ePs 110:1
48:14
fGe 41:51
48:15
gGe 17:1
hGe 49:24
48:16
iHeb 11:21
jGe 28:13

ᵃ31 Or *Israel bowed down at the head of his bed*   ᵇ3 Hebrew *El-Shaddai*   ᶜ7 That is, Northwest Mesopotamia

[17]When Joseph saw his father placing his right hand on Ephraim's head[k] he was displeased; so he took hold of his father's hand to move it from Ephraim's head to Manasseh's head. [18]Joseph said to him, "No, my father, this one is the firstborn; put your right hand on his head."

[19]But his father refused and said, "I know, my son, I know. He too will become a people, and he too will become great.[l] Nevertheless, his younger brother will be greater than he,[m] and his descendants will become a group of nations." [20]He blessed them that day and said,

> "In your[a] name will Israel pronounce this blessing:
> 'May God make you like Ephraim[n] and Manasseh.[o]' "

So he put Ephraim ahead of Manasseh.

[21]Then Israel said to Joseph, "I am about to die, but God will be with you[bp] and take you[b] back to the land of your[b] fathers.[q] [22]And to you, as one who is over your brothers,[r] I give the ridge of land[cs] I took from the Amorites with my sword and my bow."

Jacob Blesses His Sons

49:1–28Ref — Dt 33:1–29

49 Then Jacob called for his sons and said: "Gather around so I can tell you what will happen to you in days to come.[t]

> [2]"Assemble and listen, sons of Jacob;
>   listen to your father Israel.[u]
>
> [3]"Reuben, you are my firstborn,[v]
>   my might, the first sign of my strength,[w]
>   excelling in honor, excelling in power.
> [4]Turbulent as the waters,[x] you will no longer excel,
>   for you went up onto your father's bed,
>   onto my couch and defiled it.[y]
>
> [5]"Simeon and Levi are brothers—
>   their swords[d] are weapons of violence.[z]
> [6]Let me not enter their council,
>   let me not join their assembly,[a]
> for they have killed men in their anger[b]
>   and hamstrung oxen as they pleased.
> [7]Cursed be their anger, so fierce,
>   and their fury, so cruel!
> I will scatter them in Jacob
>   and disperse them in Israel.[c]
>
> [8]"Judah,[e] your brothers will praise you;
>   your hand will be on the neck of your enemies;
>   your father's sons will bow down to you.[d]
> [9]You are a lion[e]'s cub, O Judah;[f]
>   you return from the prey, my son.
> Like a lion he crouches and lies down,
>   like a lioness—who dares to rouse him?

48:17
kver 14
48:19
lGe 17:20
mGe 25:23
48:20
nNu 2:18
oNu 2:20;
Ru 4:11
48:21
pGe 26:3; 46:4
qGe 28:13;
50:24
48:22
rIsa 37:8
sJos 24:32;
Jn 4:5
49:1
tNu 24:14;
Jer 23:20
49:2
uPs 34:11
49:3
vGe 29:32
wDt 21:17;
Ps 78:51
49:4
xIsa 57:20
yGe 35:22;
Dt 27:20
49:5
zGe 34:25;
Pr 4:17
49:6
aPr 1:15;
Eph 5:11
bGe 34:26
49:7
cJos 19:1,9;
21:1-42
49:8
dDt 33:7;
1Ch 5:2
49:9
eNu 24:9;
Eze 19:5;
Mic 5:8
fRev 5:5

---

[a]20 The Hebrew is singular.   [b]21 The Hebrew is plural.   [c]22 Or *And to you I give one portion more than to your brothers—the portion*   [d]5 The meaning of the Hebrew for this word is uncertain.   [e]8 *Judah* sounds like and may be derived from the Hebrew for *praise*.

¹⁰The scepter will not depart from Judah,^g
  nor the ruler's staff from between his feet,
until he comes to whom it belongs^a
  and the obedience of the nations is his.^h
¹¹He will tether his donkey to a vine,
  his colt to the choicest branch;
he will wash his garments in wine,
  his robes in the blood of grapes.
¹²His eyes will be darker than wine,
  his teeth whiter than milk.^b

¹³"Zebulunⁱ will live by the seashore
  and become a haven for ships;
  his border will extend toward Sidon.

¹⁴"Issachar^j is a rawboned^c donkey
  lying down between two saddlebags.^d
¹⁵When he sees how good is his resting place
  and how pleasant is his land,
he will bend his shoulder to the burden
  and submit to forced labor.

¹⁶"Dan^{ek} will provide justice for his people
  as one of the tribes of Israel.
¹⁷Dan^l will be a serpent by the roadside,
  a viper along the path,
that bites the horse's heels
  so that its rider tumbles backward.

¹⁸"I look for your deliverance, O LORD.^m

¹⁹"Gad^{fn} will be attacked by a band of raiders,
  but he will attack them at their heels.

²⁰"Asher's^o food will be rich;
  he will provide delicacies fit for a king.

²¹"Naphtali^p is a doe set free
  that bears beautiful fawns.^g

²²"Joseph^q is a fruitful vine,
  a fruitful vine near a spring,
  whose branches climb over a wall.^h
²³With bitterness archers attacked him;
  they shot at him with hostility.^r
²⁴But his bow remained steady,
  his strong arms^s stayedⁱ limber,
because of the hand of the Mighty One of Jacob,^t
  because of the Shepherd, the Rock of Israel,^u
²⁵because of your father's God,^v who helps you,
  because of the Almighty,^j who blesses you

49:10
gNu 24:17,19;
Ps 60:7 hPs 2:9;
Isa 42:1,4
49:13
iGe 30:20;
Dt 33:18-19;
Jos 19:10-11
49:14
jGe 30:18
49:16
kGe 30:6;
Dt 33:22;
Jdg 18:26-27
49:17
lJdg 18:27
49:18
mPs 119:166,
174
49:19
nGe 30:11;
Dt 33:20;
1Ch 5:18
49:20
oGe 30:13;
Dt 33:24
49:21
pGe 30:8;
Dt 33:23
49:22
qGe 30:24;
Dt 33:13-17
49:23
rGe 37:24
49:24
sPs 18:34
tPs 132:2,5;
Isa 1:24; 41:10
uIsa 28:16
49:25
vGe 28:13

---

^a10 Or *until Shiloh comes; or until he comes to whom tribute belongs*   ^b12 Or *will be dull from wine, / his teeth white from milk*   ^c14 Or *strong*   ^d14 Or *campfires*   ^e16 *Dan* here means *he provides justice.*   ^f19 *Gad* can mean *attack* and *band of raiders.*   ^g21 Or *free; / he utters beautiful words*   ^h22 Or *Joseph is a wild colt, / a wild colt near a spring, / a wild donkey on a terraced hill*   ⁱ23,24 Or *archers will attack . . . will shoot . . . will remain . . . will stay*   ^j25 Hebrew *Shaddai*

> with blessings of the heavens above,
>> blessings of the deep that lies below, [w]
>> blessings of the breast and womb.
> 26Your father's blessings are greater
>> than the blessings of the ancient mountains,
>> than [a] the bounty of the age-old hills.
> Let all these rest on the head of Joseph,
>> on the brow of the prince among [b] his brothers. [x]

> 27"Benjamin [y] is a ravenous wolf;
>> in the morning he devours the prey,
>> in the evening he divides the plunder."

28All these are the twelve tribes of Israel, and this is what their father said to them when he blessed them, giving each the blessing appropriate to him.

The Death of Jacob

29Then he gave them these instructions: [z] "I am about to be gathered to my people. [a] Bury me with my fathers [b] in the cave in the field of Ephron the Hittite, 30the cave in the field of Machpelah, [c] near Mamre in Canaan, which Abraham bought as a burial place from Ephron the Hittite, along with the field. [d] 31There Abraham [e] and his wife Sarah [f] were buried, there Isaac and his wife Rebekah [g] were buried, and there I buried Leah. 32The field and the cave in it were bought from the Hittites. [c]"

33When Jacob had finished giving instructions to his sons, he drew his feet up into the bed, breathed his last and was gathered to his people. [h]

50 Joseph threw himself upon his father and wept over him and kissed him. [i] 2Then Joseph directed the physicians in his service to embalm his father Israel. So the physicians embalmed him, [j] 3taking a full forty days, for that was the time required for embalming. And the Egyptians mourned for him seventy days. [k]

4When the days of mourning had passed, Joseph said to Pharaoh's court, "If I have found favor in your eyes, speak to Pharaoh for me. Tell him, 5'My father made me swear an oath[1] and said, "I am about to die; bury me in the tomb I dug for myself [m] in the land of Canaan." [n] Now let me go up and bury my father; then I will return.' "

6Pharaoh said, "Go up and bury your father, as he made you swear to do."

7So Joseph went up to bury his father. All Pharaoh's officials accompanied him—the dignitaries of his court and all the dignitaries of Egypt— 8besides all the members of Joseph's household and his brothers and those belonging to his father's household. Only their children and their flocks and herds were left in Goshen. 9Chariots and horsemen [d] also went up with him. It was a very large company.

10When they reached the threshing floor of Atad, near the Jordan, they lamented loudly and bitterly; [o] and there Joseph observed a seven-day period [p] of mourning for his father. 11When the Canaanites who

49:25
w Ge 27:28
49:26
x Dt 33:15-16
49:27
y Ge 35:18;
Jdg 20:12-13
49:29
z Ge 50:16
a Ge 25:8
b Ge 15:15;
47:30; 50:13
49:30
c Ge 23:9
d Ge 23:20
49:31
e Ge 25:9
f Ge 23:19
g Ge 35:29
49:33
h ver 29;
Ge 25:8;
Ac 7:15
50:1
i Ge 46:4
50:2
j ver 26;
2Ch 16:14
50:3
k Ge 37:34;
Nu 20:29;
Dt 34:8
50:5
l Ge 47:31
m 2Ch 16:14;
Isa 22:16
n Ge 47:31
50:10
o 2Sa 1:17;
Ac 8:2
p 1Sa 31:13;
Job 2:13

---

*a*26 Or *of my progenitors, / as great as*   *b*26 Or *the one separated from*   *c*32 Or *the sons of Heth*
*d*9 Or *charioteers*

lived there saw the mourning at the threshing floor of Atad, they said, "The Egyptians are holding a solemn ceremony of mourning." That is why that place near the Jordan is called Abel Mizraim. *a*

¹²So Jacob's sons did as he had commanded them: ¹³They carried him to the land of Canaan and buried him in the cave in the field of Machpelah, near Mamre, which Abraham had bought as a burial place from Ephron the Hittite, along with the field.^q ¹⁴After burying his father, Joseph returned to Egypt, together with his brothers and all the others who had gone with him to bury his father.

Joseph Reassures His Brothers

¹⁵When Joseph's brothers saw that their father was dead, they said, "What if Joseph holds a grudge against us and pays us back for all the wrongs we did to him?"^r ¹⁶So they sent word to Joseph, saying, "Your father left these instructions before he died: ¹⁷'This is what you are to say to Joseph: I ask you to forgive your brothers the sins and the wrongs they committed in treating you so badly.' Now please forgive the sins of the servants of the God of your father." When their message came to him, Joseph wept.

¹⁸His brothers then came and threw themselves down before him.^s "We are your slaves,"^t they said.

¹⁹But Joseph said to them, "Don't be afraid. Am I in the place of God?^u ²⁰You intended to harm me,^v but God intended^w it for good^x to accomplish what is now being done, the saving of many lives.^y ²¹So then, don't be afraid. I will provide for you and your children.^z" And he reassured them and spoke kindly to them.

The Death of Joseph

²²Joseph stayed in Egypt, along with all his father's family. He lived a hundred and ten years^a ²³and saw the third generation^b of Ephraim's children. Also the children of Makir^c son of Manasseh were placed at birth on Joseph's knees.^b

²⁴Then Joseph said to his brothers, "I am about to die.^d But God will surely come to your aid^e and take you up out of this land to the land^f he promised on oath to Abraham, Isaac and Jacob."^g ²⁵And Joseph made the sons of Israel swear an oath and said, "God will surely come to your aid, and then you must carry my bones up from this place."^h

²⁶So Joseph died at the age of a hundred and ten. And after they embalmed him,ⁱ he was placed in a coffin in Egypt.

50:13
^qGe 23:20;
Ac 7:16
50:15
^rGe 37:28;
42:21-22
50:18
^sGe 37:7
^tGe 43:18
50:19
^uRo 12:19;
Heb 10:30
50:20
^vGe 37:20
^wMic 4:11-12
^xRo 8:28
^yGe 45:5
50:21
^zGe 45:11;
47:12
50:22
^aGe 25:7;
Jos 24:29
50:23
^bJob 42:16
^cNu 32:39,40
50:24
^dGe 48:21
^eEx 3:16-17
^fGe 15:14
^gGe 12:7; 26:3;
28:13; 35:12
50:25
^hGe 47:29-30;
Ex 13:19;
Jos 24:32;
Heb 11:22
50:26
ⁱver 2

---

^a11 *Abel Mizraim* means *mourning of the Egyptians.*   ^b23 That is, were counted as his

Exodus

Title and Background

"Exodus" is a Latin word (derived from the Greek) that means "exit," "departure," and describes the greatest miracle in the Old Testament record of Israel's history—the "going out" from Egypt and slavery. While the story of the Israelites began with Abraham in Genesis, Exodus is the history of their early years as God's chosen nation, committed to him according to the terms of the Mosaic covenant given at Mount Sinai. The book of Exodus was not intended to exist separately, but was thought of as a continuation of a narrative that began in Genesis and continues through Leviticus, Numbers and Deuteronomy.

Author and Date of Writing

Several statements in Exodus indicate that Moses wrote certain sections of the book (see 17:14; 24:4; 34:27). The New Testament also claims Mosaic authorship for various passages in Exodus (see, for example, Mk 7:10; 12:26; Lk 2:22-23). Taken together, these references strongly suggest that Moses was largely responsible for writing the book of Exodus.

According to 1 Kings 6:1, the exodus took place 480 years before "the fourth year of Solomon's reign over Israel." Since that year was about 966 B.C., the exodus occurred about 1446 B.C. The book of Exodus was most likely written after the exodus from Egypt (about 1446 B.C.) and before the death of Moses (about 1406 B.C.).

Theme and Message

Exodus lays the foundation for a theology of God's revelation of his name, his attributes, his redemption, his law and his worship. It also reports the appointment and work of the first covenant mediator (Moses), describes the beginning of the priesthood, defines the role of the prophet and relates how the ancient covenant relationship between God and his people came under a new administration (the Sinai covenant).

Outline

I. Preparation for Israel's Deliverance From Bondage (1:1-4:31)
II. Israel's Deliverance from Egyptian Bondage (5:1-18:27)
    A. Pharaoh's Resistance and the Lord's Reassurance (5:1-6:27)
    B. Plagues on Egypt (6:28-12:36)
    C. The Exodus: From Egypt to Mount Sinai (12:37-18:27)
III. Covenant at Sinai (19:1-24:18)
IV. The Tabernacle for Worship (25:1-40:38)

The Israelites Oppressed

1 These are the names of the sons of Israelª who went to Egypt with Jacob, each with his family: ²Reuben, Simeon, Levi and Judah; ³Issachar, Zebulun and Benjamin; ⁴Dan and Naphtali; Gad and Asher.

1:1
ªGe 46:8

⁵The descendants of Jacob numbered seventy*ᵃ* in all;*ᵇ* Joseph was already in Egypt.

⁶Now Joseph and all his brothers and all that generation died,*ᶜ* ⁷but the Israelites were fruitful and multiplied greatly and became exceedingly numerous,*ᵈ* so that the land was filled with them.

⁸Then a new king, who did not know about Joseph, came to power in Egypt. ⁹"Look," he said to his people, "the Israelites have become much too numerous*ᵉ* for us. ¹⁰Come, we must deal shrewdly*ᶠ* with them or they will become even more numerous and, if war breaks out, will join our enemies, fight against us and leave the country."*ᵍ*

¹¹So they put slave masters*ʰ* over them to oppress them with forced labor,*ⁱ* and they built Pithom and Rameses*ʲ* as store cities*ᵏ* for Pharaoh. ¹²But the more they were oppressed, the more they multiplied and spread; so the Egyptians came to dread the Israelites ¹³and worked them ruthlessly.*ˡ* ¹⁴They made their lives bitter with hard labor in brick and mortar and with all kinds of work in the fields; in all their hard labor the Egyptians used them ruthlessly.*ᵐ*

¹⁵The king of Egypt said to the Hebrew midwives, whose names were Shiphrah and Puah, ¹⁶"When you help the Hebrew women in childbirth and observe them on the delivery stool, if it is a boy, kill him; but if it is a girl, let her live." ¹⁷The midwives, however, feared*ⁿ* God and did not do what the king of Egypt had told them to do;*ᵒ* they let the boys live. ¹⁸Then the king of Egypt summoned the midwives and asked them, "Why have you done this? Why have you let the boys live?"

¹⁹The midwives answered Pharaoh, "Hebrew women are not like Egyptian women; they are vigorous and give birth before the midwives arrive."*ᵖ*

²⁰So God was kind to the midwives*�q* and the people increased and became even more numerous. ²¹And because the midwives feared God, he gave them families*ʳ* of their own.

²²Then Pharaoh gave this order to all his people: "Every boy that is born*ᵇ* you must throw into the Nile, but let every girl live."*ˢ*

The Birth of Moses

2 Now a man of the house of Levi married a Levite woman,*ᵗ* ²and she became pregnant and gave birth to a son. When she saw that he was a fine child, she hid him for three months.*ᵘ* ³But when she could hide him no longer, she got a papyrus basket for him and coated it with tar and pitch. Then she placed the child in it and put it among the reeds along the bank of the Nile. ⁴His sister*ᵛ* stood at a distance to see what would happen to him.

⁵Then Pharaoh's daughter went down to the Nile to bathe, and her attendants were walking along the river bank.*ʷ* She saw the basket among the reeds and sent her slave girl to get it. ⁶She opened it and saw the baby. He was crying, and she felt sorry for him. "This is one of the Hebrew babies," she said.

⁷Then his sister asked Pharaoh's daughter, "Shall I go and get one of the Hebrew women to nurse the baby for you?"

1:5
ᵇGe 46:26
1:6
ᶜGe 50:26
1:7
ᵈGe 46:3;
Dt 26:5;
Ac 7:17
1:9
ᵉPs 105:24-25
1:10
ᶠPs 83:3
ᵍAc 7:17-19
1:11
ʰEx 3:7
ⁱGe 15:13;
Ex 2:11; 5:4;
6:6-7 ʲGe 47:11
ᵏ1Ki 9:19;
2Ch 8:4
1:13
ˡDt 4:20
1:14
ᵐEx 2:23; 6:9;
Nu 20:15;
Ps 81:6; Ac 7:19
1:17
ⁿver 21; Pr 16:6
ᵒDa 3:16-18;
Ac 4:18-20;
5:29
1:19
ᵖJos 2:4-6;
2Sa 17:20
1:20
qver 12;
Pr 11:18;
Isa 3:10
1:21
ʳ1Sa 2:35;
2Sa 7:11,27-29;
1Ki 11:38
1:22
ˢAc 7:19
2:1
ᵗEx 6:20;
Nu 26:59
2:2
ᵘAc 7:20;
Heb 11:23
2:4
ᵛEx 15:20;
Nu 26:59
2:5
ʷEx 7:15; 8:20

ᵃ5 Masoretic Text (see also Gen. 46:27); Dead Sea Scrolls and Septuagint (see also Acts 7:14 and note at Gen. 46:27) *seventy-five*   *ᵇ22* Masoretic Text; Samaritan Pentateuch, Septuagint and Targums *born to the Hebrews*

8"Yes, go," she answered. And the girl went and got the baby's mother. 9Pharaoh's daughter said to her, "Take this baby and nurse him for me, and I will pay you." So the woman took the baby and nursed him. 10When the child grew older, she took him to Pharaoh's daughter and he became her son. She named him Moses,*a* saying, "I drew him out of the water."

Moses Flees to Midian

11One day, after Moses had grown up, he went out to where his own people*x* were and watched them at their hard labor. He saw an Egyptian beating a Hebrew, one of his own people. 12Glancing this way and that and seeing no one, he killed the Egyptian and hid him in the sand. 13The next day he went out and saw two Hebrews fighting. He asked the one in the wrong, "Why are you hitting your fellow Hebrew?"*y*

14The man said, "Who made you ruler and judge over us?*z* Are you thinking of killing me as you killed the Egyptian?" Then Moses was afraid and thought, "What I did must have become known."

15When Pharaoh heard of this, he tried to kill Moses, but Moses fled from Pharaoh and went to live in Midian,*a* where he sat down by a well. 16Now a priest of Midian*b* had seven daughters, and they came to draw water*c* and fill the troughs to water their father's flock. 17Some shepherds came along and drove them away, but Moses got up and came to their rescue and watered their flock. *d*

18When the girls returned to Reuel*e* their father, he asked them, "Why have you returned so early today?"

19They answered, "An Egyptian rescued us from the shepherds. He even drew water for us and watered the flock."

20"And where is he?" he asked his daughters. "Why did you leave him? Invite him to have something to eat."*f*

21Moses agreed to stay with the man, who gave his daughter Zipporah*g* to Moses in marriage. 22Zipporah gave birth to a son, and Moses named him Gershom,*b* saying, "I have become an alien*h* in a foreign land."

23During that long period,*i* the king of Egypt died. The Israelites groaned in their slavery and cried out, and their cry*j* for help because of their slavery went up to God. 24God heard their groaning and he remembered his covenant*k* with Abraham, with Isaac and with Jacob. 25So God looked on the Israelites and was concerned*l* about them.

Moses and the Burning Bush

3 Now Moses was tending the flock of Jethro*m* his father-in-law, the priest of Midian, and he led the flock to the far side of the desert and came to Horeb,*n* the mountain*o* of God. 2There the angel of the LORD*p* appeared to him in flames of fire from within a bush. *q* Moses saw that though the bush was on fire it did not burn up. 3So Moses thought, "I will go over and see this strange sight—why the bush does not burn up."

4When the LORD saw that he had gone over to look, God called to him from within the bush, "Moses! Moses!"

2:11
xAc 7:23;
Heb 11:24-26
2:13
yAc 7:26
2:14
zAc 7:27*
2:15
aAc 7:29;
Heb 11:27
2:16
bEx 3:1
cGe 24:11
2:17
dGe 29:10
2:18
eNu 10:29
2:20
fGe 31:54
2:21
gEx 18:2
2:22
hEx 18:3-4;
Heb 11:13
2:23
iAc 7:30
jEx 3:7,9;
Dt 26:7; Jas 5:4
2:24
kEx 6:5;
Ps 105:10,42
2:25
lEx 3:7; 4:31
3:1
mEx 2:18
n1Ki 19:8
oEx 18:5
3:2
pGe 16:7
qDt 33:16;
Mk 12:26;
Ac 7:30

---

a10 Moses sounds like the Hebrew for *draw out.*   *b22 Gershom* sounds like the Hebrew for *an alien there.*

And Moses said, "Here I am."

5"Do not come any closer," God said. "Take off your sandals, for the place where you are standing is holy ground."[r] 6Then he said, "I am the God of your father, the God of Abraham, the God of Isaac and the God of Jacob."[s] At this, Moses hid his face, because he was afraid to look at God.

7The LORD said, "I have indeed seen the misery of my people in Egypt. I have heard them crying out because of their slave drivers, and I am concerned[t] about their suffering. 8So I have come down[u] to rescue them from the hand of the Egyptians and to bring them up out of that land into a good and spacious land, a land flowing with milk and honey[v]—the home of the Canaanites, Hittites, Amorites, Perizzites, Hivites and Jebusites.[w] 9And now the cry of the Israelites has reached me, and I have seen the way the Egyptians are oppressing[x] them. 10So now, go. I am sending you to Pharaoh to bring my people the Israelites out of Egypt."[y]

11But Moses said to God, "Who am I,[z] that I should go to Pharaoh and bring the Israelites out of Egypt?"

12And God said, "I will be with you.[a] And this will be the sign to you that it is I who have sent you: When you have brought the people out of Egypt, you[a] will worship God on this mountain."

13Moses said to God, "Suppose I go to the Israelites and say to them, 'The God of your fathers has sent me to you,' and they ask me, 'What is his name?' Then what shall I tell them?"

14God said to Moses, "I AM WHO I AM.[b] This is what you are to say to the Israelites: 'I AM[b] has sent me to you.'"

15God also said to Moses, "Say to the Israelites, 'The LORD,[c] the God of your fathers—the God of Abraham, the God of Isaac and the God of Jacob—has sent me to you.' This is my name[c] forever, the name by which I am to be remembered from generation to generation.

16"Go, assemble the elders[d] of Israel and say to them, 'The LORD, the God of your fathers—the God of Abraham, Isaac and Jacob— appeared to me and said: I have watched over you and have seen what has been done to you in Egypt. 17And I have promised to bring you up out of your misery in Egypt[e] into the land of the Canaanites, Hittites, Amorites, Perizzites, Hivites and Jebusites—a land flowing with milk and honey.'

18"The elders of Israel will listen[f] to you. Then you and the elders are to go to the king of Egypt and say to him, 'The LORD, the God of the Hebrews, has met with us. Let us take a three-day journey into the desert to offer sacrifices[g] to the LORD our God.' 19But I know that the king of Egypt will not let you go unless a mighty hand[h] compels him. 20So I will stretch out my hand[i] and strike the Egyptians with all the wonders[j] that I will perform among them. After that, he will let you go.[k]

21"And I will make the Egyptians favorably disposed[l] toward this people, so that when you leave you will not go empty-handed.[m] 22Every woman is to ask her neighbor and any woman living in her house for articles of silver and gold[n] and for clothing, which you will put on

**Cross references (left margin):**

3:5
r Ge 28:17;
Jos 5:15;
Ac 7:33*

3:6
s Ex 4:5;
Mt 22:32*;
Mk 12:26*;
Lk 20:37*;
Ac 7:32*

3:7
t Ex 2:25

3:8
u Ge 50:24
v ver 17;
Ex 13:5; Dt 1:25
w Ge 15:18-21

3:9
x Ex 1:14; 2:23

3:10
y Mic 6:4

3:11
z Ex 6:12,30;
1Sa 18:18

3:12
a Ge 31:3;
Jos 1:5; Ro 8:31

3:14
b Ex 6:2-3;
Jn 8:58;
Heb 13:8

3:15
c Ps 135:13;
Hos 12:5

3:16
d Ex 4:29

3:17
e Ge 15:16;
Jos 24:11

3:18
f Ex 4:1,8,31
g Ex 5:1,3

3:19
h Ex 4:21; 5:2

3:20
i Ex 6:1,6; 9:15
j Dt 6:22;
Ne 9:10;
Ac 7:36
k Ex 12:31-33

3:21
l Ex 12:36
m Ps 105:37

3:22
n Ex 11:2

---

[a]12 The Hebrew is plural.   [b]14 Or *I WILL BE WHAT I WILL BE*   [c]15 The Hebrew for LORD sounds like and may be derived from the Hebrew for *I AM* in verse 14.

your sons and daughters. And so you will plunder⁰ the Egyptians."

Signs for Moses

4 Moses answered, "What if they do not believe me or listenᴾ to me and say, 'The LORD did not appear to you'?"

²Then the LORD said to him, "What is that in your hand?"

"A staff," q he replied.

³The LORD said, "Throw it on the ground."

Moses threw it on the ground and it became a snake, and he ran from it. ⁴Then the LORD said to him, "Reach out your hand and take it by the tail." So Moses reached out and took hold of the snake and it turned back into a staff in his hand. ⁵"This," said the LORD, "is so that they may believeʳ that the LORD, the God of their fathers—the God of Abraham, the God of Isaac and the God of Jacob—has appeared to you."

⁶Then the LORD said, "Put your hand inside your cloak." So Moses put his hand into his cloak, and when he took it out, it was leprous,ᵃ like snow.ˢ

⁷"Now put it back into your cloak," he said. So Moses put his hand back into his cloak, and when he took it out, it was restored,ᵗ like the rest of his flesh.

⁸Then the LORD said, "If they do not believe you or pay attention to the first miraculous sign, they may believe the second. ⁹But if they do not believe these two signs or listen to you, take some water from the Nile and pour it on the dry ground. The water you take from the river will become bloodᵘ on the ground."

¹⁰Moses said to the LORD, "O Lord, I have never been eloquent, neither in the past nor since you have spoken to your servant. I am slow of speech and tongue."ᵛ

¹¹The LORD said to him, "Who gave man his mouth? Who makes him deaf or mute? Who gives him sight or makes him blind?ʷ Is it not I, the LORD? ¹²Now go; I will help you speak and will teach you what to say."ˣ

¹³But Moses said, "O Lord, please send someone else to do it."

¹⁴Then the LORD's anger burned against Moses and he said, "What about your brother, Aaron the Levite? I know he can speak well. He is already on his way to meetʸ you, and his heart will be glad when he sees you. ¹⁵You shall speak to him and put words in his mouth;ᶻ I will help both of you speak and will teach you what to do. ¹⁶He will speak to the people for you, and it will be as if he were your mouthᵃ and as if you were God to him. ¹⁷But take this staffᵇ in your hand so you can perform miraculous signsᶜ with it."

Moses Returns to Egypt

¹⁸Then Moses went back to Jethro his father-in-law and said to him, "Let me go back to my own people in Egypt to see if any of them are still alive."

Jethro said, "Go, and I wish you well."

¹⁹Now the LORD had said to Moses in Midian, "Go back to Egypt, for all the men who wanted to killᵈ you are dead.ᵉ" ²⁰So Moses took his

3:22
oEze 39:10
4:1
pEx 3:18; 6:30
4:2
qver 17,20
4:5
rEx 19:9
4:6
sNu 12:10;
2Ki 5:1,27
4:7
tNu 12:13-15;
Dt 32:39;
2Ki 5:14; Mt 8:3
4:9
uEx 7:17-21
4:10
vEx 6:12;
Jer 1:6
4:11
wPs 94:9;
Mt 11:5
4:12
xIsa 50:4;
Jer 1:9;
Mt 10:19-20;
Mk 13:11;
Lk 12:12;
21:14-15
4:14
yver 27
4:15
zNu 23:5,12,16
4:16
aEx 7:1-2
4:17
bver 2
cEx 7:9-21
4:19
dEx 2:15
eEx 2:23

ᵃ6 The Hebrew word was used for various diseases affecting the skin—not necessarily leprosy.

wife and sons, put them on a donkey and started back to Egypt. And he took the staff[f] of God in his hand.

[21]The LORD said to Moses, "When you return to Egypt, see that you perform before Pharaoh all the wonders[g] I have given you the power to do. But I will harden his heart[h] so that he will not let the people go. [22]Then say to Pharaoh, 'This is what the LORD says: Israel is my first-born son,[i] [23]and I told you, "Let my son go,[j] so he may worship me." But you refused to let him go; so I will kill your firstborn son.'"[k]

[24]At a lodging place on the way, the LORD met ͺMoses,[a] and was about to kill[l] him. [25]But Zipporah took a flint knife, cut off her son's foreskin[m] and touched ͺMoses,ͺ feet with it.[b] "Surely you are a bride-groom of blood to me," she said. [26]So the LORD let him alone. (At that time she said "bridegroom of blood," referring to circumcision.)

[27]The LORD said to Aaron, "Go into the desert to meet Moses." So he met Moses at the mountain[n] of God and kissed[o] him. [28]Then Moses told Aaron everything the LORD had sent him to say,[p] and also about all the miraculous signs he had commanded him to perform.

[29]Moses and Aaron brought together all the elders[q] of the Israelites, [30]and Aaron told them everything the LORD had said to Moses. He also performed the signs before the people, [31]and they believed.[r] And when they heard that the LORD was concerned[s] about them and had seen their misery, they bowed down and worshiped.

Bricks Without Straw

5 Afterward Moses and Aaron went to Pharaoh and said, "This is what the LORD, the God of Israel, says: 'Let my people go, so that they may hold a festival[t] to me in the desert.'"

[2]Pharaoh said, "Who is the LORD,[u] that I should obey him and let Israel go? I do not know the LORD and I will not let Israel go."[v]

[3]Then they said, "The God of the Hebrews has met with us. Now let us take a three-day journey into the desert to offer sacrifices to the LORD our God, or he may strike us with plagues[w] or with the sword."

[4]But the king of Egypt said, "Moses and Aaron, why are you taking the people away from their labor?[x] Get back to your work!" [5]Then Pharaoh said, "Look, the people of the land are now numerous,[y] and you are stopping them from working."

[6]That same day Pharaoh gave this order to the slave drivers and foremen in charge of the people: [7]"You are no longer to supply the people with straw for making bricks; let them go and gather their own straw. [8]But require them to make the same number of bricks as before; don't reduce the quota. They are lazy; that is why they are crying out, 'Let us go and sacrifice to our God.' [9]Make the work harder for the men so that they keep working and pay no attention to lies."

[10]Then the slave drivers and the foremen went out and said to the people, "This is what Pharaoh says: 'I will not give you any more straw. [11]Go and get your own straw wherever you can find it, but your work will not be reduced at all.'" [12]So the people scattered all over Egypt to gather stubble to use for straw. [13]The slave drivers kept pressing them, saying, "Complete the work required of you for each day, just as when you had straw." [14]The Israelite foremen appointed by Pharaoh's slave

4:20
fEx 17:9;
Nu 20:8-9,11
4:21
gEx 3:19,20
hEx 7:3,13;
9:12,35; 14:4,8;
Dt 2:30;
Isa 63:17;
Jn 12:40;
Ro 9:18
4:22
iIsa 63:16;
64:8; Jer 31:9;
Hos 11:1;
Ro 9:4
4:23
jEx 5:1; 7:16
kEx 11:5;
12:12,29
4:24
lNu 22:22
4:25
mGe 17:14;
Jos 5:2,3
4:27
nEx 3:1 over 14
4:28
pver 8-9,16
4:29
qEx 3:16
4:31
rver 8; Ex 3:18
sEx 2:25
5:1
tEx 3:18
5:2
u2Ki 18:35;
Job 21:15
vEx 3:19
5:3
wEx 3:18
5:4
xEx 1:11
5:5
yEx 1:7,9

---

[a]24 Or ͺMoses' son;ͺ Hebrew *him*   [b]25 Or *and drew near* ͺMoses',ͺ *feet*

drivers were beaten[z] and were asked, "Why didn't you meet your quota of bricks yesterday or today, as before?"

[15]Then the Israelite foremen went and appealed to Pharaoh: "Why have you treated your servants this way? [16]Your servants are given no straw, yet we are told, 'Make bricks!' Your servants are being beaten, but the fault is with your own people."

[17]Pharaoh said, "Lazy, that's what you are—lazy![a] That is why you keep saying, 'Let us go and sacrifice to the LORD.' [18]Now get to work. You will not be given any straw, yet you must produce your full quota of bricks."

[19]The Israelite foremen realized they were in trouble when they were told, "You are not to reduce the number of bricks required of you for each day." [20]When they left Pharaoh, they found Moses and Aaron waiting to meet them, [21]and they said, "May the LORD look upon you and judge you! You have made us a stench[b] to Pharaoh and his officials and have put a sword in their hand to kill us."[c]

God Promises Deliverance

[22]Moses returned to the LORD and said, "O Lord, why have you brought trouble upon this people?[d] Is this why you sent me? [23]Ever since I went to Pharaoh to speak in your name, he has brought trouble upon this people, and you have not rescued[e] your people at all."

6 Then the LORD said to Moses, "Now you will see what I will do to Pharaoh: Because of my mighty hand[f] he will let them go;[g] because of my mighty hand he will drive them out of his country."[h]

[2]God also said to Moses, "I am the LORD. [3]I appeared to Abraham, to Isaac and to Jacob as God Almighty,[a][i] but by my name[j] the LORD[b][k] I did not make myself known to them.[c] [4]I also established my covenant[l] with them to give them the land of Canaan, where they lived as aliens.[m] [5]Moreover, I have heard the groaning[n] of the Israelites, whom the Egyptians are enslaving, and I have remembered my covenant.

[6]"Therefore, say to the Israelites: 'I am the LORD, and I will bring you out from under the yoke of the Egyptians. I will free you from being slaves to them, and I will redeem[o] you with an outstretched arm[p] and with mighty acts of judgment. [7]I will take you as my own people, and I will be your God.[q] Then you will know[r] that I am the LORD your God, who brought you out from under the yoke of the Egyptians. [8]And I will bring you to the land[s] I swore with uplifted hand[t] to give to Abraham, to Isaac and to Jacob.[u] I will give it to you as a possession. I am the LORD.'"

[9]Moses reported this to the Israelites, but they did not listen to him because of their discouragement and cruel bondage.

[10]Then the LORD said to Moses, [11]"Go, tell Pharaoh king of Egypt to let the Israelites go out of his country."

[12]But Moses said to the LORD, "If the Israelites will not listen to me, why would Pharaoh listen to me, since I speak with faltering lips[d]?"[v]

5:14
z Isa 10:24
5:17
a ver 8
5:21
b Ge 34:30
c Ex 14:11
5:22
d Nu 11:11
5:23
e Jer 4:10
6:1
f Ex 3:19
g Ex 3:20
h Ex 12:31,33,39
6:3
i Ge 17:1
j Ps 68:4; 83:18;
Isa 52:6
k Ex 3:14
6:4
l Ge 15:18
m Ge 28:4,13
6:5
n Ex 2:23
6:6
o Dt 7:8;
1Ch 17:21
p Dt 26:8
6:7
q Dt 4:20;
2Sa 7:24
r Ex 16:12;
Isa 41:20
6:8
s Ge 15:18; 26:3
t Ge 14:22
u Ps 136:21-22
6:12
v ver 30;
Ex 4:10; Jer 1:6

a3 Hebrew *El-Shaddai*   *b3* See note at Exodus 3:15.   *c3* Or *Almighty, and by my name the LORD did I not let myself be known to them?*   *d12* Hebrew *I am uncircumcised of lips; also in verse 30*

Family Record of Moses and Aaron

¹³Now the LORD spoke to Moses and Aaron about the Israelites and Pharaoh king of Egypt, and he commanded them to bring the Israelites out of Egypt.

¹⁴These were the heads of their families[a]:[w]

The sons of Reuben the firstborn son of Israel were Hanoch and Pallu, Hezron and Carmi. These were the clans of Reuben. ¹⁵The sons of Simeon[x] were Jemuel, Jamin, Ohad, Jakin, Zohar and Shaul the son of a Canaanite woman. These were the clans of Simeon.

¹⁶These were the names of the sons of Levi according to their records: Gershon,[y] Kohath and Merari.[z] Levi lived 137 years. ¹⁷The sons of Gershon, by clans, were Libni and Shimei.[a] ¹⁸The sons of Kohath were Amram, Izhar, Hebron and Uzziel.[b] Kohath lived 133 years. ¹⁹The sons of Merari were Mahli and Mushi.[c]

These were the clans of Levi according to their records. ²⁰Amram married his father's sister Jochebed, who bore him Aaron and Moses.[d] Amram lived 137 years. ²¹The sons of Izhar[e] were Korah, Nepheg and Zicri. ²²The sons of Uzziel were Mishael, Elzaphan[f] and Sithri. ²³Aaron married Elisheba, daughter of Amminadab[g] and sister of Nahshon, and she bore him Nadab and Abihu,[h] Eleazar[i] and Ithamar.[j] ²⁴The sons of Korah[k] were Assir, Elkanah and Abiasaph. These were the Korahite clans. ²⁵Eleazar son of Aaron married one of the daughters of Putiel, and she bore him Phinehas.[l]

These were the heads of the Levite families, clan by clan.

²⁶It was this same Aaron and Moses to whom the LORD said, "Bring the Israelites out of Egypt by their divisions."[m] ²⁷They were the ones who spoke to Pharaoh king of Egypt about bringing the Israelites out of Egypt. It was the same Moses and Aaron.

Aaron to Speak for Moses

²⁸Now when the LORD spoke to Moses in Egypt, ²⁹he said to him, "I am the LORD.[n] Tell Pharaoh king of Egypt everything I tell you." ³⁰But Moses said to the LORD, "Since I speak with faltering lips,[o] why would Pharaoh listen to me?"

7 Then the LORD said to Moses, "See, I have made you like God[p] to Pharaoh, and your brother Aaron will be your prophet. ²You are to say everything I command you, and your brother Aaron is to tell Pharaoh to let the Israelites go out of his country. ³But I will harden Pharaoh's heart,[q] and though I multiply my miraculous signs and wonders in Egypt, ⁴he will not listen[r] to you. Then I will lay my hand on Egypt and with mighty acts of judgment[s] I will bring out my divisions, my people the Israelites. ⁵And the Egyptians will know that

Side references:

6:14 wGe 46:9
6:15 xGe 46:10; 1Ch 4:24
6:16 yGe 46:11 zNu 3:17
6:17 a1Ch 6:17
6:18 b1Ch 6:2,18
6:19 c1Ch 6:19; 23:21
6:20 dEx 2:1-2; Nu 26:59
6:21 e1Ch 6:38
6:22 fLev 10:4; Nu 3:30
6:23 gRu 4:19,20 hLev 10:1 iNu 3:2,32 jNu 26:60
6:24 kNu 26:11
6:25 lNu 25:7,11; Jos 24:33; Ps 106:30
6:26 mEx 7:4; 12:17, 41,51
6:29 nver 11; Ex 7:2
6:30 over 12; Ex 4:10
7:1 pEx 4:16
7:3 qEx 4:21; 11:9
7:4 rEx 11:9 sEx 3:20; 6:6

---

[a]14 The Hebrew for *families* here and in verse 25 refers to units larger than clans.

I am the LORD[t] when I stretch out my hand[u] against Egypt and bring the Israelites out of it."

[6]Moses and Aaron did just as the LORD commanded[v] them. [7]Moses was eighty years old[w] and Aaron eighty-three when they spoke to Pharaoh.

Aaron's Staff Becomes a Snake

[8]The LORD said to Moses and Aaron, [9]"When Pharaoh says to you, 'Perform a miracle,[x]' then say to Aaron, 'Take your staff and throw it down before Pharaoh,' and it will become a snake."[y]

[10]So Moses and Aaron went to Pharaoh and did just as the LORD commanded. Aaron threw his staff down in front of Pharaoh and his officials, and it became a snake. [11]Pharaoh then summoned wise men and sorcerers, and the Egyptian magicians[z] also did the same things by their secret arts:[a] [12]Each one threw down his staff and it became a snake. But Aaron's staff swallowed up their staffs. [13]Yet Pharaoh's heart[b] became hard and he would not listen to them, just as the LORD had said.

The Plague of Blood

[14]Then the LORD said to Moses, "Pharaoh's heart is unyielding;[c] he refuses to let the people go. [15]Go to Pharaoh in the morning as he goes out to the water. Wait on the bank of the Nile to meet him, and take in your hand the staff that was changed into a snake. [16]Then say to him, 'The LORD, the God of the Hebrews, has sent me to say to you: Let my people go, so that they may worship[d] me in the desert. But until now you have not listened. [17]This is what the LORD says: By this you will know that I am the LORD:[e] With the staff that is in my hand I will strike the water of the Nile, and it will be changed into blood.[f] [18]The fish in the Nile will die, and the river will stink; the Egyptians will not be able to drink its water.' "[g]

[19]The LORD said to Moses, "Tell Aaron, 'Take your staff and stretch out your hand[h] over the waters of Egypt—over the streams and canals, over the ponds and all the reservoirs'—and they will turn to blood. Blood will be everywhere in Egypt, even in the wooden buckets and stone jars."

[20]Moses and Aaron did just as the LORD had commanded. He raised his staff in the presence of Pharaoh and his officials and struck the water of the Nile,[i] and all the water was changed into blood.[j] [21]The fish in the Nile died, and the river smelled so bad that the Egyptians could not drink its water. Blood was everywhere in Egypt.

[22]But the Egyptian magicians did the same things by their secret arts,[k] and Pharaoh's heart became hard; he would not listen to Moses and Aaron, just as the LORD had said. [23]Instead, he turned and went into his palace, and did not take even this to heart. [24]And all the Egyptians dug along the Nile to get drinking water, because they could not drink the water of the river.

The Plague of Frogs

8 [25]Seven days passed after the LORD struck the Nile. [1]Then the LORD said to Moses, "Go to Pharaoh and say to him, 'This is what the LORD says: Let my people go, so that they may worship[1] me. [2]If you

7:5
tver 17; Ex 8:19, 22 uEx 3:20
7:6
vver 2
7:7
wDt 31:2; 34:7; Ac 7:23,30
7:9
xIsa 7:11; Jn 2:18
yEx 4:2-5
7:11
zGe 41:8; 2Ti 3:8 aver 22; Ex 8:7,18
7:13
bEx 4:21
7:14
cEx 8:15,32; 10:1,20,27
7:16
dEx 3:18; 5:1,3
7:17
eEx 5:2 fEx 4:9; Rev 11:6; 16:4
7:18
gver 21,24
7:19
hEx 8:5-6,16; 9:22; 10:12,21; 14:21
7:20
iEx 17:5 jPs 78:44; 105:29
7:22
kver 11
8:1
lEx 3:12,18; 4:23

refuse to let them go, I will plague your whole country with frogs. ³The Nile will teem with frogs. They will come up into your palace and your bedroom and onto your bed, into the houses of your officials and on your people,ᵐ and into your ovens and kneading troughs. ⁴The frogs will go up on you and your people and all your officials.' "

⁵Then the LORD said to Moses, "Tell Aaron, 'Stretch out your hand with your staffⁿ over the streams and canals and ponds, and make frogs come up on the land of Egypt.' "

⁶So Aaron stretched out his hand over the waters of Egypt, and the frogsᵒ came up and covered the land. ⁷But the magicians did the same things by their secret arts;ᵖ they also made frogs come up on the land of Egypt.

⁸Pharaoh summoned Moses and Aaron and said, "Pray�q to the LORD to take the frogs away from me and my people, and I will let your people go to offer sacrificesʳ to the LORD."

⁹Moses said to Pharaoh, "I leave to you the honor of setting the time for me to pray for you and your officials and your people that you and your houses may be rid of the frogs, except for those that remain in the Nile."

¹⁰"Tomorrow," Pharaoh said.

Moses replied, "It will be as you say, so that you may know there is no one like the LORD our God.ˢ ¹¹The frogs will leave you and your houses, your officials and your people; they will remain only in the Nile."

¹²After Moses and Aaron left Pharaoh, Moses cried out to the LORD about the frogs he had brought on Pharaoh. ¹³And the LORD did what Moses asked. The frogs died in the houses, in the courtyards and in the fields. ¹⁴They were piled into heaps, and the land reeked of them. ¹⁵But when Pharaoh saw that there was relief, he hardened his heartᵗ and would not listen to Moses and Aaron, just as the LORD had said.

The Plague of Gnats

¹⁶Then the LORD said to Moses, "Tell Aaron, 'Stretch out your staff and strike the dust of the ground,' and throughout the land of Egypt the dust will become gnats." ¹⁷They did this, and when Aaron stretched out his hand with the staff and struck the dust of the ground, gnatsᵘ came upon men and animals. All the dust throughout the land of Egypt became gnats. ¹⁸But when the magiciansᵛ tried to produce gnats by their secret arts,ʷ they could not. And the gnats were on men and animals.

¹⁹The magicians said to Pharaoh, "This is the fingerˣ of God." But Pharaoh's heart was hard and he would not listen, just as the LORD had said.

The Plague of Flies

²⁰Then the LORD said to Moses, "Get up early in the morningʸ and confront Pharaoh as he goes to the water and say to him, 'This is what the LORD says: Let my people go, so that they may worshipᶻ me. ²¹If you do not let my people go, I will send swarms of flies on you and your officials, on your people and into your houses. The houses of the Egyptians will be full of flies, and even the ground where they are. ²²" 'But on that day I will deal differently with the land of Goshen,

---

8:3
ᵐEx 10:6
8:5
ⁿEx 7:19
8:6
ᵒPs 78:45;
105:30
8:7
ᵖEx 7:11
8:8
qver 28;
Ex 9:28; 10:17
ʳver 25
8:10
ˢEx 9:14;
Dt 4:35; 33:26;
2Sa 7:22;
1Ch 17:20;
Ps 86:8;
Isa 46:9;
Jer 10:6
8:15
ᵗEx 7:14
8:17
ᵘPs 105:31
8:18
ᵛEx 9:11;
Da 5:8 ʷEx 7:11
8:19
ˣEx 7:5; 10:7;
Ps 8:3; Lk 11:20
8:20
ʸEx 7:15; 9:13
ᶻver 1; Ex 3:18

where my people live;[a] no swarms of flies will be there, so that you will know[b] that I, the LORD, am in this land. [23]I will make a distinction[a] between my people and your people. This miraculous sign will occur tomorrow.' "

[24]And the LORD did this. Dense swarms of flies poured into Pharaoh's palace and into the houses of his officials, and throughout Egypt the land was ruined by the flies.[c]

[25]Then Pharaoh summoned[d] Moses and Aaron and said, "Go, sacrifice to your God here in the land."

[26]But Moses said, "That would not be right. The sacrifices we offer the LORD our God would be detestable to the Egyptians.[e] And if we offer sacrifices that are detestable in their eyes, will they not stone us? [27]We must take a three-day journey into the desert to offer sacrifices[f] to the LORD our God, as he commands us."

[28]Pharaoh said, "I will let you go to offer sacrifices to the LORD your God in the desert, but you must not go very far. Now pray[g] for me."

[29]Moses answered, "As soon as I leave you, I will pray to the LORD, and tomorrow the flies will leave Pharaoh and his officials and his people. Only be sure that Pharaoh does not act deceitfully[h] again by not letting the people go to offer sacrifices to the LORD."

[30]Then Moses left Pharaoh and prayed to the LORD,[i] [31]and the LORD did what Moses asked: The flies left Pharaoh and his officials and his people; not a fly remained. [32]But this time also Pharaoh hardened his heart[j] and would not let the people go.

The Plague on Livestock

9 Then the LORD said to Moses, "Go to Pharaoh and say to him, 'This is what the LORD, the God of the Hebrews, says: "Let my people go, so that they may worship[k] me." [2]If you refuse to let them go and continue to hold them back, [3]the hand[l] of the LORD will bring a terrible plague on your livestock in the field—on your horses and donkeys and camels and on your cattle and sheep and goats. [4]But the LORD will make a distinction between the livestock of Israel and that of Egypt,[m] so that no animal belonging to the Israelites will die.' "

[5]The LORD set a time and said, "Tomorrow the LORD will do this in the land." [6]And the next day the LORD did it: All the livestock[n] of the Egyptians died,[o] but not one animal belonging to the Israelites died. [7]Pharaoh sent men to investigate and found that not even one of the animals of the Israelites had died. Yet his heart was unyielding and he would not let the people go.[p]

The Plague of Boils

[8]Then the LORD said to Moses and Aaron, "Take handfuls of soot from a furnace and have Moses toss it into the air in the presence of Pharaoh. [9]It will become fine dust over the whole land of Egypt, and festering boils[q] will break out on men and animals throughout the land."

[10]So they took soot from a furnace and stood before Pharaoh. Moses tossed it into the air, and festering boils broke out on men and animals. [11]The magicians[r] could not stand before Moses because of the boils that

---

8:22
[a]Ex 9:4,6,26; 10:23; 11:7
[b]Ex 7:5; 9:29
8:24
[c]Ps 78:45; 105:31
8:25
[d]ver 8; Ex 9:27
8:26
[e]Ge 43:32; 46:34
8:27
[f]Ex 3:18
8:28
[g]ver 8; Ex 9:28; 1Ki 13:6
8:29
[h]ver 15
8:30
[i]ver 12
8:32
[j]ver 8,15; Ex 4:21
9:1
[k]Ex 8:1
9:3
[l]Ex 7:4
9:4
[m]ver 26; Ex 8:22
9:6
[n]ver 19-21; Ex 11:5
[o]Ps 78:48-50
9:7
[p]Ex 7:14; 8:32
9:9
[q]Dt 28:27,35; Rev 16:2
9:11
[r]Ex 8:18

---

[a]23 Septuagint and Vulgate; Hebrew *will put a deliverance*

were on them and on all the Egyptians. [12]But the LORD hardened Pharaoh's heart[s] and he would not listen to Moses and Aaron, just as the LORD had said to Moses.

The Plague of Hail

[13]Then the LORD said to Moses, "Get up early in the morning, confront Pharaoh and say to him, 'This is what the LORD, the God of the Hebrews, says: Let my people go, so that they may worship[t] me, [14]or this time I will send the full force of my plagues against you and against your officials and your people, so you may know[u] that there is no one like[v] me in all the earth. [15]For by now I could have stretched out my hand and struck you and your people[w] with a plague that would have wiped you off the earth. [16]But I have raised you up[a] for this very purpose,[x] that I might show you my power[y] and that my name might be proclaimed in all the earth. [17]You still set yourself against my people and will not let them go. [18]Therefore, at this time tomorrow I will send the worst hailstorm[z] that has ever fallen on Egypt, from the day it was founded till now.[a] [19]Give an order now to bring your livestock and everything you have in the field to a place of shelter, because the hail will fall on every man and animal that has not been brought in and is still out in the field, and they will die.'"

[20]Those officials of Pharaoh who feared[b] the word of the LORD hurried to bring their slaves and their livestock inside. [21]But those who ignored the word of the LORD left their slaves and livestock in the field.

[22]Then the LORD said to Moses, "Stretch out your hand toward the sky so that hail will fall all over Egypt—on men and animals and on everything growing in the fields of Egypt." [23]When Moses stretched out his staff toward the sky, the LORD sent thunder[c] and hail,[d] and lightning flashed down to the ground. So the LORD rained hail on the land of Egypt; [24]hail fell and lightning flashed back and forth. It was the worst storm in all the land of Egypt since it had become a nation. [25]Throughout Egypt hail struck everything in the fields—both men and animals; it beat down everything growing in the fields and stripped every tree.[e] [26]The only place it did not hail was the land of Goshen,[f] where the Israelites were.[g]

[27]Then Pharaoh summoned Moses and Aaron. "This time I have sinned,"[h] he said to them. "The LORD is in the right,[i] and I and my people are in the wrong. [28]Pray[j] to the LORD, for we have had enough thunder and hail. I will let you go;[k] you don't have to stay any longer."

[29]Moses replied, "When I have gone out of the city, I will spread out my hands[l] in prayer to the LORD. The thunder will stop and there will be no more hail, so you may know that the earth[m] is the LORD's. [30]But I know that you and your officials still do not fear the LORD God."

[31](The flax and barley[n] were destroyed, since the barley had headed and the flax was in bloom. [32]The wheat and spelt, however, were not destroyed, because they ripen later.)

[33]Then Moses left Pharaoh and went out of the city. He spread out his hands toward the LORD; the thunder and hail stopped, and the rain no longer poured down on the land. [34]When Pharaoh saw that the rain and hail and thunder had stopped, he sinned again: He and his officials

9:12
sEx 4:21
9:13
tEx 8:20
9:14
uEx 8:10
v2Sa 7:22;
1Ch 17:20;
Ps 86:8;
Isa 46:9;
Jer 10:6
9:15
wEx 3:20
9:16
xPr 16:4
yRo 9:17*
9:18
zver 23 aver 24
9:20
bPr 13:13
9:23
cPs 18:13
dJos 10:11;
Ps 78:47;
105:32;
Isa 30:30;
Eze 38:22;
Rev 8:7; 16:21
9:25
ePs 105:32-33
9:26
fver 4 gEx 8:22;
10:23; 11:7;
12:13
9:27
hEx 10:16
i2Ch 12:6;
Ps 129:4;
La 1:18
9:28
jEx 10:17
kEx 8:8
9:29
l1Ki 8:22,38;
Ps 143:6;
Isa 1:15
mEx 19:5;
Ps 24:1;
1Co 10:26
9:31
nRu 1:22; 2:23

---

[a]16 Or *have spared you*

hardened their hearts. 35So Pharaoh's heart° was hard and he would not let the Israelites go, just as the LORD had said through Moses.

The Plague of Locusts

10 Then the LORD said to Moses, "Go to Pharaoh, for I have hardened his heartᵖ and the hearts of his officials so that I may perform these miraculous signs�q of mine among them 2that you may tell your childrenʳ and grandchildren how I dealt harshly with the Egyptians and how I performed my signs among them, and that you may know that I am the LORD."

3So Moses and Aaron went to Pharaoh and said to him, "This is what the LORD, the God of the Hebrews, says: 'How long will you refuse to humbleˢ yourself before me? Let my people go, so that they may worship me. 4If you refuse to let them go, I will bring locustsᵗ into your country tomorrow. 5They will cover the face of the ground so that it cannot be seen. They will devour what little you have leftᵘ after the hail, including every tree that is growing in your fields. 6They will fill your houses and those of all your officials and all the Egyptians—something neither your fathers nor your forefathers have ever seen from the day they settled in this land till now.' " Then Moses turned and left Pharaoh.

7Pharaoh's officials said to him, "How long will this man be a snareᵛ to us? Let the people go, so that they may worship the LORD their God. Do you not yet realize that Egypt is ruined?"ʷ

8Then Moses and Aaron were brought back to Pharaoh. "Go, worshipˣ the LORD your God," he said. "But just who will be going?"

9Moses answered, "We will go with our young and old, with our sons and daughters, and with our flocks and herds, because we are to celebrate a festival to the LORD."

10Pharaoh said, "The LORD be with you—if I let you go, along with your women and children! Clearly you are bent on evil.ᵃ 11No! Have only the men go; and worship the LORD, since that's what you have been asking for." Then Moses and Aaron were driven out of Pharaoh's presence.

12And the LORD said to Moses, "Stretch out your handʸ over Egypt so that locusts will swarm over the land and devour everything growing in the fields, everything left by the hail."

13So Moses stretched out his staff over Egypt, and the LORD made an east wind blow across the land all that day and all that night. By morning the wind had brought the locusts;ᶻ 14they invaded all Egypt and settled down in every area of the country in great numbers. Never before had there been such a plague of locusts,ᵃ nor will there ever be again. 15They covered all the ground until it was black. They devouredᵇ all that was left after the hail—everything growing in the fields and the fruit on the trees. Nothing green remained on tree or plant in all the land of Egypt.

16Pharaoh quickly summoned Moses and Aaron and said, "I have sinnedᶜ against the LORD your God and against you. 17Now forgive my sin once more and prayᵈ to the LORD your God to take this deadly plague away from me."

ᵃ10 Or *Be careful, trouble is in store for you!*

9:35
oEx 4:21
10:1
pEx 4:21 qEx 7:3
10:2
rEx 12:26-27;
13:8,14; Dt 4:9;
Ps 44:1; 78:4,5;
Joel 1:3
10:3
s1Ki 21:29;
Jas 4:10;
1Pe 5:6
10:4
tRev 9:3
10:5
uEx 9:32;
Joel 1:4
10:7
vEx 23:33;
Jos 23:7-13;
1Sa 18:21;
Ecc 7:26
wEx 8:19
10:8
xEx 8:8
10:12
yEx 7:19
10:13
zPs 105:34
10:14
aPs 78:46;
Joel 2:1-11,25
10:15
bver 5;
Ps 105:34-35
10:16
cEx 9:27
10:17
dEx 8:8

¹⁸Moses then left Pharaoh and prayed to the LORD. ᵉ ¹⁹And the LORD changed the wind to a very strong west wind, which caught up the locusts and carried them into the Red Sea.ᵃ Not a locust was left anywhere in Egypt. ²⁰But the LORD hardened Pharaoh's heart, ᶠ and he would not let the Israelites go.

The Plague of Darkness

²¹Then the LORD said to Moses, "Stretch out your hand toward the sky so that darknessᵍ will spread over Egypt—darkness that can be felt." ²²So Moses stretched out his hand toward the sky, and total darknessʰ covered all Egypt for three days. ²³No one could see anyone else or leave his place for three days. Yet all the Israelites had light in the places where they lived. ⁱ

²⁴Then Pharaoh summoned Moses and said, "Go, worship the LORD. Even your women and childrenʲ may go with you; only leave your flocks and herds behind."

²⁵But Moses said, "You must allow us to have sacrifices and burnt offerings to present to the LORD our God. ²⁶Our livestock too must go with us; not a hoof is to be left behind. We have to use some of them in worshiping the LORD our God, and until we get there we will not know what we are to use to worship the LORD."

²⁷But the LORD hardened Pharaoh's heart, ᵏ and he was not willing to let them go. ²⁸Pharaoh said to Moses, "Get out of my sight! Make sure you do not appear before me again! The day you see my face you will die."

²⁹"Just as you say," Moses replied, "I will never appearˡ before you again."

The Plague on the Firstborn

11 Now the LORD had said to Moses, "I will bring one more plague on Pharaoh and on Egypt. After that, he will let you go from here, and when he does, he will drive you out completely. ²Tell the people that men and women alike are to ask their neighbors for articles of silver and gold."ᵐ ³(The LORD made the Egyptians favorably disposed toward the people, and Moses himself was highly regardedⁿ in Egypt by Pharaoh's officials and by the people.)

⁴So Moses said, "This is what the LORD says: 'About midnightᵒ I will go throughout Egypt. ⁵Every firstbornᵖ son in Egypt will die, from the firstborn son of Pharaoh, who sits on the throne, to the firstborn son of the slave girl, who is at her hand mill, and all the firstborn of the cattle as well. ⁶There will be loud wailing�q throughout Egypt—worse than there has ever been or ever will be again. ⁷But among the Israelites not a dog will bark at any man or animal.' Then you will know that the LORD makes a distinctionʳ between Egypt and Israel. ⁸All these officials of yours will come to me, bowing down before me and saying, 'Go, ˢ you and all the people who follow you!' After that I will leave." Then Moses, hot with anger, left Pharaoh.

⁹The LORD had said to Moses, "Pharaoh will refuse to listenᵗ to you—so that my wonders may be multiplied in Egypt." ¹⁰Moses and Aaron performed all these wonders before Pharaoh, but the LORD

10:18
eEx 8:30
10:20
fEx 4:21; 11:10
10:21
gDt 28:29
10:22
hPs 105:28;
Rev 16:10
10:23
iEx 8:22
10:24
jver 8-10
10:27
kver 20; Ex 4:21
10:29
lHeb 11:27
11:2
mEx 3:21,22
11:3
nDt 34:11
11:4
oEx 12:29
11:5
pEx 4:23;
Ps 78:51
11:6
qEx 12:30
11:7
rEx 8:22
11:8
sEx 12:31-33
11:9
tEx 7:4

ᵃ19 Hebrew *Yam Suph*; that is, Sea of Reeds

hardened Pharaoh's heart, ᵘ and he would not let the Israelites go out of his country.

The Passover

12:14–20pp — Lev 23:4–8; Nu 28:16–25; Dt 16:1–8

12 The LORD said to Moses and Aaron in Egypt, ²"This month is to be for you the first month, ᵛ the first month of your year. ³Tell the whole community of Israel that on the tenth day of this month each man is to take a lambᵃ for his family, one for each household. ⁴If any household is too small for a whole lamb, they must share one with their nearest neighbor, having taken into account the number of people there are. You are to determine the amount of lamb needed in accordance with what each person will eat. ⁵The animals you choose must be year-old males without defect, ʷ and you may take them from the sheep or the goats. ⁶Take care of them until the fourteenth day of the month, ˣ when all the people of the community of Israel must slaughter them at twilight. ʸ ⁷Then they are to take some of the blood and put it on the sides and tops of the doorframes of the houses where they eat the lambs. ⁸That same nightᶻ they are to eat the meat roastedᵃ over the fire, along with bitter herbs, ᵇ and bread made without yeast. ᶜ ⁹Do not eat the meat raw or cooked in water, but roast it over the fire—head, legs and inner parts. ¹⁰Do not leave any of it till morning; ᵈ if some is left till morning, you must burn it. ¹¹This is how you are to eat it: with your cloak tucked into your belt, your sandals on your feet and your staff in your hand. Eat it in haste; ᵉ it is the LORD's Passover. ᶠ

¹²"On that same night I will pass throughᵍ Egypt and strike down every firstborn—both men and animals—and I will bring judgment on all the godsʰ of Egypt. I am the LORD. ⁱ ¹³The blood will be a sign for you on the houses where you are; and when I see the blood, I will pass over you. No destructive plague will touch you when I strike Egypt.

¹⁴"This is a day you are to commemorate; ʲ for the generations to come you shall celebrate it as a festival to the LORD—a lasting ordinance. ᵏ ¹⁵For seven days you are to eat bread made without yeast. ˡ On the first day remove the yeast from your houses, for whoever eats anything with yeast in it from the first day through the seventh must be cut offᵐ from Israel. ¹⁶On the first day hold a sacred assembly, and another one on the seventh day. Do no work at all on these days, except to prepare food for everyone to eat—that is all you may do.

¹⁷"Celebrate the Feast of Unleavened Bread, because it was on this very day that I brought your divisions out of Egypt. ⁿ Celebrate this day as a lasting ordinance for the generations to come. ¹⁸In the first monthᵒ you are to eat bread made without yeast, from the evening of the fourteenth day until the evening of the twenty-first day. ¹⁹For seven days no yeast is to be found in your houses. And whoever eats anything with yeast in it must be cut off from the community of Israel, whether he is an alien or native-born. ²⁰Eat nothing made with yeast. Wherever you live, you must eat unleavened bread."

²¹Then Moses summoned all the elders of Israel and said to them, "Go at once and select the animals for your families and slaughter the Passoverᵖ lamb. ²²Take a bunch of hyssop, dip it into the blood in the

---

ᵃ3 The Hebrew word can mean both *lamb* or *kid*; also in verse 4.

11:10
uEx 4:21; 10:20, 27

12:2
vEx 13:4;
Dt 16:1

12:5
wLev 22:18-21;
Heb 9:14

12:6
xLev 23:5;
Nu 9:1-3,5,11
yEx 16:12;
Dt 16:4,6

12:8
zEx 34:25;
Nu 9:12
aDt 16:7
bNu 9:11
cDt 16:3-4;
1Co 5:8

12:10
dEx 23:18;
34:25

12:11
eDt 16:3
fver 13,21,27,
43; Dt 16:1

12:12
gEx 11:4;
Am 5:17
hNu 33:4
iEx 6:2

12:14
jEx 13:9
kver 17,24;
Ex 13:5,10;
2Ki 23:21

12:15
lEx 13:6-7;
23:15; 34:18;
Lev 23:6;
Dt 16:3
mGe 17:14;
Nu 9:13

12:17
nver 41; Ex 13:3

12:18
over 2;
Lev 23:5-8;
Nu 28:16-25

12:21
pver 11;
Mk 14:12-16

basin and put some of the blood[q] on the top and on both sides of the doorframe. Not one of you shall go out the door of his house until morning. [23]When the LORD goes through the land to strike down the Egyptians, he will see the blood[r] on the top and sides of the doorframe and will pass over[s] that doorway, and he will not permit the destroyer[t] to enter your houses and strike you down.

[24]"Obey these instructions as a lasting ordinance for you and your descendants. [25]When you enter the land that the LORD will give you as he promised, observe this ceremony. [26]And when your children[u] ask you, 'What does this ceremony mean to you?' [27]then tell them, 'It is the Passover[v] sacrifice to the LORD, who passed over the houses of the Israelites in Egypt and spared our homes when he struck down the Egyptians.'" Then the people bowed down and worshiped. [w] [28]The Israelites did just what the LORD commanded Moses and Aaron.

[29]At midnight[x] the LORD struck down all the firstborn[y] in Egypt, from the firstborn of Pharaoh, who sat on the throne, to the firstborn of the prisoner, who was in the dungeon, and the firstborn of all the livestock[z] as well. [30]Pharaoh and all his officials and all the Egyptians got up during the night, and there was loud wailing[a] in Egypt, for there was not a house without someone dead.

The Exodus

[31]During the night Pharaoh summoned Moses and Aaron and said, "Up! Leave my people, you and the Israelites! Go, worship[b] the LORD as you have requested. [32]Take your flocks and herds,[c] as you have said, and go. And also bless me."

[33]The Egyptians urged the people to hurry and leave[d] the country. "For otherwise," they said, "we will all die!" [34]So the people took their dough before the yeast was added, and carried it on their shoulders in kneading troughs wrapped in clothing. [35]The Israelites did as Moses instructed and asked the Egyptians for articles of silver and gold[e] and for clothing. [36]The LORD had made the Egyptians favorably disposed toward the people, and they gave them what they asked for; so they plundered[f] the Egyptians.

[37]The Israelites journeyed from Rameses to Succoth.[g] There were about six hundred thousand men[h] on foot, besides women and children. [38]Many other people[i] went up with them, as well as large droves of livestock, both flocks and herds. [39]With the dough they had brought from Egypt, they baked cakes of unleavened bread. The dough was without yeast because they had been driven out[j] of Egypt and did not have time to prepare food for themselves.

[40]Now the length of time the Israelite people lived in Egypt[a] was 430 years. [k] [41]At the end of the 430 years, to the very day, all the LORD's divisions[l] left Egypt. [m] [42]Because the LORD kept vigil that night to bring them out of Egypt, on this night all the Israelites are to keep vigil to honor the LORD for the generations to come. [n]

Passover Restrictions

[43]The LORD said to Moses and Aaron, "These are the regulations for the Passover:[o]

12:22
q ver 7;
Heb 11:28
12:23
r Rev 7:3 s ver 13
t 1Co 10:10;
Heb 11:28
12:26
u Ex 10:2; 13:8,
14-15; Jos 4:6
12:27
v ver 11
w Ex 4:31
12:29
x Ex 11:4
y Ex 4:23;
Ps 78:51 z Ex 9:6
12:30
a Ex 11:6
12:31
b Ex 8:8
12:32
c Ex 10:9,26
12:33
d Ps 105:38
12:35
e Ex 3:22
12:36
f Ex 3:22
12:37
g Nu 33:3-5
h Ex 38:26;
Nu 1:46;
11:13,21
12:38
i Nu 11:4
12:39
j ver 31-33;
Ex 6:1; 11:1
12:40
k Ge 15:13;
Ac 7:6; Gal 3:17
12:41
l ver 17; Ex 6:26
m Ex 3:10
12:42
n Ex 13:10;
Dt 16:1,6
12:43
o ver 11

---

a40 Masoretic Text; Samaritan Pentateuch and Septuagint *Egypt and Canaan*

"No foreigner[p] is to eat of it. [44]Any slave you have bought may eat of it after you have circumcised[q] him, [45]but a temporary resident and a hired worker[r] may not eat of it.

[46]"It must be eaten inside one house; take none of the meat outside the house. Do not break any of the bones.[s] [47]The whole community of Israel must celebrate it.

[48]"An alien living among you who wants to celebrate the LORD's Passover must have all the males in his household circumcised; then he may take part like one born in the land.[t] No uncircumcised male may eat of it. [49]The same law applies to the native-born and to the alien[u] living among you."

[50]All the Israelites did just what the LORD had commanded Moses and Aaron. [51]And on that very day the LORD brought the Israelites out of Egypt by their divisions.[v]

Consecration of the Firstborn

13 The LORD said to Moses, [2]"Consecrate to me every firstborn male.[w] The first offspring of every womb among the Israelites belongs to me, whether man or animal."

[3]Then Moses said to the people, "Commemorate this day, the day you came out of Egypt, out of the land of slavery, because the LORD brought you out of it with a mighty hand.[x] Eat nothing containing yeast.[y] [4]Today, in the month of Abib,[z] you are leaving. [5]When the LORD brings you into the land of the Canaanites, Hittites, Amorites, Hivites and Jebusites[a]—the land he swore to your forefathers to give you, a land flowing with milk and honey—you are to observe this ceremony[b] in this month: [6]For seven days eat bread made without yeast and on the seventh day hold a festival[c] to the LORD. [7]Eat unleavened bread during those seven days; nothing with yeast in it is to be seen among you, nor shall any yeast be seen anywhere within your borders. [8]On that day tell your son,[d] 'I do this because of what the LORD did for me when I came out of Egypt.' [9]This observance will be for you like a sign on your hand and a reminder on your forehead[e] that the law of the LORD is to be on your lips. For the LORD brought you out of Egypt with his mighty hand. [10]You must keep this ordinance[f] at the appointed time year after year.

[11]"After the LORD brings you into the land of the Canaanites and gives it to you, as he promised on oath to you and your forefathers, [12]you are to give over to the LORD the first offspring of every womb. All the firstborn males of your livestock belong to the LORD.[g] [13]Redeem with a lamb every firstborn donkey, but if you do not redeem it, break its neck.[h] Redeem every firstborn among your sons.[i]

[14]"In days to come, when your son[j] asks you, 'What does this mean?' say to him, 'With a mighty hand the LORD brought us out of Egypt, out of the land of slavery.[k] [15]When Pharaoh stubbornly refused to let us go, the LORD killed every firstborn in Egypt, both man and animal. This is why I sacrifice to the LORD the first male offspring of every womb and redeem each of my firstborn sons.'[l] [16]And it will be like a sign on your hand and a symbol on your forehead[m] that the LORD brought us out of Egypt with his mighty hand."

12:43
p ver 48;
Nu 9:14
12:44
q Ge 17:12-13
12:45
r Lev 22:10
12:46
s Nu 9:12;
Jn 19:36*
12:48
t Nu 9:14
12:49
u Nu 15:15-16,
29; Gal 3:28
12:51
v ver 41; Ex 6:26
13:2
w ver 12,13,15;
Ex 22:29;
Nu 3:13;
Dt 15:19;
Lk 2:23*
13:3
x Ex 3:20; 6:1
y Ex 12:19
13:4
z Ex 12:2
13:5
a Ex 3:8
b Ex 12:25-26
13:6
c Ex 12:15-20
13:8
d ver 14;
Ex 10:2;
Ps 78:5-6
13:9
e ver 16; Dt 6:8;
11:18
13:10
f Ex 12:24-25
13:12
g Lev 27:26;
Lk 2:23*
13:13
h Ex 34:20
i Nu 18:15
13:14
j Ex 10:2;
12:26-27;
Dt 6:20 k ver 3,9
13:15
l Ex 12:29
13:16
m ver 9

Crossing the Sea

[17]When Pharaoh let the people go, God did not lead them on the road through the Philistine country, though that was shorter. For God said, "If they face war, they might change their minds and return to Egypt."[n] [18]So God led[o] the people around by the desert road toward the Red Sea.[a] The Israelites went up out of Egypt armed for battle.[p]

[19]Moses took the bones of Joseph[q] with him because Joseph had made the sons of Israel swear an oath. He had said, "God will surely come to your aid, and then you must carry my bones up with you from this place."[b r]

[20]After leaving Succoth they camped at Etham on the edge of the desert.[s] [21]By day the LORD went ahead of them in a pillar of cloud[t] to guide them on their way and by night in a pillar of fire to give them light, so that they could travel by day or night. [22]Neither the pillar of cloud by day nor the pillar of fire by night left its place in front of the people.

14 Then the LORD said to Moses, [2]"Tell the Israelites to turn back and encamp near Pi Hahiroth, between Migdol[u] and the sea. They are to encamp by the sea, directly opposite Baal Zephon. [3]Pharaoh will think, 'The Israelites are wandering around the land in confusion, hemmed in by the desert.' [4]And I will harden Pharaoh's heart,[v] and he will pursue them. But I will gain glory[w] for myself through Pharaoh and all his army, and the Egyptians will know that I am the LORD."[x] So the Israelites did this.

[5]When the king of Egypt was told that the people had fled, Pharaoh and his officials changed their minds about them and said, "What have we done? We have let the Israelites go and have lost their services!" [6]So he had his chariot made ready and took his army with him. [7]He took six hundred of the best chariots, along with all the other chariots of Egypt, with officers over all of them. [8]The LORD hardened the heart[y] of Pharaoh king of Egypt, so that he pursued the Israelites, who were marching out boldly.[z] [9]The Egyptians—all Pharaoh's horses and chariots, horsemen[c] and troops—pursued the Israelites and overtook[a] them as they camped by the sea near Pi Hahiroth, opposite Baal Zephon.

[10]As Pharaoh approached, the Israelites looked up, and there were the Egyptians, marching after them. They were terrified and cried[b] out to the LORD. [11]They said to Moses, "Was it because there were no graves in Egypt that you brought us to the desert to die?[c] What have you done to us by bringing us out of Egypt? [12]Didn't we say to you in Egypt, 'Leave us alone; let us serve the Egyptians'? It would have been better for us to serve the Egyptians than to die in the desert!"

[13]Moses answered the people, "Do not be afraid.[d] Stand firm and you will see[e] the deliverance the LORD will bring you today. The Egyptians you see today you will never see[f] again. [14]The LORD will fight[g] for you; you need only to be still."[h]

[15]Then the LORD said to Moses, "Why are you crying out to me? Tell the Israelites to move on. [16]Raise your staff[i] and stretch out your hand over the sea to divide the water[j] so that the Israelites can go through the sea on dry ground. [17]I will harden the hearts of the Egyptians so that

13:17
n Ex 14:11;
Nu 14:1-4;
Dt 17:16
13:18
o Ps 136:16
p Jos 1:14
13:19
q Jos 24:32;
Ac 7:16
r Ge 50:24-25
13:20
s Nu 33:6
13:21
t Ex 14:19,24;
33:9-10;
Nu 9:16;
Dt 1:33;
Ne 9:12,19;
Ps 78:14; 99:7;
105:39; Isa 4:5;
1Co 10:1
14:2
u Nu 33:7;
Jer 44:1
14:4
v Ex 4:21
w Ro 9:17,22-23
x Ex 7:5
14:8
y ver 4; Ex 11:10
z Nu 33:3;
Ac 13:17
14:9
a Ex 15:9
14:10
b Jos 24:7;
Ne 9:9;
Ps 34:17
14:11
c Ps 106:7-8
14:13
d Ge 15:1
e 2Ch 20:17;
Isa 41:10,13-14
f ver 30
14:14
g ver 25;
Ex 15:3;
Dt 1:30; 3:22;
2Ch 20:29
h Ps 37:7;
46:10; Isa 30:15
14:16
i Ex 4:17;
Nu 20:8-9,11
j Isa 10:26

---

[a]18 Hebrew *Yam Suph*; that is, Sea of Reeds   [b]19 See Gen. 50:25.   [c]9 Or *charioteers*; also in verses 17, 18, 23, 26 and 28

they will go in after them.ᵏ And I will gain glory through Pharaoh and all his army, through his chariots and his horsemen. ¹⁸The Egyptians will know that I am the LORD when I gain glory through Pharaoh, his chariots and his horsemen."

¹⁹Then the angel of God, who had been traveling in front of Israel's army, withdrew and went behind them. The pillar of cloud¹ also moved from in front and stood behind them, ²⁰coming between the armies of Egypt and Israel. Throughout the night the cloud brought darkness to the one side and light to the other side; so neither went near the other all night long.

²¹Then Moses stretched out his hand over the sea, and all that night the LORD drove the sea back with a strong east windᵐ and turned it into dry land. The waters were divided,ⁿ ²²and the Israelites went through the sea on dry ground,ᵒ with a wall of water on their right and on their left.

²³The Egyptians pursued them, and all Pharaoh's horses and chariots and horsemen followed them into the sea. ²⁴During the last watch of the night the LORD looked down from the pillar of fire and cloudᴾ at the Egyptian army and threw it into confusion. ²⁵He made the wheels of their chariots come offᵃ so that they had difficulty driving. And the Egyptians said, "Let's get away from the Israelites! The LORD is fighting�q for them against Egypt."

²⁶Then the LORD said to Moses, "Stretch out your hand over the sea so that the waters may flow back over the Egyptians and their chariots and horsemen." ²⁷Moses stretched out his hand over the sea, and at daybreak the sea went back to its place.ʳ The Egyptians were fleeing towardᵇ it, and the LORD swept them into the sea.ˢ ²⁸The water flowed back and covered the chariots and horsemen—the entire army of Pharaoh that had followed the Israelites into the sea. Not one of them survived.

²⁹But the Israelites went through the sea on dry ground,ᵗ with a wall of water on their right and on their left. ³⁰That day the LORD savedᵘ Israel from the hands of the Egyptians, and Israel saw the Egyptians lying dead on the shore. ³¹And when the Israelites saw the great power the LORD displayed against the Egyptians, the people feared the LORD and put their trustᵛ in him and in Moses his servant.

The Song of Moses and Miriam

15 Then Moses and the Israelites sang this songʷ to the LORD:

"I will singˣ to the LORD,
  for he is highly exalted.
The horse and its rider
  he has hurled into the sea.
²The LORD is my strengthʸ and my song;
  he has become my salvation.ᶻ
He is my God,ᵃ and I will praise him,
  my father's God, and I will exaltᵇ him.
³The LORD is a warrior;ᶜ

ᵃ25 Or *He jammed the wheels of their chariots* (see Samaritan Pentateuch, Septuagint and Syriac)
ᵇ27 Or *from*

14:17
kver 4
14:19
lEx 13:21
14:21
mEx 15:8
nPs 74:13;
114:5; Isa 63:12
14:22
oEx 15:19;
Ne 9:11;
Ps 66:6;
Heb 11:29
14:24
pEx 13:21
14:25
qver 14
14:27
rJos 4:18
sEx 15:1,21;
Ps 78:53;
106:11
14:29
tver 22
14:30
uPs 106:8,10,21
14:31
vPs 106:12;
Jn 2:11
15:1
wRev 15:3
xPs 106:12
15:2
yPs 59:17
zPs 18:2,46;
Isa 12:2;
Hab 3:18
aGe 28:21
bEx 3:6,15-16;
Isa 25:1
15:3
cEx 14:14;
Ps 24:8;
Rev 19:11

the LORD is his name. [d]
[4]Pharaoh's chariots and his army[e]
    he has hurled into the sea.
The best of Pharaoh's officers
    are drowned in the Red Sea. [a]
[5]The deep waters have covered them;
    they sank to the depths like a stone. [f]

[6]"Your right hand, [g] O LORD,
    was majestic in power.
Your right hand, O LORD,
    shattered the enemy.
[7]In the greatness of your majesty
    you threw down those who opposed you.
You unleashed your burning anger;[h]
    it consumed them like stubble.
[8]By the blast of your nostrils[i]
    the waters piled up. [j]
The surging waters stood firm like a wall;[k]
    the deep waters congealed in the heart of the sea.

[9]"The enemy boasted,
    'I will pursue, [l] I will overtake them.
I will divide the spoils;[m]
    I will gorge myself on them.
I will draw my sword
    and my hand will destroy them.'
[10]But you blew with your breath,
    and the sea covered them.
They sank like lead
    in the mighty waters. [n]

[11]"Who among the gods is like you, [o] O LORD?
    Who is like you—
    majestic in holiness, [p]
    awesome in glory, [q]
    working wonders?
[12]You stretched out your right hand
    and the earth swallowed them.

[13]"In your unfailing love you will lead[r]
    the people you have redeemed.
In your strength you will guide them
    to your holy dwelling. [s]
[14]The nations will hear and tremble;[t]
    anguish will grip the people of Philistia.
[15]The chiefs[u] of Edom will be terrified,
    the leaders of Moab will be seized with trembling, [v]
the people[b] of Canaan will melt[w] away;
[16]   terror[x] and dread will fall upon them.
By the power of your arm
    they will be as still as a stone[y]—

15:3
dEx 6:2-3,7-8;
Ps 83:18
15:4
eEx 14:6-7
15:5
fver 10; Ne 9:11
15:6
gPs 118:15
15:7
hPs 78:49-50
15:8
iEx 14:21
jPs 78:13
kEx 14:22
15:9
lEx 14:5-9
mJdg 5:30;
Isa 53:12
15:10
nver 5;
Ex 14:27-28
15:11
oEx 8:10;
Dt 3:24;
Ps 77:13
pIsa 6:3;
Rev 4:8 qPs 8:1
15:13
rNe 9:12;
Ps 77:20
sPs 78:54
15:14
tDt 2:25
15:15
uGe 36:15
vNu 22:3
wJos 5:1
15:16
xEx 23:27;
Jos 2:9
y1Sa 25:37

---

a4 Hebrew *Yam Suph*; that is, Sea of Reeds; also in verse 22   *b15* Or *rulers*

until your people pass by, O LORD,
    until the people you bought[az] pass by.
[17]You will bring them in and plant[a] them
    on the mountain[b] of your inheritance—
the place, O LORD, you made for your dwelling,
    the sanctuary, O Lord, your hands established.
[18]The LORD will reign
    for ever and ever."

[19]When Pharaoh's horses, chariots and horsemen[b] went into the sea,[c] the LORD brought the waters of the sea back over them, but the Israelites walked through the sea on dry ground.[d] [20]Then Miriam[e] the prophetess,[f] Aaron's sister, took a tambourine in her hand, and all the women followed her, with tambourines and dancing.[g] [21]Miriam sang to them:

"Sing to the LORD,
    for he is highly exalted.
The horse and its rider
    he has hurled into the sea."[h]

The Waters of Marah and Elim

[22]Then Moses led Israel from the Red Sea and they went into the Desert of Shur. For three days they traveled in the desert without finding water. [23]When they came to Marah, they could not drink its water because it was bitter. (That is why the place is called Marah.[c i]) [24]So the people grumbled[j] against Moses, saying, "What are we to drink?"

[25]Then Moses cried out[k] to the LORD, and the LORD showed him a piece of wood. He threw it into the water, and the water became sweet.

There the LORD made a decree and a law for them, and there he tested[l] them. [26]He said, "If you listen carefully to the voice of the LORD your God and do what is right in his eyes, if you pay attention to his commands and keep all his decrees,[m] I will not bring on you any of the diseases[n] I brought on the Egyptians, for I am the LORD, who heals[o] you."

[27]Then they came to Elim, where there were twelve springs and seventy palm trees, and they camped[p] there near the water.

Manna and Quail

16 The whole Israelite community set out from Elim and came to the Desert of Sin,[q] which is between Elim and Sinai, on the fifteenth day of the second month after they had come out of Egypt. [2]In the desert the whole community grumbled[r] against Moses and Aaron. [3]The Israelites said to them, "If only we had died by the LORD's hand in Egypt![s] There we sat around pots of meat and ate all the food[t] we wanted, but you have brought us out into this desert to starve this entire assembly to death."

[4]Then the LORD said to Moses, "I will rain down bread from heaven[u] for you. The people are to go out each day and gather enough for that day. In this way I will test them and see whether they will follow my

---

[a]16 Or *created*   [b]19 Or *charioteers*   [c]23 *Marah* means *bitter.*

15:16
z Ps 74:2
15:17
a Ps 44:2
b Ps 78:54,68
15:19
c Ex 14:28
d Ex 14:22
15:20
e Nu 26:59
f Jdg 4:4
g Jdg 11:34;
1Sa 18:6;
Ps 30:11; 150:4
15:21
h ver 1; Ex 14:27
15:23
i Nu 33:8
15:24
j Ex 14:12; 16:2
15:25
k Ex 14:10
l Jdg 3:4
15:26
m Dt 7:12
n Dt 28:27,58-60
o Ex 23:25-26
15:27
p Nu 33:9
16:1
q Nu 33:11,12
16:2
r Ex 14:11;
15:24;
1Co 10:10
16:3
s Ex 17:3
t Nu 11:4,34
16:4
u Dt 8:3;
Jn 6:31*

instructions. ⁵On the sixth day they are to prepare what they bring in, and that is to be twice[v] as much as they gather on the other days."

⁶So Moses and Aaron said to all the Israelites, "In the evening you will know that it was the LORD who brought you out of Egypt,[w] ⁷and in the morning you will see the glory[x] of the LORD, because he has heard your grumbling[y] against him. Who are we, that you should grumble against us?"[z] ⁸Moses also said, "You will know that it was the LORD when he gives you meat to eat in the evening and all the bread you want in the morning, because he has heard your grumbling against him. Who are we? You are not grumbling against us, but against the LORD."[a]

⁹Then Moses told Aaron, "Say to the entire Israelite community, 'Come before the LORD, for he has heard your grumbling.' "

¹⁰While Aaron was speaking to the whole Israelite community, they looked toward the desert, and there was the glory[b] of the LORD appearing in the cloud.[c]

¹¹The LORD said to Moses, ¹²"I have heard the grumbling[d] of the Israelites. Tell them, 'At twilight you will eat meat, and in the morning you will be filled with bread. Then you will know that I am the LORD your God.' "

¹³That evening quail[e] came and covered the camp, and in the morning there was a layer of dew[f] around the camp. ¹⁴When the dew was gone, thin flakes like frost[g] on the ground appeared on the desert floor. ¹⁵When the Israelites saw it, they said to each other, "What is it?" For they did not know what it was.

Moses said to them, "It is the bread[h] the LORD has given you to eat. ¹⁶This is what the LORD has commanded: 'Each one is to gather as much as he needs. Take an omer[a][i] for each person you have in your tent.' "

¹⁷The Israelites did as they were told; some gathered much, some little. ¹⁸And when they measured it by the omer, he who gathered much did not have too much, and he who gathered little did not have too little.[j] Each one gathered as much as he needed.

¹⁹Then Moses said to them, "No one is to keep any of it until morning."[k]

²⁰However, some of them paid no attention to Moses; they kept part of it until morning, but it was full of maggots and began to smell. So Moses was angry with them.

²¹Each morning everyone gathered as much as he needed, and when the sun grew hot, it melted away. ²²On the sixth day, they gathered twice[l] as much—two omers[b] for each person—and the leaders of the community[m] came and reported this to Moses. ²³He said to them, "This is what the LORD commanded: 'Tomorrow is to be a day of rest, a holy Sabbath[n] to the LORD. So bake what you want to bake and boil what you want to boil. Save whatever is left and keep it until morning.' "

²⁴So they saved it until morning, as Moses commanded, and it did not stink or get maggots in it. ²⁵"Eat it today," Moses said, "because today is a Sabbath to the LORD. You will not find any of it on the ground today. ²⁶Six days you are to gather it, but on the seventh day, the Sabbath,[o] there will not be any."

16:5
vver 22
16:6
wEx 6:6
16:7
xver 10;
Isa 35:2; 40:5
yver 12;
Nu 14:2,27,28
zNu 16:11
16:8
a1Sa 8:7;
Ro 13:2
16:10
bver 7;
Nu 16:19
cEx 13:21;
1Ki 8:10
16:12
dver 7
16:13
eNu 11:31;
Ps 78:27-28;
105:40 fNu 11:9
16:14
gver 31;
Nu 11:7-9;
Ps 105:40
16:15
hver 4; Jn 6:31
16:16
iver 32,36
16:18
j2Co 8:15*
16:19
kver 23;
Ex 12:10; 23:18
16:22
lver 5 mEx 34:31
16:23
nGe 2:3;
Ex 20:8; 23:12;
Lev 23:3
16:26
oEx 20:9-10

---

[a]16 That is, probably about 2 quarts (about 2 liters); also in verses 18, 32, 33 and 36   [b]22 That is, probably about 4 quarts (about 4.5 liters)

27Nevertheless, some of the people went out on the seventh day to gather it, but they found none. 28Then the LORD said to Moses, "How long will you[a] refuse to keep my commands[p] and my instructions? 29Bear in mind that the LORD has given you the Sabbath; that is why on the sixth day he gives you bread for two days. Everyone is to stay where he is on the seventh day; no one is to go out." 30So the people rested on the seventh day.

31The people of Israel called the bread manna.[b][q] It was white like coriander seed and tasted like wafers made with honey. 32Moses said, "This is what the LORD has commanded: 'Take an omer of manna and keep it for the generations to come, so they can see the bread I gave you to eat in the desert when I brought you out of Egypt.' "

33So Moses said to Aaron, "Take a jar and put an omer of manna[r] in it. Then place it before the LORD to be kept for the generations to come."

34As the LORD commanded Moses, Aaron put the manna in front of the Testimony,[s] that it might be kept. 35The Israelites ate manna[t] forty years,[u] until they came to a land that was settled; they ate manna until they reached the border of Canaan.[v]

36(An omer is one tenth of an ephah.)

Water From the Rock

17 The whole Israelite community set out from the Desert of Sin,[w] traveling from place to place as the LORD commanded. They camped at Rephidim, but there was no water[x] for the people to drink. 2So they quarreled with Moses and said, "Give us water[y] to drink."

Moses replied, "Why do you quarrel with me? Why do you put the LORD to the test?"[z]

3But the people were thirsty for water there, and they grumbled[a] against Moses. They said, "Why did you bring us up out of Egypt to make us and our children and livestock die of thirst?"

4Then Moses cried out to the LORD, "What am I to do with these people? They are almost ready to stone[b] me."

5The LORD answered Moses, "Walk on ahead of the people. Take with you some of the elders of Israel and take in your hand the staff with which you struck the Nile,[c] and go. 6I will stand there before you by the rock at Horeb. Strike the rock, and water[d] will come out of it for the people to drink." So Moses did this in the sight of the elders of Israel. 7And he called the place Massah[c] and Meribah[d][e] because the Israelites quarreled and because they tested the LORD saying, "Is the LORD among us or not?"

The Amalekites Defeated

8The Amalekites[f] came and attacked the Israelites at Rephidim. 9Moses said to Joshua, "Choose some of our men and go out to fight the Amalekites. Tomorrow I will stand on top of the hill with the staff[g] of God in my hands."

10So Joshua fought the Amalekites as Moses had ordered, and Moses, Aaron and Hur[h] went to the top of the hill. 11As long as Moses held up his hands, the Israelites were winning,[i] but whenever he lowered his

16:28
p 2Ki 17:14;
Ps 78:10;
106:13
16:31
q Nu 11:7-9
16:33
r Heb 9:4
16:34
s Ex 25:16,21,22;
40:20; Nu 17:4,
10
16:35
t Jn 6:31,49
u Ne 9:21
v Jos 5:12
17:1
w Ex 16:1
x Nu 33:14
17:2
y Nu 20:2
z Dt 6:16;
Ps 78:18,41;
1Co 10:9
17:3
a Ex 15:24;
16:2-3
17:4
b Nu 14:10;
1Sa 30:6
17:5
c Ex 7:20
17:6
d Nu 20:11;
Ps 114:8;
1Co 10:4
17:7
e Nu 20:13,24;
Ps 81:7
17:8
f Ge 36:12;
Dt 25:17-19
17:9
g Ex 4:17
17:10
h Ex 24:14
17:11
i Jas 5:16

---

a28 The Hebrew is plural.   *b31* *Manna* means *What is it?* (see verse 15).   *c7* *Massah* means *testing.*   *d7* *Meribah* means *quarreling.*

hands, the Amalekites were winning. [12]When Moses' hands grew tired, they took a stone and put it under him and he sat on it. Aaron and Hur held his hands up—one on one side, one on the other—so that his hands remained steady till sunset. [13]So Joshua overcame the Amalekite army with the sword.

[14]Then the LORD said to Moses, "Write[j] this on a scroll as something to be remembered and make sure that Joshua hears it, because I will completely blot out the memory of Amalek[k] from under heaven."

[15]Moses built an altar and called it The LORD is my Banner. [16]He said, "For hands were lifted up to the throne of the LORD. The[a] LORD will be at war against the Amalekites from generation to generation."

Jethro Visits Moses

18 Now Jethro, the priest of Midian[l] and father-in-law of Moses, heard of everything God had done for Moses and for his people Israel, and how the LORD had brought Israel out of Egypt.

[2]After Moses had sent away his wife Zipporah,[m] his father-in-law Jethro received her [3]and her two sons.[n] One son was named Gershom,[b] for Moses said, "I have become an alien in a foreign land";[o] [4]and the other was named Eliezer,[c][p] for he said, "My father's God was my helper; he saved me from the sword of Pharaoh."

[5]Jethro, Moses' father-in-law, together with Moses' sons and wife, came to him in the desert, where he was camped near the mountain[q] of God. [6]Jethro had sent word to him, "I, your father-in-law Jethro, am coming to you with your wife and her two sons."

[7]So Moses went out to meet his father-in-law and bowed down[r] and kissed[s] him. They greeted each other and then went into the tent. [8]Moses told his father-in-law about everything the LORD had done to Pharaoh and the Egyptians for Israel's sake and about all the hardships they had met along the way and how the LORD had saved[t] them.

[9]Jethro was delighted to hear about all the good things the LORD had done for Israel in rescuing them from the hand of the Egyptians. [10]He said, "Praise be to the LORD,[u] who rescued you from the hand of the Egyptians and of Pharaoh, and who rescued the people from the hand of the Egyptians. [11]Now I know that the LORD is greater than all other gods,[v] for he did this to those who had treated Israel arrogantly."[w] [12]Then Jethro, Moses' father-in-law, brought a burnt offering and other sacrifices to God, and Aaron came with all the elders of Israel to eat bread with Moses' father-in-law in the presence[x] of God.

[13]The next day Moses took his seat to serve as judge for the people, and they stood around him from morning till evening. [14]When his father-in-law saw all that Moses was doing for the people, he said, "What is this you are doing for the people? Why do you alone sit as judge, while all these people stand around you from morning till evening?"

[15]Moses answered him, "Because the people come to me to seek God's will.[y] [16]Whenever they have a dispute, it is brought to me, and I decide between the parties and inform them of God's decrees and laws."[z]

Cross references

17:14
jEx 24:4; 34:27;
Nu 33:2
kSa 15:3;
30:17-18
18:1
lEx 2:16; 3:1
18:2
mEx 2:21; 4:25
18:3
nEx 4:20;
Ac 7:29
oEx 2:22
18:4
p1Ch 23:15
18:5
qEx 3:1
18:7
rGe 43:28
sGe 29:13
18:8
tEx 15:6,16;
Ps 81:7
18:10
uGe 14:20;
Ps 68:19-20
18:11
vEx 12:12;
15:11; 2Ch 2:5
wLk 1:51
18:12
xDt 12:7
18:15
yNu 9:6,8;
Dt 17:8-13
18:16
zLev 24:12

---

[a]16 Or "Because a hand was against the throne of the LORD, the   [b]3 Gershom sounds like the Hebrew for an alien there.   [c]4 Eliezer means my God is helper.

¹⁷Moses' father-in-law replied, "What you are doing is not good. ¹⁸You and these people who come to you will only wear yourselves out. The work is too heavy for you; you cannot handle it alone.ᵃ ¹⁹Listen now to me and I will give you some advice, and may God be with you.ᵇ You must be the people's representative before God and bring their disputesᶜ to him. ²⁰Teach them the decrees and laws,ᵈ and show them the way to liveᵉ and the duties they are to perform.ᶠ ²¹But select capable menᵍ from all the people—men who fear God, trustworthy men who hate dishonest gainʰ—and appoint them as officialsⁱ over thousands, hundreds, fifties and tens. ²²Have them serve as judges for the people at all times, but have them bring every difficult caseʲ to you; the simple cases they can decide themselves. That will make your load lighter, because they will shareᵏ it with you. ²³If you do this and God so commands, you will be able to stand the strain, and all these people will go home satisfied."

²⁴Moses listened to his father-in-law and did everything he said. ²⁵He chose capable men from all Israel and made them leaders of the people, officials over thousands, hundreds, fifties and tens.ˡ ²⁶They served as judges for the people at all times. The difficult cases they brought to Moses, but the simple ones they decided themselves.ᵐ

²⁷Then Moses sent his father-in-law on his way, and Jethro returned to his own country.ⁿ

At Mount Sinai

19 In the third month after the Israelites left Egypt—on the very day—they came to the Desert of Sinai. ²After they set out from Rephidim,ᵒ they entered the Desert of Sinai, and Israel camped there in the desert in front of the mountain.ᵖ

³Then Moses went up to God, and the Lord calledᑫ to him from the mountain and said, "This is what you are to say to the house of Jacob and what you are to tell the people of Israel: ⁴'You yourselves have seen what I did to Egypt,ʳ and how I carried you on eagles' wingsˢ and brought you to myself. ⁵Now if you obey me fullyᵗ and keep my covenant,ᵘ then out of all nations you will be my treasured possession.ᵛ Although the whole earthʷ is mine, ⁶youᵃ will be for me a kingdom of priestsˣ and a holy nation.'ʸ These are the words you are to speak to the Israelites."

⁷So Moses went back and summoned the elders of the people and set before them all the words the Lord had commanded him to speak. ⁸The people all responded together, "We will do everything the Lord has said."ᶻ So Moses brought their answer back to the Lord.

⁹The Lord said to Moses, "I am going to come to you in a dense cloud,ᵃ so that the people will hear me speakingᵇ with you and will always put their trust in you." Then Moses told the Lord what the people had said.

¹⁰And the Lord said to Moses, "Go to the people and consecrateᶜ them today and tomorrow. Have them wash their clothesᵈ ¹¹and be ready by the third day,ᵉ because on that day the Lord will come down on Mount Sinai in the sight of all the people. ¹²Put limits for the people around the mountain and tell them, 'Be careful that you do not go up

ᵃ5,6 Or *possession, for the whole earth is mine.* ⁶*You*

18:18
a Nu 11:11,14,17
18:19
b Ex 3:12
c Nu 27:5
18:20
d Dt 5:1
e Ps 143:8
f Dt 1:18
18:21
g Ac 6:3
h Dt 16:19;
Ps 15:5;
Eze 18:8
i Dt 1:13,15;
2Ch 19:5-10
18:22
j Dt 1:17-18
k Nu 11:17
18:25
l Dt 1:13-15
18:26
m ver 22
18:27
n Nu 10:29-30
19:2
o Ex 17:1 p Ex 3:1
19:3
q Ex 3:4;
Ac 7:38
19:4
r Dt 29:2
s Isa 63:9
19:5
t Ex 15:26
u Dt 5:2
v Dt 14:2;
Ps 135:4
w Ex 9:29;
Dt 10:14
19:6
x 1Pe 2:5
y Dt 7:6; 26:19;
Isa 62:12
19:8
z Ex 24:3,7;
Dt 5:27
19:9
a ver 16;
Ex 24:15-16
b Dt 4:12,36
19:10
c Lev 11:44;
Heb 10:22
d Ge 35:2
19:11
e ver 16

the mountain or touch the foot of it. Whoever touches the mountain shall surely be put to death. ¹³He shall surely be stoned[f] or shot with arrows; not a hand is to be laid on him. Whether man or animal, he shall not be permitted to live.' Only when the ram's horn sounds a long blast may they go up to the mountain."

¹⁴After Moses had gone down the mountain to the people, he consecrated them, and they washed their clothes. ¹⁵Then he said to the people, "Prepare yourselves for the third day. Abstain from sexual relations."

¹⁶On the morning of the third day there was thunder and lightning, with a thick cloud over the mountain, and a very loud trumpet blast.[g] Everyone in the camp trembled.[h] ¹⁷Then Moses led the people out of the camp to meet with God, and they stood at the foot of the mountain. ¹⁸Mount Sinai was covered with smoke,[i] because the LORD descended on it in fire.[j] The smoke billowed up from it like smoke from a furnace,[k] the whole mountain[a] trembled[l] violently, ¹⁹and the sound of the trumpet grew louder and louder. Then Moses spoke and the voice[m] of God answered[n] him.[b]

²⁰The LORD descended to the top of Mount Sinai and called Moses to the top of the mountain. So Moses went up ²¹and the LORD said to him, "Go down and warn the people so they do not force their way through to see[o] the LORD and many of them perish. ²²Even the priests, who approach[p] the LORD, must consecrate themselves, or the LORD will break out against them."[q]

²³Moses said to the LORD, "The people cannot come up Mount Sinai, because you yourself warned us, 'Put limits[r] around the mountain and set it apart as holy.' "

²⁴The LORD replied, "Go down and bring Aaron[s] up with you. But the priests and the people must not force their way through to come up to the LORD, or he will break out against them."

²⁵So Moses went down to the people and told them.

The Ten Commandments

20:1–17pp — Dt 5:6–21

20 And God spoke all these words:

> ²"I am the LORD your God, who brought you out of Egypt, out of the land of slavery.[t]
>
> ³"You shall have no other gods before[c] me.[u]
>
> ⁴"You shall not make for yourself an idol[v] in the form of anything in heaven above or on the earth beneath or in the waters below. ⁵You shall not bow down to them or worship[w] them; for I, the LORD your God, am a jealous God,[x] punishing the children for the sin of the fathers to the third and fourth generation[y] of those who hate me, ⁶but showing love to a thousand[z] ⌊generations⌋ of those who love me and keep my commandments.
>
> ⁷"You shall not misuse the name of the LORD your God, for the LORD will not hold anyone guiltless who misuses his name.[a]

Cross references (margin):

19:13 fHeb 12:20*
19:16 gHeb 12:18-19; Rev 4:1 hHeb 12:21
19:18 iPs 104:32 jEx 3:2; 24:17; Dt 4:11; 2Ch 7:1; Ps 18:8; Heb 12:18 kGe 19:28 lJdg 5:5; Ps 68:8; Jer 4:24
19:19 mNe 9:13 nPs 81:7
19:21 oEx 3:5; 1Sa 6:19
19:22 pLev 10:3 q2Sa 6:7
19:23 rver 12
19:24 sEx 24:1,9
20:2 tEx 13:3
20:3 uDt 6:14; Jer 35:15
20:4 vLev 26:1; Dt 4:15-19,23; 27:15
20:5 wIsa 44:15,17, 19 xEx 34:14; Dt 4:24 yNu 14:18; Jer 32:18
20:6 zDt 7:9
20:7 aLev 19:12; Mt 5:33

---

[a]18 Most Hebrew manuscripts; a few Hebrew manuscripts and Septuagint *all the people*　　[b]19 Or *and God answered him with thunder*　　[c]3 Or *besides*

8"Remember the Sabbath[b] day by keeping it holy. 9Six days you shall labor and do all your work,[c] 10but the seventh day is a Sabbath to the LORD your God. On it you shall not do any work, neither you, nor your son or daughter, nor your manservant or maidservant, nor your animals, nor the alien within your gates. 11For in six days the LORD made the heavens and the earth, the sea, and all that is in them, but he rested[d] on the seventh day. Therefore the LORD blessed the Sabbath day and made it holy.

12"Honor your father and your mother,[e] so that you may live long in the land the LORD your God is giving you.

13"You shall not murder.[f]

14"You shall not commit adultery.[g]

15"You shall not steal.[h]

16"You shall not give false testimony against your neighbor.[i]

17"You shall not covet[j] your neighbor's house. You shall not covet your neighbor's wife, or his manservant or maidservant, his ox or donkey, or anything that belongs to your neighbor."

18When the people saw the thunder and lightning and heard the trumpet[k] and saw the mountain in smoke, they trembled with fear. They stayed at a distance 19and said to Moses, "Speak to us yourself and we will listen. But do not have God speak to us or we will die."[l]

20Moses said to the people, "Do not be afraid. God has come to test you, so that the fear[m] of God will be with you to keep you from sinning."[n]

21The people remained at a distance, while Moses approached the thick darkness[o] where God was.

Idols and Altars

22Then the LORD said to Moses, "Tell the Israelites this: 'You have seen for yourselves that I have spoken to you from heaven:[p] 23Do not make any gods to be alongside me;[q] do not make for yourselves gods of silver or gods of gold.[r]

24" 'Make an altar of earth for me and sacrifice on it your burnt offerings and fellowship offerings,[a] your sheep and goats and your cattle. Wherever I cause my name[s] to be honored, I will come to you and bless[t] you. 25If you make an altar of stones for me, do not build it with dressed stones, for you will defile it if you use a tool[u] on it. 26And do not go up to my altar on steps, lest your nakedness be exposed on it.'

21
"These are the laws[v] you are to set before them:

Hebrew Servants

21:2–6pp — Dt 15:12–18
21:2–11Ref — Lev 25:39–55

2"If you buy a Hebrew servant, he is to serve you for six years. But in the seventh year, he shall go free,[w] without paying anything. 3If he comes alone, he is to go free alone; but if he has a wife when he comes, she is to go with him. 4If his master gives him a wife and she bears him

[a]24 Traditionally *peace offerings*

20:8
bEx 31:13-16;
Lev 26:2
20:9
cEx 34:21;
Lk 13:14
20:11
dGe 2:2
20:12
eMt 15:4*;
Mk 7:10*;
Eph 6:2
20:13
fMt 5:21*;
Ro 13:9*
20:14
gMt 19:18*
20:15
hLev 19:11,13;
Mt 19:18*
20:16
iEx 23:1,7;
Mt 19:18*
20:17
jRo 7:7*;
13:9*; Eph 5:3
20:18
kEx 19:16-19;
Heb 12:18-19
20:19
lDt 5:5,23-27;
Gal 3:19
20:20
mDt 4:10;
Isa 8:13
nPr 16:6
20:21
oDt 5:22
20:22
pNe 9:13
20:23
qver 3 rEx 32:4,
8,31
20:24
sDt 12:5; 16:6,
11; 2Ch 6:6
tGe 12:2
20:25
uDt 27:5-6
21:1
vDt 4:14
21:2
wJer 34:8,14

sons or daughters, the woman and her children shall belong to her master, and only the man shall go free.

⁵"But if the servant declares, 'I love my master and my wife and children and do not want to go free,'ˣ ⁶then his master must take him before the judges.ᵃʸ He shall take him to the door or the doorpost and pierce his ear with an awl. Then he will be his servant for life.ᶻ

⁷"If a man sells his daughter as a servant, she is not to go free as menservants do. ⁸If she does not please the master who has selected her for himself,ᵇ he must let her be redeemed. He has no right to sell her to foreigners, because he has broken faith with her. ⁹If he selects her for his son, he must grant her the rights of a daughter. ¹⁰If he marries another woman, he must not deprive the first one of her food, clothing and marital rights.ᵃ ¹¹If he does not provide her with these three things, she is to go free, without any payment of money.

Personal Injuries

¹²"Anyone who strikes a man and kills him shall surely be put to death.ᵇ ¹³However, if he does not do it intentionally, but God lets it happen, he is to flee to a placeᶜ I will designate. ¹⁴But if a man schemes and kills another man deliberately,ᵈ take him away from my altar and put him to death.ᵉ

¹⁵"Anyone who attacksᶜ his father or his mother must be put to death.

¹⁶"Anyone who kidnaps another and either sellsᶠ him or still has him when he is caught must be put to death.ᵍ

¹⁷"Anyone who curses his father or mother must be put to death.ʰ

¹⁸"If men quarrel and one hits the other with a stone or with his fistᵈ and he does not die but is confined to bed, ¹⁹the one who struck the blow will not be held responsible if the other gets up and walks around outside with his staff; however, he must pay the injured man for the loss of his time and see that he is completely healed.

²⁰"If a man beats his male or female slave with a rod and the slave dies as a direct result, he must be punished, ²¹but he is not to be punished if the slave gets up after a day or two, since the slave is his property.ⁱ

²²"If men who are fighting hit a pregnant woman and she gives birth prematurelyᵉ but there is no serious injury, the offender must be fined whatever the woman's husband demandsʲ and the court allows. ²³But if there is serious injury, you are to take life for life,ᵏ ²⁴eye for eye, tooth for tooth,ˡ hand for hand, foot for foot, ²⁵burn for burn, wound for wound, bruise for bruise.

²⁶"If a man hits a manservant or maidservant in the eye and destroys it, he must let the servant go free to compensate for the eye. ²⁷And if he knocks out the tooth of a manservant or maidservant, he must let the servant go free to compensate for the tooth.

²⁸"If a bull gores a man or a woman to death, the bull must be stoned to death,ᵐ and its meat must not be eaten. But the owner of the bull will not be held responsible. ²⁹If, however, the bull has had the habit of goring and the owner has been warned but has not kept it penned up and it kills a man or woman, the bull must be stoned and the owner also

21:5
ˣDt 15:16
21:6
ʸEx 22:8-9
ᶻNe 5:5
21:10
ᵃ1Co 7:3-5
21:12
ᵇGe 9:6;
Mt 26:52
21:13
ᶜNu 35:10-34;
Dt 19:2-13;
Jos 20:9;
1Sa 24:4,10,18
21:14
ᵈHeb 10:26
ᵉDt 19:11-12;
1Ki 2:28-34
21:16
ᶠGe 37:28
ᵍEx 22:4;
Dt 24:7
21:17
ʰLev 20:9-10;
Mt 15:4*;
Mk 7:10*
21:21
ⁱLev 25:44-46
21:22
ʲver 30;
Dt 22:18-19
21:23
ᵏLev 24:19;
Dt 19:21
21:24
ˡMt 5:38*
21:28
ᵐver 32; Ge 9:5

ᵃ6 Or *before God*   ᵇ8 Or *master so that he does not choose her*   ᶜ15 Or *kills*   ᵈ18 Or *with a tool*   ᵉ22 Or *she has a miscarriage* must be put to death. [30]However, if payment is demanded of him, he may redeem his life by paying whatever is demanded. [n] [31]This law also applies if the bull gores a son or daughter. [32]If the bull gores a male or female slave, the owner must pay thirty shekels[ao] of silver to the master of the slave, and the bull must be stoned.

[33]"If a man uncovers a pit or digs one and fails to cover it and an ox or a donkey falls into it, [34]the owner of the pit must pay for the loss; he must pay its owner, and the dead animal will be his.

[35]"If a man's bull injures the bull of another and it dies, they are to sell the live one and divide both the money and the dead animal equally. [36]However, if it was known that the bull had the habit of goring, yet the owner did not keep it penned up, the owner must pay, animal for animal, and the dead animal will be his.

Protection of Property

22 "If a man steals an ox or a sheep and slaughters it or sells it, he must pay back[p] five head of cattle for the ox and four sheep for the sheep.

[2]"If a thief is caught breaking in[q] and is struck so that he dies, the defender is not guilty of bloodshed;[r] [3]but if it happens[b] after sunrise, he is guilty of bloodshed.

"A thief must certainly make restitution, but if he has nothing, he must be sold[s] to pay for his theft.

[4]"If the stolen animal is found alive in his possession—whether ox or donkey or sheep—he must pay back double. [t]

[5]"If a man grazes his livestock in a field or vineyard and lets them stray and they graze in another man's field, he must make restitution from the best of his own field or vineyard.

[6]"If a fire breaks out and spreads into thornbushes so that it burns shocks of grain or standing grain or the whole field, the one who started the fire must make restitution.

[7]"If a man gives his neighbor silver or goods for safekeeping and they are stolen from the neighbor's house, the thief, if he is caught, must pay back double. [u] [8]But if the thief is not found, the owner of the house must appear before the judges[cv] to determine whether he has laid his hands on the other man's property. [9]In all cases of illegal possession of an ox, a donkey, a sheep, a garment, or any other lost property about which somebody says, 'This is mine,' both parties are to bring their cases before the judges. [w] The one whom the judges declare[d] guilty must pay back double to his neighbor.

[10]"If a man gives a donkey, an ox, a sheep or any other animal to his neighbor for safekeeping and it dies or is injured or is taken away while no one is looking, [11]the issue between them will be settled by the taking of an oath[x] before the LORD that the neighbor did not lay hands on the other person's property. The owner is to accept this, and no restitution is required. [12]But if the animal was stolen from the neighbor, he must make restitution to the owner. [13]If it was torn to pieces by a wild animal, he shall bring in the remains as evidence and he will not be required to pay for the torn animal. [y]

---

[a]32 That is, about 12 ounces (about 0.3 kilogram)   [b]3 Or *if he strikes him*   [c]8 Or *before God;* also in verse 9   [d]9 Or *whom God declares*

21:30
[n]ver 22;
Nu 35:31
21:32
[o]Zec 11:12-13;
Mt 26:15;
27:3,9
22:1
[p]2Sa 12:6;
Pr 6:31; Lk 19:8
22:2
[q]Mt 6:19-20;
24:43 [r]Nu 35:27
22:3
[s]Ex 21:2;
Mt 18:25
22:4
[t]Ge 43:12
22:7
[u]ver 4
22:8
[v]Ex 21:6;
Dt 17:8-9; 19:17
22:9
[w]ver 28;
Dt 25:1
22:11
[x]Heb 6:16
22:13
[y]Ge 31:39

[14]"If a man borrows an animal from his neighbor and it is injured or dies while the owner is not present, he must make restitution. [15]But if the owner is with the animal, the borrower will not have to pay. If the animal was hired, the money paid for the hire covers the loss.

Social Responsibility

[16]"If a man seduces a virgin[z] who is not pledged to be married and sleeps with her, he must pay the bride-price, and she shall be his wife. [17]If her father absolutely refuses to give her to him, he must still pay the bride-price for virgins.

[18]"Do not allow a sorceress[a] to live.

[19]"Anyone who has sexual relations with an animal[b] must be put to death.

[20]"Whoever sacrifices to any god other than the LORD must be destroyed.[a c]

[21]"Do not mistreat an alien[d] or oppress him, for you were aliens[e] in Egypt.

[22]"Do not take advantage of a widow or an orphan.[f] [23]If you do and they cry out[g] to me, I will certainly hear their cry.[h] [24]My anger will be aroused, and I will kill you with the sword; your wives will become widows and your children fatherless.[i]

[25]"If you lend money to one of my people among you who is needy, do not be like a moneylender; charge him no interest.[b j] [26]If you take your neighbor's cloak as a pledge,[k] return it to him by sunset, [27]because his cloak is the only covering he has for his body. What else will he sleep in? When he cries out to me, I will hear, for I am compassionate.[l]

[28]"Do not blaspheme God[c m] or curse the ruler of your people.[n]

[29]"Do not hold back offerings[o] from your granaries or your vats.[d]

"You must give me the firstborn of your sons.[p] [30]Do the same with your cattle and your sheep.[q] Let them stay with their mothers for seven days, but give them to me on the eighth day.[r]

[31]"You are to be my holy people.[s] So do not eat the meat of an animal torn by wild beasts;[t] throw it to the dogs.

Laws of Justice and Mercy

23 "Do not spread false reports.[u] Do not help a wicked man by being a malicious witness.[v]

[2]"Do not follow the crowd in doing wrong. When you give testimony in a lawsuit, do not pervert justice[w] by siding with the crowd, [3]and do not show favoritism to a poor man in his lawsuit.

[4]"If you come across your enemy's ox or donkey wandering off, be sure to take it back to him.[x] [5]If you see the donkey[y] of someone who hates you fallen down under its load, do not leave it there; be sure you help him with it.

[6]"Do not deny justice[z] to your poor people in their lawsuits. [7]Have nothing to do with a false charge[a] and do not put an innocent or honest person to death, for I will not acquit the guilty.

Cross references (left margin):

22:16 z Dt 22:28
22:18 a Lev 20:27; Dt 18:11; 1Sa 28:3
22:19 b Lev 18:23; Dt 27:21
22:20 c Dt 17:2-5
22:21 d Lev 19:33 e Dt 10:19
22:22 f Dt 24:6,10, 12,17
22:23 g Lk 18:7 h Dt 15:9; Ps 18:6
22:24 i Ps 69:24; 109:9
22:25 j Lev 25:35-37; Dt 23:20; Ps 55:5
22:26 k Dt 24:6
22:27 l Ex 34:6
22:28 m Ecc 24:11,16 n Ecc 10:20; Ac 23:5*
22:29 o Ex 23:15,16,19 p Ex 13:2
22:30 q Ex 13:12; Dt 15:19 r Lev 22:27
22:31 s Lev 19:2 t Eze 4:14
23:1 u Ex 20:16; Ps 101:5 v Ps 35:11; Ac 6:11
23:2 w Dt 16:19
23:4 x Dt 22:1-3
23:5 y Dt 22:4
23:6 z ver 2
23:7 a Eph 4:25

---

[a]20 The Hebrew term refers to the irrevocable giving over of things or persons to the LORD, often by totally destroying them.   [b]25 Or *excessive interest*   [c]28 Or *Do not revile the judges*
[d]29 The meaning of the Hebrew for this phrase is uncertain.

8"Do not accept a bribe,[b] for a bribe blinds those who see and twists the words of the righteous.

9"Do not oppress an alien;[c] you yourselves know how it feels to be aliens, because you were aliens in Egypt.

Sabbath Laws

10"For six years you are to sow your fields and harvest the crops, 11but during the seventh year let the land lie unplowed and unused. Then the poor among your people may get food from it, and the wild animals may eat what they leave. Do the same with your vineyard and your olive grove.

12"Six days do your work,[d] but on the seventh day do not work, so that your ox and your donkey may rest and the slave born in your household, and the alien as well, may be refreshed.

13"Be careful[e] to do everything I have said to you. Do not invoke the names of other gods; do not let them be heard on your lips.

The Three Annual Festivals

14"Three times[f] a year you are to celebrate a festival to me.

15"Celebrate the Feast of Unleavened Bread;[g] for seven days eat bread made without yeast, as I commanded you. Do this at the appointed time in the month of Abib, for in that month you came out of Egypt.

"No one is to appear before me empty-handed.[h]

16"Celebrate the Feast of Harvest with the firstfruits[i] of the crops you sow in your field.

"Celebrate the Feast of Ingathering at the end of the year, when you gather in your crops from the field.[j]

17"Three times[k] a year all the men are to appear before the Sovereign LORD.

18"Do not offer the blood of a sacrifice to me along with anything containing yeast.[l]

"The fat of my festival offerings must not be kept until morning.[m]

19"Bring the best of the firstfruits[n] of your soil to the house of the LORD your God.

"Do not cook a young goat in its mother's milk.[o]

God's Angel to Prepare the Way

20"See, I am sending an angel[p] ahead of you to guard you along the way and to bring you to the place I have prepared.[q] 21Pay attention to him and listen[r] to what he says. Do not rebel against him; he will not forgive your rebellion,[s] since my Name is in him. 22If you listen carefully to what he says and do all that I say, I will be an enemy[t] to your enemies and will oppose those who oppose you. 23My angel will go ahead of you and bring you into the land of the Amorites, Hittites, Perizzites, Canaanites, Hivites and Jebusites,[u] and I will wipe them out. 24Do not bow down before their gods or worship[v] them or follow their practices.[w] You must demolish[x] them and break their sacred stones to pieces. 25Worship the LORD your God,[y] and his blessing[z] will be on your food and water. I will take away sickness[a] from among you, 26and none will miscarry or be barren[b] in your land. I will give you a full life span.[c]

27"I will send my terror[d] ahead of you and throw into confusion[e]

23:8
b Dt 10:17; 16:19; Pr 15:27
23:9
c Ex 22:21
23:12
d Ex 20:9
23:13
e 1Ti 4:16
23:14
f Ex 34:23,24
23:15
g Ex 12:17
h Ex 34:20
23:16
i Ex 34:22
j Dt 16:13
23:17
k Dt 16:16
23:18
l Ex 34:25
m Dt 16:4
23:19
n Ex 22:29; Dt 26:2,10
o Dt 14:21
23:20
p Ex 14:19; 32:34 q Ex 15:17
23:21
r Nu 14:11; Dt 18:19
s Ps 78:8,40,56
23:22
t Ge 12:3; Dt 30:7
23:23
u ver 20; Jos 24:8,11
23:24
v Ex 20:5
w Dt 12:30-31
x Ex 34:13; Nu 33:52
23:25
y Dt 6:13; Mt 4:10
z Dt 7:12-15; 28:1-14
a Ex 15:26
23:26
b Dt 7:14; Mal 3:11
c Job 5:26
23:27
d Ex 15:14; Dt 2:25
e Dt 7:23

every nation you encounter. I will make all your enemies turn their backs and run. 28I will send the hornet[f] ahead of you to drive the Hivites, Canaanites and Hittites out of your way. 29But I will not drive them out in a single year, because the land would become desolate and the wild animals[g] too numerous for you. 30Little by little I will drive them out before you, until you have increased enough to take possession of the land.

31"I will establish your borders from the Red Sea[a] to the Sea of the Philistines,[b] and from the desert to the River.[c][h] I will hand over to you the people who live in the land and you will drive them out[i] before you. 32Do not make a covenant[j] with them or with their gods. 33Do not let them live in your land, or they will cause you to sin against me, because the worship of their gods will certainly be a snare[k] to you."

The Covenant Confirmed

24 Then he said to Moses, "Come up to the LORD, you and Aaron, Nadab and Abihu,[l] and seventy of the elders[m] of Israel. You are to worship at a distance, 2but Moses alone is to approach the LORD; the others must not come near. And the people may not come up with him."

3When Moses went and told the people all the LORD's words and laws, they responded with one voice, "Everything the LORD has said we will do."[n] 4Moses then wrote[o] down everything the LORD had said.

He got up early the next morning and built an altar at the foot of the mountain and set up twelve stone pillars[p] representing the twelve tribes of Israel. 5Then he sent young Israelite men, and they offered burnt offerings and sacrificed young bulls as fellowship offerings[d] to the LORD. 6Moses took half of the blood[q] and put it in bowls, and the other half he sprinkled on the altar. 7Then he took the Book of the Covenant[r] and read it to the people. They responded, "We will do everything the LORD has said; we will obey."

8Moses then took the blood, sprinkled it on the people and said, "This is the blood of the covenant[s] that the LORD has made with you in accordance with all these words."

9Moses and Aaron, Nadab and Abihu, and the seventy elders[t] of Israel went up 10and saw[u] the God of Israel. Under his feet was something like a pavement made of sapphire,[e][v] clear as the sky[w] itself. 11But God did not raise his hand against these leaders of the Israelites; they saw[x] God, and they ate and drank.

12The LORD said to Moses, "Come up to me on the mountain and stay here, and I will give you the tablets of stone,[y] with the law and commands I have written for their instruction."

13Then Moses set out with Joshua[z] his aide, and Moses went up on the mountain[a] of God. 14He said to the elders, "Wait here for us until we come back to you. Aaron and Hur are with you, and anyone involved in a dispute can go to them."

15When Moses went up on the mountain, the cloud[b] covered it, 16and the glory[c] of the LORD settled on Mount Sinai. For six days the cloud covered the mountain, and on the seventh day the LORD called to

---

23:28
fDt 7:20;
Jos 24:12
23:29
gDt 7:22
23:31
hGe 15:18
iJos 21:44;
24:12,18
23:32
jEx 34:12;
Dt 7:2
23:33
kDt 7:16;
Ps 106:36
24:1
lEx 6:23;
Lev 10:1-2
mNu 11:16
24:3
nEx 19:8;
Dt 5:27
24:4
oDt 31:9
pGe 28:18
24:6
qHeb 9:18
24:7
rHeb 9:19
24:8
sHeb 9:20*;
1Pe 1:2
24:9
tver 1
24:10
uMt 17:2;
Jn 1:18; 6:46
vEze 1:26
wRev 4:3
24:11
xGe 32:30;
Ex 19:21
24:12
yEx 32:15-16
24:13
zEx 17:9 aEx 3:1
24:15
bEx 19:9
24:16
cEx 16:10

---

a31 Hebrew Yam Suph; *that is, Sea of Reeds*   *b31 That is, the Mediterranean*   *c31 That is, the Euphrates*   *d5 Traditionally* peace offerings   *e10 Or lapis lazuli*

Moses from within the cloud. [d] [17]To the Israelites the glory of the LORD looked like a consuming fire[e] on top of the mountain. [18]Then Moses entered the cloud as he went on up the mountain. And he stayed on the mountain forty[f] days and forty nights. [g]

Offerings for the Tabernacle

25:1–7pp — Ex 35:4–9

25 The LORD said to Moses, [2]"Tell the Israelites to bring me an offering. You are to receive the offering for me from each man whose heart prompts[h] him to give. [3]These are the offerings you are to receive from them: gold, silver and bronze; [4]blue, purple and scarlet yarn and fine linen; goat hair; [5]ram skins dyed red and hides of sea cows[a]; acacia wood; [6]olive oil[i] for the light; spices for the anointing oil and for the fragrant incense; [7]and onyx stones and other gems to be mounted on the ephod[j] and breastpiece. [k]

[8]"Then have them make a sanctuary[l] for me, and I will dwell[m] among them. [9]Make this tabernacle and all its furnishings exactly like the pattern[n] I will show you.

The Ark

25:10–20pp — Ex 37:1–9

[10]"Have them make a chest[o] of acacia wood—two and a half cubits long, a cubit and a half wide, and a cubit and a half high. [b] [11]Overlay it with pure gold, both inside and out, and make a gold molding around it. [12]Cast four gold rings for it and fasten them to its four feet, with two rings on one side and two rings on the other. [13]Then make poles of acacia wood and overlay them with gold. [14]Insert the poles into the rings on the sides of the chest to carry it. [15]The poles are to remain in the rings of this ark; they are not to be removed. [p] [16]Then put in the ark the Testimony, [q] which I will give you.

[17]"Make an atonement cover[c][r] of pure gold—two and a half cubits long and a cubit and a half wide. [d] [18]And make two cherubim out of hammered gold at the ends of the cover. [19]Make one cherub on one end and the second cherub on the other; make the cherubim of one piece with the cover, at the two ends. [20]The cherubim are to have their wings spread upward, overshadowing[s] the cover with them. The cherubim are to face each other, looking toward the cover. [21]Place the cover on top of the ark[t] and put in the ark the Testimony, [u] which I will give you. [22]There, above the cover between the two cherubim[v] that are over the ark of the Testimony, I will meet[w] with you and give you all my commands for the Israelites.

The Table

25:23–29pp — Ex 37:10–16

[23]"Make a table[x] of acacia wood—two cubits long, a cubit wide and a cubit and a half high. [e] [24]Overlay it with pure gold and make a gold molding around it. [25]Also make around it a rim a handbreadth[f] wide

---

[a]5 That is, dugongs   [b]10 That is, about 3 3/4 feet (about 1.1 meters) long and 2 1/4 feet (about 0.7 meter) wide and high   [c]17 Traditionally *a mercy seat*   [d]17 That is, about 3 3/4 feet (about 1.1 meters) long and 2 1/4 feet (about 0.7 meter) wide   [e]23 That is, about 3 feet (about 0.9 meter) long and 1 1/2 feet (about 0.5 meter) wide and 2 1/4 feet (about 0.7 meter) high   [f]25 That is, about 3 inches (about 8 centimeters)

24:16
d Ps 99:7
24:17
e Ex 3:2;
Dt 4:36;
Heb 12:18,29
24:18
f Dt 9:9
g Ex 34:28
25:2
h Ex 35:21;
1Ch 29:5,7,9;
Ezr 2:68;
2Co 8:11-12;
9:7
25:6
i Ex 27:20;
30:22-32
25:7
j Ex 28:4,6-14
k Ex 28:15-30
25:8
l Ex 36:1-5;
Heb 9:1-2
m Ex 29:45;
1Ki 6:13;
2Co 6:16;
Rev 21:3
25:9
n ver 40;
Ac 7:44;
Heb 8:5
25:10
o Dt 10:1-5;
Heb 9:4
25:15
p 1Ki 8:8
25:16
q Dt 31:26;
Heb 9:4
25:17
r Ro 3:25
25:20
s 1Ki 8:7;
1Ch 28:18;
Heb 9:5
25:21
t Ex 26:34
u ver 16
25:22
v Nu 7:89;
1Sa 4:4;
2Sa 6:2;
2Ki 19:15;
Ps 80:1;
Isa 37:16
w Ex 29:42-43
25:23
x Heb 9:2

and put a gold molding on the rim. 26Make four gold rings for the table and fasten them to the four corners, where the four legs are. 27The rings are to be close to the rim to hold the poles used in carrying the table. 28Make the poles of acacia wood, overlay them with gold and carry the table with them. 29And make its plates and dishes of pure gold, as well as its pitchers and bowls for the pouring out of offerings.y 30Put the bread of the Presencez on this table to be before me at all times.

The Lampstand

25:31–39pp — Ex 37:17–24

31"Make a lampstanda of pure gold and hammer it out, base and shaft; its flowerlike cups, buds and blossoms shall be of one piece with it. 32Six branches are to extend from the sides of the lampstand—three on one side and three on the other. 33Three cups shaped like almond flowers with buds and blossoms are to be on one branch, three on the next branch, and the same for all six branches extending from the lampstand. 34And on the lampstand there are to be four cups shaped like almond flowers with buds and blossoms. 35One bud shall be under the first pair of branches extending from the lampstand, a second bud under the second pair, and a third bud under the third pair—six branches in all. 36The buds and branches shall all be of one piece with the lampstand, hammered out of pure gold.

37"Then make its seven lampsb and set them up on it so that they light the space in front of it. 38Its wick trimmers and trays are to be of pure gold. 39A talenta of pure gold is to be used for the lampstand and all these accessories. 40See that you make them according to the patternc shown you on the mountain.

The Tabernacle

26:1–37pp — Ex 36:8–38

26 "Make the tabernacle with ten curtains of finely twisted linen and blue, purple and scarlet yarn, with cherubim worked into them by a skilled craftsman. 2All the curtains are to be the same size —twenty-eight cubits long and four cubits wide.b 3Join five of the curtains together, and do the same with the other five. 4Make loops of blue material along the edge of the end curtain in one set, and do the same with the end curtain in the other set. 5Make fifty loops on one curtain and fifty loops on the end curtain of the other set, with the loops opposite each other. 6Then make fifty gold clasps and use them to fasten the curtains together so that the tabernacle is a unit.

7"Make curtains of goat hair for the tent over the tabernacle—eleven altogether. 8All eleven curtains are to be the same size—thirty cubits long and four cubits wide.c 9Join five of the curtains together into one set and the other six into another set. Fold the sixth curtain double at the front of the tent. 10Make fifty loops along the edge of the end curtain in one set and also along the edge of the end curtain in the other set. 11Then make fifty bronze clasps and put them in the loops to fasten the tent together as a unit. 12As for the additional length of the tent cur-

### Cross references (margin)

25:29
y Nu 4:7
25:30
z Lev 24:5-9
25:31
a 1Ki 7:49;
Zec 4:2;
Heb 9:2;
Rev 1:12
25:37
b Ex 27:21;
Lev 24:3-4;
Nu 8:2
25:40
c Ex 26:30;
Nu 8:4;
Ac 7:44;
Heb 8:5*

---

a39 That is, about 75 pounds (about 34 kilograms)   b2 That is, about 42 feet (about 12.5 meters) long and 6 feet (about 1.8 meters) wide   c8 That is, about 45 feet (about 13.5 meters) long and 6 feet (about 1.8 meters) wide tains, the half curtain that is left over is to hang down at the rear of the tabernacle. [13]The tent curtains will be a cubit[a] longer on both sides; what is left will hang over the sides of the tabernacle so as to cover it. [14]Make for the tent a covering of ram skins dyed red, and over that a covering of hides of sea cows.[b][d]

[15]"Make upright frames of acacia wood for the tabernacle. [16]Each frame is to be ten cubits long and a cubit and a half wide,[c] [17]with two projections set parallel to each other. Make all the frames of the tabernacle in this way. [18]Make twenty frames for the south side of the tabernacle [19]and make forty silver bases to go under them—two bases for each frame, one under each projection. [20]For the other side, the north side of the tabernacle, make twenty frames [21]and forty silver bases—two under each frame. [22]Make six frames for the far end, that is, the west end of the tabernacle, [23]and make two frames for the corners at the far end. [24]At these two corners they must be double from the bottom all the way to the top, and fitted into a single ring; both shall be like that. [25]So there will be eight frames and sixteen silver bases—two under each frame.

[26]"Also make crossbars of acacia wood: five for the frames on one side of the tabernacle, [27]five for those on the other side, and five for the frames on the west, at the far end of the tabernacle. [28]The center crossbar is to extend from end to end at the middle of the frames. [29]Overlay the frames with gold and make gold rings to hold the crossbars. Also overlay the crossbars with gold.

[30]"Set up the tabernacle according to the plan[e] shown you on the mountain.

[31]"Make a curtain[f] of blue, purple and scarlet yarn and finely twisted linen, with cherubim[g] worked into it by a skilled craftsman. [32]Hang it with gold hooks on four posts of acacia wood overlaid with gold and standing on four silver bases. [33]Hang the curtain from the clasps and place the ark of the Testimony behind the curtain.[h] The curtain will separate the Holy Place from the Most Holy Place.[i] [34]Put the atonement cover[j] on the ark of the Testimony in the Most Holy Place. [35]Place the table[k] outside the curtain on the north side of the tabernacle and put the lampstand[l] opposite it on the south side.

[36]"For the entrance to the tent make a curtain of blue, purple and scarlet yarn and finely twisted linen—the work of an embroiderer. [37]Make gold hooks for this curtain and five posts of acacia wood overlaid with gold. And cast five bronze bases for them.

The Altar of Burnt Offering

27:1–8pp — Ex 38:1–7

27 "Build an altar[m] of acacia wood, three cubits[d] high; it is to be square, five cubits long and five cubits wide.[e] [2]Make a horn[n] at each of the four corners, so that the horns and the altar are of one piece, and overlay the altar with bronze. [3]Make all its utensils of bronze—its pots to remove the ashes, and its shovels, sprinkling bowls, meat forks and firepans. [4]Make a grating for it, a bronze network, and make a

26:14
dEx 36:19;
Nu 4:25
26:30
eEx 25:9,40;
Ac 7:44;
Heb 8:5
26:31
f2Ch 3:14;
Mt 27:51;
Heb 9:3
gEx 36:35
26:33
hEx 40:3,21;
Lev 16:2
iHeb 9:2-3
26:34
jEx 25:21;
40:20; Heb 9:5
26:35
kHeb 9:2
lEx 40:22,24
27:1
mEze 43:13
27:2
nPs 118:27

a13 That is, about 1 1/2 feet (about 0.5 meter)   *b14* That is, dugongs   *c16* That is, about 15 feet (about 4.5 meters) long and 2 1/4 feet (about 0.7 meter) wide   *d1* That is, about 4 1/2 feet (about 1.3 meters)   *e1* That is, about 7 1/2 feet (about 2.3 meters) long and wide bronze ring at each of the four corners of the network. [5]Put it under the ledge of the altar so that it is halfway up the altar. [6]Make poles of acacia wood for the altar and overlay them with bronze. [7]The poles are to be inserted into the rings so they will be on two sides of the altar when it is carried. [8]Make the altar hollow, out of boards. It is to be made just as you were shown[o] on the mountain.

The Courtyard

27:9–19pp — Ex 38:9–20

[9]"Make a courtyard for the tabernacle. The south side shall be a hundred cubits[a] long and is to have curtains of finely twisted linen, [10]with twenty posts and twenty bronze bases and with silver hooks and bands on the posts. [11]The north side shall also be a hundred cubits long and is to have curtains, with twenty posts and twenty bronze bases and with silver hooks and bands on the posts.

[12]"The west end of the courtyard shall be fifty cubits[b] wide and have curtains, with ten posts and ten bases. [13]On the east end, toward the sunrise, the courtyard shall also be fifty cubits wide. [14]Curtains fifteen cubits[c] long are to be on one side of the entrance, with three posts and three bases, [15]and curtains fifteen cubits long are to be on the other side, with three posts and three bases.

[16]"For the entrance to the courtyard, provide a curtain twenty cubits[d] long, of blue, purple and scarlet yarn and finely twisted linen—the work of an embroiderer—with four posts and four bases. [17]All the posts around the courtyard are to have silver bands and hooks, and bronze bases. [18]The courtyard shall be a hundred cubits long and fifty cubits wide,[e] with curtains of finely twisted linen five cubits[f] high, and with bronze bases. [19]All the other articles used in the service of the tabernacle, whatever their function, including all the tent pegs for it and those for the courtyard, are to be of bronze.

Oil for the Lampstand

27:20–21pp — Lev 24:1–3

[20]"Command the Israelites to bring you clear oil of pressed olives for the light so that the lamps may be kept burning. [21]In the Tent of Meeting,[p] outside the curtain that is in front of the Testimony,[q] Aaron and his sons are to keep the lamps[r] burning before the LORD from evening till morning. This is to be a lasting ordinance[s] among the Israelites for the generations to come.

The Priestly Garments

28 "Have Aaron[t] your brother brought to you from among the Israelites, along with his sons Nadab and Abihu, Eleazar and Ithamar, so they may serve me as priests.[u] [2]Make sacred garments[v] for your brother Aaron, to give him dignity and honor. [3]Tell all the skilled men[w] to whom I have given wisdom[x] in such matters that they are to make garments for Aaron, for his consecration, so he may serve me as priest. [4]These are the garments they are to make: a breastpiece,[y] an

27:8
o Ex 25:9,40
27:21
p Ex 28:43
q Ex 26:31,33
r Ex 25:37; 30:8;
1Sa 3:3;
2Ch 13:11
s Ex 29:9;
Lev 3:17;
16:34;
Nu 18:23; 19:21
28:1
t Heb 5:4
u Nu 18:1-7;
Heb 5:1
28:2
v Ex 29:5,29;
31:10; 39:1;
Lev 8:7-9,30
28:3
w Ex 31:6; 36:1
x Ex 31:3
28:4
y ver 15-30

---

[a]9 That is, about 150 feet (about 46 meters); also in verse 11   [b]12 That is, about 75 feet (about 23 meters); also in verse 13   [c]14 That is, about 22 1/2 feet (about 6.9 meters); also in verse 15   [d]16 That is, about 30 feet (about 9 meters)   [e]18 That is, about 150 feet (about 46 meters) long and 75 feet (about 23 meters) wide   [f]18 That is, about 7 1/2 feet (about 2.3 meters)

ephod, a robe,ᶻ a woven tunic,ᵃ a turban and a sash. They are to make these sacred garments for your brother Aaron and his sons, so they may serve me as priests. ⁵Have them use gold, and blue, purple and scarlet yarn, and fine linen.

The Ephod

28:6–14pp — Ex 39:2–7

⁶"Make the ephod of gold, and of blue, purple and scarlet yarn, and of finely twisted linen—the work of a skilled craftsman. ⁷It is to have two shoulder pieces attached to two of its corners, so it can be fastened. ⁸Its skillfully woven waistband is to be like it—of one piece with the ephod and made with gold, and with blue, purple and scarlet yarn, and with finely twisted linen.

⁹"Take two onyx stones and engrave on them the names of the sons of Israel ¹⁰in the order of their birth—six names on one stone and the remaining six on the other. ¹¹Engrave the names of the sons of Israel on the two stones the way a gem cutter engraves a seal. Then mount the stones in gold filigree settings ¹²and fasten them on the shoulder pieces of the ephod as memorial stones for the sons of Israel. Aaron is to bear the names on his shoulders as a memorial before the LORD. ¹³Make gold filigree settings ¹⁴and two braided chains of pure gold, like a rope, and attach the chains to the settings.

The Breastpiece

28:15–28pp — Ex 39:8–21

¹⁵"Fashion a breastpiece for making decisions—the work of a skilled craftsman. Make it like the ephod: of gold, and of blue, purple and scarlet yarn, and of finely twisted linen. ¹⁶It is to be square—a spanᵃ long and a span wide—and folded double. ¹⁷Then mount four rows of precious stones on it. In the first row there shall be a ruby, a topaz and a beryl; ¹⁸in the second row a turquoise, a sapphireᵇ and an emerald; ¹⁹in the third row a jacinth, an agate and an amethyst; ²⁰in the fourth row a chrysolite, an onyx and a jasper.ᶜ Mount them in gold filigree settings. ²¹There are to be twelve stones, one for each of the names of the sons of Israel, each engraved like a seal with the name of one of the twelve tribes.

²²"For the breastpiece make braided chains of pure gold, like a rope. ²³Make two gold rings for it and fasten them to two corners of the breastpiece. ²⁴Fasten the two gold chains to the rings at the corners of the breastpiece, ²⁵and the other ends of the chains to the two settings, attaching them to the shoulder pieces of the ephod at the front. ²⁶Make two gold rings and attach them to the other two corners of the breastpiece on the inside edge next to the ephod. ²⁷Make two more gold rings and attach them to the bottom of the shoulder pieces on the front of the ephod, close to the seam just above the waistband of the ephod. ²⁸The rings of the breastpiece are to be tied to the rings of the ephod with blue cord, connecting it to the waistband, so that the breastpiece will not swing out from the ephod.

²⁹"Whenever Aaron enters the Holy Place,ᵇ he will bear the names of

---

28:4
ᶻver 31-35
ᵃver 39
28:29
ᵇver 12

ᵃ16 That is, about 9 inches (about 22 centimeters)   ᵇ18 Or *lapis lazuli*   ᶜ20 The precise identification of some of these precious stones is uncertain.

the sons of Israel over his heart on the breastpiece of decision as a continuing memorial before the LORD. [30]Also put the Urim and the Thummim[c] in the breastpiece, so they may be over Aaron's heart whenever he enters the presence of the LORD. Thus Aaron will always bear the means of making decisions for the Israelites over his heart before the LORD.

Other Priestly Garments

28:31–43pp — Ex 39:22–31

[31]"Make the robe of the ephod entirely of blue cloth, [32]with an opening for the head in its center. There shall be a woven edge like a collar[a] around this opening, so that it will not tear. [33]Make pomegranates of blue, purple and scarlet yarn around the hem of the robe, with gold bells between them. [34]The gold bells and the pomegranates are to alternate around the hem of the robe. [35]Aaron must wear it when he ministers. The sound of the bells will be heard when he enters the Holy Place before the LORD and when he comes out, so that he will not die.

[36]"Make a plate of pure gold and engrave on it as on a seal: HOLY TO THE LORD. [d] [37]Fasten a blue cord to it to attach it to the turban; it is to be on the front of the turban. [38]It will be on Aaron's forehead, and he will bear the guilt[e] involved in the sacred gifts the Israelites consecrate, whatever their gifts may be. It will be on Aaron's forehead continually so that they will be acceptable to the LORD.

[39]"Weave the tunic of fine linen and make the turban of fine linen. The sash is to be the work of an embroiderer. [40]Make tunics, sashes and headbands for Aaron's sons,[f] to give them dignity and honor. [41]After you put these clothes on your brother Aaron and his sons, anoint[g] and ordain them. Consecrate them so they may serve me as priests. [h]

[42]"Make linen undergarments[i] as a covering for the body, reaching from the waist to the thigh. [43]Aaron and his sons must wear them whenever they enter the Tent of Meeting[j] or approach the altar to minister in the Holy Place, so that they will not incur guilt and die. [k]

"This is to be a lasting ordinance[l] for Aaron and his descendants.

Consecration of the Priests

29:1–37pp — Lev 8:1–36

29 "This is what you are to do to consecrate them, so they may serve me as priests: Take a young bull and two rams without defect. [2]And from fine wheat flour, without yeast, make bread, and cakes mixed with oil, and wafers spread with oil. [m] [3]Put them in a basket and present them in it—along with the bull and the two rams. [4]Then bring Aaron and his sons to the entrance to the Tent of Meeting and wash them with water. [n] [5]Take the garments[o] and dress Aaron with the tunic, the robe of the ephod, the ephod itself and the breastpiece. Fasten the ephod on him by its skillfully woven waistband. [p] [6]Put the turban on his head and attach the sacred diadem[q] to the turban. [7]Take the anointing oil[r] and anoint him by pouring it on his head. [8]Bring his sons and dress them in tunics [9]and put headbands on them. Then tie sashes on Aaron and his sons. [b][s] The priesthood is theirs by a lasting ordinance. [t] In this way you shall ordain Aaron and his sons.

---

[a]32 The meaning of the Hebrew for this word is uncertain.   [b]9 Hebrew; Septuagint *on them*

28:30
c Lev 8:8;
Nu 27:21;
Dt 33:8;
Ezr 2:63;
Ne 7:65
28:36
d Zec 14:20
28:38
e Lev 10:17;
22:9,16;
Nu 18:1;
Heb 9:28;
1Pe 2:24
28:40
f ver 4; Ex 39:41
28:41
g Ex 29:7;
Lev 10:7
h Ex 29:7-9;
30:30; 40:15;
Lev 8:1-36;
Heb 7:28
28:42
i Lev 6:10; 16:4,
23; Eze 44:18
28:43
j Ex 27:21
k Ex 20:26
l Lev 17:7
29:2
m Lev 2:1,4;
6:19-23
29:4
n Ex 40:12;
Heb 10:22
29:5
o Ex 28:2;
Lev 8:7 p Ex 28:8
29:6
q Lev 8:9
29:7
r Ex 30:25,30,31;
Lev 8:12;
21:10;
Nu 35:25;
Ps 133:2
29:9
s Ex 28:40
t Ex 40:15;
Nu 3:10; 18:7;
25:13; Dt 18:5

¹⁰"Bring the bull to the front of the Tent of Meeting, and Aaron and his sons shall lay their hands on its head.^u ¹¹Slaughter it in the LORD's presence at the entrance to the Tent of Meeting. ¹²Take some of the bull's blood and put it on the horns^v of the altar with your finger, and pour out the rest of it at the base of the altar. ¹³Then take all the fat^w around the inner parts, the covering of the liver, and both kidneys with the fat around them, and burn them on the altar. ¹⁴But burn the bull's flesh and its hide and its offal outside the camp.^x It is a sin offering.

¹⁵"Take one of the rams, and Aaron and his sons shall lay their hands on its head. ¹⁶Slaughter it and take the blood and sprinkle it against the altar on all sides. ¹⁷Cut the ram into pieces and wash the inner parts and the legs, putting them with the head and the other pieces. ¹⁸Then burn the entire ram on the altar. It is a burnt offering to the LORD, a pleasing aroma,^y an offering made to the LORD by fire.

¹⁹"Take the other ram,^z and Aaron and his sons shall lay their hands on its head. ²⁰Slaughter it, take some of its blood and put it on the lobes of the right ears of Aaron and his sons, on the thumbs of their right hands, and on the big toes of their right feet. Then sprinkle blood against the altar on all sides. ²¹And take some of the blood^a on the altar and some of the anointing oil^b and sprinkle it on Aaron and his garments and on his sons and their garments. Then he and his sons and their garments will be consecrated.^c

²²"Take from this ram the fat, the fat tail, the fat around the inner parts, the covering of the liver, both kidneys with the fat around them, and the right thigh. (This is the ram for the ordination.) ²³From the basket of bread made without yeast, which is before the LORD, take a loaf, and a cake made with oil, and a wafer. ²⁴Put all these in the hands of Aaron and his sons and wave them before the LORD as a wave offering.^d ²⁵Then take them from their hands and burn them on the altar along with the burnt offering for a pleasing aroma to the LORD, an offering made to the LORD by fire. ²⁶After you take the breast of the ram for Aaron's ordination, wave it before the LORD as a wave offering, and it will be your share.^e

²⁷"Consecrate those parts of the ordination ram that belong to Aaron and his sons:^f the breast that was waved and the thigh that was presented. ²⁸This is always to be the regular share from the Israelites for Aaron and his sons. It is the contribution the Israelites are to make to the LORD from their fellowship offerings.^a ^g

²⁹"Aaron's sacred garments will belong to his descendants so that they can be anointed and ordained in them.^h ³⁰The sonⁱ who succeeds him as priest and comes to the Tent of Meeting to minister in the Holy Place is to wear them seven days.

³¹"Take the ram for the ordination and cook the meat in a sacred place. ³²At the entrance to the Tent of Meeting, Aaron and his sons are to eat the meat of the ram and the bread^j that is in the basket. ³³They are to eat these offerings by which atonement was made for their ordination and consecration. But no one else may eat^k them, because they are sacred. ³⁴And if any of the meat of the ordination ram or any bread is left over till morning,^l burn it up. It must not be eaten, because it is sacred.

---

^a28 Traditionally *peace offerings*

29:10
uLev 1:4
29:12
vEx 27:2
29:13
wLev 3:3,5,9
29:14
xLev 4:11-12, 21; Heb 13:11
29:18
yGe 8:21
29:19
zver 3
29:21
aHeb 9:22
bEx 30:25,31
cver 1
29:24
dLev 7:30
29:26
eLev 7:31-34
29:27
fLev 7:31,34; Dt 18:3
29:28
gLev 10:15
29:29
hNu 20:26,28
29:30
iNu 20:28
29:32
jMt 12:4
29:33
kLev 10:14; 22:10,13
29:34
lEx 12:10

35"Do for Aaron and his sons everything I have commanded you, taking seven days to ordain them. 36Sacrifice a bull each day[m] as a sin offering to make atonement. Purify the altar by making atonement for it, and anoint it to consecrate[n] it. 37For seven days make atonement for the altar and consecrate it. Then the altar will be most holy, and whatever touches it will be holy.[o]

38"This is what you are to offer on the altar regularly each day:[p] two lambs a year old. 39Offer one in the morning and the other at twilight. [q] 40With the first lamb offer a tenth of an ephah[a] of fine flour mixed with a quarter of a hin[b] of oil from pressed olives, and a quarter of a hin of wine as a drink offering. 41Sacrifice the other lamb at twilight with the same grain offering and its drink offering as in the morning—a pleasing aroma, an offering made to the LORD by fire.

42"For the generations to come[r] this burnt offering is to be made regularly at the entrance to the Tent of Meeting before the LORD. There I will meet you and speak to you;[s] 43there also I will meet with the Israelites, and the place will be consecrated by my glory.[t]

44"So I will consecrate the Tent of Meeting and the altar and will consecrate Aaron and his sons to serve me as priests. [u] 45Then I will dwell[v] among the Israelites and be their God. [w] 46They will know that I am the LORD their God, who brought them out of Egypt so that I might dwell among them. I am the LORD their God. [x]

The Altar of Incense

30:1–5pp — Ex 37:25–28

30 "Make an altar[y] of acacia wood for burning incense. [z] 2It is to be square, a cubit long and a cubit wide, and two cubits high[c]—its horns[a] of one piece with it. 3Overlay the top and all the sides and the horns with pure gold, and make a gold molding around it. 4Make two gold rings for the altar below the molding—two on opposite sides—to hold the poles used to carry it. 5Make the poles of acacia wood and overlay them with gold. 6Put the altar in front of the curtain that is before the ark of the Testimony—before the atonement cover[b] that is over the Testimony—where I will meet with you.

7"Aaron must burn fragrant incense[c] on the altar every morning when he tends the lamps. 8He must burn incense again when he lights the lamps at twilight so incense will burn regularly before the LORD for the generations to come. 9Do not offer on this altar any other incense[d] or any burnt offering or grain offering, and do not pour a drink offering on it. 10Once a year Aaron shall make atonement[e] on its horns. This annual atonement must be made with the blood of the atoning sin offering for the generations to come. It is most holy to the LORD."

Atonement Money

11Then the LORD said to Moses, 12"When you take a census[f] of the Israelites to count them, each one must pay the LORD a ransom[g] for his life at the time he is counted. Then no plague[h] will come on them when you number them. 13Each one who crosses over to those already count-

### Cross references (margin)

29:36
[m]Heb 10:11
[n]Ex 40:10

29:37
[o]Ex 30:28-29;
40:10; Mt 23:19

29:38
[p]Nu 28:3-8;
1Ch 16:40;
Da 12:11

29:39
[q]Eze 46:13-15

29:42
[r]Ex 30:8
[s]Ex 25:22

29:43
[t]1Ki 8:11

29:44
[u]Lev 21:15

29:45
[v]Ex 25:8;
Lev 26:12;
Zec 2:10;
Jn 14:17
[w]2Co 6:16;
Rev 21:3

29:46
[x]Ex 20:2

30:1
[y]Ex 37:25
[z]Rev 8:3

30:2
[a]Ex 27:2

30:6
[b]Ex 25:22;
26:34

30:7
[c]ver 34-35;
Ex 27:21;
1Sa 2:28

30:9
[d]Lev 10:1

30:10
[e]Lev 16:18-19,
30

30:12
[f]Ex 38:25;
Nu 1:2,49;
2Sa 24:1
[g]Nu 31:50;
Mt 20:28
[h]2Sa 24:13

---

[a]40 That is, probably about 2 quarts (about 2 liters)   [b]40 That is, probably about 1 quart (about 1 liter)   [c]2 That is, about 1 1/2 feet (about 0.5 meter) long and wide and about 3 feet (about 0.9 meter) high

ed is to give a half shekel,ᵃ according to the sanctuary shekel,ⁱ which weighs twenty gerahs. This half shekel is an offering to the LORD. ¹⁴All who cross over, those twenty years old or more, are to give an offering to the LORD. ¹⁵The rich are not to give more than a half shekel and the poor are not to give lessʲ when you make the offering to the LORD to atone for your lives. ¹⁶Receive the atonement money from the Israelites and use it for the service of the Tent of Meeting.ᵏ It will be a memorial for the Israelites before the LORD, making atonement for your lives."

Basin for Washing

¹⁷Then the LORD said to Moses, ¹⁸"Make a bronze basin,ˡ with its bronze stand, for washing. Place it between the Tent of Meeting and the altar, and put water in it. ¹⁹Aaron and his sons are to wash their hands and feetᵐ with waterⁿ from it. ²⁰Whenever they enter the Tent of Meeting, they shall wash with water so that they will not die. Also, when they approach the altar to minister by presenting an offering made to the LORD by fire, ²¹they shall wash their hands and feet so that they will not die. This is to be a lasting ordinanceᵒ for Aaron and his descendants for the generations to come."

Anointing Oil

²²Then the LORD said to Moses, ²³"Take the following fine spices: 500 shekelsᵇ of liquid myrrh,ᵖ half as much (that is, 250 shekels) of fragrant cinnamon, 250 shekels of fragrant cane, ²⁴500 shekels of cassia�q—all according to the sanctuary shekel—and a hinᶜ of olive oil. ²⁵Make these into a sacred anointing oil, a fragrant blend, the work of a perfumer.ʳ It will be the sacred anointing oil.ˢ ²⁶Then use it to anointᵗ the Tent of Meeting, the ark of the Testimony, ²⁷the table and all its articles, the lampstand and its accessories, the altar of incense, ²⁸the altar of burnt offering and all its utensils, and the basin with its stand. ²⁹You shall consecrate them so they will be most holy, and whatever touches them will be holy.ᵘ

³⁰"Anoint Aaron and his sons and consecrateᵛ them so they may serve me as priests. ³¹Say to the Israelites, 'This is to be my sacred anointing oil for the generations to come. ³²Do not pour it on men's bodies and do not make any oil with the same formula. It is sacred, and you are to consider it sacred.ʷ ³³Whoever makes perfume like it and whoever puts it on anyone other than a priest must be cut offˣ from his people.' "

Incense

³⁴Then the LORD said to Moses, "Take fragrant spices—gum resin, onycha and galbanum—and pure frankincense, all in equal amounts, ³⁵and make a fragrant blend of incense, the work of a perfumer.ʸ It is to be salted and pure and sacred. ³⁶Grind some of it to powder and place it in front of the Testimony in the Tent of Meeting, where I will meet with you. It shall be most holyᶻ to you. ³⁷Do not make any incense with this formula for yourselves; consider it holyᵃ to the LORD. ³⁸Whoev-

30:13
iNu 3:47;
Mt 17:24

30:15
jPr 22:2;
Eph 6:9

30:16
kEx 38:25-28

30:18
lEx 38:8;
40:7,30

30:19
mEx 40:31-32;
Isa 52:11
nPs 26:6

30:21
oEx 27:21;
28:43

30:23
pGe 37:25

30:24
qPs 45:8

30:25
rEx 37:29
sEx 40:9

30:26
tEx 40:9;
Lev 8:10;
Nu 7:1

30:29
uEx 29:37

30:30
vEx 29:7;
Lev 8:2,12,30

30:32
wver 25,37

30:33
xver 38;
Ge 17:14

30:35
yver 25

30:36
zver 32;
Ex 29:37;
Lev 2:3

30:37
aver 32

ᵃ13 That is, about 1/5 ounce (about 6 grams); also in verse 15   ᵇ23 That is, about 12 1/2 pounds (about 6 kilograms)   ᶜ24 That is, probably about 4 quarts (about 4 liters) er makes any like it to enjoy its fragrance must be cut off[b] from his people."

Bezalel and Oholiab

31:2-6pp — Ex 35:30-35

31 Then the LORD said to Moses, [2]"See, I have chosen Bezalel[c] son of Uri, the son of Hur, of the tribe of Judah, [3]and I have filled him with the Spirit of God, with skill, ability and knowledge in all kinds of crafts[d]— [4]to make artistic designs for work in gold, silver and bronze, [5]to cut and set stones, to work in wood, and to engage in all kinds of craftsmanship. [6]Moreover, I have appointed Oholiab son of Ahisamach, of the tribe of Dan, to help him. Also I have given skill to all the craftsmen to make everything I have commanded you: [7]the Tent of Meeting,[e] the ark of the Testimony[f] with the atonement cover[g] on it, and all the other furnishings of the tent— [8]the table[h] and its articles, the pure gold lampstand[i] and all its accessories, the altar of incense, [9]the altar of burnt offering and all its utensils, the basin with its stand— [10]and also the woven garments[j], both the sacred garments for Aaron the priest and the garments for his sons when they serve as priests, [11]and the anointing oil[k] and fragrant incense for the Holy Place. They are to make them just as I commanded you."

The Sabbath

[12]Then the LORD said to Moses, [13]"Say to the Israelites, 'You must observe my Sabbaths.[l] This will be a sign[m] between me and you for the generations to come, so you may know that I am the LORD, who makes you holy.[a] [n]

[14]' 'Observe the Sabbath, because it is holy to you. Anyone who desecrates it must be put to death;[o] whoever does any work on that day must be cut off from his people. [15]For six days, work[p] is to be done, but the seventh day is a Sabbath of rest,[q] holy to the LORD. Whoever does any work on the Sabbath day must be put to death. [16]The Israelites are to observe the Sabbath, celebrating it for the generations to come as a lasting covenant. [17]It will be a sign[r] between me and the Israelites forever, for in six days the LORD made the heavens and the earth, and on the seventh day he abstained from work and rested.[s] ' "

[18]When the LORD finished speaking to Moses on Mount Sinai, he gave him the two tablets of the Testimony, the tablets of stone[t] inscribed by the finger of God.[u]

The Golden Calf

32 When the people saw that Moses was so long in coming down from the mountain,[v] they gathered around Aaron and said, "Come, make us gods[b] who will go before us. As for this fellow Moses who brought us up out of Egypt, we don't know what has happened to him."[w]

[2]Aaron answered them, "Take off the gold earrings[x] that your wives, your sons and your daughters are wearing, and bring them to me." [3]So all the people took off their earrings and brought them to Aaron. [4]He took what they handed him and made it into an idol cast in the shape of

30:38
b ver 33
31:2
c Ex 36:1,2;
1Ch 2:20
31:3
d 1Ki 7:14
31:7
e Ex 36:8-38
f Ex 37:1-5
g Ex 37:6
31:8
h Ex 37:10-16
i Ex 37:17-24
31:10
j Ex 28:2;
39:1,41
31:11
k Ex 30:22-32
31:13
l Ex 20:8;
Lev 19:3,30
m Eze 20:12,20
n Lev 11:44
31:14
o Nu 15:32-36
31:15
p Ex 20:8-11
q Ge 2:3;
Ex 16:23
31:17
r ver 13
s Ge 2:2-3
31:18
t Ex 24:12
u Ex 32:15-16;
34:1,28;
Dt 4:13; 5:22
32:1
v Ex 24:18;
Dt 9:9-12
w Ac 7:40*
32:2
x Ex 35:22

---

[a]13 Or *who sanctifies you; or who sets you apart as holy*   [b]1 Or *a god;* also in verses 23 and 31

a calf,ʸ fashioning it with a tool. Then they said, "These are your gods,ᵃ O Israel, who brought you up out of Egypt."

⁵When Aaron saw this, he built an altar in front of the calf and announced, "Tomorrow there will be a festivalᶻ to the LORD." ⁶So the next day the people rose early and sacrificed burnt offerings and presented fellowship offerings.ᵇᵃ Afterward they sat down to eat and drink and got up to indulge in revelry.ᵇ

⁷Then the LORD said to Moses, "Go down, because your people, whom you brought up out of Egypt,ᶜ have become corrupt.ᵈ ⁸They have been quick to turn away from what I commanded them and have made themselves an idolᵉ cast in the shape of a calf. They have bowed down to it and sacrificedᶠ to it and have said, 'These are your gods, O Israel, who brought you up out of Egypt.'ᵍ

⁹"I have seen these people," the LORD said to Moses, "and they are a stiff-neckedʰ people. ¹⁰Now leave me alone so that my anger may burn against them and that I may destroy them. Then I will make you into a great nation."ⁱ

¹¹But Moses sought the favorʲ of the LORD his God. "O LORD," he said, "why should your anger burn against your people, whom you brought out of Egypt with great power and a mighty hand?ᵏ ¹²Why should the Egyptians say, 'It was with evil intent that he brought them out, to kill them in the mountains and to wipe them off the face of the earth'?ˡ Turn from your fierce anger; relent and do not bring disaster on your people. ¹³Rememberᵐ your servants Abraham, Isaac and Israel, to whom you swore by your own self:ⁿ 'I will make your descendants as numerous as the starsᵒ in the sky and I will give your descendants all this landᵖ I promised them, and it will be their inheritance forever.' "

¹⁴Then the LORD relented�q and did not bring on his people the disaster he had threatened.

¹⁵Moses turned and went down the mountain with the two tablets of the Testimonyʳ in his hands.ˢ They were inscribed on both sides, front and back. ¹⁶The tablets were the work of God; the writing was the writing of God, engraved on the tablets.ᵗ

¹⁷When Joshua heard the noise of the people shouting, he said to Moses, "There is the sound of war in the camp."

¹⁸Moses replied:

> "It is not the sound of victory,
>   it is not the sound of defeat;
>   it is the sound of singing that I hear."

¹⁹When Moses approached the camp and saw the calfᵘ and the dancing, his anger burned and he threw the tablets out of his hands, breaking them to piecesᵛ at the foot of the mountain. ²⁰And he took the calf they had made and burned it in the fire; then he ground it to powder, scattered it on the waterʷ and made the Israelites drink it.

²¹He said to Aaron, "What did these people do to you, that you led them into such great sin?"

²²"Do not be angry, my lord," Aaron answered. "You know how prone these people are to evil.ˣ ²³They said to me, 'Make us gods who will go before us. As for this fellow Moses who brought us up out of

---

²⁴ Or *This is your god*; also in verse 8   ᵇ6 Traditionally *peace offerings*

32:4
ʸDt 9:16;
Ne 9:18;
Ps 106:19;
Ac 7:41
32:5
ᶻLev 23:2,37;
2Ki 10:20
32:6
ᵃNu 25:2;
Ac 7:41
ᵇver 17-19;
1Co 10:7*
32:7
ᶜver 4,11
ᵈGe 6:11-12;
Dt 9:12
32:8
ᵉEx 20:4
ᶠEx 22:20
ᵍ1Ki 12:28
32:9
ʰEx 33:3,5;
34:9; Isa 48:4;
Ac 7:51
32:10
ⁱNu 14:12;
Dt 9:14
32:11
ʲDt 9:18
ᵏDt 9:26
32:12
ˡNu 14:13-16;
Dt 9:28
32:13
ᵐEx 2:24
ⁿGe 22:16;
Heb 6:13
ᵒGe 15:5; 26:4
ᵖGe 12:7
32:14
q2Sa 24:16;
Ps 106:45
32:15
ʳEx 31:18
ˢDt 9:15
32:16
ᵗEx 31:18
32:19
ᵘDt 9:16
ᵛDt 9:17
32:20
ʷDt 9:21
32:22
ˣDt 9:24

Egypt, we don't know what has happened to him.'ʸ ²⁴So I told them, 'Whoever has any gold jewelry, take it off.' Then they gave me the gold, and I threw it into the fire, and out came this calf!"ᶻ

²⁵Moses saw that the people were running wild and that Aaron had let them get out of control and so become a laughingstock to their enemies. ²⁶So he stood at the entrance to the camp and said, "Whoever is for the LORD, come to me." And all the Levites rallied to him.

²⁷Then he said to them, "This is what the LORD, the God of Israel, says: 'Each man strap a sword to his side. Go back and forth through the camp from one end to the other, each killing his brother and friend and neighbor.' "ᵃ ²⁸The Levites did as Moses commanded, and that day about three thousand of the people died. ²⁹Then Moses said, "You have been set apart to the LORD today, for you were against your own sons and brothers, and he has blessed you this day."

³⁰The next day Moses said to the people, "You have committed a great sin.ᵇ But now I will go up to the LORD; perhaps I can make atonementᶜ for your sin."

³¹So Moses went back to the LORD and said, "Oh, what a great sin these people have committed!ᵈ They have made themselves gods of gold.ᵉ ³²But now, please forgive their sin—but if not, then blot meᶠ out of the bookᵍ you have written."

³³The LORD replied to Moses, "Whoever has sinned against me I will blot outʰ of my book. ³⁴Now go, lead the people to the placeⁱ I spoke of, and my angelʲ will go before you. However, when the time comes for me to punish,ᵏ I will punish them for their sin."

³⁵And the LORD struck the people with a plague because of what they did with the calfˡ Aaron had made.

33 Then the LORD said to Moses, "Leave this place, you and the people you brought up out of Egypt, and go up to the land I promised on oath to Abraham, Isaac and Jacob, saying, 'I will give it to your descendants.'ᵐ ²I will send an angelⁿ before you and drive out the Canaanites, Amorites, Hittites, Perizzites, Hivites and Jebusites.ᵒ ³Go up to the land flowing with milk and honey.ᵖ But I will not go with you, because you are a stiff-necked�q people and I might destroyʳ you on the way."

⁴When the people heard these distressing words, they began to mournˢ and no one put on any ornaments. ⁵For the LORD had said to Moses, "Tell the Israelites, 'You are a stiff-necked people. If I were to go with you even for a moment, I might destroy you. Now take off your ornaments and I will decide what to do with you.' " ⁶So the Israelites stripped off their ornaments at Mount Horeb.

The Tent of Meeting

⁷Now Moses used to take a tent and pitch it outside the camp some distance away, calling it the "tent of meeting."ᵗ Anyone inquiring of the LORD would go to the tent of meeting outside the camp. ⁸And whenever Moses went out to the tent, all the people rose and stood at the entrances to their tents,ᵘ watching Moses until he entered the tent. ⁹As Moses went into the tent, the pillar of cloudᵛ would come down and stay at the entrance, while the LORD spokeʷ with Moses. ¹⁰Whenever the people saw the pillar of cloud standing at the entrance to the tent, they all stood and worshiped, each at the entrance to his tent.

[11]The LORD would speak to Moses face to face,[x] as a man speaks with his friend. Then Moses would return to the camp, but his young aide Joshua son of Nun did not leave the tent.

Moses and the Glory of the LORD

[12]Moses said to the LORD, "You have been telling me, 'Lead these people,'[y] but you have not let me know whom you will send with me. You have said, 'I know you by name[z] and you have found favor with me.' [13]If you are pleased with me, teach me your ways[a] so I may know you and continue to find favor with you. Remember that this nation is your people."[b]

[14]The LORD replied, "My Presence[c] will go with you, and I will give you rest."[d]

[15]Then Moses said to him, "If your Presence does not go with us, do not send us up from here. [16]How will anyone know that you are pleased with me and with your people unless you go with us?[e] What else will distinguish me and your people from all the other people on the face of the earth?"[f]

[17]And the LORD said to Moses, "I will do the very thing you have asked, because I am pleased with you and I know you by name."

[18]Then Moses said, "Now show me your glory."

[19]And the LORD said, "I will cause all my goodness to pass in front of you, and I will proclaim my name, the LORD, in your presence. I will have mercy on whom I will have mercy, and I will have compassion on whom I will have compassion.[g] [20]But," he said, "you cannot see my face, for no one may see[h] me and live."

[21]Then the LORD said, "There is a place near me where you may stand on a rock. [22]When my glory passes by, I will put you in a cleft in the rock and cover you with my hand[i] until I have passed by. [23]Then I will remove my hand and you will see my back; but my face must not be seen."

The New Stone Tablets

34 The LORD said to Moses, "Chisel out two stone tablets like the first ones, and I will write on them the words that were on the first tablets,[j] which you broke.[k] [2]Be ready in the morning, and then come up on Mount Sinai.[l] Present yourself to me there on top of the mountain. [3]No one is to come with you or be seen anywhere on the mountain;[m] not even the flocks and herds may graze in front of the mountain."

[4]So Moses chiseled out two stone tablets like the first ones and went up Mount Sinai early in the morning, as the LORD had commanded him; and he carried the two stone tablets in his hands. [5]Then the LORD came down in the cloud and stood there with him and proclaimed his name, the LORD.[n] [6]And he passed in front of Moses, proclaiming, "The LORD, the LORD, the compassionate[o] and gracious God, slow to anger,[p] abounding in love[q] and faithfulness,[r] [7]maintaining love to thousands,[s] and forgiving wickedness, rebellion and sin.[t] Yet he does not leave the guilty unpunished;[u] he punishes the children and their children for the sin of the fathers to the third and fourth generation."

[8]Moses bowed to the ground at once and worshiped. [9]"O Lord, if I have found favor in your eyes," he said, "then let the Lord go with us.[v]

33:11
xNu 12:8;
Dt 34:10
33:12
yEx 3:10
zver 17;
Jn 10:14-15;
2Ti 2:19
33:13
aPs 25:4; 86:11;
119:33
bEx 34:9;
Dt 9:26,29
33:14
cIsa 63:9
dJos 21:44; 22:4
33:16
eNu 14:14
fEx 34:10
33:19
gRo 9:15*
33:20
hGe 32:30;
Isa 6:5
33:22
iPs 91:4
34:1
jDt 10:2,4
kEx 32:19
34:2
lEx 19:11
34:3
mEx 19:12-13,21
34:5
nEx 33:19
34:6
oPs 86:15
pNu 14:18;
Ro 2:4
qNe 9:17;
Ps 103:8;
Joel 2:13
rPs 108:4
34:7
sEx 20:6
tPs 103:3;
130:4,8;
Da 9:9; 1Jn 1:9
uJob 10:14;
Na 1:3
34:9
vEx 33:15

Although this is a stiff-necked people, forgive our wickedness and our sin, and take us as your inheritance." w

[10]Then the LORD said: "I am making a covenant x with you. Before all your people I will do wonders never before done in any nation in all the world. y The people you live among will see how awesome is the work that I, the LORD, will do for you. [11]Obey what I command you today. I will drive out before you the Amorites, Canaanites, Hittites, Perizzites, Hivites and Jebusites. z [12]Be careful not to make a treaty with those who live in the land where you are going, or they will be a snare a among you. [13]Break down their altars, smash their sacred stones and cut down their Asherah poles. a b [14]Do not worship any other god, c for the LORD, whose name is Jealous, is a jealous God. d

[15]"Be careful not to make a treaty with those who live in the land; for when they prostitute e themselves to their gods and sacrifice to them, they will invite you and you will eat their sacrifices. f [16]And when you choose some of their daughters as wives g for your sons and those daughters prostitute themselves to their gods, h they will lead your sons to do the same.

[17]"Do not make cast idols. i

[18]"Celebrate the Feast of Unleavened Bread. j For seven days eat bread made without yeast, k as I commanded you. Do this at the appointed time in the month of Abib, l for in that month you came out of Egypt.

[19]"The first offspring m of every womb belongs to me, including all the firstborn males of your livestock, whether from herd or flock. [20]Redeem the firstborn donkey with a lamb, but if you do not redeem it, break its neck. n Redeem all your firstborn sons.

"No one is to appear before me empty-handed. o

[21]"Six days you shall labor, but on the seventh day you shall rest; p even during the plowing season and harvest you must rest.

[22]"Celebrate the Feast of Weeks with the firstfruits of the wheat harvest, and the Feast of Ingathering q at the turn of the year. b [23]Three times r a year all your men are to appear before the Sovereign LORD, the God of Israel. [24]I will drive out nations s before you and enlarge your territory, and no one will covet your land when you go up three times each year to appear before the LORD your God.

[25]"Do not offer the blood of a sacrifice to me along with anything containing yeast, t and do not let any of the sacrifice from the Passover Feast remain until morning. u

[26]"Bring the best of the firstfruits of your soil to the house of the LORD your God.

"Do not cook a young goat in its mother's milk." v

[27]Then the LORD said to Moses, "Write w down these words, for in accordance with these words I have made a covenant with you and with Israel." [28]Moses was there with the LORD forty days and forty nights x without eating bread or drinking water. And he wrote on the tablets y the words of the covenant—the Ten Commandments. z

The Radiant Face of Moses

[29]When Moses came down from Mount Sinai with the two tablets of

---

34:9
w Ps 33:12
34:10
x Dt 5:2-3
y Ex 33:16;
Dt 4:32
34:11
z Ex 33:2
34:12
a Ex 23:32-33
34:13
b Ex 23:24;
Dt 12:3;
2Ki 18:4
34:14
c Ex 20:3
d Ex 20:5;
Dt 4:24
34:15
e Jdg 2:17
f Nu 25:2;
1Co 8:4
34:16
g Dt 7:3
h 1Ki 11:4
34:17
i Ex 32:8
34:18
j Ex 12:17
k Ex 12:15
l Ex 12:2
34:19
m Ex 13:2
34:20
n Ex 13:13,15
o Ex 23:15;
Dt 16:16
34:21
p Ex 20:9;
Lk 13:14
34:22
q Ex 23:16
34:23
r Ex 23:14
34:24
s Ex 23:28; 33:2;
Ps 78:55
34:25
t Ex 23:18
u Ex 12:8,10
34:26
v Ex 23:19
34:27
w Ex 17:14; 24:4
34:28
x Ge 7:4;
Ex 24:18;
Mt 4:2 y ver 1;
Ex 31:18
z Dt 4:13; 10:4

---

a13 That is, symbols of the goddess Asherah   b22 That is, in the fall the Testimony in his hands,ᵃ he was not aware that his face was radiantᵇ because he had spoken with the LORD. ³⁰When Aaron and all the Israelites saw Moses, his face was radiant, and they were afraid to come near him. ³¹But Moses called to them; so Aaron and all the leaders of the community came back to him, and he spoke to them. ³²Afterward all the Israelites came near him, and he gave them all the commandsᶜ the LORD had given him on Mount Sinai.

³³When Moses finished speaking to them, he put a veilᵈ over his face. ³⁴But whenever he entered the LORD's presence to speak with him, he removed the veil until he came out. And when he came out and told the Israelites what he had been commanded, ³⁵they saw that his face was radiant. Then Moses would put the veil back over his face until he went in to speak with the LORD.

Sabbath Regulations

35 Moses assembled the whole Israelite community and said to them, "These are the things the LORD has commandedᵉ you to do: ²For six days, work is to be done, but the seventh day shall be your holy day, a Sabbathᶠ of rest to the LORD. Whoever does any work on it must be put to death. ³Do not light a fire in any of your dwellings on the Sabbath day.ᵍ"

Materials for the Tabernacle

35:4–9pp — Ex 25:1–7
35:10–19pp — Ex 39:32–41

⁴Moses said to the whole Israelite community, "This is what the LORD has commanded: ⁵From what you have, take an offering for the LORD. Everyone who is willing is to bring to the LORD an offering of gold, silver and bronze; ⁶blue, purple and scarlet yarn and fine linen; goat hair; ⁷ram skins dyed red and hides of sea cowsᵃ; acacia wood; ⁸olive oil for the light; spices for the anointing oil and for the fragrant incense; ⁹and onyx stones and other gems to be mounted on the ephod and breastpiece.

¹⁰"All who are skilled among you are to come and make everything the LORD has commanded:ʰ ¹¹the tabernacleⁱ with its tent and its covering, clasps, frames, crossbars, posts and bases; ¹²the arkʲ with its poles and the atonement cover and the curtain that shields it; ¹³the tableᵏ with its poles and all its articles and the bread of the Presence; ¹⁴the lampstandˡ that is for light with its accessories, lamps and oil for the light; ¹⁵the altarᵐ of incense with its poles, the anointing oilⁿ and the fragrant incense;ᵒ the curtain for the doorway at the entrance to the tabernacle; ¹⁶the altarᵖ of burnt offering with its bronze grating, its poles and all its utensils; the bronze basin with its stand; ¹⁷the curtains of the courtyard with its posts and bases, and the curtain for the entrance to the courtyard;�q ¹⁸the tent pegs for the tabernacle and for the courtyard, and their ropes; ¹⁹the woven garments worn for ministering in the sanctuary—both the sacred garmentsʳ for Aaron the priest and the garments for his sons when they serve as priests."

²⁰Then the whole Israelite community withdrew from Moses' presence, ²¹and everyone who was willing and whose heart moved him

---

ᵃ7 That is, dugongs; also in verse 23

34:29
ᵃEx 32:15
ᵇPs 34:5;
Mt 17:2;
2Co 3:7,13
34:32
ᶜEx 24:3
34:33
ᵈ2Co 3:13
35:1
ᵉEx 34:32
35:2
ᶠEx 20:9-10;
34:21;
Lev 23:3
35:3
ᵍEx 16:23
35:10
ʰEx 31:6
35:11
ⁱEx 26:1-37
35:12
ʲEx 25:10-22
35:13
ᵏEx 25:23-30;
Lev 24:5-6
35:14
ˡEx 25:31
35:15
ᵐEx 30:1-6
ⁿEx 30:25
ᵒEx 30:34-38
35:16
ᵖEx 27:1-8
35:17
qEx 27:9
35:19
ʳEx 28:2; 31:10;
39:1

came and brought an offering to the LORD for the work on the Tent of Meeting, for all its service, and for the sacred garments. ²²All who were willing, men and women alike, came and brought gold jewelry of all kinds: brooches, earrings, rings and ornaments. They all presented their gold as a wave offering to the LORD. ²³Everyone who had blue, purple or scarlet yarn⁵ or fine linen, or goat hair, ram skins dyed red or hides of sea cows brought them. ²⁴Those presenting an offering of silver or bronze brought it as an offering to the LORD, and everyone who had acacia wood for any part of the work brought it. ²⁵Every skilled woman¹ spun with her hands and brought what she had spun—blue, purple or scarlet yarn or fine linen. ²⁶And all the women who were willing and had the skill spun the goat hair. ²⁷The leaders" brought onyx stones and other gems to be mounted on the ephod and breastpiece. ²⁸They also brought spices and olive oil for the light and for the anointing oil and for the fragrant incense.ᵛ ²⁹All the Israelite men and women who were willingʷ brought to the LORD freewill offeringsˣ for all the work the LORD through Moses had commanded them to do.

Bezalel and Oholiab

35:30–35pp — Ex 31:2–6

³⁰Then Moses said to the Israelites, "See, the LORD has chosen Bezalel son of Uri, the son of Hur, of the tribe of Judah, ³¹and he has filled him with the Spirit of God, with skill, ability and knowledge in all kinds of craftsʸ— ³²to make artistic designs for work in gold, silver and bronze, ³³to cut and set stones, to work in wood and to engage in all kinds of artistic craftsmanship. ³⁴And he has given both him and Oholiabᶻ son of Ahisamach, of the tribe of Dan, the ability to teachᵃ others. ³⁵He has filled them with skill to do all kinds of workᵇ as craftsmen, designers, embroiderers in blue, purple and scarlet yarn and fine linen, and

36 weavers—all of them master craftsmen and designers. ¹So Bezalel, Oholiab and every skilled personᶜ to whom the LORD has given skill and ability to know how to carry out all the work of constructing the sanctuaryᵈ are to do the work just as the Lord has commanded."

²Then Moses summoned Bezalelᵉ and Oholiabᶠ and every skilled person to whom the LORD had given ability and who was willingᵍ to come and do the work. ³They received from Moses all the offeringsʰ the Israelites had brought to carry out the work of constructing the sanctuary. And the people continued to bring freewill offerings morning after morning. ⁴So all the skilled craftsmen who were doing all the work on the sanctuary left their work ⁵and said to Moses, "The people are bringing more than enoughⁱ for doing the work the LORD commanded to be done."

⁶Then Moses gave an order and they sent this word throughout the camp: "No man or woman is to make anything else as an offering for the sanctuary." And so the people were restrained from bringing more, ⁷because what they already had was moreʲ than enough to do all the work.

The Tabernacle

36:8–38pp — Ex 26:1–37

⁸All the skilled men among the workmen made the tabernacle with

35:23
ˢ1Ch 29:8

35:25
ᵗEx 28:3

35:27
ᵘ1Ch 29:6;
Ezr 2:68

35:28
ᵛEx 25:6

35:29
ʷver 21;
1Ch 29:9
ˣver 4-9;
Ex 25:1-7; 36:3;
2Ki 12:4

35:31
ʸver 35;
2Ch 2:7,14

35:34
ᶻEx 31:6
ᵃ2Ch 2:14

35:35
ᵇver 31;
Ex 31:3,6;
1Ki 7:14

36:1
ᶜEx 28:3
ᵈEx 25:8

36:2
ᵉEx 31:2
ᶠEx 31:6
ᵍEx 25:2; 35:21,
26; 1Ch 29:5

36:3
ʰEx 35:29

36:5
ⁱ2Ch 24:14;
31:10;
2Co 8:2-3

36:7
ʲ1Ki 7:47

ten curtains of finely twisted linen and blue, purple and scarlet yarn, with cherubim worked into them by a skilled craftsman. [9]All the curtains were the same size—twenty-eight cubits long and four cubits wide.[a] [10]They joined five of the curtains together and did the same with the other five. [11]Then they made loops of blue material along the edge of the end curtain in one set, and the same was done with the end curtain in the other set. [12]They also made fifty loops on one curtain and fifty loops on the end curtain of the other set, with the loops opposite each other. [13]Then they made fifty gold clasps and used them to fasten the two sets of curtains together so that the tabernacle was a unit.[k]

[14]They made curtains of goat hair for the tent over the tabernacle—eleven altogether. [15]All eleven curtains were the same size—thirty cubits long and four cubits wide.[b] [16]They joined five of the curtains into one set and the other six into another set. [17]Then they made fifty loops along the edge of the end curtain in one set and also along the edge of the end curtain in the other set. [18]They made fifty bronze clasps to fasten the tent together as a unit.[l] [19]Then they made for the tent a covering of ram skins dyed red, and over that a covering of hides of sea cows.[c]

[20]They made upright frames of acacia wood for the tabernacle. [21]Each frame was ten cubits long and a cubit and a half wide,[d] [22]with two projections set parallel to each other. They made all the frames of the tabernacle in this way. [23]They made twenty frames for the south side of the tabernacle [24]and made forty silver bases to go under them—two bases for each frame, one under each projection. [25]For the other side, the north side of the tabernacle, they made twenty frames [26]and forty silver bases—two under each frame. [27]They made six frames for the far end, that is, the west end of the tabernacle, [28]and two frames were made for the corners of the tabernacle at the far end. [29]At these two corners the frames were double from the bottom all the way to the top and fitted into a single ring; both were made alike. [30]So there were eight frames and sixteen silver bases—two under each frame.

[31]They also made crossbars of acacia wood: five for the frames on one side of the tabernacle, [32]five for those on the other side, and five for the frames on the west, at the far end of the tabernacle. [33]They made the center crossbar so that it extended from end to end at the middle of the frames. [34]They overlaid the frames with gold and made gold rings to hold the crossbars. They also overlaid the crossbars with gold.

[35]They made the curtain[m] of blue, purple and scarlet yarn and finely twisted linen, with cherubim worked into it by a skilled craftsman. [36]They made four posts of acacia wood for it and overlaid them with gold. They made gold hooks for them and cast their four silver bases. [37]For the entrance to the tent they made a curtain of blue, purple and scarlet yarn and finely twisted linen—the work of an embroiderer;[n] [38]and they made five posts with hooks for them. They overlaid the tops of the posts and their bands with gold and made their five bases of bronze.

36:13
k ver 18
36:18
l ver 13
36:35
m Ex 39:38;
Mt 27:51;
Lk 23:45;
Heb 9:3
36:37
n Ex 27:16

---

a9 That is, about 42 feet (about 12.5 meters) long and 6 feet (about 1.8 meters) wide   b15 That is, about 45 feet (about 13.5 meters) long and 6 feet (about 1.8 meters) wide   c19 That is, dugongs   d21 That is, about 15 feet (about 4.5 meters) long and 2 1/4 feet (about 0.7 meter) wide

The Ark

37:1–9pp — Ex 25:10–20

37 Bezalel[o] made the ark[p] of acacia wood—two and a half cubits long, a cubit and a half wide, and a cubit and a half high.[a] [2]He overlaid it with pure gold,[q] both inside and out, and made a gold molding around it. [3]He cast four gold rings for it and fastened them to its four feet, with two rings on one side and two rings on the other. [4]Then he made poles of acacia wood and overlaid them with gold. [5]And he inserted the poles into the rings on the sides of the ark to carry it.

[6]He made the atonement cover[r] of pure gold—two and a half cubits long and a cubit and a half wide.[b] [7]Then he made two cherubim[s] out of hammered gold at the ends of the cover. [8]He made one cherub on one end and the second cherub on the other; at the two ends he made them of one piece with the cover. [9]The cherubim had their wings spread upward, overshadowing[t] the cover with them. The cherubim faced each other, looking toward the cover.[u]

The Table

37:10–16pp — Ex 25:23–29

[10]They[c] made the table[v] of acacia wood—two cubits long, a cubit wide, and a cubit and a half high.[d] [11]Then they overlaid it with pure gold[w] and made a gold molding around it. [12]They also made around it a rim a handbreadth[e] wide and put a gold molding on the rim. [13]They cast four gold rings for the table and fastened them to the four corners, where the four legs were. [14]The rings[x] were put close to the rim to hold the poles used in carrying the table. [15]The poles for carrying the table were made of acacia wood and were overlaid with gold. [16]And they made from pure gold the articles for the table—its plates and dishes and bowls and its pitchers for the pouring out of drink offerings.

The Lampstand

37:17–24pp — Ex 25:31–39

[17]They made the lampstand[y] of pure gold and hammered it out, base and shaft; its flowerlike cups, buds and blossoms were of one piece with it. [18]Six branches extended from the sides of the lampstand—three on one side and three on the other. [19]Three cups shaped like almond flowers with buds and blossoms were on one branch, three on the next branch and the same for all six branches extending from the lampstand. [20]And on the lampstand were four cups shaped like almond flowers with buds and blossoms. [21]One bud was under the first pair of branches extending from the lampstand, a second bud under the second pair, and a third bud under the third pair—six branches in all. [22]The buds and the branches were all of one piece with the lampstand, hammered out of pure gold.[z]

[23]They made its seven lamps,[a] as well as its wick trimmers and trays,

---

37:1
oEx 31:2
pEx 30:6;
39:35; Dt 10:3
37:2
qver 11,26
37:6
rEx 26:34; 31:7;
Heb 9:5
37:7
sEze 41:18
37:9
tHeb 9:5
uDt 10:3
37:10
vHeb 9:2
37:11
wver 2
37:14
xver 27
37:17
yHeb 9:2;
Rev 1:12
37:22
zver 17; Nu 8:4
37:23
aEx 40:4,25

---

[a]1 That is, about 3 3/4 feet (about 1.1 meters) long and 2 1/4 feet (about 0.7 meter) wide and high
[b]6 That is, about 3 3/4 feet (about 1.1 meters) long and 2 1/4 feet (about 0.7 meter) wide   [c]10 Or
He; also in verses 11-29   [d]10 That is, about 3 feet (about 0.9 meter) long, 1 1/2 feet (about 0.5 meter) wide, and 2 1/4 feet (about 0.7 meter) high   [e]12 That is, about 3 inches (about 8 centimeters)

of pure gold. [24]They made the lampstand and all its accessories from one talent[a] of pure gold.

The Altar of Incense

37:25–28pp — Ex 30:1–5

[25]They made the altar of incense[b] out of acacia wood. It was square, a cubit long and a cubit wide, and two cubits high[b]—its horns[c] of one piece with it. [26]They overlaid the top and all the sides and the horns with pure gold, and made a gold molding around it. [27]They made two gold rings[d] below the molding—two on opposite sides—to hold the poles used to carry it. [28]They made the poles of acacia wood and overlaid them with gold. [e]

[29]They also made the sacred anointing oil[f] and the pure, fragrant incense[g]—the work of a perfumer.

The Altar of Burnt Offering

38:1–7pp — Ex 27:1–8

38 They[c] built the altar of burnt offering of acacia wood, three cubits[d] high; it was square, five cubits long and five cubits wide. [e] [2]They made a horn at each of the four corners, so that the horns and the altar were of one piece, and they overlaid the altar with bronze.[h] [3]They made all its utensils[i] of bronze—its pots, shovels, sprinkling bowls, meat forks and firepans. [4]They made a grating for the altar, a bronze network, to be under its ledge, halfway up the altar. [5]They cast bronze rings to hold the poles for the four corners of the bronze grating. [6]They made the poles of acacia wood and overlaid them with bronze. [7]They inserted the poles into the rings so they would be on the sides of the altar for carrying it. They made it hollow, out of boards.

Basin for Washing

[8]They made the bronze basin[j] and its bronze stand from the mirrors of the women[k] who served at the entrance to the Tent of Meeting.

The Courtyard

38:9–20pp — Ex 27:9–19

[9]Next they made the courtyard. The south side was a hundred cubits[f] long and had curtains of finely twisted linen, [10]with twenty posts and twenty bronze bases, and with silver hooks and bands on the posts. [11]The north side was also a hundred cubits long and had twenty posts and twenty bronze bases, with silver hooks and bands on the posts.

[12]The west end was fifty cubits[g] wide and had curtains, with ten posts and ten bases, with silver hooks and bands on the posts. [13]The east end, toward the sunrise, was also fifty cubits wide. [14]Curtains fifteen cubits[h] long were on one side of the entrance, with three posts and three bases, [15]and curtains fifteen cubits long were on the other

37:25
b Ex 30:34-36;
Lk 1:11;
Heb 9:4;
Rev 8:3
c Ex 27:2;
Rev 9:13
37:27
d ver 14
37:28
e Ex 25:13
37:29
f Ex 31:11
g Ex 30:1,25;
39:38
38:2
h 2Ch 1:5
38:3
i Ex 31:9
38:8
j Ex 30:18; 40:7
k Dt 23:17;
1Sa 2:22;
1Ki 14:24

---

a24 That is, about 75 pounds (about 34 kilograms)   *b25* That is, about 1 1/2 feet (about 0.5 meter) long and wide, and about 3 feet (about 0.9 meter) high   *c1* Or *He*; also in verses 2-9   *d1* That is, about 4 1/2 feet (about 1.3 meters)   *e1* That is, about 7 1/2 feet (about 2.3 meters) long and wide   *f9* That is, about 150 feet (about 46 meters)   *g12* That is, about 75 feet (about 23 meters)   *h14* That is, about 22 1/2 feet (about 6.9 meters) side of the entrance to the courtyard, with three posts and three bases. [16]All the curtains around the courtyard were of finely twisted linen. [17]The bases for the posts were bronze. The hooks and bands on the posts were silver, and their tops were overlaid with silver; so all the posts of the courtyard had silver bands.

[18]The curtain for the entrance to the courtyard was of blue, purple and scarlet yarn and finely twisted linen—the work of an embroiderer. It was twenty cubits[a] long and, like the curtains of the courtyard, five cubits[b] high, [19]with four posts and four bronze bases. Their hooks and bands were silver, and their tops were overlaid with silver. [20]All the tent pegs[1] of the tabernacle and of the surrounding courtyard were bronze.

The Materials Used

[21]These are the amounts of the materials used for the tabernacle, the tabernacle of the Testimony,[m] which were recorded at Moses' command by the Levites under the direction of Ithamar[n] son of Aaron, the priest. [22](Bezalel[o] son of Uri, the son of Hur, of the tribe of Judah, made everything the LORD commanded Moses; [23]with him was Oholiab[p] son of Ahisamach, of the tribe of Dan—a craftsman and designer, and an embroiderer in blue, purple and scarlet yarn and fine linen.) [24]The total amount of the gold from the wave offering used for all the work on the sanctuary[q] was 29 talents and 730 shekels,[c] according to the sanctuary shekel.[r]

[25]The silver obtained from those of the community who were counted in the census[s] was 100 talents and 1,775 shekels,[d] according to the sanctuary shekel— [26]one beka per person,[t] that is, half a shekel,[e] according to the sanctuary shekel,[u] from everyone who had crossed over to those counted, twenty years old or more,[v] a total of 603,550 men.[w] [27]The 100 talents[f] of silver were used to cast the bases[x] for the sanctuary and for the curtain—100 bases from the 100 talents, one talent for each base. [28]They used the 1,775 shekels[g] to make the hooks for the posts, to overlay the tops of the posts, and to make their bands.

[29]The bronze from the wave offering was 70 talents and 2,400 shekels.[h] [30]They used it to make the bases for the entrance to the Tent of Meeting, the bronze altar with its bronze grating and all its utensils, [31]the bases for the surrounding courtyard and those for its entrance and all the tent pegs for the tabernacle and those for the surrounding courtyard.

The Priestly Garments

39 From the blue, purple and scarlet yarn[y] they made woven garments for ministering in the sanctuary.[z] They also made sacred garments[a] for Aaron, as the LORD commanded Moses.

38:20
l Ex 35:18
38:21
m Nu 1:50,53;
8:24; 9:15;
10:11; 17:7;
1Ch 23:32;
2Ch 24:6;
Ac 7:44;
Rev 15:5
n Nu 4:28,33
38:22
o Ex 31:2
38:23
p Ex 31:6
38:24
q Ex 30:16
r Ex 30:13;
Lev 27:25;
Nu 3:47; 18:16
38:25
s Ex 30:12
38:26
t Ex 30:12
u Ex 30:13
v Ex 30:14
w Ex 12:37;
Nu 1:46
38:27
x Ex 26:19
39:1
y Ex 35:23
z Ex 35:19
a ver 41; Ex 28:2

[a]18 That is, about 30 feet (about 9 meters)   [b]18 That is, about 7 1/2 feet (about 2.3 meters)   [c]24 The weight of the gold was a little over one ton (about 1 metric ton).   [d]25 The weight of the silver was a little over 3 3/4 tons (about 3.4 metric tons).   [e]26 That is, about 1/5 ounce (about 5.5 grams)   [f]27 That is, about 3 3/4 tons (about 3.4 metric tons)   [g]28 That is, about 45 pounds (about 20 kilograms)   [h]29 The weight of the bronze was about 2 1/2 tons (about 2.4 metric tons).

The Ephod

39:2–7pp — Ex 28:6–14

[2]They[a] made the ephod of gold, and of blue, purple and scarlet yarn, and of finely twisted linen. [3]They hammered out thin sheets of gold and cut strands to be worked into the blue, purple and scarlet yarn and fine linen—the work of a skilled craftsman. [4]They made shoulder pieces for the ephod, which were attached to two of its corners, so it could be fastened. [5]Its skillfully woven waistband was like it—of one piece with the ephod and made with gold, and with blue, purple and scarlet yarn, and with finely twisted linen, as the LORD commanded Moses.

[6]They mounted the onyx stones in gold filigree settings and engraved them like a seal with the names of the sons of Israel. [7]Then they fastened them on the shoulder pieces of the ephod as memorial[b] stones for the sons of Israel, as the LORD commanded Moses.

The Breastpiece

39:8–21pp — Ex 28:15–28

[8]They fashioned the breastpiece[c]—the work of a skilled craftsman. They made it like the ephod: of gold, and of blue, purple and scarlet yarn, and of finely twisted linen. [9]It was square—a span[b] long and a span wide—and folded double. [10]Then they mounted four rows of precious stones on it. In the first row there was a ruby, a topaz and a beryl; [11]in the second row a turquoise, a sapphire[c] and an emerald; [12]in the third row a jacinth, an agate and an amethyst; [13]in the fourth row a chrysolite, an onyx and a jasper.[d] They were mounted in gold filigree settings. [14]There were twelve stones, one for each of the names of the sons of Israel, each engraved like a seal with the name of one of the twelve tribes.[d]

[15]For the breastpiece they made braided chains of pure gold, like a rope. [16]They made two gold filigree settings and two gold rings, and fastened the rings to two of the corners of the breastpiece. [17]They fastened the two gold chains to the rings at the corners of the breastpiece, [18]and the other ends of the chains to the two settings, attaching them to the shoulder pieces of the ephod at the front. [19]They made two gold rings and attached them to the other two corners of the breastpiece on the inside edge next to the ephod. [20]Then they made two more gold rings and attached them to the bottom of the shoulder pieces on the front of the ephod, close to the seam just above the waistband of the ephod. [21]They tied the rings of the breastpiece to the rings of the ephod with blue cord, connecting it to the waistband so that the breastpiece would not swing out from the ephod—as the LORD commanded Moses.

Other Priestly Garments

39:22–31pp — Ex 28:31–43

[22]They made the robe of the ephod entirely of blue cloth—the work of a weaver— [23]with an opening in the center of the robe like the opening of a collar,[e] and a band around this opening, so that it would not tear.

39:7
b Lev 24:7;
Jos 4:7
39:8
c Lev 8:8
39:14
d Rev 21:12

---

[a]2 Or *He*; also in verses 7, 8 and 22   [b]9 That is, about 9 inches (about 22 centimeters)
[c]11 Or *lapis lazuli*   [d]13 The precise identification of some of these precious stones is uncertain.
[e]23 The meaning of the Hebrew for this word is uncertain.

²⁴They made pomegranates of blue, purple and scarlet yarn and finely twisted linen around the hem of the robe. ²⁵And they made bells of pure gold and attached them around the hem between the pomegranates. ²⁶The bells and pomegranates alternated around the hem of the robe to be worn for ministering, as the LORD commanded Moses.

²⁷For Aaron and his sons, they made tunics of fine linen e—the work of a weaver— ²⁸and the turban f of fine linen, the linen headbands and the undergarments of finely twisted linen. ²⁹The sash was of finely twisted linen and blue, purple and scarlet yarn—the work of an embroiderer—as the LORD commanded Moses.

³⁰They made the plate, the sacred diadem, out of pure gold and engraved on it, like an inscription on a seal: HOLY TO THE LORD. ³¹Then they fastened a blue cord to it to attach it to the turban, as the LORD commanded Moses.

Moses Inspects the Tabernacle

39:32–41pp — Ex 35:10–19

³²So all the work on the tabernacle, the Tent of Meeting, was completed. The Israelites did everything just as the LORD commanded Moses. g ³³Then they brought the tabernacle to Moses: the tent and all its furnishings, its clasps, frames, crossbars, posts and bases; ³⁴the covering of ram skins dyed red, the covering of hides of sea cows a and the shielding curtain; ³⁵the ark of the Testimony h with its poles and the atonement cover; ³⁶the table with all its articles and the bread of the Presence; ³⁷the pure gold lampstand i with its row of lamps and all its accessories, and the oil for the light; ³⁸the gold altar, j the anointing oil, the fragrant incense, and the curtain k for the entrance to the tent; ³⁹the bronze altar with its bronze grating, its poles and all its utensils; the basin with its stand; ⁴⁰the curtains of the courtyard with its posts and bases, and the curtain for the entrance to the courtyard; l the ropes and tent pegs for the courtyard; all the furnishings for the tabernacle, the Tent of Meeting; ⁴¹and the woven garments worn for ministering in the sanctuary, both the sacred garments for Aaron the priest and the garments for his sons when serving as priests.

⁴²The Israelites had done all the work just as the LORD had commanded Moses. m ⁴³Moses inspected the work and saw that they had done it just as the LORD had commanded. So Moses blessed n them.

Setting Up the Tabernacle

40 Then the LORD said to Moses: ²"Set up the tabernacle, the Tent of Meeting, o on the first day of the first month. p ³Place the ark q of the Testimony in it and shield the ark with the curtain. ⁴Bring in the table and set out what belongs on it. r Then bring in the lampstand s and set up its lamps. ⁵Place the gold altar t of incense in front of the ark of the Testimony and put the curtain at the entrance to the tabernacle.

⁶"Place the altar of burnt offering in front of the entrance to the tabernacle, the Tent of Meeting; ⁷place the basin u between the Tent of Meeting and the altar and put water in it. ⁸Set up the courtyard around it and put the curtain at the entrance to the courtyard.

⁹"Take the anointing oil and anoint v the tabernacle and everything in

39:27
e Lev 6:10
39:28
f Ex 28:4
39:32
g ver 42-43;
Ex 25:9
39:35
h Ex 30:6
39:37
i Ex 25:31
39:38
j Ex 30:1-10
k Ex 36:35
39:40
l Ex 27:9-19
39:42
m Ex 25:9
39:43
n Lev 9:22,23;
Nu 6:23-27;
2Sa 6:18;
1Ki 8:14,55;
2Ch 30:27
40:2
o Nu 1:1
p ver 17; Ex 12:2
40:3
q ver 21;
Nu 4:5;
Ex 26:33
40:4
r Ex 25:30
s ver 22-25;
Ex 26:35
40:5
t ver 26; Ex 30:1
40:7
u ver 30;
Ex 30:18
40:9
v Ex 30:26;
Lev 8:10

a34 That is, dugongs

it; consecrate it and all its furnishings, and it will be holy. [10]Then anoint the altar of burnt offering and all its utensils; consecrate[w] the altar, and it will be most holy. [11]Anoint the basin and its stand and consecrate them.

[12]"Bring Aaron and his sons to the entrance to the Tent of Meeting and wash them with water.[x] [13]Then dress Aaron in the sacred garments,[y] anoint him and consecrate[z] him so he may serve me as priest. [14]Bring his sons and dress them in tunics. [15]Anoint them just as you anointed their father, so they may serve me as priests. Their anointing will be to a priesthood that will continue for all generations to come.[a]"

[16]Moses did everything just as the LORD commanded him.

[17]So the tabernacle[b] was set up on the first day of the first month[c] in the second year. [18]When Moses set up the tabernacle, he put the bases in place, erected the frames, inserted the crossbars and set up the posts. [19]Then he spread the tent over the tabernacle and put the covering over the tent, as the LORD commanded him.

[20]He took the Testimony[d] and placed it in the ark, attached the poles to the ark and put the atonement cover over it. [21]Then he brought the ark into the tabernacle and hung the shielding curtain[e] and shielded the ark of the Testimony, as the LORD commanded him.

[22]Moses placed the table[f] in the Tent of Meeting on the north side of the tabernacle outside the curtain [23]and set out the bread[g] on it before the LORD, as the LORD commanded him.

[24]He placed the lampstand[h] in the Tent of Meeting opposite the table on the south side of the tabernacle [25]and set up the lamps[i] before the LORD, as the LORD commanded him.

[26]Moses placed the gold altar[j] in the Tent of Meeting in front of the curtain [27]and burned fragrant incense on it, as the LORD commanded[k] him. [28]Then he put up the curtain[l] at the entrance to the tabernacle.

[29]He set the altar of burnt offering near the entrance to the tabernacle, the Tent of Meeting, and offered on it burnt offerings and grain offerings,[m] as the LORD commanded him.

[30]He placed the basin[n] between the Tent of Meeting and the altar and put water in it for washing, [31]and Moses and Aaron and his sons used it to wash their hands and feet. [32]They washed whenever they entered the Tent of Meeting or approached the altar,[o] as the LORD commanded Moses.

[33]Then Moses set up the courtyard[p] around the tabernacle and altar and put up the curtain[q] at the entrance to the courtyard. And so Moses finished the work.

The Glory of the LORD

[34]Then the cloud[r] covered the Tent of Meeting, and the glory of the LORD filled the tabernacle. [35]Moses could not enter the Tent of Meeting because the cloud had settled upon it, and the glory of the LORD filled the tabernacle.[s]

[36]In all the travels of the Israelites, whenever the cloud lifted from above the tabernacle, they would set out;[t] [37]but if the cloud did not lift, they did not set out—until the day it lifted. [38]So the cloud[u] of the LORD was over the tabernacle by day, and fire was in the cloud by night, in the sight of all the house of Israel during all their travels.

40:10
w Ex 29:36
40:12
x Lev 8:1-13
40:13
y Ex 28:41
z Lev 8:12
40:15
a Ex 29:9;
Nu 25:13
40:17
b Nu 7:1 c ver 2
40:20
d Ex 16:34;
25:16; Dt 10:5;
1Ki 8:9;
Heb 9:4
40:21
e Ex 26:33
40:22
f Ex 26:35
40:23
g ver 4
40:24
h Ex 26:35
40:25
i ver 4; Ex 25:37
40:26
j ver 5; Ex 30:6
40:27
k Ex 30:7
40:28
l Ex 26:36
40:29
m ver 6;
Ex 29:38-42
40:30
n ver 7
40:32
o Ex 30:20
40:33
p Ex 27:9 q ver 8
40:34
r Nu 9:15-23;
1Ki 8:12
40:35
s 1Ki 8:11;
2Ch 5:13-14
40:36
t Nu 9:17-23;
10:13; Ne 9:19
40:38
u Ex 13:21;
Nu 9:15;
1Co 10:1

Leviticus

Title and Background

Leviticus receives its name from the Septuagint (the Greek translation of the Old Testament) and means "relating to the Levites." Although Leviticus does not deal only with the special duties of the Levites, it is so named because it is concerned mainly with the service of worship at the tabernacle. Exodus had given the directions for building the tabernacle. Leviticus gives the laws and regulations for worship at the tabernacle, along with instructions on ceremonial cleanness, moral laws, holy days, the sabbath year, and the Year of Jubilee.

Author and Date of Writing

Leviticus 1:1 states that the contents of Leviticus were given to Moses by God. In more than fifty places in the book it is said that the Lord spoke to Moses. The date for the writing of the book by Moses would appear to be between about 1446 and about 1406 B.C.

Theme and Message

The key thought of Leviticus is holiness—the holiness of God and of man. The command to be holy is stated in 11:45—"be holy, because I am holy." The instructions or laws in the book were given to help the Israelites worship and live as God's holy people. Some of the instructions deal with such things as offering sacrifices, handling everyday problems concerning cleanliness, and observing special holidays. The Levitical priests are also given special instructions for making sacrifices and carrying out God's commands.

Outline

   I. Laws and Instructions for Offerings (1:1-7:38)
  II. Appointment of Aaron and His Sons as God's Priests (8:1-10:20)
 III. Rules for Holy Living (11:1-15:33)
 IV. The Day of Atonement (16:1-34)
  V. Practical Holiness (17:1-22:33)
 VI. The Sabbath, Feasts and Seasons (23:1-25:55)
VII. Conditions for God's Blessings (26:1-27:34)

The Burnt Offering

1:1
aEx 19:3; 25:22
bNu 7:89
1:2
cLev 22:18-19
1:3
dEx 12:5;
Dt 15:21;
Heb 9:14;
1Pe 1:9
eLev 17:9
1:4
fEx 29:10,15;
Lev 3:2

1 The Lord called to Moses^a and spoke to him from the Tent of Meeting. ^b He said, ²"Speak to the Israelites and say to them: 'When any of you brings an offering to the Lord, bring as your offering an animal from either the herd or the flock.^c

³" 'If the offering is a burnt offering from the herd, he is to offer a male without defect. ^d He must present it at the entrance to the Tent^e of Meeting so that it^a will be acceptable to the Lord. ⁴He is to lay his hand on the head^f of the burnt offering, and it will be accepted on his behalf

^a3 Or *he*

to make atonement[g] for him. [5]He is to slaughter[h] the young bull before the Lord, and then Aaron's sons the priests shall bring the blood and sprinkle it against the altar on all sides[i] at the entrance to the Tent of Meeting. [6]He is to skin[j] the burnt offering and cut it into pieces. [7]The sons of Aaron the priest are to put fire on the altar and arrange wood[k] on the fire. [8]Then Aaron's sons the priests shall arrange the pieces, including the head and the fat,[l] on the burning wood that is on the altar. [9]He is to wash the inner parts and the legs with water, and the priest is to burn all of it on the altar.[m] It is a burnt offering, an offering made by fire, an aroma pleasing to the Lord.[n]

[10]" 'If the offering is a burnt offering from the flock, from either the sheep or the goats,[o] he is to offer a male without defect. [11]He is to slaughter it at the north side of the altar before the Lord, and Aaron's sons the priests shall sprinkle its blood against the altar on all sides.[p] [12]He is to cut it into pieces, and the priest shall arrange them, including the head and the fat, on the burning wood that is on the altar. [13]He is to wash the inner parts and the legs with water, and the priest is to bring all of it and burn it on the altar. It is a burnt offering, an offering made by fire, an aroma pleasing to the Lord.

[14]" 'If the offering to the Lord is a burnt offering of birds, he is to offer a dove or a young pigeon.[q] [15]The priest shall bring it to the altar, wring off the head and burn it on the altar; its blood shall be drained out on the side of the altar.[r] [16]He is to remove the crop with its contents[a] and throw it to the east side of the altar, where the ashes[s] are. [17]He shall tear it open by the wings, not severing it completely,[t] and then the priest shall burn it on the wood[u] that is on the fire on the altar. It is a burnt offering, an offering made by fire, an aroma pleasing to the Lord.

The Grain Offering

2 " 'When someone brings a grain offering[v] to the Lord, his offering is to be of fine flour. He is to pour oil[w] on it, put incense on it [2]and take it to Aaron's sons the priests. The priest shall take a handful of the fine flour[x] and oil, together with all the incense,[y] and burn this as a memorial portion[z] on the altar, an offering made by fire, an aroma pleasing to the Lord. [3]The rest of the grain offering belongs to Aaron and his sons;[a] it is a most holy part of the offerings made to the Lord by fire.

[4]" 'If you bring a grain offering baked in an oven, it is to consist of fine flour: cakes made without yeast and mixed with oil, or[b] wafers made without yeast and spread with oil.[b] [5]If your grain offering is prepared on a griddle, it is to be made of fine flour mixed with oil, and without yeast. [6]Crumble it and pour oil on it; it is a grain offering. [7]If your grain offering is cooked in a pan,[c] it is to be made of fine flour and oil. [8]Bring the grain offering made of these things to the Lord; present it to the priest, who shall take it to the altar. [9]He shall take out the memorial portion[d] from the grain offering and burn it on the altar as an offering made by fire, an aroma pleasing to the Lord.[e] [10]The rest of the grain offering belongs to Aaron and his sons;[f] it is a most holy part of the offerings made to the Lord by fire.

---

[a]16 Or *crop and the feathers*; the meaning of the Hebrew for this word is uncertain.   [b]4 Or *and*

1:4
g 2Ch 29:23-24
1:5
h Lev 3:2,8
i Heb 12:24;
1Pe 1:2
1:6
j Lev 7:8
1:7
k Lev 6:12
1:8
l ver 12
1:9
m Ex 29:18
n ver 13;
Ge 8:21;
Nu 15:8-10;
Eph 5:2
1:10
o ver 3; Ex 12:5
1:11
p ver 5
1:14
q Ge 15:9;
Lev 5:7; Lk 2:24
1:15
r Lev 5:9
1:16
s Lev 6:10
1:17
t Ge 15:10
u Lev 5:8
2:1
v Lev 6:14-18
w Nu 15:4
2:2
x Lev 5:11
y Lev 6:15;
Isa 66:3 z ver 9,
16; Lev 5:12;
6:15; 24:7;
Ac 10:4
2:3
a ver 10;
Lev 6:16;
10:12,13
2:4
b Ex 29:2
2:7
c Lev 7:9
2:9
d ver 2
e Ex 29:18;
Lev 6:15
2:10
f ver 3

¹¹' 'Every grain offering you bring to the Lord must be made without yeast,ᵍ for you are not to burn any yeast or honey in an offering made to the Lord by fire. ¹²You may bring them to the Lord as an offering of the firstfruits,ʰ but they are not to be offered on the altar as a pleasing aroma. ¹³Season all your grain offerings with salt. Do not leave the salt of the covenantⁱ of your God out of your grain offerings; add salt to all your offerings.

¹⁴' 'If you bring a grain offering of firstfruitsʲ to the Lord, offer crushed heads of new grain roasted in the fire. ¹⁵Put oil and incense on it; it is a grain offering. ¹⁶The priest shall burn the memorial portionᵏ of the crushed grain and the oil, together with all the incense, as an offering made to the Lord by fire.

The Fellowship Offering

3 " 'If someone's offering is a fellowship offering,ᵃˡ and he offers an animal from the herd, whether male or female, he is to present before the Lord an animal without defect. ᵐ²He is to lay his hand on the headⁿ of his offering and slaughter itᵒ at the entrance to the Tent of Meeting. Then Aaron's sons the priests shall sprinkle the blood against the altar on all sides. ³From the fellowship offering he is to bring a sacrifice made to the Lord by fire: all the fatᵖ that covers the inner parts or is connected to them, ⁴both kidneys with the fat on them near the loins, and the covering of the liver, which he will remove with the kidneys. ⁵Then Aaron's sons�q are to burn it on the altar on top of the burnt offeringʳ that is on the burning wood, as an offering made by fire, an aroma pleasing to the Lord.

⁶' 'If he offers an animal from the flock as a fellowship offeringˢ to the Lord, he is to offer a male or female without defect. ⁷If he offers a lamb, he is to present it before the Lord.ᵗ ⁸He is to lay his hand on the head of his offering and slaughter itᵘ in front of the Tent of Meeting. Then Aaron's sons shall sprinkle its blood against the altar on all sides. ⁹From the fellowship offering he is to bring a sacrifice made to the Lord by fire: its fat, the entire fat tail cut off close to the backbone, all the fat that covers the inner parts or is connected to them, ¹⁰both kidneys with the fat on them near the loins, and the covering of the liver, which he will remove with the kidneys. ¹¹The priest shall burn them on the altarᵛ as food,ʷ an offering made to the Lord by fire.

¹²' 'If his offering is a goat, he is to present it before the Lord. ¹³He is to lay his hand on its head and slaughter it in front of the Tent of Meeting. Then Aaron's sons shall sprinkleˣ its blood against the altar on all sides. ¹⁴From what he offers he is to make this offering to the Lord by fire: all the fat that covers the inner parts or is connected to them, ¹⁵both kidneys with the fat on them near the loins, and the covering of the liver, which he will remove with the kidneys. ¹⁶The priest shall burn them on the altar as food, an offering made by fire, a pleasing aroma. All the fat is the Lord's.ʸ

¹⁷' 'This is a lasting ordinance for the generations to come,ᶻ wherever you live: You must not eat any fat or any blood.ᵃ' "

2:11
ᵍEx 23:18;
34:25; Lev 6:16
2:12
ʰLev 7:13;
23:10
2:13
ⁱNu 18:19;
Eze 43:24
2:14
ʲLev 23:10
2:16
ᵏver 2
3:1
ˡLev 7:11-34
ᵐLev 1:3; 22:21
3:2
ⁿEx 29:10,15
ᵒLev 1:5
3:3
ᵖEx 29:13
3:5
qLev 7:29-34
ʳEx 29:13,38-42
3:6
ˢver 1
3:7
ᵗLev 17:8-9
3:8
ᵘver 2; Lev 1:5
3:11
ᵛver 5 ʷver 16;
Lev 21:6,17
3:13
ˣEx 24:6
3:16
ʸ1Sa 2:16
3:17
ᶻLev 6:18; 17:7
ᵃGe 9:4;
Lev 7:25-26;
17:10-16;
Dt 12:16;
Ac 15:20

ᵃ1 Traditionally *peace offering*; also in verses 3, 6 and 9

The Sin Offering

4 The Lord said to Moses, [2]"Say to the Israelites: 'When anyone sins unintentionally[b] and does what is forbidden in any of the Lord's commands—

[3]" 'If the anointed priest sins, bringing guilt on the people, he must bring to the Lord a young bull[c] without defect as a sin offering[d] for the sin he has committed. [4]He is to present the bull at the entrance to the Tent of Meeting before the Lord. [e] He is to lay his hand on its head and slaughter it before the Lord. [5]Then the anointed priest shall take some of the bull's blood[f] and carry it into the Tent of Meeting. [6]He is to dip his finger into the blood and sprinkle some of it seven times before the Lord, in front of the curtain of the sanctuary. [7]The priest shall then put some of the blood on the horns of the altar of fragrant incense that is before the Lord in the Tent of Meeting. The rest of the bull's blood he shall pour out at the base of the altar[g] of burnt offering[h] at the entrance to the Tent of Meeting. [8]He shall remove all the fat[i] from the bull of the sin offering—the fat that covers the inner parts or is connected to them, [9]both kidneys with the fat on them near the loins, and the covering of the liver, which he will remove with the kidneys[j]— [10]just as the fat is removed from the ox[a] sacrificed as a fellowship offering.[b] Then the priest shall burn them on the altar of burnt offering. [11]But the hide of the bull and all its flesh, as well as the head and legs, the inner parts and offal[k]— [12]that is, all the rest of the bull—he must take outside the camp[l] to a place ceremonially clean,[m] where the ashes are thrown, and burn it in a wood fire on the ash heap.

[13]" 'If the whole Israelite community sins unintentionally[n] and does what is forbidden in any of the Lord's commands, even though the community is unaware of the matter, they are guilty. [14]When they become aware of the sin they committed, the assembly must bring a young bull[o] as a sin offering[p] and present it before the Tent of Meeting. [15]The elders of the community are to lay their hands on the bull's head[q] before the Lord, and the bull shall be slaughtered before the Lord. [16]Then the anointed priest is to take some of the bull's blood[r] into the Tent of Meeting. [17]He shall dip his finger into the blood and sprinkle it before the Lord[s] seven times in front of the curtain. [18]He is to put some of the blood on the horns of the altar that is before the Lord[t] in the Tent of Meeting. The rest of the blood he shall pour out at the base of the altar of burnt offering at the entrance to the Tent of Meeting. [19]He shall remove all the fat[u] from it and burn it on the altar, [20]and do with this bull just as he did with the bull for the sin offering. In this way the priest will make atonement[v] for them, and they will be forgiven.[w] [21]Then he shall take the bull outside the camp and burn it as he burned the first bull. This is the sin offering for the community.[x]

[22]" 'When a leader[y] sins unintentionally[z] and does what is forbidden in any of the commands of the Lord his God, he is guilty. [23]When he is made aware of the sin he committed, he must bring as his offering a male goat without defect. [24]He is to lay his hand on the goat's head and

---

4:2
[b]Lev 5:15-18;
Ps 19:12;
Heb 9:7
4:3
[c]ver 14;
Ps 66:15
[d]Lev 9:2-22;
Heb 9:13-14
4:4
[e]Lev 1:3
4:5
[f]Lev 16:14
4:7
[g]ver 34;
Lev 8:15
[h]ver 18,30;
Lev 5:9; 9:9;
16:18
4:8
[i]Lev 3:3-5
4:9
[j]Lev 3:4
4:11
[k]Ex 29:14;
Lev 9:11;
Nu 19:5
4:12
[l]Heb 13:11
[m]Lev 6:11
4:13
[n]ver 2;
Lev 5:2-4,17;
Nu 15:24-26
4:14
[o]ver 3
[p]ver 23,28
4:15
[q]Lev 1:4; 8:14,
22; Nu 8:10
4:16
[r]ver 5
4:17
[s]ver 6
4:18
[t]ver 7
4:19
[u]ver 8
4:20
[v]Heb 10:10-12
[w]Nu 15:25
4:21
[x]Lev 16:5,15
4:22
[y]Nu 31:13
[z]ver 2

---

[a]10 The Hebrew word can include both male and female.   [b]10 Traditionally *peace offering*; also in verses 26, 31 and 35

slaughter it at the place where the burnt offering is slaughtered before the LORD. It is a sin offering. 25Then the priest shall take some of the blood of the sin offering with his finger and put it on the horns of the altar of burnt offering and pour out the rest of the blood at the base of the altar. [a] 26He shall burn all the fat on the altar as he burned the fat of the fellowship offering. In this way the priest will make atonement for the man's sin, and he will be forgiven. [b]

27" 'If a member of the community sins unintentionally[c] and does what is forbidden in any of the LORD's commands, he is guilty. 28When he is made aware of the sin he committed, he must bring as his offering[d] for the sin he committed a female goat[e] without defect. 29He is to lay his hand on the head[f] of the sin offering[g] and slaughter it at the place of the burnt offering. 30Then the priest is to take some of the blood with his finger and put it on the horns of the altar of burnt offering[h] and pour out the rest of the blood at the base of the altar. 31He shall remove all the fat, just as the fat is removed from the fellowship offering, and the priest shall burn it on the altar as an aroma pleasing to the LORD. [i] In this way the priest will make atonement for him, and he will be forgiven.

32" 'If he brings a lamb as his sin offering, he is to bring a female without defect.[j] 33He is to lay his hand on its head and slaughter it for a sin offering at the place where the burnt offering is slaughtered.[k] 34Then the priest shall take some of the blood of the sin offering with his finger and put it on the horns of the altar of burnt offering and pour out the rest of the blood at the base of the altar.[l] 35He shall remove all the fat, just as the fat is removed from the lamb of the fellowship offering, and the priest shall burn it on the altar[m] on top of the offerings made to the LORD by fire. In this way the priest will make atonement for him for the sin he has committed, and he will be forgiven.

5 " 'If a person sins because he does not speak up when he hears a public charge to testify[n] regarding something he has seen or learned about, he will be held responsible. [o]

2" 'Or if a person touches anything ceremonially unclean—whether the carcasses of unclean wild animals or of unclean livestock or of unclean creatures that move along the ground[p]—even though he is unaware of it, he has become unclean and is guilty.

3" 'Or if he touches human uncleanness[q]—anything that would make him unclean—even though he is unaware of it, when he learns of it he will be guilty.

4" 'Or if a person thoughtlessly takes an oath[r] to do anything, whether good or evil—in any matter one might carelessly swear about—even though he is unaware of it, in any case when he learns of it he will be guilty.

5" 'When anyone is guilty in any of these ways, he must confess[s] in what way he has sinned 6and, as a penalty for the sin he has committed, he must bring to the LORD a female lamb or goat from the flock as a sin offering;[t] and the priest shall make atonement for him for his sin.

7" 'If he cannot afford[u] a lamb, he is to bring two doves or two young pigeons to the LORD as a penalty for his sin—one for a sin offering and the other for a burnt offering. 8He is to bring them to the priest, who shall first offer the one for the sin offering. He is to wring its head from

4:25
a ver 7,18,30,34;
Lev 9:9
4:26
b Lev 5:10
4:27
c ver 2;
Nu 15:27
4:28
d ver 23 e ver 3
4:29
f ver 4,24
g Lev 1:4
4:30
h ver 7
4:31
i Ge 8:21
4:32
j ver 28
4:33
k ver 29
4:34
l ver 7
4:35
m ver 26,31
5:1
n Pr 29:24
o ver 17
5:2
p Lev 11:11,
24-40; Dt 14:8
5:3
q Nu 19:11-16
5:4
r Nu 30:6,8
5:5
s Lev 16:21;
26:40; Nu 5:7;
Pr 28:13
5:6
t Lev 4:28
5:7
u Lev 12:8;
14:21

its neck,[v] not severing it completely,[w] [9]and is to sprinkle some of the blood of the sin offering against the side of the altar; the rest of the blood must be drained out at the base of the altar.[x] It is a sin offering. [10]The priest shall then offer the other as a burnt offering in the prescribed way[y] and make atonement for him for the sin he has committed, and he will be forgiven.[z]

[11]" 'If, however, he cannot afford two doves or two young pigeons, he is to bring as an offering for his sin a tenth of an ephah[a] of fine flour[a] for a sin offering. He must not put oil or incense on it, because it is a sin offering. [12]He is to bring it to the priest, who shall take a handful of it as a memorial portion and burn it on the altar on top of the offerings made to the LORD by fire. It is a sin offering. [13]In this way the priest will make atonement[b] for him for any of these sins he has committed, and he will be forgiven. The rest of the offering will belong to the priest,[c] as in the case of the grain offering.' "

The Guilt Offering

[14]The LORD said to Moses: [15]"When a person commits a violation and sins unintentionally in regard to any of the LORD's holy things, he is to bring to the LORD as a penalty[d] a ram[e] from the flock, one without defect and of the proper value in silver, according to the sanctuary shekel.[b][f] It is a guilt offering. [16]He must make restitution[g] for what he has failed to do in regard to the holy things, add a fifth of the value[h] to that and give it all to the priest, who will make atonement for him with the ram as a guilt offering, and he will be forgiven.

[17]"If a person sins and does what is forbidden in any of the LORD's commands, even though he does not know it,[i] he is guilty and will be held responsible. [18]He is to bring to the priest as a guilt offering a ram from the flock, one without defect and of the proper value. In this way the priest will make atonement for him for the wrong he has committed unintentionally, and he will be forgiven.[j] [19]It is a guilt offering; he has been guilty of[c] wrongdoing against the LORD."

6 The LORD said to Moses: [2]"If anyone sins and is unfaithful to the LORD[k] by deceiving his neighbor[l] about something entrusted to him or left in his care[m] or stolen, or if he cheats him, [3]or if he finds lost property and lies about it,[n] or if he swears falsely, or if he commits any such sin that people may do— [4]when he thus sins and becomes guilty, he must return[o] what he has stolen or taken by extortion, or what was entrusted to him, or the lost property he found, [5]or whatever it was he swore falsely about. He must make restitution[p] in full, add a fifth of the value to it and give it all to the owner on the day he presents his guilt offering. [q] [6]And as a penalty he must bring to the priest, that is, to the LORD, his guilt offering,[r] a ram from the flock, one without defect and of the proper value. [7]In this way the priest will make atonement[s] for him before the LORD, and he will be forgiven for any of these things he did that made him guilty."

The Burnt Offering

[8]The LORD said to Moses: [9]"Give Aaron and his sons this command:

5:8
vLev 1:15
wLev 1:17
5:9
xLev 4:7,18
5:10
yLev 1:14-17
zLev 4:26
5:11
aLev 2:1
5:13
bLev 4:26
cLev 2:3
5:15
dLev 22:14
eNu 5:8
fEx 30:13
5:16
gLev 6:4
hLev 22:14; Nu 5:7
5:17
iver 15; Lev 4:2
5:18
jver 15
6:2
kNu 5:6; Ac 5:4; Col 3:9
lPr 24:28
mEx 22:7
6:3
nDt 22:1-3
6:4
oLk 19:8
6:5
pNu 5:7
qLev 5:15
6:6
rLev 5:15
6:7
sLev 4:26

---

[a]11 That is, probably about 2 quarts (about 2 liters) [b]15 That is, about 2/5 ounce (about 11.5 grams) [c]19 Or *has made full expiation for his*

'These are the regulations for the burnt offering: The burnt offering is to remain on the altar hearth throughout the night, till morning, and the fire must be kept burning on the altar. ¹⁰The priest shall then put on his linen clothes, with linen undergarments next to his body,ᵗ and shall remove the ashes of the burnt offering that the fire has consumed on the altar and place them beside the altar. ¹¹Then he is to take off these clothes and put on others, and carry the ashes outside the camp to a place that is ceremonially clean.ᵘ ¹²The fire on the altar must be kept burning; it must not go out. Every morning the priest is to add firewood and arrange the burnt offering on the fire and burn the fat of the fellowship offeringsᵃ on it. ¹³The fire must be kept burning on the altar continuously; it must not go out.

The Grain Offering

¹⁴'' 'These are the regulations for the grain offering:ᵛ Aaron's sons are to bring it before the LORD, in front of the altar. ¹⁵The priest is to take a handful of fine flour and oil, together with all the incense on the grain offering,ʷ and burn the memorial portionˣ on the altar as an aroma pleasing to the LORD. ¹⁶Aaron and his sonsʸ shall eat the restᶻ of it, but it is to be eaten without yeastᵃ in a holy place;ᵇ they are to eat it in the courtyard of the Tent of Meeting. ¹⁷It must not be baked with yeast; I have given it as their share of the offerings made to me by fire. Like the sin offering and the guilt offering, it is most holy.ᶜ ¹⁸Any male descendant of Aaron may eat it.ᵈ It is his regular share of the offerings made to the LORD by fire for the generations to come. Whatever touches them will become holy.ᵇ ᵉ' ''

¹⁹The LORD also said to Moses, ²⁰"This is the offering Aaron and his sons are to bring to the LORD on the day heᶜ is anointed: a tenth of an ephahᵈ ᶠ of fine flour as a regular grain offering,ᵍ half of it in the morning and half in the evening. ²¹Prepare it with oil on a griddle;ʰ bring it well-mixed and present the grain offering brokenᵉ in pieces as an aroma pleasing to the LORD. ²²The son who is to succeed him as anointed priest shall prepare it. It is the LORD's regular share and is to be burned completely. ²³Every grain offering of a priest shall be burned completely; it must not be eaten."

The Sin Offering

²⁴The LORD said to Moses, ²⁵"Say to Aaron and his sons: 'These are the regulations for the sin offering: The sin offering is to be slaughtered before the LORDⁱ in the placeʲ the burnt offering is slaughtered; it is most holy. ²⁶The priest who offers it shall eat it; it is to be eaten in a holy place,ᵏ in the courtyardˡ of the Tent of Meeting. ²⁷Whatever touches any of the flesh will become holy,ᵐ and if any of the blood is spattered on a garment, you must wash it in a holy place. ²⁸The clay potⁿ the meat is cooked in must be broken; but if it is cooked in a bronze pot, the pot is to be scoured and rinsed with water. ²⁹Any male in a priest's family may eat it;ᵒ it is most holy.ᵖ ³⁰But any sin offering whose blood is

6:10
ᵗEx 28:39-42,43; 39:28
6:11
ᵘLev 4:12
6:14
ᵛLev 2:1; 15:4
6:15
ʷLev 2:9
ˣLev 2:2
6:16
ʸLev 2:3
ᶻEze 44:29
ᵃLev 2:11
ᵇLev 10:13
6:17
ᶜver 29; Ex 40:10; Nu 18:9,10
6:18
ᵈver 29; Nu 18:9-10
ᵉver 27
6:20
ᶠEx 16:36
ᵍEx 29:2
6:21
ʰLev 2:5
6:25
ⁱLev 1:3
ʲLev 1:5,11
6:26
ᵏver 16
ˡLev 10:17-18
6:27
ᵐEx 29:37
6:28
ⁿLev 11:33; 15:12
6:29
ᵒver 18 ᵖver 17

ᵃ12 Traditionally *peace offerings*   ᵇ18 Or *Whoever touches them must be holy* ; similarly in verse 27   ᶜ20 Or *each*   ᵈ20 That is, probably about 2 quarts (about 2 liters)   ᵉ21 The meaning of the Hebrew for this word is uncertain.

brought into the Tent of Meeting to make atonement in the Holy Place⁹ must not be eaten; it must be burned. ʳ

The Guilt Offering

7 " 'These are the regulations for the guilt offering,ˢ which is most holy: ²The guilt offering is to be slaughtered in the place where the burnt offering is slaughtered, and its blood is to be sprinkled against the altar on all sides. ³All its fatᵗ shall be offered: the fat tail and the fat that covers the inner parts, ⁴both kidneys with the fat on them near the loins, and the covering of the liver, which is to be removed with the kidneys. ⁵The priest shall burn them on the altar as an offering made to the LORD by fire. It is a guilt offering. ⁶Any male in a priest's family may eat it,ᵘ but it must be eaten in a holy place; it is most holy. ᵛ

⁷" 'The same law applies to both the sin offering and the guilt offering: They belong to the priestᵂ who makes atonement with them. ⁸The priest who offers a burnt offering for anyone may keep its hide for himself. ⁹Every grain offering baked in an oven or cooked in a pan or on a griddleˣ belongs to the priest who offers it, ¹⁰and every grain offering, whether mixed with oil or dry, belongs equally to all the sons of Aaron.

The Fellowship Offering

¹¹" 'These are the regulations for the fellowship offeringᵃ a person may present to the LORD:

¹²" 'If he offers it as an expression of thankfulness, then along with this thank offeringʸ he is to offer cakes of bread made without yeast and mixed with oil, wafersᶻ made without yeast and spread with oil, and cakes of fine flour well-kneaded and mixed with oil. ¹³Along with his fellowship offering of thanksgiving he is to present an offering with cakes of bread made with yeast. ᵃ ¹⁴He is to bring one of each kind as an offering, a contribution to the LORD; it belongs to the priest who sprinkles the blood of the fellowship offerings. ¹⁵The meat of his fellowship offering of thanksgiving must be eaten on the day it is offered; he must leave none of it till morning. ᵇ

¹⁶" 'If, however, his offering is the result of a vow or is a freewill offering, the sacrifice shall be eaten on the day he offers it, but anything left over may be eaten on the next day. ᶜ ¹⁷Any meat of the sacrifice left over till the third day must be burned up. ¹⁸If any meat of the fellowship offering is eaten on the third day, it will not be accepted. ᵈ It will not be creditedᵉ to the one who offered it, for it is impure; the person who eats any of it will be held responsible.

¹⁹" 'Meat that touches anything ceremonially unclean must not be eaten; it must be burned up. As for other meat, anyone ceremonially clean may eat it. ²⁰But if anyone who is unclean eats any meat of the fellowship offering belonging to the LORD, that person must be cut off from his people. ᶠ ²¹If anyone touches something uncleanᵍ—whether human uncleanness or an unclean animal or any unclean, detestable thing—and then eats any of the meat of the fellowship offering belonging to the LORD, that person must be cut off from his people.' "

6:30
qLev 4:18
rLev 4:12
7:1
sLev 5:14-6:7
7:3
tEx 29:13;
Lev 3:4,9
7:6
uLev 6:18;
Nu 18:9-10
vLev 2:3
7:7
wLev 6:17,26;
1Co 9:13
7:9
xLev 2:5
7:12
yver 13,15
zLev 2:4;
Nu 6:15
7:13
aLev 23:17;
Am 4:5
7:15
bLev 22:30
7:16
cLev 19:5-8
7:18
dLev 19:7
eNu 18:27
7:20
fLev 22:3-7
7:21
gLev 5:2;
11:24,28

ᵃ11 Traditionally *peace offering*; also in verses 13-37

Eating Fat and Blood Forbidden

²²The Lord said to Moses, ²³"Say to the Israelites: 'Do not eat any of the fat of cattle, sheep or goats. ^h ²⁴The fat of an animal found dead or torn by wild animalsⁱ may be used for any other purpose, but you must not eat it. ²⁵Anyone who eats the fat of an animal from which an offering by fire may be^a made to the Lord must be cut off from his people. ²⁶And wherever you live, you must not eat the blood^j of any bird or animal. ²⁷If anyone eats blood, ^k that person must be cut off from his people.' "

The Priests' Share

²⁸The Lord said to Moses, ²⁹"Say to the Israelites: 'Anyone who brings a fellowship offering to the Lord is to bring part of it as his sacrifice to the Lord. ³⁰With his own hands he is to bring the offering made to the Lord by fire; he is to bring the fat, together with the breast, and wave the breast before the Lord as a wave offering.^l ³¹The priest shall burn the fat on the altar, but the breast belongs to Aaron and his sons. ^m ³²You are to give the right thigh of your fellowship offerings to the priest as a contribution. ⁿ ³³The son of Aaron who offers the blood and the fat of the fellowship offering shall have the right thigh as his share. ³⁴From the fellowship offerings of the Israelites, I have taken the breast that is waved and the thigh^o that is presented and have given them to Aaron the priest and his sons^p as their regular share from the Israelites.' "

³⁵This is the portion of the offerings made to the Lord by fire that were allotted to Aaron and his sons on the day they were presented to serve the Lord as priests. ³⁶On the day they were anointed, ^q the Lord commanded that the Israelites give this to them as their regular share for the generations to come.

³⁷These, then, are the regulations for the burnt offering,^r the grain offering,^s the sin offering, the guilt offering, the ordination offering^t and the fellowship offering, ³⁸which the Lord gave Moses on Mount Sinai on the day he commanded the Israelites to bring their offerings to the Lord, ^u in the Desert of Sinai.

The Ordination of Aaron and His Sons

8:1–36pp — Ex 29:1–37

8 The Lord said to Moses, ²"Bring Aaron and his sons, their garments, the anointing oil,^v the bull for the sin offering, the two rams and the basket containing bread made without yeast,^w ³and gather the entire assembly^x at the entrance to the Tent of Meeting." ⁴Moses did as the Lord commanded him, and the assembly gathered at the entrance to the Tent of Meeting.

⁵Moses said to the assembly, "This is what the Lord has commanded to be done." ⁶Then Moses brought Aaron and his sons forward and washed them with water.^y ⁷He put the tunic on Aaron, tied the sash around him, clothed him with the robe and put the ephod on him. He also tied the ephod to him by its skillfully woven waistband; so it was fastened on him.^z ⁸He placed the breastpiece on him and put the Urim

### Cross references (margin)

7:23
h Lev 3:17;
17:13-14
7:24
i Ex 22:31
7:26
j Ge 9:4
7:27
k Lev 17:10-24;
Ac 15:20,29
7:30
l Ex 29:24;
Nu 6:20
7:31
m ver 34
7:32
n ver 34;
Lev 9:21;
Nu 6:20
7:34
o Lev 10:15
p Ex 29:27;
Nu 18:18-19
7:36
q Ex 40:13,15;
Lev 8:12,30
7:37
r Lev 6:9
s Lev 6:14
t ver 1,11
7:38
u Lev 1:2
8:2
v Ex 30:23-25,30
w Ex 29:2-3
8:3
x Nu 8:9
8:6
y Ex 29:4;
30:19; Ps 26:6;
Ac 22:16;
1Co 6:11;
Eph 5:26
8:7
z Ex 28:4

---

^a25 Or *fire is*

and Thummim[a] in the breastpiece. [9]Then he placed the turban on Aaron's head and set the gold plate, the sacred diadem,[b] on the front of it, as the LORD commanded Moses.

[10]Then Moses took the anointing oil[c] and anointed[d] the tabernacle and everything in it, and so consecrated them. [11]He sprinkled some of the oil on the altar seven times, anointing the altar and all its utensils and the basin with its stand, to consecrate them.[e] [12]He poured some of the anointing oil on Aaron's head and anointed[f] him to consecrate him.[g] [13]Then he brought Aaron's sons forward, put tunics on them, tied sashes around them and put headbands on them, as the LORD commanded Moses.

[14]He then presented the bull[h] for the sin offering,[i] and Aaron and his sons laid their hands on its head. [15]Moses slaughtered the bull and took some of the blood, and with his finger he put it on all the horns of the altar[j] to purify the altar.[k] He poured out the rest of the blood at the base of the altar. So he consecrated it to make atonement for it.[l] [16]Moses also took all the fat around the inner parts, the covering of the liver, and both kidneys and their fat, and burned it on the altar. [17]But the bull with its hide and its flesh and its offal[m] he burned up outside the camp,[n] as the LORD commanded Moses.

[18]He then presented the ram[o] for the burnt offering, and Aaron and his sons laid their hands on its head. [19]Then Moses slaughtered the ram and sprinkled the blood against the altar on all sides. [20]He cut the ram into pieces and burned the head, the pieces and the fat. [21]He washed the inner parts and the legs with water and burned the whole ram on the altar as a burnt offering, a pleasing aroma, an offering made to the LORD by fire, as the LORD commanded Moses.

[22]He then presented the other ram, the ram for the ordination,[p] and Aaron and his sons laid their hands on its head. [23]Moses slaughtered the ram and took some of its blood and put it on the lobe of Aaron's right ear, on the thumb of his right hand and on the big toe of his right foot. [24]Moses also brought Aaron's sons forward and put some of the blood on the lobes of their right ears, on the thumbs of their right hands and on the big toes of their right feet. Then he sprinkled blood against the altar on all sides.[q] [25]He took the fat, the fat tail, all the fat around the inner parts, the covering of the liver, both kidneys and their fat and the right thigh. [26]Then from the basket of bread made without yeast, which was before the LORD, he took a cake of bread, and one made with oil, and a wafer; he put these on the fat portions and on the right thigh. [27]He put all these in the hands of Aaron and his sons and waved them before the LORD as a wave offering. [28]Then Moses took them from their hands and burned them on the altar on top of the burnt offering as an ordination offering, a pleasing aroma, an offering made to the LORD by fire. [29]He also took the breast—Moses' share of the ordination ram[r]— and waved it before the LORD as a wave offering, as the LORD commanded Moses.

[30]Then Moses took some of the anointing oil and some of the blood from the altar and sprinkled them on Aaron and his garments[s] and on his sons and their garments. So he consecrated[t] Aaron and his garments and his sons and their garments.

[31]Moses then said to Aaron and his sons, "Cook the meat at the entrance to the Tent of Meeting and eat it there with the bread from the

8:8
a Ex 28:30
8:9
b Ex 28:36
8:10
c ver 2 d Ex 30:26
8:11
e Ex 30:29
8:12
f Lev 21:10,12
g Ex 30:30
8:14
h Lev 4:3
i Ps 66:15;
Eze 43:19
8:15
j Lev 4:7
k Heb 9:22
l Eze 43:20
8:17
m Lev 4:11
n Lev 4:12
8:18
o ver 2
8:22
p ver 2
8:24
q Heb 9:18-22
8:29
r Lev 7:31-34
8:30
s Ex 28:2
t Nu 3:3

basket of ordination offerings, as I commanded, saying,[a] 'Aaron and his sons are to eat it.' 32Then burn up the rest of the meat and the bread. 33Do not leave the entrance to the Tent of Meeting for seven days, until the days of your ordination are completed, for your ordination will last seven days. 34What has been done today was commanded by the LORD[u] to make atonement for you. 35You must stay at the entrance to the Tent of Meeting day and night for seven days and do what the LORD requires,[v] so you will not die; for that is what I have been commanded." 36So Aaron and his sons did everything the LORD commanded through Moses.

The Priests Begin Their Ministry

9 On the eighth day[w] Moses summoned Aaron and his sons and the elders of Israel. 2He said to Aaron, "Take a bull calf for your sin offering and a ram for your burnt offering, both without defect, and present them before the LORD. 3Then say to the Israelites: 'Take a male goat for a sin offering, a calf and a lamb—both a year old and without defect—for a burnt offering, 4and an ox[b] and a ram for a fellowship offering[c] to sacrifice before the LORD, together with a grain offering mixed with oil. For today the LORD will appear to you.[x]' "

5They took the things Moses commanded to the front of the Tent of Meeting, and the entire assembly came near and stood before the LORD. 6Then Moses said, "This is what the LORD has commanded you to do, so that the glory of the LORD[y] may appear to you."

7Moses said to Aaron, "Come to the altar and sacrifice your sin offering and your burnt offering and make atonement for yourself and the people; sacrifice the offering that is for the people and make atonement for them, as the LORD has commanded.[z]"

8So Aaron came to the altar and slaughtered the calf as a sin offering[a] for himself. 9His sons brought the blood to him,[b] and he dipped his finger into the blood and put it on the horns of the altar; the rest of the blood he poured out at the base of the altar.[c] 10On the altar he burned the fat, the kidneys and the covering of the liver from the sin offering, as the LORD commanded Moses; 11the flesh and the hide[d] he burned up outside the camp.[e]

12Then he slaughtered the burnt offering. His sons handed him the blood, and he sprinkled it against the altar on all sides. 13They handed him the burnt offering piece by piece, including the head, and he burned them on the altar.[f] 14He washed the inner parts and the legs and burned them on top of the burnt offering on the altar.

15Aaron then brought the offering that was for the people.[g] He took the goat for the people's sin offering and slaughtered it and offered it for a sin offering as he did with the first one.

16He brought the burnt offering and offered it in the prescribed way.[h] 17He also brought the grain offering, took a handful of it and burned it on the altar in addition to the morning's burnt offering.[i]

18He slaughtered the ox and the ram as the fellowship offering for the people.[j] His sons handed him the blood, and he sprinkled it against the altar on all sides. 19But the fat portions of the ox and the ram—the

8:34
u Heb 7:16
8:35
v Nu 3:7; 9:19;
Dt 11:1;
1Ki 2:3;
Eze 48:11
9:1
w Eze 43:27
9:4
x Ex 29:43
9:6
y ver 23;
Ex 24:16
9:7
z Heb 5:1,3;
7:27
9:8
a Lev 4:1-12
9:9
b ver 12,18
c Lev 4:7
9:11
d Lev 4:11
e Lev 4:12; 8:17
9:13
f Lev 1:8
9:15
g Lev 4:27-31
9:16
h Lev 1:1-13
9:17
i Lev 2:1-2; 3:5
9:18
j Lev 3:1-11

---

a31 Or *I was commanded:*　　b4 The Hebrew word can include both male and female; also in verses 18 and 19.　　c4 Traditionally *peace offering;* also in verses 18 and 22

fat tail, the layer of fat, the kidneys and the covering of the liver—
20these they laid on the breasts, and then Aaron burned the fat on the
altar. 21Aaron waved the breasts and the right thigh before the LORD as
a wave offering,k as Moses commanded.

22Then Aaron lifted his hands toward the people and blessed them.l
And having sacrificed the sin offering, the burnt offering and the
fellowship offering, he stepped down.

23Moses and Aaron then went into the Tent of Meeting. When they
came out, they blessed the people; and the glory of the LORDm appeared
to all the people. 24Firen came out from the presence of the LORD and
consumed the burnt offering and the fat portions on the altar. And
when all the people saw it, they shouted for joy and fell facedown.o

The Death of Nadab and Abihu

10 Aaron's sons Nadab and Abihup took their censers, put fire in
themq and added incense; and they offered unauthorized fire
before the LORD, contrary to his command.r 2So fire came out from the
presence of the LORD and consumed them,s and they died before the
LORD. 3Moses then said to Aaron, "This is what the LORD spoke of
when he said:

" 'Among those who approach met
   I will show myself holy;u
in the sight of all the people
   I will be honored.v' "

Aaron remained silent.

4Moses summoned Mishael and Elzaphan,w sons of Aaron's uncle
Uzziel,x and said to them, "Come here; carry your cousins outside the
camp,y away from the front of the sanctuary." 5So they came and
carried them, still in their tunics,z outside the camp, as Moses ordered.

6Then Moses said to Aaron and his sons Eleazar and Ithamar, "Do
not let your hair become unkempt,aa and do not tear your clothes, or
you will die and the LORD will be angry with the whole community.b
But your relatives, all the house of Israel, may mourn for those the
LORD has destroyed by fire. 7Do not leave the entrance to the Tent of
Meeting or you will die, because the LORD's anointing oilc is on you."
So they did as Moses said.

8Then the LORD said to Aaron, 9"You and your sons are not to drink
wined or other fermented drinke whenever you go into the Tent of
Meeting, or you will die. This is a lasting ordinance for the generations
to come. 10You must distinguish between the holy and the common,
between the unclean and the clean,f 11and you must teachg the Israelites all the decrees the LORD has given them through Moses.h"

12Moses said to Aaron and his remaining sons, Eleazar and Ithamar,
"Take the grain offering left over from the offerings made to the LORD
by fire and eat it prepared without yeast beside the altar,i for it is most
holy. 13Eat it in a holy place, because it is your share and your sons'
share of the offerings made to the LORD by fire; for so I have been
commanded. 14But you and your sons and your daughters may eat the
breast that was waved and the thigh that was presented. Eat them in a

9:21
kEx 29:24,26;
Lev 7:30-34
9:22
lNu 6:23;
Dt 21:5;
Lk 24:50
9:23
mver 6
9:24
nJdg 6:21;
2Ch 7:1
o1Ki 18:39
10:1
pEx 24:1;
Nu 3:2-4; 26:61
qLev 16:12
rEx 30:9
10:2
sNu 3:4; 16:35;
26:61
10:3
tEx 19:22
uEx 30:29;
Lev 21:6;
Eze 28:22
vIsa 49:3
10:4
wEx 6:22
xEx 6:18
yAc 5:6,9,10
10:5
zLev 8:13
10:6
aLev 21:10
bNu 1:53;
16:22; Jos 7:1;
22:18; 2Sa 24:1
10:7
cEx 28:41;
Lev 21:12
10:9
dHos 4:11
ePr 20:1;
Isa 28:7;
Eze 44:21;
Lk 1:15;
Eph 5:18;
1Ti 3:3; Tit 1:7
10:10
fLev 11:47;
20:25;
Eze 22:26
10:11
gMal 2:7
hDt 24:8
10:12
iLev 6:14-18;
21:22

---

a6 Or *Do not uncover your heads*

ceremonially clean place;ʲ they have been given to you and your children as your share of the Israelites' fellowship offerings.ᵃ ¹⁵The thighᵏ that was presented and the breast that was waved must be brought with the fat portions of the offerings made by fire, to be waved before the LORD as a wave offering. This will be the regular share for you and your children, as the LORD has commanded."

¹⁶When Moses inquired about the goat of the sin offeringˡ and found that it had been burned up, he was angry with Eleazar and Ithamar, Aaron's remaining sons, and asked, ¹⁷"Why didn't you eat the sin offeringᵐ in the sanctuary area? It is most holy; it was given to you to take away the guilt of the community by making atonement for them before the LORD. ¹⁸Since its blood was not taken into the Holy Place,ⁿ you should have eaten the goat in the sanctuary area, as I commanded."

¹⁹Aaron replied to Moses, "Today they sacrificed their sin offering and their burnt offeringᵒ before the LORD, but such things as this have happened to me. Would the LORD have been pleased if I had eaten the sin offering today?" ²⁰When Moses heard this, he was satisfied.

Clean and Unclean Food

11:1–23pp — Dt 14:3–20

11 The LORD said to Moses and Aaron, ²"Say to the Israelites: 'Of all the animals that live on land, these are the ones you may eat:ᵖ ³You may eat any animal that has a split hoof completely divided and that chews the cud.

⁴" 'There are some that only chew the cud or only have a split hoof, but you must not eat them. The camel, though it chews the cud, does not have a split hoof; it is ceremonially unclean for you. ⁵The coney,ᵇ though it chews the cud, does not have a split hoof; it is unclean for you. ⁶The rabbit, though it chews the cud, does not have a split hoof; it is unclean for you. ⁷And the pig, �q though it has a split hoof completely divided, does not chew the cud; it is unclean for you. ⁸You must not eat their meat or touch their carcasses; they are unclean for you.ʳ

⁹" 'Of all the creatures living in the water of the seas and the streams, you may eat any that have fins and scales. ¹⁰But all creatures in the seas or streams that do not have fins and scales—whether among all the swarming things or among all the other living creatures in the water—you are to detest.ˢ ¹¹And since you are to detest them, you must not eat their meat and you must detest their carcasses. ¹²Anything living in the water that does not have fins and scales is to be detestable to you.

¹³" 'These are the birds you are to detest and not eat because they are detestable: the eagle, the vulture, the black vulture, ¹⁴the red kite, any kind of black kite, ¹⁵any kind of raven, ¹⁶the horned owl, the screech owl, the gull, any kind of hawk, ¹⁷the little owl, the cormorant, the great owl, ¹⁸the white owl, the desert owl, the osprey, ¹⁹the stork, any kind of heron, the hoopoe and the bat.ᶜ

²⁰" 'All flying insects that walk on all fours are to be detestable to you.ᵗ ²¹There are, however, some winged creatures that walk on all fours that you may eat: those that have jointed legs for hopping on the

10:14
ʲEx 29:24,26-27;
Lev 7:31,34;
Nu 18:11
10:15
ᵏLev 7:34
10:16
ˡLev 9:3
10:17
ᵐLev 6:24-30
10:18
ⁿLev 6:26,30
10:19
ᵒLev 9:12
11:2
ᵖAc 10:12-14
11:7
qIsa 65:4;
66:3,17
11:8
ʳIsa 52:11;
Heb 9:10
11:10
ˢLev 7:18
11:20
ᵗAc 10:14

ᵃ14 Traditionally *peace offerings*   ᵇ5 That is, the hyrax or rock badger   ᶜ19 The precise identification of some of the birds, insects and animals in this chapter is uncertain.

ground. ²²Of these you may eat any kind of locust,ᵘ katydid, cricket or grasshopper. ²³But all other winged creatures that have four legs you are to detest.

²⁴" 'You will make yourselves unclean by these; whoever touches their carcasses will be unclean till evening. ²⁵Whoever picks up one of their carcasses must wash his clothes,ᵛ and he will be unclean till evening.ʷ

²⁶" 'Every animal that has a split hoof not completely divided or that does not chew the cud is unclean for you; whoever touches ˌthe carcass ofˌ any of them will be unclean. ²⁷Of all the animals that walk on all fours, those that walk on their paws are unclean for you; whoever touches their carcasses will be unclean till evening. ²⁸Anyone who picks up their carcasses must wash his clothes, and he will be unclean till evening. They are unclean for you.

²⁹" 'Of the animals that move about on the ground, these are unclean for you: the weasel, the rat,ˣ any kind of great lizard, ³⁰the gecko, the monitor lizard, the wall lizard, the skink and the chameleon. ³¹Of all those that move along the ground, these are unclean for you. Whoever touches them when they are dead will be unclean till evening. ³²When one of them dies and falls on something, that article, whatever its use, will be unclean, whether it is made of wood, cloth, hide or sackcloth.ʸ Put it in water; it will be unclean till evening, and then it will be clean. ³³If one of them falls into a clay pot, everything in it will be unclean, and you must break the pot.ᶻ ³⁴Any food that could be eaten but has water on it from such a pot is unclean, and any liquid that could be drunk from it is unclean. ³⁵Anything that one of their carcasses falls on becomes unclean; an oven or cooking pot must be broken up. They are unclean, and you are to regard them as unclean. ³⁶A spring, however, or a cistern for collecting water remains clean, but anyone who touches one of these carcasses is unclean. ³⁷If a carcass falls on any seeds that are to be planted, they remain clean. ³⁸But if water has been put on the seed and a carcass falls on it, it is unclean for you.

³⁹" 'If an animal that you are allowed to eat dies, anyone who touches the carcass will be unclean till evening. ⁴⁰Anyone who eats some of the carcass must wash his clothes, and he will be unclean till evening.ᵃ Anyone who picks up the carcass must wash his clothes, and he will be unclean till evening.

⁴¹" 'Every creature that moves about on the ground is detestable; it is not to be eaten. ⁴²You are not to eat any creature that moves about on the ground, whether it moves on its belly or walks on all fours or on many feet; it is detestable. ⁴³Do not defile yourselves by any of these creatures.ᵇ Do not make yourselves unclean by means of them or be made unclean by them. ⁴⁴I am the LORD your God;ᶜ consecrate yourselvesᵈ and be holy,ᵉ because I am holy.ᶠ Do not make yourselves unclean by any creature that moves about on the ground. ⁴⁵I am the LORD who brought you up out of Egyptᵍ to be your God;ʰ therefore be holy, because I am holy.ⁱ

⁴⁶" 'These are the regulations concerning animals, birds, every living thing that moves in the water and every creature that moves about on the ground. ⁴⁷You must distinguish between the unclean and the clean, between living creatures that may be eaten and those that may not be eaten.ʲ ' "

11:22
ᵘMt 3:4;
Mk 1:6
11:25
ᵛLev 14:8,47;
15:5 ʷver 40;
Nu 31:24
11:29
ˣIsa 66:17
11:32
ʸLev 15:12
11:33
ᶻLev 6:28;
15:12
11:40
ᵃLev 17:15;
22:8; Eze 44:31
11:43
ᵇLev 20:25
11:44
ᶜEx 6:2,7;
Isa 43:3; 51:15
ᵈLev 20:7
ᵉEx 19:6
ᶠLev 19:2;
Ps 99:3;
Eph 1:4;
1Th 4:7;
1Pe 1:15,16*
11:45
ᵍLev 25:38,55;
Ex 6:7; 20:2
ʰGe 17:7
ⁱEx 19:6;
1Pe 1:16*
11:47
ʲLev 10:10

Purification After Childbirth

12 The LORD said to Moses, [2]"Say to the Israelites: 'A woman who becomes pregnant and gives birth to a son will be ceremonially unclean for seven days, just as she is unclean during her monthly period.[k] [3]On the eighth day the boy is to be circumcised.[l] [4]Then the woman must wait thirty-three days to be purified from her bleeding. She must not touch anything sacred or go to the sanctuary until the days of her purification are over. [5]If she gives birth to a daughter, for two weeks the woman will be unclean, as during her period. Then she must wait sixty-six days to be purified from her bleeding.

[6]" 'When the days of her purification for a son or daughter are over,[m] she is to bring to the priest at the entrance to the Tent of Meeting a year-old lamb[n] for a burnt offering and a young pigeon or a dove for a sin offering.[o] [7]He shall offer them before the LORD to make atonement for her, and then she will be ceremonially clean from her flow of blood.

" 'These are the regulations for the woman who gives birth to a boy or a girl. [8]If she cannot afford a lamb, she is to bring two doves or two young pigeons,[p] one for a burnt offering and the other for a sin offering. [q] In this way the priest will make atonement for her, and she will be clean.[r]' "

Regulations About Infectious Skin Diseases

13 The LORD said to Moses and Aaron, [2]"When anyone has a swelling[s] or a rash or a bright spot[t] on his skin that may become an infectious skin disease,[a][u] he must be brought to Aaron the priest[v] or to one of his sons[b] who is a priest. [3]The priest is to examine the sore on his skin, and if the hair in the sore has turned white and the sore appears to be more than skin deep,[c] it is an infectious skin disease. When the priest examines him, he shall pronounce him ceremonially unclean.[w] [4]If the spot[x] on his skin is white but does not appear to be more than skin deep and the hair in it has not turned white, the priest is to put the infected person in isolation for seven days.[y] [5]On the seventh day[z] the priest is to examine him,[a] and if he sees that the sore is unchanged and has not spread in the skin, he is to keep him in isolation another seven days. [6]On the seventh day the priest is to examine him again, and if the sore has faded and has not spread in the skin, the priest shall pronounce him clean;[b] it is only a rash. The man must wash his clothes,[c] and he will be clean.[d] [7]But if the rash does spread in his skin after he has shown himself to the priest to be pronounced clean, he must appear before the priest again.[e] [8]The priest is to examine him, and if the rash has spread in the skin, he shall pronounce him unclean; it is an infectious disease.

[9]"When anyone has an infectious skin disease, he must be brought to the priest. [10]The priest is to examine him, and if there is a white swelling in the skin that has turned the hair white and if there is raw flesh in the swelling, [11]it is a chronic skin disease[f] and the priest shall pronounce him unclean. He is not to put him in isolation, because he is already unclean.

---

[a]2 Traditionally *leprosy*; the Hebrew word was used for various diseases affecting the skin—not necessarily leprosy; also elsewhere in this chapter.   [b]2 Or *descendants*   [c]3 Or *be lower than the rest of the skin*; also elsewhere in this chapter

12:2
kLev 15:19;
18:19
12:3
lGe 17:12;
Lk 1:59; 2:21
12:6
mLk 2:22
nEx 29:38;
Lev 23:12;
Nu 6:12,14;
7:15 oLev 5:7
12:8
pGe 15:9;
Lev 14:22
qLev 5:7;
Lk 2:22-24*
rLev 4:26
13:2
sver 10,19,28,43
tver 4,38,39;
Lev 14:56
uver 3,9,15;
Ex 4:6;
Lev 14:3,32;
Nu 5:2; Dt 24:8
vDt 24:8
13:3
wver 8,11,20,
30; Lev 21:1;
Nu 9:6
13:4
xver 2
yver 5,21,26,
33,46;
Lev 14:38;
Nu 12:14,15;
Dt 24:9
13:5
zLev 14:9
aver 27,32,34,51
13:6
bver 13,17,23,
28,34; Mt 8:3;
Lk 5:12-14
cLev 11:25
dLev 11:25;
14:8,9,20,48;
15:8; Nu 8:7
13:7
eLk 5:14
13:11
fEx 4:6;
Lev 14:8;
Nu 12:10;
Mt 8:2

12"If the disease breaks out all over his skin and, so far as the priest can see, it covers all the skin of the infected person from head to foot, 13the priest is to examine him, and if the disease has covered his whole body, he shall pronounce that person clean. Since it has all turned white, he is clean. 14But whenever raw flesh appears on him, he will be unclean. 15When the priest sees the raw flesh, he shall pronounce him unclean. The raw flesh is unclean; he has an infectious disease. g 16Should the raw flesh change and turn white, he must go to the priest. 17The priest is to examine him, and if the sores have turned white, the priest shall pronounce the infected person clean; h then he will be clean.

18"When someone has a boil i on his skin and it heals, 19and in the place where the boil was, a white swelling or reddish-white j spot k appears, he must present himself to the priest. 20The priest is to examine it, and if it appears to be more than skin deep and the hair in it has turned white, the priest shall pronounce him unclean. It is an infectious skin disease l that has broken out where the boil was. 21But if, when the priest examines it, there is no white hair in it and it is not more than skin deep and has faded, then the priest is to put him in isolation for seven days. 22If it is spreading in the skin, the priest shall pronounce him unclean; it is infectious. 23But if the spot is unchanged and has not spread, it is only a scar from the boil, and the priest shall pronounce him clean. m

24"When someone has a burn on his skin and a reddish-white or white spot appears in the raw flesh of the burn, 25the priest is to examine the spot, and if the hair in it has turned white, and it appears to be more than skin deep, it is an infectious disease that has broken out in the burn. The priest shall pronounce him unclean; it is an infectious skin disease. n 26But if the priest examines it and there is no white hair in the spot and if it is not more than skin deep and has faded, then the priest is to put him in isolation for seven days. o 27On the seventh day the priest is to examine him, p and if it is spreading in the skin, the priest shall pronounce him unclean; it is an infectious skin disease. 28If, however, the spot is unchanged and has not spread in the skin but has faded, it is a swelling from the burn, and the priest shall pronounce him clean; it is only a scar from the burn. q

29"If a man or woman has a sore on the head r or on the chin, 30the priest is to examine the sore, and if it appears to be more than skin deep and the hair in it is yellow and thin, the priest shall pronounce that person unclean; it is an itch, an infectious disease of the head or chin. 31But if, when the priest examines this kind of sore, it does not seem to be more than skin deep and there is no black hair in it, then the priest is to put the infected person in isolation for seven days. s 32On the seventh day the priest is to examine the sore, t and if the itch has not spread and there is no yellow hair in it and it does not appear to be more than skin deep, 33he must be shaved except for the diseased area, and the priest is to keep him in isolation another seven days. 34On the seventh day the priest is to examine the itch, u and if it has not spread in the skin and appears to be no more than skin deep, the priest shall pronounce him clean. He must wash his clothes, and he will be clean. v 35But if the itch does spread in the skin after he is pronounced clean, 36the priest is to examine him, and if the itch has spread in the skin, the priest does not need to look for yellow hair; the person is unclean. w 37If,

13:15
g ver 2
13:17
h ver 6
13:18
i Ex 9:9
13:19
j ver 24,42;
Lev 14:37 k ver 2
13:20
l ver 2
13:23
m ver 6
13:25
n ver 11
13:26
o ver 4
13:27
p ver 5
13:28
q ver 2
13:29
r ver 43,44
13:31
s ver 4
13:32
t ver 5
13:34
u ver 5
v Lev 11:25
13:36
w ver 30

however, in his judgment it is unchanged and black hair has grown in it, the itch is healed. He is clean, and the priest shall pronounce him clean.

38"When a man or woman has white spots on the skin, 39the priest is to examine them, and if the spots are dull white, it is a harmless rash that has broken out on the skin; that person is clean.

40"When a man has lost his hair and is bald,x he is clean. 41If he has lost his hair from the front of his scalp and has a bald forehead, he is clean. 42But if he has a reddish-white sore on his bald head or forehead, it is an infectious disease breaking out on his head or forehead. 43The priest is to examine him, and if the swollen sore on his head or forehead is reddish-white like an infectious skin disease, 44the man is diseased and is unclean. The priest shall pronounce him unclean because of the sore on his head.

45"The person with such an infectious disease must wear torn clothes,y let his hair be unkempt,a cover the lower part of his facez and cry out, 'Unclean! Unclean!'a 46As long as he has the infection he remains unclean. He must live alone; he must live outside the camp.b

Regulations About Mildew

47"If any clothing is contaminated with mildew—any woolen or linen clothing, 48any woven or knitted material of linen or wool, any leather or anything made of leather— 49and if the contamination in the clothing, or leather, or woven or knitted material, or any leather article, is greenish or reddish, it is a spreading mildew and must be shown to the priest.c 50The priest is to examine the mildewd and isolate the affected article for seven days. 51On the seventh day he is to examine it,e and if the mildew has spread in the clothing, or the woven or knitted material, or the leather, whatever its use, it is a destructive mildew; the article is unclean.f 52He must burn up the clothing, or the woven or knitted material of wool or linen, or any leather article that has the contamination in it, because the mildew is destructive; the article must be burned up.g

53"But if, when the priest examines it, the mildew has not spread in the clothing, or the woven or knitted material, or the leather article, 54he shall order that the contaminated article be washed. Then he is to isolate it for another seven days. 55After the affected article has been washed, the priest is to examine it, and if the mildew has not changed its appearance, even though it has not spread, it is unclean. Burn it with fire, whether the mildew has affected one side or the other. 56If, when the priest examines it, the mildew has faded after the article has been washed, he is to tear the contaminated part out of the clothing, or the leather, or the woven or knitted material. 57But if it reappears in the clothing, or in the woven or knitted material, or in the leather article, it is spreading, and whatever has the mildew must be burned with fire. 58The clothing, or the woven or knitted material, or any leather article that has been washed and is rid of the mildew, must be washed again, and it will be clean."

59These are the regulations concerning contamination by mildew in

13:40
xLev 21:5;
2Ki 2:23;
Isa 3:24; 15:2;
22:12;
Eze 27:31;
29:18;
Am 8:10;
Mic 1:16
13:45
yLev 10:6
zEze 24:17,22;
Mic 3:7
aLev 5:2;
La 4:15;
Lk 17:12
13:46
bNu 5:1-4;
12:14; 2Ki 7:3;
15:5; Lk 17:12
13:49
cMk 1:44
13:50
dEze 44:23
13:51
ever 5
fLev 14:44
13:52
gver 55,57

a45 Or *clothes, uncover his head*

woolen or linen clothing, woven or knitted material, or any leather article, for pronouncing them clean or unclean.

Cleansing From Infectious Skin Diseases

14 The LORD said to Moses, [2]"These are the regulations for the diseased person at the time of his ceremonial cleansing, when he is brought to the priest:[h] [3]The priest is to go outside the camp and examine him.[i] If the person has been healed of his infectious skin disease,[a] [4]the priest shall order that two live clean birds and some cedar wood, scarlet yarn and hyssop be brought for the one to be cleansed.[j] [5]Then the priest shall order that one of the birds be killed over fresh water in a clay pot. [6]He is then to take the live bird and dip it, together with the cedar wood, the scarlet yarn and the hyssop, into the blood of the bird that was killed over the fresh water.[k] [7]Seven times he shall sprinkle[l] the one to be cleansed of the infectious disease and pronounce him clean. Then he is to release the live bird in the open fields.

[8]"The person to be cleansed must wash his clothes,[m] shave off all his hair and bathe with water;[n] then he will be ceremonially clean.[o] After this he may come into the camp,[p] but he must stay outside his tent for seven days. [9]On the seventh day he must shave off all his hair; he must shave his head, his beard, his eyebrows and the rest of his hair. He must wash his clothes and bathe himself with water, and he will be clean.

[10]"On the eighth day[q] he must bring two male lambs and one ewe lamb a year old, each without defect, along with three-tenths of an ephah[b] of fine flour mixed with oil for a grain offering,[r] and one log[c] of oil.[s] [11]The priest who pronounces him clean shall present both the one to be cleansed and his offerings before the LORD at the entrance to the Tent of Meeting.

[12]"Then the priest is to take one of the male lambs and offer it as a guilt offering,[t] along with the log of oil; he shall wave them before the LORD as a wave offering.[u] [13]He is to slaughter the lamb in the holy place[v] where the sin offering and the burnt offering are slaughtered. Like the sin offering, the guilt offering belongs to the priest;[w] it is most holy. [14]The priest is to take some of the blood of the guilt offering and put it on the lobe of the right ear of the one to be cleansed, on the thumb of his right hand and on the big toe of his right foot.[x] [15]The priest shall then take some of the log of oil, pour it in the palm of his own left hand, [16]dip his right forefinger into the oil in his palm, and with his finger sprinkle some of it before the LORD seven times. [17]The priest is to put some of the oil remaining in his palm on the lobe of the right ear of the one to be cleansed, on the thumb of his right hand and on the big toe of his right foot, on top of the blood of the guilt offering. [18]The rest of the oil in his palm the priest shall put on the head of the one to be cleansed and make atonement for him before the LORD.

[19]"Then the priest is to sacrifice the sin offering and make atonement for the one to be cleansed from his uncleanness. After that, the priest shall slaughter the burnt offering [20]and offer it on the altar, together

14:2
h Mt 8:2-4;
Mk 1:40-44;
Lk 5:12-14;
17:14
14:3
i Lev 13:46
14:4
j ver 6,49,51,52;
Nu 19:6;
Ps 51:7
14:6
k ver 4
14:7
l 2Ki 5:10,14;
Isa 52:15;
Eze 36:25
14:8
m Lev 11:25;
13:6 n ver 9
o ver 20
p Nu 5:2,3;
12:14,15;
2Ch 26:21
14:10
q Mt 8:4;
Mk 1:44;
Lk 5:14 r Lev 2:1
s ver 12,15,21,24
14:12
t Lev 5:18; 6:6-7
u Ex 29:24
14:13
v Ex 29:11
w Lev 6:24-30;
7:7
14:14
x Ex 29:20;
Lev 8:23

---

a3 Traditionally *leprosy*; the Hebrew word was used for various diseases affecting the skin—not necessarily leprosy; also elsewhere in this chapter.   b10 That is, probably about 6 quarts (about 6.5 liters)   c10 That is, probably about 2/3 pint (about 0.3 liter); also in verses 12, 15, 21 and 24 with the grain offering, and make atonement for him, and he will be clean.y

21"If, however, he is poorz and cannot afford these,a he must take one male lamb as a guilt offering to be waved to make atonement for him, together with a tenth of an ephaha of fine flour mixed with oil for a grain offering, a log of oil, 22and two doves or two young pigeons,b which he can afford, one for a sin offering and the other for a burnt offering.

23"On the eighth day he must bring them for his cleansing to the priest at the entrance to the Tent of Meeting, before the LORD.c 24The priest is to take the lamb for the guilt offering,d together with the log of oil,e and wave them before the LORD as a wave offering.f 25He shall slaughter the lamb for the guilt offering and take some of its blood and put it on the lobe of the right ear of the one to be cleansed, on the thumb of his right hand and on the big toe of his right foot.g 26The priest is to pour some of the oil into the palm of his own left hand,h 27and with his right forefinger sprinkle some of the oil from his palm seven times before the LORD. 28Some of the oil in his palm he is to put on the same places he put the blood of the guilt offering—on the lobe of the right ear of the one to be cleansed, on the thumb of his right hand and on the big toe of his right foot. 29The rest of the oil in his palm the priest shall put on the head of the one to be cleansed, to make atonement for him before the LORD.i 30Then he shall sacrifice the doves or the young pigeons, which the person can afford,j 31oneb as a sin offering and the other as a burnt offering,k together with the grain offering. In this way the priest will make atonement before the LORD on behalf of the one to be cleansed.l"

32These are the regulations for anyone who has an infectious skin diseasem and who cannot afford the regular offeringsn for his cleansing.

Cleansing From Mildew

33The LORD said to Moses and Aaron, 34"When you enter the land of Canaan,o which I am giving you as your possession,p and I put a spreading mildew in a house in that land, 35the owner of the house must go and tell the priest, 'I have seen something that looks like mildew in my house.' 36The priest is to order the house to be emptied before he goes in to examine the mildew, so that nothing in the house will be pronounced unclean. After this the priest is to go in and inspect the house. 37He is to examine the mildew on the walls, and if it has greenish or reddishq depressions that appear to be deeper than the surface of the wall, 38the priest shall go out the doorway of the house and close it up for seven days.r 39On the seventh days the priest shall return to inspect the house. If the mildew has spread on the walls, 40he is to order that the contaminated stones be torn out and thrown into an unclean place outside the town.t 41He must have all the inside walls of the house scraped and the material that is scraped off dumped into an unclean place outside the town. 42Then they are to take other stones to replace these and take new clay and plaster the house.

14:20
yver 8
14:21
zLev 5:7; 12:8
aver 22,32
14:22
bLev 5:7
14:23
cver 10,11
14:24
dNu 6:14
ever 10 fver 12
14:25
gver 14;
Ex 29:20
14:26
hver 15
14:29
iver 18
14:30
jLev 5:7
14:31
kver 22;
Lev 5:7;
15:15,30
lver 18,19
14:32
mLev 13:2
nver 21
14:34
oGe 12:5;
Ex 6:4; Nu 13:2
pGe 17:8; 48:4;
Nu 27:12;
32:22; Dt 3:27;
7:1; 32:49
14:37
qLev 13:19
14:38
rLev 13:4
14:39
sLev 13:5
14:40
tver 45

---

a21 That is, probably about 2 quarts (about 2 liters)   b31 Septuagint and Syriac; Hebrew 31such as the person can afford, one

43"If the mildew reappears in the house after the stones have been torn out and the house scraped and plastered, 44the priest is to go and examine it and, if the mildew has spread in the house, it is a destructive mildew; the house is unclean.ᵘ 45It must be torn down—its stones, timbers and all the plaster—and taken out of the town to an unclean place.

46"Anyone who goes into the house while it is closed up will be unclean till evening.ᵛ 47Anyone who sleeps or eats in the house must wash his clothes.ʷ

48"But if the priest comes to examine it and the mildew has not spread after the house has been plastered, he shall pronounce the house clean,ˣ because the mildew is gone. 49To purify the house he is to take two birds and some cedar wood, scarlet yarn and hyssop.ʸ 50He shall kill one of the birds over fresh water in a clay pot.ᶻ 51Then he is to take the cedar wood, the hyssop,ᵃ the scarlet yarn and the live bird, dip them into the blood of the dead bird and the fresh water, and sprinkle the house seven times.ᵇ 52He shall purify the house with the bird's blood, the fresh water, the live bird, the cedar wood, the hyssop and the scarlet yarn. 53Then he is to release the live bird in the open fieldsᶜ outside the town. In this way he will make atonement for the house, and it will be clean.ᵈ"

54These are the regulations for any infectious skin disease,ᵉ for an itch, 55for mildewᶠ in clothing or in a house, 56and for a swelling, a rash or a bright spot,ᵍ 57to determine when something is clean or unclean.

These are the regulations for infectious skin diseases and mildew.ʰ

Discharges Causing Uncleanness

15 The LORD said to Moses and Aaron, 2"Speak to the Israelites and say to them: 'When any man has a bodily discharge,ⁱ the discharge is unclean. 3Whether it continues flowing from his body or is blocked, it will make him unclean. This is how his discharge will bring about uncleanness:

4"'Any bed the man with a discharge lies on will be unclean, and anything he sits on will be unclean. 5Anyone who touches his bed must wash his clothesʲ and bathe with water,ᵏ and he will be unclean till evening.ˡ 6Whoever sits on anything that the man with a discharge sat on must wash his clothes and bathe with water, and he will be unclean till evening.

7"'Whoever touches the manᵐ who has a dischargeⁿ must wash his clothes and bathe with water, and he will be unclean till evening.

8"'If the man with the discharge spitsᵒ on someone who is clean, that person must wash his clothes and bathe with water, and he will be unclean till evening.

9"'Everything the man sits on when riding will be unclean, 10and whoever touches any of the things that were under him will be unclean till evening; whoever picks up those thingsᵖ must wash his clothes and bathe with water, and he will be unclean till evening.

11"'Anyone the man with a discharge touches without rinsing his hands with water must wash his clothes and bathe with water, and he will be unclean till evening.

14:44
uLev 13:51
14:46
vLev 11:24
14:47
wLev 11:25
14:48
xLev 13:6
14:49
yver 4; 1Ki 4:33
14:50
zver 5
14:51
aver 6; Ps 51:7
bver 4,7
14:53
cver 7 dver 20
14:54
eLev 13:2,30
14:55
fLev 13:47-52
14:56
gLev 13:2
14:57
hLev 10:10
15:2
iver 16,32;
Lev 22:4;
Nu 5:2;
2Sa 3:29;
Mt 9:20
15:5
jLev 11:25
kLev 14:8
lLev 11:24
15:7
mver 19;
Lev 22:5
nver 16;
Lev 22:4
15:8
oNu 12:14
15:10
pNu 19:10

12" 'A clay pot[q] that the man touches must be broken, and any wooden article[r] is to be rinsed with water.

13" 'When a man is cleansed from his discharge, he is to count off seven days[s] for his ceremonial cleansing; he must wash his clothes and bathe himself with fresh water, and he will be clean.[t] 14On the eighth day he must take two doves or two young pigeons[u] and come before the LORD to the entrance to the Tent of Meeting and give them to the priest. 15The priest is to sacrifice them, the one for a sin offering[v] and the other for a burnt offering.[w] In this way he will make atonement before the LORD for the man because of his discharge.[x]

16" 'When a man has an emission of semen,[y] he must bathe his whole body with water, and he will be unclean till evening.[z] 17Any clothing or leather that has semen on it must be washed with water, and it will be unclean till evening. 18When a man lies with a woman and there is an emission of semen,[a] both must bathe with water, and they will be unclean till evening.

19" 'When a woman has her regular flow of blood, the impurity of her monthly period[b] will last seven days, and anyone who touches her will be unclean till evening.

20" 'Anything she lies on during her period will be unclean, and anything she sits on will be unclean. 21Whoever touches her bed must wash his clothes and bathe with water, and he will be unclean till evening.[c] 22Whoever touches anything she sits on must wash his clothes and bathe with water, and he will be unclean till evening. 23Whether it is the bed or anything she was sitting on, when anyone touches it, he will be unclean till evening.

24" 'If a man lies with her and her monthly flow[d] touches him, he will be unclean for seven days; any bed he lies on will be unclean.

25" 'When a woman has a discharge of blood for many days at a time other than her monthly period[e] or has a discharge that continues beyond her period, she will be unclean as long as she has the discharge, just as in the days of her period. 26Any bed she lies on while her discharge continues will be unclean, as is her bed during her monthly period, and anything she sits on will be unclean, as during her period. 27Whoever touches them will be unclean; he must wash his clothes and bathe with water, and he will be unclean till evening.

28" 'When she is cleansed from her discharge, she must count off seven days, and after that she will be ceremonially clean. 29On the eighth day she must take two doves or two young pigeons[f] and bring them to the priest at the entrance to the Tent of Meeting. 30The priest is to sacrifice one for a sin offering and the other for a burnt offering. In this way he will make atonement for her before the LORD for the uncleanness of her discharge.[g]

31" 'You must keep the Israelites separate from things that make them unclean, so they will not die in their uncleanness for defiling my dwelling place,[a][h] which is among them.' "

32These are the regulations for a man with a discharge, for anyone made unclean by an emission of semen,[i] 33for a woman in her monthly period, for a man or a woman with a discharge, and for a man who lies with a woman who is ceremonially unclean.[j]

15:12
qLev 6:28
rLev 11:32
15:13
sLev 8:33 tver 5
15:14
uLev 14:22
15:15
vLev 5:7
wLev 14:31
xLev 14:18,19
15:16
yver 2;
Lev 22:4;
Dt 23:10 zver 5;
Dt 23:11
15:18
a1Sa 21:4
15:19
bver 24;
Lev 12:2
15:21
cver 27
15:24
dver 19;
Lev 12:2;
18:19; 20:18;
Eze 18:6
15:25
eMt 9:20;
Mk 5:25;
Lk 8:43
15:29
fLev 14:22
15:30
gLev 5:10;
14:20,31;
18:19;
2Sa 11:4;
Mk 5:25;
Lk 8:43
15:31
hLev 20:3;
Nu 5:3; 19:13,
20; 2Sa 15:25;
2Ki 21:7;
Ps 33:14; 74:7;
76:2; Eze 5:11;
23:38
15:32
iver 2
15:33
jver 19,24,25

a31 Or *my tabernacle*

The Day of Atonement

16:2-34pp — Lev 23:26-32; Nu 29:7-11

16 The LORD spoke to Moses after the death of the two sons of Aaron who died when they approached the LORD.[k] [2]The LORD said to Moses: "Tell your brother Aaron not to come whenever he chooses[1] into the Most Holy Place[m] behind the curtain in front of the atonement cover on the ark, or else he will die, because I appear[n] in the cloud[o] over the atonement cover.

[3]"This is how Aaron is to enter the sanctuary area:[p] with a young bull for a sin offering and a ram for a burnt offering. [4]He is to put on the sacred linen tunic, with linen undergarments next to his body; he is to tie the linen sash around him and put on the linen turban.[q] These are sacred garments;[r] so he must bathe himself with water[s] before he puts them on. [5]From the Israelite community[t] he is to take two male goats[u] for a sin offering and a ram for a burnt offering.

[6]"Aaron is to offer the bull for his own sin offering to make atonement for himself and his household.[v] [7]Then he is to take the two goats and present them before the LORD at the entrance to the Tent of Meeting. [8]He is to cast lots for the two goats—one lot for the LORD and the other for the scapegoat.[a] [9]Aaron shall bring the goat whose lot falls to the LORD and sacrifice it for a sin offering. [10]But the goat chosen by lot as the scapegoat shall be presented alive before the LORD to be used for making atonement[w] by sending it into the desert as a scapegoat.

[11]"Aaron shall bring the bull for his own sin offering to make atonement for himself and his household,[x] and he is to slaughter the bull for his own sin offering. [12]He is to take a censer full of burning coals[y] from the altar before the LORD and two handfuls of finely ground fragrant incense[z] and take them behind the curtain. [13]He is to put the incense on the fire before the LORD, and the smoke of the incense will conceal the atonement cover above the Testimony, so that he will not die.[a] [14]He is to take some of the bull's blood[b] and with his finger sprinkle it on the front of the atonement cover; then he shall sprinkle some of it with his finger seven times before the atonement cover.[c]

[15]"He shall then slaughter the goat for the sin offering for the people[d] and take its blood behind the curtain[e] and do with it as he did with the bull's blood: He shall sprinkle it on the atonement cover and in front of it. [16]In this way he will make atonement[f] for the Most Holy Place because of the uncleanness and rebellion of the Israelites, whatever their sins have been. He is to do the same for the Tent of Meeting, which is among them in the midst of their uncleanness. [17]No one is to be in the Tent of Meeting from the time Aaron goes in to make atonement in the Most Holy Place until he comes out, having made atonement for himself, his household and the whole community of Israel.

[18]"Then he shall come out to the altar[g] that is before the LORD and make atonement for it. He shall take some of the bull's blood and some of the goat's blood and put it on all the horns of the altar.[h] [19]He shall sprinkle some of the blood on it with his finger seven times to cleanse it and to consecrate it from the uncleanness of the Israelites.[i]

[20]"When Aaron has finished making atonement for the Most Holy

16:1
k Lev 10:1
16:2
l Ex 30:10;
Heb 9:7
m Heb 9:25;
10:19 n Ex 25:22
o Ex 40:34
16:3
p Heb 9:24,25
16:4
q Ex 28:39
r Ex 28:42
s ver 24;
Heb 10:22
16:5
t Lev 4:13-21
u 2Ch 29:23
16:6
v Lev 9:7;
Heb 5:3; 7:27;
9:7,12
16:10
w Isa 53:4-10;
Ro 3:25; 1Jn 2:2
16:11
x Heb 7:27; 9:7
16:12
y Lev 10:1
z Ex 30:34-38
16:13
a Ex 28:43;
Lev 22:9
16:14
b Lev 4:5;
Heb 9:7,13,25
c Lev 4:6
16:15
d Heb 9:7,12
e Heb 9:3
16:16
f Ex 29:36
16:18
g Lev 4:7
h Lev 4:25
16:19
i Eze 43:20

_a8_ That is, the goat of removal; Hebrew _azazel_; also in verses 10 and 26

Place, the Tent of Meeting and the altar, he shall bring forward the live goat. [21]He is to lay both hands on the head of the live goat and confess[j] over it all the wickedness and rebellion of the Israelites—all their sins —and put them on the goat's head. He shall send the goat away into the desert in the care of a man appointed for the task. [22]The goat will carry on itself all their sins[k] to a solitary place; and the man shall release it in the desert.

[23]"Then Aaron is to go into the Tent of Meeting and take off the linen garments he put on before he entered the Most Holy Place, and he is to leave them there.[l] [24]He shall bathe himself with water in a holy place and put on his regular garments.[m] Then he shall come out and sacrifice the burnt offering for himself and the burnt offering for the people, to make atonement for himself and for the people. [25]He shall also burn the fat of the sin offering on the altar.

[26]"The man who releases the goat as a scapegoat must wash his clothes[n] and bathe himself with water; afterward he may come into the camp. [27]The bull and the goat for the sin offerings, whose blood was brought into the Most Holy Place to make atonement, must be taken outside the camp;[o] their hides, flesh and offal are to be burned up. [28]The man who burns them must wash his clothes and bathe himself with water; afterward he may come into the camp.

[29]"This is to be a lasting ordinance for you: On the tenth day of the seventh month you must deny yourselves[a][p] and not do any work— whether native-born or an alien living among you— [30]because on this day atonement will be made for you, to cleanse you. Then, before the LORD, you will be clean from all your sins. [q] [31]It is a sabbath of rest, and you must deny yourselves;[r] it is a lasting ordinance. [32]The priest who is anointed and ordained to succeed his father as high priest is to make atonement. He is to put on the sacred linen garments[s] [33]and make atonement for the Most Holy Place, for the Tent of Meeting and the altar, and for the priests and all the people of the community.[t]

[34]"This is to be a lasting ordinance for you: Atonement is to be made once a year[u] for all the sins of the Israelites."

And it was done, as the LORD commanded Moses.

Eating Blood Forbidden

17 The LORD said to Moses, [2]"Speak to Aaron and his sons and to all the Israelites and say to them: 'This is what the LORD has commanded: [3]Any Israelite who sacrifices an ox,[b] a lamb or a goat in the camp or outside of it [4]instead of bringing it to the entrance to the Tent of Meeting to present it as an offering to the LORD in front of the tabernacle of the LORD[v]—that man shall be considered guilty of bloodshed; he has shed blood and must be cut off from his people.[w] [5]This is so the Israelites will bring to the LORD the sacrifices they are now making in the open fields. They must bring them to the priest, that is, to the LORD, at the entrance to the Tent of Meeting and sacrifice them as fellowship offerings.[c] [6]The priest is to sprinkle the blood against the altar of the LORD[x] at the entrance to the Tent of Meeting and burn the fat as an aroma pleasing to the LORD. [y] [7]They must no longer offer any

16:21
j Lev 5:5
16:22
k Isa 53:12
16:23
l Eze 42:14; 44:19
16:24
m ver 3-5
16:26
n Lev 11:25
16:27
o Lev 4:12,21; Heb 13:11
16:29
p Lev 23:27,32; Nu 29:7; Isa 58:3
16:30
q Jer 33:8; Eph 5:26
16:31
r Isa 58:3,5
16:32
s ver 4; Nu 20:26,28
16:33
t ver 11,16-18
16:34
u Heb 9:7,25
17:4
v Dt 12:5-21
w Ge 17:14
17:6
x Lev 3:2
y Nu 18:17

[a]29 Or *must fast*; also in verse 31   [b]3 The Hebrew word can include both male and female.
[c]5 Traditionally *peace offerings*

of their sacrifices to the goat idols *a z* to whom they prostitute themselves.*a* This is to be a lasting ordinance for them and for the generations to come.'

8"Say to them: 'Any Israelite or any alien living among them who offers a burnt offering or sacrifice ⁹and does not bring it to the entrance to the Tent of Meeting*b* to sacrifice it to the Lᴏʀᴅ—that man must be cut off from his people.

10" 'Any Israelite or any alien living among them who eats any blood—I will set my face against that person who eats blood*c* and will cut him off from his people. ¹¹For the life of a creature is in the blood,*d* and I have given it to you to make atonement for yourselves on the altar; it is the blood that makes atonement for one's life.*e* ¹²Therefore I say to the Israelites, "None of you may eat blood, nor may an alien living among you eat blood."

13" 'Any Israelite or any alien living among you who hunts any animal or bird that may be eaten must drain out the blood and cover it with earth,*f* ¹⁴because the life of every creature is its blood. That is why I have said to the Israelites, "You must not eat the blood of any creature, because the life of every creature is its blood; anyone who eats it must be cut off."*g*

15" 'Anyone, whether native-born or alien, who eats anything found dead or torn by wild animals*h* must wash his clothes and bathe with water, and he will be ceremonially unclean till evening; then he will be clean. ¹⁶But if he does not wash his clothes and bathe himself, he will be held responsible.' "

Unlawful Sexual Relations

18 The Lᴏʀᴅ said to Moses, ²"Speak to the Israelites and say to them: 'I am the Lᴏʀᴅ your God.*i* ³You must not do as they do in Egypt, where you used to live, and you must not do as they do in the land of Canaan, where I am bringing you. Do not follow their practices.*j* ⁴You must obey my laws and be careful to follow my decrees. I am the Lᴏʀᴅ your God.*k* ⁵Keep my decrees and laws, for the man who obeys them will live by them.*l* I am the Lᴏʀᴅ.

6" 'No one is to approach any close relative to have sexual relations. I am the Lᴏʀᴅ.

7" 'Do not dishonor your father*m* by having sexual relations with your mother.*n* She is your mother; do not have relations with her.

8" 'Do not have sexual relations with your father's wife;*o* that would dishonor your father.*p*

9" 'Do not have sexual relations with your sister,*q* either your father's daughter or your mother's daughter, whether she was born in the same home or elsewhere.

10" 'Do not have sexual relations with your son's daughter or your daughter's daughter; that would dishonor you.

11" 'Do not have sexual relations with the daughter of your father's wife, born to your father; she is your sister.

12" 'Do not have sexual relations with your father's sister;*r* she is your father's close relative.

17:7
zEx 22:20;
2Ch 11:15
aEx 32:8; 34:15;
Dt 32:17;
1Co 10:20
17:9
bver 4
17:10
cGe 9:4;
Lev 3:17;
Dt 12:16,23;
1Sa 14:33
17:11
dver 14; Ge 9:4
eHeb 9:22
17:13
fLev 7:26;
Dt 12:16
17:14
gver 11; Ge 9:4
17:15
hEx 22:31;
Dt 14:21
18:2
iEx 6:7;
Lev 11:44;
Eze 20:5
18:3
jver 24-30;
Ex 23:24;
Lev 20:23
18:4
kver 2
18:5
lEze 20:11;
Ro 10:5*;
Gal 3:12*
18:7
mLev 20:11
nEze 22:10
18:8
o1Co 5:1
pLev 20:11
18:9
qLev 20:17
18:12
rLev 20:19

---

a7 Or demons

¹³" 'Do not have sexual relations with your mother's sister, because she is your mother's close relative.

¹⁴" 'Do not dishonor your father's brother by approaching his wife to have sexual relations; she is your aunt. ˢ

¹⁵" 'Do not have sexual relations with your daughter-in-law. ᵗ She is your son's wife; do not have relations with her.

¹⁶" 'Do not have sexual relations with your brother's wife;ᵘ that would dishonor your brother.

¹⁷" 'Do not have sexual relations with both a woman and her daughter. ᵛ Do not have sexual relations with either her son's daughter or her daughter's daughter; they are her close relatives. That is wickedness.

¹⁸" 'Do not take your wife's sister as a rival wife and have sexual relations with her while your wife is living.

¹⁹" 'Do not approach a woman to have sexual relations during the uncleanness of her monthly period. ʷ

²⁰" 'Do not have sexual relations with your neighbor's wifeˣ and defile yourself with her.

²¹" 'Do not give any of your childrenʸ to be sacrificedᵃ to Molech,ᶻ for you must not profane the name of your God. ᵃ I am the LORD.

²²" 'Do not lie with a man as one lies with a woman;ᵇ that is detestable.

²³" 'Do not have sexual relations with an animal and defile yourself with it. A woman must not present herself to an animal to have sexual relations with it; that is a perversion. ᶜ

²⁴" 'Do not defile yourselves in any of these ways, because this is how the nations that I am going to drive out before youᵈ became defiled. ᵉ ²⁵Even the land was defiled; so I punished it for its sin, ᶠ and the land vomited out its inhabitants. ᵍ ²⁶But you must keep my decrees and my laws. The native-born and the aliens living among you must not do any of these detestable things, ²⁷for all these things were done by the people who lived in the land before you, and the land became defiled. ²⁸And if you defile the land, it will vomit you out as it vomited out the nations that were before you.

²⁹" 'Everyone who does any of these detestable things—such persons must be cut off from their people. ³⁰Keep my requirementsʰ and do not follow any of the detestable customs that were practiced before you came and do not defile yourselves with them. I am the LORD your God. ⁱ ' "

Various Laws

19 The LORD said to Moses, ²"Speak to the entire assembly of Israel and say to them: 'Be holy because I, the LORD your God, am holy. ʲ

³" 'Each of you must respect his mother and father, ᵏ and you must observe my Sabbaths. I am the LORD your God. ˡ

⁴" 'Do not turn to idols or make gods of cast metal for yourselves. ᵐ I am the LORD your God.

⁵" 'When you sacrifice a fellowship offeringᵇ to the LORD, sacrifice it in such a way that it will be accepted on your behalf. ⁶It shall be eaten on the day you sacrifice it or on the next day; anything left over until the

---

*Cross references (left margin):*

18:14
ˢLev 20:20
18:15
ᵗLev 20:12
18:16
ᵘLev 20:21
18:17
ᵛLev 20:14
18:19
ʷLev 15:24;
20:18
18:20
ˣEx 20:14;
Lev 20:10;
Mt 5:27,28;
1Co 6:9;
Heb 13:4
18:21
ʸDt 12:31
ᶻLev 20:2-5
ᵃLev 19:12;
21:6; Eze 36:20
18:22
ᵇLev 20:13;
Dt 23:18;
Ro 1:27
18:23
ᶜEx 22:19;
Lev 20:15;
Dt 27:21
18:24
ᵈver 3,27,30
ᵉDt 18:12
18:25
ᶠLev 20:23;
Dt 9:5; 18:12
ᵍver 28;
Lev 20:22
18:30
ʰDt 11:1 iver 2
19:2
ʲ1Pe 1:16*;
Lev 11:44
19:3
ᵏEx 20:12
ˡLev 11:44
19:4
ᵐEx 20:4,23;
34:17;
Lev 26:1;
Ps 96:5; 115:4-7

ᵃ21 Or *to be passed through the fire*   ᵇ5 Traditionally *peace offering* third day must be burned up. 7If any of it is eaten on the third day, it is impure and will not be accepted. 8Whoever eats it will be held responsible because he has desecrated what is holy to the LORD; that person must be cut off from his people.

9″ 'When you reap the harvest of your land, do not reap to the very edges of your field or gather the gleanings of your harvest. ⁿ 10Do not go over your vineyard a second time or pick up the grapes that have fallen. Leave them for the poor and the alien. I am the LORD your God.

11″ 'Do not steal. º

″ 'Do not lie. ᴾ

″ 'Do not deceive one another.

12″ 'Do not swear falsely by my name�q and so profane the name of your God. I am the LORD.

13″ 'Do not defraud your neighbor or rob him. ʳ

″ 'Do not hold back the wages of a hired man overnight. ˢ

14″ 'Do not curse the deaf or put a stumbling block in front of the blind,ᵗ but fear your God. I am the LORD.

15″ 'Do not pervert justice;ᵘ do not show partialityᵛ to the poor or favoritism to the great, but judge your neighbor fairly.

16″ 'Do not go about spreading slanderʷ among your people.

″ 'Do not do anything that endangers your neighbor's life.ˣ I am the LORD.

17″ 'Do not hate your brother in your heart.ʸ Rebuke your neighbor franklyᶻ so you will not share in his guilt.

18″ 'Do not seek revengeᵃ or bear a grudgeᵇ against one of your people, but love your neighbor as yourself. ᶜ I am the LORD.

19″ 'Keep my decrees.

″ 'Do not mate different kinds of animals.

″ 'Do not plant your field with two kinds of seed. ᵈ

″ 'Do not wear clothing woven of two kinds of material. ᵉ

20″ 'If a man sleeps with a woman who is a slave girl promised to another man but who has not been ransomed or given her freedom, there must be due punishment. Yet they are not to be put to death, because she had not been freed. 21The man, however, must bring a ram to the entrance to the Tent of Meeting for a guilt offering to the LORD.ᶠ 22With the ram of the guilt offering the priest is to make atonement for him before the LORD for the sin he has committed, and his sin will be forgiven.

23″ 'When you enter the land and plant any kind of fruit tree, regard its fruit as forbidden. ᵃ For three years you are to consider it forbiddenᵃ; it must not be eaten. 24In the fourth year all its fruit will be holy,ᵍ an offering of praise to the LORD. 25But in the fifth year you may eat its fruit. In this way your harvest will be increased. I am the LORD your God.

26″ 'Do not eat any meat with the blood still in it. ʰ

″ 'Do not practice divination or sorcery. ⁱ

27″ 'Do not cut the hair at the sides of your head or clip off the edges of your beard.ʲ

28″ 'Do not cut your bodies for the dead or put tattoo marks on yourselves. I am the LORD.

ᵃ23 Hebrew *uncircumcised*

19:9
ⁿLev 23:10,22;
Dt 24:19-22
19:11
ºEx 20:15
ᴾEph 4:25
19:12
qEx 20:7;
Mt 5:33
19:13
ʳEx 22:15,25-27
ˢDt 24:15;
Jas 5:4
19:14
ᵗDt 27:18
19:15
ᵘEx 23:2,6
ᵛDt 1:17
19:16
ʷPs 15:3;
Eze 22:9
ˣEx 23:7
19:17
ʸ1Jn 2:9; 3:15
ᶻMt 18:15;
Lk 17:3
19:18
ᵃRo 12:19
ᵇPs 103:9
ᶜMt 5:43*;
19:16*; 22:39*;
Mk 12:31*;
Lk 10:27*;
Jn 13:34;
Ro 13:9*;
Gal 5:14*;
Jas 2:8*
19:19
ᵈDt 22:9
ᵉDt 22:11
19:21
ᶠLev 5:15
19:24
ᵍPr 3:9
19:26
ʰLev 17:10
ⁱDt 18:10
19:27
ʲLev 21:5

^{29'} 'Do not degrade your daughter by making her a prostitute,^k or the land will turn to prostitution and be filled with wickedness.

^{30'} 'Observe my Sabbaths and have reverence for my sanctuary. I am the Lord.^l

^{31'} 'Do not turn to mediums or seek out spiritists,^m for you will be defiled by them. I am the Lord your God.

^{32'} 'Rise in the presence of the aged, show respect for the elderlyⁿ and revere your God. I am the Lord.

^{33'} 'When an alien lives with you in your land, do not mistreat him. ³⁴The alien living with you must be treated as one of your native-born.^o Love him as yourself, for you were aliens in Egypt.^p I am the Lord your God.

^{35'} 'Do not use dishonest standards when measuring length, weight or quantity. ³⁶Use honest scales and honest weights, an honest ephah^a and an honest hin.^{bq} I am the Lord your God, who brought you out of Egypt.

^{37'} 'Keep all my decrees and all my laws and follow them. I am the Lord.' "

Punishments for Sin

20 The Lord said to Moses, ²"Say to the Israelites: 'Any Israelite or any alien living in Israel who gives^c any of his children to Molech must be put to death. The people of the community are to stone him. ³I will set my face against that man and I will cut him off from his people; for by giving his children to Molech, he has defiled my sanctuary^r and profaned my holy name.^s ⁴If the people of the community close their eyes when that man gives one of his children to Molech and they fail to put him to death,^t ⁵I will set my face against that man and his family and will cut off from their people both him and all who follow him in prostituting themselves to Molech.

^{6'} 'I will set my face against the person who turns to mediums and spiritists to prostitute himself by following them, and I will cut him off from his people.^u

^{7'} 'Consecrate yourselves and be holy,^v because I am the Lord your God. ⁸Keep my decrees and follow them. I am the Lord, who makes you holy.^{dw}

^{9'} 'If anyone curses his father or mother,^x he must be put to death.^y He has cursed his father or his mother, and his blood will be on his own head.^z

^{10'} 'If a man commits adultery with another man's wife^a—with the wife of his neighbor—both the adulterer and the adulteress must be put to death.

^{11'} 'If a man sleeps with his father's wife, he has dishonored his father.^b Both the man and the woman must be put to death; their blood will be on their own heads.

^{12'} 'If a man sleeps with his daughter-in-law,^c both of them must be put to death. What they have done is a perversion; their blood will be on their own heads.

^{13'} 'If a man lies with a man as one lies with a woman, both of them

19:29
k Dt 23:18
19:30
l Lev 26:2
19:31
m Lev 20:6;
Isa 8:19
19:32
n 1Ti 5:1
19:34
o Ex 12:48
p Dt 10:19
19:36
q Dt 25:13-15
20:3
r Lev 15:31
s Lev 18:21
20:4
t Dt 17:2-5
20:6
u Lev 19:31
20:7
v Eph 1:4;
1Pe 1:16*
20:8
w Ex 31:13
20:9
x Dt 27:16
y Ex 21:17;
Mt 15:4*;
Mk 7:10*
z ver 11;
2Sa 1:16
20:10
a Ex 20:14;
Dt 5:18; 22:22
20:11
b Lev 18:7;
Dt 27:23
20:12
c Lev 18:15

---

^a36 An ephah was a dry measure.   ^b36 A hin was a liquid measure.   ^c2 Or *sacrifices*; also in verses 3 and 4   ^d8 Or *who sanctifies you; or who sets you apart as holy*

have done what is detestable. ᵈ They must be put to death; their blood will be on their own heads.

¹⁴″ 'If a man marries both a woman and her mother, ᵉ it is wicked. Both he and they must be burned in the fire, so that no wickedness will be among you. ᶠ

¹⁵″ 'If a man has sexual relations with an animal, ᵍ he must be put to death, and you must kill the animal.

¹⁶″ 'If a woman approaches an animal to have sexual relations with it, kill both the woman and the animal. They must be put to death; their blood will be on their own heads.

¹⁷″ 'If a man marries his sisterʰ, the daughter of either his father or his mother, and they have sexual relations, it is a disgrace. They must be cut off before the eyes of their people. He has dishonored his sister and will be held responsible.

¹⁸″ 'If a man lies with a woman during her monthly periodⁱ and has sexual relations with her, he has exposed the source of her flow, and she has also uncovered it. Both of them must be cut off from their people.

¹⁹″ 'Do not have sexual relations with the sister of either your mother or your father, ʲ for that would dishonor a close relative; both of you would be held responsible.

²⁰″ 'If a man sleeps with his aunt, ᵏ he has dishonored his uncle. They will be held responsible; they will die childless.

²¹″ 'If a man marries his brother's wife, ˡ it is an act of impurity; he has dishonored his brother. They will be childless.

²²″ 'Keep all my decrees and laws and follow them, so that the landᵐ where I am bringing you to live may not vomit you out. ²³You must not live according to the customs of the nationsⁿ I am going to drive out before you. ᵒ Because they did all these things, I abhorred them. ²⁴But I said to you, "You will possess their land; I will give it to you as an inheritance, a land flowing with milk and honey."ᵖ I am the LORD your God, who has set you apart from the nations. �q

²⁵″ 'You must therefore make a distinction between clean and unclean animals and between unclean and clean birds. ʳ Do not defile yourselves by any animal or bird or anything that moves along the ground—those which I have set apart as unclean for you. ²⁶You are to be holy to meᵃ because I, the LORD, am holy, ˢ and I have set you apart from the nations to be my own.

²⁷″ 'A man or woman who is a medium or spiritist among you must be put to death. ᵗ You are to stone them; their blood will be on their own heads.' ″

Rules for Priests

21 The LORD said to Moses, "Speak to the priests, the sons of Aaron, and say to them: 'A priest must not make himself ceremonially unclean for any of his people who die, ᵘ ²except for a close relative, such as his mother or father, his son or daughter, his brother, ³or an unmarried sister who is dependent on him since she has no husband—for her he may make himself unclean. ⁴He must not make

20:13
dLev 18:22
20:14
eLev 18:17
fDt 27:23
20:15
gLev 18:23
20:17
hLev 18:9
20:18
iLev 15:24;
18:19
20:19
jLev 18:12-13
20:20
kLev 18:14
20:21
lLev 18:16
20:22
mLev 18:25-28
20:23
nLev 18:3
oLev 18:24,
27,30
20:24
pEx 3:8; 13:5;
33:3 qEx 33:16
20:25
rLev 11:1-47;
Dt 14:3-21
20:26
sLev 19:2
20:27
tLev 19:31
21:1
uEze 44:25

ᵃ26 Or *be my holy ones*

himself unclean for people related to him by marriage,ª and so defile himself.

⁵'' 'Priests must not shave their heads or shave off the edges of their beardsᵛ or cut their bodies. ʷ ⁶They must be holy to their God and must not profane the name of their God. ˣ Because they present the offerings made to the LORD by fire,ʸ the food of their God, they are to be holy.

⁷'' 'They must not marry women defiled by prostitution or divorced from their husbands,ᶻ because priests are holy to their God. ª ⁸Regard them as holy,ᵇ because they offer up the food of your God. Consider them holy, because I the LORD am holy—I who make you holy. ᵇ

⁹'' 'If a priest's daughter defiles herself by becoming a prostitute, she disgraces her father; she must be burned in the fire. ᶜ

¹⁰'' 'The high priest, the one among his brothers who has had the anointing oil poured on his head and who has been ordained to wear the priestly garments, ᵈ must not let his hair become unkemptᶜ or tear his clothes. ᵉ ¹¹He must not enter a place where there is a dead body. ᶠ He must not make himself unclean, ᵍ even for his father or mother, ¹²nor leave the sanctuary of his God or desecrate it, because he has been dedicated by the anointing oilʰ of his God. I am the LORD.

¹³'' 'The woman he marries must be a virgin. ⁱ ¹⁴He must not marry a widow, a divorced woman, or a woman defiled by prostitution, but only a virgin from his own people, ¹⁵so he will not defile his offspring among his people. I am the LORD, who makes him holy. ᵈ ' ''

¹⁶The LORD said to Moses, ¹⁷''Say to Aaron: 'For the generations to come none of your descendants who has a defect may come near to offer the food of his God. ʲ ¹⁸No man who has any defectᵏ may come near: no man who is blind or lame, disfigured or deformed; ¹⁹no man with a crippled foot or hand, ²⁰or who is hunchbacked or dwarfed, or who has any eye defect, or who has festering or running sores or damaged testicles. ˡ ²¹No descendant of Aaron the priest who has any defect is to come near to present the offerings made to the LORD by fire. He has a defect; he must not come near to offer the food of his God. ²²He may eat the most holy food of his God, ᵐ as well as the holy food; ²³yet because of his defect, he must not go near the curtain or approach the altar, and so desecrate my sanctuary. I am the LORD, who makes them holy. ᵉ ' ''

²⁴So Moses told this to Aaron and his sons and to all the Israelites.

22 The LORD said to Moses, ²''Tell Aaron and his sons to treat with respect the sacred offerings the Israelites consecrate to me, so they will not profane my holy name. I am the LORD.

³''Say to them: 'For the generations to come, if any of your descendants is ceremonially unclean and yet comes near the sacred offerings that the Israelites consecrate to the LORD, that person must be cut off from my presence. ⁿ I am the LORD.

⁴'' 'If a descendant of Aaron has an infectious skin diseaseᶠ or a bodily discharge, ᵒ he may not eat the sacred offerings until he is cleansed. He will also be unclean if he touches something defiled by a corpseᵖ or by anyone who has an emission of semen, ⁵or if he touches

21:5
vEze 44:20
wLev 19:28;
Dt 14:1
21:6
xLev 18:21
yLev 3:11
21:7
zver 13,14
aEze 44:22
21:8
bver 6
21:9
cGe 38:24;
Lev 19:29
21:10
dLev 16:32
eLev 10:6
21:11
fNu 19:11,13,14
gLev 19:28
21:12
hEx 29:6-7;
Lev 10:7
21:13
iEze 44:22
21:17
jver 6
21:18
kLev 22:19-25
21:20
lDt 23:1;
Isa 56:3
21:22
m1Co 9:13
22:3
nLev 7:20,21;
Nu 19:13
22:4
oLev 14:1-32;
15:2-15
pLev 11:24-28,
39

ª4 Or *unclean as a leader among his people*   ᵇ8 Or *who sanctify you; or who set you apart as holy*
ᶜ10 Or *not uncover his head*   ᵈ15 Or *who sanctifies him; or who sets him apart as holy*   ᵉ23 Or *who sanctifies them; or who sets them apart as holy*   ᶠ4 Traditionally *leprosy;* the Hebrew word was used for various diseases affecting the skin—not necessarily leprosy.

any crawling thing^q that makes him unclean, or any person^r who makes him unclean, whatever the uncleanness may be. ⁶The one who touches any such thing will be unclean till evening. He must not eat any of the sacred offerings unless he has bathed himself with water. ⁷When the sun goes down, he will be clean, and after that he may eat the sacred offerings, for they are his food.^s ⁸He must not eat anything found dead^t or torn by wild animals,^u and so become unclean^v through it. I am the LORD.

⁹" 'The priests are to keep my requirements so that they do not become guilty and die^w for treating them with contempt. I am the LORD, who makes them holy.^a

¹⁰" 'No one outside a priest's family may eat the sacred offering, nor may the guest of a priest or his hired worker eat it. ¹¹But if a priest buys a slave with money, or if a slave is born in his household, that slave may eat his food.^x ¹²If a priest's daughter marries anyone other than a priest, she may not eat any of the sacred contributions. ¹³But if a priest's daughter becomes a widow or is divorced, yet has no children, and she returns to live in her father's house as in her youth, she may eat of her father's food. No unauthorized person, however, may eat any of it.

¹⁴" 'If anyone eats a sacred offering by mistake, he must make restitution to the priest for the offering and add a fifth of the value^y to it. ¹⁵The priests must not desecrate the sacred offerings the Israelites present to the LORD^z ¹⁶by allowing them to eat the sacred offerings and so bring upon them guilt requiring payment.^a I am the LORD, who makes them holy.' "

Unacceptable Sacrifices

¹⁷The LORD said to Moses, ¹⁸"Speak to Aaron and his sons and to all the Israelites and say to them: 'If any of you—either an Israelite or an alien living in Israel—presents a gift^b for a burnt offering to the LORD, either to fulfill a vow or as a freewill offering, ¹⁹you must present a male without defect^c from the cattle, sheep or goats in order that it may be accepted on your behalf. ²⁰Do not bring anything with a defect,^d because it will not be accepted on your behalf. ²¹When anyone brings from the herd or flock a fellowship offering^{be} to the LORD to fulfill a special vow or as a freewill offering, it must be without defect or blemish to be acceptable. ²²Do not offer to the LORD the blind, the injured or the maimed, or anything with warts or festering or running sores. Do not place any of these on the altar as an offering made to the LORD by fire. ²³You may, however, present as a freewill offering an ox^c or a sheep that is deformed or stunted, but it will not be accepted in fulfillment of a vow. ²⁴You must not offer to the LORD an animal whose testicles are bruised, crushed, torn or cut.^f You must not do this in your own land, ²⁵and you must not accept such animals from the hand of a foreigner and offer them as the food of your God.^g They will not be accepted on your behalf, because they are deformed and have defects.' "

²⁶The LORD said to Moses, ²⁷"When a calf, a lamb or a goat is born, it is to remain with its mother for seven days.^h From the eighth day on, it

22:5
qLev 11:24-28,
43 rLev 15:7
22:7
sNu 18:11
22:8
tLev 11:39
uEx 22:31;
Lev 17:15
vLev 11:40
22:9
wver 16;
Ex 28:43
22:11
xGe 17:13;
Ex 12:44
22:14
yLev 5:15
22:15
zNu 18:32
22:16
aver 9
22:18
bLev 1:2
22:19
cLev 1:3
22:20
dDt 15:21;
17:1; Mal 1:8,
14; Heb 9:14;
1Pe 1:19
22:21
eLev 3:6;
Nu 15:3,8
22:24
fLev 21:20
22:25
gLev 21:6
22:27
hEx 22:30

---

^a9 Or *who sanctifies them;* or *who sets them apart as holy;* also in verse 16   ^b21 Traditionally *peace offering*   ^c23 The Hebrew word can include both male and female.

will be acceptable as an offering made to the LORD by fire. [28]Do not slaughter a cow or a sheep and its young on the same day.[i]

[29]"When you sacrifice a thank offering[j] to the LORD, sacrifice it in such a way that it will be accepted on your behalf. [30]It must be eaten that same day; leave none of it till morning.[k] I am the LORD.

[31]"Keep[l] my commands and follow them. I am the LORD. [32]Do not profane my holy name.[m] I must be acknowledged as holy by the Israelites.[n] I am the LORD, who makes[a] you holy[b] [33]and who brought you out of Egypt to be your God.[o] I am the LORD."

23

The LORD said to Moses, [2]"Speak to the Israelites and say to them: 'These are my appointed feasts,[p] the appointed feasts of the LORD, which you are to proclaim as sacred assemblies.[q]

The Sabbath

[3]" 'There are six days when you may work,[r] but the seventh day is a Sabbath of rest,[s] a day of sacred assembly. You are not to do any work; wherever you live, it is a Sabbath to the LORD.

The Passover and Unleavened Bread

23:4–8pp — Ex 12:14–20; Nu 28:16–25; Dt 16:1–8

[4]" 'These are the LORD's appointed feasts, the sacred assemblies you are to proclaim at their appointed times: [5]The LORD's Passover begins at twilight on the fourteenth day of the first month.[t] [6]On the fifteenth day of that month the LORD's Feast of Unleavened Bread begins; for seven days you must eat bread made without yeast. [7]On the first day hold a sacred assembly[u] and do no regular work. [8]For seven days present an offering made to the LORD by fire. And on the seventh day hold a sacred assembly and do no regular work.' "

Firstfruits

[9]The LORD said to Moses, [10]"Speak to the Israelites and say to them: 'When you enter the land I am going to give you and you reap its harvest, bring to the priest a sheaf[v] of the first grain you harvest. [11]He is to wave the sheaf before the LORD[w] so it will be accepted on your behalf; the priest is to wave it on the day after the Sabbath. [12]On the day you wave the sheaf, you must sacrifice as a burnt offering to the LORD a lamb a year old without defect, [13]together with its grain offering[x] of two-tenths of an ephah[c] of fine flour mixed with oil—an offering made to the LORD by fire, a pleasing aroma—and its drink offering of a quarter of a hin[d] of wine. [14]You must not eat any bread, or roasted or new grain, until the very day you bring this offering to your God.[y] This is to be a lasting ordinance for the generations to come,[z] wherever you live.

Feast of Weeks

23:15–22pp — Nu 28:26–31; Dt 16:9–12

[15]" 'From the day after the Sabbath, the day you brought the sheaf of

---

22:28
iDt 22:6,7
22:29
jLev 7:12;
Ps 107:22
22:30
kLev 7:15
22:31
lDt 4:2,40;
Ps 105:45
22:32
mLev 18:21
nLev 10:3
22:33
oLev 11:45
23:2
pver 4,37,44;
Nu 29:39
qver 21,27
23:3
rEx 20:9
sEx 20:10;
31:13-17;
Lev 19:3;
Dt 5:13;
Heb 4:9,10
23:5
tEx 12:18-19;
Nu 28:16-17;
Dt 16:1-8
23:7
uver 3,8
23:10
vEx 23:16,19;
34:26
23:11
wEx 29:24
23:13
xLev 2:14-16;
6:20
23:14
yEx 34:26
zNu 15:21

[a]32 Or *made*   [b]32 Or *who sanctifies you; or who sets you apart as holy*   [c]13 That is, probably about 4 quarts (about 4.5 liters); also in verse 17   [d]13 That is, probably about 1 quart (about 1 liter)

the wave offering, count off seven full weeks. [16]Count off fifty days up to the day after the seventh Sabbath,[a] and then present an offering of new grain to the LORD. [17]From wherever you live, bring two loaves made of two-tenths of an ephah of fine flour, baked with yeast, as a wave offering of firstfruits[b] to the LORD. [18]Present with this bread seven male lambs, each a year old and without defect, one young bull and two rams. They will be a burnt offering to the LORD, together with their grain offerings and drink offerings—an offering made by fire, an aroma pleasing to the LORD. [19]Then sacrifice one male goat for a sin offering and two lambs, each a year old, for a fellowship offering.[a] [20]The priest is to wave the two lambs before the LORD as a wave offering, together with the bread of the firstfruits. They are a sacred offering to the LORD for the priest. [21]On that same day you are to proclaim a sacred assembly[c] and do no regular work.[d] This is to be a lasting ordinance for the generations to come, wherever you live.

[22]" 'When you reap the harvest[e] of your land, do not reap to the very edges of your field or gather the gleanings of your harvest.[f] Leave them for the poor and the alien. I am the LORD your God.' "

Feast of Trumpets

23:23–25pp — Nu 29:1–6

[23]The LORD said to Moses, [24]"Say to the Israelites: 'On the first day of the seventh month you are to have a day of rest, a sacred assembly commemorated with trumpet blasts.[g] [25]Do no regular work,[h] but present an offering made to the LORD by fire.' "

Day of Atonement

23:26–32pp — Lev 16:2–34; Nu 29:7–11

[26]The LORD said to Moses, [27]"The tenth day of this seventh month[i] is the Day of Atonement.[j] Hold a sacred assembly[k] and deny yourselves,[b] and present an offering made to the LORD by fire. [28]Do no work on that day, because it is the Day of Atonement, when atonement is made for you before the LORD your God. [29]Anyone who does not deny himself on that day must be cut off from his people.[l] [30]I will destroy from among his people[m] anyone who does any work on that day. [31]You shall do no work at all. This is to be a lasting ordinance for the generations to come, wherever you live. [32]It is a sabbath of rest for you, and you must deny yourselves. From the evening of the ninth day of the month until the following evening you are to observe your sabbath."

Feast of Tabernacles

23:33–43pp — Nu 29:12–39; Dt 16:13–17

[33]The LORD said to Moses, [34]"Say to the Israelites: 'On the fifteenth day of the seventh month the LORD's Feast of Tabernacles[n] begins, and it lasts for seven days. [35]The first day is a sacred assembly; do no regular work. [36]For seven days present offerings made to the LORD by fire, and on the eighth day hold a sacred assembly[o] and present an offering made to the LORD by fire. It is the closing assembly; do no regular work.

[37](" 'These are the LORD's appointed feasts, which you are to proclaim as sacred assemblies for bringing offerings made to the LORD by

23:16
aNu 28:26;
Ac 2:1
23:17
bEx 34:22;
Lev 2:12
23:21
cver 2 dver 3
23:22
eLev 19:9
fLev 19:10;
Dt 24:19-21;
Ru 2:15
23:24
gLev 25:9;
Nu 10:9,10;
29:1
23:25
hver 21
23:27
iLev 16:29
jEx 30:10
kNu 29:7
23:29
lGe 17:14;
Nu 5:2
23:30
mLev 20:3
23:34
nEx 23:16;
Dt 16:13;
Ezr 3:4;
Ne 8:14;
Zec 14:16;
Jn 7:2
23:36
o2Ch 7:9;
Ne 8:18;
Jn 7:37

---

[a]19 Traditionally *peace offering*   [b]27 Or *and fast; also in verses 29 and 32*

fire—the burnt offerings and grain offerings, sacrifices and drink offerings[p] required for each day. [38]These offerings are in addition to those for the LORD's Sabbaths[q] and[a] in addition to your gifts and whatever you have vowed and all the freewill offerings you give to the LORD.)

[39]" 'So beginning with the fifteenth day of the seventh month, after you have gathered the crops of the land, celebrate the festival to the LORD for seven days;[r] the first day is a day of rest, and the eighth day also is a day of rest. [40]On the first day you are to take choice fruit from the trees, and palm fronds, leafy branches and poplars,[s] and rejoice before the LORD your God for seven days. [41]Celebrate this as a festival to the LORD for seven days each year. This is to be a lasting ordinance for the generations to come; celebrate it in the seventh month. [42]Live in booths[t] for seven days: All native-born Israelites are to live in booths [43]so your descendants will know[u] that I had the Israelites live in booths when I brought them out of Egypt. I am the LORD your God.' "

[44]So Moses announced to the Israelites the appointed feasts of the LORD.

Oil and Bread Set Before the LORD

24:1–3pp — Ex 27:20–21

24 The LORD said to Moses, [2]"Command the Israelites to bring you clear oil of pressed olives for the light so that the lamps may be kept burning continually. [3]Outside the curtain of the Testimony in the Tent of Meeting, Aaron is to tend the lamps before the LORD from evening till morning, continually. This is to be a lasting ordinance for the generations to come. [4]The lamps on the pure gold lampstand[v] before the LORD must be tended continually.

[5]"Take fine flour and bake twelve loaves of bread,[w] using two-tenths of an ephah[b] for each loaf. [6]Set them in two rows, six in each row, on the table of pure gold[x] before the LORD. [7]Along each row put some pure incense as a memorial portion[y] to represent the bread and to be an offering made to the LORD by fire. [8]This bread is to be set out before the LORD regularly,[z] Sabbath after Sabbath,[a] on behalf of the Israelites, as a lasting covenant. [9]It belongs to Aaron and his sons,[b] who are to eat it in a holy place, because it is a most holy part of their regular share of the offerings made to the LORD by fire."

A Blasphemer Stoned

[10]Now the son of an Israelite mother and an Egyptian father went out among the Israelites, and a fight broke out in the camp between him and an Israelite. [11]The son of the Israelite woman blasphemed the Name[c] with a curse; so they brought him to Moses. (His mother's name was Shelomith, the daughter of Dibri the Danite.) [12]They put him in custody until the will of the LORD should be made clear to them. [d]

[13]Then the LORD said to Moses: [14]"Take the blasphemer outside the camp. All those who heard him are to lay their hands on his head, and the entire assembly is to stone him. [e] [15]Say to the Israelites: 'If anyone curses his God, [f] he will be held responsible; [16]anyone who blasphemes the name of the LORD must be put to death. [g] The entire assembly must

23:37
p ver 2,4
23:38
q Eze 45:17
23:39
r Ex 23:16;
Dt 16:13
23:40
s Ne 8:14-17
23:42
t Ne 8:14-16
23:43
u Dt 31:13;
Ps 78:5
24:4
v Ex 25:31; 31:8
24:5
w Ex 25:30
24:6
x Ex 25:23-30;
1Ki 7:48
24:7
y Lev 2:2
24:8
z Nu 4:7;
1Ch 9:32;
2Ch 2:4
a Mt 12:5
24:9
b Lev 8:31;
Mt 12:4;
Mk 2:26; Lk 6:4
24:11
c Ex 3:15
24:12
d Ex 18:16;
Nu 15:34
24:14
e Lev 20:27;
Dt 13:9; 17:5,7;
21:21
24:15
f Ex 22:28
24:16
g 1Ki 21:10,13;
Mt 26:66

---

[a]38 Or *These feasts are in addition to the* LORD's *Sabbaths, and these offerings are*   [b]5 That is, probably about 4 quarts (about 4.5 liters)

stone him. Whether an alien or native-born, when he blasphemes the Name, he must be put to death.

17" 'If anyone takes the life of a human being, he must be put to death. [h] 18Anyone who takes the life of someone's animal must make restitution[i]—life for life. 19If anyone injures his neighbor, whatever he has done must be done to him: 20fracture for fracture, eye for eye, tooth for tooth. [j] As he has injured the other, so he is to be injured. 21Whoever kills an animal must make restitution, but whoever kills a man must be put to death. [k] 22You are to have the same law for the alien[l] and the native-born. [m] I am the LORD your God.' "

23Then Moses spoke to the Israelites, and they took the blasphemer outside the camp and stoned him. The Israelites did as the LORD commanded Moses.

The Sabbath Year

25 The LORD said to Moses on Mount Sinai, 2"Speak to the Israelites and say to them: 'When you enter the land I am going to give you, the land itself must observe a sabbath to the LORD. 3For six years sow your fields, and for six years prune your vineyards and gather their crops. [n] 4But in the seventh year the land is to have a sabbath of rest, a sabbath to the LORD. Do not sow your fields or prune your vineyards. 5Do not reap what grows of itself or harvest the grapes of your untended vines. The land is to have a year of rest. 6Whatever the land yields during the sabbath year[o] will be food for you—for yourself, your manservant and maidservant, and the hired worker and temporary resident who live among you, 7as well as for your livestock and the wild animals in your land. Whatever the land produces may be eaten.

The Year of Jubilee

25:8–38Ref — Dt 15:1–11
25:39–55Ref — Ex 21:2–11; Dt 15:12–18

8" 'Count off seven sabbaths of years—seven times seven years—so that the seven sabbaths of years amount to a period of forty-nine years. 9Then have the trumpet[p] sounded everywhere on the tenth day of the seventh month; on the Day of Atonement sound the trumpet throughout your land. 10Consecrate the fiftieth year and proclaim liberty[q] throughout the land to all its inhabitants. It shall be a jubilee[r] for you; each one of you is to return to his family property and each to his own clan. 11The fiftieth year shall be a jubilee for you; do not sow and do not reap what grows of itself or harvest the untended vines. 12For it is a jubilee and is to be holy for you; eat only what is taken directly from the fields.

13" 'In this Year of Jubilee[s] everyone is to return to his own property.

14" 'If you sell land to one of your countrymen or buy any from him, do not take advantage of each other. [t] 15You are to buy from your countryman on the basis of the number of years[u] since the Jubilee. And he is to sell to you on the basis of the number of years left for harvesting crops. 16When the years are many, you are to increase the price, and when the years are few, you are to decrease the price, [v] because what he is really selling you is the number of crops. 17Do not take advantage of each other, [w] but fear your God. [x] I am the LORD your God. [y]

18" 'Follow my decrees and be careful to obey my laws, and you will

24:17
hGe 9:6;
Ex 21:12;
Nu 35:30-31;
Dt 27:24
24:18
iver 21
24:20
jEx 21:24;
Mt 5:38*
24:21
kver 17
24:22
lEx 12:49
mNu 9:14;
15:16
25:3
nEx 23:10
25:6
over 20
25:9
pLev 23:24
25:10
qIsa 61:1;
Jer 34:8,15,17;
Lk 4:19
rNu 36:4
25:13
sver 10
25:14
tLev 19:13;
1Sa 12:3,4
25:15
uLev 27:18,23
25:16
vver 27,51,52
25:17
wPr 22:22;
Jer 7:5,6;
1Th 4:6
xLev 19:14
yLev 19:32

live safely in the land. z 19Then the land will yield its fruit, a and you will eat your fill and live there in safety. 20You may ask, "What will we eat in the seventh yearb if we do not plant or harvest our crops?" 21I will send you such a blessingc in the sixth year that the land will yield enough for three years. 22While you plant during the eighth year, you will eat from the old crop and will continue to eat from it until the harvest of the ninth year comes in. d

23" 'The land must not be sold permanently, because the land is minee and you are but aliensf and my tenants. 24Throughout the country that you hold as a possession, you must provide for the redemptiong of the land.

25" 'If one of your countrymen becomes poor and sells some of his property, his nearest relativeh is to come and redeemi what his countryman has sold. 26If, however, a man has no one to redeem it for him but he himself prospers and acquires sufficient means to redeem it, 27he is to determine the value for the years since he sold it and refund the balance to the man to whom he sold it; he can then go back to his own property. 28But if he does not acquire the means to repay him, what he sold will remain in the possession of the buyer until the Year of Jubilee. It will be returned in the Jubilee, and he can then go back to his property. i

29" 'If a man sells a house in a walled city, he retains the right of redemption a full year after its sale. During that time he may redeem it. 30If it is not redeemed before a full year has passed, the house in the walled city shall belong permanently to the buyer and his descendants. It is not to be returned in the Jubilee. 31But houses in villages without walls around them are to be considered as open country. They can be redeemed, and they are to be returned in the Jubilee.

32" 'The Levites always have the right to redeem their houses in the Levitical towns, k which they possess. 33So the property of the Levites is redeemable—that is, a house sold in any town they hold—and is to be returned in the Jubilee, because the houses in the towns of the Levites are their property among the Israelites. 34But the pastureland belonging to their towns must not be sold; it is their permanent possession. l

35" 'If one of your countrymen becomes poorm and is unable to support himself among you, help himn as you would an alien or a temporary resident, so he can continue to live among you. 36Do not take interesto of any kinda from him, but fear your God, so that your countryman may continue to live among you. 37You must not lend him money at interest or sell him food at a profit. 38I am the LORD your God, who brought you out of Egypt to give you the land of Canaan and to be your God. p

39" 'If one of your countrymen becomes poor among you and sells himself to you, do not make him work as a slave. q 40He is to be treated as a hired worker or a temporary resident among you; he is to work for you until the Year of Jubilee. 41Then he and his children are to be released, and he will go back to his own clan and to the propertyr of his forefathers. 42Because the Israelites are my servants, whom I brought out of Egypt, they must not be sold as slaves. 43Do not rule over them ruthlessly, s but fear your God.

a36 Or *take excessive interest*; similarly in verse 37

25:18
zLev 26:4,5;
Dt 12:10;
Ps 4:8; Jer 23:6
25:19
aLev 26:4
25:20
bver 4
25:21
cDt 28:8,12;
Hag 2:19;
Mal 3:10
25:22
dLev 26:10
25:23
eEx 19:5
fGe 23:4;
1Ch 29:15;
Ps 39:12;
Heb 11:13;
1Pe 2:11
25:24
gver 29,48;
Ru 4:7
25:25
hRu 2:20;
Jer 32:7
iLev 27:13,19,
31; Ru 4:4
25:28
jver 10
25:32
kNu 35:1-8;
Jos 21:2
25:34
lNu 35:2-5
25:35
mDt 24:14,15
nDt 15:8;
Ps 37:21,26;
Lk 6:35
25:36
oEx 22:25;
Dt 23:19-20
25:38
pGe 17:7;
Lev 11:45
25:39
qEx 21:2;
Dt 15:12;
1Ki 9:22
25:41
rver 28
25:43
sEx 1:13;
Eze 34:4;
Col 4:1

44″ 'Your male and female slaves are to come from the nations around you; from them you may buy slaves. 45You may also buy some of the temporary residents living among you and members of their clans born in your country, and they will become your property. 46You can will them to your children as inherited property and can make them slaves for life, but you must not rule over your fellow Israelites ruthlessly.

47″ 'If an alien or a temporary resident among you becomes rich and one of your countrymen becomes poor and sells himself to the alien living among you or to a member of the alien's clan, 48he retains the right of redemption after he has sold himself. One of his relatives^t may redeem him: 49An uncle or a cousin or any blood relative in his clan may redeem him. Or if he prospers,^u he may redeem himself. 50He and his buyer are to count the time from the year he sold himself up to the Year of Jubilee. The price for his release is to be based on the rate paid to a hired man^v for that number of years. 51If many years remain, he must pay for his redemption a larger share of the price paid for him. 52If only a few years remain until the Year of Jubilee, he is to compute that and pay for his redemption accordingly. 53He is to be treated as a man hired from year to year; you must see to it that his owner does not rule over him ruthlessly.

54″ 'Even if he is not redeemed in any of these ways, he and his children are to be released in the Year of Jubilee, 55for the Israelites belong to me as servants. They are my servants, whom I brought out of Egypt. I am the LORD your God.

Reward for Obedience

26 ″ 'Do not make idols^w or set up an image or a sacred stone^x for yourselves, and do not place a carved stone^y in your land to bow down before it. I am the LORD your God.

2″ 'Observe my Sabbaths and have reverence for my sanctuary.^z I am the LORD.

3″ 'If you follow my decrees and are careful to obey^a my commands, 4I will send you rain^b in its season, and the ground will yield its crops and the trees of the field their fruit.^c 5Your threshing will continue until grape harvest and the grape harvest will continue until planting, and you will eat all the food you want^d and live in safety in your land.^e

6″ 'I will grant peace in the land,^f and you will lie down^g and no one will make you afraid.^h I will remove savage beastsⁱ from the land, and the sword will not pass through your country. 7You will pursue your enemies, and they will fall by the sword before you. 8Five of you will chase a hundred, and a hundred of you will chase ten thousand, and your enemies will fall by the sword before you.^j

9″ 'I will look on you with favor and make you fruitful and increase your numbers,^k and I will keep my covenant^l with you. 10You will still be eating last year's harvest when you will have to move it out to make room for the new.^m 11I will put my dwelling place^{a n} among you, and I will not abhor you. 12I will walk^o among you and be your God, and you will be my people.^p 13I am the LORD your God, who brought you out of Egypt so that you would no longer be slaves to the Egyptians; I broke the bars of your yoke^q and enabled you to walk with heads held high.

a11 Or my tabernacle

25:48
tNe 5:5
25:49
uver 26
25:50
vJob 7:1;
Isa 16:14; 21:16
26:1
wEx 20:4;
Lev 19:4; Dt 5:8
xEx 23:24
yNu 33:52
26:2
zLev 19:30
26:3
aDt 7:12; 11:13,
22; 28:1,9
26:4
bDt 11:14
cPs 67:6
26:5
dDt 11:15;
Joel 2:19,26;
Am 9:13
eLev 25:18
26:6
fPs 29:11; 85:8;
147:14 gPs 4:8
hZep 3:13
iver 22
26:8
jDt 32:30;
Jos 23:10
26:9
kGe 17:6;
Ne 9:23
lGe 17:7
26:10
mLev 25:22
26:11
nEx 25:8;
Ps 76:2;
Eze 37:27
26:12
oGe 3:8
p2Co 6:16*
26:13
qEze 34:27

Punishment for Disobedience

14'' 'But if you will not listen to me and carry out all these commands,ʳ ¹⁵and if you reject my decrees and abhor my laws and fail to carry out all my commands and so violate my covenant, ¹⁶then I will do this to you: I will bring upon you sudden terror, wasting diseases and feverˢ that will destroy your sight and drain away your life.ᵗ You will plant seed in vain, because your enemies will eat it.ᵘ ¹⁷I will set my faceᵛ against you so that you will be defeated by your enemies; those who hate you will rule over you,ʷ and you will flee even when no one is pursuing you.ˣ

18'' 'If after all this you will not listen to me, I will punish you for your sins seven times over.ʸ ¹⁹I will break down your stubborn prideᶻ and make the sky above you like iron and the ground beneath you like bronze.ᵃ ²⁰Your strength will be spent in vain,ᵇ because your soil will not yield its crops, nor will the trees of the land yield their fruit.ᶜ

21'' 'If you remain hostile toward me and refuse to listen to me, I will multiply your afflictions seven times over,ᵈ as your sins deserve. ²²I will send wild animalsᵉ against you, and they will rob you of your children, destroy your cattle and make you so few in number that your roads will be deserted.

23'' 'If in spite of these things you do not accept my correctionᶠ but continue to be hostile toward me, ²⁴I myself will be hostile toward you and will afflict you for your sins seven times over. ²⁵And I will bring the sword upon you to avenge the breaking of the covenant. When you withdraw into your cities, I will send a plagueᵍ among you, and you will be given into enemy hands. ²⁶When I cut off your supply of bread,ʰ ten women will be able to bake your bread in one oven, and they will dole out the bread by weight. You will eat, but you will not be satisfied.

27'' 'If in spite of this you still do not listen to me but continue to be hostile toward me, ²⁸then in my anger I will be hostile toward you, and I myself will punish you for your sins seven times over. ²⁹You will eat the flesh of your sons and the flesh of your daughters.ⁱ ³⁰I will destroy your high places,ʲ cut down your incense altarsᵏ and pile your dead bodies on the lifeless forms of your idols,ˡ and I will abhor you. ³¹I will turn your cities into ruins and lay waste your sanctuaries,ᵐ and I will take no delight in the pleasing aroma of your offerings. ³²I will lay waste the land,ⁿ so that your enemies who live there will be appalled. ³³I will scatter you among the nationsᵒ and will draw out my sword and pursue you. Your land will be laid waste, and your cities will lie in ruins. ³⁴Then the land will enjoy its sabbath years all the time that it lies desolate and you are in the country of your enemies;ᵖ then the land will rest and enjoy its sabbaths. ³⁵All the time that it lies desolate, the land will have the rest it did not have during the sabbaths you lived in it.

36'' 'As for those of you who are left, I will make their hearts so fearful in the lands of their enemies that the sound of a windblown leaf will put them to flight.�vq They will run as though fleeing from the sword, and they will fall, even though no one is pursuing them. ³⁷They will stumble over one another as though fleeing from the sword, even though no one is pursuing them. So you will not be able to stand before your enemies.ʳ ³⁸You will perish among the nations; the land of your enemies will devour you.ˢ ³⁹Those of you who are left will waste away in

---

26:14
ʳDt 28:15-68;
Mal 2:2

26:16
ˢDt 28:22,35
ᵗ1Sa 2:33
ᵘJob 31:8

26:17
ᵛLev 17:10
ʷPs 106:41
ˣver 36,37;
Dt 28:7,25;
Ps 53:5

26:18
ʸver 21

26:19
ᶻIsa 25:11
ᵃDt 28:23

26:20
ᵇPs 127:1;
Isa 17:11
ᶜDt 11:17

26:21
ᵈver 18

26:22
ᵉDt 32:24

26:23
ᶠJer 2:30; 5:3

26:25
ᵍNu 14:12;
Eze 5:17

26:26
ʰPs 105:16;
Isa 3:1;
Mic 6:14

26:29
ⁱDt 28:53

26:30
ʲ2Ch 34:3;
Eze 6:3
ᵏEze 6:6
ˡEze 6:13

26:31
ᵐPs 74:3-7

26:32
ⁿJer 9:11

26:33
ᵒDt 4:27;
Eze 12:15;
20:23; Zec 7:14

26:34
ᵖver 43;
2Ch 36:21

26:36
qEze 21:7

26:37
ʳJos 7:12

26:38
ˢDt 4:26

the lands of their enemies because of their sins; also because of their fathers' sins they will waste away.ᵗ

⁴⁰" 'But if they will confess their sins and the sins of their fathersᵘ —their treachery against me and their hostility toward me, ⁴¹which made me hostile toward them so that I sent them into the land of their enemies—then when their uncircumcised heartsᵛ are humbled and they pay for their sin, ⁴²I will remember my covenant with Jacobʷ and my covenant with Isaacˣ and my covenant with Abraham, and I will remember the land. ⁴³For the land will be deserted by them and will enjoy its sabbaths while it lies desolate without them. They will pay for their sins because they rejected my laws and abhorred my decrees. ⁴⁴Yet in spite of this, when they are in the land of their enemies, I will not reject them or abhorʸ them so as to destroy them completely,ᶻ breaking my covenantᵃ with them. I am the LORD their God. ⁴⁵But for their sake I will rememberᵇ the covenant with their ancestors whom I brought out of Egyptᶜ in the sight of the nations to be their God. I am the LORD.' "

⁴⁶These are the decrees, the laws and the regulations that the LORD established on Mount Sinai between himself and the Israelites through Moses. ᵈ

Redeeming What Is the LORD's

27 The LORD said to Moses, ²"Speak to the Israelites and say to them: 'If anyone makes a special vowᵉ to dedicate persons to the LORD by giving equivalent values, ³set the value of a male between the ages of twenty and sixty at fifty shekelsᵃ of silver, according to the sanctuary shekelᵇ;ᶠ ⁴and if it is a female, set her value at thirty shekels. ᶜ ⁵If it is a person between the ages of five and twenty, set the value of a male at twenty shekelsᵈ and of a female at ten shekels.ᵉ ⁶If it is a person between one month and five years, set the value of a male at five shekelsᶠ;ᵍ of silver and that of a female at three shekelsᵍ of silver. ⁷If it is a person sixty years old or more, set the value of a male at fifteen shekelsʰ and of a female at ten shekels. ⁸If anyone making the vow is too poor to payʰ the specified amount, he is to present the person to the priest, who will set the valueⁱ for him according to what the man making the vow can afford.

⁹" 'If what he vowed is an animal that is acceptable as an offering to the LORD, such an animal given to the LORD becomes holy. ¹⁰He must not exchange it or substitute a good one for a bad one, or a bad one for a good one;ʲ if he should substitute one animal for another, both it and the substitute become holy. ¹¹If what he vowed is a ceremonially unclean animal—one that is not acceptable as an offering to the LORD—the animal must be presented to the priest, ¹²who will judge its quality as good or bad. Whatever value the priest then sets, that is what it will be. ¹³If the owner wishes to redeemᵏ the animal, he must add a fifth to its value.

¹⁴" 'If a man dedicates his house as something holy to the LORD, the

26:39
tEze 4:17
26:40
uJer 3:12-15;
Lk 15:18;
1Jn 1:9
26:41
vEze 44:7,9;
Ac 7:51
26:42
wGe 22:15-18;
28:15 xGe 26:5
26:44
yRo 11:2
zDt 4:31;
Jer 30:11
aJer 33:26
26:45
bGe 17:7
cEx 6:8;
Lev 25:38
26:46
dLev 7:38;
27:34
27:2
eNu 6:2
27:3
fEx 30:13;
Nu 3:47; 18:16
27:6
gNu 18:16
27:8
hLev 5:11
iver 12,14
27:10
jver 33
27:13
kver 15,19;
Lev 25:25

ᵃ3 That is, about 1 1/4 pounds (about 0.6 kilogram); also in verse 16　　ᵇ3 That is, about 2/5 ounce (about 11.5 grams); also in verse 25　　ᶜ4 That is, about 12 ounces (about 0.3 kilogram) ᵈ5 That is, about 8 ounces (about 0.2 kilogram)　　ᵉ5 That is, about 4 ounces (about 110 grams); also in verse 7　　ᶠ6 That is, about 2 ounces (about 55 grams)　　ᵍ6 That is, about 1 1/4 ounces (about 35 grams)　　ʰ7 That is, about 6 ounces (about 170 grams) priest will judge its quality as good or bad. Whatever value the priest then sets, so it will remain. ¹⁵If the man who dedicates his house redeems it,[1] he must add a fifth to its value, and the house will again become his.

¹⁶" 'If a man dedicates to the Lord part of his family land, its value is to be set according to the amount of seed required for it—fifty shekels of silver to a homer[a] of barley seed. ¹⁷If he dedicates his field during the Year of Jubilee, the value that has been set remains. ¹⁸But if he dedicates his field after the Jubilee, the priest will determine the value according to the number of years that remain[m] until the next Year of Jubilee, and its set value will be reduced. ¹⁹If the man who dedicates the field wishes to redeem it, he must add a fifth to its value, and the field will again become his. ²⁰If, however, he does not redeem the field, or if he has sold it to someone else, it can never be redeemed. ²¹When the field is released in the Jubilee,[n] it will become holy, like a field devoted to the Lord;[o] it will become the property of the priests.[b]

²²" 'If a man dedicates to the Lord a field he has bought, which is not part of his family land, ²³the priest will determine its value up to the Year of Jubilee, and the man must pay its value on that day as something holy to the Lord. ²⁴In the Year of Jubilee the field will revert to the person from whom he bought it,[p] the one whose land it was. ²⁵Every value is to be set according to the sanctuary shekel,[q] twenty gerahs[r] to the shekel.

²⁶" 'No one, however, may dedicate the firstborn of an animal, since the firstborn already belongs to the Lord;[s] whether an ox[c] or a sheep, it is the Lord's. ²⁷If it is one of the unclean animals,[t] he may buy it back at its set value, adding a fifth of the value to it. If he does not redeem it, it is to be sold at its set value.

²⁸" 'But nothing that a man owns and devotes[du] to the Lord— whether man or animal or family land—may be sold or redeemed; everything so devoted is most holy to the Lord.

²⁹" 'No person devoted to destruction[e] may be ransomed; he must be put to death.

³⁰" 'A tithe[v] of everything from the land, whether grain from the soil or fruit from the trees, belongs to the Lord; it is holy to the Lord. ³¹If a man redeems any of his tithe, he must add a fifth of the value to it. ³²The entire tithe of the herd and flock—every tenth animal that passes under the shepherd's rod[w]—will be holy to the Lord. ³³He must not pick out the good from the bad or make any substitution.[x] If he does make a substitution, both the animal and its substitute become holy and cannot be redeemed.' "

³⁴These are the commands the Lord gave Moses on Mount Sinai for the Israelites.[y]

27:15
l ver 13,20
27:18
m Lev 25:15
27:21
n Lev 25:10
over 28;
Nu 18:14;
Eze 44:29
27:24
p Lev 25:28
27:25
q Ex 30:13;
Nu 18:16
r Nu 3:47;
Eze 45:12
27:26
s Ex 13:2,12
27:27
t ver 11
27:28
u Nu 18:14;
Jos 6:17-19
27:30
v Ge 28:22;
2Ch 31:6;
Mal 3:8
27:32
w Jer 33:13;
Eze 20:37
27:33
x ver 10
27:34
y Lev 26:46;
Dt 4:5

a16 That is, probably about 6 bushels (about 220 liters)   *b21* Or *priest*   *c26* The Hebrew word can include both male and female.   *d28* The Hebrew term refers to the irrevocable giving over of things or persons to the Lord.   *e29* The Hebrew term refers to the irrevocable giving over of things or persons to the Lord, often by totally destroying them.

Numbers

Title and Background

The book of Numbers gets its name from the two numberings or countings of the Israelites during their 38 years of wandering in the wilderness. These countings are found in chapters 1 and 26. Numbers presents an account of that wandering in the desert following the establishment of the covenant at Sinai.

Author and Date of Writing

Numbers has been traditionally ascribed to Moses. This assignment is based on: (1) the statements concerning Moses' writing activity (e.g., 33:1-2; Ex 17:14; 24:4; 34:27); (2) the assumption that the Pentateuch is a unity and comes from one great author; and (3) the New Testament's ascription of quotations from the Pentateuch to Moses (e.g., Mt 19:8; Jn 5:46-47; Ro 10:5). Numbers was written by Moses shortly before his death in 1406 B.C.

Theme and Message

Numbers relates the story of Israel's journey from Mount Sinai to the plains of Moab on the border of Canaan. It tells of the murmuring and rebellion of God's people and of their subsequent judgment. They were condemned to live out their lives in the desert; only their children would enjoy the fulfillment of the promise that had originally been theirs. Throughout the years in the desert, one thing became clear to Israel—God's constant care for them. Not only did he meet their needs, but he also loved and forgave his people continually.

Outline

   I. Israel at Sinai, Preparing to Go to Canaan (1:1-10:10)
  II. From Sinai to Kadesh Barnea (10:11-12:16)
 III. Israel at Kadesh, the Delay Resulting From Rebellion (13:1-20:13)
  IV. From Kadesh to the Plains of Moab (20:14-22:1)
   V. Israel on the Plains of Moab, Anticipating the Taking of Canaan (22:2-32:42)
  VI. Supplements Dealing With Various Matters (33:1-36:13)

The Census

1 The LORD spoke to Moses in the Tent of Meeting[a] in the Desert of Sinai[b] on the first day of the second month[c] of the second year after the Israelites came out of Egypt. He said: ²"Take a census[d] of the whole Israelite community by their clans and families, listing every man by name, one by one. ³You and Aaron are to number by their divisions all the men in Israel twenty years old or more[e] who are able to serve in the army. ⁴One man from each tribe, each the head of his family,[f] is to help you.[g] ⁵These are the names of the men who are to assist you:

from Reuben,[h] Elizur son of Shedeur;
⁶from Simeon, Shelumiel son of Zurishaddai;
⁷from Judah,[i] Nahshon son of Amminadab;[j]

1:1
aEx 40:2
bEx 19:1
cEx 40:17
1:2
dEx 30:11-16;
Nu 26:2
1:3
eEx 30:14
1:4
fver 16
gEx 18:21;
Dt 1:15
1:5
hGe 29:32;
Dt 33:6
1:7
iGe 29:35;
Ps 78:68
jRu 4:20;
Lk 3:32

⁸from Issachar,ᵏ Nethanel son of Zuar;
⁹from Zebulun,ˡ Eliab son of Helon;
¹⁰from the sons of Joseph:
    from Ephraim,ᵐ Elishama son of Ammihud;
    from Manasseh, Gamaliel son of Pedahzur;
¹¹from Benjamin, Abidan son of Gideoni;
¹²from Dan,ⁿ Ahiezer son of Ammishaddai;
¹³from Asher,ᵒ Pagiel son of Ocran;
¹⁴from Gad, Eliasaph son of Deuel;ᵖ
¹⁵from Naphtali,�q Ahira son of Enan."

1:8
kGe 30:18
1:9
lver 30
1:10
mver 32
1:12
nver 38
1:13
over 40
1:14
pNu 2:14
1:15
qver 42
1:16
rEx 18:25
sver 4;
Ex 18:21;
Nu 7:2
1:18
tver 1
uEzr 2:59;
Heb 7:3
1:20
vNu 26:5-11;
Rev 7:5
1:22
wNu 26:12-14;
Rev 7:7
1:24
xGe 30:11;
Nu 26:15-18;
Rev 7:5
1:26
yGe 29:35;
Nu 26:19-22;
Mt 1:2; Rev 7:5
1:28
zNu 26:23-25;
Rev 7:7
1:30
aNu 26:26-27;
Rev 7:8

¹⁶These were the men appointed from the community, the leadersʳ of their ancestral tribes. They were the heads of the clans of Israel.ˢ

¹⁷Moses and Aaron took these men whose names had been given, ¹⁸and they called the whole community together on the first day of the second month.ᵗ The people indicated their ancestryᵘ by their clans and families, and the men twenty years old or more were listed by name, one by one, ¹⁹as the LORD commanded Moses. And so he counted them in the Desert of Sinai:

²⁰From the descendants of Reubenᵛ the firstborn son of Israel:
    All the men twenty years old or more who were able to serve in the army were listed by name, one by one, according to the records of their clans and families. ²¹The number from the tribe of Reuben was 46,500.

²²From the descendants of Simeon:ʷ
    All the men twenty years old or more who were able to serve in the army were counted and listed by name, one by one, according to the records of their clans and families. ²³The number from the tribe of Simeon was 59,300.

²⁴From the descendants of Gad:ˣ
    All the men twenty years old or more who were able to serve in the army were listed by name, according to the records of their clans and families. ²⁵The number from the tribe of Gad was 45,650.

²⁶From the descendants of Judah:ʸ
    All the men twenty years old or more who were able to serve in the army were listed by name, according to the records of their clans and families. ²⁷The number from the tribe of Judah was 74,600.

²⁸From the descendants of Issachar:ᶻ
    All the men twenty years old or more who were able to serve in the army were listed by name, according to the records of their clans and families. ²⁹The number from the tribe of Issachar was 54,400.

³⁰From the descendants of Zebulun:ᵃ
    All the men twenty years old or more who were able to serve in the army were listed by name, according to the records of their clans and families. ³¹The number from the tribe of Zebulun was 57,400.

³²From the sons of Joseph:

From the descendants of Ephraim: ᵇ

All the men twenty years old or more who were able to serve in the army were listed by name, according to the records of their clans and families. ³³The number from the tribe of Ephraim was 40,500.

³⁴From the descendants of Manasseh: ᶜ

All the men twenty years old or more who were able to serve in the army were listed by name, according to the records of their clans and families. ³⁵The number from the tribe of Manasseh was 32,200.

³⁶From the descendants of Benjamin: ᵈ

All the men twenty years old or more who were able to serve in the army were listed by name, according to the records of their clans and families. ³⁷The number from the tribe of Benjamin was 35,400.

³⁸From the descendants of Dan: ᵉ

All the men twenty years old or more who were able to serve in the army were listed by name, according to the records of their clans and families. ³⁹The number from the tribe of Dan was 62,700.

⁴⁰From the descendants of Asher: ᶠ

All the men twenty years old or more who were able to serve in the army were listed by name, according to the records of their clans and families. ⁴¹The number from the tribe of Asher was 41,500.

⁴²From the descendants of Naphtali: ᵍ

All the men twenty years old or more who were able to serve in the army were listed by name, according to the records of their clans and families. ⁴³The number from the tribe of Naphtali was 53,400.

⁴⁴These were the men counted by Moses and Aaron ʰ and the twelve leaders of Israel, each one representing his family. ⁴⁵All the Israelites twenty years old or more who were able to serve in Israel's army were counted according to their families. ⁴⁶The total number was 603,550. ⁱ

⁴⁷The families of the tribe of Levi, ʲ however, were not counted ᵏ along with the others. ⁴⁸The LORD had said to Moses: ⁴⁹"You must not count the tribe of Levi or include them in the census of the other Israelites. ⁵⁰Instead, appoint the Levites to be in charge of the tabernacle of the Testimony ˡ—over all its furnishings and everything belonging to it. They are to carry the tabernacle and all its furnishings; they are to take care of it and encamp around it. ⁵¹Whenever the tabernacle is to move, the Levites are to take it down, and whenever the tabernacle is to be set up, the Levites shall do it. ᵐ Anyone else who goes near it shall be put to death. ⁵²The Israelites are to set up their tents by divisions, each man in his own camp under his own standard. ⁿ ⁵³The Levites, however, are to set up their tents around the tabernacle of the Testimony so that wrath will not fall ° on the Israelite community. The Levites are to be responsible for the care of the tabernacle of the Testimony. ᵖ"

1:32
ᵇNu 26:35-37
1:34
ᶜNu 26:28-34;
Rev 7:6
1:36
ᵈNu 26:38-41;
2Ch 17:17;
Rev 7:8
1:38
ᵉGe 30:6;
Nu 26:42-43
1:40
ᶠNu 26:44-47;
Rev 7:6
1:42
ᵍNu 26:48-50;
Rev 7:6
1:44
ʰNu 26:64
1:46
ⁱEx 12:37;
38:26; Nu 2:32;
26:51
1:47
ʲNu 2:33; 26:57
ᵏNu 4:3,49
1:50
ˡEx 38:21;
Ac 7:44
1:51
ᵐNu 3:38;
4:1-33
1:52
ⁿNu 2:2;
Ps 20:5
1:53
°Lev 10:6;
Nu 16:46; 18:5
ᵖNu 18:2-4

⁵⁴The Israelites did all this just as the LORD commanded Moses.

The Arrangement of the Tribal Camps

2 The LORD said to Moses and Aaron: ²"The Israelites are to camp around the Tent of Meeting some distance from it, each man under his standard q with the banners of his family."

³On the east, toward the sunrise, the divisions of the camp of Judah are to encamp under their standard. The leader of the people of Judah is Nahshon son of Amminadab.ʳ ⁴His division numbers 74,600.

⁵The tribe of Issachar will camp next to them. The leader of the people of Issachar is Nethanel son of Zuar.ˢ ⁶His division numbers 54,400.

⁷The tribe of Zebulun will be next. The leader of the people of Zebulun is Eliab son of Helon.ᵗ ⁸His division numbers 57,400.

⁹All the men assigned to the camp of Judah, according to their divisions, number 186,400. They will set out first.ᵘ

¹⁰On the south will be the divisions of the camp of Reuben under their standard. The leader of the people of Reuben is Elizur son of Shedeur.ᵛ ¹¹His division numbers 46,500.

¹²The tribe of Simeon will camp next to them. The leader of the people of Simeon is Shelumiel son of Zurishaddai.ʷ ¹³His division numbers 59,300.

¹⁴The tribe of Gad will be next. The leader of the people of Gad is Eliasaph son of Deuel.ᵃˣ ¹⁵His division numbers 45,650.

¹⁶All the men assigned to the camp of Reuben,ʸ according to their divisions, number 151,450. They will set out second.

¹⁷Then the Tent of Meeting and the camp of the Levitesᶻ will set out in the middle of the camps. They will set out in the same order as they encamp, each in his own place under his standard.

¹⁸On the west will be the divisions of the camp of Ephraimᵃ under their standard. The leader of the people of Ephraim is Elishama son of Ammihud.ᵇ ¹⁹His division numbers 40,500.

²⁰The tribe of Manasseh will be next to them. The leader of the people of Manasseh is Gamaliel son of Pedahzur.ᶜ ²¹His division numbers 32,200.

²²The tribe of Benjamin will be next. The leader of the people of Benjamin is Abidan son of Gideoni.ᵈ ²³His division numbers 35,400.

²⁴All the men assigned to the camp of Ephraim,ᵉ according to their divisions, number 108,100. They will set out third.ᶠ

²⁵On the north will be the divisions of the camp of Dan, under their standard. The leader of the people of Dan is Ahiezer son of Ammishaddai.ᵍ ²⁶His division numbers 62,700.

²⁷The tribe of Asher will camp next to them. The leader of the

ᵃ14 Many manuscripts of the Masoretic Text, Samaritan Pentateuch and Vulgate (see also Num. 1:14); most manuscripts of the Masoretic Text *Reuel* people of Asher is Pagiel son of Ocran. [h] 28His division numbers 41,500.

29The tribe of Naphtali will be next. The leader of the people of Naphtali is Ahira son of Enan. [i] 30His division numbers 53,400.

31All the men assigned to the camp of Dan number 157,600. They will set out last, [j] under their standards.

32These are the Israelites, counted according to their families. All those in the camps, by their divisions, number 603,550. [k] 33The Levites, however, were not counted [l] along with the other Israelites, as the LORD commanded Moses.

34So the Israelites did everything the LORD commanded Moses; that is the way they encamped under their standards, and that is the way they set out, each with his clan and family.

The Levites

3 This is the account of the family of Aaron and Moses [m] at the time the LORD talked with Moses on Mount Sinai.

2The names of the sons of Aaron were Nadab the firstborn and Abihu, Eleazar and Ithamar. [n] 3Those were the names of Aaron's sons, the anointed priests, [o] who were ordained to serve as priests. 4Nadab and Abihu, however, fell dead before the LORD [p] when they made an offering with unauthorized fire before him in the Desert of Sinai. [q] They had no sons; so only Eleazar and Ithamar served as priests during the lifetime of their father Aaron. [r]

5The LORD said to Moses, 6"Bring the tribe of Levi [s] and present them to Aaron the priest to assist him. [t] 7They are to perform duties for him and for the whole community at the Tent of Meeting by doing the work [u] of the tabernacle. 8They are to take care of all the furnishings of the Tent of Meeting, fulfilling the obligations of the Israelites by doing the work of the tabernacle. 9Give the Levites to Aaron and his sons; [v] they are the Israelites who are to be given wholly to him. [a] 10Appoint Aaron and his sons to serve as priests; [w] anyone else who approaches the sanctuary must be put to death." [x]

11The LORD also said to Moses, 12"I have taken the Levites [y] from among the Israelites in place of the first male offspring [z] of every Israelite woman. The Levites are mine, [a] 13for all the firstborn are mine. [b] When I struck down all the firstborn in Egypt, I set apart for myself every firstborn in Israel, whether man or animal. They are to be mine. I am the LORD."

14The LORD said to Moses in the Desert of Sinai, 15"Count [c] the Levites by their families and clans. Count every male a month old or more." [d] 16So Moses counted them, as he was commanded by the word of the LORD.

17These were the names of the sons of Levi: [e]

Gershon, Kohath and Merari. [f]

18These were the names of the Gershonite clans:

Libni and Shimei. [g]

19The Kohathite clans:

2:27
hNu 1:13
2:29
iNu 1:15
2:31
jNu 10:25
2:32
kEx 38:26;
Nu 1:46
2:33
lNu 1:47;
26:57-62
3:1
mEx 6:27
3:2
nEx 6:23;
Nu 26:60
3:3
oEx 28:41
3:4
pLev 10:2
qLev 10:1
r1Ch 24:1
3:6
sDt 10:8; 31:9;
1Ch 15:2
tNu 8:6-22;
18:1-7;
2Ch 29:11
3:7
uLev 8:35;
Nu 1:50
3:9
vNu 8:19; 18:6
3:10
wEx 29:9
xNu 1:51
3:12
yMal 2:4
zver 41;
Nu 8:16,18
aEx 13:2
3:13
bEx 13:12
3:15
cver 39
dNu 26:62
3:17
eGe 46:11
fEx 6:16
3:18
gEx 6:17

---

a9 Most manuscripts of the Masoretic Text; some manuscripts of the Masoretic Text, Samaritan Pentateuch and Septuagint (see also Num. 8:16) *to me*

Amram, Izhar, Hebron and Uzziel. [h]
20The Merarite clans: [i]
Mahli and Mushi. [j]
These were the Levite clans, according to their families.

21To Gershon belonged the clans of the Libnites and Shimeites; [k] these were the Gershonite clans. 22The number of all the males a month old or more who were counted was 7,500. 23The Gershonite clans were to camp on the west, behind the tabernacle. 24The leader of the families of the Gershonites was Eliasaph son of Lael. 25At the Tent of Meeting the Gershonites were responsible for the care of the tabernacle[l] and tent, its coverings, [m] the curtain at the entrance[n] to the Tent of Meeting, 26the curtains of the courtyard[o], the curtain at the entrance to the courtyard surrounding the tabernacle and altar, and the ropes[p]—and everything related to their use.

27To Kohath belonged the clans of the Amramites, Izharites, Hebronites and Uzzielites; [q] these were the Kohathite clans. 28The number of all the males a month old or more was 8,600. [a] The Kohathites were responsible for the care of the sanctuary. 29The Kohathite clans were to camp on the south side[r] of the tabernacle. 30The leader of the families of the Kohathite clans was Elizaphan son of Uzziel. 31They were responsible for the care of the ark, [s] the table, [t] the lampstand, [u] the altars, [v] the articles of the sanctuary used in ministering, the curtain, [w] and everything related to their use. [x] 32The chief leader of the Levites was Eleazar son of Aaron, the priest. He was appointed over those who were responsible for the care of the sanctuary.

33To Merari belonged the clans of the Mahlites and the Mushites; [y] these were the Merarite clans. 34The number of all the males a month old or more who were counted was 6,200. 35The leader of the families of the Merarite clans was Zuriel son of Abihail; they were to camp on the north side of the tabernacle. [z] 36The Merarites were appointed[a] to take care of the frames of the tabernacle, its crossbars, posts, bases, all its equipment, and everything related to their use, 37as well as the posts of the surrounding courtyard with their bases, tent pegs and ropes.

38Moses and Aaron and his sons were to camp to the east[b] of the tabernacle, toward the sunrise, in front of the Tent of Meeting. [c] They were responsible for the care of the sanctuary[d] on behalf of the Israelites. Anyone else who approached the sanctuary was to be put to death. [e]

39The total number of Levites counted at the LORD's command by Moses and Aaron according to their clans, including every male a month old or more, was 22,000. [f]

40The LORD said to Moses, "Count all the firstborn Israelite males who are a month old or more[g] and make a list of their names. 41Take the Levites for me in place of all the firstborn of the Israelites, [h] and the

3:19
hEx 6:18
3:20
iGe 46:11
jEx 6:19
3:21
kEx 6:17
3:25
lEx 25:9
mEx 26:14
nEx 26:36;
Nu 4:25
3:26
oEx 27:9
pEx 35:18
3:27
q1Ch 26:23
3:29
rNu 1:53
3:31
sEx 25:10-22
tEx 25:23
uEx 25:31
vEx 27:1; 30:1
wEx 26:33
xNu 4:15
3:33
yEx 6:19
3:35
zNu 1:53; 2:25
3:36
aNu 4:32
3:38
bNu 2:3
cNu 1:53
dver 7; Nu 18:5
ever 10;
Nu 1:51
3:39
fNu 26:62
3:40
gver 15
3:41
hver 12

---

a28 Hebrew; some Septuagint manuscripts 8,300

livestock of the Levites in place of all the firstborn of the livestock of the Israelites. I am the LORD."

⁴²So Moses counted all the firstborn of the Israelites, as the LORD commanded him. ⁴³The total number of firstborn males a month old or more, listed by name, was 22,273. ⁱ

⁴⁴The LORD also said to Moses, ⁴⁵"Take the Levites in place of all the firstborn of Israel, and the livestock of the Levites in place of their livestock. The Levites are to be mine. I am the LORD. ⁴⁶To redeemʲ the 273 firstborn Israelites who exceed the number of the Levites, ⁴⁷collect five shekelsᵃᵏ for each one, according to the sanctuary shekel,ˡ which weighs twenty gerahs. ᵐ ⁴⁸Give the money for the redemption of the additional Israelites to Aaron and his sons."

⁴⁹So Moses collected the redemption money from those who exceeded the number redeemed by the Levites. ⁵⁰From the firstborn of the Israelites he collected silver weighing 1,365 shekels,ᵇⁿ according to the sanctuary shekel. ⁵¹Moses gave the redemption money to Aaron and his sons, as he was commanded by the word of the LORD.

The Kohathites

4 The LORD said to Moses and Aaron: ²"Take a censusᵒ of the Kohathite branch of the Levites by their clans and families. ³Count all the men from thirty to fifty years of ageᵖ who come to serve in the work in the Tent of Meeting.

⁴"This is the work of the Kohathites in the Tent of Meeting: the care of the most holy things. �q ⁵When the camp is to move, Aaron and his sons are to go in and take down the shielding curtainʳ and cover the ark of the Testimony with it. ˢ ⁶Then they are to cover this with hides of sea cows,ᶜ spread a cloth of solid blue over that and put the polesᵗ in place.

⁷"Over the table of the Presenceᵘ they are to spread a blue cloth and put on it the plates, dishes and bowls, and the jars for drink offerings; the bread that is continually thereᵛ is to remain on it. ⁸Over these they are to spread a scarlet cloth, cover that with hides of sea cows and put its poles in place.

⁹"They are to take a blue cloth and cover the lampstand that is for light, together with its lamps, its wick trimmers and trays,ʷ and all its jars for the oil used to supply it. ¹⁰Then they are to wrap it and all its accessories in a covering of hides of sea cows and put it on a carrying frame.

¹¹"Over the gold altarˣ they are to spread a blue cloth and cover that with hides of sea cows and put its poles in place.

¹²"They are to take all the articles used for ministering in the sanctuary, wrap them in a blue cloth, cover that with hides of sea cows and put them on a carrying frame.

¹³"They are to remove the ashes from the bronze altarʸ and spread a purple cloth over it. ¹⁴Then they are to place on it all the utensils used for ministering at the altar, including the firepans, meat forks,ᶻ shovels and sprinkling bowls. ᵃ Over it they are to spread a covering of hides of sea cows and put its polesᵇ in place.

¹⁵"After Aaron and his sons have finished covering the holy furnish-

3:43
ⁱver 39
3:46
ʲEx 13:13;
Nu 18:15
3:47
ᵏLev 27:6
ˡEx 30:13
ᵐLev 27:25
3:50
ⁿver 46-48
4:2
ᵒEx 30:12
4:3
ᵖver 23;
Nu 8:25;
1Ch 23:3,24,27;
Ezr 3:8
4:4
�q ver 19
4:5
ʳEx 26:31,33
ˢEx 25:10,16
4:6
ᵗEx 25:13-15;
1Ki 8:7; 2Ch 5:8
4:7
ᵘEx 25:23,29;
Lev 24:6
ᵛEx 25:30
4:9
ʷEx 25:31,37,38
4:11
ˣEx 30:1
4:13
ʸEx 27:1-8
4:14
ᶻ2Ch 4:16
ᵃJer 52:18
ᵇEx 27:6

ᵃ47 That is, about 2 ounces (about 55 grams)   ᵇ50 That is, about 35 pounds (about 15.5 kilograms)   ᶜ6 That is, dugongs; also in verses 8, 10, 11, 12, 14 and 25 ings and all the holy articles, and when the camp is ready to move, the Kohathites are to come to do the carrying.[c] But they must not touch the holy things or they will die.[d] The Kohathites are to carry those things that are in the Tent of Meeting.

16"Eleazar[e] son of Aaron, the priest, is to have charge of the oil for the light,[f] the fragrant incense, the regular grain offering[g] and the anointing oil. He is to be in charge of the entire tabernacle and everything in it, including its holy furnishings and articles."

17The LORD said to Moses and Aaron, 18"See that the Kohathite tribal clans are not cut off from the Levites. 19So that they may live and not die when they come near the most holy things,[h] do this for them: Aaron and his sons are to go into the sanctuary and assign to each man his work and what he is to carry. 20But the Kohathites must not go in to look[i] at the holy things, even for a moment, or they will die."

The Gershonites

21The LORD said to Moses, 22"Take a census also of the Gershonites by their families and clans. 23Count all the men from thirty to fifty years of age[j] who come to serve in the work at the Tent of Meeting.

24"This is the service of the Gershonite clans as they work and carry burdens: 25They are to carry the curtains of the tabernacle,[k] the Tent of Meeting,[l] its covering[m] and the outer covering of hides of sea cows, the curtains for the entrance to the Tent of Meeting, 26the curtains of the courtyard surrounding the tabernacle and altar, the curtain for the entrance, the ropes and all the equipment used in its service. The Gershonites are to do all that needs to be done with these things. 27All their service, whether carrying or doing other work, is to be done under the direction of Aaron and his sons. You shall assign to them as their responsibility all they are to carry. 28This is the service of the Gershonite clans[n] at the Tent of Meeting. Their duties are to be under the direction of Ithamar son of Aaron, the priest.

The Merarites

29"Count the Merarites by their clans and families.[o] 30Count all the men from thirty to fifty years of age who come to serve in the work at the Tent of Meeting. 31This is their duty as they perform service at the Tent of Meeting: to carry the frames of the tabernacle, its crossbars, posts and bases,[p] 32as well as the posts of the surrounding courtyard with their bases, tent pegs, ropes, all their equipment and everything related to their use. Assign to each man the specific things he is to carry. 33This is the service of the Merarite clans as they work at the Tent of Meeting under the direction of Ithamar son of Aaron, the priest."

The Numbering of the Levite Clans

34Moses, Aaron and the leaders of the community counted the Kohathites[q] by their clans and families. 35All the men from thirty to fifty years of age who came to serve in the work in the Tent of Meeting, 36counted by clans, were 2,750. 37This was the total of all those in the Kohathite clans[r] who served in the Tent of Meeting. Moses and Aaron counted them according to the LORD's command through Moses.

38The Gershonites[s] were counted by their clans and families. 39All the men from thirty to fifty years of age who came to serve in the work at

4:15
c Nu 7:9
d Nu 1:51;
2Sa 6:6,7
4:16
e Lev 10:6
f Ex 25:6
g Ex 29:41;
Lev 6:14-23
4:19
h ver 15
4:20
i Ex 19:21;
1Sa 6:19
4:23
j ver 3;
1Ch 23:3,24,27
4:25
k Ex 27:10-18;
Nu 3:26
l Nu 3:25
m Ex 26:14
4:28
n Nu 7:7
4:29
o Ge 46:11
4:31
p Nu 3:36
4:34
q ver 2
4:37
r Nu 3:27
4:38
s Ge 46:11

the Tent of Meeting, [40]counted by their clans and families, were 2,630. [41]This was the total of those in the Gershonite clans who served at the Tent of Meeting. Moses and Aaron counted them according to the LORD's command.

[42]The Merarites were counted by their clans and families. [43]All the men from thirty to fifty years of age who came to serve in the work at the Tent of Meeting, [44]counted by their clans, were 3,200. [45]This was the total of those in the Merarite clans.[t] Moses and Aaron counted them according to the LORD's command through Moses.

[46]So Moses, Aaron and the leaders of Israel counted all the Levites by their clans and families. [47]All the men from thirty to fifty years of age[u] who came to do the work of serving and carrying the Tent of Meeting [48]numbered 8,580.[v] [49]At the LORD's command through Moses, each was assigned his work and told what to carry.

Thus they were counted,[w] as the LORD commanded Moses.

The Purity of the Camp

5 The LORD said to Moses, [2]"Command the Israelites to send away from the camp anyone who has an infectious skin disease[a][x] or a discharge[y] of any kind, or who is ceremonially unclean[z] because of a dead body. [3]Send away male and female alike; send them outside the camp so they will not defile their camp, where I dwell among them.[a]" [4]The Israelites did this; they sent them outside the camp. They did just as the LORD had instructed Moses.

Restitution for Wrongs

[5]The LORD said to Moses, [6]"Say to the Israelites: 'When a man or woman wrongs another in any way[b] and so is unfaithful[b] to the LORD, that person is guilty[c] [7]and must confess[d] the sin he has committed. He must make full restitution[e] for his wrong, add one fifth to it and give it all to the person he has wronged. [8]But if that person has no close relative to whom restitution can be made for the wrong, the restitution belongs to the LORD and must be given to the priest, along with the ram with which atonement is made for him.[f] [9]All the sacred contributions the Israelites bring to a priest will belong to him.[g] [10]Each man's sacred gifts are his own, but what he gives to the priest will belong to the priest.[h]' "

The Test for an Unfaithful Wife

[11]Then the LORD said to Moses, [12]"Speak to the Israelites and say to them: 'If a man's wife goes astray[i] and is unfaithful to him [13]by sleeping with another man,[j] and this is hidden from her husband and her impurity is undetected (since there is no witness against her and she has not been caught in the act), [14]and if feelings of jealousy[k] come over her husband and he suspects his wife and she is impure—or if he is jealous and suspects her even though she is not impure— [15]then he is to take his wife to the priest. He must also take an offering of a tenth of an ephah[c1] of barley flour[m] on her behalf. He must not pour oil on it

4:45
tver 29
4:47
uver 3
4:48
vNu 3:39
4:49
wNu 1:47
5:2
xLev 13:46
yLev 15:2;
Mt 9:20
zLev 13:3;
Nu 9:6-10
5:3
aLev 26:12;
Nu 35:34;
2Co 6:16
5:6
bLev 6:2
cLev 5:14-6:7
5:7
dLev 5:5;
26:40; Jos 7:19;
Lk 19:8 eLev 6:5
5:8
fLev 6:6,7; 7:7
5:9
gLev 6:17;
7:6-14
5:10
hLev 10:13
5:12
iEx 20:14
5:13
jLev 18:20;
20:10
5:14
kPr 6:34; SS 8:6
5:15
lEx 16:36
mLev 6:20

---

[a]2 Traditionally *leprosy*; the Hebrew word was used for various diseases affecting the skin—not necessarily leprosy.   [b]6 Or *woman commits any wrong common to mankind*   [c]15 That is, probably about 2 quarts (about 2 liters)

or put incense on it, because it is a grain offering for jealousy, a reminder[n] offering to draw attention to guilt.

¹⁶" 'The priest shall bring her and have her stand before the LORD. ¹⁷Then he shall take some holy water in a clay jar and put some dust from the tabernacle floor into the water. ¹⁸After the priest has had the woman stand before the LORD, he shall loosen her hair[o] and place in her hands the reminder offering, the grain offering for jealousy, while he himself holds the bitter water that brings a curse. ¹⁹Then the priest shall put the woman under oath and say to her, "If no other man has slept with you and you have not gone astray[p] and become impure while married to your husband, may this bitter water that brings a curse not harm you. ²⁰But if you have gone astray[q] while married to your husband and you have defiled yourself by sleeping with a man other than your husband"— ²¹here the priest is to put the woman under this curse of the oath[r]—"may the LORD cause your people to curse and denounce you when he causes your thigh to waste away and your abdomen to swell.[a] ²²May this water[s] that brings a curse[t] enter your body so that your abdomen swells and your thigh wastes away.[b] "

" 'Then the woman is to say, "Amen. So be it.[u]"

²³" 'The priest is to write these curses on a scroll[v] and then wash them off into the bitter water. ²⁴He shall have the woman drink the bitter water that brings a curse, and this water will enter her and cause bitter suffering. ²⁵The priest is to take from her hands the grain offering for jealousy, wave it before the LORD[w] and bring it to the altar. ²⁶The priest is then to take a handful of the grain offering as a memorial offering and burn it on the altar; after that, he is to have the woman drink the water. ²⁷If she has defiled herself and been unfaithful to her husband, then when she is made to drink the water that brings a curse, it will go into her and cause bitter suffering; her abdomen will swell and her thigh waste away,[c] and she will become accursed[x] among her people. ²⁸If, however, the woman has not defiled herself and is free from impurity, she will be cleared of guilt and will be able to have children.

²⁹" 'This, then, is the law of jealousy when a woman goes astray[y] and defiles herself while married to her husband, ³⁰or when feelings of jealousy come over a man because he suspects his wife. The priest is to have her stand before the LORD and is to apply this entire law to her. ³¹The husband will be innocent of any wrongdoing, but the woman will bear the consequences[z] of her sin.' "

The Nazirite

6 The LORD said to Moses, ²"Speak to the Israelites and say to them: 'If a man or woman wants to make a special vow[a], a vow of separation to the LORD as a Nazirite,[b] ³he must abstain from wine[c] and other fermented drink and must not drink vinegar[d] made from wine or from other fermented drink. He must not drink grape juice or eat grapes or raisins. ⁴As long as he is a Nazirite, he must not eat anything that comes from the grapevine, not even the seeds or skins.

⁵" 'During the entire period of his vow of separation no razor[e] may

---

5:15
[n]Eze 29:16
5:18
[o]Lev 10:6;
1Co 11:6
5:19
[p]ver 12,29
5:20
[q]ver 12
5:21
[r]Jos 6:26;
1Sa 14:24;
Ne 10:29
5:22
[s]Ps 109:18
[t]ver 18
[u]Dt 27:15
5:23
[v]Jer 45:1
5:25
[w]Lev 8:27
5:27
[x]Isa 43:28;
65:15; Jer 26:6;
29:18; 42:18;
44:12,22;
Zec 8:13
5:29
[y]ver 19
5:31
[z]Lev 5:1; 20:17
6:2
[a]Ge 28:20;
Ac 21:23
[b]Jdg 13:5;
16:17;
Am 2:11,12
6:3
[c]Lk 1:15
[d]Ru 2:14;
Ps 69:21;
Pr 10:26
6:5
[e]Ps 52:2; 57:4;
59:7; Isa 7:20;
Eze 5:1

---

[a]21 Or *causes you to have a miscarrying womb and barrenness*   [b]22 Or *body and cause you to be barren and have a miscarrying womb*   [c]27 Or *suffering; she will have barrenness and a miscarrying womb*

be used on his head. [f] He must be holy until the period of his separation to the LORD is over; he must let the hair of his head grow long. [6]Throughout the period of his separation to the LORD he must not go near a dead body. [g] [7]Even if his own father or mother or brother or sister dies, he must not make himself ceremonially unclean[h] on account of them, because the symbol of his separation to God is on his head. [8]Throughout the period of his separation he is consecrated to the LORD.

[9]" 'If someone dies suddenly in his presence, thus defiling the hair he has dedicated,[i] he must shave his head on the day of his cleansing[j] —the seventh day. [10]Then on the eighth day he must bring two doves or two young pigeons[k] to the priest at the entrance to the Tent of Meeting. [11]The priest is to offer one as a sin offering and the other as a burnt offering[l] to make atonement[m] for him because he sinned by being in the presence of the dead body. That same day he is to consecrate his head. [12]He must dedicate himself to the LORD for the period of his separation and must bring a year-old male lamb as a guilt offering. The previous days do not count, because he became defiled during his separation.

[13]" 'Now this is the law for the Nazirite when the period of his separation is over.[n] He is to be brought to the entrance to the Tent of Meeting. [14]There he is to present his offerings to the LORD: a year-old male lamb without defect for a burnt offering, a year-old ewe lamb without defect for a sin offering,[o] a ram without defect for a fellowship offering,[a] [15]together with their grain offerings and drink offerings,[p] and a basket of bread made without yeast—cakes made of fine flour mixed with oil, and wafers spread with oil.[q]

[16]" 'The priest is to present them before the LORD and make the sin offering and the burnt offering. [17]He is to present the basket of unleavened bread and is to sacrifice the ram as a fellowship offering to the LORD, together with its grain offering and drink offering.

[18]" 'Then at the entrance to the Tent of Meeting, the Nazirite must shave off the hair that he dedicated.[r] He is to take the hair and put it in the fire that is under the sacrifice of the fellowship offering.

[19]" 'After the Nazirite has shaved off the hair of his dedication, the priest is to place in his hands a boiled shoulder of the ram, and a cake and a wafer from the basket, both made without yeast. [20]The priest shall then wave them before the LORD as a wave offering; they are holy and belong to the priest, together with the breast that was waved and the thigh that was presented. After that, the Nazirite may drink wine.[s]

[21]" 'This is the law of the Nazirite who vows his offering to the LORD in accordance with his separation, in addition to whatever else he can afford. He must fulfill the vow he has made, according to the law of the Nazirite.' "

The Priestly Blessing

[22]The LORD said to Moses, [23]"Tell Aaron and his sons, 'This is how you are to bless[t] the Israelites. Say to them:

> [24]" ' "The LORD bless you[u]
>   and keep you;[v]

---

[a]14 Traditionally *peace offering*; also in verses 17 and 18

6:5
f 1Sa 1:11
6:6
g Lev 21:1-3;
Nu 19:11-22
6:7
h Nu 9:6
6:9
i ver 18
j Lev 14:9
6:10
k Lev 5:7; 14:22
6:11
l Ge 8:20
m Ex 29:36
6:13
n Ac 21:26
6:14
o Lev 14:10;
Nu 15:27
6:15
p Nu 15:1-7
q Ex 29:2;
Lev 2:4
6:18
r ver 9; Ac 21:24
6:20
s Ecc 9:7
6:23
t Dt 21:5;
1Ch 23:13
6:24
u Dt 28:3-6;
Ps 28:9
v 1Sa 2:9;
Ps 17:8

> ²⁵the LORD make his face shine upon you[w]
> and be gracious to you;[x]
> ²⁶the LORD turn his face[y] toward you
> and give you peace.[z]" '

²⁷"So they will put my name[a] on the Israelites, and I will bless them."

Offerings at the Dedication of the Tabernacle

7 When Moses finished setting up the tabernacle,[b] he anointed it and consecrated it and all its furnishings.[c] He also anointed and consecrated the altar and all its utensils.[d] ²Then the leaders of Israel,[e] the heads of families who were the tribal leaders in charge of those who were counted, made offerings. ³They brought as their gifts before the LORD six covered carts and twelve oxen—an ox from each leader and a cart from every two. These they presented before the tabernacle.

⁴The LORD said to Moses, ⁵"Accept these from them, that they may be used in the work at the Tent of Meeting. Give them to the Levites as each man's work requires."

⁶So Moses took the carts and oxen and gave them to the Levites. ⁷He gave two carts and four oxen to the Gershonites,[f] as their work required, ⁸and he gave four carts and eight oxen to the Merarites,[g] as their work required. They were all under the direction of Ithamar son of Aaron, the priest. ⁹But Moses did not give any to the Kohathites, because they were to carry on their shoulders[h] the holy things, for which they were responsible.

¹⁰When the altar was anointed,[i] the leaders brought their offerings for its dedication[j] and presented them before the altar. ¹¹For the LORD had said to Moses, "Each day one leader is to bring his offering for the dedication of the altar."

¹²The one who brought his offering on the first day was Nahshon son of Amminadab of the tribe of Judah.

¹³His offering was one silver plate weighing a hundred and thirty shekels,[a] and one silver sprinkling bowl weighing seventy shekels,[b] both according to the sanctuary shekel,[k] each filled with fine flour mixed with oil as a grain offering;[l] ¹⁴one gold dish weighing ten shekels,[c] filled with incense;[m] ¹⁵one young bull,[n] one ram and one male lamb a year old, for a burnt offering;[o] ¹⁶one male goat for a sin offering;[p] ¹⁷and two oxen, five rams, five male goats and five male lambs a year old, to be sacrificed as a fellowship offering.[d][q] This was the offering of Nahshon son of Amminadab.[r]

¹⁸On the second day Nethanel son of Zuar,[s] the leader of Issachar, brought his offering.

¹⁹The offering he brought was one silver plate weighing a hundred and thirty shekels, and one silver sprinkling bowl weighing seventy shekels, both according to the sanctuary shekel, each filled with fine flour mixed with oil as a grain offering; ²⁰one gold

---

6:25
w Job 29:24;
Ps 31:16; 80:3;
119:135
x Ge 43:29;
Ps 25:16; 86:16
6:26
y Ps 4:6; 44:3
z Ps 29:11;
37:11,37;
Jn 14:27
6:27
a Dt 28:10;
2Sa 7:23;
2Ch 7:14;
Ne 9:10;
Jer 25:29
7:1
b Ex 40:17
c Ex 40:9
d ver 84,88;
Ex 40:10
7:2
e Nu 1:5-16
7:7
f Nu 4:24-26,28
7:8
g Nu 4:31-33
7:9
h Nu 4:15
7:10
i ver 1
j 2Ch 7:9
7:13
k Ex 30:13;
Nu 3:47
l Lev 2:1
7:14
m Ex 30:34
7:15
n Ex 24:5; 29:3;
Nu 28:11
o Lev 1:3
7:16
p Lev 4:3,23
7:17
q Lev 3:1
r Nu 1:7
7:18
s Nu 1:8

---

[a]13 That is, about 3 1/4 pounds (about 1.5 kilograms); also elsewhere in this chapter   [b]13 That is, about 1 3/4 pounds (about 0.8 kilogram); also elsewhere in this chapter   [c]14 That is, about 4 ounces (about 110 grams); also elsewhere in this chapter   [d]17 Traditionally *peace offering*; also elsewhere in this chapter

dish[t] weighing ten shekels, filled with incense; [21]one young bull, one ram and one male lamb a year old, for a burnt offering; [22]one male goat for a sin offering; [23]and two oxen, five rams, five male goats and five male lambs a year old, to be sacrificed as a fellowship offering. This was the offering of Nethanel son of Zuar.

[24]On the third day, Eliab son of Helon,[u] the leader of the people of Zebulun, brought his offering.

[25]His offering was one silver plate weighing a hundred and thirty shekels, and one silver sprinkling bowl weighing seventy shekels, both according to the sanctuary shekel, each filled with fine flour mixed with oil as a grain offering; [26]one gold dish weighing ten shekels, filled with incense; [27]one young bull, one ram and one male lamb a year old, for a burnt offering; [28]one male goat for a sin offering; [29]and two oxen, five rams, five male goats and five male lambs a year old, to be sacrificed as a fellowship offering. This was the offering of Eliab son of Helon.

[30]On the fourth day Elizur son of Shedeur,[v] the leader of the people of Reuben, brought his offering.

[31]His offering was one silver plate weighing a hundred and thirty shekels, and one silver sprinkling bowl weighing seventy shekels, both according to the sanctuary shekel, each filled with fine flour mixed with oil as a grain offering; [32]one gold dish weighing ten shekels, filled with incense; [33]one young bull, one ram and one male lamb a year old, for a burnt offering; [34]one male goat for a sin offering; [35]and two oxen, five rams, five male goats and five male lambs a year old, to be sacrificed as a fellowship offering. This was the offering of Elizur son of Shedeur.

[36]On the fifth day Shelumiel son of Zurishaddai,[w] the leader of the people of Simeon, brought his offering.

[37]His offering was one silver plate weighing a hundred and thirty shekels, and one silver sprinkling bowl weighing seventy shekels, both according to the sanctuary shekel, each filled with fine flour mixed with oil as a grain offering; [38]one gold dish weighing ten shekels, filled with incense; [39]one young bull, one ram and one male lamb a year old, for a burnt offering; [40]one male goat for a sin offering; [41]and two oxen, five rams, five male goats and five male lambs a year old, to be sacrificed as a fellowship offering. This was the offering of Shelumiel son of Zurishaddai.

[42]On the sixth day Eliasaph son of Deuel,[x] the leader of the people of Gad, brought his offering.

[43]His offering was one silver plate weighing a hundred and thirty shekels, and one silver sprinkling bowl weighing seventy shekels, both according to the sanctuary shekel, each filled with fine flour mixed with oil as a grain offering; [44]one gold dish weighing ten shekels, filled with incense; [45]one young bull, one ram and one male lamb a year old, for a burnt offering; [46]one male goat for a sin offering; [47]and two oxen, five rams, five male goats and five male lambs a year old, to be sacrificed as a fellowship offering. This was the offering of Eliasaph son of Deuel.

7:20
[t]ver 14
7:24
[u]Nu 1:9
7:30
[v]Nu 1:5
7:36
[w]Nu 1:6
7:42
[x]Nu 1:14

⁴⁸On the seventh day Elishama son of Ammihud,ʸ the leader of the people of Ephraim, brought his offering.
⁴⁹His offering was one silver plate weighing a hundred and thirty shekels, and one silver sprinkling bowl weighing seventy shekels, both according to the sanctuary shekel, each filled with fine flour mixed with oil as a grain offering; ⁵⁰one gold dish weighing ten shekels, filled with incense; ⁵¹one young bull, one ram and one male lamb a year old, for a burnt offering; ⁵²one male goat for a sin offering; ⁵³and two oxen, five rams, five male goats and five male lambs a year old, to be sacrificed as a fellowship offering. This was the offering of Elishama son of Ammihud.ᶻ

⁵⁴On the eighth day Gamaliel son of Pedahzur,ᵃ the leader of the people of Manasseh, brought his offering.
⁵⁵His offering was one silver plate weighing a hundred and thirty shekels, and one silver sprinkling bowl weighing seventy shekels, both according to the sanctuary shekel, each filled with fine flour mixed with oil as a grain offering; ⁵⁶one gold dish weighing ten shekels, filled with incense; ⁵⁷one young bull, one ram and one male lamb a year old, for a burnt offering; ⁵⁸one male goat for a sin offering; ⁵⁹and two oxen, five rams, five male goats and five male lambs a year old, to be sacrificed as a fellowship offering. This was the offering of Gamaliel son of Pedahzur.

⁶⁰On the ninth day Abidan son of Gideoni,ᵇ the leader of the people of Benjamin, brought his offering.
⁶¹His offering was one silver plate weighing a hundred and thirty shekels, and one silver sprinkling bowl weighing seventy shekels, both according to the sanctuary shekel, each filled with fine flour mixed with oil as a grain offering; ⁶²one gold dish weighing ten shekels, filled with incense; ⁶³one young bull, one ram and one male lamb a year old, for a burnt offering; ⁶⁴one male goat for a sin offering; ⁶⁵and two oxen, five rams, five male goats and five male lambs a year old, to be sacrificed as a fellowship offering. This was the offering of Abidan son of Gideoni.

⁶⁶On the tenth day Ahiezer son of Ammishaddai,ᶜ the leader of the people of Dan, brought his offering.
⁶⁷His offering was one silver plate weighing a hundred and thirty shekels, and one silver sprinkling bowl weighing seventy shekels, both according to the sanctuary shekel, each filled with fine flour mixed with oil as a grain offering; ⁶⁸one gold dish weighing ten shekels, filled with incense; ⁶⁹one young bull, one ram and one male lamb a year old, for a burnt offering; ⁷⁰one male goat for a sin offering; ⁷¹and two oxen, five rams, five male goats and five male lambs a year old, to be sacrificed as a fellowship offering. This was the offering of Ahiezer son of Ammishaddai.

⁷²On the eleventh day Pagiel son of Ocran,ᵈ the leader of the people of Asher, brought his offering.
⁷³His offering was one silver plate weighing a hundred and thirty shekels, and one silver sprinkling bowl weighing seventy shekels, both according to the sanctuary shekel, each filled with fine flour mixed with oil as a grain offering; ⁷⁴one gold dish weighing

7:48
yNu 1:10
7:53
zNu 1:10
7:54
aNu 1:10; 2:20
7:60
bNu 1:11
7:66
cNu 1:12; 2:25
7:72
dNu 1:13

ten shekels, filled with incense; 75one young bull, one ram and one male lamb a year old, for a burnt offering; 76one male goat for a sin offering; 77and two oxen, five rams, five male goats and five male lambs a year old, to be sacrificed as a fellowship offering. This was the offering of Pagiel son of Ocran.

78On the twelfth day Ahira son of Enan,ᵉ the leader of the people of Naphtali, brought his offering.

79His offering was one silver plate weighing a hundred and thirty shekels, and one silver sprinkling bowl weighing seventy shekels, both according to the sanctuary shekel, each filled with fine flour mixed with oil as a grain offering; 80one gold dish weighing ten shekels, filled with incense; 81one young bull, one ram and one male lamb a year old, for a burnt offering; 82one male goat for a sin offering; 83and two oxen, five rams, five male goats and five male lambs a year old, to be sacrificed as a fellowship offering. This was the offering of Ahira son of Enan.

84These were the offerings of the Israelite leaders for the dedication of the altar when it was anointed:ᶠ twelve silver plates, twelve silver sprinkling bowlsᵍ and twelve gold dishes.ʰ 85Each silver plate weighed a hundred and thirty shekels, and each sprinkling bowl seventy shekels. Altogether, the silver dishes weighed two thousand four hundred shekels,ᵃ according to the sanctuary shekel. 86The twelve gold dishes filled with incense weighed ten shekels each, according to the sanctuary shekel. Altogether, the gold dishes weighed a hundred and twenty shekels.ᵇ 87The total number of animals for the burnt offering came to twelve young bulls, twelve rams and twelve male lambs a year old, together with their grain offering. Twelve male goats were used for the sin offering. 88The total number of animals for the sacrifice of the fellowship offering came to twenty-four oxen, sixty rams, sixty male goats and sixty male lambs a year old. These were the offerings for the dedication of the altar after it was anointed.ⁱ

89When Moses entered the Tent of Meeting to speak with the Lord,ʲ he heard the voice speaking to him from between the two cherubim above the atonement coverᵏ on the ark of the Testimony. And he spoke with him.

Setting Up the Lamps

8 The Lord said to Moses, 2"Speak to Aaron and say to him, 'When you set up the seven lamps, they are to light the area in front of the lampstand.ˡ'"

3Aaron did so; he set up the lamps so that they faced forward on the lampstand, just as the Lord commanded Moses. 4This is how the lampstand was made: It was made of hammered goldᵐ—from its base to its blossoms. The lampstand was made exactly like the patternⁿ the Lord had shown Moses.

The Setting Apart of the Levites

5The Lord said to Moses: 6"Take the Levites from among the other

7:78
eNu 1:15; 2:29
7:84
fver 1,10
gNu 4:14
hver 14
7:88
iver 1,10
7:89
jEx 25:21,22;
33:9,11
kPs 80:1; 99:1
8:2
lEx 25:37;
Lev 24:2,4
8:4
mEx 25:18,36
nEx 25:9

ᵃ85 That is, about 60 pounds (about 28 kilograms)   ᵇ86 That is, about 3 pounds (about 1.4 kilograms)

Israelites and make them ceremonially clean. º 7To purify them, do this: Sprinkle the water of cleansingᴾ on them; then have them shave their whole bodies�q and wash their clothes,ʳ and so purify themselves. 8Have them take a young bull with its grain offering of fine flour mixed with oil;ˢ then you are to take a second young bull for a sin offering. 9Bring the Levites to the front of the Tent of Meetingᵗ and assemble the whole Israelite community. ᵘ 10You are to bring the Levites before the LORD, and the Israelites are to lay their hands on them. ᵛ 11Aaron is to present the Levites before the LORD as a wave offeringʷ from the Israelites, so that they may be ready to do the work of the LORD.

12"After the Levites lay their hands on the heads of the bulls, ˣ use the one for a sin offering to the LORD and the other for a burnt offering, to make atonementʸ for the Levites. 13Have the Levites stand in front of Aaron and his sons and then present them as a wave offering to the LORD. 14In this way you are to set the Levites apart from the other Israelites, and the Levites will be mine. ᶻ

15"After you have purified the Levites and presented them as a wave offering, ᵃ they are to come to do their work at the Tent of Meeting. 16They are the Israelites who are to be given wholly to me. I have taken them as my own in place of the firstborn, the first male offspringᵇ from every Israelite woman. 17Every firstborn male in Israel, whether man or animal, ᶜ is mine. When I struck down all the firstborn in Egypt, I set them apart for myself. ᵈ 18And I have taken the Levites in place of all the firstborn sons in Israel. ᵉ 19Of all the Israelites, I have given the Levites as gifts to Aaron and his sonsᶠ to do the work at the Tent of Meeting on behalf of the Israelitesᵍ and to make atonement for themʰ so that no plague will strike the Israelites when they go near the sanctuary."

20Moses, Aaron and the whole Israelite community did with the Levites just as the LORD commanded Moses. 21The Levites purified themselves and washed their clothes. ⁱ Then Aaron presented them as a wave offering before the LORD and made atonement for them to purify them.ʲ 22After that, the Levites came to do their work at the Tent of Meeting under the supervision of Aaron and his sons. They did with the Levites just as the LORD commanded Moses.

23The LORD said to Moses, 24"This applies to the Levites: Men twenty-five years old or moreᵏ shall come to take part in the work at the Tent of Meeting,ˡ 25but at the age of fifty, they must retire from their regular service and work no longer. 26They may assist their brothers in performing their duties at the Tent of Meeting, but they themselves must not do the work. This, then, is how you are to assign the responsibilities of the Levites."

The Passover

9 The LORD spoke to Moses in the Desert of Sinai in the first monthᵐ of the second year after they came out of Egypt. ⁿ He said, 2"Have the Israelites celebrate the Passover at the appointed time. 3Celebrate it at the appointed time, at twilight on the fourteenth day of this month, in accordance with all its rules and regulations.º"

4So Moses told the Israelites to celebrate the Passover, 5and they did so in the Desert of Sinai at twilight on the fourteenth day of the first month.ᴾ The Israelites did everything just as the LORD commanded Moses.

8:6
oLev 22:2;
Isa 1:16; 52:11
8:7
pNu 19:9,17
qLev 14:9;
Dt 21:12
rLev 14:8
8:8
sLev 2:1;
Nu 15:8-10
8:9
tEx 40:12
uLev 8:3
8:10
vAc 6:6
8:11
wLev 7:30
8:12
xEx 29:10
yEx 29:36
8:14
zNu 3:12
8:15
aEx 29:24
8:16
bNu 3:12
8:17
cEx 4:23
dEx 13:2;
Lk 2:23
8:18
eNu 3:12
8:19
fNu 3:9
gNu 1:53
hNu 16:46
8:21
iver 7
jver 12
8:24
k1Ch 23:3
lEx 38:21;
Nu 4:3
9:1
mEx 40:2
nNu 1:1
9:3
oEx 12:2-11,
43-49;
Lev 23:5-8;
Dt 16:1-8
9:5
pEx 12:1-13;
Jos 5:10

⁶But some of them could not celebrate the Passover on that day because they were ceremonially unclean ᑫ on account of a dead body. So they came to Moses and Aaron ʳ that same day ⁷and said to Moses, "We have become unclean because of a dead body, but why should we be kept from presenting the Lord's offering with the other Israelites at the appointed time?"

⁸Moses answered them, "Wait until I find out what the Lord commands concerning you." ˢ

⁹Then the Lord said to Moses, ¹⁰"Tell the Israelites: 'When any of you or your descendants are unclean because of a dead body or are away on a journey, they may still celebrate ᵗ the Lord's Passover. ¹¹They are to celebrate it on the fourteenth day of the second month at twilight. They are to eat the lamb, together with unleavened bread and bitter herbs. ᵘ ¹²They must not leave any of it till morning ᵛ or break any of its bones. ʷ When they celebrate the Passover, they must follow all the regulations. ¹³But if a man who is ceremonially clean and not on a journey fails to celebrate the Passover, that person must be cut off from his people ˣ because he did not present the Lord's offering at the appointed time. That man will bear the consequences of his sin.

¹⁴" 'An alien ʸ living among you who wants to celebrate the Lord's Passover must do so in accordance with its rules and regulations. You must have the same regulations for the alien and the native-born.' "

The Cloud Above the Tabernacle

¹⁵On the day the tabernacle, the Tent of the Testimony, was set up, the cloud ᶻ covered it. From evening till morning the cloud above the tabernacle looked like fire. ᵃ ¹⁶That is how it continued to be; the cloud covered it, and at night it looked like fire. ¹⁷Whenever the cloud lifted from above the Tent, the Israelites set out; wherever the cloud settled, the Israelites encamped. ᵇ ¹⁸At the Lord's command the Israelites set out, and at his command they encamped. As long as the cloud stayed over the tabernacle, they remained in camp. ¹⁹When the cloud remained over the tabernacle a long time, the Israelites obeyed the Lord's order and did not set out. ²⁰Sometimes the cloud was over the tabernacle only a few days; at the Lord's command they would encamp, and then at his command they would set out. ²¹Sometimes the cloud stayed only from evening till morning, and when it lifted in the morning, they set out. Whether by day or by night, whenever the cloud lifted, they set out. ²²Whether the cloud stayed over the tabernacle for two days or a month or a year, the Israelites would remain in camp and not set out; but when it lifted, they would set out. ²³At the Lord's command they encamped, and at the Lord's command they set out. They obeyed the Lord's order, in accordance with his command through Moses.

The Silver Trumpets

10 The Lord said to Moses: ²"Make two trumpets ᶜ of hammered silver, and use them for calling the community ᵈ together and for having the camps set out. ³When both are sounded, the whole community is to assemble before you at the entrance to the Tent of Meeting. ⁴If only one is sounded, the leaders ᵉ—the heads of the clans of Israel—are to assemble before you. ⁵When a trumpet blast is sounded, the tribes

9:6
ᑫLev 5:3
ʳEx 18:15;
Nu 27:2
9:8
ˢEx 18:15;
Nu 27:5,21;
Ps 85:8
9:10
ᵗ2Ch 30:2
9:11
ᵘEx 12:8
9:12
ᵛEx 12:10,43
ʷEx 12:46;
Jn 19:36*
9:13
ˣGe 17:14;
Ex 12:15
9:14
ʸEx 12:48,49
9:15
ᶻEx 40:34
ᵃEx 13:21
9:17
ᵇEx 40:36-38;
Nu 10:11,12;
1Co 10:1
10:2
ᶜNe 12:35;
Ps 47:5
ᵈJer 4:5,19;
6:1; Hos 5:8;
Joel 2:1,15;
Am 3:6
10:4
ᵉEx 18:21;
Nu 1:16; 7:2

camping on the east are to set out. [f] [6]At the sounding of a second blast, the camps on the south are to set out. [g] The blast will be the signal for setting out. [7]To gather the assembly, blow the trumpets, [h] but not with the same signal. [i]

[8]"The sons of Aaron, the priests, are to blow the trumpets. This is to be a lasting ordinance for you and the generations to come. [j] [9]When you go into battle in your own land against an enemy who is oppressing you, [k] sound a blast on the trumpets. Then you will be remembered[l] by the LORD your God and rescued from your enemies. [m] [10]Also at your times of rejoicing—your appointed feasts and New Moon festivals[n]—you are to sound the trumpets[o] over your burnt offerings and fellowship offerings, [a] and they will be a memorial for you before your God. I am the LORD your God."

The Israelites Leave Sinai

[11]On the twentieth day of the second month of the second year, [p] the cloud lifted[q] from above the tabernacle of the Testimony. [12]Then the Israelites set out from the Desert of Sinai and traveled from place to place until the cloud came to rest in the Desert of Paran. [13]They set out, this first time, at the LORD's command through Moses. [r]

[14]The divisions of the camp of Judah went first, under their standard. [s] Nahshon son of Amminadab[t] was in command. [15]Nethanel son of Zuar was over the division of the tribe of Issachar, [16]and Eliab son of Helon was over the division of the tribe of Zebulun. [17]Then the tabernacle was taken down, and the Gershonites and Merarites, who carried it, set out. [u]

[18]The divisions of the camp of Reuben went next, under their standard. [v] Elizur son of Shedeur was in command. [19]Shelumiel son of Zurishaddai was over the division of the tribe of Simeon, [20]and Eliasaph son of Deuel was over the division of the tribe of Gad. [21]Then the Kohathites set out, carrying the holy things. [w] The tabernacle was to be set up before they arrived. [x]

[22]The divisions of the camp of Ephraim[y] went next, under their standard. Elishama son of Ammihud was in command. [23]Gamaliel son of Pedahzur was over the division of the tribe of Manasseh, [24]and Abidan son of Gideoni was over the division of the tribe of Benjamin.

[25]Finally, as the rear guard[z] for all the units, the divisions of the camp of Dan set out, under their standard. Ahiezer son of Ammishaddai was in command. [26]Pagiel son of Ocran was over the division of the tribe of Asher, [27]and Ahira son of Enan was over the division of the tribe of Naphtali. [28]This was the order of march for the Israelite divisions as they set out.

[29]Now Moses said to Hobab[a] son of Reuel[b] the Midianite, Moses' father-in-law, [c] "We are setting out for the place about which the LORD said, 'I will give it to you.'[d] Come with us and we will treat you well, for the LORD has promised good things to Israel."

[30]He answered, "No, I will not go;[e] I am going back to my own land and my own people."

[31]But Moses said, "Please do not leave us. You know where we

10:5
fver 14
10:6
gver 18
10:7
hEze 33:3;
Joel 2:1
i1Co 14:8
10:8
jNu 31:6
10:9
kJdg 2:18; 6:9;
1Sa 10:18;
Ps 106:42
lGe 8:1
mPs 106:4
10:10
nPs 81:3
oLev 23:24
10:11
pEx 40:17
qNu 9:17
10:13
rDt 1:6
10:14
sNu 2:3-9
tNu 1:7
10:17
uNu 4:21-32
10:18
vNu 2:10-16
10:21
wNu 4:20
xver 17
10:22
yNu 2:24
10:25
zNu 2:31;
Jos 6:9
10:29
aJdg 4:11
bEx 2:18 cEx 3:1
dGe 12:7
10:30
eMt 21:29

a10 Traditionally peace offerings

should camp in the desert, and you can be our eyes. [f] [32]If you come with us, we will share with you[g] whatever good things the L<small>ORD</small> gives us. [h]"

[33]So they set out[i] from the mountain of the L<small>ORD</small> and traveled for three days. The ark of the covenant of the L<small>ORD</small>[j] went before them during those three days to find them a place to rest. [34]The cloud of the L<small>ORD</small> was over them by day when they set out from the camp. [k]

[35]Whenever the ark set out, Moses said,

> "Rise up, O L<small>ORD</small>!
> May your enemies be scattered;[l]
> may your foes flee before you.[m]"

[36]Whenever it came to rest, he said,

> "Return,[n] O L<small>ORD</small>,
> to the countless thousands of Israel.[o]"

Fire From the L<small>ORD</small>

11 Now the people complained about their hardships in the hearing of the L<small>ORD</small>, and when he heard them his anger was aroused. Then fire from the L<small>ORD</small> burned among them[p] and consumed some of the outskirts of the camp. [2]When the people cried out to Moses, he prayed to the L<small>ORD</small>[q] and the fire died down. [3]So that place was called Taberah,[a] [r] because fire from the L<small>ORD</small> had burned among them.

Quail From the L<small>ORD</small>

[4]The rabble with them began to crave other food,[s] and again the Israelites started wailing[t] and said, "If only we had meat to eat! [5]We remember the fish we ate in Egypt at no cost—also the cucumbers, melons, leeks, onions and garlic. [u] [6]But now we have lost our appetite; we never see anything but this manna!"

[7]The manna was like coriander seed[v] and looked like resin. [w] [8]The people went around gathering it, and then ground it in a handmill or crushed it in a mortar. They cooked it in a pot or made it into cakes. And it tasted like something made with olive oil. [9]When the dew[x] settled on the camp at night, the manna also came down.

[10]Moses heard the people of every family wailing, each at the entrance to his tent. The L<small>ORD</small> became exceedingly angry, and Moses was troubled. [11]He asked the L<small>ORD</small>, "Why have you brought this trouble on your servant? What have I done to displease you that you put the burden of all these people on me?[y] [12]Did I conceive all these people? Did I give them birth? Why do you tell me to carry them in my arms, as a nurse carries an infant,[z] to the land you promised on oath to their forefathers?[a] [13]Where can I get meat for all these people?[b] They keep wailing to me, 'Give us meat to eat!' [14]I cannot carry all these people by myself; the burden is too heavy for me. [c] [15]If this is how you are going to treat me, put me to death[d] right now[e]—if I have found favor in your eyes—and do not let me face my own ruin."

[16]The L<small>ORD</small> said to Moses: "Bring me seventy of Israel's elders who

---

[a]3 *Taberah* means *burning.*

10:31
f Job 29:15
10:32
g Dt 10:18
h Ps 22:27-31;
67:5-7
10:33
i ver 12; Dt 1:33
j Jos 3:3
10:34
k Nu 9:15-23
10:35
l Ps 68:1
m Dt 7:10;
32:41; Ps 68:2;
Isa 17:12-14
10:36
n Isa 63:17
o Dt 1:10
11:1
p Lev 10:2
11:2
q Nu 21:7
11:3
r Dt 9:22
11:4
s Ex 12:38
t Ps 78:18;
1Co 10:6
11:5
u Ex 16:3
11:7
v Ex 16:31
w Ge 2:12
11:9
x Ex 16:13
11:11
y Ex 5:22
11:12
z Isa 40:11;
49:23 a Ex 13:5
11:13
b Jn 6:5-9
11:14
c Ex 18:18
11:15
d Ex 32:32
e 1Ki 19:4;
Jnh 4:3

are known to you as leaders and officials among the people. Have them come to the Tent of Meeting, that they may stand there with you. 17I will come down and speak with you there, and I will take of the Spirit that is on you and put the Spirit on them.f They will help you carry the burden of the people so that you will not have to carry it alone.

18"Tell the people: 'Consecrate yourselvesg in preparation for tomorrow, when you will eat meat. The LORD heard you when you wailed,h "If only we had meat to eat! We were better off in Egypt!"i Now the LORD will give you meat, and you will eat it. 19You will not eat it for just one day, or two days, or five, ten or twenty days, 20but for a whole month—until it comes out of your nostrils and you loathe itj —because you have rejected the LORD,k who is among you, and have wailed before him, saying, "Why did we ever leave Egypt?"' "

21But Moses said, "Here I am among six hundred thousand menl on foot, and you say, 'I will give them meat to eat for a whole month!' 22Would they have enough if flocks and herds were slaughtered for them? Would they have enough if all the fish in the sea were caught for them?"m

23The LORD answered Moses, "Is the LORD's arm too short?n You will now see whether or not what I say will come true for you.o"

24So Moses went out and told the people what the LORD had said. He brought together seventy of their elders and had them stand around the Tent. 25Then the LORD came down in the cloudp and spoke with him,q and he took of the Spiritr that was on him and put the Spirit on the seventy elders.s When the Spirit rested on them, they prophesied,t but they did not do so again.ᵃ

26However, two men, whose names were Eldad and Medad, had remained in the camp. They were listed among the elders, but did not go out to the Tent. Yet the Spirit also rested on them, and they prophesied in the camp. 27A young man ran and told Moses, "Eldad and Medad are prophesying in the camp."

28Joshua son of Nun, who had been Moses' aideu since youth, spoke up and said, "Moses, my lord, stop them!"v

29But Moses replied, "Are you jealous for my sake? I wish that all the LORD's people were prophetsw and that the LORD would put his Spirit on them!" 30Then Moses and the elders of Israel returned to the camp.

31Now a wind went out from the LORD and drove quailx in from the sea. It brought themᵇ down all around the camp to about three feetᶜ above the ground, as far as a day's walk in any direction. 32All that day and night and all the next day the people went out and gathered quail. No one gathered less than ten homers.ᵈ Then they spread them out all around the camp. 33But while the meat was still between their teethy and before it could be consumed, the anger of the LORD burned against the people, and he struck them with a severe plague.z 34Therefore the place was named Kibroth Hattaavah,ᵉᵃ because there they buried the people who had craved other food.

35From Kibroth Hattaavah the people traveled to Hazerothᵇ and stayed there.

11:17
f ver 25,29;
1Sa 10:6;
2Ki 2:9,15;
Joel 2:28
11:18
g Ex 19:10
h Ex 16:7 i ver 5;
Ac 7:39
11:20
j Ps 78:29;
106:14,15
k Jos 24:27;
1Sa 10:19
11:21
l Ex 12:37
11:22
m Mt 15:33
11:23
n Isa 50:2; 59:1
o Nu 23:19;
Eze 12:25;
24:14
11:25
p Nu 12:5
q ver 17
r 1Sa 10:6
s Ac 2:17
t 1Sa 10:10
11:28
u Ex 33:11;
Jos 1:1
v Mk 9:38-40
11:29
w 1Co 14:5
11:31
x Ex 16:13;
Ps 78:26-28
11:33
y Ps 78:30
z Ps 106:15
11:34
a Dt 9:22
11:35
b Nu 33:17

ᵃ25 Or *prophesied and continued to do so*   ᵇ31 Or *They flew*   ᶜ31 Hebrew *two cubits* (about 1 meter)   ᵈ32 That is, probably about 60 bushels (about 2.2 kiloliters)   ᵉ34 *Kibroth Hattaavah* means *graves of craving.*

Miriam and Aaron Oppose Moses

12 Miriam and Aaron began to talk against Moses because of his Cushite wife,^c for he had married a Cushite. 2"Has the LORD spoken only through Moses?" they asked. "Hasn't he also spoken through us?"^d And the LORD heard this.^e

3(Now Moses was a very humble man,^f more humble than anyone else on the face of the earth.)

4At once the LORD said to Moses, Aaron and Miriam, "Come out to the Tent of Meeting, all three of you." So the three of them came out. 5Then the LORD came down in a pillar of cloud;^g he stood at the entrance to the Tent and summoned Aaron and Miriam. When both of them stepped forward, 6he said, "Listen to my words:

> "When a prophet of the LORD is among you,
> I reveal myself to him in visions,^h
> I speak to him in dreams.ⁱ
> 7But this is not true of my servant Moses;^j
> he is faithful in all my house.^k
> 8With him I speak face to face,
> clearly and not in riddles;^l
> he sees the form of the LORD.^m
> Why then were you not afraid
> to speak against my servant Moses?"

9The anger of the LORD burned against them, and he left them.ⁿ 10When the cloud lifted from above the Tent, there stood Miriam— leprous,^a like snow.^o Aaron turned toward her and saw that she had leprosy;^p 11and he said to Moses, "Please, my lord, do not hold against us the sin we have so foolishly committed.^q 12Do not let her be like a stillborn infant coming from its mother's womb with its flesh half eaten away."

13So Moses cried out to the LORD, "O God, please heal her!^r"

14The LORD replied to Moses, "If her father had spit in her face,^s would she not have been in disgrace for seven days? Confine her outside the camp^t for seven days; after that she can be brought back." 15So Miriam was confined outside the camp for seven days, and the people did not move on till she was brought back.

16After that, the people left Hazeroth^u and encamped in the Desert of Paran.

Exploring Canaan

13 The LORD said to Moses, 2"Send some men to explore^v the land of Canaan, which I am giving to the Israelites. From each ancestral tribe send one of its leaders."

3So at the LORD's command Moses sent them out from the Desert of Paran. All of them were leaders of the Israelites. 4These are their names:

from the tribe of Reuben, Shammua son of Zaccur;
5from the tribe of Simeon, Shaphat son of Hori;
6from the tribe of Judah, Caleb son of Jephunneh;^w
7from the tribe of Issachar, Igal son of Joseph;

---

^a10 The Hebrew word was used for various diseases affecting the skin—not necessarily leprosy.

12:1
cEx 2:21
12:2
dNu 16:3
eNu 11:1
12:3
fMt 11:29
12:5
gNu 11:25
12:6
hGe 15:1; 46:2
iGe 31:10;
1Ki 3:5;
Heb 1:1
12:7
jJos 1:1-2;
Ps 105:26
kHeb 3:2,5
12:8
lDt 34:10
mEx 20:4;
Ps 17:15
12:9
nGe 17:22
12:10
oEx 4:6; Dt 24:9
p2Ki 5:1,27
12:11
q2Sa 19:19;
24:10
12:13
rIsa 30:26;
Jer 17:14
12:14
sDt 25:9;
Job 17:6;
30:9-10;
Isa 50:6
tLev 13:46;
Nu 5:2-3
12:16
uNu 11:35
13:2
vDt 1:22
13:6
wver 30;
Nu 14:6,24;
34:19;
Jdg 1:12-15

8from the tribe of Ephraim, Hoshea son of Nun;
9from the tribe of Benjamin, Palti son of Raphu;
10from the tribe of Zebulun, Gaddiel son of Sodi;
11from the tribe of Manasseh (a tribe of Joseph), Gaddi son of Susi;
12from the tribe of Dan, Ammiel son of Gemalli;
13from the tribe of Asher, Sethur son of Michael;
14from the tribe of Naphtali, Nahbi son of Vophsi;
15from the tribe of Gad, Geuel son of Maki.

16These are the names of the men Moses sent to explore the land. (Moses gave Hoshea son of Nunˣ the name Joshua.)ʸ

17When Moses sent them to explore Canaan, he said, "Go up through the Negevᶻ and on into the hill country.ᵃ 18See what the land is like and whether the people who live there are strong or weak, few or many. 19What kind of land do they live in? Is it good or bad? What kind of towns do they live in? Are they unwalled or fortified? 20How is the soil? Is it fertile or poor? Are there trees on it or not? Do your best to bring back some of the fruit of the land.ᵇ" (It was the season for the first ripe grapes.)

21So they went up and explored the land from the Desert of Zinᶜ as far as Rehob,ᵈ toward Leboᵃ Hamath.ᵉ 22They went up through the Negev and came to Hebron, where Ahiman, Sheshai and Talmai,ᶠ the descendants of Anak,ᵍ lived. (Hebron had been built seven years before Zoan in Egypt.)ʰ 23When they reached the Valley of Eshcol,ᵇ they cut off a branch bearing a single cluster of grapes. Two of them carried it on a pole between them, along with some pomegranates and figs. 24That place was called the Valley of Eshcol because of the cluster of grapes the Israelites cut off there. 25At the end of forty days they returned from exploring the land.

Report on the Exploration

26They came back to Moses and Aaron and the whole Israelite community at Kadesh in the Desert of Paran. There they reported to themⁱ and to the whole assembly and showed them the fruit of the land. 27They gave Moses this account: "We went into the land to which you sent us, and it does flow with milk and honey!ʲ Here is its fruit.ᵏ 28But the people who live there are powerful, and the cities are fortified and very large.ˡ We even saw descendants of Anak there. 29The Amalekites live in the Negev; the Hittites, Jebusites and Amorites live in the hill country; and the Canaanites live near the sea and along the Jordan."

30Then Caleb silenced the people before Moses and said, "We should go up and take possession of the land, for we can certainly do it."

31But the men who had gone up with him said, "We can't attack those people; they are stronger than we are."ᵐ 32And they spread among the Israelites a bad reportⁿ about the land they had explored. They said, "The land we explored devoursᵒ those living in it. All the people we saw there are of great size.ᵖ 33We saw the Nephilim�q there (the descendants of Anakʳ come from the Nephilim). We seemed like grasshoppers in our own eyes, and we looked the same to them."

ᵃ21 Or *toward the entrance to*   ᵇ23 *Eshcol* means *cluster*; also in verse 24.

13:16
xver 8 yDt 32:44
13:17
zGe 12:9
aJdg 1:9
13:20
bDt 1:25
13:21
cNu 20:1;
27:14; 33:36;
Jos 15:1
dJos 19:28
eJos 13:5
13:22
fJos 15:14
gJos 15:13
hPs 78:12,43;
Isa 19:11,13
13:26
iNu 32:8
13:27
jEx 3:8 kDt 1:25
13:28
lDt 1:28; 9:1,2
13:31
mDt 1:28; 9:1;
Jos 14:8
13:32
nNu 14:36,37
oEze 36:13,14
pAm 2:9
13:33
qGe 6:4
rDt 1:28

The People Rebel

14 That night all the people of the community raised their voices and wept aloud. [2]All the Israelites grumbled against Moses and Aaron, and the whole assembly said to them, "If only we had died in Egypt! Or in this desert![s] [3]Why is the LORD bringing us to this land only to let us fall by the sword? Our wives and children will be taken as plunder. Wouldn't it be better for us to go back to Egypt?" [4]And they said to each other, "We should choose a leader and go back to Egypt.[t] "

[5]Then Moses and Aaron fell facedown[u] in front of the whole Israelite assembly gathered there. [6]Joshua son of Nun and Caleb son of Jephunneh, who were among those who had explored the land, tore their clothes [7]and said to the entire Israelite assembly, "The land we passed through and explored is exceedingly good.[v] [8]If the LORD is pleased with us,[w] he will lead us into that land, a land flowing with milk and honey,[x] and will give it to us. [9]Only do not rebel[y] against the LORD. And do not be afraid of the people of the land,[z] because we will swallow them up. Their protection is gone, but the LORD is with us. Do not be afraid of them."

[10]But the whole assembly talked about stoning[a] them. Then the glory of the LORD[b] appeared at the Tent of Meeting to all the Israelites. [11]The LORD said to Moses, "How long will these people treat me with contempt? How long will they refuse to believe in me,[c] in spite of all the miraculous signs I have performed among them? [12]I will strike them down with a plague and destroy them, but I will make you into a nation[d] greater and stronger than they."

[13]Moses said to the LORD, "Then the Egyptians will hear about it! By your power you brought these people up from among them.[e] [14]And they will tell the inhabitants of this land about it. They have already heard[f] that you, O LORD, are with these people and that you, O LORD, have been seen face to face, that your cloud stays over them, and that you go before them in a pillar of cloud by day and a pillar of fire by night.[g] [15]If you put these people to death all at one time, the nations who have heard this report about you will say, [16]'The LORD was not able to bring these people into the land he promised them on oath; so he slaughtered them in the desert.'[h]

[17]"Now may the Lord's strength be displayed, just as you have declared: [18]'The LORD is slow to anger, abounding in love and forgiving sin and rebellion.[i] Yet he does not leave the guilty unpunished; he punishes the children for the sin of the fathers to the third and fourth generation.'[j] [19]In accordance with your great love, forgive[k] the sin of these people,[l] just as you have pardoned them from the time they left Egypt until now."[m]

[20]The LORD replied, "I have forgiven them,[n] as you asked. [21]Nevertheless, as surely as I live[o] and as surely as the glory of the LORD fills the whole earth,[p] [22]not one of the men who saw my glory and the miraculous signs I performed in Egypt and in the desert but who disobeyed me and tested me ten times[q]— [23]not one of them will ever see the land I promised on oath[r] to their forefathers. No one who has treated me with contempt will ever see it.[s] [24]But because my servant Caleb has a different spirit and follows me wholeheartedly,[t] I will bring him into the land he went to, and his descendants will inherit it.[u] [25]Since the

---

14:2
[s]Nu 11:1
14:4
[t]Ne 9:17
14:5
[u]Nu 16:4,22,45
14:7
[v]Nu 13:27;
Dt 1:25
14:8
[w]Dt 10:15
[x]Nu 13:27
14:9
[y]Dt 1:26; 9:7,
23,24 [z]Dt 1:21;
7:18; 20:1
14:10
[a]Ex 17:4
[b]Lev 9:23
14:11
[c]Ps 78:22;
106:24
14:12
[d]Ex 32:10
14:13
[e]Ex 32:11-14;
Ps 106:23
14:14
[f]Ex 15:14
[g]Ex 13:21
14:16
[h]Jos 7:7
14:18
[i]Ex 34:6;
Ps 145:8;
Jnh 4:2 [j]Ex 20:5
14:19
[k]Ex 34:9
[l]Ps 106:45
[m]Ps 78:38
14:20
[n]Ps 106:23;
Mic 7:18-20
14:21
[o]Dt 32:40;
Isa 49:18
[p]Ps 72:19;
Isa 6:3;
Hab 2:14
14:22
[q]Ex 14:11;
32:1; 1Co 10:5
14:23
[r]Nu 32:11
[s]Heb 3:18
14:24
[t]ver 6-9;
Jos 14:8,14
[u]Nu 32:12

Amalekites and Canaanites are living in the valleys, turn[v] back tomorrow and set out toward the desert along the route to the Red Sea.[a]"

26The LORD said to Moses and Aaron: 27"How long will this wicked community grumble against me? I have heard the complaints of these grumbling Israelites.[w] 28So tell them, 'As surely as I live,[x] declares the LORD, I will do to you the very things I heard you say: 29In this desert your bodies will fall[y]—every one of you twenty years old or more[z] who was counted in the census and who has grumbled against me. 30Not one of you will enter the land I swore with uplifted hand to make your home, except Caleb son of Jephunneh and Joshua son of Nun. 31As for your children that you said would be taken as plunder, I will bring them in to enjoy the land you have rejected.[a] 32But you—your bodies will fall[b] in this desert. 33Your children will be shepherds here for forty years, suffering for your unfaithfulness, until the last of your bodies lies in the desert. 34For forty years—one year for each of the forty days you explored the land[c]—you will suffer for your sins and know what it is like to have me against you.' 35I, the LORD, have spoken, and I will surely do these things[d] to this whole wicked community, which has banded together against me. They will meet their end in this desert; here they will die."

36So the men Moses had sent[e] to explore the land, who returned and made the whole community grumble against him by spreading a bad report[f] about it— 37these men responsible for spreading the bad report[g] about the land were struck down and died of a plague[h] before the LORD. 38Of the men who went to explore the land, only Joshua son of Nun and Caleb son of Jephunneh survived.[i]

39When Moses reported this to all the Israelites, they mourned[j] bitterly. 40Early the next morning they went up toward the high hill country. "We have sinned[k]," they said. "We will go up to the place the LORD promised."

41But Moses said, "Why are you disobeying the LORD's command? This will not succeed![l] 42Do not go up, because the LORD is not with you. You will be defeated by your enemies,[m] 43for the Amalekites and Canaanites will face you there. Because you have turned away from the LORD, he will not be with you and you will fall by the sword."

44Nevertheless, in their presumption they went up[n] toward the high hill country, though neither Moses nor the ark of the LORD's covenant moved from the camp.[o] 45Then the Amalekites and Canaanites who lived in that hill country came down and attacked them and beat them down all the way to Hormah.[p]

Supplementary Offerings

15 The LORD said to Moses, 2"Speak to the Israelites and say to them: 'After you enter the land I am giving you[q] as a home 3and you present to the LORD offerings made by fire, from the herd or the flock,[r] as an aroma pleasing to the LORD[s]—whether burnt offerings[t] or sacrifices, for special vows or freewill offerings[u] or festival offerings[v]— 4then the one who brings his offering shall present to the LORD a grain offering[w] of a tenth of an ephah[b] of fine flour mixed with a

---

Cross references (left margin):

14:25
v Dt 1:40
14:27
w Ex 16:12
14:28
x ver 21
14:29
y Nu 26:65
z Nu 1:45
14:31
a Ps 106:24
14:32
b 1Co 10:5
14:34
c Nu 13:25
14:35
d Nu 23:19
14:36
e Nu 13:4-16
f Nu 13:32
14:37
g 1Co 10:10
h Nu 16:49
14:38
i Jos 14:6
14:39
j Ex 33:4
14:40
k Dt 1:41
14:41
l 2Ch 24:20
14:42
m Dt 1:42
14:44
n Dt 1:43
o Nu 31:6
14:45
p Nu 21:3;
Dt 1:44;
Jdg 1:17
15:2
q Lev 23:10
15:3
r Lev 1:2
s ver 24;
Ge 8:21;
Ex 29:18
t Nu 28:19,27
u Lev 22:18,21;
Ezr 1:4
v Lev 23:1-44
15:4
w Lev 2:1; 6:14

---

[a]25 Hebrew *Yam Suph*; that is, Sea of Reeds   [b]4 That is, probably about 2 quarts (about 2 liters)

quarter of a hin*ª* of oil. [5]With each lamb for the burnt offering or the sacrifice, prepare a quarter of a hin of wine*ˣ* as a drink offering.

[6]" 'With a ram*ʸ* prepare a grain offering*ᶻ* of two-tenths of an ephah*ᵇ* of fine flour mixed with a third of a hin*ᶜ* of oil,*ª* [7]and a third of a hin of wine as a drink offering. Offer it as an aroma pleasing to the LORD.

[8]" 'When you prepare a young bull as a burnt offering or sacrifice, for a special vow or a fellowship offering*ᵈᵇ* to the LORD, [9]bring with the bull a grain offering of three-tenths of an ephah*ᵉᶜ* of fine flour mixed with half a hin*ᶠ* of oil. [10]Also bring half a hin of wine as a drink offering. It will be an offering made by fire, an aroma pleasing to the LORD. [11]Each bull or ram, each lamb or young goat, is to be prepared in this manner. [12]Do this for each one, for as many as you prepare.

[13]" 'Everyone who is native-born*ᵈ* must do these things in this way when he brings an offering made by fire as an aroma pleasing to the LORD. [14]For the generations to come, whenever an alien or anyone else living among you presents an offering made by fire as an aroma pleasing to the LORD, he must do exactly as you do. [15]The community is to have the same rules for you and for the alien living among you; this is a lasting ordinance for the generations to come.*ᵉ* You and the alien shall be the same before the LORD: [16]The same laws and regulations will apply both to you and to the alien living among you.*ᶠ* '"

[17]The LORD said to Moses, [18]"Speak to the Israelites and say to them: 'When you enter the land to which I am taking you [19]and you eat the food of the land,*ᵍ* present a portion as an offering to the LORD. [20]Present a cake from the first of your ground meal*ʰ* and present it as an offering from the threshing floor.*ⁱ* [21]Throughout the generations to come you are to give this offering to the LORD from the first of your ground meal.*ʲ*

Offerings for Unintentional Sins

[22]" 'Now if you unintentionally fail to keep any of these commands the LORD gave Moses*ᵏ*— [23]any of the LORD's commands to you through him, from the day the LORD gave them and continuing through the generations to come— [24]and if this is done unintentionally without the community being aware of it,[1] then the whole community is to offer a young bull for a burnt offering*ᵐ* as an aroma pleasing to the LORD, along with its prescribed grain offering and drink offering, and a male goat for a sin offering.*ⁿ* [25]The priest is to make atonement for the whole Israelite community, and they will be forgiven,*ᵒ* for it was not intentional and they have brought to the LORD for their wrong an offering made by fire and a sin offering. [26]The whole Israelite community and the aliens living among them will be forgiven, because all the people were involved in the unintentional wrong.*ᵖ*

[27]" 'But if just one person sins unintentionally,*�q* he must bring a year-old female goat for a sin offering. [28]The priest is to make atonement before the LORD for the one who erred by sinning unintentionally, and when atonement has been made for him, he will be forgiven.*ʳ*

ª4 That is, probably about 1 quart (about 1 liter); also in verse 5   ᵇ6 That is, probably about 4 quarts (about 4.5 liters)   ᶜ6 That is, probably about 1 1/4 quarts (about 1.2 liters); also in verse 7   ᵈ8 Traditionally peace offering   *ᵉ9 That is, probably about 6 quarts (about 6.5 liters) ᶠ9 That is, probably about 2 quarts (about 2 liters); also in verse 10*

15:5
ˣNu 28:7,14

15:6
ʸLev 5:15
ᶻNu 28:12
ªEze 46:14

15:8
ᵇLev 1:3; 3:1

15:9
ᶜLev 14:10

15:13
ᵈLev 16:29

15:15
ᵉver 29;
Nu 9:14

15:16
ᶠNu 9:14

15:19
ᵍJos 5:11,12

15:20
ʰEx 34:26;
Lev 23:14;
Dt 26:2,10
ⁱLev 2:14

15:21
ʲRo 11:16

15:22
ᵏLev 4:2

15:24
ˡLev 5:15
ᵐLev 4:14
ⁿLev 4:3

15:25
ᵒLev 4:20;
Ro 3:25;
Heb 2:17

15:26
ᵖver 24

15:27
qLev 4:27

15:28
ʳLev 4:35

[29]One and the same law applies to everyone who sins unintentionally, whether he is a native-born Israelite or an alien.

[30]" 'But anyone who sins defiantly,[s] whether native-born or alien,[t] blasphemes the LORD, and that person must be cut off from his people. [31]Because he has despised the LORD's word and broken his commands,[u] that person must surely be cut off; his guilt remains on him.[v] '"

The Sabbath-Breaker Put to Death

[32]While the Israelites were in the desert, a man was found gathering wood on the Sabbath day.[w] [33]Those who found him gathering wood brought him to Moses and Aaron and the whole assembly, [34]and they kept him in custody, because it was not clear what should be done to him.[x] [35]Then the LORD said to Moses, "The man must die.[y] The whole assembly must stone him outside the camp.[z]" [36]So the assembly took him outside the camp and stoned him to death, as the LORD commanded Moses.

Tassels on Garments

[37]The LORD said to Moses, [38]"Speak to the Israelites and say to them: 'Throughout the generations to come you are to make tassels on the corners of your garments,[a] with a blue cord on each tassel. [39]You will have these tassels to look at and so you will remember[b] all the commands of the LORD, that you may obey them and not prostitute yourselves by going after the lusts of your own hearts and eyes. [40]Then you will remember to obey all my commands and will be consecrated to your God.[c] [41]I am the LORD your God, who brought you out of Egypt to be your God. I am the LORD your God.' "

Korah, Dathan and Abiram

16 Korah[d] son of Izhar, the son of Kohath, the son of Levi, and certain Reubenites—Dathan and Abiram, sons of Eliab,[e] and On son of Peleth—became insolent[a] [2]and rose up against Moses. With them were 250 Israelite men, well-known community leaders who had been appointed members of the council.[f] [3]They came as a group to oppose Moses and Aaron[g] and said to them, "You have gone too far! The whole community is holy,[h] every one of them, and the LORD is with them.[i] Why then do you set yourselves above the LORD's assembly?"[j]

[4]When Moses heard this, he fell facedown.[k] [5]Then he said to Korah and all his followers: "In the morning the LORD will show who belongs to him and who is holy,[l] and he will have that person come near him. The man he chooses[m] he will cause to come near him. [6]You, Korah, and all your followers are to do this: Take censers [7]and tomorrow put fire and incense in them before the LORD. The man the LORD chooses will be the one who is holy. You Levites have gone too far!"

[8]Moses also said to Korah, "Now listen, you Levites! [9]Isn't it enough for you that the God of Israel has separated you from the rest of the Israelite community and brought you near himself to do the work at the LORD's tabernacle and to stand before the community and minister to

15:30
sNu 14:40-44;
Dt 1:43; 17:13;
Ps 19:13 tver 14
15:31
u2Sa 12:9;
Ps 119:126;
Pr 13:13
vLev 5:1;
Eze 18:20
15:32
wEx 31:14,15;
35:2,3
15:34
xNu 9:8
15:35
yEx 31:14,15;
Dt 21:21
zLev 20:2;
24:14; Ac 7:58
15:38
aDt 22:12;
Mt 23:5
15:39
bDt 4:23; 6:12;
Ps 73:27
15:40
cLev 11:44;
Ro 12:1;
Col 1:22;
1Pe 1:15

16:1
dJude 1:11
eNu 26:8;
Dt 11:6
16:2
fNu 1:16; 26:9
16:3
gver 7;
Ps 106:16
hEx 19:6
iNu 14:14
jNu 12:2
16:4
kNu 14:5
16:5
lLev 10:3;
2Ti 2:19*
mNu 17:5;
Ps 65:4

---

[a]1 Or *Peleth—took men,*

them?ⁿ ¹⁰He has brought you and all your fellow Levites near himself, but now you are trying to get the priesthood too.ᵒ ¹¹It is against the LORD that you and all your followers have banded together. Who is Aaron that you should grumbleᵖ against him?�q"

¹²Then Moses summoned Dathan and Abiram, the sons of Eliab. But they said, "We will not come! ¹³Isn't it enough that you have brought us up out of a land flowing with milk and honey to kill us in the desert?ʳ And now you also want to lord it over us?ˢ ¹⁴Moreover, you haven't brought us into a land flowing with milk and honeyᵗ or given us an inheritance of fields and vineyards.ᵘ Will you gouge out the eyes ofᵃ these men?ᵛ No, we will not come!"

¹⁵Then Moses became very angry and said to the LORD, "Do not accept their offering. I have not taken so much as a donkeyʷ from them, nor have I wronged any of them."

¹⁶Moses said to Korah, "You and all your followers are to appear before the LORD tomorrow—you and they and Aaron.ˣ ¹⁷Each man is to take his censer and put incense in it—250 censers in all—and present it before the LORD. You and Aaron are to present your censers also." ¹⁸So each man took his censer, put fire and incense in it, and stood with Moses and Aaron at the entrance to the Tent of Meeting. ¹⁹When Korah had gathered all his followers in opposition to themʸ at the entrance to the Tent of Meeting, the glory of the LORDᶻ appeared to the entire assembly. ²⁰The LORD said to Moses and Aaron, ²¹"Separate yourselves from this assembly so I can put an end to them at once."ᵃ

²²But Moses and Aaron fell facedownᵇ and cried out, "O God, God of the spirits of all mankind,ᶜ will you be angry with the entire assembly when only one man sins?"ᵈ

²³Then the LORD said to Moses, ²⁴"Say to the assembly, 'Move away from the tents of Korah, Dathan and Abiram.' "

²⁵Moses got up and went to Dathan and Abiram, and the elders of Israel followed him. ²⁶He warned the assembly, "Move back from the tents of these wicked men!ᵉ Do not touch anything belonging to them, or you will be swept awayᶠ because of all their sins." ²⁷So they moved away from the tents of Korah, Dathan and Abiram. Dathan and Abiram had come out and were standing with their wives, children and little ones at the entrances to their tents.

²⁸Then Moses said, "This is how you will know that the LORD has sent meᵍ to do all these things and that it was not my idea: ²⁹If these men die a natural death and experience only what usually happens to men, then the LORD has not sent me.ʰ ³⁰But if the LORD brings about something totally new, and the earth opens its mouth and swallows them, with everything that belongs to them, and they go down alive into the grave,ᵇⁱ then you will know that these men have treated the LORD with contempt."

³¹As soon as he finished saying all this, the ground under them split apartʲ ³²and the earth opened its mouth and swallowed them,ᵏ with their households and all Korah's men and all their possessions. ³³They went down alive into the grave, with everything they owned; the earth closed over them, and they perished and were gone from the commu-

16:9
ⁿNu 3:6;
Dt 10:8
16:10
ᵒNu 3:10; 18:7
16:11
ᵖ1Co 10:10
qEx 16:7
16:13
ʳNu 14:2
ˢAc 7:27,35
16:14
ᵗLev 20:24
ᵘEx 22:5;
23:11; Nu 20:5
ᵛJdg 16:21;
1Sa 11:2
16:15
ʷ1Sa 12:3
16:16
ˣver 6
16:19
ʸver 42
ᶻEx 16:7;
Nu 14:10; 20:6
16:21
ᵃEx 32:10
16:22
ᵇNu 14:5
ᶜNu 27:16;
Job 12:10;
Heb 12:9
ᵈGe 18:23
16:26
ᵉIsa 52:11
ᶠGe 19:15
16:28
ᵍEx 3:12;
Jn 5:36; 6:38
16:29
ʰEcc 3:19
16:30
ⁱver 33;
Ps 55:15
16:31
ʲMic 1:3-4
16:32
ᵏNu 26:11;
Dt 11:6;
Ps 106:17

ᵃ14 Or *you make slaves of* ; or *you deceive*   ᵇ30 Hebrew *Sheol*; also in verse 33 nity. [34]At their cries, all the Israelites around them fled, shouting, "The earth is going to swallow us too!"

[35]And fire came out from the LORD[1] and consumed[m] the 250 men who were offering the incense.

[36]The LORD said to Moses, [37]"Tell Eleazar son of Aaron, the priest, to take the censers out of the smoldering remains and scatter the coals some distance away, for the censers are holy— [38]the censers of the men who sinned at the cost of their lives.[n] Hammer the censers into sheets to overlay the altar, for they were presented before the LORD and have become holy. Let them be a sign[o] to the Israelites."

[39]So Eleazar the priest collected the bronze censers brought by those who had been burned up, and he had them hammered out to overlay the altar, [40]as the LORD directed him through Moses. This was to remind the Israelites that no one except a descendant of Aaron should come to burn incense[p] before the LORD,[q] or he would become like Korah and his followers.[r]

[41]The next day the whole Israelite community grumbled against Moses and Aaron. "You have killed the LORD's people," they said.

[42]But when the assembly gathered in opposition[s] to Moses and Aaron and turned toward the Tent of Meeting, suddenly the cloud covered it and the glory of the LORD appeared. [43]Then Moses and Aaron went to the front of the Tent of Meeting, [44]and the LORD said to Moses, [45]"Get away from this assembly so I can put an end to them at once." And they fell facedown.

[46]Then Moses said to Aaron, "Take your censer and put incense in it, along with fire from the altar, and hurry to the assembly[t] to make atonement[u] for them. Wrath has come out from the LORD; the plague[v] has started." [47]So Aaron did as Moses said, and ran into the midst of the assembly. The plague had already started among the people,[w] but Aaron offered the incense and made atonement for them. [48]He stood between the living and the dead, and the plague stopped.[x] [49]But 14,700 people died from the plague, in addition to those who had died because of Korah.[y] [50]Then Aaron returned to Moses at the entrance to the Tent of Meeting, for the plague had stopped.

The Budding of Aaron's Staff

17 The LORD said to Moses, [2]"Speak to the Israelites and get twelve staffs from them, one from the leader of each of their ancestral tribes. Write the name of each man on his staff. [3]On the staff of Levi write Aaron's name,[z] for there must be one staff for the head of each ancestral tribe. [4]Place them in the Tent of Meeting in front of the Testimony,[a] where I meet with you.[b] [5]The staff belonging to the man I choose[c] will sprout, and I will rid myself of this constant grumbling against you by the Israelites."

[6]So Moses spoke to the Israelites, and their leaders gave him twelve staffs, one for the leader of each of their ancestral tribes, and Aaron's staff was among them. [7]Moses placed the staffs before the LORD in the Tent of the Testimony.[d]

[8]The next day Moses entered the Tent of the Testimony and saw that Aaron's staff, which represented the house of Levi, had not only sprouted but had budded, blossomed and produced almonds.[e] [9]Then Moses brought out all the staffs from the LORD's presence to all the

16:35
lNu 11:1-3;
26:10 mLev 10:2
16:38
nPr 20:2
oNu 26:10;
Eze 14:8;
2Pe 2:6
16:40
pEx 30:7-10;
Nu 1:51
q2Ch 26:18
rNu 3:10
16:42
sver 19;
Nu 20:6
16:46
tLev 10:6
uNu 18:5;
25:13; Dt 9:22
vNu 8:19;
Ps 106:29
16:47
wNu 25:6-8
16:48
xNu 25:8;
Ps 106:30
16:49
yver 32
17:3
zNu 1:3
17:4
aver 7 bEx 25:22
17:5
cNu 16:5
17:7
dEx 38:21;
Ac 7:44
17:8
eEze 17:24;
Heb 9:4

Israelites. They looked at them, and each man took his own staff. [10]The LORD said to Moses, "Put back Aaron's staff in front of the Testimony, to be kept as a sign to the rebellious. [f] This will put an end to their grumbling against me, so that they will not die." [11]Moses did just as the LORD commanded him.

[12]The Israelites said to Moses, "We will die! We are lost, we are all lost! [g] [13]Anyone who even comes near the tabernacle of the LORD will die. [h] Are we all going to die?"

Duties of Priests and Levites

18 The LORD said to Aaron, "You, your sons and your father's family are to bear the responsibility for offenses against the sanctuary, [i] and you and your sons alone are to bear the responsibility for offenses against the priesthood. [2]Bring your fellow Levites from your ancestral tribe to join you and assist you when you and your sons minister [j] before the Tent of the Testimony. [3]They are to be responsible to you and are to perform all the duties of the Tent, [k] but they must not go near the furnishings of the sanctuary or the altar, or both they and you will die. [l] [4]They are to join you and be responsible for the care of the Tent of Meeting—all the work at the Tent—and no one else may come near where you are.

[5]"You are to be responsible for the care of the sanctuary and the altar, [m] so that wrath will not fall on the Israelites again. [6]I myself have selected your fellow Levites from among the Israelites as a gift to you, [n] dedicated to the LORD to do the work at the Tent of Meeting. [7]But only you and your sons may serve as priests in connection with everything at the altar and inside the curtain. [o] I am giving you the service of the priesthood as a gift. [p] Anyone else who comes near the sanctuary must be put to death. [q]"

Offerings for Priests and Levites

[8]Then the LORD said to Aaron, "I myself have put you in charge of the offerings presented to me; all the holy offerings the Israelites give me I give to you and your sons as your portion and regular share. [r] [9]You are to have the part of the most holy offerings that is kept from the fire. From all the gifts they bring me as most holy offerings, whether grain [s] or sin [t] or guilt offerings, [u] that part belongs to you and your sons. [10]Eat it as something most holy; every male shall eat it. [v] You must regard it as holy.

[11]"This also is yours: whatever is set aside from the gifts of all the wave offerings [w] of the Israelites. I give this to you and your sons and daughters as your regular share. Everyone in your household who is ceremonially clean [x] may eat it.

[12]"I give you all the finest olive oil and all the finest new wine and grain they give the LORD as the firstfruits of their harvest. [y] [13]All the land's firstfruits that they bring to the LORD will be yours. [z] Everyone in your household who is ceremonially clean may eat it.

[14]"Everything in Israel that is devoted [a] to the LORD[a] is yours. [15]The first offspring of every womb, both man and animal, that is offered to

17:10
f Dt 9:24
17:12
g Isa 6:5
17:13
h Nu 1:51
18:1
i Ex 28:38
18:2
j Nu 3:10
18:3
k Nu 3:51
l ver 7; Nu 4:15
18:5
m Nu 16:46
18:6
n Nu 3:9
18:7
o Heb 9:3,6
p ver 20; Ex 29:9
q Nu 3:10
18:8
r Lev 6:16; 7:6, 31-34,36
18:9
s Lev 2:1
t Lev 6:25
u Lev 5:15; 7:7
18:10
v Lev 6:16
18:11
w Ex 29:26
x Lev 22:1-16
18:12
y Ex 23:19; Ne 10:35
18:13
z Ex 22:29; 23:19
18:14
a Lev 27:28

---

[a]14 The Hebrew term refers to the irrevocable giving over of things or persons to the LORD, often by totally destroying them.

the LORD is yours.ᵇ But you must redeemᶜ every firstborn son and every firstborn male of unclean animals.ᵈ ¹⁶When they are a month old, you must redeem them at the redemption price set at five shekelsᵃᵉ of silver, according to the sanctuary shekel,ᶠ which weighs twenty gerahs.

¹⁷"But you must not redeem the firstborn of an ox, a sheep or a goat; they are holy.ᵍ Sprinkle their bloodʰ on the altar and burn their fat as an offering made by fire, an aroma pleasing to the LORD. ¹⁸Their meat is to be yours, just as the breast of the wave offeringⁱ and the right thigh are yours. ¹⁹Whatever is set aside from the holy offerings the Israelites present to the LORD I give to you and your sons and daughters as your regular share. It is an everlasting covenant of saltʲ before the LORD for both you and your offspring."

²⁰The LORD said to Aaron, "You will have no inheritance in their land, nor will you have any share among them;ᵏ I am your share and your inheritanceˡ among the Israelites.

²¹"I give to the Levites all the tithesᵐ in Israel as their inheritanceⁿ in return for the work they do while serving at the Tent of Meeting. ²²From now on the Israelites must not go near the Tent of Meeting, or they will bear the consequences of their sin and will die.º ²³It is the Levites who are to do the work at the Tent of Meeting and bear the responsibility for offenses against it. This is a lasting ordinance for the generations to come. They will receive no inheritanceᵖ among the Israelites. ²⁴Instead, I give to the Levites as their inheritance the tithes that the Israelites present as an offering to the LORD. That is why I said concerning them: 'They will have no inheritance among the Israelites.'"

²⁵The LORD said to Moses, ²⁶"Speak to the Levites and say to them: 'When you receive from the Israelites the tithe I give you�q as your inheritance, you must present a tenth of that tithe as the LORD's offering.ʳ ²⁷Your offering will be reckoned to you as grain from the threshing floor or juice from the winepress. ²⁸In this way you also will present an offering to the LORD from all the tithesˢ you receive from the Israelites. From these tithes you must give the LORD's portion to Aaron the priest. ²⁹You must present as the LORD's portion the best and holiest part of everything given to you.'

³⁰"Say to the Levites: 'When you present the best part, it will be reckoned to you as the product of the threshing floor or the winepress.ᵗ ³¹You and your households may eat the rest of it anywhere, for it is your wages for your work at the Tent of Meeting. ³²By presenting the best partᵘ of it you will not be guilty in this matter; then you will not defile the holy offeringsᵛ of the Israelites, and you will not die.'"

The Water of Cleansing

19 The LORD said to Moses and Aaron: ²"This is a requirement of the law that the LORD has commanded: Tell the Israelites to bring you a red heiferʷ without defect or blemishˣ and that has never been under a yoke.ʸ ³Give it to Eleazarᶻ the priest; it is to be taken outside

18:15
ᵇEx 13:2
ᶜNu 3:46
ᵈEx 13:13
18:16
ᵉLev 27:6
ᶠEx 30:13
18:17
ᵍDt 15:19
ʰLev 3:2
18:18
ⁱLev 7:30
18:19
ʲLev 2:13;
2Ch 13:5
18:20
ᵏDt 12:12
ˡDt 10:9; 14:27;
18:1-2;
Jos 13:33;
Eze 44:28
18:21
ᵐDt 14:22;
Mal 3:8
ⁿLev 27:30-33;
Heb 7:5
18:22
ºLev 22:9;
Nu 1:51
18:23
ᵖver 20
18:26
𝑞ver 21
ʳNe 10:38
18:28
ˢMal 3:8
18:30
ᵗver 27
18:32
ᵘLev 22:15
ᵛLev 19:8
19:2
ʷGe 15:9;
Heb 9:13
ˣLev 22:19-25
ʸDt 21:3;
1Sa 6:7
19:3
ᶻNu 3:4

ᵃ16 That is, about 2 ounces (about 55 grams)

the camp[a] and slaughtered in his presence. [4]Then Eleazar the priest is to take some of its blood on his finger and sprinkle[b] it seven times toward the front of the Tent of Meeting. [5]While he watches, the heifer is to be burned—its hide, flesh, blood and offal.[c] [6]The priest is to take some cedar wood, hyssop[d] and scarlet wool[e] and throw them onto the burning heifer. [7]After that, the priest must wash his clothes and bathe himself with water.[f] He may then come into the camp, but he will be ceremonially unclean till evening. [8]The man who burns it must also wash his clothes and bathe with water, and he too will be unclean till evening.

[9]"A man who is clean shall gather up the ashes of the heifer[g] and put them in a ceremonially clean place outside the camp. They shall be kept by the Israelite community for use in the water of cleansing;[h] it is for purification from sin. [10]The man who gathers up the ashes of the heifer must also wash his clothes, and he too will be unclean till evening. This will be a lasting ordinance both for the Israelites and for the aliens living among them.

[11]"Whoever touches the dead body[i] of anyone will be unclean for seven days.[j] [12]He must purify himself with the water on the third day and on the seventh day;[k] then he will be clean. But if he does not purify himself on the third and seventh days, he will not be clean. [13]Whoever touches the dead body[l] of anyone and fails to purify himself defiles the Lord's tabernacle.[m] That person must be cut off from Israel.[n] Because the water of cleansing has not been sprinkled on him, he is unclean;[o] his uncleanness remains on him.

[14]"This is the law that applies when a person dies in a tent: Anyone who enters the tent and anyone who is in it will be unclean for seven days, [15]and every open container without a lid fastened on it will be unclean.

[16]"Anyone out in the open who touches someone who has been killed with a sword or someone who has died a natural death,[p] or anyone who touches a human bone or a grave,[q] will be unclean for seven days.

[17]"For the unclean person, put some ashes[r] from the burned purification offering into a jar and pour fresh water over them. [18]Then a man who is ceremonially clean is to take some hyssop,[s] dip it in the water and sprinkle the tent and all the furnishings and the people who were there. He must also sprinkle anyone who has touched a human bone or a grave or someone who has been killed or someone who has died a natural death. [19]The man who is clean is to sprinkle the unclean person on the third and seventh days, and on the seventh day he is to purify him.[t] The person being cleansed must wash his clothes and bathe with water, and that evening he will be clean. [20]But if a person who is unclean does not purify himself, he must be cut off from the community, because he has defiled the sanctuary of the Lord. The water of cleansing has not been sprinkled on him, and he is unclean. [21]This is a lasting ordinance for them.

"The man who sprinkles the water of cleansing must also wash his clothes, and anyone who touches the water of cleansing will be unclean till evening. [22]Anything that an unclean[u] person touches becomes unclean, and anyone who touches it becomes unclean till evening."

19:3
aLev 4:12,21;
Heb 13:11
19:4
bLev 4:17
19:5
cEx 29:14
19:6
dver 18; Ps 51:7
eLev 14:4
19:7
fLev 11:25;
16:26,28; 22:6
19:9
gHeb 9:13
hver 13; Nu 8:7
19:11
iLev 21:1;
Nu 5:2
jNu 31:19
19:12
kver 19;
Nu 31:19
19:13
lLev 20:3
mLev 15:31;
2Ch 36:14
nLev 7:20; 22:3
oHag 2:13
19:16
pNu 31:19
qMt 23:27
19:17
rver 9
19:18
sver 6
19:19
tEze 36:25;
Heb 10:22
19:22
uLev 5:2;
Hag 2:13,14

Water From the Rock

20 In the first month the whole Israelite community arrived at the Desert of Zin,ᵛ and they stayed at Kadesh. ʷThere Miriamˣ died and was buried.

²Now there was no water for the community,ʸ and the people gathered in oppositionᶻ to Moses and Aaron. ³They quarreledᵃ with Moses and said, "If only we had died when our brothers fell dead before the LORD!ᵇ ⁴Why did you bring the LORD's community into this desert, that we and our livestock should die here?ᶜ ⁵Why did you bring us up out of Egypt to this terrible place? It has no grain or figs, grapevines or pomegranates.ᵈ And there is no water to drink!"

⁶Moses and Aaron went from the assembly to the entrance to the Tent of Meeting and fell facedown,ᵉ and the glory of the LORDᶠ appeared to them. ⁷The LORD said to Moses, ⁸"Take the staff,ᵍ and you and your brother Aaron gather the assembly together. Speak to that rock before their eyes and it will pour out its water.ʰ You will bring water out of the rock for the community so they and their livestock can drink."

⁹So Moses took the staff from the LORD's presence,ⁱ just as he commanded him. ¹⁰He and Aaron gathered the assembly together in front of the rock and Moses said to them, "Listen, you rebels, must we bring you water out of this rock?"ʲ ¹¹Then Moses raised his arm and struck the rock twice with his staff. Waterᵏ gushed out, and the community and their livestock drank.

¹²But the LORD said to Moses and Aaron, "Because you did not trust in me enough to honor me as holyˡ in the sight of the Israelites, you will not bring this community into the land I give them."ᵐ

¹³These were the waters of Meribah,ᵃⁿ where the Israelites quarreledᵒ with the LORD and where he showed himself holy among them.

Edom Denies Israel Passage

¹⁴Moses sent messengers from Kadeshᵖ to the king of Edom,�q saying:

"This is what your brother Israel says: You knowʳ about all the hardships that have come upon us. ¹⁵Our forefathers went down into Egypt,ˢ and we lived there many years.ᵗ The Egyptians mistreatedᵘ us and our fathers, ¹⁶but when we cried out to the LORD, he heard our cryᵛ and sent an angelʷ and brought us out of Egypt.

"Now we are here at Kadesh, a town on the edge of your territory. ¹⁷Please let us pass through your country. We will not go through any field or vineyard, or drink water from any well. We will travel along the king's highway and not turn to the right or to the left until we have passed through your territory.ˣ"

¹⁸But Edom answered:

"You may not pass through here; if you try, we will march out and attack you with the sword."

ᵃ13 *Meribah* means *quarreling*.

20:1
vNu 13:21
wNu 33:36
xEx 15:20

20:2
yEx 17:1
zNu 16:19

20:3
aEx 17:2
bNu 14:2;
16:31-35

20:4
cEx 14:11; 17:3;
Nu 14:3; 16:13

20:5
dNu 16:14

20:6
eNu 14:5
fNu 16:19

20:8
gEx 4:17,20
hEx 17:6;
Isa 43:20

20:9
iNu 17:10

20:10
jPs 106:32,33

20:11
kEx 17:6;
Dt 8:15;
Ps 78:16;
Isa 48:2;
1Co 10:4

20:12
lNu 27:14
mver 24;
Dt 1:37; 3:27

20:13
nEx 17:7
oDt 33:8;
Ps 95:8; 106:32

20:14
pJdg 11:16-17
qDt 2:4
rJos 2:11; 9:9

20:15
sGe 46:6
tGe 15:13;
Ex 12:40
uEx 1:11;
Dt 26:6

20:16
vEx 2:23; 3:7
wEx 14:19

20:17
xNu 21:22

¹⁹The Israelites replied:

"We will go along the main road, and if we or our livestock^y drink any of your water, we will pay for it.^z We only want to pass through on foot—nothing else."

²⁰Again they answered:

"You may not pass through."

Then Edom came out against them with a large and powerful army. ²¹Since Edom refused to let them go through their territory, Israel turned away from them.^a

The Death of Aaron

²²The whole Israelite community set out from Kadesh and came to Mount Hor.^b ²³At Mount Hor, near the border of Edom,^c the LORD said to Moses and Aaron, ²⁴"Aaron will be gathered to his people.^d He will not enter the land I give the Israelites, because both of you rebelled against my command^e at the waters of Meribah. ²⁵Get Aaron and his son Eleazar and take them up Mount Hor.^f ²⁶Remove Aaron's garments and put them on his son Eleazar, for Aaron will be gathered to his people;^g he will die there."

²⁷Moses did as the LORD commanded: They went up Mount Hor in the sight of the whole community. ²⁸Moses removed Aaron's garments and put them on his son Eleazar.^h And Aaron died thereⁱ on top of the mountain. Then Moses and Eleazar came down from the mountain, ²⁹and when the whole community learned that Aaron had died, the entire house of Israel mourned for him^j thirty days.

Arad Destroyed

21 When the Canaanite king of Arad,^k who lived in the Negev,^l heard that Israel was coming along the road to Atharim, he attacked the Israelites and captured some of them. ²Then Israel made this vow to the LORD: "If you will deliver these people into our hands, we will totally destroy^a their cities." ³The LORD listened to Israel's plea and gave the Canaanites over to them. They completely destroyed them and their towns; so the place was named Hormah.^b

The Bronze Snake

⁴They traveled from Mount Hor^m along the route to the Red Sea,^c to go around Edom. But the people grew impatient on the way;ⁿ ⁵they spoke against God^o and against Moses, and said, "Why have you brought us up out of Egypt to die in the desert?^p There is no bread! There is no water! And we detest this miserable food!"^q

⁶Then the LORD sent venomous snakes^r among them; they bit the people and many Israelites died.^s ⁷The people came to Moses^t and said, "We sinned when we spoke against the LORD and against you. Pray that the LORD^u will take the snakes away from us." So Moses prayed^v for the people.

^a2 The Hebrew term refers to the irrevocable giving over of things or persons to the LORD, often by totally destroying them; also in verse 3. ^b3 *Hormah* means *destruction.* ^c4 Hebrew *Yam Suph;* that is, Sea of Reeds

20:19 yEx 12:38 zDt 2:6,28
20:21 aDt 2:8; Jdg 11:18
20:22 bNu 33:37
20:23 cNu 33:37
20:24 dGe 25:8 ever 10
20:25 fNu 33:38
20:26 gver 24
20:28 hEx 29:29 iNu 33:38; Dt 10:6; 32:50
20:29 jDt 34:8
21:1 kNu 33:40; Jos 12:14 lJdg 1:9,16
21:4 mNu 20:22 nDt 2:8; Jdg 11:18
21:5 oPs 78:19 pNu 14:2,3 qNu 11:6
21:6 rDt 8:15; Jer 8:17 s1Co 10:9
21:7 tPs 78:34; Hos 5:15 uEx 8:8; Ac 8:24 vNu 11:2

[8]The LORD said to Moses, "Make a snake and put it up on a pole;[w] anyone who is bitten can look at it and live." [9]So Moses made a bronze snake[x] and put it up on a pole. Then when anyone was bitten by a snake and looked at the bronze snake, he lived.[y]

The Journey to Moab

[10]The Israelites moved on and camped at Oboth.[z] [11]Then they set out from Oboth and camped in Iye Abarim, in the desert that faces Moab[a] toward the sunrise. [12]From there they moved on and camped in the Zered Valley.[b] [13]They set out from there and camped alongside the Arnon[c], which is in the desert extending into Amorite territory. The Arnon is the border of Moab, between Moab and the Amorites. [14]That is why the Book of the Wars of the LORD says:

> ". . . Waheb in Suphah[a] and the ravines,
>> the Arnon [15]and[b] the slopes of the ravines
> that lead to the site of Ar[d]
>> and lie along the border of Moab."

[16]From there they continued on to Beer,[e] the well where the LORD said to Moses, "Gather the people together and I will give them water." [17]Then Israel sang this song:[f]

> "Spring up, O well!
>> Sing about it,
> [18]about the well that the princes dug,
>> that the nobles of the people sank—
>> the nobles with scepters and staffs."

Then they went from the desert to Mattanah, [19]from Mattanah to Nahaliel, from Nahaliel to Bamoth, [20]and from Bamoth to the valley in Moab where the top of Pisgah overlooks the wasteland.

Defeat of Sihon and Og

[21]Israel sent messengers to say to Sihon[g] king of the Amorites:

[22]"Let us pass through your country. We will not turn aside into any field or vineyard, or drink water from any well. We will travel along the king's highway until we have passed through your territory.[h]"

[23]But Sihon would not let Israel pass through his territory.[i] He mustered his entire army and marched out into the desert against Israel. When he reached Jahaz,[j] he fought with Israel. [24]Israel, however, put him to the sword[k] and took over his land from the Arnon to the Jabbok, but only as far as the Ammonites,[l] because their border was fortified. [25]Israel captured all the cities of the Amorites[m] and occupied them, including Heshbon and all its surrounding settlements. [26]Heshbon was the city of Sihon[n] king of the Amorites, who had fought against the former king of Moab and had taken from him all his land as far as the Arnon.

[27]That is why the poets say:

### Cross references (margin)

21:8
w Jn 3:14

21:9
x 2Ki 18:4
y Jn 3:14-15

21:10
z Nu 33:43

21:11
a Nu 33:44

21:12
b Dt 2:13,14

21:13
c Nu 22:36;
Jdg 11:13,18

21:15
d ver 28;
Dt 2:9,18

21:16
e Jdg 9:21

21:17
f Ex 15:1

21:21
g Dt 1:4;
2:26-27;
Jdg 11:19-21

21:22
h Nu 20:17

21:23
i Nu 20:21
j Dt 2:32;
Jdg 11:20

21:24
k Dt 2:33;
Ps 135:10-11;
Am 2:9 l Dt 2:37

21:25
m Nu 13:29;
Jdg 10:11;
Am 2:10

21:26
n Dt 29:7;
Ps 135:11

---

[a]14 The meaning of the Hebrew for this phrase is uncertain.   [b]14,15 Or *"I have been given from Suphah and the ravines / of the Arnon [15]to*

"Come to Heshbon and let it be rebuilt;
let Sihon's city be restored.

²⁸"Fire went out from Heshbon,
a blaze from the city of Sihon.°
It consumed Arᵖ of Moab,
the citizens of Arnon's heights.ۥ
²⁹Woe to you, O Moab!ʳ
You are destroyed, O people of Chemosh!ˢ
He has given up his sons as fugitivesᵗ
and his daughters as captivesᵘ
to Sihon king of the Amorites.

³⁰"But we have overthrown them;
Heshbon is destroyed all the way to Dibon.ᵛ
We have demolished them as far as Nophah,
which extends to Medeba."

³¹So Israel settled in the land of the Amorites.

³²After Moses had sent spies to Jazer,ʷ the Israelites captured its surrounding settlements and drove out the Amorites who were there. ³³Then they turned and went up along the road toward Bashanˣ,ʸ and Og king of Bashan and his whole army marched out to meet them in battle at Edrei.ᶻ

³⁴The Lord said to Moses, "Do not be afraid of him, for I have handed him over to you, with his whole army and his land. Do to him what you did to Sihon king of the Amorites, who reigned in Heshbon.ᵃ"

³⁵So they struck him down, together with his sons and his whole army, leaving them no survivors. And they took possession of his land.

Balak Summons Balaam

22 Then the Israelites traveled to the plains of Moab and camped along the Jordan across from Jericho.ᵃ ᵇ

²Now Balak son of Zipporᶜ saw all that Israel had done to the Amorites, ³and Moab was terrified because there were so many people. Indeed, Moab was filled with dreadᵈ because of the Israelites.

⁴The Moabites said to the elders of Midian, "This horde is going to lick up everything around us, as an ox licks up the grass of the field."

So Balak son of Zippor, who was king of Moab at that time, ⁵sent messengers to summon Balaam son of Beor,ᵉ who was at Pethor, near the River,ᵇ in his native land. Balak said:

"A people has come out of Egypt; they cover the face of the land and have settled next to me. ⁶Now come and put a curseᶠ on these people, because they are too powerful for me. Perhaps then I will be able to defeat them and drive them out of the country. For I know that those you bless are blessed, and those you curse are cursed."

⁷The elders of Moab and Midian left, taking with them the fee for

21:28
oJer 48:45
pver 15
qNu 22:41;
Isa 15:2
21:29
rIsa 25:10;
Jer 48:46
sJdg 11:24;
1Ki 11:7,33;
2Ki 23:13;
Jer 48:7,46
tIsa 15:5
uIsa 16:2
21:30
vNu 32:3;
Isa 15:2;
Jer 48:18,22
21:32
wNu 32:1,3,35;
Jer 48:32
21:33
xDt 3:3 yDt 3:4
zDt 1:4; 3:1,10;
Jos 13:12,31
21:34
aDt 3:2
22:1
bNu 33:48
22:2
cJdg 11:25
22:3
dEx 15:15
22:5
eDt 23:4;
Jos 13:22; 24:9;
Ne 13:2;
Mic 6:5;
2Pe 2:15
22:6
fver 12,17;
Nu 23:7,11,13

ᵃ1 Hebrew *Jordan of Jericho*; possibly an ancient name for the Jordan River   ᵇ5 That is, the Euphrates divination.ᵍ When they came to Balaam, they told him what Balak had said.

⁸"Spend the night here," Balaam said to them, "and I will bring you back the answer the LORD gives me.ʰ" So the Moabite princes stayed with him.

⁹God came to Balaamⁱ and asked,ʲ "Who are these men with you?"

¹⁰Balaam said to God, "Balak son of Zippor, king of Moab, sent me this message: ¹¹'A people that has come out of Egypt covers the face of the land. Now come and put a curse on them for me. Perhaps then I will be able to fight them and drive them away.'"

¹²But God said to Balaam, "Do not go with them. You must not put a curse on those people, because they are blessed.ᵏ"

¹³The next morning Balaam got up and said to Balak's princes, "Go back to your own country, for the LORD has refused to let me go with you."

¹⁴So the Moabite princes returned to Balak and said, "Balaam refused to come with us."

¹⁵Then Balak sent other princes, more numerous and more distinguished than the first. ¹⁶They came to Balaam and said:

"This is what Balak son of Zippor says: Do not let anything keep you from coming to me, ¹⁷because I will reward you handsomelyˡ and do whatever you say. Come and put a curseᵐ on these people for me."

¹⁸But Balaam answered them, "Even if Balak gave me his palace filled with silver and gold, I could not do anything great or small to go beyond the command of the LORD my God.ⁿ ¹⁹Now stay here tonight as the others did, and I will find out what else the LORD will tell me.ᵒ"

²⁰That night God came to Balaamᵖ and said, "Since these men have come to summon you, go with them, but do only what I tell you."�q

Balaam's Donkey

²¹Balaam got up in the morning, saddled his donkey and went with the princes of Moab. ²²But God was very angryʳ when he went, and the angel of the LORDˢ stood in the road to oppose him. Balaam was riding on his donkey, and his two servants were with him. ²³When the donkey saw the angel of the LORD standing in the road with a drawn swordᵗ in his hand, she turned off the road into a field. Balaam beat herᵘ to get her back on the road.

²⁴Then the angel of the LORD stood in a narrow path between two vineyards, with walls on both sides. ²⁵When the donkey saw the angel of the LORD, she pressed close to the wall, crushing Balaam's foot against it. So he beat her again.

²⁶Then the angel of the LORD moved on ahead and stood in a narrow place where there was no room to turn, either to the right or to the left. ²⁷When the donkey saw the angel of the LORD, she lay down under Balaam, and he was angryᵛ and beat her with his staff. ²⁸Then the LORD opened the donkey's mouth,ʷ and she said to Balaam, "What have I done to you to make you beat me these three times?ˣ"

²⁹Balaam answered the donkey, "You have made a fool of me! If I had a sword in my hand, I would kill you right now.ʸ"

³⁰The donkey said to Balaam, "Am I not your own donkey, which

22:7
ᵍNu 23:23; 24:1
22:8
ʰver 19
22:9
ⁱGe 20:3 ʲver 20
22:12
ᵏGe 12:2;
22:17; Nu 23:20
22:17
ˡver 37;
Nu 24:11
ᵐver 6
22:18
ⁿver 38;
Nu 23:12,26;
24:13;
1Ki 22:14;
2Ch 18:13;
Jer 42:4
22:19
ᵒver 8
22:20
ᵖGe 20:3
qver 35,38;
Nu 23:5,12,16,
26; 24:13;
2Ch 18:13
22:22
ʳEx 4:14
ˢGe 16:7;
Ex 23:20;
Jdg 13:3,6,13
22:23
ᵗJos 5:13
ᵘver 25,27
22:27
ᵛNu 11:1;
Jas 1:19
22:28
ʷ2Pe 2:16
ˣver 32
22:29
ʸDt 25:4;
Pr 12:10;
27:23-27;
Mt 15:19

you have always ridden, to this day? Have I been in the habit of doing this to you?"

"No," he said.

[31]Then the LORD opened Balaam's eyes,[z] and he saw the angel of the LORD standing in the road with his sword drawn. So he bowed low and fell facedown.

[32]The angel of the LORD asked him, "Why have you beaten your donkey these three times? I have come here to oppose you because your path is a reckless one before me.[a] [33]The donkey saw me and turned away from me these three times. If she had not turned away, I would certainly have killed you by now,[a] but I would have spared her."

[34]Balaam said to the angel of the LORD, "I have sinned.[b] I did not realize you were standing in the road to oppose me. Now if you are displeased, I will go back."

[35]The angel of the LORD said to Balaam, "Go with the men, but speak only what I tell you." So Balaam went with the princes of Balak.

[36]When Balak heard that Balaam was coming, he went out to meet him at the Moabite town on the Arnon[c] border, at the edge of his territory. [37]Balak said to Balaam, "Did I not send you an urgent summons? Why didn't you come to me? Am I really not able to reward you?"

[38]"Well, I have come to you now," Balaam replied. "But can I say just anything? I must speak only what God puts in my mouth."[d]

[39]Then Balaam went with Balak to Kiriath Huzoth. [40]Balak sacrificed cattle and sheep,[e] and gave some to Balaam and the princes who were with him. [41]The next morning Balak took Balaam up to Bamoth Baal,[f] and from there he saw part of the people.[g]

Balaam's First Oracle

23 Balaam said, "Build me seven altars here, and prepare seven bulls and seven rams[h] for me." [2]Balak did as Balaam said, and the two of them offered a bull and a ram on each altar.[i]

[3]Then Balaam said to Balak, "Stay here beside your offering while I go aside. Perhaps the LORD will come to meet with me.[j] Whatever he reveals to me I will tell you." Then he went off to a barren height.

[4]God met with him,[k] and Balaam said, "I have prepared seven altars, and on each altar I have offered a bull and a ram."

[5]The LORD put a message in Balaam's mouth[l] and said, "Go back to Balak and give him this message."[m]

[6]So he went back to him and found him standing beside his offering, with all the princes of Moab.[n] [7]Then Balaam[o] uttered his oracle:[p]

"Balak brought me from Aram,
    the king of Moab from the eastern mountains.
'Come,' he said, 'curse Jacob for me;
    come, denounce Israel.'[q]
[8]How can I curse
    those whom God has not cursed?[r]
How can I denounce

22:31
zGe 21:19
22:33
aver 29
22:34
bGe 39:9;
Nu 14:40;
1Sa 15:24,30;
2Sa 12:13;
24:10;
Job 33:27;
Ps 51:4
22:36
cNu 21:13
22:38
dNu 23:5,16,26
22:40
eNu 23:1,14,29;
Eze 45:23
22:41
fNu 21:28
gNu 23:13
23:1
hNu 22:40
23:2
iver 14,30
23:3
jver 15
23:4
kver 16
23:5
lDt 18:18;
Jer 1:9
mNu 22:20
23:6
nver 17
23:7
oNu 22:5
pver 18;
Nu 24:3,21
qNu 22:6;
Dt 23:4
23:8
rNu 22:12

---

a32 The meaning of the Hebrew for this clause is uncertain.

those whom the LORD has not denounced?
9From the rocky peaks I see them,
　from the heights I view them.
I see a people who live apart
　and do not consider themselves one of the nations. s
10Who can count the dust of Jacobt
　or number the fourth part of Israel?
Let me die the death of the righteous, u
　and may my end be like theirs!v"

11Balak said to Balaam, "What have you done to me? I brought you to curse my enemies, but you have done nothing but bless them!"w

12He answered, "Must I not speak what the LORD puts in my mouth?"x

Balaam's Second Oracle

13Then Balak said to him, "Come with me to another place where you can see them; you will see only a part but not all of them. And from there, curse them for me." 14So he took him to the field of Zophim on the top of Pisgah, and there he built seven altars and offered a bull and a ram on each altar. y

15Balaam said to Balak, "Stay here beside your offering while I meet with him over there."

16The LORD met with Balaam and put a message in his mouthz and said, "Go back to Balak and give him this message."

17So he went to him and found him standing beside his offering, with the princes of Moab. Balak asked him, "What did the LORD say?"

18Then he uttered his oracle:

"Arise, Balak, and listen;
　hear me, son of Zippor.
19God is not a man, a that he should lie,
　nor a son of man, that he should change his
　　mind. b
Does he speak and then not act?
　Does he promise and not fulfill?
20I have received a command to bless;
　he has blessed, c and I cannot change it. d

21"No misfortune is seen in Jacob, e
　no misery observed in Israel. a f
The LORD their God is with them; g
　the shout of the Kingh is among them.
22God brought them out of Egypt; i
　they have the strength of a wild ox. j
23There is no sorcery against Jacob,
　no divinationk against Israel.
It will now be said of Jacob
　and of Israel, 'See what God has done!'
24The people rise like a lioness; l
　they rouse themselves like a lionm

---

a21 Or He has not looked on Jacob's offenses / or on the wrongs found in Israel.

23:9
sEx 33:16;
Dt 32:8; 33:28
23:10
tGe 13:16
uPs 116:15;
Isa 57:1
vPs 37:37
23:11
wNu 24:10;
Ne 13:2
23:12
xNu 22:20,38
23:14
yver 2
23:16
zNu 22:38
23:19
aIsa 55:9;
Hos 11:9
b1Sa 15:29;
Mal 3:6;
Tit 1:2; Jas 1:17
23:20
cGe 22:17;
Nu 22:12
dIsa 43:13
23:21
ePs 32:2,5;
Ro 4:7-8
fIsa 40:2;
Jer 50:20
gEx 29:45,46;
Ps 145:18
hDt 33:5;
Ps 89:15-18
23:22
iNu 24:8
jDt 33:17;
Job 39:9
23:23
kNu 24:1;
Jos 13:22
23:24
lNa 2:11
mGe 49:9

that does not rest till he devours his prey
and drinks the blood of his victims.''

25Then Balak said to Balaam, ''Neither curse them at all nor bless them at all!''

26Balaam answered, ''Did I not tell you I must do whatever the LORD says?''

Balaam's Third Oracle

27Then Balak said to Balaam, ''Come, let me take you to another place. Perhaps it will please God to let you curse them for me from there.'' 28And Balak took Balaam to the top of Peor, overlooking the wasteland.

29Balaam said, ''Build me seven altars here, and prepare seven bulls and seven rams for me.'' 30Balak did as Balaam had said, and offered a bull and a ram on each altar.

24 Now when Balaam saw that it pleased the LORD to bless Israel, he did not resort to sorcery as at other times, but turned his face toward the desert. 2When Balaam looked out and saw Israel encamped tribe by tribe, the Spirit of God came upon him 3and he uttered his oracle:

"The oracle of Balaam son of Beor,
the oracle of one whose eye sees clearly,
4the oracle of one who hears the words of God,
who sees a vision from the Almighty, [a]
who falls prostrate, and whose eyes are opened:

5"How beautiful are your tents, O Jacob,
your dwelling places, O Israel!

6"Like valleys they spread out,
like gardens beside a river,
like aloes planted by the LORD,
like cedars beside the waters.

7Water will flow from their buckets;
their seed will have abundant water.

"Their king will be greater than Agag;
their kingdom will be exalted.

8"God brought them out of Egypt;
they have the strength of a wild ox.
They devour hostile nations
and break their bones in pieces;
with their arrows they pierce them.
9Like a lion they crouch and lie down,
like a lioness—who dares to rouse them?

"May those who bless you be blessed
and those who curse you be cursed!"

10Then Balak's anger burned against Balaam. He struck his hands together and said to him, ''I summoned you to curse my enemies, but

---

[a]4 Hebrew *Shaddai*; also in verse 16

23:27
nver 13
23:28
oPs 106:28
24:1
pNu 23:23
qNu 23:28
24:2
rNu 11:25,26;
1Sa 10:10;
19:20; 2Ch 15:1
24:4
sNu 22:20
tGe 15:1
24:6
uPs 45:8
vPs 1:3; 104:16
24:7
w1Sa 15:8
x2Sa 5:12;
1Ch 14:2;
Ps 145:11-13
24:8
yPs 2:9
Jer 50:17
zPs 45:5
24:9
aGe 49:9;
Nu 23:24
bGe 12:3
24:10
cEze 21:14

you have blessed them^d these three times. ^e ¹¹Now leave at once and go home! I said I would reward you handsomely,^f but the Lord has kept you from being rewarded."

¹²Balaam answered Balak, "Did I not tell the messengers you sent me,^g ¹³'Even if Balak gave me his palace filled with silver and gold, I could not do anything of my own accord, good or bad, to go beyond the command of the Lord^h—and I must say only what the Lord says'?ⁱ ¹⁴Now I am going back to my people, but come, let me warn you of what this people will do to your people in days to come."^j

Balaam's Fourth Oracle

¹⁵Then he uttered his oracle:

"The oracle of Balaam son of Beor,
    the oracle of one whose eye sees clearly,
¹⁶the oracle of one who hears the words of God,
    who has knowledge from the Most High,
who sees a vision from the Almighty,
    who falls prostrate, and whose eyes are opened:

¹⁷"I see him, but not now;
    I behold him, but not near.^k
A star will come out of Jacob;^l
    a scepter will rise out of Israel.^m
He will crush the foreheads of Moab,ⁿ
    the skulls^a of^b all the sons of Sheth.^c
¹⁸Edom^o will be conquered;
    Seir, his enemy, will be conquered,
    but Israel will grow strong.
¹⁹A ruler will come out of Jacob^p
    and destroy the survivors of the city."

Balaam's Final Oracles

²⁰Then Balaam saw Amalek^q and uttered his oracle:

"Amalek was first among the nations,
    but he will come to ruin at last."

²¹Then he saw the Kenites^r and uttered his oracle:

"Your dwelling place is secure,
    your nest is set in a rock;
²²yet you Kenites will be destroyed
    when Asshur^s takes you captive."

²³Then he uttered his oracle:

"Ah, who can live when God does this?^d
²⁴   Ships will come from the shores of Kittim;^t
    they will subdue Asshur and Eber,^u
    but they too will come to ruin.^v"

24:10
^dNu 23:11
^eNe 13:2
24:11
^fNu 22:17
24:12
^gNu 22:18
24:13
^hNu 22:18
ⁱNu 22:20
24:14
^jGe 49:1;
Nu 31:8,16;
Da 2:28;
Mic 6:5
24:17
^kRev 1:7
^lMt 2:2
^mGe 49:10
ⁿNu 21:29;
Isa 15:1-16:14
24:18
^oAm 9:12
24:19
^pGe 49:10;
Mic 5:2
24:20
^qEx 17:14
24:21
^rGe 15:19
24:22
^sGe 10:22
24:24
^tGe 10:4
^uGe 10:21
^vver 20

^a17 Samaritan Pentateuch (see also Jer. 48:45); the meaning of the word in the Masoretic Text is uncertain.   ^b17 Or possibly *Moab, / batter*   ^c17 Or *all the noisy boasters*   ^d23 Masoretic Text; with a different word division of the Hebrew *A people will gather from the north.*

²⁵Then Balaam^w got up and returned home and Balak went his own way.

Moab Seduces Israel

25 While Israel was staying in Shittim,^x the men began to indulge in sexual immorality^y with Moabite women,^z ²who invited them to the sacrifices^a to their gods.^b The people ate and bowed down before these gods. ³So Israel joined in worshiping the Baal of Peor.^c And the LORD's anger burned against them.

⁴The LORD said to Moses, "Take all the leaders of these people, kill them and expose them in broad daylight before the LORD,^d so that the LORD's fierce anger^e may turn away from Israel."

⁵So Moses said to Israel's judges, "Each of you must put to death^f those of your men who have joined in worshiping the Baal of Peor."

⁶Then an Israelite man brought to his family a Midianite woman right before the eyes of Moses and the whole assembly of Israel while they were weeping at the entrance to the Tent of Meeting. ⁷When Phinehas son of Eleazar, the son of Aaron, the priest, saw this, he left the assembly, took a spear in his hand ⁸and followed the Israelite into the tent. He drove the spear through both of them—through the Israelite and into the woman's body. Then the plague against the Israelites was stopped;^g ⁹but those who died in the plague^h numbered 24,000.ⁱ

¹⁰The LORD said to Moses, ¹¹"Phinehas son of Eleazar, the son of Aaron, the priest, has turned my anger away from the Israelites;^j for he was as zealous as I am for my honor^k among them, so that in my zeal I did not put an end to them. ¹²Therefore tell him I am making my covenant of peace^l with him. ¹³He and his descendants will have a covenant of a lasting priesthood,^m because he was zealous for the honor of his God and made atonementⁿ for the Israelites."

¹⁴The name of the Israelite who was killed with the Midianite woman was Zimri son of Salu, the leader of a Simeonite family. ¹⁵And the name of the Midianite woman who was put to death was Cozbi^o daughter of Zur, a tribal chief of a Midianite family.^p

¹⁶The LORD said to Moses, ¹⁷"Treat the Midianites^q as enemies and kill them, ¹⁸because they treated you as enemies when they deceived you in the affair of Peor^r and their sister Cozbi, the daughter of a Midianite leader, the woman who was killed when the plague came as a result of Peor."

The Second Census

26 After the plague the LORD said to Moses and Eleazar son of Aaron, the priest, ²"Take a census^s of the whole Israelite community by families—all those twenty years old or more who are able to serve in the army^t of Israel." ³So on the plains of Moab^u by the Jordan across from Jericho,^{a,v} Moses and Eleazar the priest spoke with them and said, ⁴"Take a census of the men twenty years old or more, as the LORD commanded Moses."

These were the Israelites who came out of Egypt:

⁵The descendants of Reuben, the firstborn son of Israel, were:

24:25
w Nu 31:8
25:1
x Jos 2:1;
Mic 6:5
y 1Co 10:8;
Rev 2:14
z Nu 31:16
25:2
a Ex 34:15
b Ex 20:5;
Dt 32:38;
1Co 10:20
25:3
c Ps 106:28;
Hos 9:10
25:4
d Dt 4:3
e Dt 13:17
25:5
f Ex 32:27
25:8
g Nu 16:46-48;
Ps 106:30
25:9
h Nu 14:37;
1Co 10:8
i Nu 31:16
25:11
j Ps 106:30
k Ex 20:5;
Dt 32:16,21;
Ps 78:58
25:12
l Isa 54:10;
Eze 34:25;
Mal 2:4,5
25:13
m Ex 29:9
n Nu 16:46
25:15
o ver 18
p Nu 31:8;
Jos 13:21
25:17
q Nu 31:1-3
25:18
r Nu 31:16
26:2
s Ex 30:11-16;
38:25-26;
Nu 1:2 t Nu 1:3
26:3
u Nu 33:48
v Nu 22:1

---

a3 Hebrew Jordan of Jericho; *possibly an ancient name for the Jordan River; also in verse 63*

through Hanoch, [w] the Hanochite clan;
through Pallu, [x] the Palluite clan;
[6]through Hezron, the Hezronite clan;
through Carmi, the Carmite clan.

[7]These were the clans of Reuben; those numbered were 43,730.

[8]The son of Pallu was Eliab, [9]and the sons of Eliab [y] were Nemuel, Dathan and Abiram. The same Dathan and Abiram were the community [z] officials who rebelled against Moses and Aaron and were among Korah's followers when they rebelled against the LORD. [a] [10]The earth opened its mouth and swallowed them along with Korah, whose followers died when the fire devoured the 250 men. And they served as a warning sign. [b] [11]The line of Korah, [c] however, did not die out. [d]

[12]The descendants of Simeon by their clans were:
through Nemuel, the Nemuelite clan;
through Jamin, [e] the Jaminite clan;
through Jakin, the Jakinite clan;
[13]through Zerah, [f] the Zerahite clan;
through Shaul, the Shaulite clan.

[14]These were the clans of Simeon; there were 22,200 men. [g]

[15]The descendants of Gad by their clans were:
through Zephon, [h] the Zephonite clan;
through Haggi, the Haggite clan;
through Shuni, the Shunite clan;
[16]through Ozni, the Oznite clan;
through Eri, the Erite clan;
[17]through Arodi, [a] the Arodite clan;
through Areli, the Arelite clan.

[18]These were the clans of Gad; [i] those numbered were 40,500.

[19]Er and Onan were sons of Judah, but they died [j] in Canaan.
[20]The descendants of Judah by their clans were:
through Shelah, [k] the Shelanite clan;
through Perez, the Perezite clan;
through Zerah, the Zerahite clan. [l]
[21]The descendants of Perez were:
through Hezron, [m] the Hezronite clan;
through Hamul, the Hamulite clan.

[22]These were the clans of Judah; [n] those numbered were 76,500.

[23]The descendants of Issachar by their clans were:
through Tola, [o] the Tolaite clan;
through Puah, the Puite [b] clan;
[24]through Jashub, [p] the Jashubite clan;
through Shimron, the Shimronite clan.

[25]These were the clans of Issachar; [q] those numbered were 64,300.

[26]The descendants of Zebulun by their clans were:
through Sered, the Seredite clan;
through Elon, the Elonite clan;

26:5
wGe 46:9
x1Ch 5:3
26:9
yNu 16:1
zNu 1:16
aNu 16:2
26:10
bNu 16:35,38
26:11
cEx 6:24
dNu 16:33;
Dt 24:16
26:12
e1Ch 4:24
26:13
fGe 46:10
26:14
gNu 1:23
26:15
hGe 46:16
26:18
iNu 1:25;
Jos 13:24-28
26:19
jGe 38:2-10;
46:12
26:20
k1Ch 2:3
lJos 7:17
26:21
mRu 4:19;
1Ch 2:9
26:22
nNu 1:27
26:23
oGe 46:13;
1Ch 7:1
26:24
pGe 46:13
26:25
qNu 1:29

[a]17 Samaritan Pentateuch and Syriac (see also Gen. 46:16); Masoretic Text *Arod* [b]23 Samaritan Pentateuch, Septuagint, Vulgate and Syriac (see also 1 Chron. 7:1); Masoretic Text *through Puvah, the Punite*

through Jahleel, the Jahleelite clan.
²⁷These were the clans of Zebulun;ʳ those numbered were 60,500.

²⁸The descendants of Joseph by their clans through Manasseh and Ephraim were:

²⁹The descendants of Manasseh:
    through Makir,ˢ the Makirite clan (Makir was the father of Gileadᵗ);
    through Gilead, the Gileadite clan.
    ³⁰These were the descendants of Gilead:
        through Iezer,ᵘ the Iezerite clan;
        through Helek, the Helekite clan;
    ³¹through Asriel, the Asrielite clan;
    through Shechem, the Shechemite clan;
    ³²through Shemida, the Shemidaite clan;
    through Hepher, the Hepherite clan.
    ³³(Zelophehadᵛ son of Hepher had no sons; he had only daughters, whose names were Mahlah, Noah, Hoglah, Milcah and Tirzah.)ʷ
³⁴These were the clans of Manasseh; those numbered were 52,700.ˣ

³⁵These were the descendants of Ephraim by their clans:
    through Shuthelah, the Shuthelahite clan;
    through Beker, the Bekerite clan;
    through Tahan, the Tahanite clan.
    ³⁶These were the descendants of Shuthelah:
        through Eran, the Eranite clan.
³⁷These were the clans of Ephraim;ʸ those numbered were 32,500.

These were the descendants of Joseph by their clans.

³⁸The descendants of Benjaminᶻ by their clans were:
    through Bela, the Belaite clan;
    through Ashbel, the Ashbelite clan;
    through Ahiram, the Ahiramite clan;
    ³⁹through Shupham,ᵃ the Shuphamite clan;
    through Hupham, the Huphamite clan.
    ⁴⁰The descendants of Bela through Ardᵃ and Naaman were:
        through Ard,ᵇ the Ardite clan;
        through Naaman, the Naamite clan.
⁴¹These were the clans of Benjamin;ᵇ those numbered were 45,600.

⁴²These were the descendants of Dan by their clans:
    through Shuham,ᶜ the Shuhamite clan.
These were the clans of Dan: ⁴³All of them were Shuhamite clans; and those numbered were 64,400.

⁴⁴The descendants of Asher by their clans were:
    through Imnah, the Imnite clan;
    through Ishvi, the Ishvite clan;
    through Beriah, the Beriite clan;

26:27
ʳNu 1:31
26:29
ˢJos 17:1
ᵗJdg 11:1
26:30
ᵘJos 17:2;
Jdg 6:11
26:33
ᵛNu 27:1
ʷNu 36:11
26:34
ˣNu 1:35
26:37
ʸNu 1:33
26:38
ᶻGe 46:21;
1Ch 7:6
26:40
ᵃGe 46:21;
1Ch 8:3
26:41
ᵇNu 1:37
26:42
ᶜGe 46:23

ᵃ39 A few manuscripts of the Masoretic Text, Samaritan Pentateuch, Vulgate and Syriac (see also Septuagint); most manuscripts of the Masoretic Text *Shephupham*   ᵇ40 Samaritan Pentateuch and Vulgate (see also Septuagint); Masoretic Text does not have *through Ard.*

⁴⁵and through the descendants of Beriah:
  through Heber, the Heberite clan;
  through Malkiel, the Malkielite clan.
⁴⁶(Asher had a daughter named Serah.)
⁴⁷These were the clans of Asher;ᵈ those numbered were 53,400.

⁴⁸The descendants of Naphtaliᵉ by their clans were:
  through Jahzeel, the Jahzeelite clan;
  through Guni, the Gunite clan;
    ⁴⁹through Jezer, the Jezerite clan;
  through Shillem, the Shillemite clan.
⁵⁰These were the clans of Naphtali;ᶠ those numbered were 45,400.

⁵¹The total number of the men of Israel was 601,730.ᵍ

⁵²The LORD said to Moses, ⁵³"The land is to be allotted to them as an inheritance based on the number of names.ʰ ⁵⁴To a larger group give a larger inheritance, and to a smaller group a smaller one; each is to receive its inheritance according to the numberⁱ of those listed. ⁵⁵Be sure that the land is distributed by lot.ʲ What each group inherits will be according to the names for its ancestral tribe. ⁵⁶Each inheritance is to be distributed by lot among the larger and smaller groups."

⁵⁷These were the Levitesᵏ who were counted by their clans:
  through Gershon, the Gershonite clan;
  through Kohath, the Kohathite clan;
  through Merari, the Merarite clan.
⁵⁸These also were Levite clans:
  the Libnite clan,
  the Hebronite clan,
  the Mahlite clan,
  the Mushite clan,
  the Korahite clan.
(Kohath was the forefather of Amram;ˡ ⁵⁹the name of Amram's wife was Jochebed,ᵐ a descendant of Levi, who was born to the Levitesᵃ in Egypt. To Amram she bore Aaron, Mosesⁿ and their sister Miriam. ⁶⁰Aaron was the father of Nadab and Abihu, Eleazar and Ithamar.ᵒ ⁶¹But Nadab and Abihuᵖ died when they made an offering before the LORD with unauthorized fire.)�q

⁶²All the male Levites a month old or more numbered 23,000.ʳ They were not countedˢ along with the other Israelites because they received no inheritanceᵗ among them.ᵘ

⁶³These are the ones counted by Moses and Eleazar the priest when they counted the Israelites on the plains of Moab�v by the Jordan across from Jericho. ⁶⁴Not one of them was among those countedʷ by Moses and Aaron the priest when they counted the Israelites in the Desert of Sinai. ⁶⁵For the LORD had told those Israelites they would surely die in the desert,ˣ and not one of them was left except Caleb son of Jephunneh and Joshua son of Nun.ʸ

ᵃ59 Or *Jochebed, a daughter of Levi, who was born to Levi*

26:47
dNu 1:41
26:48
eGe 46:24;
1Ch 7:13
26:50
fNu 1:43
26:51
gEx 12:37;
38:26; Nu 1:46;
11:21
26:53
hJos 11:23;
14:1; Eze 45:8
26:54
iNu 33:54
26:55
jNu 34:14
26:57
kGe 46:11;
Ex 6:16-19
26:58
lEx 6:20
26:59
mEx 2:1
nEx 6:20
26:60
oNu 3:2
26:61
pLev 10:1-2
qNu 3:4
26:62
rNu 3:39
sNu 1:47
tNu 18:23
uNu 2:33;
Dt 10:9
26:63
vver 3
26:64
wNu 14:29;
Dt 2:14-15;
Heb 3:17
26:65
xNu 14:28;
1Co 10:5
yJos 14:6-10

Zelophehad's Daughters

27:1–11pp — Nu 36:1–12

27 The daughters of Zelophehad[z] son of Hepher,[a] the son of Gilead, the son of Makir,[b] the son of Manasseh, belonged to the clans of Manasseh son of Joseph. The names of the daughters were Mahlah, Noah, Hoglah, Milcah and Tirzah. They approached [2]the entrance to the Tent of Meeting and stood before Moses, Eleazar the priest, the leaders and the whole assembly, and said, [3]"Our father died in the desert.[c] He was not among Korah's followers, who banded together against the LORD,[d] but he died for his own sin and left no sons.[e] [4]Why should our father's name disappear from his clan because he had no son? Give us property among our father's relatives."

[5]So Moses brought their case[f] before the LORD[g] [6]and the LORD said to him, [7]"What Zelophehad's daughters are saying is right. You must certainly give them property as an inheritance[h] among their father's relatives and turn their father's inheritance over to them.[i]

[8]"Say to the Israelites, 'If a man dies and leaves no son, turn his inheritance over to his daughter. [9]If he has no daughter, give his inheritance to his brothers. [10]If he has no brothers, give his inheritance to his father's brothers. [11]If his father had no brothers, give his inheritance to the nearest relative in his clan, that he may possess it. This is to be a legal requirement[j] for the Israelites, as the LORD commanded Moses.' "

Joshua to Succeed Moses

[12]Then the LORD said to Moses, "Go up this mountain in the Abarim range[k] and see the land[l] I have given the Israelites. [13]After you have seen it, you too will be gathered to your people,[m] as your brother Aaron[n] was, [14]for when the community rebelled at the waters in the Desert of Zin, both of you disobeyed my command to honor me as holy[o] before their eyes." (These were the waters of Meribah[p] Kadesh, in the Desert of Zin.)

[15]Moses said to the LORD, [16]"May the LORD, the God of the spirits of all mankind,[q] appoint a man over this community [17]to go out and come in before them, one who will lead them out and bring them in, so the LORD's people will not be like sheep without a shepherd."[r]

[18]So the LORD said to Moses, "Take Joshua son of Nun, a man in whom is the spirit,[a][s] and lay your hand on him.[t] [19]Have him stand before Eleazar the priest and the entire assembly and commission him[u] in their presence.[v] [20]Give him some of your authority so the whole Israelite community will obey him.[w] [21]He is to stand before Eleazar the priest, who will obtain decisions for him by inquiring[x] of the Urim[y] before the LORD. At his command he and the entire community of the Israelites will go out, and at his command they will come in."

[22]Moses did as the LORD commanded him. He took Joshua and had him stand before Eleazar the priest and the whole assembly. [23]Then he laid his hands on him and commissioned him, as the LORD instructed through Moses.

[a]18 Or *Spirit*

27:1
zNu 26:33
aJos 17:2,3
bNu 36:1
27:3
cNu 26:65
dNu 16:2
eNu 26:33
27:5
fEx 18:19
gNu 9:8
27:7
hJob 42:15
iJos 17:4
27:11
jNu 35:29
27:12
kNu 33:47;
Jer 22:20
lDt 3:23-27;
32:48-52
27:13
mNu 31:2
nNu 20:28
27:14
oNu 20:12
pEx 17:7;
Dt 32:51;
Ps 106:32
27:16
qNu 16:22
27:17
rDt 31:2;
1Ki 22:17;
Eze 34:5;
Zec 10:2;
Mt 9:36;
Mk 6:34
27:18
sGe 41:38;
Nu 11:25-29
tver 23; Dt 34:9
27:19
uDt 3:28;
31:14,23
vDt 31:7
27:20
wJos 1:16,17
27:21
xJos 9:14
yEx 28:30

Daily Offerings

28 The LORD said to Moses, 2"Give this command to the Israelites and say to them: 'See that you present to me at the appointed time the food[z] for my offerings made by fire, as an aroma pleasing to me.' 3Say to them: 'This is the offering made by fire that you are to present to the LORD: two lambs a year old without defect, as a regular burnt offering each day.[a] 4Prepare one lamb in the morning and the other at twilight, 5together with a grain offering of a tenth of an ephah[a] of fine flour mixed with a quarter of a hin[b] of oil[b] from pressed olives. 6This is the regular burnt offering instituted at Mount Sinai[c] as a pleasing aroma, an offering made to the LORD by fire. 7The accompanying drink offering[d] is to be a quarter of a hin of fermented drink with each lamb. Pour out the drink offering to the LORD at the sanctuary.[e] 8Prepare the second lamb at twilight, along with the same kind of grain offering and drink offering that you prepare in the morning. This is an offering made by fire, an aroma pleasing to the LORD.[f]

Sabbath Offerings

9" 'On the Sabbath[g] day, make an offering of two lambs a year old without defect, together with its drink offering and a grain offering of two-tenths of an ephah[c][h] of fine flour mixed with oil. 10This is the burnt offering for every Sabbath, in addition to the regular burnt offering[i] and its drink offering.

Monthly Offerings

11" 'On the first of every month,[j] present to the LORD a burnt offering of two young bulls, one ram and seven male lambs a year old, all without defect.[k] 12With each bull there is to be a grain offering[l] of three-tenths of an ephah[d][m] of fine flour mixed with oil; with the ram, a grain offering of two-tenths of an ephah of fine flour mixed with oil; 13and with each lamb, a grain offering[n] of a tenth of an ephah of fine flour mixed with oil. This is for a burnt offering, a pleasing aroma, an offering made to the LORD by fire. 14With each bull there is to be a drink offering[o] of half a hin[e] of wine; with the ram, a third of a hin[f]; and with each lamb, a quarter of a hin. This is the monthly burnt offering to be made at each new moon[p] during the year. 15Besides the regular burnt offering[q] with its drink offering, one male goat is to be presented to the LORD as a sin offering.[r]

The Passover

28:16-25pp — Ex 12:14-20; Lev 23:4-8; Dt 16:1-8

16" 'On the fourteenth day of the first month the LORD's Passover[s] is to be held. 17On the fifteenth day of this month there is to be a festival; for seven days[t] eat bread made without yeast.[u] 18On the first day hold a sacred assembly and do no regular work.[v] 19Present to the LORD an offering made by fire, a burnt offering of two young bulls, one ram and

Cross references:
28:2 zLev 3:11
28:3 aEx 29:38
28:5 bLev 2:1; Nu 15:4
28:6 cEx 19:3
28:7 dEx 29:41 eLev 3:7
28:8 fLev 1:9
28:9 gEx 20:10 hLev 23:13
28:10 iver 3
28:11 jNu 10:10 kLev 1:3
28:12 lNu 15:6 mNu 15:9
28:13 nLev 6:14
28:14 oNu 15:7 pEzr 3:5
28:15 qver 3,23,24 rLev 4:3
28:16 sEx 12:6,18; Lev 23:5; Dt 16:1
28:17 tEx 12:19 uEx 23:15; 34:18; Lev 23:6; Dt 16:3-8
28:18 vEx 12:16; Lev 23:7

---

[a]5 That is, probably about 2 quarts (about 2 liters); also in verses 13, 21 and 29   [b]5 That is, probably about 1 quart (about 1 liter); also in verses 7 and 14   [c]9 That is, probably about 4 quarts (about 4.5 liters); also in verses 12, 20 and 28   [d]12 That is, probably about 6 quarts (about 6.5 liters); also in verses 20 and 28   [e]14 That is, probably about 2 quarts (about 2 liters)   [f]14 That is, probably about 1 1/4 quarts (about 1.2 liters)

seven male lambs a year old, all without defect. [20]With each bull prepare a grain offering of three-tenths of an ephah[w] of fine flour mixed with oil; with the ram, two-tenths; [21]and with each of the seven lambs, one-tenth. [22]Include one male goat as a sin offering[x] to make atonement for you.[y] [23]Prepare these in addition to the regular morning burnt offering. [24]In this way prepare the food for the offering made by fire every day for seven days as an aroma pleasing to the LORD; it is to be prepared in addition to the regular burnt offering and its drink offering. [25]On the seventh day hold a sacred assembly and do no regular work.

Feast of Weeks
28:26–31pp — Lev 23:15–22; Dt 16:9–12

[26]'' 'On the day of firstfruits,[z] when you present to the LORD an offering of new grain during the Feast of Weeks,[a] hold a sacred assembly and do no regular work.[b] [27]Present a burnt offering of two young bulls, one ram and seven male lambs a year old as an aroma pleasing to the LORD. [28]With each bull there is to be a grain offering of three-tenths of an ephah of fine flour mixed with oil; with the ram, two-tenths; [29]and with each of the seven lambs, one-tenth.[c] [30]Include one male goat to make atonement for you. [31]Prepare these together with their drink offerings, in addition to the regular burnt offering[d] and its grain offering. Be sure the animals are without defect.

Feast of Trumpets
29:1–6pp — Lev 23:23–25

29 '' 'On the first day of the seventh month hold a sacred assembly and do no regular work.[e] It is a day for you to sound the trumpets. [2]As an aroma pleasing to the LORD,[f] prepare a burnt offering of one young bull, one ram and seven male lambs a year old, all without defect.[g] [3]With the bull prepare a grain offering of three-tenths of an ephah[a] of fine flour mixed with oil; with the ram, two-tenths[b]; [4]and with each of the seven lambs, one-tenth.[c] [5]Include one male goat[h] as a sin offering to make atonement for you. [6]These are in addition to the monthly[i] and daily burnt offerings[j] with their grain offerings and drink offerings as specified. They are offerings made to the LORD by fire—a pleasing aroma.

Day of Atonement
29:7–11pp — Lev 16:2–34; 23:26–32

[7]'' 'On the tenth day of this seventh month hold a sacred assembly. You must deny yourselves[d][k] and do no work.[l] [8]Present as an aroma pleasing to the LORD a burnt offering of one young bull, one ram and seven male lambs a year old, all without defect. [9]With the bull prepare a grain offering[m] of three-tenths of an ephah of fine flour mixed with oil; with the ram, two-tenths; [10]and with each of the seven lambs, one-tenth.[n] [11]Include one male goat as a sin offering, in addition to the sin offering for atonement and the regular burnt offering[o] with its grain offering, and their drink offerings.

28:20
wLev 14:10
28:22
xRo 8:3
yNu 15:28
28:26
zEx 34:22
aEx 23:16
bver 18;
Dt 16:10
28:29
cver 13
28:31
dver 3,19
29:1
eLev 23:24
29:2
fNu 28:2
gNu 28:3
29:5
hNu 28:15
29:6
iNu 28:11
jNu 28:3
29:7
kAc 27:9
lEx 31:15;
Lev 16:29;
23:26-32
29:9
mver 3,18
29:10
nNu 28:13
29:11
oLev 16:3;
Nu 28:3

---

[a]3 That is, probably about 6 quarts (about 6.5 liters); also in verses 9 and 14   [b]3 That is, probably about 4 quarts (about 4.5 liters); also in verses 9 and 14   [c]4 That is, probably about 2 quarts (about 2 liters); also in verses 10 and 15   [d]7 Or *must fast*

Feast of Tabernacles

29:12–39pp — Lev 23:33–43; Dt 16:13–17

[12] " 'On the fifteenth day of the seventh[p] month,[q] hold a sacred assembly and do no regular work. Celebrate a festival to the LORD for seven days. [13]Present an offering made by fire as an aroma pleasing to the LORD, a burnt offering of thirteen young bulls, two rams and fourteen male lambs a year old, all without defect. [14]With each of the thirteen bulls prepare a grain offering[r] of three-tenths of an ephah of fine flour mixed with oil; with each of the two rams, two-tenths; [15]and with each of the fourteen lambs, one-tenth. [16]Include one male goat as a sin offering, in addition to the regular burnt offering with its grain offering and drink offering.[s]

[17] " 'On the second day[t] prepare twelve young bulls, two rams and fourteen male lambs a year old, all without defect.[u] [18]With the bulls, rams and lambs, prepare their grain offerings[v] and drink offerings[w] according to the number specified.[x] [19]Include one male goat as a sin offering,[y] in addition to the regular burnt offering with its grain offering, and their drink offerings.

[20] " 'On the third day prepare eleven bulls, two rams and fourteen male lambs a year old, all without defect.[z] [21]With the bulls, rams and lambs, prepare their grain offerings and drink offerings according to the number specified.[a] [22]Include one male goat as a sin offering, in addition to the regular burnt offering with its grain offering and drink offering.

[23] " 'On the fourth day prepare ten bulls, two rams and fourteen male lambs a year old, all without defect. [24]With the bulls, rams and lambs, prepare their grain offerings and drink offerings according to the number specified. [25]Include one male goat as a sin offering, in addition to the regular burnt offering with its grain offering and drink offering.

[26] " 'On the fifth day prepare nine bulls, two rams and fourteen male lambs a year old, all without defect. [27]With the bulls, rams and lambs, prepare their grain offerings and drink offerings according to the number specified. [28]Include one male goat as a sin offering, in addition to the regular burnt offering with its grain offering and drink offering.

[29] " 'On the sixth day prepare eight bulls, two rams and fourteen male lambs a year old, all without defect. [30]With the bulls, rams and lambs, prepare their grain offerings and drink offerings according to the number specified. [31]Include one male goat as a sin offering, in addition to the regular burnt offering with its grain offering and drink offering.

[32] " 'On the seventh day prepare seven bulls, two rams and fourteen male lambs a year old, all without defect. [33]With the bulls, rams and lambs, prepare their grain offerings and drink offerings according to the number specified. [34]Include one male goat as a sin offering, in addition to the regular burnt offering with its grain offering and drink offering.

[35] " 'On the eighth day hold an assembly[b] and do no regular work. [36]Present an offering made by fire as an aroma pleasing to the LORD,[c] a burnt offering of one bull, one ram and seven male lambs a year old,[d] all without defect. [37]With the bull, the ram and the lambs, prepare their grain offerings and drink offerings according to the number specified.

29:12
p1Ki 8:2
qLev 23:24
29:14
rver 3
29:16
sver 6
29:17
tLev 23:36
uNu 28:3
29:18
vver 9
wNu 28:7
xNu 15:4-12
29:19
yNu 28:15
29:20
zver 17
29:21
aver 18
29:35
bLev 23:36
29:36
cLev 1:9 dver 2

38Include one male goat as a sin offering, in addition to the regular burnt offering with its grain offering and drink offering.

39" 'In addition to what you vow[e] and your freewill offerings, prepare these for the LORD at your appointed feasts:[f] your burnt offerings,[g] grain offerings, drink offerings and fellowship offerings.[a]' "

40Moses told the Israelites all that the LORD commanded him.

Vows

30 Moses said to the heads of the tribes of Israel:[h] "This is what the LORD commands: 2When a man makes a vow to the LORD or takes an oath to obligate himself by a pledge, he must not break his word but must do everything he said.[i]

3"When a young woman still living in her father's house makes a vow to the LORD or obligates herself by a pledge 4and her father hears about her vow or pledge but says nothing to her, then all her vows and every pledge by which she obligated herself will stand.[j] 5But if her father forbids her when he hears about it, none of her vows or the pledges by which she obligated herself will stand; the LORD will release her because her father has forbidden her.

6"If she marries after she makes a vow[k] or after her lips utter a rash promise by which she obligates herself 7and her husband hears about it but says nothing to her, then her vows or the pledges by which she obligated herself will stand. 8But if her husband[l] forbids her when he hears about it, he nullifies the vow that obligates her or the rash promise by which she obligates herself, and the LORD will release her.

9"Any vow or obligation taken by a widow or divorced woman will be binding on her.

10"If a woman living with her husband makes a vow or obligates herself by a pledge under oath 11and her husband hears about it but says nothing to her and does not forbid her, then all her vows or the pledges by which she obligated herself will stand. 12But if her husband nullifies them when he hears about them, then none of the vows or pledges that came from her lips will stand.[m] Her husband has nullified them, and the LORD will release her. 13Her husband may confirm or nullify any vow she makes or any sworn pledge to deny herself. 14But if her husband says nothing to her about it from day to day, then he confirms all her vows or the pledges binding on her. He confirms them by saying nothing to her when he hears about them. 15If, however, he nullifies them some time after he hears about them, then he is responsible for her guilt."

16These are the regulations the LORD gave Moses concerning relationships between a man and his wife, and between a father and his young daughter still living in his house.

Vengeance on the Midianites

31 The LORD said to Moses, 2"Take vengeance on the Midianites[n] for the Israelites. After that, you will be gathered to your people.[o]"

3So Moses said to the people, "Arm some of your men to go to war against the Midianites and to carry out the LORD's vengeance[p] on them.

---

a39 Traditionally *peace offerings*

29:39
eNu 6:2
fLev 23:2
gLev 1:3;
1Ch 23:31;
2Ch 31:3
30:1
hNu 1:4
30:2
iDt 23:21-23;
Jdg 11:35;
Job 22:27;
Ps 22:25; 50:14;
116:14;
Pr 20:25;
Ecc 5:4,5;
Jnh 1:16
30:4
jver 7
30:6
kLev 5:4
30:8
lGe 3:16
30:12
mEph 5:22;
Col 3:18
31:2
nGe 25:2
oNu 20:26;
27:13
31:3
pJdg 11:36;
1Sa 24:12;
2Sa 4:8; 22:48;
Ps 94:1; 149:7

4Send into battle a thousand men from each of the tribes of Israel." 5So twelve thousand men armed for battle, a thousand from each tribe, were supplied from the clans of Israel. 6Moses sent them into battle, a thousand from each tribe, along with Phinehas son of Eleazar, the priest, who took with him articles from the sanctuary�q and the trumpetsʳ for signaling.

7They fought against Midian, as the LORD commanded Moses, and killed every man.ˢ 8Among their victims were Evi, Rekem, Zur, Hur and Rebaᵗ—the five kings of Midian.ᵘ They also killed Balaam son of Beor with the sword.ᵛ 9The Israelites captured the Midianite women and children and took all the Midianite herds, flocks and goods as plunder. 10They burned all the towns where the Midianites had settled, as well as all their camps.ʷ 11They took all the plunder and spoils, including the people and animals,ˣ 12and brought the captives, spoils and plunder to Moses and Eleazar the priest and the Israelite assemblyʸ at their camp on the plains of Moab, by the Jordan across from Jericho.ᵃ

13Moses, Eleazar the priest and all the leaders of the community went to meet them outside the camp. 14Moses was angry with the officers of the armyᶻ—the commanders of thousands and commanders of hundreds—who returned from the battle.

15"Have you allowed all the women to live?" he asked them. 16"They were the ones who followed Balaam's adviceᵃ and were the means of turning the Israelites away from the LORD in what happened at Peor,ᵇ so that a plague struck the LORD's people. 17Now kill all the boys. And kill every woman who has slept with a man,ᶜ 18but save for yourselves every girl who has never slept with a man.

19"All of you who have killed anyone or touched anyone who was killedᵈ must stay outside the camp seven days. On the third and seventh days you must purify yourselvesᵉ and your captives. 20Purify every garmentᶠ as well as everything made of leather, goat hair or wood."

21Then Eleazar the priest said to the soldiers who had gone into battle, "This is the requirement of the law that the LORD gave Moses: 22Gold, silver, bronze, iron,ᵍ tin, lead 23and anything else that can withstand fire must be put through the fire,ʰ and then it will be clean. But it must also be purified with the water of cleansing.ⁱ And whatever cannot withstand fire must be put through that water. 24On the seventh day wash your clothes and you will be clean.ʲ Then you may come into the camp."

Dividing the Spoils

25The LORD said to Moses, 26"You and Eleazar the priest and the family heads of the community are to count all the peopleᵏ and animals that were captured. 27Divideˡ the spoils between the soldiers who took part in the battle and the rest of the community. 28From the soldiers who fought in the battle, set apart as tribute for the LORDᵐ one out of every five hundred, whether persons, cattle, donkeys, sheep or goats. 29Take this tribute from their half share and give it to Eleazar the priest as the LORD's part. 30From the Israelites' half, select one out of every fifty, whether persons, cattle, donkeys, sheep, goats or other animals.

31:6
qNu 14:44
rNu 10:9
31:7
sDt 20:13;
Jdg 21:11;
1Ki 11:15,16
31:8
tJos 13:21
uNu 25:15
vJos 13:22
31:10
wGe 25:16;
1Ch 6:54;
Ps 69:25;
Eze 25:4
31:11
xDt 20:14
31:12
yNu 27:2
31:14
zver 48;
Ex 18:21;
Dt 1:15
31:16
a2Pe 2:15;
Rev 2:14
bNu 25:1-9
31:17
cDt 7:2;
20:16-18;
Jdg 21:11
31:19
dNu 19:16
eNu 19:12
31:20
fNu 19:19
31:22
gJos 6:19; 22:8
31:23
h1Co 3:13
iNu 19:9,17
31:24
jLev 11:25
31:26
kNu 1:19
31:27
lJos 22:8;
1Sa 30:24
31:28
mNu 18:21

ᵃ12 Hebrew *Jordan of Jericho*; possibly an ancient name for the Jordan River

Give them to the Levites, who are responsible for the care of the LORD's tabernacle. [n]'' [31]So Moses and Eleazar the priest did as the LORD commanded Moses.

[32]The plunder remaining from the spoils that the soldiers took was 675,000 sheep, [33]72,000 cattle, [34]61,000 donkeys [35]and 32,000 women who had never slept with a man.

[36]The half share of those who fought in the battle was:

337,500 sheep, [37]of which the tribute for the LORD[o] was 675;
[38]36,000 cattle, of which the tribute for the LORD was 72;
[39]30,500 donkeys, of which the tribute for the LORD was 61;
[40]16,000 people, of which the tribute for the LORD was 32.

[41]Moses gave the tribute to Eleazar the priest as the LORD's part, [p] as the LORD commanded Moses.

[42]The half belonging to the Israelites, which Moses set apart from that of the fighting men— [43]the community's half—was 337,500 sheep, [44]36,000 cattle, [45]30,500 donkeys [46]and 16,000 people. [47]From the Israelites' half, Moses selected one out of every fifty persons and animals, as the LORD commanded him, and gave them to the Levites, who were responsible for the care of the LORD's tabernacle.

[48]Then the officers who were over the units of the army—the commanders of thousands and commanders of hundreds—went to Moses [49]and said to him, "Your servants have counted the soldiers under our command, and not one is missing. [q] [50]So we have brought as an offering to the LORD the gold articles each of us acquired—armlets, bracelets, signet rings, earrings and necklaces—to make atonement for ourselves[r] before the LORD."

[51]Moses and Eleazar the priest accepted from them the gold—all the crafted articles. [52]All the gold from the commanders of thousands and commanders of hundreds that Moses and Eleazar presented as a gift to the LORD weighed 16,750 shekels.[a] [53]Each soldier had taken plunder[s] for himself. [54]Moses and Eleazar the priest accepted the gold from the commanders of thousands and commanders of hundreds and brought it into the Tent of Meeting as a memorial[t] for the Israelites before the LORD.

The Transjordan Tribes

32 The Reubenites and Gadites, who had very large herds and flocks, saw that the lands of Jazer[u] and Gilead were suitable for livestock.[v] [2]So they came to Moses and Eleazar the priest and to the leaders of the community, and said, [3]"Ataroth,[w] Dibon, Jazer, Nimrah,[x] Heshbon, Elealeh,[y] Sebam, Nebo and Beon[z]— [4]the land the LORD subdued[a] before the people of Israel—are suitable for livestock,[b] and your servants have livestock. [5]If we have found favor in your eyes," they said, "let this land be given to your servants as our possession. Do not make us cross the Jordan."

[6]Moses said to the Gadites and Reubenites, "Shall your countrymen go to war while you sit here? [7]Why do you discourage the Israelites from going over into the land the LORD has given them?[c] [8]This is what your fathers did when I sent them from Kadesh Barnea to look over the

a52 That is, about 420 pounds (about 190 kilograms)

31:30
nNu 3:7; 18:3
31:37
over 38-41
31:41
pNu 5:9; 18:8
31:49
qJer 23:4
31:50
rEx 30:16
31:53
sDt 20:14
31:54
tEx 28:12
32:1
uNu 21:32
vEx 12:38
32:3
wver 34
xver 36
yver 37;
Isa 15:4; 16:9;
Jer 48:34
zver 38;
Jos 13:17;
Eze 25:9
32:4
aNu 21:34
bEx 12:38
32:7
cNu 13:27-14:4

land. d 9After they went up to the Valley of Eshcole and viewed the land, they discouraged the Israelites from entering the land the LORD had given them. 10The LORD's anger was aroused f that day and he swore this oath: 11'Because they have not followed me wholeheartedly, not one of the men twenty years old or more g who came up out of Egypt will see the land I promised on oath h to Abraham, Isaac and Jacob i— 12not one except Caleb son of Jephunneh the Kenizzite and Joshua son of Nun, for they followed the LORD wholeheartedly.' j 13The LORD's anger burned against Israel k and he made them wander in the desert forty years, until the whole generation of those who had done evil in his sight was gone. l

14"And here you are, a brood of sinners, standing in the place of your fathers and making the LORD even more angry with Israel. m 15If you turn away from following him, he will again leave all this people in the desert, and you will be the cause of their destruction. n"

16Then they came up to him and said, "We would like to build pens here for our livestock o and cities for our women and children. 17But we are ready to arm ourselves and go ahead of the Israelites p until we have brought them to their place. q Meanwhile our women and children will live in fortified cities, for protection from the inhabitants of the land. 18We will not return to our homes until every Israelite has received his inheritance. r 19We will not receive any inheritance with them on the other side of the Jordan, because our inheritance has come to us on the east side of the Jordan." s

20Then Moses said to them, "If you will do this—if you will arm yourselves before the LORD for battle, t 21and if all of you will go armed over the Jordan before the LORD until he has driven his enemies out before him— 22then when the land is subdued before the LORD, you may return u and be free from your obligation to the LORD and to Israel. And this land will be your possession before the LORD. v

23"But if you fail to do this, you will be sinning against the LORD; and you may be sure that your sin will find you out. w 24Build cities for your women and children, and pens for your flocks, x but do what you have promised. y"

25The Gadites and Reubenites said to Moses, "We your servants will do as our lord commands. 26Our children and wives, our flocks and herds will remain here in the cities of Gilead. z 27But your servants, every man armed for battle, will cross over to fight before the LORD, just as our lord says."

28Then Moses gave orders about them a to Eleazar the priest and Joshua son of Nun and to the family heads of the Israelite tribes. 29He said to them, "If the Gadites and Reubenites, every man armed for battle, cross over the Jordan with you before the LORD, then when the land is subdued before you, give them the land of Gilead as their possession. 30But if they do not cross over with you armed, they must accept their possession with you in Canaan."

31The Gadites and Reubenites answered, "Your servants will do what the LORD has said. b 32We will cross over before the LORD into Canaan armed, but the property we inherit will be on this side of the Jordan."

33Then Moses gave to the Gadites, c the Reubenites and the half-tribe of Manasseh son of Joseph the kingdom of Sihon king of the Amorites d

32:8
dNu 13:3,26;
Dt 1:19-25

32:9
eNu 13:23;
Dt 1:24

32:10
fNu 11:1

32:11
gEx 30:14
hNu 14:23
iNu 14:28-30

32:12
jNu 14:24,30;
Dt 1:36; Ps 63:8

32:13
kEx 4:14
lNu 14:28-35;
26:64,65

32:14
mver 10;
Dt 1:34;
Ps 78:59

32:15
nDt 30:17-18;
2Ch 7:20

32:16
oEx 12:38;
Dt 3:19

32:17
pJos 4:12,13
qNu 22:4;
Dt 3:20

32:18
rJos 22:1-4

32:19
sJos 12:1

32:20
tDt 3:18

32:22
uJos 22:4
vDt 3:18-20

32:23
wGe 4:7;
44:16; Isa 59:12

32:24
xver 1,16
yNu 30:2

32:26
zJos 1:14

32:28
aDt 3:18-20;
Jos 1:13

32:31
bver 29

32:33
cJos 13:24-28;
1Sa 13:7
dDt 2:26

and the kingdom of Og king of Bashan—the whole land with its cities and the territory around them. [e]

[34]The Gadites built up Dibon, Ataroth, Aroer, [f] [35]Atroth Shophan, Jazer, [g] Jogbehah, [36]Beth Nimrah [h] and Beth Haran as fortified cities, and built pens for their flocks. [37]And the Reubenites rebuilt Heshbon, Elealeh and Kiriathaim, [38]as well as Nebo [i] and Baal Meon (these names were changed) and Sibmah. They gave names to the cities they rebuilt.

[39]The descendants of Makir [j] son of Manasseh went to Gilead, captured it and drove out the Amorites who were there. [40]So Moses gave Gilead to the Makirites, [k] the descendants of Manasseh, and they settled there. [41]Jair, a descendant of Manasseh, captured their settlements and called them Havvoth Jair. [a1] [42]And Nobah captured Kenath and its surrounding settlements and called it Nobah after himself. [m]

Stages in Israel's Journey

33 Here are the stages in the journey of the Israelites when they came out of Egypt [n] by divisions under the leadership of Moses and Aaron. [o] [2]At the LORD's command Moses recorded the stages in their journey. This is their journey by stages:

[3]The Israelites set out from Rameses on the fifteenth day of the first month, the day after the Passover. [p] They marched out boldly [q] in full view of all the Egyptians, [4]who were burying all their firstborn, whom the LORD had struck down among them; for the LORD had brought judgment on their gods. [r]

[5]The Israelites left Rameses and camped at Succoth. [s]

[6]They left Succoth and camped at Etham, on the edge of the desert. [t]

[7]They left Etham, turned back to Pi Hahiroth, to the east of Baal Zephon, [u] and camped near Migdol. [v]

[8]They left Pi Hahiroth [b] and passed through the sea [w] into the desert, and when they had traveled for three days in the Desert of Etham, they camped at Marah. [x]

[9]They left Marah and went to Elim, where there were twelve springs and seventy palm trees, and they camped [y] there.

[10]They left Elim and camped by the Red Sea. [c]

[11]They left the Red Sea and camped in the Desert of Sin. [z]

[12]They left the Desert of Sin and camped at Dophkah.

[13]They left Dophkah and camped at Alush.

[14]They left Alush and camped at Rephidim, where there was no water for the people to drink.

[15]They left Rephidim [a] and camped in the Desert of Sinai. [b]

[16]They left the Desert of Sinai and camped at Kibroth Hattaavah. [c]

[17]They left Kibroth Hattaavah and camped at Hazeroth. [d]

[18]They left Hazeroth and camped at Rithmah.

[19]They left Rithmah and camped at Rimmon Perez.

[20]They left Rimmon Perez and camped at Libnah. [e]

[21]They left Libnah and camped at Rissah.

32:33
eNu 21:24;
Jos 12:6

32:34
fDt 2:36;
Jdg 11:26

32:35
gver 3

32:36
hver 3

32:38
iver 3; Isa 15:2;
Jer 48:1,22

32:39
jGe 50:23

32:40
kDt 3:15;
Jos 17:1

32:41
lDt 3:14;
Jos 13:30;
Jdg 10:4;
1Ch 2:23

32:42
m2Sa 18:18;
Ps 49:11

33:1
nMic 6:4
oPs 77:20

33:3
pEx 13:4
qEx 14:8

33:4
rEx 12:12

33:5
sEx 12:37

33:6
tEx 13:20

33:7
uEx 14:9
vEx 14:2

33:8
wEx 14:22
xEx 15:23

33:9
yEx 15:27

33:11
zEx 16:1

33:15
aEx 17:1
bEx 19:1

33:16
cNu 11:34

33:17
dNu 11:35

33:20
eJos 10:29

---

a41 Or *them the settlements of Jair*   b8 Many manuscripts of the Masoretic Text, Samaritan Pentateuch and Vulgate; most manuscripts of the Masoretic Text *left from before Hahiroth*
c10 Hebrew *Yam Suph*; that is, Sea of Reeds; also in verse 11

²²They left Rissah and camped at Kehelathah.

²³They left Kehelathah and camped at Mount Shepher.

²⁴They left Mount Shepher and camped at Haradah.

²⁵They left Haradah and camped at Makheloth.

²⁶They left Makheloth and camped at Tahath.

²⁷They left Tahath and camped at Terah.

²⁸They left Terah and camped at Mithcah.

²⁹They left Mithcah and camped at Hashmonah.

³⁰They left Hashmonah and camped at Moseroth. f

³¹They left Moseroth and camped at Bene Jaakan.

³²They left Bene Jaakan and camped at Hor Haggidgad.

³³They left Hor Haggidgad and camped at Jotbathah. g

³⁴They left Jotbathah and camped at Abronah.

³⁵They left Abronah and camped at Ezion Geber. h

³⁶They left Ezion Geber and camped at Kadesh, in the Desert of Zin. i

³⁷They left Kadesh and camped at Mount Hor, j on the border of Edom. k ³⁸At the LORD's command Aaron the priest went up Mount Hor, where he died l on the first day of the fifth month of the fortieth year after the Israelites came out of Egypt. m ³⁹Aaron was a hundred and twenty-three years old when he died on Mount Hor.

⁴⁰The Canaanite king of Arad, n who lived in the Negev of Canaan, heard that the Israelites were coming.

⁴¹They left Mount Hor and camped at Zalmonah.

⁴²They left Zalmonah and camped at Punon.

⁴³They left Punon and camped at Oboth. o

⁴⁴They left Oboth and camped at Iye Abarim, on the border of Moab. p

⁴⁵They left Iyim a and camped at Dibon Gad.

⁴⁶They left Dibon Gad and camped at Almon Diblathaim.

⁴⁷They left Almon Diblathaim and camped in the mountains of Abarim, q near Nebo.

⁴⁸They left the mountains of Abarim and camped on the plains of Moab by the Jordan across from Jericho. b r ⁴⁹There on the plains of Moab they camped along the Jordan from Beth Jeshimoth to Abel Shittim. s

⁵⁰On the plains of Moab by the Jordan across from Jericho the LORD said to Moses, ⁵¹"Speak to the Israelites and say to them: 'When you cross the Jordan into Canaan, t ⁵²drive out all the inhabitants of the land before you. Destroy all their carved images and their cast idols, and demolish all their high places. u ⁵³Take possession of the land and settle in it, for I have given you the land to possess. v ⁵⁴Distribute the land by lot, according to your clans. w To a larger group give a larger inheritance, and to a smaller group a smaller one. Whatever falls to them by lot will be theirs. Distribute it according to your ancestral tribes.

⁵⁵" 'But if you do not drive out the inhabitants of the land, those you allow to remain will become barbs in your eyes and thorns x in your

33:30
fDt 10:6
33:33
gDt 10:7
33:35
hDt 2:8;
1Ki 9:26; 22:48
33:36
iNu 20:1
33:37
jNu 20:22
kNu 20:16; 21:4
33:38
lDt 10:6
mNu 20:25-28
33:40
nNu 21:1
33:43
oNu 21:10
33:44
pNu 21:11
33:47
qNu 27:12
33:48
rNu 22:1
33:49
sNu 25:1
33:51
tJos 3:17
33:52
uEx 23:24;
34:13;
Lev 26:1;
Dt 7:2,5; 12:3;
Jos 11:12;
Ps 106:34-36
33:53
vDt 11:31;
Jos 21:43
33:54
wNu 26:54
33:55
xJos 23:13;
Jdg 2:3;
Ps 106:36

ᵃ45 That is, Iye Abarim   ᵇ48 Hebrew *Jordan of Jericho*; possibly an ancient name for the Jordan River; also in verse 50 sides. They will give you trouble in the land where you will live. [56]And then I will do to you what I plan to do to them.' "

Boundaries of Canaan

34 The LORD said to Moses, [2]"Command the Israelites and say to them: 'When you enter Canaan, the land that will be allotted to you as an inheritance[y] will have these boundaries:[z]

[3]" 'Your southern side will include some of the Desert of Zin[a] along the border of Edom. On the east, your southern boundary will start from the end of the Salt Sea,[ab] [4]cross south of Scorpion[b] Pass,[c] continue on to Zin and go south of Kadesh Barnea.[d] Then it will go to Hazar Addar and over to Azmon, [5]where it will turn, join the Wadi of Egypt[e] and end at the Sea.[c]

[6]" 'Your western boundary will be the coast of the Great Sea. This will be your boundary on the west.

[7]" 'For your northern boundary,[f] run a line from the Great Sea to Mount Hor [8]and from Mount Hor to Lebo[d] Hamath.[g] Then the boundary will go to Zedad, [9]continue to Ziphron and end at Hazar Enan. This will be your boundary on the north.

[10]" 'For your eastern boundary, run a line from Hazar Enan to Shepham. [11]The boundary will go down from Shepham to Riblah[h] on the east side of Ain and continue along the slopes east of the Sea of Kinnereth.[ei] [12]Then the boundary will go down along the Jordan and end at the Salt Sea.

" 'This will be your land, with its boundaries on every side.' "

[13]Moses commanded the Israelites: "Assign this land by lot as an inheritance.[j] The LORD has ordered that it be given to the nine and a half tribes, [14]because the families of the tribe of Reuben, the tribe of Gad and the half-tribe of Manasseh have received their inheritance.[k] [15]These two and a half tribes have received their inheritance on the east side of the Jordan of Jericho,[f] toward the sunrise."

[16]The LORD said to Moses, [17]"These are the names of the men who are to assign the land for you as an inheritance: Eleazar the priest and Joshua[l] son of Nun. [18]And appoint one leader from each tribe to help[m] assign the land. [19]These are their names:

Caleb[n] son of Jephunneh,
　　from the tribe of Judah;[o]
[20]Shemuel son of Ammihud,
　　from the tribe of Simeon;[p]
[21]Elidad son of Kislon,
　　from the tribe of Benjamin;[q]
[22]Bukki son of Jogli,
　　the leader from the tribe of Dan;
[23]Hanniel son of Ephod,
　　the leader from the tribe of Manasseh son of Joseph;
[24]Kemuel son of Shiphtan,
　　the leader from the tribe of Ephraim son of Joseph;

34:2
yGe 17:8;
Dt 1:7-8;
Ps 78:54-55
zEze 47:15
34:3
aJos 15:1-3
bGe 14:3
34:4
cJos 15:3
dNu 32:8
34:5
eGe 15:18;
Jos 15:4
34:7
fEze 47:15-17
34:8
gNu 13:21;
Jos 13:5
34:11
h2Ki 23:33;
Jer 39:5
iDt 3:17;
Jos 11:2; 13:27
34:13
jJos 14:1-5
34:14
kNu 32:33;
Jos 14:3
34:17
lJos 14:1
34:18
mNu 1:4,16
34:19
nNu 26:65
oGe 29:35;
Dt 33:7
34:20
pGe 49:5
34:21
qGe 49:27;
Ps 68:27

---

[a]3 That is, the Dead Sea; also in verse 12　　[b]4 Hebrew *Akrabbim*　　[c]5 That is, the Mediterranean; also in verses 6 and 7　　[d]8 Or *to the entrance to*　　[e]11 That is, Galilee [f]15 *Jordan of Jericho* was possibly an ancient name for the Jordan River.

²⁵Elizaphan son of Parnach,
the leader from the tribe of Zebulun;
²⁶Paltiel son of Azzan,
the leader from the tribe of Issachar;
²⁷Ahihud son of Shelomi,
the leader from the tribe of Asher;ʳ
²⁸Pedahel son of Ammihud,
the leader from the tribe of Naphtali."

²⁹These are the men the LORD commanded to assign the inheritance to the Israelites in the land of Canaan.

Towns for the Levites

35 On the plains of Moab by the Jordan across from Jericho,ᵃ the LORD said to Moses, ²"Command the Israelites to give the Levites towns to live inˢ from the inheritance the Israelites will possess. And give them pasturelands around the towns. ³Then they will have towns to live in and pasturelands for their cattle, flocks and all their other livestock.

⁴"The pasturelands around the towns that you give the Levites will extend out fifteen hundred feetᵇ from the town wall. ⁵Outside the town, measure three thousand feetᶜ on the east side, three thousand on the south side, three thousand on the west and three thousand on the north, with the town in the center. They will have this area as pastureland for the towns.

Cities of Refuge

35:6–34Ref — Dt 4:41–43; 19:1–14; Jos 20:1–9

⁶"Six of the towns you give the Levites will be cities of refuge, to which a person who has killed someone may flee.ᵗ In addition, give them forty-two other towns. ⁷In all you must give the Levites forty-eight towns, together with their pasturelands. ⁸The towns you give the Levites from the land the Israelites possess are to be given in proportion to the inheritance of each tribe: Take many towns from a tribe that has many, but few from one that has few."ᵘ

⁹Then the LORD said to Moses: ¹⁰"Speak to the Israelites and say to them: 'When you cross the Jordan into Canaan,ᵛ ¹¹select some towns to be your cities of refuge, to which a person who has killed someoneʷ accidentallyˣ may flee. ¹²They will be places of refuge from the avenger,ʸ so that a person accused of murder may not die before he stands trial before the assembly. ¹³These six towns you give will be your cities of refuge. ¹⁴Give three on this side of the Jordan and three in Canaan as cities of refuge. ¹⁵These six towns will be a place of refuge for Israelites, aliens and any other people living among them, so that anyone who has killed another accidentally can flee there.

¹⁶" 'If a man strikes someone with an iron object so that he dies, he is a murderer; the murderer shall be put to death.ᶻ ¹⁷Or if anyone has a stone in his hand that could kill, and he strikes someone so that he dies, he is a murderer; the murderer shall be put to death. ¹⁸Or if anyone has a wooden object in his hand that could kill, and he hits someone so that

### Cross references (margin)

34:27
ʳNu 1:40
35:2
ˢLev 25:32-34;
Jos 14:3,4
35:6
ᵗJos 20:7-9;
21:3,13
35:8
ᵘNu 26:54;
33:54;
Jos 21:1-42
35:10
ᵛJos 20:2
35:11
ʷver 22-25
ˣEx 21:13;
Dt 19:1-13
35:12
ʸDt 19:6;
Jos 20:3
35:16
ᶻEx 21:12;
Lev 24:17

ᵃ1 Hebrew *Jordan of Jericho*; possibly an ancient name for the Jordan River   ᵇ4 Hebrew *a thousand cubits* (about 450 meters)   ᶜ5 Hebrew *two thousand cubits* (about 900 meters) he dies, he is a murderer; the murderer shall be put to death. [19]The avenger of blood shall put the murderer to death; when he meets him, he shall put him to death.[a] [20]If anyone with malice aforethought shoves another or throws something at him intentionally[b] so that he dies [21]or if in hostility he hits him with his fist so that he dies, that person shall be put to death; he is a murderer. The avenger of blood shall put the murderer to death when he meets him.

[22]" 'But if without hostility someone suddenly shoves another or throws something at him unintentionally[c] [23]or, without seeing him, drops a stone on him that could kill him, and he dies, then since he was not his enemy and he did not intend to harm him, [24]the assembly[d] must judge between him and the avenger of blood according to these regulations. [25]The assembly must protect the one accused of murder from the avenger of blood and send him back to the city of refuge to which he fled. He must stay there until the death of the high priest, who was anointed with the holy oil.[e]

[26]" 'But if the accused ever goes outside the limits of the city of refuge to which he has fled [27]and the avenger of blood finds him outside the city, the avenger of blood may kill the accused without being guilty of murder. [28]The accused must stay in his city of refuge until the death of the high priest; only after the death of the high priest may he return to his own property.

[29]" 'These are to be legal requirements[f] for you throughout the generations to come, wherever you live.

[30]" 'Anyone who kills a person is to be put to death as a murderer only on the testimony of witnesses. But no one is to be put to death on the testimony of only one witness.[g]

[31]" 'Do not accept a ransom for the life of a murderer, who deserves to die. He must surely be put to death.

[32]" 'Do not accept a ransom for anyone who has fled to a city of refuge and so allow him to go back and live on his own land before the death of the high priest.

[33]" 'Do not pollute the land where you are. Bloodshed pollutes the land,[h] and atonement cannot be made for the land on which blood has been shed, except by the blood of the one who shed it. [34]Do not defile the land[i] where you live and where I dwell,[j] for I, the LORD, dwell among the Israelites.' "

Inheritance of Zelophehad's Daughters

36:1–12pp — Nu 27:1–11

36 The family heads of the clan of Gilead[k] son of Makir, the son of Manasseh, who were from the clans of the descendants of Joseph, came and spoke before Moses and the leaders,[l] the heads of the Israelite families. [2]They said, "When the LORD commanded my lord to give the land as an inheritance to the Israelites by lot, he ordered you to give the inheritance of our brother Zelophehad[m] to his daughters. [3]Now suppose they marry men from other Israelite tribes; then their inheritance will be taken from our ancestral inheritance and added to that of the tribe they marry into. And so part of the inheritance allotted to us will be taken away. [4]When the Year of Jubilee[n] for the Israelites comes, their inheritance will be added to that of the tribe into which

35:19
a ver 21
35:20
b Ge 4:8;
Ex 21:14;
Dt 19:11;
2Sa 3:27; 20:10
35:22
c ver 11;
Ex 21:13
35:24
d ver 12;
Jos 20:6
35:25
e Ex 29:7
35:29
f Nu 27:11
35:30
g ver 16;
Dt 17:6; 19:15;
Mt 18:16;
Jn 7:51;
2Co 13:1;
Heb 10:28
35:33
h Ge 9:6;
Ps 106:38;
Mic 4:11
35:34
i Lev 18:24,25
j Ex 29:45
36:1
k Nu 26:29
l Nu 27:2
36:2
m Nu 26:33;
27:1,7
36:4
n Lev 25:10

they marry, and their property will be taken from the tribal inheritance of our forefathers."

⁵Then at the LORD's command Moses gave this order to the Israelites: "What the tribe of the descendants of Joseph is saying is right. ⁶This is what the LORD commands for Zelophehad's daughters: They may marry anyone they please as long as they marry within the tribal clan of their father. ⁷No inheritance° in Israel is to pass from tribe to tribe, for every Israelite shall keep the tribal land inherited from his forefathers. ⁸Every daughter who inherits land in any Israelite tribe must marry someone in her father's tribal clan, ᴾ so that every Israelite will possess the inheritance of his fathers. ⁹No inheritance may pass from tribe to tribe, for each Israelite tribe is to keep the land it inherits."

¹⁰So Zelophehad's daughters did as the LORD commanded Moses. ¹¹Zelophehad's daughters—Mahlah, Tirzah, Hoglah, Milcah and Noah�q—married their cousins on their father's side. ¹²They married within the clans of the descendants of Manasseh son of Joseph, and their inheritance remained in their father's clan and tribe.

¹³These are the commands and regulations the LORD gave through Mosesʳ to the Israelites on the plains of Moab by the Jordan across from Jericho. ª ˢ

36:7
o1Ki 21:3
36:8
p1Ch 23:22
36:11
qNu 26:33; 27:1
36:13
rLev 26:46;
27:34 sNu 22:1

ª13 Hebrew *Jordan of Jericho*; possibly an ancient name for the Jordan River

Deuteronomy

Title and Background

The word "Deuteronomy" means "repetition of the law." After forty years the Israelites were about to enter Canaan. But before they did, Moses wanted to remind them of their history, all that God had done for them, and the laws they had to continue to obey as God's chosen people.

Author and Date of Writing

The book itself testifies that, for the most part, Moses wrote it (1:5; 31:9,22,24) as other Old Testament books agree (1Ki 2:3; 8:53; 2Ki 14:6; 18:12). Jesus bears the same testimony (Mt 19:7-8; Mk 10:3-5; Jn 5:45-47), and so do other New Testament writers (Ac 3:22-23; 7:37-38; Ro 10:19). Moreover, Jesus quotes Deuteronomy as authoritative (Mt 4:4,7,10). The book was written shortly before Moses' death in about 1406 B.C.

Theme and Message

Moses reminded the people of God's goodness to them throughout their journey and of his giving to them the land of Canaan. He also summarized God's laws, including the Ten Commandments. One subject that pervades the whole book is the love relationship of the Lord to his people and that of the people to the Lord as their sovereign God.

Outline

I. Preamble (1:1-5)
II. Historical Prologue (1:6-4:43)
III. Stipulations of the Covenant (4:44-26:19)
   A. Primary Demands (4:44-11:32)
   B. Supplementary Requirements (12:1-26:19)
IV. Ratification, and Curses and Blessings (27:1-30:20)
V. Succession Under the Covenant (31:1-34:12)

The Command to Leave Horeb

1 These are the words Moses spoke to all Israel in the desert east of the Jordan—that is, in the Arabah—opposite Suph, between Paran and Tophel, Laban, Hazeroth and Dizahab. ²(It takes eleven days to go from Horeb[a] to Kadesh Barnea[b] by the Mount Seir road.)

³In the fortieth year,[c] on the first day of the eleventh month, Moses proclaimed[d] to the Israelites all that the LORD had commanded him concerning them. ⁴This was after he had defeated Sihon[e] king of the Amorites, who reigned in Heshbon,[f] and at Edrei had defeated Og[g] king of Bashan, who reigned in Ashtaroth.

⁵East of the Jordan in the territory of Moab, Moses began to expound this law, saying:

⁶The LORD our God said to us[h] at Horeb,[i] "You have stayed long enough at this mountain. ⁷Break camp and advance into the hill coun-

1:2
aEx 3:1
bNu 13:26;
Dt 9:23

1:3
cNu 33:38
dDt 4:1-2

1:4
eNu 21:21-26
fNu 21:25
gNu 21:33-35;
Jos 13:12

1:6
hNu 10:13
iEx 3:1

try of the Amorites; go to all the neighboring peoples in the Arabah, in the mountains, in the western foothills, in the Negev[j] and along the coast, to the land of the Canaanites and to Lebanon,[k] as far as the great river, the Euphrates. [8]See, I have given you this land. Go in and take possession of the land that the LORD swore[1] he would give to your fathers—to Abraham, Isaac and Jacob—and to their descendants after them."

The Appointment of Leaders

[9]At that time I said to you, "You are too heavy a burden for me to carry alone. [m] [10]The LORD your God has increased your numbers so that today you are as many[n] as the stars in the sky. [o] [11]May the LORD, the God of your fathers, increase you a thousand times and bless you as he has promised![p] [12]But how can I bear your problems and your burdens and your disputes all by myself? [13]Choose some wise, understanding and respected men[q] from each of your tribes, and I will set them over you."

[14]You answered me, "What you propose to do is good."

[15]So I took[r] the leading men of your tribes, wise and respected men, and appointed them to have authority over you—as commanders of thousands, of hundreds, of fifties and of tens and as tribal officials. [16]And I charged your judges at that time: Hear the disputes between your brothers and judge fairly,[s] whether the case is between brother Israelites or between one of them and an alien. [t] [17]Do not show partiality[u] in judging; hear both small and great alike. Do not be afraid of any man,[v] for judgment belongs to God. Bring me any case too hard for you, and I will hear it. [w] [18]And at that time I told you everything you were to do.

Spies Sent Out

[19]Then, as the LORD our God commanded us, we set out from Horeb and went toward the hill country of the Amorites through all that vast and dreadful desert[x] that you have seen, and so we reached Kadesh Barnea. [y] [20]Then I said to you, "You have reached the hill country of the Amorites, which the LORD our God is giving us. [21]See, the LORD your God has given you the land. Go up and take possession of it as the LORD, the God of your fathers, told you. Do not be afraid;[z] do not be discouraged."

[22]Then all of you came to me and said, "Let us send men ahead to spy out the land for us and bring back a report about the route we are to take and the towns we will come to."

[23]The idea seemed good to me; so I selected[a] twelve of you, one man from each tribe. [24]They left and went up into the hill country, and came to the Valley of Eshcol[b] and explored it. [25]Taking with them some of the fruit of the land, they brought it down to us and reported,[c] "It is a good land that the LORD our God is giving us."

Rebellion Against the LORD

[26]But you were unwilling to go up;[d] you rebelled against the command of the LORD your God. [27]You grumbled[e] in your tents and said, "The LORD hates us; so he brought us out of Egypt to deliver us into the hands of the Amorites to destroy us. [28]Where can we go? Our brothers

1:7
jJos 10:40
kDt 11:24
1:8
lGe 12:7;
15:18; 17:7- 8;
26:4; 28:13
1:9
mEx 18:18
1:10
nGe 15:5
oDt 10:22;
28:62
1:11
pGe 22:17;
Ex 32:13
1:13
qEx 18:21
1:15
rEx 18:25
1:16
sDt 16:18;
Jn 7:24
tLev 24:22
1:17
uLev 19:15;
Dt 16:19;
Pr 24:23; Jas 2:1
v2Ch 19:6
wEx 18:26
1:19
xDt 8:15;
Jer 2:2,6
yver 2;
Nu 13:26
1:21
zJos 1:6,9,18
1:23
aNu 13:1-3
1:24
bNu 13:21-25
1:25
cNu 13:27
1:26
dNu 14:1-4
1:27
eDt 9:28;
Ps 106:25

have made us lose heart. They say, 'The people are stronger and taller[f] than we are; the cities are large, with walls up to the sky. We even saw the Anakites[g] there.'"

29Then I said to you, "Do not be terrified; do not be afraid of them. 30The LORD your God, who is going before you, will fight[h] for you, as he did for you in Egypt, before your very eyes, 31and in the desert. There you saw how the LORD your God carried[i] you, as a father carries his son, all the way you went until you reached this place."

32In spite of this, you did not trust[j] in the LORD your God, 33who went ahead of you on your journey, in fire by night and in a cloud by day,[k] to search[l] out places for you to camp and to show you the way you should go.

34When the LORD heard what you said, he was angry and solemnly swore:[m] 35"Not a man of this evil generation shall see the good land[n] I swore to give your forefathers, 36except Caleb son of Jephunneh. He will see it, and I will give him and his descendants the land he set his feet on, because he followed the LORD wholeheartedly.[o]"

37Because of you the LORD became angry[p] with me also and said, "You shall not enter[q] it, either. 38But your assistant, Joshua[r] son of Nun, will enter it. Encourage[s] him, because he will lead[t] Israel to inherit it. 39And the little ones that you said would be taken captive,[u] your children who do not yet know[v] good from bad—they will enter the land. I will give it to them and they will take possession of it. 40But as for you, turn around and set out toward the desert along the route to the Red Sea.[a][w]"

41Then you replied, "We have sinned against the LORD. We will go up and fight, as the LORD our God commanded us." So every one of you put on his weapons, thinking it easy to go up into the hill country.

42But the LORD said to me, "Tell them, 'Do not go up and fight, because I will not be with you. You will be defeated by your enemies.'"[x]

43So I told you, but you would not listen. You rebelled against the LORD's command and in your arrogance you marched up into the hill country. 44The Amorites who lived in those hills came out against you; they chased you like a swarm of bees[y] and beat you down from Seir all the way to Hormah. 45You came back and wept before the LORD, but he paid no attention to your weeping and turned a deaf ear to you. 46And so you stayed in Kadesh[z] many days—all the time you spent there.

Wanderings in the Desert

2 Then we turned back and set out toward the desert along the route to the Red Sea,[aa] as the LORD had directed me. For a long time we made our way around the hill country of Seir.

2Then the LORD said to me, 3"You have made your way around this hill country long enough; now turn north. 4Give the people these orders:[b] 'You are about to pass through the territory of your brothers the descendants of Esau, who live in Seir. They will be afraid of you, but be very careful. 5Do not provoke them to war, for I will not give you any of their land, not even enough to put your foot on. I have given

---

1:28
f Nu 13:32
g Nu 13:33;
Dt 9:1-3
1:30
h Ex 14:14;
Dt 3:22;
Ne 4:20
1:31
i Dt 32:10-12;
Isa 46:3-4;
63:9; Hos 11:3;
Ac 13:18
1:32
j Ps 106:24;
Jude 1:5
1:33
k Ex 13:21;
Ps 78:14
l Nu 10:33
1:34
m Nu 14:23,
28-30
1:35
n Ps 95:11
1:36
o Nu 14:24;
Jos 14:9
1:37
p Dt 3:26; 4:21
q Nu 20:12
1:38
r Nu 14:30
s Dt 31:7
t Dt 3:28
1:39
u Nu 14:3
v Isa 7:15-16
1:40
w Nu 14:25
1:42
x Nu 14:41-43
1:44
y Ps 118:12
1:46
z Nu 20:1;
Jdg 11:17
2:1
a Nu 21:4
2:4
b Nu 20:14-21

---

a40,1 Hebrew *Yam Suph*; that is, Sea of Reeds

Esau the hill country of Seir as his own.[c] ⁶You are to pay them in silver for the food you eat and the water you drink.' "

⁷The LORD your God has blessed you in all the work of your hands. He has watched[d] over your journey through this vast desert. These forty years the LORD your God has been with you, and you have not lacked anything.

⁸So we went on past our brothers the descendants of Esau, who live in Seir. We turned from the Arabah road, which comes up from Elath and Ezion Geber,[e] and traveled along the desert road of Moab.[f]

⁹Then the LORD said to me, "Do not harass the Moabites or provoke them to war, for I will not give you any part of their land. I have given Ar[g] to the descendants of Lot[h] as a possession."

¹⁰(The Emites[i] used to live there—a people strong and numerous, and as tall as the Anakites.[j] ¹¹Like the Anakites, they too were considered Rephaites, but the Moabites called them Emites. ¹²Horites used to live in Seir, but the descendants of Esau drove them out. They destroyed the Horites from before them and settled in their place, just as Israel did[k] in the land the LORD gave them as their possession.)

¹³And the LORD said, "Now get up and cross the Zered Valley." So we crossed the valley.

¹⁴Thirty-eight years passed from the time we left Kadesh Barnea[l] until we crossed the Zered Valley. By then, that entire generation[m] of fighting men had perished from the camp, as the LORD had sworn to them.[n] ¹⁵The LORD's hand was against them until he had completely eliminated[o] them from the camp.

¹⁶Now when the last of these fighting men among the people had died, ¹⁷the LORD said to me, ¹⁸"Today you are to pass by the region of Moab at Ar. ¹⁹When you come to the Ammonites,[p] do not harass them or provoke them to war, for I will not give you possession of any land belonging to the Ammonites. I have given it as a possession to the descendants of Lot.[q]"

²⁰(That too was considered a land of the Rephaites, who used to live there; but the Ammonites called them Zamzummites. ²¹They were a people strong and numerous, and as tall as the Anakites.[r] The LORD destroyed them from before the Ammonites, who drove them out and settled in their place. ²²The LORD had done the same for the descendants of Esau, who lived in Seir,[s] when he destroyed the Horites from before them. They drove them out and have lived in their place to this day. ²³And as for the Avvites[t] who lived in villages as far as Gaza, the Caphtorites[u] coming out from Caphtor[a v] destroyed them and settled in their place.)

Defeat of Sihon King of Heshbon

²⁴"Set out now and cross the Arnon Gorge.[w] See, I have given into your hand Sihon the Amorite, king of Heshbon, and his country. Begin to take possession of it and engage him in battle. ²⁵This very day I will begin to put the terror[x] and fear[y] of you on all the nations under heaven. They will hear reports of you and will tremble[z] and be in anguish because of you."

²⁶From the desert of Kedemoth I sent messengers to Sihon king of

**Cross references (left margin):**

2:5
[c] Ge 36:8; Jos 24:4
2:7
[d] Dt 8:2-4
2:8
[e] 1Ki 9:26
[f] Jdg 11:18
2:9
[g] Nu 21:15
[h] Ge 19:36-38
2:10
[i] Ge 14:5
[j] Nu 13:22,33
2:12
[k] ver 22
2:14
[l] Nu 13:26
[m] Nu 14:29-35
[n] Dt 1:34-35
2:15
[o] Ps 106:26
2:19
[p] Ge 19:38
[q] ver 9
2:21
[r] ver 10
2:22
[s] Ge 36:8
2:23
[t] Jos 13:3
[u] Ge 10:14
[v] Am 9:7
2:24
[w] Nu 21:13-14; Jdg 11:13,18
2:25
[x] Dt 11:25
[y] Jos 2:9,11
[z] Ex 15:14-16

---

[a]23 That is, Crete

Heshbon offering peace and saying, [27]"Let us pass through your country. We will stay on the main road; we will not turn aside to the right or to the left.[a] [28]Sell us food to eat and water to drink for their price in silver. Only let us pass through on foot[b]— [29]as the descendants of Esau, who live in Seir, and the Moabites, who live in Ar, did for us—until we cross the Jordan into the land the LORD our God is giving us." [30]But Sihon king of Heshbon refused to let us pass through. For the LORD[c] your God had made his spirit stubborn[d] and his heart obstinate in order to give him into your hands, as he has now done.

[31]The LORD said to me, "See, I have begun to deliver Sihon and his country over to you. Now begin to conquer and possess his land."[e]

[32]When Sihon and all his army came out to meet us in battle[f] at Jahaz, [33]the LORD our God delivered him over to us and we struck him down,[g] together with his sons and his whole army. [34]At that time we took all his towns and completely destroyed[a][h] them—men, women and children. We left no survivors. [35]But the livestock and the plunder from the towns we had captured we carried off for ourselves. [36]From Aroer[i] on the rim of the Arnon Gorge, and from the town in the gorge, even as far as Gilead, not one town was too strong for us. The LORD our God gave[j] us all of them. [37]But in accordance with the command of the LORD our God,[k] you did not encroach on any of the land of the Ammonites,[l] neither the land along the course of the Jabbok[m] nor that around the towns in the hills.

Defeat of Og King of Bashan

3 Next we turned and went up along the road toward Bashan, and Og king of Bashan with his whole army marched out to meet us in battle at Edrei.[n] [2]The LORD said to me, "Do not be afraid[o] of him, for I have handed him over to you with his whole army and his land. Do to him what you did to Sihon king of the Amorites, who reigned in Heshbon."

[3]So the LORD our God also gave into our hands Og king of Bashan and all his army. We struck them down, leaving no survivors.[p] [4]At that time we took all his cities. There was not one of the sixty cities that we did not take from them—the whole region of Argob, Og's kingdom in Bashan.[q] [5]All these cities were fortified with high walls and with gates and bars, and there were also a great many unwalled villages. [6]We completely destroyed[a] them, as we had done with Sihon king of Heshbon, destroying[a][r] every city—men, women and children. [7]But all the livestock and the plunder from their cities we carried off for ourselves.

[8]So at that time we took from these two kings of the Amorites the territory east of the Jordan, from the Arnon Gorge as far as Mount Hermon. [9](Hermon is called Sirion[s] by the Sidonians; the Amorites call it Senir.)[t] [10]We took all the towns on the plateau, and all Gilead, and all Bashan as far as Salecah[u] and Edrei, towns of Og's kingdom in Bashan. [11](Only Og king of Bashan was left of the remnant of the Rephaites.[v] His bed[b] was made of iron and was more than thirteen feet long and six feet wide.[c] It is still in Rabbah[w] of the Ammonites.)

2:27
aNu 21:21-22
2:28
bNu 20:19
2:30
cJos 11:20
dEx 4:21;
Nu 21:23;
Ro 9:18
2:31
eDt 1:8
2:32
fNu 21:23
2:33
gNu 29:7
2:34
hDt 3:6; 7:2
2:36
iDt 3:12; 4:48;
Jos 13:9
jPs 44:3
2:37
kver 18-19
lNu 21:24
mGe 32:22;
Dt 3:16
3:1
nNu 21:33
3:2
oNu 21:34
3:3
pNu 21:35
3:4
q1Ki 4:13
3:6
rDt 2:24,34
3:9
sDt 4:48;
Ps 29:6
t1Ch 5:23
3:10
uJos 13:11
3:11
vGe 14:5
w2Sa 12:26;
Jer 49:2

---

a34,6 The Hebrew term refers to the irrevocable giving over of things or persons to the LORD, often by totally destroying them.   *b11* Or *sarcophagus*   *c11* Hebrew *nine cubits long and four cubits wide* (about 4 meters long and 1.8 meters wide)

Division of the Land

¹²Of the land that we took over at that time, I gave the Reubenites and the Gadites the territory north of Aroer[x] by the Arnon Gorge, including half the hill country of Gilead, together with its towns. ¹³The rest of Gilead and also all of Bashan, the kingdom of Og, I gave to the half tribe of Manasseh. (The whole region of Argob in Bashan used to be known as a land of the Rephaites. ¹⁴Jair,[y] a descendant of Manasseh, took the whole region of Argob as far as the border of the Geshurites and the Maacathites; it was named after him, so that to this day Bashan is called Havvoth Jair.[a]) ¹⁵And I gave Gilead to Makir.[z] ¹⁶But to the Reubenites and the Gadites I gave the territory extending from Gilead down to the Arnon Gorge (the middle of the gorge being the border) and out to the Jabbok River,[a] which is the border of the Ammonites. ¹⁷Its western border was the Jordan in the Arabah, from Kinnereth[b] to the Sea of the Arabah (the Salt Sea[bc]), below the slopes of Pisgah.

¹⁸I commanded you at that time: "The LORD your God has given you this land to take possession of it. But all your able-bodied men, armed for battle, must cross over ahead of your brother Israelites.[d] ¹⁹However, your wives, your children and your livestock (I know you have much livestock) may stay in the towns I have given you, ²⁰until the LORD gives rest to your brothers as he has to you, and they too have taken over the land that the LORD your God is giving them, across the Jordan. After that, each of you may go back to the possession I have given you."

Moses Forbidden to Cross the Jordan

²¹At that time I commanded Joshua: "You have seen with your own eyes all that the LORD your God has done to these two kings. The LORD will do the same to all the kingdoms over there where you are going. ²²Do not be afraid[e] of them; the LORD your God himself will fight[f] for you."

²³At that time I pleaded with the LORD: ²⁴"O Sovereign LORD, you have begun to show to your servant your greatness[g] and your strong hand. For what god[h] is there in heaven or on earth who can do the deeds and mighty works[i] you do?[j] ²⁵Let me go over and see the good land[k] beyond the Jordan—that fine hill country and Lebanon."

²⁶But because of you the LORD was angry[l] with me and would not listen to me. "That is enough," the LORD said. "Do not speak to me anymore about this matter. ²⁷Go up to the top of Pisgah and look west and north and south and east. Look at the land with your own eyes, since you are not going to cross this Jordan.[m] ²⁸But commission[n] Joshua, and encourage and strengthen him, for he will lead this people across[o] and will cause them to inherit the land that you will see." ²⁹So we stayed in the valley near Beth Peor.[p]

Obedience Commanded

4 Hear now, O Israel, the decrees and laws I am about to teach you. Follow them so that you may live[q] and may go in and take possession of the land that the LORD, the God of your fathers, is giving you.

3:12
xNu 32:32-38;
Dt 2:36;
Jos 13:8-13
3:14
yNu 32:41;
1Ch 2:22
3:15
zNu 32:39-40
3:16
aNu 21:24
3:17
bNu 34:11;
Jos 13:27
cGe 14:3;
Jos 12:3
3:18
dNu 32:17
3:22
eDt 1:29
fEx 14:14;
Dt 20:4
3:24
gDt 11:2
hEx 15:11;
Ps 86:8
iPs 71:16,19
j2Sa 7:22
3:25
kDt 4:22
3:26
lDt 1:37; 31:2
3:27
mNu 27:12
3:28
nNu 27:18-23
oDt 31:3,23
3:29
pDt 4:46; 34:6
4:1
qDt 5:33; 8:1;
16:20;
30:15-20;
Eze 20:11;
Ro 10:5

---

[a]14 Or *called the settlements of Jair*   [b]17 That is, the Dead Sea

[2]Do not add[r] to what I command you and do not subtract from it, but keep the commands of the Lord your God that I give you.

[3]You saw with your own eyes what the Lord did at Baal Peor.[s] The Lord your God destroyed from among you everyone who followed the Baal of Peor, [4]but all of you who held fast to the Lord your God are still alive today.

[5]See, I have taught you decrees and laws as the Lord my God commanded me, so that you may follow them in the land you are entering to take possession of it. [6]Observe them carefully, for this will show your wisdom[t] and understanding to the nations, who will hear about all these decrees and say, "Surely this great nation is a wise and understanding people."[u] [7]What other nation is so great[v] as to have their gods near[w] them the way the Lord our God is near us whenever we pray to him? [8]And what other nation is so great as to have such righteous decrees and laws as this body of laws I am setting before you today?

[9]Only be careful,[x] and watch yourselves closely so that you do not forget the things your eyes have seen or let them slip from your heart as long as you live. Teach[y] them to your children[z] and to their children after them. [10]Remember the day you stood before the Lord your God at Horeb,[a] when he said to me, "Assemble the people before me to hear my words so that they may learn to revere me as long as they live in the land and may teach them to their children." [11]You came near and stood at the foot of the mountain while it blazed with fire[b] to the very heavens, with black clouds and deep darkness. [12]Then the Lord spoke[c] to you out of the fire. You heard the sound of words but saw no form; there was only a voice. [13]He declared to you his covenant,[d] the Ten Commandments,[e] which he commanded you to follow and then wrote them on two stone tablets. [14]And the Lord directed me at that time to teach you the decrees and laws you are to follow in the land that you are crossing the Jordan to possess.

Idolatry Forbidden

[15]You saw no form[f] of any kind the day the Lord spoke to you at Horeb out of the fire. Therefore watch yourselves very carefully,[g] [16]so that you do not become corrupt and make for yourselves an idol,[h] an image of any shape, whether formed like a man or a woman, [17]or like any animal on earth or any bird that flies in the air, [18]or like any creature that moves along the ground or any fish in the waters below. [19]And when you look up to the sky and see the sun,[i] the moon and the stars—all the heavenly array[j]—do not be enticed into bowing down to them and worshiping things the Lord your God has apportioned to all the nations under heaven. [20]But as for you, the Lord took you and brought you out of the iron-smelting furnace,[k] out of Egypt, to be the people of his inheritance,[l] as you now are.

[21]The Lord was angry with me[m] because of you, and he solemnly swore that I would not cross the Jordan and enter the good land the Lord your God is giving you as your inheritance. [22]I will die in this land; I will not cross the Jordan; but you are about to cross over and take possession of that good land.[n] [23]Be careful not to forget the covenant[o] of the Lord your God that he made with you; do not make for yourselves an idol[p] in the form of anything the Lord your God has forbid-

4:2
rDt 12:32;
Jos 1:7;
Rev 22:18-19
4:3
sNu 25:1-9;
Ps 106:28
4:6
tDt 30:19-20;
Ps 19:7; Pr 1:7
uJob 28:28
4:7
v2Sa 7:23
wPs 46:1;
Isa 55:6
4:9
xPr 4:23
yGe 18:19;
Eph 6:4
zPs 78:5-6
4:10
aEx 19:9,16
4:11
bEx 19:18;
Heb 12:18-19
4:12
cEx 20:22;
Dt 5:4,22
4:13
dDt 9:9,11
eEx 24:12;
31:18; 34:28
4:15
fIsa 40:18
gJos 23:11
4:16
hEx 20:4-5;
32:7; Dt 5:8;
Ro 1:23
4:19
iDt 17:3;
Job 31:26
j2Ki 17:16;
21:3; Ro 1:25
4:20
k1Ki 8:51;
Jer 11:4
lEx 19:5;
Dt 9:29
4:21
mNu 20:12;
Dt 1:37
4:22
nDt 3:25
4:23
over 9,16
pEx 20:4

den. ²⁴For the LORD your God is a consuming fire,�q a jealous God.

²⁵After you have had children and grandchildren and have lived in the land a long time—if you then become corrupt and make any kind of idol, doing evilʳ in the eyes of the LORD your God and provoking him to anger, ²⁶I call heaven and earth as witnesses against youˢ this day that you will quickly perish from the land that you are crossing the Jordan to possess. You will not live there long but will certainly be destroyed. ²⁷The LORD will scatterᵗ you among the peoples, and only a few of you will survive among the nations to which the LORD will drive you. ²⁸There you will worship man-made godsᵘ of wood and stone, which cannot see or hear or eat or smell.ᵛ ²⁹But if from there you seekʷ the LORD your God, you will find him if you look for him with all your heartˣ and with all your soul.ʸ ³⁰When you are in distress and all these things have happened to you, then in later daysᶻ you will return to the LORD your God and obey him. ³¹For the LORD your God is a mercifulᵃ God; he will not abandon or destroy you or forget the covenant with your forefathers, which he confirmed to them by oath.

The LORD Is God

³²Askᵇ now about the former days, long before your time, from the day God created man on the earth;ᶜ ask from one end of the heavens to the other.ᵈ Has anything so great as this ever happened, or has anything like it ever been heard of? ³³Has any other people heard the voice of Godᵃ speaking out of fire, as you have, and lived?ᵉ ³⁴Has any god ever tried to take for himself one nation out of another nation,ᶠ by testings, by miraculous signsᵍ and wonders,ʰ by war, by a mighty hand and an outstretched arm,ⁱ or by great and awesome deeds,ʲ like all the things the LORD your God did for you in Egypt before your very eyes?

³⁵You were shown these things so that you might know that the LORD is God; besides him there is no other.ᵏ ³⁶From heaven he made you hear his voiceˡ to discipline you. On earth he showed you his great fire, and you heard his words from out of the fire. ³⁷Because he lovedᵐ your forefathers and chose their descendants after them, he brought you out of Egypt by his Presence and his great strength,ⁿ ³⁸to drive out before you nations greater and stronger than you and to bring you into their land to give it to you for your inheritance,ᵒ as it is today.

³⁹Acknowledge and take to heart this day that the LORD is God in heaven above and on the earth below. There is no other.ᵖ ⁴⁰Keep�q his decrees and commands, which I am giving you today, so that it may go wellʳ with you and your children after you and that you may live longˢ in the land the LORD your God gives you for all time.

Cities of Refuge

4:41–43Ref — Nu 35:6–34; Dt 19:1–14; Jos 20:1–9

⁴¹Then Moses set aside three cities east of the Jordan, ⁴²to which anyone who had killed a person could flee if he had unintentionally killed his neighbor without malice aforethought. He could flee into one of these cities and save his life. ⁴³The cities were these: Bezer in the

ᵃ33 Or *of a god*

### Cross references (margin)

4:24
qEx 24:17;
Dt 9:3;
Heb 12:29

4:25
r2Ki 17:2,17

4:26
sDt 30:18-19;
Isa 1:2; Mic 6:2

4:27
tLev 26:33;
Dt 28:36,64;
Ne 1:8

4:28
uDt 28:36,64;
1Sa 26:19;
Jer 16:13
vPs 115:4-8;
135:15-18

4:29
w2Ch 15:4;
Isa 55:6
xJer 29:13
yDt 30:1-3,10

4:30
zDt 31:29;
Jer 23:20;
Hos 3:5

4:31
a2Ch 30:9;
Ne 9:31;
Ps 116:5;
Jnh 4:2

4:32
bDt 32:7;
Job 8:8
cGe 1:27
dMt 24:31

4:33
eEx 20:22;
Dt 5:24-26

4:34
fEx 6:6 gEx 7:3
hDt 7:19; 26:8
iEx 13:3
jDt 34:12

4:35
kDt 32:39;
1Sa 2:2;
Isa 45:5,18

4:36
lEx 19:9,19

4:37
mDt 10:15
nEx 13:3,9,14

4:38
oDt 7:1; 9:5

4:39
pver 35;
Jos 2:11

4:40
qLev 22:31;
Dt 5:33 rDt 5:16
sDt 6:3,18;
Eph 6:2-3

desert plateau, for the Reubenites; Ramoth in Gilead, for the Gadites; and Golan in Bashan, for the Manassites.

Introduction to the Law

⁴⁴This is the law Moses set before the Israelites. ⁴⁵These are the stipulations, decrees and laws Moses gave them when they came out of Egypt ⁴⁶and were in the valley near Beth Peor east of the Jordan, in the land of Sihonᵗ king of the Amorites, who reigned in Heshbon and was defeated by Moses and the Israelites as they came out of Egypt. ⁴⁷They took possession of his land and the land of Og king of Bashan, the two Amorite kings east of the Jordan. ⁴⁸This land extended from Aroerᵘ on the rim of the Arnon Gorge to Mount Siyonᵃᵛ (that is, Hermon), ⁴⁹and included all the Arabah east of the Jordan, as far as the Sea of the Arabah,ᵇ below the slopes of Pisgah.

The Ten Commandments

5:6–21pp — Ex 20:1–17

5 Moses summoned all Israel and said:

Hear, O Israel, the decrees and laws I declare in your hearing today. Learn them and be sure to follow them. ²The LORD our God made a covenantʷ with us at Horeb. ³It was not with our fathers that the LORD made this covenant, but with us, with all of us who are alive here today.ˣ ⁴The LORD spokeʸ to you face to face out of the fire on the mountain. ⁵(At that time I stood betweenᶻ the LORD and you to declare to you the word of the LORD, because you were afraidᵃ of the fire and did not go up the mountain.) And he said:

⁶"I am the LORD your God, who brought you out of Egypt, out of the land of slavery.

⁷"You shall have no other gods beforeᶜ me.

⁸"You shall not make for yourself an idol in the form of anything in heaven above or on the earth beneath or in the waters below. ⁹You shall not bow down to them or worship them; for I, the LORD your God, am a jealous God, punishing the children for the sin of the fathers to the third and fourth generation of those who hate me,ᵇ ¹⁰but showing love to a thousand ⌐generations⌐ of those who love me and keep my commandments.ᶜ

¹¹"You shall not misuse the name of the LORD your God, for the LORD will not hold anyone guiltless who misuses his name.ᵈ

¹²"Observe the Sabbath day by keeping it holy,ᵉ as the LORD your God has commanded you. ¹³Six days you shall labor and do all your work, ¹⁴but the seventh dayᶠ is a Sabbath to the LORD your God. On it you shall not do any work, neither you, nor your son or daughter, nor your manservant or maidservant, nor your ox, your donkey or any of your animals, nor the alien within your gates, so that your manservant and maidservant may rest, as you do. ¹⁵Remember that you were slaves in Egypt and that the LORD your God brought you out of there with a mighty hand and an outstretched arm.ᵍ

4:46
tNu 21:26;
Dt 3:29
4:48
uDt 2:36
vDt 3:9
5:2
wEx 19:5
5:3
xHeb 8:9
5:4
yDt 4:12,33,36
5:5
zGal 3:19
aEx 20:18,21
5:9
bEx 34:7
5:10
cJer 32:18
5:11
dLev 19:12;
Mt 5:33-37
5:12
eEx 20:8
5:14
fGe 2:2;
Heb 4:4
5:15
gDt 4:34

ᵃ48 Hebrew; Syriac (see also Deut. 3:9) *Sirion*   ᵇ49 That is, the Dead Sea   ᶜ7 Or *besides*

Therefore the LORD your God has commanded you to observe the Sabbath day.

16"Honor your father and your mother,[h] as the LORD your God has commanded you, so that you may live long[i] and that it may go well with you in the land the LORD your God is giving you.

17"You shall not murder.[j]

18"You shall not commit adultery.[k]

19"You shall not steal.

20"You shall not give false testimony against your neighbor.

21"You shall not covet your neighbor's wife. You shall not set your desire on your neighbor's house or land, his manservant or maidservant, his ox or donkey, or anything that belongs to your neighbor."[l]

22These are the commandments the LORD proclaimed in a loud voice to your whole assembly there on the mountain from out of the fire, the cloud and the deep darkness; and he added nothing more. Then he wrote them on two stone tablets[m] and gave them to me.

23When you heard the voice out of the darkness, while the mountain was ablaze with fire, all the leading men of your tribes and your elders came to me. 24And you said, "The LORD our God has shown us his glory and his majesty, and we have heard his voice from the fire. Today we have seen that a man can live even if God speaks with him.[n] 25But now, why should we die? This great fire will consume us, and we will die if we hear the voice of the LORD our God any longer.[o] 26For what mortal man has ever heard the voice of the living God speaking out of fire, as we have, and survived?[p] 27Go near and listen to all that the LORD our God says. Then tell us whatever the LORD our God tells you. We will listen and obey."

28The LORD heard you when you spoke to me and the LORD said to me, "I have heard what this people said to you. Everything they said was good.[q] 29Oh, that their hearts would be inclined to fear me[r] and keep all my commands[s] always, so that it might go well with them and their children forever![t]

30"Go, tell them to return to their tents. 31But you stay here[u] with me so that I may give you all the commands, decrees and laws you are to teach them to follow in the land I am giving them to possess."

32So be careful to do what the LORD your God has commanded you; do not turn aside to the right or to the left.[v] 33Walk in all the way that the LORD your God has commanded you,[w] so that you may live and prosper and prolong your days[x] in the land that you will possess.

Love the LORD Your God

6 These are the commands, decrees and laws the LORD your God directed me to teach you to observe in the land that you are crossing the Jordan to possess, 2so that you, your children and their children after them may fear[y] the LORD your God as long as you live by keeping all his decrees and commands that I give you, and so that you may enjoy long life. 3Hear, O Israel, and be careful to obey so that it may go well with you and that you may increase greatly[z] in a land flowing with milk and honey,[a] just as the LORD, the God of your fathers, promised you.

5:16
h Ex 20:12;
Lev 19:3;
Dt 27:16;
Eph 6:2-3*;
Col 3:20
i Dt 4:40
5:17
j Mt 5:21-22*
5:18
k Mt 5:27-30;
Lk 18:20*;
Jas 2:11*
5:21
l Ro 7:7*; 13:9*
5:22
m Ex 24:12;
31:18; Dt 4:13
5:24
n Ex 19:19
5:25
o Dt 18:16
5:26
p Dt 4:33
5:28
q Dt 18:17
5:29
r Ps 81:8,13
s Dt 11:1;
Isa 48:18
t Dt 4:1,40
5:31
u Ex 24:12
5:32
v Dt 17:11,20;
28:14; Jos 1:7;
23:6; Pr 4:27
5:33
w Jer 7:23
x Dt 4:40
6:2
y Ex 20:20;
Dt 10:12-13
6:3
z Dt 5:33 a Ex 3:8

[4]Hear, O Israel: The LORD our God, the LORD is one.[ab] [5]Love[c] the LORD your God with all your heart and with all your soul and with all your strength.[d] [6]These commandments that I give you today are to be upon your hearts.[e] [7]Impress them on your children. Talk about them when you sit at home and when you walk along the road, when you lie down and when you get up.[f] [8]Tie them as symbols on your hands and bind them on your foreheads.[g] [9]Write them on the doorframes of your houses and on your gates.[h]

[10]When the LORD your God brings you into the land he swore to your fathers, to Abraham, Isaac and Jacob, to give you—a land with large, flourishing cities you did not build,[i] [11]houses filled with all kinds of good things you did not provide, wells you did not dig, and vineyards and olive groves you did not plant—then when you eat and are satisfied,[j] [12]be careful that you do not forget the LORD, who brought you out of Egypt, out of the land of slavery.

[13]Fear the LORD[k] your God, serve him only[l] and take your oaths in his name. [14]Do not follow other gods, the gods of the peoples around you; [15]for the LORD your God[m], who is among you, is a jealous God and his anger will burn against you, and he will destroy you from the face of the land. [16]Do not test the LORD your God[n] as you did at Massah. [17]Be sure to keep the commands of the LORD your God and the stipulations and decrees he has given you.[o] [18]Do what is right and good in the LORD's sight, so that it may go well[p] with you and you may go in and take over the good land that the LORD promised on oath to your forefathers, [19]thrusting out all your enemies before you, as the LORD said.

[20]In the future, when your son asks you,[q] "What is the meaning of the stipulations, decrees and laws the LORD our God has commanded you?" [21]tell him: "We were slaves of Pharaoh in Egypt, but the LORD brought us out of Egypt with a mighty hand. [22]Before our eyes the LORD sent miraculous signs and wonders—great and terrible—upon Egypt and Pharaoh and his whole household. [23]But he brought us out from there to bring us in and give us the land that he promised on oath to our forefathers. [24]The LORD commanded us to obey all these decrees and to fear the LORD our God,[r] so that we might always prosper and be kept alive, as is the case today.[s] [25]And if we are careful to obey all this law before the LORD our God, as he has commanded us, that will be our righteousness.[t]"

Driving Out the Nations

7 When the LORD your God brings you into the land you are entering to possess and drives out before you many nations[u]—the Hittites, Girgashites, Amorites, Canaanites, Perizzites, Hivites and Jebusites, seven nations larger and stronger than you— [2]and when the LORD your God has delivered them over to you and you have defeated them, then you must destroy them totally.[b] Make no treaty[v] with them, and show them no mercy.[w] [3]Do not intermarry with them.[x] Do not give your daughters to their sons or take their daughters for your sons, [4]for they will turn your sons away from following me to serve other gods, and

6:4
bMk 12:29*;
1Co 8:4
6:5
cMt 22:37*;
Mk 12:30*;
Lk 10:27*
dDt 10:12
6:6
eDt 11:18
6:7
fDt 4:9; 11:19;
Eph 6:4
6:8
gEx 13:9,16;
Dt 11:18
6:9
hDt 11:20
6:10
iJos 24:13
6:11
jDt 8:10
6:13
kDt 10:20
lMt 4:10*;
Lk 4:8
6:15
mDt 4:24
6:16
nEx 17:7;
Mt 4:7*;
Lk 4:12*
6:17
oDt 11:22;
Ps 119:4
6:18
pDt 4:40
6:20
qEx 13:14
6:24
rDt 10:12;
Jer 32:39
sPs 41:2
6:25
tDt 24:13;
Ro 10:3,5
7:1
uDt 31:3;
Ac 13:19
7:2
vEx 23:32
wDt 13:8
7:3
xEx 34:15-16;
Ezr 9:2

a4 Or *The LORD our God is one LORD;* or *The LORD is our God, the LORD is one;* or *The LORD is our God, the LORD alone*   b2 The Hebrew term refers to the irrevocable giving over of things or persons to the LORD, often by totally destroying them; also in verse 26.

the LORD's anger will burn against you and will quickly destroy[y] you. [5]This is what you are to do to them: Break down their altars, smash their sacred stones, cut down their Asherah poles[a] and burn their idols in the fire.[z] [6]For you are a people holy[a] to the LORD your God.[b] The LORD your God has chosen[c] you out of all the peoples on the face of the earth to be his people, his treasured possession.

[7]The LORD did not set his affection on you and choose you because you were more numerous than other peoples, for you were the fewest of all peoples.[d] [8]But it was because the LORD loved[e] you and kept the oath he swore[f] to your forefathers that he brought you out with a mighty hand and redeemed you from the land of slavery,[g] from the power of Pharaoh king of Egypt. [9]Know therefore that the LORD your God is God;[h] he is the faithful God,[i] keeping his covenant of love[j] to a thousand generations of those who love him and keep his commands. [10]But

> those who hate him he will repay to their face by
> destruction;
> he will not be slow to repay to their face those who
> hate him.

[11]Therefore, take care to follow the commands, decrees and laws I give you today.

[12]If you pay attention to these laws and are careful to follow them, then the LORD your God will keep his covenant of love with you, as he swore to your forefathers.[k] [13]He will love you and bless you[l] and increase your numbers. He will bless the fruit of your womb, the crops of your land—your grain, new wine and oil—the calves of your herds and the lambs of your flocks in the land that he swore to your forefathers to give you.[m] [14]You will be blessed more than any other people; none of your men or women will be childless, nor any of your livestock without young.[n] [15]The LORD will keep you free from every disease.[o] He will not inflict on you the horrible diseases you knew in Egypt, but he will inflict them on all who hate you. [16]You must destroy all the peoples the LORD your God gives over to you. Do not look on them with pity[p] and do not serve their gods, for that will be a snare[q] to you.

[17]You may say to yourselves, "These nations are stronger than we are. How can we drive them out?"[r] [18]But do not be afraid[s] of them; remember well what the LORD your God did to Pharaoh and to all Egypt.[t] [19]You saw with your own eyes the great trials, the miraculous signs and wonders, the mighty hand and outstretched arm, with which the LORD your God brought you out. The LORD your God will do the same to all the peoples you now fear.[u] [20]Moreover, the LORD your God will send the hornet[v] among them until even the survivors who hide from you have perished. [21]Do not be terrified by them, for the LORD your God, who is among you,[w] is a great and awesome God.[x] [22]The LORD your God will drive out those nations before you, little by little.[y] You will not be allowed to eliminate them all at once, or the wild animals will multiply around you. [23]But the LORD your God will deliver them over to you, throwing them into great confusion until they are

7:4
y Dt 6:15
7:5
z Ex 23:24;
Dt 12:2-3
7:6
a Ex 19:5-6;
1Pe 2:9
b Ps 50:5;
Jer 2:3 c Dt 14:2
7:7
d Dt 10:22
7:8
e Dt 10:15
f Ex 32:13
g Ex 13:14
7:9
h Dt 4:35
i 1Co 1:9;
2Ti 2:13
j Ne 1:5; Da 9:4
7:12
k Lev 26:3-13;
Dt 28:1-14;
Ps 105:8-9
7:13
l Jn 14:21
m Dt 28:4
7:14
n Ex 23:26
7:15
o Ex 15:26
7:16
p ver 2; Ex 23:33
q Jdg 8:27
7:17
r Nu 33:53
7:18
s Dt 31:6
t Ps 105:5
7:19
u Dt 4:34
7:20
v Ex 23:28;
Jos 24:12
7:21
w Jos 3:10
x Dt 10:17;
Ne 9:32
7:22
y Ex 23:28-30

[a]5 That is, symbols of the goddess Asherah; here and elsewhere in Deuteronomy

destroyed. [24]He will give their kings into your hand, and you will wipe out their names from under heaven. No one will be able to stand up against you;[z] you will destroy them. [25]The images of their gods you are to burn[a] in the fire. Do not covet[b] the silver and gold on them, and do not take it for yourselves, or you will be ensnared[c] by it, for it is detestable[d] to the LORD your God. [26]Do not bring a detestable thing into your house or you, like it, will be set apart for destruction.[e] Utterly abhor and detest it, for it is set apart for destruction.

Do Not Forget the LORD

8 Be careful to follow every command I am giving you today, so that you may live[f] and increase and may enter and possess the land that the LORD promised on oath to your forefathers. [2]Remember how the LORD your God led[g] you all the way in the desert these forty years, to humble you and to test you in order to know what was in your heart, whether or not you would keep his commands. [3]He humbled you, causing you to hunger and then feeding you with manna,[h] which neither you nor your fathers had known, to teach you that man does not live on bread alone but on every word that comes from the mouth of the LORD.[i] [4]Your clothes did not wear out and your feet did not swell during these forty years.[j] [5]Know then in your heart that as a man disciplines his son, so the LORD your God disciplines you.[k]

[6]Observe the commands of the LORD your God, walking in his ways and revering him.[l] [7]For the LORD your God is bringing you into a good land—a land with streams and pools of water, with springs flowing in the valleys and hills;[m] [8]a land with wheat and barley, vines and fig trees, pomegranates, olive oil and honey; [9]a land where bread will not be scarce and you will lack nothing; a land where the rocks are iron and you can dig copper out of the hills.

[10]When you have eaten and are satisfied,[n] praise the LORD your God for the good land he has given you. [11]Be careful that you do not forget the LORD your God, failing to observe his commands, his laws and his decrees that I am giving you this day. [12]Otherwise, when you eat and are satisfied, when you build fine houses and settle down,[o] [13]and when your herds and flocks grow large and your silver and gold increase and all you have is multiplied, [14]then your heart will become proud and you will forget[p] the LORD your God, who brought you out of Egypt, out of the land of slavery. [15]He led you through the vast and dreadful desert,[q] that thirsty and waterless land, with its venomous snakes[r] and scorpions. He brought you water out of hard rock.[s] [16]He gave you manna to eat in the desert, something your fathers had never known,[t] to humble and to test you so that in the end it might go well with you. [17]You may say to yourself,[u] "My power and the strength of my hands have produced this wealth for me." [18]But remember the LORD your God, for it is he who gives you the ability to produce wealth,[v] and so confirms his covenant, which he swore to your forefathers, as it is today.

[19]If you ever forget the LORD your God and follow other gods and worship and bow down to them, I testify against you today that you will surely be destroyed. [w] [20]Like the nations the LORD destroyed before you, so you will be destroyed for not obeying the LORD your God.

7:24
z Jos 23:9

7:25
a Ex 32:20;
1Ch 14:12
b Jos 7:21
c Jdg 8:27
d Dt 17:1

7:26
e Lev 27:28-29

8:1
f Dt 4:1

8:2
g Am 2:10

8:3
h Ex 16:12,14,35
i Ex 16:2-3;
Mt 4:4*;
Lk 4:4*

8:4
j Dt 29:5;
Ne 9:21

8:5
k 2Sa 7:14;
Pr 3:11-12;
Heb 12:5-11;
Rev 3:19

8:6
l Dt 5:33

8:7
m Dt 11:9-12

8:10
n Dt 6:10-12

8:12
o Hos 13:6

8:14
p Ps 106:21

8:15
q Jer 2:6
r Nu 21:6
s Nu 20:11;
Ps 78:15; 114:8

8:16
t Ex 16:15

8:17
u Dt 9:4,7,24

8:18
v Pr 10:22;
Hos 2:8

8:19
w Dt 4:26; 30:18

Not Because of Israel's Righteousness

9 Hear, O Israel. You are now about to cross the Jordan to go in and dispossess nations greater and stronger than you,ˣ with large cities that have walls up to the sky.ʸ ²The people are strong and tall—Anakites! You know about them and have heard it said: "Who can stand up against the Anakites?"ᶻ ³But be assured today that the LORD your God is the one who goes across ahead of youᵃ like a devouring fire.ᵇ He will destroy them; he will subdue them before you. And you will drive them out and annihilate them quickly,ᶜ as the LORD has promised you.

⁴After the LORD your God has driven them out before you, do not say to yourself,ᵈ "The LORD has brought me here to take possession of this land because of my righteousness." No, it is on account of the wickedness of these nationsᵉ that the LORD is going to drive them out before you. ⁵It is not because of your righteousness or your integrityᶠ that you are going in to take possession of their land; but on account of the wickedness of these nations, the LORD your God will drive them out before you, to accomplish what he sworeᵍ to your fathers, to Abraham, Isaac and Jacob. ⁶Understand, then, that it is not because of your righteousness that the LORD your God is giving you this good land to possess, for you are a stiff-necked people.ʰ

The Golden Calf

⁷Remember this and never forget how you provoked the LORD your God to anger in the desert. From the day you left Egypt until you arrived here, you have been rebellious against the LORD. ⁸At Horeb you aroused the LORD's wrath so that he was angry enough to destroy you.ⁱ ⁹When I went up on the mountain to receive the tablets of stone, the tablets of the covenant that the LORD had made with you, I stayed on the mountain forty days and forty nights; I ate no bread and drank no water.ʲ ¹⁰The LORD gave me two stone tablets inscribed by the finger of God.ᵏ On them were all the commandments the LORD proclaimed to you on the mountain out of the fire, on the day of the assembly.

¹¹At the end of the forty days and forty nights, the LORD gave me the two stone tablets, the tablets of the covenant. ¹²Then the LORD told me, "Go down from here at once, because your people whom you brought out of Egypt have become corrupt.ˡ They have turned away quicklyᵐ from what I commanded them and have made a cast idol for themselves."

¹³And the LORD said to me, "I have seen this peopleⁿ, and they are a stiff-necked people indeed! ¹⁴Let me alone,ᵒ so that I may destroy them and blot outᵖ their name from under heaven. And I will make you into a nation stronger and more numerous than they."

¹⁵So I turned and went down from the mountain while it was ablaze with fire. And the two tablets of the covenant were in my hands.ᵃ �q ¹⁶When I looked, I saw that you had sinned against the LORD your God; you had made for yourselves an idol cast in the shape of a calf.ʳ You had turned aside quickly from the way that the LORD had commanded you. ¹⁷So I took the two tablets and threw them out of my hands, breaking them to pieces before your eyes.

ᵃ15 Or *And I had the two tablets of the covenant with me, one in each hand*

9:1
ˣDt 4:38; 11:23, 31 ʸDt 1:28

9:2
ᶻNu 13:22,28, 32-33

9:3
ᵃDt 31:3; Jos 3:11 ᵇDt 4:24; Heb 12:29 ᶜEx 23:31; Dt 7:23-24

9:4
ᵈDt 8:17 ᵉLev 18:21, 24-30; Dt 18:9-14

9:5
ᶠTit 3:5 ᵍGe 12:7; 13:15; 15:7; 17:8; 26:4

9:6
ʰver 13; Ex 32:9; Dt 31:27

9:8
ⁱEx 32:7-10; Ps 106:19

9:9
ʲEx 24:12,15,18; 34:28

9:10
ᵏEx 31:18; Dt 4:13

9:12
ˡEx 32:7-8; Dt 31:29 ᵐJdg 2:17

9:13
ⁿver 6; Ex 32:9; Dt 10:16

9:14
ᵒEx 32:10 ᵖNu 14:12; Dt 29:20

9:15
qEx 19:18; 32:15

9:16
ʳEx 32:19

[18]Then once again I fell[s] prostrate before the LORD for forty days and forty nights; I ate no bread and drank no water, because of all the sin you had committed, doing what was evil in the LORD's sight and so provoking him to anger. [19]I feared the anger and wrath of the LORD, for he was angry enough with you to destroy you.[t] But again the LORD listened to me.[u] [20]And the LORD was angry enough with Aaron to destroy him, but at that time I prayed for Aaron too. [21]Also I took that sinful thing of yours, the calf you had made, and burned it in the fire. Then I crushed it and ground it to powder as fine as dust and threw the dust into a stream that flowed down the mountain.[v]

[22]You also made the LORD angry at Taberah,[w] at Massah[x] and at Kibroth Hattaavah.[y]

[23]And when the LORD sent you out from Kadesh Barnea, he said, "Go up and take possession of the land I have given you." But you rebelled against the command of the LORD your God. You did not trust[z] him or obey him. [24]You have been rebellious against the LORD ever since I have known you.[a]

[25]I lay prostrate before the LORD those forty days and forty nights because the LORD had said he would destroy you.[b] [26]I prayed to the LORD and said, "O Sovereign LORD, do not destroy your people, your own inheritance that you redeemed by your great power and brought out of Egypt with a mighty hand.[c] [27]Remember your servants Abraham, Isaac and Jacob. Overlook the stubbornness of this people, their wickedness and their sin. [28]Otherwise, the country from which you brought us will say, 'Because the LORD was not able to take them into the land he had promised them, and because he hated them, he brought them out to put them to death in the desert.'[d] [29]But they are your people, your inheritance[e] that you brought out by your great power and your outstretched arm.[f]"

Tablets Like the First Ones

10 At that time the LORD said to me, "Chisel out two stone tablets[g] like the first ones and come up to me on the mountain. Also make a wooden chest.[a] [2]I will write on the tablets the words that were on the first tablets, which you broke. Then you are to put them in the chest."[h]

[3]So I made the ark out of acacia wood[i] and chiseled[j] out two stone tablets like the first ones, and I went up on the mountain with the two tablets in my hands. [4]The LORD wrote on these tablets what he had written before, the Ten Commandments he had proclaimed[k] to you on the mountain, out of the fire, on the day of the assembly. And the LORD gave them to me. [5]Then I came back down the mountain[l] and put the tablets in the ark[m] I had made, as the LORD commanded me, and they are there now.[n]

[6](The Israelites traveled from the wells of the Jaakanites to Moserah.[o] There Aaron died and was buried, and Eleazar his son succeeded him as priest.[p] [7]From there they traveled to Gudgodah and on to Jotbathah, a land with streams of water.[q] [8]At that time the LORD set apart the tribe of Levi[r] to carry the ark of the covenant of the LORD, to stand before the LORD to minister[s] and to pronounce blessings[t] in his name, as they still

---

[a]1 That is, an ark

9:18
s Ex 34:28
9:19
t Ex 32:10-11,14
u Dt 10:10
9:21
v Ex 32:20
9:22
w Nu 11:3
x Ex 17:7
y Nu 11:34
9:23
z Ps 106:24
9:24
a ver 7; Dt 31:27
9:25
b ver 18
9:26
c Ex 32:11
9:28
d Ex 32:12;
Nu 14:16
9:29
e Dt 4:20;
1Ki 8:51
f Dt 4:34;
Ne 1:10
10:1
g Ex 25:10;
34:1-2
10:2
h Ex 25:16,21;
Dt 4:13
10:3
i Ex 25:5,10;
37:1-9 j Ex 34:4
10:4
k Ex 20:1
10:5
l Ex 34:29
m Ex 40:20
n 1Ki 8:9
10:6
o Nu 33:30-31,38
p Nu 20:25-28
10:7
q Nu 33:32-34
10:8
r Nu 3:6
s Dt 18:5
t Dt 21:5

do today. ⁹That is why the Levites have no share or inheritance among their brothers; the L<small>ORD</small> is their inheritance,ᵘ as the L<small>ORD</small> your God told them.)

¹⁰Now I had stayed on the mountain forty days and nights, as I did the first time, and the L<small>ORD</small> listened to me at this time also. It was not his will to destroy you.ᵛ ¹¹"Go," the L<small>ORD</small> said to me, "and lead the people on their way, so that they may enter and possess the land that I swore to their fathers to give them."

Fear the L<small>ORD</small>

¹²And now, O Israel, what does the L<small>ORD</small> your God ask of youʷ but to fear the L<small>ORD</small> your God, to walk in all his ways, to love him,ˣ to serve the L<small>ORD</small> your God with all your heartʸ and with all your soul, ¹³and to observe the L<small>ORD</small>'s commands and decrees that I am giving you today for your own good?

¹⁴To the L<small>ORD</small> your God belong the heavens, even the highest heavens,ᶻ the earth and everything in it.ᵃ ¹⁵Yet the L<small>ORD</small> set his affection on your forefathers and lovedᵇ them, and he chose you, their descendants, above all the nations, as it is today. ¹⁶Circumciseᶜ your hearts, therefore, and do not be stiff-neckedᵈ any longer. ¹⁷For the L<small>ORD</small> your God is God of godsᵉ and Lord of lords, the great God, mighty and awesome, who shows no partialityᶠ and accepts no bribes. ¹⁸He defends the cause of the fatherless and the widow,ᵍ and loves the alien, giving him food and clothing. ¹⁹And you are to love those who are aliens, for you yourselves were aliens in Egypt.ʰ ²⁰Fear the L<small>ORD</small> your God and serve him.ⁱ Hold fastʲ to him and take your oaths in his name.ᵏ ²¹He is your praise;ˡ he is your God, who performed for you those great and awesome wondersᵐ you saw with your own eyes. ²²Your forefathers who went down into Egypt were seventy in all,ⁿ and now the L<small>ORD</small> your God has made you as numerous as the stars in the sky.ᵒ

Love and Obey the L<small>ORD</small>

11 Loveᵖ the L<small>ORD</small> your God and keep his requirements, his decrees, his laws and his commands always.�q ²Remember today that your children were not the ones who saw and experienced the discipline of the L<small>ORD</small> your God:ʳ his majesty, his mighty hand, his outstretched arm; ³the signs he performed and the things he did in the heart of Egypt, both to Pharaoh king of Egypt and to his whole country; ⁴what he did to the Egyptian army, to its horses and chariots, how he overwhelmed them with the waters of the Red Seaᵃˢ as they were pursuing you, and how the L<small>ORD</small> brought lasting ruin on them. ⁵It was not your children who saw what he did for you in the desert until you arrived at this place, ⁶and what he didᵗ to Dathan and Abiram, sons of Eliab the Reubenite, when the earth opened its mouth right in the middle of all Israel and swallowed them up with their households, their tents and every living thing that belonged to them. ⁷But it was your own eyes that saw all these great things the L<small>ORD</small> has done.

⁸Observe therefore all the commands I am giving you today, so that

---

10:9
uNu 18:20;
Dt 18:1-2;
Eze 44:28
10:10
vEx 33:17;
34:28;
Dt 9:18-19,25
10:12
wMic 6:8
xDt 5:33; 6:13;
Mt 22:37
yDt 6:5
10:14
z1Ki 8:27
aEx 19:5
10:15
bDt 4:37
10:16
cJer 4:4 dDt 9:6
10:17
eJos 22:22;
Da 2:47
fAc 10:34;
Ro 2:11;
Eph 6:9
10:18
gPs 68:5
10:19
hLev 19:34
10:20
iMt 4:10
jDt 11:22
kPs 63:11
10:21
lEx 15:2;
Jer 17:14
mPs 106:21-22
10:22
nGe 46:26-27
oGe 15:5;
Dt 1:10
11:1
pDt 10:12
qZec 3:7
11:2
rDt 5:24; 8:5
11:4
sEx 14:27
11:6
tNu 16:1-35

ᵃ4 Hebrew *Yam Suph*; that is, Sea of Reeds

you may have the strength to go in and take over the land that you are crossing the Jordan to possess,ᵘ ⁹and so that you may live longᵛ in the land that the Lord sworeʷ to your forefathers to give to them and their descendants, a land flowing with milk and honey.ˣ ¹⁰The land you are entering to take over is not like the land of Egypt, from which you have come, where you planted your seed and irrigated it by foot as in a vegetable garden. ¹¹But the land you are crossing the Jordan to take possession of is a land of mountains and valleys that drinks rain from heaven.ʸ ¹²It is a land the Lord your God cares for; the eyesᶻ of the Lord your God are continually on it from the beginning of the year to its end.

¹³So if you faithfully obeyᵃ the commands I am giving you today—to loveᵇ the Lord your God and to serve him with all your heart and with all your soul— ¹⁴then I will send rainᶜ on your land in its season, both autumn and spring rains,ᵈ so that you may gather in your grain, new wine and oil. ¹⁵I will provide grassᵉ in the fields for your cattle, and you will eat and be satisfied.ᶠ

¹⁶Be careful, or you will be enticed to turn away and worship other gods and bow down to them.ᵍ ¹⁷Then the Lord's angerʰ will burn against you, and he will shutⁱ the heavens so that it will not rain and the ground will yield no produce, and you will soon perishʲ from the good land the Lord is giving you. ¹⁸Fix these words of mine in your hearts and minds; tie them as symbols on your hands and bind them on your foreheads.ᵏ ¹⁹Teach them to your children,ˡ talking about them when you sit at home and when you walk along the road, when you lie down and when you get up.ᵐ ²⁰Write them on the doorframes of your houses and on your gates,ⁿ ²¹so that your days and the days of your children may be manyᵒ in the land that the Lord swore to give your forefathers, as many as the days that the heavens are above the earth.ᵖ

²²If you carefully observeᑫ all these commands I am giving you to follow—to love the Lord your God, to walk in all his ways and to hold fastʳ to him— ²³then the Lord will drive out all these nations before you, and you will dispossess nations larger and stronger than you.ˢ ²⁴Every place where you set your foot will be yours:ᵗ Your territory will extend from the desert to Lebanon, and from the Euphrates River to the western sea.ᵃ ²⁵No man will be able to stand against you. The Lord your God, as he promised you, will put the terror and fear of you on the whole land, wherever you go.ᵘ

²⁶See, I am setting before you today a blessing and a curseᵛ— ²⁷the blessingʷ if you obey the commands of the Lord your God that I am giving you today; ²⁸the curse if you disobeyˣ the commands of the Lord your God and turn from the way that I command you today by following other gods, which you have not known. ²⁹When the Lord your God has brought you into the land you are entering to possess, you are to proclaim on Mount Gerizim the blessings, and on Mount Ebal the curses.ʸ ³⁰As you know, these mountains are across the Jordan, west of the road,ᵇ toward the setting sun, near the great trees of Moreh,ᶻ in the territory of those Canaanites living in the Arabah in the vicinity of Gilgal.ᵃ ³¹You are about to cross the Jordan to enter and take possessionᵇ of the land the Lord your God is giving you. When you have

---

ᵃ24 That is, the Mediterranean   ᵇ30 Or *Jordan, westward*

11:8
uJos 1:7
11:9
vDt 4:40;
Pr 10:27
wDt 9:5 xEx 3:8
11:11
yDt 8:7
11:12
z1Ki 9:3
11:13
aDt 6:17
bDt 10:12
11:14
cLev 26:4;
Dt 28:12
dJoel 2:23;
Jas 5:7
11:15
ePs 104:14
fDt 6:11
11:16
gDt 8:19;
29:18;
Job 31:9,27
11:17
hDt 6:15
i1Ki 8:35;
2Ch 6:26
jDt 4:26
11:18
kDt 6:6-8
11:19
lDt 6:7
mDt 4:9-10
11:20
nDt 6:9
11:21
oPr 3:2; 4:10
pPs 72:5
11:22
qDt 6:17
rDt 10:20
11:23
sDt 4:38; 9:1
11:24
tGe 15:18;
Ex 23:31;
Jos 1:3; 14:9
11:25
uEx 23:27;
Dt 7:24
11:26
vDt 30:1,15,19
11:27
wDt 28:1-14
11:28
xDt 28:15
11:29
yDt 27:12-13;
Jos 8:33
11:30
zGe 12:6
aJos 4:19
11:31
bDt 9:1;
Jos 1:11

taken it over and are living there, [32]be sure that you obey all the decrees and laws I am setting before you today.

The One Place of Worship

12 These are the decrees and laws you must be careful to follow in the land that the LORD, the God of your fathers, has given you to possess—as long as you live in the land.[c] [2]Destroy completely all the places on the high mountains and on the hills and under every spreading tree[d] where the nations you are dispossessing worship their gods. [3]Break down their altars, smash[e] their sacred stones and burn their Asherah poles in the fire; cut down the idols of their gods and wipe out their names from those places.

[4]You must not worship the LORD your God in their way. [5]But you are to seek the place the LORD your God will choose from among all your tribes to put his Name there for his dwelling.[f] To that place you must go; [6]there bring your burnt offerings and sacrifices, your tithes[g] and special gifts, what you have vowed to give and your freewill offerings, and the firstborn of your herds and flocks. [7]There, in the presence of the LORD your God, you and your families shall eat and shall rejoice[h] in everything you have put your hand to, because the LORD your God has blessed you.

[8]You are not to do as we do here today, everyone as he sees fit, [9]since you have not yet reached the resting place and the inheritance the LORD your God is giving you. [10]But you will cross the Jordan and settle in the land the LORD your God is giving[i] you as an inheritance, and he will give you rest from all your enemies around you so that you will live in safety. [11]Then to the place the LORD your God will choose as a dwelling for his Name[j]—there you are to bring everything I command you: your burnt offerings and sacrifices, your tithes and special gifts, and all the choice possessions you have vowed to the LORD. [12]And there rejoice[k] before the LORD your God, you, your sons and daughters, your menservants and maidservants, and the Levites from your towns, who have no allotment or inheritance[l] of their own. [13]Be careful not to sacrifice your burnt offerings anywhere you please. [14]Offer them only at the place the LORD will choose[m] in one of your tribes, and there observe everything I command you.

[15]Nevertheless, you may slaughter your animals in any of your towns and eat as much of the meat as you want, as if it were gazelle or deer,[n] according to the blessing the LORD your God gives you. Both the ceremonially unclean and the clean may eat it. [16]But you must not eat the blood;[o] pour it out on the ground like water.[p] [17]You must not eat in your own towns the tithe of your grain and new wine and oil, or the firstborn of your herds and flocks, or whatever you have vowed to give, or your freewill offerings or special gifts. [18]Instead, you are to eat[q] them in the presence of the LORD your God at the place the LORD your God will choose[r]—you, your sons and daughters, your menservants and maidservants, and the Levites from your towns—and you are to rejoice[s] before the LORD your God in everything you put your hand to. [19]Be careful not to neglect the Levites[t] as long as you live in your land.

[20]When the LORD your God has enlarged your territory[u] as he promised[v] you, and you crave meat and say, "I would like some meat," then you may eat as much of it as you want. [21]If the place where the LORD

12:1
cDt 4:9-10;
1Ki 8:40
12:2
d2Ki 16:4; 17:10
12:3
eNu 33:52;
Dt 7:5; Jdg 2:2
12:5
fver 11,13;
2Ch 7:12,16
12:6
gDt 14:22-23
12:7
hver 12,18;
Lev 23:40;
Dt 14:26
12:10
iDt 11:31
12:11
jver 5;
Dt 15:20; 16:2
12:12
kver 7 lDt 10:9;
14:29
12:14
mver 11
12:15
nver 20-23;
Dt 14:5; 15:22
12:16
oGe 9:4;
Lev 7:26;
17:10-12
pDt 15:23
12:18
qDt 14:23 rver 5
sver 7,12
12:19
tDt 14:27
12:20
uDt 19:8
vGe 15:18;
Dt 11:24

your God chooses to put his Name is too far away from you, you may slaughter animals from the herds and flocks the LORD has given you, as I have commanded you, and in your own towns you may eat as much of them as you want. [22]Eat them as you would gazelle or deer. [w] Both the ceremonially unclean and the clean may eat. [23]But be sure you do not eat the blood, [x] because the blood is the life, and you must not eat the life with the meat. [24]You must not eat the blood; pour it out on the ground like water. [25]Do not eat it, so that it may go well [y] with you and your children after you, because you will be doing what is right [z] in the eyes of the LORD.

[26]But take your consecrated things and whatever you have vowed to give, [a] and go to the place the LORD will choose. [27]Present your burnt offerings [b] on the altar of the LORD your God, both the meat and the blood. The blood of your sacrifices must be poured beside the altar of the LORD your God, but you may eat the meat. [28]Be careful to obey all these regulations I am giving you, so that it may always go well [c] with you and your children after you, because you will be doing what is good and right in the eyes of the LORD your God.

[29]The LORD your God will cut off [d] before you the nations you are about to invade and dispossess. But when you have driven them out and settled in their land, [30]and after they have been destroyed before you, be careful not to be ensnared by inquiring about their gods, saying, "How do these nations serve their gods? We will do the same." [31]You must not worship the LORD your God in their way, because in worshiping their gods, they do all kinds of detestable things the LORD hates. [e] They even burn their sons [f] and daughters in the fire as sacrifices to their gods.

[32]See that you do all I command you; do not add [g] to it or take away from it.

Worshiping Other Gods

13 If a prophet, [h] or one who foretells by dreams, appears among you and announces to you a miraculous sign or wonder, [2]and if the sign or wonder of which he has spoken takes place, and he says, "Let us follow other gods" [i] (gods you have not known) "and let us worship them," [3]you must not listen to the words of that prophet or dreamer. The LORD your God is testing [j] you to find out whether you love him with all your heart and with all your soul. [4]It is the LORD your God you must follow, [k] and him you must revere. Keep his commands and obey him; serve him and hold fast [l] to him. [5]That prophet or dreamer must be put to death, because he preached rebellion against the LORD your God, who brought you out of Egypt and redeemed you from the land of slavery; he has tried to turn you from the way the LORD your God commanded you to follow. You must purge the evil [m] from among you.

[6]If your very own brother, or your son or daughter, or the wife you love, or your closest friend secretly entices [n] you, saying, "Let us go and worship other gods" (gods that neither you nor your fathers have known, [7]gods of the peoples around you, whether near or far, from one end of the land to the other), [8]do not yield [o] to him or listen to him. Show him no pity. Do not spare him or shield him. [9]You must certainly put him to death. [p] Your hand must be the first in putting him to death,

12:22
w ver 15
12:23
x ver 16;
Ge 9:4;
Lev 17:11,14
12:25
y Dt 4:40;
Isa 3:10
z Ex 15:26;
Dt 13:18;
1Ki 11:38
12:26
a ver 17;
Nu 5:9-10
12:27
b Lev 1:5,9,13
12:28
c ver 25; Dt 4:40
12:29
d Jos 23:4
12:31
e Dt 9:5
f Dt 18:10;
Jer 32:35
12:32
g Dt 4:2;
Jos 1:7;
Rev 22:18-19
13:1
h Mt 24:24;
Mk 13:22;
2Th 2:9
13:2
i ver 6,13
13:3
j Dt 8:2,16
13:4
k 2Ki 23:3;
2Ch 34:31
l Dt 10:20
13:5
m Dt 17:7,12;
1Co 5:13
13:6
n Dt 17:2-7;
29:18
13:8
o Pr 1:10
13:9
p Dt 17:5,7

and then the hands of all the people. [10]Stone him to death, because he tried to turn you away from the LORD your God, who brought you out of Egypt, out of the land of slavery. [11]Then all Israel will hear and be afraid,[q] and no one among you will do such an evil thing again.

[12]If you hear it said about one of the towns the LORD your God is giving you to live in [13]that wicked men[r] have arisen among you and have led the people of their town astray, saying, "Let us go and worship other gods" (gods you have not known), [14]then you must inquire, probe and investigate it thoroughly. And if it is true and it has been proved that this detestable thing has been done among you, [15]you must certainly put to the sword all who live in that town. Destroy it completely,[a] both its people and its livestock. [16]Gather all the plunder of the town into the middle of the public square and completely burn the town and all its plunder as a whole burnt offering to the LORD your God.[s] It is to remain a ruin[t] forever, never to be rebuilt. [17]None of those condemned things[a] shall be found in your hands, so that the LORD will turn from his fierce anger;[u] he will show you mercy, have compassion[v] on you, and increase your numbers,[w] as he promised[x] on oath to your forefathers, [18]because you obey the LORD your God, keeping all his commands that I am giving you today and doing what is right[y] in his eyes.

Clean and Unclean Food

14:3–20pp — Lev 11:1–23

14 You are the children[z] of the LORD your God. Do not cut yourselves or shave the front of your heads for the dead, [2]for you are a people holy to the LORD your God.[a] Out of all the peoples on the face of the earth, the LORD has chosen you to be his treasured possession.[b]

[3]Do not eat any detestable thing.[c] [4]These are the animals you may eat:[d] the ox, the sheep, the goat, [5]the deer, the gazelle, the roe deer, the wild goat, the ibex, the antelope and the mountain sheep.[b] [6]You may eat any animal that has a split hoof divided in two and that chews the cud. [7]However, of those that chew the cud or that have a split hoof completely divided you may not eat the camel, the rabbit or the coney.[c] Although they chew the cud, they do not have a split hoof; they are ceremonially unclean for you. [8]The pig is also unclean; although it has a split hoof, it does not chew the cud. You are not to eat their meat or touch their carcasses.[e]

[9]Of all the creatures living in the water, you may eat any that has fins and scales. [10]But anything that does not have fins and scales you may not eat; for you it is unclean.

[11]You may eat any clean bird. [12]But these you may not eat: the eagle, the vulture, the black vulture, [13]the red kite, the black kite, any kind of falcon, [14]any kind of raven, [15]the horned owl, the screech owl, the gull, any kind of hawk, [16]the little owl, the great owl, the white owl, [17]the desert owl, the osprey, the cormorant, [18]the stork, any kind of heron, the hoopoe and the bat.

13:11
qDt 19:20
13:13
rver 2,6;
1Jn 2:19
13:16
sJos 6:24
tJos 8:28;
Jer 49:2
13:17
uNu 25:4
vDt 30:3
wDt 7:13
xGe 22:17; 26:4,
24; 28:14
13:18
yDt 12:25,28
14:1
zLev 19:28;
21:5; Jer 16:6;
41:5; Ro 8:14;
9:8; Gal 3:26
14:2
aLev 20:26
bDt 7:6;
26:18-19
14:3
cEze 4:14
14:4
dLev 11:2-45;
Ac 10:14
14:8
eLev 11:26-27

---

[a]15,17 The Hebrew term refers to the irrevocable giving over of things or persons to the LORD, often by totally destroying them.　　[b]5 The precise identification of some of the birds and animals in this chapter is uncertain.　　[c]7 That is, the hyrax or rock badger

¹⁹All flying insects that swarm are unclean to you; do not eat them. ²⁰But any winged creature that is clean you may eat.

²¹Do not eat anything you find already dead.ᶠ You may give it to an alien living in any of your towns, and he may eat it, or you may sell it to a foreigner. But you are a people holy to the LORD your God.ᵍ Do not cook a young goat in its mother's milk.ʰ

Tithes

²²Be sure to set aside a tenthⁱ of all that your fields produce each year. ²³Eat the tithe of your grain, new wine and oil, and the firstborn of your herds and flocks in the presence of the LORD your God at the place he will choose as a dwelling for his Name,ʲ so that you may learnᵏ to revere the LORD your God always. ²⁴But if that place is too distant and you have been blessed by the LORD your God and cannot carry your tithe (because the place where the LORD will choose to put his Name is so far away), ²⁵then exchange your tithe for silver, and take the silver with you and go to the place the LORD your God will choose. ²⁶Use the silver to buy whatever you like: cattle, sheep, wine or other fermented drink, or anything you wish. Then you and your household shall eat there in the presence of the LORD your God and rejoice.ˡ ²⁷And do not neglect the Levitesᵐ living in your towns, for they have no allotment or inheritance of their own.ⁿ

²⁸At the end of every three years, bring all the tithes of that year's produce and store it in your towns,ᵒ ²⁹so that the Levites (who have no allotmentᵖ or inheritance of their own) and the aliens,�q the fatherless and the widows who live in your towns may come and eat and be satisfied, and so that the LORD your God may blessʳ you in all the work of your hands.

The Year for Canceling Debts

15:1–11Ref — Lev 25:8–38

15 At the end of every seven years you must cancel debts.ˢ ²This is how it is to be done: Every creditor shall cancel the loan he has made to his fellow Israelite. He shall not require payment from his fellow Israelite or brother, because the LORD's time for canceling debts has been proclaimed. ³You may require payment from a foreigner,ᵗ but you must cancel any debt your brother owes you. ⁴However, there should be no poor among you, for in the land the LORD your God is giving you to possess as your inheritance, he will richly blessᵘ you, ⁵if only you fully obey the LORD your God and are careful to followᵛ all these commands I am giving you today. ⁶For the LORD your God will bless you as he has promised, and you will lend to many nations but will borrow from none. You will rule over many nations but none will rule over you.ʷ

⁷If there is a poor man among your brothers in any of the towns of the land that the LORD your God is giving you, do not be hardhearted or tightfistedˣ toward your poor brother. ⁸Rather be openhandedʸ and freely lend him whatever he needs. ⁹Be careful not to harbor this wicked thought: "The seventh year, the year for canceling debts,ᶻ is near," so that you do not show ill willᵃ toward your needy brother and give him nothing. He may then appeal to the LORD against you, and you will be found guilty of sin.ᵇ ¹⁰Give generously to him and do so without a

14:21
fLev 17:15; 22:8
gver 2
hEx 23:19;
34:26
14:22
iLev 27:30;
Dt 12:6,17;
Ne 10:37
14:23
jDt 12:5
kDt 4:10
14:26
lDt 12:7-8
14:27
mDt 12:19
nNu 18:20
14:28
oDt 26:12
14:29
pver 27
qDt 26:12
rDt 15:10;
Mal 3:10
15:1
sDt 31:10
15:3
tDt 23:20
15:4
uDt 28:8
15:5
vDt 28:1
15:6
wDt 28:12-13,44
15:7
x1Jn 3:17
15:8
yMt 5:42;
Lk 6:34
15:9
zver 1
aMt 20:15
bDt 24:15

grudging heart;[c] then because of this the LORD your God will bless[d] you in all your work and in everything you put your hand to. [11]There will always be poor people in the land. Therefore I command you to be openhanded toward your brothers and toward the poor and needy in your land.[e]

Freeing Servants

15:12–18pp — Ex 21:2–6
15:12–18Ref — Lev 25:38–55

[12]If a fellow Hebrew, a man or a woman, sells himself to you and serves you six years, in the seventh year you must let him go free.[f] [13]And when you release him, do not send him away empty-handed. [14]Supply him liberally from your flock, your threshing floor and your winepress. Give to him as the LORD your God has blessed you. [15]Remember that you were slaves[g] in Egypt and the LORD your God redeemed you.[h] That is why I give you this command today.

[16]But if your servant says to you, "I do not want to leave you," because he loves you and your family and is well off with you, [17]then take an awl and push it through his ear lobe into the door, and he will become your servant for life. Do the same for your maidservant.

[18]Do not consider it a hardship to set your servant free, because his service to you these six years has been worth twice as much as that of a hired hand. And the LORD your God will bless you in everything you do.

The Firstborn Animals

[19]Set apart for the LORD your God every firstborn male[i] of your herds and flocks. Do not put the firstborn of your oxen to work, and do not shear the firstborn of your sheep. [20]Each year you and your family are to eat them in the presence of the LORD your God at the place he will choose.[j] [21]If an animal has a defect, is lame or blind, or has any serious flaw, you must not sacrifice it to the LORD your God.[k] [22]You are to eat it in your own towns. Both the ceremonially unclean and the clean may eat it, as if it were gazelle or deer.[l] [23]But you must not eat the blood; pour it out on the ground like water.[m]

Passover

16:1–8pp — Ex 12:14–20; Lev 23:4–8; Nu 28:16–25

16 Observe the month of Abib[n] and celebrate the Passover of the LORD your God, because in the month of Abib he brought you out of Egypt by night. [2]Sacrifice as the Passover to the LORD your God an animal from your flock or herd at the place the LORD will choose as a dwelling for his Name.[o] [3]Do not eat it with bread made with yeast, but for seven days eat unleavened bread, the bread of affliction,[p] because you left Egypt in haste[q]—so that all the days of your life you may remember the time of your departure from Egypt.[r] [4]Let no yeast be found in your possession in all your land for seven days. Do not let any of the meat you sacrifice on the evening of the first day remain until morning.[s]

[5]You must not sacrifice the Passover in any town the LORD your God gives you [6]except in the place he will choose as a dwelling for his Name. There you must sacrifice the Passover in the evening, when the sun

---

15:10
c 2Co 9:5
d Dt 14:29;
24:19
15:11
e Mt 26:11;
Mk 14:7;
Jn 12:8
15:12
f Ex 21:2;
Lev 25:39;
Jer 34:14
15:15
g Dt 5:15
h Dt 16:12
15:19
i Ex 13:2
15:20
j Dt 12:5-7,17,
18; 14:23
15:21
k Lev 22:19-25
15:22
l Dt 12:15,22
15:23
m Dt 12:16
16:1
n Ex 12:2; 13:4
16:2
o Dt 12:5,26
16:3
p Ex 12:8,39;
34:18 q Ex 12:11,
15,19 r Ex 13:3,
6-7
16:4
s Ex 12:10; 34:25

goes down, on the anniversary[at] of your departure from Egypt. [7]Roast[u] it and eat it at the place the LORD your God will choose. Then in the morning return to your tents. [8]For six days eat unleavened bread and on the seventh day hold an assembly[v] to the LORD your God and do no work.

Feast of Weeks
16:9–12pp — Lev 23:15–22; Nu 28:26–31

[9]Count off seven weeks[w] from the time you begin to put the sickle to the standing grain.[x] [10]Then celebrate the Feast of Weeks to the LORD your God by giving a freewill offering in proportion to the blessings the LORD your God has given you. [11]And rejoice[y] before the LORD your God at the place he will choose as a dwelling for his Name—you, your sons and daughters, your menservants and maidservants, the Levites[z] in your towns, and the aliens, the fatherless and the widows living among you. [12]Remember that you were slaves in Egypt,[a] and follow carefully these decrees.

Feast of Tabernacles
16:13–17pp — Lev 23:33–43; Nu 29:12–39

[13]Celebrate the Feast of Tabernacles for seven days after you have gathered the produce of your threshing floor[b] and your winepress.[c] [14]Be joyful[d] at your Feast—you, your sons and daughters, your menservants and maidservants, and the Levites, the aliens, the fatherless and the widows who live in your towns. [15]For seven days celebrate the Feast to the LORD your God at the place the LORD will choose. For the LORD your God will bless you in all your harvest and in all the work of your hands, and your joy[e] will be complete.

[16]Three times a year all your men must appear before the LORD your God at the place he will choose: at the Feast of Unleavened Bread, the Feast of Weeks and the Feast of Tabernacles.[f] No man should appear before the LORD empty-handed:[g] [17]Each of you must bring a gift in proportion to the way the LORD your God has blessed you.

Judges

[18]Appoint judges[h] and officials for each of your tribes in every town the LORD your God is giving you, and they shall judge the people fairly. [19]Do not pervert justice[i] or show partiality.[j] Do not accept a bribe,[k] for a bribe blinds the eyes of the wise and twists the words of the righteous. [20]Follow justice and justice alone, so that you may live and possess the land the LORD your God is giving you.

Worshiping Other Gods

[21]Do not set up any wooden Asherah pole[b1] beside the altar you build to the LORD your God,[m] [22]and do not erect a sacred stone,[n] for these the LORD your God hates.

17 Do not sacrifice to the LORD your God an ox or a sheep that has any defect[o] or flaw in it, for that would be detestable to him.[p]

[2]If a man or woman living among you in one of the towns the LORD gives you is found doing evil in the eyes of the LORD your God in

---

16:6
tEx 12:6;
Dt 12:5
16:7
uEx 12:8;
2Ch 35:13
16:8
vEx 12:16;
13:6; Lev 23:8
16:9
wEx 34:22;
Lev 23:15
xEx 23:16;
Nu 28:26
16:11
yDt 12:7
zDt 12:12
16:12
aDt 15:15
16:13
bLev 23:34
cEx 23:16
16:14
dver 11
16:15
eLev 23:39
16:16
fEx 23:14,16
gEx 34:20
16:18
hDt 1:16
16:19
iEx 23:2,8
jLev 19:15;
Dt 1:17
kEcc 7:7
16:21
lDt 7:5
mEx 34:13;
2Ki 17:16; 21:3;
2Ch 33:3
16:22
nLev 26:1
17:1
oMal 1:8,13
pDt 15:21

---

[a]6 Or *down, at the time of day*   [b]21 Or *Do not plant any tree dedicated to Asherah*

violation of his covenant, q 3and contrary to my command r has worshiped other gods, bowing down to them or to the sun s or the moon or the stars of the sky, 4and this has been brought to your attention, then you must investigate it thoroughly. If it is true and it has been proved that this detestable thing has been done in Israel, t 5take the man or woman who has done this evil deed to your city gate and stone that person to death. u 6On the testimony of two or three witnesses a man shall be put to death, but no one shall be put to death on the testimony of only one witness. v 7The hands of the witnesses must be the first in putting him to death, and then the hands of all the people. You must purge the evil w from among you.

Law Courts

8If cases come before your courts that are too difficult for you to judge—whether bloodshed, lawsuits or assaults x—take them to the place the LORD your God will choose. y 9Go to the priests, who are Levites, and to the judge who is in office at that time. Inquire of them and they will give you the verdict. z 10You must act according to the decisions they give you at the place the LORD will choose. Be careful to do everything they direct you to do. 11Act according to the law they teach you and the decisions they give you. Do not turn aside from what they tell you, to the right or to the left. a 12The man who shows contempt b for the judge or for the priest who stands ministering there to the LORD your God must be put to death. You must purge the evil from Israel. 13All the people will hear and be afraid, and will not be contemptuous again. c

The King

14When you enter the land the LORD your God is giving you and have taken possession of it and settled in it, and you say, "Let us set a king over us like all the nations around us," d 15be sure to appoint over you the king the LORD your God chooses. He must be from among your own brothers. e Do not place a foreigner over you, one who is not a brother Israelite. 16The king, moreover, must not acquire great numbers of horses for himself f or make the people return to Egypt g to get more of them, h for the LORD has told you, "You are not to go back that way again." i 17He must not take many wives, j or his heart will be led astray. He must not accumulate large amounts of silver and gold.

18When he takes the throne of his kingdom, he is to write k for himself on a scroll a copy of this law, taken from that of the priests, who are Levites. 19It is to be with him, and he is to read it all the days of his life l so that he may learn to revere the LORD his God and follow carefully all the words of this law and these decrees 20and not consider himself better than his brothers and turn from the law m to the right or to the left. n Then he and his descendants will reign a long time over his kingdom in Israel.

Offerings for Priests and Levites

18 The priests, who are Levites—indeed the whole tribe of Levi— are to have no allotment or inheritance with Israel. They shall

17:2
qDt 13:6-11
17:3
rJer 7:22-23
sJob 31:26
17:4
tDt 13:12-14
17:5
uLev 24:14
17:6
vNu 35:30;
Dt 19:15;
Jos 7:25;
Mt 18:16;
Jn 8:17;
2Co 13:1;
1Ti 5:19;
Heb 10:28
17:7
wDt 13:5,9
17:8
x2Ch 19:10
yDt 12:5;
Hag 2:11
17:9
zDt 19:17;
Eze 44:24
17:11
aDt 25:1
17:12
bNu 15:30
17:13
cDt 13:11;
19:20
17:14
dDt 11:31;
1Sa 8:5,19-20
17:15
eJer 30:21
17:16
f1Ki 4:26; 10:26
gIsa 31:1;
Hos 11:5
h1Ki 10:28;
Eze 17:15
iEx 13:17
17:17
j1Ki 11:3
17:18
kDt 31:22,24
17:19
lJos 1:8
17:20
m1Ki 15:5
nDt 5:32

live on the offerings made to the LORD by fire, for that is their inheritance. ° ²They shall have no inheritance among their brothers; the LORD is their inheritance, as he promised them.

³This is the share due the priests from the people who sacrifice a bull or a sheep: the shoulder, the jowls and the inner parts. ᵖ ⁴You are to give them the firstfruits of your grain, new wine and oil, and the first wool from the shearing of your sheep, �q ⁵for the LORD your God has chosen them ʳ and their descendants out of all your tribes to stand and minister ˢ in the LORD's name always.

⁶If a Levite moves from one of your towns anywhere in Israel where he is living, and comes in all earnestness to the place the LORD will choose, ᵗ ⁷he may minister in the name of the LORD his God like all his fellow Levites who serve there in the presence of the LORD. ⁸He is to share equally in their benefits, even though he has received money from the sale of family possessions. ᵘ

Detestable Practices

⁹When you enter the land the LORD your God is giving you, do not learn to imitate ᵛ the detestable ways of the nations there. ¹⁰Let no one be found among you who sacrifices his son or daughter in ᵃ the fire, who practices divination ʷ or sorcery, interprets omens, engages in witchcraft, ˣ ¹¹or casts spells, or who is a medium or spiritist or who consults the dead. ¹²Anyone who does these things is detestable to the LORD, and because of these detestable practices the LORD your God will drive out those nations before you. ʸ ¹³You must be blameless before the LORD your God.

The Prophet

¹⁴The nations you will dispossess listen to those who practice sorcery or divination. But as for you, the LORD your God has not permitted you to do so. ¹⁵The LORD your God will raise up for you a prophet like me from among your own brothers. ᶻ You must listen to him. ¹⁶For this is what you asked of the LORD your God at Horeb on the day of the assembly when you said, "Let us not hear the voice of the LORD our God nor see this great fire anymore, or we will die." ᵃ

¹⁷The LORD said to me: "What they say is good. ¹⁸I will raise up for them a prophet like you from among their brothers; I will put my words ᵇ in his mouth, and he will tell them everything I command him. ᶜ ¹⁹If anyone does not listen to my words that the prophet speaks in my name, I myself will call him to account. ᵈ ²⁰But a prophet who presumes to speak in my name anything I have not commanded him to say, or a prophet who speaks in the name of other gods, ᵉ must be put to death." ᶠ

²¹You may say to yourselves, "How can we know when a message has not been spoken by the LORD?" ²²If what a prophet proclaims in the name of the LORD does not take place or come true, that is a message the LORD has not spoken. ᵍ That prophet has spoken presumptuously. ʰ Do not be afraid of him.

ᵃ10 Or *who makes his son or daughter pass through*

18:1
oDt 10:9;
1Co 9:13
18:3
pLev 7:28-34
18:4
qEx 22:29;
Nu 18:12
18:5
rEx 28:1
sDt 10:8
18:6
tNu 35:2-3
18:8
u2Ch 31:4;
Ne 12:44,47
18:9
vDt 12:29-31
18:10
wDt 12:31
xLev 19:31
18:12
yLev 18:24;
Dt 9:4
18:15
zJn 1:21;
Ac 3:22*; 7:37*
18:16
aEx 20:19;
Dt 5:23-27
18:18
bIsa 51:16;
Jn 17:8
cJn 4:25-26;
8:28; 12:49-50
18:19
dAc 3:23*
18:20
eJer 14:14
fDt 13:1-5
18:22
gJer 28:9
hver 20

Cities of Refuge

19:1–14Ref — Nu 35:6–34; Dt 4:41–43; Jos 20:1–9

19 When the LORD your God has destroyed the nations whose land he is giving you, and when you have driven them out and settled in their towns and houses,[i] [2]then set aside for yourselves three cities centrally located in the land the LORD your God is giving you to possess. [3]Build roads to them and divide into three parts the land the LORD your God is giving you as an inheritance, so that anyone who kills a man may flee there.

[4]This is the rule concerning the man who kills another and flees there to save his life—one who kills his neighbor unintentionally, without malice aforethought. [5]For instance, a man may go into the forest with his neighbor to cut wood, and as he swings his ax to fell a tree, the head may fly off and hit his neighbor and kill him. That man may flee to one of these cities and save his life. [6]Otherwise, the avenger of blood[j] might pursue him in a rage, overtake him if the distance is too great, and kill him even though he is not deserving of death, since he did it to his neighbor without malice aforethought. [7]This is why I command you to set aside for yourselves three cities.

[8]If the LORD your God enlarges your territory, as he promised on oath to your forefathers, and gives you the whole land he promised them, [9]because you carefully follow all these laws I command you today—to love the LORD your God and to walk always in his ways[k]—then you are to set aside three more cities. [10]Do this so that innocent blood will not be shed in your land, which the LORD your God is giving you as your inheritance, and so that you will not be guilty of bloodshed.[l]

[11]But if a man hates his neighbor and lies in wait for him, assaults and kills him,[m] and then flees to one of these cities, [12]the elders of his town shall send for him, bring him back from the city, and hand him over to the avenger of blood to die. [13]Show him no pity.[n] You must purge from Israel the guilt of shedding innocent blood,[o] so that it may go well with you.

[14]Do not move your neighbor's boundary stone set up by your predecessors in the inheritance you receive in the land the LORD your God is giving you to possess.[p]

Witnesses

[15]One witness is not enough to convict a man accused of any crime or offense he may have committed. A matter must be established by the testimony of two or three witnesses.[q]

[16]If a malicious witness[r] takes the stand to accuse a man of a crime, [17]the two men involved in the dispute must stand in the presence of the LORD before the priests and the judges[s] who are in office at the time. [18]The judges must make a thorough investigation, and if the witness proves to be a liar, giving false testimony against his brother, [19]then do to him as he intended to do to his brother.[t] You must purge the evil from among you. [20]The rest of the people will hear of this and be afraid,[u] and never again will such an evil thing be done among you. [21]Show no pity:[v] life for life, eye for eye, tooth for tooth, hand for hand, foot for foot.[w]

19:1
i Dt 12:29
19:6
j Nu 35:12
19:9
k Jos 20:7-8
19:10
l Nu 35:33;
Dt 21:1-9
19:11
m Nu 35:16
19:13
n Dt 7:2
o 1Ki 2:31
19:14
p Dt 27:17;
Pr 22:28;
Hos 5:10
19:15
q Nu 35:30;
Dt 17:6;
Mt 18:16*;
Jn 8:17;
2Co 13:1*;
1Ti 5:19;
Heb 10:28
19:16
r Ex 23:1;
Ps 27:12
19:17
s Dt 17:9
19:19
t Pr 19:5,9
19:20
u Dt 17:13;
21:21
19:21
v ver 13
w Ex 21:24;
Lev 24:20;
Mt 5:38*

Going to War

20 When you go to war against your enemies and see horses and chariots and an army greater than yours,ˣ do not be afraidʸ of them,ᶻ because the LORD your God, who brought you up out of Egypt, will be with you. ²When you are about to go into battle, the priest shall come forward and address the army. ³He shall say: "Hear, O Israel, today you are going into battle against your enemies. Do not be faint-heartedᵃ or afraid; do not be terrified or give way to panic before them. ⁴For the LORD your God is the one who goes with you to fightᵇ for you against your enemies to give you victory."

⁵The officers shall say to the army: "Has anyone built a new house and not dedicatedᶜ it? Let him go home, or he may die in battle and someone else may dedicate it. ⁶Has anyone planted a vineyard and not begun to enjoy it? Let him go home, or he may die in battle and someone else enjoy it. ⁷Has anyone become pledged to a woman and not married her? Let him go home, or he may die in battle and someone else marry her.ᵈ" ⁸Then the officers shall add, "Is any man afraid or fainthearted? Let him go home so that his brothers will not become disheartened too."ᵉ ⁹When the officers have finished speaking to the army, they shall appoint commanders over it.

¹⁰When you march up to attack a city, make its people an offer of peace.ᶠ ¹¹If they accept and open their gates, all the people in it shall be subject to forced laborᵍ and shall work for you. ¹²If they refuse to make peace and they engage you in battle, lay siege to that city. ¹³When the LORD your God delivers it into your hand, put to the sword all the men in it.ʰ ¹⁴As for the women, the children, the livestockⁱ and everything else in the city, you may take these as plunder for yourselves. And you may use the plunder the LORD your God gives you from your enemies. ¹⁵This is how you are to treat all the cities that are at a distance from you and do not belong to the nations nearby.

¹⁶However, in the cities of the nations the LORD your God is giving you as an inheritance, do not leave alive anything that breathes.ʲ ¹⁷Completely destroyᵃ them—the Hittites, Amorites, Canaanites, Perizzites, Hivites and Jebusites—as the LORD your God has commanded you. ¹⁸Otherwise, they will teach you to follow all the detestable things they do in worshiping their gods,ᵏ and you will sinˡ against the LORD your God.

¹⁹When you lay siege to a city for a long time, fighting against it to capture it, do not destroy its trees by putting an ax to them, because you can eat their fruit. Do not cut them down. Are the trees of the field people, that you should besiege them?ᵇ ²⁰However, you may cut down trees that you know are not fruit trees and use them to build siege works until the city at war with you falls.

Atonement for an Unsolved Murder

21 If a man is found slain, lying in a field in the land the LORD your God is giving you to possess, and it is not known who killed him, ²your elders and judges shall go out and measure the distance

---

aʲ17 The Hebrew term refers to the irrevocable giving over of things or persons to the LORD, often by totally destroying them.   b19 Or *down to use in the siege, for the fruit trees are for the benefit of man.*

20:1
ˣPs 20:7;
Isa 31:1
ʸDt 31:6,8
ᶻ2Ch 32:7-8
20:3
ᵃJos 23:10
20:4
ᵇDt 1:30; 3:22;
Jos 23:10
20:5
ᶜNe 12:27
20:7
ᵈDt 24:5
20:8
ᵉJdg 7:3
20:10
ᶠLk 14:31-32
20:11
ᵍ1Ki 9:21
20:13
ʰNu 31:7
20:14
ⁱJos 8:2; 22:8
20:16
ʲEx 23:31-33;
Nu 21:2-3;
Dt 7:2;
Jos 11:14
20:18
ᵏEx 34:16;
Dt 7:4; 12:30-31
ˡEx 23:33

from the body to the neighboring towns. [3]Then the elders of the town nearest the body shall take a heifer that has never been worked and has never worn a yoke [4]and lead her down to a valley that has not been plowed or planted and where there is a flowing stream. There in the valley they are to break the heifer's neck. [5]The priests, the sons of Levi, shall step forward, for the LORD your God has chosen them to minister and to pronounce blessings[m] in the name of the LORD and to decide all cases of dispute and assault. [n] [6]Then all the elders of the town nearest the body shall wash their hands[o] over the heifer whose neck was broken in the valley, [7]and they shall declare: "Our hands did not shed this blood, nor did our eyes see it done. [8]Accept this atonement for your people Israel, whom you have redeemed, O LORD, and do not hold your people guilty of the blood of an innocent man." And the bloodshed will be atoned for. [p] [9]So you will purge[q] from yourselves the guilt of shedding innocent blood, since you have done what is right in the eyes of the LORD.

Marrying a Captive Woman

[10]When you go to war against your enemies and the LORD your God delivers them into your hands[r] and you take captives, [11]if you notice among the captives a beautiful woman and are attracted to her, you may take her as your wife. [12]Bring her into your home and have her shave her head,[s] trim her nails [13]and put aside the clothes she was wearing when captured. After she has lived in your house and mourned her father and mother for a full month,[t] then you may go to her and be her husband and she shall be your wife. [14]If you are not pleased with her, let her go wherever she wishes. You must not sell her or treat her as a slave, since you have dishonored her. [u]

The Right of the Firstborn

[15]If a man has two wives, and he loves one but not the other, and both bear him sons but the firstborn is the son of the wife he does not love, [v] [16]when he wills his property to his sons, he must not give the rights of the firstborn to the son of the wife he loves in preference to his actual firstborn, the son of the wife he does not love. [w] [17]He must acknowledge the son of his unloved wife as the firstborn by giving him a double share of all he has. That son is the first sign of his father's strength. [x] The right of the firstborn belongs to him. [y]

A Rebellious Son

[18]If a man has a stubborn and rebellious son who does not obey his father and mother[z] and will not listen to them when they discipline him, [19]his father and mother shall take hold of him and bring him to the elders at the gate of his town. [20]They shall say to the elders, "This son of ours is stubborn and rebellious. He will not obey us. He is a profligate and a drunkard." [21]Then all the men of his town shall stone him to death. You must purge the evil[a] from among you. All Israel will hear of it and be afraid. [b]

Various Laws

[22]If a man guilty of a capital offense[c] is put to death and his body is hung on a tree, [23]you must not leave his body on the tree overnight. [d] Be

21:5
m 1Ch 23:13
n Dt 17:8-11
21:6
o Mt 27:24
21:8
p Nu 35:33-34
21:9
q Dt 19:13
21:10
r Jos 21:44
21:12
s Lev 14:9;
Nu 6:9
21:13
t Ps 45:10
21:14
u Ge 34:2
21:15
v Ge 29:33
21:16
w 1Ch 26:10
21:17
x Ge 49:3
y Ge 25:31
21:18
z Pr 1:8;
Isa 30:1;
Eph 6:1-3
21:21
a Dt 19:19
b Dt 13:11
21:22
c Dt 22:26;
Mk 14:64;
Ac 23:29
21:23
d Jos 8:29;
10:27; Jn 19:31

sure to bury him that same day, because anyone who is hung on a tree is under God's curse.ᵉ You must not desecrateᶠ the land the LORD your God is giving you as an inheritance.

22 If you see your brother's ox or sheep straying, do not ignore it but be sure to take it back to him.ᵍ ²If the brother does not live near you or if you do not know who he is, take it home with you and keep it until he comes looking for it. Then give it back to him. ³Do the same if you find your brother's donkey or his cloak or anything he loses. Do not ignore it.

⁴If you see your brother's donkeyʰ or his ox fallen on the road, do not ignore it. Help him get it to its feet.

⁵A woman must not wear men's clothing, nor a man wear women's clothing, for the LORD your God detests anyone who does this.

⁶If you come across a bird's nest beside the road, either in a tree or on the ground, and the mother is sitting on the young or on the eggs, do not take the mother with the young.ⁱ ⁷You may take the young, but be sure to let the mother go, so that it may go well with you and you may have a long life.ʲ

⁸When you build a new house, make a parapet around your roof so that you may not bring the guilt of bloodshed on your house if someone falls from the roof.

⁹Do not plant two kinds of seed in your vineyard;ᵏ if you do, not only the crops you plant but also the fruit of the vineyard will be defiled.ᵃ

¹⁰Do not plow with an ox and a donkey yoked together.ˡ

¹¹Do not wear clothes of wool and linen woven together.ᵐ

¹²Make tassels on the four corners of the cloak you wear.ⁿ

Marriage Violations

¹³If a man takes a wife and, after lying with herᵒ, dislikes her ¹⁴and slanders her and gives her a bad name, saying, "I married this woman, but when I approached her, I did not find proof of her virginity," ¹⁵then the girl's father and mother shall bring proof that she was a virgin to the town elders at the gate. ¹⁶The girl's father will say to the elders, "I gave my daughter in marriage to this man, but he dislikes her. ¹⁷Now he has slandered her and said, 'I did not find your daughter to be a virgin.' But here is the proof of my daughter's virginity." Then her parents shall display the cloth before the elders of the town, ¹⁸and the eldersᵖ shall take the man and punish him. ¹⁹They shall fine him a hundred shekels of silverᵇ and give them to the girl's father, because this man has given an Israelite virgin a bad name. She shall continue to be his wife; he must not divorce her as long as he lives.

²⁰If, however, the charge is true and no proof of the girl's virginity can be found, ²¹she shall be brought to the door of her father's house and there the men of her town shall stone her to death. She has done a disgraceful thing�q in Israel by being promiscuous while still in her father's house. You must purge the evil from among you.

²²If a man is found sleeping with another man's wife, both the man who slept with her and the woman must die.ʳ You must purge the evil from Israel.

²³If a man happens to meet in a town a virgin pledged to be married

21:23
eGal 3:13*
fLev 18:25;
Nu 35:34
22:1
gEx 23:4-5
22:4
hEx 23:5
22:6
iLev 22:28
22:7
jDt 4:40
22:9
kLev 19:19
22:10
l2Co 6:14
22:11
mLev 19:19
22:12
nNu 15:37-41;
Mt 23:5
22:13
oDt 24:1
22:18
pEx 18:21
22:21
qGe 34:7;
Dt 13:5;
23:17-18;
Jdg 20:6;
2Sa 13:12
22:22
rLev 20:10;
Jn 8:5

ᵃ9 Or *be forfeited to the sanctuary*   ᵇ19 That is, about 2 1/2 pounds (about 1 kilogram) and he sleeps with her, 24you shall take both of them to the gate of that town and stone them to death—the girl because she was in a town and did not scream for help, and the man because he violated another man's wife. You must purge the evil from among you. s

25But if out in the country a man happens to meet a girl pledged to be married and rapes her, only the man who has done this shall die. 26Do nothing to the girl; she has committed no sin deserving death. This case is like that of someone who attacks and murders his neighbor, 27for the man found the girl out in the country, and though the betrothed girl screamed, there was no one to rescue her.

28If a man happens to meet a virgin who is not pledged to be married and rapes her and they are discovered, t 29he shall pay the girl's father fifty shekels of silver. a He must marry the girl, for he has violated her. He can never divorce her as long as he lives.

30A man is not to marry his father's wife; he must not dishonor his father's bed. u

Exclusion From the Assembly

23 No one who has been emasculated by crushing or cutting may enter the assembly of the LORD.

2No one born of a forbidden marriage b nor any of his descendants may enter the assembly of the LORD, even down to the tenth generation.

3No Ammonite or Moabite or any of his descendants may enter the assembly of the LORD, even down to the tenth generation. v 4For they did not come to meet you with bread and water on your way when you came out of Egypt, and they hired Balaam w son of Beor from Pethor in Aram Naharaim c to pronounce a curse on you. 5However, the LORD your God would not listen to Balaam but turned the curse x into a blessing for you, because the LORD your God loves you. 6Do not seek a treaty of friendship with them as long as you live. y

7Do not abhor an Edomite, for he is your brother. z Do not abhor an Egyptian, because you lived as an alien in his country. a 8The third generation of children born to them may enter the assembly of the LORD.

Uncleanness in the Camp

9When you are encamped against your enemies, keep away from everything impure. 10If one of your men is unclean because of a nocturnal emission, he is to go outside the camp and stay there. b 11But as evening approaches he is to wash himself, and at sunset he may return to the camp.

12Designate a place outside the camp where you can go to relieve yourself. 13As part of your equipment have something to dig with, and when you relieve yourself, dig a hole and cover up your excrement. 14For the LORD your God moves c about in your camp to protect you and to deliver your enemies to you. Your camp must be holy, d so that he will not see among you anything indecent and turn away from you.

22:24
s ver 21-22;
1Co 5:13*
22:28
t Ex 22:16
22:30
u Lev 18:8;
20:11;
Dt 27:20;
1Co 5:1
23:3
v Ne 13:2
23:4
w Nu 22:5-6;
23:7; 2Pe 2:15
23:5
x Pr 26:2
23:6
y Ezr 9:12
23:7
z Ge 25:26;
Ob 1:10,12
a Ex 22:21; 23:9;
Lev 19:34;
Dt 10:19
23:10
b Lev 15:16
23:14
c Lev 26:12
d Ex 3:5

a29 That is, about 1 1/4 pounds (about 0.6 kilogram)   b2 Or *one of illegitimate birth*   c4 That is, Northwest Mesopotamia

Miscellaneous Laws

[15]If a slave has taken refuge with you, do not hand him over to his master.[e] [16]Let him live among you wherever he likes and in whatever town he chooses. Do not oppress[f] him.

[17]No Israelite man[g] or woman is to become a shrine prostitute.[h] [18]You must not bring the earnings of a female prostitute or of a male prostitute[a] into the house of the LORD your God to pay any vow, because the LORD your God detests them both.

[19]Do not charge your brother interest, whether on money or food or anything else that may earn interest.[i] [20]You may charge a foreigner interest, but not a brother Israelite, so that the LORD your God may bless[j] you in everything you put your hand to in the land you are entering to possess.

[21]If you make a vow to the LORD your God, do not be slow to pay it, for the LORD your God will certainly demand it of you and you will be guilty of sin.[k] [22]But if you refrain from making a vow, you will not be guilty. [23]Whatever your lips utter you must be sure to do, because you made your vow freely to the LORD your God with your own mouth.

[24]If you enter your neighbor's vineyard, you may eat all the grapes you want, but do not put any in your basket. [25]If you enter your neighbor's grainfield, you may pick kernels with your hands, but you must not put a sickle to his standing grain.[l]

24 If a man marries a woman who becomes displeasing to him[m] because he finds something indecent about her, and he writes her a certificate of divorce,[n] gives it to her and sends her from his house, [2]and if after she leaves his house she becomes the wife of another man, [3]and her second husband dislikes her and writes her a certificate of divorce, gives it to her and sends her from his house, or if he dies, [4]then her first husband, who divorced her, is not allowed to marry her again after she has been defiled. That would be detestable in the eyes of the LORD. Do not bring sin upon the land the LORD[o] your God is giving you as an inheritance.

[5]If a man has recently married, he must not be sent to war or have any other duty laid on him. For one year he is to be free to stay at home and bring happiness to the wife he has married.[p]

[6]Do not take a pair of millstones—not even the upper one—as security for a debt, because that would be taking a man's livelihood as security.

[7]If a man is caught kidnapping one of his brother Israelites and treats him as a slave or sells him, the kidnapper must die.[q] You must purge the evil from among you.

[8]In cases of leprous[b] diseases be very careful to do exactly as the priests, who are Levites, instruct you. You must follow carefully what I have commanded them.[r] [9]Remember what the LORD your God did to Miriam along the way after you came out of Egypt.[s]

[10]When you make a loan of any kind to your neighbor, do not go into his house to get what he is offering as a pledge. [11]Stay outside and let the man to whom you are making the loan bring the pledge out to you. [12]If the man is poor, do not go to sleep with his pledge in your posses-

---

23:15
e 1Sa 30:15
23:16
f Ex 22:21
23:17
g Ge 19:25;
2Ki 23:7
h Lev 19:29;
Dt 22:21
23:19
i Ex 22:25;
Lev 25:35-37
23:20
j Dt 15:10; 28:12
23:21
k Nu 30:1-2;
Ecc 5:4-5;
Mt 5:33
23:25
l Mt 12:1;
Mk 2:23; Lk 6:1
24:1
m Dt 22:13
n Mt 5:31*;
19:7-9;
Mk 10:4-5
24:4
o Jer 3:1
24:5
p Dt 20:7
24:7
q Ex 21:16
24:8
r Lev 13:1-46;
14:2
24:9
s Nu 12:10

---

*a18 Hebrew *of a dog*   *b8 The Hebrew word was used for various diseases affecting the skin—not necessarily leprosy.

sion. [13]Return his cloak to him by sunset[t] so that he may sleep in it. Then he will thank you, and it will be regarded as a righteous act in the sight of the LORD your God. [u]

[14]Do not take advantage of a hired man who is poor and needy, whether he is a brother Israelite or an alien living in one of your towns. [v] [15]Pay him his wages each day before sunset, because he is poor[w] and is counting on it. [x] Otherwise he may cry to the LORD against you, and you will be guilty of sin. [y]

[16]Fathers shall not be put to death for their children, nor children put to death for their fathers; each is to die for his own sin. [z]

[17]Do not deprive the alien or the fatherless of justice, [a] or take the cloak of the widow as a pledge. [18]Remember that you were slaves in Egypt and the LORD your God redeemed you from there. That is why I command you to do this.

[19]When you are harvesting in your field and you overlook a sheaf, do not go back to get it. [b] Leave it for the alien, the fatherless and the widow, so that the LORD your God may bless[c] you in all the work of your hands. [20]When you beat the olives from your trees, do not go over the branches a second time. [d] Leave what remains for the alien, the fatherless and the widow. [21]When you harvest the grapes in your vineyard, do not go over the vines again. Leave what remains for the alien, the fatherless and the widow. [22]Remember that you were slaves in Egypt. That is why I command you to do this. [e]

25 When men have a dispute, they are to take it to court and the judges will decide the case, [f] acquitting the innocent and condemning the guilty. [g] [2]If the guilty man deserves to be beaten, [h] the judge shall make him lie down and have him flogged in his presence with the number of lashes his crime deserves, [3]but he must not give him more than forty lashes. [i] If he is flogged more than that, your brother will be degraded in your eyes. [j]

[4]Do not muzzle an ox while it is treading out the grain. [k]

[5]If brothers are living together and one of them dies without a son, his widow must not marry outside the family. Her husband's brother shall take her and marry her and fulfill the duty of a brother-in-law to her. [l] [6]The first son she bears shall carry on the name of the dead brother so that his name will not be blotted out from Israel. [m]

[7]However, if a man does not want to marry his brother's wife, she shall go to the elders at the town gate and say, "My husband's brother refuses to carry on his brother's name in Israel. He will not fulfill the duty of a brother-in-law to me."[n] [8]Then the elders of his town shall summon him and talk to him. If he persists in saying, "I do not want to marry her," [9]his brother's widow shall go up to him in the presence of the elders, take off one of his sandals, [o] spit in his face and say, "This is what is done to the man who will not build up his brother's family line." [10]That man's line shall be known in Israel as The Family of the Unsandaled.

[11]If two men are fighting and the wife of one of them comes to rescue her husband from his assailant, and she reaches out and seizes him by his private parts, [12]you shall cut off her hand. Show her no pity. [p]

[13]Do not have two differing weights in your bag—one heavy, one light. [q] [14]Do not have two differing measures in your house—one large, one small. [15]You must have accurate and honest weights and measures,

24:13
tEx 22:26
uDt 6:25;
Da 4:27
24:14
vLev 25:35-43;
Dt 15:12-18
24:15
wJer 22:13
xLev 19:13
yDt 15:9;
Jas 5:4
24:16
zZKi 14:6;
2Ch 25:4;
Jer 31:29-30;
Eze 18:20
24:17
aDt 1:17;
10:17-18; 16:19
24:19
bLev 19:9;
23:22 cPr 19:17
24:20
dLev 19:10
24:22
ever 18
25:1
fDt 19:17
gDt 1:16-17
25:2
hLk 12:47-48
25:3
i2Co 11:24
jJob 18:3
25:4
kPr 12:10;
1Co 9:9*;
1Ti 5:18*
25:5
lMt 22:24;
Mk 12:19;
Lk 20:28
25:6
mGe 38:9;
Ru 4:5,10
25:7
nRu 4:1-2,5-6
25:9
oRu 4:7-8,11
25:12
pDt 19:13
25:13
qLev 19:35-37;
Pr 11:1;
Eze 45:10;
Mic 6:11

so that you may live long[r] in the land the Lord your God is giving you. [16]For the Lord your God detests anyone who does these things, anyone who deals dishonestly.[s]

[17]Remember what the Amalekites[t] did to you along the way when you came out of Egypt. [18]When you were weary and worn out, they met you on your journey and cut off all who were lagging behind; they had no fear of God.[u] [19]When the Lord your God gives you rest from all the enemies around you in the land he is giving you to possess as an inheritance, you shall blot out the memory of Amalek[v] from under heaven. Do not forget!

Firstfruits and Tithes

26 When you have entered the land the Lord your God is giving you as an inheritance and have taken possession of it and settled in it, [2]take some of the firstfruits[w] of all that you produce from the soil of the land the Lord your God is giving you and put them in a basket. Then go to the place the Lord your God will choose as a dwelling for his Name[x] [3]and say to the priest in office at the time, "I declare today to the Lord your God that I have come to the land the Lord swore to our forefathers to give us." [4]The priest shall take the basket from your hands and set it down in front of the altar of the Lord your God. [5]Then you shall declare before the Lord your God: "My father was a wandering Aramean,[y] and he went down into Egypt with a few people[z] and lived there and became a great nation, powerful and numerous. [6]But the Egyptians mistreated us and made us suffer,[a] putting us to hard labor. [7]Then we cried out to the Lord, the God of our fathers, and the Lord heard our voice[b] and saw[c] our misery, toil and oppression. [8]So the Lord brought us out of Egypt with a mighty hand and an outstretched arm, with great terror and with miraculous signs and wonders.[d] [9]He brought us to this place and gave us this land, a land flowing with milk and honey;[e] [10]and now I bring the firstfruits of the soil that you, O Lord, have given me." Place the basket before the Lord your God and bow down before him. [11]And you and the Levites[f] and the aliens among you shall rejoice[g] in all the good things the Lord your God has given to you and your household.

[12]When you have finished setting aside a tenth[h] of all your produce in the third year, the year of the tithe,[i] you shall give it to the Levite, the alien, the fatherless and the widow, so that they may eat in your towns and be satisfied. [13]Then say to the Lord your God: "I have removed from my house the sacred portion and have given it to the Levite, the alien, the fatherless and the widow, according to all you commanded. I have not turned aside from your commands nor have I forgotten any of them.[j] [14]I have not eaten any of the sacred portion while I was in mourning, nor have I removed any of it while I was unclean,[k] nor have I offered any of it to the dead. I have obeyed the Lord my God; I have done everything you commanded me. [15]Look down from heaven,[l] your holy dwelling place, and bless your people Israel and the land you have given us as you promised on oath to our forefathers, a land flowing with milk and honey."

Follow the Lord's Commands

[16]The Lord your God commands you this day to follow these decrees

25:15
r Ex 20:12
25:16
s Pr 11:1
25:17
t Ex 17:8
25:18
u Ps 36:1;
Ro 3:18
25:19
v 1Sa 15:2-3
26:2
w Ex 22:29;
23:16,19;
Nu 18:13;
Pr 3:9 x Dt 12:5
26:5
y Hos 12:12
z Ge 43:1-2;
45:7,11; 46:27;
Dt 10:22
26:6
a Ex 1:11,14
26:7
b Ex 2:23-25
c Ex 3:9
26:8
d Dt 4:34
26:9
e Dt 3:8
26:11
f Dt 12:7
g Dt 16:11
26:12
h Lev 27:30
i Nu 18:24;
Dt 14:28-29;
Heb 7:5,9
26:13
j Ps 119:141,
153,176
26:14
k Lev 7:20;
Hos 9:4
26:15
l Isa 63:15;
Zec 2:13

and laws; carefully observe them with all your heart and with all your soul. [m] [17]You have declared this day that the LORD is your God and that you will walk in his ways, that you will keep his decrees, commands and laws, and that you will obey him. [18]And the LORD has declared this day that you are his people, his treasured possession[n] as he promised, and that you are to keep all his commands. [19]He has declared that he will set you in praise, fame and honor high above all the nations[o] he has made and that you will be a people holy[p] to the LORD your God, as he promised.

The Altar on Mount Ebal

27 Moses and the elders of Israel commanded the people: "Keep all these commands that I give you today. [2]When you have crossed the Jordan into the land the LORD your God is giving you, set up some large stones and coat them with plaster. [q] [3]Write on them all the words of this law when you have crossed over to enter the land the LORD your God is giving you, a land flowing with milk and honey,[r] just as the LORD, the God of your fathers, promised you. [4]And when you have crossed the Jordan, set up these stones on Mount Ebal,[s] as I command you today, and coat them with plaster. [5]Build there an altar[t] to the LORD your God, an altar of stones. Do not use any iron tool[u] upon them. [6]Build the altar of the LORD your God with fieldstones and offer burnt offerings on it to the LORD your God. [7]Sacrifice fellowship offerings[a] there, eating them and rejoicing in the presence of the LORD your God. [8]And you shall write very clearly all the words of this law on these stones you have set up."

Curses From Mount Ebal

[9]Then Moses and the priests, who are Levites, said to all Israel, "Be silent, O Israel, and listen! You have now become the people of the LORD your God. [v] [10]Obey the LORD your God and follow his commands and decrees that I give you today."

[11]On the same day Moses commanded the people:

[12]When you have crossed the Jordan, these tribes shall stand on Mount Gerizim[w] to bless the people: Simeon, Levi, Judah, Issachar, Joseph and Benjamin. [x] [13]And these tribes shall stand on Mount Ebal to pronounce curses: Reuben, Gad, Asher, Zebulun, Dan and Naphtali. [14]The Levites shall recite to all the people of Israel in a loud voice:

[15]"Cursed is the man who carves an image or casts an idol[y]—a thing detestable to the LORD, the work of the craftsman's hands —and sets it up in secret."

Then all the people shall say, "Amen!"

[16]"Cursed is the man who dishonors his father or his mother."[z]

Then all the people shall say, "Amen!"

[17]"Cursed is the man who moves his neighbor's boundary stone."[a]

Then all the people shall say, "Amen!"

[18]"Cursed is the man who leads the blind astray on the road."[b]

Then all the people shall say, "Amen!"

26:16
[m]Dt 4:29
26:18
[n]Ex 6:7; 19:5;
Dt 7:6; 14:2;
28:9
26:19
[o]Dt 4:7-8; 28:1,
13,44 [p]Ex 19:6;
Dt 7:6; 1Pe 2:9
27:2
[q]Jos 8:31
27:3
[r]Dt 26:9
27:4
[s]Dt 11:29
27:5
[t]Jos 8:31
[u]Ex 20:25
27:9
[v]Dt 26:18
27:12
[w]Dt 11:29
[x]Jos 8:35
27:15
[y]Ex 20:4;
34:17;
Lev 19:4; 26:1;
Dt 4:16,23; 5:8;
Isa 44:9
27:16
[z]Ex 20:12;
21:17;
Lev 19:3; 20:9
27:17
[a]Dt 19:14;
Pr 22:28
27:18
[b]Lev 19:14

[a]7 Traditionally *peace offerings*

[19]"Cursed is the man who withholds justice from the alien,[c] the fatherless or the widow."[d]

Then all the people shall say, "Amen!"

[20]"Cursed is the man who sleeps with his father's wife, for he dishonors his father's bed."[e]

Then all the people shall say, "Amen!"

[21]"Cursed is the man who has sexual relations with any animal."[f]

Then all the people shall say, "Amen!"

[22]"Cursed is the man who sleeps with his sister, the daughter of his father or the daughter of his mother."[g]

Then all the people shall say, "Amen!"

[23]"Cursed is the man who sleeps with his mother-in-law."[h]

Then all the people shall say, "Amen!"

[24]"Cursed is the man who kills[i] his neighbor secretly."

Then all the people shall say, "Amen!"

[25]"Cursed is the man who accepts a bribe to kill an innocent person."[j]

Then all the people shall say, "Amen!"

[26]"Cursed is the man who does not uphold the words of this law by carrying them out."[k]

Then all the people shall say, "Amen!"

Blessings for Obedience

28 If you fully obey the LORD your God and carefully follow all his commands[l] I give you today, the LORD your God will set you high above all the nations on earth.[m] [2]All these blessings will come upon you[n] and accompany you if you obey the LORD your God:

[3]You will be blessed[o] in the city and blessed in the country.[p]

[4]The fruit of your womb will be blessed, and the crops of your land and the young of your livestock—the calves of your herds and the lambs of your flocks.[q]

[5]Your basket and your kneading trough will be blessed.

[6]You will be blessed when you come in and blessed when you go out.[r]

[7]The LORD will grant that the enemies who rise up against you will be defeated before you. They will come at you from one direction but flee from you in seven.[s]

[8]The LORD will send a blessing on your barns and on everything you put your hand to. The LORD your God will bless you in the land he is giving you.

[9]The LORD will establish you as his holy people,[t] as he promised you on oath, if you keep the commands of the LORD your God and walk in his ways. [10]Then all the peoples on earth will see that you are called by the name[u] of the LORD, and they will fear you. [11]The LORD will grant you abundant prosperity—in the fruit of your womb, the young of your livestock and the crops of your ground—in the land he swore to your forefathers to give you.[v]

[12]The LORD will open the heavens, the storehouse of his bounty, to send rain[w] on your land in season and to bless all the work of your hands. You will lend to many nations but will borrow from none.[x]

27:19
c Ex 22:21;
Dt 24:19
d Dt 10:18
27:20
e Lev 18:7;
Dt 22:30
27:21
f Lev 18:23
27:22
g Lev 18:9;
20:17
27:23
h Lev 20:14
27:24
i Lev 24:17;
Nu 35:31
27:25
j Ex 23:7-8;
Dt 10:17;
Eze 22:12
27:26
k Jer 11:3;
Gal 3:10*
28:1
l Ex 15:26;
Lev 26:3;
Dt 7:12-26
m Dt 26:19
28:2
n Zec 1:6
28:3
o Ps 128:1,4
p Ge 39:5
28:4
q Ge 49:25;
Pr 10:22
28:6
r Ps 121:8
28:7
s Lev 26:8,17
28:9
t Ex 19:6; Dt 7:6
28:10
u 2Ch 7:14
28:11
v Dt 30:9;
Pr 10:22
28:12
w Lev 26:4
x Dt 15:3,6

[13]The LORD will make you the head, not the tail. If you pay attention to the commands of the LORD your God that I give you this day and carefully follow them, you will always be at the top, never at the bottom. [14]Do not turn aside from any of the commands I give you today, to the right or to the left,[y] following other gods and serving them.

Curses for Disobedience

[15]However, if you do not obey[z] the LORD your God and do not carefully follow all his commands and decrees I am giving you today, all these curses will come upon you and overtake you:[a]

[16]You will be cursed in the city and cursed in the country.
[17]Your basket and your kneading trough will be cursed.
[18]The fruit of your womb will be cursed, and the crops of your land, and the calves of your herds and the lambs of your flocks.
[19]You will be cursed when you come in and cursed when you go out.

[20]The LORD will send on you curses,[b] confusion and rebuke[c] in everything you put your hand to, until you are destroyed and come to sudden ruin[d] because of the evil you have done in forsaking him.[a] [21]The LORD will plague you with diseases until he has destroyed you from the land you are entering to possess.[e] [22]The LORD will strike you with wasting disease, with fever and inflammation, with scorching heat and drought,[f] with blight and mildew, which will plague you until you perish.[g] [23]The sky over your head will be bronze, the ground beneath you iron.[h] [24]The LORD will turn the rain of your country into dust and powder; it will come down from the skies until you are destroyed.

[25]The LORD will cause you to be defeated before your enemies. You will come at them from one direction but flee from them in seven,[i] and you will become a thing of horror to all the kingdoms on earth.[j] [26]Your carcasses will be food for all the birds of the air and the beasts of the earth, and there will be no one to frighten them away.[k] [27]The LORD will afflict you with the boils of Egypt[l] and with tumors, festering sores and the itch, from which you cannot be cured. [28]The LORD will afflict you with madness, blindness and confusion of mind. [29]At midday you will grope[m] about like a blind man in the dark. You will be unsuccessful in everything you do; day after day you will be oppressed and robbed, with no one to rescue you.

[30]You will be pledged to be married to a woman, but another will take her and ravish her.[n] You will build a house, but you will not live in it.[o] You will plant a vineyard, but you will not even begin to enjoy its fruit.[p] [31]Your ox will be slaughtered before your eyes, but you will eat none of it. Your donkey will be forcibly taken from you and will not be returned. Your sheep will be given to your enemies, and no one will rescue them. [32]Your sons and daughters will be given to another nation,[q] and you will wear out your eyes watching for them day after day, powerless to lift a hand. [33]A people that you do not know will eat what your land and labor produce, and you will have nothing but cruel

---

28:14
y Dt 5:32
28:15
z Lev 26:14
a Jos 23:15;
Da 9:11;
Mal 2:2
28:20
b Mal 2:2
c Isa 51:20;
66:15 d Dt 4:26
28:21
e Lev 26:25;
Jer 24:10
28:22
f Lev 26:16
g Am 4:9
28:23
h Lev 26:19
28:25
i Isa 30:17
j Jer 15:4; 24:9;
Eze 23:46
28:26
k Jer 7:33; 16:4;
34:20
28:27
l ver 60-61;
1Sa 5:6
28:29
m Job 5:14;
Isa 59:10
28:30
n Job 31:10;
Jer 8:10
o Am 5:11
p Jer 12:13
28:32
q ver 41

---

[a]20 Hebrew *me*

oppression all your days.ʳ ³⁴The sights you see will drive you mad. ³⁵The Lᴏʀᴅ will afflict your knees and legs with painful boilsˢ that cannot be cured, spreading from the soles of your feet to the top of your head.

³⁶The Lᴏʀᴅ will drive you and the kingᵗ you set over you to a nation unknown to you or your fathers.ᵘ There you will worship other gods, gods of wood and stone.ᵛ ³⁷You will become a thing of horror and an object of scorn and ridicule to all the nations where the Lᴏʀᴅ will drive you.ʷ

³⁸You will sow much seed in the field but you will harvest little,ˣ because locusts will devourʸ it. ³⁹You will plant vineyards and cultivate them but you will not drink the wine or gather the grapes, because worms will eat them.ᶻ ⁴⁰You will have olive trees throughout your country but you will not use the oil, because the olives will drop off.ᵃ ⁴¹You will have sons and daughters but you will not keep them, because they will go into captivity.ᵇ ⁴²Swarms of locusts will take over all your trees and the crops of your land.

⁴³The alien who lives among you will rise above you higher and higher, but you will sink lower and lower.ᶜ ⁴⁴He will lend to you, but you will not lend to him.ᵈ He will be the head, but you will be the tail.ᵉ

⁴⁵All these curses will come upon you. They will pursue you and overtake you until you are destroyed,ᶠ because you did not obey the Lᴏʀᴅ your God and observe the commands and decrees he gave you. ⁴⁶They will be a sign and a wonder to you and your descendants forever.ᵍ ⁴⁷Because you did not serveʰ the Lᴏʀᴅ your God joyfully and gladlyⁱ in the time of prosperity, ⁴⁸therefore in hunger and thirst, in nakedness and dire poverty, you will serve the enemies the Lᴏʀᴅ sends against you. He will put an iron yokeʲ on your neck until he has destroyed you.

⁴⁹The Lᴏʀᴅ will bring a nation against you from far away, from the ends of the earth,ᵏ like an eagleˡ swooping down, a nation whose language you will not understand, ⁵⁰a fierce-looking nation without respect for the oldᵐ or pity for the young. ⁵¹They will devour the young of your livestock and the crops of your land until you are destroyed. They will leave you no grain, new wine or oil, nor any calves of your herds or lambs of your flocks until you are ruined.ⁿ ⁵²They will lay siege to all the cities throughout your land until the high fortified walls in which you trust fall down. They will besiege all the cities throughout the land the Lᴏʀᴅ your God is giving you.ᵒ

⁵³Because of the suffering that your enemy will inflict on you during the siege, you will eat the fruit of the womb, the flesh of the sons and daughters the Lᴏʀᴅ your God has given you.ᵖ ⁵⁴Even the most gentle and sensitive man among you will have no compassion on his own brother or the wife he loves or his surviving children, ⁵⁵and he will not give to one of them any of the flesh of his children that he is eating. It will be all he has left because of the suffering your enemy will inflict on you during the siege of all your cities. ⁵⁶The most gentle and sensitive�q woman among you—so sensitive and gentle that she would not venture to touch the ground with the sole of her foot—will begrudge the husband she loves and her own son or daughter ⁵⁷the afterbirth from her womb and the children she bears. For she intends to eat them

28:33
ʳJer 5:15-17
28:35
ˢver 27
28:36
ᵗ2Ki 17:4,6;
24:12,14; 25:7,
11 ᵘJer 16:13
ᵛDt 4:28
28:37
ʷJer 24:9
28:38
ˣMic 6:15;
Hag 1:6,9
ʸJoel 1:4
28:39
ᶻIsa 5:10;
17:10-11
28:40
ᵃMic 6:15
28:41
ᵇver 32
28:43
ᶜver 13
28:44
ᵈver 12 ᵉver 13
28:45
ᶠver 15
28:46
ᵍIsa 8:18;
Eze 14:8
28:47
ʰDt 32:15
ⁱNe 9:35
28:48
ʲJer 28:13-14
28:49
ᵏJer 5:15; 6:22
ˡLa 4:19;
Hos 8:1
28:50
ᵐIsa 47:6
28:51
ⁿver 33
28:52
ᵒJer 10:18;
Zep 1:14-16,17
28:53
ᵖLev 26:29;
2Ki 6:28-29;
Jer 19:9;
La 2:20; 4:10
28:56
qver 54

secretly during the siege and in the distress that your enemy will inflict on you in your cities.

58If you do not carefully follow all the words of this law, which are written in this book, and do not revere[r] this glorious and awesome name[s]—the Lord your God— 59the Lord will send fearful plagues on you and your descendants, harsh and prolonged disasters, and severe and lingering illnesses. 60He will bring upon you all the diseases of Egypt[t] that you dreaded, and they will cling to you. 61The Lord will also bring on you every kind of sickness and disaster not recorded in this Book of the Law, until you are destroyed.[u] 62You who were as numerous as the stars in the sky[v] will be left but few in number, because you did not obey the Lord your God. 63Just as it pleased[w] the Lord to make you prosper and increase in number, so it will please[x] him to ruin and destroy you. You will be uprooted[y] from the land you are entering to possess.

64Then the Lord will scatter[z] you among all nations,[a] from one end of the earth to the other. There you will worship other gods—gods of wood and stone, which neither you nor your fathers have known. 65Among those nations you will find no repose, no resting place for the sole of your foot. There the Lord will give you an anxious mind, eyes weary with longing, and a despairing heart.[b] 66You will live in constant suspense, filled with dread both night and day, never sure of your life. 67In the morning you will say, "If only it were evening!" and in the evening, "If only it were morning!"—because of the terror that will fill your hearts and the sights that your eyes will see.[c] 68The Lord will send you back in ships to Egypt on a journey I said you should never make again. There you will offer yourselves for sale to your enemies as male and female slaves, but no one will buy you.

Renewal of the Covenant

29 These are the terms of the covenant the Lord commanded Moses to make with the Israelites in Moab, in addition to the covenant he had made with them at Horeb.[d]

2Moses summoned all the Israelites and said to them:

Your eyes have seen all that the Lord did in Egypt to Pharaoh, to all his officials and to all his land.[e] 3With your own eyes you saw those great trials, those miraculous signs and great wonders.[f] 4But to this day the Lord has not given you a mind that understands or eyes that see or ears that hear.[g] 5During the forty years that I led you through the desert, your clothes did not wear out, nor did the sandals on your feet.[h] 6You ate no bread and drank no wine or other fermented drink. I did this so that you might know that I am the Lord your God.[i]

7When you reached this place, Sihon[j] king of Heshbon and Og king of Bashan came out to fight against us, but we defeated them.[k] 8We took their land and gave it as an inheritance to the Reubenites, the Gadites and the half-tribe of Manasseh.[l]

9Carefully follow[m] the terms of this covenant, so that you may prosper in everything you do.[n] 10All of you are standing today in the presence of the Lord your God—your leaders and chief men, your elders and officials, and all the other men of Israel, 11together with your children and your wives, and the aliens living in your camps who chop

28:58
rMal 1:14
sEx 6:3
28:60
tver 27
28:61
uDt 4:25-26
28:62
vDt 4:27;
10:22; Ne 9:23
28:63
wJer 32:41
xPr 1:26
yJer 12:14; 45:4
28:64
zLev 26:33;
Dt 4:27 aNe 1:8
28:65
bLev 26:16,36
28:67
cver 34; Job 7:4
29:1
dDt 5:2-3
29:2
eEx 19:4
29:3
fDt 4:34; 7:19
29:4
gIsa 6:10;
Ac 28:26-27;
Ro 11:8*;
Eph 4:18
29:5
hDt 8:4
29:6
iDt 8:3
29:7
jDt 2:32; 3:1
kNu 21:21-24,
33-35
29:8
lNu 32:33;
Dt 3:12-13
29:9
mDt 4:6;
Jos 1:7 n1Ki 2:3

your wood and carry your water.° ¹²You are standing here in order to enter into a covenant with the LORD your God, a covenant the LORD is making with you this day and sealing with an oath, ¹³to confirm you this day as his people,ᵖ that he may be your God�q as he promised you and as he swore to your fathers, Abraham, Isaac and Jacob. ¹⁴I am making this covenant,ʳ with its oath, not only with you ¹⁵who are standing here with us today in the presence of the LORD our God but also with those who are not here today.ˢ

¹⁶You yourselves know how we lived in Egypt and how we passed through the countries on the way here. ¹⁷You saw among them their detestable images and idols of wood and stone, of silver and gold.ᵗ ¹⁸Make sure there is no man or woman, clan or tribe among you today whose heart turns away from the LORD our God to go and worship the gods of those nations; make sure there is no root among you that produces such bitter poison.ᵘ

¹⁹When such a person hears the words of this oath, he invokes a blessing on himself and therefore thinks, "I will be safe, even though I persist in going my own way." This will bring disaster on the watered land as well as the dry.ᵃ ²⁰The LORD will never be willing to forgive him; his wrath and zealᵛ will burnʷ against that man. All the curses written in this book will fall upon him, and the LORD will blotˣ out his name from under heaven. ²¹The LORD will single him out from all the tribes of Israel for disaster, according to all the curses of the covenant written in this Book of the Law.

²²Your children who follow you in later generations and foreigners who come from distant lands will see the calamities that have fallen on the land and the diseases with which the LORD has afflicted it.ʸ ²³The whole land will be a burning wasteᶻ of saltᵃ and sulfur—nothing planted, nothing sprouting, no vegetation growing on it. It will be like the destruction of Sodom and Gomorrah,ᵇ Admah and Zeboiim, which the LORD overthrew in fierce anger. ²⁴All the nations will ask: "Why has the LORD done this to this land?ᶜ Why this fierce, burning anger?"

²⁵And the answer will be: "It is because this people abandoned the covenant of the LORD, the God of their fathers, the covenant he made with them when he brought them out of Egypt. ²⁶They went off and worshiped other gods and bowed down to them, gods they did not know, gods he had not given them. ²⁷Therefore the LORD's anger burned against this land, so that he brought on it all the curses written in this book.ᵈ ²⁸In furious anger and in great wrath the LORD uprootedᵉ them from their land and thrust them into another land, as it is now."

²⁹The secret things belong to the LORD our God, but the things revealed belong to us and to our children forever, that we may follow all the words of this law.

Prosperity After Turning to the LORD

30 When all these blessings and cursesᶠ I have set before you come upon you and you take them to heart wherever the LORD your God disperses you among the nations,ᵍ ²and when you and your children returnʰ to the LORD your God and obey him with all your heart and with all your soul according to everything I command you today,

---

ᵃ19 Or *way, in order to add drunkenness to thirst."*

29:11
ᵒJos 9:21,23,27
29:13
ᵖDt 28:9
qGe 17:7;
Ex 6:7
29:14
ʳJer 31:31
29:15
ˢAc 2:39
29:17
ᵗDt 28:36
29:18
ᵘDt 11:16;
Heb 12:15
29:20
ᵛEze 23:25
ʷPs 74:1; 79:5
ˣEx 32:33;
Dt 9:14
29:22
ʸJer 19:8
29:23
ᶻIsa 34:9
ᵃJer 17:6
ᵇGe 19:24,25;
Zep 2:9
29:24
ᶜ1Ki 9:8;
Jer 22:8-9
29:27
ᵈDa 9:11,13,14
29:28
ᵉ1Ki 14:15;
2Ch 7:20;
Ps 52:5; Pr 2:22
30:1
ᶠver 15,19;
Dt 11:26
gLev 26:40-45;
Dt 28:64;
29:28; 1Ki 8:47
30:2
ʰDt 4:30;
Ne 1:9

[3]then the LORD your God will restore your fortunes[a][i] and have compassion on you and gather[j] you again from all the nations where he scattered you.[k] [4]Even if you have been banished to the most distant land under the heavens, from there the LORD your God will gather you and bring you back.[l] [5]He will bring[m] you to the land that belonged to your fathers, and you will take possession of it. He will make you more prosperous and numerous than your fathers. [6]The LORD your God will circumcise your hearts and the hearts of your descendants,[n] so that you may love him with all your heart and with all your soul, and live. [7]The LORD your God will put all these curses on your enemies who hate and persecute you.[o] [8]You will again obey the LORD and follow all his commands I am giving you today. [9]Then the LORD your God will make you most prosperous in all the work of your hands and in the fruit of your womb, the young of your livestock and the crops of your land.[p] The LORD will again delight in you and make you prosperous, just as he delighted in your fathers, [10]if you obey the LORD your God and keep his commands and decrees that are written in this Book of the Law and turn to the LORD your God with all your heart and with all your soul.[q]

The Offer of Life or Death

[11]Now what I am commanding you today is not too difficult for you or beyond your reach.[r] [12]It is not up in heaven, so that you have to ask, "Who will ascend into heaven to get it and proclaim it to us so we may obey it?"[s] [13]Nor is it beyond the sea, so that you have to ask, "Who will cross the sea to get it and proclaim it to us so we may obey it?" [14]No, the word is very near you; it is in your mouth and in your heart so you may obey it.

[15]See, I set before you today life and prosperity, death and destruction.[t] [16]For I command you today to love the LORD your God, to walk in his ways, and to keep his commands, decrees and laws; then you will live and increase, and the LORD your God will bless you in the land you are entering to possess.

[17]But if your heart turns away and you are not obedient, and if you are drawn away to bow down to other gods and worship them, [18]I declare to you this day that you will certainly be destroyed.[u] You will not live long in the land you are crossing the Jordan to enter and possess.

[19]This day I call heaven and earth as witnesses against you[v] that I have set before you life and death, blessings and curses.[w] Now choose life, so that you and your children may live [20]and that you may love[x] the LORD your God, listen to his voice, and hold fast to him. For the LORD is your life,[y] and he will give you many years in the land he swore to give to your fathers, Abraham, Isaac and Jacob.

Joshua to Succeed Moses

31 Then Moses went out and spoke these words to all Israel: [2]"I am now a hundred and twenty years old[z] and I am no longer able to lead you.[a] The LORD has said to me, 'You shall not cross the Jordan.'[b] [3]The LORD your God himself will cross[c] over ahead of you.[d] He will destroy these nations before you, and you will take possession of their

30:3
iPs 126:4
jPs 147:2;
Jer 32:37;
Eze 34:13
kJer 29:14
30:4
lNe 1:8-9;
Isa 43:6
30:5
mJer 29:14
30:6
nDt 10:16;
Jer 32:39
30:7
oDt 7:15
30:9
pDt 28:11;
Jer 31:28; 32:41
30:10
qDt 4:29
30:11
rIsa 45:19,23
30:12
sRo 10:6*
30:15
tDt 11:26
30:18
uDt 8:19
30:19
vDt 4:26 wver 1
30:20
xDt 6:5; 10:20
yPs 27:1;
Jn 11:25
31:2
zDt 34:7
aNu 27:17;
1Ki 3:7
bDt 3:23,26
31:3
cNu 27:18
dDt 9:3

---

[a]3 Or *will bring you back from captivity*

land. Joshua also will cross[e] over ahead of you, as the LORD said. [4]And the LORD will do to them what he did to Sihon and Og, the kings of the Amorites, whom he destroyed along with their land. [5]The LORD will deliver[f] them to you, and you must do to them all that I have commanded you. [6]Be strong and courageous.[g] Do not be afraid or terrified[h] because of them, for the LORD your God goes with you;[i] he will never leave you[j] nor forsake[k] you."

[7]Then Moses summoned Joshua and said[l] to him in the presence of all Israel, "Be strong and courageous, for you must go with this people into the land that the LORD swore to their forefathers to give them, and you must divide it among them as their inheritance. [8]The LORD himself goes before you and will be with you;[m] he will never leave you nor forsake you. Do not be afraid; do not be discouraged."

The Reading of the Law

[9]So Moses wrote down this law and gave it to the priests, the sons of Levi, who carried[n] the ark of the covenant of the LORD, and to all the elders of Israel. [10]Then Moses commanded them: "At the end of every seven years, in the year for canceling debts,[o] during the Feast of Tabernacles,[p] [11]when all Israel comes to appear[q] before the LORD your God at the place he will choose, you shall read this law[r] before them in their hearing. [12]Assemble the people—men, women and children, and the aliens living in your towns—so they can listen and learn[s] to fear the LORD your God and follow carefully all the words of this law. [13]Their children,[t] who do not know this law, must hear it and learn to fear the LORD your God as long as you live in the land you are crossing the Jordan to possess."

Israel's Rebellion Predicted

[14]The LORD said to Moses, "Now the day of your death[u] is near. Call Joshua and present yourselves at the Tent of Meeting, where I will commission him." So Moses and Joshua came and presented themselves at the Tent of Meeting.

[15]Then the LORD appeared at the Tent in a pillar of cloud, and the cloud stood over the entrance to the Tent.[v] [16]And the LORD said to Moses: "You are going to rest with your fathers, and these people will soon prostitute[w] themselves to the foreign gods of the land they are entering. They will forsake[x] me and break the covenant I made with them. [17]On that day I will become angry[y] with them and forsake[z] them; I will hide[a] my face from them, and they will be destroyed. Many disasters and difficulties will come upon them, and on that day they will ask, 'Have not these disasters come upon us because our God is not with us?'[b] [18]And I will certainly hide my face on that day because of all their wickedness in turning to other gods.

[19]"Now write down for yourselves this song and teach it to the Israelites and have them sing it, so that it may be a witness for me against them. [20]When I have brought them into the land flowing with milk and honey, the land I promised on oath to their forefathers,[c] and when they eat their fill and thrive, they will turn to other gods[d] and worship them, rejecting me and breaking my covenant.[e] [21]And when many disasters and difficulties come upon them,[f] this song will testify against them, because it will not be forgotten by their descendants. I

31:3
eDt 3:28
31:5
fDt 7:2
31:6
gJos 10:25;
1Ch 22:13
hDt 7:18
iDt 1:29; 20:4
jJos 1:5
kHeb 13:5*
31:7
lDt 1:38; 3:28
31:8
mEx 13:21;
33:14
31:9
nver 25;
Nu 4:15;
Jos 3:3
31:10
oDt 15:1
pLev 23:34
31:11
qDt 16:16
rJos 8:34-35;
2Ki 23:2
31:12
sDt 4:10
31:13
tDt 11:2;
Ps 78:6-7
31:14
uNu 27:13;
Dt 32:49-50
31:15
vEx 33:9
31:16
wJdg 2:12
xJdg 10:6,13
31:17
yJdg 2:14,20
zJdg 6:13;
2Ch 15:2
aDt 32:20;
Isa 1:15; 8:17
bNu 14:42
31:20
cDt 6:10-12
dDt 32:15-17
ever 16
31:21
fver 17

know what they are disposed to do,⁸ even before I bring them into the land I promised them on oath." ²²So Moses wroteʰ down this song that day and taught it to the Israelites.

²³The LORD gave this commandⁱ to Joshua son of Nun: "Be strong and courageous,ʲ for you will bring the Israelites into the land I promised them on oath, and I myself will be with you."

²⁴After Moses finished writing in a book the words of this law from beginning to end, ²⁵he gave this command to the Levites who carried the ark of the covenant of the LORD: ²⁶"Take this Book of the Law and place it beside the ark of the covenant of the LORD your God. There it will remain as a witness against you.ᵏ ²⁷For I know how rebellious and stiff-neckedˡ you are. If you have been rebellious against the LORD while I am still alive and with you, how much more will you rebel after I die! ²⁸Assemble before me all the elders of your tribes and all your officials, so that I can speak these words in their hearing and call heaven and earth to testify against them.ᵐ ²⁹For I know that after my death you are sure to become utterly corruptⁿ and to turn from the way I have commanded you. In days to come, disasterᵒ will fall upon you because you will do evil in the sight of the LORD and provoke him to anger by what your hands have made."

The Song of Moses

³⁰And Moses recited the words of this song from beginning to end in the hearing of the whole assembly of Israel:

32 Listen, O heavens,ᵖ and I will speak;
      hear, O earth, the words of my mouth.
  ²Let my teaching fall like rain
      and my words descend like dew, q
  like showersʳ on new grass,
      like abundant rain on tender plants.

  ³I will proclaim the name of the LORD.ˢ
      Oh, praise the greatnessᵗ of our God!
  ⁴He is the Rock,ᵘ his works are perfect,ᵛ
      and all his ways are just.
  A faithful Godʷ who does no wrong,
      upright and just is he.

  ⁵They have acted corruptly toward him;
      to their shame they are no longer his children,
      but a warped and crooked generation.ᵃ ˣ
  ⁶Is this the way you repayʸ the LORD,
      O foolish and unwise people?ᶻ
  Is he not your Father,ᵃ your Creator,ᵇ
      who made you and formed you?ᵇ

  ⁷Remember the days of old;
      consider the generations long past.
  Ask your father and he will tell you,
      your elders, and they will explain to you.ᶜ

31:21
gHos 5:3
31:22
hver 19
31:23
iver 7 jJos 1:6
31:26
kver 19
31:27
lEx 32:9;
Dt 9:6,24
31:28
mDt 4:26;
30:19; 32:1
31:29
nDt 32:5;
Jdg 2:19
oDt 28:15
32:1
pIsa 1:2
32:2
qIsa 55:11
rPs 72:6
32:3
sEx 33:19
tDt 3:24
32:4
uver 15,18,30
v2Sa 22:31
wDt 7:9
32:5
xDt 31:29
32:6
yPs 116:12
zPs 74:2
aDt 1:31;
Isa 63:16
bver 15
32:7
cEx 13:14

ᵃ5 Or *Corrupt are they and not his children, / a generation warped and twisted to their shame*   ᵇ6 Or *Father, who bought you*

⁸When the Most High gave the nations their inheritance,
    when he divided all mankind,ᵈ
  he set up boundaries for the peoples
    according to the number of the sons of Israel.ᵃ
⁹For the LORD's portionᵉ is his people,
    Jacob his allotted inheritance.ᶠ

¹⁰In a desertᵍ land he found him,
    in a barren and howling waste.
  He shielded him and cared for him;
    he guarded him as the apple of his eye,ʰ
¹¹like an eagle that stirs up its nest
    and hovers over its young,ⁱ
  that spreads its wings to catch them
    and carries them on its pinions.
¹²The LORD alone led him;
    no foreign god was with him.ʲ

¹³He made him ride on the heightsᵏ of the land
    and fed him with the fruit of the fields.
  He nourished him with honey from the rock,
    and with oilˡ from the flinty crag,
¹⁴with curds and milk from herd and flock
    and with fattened lambs and goats,
  with choice rams of Bashan
    and the finest kernels of wheat.ᵐ
  You drank the foaming blood of the grape.ⁿ

¹⁵Jeshurunᵇ grew fatᵒ and kicked;
    filled with food, he became heavy and sleek.
  He abandonedᵖ the God who made him
    and rejected the Rock�q his Savior.
¹⁶They made him jealousʳ with their foreign gods
    and angeredˢ him with their detestable idols.
¹⁷They sacrificed to demons, which are not God—
    gods they had not known,ᵗ
  gods that recently appeared,ᵘ
    gods your fathers did not fear.
¹⁸You deserted the Rock, who fathered you;
    you forgotᵛ the God who gave you birth.

¹⁹The LORD saw this and rejected themʷ
    because he was angered by his sons and daughters.ˣ
²⁰"I will hide my faceʸ from them," he said,
    "and see what their end will be;
  for they are a perverse generation,ᶻ
    children who are unfaithful.
²¹They made me jealousᵃ by what is no god
    and angered me with their worthless idols.ᵇ

32:8
dGe 11:8;
Ac 17:26
32:9
eJer 10:16
f1Ki 8:51,53
32:10
gJer 2:6
hPs 17:8;
Zec 2:8
32:11
iEx 19:4
32:12
jver 39
32:13
kIsa 58:14
lJob 29:6
32:14
mPs 81:16;
147:14
nGe 49:11
32:15
oDt 31:20
pver 6; Isa 1:4,
28 qver 4
32:16
r1Co 10:22
sPs 78:58
32:17
tDt 28:64
uJdg 5:8
32:18
vIsa 17:10
32:19
wJer 44:21-23
xPs 106:40
32:20
yDt 31:17,29
zver 5
32:21
a1Co 10:22
b1Ki 16:13,26

ᵃ8 Masoretic Text; Dead Sea Scrolls (see also Septuagint) *sons of God*   ᵇ15 *Jeshurun* means *the upright one,* that is, Israel.

I will make them envious by those who are not a people;
I will make them angry by a nation that has no
understanding. [c]

[22]For a fire has been kindled by my wrath,
one that burns to the realm of death[a] below. [d]
It will devour the earth and its harvests
and set afire the foundations of the mountains.

[23]"I will heap calamities[e] upon them
and spend my arrows[f] against them.
[24]I will send wasting famine against them,
consuming pestilence[g] and deadly plague;[h]
I will send against them the fangs of wild beasts, [i]
the venom of vipers[j] that glide in the dust.
[25]In the street the sword will make them childless;
in their homes terror will reign.[k]
Young men and young women will perish,
infants and gray-haired men. [l]
[26]I said I would scatter[m] them
and blot out their memory from mankind, [n]
[27]but I dreaded the taunt of the enemy,
lest the adversary misunderstand
and say, 'Our hand has triumphed;
the LORD has not done all this.' "[o]

[28]They are a nation without sense,
there is no discernment in them.
[29]If only they were wise and would understand
this[p]
and discern what their end will be!
[30]How could one man chase a thousand,
or two put ten thousand to flight, [q]
unless their Rock had sold them,
unless the LORD had given them up?[r]
[31]For their rock is not like our Rock,
as even our enemies concede.
[32]Their vine comes from the vine of Sodom
and from the fields of Gomorrah.
Their grapes are filled with poison,
and their clusters with bitterness.
[33]Their wine is the venom of serpents,
the deadly poison of cobras. [s]

[34]"Have I not kept this in reserve
and sealed it in my vaults?[t]
[35]It is mine to avenge; I will repay. [u]
In due time their foot will slip;[v]
their day of disaster is near
and their doom rushes upon them. [w]"

[36]The LORD will judge his people

32:21
cRo 10:19*
32:22
dPs 18:7-8;
Jer 15:14;
La 4:11
32:23
eDt 29:21
fPs 7:13;
Eze 5:16
32:24
gDt 28:22
hPs 91:6
iLev 26:22
jAm 5:18-19
32:25
kEze 7:15
l2Ch 36:17;
La 2:21
32:26
mDt 4:27
nPs 34:16
32:27
oIsa 10:13
32:29
pDt 5:29;
Ps 81:13
32:30
qLev 26:8
rPs 44:12
32:33
sPs 58:4
32:34
tJer 2:22;
Hos 13:12
32:35
uRo 12:19*;
Heb 10:30*
vJer 23:12
wEze 7:8-9

[a]22 Hebrew *to Sheol*

and have compassion on his servants[x]
when he sees their strength is gone
and no one is left, slave or free.
[37]He will say: "Now where are their gods,
the rock they took refuge in,[y]
[38]the gods who ate the fat of their sacrifices
and drank the wine of their drink offerings?
Let them rise up to help you!
Let them give you shelter!

[39]"See now that I myself am He![z]
There is no god besides me.[a]
I put to death and I bring to life,[b]
I have wounded and I will heal,[c]
and no one can deliver out of my hand.[d]
[40]I lift my hand to heaven and declare:
As surely as I live forever,
[41]when I sharpen my flashing sword[e]
and my hand grasps it in judgment,
I will take vengeance on my adversaries
and repay those who hate me.[f]
[42]I will make my arrows drunk with blood,[g]
while my sword devours flesh:[h]
the blood of the slain and the captives,
the heads of the enemy leaders."

[43]Rejoice,[i] O nations, with his people,[a,b]
for he will avenge the blood of his servants;[j]
he will take vengeance on his enemies
and make atonement for his land and people.[k]

[44]Moses came with Joshua[c1] son of Nun and spoke all the words of this song in the hearing of the people. [45]When Moses finished reciting all these words to all Israel, [46]he said to them, "Take to heart all the words I have solemnly declared to you this day,[m] so that you may command your children to obey carefully all the words of this law. [47]They are not just idle words for you—they are your life.[n] By them you will live long in the land you are crossing the Jordan to possess."

Moses to Die on Mount Nebo

[48]On that same day the LORD told Moses, [49]"Go up into the Abarim[o] Range to Mount Nebo in Moab, across from Jericho, and view Canaan, the land I am giving the Israelites as their own possession. [50]There on the mountain that you have climbed you will die[p] and be gathered to your people, just as your brother Aaron died on Mount Hor and was gathered to his people. [51]This is because both of you broke faith with me in the presence of the Israelites at the waters of Meribah Kadesh in the Desert of Zin[q] and because you did not uphold my holiness among the Israelites.[r] [52]Therefore, you will see the land only from a distance;[s] you will not enter[t] the land I am giving to the people of Israel."

32:36
x Dt 30:1-3;
Ps 135:14;
Joel 2:14
32:37
y Jdg 10:14;
Jer 2:28
32:39
z Isa 41:4
a Isa 45:5
b 1Sa 2:6;
Ps 68:20
c Hos 6:1
d Ps 50:22
32:41
e Isa 34:6;
66:16;
Eze 21:9-10
f Jer 50:29
32:42
g ver 23
h Jer 46:10,14
32:43
i Ro 15:10*
j 2Ki 9:7
k Ps 65:3; 85:1;
Rev 19:2
32:44
l Nu 13:8,16
32:46
m Eze 40:4
32:47
n Dt 30:20
32:49
o Nu 27:12
32:50
p Ge 25:8
32:51
q Nu 20:11-13
r Nu 27:14
32:52
s Dt 34:1-3
t Dt 1:37

---

a43 Or *Make his people rejoice, O nations*   b43 Masoretic Text; Dead Sea Scrolls (see also Septuagint) *people, / and let all the angels worship him /*   c44 Hebrew *Hoshea,* a variant of *Joshua*

Moses Blesses the Tribes

33:1–29Ref — Ge 49:1–28

33 This is the blessing that Moses the man of God[u] pronounced on the Israelites before his death. [2]He said:

"The LORD came from Sinai[v]
    and dawned over them from Seir;[w]
    he shone forth from Mount Paran.[x]
He came with[a] myriads of holy ones[y]
    from the south, from his mountain slopes.[b]
    [3]Surely it is you who love[z] the people;
    all the holy ones are in your hand.[a]
At your feet they all bow down,[b]
    and from you receive instruction,
    [4]the law that Moses gave us,[c]
    the possession of the assembly of Jacob.[d]
    [5]He was king over Jeshurun[e]
    when the leaders of the people assembled,
    along with the tribes of Israel.

[6]"Let Reuben live and not die,
    nor[d] his men be few."

[7]And this he said about Judah:[e]

"Hear, O LORD, the cry of Judah;
    bring him to his people.
With his own hands he defends his cause.
    Oh, be his help against his foes!"

[8]About Levi he said:

"Your Thummim and Urim[f] belong
    to the man you favored.
You tested him at Massah;
    you contended with him at the waters of
        Meribah.[g]
    [9]He said of his father and mother,[h]
    'I have no regard for them.'
He did not recognize his brothers
    or acknowledge his own children,
but he watched over your word
    and guarded your covenant.[i]
    [10]He teaches your precepts to Jacob
    and your law to Israel.[j]
He offers incense before you
    and whole burnt offerings on your altar.[k]
    [11]Bless all his skills, O LORD,
    and be pleased with the work of his hands.[l]

33:1
u Jos 14:6
33:2
v Ex 19:18;
Ps 68:8
w Jdg 5:4
x Hab 3:3
y Da 7:10;
Ac 7:53;
Rev 5:11
33:3
z Hos 11:1
a Dt 14:2
b Lk 10:39
33:4
c Jn 1:17
d Ps 119:111
33:7
e Ge 49:10
33:8
f Ex 28:30
g Ex 17:7
33:9
h Ex 32:26-29
i Mal 2:5
33:10
j Lev 10:11;
Dt 31:9-13
k Ps 51:19
33:11
l 2Sa 24:23

---

a2 Or *from*   b2 The meaning of the Hebrew for this phrase is uncertain.   c5 *Jeshurun* means *the upright one,* that is, Israel; also in verse 26.   d6 Or *but let*

Smite the loins of those who rise up against him;
    strike his foes till they rise no more."

12About Benjamin he said:

"Let the beloved of the LORD rest secure in him, m
    for he shields him all day long,
and the one the LORD loves rests between his
    shoulders. n"

13About Joseph o he said:

"May the LORD bless his land
    with the precious dew from heaven above
    and with the deep waters that lie below; p
14with the best the sun brings forth
    and the finest the moon can yield;
15with the choicest gifts of the ancient mountains q
    and the fruitfulness of the everlasting hills;
16with the best gifts of the earth and its fullness
    and the favor of him who dwelt in the burning
       bush. r
Let all these rest on the head of Joseph,
    on the brow of the prince among a his brothers.
17In majesty he is like a firstborn bull;
    his horns are the horns of a wild ox. s
With them he will gore t the nations,
    even those at the ends of the earth.
Such are the ten thousands of Ephraim;
    such are the thousands of Manasseh."

18About Zebulun u he said:

"Rejoice, Zebulun, in your going out,
    and you, Issachar, in your tents.
19They will summon peoples to the mountain v
    and there offer sacrifices of righteousness; w
they will feast on the abundance of the seas, x
    on the treasures hidden in the sand."

20About Gad y he said:

"Blessed is he who enlarges Gad's domain!
Gad lives there like a lion,
    tearing at arm or head.
21He chose the best land for himself; z
    the leader's portion was kept for him.
When the heads of the people assembled,
    he carried out the LORD's righteous will, a
    and his judgments concerning Israel."

22About Dan b he said:

"Dan is a lion's cub,
    springing out of Bashan."

a16 Or *of the one separated from*

33:12
mDt 12:10
nEx 28:12
33:13
oGe 49:25
pGe 27:28
33:15
qHab 3:6
33:16
rEx 3:2
33:17
sNu 23:22
t1Ki 22:11;
Ps 44:5
33:18
uGe 49:13-15
33:19
vEx 15:17;
Isa 2:3 wPs 4:5
xIsa 60:5,11
33:20
yGe 49:19
33:21
zNu 32:1-5,
31-32 aJos 4:12;
22:1-3
33:22
bGe 49:16

23About Naphtali he said:

"Naphtali is abounding with the favor of the Lord
  and is full of his blessing;
  he will inherit southward to the lake."

24About Asherᶜ he said:

"Most blessed of sons is Asher;
  let him be favored by his brothers,
  and let him bathe his feet in oil. ᵈ
25The bolts of your gates will be iron and bronze,
  and your strength will equal your days. ᵉ

26"There is no one like the God of Jeshurun, ᶠ
  who rides on the heavens to help youᵍ
  and on the clouds in his majesty.
27The eternal God is your refuge, ʰ
  and underneath are the everlasting arms.
He will drive out your enemy before you, ⁱ
  saying, 'Destroy him!'ʲ
28So Israel will live in safety alone;ᵏ
  Jacob's spring is secure
in a land of grain and new wine,
  where the heavens drop dew.ˡ
29Blessed are you, O Israel!ᵐ
  Who is like you,ⁿ
  a people saved by the Lord?ᵒ
He is your shield and helperᵖ
  and your glorious sword.
Your enemies will cower before you,
  and you will trample down their high places.ᵃ ᑫ"

The Death of Moses

34 Then Moses climbed Mount Nebo from the plains of Moab to the top of Pisgah, across from Jericho.ʳ There the Lord showedˢ him the whole land—from Gilead to Dan, 2all of Naphtali, the territory of Ephraim and Manasseh, all the land of Judah as far as the western sea,ᵇᵗ 3the Negev and the whole region from the Valley of Jericho, the City of Palms,ᵘ as far as Zoar. 4Then the Lord said to him, "This is the land I promised on oathᵛ to Abraham, Isaac and Jacob when I said, 'I will give itʷ to your descendants.' I have let you see it with your eyes, but you will not crossˣ over into it."

5And Moses the servant of the Lordʸ diedᶻ there in Moab, as the Lord had said. 6He buried himᶜ in Moab, in the valley opposite Beth Peor,ᵃ but to this day no one knows where his grave is. ᵇ 7Moses was a hundred and twenty years oldᶜ when he died, yet his eyes were not weakᵈ nor his strength gone. 8The Israelites grieved for Moses in the plains of Moab thirty days, until the time of weeping and mourningᵉ was over.

9Now Joshua son of Nun was filled with the spiritᵈ of wisdomᶠ

ᵃ29 Or *will tread upon their bodies*   ᵇ2 That is, the Mediterranean   ᶜ6 Or *He was buried*
ᵈ9 Or *Spirit*

33:24
cGe 49:21
dGe 49:20;
Job 29:6
33:25
eDt 4:40; 32:47
33:26
fEx 15:11
gPs 104:3
33:27
hPs 90:1
iJos 24:18
jDt 7:2
33:28
kNu 23:9;
Jer 23:6
lGe 27:28
33:29
mPs 144:15
nPs 18:44
o2Sa 7:23
pPs 115:9-11
qDt 32:13
34:1
rDt 32:49
sDt 32:52
34:2
tDt 11:24
34:3
uJdg 1:16;
3:13; 2Ch 28:15
34:4
vGe 28:13
wGe 12:7
xDt 3:27
34:5
yNu 12:7
zDt 32:50;
Jos 1:1-2
34:6
aDt 3:29
bJude 1:9
34:7
cDt 31:2
dGe 27:1
34:8
eGe 50:3,10;
2Sa 11:27
34:9
fGe 41:38;
Isa 11:2; Da 6:3

because Moses had laid his hands on him. **g** So the Israelites listened to him and did what the LORD had commanded Moses.

10Since then, no prophet has risen in Israel like Moses, **h** whom the LORD knew face to face, **i** 11who did all those miraculous signs and wonders **j** the LORD sent him to do in Egypt—to Pharaoh and to all his officials **k** and to his whole land. 12For no one has ever shown the mighty power or performed the awesome deeds that Moses did in the sight of all Israel.

34:9
gNu 27:18,23
34:10
hDt 18:15,18
iEx 33:11;
Nu 12:6,8;
Dt 5:4
34:11
jDt 4:34
kDt 7:19

Joshua

Title and Background

This book is named after its leading character, Joshua, whom God named as Israel's leader before Moses' death. Where Deuteronomy ends, the book of Joshua begins—with the tribes still camped on the east side of the Jordan River.

Author and Date of Writing

The earliest Jewish traditions (Talmud) claim that Joshua wrote his own book except for the final section about his funeral, which is assigned to Eleazar son of Aaron. Others think that Samuel may have shaped or compiled the materials of the book. However, we have no sure knowledge of who the author was. The book of Joshua was written sometime before 1000 B.C.

Theme and Message

The theme of the book is the establishment of Israel in the promised land. With God's help the people crossed the Jordan River and took possession of all the main areas of Canaan. Toward the end of the book Joshua reminded the people of God's covenant promises to them and instructed them to keep on loving and obeying God.

Outline

   I. Preparation for Possession of Canaan (1:1-5:12)
  II. The Conquest of Canaan (5:13-12:24)
 III. The Division of Land by Tribes (13:1-21:45)
  IV. Farewell and Death of Joshua (22:1-24:33)

The LORD Commands Joshua

1 After the death of Moses the servant of the LORD,ᵃ the LORD said to Joshuaᵇ son of Nun, Moses' aide: ²"Moses my servant is dead. Now then, you and all these people, get ready to cross the Jordan Riverᶜ into the land I am about to give to them—to the Israelites. ³I will give you every place where you set your foot,ᵈ as I promised Moses. ⁴Your territory will extend from the desert to Lebanon, and from the great river, the Euphratesᵉ—all the Hittite country—to the Great Seaᵃ on the west.ᶠ ⁵No one will be able to stand up against youᵍ all the days of your life. As I was withʰ Moses, so I will be with you; I will never leave you nor forsakeⁱ you.

⁶"Be strong and courageous, because you will lead these people to inherit the land I swore to their forefathersʲ to give them. ⁷Be strong and very courageous. Be careful to obey all the law my servant Moses gave you; do not turn from it to the right or to the left,ᵏ that you may be successful wherever you go.ˡ ⁸Do not let this Book of the Law depart from your mouth; meditate on it day and night, so that you may be careful to do everything written in it. Then you will be prosperous and

1:1
aNu 12:7;
Dt 34:5
bEx 24:13;
Dt 1:38
1:2
cver 11
1:3
dDt 11:24
1:4
eGe 15:18
fNu 34:2-12
1:5
gDt 7:24
hJos 3:7; 6:27
iDt 31:6-8
1:6
jDt 31:23
1:7
kDt 5:32; 28:14
lJos 11:15

ᵃ4 That is, the Mediterranean

successful.ᵐ ⁹Have I not commanded you? Be strong and courageous. Do not be terrified;ⁿ do not be discouraged, for the LORD your God will be with you wherever you go."ᵒ

¹⁰So Joshua ordered the officers of the people: ¹¹"Go through the camp and tell the people, 'Get your supplies ready. Three days from now you will cross the Jordan here to go in and take possessionᵖ of the land the LORD your God is giving you for your own.'"

¹²But to the Reubenites, the Gadites and the half-tribe of Manasseh,�q Joshua said, ¹³"Remember the command that Moses the servant of the LORD gave you: 'The LORD your God is giving you restʳ and has granted you this land.' ¹⁴Your wives, your children and your livestock may stay in the land that Moses gave you east of the Jordan, but all your fighting men, fully armed, must cross over ahead of your brothers. You are to help your brothers ¹⁵until the LORD gives them rest, as he has done for you, and until they too have taken possession of the land that the LORD your God is giving them. After that, you may go back and occupy your own land, which Moses the servant of the LORD gave you east of the Jordan toward the sunrise."ˢ

¹⁶Then they answered Joshua, "Whatever you have commanded us we will do, and wherever you send us we will go. ¹⁷Just as we fully obeyed Moses, so we will obey you.ᵗ Only may the LORD your God be with you as he was with Moses. ¹⁸Whoever rebels against your word and does not obey your words, whatever you may command them, will be put to death. Only be strong and courageous!"

Rahab and the Spies

2 Then Joshua son of Nun secretly sent two spiesᵘ from Shittim.ᵛ "Go, look over the land," he said, "especially Jericho." So they went and entered the house of a prostituteᵃ named Rahabʷ and stayed there.

²The king of Jericho was told, "Look! Some of the Israelites have come here tonight to spy out the land." ³So the king of Jericho sent this message to Rahab: "Bring out the men who came to you and entered your house, because they have come to spy out the whole land."

⁴But the woman had taken the two men and hidden them.ˣ She said, "Yes, the men came to me, but I did not know where they had come from. ⁵At dusk, when it was time to close the city gate, the men left. I don't know which way they went. Go after them quickly. You may catch up with them." ⁶(But she had taken them up to the roof and hidden them under the stalks of flaxʸ she had laid out on the roof.)ᶻ ⁷So the men set out in pursuit of the spies on the road that leads to the fords of the Jordan, and as soon as the pursuers had gone out, the gate was shut.

⁸Before the spies lay down for the night, she went up on the roof ⁹and said to them, "I know that the LORD has given this land to you and that a great fearᵃ of you has fallen on us, so that all who live in this country are melting in fear because of you. ¹⁰We have heard how the LORD dried upᵇ the water of the Red Seaᵇ for you when you came out of Egypt,ᶜ and what you did to Sihon and Og,ᵈ the two kings of the Amorites east

1:8
ᵐDt 29:9;
Ps 1:1-3
1:9
ⁿPs 27:1 over 7;
Dt 31:7-8;
Jer 1:8
1:11
ᵖJoel 3:2
1:12
qNu 32:20-22
1:13
ʳDt 3:18-20
1:15
ˢJos 22:1-4
1:17
ᵗver 5,9
2:1
ᵘJas 2:25
ᵛNu 25:1;
Jos 3:1
ʷHeb 11:31
2:4
ˣ2Sa 17:19-20
2:6
ʸJas 2:25
ᶻEx 1:17,19;
2Sa 17:19
2:9
ᵃGe 35:5;
Ex 23:27;
Dt 2:25
2:10
ᵇEx 14:21
ᶜNu 23:22
ᵈNu 21:21,24,
34-35

ᵃ1 Or possibly *an innkeeper*   ᵇ10 Hebrew *Yam Suph;* that is, Sea of Reeds of the Jordan, whom you completely destroyed.ª ¹¹When we heard of it, our hearts melted and everyone's courage failed because of you,ᵉ for the LORD your God is God in heaven above and on the earthᶠ below. ¹²Now then, please swear to me by the LORD that you will show kindness to my family, because I have shown kindness to you. Give me a sure signᵍ ¹³that you will spare the lives of my father and mother, my brothers and sisters, and all who belong to them, and that you will save us from death."

¹⁴"Our lives for your lives!" the men assured her. "If you don't tell what we are doing, we will treat you kindly and faithfullyʰ when the LORD gives us the land."

¹⁵So she let them down by a rope through the window,ⁱ for the house she lived in was part of the city wall. ¹⁶Now she had said to them, "Go to the hills so the pursuers will not find you. Hide yourselves there three daysʲ until they return, and then go on your way."ᵏ

¹⁷The men said to her, "This oathˡ you made us swear will not be binding on us ¹⁸unless, when we enter the land, you have tied this scarlet cord in the window through which you let us down, and unless you have brought your father and mother, your brothers and all your familyᵐ into your house. ¹⁹If anyone goes outside your house into the street, his blood will be on his own head;ⁿ we will not be responsible. As for anyone who is in the house with you, his blood will be on our headᵒ if a hand is laid on him. ²⁰But if you tell what we are doing, we will be released from the oath you made us swear."

²¹"Agreed," she replied. "Let it be as you say." So she sent them away and they departed. And she tied the scarlet cord in the window.

²²When they left, they went into the hills and stayed there three days, until the pursuers had searched all along the road and returned without finding them. ²³Then the two men started back. They went down out of the hills, forded the river and came to Joshua son of Nun and told him everything that had happened to them. ²⁴They said to Joshua, "The LORD has surely given the whole land into our hands;ᵖ all the people are melting in fear because of us."

Crossing the Jordan

3 Early in the morning Joshua and all the Israelites set out from Shittim�q and went to the Jordan, where they camped before crossing over. ²After three days the officers went throughout the camp,ʳ ³giving orders to the people: "When you see the ark of the covenantˢ of the LORD your God, and the priests,ᵗ who are Levites, carrying it, you are to move out from your positions and follow it. ⁴Then you will know which way to go, since you have never been this way before. But keep a distance of about a thousand yardsᵇ between you and the ark; do not go near it."

⁵Joshua told the people, "Consecrate yourselves,ᵘ for tomorrow the LORD will do amazing things among you."

⁶Joshua said to the priests, "Take up the ark of the covenant and pass on ahead of the people." So they took it up and went ahead of them. ⁷And the LORD said to Joshua, "Today I will begin to exalt youᵛ in the

2:11
eEx 15:14;
Jos 5:1; 7:5;
Ps 22:14;
Isa 13:7
fDt 4:39
2:12
gver 18
2:14
hJdg 1:24;
Mt 5:7
2:15
iAc 9:25
2:16
jJas 2:25
kHeb 11:31
2:17
lGe 24:8
2:18
mver 12;
Jos 6:23
2:19
nEze 33:4
oMt 27:25
2:24
pver 9; Jos 6:2
3:1
qJos 2:1
3:2
rJos 1:11
3:3
sNu 10:33
tDt 31:9
3:5
uEx 19:10,14;
Lev 20:7;
Jos 7:13;
1Sa 16:5;
Joel 2:16
3:7
vJos 4:14;
1Ch 29:25

ª10 The Hebrew term refers to the irrevocable giving over of things or persons to the LORD, often by totally destroying them.   ᵇ4 Hebrew *about two thousand cubits* (about 900 meters) eyes of all Israel, so they may know that I am with you as I was with Moses. ʷ ⁸Tell the priestsˣ who carry the ark of the covenant: 'When you reach the edge of the Jordan's waters, go and stand in the river.'"

⁹Joshua said to the Israelites, "Come here and listen to the words of the LORD your God. ¹⁰This is how you will know that the living Godʸ is among you and that he will certainly drive out before you the Canaanites, Hittites, Hivites, Perizzites, Girgashites, Amorites and Jebusites. ᶻ ¹¹See, the ark of the covenant of the Lord of all the earthᵃ will go into the Jordan ahead of you. ¹²Now then, choose twelve menᵇ from the tribes of Israel, one from each tribe. ¹³And as soon as the priests who carry the ark of the LORD—the Lord of all the earthᶜ—set foot in the Jordan, its waters flowing downstreamᵈ will be cut off and stand up in a heap. ᵉ"

¹⁴So when the people broke camp to cross the Jordan, the priests carrying the ark of the covenantᶠ went aheadᵍ of them. ¹⁵Now the Jordan is at flood stageʰ all during harvest. Yet as soon as the priests who carried the ark reached the Jordan and their feet touched the water's edge, ¹⁶the water from upstream stopped flowing.ⁱ It piled up in a heap a great distance away, at a town called Adam in the vicinity of Zarethan,ʲ while the water flowing downᵏ to the Sea of the Arabahˡ (the Salt Sea ᵃᵐ) was completely cut off. So the people crossed over opposite Jericho. ¹⁷The priests who carried the ark of the covenant of the LORD stood firm on dry ground in the middle of the Jordan, while all Israel passed by until the whole nation had completed the crossing on dry ground. ⁿ

4 When the whole nation had finished crossing the Jordan,ᵒ the LORD said to Joshua, ²"Choose twelve menᵖ from among the people, one from each tribe, ³and tell them to take up twelve stonesᵠ from the middle of the Jordan from right where the priests stood and to carry them over with you and put them down at the place where you stay tonight.ʳ"

⁴So Joshua called together the twelve men he had appointed from the Israelites, one from each tribe, ⁵and said to them, "Go over before the ark of the LORD your God into the middle of the Jordan. Each of you is to take up a stone on his shoulder, according to the number of the tribes of the Israelites, ⁶to serve as a sign among you. In the future, when your children ask you, 'What do these stones mean?'ˢ ⁷tell them that the flow of the Jordan was cut offᵗ before the ark of the covenant of the LORD. When it crossed the Jordan, the waters of the Jordan were cut off. These stones are to be a memorialᵘ to the people of Israel forever."

⁸So the Israelites did as Joshua commanded them. They took twelve stones from the middle of the Jordan, according to the number of the tribes of the Israelites, as the LORD had told Joshua;ᵛ and they carried them over with them to their camp, where they put them down. ⁹Joshua set up the twelve stonesʷ that had beenᵇ in the middle of the Jordan at the spot where the priests who carried the ark of the covenant had stood. And they are there to this day.

¹⁰Now the priests who carried the ark remained standing in the middle of the Jordan until everything the LORD had commanded Joshua was done by the people, just as Moses had directed Joshua. The people

3:7
w Jos 1:5
3:8
x ver 3
3:10
y Dt 5:26;
1Sa 17:26,36;
2Ki 19:4,16;
Hos 1:10;
Mt 16:16;
1Th 1:9
z Ex 33:2; Dt 7:1
3:11
a ver 13;
Job 41:11;
Zec 6:5
3:12
b Jos 4:2,4
3:13
c ver 11 d ver 16
e Ex 15:8;
Ps 78:13
3:14
f Ps 132:8
g Ac 7:44-45
3:15
h Jos 4:18;
1Ch 12:15
3:16
i Ps 66:6; 74:15
j 1Ki 4:12; 7:46
k ver 13 l Dt 1:1
m Ge 14:3
3:17
n Ex 14:22,29
4:1
o Dt 27:2
4:2
p Jos 3:12
4:3
q ver 20 r ver 19
4:6
s ver 21;
Ex 12:26; 13:14
4:7
t Jos 3:13
u Ex 12:14
4:8
v ver 20
4:9
w Ge 28:18;
Jos 24:26;
1Sa 7:12

ᵃ16 That is, the Dead Sea   ᵇ9 Or *Joshua also set up twelve stones* hurried over, [11]and as soon as all of them had crossed, the ark of the LORD and the priests came to the other side while the people watched. [12]The men of Reuben, Gad and the half-tribe of Manasseh crossed over, armed, in front of the Israelites,[x] as Moses had directed them. [13]About forty thousand armed for battle crossed over before the LORD to the plains of Jericho for war.

[14]That day the LORD exalted[y] Joshua in the sight of all Israel; and they revered him all the days of his life, just as they had revered Moses.

[15]Then the LORD said to Joshua, [16]"Command the priests carrying the ark of the Testimony[z] to come up out of the Jordan."

[17]So Joshua commanded the priests, "Come up out of the Jordan."

[18]And the priests came up out of the river carrying the ark of the covenant of the LORD. No sooner had they set their feet on the dry ground than the waters of the Jordan returned to their place and ran at flood stage[a] as before.

[19]On the tenth day of the first month the people went up from the Jordan and camped at Gilgal[b] on the eastern border of Jericho. [20]And Joshua set up at Gilgal the twelve stones[c] they had taken out of the Jordan. [21]He said to the Israelites, "In the future when your descendants ask their fathers, 'What do these stones mean?'[d] [22]tell them, 'Israel crossed the Jordan on dry ground.'[e] [23]For the LORD your God dried up the Jordan before you until you had crossed over. The LORD your God did to the Jordan just what he had done to the Red Sea[a] when he dried it up before us until we had crossed over.[f] [24]He did this so that all the peoples of the earth might know[g] that the hand of the LORD is powerful[h] and so that you might always fear the LORD your God.[i]"

Circumcision at Gilgal

5 Now when all the Amorite kings west of the Jordan and all the Canaanite kings along the coast[j] heard how the LORD had dried up the Jordan before the Israelites until we had crossed over, their hearts melted[k] and they no longer had the courage to face the Israelites.

[2]At that time the LORD said to Joshua, "Make flint knives[l] and circumcise the Israelites again." [3]So Joshua made flint knives and circumcised the Israelites at Gibeath Haaraloth.[b]

[4]Now this is why he did so: All those who came out of Egypt—all the men of military age—died in the desert on the way after leaving Egypt.[m] [5]All the people that came out had been circumcised, but all the people born in the desert during the journey from Egypt had not. [6]The Israelites had moved about in the desert forty years[n] until all the men who were of military age when they left Egypt had died, since they had not obeyed the LORD. For the LORD had sworn to them that they would not see the land that he had solemnly promised their fathers to give us,[o] a land flowing with milk and honey.[p] [7]So he raised up their sons in their place, and these were the ones Joshua circumcised. They were still uncircumcised because they had not been circumcised on the way. [8]And after the whole nation had been circumcised, they remained where they were in camp until they were healed.[q]

[9]Then the LORD said to Joshua, "Today I have rolled away the re-

### Cross references (margin)

4:12
xNu 32:27
4:14
yJos 3:7
4:16
zEx 25:22
4:18
aJos 3:15
4:19
bJos 5:9
4:20
cver 3,8
4:21
dver 6
4:22
eJos 3:17
4:23
fEx 14:21
4:24
g1Ki 8:42-43;
2Ki 19:19;
Ps 106:8;
Jer 10:7
hEx 15:16;
1Ch 29:12;
Ps 89:13
iEx 14:31
5:1
jNu 13:29
kJos 2:9-11
5:2
lEx 4:25
5:4
mDt 2:14
5:6
nDt 2:7
oNu 14:23,
29-35; Dt 2:14
pEx 3:8
5:8
qGe 34:25

---

[a]23 Hebrew *Yam Suph*; that is, Sea of Reeds   [b]3 *Gibeath Haaraloth* means *hill of foreskins.*

proach of Egypt from you." So the place has been called Gilgal*ᵃ* to this day.

¹⁰On the evening of the fourteenth day of the month,ʳ while camped at Gilgal on the plains of Jericho, the Israelites celebrated the Passover. ¹¹The day after the Passover, that very day, they ate some of the produce of the land:ˢ unleavened bread and roasted grain.ᵗ ¹²The manna stopped the day afterᵇ they ate this food from the land; there was no longer any manna for the Israelites, but that year they ate of the produce of Canaan.ᵘ

The Fall of Jericho

¹³Now when Joshua was near Jericho, he looked up and saw a manᵛ standing in front of him with a drawn swordʷ in his hand. Joshua went up to him and asked, "Are you for us or for our enemies?"

¹⁴"Neither," he replied, "but as commander of the army of the LORD I have now come." Then Joshua fell facedownˣ to the ground in reverence, and asked him, "What message does my Lordᶜ have for his servant?"

¹⁵The commander of the LORD's army replied, "Take off your sandals, for the place where you are standing is holy."ʸ And Joshua did so.

6 Now Jerichoᶻ was tightly shut up because of the Israelites. No one went out and no one came in.

²Then the LORD said to Joshua, "See, I have deliveredᵃ Jericho into your hands, along with its king and its fighting men. ³March around the city once with all the armed men. Do this for six days. ⁴Have seven priests carry trumpets of rams' horns in front of the ark. On the seventh day, march around the city seven times, with the priests blowing the trumpets. ᵇ ⁵When you hear them sound a long blastᶜ on the trumpets, have all the people give a loud shout;ᵈ then the wall of the city will collapse and the people will go up, every man straight in."

⁶So Joshua son of Nun called the priests and said to them, "Take up the ark of the covenant of the LORD and have seven priests carry trumpets in front of it." ⁷And he ordered the people, "Advanceᵉ! March around the city, with the armed guard going ahead of the ark of the LORD."

⁸When Joshua had spoken to the people, the seven priests carrying the seven trumpets before the LORD went forward, blowing their trumpets, and the ark of the LORD's covenant followed them. ⁹The armed guard marched ahead of the priests who blew the trumpets, and the rear guardᶠ followed the ark. All this time the trumpets were sounding. ¹⁰But Joshua had commanded the people, "Do not give a war cry, do not raise your voices, do not say a word until the day I tell you to shout. Then shout!ᵍ" ¹¹So he had the ark of the LORD carried around the city, circling it once. Then the people returned to camp and spent the night there.

¹²Joshua got up early the next morning and the priests took up the ark of the LORD. ¹³The seven priests carrying the seven trumpets went forward, marching before the ark of the LORD and blowing the trumpets. The armed men went ahead of them and the rear guard followed the ark of the LORD, while the trumpets kept sounding. ¹⁴So on the

5:10
rEx 12:6
5:11
sNu 15:19
tLev 23:14
5:12
uEx 16:35
5:13
vGe 18:2; 32:24
wNu 22:23
5:14
xGe 17:3
5:15
yEx 3:5; Ac 7:33
6:1
zJos 24:11
6:2
aDt 7:24;
Jos 2:9,24; 8:1
6:4
bLev 25:9;
Nu 10:8
6:5
cEx 19:13
dver 20;
1Sa 4:5;
Ps 42:4;
Isa 42:13
6:7
eEx 14:15
6:9
fver 13;
Isa 52:12
6:10
gver 20

ᵃ9 *Gilgal sounds like the Hebrew for* roll.   *ᵇ12* Or *the day*   *ᶜ14* Or lord second day they marched around the city once and returned to the camp. They did this for six days.

¹⁵On the seventh day, they got up at daybreak and marched around the city seven times in the same manner, except that on that day they circled the city seven times.ʰ ¹⁶The seventh time around, when the priests sounded the trumpet blast, Joshua commanded the people, "Shout! For the LORD has given you the city! ¹⁷The city and all that is in it are to be devotedᵃⁱ to the LORD. Only Rahab the prostituteᵇ and all who are with her in her house shall be spared, because she hidʲ the spies we sent. ¹⁸But keep away from the devoted things,ᵏ so that you will not bring about your own destruction by taking any of them. Otherwise you will make the camp of Israel liable to destructionˡ and bring troubleᵐ on it. ¹⁹All the silver and gold and the articles of bronze and ironⁿ are sacred to the LORD and must go into his treasury."

²⁰When the trumpets sounded,ᵒ the people shouted, and at the sound of the trumpet, when the people gave a loud shout,ᵖ the wall collapsed; so every man charged straight in, and they took the city.�q ²¹They devoted the city to the LORD and destroyedʳ with the sword every living thing in it—men and women, young and old, cattle, sheep and donkeys.

²²Joshua said to the two men who had spied out the land, "Go into the prostitute's house and bring her out and all who belong to her, in accordance with your oath to her.ˢ" ²³So the young men who had done the spying went in and brought out Rahab, her father and mother and brothers and all who belonged to her.ᵗ They brought out her entire family and put them in a place outside the camp of Israel.

²⁴Then they burned the whole city and everything in it, but they put the silver and gold and the articles of bronze and ironᵘ into the treasury of the LORD's house. ²⁵But Joshua spared Rahab the prostitute,ᵛ with her family and all who belonged to her, because she hid the men Joshua had sent as spies to Jerichoʷ—and she lives among the Israelites to this day.

²⁶At that time Joshua pronounced this solemn oath: "Cursed before the LORD is the man who undertakes to rebuild this city, Jericho:

> "At the cost of his firstborn son
>   will he lay its foundations;
> at the cost of his youngest
>   will he set up its gates."ˣ

²⁷So the LORD was with Joshua,ʸ and his fame spreadᶻ throughout the land.

Achan's Sin

7 But the Israelites acted unfaithfully in regard to the devoted thingsᶜ;ᵃ Achan son of Carmi, the son of Zimri,ᵈ the son of Zerah,ᵇ of the tribe of Judah, took some of them. So the LORD's anger burned against Israel.

6:15
h 1Ki 18:44
6:17
i Lev 27:28;
Dt 20:17
j Jos 2:4
6:18
k Jos 7:1
l Jos 7:12
m Jos 7:25,26
6:19
n ver 24;
Nu 31:22
6:20
o Jdg 6:34;
Jer 4:21;
Am 2:2 pver 5
q Heb 11:30
6:21
r Dt 20:16
6:22
s Jos 2:14;
Heb 11:31
6:23
t Jos 2:13
6:24
u ver 19
6:25
v Heb 11:31
w Jos 2:6
6:26
x 1Ki 16:34
6:27
y Ge 39:2;
Jos 1:5 z Jos 9:1
7:1
a Jos 6:18
b Jos 22:20

ᵃ17 The Hebrew term refers to the irrevocable giving over of things or persons to the LORD, often by totally destroying them; also in verses 18 and 21.   ᵇ17 Or possibly *innkeeper*; also in verses 22 and 25   ᶜ1 The Hebrew term refers to the irrevocable giving of things or persons to the LORD, often by totally destroying them; also in verses 11, 12, 13 and 15.   ᵈ1 See Septuagint and 1 Chron. 2:6; Hebrew *Zabdi*; also in verses 17 and 18.

²Now Joshua sent men from Jericho to Ai, which is near Beth Aven[c] to the east of Bethel, and told them, "Go up and spy out the region." So the men went up and spied out Ai.

³When they returned to Joshua, they said, "Not all the people will have to go up against Ai. Send two or three thousand men to take it and do not weary all the people, for only a few men are there." ⁴So about three thousand men went up; but they were routed by the men of Ai,[d] ⁵who killed about thirty-six of them. They chased the Israelites from the city gate as far as the stone quarries[a] and struck them down on the slopes. At this the hearts of the people melted[e] and became like water.

⁶Then Joshua tore his clothes[f] and fell facedown to the ground before the ark of the LORD, remaining there till evening. The elders of Israel did the same, and sprinkled dust[g] on their heads. ⁷And Joshua said, "Ah, Sovereign LORD, why did you ever bring this people across the Jordan to deliver us into the hands of the Amorites to destroy us?[h] If only we had been content to stay on the other side of the Jordan! ⁸O Lord, what can I say, now that Israel has been routed by its enemies? ⁹The Canaanites and the other people of the country will hear about this and they will surround us and wipe out our name from the earth.[i] What then will you do for your own great name?"

¹⁰The LORD said to Joshua, "Stand up! What are you doing down on your face? ¹¹Israel has sinned; they have violated my covenant,[j] which I commanded them to keep. They have taken some of the devoted things; they have stolen, they have lied,[k] they have put them with their own possessions. ¹²That is why the Israelites cannot stand against their enemies;[l] they turn their backs and run because they have been made liable to destruction.[m] I will not be with you anymore unless you destroy whatever among you is devoted to destruction.

¹³"Go, consecrate the people. Tell them, 'Consecrate yourselves[n] in preparation for tomorrow; for this is what the LORD, the God of Israel, says: That which is devoted is among you, O Israel. You cannot stand against your enemies until you remove it.

¹⁴" 'In the morning, present yourselves tribe by tribe. The tribe that the LORD takes[o] shall come forward clan by clan; the clan that the LORD takes shall come forward family by family; and the family that the LORD takes shall come forward man by man. ¹⁵He who is caught with the devoted things shall be destroyed by fire, along with all that belongs to him.[p] He has violated the covenant[q] of the LORD and has done a disgraceful thing in Israel!' "[r]

¹⁶Early the next morning Joshua had Israel come forward by tribes, and Judah was taken. ¹⁷The clans of Judah came forward, and he took the Zerahites.[s] He had the clan of the Zerahites come forward by families, and Zimri was taken. ¹⁸Joshua had his family come forward man by man, and Achan son of Carmi, the son of Zimri, the son of Zerah, of the tribe of Judah, was taken.

¹⁹Then Joshua said to Achan, "My son, give glory[t] to the LORD,[b] the God of Israel, and give him the praise.[c] Tell[u] me what you have done; do not hide it from me."

²⁰Achan replied, "It is true! I have sinned against the LORD, the God of Israel. This is what I have done: ²¹When I saw in the plunder a

7:2	
c Jos 18:12;	
1Sa 13:5; 14:23	
7:4	
d Lev 26:17;	
Dt 28:25	
7:5	
e Lev 26:36;	
Jos 2:9,11;	
Eze 21:7;	
Na 2:10	
7:6	
f Ge 37:29	
g 1Sa 4:12;	
2Sa 13:19;	
Ne 9:1;	
Job 2:12;	
La 2:10;	
Rev 18:19	
7:7	
h Ex 5:22	
7:9	
i Ex 32:12;	
Dt 9:28	
7:11	
j Jos 6:17-19	
k Ac 5:1-2	
7:12	
l Nu 14:45;	
Jdg 2:14	
m Jos 6:18	
7:13	
n Jos 3:5; 6:18	
7:14	
o Pr 16:33	
7:15	
p 1Sa 14:39	
q ver 11	
r Ge 34:7	
7:17	
s Nu 26:20	
7:19	
t 1Sa 6:5;	
Jer 13:16;	
Jn 9:24*	
u 1Sa 14:43	

---

[a]5 Or *as far as Shebarim*   [b]19 A solemn charge to tell the truth   [c]19 Or *and confess to him*

beautiful robe from Babylonia,*a* two hundred shekels*b* of silver and a wedge of gold weighing fifty shekels,*c* I coveted*v* them and took them. They are hidden in the ground inside my tent, with the silver underneath."

22So Joshua sent messengers, and they ran to the tent, and there it was, hidden in his tent, with the silver underneath. 23They took the things from the tent, brought them to Joshua and all the Israelites and spread them out before the LORD.

24Then Joshua, together with all Israel, took Achan son of Zerah, the silver, the robe, the gold wedge, his sons and daughters, his cattle, donkeys and sheep, his tent and all that he had, to the Valley of Achor.*w* 25Joshua said, "Why have you brought this trouble*x* on us? The LORD will bring trouble on you today."

Then all Israel stoned him,*y* and after they had stoned the rest, they burned them. 26Over Achan they heaped up a large pile of rocks, which remains to this day. Then the LORD turned from his fierce anger.*z* Therefore that place has been called the Valley of Achor*da* ever since.

Ai Destroyed

8 Then the LORD said to Joshua, "Do not be afraid;*b* do not be discouraged.*c* Take the whole army*d* with you, and go up and attack Ai. For I have delivered*e* into your hands the king of Ai, his people, his city and his land. 2You shall do to Ai and its king as you did to Jericho and its king, except that you may carry off their plunder and livestock for yourselves.*f* Set an ambush behind the city."

3So Joshua and the whole army moved out to attack Ai. He chose thirty thousand of his best fighting men and sent them out at night 4with these orders: "Listen carefully. You are to set an ambush behind the city. Don't go very far from it. All of you be on the alert. 5I and all those with me will advance on the city, and when the men come out against us, as they did before, we will flee from them. 6They will pursue us until we have lured them away from the city, for they will say, 'They are running away from us as they did before.' So when we flee from them, 7you are to rise up from ambush and take the city. The LORD your God will give it into your hand.*g* 8When you have taken the city, set it on fire.*h* Do what the LORD has commanded.*i* See to it; you have my orders."

9Then Joshua sent them off, and they went to the place of ambush*j* and lay in wait between Bethel and Ai, to the west of Ai—but Joshua spent that night with the people.

10Early the next morning*k* Joshua mustered his men, and he and the leaders of Israel*l* marched before them to Ai. 11The entire force that was with him marched up and approached the city and arrived in front of it. They set up camp north of Ai, with the valley between them and the city. 12Joshua had taken about five thousand men and set them in ambush between Bethel and Ai, to the west of the city. 13They had the soldiers take up their positions—all those in the camp to the north of the city and the ambush to the west of it. That night Joshua went into the valley.

7:21
vDt 7:25;
Eph 5:5;
1Ti 6:10
7:24
wver 26;
Jos 15:7
7:25
xJos 6:18
yDt 17:5
7:26
zNu 25:4;
Dt 13:17
aver 24;
Isa 65:10;
Hos 2:15
8:1
bDt 31:6
cDt 1:21; 7:18;
Jos 1:9
dJos 10:7
eJos 6:2
8:2
fver 27;
Dt 20:14
8:7
gJdg 7:7;
1Sa 23:4
8:8
hJdg 20:29-38
iver 19
8:9
j2Ch 13:13
8:10
kGe 22:3
lJos 7:6

a21 Hebrew Shinar   b21 That is, about 5 pounds (about 2.3 kilograms)   c21 That is, about 1 1/4 pounds (about 0.6 kilogram)   d26 Achor means trouble.

[14]When the king of Ai saw this, he and all the men of the city hurried out early in the morning to meet Israel in battle at a certain place overlooking the Arabah.[m] But he did not know[n] that an ambush had been set against him behind the city. [15]Joshua and all Israel let themselves be driven back[o] before them, and they fled toward the desert.[p] [16]All the men of Ai were called to pursue them, and they pursued Joshua and were lured away[q] from the city. [17]Not a man remained in Ai or Bethel who did not go after Israel. They left the city open and went in pursuit of Israel.

[18]Then the LORD said to Joshua, "Hold out toward Ai the javelin[r] that is in your hand,[s] for into your hand I will deliver the city." So Joshua held out his javelin[t] toward Ai. [19]As soon as he did this, the men in the ambush rose quickly[u] from their position and rushed forward. They entered the city and captured it and quickly set it on fire.[v]

[20]The men of Ai looked back and saw the smoke of the city rising against the sky,[w] but they had no chance to escape in any direction, for the Israelites who had been fleeing toward the desert had turned back against their pursuers. [21]For when Joshua and all Israel saw that the ambush had taken the city and that smoke was going up from the city, they turned around and attacked the men of Ai. [22]The men of the ambush also came out of the city against them, so that they were caught in the middle, with Israelites on both sides. Israel cut them down, leaving them neither survivors nor fugitives.[x] [23]But they took the king of Ai alive[y] and brought him to Joshua.

[24]When Israel had finished killing all the men of Ai in the fields and in the desert where they had chased them, and when every one of them had been put to the sword, all the Israelites returned to Ai and killed those who were in it. [25]Twelve thousand men and women fell that day—all the people of Ai.[z] [26]For Joshua did not draw back the hand that held out his javelin until he had destroyed[aa] all who lived in Ai.[b] [27]But Israel did carry off for themselves the livestock and plunder of this city, as the LORD had instructed Joshua.[c]

[28]So Joshua burned[d] Ai[e] and made it a permanent heap of ruins,[f] a desolate place to this day.[g] [29]He hung the king of Ai on a tree and left him there until evening. At sunset,[h] Joshua ordered them to take his body from the tree and throw it down at the entrance of the city gate. And they raised a large pile of rocks[i] over it, which remains to this day.

The Covenant Renewed at Mount Ebal

[30]Then Joshua built on Mount Ebal[j] an altar[k] to the LORD, the God of Israel, [31]as Moses the servant of the LORD had commanded the Israelites. He built it according to what is written in the Book of the Law of Moses—an altar of uncut stones, on which no iron tool[l] had been used. On it they offered to the LORD burnt offerings and sacrificed fellowship offerings.[b][m] [32]There, in the presence of the Israelites, Joshua copied on stones the law of Moses, which he had written.[n] [33]All Israel, aliens and citizens[o] alike, with their elders, officials and judges, were standing on both sides of the ark of the covenant of the LORD, facing those who carried it—the priests, who were Levites.[p] Half of the people stood in

8:14
mDt 1:1
nJdg 20:34
8:15
oJdg 20:36
pJos 15:61;
16:1; 18:12
8:16
qJdg 20:31
8:18
rJob 41:26;
Ps 35:3 sEx 4:2;
14:16; 17:9-12
tver 26
8:19
uJdg 20:33
vver 8
8:20
wJdg 20:40
8:22
xDt 7:2;
Jos 10:1
8:23
y1Sa 15:8
8:25
zDt 20:16-18
8:26
aNu 21:2
bEx 17:12
8:27
cver 2
8:28
dNu 31:10
eJos 7:2;
Jer 49:3
fDt 13:16;
Jos 10:1
gGe 35:20
8:29
hDt 21:23;
Jn 19:31
i2Sa 18:17
8:30
jDt 11:29
kEx 20:24
8:31
lEx 20:25
mDt 27:6-7
8:32
nDt 27:8
8:33
oLev 16:29
pDt 31:12

---

[a]26 The Hebrew term refers to the irrevocable giving over of things or persons to the LORD, often by totally destroying them.   [b]31 Traditionally *peace offerings*

front of Mount Gerizim and half of them in front of Mount Ebal,�q as Moses the servant of the LORD had formerly commanded when he gave instructions to bless the people of Israel.

³⁴Afterward, Joshua read all the words of the law—the blessings and the curses—just as it is written in the Book of the Law.ʳ ³⁵There was not a word of all that Moses had commanded that Joshua did not read to the whole assembly of Israel, including the women and children, and the aliens who lived among them.ˢ

The Gibeonite Deception

9 Now when all the kings west of the Jordan heard about these things—those in the hill country, in the western foothills, and along the entire coast of the Great Seaᵃᵗ as far as Lebanon (the kings of the Hittites, Amorites, Canaanites, Perizzites, Hivites and Jebusites)ᵘ— ²they came together to make war against Joshua and Israel.

³However, when the people of Gibeonᵛ heard what Joshua had done to Jericho and Ai, ⁴they resorted to a ruse: They went as a delegation whose donkeys were loadedᵇ with worn-out sacks and old wineskins, cracked and mended. ⁵The men put worn and patched sandals on their feet and wore old clothes. All the bread of their food supply was dry and moldy. ⁶Then they went to Joshua in the camp at Gilgalʷ and said to him and the men of Israel, "We have come from a distant country; make a treaty with us."

⁷The men of Israel said to the Hivites,ˣ "But perhaps you live near us. How then can we make a treatyʸ with you?"

⁸"We are your servants,ᶻ" they said to Joshua.

But Joshua asked, "Who are you and where do you come from?"

⁹They answered: "Your servants have come from a very distant countryᵃ because of the fame of the LORD your God. For we have heard reportsᵇ of him: all that he did in Egypt, ¹⁰and all that he did to the two kings of the Amorites east of the Jordan—Sihon king of Heshbon, and Og king of Bashan,ᶜ who reigned in Ashtaroth.ᵈ ¹¹And our elders and all those living in our country said to us, 'Take provisions for your journey; go and meet them and say to them, "We are your servants; make a treaty with us."' ¹²This bread of ours was warm when we packed it at home on the day we left to come to you. But now see how dry and moldy it is. ¹³And these wineskins that we filled were new, but see how cracked they are. And our clothes and sandals are worn out by the very long journey."

¹⁴The men of Israel sampled their provisions but did not inquireᵉ of the LORD. ¹⁵Then Joshua made a treaty of peaceᶠ with them to let them live, and the leaders of the assembly ratified it by oath.

¹⁶Three days after they made the treaty with the Gibeonites, the Israelites heard that they were neighbors, living near them. ¹⁷So the Israelites set out and on the third day came to their cities: Gibeon, Kephirah, Beerothᵍ and Kiriath Jearim.ʰ ¹⁸But the Israelites did not attack them, because the leaders of the assembly had sworn an oathⁱ to them by the LORD, the God of Israel.

The whole assembly grumbledʲ against the leaders, ¹⁹but all the

8:33
qDt 11:29;
27:11-14
8:34
rDt 28:61;
31:11; Jos 1:8
8:35
sEx 12:38;
Dt 31:12
9:1
tNu 34:6
uEx 3:17;
Jos 3:10
9:3
vver 17;
Jos 10:2;
2Sa 2:12;
2Ch 1:3;
Isa 28:21
9:6
wJos 5:10
9:7
xver 1;
Jos 11:19
yEx 23:32;
Dt 7:2
9:8
zDt 20:11;
2Ki 10:5
9:9
aDt 20:15
bver 24; Jos 2:9
9:10
cNu 21:33
dNu 21:24,35
9:14
eNu 27:21
9:15
fEx 23:32;
Jos 11:19;
2Sa 21:2
9:17
gJos 18:25
h1Sa 7:1-2
9:18
iPs 15:4
jEx 15:24

ᵃ1 That is, the Mediterranean   ᵇ4 Most Hebrew manuscripts; some Hebrew manuscripts, Vulgate and Syriac (see also Septuagint) *They prepared provisions and loaded their donkeys* leaders answered, "We have given them our oath by the LORD, the God of Israel, and we cannot touch them now. 20This is what we will do to them: We will let them live, so that wrath will not fall on us for breaking the oath we swore to them." 21They continued, "Let them live,[k] but let them be woodcutters and water carriers[l] for the entire community." So the leaders' promise to them was kept.

22Then Joshua summoned the Gibeonites and said, "Why did you deceive us by saying, 'We live a long way[m] from you,' while actually you live near[n] us? 23You are now under a curse:[o] You will never cease to serve as woodcutters and water carriers for the house of my God."

24They answered Joshua, "Your servants were clearly told[p] how the LORD your God had commanded his servant Moses to give you the whole land and to wipe out all its inhabitants from before you. So we feared for our lives because of you, and that is why we did this. 25We are now in your hands.[q] Do to us whatever seems good and right to you."

26So Joshua saved them from the Israelites, and they did not kill them. 27That day he made the Gibeonites woodcutters and water carriers for the community and for the altar of the LORD at the place the LORD would choose.[r] And that is what they are to this day.

The Sun Stands Still

10 Now Adoni-Zedek king of Jerusalem[s] heard that Joshua had taken Ai[t] and totally destroyed[au] it, doing to Ai and its king as he had done to Jericho and its king, and that the people of Gibeon had made a treaty of peace[v] with Israel and were living near them. 2He and his people were very much alarmed at this, because Gibeon was an important city, like one of the royal cities; it was larger than Ai, and all its men were good fighters. 3So Adoni-Zedek king of Jerusalem appealed to Hoham king of Hebron,[w] Piram king of Jarmuth, Japhia king of Lachish[x] and Debir king of Eglon. 4"Come up and help me attack Gibeon," he said, "because it has made peace[y] with Joshua and the Israelites."

5Then the five kings of the Amorites[z]—the kings of Jerusalem, Hebron, Jarmuth, Lachish and Eglon—joined forces. They moved up with all their troops and took up positions against Gibeon and attacked it.

6The Gibeonites then sent word to Joshua in the camp at Gilgal: "Do not abandon your servants. Come up to us quickly and save us! Help us, because all the Amorite kings from the hill country have joined forces against us."

7So Joshua marched up from Gilgal with his entire army,[a] including all the best fighting men. 8The LORD said to Joshua, "Do not be afraid[b] of them; I have given them into your hand. Not one of them will be able to withstand you."

9After an all-night march from Gilgal, Joshua took them by surprise. 10The LORD threw them into confusion before Israel,[c] who defeated them in a great victory at Gibeon. Israel pursued them along the road going up to Beth Horon[d] and cut them down all the way to Azekah[e] and Makkedah. 11As they fled before Israel on the road down from Beth Horon to Azekah, the LORD hurled large hailstones[f] down on them

9:21
k ver 15
l Dt 29:11
9:22
m ver 6 n ver 16
9:23
o Ge 9:25
9:24
p ver 9
9:25
q Ge 16:6
9:27
r Dt 12:5
10:1
s Jdg 1:7
t Jos 8:1
u Dt 20:16;
Jos 8:22
v Jos 9:15
10:3
w Ge 13:18
x 2Ch 11:9;
25:27;
Ne 11:30;
Isa 36:2; 37:8;
Jer 34:7;
Mic 1:13
10:4
y Jos 9:15
10:5
z Nu 13:29
10:7
a Jos 8:1
10:8
b Dt 3:2; Jos 1:9
10:10
c Dt 7:23
d Jos 16:3,5
e Jos 15:35
10:11
f Ps 18:12;
Isa 28:2,17

a1 The Hebrew term refers to the irrevocable giving over of things or persons to the LORD, often by totally destroying them; also in verses 28, 35, 37, 39 and 40.

from the sky, and more of them died from the hailstones than were killed by the swords of the Israelites.

¹²On the day the LORD gave the Amorites⁸ over to Israel, Joshua said to the LORD in the presence of Israel:

> "O sun, stand still over Gibeon,
> O moon, over the Valley of Aijalon.ʰ"
> ¹³So the sun stood still,ⁱ
> and the moon stopped,
> till the nation avenged itself onᵃ its enemies,

as it is written in the Book of Jashar.ʲ

The sun stoppedᵏ in the middle of the sky and delayed going down about a full day. ¹⁴There has never been a day like it before or since, a day when the LORD listened to a man. Surely the LORD was fighting¹ for Israel!

¹⁵Then Joshua returned with all Israel to the camp at Gilgal.ᵐ

Five Amorite Kings Killed

¹⁶Now the five kings had fled and hidden in the cave at Makkedah. ¹⁷When Joshua was told that the five kings had been found hiding in the cave at Makkedah, ¹⁸he said, "Roll large rocks up to the mouth of the cave, and post some men there to guard it. ¹⁹But don't stop! Pursue your enemies, attack them from the rear and don't let them reach their cities, for the LORD your God has given them into your hand."

²⁰So Joshua and the Israelites destroyed them completelyⁿ—almost to a man—but the few who were left reached their fortified cities. ²¹The whole army then returned safely to Joshua in the camp at Makkedah, and no one uttered a word against the Israelites.

²²Joshua said, "Open the mouth of the cave and bring those five kings out to me." ²³So they brought the five kings out of the cave—the kings of Jerusalem, Hebron, Jarmuth, Lachish and Eglon. ²⁴When they had brought these kings to Joshua, he summoned all the men of Israel and said to the army commanders who had come with him, "Come here and put your feetᵒ on the necks of these kings." So they came forward and placed their feetᵖ on their necks.

²⁵Joshua said to them, "Do not be afraid; do not be discouraged. Be strong and courageous.�q This is what the LORD will do to all the enemies you are going to fight." ²⁶Then Joshua struck and killed the kings and hung them on five trees, and they were left hanging on the trees until evening.

²⁷At sunsetʳ Joshua gave the order and they took them down from the trees and threw them into the cave where they had been hiding. At the mouth of the cave they placed large rocks, which are there to this day.

²⁸That day Joshua took Makkedah. He put the city and its king to the sword and totally destroyed everyone in it. He left no survivors.ˢ And he did to the king of Makkedah as he had done to the king of Jericho.ᵗ

Southern Cities Conquered

²⁹Then Joshua and all Israel with him moved on from Makkedah to

10:12
ᵍAm 2:9
ʰJdg 1:35;
12:12
10:13
ⁱHab 3:11
ʲ2Sa 1:18
ᵏIsa 38:8
10:14
ˡver 42;
Ex 14:14;
Dt 1:30;
Ps 106:43;
136:24
10:15
ᵐver 43
10:20
ⁿDt 20:16
10:24
ᵒMal 4:3
ᵖPs 110:1
10:25
qDt 31:6
10:27
ʳDt 21:23;
Jos 8:9,29
10:28
ˢDt 20:16
ᵗJos 6:21

ᵃ13 Or *nation triumphed over*

Libnah and attacked it. ³⁰The LORD also gave that city and its king into Israel's hand. The city and everyone in it Joshua put to the sword. He left no survivors there. And he did to its king as he had done to the king of Jericho.

³¹Then Joshua and all Israel with him moved on from Libnah to Lachish; he took up positions against it and attacked it. ³²The LORD handed Lachish over to Israel, and Joshua took it on the second day. The city and everyone in it he put to the sword, just as he had done to Libnah. ³³Meanwhile, Horam king of Gezer^u had come up to help Lachish, but Joshua defeated him and his army—until no survivors were left.

³⁴Then Joshua and all Israel with him moved on from Lachish to Eglon; they took up positions against it and attacked it. ³⁵They captured it that same day and put it to the sword and totally destroyed everyone in it, just as they had done to Lachish.

³⁶Then Joshua and all Israel with him went up from Eglon to Hebron^v and attacked it. ³⁷They took the city and put it to the sword, together with its king, its villages and everyone in it. They left no survivors. Just as at Eglon, they totally destroyed it and everyone in it.

³⁸Then Joshua and all Israel with him turned around and attacked Debir.^w ³⁹They took the city, its king and its villages, and put them to the sword. Everyone in it they totally destroyed. They left no survivors. They did to Debir and its king as they had done to Libnah and its king and to Hebron.

⁴⁰So Joshua subdued the whole region, including the hill country, the Negev,^x the western foothills and the mountain slopes,^y together with all their kings.^z He left no survivors. He totally destroyed all who breathed, just as the LORD, the God of Israel, had commanded.^a ⁴¹Joshua subdued them from Kadesh Barnea^b to Gaza^c and from the whole region of Goshen^d to Gibeon. ⁴²All these kings and their lands Joshua conquered in one campaign, because the LORD, the God of Israel, fought^e for Israel.

⁴³Then Joshua returned with all Israel to the camp at Gilgal.^f

Northern Kings Defeated

11 When Jabin^g king of Hazor^h heard of this, he sent word to Jobab king of Madon, to the kings of Shimronⁱ and Acshaph, ²and to the northern kings who were in the mountains, in the Arabah^j south of Kinnereth,^k in the western foothills and in Naphoth Dor^{a1} on the west; ³to the Canaanites in the east and west; to the Amorites, Hittites, Perizzites and Jebusites in the hill country; and to the Hivites^m below Hermon in the region of Mizpah.ⁿ ⁴They came out with all their troops and a large number of horses and chariots—a huge army, as numerous as the sand on the seashore.^o ⁵All these kings joined forces^p and made camp together at the Waters of Merom, to fight against Israel.

⁶The LORD said to Joshua, "Do not be afraid of them, because by this time tomorrow I will hand all of them over^q to Israel, slain. You are to hamstring^r their horses and burn their chariots."

⁷So Joshua and his whole army came against them suddenly at the Waters of Merom and attacked them, ⁸and the LORD gave them into the

---

10:33
uJos 16:3,10;
Jdg 1:29;
1Ki 9:15

10:36
vJos 14:13;
15:13; Jdg 1:10

10:38
wJos 15:15;
Jdg 1:11

10:40
xGe 12:9;
Jos 12:8 yDt 1:7
zDt 7:24
aDt 20:16-17

10:41
bGe 14:7
cGe 10:19
dJos 11:16;
15:51

10:42
ever 14

10:43
fver 15; Jos 5:9

11:1
gJdg 4:2,7,23
hver 10;
1Sa 12:9
iJos 19:15

11:2
jJos 12:3
kNu 34:11
lJos 17:11;
Jdg 1:27;
1Ki 4:11

11:3
mDt 7:1;
Jdg 3:3,5;
1Ki 9:20
nGe 31:49;
Jos 15:38; 18:26

11:4
oJdg 7:12;
1Sa 13:5

11:5
pJdg 5:19

11:6
qJos 10:8
r2Sa 8:4

---

^a2 Or *in the heights of Dor*

hand of Israel. They defeated them and pursued them all the way to Greater Sidon, to Misrephoth Maim, ˢ and to the Valley of Mizpah on the east, until no survivors were left. ⁹Joshua did to them as the LORD had directed: He hamstrung their horses and burned their chariots.

¹⁰At that time Joshua turned back and captured Hazor and put its king to the sword. (Hazor had been the head of all these kingdoms.) ¹¹Everyone in it they put to the sword. They totally destroyedᵃ them, not sparing anything that breathed,ᵗ and he burned up Hazor itself.

¹²Joshua took all these royal cities and their kings and put them to the sword. He totally destroyed them, as Moses the servant of the LORD had commanded.ᵘ ¹³Yet Israel did not burn any of the cities built on their mounds—except Hazor, which Joshua burned. ¹⁴The Israelites carried off for themselves all the plunder and livestock of these cities, but all the people they put to the sword until they completely destroyed them, not sparing anyone that breathed.ᵛ ¹⁵As the LORD commanded his servant Moses, so Moses commanded Joshua, and Joshua did it; he left nothing undone of all that the LORD commanded Moses.ʷ

¹⁶So Joshua took this entire land: the hill country, all the Negev, the whole region of Goshen, the western foothills,ˣ the Arabah and the mountains of Israel with their foothills, ¹⁷from Mount Halak, which rises toward Seir, to Baal Gad in the Valley of Lebanonʸ below Mount Hermon. He captured all their kings and struck them down, putting them to death.ᶻ ¹⁸Joshua waged war against all these kings for a long time. ¹⁹Except for the Hivites living in Gibeon,ᵃ not one city made a treaty of peace with the Israelites, who took them all in battle. ²⁰For it was the LORD himself who hardened their heartsᵇ to wage war against Israel, so that he might destroy them totally, exterminating them without mercy, as the LORD had commanded Moses.ᶜ

²¹At that time Joshua went and destroyed the Anakitesᵈ from the hill country: from Hebron, Debir and Anab, from all the hill country of Judah, and from all the hill country of Israel. Joshua totally destroyed them and their towns. ²²No Anakites were left in Israelite territory; only in Gaza, Gatheᵉ and Ashdodᶠ did any survive. ²³So Joshua took the entire land,ᵍ just as the LORD had directed Moses, and he gave it as an inheritanceʰ to Israel according to their tribal divisions.ⁱ

Then the land had rest from war.ʲ

List of Defeated Kings

12 These are the kings of the land whom the Israelites had defeated and whose territory they took over east of the Jordan, from the Arnon Gorge to Mount Hermon,ᵏ including all the eastern side of the Arabah:

²Sihon king of the Amorites,
    who reigned in Heshbon. He ruled from Aroer on the rim of the Arnon Gorge—from the middle of the gorge—to the Jabbok River, which is the border of the Ammonites. This included half of Gilead.ˡ ³He also ruled over the eastern Arabah from the Sea of Kinnerethᵇᵐ to the Sea of the Arabah (the Salt Seaᶜ), to Beth

Cross references (side column)

11:8
ˢJos 13:6
11:11
ᵗDt 20:16-17
11:12
ᵘNu 33:50-52;
Dt 7:2
11:14
ᵛNu 31:11-12
11:15
ʷEx 34:11;
Jos 1:7
11:16
ˣJos 10:41
11:17
ʸJos 12:7
ᶻDt 7:24
11:19
ᵃJos 9:3
11:20
ᵇEx 14:17;
Ro 9:18
ᶜDt 7:16;
Jdg 14:4
11:21
ᵈNu 13:22,33;
Dt 9:2
11:22
ᵉ1Sa 17:4;
1Ki 2:39;
1Ch 8:13
ᶠ1Sa 5:1;
Isa 20:1
11:23
ᵍJos 21:43-45
ʰDt 1:38;
12:9-10; 25:19
ⁱNu 26:53
ʲJos 14:15
12:1
ᵏDt 3:8
12:2
ˡDt 2:36
12:3
ᵐJos 11:2

ᵃ11 The Hebrew term refers to the irrevocable giving over of things or persons to the LORD, often by totally destroying them; also in verses 12, 20 and 21.   ᵇ3 That is, Galilee   ᶜ3 That is, the Dead Sea

Jeshimoth,[n] and then southward below the slopes of Pisgah.

[4]And the territory of Og king of Bashan,[o] one of the last of the Rephaites, who reigned in Ashtaroth[p] and Edrei. [5]He ruled over Mount Hermon, Salecah,[q] all of Bashan to the border of the people of Geshur[r] and Maacah,[s] and half of Gilead to the border of Sihon king of Heshbon.

[6]Moses, the servant of the LORD, and the Israelites conquered them. And Moses the servant of the LORD gave their land to the Reubenites, the Gadites and the half-tribe of Manasseh to be their possession.[t]

[7]These are the kings of the land that Joshua and the Israelites conquered on the west side of the Jordan, from Baal Gad in the Valley of Lebanon[u] to Mount Halak, which rises toward Seir (their lands Joshua gave as an inheritance to the tribes of Israel according to their tribal divisions— [8]the hill country, the western foothills, the Arabah, the mountain slopes, the desert and the Negev[v]—the lands of the Hittites, Amorites, Canaanites, Perizzites, Hivites and Jebusites):

[9]the king of Jericho[w]	one
the king of Ai[x] (near Bethel)	one
[10]the king of Jerusalem[y]	one
the king of Hebron	one
[11]the king of Jarmuth	one
the king of Lachish	one
[12]the king of Eglon	one
the king of Gezer[z]	one
[13]the king of Debir	one
the king of Geder	one
[14]the king of Hormah	one
the king of Arad[a]	one
[15]the king of Libnah	one
the king of Adullam	one
[16]the king of Makkedah	one
the king of Bethel[b]	one
[17]the king of Tappuah	one
the king of Hepher[c]	one
[18]the king of Aphek[d]	one
the king of Lasharon	one
[19]the king of Madon	one
the king of Hazor	one
[20]the king of Shimron Meron	one
the king of Acshaph[e]	one
[21]the king of Taanach	one
the king of Megiddo	one
[22]the king of Kedesh[f]	one
the king of Jokneam in Carmel[g]	one
[23]the king of Dor (in Naphoth Dor[a] [h])	one
the king of Goyim in Gilgal	one
[24]the king of Tirzah	one

thirty-one kings in all.[i]

[a]23 Or in the heights of Dor

12:3
nJos 13:20
12:4
oNu 21:21,33;
Dt 3:11 pDt 1:4
12:5
qDt 3:10
r1Sa 27:8
sDt 3:14
12:6
tNu 32:29,33;
Jos 13:8
12:7
uJos 11:17
12:8
vJos 11:16
12:9
wJos 6:2
xJos 8:29
12:10
yJos 10:23
12:12
zJos 10:33
12:14
aNu 21:1
12:16
bJos 7:2
12:17
c1Ki 4:10
12:18
dJos 13:4
12:20
eJos 11:1
12:22
fJos 19:37;
20:7; 21:32
g1Sa 15:12
12:23
hJos 11:2
12:24
iPs 135:11;
Dt 7:24

Land Still to Be Taken

13 When Joshua was old and well advanced in years,[j] the LORD said to him, "You are very old, and there are still very large areas of land to be taken over.

2"This is the land that remains: all the regions of the Philistines and Geshurites: 3from the Shihor River[k] on the east of Egypt to the territory of Ekron[l] on the north, all of it counted as Canaanite (the territory of the five Philistine rulers[m] in Gaza, Ashdod, Ashkelon, Gath and Ekron—that of the Avvites);[n] 4from the south, all the land of the Canaanites, from Arah of the Sidonians as far as Aphek,[o] the region of the Amorites,[p] 5the area of the Gebalites[a];[q] and all Lebanon[r] to the east, from Baal Gad below Mount Hermon to Lebo[b] Hamath.

6"As for all the inhabitants of the mountain regions from Lebanon to Misrephoth Maim,[s] that is, all the Sidonians, I myself will drive them out before the Israelites. Be sure to allocate this land to Israel for an inheritance, as I have instructed you,[t] 7and divide it as an inheritance[u] among the nine tribes and half of the tribe of Manasseh."

Division of the Land East of the Jordan

8The other half of Manasseh,[c] the Reubenites and the Gadites had received the inheritance that Moses had given them east of the Jordan, as he, the servant of the LORD, had assigned[v] it to them.

9It extended from Aroer[w] on the rim of the Arnon Gorge, and from the town in the middle of the gorge, and included the whole plateau[x] of Medeba as far as Dibon,[y] 10and all the towns of Sihon king of the Amorites, who ruled in Heshbon, out to the border of the Ammonites.[z] 11It also included Gilead, the territory of the people of Geshur and Maacah, all of Mount Hermon and all Bashan as far as Salecah[a]— 12that is, the whole kingdom of Og in Bashan,[b] who had reigned in Ashtaroth[c] and Edrei and had survived as one of the last of the Rephaites.[d] Moses had defeated them and taken over their land. 13But the Israelites did not drive out the people of Geshur[e] and Maacah,[f] so they continue to live among the Israelites to this day.

14But to the tribe of Levi he gave no inheritance, since the offerings made by fire to the LORD, the God of Israel, are their inheritance, as he promised them.[g]

15This is what Moses had given to the tribe of Reuben, clan by clan:

16The territory from Aroer[h] on the rim of the Arnon Gorge, and from the town in the middle of the gorge, and the whole plateau past Medeba[i] 17to Heshbon and all its towns on the plateau, including Dibon,[j] Bamoth Baal, Beth Baal Meon,[k] 18Jahaz,[l] Kedemoth, Mephaath,[m] 19Kiriathaim,[n] Sibmah, Zereth Shahar on the hill in the valley, 20Beth Peor,[o] the slopes of Pisgah, and Beth Jeshimoth 21—all the towns on the plateau and the entire realm of

---

13:1
j Ge 24:1;
Jos 14:10
13:3
k Jer 2:18
l Jdg 1:18
m Jdg 3:3
n Dt 2:23
13:4
o Jos 12:18;
19:30 p Am 2:10
13:5
q 1Ki 5:18;
Ps 83:7;
Eze 27:9
r Jos 12:7
13:6
s Jos 11:8
t Nu 33:54
13:7
u Jos 11:23;
Ps 78:55
13:8
v Jos 12:6
13:9
w ver 16;
Jdg 11:26
x Jer 48:8,21
y Nu 21:30
13:10
z Nu 21:24
13:11
a Jos 12:5
13:12
b Dt 3:11
c Jos 12:4
d Ge 14:5
13:13
e Jos 12:5
f Dt 3:14
13:14
g ver 33;
Dt 18:1-2
13:16
h ver 9; Jos 12:2
i Nu 21:30
13:17
j Nu 32:3
k 1Ch 5:8
13:18
l Nu 21:23
m Jer 48:21
13:19
n Nu 32:37
13:20
o Dt 3:29

---

a5 That is, the area of Byblos   b5 Or *to the entrance to*   c8 Hebrew *With it* (that is, with the other half of Manasseh)

Sihon king of the Amorites, who ruled at Heshbon. Moses had defeated him and the Midianite chiefs,ᴾ Evi, Rekem, Zur, Hur and Reba�q—princes allied with Sihon—who lived in that country. ²²In addition to those slain in battle, the Israelites had put to the sword Balaam son of Beor,ʳ who practiced divination. ²³The boundary of the Reubenites was the bank of the Jordan. These towns and their villages were the inheritance of the Reubenites, clan by clan.

²⁴This is what Moses had given to the tribe of Gad, clan by clan:

²⁵The territory of Jazer,ˢ all the towns of Gilead and half the Ammonite country as far as Aroer, near Rabbah; ²⁶and from Heshbonᵗ to Ramath Mizpah and Betonim, and from Mahanaim to the territory of Debir;ᵘ ²⁷and in the valley, Beth Haram, Beth Nimrah, Succothᵛ and Zaphon with the rest of the realm of Sihon king of Heshbon (the east side of the Jordan, the territory up to the end of the Sea of Kinnerethᵃʷ). ²⁸These towns and their villages were the inheritance of the Gadites,ˣ clan by clan.

²⁹This is what Moses had given to the half-tribe of Manasseh, that is, to half the family of the descendants of Manasseh, clan by clan:

³⁰The territory extending from Mahanaimʸ and including all of Bashan, the entire realm of Og king of Bashan—all the settlements of Jairᶻ in Bashan, sixty towns, ³¹half of Gilead, and Ashtaroth and Edrei (the royal cities of Og in Bashan). This was for the descendants of Makirᵃ son of Manasseh—for half of the sons of Makir, clan by clan.

³²This is the inheritance Moses had given when he was in the plains of Moab across the Jordan east of Jericho. ³³But to the tribe of Levi, Moses had given no inheritance; the LORD, the God of Israel, is their inheritance,ᵇ as he promised them.ᶜ

Division of the Land West of the Jordan

14 Now these are the areas the Israelites received as an inheritance in the land of Canaan, which Eleazar the priest, Joshua son of Nun and the heads of the tribal clans of Israel allotted to them.ᵈ ²Their inheritances were assigned by lotᵉ to the nine-and-a-half tribes, as the LORD had commanded through Moses. ³Moses had granted the two-and-a-half tribes their inheritance east of the Jordanᶠ but had not granted the Levites an inheritance among the rest,ᵍ ⁴for the sons of Joseph had become two tribes—Manasseh and Ephraim.ʰ The Levites received no share of the land but only towns to live in, with pasturelands for their flocks and herds. ⁵So the Israelites divided the land, just as the LORD had commanded Moses.ⁱ

Hebron Given to Caleb

⁶Now the men of Judah approached Joshua at Gilgal, and Caleb son of Jephunnehʲ the Kenizzite said to him, "You know what the LORD said to Moses the man of God at Kadesh Barneaᵏ about you and me. ⁷I

13:21
pNu 25:15
qNu 31:8
13:22
rNu 22:5; 31:8
13:25
sNu 21:32;
Jos 21:39
13:26
tNu 21:25;
Jer 49:3
uJos 10:3
13:27
vGe 33:17
wNu 34:11
13:28
xNu 32:33
13:30
yGe 32:2
zNu 32:41
13:31
aGe 50:23
13:33
bNu 18:20
cver 14;
Jos 18:7
14:1
dNu 34:17-18
14:2
eNu 26:55
14:3
fNu 32:33
gJos 13:14
14:4
hGe 41:52; 48:5
14:5
iNu 34:13;
35:2; Jos 21:2
14:6
jNu 13:6; 14:30
kNu 13:26

was forty years old when Moses the servant of the LORD sent me from Kadesh Barnea to explore the land.[l] And I brought him back a report according to my convictions,[m] [8]but my brothers who went up with me made the hearts of the people melt with fear.[n] I, however, followed the LORD my God wholeheartedly.[o] [9]So on that day Moses swore to me, 'The land on which your feet have walked will be your inheritance and that of your children[p] forever, because you have followed the LORD my God wholeheartedly.'[a]

[10]"Now then, just as the LORD promised,[q] he has kept me alive for forty-five years since the time he said this to Moses, while Israel moved about in the desert. So here I am today, eighty-five years old! [11]I am still as strong[r] today as the day Moses sent me out; I'm just as vigorous to go out to battle now as I was then. [12]Now give me this hill country that the LORD promised me that day. You yourself heard then that the Anakites[s] were there and their cities were large and fortified,[t] but, the LORD helping me, I will drive them out just as he said."

[13]Then Joshua blessed[u] Caleb son of Jephunneh and gave him Hebron[v] as his inheritance.[w] [14]So Hebron has belonged to Caleb son of Jephunneh the Kenizzite ever since, because he followed the LORD, the God of Israel, wholeheartedly. [15](Hebron used to be called Kiriath Arba[x] after Arba,[y] who was the greatest man among the Anakites.)

Then the land had rest[z] from war.

Allotment for Judah

15:15-19pp — Jdg 1:11-15

15 The allotment for the tribe of Judah, clan by clan, extended down to the territory of Edom,[a] to the Desert of Zin[b] in the extreme south.

[2]Their southern boundary started from the bay at the southern end of the Salt Sea,[b] [3]crossed south of Scorpion[c] Pass,[c] continued on to Zin and went over to the south of Kadesh Barnea. Then it ran past Hezron up to Addar and curved around to Karka. [4]It then passed along to Azmon[d] and joined the Wadi of Egypt,[e] ending at the sea. This is their[d] southern boundary.

[5]The eastern boundary[f] is the Salt Sea as far as the mouth of the Jordan.

The northern boundary[g] started from the bay of the sea at the mouth of the Jordan, [6]went up to Beth Hoglah[h] and continued north of Beth Arabah to the Stone of Bohan[i] son of Reuben. [7]The boundary then went up to Debir from the Valley of Achor[j] and turned north to Gilgal, which faces the Pass of Adummim south of the gorge. It continued along to the waters of En Shemesh and came out at En Rogel.[k] [8]Then it ran up the Valley of Ben Hinnom along the southern slope of the Jebusite[l] city (that is, Jerusalem). From there it climbed to the top of the hill west of the Hinnom Valley at the northern end of the Valley of Rephaim. [9]From the hilltop the boundary headed toward the spring of the waters of Nephtoah,[m] came out at the towns of Mount Ephron and went down toward Baalah[n] (that is, Kiriath Jearim). [10]Then it curved

14:7
lNu 13:17
mNu 13:30;
14:6-9
14:8
nNu 13:31
oNu 14:24
14:9
pNu 14:24;
Dt 1:36
14:10
qNu 14:30
14:11
rDt 34:7
14:12
sNu 13:33
tNu 13:28
14:13
uJos 22:6,7
vJos 10:36
wJdg 1:20;
1Ch 6:56
14:15
xGe 23:2
yJos 15:13
zJos 11:23
15:1
aNu 34:3
bNu 33:36
15:3
cNu 34:4
15:4
dNu 34:5
eGe 15:18
15:5
fNu 34:10
gJos 18:15-19
15:6
hJos 18:19,21
iJos 18:17
15:7
jJos 7:24
k2Sa 17:17;
1Ki 1:9
15:8
lver 63;
Jos 18:16,28;
Jdg 1:21; 19:10
15:9
mJos 18:15
n1Ch 13:6

---

[a]9 Deut. 1:36   [b]2 That is, the Dead Sea; also in verse 5   [c]3 Hebrew *Akrabbim*
[d]4 Hebrew *your*

westward from Baalah to Mount Seir, ran along the northern slope of Mount Jearim (that is, Kesalon), continued down to Beth Shemesh and crossed to Timnah. [o] [11]It went to the northern slope of Ekron, turned toward Shikkeron, passed along to Mount Baalah and reached Jabneel. [p] The boundary ended at the sea.

[12]The western boundary is the coastline of the Great Sea. [a] [q] These are the boundaries around the people of Judah by their clans.

[13]In accordance with the LORD's command to him, Joshua gave to Caleb son of Jephunneh a portion in Judah—Kiriath Arba, that is, Hebron. (Arba was the forefather of Anak.) [r] [14]From Hebron Caleb drove out the three Anakites [s]—Sheshai, Ahiman and Talmai [t]—descendants of Anak. [u] [15]From there he marched against the people living in Debir (formerly called Kiriath Sepher). [16]And Caleb said, "I will give my daughter Acsah [v] in marriage to the man who attacks and captures Kiriath Sepher." [17]Othniel [w] son of Kenaz, Caleb's brother, took it; so Caleb gave his daughter Acsah to him in marriage.

[18]One day when she came to Othniel, she urged him [b] to ask her father for a field. When she got off her donkey, Caleb asked her, "What can I do for you?"

[19]She replied, "Do me a special favor. Since you have given me land in the Negev, give me also springs of water." So Caleb gave her the upper and lower springs.

[20]This is the inheritance of the tribe of Judah, clan by clan:

[21]The southernmost towns of the tribe of Judah in the Negev toward the boundary of Edom were:

Kabzeel, Eder, [x] Jagur, [22]Kinah, Dimonah, Adadah, [23]Kedesh, Hazor, Ithnan, [24]Ziph, [y] Telem, Bealoth, [25]Hazor Hadattah, Kerioth Hezron (that is, Hazor), [26]Amam, Shema, Moladah, [z] [27]Hazar Gaddah, Heshmon, Beth Pelet, [28]Hazar Shual, Beersheba, [a] Biziothiah, [29]Baalah, [b] Iim, Ezem, [30]Eltolad, [c] Kesil, Hormah, [31]Ziklag, [d] Madmannah, Sansannah, [32]Lebaoth, Shilhim, Ain and Rimmon [e]—a total of twenty-nine towns and their villages.

[33]In the western foothills:

Eshtaol, [f] Zorah, Ashnah, [34]Zanoah, [g] En Gannim, Tappuah, Enam, [35]Jarmuth, [h] Adullam, [i] Socoh, Azekah, [36]Shaaraim, Adithaim and Gederah [j] (or Gederothaim) [c]—fourteen towns and their villages.

[37]Zenan, Hadashah, Migdal Gad, [38]Dilean, Mizpah, Joktheel, [k] [39]Lachish, [l] Bozkath, [m] Eglon, [40]Cabbon, Lahmas, Kitlish, [41]Gederoth, Beth Dagon, Naamah and Makkedah [n]—sixteen towns and their villages.

[42]Libnah, Ether, Ashan, [o] [43]Iphtah, Ashnah, Nezib, [44]Keilah, Aczib [p] and Mareshah [q]—nine towns and their villages.

[45]Ekron, with its surrounding settlements and villages; [46]west of Ekron, all that were in the vicinity of Ashdod, together with their villages; [47]Ashdod, [r] its surrounding settlements and villages; and

---

[a]12 That is, the Mediterranean; also in verse 47   [b]18 Hebrew and some Septuagint manuscripts; other Septuagint manuscripts (see also note at Judges 1:14) *Othniel, he urged her* [c]36 Or *Gederah and Gederothaim*

15:10
oGe 38:12;
Jdg 14:1
15:11
pJos 19:33
15:12
qNu 34:6
15:13
rJos 14:13-15
15:14
sNu 13:33
tNu 13:22
uJdg 1:10,20
15:16
vJdg 1:12
15:17
wJdg 3:9,11
15:21
xGe 35:21
15:24
y1Sa 23:14
15:26
z1Ch 4:28
15:28
aGe 21:31
15:29
bver 9
15:30
cJos 19:4
15:31
d1Sa 27:6
15:32
eJdg 20:45
15:33
fJdg 13:25;
16:31
15:34
g1Ch 4:18;
Ne 3:13
15:35
hJos 10:3
i1Sa 22:1
15:36
j1Ch 12:4
15:38
k2Ki 14:7
15:39
lJos 10:3;
2Ki 14:19
m2Ki 22:1
15:41
nJos 10:10
15:42
o1Sa 30:30
15:44
pJdg 1:31
qMic 1:15
15:47
rJos 11:22

Gaza, its settlements and villages, as far as the Wadi of Egypt[s] and the coastline of the Great Sea.[t]

48In the hill country:

Shamir, Jattir,[u] Socoh, 49Dannah, Kiriath Sannah (that is, Debir[v]), 50Anab, Eshtemoh,[w] Anim, 51Goshen,[x] Holon and Giloh —eleven towns and their villages.

52Arab, Dumah,[y] Eshan, 53Janim, Beth Tappuah, Aphekah, 54Humtah, Kiriath Arba (that is, Hebron) and Zior—nine towns and their villages.

55Maon, Carmel,[z] Ziph, Juttah, 56Jezreel,[a] Jokdeam, Zanoah, 57Kain, Gibeah[b] and Timnah—ten towns and their villages.

58Halhul, Beth Zur,[c] Gedor, 59Maarath, Beth Anoth and Eltekon—six towns and their villages.

60Kiriath Baal (that is, Kiriath Jearim[d]) and Rabbah[e]—two towns and their villages.

61In the desert:

Beth Arabah, Middin, Secacah, 62Nibshan, the City of Salt and En Gedi[f]—six towns and their villages.

63Judah could not[g] dislodge the Jebusites[h], who were living in Jerusalem; to this day the Jebusites live there with the people of Judah.

Allotment for Ephraim and Manasseh

16 The allotment for Joseph began at the Jordan of Jericho,[a] east of the waters of Jericho, and went up from there through the desert[i] into the hill country of Bethel. 2It went on from Bethel (that is, Luz[j]),[b] crossed over to the territory of the Arkites in Ataroth, 3descended westward to the territory of the Japhletites as far as the region of Lower Beth Horon[k] and on to Gezer,[l] ending at the sea.

4So Manasseh and Ephraim, the descendants of Joseph, received their inheritance.[m]

5This was the territory of Ephraim, clan by clan:

The boundary of their inheritance went from Ataroth Addar[n] in the east to Upper Beth Horon 6and continued to the sea. From Micmethath[o] on the north it curved eastward to Taanath Shiloh, passing by it to Janoah on the east. 7Then it went down from Janoah to Ataroth[p] and Naarah, touched Jericho and came out at the Jordan. 8From Tappuah the border went west to the Kanah Ravine[q] and ended at the sea. This was the inheritance of the tribe of the Ephraimites, clan by clan. 9It also included all the towns and their villages that were set aside for the Ephraimites within the inheritance of the Manassites.

10They did not dislodge the Canaanites living in Gezer; to this day the Canaanites live among the people of Ephraim but are required to do forced labor.[r]

17 This was the allotment for the tribe of Manasseh as Joseph's firstborn,[s] that is, for Makir,[t] Manasseh's firstborn. Makir was

15:47
sver 4 tNu 34:6
15:48
u1Sa 30:27
15:49
vJos 10:3
15:50
wJos 21:14
15:51
xJos 10:41;
11:16
15:52
yGe 25:14
15:55
zJos 12:22
15:56
aJos 17:16
15:57
bJos 18:28;
Jdg 19:12
15:58
c1Ch 2:45
15:60
dJos 18:14
eDt 3:11
15:62
f1Sa 23:29
15:63
gJdg 1:21
h2Sa 5:6
16:1
iJos 8:15; 18:12
16:2
jJos 18:13
16:3
k2Ch 8:5
lJos 10:33;
1Ki 9:15
16:4
mJos 17:14
16:5
nJos 18:13
16:6
oJos 17:7
16:7
p1Ch 7:28
16:8
qJos 17:9
16:10
rJos 17:13;
Jdg 1:28-29;
1Ki 9:16
17:1
sGe 41:51
tGe 50:23

---

[a]1 *Jordan of Jericho* was possibly an ancient name for the Jordan River.   [b]2 Septuagint; Hebrew *Bethel to Luz*

the ancestor of the Gileadites, who had received Gilead and Bashan because the Makirites were great soldiers. ²So this allotment was for the rest of the people of Manasseh—the clans of Abiezer,ᵘ Helek, Asriel, Shechem, Hepher and Shemida. These are the other male descendants of Manasseh son of Joseph by their clans.

³Now Zelophehad son of Hepher,ᵛ the son of Gilead, the son of Makir, the son of Manasseh, had no sons but only daughters,ʷ whose names were Mahlah, Noah, Hoglah, Milcah and Tirzah. ⁴They went to Eleazar the priest, Joshua son of Nun, and the leaders and said, "The Lᴏʀᴅ commanded Moses to give us an inheritance among our brothers." So Joshua gave them an inheritance along with the brothers of their father, according to the Lᴏʀᴅ's command.ˣ ⁵Manasseh's share consisted of ten tracts of land besides Gilead and Bashan east of the Jordan, ⁶because the daughters of the tribe of Manasseh received an inheritance among the sons. The land of Gilead belonged to the rest of the descendants of Manasseh.

⁷The territory of Manasseh extended from Asher to Micmethathʸ east of Shechem.ᶻ The boundary ran southward from there to include the people living at En Tappuah. ⁸(Manasseh had the land of Tappuah, but Tappuahᵃ itself, on the boundary of Manasseh, belonged to the Ephraimites.) ⁹Then the boundary continued south to the Kanah Ravine.ᵇ There were towns belonging to Ephraim lying among the towns of Manasseh, but the boundary of Manasseh was the northern side of the ravine and ended at the sea. ¹⁰On the south the land belonged to Ephraim, on the north to Manasseh. The territory of Manasseh reached the sea and bordered Asher on the north and Issacharᶜ on the east.

¹¹Within Issachar and Asher, Manasseh also had Beth Shan,ᵈ Ibleam and the people of Dor,ᵉ Endor,ᶠ Taanach and Megiddo,ᵍ together with their surrounding settlements (the third in the list is Naphothᵃ).

¹²Yet the Manassites were not ableʰ to occupy these towns, for the Canaanites were determined to live in that region. ¹³However, when the Israelites grew stronger, they subjected the Canaanites to forced labor but did not drive them out completely.ⁱ

¹⁴The people of Joseph said to Joshua, "Why have you given us only one allotment and one portion for an inheritance? We are a numerous people and the Lᴏʀᴅ has blessed us abundantly."ʲ

¹⁵"If you are so numerous," Joshua answered, "and if the hill country of Ephraim is too small for you, go up into the forest and clear land for yourselves there in the land of the Perizzites and Rephaites.ᵏ"

¹⁶The people of Joseph replied, "The hill country is not enough for us, and all the Canaanites who live in the plain have iron chariots,ˡ both those in Beth Shan and its settlements and those in the Valley of Jezreel."

¹⁷But Joshua said to the house of Joseph—to Ephraim and Manasseh—"You are numerous and very powerful. You will have not only one allotment ¹⁸but the forested hill country as well. Clear it, and its farthest limits will be yours; though the Canaanites have iron chariotsᵐ and though they are strong, you can drive them out."

17:2
uNu 26:30;
1Ch 7:18
17:3
vNu 27:1
wNu 26:33
17:4
xNu 27:5-7
17:7
yJos 16:6
zGe 12:6;
Jos 21:21
17:8
aJos 16:8
17:9
bJos 16:8
17:10
cGe 30:18
17:11
d1Sa 31:10;
1Ki 4:12;
1Ch 7:29
eJos 11:2
f1Sa 28:7;
Ps 83:10
g1Ki 9:15
17:12
hJdg 1:27
17:13
iJos 16:10
17:14
jNu 26:28-37
17:15
kGe 14:5
17:16
lJdg 1:19;
4:3,13
17:18
mver 16

ᵃ11 That is, Naphoth Dor

Division of the Rest of the Land

18 The whole assembly of the Israelites gathered at Shiloh[n] and set up the Tent of Meeting[o] there. The country was brought under their control, [2]but there were still seven Israelite tribes who had not yet received their inheritance.

[3]So Joshua said to the Israelites: "How long will you wait before you begin to take possession of the land that the LORD, the God of your fathers, has given you? [4]Appoint three men from each tribe. I will send them out to make a survey of the land and to write a description of it, according to the inheritance of each.[p] Then they will return to me. [5]You are to divide the land into seven parts. Judah is to remain in its territory on the south[q] and the house of Joseph in its territory on the north.[r] [6]After you have written descriptions of the seven parts of the land, bring them here to me and I will cast lots[s] for you in the presence of the LORD our God. [7]The Levites, however, do not get a portion among you, because the priestly service of the LORD is their inheritance.[t] And Gad, Reuben and the half-tribe of Manasseh have already received their inheritance on the east side of the Jordan. Moses the servant of the LORD gave it to them.[u]"

[8]As the men started on their way to map out the land, Joshua instructed them, "Go and make a survey of the land and write a description of it. Then return to me, and I will cast lots for you here at Shiloh[v] in the presence of the LORD." [9]So the men left and went through the land. They wrote its description on a scroll, town by town, in seven parts, and returned to Joshua in the camp at Shiloh. [10]Joshua then cast lots[w] for them in Shiloh in the presence[x] of the LORD, and there he distributed the land to the Israelites according to their tribal divisions.[y]

Allotment for Benjamin

[11]The lot came up for the tribe of Benjamin, clan by clan. Their allotted territory lay between the tribes of Judah and Joseph:

[12]On the north side their boundary began at the Jordan, passed the northern slope of Jericho and headed west into the hill country, coming out at the desert[z] of Beth Aven.[a] [13]From there it crossed to the south slope of Luz[b] (that is, Bethel[c]) and went down to Ataroth Addar[d] on the hill south of Lower Beth Horon.

[14]From the hill facing Beth Horon[e] on the south the boundary turned south along the western side and came out at Kiriath Baal (that is, Kiriath Jearim), a town of the people of Judah. This was the western side.

[15]The southern side began at the outskirts of Kiriath Jearim on the west, and the boundary came out at the spring of the waters of Nephtoah.[f] [16]The boundary went down to the foot of the hill facing the Valley of Ben Hinnom, north of the Valley of Rephaim. It continued down the Hinnom Valley[g] along the southern slope of the Jebusite city and so to En Rogel.[h] [17]It then curved north, went to En Shemesh, continued to Geliloth, which faces the Pass of Adummim, and ran down to the Stone of Bohan[i] son of Reuben. [18]It continued to the northern slope of Beth Arabah[a] [j]

18:1
n Jos 19:51;
21:2; Jdg 18:31;
21:12,19;
1Sa 1:3; 4:3;
Jer 7:12; 26:6
o Ex 27:21
18:4
p Mic 2:5
18:5
q Jos 15:1
r Jos 16:1-4
18:6
s Jos 14:2
18:7
t Jos 13:33
u Jos 13:8
18:8
v ver 1
18:10
w Nu 34:13
x ver 1; Jer 7:12
y Nu 33:54;
Jos 19:51
18:12
z Jos 16:1
a Jos 7:2
18:13
b Ge 28:19
c Jdg 1:23
d Jos 16:5
18:14
e Jos 10:10
18:15
f Jos 15:9
18:16
g Jos 15:8;
2Ki 23:10
h Jos 15:7
18:17
i Jos 15:6
18:18
j Jos 15:6

---

a18 Septuagint; Hebrew *slope facing the Arabah*

and on down into the Arabah. [19]It then went to the northern slope of Beth Hoglah and came out at the northern bay of the Salt Sea,[a][k] at the mouth of the Jordan in the south. This was the southern boundary.

[20]The Jordan formed the boundary on the eastern side.

These were the boundaries that marked out the inheritance of the clans of Benjamin on all sides.[l]

[21]The tribe of Benjamin, clan by clan, had the following cities:

Jericho, Beth Hoglah, Emek Keziz, [22]Beth Arabah, Zemaraim, Bethel,[m] [23]Avvim, Parah, Ophrah, [24]Kephar Ammoni, Ophni and Geba[n]—twelve towns and their villages.

[25]Gibeon,[o] Ramah,[p] Beeroth,[q] [26]Mizpah,[r] Kephirah, Mozah, [27]Rekem, Irpeel, Taralah, [28]Zelah,[s] Haeleph, the Jebusite city[t] (that is, Jerusalem[u]), Gibeah[v] and Kiriath—fourteen towns and their villages.

This was the inheritance of Benjamin for its clans.

Allotment for Simeon

19:2–10pp — 1Ch 4:28–33

19 The second lot came out for the tribe of Simeon, clan by clan. Their inheritance lay within the territory of Judah.[w] [2]It included:

Beersheba[x] (or Sheba),[b] Moladah, [3]Hazar Shual, Balah, Ezem, [4]Eltolad, Bethul, Hormah, [5]Ziklag, Beth Marcaboth, Hazar Susah, [6]Beth Lebaoth and Sharuhen—thirteen towns and their villages;

[7]Ain, Rimmon, Ether and Ashan[y]—four towns and their villages— [8]and all the villages around these towns as far as Baalath Beer (Ramah in the Negev).[z]

This was the inheritance of the tribe of the Simeonites, clan by clan. [9]The inheritance of the Simeonites was taken from the share of Judah,[a] because Judah's portion was more than they needed. So the Simeonites received their inheritance within the territory of Judah.[b]

Allotment for Zebulun

[10]The third lot came up for Zebulun,[c] clan by clan:

The boundary of their inheritance went as far as Sarid. [11]Going west it ran to Maralah, touched Dabbesheth, and extended to the ravine near Jokneam.[d] [12]It turned east from Sarid toward the sunrise to the territory of Kisloth Tabor and went on to Daberath and up to Japhia. [13]Then it continued eastward to Gath Hepher and Eth Kazin; it came out at Rimmon[e] and turned toward Neah. [14]There the boundary went around on the north to Hannathon and ended at the Valley of Iphtah El. [15]Included were Kattath, Nahalal, Shimron, Idalah and Bethlehem.[f] There were twelve towns and their villages.

[16]These towns and their villages were the inheritance of Zebulun,[g] clan by clan.[h]

18:19
k Ge 14:3
18:20
l Jos 21:4,17; 1Sa 9:1
18:22
m Jos 16:1
18:24
n Isa 10:29
18:25
o Jos 9:3
p Jdg 4:5
q Jos 9:17
18:26
r Jos 11:3
18:28
s 2Sa 21:14
t Jos 15:8
u Jos 10:1
v Jos 15:57
19:1
w ver 9; Ge 49:7
19:2
x Ge 21:14; 1Ki 19:3
19:7
y Jos 15:42
19:8
z Jos 10:40
19:9
a Ge 49:7
b Eze 48:24
19:10
c Jos 21:7,34
19:11
d Jos 12:22
19:13
e Jos 15:32
19:15
f Ge 35:19
19:16
g ver 10; Jos 21:7
h Eze 48:26

---

[a]19 That is, the Dead Sea   [b]2 Or *Beersheba, Sheba*; 1 Chron. 4:28 does not have *Sheba*.

Allotment for Issachar

[17]The fourth lot came out for Issachar,[i] clan by clan. [18]Their territory included:

Jezreel,[j] Kesulloth, Shunem,[k] [19]Hapharaim, Shion, Anaharath, [20]Rabbith, Kishion, Ebez, [21]Remeth, En Gannim, En Haddah and Beth Pazzez. [22]The boundary touched Tabor,[l] Shahazumah and Beth Shemesh,[m] and ended at the Jordan. There were sixteen towns and their villages.

[23]These towns and their villages were the inheritance of the tribe of Issachar,[n] clan by clan.[o]

Allotment for Asher

[24]The fifth lot came out for the tribe of Asher,[p] clan by clan. [25]Their territory included:

Helkath, Hali, Beten, Acshaph, [26]Allammelech, Amad and Mishal. On the west the boundary touched Carmel[q] and Shihor Libnath. [27]It then turned east toward Beth Dagon, touched Zebulun[r] and the Valley of Iphtah El, and went north to Beth Emek and Neiel, passing Cabul[s] on the left. [28]It went to Abdon,[a] Rehob,[t] Hammon[u] and Kanah, as far as Greater Sidon.[v] [29]The boundary then turned back toward Ramah[w] and went to the fortified city of Tyre,[x] turned toward Hosah and came out at the sea in the region of Aczib,[y] [30]Ummah, Aphek and Rehob. There were twenty-two towns and their villages.

[31]These towns and their villages were the inheritance of the tribe of Asher,[z] clan by clan.

Allotment for Naphtali

[32]The sixth lot came out for Naphtali, clan by clan:

[33]Their boundary went from Heleph and the large tree in Zaanannim, passing Adami Nekeb and Jabneel to Lakkum and ending at the Jordan. [34]The boundary ran west through Aznoth Tabor and came out at Hukkok. It touched Zebulun on the south, Asher on the west and the Jordan[b] on the east. [35]The fortified cities were Ziddim, Zer, Hammath, Rakkath, Kinnereth,[a] [36]Adamah, Ramah,[b] Hazor,[c] [37]Kedesh, Edrei,[d] En Hazor, [38]Iron, Migdal El, Horem, Beth Anath and Beth Shemesh. There were nineteen towns and their villages.

[39]These towns and their villages were the inheritance of the tribe of Naphtali, clan by clan.[e]

Allotment for Dan

[40]The seventh lot came out for the tribe of Dan, clan by clan. [41]The territory of their inheritance included:

Zorah, Eshtaol, Ir Shemesh, [42]Shaalabbin, Aijalon,[f] Ithlah, [43]Elon, Timnah,[g] Ekron, [44]Eltekeh, Gibbethon, Baalath, [45]Jehud, Bene Berak, Gath Rimmon,[h] [46]Me Jarkon and Rakkon, with the area facing Joppa.[i]

[47](But the Danites had difficulty taking possession of their territory,[j]

19:17
iGe 30:18
19:18
jJos 15:56
k1Sa 28:4;
2Ki 4:8
19:22
lJdg 4:6,12;
Ps 89:12
mJos 15:10
19:23
nJos 17:10
oGe 49:15;
Eze 48:25
19:24
pJos 17:7
19:26
qJos 12:22
19:27
rver 10
s1Ki 9:13
19:28
tJdg 1:31
u1Ch 6:76
vGe 10:19;
Jos 11:8
19:29
wJos 18:25
x2Sa 5:11;
24:7; Isa 23:1;
Jer 25:22;
Eze 26:2
yJdg 1:31
19:31
zGe 30:13;
Eze 48:2
19:35
aJos 11:2
19:36
bJos 18:25
cJos 11:1
19:37
dNu 21:33
19:39
eDt 33:23;
Eze 48:3
19:42
fJdg 1:35
19:43
gGe 38:12
19:45
hJos 21:24;
1Ch 6:69
19:46
i2Ch 2:16;
Jnh 1:3
19:47
jJdg 18:1

---

[a]28 Some Hebrew manuscripts (see also Joshua 21:30); most Hebrew manuscripts *Ebron*
[b]34 Septuagint; Hebrew *west, and Judah, the Jordan,*

so they went up and attacked Leshem[k], took it, put it to the sword and occupied it. They settled in Leshem and named it Dan after their forefather.)[l] [48]These towns and their villages were the inheritance of the tribe of Dan,[m] clan by clan.

Allotment for Joshua

[49]When they had finished dividing the land into its allotted portions, the Israelites gave Joshua son of Nun an inheritance among them, [50]as the LORD had commanded. They gave him the town he asked for—Timnath Serah[an] in the hill country of Ephraim. And he built up the town and settled there.

[51]These are the territories that Eleazar the priest, Joshua son of Nun and the heads of the tribal clans of Israel assigned by lot at Shiloh in the presence of the LORD at the entrance to the Tent of Meeting. And so they finished dividing the land.[o]

Cities of Refuge

20:1–9Ref — Nu 35:9–34; Dt 4:41–43; 19:1–14

20 Then the LORD said to Joshua: [2]"Tell the Israelites to designate the cities of refuge, as I instructed you through Moses, [3]so that anyone who kills a person accidentally and unintentionally[p] may flee there and find protection from the avenger of blood.[q]

[4]"When he flees to one of these cities, he is to stand in the entrance of the city gate[r] and state his case before the elders[s] of that city. Then they are to admit him into their city and give him a place to live with them. [5]If the avenger of blood pursues him, they must not surrender the one accused, because he killed his neighbor unintentionally and without malice aforethought. [6]He is to stay in that city until he has stood trial before the assembly[t] and until the death of the high priest who is serving at that time. Then he may go back to his own home in the town from which he fled."

[7]So they set apart Kedesh[u] in Galilee in the hill country of Naphtali, Shechem[v] in the hill country of Ephraim, and Kiriath Arba (that is, Hebron[w]) in the hill country of Judah.[x] [8]On the east side of the Jordan of Jericho[b] they designated Bezer[y] in the desert on the plateau in the tribe of Reuben, Ramoth in Gilead[z] in the tribe of Gad, and Golan in Bashan in the tribe of Manasseh. [9]Any of the Israelites or any alien living among them who killed someone accidentally could flee to these designated cities and not be killed by the avenger of blood prior to standing trial before the assembly.[a]

Towns for the Levites

21:4–39pp — 1Ch 6:54–80

21 Now the family heads of the Levites approached Eleazar the priest, Joshua son of Nun, and the heads of the other tribal families of Israel[b] [2]at Shiloh[c] in Canaan and said to them, "The LORD commanded through Moses that you give us towns to live in, with pasturelands for our livestock."[d] [3]So, as the LORD had commanded, the

---

[a]50 Also known as Timnath Heres (see Judges 2:9)   [b]8 Jordan of Jericho was possibly an ancient name for the Jordan River.

Israelites gave the Levites the following towns and pasturelands out of their own inheritance:

⁴The first lot came out for the Kohathites, clan by clan. The Levites who were descendants of Aaron the priest were allotted thirteen towns from the tribes of Judah, Simeon and Benjamin.ᵉ ⁵The rest of Kohath's descendants were allotted ten towns from the clans of the tribes of Ephraim, Dan and half of Manasseh.ᶠ

⁶The descendants of Gershon were allotted thirteen towns from the clans of the tribes of Issachar,ᵍ Asher, Naphtali and the half-tribe of Manasseh in Bashan.

⁷The descendants of Merari,ʰ clan by clan, received twelve towns from the tribes of Reuben, Gad and Zebulun.ⁱ

⁸So the Israelites allotted to the Levites these towns and their pasturelands, as the LORD had commanded through Moses.

⁹From the tribes of Judah and Simeon they allotted the following towns by name ¹⁰(these towns were assigned to the descendants of Aaron who were from the Kohathite clans of the Levites, because the first lot fell to them):

¹¹They gave them Kiriath Arba (that is, Hebronʲ), with its surrounding pastureland, in the hill country of Judah. (Arba was the forefather of Anak.) ¹²But the fields and villages around the city they had given to Caleb son of Jephunneh as his possession.

¹³So to the descendants of Aaron the priest they gave Hebron (a city of refuge for one accused of murder), Libnah,ᵏ ¹⁴Jattir,ˡ Eshtemoa,ᵐ ¹⁵Holon,ⁿ Debir, ¹⁶Ain, Juttahᵒ and Beth Shemesh,ᵖ together with their pasturelands—nine towns from these two tribes.

¹⁷And from the tribe of Benjamin they gave them Gibeon, Geba,�q ¹⁸Anathoth and Almon, together with their pasturelands —four towns.

¹⁹All the towns for the priests, the descendants of Aaron, were thirteen, together with their pasturelands.

²⁰The rest of the Kohathite clans of the Levites were allotted towns from the tribe of Ephraim:

²¹In the hill country of Ephraim they were given Shechemʳ (a city of refuge for one accused of murder) and Gezer, ²²Kibzaim and Beth Horon,ˢ together with their pasturelands—four towns.ᵗ

²³Also from the tribe of Dan they received Eltekeh, Gibbethon, ²⁴Aijalon and Gath Rimmon,ᵘ together with their pasturelands —four towns.

²⁵From half the tribe of Manasseh they received Taanach and Gath Rimmon, together with their pasturelands—two towns.

²⁶All these ten towns and their pasturelands were given to the rest of the Kohathite clans.

²⁷The Levite clans of the Gershonites were given:
from the half-tribe of Manasseh,
Golan in Bashanᵛ (a city of refuge for one accused of murderʷ)
and Be Eshtarah, together with their pasturelands—two towns;
²⁸from the tribe of Issachar,ˣ

21:4
ever 19
21:5
fver 26
21:6
gGe 30:18
21:7
hEx 6:16
iJos 19:10
21:11
jJos 15:13;
1Ch 6:55
21:13
kJos 15:42;
1Ch 6:57
21:14
lJos 15:48
mJos 15:50
21:15
nJos 15:51
21:16
oJos 15:55
pJos 15:10
21:17
qJos 18:24
21:21
rJos 17:7; 20:7
21:22
sJos 10:10
t1Sa 1:1
21:24
uJos 19:45
21:27
vJos 12:5
wNu 35:6
21:28
xGe 30:18

Kishion, Daberath, [29]Jarmuth and En Gannim, together with their pasturelands—four towns;
[30]from the tribe of Asher, [y]
Mishal, Abdon, [31]Helkath and Rehob, together with their pasturelands—four towns;
[32]from the tribe of Naphtali,
Kedesh[z] in Galilee (a city of refuge for one accused of murder[a]),
Hammoth Dor and Kartan, together with their pasturelands—three towns.
[33]All the towns of the Gershonite[b] clans were thirteen, together with their pasturelands.

[34]The Merarite clans (the rest of the Levites) were given:
from the tribe of Zebulun, [c]
Jokneam, Kartah, [35]Dimnah and Nahalal, together with their pasturelands—four towns;
[36]from the tribe of Reuben,
Bezer, [d] Jahaz, [37]Kedemoth and Mephaath, together with their pasturelands—four towns;
[38]from the tribe of Gad,
Ramoth[e] in Gilead (a city of refuge for one accused of murder),
Mahanaim, [f] [39]Heshbon and Jazer, together with their pasturelands—four towns in all.
[40]All the towns allotted to the Merarite clans, who were the rest of the Levites, were twelve.
[41]The towns of the Levites in the territory held by the Israelites were forty-eight in all, together with their pasturelands. [g] [42]Each of these towns had pasturelands surrounding it; this was true for all these towns.

[43]So the LORD gave Israel all the land he had sworn to give their forefathers, [h] and they took possession[i] of it and settled there. [j] [44]The LORD gave them rest[k] on every side, just as he had sworn to their forefathers. Not one of their enemies[l] withstood them; the LORD handed all their enemies[m] over to them. [n] [45]Not one of all the LORD's good promises[o] to the house of Israel failed; every one was fulfilled.

Eastern Tribes Return Home

22 Then Joshua summoned the Reubenites, the Gadites and the half-tribe of Manasseh [2]and said to them, "You have done all that Moses the servant of the LORD commanded, [p] and you have obeyed me in everything I commanded. [3]For a long time now—to this very day—you have not deserted your brothers but have carried out the mission the LORD your God gave you. [4]Now that the LORD your God has given your brothers rest as he promised, return to your homes[q] in the land that Moses the servant of the LORD gave you on the other side of the Jordan. [r] [5]But be very careful to keep the commandment[s] and the law that Moses the servant of the LORD gave you: to love the LORD your God, to walk in all his ways, to obey his commands, [t] to hold fast to him and to serve him with all your heart and all your soul. [u]"

[6]Then Joshua blessed[v] them and sent them away, and they went to their homes. [7](To the half-tribe of Manasseh Moses had given land in Bashan, [w] and to the other half of the tribe Joshua gave land on the west

21:30
y Jos 17:7
21:32
z Jos 12:22
a Nu 35:6;
Jos 20:7
21:33
b ver 6
21:34
c Jos 19:10;
1Ch 6:77
21:36
d Jos 20:8
21:38
e Dt 4:43
f Ge 32:2
21:41
g Nu 35:7
21:43
h Dt 34:4
i Dt 11:31
j Dt 17:14
21:44
k Ex 33:14;
Jos 1:13
l Dt 6:19
m Ex 23:31
n Dt 7:24; 21:10
21:45
o Jos 23:14;
Ne 9:8
22:2
p Nu 32:25
22:4
q Nu 32:22;
Dt 3:20
r Nu 32:18;
Jos 1:13-15
22:5
s Isa 43:22
t Dt 5:29 ·
u Dt 6:6,17
22:6
v Ex 39:43
22:7
w Nu 32:33;
Jos 12:5

side^x of the Jordan with their brothers.) When Joshua sent them home, he blessed them, ⁸saying, "Return to your homes with your great wealth—with large herds of livestock,^y with silver, gold, bronze and iron, and a great quantity of clothing—and divide^z with your brothers the plunder^a from your enemies."

⁹So the Reubenites, the Gadites and the half-tribe of Manasseh left the Israelites at Shiloh in Canaan to return to Gilead,^b their own land, which they had acquired in accordance with the command of the Lord through Moses.

¹⁰When they came to Geliloth near the Jordan in the land of Canaan, the Reubenites, the Gadites and the half-tribe of Manasseh built an imposing altar there by the Jordan. ¹¹And when the Israelites heard that they had built the altar on the border of Canaan at Geliloth near the Jordan on the Israelite side, ¹²the whole assembly of Israel gathered at Shiloh^c to go to war against them.

¹³So the Israelites sent Phinehas^d son of Eleazar,^e the priest, to the land of Gilead—to Reuben, Gad and the half-tribe of Manasseh. ¹⁴With him they sent ten of the chief men, one for each of the tribes of Israel, each the head of a family division among the Israelite clans.^f

¹⁵When they went to Gilead—to Reuben, Gad and the half-tribe of Manasseh—they said to them: ¹⁶"The whole assembly of the Lord says: 'How could you break faith^g with the God of Israel like this? How could you turn away from the Lord and build yourselves an altar in rebellion^h against him now? ¹⁷Was not the sin of Peorⁱ enough for us? Up to this very day we have not cleansed ourselves from that sin, even though a plague fell on the community of the Lord! ¹⁸And are you now turning away from the Lord?

" 'If you rebel against the Lord today, tomorrow he will be angry with the whole community^j of Israel. ¹⁹If the land you possess is defiled, come over to the Lord's land, where the Lord's tabernacle stands, and share the land with us. But do not rebel against the Lord or against us by building an altar for yourselves, other than the altar of the Lord our God. ²⁰When Achan son of Zerah acted unfaithfully regarding the devoted things,^{a k} did not wrath^l come upon the whole community of Israel? He was not the only one who died for his sin.' "^m

²¹Then Reuben, Gad and the half-tribe of Manasseh replied to the heads of the clans of Israel: ²²"The Mighty One, God, the Lord! The Mighty One, God,ⁿ the Lord!^o He knows!^p And let Israel know! If this has been in rebellion or disobedience to the Lord, do not spare us this day. ²³If we have built our own altar to turn away from the Lord and to offer burnt offerings and grain offerings,^q or to sacrifice fellowship offerings^b on it, may the Lord himself call us to account.^r

²⁴"No! We did it for fear that some day your descendants might say to ours, 'What do you have to do with the Lord, the God of Israel? ²⁵The Lord has made the Jordan a boundary between us and you—you Reubenites and Gadites! You have no share in the Lord.' So your descendants might cause ours to stop fearing the Lord.

²⁶"That is why we said, 'Let us get ready and build an altar—but not for burnt offerings or sacrifices.' ²⁷On the contrary, it is to be a witness^s

22:7
xJos 17:2,5
22:8
yDt 20:14
zNu 31:27
aGe 49:27;
1Sa 30:16;
Isa 9:3
22:9
bNu 32:26,29
22:12
cJos 18:1
22:13
dNu 25:7
eNu 3:32;
Jos 24:33
22:14
fNu 1:4
22:16
gDt 13:14
hDt 12:13-14
22:17
iNu 25:1-9
22:18
jLev 10:6;
Nu 16:22
22:20
kJos 7:1
lPs 7:11
mJos 7:5
22:22
nDt 10:17
oPs 50:1
p1Ki 8:39;
Job 10:7;
Ps 44:21;
Jer 17:10
22:23
qJer 41:5
rDt 12:11;
18:19;
1Sa 20:16
22:27
sGe 21:30;
Jos 24:27

^a20 The Hebrew term refers to the irrevocable giving over of things or persons to the Lord, often by totally destroying them.   ^b23 Traditionally *peace offerings*; also in verse 27

between us and you and the generations that follow, that we will worship the LORD at his sanctuary with our burnt offerings, sacrifices and fellowship offerings.ᵗ Then in the future your descendants will not be able to say to ours, 'You have no share in the LORD.'

²⁸"And we said, 'If they ever say this to us, or to our descendants, we will answer: Look at the replica of the LORD's altar, which our fathers built, not for burnt offerings and sacrifices, but as a witness between us and you.'

²⁹"Far be it from us to rebelᵘ against the LORD and turn away from him today by building an altar for burnt offerings, grain offerings and sacrifices, other than the altar of the LORD our God that stands before his tabernacle.ᵛ"

³⁰When Phinehas the priest and the leaders of the community—the heads of the clans of the Israelites—heard what Reuben, Gad and Manasseh had to say, they were pleased. ³¹And Phinehas son of Eleazar, the priest, said to Reuben, Gad and Manasseh, "Today we know that the LORD is with us,ʷ because you have not acted unfaithfully toward the LORD in this matter. Now you have rescued the Israelites from the LORD's hand."

³²Then Phinehas son of Eleazar, the priest, and the leaders returned to Canaan from their meeting with the Reubenites and Gadites in Gilead and reported to the Israelites. ³³They were glad to hear the report and praised God.ˣ And they talked no more about going to war against them to devastate the country where the Reubenites and the Gadites lived.

³⁴And the Reubenites and the Gadites gave the altar this name: A Witnessʸ Between Us that the LORD is God.

Joshua's Farewell to the Leaders

23 After a long time had passed and the LORD had given Israel restᶻ from all their enemies around them, Joshua, by then old and well advanced in years,ᵃ ²summoned all Israel—their elders,ᵇ leaders, judges and officialsᶜ—and said to them: "I am old and well advanced in years. ³You yourselves have seen everything the LORD your God has done to all these nations for your sake; it was the LORD your God who fought for you.ᵈ ⁴Remember how I have allottedᵉ as an inheritance for your tribes all the land of the nations that remain—the nations I conquered—between the Jordan and the Great Seaᵃᶠ in the west. ⁵The LORD your God himself will drive them out of your way. He will push them out before you, and you will take possession of their land, as the LORD your God promised you.ᵍ

⁶"Be very strong; be careful to obey all that is written in the Book of the Law of Moses, without turning aside to the right or to the left.ʰ ⁷Do not associate with these nations that remain among you; do not invoke the names of their gods or swearⁱ by them. You must not serve them or bow downʲ to them. ⁸But you are to hold fast to the LORDᵏ your God, as you have until now.

⁹"The LORD has driven out before you great and powerful nations;ˡ to this day no one has been able to withstand you.ᵐ ¹⁰One of you routs

ᵃ4 That is, the Mediterranean

22:27
ᵗDt 12:6
22:29
ᵘJos 24:16
ᵛDt 12:13-14
22:31
ʷLev 26:11-12;
2Ch 15:2
22:33
ˣ1Ch 29:20;
Da 2:19;
Lk 2:28
22:34
ʸGe 21:30
23:1
ᶻDt 12:9;
Jos 21:44
ᵃJos 13:1
23:2
ᵇJos 7:6
ᶜJos 24:1
23:3
ᵈEx 14:14
23:4
ᵉJos 19:51
ᶠNu 34:6
23:5
ᵍEx 23:30;
Nu 33:53
23:6
ʰDt 5:32;
Jos 1:7
23:7
ⁱEx 23:13;
Ps 16:4; Jer 5:7
ʲEx 20:5
23:8
ᵏDt 10:20
23:9
ˡDt 11:23
ᵐDt 7:24

a thousand,[n] because the LORD your God fights for you,[o] just as he promised. [11]So be very careful to love the LORD[p] your God.

[12]"But if you turn away and ally yourselves with the survivors of these nations that remain among you and if you intermarry with them[q] and associate with them,[r] [13]then you may be sure that the LORD your God will no longer drive out these nations before you. Instead, they will become snares[s] and traps for you, whips on your backs and thorns in your eyes,[t] until you perish from this good land, which the LORD your God has given you.

[14]"Now I am about to go the way of all the earth.[u] You know with all your heart and soul that not one of all the good promises the LORD your God gave you has failed. Every promise has been fulfilled; not one has failed.[v] [15]But just as every good promise of the LORD your God has come true, so the LORD will bring on you all the evil he has threatened, until he has destroyed you from this good land he has given you.[w] [16]If you violate the covenant of the LORD your God, which he commanded you, and go and serve other gods and bow down to them, the LORD's anger will burn against you, and you will quickly perish from the good land he has given you.[x]"

The Covenant Renewed at Shechem

24 Then Joshua assembled all the tribes of Israel at Shechem. He summoned the elders, leaders, judges and officials of Israel,[y] and they presented themselves before God.

[2]Joshua said to all the people, "This is what the LORD, the God of Israel, says: 'Long ago your forefathers, including Terah the father of Abraham and Nahor, lived beyond the River[a] and worshiped other gods.[z] [3]But I took your father Abraham from the land beyond the River and led him throughout Canaan[a] and gave him many descendants.[b] I gave him Isaac,[c] [4]and to Isaac I gave Jacob and Esau.[d] I assigned the hill country of Seir[e] to Esau, but Jacob and his sons went down to Egypt.[f]

[5]"'Then I sent Moses and Aaron,[g] and I afflicted the Egyptians by what I did there, and I brought you out. [6]When I brought your fathers out of Egypt, you came to the sea, and the Egyptians pursued them with chariots and horsemen[b][h] as far as the Red Sea.[c] [7]But they cried to the LORD for help, and he put darkness[i] between you and the Egyptians; he brought the sea over them and covered them.[j] You saw with your own eyes what I did to the Egyptians. Then you lived in the desert for a long time.[k]

[8]"'I brought you to the land of the Amorites who lived east of the Jordan. They fought against you, but I gave them into your hands. I destroyed them from before you, and you took possession of their land.[l] [9]When Balak son of Zippor,[m] the king of Moab, prepared to fight against Israel, he sent for Balaam son of Beor to put a curse on you.[n] [10]But I would not listen to Balaam, so he blessed you[o] again and again, and I delivered you out of his hand.

[11]"'Then you crossed the Jordan[p] and came to Jericho.[q] The citizens of Jericho fought against you, as did also the Amorites, Perizzites,

---

23:10
n Lev 26:8
o Ex 14:14;
  Dt 3:22
23:11
p Jos 22:5
23:12
q Dt 7:3
r Ex 34:16;
  Ps 106:34-35
23:13
s Ex 23:33
t Nu 33:55
23:14
u 1Ki 2:2
v Jos 21:45
23:15
w Lev 26:17;
  Dt 28:15
23:16
x Dt 4:25-26
24:1
y Jos 23:2
24:2
z Ge 11:32
24:3
a Ge 12:1
b Ge 15:5
c Ge 21:3
24:4
d Ge 25:26
e Dt 2:5
f Ge 46:5-6
24:5
g Ex 3:10
24:6
h Ex 14:9
24:7
i Ex 14:20
j Ex 14:28
k Dt 1:46
24:8
l Nu 21:31
24:9
m Nu 22:2
n Nu 22:6
24:10
o Nu 23:11;
  Dt 23:5
24:11
p Jos 3:16-17
q Jos 6:1

---

[a]2 That is, the Euphrates; also in verses 3, 14 and 15   [b]6 Or *charioteers*   [c]6 Hebrew *Yam Suph*; that is, Sea of Reeds

Canaanites, Hittites, Girgashites, Hivites and Jebusites, but I gave them into your hands.ʳ ¹²I sent the hornetˢ ahead of you, which drove them out before you—also the two Amorite kings. You did not do it with your own sword and bow. ¹³So I gave you a land on which you did not toil and cities you did not build; and you live in them and eat from vineyards and olive groves that you did not plant.'ᵗ

¹⁴"Now fear the LORD and serve him with all faithfulness.ᵘ Throw away the godsᵛ your forefathers worshiped beyond the River and in Egypt,ʷ and serve the LORD. ¹⁵But if serving the LORD seems undesirable to you, then choose for yourselves this day whom you will serve, whether the gods your forefathers served beyond the River, or the gods of the Amorites,ˣ in whose land you are living. But as for me and my household, we will serve the LORD."ʸ

¹⁶Then the people answered, "Far be it from us to forsake the LORD to serve other gods! ¹⁷It was the LORD our God himself who brought us and our fathers up out of Egypt, from that land of slavery, and performed those great signs before our eyes. He protected us on our entire journey and among all the nations through which we traveled. ¹⁸And the LORD drove out before us all the nations, including the Amorites, who lived in the land. We too will serve the LORD, because he is our God."

¹⁹Joshua said to the people, "You are not able to serve the LORD. He is a holy God;ᶻ he is a jealous God.ᵃ He will not forgive your rebellionᵇ and your sins. ²⁰If you forsake the LORDᶜ and serve foreign gods, he will turnᵈ and bring disaster on you and make an end of you,ᵉ after he has been good to you."

²¹But the people said to Joshua, "No! We will serve the LORD." ²²Then Joshua said, "You are witnesses against yourselves that you have chosenᶠ to serve the LORD."

"Yes, we are witnesses," they replied.

²³"Now then," said Joshua, "throw away the foreign godsᵍ that are among you and yield your heartsʰ to the LORD, the God of Israel."

²⁴And the people said to Joshua, "We will serve the LORD our God and obey him."ⁱ

²⁵On that day Joshua made a covenantʲ for the people, and there at Shechem he drew up for them decrees and laws.ᵏ ²⁶And Joshua recorded these things in the Book of the Law of God.ˡ Then he took a large stoneᵐ and set it up there under the oak near the holy place of the LORD.

²⁷"See!" he said to all the people. "This stone will be a witnessⁿ against us. It has heard all the words the LORD has said to us. It will be a witness against you if you are untrue to your God."

Buried in the Promised Land

24:29-31pp — Jdg 2:6-9

²⁸Then Joshua sent the people away, each to his own inheritance.

²⁹After these things, Joshua son of Nun, the servant of the LORD, died at the age of a hundred and ten.ᵒ ³⁰And they buried him in the land of his inheritance, at Timnath Serahᵃᵖ in the hill country of Ephraim, north of Mount Gaash.

³¹Israel served the LORD throughout the lifetime of Joshua and of the

ᵃ30 Also known as *Timnath Heres* (see Judges 2:9)

24:11
ʳEx 23:23;
Dt 7:1
24:12
ˢEx 23:28;
Dt 7:20;
Ps 44:3,6-7
24:13
ᵗDt 6:10-11
24:14
ᵘDt 10:12;
18:13;
1Sa 12:24;
2Co 1:12
ᵛver 23
ʷEze 23:3
24:15
ˣJdg 6:10;
Ru 1:15
ʸRu 1:16;
1Ki 18:21
24:19
ᶻLev 19:2;
20:26
ᵃEx 20:5
ᵇEx 23:21
24:20
ᶜ1Ch 28:9,20
ᵈAc 7:42
ᵉJos 23:15
24:22
ᶠPs 119:30,173
24:23
ᵍver 14
ʰ1Ki 8:58;
Ps 119:36;
141:4
24:24
ⁱEx 19:8; 24:3,
7; Dt 5:27
24:25
ʲEx 24:8
ᵏEx 15:25
24:26
ˡDt 31:24
ᵐGe 28:18
24:27
ⁿJos 22:27
24:29
ᵒJdg 2:8
24:30
ᵖJos 19:50

24:31
qJdg 2:7
24:32
rGe 50:25;
Ex 13:19
sGe 33:19;
Jn 4:5; Ac 7:16
24:33
tJos 22:13
uEx 6:25

elders[q] who outlived him and who had experienced everything the LORD had done for Israel.

[32]And Joseph's bones, which the Israelites had brought up from Egypt,[r] were buried at Shechem in the tract of land[s] that Jacob bought for a hundred pieces of silver[a] from the sons of Hamor, the father of Shechem. This became the inheritance of Joseph's descendants.

[33]And Eleazar son of Aaron[t] died and was buried at Gibeah, which had been allotted to his son Phinehas[u] in the hill country of Ephraim.

---

[a]32 Hebrew *hundred kesitahs*; a kesitah was a unit of money of unknown weight and value.

Judges

Title and Background

The title describes the type of leaders Israel had from the time of the elders who outlived Joshua until the time of the monarchy. Their principal purpose for having these leaders is best expressed in 2:16: "Then the LORD raised up judges, who saved them out of the hands of these raiders." The book tells of Israel's history for the period between the death of Joshua and the ministry of Samuel.

Author and Date of Writing

According to tradition, Samuel wrote the book, but actual authorship is uncertain. It is possible that Samuel assembled some of the accounts from the period of the judges and that some of the prophets had a hand in shaping and editing the material (see 1Ch 29:29). The date of composition was undoubtedly sometime after 1000 B.C.

Theme and Message

On the one hand, the book of Judges is an account of frequent apostasy, provoking divine chastening. On the other hand, it tells of urgent appeals to God in times of crisis, moving the Lord to raise up leaders (judges) through whom he throws off foreign oppressors and restores the land to peace. It is a number of accounts of recurring cycles (apostasy, oppression, distress and deliverance). Judges reveals an age when "Israel had no king; everyone did as he saw fit" (17:6).

Outline

Israel Fights the Remaining Canaanites

1:11-15pp — Jos 15:15-19

1 After the death^a of Joshua, the Israelites asked the LORD, "Who will be the first^b to go up and fight for us against the Canaanites?^c"
²The LORD answered, "Judah^d is to go; I have given the land into their hands.^e"
³Then the men of Judah said to the Simeonites their brothers, "Come up with us into the territory allotted to us, to fight against the Canaanites. We in turn will go with you into yours." So the Simeonites^f went with them.
⁴When Judah attacked, the LORD gave the Canaanites and Perizzites^g into their hands and they struck down ten thousand men at Bezek.^h ⁵It was there that they found Adoni-Bezek and fought against him, put-

1:1 a Jos 24:29 b Nu 27:21 c ver 27; Jdg 3:1-6
1:2 d Ge 49:8 e ver 4; Jdg 3:28
1:3 f ver 17
1:4 g Ge 13:7; Jos 3:10 h 1Sa 11:8

ting to rout the Canaanites and Perizzites. 6Adoni-Bezek fled, but they chased him and caught him, and cut off his thumbs and big toes.

7Then Adoni-Bezek said, "Seventy kings with their thumbs and big toes cut off have picked up scraps under my table. Now God has paid me back[i] for what I did to them." They brought him to Jerusalem, and he died there.

8The men of Judah attacked Jerusalem[j] also and took it. They put the city to the sword and set it on fire.

9After that, the men of Judah went down to fight against the Canaanites living in the hill country,[k] the Negev[l] and the western foothills. 10They advanced against the Canaanites living in Hebron[m] (formerly called Kiriath Arba[n]) and defeated Sheshai, Ahiman and Talmai.[o]

11From there they advanced against the people living in Debir[p] (formerly called Kiriath Sepher). 12And Caleb said, "I will give my daughter Acsah in marriage to the man who attacks and captures Kiriath Sepher." 13Othniel son of Kenaz, Caleb's younger brother, took it; so Caleb gave his daughter Acsah to him in marriage.

14One day when she came to Othniel, she urged him[a] to ask her father for a field. When she got off her donkey, Caleb asked her, "What can I do for you?"

15She replied, "Do me a special favor. Since you have given me land in the Negev, give me also springs of water." Then Caleb gave her the upper and lower springs.

16The descendants of Moses' father-in-law,[q] the Kenite,[r] went up from the City of Palms[bs] with the men of Judah to live among the people of the Desert of Judah in the Negev near Arad.[t]

17Then the men of Judah went with the Simeonites[u] their brothers and attacked the Canaanites living in Zephath, and they totally destroyed[c] the city. Therefore it was called Hormah.[dv] 18The men of Judah also took[e] Gaza,[w] Ashkelon and Ekron—each city with its territory.

19The LORD was with[x] the men of Judah. They took possession of the hill country, but they were unable to drive the people from the plains, because they had iron chariots.[y] 20As Moses had promised, Hebron[z] was given to Caleb, who drove from it the three sons of Anak.[a] 21The Benjamites, however, failed[b] to dislodge the Jebusites, who were living in Jerusalem;[c] to this day the Jebusites live there with the Benjamites.

22Now the house of Joseph attacked Bethel, and the LORD was with them. 23When they sent men to spy out Bethel (formerly called Luz),[d] 24the spies saw a man coming out of the city and they said to him, "Show us how to get into the city and we will see that you are treated well.[e]" 25So he showed them, and they put the city to the sword but spared[f] the man and his whole family. 26He then went to the land of the Hittites, where he built a city and called it Luz, which is its name to this day.

27But Manasseh did not drive out the people of Beth Shan or Taanach or Dor or Ibleam[g] or Megiddo and their surrounding settlements, for the Canaanites[h] were determined to live in that land. 28When Israel

---

1:7
i Lev 24:19
1:8
j ver 21;
Jos 15:63
1:9
k Nu 13:17
l Nu 21:1
1:10
m Ge 13:18
n Ge 35:27
o Jos 15:14
1:11
p Jos 15:15
1:16
q Nu 10:29
r Ge 15:19;
Jdg 4:11
s Dt 34:3;
Jdg 3:13
t Nu 21:1
1:17
u ver 3 v Nu 21:3
1:18
w Jos 11:22
1:19
x ver 2
y Jos 17:16
1:20
z Jos 14:9;
15:13-14
a ver 10;
Jos 14:13
1:21
b Jos 15:63
c ver 8
1:23
d Ge 28:19
1:24
e Jos 2:12,14
1:25
f Jos 6:25
1:27
g Jos 17:11
h ver 1

---

[a]14 Hebrew; Septuagint and Vulgate *Othniel, he urged her*   [b]16 That is, Jericho   [c]17 The Hebrew term refers to the irrevocable giving over of things or persons to the LORD, often by totally destroying them.   [d]17 *Hormah* means *destruction*.   [e]18 Hebrew; Septuagint *Judah did not take*

became strong, they pressed the Canaanites into forced labor but never drove them out completely. [29]Nor did Ephraim drive out the Canaanites living in Gezer,[i] but the Canaanites continued to live there among them.[j] [30]Neither did Zebulun drive out the Canaanites living in Kitron or Nahalol, who remained among them; but they did subject them to forced labor. [31]Nor did Asher drive out those living in Acco or Sidon or Ahlab or Aczib[k] or Helbah or Aphek or Rehob, [32]and because of this the people of Asher lived among the Canaanite inhabitants of the land. [33]Neither did Naphtali drive out those living in Beth Shemesh or Beth Anath[l]; but the Naphtalites too lived among the Canaanite inhabitants of the land, and those living in Beth Shemesh and Beth Anath became forced laborers for them. [34]The Amorites[m] confined the Danites to the hill country, not allowing them to come down into the plain. [35]And the Amorites were determined also to hold out in Mount Heres, Aijalon[n] and Shaalbim, but when the power of the house of Joseph increased, they too were pressed into forced labor. [36]The boundary of the Amorites was from Scorpion[a] Pass[o] to Sela and beyond.

The Angel of the LORD at Bokim

2 The angel of the LORD[p] went up from Gilgal to Bokim[q] and said, "I brought you up out of Egypt[r] and led you into the land that I swore to give to your forefathers.[s] I said, 'I will never break my covenant with you,[t] [2]and you shall not make a covenant with the people of this land,[u] but you shall break down their altars.'[v] Yet you have disobeyed me. Why have you done this? [3]Now therefore I tell you that I will not drive them out before you;[w] they will be ‚thorns‚[x] in your sides and their gods will be a snare[y] to you."

[4]When the angel of the LORD had spoken these things to all the Israelites, the people wept aloud, [5]and they called that place Bokim.[b] There they offered sacrifices to the LORD.

Disobedience and Defeat

2:6–9pp — Jos 24:29–31

[6]After Joshua had dismissed the Israelites, they went to take possession of the land, each to his own inheritance. [7]The people served the LORD throughout the lifetime of Joshua and of the elders who outlived him and who had seen all the great things the LORD had done for Israel.

[8]Joshua son of Nun, the servant of the LORD, died at the age of a hundred and ten. [9]And they buried him in the land of his inheritance, at Timnath Heres[cz] in the hill country of Ephraim, north of Mount Gaash.

[10]After that whole generation had been gathered to their fathers, another generation grew up, who knew neither the LORD nor what he had done for Israel.[a] [11]Then the Israelites did evil in the eyes of the LORD[b] and served the Baals.[c] [12]They forsook the LORD, the God of their fathers, who had brought them out of Egypt. They followed and worshiped various gods[d] of the peoples around them.[e] They provoked the LORD to anger [13]because they forsook him and served Baal and the

1:29
i 1Ki 9:16
j Jos 16:10
1:31
k Jdg 10:6
1:33
l Jos 19:38
1:34
m Ex 3:17
1:35
n Jos 19:42
1:36
o Jos 15:3
2:1
p Jdg 6:11 q ver 5
r Ex 20:2
s Ge 17:8
t Lev 26:42-44;
Dt 7:9
2:2
u Ex 23:32;
34:12; Dt 7:2
v Ex 34:13
2:3
w Jos 23:13
x Nu 33:55
y Dt 7:16;
Jdg 3:6;
Ps 106:36
2:9
z Jos 19:50
2:10
a Ex 5:2;
1Sa 2:12;
1Ch 28:9;
Gal 4:8
2:11
b Jdg 3:12; 4:1;
6:1; 10:6
c Jdg 3:7; 8:33
2:12
d Ps 106:36
e Dt 31:16;
Jdg 10:6

---

[a]36 Hebrew *Akrabbim*   [b]5 *Bokim* means *weepers*.   [c]9 Also known as *Timnath Serah* (see Joshua 19:50 and 24:30)

Ashtoreths. f 14In his anger g against Israel the LORD handed them over h to raiders who plundered them. He sold them i to their enemies all around, whom they were no longer able to resist. j 15Whenever Israel went out to fight, the hand of the LORD was against them to defeat them, just as he had sworn to them. They were in great distress.

16Then the LORD raised up judges, a k who saved l them out of the hands of these raiders. 17Yet they would not listen to their judges but prostituted m themselves to other gods and worshiped them. Unlike their fathers, they quickly turned from the way in which their fathers had walked, the way of obedience to the LORD's commands. n 18Whenever the LORD raised up a judge for them, he was with the judge and saved them out of the hands of their enemies as long as the judge lived; for the LORD had compassion o on them as they groaned p under those who oppressed and afflicted them. 19But when the judge died, the people returned to ways even more corrupt q than those of their fathers, following other gods and serving and worshiping them. r They refused to give up their evil practices and stubborn ways.

20Therefore the LORD was very angry s with Israel and said, "Because this nation has violated the covenant that I laid down for their forefathers and has not listened to me, 21I will no longer drive out t before them any of the nations Joshua left when he died. 22I will use them to test u Israel and see whether they will keep the way of the LORD and walk in it as their forefathers did." 23The LORD had allowed those nations to remain; he did not drive them out at once by giving them into the hands of Joshua.

3 These are the nations the LORD left to test v all those Israelites who had not experienced any of the wars in Canaan 2(he did this only to teach warfare to the descendants of the Israelites who had not had previous battle experience): 3the five w rulers of the Philistines, all the Canaanites, the Sidonians, and the Hivites living in the Lebanon mountains from Mount Baal Hermon to Lebo b Hamath. 4They were left to test x the Israelites to see whether they would obey the LORD's commands, which he had given their forefathers through Moses.

5The Israelites lived y among the Canaanites, Hittites, Amorites, Perizzites, Hivites and Jebusites. 6They took their daughters in marriage and gave their own daughters to their sons, and served their gods. z

Othniel

7The Israelites did evil in the eyes of the LORD; they forgot the LORD a their God and served the Baals and the Asherahs. b 8The anger of the LORD burned against Israel so that he sold c them into the hands of Cushan-Rishathaim king of Aram Naharaim, c to whom the Israelites were subject for eight years. 9But when they cried out d to the LORD, he raised up for them a deliverer, Othniel e son of Kenaz, Caleb's younger brother, who saved them. 10The Spirit of the LORD came upon him, f so that he became Israel's judge d and went to war. The LORD gave Cushan-Rishathaim king of Aram into the hands of Othniel, who over-

2:13
f Jdg 10:6
2:14
g Dt 31:17
h Ps 106:41
i Dt 32:30;
Jdg 3:8
j Dt 28:25
2:16
k Ac 13:20
l Ps 106:43
2:17
m Ex 34:15
n ver 7
2:18
o Dt 32:36;
Jos 1:5
p Ps 106:44
2:19
q Jdg 3:12
r Jdg 4:1; 8:33
2:20
s ver 14;
Jos 23:16
2:21
t Jos 23:13
2:22
u Dt 8:2,16;
Jdg 3:1,14
3:1
v Jdg 2:21-22
3:3
w Jos 13:3
3:4
x Dt 8:2;
Jdg 2:22
3:5
y Ps 106:35
3:6
z Ex 34:16;
Dt 7:3-4
3:7
a Dt 4:9
b Ex 34:13;
Jdg 2:11,13
3:8
c Jdg 2:14
3:9
d ver 15;
Jdg 6:6,7;
10:10;
Ps 106:44
e Jdg 1:13
3:10
f Nu 11:25,29;
24:2; Jdg 6:34;
11:29; 13:25;
14:6,19;
1Sa 11:6

a16 Or *leaders*; similarly in verses 17-19   b3 Or *to the entrance to*   c8 That is, Northwest Mesopotamia   d10 Or *leader* powered him. [11]So the land had peace for forty years, until Othniel son of Kenaz died.

Ehud

[12]Once again the Israelites did evil in the eyes of the LORD,[g] and because they did this evil the LORD gave Eglon king of Moab[h] power over Israel. [13]Getting the Ammonites and Amalekites to join him, Eglon came and attacked Israel, and they took possession of the City of Palms.[a][i] [14]The Israelites were subject to Eglon king of Moab for eighteen years.

[15]Again the Israelites cried out to the LORD, and he gave them a deliverer[j]—Ehud, a left-handed man, the son of Gera the Benjamite. The Israelites sent him with tribute to Eglon king of Moab. [16]Now Ehud had made a double-edged sword about a foot and a half[b] long, which he strapped to his right thigh under his clothing. [17]He presented the tribute to Eglon king of Moab, who was a very fat man.[k] [18]After Ehud had presented the tribute, he sent on their way the men who had carried it. [19]At the idols[c] near Gilgal he himself turned back and said, "I have a secret message for you, O king."

The king said, "Quiet!" And all his attendants left him.

[20]Ehud then approached him while he was sitting alone in the upper room of his summer palace[d] and said, "I have a message from God for you." As the king rose from his seat, [21]Ehud reached with his left hand, drew the sword from his right thigh and plunged it into the king's belly. [22]Even the handle sank in after the blade, which came out his back. Ehud did not pull the sword out, and the fat closed in over it. [23]Then Ehud went out to the porch[e]; he shut the doors of the upper room behind him and locked them.

[24]After he had gone, the servants came and found the doors of the upper room locked. They said, "He must be relieving himself[l] in the inner room of the house." [25]They waited to the point of embarrassment,[m] but when he did not open the doors of the room, they took a key and unlocked them. There they saw their lord fallen to the floor, dead.

[26]While they waited, Ehud got away. He passed by the idols and escaped to Seirah. [27]When he arrived there, he blew a trumpet[n] in the hill country of Ephraim, and the Israelites went down with him from the hills, with him leading them.

[28]"Follow me," he ordered, "for the LORD has given Moab, your enemy, into your hands.[o]" So they followed him down and, taking possession of the fords of the Jordan[p] that led to Moab, they allowed no one to cross over. [29]At that time they struck down about ten thousand Moabites, all vigorous and strong; not a man escaped. [30]That day Moab was made subject to Israel, and the land had peace[q] for eighty years.

Shamgar

[31]After Ehud came Shamgar son of Anath,[r] who struck down six hundred[s] Philistines with an oxgoad. He too saved Israel.

3:12
g Jdg 2:11,14
h 1Sa 12:9
3:13
i Jdg 1:16
3:15
j ver 9;
Ps 78:34;
107:13
3:17
k ver 12
3:24
l 1Sa 24:3
3:25
m 2Ki 2:17; 8:11
3:27
n Jdg 6:34;
1Sa 13:3
3:28
o Jdg 7:9,15
p Jos 2:7;
Jdg 7:24; 12:5
3:30
q ver 11
3:31
r Jdg 5:6
s Jos 23:10

---

a13 That is, Jericho   *b16* Hebrew *a cubit* (about 0.5 meter)   *c19* Or *the stone quarries*; also in verse 26   *d20* The meaning of the Hebrew for this phrase is uncertain.   *e23* The meaning of the Hebrew for this word is uncertain.

Deborah

4 After Ehud died, the Israelites once again did evil[t] in the eyes of the LORD. [2]So the LORD sold them into the hands of Jabin, a king of Canaan, who reigned in Hazor.[u] The commander of his army was Sisera,[v] who lived in Harosheth Haggoyim. [3]Because he had nine hundred iron chariots[w] and had cruelly oppressed[x] the Israelites for twenty years, they cried to the LORD for help.

[4]Deborah, a prophetess, the wife of Lappidoth, was leading[a] Israel at that time. [5]She held court under the Palm of Deborah between Ramah and Bethel[y] in the hill country of Ephraim, and the Israelites came to her to have their disputes decided. [6]She sent for Barak son of Abinoam[z] from Kedesh in Naphtali and said to him, "The LORD, the God of Israel, commands you: 'Go, take with you ten thousand men of Naphtali and Zebulun and lead the way to Mount Tabor. [7]I will lure Sisera, the commander of Jabin's army, with his chariots and his troops to the Kishon River[a] and give him into your hands.'"

[8]Barak said to her, "If you go with me, I will go; but if you don't go with me, I won't go."

[9]"Very well," Deborah said, "I will go with you. But because of the way you are going about this,[b] the honor will not be yours, for the LORD will hand Sisera over to a woman." So Deborah went with Barak to Kedesh,[b] [10]where he summoned[c] Zebulun and Naphtali. Ten thousand men followed him, and Deborah also went with him.

[11]Now Heber the Kenite had left the other Kenites,[d] the descendants of Hobab,[e] Moses' brother-in-law,[c] and pitched his tent by the great tree in Zaanannim[f] near Kedesh.

[12]When they told Sisera that Barak son of Abinoam had gone up to Mount Tabor, [13]Sisera gathered together his nine hundred iron chariots[g] and all the men with him, from Harosheth Haggoyim to the Kishon River.

[14]Then Deborah said to Barak, "Go! This is the day the LORD has given Sisera into your hands. Has not the LORD gone ahead[h] of you?" So Barak went down Mount Tabor, followed by ten thousand men. [15]At Barak's advance, the LORD routed[i] Sisera and all his chariots and army by the sword, and Sisera abandoned his chariot and fled on foot. [16]But Barak pursued the chariots and army as far as Harosheth Haggoyim. All the troops of Sisera fell by the sword; not a man was left.[j]

[17]Sisera, however, fled on foot to the tent of Jael, the wife of Heber the Kenite, because there were friendly relations between Jabin king of Hazor and the clan of Heber the Kenite.

[18]Jael went out to meet Sisera and said to him, "Come, my lord, come right in. Don't be afraid." So he entered her tent, and she put a covering over him.

[19]"I'm thirsty," he said. "Please give me some water." She opened a skin of milk,[k] gave him a drink, and covered him up.

[20]"Stand in the doorway of the tent," he told her. "If someone comes by and asks you, 'Is anyone here?' say 'No.'"

[21]But Jael, Heber's wife, picked up a tent peg and a hammer and went

4:1
t Jdg 2:19
4:2
u Jos 11:1
v ver 13,16;
1Sa 12:9;
Ps 83:9
4:3
w Jdg 1:19
x Ps 106:42
4:5
y Ge 35:8
4:6
z Heb 11:32
4:7
a Ps 83:9
4:9
b ver 21;
Jdg 2:14
4:10
c ver 14;
Jdg 5:15,18
4:11
d Jdg 1:16
e Nu 10:29
f Jos 19:33
4:13
g ver 3
4:14
h Dt 9:3;
2Sa 5:24;
Ps 68:7
4:15
Jos 10:10;
Ps 83:9-10
4:16
i Ex 14:28;
Ps 83:9
4:19
k Jdg 5:25

a4 Traditionally *judging*   b9 Or *But on the expedition you are undertaking*   c11 Or *father-in-law* quietly to him while he lay fast asleep, exhausted. She drove the peg through his temple into the ground, and he died.[1]

[22]Barak came by in pursuit of Sisera, and Jael went out to meet him. "Come," she said, "I will show you the man you're looking for." So he went in with her, and there lay Sisera with the tent peg through his temple—dead.

[23]On that day God subdued[m] Jabin, the Canaanite king, before the Israelites. [24]And the hand of the Israelites grew stronger and stronger against Jabin, the Canaanite king, until they destroyed him.

The Song of Deborah

5 On that day Deborah and Barak son of Abinoam sang this song:[n]

[2]"When the princes in Israel take the lead,
　　when the people willingly offer[o] themselves—
　　praise the LORD![p]

[3]"Hear this, you kings! Listen, you rulers!
　　I will sing to[a] the LORD, I will sing;
　　I will make music to[b] the LORD, the God of Israel. [q]

[4]"O LORD, when you went out from Seir,[r]
　　when you marched from the land of Edom,
　the earth shook, the heavens poured,
　　the clouds poured down water.[s]
[5]The mountains quaked[t] before the LORD, the One of
　　Sinai,
　　before the LORD, the God of Israel.

[6]"In the days of Shamgar son of Anath,[u]
　　in the days of Jael,[v] the roads[w] were abandoned;
　　travelers took to winding paths.
[7]Village life[c] in Israel ceased,
　　ceased until I,[d] Deborah, arose,
　　arose a mother in Israel.
[8]When they chose new gods,[x]
　　war came to the city gates,
　and not a shield or spear was seen
　　among forty thousand in Israel.
[9]My heart is with Israel's princes,
　　with the willing volunteers[y] among the people.
　　Praise the LORD!

[10]"You who ride on white donkeys,[z]
　　sitting on your saddle blankets,
　　and you who walk along the road,
　consider [11]the voice of the singers[e] at the watering
　　places.
　　They recite the righteous acts[a] of the LORD,
　　the righteous acts of his warriors[f] in Israel.

4:21
l Jdg 5:26
4:23
m Ne 9:24;
Ps 18:47
5:1
n Ex 15:1
5:2
o 2Ch 17:16;
Ps 110:3 pver 9
5:3
q Ps 27:6
5:4
r Dt 33:2
s Ps 68:8
5:5
t Ex 19:18;
Ps 68:8; 97:5;
Isa 64:3
5:6
u Jdg 3:31
v Jdg 4:17
w Isa 33:8
5:8
x Dt 32:17
5:9
y ver 2
5:10
z Jdg 10:4;
12:14
5:11
a 1Sa 12:7;
Mic 6:5

a3 Or *of*　b3 Or *I with song I will praise*　c7 Or *Warriors*　d7 Or *you*　e11 Or *archers;*
the meaning of the Hebrew for this word is uncertain.　f11 Or *villagers*

"Then the people of the LORD
   went down to the city gates.[b]
12'Wake up,[c] wake up, Deborah!
   Wake up, wake up, break out in song!
Arise, O Barak!
   Take captive your captives,[d] O son of Abinoam.'

13"Then the men who were left
   came down to the nobles;
the people of the LORD
   came to me with the mighty.
14Some came from Ephraim, whose roots were in
      Amalek;[e]
   Benjamin was with the people who followed you.
From Makir captains came down,
   from Zebulun those who bear a commander's staff.
15The princes of Issachar were with Deborah;[f]
   yes, Issachar was with Barak,
   rushing after him into the valley.
In the districts of Reuben
   there was much searching of heart.
16Why did you stay among the campfires[a]
   to hear the whistling for the flocks?[g]
In the districts of Reuben
   there was much searching of heart.
17Gilead stayed beyond the Jordan.
   And Dan, why did he linger by the ships?
Asher remained on the coast[h]
   and stayed in his coves.
18The people of Zebulun risked their very lives;
   so did Naphtali on the heights of the field.[i]

19"Kings came[j], they fought;
   the kings of Canaan fought
at Taanach by the waters of Megiddo,[k]
   but they carried off no silver, no plunder.[l]
20From the heavens[m] the stars fought,
   from their courses they fought against Sisera.
21The river Kishon[n] swept them away,
   the age-old river, the river Kishon.
March on, my soul; be strong!
22Then thundered the horses' hoofs—
   galloping, galloping go his mighty steeds.
23'Curse Meroz,' said the angel of the LORD.
   'Curse its people bitterly,
because they did not come to help the LORD,
   to help the LORD against the mighty.'

24"Most blessed of women be Jael,[o]
   the wife of Heber the Kenite,
   most blessed of tent-dwelling women.

5:11
b ver 8
5:12
c Ps 57:8
d Ps 68:18;
Eph 4:8
5:14
e Jdg 3:13
5:15
f Jdg 4:10
5:16
g Nu 32:1
5:17
h Jos 19:29
5:18
i Jdg 4:6,10
5:19
j Jos 11:5;
Jdg 4:13
k Jdg 1:27
l ver 30
5:20
m Jos 10:11
5:21
n Jdg 4:7
5:24
o Jdg 4:17

[a]16 Or *saddlebags*

²⁵He asked for water, and she gave him milk;^p
    in a bowl fit for nobles she brought him curdled milk.
²⁶Her hand reached for the tent peg,
    her right hand for the workman's hammer.
She struck Sisera, she crushed his head,
    she shattered and pierced his temple. ^q
²⁷At her feet he sank,
    he fell; there he lay.
At her feet he sank, he fell;
    where he sank, there he fell—dead.

²⁸"Through the window peered Sisera's mother;
    behind the lattice she cried out,^r
'Why is his chariot so long in coming?
    Why is the clatter of his chariots delayed?'
²⁹The wisest of her ladies answer her;
    indeed, she keeps saying to herself,
³⁰'Are they not finding and dividing the spoils:^s
    a girl or two for each man,
    colorful garments as plunder for Sisera,
    colorful garments embroidered,
    highly embroidered garments for my neck—
all this as plunder?'

³¹"So may all your enemies perish, O LORD!
    But may they who love you be like the sun^t
    when it rises in its strength.''

Then the land had peace^u forty years.

Gideon

6 Again the Israelites did evil in the eyes of the LORD,^v and for seven years he gave them into the hands of the Midianites. ^w ²Because the power of Midian was so oppressive,^x the Israelites prepared shelters for themselves in mountain clefts, caves and strongholds.^y ³Whenever the Israelites planted their crops, the Midianites, Amalekites^z and other eastern peoples invaded the country. ⁴They camped on the land and ruined the crops^a all the way to Gaza and did not spare a living thing for Israel, neither sheep nor cattle nor donkeys. ⁵They came up with their livestock and their tents like swarms of locusts. ^b It was impossible to count the men and their camels;^c they invaded the land to ravage it. ⁶Midian so impoverished the Israelites that they cried out^d to the LORD for help.

⁷When the Israelites cried to the LORD because of Midian, ⁸he sent them a prophet, who said, ''This is what the LORD, the God of Israel, says: I brought you up out of Egypt,^e out of the land of slavery. ⁹I snatched you from the power of Egypt and from the hand of all your oppressors. I drove them from before you and gave you their land.^f ¹⁰I said to you, 'I am the LORD your God; do not worship^g the gods of the Amorites,^h in whose land you live.' But you have not listened to me.''

¹¹The angel of the LORDⁱ came and sat down under the oak in Ophrah that belonged to Joash the Abiezrite,^j where his son Gideon^k was threshing wheat in a winepress to keep it from the Midianites.

5:25
p Jdg 4:19
5:26
q Jdg 4:21
5:28
r Pr 7:6
5:30
s Ex 15:9;
1Sa 30:24
5:31
t 2Sa 23:4;
Ps 19:4; 89:36
u Jdg 3:11
6:1
v Jdg 2:11
w Nu 25:15-18;
31:1-3
6:2
x 1Sa 13:6;
Isa 8:21
y Heb 11:38
6:3
z Jdg 3:13
6:4
a Lev 26:16;
Dt 28:30,51
6:5
b Jdg 7:12
c Jdg 8:10
6:6
d Jdg 3:9
6:8
e Jdg 2:1
6:9
f Ps 44:2
6:10
g 2Ki 17:35
h Jer 10:2
6:11
i Ge 16:7
j Jos 17:2
k Heb 11:32

¹²When the angel of the LORD appeared to Gideon, he said, "The LORD is with you,¹ mighty warrior."

¹³"But sir," Gideon replied, "if the LORD is with us, why has all this happened to us? Where are all his wonders that our fathers told^m us about when they said, 'Did not the LORD bring us up out of Egypt?' But now the LORD has abandonedⁿ us and put us into the hand of Midian."

¹⁴The LORD turned to him and said, "Go in the strength you have^o and save Israel out of Midian's hand. Am I not sending you?"

¹⁵"But Lord,^a" Gideon asked, "how can I save Israel? My clan is the weakest in Manasseh, and I am the least in my family.^p"

¹⁶The LORD answered, "I will be with you^q, and you will strike down all the Midianites together."

¹⁷Gideon replied, "If now I have found favor in your eyes, give me a sign^r that it is really you talking to me. ¹⁸Please do not go away until I come back and bring my offering and set it before you."

And the LORD said, "I will wait until you return."

¹⁹Gideon went in, prepared a young goat, and from an ephah^b of flour he made bread without yeast. Putting the meat in a basket and its broth in a pot, he brought them out and offered them to him under the oak.^s

²⁰The angel of God said to him, "Take the meat and the unleavened bread, place them on this rock,^t and pour out the broth." And Gideon did so. ²¹With the tip of the staff that was in his hand, the angel of the LORD touched the meat and the unleavened bread.^u Fire flared from the rock, consuming the meat and the bread. And the angel of the LORD disappeared. ²²When Gideon realized^v that it was the angel of the LORD, he exclaimed, "Ah, Sovereign LORD! I have seen the angel of the LORD face to face!"^w

²³But the LORD said to him, "Peace! Do not be afraid.^x You are not going to die."

²⁴So Gideon built an altar to the LORD there and called^y it The LORD is Peace. To this day it stands in Ophrah^z of the Abiezrites.

²⁵That same night the LORD said to him, "Take the second bull from your father's herd, the one seven years old.^c Tear down your father's altar to Baal and cut down the Asherah pole^{d a} beside it. ²⁶Then build a proper kind of^e altar to the LORD your God on the top of this height. Using the wood of the Asherah pole that you cut down, offer the second^f bull as a burnt offering."

²⁷So Gideon took ten of his servants and did as the LORD told him. But because he was afraid of his family and the men of the town, he did it at night rather than in the daytime.

²⁸In the morning when the men of the town got up, there was Baal's altar,^b demolished, with the Asherah pole beside it cut down and the second bull sacrificed on the newly built altar!

²⁹They asked each other, "Who did this?"

When they carefully investigated, they were told, "Gideon son of Joash did it."

³⁰The men of the town demanded of Joash, "Bring out your son. He

6:12
¹Jos 1:5;
Jdg 13:3;
Lk 1:11,28
6:13
mPs 44:1
n2Ch 15:2
6:14
oHeb 11:34
6:15
pEx 3:11;
1Sa 9:21
6:16
qEx 3:12;
Jos 1:5
6:17
rver 36-37;
Ge 24:14;
Isa 38:7-8
6:19
sGe 18:7-8
6:20
tJdg 13:19
6:21
uLev 9:24
6:22
vJdg 13:16,21
wGe 32:30;
Ex 33:20;
Jdg 13:22
6:23
xDa 10:19
6:24
yGe 22:14
zJdg 8:32
6:25
aEx 34:13;
Dt 7:5
6:28
b1Ki 16:32

^a15 Or *sir*   ^b19 That is, probably about 3/5 bushel (about 22 liters)   ^c25 Or *Take a full-grown, mature bull from your father's herd*   ^d25 That is, a symbol of the goddess Asherah; here and elsewhere in Judges   ^e26 Or *build with layers of stone an*   ^f26 Or *full-grown*; also in verse 28

must die, because he has broken down Baal's altar and cut down the Asherah pole beside it."

³¹But Joash replied to the hostile crowd around him, "Are you going to plead Baal's cause? Are you trying to save him? Whoever fights for him shall be put to death by morning! If Baal really is a god, he can defend himself when someone breaks down his altar." ³²So that day they called Gideon "Jerub-Baal,ᵃᶜ" saying, "Let Baal contend with him," because he broke down Baal's altar.

³³Now all the Midianites, Amalekites and other eastern peoplesᵈ joined forces and crossed over the Jordan and camped in the Valley of Jezreel.ᵉ ³⁴Then the Spirit of the LORD came uponᶠ Gideon, and he blew a trumpet,ᵍ summoning the Abiezrites to follow him. ³⁵He sent messengers throughout Manasseh, calling them to arms, and also into Asher, Zebulun and Naphtali,ʰ so that they too went up to meet them.

³⁶Gideon said to God, "If you will saveⁱ Israel by my hand as you have promised— ³⁷look, I will place a wool fleece on the threshing floor.ʲ If there is dew only on the fleece and all the ground is dry, then I will knowᵏ that you will save Israel by my hand, as you said." ³⁸And that is what happened. Gideon rose early the next day; he squeezed the fleece and wrung out the dew—a bowlful of water.

³⁹Then Gideon said to God, "Do not be angry with me. Let me make just one more request.ˡ Allow me one more test with the fleece. This time make the fleece dry and the ground covered with dew." ⁴⁰That night God did so. Only the fleece was dry; all the ground was covered with dew.

Gideon Defeats the Midianites

7 Early in the morning, Jerub-Baalᵐ (that is, Gideon) and all his men camped at the spring of Harod. The camp of Midian was north of them in the valley near the hill of Moreh.ⁿ ²The LORD said to Gideon, "You have too many men for me to deliver Midian into their hands. In order that Israel may not boast against me that her own strengthᵒ has saved her, ³announce now to the people, 'Anyone who trembles with fear may turn back and leave Mount Gilead.ᵖ'" So twenty-two thousand men left, while ten thousand remained.

⁴But the LORD said to Gideon, "There are still too many�q men. Take them down to the water, and I will sift them for you there. If I say, 'This one shall go with you,' he shall go; but if I say, 'This one shall not go with you,' he shall not go."

⁵So Gideon took the men down to the water. There the LORD told him, "Separate those who lap the water with their tongues like a dog from those who kneel down to drink." ⁶Three hundred men lapped with their hands to their mouths. All the rest got down on their knees to drink.

⁷The LORD said to Gideon, "With the three hundred men that lapped I will save you and give the Midianites into your hands. Let all the other men go, each to his own place."ʳ ⁸So Gideon sent the rest of the Israelites to their tents but kept the three hundred, who took over the provisions and trumpets of the others.

Now the camp of Midian lay below him in the valley. ⁹During that

6:32
cJdg 7:1; 8:29, 35; 1Sa 12:11
6:33
dver 3
eJos 17:16
6:34
fJdg 3:10;
1Ch 12:18;
2Ch 24:20
gJdg 3:27
6:35
hJdg 4:6
6:36
iver 14
6:37
jEx 4:3-7
kGe 24:14
6:39
lGe 18:32
7:1
mJdg 6:32
nGe 12:6
7:2
oDt 8:17;
2Co 4:7
7:3
pDt 20:8
7:4
q1Sa 14:6
7:7
r1Sa 14:6

ᵃ32 *Jerub-Baal* means *let Baal contend.*

night the LORD said to Gideon, "Get up, go down against the camp, because I am going to give it into your hands.ˢ ¹⁰If you are afraid to attack, go down to the camp with your servant Purah ¹¹and listen to what they are saying. Afterward, you will be encouraged to attack the camp." So he and Purah his servant went down to the outposts of the camp. ¹²The Midianites, the Amalekitesᵗ and all the other eastern peoples had settled in the valley, thick as locusts.ᵘ Their camelsᵛ could no more be counted than the sand on the seashore.ʷ

¹³Gideon arrived just as a man was telling a friend his dream. "I had a dream," he was saying. "A round loaf of barley bread came tumbling into the Midianite camp. It struck the tent with such force that the tent overturned and collapsed."

¹⁴His friend responded, "This can be nothing other than the sword of Gideon son of Joash, the Israelite. God has given the Midianites and the whole camp into his hands."

¹⁵When Gideon heard the dream and its interpretation, he worshiped God.ˣ He returned to the camp of Israel and called out, "Get up! The LORD has given the Midianite camp into your hands." ¹⁶Dividing the three hundred menʸ into three companies,ᶻ he placed trumpets and empty jars in the hands of all of them, with torches inside.

¹⁷"Watch me," he told them. "Follow my lead. When I get to the edge of the camp, do exactly as I do. ¹⁸When I and all who are with me blow our trumpets,ᵃ then from all around the camp blow yours and shout, 'For the LORD and for Gideon.'"

¹⁹Gideon and the hundred men with him reached the edge of the camp at the beginning of the middle watch, just after they had changed the guard. They blew their trumpets and broke the jars that were in their hands. ²⁰The three companies blew the trumpets and smashed the jars. Grasping the torches in their left hands and holding in their right hands the trumpets they were to blow, they shouted, "A swordᵇ for the LORD and for Gideon!" ²¹While each man held his position around the camp, all the Midianites ran, crying out as they fled.ᶜ

²²When the three hundred trumpets sounded,ᵈ the LORD caused the men throughout the camp to turn on each otherᵉ with their swords. The army fled to Beth Shittah toward Zererah as far as the border of Abel Meholahᶠ near Tabbath. ²³Israelites from Naphtali, Asher and all Manasseh were called out,ᵍ and they pursued the Midianites. ²⁴Gideon sent messengers throughout the hill country of Ephraim, saying, "Come down against the Midianites and seize the waters of the Jordanʰ ahead of them as far as Beth Barah."

So all the men of Ephraim were called out and they took the waters of the Jordan as far as Beth Barah. ²⁵They also captured two of the Midianite leaders, Oreb and Zeebⁱ. They killed Oreb at the rock of Oreb,ʲ and Zeeb at the winepress of Zeeb. They pursued the Midianites and brought the heads of Oreb and Zeeb to Gideon, who was by the Jordan.ᵏ

Zebah and Zalmunna

8 Now the Ephraimites asked Gideon, "Why have you treated us like this? Why didn't you call us when you went to fight Midian?"ˡ And they criticized him sharply.ᵐ

²But he answered them, "What have I accomplished compared to

7:9
ˢ Jos 2:24; 10:8;
11:6

7:12
ᵗ Jdg 8:10
ᵘ Jdg 6:5
ᵛ Jer 49:29
ʷ Jos 11:4

7:15
ˣ 1Sa 15:31

7:16
ʸ Ge 14:15
ᶻ 2Sa 18:2

7:18
ᵃ Jdg 3:27

7:20
ᵇ ver 14

7:21
ᶜ 2Ki 7:7

7:22
ᵈ Jos 6:20
ᵉ 1Sa 14:20;
2Ch 20:23
ᶠ 1Ki 4:12; 19:16

7:23
ᵍ Jdg 6:35

7:24
ʰ Jdg 3:28

7:25
ⁱ Jdg 8:3;
Ps 83:11
ʲ Isa 10:26
ᵏ Jdg 8:4

8:1
ˡ Jdg 12:1
ᵐ 2Sa 19:41

you? Aren't the gleanings of Ephraim's grapes better than the full grape harvest of Abiezer? [3]God gave Oreb and Zeeb,[n] the Midianite leaders, into your hands. What was I able to do compared to you?" At this, their resentment against him subsided.

[4]Gideon and his three hundred men, exhausted yet keeping up the pursuit, came to the Jordan[o] and crossed it. [5]He said to the men of Succoth,[p] "Give my troops some bread; they are worn out, and I am still pursuing Zebah and Zalmunna,[q] the kings of Midian."

[6]But the officials of Succoth said, "Do you already have the hands of Zebah and Zalmunna in your possession? Why should we give bread[r] to your troops?"[s]

[7]Then Gideon replied, "Just for that, when the LORD has given Zebah and Zalmunna[t] into my hand, I will tear your flesh with desert thorns and briers."

[8]From there he went up to Peniel[au] and made the same request of them, but they answered as the men of Succoth had. [9]So he said to the men of Peniel, "When I return in triumph, I will tear down this tower."[v]

[10]Now Zebah and Zalmunna were in Karkor with a force of about fifteen thousand men, all that were left of the armies of the eastern peoples; a hundred and twenty thousand swordsmen had fallen.[w] [11]Gideon went up by the route of the nomads east of Nobah[x] and Jogbehah[y] and fell upon the unsuspecting army. [12]Zebah and Zalmunna, the two kings of Midian, fled, but he pursued them and captured them, routing their entire army.

[13]Gideon son of Joash then returned from the battle by the Pass of Heres. [14]He caught a young man of Succoth and questioned him, and the young man wrote down for him the names of the seventy-seven officials of Succoth, the elders of the town. [15]Then Gideon came and said to the men of Succoth, "Here are Zebah and Zalmunna, about whom you taunted me by saying, 'Do you already have the hands of Zebah and Zalmunna in your possession? Why should we give bread to your exhausted men?[z]' " [16]He took the elders of the town and taught the men of Succoth a lesson[a] by punishing them with desert thorns and briers. [17]He also pulled down the tower of Peniel and killed the men of the town.[b]

[18]Then he asked Zebah and Zalmunna, "What kind of men did you kill at Tabor?[c]"

"Men like you," they answered, "each one with the bearing of a prince."

[19]Gideon replied, "Those were my brothers, the sons of my own mother. As surely as the LORD lives, if you had spared their lives, I would not kill you." [20]Turning to Jether, his oldest son, he said, "Kill them!" But Jether did not draw his sword, because he was only a boy and was afraid.

[21]Zebah and Zalmunna said, "Come, do it yourself. 'As is the man, so is his strength.' " So Gideon stepped forward and killed them, and took the ornaments[d] off their camels' necks.

---

[a]8 Hebrew *Penuel*, a variant of *Peniel*; also in verses 9 and 17

8:3
nJdg 7:25;
Pr 15:1
8:4
oJdg 7:25
8:5
pGe 33:17
qPs 83:11
8:6
r1Sa 25:11
sver 15
8:7
tJdg 7:15
8:8
uGe 32:30;
1Ki 12:25
8:9
vver 17
8:10
wJdg 6:5; 7:12;
Isa 9:4
8:11
xNu 32:42
yNu 32:35
8:15
zver 6
8:16
aver 7
8:17
bver 9
8:18
cJos 19:22;
Jdg 4:6
8:21
dver 26;
Ps 83:11

Gideon's Ephod

22The Israelites said to Gideon, "Rule over us—you, your son and your grandson—because you have saved us out of the hand of Midian."

23But Gideon told them, "I will not rule over you, nor will my son rule over you. The LORD will rule[e] over you." 24And he said, "I do have one request, that each of you give me an earring from your share of the plunder." (It was the custom of the Ishmaelites[f] to wear gold earrings.)

25They answered, "We'll be glad to give them." So they spread out a garment, and each man threw a ring from his plunder onto it. 26The weight of the gold rings he asked for came to seventeen hundred shekels,[a] not counting the ornaments, the pendants and the purple garments worn by the kings of Midian or the chains that were on their camels' necks. 27Gideon made the gold into an ephod,[g] which he placed in Ophrah, his town. All Israel prostituted themselves by worshiping it there, and it became a snare[h] to Gideon and his family.

Gideon's Death

28Thus Midian was subdued before the Israelites and did not raise its head again. During Gideon's lifetime, the land enjoyed peace[i] forty years.

29Jerub-Baal[j] son of Joash went back home to live. 30He had seventy sons[k] of his own, for he had many wives. 31His concubine, who lived in Shechem, also bore him a son, whom he named Abimelech.[l] 32Gideon son of Joash died at a good old age[m] and was buried in the tomb of his father Joash in Ophrah of the Abiezrites.

33No sooner had Gideon died than the Israelites again prostituted themselves to the Baals.[n] They set up Baal-Berith[o] as their god[p] and 34did not remember[q] the LORD their God, who had rescued them from the hands of all their enemies on every side. 35They also failed to show kindness to the family of Jerub-Baal (that is, Gideon) for all the good things he had done for them.[r]

Abimelech

9 Abimelech[s] son of Jerub-Baal went to his mother's brothers in Shechem and said to them and to all his mother's clan, 2"Ask all the citizens of Shechem, 'Which is better for you: to have all seventy of Jerub-Baal's sons rule over you, or just one man?' Remember, I am your flesh and blood.[t]"

3When the brothers repeated all this to the citizens of Shechem, they were inclined to follow Abimelech, for they said, "He is our brother." 4They gave him seventy shekels[b] of silver from the temple of Baal-Berith,[u] and Abimelech used it to hire reckless adventurers,[v] who became his followers. 5He went to his father's home in Ophrah and on one stone murdered his seventy brothers,[w] the sons of Jerub-Baal. But Jotham, the youngest son of Jerub-Baal, escaped by hiding.[x] 6Then all the citizens of Shechem and Beth Millo gathered beside the great tree at the pillar in Shechem to crown Abimelech king.

7When Jotham was told about this, he climbed up on the top of

---

8:23
eEx 16:8;
1Sa 8:7; 10:19;
12:12
8:24
fGe 25:13
8:27
gJdg 17:5;
18:14 hDt 7:16;
Ps 106:39
8:28
iJdg 5:31
8:29
jJdg 7:1
8:30
kJdg 9:2,5,18,24
8:31
lJdg 9:1
8:32
mGe 25:8
8:33
nJdg 2:11,13,19
oJdg 9:4
pJdg 9:27,46
8:34
qJdg 3:7;
Dt 4:9;
Ps 78:11,42
8:35
rJdg 9:16
9:1
sJdg 8:31
9:2
tGe 29:14;
Jdg 8:30
9:4
uJdg 8:33
vJdg 11:3;
2Ch 13:7
9:5
wver 2;
Jdg 8:30
x2Ki 11:2

---

a26 That is, about 43 pounds (about 19.5 kilograms)   b4 That is, about 1 3/4 pounds (about 0.8 kilogram)

Mount Gerizim[y] and shouted to them, "Listen to me, citizens of Shechem, so that God may listen to you. [8]One day the trees went out to anoint a king for themselves. They said to the olive tree, 'Be our king.'

[9]"But the olive tree answered, 'Should I give up my oil, by which both gods and men are honored, to hold sway over the trees?'

[10]"Next, the trees said to the fig tree, 'Come and be our king.'

[11]"But the fig tree replied, 'Should I give up my fruit, so good and sweet, to hold sway over the trees?'

[12]"Then the trees said to the vine, 'Come and be our king.'

[13]"But the vine answered, 'Should I give up my wine,[z] which cheers both gods and men, to hold sway over the trees?'

[14]"Finally all the trees said to the thornbush, 'Come and be our king.'

[15]"The thornbush said to the trees, 'If you really want to anoint me king over you, come and take refuge in my shade;[a] but if not, then let fire come out[b] of the thornbush and consume the cedars of Lebanon!'[c]

[16]"Now if you have acted honorably and in good faith when you made Abimelech king, and if you have been fair to Jerub-Baal and his family, and if you have treated him as he deserves— [17]and to think that my father fought for you, risked his life to rescue you from the hand of Midian [18](but today you have revolted against my father's family, murdered his seventy sons[d] on a single stone, and made Abimelech, the son of his slave girl, king over the citizens of Shechem because he is your brother)— [19]if then you have acted honorably and in good faith toward Jerub-Baal and his family today, may Abimelech be your joy, and may you be his, too! [20]But if you have not, let fire come out[e] from Abimelech and consume you, citizens of Shechem and Beth Millo, and let fire come out from you, citizens of Shechem and Beth Millo, and consume Abimelech!"

[21]Then Jotham fled, escaping to Beer, and he lived there because he was afraid of his brother Abimelech.

[22]After Abimelech had governed Israel three years, [23]God sent an evil spirit[f] between Abimelech and the citizens of Shechem, who acted treacherously against Abimelech. [24]God did this in order that the crime against Jerub-Baal's seventy sons, the shedding[g] of their blood, might be avenged[h] on their brother Abimelech and on the citizens of Shechem, who had helped him[i] murder his brothers. [25]In opposition to him these citizens of Shechem set men on the hilltops to ambush and rob everyone who passed by, and this was reported to Abimelech.

[26]Now Gaal son of Ebed moved with his brothers into Shechem, and its citizens put their confidence in him. [27]After they had gone out into the fields and gathered the grapes and trodden[j] them, they held a festival in the temple of their god.[k] While they were eating and drinking, they cursed Abimelech. [28]Then Gaal son of Ebed said, "Who[l] is Abimelech, and who is Shechem, that we should be subject to him? Isn't he Jerub-Baal's son, and isn't Zebul his deputy? Serve the men of Hamor,[m] Shechem's father! Why should we serve Abimelech? [29]If only this people were under my command![n] Then I would get rid of him. I would say to Abimelech, 'Call out your whole army!' "[a]

[30]When Zebul the governor of the city heard what Gaal son of Ebed said, he was very angry. [31]Under cover he sent messengers to Abime-

9:7
y Dt 11:29;
27:12; Jn 4:20
9:13
z Ecc 2:3
9:15
a Isa 30:2
b ver 20
c Isa 2:13
9:18
d ver 5-6;
Jdg 8:30
9:20
e ver 15
9:23
f 1Sa 16:14,23;
18:10;
1Ki 22:22;
Isa 19:14; 33:1
9:24
g Nu 35:33;
1Ki 2:32
h ver 56-57
i Dt 27:25
9:27
j Am 9:13
k Jdg 8:33
9:28
l 1Sa 25:10;
1Ki 12:16
m Ge 34:2,6
9:29
n 2Sa 15:4

---

[a]29 Septuagint; Hebrew *him." Then he said to Abimelech, "Call out your whole army!"*

lech, saying, "Gaal son of Ebed and his brothers have come to Shechem and are stirring up the city against you. ³²Now then, during the night you and your men should come and lie in wait° in the fields. ³³In the morning at sunrise, advance against the city. When Gaal and his men come out against you, do whatever your hand finds to do.ᴾ"

³⁴So Abimelech and all his troops set out by night and took up concealed positions near Shechem in four companies. ³⁵Now Gaal son of Ebed had gone out and was standing at the entrance to the city gate just as Abimelech and his soldiers came out from their hiding place.�q

³⁶When Gaal saw them, he said to Zebul, "Look, people are coming down from the tops of the mountains!"

Zebul replied, "You mistake the shadows of the mountains for men."

³⁷But Gaal spoke up again: "Look, people are coming down from the center of the land, and a company is coming from the direction of the soothsayers' tree."

³⁸Then Zebul said to him, "Where is your big talk now, you who said, 'Who is Abimelech that we should be subject to him?' Aren't these the men you ridiculed?ʳ Go out and fight them!"

³⁹So Gaal led outª the citizens of Shechem and fought Abimelech. ⁴⁰Abimelech chased him, and many fell wounded in the flight—all the way to the entrance to the gate. ⁴¹Abimelech stayed in Arumah, and Zebul drove Gaal and his brothers out of Shechem.

⁴²The next day the people of Shechem went out to the fields, and this was reported to Abimelech. ⁴³So he took his men, divided them into three companiesˢ and set an ambush in the fields. When he saw the people coming out of the city, he rose to attack them. ⁴⁴Abimelech and the companies with him rushed forward to a position at the entrance to the city gate. Then two companies rushed upon those in the fields and struck them down. ⁴⁵All that day Abimelech pressed his attack against the city until he had captured it and killed its people. Then he destroyed the cityᵗ and scattered saltᵘ over it.

⁴⁶On hearing this, the citizens in the tower of Shechem went into the stronghold of the templeᵛ of El-Berith. ⁴⁷When Abimelech heard that they had assembled there, ⁴⁸he and all his men went up Mount Zalmon.ʷ He took an ax and cut off some branches, which he lifted to his shoulders. He ordered the men with him, "Quick! Do what you have seen me do!" ⁴⁹So all the men cut branches and followed Abimelech. They piled them against the stronghold and set it on fire over the people inside. So all the people in the tower of Shechem, about a thousand men and women, also died.

⁵⁰Next Abimelech went to Thebezˣ and besieged it and captured it. ⁵¹Inside the city, however, was a strong tower, to which all the men and women—all the people of the city—fled. They locked themselves in and climbed up on the tower roof. ⁵²Abimelech went to the tower and stormed it. But as he approached the entrance to the tower to set it on fire, ⁵³a woman dropped an upper millstone on his head and cracked his skull.ʸ

⁵⁴Hurriedly he called to his armor-bearer, "Draw your sword and kill me,ᶻ so that they can't say, 'A woman killed him.' " So his servant ran

9:32
oJos 8:2
9:33
p1Sa 10:7
9:35
qPs 32:7;
Jer 49:10
9:38
rver 28-29
9:43
sJdg 7:16
9:45
tver 20;
2Ki 3:25
uDt 29:23
9:46
vJdg 8:33
9:48
wPs 68:14
9:50
x2Sa 11:21
9:53
y2Sa 11:21
9:54
z1Sa 31:4;
2Sa 1:9

ª39 Or *Gaal went out in the sight of*

him through, and he died. ⁵⁵When the Israelites saw that Abimelech was dead, they went home.

⁵⁶Thus God repaid the wickedness that Abimelech had done to his father by murdering his seventy brothers. ⁵⁷God also made the men of Shechem pay for all their wickedness.ᵃ The curse of Jotham son of Jerub-Baal came on them.

Tola

10 After the time of Abimelech a man of Issachar,ᵇ Tola son of Puah,ᶜ the son of Dodo, rose to saveᵈ Israel. He lived in Shamir, in the hill country of Ephraim. ²He ledᵃ Israel twenty-three years; then he died, and was buried in Shamir.

Jair

³He was followed by Jair of Gilead, who led Israel twenty-two years. ⁴He had thirty sons, who rode thirty donkeys. They controlled thirty towns in Gilead, which to this day are called Havvoth Jair.ᵇᵉ ⁵When Jair died, he was buried in Kamon.

Jephthah

⁶Again the Israelites did evil in the eyes of the Lord.ᶠ They served the Baals and the Ashtoreths,ᵍ and the gods of Aram, the gods of Sidon, the gods of Moab, the gods of the Ammonites and the gods of the Philistines.ʰ And because the Israelites forsook the Lordⁱ and no longer served him, ⁷he became angryʲ with them. He sold themᵏ into the hands of the Philistines and the Ammonites, ⁸who that year shattered and crushed them. For eighteen years they oppressed all the Israelites on the east side of the Jordan in Gilead, the land of the Amorites. ⁹The Ammonites also crossed the Jordan to fight against Judah, Benjamin and the house of Ephraim; and Israel was in great distress. ¹⁰Then the Israelites cried out to the Lord, "We have sinned against you, forsaking our God and serving the Baals."ˡ

¹¹The Lord replied, "When the Egyptians,ᵐ the Amorites, the Ammonites,ⁿ the Philistines,ᵒ ¹²the Sidonians, the Amalekites and the Maonitesᶜ oppressed youᵖ and you cried to me for help, did I not save you from their hands? ¹³But you have forsaken me and served other gods, so I will no longer save you. ¹⁴Go and cry out to the gods you have chosen. Let them save you when you are in trouble!ᑫ"

¹⁵But the Israelites said to the Lord, "We have sinned. Do with us whatever you think best,ʳ but please rescue us now." ¹⁶Then they got rid of the foreign gods among them and served the Lord.ˢ And he could bear Israel's miseryᵗ no longer.ᵘ

¹⁷When the Ammonites were called to arms and camped in Gilead, the Israelites assembled and camped at Mizpah.ᵛ ¹⁸The leaders of the people of Gilead said to each other, "Whoever will launch the attack against the Ammonites will be the headʷ of all those living in Gilead."

11 Jephthahˣ the Gileadite was a mighty warrior.ʸ His father was Gilead; his mother was a prostitute. ²Gilead's wife also bore him sons, and when they were grown up, they drove Jephthah away. "You

9:57
ᵃver 20
10:1
ᵇGe 30:18
ᶜGe 46:13
ᵈJdg 2:16; 6:14
10:4
ᵉNu 32:41
10:6
ᶠJdg 2:11
ᵍJdg 2:13
ʰJdg 2:12
ⁱDt 32:15
10:7
ʲDt 31:17
ᵏDt 32:30; Jdg 2:14; 1Sa 12:9
10:10
ˡ1Sa 12:10
10:11
ᵐEx 14:30
ⁿNu 21:21; Jdg 3:13
ᵒJdg 3:31
10:12
ᵖPs 106:42
10:14
ᑫDt 32:37
10:15
ʳ1Sa 3:18; 2Sa 15:26
10:16
ˢJos 24:23; Jer 18:8
ᵗIsa 63:9
ᵘDt 32:36; Ps 106:44-45
10:17
ᵛGe 31:49; Jdg 11:29
10:18
ʷJdg 11:8,9
11:1
ˣHeb 11:32
ʸJdg 6:12

ᵃ2 Traditionally *judged*; also in verse 3   ᵇ4 Or *called the settlements of Jair*   ᶜ12 Hebrew; some Septuagint manuscripts *Midianites* are not going to get any inheritance in our family," they said, "because you are the son of another woman." [3]So Jephthah fled from his brothers and settled in the land of Tob,[z] where a group of adventurers[a] gathered around him and followed him.

[4]Some time later, when the Ammonites[b] made war on Israel, [5]the elders of Gilead went to get Jephthah from the land of Tob. [6]"Come," they said, "be our commander, so we can fight the Ammonites."

[7]Jephthah said to them, "Didn't you hate me and drive me from my father's house?[c] Why do you come to me now, when you're in trouble?"

[8]The elders of Gilead said to him, "Nevertheless, we are turning to you now; come with us to fight the Ammonites, and you will be our head[d] over all who live in Gilead."

[9]Jephthah answered, "Suppose you take me back to fight the Ammonites and the LORD gives them to me—will I really be your head?"

[10]The elders of Gilead replied, "The LORD is our witness;[e] we will certainly do as you say." [11]So Jephthah went with the elders of Gilead, and the people made him head and commander over them. And he repeated all his words before the LORD in Mizpah. [f]

[12]Then Jephthah sent messengers to the Ammonite king with the question: "What do you have against us that you have attacked our country?"

[13]The king of the Ammonites answered Jephthah's messengers, "When Israel came up out of Egypt, they took away my land from the Arnon to the Jabbok,[g] all the way to the Jordan. Now give it back peaceably."

[14]Jephthah sent back messengers to the Ammonite king, [15]saying:

"This is what Jephthah says: Israel did not take the land of Moab[h] or the land of the Ammonites.[i] [16]But when they came up out of Egypt, Israel went through the desert to the Red Sea[a][j] and on to Kadesh.[k] [17]Then Israel sent messengers[l] to the king of Edom, saying, 'Give us permission to go through your country,'[m] but the king of Edom would not listen. They sent also to the king of Moab, and he refused.[n] So Israel stayed at Kadesh.

[18]"Next they traveled through the desert, skirted the lands of Edom[o] and Moab, passed along the eastern side[p] of the country of Moab, and camped on the other side of the Arnon.[q] They did not enter the territory of Moab, for the Arnon was its border.

[19]"Then Israel sent messengers to Sihon king of the Amorites, who ruled in Heshbon, and said to him, 'Let us pass through your country to our own place.'[r] [20]Sihon, however, did not trust Israel[b] to pass through his territory. He mustered all his men and encamped at Jahaz and fought with Israel.[s]

[21]"Then the LORD, the God of Israel, gave Sihon and all his men into Israel's hands, and they defeated them. Israel took over all the land of the Amorites who lived in that country, [22]capturing all of it from the Arnon to the Jabbok and from the desert to the Jordan.[t]

11:3
z 2Sa 10:6,8
a Jdg 9:4
11:4
b Jdg 10:9
11:7
c Ge 26:27
11:8
d Jdg 10:18
11:10
e Ge 31:50;
Jer 42:5
11:11
f Jos 11:3;
Jdg 10:17; 20:1;
1Sa 10:17
11:13
g Ge 32:22;
Nu 21:24
11:15
h Dt 2:9 i Dt 2:19
11:16
j Nu 14:25;
Dt 1:40
k Nu 20:1
11:17
l Nu 20:14
m Nu 20:18,21
n Jos 24:9
11:18
o Nu 21:4
p Dt 2:8
q Nu 21:13
11:19
r Nu 21:21-22;
Dt 2:26-27
11:20
s Nu 21:23;
Dt 2:32
11:22
t Dt 2:36

---

[a]16 Hebrew *Yam Suph*; that is, Sea of Reeds   [b]20 Or *however, would not make an agreement for Israel*

²³"Now since the LORD, the God of Israel, has driven the Amorites out before his people Israel, what right have you to take it over? ²⁴Will you not take what your god Chemosh⁽ᵘ⁾ gives you? Likewise, whatever the LORD our God has given us, we will possess. ²⁵Are you better than Balak son of Zippor,⁽ᵛ⁾ king of Moab? Did he ever quarrel with Israel or fight with them?⁽ʷ⁾ ²⁶For three hundred years Israel occupied⁽ˣ⁾ Heshbon, Aroer, the surrounding settlements and all the towns along the Arnon. Why didn't you retake them during that time? ²⁷I have not wronged you, but you are doing me wrong by waging war against me. Let the LORD, the Judge,⁽ᵃ⁾⁽ʸ⁾ decide⁽ᶻ⁾ the dispute this day between the Israelites and the Ammonites."

²⁸The king of Ammon, however, paid no attention to the message Jephthah sent him.

²⁹Then the Spirit⁽ᵃ⁾ of the LORD came upon Jephthah. He crossed Gilead and Manasseh, passed through Mizpah of Gilead, and from there he advanced against the Ammonites. ³⁰And Jephthah made a vow⁽ᵇ⁾ to the LORD: "If you give the Ammonites into my hands, ³¹whatever comes out of the door of my house to meet me when I return in triumph from the Ammonites will be the LORD's, and I will sacrifice it as a burnt offering."

³²Then Jephthah went over to fight the Ammonites, and the LORD gave them into his hands. ³³He devastated twenty towns from Aroer to the vicinity of Minnith,⁽ᶜ⁾ as far as Abel Keramim. Thus Israel subdued Ammon.

³⁴When Jephthah returned to his home in Mizpah, who should come out to meet him but his daughter, dancing to the sound of tambourines!⁽ᵈ⁾ She was an only child. Except for her he had neither son nor daughter. ³⁵When he saw her, he tore his clothes and cried, "Oh! My daughter! You have made me miserable and wretched, because I have made a vow to the LORD that I cannot break.⁽ᵉ⁾"

³⁶"My father," she replied, "you have given your word to the LORD. Do to me just as you promised,⁽ᶠ⁾ now that the LORD has avenged you of your enemies,⁽ᵍ⁾ the Ammonites. ³⁷But grant me this one request," she said. "Give me two months to roam the hills and weep with my friends, because I will never marry."

³⁸"You may go," he said. And he let her go for two months. She and the girls went into the hills and wept because she would never marry. ³⁹After the two months, she returned to her father and he did to her as he had vowed. And she was a virgin.

From this comes the Israelite custom ⁴⁰that each year the young women of Israel go out for four days to commemorate the daughter of Jephthah the Gileadite.

Jephthah and Ephraim

12 The men of Ephraim called out their forces, crossed over to Zaphon and said to Jephthah, "Why did you go to fight the Ammonites without calling us to go with you?⁽ʰ⁾ We're going to burn down your house over your head."

ᵃ27 Or Ruler

11:24
u Nu 21:29;
Jos 3:10;
1Ki 11:7
11:25
v Nu 22:2
w Jos 24:9
11:26
x Nu 21:25
11:27
y Ge 18:25
z Ge 16:5;
31:53;
1Sa 24:12,15
11:29
a Nu 11:25;
Jdg 3:10; 6:34;
14:6,19; 15:14;
1Sa 11:6;
16:13; Isa 11:2
11:30
b Ge 28:20
11:33
c Eze 27:17
11:34
d Ex 15:20;
Jer 31:4
11:35
e Nu 30:2;
Ecc 5:2,4,5
11:36
f Lk 1:38
g 2Sa 18:19
12:1
h Jdg 8:1

²Jephthah answered, "I and my people were engaged in a great struggle with the Ammonites, and although I called, you didn't save me out of their hands. ³When I saw that you wouldn't help, I took my life in my hands[i] and crossed over to fight the Ammonites, and the LORD gave me the victory over them. Now why have you come up today to fight me?"

⁴Jephthah then called together the men of Gilead and fought against Ephraim. The Gileadites struck them down because the Ephraimites had said, "You Gileadites are renegades from Ephraim and Manasseh." ⁵The Gileadites captured the fords of the Jordan[j] leading to Ephraim, and whenever a survivor of Ephraim said, "Let me cross over," the men of Gilead asked him, "Are you an Ephraimite?" If he replied, "No," ⁶they said, "All right, say 'Shibboleth.' " If he said, "Sibboleth," because he could not pronounce the word correctly, they seized him and killed him at the fords of the Jordan. Forty-two thousand Ephraimites were killed at that time.

⁷Jephthah led[a] Israel six years. Then Jephthah the Gileadite died, and was buried in a town in Gilead.

Ibzan, Elon and Abdon

⁸After him, Ibzan of Bethlehem led Israel. ⁹He had thirty sons and thirty daughters. He gave his daughters away in marriage to those outside his clan, and for his sons he brought in thirty young women as wives from outside his clan. Ibzan led Israel seven years. ¹⁰Then Ibzan died, and was buried in Bethlehem.

¹¹After him, Elon the Zebulunite led Israel ten years. ¹²Then Elon died, and was buried in Aijalon in the land of Zebulun.

¹³After him, Abdon son of Hillel, from Pirathon, led Israel. ¹⁴He had forty sons and thirty grandsons,[k] who rode on seventy donkeys.[l] He led Israel eight years. ¹⁵Then Abdon son of Hillel died, and was buried at Pirathon in Ephraim, in the hill country of the Amalekites.[m]

The Birth of Samson

13 Again the Israelites did evil in the eyes of the LORD, so the LORD delivered them into the hands of the Philistines[n] for forty years.

²A certain man of Zorah,[o] named Manoah, from the clan of the Danites, had a wife who was sterile and remained childless. ³The angel of the LORD[p] appeared to her[q] and said, "You are sterile and childless, but you are going to conceive and have a son.[r] ⁴Now see to it that you drink no wine or other fermented drink and that you do not eat anything unclean,[s] ⁵because you will conceive and give birth to a son. No razor[t] may be used on his head, because the boy is to be a Nazirite,[u] set apart to God from birth, and he will begin[v] the deliverance of Israel from the hands of the Philistines."

⁶Then the woman went to her husband and told him, "A man of God[w] came to me. He looked like an angel of God,[x] very awesome. I didn't ask him where he came from, and he didn't tell me his name. ⁷But he said to me, 'You will conceive and give birth to a son. Now then, drink no wine or other fermented drink and do not eat anything

12:3
i1Sa 19:5;
28:21;
Job 13:14
12:5
jJos 22:11;
Jdg 3:28
12:14
kJdg 10:4
lJdg 5:10
12:15
mJdg 5:14
13:1
nJdg 2:11;
1Sa 12:9
13:2
oJos 15:33;
19:41
13:3
pver 6,8;
Jdg 6:12 qver 10
rLk 1:13
13:4
sver 14;
Nu 6:2-4;
Lk 1:15
13:5
tNu 6:5;
1Sa 1:11
uNu 6:2,13
v1Sa 7:13
13:6
wver 8;
1Sa 2:27; 9:6
xver 17-18;
Mt 28:3

---

[a]7 Traditionally *judged*; also in verses 8-14

unclean, because the boy will be a Nazirite of God from birth until the day of his death.' "

8Then Manoah prayed to the LORD: "O Lord, I beg you, let the man of God you sent to us come again to teach us how to bring up the boy who is to be born."

9God heard Manoah, and the angel of God came again to the woman while she was out in the field; but her husband Manoah was not with her. 10The woman hurried to tell her husband, "He's here! The man who appeared to me the other day!"

11Manoah got up and followed his wife. When he came to the man, he said, "Are you the one who talked to my wife?"

"I am," he said.

12So Manoah asked him, "When your words are fulfilled, what is to be the rule for the boy's life and work?"

13The angel of the LORD answered, "Your wife must do all that I have told her. 14She must not eat anything that comes from the grapevine, nor drink any wine or other fermented drinky nor eat anything unclean.z She must do everything I have commanded her."

15Manoah said to the angel of the LORD, "We would like you to stay until we prepare a young goata for you."

16The angel of the LORD replied, "Even though you detain me, I will not eat any of your food. But if you prepare a burnt offering,b offer it to the LORD." (Manoah did not realize that it was the angel of the LORD.)

17Then Manoah inquired of the angel of the LORD, "What is your name,c so that we may honor you when your word comes true?"

18He replied, "Why do you ask my name?d It is beyond understanding.a" 19Then Manoah took a young goat, together with the grain offering, and sacrificed it on a rocke to the LORD. And the LORD did an amazing thing while Manoah and his wife watched: 20As the flamef blazed up from the altar toward heaven, the angel of the LORD ascended in the flame. Seeing this, Manoah and his wife fell with their faces to the ground.g 21When the angel of the LORD did not show himself again to Manoah and his wife, Manoah realizedh that it was the angel of the LORD.

22"We are doomedi to die!" he said to his wife. "We have seenj God!"

23But his wife answered, "If the LORD had meant to kill us, he would not have accepted a burnt offering and grain offering from our hands, nor shown us all these things or now told us this."k

24The woman gave birth to a boy and named him Samson.l He grewm and the LORD blessed him,n 25and the Spirit of the LORD began to stiro him while he was in Mahaneh Dan,p between Zorah and Eshtaol.

Samson's Marriage

14 Samson went down to Timnahq and saw there a young Philistine woman. 2When he returned, he said to his father and mother, "I have seen a Philistine woman in Timnah; now get her for me as my wife."r

3His father and mother replied, "Isn't there an acceptable woman

13:14
yNu 6:4 zver 4
13:15
aver 3; Jdg 6:19
13:16
bJdg 6:20
13:17
cGe 32:29
13:18
dIsa 9:6
13:19
eJdg 6:20
13:20
fLev 9:24
g1Ch 21:16;
Eze 1:28;
Mt 17:6
13:21
hver 16;
Jdg 6:22
13:22
iDt 5:26
jGe 32:30;
Jdg 6:22
13:23
kPs 25:14
13:24
lHeb 11:32
m1Sa 3:19
nLk 1:80
13:25
oJdg 3:10
pJdg 18:12
14:1
qGe 38:12
14:2
rGe 21:21; 34:4

a18 Or is wonderful

among your relatives or among all our people?ˢ Must you go to the uncircumcisedᵗ Philistines to get a wife?ᵘ"

But Samson said to his father, "Get her for me. She's the right one for me." ⁴(His parents did not know that this was from the LORD, who was seeking an occasion to confront the Philistines;ᵛ for at that time they were ruling over Israel.)ʷ ⁵Samson went down to Timnah together with his father and mother. As they approached the vineyards of Timnah, suddenly a young lion came roaring toward him. ⁶The Spirit of the LORD came upon him in powerˣ so that he tore the lion apart with his bare hands as he might have torn a young goat. But he told neither his father nor his mother what he had done. ⁷Then he went down and talked with the woman, and he liked her.

⁸Some time later, when he went back to marry her, he turned aside to look at the lion's carcass. In it was a swarm of bees and some honey, ⁹which he scooped out with his hands and ate as he went along. When he rejoined his parents, he gave them some, and they too ate it. But he did not tell them that he had taken the honey from the lion's carcass.

¹⁰Now his father went down to see the woman. And Samson made a feast there, as was customary for bridegrooms. ¹¹When he appeared, he was given thirty companions.

¹²"Let me tell you a riddle,ʸ" Samson said to them. "If you can give me the answer within the seven days of the feast,ᶻ I will give you thirty linen garments and thirty sets of clothes.ᵃ ¹³If you can't tell me the answer, you must give me thirty linen garments and thirty sets of clothes."

"Tell us your riddle," they said. "Let's hear it."
¹⁴He replied,

> "Out of the eater, something to eat;
> out of the strong, something sweet."

For three days they could not give the answer.

¹⁵On the fourthᵃ day, they said to Samson's wife, "Coaxᵇ your husband into explaining the riddle for us, or we will burn you and your father's household to death.ᶜ Did you invite us here to rob us?"

¹⁶Then Samson's wife threw herself on him, sobbing, "You hate me! You don't really love me.ᵈ You've given my people a riddle, but you haven't told me the answer."

"I haven't even explained it to my father or mother," he replied, "so why should I explain it to you?" ¹⁷She cried the whole seven daysᵉ of the feast. So on the seventh day he finally told her, because she continued to press him. She in turn explained the riddle to her people.

¹⁸Before sunset on the seventh day the men of the town said to him,

> "What is sweeter than honey?
> What is stronger than a lion?"ᶠ

Samson said to them,

> "If you had not plowed with my heifer,
> you would not have solved my riddle."

14:3
ˢGe 24:4
ᵗDt 7:3
ᵘEx 34:16
14:4
ᵛJos 11:20
ʷJdg 13:1
14:6
ˣJdg 3:10;
13:25
14:12
ʸ1Ki 10:1;
Eze 17:2
ᶻGe 29:27
ᵃGe 45:22;
2Ki 5:5
14:15
ᵇJdg 16:5;
Ecc 7:26
ᶜJdg 15:6
14:16
ᵈJdg 16:15
14:17
ᵉEst 1:5
14:18
ᶠver 14

ᵃ15 Some Septuagint manuscripts and Syriac; Hebrew *seventh*

¹⁹Then the Spirit of the LORD came upon him in power.[g] He went down to Ashkelon, struck down thirty of their men, stripped them of their belongings and gave their clothes to those who had explained the riddle. Burning with anger,[h] he went up to his father's house. ²⁰And Samson's wife was given to the friend[i] who had attended him at his wedding.

Samson's Vengeance on the Philistines

15 Later on, at the time of wheat harvest, Samson took a young goat[j] and went to visit his wife. He said, "I'm going to my wife's room." But her father would not let him go in.

²"I was so sure you thoroughly hated her," he said, "that I gave her to your friend.[k] Isn't her younger sister more attractive? Take her instead."

³Samson said to them, "This time I have a right to get even with the Philistines; I will really harm them." ⁴So he went out and caught three hundred foxes and tied them tail to tail in pairs. He then fastened a torch to every pair of tails, ⁵lit the torches and let the foxes loose in the standing grain of the Philistines. He burned up the shocks and standing grain, together with the vineyards and olive groves.

⁶When the Philistines asked, "Who did this?" they were told, "Samson, the Timnite's son-in-law, because his wife was given to his friend."

So the Philistines went up and burned her and her father to death.[l] ⁷Samson said to them, "Since you've acted like this, I won't stop until I get my revenge on you." ⁸He attacked them viciously and slaughtered many of them. Then he went down and stayed in a cave in the rock of Etam.

⁹The Philistines went up and camped in Judah, spreading out near Lehi.[m] ¹⁰The men of Judah asked, "Why have you come to fight us?"

"We have come to take Samson prisoner," they answered, "to do to him as he did to us."

¹¹Then three thousand men from Judah went down to the cave in the rock of Etam and said to Samson, "Don't you realize that the Philistines are rulers over us?[n] What have you done to us?"

He answered, "I merely did to them what they did to me."

¹²They said to him, "We've come to tie you up and hand you over to the Philistines."

Samson said, "Swear to me that you won't kill me yourselves."

¹³"Agreed," they answered. "We will only tie you up and hand you over to them. We will not kill you." So they bound him with two new ropes and led him up from the rock. ¹⁴As he approached Lehi, the Philistines came toward him shouting. The Spirit of the LORD came upon him in power.[o] The ropes on his arms became like charred flax, and the bindings dropped from his hands. ¹⁵Finding a fresh jawbone of a donkey, he grabbed it and struck down a thousand men.[p]

¹⁶Then Samson said,

> "With a donkey's jawbone
> I have made donkeys of them.[a]

---

[a]16 Or *made a heap or two*; the Hebrew for *donkey* sounds like the Hebrew for *heap*.

14:19
gNu 11:25;
Jdg 3:10; 6:34;
11:29; 13:25;
15:14;
1Sa 11:6;
16:13;
1Ki 18:46;
2Ch 24:20;
Isa 11:2
h1Sa 11:6

14:20
iJdg 15:2,6;
Jn 3:29

15:1
jGe 38:17

15:2
kJdg 14:20

15:6
lJdg 14:15

15:9
mver 14,17,19

15:11
nJdg 13:1;
14:4;
Ps 106:40-42

15:14
oJdg 3:10;
14:19; 1Sa 11:6

15:15
pLev 26:8;
Jos 23:10;
Jdg 3:31

> With a donkey's jawbone
> I have killed a thousand men."

¹⁷When he finished speaking, he threw away the jawbone; and the place was called Ramath Lehi.ᵃ

¹⁸Because he was very thirsty, he cried out to the LORD,�q "You have given your servant this great victory. Must I now die of thirst and fall into the hands of the uncircumcised?" ¹⁹Then God opened up the hollow place in Lehi, and water came out of it. When Samson drank, his strength returned and he revived.ʳ So the spring was called En Hakkore,ᵇ and it is still there in Lehi.

²⁰Samson ledᶜ Israel for twenty yearsˢ in the days of the Philistines.

Samson and Delilah

16 One day Samson went to Gaza, where he saw a prostitute. He went in to spend the night with her. ²The people of Gaza were told, "Samson is here!" So they surrounded the place and lay in wait for him all night at the city gate.ᵗ They made no move during the night, saying, "At dawn we'll kill him."

³But Samson lay there only until the middle of the night. Then he got up and took hold of the doors of the city gate, together with the two posts, and tore them loose, bar and all. He lifted them to his shoulders and carried them to the top of the hill that faces Hebron.ᵘ

⁴Some time later, he fell in loveᵛ with a woman in the Valley of Sorek whose name was Delilah. ⁵The rulers of the Philistinesʷ went to her and said, "See if you can lureˣ him into showing you the secret of his great strength and how we can overpower him so we may tie him up and subdue him. Each one of us will give you eleven hundred shekelsᵈ of silver."ʸ

⁶So Delilah said to Samson, "Tell me the secret of your great strength and how you can be tied up and subdued."

⁷Samson answered her, "If anyone ties me with seven fresh thongsᵉ that have not been dried, I'll become as weak as any other man."

⁸Then the rulers of the Philistines brought her seven fresh thongs that had not been dried, and she tied him with them. ⁹With men hidden in the room,ᶻ she called to him, "Samson, the Philistines are upon you!" But he snapped the thongs as easily as a piece of string snaps when it comes close to a flame. So the secret of his strength was not discovered.

¹⁰Then Delilah said to Samson, "You have made a fool of me;ᵃ you lied to me. Come now, tell me how you can be tied."

¹¹He said, "If anyone ties me securely with new ropesᵇ that have never been used, I'll become as weak as any other man."

¹²So Delilah took new ropes and tied him with them. Then, with men hidden in the room, she called to him, "Samson, the Philistines are upon you!" But he snapped the ropes off his arms as if they were threads.

¹³Delilah then said to Samson, "Until now, you have been making a fool of me and lying to me. Tell me how you can be tied."

15:18
qJdg 16:28
15:19
rGe 45:27;
Isa 40:29
15:20
sJdg 13:1;
16:31;
Heb 11:32
16:2
t1Sa 23:26;
Ps 118:10-12;
Ac 9:24
16:3
uJos 10:36
16:4
vGe 24:67
16:5
wJos 13:3
xEx 10:7;
Jdg 14:15
yver 18
16:9
zver 12
16:10
aver 13
16:11
bJdg 15:13

ᵃ*17 Ramath Lehi* means *jawbone hill.*   ᵇ*19 En Hakkore* means *caller's spring.*   ᶜ*20 Traditionally judged*   ᵈ*5 That is, about 28 pounds (about 13 kilograms)*   ᵉ*7 Or bowstrings; also in verses 8 and 9*

He replied, "If you weave the seven braids of my head into the fabric on the loom, and tighten it with the pin, I'll become as weak as any other man." So while he was sleeping, Delilah took the seven braids of his head, wove them into the fabric [14]and[a] tightened it with the pin.

Again she called to him, "Samson, the Philistines are upon you!"[c] He awoke from his sleep and pulled up the pin and the loom, with the fabric.

[15]Then she said to him, "How can you say, 'I love you,'[d] when you won't confide in me? This is the third time[e] you have made a fool of me and haven't told me the secret of your great strength."[f] [16]With such nagging she prodded him day after day until he was tired to death.

[17]So he told her everything.[g] "No razor has ever been used on my head," he said, "because I have been a Nazirite[h] set apart to God since birth. If my head were shaved, my strength would leave me, and I would become as weak as any other man."

[18]When Delilah saw that he had told her everything, she sent word to the rulers of the Philistines[i], "Come back once more; he has told me everything." So the rulers of the Philistines returned with the silver in their hands. [19]Having put him to sleep on her lap, she called a man to shave off the seven braids of his hair, and so began to subdue him.[b] And his strength left him.[j]

[20]Then she called, "Samson, the Philistines are upon you!"

He awoke from his sleep and thought, "I'll go out as before and shake myself free." But he did not know that the LORD had left him.[k]

[21]Then the Philistines[l] seized him, gouged out his eyes[m] and took him down to Gaza. Binding him with bronze shackles, they set him to grinding[n] in the prison. [22]But the hair on his head began to grow again after it had been shaved.

The Death of Samson

[23]Now the rulers of the Philistines assembled to offer a great sacrifice to Dagon[o] their god and to celebrate, saying, "Our god has delivered Samson, our enemy, into our hands."

[24]When the people saw him, they praised their god,[p] saying,

"Our god has delivered our enemy
    into our hands,[q]
the one who laid waste our land
    and multiplied our slain."

[25]While they were in high spirits,[r] they shouted, "Bring out Samson to entertain us." So they called Samson out of the prison, and he performed for them.

When they stood him among the pillars, [26]Samson said to the servant who held his hand, "Put me where I can feel the pillars that support the temple, so that I may lean against them." [27]Now the temple was crowded with men and women; all the rulers of the Philistines were there, and on the roof[s] were about three thousand men and women watching Samson perform. [28]Then Samson prayed to the LORD,[t] "O Sovereign LORD, remember me. O God, please strengthen me just once more, and

16:14
[c]ver 9,20
16:15
[d]Jdg 14:16
[e]Nu 24:10
[f]ver 5
16:17
[g]Mic 7:5
[h]Nu 6:2,5;
Jdg 13:5
16:18
[i]Jos 13:3;
1Sa 5:8
16:19
[j]Pr 7:26-27
16:20
[k]Nu 14:42;
Jos 7:12;
1Sa 16:14;
18:12; 28:15
16:21
[l]Jer 47:1
[m]Nu 16:14
[n]Job 31:10;
Isa 47:2
16:23
[o]1Sa 5:2;
1Ch 10:10
16:24
[p]Da 5:4
[q]1Sa 31:9;
1Ch 10:9
16:25
[r]Jdg 9:27;
Ru 3:7; Est 1:10
16:27
[s]Dt 22:8;
Jos 2:8
16:28
[t]Jdg 15:18

---

[a]13,14 Some Septuagint manuscripts; Hebrew *"I can, if you weave the seven braids of my head into the fabric on the loom."* [14]*So she*   [b]19 Hebrew; some Septuagint manuscripts *and he began to weaken*

let me with one blow get revenge[u] on the Philistines for my two eyes." [29]Then Samson reached toward the two central pillars on which the temple stood. Bracing himself against them, his right hand on the one and his left hand on the other, [30]Samson said, "Let me die with the Philistines!" Then he pushed with all his might, and down came the temple on the rulers and all the people in it. Thus he killed many more when he died than while he lived.

[31]Then his brothers and his father's whole family went down to get him. They brought him back and buried him between Zorah and Eshtaol in the tomb of Manoah[v] his father. He had led[aw] Israel twenty years.[x]

Micah's Idols

17 Now a man named Micah[y] from the hill country of Ephraim [2]said to his mother, "The eleven hundred shekels[b] of silver that were taken from you and about which I heard you utter a curse—I have that silver with me; I took it."

Then his mother said, "The Lord bless you,[z] my son!"

[3]When he returned the eleven hundred shekels of silver to his mother, she said, "I solemnly consecrate my silver to the Lord for my son to make a carved image and a cast idol.[a] I will give it back to you."

[4]So he returned the silver to his mother, and she took two hundred shekels[c] of silver and gave them to a silversmith, who made them into the image and the idol.[b] And they were put in Micah's house.

[5]Now this man Micah had a shrine,[c] and he made an ephod[d] and some idols[e] and installed[f] one of his sons as his priest.[g] [6]In those days Israel had no king;[h] everyone did as he saw fit.[i]

[7]A young Levite from Bethlehem in Judah,[j] who had been living within the clan of Judah, [8]left that town in search of some other place to stay. On his way[d] he came to Micah's house in the hill country of Ephraim.

[9]Micah asked him, "Where are you from?"

"I'm a Levite from Bethlehem in Judah," he said, "and I'm looking for a place to stay."

[10]Then Micah said to him, "Live with me and be my father and priest,[k] and I'll give you ten shekels[e] of silver a year, your clothes and your food." [11]So the Levite agreed to live with him, and the young man was to him like one of his sons. [12]Then Micah installed[l] the Levite, and the young man became his priest and lived in his house. [13]And Micah said, "Now I know that the Lord will be good to me, since this Levite has become my priest."

Danites Settle in Laish

18 In those days Israel had no king.[m] And in those days the tribe of the Danites was seeking a place of their own where they might settle, because they had not yet come into an inheritance among the tribes of Israel.[n] [2]So the Danites[o] sent five warriors from Zorah and Eshtaol to spy out the land and explore it.

16:28
u Jer 15:15

16:31
v Jdg 13:2
w Ru 1:1;
1Sa 4:18
x Jdg 15:20

17:1
y Jdg 18:2,13

17:2
z Ru 2:20;
1Sa 15:13;
2Sa 2:5

17:3
a Ex 20:4,23;
34:17; Lev 19:4

17:4
b Ex 32:4;
Isa 17:8

17:5
c Isa 44:13;
Eze 8:10
d Jdg 8:27
e Ge 31:19;
Jdg 18:14
f Nu 16:10
g Ex 29:9;
Jdg 18:24

17:6
h Jdg 18:1;
19:1; 21:25
i Dt 12:8

17:7
j Jdg 19:1;
Ru 1:1-2;
Mic 5:2; Mt 2:1

17:10
k Jdg 18:19

17:12
l Nu 16:10

18:1
m Jdg 17:6; 19:1
n Jos 19:47

18:2
o Jdg 13:25

---

[a]31 Traditionally *judged*　　[b]2 That is, about 28 pounds (about 13 kilograms)　　[c]4 That is, about 5 pounds (about 2.3 kilograms)　　[d]8 Or *To carry on his profession*　　[e]10 That is, about 4 ounces (about 110 grams)

These men represented all their clans. They told them, "Go, explore the land."[p]

The men entered the hill country of Ephraim and came to the house of Micah,[q] where they spent the night. [3]When they were near Micah's house, they recognized the voice of the young Levite; so they turned in there and asked him, "Who brought you here? What are you doing in this place? Why are you here?"

[4]He told them what Micah had done for him, and said, "He has hired me and I am his priest.[r]"

[5]Then they said to him, "Please inquire of God[s] to learn whether our journey will be successful."

[6]The priest answered them, "Go in peace[t]. Your journey has the LORD's approval."

[7]So the five men left and came to Laish,[u] where they saw that the people were living in safety, like the Sidonians, unsuspecting and secure. And since their land lacked nothing, they were prosperous.[a] Also, they lived a long way from the Sidonians[v] and had no relationship with anyone else.[b]

[8]When they returned to Zorah and Eshtaol, their brothers asked them, "How did you find things?"

[9]They answered, "Come on, let's attack them! We have seen that the land is very good. Aren't you going to do something? Don't hesitate to go there and take it over.[w] [10]When you get there, you will find an unsuspecting people and a spacious land that God has put into your hands, a land that lacks nothing[x] whatever.[y]"

[11]Then six hundred men[z] from the clan of the Danites,[a] armed for battle, set out from Zorah and Eshtaol. [12]On their way they set up camp near Kiriath Jearim in Judah. This is why the place west of Kiriath Jearim is called Mahaneh Dan[cb] to this day. [13]From there they went on to the hill country of Ephraim and came to Micah's house.

[14]Then the five men who had spied out the land of Laish said to their brothers, "Do you know that one of these houses has an ephod, other household gods, a carved image and a cast idol?[c] Now you know what to do." [15]So they turned in there and went to the house of the young Levite at Micah's place and greeted him. [16]The six hundred Danites,[d] armed for battle, stood at the entrance to the gate. [17]The five men who had spied out the land went inside and took the carved image, the ephod, the other household gods[e] and the cast idol while the priest and the six hundred armed men stood at the entrance to the gate.

[18]When these men went into Micah's house and took[f] the carved image, the ephod, the other household gods and the cast idol, the priest said to them, "What are you doing?"

[19]They answered him, "Be quiet![g] Don't say a word. Come with us, and be our father and priest.[h] Isn't it better that you serve a tribe and clan in Israel as priest rather than just one man's household?" [20]Then the priest was glad. He took the ephod, the other household gods and the carved image and went along with the people. [21]Putting their little children, their livestock and their possessions in front of them, they turned away and left.

18:2
p Jos 2:1
q Jdg 17:1
18:4
r Jdg 17:12
18:5
s 1Ki 22:5
18:6
t 1Ki 22:6
18:7
u Jos 19:47
v ver 28
18:9
w Nu 13:30;
1Ki 22:3
18:10
x ver 7,27;
Dt 8:9
y 1Ch 4:40
18:11
z ver 16,17
a Jdg 13:2
18:12
b Jdg 13:25
18:14
c Ge 31:19;
Jdg 17:5
18:16
d ver 11
18:17
e Ge 31:19;
Mic 5:13
18:18
f Isa 46:2;
Jer 43:11;
Hos 10:5
18:19
g Job 21:5;
29:9; 40:4;
Mic 7:16
h Jdg 17:10

---

a7 The meaning of the Hebrew for this clause is uncertain.   *b7* Hebrew; some Septuagint manuscripts *with the Arameans*   *c12 Mahaneh Dan means Dan's camp.*

22When they had gone some distance from Micah's house, the men who lived near Micah were called together and overtook the Danites. 23As they shouted after them, the Danites turned and said to Micah, "What's the matter with you that you called out your men to fight?"

24He replied, "You took the gods I made, and my priest, and went away. What else do I have? How can you ask, 'What's the matter with you?'"

25The Danites answered, "Don't argue with us, or some hot-tempered men will attack you, and you and your family will lose your lives." 26So the Danites went their way, and Micah, seeing that they were too strong for him,[i] turned around and went back home.

27Then they took what Micah had made, and his priest, and went on to Laish, against a peaceful and unsuspecting people.[j] They attacked them with the sword and burned down their city.[k] 28There was no one to rescue them because they lived a long way from Sidon[l] and had no relationship with anyone else. The city was in a valley near Beth Rehob.[m]

The Danites rebuilt the city and settled there. 29They named it Dan[n] after their forefather Dan, who was born to Israel—though the city used to be called Laish.[o] 30There the Danites set up for themselves the idols, and Jonathan son of Gershom,[p] the son of Moses,[a] and his sons were priests for the tribe of Dan until the time of the captivity of the land. 31They continued to use the idols Micah had made, all the time the house of God[q] was in Shiloh.[r]

A Levite and His Concubine

19 In those days Israel had no king.
Now a Levite who lived in a remote area in the hill country of Ephraim[s] took a concubine from Bethlehem in Judah.[t] 2But she was unfaithful to him. She left him and went back to her father's house in Bethlehem, Judah. After she had been there four months, 3her husband went to her to persuade her to return. He had with him his servant and two donkeys. She took him into her father's house, and when her father saw him, he gladly welcomed him. 4His father-in-law, the girl's father, prevailed upon him to stay; so he remained with him three days, eating and drinking,[u] and sleeping there.

5On the fourth day they got up early and he prepared to leave, but the girl's father said to his son-in-law, "Refresh yourself[v] with something to eat; then you can go." 6So the two of them sat down to eat and drink together. Afterward the girl's father said, "Please stay tonight and enjoy yourself.[w]" 7And when the man got up to go, his father-in-law persuaded him, so he stayed there that night. 8On the morning of the fifth day, when he rose to go, the girl's father said, "Refresh yourself. Wait till afternoon!" So the two of them ate together.

9Then when the man, with his concubine and his servant, got up to leave, his father-in-law, the girl's father, said, "Now look, it's almost evening. Spend the night here; the day is nearly over. Stay and enjoy yourself. Early tomorrow morning you can get up and be on your way home." 10But, unwilling to stay another night, the man left and went

18:26
iPs 18:17; 35:10
18:27
jver 7,10
kGe 49:17;
Jos 19:47
18:28
lver 7
mNu 13:21;
2Sa 10:6
18:29
nGe 14:14
oJos 19:47;
1Ki 15:20
18:30
pEx 2:22;
Jdg 17:3,5
18:31
qJdg 19:18
rJos 18:1;
Jer 7:14
19:1
sJdg 18:1
tRu 1:1
19:4
uEx 32:6
19:5
vver 8; Ge 18:5
19:6
wver 9,22;
Jdg 16:25

---

a30 An ancient Hebrew scribal tradition, some Septuagint manuscripts and Vulgate; Masoretic Text *Manasseh* toward Jebus[x] (that is, Jerusalem), with his two saddled donkeys and his concubine.

[11]When they were near Jebus and the day was almost gone, the servant said to his master, "Come, let's stop at this city of the Jebusites[y] and spend the night."

[12]His master replied, "No. We won't go into an alien city, whose people are not Israelites. We will go on to Gibeah." [13]He added, "Come, let's try to reach Gibeah or Ramah[z] and spend the night in one of those places." [14]So they went on, and the sun set as they neared Gibeah in Benjamin.[a] [15]There they stopped to spend the night. They went and sat in the city square,[b] but no one took them into his home for the night.

[16]That evening[c] an old man from the hill country of Ephraim,[d] who was living in Gibeah (the men of the place were Benjamites), came in from his work in the fields. [17]When he looked and saw the traveler in the city square, the old man asked, "Where are you going? Where did you come from?"[e]

[18]He answered, "We are on our way from Bethlehem in Judah to a remote area in the hill country of Ephraim where I live. I have been to Bethlehem in Judah and now I am going to the house of the LORD.[f] No one has taken me into his house. [19]We have both straw and fodder[g] for our donkeys and bread and wine[h] for ourselves your servants—me, your maidservant, and the young man with us. We don't need anything."

[20]"You are welcome at my house," the old man said. "Let me supply whatever you need. Only don't spend the night in the square." [21]So he took him into his house and fed his donkeys. After they had washed their feet, they had something to eat and drink.[i]

[22]While they were enjoying themselves,[j] some of the wicked men[k] of the city surrounded the house. Pounding on the door, they shouted to the old man who owned the house, "Bring out the man who came to your house so we can have sex with him.[l]"

[23]The owner of the house went outside[m] and said to them, "No, my friends, don't be so vile. Since this man is my guest, don't do this disgraceful thing.[n] [24]Look, here is my virgin daughter,[o] and his concubine. I will bring them out to you now, and you can use them and do to them whatever you wish. But to this man, don't do such a disgraceful thing."

[25]But the men would not listen to him. So the man took his concubine and sent her outside to them, and they raped her and abused her[p] throughout the night, and at dawn they let her go. [26]At daybreak the woman went back to the house where her master was staying, fell down at the door and lay there until daylight.

[27]When her master got up in the morning and opened the door of the house and stepped out to continue on his way, there lay his concubine, fallen in the doorway of the house, with her hands on the threshold. [28]He said to her, "Get up; let's go." But there was no answer. Then the man put her on his donkey and set out for home.

[29]When he reached home, he took a knife[q] and cut up his concubine, limb by limb, into twelve parts and sent them into all the areas of Israel.[r] [30]Everyone who saw it said, "Such a thing has never been seen

19:10
xGe 10:16;
Jos 15:8;
1Ch 11:4-5

19:11
yJos 3:10

19:13
zJos 18:25

19:14
a1Sa 10:26;
Isa 10:29

19:15
bGe 19:2

19:16
cPs 104:23
dver 1

19:17
eGe 29:4

19:18
fJdg 18:31

19:19
gGe 24:25
hGe 14:18

19:21
iGe 24:32-33;
Lk 7:44

19:22
jJdg 16:25
kDt 13:13
lGe 19:4-5;
Jdg 20:5;
Ro 1:26-27

19:23
mGe 19:6
nGe 34:7;
Lev 19:29;
Dt 22:21;
Jdg 20:6;
2Sa 13:12;
Ro 1:27

19:24
oGe 19:8;
Dt 21:14

19:25
p1Sa 31:4

19:29
qGe 22:6
rJdg 20:6;
1Sa 11:7

or done, not since the day the Israelites came up out of Egypt.[s] Think about it! Consider it! Tell us what to do![t]"

Israelites Fight the Benjamites

20 Then all the Israelites[u] from Dan to Beersheba[v] and from the land of Gilead came out as one man[w] and assembled[x] before the LORD in Mizpah. [2]The leaders of all the people of the tribes of Israel took their places in the assembly of the people of God, four hundred thousand soldiers[y] armed with swords. [3](The Benjamites heard that the Israelites had gone up to Mizpah.) Then the Israelites said, "Tell us how this awful thing happened."

[4]So the Levite, the husband of the murdered woman, said, "I and my concubine came to Gibeah[z] in Benjamin to spend the night.[a] [5]During the night the men of Gibeah came after me and surrounded the house, intending to kill me.[b] They raped my concubine, and she died.[c] [6]I took my concubine, cut her into pieces and sent one piece to each region of Israel's inheritance,[d] because they committed this lewd and disgraceful act[e] in Israel. [7]Now, all you Israelites, speak up and give your verdict.[f]"

[8]All the people rose as one man, saying, "None of us will go home. No, not one of us will return to his house. [9]But now this is what we'll do to Gibeah: We'll go up against it as the lot directs.[g] [10]We'll take ten men out of every hundred from all the tribes of Israel, and a hundred from a thousand, and a thousand from ten thousand, to get provisions for the army. Then, when the army arrives at Gibeah[a] in Benjamin, it can give them what they deserve for all this vileness done in Israel." [11]So all the men of Israel got together and united as one man[h] against the city.

[12]The tribes of Israel sent men throughout the tribe of Benjamin, saying, "What about this awful crime that was committed among you? [13]Now surrender those wicked men[i] of Gibeah so that we may put them to death and purge the evil from Israel.[j]"

But the Benjamites would not listen to their fellow Israelites. [14]From their towns they came together at Gibeah to fight against the Israelites. [15]At once the Benjamites mobilized twenty-six thousand swordsmen from their towns, in addition to seven hundred chosen men from those living in Gibeah. [16]Among all these soldiers there were seven hundred chosen men who were left-handed,[k] each of whom could sling a stone at a hair and not miss.

[17]Israel, apart from Benjamin, mustered four hundred thousand swordsmen, all of them fighting men.

[18]The Israelites went up to Bethel[b] and inquired of God.[l] They said, "Who of us shall go first to fight[m] against the Benjamites?"

The LORD replied, "Judah shall go first."

[19]The next morning the Israelites got up and pitched camp near Gibeah. [20]The men of Israel went out to fight the Benjamites and took up battle positions against them at Gibeah. [21]The Benjamites came out of Gibeah and cut down twenty-two thousand Israelites[n] on the battlefield that day. [22]But the men of Israel encouraged one another and again took up their positions where they had stationed themselves the first

---

19:30
sHos 9:9
tJdg 20:7;
Pr 13:10

20:1
uJdg 21:5
v1Sa 3:20;
2Sa 3:10;
1Ki 4:25
w1Sa 11:7
x1Sa 7:5

20:2
yJdg 8:10

20:4
zJos 15:57
aJdg 19:15

20:5
bJdg 19:22
cJdg 19:25-26

20:6
dJdg 19:29
eJos 7:15;
Jdg 19:23

20:7
fJdg 19:30

20:9
gLev 16:8

20:11
hver 1

20:13
iDt 13:13;
Jdg 19:22
jDt 17:12

20:16
kJdg 3:15;
1Ch 12:2

20:18
lver 26-27;
Nu 27:21
mver 23,28

20:21
nver 25

---

[a]10 One Hebrew manuscript; most Hebrew manuscripts *Geba,* a variant of *Gibeah*   [b]18 Or *to the house of God;* also in verse 26

day. ²³The Israelites went up and wept before the LORD until evening,ᵒ and they inquired of the LORD. They said, "Shall we go up again to battleᵖ against the Benjamites, our brothers?"

The LORD answered, "Go up against them."

²⁴Then the Israelites drew near to Benjamin the second day. ²⁵This time, when the Benjamites came out from Gibeah to oppose them, they cut down another eighteen thousand Israelites,�q all of them armed with swords.

²⁶Then the Israelites, all the people, went up to Bethel, and there they sat weeping before the LORD.ʳ They fasted that day until evening and presented burnt offerings and fellowship offeringsᵃ to the LORD.ˢ ²⁷And the Israelites inquired of the LORD. (In those days the ark of the covenant of Godᵗ was there, ²⁸with Phinehas son of Eleazar,ᵘ the son of Aaron, ministering before it.)ᵛ They asked, "Shall we go up again to battle with Benjamin our brother, or not?"

The LORD responded, "Go, for tomorrow I will give them into your hands.ʷ"

²⁹Then Israel set an ambushˣ around Gibeah. ³⁰They went up against the Benjamites on the third day and took up positions against Gibeah as they had done before. ³¹The Benjamites came out to meet them and were drawn awayy from the city. They began to inflict casualties on the Israelites as before, so that about thirty men fell in the open field and on the roads—the one leading to Bethel and the other to Gibeah.

³²While the Benjamites were saying, "We are defeating them as before,"ᶻ the Israelites were saying, "Let's retreat and draw them away from the city to the roads."

³³All the men of Israel moved from their places and took up positions at Baal Tamar, and the Israelite ambush charged out of its placeᵃ on the westᵇ of Gibeah.ᶜ ³⁴Then ten thousand of Israel's finest men made a frontal attack on Gibeah. The fighting was so heavy that the Benjamites did not realizeᵇ how near disaster was.ᶜ ³⁵The LORD defeated Benjaminᵈ before Israel, and on that day the Israelites struck down 25,100 Benjamites, all armed with swords. ³⁶Then the Benjamites saw that they were beaten.

Now the men of Israel had given wayᵉ before Benjamin, because they relied on the ambush they had set near Gibeah. ³⁷The men who had been in ambush made a sudden dash into Gibeah, spread out and put the whole city to the sword.ᶠ ³⁸The men of Israel had arranged with the ambush that they should send up a great cloud of smokeᵍ from the city, ³⁹and then the men of Israel would turn in the battle.

The Benjamites had begun to inflict casualties on the men of Israel (about thirty), and they said, "We are defeating them as in the first battle."ʰ ⁴⁰But when the column of smoke began to rise from the city, the Benjamites turned and saw the smoke of the whole city going up into the sky.ⁱ ⁴¹Then the men of Israel turned on them, and the men of Benjamin were terrified, because they realized that disaster had come upon them. ⁴²So they fled before the Israelites in the direction of the desert, but they could not escape the battle. And the men of Israel who came out of the towns cut them down there. ⁴³They surrounded the

20:23
ᵒJos 7:6 ᵖver 18
20:25
qver 21
20:26
ʳver 23
ˢJdg 21:4
20:27
ᵗJos 18:1
20:28
ᵘJos 24:33
ᵛDt 18:5
ʷJdg 7:9
20:29
ˣJos 8:2,4
20:31
ʸJos 8:16
20:32
ᶻver 39
20:33
ᵃJos 8:19
20:34
ᵇJos 8:14
ᶜIsa 47:11
20:35
ᵈ1Sa 9:21
20:36
ᵉJos 8:15
20:37
ᶠJos 8:19
20:38
ᵍJos 8:20
20:39
ʰver 32
20:40
ⁱJos 8:20

ᵃ26 Traditionally *peace offerings*   ᵇ33 Some Septuagint manuscripts and Vulgate; the meaning of the Hebrew for this word is uncertain.   ᶜ33 Hebrew *Geba,* a variant of *Gibeah*

Benjamites, chased them and easily[a] overran them in the vicinity of Gibeah on the east. [44]Eighteen thousand Benjamites fell, all of them valiant fighters.[j] [45]As they turned and fled toward the desert to the rock of Rimmon,[k] the Israelites cut down five thousand men along the roads. They kept pressing after the Benjamites as far as Gidom and struck down two thousand more.

[46]On that day twenty-five thousand Benjamite swordsmen fell, all of them valiant fighters. [47]But six hundred men turned and fled into the desert to the rock of Rimmon, where they stayed four months. [48]The men of Israel went back to Benjamin and put all the towns to the sword, including the animals and everything else they found. All the towns they came across they set on fire.[l]

Wives for the Benjamites

21 The men of Israel had taken an oath[m] at Mizpah:[n] "Not one of us will give[o] his daughter in marriage to a Benjamite."

[2]The people went to Bethel,[b] where they sat before God until evening, raising their voices and weeping bitterly. [3]"O LORD, the God of Israel," they cried, "why has this happened to Israel? Why should one tribe be missing from Israel today?"

[4]Early the next day the people built an altar and presented burnt offerings and fellowship offerings.[c] [p]

[5]Then the Israelites asked, "Who from all the tribes of Israel[q] has failed to assemble before the LORD?" For they had taken a solemn oath that anyone who failed to assemble before the LORD at Mizpah should certainly be put to death.

[6]Now the Israelites grieved for their brothers, the Benjamites. "Today one tribe is cut off from Israel," they said. [7]"How can we provide wives for those who are left, since we have taken an oath[r] by the LORD not to give them any of our daughters in marriage?" [8]Then they asked, "Which one of the tribes of Israel failed to assemble before the LORD at Mizpah?" They discovered that no one from Jabesh Gilead[s] had come to the camp for the assembly. [9]For when they counted the people, they found that none of the people of Jabesh Gilead were there.

[10]So the assembly sent twelve thousand fighting men with instructions to go to Jabesh Gilead and put to the sword those living there, including the women and children. [11]"This is what you are to do," they said. "Kill every male and every woman who is not a virgin.[t]" [12]They found among the people living in Jabesh Gilead four hundred young women who had never slept with a man, and they took them to the camp at Shiloh[u] in Canaan.

[13]Then the whole assembly sent an offer of peace[v] to the Benjamites at the rock of Rimmon.[w] [14]So the Benjamites returned at that time and were given the women of Jabesh Gilead who had been spared. But there were not enough for all of them.

[15]The people grieved for Benjamin,[x] because the LORD had made a gap in the tribes of Israel. [16]And the elders of the assembly said, "With the women of Benjamin destroyed, how shall we provide wives for the men who are left? [17]The Benjamite survivors must have heirs," they

20:44
j Ps 76:5
20:45
k Jos 15:32;
Jdg 21:13
20:48
l Jdg 21:23
21:1
m Jos 9:18
n Jdg 20:1
o ver 7,18
21:4
p Jdg 20:26;
2Sa 24:25
21:5
q Jdg 5:23; 20:1
21:7
r ver 1
21:8
s 1Sa 11:1;
31:11
21:11
t Nu 31:17-18
21:12
u Jos 18:1
21:13
v Dt 20:10
w Jdg 20:47
21:15
x ver 6

---

[a]43 The meaning of the Hebrew for this word is uncertain.   [b]2 Or *to the house of God*
[c]4 Traditionally *peace offerings*

said, "so that a tribe of Israel will not be wiped out. [18]We can't give them our daughters as wives, since we Israelites have taken this oath: 'Cursed be anyone who gives[y] a wife to a Benjamite.' [19]But look, there is the annual festival of the Lord in Shiloh,[z] to the north of Bethel, and east of the road that goes from Bethel to Shechem, and to the south of Lebonah."

[20]So they instructed the Benjamites, saying, "Go and hide in the vineyards [21]and watch. When the girls of Shiloh come out to join in the dancing,[a] then rush from the vineyards and each of you seize a wife from the girls of Shiloh and go to the land of Benjamin. [22]When their fathers or brothers complain to us, we will say to them, 'Do us a kindness by helping them, because we did not get wives for them during the war, and you are innocent, since you did not give[b] your daughters to them.'"

[23]So that is what the Benjamites did. While the girls were dancing, each man caught one and carried her off to be his wife. Then they returned to their inheritance and rebuilt the towns and settled in them.[c]

[24]At that time the Israelites left that place and went home to their tribes and clans, each to his own inheritance.

[25]In those days Israel had no king; everyone did as he saw fit.[d]

21:18
yver 1

21:19
zJos 18:1;
Jdg 18:31;
1Sa 1:3

21:21
aEx 15:20;
Jdg 11:34

21:22
bver 1,18

21:23
cJdg 20:48

21:25
dDt 12:8;
Jdg 17:6; 18:1;
19:1

Ruth

Title and Background

This book is named after the leading character whose story is told here. Ruth was the great-grandmother of David and an ancestress of Jesus (Mt 1:1,5). The story is set in the time of the judges and reflects a temporary time of peace between Israel and Moab. It gives a series of intimate glances into the private lives of the members of an Israelite family and presents a delightful account of the remnant of true faith and piety during this period.

Author and Date of Writing

The author is unknown, although Jewish tradition points to Samuel. This is unlikely because the mention of David (4:17,22) implies a later date. The literary style of Hebrew used suggests that it was written during the monarchy, probably sometime after 1000 B.C.

Theme and Message

Redemption is a key concept throughout the book; the Hebrew word in its various forms occurs twenty-three times. The word shows how God is working out his plan for salvation. The book of Ruth also illustrates love and devotion—self-giving love that fulfills God's law, and God's love in blessing the lives of his children.

Outline

I. Introduction: Naomi Emptied (1:1-5)
II. Naomi Returns From Moab (1:6-22)
III. Ruth and Boaz Meet in the Harvest Fields (2:1-23)
IV. Ruth Goes to Boaz at the Threshing Floor (3:1-18)
V. Boaz Arranges to Marry Ruth (4:1-12)
VI. Conclusion: Naomi Filled (4:13-17)
VII. Epilogue: Genealogy of David (4:18-22)

Naomi and Ruth

1 In the days when the judges ruled,[a] there was a famine in the land,[b] and a man from Bethlehem in Judah, together with his wife and two sons, went to live for a while in the country of Moab.[c] 2The man's name was Elimelech, his wife's name Naomi, and the names of his two sons were Mahlon and Kilion. They were Ephrathites from Bethlehem,[d] Judah. And they went to Moab and lived there.

3Now Elimelech, Naomi's husband, died, and she was left with her two sons. 4They married Moabite women, one named Orpah and the other Ruth.[e] After they had lived there about ten years, 5both Mahlon and Kilion also died, and Naomi was left without her two sons and her husband.

6When she heard in Moab that the LORD had come to the aid of his

1:1
a Jdg 2:16-18
b Ge 12:10;
Ps 105:16
c Jdg 3:30
1:2
d Ge 35:19
1:4
e Mt 1:5

a1 Traditionally judged

people[f] by providing food[g] for them, Naomi and her daughters-in-law prepared to return home from there. [7]With her two daughters-in-law she left the place where she had been living and set out on the road that would take them back to the land of Judah.

[8]Then Naomi said to her two daughters-in-law, "Go back, each of you, to your mother's home. May the LORD show kindness[h] to you, as you have shown to your dead[i] and to me. [9]May the LORD grant that each of you will find rest[j] in the home of another husband."

Then she kissed them and they wept aloud [10]and said to her, "We will go back with you to your people."

[11]But Naomi said, "Return home, my daughters. Why would you come with me? Am I going to have any more sons, who could become your husbands?[k] [12]Return home, my daughters; I am too old to have another husband. Even if I thought there was still hope for me—even if I had a husband tonight and then gave birth to sons— [13]would you wait until they grew up? Would you remain unmarried for them? No, my daughters. It is more bitter for me than for you, because the LORD's hand has gone out against me![l] "

[14]At this they wept again. Then Orpah kissed her mother-in-law[m] good-by, but Ruth clung to her.[n]

[15]"Look," said Naomi, "your sister-in-law is going back to her people and her gods.[o] Go back with her."

[16]But Ruth replied, "Don't urge me to leave you[p] or to turn back from you. Where you go I will go, and where you stay I will stay. Your people will be my people and your God my God.[q] [17]Where you die I will die, and there I will be buried. May the LORD deal with me, be it ever so severely,[r] if anything but death separates you and me." [18]When Naomi realized that Ruth was determined to go with her, she stopped urging her.[s]

[19]So the two women went on until they came to Bethlehem. When they arrived in Bethlehem, the whole town was stirred[t] because of them, and the women exclaimed, "Can this be Naomi?"

[20]"Don't call me Naomi,[a]" she told them. "Call me Mara,[b] because the Almighty[cu] has made my life very bitter.[v] [21]I went away full, but the LORD has brought me back empty.[w] Why call me Naomi? The LORD has afflicted[d] me; the Almighty has brought misfortune upon me."

[22]So Naomi returned from Moab accompanied by Ruth the Moabitess, her daughter-in-law, arriving in Bethlehem as the barley harvest[x] was beginning.[y]

Ruth Meets Boaz

2 Now Naomi had a relative[z] on her husband's side, from the clan of Elimelech,[a] a man of standing, whose name was Boaz.[b]

[2]And Ruth the Moabitess said to Naomi, "Let me go to the fields and pick up the leftover grain[c] behind anyone in whose eyes I find favor."

Naomi said to her, "Go ahead, my daughter." [3]So she went out and began to glean in the fields behind the harvesters. As it turned out, she found herself working in a field belonging to Boaz, who was from the clan of Elimelech.

1:6
fEx 4:31;
Jer 29:10;
Zep 2:7
gPs 132:15;
Mt 6:11
1:8
hRu 2:20;
2Ti 1:16 iver 5
1:9
jRu 3:1
1:11
kGe 38:11;
Dt 25:5
1:13
lJdg 2:15;
Job 4:5; 19:21;
Ps 32:4
1:14
mRu 2:11
nPr 17:17;
18:24
1:15
oJos 24:14;
Jdg 11:24
1:16
p2Ki 2:2
qRu 2:11,12
1:17
r1Sa 3:17;
25:22;
2Sa 19:13;
2Ki 6:31
1:18
sAc 21:14
1:19
tMt 21:10
1:20
uEx 6:3 vver 13;
Job 6:4
1:21
wJob 1:21
1:22
xEx 9:31;
Ru 2:23
y2Sa 21:9
2:1
zRu 3:2,12
aRu 1:2
bRu 4:21
2:2
cver 7;
Lev 19:9;
23:22; Dt 24:19

---

[a]20 *Naomi* means *pleasant*; also in verse 21.　　[b]20 *Mara* means *bitter*.　　[c]20 Hebrew *Shaddai*; also in verse 21　　[d]21 Or *has testified against*

⁴Just then Boaz arrived from Bethlehem and greeted the harvesters, "The Lᴏʀᴅ be with you!ᵈ"

"The Lᴏʀᴅ bless you!ᵉ" they called back.

⁵Boaz asked the foreman of his harvesters, "Whose young woman is that?"

⁶The foreman replied, "She is the Moabitessᶠ who came back from Moab with Naomi. ⁷She said, 'Please let me glean and gather among the sheaves behind the harvesters.' She went into the field and has worked steadily from morning till now, except for a short rest in the shelter."

⁸So Boaz said to Ruth, "My daughter, listen to me. Don't go and glean in another field and don't go away from here. Stay here with my servant girls. ⁹Watch the field where the men are harvesting, and follow along after the girls. I have told the men not to touch you. And whenever you are thirsty, go and get a drink from the water jars the men have filled."

¹⁰At this, she bowed down with her face to the ground.ᵍ She exclaimed, "Why have I found such favor in your eyes that you notice meʰ—a foreigner?ⁱ"

¹¹Boaz replied, "I've been told all about what you have done for your mother-in-lawʲ since the death of your husband—how you left your father and mother and your homeland and came to live with a people you did not know before.ᵏ ¹²May the Lᴏʀᴅ repay you for what you have done. May you be richly rewarded by the Lᴏʀᴅ,ˡ the God of Israel, under whose wingsᵐ you have come to take refuge.ⁿ"

¹³"May I continue to find favor in your eyes, my lord," she said. "You have given me comfort and have spoken kindly to your servant—though I do not have the standing of one of your servant girls."

¹⁴At mealtime Boaz said to her, "Come over here. Have some bread and dip it in the wine vinegar."

When she sat down with the harvesters, he offered her some roasted grain. She ate all she wanted and had some left over.ᵒ ¹⁵As she got up to glean, Boaz gave orders to his men, "Even if she gathers among the sheaves, don't embarrass her. ¹⁶Rather, pull out some stalks for her from the bundles and leave them for her to pick up, and don't rebuke her."

¹⁷So Ruth gleaned in the field until evening. Then she threshed the barley she had gathered, and it amounted to about an ephah.ᵃ ¹⁸She carried it back to town, and her mother-in-law saw how much she had gathered. Ruth also brought out and gave her what she had left overᵖ after she had eaten enough.

¹⁹Her mother-in-law asked her, "Where did you glean today? Where did you work? Blessed be the man who took notice of you!�q"

Then Ruth told her mother-in-law about the one at whose place she had been working. "The name of the man I worked with today is Boaz," she said.

²⁰"The Lᴏʀᴅ bless him!" Naomi said to her daughter-in-law. "He has not stopped showing his kindnessʳ to the living and the dead." She added, "That man is our close relative; he is one of our kinsman-redeemers.ˢ"

2:4
ᵈJdg 6:12;
Lk 1:28;
2Th 3:16
ᵉPs 129:7-8
2:6
ᶠRu 1:22
2:10
ᵍ1Sa 25:23
ʰPs 41:1
ⁱDt 15:3
2:11
ʲRu 1:14
ᵏRu 1:16-17
2:12
ˡ1Sa 24:19
ᵐPs 17:8; 36:7;
57:1; 61:4;
63:7; 91:4
ⁿRu 1:16
2:14
ᵒver 18
2:18
ᵖver 14
2:19
qver 10; Ps 41:1
2:20
ʳRu 3:10;
2Sa 2:5;
Pr 17:17
ˢRu 3:9,12;
4:1,14

ᵃ17 That is, probably about 3/5 bushel (about 22 liters)

21Then Ruth the Moabitess said, "He even said to me, 'Stay with my workers until they finish harvesting all my grain.'"

22Naomi said to Ruth her daughter-in-law, "It will be good for you, my daughter, to go with his girls, because in someone else's field you might be harmed."

23So Ruth stayed close to the servant girls of Boaz to glean until the barley and wheat harvests[t] were finished. And she lived with her mother-in-law.

Ruth and Boaz at the Threshing Floor

3 One day Naomi her mother-in-law said to her, "My daughter, should I not try to find a home[a][u] for you, where you will be well provided for? 2Is not Boaz, with whose servant girls you have been, a kinsman[v] of ours? Tonight he will be winnowing barley on the threshing floor. 3Wash and perfume yourself,[w] and put on your best clothes. Then go down to the threshing floor, but don't let him know you are there until he has finished eating and drinking. 4When he lies down, note the place where he is lying. Then go and uncover his feet and lie down. He will tell you what to do."

5"I will do whatever you say,"[x] Ruth answered. 6So she went down to the threshing floor and did everything her mother-in-law told her to do.

7When Boaz had finished eating and drinking and was in good spirits,[y] he went over to lie down at the far end of the grain pile. Ruth approached quietly, uncovered his feet and lay down. 8In the middle of the night something startled the man, and he turned and discovered a woman lying at his feet.

9"Who are you?" he asked.

"I am your servant Ruth," she said. "Spread the corner of your garment[z] over me, since you are a kinsman-redeemer.[a]"

10"The LORD bless you, my daughter," he replied. "This kindness is greater than that which you showed earlier: You have not run after the younger men, whether rich or poor. 11And now, my daughter, don't be afraid. I will do for you all you ask. All my fellow townsmen know that you are a woman of noble character.[b] 12Although it is true that I am near of kin, there is a kinsman-redeemer[c] nearer than[d] I. 13Stay here for the night, and in the morning if he wants to redeem,[e] good; let him redeem. But if he is not willing, as surely as the LORD lives[f] I will do it. Lie here until morning."

14So she lay at his feet until morning, but got up before anyone could be recognized; and he said, "Don't let it be known that a woman came to the threshing floor."[g]

15He also said, "Bring me the shawl you are wearing and hold it out." When she did so, he poured into it six measures of barley and put it on her. Then he[b] went back to town.

16When Ruth came to her mother-in-law, Naomi asked, "How did it go, my daughter?"

Then she told her everything Boaz had done for her 17and added,

2:23
tDt 16:9
3:1
uRu 1:9
3:2
vDt 25:5-10;
Ru 2:1
3:3
w2Sa 14:2
3:5
xEph 6:1;
Col 3:20
3:7
yJdg 19:6,9,22;
2Sa 13:28;
1Ki 21:7;
Est 1:10
3:9
zEze 16:8
aver 12; Ru 2:20
3:11
bPr 12:4; 31:10
3:12
cver 9 dRu 4:1
3:13
eDt 25:5;
Ru 4:5;
Mt 22:24
fJdg 8:19;
Jer 4:2
3:14
gRo 14:16;
2Co 8:21

---

a1 Hebrew *find rest* (see Ruth 1:9)   *b15* Most Hebrew manuscripts; many Hebrew manuscripts, Vulgate and Syriac *she*

"He gave me these six measures of barley, saying, 'Don't go back to your mother-in-law empty-handed.'"

[18]Then Naomi said, "Wait, my daughter, until you find out what happens. For the man will not rest until the matter is settled today."[h]

Boaz Marries Ruth

4 Meanwhile Boaz went up to the town gate and sat there. When the kinsman-redeemer he had mentioned[i] came along, Boaz said, "Come over here, my friend, and sit down." So he went over and sat down.

[2]Boaz took ten of the elders[j] of the town and said, "Sit here," and they did so. [3]Then he said to the kinsman-redeemer, "Naomi, who has come back from Moab, is selling the piece of land that belonged to our brother Elimelech. [4]I thought I should bring the matter to your attention and suggest that you buy it in the presence of these seated here and in the presence of the elders of my people. If you will redeem it, do so. But if you[a] will not, tell me, so I will know. For no one has the right to do it except you,[k] and I am next in line."

"I will redeem it," he said.

[5]Then Boaz said, "On the day you buy the land from Naomi and from Ruth the Moabitess, you acquire[b] the dead man's widow, in order to maintain the name of the dead with his property."[l]

[6]At this, the kinsman-redeemer said, "Then I cannot redeem[m] it because I might endanger my own estate. You redeem it yourself. I cannot do it."

[7](Now in earlier times in Israel, for the redemption and transfer of property to become final, one party took off his sandal and gave it to the other. This was the method of legalizing transactions in Israel.)[n]

[8]So the kinsman-redeemer said to Boaz, "Buy it yourself." And he removed his sandal.

[9]Then Boaz announced to the elders and all the people, "Today you are witnesses that I have bought from Naomi all the property of Elimelech, Kilion and Mahlon. [10]I have also acquired Ruth the Moabitess, Mahlon's widow, as my wife, in order to maintain the name of the dead with his property, so that his name will not disappear from among his family or from the town records.[o] Today you are witnesses!"

[11]Then the elders and all those at the gate said, "We are witnesses.[p] May the LORD make the woman who is coming into your home like Rachel and Leah,[q] who together built up the house of Israel. May you have standing in Ephrathah[r] and be famous in Bethlehem. [12]Through the offspring the LORD gives you by this young woman, may your family be like that of Perez,[s] whom Tamar bore to Judah."

The Genealogy of David

4:18–22pp — 1Ch 2:5–15; Mt 1:3–6; Lk 3:31–33

[13]So Boaz took Ruth and she became his wife. Then he went to her, and the LORD enabled her to conceive,[t] and she gave birth to a son. [14]The women[u] said to Naomi: "Praise be to the LORD, who this day has not left you without a kinsman-redeemer. May he become famous

3:18
hPs 37:3-5
4:1
iRu 3:12
4:2
j1Ki 21:8;
Pr 31:23
4:4
kLev 25:25;
Jer 32:7-8
4:5
lGe 38:8;
Dt 25:5-6;
Ru 3:13;
Mt 22:24
4:6
mLev 25:25;
Ru 3:13
4:7
nDt 25:7-9
4:10
oDt 25:6
4:11
pDt 25:9
qPs 127:3;
128:3 rGe 35:16
4:12
sver 18;
Ge 38:29
4:13
tGe 29:31;
33:5; Ru 3:11
4:14
uLk 1:58

---

[a]4 Many Hebrew manuscripts, Septuagint, Vulgate and Syriac; most Hebrew manuscripts *he*
[b]5 Hebrew; Vulgate and Syriac *Naomi, you acquire Ruth the Moabitess,*

throughout Israel! [15]He will renew your life and sustain you in your old age. For your daughter-in-law, who loves you and who is better to you than seven sons,[v] has given him birth.''

[16]Then Naomi took the child, laid him in her lap and cared for him. [17]The women living there said, ''Naomi has a son.'' And they named him Obed. He was the father of Jesse,[w] the father of David.

[18]This, then, is the family line of Perez[x]:

Perez was the father of Hezron,
[19]Hezron the father of Ram,
Ram the father of Amminadab,[y]
[20]Amminadab the father of Nahshon,
Nahshon the father of Salmon,[a]
[21]Salmon the father of Boaz,[z]
Boaz the father of Obed,
[22]Obed the father of Jesse,
and Jesse the father of David.

4:15
vRu 1:16-17;
2:11-12; 1Sa 1:8
4:17
wver 22;
1Sa 16:1,18;
1Ch 2:12,13
4:18
xMt 1:3-6
4:19
yEx 6:23
4:21
zRu 2:1

---

[a]20 A few Hebrew manuscripts, some Septuagint manuscripts and Vulgate (see also verse 21 and Septuagint of 1 Chron. 2:11); most Hebrew manuscripts *Salma*

1 Samuel

Title and Background

1 and 2 Samuel are named after the individual whom God used to establish kingship in Israel. These two books were originally one book, but it was divided into two parts by the translators of the Septuagint (the Greek translation of the Old Testament). The book of 1 Samuel records the lives of Samuel and Saul, and much of the life of David.

Author and Date of Writing

Who the author was is uncertain because the book itself gives no indication as to his identity. The author probably wrote shortly after the division of the kingdom that followed upon the death of Solomon in 930 B.C.

Theme and Message

1 Samuel portrays the establishment of kingship in Israel. When the people demanded a king, Samuel, by God's leading, anointed Saul to be the first king of Israel. But Saul was disobedient to God, and God rejected him as king. Then Samuel secretly anointed David to take Saul's place. The struggles between Saul and David make up the rest of the book. The weaknesses and sins of these men are shown, as well as the goodness of Samuel and David and their obedience to God.

Outline

   I. Background for the Establishment of Kingship in Israel (1:1-7:17)
  II. Establishment of Kingship in Israel (8:1-12:25)
 III. Failure of Saul's Kingship (13:1-15:35)
 IV. David and Saul (16:1-30:31)
  V. Death of Saul (31:1-13)

The Birth of Samuel

1 There was a certain man from Ramathaim, a Zuphite[a] from the hill country[a] of Ephraim, whose name was Elkanah[b] son of Jeroham, the son of Elihu, the son of Tohu, the son of Zuph, an Ephraimite. [2]He had two wives;[c] one was called Hannah and the other Peninnah. Peninnah had children, but Hannah had none.

[3]Year after year[d] this man went up from his town to worship[e] and sacrifice to the LORD Almighty at Shiloh,[f] where Hophni and Phinehas, the two sons of Eli, were priests of the LORD. [4]Whenever the day came for Elkanah to sacrifice,[g] he would give portions of the meat to his wife Peninnah and to all her sons and daughters. [5]But to Hannah he gave a double portion because he loved her, and the LORD had closed her womb.[h] [6]And because the LORD had closed her womb, her rival kept provoking her in order to irritate her.[i] [7]This went on year after year. Whenever Hannah went up to the house of the LORD, her rival provoked her till she wept and would not eat. [8]Elkanah her husband

1:1
a Jos 17:17-18
b 1Ch 6:27,34
1:2
c Dt 21:15-17;
Lk 2:36
1:3
d ver 21;
Ex 23:14; 34:23;
Lk 2:41
e Dt 12:5-7
f Jos 18:1
1:4
g Dt 12:17-18
1:5
h Ge 16:1; 30:2
1:6
i Job 24:21

a 1 Or from Ramathaim Zuphim

would say to her, "Hannah, why are you weeping? Why don't you eat? Why are you downhearted? Don't I mean more to you than ten sons?[j] "

[9]Once when they had finished eating and drinking in Shiloh, Hannah stood up. Now Eli the priest was sitting on a chair by the doorpost of the LORD's temple.[a][k] [10]In bitterness of soul[l] Hannah wept much and prayed to the LORD. [11]And she made a vow, saying, "O LORD Almighty, if you will only look upon your servant's misery and remember[m] me, and not forget your servant but give her a son, then I will give him to the LORD for all the days of his life, and no razor[n] will ever be used on his head."

[12]As she kept on praying to the LORD, Eli observed her mouth. [13]Hannah was praying in her heart, and her lips were moving but her voice was not heard. Eli thought she was drunk [14]and said to her, "How long will you keep on getting drunk? Get rid of your wine."

[15]"Not so, my lord," Hannah replied, "I am a woman who is deeply troubled. I have not been drinking wine or beer; I was pouring[o] out my soul to the LORD. [16]Do not take your servant for a wicked woman; I have been praying here out of my great anguish and grief."

[17]Eli answered, "Go in peace,[p] and may the God of Israel grant you what you have asked of him.[q]"

[18]She said, "May your servant find favor in your eyes.[r]" Then she went her way and ate something, and her face was no longer downcast.[s]

[19]Early the next morning they arose and worshiped before the LORD and then went back to their home at Ramah. Elkanah lay with Hannah his wife, and the LORD remembered[t] her. [20]So in the course of time Hannah conceived and gave birth to a son. She named[u] him Samuel,[b] saying, "Because I asked the LORD for him."

Hannah Dedicates Samuel

[21]When the man Elkanah went up with all his family to offer the annual[v] sacrifice to the LORD and to fulfill his vow,[w] [22]Hannah did not go. She said to her husband, "After the boy is weaned, I will take him and present[x] him before the LORD, and he will live there always."

[23]"Do what seems best to you," Elkanah her husband told her. "Stay here until you have weaned him; only may the LORD make good[y] his[c] word." So the woman stayed at home and nursed her son until she had weaned him.

[24]After he was weaned, she took the boy with her, young as he was, along with a three-year-old bull,[d][z] an ephah[e] of flour and a skin of wine, and brought him to the house of the LORD at Shiloh. [25]When they had slaughtered the bull, they brought the boy to Eli, [26]and she said to him, "As surely as you live, my lord, I am the woman who stood here beside you praying to the LORD. [27]I prayed[a] for this child, and the LORD has granted me what I asked of him. [28]So now I give him to the LORD. For his whole life[b] he will be given over to the LORD." And he worshiped the LORD there.

---

[a]9 That is, tabernacle   [b]20 *Samuel* sounds like the Hebrew for *heard of God.*   [c]23 Masoretic Text; Dead Sea Scrolls, Septuagint and Syriac *your*   [d]24 Dead Sea Scrolls, Septuagint and Syriac; Masoretic Text *with three bulls*   [e]24 That is, probably about 3/5 bushel (about 22 liters)

1:8
jRu 4:15
1:9
k1Sa 3:3
1:10
lJob 7:11
1:11
mGe 8:1;
28:20; 29:32
nNu 6:1-21;
Jdg 13:5
1:15
oPs 42:4; 62:8;
La 2:19
1:17
pJdg 18:6;
1Sa 25:35;
2Ki 5:19;
Mk 5:34
qPs 20:3-5
1:18
rRu 2:13
sEcc 9:7;
Ro 15:13
1:19
tGe 4:1; 30:22
1:20
uGe 41:51-52;
Ex 2:10,22;
Mt 1:21
1:21
vver 3
wDt 12:11
1:22
xver 11,28;
Lk 2:22
1:23
yver 17;
Nu 30:7
1:24
zNu 15:8-10;
Dt 12:5;
Jos 18:1
1:27
aver 11-13;
Ps 66:19-20
1:28
bver 11,22;
Ge 24:26,52

Hannah's Prayer

2 Then Hannah prayed and said:[c]

"My heart rejoices[d] in the LORD;
  in the LORD my horn[a][e] is lifted high.
My mouth boasts over my enemies,
  for I delight in your deliverance.

2"There is no one holy[b][f] like the LORD;
  there is no one besides you;
  there is no Rock[g] like our God.

3"Do not keep talking so proudly
  or let your mouth speak such arrogance,[h]
for the LORD is a God who knows,
  and by him deeds[i] are weighed.[j]

4"The bows of the warriors are broken,[k]
  but those who stumbled are armed with strength.
5Those who were full hire themselves out for food,
  but those who were hungry hunger no more.
She who was barren[l] has borne seven children,
  but she who has had many sons pines away.

6"The LORD brings death and makes alive;[m]
  he brings down to the grave[c] and raises up.[n]
7The LORD sends poverty and wealth;[o]
  he humbles and he exalts.[p]
8He raises[q] the poor from the dust
  and lifts the needy from the ash heap;
he seats them with princes
  and has them inherit a throne of honor.[r]

"For the foundations[s] of the earth are the LORD's;
  upon them he has set the world.
9He will guard the feet[t] of his saints,
  but the wicked will be silenced in darkness.[u]

"It is not by strength[v] that one prevails;
10 those who oppose the LORD will be shattered.[w]
He will thunder[x] against them from heaven;
  the LORD will judge[y] the ends of the earth.

"He will give strength[z] to his king
  and exalt the horn[a] of his anointed."

11Then Elkanah went home to Ramah, but the boy ministered[b] before the LORD under Eli the priest.

Eli's Wicked Sons

12Eli's sons were wicked men; they had no regard[c] for the LORD. 13Now it was the practice of the priests with the people that whenever anyone offered a sacrifice and while the meat[d] was being boiled, the servant of the priest would come with a three-pronged fork in his hand.

---

[a]1 *Horn* here symbolizes strength; also in verse 10.   [b]2 Or *no Holy One*   [c]6 Hebrew *Sheol*

2:1
cLk 1:46-55
dPs 9:14; 13:5
ePs 89:17,24;
 92:10;
Isa 12:2-3
2:2
fEx 15:11;
Lev 19:2
gDt 32:30-31;
2Sa 22:2,32
2:3
hPr 8:13
iISa 16:7;
1Ki 8:39
jPr 16:2;
24:11-12
2:4
kPs 37:15
2:5
lPs 113:9;
Jer 15:9
2:6
mDt 32:39
nIsa 26:19
2:7
oDt 8:18
pJob 5:11;
Ps 75:7
2:8
qPs 113:7-8
rJob 36:7
sJob 38:4
2:9
tPs 91:12
uMt 8:12
vPs 33:16-17
2:10
wPs 2:9
xPs 18:13
yPs 96:13
zPs 21:1
aPs 89:24
2:11
bver 18; 1Sa 3:1
2:12
cJer 2:8; 9:6
2:13
dLev 7:29-34

¹⁴He would plunge it into the pan or kettle or caldron or pot, and the priest would take for himself whatever the fork brought up. This is how they treated all the Israelites who came to Shiloh. ¹⁵But even before the fat was burned, the servant of the priest would come and say to the man who was sacrificing, "Give the priest some meat to roast; he won't accept boiled meat from you, but only raw."

¹⁶If the man said to him, "Let the fat be burned up first, and then take whatever you want," the servant would then answer, "No, hand it over now; if you don't, I'll take it by force."

¹⁷This sin of the young men was very great in the LORD's sight, for they[a] were treating the LORD's offering with contempt.[e]

¹⁸But Samuel was ministering[f] before the LORD—a boy wearing a linen ephod.[g] ¹⁹Each year his mother made him a little robe and took it to him when she went up with her husband to offer the annual[h] sacrifice. ²⁰Eli would bless Elkanah and his wife, saying, "May the LORD give you children by this woman to take the place of the one she prayed[i] for and gave to the LORD." Then they would go home. ²¹And the LORD was gracious to Hannah;[j] she conceived and gave birth to three sons and two daughters. Meanwhile, the boy Samuel grew[k] up in the presence of the LORD.

²²Now Eli, who was very old, heard about everything his sons were doing to all Israel and how they slept with the women[l] who served at the entrance to the Tent of Meeting. ²³So he said to them, "Why do you do such things? I hear from all the people about these wicked deeds of yours. ²⁴No, my sons; it is not a good report that I hear spreading among the LORD's people. ²⁵If a man sins against another man, God[b] may mediate for him; but if a man sins against the LORD, who will[m] intercede[n] for him?" His sons, however, did not listen to their father's rebuke, for it was the LORD's will to put them to death.

²⁶And the boy Samuel continued to grow[o] in stature and in favor with the LORD and with men.

Prophecy Against the House of Eli

²⁷Now a man of God[p] came to Eli and said to him, "This is what the LORD says: 'Did I not clearly reveal myself to your father's house when they were in Egypt under Pharaoh? ²⁸I chose[q] your father out of all the tribes of Israel to be my priest, to go up to my altar, to burn incense, and to wear an ephod[r] in my presence. I also gave your father's house all the offerings made with fire by the Israelites. ²⁹Why do you[c] scorn my sacrifice and offering[s] that I prescribed for my dwelling?[t] Why do you honor your sons more than me by fattening yourselves on the choice parts of every offering made by my people Israel?'

³⁰"Therefore the LORD, the God of Israel, declares: 'I promised that your house and your father's house would minister before me forever.[u]' But now the LORD declares: 'Far be it from me! Those who honor me I will honor,[v] but those who despise[w] me will be disdained. ³¹The time is coming when I will cut short your strength and the strength of your father's house, so that there will not be an old man in your family line[x] ³²and you will see distress in my dwelling. Although good will be done to Israel, in your family line there will never be an old man.[y]

2:17
[e] Mal 2:7-9
2:18
[f] ver 11; 1Sa 3:1
[g] ver 28
2:19
[h] 1Sa 1:3
2:20
[i] 1Sa 1:11,27-28;
Lk 2:34
2:21
[j] Ge 21:1
[k] ver 26;
Jdg 13:24;
1Sa 3:19;
Lk 2:40
2:22
[l] Ex 38:8
2:25
[m] Nu 15:30;
Jos 11:20
[n] Dt 1:17;
1Sa 3:14;
Heb 10:26
2:26
[o] ver 21; Lk 2:52
2:27
[p] Ex 4:14-16;
1Ki 13:1
2:28
[q] Ex 28:1
[r] Lev 8:7-8
2:29
[s] ver 12-17
[t] Dt 12:5;
Mt 10:37
2:30
[u] Ex 29:9
[v] Ps 50:23;
91:15 [w] Mal 2:9
2:31
[x] 1Sa 4:11-18;
22:16-20
2:32
[y] 1Ki 2:26-27;
Zec 8:4

---

[a]17 Or *men*   [b]25 Or *the judges*   [c]29 The Hebrew is plural.

33Every one of you that I do not cut off from my altar will be spared only to blind your eyes with tears and to grieve your heart, and all your descendants will die in the prime of life.

34" 'And what happens to your two sons, Hophni and Phinehas, will be a sign to you—they will both die[z] on the same day.[a] 35I will raise up for myself a faithful priest,[b] who will do according to what is in my heart and mind. I will firmly establish his house, and he will minister before my anointed[c] one always. 36Then everyone left in your family line will come and bow down before him for a piece of silver and a crust of bread and plead, "Appoint me to some priestly office so I can have food to eat.[d]" ' "

The Lord Calls Samuel

3 The boy Samuel ministered[e] before the Lord under Eli. In those days the word of the Lord was rare;[f] there were not many visions.[g]

2One night Eli, whose eyes[h] were becoming so weak that he could barely see, was lying down in his usual place. 3The lamp[i] of God had not yet gone out, and Samuel was lying down in the temple[a] of the Lord, where the ark of God was. 4Then the Lord called Samuel.

Samuel answered, "Here I am.[j]" 5And he ran to Eli and said, "Here I am; you called me."

But Eli said, "I did not call; go back and lie down." So he went and lay down.

6Again the Lord called, "Samuel!" And Samuel got up and went to Eli and said, "Here I am; you called me."

"My son," Eli said, "I did not call; go back and lie down."

7Now Samuel did not yet know the Lord: The word of the Lord had not yet been revealed[k] to him.

8The Lord called Samuel a third time, and Samuel got up and went to Eli and said, "Here I am; you called me."

Then Eli realized that the Lord was calling the boy. 9So Eli told Samuel, "Go and lie down, and if he calls you, say, 'Speak, Lord, for your servant is listening.' " So Samuel went and lay down in his place.

10The Lord came and stood there, calling as at the other times, "Samuel! Samuel!"

Then Samuel said, "Speak, for your servant is listening."

11And the Lord said to Samuel: "See, I am about to do something in Israel that will make the ears of everyone who hears of it tingle.[l] 12At that time I will carry out against Eli everything[m] I spoke against his family—from beginning to end. 13For I told him that I would judge his family forever because of the sin he knew about; his sons made themselves contemptible,[b] and he failed to restrain[n] them. 14Therefore, I swore to the house of Eli, 'The guilt of Eli's house will never be atoned[o] for by sacrifice or offering.' "

15Samuel lay down until morning and then opened the doors of the house of the Lord. He was afraid to tell Eli the vision, 16but Eli called him and said, "Samuel, my son."

Samuel answered, "Here I am."

2:34
z1Sa 4:11
a1Ki 13:3
2:35
b1Sa 12:3;
1Ki 2:35
c1Sa 16:13;
2Sa 7:11,27;
1Ki 11:38
2:36
d1Ki 2:27
3:1
e1Sa 2:11
fPs 74:9
gAm 8:11
3:2
h1Sa 4:15
3:3
iLev 24:1-4
3:4
jIsa 6:8
3:7
kAc 19:12
3:11
l2Ki 21:12;
Jer 19:3
3:12
m1Sa 2:27-36
3:13
n1Sa 2:12,17,22,
29-31
3:14
oLev 15:30-31;
1Sa 2:25;
Isa 22:14

---

[a]3 That is, tabernacle   [b]13 Masoretic Text; an ancient Hebrew scribal tradition and Septuagint *sons blasphemed God*

[17]"What was it he said to you?" Eli asked. "Do not hide it from me. May God deal with you, be it ever so severely,[p] if you hide from me anything he told you." [18]So Samuel told him everything, hiding nothing from him. Then Eli said, "He is the LORD; let him do what is good in his eyes."[q]

[19]The LORD was with[r] Samuel as he grew[s] up, and he let none[t] of his words fall to the ground. [20]And all Israel from Dan to Beersheba[u] recognized that Samuel was attested as a prophet of the LORD. [21]The LORD continued to appear at Shiloh, and there he revealed[v] himself to Samuel through his word.

4 And Samuel's word came to all Israel.

The Philistines Capture the Ark

Now the Israelites went out to fight against the Philistines. The Israelites camped at Ebenezer,[w] and the Philistines at Aphek.[x] [2]The Philistines deployed their forces to meet Israel, and as the battle spread, Israel was defeated by the Philistines, who killed about four thousand of them on the battlefield. [3]When the soldiers returned to camp, the elders of Israel asked, "Why[y] did the LORD bring defeat upon us today before the Philistines? Let us bring the ark[z] of the LORD's covenant from Shiloh, so that it[a] may go with us and save us from the hand of our enemies."

[4]So the people sent men to Shiloh, and they brought back the ark of the covenant of the LORD Almighty, who is enthroned between the cherubim.[a] And Eli's two sons, Hophni and Phinehas, were there with the ark of the covenant of God.

[5]When the ark of the LORD's covenant came into the camp, all Israel raised such a great shout[b] that the ground shook. [6]Hearing the uproar, the Philistines asked, "What's all this shouting in the Hebrew camp?"

When they learned that the ark of the LORD had come into the camp, [7]the Philistines were afraid.[c] "A god has come into the camp," they said. "We're in trouble! Nothing like this has happened before. [8]Woe to us! Who will deliver us from the hand of these mighty gods? They are the gods who struck the Egyptians with all kinds of plagues in the desert. [9]Be strong, Philistines! Be men, or you will be subject to the Hebrews, as they[d] have been to you. Be men, and fight!"

[10]So the Philistines fought, and the Israelites were defeated[e] and every man fled to his tent. The slaughter was very great; Israel lost thirty thousand foot soldiers. [11]The ark of God was captured, and Eli's two sons, Hophni and Phinehas, died.[f]

Death of Eli

[12]That same day a Benjamite ran from the battle line and went to Shiloh, his clothes torn and dust[g] on his head. [13]When he arrived, there was Eli[h] sitting on his chair by the side of the road, watching, because his heart feared for the ark of God. When the man entered the town and told what had happened, the whole town sent up a cry.

[14]Eli heard the outcry and asked, "What is the meaning of this uproar?"

The man hurried over to Eli, [15]who was ninety-eight years old and

3:17
p Ru 1:17;
2Sa 3:35
3:18
q Job 2:10;
Isa 39:8
3:19
r Ge 21:22; 39:2
s 1Sa 2:21
t 1Sa 9:6
3:20
u Jdg 20:1
3:21
v ver 10
4:1
w 1Sa 7:12
x Jos 12:18;
1Sa 29:1
4:3
y Jos 7:7
z Nu 10:35;
Jos 6:7
4:4
a Ex 25:22;
2Sa 6:2
4:5
b Jos 6:5,10
4:7
c Ex 15:14
4:9
d Jdg 13:1;
1Co 16:13
4:10
e ver 2;
Dt 28:25;
2Sa 18:17;
2Ki 14:12
4:11
f 1Sa 2:34;
Ps 78:61,64
4:12
g Jos 7:6;
2Sa 1:2; 15:32;
Ne 9:1;
Job 2:12
4:13
h ver 18; 1Sa 1:9

a3 Or he

whose eyes[i] were set so that he could not see. [16]He told Eli, "I have just come from the battle line; I fled from it this very day."

Eli asked, "What happened, my son?"

[17]The man who brought the news replied, "Israel fled before the Philistines, and the army has suffered heavy losses. Also your two sons, Hophni and Phinehas, are dead, and the ark of God has been captured."

[18]When he mentioned the ark of God, Eli fell backward off his chair by the side of the gate. His neck was broken and he died, for he was an old man and heavy. He had led[aj] Israel forty years.

[19]His daughter-in-law, the wife of Phinehas, was pregnant and near the time of delivery. When she heard the news that the ark of God had been captured and that her father-in-law and her husband were dead, she went into labor and gave birth, but was overcome by her labor pains. [20]As she was dying, the women attending her said, "Don't despair; you have given birth to a son." But she did not respond or pay any attention.

[21]She named the boy Ichabod,[bk] saying, "The glory[l] has departed from Israel"—because of the capture of the ark of God and the deaths of her father-in-law and her husband. [22]She said, "The glory has departed from Israel, for the ark of God has been captured."

The Ark in Ashdod and Ekron

5 After the Philistines had captured the ark of God, they took it from Ebenezer[m] to Ashdod.[n] [2]Then they carried the ark into Dagon's temple and set it beside Dagon.[o] [3]When the people of Ashdod rose early the next day, there was Dagon, fallen[p] on his face on the ground before the ark of the LORD! They took Dagon and put him back in his place. [4]But the following morning when they rose, there was Dagon, fallen on his face on the ground before the ark of the LORD! His head and hands had been broken[q] off and were lying on the threshold; only his body remained. [5]That is why to this day neither the priests of Dagon nor any others who enter Dagon's temple at Ashdod step on the threshold.[r]

[6]The LORD's hand[s] was heavy upon the people of Ashdod and its vicinity; he brought devastation[t] upon them and afflicted them with tumors.[cu] [7]When the men of Ashdod saw what was happening, they said, "The ark of the god of Israel must not stay here with us, because his hand is heavy upon us and upon Dagon our god." [8]So they called together all the rulers of the Philistines and asked them, "What shall we do with the ark of the god of Israel?"

They answered, "Have the ark of the god of Israel moved to Gath.[v]" So they moved the ark of the God of Israel.

[9]But after they had moved it, the LORD's hand was against that city, throwing it into a great panic.[w] He afflicted the people of the city, both young and old, with an outbreak of tumors.[d] [10]So they sent the ark of God to Ekron.

As the ark of God was entering Ekron, the people of Ekron cried out,

4:15
i 1Sa 3:2
4:18
j ver 13
4:21
k Ge 35:18
l Ps 26:8;
Jer 2:11
5:1
m 1Sa 4:1; 7:12
n Jos 13:3
5:2
o Jdg 16:23
5:3
p Isa 19:1; 46:7
5:4
q Eze 6:6;
Mic 1:7
5:5
r Zep 1:9
5:6
s ver 7; Ex 9:3;
Ps 32:4;
Ac 13:11
t ver 11;
Ps 78:66
u Dt 28:27;
1Sa 6:5
5:8
v ver 11
5:9
w ver 6,11;
Dt 2:15;
1Sa 7:13;
Ps 78:66

---

a18 Traditionally *judged*   *b21 Ichabod* means *no glory.*   *c6* Hebrew; Septuagint and Vulgate *tumors. And rats appeared in their land, and death and destruction were throughout the city*   *d9* Or *with tumors in the groin* (see Septuagint)

"They have brought the ark of the god of Israel around to us to kill us and our people." [11]So they called together all the rulers[x] of the Philistines and said, "Send the ark of the god of Israel away; let it go back to its own place, or it[a] will kill us and our people." For death had filled the city with panic; God's hand was very heavy upon it. [12]Those who did not die were afflicted with tumors, and the outcry of the city went up to heaven.

The Ark Returned to Israel

6 When the ark of the LORD had been in Philistine territory seven months, [2]the Philistines called for the priests and the diviners[y] and said, "What shall we do with the ark of the LORD? Tell us how we should send it back to its place."

[3]They answered, "If you return the ark of the god of Israel, do not send it away empty,[z] but by all means send a guilt offering[a] to him. Then you will be healed, and you will know why his hand[b] has not been lifted from you."

[4]The Philistines asked, "What guilt offering should we send to him?"

They replied, "Five gold tumors and five gold rats, according to the number[c] of the Philistine rulers, because the same plague has struck both you and your rulers. [5]Make models of the tumors[d] and of the rats that are destroying the country, and pay honor[e] to Israel's god. Perhaps he will lift his hand from you and your gods and your land. [6]Why do you harden[f] your hearts as the Egyptians and Pharaoh did? When he[b] treated them harshly, did they[g] not send the Israelites out so they could go on their way?

[7]"Now then, get a new cart[h] ready, with two cows that have calved and have never been yoked.[i] Hitch the cows to the cart, but take their calves away and pen them up. [8]Take the ark of the LORD and put it on the cart, and in a chest beside it put the gold objects you are sending back to him as a guilt offering. Send it on its way, [9]but keep watching it. If it goes up to its own territory, toward Beth Shemesh,[j] then the LORD has brought this great disaster on us. But if it does not, then we will know that it was not his hand that struck us and that it happened to us by chance."

[10]So they did this. They took two such cows and hitched them to the cart and penned up their calves. [11]They placed the ark of the LORD on the cart and along with it the chest containing the gold rats and the models of the tumors. [12]Then the cows went straight up toward Beth Shemesh, keeping on the road and lowing all the way; they did not turn to the right or to the left. The rulers of the Philistines followed them as far as the border of Beth Shemesh.

[13]Now the people of Beth Shemesh were harvesting their wheat in the valley, and when they looked up and saw the ark, they rejoiced at the sight. [14]The cart came to the field of Joshua of Beth Shemesh, and there it stopped beside a large rock. The people chopped up the wood of the cart and sacrificed the cows as a burnt offering[k] to the LORD. [15]The Levites[l] took down the ark of the LORD, together with the chest containing the gold objects, and placed them on the large rock. On that day the people of Beth Shemesh offered burnt offerings and made

5:11
x ver 6,8-9
6:2
y Ge 41:8;
Ex 7:11; Isa 2:6
6:3
z Ex 23:15;
Dt 16:16
a Lev 5:15 b ver 9
6:4
c ver 17-18;
Jos 13:3;
Jdg 3:3
6:5
d 1Sa 5:6-11
e Jos 7:19;
Isa 42:12;
Jn 9:24;
Rev 14:7
6:6
f Ex 7:13; 8:15;
9:34; 14:17
g Ex 12:31,33
6:7
h 2Sa 6:3
i Nu 19:2
6:9
j ver 3;
Jos 15:10; 21:16
6:14
k 2Sa 24:22;
1Ki 19:21
6:15
l Jos 3:3

---

[a]11 Or *he*   [b]6 That is, God

sacrifices to the LORD. ¹⁶The five rulers of the Philistines saw all this and then returned that same day to Ekron.

¹⁷These are the gold tumors the Philistines sent as a guilt offering to the LORD—one each^m for Ashdod, Gaza, Ashkelon, Gath and Ekron. ¹⁸And the number of the gold rats was according to the number of Philistine towns belonging to the five rulers—the fortified towns with their country villages. The large rock, on which^a they set the ark of the LORD, is a witness to this day in the field of Joshua of Beth Shemesh.

¹⁹But God struck downⁿ some of the men of Beth Shemesh, putting seventy^b of them to death because they had looked^o into the ark of the LORD. The people mourned because of the heavy blow the LORD had dealt them, ²⁰and the men of Beth Shemesh asked, "Who can stand^p in the presence of the LORD, this holy^q God? To whom will the ark go up from here?"

²¹Then they sent messengers to the people of Kiriath Jearim,^r saying, "The Philistines have returned the ark of the LORD. Come down and take it up to your place." ¹So the men of Kiriath Jearim came and took up the ark of the LORD. They took it to Abinadab's^s house on the hill and consecrated Eleazar his son to guard the ark of the LORD.

Samuel Subdues the Philistines at Mizpah

²It was a long time, twenty years in all, that the ark remained at Kiriath Jearim, and all the people of Israel mourned and sought after the LORD. ³And Samuel said to the whole house of Israel, "If you are returning^t to the LORD with all your hearts, then rid^u yourselves of the foreign gods and the Ashtoreths^v and commit^w yourselves to the LORD and serve him only,^x and he will deliver you out of the hand of the Philistines." ⁴So the Israelites put away their Baals and Ashtoreths, and served the LORD only.

⁵Then Samuel said, "Assemble all Israel at Mizpah^y and I will intercede with the LORD for you." ⁶When they had assembled at Mizpah, they drew water and poured^z it out before the LORD. On that day they fasted and there they confessed, "We have sinned against the LORD." And Samuel was leader^{ca} of Israel at Mizpah.

⁷When the Philistines heard that Israel had assembled at Mizpah, the rulers of the Philistines came up to attack them. And when the Israelites heard of it, they were afraid^b because of the Philistines. ⁸They said to Samuel, "Do not stop crying^c out to the LORD our God for us, that he may rescue us from the hand of the Philistines." ⁹Then Samuel^d took a suckling lamb and offered it up as a whole burnt offering to the LORD. He cried out to the LORD on Israel's behalf, and the LORD answered him.^e

¹⁰While Samuel was sacrificing the burnt offering, the Philistines drew near to engage Israel in battle. But that day the LORD thundered^f with loud thunder against the Philistines and threw them into such a panic^g that they were routed before the Israelites. ¹¹The men of Israel rushed out of Mizpah and pursued the Philistines, slaughtering them along the way to a point below Beth Car.

6:17
m ver 4
6:19
n 2Sa 6:7
o Ex 19:21;
Nu 4:5,15,20
6:20
p 2Sa 6:9;
Mal 3:2;
Rev 6:17
q Lev 11:45
6:21
r Jos 9:17; 15:9,
60; 1Ch 13:5-6
7:1
s 2Sa 6:3
7:3
t Dt 30:10;
Isa 55:7;
Hos 6:1
u Ge 35:2;
Jos 24:14
v Jdg 2:12-13;
1Sa 31:10
w Joel 2:12
x Dt 6:13;
Mt 4:10; Lk 4:8
7:5
y Jdg 20:1
7:6
z Ps 62:8;
La 2:19
a Jdg 10:10;
Ne 9:1;
Ps 106:6
7:7
b 1Sa 17:11
7:8
c 1Sa 12:19,23;
Isa 37:4;
Jer 15:1
7:9
d Ps 99:6
e Jer 15:1
7:10
f 1Sa 2:10;
2Sa 22:14-15
g Jos 10:10

---

^a18 A few Hebrew manuscripts (see also Septuagint); most Hebrew manuscripts *villages as far as Greater Abel, where*   ^b19 A few Hebrew manuscripts; most Hebrew manuscripts and Septuagint *50,070*   ^c6 Traditionally *judge*.

¹²Then Samuel took a stone[h] and set it up between Mizpah and Shen. He named it Ebenezer,[a] saying, "Thus far has the LORD helped us." ¹³So the Philistines were subdued[i] and did not invade Israelite territory again.

Throughout Samuel's lifetime, the hand of the LORD was against the Philistines. ¹⁴The towns from Ekron to Gath that the Philistines had captured from Israel were restored to her, and Israel delivered the neighboring territory from the power of the Philistines. And there was peace between Israel and the Amorites.

¹⁵Samuel[j] continued as judge over Israel all the days of his life. ¹⁶From year to year he went on a circuit from Bethel to Gilgal to Mizpah, judging Israel in all those places. ¹⁷But he always went back to Ramah,[k] where his home was, and there he also judged Israel. And he built an altar[l] there to the LORD.

Israel Asks for a King

8 When Samuel grew old, he appointed[m] his sons as judges for Israel. ²The name of his firstborn was Joel and the name of his second was Abijah, and they served at Beersheba.[n] ³But his sons did not walk in his ways. They turned aside after dishonest gain and accepted bribes[o] and perverted justice.

⁴So all the elders of Israel gathered together and came to Samuel at Ramah.[p] ⁵They said to him, "You are old, and your sons do not walk in your ways; now appoint a king[q] to lead[b] us, such as all the other nations have."

⁶But when they said, "Give us a king to lead us," this displeased[r] Samuel; so he prayed to the LORD. ⁷And the LORD told him: "Listen to all that the people are saying to you; it is not you they have rejected, but they have rejected me as their king.[s] ⁸As they have done from the day I brought them up out of Egypt until this day, forsaking me and serving other gods, so they are doing to you. ⁹Now listen to them; but warn them solemnly and let them know[t] what the king who will reign over them will do."

¹⁰Samuel told all the words of the LORD to the people who were asking him for a king. ¹¹He said, "This is what the king who will reign over you will do: He will take[u] your sons and make them serve with his chariots and horses, and they will run in front of his chariots.[v] ¹²Some he will assign to be commanders[w] of thousands and commanders of fifties, and others to plow his ground and reap his harvest, and still others to make weapons of war and equipment for his chariots. ¹³He will take your daughters to be perfumers and cooks and bakers. ¹⁴He will take the best of your[x] fields and vineyards[y] and olive groves and give them to his attendants. ¹⁵He will take a tenth of your grain and of your vintage and give it to his officials and attendants. ¹⁶Your menservants and maidservants and the best of your cattle[c] and donkeys he will take for his own use. ¹⁷He will take a tenth of your flocks, and you yourselves will become his slaves. ¹⁸When that day comes, you will cry out for relief from the king you have chosen, and the LORD will not answer[z] you in that day."

7:12
h Ge 35:14;
Jos 4:9
7:13
i Jdg 13:1,5;
1Sa 13:5
7:15
j ver 6;
1Sa 12:11
7:17
k 1Sa 1:19; 8:4
l Jdg 21:4
8:1
m Dt 16:18-19
8:2
n Ge 22:19;
1Ki 19:3;
Am 5:4-5
8:3
o Ex 23:8;
Dt 16:19;
Ps 15:5
8:4
p 1Sa 7:17
8:5
q Dt 17:14-20
8:6
r 1Sa 15:11
8:7
s Ex 16:8;
1Sa 10:19
8:9
t ver 11-18;
1Sa 10:25
8:11
u 1Sa 10:25;
14:52
v Dt 17:16;
2Sa 15:1
8:12
w 1Sa 22:7
8:14
x Eze 46:18
y 1Ki 21:7,15
8:18
z Pr 1:28;
Isa 1:15;
Mic 3:4

---

a12 Ebenezer means stone of help.   *b5 Traditionally judge; also in verses 6 and 20*
c16 Septuagint; Hebrew young men

¹⁹But the people refused[a] to listen to Samuel. "No!" they said. "We want a king over us. ²⁰Then we will be like all the other nations,[b] with a king to lead us and to go out before us and fight our battles."

²¹When Samuel heard all that the people said, he repeated[c] it before the LORD. ²²The LORD answered, "Listen[d] to them and give them a king."

Then Samuel said to the men of Israel, "Everyone go back to his town."

Samuel Anoints Saul

9 There was a Benjamite, a man of standing, whose name was Kish[e] son of Abiel, the son of Zeror, the son of Becorath, the son of Aphiah of Benjamin. ²He had a son named Saul, an impressive young man without equal[f] among the Israelites—a head taller[g] than any of the others.

³Now the donkeys belonging to Saul's father Kish were lost, and Kish said to his son Saul, "Take one of the servants with you and go and look for the donkeys." ⁴So he passed through the hill[h] country of Ephraim and through the area around Shalisha,[i] but they did not find them. They went on into the district of Shaalim, but the donkeys were not there. Then he passed through the territory of Benjamin, but they did not find them.

⁵When they reached the district of Zuph,[j] Saul said to the servant who was with him, "Come, let's go back, or my father will stop thinking about the donkeys and start worrying[k] about us."

⁶But the servant replied, "Look, in this town there is a man of God;[l] he is highly respected, and everything[m] he says comes true. Let's go there now. Perhaps he will tell us what way to take."

⁷Saul said to his servant, "If we go, what can we give the man? The food in our sacks is gone. We have no gift[n] to take to the man of God. What do we have?"

⁸The servant answered him again. "Look," he said, "I have a quarter of a shekel[a] of silver. I will give it to the man of God so that he will tell us what way to take." ⁹(Formerly in Israel, if a man went to inquire of God, he would say, "Come, let us go to the seer," because the prophet of today used to be called a seer.)[o]

¹⁰"Good," Saul said to his servant. "Come, let's go." So they set out for the town where the man of God was.

¹¹As they were going up the hill to the town, they met some girls coming out to draw[p] water, and they asked them, "Is the seer here?"

¹²"He is," they answered. "He's ahead of you. Hurry now; he has just come to our town today, for the people have a sacrifice[q] at the high place.[r] ¹³As soon as you enter the town, you will find him before he goes up to the high place to eat. The people will not begin eating until he comes, because he must bless the sacrifice; afterward, those who are invited will eat. Go up now; you should find him about this time."

¹⁴They went up to the town, and as they were entering it, there was Samuel, coming toward them on his way up to the high place.

¹⁵Now the day before Saul came, the LORD had revealed this to Samuel: ¹⁶"About this time tomorrow I will send you a man from the

Cross references

8:19
[a] Isa 66:4;
Jer 44:16
8:20
[b] ver 5
8:21
[c] Jdg 11:11
8:22
[d] ver 7
9:1
[e] 1Sa 14:51;
1Ch 8:33; 9:39
9:2
[f] 1Sa 10:24
[g] 1Sa 10:23
9:4
[h] Jos 24:33
[i] 2Ki 4:42
9:5
[j] 1Sa 1:1
[k] 1Sa 10:2
9:6
[l] Dt 33:1;
1Ki 13:1
[m] 1Sa 3:19
9:7
[n] 1Ki 14:3;
2Ki 5:5,15; 8:8
9:9
[o] 2Sa 24:11;
2Ki 17:13;
1Ch 9:22;
26:28; 29:29;
Isa 30:10;
Am 7:12
9:11
[p] Ge 24:11,13
9:12
[q] Nu 28:11-15;
1Sa 7:17
[r] Ge 31:54;
1Sa 10:5;
1Ki 3:2

---

[a]8 That is, about 1/10 ounce (about 3 grams)

land of Benjamin. Anoint^s him leader over my people Israel; he will deliver^t my people from the hand of the Philistines. I have looked upon my people, for their cry has reached me."

¹⁷When Samuel caught sight of Saul, the Lᴏʀᴅ said to him, "This^u is the man I spoke to you about; he will govern my people."

¹⁸Saul approached Samuel in the gateway and asked, "Would you please tell me where the seer's house is?"

¹⁹"I am the seer," Samuel replied. "Go up ahead of me to the high place, for today you are to eat with me, and in the morning I will let you go and will tell you all that is in your heart. ²⁰As for the donkeys^v you lost three days ago, do not worry about them; they have been found. And to whom is all the desire^w of Israel turned, if not to you and all your father's family?"

²¹Saul answered, "But am I not a Benjamite, from the smallest tribe^x of Israel, and is not my clan the least of all the clans of the tribe of Benjamin?^y Why do you say such a thing to me?"

²²Then Samuel brought Saul and his servant into the hall and seated them at the head of those who were invited—about thirty in number. ²³Samuel said to the cook, "Bring the piece of meat I gave you, the one I told you to lay aside."

²⁴So the cook took up the leg^z with what was on it and set it in front of Saul. Samuel said, "Here is what has been kept for you. Eat, because it was set aside for you for this occasion, from the time I said, 'I have invited guests.' " And Saul dined with Samuel that day.

²⁵After they came down from the high place to the town, Samuel talked with Saul on the roof^a of his house. ²⁶They rose about daybreak and Samuel called to Saul on the roof, "Get ready, and I will send you on your way." When Saul got ready, he and Samuel went outside together. ²⁷As they were going down to the edge of the town, Samuel said to Saul, "Tell the servant to go on ahead of us"—and the servant did so—"but you stay here awhile, so that I may give you a message from God."

10 Then Samuel took a flask^b of oil and poured it on Saul's head and kissed him, saying, "Has not the Lᴏʀᴅ anointed^c you leader over his inheritance?^{ad} ²When you leave me today, you will meet two men near Rachel's tomb,^e at Zelzah on the border of Benjamin. They will say to you, 'The donkeys^f you set out to look for have been found. And now your father has stopped thinking about them and is worried^g about you. He is asking, "What shall I do about my son?" '

³"Then you will go on from there until you reach the great tree of Tabor. Three men going up to God at Bethel^h will meet you there. One will be carrying three young goats, another three loaves of bread, and another a skin of wine. ⁴They will greet you and offer you two loaves of bread, which you will accept from them.

⁵"After that you will go to Gibeah of God, where there is a Philistine outpost.ⁱ As you approach the town, you will meet a procession of prophets coming down from the high place^j with lyres, tambourines, flutes and harps^k being played before them, and they will be prophesy-

---

9:16
s1Sa 10:1
tEx 3:7-9
9:17
u1Sa 16:12
9:20
vver 3
w1Sa 8:5; 12:13
9:21
x1Sa 15:17
yJdg 20:35,46
9:24
zLev 7:32-34;
Nu 18:18
9:25
aDt 22:8;
Ac 10:9
10:1
b1Sa 16:13;
2Ki 9:1,3,6
cPs 2:12
dDt 32:9;
Ps 78:62,71
10:2
eGe 35:20
f1Sa 9:4
g1Sa 9:5
10:3
hGe 28:22;
35:7-8
10:5
i1Sa 13:3
j1Sa 9:12
k2Ki 3:15

---

^a1 Hebrew; Septuagint and Vulgate *over his people Israel? You will reign over the* Lᴏʀᴅ's *people and save them from the power of their enemies round about. And this will be a sign to you that the* Lᴏʀᴅ *has anointed you leader over his inheritance:*

ing.[l] [6]The Spirit[m] of the LORD will come upon you in power, and you will prophesy with them; and you will be changed into a different person. [7]Once these signs are fulfilled, do whatever[n] your hand finds to do, for God is with[o] you.

[8]"Go down ahead of me to Gilgal.[p] I will surely come down to you to sacrifice burnt offerings and fellowship offerings,[a] but you must wait seven days until I come to you and tell you what you are to do."

Saul Made King

[9]As Saul turned to leave Samuel, God changed[q] Saul's heart, and all these signs were fulfilled that day. [10]When they arrived at Gibeah, a procession of prophets met him; the Spirit of God came upon him in power, and he joined in their prophesying.[r] [11]When all those who had formerly known him saw him prophesying with the prophets, they asked each other, "What is this[s] that has happened to the son of Kish? Is Saul also among the prophets?"[t]

[12]A man who lived there answered, "And who is their father?" So it became a saying: "Is Saul also among the prophets?" [13]After Saul stopped prophesying, he went to the high place.

[14]Now Saul's uncle[u] asked him and his servant, "Where have you been?"

"Looking for the donkeys," he said. "But when we saw they were not to be found, we went to Samuel."

[15]Saul's uncle said, "Tell me what Samuel said to you."

[16]Saul replied, "He assured us that the donkeys[v] had been found." But he did not tell his uncle what Samuel had said about the kingship.

[17]Samuel summoned the people of Israel to the LORD at Mizpah[w] [18]and said to them, "This is what the LORD, the God of Israel, says: 'I brought Israel up out of Egypt, and I delivered you from the power of Egypt and all the kingdoms that oppressed[x] you.' [19]But you have now rejected your God, who saves you out of all your calamities and distresses. And you have said, 'No, set a king[y] over us.' So now present[z] yourselves before the LORD by your tribes and clans."

[20]When Samuel brought all the tribes of Israel near, the tribe of Benjamin was chosen. [21]Then he brought forward the tribe of Benjamin, clan by clan, and Matri's clan was chosen. Finally Saul son of Kish was chosen. But when they looked for him, he was not to be found. [22]So they inquired[a] further of the LORD, "Has the man come here yet?"

And the LORD said, "Yes, he has hidden himself among the baggage."

[23]They ran and brought him out, and as he stood among the people he was a head taller[b] than any of the others. [24]Samuel said to all the people, "Do you see the man the LORD has chosen?[c] There is no one like him among all the people."

Then the people shouted, "Long live[d] the king!"

[25]Samuel explained to the people the regulations[e] of the kingship. He wrote them down on a scroll and deposited it before the LORD. Then Samuel dismissed the people, each to his own home.

[26]Saul also went to his home in Gibeah,[f] accompanied by valiant men whose hearts God had touched. [27]But some troublemakers[g] said,

10:5
l 1Sa 19:20;
1Co 14:1
10:6
m ver 10;
Nu 11:25;
1Sa 19:23-24
10:7
n Ecc 9:10
o Jos 1:5;
Jdg 6:12;
Heb 13:5
10:8
p 1Sa 11:14-15
10:9
q ver 6
10:10
r ver 5-6;
1Sa 19:20
10:11
s Mt 13:54;
Jn 7:15
t 1Sa 19:24
10:14
u 1Sa 14:50
10:16
v 1Sa 9:20
10:17
w Jdg 20:1;
1Sa 7:5
10:18
x Jdg 6:8-9
10:19
y 1Sa 8:5-7;
12:12 z Jos 7:14;
24:1
10:22
a 1Sa 23:2,4,9-11
10:23
b 1Sa 9:2
10:24
c Dt 17:15;
2Sa 21:6
d 1Ki 1:25,34,39
10:25
e Dt 17:14-20;
1Sa 8:11-18
10:26
f 1Sa 11:4
10:27
g Dt 13:13

a8 Traditionally *peace offerings*

"How can this fellow save us?" They despised him and brought him no gifts. h But Saul kept silent.

Saul Rescues the City of Jabesh

11 Nahash i the Ammonite went up and besieged Jabesh Gilead. j And all the men of Jabesh said to him, "Make a treaty k with us, and we will be subject to you."

²But Nahash the Ammonite replied, "I will make a treaty with you only on the condition that I gouge l out the right eye of every one of you and so bring disgrace m on all Israel."

³The elders of Jabesh said to him, "Give us seven days so we can send messengers throughout Israel; if no one comes to rescue us, we will surrender to you."

⁴When the messengers came to Gibeah n of Saul and reported these terms to the people, they all wept o aloud. ⁵Just then Saul was returning from the fields, behind his oxen, and he asked, "What is wrong with the people? Why are they weeping?" Then they repeated to him what the men of Jabesh had said.

⁶When Saul heard their words, the Spirit p of God came upon him in power, and he burned with anger. ⁷He took a pair of oxen, cut them into pieces, and sent the pieces by messengers throughout Israel, q proclaiming, "This is what will be done to the oxen of anyone r who does not follow Saul and Samuel." Then the terror of the LORD fell on the people, and they turned out as one man. ⁸When Saul mustered s them at Bezek, t the men of Israel numbered three hundred thousand and the men of Judah thirty thousand.

⁹They told the messengers who had come, "Say to the men of Jabesh Gilead, 'By the time the sun is hot tomorrow, you will be delivered.'" When the messengers went and reported this to the men of Jabesh, they were elated. ¹⁰They said to the Ammonites, "Tomorrow we will surrender u to you, and you can do to us whatever seems good to you."

¹¹The next day Saul separated his men into three divisions; v during the last watch of the night they broke into the camp of the Ammonites and slaughtered them until the heat of the day. Those who survived were scattered, so that no two of them were left together.

Saul Confirmed as King

¹²The people then said to Samuel, "Who w was it that asked, 'Shall Saul reign over us?' Bring these men to us and we will put them to death."

¹³But Saul said, "No one shall be put to death today, x for this day the LORD has rescued y Israel."

¹⁴Then Samuel said to the people, "Come, let us go to Gilgal z and there reaffirm the kingship. a" ¹⁵So all the people went to Gilgal b and confirmed Saul as king in the presence of the LORD. There they sacrificed fellowship offerings a before the LORD, and Saul and all the Israelites held a great celebration.

a15 Traditionally *peace offerings*

10:27
h 1Ki 10:25;
2Ch 17:5
11:1
i 1Sa 12:12
j Jdg 21:8
k 1Ki 20:34;
Eze 17:13
11:2
l Nu 16:14
m 1Sa 17:26
11:4
n 1Sa 10:5,26;
15:34 o Jdg 2:4;
1Sa 30:4
11:6
p Jdg 3:10;
6:34; 13:25;
14:6;
1Sa 10:10;
16:13
11:7
q Jdg 19:29
r Jdg 21:5
11:8
s Jdg 20:2
t Jdg 1:4
11:10
u ver 3
11:11
v Jdg 7:16
11:12
w 1Sa 10:27;
Lk 19:27
11:13
x 2Sa 19:22
y Ex 14:13;
1Sa 19:5
11:14
z 1Sa 10:8
a 1Sa 10:25
11:15
b 1Sa 10:8,17

Samuel's Farewell Speech

12 Samuel said to all Israel, "I have listened[c] to everything you said to me and have set a king[d] over you. ²Now you have a king as your leader.[e] As for me, I am old and gray, and my sons are here with you. I have been your leader from my youth until this day. ³Here I stand. Testify against me in the presence of the LORD and his anointed.[f] Whose ox have I taken? Whose donkey[g] have I taken? Whom have I cheated? Whom have I oppressed? From whose hand have I accepted a bribe[h] to make me shut my eyes? If I have done[i] any of these, I will make it right."

⁴"You have not cheated or oppressed us," they replied. "You have not taken anything from anyone's hand."

⁵Samuel said to them, "The LORD is witness against you, and also his anointed is witness this day, that you have not found anything[j] in my hand.[k]"

"He is witness," they said.

⁶Then Samuel said to the people, "It is the LORD who appointed Moses and Aaron and brought[l] your forefathers up out of Egypt. ⁷Now then, stand here, because I am going to confront[m] you with evidence before the LORD as to all the righteous acts performed by the LORD for you and your fathers.

⁸"After Jacob entered Egypt, they cried[n] to the LORD for help, and the LORD sent[o] Moses and Aaron, who brought your forefathers out of Egypt and settled them in this place.

⁹"But they forgot[p] the LORD their God; so he sold them into the hand of Sisera,[q] the commander of the army of Hazor, and into the hands of the Philistines[r] and the king of Moab,[s] who fought against them. ¹⁰They cried out to the LORD and said, 'We have sinned; we have forsaken[t] the LORD and served the Baals and the Ashtoreths.[u] But now deliver us from the hands of our enemies, and we will serve you.' ¹¹Then the LORD sent Jerub-Baal,[a][v] Barak,[b][w] Jephthah[x] and Samuel,[c] and he delivered you from the hands of your enemies on every side, so that you lived securely.

¹²"But when you saw that Nahash[y] king[z] of the Ammonites was moving against you, you said to me, 'No, we want a king to rule[a] over us'—even though the LORD your God was your king. ¹³Now here is the king[b] you have chosen, the one you asked[c] for; see, the LORD has set a king over you. ¹⁴If you fear[d] the LORD and serve and obey him and do not rebel against his commands, and if both you and the king who reigns over you follow the LORD your God—good! ¹⁵But if you do not obey the LORD, and if you rebel against[e] his commands, his hand will be against you, as it was against your fathers.

¹⁶"Now then, stand still and see[f] this great thing the LORD is about to do before your eyes! ¹⁷Is it not wheat harvest[g] now? I will call[h] upon the LORD to send thunder and rain.[i] And you will realize what an evil[j] thing you did in the eyes of the LORD when you asked for a king."

¹⁸Then Samuel called upon the LORD, and that same day the LORD sent thunder and rain. So all the people stood in awe[k] of the LORD and of Samuel.

Cross references

12:1
c 1Sa 8:7
d 1Sa 10:24;
11:15

12:2
e 1Sa 8:5

12:3
f 1Sa 10:1; 24:6;
2Sa 1:14
g Nu 16:15
h Dt 16:19
i Ac 20:33

12:5
j Ac 23:9; 24:20
k Ex 22:4

12:6
l Ex 6:26;
Mic 6:4

12:7
m Isa 1:18;
Mic 6:1-5

12:8
n Ex 2:23
o Ex 3:10; 4:16

12:9
p Jdg 3:7
q Jdg 4:2
r Jdg 10:7; 13:1
s Jdg 3:12

12:10
t Jdg 10:10,15
u Jdg 2:13

12:11
v Jdg 6:14,32
w Jdg 4:6
x Jdg 11:1

12:12
y 1Sa 11:1
z 1Sa 8:5
a Jdg 8:23;
1Sa 8:6,19

12:13
b 1Sa 8:5;
Hos 13:11
c 1Sa 10:24

12:14
d Jos 24:14

12:15
e ver 9;
Jos 24:20;
Isa 1:20

12:16
f Ex 14:13

12:17
g 1Sa 7:9-10
h Jas 5:18
i Pr 26:1
j 1Sa 8:6-7

12:18
k Ex 14:31

---

a11 Also called *Gideon*   *b11* Some Septuagint manuscripts and Syriac; Hebrew *Bedan*
c11 Hebrew; some Septuagint manuscripts and Syriac *Samson*

[19]The people all said to Samuel, "Pray[l] to the LORD your God for your servants so that we will not die, for we have added to all our other sins the evil of asking for a king."

[20]"Do not be afraid," Samuel replied. "You have done all this evil; yet do not turn away from the LORD, but serve the LORD with all your heart. [21]Do not turn away after useless[m] idols.[n] They can do you no good, nor can they rescue you, because they are useless. [22]For the sake[o] of his great name[p] the LORD will not reject[q] his people, because the LORD was pleased to make[r] you his own. [23]As for me, far be it from me that I should sin against the LORD by failing to pray[s] for you. And I will teach[t] you the way that is good and right. [24]But be sure to fear[u] the LORD and serve him faithfully with all your heart; consider[v] what great[w] things he has done for you. [25]Yet if you persist[x] in doing evil, both you and your king will be swept[y] away."

Samuel Rebukes Saul

13 Saul was ⌊thirty⌋[a] years old when he became king, and he reigned over Israel ⌊forty-⌋[b] two years.

[2]Saul[c] chose three thousand men from Israel; two thousand were with him at Micmash and in the hill country of Bethel, and a thousand were with Jonathan at Gibeah[z] in Benjamin. The rest of the men he sent back to their homes.

[3]Jonathan attacked the Philistine outpost[a] at Geba, and the Philistines heard about it. Then Saul had the trumpet blown throughout the land and said, "Let the Hebrews hear!" [4]So all Israel heard the news: "Saul has attacked the Philistine outpost, and now Israel has become a stench[b] to the Philistines." And the people were summoned to join Saul at Gilgal.

[5]The Philistines assembled to fight Israel, with three thousand[d] chariots, six thousand charioteers, and soldiers as numerous as the sand[c] on the seashore. They went up and camped at Micmash, east of Beth Aven. [6]When the men of Israel saw that their situation was critical and that their army was hard pressed, they hid in caves and thickets, among the rocks, and in pits and cisterns.[d] [7]Some Hebrews even crossed the Jordan to the land of Gad[e] and Gilead.

Saul remained at Gilgal, and all the troops with him were quaking with fear. [8]He waited seven[f] days, the time set by Samuel; but Samuel did not come to Gilgal, and Saul's men began to scatter. [9]So he said, "Bring me the burnt offering and the fellowship offerings.[e]" And Saul offered[g] up the burnt offering. [10]Just as he finished making the offering, Samuel[h] arrived, and Saul went out to greet him.

[11]"What have you done?" asked Samuel.

Saul replied, "When I saw that the men were scattering, and that you did not come at the set time, and that the Philistines were assembling at Micmash,[i] [12]I thought, 'Now the Philistines will come down against me at Gilgal, and I have not sought the LORD's favor.[j]' So I felt compelled to offer the burnt offering."

[13]"You acted foolishly,[k]" Samuel said. "You have not kept[l] the

### Cross references (margin)

12:19
lver 23;
Ex 9:28;
Jas 5:18;
1Jn 5:16
12:21
mIsa 41:24,29;
Jer 16:19;
Hab 2:18
nDt 11:16
12:22
oPs 106:8
pJos 7:9
qIKi 6:13
rDt 7:7; 1Pe 2:9
12:23
sRo 1:9-10;
Col 1:9; 2Ti 1:3
tIKi 8:36;
Ps 34:11;
Pr 4:11
12:24
uEcc 12:13
vIsa 5:12
wDt 10:21
12:25
xISa 31:1-5
yJos 24:20
13:2
zISa 10:26
13:3
aISa 10:5
13:4
bGe 34:30
13:5
cJos 11:4
13:6
dJdg 6:2
13:7
eNu 32:33
13:8
fISa 10:8
13:9
g2Sa 24:25;
1Ki 3:4
13:10
hISa 15:13
13:11
iver 2,5,16,23
13:12
jJer 26:19
13:13
k2Ch 16:9
lISa 15:23,24

---

[a]1 A few late manuscripts of the Septuagint; Hebrew does not have *thirty*.   [b]1 See the round number in Acts 13:21; Hebrew does not have *forty-*.   [c]1,2 Or *and when he had reigned over Israel two years,* [2]*he*   [d]5 Some Septuagint manuscripts and Syriac; Hebrew *thirty thousand*   [e]9 Traditionally *peace offerings*

command the LORD your God gave you; if you had, he would have established your kingdom over Israel for all time. [14]But now your kingdom[m] will not endure; the LORD has sought out a man after his own heart[n] and appointed[o] him leader of his people, because you have not kept the LORD's command."

[15]Then Samuel left Gilgal[a] and went up to Gibeah[p] in Benjamin, and Saul counted the men who were with him. They numbered about six hundred.

Israel Without Weapons

[16]Saul and his son Jonathan and the men with them were staying in Gibeah[b] in Benjamin, while the Philistines camped at Micmash. [17]Raiding[q] parties went out from the Philistine camp in three detachments. One turned toward Ophrah[r] in the vicinity of Shual, [18]another toward Beth Horon,[s] and the third toward the borderland overlooking the Valley of Zeboim[t] facing the desert.

[19]Not a blacksmith[u] could be found in the whole land of Israel, because the Philistines had said, "Otherwise the Hebrews will make swords or spears!" [20]So all Israel went down to the Philistines to have their plowshares, mattocks, axes and sickles[c] sharpened. [21]The price was two thirds of a shekel[d] for sharpening plowshares and mattocks, and a third of a shekel[e] for sharpening forks and axes and for repointing goads.

[22]So on the day of the battle not a soldier with Saul and Jonathan[v] had a sword or spear[w] in his hand; only Saul and his son Jonathan had them.

Jonathan Attacks the Philistines

[23]Now a detachment of Philistines had gone out to the pass[x] at

14 Micmash. [1]One day Jonathan son of Saul said to the young man bearing his armor, "Come, let's go over to the Philistine outpost on the other side." But he did not tell his father.

[2]Saul was staying on the outskirts of Gibeah[y] under a pomegranate tree in Migron.[z] With him were about six hundred men, [3]among whom was Ahijah, who was wearing an ephod. He was a son of Ichabod's[a] brother Ahitub[b] son of Phinehas, the son of Eli,[c] the LORD's priest in Shiloh. No one was aware that Jonathan had left.

[4]On each side of the pass[d] that Jonathan intended to cross to reach the Philistine outpost was a cliff; one was called Bozez, and the other Seneh. [5]One cliff stood to the north toward Micmash, the other to the south toward Geba.

[6]Jonathan said to his young armor-bearer, "Come, let's go over to the outpost of those uncircumcised[e] fellows. Perhaps the LORD will act in our behalf. Nothing[f] can hinder the LORD from saving, whether by many[g] or by few.[h]"

[7]"Do all that you have in mind," his armor-bearer said. "Go ahead; I am with you heart and soul."

[8]Jonathan said, "Come, then; we will cross over toward the men and

13:14
m 1Sa 15:28
n Ac 7:46; 13:22
o 2Sa 6:21
13:15
p 1Sa 14:2
13:17
q 1Sa 14:15
r Jos 18:23
13:18
s Jos 18:13-14
t Ne 11:34
13:19
u 2Ki 24:14;
Jer 24:1
13:22
v 1Ch 9:39
w Jdg 5:8
13:23
x 1Sa 14:4
14:2
y 1Sa 13:15
z Isa 10:28
14:3
a 1Sa 4:21
b 1Sa 22:11,20
c 1Sa 2:28
14:4
d 1Sa 13:23
14:6
e 1Sa 17:26,36;
Jer 9:26
f Heb 11:34
g Jdg 7:4
h 1Sa 17:46-47

---

[a]15 Hebrew; Septuagint *Gilgal and went his way; the rest of the people went after Saul to meet the army, and they went out of Gilgal*   [b]16 Two Hebrew manuscripts; most Hebrew manuscripts *Geba,* a variant of *Gibeah*   [c]20 Septuagint; Hebrew *plowshares*   [d]21 Hebrew *pim;* that is, about 1/4 ounce (about 8 grams)   [e]21 That is, about 1/8 ounce (about 4 grams)

let them see us. [9]If they say to us, 'Wait there until we come to you,' we will stay where we are and not go up to them. [10]But if they say, 'Come up to us,' we will climb up, because that will be our sign[i] that the LORD has given them into our hands."

[11]So both of them showed themselves to the Philistine outpost. "Look!" said the Philistines. "The Hebrews are crawling out of the holes they were hiding[j] in." [12]The men of the outpost shouted to Jonathan and his armor-bearer, "Come up to us and we'll teach you a lesson.[k]"

So Jonathan said to his armor-bearer, "Climb up after me; the LORD has given them into the hand[l] of Israel."

[13]Jonathan climbed up, using his hands and feet, with his armor-bearer right behind him. The Philistines fell before Jonathan, and his armor-bearer followed and killed behind him. [14]In that first attack Jonathan and his armor-bearer killed some twenty men in an area of about half an acre.[a]

Israel Routs the Philistines

[15]Then panic[m] struck the whole army—those in the camp and field, and those in the outposts and raiding[n] parties—and the ground shook. It was a panic sent by God.[b]

[16]Saul's lookouts[o] at Gibeah of Benjamin saw the army melting away in all directions. [17]Then Saul said to the men who were with him, "Muster the forces and see who has left us." When they did, it was Jonathan and his armor-bearer who were not there.

[18]Saul said to Ahijah, "Bring[p] the ark of God." (At that time it was with the Israelites.)[c] [19]While Saul was talking to the priest, the tumult in the Philistine camp increased more and more. So Saul said to the priest,[q] "Withdraw your hand."

[20]Then Saul and all his men assembled and went to the battle. They found the Philistines in total confusion, striking[r] each other with their swords. [21]Those Hebrews who had previously been with the Philistines and had gone up with them to their camp went[s] over to the Israelites who were with Saul and Jonathan. [22]When all the Israelites who had hidden[t] in the hill country of Ephraim heard that the Philistines were on the run, they joined the battle in hot pursuit. [23]So the LORD rescued[u] Israel that day, and the battle moved on beyond Beth Aven.[v]

Jonathan Eats Honey

[24]Now the men of Israel were in distress that day, because Saul had bound the people under an oath,[w] saying, "Cursed be any man who eats food before evening comes, before I have avenged myself on my enemies!" So none of the troops tasted food.

[25]The entire army[d] entered the woods, and there was honey on the ground. [26]When they went into the woods, they saw the honey oozing out, yet no one put his hand to his mouth, because they feared the oath. [27]But Jonathan had not heard that his father had bound the people with the oath, so he reached out the end of the staff that was in his hand and

14:10
i Ge 24:14;
Jdg 6:36-37
14:11
j 1Sa 13:6
14:12
k 1Sa 17:43-44
l 2Sa 5:24
14:15
m Ge 35:5;
2Ki 7:5-7
n 1Sa 13:17
14:16
o 2Sa 18:24
14:18
p 1Sa 30:7
14:19
q Nu 27:21
14:20
r Jdg 7:22;
2Ch 20:23
14:21
s 1Sa 29:4
14:22
t 1Sa 13:6
14:23
u Ex 14:30;
Ps 44:6-7
v 1Sa 13:5
14:24
w Jos 6:26

---

[a]14 Hebrew *half a yoke*; a "yoke" was the land plowed by a yoke of oxen in one day.   [b]15 Or *a terrible panic*   [c]18 Hebrew; Septuagint *"Bring the ephod."* (At that time he wore the ephod before the Israelites.)   [d]25 Or *Now all the people of the land*

dipped it into the honeycomb.ˣ He raised his hand to his mouth, and his eyes brightened.ᵃ ²⁸Then one of the soldiers told him, "Your father bound the army under a strict oath, saying, 'Cursed be any man who eats food today!' That is why the men are faint."

²⁹Jonathan said, "My father has made troubleʸ for the country. See how my eyes brightenedᵇ when I tasted a little of this honey. ³⁰How much better it would have been if the men had eaten today some of the plunder they took from their enemies. Would not the slaughter of the Philistines have been even greater?"

³¹That day, after the Israelites had struck down the Philistines from Micmash to Aijalon,ᶻ they were exhausted. ³²They pounced on the plunderᵃ and, taking sheep, cattle and calves, they butchered them on the ground and ate them, together with the blood.ᵇ ³³Then someone said to Saul, "Look, the men are sinning against the LORD by eating meat that has blood in it."

"You have broken faith," he said. "Roll a large stone over here at once." ³⁴Then he said, "Go out among the men and tell them, 'Each of you bring me your cattle and sheep, and slaughter them here and eat them. Do not sin against the LORD by eating meat with blood still in it.'"

So everyone brought his ox that night and slaughtered it there. ³⁵Then Saul built an altarᶜ to the LORD; it was the first time he had done this.

³⁶Saul said, "Let us go down after the Philistines by night and plunder them till dawn, and let us not leave one of them alive."

"Do whatever seems best to you," they replied.

But the priest said, "Let us inquire of God here."

³⁷So Saul asked God, "Shall I go down after the Philistines? Will you give them into Israel's hand?" But God did not answerᵈ him that day.

³⁸Saul therefore said, "Come here, all you who are leaders of the army, and let us find out what sin has been committedᵉ today. ³⁹As surely as the LORD who rescues Israel lives,ᶠ even if it lies with my son Jonathan, he must die." But not one of the men said a word.

⁴⁰Saul then said to all the Israelites, "You stand over there; I and Jonathan my son will stand over here."

"Do what seems best to you," the men replied.

⁴¹Then Saul prayed to the LORD, the God of Israel, "Giveᵍ me the rightʰ answer."ᶜ And Jonathan and Saul were taken by lot, and the men were cleared. ⁴²Saul said, "Cast the lot between me and Jonathan my son." And Jonathan was taken.

⁴³Then Saul said to Jonathan, "Tell me what you have done."ⁱ

So Jonathan told him, "I merely tasted a little honeyʲ with the end of my staff. And now must I die?"

⁴⁴Saul said, "May God deal with me, be it ever so severely,ᵏ if you do not die, Jonathan.ˡ"

⁴⁵But the men said to Saul, "Should Jonathan die—he who has brought about this great deliverance in Israel? Never! As surely as the LORD lives, not a hairᵐ of his head will fall to the ground, for he did this

14:27
ˣver 43;
1Sa 30:12
14:29
ʸJos 7:25;
1Ki 18:18
14:31
ᶻJos 10:12
14:32
ᵃ1Sa 15:19
ᵇGe 9:4;
Lev 3:17; 7:26;
17:10-14;
19:26; Dt 12:16,
23-24
14:35
ᶜ1Sa 7:17
14:37
ᵈ1Sa 10:22;
28:6,15
14:38
ᵉJos 7:11;
1Sa 10:19
14:39
ᶠ2Sa 12:5
14:41
ᵍAc 1:24
ʰPr 16:33
14:43
ⁱJos 7:19 jver 27
14:44
ᵏRu 1:17 ˡver 39
14:45
ᵐ1Ki 1:52;
Lk 21:18;
Ac 27:34

ᵃ27 Or *his strength was renewed*   ᵇ29 Or *my strength was renewed*   ᶜ41 Hebrew; Septuagint *"Why have you not answered your servant today? If the fault is in me or my son Jonathan, respond with Urim, but if the men of Israel are at fault, respond with Thummim."*

today with God's help." So the men rescued[n] Jonathan, and he was not put to death.

[46]Then Saul stopped pursuing the Philistines, and they withdrew to their own land.

[47]After Saul had assumed rule over Israel, he fought against their enemies on every side: Moab, the Ammonites,[o] Edom, the kings[a] of Zobah,[p] and the Philistines. Wherever he turned, he inflicted punishment on them.[b] [48]He fought valiantly and defeated the Amalekites,[q] delivering Israel from the hands of those who had plundered them.

Saul's Family

[49]Saul's sons were Jonathan, Ishvi and Malki-Shua.[r] The name of his older daughter was Merab, and that of the younger was Michal.[s] [50]His wife's name was Ahinoam daughter of Ahimaaz. The name of the commander of Saul's army was Abner son of Ner, and Ner was Saul's uncle. [51]Saul's father Kish[t] and Abner's father Ner were sons of Abiel.

[52]All the days of Saul there was bitter war with the Philistines, and whenever Saul saw a mighty or brave man, he took[u] him into his service.

The Lord Rejects Saul as King

15 Samuel said to Saul, "I am the one the Lord sent to anoint[v] you king over his people Israel; so listen now to the message from the Lord. [2]This is what the Lord Almighty says: 'I will punish the Amalekites[w] for what they did to Israel when they waylaid them as they came up from Egypt. [3]Now go, attack the Amalekites and totally[x] destroy[c] everything that belongs to them. Do not spare them; put to death men and women, children and infants, cattle and sheep, camels and donkeys.' "

[4]So Saul summoned the men and mustered them at Telaim—two hundred thousand foot soldiers and ten thousand men from Judah. [5]Saul went to the city of Amalek and set an ambush in the ravine. [6]Then he said to the Kenites,[y] "Go away, leave the Amalekites so that I do not destroy you along with them; for you showed kindness to all the Israelites when they came up out of Egypt." So the Kenites moved away from the Amalekites.

[7]Then Saul attacked the Amalekites[z] all the way from Havilah to Shur,[a] to the east of Egypt. [8]He took Agag king of the Amalekites alive,[b] and all his people he totally destroyed with the sword. [9]But Saul and the army spared[c] Agag and the best of the sheep and cattle, the fat calves[d] and lambs—everything that was good. These they were unwilling to destroy completely, but everything that was despised and weak they totally destroyed.

[10]Then the word of the Lord came to Samuel: [11]"I am grieved[d] that I have made Saul king, because he has turned[e] away from me and has not carried out my instructions."[f] Samuel was troubled,[g] and he cried out to the Lord all that night.

[12]Early in the morning Samuel got up and went to meet Saul, but he

14:45
n2Sa 14:11
14:47
o1Sa 11:1-13
pver 52;
2Sa 10:6
14:48
q1Sa 15:2,7
14:49
r1Sa 31:2;
1Ch 8:33
s1Sa 18:17-20
14:51
t1Sa 9:1
14:52
u1Sa 8:11
15:1
v1Sa 9:16
15:2
wEx 17:8-14;
Nu 24:20;
Dt 25:17-19
15:3
xNu 24:20;
Dt 20:16-18;
Jos 6:17;
1Sa 22:19
15:6
yEx 18:10,19;
Nu 10:29-32;
24:22; Jdg 1:16;
4:1
15:7
z1Sa 14:48
aGe 16:7;
25:17-18;
Ex 15:22
15:8
b1Sa 30:1
15:9
cver 3,15
15:11
dGe 6:6;
2Sa 24:16
eJos 22:16
f1Sa 13:13;
1Ki 9:6-7
gver 35

---

[a]47 Masoretic Text; Dead Sea Scrolls and Septuagint *king*   [b]47 Hebrew; Septuagint *he was victorious*   [c]3 The Hebrew term refers to the irrevocable giving over of things or persons to the Lord, often by totally destroying them; also in verses 8, 9, 15, 18, 20 and 21.   [d]9 Or *the grown bulls*; the meaning of the Hebrew for this phrase is uncertain.

was told, "Saul has gone to Carmel. [h] There he has set up a monument in his own honor and has turned and gone on down to Gilgal."

[13]When Samuel reached him, Saul said, "The Lord bless you! I have carried out the Lord's instructions."

[14]But Samuel said, "What then is this bleating of sheep in my ears? What is this lowing of cattle that I hear?"

[15]Saul answered, "The soldiers brought them from the Amalekites; they spared the best of the sheep and cattle to sacrifice to the Lord your God, but we totally destroyed the rest."

[16]"Stop!" Samuel said to Saul. "Let me tell you what the Lord said to me last night."

"Tell me," Saul replied.

[17]Samuel said, "Although you were once small[i] in your own eyes, did you not become the head of the tribes of Israel? The Lord anointed you king over Israel. [18]And he sent you on a mission, saying, 'Go and completely destroy those wicked people, the Amalekites; make war on them until you have wiped them out.' [19]Why did you not obey the Lord? Why did you pounce on the plunder[j] and do evil in the eyes of the Lord?"

[20]"But I did obey[k] the Lord," Saul said. "I went on the mission the Lord assigned me. I completely destroyed the Amalekites and brought back Agag their king. [21]The soldiers took sheep and cattle from the plunder, the best of what was devoted to God, in order to sacrifice them to the Lord your God at Gilgal."

[22]But Samuel replied:

> "Does the Lord delight in burnt offerings and sacrifices
>   as much as in obeying the voice of the Lord?
> To obey is better than sacrifice,[l]
>   and to heed is better than the fat of rams.
> [23]For rebellion is like the sin of divination,[m]
>   and arrogance like the evil of idolatry.
> Because you have rejected[n] the word of the Lord,
>   he has rejected you as king."

[24]Then Saul said to Samuel, "I have sinned. [o] I violated the Lord's command and your instructions. I was afraid[p] of the people and so I gave in to them. [25]Now I beg you, forgive[q] my sin and come back with me, so that I may worship the Lord."

[26]But Samuel said to him, "I will not go back with you. You have rejected[r] the word of the Lord, and the Lord has rejected you as king over Israel!"

[27]As Samuel turned to leave, Saul caught hold of the hem of his robe, and it tore. [s] [28]Samuel said to him, "The Lord has torn[t] the kingdom of Israel from you today and has given it to one of your neighbors—to one better than you. [29]He who is the Glory of Israel does not lie[u] or change[v] his mind; for he is not a man, that he should change his mind."

[30]Saul replied, "I have sinned. But please honor[w] me before the elders of my people and before Israel; come back with me, so that I may worship the Lord your God." [31]So Samuel went back with Saul, and Saul worshiped the Lord.

[32]Then Samuel said, "Bring me Agag king of the Amalekites."

15:12
h Jos 15:55
15:17
i 1Sa 9:21
15:19
j 1Sa 14:32
15:20
k ver 13
15:22
l Ps 40:6-8;
51:16;
Isa 1:11-15;
Jer 7:22;
Hos 6:6;
Mic 6:6-8;
Mt 12:7;
Mk 12:33;
Heb 10:6-9
15:23
m Dt 18:10
n 1Sa 13:13
15:24
o 2Sa 12:13
p Pr 29:25;
Isa 51:12-13
15:25
q Ex 10:17
15:26
r 1Sa 13:14
15:27
s 1Ki 11:11,31
15:28
t 1Sa 28:17;
1Ki 11:31
15:29
u 1Ch 29:11;
Tit 1:2
v Nu 23:19;
Eze 24:14
15:30
w Isa 29:13;
Jn 5:44; 12:43

Agag came to him confidently,[a] thinking, "Surely the bitterness of death is past."

[33]But Samuel said,

"As your sword has made women childless,
    so will your mother be childless among women."[x]

And Samuel put Agag to death before the LORD at Gilgal.

[34]Then Samuel left for Ramah,[y] but Saul went up to his home in Gibeah[z] of Saul. [35]Until the day Samuel[a] died, he did not go to see Saul again, though Samuel mourned[b] for him. And the LORD was grieved that he had made Saul king over Israel.

Samuel Anoints David

16 The LORD said to Samuel, "How long will you mourn[c] for Saul, since I have rejected[d] him as king over Israel? Fill your horn with oil[e] and be on your way; I am sending you to Jesse[f] of Bethlehem. I have chosen[g] one of his sons to be king."

[2]But Samuel said, "How can I go? Saul will hear about it and kill me."

The LORD said, "Take a heifer with you and say, 'I have come to sacrifice to the LORD.' [3]Invite Jesse to the sacrifice, and I will show[h] you what to do. You are to anoint[i] for me the one I indicate."

[4]Samuel did what the LORD said. When he arrived at Bethlehem,[j] the elders of the town trembled when they met him. They asked, "Do you come in peace?[k]"

[5]Samuel replied, "Yes, in peace; I have come to sacrifice to the LORD. Consecrate[l] yourselves and come to the sacrifice with me." Then he consecrated Jesse and his sons and invited them to the sacrifice.

[6]When they arrived, Samuel saw Eliab[m] and thought, "Surely the LORD's anointed stands here before the LORD."

[7]But the LORD said to Samuel, "Do not consider his appearance or his height, for I have rejected him. The LORD does not look at the things man looks at. Man looks at the outward appearance,[n] but the LORD looks at the heart."[o]

[8]Then Jesse called Abinadab[p] and had him pass in front of Samuel. But Samuel said, "The LORD has not chosen this one either." [9]Jesse then had Shammah pass by, but Samuel said, "Nor has the LORD chosen this one." [10]Jesse had seven of his sons pass before Samuel, but Samuel said to him, "The LORD has not chosen these." [11]So he asked Jesse, "Are these all[q] the sons you have?"

"There is still the youngest," Jesse answered, "but he is tending the sheep."

Samuel said, "Send for him; we will not sit down[b] until he arrives."

[12]So he[r] sent and had him brought in. He was ruddy, with a fine appearance and handsome[s] features.

Then the LORD said, "Rise and anoint him; he is the one."

[13]So Samuel took the horn of oil and anointed him in the presence of his brothers, and from that day on the Spirit of the LORD[t] came upon David in power.[u] Samuel then went to Ramah.

---

[a]32 Or *him trembling, yet*   [b]11 Some Septuagint manuscripts; Hebrew *not gather around*

15:33
xGe 9:6;
Jdg 1:7
15:34
y1Sa 7:17
z1Sa 11:4
15:35
a1Sa 19:24
b1Sa 16:1
16:1
c1Sa 15:35
d1Sa 15:23
e2Ki 9:1
fRu 4:17;
1Sa 9:16
g Ps 78:70;
Ac 13:22
16:3
hEx 4:15
iDt 17:15;
1Sa 9:16
16:4
jGe 48:7;
Lk 2:4
k1Ki 2:13;
2Ki 9:17
16:5
lEx 19:10,22
16:6
m1Sa 17:13
16:7
nPs 147:10
o1Ki 8:39;
1Ch 28:9;
Isa 55:8
16:8
p1Sa 17:13
16:11
q1Sa 17:12
16:12
r1Sa 9:17
sGe 39:6;
1Sa 17:42
16:13
tNu 27:18;
Jdg 11:29
u1Sa 10:1,6,
9-10; 11:6

David in Saul's Service

14Now the Spirit of the LORD had departed[v] from Saul, and an evil[a] spirit[w] from the LORD tormented him.

15Saul's attendants said to him, "See, an evil spirit from God is tormenting you. 16Let our lord command his servants here to search for someone who can play the harp.[x] He will play when the evil spirit from God comes upon you, and you will feel better."

17So Saul said to his attendants, "Find someone who plays well and bring him to me."

18One of the servants answered, "I have seen a son of Jesse of Bethlehem who knows how to play the harp. He is a brave man and a warrior. He speaks well and is a fine-looking man. And the LORD is with[y] him."

19Then Saul sent messengers to Jesse and said, "Send me your son David, who is with the sheep." 20So Jesse took a donkey loaded with bread,[z] a skin of wine and a young goat and sent them with his son David to Saul.

21David came to Saul and entered his service.[a] Saul liked him very much, and David became one of his armor-bearers. 22Then Saul sent word to Jesse, saying, "Allow David to remain in my service, for I am pleased with him."

23Whenever the spirit from God came upon Saul, David would take his harp and play. Then relief would come to Saul; he would feel better, and the evil spirit[b] would leave him.

David and Goliath

17 Now the Philistines gathered their forces for war and assembled[c] at Socoh in Judah. They pitched camp at Ephes Dammim, between Socoh[d] and Azekah. 2Saul and the Israelites assembled and camped in the Valley of Elah[e] and drew up their battle line to meet the Philistines. 3The Philistines occupied one hill and the Israelites another, with the valley between them.

4A champion named Goliath,[f] who was from Gath, came out of the Philistine camp. He was over nine feet[b] tall. 5He had a bronze helmet on his head and wore a coat of scale armor of bronze weighing five thousand shekels[c]; 6on his legs he wore bronze greaves, and a bronze javelin[g] was slung on his back. 7His spear shaft was like a weaver's rod,[h] and its iron point weighed six hundred shekels.[d] His shield bearer[i] went ahead of him.

8Goliath stood and shouted to the ranks of Israel, "Why do you come out and line up for battle? Am I not a Philistine, and are you not the servants of Saul? Choose[j] a man and have him come down to me. 9If he is able to fight and kill me, we will become your subjects; but if I overcome him and kill him, you will become our subjects and serve us." 10Then the Philistine said, "This day I defy[k] the ranks of Israel! Give me a man and let us fight each other." 11On hearing the Philistine's words, Saul and all the Israelites were dismayed and terrified.

12Now David was the son of an Ephrathite named Jesse,[l] who was

---

16:14
v Jdg 16:20
w Jdg 9:23;
1Sa 18:10
16:16
x ver 23;
1Sa 18:10;
19:9; 2Ki 3:15
16:18
y 1Sa 3:19;
17:32-37
16:20
z 1Sa 10:27;
Pr 18:16
16:21
a Ge 41:46;
Pr 22:29
16:23
b ver 14-16
17:1
c 1Sa 13:5
d Jos 15:35;
2Ch 28:18
17:2
e 1Sa 21:9
17:4
f Jos 11:21-22;
2Sa 21:19
17:6
g ver 45
17:7
h 2Sa 21:19
i ver 41
17:8
j 1Sa 8:17
17:10
k ver 26,45;
2Sa 21:21
17:12
l Ru 4:17;
1Ch 2:13-15

---

a14 Or *injurious*; also in verses 15, 16 and 23   b4 Hebrew *was six cubits and a span* (about 3 meters)   c5 That is, about 125 pounds (about 57 kilograms)   d7 That is, about 15 pounds (about 7 kilograms) from Bethlehem ᵐ in Judah. Jesse had eight ⁿ sons, and in Saul's time he was old and well advanced in years. ¹³Jesse's three oldest sons had followed Saul to the war: The firstborn was Eliab; ᵒ the second, Abinadab; and the third, Shammah. ᵖ ¹⁴David was the youngest. The three oldest followed Saul, ¹⁵but David went back and forth from Saul to tend his father's sheep ᑫ at Bethlehem.

¹⁶For forty days the Philistine came forward every morning and evening and took his stand.

¹⁷Now Jesse said to his son David, "Take this ephah ᵃ of roasted grain ʳ and these ten loaves of bread for your brothers and hurry to their camp. ¹⁸Take along these ten cheeses to the commander of their unit. ᵇ See how your brothers ˢ are and bring back some assurance ᶜ from them. ¹⁹They are with Saul and all the men of Israel in the Valley of Elah, fighting against the Philistines."

²⁰Early in the morning David left the flock with a shepherd, loaded up and set out, as Jesse had directed. He reached the camp as the army was going out to its battle positions, shouting the war cry. ²¹Israel and the Philistines were drawing up their lines facing each other. ²²David left his things with the keeper of supplies, ran to the battle lines and greeted his brothers. ²³As he was talking with them, Goliath, the Philistine champion from Gath, stepped out from his lines and shouted his usual ᵗ defiance, and David heard it. ²⁴When the Israelites saw the man, they all ran from him in great fear.

²⁵Now the Israelites had been saying, "Do you see how this man keeps coming out? He comes out to defy Israel. The king will give great wealth to the man who kills him. He will also give him his daughter ᵘ in marriage and will exempt his father's family from taxes in Israel."

²⁶David asked the men standing near him, "What will be done for the man who kills this Philistine and removes this disgrace ᵛ from Israel? Who is this uncircumcised ʷ Philistine that he should defy ˣ the armies of the living ʸ God?"

²⁷They repeated to him what they had been saying and told him, "This is what will be done for the man who kills him."

²⁸When Eliab, David's oldest brother, heard him speaking with the men, he burned with anger ᶻ at him and asked, "Why have you come down here? And with whom did you leave those few sheep in the desert? I know how conceited you are and how wicked your heart is; you came down only to watch the battle."

²⁹"Now what have I done?" said David. "Can't I even speak?" ³⁰He then turned away to someone else and brought up the same matter, and the men answered him as before. ³¹What David said was overheard and reported to Saul, and Saul sent for him.

³²David said to Saul, "Let no one lose heart ᵃ on account of this Philistine; your servant will go and fight him."

³³Saul replied, ᵇ "You are not able to go out against this Philistine and fight him; you are only a boy, and he has been a fighting man from his youth."

³⁴But David said to Saul, "Your servant has been keeping his father's sheep. When a lion ᶜ or a bear came and carried off a sheep from the

17:12
m Ge 35:19
n 1Sa 16:11
17:13
o 1Sa 16:6
p 1Sa 16:9
17:15
q 1Sa 16:19
17:17
r 1Sa 25:18
17:18
s Ge 37:14
17:23
t ver 8-10
17:25
u Jos 15:16;
1Sa 18:17
17:26
v 1Sa 11:2
w 1Sa 14:6
x ver 10 y Dt 5:26
17:28
z Ge 37:4,8,11;
Pr 18:19;
Mt 10:36
17:32
a Dt 20:3;
1Sa 16:18
17:33
b Nu 13:31
17:34
c Jer 49:19;
Am 3:12

ᵃ17 That is, probably about 3/5 bushel (about 22 liters)   ᵇ18 Hebrew *thousand*   ᶜ18 Or *some token; or some pledge of spoils* flock, 35I went after it, struck it and rescued the sheep from its mouth. When it turned on me, I seized it by its hair, struck it and killed it. 36Your servant has killed both the lion and the bear; this uncircumcised Philistine will be like one of them, because he has defied the armies of the living God. 37The LORD who delivered[d] me from the paw of the lion[e] and the paw of the bear will deliver me from the hand of this Philistine."

Saul said to David, "Go, and the LORD be with[f] you."

38Then Saul dressed David in his own tunic. He put a coat of armor on him and a bronze helmet on his head. 39David fastened on his sword over the tunic and tried walking around, because he was not used to them.

"I cannot go in these," he said to Saul, "because I am not used to them." So he took them off. 40Then he took his staff in his hand, chose five smooth stones from the stream, put them in the pouch of his shepherd's bag and, with his sling in his hand, approached the Philistine.

41Meanwhile, the Philistine, with his shield bearer in front of him, kept coming closer to David. 42He looked David over and saw that he was only a boy, ruddy and handsome,[g] and he despised[h] him. 43He said to David, "Am I a dog,[i] that you come at me with sticks?" And the Philistine cursed David by his gods. 44"Come here," he said, "and I'll give your flesh to the birds of the air and the beasts of the field![j]"

45David said to the Philistine, "You come against me with sword and spear and javelin, but I come against you in the name[k] of the LORD Almighty, the God of the armies of Israel, whom you have defied.[l] 46This day the LORD will hand you over to me, and I'll strike you down and cut off your head. Today I will give the carcasses[m] of the Philistine army to the birds of the air and the beasts of the earth, and the whole world[n] will know that there is a God in Israel.[o] 47All those gathered here will know that it is not by sword[p] or spear that the LORD saves;[q] for the battle[r] is the LORD's, and he will give all of you into our hands."

48As the Philistine moved closer to attack him, David ran quickly toward the battle line to meet him. 49Reaching into his bag and taking out a stone, he slung it and struck the Philistine on the forehead. The stone sank into his forehead, and he fell facedown on the ground.

50So David triumphed over the Philistine with a sling[s] and a stone; without a sword in his hand he struck down the Philistine and killed him.

51David ran and stood over him. He took hold of the Philistine's sword and drew it from the scabbard. After he killed him, he cut[t] off his head with the sword.[u]

When the Philistines saw that their hero was dead, they turned and ran. 52Then the men of Israel and Judah surged forward with a shout and pursued the Philistines to the entrance of Gath[a] and to the gates of Ekron.[v] Their dead were strewn along the Shaaraim[w] road to Gath and Ekron. 53When the Israelites returned from chasing the Philistines, they plundered their camp. 54David took the Philistine's head and brought it to Jerusalem, and he put the Philistine's weapons in his own tent.

55As Saul watched David[x] going out to meet the Philistine, he said to

17:37
d 2Co 1:10
e 2Ti 4:17
f 1Sa 20:13;
1Ch 22:11,16
17:42
g 1Sa 16:12
h Ps 123:3-4;
Pr 16:18
17:43
i 1Sa 24:14;
2Sa 3:8; 9:8;
2Ki 8:13
17:44
j 1Ki 20:10-11
17:45
k 2Sa 22:33,35;
2Ch 32:8;
Ps 124:8;
Heb 11:32-34
l ver 10
17:46
m Dt 28:26
n Jos 4:24;
1Ki 8:43;
Isa 52:10
o 1Ki 18:36;
2Ki 19:19;
Isa 37:20
17:47
p Hos 1:7;
Zec 4:6
q 1Sa 14:6;
2Ch 14:11
r 2Ch 20:15;
Ps 44:6-7
17:50
s 2Sa 23:21
17:51
t Heb 11:34
u 1Sa 21:9
17:52
v Jos 15:11
w Jos 15:36
17:55
x 1Sa 16:21

---

a52 Some Septuagint manuscripts; Hebrew *a valley*

Abner, commander of the army, "Abner, whose son is that young man?"

Abner replied, "As surely as you live, O king, I don't know."

⁵⁶The king said, "Find out whose son this young man is."

⁵⁷As soon as David returned from killing the Philistine, Abner took him and brought him before Saul, with David still holding the Philistine's head.

⁵⁸"Whose son are you, young man?" Saul asked him.

David said, "I am the son of your servant Jesseʸ of Bethlehem."

Saul's Jealousy of David

18 After David had finished talking with Saul, Jonathan became one in spirit with David, and he lovedᶻ him as himself.ᵃ ²From that day Saul kept David with him and did not let him return to his father's house. ³And Jonathan made a covenantᵇ with David because he loved him as himself. ⁴Jonathan took off the robeᶜ he was wearing and gave it to David, along with his tunic, and even his sword, his bow and his belt.

⁵Whatever Saul sent him to do, David did it so successfullyᵃ that Saul gave him a high rank in the army. This pleased all the people, and Saul's officers as well.

⁶When the men were returning home after David had killed the Philistine, the women came out from all the towns of Israel to meet King Saul with singing and dancing,ᵈ with joyful songs and with tambourinesᵉ and lutes. ⁷As they danced, they sang:ᶠ

"Saul has slain his thousands,
    and David his tensᵍ of thousands."

⁸Saul was very angry; this refrain galled him. "They have credited David with tens of thousands," he thought, "but me with only thousands. What more can he get but the kingdom?ʰ" ⁹And from that time on Saul kept a jealous eye on David.

¹⁰The next day an evilᵇ spiritⁱ from God came forcefully upon Saul. He was prophesying in his house, while David was playing the harp, as he usuallyʲ did. Saul had a spear in his hand ¹¹and he hurled it, saying to himself,ᵏ "I'll pin David to the wall." But David eludedˡ him twice.

¹²Saul was afraidᵐ of David, because the LORDⁿ was withᵒ David but had left Saul. ¹³So he sent David away from him and gave him command over a thousand men, and David ledᵖ the troops in their campaigns.�q ¹⁴In everything he did he had great success,ᶜʳ because the LORD was withˢ him. ¹⁵When Saul saw how successfulᵈ he was, he was afraid of him. ¹⁶But all Israel and Judah loved David, because he led them in their campaigns.ᵗ

¹⁷Saul said to David, "Here is my older daughterᵘ Merab. I will give her to you in marriage; only serve me bravely and fight the battlesᵛ of the LORD." For Saul said to himself,ʷ "I will not raise a hand against him. Let the Philistines do that!"

¹⁸But David said to Saul, "Who am I,ˣ and what is my family or my father's clan in Israel, that I should become the king's son-in-law?ʸ"

17:58
yver 12
18:1
z2Sa 1:26
aGe 44:30
18:3
b1Sa 20:8,16,
17,42
18:4
cGe 41:42
18:6
dEx 15:20
eJdg 11:34;
Ps 68:25
18:7
f1Sa 15:21
g1Sa 21:11;
29:5
18:8
h1Sa 15:8
18:10
i1Sa 16:14
j1Sa 19:7
18:11
k1Sa 20:7,33
l1Sa 19:10
18:12
mver 15,29
n1Sa 16:13
o1Sa 28:15
18:13
pver 16;
Nu 27:17
q2Sa 5:2
18:14
rGe 39:3
s Ge 39:2,23;
Jos 6:27;
1Sa 16:18
18:16
tver 5
18:17
u1Sa 17:25
vNu 21:14;
1Sa 25:28
wver 25
18:18
x1Sa 9:21;
2Sa 7:18
yver 23

ᵃ5 Or *wisely*   ᵇ10 Or *injurious*   ᶜ14 Or *he was very wise*   ᵈ15 Or *wise*

[19]So[a] when the time came for Merab,[z] Saul's daughter, to be given to David, she was given in marriage to Adriel of Meholah.[a]

[20]Now Saul's daughter Michal[b] was in love with David, and when they told Saul about it, he was pleased. [21]"I will give her to him," he thought, "so that she may be a snare[c] to him and so that the hand of the Philistines may be against him." So Saul said to David, "Now you have a second opportunity to become my son-in-law."

[22]Then Saul ordered his attendants: "Speak to David privately and say, 'Look, the king is pleased with you, and his attendants all like you; now become his son-in-law.'"

[23]They repeated these words to David. But David said, "Do you think it is a small matter to become the king's son-in-law? I'm only a poor man and little known."

[24]When Saul's servants told him what David had said, [25]Saul replied, "Say to David, 'The king wants no other price[d] for the bride than a hundred Philistine foreskins, to take revenge on his enemies.'" Saul's plan[e] was to have David fall by the hands of the Philistines.

[26]When the attendants told David these things, he was pleased to become the king's son-in-law. So before the allotted time elapsed, [27]David and his men went out and killed two hundred Philistines. He brought their foreskins and presented the full number to the king so that he might become the king's son-in-law. Then Saul gave him his daughter Michal[f] in marriage.

[28]When Saul realized that the LORD was with David and that his daughter Michal loved David, [29]Saul became still more afraid of him, and he remained his enemy the rest of his days.

[30]The Philistine commanders continued to go out to battle, and as often as they did, David met with more success[b][g] than the rest of Saul's officers, and his name became well known.

Saul Tries to Kill David

19 Saul told his son Jonathan[h] and all the attendants to kill[i] David. But Jonathan was very fond of David [2]and warned him, "My father Saul is looking for a chance to kill you. Be on your guard tomorrow morning; go into hiding and stay there. [3]I will go out and stand with my father in the field where you are. I'll speak[j] to him about you and will tell you what I find out."

[4]Jonathan spoke[k] well of David to Saul his father and said to him, "Let not the king do wrong[l] to his servant David; he has not wronged you, and what he has done has benefited you greatly. [5]He took his life in his hands when he killed the Philistine. The LORD won a great victory[m] for all Israel, and you saw it and were glad. Why then would you do wrong to an innocent[n] man like David by killing him for no reason?"

[6]Saul listened to Jonathan and took this oath: "As surely as the LORD lives, David will not be put to death."

[7]So Jonathan called David and told him the whole conversation. He brought him to Saul, and David was with Saul as before.[o]

[8]Once more war broke out, and David went out and fought the Philistines. He struck them with such force that they fled before him.

Side references

18:19
z 2Sa 21:8
a Jdg 7:22
18:20
b ver 28
18:21
c ver 17,26
18:25
d Ge 34:12;
Ex 22:17;
1Sa 14:24
e ver 17
18:27
f ver 13;
2Sa 3:14
18:30
g ver 5; 2Sa 11:1
19:1
h 1Sa 18:1
i 1Sa 18:9
19:3
j 1Sa 20:12
19:4
k 1Sa 20:32;
Pr 31:8,9;
Jer 18:20
l Ge 42:22;
Pr 17:13
19:5
m 1Sa 11:13;
17:49-50;
1Ch 11:14
n Dt 19:10-13;
1Sa 20:32;
Mt 27:4
19:7
o 1Sa 16:21;
18:2,13

---

[a]19 Or *However*,   [b]30 Or *David acted more wisely*

⁹But an evil*ᵃ* spirit*ᵖ* from the LORD came upon Saul as he was sitting in his house with his spear in his hand. While David was playing the harp, ¹⁰Saul tried to pin him to the wall with his spear, but David eluded*�q* him as Saul drove the spear into the wall. That night David made good his escape.

¹¹Saul sent men to David's house to watch*ʳ* it and to kill him in the morning. But Michal, David's wife, warned him, "If you don't run for your life tonight, tomorrow you'll be killed." ¹²So Michal let David down through a window,*ˢ* and he fled and escaped. ¹³Then Michal took an idol*ᵇ* and laid it on the bed, covering it with a garment and putting some goats' hair at the head.

¹⁴When Saul sent the men to capture David, Michal said,*ᵗ* "He is ill."

¹⁵Then Saul sent the men back to see David and told them, "Bring him up to me in his bed so that I may kill him." ¹⁶But when the men entered, there was the idol in the bed, and at the head was some goats' hair.

¹⁷Saul said to Michal, "Why did you deceive me like this and send my enemy away so that he escaped?"

Michal told him, "He said to me, 'Let me get away. Why should I kill you?' "

¹⁸When David had fled and made his escape, he went to Samuel at Ramah*ᵘ* and told him all that Saul had done to him. Then he and Samuel went to Naioth and stayed there. ¹⁹Word came to Saul: "David is in Naioth at Ramah"; ²⁰so he sent men to capture him. But when they saw a group of prophets*ᵛ* prophesying, with Samuel standing there as their leader, the Spirit of God came upon*ʷ* Saul's men and they also prophesied.*ˣ* ²¹Saul was told about it, and he sent more men, and they prophesied too. Saul sent men a third time, and they also prophesied. ²²Finally, he himself left for Ramah and went to the great cistern at Secu. And he asked, "Where are Samuel and David?"

"Over in Naioth at Ramah," they said.

²³So Saul went to Naioth at Ramah. But the Spirit of God came even upon him, and he walked along prophesying*ʸ* until he came to Naioth. ²⁴He stripped*ᶻ* off his robes and also prophesied in Samuel's presence. He lay that way all that day and night. This is why people say, "Is Saul also among the prophets?"*ᵃ*

David and Jonathan

20 Then David fled from Naioth at Ramah and went to Jonathan and asked, "What have I done? What is my crime? How have I wronged*ᵇ* your father, that he is trying to take my life?"

²"Never!" Jonathan replied. "You are not going to die! Look, my father doesn't do anything, great or small, without confiding in me. Why would he hide this from me? It's not so!"

³But David took an oath*ᶜ* and said, "Your father knows very well that I have found favor in your eyes, and he has said to himself, 'Jonathan must not know this or he will be grieved.' Yet as surely as the LORD lives and as you live, there is only a step between me and death."

⁴Jonathan said to David, "Whatever you want me to do, I'll do for you."

ᵃ9 Or injurious   *ᵇ13 Hebrew teraphim; also in verse 16*

19:9
ᵖ1Sa 16:14;
18:10-11
19:10
q1Sa 18:11
19:11
ʳPs 59 Title
19:12
ˢJos 2:15;
Ac 9:25
19:14
ᵗJos 2:4
19:18
ᵘ1Sa 7:17
19:20
ᵛver 11,14;
Jn 7:32,45
ʷNu 11:25
ˣ1Sa 10:5;
Joel 2:28
19:23
ʸ1Sa 10:13
19:24
ᶻ2Sa 6:20;
Isa 20:2;
Mic 1:8
ᵃ1Sa 10:11
20:1
ᵇ1Sa 24:9
20:3
ᶜDt 6:13

[5]So David said, "Look, tomorrow is the New Moon festival,[d] and I am supposed to dine with the king; but let me go and hide[e] in the field until the evening of the day after tomorrow. [6]If your father misses me at all, tell him, 'David earnestly asked my permission to hurry to Bethlehem,[f] his hometown, because an annual[g] sacrifice is being made there for his whole clan.' [7]If he says, 'Very well,' then your servant is safe. But if he loses his temper,[h] you can be sure that he is determined to harm me. [8]As for you, show kindness to your servant, for you have brought him into a covenant[i] with you before the LORD. If I am guilty, then kill[j] me yourself! Why hand me over to your father?"

[9]"Never!" Jonathan said. "If I had the least inkling that my father was determined to harm you, wouldn't I tell you?"

[10]David asked, "Who will tell me if your father answers you harshly?"

[11]"Come," Jonathan said, "let's go out into the field." So they went there together.

[12]Then Jonathan said to David: "By the LORD, the God of Israel, I will surely sound out my father by this time the day after tomorrow! If he is favorably disposed toward you, will I not send you word and let you know? [13]But if my father is inclined to harm you, may the LORD deal with me, be it ever so severely,[k] if I do not let you know and send you away safely. May the LORD be with[l] you as he has been with my father. [14]But show me unfailing kindness like that of the LORD as long as I live, so that I may not be killed, [15]and do not ever cut off your kindness from my family[m]—not even when the LORD has cut off every one of David's enemies from the face of the earth."

[16]So Jonathan made a covenant[n] with the house of David, saying, "May the LORD call David's enemies to account." [17]And Jonathan had David reaffirm his oath[o] out of love for him, because he loved him as he loved himself.

[18]Then Jonathan said to David: "Tomorrow is the New Moon festival. You will be missed, because your seat will be empty.[p] [19]The day after tomorrow, toward evening, go to the place where you hid[q] when this trouble began, and wait by the stone Ezel. [20]I will shoot three arrows to the side of it, as though I were shooting at a target. [21]Then I will send a boy and say, 'Go, find the arrows.' If I say to him, 'Look, the arrows are on this side of you; bring them here,' then come, because, as surely as the LORD lives, you are safe; there is no danger. [22]But if I say to the boy, 'Look, the arrows are beyond[r] you,' then you must go, because the LORD has sent you away. [23]And about the matter you and I discussed —remember, the LORD is witness[s] between you and me forever."

[24]So David hid in the field, and when the New Moon festival came, the king sat down to eat. [25]He sat in his customary place by the wall, opposite Jonathan,[a] and Abner sat next to Saul, but David's place was empty.[t] [26]Saul said nothing that day, for he thought, "Something must have happened to David to make him ceremonially unclean—surely he is unclean.[u]" [27]But the next day, the second day of the month, David's place was empty again. Then Saul said to his son Jonathan, "Why hasn't the son of Jesse come to the meal, either yesterday or today?"

[28]Jonathan answered, "David earnestly asked me for permission[v] to

20:5
d Nu 10:10;
28:11 e 1Sa 19:2

20:6
f 1Sa 17:58
g Dt 12:5

20:7
h 1Sa 25:17

20:8
i 1Sa 18:3; 23:18
j 2Sa 14:32

20:13
k Ru 1:17;
1Sa 3:17
l Jos 1:5;
1Sa 17:37;
18:12;
1Ch 22:11,16

20:15
m 2Sa 9:7

20:16
n 1Sa 25:22

20:17
o 1Sa 18:3

20:18
p ver 5,25

20:19
q 1Sa 19:2

20:22
r ver 37

20:23
s ver 14-15;
Ge 31:50

20:25
t ver 18

20:26
u Lev 7:20-21;
15:5; 1Sa 16:5

20:28
v ver 6

---

[a]25 Septuagint; Hebrew *wall. Jonathan arose*

go to Bethlehem. [29]He said, 'Let me go, because our family is observing a sacrifice in the town and my brother has ordered me to be there. If I have found favor in your eyes, let me get away to see my brothers.' That is why he has not come to the king's table."

[30]Saul's anger flared up at Jonathan and he said to him, "You son of a perverse and rebellious woman! Don't I know that you have sided with the son of Jesse to your own shame and to the shame of the mother who bore you? [31]As long as the son of Jesse lives on this earth, neither you nor your kingdom will be established. Now send and bring him to me, for he must die!"

[32]"Why[w] should he be put to death? What[x] has he done?" Jonathan asked his father. [33]But Saul hurled his spear at him to kill him. Then Jonathan knew that his father intended[y] to kill David.

[34]Jonathan got up from the table in fierce anger; on that second day of the month he did not eat, because he was grieved at his father's shameful treatment of David.

[35]In the morning Jonathan went out to the field for his meeting with David. He had a small boy with him, [36]and he said to the boy, "Run and find the arrows I shoot." As the boy ran, he shot an arrow beyond him. [37]When the boy came to the place where Jonathan's arrow had fallen, Jonathan called out after him, "Isn't the arrow beyond[z] you?" [38]Then he shouted, "Hurry! Go quickly! Don't stop!" The boy picked up the arrow and returned to his master. [39](The boy knew nothing of all this; only Jonathan and David knew.) [40]Then Jonathan gave his weapons to the boy and said, "Go, carry them back to town."

[41]After the boy had gone, David got up from the south side of the stone, and bowed down before Jonathan three times, with his face to the ground. Then they kissed each other and wept together—but David wept the most.

[42]Jonathan said to David, "Go in peace,[a] for we have sworn friendship[b] with each other in the name of the LORD, saying, 'The LORD is witness between you and me, and between your descendants and my descendants forever.'" Then David left, and Jonathan went back to the town.

David at Nob

21 David went to Nob,[c] to Ahimelech the priest. Ahimelech trembled[d] when he met him, and asked, "Why are you alone? Why is no one with you?"

[2]David answered Ahimelech the priest, "The king charged me with a certain matter and said to me, 'No one is to know anything about your mission and your instructions.' As for my men, I have told them to meet me at a certain place. [3]Now then, what do you have on hand? Give me five loaves of bread, or whatever you can find."

[4]But the priest answered David, "I don't have any ordinary bread[e] on hand; however, there is some consecrated[f] bread here—provided the men have kept[g] themselves from women."

[5]David replied, "Indeed women have been kept from us, as usual whenever[a] I set out. The men's things[b] are holy[h] even on missions that are not holy. How much more so today!" [6]So the priest gave him the

---

20:32
w1Sa 19:4;
Mt 27:23
xGe 31:36;
Lk 23:22
20:33
yver 7;
1Sa 18:11,17
20:37
zver 22
20:42
aver 22;
1Sa 1:17
b2Sa 1:26;
Pr 18:24
21:1
c1Sa 14:3; 22:9,
19; Ne 11:32;
Isa 10:32
d1Sa 16:4
21:4
eLev 24:8-9
fEx 25:30;
Mt 12:4
gEx 19:15
21:5
h1Th 4:4

---

a5 Or from us in the past few days since　　　*b5 Or bodies*

consecrated bread,[i] since there was no bread there except the bread of the Presence that had been removed from before the LORD and replaced by hot bread on the day it was taken away.

[7]Now one of Saul's servants was there that day, detained before the LORD; he was Doeg[j] the Edomite,[k] Saul's head shepherd.

[8]David asked Ahimelech, "Don't you have a spear or a sword here? I haven't brought my sword or any other weapon, because the king's business was urgent."

[9]The priest replied, "The sword[l] of Goliath the Philistine, whom you killed in the Valley of Elah,[m] is here; it is wrapped in a cloth behind the ephod. If you want it, take it; there is no sword here but that one."

David said, "There is none like it; give it to me."

David at Gath

[10]That day David fled from Saul and went[n] to Achish king of Gath. [11]But the servants of Achish said to him, "Isn't this David, the king of the land? Isn't he the one they sing about in their dances:

> " 'Saul has slain his thousands,
>   and David his tens of thousands'?"[o]

[12]David took these words to heart and was very much afraid of Achish king of Gath. [13]So he pretended to be insane[p] in their presence; and while he was in their hands he acted like a madman, making marks on the doors of the gate and letting saliva run down his beard.

[14]Achish said to his servants, "Look at the man! He is insane! Why bring him to me? [15]Am I so short of madmen that you have to bring this fellow here to carry on like this in front of me? Must this man come into my house?"

David at Adullam and Mizpah

22 David left Gath and escaped to the cave[q] of Adullam. When his brothers and his father's household heard about it, they went down to him there. [2]All those who were in distress or in debt or discontented gathered[r] around him, and he became their leader. About four hundred men were with him.

[3]From there David went to Mizpah in Moab and said to the king of Moab, "Would you let my father and mother come and stay with you until I learn what God will do for me?" [4]So he left them with the king of Moab, and they stayed with him as long as David was in the stronghold.

[5]But the prophet Gad[s] said to David, "Do not stay in the stronghold. Go into the land of Judah." So David left and went to the forest of Hereth.

Saul Kills the Priests of Nob

[6]Now Saul heard that David and his men had been discovered. And Saul, spear in hand, was seated[t] under the tamarisk[u] tree on the hill at Gibeah, with all his officials standing around him. [7]Saul said to them, "Listen, men of Benjamin! Will the son of Jesse give all of you fields and vineyards? Will he make all of you commanders[v] of thousands and commanders of hundreds? [8]Is that why you have all conspired against me? No one tells me when my son makes a covenant[w] with the son of

Jesse. None of you is concerned[x] about me or tells me that my son has incited my servant to lie in wait for me, as he does today."

[9]But Doeg[y] the Edomite, who was standing with Saul's officials, said, "I saw the son of Jesse come to Ahimelech son of Ahitub at Nob.[z] [10]Ahimelech inquired[a] of the Lord for him; he also gave him provisions[b] and the sword of Goliath the Philistine."

[11]Then the king sent for the priest Ahimelech son of Ahitub and his father's whole family, who were the priests at Nob, and they all came to the king. [12]Saul said, "Listen now, son of Ahitub."

"Yes, my lord," he answered.

[13]Saul said to him, "Why have you conspired[c] against me, you and the son of Jesse, giving him bread and a sword and inquiring of God for him, so that he has rebelled against me and lies in wait for me, as he does today?"

[14]Ahimelech answered the king, "Who[d] of all your servants is as loyal as David, the king's son-in-law, captain of your bodyguard and highly respected in your household? [15]Was that day the first time I inquired of God for him? Of course not! Let not the king accuse your servant or any of his father's family, for your servant knows nothing at all about this whole affair."

[16]But the king said, "You will surely die, Ahimelech, you and your father's whole family."

[17]Then the king ordered the guards at his side: "Turn and kill the priests of the Lord, because they too have sided with David. They knew he was fleeing, yet they did not tell me."

But the king's officials were not willing[e] to raise a hand to strike the priests of the Lord.

[18]The king then ordered Doeg, "You turn and strike down the priests." So Doeg the Edomite turned and struck them down. That day he killed eighty-five men who wore the linen ephod.[f] [19]He also put to the sword[g] Nob, the town of the priests, with its men and women, its children and infants, and its cattle, donkeys and sheep.

[20]But Abiathar,[h] a son of Ahimelech son of Ahitub, escaped and fled to join David.[i] [21]He told David that Saul had killed the priests of the Lord. [22]Then David said to Abiathar: "That day, when Doeg[j] the Edomite was there, I knew he would be sure to tell Saul. I am responsible for the death of your father's whole family. [23]Stay with me; don't be afraid; the man who is seeking your life[k] is seeking mine also. You will be safe with me."

David Saves Keilah

23 When David was told, "Look, the Philistines are fighting against Keilah[l] and are looting the threshing floors," [2]he inquired[m] of the Lord, saying, "Shall I go and attack these Philistines?"

The Lord answered him, "Go, attack the Philistines and save Keilah."

[3]But David's men said to him, "Here in Judah we are afraid. How much more, then, if we go to Keilah against the Philistine forces!"

[4]Once again David inquired of the Lord, and the Lord answered him, "Go down to Keilah, for I am going to give the Philistines into your hand.[n]" [5]So David and his men went to Keilah, fought the Philistines and carried off their livestock. He inflicted heavy losses on the

22:8
x1Sa 23:21
22:9
y1Sa 21:7; Ps 52
Title z1Sa 21:1
22:10
aNu 27:21;
1Sa 10:22
b1Sa 21:6
22:13
cver 8
22:14
d1Sa 19:4
22:17
eEx 1:17
22:18
f1Sa 2:18,31
22:19
g1Sa 15:3
22:20
h1Sa 23:6,9;
30:7; 1Ki 2:22,
26,27 i1Sa 2:32
22:22
j1Sa 21:7
22:23
k1Ki 2:26
23:1
lJos 15:44
23:2
mver 4,12;
1Sa 30:8;
2Sa 5:19,23
23:4
nJos 8:7;
Jdg 7:7

Philistines and saved the people of Keilah. ⁶(Now Abiathar° son of Ahimelech had brought the ephod down with him when he fled to David at Keilah.)

Saul Pursues David

⁷Saul was told that David had gone to Keilah, and he said, "God has handed him over to me, for David has imprisoned himself by entering a town with gates and bars." ⁸And Saul called up all his forces for battle, to go down to Keilah to besiege David and his men.

⁹When David learned that Saul was plotting against him, he said to Abiatharᵖ the priest, "Bring the ephod." ¹⁰David said, "O LORD, God of Israel, your servant has heard definitely that Saul plans to come to Keilah and destroy the town on account of me. ¹¹Will the citizens of Keilah surrender me to him? Will Saul come down, as your servant has heard? O LORD, God of Israel, tell your servant."

And the LORD said, "He will."

¹²Again David asked, "Will the citizens of Keilah surrender�q me and my men to Saul?"

And the LORD said, "They will."

¹³So David and his men,ʳ about six hundred in number, left Keilah and kept moving from place to place. When Saul was told that David had escaped from Keilah, he did not go there.

¹⁴David stayed in the desert strongholds and in the hills of the Desert of Ziph.ˢ Day after day Saul searchedᵗ for him, but God did notᵘ give David into his hands.

¹⁵While David was at Horesh in the Desert of Ziph, he learned that Saul had come out to take his life. ¹⁶And Saul's son Jonathan went to David at Horesh and helped him find strengthᵛ in God. ¹⁷"Don't be afraid," he said. "My father Saul will not lay a hand on you. You will be kingʷ over Israel, and I will be second to you. Even my father Saul knows this." ¹⁸The two of them made a covenantˣ before the LORD. Then Jonathan went home, but David remained at Horesh.

¹⁹The Ziphitesʸ went up to Saul at Gibeah and said, "Is not David hiding among usᶻ in the strongholds at Horesh, on the hill of Hakilah,ᵃ south of Jeshimon? ²⁰Now, O king, come down whenever it pleases you to do so, and we will be responsible for handingᵇ him over to the king."

²¹Saul replied, "The LORD bless you for your concernᶜ for me. ²²Go and make further preparation. Find out where David usually goes and who has seen him there. They tell me he is very crafty. ²³Find out about all the hiding places he uses and come back to me with definite information.ᵃ Then I will go with you; if he is in the area, I will track him down among all the clans of Judah."

²⁴So they set out and went to Ziph ahead of Saul. Now David and his men were in the Desert of Maon,ᵈ in the Arabah south of Jeshimon. ²⁵Saul and his men began the search, and when David was told about it, he went down to the rock and stayed in the Desert of Maon. When Saul heard this, he went into the Desert of Maon in pursuit of David. ²⁶Saulᵉ was going along one side of the mountain, and David and his men were on the other side, hurrying to get away from Saul. As Saul

ᵃ23 Or me at Nacon

### Cross references (margin)

23:6
o 1Sa 22:20
23:9
p ver 6;
1Sa 22:20; 30:7
23:12
q ver 20
23:13
r 1Sa 22:2; 25:13
23:14
s Jos 15:24,55
t Ps 54:3-4
u Ps 32:7
23:16
v 1Sa 30:6
23:17
w 1Sa 20:31;
24:20
23:18
x 1Sa 18:3;
20:16,42;
2Sa 9:1; 21:7
23:19
y 1Sa 26:1 z Ps 54
Title a 1Sa 26:3
23:20
b ver 12
23:21
c 1Sa 22:8
23:24
d Jos 15:55;
1Sa 25:2
23:26
e Ps 17:9

and his forces were closing in on David and his men to capture them, [27]a messenger came to Saul, saying, "Come quickly! The Philistines are raiding the land." [28]Then Saul broke off his pursuit of David and went to meet the Philistines. That is why they call this place Sela Hammahlekoth.[a] [29]And David went up from there and lived in the strongholds of En Gedi.[f]

David Spares Saul's Life

24 After Saul returned from pursuing the Philistines, he was told, "David is in the Desert of En Gedi.[g]" [2]So Saul took three thousand chosen men from all Israel and set out to look[h] for David and his men near the Crags of the Wild Goats.

[3]He came to the sheep pens along the way; a cave[i] was there, and Saul went in to relieve[j] himself. David and his men were far back in the cave. [4]The men said, "This is the day the LORD spoke[k] of when he said[b] to you, 'I will give your enemy into your hands for you to deal with as you wish.'"[l] Then David crept up unnoticed and cut off a corner of Saul's robe.

[5]Afterward, David was conscience-stricken[m] for having cut off a corner of his robe. [6]He said to his men, "The LORD forbid that I should do such a thing to my master, the LORD's anointed,[n] or lift my hand against him; for he is the anointed of the LORD." [7]With these words David rebuked his men and did not allow them to attack Saul. And Saul left the cave and went his way.

[8]Then David went out of the cave and called out to Saul, "My lord the king!" When Saul looked behind him, David bowed down and prostrated himself with his face to the ground.[o] [9]He said to Saul, "Why do you listen when men say, 'David is bent on harming you'? [10]This day you have seen with your own eyes how the LORD delivered you into my hands in the cave. Some urged me to kill you, but I spared you; I said, 'I will not lift my hand against my master, because he is the LORD's anointed.' [11]See, my father, look at this piece of your robe in my hand! I cut off the corner of your robe but did not kill you. Now understand and recognize that I am not guilty[p] of wrongdoing or rebellion. I have not wronged you, but you are hunting[q] me down to take my life. [12]May the LORD judge[r] between you and me. And may the LORD avenge[s] the wrongs you have done to me, but my hand will not touch you. [13]As the old saying goes, 'From evildoers come evil deeds,'[t] so my hand will not touch you.

[14]"Against whom has the king of Israel come out? Whom are you pursuing? A dead dog?[u] A flea?[v] [15]May the LORD be our judge[w] and decide between us. May he consider my cause and uphold[x] it; may he vindicate[y] me by delivering[z] me from your hand."

[16]When David finished saying this, Saul asked, "Is that your voice,[a] David my son?" And he wept aloud. [17]"You are more righteous than I,"[b] he said. "You have treated me well,[c] but I have treated you badly. [18]You have just now told me of the good you did to me; the LORD delivered[d] me into your hands, but you did not kill me. [19]When a man finds his enemy, does he let him get away unharmed? May the LORD reward you well for the way you treated me today. [20]I know that you

---

23:29
f 2Ch 20:2

24:1
g 1Sa 23:28-29

24:2
h 1Sa 26:2

24:3
i Ps 57 Title; 142 Title j Jdg 3:24

24:4
k 1Sa 25:28-30 l 1Sa 23:17; 26:8

24:5
m 2Sa 24:10

24:6
n 1Sa 26:11

24:8
o 1Sa 25:23-24

24:11
p Ps 7:3 q 1Sa 23:14,23; 1Sa 26:20

24:12
r Ge 16:5; 31:53; Job 5:8 s Jdg 11:27; 1Sa 26:10

24:13
t Mt 7:20

24:14
u 1Sa 17:43; 2Sa 9:8 v 1Sa 26:20

24:15
w ver 12 x Ps 35:1,23; Mic 7:9 y Ps 43:1 z Ps 119:134,154

24:16
a 1Sa 26:17

24:17
b Ge 38:26; 1Sa 26:21 c Mt 5:44

24:18
d 1Sa 26:23

---

a28 Sela Hammahlekoth means rock of parting.   *b4 Or "Today the LORD is saying* will surely be king[e] and that the kingdom[f] of Israel will be established in your hands. [21]Now swear[g] to me by the LORD that you will not cut off my descendants or wipe out my name from my father's family.[h]"

[22]So David gave his oath to Saul. Then Saul returned home, but David and his men went up to the stronghold.[i]

David, Nabal and Abigail

25 Now Samuel died,[j] and all Israel assembled and mourned[k] for him; and they buried him at his home in Ramah.[l]

Then David moved down into the Desert of Maon.[a] [2]A certain man in Maon,[m] who had property there at Carmel, was very wealthy. He had a thousand goats and three thousand sheep, which he was shearing in Carmel. [3]His name was Nabal and his wife's name was Abigail.[n] She was an intelligent and beautiful woman, but her husband, a Calebite,[o] was surly and mean in his dealings.

[4]While David was in the desert, he heard that Nabal was shearing sheep. [5]So he sent ten young men and said to them, "Go up to Nabal at Carmel and greet him in my name. [6]Say to him: 'Long life to you! Good health[p] to you and your household! And good health to all that is yours![q]

[7]" 'Now I hear that it is sheep-shearing time. When your shepherds were with us, we did not mistreat[r] them, and the whole time they were at Carmel nothing of theirs was missing. [8]Ask your own servants and they will tell you. Therefore be favorable toward my young men, since we come at a festive time. Please give your servants and your son David whatever[s] you can find for them.' "

[9]When David's men arrived, they gave Nabal this message in David's name. Then they waited.

[10]Nabal answered David's servants, "Who[t] is this David? Who is this son of Jesse? Many servants are breaking away from their masters these days. [11]Why should I take my bread[u] and water, and the meat I have slaughtered for my shearers, and give it to men coming from who knows where?"

[12]David's men turned around and went back. When they arrived, they reported every word. [13]David said to his men, "Put on your swords!" So they put on their swords, and David put on his. About four hundred men went[v] up with David, while two hundred stayed with the supplies.[w]

[14]One of the servants told Nabal's wife Abigail: "David sent messengers from the desert to give our master his greetings,[x] but he hurled insults at them. [15]Yet these men were very good to us. They did not mistreat[y] us, and the whole time we were out in the fields near them nothing was missing.[z] [16]Night and day they were a wall[a] around us all the time we were herding our sheep near them. [17]Now think it over and see what you can do, because disaster is hanging over our master and his whole household. He is such a wicked[b] man that no one can talk to him."

[18]Abigail lost no time. She took two hundred loaves of bread, two skins of wine, five dressed sheep, five seahs[b] of roasted grain, a hun-

---

24:20
e 1Sa 23:17
f 1Sa 13:14

24:21
g Ge 21:23;
2Sa 21:1-9
h 1Sa 20:14-15

24:22
i 1Sa 23:29

25:1
j 1Sa 28:3
k Nu 20:29;
Dt 34:8
l Ge 21:21;
2Ch 33:20

25:2
m Jos 15:55;
1Sa 23:24

25:3
n Pr 31:10
o Jos 15:13

25:6
p Ps 122:7;
Lk 10:5
q 1Ch 12:18

25:7
r ver 15

25:8
s Ne 8:10

25:10
t Jdg 9:28

25:11
u Jdg 8:6

25:13
v 1Sa 23:13
w 1Sa 30:24

25:14
x 1Sa 13:10

25:15
y ver 7 z ver 21

25:16
a Ex 14:22;
Job 1:10

25:17
b 1Sa 20:7

---

a1 Some Septuagint manuscripts; Hebrew *Paran*   *b18* That is, probably about a bushel (about 37 liters) dred cakes of raisins[c] and two hundred cakes of pressed figs, and loaded them on donkeys.[d] [19]Then she told her servants, "Go on ahead;[e] I'll follow you." But she did not tell her husband Nabal.

[20]As she came riding her donkey into a mountain ravine, there were David and his men descending toward her, and she met them. [21]David had just said, "It's been useless—all my watching over this fellow's property in the desert so that nothing of his was missing. He has paid[f] me back evil for good. [22]May God deal with David,[a] be it ever so severely,[g] if by morning I leave alive one male[h] of all who belong to him!"

[23]When Abigail saw David, she quickly got off her donkey and bowed down before David with her face to the ground.[i] [24]She fell at his feet and said: "My lord, let the blame be on me alone. Please let your servant speak to you; hear what your servant has to say. [25]May my lord pay no attention to that wicked man Nabal. He is just like his name— his name is Fool,[j] and folly goes with him. But as for me, your servant, I did not see the men my master sent.

[26]"Now since the LORD has kept you, my master, from bloodshed[k] and from avenging[l] yourself with your own hands, as surely as the LORD lives and as you live, may your enemies and all who intend to harm my master be like Nabal.[m] [27]And let this gift,[n] which your servant has brought to my master, be given to the men who follow you. [28]Please forgive[o] your servant's offense, for the LORD will certainly make a lasting[p] dynasty for my master, because he fights the LORD's battles.[q] Let no wrongdoing[r] be found in you as long as you live. [29]Even though someone is pursuing you to take your life, the life of my master will be bound securely in the bundle of the living by the LORD your God. But the lives of your enemies he will hurl[s] away as from the pocket of a sling. [30]When the LORD has done for my master every good thing he promised concerning him and has appointed him leader[t] over Israel, [31]my master will not have on his conscience the staggering burden of needless bloodshed or of having avenged himself. And when the LORD has brought my master success, remember[u] your servant."

[32]David said to Abigail, "Praise[v] be to the LORD, the God of Israel, who has sent you today to meet me. [33]May you be blessed for your good judgment and for keeping me from bloodshed[w] this day and from avenging myself with my own hands. [34]Otherwise, as surely as the LORD, the God of Israel, lives, who has kept me from harming you, if you had not come quickly to meet me, not one male belonging to Nabal would have been left alive by daybreak."

[35]Then David accepted from her hand what she had brought him and said, "Go home in peace. I have heard your words and granted[x] your request."

[36]When Abigail went to Nabal, he was in the house holding a banquet like that of a king. He was in high[y] spirits and very drunk.[z] So she told[a] him nothing until daybreak. [37]Then in the morning, when Nabal was sober, his wife told him all these things, and his heart failed him and he became like a stone. [38]About ten days later, the LORD struck[b] Nabal and he died.

[39]When David heard that Nabal was dead, he said, "Praise be to the

25:18
c 1Ch 12:40
d 2Sa 16:1
25:19
e Ge 32:20
25:21
f Ps 109:5
25:22
g 1Sa 3:17;
20:13
h 1Ki 14:10;
21:21; 2Ki 9:8
25:23
i 1Sa 20:41
25:25
j Pr 14:16
25:26
k ver 33
l Heb 10:30
m 2Sa 18:32
25:27
n Ge 33:11;
1Sa 30:26
25:28
o ver 24
p 2Sa 7:11,26
q 1Sa 18:17
r 1Sa 24:11
25:29
s Jer 10:18
25:30
t 1Sa 13:14
25:31
u Ge 40:14
25:32
v Ge 24:27;
Ex 18:10;
Lk 1:68
25:33
w ver 26
25:35
x Ge 19:21;
1Sa 20:42;
2Ki 5:19
25:36
y 2Sa 13:23
z Pr 20:1;
Isa 5:11,22;
Hos 4:11
a ver 19
25:38
b 1Sa 26:10;
2Sa 6:7

a22 Some Septuagint manuscripts; Hebrew *with David's enemies*

LORD, who has upheld my cause against Nabal for treating me with contempt. He has kept his servant from doing wrong and has brought Nabal's wrongdoing down on his own head."

Then David sent word to Abigail, asking her to become his wife. [40]His servants went to Carmel and said to Abigail, "David has sent us to you to take you to become his wife."

[41]She bowed down with her face to the ground and said, "Here is your maidservant, ready to serve you and wash the feet of my master's servants." [42]Abigail[c] quickly got on a donkey and, attended by her five maids, went with David's messengers and became his wife. [43]David had also married Ahinoam[d] of Jezreel, and they both were his wives.[e] [44]But Saul had given his daughter Michal, David's wife, to Paltiel[af] son of Laish, who was from Gallim.[g]

David Again Spares Saul's Life

26 The Ziphites[h] went to Saul at Gibeah and said, "Is not David hiding[i] on the hill of Hakilah, which faces Jeshimon?" [2]So Saul went down to the Desert of Ziph, with his three thousand chosen men of Israel, to search[j] there for David. [3]Saul made his camp beside the road on the hill of Hakilah facing Jeshimon, but David stayed in the desert. When he saw that Saul had followed him there, [4]he sent out scouts and learned that Saul had definitely arrived.[b]

[5]Then David set out and went to the place where Saul had camped. He saw where Saul and Abner[k] son of Ner, the commander of the army, had lain down. Saul was lying inside the camp, with the army encamped around him.

[6]David then asked Ahimelech the Hittite and Abishai son of Zeruiah,[l] Joab's brother, "Who will go down into the camp with me to Saul?"

"I'll go with you," said Abishai.

[7]So David and Abishai went to the army by night, and there was Saul, lying asleep inside the camp with his spear stuck in the ground near his head. Abner and the soldiers were lying around him.

[8]Abishai said to David, "Today God has delivered your enemy into your hands. Now let me pin him to the ground with one thrust of my spear; I won't strike him twice."

[9]But David said to Abishai, "Don't destroy him! Who can lay a hand on the LORD's anointed[m] and be guiltless?[n] [10]As surely as the LORD lives," he said, "the LORD himself will strike[o] him; either his time[p] will come and he will die,[q] or he will go into battle and perish. [11]But the LORD forbid that I should lay a hand on the LORD's anointed. Now get the spear and water jug that are near his head, and let's go."

[12]So David took the spear and water jug near Saul's head, and they left. No one saw or knew about it, nor did anyone wake up. They were all sleeping, because the LORD had put them into a deep sleep.[r]

[13]Then David crossed over to the other side and stood on top of the hill some distance away; there was a wide space between them. [14]He called out to the army and to Abner son of Ner, "Aren't you going to answer me, Abner?"

Abner replied, "Who are you who calls to the king?"

---

[a]44 Hebrew *Palti*, a variant of *Paltiel*   [b]4 Or *had come to Nacon*

25:42
cGe 24:61-67
25:43
dJos 15:56
e1Sa 27:3; 30:5
25:44
f2Sa 3:15
gIsa 10:30
26:1
h1Sa 23:19
iPs 54 Title
26:2
j1Sa 13:2; 24:2
26:5
k1Sa 14:50; 17:55
26:6
lJdg 7:10-11; 1Ch 2:16
26:9
m2Sa 1:14
n1Sa 24:5
26:10
o1Sa 25:38; Ro 12:19
pGe 47:29; Dt 31:14; Ps 37:13
q1Sa 31:6; 2Sa 1:1
26:12
rGe 2:21; 15:12

¹⁵David said, "You're a man, aren't you? And who is like you in Israel? Why didn't you guard your lord the king? Someone came to destroy your lord the king. ¹⁶What you have done is not good. As surely as the LORD lives, you and your men deserve to die, because you did not guard your master, the LORD's anointed. Look around you. Where are the king's spear and water jug that were near his head?"

¹⁷Saul recognized David's voice and said, "Is that your voice,ˢ David my son?"

David replied, "Yes it is, my lord the king." ¹⁸And he added, "Why is my lord pursuing his servant? What have I done, and what wrongᵗ am I guilty of? ¹⁹Now let my lord the king listen to his servant's words. If the LORD has incited you against me, then may he accept an offering.ᵘ If, however, men have done it, may they be cursed before the LORD! They have now driven me from my share in the LORD's inheritanceᵛ and have said, 'Go, serve other gods.' ²⁰Now do not let my blood fall to the ground far from the presence of the LORD. The king of Israel has come out to look for a fleaʷ—as one hunts a partridge in the mountains."

²¹Then Saul said, "I have sinned.ˣ Come back, David my son. Because you considered my life preciousʸ today, I will not try to harm you again. Surely I have acted like a fool and have erred greatly."

²²"Here is the king's spear," David answered. "Let one of your young men come over and get it. ²³The LORD rewardsᶻ every man for his righteousnessᵃ and faithfulness. The LORD delivered you into my hands today, but I would not lay a hand on the LORD's anointed. ²⁴As surely as I valued your life today, so may the LORD value my life and deliverᵇ me from all trouble."

²⁵Then Saul said to David, "May you be blessed, my son David; you will do great things and surely triumph."

So David went on his way, and Saul returned home.

David Among the Philistines

27 But David thought to himself, "One of these days I will be destroyed by the hand of Saul. The best thing I can do is to escape to the land of the Philistines. Then Saul will give up searching for me anywhere in Israel, and I will slip out of his hand."

²So David and the six hundred menᶜ with him left and wentᵈ over to Achishᵉ son of Maoch king of Gath. ³David and his men settled in Gath with Achish. Each man had his family with him, and David had his two wives:ᶠ Ahinoam of Jezreel and Abigail of Carmel, the widow of Nabal. ⁴When Saul was told that David had fled to Gath, he no longer searched for him.

⁵Then David said to Achish, "If I have found favor in your eyes, let a place be assigned to me in one of the country towns, that I may live there. Why should your servant live in the royal city with you?"

⁶So on that day Achish gave him Ziklag,ᵍ and it has belonged to the kings of Judah ever since. ⁷David livedʰ in Philistine territory a year and four months.

⁸Now David and his men went up and raided the Geshurites,ⁱ the Girzites and the Amalekites.ʲ (From ancient times these peoples had lived in the land extending to Shurᵏ and Egypt.) ⁹Whenever David attacked an area, he did not leave a man or woman alive,ˡ but took

26:17
s1Sa 24:16
26:18
t1Sa 24:9,11-14
26:19
u2Sa 16:11
v2Sa 14:16
26:20
w1Sa 24:14
26:21
xEx 9:27;
1Sa 15:24
y1Sa 24:17
26:23
zPs 62:12
aPs 7:8;
18:20,24
26:24
bPs 54:7
27:2
c1Sa 25:13
d1Sa 21:10
e1Ki 2:39
27:3
f1Sa 25:43; 30:3
27:6
gJos 15:31;
19:5; Ne 11:28
27:7
h1Sa 29:3
27:8
iJos 13:2,13
jEx 17:8;
1Sa 15:7-8
kEx 15:22
27:9
l1Sa 15:3

sheep and cattle, donkeys and camels, and clothes. Then he returned to Achish.

¹⁰When Achish asked, "Where did you go raiding today?" David would say, "Against the Negev of Judah" or "Against the Negev of Jerahmeel^m" or "Against the Negev of the Kenites.^n" ¹¹He did not leave a man or woman alive to be brought to Gath, for he thought, "They might inform on us and say, 'This is what David did.'" And such was his practice as long as he lived in Philistine territory. ¹²Achish trusted David and said to himself, "He has become so odious to his people, the Israelites, that he will be my servant forever."

Saul and the Witch of Endor

28 In those days the Philistines gathered^o their forces to fight against Israel. Achish said to David, "You must understand that you and your men will accompany me in the army."

²David said, "Then you will see for yourself what your servant can do."

Achish replied, "Very well, I will make you my bodyguard for life."

³Now Samuel was dead,^p and all Israel had mourned for him and buried him in his own town of Ramah. ^q Saul had expelled the mediums and spiritists^r from the land.

⁴The Philistines assembled and came and set up camp at Shunem,^s while Saul gathered all the Israelites and set up camp at Gilboa.^t ⁵When Saul saw the Philistine army, he was afraid; terror filled his heart. ⁶He inquired^u of the LORD, but the LORD did not answer him by dreams^v or Urim^w or prophets. ⁷Saul then said to his attendants, "Find me a woman who is a medium,^x so I may go and inquire of her."

"There is one in Endor,^y" they said.

⁸So Saul disguised^z himself, putting on other clothes, and at night he and two men went to the woman. "Consult^a a spirit for me," he said, "and bring up for me the one I name."

⁹But the woman said to him, "Surely you know what Saul has done. He has cut off^b the mediums and spiritists from the land. Why have you set a trap for my life to bring about my death?"

¹⁰Saul swore to her by the LORD, "As surely as the LORD lives, you will not be punished for this."

¹¹Then the woman asked, "Whom shall I bring up for you?"

"Bring up Samuel," he said.

¹²When the woman saw Samuel, she cried out at the top of her voice and said to Saul, "Why have you deceived me? You are Saul!"

¹³The king said to her, "Don't be afraid. What do you see?"

The woman said, "I see a spirit^a coming up out of the ground."

¹⁴"What does he look like?" he asked.

"An old man wearing a robe^c is coming up," she said.

Then Saul knew it was Samuel, and he bowed down and prostrated himself with his face to the ground.

¹⁵Samuel said to Saul, "Why have you disturbed me by bringing me up?"

"I am in great distress," Saul said. "The Philistines are fighting against me, and God has turned^d away from me. He no longer answers

---

27:10
^m 1Sa 30:29;
1Ch 2:9,25
^n Jdg 1:16
28:1
^o 1Sa 29:1
28:3
^p 1Sa 25:1
^q 1Sa 7:17
^r Ex 22:18;
Lev 19:31;
20:27;
Dt 18:10-11;
1Sa 15:23
28:4
^s Jos 19:18;
2Ki 4:8
^t 1Sa 31:1,3
28:6
^u 1Sa 14:37;
1Ch 10:13-14;
Pr 1:28
^v Nu 12:6
^w Ex 28:30;
Nu 27:21
28:7
^x Ac 16:16
^y Jos 17:11
28:8
^z 2Ch 18:29;
35:22
^a Dt 18:10-11;
1Ch 10:13;
Isa 8:19
28:9
^b ver 3
28:14
^c 1Sa 15:27;
24:8
28:15
^d ver 6;
1Sa 18:12

---

^a 13 Or *see spirits; or see gods*

me, either by prophets or by dreams. So I have called on you to tell me what to do."

[16]Samuel said, "Why do you consult me, now that the LORD has turned away from you and become your enemy? [17]The LORD has done what he predicted through me. The LORD has torn[e] the kingdom out of your hands and given it to one of your neighbors—to David. [18]Because you did not obey[f] the LORD or carry out his fierce wrath[g] against the Amalekites, the LORD has done this to you today. [19]The LORD will hand over both Israel and you to the Philistines, and tomorrow you and your sons[h] will be with me. The LORD will also hand over the army of Israel to the Philistines."

[20]Immediately Saul fell full length on the ground, filled with fear because of Samuel's words. His strength was gone, for he had eaten nothing all that day and night.

[21]When the woman came to Saul and saw that he was greatly shaken, she said, "Look, your maidservant has obeyed you. I took my life[i] in my hands and did what you told me to do. [22]Now please listen to your servant and let me give you some food so you may eat and have the strength to go on your way."

[23]He refused[j] and said, "I will not eat."

But his men joined the woman in urging him, and he listened to them. He got up from the ground and sat on the couch.

[24]The woman had a fattened calf at the house, which she butchered at once. She took some flour, kneaded it and baked bread without yeast. [25]Then she set it before Saul and his men, and they ate. That same night they got up and left.

Achish Sends David Back to Ziklag

29 The Philistines gathered[k] all their forces at Aphek,[l] and Israel camped by the spring in Jezreel.[m] [2]As the Philistine rulers marched with their units of hundreds and thousands, David and his men were marching at the rear[n] with Achish. [3]The commanders of the Philistines asked, "What about these Hebrews?"

Achish replied, "Is this not David, who was an officer of Saul king of Israel? He has already been with me for over a year,[o] and from the day he left Saul until now, I have found no fault in him."

[4]But the Philistine commanders were angry with him and said, "Send[p] the man back, that he may return to the place you assigned him. He must not go with us into battle, or he will turn[q] against us during the fighting. How better could he regain his master's favor than by taking the heads of our own men? [5]Isn't this the David they sang about in their dances:

" 'Saul has slain his thousands,
     and David his tens of thousands'?"[r]

[6]So Achish called David and said to him, "As surely as the LORD lives, you have been reliable, and I would be pleased to have you serve with me in the army. From the day[s] you came to me until now, I have found no fault in you, but the rulers[t] don't approve of you. [7]Turn back and go in peace; do nothing to displease the Philistine rulers."

28:17
e1Sa 15:28
28:18
f1Sa 15:20
g1Ki 20:42
28:19
h1Sa 31:2
28:21
iJdg 12:3;
1Sa 19:5;
Job 13:14
28:23
j2Ki 5:13
29:1
k1Sa 28:1
lJos 12:18;
1Sa 4:1
m2Ki 9:30
29:2
n1Sa 28:2
29:3
o1Sa 27:7;
Da 6:5
29:4
p1Ch 12:19
q1Sa 14:21
29:5
r1Sa 18:7; 21:11
29:6
s1Sa 27:8-12
tver 3

8"But what have I done?" asked David. "What have you found against your servant from the day I came to you until now? Why can't I go and fight against the enemies of my lord the king?"

9Achish answered, "I know that you have been as pleasing in my eyes as an angelᵘ of God; nevertheless, the Philistine commandersᵛ have said, 'He must not go up with us into battle.' 10Now get up early, along with your master's servants who have come with you, and leaveʷ in the morning as soon as it is light."

11So David and his men got up early in the morning to go back to the land of the Philistines, and the Philistines went up to Jezreel.

David Destroys the Amalekites

30 David and his men reached Ziklagˣ on the third day. Now the Amalekitesʸ had raided the Negev and Ziklag. They had attacked Ziklag and burned it, 2and had taken captive the women and all who were in it, both young and old. They killed none of them, but carried them off as they went on their way.

3When David and his men came to Ziklag, they found it destroyed by fire and their wives and sons and daughters taken captive. 4So David and his men wept aloud until they had no strength left to weep. 5David's two wivesᶻ had been captured—Ahinoam of Jezreel and Abigail, the widow of Nabal of Carmel. 6David was greatly distressed because the men were talking of stoningᵃ him; each one was bitter in spirit because of his sons and daughters. But David found strengthᵇ in the LORD his God.

7Then David said to Abiatharᶜ the priest, the son of Ahimelech, "Bring me the ephod.ᵈ" Abiathar brought it to him, 8and David inquiredᵉ of the LORD, "Shall I pursue this raiding party? Will I overtake them?"

"Pursue them," he answered. "You will certainly overtake them and succeedᶠ in the rescue."

9David and the six hundred menᵍ with him came to the Besor Ravine, where some stayed behind, 10for two hundred men were too exhaustedʰ to cross the ravine. But David and four hundred men continued the pursuit.

11They found an Egyptian in a field and brought him to David. They gave him water to drink and food to eat— 12part of a cake of pressed figs and two cakes of raisins. He ate and was revived,ⁱ for he had not eaten any food or drunk any water for three days and three nights.

13David asked him, "To whom do you belong, and where do you come from?"

He said, "I am an Egyptian, the slave of an Amalekite. My master abandoned me when I became ill three days ago. 14We raided the Negev of the Kerethitesʲ and the territory belonging to Judah and the Negev of Caleb.ᵏ And we burnedˡ Ziklag."

15David asked him, "Can you lead me down to this raiding party?"

He answered, "Swear to me before God that you will not kill me or hand me over to my master, and I will take you down to them."

16He led David down, and there they were, scattered over the countryside, eating, drinking and revelingᵐ because of the great amount of plunderⁿ they had taken from the land of the Philistines and from

29:9
u2Sa 14:17,20;
19:27 vver 4
29:10
w1Ch 12:19
30:1
x1Sa 29:4,11
y1Sa 15:7; 27:8
30:5
z1Sa 25:43;
2Sa 2:2
30:6
aEx 17:4;
Jn 8:59
bPs 27:14;
56:3-4,11;
Ro 4:20
30:7
c1Sa 22:20
d1Sa 23:9
30:8
e1Sa 23:2
fver 18
30:9
g1Sa 27:2
30:10
hver 9,21
30:12
iJdg 15:19
30:14
j2Sa 8:18;
1Ki 1:38,44;
Eze 25:16;
Zep 2:5
kver 16;
Jos 14:13; 15:13
lver 1
30:16
mLk 12:19
nver 14

Judah. [17]David fought[o] them from dusk until the evening of the next day, and none of them got away, except four hundred young men who rode off on camels and fled.[p] [18]David recovered[q] everything the Amalekites had taken, including his two wives. [19]Nothing was missing: young or old, boy or girl, plunder or anything else they had taken. David brought everything back. [20]He took all the flocks and herds, and his men drove them ahead of the other livestock, saying, "This is David's plunder."

[21]Then David came to the two hundred men who had been too exhausted[r] to follow him and who were left behind at the Besor Ravine. They came out to meet David and the people with him. As David and his men approached, he greeted them. [22]But all the evil men and troublemakers among David's followers said, "Because they did not go out with us, we will not share with them the plunder we recovered. However, each man may take his wife and children and go."

[23]David replied, "No, my brothers, you must not do that with what the LORD has given us. He has protected us and handed over to us the forces that came against us. [24]Who will listen to what you say? The share of the man who stayed with the supplies is to be the same as that of him who went down to the battle. All will share alike.[s]" [25]David made this a statute and ordinance for Israel from that day to this.

[26]When David arrived in Ziklag, he sent some of the plunder to the elders of Judah, who were his friends, saying, "Here is a present for you from the plunder of the LORD's enemies."

[27]He sent it to those who were in Bethel,[t] Ramoth[u] Negev and Jattir;[v] [28]to those in Aroer,[w] Siphmoth, Eshtemoa[x] [29]and Racal; to those in the towns of the Jerahmeelites[y] and the Kenites;[z] [30]to those in Hormah,[a] Bor Ashan,[b] Athach [31]and Hebron;[c] and to those in all the other places where David and his men had roamed.

Saul Takes His Life

31:1–13pp — 2Sa 1:4–12; 1Ch 10:1–12

31 Now the Philistines fought against Israel; the Israelites fled before them, and many fell slain on Mount Gilboa.[d] [2]The Philistines pressed hard after Saul and his sons, and they killed his sons Jonathan, Abinadab and Malki-Shua. [3]The fighting grew fierce around Saul, and when the archers overtook him, they wounded[e] him critically.

[4]Saul said to his armor-bearer, "Draw your sword and run me through,[f] or these uncircumcised[g] fellows will come and run me through and abuse me."

But his armor-bearer was terrified and would not do it; so Saul took his own sword and fell on it. [5]When the armor-bearer saw that Saul was dead, he too fell on his sword and died with him. [6]So Saul and his three sons and his armor-bearer and all his men died together that same day.

[7]When the Israelites along the valley and those across the Jordan saw that the Israelite army had fled and that Saul and his sons had died, they abandoned their towns and fled. And the Philistines came and occupied them.

[8]The next day, when the Philistines came to strip the dead, they

30:17
o1Sa 11:11
p1Sa 15:3
30:18
qGe 14:16
30:21
rver 10
30:24
sNu 31:27;
Jos 22:8
30:27
tJos 7:2
uJos 19:8
vJos 15:48
30:28
wJos 13:16
xJos 15:50
30:29
y1Sa 27:10
zJdg 1:16;
1Sa 15:6
30:30
aNu 14:45;
Jdg 1:17
bJos 15:42
30:31
cJos 14:13;
2Sa 2:1,4
31:1
d1Sa 28:4;
1Ch 10:1-12
31:3
e2Sa 1:6
31:4
fJdg 9:54;
2Sa 1:6,10
g1Sa 14:6

found Saul and his three sons fallen on Mount Gilboa. [9]They cut off his head and stripped off his armor, and they sent messengers throughout the land of the Philistines to proclaim the news[h] in the temple of their idols and among their people.[i] [10]They put his armor in the temple of the Ashtoreths[j] and fastened his body to the wall of Beth Shan.[k]

[11]When the people of Jabesh Gilead[l] heard of what the Philistines had done to Saul, [12]all their valiant men journeyed through the night to Beth Shan. They took down the bodies of Saul and his sons from the wall of Beth Shan and went to Jabesh, where they burned[m] them. [13]Then they took their bones[n] and buried them under a tamarisk[o] tree at Jabesh, and they fasted[p] seven days.[q]

2 Samuel

Title and Background

1 and 2 Samuel were originally one book (see Introduction to 1 Samuel).

Author and Date of Writing

See Introduction to 1 Samuel.

Theme and Message

2 Samuel depicts David as a true (though imperfect) representative of the ideal theocratic king. Under David's rule the Lord caused the nation to prosper and to defeat its enemies. In chapter 7 we read of the Lord's promise that David's dynasty would endure forever and of the establishment of the Davidic covenant.

Outline

I. David Becomes King Over Judah (1:1-4:12)
II. David Becomes King Over All Israel (5:1-5)
III. David's Kingship in Its Accomplishments and Glory (5:6-9:12)
IV. David's Kingship in Its Weaknesses and Failures (10:1-20:16)
V. Final Reflections on David's Reign (21:1-24:25)

David Hears of Saul's Death

1:4–12pp — 1Sa 31:1–13; 1Ch 10:1–12

1 After the death[a] of Saul, David returned from defeating[b] the Amalekites and stayed in Ziklag two days. [2]On the third day a man[c] arrived from Saul's camp, with his clothes torn and with dust on his head. [d] When he came to David, he fell to the ground to pay him honor.

[3]"Where have you come from?" David asked him.

He answered, "I have escaped from the Israelite camp."

[4]"What happened?" David asked. "Tell me."

He said, "The men fled from the battle. Many of them fell and died. And Saul and his son Jonathan are dead."

[5]Then David said to the young man who brought him the report, "How do you know that Saul and his son Jonathan are dead?"

[6]"I happened to be on Mount Gilboa, [e]" the young man said, "and there was Saul, leaning on his spear, with the chariots and riders almost upon him. [7]When he turned around and saw me, he called out to me, and I said, 'What can I do?'

[8]"He asked me, 'Who are you?'

" 'An Amalekite,[f]' I answered.

[9]"Then he said to me, 'Stand over me and kill me! I am in the throes of death, but I'm still alive.'

[10]"So I stood over him and killed him, because I knew that after he had fallen he could not survive. And I took the crown[g] that was on his head and the band on his arm and have brought them here to my lord."

1:1
a 1Sa 31:6
b 1Sa 30:17

1:2
c 2Sa 4:10
d 1Sa 4:12

1:6
e 1Sa 28:4;
31:2-4

1:8
f 1Sa 15:2;
30:13,17

1:10
g Jdg 9:54;
2Ki 11:12

¹¹Then David and all the men with him took hold of their clothes and tore[h] them. ¹²They mourned and wept and fasted till evening for Saul and his son Jonathan, and for the army of the LORD and the house of Israel, because they had fallen by the sword.

¹³David said to the young man who brought him the report, "Where are you from?"

"I am the son of an alien, an Amalekite,[i]" he answered.

¹⁴David asked him, "Why were you not afraid to lift your hand to destroy the LORD's anointed?[j]"

¹⁵Then David called one of his men and said, "Go, strike him down!"[k] So he struck him down, and he died.[l] ¹⁶For David had said to him, "Your blood be on your own head.[m] Your own mouth testified against you when you said, 'I killed the LORD's anointed.'"

David's Lament for Saul and Jonathan

¹⁷David took up this lament[n] concerning Saul and his son Jonathan, ¹⁸and ordered that the men of Judah be taught this lament of the bow (it is written in the Book of Jashar):[o]

¹⁹"Your glory, O Israel, lies slain on your heights.
    How the mighty have fallen![p]

²⁰"Tell it not in Gath,[q]
    proclaim it not in the streets of Ashkelon,
lest the daughters of the Philistines[r] be glad,
    lest the daughters of the uncircumcised rejoice.[s]

²¹"O mountains of Gilboa,[t]
    may you have neither dew nor rain,
    nor fields that yield offerings[u] ͺof grainͺ.
For there the shield of the mighty was defiled,
    the shield of Saul—no longer rubbed with oil.[v]
²²From the blood[w] of the slain,
    from the flesh of the mighty,
the bow[x] of Jonathan did not turn back,
    the sword of Saul did not return unsatisfied.

²³"Saul and Jonathan—
    in life they were loved and gracious,
    and in death they were not parted.
They were swifter than eagles,[y]
    they were stronger than lions.[z]

²⁴"O daughters of Israel,
    weep for Saul,
who clothed you in scarlet and finery,
    who adorned your garments with ornaments of gold.

²⁵"How the mighty have fallen in battle!
    Jonathan lies slain on your heights.
²⁶I grieve for you, Jonathan my brother;[a]
    you were very dear to me.
Your love for me was wonderful,[b]
    more wonderful than that of women.

1:11
h Ge 37:29;
2Sa 3:31; 13:31
1:13
i ver 8
1:14
j 1Sa 24:6; 26:9
1:15
k 2Sa 4:12
l 2Sa 4:10
1:16
m Lev 20:9;
2Sa 3:28-29;
1Ki 2:32;
Mt 27:24-25;
Ac 18:6
1:17
n 2Ch 35:25
1:18
o Jos 10:13;
1Sa 31:3
1:19
p ver 27
1:20
q Mic 1:10
r 1Sa 31:8
s Ex 15:20;
1Sa 18:6
1:21
t ver 6; 1Sa 31:1
u Eze 31:15
v Isa 21:5
1:22
w Isa 34:3,7
x Dt 32:42;
1Sa 18:4
1:23
y Dt 28:49;
Jer 4:13
z Jdg 14:18
1:26
a 1Sa 20:42
b 1Sa 18:1

²⁷"How the mighty have fallen!
The weapons of war have perished!"ᶜ

David Anointed King Over Judah

2 In the course of time, David inquiredᵈ of the LORD. "Shall I go up to one of the towns of Judah?" he asked.

The LORD said, "Go up."

David asked, "Where shall I go?"

"To Hebron,"ᵉ the LORD answered.

²So David went up there with his two wives,ᶠ Ahinoam of Jezreel and Abigail,ᵍ the widow of Nabal of Carmel. ³David also took the men who were with him,ʰ each with his family, and they settled in Hebron and its towns. ⁴Then the men of Judah came to Hebronⁱ and there they anointedʲ David king over the house of Judah.

When David was told that it was the men of Jabesh Gileadᵏ who had buried Saul, ⁵he sent messengers to the men of Jabesh Gilead to say to them, "The LORD blessˡ you for showing this kindness to Saul your master by burying him. ⁶May the LORD now show you kindness and faithfulness,ᵐ and I too will show you the same favor because you have done this. ⁷Now then, be strong and brave, for Saul your master is dead, and the house of Judah has anointed me king over them."

War Between the Houses of David and Saul

3:2–5pp — 1Ch 3:1–4

⁸Meanwhile, Abnerⁿ son of Ner, the commander of Saul's army, had taken Ish-Bosheth son of Saul and brought him over to Mahanaim.ᵒ ⁹He made him king over Gilead,ᵖ Ashuriᵃ�q and Jezreel, and also over Ephraim, Benjamin and all Israel.ʳ

¹⁰Ish-Bosheth son of Saul was forty years old when he became king over Israel, and he reigned two years. The house of Judah, however, followed David. ¹¹The length of time David was king in Hebron over the house of Judah was seven years and six months.ˢ

¹²Abner son of Ner, together with the men of Ish-Bosheth son of Saul, left Mahanaim and went to Gibeon.ᵗ ¹³Joabᵘ son of Zeruiah and David's men went out and met them at the pool of Gibeon. One group sat down on one side of the pool and one group on the other side.

¹⁴Then Abner said to Joab, "Let's have some of the young men get up and fight hand to hand in front of us."

"All right, let them do it," Joab said.

¹⁵So they stood up and were counted off—twelve men for Benjamin and Ish-Bosheth son of Saul, and twelve for David. ¹⁶Then each man grabbed his opponent by the head and thrust his dagger into his opponent's side, and they fell down together. So that place in Gibeon was called Helkath Hazzurim.ᵇ

¹⁷The battle that day was very fierce, and Abner and the men of Israel were defeatedᵛ by David's men.

¹⁸The three sons of Zeruiahʷ were there: Joab,ˣ Abishaiʸ and Asahel.ᶻ Now Asahel was as fleet-footed as a wild gazelle.ᵃ ¹⁹He chased Abner, turning neither to the right nor to the left as he pursued him. ²⁰Abner looked behind him and asked, "Is that you, Asahel?"

1:27
c ver 19,25;
1Sa 2:4

2:1
d 1Sa 23:2,11-12
e Ge 13:18;
1Sa 30:31

2:2
f 1Sa 25:43; 30:5
g 1Sa 25:42

2:3
h 1Sa 27:2; 30:9

2:4
i 1Sa 30:31
j 1Sa 2:35;
2Sa 5:3-5
k 1Sa 31:11-13

2:5
l 1Sa 23:21

2:6
m Ex 34:6;
1Ti 1:16

2:8
n 1Sa 14:50
o Ge 32:2

2:9
p Nu 32:26
q Jdg 1:32
r 1Ch 12:29

2:11
s 2Sa 5:5

2:12
t Jos 18:25

2:13
u 2Sa 8:16;
1Ch 2:16; 11:6

2:17
v 2Sa 3:1

2:18
w 2Sa 3:39
x 2Sa 3:30
y 1Sa 26:6
z 1Ch 2:16
a 1Ch 12:8

ᵃ9 Or *Asher*   ᵇ16 *Helkath Hazzurim* means *field of daggers* or *field of hostilities.*

"It is," he answered.

²¹Then Abner said to him, "Turn aside to the right or to the left; take on one of the young men and strip him of his weapons." But Asahel would not stop chasing him.

²²Again Abner warned Asahel, "Stop chasing me! Why should I strike you down? How could I look your brother Joab in the face?"[b]

²³But Asahel refused to give up the pursuit; so Abner thrust the butt of his spear into Asahel's stomach,[c] and the spear came out through his back. He fell there and died on the spot. And every man stopped when he came to the place where Asahel had fallen and died.[d]

²⁴But Joab and Abishai pursued Abner, and as the sun was setting, they came to the hill of Ammah, near Giah on the way to the wasteland of Gibeon. ²⁵Then the men of Benjamin rallied behind Abner. They formed themselves into a group and took their stand on top of a hill.

²⁶Abner called out to Joab, "Must the sword devour[e] forever? Don't you realize that this will end in bitterness? How long before you order your men to stop pursuing their brothers?"

²⁷Joab answered, "As surely as God lives, if you had not spoken, the men would have continued the pursuit of their brothers until morning.[a]"

²⁸So Joab[f] blew the trumpet,[g] and all the men came to a halt; they no longer pursued Israel, nor did they fight anymore.

²⁹All that night Abner and his men marched through the Arabah. They crossed the Jordan, continued through the whole Bithron[b] and came to Mahanaim.[h]

³⁰Then Joab returned from pursuing Abner and assembled all his men. Besides Asahel, nineteen of David's men were found missing. ³¹But David's men had killed three hundred and sixty Benjamites who were with Abner. ³²They took Asahel and buried him in his father's tomb[i] at Bethlehem. Then Joab and his men marched all night and arrived at Hebron by daybreak.

3 The war between the house of Saul and the house of David lasted a long time.[j] David grew stronger and stronger,[k] while the house of Saul grew weaker and weaker.[l]

²Sons were born to David in Hebron:

His firstborn was Amnon the son of Ahinoam[m] of Jezreel;

³his second, Kileab the son of Abigail[n] the widow of Nabal of Carmel;

the third, Absalom[o] the son of Maacah daughter of Talmai king of Geshur;[p]

⁴the fourth, Adonijah[q] the son of Haggith;

the fifth, Shephatiah the son of Abital;

⁵and the sixth, Ithream the son of David's wife Eglah.

These were born to David in Hebron.

Abner Goes Over to David

⁶During the war between the house of Saul and the house of David, Abner had been strengthening his own position in the house of Saul.

2:22
b 2Sa 3:27

2:23
c 2Sa 3:27; 4:6
d 2Sa 20:12

2:26
e Dt 32:42;
Jer 46:10,14

2:28
f 2Sa 18:16
g Jdg 3:27

2:29
h ver 8

2:32
i Ge 49:29

3:1
j 1Ki 14:30
k 2Sa 5:10
l 2Sa 2:17

3:2
m 1Sa 25:43;
1Ch 3:1-3

3:3
n 1Sa 25:42
o 2Sa 13:1,28
p 1Sa 27:8;
2Sa 13:37;
14:32; 15:8

3:4
q 1Ki 1:5,11

---

[a]27 Or *spoken this morning, the men would not have taken up the pursuit of their brothers; or spoken, the men would have given up the pursuit of their brothers by morning*   [b]29 Or *morning;* or *ravine;* the meaning of the Hebrew for this word is uncertain.

7Now Saul had had a concubine^r named Rizpah^s daughter of Aiah. And Ish-Bosheth said to Abner, "Why did you sleep with my father's concubine?"

8Abner was very angry because of what Ish-Bosheth said and he answered, "Am I a dog's head^t—on Judah's side? This very day I am loyal to the house of your father Saul and to his family and friends. I haven't handed you over to David. Yet now you accuse me of an offense involving this woman! 9May God deal with Abner, be it ever so severely, if I do not do for David what the Lord promised^u him on oath 10and transfer the kingdom from the house of Saul and establish David's throne over Israel and Judah from Dan to Beersheba."^v 11Ish-Bosheth did not dare to say another word to Abner, because he was afraid of him.

12Then Abner sent messengers on his behalf to say to David, "Whose land is it? Make an agreement with me, and I will help you bring all Israel over to you."

13"Good," said David. "I will make an agreement with you. But I demand one thing of you: Do not come into my presence unless you bring Michal daughter of Saul when you come to see me."^w 14Then David sent messengers to Ish-Bosheth son of Saul, demanding, "Give me my wife Michal,^x whom I betrothed to myself for the price of a hundred Philistine foreskins."

15So Ish-Bosheth gave orders and had her taken away from her husband^y Paltiel^z son of Laish. 16Her husband, however, went with her, weeping behind her all the way to Bahurim.^a Then Abner said to him, "Go back home!" So he went back.

17Abner conferred with the elders^b of Israel and said, "For some time you have wanted to make David your king. 18Now do it! For the Lord promised David, 'By my servant David I will rescue my people Israel from the hand of the Philistines^c and from the hand of all their enemies.^d'"

19Abner also spoke to the Benjamites in person. Then he went to Hebron to tell David everything that Israel and the whole house of Benjamin^e wanted to do. 20When Abner, who had twenty men with him, came to David at Hebron, David prepared a feast for him and his men. 21Then Abner said to David, "Let me go at once and assemble all Israel for my lord the king, so that they may make a compact^f with you, and that you may rule over all that your heart desires."^g So David sent Abner away, and he went in peace.

Joab Murders Abner

22Just then David's men and Joab returned from a raid and brought with them a great deal of plunder. But Abner was no longer with David in Hebron, because David had sent him away, and he had gone in peace. 23When Joab and all the soldiers with him arrived, he was told that Abner son of Ner had come to the king and that the king had sent him away and that he had gone in peace.

24So Joab went to the king and said, "What have you done? Look, Abner came to you. Why did you let him go? Now he is gone! 25You know Abner son of Ner; he came to deceive you and observe your movements and find out everything you are doing."

26Joab then left David and sent messengers after Abner, and they

3:7
r2Sa 16:21-22
s2Sa 21:8-11

3:8
t1Sa 24:14;
2Sa 9:8; 16:9

3:9
u1Sa 15:28;
1Ki 19:2

3:10
vJdg 20:1;
1Sa 3:20

3:13
wGe 43:5;
1Sa 18:20

3:14
x1Sa 18:27

3:15
yDt 24:1-4
z1Sa 25:44

3:16
a2Sa 16:5;
19:16

3:17
bJdg 11:11

3:18
c1Sa 9:16
d1Sa 15:28;
2Sa 8:6

3:19
e1Sa 10:20-21;
1Ch 12:2,16,29

3:21
fver 10,12
g1Ki 11:37

brought him back from the well of Sirah. But David did not know it.
27Now when Abner[h] returned to Hebron, Joab took him aside into the
gateway, as though to speak with him privately. And there, to avenge
the blood of his brother Asahel, Joab stabbed him in the stomach, and
he died.[i]

28Later, when David heard about this, he said, "I and my kingdom
are forever innocent[j] before the LORD concerning the blood of Abner
son of Ner. 29May his blood[k] fall upon the head of Joab and upon all his
father's house![l] May Joab's house never be without someone who has
a running sore[m] or leprosy[a] or who leans on a crutch or who falls by the
sword or who lacks food."

30(Joab and his brother Abishai murdered Abner because he had
killed their brother Asahel in the battle at Gibeon.)

31Then David said to Joab and all the people with him, "Tear your
clothes and put on sackcloth[n] and walk in mourning[o] in front of
Abner." King David himself walked behind the bier. 32They buried
Abner in Hebron, and the king wept[p] aloud at Abner's tomb. All the
people wept also.

33The king sang this lament[q] for Abner:

> "Should Abner have died as the lawless die?
> 34 Your hands were not bound,
>   your feet were not fettered.
>   You fell as one falls before wicked men."

And all the people wept over him again.

35Then they all came and urged David to eat something while it was
still day; but David took an oath, saying, "May God deal with me, be it
ever so severely,[r] if I taste bread[s] or anything else before the sun sets!"

36All the people took note and were pleased; indeed, everything the
king did pleased them. 37So on that day all the people and all Israel
knew that the king had no part[t] in the murder of Abner son of Ner.

38Then the king said to his men, "Do you not realize that a prince and
a great man has fallen[u] in Israel this day? 39And today, though I am the
anointed king, I am weak, and these sons of Zeruiah[v] are too strong for
me.[w] May the LORD repay[x] the evildoer according to his evil deeds!"

Ish-Bosheth Murdered

4 When Ish-Bosheth son of Saul heard that Abner[y] had died in
Hebron, he lost courage, and all Israel became alarmed. 2Now
Saul's son had two men who were leaders of raiding bands. One was
named Baanah and the other Recab; they were sons of Rimmon the
Beerothite from the tribe of Benjamin—Beeroth[z] is considered part of
Benjamin, 3because the people of Beeroth fled to Gittaim[a] and have
lived there as aliens to this day.

4(Jonathan[b] son of Saul had a son who was lame in both feet. He was
five years old when the news[c] about Saul and Jonathan came from
Jezreel. His nurse picked him up and fled, but as she hurried to leave,
he fell and became crippled.[d] His name was Mephibosheth.)[e]

5Now Recab and Baanah, the sons of Rimmon the Beerothite, set out
for the house of Ish-Bosheth,[f] and they arrived there in the heat of the

---

3:27
h2Sa 2:8
i2Sa 2:22;
20:9-10; 1Ki 2:5
3:28
jver 37; Dt 21:9
3:29
kLev 20:9
l1Ki 2:31-33
mLev 15:2
3:31
n2Sa 1:2,11;
Ps 30:11;
Isa 20:2
oGe 37:34
3:32
pNu 14:1;
Pr 24:17
3:33
q2Sa 1:17
3:35
rRu 1:17;
1Sa 3:17
s1Sa 31:13;
2Sa 1:12;
12:17; Jer 16:7
3:37
tver 28
3:38
u2Sa 1:19
3:39
v2Sa 2:18
w2Sa 19:5-7
x1Ki 2:5-6,
33-34; Ps 41:10;
101:8
4:1
y2Sa 3:27;
Ezr 4:4
4:2
zJos 9:17; 18:25
4:3
aNe 11:33
4:4
b1Sa 18:1
c1Sa 31:1-4
dLev 21:18
e2Sa 9:3,6;
1Ch 8:34; 9:40
4:5
f2Sa 2:8

---

a29 The Hebrew word was used for various diseases affecting the skin—not necessarily leprosy.

day while he was taking his noonday rest. 6They went into the inner part of the house as if to get some wheat, and they stabbed⁸ him in the stomach. Then Recab and his brother Baanah slipped away.

7They had gone into the house while he was lying on the bed in his bedroom. After they stabbed and killed him, they cut off his head. Taking it with them, they traveled all night by way of the Arabah. 8They brought the head of Ish-Bosheth to David at Hebron and said to the king, "Here is the head of Ish-Bosheth son of Saul,ʰ your enemy, who tried to take your life. This day the LORD has avenged my lord the king against Saul and his offspring."

9David answered Recab and his brother Baanah, the sons of Rimmon the Beerothite, "As surely as the LORD lives, who has deliveredⁱ me out of all trouble, 10when a man told me, 'Saul is dead,' and thought he was bringing good news, I seized him and put him to death in Ziklag.ʲ That was the reward I gave him for his news! 11How much more—when wicked men have killed an innocent man in his own house and on his own bed—should I not now demand his bloodᵏ from your hand and rid the earth of you!"

12So David gave an order to his men, and they killed them.ˡ They cut off their hands and feet and hung the bodies by the pool in Hebron. But they took the head of Ish-Bosheth and buried it in Abner's tomb at Hebron.

David Becomes King Over Israel

5:1–3pp — 1Ch 11:1–3

5 All the tribes of Israelᵐ came to David at Hebron and said, "We are your own flesh and blood.ⁿ 2In the past, while Saul was king over us, you were the one who led Israel on their military campaigns.ᵒ And the LORD said to you, 'You will shepherdᵖ my people Israel, and you will become their ruler.�q' "

3When all the elders of Israel had come to King David at Hebron, the king made a compactʳ with them at Hebron before the LORD, and they anointedˢ David king over Israel.

4David was thirty years oldᵗ when he became king, and he reignedᵘ fortyᵛ years. 5In Hebron he reigned over Judah seven years and six months,ʷ and in Jerusalem he reigned over all Israel and Judah thirty-three years.

David Conquers Jerusalem

5:6–10pp — 1Ch 11:4–9
5:11–16pp — 1Ch 3:5–9; 14:1–7

6The king and his men marched to Jerusalemˣ to attack the Jebusites,ʸ who lived there. The Jebusites said to David, "You will not get in here; even the blind and the lame can ward you off." They thought, "David cannot get in here." 7Nevertheless, David captured the fortress of Zion, the City of David.ᶻ

8On that day, David said, "Anyone who conquers the Jebusites will have to use the water shaftᵃ to reach those 'lame and blind' who are David's enemies.ᵇ" That is why they say, "The 'blind and lame' will not enter the palace."

ᵃ8 Or *use scaling hooks*   ᵇ8 Or *are hated by David*

4:6
g2Sa 2:23
4:8
h1Sa 24:4;
25:29
4:9
iGe 48:16;
1Ki 1:29
4:10
j2Sa 1:2-16
4:11
kGe 9:5;
Ps 9:12
4:12
l2Sa 1:15
5:1
m2Sa 19:43
n1Ch 11:1
5:2
o1Sa 18:5,13,16
p1Sa 16:1;
2Sa 7:7
q1Sa 25:30
5:3
r2Sa 3:21
s2Sa 2:4
5:4
tLk 3:23
u1Ki 2:11;
1Ch 3:4
v1Ch 26:31;
29:27
5:5
w2Sa 2:11;
1Ch 3:4
5:6
xJdg 1:8
yJos 15:8
5:7
z2Sa 6:12,16;
1Ki 2:10

9David then took up residence in the fortress and called it the City of David. He built up the area around it, from the supporting terraces*a a* inward. 10And he became more and more powerful,*b* because the LORD God Almighty was with him.

11Now Hiram*c* king of Tyre sent messengers to David, along with cedar logs and carpenters and stonemasons, and they built a palace for David. 12And David knew that the LORD had established him as king over Israel and had exalted his kingdom for the sake of his people Israel.

13After he left Hebron, David took more concubines and wives*d* in Jerusalem, and more sons and daughters were born to him. 14These are the names of the children born to him there:*e* Shammua, Shobab, Nathan, Solomon, 15Ibhar, Elishua, Nepheg, Japhia, 16Elishama, Eliada and Eliphelet.

David Defeats the Philistines

5:17–25pp — 1Ch 14:8–17

17When the Philistines heard that David had been anointed king over Israel, they went up in full force to search for him, but David heard about it and went down to the stronghold.*f* 18Now the Philistines had come and spread out in the Valley of Rephaim;*g* 19so David inquired*h* of the LORD, "Shall I go and attack the Philistines? Will you hand them over to me?"

The LORD answered him, "Go, for I will surely hand the Philistines over to you."

20So David went to Baal Perazim, and there he defeated them. He said, "As waters break out, the LORD has broken out against my enemies before me." So that place was called Baal Perazim.*b i* 21The Philistines abandoned their idols there, and David and his men carried them off.*j*

22Once more the Philistines came up and spread out in the Valley of Rephaim; 23so David inquired of the LORD, and he answered, "Do not go straight up, but circle around behind them and attack them in front of the balsam trees. 24As soon as you hear the sound*k* of marching in the tops of the balsam trees, move quickly, because that will mean the LORD has gone out in front*l* of you to strike the Philistine army." 25So David did as the LORD commanded him, and he struck down the Philistines all the way from Gibeon*c m* to Gezer.*n*

The Ark Brought to Jerusalem

6:1–11pp — 1Ch 13:1–14
6:12–19pp — 1Ch 15:25–16:3

6 David again brought together out of Israel chosen men, thirty thousand in all. 2He and all his men set out from Baalah*o* of Judah*d* to bring up from there the ark*p* of God, which is called by the Name,*e q* the name of the LORD Almighty, who is enthroned*r* between the cherubim*s* that are on the ark. 3They set the ark of God on a new cart*t* and brought it from the house of Abinadab, which was on the hill. Uzzah and Ahio, sons of Abinadab, were guiding the new cart 4with the ark of

Side references

5:9
aver 7;
1Ki 9:15,24
5:10
b2Sa 3:1
5:11
c1Ki 5:1,18;
1Ch 14:1
5:13
dDt 17:17;
1Ch 3:9
5:14
e1Ch 3:5
5:17
f2Sa 23:14;
1Ch 11:16
5:18
gJos 15:8;
17:15; 18:16
5:19
h1Sa 23:2;
2Sa 2:1
5:20
iIsa 28:21
5:21
jDt 7:5;
1Ch 14:12;
Isa 46:2
5:24
k2Ki 7:6
1Jdg 4:14
5:25
mIsa 28:21
n1Ch 14:16
6:2
oJos 15:9
p1Sa 4:4; 7:1
qLev 24:16;
Isa 63:14
rPs 99:1
sEx 25:22;
1Ch 13:5-6
6:3
tNu 7:4-9;
1Sa 6:7

---

*a*9 Or *the Millo*   *b*20 *Baal Perazim* means *the lord who breaks out.*   *c*25 Septuagint (see also 1 Chron. 14:16); Hebrew *Geba*   *d*2 That is, Kiriath Jearim; Hebrew *Baale Judah,* a variant of *Baalah of Judah*   *e*2 Hebrew; Septuagint and Vulgate do not have *the Name.*

God on it,[a] and Ahio was walking in front of it. [5]David and the whole house of Israel were celebrating with all their might before the LORD, with songs[b] and with harps, lyres, tambourines, sistrums and cymbals.[u]

[6]When they came to the threshing floor of Nacon, Uzzah reached out and took hold of[v] the ark of God, because the oxen stumbled. [7]The LORD's anger burned against Uzzah because of his irreverent act;[w] therefore God struck him down[x] and he died there beside the ark of God.

[8]Then David was angry because the LORD's wrath[y] had broken out against Uzzah, and to this day that place is called Perez Uzzah.[c] [z]

[9]David was afraid of the LORD that day and said, "How[a] can the ark of the LORD ever come to me?" [10]He was not willing to take the ark of the LORD to be with him in the City of David. Instead, he took it aside to the house of Obed-Edom[b] the Gittite. [11]The ark of the LORD remained in the house of Obed-Edom the Gittite for three months, and the LORD blessed him and his entire household.[c]

[12]Now King David[d] was told, "The LORD has blessed the household of Obed-Edom and everything he has, because of the ark of God." So David went down and brought up the ark of God from the house of Obed-Edom to the City of David with rejoicing. [13]When those who were carrying the ark of the LORD had taken six steps, he sacrificed[e] a bull and a fattened calf. [14]David, wearing a linen ephod,[f] danced[g] before the LORD with all his might, [15]while he and the entire house of Israel brought up the ark of the LORD with shouts and the sound of trumpets.[h]

[16]As the ark of the LORD was entering the City of David,[i] Michal daughter of Saul watched from a window. And when she saw King David leaping and dancing before the LORD, she despised him in her heart.

[17]They brought the ark of the LORD and set it in its place inside the tent that David had pitched for it,[j] and David sacrificed burnt offerings[k] and fellowship offerings[d] before the LORD. [18]After he had finished sacrificing[l] the burnt offerings and fellowship offerings, he blessed the people in the name of the LORD Almighty. [19]Then he gave a loaf of bread, a cake of dates and a cake of raisins[m] to each person in the whole crowd of Israelites, both men and women.[n] And all the people went to their homes.

[20]When David returned home to bless his household, Michal daughter of Saul came out to meet him and said, "How the king of Israel has distinguished himself today, disrobing[o] in the sight of the slave girls of his servants as any vulgar fellow would!"

[21]David said to Michal, "It was before the LORD, who chose me rather than your father or anyone from his house when he appointed[p] me ruler over the LORD's people Israel—I will celebrate before the LORD. [22]I will become even more undignified than this, and I will be humiliated

---

6:5
u1Sa 18:6-7;
Ezr 3:10;
Ps 150:5
6:6
vNu 4:15,19-20;
1Ch 13:9
6:7
w1Ch 15:13-15
xEx 19:22;
1Sa 6:19
6:8
yPs 7:11
zGe 38:29
6:9
aPs 119:120
6:10
b1Ch 13:13;
26:4-5
6:11
cGe 30:27; 39:5
6:12
d1Ki 8:1;
1Ch 15:25
6:13
e1Ki 8:5,62
6:14
fEx 19:6;
1Sa 2:18
gEx 15:20
6:15
hPs 47:5; 98:6
6:16
i2Sa 5:7
6:17
j1Ch 15:1;
2Ch 1:4
kLev 1:1-17;
1Ki 8:62-64
6:18
l1Ki 8:22
6:19
mHos 3:1
nNe 8:10
6:20
over 14,16
6:21
p1Sa 13:14;
15:28

---

[a]3,4 Dead Sea Scrolls and some Septuagint manuscripts; Masoretic Text *cart* [4]*and they brought it with the ark of God from the house of Abinadab, which was on the hill* [b]5 See Dead Sea Scrolls, Septuagint and 1 Chronicles 13:8; Masoretic Text *celebrating before the LORD with all kinds of instruments made of pine.* [c]8 *Perez Uzzah* means *outbreak against Uzzah.* [d]17 Traditionally *peace offerings;* also in verse 18

in my own eyes. But by these slave girls you spoke of, I will be held in honor."

²³And Michal daughter of Saul had no children to the day of her death.

God's Promise to David

7:1–17pp — 1Ch 17:1–15

7 After the king was settled in his palace[q] and the LORD had given him rest from all his enemies around him, ²he said to Nathan the prophet, "Here I am, living in a palace[r] of cedar, while the ark of God remains in a tent."[s]

³Nathan replied to the king, "Whatever you have in mind, go ahead and do it, for the LORD is with you."

⁴That night the word of the LORD came to Nathan, saying:

⁵"Go and tell my servant David, 'This is what the LORD says: Are you[t] the one to build me a house to dwell in?[u] ⁶I have not dwelt in a house from the day I brought the Israelites up out of Egypt to this day. I have been moving from place to place with a tent[v] as my dwelling.[w] ⁷Wherever I have moved with all the Israelites,[x] did I ever say to any of their rulers whom I commanded to shepherd[y] my people Israel, "Why have you not built me a house of cedar?[z]"'

⁸"Now then, tell my servant David, 'This is what the LORD Almighty says: I took you from the pasture and from following the flock[a] to be ruler[b] over my people Israel.[c] ⁹I have been with you wherever you have gone,[d] and I have cut off all your enemies from before you.[e] Now I will make your name great, like the names of the greatest men of the earth. ¹⁰And I will provide a place for my people Israel and will plant[f] them so that they can have a home of their own and no longer be disturbed. Wicked[g] people will not oppress them anymore,[h] as they did at the beginning ¹¹and have done ever since the time I appointed leaders[a][i] over my people Israel. I will also give you rest from all your enemies.[j]

" 'The LORD declares to you that the LORD himself will establish[k] a house[l] for you: ¹²When your days are over and you rest[m] with your fathers, I will raise up your offspring to succeed you, who will come from your own body,[n] and I will establish his kingdom. ¹³He is the one who will build a house for my Name,[o] and I will establish the throne of his kingdom forever.[p] ¹⁴I will be his father, and he will be my son.[q] When he does wrong, I will punish him with the rod[r] of men, with floggings inflicted by men. ¹⁵But my love will never be taken away from him, as I took it away from Saul,[s] whom I removed from before you. ¹⁶Your house and your kingdom will endure forever before me[b]; your throne[t] will be established forever.[u]' "

¹⁷Nathan reported to David all the words of this entire revelation.

ₐ11 Traditionally judges *ᵇ16 Some Hebrew manuscripts and Septuagint; most Hebrew manuscripts you*

### Cross references (margin)

7:1
q1Ch 17:1

7:2
r2Sa 5:11
sEx 26:1;
Ac 7:45-46

7:5
t1Ki 8:19;
1Ch 22:8
u1Ki 5:3-5

7:6
vEx 40:18,34
w1Ki 8:16

7:7
xDt 23:14
y2Sa 5:2
zLev 26:11-12

7:8
a1Sa 16:11
b2Sa 6:21
cPs 78:70-72;
2Co 6:18*

7:9
d2Sa 5:10
ePs 18:37-42

7:10
fEx 15:17;
Isa 5:1-7
gPs 89:22-23
hIsa 60:18

7:11
iJdg 2:16;
1Sa 12:9-11
jver 1
k1Sa 25:28
lver 27

7:12
m1Ki 2:1
nPs 132:11-12

7:13
o1Ki 5:5;
8:19,29
pIsa 9:7

7:14
qPs 89:26;
Heb 1:5*
rPs 89:30-33

7:15
s1Sa 15:23,28

7:16
tPs 89:36-37
uver 13

David's Prayer
7:18–29pp — 1Ch 17:16–27

[18]Then King David went in and sat before the LORD, and he said:

"Who am I,[v] O Sovereign LORD, and what is my family, that you have brought me this far? [19]And as if this were not enough in your sight, O Sovereign LORD, you have also spoken about the future of the house of your servant. Is this your usual way of dealing with man,[w] O Sovereign LORD?

[20]"What more can David say to you? For you know[x] your servant,[y] O Sovereign LORD. [21]For the sake of your word and according to your will, you have done this great thing and made it known to your servant.

[22]"How great[z] you are,[a] O Sovereign LORD! There is no one like you, and there is no God[b] but you, as we have heard with our own ears.[c] [23]And who is like your people Israel[d]—the one nation on earth that God went out to redeem as a people for himself, and to make a name for himself, and to perform great and awesome wonders[e] by driving out nations and their gods from before your people, whom you redeemed[f] from Egypt?[a] [24]You have established your people Israel as your very own[g] forever, and you, O LORD, have become their God.[h]

[25]"And now, LORD God, keep forever the promise you have made concerning your servant and his house. Do as you promised, [26]so that your name will be great forever. Then men will say, 'The LORD Almighty is God over Israel!' And the house of your servant David will be established before you.

[27]"O LORD Almighty, God of Israel, you have revealed this to your servant, saying, 'I will build a house for you.' So your servant has found courage to offer you this prayer. [28]O Sovereign LORD, you are God! Your words are trustworthy,[i] and you have promised these good things to your servant. [29]Now be pleased to bless the house of your servant, that it may continue forever in your sight; for you, O Sovereign LORD, have spoken, and with your blessing[j] the house of your servant will be blessed forever."

David's Victories
8:1–14pp — 1Ch 18:1–13

8 In the course of time, David defeated the Philistines and subdued them, and he took Metheg Ammah from the control of the Philistines.

[2]David also defeated the Moabites.[k] He made them lie down on the ground and measured them off with a length of cord. Every two lengths of them were put to death, and the third length was allowed to live. So the Moabites became subject to David and brought tribute.

[3]Moreover, David fought Hadadezer[l] son of Rehob, king of Zobah,[m] when he went to restore his control along the Euphrates River. [4]David captured a thousand of his chariots, seven thousand charioteers[b] and

7:18
vEx 3:11;
1Sa 18:18
7:19
wIsa 55:8-9
7:20
xJn 21:17
y1Sa 16:7
7:22
zPs 48:1; 86:10;
Jer 10:6
aDt 3:24
bEx 15:11
cEx 10:2;
Ps 44:1
7:23
dDt 4:32-38
eDt 10:21
fDt 9:26; 15:15
7:24
gDt 26:18
hEx 6:6-7;
Ps 48:14
7:28
iEx 34:6;
Jn 17:17
7:29
jNu 6:23-27
8:2
kGe 19:37;
Nu 24:17
8:3
l2Sa 10:16,19
m1Sa 14:47

---

[a]23 See Septuagint and 1 Chron. 17:21; Hebrew *wonders for your land and before your people, whom you redeemed from Egypt, from the nations and their gods.*   [b]4 Septuagint (see also Dead Sea Scrolls and 1 Chron. 18:4); Masoretic Text *captured seventeen hundred of his charioteers*

twenty thousand foot soldiers. He hamstrung[n] all but a hundred of the chariot horses.

5When the Arameans of Damascus[o] came to help Hadadezer king of Zobah, David struck down twenty-two thousand of them. 6He put garrisons in the Aramean kingdom of Damascus, and the Arameans became subject to him and brought tribute. The LORD gave David victory wherever he went. [p]

7David took the gold shields[q] that belonged to the officers of Hadadezer and brought them to Jerusalem. 8From Tebah[a] and Berothai,[r] towns that belonged to Hadadezer, King David took a great quantity of bronze.

9When Tou[b] king of Hamath[s] heard that David had defeated the entire army of Hadadezer, 10he sent his son Joram[c] to King David to greet him and congratulate him on his victory in battle over Hadadezer, who had been at war with Tou. Joram brought with him articles of silver and gold and bronze.

11King David dedicated[t] these articles to the LORD, as he had done with the silver and gold from all the nations he had subdued: 12Edom[d] and Moab,[u] the Ammonites[v] and the Philistines,[w] and Amalek.[x] He also dedicated the plunder taken from Hadadezer son of Rehob, king of Zobah.

13And David became famous[y] after he returned from striking down eighteen thousand Edomites[e] in the Valley of Salt.[z]

14He put garrisons throughout Edom, and all the Edomites[a] became subject to David.[b] The LORD gave David victory wherever he went.[c]

David's Officials

8:15–18pp — 1Ch 18:14–17

15David reigned over all Israel, doing what was just and right for all his people. 16Joab[d] son of Zeruiah was over the army; Jehoshaphat[e] son of Ahilud was recorder; 17Zadok[f] son of Ahitub and Ahimelech son of Abiathar were priests; Seraiah was secretary;[g] 18Benaiah[h] son of Jehoiada was over the Kerethites[i] and Pelethites; and David's sons were royal advisers.[f]

David and Mephibosheth

9 David asked, "Is there anyone still left of the house of Saul to whom I can show kindness for Jonathan's sake?"[j]

2Now there was a servant of Saul's household named Ziba.[k] They called him to appear before David, and the king said to him, "Are you Ziba?"

"Your servant," he replied.

3The king asked, "Is there no one still left of the house of Saul to whom I can show God's kindness?"

Ziba answered the king, "There is still a son of Jonathan;[l] he is crippled[m] in both feet."

4"Where is he?" the king asked.

### Cross references (margin)

8:4
nJos 11:9

8:5
o1Ki 11:24

8:6
pver 14;
2Sa 3:18; 7:9

8:7
q1Ki 10:16

8:8
rEze 47:16

8:9
s1Ki 8:65;
2Ch 8:4

8:11
t1Ki 7:51;
1Ch 26:26

8:12
uver 2
v2Sa 10:14
w2Sa 5:25
x1Sa 27:8

8:13
y2Sa 7:9
z2Ki 14:7;
1Ch 18:12

8:14
aNu 24:17-18
bGe 27:29,37-40
cver 6

8:16
d2Sa 19:13;
1Ch 11:6
e2Sa 20:24;
1Ki 4:3

8:17
f2Sa 15:24,29;
1Ch 16:39; 24:3
g1Ki 4:3;
2Ki 12:10

8:18
h2Sa 20:23;
1Ki 1:8,38;
1Ch 18:17
i1Sa 30:14

9:1
j1Sa 20:14-17,42

9:2
k2Sa 16:1-4;
19:17,26,29

9:3
l1Sa 20:14
m2Sa 4:4

---

[a]8 See some Septuagint manuscripts (see also 1 Chron. 18:8); Hebrew *Betah*.   [b]9 Hebrew *Toi*, a variant of *Tou*; also in verse 10   [c]10 A variant of *Hadoram*   [d]12 Some Hebrew manuscripts, Septuagint and Syriac (see also 1 Chron. 18:11); most Hebrew manuscripts *Aram*   [e]13 A few Hebrew manuscripts, Septuagint and Syriac (see also 1 Chron. 18:12); most Hebrew manuscripts *Aram* (that is, Arameans)   [f]18 Or *were priests*

Ziba answered, "He is at the house of Makir[n] son of Ammiel in Lo Debar."

[5]So King David had him brought from Lo Debar, from the house of Makir son of Ammiel.

[6]When Mephibosheth son of Jonathan, the son of Saul, came to David, he bowed down to pay him honor.[o]

David said, "Mephibosheth!"

"Your servant," he replied.

[7]"Don't be afraid," David said to him, "for I will surely show you kindness for the sake of your father Jonathan. I will restore to you all the land that belonged to your grandfather Saul, and you will always eat at my table.[p]"

[8]Mephibosheth bowed down and said, "What is your servant, that you should notice a dead dog[q] like me?"

[9]Then the king summoned Ziba, Saul's servant, and said to him, "I have given your master's grandson everything that belonged to Saul and his family. [10]You and your sons and your servants are to farm the land for him and bring in the crops, so that your master's grandson[r] may be provided for. And Mephibosheth, grandson of your master, will always eat at my table." (Now Ziba had fifteen sons and twenty servants.)

[11]Then Ziba said to the king, "Your servant will do whatever my lord the king commands his servant to do." So Mephibosheth ate at David's[a] table like one of the king's sons.[s]

[12]Mephibosheth had a young son named Mica, and all the members of Ziba's household were servants of Mephibosheth.[t] [13]And Mephibosheth lived in Jerusalem, because he always ate at the king's table, and he was crippled in both feet.

David Defeats the Ammonites

10:1-19pp — 1Ch 19:1-19

10 In the course of time, the king of the Ammonites died, and his son Hanun succeeded him as king. [2]David thought, "I will show kindness to Hanun son of Nahash,[u] just as his father showed kindness to me." So David sent a delegation to express his sympathy to Hanun concerning his father.

When David's men came to the land of the Ammonites, [3]the Ammonite nobles said to Hanun their lord, "Do you think David is honoring your father by sending men to you to express sympathy? Hasn't David sent them to you to explore the city and spy it out and overthrow it?" [4]So Hanun seized David's men, shaved off half of each man's beard,[v] cut off their garments in the middle at the buttocks,[w] and sent them away.

[5]When David was told about this, he sent messengers to meet the men, for they were greatly humiliated. The king said, "Stay at Jericho till your beards have grown, and then come back."

[6]When the Ammonites realized that they had become a stench[x] in David's nostrils, they hired twenty thousand Aramean[y] foot soldiers from Beth Rehob[z] and Zobah, as well as the king of Maacah[a] with a thousand men, and also twelve thousand men from Tob.

9:4
n2Sa 17:27-29
9:6
o2Sa 16:4;
19:24-30
9:7
pver 1,3;
2Sa 12:8;
19:28; 1Ki 2:7;
2Ki 25:29
9:8
q2Sa 16:9
9:10
rver 7,11,13;
2Sa 19:28
9:11
sJob 36:7;
Ps 113:8
9:12
t1Ch 8:34
10:2
u1Sa 11:1
10:4
vLev 19:27;
Isa 15:2;
Jer 48:37
wIsa 20:4
10:6
xGe 34:30
y2Sa 8:5
zJdg 18:28
aDt 3:14

---

[a]11 Septuagint; Hebrew *my*

7On hearing this, David sent Joab out with the entire army of fighting men. 8The Ammonites came out and drew up in battle formation at the entrance to their city gate, while the Arameans of Zobah and Rehob and the men of Tob and Maacah were by themselves in the open country.

9Joab saw that there were battle lines in front of him and behind him; so he selected some of the best troops in Israel and deployed them against the Arameans. 10He put the rest of the men under the command of Abishai his brother and deployed them against the Ammonites. 11Joab said, "If the Arameans are too strong for me, then you are to come to my rescue; but if the Ammonites are too strong for you, then I will come to rescue you. 12Be strong[b] and let us fight bravely for our people and the cities of our God. The LORD will do what is good in his sight."[c]

10:12
bDt 31:6;
1Co 16:13;
Eph 6:10
cJdg 10:15;
1Sa 3:18;
Ne 4:14
10:19
d2Sa 8:6
e1Ki 11:25;
2Ki 5:1
11:1
f1Ki 20:22,26
g2Sa 2:18
h1Ch 20:1
i2Sa 12:26-28
11:2
jDt 22:8;
Jos 2:8
kMt 5:28
11:3
l1Ch 3:5
m2Sa 23:34
n2Sa 23:39
11:4
oLev 20:10;
Ps 51 Title;
Jas 1:14-15
pDt 22:22
qLev 15:25-30;
18:19
11:6
r1Ch 11:41

13Then Joab and the troops with him advanced to fight the Arameans, and they fled before him. 14When the Ammonites saw that the Arameans were fleeing, they fled before Abishai and went inside the city. So Joab returned from fighting the Ammonites and came to Jerusalem.

15After the Arameans saw that they had been routed by Israel, they regrouped. 16Hadadezer had Arameans brought from beyond the River[a]; they went to Helam, with Shobach the commander of Hadadezer's army leading them.

17When David was told of this, he gathered all Israel, crossed the Jordan and went to Helam. The Arameans formed their battle lines to meet David and fought against him. 18But they fled before Israel, and David killed seven hundred of their charioteers and forty thousand of their foot soldiers.[b] He also struck down Shobach the commander of their army, and he died there. 19When all the kings who were vassals of Hadadezer saw that they had been defeated by Israel, they made peace with the Israelites and became subject[d] to them.

So the Arameans[e] were afraid to help the Ammonites anymore.

David and Bathsheba

11 In the spring,[f] at the time when kings go off to war, David sent Joab[g] out with the king's men and the whole Israelite army.[h] They destroyed the Ammonites and besieged Rabbah.[i] But David remained in Jerusalem.

2One evening David got up from his bed and walked around on the roof[j] of the palace. From the roof he saw[k] a woman bathing. The woman was very beautiful, 3and David sent someone to find out about her. The man said, "Isn't this Bathsheba,[l] the daughter of Eliam[m] and the wife of Uriah[n] the Hittite?" 4Then David sent messengers to get her.[o] She came to him, and he slept[p] with her. (She had purified herself from her uncleanness.)[q] Then[c] she went back home. 5The woman conceived and sent word to David, saying, "I am pregnant."

6So David sent this word to Joab: "Send me Uriah[r] the Hittite." And Joab sent him to David. 7When Uriah came to him, David asked him how Joab was, how the soldiers were and how the war was going. 8Then David said to Uriah, "Go down to your house and wash your

---

a16 That is, the Euphrates   b18 Some Septuagint manuscripts (see also 1 Chron. 19:18);
Hebrew *horsemen*   c4 Or *with her. When she purified herself from her uncleanness,*

feet."[s] So Uriah left the palace, and a gift from the king was sent after him. [9]But Uriah slept at the entrance to the palace with all his master's servants and did not go down to his house.

[10]When David was told, "Uriah did not go home," he asked him, "Haven't you just come from a distance? Why didn't you go home?"

[11]Uriah said to David, "The ark[t] and Israel and Judah are staying in tents, and my master Joab and my lord's men are camped in the open fields. How could I go to my house to eat and drink and lie with my wife? As surely as you live, I will not do such a thing!"

[12]Then David said to him, "Stay here one more day, and tomorrow I will send you back." So Uriah remained in Jerusalem that day and the next. [13]At David's invitation, he ate and drank with him, and David made him drunk. But in the evening Uriah went out to sleep on his mat among his master's servants; he did not go home.

[14]In the morning David wrote a letter[u] to Joab and sent it with Uriah. [15]In it he wrote, "Put Uriah in the front line where the fighting is fiercest. Then withdraw from him so he will be struck down[v] and die.[w]"

[16]So while Joab had the city under siege, he put Uriah at a place where he knew the strongest defenders were. [17]When the men of the city came out and fought against Joab, some of the men in David's army fell; moreover, Uriah the Hittite was dead.

[18]Joab sent David a full account of the battle. [19]He instructed the messenger: "When you have finished giving the king this account of the battle, [20]the king's anger may flare up, and he may ask you, 'Why did you get so close to the city to fight? Didn't you know they would shoot arrows from the wall? [21]Who killed Abimelech[x] son of Jerub-Besheth[a]? Didn't a woman throw an upper millstone on him from the wall,[y] so that he died in Thebez? Why did you get so close to the wall?' If he asks you this, then say to him, 'Also, your servant Uriah the Hittite is dead.'"

[22]The messenger set out, and when he arrived he told David everything Joab had sent him to say. [23]The messenger said to David, "The men overpowered us and came out against us in the open, but we drove them back to the entrance to the city gate. [24]Then the archers shot arrows at your servants from the wall, and some of the king's men died. Moreover, your servant Uriah the Hittite is dead."

[25]David told the messenger, "Say this to Joab: 'Don't let this upset you; the sword devours one as well as another. Press the attack against the city and destroy it.' Say this to encourage Joab."

[26]When Uriah's wife heard that her husband was dead, she mourned for him. [27]After the time of mourning was over, David had her brought to his house, and she became his wife and bore him a son. But the thing David had done displeased[z] the LORD.

Nathan Rebukes David

11:1; 12:29-31pp — 1Ch 20:1-3

12 The LORD sent Nathan[a] to David.[b] When he came to him,[c] he said, "There were two men in a certain town, one rich and the other poor. [2]The rich man had a very large number of sheep and cattle,

---

11:8
sGe 18:4;
43:24; Lk 7:44
11:11
t2Sa 7:2
11:14
u1Ki 21:8
11:15
v2Sa 12:9
w2Sa 12:12
11:21
xJdg 8:31
yJdg 9:50-54
11:27
z2Sa 12:9;
Ps 51:4-5
12:1
a2Sa 7:2;
1Ki 20:35-41
bPs 51 Title
c2Sa 14:4

---

[a]21 Also known as *Jerub-Baal* (that is, Gideon)

³but the poor man had nothing except one little ewe lamb he had bought. He raised it, and it grew up with him and his children. It shared his food, drank from his cup and even slept in his arms. It was like a daughter to him.

⁴"Now a traveler came to the rich man, but the rich man refrained from taking one of his own sheep or cattle to prepare a meal for the traveler who had come to him. Instead, he took the ewe lamb that belonged to the poor man and prepared it for the one who had come to him."

⁵David[d] burned with anger against the man and said to Nathan, "As surely as the LORD lives, the man who did this deserves to die! ⁶He must pay for that lamb four times over,[e] because he did such a thing and had no pity."

⁷Then Nathan said to David, "You are the man! This is what the LORD, the God of Israel, says: 'I anointed[f] you[g] king over Israel, and I delivered you from the hand of Saul. ⁸I gave your master's house to you,[h] and your master's wives into your arms. I gave you the house of Israel and Judah. And if all this had been too little, I would have given you even more. ⁹Why did you despise[i] the word of the LORD by doing what is evil in his eyes? You struck down[j] Uriah the Hittite with the sword and took his wife to be your own. You killed him with the sword of the Ammonites. ¹⁰Now, therefore, the sword[k] will never depart from your house, because you despised me and took the wife of Uriah the Hittite to be your own.'

¹¹"This is what the LORD says: 'Out of your own household I am going to bring calamity upon you.[l] Before your very eyes I will take your wives and give them to one who is close to you, and he will lie with your wives in broad daylight. ¹²You did it in secret,[m] but I will do this thing in broad daylight[n] before all Israel.'"

¹³Then David said to Nathan, "I have sinned[o] against the LORD."

Nathan replied, "The LORD has taken away[p] your sin.[q] You are not going to die.[r] ¹⁴But because by doing this you have made the enemies of the LORD show utter contempt,[a][s] the son born to you will die."

¹⁵After Nathan had gone home, the LORD struck[t] the child that Uriah's wife had borne to David, and he became ill. ¹⁶David pleaded with God for the child. He fasted and went into his house and spent the nights lying[u] on the ground. ¹⁷The elders of his household stood beside him to get him up from the ground, but he refused, and he would not eat any food with them.[v]

¹⁸On the seventh day the child died. David's servants were afraid to tell him that the child was dead, for they thought, "While the child was still living, we spoke to David but he would not listen to us. How can we tell him the child is dead? He may do something desperate."

¹⁹David noticed that his servants were whispering among themselves and he realized the child was dead. "Is the child dead?" he asked.

"Yes," they replied, "he is dead."

²⁰Then David got up from the ground. After he had washed,[w] put on lotions and changed his clothes,[x] he went into the house of the LORD

12:5
d 1Ki 20:40

12:6
e Ex 22:1;
Lk 19:8

12:7
f 1Sa 16:13
g 1Ki 20:42

12:8
h 2Sa 9:7

12:9
i Nu 15:31;
1Sa 15:19
j 2Sa 11:15

12:10
k 2Sa 13:28;
18:14-15;
1Ki 2:25

12:11
l Dt 28:30;
2Sa 16:21-22

12:12
m 2Sa 11:4-15
n 2Sa 16:22

12:13
o Ge 13:13;
Nu 22:34;
1Sa 15:24;
2Sa 24:10
p Ps 32:1-5;
51:1,9; 103:12;
Zec 3:4,9
q Pr 28:13;
Mic 7:18-19
r Lev 20:10;
24:17

12:14
s Isa 52:5;
Ro 2:24

12:15
t 1Sa 25:38

12:16
u 2Sa 13:31;
Ps 5:7

12:17
v 2Sa 3:35

12:20
w Mt 6:17
x Job 1:20

---

a14 Masoretic Text; an ancient Hebrew scribal tradition this you have shown utter contempt for the LORD and worshiped. Then he went to his own house, and at his request they served him food, and he ate.

[21]His servants asked him, "Why are you acting this way? While the child was alive, you fasted and wept, [y] but now that the child is dead, you get up and eat!"

[22]He answered, "While the child was still alive, I fasted and wept. I thought, 'Who knows?[z] The LORD may be gracious to me and let the child live.'[a] [23]But now that he is dead, why should I fast? Can I bring him back again? I will go to him,[b] but he will not return to me."[c]

[24]Then David comforted his wife Bathsheba,[d] and he went to her and lay with her. She gave birth to a son, and they named him Solomon.[e] The LORD loved him; [25]and because the LORD loved him, he sent word through Nathan the prophet to name him Jedidiah.[a][f]

[26]Meanwhile Joab fought against Rabbah[g] of the Ammonites and captured the royal citadel. [27]Joab then sent messengers to David, saying, "I have fought against Rabbah and taken its water supply. [28]Now muster the rest of the troops and besiege the city and capture it. Otherwise I will take the city, and it will be named after me."

[29]So David mustered the entire army and went to Rabbah, and attacked and captured it. [30]He took the crown[h] from the head of their king[b]—its weight was a talent[c] of gold, and it was set with precious stones—and it was placed on David's head. He took a great quantity of plunder from the city [31]and brought out the people who were there, consigning them to labor with saws and with iron picks and axes, and he made them work at brickmaking.[d] He did this to all the Ammonite[i] towns. Then David and his entire army returned to Jerusalem.

Amnon and Tamar

13 In the course of time, Amnon[j] son of David fell in love with Tamar,[k] the beautiful sister of Absalom[l] son of David.

[2]Amnon became frustrated to the point of illness on account of his sister Tamar, for she was a virgin, and it seemed impossible for him to do anything to her.

[3]Now Amnon had a friend named Jonadab son of Shimeah,[m] David's brother. Jonadab was a very shrewd man. [4]He asked Amnon, "Why do you, the king's son, look so haggard morning after morning? Won't you tell me?"

Amnon said to him, "I'm in love with Tamar, my brother Absalom's sister."

[5]"Go to bed and pretend to be ill," Jonadab said. "When your father comes to see you, say to him, 'I would like my sister Tamar to come and give me something to eat. Let her prepare the food in my sight so I may watch her and then eat it from her hand.'"

[6]So Amnon lay down and pretended to be ill. When the king came to see him, Amnon said to him, "I would like my sister Tamar to come and make some special bread in my sight, so I may eat from her hand."

[7]David sent word to Tamar at the palace: "Go to the house of your brother Amnon and prepare some food for him." [8]So Tamar went to the house of her brother Amnon, who was lying down. She took some

12:21
yJdg 20:26
12:22
zJnh 3:9
aIsa 38:1-5
12:23
bGe 37:35
c1Sa 31:13;
2Sa 13:39;
Job 7:10; 10:21
12:24
d1Ki 1:11
e1Ki 1:10;
1Ch 22:9; 28:5;
Mt 1:6
12:25
fNe 13:26
12:26
gDt 3:11;
1Ch 20:1-3
12:30
h1Ch 20:2;
Est 8:15;
Ps 21:3; 132:18
12:31
i1Sa 14:47
13:1
j2Sa 3:2
k2Sa 14:27;
1Ch 3:9
l2Sa 3:3
13:3
m1Sa 16:9

---

[a]25 *Jedidiah* means *loved by the* LORD.   [b]30 Or *of Milcom* (that is, Molech)   [c]30 That is, about 75 pounds (about 34 kilograms)   [d]31 The meaning of the Hebrew for this clause is uncertain.

dough, kneaded it, made the bread in his sight and baked it. [9]Then she took the pan and served him the bread, but he refused to eat.

"Send everyone out of here,"[n] Amnon said. So everyone left him. [10]Then Amnon said to Tamar, "Bring the food here into my bedroom so I may eat from your hand." And Tamar took the bread she had prepared and brought it to her brother Amnon in his bedroom. [11]But when she took it to him to eat, he grabbed[o] her and said, "Come to bed with me, my sister."[p]

[12]"Don't, my brother!" she said to him. "Don't force me. Such a thing should not be done in Israel![q] Don't do this wicked thing.[r] [13]What about me?[s] Where could I get rid of my disgrace? And what about you? You would be like one of the wicked fools in Israel. Please speak to the king; he will not keep me from being married to you." [14]But he refused to listen to her, and since he was stronger than she, he raped her.[t]

[15]Then Amnon hated her with intense hatred. In fact, he hated her more than he had loved her. Amnon said to her, "Get up and get out!"

[16]"No!" she said to him. "Sending me away would be a greater wrong than what you have already done to me."

But he refused to listen to her. [17]He called his personal servant and said, "Get this woman out of here and bolt the door after her." [18]So his servant put her out and bolted the door after her. She was wearing a richly ornamented[a] robe,[u] for this was the kind of garment the virgin daughters of the king wore. [19]Tamar put ashes[v] on her head and tore the ornamented[b] robe she was wearing. She put her hand on her head and went away, weeping aloud as she went.

[20]Her brother Absalom said to her, "Has that Amnon, your brother, been with you? Be quiet now, my sister; he is your brother. Don't take this thing to heart." And Tamar lived in her brother Absalom's house, a desolate woman.

[21]When King David heard all this, he was furious.[w] [22]Absalom never said a word to Amnon, either good or bad;[x] he hated[y] Amnon because he had disgraced his sister Tamar.

Absalom Kills Amnon

[23]Two years later, when Absalom's sheepshearers[z] were at Baal Hazor near the border of Ephraim, he invited all the king's sons to come there. [24]Absalom went to the king and said, "Your servant has had shearers come. Will the king and his officials please join me?"

[25]"No, my son," the king replied. "All of us should not go; we would only be a burden to you." Although Absalom urged him, he still refused to go, but gave him his blessing.

[26]Then Absalom said, "If not, please let my brother Amnon come with us."

The king asked him, "Why should he go with you?" [27]But Absalom urged him, so he sent with him Amnon and the rest of the king's sons.

[28]Absalom[a] ordered his men, "Listen! When Amnon is in high[b] spirits from drinking wine and I say to you, 'Strike Amnon down,' then kill him. Don't be afraid. Have not I given you this order? Be strong and brave.[c]" [29]So Absalom's men did to Amnon what Absalom had or-

13:9
n Ge 45:1
13:11
o Ge 39:12
p Ge 38:16
13:12
q Lev 20:17;
Jdg 20:6
r Ge 34:7;
Jdg 19:23
13:13
s Ge 20:12;
Lev 18:9;
Dt 22:21,23-24
13:14
t Ge 34:2;
Dt 22:25;
Eze 22:11
13:18
u Ge 37:23;
Jdg 5:30
13:19
v Jos 7:6;
1Sa 4:12;
2Sa 1:2;
Est 4:1; Da 9:3
13:21
w Ge 34:7
13:22
x Ge 31:24
y Lev 19:17-18;
1Jn 2:9-11
13:23
z 1Sa 25:7
13:28
a 2Sa 3:3
b Jdg 19:6,9,22;
Ru 3:7;
1Sa 25:36
c 2Sa 12:10

---

[a]18 The meaning of the Hebrew for this phrase is uncertain.   [b]19 The meaning of the Hebrew for this word is uncertain.

dered. Then all the king's sons got up, mounted their mules and fled.

[30]While they were on their way, the report came to David: "Absalom has struck down all the king's sons; not one of them is left." [31]The king stood up, tore[d] his clothes and lay down on the ground; and all his servants stood by with their clothes torn.

[32]But Jonadab son of Shimeah, David's brother, said, "My lord should not think that they killed all the princes; only Amnon is dead. This has been Absalom's expressed intention ever since the day Amnon raped his sister Tamar. [33]My lord the king should not be concerned about the report that all the king's sons are dead. Only Amnon is dead."

[34]Meanwhile, Absalom had fled.

Now the man standing watch looked up and saw many people on the road west of him, coming down the side of the hill. The watchman went and told the king, "I see men in the direction of Horonaim, on the side of the hill."[a]

[35]Jonadab said to the king, "See, the king's sons are here; it has happened just as your servant said."

[36]As he finished speaking, the king's sons came in, wailing loudly. The king, too, and all his servants wept very bitterly.

[37]Absalom fled and went to Talmai[e] son of Ammihud, the king of Geshur. But King David mourned for his son every day.

[38]After Absalom fled and went to Geshur, he stayed there three years. [39]And the spirit of the king[b] longed to go to Absalom,[f] for he was consoled[g] concerning Amnon's death.

Absalom Returns to Jerusalem

14 Joab[h] son of Zeruiah knew that the king's heart longed for Absalom. [2]So Joab sent someone to Tekoa[i] and had a wise woman[j] brought from there. He said to her, "Pretend you are in mourning. Dress in mourning clothes, and don't use any cosmetic lotions.[k] Act like a woman who has spent many days grieving for the dead. [3]Then go to the king and speak these words to him." And Joab[l] put the words in her mouth.

[4]When the woman from Tekoa went[c] to the king, she fell with her face to the ground to pay him honor, and she said, "Help me, O king!"

[5]The king asked her, "What is troubling you?"

She said, "I am indeed a widow; my husband is dead. [6]I your servant had two sons. They got into a fight with each other in the field, and no one was there to separate them. One struck the other and killed him. [7]Now the whole clan has risen up against your servant; they say, 'Hand over the one who struck his brother down, so that we may put him to death[m] for the life of his brother whom he killed; then we will get rid of the heir[n] as well.' They would put out the only burning coal I have left,[o] leaving my husband neither name nor descendant on the face of the earth."

[8]The king said to the woman, "Go home,[p] and I will issue an order in your behalf."

13:31
dNu 14:6;
2Sa 1:11; 12:16
13:37
ever 34;
2Sa 3:3;
14:23,32
13:39
f2Sa 14:13
g2Sa 12:19-23
14:1
h2Sa 2:18
14:2
i2Ch 11:6;
Ne 3:5; Jer 6:1;
Am 1:1
j2Sa 20:16
kRu 3:3;
2Sa 12:20;
Isa 1:6
14:3
lver 19
14:7
mNu 35:19
nMt 21:38
oDt 19:10-13
14:8
p1Sa 25:35

---

[a]34 Septuagint; Hebrew does not have this sentence.   [b]39 Dead Sea Scrolls and some Septuagint manuscripts; Masoretic Text *But the spirit of David the king*   [c]4 Many Hebrew manuscripts, Septuagint, Vulgate and Syriac; most Hebrew manuscripts *spoke*

⁹But the woman from Tekoa said to him, "My lord the king, let the blame�q rest on me and on my father's family,ʳ and let the king and his throne be without guilt.ˢ"

¹⁰The king replied, "If anyone says anything to you, bring him to me, and he will not bother you again."

¹¹She said, "Then let the king invoke the Lord his God to prevent the avengerᵗ of blood from adding to the destruction, so that my son will not be destroyed."

"As surely as the Lord lives," he said, "not one hairᵘ of your son's head will fall to the ground.ᵛ"

¹²Then the woman said, "Let your servant speak a word to my lord the king."

"Speak," he replied.

¹³The woman said, "Why then have you devised a thing like this against the people of God? When the king says this, does he not convict himself,ʷ for the king has not brought back his banished son?ˣ ¹⁴Like waterʸ spilled on the ground, which cannot be recovered, so we must die.ᶻ But God does not take away life; instead, he devises ways so that a banished personᵃ may not remain estranged from him.

¹⁵"And now I have come to say this to my lord the king because the people have made me afraid. Your servant thought, 'I will speak to the king; perhaps he will do what his servant asks. ¹⁶Perhaps the king will agree to deliver his servant from the hand of the man who is trying to cut off both me and my son from the inheritanceᵇ God gave us.'

¹⁷"And now your servant says, 'May the word of my lord the king bring me rest, for my lord the king is like an angelᶜ of God in discerningᵈ good and evil. May the Lord your God be with you.'"

¹⁸Then the king said to the woman, "Do not keep from me the answer to what I am going to ask you."

"Let my lord the king speak," the woman said.

¹⁹The king asked, "Isn't the hand of Joabᵉ with you in all this?"

The woman answered, "As surely as you live, my lord the king, no one can turn to the right or to the left from anything my lord the king says. Yes, it was your servant Joab who instructed me to do this and who put all these words into the mouth of your servant. ²⁰Your servant Joab did this to change the present situation. My lord has wisdomᶠ like that of an angel of God—he knows everything that happens in the land.ᵍ"

²¹The king said to Joab, "Very well, I will do it. Go, bring back the young man Absalom."

²²Joab fell with his face to the ground to pay him honor, and he blessed the king.ʰ Joab said, "Today your servant knows that he has found favor in your eyes, my lord the king, because the king has granted his servant's request."

²³Then Joab went to Geshur and brought Absalom back to Jerusalem. ²⁴But the king said, "He must go to his own house; he must not see my face." So Absalom went to his own house and did not see the face of the king.

²⁵In all Israel there was not a man so highly praised for his handsome appearance as Absalom. From the top of his head to the sole of his foot there was no blemish in him. ²⁶Whenever he cut the hair of his headⁱ —he used to cut his hair from time to time when it became too heavy for

14:9
q 1Sa 25:24
r Mt 27:25
s 1Sa 25:28;
1Ki 2:33
14:11
t Nu 35:12,21
u Mt 10:30
v 1Sa 14:45
14:13
w 2Sa 12:7;
1Ki 20:40
x 2Sa 13:38-39
14:14
y Job 14:11;
Ps 58:7;
Isa 19:5
z Job 10:8;
17:13; 30:23;
Ps 22:15;
Heb 9:27
a Nu 35:15,
25-28; Job 34:15
14:16
b Ex 34:9;
1Sa 26:19
14:17
c ver 20;
1Sa 29:9;
2Sa 19:27
d 1Ki 3:9;
Da 2:21
14:19
e ver 3
14:20
f 1Ki 3:12,28;
Isa 28:6
g ver 17;
2Sa 18:13;
19:27
14:22
h Ge 47:7
14:26
i 2Sa 18:9;
Eze 44:20

him—he would weigh it, and its weight was two hundred shekels[a] by the royal standard.

27Three sons[j] and a daughter were born to Absalom. The daughter's name was Tamar,[k] and she became a beautiful woman.

28Absalom lived two years in Jerusalem without seeing the king's face. 29Then Absalom sent for Joab in order to send him to the king, but Joab refused to come to him. So he sent a second time, but he refused to come. 30Then he said to his servants, "Look, Joab's field is next to mine, and he has barley[l] there. Go and set it on fire." So Absalom's servants set the field on fire.

31Then Joab did go to Absalom's house and he said to him, "Why have your servants set my field on fire?[m]"

32Absalom said to Joab, "Look, I sent word to you and said, 'Come here so I can send you to the king to ask, "Why have I come from Geshur?[n] It would be better for me if I were still there!" ' Now then, I want to see the king's face, and if I am guilty of anything, let him put me to death."[o]

33So Joab went to the king and told him this. Then the king summoned Absalom, and he came in and bowed down with his face to the ground before the king. And the king kissed[p] Absalom.

Absalom's Conspiracy

15 In the course of time,[q] Absalom provided himself with a chariot[r] and horses and with fifty men to run ahead of him. 2He would get up early and stand by the side of the road leading to the city gate.[s] Whenever anyone came with a complaint to be placed before the king for a decision, Absalom would call out to him, "What town are you from?" He would answer, "Your servant is from one of the tribes of Israel." 3Then Absalom would say to him, "Look, your claims are valid and proper, but there is no representative of the king to hear you."[t] 4And Absalom would add, "If only I were appointed judge in the land![u] Then everyone who has a complaint or case could come to me and I would see that he gets justice."

5Also, whenever anyone approached him to bow down before him, Absalom would reach out his hand, take hold of him and kiss him. 6Absalom behaved in this way toward all the Israelites who came to the king asking for justice, and so he stole the hearts[v] of the men of Israel.

7At the end of four[b] years, Absalom said to the king, "Let me go to Hebron and fulfill a vow I made to the LORD. 8While your servant was living at Geshur[w] in Aram, I made this vow:[x] 'If the LORD takes me back to Jerusalem, I will worship the LORD in Hebron.[c] ' "

9The king said to him, "Go in peace." So he went to Hebron.

10Then Absalom sent secret messengers throughout the tribes of Israel to say, "As soon as you hear the sound of the trumpets,[y] then say, 'Absalom is king in Hebron.' " 11Two hundred men from Jerusalem had accompanied Absalom. They had been invited as guests and went quite innocently, knowing nothing about the matter. 12While Absalom was offering sacrifices, he also sent for Ahithophel[z] the Gilonite, David's counselor,[a] to come from Giloh,[b] his hometown. And so

14:27
j2Sa 18:18
k2Sa 13:1

14:30
lEx 9:31

14:31
mJdg 15:5

14:32
n2Sa 3:3
o1Sa 20:8

14:33
pGe 33:4;
Lk 15:20

15:1
q2Sa 12:11
r1Sa 8:11;
1Ki 1:5

15:2
sGe 23:10;
2Sa 19:8

15:3
tPr 12:2

15:4
uJdg 9:29

15:6
vRo 16:18

15:8
w2Sa 3:3;
13:37-38
xGe 28:20

15:10
y1Ki 1:34,39;
2Ki 9:13

15:12
zver 31,34;
2Sa 16:15,23;
1Ch 27:33
aJob 19:14;
Ps 41:9; 55:13;
Jer 9:4
bJos 15:51

---

a26 That is, about 5 pounds (about 2.3 kilograms)   *b7* Some Septuagint manuscripts, Syriac and Josephus; Hebrew *forty*   *c8* Some Septuagint manuscripts; Hebrew does not have *in Hebron*.

the conspiracy gained strength, and Absalom's following kept on increasing.[c]

David Flees

[13]A messenger came and told David, "The hearts of the men of Israel are with Absalom."

[14]Then David said to all his officials who were with him in Jerusalem, "Come! We must flee,[d] or none of us will escape from Absalom.[e] We must leave immediately, or he will move quickly to overtake us and bring ruin upon us and put the city to the sword."

[15]The king's officials answered him, "Your servants are ready to do whatever our lord the king chooses."

[16]The king set out, with his entire household following him; but he left ten concubines[f] to take care of the palace. [17]So the king set out, with all the people following him, and they halted at a place some distance away. [18]All his men marched past him, along with all the Kerethites[g] and Pelethites; and all the six hundred Gittites who had accompanied him from Gath marched before the king.

[19]The king said to Ittai[h] the Gittite, "Why should you come along with us? Go back and stay with King Absalom. You are a foreigner,[i] an exile from your homeland. [20]You came only yesterday. And today shall I make you wander[j] about with us, when I do not know where I am going? Go back, and take your countrymen. May kindness and faithfulness[k] be with you."

[21]But Ittai replied to the king, "As surely as the LORD lives, and as my lord the king lives, wherever my lord the king may be, whether it means life or death, there will your servant be."[l]

[22]David said to Ittai, "Go ahead, march on." So Ittai the Gittite marched on with all his men and the families that were with him.

[23]The whole countryside wept aloud as all the people passed by. The king also crossed the Kidron Valley,[m] and all the people moved on toward the desert.

[24]Zadok[n] was there, too, and all the Levites who were with him were carrying the ark[o] of the covenant of God. They set down the ark of God, and Abiathar[p] offered sacrifices[a] until all the people had finished leaving the city.

[25]Then the king said to Zadok, "Take the ark of God back into the city. If I find favor in the LORD's eyes, he will bring me back and let me see it and his dwelling place[q] again. [26]But if he says, 'I am not pleased with you,' then I am ready; let him do to me whatever seems good to him.[r]"

[27]The king also said to Zadok the priest, "Aren't you a seer?[s] Go back to the city in peace, with your son Ahimaaz and Jonathan[t] son of Abiathar. You and Abiathar take your two sons with you. [28]I will wait at the fords[u] in the desert until word comes from you to inform me." [29]So Zadok and Abiathar took the ark of God back to Jerusalem and stayed there.

[30]But David continued up the Mount of Olives, weeping[v] as he went; his head[w] was covered and he was barefoot. All the people with him covered their heads too and were weeping as they went up. [31]Now

15:12
cPs 3:1
15:14
d2Sa 12:11;
1Ki 2:26;
Ps 132:1; Ps 3
Title e2Sa 19:9
15:16
f2Sa 16:21-22;
20:3
15:18
g1Sa 30:14;
2Sa 8:18; 20:7,
23; 1Ki 1:38,44;
1Ch 18:17
15:19
h2Sa 18:2
iGe 31:15
15:20
j1Sa 23:13
k2Sa 2:6
15:21
lRu 1:16-17;
Pr 17:17
15:23
m2Ch 29:16
15:24
n2Sa 8:17
oNu 4:15
p1Sa 22:20
15:25
qEx 15:13;
Ps 43:3;
Jer 25:30
15:26
r1Sa 3:18;
2Sa 22:20;
1Ki 10:9
15:27
s1Sa 9:9
t2Sa 17:17
15:28
u2Sa 17:16
15:30
v2Sa 19:4;
Ps 126:6
wEst 6:12;
Isa 20:2-4

[a]24 Or Abiathar went up

David had been told, "Ahithophel[x] is among the conspirators with Absalom." So David prayed, "O LORD, turn Ahithophel's counsel into foolishness."

[32]When David arrived at the summit, where people used to worship God, Hushai the Arkite[y] was there to meet him, his robe torn and dust[z] on his head. [33]David said to him, "If you go with me, you will be a burden[a] to me. [34]But if you return to the city and say to Absalom, 'I will be your servant, O king; I was your father's servant in the past, but now I will be your servant,'[b] then you can help me by frustrating Ahithophel's advice. [35]Won't the priests Zadok and Abiathar be there with you? Tell them anything you hear in the king's palace.[c] [36]Their two sons, Ahimaaz son of Zadok and Jonathan[d] son of Abiathar, are there with them. Send them to me with anything you hear."

[37]So David's friend Hushai[e] arrived at Jerusalem as Absalom[f] was entering the city.

David and Ziba

16 When David had gone a short distance beyond the summit, there was Ziba,[g] the steward of Mephibosheth, waiting to meet him. He had a string of donkeys saddled and loaded with two hundred loaves of bread, a hundred cakes of raisins, a hundred cakes of figs and a skin of wine.[h]

[2]The king asked Ziba, "Why have you brought these?"

Ziba answered, "The donkeys are for the king's household to ride on, the bread and fruit are for the men to eat, and the wine is to refresh[i] those who become exhausted in the desert."

[3]The king then asked, "Where is your master's grandson?"[i]

Ziba said to him, "He is staying in Jerusalem, because he thinks, 'Today the house of Israel will give me back my grandfather's kingdom.'"

[4]Then the king said to Ziba, "All that belonged to Mephibosheth is now yours."

"I humbly bow," Ziba said. "May I find favor in your eyes, my lord the king."

Shimei Curses David

[5]As King David approached Bahurim,[k] a man from the same clan as Saul's family came out from there. His name was Shimei[l] son of Gera, and he cursed[m] as he came out. [6]He pelted David and all the king's officials with stones, though all the troops and the special guard were on David's right and left. [7]As he cursed, Shimei said, "Get out, get out, you man of blood, you scoundrel! [8]The LORD has repaid you for all the blood you shed in the household of Saul, in whose place you have reigned.[n] The LORD has handed the kingdom over to your son Absalom. You have come to ruin because you are a man of blood!"

[9]Then Abishai[o] son of Zeruiah said to the king, "Why should this dead dog curse my lord the king? Let me go over and cut off his head."[p]

[10]But the king said, "What do you and I have in common, you sons of Zeruiah?[q] If he is cursing because the LORD said to him, 'Curse David,' who can ask, 'Why do you do this?'"[r]

[11]David then said to Abishai and all his officials, "My son,[s] who is of

15:31
xver 12;
2Sa 16:23;
17:14,23
15:32
yJos 16:2
z2Sa 1:2
15:33
a2Sa 19:35
15:34
b2Sa 16:19
15:35
c2Sa 17:15-16
15:36
dver 27;
2Sa 17:17
15:37
e2Sa 16:16-17;
1Ch 27:33
f2Sa 16:15
16:1
g2Sa 9:1-13
h1Sa 25:18
16:2
i2Sa 17:27-29
16:3
j2Sa 9:9-10;
19:26-27
16:5
k2Sa 3:16
l2Sa 19:16-23;
1Ki 2:8-9,36,44
mEx 22:28
16:8
n2Sa 21:9
16:9
o2Sa 9:8
pEx 22:28;
Lk 9:54
16:10
q2Sa 19:22
rRo 9:20
16:11
s2Sa 12:11

my own flesh, is trying to take my life. How much more, then, this Benjamite! Leave him alone; let him curse, for the LORD has told him to.[t] [12]It may be that the LORD will see my distress[u] and repay me with good[v] for the cursing I am receiving today.[w]"

[13]So David and his men continued along the road while Shimei was going along the hillside opposite him, cursing as he went and throwing stones at him and showering him with dirt. [14]The king and all the people with him arrived at their destination exhausted.[x] And there he refreshed himself.

The Advice of Hushai and Ahithophel

[15]Meanwhile, Absalom[y] and all the men of Israel came to Jerusalem, and Ahithophel[z] was with him. [16]Then Hushai[a] the Arkite, David's friend, went to Absalom and said to him, "Long live the king! Long live the king!"

[17]Absalom asked Hushai, "Is this the love you show your friend? Why didn't you go with your friend?"[b]

[18]Hushai said to Absalom, "No, the one chosen by the LORD, by these people, and by all the men of Israel—his I will be, and I will remain with him. [19]Furthermore, whom should I serve? Should I not serve the son? Just as I served your father, so I will serve you."[c]

[20]Absalom said to Ahithophel, "Give us your advice. What should we do?"

[21]Ahithophel answered, "Lie with your father's concubines whom he left to take care of the palace. Then all Israel will hear that you have made yourself a stench in your father's nostrils, and the hands of everyone with you will be strengthened." [22]So they pitched a tent for Absalom on the roof, and he lay with his father's concubines in the sight of all Israel.[d]

[23]Now in those days the advice[e] Ahithophel gave was like that of one who inquires of God. That was how both David[f] and Absalom regarded all of Ahithophel's advice.

17 Ahithophel said to Absalom, "I would[a] choose twelve thousand men and set out tonight in pursuit of David. [2]I would[b] attack him while he is weary and weak.[g] I would[b] strike him with terror, and then all the people with him will flee. I would[b] strike down only the king[h] [3]and bring all the people back to you. The death of the man you seek will mean the return of all; all the people will be unharmed." [4]This plan seemed good to Absalom and to all the elders of Israel.

[5]But Absalom said, "Summon also Hushai[i] the Arkite, so we can hear what he has to say." [6]When Hushai came to him, Absalom said, "Ahithophel has given this advice. Should we do what he says? If not, give us your opinion."

[7]Hushai replied to Absalom, "The advice Ahithophel has given is not good this time. [8]You know your father and his men; they are fighters, and as fierce as a wild bear robbed of her cubs.[j] Besides, your father is an experienced fighter;[k] he will not spend the night with the troops. [9]Even now, he is hidden in a cave or some other place.[l] If he should attack your troops first,[c] whoever hears about it will say, 'There has been a slaughter among the troops who follow Absalom.' [10]Then even

---

16:11
tGe 45:5
16:12
uPs 4:1; 25:18
vDt 23:5;
Ro 8:28
wPs 109:28
16:14
x2Sa 17:2
16:15
y2Sa 15:37
z2Sa 15:12
16:16
a2Sa 15:37
16:17
b2Sa 19:25
16:19
c2Sa 15:34
16:22
d2Sa 12:11-12;
15:16
16:23
e2Sa 17:14,23
f2Sa 15:12
17:2
g2Sa 16:14
h1Ki 22:31;
Zec 13:7
17:5
i2Sa 15:32
17:8
jHos 13:8
k1Sa 16:18
17:9
lJer 41:9

---

[a]1 Or *Let me*   [b]2 Or *will*   [c]9 Or *When some of the men fall at the first attack*

the bravest soldier, whose heart is like the heart of a lion,[m] will melt[n] with fear, for all Israel knows that your father is a fighter and that those with him are brave.[o]

[11]"So I advise you: Let all Israel, from Dan to Beersheba[p]—as numerous as the sand[q] on the seashore—be gathered to you, with you yourself leading them into battle. [12]Then we will attack him wherever he may be found, and we will fall on him as dew settles on the ground. Neither he nor any of his men will be left alive. [13]If he withdraws into a city, then all Israel will bring ropes to that city, and we will drag it down to the valley[r] until not even a piece of it can be found."

[14]Absalom and all the men of Israel said, "The advice[s] of Hushai the Arkite is better than that of Ahithophel."[t] For the LORD had determined to frustrate[u] the good advice of Ahithophel in order to bring disaster[v] on Absalom.[w]

[15]Hushai told Zadok and Abiathar, the priests, "Ahithophel has advised Absalom and the elders of Israel to do such and such, but I have advised them to do so and so. [16]Now send a message immediately and tell David, 'Do not spend the night at the fords in the desert;[x] cross over without fail, or the king and all the people with him will be swallowed up.[y]'"

[17]Jonathan[z] and Ahimaaz were staying at En Rogel.[a] A servant girl was to go and inform them, and they were to go and tell King David, for they could not risk being seen entering the city. [18]But a young man saw them and told Absalom. So the two of them left quickly and went to the house of a man in Bahurim.[b] He had a well in his courtyard, and they climbed down into it. [19]His wife took a covering and spread it out over the opening of the well and scattered grain over it. No one knew anything about it.[c]

[20]When Absalom's men came to the woman[d] at the house, they asked, "Where are Ahimaaz and Jonathan?"

The woman answered them, "They crossed over the brook."[a] The men searched but found no one, so they returned to Jerusalem.

[21]After the men had gone, the two climbed out of the well and went to inform King David. They said to him, "Set out and cross the river at once; Ahithophel has advised such and such against you." [22]So David and all the people with him set out and crossed the Jordan. By daybreak, no one was left who had not crossed the Jordan.

[23]When Ahithophel saw that his advice[e] had not been followed, he saddled his donkey and set out for his house in his hometown. He put his house in order[f] and then hanged himself. So he died and was buried in his father's tomb.

[24]David went to Mahanaim,[g] and Absalom crossed the Jordan with all the men of Israel. [25]Absalom had appointed Amasa[h] over the army in place of Joab. Amasa was the son of a man named Jether,[bi] an Israelite[c] who had married Abigail,[d] the daughter of Nahash and sister of Zeruiah the mother of Joab. [26]The Israelites and Absalom camped in the land of Gilead.

[27]When David came to Mahanaim, Shobi son of Nahash[j] from Rab-

---

17:10
m1Ch 12:8
nJos 2:9,11;
Eze 21:15
o2Sa 23:8;
1Ch 11:11
17:11
pJdg 20:1
qGe 12:2;
22:17; Jos 11:4
17:13
rMic 1:6
17:14
s2Sa 16:23
t2Sa 15:12
u2Sa 15:34;
Ne 4:15
vPs 9:16
w2Ch 10:8
17:16
x2Sa 15:28
y2Sa 15:35
17:17
z2Sa 15:27,36
aJos 15:7; 18:16
17:18
b2Sa 3:16; 16:5
17:19
cJos 2:6
17:20
dEx 1:19;
Jos 2:3-5;
1Sa 19:12-17
17:23
e2Sa 15:12;
16:23 f2Ki 20:1;
Mt 27:5
17:24
gGe 32:2;
2Sa 2:8
17:25
h2Sa 19:13;
20:4,9-12;
1Ki 2:5,32;
1Ch 12:18
i1Ch 2:13-17
17:27
j1Sa 11:1

---

*a20 Or "They passed by the sheep pen toward the water."   b25 Hebrew Ithra, a variant of Jether
c25 Hebrew and some Septuagint manuscripts; other Septuagint manuscripts (see also 1 Chron.
2:17) Ishmaelite or Jezreelite   d25 Hebrew Abigal, a variant of Abigail*

bah[k] of the Ammonites, and Makir[l] son of Ammiel from Lo Debar, and Barzillai[m] the Gileadite[n] from Rogelim [28]brought bedding and bowls and articles of pottery. They also brought wheat and barley, flour and roasted grain, beans and lentils,[a] [29]honey and curds, sheep, and cheese from cows' milk for David and his people to eat.[o] For they said, "The people have become hungry and tired and thirsty in the desert.[p]"

Absalom's Death

18 David mustered the men who were with him and appointed over them commanders of thousands and commanders of hundreds. [2]David sent the troops out[q]—a third under the command of Joab, a third under Joab's brother Abishai[r] son of Zeruiah, and a third under Ittai[s] the Gittite. The king told the troops, "I myself will surely march out with you."

[3]But the men said, "You must not go out; if we are forced to flee, they won't care about us. Even if half of us die, they won't care; but you are worth ten[t] thousand of us.[b] It would be better now for you to give us support from the city."[u]

[4]The king answered, "I will do whatever seems best to you."

So the king stood beside the gate while all the men marched out in units of hundreds and of thousands. [5]The king commanded Joab, Abishai and Ittai, "Be gentle with the young man Absalom for my sake." And all the troops heard the king giving orders concerning Absalom to each of the commanders.

[6]The army marched into the field to fight Israel, and the battle took place in the forest[v] of Ephraim. [7]There the army of Israel was defeated by David's men, and the casualties that day were great—twenty thousand men. [8]The battle spread out over the whole countryside, and the forest claimed more lives that day than the sword.

[9]Now Absalom happened to meet David's men. He was riding his mule, and as the mule went under the thick branches of a large oak, Absalom's head[w] got caught in the tree. He was left hanging in midair, while the mule he was riding kept on going.

[10]When one of the men saw this, he told Joab, "I just saw Absalom hanging in an oak tree."

[11]Joab said to the man who had told him this, "What! You saw him? Why didn't you strike[x] him to the ground right there? Then I would have had to give you ten shekels[c] of silver and a warrior's belt.[y]"

[12]But the man replied, "Even if a thousand shekels[d] were weighed out into my hands, I would not lift my hand against the king's son. In our hearing the king commanded you and Abishai and Ittai, 'Protect the young man Absalom for my sake.[e]' [13]And if I had put my life in jeopardy[f]—and nothing is hidden from the king[z]—you would have kept your distance from me."

[14]Joab[a] said, "I'm not going to wait like this for you." So he took three javelins in his hand and plunged them into Absalom's heart while

17:27
k Dt 3:11;
2Sa 10:1-2;
12:26,29
l 2Sa 9:4
m 2Sa 19:31-39;
1Ki 2:7
n 2Sa 19:31;
Ezr 2:61
17:29
o 1Ch 12:40
p 2Sa 16:2;
Ro 12:13
18:2
q Jdg 7:16;
1Sa 11:11
r 1Sa 26:6
s 2Sa 15:19
18:3
t 1Sa 18:7
u 2Sa 21:17
18:6
v Jos 17:18
18:9
w 2Sa 14:26
18:11
x 2Sa 3:39
y 1Sa 18:4
18:13
z 2Sa 14:19-20
18:14
a 2Sa 2:18;
14:30

---

a28 Most Septuagint manuscripts and Syriac; Hebrew *lentils, and roasted grain*   *b3* Two Hebrew manuscripts, some Septuagint manuscripts and Vulgate; most Hebrew manuscripts *care; for now there are ten thousand like us*   *c11* That is, about 4 ounces (about 115 grams)   *d12* That is, about 25 pounds (about 11 kilograms)   *e12* A few Hebrew manuscripts, Septuagint, Vulgate and Syriac; most Hebrew manuscripts may be translated *Absalom, whoever you may be.*   *f13* Or *Otherwise, if I had acted treacherously toward him*

Absalom was still alive in the oak tree. ¹⁵And ten of Joab's armor-bearers surrounded Absalom, struck him and killed him. ᵇ

¹⁶Then Joabᶜ sounded the trumpet, and the troops stopped pursuing Israel, for Joab halted them. ¹⁷They took Absalom, threw him into a big pit in the forest and piled upᵈ a large heap of rocksᵉ over him. Meanwhile, all the Israelites fled to their homes.

¹⁸During his lifetime Absalom had taken a pillar and erected it in the King's Valleyᶠ as a monumentᵍ to himself, for he thought, "I have no sonʰ to carry on the memory of my name." He named the pillar after himself, and it is called Absalom's Monument to this day.

David Mourns

¹⁹Now Ahimaazⁱ son of Zadok said, "Let me run and take the news to the king that the LORD has delivered him from the hand of his enemies.ʲ"

²⁰"You are not the one to take the news today," Joab told him. "You may take the news another time, but you must not do so today, because the king's son is dead."

²¹Then Joab said to a Cushite, "Go, tell the king what you have seen." The Cushite bowed down before Joab and ran off.

²²Ahimaaz son of Zadok again said to Joab, "Come what may, please let me run behind the Cushite."

But Joab replied, "My son, why do you want to go? You don't have any news that will bring you a reward."

²³He said, "Come what may, I want to run."

So Joab said, "Run!" Then Ahimaaz ran by way of the plainᵃ and outran the Cushite.

²⁴While David was sitting between the inner and outer gates, the watchmanᵏ went up to the roof of the gateway by the wall. As he looked out, he saw a man running alone. ²⁵The watchman called out to the king and reported it.

The king said, "If he is alone, he must have good news." And the man came closer and closer.

²⁶Then the watchman saw another man running, and he called down to the gatekeeper, "Look, another man running alone!"

The king said, "He must be bringing good news,ˡ too."

²⁷The watchman said, "It seems to me that the first one runs likeᵐ Ahimaaz son of Zadok."

"He's a good man," the king said. "He comes with good news."

²⁸Then Ahimaaz called out to the king, "All is well!" He bowed down before the king with his face to the ground and said, "Praise be to the LORD your God! He has delivered up the men who lifted their hands against my lord the king."

²⁹The king asked, "Is the young man Absalom safe?"

Ahimaaz answered, "I saw great confusion just as Joab was about to send the king's servant and me, your servant, but I don't know what it was."

³⁰The king said, "Stand aside and wait here." So he stepped aside and stood there.

³¹Then the Cushite arrived and said, "My lord the king, hear the

---

18:15
b 2Sa 12:10

18:16
c 2Sa 2:28;
20:22

18:17
d Jos 7:26
e Jos 8:29

18:18
f Ge 14:17
g Ge 50:5;
Nu 32:42;
1Sa 15:12
h 2Sa 14:27

18:19
i 2Sa 15:36
j ver 31;
Jdg 11:36

18:24
k 1Sa 14:16;
2Sa 19:8;
2Ki 9:17;
Jer 51:12

18:26
l 1Ki 1:42;
Isa 52:7; 61:1

18:27
m 2Ki 9:20

ᵃ 23 That is, the plain of the Jordan

good news! The LORD has delivered you today from all who rose up against you."

[32]The king asked the Cushite, "Is the young man Absalom safe?"

The Cushite replied, "May the enemies of my lord the king and all who rise up to harm you be like that young man."[n]

[33]The king was shaken. He went up to the room over the gateway and wept. As he went, he said: "O my son Absalom! My son, my son Absalom! If only I had died[o] instead of you—O Absalom, my son, my son!"[p]

19 Joab was told, "The king is weeping and mourning for Absalom." [2]And for the whole army the victory that day was turned into mourning, because on that day the troops heard it said, "The king is grieving for his son." [3]The men stole into the city that day as men steal in who are ashamed when they flee from battle. [4]The king covered his face and cried aloud, "O my son Absalom! O Absalom, my son, my son!"

[5]Then Joab went into the house to the king and said, "Today you have humiliated all your men, who have just saved your life and the lives of your sons and daughters and the lives of your wives and concubines. [6]You love those who hate you and hate those who love you. You have made it clear today that the commanders and their men mean nothing to you. I see that you would be pleased if Absalom were alive today and all of us were dead. [7]Now go out and encourage your men. I swear by the LORD that if you don't go out, not a man will be left with you by nightfall. This will be worse for you than all the calamities that have come upon you from your youth till now."[q]

[8]So the king got up and took his seat in the gateway. When the men were told, "The king is sitting in the gateway,[r]" they all came before him.

David Returns to Jerusalem

Meanwhile, the Israelites had fled to their homes. [9]Throughout the tribes of Israel, the people were all arguing with each other, saying, "The king delivered us from the hand of our enemies; he is the one who rescued us from the hand of the Philistines.[s] But now he has fled the country because of Absalom;[t] [10]and Absalom, whom we anointed to rule over us, has died in battle. So why do you say nothing about bringing the king back?"

[11]King David sent this message to Zadok[u] and Abiathar, the priests: "Ask the elders of Judah, 'Why should you be the last to bring the king back to his palace, since what is being said throughout Israel has reached the king at his quarters? [12]You are my brothers, my own flesh and blood. So why should you be the last to bring back the king?' [13]And say to Amasa,[v] 'Are you not my own flesh and blood?[w] May God deal with me, be it ever so severely,[x] if from now on you are not the commander of my army in place of Joab.[y]'"

[14]He won over the hearts of all the men of Judah as though they were one man. They sent word to the king, "Return, you and all your men." [15]Then the king returned and went as far as the Jordan.

Now the men of Judah had come to Gilgal[z] to go out and meet the king and bring him across the Jordan. [16]Shimei[a] son of Gera, the Benjamite from Bahurim, hurried down with the men of Judah to meet

18:32
nJdg 5:31;
1Sa 25:26
18:33
oEx 32:32
pGe 43:14;
2Sa 19:4;
Ro 9:3
19:7
qPr 14:28
19:8
r2Sa 15:2
19:9
s2Sa 8:1-14
t2Sa 15:14
19:11
u2Sa 15:24
19:13
v2Sa 17:25
wGe 29:14
xRu 1:17;
1Ki 19:2; 8:16
y2Sa 2:13
19:15
zJos 5:9;
1Sa 11:15
19:16
a2Sa 16:5-13;
1Ki 2:8

King David. [17]With him were a thousand Benjamites, along with Ziba, [b] the steward of Saul's household, [c] and his fifteen sons and twenty servants. They rushed to the Jordan, where the king was. [18]They crossed at the ford to take the king's household over and to do whatever he wished.

When Shimei son of Gera crossed the Jordan, he fell prostrate before the king [19]and said to him, "May my lord not hold me guilty. Do not remember how your servant did wrong on the day my lord the king left Jerusalem. [d] May the king put it out of his mind. [20]For I your servant know that I have sinned, but today I have come here as the first of the whole house of Joseph to come down and meet my lord the king."

[21]Then Abishai [e] son of Zeruiah said, "Shouldn't Shimei be put to death for this? He cursed [f] the LORD's anointed." [g]

[22]David replied, "What do you and I have in common, you sons of Zeruiah? [h] This day you have become my adversaries! Should anyone be put to death in Israel today? [i] Do I not know that today I am king over Israel?" [23]So the king said to Shimei, "You shall not die." And the king promised him on oath. [j]

[24]Mephibosheth, [k] Saul's grandson, also went down to meet the king. He had not taken care of his feet or trimmed his mustache or washed his clothes from the day the king left until the day he returned safely. [25]When he came from Jerusalem to meet the king, the king asked him, "Why didn't you go with me, [l] Mephibosheth?"

[26]He said, "My lord the king, since I your servant am lame, [m] I said, 'I will have my donkey saddled and will ride on it, so I can go with the king.' But Ziba [n] my servant betrayed me. [27]And he has slandered your servant to my lord the king. My lord the king is like an angel [o] of God; so do whatever pleases you. [28]All my grandfather's descendants deserved nothing but death [p] from my lord the king, but you gave your servant a place among those who sat at your table. [q] So what right do I have to make any more appeals to the king?"

[29]The king said to him, "Why say more? I order you and Ziba to divide the fields."

[30]Mephibosheth said to the king, "Let him take everything, now that my lord the king has arrived home safely."

[31]Barzillai [r] the Gileadite also came down from Rogelim to cross the Jordan with the king and to send him on his way from there. [32]Now Barzillai was a very old man, eighty years of age. He had provided for the king during his stay in Mahanaim, for he was a very wealthy [s] man. [33]The king said to Barzillai, "Cross over with me and stay with me in Jerusalem, and I will provide for you."

[34]But Barzillai answered the king, "How many more years will I live, that I should go up to Jerusalem with the king? [35]I am now eighty [t] years old. Can I tell the difference between what is good and what is not? Can your servant taste what he eats and drinks? Can I still hear the voices of men and women singers? [u] Why should your servant be an added [v] burden to my lord the king? [36]Your servant will cross over the Jordan with the king for a short distance, but why should the king reward me in this way? [37]Let your servant return, that I may die in my own town near the tomb of my father [w] and mother. But here is your servant Kimham. [x] Let him cross over with my lord the king. Do for him whatever pleases you."

19:17
b 2Sa 9:2; 16:1-2
c Ge 43:16
19:19
d 1Sa 22:15;
2Sa 16:6-8
19:21
e 1Sa 26:6
f Ex 22:28
g 1Sa 12:3;
26:9; 2Sa 16:7-8
19:22
h 2Sa 2:18;
16:10 i 1Sa 11:13
19:23
j 1Ki 2:8,42
19:24
k 2Sa 4:4; 9:6-10
19:25
l 2Sa 16:17
19:26
m Lev 21:18
n 2Sa 9:2
19:27
o 1Sa 29:9;
2Sa 14:17,20
19:28
p 2Sa 16:8;
21:6-9 q 2Sa 9:7,
13
19:31
r 2Sa 17:27-29,
27; 1Ki 2:7
19:32
s 1Sa 25:2;
2Sa 17:27
19:35
t Ps 90:10
u 2Ch 35:25;
Ezr 2:65;
Ecc 2:8; 12:1;
Isa 5:11-12
v 2Sa 15:33
19:37
w Ge 49:29;
1Ki 2:7 x ver 40;
Jer 41:17

38The king said, "Kimham shall cross over with me, and I will do for him whatever pleases you. And anything you desire from me I will do for you."

39So all the people crossed the Jordan, and then the king crossed over. The king kissed Barzillai and gave him his blessing, y and Barzillai returned to his home.

40When the king crossed over to Gilgal, Kimham crossed with him. All the troops of Judah and half the troops of Israel had taken the king over.

41Soon all the men of Israel were coming to the king and saying to him, "Why did our brothers, the men of Judah, steal the king away and bring him and his household across the Jordan, together with all his men?" z

42All the men of Judah answered the men of Israel, "We did this because the king is closely related to us. Why are you angry about it? Have we eaten any of the king's provisions? Have we taken anything for ourselves?"

43Then the men of Israel a answered the men of Judah, "We have ten shares in the king; and besides, we have a greater claim on David than you have. So why do you treat us with contempt? Were we not the first to speak of bringing back our king?"

But the men of Judah responded even more harshly than the men of Israel.

Sheba Rebels Against David

20 Now a troublemaker named Sheba son of Bicri, a Benjamite, happened to be there. He sounded the trumpet and shouted,

> "We have no share b in David, c
>   no part in Jesse's son! d
> Every man to his tent, O Israel!"

2So all the men of Israel deserted David to follow Sheba son of Bicri. But the men of Judah stayed by their king all the way from the Jordan to Jerusalem.

3When David returned to his palace in Jerusalem, he took the ten concubines e he had left to take care of the palace and put them in a house under guard. He provided for them, but did not lie with them. They were kept in confinement till the day of their death, living as widows.

4Then the king said to Amasa, f "Summon the men of Judah to come to me within three days, and be here yourself." 5But when Amasa went to summon Judah, he took longer than the time the king had set for him.

6David said to Abishai, g "Now Sheba son of Bicri will do us more harm than Absalom did. Take your master's men and pursue him, or he will find fortified cities and escape from us." 7So Joab's men and the Kerethites h and Pelethites and all the mighty warriors went out under the command of Abishai. They marched out from Jerusalem to pursue Sheba son of Bicri.

8While they were at the great rock in Gibeon, i Amasa came to meet them. Joab j was wearing his military tunic, and strapped over it at his

19:39
yGe 31:55;
Ge 47:7
19:41
zJdg 8:1; 12:1
19:43
a2Sa 5:1
20:1
bGe 31:14
cGe 29:14;
1Ki 12:16
d1Sa 22:7-8;
2Ch 10:16
20:3
e2Sa 15:16;
16:21-22
20:4
f2Sa 17:25;
19:13
20:6
g2Sa 21:17
20:7
h1Sa 30:14;
2Sa 8:18;
15:18; 1Ki 1:38
20:8
iJos 9:3
j2Sa 2:18

waist was a belt with a dagger in its sheath. As he stepped forward, it dropped out of its sheath.

⁹Joab said to Amasa, "How are you, my brother?" Then Joab took Amasa by the beard with his right hand to kiss him. ¹⁰Amasa was not on his guard against the dagger[k] in Joab'[l]s hand, and Joab plunged it into his belly, and his intestines spilled out on the ground. Without being stabbed again, Amasa died. Then Joab and his brother Abishai pursued Sheba son of Bicri.

¹¹One of Joab's men stood beside Amasa and said, "Whoever favors Joab, and whoever is for David, let him follow Joab!" ¹²Amasa lay wallowing in his blood in the middle of the road, and the man saw that all the troops came to a halt[m] there. When he realized that everyone who came up to Amasa stopped, he dragged him from the road into a field and threw a garment over him. ¹³After Amasa had been removed from the road, all the men went on with Joab to pursue Sheba son of Bicri.

¹⁴Sheba passed through all the tribes of Israel to Abel Beth Maacah[a] and through the entire region of the Berites,[n] who gathered together and followed him. ¹⁵All the troops with Joab came and besieged Sheba in Abel Beth Maacah.[o] They built a siege ramp[p] up to the city, and it stood against the outer fortifications. While they were battering the wall to bring it down, ¹⁶a wise woman[q] called from the city, "Listen! Listen! Tell Joab to come here so I can speak to him." ¹⁷He went toward her, and she asked, "Are you Joab?"

"I am," he answered.

She said, "Listen to what your servant has to say."

"I'm listening," he said.

¹⁸She continued, "Long ago they used to say, 'Get your answer at Abel,' and that settled it. ¹⁹We are the peaceful[r] and faithful in Israel. You are trying to destroy a city that is a mother in Israel. Why do you want to swallow up the LORD's inheritance?"[s]

²⁰"Far be it from me!" Joab replied, "Far be it from me to swallow up or destroy! ²¹That is not the case. A man named Sheba son of Bicri, from the hill country of Ephraim, has lifted up his hand against the king, against David. Hand over this one man, and I'll withdraw from the city."

The woman said to Joab, "His head[t] will be thrown to you from the wall."

²²Then the woman went to all the people with her wise advice,[u] and they cut off the head of Sheba son of Bicri and threw it to Joab. So he sounded the trumpet, and his men dispersed from the city, each returning to his home. And Joab went back to the king in Jerusalem.

²³Joab[v] was over Israel's entire army; Benaiah son of Jehoiada was over the Kerethites and Pelethites; ²⁴Adoniram[b][w] was in charge of forced labor; Jehoshaphat[x] son of Ahilud was recorder; ²⁵Sheva was secretary; Zadok[y] and Abiathar were priests; ²⁶and Ira the Jairite was David's priest.

20:10
k Jdg 3:21;
2Sa 2:23; 3:27
l 1Ki 2:5
20:12
m 2Sa 2:23
20:14
n Nu 21:16
20:15
o 1Ki 15:20;
2Ki 15:29
p 2Ki 19:32;
Isa 37:33;
Jer 6:6; 32:24
20:16
q 2Sa 14:2
20:19
r Dt 2:26
s 1Sa 26:19;
2Sa 21:3
20:21
t 2Sa 4:8
20:22
u Ecc 9:13
20:23
v 2Sa 2:28;
8:16-18; 24:2
20:24
w 1Ki 4:6; 5:14;
12:18;
2Ch 10:18
x 2Sa 8:16;
1Ki 4:3
20:25
y 1Sa 2:35;
2Sa 8:17

---

[a]14 Or *Abel, even Beth Maacah*; also in verse 15   [b]24 Some Septuagint manuscripts (see also 1 Kings 4:6 and 5:14); Hebrew *Adoram*

The Gibeonites Avenged

21 During the reign of David, there was a famine[z] for three successive years; so David sought[a] the face of the LORD. The LORD said, "It is on account of Saul and his blood-stained house; it is because he put the Gibeonites to death."

[2]The king summoned the Gibeonites[b] and spoke to them. (Now the Gibeonites were not a part of Israel but were survivors of the Amorites; the Israelites had sworn to spare, them, but Saul in his zeal for Israel and Judah had tried to annihilate them.) [3]David asked the Gibeonites, "What shall I do for you? How shall I make amends so that you will bless the LORD's inheritance?"[c]

[4]The Gibeonites answered him, "We have no right to demand silver or gold from Saul or his family, nor do we have the right to put anyone in Israel to death."[d]

"What do you want me to do for you?" David asked.

[5]They answered the king, "As for the man who destroyed us and plotted against us so that we have been decimated and have no place anywhere in Israel, [6]let seven of his male descendants be given to us to be killed and exposed[e] before the LORD at Gibeah of Saul—the Lord's chosen[f] one."

So the king said, "I will give them to you."

[7]The king spared Mephibosheth[g] son of Jonathan, the son of Saul, because of the oath[h] before the LORD between David and Jonathan son of Saul. [8]But the king took Armoni and Mephibosheth, the two sons of Aiah's daughter Rizpah,[i] whom she had borne to Saul, together with the five sons of Saul's daughter Merab,[a] whom she had borne to Adriel son of Barzillai the Meholathite.[j] [9]He handed them over to the Gibeonites, who killed and exposed them on a hill before the LORD. All seven of them fell together; they were put to death[k] during the first days of the harvest, just as the barley harvest was beginning.[l]

[10]Rizpah daughter of Aiah took sackcloth and spread it out for herself on a rock. From the beginning of the harvest till the rain poured down from the heavens on the bodies, she did not let the birds of the air touch them by day or the wild animals by night.[m] [11]When David was told what Aiah's daughter Rizpah, Saul's concubine, had done, [12]he went and took the bones of Saul[n] and his son Jonathan from the citizens of Jabesh Gilead. (They had taken them secretly from the public square at Beth Shan,[o] where the Philistines had hung[p] them after they struck Saul down on Gilboa.) [13]David brought the bones of Saul and his son Jonathan from there, and the bones of those who had been killed and exposed were gathered up.

[14]They buried the bones of Saul and his son Jonathan in the tomb of Saul's father Kish, at Zela[q] in Benjamin, and did everything the king commanded. After that,[r] God answered prayer[s] in behalf of the land.

Wars Against the Philistines

21:15–22pp — 1Ch 20:4–8

[15]Once again there was a battle between the Philistines[t] and Israel. David went down with his men to fight against the Philistines, and he

### Cross references (margin)

21:1
z Ge 12:10;
Dt 32:24
a Ex 32:11

21:2
b Jos 9:15

21:3
c 1Sa 26:19;
2Sa 20:19

21:4
d Nu 35:33-34

21:6
e Nu 25:4
f 1Sa 10:24

21:7
g 2Sa 4:4
h 1Sa 18:3; 20:8,
15; 2Sa 9:7

21:8
i 2Sa 3:7
j 1Sa 18:19

21:9
k 2Sa 16:8
l Ru 1:22

21:10
m ver 8;
Dt 21:23;
1Sa 17:44

21:12
n 1Sa 31:11-13
o Jos 17:11
p 1Sa 31:10

21:14
q Jos 18:28
r Jos 7:26
s 2Sa 24:25

21:15
t 2Sa 5:25

---

a8 Two Hebrew manuscripts, some Septuagint manuscripts and Syriac (see also 1 Samuel 18:19); most Hebrew and Septuagint manuscripts *Michal* became exhausted. [16]And Ishbi-Benob, one of the descendants of Rapha, whose bronze spearhead weighed three hundred shekels[a] and who was armed with a new sword, said he would kill David. [17]But Abishai[u] son of Zeruiah came to David's rescue; he struck the Philistine down and killed him. Then David's men swore to him, saying, "Never again will you go out with us to battle, so that the lamp[v] of Israel will not be extinguished.[w]"

[18]In the course of time, there was another battle with the Philistines, at Gob. At that time Sibbecai[x] the Hushathite killed Saph, one of the descendants of Rapha.

[19]In another battle with the Philistines at Gob, Elhanan son of Jaare-Oregim[b] the Bethlehemite killed Goliath[c] the Gittite, who had a spear with a shaft like a weaver's rod.[y]

[20]In still another battle, which took place at Gath, there was a huge man with six fingers on each hand and six toes on each foot—twenty-four in all. He also was descended from Rapha. [21]When he taunted Israel, Jonathan son of Shimeah,[z] David's brother, killed him.

[22]These four were descendants of Rapha in Gath, and they fell at the hands of David and his men.

David's Song of Praise

22:1-51pp — Ps 18:1-50

22 David sang[a] to the LORD the words of this song when the LORD delivered him from the hand of all his enemies and from the hand of Saul. [2]He said:

> "The LORD is my rock,[b] my fortress[c] and my deliverer;[d]
> 3   my God is my rock, in whom I take refuge,[e]
>   my shield[f] and the horn[d][g] of my salvation.
> He is my stronghold,[h] my refuge and my savior—
>   from violent men you save me.
> [4]I call to the LORD, who is worthy[i] of praise,
>   and I am saved from my enemies.
>
> [5]"The waves[j] of death swirled about me;
>   the torrents of destruction overwhelmed me.
> [6]The cords of the grave[e][k] coiled around me;
>   the snares of death confronted me.
> [7]In my distress[l] I called[m] to the LORD;
>   I called out to my God.
> From his temple he heard my voice;
>   my cry came to his ears.
>
> [8]"The earth[n] trembled and quaked,[o]
>   the foundations[p] of the heavens[f] shook;
>   they trembled because he was angry.
> [9]Smoke rose from his nostrils;
>   consuming fire[q] came from his mouth,
>   burning coals blazed out of it.

21:17
u2Sa 20:6
v1Ki 11:36
w2Sa 18:3
21:18
x1Ch 11:29;
20:4; 27:11
21:19
y1Sa 17:7
21:21
z1Sa 16:9
22:1
aEx 15:1;
Jdg 5:1;
Ps 18:2-50
22:2
bDt 32:4;
Ps 71:3
cPs 31:3; 91:2
dPs 144:2
22:3
eDt 32:37;
Jer 16:19
fGe 15:1
gLk 1:69
hPs 9:9
22:4
iPs 48:1; 96:4
22:5
jPs 69:14-15;
93:4; Jnh 2:3
22:6
kPs 116:3
22:7
lPs 120:1
mPs 34:6,15;
116:4
22:8
nJdg 5:4;
Ps 97:4
oPs 77:18
pJob 26:11
22:9
qPs 97:3;
Heb 12:29

---

[a]16 That is, about 7 1/2 pounds (about 3.5 kilograms)   [b]19 Or *son of Jair the weaver*
[c]19 Hebrew and Septuagint; 1 Chron. 20:5 *son of Jair killed Lahmi the brother of Goliath*   [d]3 *Horn* here symbolizes strength.   [e]6 Hebrew *Sheol*   [f]8 Hebrew; Vulgate and Syriac (see also Psalm 18:7) *mountains*

[10]He parted the heavens and came down;
　　dark clouds[r] were under his feet.
[11]He mounted the cherubim and flew;
　　he soared[a] on the wings of the wind.[s]
[12]He made darkness his canopy around him—
　　the dark[b] rain clouds of the sky.
[13]Out of the brightness of his presence
　　bolts of lightning[t] blazed forth.
[14]The LORD thundered[u] from heaven;
　　the voice of the Most High resounded.
[15]He shot arrows[v] and scattered the enemies,,
　　bolts of lightning and routed them.
[16]The valleys of the sea were exposed
　　and the foundations of the earth laid bare
　at the rebuke[w] of the LORD,
　　at the blast of breath from his nostrils.

[17]"He reached down from on high[x] and took hold of me;
　　he drew[y] me out of deep waters.
[18]He rescued me from my powerful enemy,
　　from my foes, who were too strong for me.
[19]They confronted me in the day of my disaster,
　　but the LORD was my support.[z]
[20]He brought me out into a spacious[a] place;
　　he rescued[b] me because he delighted[c] in me.[d]

[21]"The LORD has dealt with me according to my
　　righteousness;[e]
　according to the cleanness of my hands[f] he has
　　rewarded me.
[22]For I have kept[g] the ways of the LORD;
　　I have not done evil by turning from my God.
[23]All his laws are before me;[h]
　　I have not turned[i] away from his decrees.
[24]I have been blameless[j] before him
　　and have kept myself from sin.
[25]The LORD has rewarded me according to my
　　righteousness,[k]
　according to my cleanness[c] in his sight.

[26]"To the faithful you show yourself faithful,
　　to the blameless you show yourself blameless,
[27]to the pure[l] you show yourself pure,
　　but to the crooked you show yourself shrewd.[m]
[28]You save the humble,[n]
　　but your eyes are on the haughty to bring them low.[o]
[29]You are my lamp,[p] O LORD;
　　the LORD turns my darkness into light.
[30]With your help I can advance against a troop[d];
　　with my God I can scale a wall.

---

[a]11 Many Hebrew manuscripts (see also Psalm 18:10); most Hebrew manuscripts *appeared*
[b]12 Septuagint and Vulgate (see also Psalm 18:11); Hebrew *massed*　　[c]25 Hebrew; Septuagint
and Vulgate (see also Psalm 18:24) *to the cleanness of my hands*　　[d]30 Or *can run through a barricade*

22:10
r1Ki 8:12;
Na 1:3
22:11
sPs 104:3
22:13
tver 9
22:14
u1Sa 2:10
22:15
vDt 32:23
22:16
wNa 1:4
22:17
xPs 144:7
yEx 2:10
22:19
zPs 23:4
22:20
aPs 31:8
bPs 118:5
cPs 22:8
d2Sa 15:26
22:21
e1Sa 26:23
fPs 24:4
22:22
gGe 18:19;
Ps 128:1;
Pr 8:32
22:23
hDt 6:4-9;
Ps 119:30-32
iPs 119:102
22:24
jGe 6:9;
Eph 1:4
22:25
kver 21
22:27
lMt 5:8
mLev 26:23-24
22:28
nEx 3:8;
Ps 72:12-13
oIsa 2:12,17;
5:15
22:29
pPs 27:1

31"As for God, his way is perfect;^q
    the word of the LORD is flawless.^r
He is a shield
    for all who take refuge in him.
32For who is God besides the LORD?
    And who is the Rock^s except our God?
33It is God who arms me with strength^a
    and makes my way perfect.
34He makes my feet like the feet of a deer;^t
    he enables me to stand on the heights.^u
35He trains my hands^v for battle;
    my arms can bend a bow of bronze.
36You give me your shield^w of victory;
    you stoop down to make me great.
37You broaden the path^x beneath me,
    so that my ankles do not turn.

38"I pursued my enemies and crushed them;
    I did not turn back till they were destroyed.
39I crushed^y them completely, and they could not rise;
    they fell beneath my feet.
40You armed me with strength for battle;
    you made my adversaries bow at my feet.^z
41You made my enemies turn their backs^a in flight,
    and I destroyed my foes.
42They cried for help,^b but there was no one to save
    them—^c
to the LORD, but he did not answer.
43I beat them as fine as the dust of the earth;
    I pounded and trampled^d them like mud^e in the
    streets.

44"You have delivered^f me from the attacks of my people;
    you have preserved^g me as the head of nations.
People^h I did not know are subject to me,
45   and foreigners come cringingⁱ to me;
    as soon as they hear me, they obey me.
46They all lose heart;
    they come trembling^{bj} from their strongholds.

47"The LORD lives! Praise be to my Rock!
    Exalted be God, the Rock, my Savior!^k
48He is the God who avenges me,^l
    who puts the nations under me,
49   who sets me free from my enemies.^m
You exalted me above my foes;
    from violent men you rescued me.
50Therefore I will praise you, O LORD, among the nations;
    I will sing praises to your name.ⁿ
51He gives his king great victories;^o

22:31
qDt 32:4;
Mt 5:48
rPs 12:6;
119:140;
Pr 30:5-6
22:32
s1Sa 2:2
22:34
tHab 3:19
uDt 32:13
22:35
vPs 144:1
22:36
wEph 6:16
22:37
xPr 4:11
22:39
yMal 4:3
22:40
zPs 44:5
22:41
aEx 23:27
22:42
bIsa 1:15
cPs 50:22
22:43
dMic 7:10
eIsa 10:6;
Mic 7:10
22:44
f2Sa 3:1
gDt 28:13
h2Sa 8:1-14;
Isa 55:3-5
22:45
iPs 66:3; 81:15
22:46
jMic 7:17
22:47
kPs 89:26
22:48
lPs 94:1; 144:2;
1Sa 25:39
22:49
mPs 140:1,4
22:50
nRo 15:9*
22:51
oPs 144:9-10

---

^a33 Dead Sea Scrolls, some Septuagint manuscripts, Vulgate and Syriac (see also Psalm 18:32);
Masoretic Text *who is my strong refuge*   ^b46 Some Septuagint manuscripts and Vulgate (see also
Psalm 18:45); Masoretic Text *they arm themselves.*

he shows unfailing kindness to his anointed, P
to David q and his descendants forever." r

The Last Words of David

23 These are the last words of David:

"The oracle of David son of Jesse,
   the oracle of the man exalted s by the Most High,
the man anointed t by the God of Jacob,
   Israel's singer of songs a :

2"The Spirit u of the LORD spoke through me;
   his word was on my tongue.
3The God of Israel spoke,
   the Rock v of Israel said to me:
'When one rules over men in righteousness, w
   when he rules in the fear of God, x
4he is like the light of morning at sunrise y
   on a cloudless morning,
like the brightness after rain
   that brings the grass from the earth.'

5"Is not my house right with God?
   Has he not made with me an everlasting covenant, z
   arranged and secured in every part?
Will he not bring to fruition my salvation
   and grant me my every desire?
6But evil men are all to be cast aside like thorns, a
   which are not gathered with the hand.
7Whoever touches thorns
   uses a tool of iron or the shaft of a spear;
   they are burned up where they lie."

David's Mighty Men

23:8-39pp — 1Ch 11:10-41

8These are the names of David's mighty men:

Josheb-Basshebeth, b a Tahkemonite, c was chief of the Three; he raised his spear against eight hundred men, whom he killed d in one encounter.

9Next to him was Eleazar son of Dodai b the Ahohite. c As one of the three mighty men, he was with David when they taunted the Philistines gathered at Pas Dammim, e for battle. Then the men of Israel retreated, 10but he stood his ground and struck down the Philistines till his hand grew tired and froze to the sword. The LORD brought about a great victory that day. The troops returned to Eleazar, but only to strip the dead.

11Next to him was Shammah son of Agee the Hararite. When the Philistines banded together at a place where there was a field full of

---

Left margin cross-references:

22:51
p Ps 89:20
q 2Sa 7:13
r Ps 89:24,29

23:1
s 2Sa 7:8-9;
Ps 78:70-71;
89:27
t 1Sa 16:12-13;
Ps 89:20

23:2
u Mt 22:43;
2Pe 1:21

23:3
v Dt 32:4;
2Sa 22:2,32
w Ps 72:3
x 2Ch 19:7,9;
Isa 11:1-5

23:4
y Jdg 5:31;
Ps 89:36

23:5
z Ps 89:29;
Isa 55:3

23:6
a Mt 13:40-41

23:9
b 1Ch 27:4
c 1Ch 8:4

---

a1 Or *Israel's beloved singer*   b8 Hebrew; some Septuagint manuscripts suggest *Ish-Bosheth,* that is, *Esh-Baal* (see also 1 Chron. 11:11 *Jashobeam*).   c8 Probably a variant of *Hacmonite* (see 1 Chron. 11:11)   d8 Some Septuagint manuscripts (see also 1 Chron. 11:11); Hebrew and other Septuagint manuscripts *Three; it was Adino the Eznite who killed eight hundred men*   e9 See 1 Chron. 11:13; Hebrew *gathered there.*

lentils, Israel's troops fled from them. [12]But Shammah took his stand in the middle of the field. He defended it and struck the Philistines down, and the LORD brought about a great victory.

[13]During harvest time, three of the thirty chief men came down to David at the cave of Adullam,[d] while a band of Philistines was encamped in the Valley of Rephaim.[e] [14]At that time David was in the stronghold,[f] and the Philistine garrison was at Bethlehem.[g] [15]David longed for water and said, "Oh, that someone would get me a drink of water from the well near the gate of Bethlehem!" [16]So the three mighty men broke through the Philistine lines, drew water from the well near the gate of Bethlehem and carried it back to David. But he refused to drink it; instead, he poured[h] it out before the LORD. [17]"Far be it from me, O LORD, to do this!" he said. "Is it not the blood[i] of men who went at the risk of their lives?" And David would not drink it.

Such were the exploits of the three mighty men.

[18]Abishai[j] the brother of Joab son of Zeruiah was chief of the Three.[a] He raised his spear against three hundred men, whom he killed, and so he became as famous as the Three. [19]Was he not held in greater honor than the Three? He became their commander, even though he was not included among them.

[20]Benaiah[k] son of Jehoiada was a valiant fighter from Kabzeel,[l] who performed great exploits. He struck down two of Moab's best men. He also went down into a pit on a snowy day and killed a lion. [21]And he struck down a huge Egyptian. Although the Egyptian had a spear in his hand, Benaiah went against him with a club. He snatched the spear from the Egyptian's hand and killed him with his own spear. [22]Such were the exploits of Benaiah son of Jehoiada; he too was as famous as the three mighty men. [23]He was held in greater honor than any of the Thirty, but he was not included among the Three. And David put him in charge of his bodyguard.

[24]Among the Thirty were:
    Asahel[m] the brother of Joab,
    Elhanan son of Dodo from Bethlehem,
  [25]Shammah the Harodite,[n]
    Elika the Harodite,
  [26]Helez[o] the Paltite,
    Ira son of Ikkesh from Tekoa,
  [27]Abiezer from Anathoth,[p]
    Mebunnai[b] the Hushathite,
  [28]Zalmon the Ahohite,
    Maharai[q] the Netophathite,[r]
  [29]Heled[c] son of Baanah the Netophathite,
    Ithai son of Ribai from Gibeah[s] in Benjamin,
  [30]Benaiah the Pirathonite,[t]
    Hiddai[d] from the ravines of Gaash,[u]
  [31]Abi-Albon the Arbathite,
    Azmaveth the Barhumite,[v]

23:13
d1Sa 22:1
e2Sa 5:18
23:14
f1Sa 22:4-5
gRu 1:19
23:16
hGe 35:14
23:17
iLev 17:10-12
23:18
j2Sa 10:10,14;
1Ch 11:20
23:20
k2Sa 8:18;
20:23 lJos 15:21
23:24
m2Sa 2:18
23:25
nJdg 7:1;
1Ch 11:27
23:26
o1Ch 27:10
23:27
pJos 21:18
23:28
q1Ch 27:13
r2Ki 25:23;
Ne 7:26
23:29
sJos 15:57
23:30
tJdg 12:13
uJos 24:30
23:31
v2Sa 3:16

---

[a]18 Most Hebrew manuscripts (see also 1 Chron. 11:20); two Hebrew manuscripts and Syriac *Thirty*
[b]27 Hebrew; some Septuagint manuscripts (see also 1 Chron. 11:29) *Sibbecai*   [c]29 Some Hebrew manuscripts and Vulgate (see also 1 Chron. 11:30); most Hebrew manuscripts *Heleb*
[d]30 Hebrew; some Septuagint manuscripts (see also 1 Chron. 11:32) *Hurai*

³²Eliahba the Shaalbonite,
　the sons of Jashen,
　Jonathan ³³son of^a Shammah the Hararite,
　Ahiam son of Sharar^b the Hararite,
³⁴Eliphelet son of Ahasbai the Maacathite,
　Eliam^w son of Ahithophel^x the Gilonite,
³⁵Hezro the Carmelite,^y
　Paarai the Arbite,
³⁶Igal son of Nathan from Zobah,^z
　the son of Hagri,^c
³⁷Zelek the Ammonite,
　Naharai the Beerothite, the armor-bearer of Joab son of Zeruiah,
³⁸Ira the Ithrite,^a
　Gareb the Ithrite
³⁹and Uriah^b the Hittite.
There were thirty-seven in all.

David Counts the Fighting Men

24:1–17pp — 1Ch 21:1–17

24 Again^c the anger of the LORD burned against Israel, and he incited David against them, saying, "Go and take a census of^d Israel and Judah."

²So the king said to Joab^e and the army commanders^d with him, "Go throughout the tribes of Israel from Dan to Beersheba^f and enroll the fighting men, so that I may know how many there are."

³But Joab replied to the king, "May the LORD your God multiply the troops a hundred times over,^g and may the eyes of my lord the king see it. But why does my lord the king want to do such a thing?"

⁴The king's word, however, overruled Joab and the army commanders; so they left the presence of the king to enroll the fighting men of Israel.

⁵After crossing the Jordan, they camped near Aroer,^h south of the town in the gorge, and then went through Gad and on to Jazer.ⁱ ⁶They went to Gilead and the region of Tahtim Hodshi, and on to Dan Jaan and around toward Sidon.^j ⁷Then they went toward the fortress of Tyre^k and all the towns of the Hivites and Canaanites. Finally, they went on to Beersheba^l in the Negev^m of Judah.

⁸After they had gone through the entire land, they came back to Jerusalem at the end of nine months and twenty days.

⁹Joab reported the number of the fighting men to the king: In Israel there were eight hundred thousand able-bodied men who could handle a sword, and in Judah five hundred thousand.ⁿ

¹⁰David was conscience-stricken^o after he had counted the fighting men, and he said to the LORD, "I have sinned^p greatly in what I have done. Now, O LORD, I beg you, take away the guilt of your servant. I have done a very foolish thing.^q"

¹¹Before David got up the next morning, the word of the LORD had come to Gad^r the prophet, David's seer:^s ¹²"Go and tell David, 'This is

23:34
w2Sa 11:3
x2Sa 15:12
23:35
yJos 12:22
23:36
z1Sa 14:47
23:38
a2Sa 20:26;
1Ch 2:53
23:39
b2Sa 11:3
24:1
cJos 9:15
d1Ch 27:23
24:2
e2Sa 20:23
fJdg 20:1;
2Sa 3:10
24:3
gDt 1:11
24:5
hDt 2:36;
Jos 13:9
iNu 21:32
24:6
jGe 10:19;
Jos 19:28;
Jdg 1:31
24:7
kJos 19:29
lGe 21:22-33
mDt 1:7;
Jos 11:3
24:9
nNu 1:44-46;
1Ch 21:5
24:10
o1Sa 24:5
p2Sa 12:13
qNu 12:11;
1Sa 13:13
24:11
r1Sa 22:5
s1Sa 9:9;
1Ch 29:29

---

^a33 Some Septuagint manuscripts (see also 1 Chron. 11:34); Hebrew does not have *son of.*
^b33 Hebrew; some Septuagint manuscripts (see also 1 Chron. 11:35) *Sacar*　　^c36 Some
Septuagint manuscripts (see also 1 Chron. 11:38); Hebrew *Haggadi*　　^d2 Septuagint (see also
verse 4 and 1 Chron. 21:2); Hebrew *Joab the army commander*

what the LORD says: I am giving you three options. Choose one of them for me to carry out against you.' "

[13]So Gad went to David and said to him, "Shall there come upon you three[a] years of famine[t] in your land? Or three months of fleeing from your enemies while they pursue you? Or three days of plague[u] in your land? Now then, think it over and decide how I should answer the one who sent me."

[14]David said to Gad, "I am in deep distress. Let us fall into the hands of the LORD, for his mercy[v] is great; but do not let me fall into the hands of men."

[15]So the LORD sent a plague on Israel from that morning until the end of the time designated, and seventy thousand of the people from Dan to Beersheba died.[w] [16]When the angel stretched out his hand to destroy Jerusalem, the LORD was grieved[x] because of the calamity and said to the angel who was afflicting the people, "Enough! Withdraw your hand." The angel of the LORD[y] was then at the threshing floor of Araunah the Jebusite.

[17]When David saw the angel who was striking down the people, he said to the LORD, "I am the one who has sinned and done wrong. These are but sheep.[z] What have they done? Let your hand fall upon me and my family."[a]

David Builds an Altar

24:18–25pp — 1Ch 21:18–26

[18]On that day Gad went to David and said to him, "Go up and build an altar to the LORD on the threshing floor of Araunah the Jebusite." [19]So David went up, as the LORD had commanded through Gad. [20]When Araunah looked and saw the king and his men coming toward him, he went out and bowed down before the king with his face to the ground.

[21]Araunah said, "Why has my lord the king come to his servant?"

"To buy your threshing floor," David answered, "so I can build an altar to the LORD, that the plague on the people may be stopped."[b]

[22]Araunah said to David, "Let my lord the king take whatever pleases him and offer it up. Here are oxen[c] for the burnt offering, and here are threshing sledges and ox yokes for the wood. [23]O king, Araunah gives[d] all this to the king." Araunah also said to him, "May the LORD your God accept you."

[24]But the king replied to Araunah, "No, I insist on paying you for it. I will not sacrifice to the LORD my God burnt offerings that cost me nothing."[e]

So David bought the threshing floor and the oxen and paid fifty shekels[b] of silver for them. [25]David built an altar[f] to the LORD there and sacrificed burnt offerings and fellowship offerings.[c] Then the LORD answered prayer[g] in behalf of the land, and the plague on Israel was stopped.

24:13
t Dt 28:38-42,48;
Eze 14:21
u Lev 26:25
24:14
v Ne 9:28;
Ps 51:1; 103:8,
13; 130:4
24:15
w 1Ch 27:24
24:16
x Ge 6:6;
1Sa 15:11
y Ex 12:23;
Ac 12:23
24:17
z Ps 74:1
a Jnh 1:12
24:21
b Nu 16:44-50
24:22
c 1Sa 6:14;
1Ki 19:21
24:23
d Eze 20:40-41
24:24
e Mal 1:13-14
24:25
f 1Sa 7:17
g 2Sa 21:14

---

[a]13 Septuagint (see also 1 Chron. 21:12); Hebrew *seven*   [b]24 That is, about 1 1/4 pounds (about 0.6 kilogram)   [c]25 Traditionally *peace offerings*

1 Kings

Title and Background

1 and 2 Kings (like 1,2 Samuel and 1,2 Chronicles) are actually one literary work, called in Hebrew tradition simply "Kings." Together Samuel and Kings relate the whole history of the monarchy, from its rise under the ministry of Samuel to its destruction at the hands of the Babylonians. Beginning with Solomon's reign, 1 Kings records the history of Israel through the divided kingdom to the death of Ahaz.

Author and Date of Writing

There is little conclusive evidence as to the identity of the author of 1,2 Kings. Whoever the author may have been, it is clear that he was familiar with the book of Deuteronomy—as were many of Israel's prophets. The book was probably written subsequent to Jehoiachin's release from prison (562 B.C.) and prior to the end of the Babylonian exile in 538.

Theme and Message

No explicit statement of purpose or theme is found in 1 or 2 Kings. In general, they describe the history of the kings of Israel and Judah in the light of God's covenants. The author was primarily concerned with Israel's faithfulness to the covenants, so he recorded the activities of each ruler as to his/her obedience to the covenant. Obedience to God brought peace and prosperity; disobedience and idol worship resulted in war and disaster.

Outline

I. Solomon's Reign (1:1-12:24)
II. Israel and Judah From Jeroboam/Rehoboam to Ahab/Asa (12:25-16:34)
III. Elijah and King Ahab (17:1-22:40)
IV. Jehoshaphat King of Judah (22:41-50)
V. Ahaziah King of Israel (22:51-53)

Adonijah Sets Himself Up as King

1 When King David was old and well advanced in years, he could not keep warm even when they put covers over him. ²So his servants said to him, "Let us look for a young virgin to attend the king and take care of him. She can lie beside him so that our lord the king may keep warm."

1:3
ªJos 19:18

1:5
ᵇ2Sa 3:4
ᶜ2Sa 15:1

³Then they searched throughout Israel for a beautiful girl and found Abishag, a Shunammite,ª and brought her to the king. ⁴The girl was very beautiful; she took care of the king and waited on him, but the king had no intimate relations with her.

⁵Now Adonijah,ᵇ whose mother was Haggith, put himself forward and said, "I will be king." So he got chariotsᶜ and horsesᵈ ready, with

---

ª5 Or charioteers

fifty men to run ahead of him. [6](His father had never interfered[d] with him by asking, "Why do you behave as you do?" He was also very handsome and was born next after Absalom.)

[7]Adonijah conferred with Joab[e] son of Zeruiah and with Abiathar[f] the priest, and they gave him their support. [8]But Zadok[g] the priest, Benaiah[h] son of Jehoiada, Nathan[i] the prophet, Shimei[j] and Rei[a] and David's special guard[k] did not join Adonijah.

[9]Adonijah then sacrificed sheep, cattle and fattened calves at the Stone of Zoheleth near En Rogel.[l] He invited all his brothers, the king's sons, and all the men of Judah who were royal officials, [10]but he did not invite Nathan the prophet or Benaiah or the special guard or his brother Solomon.[m]

[11]Then Nathan asked Bathsheba,[n] Solomon's mother, "Have you not heard that Adonijah,[o] the son of Haggith, has become king without our lord David's knowing it? [12]Now then, let me advise[p] you how you can save your own life and the life of your son Solomon. [13]Go in to King David and say to him, 'My lord the king, did you not swear[q] to me your servant: "Surely Solomon your son shall be king after me, and he will sit on my throne"? Why then has Adonijah become king?' [14]While you are still there talking to the king, I will come in and confirm what you have said."

[15]So Bathsheba went to see the aged king in his room, where Abishag[r] the Shunammite was attending him. [16]Bathsheba bowed low and knelt before the king.

"What is it you want?" the king asked.

[17]She said to him, "My lord, you yourself swore[s] to me your servant by the LORD your God: 'Solomon your son shall be king after me, and he will sit on my throne.' [18]But now Adonijah has become king, and you, my lord the king, do not know about it. [19]He has sacrificed[t] great numbers of cattle, fattened calves, and sheep, and has invited all the king's sons, Abiathar the priest and Joab the commander of the army, but he has not invited Solomon your servant. [20]My lord the king, the eyes of all Israel are on you, to learn from you who will sit on the throne of my lord the king after him. [21]Otherwise, as soon as my lord the king is laid to rest[u] with his fathers, I and my son Solomon will be treated as criminals."

[22]While she was still speaking with the king, Nathan the prophet arrived. [23]And they told the king, "Nathan the prophet is here." So he went before the king and bowed with his face to the ground.

[24]Nathan said, "Have you, my lord the king, declared that Adonijah shall be king after you, and that he will sit on your throne? [25]Today he has gone down and sacrificed great numbers of cattle, fattened calves, and sheep. He has invited all the king's sons, the commanders of the army and Abiathar the priest. Right now they are eating and drinking with him and saying, 'Long live King Adonijah!' [26]But me your servant, and Zadok the priest, and Benaiah son of Jehoiada, and your servant Solomon he did not invite.[v] [27]Is this something my lord the king has done without letting his servants know who should sit on the throne of my lord the king after him?"

1:6
d2Sa 3:3-4
1:7
e1Ki 2:22,28;
1Ch 11:6
f1Sa 22:20;
2Sa 20:25
1:8
g2Sa 20:25
h2Sa 8:18
i2Sa 12:1
j1Ki 4:18
k2Sa 23:8
1:9
l2Sa 17:17
1:10
m2Sa 12:24
1:11
n2Sa 12:24
o2Sa 3:4
1:12
pPr 15:22
1:13
qver 30;
1Ch 22:9-13
1:15
rver 1
1:17
sver 13,30
1:19
tver 9
1:21
uDt 31:16;
1Ki 2:10
1:26
vver 8,10

---

a8 Or *and his friends*

David Makes Solomon King

1:28–53pp — 1Ch 29:21-25

28Then King David said, "Call in Bathsheba." So she came into the king's presence and stood before him.

29The king then took an oath: "As surely as the LORD lives, who has delivered me out of every trouble, w 30I will surely carry out today what I swore x to you by the LORD, the God of Israel: Solomon your son shall be king after me, and he will sit on my throne in my place."

31Then Bathsheba bowed low with her face to the ground and, kneeling before the king, said, "May my lord King David live forever!"

32King David said, "Call in Zadok the priest, Nathan the prophet and Benaiah son of Jehoiada." When they came before the king, 33he said to them: "Take your lord's servants with you and set Solomon my son on my own mule y and take him down to Gihon. z 34There have Zadok the priest and Nathan the prophet anoint a him king over Israel. Blow the trumpet b and shout, 'Long live King Solomon!' 35Then you are to go up with him, and he is to come and sit on my throne and reign in my place. I have appointed him ruler over Israel and Judah."

36Benaiah son of Jehoiada answered the king, "Amen! May the LORD, the God of my lord the king, so declare it. 37As the LORD was with my lord the king, so may he be with c Solomon to make his throne even greater d than the throne of my lord King David!"

38So Zadok e the priest, Nathan the prophet, Benaiah son of Jehoiada, the Kerethites f and the Pelethites went down and put Solomon on King David's mule and escorted him to Gihon. g 39Zadok the priest took the horn of oil h from the sacred tent and anointed Solomon. Then they sounded the trumpet and all the people shouted, i "Long live King Solomon!" 40And all the people went up after him, playing flutes and rejoicing greatly, so that the ground shook with the sound.

41Adonijah and all the guests who were with him heard it as they were finishing their feast. On hearing the sound of the trumpet, Joab asked, "What's the meaning of all the noise in the city?"

42Even as he was speaking, Jonathan j son of Abiathar the priest arrived. Adonijah said, "Come in. A worthy man like you must be bringing good news." k

43"Not at all!" Jonathan answered. "Our lord King David has made Solomon king. 44The king has sent with him Zadok the priest, Nathan the prophet, Benaiah son of Jehoiada, the Kerethites and the Pelethites, and they have put him on the king's mule, 45and Zadok the priest and Nathan the prophet have anointed him king at Gihon. From there they have gone up cheering, and the city resounds l with it. That's the noise you hear. 46Moreover, Solomon has taken his seat on the royal throne. 47Also, the royal officials have come to congratulate our lord King David, saying, 'May your God make Solomon's name more famous than yours and his throne greater m than yours!' And the king bowed in worship on his bed 48and said, 'Praise be to the LORD, the God of Israel, who has allowed my eyes to see a successor n on my throne today.' "

49At this, all Adonijah's guests rose in alarm and dispersed. 50But Adonijah, in fear of Solomon, went and took hold of the horns o of the altar. 51Then Solomon was told, "Adonijah is afraid of King Solomon and is clinging to the horns of the altar. He says, 'Let King Solomon

---

1:29
w2Sa 4:9
1:30
xver 13,17
1:33
y2Sa 20:6-7
z2Ch 32:30;
33:14
1:34
a1Sa 10:1; 16:3,
12; 1Ki 19:16;
2Ki 9:3,13
bver 25;
2Sa 5:3; 15:10
1:37
cJos 1:5,17;
1Sa 20:13
dver 47
1:38
ever 8 f2Sa 8:18
gver 33
1:39
hEx 30:23-32;
Ps 89:20
iver 34;
1Sa 10:24
1:42
j2Sa 15:27,36
k2Sa 18:26
1:45
lver 40
1:47
mver 37;
Ge 47:31
1:48
n2Sa 7:12;
1Ki 3:6
1:50
o1Ki 2:28

swear to me today that he will not put his servant to death with the sword.' "

⁵²Solomon replied, "If he shows himself to be a worthy man, not a hairᵖ of his head will fall to the ground; but if evil is found in him, he will die." ⁵³Then King Solomon sent men, and they brought him down from the altar. And Adonijah came and bowed down to King Solomon, and Solomon said, "Go to your home."

David's Charge to Solomon

2:10–12pp — 1Ch 29:26–28

2 When the time drew near for David to die,�q he gave a charge to Solomon his son.

²"I am about to go the way of all the earth,"ʳ he said. "So be strong,ˢ show yourself a man, ³and observeᵗ what the LORD your God requires: Walk in his ways, and keep his decrees and commands, his laws and requirements, as written in the Law of Moses, so that you may prosperᵘ in all you do and wherever you go, ⁴and that the LORD may keep his promiseᵛ to me: 'If your descendants watch how they live, and if they walk faithfullyʷ before me with all their heart and soul, you will never fail to have a man on the throne of Israel.'

⁵"Now you yourself know what Joabˣ son of Zeruiah did to me— what he did to the two commanders of Israel's armies, Abnerʸ son of Ner and Amasaᶻ son of Jether. He killed them, shedding their blood in peacetime as if in battle, and with that blood stained the belt around his waist and the sandals on his feet. ⁶Deal with him according to your wisdom,ᵃ but do not let his gray head go down to the graveᵃ in peace.

⁷"But show kindness to the sons of Barzillaiᵇ of Gilead and let them be among those who eat at your table.ᶜ They stood by me when I fled from your brother Absalom.

⁸"And remember, you have with you Shimeiᵈ son of Gera, the Benjamite from Bahurim, who called down bitter curses on me the day I went to Mahanaim. When he came down to meet me at the Jordan, I sworeᵉ to him by the LORD: 'I will not put you to death by the sword.' ⁹But now, do not consider him innocent. You are a man of wisdom;ᶠ you will know what to do to him. Bring his gray head down to the grave in blood."

¹⁰Then David rested with his fathers and was buriedᵍ in the City of David.ʰ ¹¹He had reignedⁱ forty years over Israel—seven years in Hebron and thirty-three in Jerusalem. ¹²So Solomon sat on the throneʲ of his father David, and his rule was firmly established.ᵏ

Solomon's Throne Established

¹³Now Adonijah, the son of Haggith, went to Bathsheba, Solomon's mother. Bathsheba asked him, "Do you come peacefully?"ˡ

He answered, "Yes, peacefully." ¹⁴Then he added, "I have something to say to you."

"You may say it," she replied.

¹⁵"As you know," he said, "the kingdom was mine. All Israel looked to me as their king. But things changed, and the kingdom has gone to

---

1:52
p 1Sa 14:45;
2Sa 14:11

2:1
q Ge 47:29;
Dt 31:14

2:2
r Jos 23:14
s Dt 31:7,23;
Jos 1:6

2:3
t Dt 17:14-20;
Jos 1:7
u 1Ch 22:13

2:4
v 2Sa 7:13,25;
1Ki 8:25
w 2Ki 20:3;
Ps 132:12

2:5
x 2Sa 2:18; 18:5,
12,14 y 2Sa 3:27
z 2Sa 20:10

2:6
a ver 9

2:7
b 2Sa 17:27;
19:31-39
c 2Sa 9:7

2:8
d 2Sa 16:5-13
e 2Sa 19:18-23

2:9
f ver 6

2:10
g Ac 2:29; 13:36
h 2Sa 5:7

2:11
i 2Sa 5:4,5

2:12
j 1Ch 29:23
k 2Ch 1:1

2:13
l 1Sa 16:4

ᵃ6 Hebrew *Sheol*; also in verse 9

my brother; for it has come to him from the LORD. [16]Now I have one request to make of you. Do not refuse me."

"You may make it," she said.

[17]So he continued, "Please ask King Solomon—he will not refuse you—to give me Abishag[m] the Shunammite as my wife."

[18]"Very well," Bathsheba replied, "I will speak to the king for you."

[19]When Bathsheba went to King Solomon to speak to him for Adonijah, the king stood up to meet her, bowed down to her and sat down on his throne. He had a throne brought for the king's mother,[n] and she sat down at his right hand.[o]

[20]"I have one small request to make of you," she said. "Do not refuse me."

The king replied, "Make it, my mother; I will not refuse you."

[21]So she said, "Let Abishag[p] the Shunammite be given in marriage to your brother Adonijah."

[22]King Solomon answered his mother, "Why do you request Abishag[q] the Shunammite for Adonijah? You might as well request the kingdom for him—after all, he is my older brother[r]—yes, for him and for Abiathar the priest and Joab son of Zeruiah!"

[23]Then King Solomon swore by the LORD: "May God deal with me, be it ever so severely,[s] if Adonijah does not pay with his life for this request! [24]And now, as surely as the LORD lives—he who has established me securely on the throne of my father David and has founded a dynasty for me as he promised[t]—Adonijah shall be put to death today!" [25]So King Solomon gave orders to Benaiah[u] son of Jehoiada, and he struck down Adonijah and he died.

[26]To Abiathar[v] the priest the king said, "Go back to your fields in Anathoth.[w] You deserve to die, but I will not put you to death now, because you carried the ark[x] of the Sovereign LORD before my father David and shared all my father's hardships."[y] [27]So Solomon removed Abiathar from the priesthood of the LORD, fulfilling[z] the word the LORD had spoken at Shiloh about the house of Eli.

[28]When the news reached Joab, who had conspired with Adonijah though not with Absalom, he fled to the tent of the LORD and took hold of the horns[a] of the altar. [29]King Solomon was told that Joab had fled to the tent of the LORD and was beside the altar. Then Solomon ordered Benaiah[b] son of Jehoiada, "Go, strike him down!"

[30]So Benaiah entered the tent of the LORD and said to Joab, "The king says, 'Come out!'[c] "

But he answered, "No, I will die here."

Benaiah reported to the king, "This is how Joab answered me."

[31]Then the king commanded Benaiah, "Do as he says. Strike him down and bury him, and so clear me and my father's house of the guilt of the innocent blood[d] that Joab shed. [32]The LORD will repay[e] him for the blood he shed,[f] because without the knowledge of my father David he attacked two men and killed them with the sword. Both of them—Abner son of Ner, commander of Israel's army, and Amasa[g] son of Jether, commander of Judah's army—were better[h] men and more upright than he. [33]May the guilt of their blood rest on the head of Joab and his descendants forever. But on David and his descendants, his house and his throne, may there be the LORD's peace forever."

[34]So Benaiah son of Jehoiada went up and struck down Joab and

---

2:17
m 1Ki 1:3
2:19
n 1Ki 15:13
o Ps 45:9
2:21
p 1Ki 1:3
2:22
q 2Sa 12:8;
1Ki 1:3 r 1Ch 3:2
2:23
s Ru 1:17
2:24
t 2Sa 7:11;
1Ch 22:10
2:25
u 2Sa 8:18
2:26
v 1Sa 22:20
w Jos 21:18
x 2Sa 15:24
y 1Sa 23:6
2:27
z 1Sa 2:27-36
2:28
a 1Ki 1:7,50
2:29
b ver 25
2:30
c Ex 21:14
2:31
d Nu 35:33;
Dt 19:13; 21:8-9
2:32
e Jdg 9:57;
Ps 7:16
f Jdg 9:24
g 2Sa 3:27;
20:10
h 2Ch 21:13

killed him, and he was buried on his own land[a] in the desert. [35]The king put Benaiah[i] son of Jehoiada over the army in Joab's position and replaced Abiathar with Zadok[j] the priest.

[36]Then the king sent for Shimei[k] and said to him, "Build yourself a house in Jerusalem and live there, but do not go anywhere else. [37]The day you leave and cross the Kidron Valley,[l] you can be sure you will die; your blood will be on your own head."[m]

[38]Shimei answered the king, "What you say is good. Your servant will do as my lord the king has said." And Shimei stayed in Jerusalem for a long time.

[39]But three years later, two of Shimei's slaves ran off to Achish[n] son of Maacah, king of Gath, and Shimei was told, "Your slaves are in Gath." [40]At this, he saddled his donkey and went to Achish at Gath in search of his slaves. So Shimei went away and brought the slaves back from Gath.

[41]When Solomon was told that Shimei had gone from Jerusalem to Gath and had returned, [42]the king summoned Shimei and said to him, "Did I not make you swear by the LORD and warn you, 'On the day you leave to go anywhere else, you can be sure you will die'? At that time you said to me, 'What you say is good. I will obey.' [43]Why then did you not keep your oath to the LORD and obey the command I gave you?"

[44]The king also said to Shimei, "You know in your heart all the wrong[o] you did to my father David. Now the LORD will repay you for your wrongdoing. [45]But King Solomon will be blessed, and David's throne will remain secure[p] before the LORD forever."

[46]Then the king gave the order to Benaiah son of Jehoiada, and he went out and struck Shimei down and killed him.

The kingdom was now firmly established[q] in Solomon's hands.

Solomon Asks for Wisdom
3:4–15pp — 2Ch 1:2–13

3 Solomon made an alliance with Pharaoh king of Egypt and married[r] his daughter.[s] He brought her to the City of David[t] until he finished building his palace[u] and the temple of the LORD, and the wall around Jerusalem. [2]The people, however, were still sacrificing at the high places,[v] because a temple had not yet been built for the Name of the LORD. [3]Solomon showed his love[w] for the LORD by walking according to the statutes[x] of his father David, except that he offered sacrifices and burned incense on the high places.

[4]The king went to Gibeon[y] to offer sacrifices, for that was the most important high place, and Solomon offered a thousand burnt offerings on that altar. [5]At Gibeon the LORD appeared[z] to Solomon during the night in a dream,[a] and God said, "Ask for whatever you want me to give you."

[6]Solomon answered, "You have shown great kindness to your servant, my father David, because he was faithful[b] to you and righteous and upright in heart. You have continued this great kindness to him and have given him a son[c] to sit on his throne this very day.

[7]"Now, O LORD my God, you have made your servant king in place of my father David. But I am only a little child[d] and do not know how

---

[a]34 Or *buried in his tomb*

2:35
i1Ki 4:4 jver 27;
1Ch 29:22
2:36
kver 8; 2Sa 16:5
2:37
l2Sa 15:23
mLev 20:9;
Jos 2:19;
2Sa 1:16
2:39
n1Sa 27:2
2:44
o1Sa 25:39;
2Sa 16:5-13;
Eze 17:19
2:45
p2Sa 7:13;
Pr 25:5
2:46
qver 12;
2Ch 1:1
3:1
r1Ki 7:8
s1Ki 9:24
t2Sa 5:7
u1Ki 7:1;
9:15,19
3:2
vLev 17:3-5;
Dt 12:2,4-5;
1Ki 22:43
3:3
wDt 6:5;
Ps 31:23;
1Co 8:3
x1Ki 2:3; 9:4;
11:4,6,38
3:4
y1Ch 16:39
3:5
z1Ki 9:2
aNu 12:6;
Mt 1:20
3:6
b1Ki 2:4; 9:4
c1Ki 1:48
3:7
dNu 27:17;
1Ch 29:1

to carry out my duties. [8]Your servant is here among the people you have chosen,[e] a great people, too numerous to count or number.[f] [9]So give your servant a discerning[g] heart to govern your people and to distinguish[h] between right and wrong. For who is able[i] to govern this great people of yours?"

[10]The Lord was pleased that Solomon had asked for this. [11]So God said to him, "Since you have asked[j] for this and not for long life or wealth for yourself, nor have asked for the death of your enemies but for discernment in administering justice, [12]I will do what you have asked.[k] I will give you a wise[l] and discerning heart, so that there will never have been anyone like you, nor will there ever be. [13]Moreover, I will give you what you have not[m] asked for—both riches and honor[n] —so that in your lifetime you will have no equal[o] among kings. [14]And if you walk[p] in my ways and obey my statutes and commands as David your father did, I will give you a long life."[q] [15]Then Solomon awoke[r] —and he realized it had been a dream.

He returned to Jerusalem, stood before the ark of the Lord's covenant and sacrificed burnt offerings[s] and fellowship offerings.[a][t] Then he gave a feast[u] for all his court.

A Wise Ruling

[16]Now two prostitutes came to the king and stood before him. [17]One of them said, "My lord, this woman and I live in the same house. I had a baby while she was there with me. [18]The third day after my child was born, this woman also had a baby. We were alone; there was no one in the house but the two of us.

[19]"During the night this woman's son died because she lay on him. [20]So she got up in the middle of the night and took my son from my side while I your servant was asleep. She put him by her breast and put her dead son by my breast. [21]The next morning, I got up to nurse my son—and he was dead! But when I looked at him closely in the morning light, I saw that it wasn't the son I had borne."

[22]The other woman said, "No! The living one is my son; the dead one is yours."

But the first one insisted, "No! The dead one is yours; the living one is mine." And so they argued before the king.

[23]The king said, "This one says, 'My son is alive and your son is dead,' while that one says, 'No! Your son is dead and mine is alive.' "

[24]Then the king said, "Bring me a sword." So they brought a sword for the king. [25]He then gave an order: "Cut the living child in two and give half to one and half to the other."

[26]The woman whose son was alive was filled with compassion[v] for her son and said to the king, "Please, my lord, give her the living baby! Don't kill him!"

But the other said, "Neither I nor you shall have him. Cut him in two!"

[27]Then the king gave his ruling: "Give the living baby to the first woman. Do not kill him; she is his mother."

[28]When all Israel heard the verdict the king had given, they held the

3:8
e Dt 7:6
f Ge 15:5
3:9
g 2Sa 14:17;
Jas 1:5
h Pr 2:3-9;
Heb 5:14
i Ps 72:1-2
3:11
j Jas 4:3
3:12
k 1Jn 5:14-15
l 1Ki 4:29,30,31;
5:12; 10:23;
Ecc 1:16
3:13
m Mt 6:33;
Eph 3:20
n 1Ki 4:21-24;
Pr 3:1-2,16
o 1Ki 10:23
3:14
p ver 6;
Pr 3:1-2,16
q Ps 61:6;
91:16
3:15
r Ge 41:7
s 1Ki 8:65
t Mk 6:21
u Est 1:3,9;
Da 5:1
3:26
v Ge 43:30;
Isa 49:15;
Jer 31:20;
Hos 11:8

a15 Traditionally *peace offerings*

king in awe, because they saw that he had wisdom[w] from God to administer justice.

Solomon's Officials and Governors

4 So King Solomon ruled over all Israel. [2]And these were his chief officials:

Azariah[x] son of Zadok—the priest;
[3]Elihoreph and Ahijah, sons of Shisha—secretaries;
Jehoshaphat[y] son of Ahilud—recorder;
[4]Benaiah[z] son of Jehoiada—commander in chief;
Zadok[a] and Abiathar—priests;
[5]Azariah son of Nathan—in charge of the district officers;
Zabud son of Nathan—a priest and personal adviser to the king;
[6]Ahishar—in charge of the palace;
Adoniram son of Abda—in charge of forced labor.

[7]Solomon also had twelve district governors over all Israel, who supplied provisions for the king and the royal household. Each one had to provide supplies for one month in the year. [8]These are their names:

Ben-Hur—in the hill country[b] of Ephraim;
[9]Ben-Deker—in Makaz, Shaalbim,[c] Beth Shemesh[d] and Elon Bethhanan;
[10]Ben-Hesed—in Arubboth (Socoh[e] and all the land of Hepher[f] were his);
[11]Ben-Abinadab—in Naphoth Dor[a g] (he was married to Taphath daughter of Solomon);
[12]Baana son of Ahilud—in Taanach and Megiddo, and in all of Beth Shan[h] next to Zarethan[i] below Jezreel, from Beth Shan to Abel Meholah[j] across to Jokmeam;[k]
[13]Ben-Geber—in Ramoth Gilead (the settlements of Jair[l] son of Manasseh in Gilead were his, as well as the district of Argob in Bashan and its sixty large walled cities[m] with bronze gate bars);
[14]Ahinadab son of Iddo—in Mahanaim;[n]
[15]Ahimaaz[o]—in Naphtali (he had married Basemath daughter of Solomon);
[16]Baana son of Hushai[p]—in Asher and in Aloth;
[17]Jehoshaphat son of Paruah—in Issachar;
[18]Shimei[q] son of Ela—in Benjamin;
[19]Geber son of Uri—in Gilead (the country of Sihon king of the Amorites and the country of Og[r] king of Bashan). He was the only governor over the district.

Solomon's Daily Provisions

[20]The people of Judah and Israel were as numerous as the sand[s] on the seashore; they ate, they drank and they were happy. [21]And Solomon ruled[t] over all the kingdoms from the River[b u] to the land of the Philistines, as far as the border of Egypt.[v] These countries brought tribute[w] and were Solomon's subjects all his life.

[a]11 Or *in the heights of Dor*   [b]21 That is, the Euphrates; also in verse 24

3:28
wver 9,11-12;
Col 2:3
4:2
x1Ch 6:10
4:3
y2Sa 8:16
4:4
z1Ki 2:35
a1Ki 2:27
4:8
bJos 24:33
4:9
cJdg 1:35
dJos 21:16
4:10
eJos 15:35
fJos 12:17
4:11
gJos 11:2
4:12
hJos 17:11;
Jdg 5:19
iJos 3:16
j1Ki 19:16
k1Ch 6:68
4:13
lNu 32:41
mDt 3:4
4:14
nJos 13:26
4:15
o2Sa 15:27
4:16
p2Sa 15:32
4:18
q1Ki 1:8
4:19
rDt 3:8-10
4:20
sGe 22:17;
32:12; 1Ki 3:8
4:21
t2Ch 9:26;
Ps 72:11
uJos 1:4;
Ps 72:8
vGe 15:18
wPs 68:29

22Solomon's daily provisions were thirty cors[a] of fine flour and sixty cors[b] of meal, 23ten head of stall-fed cattle, twenty of pasture-fed cattle and a hundred sheep and goats, as well as deer, gazelles, roebucks and choice fowl. 24For he ruled over all the kingdoms west of the River, from Tiphsah[x] to Gaza, and had peace[y] on all sides. 25During Solomon's lifetime Judah and Israel, from Dan to Beersheba,[z] lived in safety,[a] each man under his own vine and fig tree.[b]

26Solomon had four[c] thousand stalls for chariot horses,[c] and twelve thousand horses.[d]

27The district officers,[d] each in his month, supplied provisions for King Solomon and all who came to the king's table. They saw to it that nothing was lacking. 28They also brought to the proper place their quotas of barley and straw for the chariot horses and the other horses.

Solomon's Wisdom

29God gave Solomon wisdom[e] and very great insight, and a breadth of understanding as measureless as the sand on the seashore. 30Solomon's wisdom was greater than the wisdom of all the men of the East,[f] and greater than all the wisdom of Egypt.[g] 31He was wiser[h] than any other man, including Ethan the Ezrahite—wiser than Heman, Calcol and Darda, the sons of Mahol. And his fame spread to all the surrounding nations. 32He spoke three thousand proverbs[i] and his songs[j] numbered a thousand and five. 33He described plant life, from the cedar of Lebanon to the hyssop that grows out of walls. He also taught about animals and birds, reptiles and fish. 34Men of all nations came to listen to Solomon's wisdom, sent by all the kings[k] of the world, who had heard of his wisdom.

Preparations for Building the Temple

5:1–16pp — 2Ch 2:1–18

5 When Hiram[1] king of Tyre heard that Solomon had been anointed king to succeed his father David, he sent his envoys to Solomon, because he had always been on friendly terms with David. 2Solomon sent back this message to Hiram:

3"You know that because of the wars[m] waged against my father David from all sides, he could not build a temple for the Name of the LORD his God until the LORD put his enemies under his feet. 4But now the LORD my God has given me rest[n] on every side, and there is no adversary or disaster. 5I intend, therefore, to build a temple[o] for the Name of the LORD my God, as the LORD told my father David, when he said, 'Your son whom I will put on the throne in your place will build the temple for my Name.'[p]

6"So give orders that cedars of Lebanon be cut for me. My men will work with yours, and I will pay you for your men whatever wages you set. You know that we have no one so skilled in felling timber as the Sidonians."

7When Hiram heard Solomon's message, he was greatly pleased and

Cross references

4:24
xPs 72:11
y1Ch 22:9

4:25
zJdg 20:1
aJer 23:6
bMic 4:4;
Zec 3:10

4:26
c1Ki 10:26;
2Ch 1:14

4:27
dver 7

4:29
e1Ki 3:12

4:30
fGe 25:6
gAc 7:22

4:31
h1Ki 3:12;
1Ch 2:6; 6:33;
15:19;
Ps 89 Title

4:32
iPr 1:1;
Ecc 12:9 jSS 1:1

4:34
k1Ki 10:1;
2Ch 9:23

5:1
lver 10,18;
2Sa 5:11;
1Ch 14:1

5:3
m1Ch 22:8;
28:3

5:4
n1Ki 4:24;
1Ch 22:9

5:5
o1Ch 17:12
p2Sa 7:13;
1Ch 22:10

---

a22 That is, probably about 185 bushels (about 6.6 kiloliters) b22 That is, probably about 375 bushels (about 13.2 kiloliters) c26 Some Septuagint manuscripts (see also 2 Chron. 9:25); Hebrew *forty* d26 Or *charioteers* said, "Praise be to the LORD today, for he has given David a wise son to rule over this great nation."

⁸So Hiram sent word to Solomon:

"I have received the message you sent me and will do all you want in providing the cedar and pine logs. ⁹My men will haul them down from Lebanon to the sea �q, and I will float them in rafts by sea to the place you specify. There I will separate them and you can take them away. And you are to grant my wish by providing food ʳ for my royal household."

¹⁰In this way Hiram kept Solomon supplied with all the cedar and pine logs he wanted, ¹¹and Solomon gave Hiram twenty thousand cors ᵃ of wheat as food for his household, in addition to twenty thousand baths ᵇᶜ of pressed olive oil. Solomon continued to do this for Hiram year after year. ¹²The LORD gave Solomon wisdom, ˢ just as he had promised him. There were peaceful relations between Hiram and Solomon, and the two of them made a treaty. ᵗ

¹³King Solomon conscripted laborers ᵘ from all Israel—thirty thousand men. ¹⁴He sent them off to Lebanon in shifts of ten thousand a month, so that they spent one month in Lebanon and two months at home. Adoniram ᵛ was in charge of the forced labor. ¹⁵Solomon had seventy thousand carriers and eighty thousand stonecutters in the hills, ¹⁶as well as thirty-three hundred ᵈ foremen ʷ who supervised the project and directed the workmen. ¹⁷At the king's command they removed from the quarry ˣ large blocks of quality stone ʸ to provide a foundation of dressed stone for the temple. ¹⁸The craftsmen of Solomon and Hiram and the men of Gebal ᵉᶻ cut and prepared the timber and stone for the building of the temple.

Solomon Builds the Temple

6:1–29pp — 2Ch 3:1–14

6 In the four hundred and eightieth ᶠ year after the Israelites had come out of Egypt, in the fourth year of Solomon's reign over Israel, in the month of Ziv, the second month, he began to build the temple of the LORD. ᵃ

²The temple ᵇ that King Solomon built for the LORD was sixty cubits long, twenty wide and thirty high. ᵍ ³The portico at the front of the main hall of the temple extended the width of the temple, that is twenty cubits, ʰ and projected ten cubits ⁱ from the front of the temple. ⁴He made narrow clerestory windows ᶜ in the temple. ⁵Against the walls of the main hall and inner sanctuary he built a structure around the building, in which there were side rooms. ᵈ ⁶The lowest floor was five cubits ʲ wide, the middle floor six cubits ᵏ and the third floor seven. ˡ He made offset ledges around the outside of the temple so that nothing would be inserted into the temple walls.

ᵃ11 That is, probably about 125,000 bushels (about 4,400 kiloliters)   ᵇ11 Septuagint (see also 2 Chron. 2:10); Hebrew *twenty cors*   ᶜ11 That is, about 115,000 gallons (about 440 kiloliters)   ᵈ16 Hebrew; some Septuagint manuscripts (see also 2 Chron. 2:2, 18) *thirty-six hundred*   ᵉ18 That is, Byblos   ᶠ1 Hebrew; Septuagint *four hundred and fortieth*   ᵍ2 That is, about 90 feet (about 27 meters) long and 30 feet (about 9 meters) wide and 45 feet (about 13.5 meters) high   ʰ3 That is, about 30 feet (about 9 meters)   ⁱ3 That is, about 15 feet (about 4.5 meters)   ʲ6 That is, about 7 1/2 feet (about 2.3 meters); also in verses 10 and 24   ᵏ6 That is, about 9 feet (about 2.7 meters)   ˡ6 That is, about 10 1/2 feet (about 3.1 meters)

5:9
q Ezr 3:7
r Eze 27:17;
Ac 12:20
5:12
s 1Ki 3:12
t Am 1:9
5:13
u 1Ki 9:15
5:14
v 1Ki 4:6;
2Ch 10:18
5:16
w 1Ki 9:23
5:17
x 1Ki 6:7
y 1Ch 22:2
5:18
z Jos 13:5
6:1
a Ac 7:47
6:2
b Eze 41:1
6:4
c Eze 40:16;
41:16
6:5
d ver 16,19-21;
Eze 41:5-6

7In building the temple, only blocks dressede at the quarry were used, and no hammer, chisel or any other iron toolf was heard at the temple site while it was being built.

8The entrance to the lowesta floor was on the south side of the temple; a stairway led up to the middle level and from there to the third. 9So he built the temple and completed it, roofing it with beams and cedarg planks. 10And he built the side rooms all along the temple. The height of each was five cubits, and they were attached to the temple by beams of cedar.

11The word of the LORD came to Solomon: 12"As for this temple you are building, if you follow my decrees, carry out my regulations and keep all my commands and obey them, I will fulfill through you the promiseh I gave to David your father. 13And I will live among the Israelites and will not abandoni my people Israel."

14So Solomon built the temple and completedj it. 15He lined its interior walls with cedar boards, paneling them from the floor of the temple to the ceiling,k and covered the floor of the temple with planks of pine. 16He partitioned off twenty cubitsb at the rear of the temple with cedar boards from floor to ceiling to form within the temple an inner sanctuary, the Most Holy Place.l 17The main hall in front of this room was forty cubitsc long. 18The inside of the temple was cedar,m carved with gourds and open flowers. Everything was cedar; no stone was to be seen.

19He prepared the inner sanctuaryn within the temple to set the ark of the covenanto of the LORD there. 20The inner sanctuaryp was twenty cubits long, twenty wide and twenty high.d He overlaid the inside with pure gold, and he also overlaid the altar of cedar. 21Solomon covered the inside of the temple with pure gold, and he extended gold chains across the front of the inner sanctuary, which was overlaid with gold. 22So he overlaid the whole interior with gold. He also overlaid with gold the altar that belonged to the inner sanctuary.

23In the inner sanctuary he made a pair of cherubimq of olive wood, each ten cubitse high. 24One wing of the first cherub was five cubits long, and the other wing five cubits—ten cubits from wing tip to wing tip. 25The second cherub also measured ten cubits, for the two cherubim were identical in size and shape. 26The height of each cherub was ten cubits. 27He placed the cherubimr inside the innermost room of the temple, with their wings spread out. The wing of one cherub touched one wall, while the wing of the other touched the other wall, and their wings touched each other in the middle of the room. 28He overlaid the cherubim with gold.

29On the walls all around the temple, in both the inner and outer rooms, he carved cherubim,s palm trees and open flowers. 30He also covered the floors of both the inner and outer rooms of the temple with gold.

31For the entrance of the inner sanctuary he made doors of olive wood with five-sided jambs. 32And on the two olive wood doors he carved cherubim, palm trees and open flowers, and overlaid the cherubim and

6:7
eEx 20:25
fDt 27:5
6:9
gver 14,38
6:12
h2Sa 7:12-16;
1Ki 2:4; 9:5
6:13
iEx 25:8;
Lev 26:11;
Dt 31:6;
Heb 13:5
6:14
jver 9,38
6:15
k1Ki 7:7
6:16
lEx 26:33;
Lev 16:2;
1Ki 8:6
6:18
m1Ki 7:24;
Ps 74:6
6:19
n1Ki 8:6
o1Sa 3:3
6:20
pEze 41:3-4
6:23
qEx 37:1-9
6:27
rEx 25:20; 37:9;
1Ki 8:7; 2Ch 5:8
6:29
sver 32,35

---

a8 Septuagint; Hebrew *middle*   b16 That is, about 30 feet (about 9 meters)   c17 That is, about 60 feet (about 18 meters)   d20 That is, about 30 feet (about 9 meters) long, wide and high   e23 That is, about 15 feet (about 4.5 meters) palm trees with beaten gold. [33]In the same way he made four-sided jambs of olive wood for the entrance to the main hall. [34]He also made two pine doors, each having two leaves that turned in sockets. [35]He carved cherubim, palm trees and open flowers on them and overlaid them with gold hammered evenly over the carvings.

[36]And he built the inner courtyard of three courses[t] of dressed stone and one course of trimmed cedar beams.

[37]The foundation of the temple of the LORD was laid in the fourth year, in the month of Ziv. [38]In the eleventh year in the month of Bul, the eighth month, the temple was finished in all its details according to its specifications. [u] He had spent seven years building it.

Solomon Builds His Palace

7 It took Solomon thirteen years, however, to complete the construction of his palace. [v] [2]He built the Palace[w] of the Forest of Lebanon[x] a hundred cubits long, fifty wide and thirty high, [a] with four rows of cedar columns supporting trimmed cedar beams. [3]It was roofed with cedar above the beams that rested on the columns—forty-five beams, fifteen to a row. [4]Its windows were placed high in sets of three, facing each other. [5]All the doorways had rectangular frames; they were in the front part in sets of three, facing each other. [b]

[6]He made a colonnade fifty cubits long and thirty wide. [c] In front of it was a portico, and in front of that were pillars and an overhanging roof.

[7]He built the throne hall, the Hall of Justice, where he was to judge, [y] and he covered it with cedar from floor to ceiling. [dz] [8]And the palace in which he was to live, set farther back, was similar in design. Solomon also made a palace like this hall for Pharaoh's daughter, whom he had married. [a]

[9]All these structures, from the outside to the great courtyard and from foundation to eaves, were made of blocks of high-grade stone cut to size and trimmed with a saw on their inner and outer faces. [10]The foundations were laid with large stones of good quality, some measuring ten cubits[e] and some eight.[f] [11]Above were high-grade stones, cut to size, and cedar beams. [12]The great courtyard was surrounded by a wall of three courses[b] of dressed stone and one course of trimmed cedar beams, as was the inner courtyard of the temple of the LORD with its portico.

The Temple's Furnishings

7:23–26pp — 2Ch 4:2–5
7:38–51pp — 2Ch 4:6,10–5:1

[13]King Solomon sent to Tyre and brought Huram, [gc] [14]whose mother was a widow from the tribe of Naphtali and whose father was a man of Tyre and a craftsman in bronze. Huram was highly skilled[d] and experienced in all kinds of bronze work. He came to King Solomon and did all[e] the work assigned to him.

[15]He cast two bronze pillars, [f] each eighteen cubits high and twelve

### Cross references (right column)

6:36
t1Ki 7:12;
Ezr 6:4

6:38
uHeb 8:5

7:1
v1Ki 9:10;
2Ch 8:1

7:2
w2Sa 7:2
x1Ki 10:17;
2Ch 9:16

7:7
yPs 122:5;
Pr 20:8
z1Ki 6:15

7:8
a1Ki 3:1;
2Ch 8:11

7:12
b1Ki 6:36

7:13
c2Ch 2:13

7:14
dEx 31:2-5;
35:31; 36:1;
2Ch 2:14
e2Ch 4:11,16

7:15
f2Ki 25:17;
2Ch 3:15; 4:12;
52:17,21

---

[a]2 That is, about 150 feet (about 46 meters) long, 75 feet (about 23 meters) wide and 45 feet (about 13.5 meters) high   [b]5 The meaning of the Hebrew for this verse is uncertain.   [c]6 That is, about 75 feet (about 23 meters) long and 45 feet (about 13.5 meters) wide   [d]7 Vulgate and Syriac; Hebrew *floor*   [e]10 That is, about 15 feet (about 4.5 meters)   [f]10 That is, about 12 feet (about 3.6 meters)   [g]13 Hebrew *Hiram*, a variant of *Huram*; also in verses 40 and 45

cubits around,[a] by line. [16]He also made two capitals[g] of cast bronze to set on the tops of the pillars; each capital was five cubits[b] high. [17]A network of interwoven chains festooned the capitals on top of the pillars, seven for each capital. [18]He made pomegranates in two rows[c] encircling each network to decorate the capitals on top of the pillars.[d] He did the same for each capital. [19]The capitals on top of the pillars in the portico were in the shape of lilies, four cubits[e] high. [20]On the capitals of both pillars, above the bowl-shaped part next to the network, were the two hundred pomegranates[h] in rows all around. [21]He erected the pillars at the portico of the temple. The pillar to the south he named Jakin[f] and the one to the north Boaz.[g][i] [22]The capitals on top were in the shape of lilies. And so the work on the pillars was completed.

[23]He made the Sea[j] of cast metal, circular in shape, measuring ten cubits[h] from rim to rim and five cubits high. It took a line of thirty cubits[i] to measure around it. [24]Below the rim, gourds encircled it—ten to a cubit. The gourds were cast in two rows in one piece with the Sea.

[25]The Sea stood on twelve bulls,[k] three facing north, three facing west, three facing south and three facing east. The Sea rested on top of them, and their hindquarters were toward the center. [26]It was a handbreadth[j] in thickness, and its rim was like the rim of a cup, like a lily blossom. It held two thousand baths.[k]

[27]He also made ten movable stands[l] of bronze; each was four cubits long, four wide and three high.[l] [28]This is how the stands were made: They had side panels attached to uprights. [29]On the panels between the uprights were lions, bulls and cherubim—and on the uprights as well. Above and below the lions and bulls were wreaths of hammered work. [30]Each stand[m] had four bronze wheels with bronze axles, and each had a basin resting on four supports, cast with wreaths on each side. [31]On the inside of the stand there was an opening that had a circular frame one cubit[m] deep. This opening was round, and with its basework it measured a cubit and a half.[n] Around its opening there was engraving. The panels of the stands were square, not round. [32]The four wheels were under the panels, and the axles of the wheels were attached to the stand. The diameter of each wheel was a cubit and a half. [33]The wheels were made like chariot wheels; the axles, rims, spokes and hubs were all of cast metal.

[34]Each stand had four handles, one on each corner, projecting from the stand. [35]At the top of the stand there was a circular band half a cubit[o] deep. The supports and panels were attached to the top of the stand. [36]He engraved cherubim, lions and palm trees on the surfaces of the supports and on the panels, in every available space, with wreaths

---

7:16
g2Ki 25:17

7:20
h2Ch 3:16;
4:13; Jer 52:23

7:21
i1Ki 6:3;
2Ch 3:17

7:23
j2Ki 25:13;
1Ch 18:8;
Jer 52:17

7:25
k2Ch 4:4-5;
Jer 52:20

7:27
lver 38;
2Ch 4:14

7:30
m2Ki 16:17

---

[a]15 That is, about 27 feet (about 8.1 meters) high and 18 feet (about 5.4 meters) around   [b]16 That is, about 7 1/2 feet (about 2.3 meters); also in verse 23   [c]18 Two Hebrew manuscripts and Septuagint; most Hebrew manuscripts *made the pillars, and there were two rows*   [d]18 Many Hebrew manuscripts and Syriac; most Hebrew manuscripts *pomegranates*   [e]19 That is, about 6 feet (about 1.8 meters); also in verse 38   [f]21 Jakin probably means *he establishes.*   [g]21 Boaz probably means *in him is strength.*   [h]23 That is, about 15 feet (about 4.5 meters)   [i]23 That is, about 45 feet (about 13.5 meters)   [j]26 That is, about 3 inches (about 8 centimeters)   [k]26 That is, probably about 11,500 gallons (about 44 kiloliters); the Septuagint does not have this sentence.   [l]27 That is, about 6 feet (about 1.8 meters) long and wide and about 4 1/2 feet (about 1.3 meters) high   [m]31 That is, about 1 1/2 feet (about 0.5 meter)   [n]31 That is, about 2 1/4 feet (about 0.7 meter); also in verse 32   [o]35 That is, about 3/4 foot (about 0.2 meter)

all around. ³⁷This is the way he made the ten stands. They were all cast in the same molds and were identical in size and shape.

³⁸He then made ten bronze basins,ⁿ each holding forty baths ͣ and measuring four cubits across, one basin to go on each of the ten stands. ³⁹He placed five of the stands on the south side of the temple and five on the north. He placed the Sea on the south side, at the southeast corner of the temple. ⁴⁰He also made the basins and shovels and sprinkling bowls.

So Huram finished all the work he had undertaken for King Solomon in the temple of the LORD:

⁴¹the two pillars;
the two bowl-shaped capitals on top of the pillars;
the two sets of network decorating the two bowl-shaped capitals on top of the pillars;
⁴²the four hundred pomegranates for the two sets of network (two rows of pomegranates for each network, decorating the bowl-shaped capitals ᵒ on top of the pillars);
⁴³the ten stands with their ten basins;
⁴⁴the Sea and the twelve bulls under it;
⁴⁵the pots, shovels and sprinkling bowls. ᵖ

All these objects that Huram made for King Solomon for the temple of the LORD were of burnished bronze. ⁴⁶The king had them cast in clay molds in the plain ꟼ of the Jordan between Succoth ͬ and Zarethan. ˢ ⁴⁷Solomon left all these things unweighed,ᵗ because there were so many; the weight of the bronze was not determined.

⁴⁸Solomon also made all the furnishings that were in the LORD's temple:

the golden altar;
the golden table ᵘ on which was the bread of the Presence;ᵛ
⁴⁹the lampstands ʷ of pure gold (five on the right and five on the left, in front of the inner sanctuary);
the gold floral work and lamps and tongs;
⁵⁰the pure gold basins, wick trimmers, sprinkling bowls, dishes and censers;ˣ
and the gold sockets for the doors of the innermost room, the Most Holy Place, and also for the doors of the main hall of the temple.

⁵¹When all the work King Solomon had done for the temple of the LORD was finished, he brought in the things his father David had dedicated ʸ—the silver and gold and the furnishings—and he placed them in the treasuries of the LORD's temple.

The Ark Brought to the Temple

8:1–21pp — 2Ch 5:2–6:11

8 Then King Solomon summoned into his presence at Jerusalem the elders of Israel, all the heads of the tribes and the chiefs ᶻ of the Israelite families, to bring up the ark ͣ of the LORD's covenant from Zion, the City of David. ᵇ ²All the men of Israel came together to King

ͣ38 That is, about 230 gallons (about 880 liters)

7:38
n Ex 30:18;
2Ch 4:6
7:42
over 20
7:45
p Ex 27:3
7:46
q 2Ch 4:17
r Ge 33:17;
Jos 13:27
s Jos 3:16
7:47
t 1Ch 22:3
7:48
u Ex 37:10
v Ex 25:30
7:49
w Ex 25:31-38
7:50
x 2Ki 25:13
7:51
y 2Sa 8:11
8:1
z Nu 7:2
a 2Sa 6:17
b 2Sa 5:7

Solomon at the time of the festival[c] in the month of Ethanim, the seventh month.[d]

[3]When all the elders of Israel had arrived, the priests[e] took up the ark, [4]and they brought up the ark of the LORD and the Tent of Meeting[f] and all the sacred furnishings in it. The priests and Levites carried them up, [5]and King Solomon and the entire assembly of Israel that had gathered about him were before the ark, sacrificing[g] so many sheep and cattle that they could not be recorded or counted.

[6]The priests then brought the ark of the LORD's covenant[h] to its place in the inner sanctuary of the temple, the Most Holy Place, and put it beneath the wings of the cherubim.[i] [7]The cherubim spread their wings over the place of the ark and overshadowed the ark and its carrying poles. [8]These poles were so long that their ends could be seen from the Holy Place in front of the inner sanctuary, but not from outside the Holy Place; and they are still there today.[j] [9]There was nothing in the ark except the two stone tablets[k] that Moses had placed in it at Horeb, where the LORD made a covenant with the Israelites after they came out of Egypt.

[10]When the priests withdrew from the Holy Place, the cloud[l] filled the temple of the LORD. [11]And the priests could not perform their service because of the cloud, for the glory of the LORD filled his temple.

[12]Then Solomon said, "The LORD has said that he would dwell in a dark cloud;[m] [13]I have indeed built a magnificent temple for you, a place for you to dwell[n] forever."

[14]While the whole assembly of Israel was standing there, the king turned around and blessed[o] them. [15]Then he said:

"Praise be to the LORD,[p] the God of Israel, who with his own hand has fulfilled what he promised with his own mouth to my father David. For he said, [16]'Since the day I brought my people Israel out of Egypt, I have not chosen a city in any tribe of Israel to have a temple built for my Name[q] to be there, but I have chosen[r] David[s] to rule my people Israel.'

[17]"My father David had it in his heart to build a temple[t] for the Name of the LORD, the God of Israel. [18]But the LORD said to my father David, 'Because it was in your heart to build a temple for my Name, you did well to have this in your heart. [19]Nevertheless, you[u] are not the one to build the temple, but your son, who is your own flesh and blood—he is the one who will build the temple for my Name.'[v]

[20]"The LORD has kept the promise he made: I have succeeded David my father and now I sit on the throne of Israel, just as the LORD promised, and I have built[w] the temple for the Name of the LORD, the God of Israel. [21]I have provided a place there for the ark, in which is the covenant of the LORD that he made with our fathers when he brought them out of Egypt."

Solomon's Prayer of Dedication

8:22–53pp — 2Ch 6:12-40

[22]Then King Solomon stood before the altar of the LORD in front of the whole assembly of Israel, spread out his hands[x] toward heaven [23]and said:

8:2
c2Ch 7:8
dLev 23:34
8:3
eNu 7:9;
Jos 3:3
8:4
f1Ki 3:4;
2Ch 1:3
8:5
g2Sa 6:13
8:6
h2Sa 6:17
i1Ki 6:19,27
8:8
jEx 25:13-15
8:9
kEx 24:7-8;
25:21; 40:20;
Dt 10:2-5;
Heb 9:4
8:10
lEx 40:34-35;
2Ch 7:1-2
8:12
mPs 18:11; 97:2
8:13
nEx 15:17;
2Sa 7:13;
Ps 132:13
8:14
o2Sa 6:18
8:15
p2Sa 7:12-13;
1Ch 29:10,20;
Ne 9:5; Lk 1:68
8:16
qDt 12:5
r1Sa 16:1
s2Sa 7:4-6,8
8:17
t2Sa 7:2;
1Ch 17:1
8:19
u2Sa 7:5
v2Sa 7:13;
1Ki 5:3,5
8:20
w1Ch 28:6
8:22
xEx 9:29;
Ezr 9:5

"O Lord, God of Israel, there is no God like[y] you in heaven above or on earth below—you who keep your covenant of love[z] with your servants who continue wholeheartedly in your way. [24]You have kept your promise to your servant David my father; with your mouth you have promised and with your hand you have fulfilled it—as it is today.

[25]"Now Lord, God of Israel, keep for your servant David my father the promises[a] you made to him when you said, 'You shall never fail to have a man to sit before me on the throne of Israel, if only your sons are careful in all they do to walk before me as you have done.' [26]And now, O God of Israel, let your word that you promised[b] your servant David my father come true.

[27]"But will God really dwell[c] on earth? The heavens, even the highest heaven, cannot contain[d] you. How much less this temple I have built! [28]Yet give attention to your servant's prayer and his plea for mercy, O Lord my God. Hear the cry and the prayer that your servant is praying in your presence this day. [29]May your eyes be open[e] toward[f] this temple night and day, this place of which you said, 'My Name[g] shall be there,' so that you will hear the prayer your servant prays toward this place. [30]Hear the supplication of your servant and of your people Israel when they pray toward this place. Hear from heaven, your dwelling place, and when you hear, forgive.[h]

[31]"When a man wrongs his neighbor and is required to take an oath and he comes and swears the oath[i] before your altar in this temple, [32]then hear from heaven and act. Judge between your servants, condemning the guilty and bringing down on his own head what he has done. Declare the innocent not guilty, and so establish his innocence.[j]

[33]"When your people Israel have been defeated[k] by an enemy because they have sinned[l] against you, and when they turn back to you and confess your name, praying and making supplication to you in this temple, [34]then hear from heaven and forgive the sin of your people Israel and bring them back to the land you gave to their fathers.

[35]"When the heavens are shut up and there is no rain[m] because your people have sinned against you, and when they pray toward this place and confess your name and turn from their sin because you have afflicted them, [36]then hear from heaven and forgive the sin of your servants, your people Israel. Teach[n] them the right way[o] to live, and send rain on the land you gave your people for an inheritance.

[37]"When famine[p] or plague comes to the land, or blight[q] or mildew, locusts or grasshoppers, or when an enemy besieges them in any of their cities, whatever disaster or disease may come, [38]and when a prayer or plea is made by any of your people Israel—each one aware of the afflictions of his own heart, and spreading out his hands toward this temple— [39]then hear from heaven, your dwelling place. Forgive and act; deal with each man according to all he does, since you know[r] his heart (for you alone know the hearts of all men), [40]so that they will fear[s] you all the time they live in the land you gave our fathers.

8:23
y 1Sa 2:2;
2Sa 7:22
z Dt 7:9,12;
Ne 1:5; 9:32;
Da 9:4
8:25
a 1Ki 2:4
8:26
b 2Sa 7:25
8:27
c Ac 7:48
d 2Ch 2:6;
Ps 139:7-16;
Isa 66:1;
Jer 23:24
8:29
e 2Ch 7:15;
Ne 1:6 f Da 6:10
g Dt 12:11
8:30
h Ps 85:2
8:31
i Ex 22:11
8:32
j Dt 25:1
8:33
k Lev 26:17;
Dt 28:25
l Lev 26:39
8:35
m Lev 26:19;
Dt 28:24
8:36
n 1Sa 12:23;
Ps 25:4; 94:12
o Ps 5:8; 27:11;
Jer 6:16
8:37
p Lev 26:26
q Dt 28:22
8:39
r 1Sa 16:7;
1Ch 28:9;
Ps 11:4;
Jer 17:10;
Jn 2:24; Ac 1:24
8:40
s Ps 130:4

41"As for the foreigner who does not belong to your people Israel but has come from a distant land because of your name— 42for men will hear of your great name and your mighty hand[t] and your outstretched arm—when he comes and prays toward this temple, 43then hear from heaven, your dwelling place, and do whatever the foreigner asks of you, so that all the peoples of the earth may know[u] your name and fear[v] you, as do your own people Israel, and may know that this house I have built bears your Name.

44"When your people go to war against their enemies, wherever you send them, and when they pray to the LORD toward the city you have chosen and the temple I have built for your Name, 45then hear from heaven their prayer and their plea, and uphold their cause.

46"When they sin against you—for there is no one who does not sin[w]—and you become angry with them and give them over to the enemy, who takes them captive[x] to his own land, far away or near; 47and if they have a change of heart in the land where they are held captive, and repent and plead[y] with you in the land of their conquerors and say, 'We have sinned, we have done wrong, we have acted wickedly';[z] 48and if they turn back to you with all their heart[a] and soul in the land of their enemies who took them captive, and pray[b] to you toward the land you gave their fathers, toward the city you have chosen and the temple[c] I have built for your Name; 49then from heaven, your dwelling place, hear their prayer and their plea, and uphold their cause. 50And forgive your people, who have sinned against you; forgive all the offenses they have committed against you, and cause their conquerors to show them mercy;[d] 51for they are your people and your inheritance,[e] whom you brought out of Egypt, out of that iron-smelting furnace.[f]

52"May your eyes be open to your servant's plea and to the plea of your people Israel, and may you listen to them whenever they cry out to you. 53For you singled them out from all the nations of the world to be your own inheritance,[g] just as you declared through your servant Moses when you, O Sovereign LORD, brought our fathers out of Egypt."

54When Solomon had finished all these prayers and supplications to the LORD, he rose from before the altar of the LORD, where he had been kneeling with his hands spread out toward heaven. 55He stood and blessed[h] the whole assembly of Israel in a loud voice, saying:

56"Praise be to the LORD, who has given rest[i] to his people Israel just as he promised. Not one word has failed of all the good promises[j] he gave through his servant Moses. 57May the LORD our God be with us as he was with our fathers; may he never leave us nor forsake[k] us. 58May he turn our hearts[l] to him, to walk in all his ways and to keep the commands, decrees and regulations he gave our fathers. 59And may these words of mine, which I have prayed before the LORD, be near to the LORD our God day and night, that he may uphold the cause of his servant and the cause of his people Israel according to each day's need, 60so that all the

8:42
[t] Dt 3:24
8:43
[u] 1Sa 17:46;
2Ki 19:19
[v] Ps 102:15
8:46
[w] Pr 20:9;
Ecc 7:20;
Ro 3:9;
1Jn 1:8-10
[x] Lev 26:33-39;
Dt 28:64
8:47
[y] Lev 26:40;
Ne 1:6
[z] Ps 106:6;
Da 9:5
8:48
[a] Dt 4:29;
Jer 29:12-14
[b] Da 6:10
[c] Jnh 2:4
8:50
[d] 2Ch 30:9;
Ps 106:46
8:51
[e] Dt 4:20; 9:29;
Ne 1:10
[f] Jer 11:4
8:53
[g] Ex 19:5;
Dt 9:26-29
8:55
[h] ver 14;
2Sa 6:18
8:56
[i] Dt 12:10
[j] Jos 21:45;
23:15
8:57
[k] Dt 31:6;
Jos 1:5;
Heb 13:5
8:58
[l] Ps 119:36

peoples[m] of the earth may know that the Lord is God and that there is no other. [n] [61]But your hearts must be fully committed[o] to the Lord our God, to live by his decrees and obey his commands, as at this time."

The Dedication of the Temple

8:62–66pp — 2Ch 7:1–10

[62]Then the king and all Israel with him offered sacrifices before the Lord. [63]Solomon offered a sacrifice of fellowship offerings[a] to the Lord: twenty-two thousand cattle and a hundred and twenty thousand sheep and goats. So the king and all the Israelites dedicated the temple of the Lord.

[64]On that same day the king consecrated the middle part of the courtyard in front of the temple of the Lord, and there he offered burnt offerings, grain offerings and the fat of the fellowship offerings, because the bronze altar[p] before the Lord was too small to hold the burnt offerings, the grain offerings and the fat of the fellowship offerings.

[65]So Solomon observed the festival[q] at that time, and all Israel with him—a vast assembly, people from Lebo[b] Hamath[r] to the Wadi of Egypt. [s] They celebrated it before the Lord our God for seven days and seven days more, fourteen days in all. [66]On the following day he sent the people away. They blessed the king and then went home, joyful and glad in heart for all the good things the Lord had done for his servant David and his people Israel.

The Lord Appears to Solomon

9:1–9pp — 2Ch 7:11–22

9 When Solomon had finished[t] building the temple of the Lord and the royal palace, and had achieved all he had desired to do, [2]the Lord appeared[u] to him a second time, as he had appeared to him at Gibeon. [3]The Lord said to him:

"I have heard[v] the prayer and plea you have made before me; I have consecrated this temple, which you have built, by putting my Name there forever. My eyes[w] and my heart will always be there.

[4]"As for you, if you walk before me in integrity of heart[x] and uprightness, as David[y] your father did, and do all I command and observe my decrees and laws, [5]I will establish[z] your royal throne over Israel forever, as I promised David your father when I said, 'You shall never fail[a] to have a man on the throne of Israel.'

[6]"But if you[c] or your sons turn away[b] from me and do not observe the commands and decrees I have given you[c] and go off to serve other gods and worship them, [7]then I will cut off Israel from the land[c] I have given them and will reject this temple I have consecrated for my Name.[d] Israel will then become a byword[e] and an object of ridicule[f] among all peoples. [8]And though this temple is now imposing, all who pass by will be appalled and will scoff and say, 'Why has the Lord done such a thing to this land

Cross references

8:60
m Jos 4:24;
1Sa 17:46
n Dt 4:35;
1Ki 18:39;
Jer 10:10-12
8:61
o 1Ki 11:4; 15:3,
14; 2Ki 20:3
8:64
p 2Ch 4:1
8:65
q ver 2;
Lev 23:34
r Nu 34:8;
Jos 13:5;
Jdg 3:3;
2Ki 14:25
s Ge 15:18
9:1
t 1Ki 7:1;
2Ch 8:6
9:2
u 1Ki 3:5
9:3
v 2Ki 20:5;
Ps 10:17
w Dt 11:12;
1Ki 8:29
9:4
x Ge 17:1
y 1Ki 15:5
9:5
z 1Ch 22:10
a 2Sa 7:15;
1Ki 2:4
9:6
b 2Sa 7:14
9:7
c 2Ki 17:23;
25:21 d Jer 7:14
e Ps 44:14
f Dt 28:37

---

[a]63 Traditionally *peace offerings*; also in verse 64   [b]65 Or *from the entrance to*   [c]6 The Hebrew is plural.

and to this temple?'ᵍ ⁹People will answer, 'Because they have forsaken the Lᴏʀᴅ their God, who brought their fathers out of Egypt, and have embraced other gods, worshiping and serving them—that is why the Lᴏʀᴅ brought all this disaster on them.' "

Solomon's Other Activities
9:10–28pp — 2Ch 8:1–18

¹⁰At the end of twenty years, during which Solomon built these two buildings—the temple of the Lᴏʀᴅ and the royal palace— ¹¹King Solomon gave twenty towns in Galilee to Hiram king of Tyre, because Hiram had supplied him with all the cedar and pine and goldʰ he wanted. ¹²But when Hiram went from Tyre to see the towns that Solomon had given him, he was not pleased with them. ¹³"What kind of towns are these you have given me, my brother?" he asked. And he called them the Land of Cabul,ᵃⁱ a name they have to this day. ¹⁴Now Hiram had sent to the king 120 talentsᵇ of gold.

¹⁵Here is the account of the forced labor King Solomon conscriptedʲ to build the Lᴏʀᴅ's temple, his own palace, the supporting terraces,ᶜ ᵏ the wall of Jerusalem, and Hazor,ˡ Megiddo and Gezer.ᵐ ¹⁶(Pharaoh king of Egypt had attacked and captured Gezer. He had set it on fire. He killed its Canaanite inhabitants and then gave it as a wedding gift to his daughter, Solomon's wife. ¹⁷And Solomon rebuilt Gezer.) He built up Lower Beth Horon,ⁿ ¹⁸Baalath,ᵒ and Tadmorᵈ in the desert, within his land, ¹⁹as well as all his store citiesᵖ and the towns for his chariots�q and for his horsesᵉ—whatever he desired to build in Jerusalem, in Lebanon and throughout all the territory he ruled.

²⁰All the people left from the Amorites, Hittites, Perizzites, Hivites and Jebusites (these peoples were not Israelites), ²¹that is, their descendantsʳ remaining in the land, whom the Israelites could not exterminateᶠˢ—these Solomon conscripted for his slave labor force,ᵗ as it is to this day. ²²But Solomon did not make slavesᵘ of any of the Israelites; they were his fighting men, his government officials, his officers, his captains, and the commanders of his chariots and charioteers. ²³They were also the chief officialsᵛ in charge of Solomon's projects—550 officials supervising the men who did the work.

²⁴After Pharaoh's daughterʷ had come up from the City of David to the palace Solomon had built for her, he constructed the supporting terraces.ˣ

²⁵Threeʸ times a year Solomon sacrificed burnt offerings and fellowship offeringsᵍ on the altar he had built for the Lᴏʀᴅ, burning incense before the Lᴏʀᴅ along with them, and so fulfilled the temple obligations.

²⁶King Solomon also built shipsᶻ at Ezion Geber,ᵃ which is near Elath in Edom, on the shore of the Red Sea.ʰ ²⁷And Hiram sent his men—sailorsᵇ who knew the sea—to serve in the fleet with Solomon's men. ²⁸They sailed to Ophirᶜ and brought back 420 talentsⁱ of gold, which they delivered to King Solomon.

9:8
ᵍDt 29:24;
Jer 22:8-9
9:11
ʰ2Ch 8:2
9:13
ⁱJos 19:27
9:15
ʲJos 16:10;
1Ki 5:13
kver 24; 2Sa 5:9
lJos 19:36
mJos 17:11
9:17
ⁿJos 16:3;
2Ch 8:5
9:18
ᵒJos 19:44
9:19
pver 1 q1Ki 4:26
9:21
ʳGe 9:25-26
ˢJos 15:63;
17:12; Jdg 1:21,
27,29
ᵗEzr 2:55,58
9:22
ᵘLev 25:39
9:23
ᵛ1Ki 5:16
9:24
ʷ1Ki 3:1; 7:8
ˣ2Sa 5:9;
1Ki 11:27;
2Ch 32:5
9:25
ʸEx 23:14;
2Ch 8:12-13,16
9:26
ᶻ1Ki 22:48
ᵃNu 33:35;
Dt 2:8
9:27
ᵇ1Ki 10:11;
Eze 27:8
9:28
ᶜ1Ch 29:4

ᵃ13 *Cabul* sounds like the Hebrew for *good-for-nothing.*   ᵇ14 That is, about 4 1/2 tons (about 4 metric tons)   ᶜ15 Or *the Millo;* also in verse 24   ᵈ18 The Hebrew may also be read *Tamar.*   ᵉ19 Or *charioteers*   ᶠ21 The Hebrew term refers to the irrevocable giving over of things or persons to the Lᴏʀᴅ, often by totally destroying them.   ᵍ25 Traditionally *peace offerings*   ʰ26 Hebrew *Yam Suph;* that is, Sea of Reeds   ⁱ28 That is, about 16 tons (about 14.5 metric tons)

The Queen of Sheba Visits Solomon

10:1–13pp — 2Ch 9:1–12

10 When the queen of Sheba[d] heard about the fame of Solomon and his relation to the name of the LORD, she came to test him with hard questions.[e] 2Arriving at Jerusalem with a very great caravan— with camels carrying spices, large quantities of gold, and precious stones—she came to Solomon and talked with him about all that she had on her mind. 3Solomon answered all her questions; nothing was too hard for the king to explain to her. 4When the queen of Sheba saw all the wisdom of Solomon and the palace he had built, 5the food on his table,[f] the seating of his officials, the attending servants in their robes, his cupbearers, and the burnt offerings he made at[a] the temple of the LORD, she was overwhelmed.

6She said to the king, "The report I heard in my own country about your achievements and your wisdom is true. 7But I did not believe these things until I came and saw with my own eyes. Indeed, not even half was told me; in wisdom and wealth[g] you have far exceeded the report I heard. 8How happy your men must be! How happy your officials, who continually stand before you and hear[h] your wisdom! 9Praise[i] be to the LORD your God, who has delighted in you and placed you on the throne of Israel. Because of the LORD's eternal love for Israel, he has made you king, to maintain justice[j] and righteousness."

10And she gave the king 120 talents[b] of gold,[k] large quantities of spices, and precious stones. Never again were so many spices brought in as those the queen of Sheba gave to King Solomon.

11(Hiram's ships brought gold from Ophir;[l] and from there they brought great cargoes of almugwood[c] and precious stones. 12The king used the almugwood to make supports for the temple of the LORD and for the royal palace, and to make harps and lyres for the musicians. So much almugwood has never been imported or seen since that day.)

13King Solomon gave the queen of Sheba all she desired and asked for, besides what he had given her out of his royal bounty. Then she left and returned with her retinue to her own country.

Solomon's Splendor

10:14–29pp — 2Ch 1:14–17; 9:13–28

14The weight of the gold[m] that Solomon received yearly was 666 talents,[d] 15not including the revenues from merchants and traders and from all the Arabian kings and the governors of the land.

16King Solomon made two hundred large shields[n] of hammered gold; six hundred bekas[e] of gold went into each shield. 17He also made three hundred small shields of hammered gold, with three minas[f] of gold in each shield. The king put them in the Palace of the Forest of Lebanon.[o]

18Then the king made a great throne inlaid with ivory and overlaid with fine gold. 19The throne had six steps, and its back had a rounded top. On both sides of the seat were armrests, with a lion standing

10:1
dGe 10:7,28;
Mt 12:42;
Lk 11:31
eJdg 14:12
10:5
f1Ch 26:16
10:7
g1Ch 29:25
10:8
hPr 8:34
10:9
i1Ki 5:7
j2Sa 8:15;
Ps 33:5; 72:2
10:10
kver 2
10:11
lGe 10:29;
1Ki 9:27-28
10:14
m1Ki 9:28
10:16
n1Ki 14:26-28
10:17
o1Ki 7:2

a5 Or *the ascent by which he went up to*   b10 That is, about 4 1/2 tons (about 4 metric tons)
c11 Probably a variant of *algumwood;* also in verse 12   d14 That is, about 25 tons (about 23 metric tons)   e16 That is, about 7 1/2 pounds (about 3.5 kilograms)   f17 That is, about 3 3/4 pounds (about 1.7 kilograms)

beside each of them. 20Twelve lions stood on the six steps, one at either end of each step. Nothing like it had ever been made for any other kingdom. 21All King Solomon's goblets were gold, and all the household articles in the Palace of the Forest of Lebanon were pure gold. Nothing was made of silver, because silver was considered of little value in Solomon's days. 22The king had a fleet of trading ships[a][p] at sea along with the ships of Hiram. Once every three years it returned, carrying gold, silver and ivory, and apes and baboons.

23King Solomon was greater in riches[q] and wisdom[r] than all the other kings of the earth. 24The whole world sought audience with Solomon to hear the wisdom[s] God had put in his heart. 25Year after year, everyone who came brought a gift—articles of silver and gold, robes, weapons and spices, and horses and mules.

26Solomon accumulated chariots and horses;[t] he had fourteen hundred chariots and twelve thousand horses,[b] which he kept in the chariot cities and also with him in Jerusalem. 27The king made silver as common[u] in Jerusalem as stones, and cedar as plentiful as sycamore-fig trees in the foothills. 28Solomon's horses were imported from Egypt[c] and from Kue[d]—the royal merchants purchased them from Kue. 29They imported a chariot from Egypt for six hundred shekels[e] of silver, and a horse for a hundred and fifty.[f] They also exported them to all the kings of the Hittites[v] and of the Arameans.

Solomon's Wives

11 King Solomon, however, loved many foreign women[w] besides Pharaoh's daughter—Moabites, Ammonites, Edomites, Sidonians and Hittites. 2They were from nations about which the LORD had told the Israelites, "You must not intermarry[x] with them, because they will surely turn your hearts after their gods." Nevertheless, Solomon held fast to them in love. 3He had seven hundred wives of royal birth and three hundred concubines, and his wives led him astray. 4As Solomon grew old, his wives turned his heart after other gods, and his heart was not fully devoted[y] to the LORD his God, as the heart of David his father had been. 5He followed Ashtoreth[z] the goddess of the Sidonians, and Molech[g][a] the detestable god of the Ammonites. 6So Solomon did evil in the eyes of the LORD; he did not follow the LORD completely, as David his father had done.

7On a hill east[b] of Jerusalem, Solomon built a high place for Chemosh[c] the detestable god of Moab, and for Molech[d] the detestable god of the Ammonites. 8He did the same for all his foreign wives, who burned incense and offered sacrifices to their gods.

9The LORD became angry with Solomon because his heart had turned away from the LORD, the God of Israel, who had appeared[e] to him twice. 10Although he had forbidden Solomon to follow other gods,[f] Solomon did not keep the LORD's command.[g] 11So the LORD said to Solomon, "Since this is your attitude and you have not kept my covenant and my decrees, which I commanded you, I will most certainly tear[h] the kingdom away from you and give it to one of your subordi-

---

### Cross references (margin)

10:22
p1Ki 9:26
10:23
q1Ki 3:13
r1Ki 4:30
10:24
s1Ki 3:9,12,28
10:26
t Dt 17:16;
1Ki 4:26; 9:19;
2Ch 1:14; 9:25
10:27
u Dt 17:17
10:29
v2Ki 7:6-7
11:1
w Dt 17:17;
Ne 13:26
11:2
xEx 34:16;
Dt 7:3-4
11:4
y1Ki 8:61; 9:4
11:5
zver 33;
Jdg 2:13;
2Ki 23:13 a ver 7
11:7
b2Ki 23:13
cNu 21:29;
Jdg 11:24
dLev 20:2-5;
Ac 7:43
11:9
ever 2-3;
1Ki 3:5; 9:2
11:10
f1Ki 9:6
g1Ki 6:12
11:11
hver 31;
1Ki 12:15-16;
2Ki 17:21

---

a22 Hebrew *of ships of Tarshish*   b26 Or *charioteers*   c28 Or possibly *Muzur*, a region in Cilicia; also in verse 29   d28 Probably *Cilicia*   e29 That is, about 15 pounds (about 7 kilograms)   f29 That is, about 3 3/4 pounds (about 1.7 kilograms)   g5 Hebrew *Milcom*; also in verse 33 nates. [12]Nevertheless, for the sake of David your father, I will not do it during your lifetime. I will tear it out of the hand of your son. [13]Yet I will not tear the whole kingdom from him, but will give him one tribe[i] for the sake[j] of David my servant and for the sake of Jerusalem, which I have chosen."[k]

Solomon's Adversaries

[14]Then the LORD raised up against Solomon an adversary, Hadad the Edomite, from the royal line of Edom. [15]Earlier when David was fighting with Edom, Joab the commander of the army, who had gone up to bury the dead, had struck down all the men in Edom.[l] [16]Joab and all the Israelites stayed there for six months, until they had destroyed all the men in Edom. [17]But Hadad, still only a boy, fled to Egypt with some Edomite officials who had served his father. [18]They set out from Midian and went to Paran.[m] Then taking men from Paran with them, they went to Egypt, to Pharaoh king of Egypt, who gave Hadad a house and land and provided him with food.

[19]Pharaoh was so pleased with Hadad that he gave him a sister of his own wife, Queen Tahpenes, in marriage. [20]The sister of Tahpenes bore him a son named Genubath, whom Tahpenes brought up in the royal palace. There Genubath lived with Pharaoh's own children.

[21]While he was in Egypt, Hadad heard that David rested with his fathers and that Joab the commander of the army was also dead. Then Hadad said to Pharaoh, "Let me go, that I may return to my own country."

[22]"What have you lacked here that you want to go back to your own country?" Pharaoh asked.

"Nothing," Hadad replied, "but do let me go!"

[23]And God raised up against Solomon another adversary,[n] Rezon son of Eliada, who had fled from his master, Hadadezer[o] king of Zobah. [24]He gathered men around him and became the leader of a band of rebels when David destroyed the forces[a] of Zobah; the rebels went to Damascus,[p] where they settled and took control. [25]Rezon was Israel's adversary as long as Solomon lived, adding to the trouble caused by Hadad. So Rezon ruled in Aram[q] and was hostile toward Israel.

Jeroboam Rebels Against Solomon

[26]Also, Jeroboam son of Nebat rebelled[r] against the king. He was one of Solomon's officials, an Ephraimite from Zeredah, and his mother was a widow named Zeruah.

[27]Here is the account of how he rebelled against the king: Solomon had built the supporting terraces[bs] and had filled in the gap in the wall of the city of David his father. [28]Now Jeroboam was a man of standing,[t] and when Solomon saw how well[u] the young man did his work, he put him in charge of the whole labor force of the house of Joseph.

[29]About that time Jeroboam was going out of Jerusalem, and Ahijah[v] the prophet of Shiloh met him on the way, wearing a new cloak. The two of them were alone out in the country, [30]and Ahijah took hold of the new cloak he was wearing and tore[w] it into twelve pieces. [31]Then he said to Jeroboam, "Take ten pieces for yourself, for this is what the

11:13
i 1Ki 12:20
j 2Sa 7:15
k Dt 12:11
11:15
l Dt 20:13;
2Sa 8:14;
1Ch 18:12
11:18
m Nu 10:12
11:23
n ver 14
o 2Sa 8:3
11:24
p 2Sa 8:5;
10:8,18
11:25
q 2Sa 10:19
11:26
r 2Sa 20:21;
1Ki 12:2;
2Ch 13:6
11:27
s 1Ki 9:24
11:28
t Ru 2:1
u Pr 22:29
11:29
v 1Ki 12:15;
14:2; 2Ch 9:29
11:30
w 1Sa 15:27

---

[a]24 Hebrew *destroyed them*   [b]27 Or *the Millo*

LORD, the God of Israel, says: 'See, I am going to tear^x the kingdom out of Solomon's hand and give you ten tribes. ³²But for the sake of my servant David and the city of Jerusalem, which I have chosen out of all the tribes of Israel, he will have one tribe. ³³I will do this because they have^a forsaken me and worshiped^y Ashtoreth the goddess of the Sidonians, Chemosh the god of the Moabites, and Molech the god of the Ammonites, and have not walked in my ways, nor done what is right in my eyes, nor kept my statutes^z and laws as David, Solomon's father, did.

³⁴" 'But I will not take the whole kingdom out of Solomon's hand; I have made him ruler all the days of his life for the sake of David my servant, whom I chose and who observed my commands and statutes. ³⁵I will take the kingdom from his son's hands and give you ten tribes. ³⁶I will give one tribe^a to his son so that David my servant may always have a lamp^b before me in Jerusalem, the city where I chose to put my Name. ³⁷However, as for you, I will take you, and you will rule over all that your heart desires;^c you will be king over Israel. ³⁸If you do whatever I command you and walk in my ways and do what is right in my eyes by keeping my statutes^d and commands, as David my servant did, I will be with you. I will build you a dynasty^e as enduring as the one I built for David and will give Israel to you. ³⁹I will humble David's descendants because of this, but not forever.' "

⁴⁰Solomon tried to kill Jeroboam, but Jeroboam fled to Egypt, to Shishak^f the king, and stayed there until Solomon's death.

Solomon's Death

11:41–43pp — 2Ch 9:29–31

⁴¹As for the other events of Solomon's reign—all he did and the wisdom he displayed—are they not written in the book of the annals of Solomon? ⁴²Solomon reigned in Jerusalem over all Israel forty years. ⁴³Then he rested with his fathers and was buried in the city of David his father. And Rehoboam^g his son succeeded him as king.

Israel Rebels Against Rehoboam

12:1–24pp — 2Ch 10:1–11:4

12 Rehoboam went to Shechem, for all the Israelites had gone there to make him king. ²When Jeroboam son of Nebat heard this (he was still in Egypt, where he had fled^h from King Solomon), he returned from^b Egypt. ³So they sent for Jeroboam, and he and the whole assembly of Israel went to Rehoboam and said to him: ⁴"Your father put a heavy yokeⁱ on us, but now lighten the harsh labor and the heavy yoke he put on us, and we will serve you."

⁵Rehoboam answered, "Go away for three days and then come back to me." So the people went away.

⁶Then King Rehoboam consulted the elders^j who had served his father Solomon during his lifetime. "How would you advise me to answer these people?" he asked.

⁷They replied, "If today you will be a servant to these people and serve them and give them a favorable answer,^k they will always be your servants."

### Cross references (margin)

11:31
xver 11

11:33
yver 5-7
z1Ki 3:3

11:36
aver 13;
1Ki 12:17
b1Ki 15:4;
2Ki 8:19

11:37
c2Sa 3:21

11:38
dDt 17:19
eJos 1:5;
2Sa 7:11,27

11:40
f2Ch 12:2

11:43
g1Ki 14:21;
Mt 1:7

12:2
h1Ki 11:40

12:4
i1Sa 8:11-18;
1Ki 4:20-28

12:6
j1Ki 4:2

12:7
kPr 15:1

---

^a33 Hebrew; Septuagint, Vulgate and Syriac *because he has*   ^b2 Or *he remained in*

8But Rehoboam rejected the advice the elders gave him and consulted the young men who had grown up with him and were serving him. 9He asked them, "What is your advice? How should we answer these people who say to me, 'Lighten the yoke your father put on us'?"

10The young men who had grown up with him replied, "Tell these people who have said to you, 'Your father put a heavy yoke on us, but make our yoke lighter'—tell them, 'My little finger is thicker than my father's waist. 11My father laid on you a heavy yoke; I will make it even heavier. My father scourged you with whips; I will scourge you with scorpions.' "

12Three days later Jeroboam and all the people returned to Rehoboam, as the king had said, "Come back to me in three days." 13The king answered the people harshly. Rejecting the advice given him by the elders, 14he followed the advice of the young men and said, "My father made your yoke heavy; I will make it even heavier. My father scourged[l] you with whips; I will scourge you with scorpions." 15So the king did not listen to the people, for this turn of events was from the Lord,[m] to fulfill the word the Lord had spoken to Jeroboam son of Nebat through Ahijah[n] the Shilonite.

16When all Israel saw that the king refused to listen to them, they answered the king:

> "What share do we have in David,
>   what part in Jesse's son?
> To your tents, O Israel![o]
>   Look after your own house, O David!"

So the Israelites went home. 17But as for the Israelites who were living in the towns of Judah,[p] Rehoboam still ruled over them.

18King Rehoboam sent out Adoniram,[a][q] who was in charge of forced labor, but all Israel stoned him to death. King Rehoboam, however, managed to get into his chariot and escape to Jerusalem. 19So Israel has been in rebellion against the house of David[r] to this day.

20When all the Israelites heard that Jeroboam had returned, they sent and called him to the assembly and made him king over all Israel. Only the tribe of Judah remained loyal to the house of David.[s]

21When Rehoboam arrived in Jerusalem, he mustered the whole house of Judah and the tribe of Benjamin—a hundred and eighty thousand fighting men—to make war[t] against the house of Israel and to regain the kingdom for Rehoboam son of Solomon.

22But this word of God came to Shemaiah[u] the man of God: 23"Say to Rehoboam son of Solomon king of Judah, to the whole house of Judah and Benjamin, and to the rest of the people, 24'This is what the Lord says: Do not go up to fight against your brothers, the Israelites. Go home, every one of you, for this is my doing.' " So they obeyed the word of the Lord and went home again, as the Lord had ordered.

Golden Calves at Bethel and Dan

25Then Jeroboam fortified Shechem[v] in the hill country of Ephraim and lived there. From there he went out and built up Peniel.[b][w]

---

a18 Some Septuagint manuscripts and Syriac (see also 1 Kings 4:6 and 5:14); Hebrew *Adoram*
b25 Hebrew *Penuel*, a variant of *Peniel*

12:14
lEx 1:14; 5:5-9,
16-18
12:15
mver 24;
Dt 2:30;
Jdg 14:4;
2Ch 22:7; 25:20
nlKi 11:29
12:16
o2Sa 20:1
12:17
p1Ki 11:13,36
12:18
q2Sa 20:24;
1Ki 4:6; 5:14
12:19
r2Ki 17:21
12:20
s1Ki 11:13,32
12:21
t2Ch 11:1
12:22
u2Ch 12:5-7
12:25
vJdg 9:45
wJdg 8:8,17

²⁶Jeroboam thought to himself, "The kingdom will now likely revert to the house of David. ²⁷If these people go up to offer sacrifices at the temple of the LORD in Jerusalem,ˣ they will again give their allegiance to their lord, Rehoboam king of Judah. They will kill me and return to King Rehoboam."

²⁸After seeking advice, the king made two golden calves.ʸ He said to the people, "It is too much for you to go up to Jerusalem. Here are your gods, O Israel, who brought you up out of Egypt."ᶻ ²⁹One he set up in Bethel,ᵃ and the other in Dan.ᵇ ³⁰And this thing became a sin;ᶜ the people went even as far as Dan to worship the one there.

³¹Jeroboam built shrinesᵈ on high places and appointed priestsᵉ from all sorts of people, even though they were not Levites. ³²He instituted a festival on the fifteenth day of the eighthᶠ month, like the festival held in Judah, and offered sacrifices on the altar. This he did in Bethel, sacrificing to the calves he had made. And at Bethel he also installed priests at the high places he had made. ³³On the fifteenth day of the eighth month, a month of his own choosing, he offered sacrifices on the altar he had built at Bethel.ᵍ So he instituted the festival for the Israelites and went up to the altar to make offerings.

The Man of God From Judah

13 By the word of the LORD a man of Godʰ came from Judah to Bethel,ⁱ as Jeroboam was standing by the altar to make an offering. ²He cried out against the altar by the word of the LORD: "O altar, altar! This is what the LORD says: 'A son named Josiahʲ will be born to the house of David. On you he will sacrifice the priests of the high places who now make offerings here, and human bones will be burned on you.' " ³That same day the man of God gave a sign:ᵏ "This is the sign the LORD has declared: The altar will be split apart and the ashes on it will be poured out."

⁴When King Jeroboam heard what the man of God cried out against the altar at Bethel, he stretched out his hand from the altar and said, "Seize him!" But the hand he stretched out toward the man shriveled up, so that he could not pull it back. ⁵Also, the altar was split apart and its ashes poured out according to the sign given by the man of God by the word of the LORD.

⁶Then the king said to the man of God, "Intercedeˡ with the LORD your God and pray for me that my hand may be restored." So the man of God interceded with the LORD, and the king's hand was restored and became as it was before.

⁷The king said to the man of God, "Come home with me and have something to eat, and I will give you a gift."ᵐ

⁸But the man of God answered the king, "Even if you were to give me half your possessions,ⁿ I would not go with you, nor would I eat breadᵒ or drink water here. ⁹For I was commanded by the word of the LORD: 'You must not eat bread or drink water or return by the way you came.' " ¹⁰So he took another road and did not return by the way he had come to Bethel.

¹¹Now there was a certain old prophet living in Bethel, whose sons came and told him all that the man of God had done there that day. They also told their father what he had said to the king. ¹²Their father asked them, "Which way did he go?" And his sons showed him which

12:27
ˣDt 12:5-6
12:28
ʸEx 32:4;
2Ki 10:29; 17:16
ᶻEx 32:8
12:29
ᵃGe 28:19
ᵇJdg 18:27-31
12:30
ᶜ1Ki 13:34;
2Ki 17:21
12:31
ᵈ1Ki 13:32
ᵉNu 3:10;
1Ki 13:33;
2Ki 17:32;
2Ch 11:14-15;
13:9
12:32
ᶠLev 23:33-34;
Nu 29:12
12:33
ᵍNu 15:39;
1Ki 13:1;
Am 7:13
13:1
ʰ2Ki 23:17
ⁱ1Ki 12:32-33
13:2
ʲ2Ki 23:15-16,20
13:3
ᵏJdg 6:17;
Isa 7:14;
Jn 2:11;
1Co 1:22
13:6
ˡEx 8:8; 9:28;
10:17;
Lk 6:27-28;
Ac 8:24;
Jas 5:16
13:7
ᵐ1Sa 9:7;
2Ki 5:15
13:8
ⁿNu 22:18;
24:13 over 16

road the man of God from Judah had taken. ¹³So he said to his sons, "Saddle the donkey for me." And when they had saddled the donkey for him, he mounted it ¹⁴and rode after the man of God. He found him sitting under an oak tree and asked, "Are you the man of God who came from Judah?"

"I am," he replied.

¹⁵So the prophet said to him, "Come home with me and eat."

¹⁶The man of God said, "I cannot turn back and go with you, nor can I eat bread[p] or drink water with you in this place. ¹⁷I have been told by the word of the LORD: 'You must not eat bread or drink water there or return by the way you came.' "

¹⁸The old prophet answered, "I too am a prophet, as you are. And an angel said to me by the word of the LORD: 'Bring him back with you to your house so that he may eat bread and drink water.' " (But he was lying[q] to him.) ¹⁹So the man of God returned with him and ate and drank in his house.

²⁰While they were sitting at the table, the word of the LORD came to the old prophet who had brought him back. ²¹He cried out to the man of God who had come from Judah, "This is what the LORD says: 'You have defied[r] the word of the LORD and have not kept the command the LORD your God gave you. ²²You came back and ate bread and drank water in the place where he told you not to eat or drink. Therefore your body will not be buried in the tomb of your fathers.' "

²³When the man of God had finished eating and drinking, the prophet who had brought him back saddled his donkey for him. ²⁴As he went on his way, a lion[s] met him on the road and killed him, and his body was thrown down on the road, with both the donkey and the lion standing beside it. ²⁵Some people who passed by saw the body thrown down there, with the lion standing beside the body, and they went and reported it in the city where the old prophet lived.

²⁶When the prophet who had brought him back from his journey heard of it, he said, "It is the man of God who defied the word of the LORD. The LORD has given him over to the lion, which has mauled him and killed him, as the word of the LORD had warned him."

²⁷The prophet said to his sons, "Saddle the donkey for me," and they did so. ²⁸Then he went out and found the body thrown down on the road, with the donkey and the lion standing beside it. The lion had neither eaten the body nor mauled the donkey. ²⁹So the prophet picked up the body of the man of God, laid it on the donkey, and brought it back to his own city to mourn for him and bury him. ³⁰Then he laid the body in his own tomb, and they mourned over him and said, "Oh, my brother!"[t]

³¹After burying him, he said to his sons, "When I die, bury me in the grave where the man of God is buried; lay my bones[u] beside his bones. ³²For the message he declared by the word of the LORD against the altar in Bethel and against all the shrines on the high places[v] in the towns of Samaria[w] will certainly come true."[x]

³³Even after this, Jeroboam did not change his evil ways, but once more appointed priests for the high places from all sorts[y] of people. Anyone who wanted to become a priest he consecrated for the high places. ³⁴This was the sin[z] of the house of Jeroboam that led to its downfall and to its destruction[a] from the face of the earth.

13:16
p ver 8
13:18
q Dt 13:3
13:21
r ver 26
13:24
s 1Ki 20:36
13:30
t Jer 22:18
13:31
u 2Ki 23:18
13:32
v ver 2;
Lev 26:30
w 1Ki 16:24,28
x 2Ki 23:16
13:33
y 1Ki 12:31;
2Ch 11:15; 13:9
13:34
z 1Ki 12:30
a 1Ki 14:10

Ahijah's Prophecy Against Jeroboam

14 At that time Abijah son of Jeroboam became ill, [2]and Jeroboam said to his wife, "Go, disguise yourself, so you won't be recognized as the wife of Jeroboam. Then go to Shiloh. Ahijah[b] the prophet is there—the one who told me I would be king over this people. [3]Take ten loaves of bread[c] with you, some cakes and a jar of honey, and go to him. He will tell you what will happen to the boy." [4]So Jeroboam's wife did what he said and went to Ahijah's house in Shiloh.

Now Ahijah could not see; his sight was gone because of his age. [5]But the LORD had told Ahijah, "Jeroboam's wife is coming to ask you about her son, for he is ill, and you are to give her such and such an answer. When she arrives, she will pretend to be someone else."

[6]So when Ahijah heard the sound of her footsteps at the door, he said, "Come in, wife of Jeroboam. Why this pretense? I have been sent to you with bad news. [7]Go, tell Jeroboam that this is what the LORD, the God of Israel, says: 'I raised you up from among the people and made you a leader[d] over my people Israel. [8]I tore[e] the kingdom away from the house of David and gave it to you, but you have not been like my servant David, who kept my commands and followed me with all his heart, doing only what was right[f] in my eyes. [9]You have done more evil than all who lived before you. You have made for yourself other gods, idols[g] made of metal; you have provoked me to anger and thrust me behind your back.[h]

[10]" 'Because of this, I am going to bring disaster on the house of Jeroboam. I will cut off from Jeroboam every last male in Israel—slave or free.[i] I will burn up the house of Jeroboam as one burns dung, until it is all gone.[j] [11]Dogs[k] will eat those belonging to Jeroboam who die in the city, and the birds of the air will feed on those who die in the country. The LORD has spoken!'

[12]"As for you, go back home. When you set foot in your city, the boy will die. [13]All Israel will mourn for him and bury him. He is the only one belonging to Jeroboam who will be buried, because he is the only one in the house of Jeroboam in whom the LORD, the God of Israel, has found anything good.[l]

[14]"The LORD will raise up for himself a king over Israel who will cut off the family of Jeroboam. This is the day! What? Yes, even now.[a] [15]And the LORD will strike Israel, so that it will be like a reed swaying in the water. He will uproot[m] Israel from this good land that he gave to their forefathers and scatter them beyond the River,[b] because they provoked[n] the LORD to anger by making Asherah[o] poles.[c] [16]And he will give Israel up because of the sins[p] Jeroboam has committed and has caused Israel to commit."

[17]Then Jeroboam's wife got up and left and went to Tirzah.[q] As soon as she stepped over the threshold of the house, the boy died. [18]They buried him, and all Israel mourned for him, as the LORD had said through his servant the prophet Ahijah.

[19]The other events of Jeroboam's reign, his wars and how he ruled, are written in the book of the annals of the kings of Israel. [20]He reigned

---

14:2
b 1Sa 28:8;
2Sa 14:2;
1Ki 11:29
14:3
c 1Sa 9:7
14:7
d 2Sa 12:7-8;
1Ki 16:2
14:8
e 1Ki 11:31,33,38
f 1Ki 15:5
14:9
g Ex 34:17;
1Ki 12:28;
2Ch 11:15
h Ne 9:26;
Ps 50:17;
Eze 23:35
14:10
i Dt 32:36;
1Ki 21:21;
2Ki 9:8-9; 14:26
j 1Ki 15:29
14:11
k 1Ki 16:4; 21:24
14:13
l 2Ch 12:12;
19:3
14:15
m Dt 29:28;
2Ki 15:29; 17:6;
Ps 52:5
n Jos 23:15-16
o Ex 34:13;
Dt 12:3
14:16
p 1Ki 12:30;
13:34; 15:30,
34; 16:2
14:17
q ver 12;
1Ki 15:33;
16:6-9

---

*a14 The meaning of the Hebrew for this sentence is uncertain.   b15 That is, the Euphrates
c15 That is, symbols of the goddess Asherah; here and elsewhere in 1 Kings*

for twenty-two years and then rested with his fathers. And Nadab his son succeeded him as king.

Rehoboam King of Judah

14:21,25–31pp — 2Ch 12:9–16

21Rehoboam son of Solomon was king in Judah. He was forty-one years old when he became king, and he reigned seventeen years in Jerusalem, the city the LORD had chosen out of all the tribes of Israel in which to put his Name. His mother's name was Naamah; she was an Ammonite. r

22Judahs did evil in the eyes of the LORD. By the sins they committed they stirred up his jealous anger t more than their fathers had done. 23They also set up for themselves high places, sacred stones u and Asherah poles on every high hill and under every spreading tree. v 24There were even male shrine prostitutes w in the land; the people engaged in all the detestable practices of the nations the LORD had driven out before the Israelites.

25In the fifth year of King Rehoboam, Shishak king of Egypt attacked x Jerusalem. 26He carried off the treasures of the temple y of the LORD and the treasures of the royal palace. He took everything, including all the gold shields z Solomon had made. 27So King Rehoboam made bronze shields to replace them and assigned these to the commanders of the guard on duty at the entrance to the royal palace. 28Whenever the king went to the LORD's temple, the guards bore the shields, and afterward they returned them to the guardroom.

29As for the other events of Rehoboam's reign, and all he did, are they not written in the book of the annals of the kings of Judah? 30There was continual warfare a between Rehoboam and Jeroboam. 31And Rehoboam rested with his fathers and was buried with them in the City of David. His mother's name was Naamah; she was an Ammonite. b And Abijah a his son succeeded him as king.

Abijah King of Judah

15:1–2,6–8pp —2Ch 13:1–2,22–14:1

15 In the eighteenth year of the reign of Jeroboam son of Nebat, Abijah b became king of Judah, 2and he reigned in Jerusalem three years. His mother's name was Maacah c daughter of Abishalom. c

3He committed all the sins his father had done before him; his heart was not fully devoted d to the LORD his God, as the heart of David his forefather had been. 4Nevertheless, for David's sake the LORD his God gave him a lamp e in Jerusalem by raising up a son to succeed him and by making Jerusalem strong. 5For David had done what was right in the eyes of the LORD and had not failed to keep f any of the LORD's commands all the days of his life—except in the case of Uriah g the Hittite.

6There was war h between Rehoboam d and Jeroboam throughout ₍Abijah's₎ lifetime. 7As for the other events of Abijah's reign, and all he did, are they not written in the book of the annals of the kings of Judah? There was war between Abijah and Jeroboam. 8And Abijah rested with

---

14:21
rver 31;
1Ki 11:1;
2Ch 12:13
14:22
s2Ch 12:1
tDt 32:21;
Ps 78:58;
1Co 10:22
14:23
uDt 16:22;
2Ki 17:9-10;
Eze 16:24-25
vDt 12:2;
Isa 57:5
14:24
wDt 23:17;
1Ki 15:12;
2Ki 23:7
14:25
x1Ki 11:40;
2Ch 12:2
14:26
y1Ki 15:15,18
z1Ki 10:17
14:30
a1Ki 12:21; 15:6
14:31
bver 21;
2Ch 12:16
15:2
c2Ch 11:20;
13:2
15:3
d1Ki 11:4;
Ps 119:80
15:4
e2Sa 21:17;
1Ki 11:36;
2Ch 21:7
15:5
f1Ki 9:4; 14:8
g2Sa 11:2-27;
12:9
15:6
h1Ki 14:30

---

a31 Some Hebrew manuscripts and Septuagint (see also 2 Chron. 12:16); most Hebrew manuscripts *Abijam* b1 Some Hebrew manuscripts and Septuagint (see also 2 Chron. 12:16); most Hebrew manuscripts *Abijam*; also in verses 7 and 8 c2 A variant of *Absalom*; also in verse 10 d6 Most Hebrew manuscripts; some Hebrew manuscripts and Syriac *Abijam* (that is, Abijah) his fathers and was buried in the City of David. And Asa his son succeeded him as king.

Asa King of Judah

15:9–22pp — 2Ch 14:2–3; 15:16–16:6
15:23–24pp — 2Ch 16:11–17:1

[9] In the twentieth year of Jeroboam king of Israel, Asa became king of Judah, [10] and he reigned in Jerusalem forty-one years. His grandmother's name was Maacah[i] daughter of Abishalom.

[11] Asa did what was right in the eyes of the LORD, as his father David had done. [12] He expelled the male shrine prostitutes[j] from the land and got rid of all the idols his fathers had made. [13] He even deposed his grandmother Maacah from her position as queen mother, because she had made a repulsive Asherah pole. Asa cut the pole down[k] and burned it in the Kidron Valley. [14] Although he did not remove the high places, Asa's heart was fully committed[l] to the LORD all his life. [15] He brought into the temple of the LORD the silver and gold and the articles that he and his father had dedicated.[m]

[16] There was war[n] between Asa and Baasha king of Israel throughout their reigns. [17] Baasha king of Israel went up against Judah and fortified Ramah[o] to prevent anyone from leaving or entering the territory of Asa king of Judah.

[18] Asa then took all the silver and gold that was left in the treasuries of the LORD's temple[p] and of his own palace. He entrusted it to his officials and sent[q] them to Ben-Hadad[r] son of Tabrimmon, the son of Hezion, the king of Aram, who was ruling in Damascus. [19] "Let there be a treaty between me and you," he said, "as there was between my father and your father. See, I am sending you a gift of silver and gold. Now break your treaty with Baasha king of Israel so he will withdraw from me."

[20] Ben-Hadad agreed with King Asa and sent the commanders of his forces against the towns of Israel. He conquered[s] Ijon, Dan, Abel Beth Maacah and all Kinnereth in addition to Naphtali. [21] When Baasha heard this, he stopped building Ramah and withdrew to Tirzah. [22] Then King Asa issued an order to all Judah—no one was exempt—and they carried away from Ramah the stones and timber Baasha had been using there. With them King Asa built up Geba[t] in Benjamin, and also Mizpah.

[23] As for all the other events of Asa's reign, all his achievements, all he did and the cities he built, are they not written in the book of the annals of the kings of Judah? In his old age, however, his feet became diseased. [24] Then Asa rested with his fathers and was buried with them in the city of his father David. And Jehoshaphat[u] his son succeeded him as king.

Nadab King of Israel

[25] Nadab son of Jeroboam became king of Israel in the second year of Asa king of Judah, and he reigned over Israel two years. [26] He did evil in the eyes of the LORD, walking in the ways of his father[v] and in his sin, which he had caused Israel to commit.

[27] Baasha son of Ahijah of the house of Issachar plotted against him, and he struck him down[w] at Gibbethon,[x] a Philistine town, while

15:10 i ver 2
15:12 j 1Ki 14:24; 22:46
15:13 k Ex 32:20
15:14 l ver 3; 1Ki 8:61; 22:43
15:15 m 1Ki 7:51
15:16 n ver 32
15:17 o Jos 18:25; 1Ki 12:27
15:18 p ver 15; 1Ki 14:26; q 2Ki 12:18; r 1Ki 11:23-24
15:20 s Jdg 18:29; 2Sa 20:14; 2Ki 15:29
15:22 t Jos 18:24; 21:17
15:24 u Mt 1:8
15:26 v 1Ki 12:30; 14:16
15:27 w 1Ki 14:14; x Jos 19:44; 21:23

Nadab and all Israel were besieging it. [28]Baasha killed Nadab in the third year of Asa king of Judah and succeeded him as king.

[29]As soon as he began to reign, he killed Jeroboam's whole family. [y] He did not leave Jeroboam anyone that breathed, but destroyed them all, according to the word of the LORD given through his servant Ahijah the Shilonite— [30]because of the sins[z] Jeroboam had committed and had caused Israel to commit, and because he provoked the LORD, the God of Israel, to anger.

[31]As for the other events of Nadab's reign, and all he did, are they not written in the book of the annals of the kings of Israel? [32]There was war[a] between Asa and Baasha king of Israel throughout their reigns.

Baasha King of Israel

[33]In the third year of Asa king of Judah, Baasha son of Ahijah became king of all Israel in Tirzah, and he reigned twenty-four years. [34]He did evil[b] in the eyes of the LORD, walking in the ways of Jeroboam and in his sin, which he had caused Israel to commit.

16 Then the word of the LORD came to Jehu[c] son of Hanani[d] against Baasha: [2]"I lifted you up from the dust[e] and made you leader[f] of my people Israel, but you walked in the ways of Jeroboam and caused[g] my people Israel to sin and to provoke me to anger by their sins. [3]So I am about to consume Baasha and his house,[h] and I will make your house like that of Jeroboam son of Nebat. [4]Dogs[i] will eat those belonging to Baasha who die in the city, and the birds of the air will feed on those who die in the country."

[5]As for the other events of Baasha's reign, what he did and his achievements, are they not written in the book of the annals[j] of the kings of Israel? [6]Baasha rested with his fathers and was buried in Tirzah.[k] And Elah his son succeeded him as king.

[7]Moreover, the word of the LORD came[l] through the prophet Jehu[m] son of Hanani to Baasha and his house, because of all the evil he had done in the eyes of the LORD, provoking him to anger by the things he did, and becoming like the house of Jeroboam—and also because he destroyed it.

Elah King of Israel

[8]In the twenty-sixth year of Asa king of Judah, Elah son of Baasha became king of Israel, and he reigned in Tirzah two years.

[9]Zimri, one of his officials, who had command of half his chariots, plotted against him. Elah was in Tirzah at the time, getting drunk[n] in the home of Arza, the man in charge[o] of the palace at Tirzah. [10]Zimri came in, struck him down and killed him in the twenty-seventh year of Asa king of Judah. Then he succeeded him as king.

[11]As soon as he began to reign and was seated on the throne, he killed off Baasha's whole family.[p] He did not spare a single male, whether relative or friend. [12]So Zimri destroyed the whole family of Baasha, in accordance with the word of the LORD spoken against Baasha through the prophet Jehu— [13]because of all the sins Baasha and his son Elah had committed and had caused Israel to commit, so that they provoked the LORD, the God of Israel, to anger by their worthless idols. [q]

[14]As for the other events of Elah's reign, and all he did, are they not written in the book of the annals of the kings of Israel?

15:29
y1Ki 14:10,14
15:30
z1Ki 14:9,16
15:32
aver 16
15:34
bver 26;
1Ki 12:28-29;
13:33; 14:16
16:1
cver 7;
2Ch 19:2; 20:34
d2Ch 16:7
16:2
e1Sa 2:8
f1Ki 14:7-9
g1Ki 15:34
16:3
hver 11;
1Ki 14:10;
15:29; 21:22
16:4
i1Ki 14:11
16:5
j1Ki 14:19;
15:31
16:6
k1Ki 14:17;
15:33
16:7
l1Ki 15:27,29
mver 1
16:9
n2Ki 9:30-33
o1Ki 18:3
16:11
pver 3
16:13
qDt 32:21;
1Sa 12:21;
Isa 41:29

Zimri King of Israel

¹⁵In the twenty-seventh year of Asa king of Judah, Zimri reigned in Tirzah seven days. The army was encamped near Gibbethon,ʳ a Philistine town. ¹⁶When the Israelites in the camp heard that Zimri had plotted against the king and murdered him, they proclaimed Omri, the commander of the army, king over Israel that very day there in the camp. ¹⁷Then Omri and all the Israelites with him withdrew from Gibbethon and laid siege to Tirzah. ¹⁸When Zimri saw that the city was taken, he went into the citadel of the royal palace and set the palace on fire around him. So he died, ¹⁹because of the sins he had committed, doing evil in the eyes of the LORD and walking in the ways of Jeroboam and in the sin he had committed and had caused Israel to commit.

²⁰As for the other events of Zimri's reign, and the rebellion he carried out, are they not written in the book of the annals of the kings of Israel?

Omri King of Israel

²¹Then the people of Israel were split into two factions; half supported Tibni son of Ginath for king, and the other half supported Omri. ²²But Omri's followers proved stronger than those of Tibni son of Ginath. So Tibni died and Omri became king.

²³In the thirty-first year of Asa king of Judah, Omri became king of Israel, and he reigned twelve years, six of them in Tirzah.ˢ ²⁴He bought the hill of Samaria from Shemer for two talentsᵃ of silver and built a city on the hill, calling it Samaria,ᵗ after Shemer, the name of the former owner of the hill.

²⁵But Omri did evilᵘ in the eyes of the LORD and sinned more than all those before him. ²⁶He walked in all the ways of Jeroboam son of Nebat and in his sin, which he had causedᵛ Israel to commit, so that they provoked the LORD, the God of Israel, to anger by their worthless idols.ʷ

²⁷As for the other events of Omri's reign, what he did and the things he achieved, are they not written in the book of the annals of the kings of Israel? ²⁸Omri rested with his fathers and was buried in Samaria. And Ahab his son succeeded him as king.

Ahab Becomes King of Israel

²⁹In the thirty-eighth year of Asa king of Judah, Ahab son of Omri became king of Israel, and he reigned in Samaria over Israel twenty-two years. ³⁰Ahab son of Omri did moreˣ evil in the eyes of the LORD than any of those before him. ³¹He not only considered it trivial to commit the sins of Jeroboam son of Nebat, but he also marriedʸ Jezebel daughterᶻ of Ethbaal king of the Sidonians, and began to serve Baalᵃ and worship him. ³²He set up an altar for Baal in the templeᵇ of Baal that he built in Samaria. ³³Ahab also made an Asherah poleᶜ and did moreᵈ to provoke the LORD, the God of Israel, to anger than did all the kings of Israel before him.

³⁴In Ahab's time, Hiel of Bethel rebuilt Jericho. He laid its foundations at the cost of his firstborn son Abiram, and he set up its gates at

---

16:15
rJos 19:44;
1Ki 15:27
16:23
s1Ki 15:21
16:24
t1Ki 13:32;
Jn 4:4
16:25
uDt 4:25;
Mic 6:16
16:26
vver 19
wDt 32:21
16:30
xver 25;
1Ki 14:9
16:31
yDt 7:3;
1Ki 11:2
zJdg 18:7;
2Ki 9:34
a2Ki 10:18;
17:16
16:32
b2Ki 10:21,27;
11:18
16:33
c2Ki 13:6
dver 29,30;
1Ki 14:9; 21:25

ᵃ24 That is, about 150 pounds (about 70 kilograms)

the cost of his youngest son Segub, in accordance with the word of the LORD spoken by Joshua son of Nun. e

Elijah Fed by Ravens

17 Now Elijah f the Tishbite, from Tishbe a in Gilead, g said to Ahab, "As the LORD, the God of Israel, lives, whom I serve, there will be neither dew nor rain h in the next few years except at my word."

²Then the word of the LORD came to Elijah: ³"Leave here, turn eastward and hide in the Kerith Ravine, east of the Jordan. ⁴You will drink from the brook, and I have ordered the ravens i to feed you there."

⁵So he did what the LORD had told him. He went to the Kerith Ravine, east of the Jordan, and stayed there. ⁶The ravens brought him bread and meat in the morning j and bread and meat in the evening, and he drank from the brook.

The Widow at Zarephath

⁷Some time later the brook dried up because there had been no rain in the land. ⁸Then the word of the LORD came to him: ⁹"Go at once to Zarephath k of Sidon and stay there. I have commanded a widow l in that place to supply you with food." ¹⁰So he went to Zarephath. When he came to the town gate, a widow was there gathering sticks. He called to her and asked, "Would you bring me a little water in a jar so I may have a drink?" m ¹¹As she was going to get it, he called, "And bring me, please, a piece of bread."

¹²"As surely as the LORD your God lives," she replied, "I don't have any bread—only a handful of flour in a jar and a little oil n in a jug. I am gathering a few sticks to take home and make a meal for myself and my son, that we may eat it—and die."

¹³Elijah said to her, "Don't be afraid. Go home and do as you have said. But first make a small cake of bread for me from what you have and bring it to me, and then make something for yourself and your son. ¹⁴For this is what the LORD, the God of Israel, says: 'The jar of flour will not be used up and the jug of oil will not run dry until the day the LORD gives rain on the land.' "

¹⁵She went away and did as Elijah had told her. So there was food every day for Elijah and for the woman and her family. ¹⁶For the jar of flour was not used up and the jug of oil did not run dry, in keeping with the word of the LORD spoken by Elijah.

¹⁷Some time later the son of the woman who owned the house became ill. He grew worse and worse, and finally stopped breathing. ¹⁸She said to Elijah, "What do you have against me, man of God? Did you come to remind me of my sin o and kill my son?"

¹⁹"Give me your son," Elijah replied. He took him from her arms, carried him to the upper room where he was staying, and laid him on his bed. ²⁰Then he cried out to the LORD, "O LORD my God, have you brought tragedy also upon this widow I am staying with, by causing her son to die?" ²¹Then he stretched p himself out on the boy three times and cried to the LORD, "O LORD my God, let this boy's life return to him!"

---

a1 Or *Tishbite, of the settlers*

16:34
e Jos 6:26
17:1
f Mal 4:5;
Jas 5:17
g Jdg 12:4
h Dt 10:8;
1Ki 18:1;
2Ki 3:14;
Lk 4:25
17:4
i Ge 8:7
17:6
j Ex 16:8
17:9
k Ob 1:20
l Lk 4:26
17:10
m Ge 24:17;
Jn 4:7
17:12
n ver 1; 2Ki 4:2
17:18
o 2Ki 3:13;
Lk 5:8
17:21
p 2Ki 4:34;
Ac 20:10

22The LORD heard Elijah's cry, and the boy's life returned to him, and he lived. 23Elijah picked up the child and carried him down from the room into the house. He gave him to his mother and said, "Look, your son is alive!"

24Then the woman said to Elijah, "Now I know⁹ that you are a man of God and that the word of the LORD from your mouth is the truth."ʳ

Elijah and Obadiah

18 After a long time, in the thirdˢ year, the word of the LORD came to Elijah: "Go and present yourself to Ahab, and I will send rainᵗ on the land." 2So Elijah went to present himself to Ahab.

Now the famine was severe in Samaria, 3and Ahab had summoned Obadiah, who was in chargeᵘ of his palace. (Obadiah was a devout believerᵛ in the LORD. 4While Jezebelʷ was killing off the LORD's prophets, Obadiah had taken a hundred prophets and hiddenˣ them in two caves, fifty in each, and had supplied them with food and water.) 5Ahab had said to Obadiah, "Go through the land to all the springs and valleys. Maybe we can find some grass to keep the horses and mules alive so we will not have to kill any of our animals." 6So they divided the land they were to cover, Ahab going in one direction and Obadiah in another.

7As Obadiah was walking along, Elijah met him. Obadiah recognizedʸ him, bowed down to the ground, and said, "Is it really you, my lord Elijah?"

8"Yes," he replied. "Go tell your master, 'Elijah is here.' "

9"What have I done wrong," asked Obadiah, "that you are handing your servant over to Ahab to be put to death? 10As surely as the LORD your God lives, there is not a nation or kingdom where my master has not sent someone to lookᶻ for you. And whenever a nation or kingdom claimed you were not there, he made them swear they could not find you. 11But now you tell me to go to my master and say, 'Elijah is here.' 12I don't know where the Spiritᵃ of the LORD may carry you when I leave you. If I go and tell Ahab and he doesn't find you, he will kill me. Yet I your servant have worshiped the LORD since my youth. 13Haven't you heard, my lord, what I did while Jezebel was killing the prophets of the LORD? I hid a hundred of the LORD's prophets in two caves, fifty in each, and supplied them with food and water. 14And now you tell me to go to my master and say, 'Elijah is here.' He will kill me!"

15Elijah said, "As the LORD Almighty lives, whom I serve, I will surely presentᵇ myself to Ahab today."

Elijah on Mount Carmel

16So Obadiah went to meet Ahab and told him, and Ahab went to meet Elijah. 17When he saw Elijah, he said to him, "Is that you, you troublerᶜ of Israel?"

18"I have not made trouble for Israel," Elijah replied. "But youᵈ and your father's family have. You have abandonedᵉ the LORD's commands and have followed the Baals. 19Now summon the people from all over Israel to meet me on Mount Carmel.ᶠ And bring the four hundred and fifty prophets of Baal and the four hundred prophets of Asherah, who eat at Jezebel's table."

20So Ahab sent word throughout all Israel and assembled the proph-

17:24
qJn 3:2; 16:30
rPs 119:43;
Jn 17:17
18:1
s1Ki 17:1;
Lk 4:25;
Jas 5:17
tDt 28:12
18:3
u1Ki 16:9
vNe 7:2
18:4
w2Ki 9:7
xver 13;
Isa 16:3
18:7
y2Ki 1:8
18:10
z1Ki 17:3
18:12
a2Ki 2:16;
Eze 3:14;
Ac 8:39
18:15
b1Ki 17:1
18:17
cJos 7:25;
1Ki 21:20;
Ac 16:20
18:18
d1Ki 16:31,33;
21:25 e2Ch 15:2
18:19
fJos 19:26

ets on Mount Carmel. 21Elijah went before the people and said, "How long will you waver[g] between two opinions? If the LORD is God, follow him; but if Baal is God, follow him."

But the people said nothing.

22Then Elijah said to them, "I am the only one of the LORD's prophets left,[h] but Baal has four hundred and fifty prophets.[i] 23Get two bulls for us. Let them choose one for themselves, and let them cut it into pieces and put it on the wood but not set fire to it. I will prepare the other bull and put it on the wood but not set fire to it. 24Then you call on the name of your god, and I will call on the name of the LORD. The god who answers by fire[j]—he is God."

Then all the people said, "What you say is good."

25Elijah said to the prophets of Baal, "Choose one of the bulls and prepare it first, since there are so many of you. Call on the name of your god, but do not light the fire." 26So they took the bull given them and prepared it.

Then they called on the name of Baal from morning till noon. "O Baal, answer us!" they shouted. But there was no response;[k] no one answered. And they danced around the altar they had made.

27At noon Elijah began to taunt them. "Shout louder!" he said. "Surely he is a god! Perhaps he is deep in thought, or busy, or traveling. Maybe he is sleeping and must be awakened."[l] 28So they shouted louder and slashed[m] themselves with swords and spears, as was their custom, until their blood flowed. 29Midday passed, and they continued their frantic prophesying until the time for the evening sacrifice.[n] But there was no response, no one answered, no one paid attention.[o]

30Then Elijah said to all the people, "Come here to me." They came to him, and he repaired the altar[p] of the LORD, which was in ruins. 31Elijah took twelve stones, one for each of the tribes descended from Jacob, to whom the word of the LORD had come, saying, "Your name shall be Israel."[q] 32With the stones he built an altar in the name[r] of the LORD, and he dug a trench around it large enough to hold two seahs[a] of seed. 33He arranged[s] the wood, cut the bull into pieces and laid it on the wood. Then he said to them, "Fill four large jars with water and pour it on the offering and on the wood."

34"Do it again," he said, and they did it again.

"Do it a third time," he ordered, and they did it the third time. 35The water ran down around the altar and even filled the trench.

36At the time of sacrifice, the prophet Elijah stepped forward and prayed: "O LORD, God of Abraham,[t] Isaac and Israel, let it be known[u] today that you are God in Israel and that I am your servant and have done all these things at your command.[v] 37Answer me, O LORD, answer me, so these people will know that you, O LORD, are God, and that you are turning their hearts back again."

38Then the fire[w] of the LORD fell and burned up the sacrifice, the wood, the stones and the soil, and also licked up the water in the trench.

39When all the people saw this, they fell prostrate and cried, "The LORD—he is God! The LORD—he is God!"[x]

40Then Elijah commanded them, "Seize the prophets of Baal. Don't

18:21
gJos 24:15;
2Ki 17:41;
Mt 6:24
18:22
h1Ki 19:10
iver 19
18:24
jver 38;
1Ch 21:26
18:26
kPs 115:4-5;
Jer 10:5;
1Co 8:4; 12:2
18:27
lHab 2:19
18:28
mLev 19:28;
Dt 14:1
18:29
nEx 29:41
over 26
18:30
p1Ki 19:10
18:31
qGe 32:28;
35:10; 2Ki 17:34
18:32
rCol 3:17
18:33
sGe 22:9;
Lev 1:6-8
18:36
tEx 3:6;
Mt 22:32
u1Ki 8:43;
2Ki 19:19
vNu 16:28
18:38
wLev 9:24;
Jdg 6:21;
1Ch 21:26;
2Ch 7:1;
Job 1:16
18:39
xver 24

---

[a]32 That is, probably about 13 quarts (about 15 liters)

let anyone get away!" They seized them, and Elijah had them brought down to the Kishon Valley[y] and slaughtered[z] there.

⁴¹And Elijah said to Ahab, "Go, eat and drink, for there is the sound of a heavy rain." ⁴²So Ahab went off to eat and drink, but Elijah climbed to the top of Carmel, bent down to the ground and put his face between his knees.[a]

⁴³"Go and look toward the sea," he told his servant. And he went up and looked.

"There is nothing there," he said.

Seven times Elijah said, "Go back."

⁴⁴The seventh time the servant reported, "A cloud[b] as small as a man's hand is rising from the sea."

So Elijah said, "Go and tell Ahab, 'Hitch up your chariot and go down before the rain stops you.'"

⁴⁵Meanwhile, the sky grew black with clouds, the wind rose, a heavy rain came on and Ahab rode off to Jezreel. ⁴⁶The power[c] of the LORD came upon Elijah and, tucking his cloak into his belt,[d] he ran ahead of Ahab all the way to Jezreel.

Elijah Flees to Horeb

19 Now Ahab told Jezebel everything Elijah had done and how he had killed[e] all the prophets with the sword. ²So Jezebel sent a messenger to Elijah to say, "May the gods deal with me, be it ever so severely,[f] if by this time tomorrow I do not make your life like that of one of them."

³Elijah was afraid[a] and ran[g] for his life. When he came to Beersheba in Judah, he left his servant there, ⁴while he himself went a day's journey into the desert. He came to a broom tree, sat down under it and prayed that he might die. "I have had enough, LORD," he said. "Take my life;[h] I am no better than my ancestors." ⁵Then he lay down under the tree and fell asleep.[i]

All at once an angel touched him and said, "Get up and eat." ⁶He looked around, and there by his head was a cake of bread baked over hot coals, and a jar of water. He ate and drank and then lay down again.

⁷The angel of the LORD came back a second time and touched him and said, "Get up and eat, for the journey is too much for you." ⁸So he got up and ate and drank. Strengthened by that food, he traveled forty[j] days and forty nights until he reached Horeb,[k] the mountain of God. ⁹There he went into a cave[l] and spent the night.

The LORD Appears to Elijah

And the word of the LORD came to him: "What are you doing here, Elijah?"

¹⁰He replied, "I have been very zealous[m] for the LORD God Almighty. The Israelites have rejected your covenant, broken down your altars, and put your prophets to death with the sword. I am the only one left,[n] and now they are trying to kill me too."

¹¹The LORD said, "Go out and stand on the mountain[o] in the presence of the LORD, for the LORD is about to pass by."

18:40
y Jdg 4:7
z Dt 13:5;
18:20;
2Ki 10:24-25
18:42
a ver 19-20;
Jas 5:18
18:44
b Lk 12:54
18:46
c 2Ki 3:15
d 2Ki 4:29; 9:1
19:1
e 1Ki 18:40
19:2
f 1Ki 20:10;
2Ki 6:31;
Ru 1:17
19:3
g Ge 31:21
19:4
h Nu 11:15;
Jer 20:18;
Jnh 4:8
19:5
i Ge 28:11
19:8
j Ex 24:18;
34:28;
Dt 9:9-11,18;
Mt 4:2 k Ex 3:1
19:9
l Ex 33:22
19:10
m Nu 25:13
n 1Ki 18:4,22;
Ro 11:3*
19:11
o Ex 24:12

---

[a] 3 Or *Elijah saw*

Then a great and powerful wind[p] tore the mountains apart and shattered the rocks before the LORD, but the LORD was not in the wind. After the wind there was an earthquake, but the LORD was not in the earthquake. [12]After the earthquake came a fire, but the LORD was not in the fire. And after the fire came a gentle whisper. [q] [13]When Elijah heard it, he pulled his cloak over his face[r] and went out and stood at the mouth of the cave.

Then a voice said to him, "What are you doing here, Elijah?"

[14]He replied, "I have been very zealous for the LORD God Almighty. The Israelites have rejected your covenant, broken down your altars, and put your prophets to death with the sword. I am the only one left,[s] and now they are trying to kill me too."

[15]The LORD said to him, "Go back the way you came, and go to the Desert of Damascus. When you get there, anoint Hazael[t] king over Aram. [16]Also, anoint[u] Jehu son of Nimshi king over Israel, and anoint Elisha[v] son of Shaphat from Abel Meholah to succeed you as prophet. [17]Jehu will put to death any who escape the sword of Hazael,[w] and Elisha will put to death any who escape the sword of Jehu. [18]Yet I reserve[x] seven thousand in Israel—all whose knees have not bowed down to Baal and all whose mouths have not kissed[y] him."

The Call of Elisha

[19]So Elijah went from there and found Elisha son of Shaphat. He was plowing with twelve yoke of oxen, and he himself was driving the twelfth pair. Elijah went up to him and threw his cloak[z] around him. [20]Elisha then left his oxen and ran after Elijah. "Let me kiss my father and mother good-by,"[a] he said, "and then I will come with you."

"Go back," Elijah replied. "What have I done to you?"

[21]So Elisha left him and went back. He took his yoke of oxen[b] and slaughtered them. He burned the plowing equipment to cook the meat and gave it to the people, and they ate. Then he set out to follow Elijah and became his attendant.[c]

Ben-Hadad Attacks Samaria

20 Now Ben-Hadad[d] king of Aram mustered his entire army. Accompanied by thirty-two kings with their horses and chariots, he went up and besieged Samaria and attacked it. [2]He sent messengers into the city to Ahab king of Israel, saying, "This is what Ben-Hadad says: [3]'Your silver and gold are mine, and the best of your wives and children are mine.'"

[4]The king of Israel answered, "Just as you say, my lord the king. I and all I have are yours."

[5]The messengers came again and said, "This is what Ben-Hadad says: 'I sent to demand your silver and gold, your wives and your children. [6]But about this time tomorrow I am going to send my officials to search your palace and the houses of your officials. They will seize everything you value and carry it away.'"

[7]The king of Israel summoned all the elders of the land and said to them, "See how this man is looking for trouble![e] When he sent for my wives and my children, my silver and my gold, I did not refuse him."

[8]The elders and the people all answered, "Don't listen to him or agree to his demands."

19:11
pEze 1:4; 37:7
19:12
qJob 4:16;
Zec 4:6
19:13
rver 9; Ex 3:6
19:14
sver 10
19:15
t2Ki 8:7-15
19:16
u2Ki 9:1-3,6
vver 21;
2Ki 2:9,15
19:17
w2Ki 8:12,29;
9:14; 13:3,7,22
19:18
xRo 11:4*
yHos 13:2
19:19
z2Ki 2:8,14
19:20
aMt 8:21-22;
Lk 9:61
19:21
b2Sa 24:22
cver 16
20:1
d1Ki 15:18;
22:31; 2Ki 6:24
20:7
e2Ki 5:7

⁹So he replied to Ben-Hadad's messengers, "Tell my lord the king, 'Your servant will do all you demanded the first time, but this demand I cannot meet.' " They left and took the answer back to Ben-Hadad.

¹⁰Then Ben-Hadad sent another message to Ahab: "May the gods deal with me, be it ever so severely, if enough dust*f* remains in Samaria to give each of my men a handful."

¹¹The king of Israel answered, "Tell him: 'One who puts on his armor should not boast*g* like one who takes it off.' "

¹²Ben-Hadad heard this message while he and the kings were drinking*h* in their tents,*a* and he ordered his men: "Prepare to attack." So they prepared to attack the city.

Ahab Defeats Ben-Hadad

¹³Meanwhile a prophet came to Ahab king of Israel and announced, "This is what the LORD says: 'Do you see this vast army? I will give it into your hand today, and then you will know*i* that I am the LORD.' "

¹⁴"But who will do this?" asked Ahab.

The prophet replied, "This is what the LORD says: 'The young officers of the provincial commanders will do it.' "

"And who will start*j* the battle?" he asked.

The prophet answered, "You will."

¹⁵So Ahab summoned the young officers of the provincial commanders, 232 men. Then he assembled the rest of the Israelites, 7,000 in all. ¹⁶They set out at noon while Ben-Hadad and the 32 kings allied with him were in their tents getting drunk.*k* ¹⁷The young officers of the provincial commanders went out first.

Now Ben-Hadad had dispatched scouts, who reported, "Men are advancing from Samaria."

¹⁸He said, "If they have come out for peace, take them alive; if they have come out for war, take them alive."

¹⁹The young officers of the provincial commanders marched out of the city with the army behind them ²⁰and each one struck down his opponent. At that, the Arameans fled, with the Israelites in pursuit. But Ben-Hadad king of Aram escaped on horseback with some of his horsemen. ²¹The king of Israel advanced and overpowered the horses and chariots and inflicted heavy losses on the Arameans.

²²Afterward, the prophet*l* came to the king of Israel and said, "Strengthen your position and see what must be done, because next spring*m* the king of Aram will attack you again."

²³Meanwhile, the officials of the king of Aram advised him, "Their gods are gods*n* of the hills. That is why they were too strong for us. But if we fight them on the plains, surely we will be stronger than they. ²⁴Do this: Remove all the kings from their commands and replace them with other officers. ²⁵You must also raise an army like the one you lost—horse for horse and chariot for chariot—so we can fight Israel on the plains. Then surely we will be stronger than they." He agreed with them and acted accordingly.

²⁶The next spring*o* Ben-Hadad mustered the Arameans and went up to Aphek*p* to fight against Israel. ²⁷When the Israelites were also mustered and given provisions, they marched out to meet them. The Israel-

---

*a*12 Or *in Succoth*; also in verse 16

20:10
f2Sa 22:43;
1Ki 19:2
20:11
gPr 27:1;
Jer 9:23
20:12
hver 16;
1Ki 16:9
20:13
iver 28; Ex 6:7
20:14
jJdg 1:1
20:16
kver 12;
1Ki 16:9
20:22
lver 13 mver 26;
2Sa 11:1
20:23
n1Ki 14:23;
Ro 1:21-23
20:26
over 22
p2Ki 13:17

ites camped opposite them like two small flocks of goats, while the Arameans covered the countryside. q

²⁸The man of God came up and told the king of Israel, "This is what the LORD says: 'Because the Arameans think the LORD is a god of the hills and not a god ʳ of the valleys, I will deliver this vast army into your hands, and you will know ˢ that I am the LORD.'"

²⁹For seven days they camped opposite each other, and on the seventh day the battle was joined. The Israelites inflicted a hundred thousand casualties on the Aramean foot soldiers in one day. ³⁰The rest of them escaped to the city of Aphek, ᵗ where the wall collapsed on twenty-seven thousand of them. And Ben-Hadad fled to the city and hid ᵘ in an inner room.

³¹His officials said to him, "Look, we have heard that the kings of the house of Israel are merciful. Let us go to the king of Israel with sackcloth ᵛ around our waists and ropes around our heads. Perhaps he will spare your life."

³²Wearing sackcloth around their waists and ropes around their heads, they went to the king of Israel and said, "Your servant Ben-Hadad says: 'Please let me live.'"

The king answered, "Is he still alive? He is my brother."

³³The men took this as a good sign and were quick to pick up his word. "Yes, your brother Ben-Hadad!" they said.

"Go and get him," the king said. When Ben-Hadad came out, Ahab had him come up into his chariot.

³⁴"I will return the cities ʷ my father took from your father," Ben-Hadad offered. "You may set up your own market areas in Damascus, ˣ as my father did in Samaria."

Ahab said, "On the basis of a treaty ʸ I will set you free." So he made a treaty with him, and let him go.

A Prophet Condemns Ahab

³⁵By the word of the LORD one of the sons of the prophets said to his companion, "Strike me with your weapon," but the man refused. ᶻ

³⁶So the prophet said, "Because you have not obeyed the LORD, as soon as you leave me a lion ᵃ will kill you." And after the man went away, a lion found him and killed him.

³⁷The prophet found another man and said, "Strike me, please." So the man struck him and wounded him. ³⁸Then the prophet went and stood by the road waiting for the king. He disguised himself with his headband down over his eyes. ³⁹As the king passed by, the prophet called out to him, "Your servant went into the thick of the battle, and someone came to me with a captive and said, 'Guard this man. If he is missing, it will be your life for his life, ᵇ or you must pay a talent ᵈ of silver.' ⁴⁰While your servant was busy here and there, the man disappeared."

"That is your sentence," the king of Israel said. "You have pronounced it yourself."

⁴¹Then the prophet quickly removed the headband from his eyes, and the king of Israel recognized him as one of the prophets. ⁴²He said to the king, "This is what the LORD says: 'You have set free a man I had

---

20:27
q Jdg 6:6;
1Sa 13:6
20:28
r ver 23 s ver 13
20:30
t ver 26
u 1Ki 22:25;
2Ch 18:24
20:31
v Ge 37:34
20:34
w 1Ki 15:20
x Jer 49:23-27
y Ex 23:32
20:35
z 1Ki 13:21;
2Ki 2:3-7
20:36
a 1Ki 13:24
20:39
b 2Ki 10:24

ᵈ39 That is, about 75 pounds (about 34 kilograms)

determined should die.*ᵃᶜ* Therefore it is your life for his life,*ᵈ* your people for his people.' " ⁴³Sullen and angry,*ᵉ* the king of Israel went to his palace in Samaria.

Naboth's Vineyard

21 Some time later there was an incident involving a vineyard belonging to Naboth*ᶠ* the Jezreelite. The vineyard was in Jezreel,*ᵍ* close to the palace of Ahab king of Samaria. ²Ahab said to Naboth, "Let me have your vineyard to use for a vegetable garden, since it is close to my palace. In exchange I will give you a better vineyard or, if you prefer, I will pay you whatever it is worth."

³But Naboth replied, "The LORD forbid that I should give you the inheritance*ʰ* of my fathers."

⁴So Ahab went home, sullen and angry*ⁱ* because Naboth the Jezreelite had said, "I will not give you the inheritance of my fathers." He lay on his bed sulking and refused to eat.

⁵His wife Jezebel came in and asked him, "Why are you so sullen? Why won't you eat?"

⁶He answered her, "Because I said to Naboth the Jezreelite, 'Sell me your vineyard; or if you prefer, I will give you another vineyard in its place.' But he said, 'I will not give you my vineyard.' "

⁷Jezebel his wife said, "Is this how you act as king over Israel? Get up and eat! Cheer up. I'll get you the vineyard*ʲ* of Naboth the Jezreelite."

⁸So she wrote letters in Ahab's name, placed his seal*ᵏ* on them, and sent them to the elders and nobles who lived in Naboth's city with him. ⁹In those letters she wrote:

> "Proclaim a day of fasting and seat Naboth in a prominent place among the people. ¹⁰But seat two scoundrels*ˡ* opposite him and have them testify that he has cursed*ᵐ* both God and the king. Then take him out and stone him to death."

¹¹So the elders and nobles who lived in Naboth's city did as Jezebel directed in the letters she had written to them. ¹²They proclaimed a fast*ⁿ* and seated Naboth in a prominent place among the people. ¹³Then two scoundrels came and sat opposite him and brought charges against Naboth before the people, saying, "Naboth has cursed both God and the king." So they took him outside the city and stoned him to death. *ᵒ* ¹⁴Then they sent word to Jezebel: "Naboth has been stoned and is dead."

¹⁵As soon as Jezebel heard that Naboth had been stoned to death, she said to Ahab, "Get up and take possession of the vineyard*ᵖ* of Naboth the Jezreelite that he refused to sell you. He is no longer alive, but dead." ¹⁶When Ahab heard that Naboth was dead, he got up and went down to take possession of Naboth's vineyard.

¹⁷Then the word of the LORD came to Elijah the Tishbite: ¹⁸"Go down to meet Ahab king of Israel, who rules in Samaria. He is now in Naboth's vineyard, where he has gone to take possession of it. ¹⁹Say to him, 'This is what the LORD says: Have you not murdered a man and seized his property?' Then say to him, 'This is what the LORD says: In

20:42
c Jer 48:10
d ver 39;
Jos 2:14;
1Ki 22:31-37

20:43
e 1Ki 21:4

21:1
f 2Ki 9:21
g 1Ki 18:45-46

21:3
h Lev 25:23;
Nu 36:7;
Eze 46:18

21:4
i 1Ki 20:43

21:7
j 1Sa 8:14

21:8
k Ge 38:18;
Est 3:12; 8:8,10

21:10
l Ac 6:11
m Ex 22:28;
Lev 24:15-16

21:12
n Isa 58:4

21:13
o 2Ki 9:26

21:15
p 1Sa 8:14

*ᵃ42 The Hebrew term refers to the irrevocable giving over of things or persons to the LORD, often by totally destroying them.

the place where dogs licked up Naboth's blood, q dogs r will lick up your blood—yes, yours!' "

20Ahab said to Elijah, "So you have found me, my enemy!" s

"I have found you," he answered, "because you have sold t yourself to do evil in the eyes of the LORD. 21'I am going to bring disaster on you. I will consume your descendants and cut off from Ahab every last male u in Israel—slave or free. 22I will make your house v like that of Jeroboam son of Nebat and that of Baasha son of Ahijah, because you have provoked me to anger and have caused Israel to sin.' w

23"And also concerning Jezebel the LORD says: 'Dogs x will devour Jezebel by the wall of a Jezreel.'

24"Dogs y will eat those belonging to Ahab who die in the city, and the birds of the air will feed on those who die in the country."

25(There was never z a man like Ahab, who sold himself to do evil in the eyes of the LORD, urged on by Jezebel his wife. 26He behaved in the vilest manner by going after idols, like the Amorites a the LORD drove out before Israel.)

27When Ahab heard these words, he tore his clothes, put on sackcloth b and fasted. He lay in sackcloth and went around meekly.

28Then the word of the LORD came to Elijah the Tishbite: 29"Have you noticed how Ahab has humbled himself before me? Because he has humbled himself, I will not bring this disaster in his day, but I will bring it on his house in the days of his son." c

Micaiah Prophesies Against Ahab
22:1–28pp — 2Ch 18:1–27

22 For three years there was no war between Aram and Israel. 2But in the third year Jehoshaphat king of Judah went down to see the king of Israel. 3The king of Israel had said to his officials, "Don't you know that Ramoth Gilead d belongs to us and yet we are doing nothing to retake it from the king of Aram?"

4So he asked Jehoshaphat, "Will you go with me to fight e against Ramoth Gilead?"

Jehoshaphat replied to the king of Israel, "I am as you are, my people as your people, my horses as your horses." 5But Jehoshaphat also said to the king of Israel, "First seek the counsel f of the LORD."

6So the king of Israel brought together the prophets—about four hundred men—and asked them, "Shall I go to war against Ramoth Gilead, or shall I refrain?"

"Go," g they answered, "for the Lord will give it into the king's hand."

7But Jehoshaphat asked, "Is there not a prophet h of the LORD here whom we can inquire of?"

8The king of Israel answered Jehoshaphat, "There is still one man through whom we can inquire of the LORD, but I hate i him because he never prophesies anything good j about me, but always bad. He is Micaiah son of Imlah."

"The king should not say that," Jehoshaphat replied.

---

a23 Most Hebrew manuscripts; a few Hebrew manuscripts, Vulgate and Syriac (see also 2 Kings 9:26) *the plot of ground at*

21:19
q2Ki 9:26;
Ps 9:12;
Isa 14:20
r1Ki 22:38
21:20
s1Ki 18:17
tver 25;
2Ki 17:17;
Ro 7:14
21:21
u1Ki 14:10;
2Ki 9:8
21:22
v1Ki 15:29; 16:3
w1Ki 12:30
21:23
x2Ki 9:10,34-36
21:24
y1Ki 14:11; 16:4
21:25
zver 20;
1Ki 16:33
21:26
aGe 15:16;
Lev 18:25-30;
2Ki 21:11
21:27
bGe 37:34;
2Sa 3:31;
2Ki 6:30
21:29
c2Ki 9:26
22:3
dDt 4:43;
Jos 21:38
22:4
e2Ki 3:7
22:5
fEx 33:7;
2Ki 3:11
22:6
g1Ki 18:19
22:7
h2Ki 3:11
22:8
iAm 5:10
jIsa 5:20

⁹So the king of Israel called one of his officials and said, "Bring Micaiah son of Imlah at once."

¹⁰Dressed in their royal robes, the king of Israel and Jehoshaphat king of Judah were sitting on their thrones at the threshing floorᵏ by the entrance of the gate of Samaria, with all the prophets prophesying before them. ¹¹Now Zedekiah son of Kenaanah had made iron hornsˡ and he declared, "This is what the LORD says: 'With these you will gore the Arameans until they are destroyed.'"

¹²All the other prophets were prophesying the same thing. "Attack Ramoth Gilead and be victorious," they said, "for the LORD will give it into the king's hand."

¹³The messenger who had gone to summon Micaiah said to him, "Look, as one man the other prophets are predicting success for the king. Let your word agree with theirs, and speak favorably."

¹⁴But Micaiah said, "As surely as the LORD lives, I can tell him only what the LORD tells me."ᵐ

¹⁵When he arrived, the king asked him, "Micaiah, shall we go to war against Ramoth Gilead, or shall I refrain?"

"Attack and be victorious," he answered, "for the LORD will give it into the king's hand."

¹⁶The king said to him, "How many times must I make you swear to tell me nothing but the truth in the name of the LORD?"

¹⁷Then Micaiah answered, "I saw all Israel scattered on the hills like sheep without a shepherd,ⁿ and the LORD said, 'These people have no master. Let each one go home in peace.'"

¹⁸The king of Israel said to Jehoshaphat, "Didn't I tell you that he never prophesies anything good about me, but only bad?"

¹⁹Micaiah continued, "Therefore hear the word of the LORD: I saw the LORD sitting on his throneᵒ with all the hostᵖ of heaven standing around him on his right and on his left. ²⁰And the LORD said, 'Who will entice Ahab into attacking Ramoth Gilead and going to his death there?'

"One suggested this, and another that. ²¹Finally, a spirit came forward, stood before the LORD and said, 'I will entice him.'

²²"'By what means?' the LORD asked.

"'I will go out and be a lyingᑫ spirit in the mouths of all his prophets,' he said.

"'You will succeed in enticing him,' said the LORD. 'Go and do it.'

²³"So now the LORD has put a lying spirit in the mouths of all these prophetsʳ of yours. The LORD has decreed disaster for you."

²⁴Then Zedekiahˢ son of Kenaanah went up and slappedᵗ Micaiah in the face. "Which way did the spirit fromᵃ the LORD go when he went from me to speak to you?" he asked.

²⁵Micaiah replied, "You will find out on the day you go to hideᵘ in an inner room."

²⁶The king of Israel then ordered, "Take Micaiah and send him back to Amon the ruler of the city and to Joash the king's son ²⁷and say, 'This is what the king says: Put this fellow in prisonᵛ and give him nothing but bread and water until I return safely.'"

²⁸Micaiah declared, "If you ever return safely, the LORD has not

22:10
kver 6
22:11
lDt 33:17;
Zec 1:18-21
22:14
mNu 22:18;
24:13;
1Ki 18:10,15
22:17
nver 34-36;
Nu 27:17;
Mt 9:36
22:19
oIsa 6:1;
Eze 1:26;
Da 7:9
pJob 1:6; 2:1;
Ps 103:20-21;
Mt 18:10;
Heb 1:7,14
22:22
qJdg 9:23;
1Sa 16:14;
18:10; 19:9;
Eze 14:9;
2Th 2:11
22:23
rEze 14:9
22:24
sver 11 tAc 23:2
22:25
u1Ki 20:30
22:27
v2Ch 16:10

ᵃ24 Or *Spirit of*

spoken^w through me." Then he added, "Mark my words, all you people!"

Ahab Killed at Ramoth Gilead

22:29–36pp — 2Ch 18:28–34

²⁹So the king of Israel and Jehoshaphat king of Judah went up to Ramoth Gilead. ³⁰The king of Israel said to Jehoshaphat, "I will enter the battle in disguise,^x but you wear your royal robes." So the king of Israel disguised himself and went into battle.

³¹Now the king of Aram had ordered his thirty-two chariot commanders, "Do not fight with anyone, small or great, except the king^y of Israel." ³²When the chariot commanders saw Jehoshaphat, they thought, "Surely this is the king of Israel." So they turned to attack him, but when Jehoshaphat cried out, ³³the chariot commanders saw that he was not the king of Israel and stopped pursuing him.

³⁴But someone drew his bow^z at random and hit the king of Israel between the sections of his armor. The king told his chariot driver, "Wheel around and get me out of the fighting. I've been wounded." ³⁵All day long the battle raged, and the king was propped up in his chariot facing the Arameans. The blood from his wound ran onto the floor of the chariot, and that evening he died. ³⁶As the sun was setting, a cry spread through the army: "Every man to his town; everyone to his land!"^a

³⁷So the king died and was brought to Samaria, and they buried him there. ³⁸They washed the chariot at a pool in Samaria (where the prostitutes bathed),^a and the dogs^b licked up his blood, as the word of the LORD had declared.

³⁹As for the other events of Ahab's reign, including all he did, the palace he built and inlaid with ivory,^c and the cities he fortified, are they not written in the book of the annals of the kings of Israel? ⁴⁰Ahab rested with his fathers. And Ahaziah his son succeeded him as king.

Jehoshaphat King of Judah

22:41–50pp — 2Ch 20:31–21:1

⁴¹Jehoshaphat son of Asa became king of Judah in the fourth year of Ahab king of Israel. ⁴²Jehoshaphat was thirty-five years old when he became king, and he reigned in Jerusalem twenty-five years. His mother's name was Azubah daughter of Shilhi. ⁴³In everything he walked in the ways of his father Asa^d and did not stray from them; he did what was right in the eyes of the LORD. The high places,^e however, were not removed, and the people continued to offer sacrifices and burn incense there. ⁴⁴Jehoshaphat was also at peace with the king of Israel.

⁴⁵As for the other events of Jehoshaphat's reign, the things he achieved and his military exploits, are they not written in the book of the annals of the kings of Judah? ⁴⁶He rid the land of the rest of the male shrine prostitutes^f who remained there even after the reign of his father Asa. ⁴⁷There was then no king^g in Edom; a deputy ruled.

⁴⁸Now Jehoshaphat built a fleet of trading ships^{bh} to go to Ophir for gold, but they never set sail—they were wrecked at Ezion Geber. ⁴⁹At

---

22:28
wDt 18:22
22:30
x2Ch 35:32
22:31
y2Sa 17:2
22:34
z2Ch 35:23
22:36
a2Ki 14:12
22:38
b1Ki 21:19
22:39
c2Ch 9:17;
Am 3:15
22:43
d2Ch 17:3
e1Ki 3:2; 15:14;
2Ki 12:3
22:46
fDt 23:17;
1Ki 14:24; 15:12
22:47
g2Sa 8:14;
2Ki 3:9; 8:20
22:48
h1Ki 9:26; 10:22

---

^a38 Or *Samaria and cleaned the weapons*   ^b48 Hebrew *of ships of Tarshish*

that time Ahaziah son of Ahab said to Jehoshaphat, "Let my men sail with your men," but Jehoshaphat refused.

50Then Jehoshaphat rested with his fathers and was buried with them in the city of David his father. And Jehoram his son succeeded him.

Ahaziah King of Israel

51Ahaziah son of Ahab became king of Israel in Samaria in the seventeenth year of Jehoshaphat king of Judah, and he reigned over Israel two years. 52He did evili in the eyes of the Lord, because he walked in the ways of his father and mother and in the ways of Jeroboam son of Nebat, who caused Israel to sin. 53He served and worshiped Baali and provoked the Lord, the God of Israel, to anger, just as his fatherk had done.

22:52
i1Ki 15:26;
21:25
22:53
jJdg 2:11
k1Ki 16:30-32

2 Kings

Title and Background

See Introduction to 1 Kings.

Author and Date of Writing

See Introduction to 1 Kings.

Theme and Message

2 Kings continues the stories of the great prophets Elijah and Elisha. It also tells the history of the northern and southern kingdoms until they were both finally conquered. In both kingdoms God's prophets continually warned the people that God would punish them if they did not repent of their sins.

Outline

  I. Elijah and Elisha (1:1-8:15)
  II. Israel and Judah From Joram/Jehoram to Israel's Exile (8:16-17:41)
  III. Judah From Hezekiah to the Babylonian Exile (18:1-25:30)

The LORD's Judgment on Ahaziah

1 After Ahab's death, Moab[a] rebelled against Israel. [2]Now Ahaziah had fallen through the lattice of his upper room in Samaria and injured himself. So he sent messengers,[b] saying to them, "Go and consult Baal-Zebub,[c] the god of Ekron,[d] to see if I will recover[e] from this injury."

[3]But the angel[f] of the LORD said to Elijah[g] the Tishbite, "Go up and meet the messengers of the king of Samaria and ask them, 'Is it because there is no God in Israel[h] that you are going off to consult Baal-Zebub, the god of Ekron?' [4]Therefore this is what the LORD says: 'You will not leave[i] the bed you are lying on. You will certainly die!' " So Elijah went.

[5]When the messengers returned to the king, he asked them, "Why have you come back?"

[6]"A man came to meet us," they replied. "And he said to us, 'Go back to the king who sent you and tell him, "This is what the LORD says: Is it because there is no God in Israel that you are sending men to consult Baal-Zebub, the god of Ekron? Therefore you will not leave the bed you are lying on. You will certainly die!"' "

[7]The king asked them, "What kind of man was it who came to meet you and told you this?"

[8]They replied, "He was a man with a garment of hair[j] and with a leather belt around his waist."

The king said, "That was Elijah the Tishbite."

[9]Then he sent[k] to Elijah a captain[l] with his company of fifty men.

1:1
[a]Ge 19:37;
2Sa 8:2; 2Ki 3:5
1:2
[b]ver 16
[c]Mk 3:22
[d]1Sa 6:2;
Isa 2:6; 14:29;
Mt 10:25
[e]Jdg 18:5;
2Ki 8:7-10
1:3
[f]ver 15; Ge 16:7
[g]1Ki 17:1
[h]1Sa 28:8
1:4
[i]ver 6,16;
Ps 41:8
1:8
[j]1Ki 18:7;
Zec 13:4;
Mt 3:4; Mk 1:6
1:9
[k]2Ki 6:14
[l]Ex 18:25;
Isa 3:3

The captain went up to Elijah, who was sitting on the top of a hill, and said to him, "Man of God, the king says, 'Come down!' "

[10]Elijah answered the captain, "If I am a man of God, may fire come down from heaven and consume you and your fifty men!" Then fire[m] fell from heaven and consumed the captain and his men.

[11]At this the king sent to Elijah another captain with his fifty men. The captain said to him, "Man of God, this is what the king says, 'Come down at once!' "

[12]"If I am a man of God," Elijah replied, "may fire come down from heaven and consume you and your fifty men!" Then the fire of God fell from heaven and consumed him and his fifty men.

[13]So the king sent a third captain with his fifty men. This third captain went up and fell on his knees before Elijah. "Man of God," he begged, "please have respect for my life[n] and the lives of these fifty men, your servants! [14]See, fire has fallen from heaven and consumed the first two captains and all their men. But now have respect for my life!"

[15]The angel[o] of the LORD said to Elijah, "Go down with him; do not be afraid[p] of him." So Elijah got up and went down with him to the king.

[16]He told the king, "This is what the LORD says: Is it because there is no God in Israel for you to consult that you have sent messengers[q] to consult Baal-Zebub, the god of Ekron? Because you have done this, you will never leave[r] the bed you are lying on. You will certainly die!" [17]So he died,[s] according to the word of the LORD that Elijah had spoken.

Because Ahaziah had no son, Joram[a][t] succeeded him as king in the second year of Jehoram son of Jehoshaphat king of Judah. [18]As for all the other events of Ahaziah's reign, and what he did, are they not written in the book of the annals of the kings of Israel?

Elijah Taken Up to Heaven

2 When the LORD was about to take[u] Elijah up to heaven in a whirlwind,[v] Elijah and Elisha[w] were on their way from Gilgal.[x] [2]Elijah said to Elisha, "Stay here;[y] the LORD has sent me to Bethel."

But Elisha said, "As surely as the LORD lives and as you live, I will not leave you."[z] So they went down to Bethel.

[3]The company[a] of the prophets at Bethel came out to Elisha and asked, "Do you know that the LORD is going to take your master from you today?"

"Yes, I know," Elisha replied, "but do not speak of it."

[4]Then Elijah said to him, "Stay here, Elisha; the LORD has sent me to Jericho.[b]"

And he replied, "As surely as the LORD lives and as you live, I will not leave you." So they went to Jericho.

[5]The company[c] of the prophets at Jericho went up to Elisha and asked him, "Do you know that the LORD is going to take your master from you today?"

"Yes, I know," he replied, "but do not speak of it."

[6]Then Elijah said to him, "Stay here;[d] the LORD has sent me to the Jordan."[e]

1:10
[m]1Ki 18:38;
Lk 9:54;
Rev 11:5; 13:13
1:13
[n]1Sa 26:21;
Ps 72:14
1:15
[o]ver 3
[p]Isa 51:12;
57:11; Jer 1:17;
Eze 2:6
1:16
[q]ver 2
[r]ver 4
1:17
[s]2Ki 8:15;
Jer 20:6; 28:17
[t]2Ki 3:1; 8:16
2:1
[u]Ge 5:24;
Heb 11:5
[v]ver 11;
1Ki 19:11;
Isa 5:28; 66:15;
Jer 4:13; Na 1:3
[w]1Ki 19:16,21
[x]Dt 11:30;
2Ki 4:38
2:2
[y]ver 6
[z]Ru 1:16;
1Sa 1:26;
2Ki 4:30
2:3
[a]1Sa 10:5;
2Ki 4:1,38
2:4
[b]Jos 3:16; 6:26
2:5
[c]ver 3
2:6
[d]ver 2 [e]Jos 3:15

And he replied, "As surely as the Lord lives and as you live, I will not leave you."[f] So the two of them walked on.

[7]Fifty men of the company of the prophets went and stood at a distance, facing the place where Elijah and Elisha had stopped at the Jordan. [8]Elijah took his cloak,[g] rolled it up and struck[h] the water with it. The water divided[i] to the right and to the left, and the two of them crossed over on dry[j] ground.

[9]When they had crossed, Elijah said to Elisha, "Tell me, what can I do for you before I am taken from you?"

"Let me inherit a double[k] portion of your spirit,"[l] Elisha replied.

[10]"You have asked a difficult thing," Elijah said, "yet if you see me when I am taken from you, it will be yours—otherwise not."

[11]As they were walking along and talking together, suddenly a chariot of fire[m] and horses of fire appeared and separated the two of them, and Elijah went up to heaven[n] in a whirlwind.[o] [12]Elisha saw this and cried out, "My father! My father! The chariots[p] and horsemen of Israel!" And Elisha saw him no more. Then he took hold of his own clothes and tore[q] them apart.

[13]He picked up the cloak that had fallen from Elijah and went back and stood on the bank of the Jordan. [14]Then he took the cloak[r] that had fallen from him and struck[s] the water with it. "Where now is the Lord, the God of Elijah?" he asked. When he struck the water, it divided to the right and to the left, and he crossed over.

[15]The company[t] of the prophets from Jericho, who were watching, said, "The spirit[u] of Elijah is resting on Elisha." And they went to meet him and bowed to the ground before him. [16]"Look," they said, "we your servants have fifty able men. Let them go and look for your master. Perhaps the Spirit[v] of the Lord has picked him up[w] and set him down on some mountain or in some valley."

"No," Elisha replied, "do not send them."

[17]But they persisted until he was too ashamed[x] to refuse. So he said, "Send them." And they sent fifty men, who searched for three days but did not find him. [18]When they returned to Elisha, who was staying in Jericho, he said to them, "Didn't I tell you not to go?"

Healing of the Water

[19]The men of the city said to Elisha, "Look, our lord, this town is well situated, as you can see, but the water is bad and the land is unproductive."

[20]"Bring me a new bowl," he said, "and put salt in it." So they brought it to him.

[21]Then he went out to the spring and threw[y] the salt into it, saying, "This is what the Lord says: 'I have healed this water. Never again will it cause death or make the land unproductive.'" [22]And the water has remained wholesome[z] to this day, according to the word Elisha had spoken.

Elisha Is Jeered

[23]From there Elisha went up to Bethel. As he was walking along the road, some youths came out of the town and jeered[a] at him. "Go on up, you baldhead!" they said. "Go on up, you baldhead!" [24]He turned around, looked at them and called down a curse[b] on them in the name[c]

2:6
[f]Ru 1:16
2:8
[g]1Ki 19:19
[h]ver 14
[i]Ex 14:21
[j]Ex 14:22,29
2:9
[k]Dt 21:17
[l]Nu 11:17
2:11
[m]2Ki 6:17;
Ps 68:17; 104:3,
4; Isa 66:15;
Hab 3:8;
Zec 6:1
[n]Ge 5:24 over 1
2:12
[p]2Ki 6:17; 13:14
[q]Ge 37:29
2:14
[r]1Ki 19:19
[s]ver 8
2:15
[t]ver 7; 1Sa 10:5
[u]Nu 11:17
2:16
[v]1Ki 18:12
[w]Ac 8:39
2:17
[x]2Ki 8:11
2:21
[y]Ex 15:25;
2Ki 4:41; 6:6
2:22
[z]Ex 15:25
2:23
[a]Ex 22:28;
2Ch 36:16;
Job 19:18;
Ps 31:18
2:24
[b]Ge 4:11;
Ne 13:25-27
[c]Dt 18:19

of the LORD. Then two bears came out of the woods and mauled forty-two of the youths. [25]And he went on to Mount Carmel[d] and from there returned to Samaria.

Moab Revolts

3 Joram[a][e] son of Ahab became king of Israel in Samaria in the eighteenth year of Jehoshaphat king of Judah, and he reigned twelve years. [2]He did evil[f] in the eyes of the LORD, but not as his father[g] and mother had done. He got rid of the sacred stone[h] of Baal that his father had made. [3]Nevertheless he clung to the sins[i] of Jeroboam son of Nebat, which he had caused Israel to commit; he did not turn away from them.

[4]Now Mesha king of Moab[j] raised sheep, and he had to supply the king of Israel with a hundred thousand lambs[k] and with the wool of a hundred thousand rams. [5]But after Ahab died, the king of Moab rebelled[l] against the king of Israel. [6]So at that time King Joram set out from Samaria and mobilized all Israel. [7]He also sent this message to Jehoshaphat king of Judah: "The king of Moab has rebelled against me. Will you go with me to fight[m] against Moab?"

"I will go with you," he replied. "I am as you are, my people as your people, my horses as your horses."

[8]"By what route shall we attack?" he asked.

"Through the Desert of Edom," he answered.

[9]So the king of Israel set out with the king of Judah and the king of Edom.[n] After a roundabout march of seven days, the army had no more water for themselves or for the animals with them.

[10]"What!" exclaimed the king of Israel. "Has the LORD called us three kings together only to hand us over to Moab?"

[11]But Jehoshaphat asked, "Is there no prophet of the LORD here, that we may inquire[o] of the LORD through him?"

An officer of the king of Israel answered, "Elisha[p] son of Shaphat is here. He used to pour water on the hands of Elijah.[b] [q]"

[12]Jehoshaphat said, "The word[r] of the LORD is with him." So the king of Israel and Jehoshaphat and the king of Edom went down to him.

[13]Elisha said to the king of Israel, "What do we have to do with each other? Go to the prophets of your father and the prophets of your mother."

"No," the king of Israel answered, "because it was the LORD who called us three kings together to hand us over to Moab."

[14]Elisha said, "As surely as the LORD Almighty lives, whom I serve, if I did not have respect for the presence of Jehoshaphat king of Judah, I would not look at you or even notice you. [15]But now bring me a harpist."[s]

While the harpist was playing, the hand[t] of the LORD came upon Elisha [16]and he said, "This is what the LORD says: Make this valley full of ditches. [17]For this is what the LORD says: You will see neither wind nor rain, yet this valley will be filled with water,[u] and you, your cattle and your other animals will drink. [18]This is an easy[v] thing in the eyes of the LORD; he will also hand Moab over to you. [19]You will overthrow

---

[a]1 Hebrew *Jehoram*, a variant of *Joram*; also in verse 6   [b]11 That is, he was Elijah's personal servant.

every fortified city and every major town. You will cut down every good tree, stop up all the springs, and ruin every good field with stones."

[20]The next morning, about the time[w] for offering the sacrifice, there it was—water flowing from the direction of Edom! And the land was filled with water.[x]

[21]Now all the Moabites had heard that the kings had come to fight against them; so every man, young and old, who could bear arms was called up and stationed on the border. [22]When they got up early in the morning, the sun was shining on the water. To the Moabites across the way, the water looked red—like blood. [23]"That's blood!" they said. "Those kings must have fought and slaughtered each other. Now to the plunder, Moab!"

[24]But when the Moabites came to the camp of Israel, the Israelites rose up and fought them until they fled. And the Israelites invaded the land and slaughtered the Moabites. [25]They destroyed the towns, and each man threw a stone on every good field until it was covered. They stopped up all the springs and cut down every good tree. Only Kir Hareseth[y] was left with its stones in place, but men armed with slings surrounded it and attacked it as well.

[26]When the king of Moab saw that the battle had gone against him, he took with him seven hundred swordsmen to break through to the king of Edom, but they failed. [27]Then he took his firstborn[z] son, who was to succeed him as king, and offered him as a sacrifice on the city wall. The fury against Israel was great; they withdrew and returned to their own land.

The Widow's Oil

4 The wife of a man from the company[a] of the prophets cried out to Elisha, "Your servant my husband is dead, and you know that he revered the LORD. But now his creditor[b] is coming to take my two boys as his slaves."

[2]Elisha replied to her, "How can I help you? Tell me, what do you have in your house?"

"Your servant has nothing there at all," she said, "except a little oil."[c]

[3]Elisha said, "Go around and ask all your neighbors for empty jars. Don't ask for just a few. [4]Then go inside and shut the door behind you and your sons. Pour oil into all the jars, and as each is filled, put it to one side."

[5]She left him and afterward shut the door behind her and her sons. They brought the jars to her and she kept pouring. [6]When all the jars were full, she said to her son, "Bring me another one."

But he replied, "There is not a jar left." Then the oil stopped flowing.

[7]She went and told the man of God,[d] and he said, "Go, sell the oil and pay your debts. You and your sons can live on what is left."

The Shunammite's Son Restored to Life

[8]One day Elisha went to Shunem.[e] And a well-to-do woman was there, who urged him to stay for a meal. So whenever he came by, he stopped there to eat. [9]She said to her husband, "I know that this man who often comes our way is a holy man of God. [10]Let's make a small

3:20
[w] Ex 29:39-40
[x] Ex 17:6
3:25
[y] ver 19;
Isa 15:1; 16:7;
Jer 48:31,36
3:27
[z] Dt 12:31;
2Ki 16:3; 21:6;
2Ch 28:3;
Ps 106:38;
Jer 19:4-5;
Am 2:1;
Mic 6:7
4:1
[a] 1Sa 10:5;
2Ki 2:3
[b] Ex 22:26;
Lev 25:39-43;
Ne 5:3-5;
Job 22:6; 24:9
4:2
[c] 1Ki 17:12
4:7
[d] 1Ki 12:22
4:8
[e] Jos 19:18

room on the roof and put in it a bed and a table, a chair and a lamp for him. Then he can stay[f] there whenever he comes to us."

[11]One day when Elisha came, he went up to his room and lay down there. [12]He said to his servant Gehazi, "Call the Shunammite."[g] So he called her, and she stood before him. [13]Elisha said to him, "Tell her, 'You have gone to all this trouble for us. Now what can be done for you? Can we speak on your behalf to the king or the commander of the army?'"

She replied, "I have a home among my own people."

[14]"What can be done for her?" Elisha asked.

Gehazi said, "Well, she has no son and her husband is old."

[15]Then Elisha said, "Call her." So he called her, and she stood in the doorway. [16]"About this time[h] next year," Elisha said, "you will hold a son in your arms."

"No, my lord," she objected. "Don't mislead your servant, O man of God!"

[17]But the woman became pregnant, and the next year about that same time she gave birth to a son, just as Elisha had told her.

[18]The child grew, and one day he went out to his father, who was with the reapers.[i] [19]"My head! My head!" he said to his father.

His father told a servant, "Carry him to his mother." [20]After the servant had lifted him up and carried him to his mother, the boy sat on her lap until noon, and then he died. [21]She went up and laid him on the bed[j] of the man of God, then shut the door and went out.

[22]She called her husband and said, "Please send me one of the servants and a donkey so I can go to the man of God quickly and return."

[23]"Why go to him today?" he asked. "It's not the New Moon[k] or the Sabbath."

"It's all right," she said.

[24]She saddled the donkey and said to her servant, "Lead on; don't slow down for me unless I tell you." [25]So she set out and came to the man of God at Mount Carmel.[l]

When he saw her in the distance, the man of God said to his servant Gehazi, "Look! There's the Shunammite! [26]Run to meet her and ask her, 'Are you all right? Is your husband all right? Is your child all right?'"

"Everything is all right," she said.

[27]When she reached the man of God at the mountain, she took hold of his feet. Gehazi came over to push her away, but the man of God said, "Leave her alone! She is in bitter distress,[m] but the LORD has hidden it from me and has not told me why."

[28]"Did I ask you for a son, my lord?" she said. "Didn't I tell you, 'Don't raise my hopes'?"

[29]Elisha said to Gehazi, "Tuck your cloak into your belt,[n] take my staff[o] in your hand and run. If you meet anyone, do not greet him, and if anyone greets you, do not answer. Lay my staff on the boy's face."

[30]But the child's mother said, "As surely as the LORD lives and as you live, I will not leave you." So he got up and followed her.

[31]Gehazi went on ahead and laid the staff on the boy's face, but there was no sound or response. So Gehazi went back to meet Elisha and told him, "The boy has not awakened."

4:10
[f]Mt 10:41;
Ro 12:13
4:12
[g]2Ki 8:1
4:16
[h]Ge 18:10
4:18
[i]Ru 2:3
4:21
[j]ver 32
4:23
[k]Nu 10:10;
1Ch 23:31;
Ps 81:3
4:25
[l]1Ki 18:20;
2Ki 2:25
4:27
[m]1Sa 1:15
4:29
[n]1Ki 18:46;
2Ki 2:8,14; 9:1
[o]Ex 4:2; 7:19;
14:16

³²When Elisha reached the house, there was the boy lying dead on his couch.ᴾ ³³He went in, shut the door on the two of them and prayed�q to the Lᴏʀᴅ. ³⁴Then he got on the bed and lay upon the boy, mouth to mouth, eyes to eyes, hands to hands. As he stretchedʳ himself out upon him, the boy's body grew warm. ³⁵Elisha turned away and walked back and forth in the room and then got on the bed and stretched out upon him once more. The boy sneezed seven timesˢ and opened his eyes.ᵗ

³⁶Elisha summoned Gehazi and said, "Call the Shunammite." And he did. When she came, he said, "Take your son."ᵘ ³⁷She came in, fell at his feet and bowed to the ground. Then she took her son and went out.

Death in the Pot

³⁸Elisha returned to Gilgalᵛ and there was a famineʷ in that region. While the company of the prophets was meeting with him, he said to his servant, "Put on the large pot and cook some stew for these men."

³⁹One of them went out into the fields to gather herbs and found a wild vine. He gathered some of its gourds and filled the fold of his cloak. When he returned, he cut them up into the pot of stew, though no one knew what they were. ⁴⁰The stew was poured out for the men, but as they began to eat it, they cried out, "O man of God, there is death in the pot!" And they could not eat it.

⁴¹Elisha said, "Get some flour." He put it into the pot and said, "Serve it to the people to eat." And there was nothing harmful in the pot.ˣ

Feeding of a Hundred

⁴²A man came from Baal Shalishah,ʸ bringing the man of God twenty loavesᶻ of barley breadᵃ baked from the first ripe grain, along with some heads of new grain. "Give it to the people to eat," Elisha said.

⁴³"How can I set this before a hundred men?" his servant asked.

But Elisha answered, "Give it to the people to eat.ᵇ For this is what the Lᴏʀᴅ says: 'They will eat and have some left over.'ᶜ " ⁴⁴Then he set it before them, and they ate and had some left over, according to the word of the Lᴏʀᴅ.

Naaman Healed of Leprosy

5 Now Naaman was commander of the army of the king of Aram.ᵈ He was a great man in the sight of his master and highly regarded, because through him the Lᴏʀᴅ had given victory to Aram. He was a valiant soldier, but he had leprosy.ᵃ ᵉ

²Now bandsᶠ from Aram had gone out and had taken captive a young girl from Israel, and she served Naaman's wife. ³She said to her mistress, "If only my master would see the prophetᵍ who is in Samaria! He would cure him of his leprosy."

⁴Naaman went to his master and told him what the girl from Israel had said. ⁵"By all means, go," the king of Aram replied. "I will send a letter to the king of Israel." So Naaman left, taking with him ten

---

4:32
pver 21
4:33
q1Ki 17:20;
Mt 6:6
4:34
r1Ki 17:21;
Ac 20:10
4:35
sJos 6:15
t2Ki 8:5
4:36
uHeb 11:35
4:38
v2Ki 2:1
wLev 26:26;
2Ki 8:1
4:41
xEx 15:25;
2Ki 2:21
4:42
y1Sa 9:4
zMt 14:17;
15:36 a1Sa 9:7
4:43
bLk 9:13
cMt 14:20;
Jn 6:12
5:1
dGe 10:22;
2Sa 10:19
eEx 4:6;
Nu 12:10;
Lk 4:27
5:2
f2Ki 6:23;
13:20; 24:2
5:3
gGe 20:7

ᵃ1 The Hebrew word was used for various diseases affecting the skin—not necessarily leprosy; also in verses 3, 6, 7, 11 and 27.

talents*a* of silver, six thousand shekels*b* of gold and ten sets of clothing. *h* 6The letter that he took to the king of Israel read: "With this letter I am sending my servant Naaman to you so that you may cure him of his leprosy."

7As soon as the king of Israel read the letter,*i* he tore his robes and said, "Am I God?*j* Can I kill and bring back to life?*k* Why does this fellow send someone to me to be cured of his leprosy? See how he is trying to pick a quarrel*l* with me!"

8When Elisha the man of God heard that the king of Israel had torn his robes, he sent him this message: "Why have you torn your robes? Have the man come to me and he will know that there is a prophet*m* in Israel." 9So Naaman went with his horses and chariots and stopped at the door of Elisha's house. 10Elisha sent a messenger to say to him, "Go, wash*n* yourself seven times*o* in the Jordan, and your flesh will be restored and you will be cleansed."

11But Naaman went away angry and said, "I thought that he would surely come out to me and stand and call on the name of the LORD his God, wave his hand*p* over the spot and cure me of my leprosy. 12Are not Abana and Pharpar, the rivers of Damascus, better than any of the waters*q* of Israel? Couldn't I wash in them and be cleansed?" So he turned and went off in a rage.*r*

13Naaman's servants went to him and said, "My father,*s* if the prophet had told you to do some great thing, would you not have done it? How much more, then, when he tells you, 'Wash and be cleansed'!" 14So he went down and dipped himself in the Jordan seven times,*t* as the man of God had told him, and his flesh was restored*u* and became clean like that of a young boy.*v*

15Then Naaman and all his attendants went back to the man of God*w*. He stood before him and said, "Now I know*x* that there is no God in all the world except in Israel. Please accept now a gift*y* from your servant."

16The prophet answered, "As surely as the LORD lives, whom I serve, I will not accept a thing." And even though Naaman urged him, he refused.*z*

17"If you will not," said Naaman, "please let me, your servant, be given as much earth*a* as a pair of mules can carry, for your servant will never again make burnt offerings and sacrifices to any other god but the LORD. 18But may the LORD forgive your servant for this one thing: When my master enters the temple of Rimmon to bow down and he is leaning*b* on my arm and I bow there also—when I bow down in the temple of Rimmon, may the LORD forgive your servant for this."

19"Go in peace,"*c* Elisha said.

After Naaman had traveled some distance, 20Gehazi, the servant of Elisha the man of God, said to himself, "My master was too easy on Naaman, this Aramean, by not accepting from him what he brought. As surely as the LORD*d* lives, I will run after him and get something from him."

21So Gehazi hurried after Naaman. When Naaman saw him running

5:5
hver 22;
Ge 24:53;
Jdg 14:12;
1Sa 9:7
5:7
i2Ki 19:14
jGe 30:2
kDt 32:39;
1Sa 2:6
l1Ki 20:7
5:8
m1Ki 22:7
5:10
nJn 9:7
oGe 33:3;
Lev 14:7
5:11
pEx 7:19
5:12
qIsa 8:6
rPr 14:17,29;
19:11; 29:11
5:13
s2Ki 6:21; 13:14
5:14
tGe 33:3;
Lev 14:7;
Jos 6:15 uEx 4:7
vJob 33:25;
Lk 4:27
5:15
wJos 2:11
xJos 4:24;
1Sa 9:7; 25:27
yJos 9:7; 25:27
5:16
zver 20,26;
Ge 14:23;
Da 5:17
5:17
aEx 20:24
5:18
b2Ki 7:2
5:19
c1Sa 1:17;
Ac 15:33
5:20
dEx 20:7

---

a5 That is, about 750 pounds (about 340 kilograms)   *b5* That is, about 150 pounds (about 70 kilograms) toward him, he got down from the chariot to meet him. "Is everything all right?" he asked.

22"Everything is all right," Gehazi answered. "My master sent me to say, 'Two young men from the company of the prophets have just come to me from the hill country of Ephraim. Please give them a talent[a] of silver and two sets of clothing.' "[e]

23"By all means, take two talents," said Naaman. He urged Gehazi to accept them, and then tied up the two talents of silver in two bags, with two sets of clothing. He gave them to two of his servants, and they carried them ahead of Gehazi. 24When Gehazi came to the hill, he took the things from the servants and put them away in the house. He sent the men away and they left. 25Then he went in and stood before his master Elisha.

"Where have you been, Gehazi?" Elisha asked.

"Your servant didn't go anywhere," Gehazi answered.

26But Elisha said to him, "Was not my spirit with you when the man got down from his chariot to meet you? Is this the time[f] to take money, or to accept clothes, olive groves, vineyards, flocks, herds, or menservants and maidservants?[g] 27Naaman's leprosy[h] will cling to you and to your descendants forever." Then Gehazi[i] went from Elisha's presence and he was leprous, as white as snow.[j]

An Axhead Floats

6 The company[k] of the prophets said to Elisha, "Look, the place where we meet with you is too small for us. 2Let us go to the Jordan, where each of us can get a pole; and let us build a place there for us to live."

And he said, "Go."

3Then one of them said, "Won't you please come with your servants?"

"I will," Elisha replied. 4And he went with them.

They went to the Jordan and began to cut down trees. 5As one of them was cutting down a tree, the iron axhead fell into the water. "Oh, my lord," he cried out, "it was borrowed!"

6The man of God asked, "Where did it fall?" When he showed him the place, Elisha cut a stick and threw[1] it there, and made the iron float. 7"Lift it out," he said. Then the man reached out his hand and took it.

Elisha Traps Blinded Arameans

8Now the king of Aram was at war with Israel. After conferring with his officers, he said, "I will set up my camp in such and such a place."

9The man of God sent word to the king[m] of Israel: "Beware of passing that place, because the Arameans are going down there." 10So the king of Israel checked on the place indicated by the man of God. Time and again Elisha warned[n] the king, so that he was on his guard in such places.

11This enraged the king of Aram. He summoned his officers and demanded of them, "Will you not tell me which of us is on the side of the king of Israel?"

12"None of us, my lord the king[o]," said one of his officers, "but

5:22 ever 5; Ge 45:22
5:26 fver 16 gJer 45:5
5:27 hNu 12:10; 2Ki 15:5 iCol 3:5 jEx 4:6
6:1 k1Sa 10:5; 2Ki 4:38
6:6 lEx 15:25; 2Ki 2:21
6:9 mver 12
6:10 nJer 11:18
6:12 over 9

Elisha, the prophet who is in Israel, tells the king of Israel the very words you speak in your bedroom."

¹³"Go, find out where he is," the king ordered, "so I can send men and capture him." The report came back: "He is in Dothan."ᵖ ¹⁴Then he sent�q horses and chariots and a strong force there. They went by night and surrounded the city.

¹⁵When the servant of the man of God got up and went out early the next morning, an army with horses and chariots had surrounded the city. "Oh, my lord, what shall we do?" the servant asked.

¹⁶"Don't be afraid,"ʳ the prophet answered. "Those who are with us are moreˢ than those who are with them."

¹⁷And Elisha prayed, "O LORD, open his eyes so he may see." Then the LORD opened the servant's eyes, and he looked and saw the hills full of horses and chariotsᵗ of fire all around Elisha.

¹⁸As the enemy came down toward him, Elisha prayed to the LORD, "Strike these people with blindness."ᵘ So he struck them with blindness, as Elisha had asked.

¹⁹Elisha told them, "This is not the road and this is not the city. Follow me, and I will lead you to the man you are looking for." And he led them to Samaria.

²⁰After they entered the city, Elisha said, "LORD, open the eyes of these men so they can see." Then the LORD opened their eyes and they looked, and there they were, inside Samaria.

²¹When the king of Israel saw them, he asked Elisha, "Shall I kill them, my father?ᵛ Shall I kill them?"

²²"Do not kill them," he answered. "Would you kill men you have capturedʷ with your own sword or bow? Set food and water before them so that they may eat and drink and then go back to their master." ²³So he prepared a great feast for them, and after they had finished eating and drinking, he sent them away, and they returned to their master. So the bandsˣ from Aram stopped raiding Israel's territory.

Famine in Besieged Samaria

²⁴Some time later, Ben-Hadadʸ king of Aram mobilized his entire army and marched up and laid siegeᶻ to Samaria. ²⁵There was a great famineª in the city; the siege lasted so long that a donkey's head sold for eighty shekelsª of silver, and a quarter of a cabᵇ of seed podsᶜᵇ for five shekels.ᵈ

²⁶As the king of Israel was passing by on the wall, a woman cried to him, "Help me, my lord the king!"

²⁷The king replied, "If the LORD does not help you, where can I get help for you? From the threshing floor? From the winepress?" ²⁸Then he asked her, "What's the matter?"

She answered, "This woman said to me, 'Give up your son so we may eat him today, and tomorrow we'll eat my son.' ²⁹So we cooked my son and ateᶜ him. The next day I said to her, 'Give up your son so we may eat him,' but she had hidden him."

³⁰When the king heard the woman's words, he toreᵈ his robes. As he went along the wall, the people looked, and there, underneath, he had

---

Cross references (left margin):

6:13
pGe 37:17
6:14
q2Ki 1:9
6:16
rGe 15:1
s2Ch 32:7;
Ps 55:18;
Ro 8:31; 1Jn 4:4
6:17
t2Ki 2:11,12;
Ps 68:17;
Zec 6:1-7
6:18
uGe 19:11;
Ac 13:11
6:21
v2Ki 5:13
6:22
wDt 20:11;
2Ch 28:8-15;
Ro 12:20
6:23
x2Ki 5:2
6:24
y1Ki 15:18;
20:1; 2Ki 8:7
zDt 28:52
6:25
aLev 26:26;
Ru 1:1
bIsa 36:12
6:29
cLev 26:29;
Dt 28:53-55
6:30
d2Ki 18:37;
Isa 22:15

ª25 That is, about 2 pounds (about 1 kilogram)   ᵇ25 That is, probably about 1/2 pint (about 0.3 liter)   ᶜ25 Or *of dove's dung*   ᵈ25 That is, about 2 ounces (about 55 grams) sackcloth[e] on his body. [31]He said, "May God deal with me, be it ever so severely, if the head of Elisha son of Shaphat remains on his shoulders today!"

[32]Now Elisha was sitting in his house, and the elders[f] were sitting with him. The king sent a messenger ahead, but before he arrived, Elisha said to the elders, "Don't you see how this murderer[g] is sending someone to cut off my head?[h] Look, when the messenger comes, shut the door and hold it shut against him. Is not the sound of his master's footsteps behind him?"

[33]While he was still talking to them, the messenger came down to him. And ˌthe kingˌ said, "This disaster is from the Lord. Why should I wait[i] for the Lord any longer?"

7 Elisha said, "Hear the word of the Lord. This is what the Lord says: About this time tomorrow, a seah[a] of flour will sell for a shekel[b] and two seahs[c] of barley for a shekel[j] at the gate of Samaria."

[2]The officer on whose arm the king was leaning[k] said to the man of God, "Look, even if the Lord should open the floodgates[l] of the heavens, could this happen?"

"You will see it with your own eyes," answered Elisha, "but you will not eat[m] any of it!"

The Siege Lifted

[3]Now there were four men with leprosy[d][n] at the entrance of the city gate. They said to each other, "Why stay here until we die? [4]If we say, 'We'll go into the city'—the famine is there, and we will die. And if we stay here, we will die. So let's go over to the camp of the Arameans and surrender. If they spare us, we live; if they kill us, then we die."

[5]At dusk they got up and went to the camp of the Arameans. When they reached the edge of the camp, not a man was there, [6]for the Lord had caused the Arameans to hear the sound[o] of chariots and horses and a great army, so that they said to one another, "Look, the king of Israel has hired[p] the Hittite[q] and Egyptian kings to attack us!" [7]So they got up and fled[r] in the dusk and abandoned their tents and their horses and donkeys. They left the camp as it was and ran for their lives.

[8]The men who had leprosy[s] reached the edge of the camp and entered one of the tents. They ate and drank, and carried away silver, gold and clothes, and went off and hid them. They returned and entered another tent and took some things from it and hid them also.

[9]Then they said to each other, "We're not doing right. This is a day of good news and we are keeping it to ourselves. If we wait until daylight, punishment will overtake us. Let's go at once and report this to the royal palace."

[10]So they went and called out to the city gatekeepers and told them, "We went into the Aramean camp and not a man was there—not a sound of anyone—only tethered horses and donkeys, and the tents left just as they were." [11]The gatekeepers shouted the news, and it was reported within the palace.

[12]The king got up in the night and said to his officers, "I will tell you

6:30
eGe 37:34;
1Ki 21:27
6:32
fEze 8:1; 14:1;
20:1 g1Ki 18:4
hver 31
6:33
iLev 24:11;
Job 2:9; 14:14;
Isa 40:31
7:1
jver 16
7:2
k2Ki 5:18
lver 19;
Ge 7:11;
Ps 78:23;
Mal 3:10
mver 17
7:3
nLev 13:45-46;
Nu 5:1-4
7:6
oEx 14:24;
2Sa 5:24;
Eze 1:24
p2Sa 10:6;
Jer 46:21
qNu 13:29
7:7
rJdg 7:21;
Ps 48:4-6;
Pr 28:1;
Isa 30:17
7:8
sIsa 33:23; 35:6

---

[a]1 That is, probably about 7 quarts (about 7.3 liters); also in verses 16 and 18   [b]1 That is, about 2/5 ounce (about 11 grams); also in verses 16 and 18   [c]1 That is, probably about 13 quarts (about 15 liters); also in verses 16 and 18   [d]3 The Hebrew word is used for various diseases affecting the skin—not necessarily leprosy; also in verse 8.

what the Arameans have done to us. They know we are starving; so they have left the camp to hide[t] in the countryside, thinking, 'They will surely come out, and then we will take them alive and get into the city.' "

13One of his officers answered, "Have some men take five of the horses that are left in the city. Their plight will be like that of all the Israelites left here—yes, they will only be like all these Israelites who are doomed. So let us send them to find out what happened."

14So they selected two chariots with their horses, and the king sent them after the Aramean army. He commanded the drivers, "Go and find out what has happened." 15They followed them as far as the Jordan, and they found the whole road strewn with the clothing and equipment the Arameans had thrown away in their headlong flight. So the messengers returned and reported to the king. 16Then the people went out and plundered[u] the camp of the Arameans. So a seah of flour sold for a shekel, and two seahs of barley sold for a shekel,[v] as the LORD had said.

17Now the king had put the officer on whose arm he leaned in charge of the gate, and the people trampled him in the gateway, and he died,[w] just as the man of God had foretold when the king came down to his house. 18It happened as the man of God had said to the king: "About this time tomorrow, a seah of flour will sell for a shekel and two seahs of barley for a shekel at the gate of Samaria."

19The officer had said to the man of God, "Look, even if the LORD should open the floodgates[x] of the heavens, could this happen?" The man of God had replied, "You will see it with your own eyes, but you will not eat any of it!" 20And that is exactly what happened to him, for the people trampled him in the gateway, and he died.

The Shunammite's Land Restored

8 Now Elisha had said to the woman[y] whose son he had restored to life, "Go away with your family and stay for a while wherever you can, because the LORD has decreed a famine[z] in the land that will last seven years."[a] 2The woman proceeded to do as the man of God said. She and her family went away and stayed in the land of the Philistines seven years.

3At the end of the seven years she came back from the land of the Philistines and went to the king to beg for her house and land. 4The king was talking to Gehazi, the servant of the man of God, and had said, "Tell me about all the great things Elisha has done." 5Just as Gehazi was telling the king how Elisha had restored[b] the dead to life, the woman whose son Elisha had brought back to life came to beg the king for her house and land.

Gehazi said, "This is the woman, my lord the king, and this is her son whom Elisha restored to life." 6The king asked the woman about it, and she told him.

Then he assigned an official to her case and said to him, "Give back everything that belonged to her, including all the income from her land from the day she left the country until now."

Hazael Murders Ben-Hadad

7Elisha went to Damascus,[c] and Ben-Hadad[d] king of Aram was ill.

7:12
t Jos 8:4;
2Ki 6:25-29
7:16
u Isa 33:4,23
v ver 1
7:17
w ver 2; 2Ki 6:32
7:19
x ver 2
8:1
y 2Ki 4:8-37
z Lev 26:26;
Dt 28:22;
Ru 1:1
a Ge 12:10;
Ps 105:16;
Hag 1:11
8:5
b 2Ki 4:35
8:7
c 2Sa 8:5;
1Ki 11:24
d 2Ki 6:24

When the king was told, "The man of God has come all the way up here," [8]he said to Hazael, [e] "Take a gift[f] with you and go to meet the man of God. Consult[g] the LORD through him; ask him, 'Will I recover from this illness?'"

[9]Hazael went to meet Elisha, taking with him as a gift forty camel-loads of all the finest wares of Damascus. He went in and stood before him, and said, "Your son Ben-Hadad king of Aram has sent me to ask, 'Will I recover from this illness?'"

[10]Elisha answered, "Go and say to him, 'You will certainly recover';[h] but[a] the LORD has revealed to me that he will in fact die." [11]He stared at him with a fixed gaze until Hazael felt ashamed.[i] Then the man of God began to weep.[j]

[12]"Why is my lord weeping?" asked Hazael.

"Because I know the harm[k] you will do to the Israelites," he answered. "You will set fire to their fortified places, kill their young men with the sword, dash[l] their little children[m] to the ground, and rip open[n] their pregnant women."

[13]Hazael said, "How could your servant, a mere dog,[o] accomplish such a feat?"

"The LORD has shown me that you will become king[p] of Aram," answered Elisha.

[14]Then Hazael left Elisha and returned to his master. When Ben-Hadad asked, "What did Elisha say to you?" Hazael replied, "He told me that you would certainly recover." [15]But the next day he took a thick cloth, soaked it in water and spread it over the king's face, so that he died.[q] Then Hazael succeeded him as king.

Jehoram King of Judah
8:16–24pp — 2Ch 21:5–10,20

[16]In the fifth year of Joram[r] son of Ahab king of Israel, when Jehoshaphat was king of Judah, Jehoram[s] son of Jehoshaphat began his reign as king of Judah. [17]He was thirty-two years old when he became king, and he reigned in Jerusalem eight years. [18]He walked in the ways of the kings of Israel, as the house of Ahab had done, for he married a daughter[t] of Ahab. He did evil in the eyes of the LORD. [19]Nevertheless, for the sake of his servant David, the LORD was not willing to destroy[u] Judah. He had promised to maintain a lamp[v] for David and his descendants forever.

[20]In the time of Jehoram, Edom rebelled against Judah and set up its own king.[w] [21]So Jehoram[b] went to Zair with all his chariots. The Edomites surrounded him and his chariot commanders, but he rose up and broke through by night; his army, however, fled back home. [22]To this day Edom has been in rebellion[x] against Judah. Libnah[y] revolted at the same time.

[23]As for the other events of Jehoram's reign, and all he did, are they not written in the book of the annals of the kings of Judah? [24]Jehoram rested with his fathers and was buried with them in the City of David. And Ahaziah his son succeeded him as king.

---

[a]10 The Hebrew may also be read *Go and say, 'You will certainly not recover,' for.*	[b]21 Hebrew *Joram,* a variant of *Jehoram*; also in verses 23 and 24

8:8
e1Ki 19:15
f Ge 32:20;
1Sa 9:7; 2Ki 1:2
g Jdg 18:5
8:10
h Isa 38:1
8:11
i Jdg 3:25
j Lk 19:41
8:12
k 1Ki 19:17;
2Ki 10:32;
12:17; 13:3,7
l Ps 137:9;
Isa 13:16;
Hos 13:16;
Na 3:10;
Lk 19:44
m Ge 34:29
n 2Ki 15:16;
Am 1:13
8:13
o 1Sa 17:43;
2Sa 3:8
p 1Ki 19:15
8:15
q 2Ki 1:17
8:16
r 2Ki 1:17; 3:1
s 2Ch 21:1-4
8:18
t ver 26;
2Ki 11:1
8:19
u Ge 6:13
v 2Sa 21:17;
7:13; 1Ki 11:36;
Rev 21:23
8:20
w 1Ki 22:47
8:22
x Ge 27:40
y Nu 33:20;
Jos 21:13;
2Ki 19:8

Ahaziah King of Judah

8:25-29pp — 2Ch 22:1-6

25In the twelfth[z] year of Joram son of Ahab king of Israel, Ahaziah son of Jehoram king of Judah began to reign. 26Ahaziah was twenty-two years old when he became king, and he reigned in Jerusalem one year. His mother's name was Athaliah,[a] a granddaughter of Omri[b] king of Israel. 27He walked in the ways of the house of Ahab[c] and did evil[d] in the eyes of the LORD, as the house of Ahab had done, for he was related by marriage to Ahab's family.

28Ahaziah went with Joram son of Ahab to war against Hazael king of Aram at Ramoth Gilead.[e] The Arameans wounded Joram; 29so King Joram returned to Jezreel[f] to recover from the wounds the Arameans had inflicted on him at Ramoth[a] in his battle with Hazael[g] king of Aram.

Then Ahaziah son of Jehoram king of Judah went down to Jezreel to see Joram son of Ahab, because he had been wounded.

Jehu Anointed King of Israel

9 The prophet Elisha summoned a man from the company[h] of the prophets and said to him, "Tuck your cloak into your belt,[i] take this flask of oil[j] with you and go to Ramoth Gilead.[k] 2When you get there, look for Jehu son of Jehoshaphat, the son of Nimshi. Go to him, get him away from his companions and take him into an inner room. 3Then take the flask and pour the oil[l] on his head and declare, 'This is what the LORD says: I anoint you king over Israel.' Then open the door and run; don't delay!"

4So the young man, the prophet, went to Ramoth Gilead. 5When he arrived, he found the army officers sitting together. "I have a message for you, commander," he said.

"For which of us?" asked Jehu.

"For you, commander," he replied.

6Jehu got up and went into the house. Then the prophet poured the oil[m] on Jehu's head and declared, "This is what the LORD, the God of Israel, says: 'I anoint you king over the LORD's people Israel. 7You are to destroy the house of Ahab your master, and I will avenge[n] the blood of my servants[o] the prophets and the blood of all the LORD's servants shed by Jezebel.[p] 8The whole house[q] of Ahab will perish. I will cut off from Ahab every last male[r] in Israel—slave or free. 9I will make the house of Ahab like the house of Jeroboam[s] son of Nebat and like the house of Baasha[t] son of Ahijah. 10As for Jezebel, dogs[u] will devour her on the plot of ground at Jezreel, and no one will bury her.'" Then he opened the door and ran.

11When Jehu went out to his fellow officers, one of them asked him, "Is everything all right? Why did this madman[v] come to you?"

"You know the man and the sort of things he says," Jehu replied.

12"That's not true!" they said. "Tell us."

Jehu said, "Here is what he told me: 'This is what the LORD says: I anoint you king over Israel.'"

13They hurried and took their cloaks and spread[w] them under him on

---

**Cross-references (margin):**

8:25
z2Ki 9:29
8:26
aver 18
b1Ki 16:23
8:27
c1Ki 16:30
d1Ki 15:26
8:28
eDt 4:43;
1Ki 22:3,29
8:29
f2Ki 9:15
g1Ki 19:15,17
9:1
h1Sa 10:5
i2Ki 4:29
j1Sa 10:1
k2Ki 8:28
9:3
l1Ki 19:16
9:6
m1Ki 19:16;
2Ch 22:7
9:7
nGe 4:24;
Rev 6:10
oDt 32:43
p1Ki 18:4; 21:15
9:8
q2Ki 10:17
rDt 32:36;
1Sa 25:22;
1Ki 21:21;
2Ki 14:26
9:9
s1Ki 14:10;
15:29; 16:3,11
t1Ki 16:3
9:10
uver 35-36;
1Ki 21:23
9:11
vJer 29:26;
Jn 10:20;
Ac 26:24
9:13
wMt 21:8;
Lk 19:36

the bare steps. Then they blew the trumpet[x] and shouted, "Jehu is king!"

Jehu Kills Joram and Ahaziah

9:21-29pp — 2Ch 22:7-9

[14]So Jehu son of Jehoshaphat, the son of Nimshi, conspired against Joram. (Now Joram and all Israel had been defending Ramoth Gilead[y] against Hazael king of Aram, [15]but King Joram[a] had returned to Jezreel to recover[z] from the wounds the Arameans had inflicted on him in the battle with Hazael king of Aram.) Jehu said, "If this is the way you feel, don't let anyone slip out of the city to go and tell the news in Jezreel." [16]Then he got into his chariot and rode to Jezreel, because Joram was resting there and Ahaziah[a] king of Judah had gone down to see him.

[17]When the lookout[b] standing on the tower in Jezreel saw Jehu's troops approaching, he called out, "I see some troops coming."

"Get a horseman," Joram ordered. "Send him to meet them and ask, 'Do you come in peace?'[c]"

[18]The horseman rode off to meet Jehu and said, "This is what the king says: 'Do you come in peace?'"

"What do you have to do with peace?" Jehu replied. "Fall in behind me."

The lookout reported, "The messenger has reached them, but he isn't coming back."

[19]So the king sent out a second horseman. When he came to them he said, "This is what the king says: 'Do you come in peace?'"

Jehu replied, "What do you have to do with peace? Fall in behind me."

[20]The lookout reported, "He has reached them, but he isn't coming back either. The driving is like[d] that of Jehu son of Nimshi—he drives like a madman."

[21]"Hitch up my chariot," Joram ordered. And when it was hitched up, Joram king of Israel and Ahaziah king of Judah rode out, each in his own chariot, to meet Jehu. They met him at the plot of ground that had belonged to Naboth[e] the Jezreelite. [22]When Joram saw Jehu he asked, "Have you come in peace, Jehu?"

"How can there be peace," Jehu replied, "as long as all the idolatry and witchcraft of your mother Jezebel[f] abound?"

[23]Joram turned about and fled, calling out to Ahaziah, "Treachery,[g] Ahaziah!"

[24]Then Jehu drew his bow[h] and shot Joram between the shoulders. The arrow pierced his heart and he slumped down in his chariot. [25]Jehu said to Bidkar, his chariot officer, "Pick him up and throw him on the field that belonged to Naboth the Jezreelite. Remember how you and I were riding together in chariots behind Ahab his father when the LORD made this prophecy[i] about him: [26]'Yesterday I saw the blood of Naboth[j] and the blood of his sons, declares the LORD, and I will surely make you pay for it on this plot of ground, declares the LORD.'[b] Now then, pick him up and throw him on that plot, in accordance with the word of the LORD."[k]

[27]When Ahaziah king of Judah saw what had happened, he fled up

9:13
x2Sa 15:10;
1Ki 1:34,39
9:14
yDt 4:43;
2Ki 8:28
9:15
z2Ki 8:29
9:16
a2Ch 22:7
9:17
bIsa 21:6
c1Sa 16:4
9:20
d2Sa 18:27
9:21
ever 26;
1Ki 21:1-7,15-19
9:22
f1Ki 16:30-33;
18:19;
2Ch 21:13;
Rev 2:20
9:23
g2Ki 11:14
9:24
h1Ki 22:34
9:25
i1Ki 21:19-22,
24-29
9:26
j1Ki 21:19
k1Ki 21:29

---

[a]15 Hebrew *Jehoram*, a variant of *Joram*; also in verses 17 and 21-24   [b]26 See 1 Kings 21:19.

the road to Beth Haggan. *a* Jehu chased him, shouting, "Kill him too!" They wounded him in his chariot on the way up to Gur near Ibleam, [l] but he escaped to Megiddo [m] and died there. [28]His servants took him by chariot [n] to Jerusalem and buried him with his fathers in his tomb in the City of David. [29](In the eleventh [o] year of Joram son of Ahab, Ahaziah had become king of Judah.)

Jezebel Killed

[30]Then Jehu went to Jezreel. When Jezebel heard about it, she painted [p] her eyes, arranged her hair and looked out of a window. [31]As Jehu entered the gate, she asked, "Have you come in peace, Zimri, [q] you murderer of your master?" [b]

[32]He looked up at the window and called out, "Who is on my side? Who?" Two or three eunuchs looked down at him. [33]"Throw her down!" Jehu said. So they threw her down, and some of her blood spattered the wall and the horses as they trampled her underfoot. [r]

[34]Jehu went in and ate and drank. "Take care of that cursed woman," he said, "and bury her, for she was a king's daughter." [s] [35]But when they went out to bury her, they found nothing except her skull, her feet and her hands. [36]They went back and told Jehu, who said, "This is the word of the LORD that he spoke through his servant Elijah the Tishbite: On the plot of ground at Jezreel dogs [t] will devour Jezebel's flesh. [c] [u] [37]Jezebel's body will be like refuse [v] on the ground in the plot at Jezreel, so that no one will be able to say, 'This is Jezebel.' "

Ahab's Family Killed

10 Now there were in Samaria [w] seventy sons [x] of the house of Ahab. So Jehu wrote letters and sent them to Samaria: to the officials of Jezreel, [d] [y] to the elders and to the guardians [z] of Ahab's children. He said, [2]"As soon as this letter reaches you, since your master's sons are with you and you have chariots and horses, a fortified city and weapons, [3]choose the best and most worthy of your master's sons and set him on his father's throne. Then fight for your master's house."

[4]But they were terrified and said, "If two kings could not resist him, how can we?"

[5]So the palace administrator, the city governor, the elders and the guardians sent this message to Jehu: "We are your servants [a] and we will do anything you say. We will not appoint anyone as king; you do whatever you think best."

[6]Then Jehu wrote them a second letter, saying, "If you are on my side and will obey me, take the heads of your master's sons and come to me in Jezreel by this time tomorrow."

Now the royal princes, seventy of them, were with the leading men of the city, who were rearing them. [7]When the letter arrived, these men took the princes and slaughtered all seventy [b] of them. They put their heads [c] in baskets and sent them to Jehu in Jezreel. [8]When the messenger arrived, he told Jehu, "They have brought the heads of the princes."

9:27
l Jdg 1:27
m 2Ki 23:29
9:28
n 2Ki 14:20;
23:30
9:29
o 2Ki 8:25
9:30
p Jer 4:30;
Eze 23:40
9:31
q 1Ki 16:9-10
9:33
r Ps 7:5
9:34
s 1Ki 16:31;
21:25
9:36
t Ps 68:23;
Jer 15:3
u 1Ki 21:23
9:37
v Ps 83:10;
Isa 5:25;
Jer 8:2; 9:22;
16:4; 25:33;
Zep 1:17
10:1
w 1Ki 13:32
x Jdg 8:30
y 1Ki 21:1 zver 5
10:5
a Jos 9:8;
1Ki 20:4,32
10:7
b 1Ki 21:21
c 2Sa 4:8

---

*a*27 Or *fled by way of the garden house*   *b*31 Or *"Did Zimri have peace, who murdered his master?"*   *c*36 See 1 Kings 21:23.   *d*1 Hebrew; some Septuagint manuscripts and Vulgate *of the city*

Then Jehu ordered, "Put them in two piles at the entrance of the city gate until morning."

[9]The next morning Jehu went out. He stood before all the people and said, "You are innocent. It was I who conspired against my master and killed him, but who killed all these? [10]Know then, that not a word the LORD has spoken against the house of Ahab will fail. The LORD has done what he promised[d] through his servant Elijah."[e] [11]So Jehu[f] killed everyone in Jezreel who remained of the house of Ahab, as well as all his chief men, his close friends and his priests, leaving him no survivor.[g]

[12]Jehu then set out and went toward Samaria. At Beth Eked of the Shepherds, [13]he met some relatives of Ahaziah king of Judah and asked, "Who are you?"

They said, "We are relatives of Ahaziah,[h] and we have come down to greet the families of the king and of the queen mother.[i]"

[14]"Take them alive!" he ordered. So they took them alive and slaughtered them by the well of Beth Eked—forty-two men. He left no survivor.

[15]After he left there, he came upon Jehonadab[j] son of Recab,[k] who was on his way to meet him. Jehu greeted him and said, "Are you in accord with me, as I am with you?"

"I am," Jehonadab answered.

"If so," said Jehu, "give me your hand."[l] So he did, and Jehu helped him up into the chariot. [16]Jehu said, "Come with me and see my zeal[m] for the LORD." Then he had him ride along in his chariot.

[17]When Jehu came to Samaria, he killed all who were left there of Ahab's family;[n] he destroyed them, according to the word of the LORD spoken to Elijah.

Ministers of Baal Killed

[18]Then Jehu brought all the people together and said to them, "Ahab served[o] Baal a little; Jehu will serve him much. [19]Now summon[p] all the prophets of Baal, all his ministers and all his priests. See that no one is missing, because I am going to hold a great sacrifice for Baal. Anyone who fails to come will no longer live." But Jehu was acting deceptively in order to destroy the ministers of Baal.

[20]Jehu said, "Call an assembly[q] in honor of Baal." So they proclaimed it. [21]Then he sent word throughout Israel, and all the ministers of Baal came; not one stayed away. They crowded into the temple of Baal until it was full from one end to the other. [22]And Jehu said to the keeper of the wardrobe, "Bring robes for all the ministers of Baal." So he brought out robes for them.

[23]Then Jehu and Jehonadab son of Recab went into the temple of Baal. Jehu said to the ministers of Baal, "Look around and see that no servants of the LORD are here with you—only ministers of Baal." [24]So they went in to make sacrifices and burnt offerings. Now Jehu had posted eighty men outside with this warning: "If one of you lets any of the men I am placing in your hands escape, it will be your life for his life."[r]

[25]As soon as Jehu had finished making the burnt offering, he ordered the guards and officers: "Go in and kill[s] them; let no one escape."[t] So they cut them down with the sword. The guards and officers threw the

---

10:10
d2Ki 9:7-10
e1Ki 21:29

10:11
fHos 1:4
gver 14;
Job 18:19

10:13
h2Ki 8:24,29;
2Ch 22:8
i1Ki 2:19

10:15
jJer 35:6,14-19
k1Ch 2:55;
Jer 35:2
lEzr 10:19;
Eze 17:18

10:16
mNu 25:13;
1Ki 19:10

10:17
n2Ki 9:8

10:18
oJdg 2:11;
1Ki 16:31-32

10:19
p1Ki 18:19; 22:6

10:20
qEx 32:5;
Joel 1:14

10:24
r1Ki 20:39

10:25
sEx 22:20;
2Ki 11:18
t1Ki 18:40

bodies out and then entered the inner shrine of the temple of Baal. ²⁶They brought the sacred stoneᵘ out of the temple of Baal and burned it. ²⁷They demolished the sacred stone of Baal and tore down the templeᵛ of Baal, and people have used it for a latrine to this day.

²⁸So Jehuʷ destroyed Baal worship in Israel. ²⁹However, he did not turn away from the sinsˣ of Jeroboam son of Nebat, which he had caused Israel to commit—the worship of the golden calvesʸ at Bethelᶻ and Dan.

³⁰The Lᴏʀᴅ said to Jehu, "Because you have done well in accomplishing what is right in my eyes and have done to the house of Ahab all I had in mind to do, your descendants will sit on the throne of Israel to the fourth generation."ᵃ ³¹Yet Jehu was not carefulᵇ to keep the law of the Lᴏʀᴅ, the God of Israel, with all his heart. He did not turn away from the sinsᶜ of Jeroboam, which he had caused Israel to commit.

³²In those days the Lᴏʀᴅ began to reduceᵈ the size of Israel. Hazaelᵉ overpowered the Israelites throughout their territory ³³east of the Jordan in all the land of Gilead (the region of Gad, Reuben and Manasseh), from Aroerᶠ by the Arnon Gorge through Gilead to Bashan.

³⁴As for the other events of Jehu's reign, all he did, and all his achievements, are they not written in the book of the annalsᵍ of the kings of Israel?

³⁵Jehu rested with his fathers and was buried in Samaria. And Jehoahaz his son succeeded him as king. ³⁶The time that Jehu reigned over Israel in Samaria was twenty-eight years.

Athaliah and Joash

11:1–21pp — 2Ch 22:10–23:21

11 When Athaliahʰ the mother of Ahaziah saw that her son was dead, she proceeded to destroy the whole royal family. ²But Jehosheba, the daughter of King Jehoramᵃ and sister of Ahaziah, took Joashⁱ son of Ahaziah and stole him away from among the royal princes, who were about to be murdered. She put him and his nurse in a bedroom to hide him from Athaliah; so he was not killed.ʲ ³He remained hidden with his nurse at the temple of the Lᴏʀᴅ for six years while Athaliah ruled the land.

⁴In the seventh year Jehoiada sent for the commanders of units of a hundred, the Caritesᵏ and the guards and had them brought to him at the temple of the Lᴏʀᴅ. He made a covenant with them and put them under oath at the temple of the Lᴏʀᴅ. Then he showed them the king's son. ⁵He commanded them, saying, "This is what you are to do: You who are in the three companies that are going on duty on the Sabbathᴸ—a third of you guarding the royal palace,ᵐ ⁶a third at the Sur Gate, and a third at the gate behind the guard, who take turns guarding the temple— ⁷and you who are in the other two companies that normally go off Sabbath duty are all to guard the temple for the king. ⁸Station yourselves around the king, each man with his weapon in his hand. Anyone who approaches your ranksᵇ must be put to death. Stay close to the king wherever he goes."

⁹The commanders of units of a hundred did just as Jehoiada the priest ordered. Each one took his men—those who were going on duty

### Cross-references (margin)

10:26
u 1Ki 14:23
10:27
v 1Ki 16:32
10:28
w 1Ki 19:17
10:29
x 1Ki 12:30
y 1Ki 12:28-29
z 1Ki 12:32
10:30
a ver 35;
2Ki 15:12
10:31
b Pr 4:23
c 1Ki 12:30
10:32
d 2Ki 13:25
e 1Ki 19:17;
2Ki 8:12
10:33
f Nu 32:34;
Dt 2:36;
Jdg 11:26;
Isa 17:2
10:34
g 1Ki 15:31
11:1
h 2Ki 8:18
11:2
i ver 21;
2Ki 12:1
j Jdg 9:5
11:4
k ver 19
11:5
l 1Ch 9:25
m 1Ki 14:27

ᵃ2 Hebrew *Joram*, a variant of *Jehoram*   ᵇ8 Or *approaches the precincts* on the Sabbath and those who were going off duty—and came to Jehoiada the priest. [10]Then he gave the commanders the spears and shields[n] that had belonged to King David and that were in the temple of the LORD. [11]The guards, each with his weapon in his hand, stationed themselves around the king—near the altar and the temple, from the south side to the north side of the temple.

[12]Jehoiada brought out the king's son and put the crown on him; he presented him with a copy of the covenant[o] and proclaimed him king. They anointed[p] him, and the people clapped their hands[q] and shouted, "Long live the king!"[r]

[13]When Athaliah heard the noise made by the guards and the people, she went to the people at the temple of the LORD. [14]She looked and there was the king, standing by the pillar,[s] as the custom was. The officers and the trumpeters were beside the king, and all the people of the land were rejoicing and blowing trumpets.[t] Then Athaliah tore[u] her robes and called out, "Treason! Treason!"[v]

[15]Jehoiada the priest ordered the commanders of units of a hundred, who were in charge of the troops: "Bring her out between the ranks[a] and put to the sword anyone who follows her." For the priest had said, "She must not be put to death in the temple[w] of the LORD." [16]So they seized her as she reached the place where the horses enter[x] the palace grounds, and there she was put to death.[y]

[17]Jehoiada then made a covenant[z] between the LORD and the king and people that they would be the LORD's people. He also made a covenant between the king and the people. [a] [18]All the people of the land went to the temple[b] of Baal and tore it down. They smashed[c] the altars and idols to pieces and killed Mattan the priest[d] of Baal in front of the altars.

Then Jehoiada the priest posted guards at the temple of the LORD. [19]He took with him the commanders of hundreds, the Carites,[e] the guards and all the people of the land, and together they brought the king down from the temple of the LORD and went into the palace, entering by way of the gate of the guards. The king then took his place on the royal throne, [20]and all the people of the land rejoiced.[f] And the city was quiet, because Athaliah had been slain with the sword at the palace.

[21]Joash[b] was seven years old when he began to reign.

Joash Repairs the Temple

12:1-21pp — 2Ch 24:1-14; 24:23-27

12 In the seventh year of Jehu, Joash[g] became king, and he reigned in Jerusalem forty years. His mother's name was Zibiah; she was from Beersheba. [2]Joash did what was right in the eyes of the LORD all the years Jehoiada the priest instructed him. [3]The high places,[h] however, were not removed; the people continued to offer sacrifices and burn incense there.

[4]Joash said to the priests, "Collect[i] all the money that is brought as sacred offerings[j] to the temple of the LORD—the money collected in the census,[k] the money received from personal vows and the money

11:10
n2Sa 8:7;
1Ch 18:7
11:12
oEx 25:16;
2Ki 23:3;
p1Sa 9:16;
1Ki 1:39
qPs 47:1; 98:8;
Isa 55:12
r1Sa 10:24
11:14
s1Ki 7:15;
2Ki 23:3;
2Ch 34:31
t1Ki 1:39
uGe 37:29
v2Ki 9:23
11:15
w1Ki 2:30
11:16
xNe 3:28;
Jer 31:40
yGe 4:14
11:17
zEx 24:8;
2Sa 5:3;
2Ch 15:12;
23:3; 29:10;
34:31; Ezr 10:3
a2Ki 23:3;
Jer 34:8
11:18
b1Ki 16:32
cDt 12:3
d1Ki 18:40;
2Ki 10:25; 23:20
11:19
ever 4
11:20
fPr 11:10;
28:12; 29:2
12:1
g2Ki 11:2
12:3
h1Ki 3:3;
2Ki 14:4; 15:35;
18:4
12:4
i2Ki 22:4
jEx 35:5
kEx 30:12

brought voluntarily[1] to the temple. [5]Let every priest receive the money from one of the treasurers, and let it be used to repair whatever damage is found in the temple."

[6]But by the twenty-third year of King Joash the priests still had not repaired the temple. [7]Therefore King Joash summoned Jehoiada the priest and the other priests and asked them, "Why aren't you repairing the damage done to the temple? Take no more money from your treasurers, but hand it over for repairing the temple." [8]The priests agreed that they would not collect any more money from the people and that they would not repair the temple themselves.

[9]Jehoiada the priest took a chest and bored a hole in its lid. He placed it beside the altar, on the right side as one enters the temple of the LORD. The priests who guarded the entrance[m] put into the chest all the money[n] that was brought to the temple of the LORD. [10]Whenever they saw that there was a large amount of money in the chest, the royal secretary[o] and the high priest came, counted the money that had been brought into the temple of the LORD and put it into bags. [11]When the amount had been determined, they gave the money to the men appointed to supervise the work on the temple. With it they paid those who worked on the temple of the LORD—the carpenters and builders, [12]the masons and stonecutters.[p] They purchased timber and dressed stone for the repair of the temple of the LORD, and met all the other expenses of restoring the temple.

[13]The money brought into the temple was not spent for making silver basins, wick trimmers, sprinkling bowls, trumpets or any other articles of gold[q] or silver for the temple of the LORD; [14]it was paid to the workmen, who used it to repair the temple. [15]They did not require an accounting from those to whom they gave the money to pay the workers, because they acted with complete honesty.[r] [16]The money from the guilt offerings[s] and sin offerings[t] was not brought into the temple of the LORD; it belonged[u] to the priests.

[17]About this time Hazael[v] king of Aram went up and attacked Gath and captured it. Then he turned to attack Jerusalem. [18]But Joash king of Judah took all the sacred objects dedicated by his fathers—Jehoshaphat, Jehoram and Ahaziah, the kings of Judah—and the gifts he himself had dedicated and all the gold found in the treasuries of the temple of the LORD and of the royal palace, and he sent[w] them to Hazael king of Aram, who then withdrew[x] from Jerusalem.

[19]As for the other events of the reign of Joash, and all he did, are they not written in the book of the annals of the kings of Judah? [20]His officials[y] conspired against him and assassinated[z] him at Beth Millo,[a] on the road down to Silla. [21]The officials who murdered him were Jozabad son of Shimeath and Jehozabad son of Shomer. He died and was buried with his fathers in the City of David. And Amaziah his son succeeded him as king.

Jehoahaz King of Israel

13 In the twenty-third year of Joash son of Ahaziah king of Judah, Jehoahaz son of Jehu became king of Israel in Samaria, and he reigned seventeen years. [2]He did evil[b] in the eyes of the LORD by following the sins of Jeroboam son of Nebat, which he had caused Israel to commit, and he did not turn away from them. [3]So the LORD's

12:4
lEx 35:29;
1Ch 29:3-9
12:9
mJer 35:4
n2Ch 24:8;
Mk 12:41;
Lk 21:1
12:10
o2Sa 8:17
12:12
p2Ki 22:5-6
12:13
q1Ki 7:48-51;
2Ch 24:14
12:15
r2Ki 22:7;
1Co 4:2
12:16
sLev 5:14-19;
Nu 18:9
tLev 4:1-35
uLev 7:7
12:17
v2Ki 8:12
12:18
w1Ki 15:18;
2Ch 21:16-17
x1Ki 15:21
12:20
y2Ki 14:5
z2Ch 24:25
aJdg 9:6
13:2
b1Ki 12:26-33

anger^c burned against Israel, and for a long time he kept them under the power^d of Hazael king of Aram and Ben-Hadad^e his son.

⁴Then Jehoahaz sought^f the LORD's favor, and the LORD listened to him, for he saw^g how severely the king of Aram was oppressing^h Israel. ⁵The LORD provided a delivererⁱ for Israel, and they escaped from the power of Aram. So the Israelites lived in their own homes as they had before. ⁶But they did not turn away from the sins^j of the house of Jeroboam, which he had caused Israel to commit; they continued in them. Also, the Asherah pole^{ak} remained standing in Samaria.

⁷Nothing had been left^l of the army of Jehoahaz except fifty horsemen, ten chariots and ten thousand foot soldiers, for the king of Aram had destroyed the rest and made them like the dust^m at threshing time.

⁸As for the other events of the reign of Jehoahaz, all he did and his achievements, are they not written in the book of the annals of the kings of Israel? ⁹Jehoahaz rested with his fathers and was buried in Samaria. And Jehoash^b his son succeeded him as king.

Jehoash King of Israel

¹⁰In the thirty-seventh year of Joash king of Judah, Jehoash son of Jehoahaz became king of Israel in Samaria, and he reigned sixteen years. ¹¹He did evil in the eyes of the LORD and did not turn away from any of the sins of Jeroboam son of Nebat, which he had caused Israel to commit; he continued in them.

¹²As for the other events of the reign of Jehoash, all he did and his achievements, including his war against Amaziahⁿ king of Judah, are they not written in the book of the annals^o of the kings of Israel? ¹³Jehoash rested with his fathers, and Jeroboam^p succeeded him on the throne. Jehoash was buried in Samaria with the kings of Israel.

¹⁴Now Elisha was suffering from the illness from which he died. Jehoash king of Israel went down to see him and wept over him. "My father! My father!" he cried. "The chariots^q and horsemen of Israel!"

¹⁵Elisha said, "Get a bow and some arrows,"^r and he did so. ¹⁶"Take the bow in your hands," he said to the king of Israel. When he had taken it, Elisha put his hands on the king's hands.

¹⁷"Open the east window," he said, and he opened it. "Shoot!"^s Elisha said, and he shot. "The LORD's arrow of victory, the arrow of victory over Aram!" Elisha declared. "You will completely destroy the Arameans at Aphek."^t

¹⁸Then he said, "Take the arrows," and the king took them. Elisha told him, "Strike the ground." He struck it three times and stopped. ¹⁹The man of God was angry with him and said, "You should have struck the ground five or six times; then you would have defeated Aram and completely destroyed it. But now you will defeat it only three times."^u

²⁰Elisha died and was buried.

Now Moabite raiders^v used to enter the country every spring. ²¹Once while some Israelites were burying a man, suddenly they saw a band of raiders; so they threw the man's body into Elisha's tomb. When the

13:3
cDt 31:17;
Jdg 2:14
d1Ki 8:12;
12:17; 19:17
ever 24
13:4
fDt 4:29;
Ps 78:34
gEx 3:7; Dt 26:7
h2Ki 14:26
13:5
iver 25;
2Ki 14:25,27
13:6
j1Ki 12:30
k1Ki 16:33
13:7
l2Ki 10:32-33
m2Sa 22:43
13:12
n2Ki 14:15
o1Ki 15:31
13:13
p2Ki 14:23;
Hos 1:1
13:14
q2Ki 2:12
13:15
r1Sa 20:20
13:17
sJos 8:18
t1Ki 20:26
13:19
uver 25
13:20
v2Ki 3:7; 24:2

---

^a6 That is, a symbol of the goddess Asherah; here and elsewhere in 2 Kings   ^b9 Hebrew *Joash*, a variant of *Jehoash*; also in verses 12-14 and 25

body touched Elisha's bones, the man came to life ʷ and stood up on his feet.

²²Hazael king of Aram oppressed ˣ Israel throughout the reign of Jehoahaz. ²³But the LORD was gracious to them and had compassion and showed concern for them because of his covenant ʸ with Abraham, Isaac and Jacob. To this day he has been unwilling to destroy ᶻ them or banish them from his presence. ᵃ

²⁴Hazael king of Aram died, and Ben-Hadad ᵇ his son succeeded him as king. ²⁵Then Jehoash son of Jehoahaz recaptured from Ben-Hadad son of Hazael the towns he had taken in battle from his father Jehoahaz. Three times ᶜ Jehoash defeated him, and so he recovered ᵈ the Israelite towns.

Amaziah King of Judah

14:1-7pp — 2Ch 25:1-4,11-12
14:8-22pp — 2Ch 25:17-26:2

14 In the second year of Jehoash ᵃ son of Jehoahaz king of Israel, Amaziah son of Joash king of Judah began to reign. ²He was twenty-five years old when he became king, and he reigned in Jerusalem twenty-nine years. His mother's name was Jehoaddin; she was from Jerusalem. ³He did what was right in the eyes of the LORD, but not as his father David had done. In everything he followed the example of his father Joash. ⁴The high places, ᵉ however, were not removed; the people continued to offer sacrifices and burn incense there.

⁵After the kingdom was firmly in his grasp, he executed ᶠ the officials ᵍ who had murdered his father the king. ⁶Yet he did not put the sons of the assassins to death, in accordance with what is written in the Book of the Law ʰ of Moses where the LORD commanded: "Fathers shall not be put to death for their children, nor children put to death for their fathers; each is to die for his own sins." ᵇ ⁱ

⁷He was the one who defeated ten thousand Edomites in the Valley of Salt ʲ and captured Sela ᵏ in battle, calling it Joktheel, the name it has to this day.

⁸Then Amaziah sent messengers to Jehoash son of Jehoahaz, the son of Jehu, king of Israel, with the challenge: "Come, meet me face to face."

⁹But Jehoash king of Israel replied to Amaziah king of Judah: "A thistle ˡ in Lebanon sent a message to a cedar in Lebanon, 'Give your daughter to my son in marriage.' Then a wild beast in Lebanon came along and trampled the thistle underfoot. ¹⁰You have indeed defeated Edom and now you are arrogant. ᵐ Glory in your victory, but stay at home! Why ask for trouble and cause your own downfall and that of Judah also?"

¹¹Amaziah, however, would not listen, so Jehoash king of Israel attacked. He and Amaziah king of Judah faced each other at Beth Shemesh ⁿ in Judah. ¹²Judah was routed by Israel, and every man fled to his home. ᵒ ¹³Jehoash king of Israel captured Amaziah king of Judah, the son of Joash, the son of Ahaziah, at Beth Shemesh. Then Jehoash went to Jerusalem and broke down the wall ᵖ of Jerusalem from the Ephraim Gate �q to the Corner Gate ʳ—a section about six hundred feet

### Cross references (margin)

13:21
ʷ Mt 27:52
13:22
ˣ 1Ki 19:17;
2Ki 8:12
13:23
ʸ Ge 13:16-17;
Ex 2:24
ᶻ Dt 29:20
ᵃ Ex 33:15;
2Ki 14:27;
17:18; 24:3,20
13:24
ᵇ ver 3
13:25
ᶜ ver 18,19
ᵈ 2Ki 10:32
14:4
ᵉ 2Ki 12:3; 16:4
14:5
ᶠ 2Ki 21:24
ᵍ 2Ki 12:20
14:6
ʰ Dt 28:61
ⁱ Nu 26:11;
Job 21:20;
Jer 31:30; 44:3;
Eze 18:4,20
14:7
ʲ 2Sa 8:13;
2Ch 25:11
ᵏ Jdg 1:36
14:9
ˡ Jdg 9:8-15
14:10
ᵐ Dt 8:14;
2Ch 26:16;
32:25
14:11
ⁿ Jos 15:10
14:12
ᵒ 2Sa 18:17
14:13
ᵖ 1Ki 3:1;
2Ch 33:14;
36:19; Jer 39:2
q Ne 8:16; 12:39
ʳ 2Ch 25:23;
Jer 31:38;
Zec 14:10

ᵃ1 Hebrew *Joash*, a variant of *Jehoash*; also in verses 13, 23 and 27   ᵇ6 Deut. 24:16

long.[a] [14]He took all the gold and silver and all the articles found in the temple of the LORD and in the treasuries of the royal palace. He also took hostages and returned to Samaria.

[15]As for the other events of the reign of Jehoash, what he did and his achievements, including his war[s] against Amaziah king of Judah, are they not written in the book of the annals of the kings of Israel? [16]Jehoash rested with his fathers and was buried in Samaria with the kings of Israel. And Jeroboam his son succeeded him as king.

[17]Amaziah son of Joash king of Judah lived for fifteen years after the death of Jehoash son of Jehoahaz king of Israel. [18]As for the other events of Amaziah's reign, are they not written in the book of the annals of the kings of Judah?

[19]They conspired[t] against him in Jerusalem, and he fled to Lachish, [u] but they sent men after him to Lachish and killed him there. [20]He was brought back by horse[v] and was buried in Jerusalem with his fathers, in the City of David.

[21]Then all the people of Judah took Azariah,[b][w] who was sixteen years old, and made him king in place of his father Amaziah. [22]He was the one who rebuilt Elath[x] and restored it to Judah after Amaziah rested with his fathers.

Jeroboam II King of Israel

[23]In the fifteenth year of Amaziah son of Joash king of Judah, Jeroboam[y] son of Jehoash king of Israel became king in Samaria, and he reigned forty-one years. [24]He did evil in the eyes of the LORD and did not turn away from any of the sins of Jeroboam son of Nebat, which he had caused Israel to commit.[z] [25]He was the one who restored the boundaries of Israel from Lebo[c] Hamath[a] to the Sea of the Arabah,[d][b] in accordance with the word of the LORD, the God of Israel, spoken through his servant Jonah[c] son of Amittai, the prophet from Gath Hepher.

[26]The LORD had seen how bitterly everyone in Israel, whether slave or free,[d] was suffering;[e] there was no one to help them.[f] [27]And since the LORD had not said he would blot out[g] the name of Israel from under heaven, he saved[h] them by the hand of Jeroboam son of Jehoash.

[28]As for the other events of Jeroboam's reign, all he did, and his military achievements, including how he recovered for Israel both Damascus[i] and Hamath,[j] which had belonged to Yaudi,[e] are they not written in the book of the annals[k] of the kings of Israel? [29]Jeroboam rested with his fathers, the kings of Israel. And Zechariah his son succeeded him as king.

Azariah King of Judah

15:1–7pp — 2Ch 26:3–4,21–23

15 In the twenty-seventh year of Jeroboam king of Israel, Azariah[1] son of Amaziah king of Judah began to reign. [2]He was sixteen years old when he became king, and he reigned in Jerusalem fifty-two years. His mother's name was Jecoliah; she was from Jerusalem. [3]He did what was right in the eyes of the LORD, just as his father Amaziah

14:15
s2Ki 13:12
14:19
t2Ki 12:20
uJos 10:3;
2Ki 18:14,17
14:20
v2Ki 9:28
14:21
w2Ki 15:1;
2Ch 26:23
14:22
x1Ki 9:26;
2Ki 16:6
14:23
y2Ki 13:13
14:24
z1Ki 15:30
14:25
aNu 13:21;
1Ki 8:65
bDt 3:17
cJnh 1:1;
Mt 12:39
14:26
dDt 32:36
e2Ki 13:4
fPs 18:41;
22:11; 72:12;
107:12;
Isa 63:5; La 1:7
14:27
g2Ki 13:23
hJdg 6:14
14:28
i2Sa 8:5;
1Ki 11:24
j2Ch 8:3
k1Ki 15:31
15:1
lver 32;
2Ki 14:21

---

[a]13 Hebrew *four hundred cubits* (about 180 meters)   [b]21 Also called *Uzziah*   [c]25 Or *from the entrance to*   [d]25 That is, the Dead Sea   [e]28 Or *Judah*

had done. 4The high places, however, were not removed; the people continued to offer sacrifices and burn incense there.

5The LORD afflicted m the king with leprosy a until the day he died, and he lived in a separate house. b n Jotham o the king's son had charge of the palace p and governed the people of the land.

6As for the other events of Azariah's reign, and all he did, are they not written in the book of the annals of the kings of Judah? 7Azariah rested q with his fathers and was buried near them in the City of David. And Jotham r his son succeeded him as king.

Zechariah King of Israel

8In the thirty-eighth year of Azariah king of Judah, Zechariah son of Jeroboam became king of Israel in Samaria, and he reigned six months. 9He did evil s in the eyes of the LORD, as his fathers had done. He did not turn away from the sins of Jeroboam son of Nebat, which he had caused Israel to commit.

10Shallum son of Jabesh conspired against Zechariah. He attacked him in front of the people, c assassinated t him and succeeded him as king. 11The other events of Zechariah's reign are written in the book of the annals u of the kings of Israel. 12So the word of the LORD spoken to Jehu was fulfilled: v "Your descendants will sit on the throne of Israel to the fourth generation." d

Shallum King of Israel

13Shallum son of Jabesh became king in the thirty-ninth year of Uzziah king of Judah, and he reigned in Samaria w one month. 14Then Menahem son of Gadi went from Tirzah x up to Samaria. He attacked Shallum son of Jabesh in Samaria, assassinated y him and succeeded him as king.

15The other events of Shallum's reign, and the conspiracy he led, are written in the book of the annals z of the kings of Israel.

16At that time Menahem, starting out from Tirzah, attacked Tiphsah a and everyone in the city and its vicinity, because they refused to open b their gates. He sacked Tiphsah and ripped open all the pregnant women.

Menahem King of Israel

17In the thirty-ninth year of Azariah king of Judah, Menahem son of Gadi became king of Israel, and he reigned in Samaria ten years. 18He did evil in the eyes of the LORD. During his entire reign he did not turn away from the sins of Jeroboam son of Nebat, which he had caused Israel to commit.

19Then Pul e c king of Assyria invaded the land, and Menahem gave him a thousand talents f of silver to gain his support and strengthen his own hold on the kingdom. 20Menahem exacted this money from Israel. Every wealthy man had to contribute fifty shekels g of silver to be given to the king of Assyria. So the king of Assyria withdrew d and stayed in the land no longer.

15:5
m Ge 12:17
n Lev 13:46
o 2Ch 27:1
p Ge 41:40
15:7
q Isa 6:1; 14:28
r ver 5
15:9
s 1Ki 15:26
15:10
t 2Ki 12:20
15:11
u 1Ki 15:31
15:12
v 2Ki 10:30
15:13
w ver 1,8
15:14
x 1Ki 14:17
y 2Ki 12:20
15:15
z 1Ki 15:31
15:16
a 1Ki 4:24
b 2Ki 8:12;
Hos 13:16
15:19
c 1Ch 5:6,26
15:20
d 2Ki 12:18

a5 The Hebrew word was used for various diseases affecting the skin—not necessarily leprosy. b5 Or *in a house where he was relieved of responsibility*   c10 Hebrew; some Septuagint manuscripts *in Ibleam*   d12 2 Kings 10:30   e19 Also called *Tiglath-Pileser*   f19 That is, about 37 tons (about 34 metric tons)   g20 That is, about 1 1/4 pounds (about 0.6 kilogram)

[21]As for the other events of Menahem's reign, and all he did, are they not written in the book of the annals of the kings of Israel? [22]Menahem rested with his fathers. And Pekahiah his son succeeded him as king.

Pekahiah King of Israel

[23]In the fiftieth year of Azariah king of Judah, Pekahiah son of Menahem became king of Israel in Samaria, and he reigned two years. [24]Pekahiah did evil in the eyes of the LORD. He did not turn away from the sins of Jeroboam son of Nebat, which he had caused Israel to commit. [25]One of his chief officers, Pekah[e] son of Remaliah, conspired against him. Taking fifty men of Gilead with him, he assassinated[f] Pekahiah, along with Argob and Arieh, in the citadel of the royal palace at Samaria. So Pekah killed Pekahiah and succeeded him as king.

[26]The other events of Pekahiah's reign, and all he did, are written in the book of the annals of the kings of Israel.

Pekah King of Israel

[27]In the fifty-second year of Azariah king of Judah, Pekah[g] son of Remaliah[h] became king of Israel in Samaria, and he reigned twenty years. [28]He did evil in the eyes of the LORD. He did not turn away from the sins of Jeroboam son of Nebat, which he had caused Israel to commit.

[29]In the time of Pekah king of Israel, Tiglath-Pileser[i] king of Assyria came and took Ijon,[j] Abel Beth Maacah, Janoah, Kedesh and Hazor. He took Gilead and Galilee, including all the land of Naphtali,[k] and deported[l] the people to Assyria. [30]Then Hoshea[m] son of Elah conspired against Pekah son of Remaliah. He attacked and assassinated[n] him, and then succeeded him as king in the twentieth year of Jotham son of Uzziah.

[31]As for the other events of Pekah's reign, and all he did, are they not written in the book of the annals of the kings of Israel?

Jotham King of Judah

15:33-38pp — 2Ch 27:1-4,7-9

[32]In the second year of Pekah son of Remaliah king of Israel, Jotham[o] son of Uzziah king of Judah began to reign. [33]He was twenty-five years old when he became king, and he reigned in Jerusalem sixteen years. His mother's name was Jerusha daughter of Zadok. [34]He did what was right[p] in the eyes of the LORD, just as his father Uzziah had done. [35]The high places,[q] however, were not removed; the people continued to offer sacrifices and burn incense there. Jotham rebuilt the Upper Gate[r] of the temple of the LORD.

[36]As for the other events of Jotham's reign, and what he did, are they not written in the book of the annals of the kings of Judah? [37](In those days the LORD began to send Rezin[s] king of Aram and Pekah son of Remaliah against Judah.) [38]Jotham rested with his fathers and was buried with them in the City of David, the city of his father. And Ahaz his son succeeded him as king.

15:25
e2Ch 28:6;
Isa 7:1
f2Ki 12:20
15:27
g2Ch 28:6;
Isa 7:1 hIsa 7:4
15:29
i2Ki 16:7; 17:6;
1Ch 5:26;
2Ch 28:20;
Jer 50:17
j1Ki 15:20
k2Ki 16:9;
17:24;
2Ch 16:4;
Isa 9:1
l2Ki 24:14-16;
1Ch 5:22;
Isa 14:6,17;
36:17; 45:13
15:30
m2Ki 17:1
n2Ki 12:20
15:32
o1Ch 5:17
15:34
pver 3;
1Ki 14:8;
2Ch 26:4-5
15:35
q2Ki 12:3
r2Ch 23:20
15:37
s2Ki 16:5;
Isa 7:1

Ahaz King of Judah

16:1–20pp — 2Ch 28:1–27

16 In the seventeenth year of Pekah son of Remaliah, Ahaz[t] son of Jotham king of Judah began to reign. ²Ahaz was twenty years old when he became king, and he reigned in Jerusalem sixteen years. Unlike David his father, he did not do what was right[u] in the eyes of the LORD his God. ³He walked in the ways of the kings of Israel and even sacrificed his son[v] in[a] the fire, following the detestable[w] ways of the nations the LORD had driven out before the Israelites. ⁴He offered sacrifices and burned incense at the high places, on the hilltops and under every spreading tree.[x]

⁵Then Rezin[y] king of Aram and Pekah son of Remaliah king of Israel marched up to fight against Jerusalem and besieged Ahaz, but they could not overpower him. ⁶At that time, Rezin[z] king of Aram recovered Elath[a] for Aram by driving out the men of Judah. Edomites then moved into Elath and have lived there to this day.

⁷Ahaz sent messengers to say to Tiglath-Pileser[b] king of Assyria, "I am your servant and vassal. Come up and save[c] me out of the hand of the king of Aram and of the king of Israel, who are attacking me." ⁸And Ahaz took the silver and gold found in the temple of the LORD and in the treasuries of the royal palace and sent it as a gift[d] to the king of Assyria. ⁹The king of Assyria complied by attacking Damascus[e] and capturing it. He deported its inhabitants to Kir[f] and put Rezin to death.

¹⁰Then King Ahaz went to Damascus to meet Tiglath-Pileser king of Assyria. He saw an altar in Damascus and sent to Uriah[g] the priest a sketch of the altar, with detailed plans for its construction. ¹¹So Uriah the priest built an altar in accordance with all the plans that King Ahaz had sent from Damascus and finished it before King Ahaz returned. ¹²When the king came back from Damascus and saw the altar, he approached it and presented offerings[b][h] on it. ¹³He offered up his burnt offering[i] and grain offering, poured out his drink offering, and sprinkled the blood of his fellowship offerings[c][j] on the altar. ¹⁴The bronze altar[k] that stood before the LORD he brought from the front of the temple—from between the new altar and the temple of the LORD —and put it on the north side of the new altar.

¹⁵King Ahaz then gave these orders to Uriah the priest: "On the large new altar, offer the morning[l] burnt offering and the evening grain offering, the king's burnt offering and his grain offering, and the burnt offering of all the people of the land, and their grain offering and their drink offering. Sprinkle on the altar all the blood of the burnt offerings and sacrifices. But I will use the bronze altar for seeking guidance."[m] ¹⁶And Uriah the priest did just as King Ahaz had ordered.

¹⁷King Ahaz took away the side panels and removed the basins from the movable stands. He removed the Sea from the bronze bulls that supported it and set it on a stone base.[n] ¹⁸He took away the Sabbath canopy[d] that had been built at the temple and removed the royal entryway outside the temple of the LORD, in deference to the king of Assyria.[o]

¹⁹As for the other events of the reign of Ahaz, and what he did, are

### Cross references (margin)

16:1
[t] Isa 1:1; 14:28
16:2
[u] 1Ki 14:8
16:3
[v] Lev 18:21; 2Ki 21:6
[w] Lev 18:3; Dt 9:4; 12:31
16:4
[x] Dt 12:2; Eze 6:13
16:5
[y] 2Ki 15:37; Isa 7:1,4
16:6
[z] Isa 9:12
[a] 2Ki 14:22; 2Ch 26:2
16:7
[b] 2Ki 15:29
[c] Isa 2:6; Jer 2:18; Eze 16:28; Hos 10:6
16:8
[d] 2Ki 12:18
16:9
[e] 2Ki 15:29
[f] Isa 22:6; Am 1:5; 9:7
16:10
[g] Isa 8:2
16:12
[h] 2Ch 26:16
16:13
[i] Lev 6:8-13
[j] Lev 7:11-21
16:14
[k] 2Ch 4:1
16:15
[l] Ex 29:38-41
[m] 1Sa 9:9
16:17
[n] 1Ki 7:27
16:18
[o] Eze 16:28

---

[a]3 Or *even made his son pass through*   [b]12 Or *and went up*   [c]13 Traditionally *peace offerings*
[d]18 Or *the dais of his throne* (see Septuagint)

they not written in the book of the annals of the kings of Judah? [20]Ahaz rested with his fathers and was buried with them in the City of David. And Hezekiah his son succeeded him as king.

Hoshea Last King of Israel

17:3–7pp — 2Ki 18:9–12

17 In the twelfth year of Ahaz king of Judah, Hoshea[p] son of Elah became king of Israel in Samaria, and he reigned nine years. [2]He did evil in the eyes of the LORD, but not like the kings of Israel who preceded him.

[3]Shalmaneser[q] king of Assyria came up to attack Hoshea, who had been Shalmaneser's vassal and had paid him tribute. [4]But the king of Assyria discovered that Hoshea was a traitor, for he had sent envoys to So[a] king of Egypt, and he no longer paid tribute to the king of Assyria, as he had done year by year. Therefore Shalmaneser seized him and put him in prison. [5]The king of Assyria invaded the entire land, marched against Samaria and laid siege[r] to it for three years. [6]In the ninth year of Hoshea, the king of Assyria captured Samaria[s] and deported[t] the Israelites to Assyria. He settled them in Halah, in Gozan[u] on the Habor River and in the towns of the Medes.

Israel Exiled Because of Sin

[7]All this took place because the Israelites had sinned[v] against the LORD their God, who had brought them up out of Egypt[w] from under the power of Pharaoh king of Egypt. They worshiped other gods [8]and followed the practices of the nations[x] the LORD had driven out before them, as well as the practices that the kings of Israel had introduced. [9]The Israelites secretly did things against the LORD their God that were not right. From watchtower to fortified city[y] they built themselves high places in all their towns. [10]They set up sacred stones and Asherah poles[z] on every high hill and under every spreading tree. [a] [11]At every high place they burned incense, as the nations whom the LORD had driven out before them had done. They did wicked things that provoked the LORD to anger. [12]They worshiped idols, [b] though the LORD had said, "You shall not do this." [b] [13]The LORD warned Israel and Judah through all his prophets and seers:[c] "Turn from your evil ways. [d] Observe my commands and decrees, in accordance with the entire Law that I commanded your fathers to obey and that I delivered to you through my servants the prophets."

[14]But they would not listen and were as stiff-necked[e] as their fathers, who did not trust in the LORD their God. [15]They rejected his decrees and the covenant[f] he had made with their fathers and the warnings he had given them. They followed worthless idols[g] and themselves became worthless. They imitated the nations[h] around them although the LORD had ordered them, "Do not do as they do," and they did the things the LORD had forbidden them to do.

[16]They forsook all the commands of the LORD their God and made for themselves two idols cast in the shape of calves,[i] and an Asherah[j] pole. They bowed down to all the starry hosts,[k] and they worshiped

17:1
p2Ki 15:30
17:3
q2Ki 18:9-12;
Hos 10:14
17:5
rHos 13:16
17:6
sHos 13:16
tDt 28:36,64;
2Ki 18:10-11
u1Ch 5:26
17:7
vJos 23:16;
Jdg 6:10
wEx 14:15-31
17:8
xLev 18:3;
Dt 18:9;
2Ki 16:3
17:9
y2Ki 18:8
17:10
zEx 34:13;
Mic 5:14
a1Ki 14:23
17:12
bEx 20:4
17:13
c1Sa 9:9
dJer 18:11;
25:5; 35:15
17:14
eEx 32:9;
Dt 31:27;
Ac 7:51
17:15
fDt 29:25
gDt 32:21;
Ro 1:21-23
hDt 12:30-31
17:16
i1Ki 12:28
j1Ki 14:15,23
k2Ki 21:3

---

a4 Or *to Sais, to the; So* is possibly an abbreviation for *Osorkon.*   *b12* Exodus 20:4, 5

Baal.[l] [17]They sacrificed[m] their sons and daughters in[a] the fire. They practiced divination and sorcery[n] and sold[o] themselves to do evil in the eyes of the LORD, provoking him to anger.

[18]So the LORD was very angry with Israel and removed them from his presence. Only the tribe of Judah was left, [19]and even Judah did not keep the commands of the LORD their God. They followed the practices Israel had introduced.[p] [20]Therefore the LORD rejected all the people of Israel; he afflicted them and gave them into the hands of plunderers,[q] until he thrust them from his presence.

[21]When he tore[r] Israel away from the house of David, they made Jeroboam son of Nebat their king.[s] Jeroboam enticed Israel away from following the LORD and caused them to commit a great sin. [22]The Israelites persisted in all the sins of Jeroboam and did not turn away from them [23]until the LORD removed them from his presence, as he had warned through all his servants the prophets. So the people of Israel were taken from their homeland into exile in Assyria, and they are still there.

Samaria Resettled

[24]The king of Assyria[t] brought people from Babylon, Cuthah, Avva, Hamath and Sepharvaim[u] and settled them in the towns of Samaria to replace the Israelites. They took over Samaria and lived in its towns. [25]When they first lived there, they did not worship the LORD; so he sent lions[v] among them and they killed some of the people. [26]It was reported to the king of Assyria: "The people you deported and resettled in the towns of Samaria do not know what the god of that country requires. He has sent lions among them, which are killing them off, because the people do not know what he requires."

[27]Then the king of Assyria gave this order: "Have one of the priests you took captive from Samaria go back to live there and teach the people what the god of the land requires." [28]So one of the priests who had been exiled from Samaria came to live in Bethel and taught them how to worship the LORD.

[29]Nevertheless, each national group made its own gods in the several towns[w] where they settled, and set them up in the shrines[x] the people of Samaria had made at the high places.[y] [30]The men from Babylon made Succoth Benoth, the men from Cuthah made Nergal, and the men from Hamath made Ashima; [31]the Avvites made Nibhaz and Tartak, and the Sepharvites burned their children in the fire as sacrifices to Adrammelech[z] and Anammelech, the gods of Sepharvaim.[a] [32]They worshiped the LORD, but they also appointed all sorts[b] of their own people to officiate for them as priests in the shrines at the high places. [33]They worshiped the LORD, but they also served their own gods in accordance with the customs of the nations from which they had been brought.

[34]To this day they persist in their former practices. They neither worship the LORD nor adhere to the decrees and ordinances, the laws and commands that the LORD gave the descendants of Jacob, whom he named Israel.[c] [35]When the LORD made a covenant with the Israelites, he commanded them: "Do not worship[d] any other gods or bow down

17:16
l 1Ki 16:31
17:17
m Dt 18:10-12;
2Ki 16:3
n Lev 19:26
o 1Ki 21:20
17:19
p 1Ki 14:22-23;
2Ki 16:3
17:20
q 2Ki 15:29
17:21
r 1Ki 11:11
s 1Ki 12:20
17:24
t Ezr 4:2,10
u 2Ki 18:34
17:25
v Ge 37:20
17:29
w Jer 2:28
x 1Ki 12:31
y Mic 4:5
17:31
z 2Ki 19:37
a ver 24
17:32
b 1Ki 12:31
17:34
c Ge 32:28;
35:10; 1Ki 18:31
17:35
d Ex 20:5;
Jdg 6:10

---

[a]17 Or *They made their sons and daughters pass through*

to them, serve them or sacrifice to them. 36But the LORD, who brought you up out of Egypt with mighty power and outstretched arm,e is the one you must worship. To him you shall bow down and to him offer sacrifices. 37You must always be carefulf to keep the decrees and ordinances, the laws and commands he wrote for you. Do not worship other gods. 38Do not forgetg the covenant I have made with you, and do not worship other gods. 39Rather, worship the LORD your God; it is he who will deliver you from the hand of all your enemies."

40They would not listen, however, but persisted in their former practices. 41Even while these people were worshiping the LORD,h they were serving their idols. To this day their children and grandchildren continue to do as their fathers did.

Hezekiah King of Judah

18:2–4pp — 2Ch 29:1–2; 31:1
18:5–7pp — 2Ch 31:20–21
18:9–12pp — 2Ki 17:3–7

18 In the third year of Hoshea son of Elah king of Israel, Hezekiahi son of Ahaz king of Judah began to reign. 2He was twenty-five years old when he became king, and he reigned in Jerusalem twenty-nine years.j His mother's name was Abijaha daughter of Zechariah. 3He did what was right in the eyes of the LORD, just as his father Davidk had done. 4He removed1 the high places, smashed the sacred stonesm and cut down the Asherah poles. He broke into pieces the bronze snaken Moses had made, for up to that time the Israelites had been burning incense to it. (It was calledb Nehushtan.c)

5Hezekiah trustedo in the LORD, the God of Israel. There was no one like him among all the kings of Judah, either before him or after him. 6He held fastp to the LORD and did not cease to follow him; he kept the commands the LORD had given Moses. 7And the LORD was with him; he was successfulq in whatever he undertook. He rebelledr against the king of Assyria and did not serve him. 8From watchtower to fortified city,s he defeated the Philistines, as far as Gaza and its territory.

9In King Hezekiah's fourth year,t which was the seventh year of Hoshea son of Elah king of Israel, Shalmaneser king of Assyria marched against Samaria and laid siege to it. 10At the end of three years the Assyrians took it. So Samaria was captured in Hezekiah's sixth year, which was the ninth year of Hoshea king of Israel. 11The kingu of Assyria deported Israel to Assyria and settled them in Halah, in Gozan on the Habor River and in towns of the Medes. 12This happened because they had not obeyed the LORD their God, but had violated his covenantv—all that Moses the servant of the LORD commanded. wThey neither listened to the commandsx nor carried them out.

13In the fourteenth year of King Hezekiah's reign, Sennacherib king of Assyria attacked all the fortified cities of Judahy and captured them. 14So Hezekiah king of Judah sent this message to the king of Assyria at Lachish: "I have done wrong.z Withdraw from me, and I will pay whatever you demand of me." The king of Assyria exacted from Hezekiah king of Judah three hundred talentsd of silver and thirty talentse of

---

a2 Hebrew *Abi*, a variant of *Abijah*   b4 Or *He called it*   c4 *Nehushtan* sounds like the Hebrew for *bronze* and *snake* and *unclean thing*.   d14 That is, about 11 tons (about 10 metric tons)
e14 That is, about 1 ton (about 1 metric ton)

gold. [15]So Hezekiah gave[a] him all the silver that was found in the temple of the LORD and in the treasuries of the royal palace.

[16]At this time Hezekiah king of Judah stripped off the gold with which he had covered the doors and doorposts of the temple of the LORD, and gave it to the king of Assyria.

Sennacherib Threatens Jerusalem

18:13, 17–37pp — Isa 36:1–22
18:17–35pp — 2Ch 32:9–19

[17]The king of Assyria sent his supreme commander,[b] his chief officer and his field commander with a large army, from Lachish to King Hezekiah at Jerusalem. They came up to Jerusalem and stopped at the aqueduct of the Upper Pool,[c] on the road to the Washerman's Field. [18]They called for the king; and Eliakim[d] son of Hilkiah the palace administrator, Shebna[e] the secretary, and Joah son of Asaph the recorder went out to them.

[19]The field commander said to them, "Tell Hezekiah:

" 'This is what the great king, the king of Assyria, says: On what are you basing this confidence of yours? [20]You say you have strategy and military strength—but you speak only empty words. On whom are you depending, that you rebel against me? [21]Look now, you are depending on Egypt,[f] that splintered reed of a staff,[g] which pierces a man's hand and wounds him if he leans on it! Such is Pharaoh king of Egypt to all who depend on him. [22]And if you say to me, "We are depending on the LORD our God"—isn't he the one whose high places and altars Hezekiah removed, saying to Judah and Jerusalem, "You must worship before this altar in Jerusalem"?

[23]" 'Come now, make a bargain with my master, the king of Assyria: I will give you two thousand horses—if you can put riders on them! [24]How can you repulse one officer[h] of the least of my master's officials, even though you are depending on Egypt for chariots and horsemen[a]? [25]Furthermore, have I come to attack and destroy this place without word from the LORD?[i] The LORD himself told me to march against this country and destroy it.' "

[26]Then Eliakim son of Hilkiah, and Shebna and Joah said to the field commander, "Please speak to your servants in Aramaic,[j] since we understand it. Don't speak to us in Hebrew in the hearing of the people on the wall."

[27]But the commander replied, "Was it only to your master and you that my master sent me to say these things, and not to the men sitting on the wall—who, like you, will have to eat their own filth and drink their own urine?"

[28]Then the commander stood and called out in Hebrew: "Hear the word of the great king, the king of Assyria! [29]This is what the king says: Do not let Hezekiah deceive[k] you. He cannot deliver you from my hand. [30]Do not let Hezekiah persuade you to trust in the LORD when he says, 'The LORD will surely deliver us; this city will not be given into the hand of the king of Assyria.'

18:15
[a]1Ki 15:18;
2Ki 16:8
18:17
[b]Isa 20:1
[c]2Ki 20:20;
2Ch 32:4,30;
Isa 7:3
18:18
[d]2Ki 19:2;
Isa 22:20
[e]Isa 22:15
18:21
[f]Isa 20:5;
Eze 29:6
[g]Isa 30:5,7
18:24
[h]Isa 10:8
18:25
[i]2Ki 19:6,22
18:26
[j]Ezr 4:7
18:29
[k]2Ki 19:10

[a]24 Or *charioteers*

³¹"Do not listen to Hezekiah. This is what the king of Assyria says: Make peace with me and come out to me. Then every one of you will eat from his own vine and fig tree¹ and drink water from his own cistern, ᵐ ³²until I come and take you to a land like your own, a land of grain and new wine, a land of bread and vineyards, a land of olive trees and honey. Choose lifeⁿ and not death!

"Do not listen to Hezekiah, for he is misleading you when he says, 'The LORD will deliver us.' ³³Has the godᵒ of any nation ever delivered his land from the hand of the king of Assyria? ³⁴Where are the gods of Hamathᵖ and Arpad?�q Where are the gods of Sepharvaim, Hena and Ivvah? Have they rescued Samaria from my hand? ³⁵Who of all the gods of these countries has been able to save his land from me? How then can the LORD deliver Jerusalem from my hand?"ʳ

³⁶But the people remained silent and said nothing in reply, because the king had commanded, "Do not answer him."

³⁷Then Eliakim son of Hilkiah the palace administrator, Shebna the secretary and Joah son of Asaph the recorder went to Hezekiah, with their clothes torn,ˢ and told him what the field commander had said.

Jerusalem's Deliverance Foretold

19:1–13pp — Isa 37:1–13

19 When King Hezekiah heard this, he toreᵗ his clothes and put on sackcloth and went into the temple of the LORD. ²He sent Eliakim the palace administrator, Shebna the secretary and the leading priests, all wearing sackcloth, to the prophet Isaiahᵘ son of Amoz. ³They told him, "This is what Hezekiah says: This day is a day of distress and rebuke and disgrace, as when children come to the point of birth and there is no strength to deliver them. ⁴It may be that the LORD your God will hear all the words of the field commander, whom his master, the king of Assyria, has sent to ridiculeᵛ the living God, and that he will rebukeʷ him for the words the LORD your God has heard. Therefore pray for the remnant that still survives."

⁵When King Hezekiah's officials came to Isaiah, ⁶Isaiah said to them, "Tell your master, 'This is what the LORD says: Do not be afraid of what you have heard—those words with which the underlings of the king of Assyria have blasphemedˣ me. ⁷Listen! I am going to put such a spirit in him that when he hears a certain report, he will return to his own country, and there I will have him cut down with the sword.ʸ ' "

⁸When the field commander heard that the king of Assyria had left Lachish,ᶻ he withdrew and found the king fighting against Libnah.

⁹Now Sennacherib received a report that Tirhakah, the Cushiteᵃ king of Egypt, was marching out to fight against him. So he again sent messengers to Hezekiah with this word: ¹⁰"Say to Hezekiah king of Judah: Do not let the god you dependᵃ on deceiveᵇ you when he says, 'Jerusalem will not be handed over to the king of Assyria.' ¹¹Surely you have heard what the kings of Assyria have done to all the countries, destroying them completely. And will you be delivered? ¹²Did the gods of the nations that were destroyed by my forefathers deliverᶜ them: the gods of Gozan, ᵈ Haran, ᵉ Rezeph and the people of Eden who were in

Cross references

18:31
lNu 13:23;
1Ki 4:25
mJer 14:3;
La 4:4
18:32
nDt 8:7-9;
30:19
18:33
o2Ki 19:12;
Isa 10:10-11
18:34
p2Ki 17:24;
19:13 qIsa 10:9
18:35
rPs 2:1-2
18:37
s2Ki 6:30
19:1
tGe 37:34;
1Ki 21:27;
2Ch 32:20-22
19:2
uIsa 1:1
19:4
v2Ki 18:35
w2Sa 16:12
19:6
x2Ki 18:25
19:7
yver 37
19:8
z2Ki 18:14
19:10
a2Ki 18:5
b2Ki 18:29
19:12
c2Ki 18:33
d2Ki 17:6
eGe 11:31

ᵃ9 That is, from the upper Nile region

Tel Assar? [13]Where is the king of Hamath, the king of Arpad, the king of the city of Sepharvaim, or of Hena or Ivvah?"[f]

Hezekiah's Prayer

19:14–19pp — Isa 37:14–20

[14]Hezekiah received the letter from the messengers and read it. Then he went up to the temple of the LORD and spread it out before the LORD. [15]And Hezekiah prayed to the LORD: "O LORD, God of Israel, enthroned between the cherubim,[g] you alone are God over all the kingdoms of the earth. You have made heaven and earth. [16]Give ear,[h] O LORD, and hear;[i] open your eyes,[j] O LORD, and see; listen to the words Sennacherib has sent to insult the living God.

[17]"It is true, O LORD, that the Assyrian kings have laid waste these nations and their lands. [18]They have thrown their gods into the fire and destroyed them, for they were not gods[k] but only wood and stone, fashioned by men's hands.[l] [19]Now, O LORD our God, deliver us from his hand, so that all kingdoms[m] on earth may know[n] that you alone, O LORD, are God."

Isaiah Prophesies Sennacherib's Fall

19:20–37pp — Isa 37:21–38
19:35–37pp — 2Ch 32:20–21

[20]Then Isaiah son of Amoz sent a message to Hezekiah: "This is what the LORD, the God of Israel, says: I have heard[o] your prayer concerning Sennacherib king of Assyria. [21]This is the word that the LORD has spoken against him:

" 'The Virgin Daughter[p] of Zion
    despises you and mocks[q] you.
The Daughter of Jerusalem
    tosses her head[r] as you flee.
[22]Who is it you have insulted and blasphemed?
    Against whom have you raised your voice
and lifted your eyes in pride?
    Against the Holy One[s] of Israel!
[23]By your messengers
    you have heaped insults on the Lord.
And you have said,[t]
    "With my many chariots[u]
I have ascended the heights of the mountains,
    the utmost heights of Lebanon.
I have cut down its tallest cedars,
    the choicest of its pines.
I have reached its remotest parts,
    the finest of its forests.
[24]I have dug wells in foreign lands
    and drunk the water there.
With the soles of my feet
    I have dried up all the streams of Egypt."

[25]" 'Have you not heard?[v]
    Long ago I ordained it.
In days of old I planned[w] it;

19:13
f2Ki 18:34
19:15
gEx 25:22
19:16
hPs 31:2
i1Ki 8:29 jver 4;
2Ch 6:40
19:18
kIsa 44:9-11;
Jer 10:3-10
lPs 115:4;
Ac 17:29
19:19
m1Ki 8:43
nPs 83:18
19:20
o2Ki 20:5
19:21
pJer 14:17;
La 2:13
qPs 22:7-8
rJob 16:4;
Ps 109:25
19:22
sPs 71:22;
Isa 5:24
19:23
tIsa 10:18
uPs 20:7
19:25
vIsa 40:21,28
wIsa 10:5; 45:7

now I have brought it to pass,
　　that you have turned fortified cities
　　　into piles of stone.[x]
[26]Their people, drained of power,
　　are dismayed[y] and put to shame.
They are like plants in the field,
　　like tender green shoots,[z]
like grass sprouting on the roof,
　　scorched[a] before it grows up.

[27]" 'But I know[b] where you stay
　　and when you come and go
　　and how you rage against me.
[28]Because you rage against me
　　and your insolence has reached my ears,
I will put my hook[c] in your nose
　　and my bit[d] in your mouth,
and I will make you return[e]
　　by the way you came.'

[29]"This will be the sign[f] for you, O Hezekiah:

"This year you will eat what grows by itself,[g]
　　and the second year what springs from that.
But in the third year sow and reap,
　　plant vineyards[h] and eat their fruit.
[30]Once more a remnant of the house of Judah
　　will take root[i] below and bear fruit above.
[31]For out of Jerusalem will come a remnant,
　　and out of Mount Zion a band of survivors.

The zeal[j] of the LORD Almighty will accomplish this.

[32]"Therefore this is what the LORD says concerning the king of Assyria:

"He will not enter this city
　　or shoot an arrow here.
He will not come before it with shield
　　or build a siege ramp against it.
[33]By the way that he came he will return;[k]
　　he will not enter this city,

　　　　　　　　　　　　　　declares the LORD.
[34]I will defend[l] this city and save it,
　　for my sake and for the sake of David[m] my servant.' "

[35]That night the angel of the LORD[n] went out and put to death a hundred and eighty-five thousand men in the Assyrian camp. When the people got up the next morning—there were all the dead bodies![o] [36]So Sennacherib king of Assyria broke camp and withdrew. He returned to Nineveh[p] and stayed there.

[37]One day, while he was worshiping in the temple of his god Nisroch, his sons Adrammelech and Sharezer cut him down with the sword,[q] and they escaped to the land of Ararat.[r] And Esarhaddon[s] his son succeeded him as king.

19:25
xMic 1:6
19:26
yPs 6:10
zIsa 4:2
aPs 129:6
19:27
bPs 139:1-4
19:28
cEze 19:9; 29:4
dIsa 30:28
ever 33
19:29
f2Ki 20:8-9;
Lk 2:12
gLev 25:5
hPs 107:37
19:30
i2Ch 32:22-23
19:31
jIsa 9:7
19:33
kver 28
19:34
l2Ki 20:6
m1Ki 11:12-13
19:35
nEx 12:23
oJob 24:24
19:36
pGe 10:11;
Jnh 1:2
19:37
qver 7 rGe 8:4
sEzr 4:2

Hezekiah's Illness

20:1–11pp — 2Ch 32:24–26; Isa 38:1–8

20 In those days Hezekiah became ill and was at the point of death. The prophet Isaiah son of Amoz went to him and said, "This is what the LORD says: Put your house in order, because you are going to die; you will not recover."

²Hezekiah turned his face to the wall and prayed to the LORD, ³"Remember,ᵗ O LORD, how I have walked before you faithfullyᵘ and with wholehearted devotion and have done what is good in your eyes." And Hezekiah wept bitterly.

⁴Before Isaiah had left the middle court, the word of the LORD came to him: ⁵"Go back and tell Hezekiah, the leader of my people, 'This is what the LORD, the God of your father David, says: I have heardᵛ your prayer and seen your tears;ʷ I will heal you. On the third day from now you will go up to the temple of the LORD. ⁶I will add fifteen years to your life. And I will deliver you and this city from the hand of the king of Assyria. I will defendˣ this city for my sake and for the sake of my servant David.' "

⁷Then Isaiah said, "Prepare a poultice of figs." They did so and applied it to the boil,ʸ and he recovered.

⁸Hezekiah had asked Isaiah, "What will be the sign that the LORD will heal me and that I will go up to the temple of the LORD on the third day from now?"

⁹Isaiah answered, "This is the LORD's signᶻ to you that the LORD will do what he has promised: Shall the shadow go forward ten steps, or shall it go back ten steps?"

¹⁰"It is a simple matter for the shadow to go forward ten steps," said Hezekiah. "Rather, have it go back ten steps."

¹¹Then the prophet Isaiah called upon the LORD, and the LORD made the shadow go backᵃ the ten steps it had gone down on the stairway of Ahaz.

Envoys From Babylon

20:12–19pp — Isa 39:1–8
20:20–21pp — 2Ch 32:32–33

¹²At that time Merodach-Baladan son of Baladan king of Babylon sent Hezekiah letters and a gift, because he had heard of Hezekiah's illness. ¹³Hezekiah received the messengers and showed them all that was in his storehouses—the silver, the gold, the spices and the fine oil—his armory and everything found among his treasures. There was nothing in his palace or in all his kingdom that Hezekiah did not show them.

¹⁴Then Isaiah the prophet went to King Hezekiah and asked, "What did those men say, and where did they come from?"

"From a distant land," Hezekiah replied. "They came from Babylon."

¹⁵The prophet asked, "What did they see in your palace?"

"They saw everything in my palace," Hezekiah said. "There is nothing among my treasures that I did not show them."

¹⁶Then Isaiah said to Hezekiah, "Hear the word of the LORD: ¹⁷The time will surely come when everything in your palace, and all that your fathers have stored up until this day, will be carried off to Babylon.ᵇ Nothing will be left, says the LORD. ¹⁸And some of your descendants,ᶜ

20:3
ᵗNe 13:22
ᵘ2Ki 18:3-6
20:5
ᵛ1Sa 9:16;
1Ki 9:3;
2Ki 19:20
ʷPs 39:12; 56:8
20:6
ˣ2Ki 19:34
20:7
ʸIsa 38:21
20:9
ᶻDt 13:2;
Jer 44:29
20:11
ᵃJos 10:13
20:17
ᵇ2Ki 24:13;
25:13;
2Ch 36:10;
Jer 27:22;
52:17-23
20:18
ᶜ2Ki 24:15;
2Ch 33:11;
Da 1:3

your own flesh and blood, that will be born to you, will be taken away, and they will become eunuchs in the palace of the king of Babylon."

¹⁹"The word of the LORD you have spoken is good," Hezekiah replied. For he thought, "Will there not be peace and security in my lifetime?"

²⁰As for the other events of Hezekiah's reign, all his achievements and how he made the pool[d] and the tunnel by which he brought water into the city, are they not written in the book of the annals of the kings of Judah? ²¹Hezekiah rested with his fathers. And Manasseh his son succeeded him as king.

Manasseh King of Judah

21:1–10pp — 2Ch 33:1–10
21:17–18pp — 2Ch 33:18–20

21 Manasseh was twelve years old when he became king, and he reigned in Jerusalem fifty-five years. His mother's name was Hephzibah.[e] ²He did evil[f] in the eyes of the LORD, following the detestable practices[g] of the nations the LORD had driven out before the Israelites. ³He rebuilt the high places[h] his father Hezekiah had destroyed; he also erected altars to Baal[i] and made an Asherah pole, as Ahab king of Israel had done. He bowed down to all the starry hosts[j] and worshiped them. ⁴He built altars[k] in the temple of the LORD, of which the LORD had said, "In Jerusalem I will put my Name."[l] ⁵In both courts[m] of the temple of the LORD, he built altars to all the starry hosts. ⁶He sacrificed his own son[n] in[a] the fire, practiced sorcery and divination, and consulted mediums and spiritists.[o] He did much evil in the eyes of the LORD, provoking him to anger.

⁷He took the carved Asherah pole[p] he had made and put it in the temple, of which the LORD had said to David and to his son Solomon, "In this temple and in Jerusalem, which I have chosen out of all the tribes of Israel, I will put my Name[q] forever. ⁸I will not again[r] make the feet of the Israelites wander from the land I gave their forefathers, if only they will be careful to do everything I commanded them and will keep the whole Law that my servant Moses[s] gave them." ⁹But the people did not listen. Manasseh led them astray, so that they did more evil[t] than the nations[u] the LORD had destroyed before the Israelites.

¹⁰The LORD said through his servants the prophets: ¹¹"Manasseh king of Judah has committed these detestable sins. He has done more evil[v] than the Amorites[w] who preceded him and has led Judah into sin with his idols. ¹²Therefore this is what the LORD, the God of Israel, says: I am going to bring such disaster[x] on Jerusalem and Judah that the ears of everyone who hears of it will tingle.[y] ¹³I will stretch out over Jerusalem the measuring line used against Samaria and the plumb line[z] used against the house of Ahab. I will wipe[a] out Jerusalem as one wipes a dish, wiping it and turning it upside down. ¹⁴I will forsake[b] the remnant[c] of my inheritance and hand them over to their enemies. They will be looted and plundered by all their foes, ¹⁵because they have done evil[d] in my eyes and have provoked[e] me to anger from the day their forefathers came out of Egypt until this day."

¹⁶Moreover, Manasseh also shed so much innocent blood[f] that he

---

20:20
d Ne 3:16
21:1
e Isa 62:4
21:2
f Jer 15:4
g 2Ki 16:3
21:3
h 2Ki 18:4
i Jdg 6:28;
1Ki 16:32
j Dt 17:3;
2Ki 17:16
21:4
k Jer 32:34
l 2Sa 7:13;
1Ki 8:29
21:5
m 1Ki 7:12;
2Ki 23:12
21:6
n Lev 18:21;
Dt 18:10;
2Ki 16:3; 17:17
o Lev 19:31
21:7
p Dt 16:21;
2Ki 23:4
q 2Sa 7:13;
1Ki 8:29; 9:3;
2Ki 23:27;
Jer 32:34
21:8
r 2Sa 7:10
s 2Ki 18:12
21:9
t Pr 29:12
u Dt 9:4
21:11
v 2Ki 24:3-4
w Ge 15:16;
1Ki 21:26
21:12
x 2Ki 23:26;
24:3; Jer 15:4
y 1Sa 3:11;
Jer 19:3
21:13
z Isa 34:11;
La 2:8;
Am 7:7-9
a 2Ki 23:27
21:14
b Ps 78:58-60
c 2Ki 19:4;
Mic 2:12
21:15
d Ex 32:22
e Jer 25:7
21:16
f 2Ki 24:4

---

a6 Or He made his own son pass through

filled Jerusalem from end to end—besides the sin that he had caused Judah to commit, so that they did evil in the eyes of the LORD.

[17]As for the other events of Manasseh's reign, and all he did, including the sin he committed, are they not written in the book of the annals of the kings of Judah? [18]Manasseh rested with his fathers and was buried in his palace garden, [g] the garden of Uzza. And Amon his son succeeded him as king.

Amon King of Judah

21:19–24pp — 2Ch 33:21–25

[19]Amon was twenty-two years old when he became king, and he reigned in Jerusalem two years. His mother's name was Meshullemeth daughter of Haruz; she was from Jotbah. [20]He did evil[h] in the eyes of the LORD, as his father Manasseh had done. [21]He walked in all the ways of his father; he worshiped the idols his father had worshiped, and bowed down to them. [22]He forsook the LORD, the God of his fathers, and did not walk[i] in the way of the LORD.

[23]Amon's officials conspired against him and assassinated[j] the king in his palace. [24]Then the people of the land killed[k] all who had plotted against King Amon, and they made Josiah his son king in his place.

[25]As for the other events of Amon's reign, and what he did, are they not written in the book of the annals of the kings of Judah? [26]He was buried in his grave in the garden[l] of Uzza. And Josiah his son succeeded him as king.

The Book of the Law Found

22:1–20pp — 2Ch 34:1–2,8–28

22 Josiah was eight years old when he became king, and he reigned in Jerusalem thirty-one years. His mother's name was Jedidah daughter of Adaiah; she was from Bozkath.[m] [2]He did what was right[n] in the eyes of the LORD and walked in all the ways of his father David, not turning aside to the right[o] or to the left.

[3]In the eighteenth year of his reign, King Josiah sent the secretary, Shaphan[p] son of Azaliah, the son of Meshullam, to the temple of the LORD. He said: [4]"Go up to Hilkiah the high priest and have him get ready the money that has been brought into the temple of the LORD, which the doorkeepers have collected[q] from the people. [5]Have them entrust it to the men appointed to supervise the work on the temple. And have these men pay the workers who repair[r] the temple of the LORD— [6]the carpenters, the builders and the masons. Also have them purchase timber and dressed stone to repair the temple.[s] [7]But they need not account for the money entrusted to them, because they are acting faithfully."[t]

[8]Hilkiah the high priest said to Shaphan the secretary, "I have found the Book of the Law[u] in the temple of the LORD." He gave it to Shaphan, who read it. [9]Then Shaphan the secretary went to the king and reported to him: "Your officials have paid out the money that was in the temple of the LORD and have entrusted it to the workers and supervisors at the temple." [10]Then Shaphan the secretary informed the king, "Hilkiah the priest has given me a book." And Shaphan read from it in the presence of the king.[v]

[11]When the king heard the words of the Book of the Law, he tore his

21:18
g ver 26
21:20
h ver 2-6
21:22
i 1Ki 11:33
21:23
j 2Ki 12:20;
2Ch 33:24-25
21:24
k 2Ki 14:5
21:26
l ver 18
22:1
m Jos 15:39
22:2
n Dt 17:19
o Dt 5:32
22:3
p 2Ch 34:20;
Jer 39:14
22:4
q 2Ki 12:4-5
22:5
r 2Ki 12:5,11-14
22:6
s 2Ki 12:11-12
22:7
t 2Ki 12:15
22:8
u Dt 31:24
22:10
v Jer 36:21

robes. [12]He gave these orders to Hilkiah the priest, Ahikam[w] son of Shaphan, Acbor son of Micaiah, Shaphan the secretary and Asaiah the king's attendant: [13]"Go and inquire of the LORD for me and for the people and for all Judah about what is written in this book that has been found. Great is the LORD's anger[x] that burns against us because our fathers have not obeyed the words of this book; they have not acted in accordance with all that is written there concerning us."

[14]Hilkiah the priest, Ahikam, Acbor, Shaphan and Asaiah went to speak to the prophetess Huldah, who was the wife of Shallum son of Tikvah, the son of Harhas, keeper of the wardrobe. She lived in Jerusalem, in the Second District.

[15]She said to them, "This is what the LORD, the God of Israel, says: Tell the man who sent you to me, [16]'This is what the LORD says: I am going to bring disaster[y] on this place and its people, according to everything written in the book[z] the king of Judah has read. [17]Because they have forsaken[a] me and burned incense to other gods and provoked me to anger by all the idols their hands have made,[a] my anger will burn against this place and will not be quenched.' [18]Tell the king of Judah, who sent you to inquire[b] of the LORD, 'This is what the LORD, the God of Israel, says concerning the words you heard: [19]Because your heart was responsive and you humbled[c] yourself before the LORD when you heard what I have spoken against this place and its people, that they would become accursed[d] and laid waste,[e] and because you tore your robes and wept in my presence, I have heard you, declares the LORD. [20]Therefore I will gather you to your fathers, and you will be buried in peace.[f] Your eyes will not see all the disaster I am going to bring on this place.'"

So they took her answer back to the king.

Josiah Renews the Covenant

23:1–3pp — 2Ch 34:29–32
23:4–20Ref — 2Ch 34:3–7,33
23:21–23pp — 2Ch 35:1,18–19
23:28–30pp — 2Ch 35:20–36:1

23 Then the king called together all the elders of Judah and Jerusalem. [2]He went up to the temple of the LORD with the men of Judah, the people of Jerusalem, the priests and the prophets—all the people from the least to the greatest. He read[g] in their hearing all the words of the Book of the Covenant, which had been found in the temple of the LORD. [3]The king stood by the pillar and renewed the covenant[h] in the presence of the LORD—to follow[i] the LORD and keep his commands, regulations and decrees with all his heart and all his soul, thus confirming the words of the covenant written in this book. Then all the people pledged themselves to the covenant.

[4]The king ordered Hilkiah the high priest, the priests next in rank and the doorkeepers[j] to remove[k] from the temple of the LORD all the articles made for Baal and Asherah and all the starry hosts. He burned them outside Jerusalem in the fields of the Kidron Valley and took the ashes to Bethel. [5]He did away with the pagan priests appointed by the kings of Judah to burn incense on the high places of the towns of Judah and on those around Jerusalem—those who burned incense to Baal, to

22:12
w 2Ki 25:22;
Jer 26:24
22:13
x Dt 29:24-28;
31:17
22:16
y Dt 31:29;
Jos 23:15
z Dt 29:27;
Da 9:11
22:17
a Dt 29:25-27
22:18
b 2Ch 34:26;
Jer 21:2
22:19
c Ex 10:3;
1Ki 21:29;
Ps 51:17;
Isa 57:15;
Mic 6:8
d Jer 26:6
e Lev 26:31
22:20
f Isa 57:1
23:2
g Dt 31:11;
2Ki 22:8
23:3
h 2Ki 11:14,17
i Dt 13:4
23:4
j 2Ki 25:18
k 2Ki 21:7

---

[a]17 Or *by everything they have done*

the sun and moon, to the constellations and to all the starry hosts.^{l} ^{6}He took the Asherah pole from the temple of the LORD to the Kidron Valley outside Jerusalem and burned it there. He ground it to powder and scattered the dust over the graves of the common people. ^{m} ^{7}He also tore down the quarters of the male shrine prostitutes,^{n} which were in the temple of the LORD and where women did weaving for Asherah.

^{8}Josiah brought all the priests from the towns of Judah and desecrated the high places, from Geba^o to Beersheba, where the priests had burned incense. He broke down the shrines^a at the gates—at the entrance to the Gate of Joshua, the city governor, which is on the left of the city gate. ^{9}Although the priests of the high places did not serve^p at the altar of the LORD in Jerusalem, they ate unleavened bread with their fellow priests.

^{10}He desecrated Topheth,^{q} which was in the Valley of Ben Hinnom,^{r} so no one could use it to sacrifice his son^s or daughter in^b the fire to Molech. ^{11}He removed from the entrance to the temple of the LORD the horses that the kings of Judah had dedicated to the sun. They were in the court near the room of an official named Nathan-Melech. Josiah then burned the chariots dedicated to the sun.^{t}

^{12}He pulled down the altars the kings of Judah had erected on the roof^u near the upper room of Ahaz, and the altars Manasseh had built in the two courts^v of the temple of the LORD. He removed them from there, smashed them to pieces and threw the rubble into the Kidron Valley. ^{13}The king also desecrated the high places that were east of Jerusalem on the south of the Hill of Corruption—the ones Solomon^w king of Israel had built for Ashtoreth the vile goddess of the Sidonians, for Chemosh the vile god of Moab, and for Molech^c the detestable god of the people of Ammon. ^{14}Josiah smashed^x the sacred stones and cut down the Asherah poles and covered the sites with human bones.

^{15}Even the altar^y at Bethel, the high place made by Jeroboam^z son of Nebat, who had caused Israel to sin—even that altar and high place he demolished. He burned the high place and ground it to powder, and burned the Asherah pole also. ^{16}Then Josiah^a looked around, and when he saw the tombs that were there on the hillside, he had the bones removed from them and burned on the altar to defile it, in accordance with the word of the LORD proclaimed by the man of God who foretold these things.

^{17}The king asked, "What is that tombstone I see?"

The men of the city said, "It marks the tomb of the man of God who came from Judah and pronounced against the altar of Bethel the very things you have done to it."

^{18}"Leave it alone," he said. "Don't let anyone disturb his bones^b." So they spared his bones and those of the prophet who had come from Samaria.

^{19}Just as he had done at Bethel, Josiah removed and defiled all the shrines at the high places that the kings of Israel had built in the towns of Samaria that had provoked the LORD to anger. ^{20}Josiah slaughtered^c all the priests of those high places on the altars and burned human bones^d on them. Then he went back to Jerusalem.

^{21}The king gave this order to all the people: "Celebrate the Passover^e

---

23:5
l 2Ki 21:3;
Jer 8:2
23:6
m Jer 26:23
23:7
n 1Ki 14:24;
15:12;
Eze 16:16
23:8
o 1Ki 15:22
23:9
p Eze 44:10-14
23:10
q Isa 30:33;
Jer 7:31,32;
19:6 r Jos 15:8
s Lev 18:21;
Dt 18:10
23:11
t Dt 4:19
23:12
u Jer 19:13;
Zep 1:5
v 2Ki 21:5
23:13
w 1Ki 11:7
23:14
x Ex 23:24;
Dt 7:5,25
23:15
y 1Ki 13:1-3
z 1Ki 12:33
23:16
a 1Ki 13:2
23:18
b 1Ki 13:31
23:20
c Ex 22:20;
2Ki 10:25; 11:18
d 1Ki 13:2
23:21
e Ex 12:11;
Nu 9:2;
Dt 16:1-8

---

^{a}8 Or *high places* ^{b}10 Or *to make his son or daughter pass through* ^{c}13 Hebrew *Milcom*

to the LORD your God, as it is written in this Book of the Covenant."
²²Not since the days of the judges who led Israel, nor throughout the
days of the kings of Israel and the kings of Judah, had any such
Passover been observed. ²³But in the eighteenth year of King Josiah,
this Passover was celebrated to the LORD in Jerusalem.

²⁴Furthermore, Josiah got rid of the mediums and spiritists,ᶠ the
household gods,ᵍ the idols and all the other detestable things seen in
Judah and Jerusalem. This he did to fulfill the requirements of the law
written in the book that Hilkiah the priest had discovered in the temple
of the LORD. ²⁵Neither before nor after Josiah was there a king like him
who turnedʰ to the LORD as he did—with all his heart and with all his
soul and with all his strength, in accordance with all the Law of Moses.

²⁶Nevertheless, the LORD did not turn away from the heat of his fierce
anger, which burned against Judah because of all that Manassehⁱ had
done to provoke him to anger. ²⁷So the LORD said, "I will removeʲ
Judah also from my presenceᵏ as I removed Israel, and I will reject
Jerusalem, the city I chose, and this temple, about which I said, 'There
shall my Name be.'ᵃ "

²⁸As for the other events of Josiah's reign, and all he did, are they not
written in the book of the annals of the kings of Judah?

²⁹While Josiah was king, Pharaoh Necoˡ king of Egypt went up to the
Euphrates River to help the king of Assyria. King Josiah marched out to
meet him in battle, but Neco faced him and killed him at Megiddo. ᵐ
³⁰Josiah's servants brought his body in a chariotⁿ from Megiddo to
Jerusalem and buried him in his own tomb. And the people of the land
took Jehoahaz son of Josiah and anointed him and made him king in
place of his father.

Jehoahaz King of Judah

23:31–34pp — 2Ch 36:2–4

³¹Jehoahazᵒ was twenty-three years old when he became king, and
he reigned in Jerusalem three months. His mother's name was Hamu-
talᵖ daughter of Jeremiah; she was from Libnah. ³²He did evil in the
eyes of the LORD, just as his fathers had done. ³³Pharaoh Neco put him
in chains at Riblahᵠ in the land of Hamathᵇʳ so that he might not reign
in Jerusalem, and he imposed on Judah a levy of a hundred talentsᶜ of
silver and a talentᵈ of gold. ³⁴Pharaoh Neco made Eliakimˢ son of
Josiah king in place of his father Josiah and changed Eliakim's name to
Jehoiakim. But he took Jehoahaz and carried him off to Egypt, and
there he died. ᵗ ³⁵Jehoiakim paid Pharaoh Neco the silver and gold he
demanded. In order to do so, he taxed the land and exacted the silver and gold from the people of the land according to their assess-
ments. ᵘ

Jehoiakim King of Judah

23:36–24:6pp — 2Ch 36:5–8

³⁶Jehoiakimᵛ was twenty-five years old when he became king, and
reigned in Jerusalem eleven years. His mother's name was Zebidah

23:24
fLev 19:31;
Dt 18:11;
2Ki 21:6
gGe 31:19
23:25
h2Ki 18:5
23:26
i2Ki 21:12;
Jer 15:4
23:27
j2Ki 21:13
k2Ki 18:11
23:29
lJer 46:2
mZec 12:11
23:30
n2Ki 9:28
23:31
o1Ch 3:15;
Jer 22:11
p2Ki 24:18
23:33
q2Ki 25:6
r1Ki 8:65
23:34
s1Ch 3:15;
2Ch 36:5-8
tJer 22:12;
Eze 19:3-4
23:35
uver 33
23:36
vJer 26:1

ᵃ27 1 Kings 8:29   ᵇ33 Hebrew; Septuagint (see also 2 Chron. 36:3) *Neco at Riblah in Hamath
removed him*   ᶜ33 That is, about 3 3/4 tons (about 3.4 metric tons)   ᵈ33 That is, about 75
pounds (about 34 kilograms)

daughter of Pedaiah; she was from Rumah. [37]And he did evil in the eyes of the LORD, just as his fathers had done.

24 During Jehoiakim's reign, Nebuchadnezzar[w] king of Babylon invaded the land, and Jehoiakim became his vassal for three years. But then he changed his mind and rebelled against Nebuchadnezzar. [2]The LORD sent Babylonian,[a] Aramean,[x] Moabite and Ammonite raiders against him. He sent them to destroy[y] Judah, in accordance with the word of the LORD proclaimed by his servants the prophets. [3]Surely these things happened to Judah according to the LORD's command,[z] in order to remove them from his presence because of the sins of Manasseh[a] and all he had done, [4]including the shedding of innocent blood.[b] For he had filled Jerusalem with innocent blood, and the LORD was not willing to forgive.

[5]As for the other events of Jehoiakim's reign, and all he did, are they not written in the book of the annals of the kings of Judah? [6]Jehoiakim rested[c] with his fathers. And Jehoiachin his son succeeded him as king.

[7]The king of Egypt[d] did not march out from his own country again, because the king of Babylon[e] had taken all his territory, from the Wadi of Egypt to the Euphrates River.

Jehoiachin King of Judah

24:8–17pp — 2Ch 36:9–10

[8]Jehoiachin[f] was eighteen years old when he became king, and he reigned in Jerusalem three months. His mother's name was Nehushta daughter of Elnathan; she was from Jerusalem. [9]He did evil in the eyes of the LORD, just as his father had done.

[10]At that time the officers of Nebuchadnezzar[g] king of Babylon advanced on Jerusalem and laid siege to it, [11]and Nebuchadnezzar himself came up to the city while his officers were besieging it. [12]Jehoiachin king of Judah, his mother, his attendants, his nobles and his officials all surrendered[h] to him.

In the eighth year of the reign of the king of Babylon, he took Jehoiachin prisoner. [13]As the LORD had declared,[i] Nebuchadnezzar removed all the treasures[j] from the temple of the LORD and from the royal palace, and took away all the gold articles[k] that Solomon[l] king of Israel had made for the temple of the LORD. [14]He carried into exile[m] all Jerusalem: all the officers and fighting men, and all the craftsmen and artisans—a total of ten thousand. Only the poorest[n] people of the land were left.

[15]Nebuchadnezzar took Jehoiachin captive to Babylon. He also took from Jerusalem to Babylon the king's mother,[o] his wives, his officials and the leading men[p] of the land. [16]The king of Babylon also deported to Babylon the entire force of seven thousand fighting men, strong and fit for war, and a thousand craftsmen and artisans.[q] [17]He made Mattaniah, Jehoiachin's uncle, king in his place and changed his name to Zedekiah.[r]

Zedekiah King of Judah

24:18–20pp — 2Ch 36:11–16; Jer 52:1–3

[18]Zedekiah[s] was twenty-one years old when he became king, and he

---

24:1
w Jer 25:1,9;
Da 1:1
24:2
x Jer 35:11
y Jer 25:9
24:3
z 2Ki 18:25
a 2Ki 21:12;
23:26
24:4
b 2Ki 21:16
24:6
c Jer 22:19
24:7
d Ge 15:18
e Jer 37:5-7;
46:2
24:8
f 1Ch 3:16
24:10
g Da 1:1
24:12
h 2Ki 25:27;
Jer 22:24-30;
24:1; 25:1;
29:2; 52:28
24:13
i 2Ki 20:17
j 2Ki 25:15;
Isa 39:6
k 2Ki 25:14;
Jer 20:5
l 1Ki 7:51
24:14
m Jer 24:1;
52:28
n 2Ki 25:12;
Jer 40:7; 52:16
24:15
o Jer 22:24-28
p Est 2:6;
Eze 17:12-14
24:16
q Jer 52:28
24:17
r 1Ch 3:15;
2Ch 36:11;
Jer 37:1
24:18
s Jer 52:1

---

a2 Or Chaldean

reigned in Jerusalem eleven years. His mother's name was Hamutal[t] daughter of Jeremiah; she was from Libnah. [19]He did evil in the eyes of the LORD, just as Jehoiakim had done. [20]It was because of the LORD's anger that all this happened to Jerusalem and Judah, and in the end he thrust[u] them from his presence.

The Fall of Jerusalem

25:1–12pp — Jer 39:1–10
25:1–21pp — 2Ch 36:17–20; Jer 52:4–27
25:22–26pp — Jer 40:7–9; 41:1–3, 16–18

Now Zedekiah rebelled against the king of Babylon.

25 So in the ninth year of Zedekiah's reign, on the tenth day of the tenth month, Nebuchadnezzar[v] king of Babylon marched against Jerusalem with his whole army. He encamped outside the city and built siege works[w] all around it. [2]The city was kept under siege until the eleventh year of King Zedekiah. [3]By the ninth day of the fourth[a] month the famine[x] in the city had become so severe that there was no food for the people to eat. [4]Then the city wall was broken through,[y] and the whole army fled at night through the gate between the two walls near the king's garden, though the Babylonians[b] were surrounding[z] the city. They fled toward the Arabah,[c] [5]but the Babylonian[d] army pursued the king and overtook him in the plains of Jericho. All his soldiers were separated from him and scattered,[a] [6]and he was captured.[b] He was taken to the king of Babylon at Riblah,[c] where sentence was pronounced on him. [7]They killed the sons of Zedekiah before his eyes. Then they put out his eyes, bound him with bronze shackles and took him to Babylon.[d]

[8]On the seventh day of the fifth month, in the nineteenth year of Nebuchadnezzar king of Babylon, Nebuzaradan commander of the imperial guard, an official of the king of Babylon, came to Jerusalem. [9]He set fire[e] to the temple of the LORD, the royal palace and all the houses of Jerusalem. Every important building he burned down.[f] [10]The whole Babylonian army, under the commander of the imperial guard, broke down the walls[g] around Jerusalem. [11]Nebuzaradan the commander of the guard carried into exile[h] the people who remained in the city, along with the rest of the populace and those who had gone over to the king of Babylon.[i] [12]But the commander left behind some of the poorest people[j] of the land to work the vineyards and fields.

[13]The Babylonians broke up the bronze pillars, the movable stands and the bronze Sea that were at the temple of the LORD and they carried the bronze to Babylon. [14]They also took away the pots, shovels, wick trimmers, dishes and all the bronze articles[k] used in the temple service. [15]The commander of the imperial guard took away the censers and sprinkling bowls—all that were made of pure gold or silver.

[16]The bronze from the two pillars, the Sea and the movable stands, which Solomon had made for the temple of the LORD, was more than could be weighed. [17]Each pillar[l] was twenty-seven feet[e] high. The bronze capital on top of one pillar was four and a half feet[f] high and

24:18
t2Ki 23:31
24:20
uDt 4:26; 29:27
25:1
vJer 34:1-7
wEze 24:2
25:3
xJer 14:18; La 4:9
25:4
yEze 33:21
zJer 4:17
25:5
aEze 12:14
25:6
bJer 34:21-22
c2Ki 23:33
25:7
dJer 21:7; 32:4-5; Eze 12:11
25:9
eIsa 60:7
fPs 74:3-8; Jer 2:15; Am 2:5; Mic 3:12
25:10
gNe 1:3
25:11
h2Ki 24:14
i2Ki 24:1
25:12
j2Ki 24:14
25:14
kEx 27:3; 1Ki 7:47-50
25:17
l1Ki 7:15-22

---

a3 See Jer. 52:6.   b4 Or *Chaldeans*; also in verses 13, 25 and 26   c4 Or *the Jordan Valley*
d5 Or *Chaldean*; also in verses 10 and 24   e17 Hebrew *eighteen cubits* (about 8.1 meters)
f17 Hebrew *three cubits* (about 1.3 meters)

was decorated with a network and pomegranates of bronze all around. The other pillar, with its network, was similar.

18The commander of the guard took as prisoners Seraiah[m] the chief priest, Zephaniah[n] the priest next in rank and the three doorkeepers. 19Of those still in the city, he took the officer in charge of the fighting men and five royal advisers. He also took the secretary who was chief officer in charge of conscripting the people of the land and sixty of his men who were found in the city. 20Nebuzaradan the commander took them all and brought them to the king of Babylon at Riblah. 21There at Riblah, in the land of Hamath, the king had them executed.

So Judah went into captivity, away from her land. [o]

22Nebuchadnezzar king of Babylon appointed Gedaliah[p] son of Ahikam, the son of Shaphan, to be over the people he had left behind in Judah. 23When all the army officers and their men heard that the king of Babylon had appointed Gedaliah as governor, they came to Gedaliah at Mizpah—Ishmael son of Nethaniah, Johanan son of Kareah, Seraiah son of Tanhumeth the Netophathite, Jaazaniah the son of the Maacathite, and their men. 24Gedaliah took an oath to reassure them and their men. "Do not be afraid of the Babylonian officials," he said. "Settle down in the land and serve the king of Babylon, and it will go well with you."

25In the seventh month, however, Ishmael son of Nethaniah, the son of Elishama, who was of royal blood, came with ten men and assassinated Gedaliah and also the men of Judah and the Babylonians who were with him at Mizpah. 26At this, all the people from the least to the greatest, together with the army officers, fled to Egypt[q] for fear of the Babylonians.

Jehoiachin Released

25:27–30pp — Jer 52:31-34

27In the thirty-seventh year of the exile of Jehoiachin king of Judah, in the year Evil-Merodach[a] became king of Babylon, he released Jehoiachin[r] from prison on the twenty-seventh day of the twelfth month. 28He spoke kindly to him and gave him a seat of honor[s] higher than those of the other kings who were with him in Babylon. 29So Jehoiachin put aside his prison clothes and for the rest of his life ate regularly at the king's table. [t] 30Day by day the king gave Jehoiachin a regular allowance as long as he lived. [u]

25:18
m1Ch 6:14;
Ezr 7:1;
Ne 11:11
nJer 21:1; 29:25
25:21
oGe 12:7;
Dt 28:64;
Jos 23:13;
2Ki 23:27
25:22
pJer 39:14;
40:5,7
25:26
qIsa 30:2;
Jer 43:7
25:27
r2Ki 24:12;
Jer 52:31-34
25:28
sEzr 5:5;
Ne 2:1; Da 2:48
25:29
t2Sa 9:7
25:30
uEst 2:9;
Jer 28:4

---

a27 Also called *Amel-Marduk*

1 Chronicles

Title and Background

The Hebrew title can be translated "the events (or annals) of the days (or years)." The Septuagint (the Greek translation of the Old Testament) translators dubbed the book "the things omitted," indicating that they regarded it as a supplement to Samuel and Kings.

Author and Date of Writing

According to ancient Jewish tradition, Ezra wrote Chronicles, but this cannot be established with certainty. A growing consensus dates Chronicles in the latter half of the fifth century B.C., thus possibly within Ezra's lifetime. It must be acknowledged that the author, if not Ezra, at least shared many basic concerns with that reforming priest.

Theme and Message

Chronicles was written for the exiles who had returned to Israel after the Babylonian captivity, to remind them that they were still God's chosen people. The burning issue was the question of continuity with the past: Is God still interested in us? Are his covenants still in force? Now that we have no Davidic king and are subject to Persia, do God's promises to David still have meaning for us?

Outline

I. Genealogies: From Creation to Restoration (1:1-9:44)
II. The Reign of David (10:1-29:30)

Historical Records From Adam to Abraham

To Noah's Sons

1 Adam,[a] Seth, Enosh, [2]Kenan,[b] Mahalalel,[c] Jared,[d] [3]Enoch,[e] Methuselah,[f] Lamech,[g] Noah.[h]

[4]The sons of Noah:[a] [i]
Shem, Ham and Japheth.[j]

The Japhethites

1:5-7pp — Ge 10:2-5

[5]The sons[b] of Japheth:
Gomer, Magog, Madai, Javan, Tubal, Meshech and Tiras.
[6]The sons of Gomer:
Ashkenaz, Riphath[c] and Togarmah.
[7]The sons of Javan:
Elishah, Tarshish, the Kittim and the Rodanim.

1:1
a Ge 5:1-32;
Lk 3:36-38
1:2
b Ge 5:9
c Ge 5:12
d Ge 5:15
1:3
e Ge 5:18;
Jude 1:14
f Ge 5:21
g Ge 5:25
h Ge 5:29
1:4
i Ge 6:10; 10:1
j Ge 5:32

a4 Septuagint; Hebrew does not have The sons of Noah: b5 Sons may mean descendants or successors or nations; also in verses 6-10, 17 and 20. c6 Many Hebrew manuscripts and Vulgate (see also Septuagint and Gen. 10:3); most Hebrew manuscripts Diphath

The Hamites

1:8–16pp — Ge 10:6–20

⁸The sons of Ham:
Cush, Mizraim,ᵃ Put and Canaan.
⁹The sons of Cush:
Seba, Havilah, Sabta, Raamah and Sabteca.
The sons of Raamah:
Sheba and Dedan.
¹⁰Cush was the fatherᵇ of
Nimrod, who grew to be a mighty warrior on earth.
¹¹Mizraim was the father of
the Ludites, Anamites, Lehabites, Naphtuhites, ¹²Pathrusites,
Casluhites (from whom the Philistines came) and Caphtorites.
¹³Canaan was the father of
Sidon his firstborn,ᶜ and of the Hittites, ¹⁴Jebusites, Amorites,
Girgashites, ¹⁵Hivites, Arkites, Sinites, ¹⁶Arvadites, Zemarites
and Hamathites.

The Semites

1:17–23pp — Ge 10:21–31; 11:10–27

¹⁷The sons of Shem:
Elam, Asshur, Arphaxad, Lud and Aram.
The sons of Aramᵈ:
Uz, Hul, Gether and Meshech.
¹⁸Arphaxad was the father of Shelah,
and Shelah the father of Eber.
¹⁹Two sons were born to Eber:
One was named Peleg,ᵉ because in his time the earth was
divided; his brother was named Joktan.
²⁰Joktan was the father of
Almodad, Sheleph, Hazarmaveth, Jerah, ²¹Hadoram, Uzal,
Diklah, ²²Obal,ᶠ Abimael, Sheba, ²³Ophir, Havilah and Jobab.
All these were sons of Joktan.

²⁴Shem,ᵏ Arphaxad,ᵍ Shelah,
²⁵Eber, Peleg, Reu,
²⁶Serug, Nahor, Terah
²⁷and Abram (that is, Abraham).

1:24
kGe 10:21-25;
Lk 3:34-36

The Family of Abraham

²⁸The sons of Abraham:
Isaac and Ishmael.

Descendants of Hagar

1:29–31pp — Ge 25:12–16

²⁹These were their descendants:

ᵃ8 That is, Egypt; also in verse 11   ᵇ10 *Father* may mean *ancestor* or *predecessor* or *founder*; also in
verses 11, 13, 18 and 20.   ᶜ13 Or *of the Sidonians, the foremost*   ᵈ17 One Hebrew manuscript
and some Septuagint manuscripts (see also Gen. 10:23); most Hebrew manuscripts do not have this
line.   ᵉ19 *Peleg* means *division*.   ᶠ22 Some Hebrew manuscripts and Syriac (see also Gen.
10:28); most Hebrew manuscripts *Ebal*   ᵍ24 Hebrew; some Septuagint manuscripts *Arphaxad,
Cainan* (see also note at Gen. 11:10)

Nebaioth the firstborn of Ishmael, Kedar, Adbeel, Mibsam, [30]Mishma, Dumah, Massa, Hadad, Tema, [31]Jetur, Naphish and Kedemah. These were the sons of Ishmael.

Descendants of Keturah

1:32–33pp — Ge 25:1–4

[32]The sons born to Keturah, Abraham's concubine:[l]
  Zimran, Jokshan, Medan, Midian, Ishbak and Shuah.
The sons of Jokshan:
  Sheba and Dedan. [m]
[33]The sons of Midian:
  Ephah, Epher, Hanoch, Abida and Eldaah.
All these were descendants of Keturah.

Descendants of Sarah

1:35–37pp — Ge 36:10–14

[34]Abraham[n] was the father of Isaac. [o]
The sons of Isaac:
  Esau and Israel. [p]

Esau's Sons

[35]The sons of Esau:[q]
  Eliphaz, Reuel,[r] Jeush, Jalam and Korah.
[36]The sons of Eliphaz:
  Teman, Omar, Zepho,[a] Gatam and Kenaz;
  by Timna: Amalek.[b][s]
[37]The sons of Reuel:[t]
  Nahath, Zerah, Shammah and Mizzah.

The People of Seir in Edom

1:38–42pp — Ge 36:20–28

[38]The sons of Seir:
  Lotan, Shobal, Zibeon, Anah, Dishon, Ezer and Dishan.
[39]The sons of Lotan:
  Hori and Homam. Timna was Lotan's sister.
[40]The sons of Shobal:
  Alvan,[c] Manahath, Ebal, Shepho and Onam.
The sons of Zibeon:
  Aiah and Anah. [u]
[41]The son of Anah:
  Dishon.
The sons of Dishon:
  Hemdan,[d] Eshban, Ithran and Keran.
[42]The sons of Ezer:
  Bilhan, Zaavan and Akan.[e]

1:32
lGe 22:24
mGe 10:7
1:34
nLk 3:34
oGe 21:2-3;
Mt 1:2; Ac 7:8
pGe 17:5;
25:25-26
1:35
qGe 36:19
rGe 36:4
1:36
sEx 17:14
1:37
tGe 36:17
1:40
uGe 36:2

---

[a]36 Many Hebrew manuscripts, some Septuagint manuscripts and Syriac (see also Gen. 36:11); most Hebrew manuscripts *Zephi*   [b]36 Some Septuagint manuscripts (see also Gen. 36:12); Hebrew *Gatam, Kenaz, Timna and Amalek*   [c]40 Many Hebrew manuscripts and some Septuagint manuscripts (see also Gen. 36:23); most Hebrew manuscripts *Alian*   [d]41 Many Hebrew manuscripts and some Septuagint manuscripts (see also Gen. 36:26); most Hebrew manuscripts *Hamran*   [e]42 Many Hebrew and Septuagint manuscripts (see also Gen. 36:27); most Hebrew manuscripts *Zaavan, Jaakan*

The sons of Dishan[a] :
Uz and Aran.

The Rulers of Edom

1:43–54pp — Ge 36:31–43

43These were the kings who reigned in Edom before any Israelite king reigned[b] :
Bela son of Beor, whose city was named Dinhabah.
44When Bela died, Jobab son of Zerah from Bozrah succeeded him as king.
45When Jobab died, Husham from the land of the Temanites[v] succeeded him as king.
46When Husham died, Hadad son of Bedad, who defeated Midian in the country of Moab, succeeded him as king. His city was named Avith.
47When Hadad died, Samlah from Masrekah succeeded him as king.
48When Samlah died, Shaul from Rehoboth on the river[c] succeeded him as king.
49When Shaul died, Baal-Hanan son of Acbor succeeded him as king.
50When Baal-Hanan died, Hadad succeeded him as king. His city was named Pau, [d] and his wife's name was Mehetabel daughter of Matred, the daughter of Me-Zahab. 51Hadad also died.

The chiefs of Edom were:
Timna, Alvah, Jetheth, 52Oholibamah, Elah, Pinon, 53Kenaz, Teman, Mibzar, 54Magdiel and Iram. These were the chiefs of Edom.

Israel's Sons

2:1–2pp — Ge 35:23–26

2 These were the sons of Israel:
Reuben, Simeon, Levi, Judah, Issachar, Zebulun, 2Dan, Joseph, Benjamin, Naphtali, Gad and Asher.

Judah

2:5–15pp — Ru 4:18–22; Mt 1:3–6

To Hezron's Sons

3The sons of Judah:[w]
Er, Onan and Shelah. [x] These three were born to him by a Canaanite woman, the daughter of Shua.[y] Er, Judah's firstborn, was wicked in the LORD's sight; so the LORD put him to death.[z] 4Tamar,[a] Judah's daughter-in-law,[b] bore him Perez[c] and Zerah. Judah had five sons in all.

5The sons of Perez:[d]
Hezron[e] and Hamul.
6The sons of Zerah:

1:45
vGe 36:11
2:3
wGe 29:35;
38:2-10
xGe 38:5
yGe 38:2
zNu 26:19
2:4
aGe 38:11-30
bGe 11:31
cGe 38:29
2:5
dGe 46:12
eNu 26:21

---

[a]42 Hebrew *Dishan*, a variant of *Dishan*   [b]43 Or *before an Israelite king reigned over them*   [c]48 Possibly the Euphrates   [d]50 Many Hebrew manuscripts, some Septuagint manuscripts, Vulgate and Syriac (see also Gen. 36:39); most Hebrew manuscripts *Pai*

Zimri, Ethan, Heman, Calcol and Darda[a]—five in all.
[7]The son of Carmi:
Achar,[b,f] who brought trouble on Israel by violating the ban on taking devoted things.[c] [8]
[8]The son of Ethan:
Azariah.
[9]The sons born to Hezron[h] were:
Jerahmeel, Ram and Caleb.[d]

From Ram Son of Hezron

[10]Ram[i] was the father of
Amminadab[j], and Amminadab the father of Nahshon,[k] the leader of the people of Judah. [11]Nahshon was the father of Salmon,[e] Salmon the father of Boaz, [12]Boaz[l] the father of Obed and Obed the father of Jesse.[m]
[13]Jesse[n] was the father of
Eliab[o] his firstborn; the second son was Abinadab, the third Shimea, [14]the fourth Nethanel, the fifth Raddai, [15]the sixth Ozem and the seventh David. [16]Their sisters were Zeruiah[p] and Abigail. Zeruiah's[q] three sons were Abishai, Joab[r] and Asahel. [17]Abigail was the mother of Amasa,[s] whose father was Jether the Ishmaelite.

Caleb Son of Hezron

[18]Caleb son of Hezron had children by his wife Azubah (and by Jerioth). These were her sons: Jesher, Shobab and Ardon. [19]When Azubah died, Caleb[t] married Ephrath, who bore him Hur. [20]Hur was the father of Uri, and Uri the father of Bezalel.[u]
[21]Later, Hezron lay with the daughter of Makir the father of Gilead[v] (he had married her when he was sixty years old), and she bore him Segub. [22]Segub was the father of Jair, who controlled twenty-three towns in Gilead. [23](But Geshur and Aram captured Havvoth Jair,[f,w] as well as Kenath[x] with its surrounding settlements—sixty towns.) All these were descendants of Makir the father of Gilead.

[24]After Hezron died in Caleb Ephrathah, Abijah the wife of Hezron bore him Ashhur[y] the father[g] of Tekoa.

Jerahmeel Son of Hezron

[25]The sons of Jerahmeel the firstborn of Hezron:
Ram his firstborn, Bunah, Oren, Ozem and[h] Ahijah. [26]Jerahmeel had another wife, whose name was Atarah; she was the mother of Onam.
[27]The sons of Ram the firstborn of Jerahmeel:
Maaz, Jamin and Eker.

[a]6 Many Hebrew manuscripts, some Septuagint manuscripts and Syriac (see also 1 Kings 4:31); most Hebrew manuscripts *Dara*   [b]7 *Achar* means *trouble; Achar* is called *Achan* in Joshua.
[c]7 The Hebrew term refers to the irrevocable giving over of things or persons to the LORD, often by totally destroying them.   [d]9 Hebrew *Kelubai,* a variant of *Caleb*   [e]11 Septuagint (see also Ruth 4:21); Hebrew *Salma*   [f]23 Or *captured the settlements of Jair*   [g]24 *Father* may mean *civic leader* or *military leader;* also in verses 42, 45, 49-52 and possibly elsewhere.   [h]25 Or *Oren and Ozem, by*

²⁸The sons of Onam:
  Shammai and Jada.
  The sons of Shammai:
  Nadab and Abishur.
²⁹Abishur's wife was named Abihail, who bore him Ahban and
  Molid.
³⁰The sons of Nadab:
  Seled and Appaim. Seled died without children.
³¹The son of Appaim:
  Ishi, who was the father of Sheshan.
  Sheshan was the father of Ahlai.
³²The sons of Jada, Shammai's brother:
  Jether and Jonathan. Jether died without children.
³³The sons of Jonathan:
  Peleth and Zaza.
  These were the descendants of Jerahmeel.
³⁴Sheshan had no sons—only daughters.
  He had an Egyptian servant named Jarha. ³⁵Sheshan gave his
  daughter in marriage to his servant Jarha, and she bore him
  Attai.
³⁶Attai was the father of Nathan,
  Nathan the father of Zabad, ᶻ
³⁷Zabad the father of Ephlal,
  Ephlal the father of Obed,
³⁸Obed the father of Jehu,
  Jehu the father of Azariah,
³⁹Azariah the father of Helez,
  Helez the father of Eleasah,
⁴⁰Eleasah the father of Sismai,
  Sismai the father of Shallum,
⁴¹Shallum the father of Jekamiah,
  and Jekamiah the father of Elishama.

The Clans of Caleb

⁴²The sons of Caleb ᵃ the brother of Jerahmeel:
  Mesha his firstborn, who was the father of Ziph, and his son
  Mareshah, ᵃ who was the father of Hebron.
⁴³The sons of Hebron:
  Korah, Tappuah, Rekem and Shema. ⁴⁴Shema was the father of
  Raham, and Raham the father of Jorkeam. Rekem was the
  father of Shammai. ⁴⁵The son of Shammai was Maon ᵇ, and
  Maon was the father of Beth Zur. ᶜ
⁴⁶Caleb's concubine Ephah was the mother of Haran, Moza and
  Gazez. Haran was the father of Gazez.
⁴⁷The sons of Jahdai:
  Regem, Jotham, Geshan, Pelet, Ephah and Shaaph.
⁴⁸Caleb's concubine Maacah was the mother of Sheber and Tirha-
  nah. ⁴⁹She also gave birth to Shaaph the father of Madmannah ᵈ
  and to Sheva the father of Macbenah and Gibea. Caleb's daughter was Acsah. ᵉ ⁵⁰These were the descendants of Caleb.

2:36
ᶻ1Ch 11:41
2:42
ᵃver 19
2:45
ᵇJos 15:55
ᶜJos 15:58
2:49
ᵈJos 15:31
ᵉJos 15:16

ᵃ42 The meaning of the Hebrew for this phrase is uncertain.

The sons of Hur[f] the firstborn of Ephrathah:
Shobal the father of Kiriath Jearim,[g] [51]Salma the father of Bethlehem, and Hareph the father of Beth Gader.
[52]The descendants of Shobal the father of Kiriath Jearim were:
Haroeh, half the Manahathites, [53]and the clans of Kiriath Jearim: the Ithrites,[h] Puthites, Shumathites and Mishraites. From these descended the Zorathites and Eshtaolites.
[54]The descendants of Salma:
Bethlehem, the Netophathites,[i] Atroth Beth Joab, half the Manahathites, the Zorites, [55]and the clans of scribes[a] who lived at Jabez: the Tirathites, Shimeathites and Sucathites. These are the Kenites[j] who came from Hammath,[k] the father of the house of Recab.[b] [l]

The Sons of David

3:1–4pp — 2Sa 3:2–5
3:5–8pp — 2Sa 5:14–16; 1Ch 14:4–7

3 These were the sons of David[m] born to him in Hebron:
The firstborn was Amnon the son of Ahinoam of Jezreel;[n] the second, Daniel the son of Abigail[o] of Carmel;
[2]the third, Absalom the son of Maacah daughter of Talmai king of Geshur;
the fourth, Adonijah[p] the son of Haggith;
[3]the fifth, Shephatiah the son of Abital;
and the sixth, Ithream, by his wife Eglah.
[4]These six were born to David in Hebron,[q] where he reigned seven years and six months.[r]
David reigned in Jerusalem thirty-three years, [5]and these were the children born to him there:
Shammua,[c] Shobab, Nathan and Solomon. These four were by Bathsheba[ds] daughter of Ammiel. [6]There were also Ibhar, Elishua,[e] Eliphelet, [7]Nogah, Nepheg, Japhia, [8]Elishama, Eliada and Eliphelet—nine in all. [9]All these were the sons of David, besides his sons by his concubines. And Tamar[t] was their sister.[u]

The Kings of Judah

[10]Solomon's son was Rehoboam,[v]
Abijah his son,
Asa his son,
Jehoshaphat[w] his son,
[11]Jehoram[fx] his son,
Ahaziah[y] his son,
Joash[z] his son,
[12]Amaziah[a] his son,
Azariah his son,
Jotham[b] his son,
[13]Ahaz[c] his son,

2:50
f1Ch 4:4
gver 19
2:53
h2Sa 23:38
2:54
iEzr 2:22;
Ne 7:26; 12:28
2:55
jGe 15:19;
Jdg 1:16;
Jdg 4:11
kJos 19:35
l2Ki 10:15,23;
Jer 35:2-19
3:1
m1Ch 14:3;
28:5 nJos 15:56
o1Sa 25:42
3:2
p1Ki 2:22
3:4
q2Sa 5:4;
1Ch 29:27
r2Sa 2:11; 5:5
3:5
s2Sa 11:3;
12:24
3:9
t2Sa 13:1
u1Ch 14:4
3:10
v1Ki 11:43;
14:21-31;
2Ch 12:16
w2Ch 17:1-21:3
3:11
x2Ki 8:16-24;
2Ch 21:1
y2Ch 22:1-10
z2Ki 11:1-12:21
3:12
a2Ki 14:1-22;
2Ch 25:1-28
bIsa 1:1;
Hos 1:1;
Mic 1:1
3:13
c2Ki 16:1-20;
2Ch 28:1;
Isa 7:1

---

[a]55 Or *of the Sopherites*   [b]55 Or *father of Beth Recab*   [c]5 Hebrew *Shimea,* a variant of *Shammua*
[d]5 One Hebrew manuscript and Vulgate (see also Septuagint and 2 Samuel 11:3); most Hebrew manuscripts *Bathshua*   [e]6 Two Hebrew manuscripts (see also 2 Samuel 5:15 and 1 Chron. 14:5); most Hebrew manuscripts *Elishama*   [f]11 Hebrew *Joram,* a variant of *Jehoram*

Hezekiah[d] his son,
Manasseh[e] his son,
[14]Amon[f] his son,
Josiah[g] his son.
[15]The sons of Josiah:
Johanan the firstborn,
Jehoiakim[h] the second son,
Zedekiah[i] the third,
Shallum[j] the fourth.
[16]The successors of Jehoiakim:
Jehoiachin[ak] his son,
and Zedekiah.[l]

The Royal Line After the Exile

[17]The descendants of Jehoiachin the captive:
Shealtiel[m] his son, [18]Malkiram, Pedaiah, Shenazzar,[n] Jekamiah,
Hoshama and Nedabiah.[o]
[19]The sons of Pedaiah:
Zerubbabel[p] and Shimei.
The sons of Zerubbabel:
Meshullam and Hananiah.
Shelomith was their sister.
[20]There were also five others:
Hashubah, Ohel, Berekiah, Hasadiah and Jushab-Hesed.
[21]The descendants of Hananiah:
Pelatiah and Jeshaiah, and the sons of Rephaiah, of Arnan, of
Obadiah and of Shecaniah.
[22]The descendants of Shecaniah:
Shemaiah and his sons:
Hattush,[q] Igal, Bariah, Neariah and Shaphat—six in all.
[23]The sons of Neariah:
Elioenai, Hizkiah and Azrikam—three in all.
[24]The sons of Elioenai:
Hodaviah, Eliashib, Pelaiah, Akkub, Johanan, Delaiah and
Anani—seven in all.

Other Clans of Judah

4 The descendants of Judah:[r]
Perez, Hezron,[s] Carmi, Hur and Shobal.
[2]Reaiah son of Shobal was the father of Jahath, and Jahath the
father of Ahumai and Lahad. These were the clans of the Zorathites.
[3]These were the sons[b] of Etam:
Jezreel, Ishma and Idbash. Their sister was named Hazzelelpo-
ni. [4]Penuel was the father of Gedor, and Ezer the father of
Hushah.
These were the descendants of Hur,[t] the firstborn of Ephrathah
and father[c] of Bethlehem.[u]

---

[a]16 Hebrew *Jeconiah*, a variant of *Jehoiachin*; also in verse 17   [b]3 Some Septuagint manuscripts
(see also Vulgate); Hebrew *father*   [c]4 *Father* may mean *civic leader* or *military leader*; also in verses
12, 14, 17, 18 and possibly elsewhere.

3:13
d2Ki 18:1-20:21;
2Ch 29:1;
Jer 26:19
e2Ch 33:1
3:14
f2Ki 21:19-26;
2Ch 33:21;
Zep 1:1
g2Ch 34:1;
Jer 1:2; 3:6;
25:3
3:15
h2Ki 23:34
iJer 37:1
j2Ki 23:31
3:16
k2Ki 24:6,8;
Mt 1:11
l2Ki 24:18
3:17
mEzr 3:2
3:18
nEzr 1:8; 5:14
oJer 22:30
3:19
pEzr 2:2; 3:2;
5:2; Ne 7:7;
12:1; Hag 1:1;
2:2; Zec 4:6
3:22
qEzr 8:2-3
4:1
rGe 29:35;
46:12; 1Ch 2:3
sNu 26:21
4:4
t1Ch 2:50
uRu 1:19

[5]Ashhur[v] the father of Tekoa had two wives, Helah and Naarah. [6]Naarah bore him Ahuzzam, Hepher, Temeni and Haahashtari. These were the descendants of Naarah. [7]The sons of Helah:

Zereth, Zohar, Ethnan, [8]and Koz, who was the father of Anub and Hazzobebah and of the clans of Aharhel son of Harum.

[9]Jabez was more honorable than his brothers. His mother had named him Jabez,[a] saying, "I gave birth to him in pain." [10]Jabez cried out to the God of Israel, "Oh, that you would bless me and enlarge my territory! Let your hand be with me, and keep me from harm so that I will be free from pain." And God granted his request.

[11]Kelub, Shuhah's brother, was the father of Mehir, who was the father of Eshton. [12]Eshton was the father of Beth Rapha, Paseah and Tehinnah the father of Ir Nahash.[b] These were the men of Recah.

[13]The sons of Kenaz:

Othniel[w] and Seraiah.

The sons of Othniel:

Hathath and Meonothai.[c] [14]Meonothai was the father of Oph- rah.

Seraiah was the father of Joab,

the father of Ge Harashim.[d] It was called this because its people were craftsmen.

[15]The sons of Caleb son of Jephunneh:

Iru, Elah and Naam.

The son of Elah:

Kenaz.

[16]The sons of Jehallelel:

Ziph, Ziphah, Tiria and Asarel.

[17]The sons of Ezrah:

Jether, Mered, Epher and Jalon. One of Mered's wives gave birth to Miriam,[x] Shammai and Ishbah the father of Eshtemoa. [18](His Judean wife gave birth to Jered the father of Gedor, Heber the father of Soco, and Jekuthiel the father of Zanoah.[y]) These were the children of Pharaoh's daughter Bithiah, whom Mered had married.

[19]The sons of Hodiah's wife, the sister of Naham:

the father of Keilah[z] the Garmite, and Eshtemoa the Maaca- thite.[a]

[20]The sons of Shimon:

Amnon, Rinnah, Ben-Hanan and Tilon.

The descendants of Ishi:

Zoheth and Ben-Zoheth.

[21]The sons of Shelah[b] son of Judah:

Er the father of Lecah, Laadah the father of Mareshah and the clans of the linen workers at Beth Ashbea, [22]Jokim, the men of Cozeba, and Joash and Saraph, who ruled in Moab and Jashubi

4:5
v1Ch 2:24
4:13
wJos 15:17
4:17
xEx 15:20
4:18
yJos 15:34
4:19
zJos 15:44
aDt 3:14
4:21
bGe 38:5

---

[a]9 *Jabez* sounds like the Hebrew for *pain.*   [b]12 Or *of the city of Nahash*   [c]13 Some Septuagint manuscripts and Vulgate; Hebrew does not have *and Meonothai.*   [d]14 *Ge Harashim* means *valley of craftsmen.*

Lehem. (These records are from ancient times.) [23]They were the potters who lived at Netaim and Gederah; they stayed there and worked for the king.

Simeon

4:28–33pp — Jos 19:2–10

[24]The descendants of Simeon:[c]
Nemuel, Jamin, Jarib,[d] Zerah and Shaul;
[25]Shallum was Shaul's son, Mibsam his son and Mishma his son.
[26]The descendants of Mishma:
Hammuel his son, Zaccur his son and Shimei his son.
[27]Shimei had sixteen sons and six daughters, but his brothers did not have many children; so their entire clan did not become as numerous as the people of Judah. [28]They lived in Beersheba,[e] Moladah,[f] Hazar Shual, [29]Bilhah, Ezem,[g] Tolad, [30]Bethuel, Hormah,[h] Ziklag, [31]Beth Marcaboth, Hazar Susim, Beth Biri and Shaaraim.[i] These were their towns until the reign of David. [32]Their surrounding villages were Etam, Ain,[j] Rimmon, Token and Ashan[k]—five towns— [33]and all the villages around these towns as far as Baalath.[a] These were their settlements. And they kept a genealogical record.

[34]Meshobab, Jamlech, Joshah son of Amaziah, [35]Joel, Jehu son of Joshibiah, the son of Seraiah, the son of Asiel, [36]also Elioenai, Jaakobah, Jeshohaiah, Asaiah, Adiel, Jesimiel, Benaiah, [37]and Ziza son of Shiphi, the son of Allon, the son of Jedaiah, the son of Shimri, the son of Shemaiah.

[38]The men listed above by name were leaders of their clans. Their families increased greatly, [39]and they went to the outskirts of Gedor[l] to the east of the valley in search of pasture for their flocks. [40]They found rich, good pasture, and the land was spacious, peaceful and quiet.[m] Some Hamites had lived there formerly.
[41]The men whose names were listed came in the days of Hezekiah king of Judah. They attacked the Hamites in their dwellings and also the Meunites[n] who were there and completely destroyed[b] them, as is evident to this day. Then they settled in their place, because there was pasture for their flocks. [42]And five hundred of these Simeonites, led by Pelatiah, Neariah, Rephaiah and Uzziel, the sons of Ishi, invaded the hill country of Seir.[o] [43]They killed the remaining Amalekites[p] who had escaped, and they have lived there to this day.

Reuben

5 The sons of Reuben[q] the firstborn of Israel (he was the firstborn, but when he defiled his father's marriage bed,[r] his rights as firstborn were given to the sons of Joseph[s] son of Israel;[t] so he could not be listed in the genealogical record in accordance with his birthright,[u] [2]and though Judah[v] was the strongest of his brothers and a ruler[w] came from him, the rights of the firstborn[x] belonged to Joseph)— [3]the sons of Reuben[y] the firstborn of Israel:

[a]33 Some Septuagint manuscripts (see also Joshua 19:8); Hebrew *Baal*   [b]41 The Hebrew term refers to the irrevocable giving over of things or persons to the LORD, often by totally destroying them.

4:24
c Ge 29:33
d Nu 26:12
4:28
e Ge 21:14
f Jos 15:26
4:29
g Jos 15:29
4:30
h Nu 14:45
4:31
i Jos 15:36
4:32
j Nu 34:11
k Jos 15:42
4:39
l Jos 15:58
4:40
m Jdg 18:7-10
4:41
n 2Ch 20:1; 26:7
4:42
o Ge 14:6
4:43
p 1Sa 15:8; 30:17; 2Sa 8:12; Est 3:1; 9:16
5:1
q Ge 29:32
r Ge 35:22; 49:4
s Ge 48:16,22; 49:26 t Ge 48:5
u 1Ch 26:10
5:2
v Ge 49:10,12
w 1Sa 9:16; 12:12; 2Sa 6:21; 1Ch 11:2; 2Ch 7:18; Ps 60:7; Mic 5:2; Mt 2:6
x Ge 25:31
5:3
y Ge 29:32; 46:9; Ex 6:14; Nu 26:5-11

Hanoch, Pallu, [z] Hezron and Carmi.

[4]The descendants of Joel:

Shemaiah his son, Gog his son,

Shimei his son, [5]Micah his son,

Reaiah his son, Baal his son,

[6]and Beerah his son, whom Tiglath-Pileser[aa] king of Assyria took into exile. Beerah was a leader of the Reubenites.

[7]Their relatives by clans, [b] listed according to their genealogical records:

Jeiel the chief, Zechariah, [8]and Bela son of Azaz, the son of Shema, the son of Joel. They settled in the area from Aroer[c] to Nebo and Baal Meon. [d] [9]To the east they occupied the land up to the edge of the desert that extends to the Euphrates River, because their livestock had increased in Gilead. [e]

[10]During Saul's reign they waged war against the Hagrites[f], who were defeated at their hands; they occupied the dwellings of the Hagrites throughout the entire region east of Gilead.

Gad

[11]The Gadites[g] lived next to them in Bashan, as far as Salecah:[h]

[12]Joel was the chief, Shapham the second, then Janai and Shaphat, in Bashan.

[13]Their relatives, by families, were:

Michael, Meshullam, Sheba, Jorai, Jacan, Zia and Eber—seven in all.

[14]These were the sons of Abihail son of Huri, the son of Jaroah, the son of Gilead, the son of Michael, the son of Jeshishai, the son of Jahdo, the son of Buz.

[15]Ahi son of Abdiel, the son of Guni, was head of their family.

[16]The Gadites lived in Gilead, in Bashan and its outlying villages, and on all the pasturelands of Sharon as far as they extended.

[17]All these were entered in the genealogical records during the reigns of Jotham[i] king of Judah and Jeroboam[j] king of Israel.

[18]The Reubenites, the Gadites and the half-tribe of Manasseh had 44,760 men ready for military service[k]—able-bodied men who could handle shield and sword, who could use a bow, and who were trained for battle. [19]They waged war against the Hagrites, Jetur,[l] Naphish and Nodab. [20]They were helped[m] in fighting them, and God handed the Hagrites and all their allies over to them, because they cried[n] out to him during the battle. He answered their prayers, because they trusted[o] in him. [21]They seized the livestock of the Hagrites—fifty thousand camels, two hundred fifty thousand sheep and two thousand donkeys. They also took one hundred thousand people captive, [22]and many others fell slain, because the battle[p] was God's. And they occupied the land until the exile. [q]

The Half-Tribe of Manasseh

[23]The people of the half-tribe of Manasseh were numerous; they

5:3
[z]Nu 26:5
5:6
[a]ver 26;
2Ki 15:19;
16:10;
2Ch 28:20
5:7
[b]ver 17
5:8
[c]Nu 32:34
[d]Jos 13:17
5:9
[e]Nu 32:26;
Jos 22:9
5:10
[f]ver 18-21
5:11
[g]Jos 13:24-28
[h]Dt 3:10;
Jos 13:11
5:17
[i]2Ki 15:32
[j]2Ki 14:16,28
5:18
[k]Nu 1:3
5:19
[l]ver 10;
Ge 25:15;
1Ch 1:31
5:20
[m]Ps 37:40
[n]1Ki 8:44;
2Ch 13:14;
14:11;
Ps 20:7-9; 22:5
[o]Ps 26:1;
Da 6:23
5:22
[p]2Ch 32:8
[q]2Ki 15:29; 17:6

---

[a]6 Hebrew *Tilgath-Pilneser*, a variant of *Tiglath-Pileser*; also in verse 26

settled in the land from Bashan to Baal Hermon, that is, to Senir (Mount Hermon). ʳ

²⁴These were the heads of their families: Epher, Ishi, Eliel, Azriel, Jeremiah, Hodaviah and Jahdiel. They were brave warriors, famous men, and heads of their families. ²⁵But they were unfaithfulˢ to the God of their fathers and prostitutedᵗ themselves to the gods of the peoples of the land, whom God had destroyed before them. ²⁶So the God of Israel stirred up the spirit of Pulᵘ king of Assyria (that is, Tiglath-Pileserᵛ king of Assyria), who took the Reubenites, the Gadites and the half-tribe of Manasseh into exile. He took them to Halah, ʷ Habor, Hara and the river of Gozan, where they are to this day.

Levi

6 The sons of Levi:ˣ
Gershon, Kohath and Merari.
²The sons of Kohath:
Amram, Izhar, Hebron and Uzziel.
³The children of Amram:
Aaron, Moses and Miriam.
The sons of Aaron:
Nadab, Abihu,ʸ Eleazar and Ithamar.
⁴Eleazar was the father of Phinehas,
Phinehas the father of Abishua,
⁵Abishua the father of Bukki,
Bukki the father of Uzzi,
⁶Uzzi the father of Zerahiah,
Zerahiah the father of Meraioth,
⁷Meraioth the father of Amariah,
Amariah the father of Ahitub,
⁸Ahitub the father of Zadok,ᶻ
Zadok the father of Ahimaaz,
⁹Ahimaaz the father of Azariah,
Azariah the father of Johanan,
¹⁰Johanan the father of Azariahᵃ (it was he who served as priest in the temple Solomon built in Jerusalem),
¹¹Azariah the father of Amariah,
Amariah the father of Ahitub,
¹²Ahitub the father of Zadok,
Zadok the father of Shallum,
¹³Shallum the father of Hilkiah,ᵇ
Hilkiah the father of Azariah,
¹⁴Azariah the father of Seraiah,ᶜ
and Seraiah the father of Jehozadak.

¹⁵Jehozadakᵈ was deported when the Lᴏʀᴅ sent Judah and Jerusalem into exile by the hand of Nebuchadnezzar.

¹⁶The sons of Levi:ᵉ
Gershon, ᵃ Kohath and Merari. ᶠ
¹⁷These are the names of the sons of Gershon:
Libni and Shimei.

5:23
ʳDt 3:8,9;
SS 4:8

5:25
ˢDt 32:15-18;
2Ki 17:7;
1Ch 9:1;
2Ch 26:16
ᵗEx 34:15

5:26
ᵘ2Ki 15:19
ᵛ2Ki 15:29
ʷ2Ki 17:6;
18:11

6:1
ˣGe 46:11;
Ex 6:16;
Nu 26:57;
1Ch 23:6

6:3
ʸLev 10:1

6:8
ᶻ2Sa 8:17;
15:27; Ezr 7:2

6:10
ᵃ1Ki 4:2; 6:1;
2Ch 3:1;
26:17-18

6:13
ᵇ2Ki 22:1-20;
2Ch 34:9; 35:8

6:14
ᶜ2Ki 25:18;
Ezr 2:2;
Ne 11:11

6:15
ᵈ2Ki 25:18;
Ne 12:1;
Hag 1:1,14;
2:2,4; Zec 6:11

6:16
ᵉGe 29:34;
Ex 6:16;
Nu 3:17-20
ᶠNu 26:57

ᵃ16 Hebrew *Gershom*, a variant of *Gershon*; also in verses 17, 20, 43, 62 and 71

18The sons of Kohath:
   Amram, Izhar, Hebron and Uzziel.
19The sons of Merari:g
   Mahli and Mushi.
These are the clans of the Levites listed according to their fathers:
20Of Gershon:
   Libni his son, Jehath his son,
   Zimmah his son, 21Joah his son,
   Iddo his son, Zerah his son
   and Jeatherai his son.
22The descendants of Kohath:
   Amminadab his son, Korahh his son,
   Assir his son, 23Elkanah his son,
   Ebiasaph his son, Assir his son,
   24Tahath his son, Urieli his son,
   Uzziah his son and Shaul his son.
25The descendants of Elkanah:
   Amasai, Ahimoth,
   26Elkanah his son,a Zophai his son,
   Nahath his son, 27Eliab his son,
   Jeroham his son, Elkanahj his son
   and Samuelk his son.b
28The sons of Samuel:
   Joelc1 the firstborn
   and Abijah the second son.
29The descendants of Merari:
   Mahli, Libni his son,
   Shimei his son, Uzzah his son,
   30Shimea his son, Haggiah his son
   and Asaiah his son.

The Temple Musicians

6:54-80pp — Jos 21:4-39

31These are the menm David put in charge of the musicn in the house of the LORD after the ark came to rest there. 32They ministered with music before the tabernacle, the Tent of Meeting, until Solomon built the temple of the LORD in Jerusalem. They performed their duties according to the regulations laid down for them.
33Here are the men who served, together with their sons:
   From the Kohathites:
   Heman,o the musician,
      the son of Joel,p the son of Samuel,
   34the son of Elkanah,q the son of Jeroham,
      the son of Eliel, the son of Toah,
   35the son of Zuph, the son of Elkanah,
      the son of Mahath, the son of Amasai,
   36the son of Elkanah, the son of Joel,
      the son of Azariah, the son of Zephaniah,

6:19
gGe 46:11;
1Ch 23:21;
24:26
6:22
hEx 6:24
6:24
i1Ch 15:5
6:27
j1Sa 1:1
k1Sa 1:20
6:28
lver 33; 1Sa 8:2
6:31
m1Ch 25:1;
2Ch 29:25-26;
Ne 12:45
n1Ch 9:33;
15:19; Ezr 3:10;
Ps 68:25
6:33
o1Ki 4:31;
1Ch 15:17; 25:1
pver 28
6:34
q1Sa 1:1

---

a26 Some Hebrew manuscripts, Septuagint and Syriac; most Hebrew manuscripts *Ahimoth* 26*and Elkanah. The sons of Elkanah:*   b27 Some Septuagint manuscripts (see also 1 Samuel 1:19,20 and 1 Chron. 6:33,34); Hebrew does not have *and Samuel his son.*   c28 Some Septuagint manuscripts and Syriac (see also 1 Samuel 8:2 and 1 Chron. 6:33); Hebrew does not have *Joel.*

³⁷the son of Tahath, the son of Assir,
  the son of Ebiasaph, the son of Korah,^r
³⁸the son of Izhar,^s the son of Kohath,
  the son of Levi, the son of Israel;
³⁹and Heman's associate Asaph,^t who served at his right hand:
  Asaph son of Berekiah, the son of Shimea,^u
⁴⁰the son of Michael, the son of Baaseiah,^a
  the son of Malkijah, ⁴¹the son of Ethni,
  the son of Zerah, the son of Adaiah,
⁴²the son of Ethan, the son of Zimmah,
  the son of Shimei, ⁴³the son of Jahath,
  the son of Gershon, the son of Levi;
⁴⁴and from their associates, the Merarites, at his left hand:
  Ethan son of Kishi, the son of Abdi,
  the son of Malluch, ⁴⁵the son of Hashabiah,
  the son of Amaziah, the son of Hilkiah,
⁴⁶the son of Amzi, the son of Bani,
  the son of Shemer, ⁴⁷the son of Mahli,
  the son of Mushi, the son of Merari,
  the son of Levi.

⁴⁸Their fellow Levites^v were assigned to all the other duties of the tabernacle, the house of God. ⁴⁹But Aaron and his descendants were the ones who presented offerings on the altar^w of burnt offering and on the altar of incense^x in connection with all that was done in the Most Holy Place, making atonement for Israel, in accordance with all that Moses the servant of God had commanded.

⁵⁰These were the descendants of Aaron:
  Eleazar his son, Phinehas his son,
  Abishua his son, ⁵¹Bukki his son,
  Uzzi his son, Zerahiah his son,
⁵²Meraioth his son, Amariah his son,
  Ahitub his son, ⁵³Zadok^y his son
  and Ahimaaz his son.

⁵⁴These were the locations of their settlements^z allotted as their territory (they were assigned to the descendants of Aaron who were from the Kohathite clan, because the first lot was for them):

⁵⁵They were given Hebron in Judah with its surrounding pasturelands. ⁵⁶But the fields and villages around the city were given to Caleb son of Jephunneh. ^a

⁵⁷So the descendants of Aaron were given Hebron (a city of refuge), and Libnah,^{bb} Jattir,^c Eshtemoa, ⁵⁸Hilen, Debir,^d ⁵⁹Ashan,^e Juttah^c and Beth Shemesh, together with their pasturelands. ⁶⁰And from the tribe of Benjamin they were given Gibeon,^d Geba, Alemeth and Anathoth,^f together with their pasturelands.

These towns, which were distributed among the Kohathite clans, were thirteen in all.

6:37
rEx 6:24
6:38
sEx 6:21
6:39
t1Ch 25:1,9;
2Ch 29:13;
Ne 11:17
u1Ch 15:17
6:48
v1Ch 23:32
6:49
wEx 27:1-8
xEx 30:1-7,10;
2Ch 26:18
6:53
y2Sa 8:17
6:54
zNu 31:10
6:56
aJos 14:13;
15:13
6:57
bNu 33:20
cJos 15:48
6:58
dJos 10:3
6:59
eJos 15:42
6:60
fJer 1:1

---

^a40 Most Hebrew manuscripts; some Hebrew manuscripts, one Septuagint manuscript and Syriac *Maaseiah*   ^b57 See Joshua 21:13; Hebrew *given the cities of refuge: Hebron, Libnah.*   ^c59 Syriac (see also Septuagint and Joshua 21:16); Hebrew does not have *Juttah.*   ^d60 See Joshua 21:17; Hebrew does not have *Gibeon.*

⁶¹The rest of Kohath's descendants were allotted ten towns from the clans of half the tribe of Manasseh.

⁶²The descendants of Gershon, clan by clan, were allotted thirteen towns from the tribes of Issachar, Asher and Naphtali, and from the part of the tribe of Manasseh that is in Bashan.

⁶³The descendants of Merari, clan by clan, were allotted twelve towns from the tribes of Reuben, Gad and Zebulun.

⁶⁴So the Israelites gave the Levites these towns⁸ and their pasturelands. ⁶⁵From the tribes of Judah, Simeon and Benjamin they allotted the previously named towns.

⁶⁶Some of the Kohathite clans were given as their territory towns from the tribe of Ephraim.

⁶⁷In the hill country of Ephraim they were given Shechem (a city of refuge), and Gezer,ᵃʰ ⁶⁸Jokmeam,ⁱ Beth Horon,ʲ ⁶⁹Aijalonᵏ and Gath Rimmon,ˡ together with their pasturelands.

⁷⁰And from half the tribe of Manasseh the Israelites gave Aner and Bileam, together with their pasturelands, to the rest of the Kohathite clans.

⁷¹The Gershonitesᵐ received the following:

From the clan of the half-tribe of Manasseh
    they received Golan in Bashanⁿ and also Ashtaroth, together with their pasturelands;

⁷²from the tribe of Issachar
    they received Kedesh, Daberath,ᵒ ⁷³Ramoth and Anem, together with their pasturelands;

⁷⁴from the tribe of Asher
    they received Mashal, Abdon,ᵖ ⁷⁵Hukokᑫ and Rehob,ʳ together with their pasturelands;

⁷⁶and from the tribe of Naphtali
    they received Kedesh in Galilee, Hammonˢ and Kiriathaim,ᵗ together with their pasturelands.

⁷⁷The Merarites (the rest of the Levites) received the following:

From the tribe of Zebulun
    they received Jokneam, Kartah,ᵇ Rimmono and Tabor, together with their pasturelands;

⁷⁸from the tribe of Reuben across the Jordan east of Jericho
    they received Bezerᵘ in the desert, Jahzah, ⁷⁹Kedemothᵛ and Mephaath, together with their pasturelands;

⁸⁰and from the tribe of Gad
    they received Ramoth in Gilead,ʷ Mahanaim,ˣ ⁸¹Heshbon and Jazer,ʸ together with their pasturelands.ᶻ

Issachar

7 The sons of Issachar:ᵃ
    Tola, Puah,ᵇ Jashub and Shimron—four in all.

²The sons of Tola:
    Uzzi, Rephaiah, Jeriel, Jahmai, Ibsam and Samuel—heads of their families. During the reign of David, the descendants of

---

6:64
ᵍNu 35:1-8;
Jos 21:3,41-42

6:67
ʰJos 10:33

6:68
ⁱ1Ki 4:12
ʲJos 10:10

6:69
ᵏJos 10:12
ˡJos 19:45

6:71
ᵐ1Ch 23:7
ⁿJos 20:8

6:72
ᵒJos 19:12

6:74
ᵖJos 19:28

6:75
ᑫJos 19:34
ʳNu 13:21

6:76
ˢJos 19:28
ᵗNu 32:37

6:78
ᵘJos 20:8

6:79
ᵛDt 2:26

6:80
ʷJos 20:8
ˣGe 32:2

6:81
ʸNu 21:32
ᶻ2Ch 11:14

7:1
ᵃGe 30:18;
Nu 26:23
ᵇGe 46:13

ᵃ67 See Joshua 21:21; Hebrew *given the cities of refuge: Shechem, Gezer*.   ᵇ77 See Septuagint and Joshua 21:34; Hebrew does not have *Jokneam, Kartah*.

Tola listed as fighting men in their genealogy numbered 22,600. ³The son of Uzzi:

Izrahiah.

The sons of Izrahiah:

Michael, Obadiah, Joel and Isshiah. All five of them were chiefs. ⁴According to their family genealogy, they had 36,000 men ready for battle, for they had many wives and children. ⁵The relatives who were fighting men belonging to all the clans of Issachar, as listed in their genealogy, were 87,000 in all.

Benjamin

⁶Three sons of Benjamin:ᶜ

Bela, Beker and Jediael.

⁷The sons of Bela:

Ezbon, Uzzi, Uzziel, Jerimoth and Iri, heads of families—five in all. Their genealogical record listed 22,034 fighting men.

⁸The sons of Beker:

Zemirah, Joash, Eliezer, Elioenai, Omri, Jeremoth, Abijah, Anathoth and Alemeth. All these were the sons of Beker. ⁹Their genealogical record listed the heads of families and 20,200 fighting men.

¹⁰The son of Jediael:

Bilhan.

The sons of Bilhan:

Jeush, Benjamin, Ehud, Kenaanah, Zethan, Tarshish and Ahishahar. ¹¹All these sons of Jediael were heads of families. There were 17,200 fighting men ready to go out to war.

¹²The Shuppites and Huppites were the descendants of Ir, and the Hushites the descendants of Aher.

Naphtali

¹³The sons of Naphtali:ᵈ

Jahziel, Guni, Jezer and Shillemᵃ—the descendants of Bilhah.

Manasseh

¹⁴The descendants of Manasseh:ᵉ

Asriel was his descendant through his Aramean concubine. She gave birth to Makir the father of Gilead.ᶠ ¹⁵Makir took a wife from among the Huppites and Shuppites. His sister's name was Maacah.

Another descendant was named Zelophehad,ᵍ who had only daughters.

¹⁶Makir's wife Maacah gave birth to a son and named him Peresh. His brother was named Sheresh, and his sons were Ulam and Rakem.

¹⁷The son of Ulam:

Bedan.

These were the sons of Gileadʰ son of Makir, the son of Manas-

---

7:6
ᶜGe 46:21;
Nu 26:38;
1Ch 8:1-40

7:13
ᵈGe 30:8; 46:24

7:14
ᵉGe 41:51;
Jos 17:1;
1Ch 5:23
ᶠNu 26:30

7:15
ᵍNu 26:33;
36:1-12

7:17
ʰNu 26:30;
1Sa 12:11

ᵃ13 Some Hebrew and Septuagint manuscripts (see also Gen. 46:24 and Num. 26:49); most Hebrew manuscripts *Shallum* seh. [18]His sister Hammoleketh gave birth to Ishhod, Abiezer[i] and Mahlah.

[19]The sons of Shemida were:

Ahian, Shechem, Likhi and Aniam.

Ephraim

[20]The descendants of Ephraim:[j]

Shuthelah, Bered his son,
Tahath his son, Eleadah his son,
Tahath his son, [21]Zabad his son
and Shuthelah his son.

Ezer and Elead were killed by the native-born men of Gath, when they went down to seize their livestock. [22]Their father Ephraim mourned for them many days, and his relatives came to comfort him. [23]Then he lay with his wife again, and she became pregnant and gave birth to a son. He named him Beriah,[a] because there had been misfortune in his family. [24]His daughter was Sheerah, who built Lower and Upper Beth Horon[k] as well as Uzzen Sheerah.

[25]Rephah was his son, Resheph his son,[b]
Telah his son, Tahan his son,
[26]Ladan his son, Ammihud his son,
Elishama his son, [27]Nun his son
and Joshua his son.

[28]Their lands and settlements included Bethel and its surrounding villages, Naaran to the east, Gezer[l] and its villages to the west, and Shechem and its villages all the way to Ayyah and its villages. [29]Along the borders of Manasseh were Beth Shan,[m] Taanach, Megiddo and Dor,[n] together with their villages. The descendants of Joseph son of Israel lived in these towns.

Asher

[30]The sons of Asher:[o]

Imnah, Ishvah, Ishvi and Beriah. Their sister was Serah.

[31]The sons of Beriah:

Heber and Malkiel, who was the father of Birzaith.

[32]Heber was the father of Japhlet, Shomer and Hotham and of their sister Shua.

[33]The sons of Japhlet:

Pasach, Bimhal and Ashvath.
These were Japhlet's sons.

[34]The sons of Shomer:

Ahi, Rohgah,[c] Hubbah and Aram.

[35]The sons of his brother Helem:

Zophah, Imna, Shelesh and Amal.

[36]The sons of Zophah:

Suah, Harnepher, Shual, Beri, Imrah, [37]Bezer, Hod, Shamma, Shilshah, Ithran[d] and Beera.

[38]The sons of Jether:

7:18
i Jos 17:2

7:20
j Ge 41:52;
Nu 1:33; 26:35

7:24
k Jos 10:10;
16:3,5

7:28
l Jos 10:33; 16:7

7:29
m Jos 17:11
n Jos 11:2

7:30
o Ge 46:17;
Nu 1:40; 26:44

---

a23 *Beriah* sounds like the Hebrew for *misfortune*.   b25 Some Septuagint manuscripts; Hebrew does not have *his son*.   c34 Or *of his brother Shomer: Rohgah*   d37 Possibly a variant of *Jether*

Jephunneh, Pispah and Ara.

39The sons of Ulla:

Arah, Hanniel and Rizia.

40All these were descendants of Asher—heads of families, choice men, brave warriors and outstanding leaders. The number of men ready for battle, as listed in their genealogy, was 26,000.

The Genealogy of Saul the Benjamite

8:28–38pp — 1Ch 9:34–44

8 Benjaminᵖ was the father of Bela his firstborn,
Ashbel the second son, Aharah the third,
2Nohah the fourth and Rapha the fifth.

3The sons of Bela were:

Addar,�q Gera, Abihud,ᵃ 4Abishua, Naaman, Ahoah,ʳ 5Gera, Shephuphan and Huram.

6These were the descendants of Ehud,ˢ who were heads of families of those living in Geba and were deported to Manahath: 7Naaman, Ahijah, and Gera, who deported them and who was the father of Uzza and Ahihud.

8Sons were born to Shaharaim in Moab after he had divorced his wives Hushim and Baara. 9By his wife Hodesh he had Jobab, Zibia, Mesha, Malcam, 10Jeuz, Sakia and Mirmah. These were his sons, heads of families. 11By Hushim he had Abitub and Elpaal.

12The sons of Elpaal:

Eber, Misham, Shemed (who built Onoᵗ and Lod with its surrounding villages), 13and Beriah and Shema, who were heads of families of those living in Aijalonᵘ and who drove out the inhabitants of Gath.ᵛ

14Ahio, Shashak, Jeremoth, 15Zebadiah, Arad, Eder, 16Michael, Ishpah and Joha were the sons of Beriah.

17Zebadiah, Meshullam, Hizki, Heber, 18Ishmerai, Izliah and Jobab were the sons of Elpaal.

19Jakim, Zicri, Zabdi, 20Elienai, Zillethai, Eliel, 21Adaiah, Beraiah and Shimrath were the sons of Shimei.

22Ishpan, Eber, Eliel, 23Abdon, Zicri, Hanan, 24Hananiah, Elam, Anthothijah, 25Iphdeiah and Penuel were the sons of Shashak.

26Shamsherai, Sheshariah, Athaliah, 27Jaareshiah, Elijah and Zicri were the sons of Jeroham.

28All these were heads of families, chiefs as listed in their genealogy, and they lived in Jerusalem.

29Jeielᵇ the fatherᶜ of Gibeon lived in Gibeon.ʷ

His wife's name was Maacah, 30and his firstborn son was Abdon, followed by Zur, Kish, Baal, Ner,ᵈ Nadab, 31Gedor, Ahio, Zeker 32and Mikloth, who was the father of Shimeah. They too lived near their relatives in Jerusalem.

33Nerˣ was the father of Kish,ʸ Kish the father of Saulᶻ, and Saul

---

8:1
pGe 46:21;
1Ch 7:6
8:3
qGe 46:21
8:4
r2Sa 23:9
8:6
sJdg 3:12-30;
1Ch 2:52
8:12
tEzr 2:33;
Ne 6:2; 7:37;
11:35
8:13
uJos 10:12
vJos 11:22
8:29
wJos 9:3
8:33
x1Sa 28:19
y1Sa 9:1
z1Sa 14:49

ᵃ3 Or *Gera the father of Ehud*   ᵇ29 Some Septuagint manuscripts (see also 1 Chron. 9:35); Hebrew does not have *Jeiel*.   ᶜ29 *Father* may mean *civic leader* or *military leader*.   ᵈ30 Some Septuagint manuscripts (see also 1 Chron. 9:36); Hebrew does not have *Ner*.

the father of Jonathan, Malki-Shua, Abinadab and Esh-Baal. *a* a

34The son of Jonathan: b

Merib-Baal, *bc* who was the father of Micah.

35The sons of Micah:

Pithon, Melech, Tarea and Ahaz.

36Ahaz was the father of Jehoaddah, Jehoaddah was the father of Alemeth, Azmaveth and Zimri, and Zimri was the father of Moza. 37Moza was the father of Binea; Raphah was his son, Eleasah his son and Azel his son.

38Azel had six sons, and these were their names:

Azrikam, Bokeru, Ishmael, Sheariah, Obadiah and Hanan. All these were the sons of Azel.

39The sons of his brother Eshek:

Ulam his firstborn, Jeush the second son and Eliphelet the third. 40The sons of Ulam were brave warriors who could handle the bow. They had many sons and grandsons—150 in all.

All these were the descendants of Benjamin. d

9 All Israel was listed in the genealogies recorded in the book of the kings of Israel.

The People in Jerusalem

9:1–17pp — Ne 11:3–19

The people of Judah were taken captive to Babylon because of their unfaithfulness. e 2Now the first to resettle on their own property in their own towns f were some Israelites, priests, Levites and temple servants. g

3Those from Judah, from Benjamin, and from Ephraim and Manasseh who lived in Jerusalem were:

4Uthai son of Ammihud, the son of Omri, the son of Imri, the son of Bani, a descendant of Perez son of Judah. h

5Of the Shilonites:

Asaiah the firstborn and his sons.

6Of the Zerahites:

Jeuel.

The people from Judah numbered 690.

7Of the Benjamites:

Sallu son of Meshullam, the son of Hodaviah, the son of Hassenuah;

8Ibneiah son of Jeroham; Elah son of Uzzi, the son of Micri; and Meshullam son of Shephatiah, the son of Reuel, the son of Ibnijah.

9The people from Benjamin, as listed in their genealogy, numbered 956. All these men were heads of their families.

10Of the priests:

Jedaiah; Jehoiarib; Jakin;

11Azariah son of Hilkiah, the son of Meshullam, the son of Zadok, the son of Meraioth, the son of Ahitub, the official in charge of the house of God;

12Adaiah son of Jeroham, the son of Pashhur, i the son of Malki-

8:33
a2Sa 2:8
8:34
b2Sa 9:12
c2Sa 4:4
8:40
dNu 26:38
9:1
e1Ch 5:25
9:2
fJos 9:27;
Ezr 2:70
gEzr 2:43,58;
8:20; Ne 7:60
9:4
hGe 38:29;
46:12
9:12
iEzr 2:38;
10:22; Ne 10:3;
Jer 21:1; 38:1

---

*a*33 Also known as *Ish-Bosheth*   *b*34 Also known as *Mephibosheth* jah; and Maasai son of Adiel, the son of Jahzerah, the son of Meshullam, the son of Meshillemith, the son of Immer.

[13]The priests, who were heads of families, numbered 1,760. They were able men, responsible for ministering in the house of God.

[14]Of the Levites:

Shemaiah son of Hasshub, the son of Azrikam, the son of Hashabiah, a Merarite; [15]Bakbakkar, Heresh, Galal and Mattaniah[j] son of Mica, the son of Zicri, the son of Asaph; [16]Obadiah son of Shemaiah, the son of Galal, the son of Jeduthun; and Berekiah son of Asa, the son of Elkanah, who lived in the villages of the Netophathites.[k]

[17]The gatekeepers:[l]

Shallum, Akkub, Talmon, Ahiman and their brothers, Shallum their chief [18]being stationed at the King's Gate[m] on the east, up to the present time. These were the gatekeepers belonging to the camp of the Levites. [19]Shallum[n] son of Kore, the son of Ebiasaph, the son of Korah, and his fellow gatekeepers from his family (the Korahites) were responsible for guarding the thresholds of the Tent[a] just as their fathers had been responsible for guarding the entrance to the dwelling of the LORD. [20]In earlier times Phinehas[o] son of Eleazar was in charge of the gatekeepers, and the LORD was with him. [21]Zechariah[p] son of Meshelemiah was the gatekeeper at the entrance to the Tent of Meeting.

[22]Altogether, those chosen to be gatekeepers[q] at the thresholds numbered 212. They were registered by genealogy in their villages. The gatekeepers had been assigned to their positions of trust by David and Samuel the seer.[r] [23]They and their descendants were in charge of guarding the gates of the house of the LORD—the house called the Tent. [24]The gatekeepers were on the four sides: east, west, north and south. [25]Their brothers in their villages had to come from time to time and share their duties for seven-day[s] periods. [26]But the four principal gatekeepers, who were Levites, were entrusted with the responsibility for the rooms and treasuries[t] in the house of God. [27]They would spend the night stationed around the house of God,[u] because they had to guard it; and they had charge of the key[v] for opening it each morning.

[28]Some of them were in charge of the articles used in the temple service; they counted them when they were brought in and when they were taken out. [29]Others were assigned to take care of the furnishings and all the other articles of the sanctuary,[w] as well as the flour and wine, and the oil, incense and spices. [30]But some[x] of the priests took care of mixing the spices. [31]A Levite named Mattithiah, the firstborn son of Shallum the Korahite, was entrusted with the responsibility for baking the offering bread. [32]Some of their Kohathite brothers were in charge of preparing for every Sabbath the bread set out on the table.[y]

[33]Those who were musicians,[z] heads of Levite families, stayed in the rooms of the temple and were exempt from other duties because they were responsible for the work day and night.[a]

[34]All these were heads of Levite families, chiefs as listed in their genealogy, and they lived in Jerusalem.

---

[a]19 That is, the temple; also in verses 21 and 23

9:15
j2Ch 20:14;
Ne 11:22
9:16
kNe 12:28
9:17
lver 22;
1Ch 26:1;
2Ch 8:14;
31:14; Ezr 2:42;
Ne 7:45
9:18
m1Ch 26:14;
Eze 43:1; 46:1
9:19
nJer 35:4
9:20
oNu 25:7-13
9:21
p1Ch 26:2,14
9:22
qver 17;
1Ch 26:1-2;
2Ch 31:15,18
r1Sa 9:9
9:25
s2Ki 11:5;
2Ch 23:8
9:26
t1Ch 26:22
9:27
uNu 3:38;
1Ch 23:30-32
vIsa 22:22
9:29
wNu 3:28;
1Ch 23:29
9:30
xEx 30:23-25
9:32
yLev 24:5-8;
1Ch 23:29;
2Ch 13:11
9:33
z1Ch 6:31;
25:1-31
aPs 134:1

The Genealogy of Saul

9:34-44pp — 1Ch 8:28-38

35Jeiel[b] the father[a] of Gibeon lived in Gibeon.

His wife's name was Maacah, 36and his firstborn son was Abdon, followed by Zur, Kish, Baal, Ner, Nadab, 37Gedor, Ahio, Zechariah and Mikloth. 38Mikloth was the father of Shimeam. They too lived near their relatives in Jerusalem.

39Ner[c] was the father of Kish,[d] Kish the father of Saul, and Saul the father of Jonathan,[e] Malki-Shua, Abinadab and Esh-Baal.[b][f]

40The son of Jonathan:

Merib-Baal,[c][g] who was the father of Micah.

41The sons of Micah:

Pithon, Melech, Tahrea and Ahaz.[d]

42Ahaz was the father of Jadah, Jadah[e] was the father of Alemeth, Azmaveth and Zimri, and Zimri was the father of Moza.

43Moza was the father of Binea; Rephaiah was his son, Eleasah his son and Azel his son.

44Azel had six sons, and these were their names:

Azrikam, Bokeru, Ishmael, Sheariah, Obadiah and Hanan. These were the sons of Azel.

Saul Takes His Life

10:1-12pp — 1Sa 31:1-13; 2Sa 1:4-12

10 Now the Philistines fought against Israel; the Israelites fled before them, and many fell slain on Mount Gilboa. 2The Philistines pressed hard after Saul and his sons, and they killed his sons Jonathan, Abinadab and Malki-Shua. 3The fighting grew fierce around Saul, and when the archers overtook him, they wounded him.

4Saul said to his armor-bearer, "Draw your sword and run me through, or these uncircumcised fellows will come and abuse me." But his armor-bearer was terrified and would not do it; so Saul took his own sword and fell on it. 5When the armor-bearer saw that Saul was dead, he too fell on his sword and died. 6So Saul and his three sons died, and all his house died together.

7When all the Israelites in the valley saw that the army had fled and that Saul and his sons had died, they abandoned their towns and fled. And the Philistines came and occupied them.

8The next day, when the Philistines came to strip the dead, they found Saul and his sons fallen on Mount Gilboa. 9They stripped him and took his head and his armor, and sent messengers throughout the land of the Philistines to proclaim the news among their idols and their people. 10They put his armor in the temple of their gods and hung up his head in the temple of Dagon.[h]

11When all the inhabitants of Jabesh Gilead[i] heard of everything the Philistines had done to Saul, 12all their valiant men went and took the bodies of Saul and his sons and brought them to Jabesh. Then they

---

9:35
b 1Ch 8:29
9:39
c 1Ch 8:33
d 1Sa 9:1
e 1Sa 13:22
f 2Sa 2:8
9:40
g 2Sa 4:4
10:10
h Jdg 16:23
10:11
i Jdg 21:8

---

a35 *Father* may mean *civic leader* or *military leader.*   b39 Also known as *Ish-Bosheth*   c40 Also known as *Mephibosheth*   d41 Vulgate and Syriac (see also Septuagint and 1 Chron. 8:35); Hebrew does not have *and Ahaz.*   e42 Some Hebrew manuscripts and Septuagint (see also 1 Chron 8:36); most Hebrew manuscripts *Jarah, Jarah* buried their bones under the great tree in Jabesh, and they fasted seven days.

[13]Saul died[j] because he was unfaithful[k] to the LORD; he did not keep[l] the word of the LORD and even consulted a medium[m] for guidance, [14]and did not inquire of the LORD. So the LORD put him to death and turned[n] the kingdom[o] over to David son of Jesse.

David Becomes King Over Israel

11:1–3pp — 2Sa 5:1–3

11 All Israel[p] came together to David at Hebron[q] and said, "We are your own flesh and blood. [2]In the past, even while Saul was king, you were the one who led Israel on their military campaigns.[r] And the LORD your God said to you, 'You will shepherd[s] my people Israel, and you will become their ruler.[t] '"

[3]When all the elders of Israel had come to King David at Hebron, he made a compact with them at Hebron before the LORD, and they anointed[u] David king over Israel, as the LORD had promised through Samuel.

David Conquers Jerusalem

11:4–9pp — 2Sa 5:6–10

[4]David and all the Israelites marched to Jerusalem (that is, Jebus). The Jebusites[v] who lived there [5]said to David, "You will not get in here." Nevertheless, David captured the fortress of Zion, the City of David.

[6]David had said, "Whoever leads the attack on the Jebusites will become commander-in-chief." Joab[w] son of Zeruiah went up first, and so he received the command.

[7]David then took up residence in the fortress, and so it was called the City of David. [8]He built up the city around it, from the supporting terraces[ax] to the surrounding wall, while Joab restored the rest of the city. [9]And David became more and more powerful,[y] because the LORD Almighty was with him.

David's Mighty Men

11:10–41pp — 2Sa 23:8–39

[10]These were the chiefs of David's mighty men—they, together with all Israel,[z] gave his kingship strong support to extend it over the whole land, as the LORD had promised[a]— [11]this is the list of David's mighty men:[b]

Jashobeam,[b] a Hacmonite, was chief of the officers[c]; he raised his spear against three hundred men, whom he killed in one encounter.

[12]Next to him was Eleazar son of Dodai the Ahohite, one of the three mighty men. [13]He was with David at Pas Dammim when the Philistines gathered there for battle. At a place where there was a field full of barley, the troops fled from the Philistines. [14]But they took their stand in the middle of the field. They defended it and struck the Philistines down, and the LORD brought about a great victory.[c]

[15]Three of the thirty chiefs came down to David to the rock at the cave of Adullam, while a band of Philistines was encamped in the Valley[d] of

---

ª8 Or *the Millo*   b11 Possibly a variant of *Jashob-Baal*   c11 Or *Thirty*; some Septuagint manuscripts *Three* (see also 2 Samuel 23:8)

Rephaim. [16]At that time David was in the stronghold, [e] and the Philistine garrison was at Bethlehem. [17]David longed for water and said, "Oh, that someone would get me a drink of water from the well near the gate of Bethlehem!" [18]So the Three broke through the Philistine lines, drew water from the well near the gate of Bethlehem and carried it back to David. But he refused to drink it; instead, he poured[f] it out before the LORD. [19]"God forbid that I should do this!" he said. "Should I drink the blood of these men who went at the risk of their lives?" Because they risked their lives to bring it back, David would not drink it.

Such were the exploits of the three mighty men.

[20]Abishai[g] the brother of Joab was chief of the Three. He raised his spear against three hundred men, whom he killed, and so he became as famous as the Three. [21]He was doubly honored above the Three and became their commander, even though he was not included among them.

[22]Benaiah son of Jehoiada was a valiant fighter from Kabzeel,[h] who performed great exploits. He struck down two of Moab's best men. He also went down into a pit on a snowy day and killed a lion.[i] [23]And he struck down an Egyptian who was seven and a half feet[a] tall. Although the Egyptian had a spear like a weaver's rod[j] in his hand, Benaiah went against him with a club. He snatched the spear from the Egyptian's hand and killed him with his own spear. [24]Such were the exploits of Benaiah son of Jehoiada; he too was as famous as the three mighty men. [25]He was held in greater honor than any of the Thirty, but he was not included among the Three. And David put him in charge of his bodyguard.

[26]The mighty men were:

    Asahel[k] the brother of Joab,
    Elhanan son of Dodo from Bethlehem,
[27] Shammoth[l] the Harorite,
    Helez the Pelonite,
[28] Ira son of Ikkesh from Tekoa,
    Abiezer[m] from Anathoth,
[29] Sibbecai[n] the Hushathite,
    Ilai the Ahohite,
[30] Maharai the Netophathite,
    Heled son of Baanah the Netophathite,
[31] Ithai son of Ribai from Gibeah in Benjamin,
    Benaiah[o] the Pirathonite, [p]
[32] Hurai from the ravines of Gaash,
    Abiel the Arbathite,
[33] Azmaveth the Baharumite,
    Eliahba the Shaalbonite,
[34] the sons of Hashem the Gizonite,
    Jonathan son of Shagee the Hararite,
[35] Ahiam son of Sacar the Hararite,
    Eliphal son of Ur,
[36] Hepher the Mekerathite,

11:16
e 2Sa 5:17
11:18
f Dt 12:16
11:20
g 1Sa 26:6
11:22
h Jos 15:21
i 1Sa 17:36
11:23
j 1Sa 17:7
11:26
k 2Sa 2:18
11:27
l 1Ch 27:8
11:28
m 1Ch 27:12
11:29
n 2Sa 21:18
11:31
o 1Ch 27:14
p Jdg 12:13

---

a23 Hebrew *five cubits* (about 2.3 meters)

> Ahijah the Pelonite,
> 37Hezro the Carmelite,
> Naarai son of Ezbai,
> 38Joel the brother of Nathan,
> Mibhar son of Hagri,
> 39Zelek the Ammonite,
> Naharai the Berothite, the armor-bearer of Joab son of Zeruiah,
> 40Ira the Ithrite,
> Gareb the Ithrite,
> 41Uriahq the Hittite,
> Zabadr son of Ahlai,
> 42Adina son of Shiza the Reubenite, who was chief of the Reubenites, and the thirty with him,
> 43Hanan son of Maacah,
> Joshaphat the Mithnite,
> 44Uzzia the Ashterathite,s
> Shama and Jeiel the sons of Hotham the Aroerite,
> 45Jediael son of Shimri,
> his brother Joha the Tizite,
> 46Eliel the Mahavite,
> Jeribai and Joshaviah the sons of Elnaam,
> Ithmah the Moabite,
> 47Eliel, Obed and Jaasiel the Mezobaite.

Warriors Join David

12 These were the men who came to David at Ziklag,t while he was banished from the presence of Saul son of Kish (they were among the warriors who helped him in battle; 2they were armed with bows and were able to shoot arrows or to sling stones right-handed or left-handed;u they were kinsmen of Saulv from the tribe of Benjamin):

3Ahiezer their chief and Joash the sons of Shemaah the Gibeathite; Jeziel and Pelet the sons of Azmaveth; Beracah, Jehu the Anathothite, 4and Ishmaiah the Gibeonite, a mighty man among the Thirty, who was a leader of the Thirty; Jeremiah, Jahaziel, Johanan, Jozabad the Gederathite, w 5Eluzai, Jerimoth, Bealiah, Shemariah and Shephatiah the Haruphite; 6Elkanah, Isshiah, Azarel, Joezer and Jashobeam the Korahites; 7and Joelah and Zebadiah the sons of Jeroham from Gedor.x

8Some Gaditesy defected to David at his stronghold in the desert. They were brave warriors, ready for battle and able to handle the shield and spear. Their faces were the faces of lions,z and they were as swift as gazellesa in the mountains.
9Ezer was the chief,
Obadiah the second in command, Eliab the third,
10Mishmannah the fourth, Jeremiah the fifth,
11Attai the sixth, Eliel the seventh,
12Johanan the eighth, Elzabad the ninth,
13Jeremiah the tenth and Macbannai the eleventh.
14These Gadites were army commanders; the least was a match for a hundred,b and the greatest for a thousand. c 15It was they who crossed the Jordan in the first month when it was overflowing all its banks,d

11:41
q2Sa 11:6
r1Ch 2:36
11:44
sDt 1:4
12:1
tJos 15:31;
1Sa 27:2-6
12:2
uJdg 3:15;
20:16 v2Sa 3:19
12:4
wJos 15:36
12:7
xJos 15:58
12:8
yGe 30:11
z2Sa 17:10
a2Sa 2:18
12:14
bLev 26:8
cDt 32:30
12:15
dJos 3:15

and they put to flight everyone living in the valleys, to the east and to the west.

16Other Benjamites[e] and some men from Judah also came to David in his stronghold. 17David went out to meet them and said to them, "If you have come to me in peace, to help me, I am ready to have you unite with me. But if you have come to betray me to my enemies when my hands are free from violence, may the God of our fathers see it and judge you."

18Then the Spirit[f] came upon Amasai,[g] chief of the Thirty, and he said:

> "We are yours, O David!
> We are with you, O son of Jesse!
> Success,[h] success to you,
>   and success to those who help you,
>   for your God will help you."

So David received them and made them leaders of his raiding bands.

19Some of the men of Manasseh defected to David when he went with the Philistines to fight against Saul. (He and his men did not help the Philistines because, after consultation, their rulers sent him away. They said, "It will cost us our heads if he deserts to his master Saul.")[i] 20When David went to Ziklag,[j] these were the men of Manasseh who defected to him: Adnah, Jozabad, Jediael, Michael, Jozabad, Elihu and Zillethai, leaders of units of a thousand in Manasseh. 21They helped David against raiding bands, for all of them were brave warriors, and they were commanders in his army. 22Day after day men came to help David, until he had a great army, like the army of God.[a]

Others Join David at Hebron

23These are the numbers of the men armed for battle who came to David at Hebron[k] to turn[l] Saul's kingdom over to him, as the LORD had said:[m]

24men of Judah, carrying shield and spear—6,800 armed for battle;

25men of Simeon, warriors ready for battle—7,100;

26men of Levi—4,600, 27including Jehoiada, leader of the family of Aaron, with 3,700 men, 28and Zadok,[n] a brave young warrior, with 22 officers from his family;

29men of Benjamin,[o] Saul's kinsmen—3,000, most[p] of whom had remained loyal to Saul's house until then;

30men of Ephraim, brave warriors, famous in their own clans—20,800;

31men of half the tribe of Manasseh, designated by name to come and make David king—18,000;

32men of Issachar, who understood the times and knew what Israel should do[q]—200 chiefs, with all their relatives under their command;

33men of Zebulun, experienced soldiers prepared for battle with every type of weapon, to help David with undivided loyalty—50,000;

12:16
e2Sa 3:19
12:18
fJdg 3:10; 6:34;
1Ch 28:12;
2Ch 15:1;
20:14; 24:20
g2Sa 17:25
h1Sa 25:5-6
12:19
i1Sa 29:2-11
12:20
j1Sa 27:6
12:23
k2Sa 2:3-4
l1Ch 10:14
m1Sa 16:1;
1Ch 11:10
12:28
n2Sa 8:17;
1Ch 6:8; 15:11;
16:39; 27:17
12:29
o2Sa 3:19
p2Sa 2:8-9
12:32
qEst 1:13

---

a22 Or *a great and mighty army*

³⁴men of Naphtali—1,000 officers, together with 37,000 men carrying shields and spears;

³⁵men of Dan, ready for battle—28,600;

³⁶men of Asher, experienced soldiers prepared for battle—40,000;

³⁷and from east of the Jordan, men of Reuben, Gad and the half-tribe of Manasseh, armed with every type of weapon—120,000.

³⁸All these were fighting men who volunteered to serve in the ranks. They came to Hebron fully determined to make David king over all Israel.ʳ All the rest of the Israelites were also of one mind to make David king. ³⁹The men spent three days there with David, eating and drinking,ˢ for their families had supplied provisions for them. ⁴⁰Also, their neighbors from as far away as Issachar, Zebulun and Naphtali came bringing food on donkeys, camels, mules and oxen. There were plentiful suppliesᵗ of flour, fig cakes, raisinᵘ cakes, wine, oil, cattle and sheep, for there was joyᵛ in Israel.

Bringing Back the Ark

13:1–14pp — 2Sa 6:1–11

13 David conferred with each of his officers, the commanders of thousands and commanders of hundreds. ²He then said to the whole assembly of Israel, "If it seems good to you and if it is the will of the LORD our God, let us send word far and wide to the rest of our brothers throughout the territories of Israel, and also to the priests and Levites who are with them in their towns and pasturelands, to come and join us. ³Let us bring the ark of our God back to us,ʷ for we did not inquireˣ ofᵃ itᵇ during the reign of Saul." ⁴The whole assembly agreed to do this, because it seemed right to all the people.

⁵So David assembled all the Israelites,ʸ from the Shihor Riverᶻ in Egypt to Leboᶜ Hamath,ᵃ to bring the ark of God from Kiriath Jearim.ᵇ ⁶David and all the Israelites with him went to Baalahᶜ of Judah (Kiriath Jearim) to bring up from there the ark of God the LORD, who is enthroned between the cherubimᵈ—the ark that is called by the Name.

⁷They moved the ark of God from Abinadab'sᵉ house on a new cart, with Uzzah and Ahio guiding it. ⁸David and all the Israelites were celebrating with all their might before God, with songs and with harps, lyres, tambourines, cymbals and trumpets.ᶠ

⁹When they came to the threshing floor of Kidon, Uzzah reached out his hand to steady the ark, because the oxen stumbled. ¹⁰The LORD's angerᵍ burned against Uzzah, and he struck him downʰ because he had put his hand on the ark. So he died there before God.

¹¹Then David was angry because the LORD's wrath had broken out against Uzzah, and to this day that place is called Perez Uzzah.ᵈ ⁱ

¹²David was afraid of God that day and asked, "How can I ever bring the ark of God to me?" ¹³He did not take the ark to be with him in the City of David. Instead, he took it aside to the house of Obed-Edomʲ the Gittite. ¹⁴The ark of God remained with the family of Obed-Edom in his house for three months, and the LORD blessed his householdᵏ and everything he had.

12:38
r2Sa 5:1-3;
1Ch 9:1
12:39
s2Sa 3:20;
Isa 25:6-8
12:40
t2Sa 16:1; 17:29
u1Sa 25:18
v1Ch 29:22
13:3
w1Sa 7:1-2
x2Ch 1:5
13:5
y1Ch 11:1; 15:3
z Jos 13:3
a Nu 13:21
b1Sa 6:21; 7:2
13:6
c Jos 15:9;
2Sa 6:2
d Ex 25:22;
2Ki 19:15
13:7
e Nu 4:15;
1Sa 7:1
13:8
f2Sa 6:5;
1Ch 15:16,19,
24; 2Ch 5:12;
Ps 92:3
13:10
g1Ch 15:13,15
h Lev 10:2
13:11
i1Ch 15:13;
Ps 7:11
13:13
j1Ch 15:18,24;
16:38; 26:4-5,15
13:14
k2Sa 6:11;
1Ch 26:4-5

ᵃ3 Or *we neglected*   ᵇ3 Or *him*   ᶜ5 Or *to the entrance to*   ᵈ11 *Perez Uzzah* means *outbreak against Uzzah.*

David's House and Family

14:1–7pp — 2Sa 5:11–16; 1Ch 3:5–8

14 Now Hiram king of Tyre sent messengers to David, along with cedar logs,[1] stonemasons and carpenters to build a palace for him. [2]And David knew that the Lord had established him as king over Israel and that his kingdom had been highly exalted[m] for the sake of his people Israel.

[3]In Jerusalem David took more wives and became the father of more sons[n] and daughters. [4]These are the names of the children born to him there:[o] Shammua, Shobab, Nathan, Solomon, [5]Ibhar, Elishua, Elpelet, [6]Nogah, Nepheg, Japhia, [7]Elishama, Beeliada[a] and Eliphelet.

David Defeats the Philistines

14:8–17pp — 2Sa 5:17–25

[8]When the Philistines heard that David had been anointed king over all Israel,[p] they went up in full force to search for him, but David heard about it and went out to meet them. [9]Now the Philistines had come and raided the Valley[q] of Rephaim; [10]so David inquired of God: "Shall I go and attack the Philistines? Will you hand them over to me?"

The Lord answered him, "Go, I will hand them over to you."

[11]So David and his men went up to Baal Perazim,[r] and there he defeated them. He said, "As waters break out, God has broken out against my enemies by my hand." So that place was called Baal Perazim.[b] [12]The Philistines had abandoned their gods there, and David gave orders to burn[s] them in the fire.[t]

[13]Once more the Philistines raided the valley;[u] [14]so David inquired of God again, and God answered him, "Do not go straight up, but circle around them and attack them in front of the balsam trees. [15]As soon as you hear the sound of marching in the tops of the balsam trees, move out to battle, because that will mean God has gone out in front of you to strike the Philistine army." [16]So David did as God commanded him, and they struck down the Philistine army, all the way from Gibeon[v] to Gezer.[w]

[17]So David's fame[x] spread throughout every land, and the Lord made all the nations fear[y] him.

The Ark Brought to Jerusalem

15:25–16:3pp — 2Sa 6:12–19

15 After David had constructed buildings for himself in the City of David, he prepared[z] a place for the ark of God and pitched[a] a tent for it. [2]Then David said, "No one but the Levites[b] may carry[c] the ark of God, because the Lord chose them to carry the ark of the Lord and to minister[d] before him forever."

[3]David assembled all Israel[e] in Jerusalem to bring up the ark of the Lord to the place he had prepared for it. [4]He called together the descendants of Aaron and the Levites:

[5]From the descendants of Kohath,
   Uriel the leader and 120 relatives;
[6]from the descendants of Merari,

14:1
l2Ch 2:3;
Ezr 3:7
14:2
mNu 24:7;
Dt 26:19
14:3
n1Ch 3:1
14:4
o1Ch 3:9
14:8
p1Ch 11:1
14:9
qver 13;
Jos 15:8;
1Ch 11:15
14:11
rIsa 28:21
14:12
sEx 32:20
tJos 7:15
14:13
uver 9
14:16
vJos 9:3
wJos 10:33
14:17
xJos 6:27;
2Ch 26:8
yEx 15:14-16;
Dt 2:25
15:1
zPs 132:1-18
a1Ch 16:1; 17:1
15:2
bNu 4:15;
Dt 10:8;
2Ch 5:5
cDt 31:9
d1Ch 23:13
15:3
e1Ki 8:1;
1Ch 13:5

Asaiah the leader and 220 relatives;
[7]from the descendants of Gershon,[a]
Joel the leader and 130 relatives;
[8]from the descendants of Elizaphan,[f]
Shemaiah the leader and 200 relatives;
[9]from the descendants of Hebron,[g]
Eliel the leader and 80 relatives;
[10]from the descendants of Uzziel,
Amminadab the leader and 112 relatives.

[11]Then David summoned Zadok[h] and Abiathar[i] the priests, and Uriel, Asaiah, Joel, Shemaiah, Eliel and Amminadab the Levites. [12]He said to them, "You are the heads of the Levitical families; you and your fellow Levites are to consecrate[j] yourselves and bring up the ark of the LORD, the God of Israel, to the place I have prepared for it. [13]It was because you, the Levites,[k] did not bring it up the first time that the LORD our God broke out in anger against us.[l] We did not inquire of him about how to do it in the prescribed way." [14]So the priests and Levites consecrated themselves in order to bring up the ark of the LORD, the God of Israel. [15]And the Levites carried the ark of God with the poles on their shoulders, as Moses had commanded[m] in accordance with the word of the LORD.

[16]David told the leaders of the Levites to appoint their brothers as singers[n] to sing joyful songs, accompanied by musical instruments: lyres, harps and cymbals.[o]

[17]So the Levites appointed Heman[p] son of Joel; from his brothers, Asaph[q] son of Berekiah; and from their brothers the Merarites,[r] Ethan son of Kushaiah; [18]and with them their brothers next in rank: Zechariah,[b] Jaaziel, Shemiramoth, Jehiel, Unni, Eliab, Benaiah, Maaseiah, Mattithiah, Eliphelehu, Mikneiah, Obed-Edom[s] and Jeiel,[c] the gatekeepers.

[19]The musicians Heman,[t] Asaph and Ethan were to sound the bronze cymbals; [20]Zechariah, Aziel, Shemiramoth, Jehiel, Unni, Eliab, Maaseiah and Benaiah were to play the lyres according to *alamoth,*[d] [21]and Mattithiah, Eliphelehu, Mikneiah, Obed-Edom, Jeiel and Azaziah were to play the harps, directing according to *sheminith.*[d] [22]Kenaniah the head Levite was in charge of the singing; that was his responsibility because he was skillful at it.

[23]Berekiah and Elkanah were to be doorkeepers for the ark. [24]Shebaniah, Joshaphat, Nethanel, Amasai, Zechariah, Benaiah and Eliezer the priests were to blow trumpets[u] before the ark of God. Obed-Edom and Jehiah were also to be doorkeepers for the ark.

[25]So David and the elders of Israel and the commanders of units of a thousand went to bring up the ark[v] of the covenant of the LORD from the house of Obed-Edom, with rejoicing. [26]Because God had helped the Levites who were carrying the ark of the covenant of the LORD, seven bulls and seven rams[w] were sacrificed. [27]Now David was clothed in a robe of fine linen, as were all the Levites who were carrying the ark, and as were the singers, and Kenaniah, who was in charge of the singing of

15:8
f Ex 6:22
15:9
g Ex 6:18
15:11
h 1Ch 12:28
i 1Sa 22:20
15:12
j Ex 19:14-15;
Lev 11:44;
2Ch 35:6
15:13
k 1Ki 8:4
l 2Sa 6:3;
1Ch 13:7-10
15:15
m Ex 25:14;
Nu 4:5,15
15:16
n Ps 68:25
o 1Ch 13:8;
25:1;
Ne 12:27,36
15:17
p 1Ch 6:33
q 1Ch 6:39
r 1Ch 6:44
15:18
s 1Ch 26:4-5
15:19
t 1Ch 25:6
15:24
u ver 28;
1Ch 16:6;
2Ch 7:6
15:25
v 1Ch 13:13;
2Ch 1:4
15:26
w Nu 23:1-4,29

---

[a]7 Hebrew *Gershom,* a variant of *Gershon*   [b]18 Three Hebrew manuscripts and most Septuagint manuscripts (see also verse 20 and 1 Chron. 16:5); most Hebrew manuscripts *Zechariah son and* or *Zechariah, Ben and*   [c]18 Hebrew; Septuagint (see also verse 21) *Jeiel and Azaziah*   [d]20,21 Probably a musical term

the choirs. David also wore a linen ephod. ²⁸So all Israel brought up the ark of the covenant of the LORD with shouts, with the sounding of rams' horns˟ and trumpets, and of cymbals, and the playing of lyres and harps.

²⁹As the ark of the covenant of the LORD was entering the City of David, Michal daughter of Saul watched from a window. And when she saw King David dancing and celebrating, she despised him in her heart.

16 They brought the ark of God and set it inside the tent that David had pitchedʸ for it, and they presented burnt offerings and fellowship offeringsᵃ before God. ²After David had finished sacrificing the burnt offerings and fellowship offerings, he blessedᶻ the people in the name of the LORD. ³Then he gave a loaf of bread, a cake of dates and a cake of raisins to each Israelite man and woman.

⁴He appointed some of the Levites to ministerᵃ before the ark of the LORD, to make petition, to give thanks, and to praise the LORD, the God of Israel: ⁵Asaph was the chief, Zechariah second, then Jeiel, Shemiramoth, Jehiel, Mattithiah, Eliab, Benaiah, Obed-Edom and Jeiel. They were to play the lyres and harps, Asaph was to sound the cymbals, ⁶and Benaiah and Jahaziel the priests were to blow the trumpets regularly before the ark of the covenant of God.

David's Psalm of Thanks

16:8–22pp — Ps 105:1–15
16:23–33pp — Ps 96:1–13
16:34–36pp — Ps 106:1,47–48

⁷That day David first committed to Asaph and his associates this psalmᵇ of thanks to the LORD:

⁸Give thanksᶜ to the LORD, call on his name;
    make known among the nationsᵈ what he has done.
⁹Sing to him, sing praiseᵉ to him;
    tell of all his wonderful acts.
¹⁰Glory in his holy name;
    let the hearts of those who seek the LORD rejoice.
¹¹Look to the LORD and his strength;
    seekᶠ his face always.
¹²Rememberᵍ the wonders he has done,
    his miracles,ʰ and the judgments he pronounced,
¹³O descendants of Israel his servant,
    O sons of Jacob, his chosen ones.

¹⁴He is the LORD our God;
    his judgmentsⁱ are in all the earth.
¹⁵He remembersᵇ his covenant forever,
    the word he commanded, for a thousand generations,
¹⁶the covenantʲ he made with Abraham,
    the oath he swore to Isaac.
¹⁷He confirmed it to Jacobᵏ as a decree,
    to Israel as an everlasting covenant:

15:28
ˣ1Ch 13:8
16:1
ʸ1Ch 15:1
16:2
ᶻEx 39:43
16:4
ᵃ1Ch 15:2
16:7
ᵇ2Sa 23:1
16:8
ᶜver 34;
Ps 136:1
ᵈ2Ki 19:19
16:9
ᵉEx 15:1
16:11
ᶠ1Ch 28:9;
2Ch 7:14;
Ps 24:6;
119:2,58
16:12
ᵍPs 77:11
ʰPs 78:43
16:14
ⁱIsa 26:9
16:16
ʲGe 12:7;
15:18; 17:2;
22:16-18; 26:3;
28:13; 35:11
16:17
ᵏGe 35:9-12

ᵃ1 Traditionally *peace offerings*; also in verse 2   ᵇ15 Some Septuagint manuscripts (see also Psalm 105:8); Hebrew *Remember*

[18]"To you I will give the land of Canaan[l]
    as the portion you will inherit."

[19]When they were but few in number,[m]
    few indeed, and strangers in it,
[20]they[a] wandered from nation to nation,
    from one kingdom to another.
[21]He allowed no man to oppress them;
    for their sake he rebuked kings:[n]
[22]"Do not touch my anointed ones;
    do my prophets[o] no harm."

[23]Sing to the LORD, all the earth;
    proclaim his salvation day after day.
[24]Declare his glory among the nations,
    his marvelous deeds among all peoples.
[25]For great is the LORD and most worthy of praise;[p]
    he is to be feared[q] above all gods.[r]
[26]For all the gods of the nations are idols,
    but the LORD made the heavens.[s]
[27]Splendor and majesty are before him;
    strength and joy in his dwelling place.
[28]Ascribe to the LORD, O families of nations,
    ascribe to the LORD glory and strength,[t]
[29] ascribe to the LORD the glory due his name.
  Bring an offering and come before him;
    worship the LORD in the splendor of his[b] holiness.[u]
[30]Tremble[v] before him, all the earth!
    The world is firmly established; it cannot be moved.
[31]Let the heavens rejoice, let the earth be glad;[w]
    let them say among the nations, "The LORD reigns!"[x]
[32]Let the sea resound, and all that is in it;[y]
    let the fields be jubilant, and everything in them!
[33]Then the trees[z] of the forest will sing,
    they will sing for joy before the LORD,
    for he comes to judge[a] the earth.

[34]Give thanks[b] to the LORD, for he is good;[c]
    his love endures forever.[d]
[35]Cry out, "Save us, O God our Savior;[e]
    gather us and deliver us from the nations,
  that we may give thanks to your holy name,
    that we may glory in your praise."
[36]Praise be to the LORD, the God of Israel,[f]
    from everlasting to everlasting.

Then all the people said "Amen" and "Praise the LORD."

[37]David left Asaph and his associates before the ark of the covenant of
the LORD to minister there regularly, according to each day's requirements.[g] [38]He also left Obed-Edom[h] and his sixty-eight associates to

16:18
lGe 13:14-17
16:19
mGe 34:30;
Dt 7:7
16:21
nGe 12:17;
20:3; Ex 7:15-18
16:22
oGe 20:7
16:25
pPs 48:1
qPs 76:7; 89:7
rDt 32:39
16:26
sLev 19:4;
Ps 102:25
16:28
tPs 29:1-2
16:29
uPs 29:1-2
16:30
vPs 114:7
16:31
wIsa 44:23;
49:13 xPs 93:1
16:32
yPs 98:7
16:33
zIsa 55:12
aPs 96:10; 98:9
16:34
bver 8 cNa 1:7
d2Ch 5:13; 7:3;
Ezr 3:11;
Ps 136:1-26;
Jer 33:11
16:35
eMic 7:7
16:36
fDt 27:15;
1Ki 8:15;
Ps 72:18-19
16:37
g2Ch 8:14
16:38
h1Ch 13:13

---

[a]18-20 One Hebrew manuscript, Septuagint and Vulgate (see also Psalm 105:12); most Hebrew
manuscripts *inherit*, / [19]*though you are but few in number*, / *few indeed, and strangers in it."* / [20]*They*
[b]29 Or LORD *with the splendor of*

minister with them. Obed-Edom son of Jeduthun, and also Hosah,[i] were gatekeepers.

[39]David left Zadok[j] the priest and his fellow priests before the tabernacle of the LORD at the high place in Gibeon[k] [40]to present burnt offerings to the LORD on the altar of burnt offering regularly, morning and evening, in accordance with everything written in the Law[l] of the LORD, which he had given Israel. [41]With them were Heman[m] and Jeduthun and the rest of those chosen and designated by name to give thanks to the LORD, "for his love endures forever." [42]Heman and Jeduthun were responsible for the sounding of the trumpets and cymbals and for the playing of the other instruments for sacred song.[n] The sons of Jeduthun were stationed at the gate.

[43]Then all the people left, each for his own home, and David returned home to bless his family.

God's Promise to David

17:1–15pp — 2Sa 7:1–17

17 After David was settled in his palace, he said to Nathan the prophet, "Here I am, living in a palace of cedar, while the ark of the covenant of the LORD is under a tent.[o]"

[2]Nathan replied to David, "Whatever you have in mind,[p] do it, for God is with you."

[3]That night the word of God came to Nathan, saying:

[4]"Go and tell my servant David, 'This is what the LORD says: You[q] are not the one to build me a house to dwell in. [5]I have not dwelt in a house from the day I brought Israel up out of Egypt to this day. I have moved from one tent site to another, from one dwelling place to another. [6]Wherever I have moved with all the Israelites, did I ever say to any of their leaders[a] whom I commanded to shepherd my people, "Why have you not built me a house of cedar?"'

[7]"Now then, tell my servant David, 'This is what the LORD Almighty says: I took you from the pasture and from following the flock, to be ruler[r] over my people Israel. [8]I have been with you wherever you have gone, and I have cut off all your enemies from before you. Now I will make your name like the names of the greatest men of the earth. [9]And I will provide a place for my people Israel and will plant them so that they can have a home of their own and no longer be disturbed. Wicked people will not oppress them anymore, as they did at the beginning [10]and have done ever since the time I appointed leaders[s] over my people Israel. I will also subdue all your enemies.

" 'I declare to you that the LORD will build a house for you: [11]When your days are over and you go to be with your fathers, I will raise up your offspring to succeed you, one of your own sons, and I will establish his kingdom. [12]He is the one who will build[t] a house for me, and I will establish his throne forever.[u] [13]I will be his father,[v] and he will be my son.[w] I will never take my love away from him, as I took it away from your predecessor. [14]I will set him

---

[a]6 Traditionally *judges*; also in verse 10

16:38
i1Ch 26:10
16:39
j2Sa 8:17;
1Ch 15:11
k1Ki 3:4;
2Ch 1:3
16:40
lEx 29:38;
Nu 28:1-8
16:41
m1Ch 6:33;
25:1-6;
2Ch 5:13
16:42
n2Ch 7:6
17:1
o1Ch 15:1
17:2
p2Ch 6:7
17:4
q1Ch 28:3
17:7
r2Sa 6:21
17:10
sJdg 2:16
17:12
t1Ki 5:5
u2Ch 7:18
17:13
v2Co 6:18
wLk 1:32;
Heb 1:5

over my house and my kingdom forever; his throne[x] will be established forever.[y]' "

[15]Nathan reported to David all the words of this entire revelation.

David's Prayer
17:16–27pp — 2Sa 7:18–29

[16]Then King David went in and sat before the LORD, and he said:

"Who am I, O LORD God, and what is my family, that you have brought me this far? [17]And as if this were not enough in your sight, O God, you have spoken about the future of the house of your servant. You have looked on me as though I were the most exalted of men, O LORD God.

[18]"What more can David say to you for honoring your servant? For you know your servant, [19]O LORD. For the sake[z] of your servant and according to your will, you have done this great thing and made known all these great promises.[a]

[20]"There is no one like you, O LORD, and there is no God but you,[b] as we have heard with our own ears. [21]And who is like your people Israel—the one nation on earth whose God went out to redeem[c] a people for himself, and to make a name for yourself, and to perform great and awesome wonders by driving out nations from before your people, whom you redeemed from Egypt? [22]You made your people Israel your very own forever,[d] and you, O LORD, have become their God.

[23]"And now, LORD, let the promise[e] you have made concerning your servant and his house be established forever. Do as you promised, [24]so that it will be established and that your name will be great forever. Then men will say, 'The LORD Almighty, the God over Israel, is Israel's God!' And the house of your servant David will be established before you.

[25]"You, my God, have revealed to your servant that you will build a house for him. So your servant has found courage to pray to you. [26]O LORD, you are God! You have promised these good things to your servant. [27]Now you have been pleased to bless the house of your servant, that it may continue forever in your sight;[f] for you, O LORD, have blessed it, and it will be blessed forever."

David's Victories
18:1–13pp — 2Sa 8:1–14

18 In the course of time, David defeated the Philistines and subdued them, and he took Gath and its surrounding villages from the control of the Philistines.

[2]David also defeated the Moabites,[g] and they became subject to him and brought tribute.

[3]Moreover, David fought Hadadezer king of Zobah,[h] as far as Hamath, when he went to establish his control along the Euphrates River.[i] [4]David captured a thousand of his chariots, seven thousand charioteers and twenty thousand foot soldiers. He hamstrung[j] all but a hundred of the chariot horses.

[5]When the Arameans of Damascus[k] came to help Hadadezer king of Zobah, David struck down twenty-two thousand of them. [6]He put

17:14
x1Ki 2:12;
1Ch 28:5
yPs 132:11;
Jer 33:17
17:19
z2Sa 7:16-17;
2Ki 20:6;
Isa 9:7; 37:35;
55:3 a2Sa 7:25
17:20
bEx 8:10; 9:14;
15:11; Isa 44:6;
46:9
17:21
cEx 6:6
17:22
dEx 19:5-6
17:23
e1Ki 8:25
17:27
fPs 16:11; 21:6
18:2
gNu 21:29
18:3
h1Ch 19:6
iGe 2:14
18:4
jGe 49:6
18:5
k2Ki 16:9;
1Ch 19:6

garrisons in the Aramean kingdom of Damascus, and the Arameans became subject to him and brought tribute. The LORD gave David victory everywhere he went.

7David took the gold shields carried by the officers of Hadadezer and brought them to Jerusalem. 8From Tebah*ᵃ* and Cun, towns that belonged to Hadadezer, David took a great quantity of bronze, which Solomon used to make the bronze Sea,*ˡ* the pillars and various bronze articles.

9When Tou king of Hamath heard that David had defeated the entire army of Hadadezer king of Zobah, 10he sent his son Hadoram to King David to greet him and congratulate him on his victory in battle over Hadadezer, who had been at war with Tou. Hadoram brought all kinds of articles of gold and silver and bronze.

11King David dedicated these articles to the LORD, as he had done with the silver and gold he had taken from all these nations: Edom*ᵐ* and Moab, the Ammonites and the Philistines, and Amalek.*ⁿ*

12Abishai son of Zeruiah struck down eighteen thousand Edomites*ᵒ* in the Valley of Salt. 13He put garrisons in Edom, and all the Edomites became subject to David. The LORD gave David victory everywhere he went.

David's Officials

18:14–17pp — 2Sa 8:15–18

14David reigned*ᵖ* over all Israel,*�q* doing what was just and right for all his people. 15Joab*ʳ* son of Zeruiah was over the army; Jehoshaphat son of Ahilud was recorder; 16Zadok*ˢ* son of Ahitub and Ahimelech*ᵇᵗ* son of Abiathar were priests; Shavsha was secretary; 17Benaiah son of Jehoiada was over the Kerethites and Pelethites;*ᵘ* and David's sons were chief officials at the king's side.

The Battle Against the Ammonites

19:1–19pp — 2Sa 10:1–19

19 In the course of time, Nahash king of the Ammonites*ᵛ* died, and his son succeeded him as king. 2David thought, "I will show kindness to Hanun son of Nahash, because his father showed kindness to me." So David sent a delegation to express his sympathy to Hanun concerning his father.

When David's men came to Hanun in the land of the Ammonites to express sympathy to him, 3the Ammonite nobles said to Hanun, "Do you think David is honoring your father by sending men to you to express sympathy? Haven't his men come to you to explore and spy out*ʷ* the country and overthrow it?" 4So Hanun seized David's men, shaved them, cut off their garments in the middle at the buttocks, and sent them away.

5When someone came and told David about the men, he sent messengers to meet them, for they were greatly humiliated. The king said, "Stay at Jericho till your beards have grown, and then come back."

6When the Ammonites realized that they had become a stench*ˣ* in

18:8
l1Ki 7:23;
2Ch 4:12,15-16
18:11
mNu 24:18
nNu 24:20
18:12
o1Ki 11:15
18:14
p1Ch 29:26
q1Ch 11:1
18:15
r2Sa 5:6-8;
1Ch 11:6
18:16
s2Sa 8:17;
1Ch 6:8
t1Ch 24:6
18:17
u1Sa 30:14;
2Sa 8:18; 15:18
19:1
vGe 19:38;
Jdg 10:17-11:33;
2Ch 20:1-2;
Zep 2:8-11
19:3
wNu 21:32
19:6
xGe 34:30

---

*ᵃ*8 Hebrew *Tibhath*, a variant of *Tebah*   *ᵇ*16 Some Hebrew manuscripts, Vulgate and Syriac (see also 2 Samuel 8:17); most Hebrew manuscripts *Abimelech*

David's nostrils, Hanun and the Ammonites sent a thousand talents[a] of silver to hire chariots and charioteers from Aram Naharaim,[b] Aram Maacah and Zobah.[y] [7]They hired thirty-two thousand chariots and charioteers, as well as the king of Maacah with his troops, who came and camped near Medeba,[z] while the Ammonites were mustered from their towns and moved out for battle.

[8]On hearing this, David sent Joab out with the entire army of fighting men. [9]The Ammonites came out and drew up in battle formation at the entrance to their city, while the kings who had come were by themselves in the open country.

[10]Joab saw that there were battle lines in front of him and behind him; so he selected some of the best troops in Israel and deployed them against the Arameans. [11]He put the rest of the men under the command of Abishai[a] his brother, and they were deployed against the Ammonites. [12]Joab said, "If the Arameans are too strong for me, then you are to rescue me; but if the Ammonites are too strong for you, then I will rescue you. [13]Be strong and let us fight bravely for our people and the cities of our God. The LORD will do what is good in his sight."

[14]Then Joab and the troops with him advanced to fight the Arameans, and they fled before him. [15]When the Ammonites saw that the Arameans were fleeing, they too fled before his brother Abishai and went inside the city. So Joab went back to Jerusalem.

[16]After the Arameans saw that they had been routed by Israel, they sent messengers and had Arameans brought from beyond the River,[c] with Shophach the commander of Hadadezer's army leading them.

[17]When David was told of this, he gathered all Israel[b] and crossed the Jordan; he advanced against them and formed his battle lines opposite them. David formed his lines to meet the Arameans in battle, and they fought against him. [18]But they fled before Israel, and David killed seven thousand of their charioteers and forty thousand of their foot soldiers. He also killed Shophach the commander of their army.

[19]When the vassals of Hadadezer saw that they had been defeated by Israel, they made peace with David and became subject to him.

So the Arameans were not willing to help the Ammonites anymore.

The Capture of Rabbah

20:1–3pp — 2Sa 11:1; 12:29–31

20 In the spring, at the time when kings go off to war, Joab led out the armed forces. He laid waste the land of the Ammonites and went to Rabbah[c] and besieged it, but David remained in Jerusalem. Joab attacked Rabbah and left it in ruins. [d] [2]David took the crown from the head of their king[d]—its weight was found to be a talent[e] of gold, and it was set with precious stones—and it was placed on David's head. He took a great quantity of plunder from the city [3]and brought out the people who were there, consigning them to labor with saws and with iron picks and axes.[e] David did this to all the Ammonite towns. Then David and his entire army returned to Jerusalem.

19:6
y 1Ch 18:3,5,9
19:7
z Nu 21:30;
Jos 13:9,16
19:11
a 1Sa 26:6
19:17
b 1Ch 9:1
20:1
c Dt 3:11;
2Sa 12:26
d Am 1:13-15
20:3
e Dt 29:11

---

[a]6 That is, about 37 tons (about 34 metric tons)   [b]6 That is, Northwest Mesopotamia
[c]16 That is, the Euphrates   [d]2 Or *of Milcom,* that is, Molech   [e]2 That is, about 75 pounds
(about 34 kilograms)

War With the Philistines

2:4-8pp — 2Sa 21:15-22

[4]In the course of time, war broke out with the Philistines, at Gezer. [f] At that time Sibbecai the Hushathite killed Sippai, one of the descendants of the Rephaites, [g] and the Philistines were subjugated.

[5]In another battle with the Philistines, Elhanan son of Jair killed Lahmi the brother of Goliath the Gittite, who had a spear with a shaft like a weaver's rod. [h]

[6]In still another battle, which took place at Gath, there was a huge man with six fingers on each hand and six toes on each foot—twenty-four in all. He also was descended from Rapha. [7]When he taunted Israel, Jonathan son of Shimea, David's brother, killed him.

[8]These were descendants of Rapha in Gath, and they fell at the hands of David and his men.

David Numbers the Fighting Men

21:1-26pp — 2Sa 24:1-25

21 Satan [i] rose up against Israel and incited David to take a census [j] of Israel. [2]So David said to Joab and the commanders of the troops, "Go and count [k] the Israelites from Beersheba to Dan. Then report back to me so that I may know how many there are."

[3]But Joab replied, "May the LORD multiply his troops a hundred times over. [l] My lord the king, are they not all my lord's subjects? Why does my lord want to do this? Why should he bring guilt on Israel?"

[4]The king's word, however, overruled Joab; so Joab left and went throughout Israel and then came back to Jerusalem. [5]Joab reported the number of the fighting men to David: In all Israel [m] there were one million one hundred thousand men who could handle a sword, including four hundred and seventy thousand in Judah.

[6]But Joab did not include Levi and Benjamin in the numbering, because the king's command was repulsive to him. [7]This command was also evil in the sight of God; so he punished Israel.

[8]Then David said to God, "I have sinned greatly by doing this. Now, I beg you, take away the guilt of your servant. I have done a very foolish thing."

[9]The LORD said to Gad, [n] David's seer, [o] [10]"Go and tell David, 'This is what the LORD says: I am giving you three options. Choose one of them for me to carry out against you.' "

[11]So Gad went to David and said to him, "This is what the LORD says: 'Take your choice: [12]three years of famine, [p] three months of being swept away[a] before your enemies, with their swords overtaking you, or three days of the sword [q] of the LORD [r]—days of plague in the land, with the angel of the LORD ravaging every part of Israel.' Now then, decide how I should answer the one who sent me."

[13]David said to Gad, "I am in deep distress. Let me fall into the hands of the LORD, for his mercy [s] is very great; but do not let me fall into the hands of men."

[14]So the LORD sent a plague on Israel, and seventy thousand men of Israel fell dead. [t] [15]And God sent an angel [u] to destroy Jerusalem. [v] But

---

a12 Hebrew; Septuagint and Vulgate (see also 2 Samuel 24:13) *of fleeing*

20:4
f Jos 10:33
g Ge 14:5
20:5
h 1Sa 17:7
21:1
i 2Ch 18:21;
Ps 109:6
j 2Ch 14:8; 25:5
21:2
k 1Ch 27:23-24
21:3
l Dt 1:11
21:5
m 1Ch 9:1
21:9
n 1Sa 22:5
o 1Sa 9:9
21:12
p Dt 32:24
q Eze 30:25
r Ge 19:13
21:13
s Ps 6:4; 86:15;
130:4,7
21:14
t 1Ch 27:24
21:15
u Ge 32:1
v Ps 125:2

as the angel was doing so, the Lord saw it and was grieved[w] because of the calamity and said to the angel who was destroying[x] the people, "Enough! Withdraw your hand." The angel of the Lord was then standing at the threshing floor of Araunah[a] the Jebusite.

[16]David looked up and saw the angel of the Lord standing between heaven and earth, with a drawn sword in his hand extended over Jerusalem. Then David and the elders, clothed in sackcloth, fell facedown.[y]

[17]David said to God, "Was it not I who ordered the fighting men to be counted? I am the one who has sinned and done wrong. These are but sheep.[z] What have they done? O Lord my God, let your hand fall upon me and my family,[a] but do not let this plague remain on your people."

[18]Then the angel of the Lord ordered Gad to tell David to go up and build an altar to the Lord on the threshing floor[b] of Araunah the Jebusite. [19]So David went up in obedience to the word that Gad had spoken in the name of the Lord.

[20]While Araunah was threshing wheat,[c] he turned and saw the angel; his four sons who were with him hid themselves. [21]Then David approached, and when Araunah looked and saw him, he left the threshing floor and bowed down before David with his face to the ground.

[22]David said to him, "Let me have the site of your threshing floor so I can build an altar to the Lord, that the plague on the people may be stopped. Sell it to me at the full price."

[23]Araunah said to David, "Take it! Let my lord the king do whatever pleases him. Look, I will give the oxen for the burnt offerings, the threshing sledges for the wood, and the wheat for the grain offering. I will give all this."

[24]But King David replied to Araunah, "No, I insist on paying the full price. I will not take for the Lord what is yours, or sacrifice a burnt offering that costs me nothing."

[25]So David paid Araunah six hundred shekels[b] of gold for the site. [26]David built an altar to the Lord there and sacrificed burnt offerings and fellowship offerings.[c] He called on the Lord, and the Lord answered him with fire[d] from heaven on the altar of burnt offering.

[27]Then the Lord spoke to the angel, and he put his sword back into its sheath. [28]At that time, when David saw that the Lord had answered him on the threshing floor of Araunah the Jebusite, he offered sacrifices there. [29]The tabernacle of the Lord, which Moses had made in the desert, and the altar of burnt offering were at that time on the high place at Gibeon.[e] [30]But David could not go before it to inquire of God, because he was afraid of the sword of the angel of the Lord.

22 Then David said, "The house of the Lord God[f] is to be here, and also the altar of burnt offering for Israel."

Preparations for the Temple

[2]So David gave orders to assemble the aliens[g] living in Israel, and from among them he appointed stonecutters[h] to prepare dressed stone for building the house of God. [3]He provided a large amount of iron to

---

*Cross references (left margin):*

21:15
wGe 6:6;
Ex 32:14
xGe 19:13
21:16
yNu 14:5;
Jos 7:6
21:17
z2Sa 7:8;
Ps 74:1
aJnh 1:12
21:18
b2Ch 3:1
21:20
cJdg 6:11
21:26
dLev 9:24;
Jdg 6:21
21:29
e1Ki 3:4;
1Ch 16:39
22:1
fGe 28:17;
1Ch 21:18-29;
2Ch 3:1
22:2
g1Ki 9:21;
Isa 56:6
h1Ki 5:17-18

---

[a]15 Hebrew *Ornan*, a variant of *Araunah*; also in verses 18-28   [b]25 That is, about 15 pounds (about 7 kilograms)   [c]26 Traditionally *peace offerings*

make nails for the doors of the gateways and for the fittings, and more bronze than could be weighed.[i] 4He also provided more cedar logs[j] than could be counted, for the Sidonians and Tyrians had brought large numbers of them to David.

5David said, "My son Solomon is young[k] and inexperienced, and the house to be built for the LORD should be of great magnificence and fame and splendor in the sight of all the nations. Therefore I will make preparations for it." So David made extensive preparations before his death.

6Then he called for his son Solomon and charged him to build[l] a house for the LORD, the God of Israel. 7David said to Solomon: "My son, I had it in my heart[m] to build[n] a house for the Name[o] of the LORD my God. 8But this word of the LORD came to me: 'You have shed much blood and have fought many wars.[p] You are not to build a house for my Name,[q] because you have shed much blood on the earth in my sight. 9But you will have a son who will be a man of peace[r] and rest, and I will give him rest from all his enemies on every side. His name will be Solomon,[a][s] and I will grant Israel peace and quiet[t] during his reign. 10He is the one who will build a house for my Name.[u] He will be my son,[v] and I will be his father. And I will establish the throne of his kingdom over Israel forever.'[w]

11"Now, my son, the LORD be with[x] you, and may you have success and build the house of the LORD your God, as he said you would. 12May the LORD give you discretion and understanding[y] when he puts you in command over Israel, so that you may keep the law of the LORD your God. 13Then you will have success if you are careful to observe the decrees and laws[z] that the LORD gave Moses for Israel. Be strong and courageous.[a] Do not be afraid or discouraged.

14"I have taken great pains to provide for the temple of the LORD a hundred thousand talents[b] of gold, a million talents[c] of silver, quantities of bronze and iron too great to be weighed, and wood and stone. And you may add to them.[b] 15You have many workmen: stonecutters, masons and carpenters, as well as men skilled in every kind of work 16in gold and silver, bronze and iron—craftsmen[c] beyond number. Now begin the work, and the LORD be with you."

17Then David ordered[d] all the leaders of Israel to help his son Solomon. 18He said to them, "Is not the LORD your God with you? And has he not granted you rest[e] on every side?[f] For he has handed the inhabitants of the land over to me, and the land is subject to the LORD and to his people. 19Now devote your heart and soul to seeking the LORD your God.[g] Begin to build the sanctuary of the LORD God, so that you may bring the ark of the covenant of the LORD and the sacred articles belonging to God into the temple that will be built for the Name of the LORD."

The Levites

23 When David was old and full of years, he made his son Solomon[h] king over Israel.[i]

2He also gathered together all the leaders of Israel, as well as the

22:3
i ver 14;
1Ki 7:47;
1Ch 29:2-5
22:4
j 1Ki 5:6
22:5
k 1Ki 3:7;
1Ch 29:1
22:6
l Ac 7:47
22:7
m 1Ch 17:2
n 2Sa 7:2;
1Ki 8:17
o Dt 12:5,11
22:8
p 1Ch 5:3
q 1Ch 28:3
22:9
r 1Ki 5:4
s 2Sa 12:24
t 1Ki 4:20
22:10
u 1Ch 17:12
v 2Sa 7:13
w 2Sa 7:14;
2Ch 6:15
22:11
x ver 16
22:12
y 1Ki 3:9-12;
2Ch 1:10
22:13
z 1Ch 28:7
a Dt 31:6;
Jos 1:6-9;
1Ch 28:20
22:14
b ver 3;
1Ch 29:2-5,19
22:16
c ver 11;
2Ch 2:7
22:17
d 1Ch 28:1-6
22:18
e ver 9;
1Ch 23:25
f 2Sa 7:1
22:19
g ver 7; 1Ki 8:6;
1Ch 28:9;
2Ch 5:7; 7:14
23:1
h 1Ki 1:33-39;
1Ch 28:5
i 1Ki 1:30;
1Ch 29:28

---

a9 *Solomon* sounds like and may be derived from the Hebrew for *peace.*   *b14* That is, about 3,750 tons (about 3,450 metric tons)   *c14* That is, about 37,500 tons (about 34,500 metric tons) priests and Levites. ³The Levites thirty years old or more[j] were counted, and the total number of men was thirty-eight thousand.[k] ⁴David said, "Of these, twenty-four thousand are to supervise[l] the work of the temple of the LORD and six thousand are to be officials and judges.[m] ⁵Four thousand are to be gatekeepers and four thousand are to praise the LORD with the musical instruments[n] I have provided for that purpose."[o]

⁶David divided[p] the Levites into groups corresponding to the sons of Levi: Gershon, Kohath and Merari.

Gershonites

⁷Belonging to the Gershonites:
　　Ladan and Shimei.
　⁸The sons of Ladan:
　　Jehiel the first, Zetham and Joel—three in all.
　⁹The sons of Shimei:
　　Shelomoth, Haziel and Haran—three in all.
　　These were the heads of the families of Ladan.
¹⁰And the sons of Shimei:
　　Jahath, Ziza,[a] Jeush and Beriah.
　　These were the sons of Shimei—four in all.
　¹¹Jahath was the first and Ziza the second, but Jeush and Beriah did not have many sons; so they were counted as one family with one assignment.

Kohathites

¹²The sons of Kohath:[q]
　　Amram, Izhar, Hebron and Uzziel—four in all.
¹³The sons of Amram:[r]
　　Aaron and Moses.
　　Aaron was set apart,[s] he and his descendants forever, to consecrate the most holy things, to offer sacrifices before the LORD, to minister before him and to pronounce blessings[t] in his name forever. ¹⁴The sons of Moses the man[u] of God were counted as part of the tribe of Levi.
¹⁵The sons of Moses:
　　Gershom and Eliezer.[v]
¹⁶The descendants of Gershom:[w]
　　Shubael was the first.
¹⁷The descendants of Eliezer:
　　Rehabiah was the first.
　　Eliezer had no other sons, but the sons of Rehabiah were very numerous.
¹⁸The sons of Izhar:
　　Shelomith was the first.
¹⁹The sons of Hebron:[x]
　　Jeriah the first, Amariah the second, Jahaziel the third and Jekameam the fourth.
²⁰The sons of Uzziel:

### Cross-references (margin)

23:3
j ver 24;
Nu 8:24
k Nu 4:3-49
23:4
l Ezr 3:8
m 1Ch 26:29;
2Ch 19:8
23:5
n 1Ch 15:16
o Ne 12:45
23:6
p 2Ch 8:14;
29:25
23:12
q Ex 6:18
23:13
r Ex 6:20; 28:1
s Ex 30:7-10;
Dt 21:5
t Nu 6:23
23:14
u Dt 33:1
23:15
v Ex 18:4
23:16
w 1Ch 26:24-28
23:19
x 1Ch 24:23

---

[a]10 One Hebrew manuscript, Septuagint and Vulgate (see also verse 11); most Hebrew manuscripts *Zina*

Micah the first and Isshiah the second.

Merarites

21The sons of Merari:y
Mahli and Mushi.
The sons of Mahli:
Eleazar and Kish.
22Eleazar died without having sons: he had only daughters. Their cousins, the sons of Kish, married them.
23The sons of Mushi:
Mahli, Eder and Jerimoth—three in all.

24These were the descendants of Levi by their families—the heads of families as they were registered under their names and counted individually, that is, the workers twenty years old or morez who served in the temple of the LORD. 25For David had said, "Since the LORD, the God of Israel, has granted resta to his people and has come to dwell in Jerusalem forever, 26the Levites no longer need to carry the tabernacle or any of the articles used in its service."b 27According to the last instructions of David, the Levites were counted from those twenty years old or more.

28The duty of the Levites was to help Aaron's descendants in the service of the temple of the LORD: to be in charge of the courtyards, the side rooms, the purificationc of all sacred things and the performance of other duties at the house of God. 29They were in charge of the bread set out on the table,d the flour for the grain offerings,e the unleavened wafers, the baking and the mixing, and all measurements of quantity and size.f 30They were also to stand every morning to thank and praise the LORD. They were to do the same in the eveningg 31and whenever burnt offerings were presented to the LORD on Sabbaths and at New Moonh festivals and at appointed feasts.i They were to serve before the LORD regularly in the proper number and in the way prescribed for them.

32And so the Levitesj carried out their responsibilities for the Tent of Meeting,k for the Holy Place and, under their brothers the descendants of Aaron, for the service of the temple of the LORD.l

The Divisions of Priests

24 These were the divisionsm of the sons of Aaron:n
The sons of Aaron were Nadab, Abihu, Eleazar and Ithamar.o
2But Nadab and Abihu died before their father did,p and they had no sons; so Eleazar and Ithamar served as the priests. 3With the help of Zadokq a descendant of Eleazar and Ahimelech a descendant of Ithamar, David separated them into divisions for their appointed order of ministering. 4A larger number of leaders were found among Eleazar's descendants than among Ithamar's, and they were divided accordingly: sixteen heads of families from Eleazar's descendants and eight heads of families from Ithamar's descendants. 5They divided them impartially by drawing lots,r for there were officials of the sanctuary and officials of God among the descendants of both Eleazar and Ithamar.

6The scribe Shemaiah son of Nethanel, a Levite, recorded their

23:21
y1Ch 24:26
23:24
zNu 4:3; 10:17, 21
23:25
a1Ch 22:9
23:26
bNu 4:5,15; 7:9; Dt 10:8
23:28
c2Ch 29:15; Ne 13:9; Mal 3:3
23:29
dEx 25:30
eLev 2:4-7; 6:20-23
fLev 19:35-36; 1Ch 9:29,32
23:30
g1Ch 9:33; Ps 134:1
23:31
h2Ki 4:23
iLev 23:4; Nu 28:9-29:39; Isa 1:13-14; Col 2:16
23:32
jNu 1:53; 1Ch 6:48
kNu 3:6-8,38
l2Ch 23:18; 31:2; Eze 44:14
24:1
m1Ch 23:6; 28:13; 2Ch 5:11; 8:14; 23:8; 31:2; 35:4,5; Ezr 6:18
nNu 3:2-4
oEx 6:23
24:2
pLev 10:1-2; Nu 3:4
24:3
q2Sa 8:17
24:5
rver 31; 1Ch 25:8

names in the presence of the king and of the officials: Zadok the priest, Ahimelech[s] son of Abiathar and the heads of families of the priests and of the Levites—one family being taken from Eleazar and then one from Ithamar.

⁷The first lot fell to Jehoiarib,
  the second to Jedaiah,[t]
⁸the third to Harim,[u]
  the fourth to Seorim,
⁹the fifth to Malkijah,
  the sixth to Mijamin,
¹⁰the seventh to Hakkoz,
  the eighth to Abijah,[v]
¹¹the ninth to Jeshua,
  the tenth to Shecaniah,
¹²the eleventh to Eliashib,
  the twelfth to Jakim,
¹³the thirteenth to Huppah,
  the fourteenth to Jeshebeab,
¹⁴the fifteenth to Bilgah,
  the sixteenth to Immer,[w]
¹⁵the seventeenth to Hezir,[x]
  the eighteenth to Happizzez,
¹⁶the nineteenth to Pethahiah,
  the twentieth to Jehezkel,
¹⁷the twenty-first to Jakin,
  the twenty-second to Gamul,
¹⁸the twenty-third to Delaiah
  and the twenty-fourth to Maaziah.

¹⁹This was their appointed order of ministering when they entered the temple of the LORD, according to the regulations prescribed for them by their forefather Aaron, as the LORD, the God of Israel, had commanded him.

The Rest of the Levites

²⁰As for the rest of the descendants of Levi:[y]
  from the sons of Amram: Shubael;
    from the sons of Shubael: Jehdeiah.
  ²¹As for Rehabiah,[z] from his sons:
    Isshiah was the first.
²²From the Izharites: Shelomoth;
  from the sons of Shelomoth: Jahath.
²³The sons of Hebron:[a] Jeriah the first,[a] Amariah the second, Jahaziel the third and Jekameam the fourth.
²⁴The son of Uzziel: Micah;
  from the sons of Micah: Shamir.
  ²⁵The brother of Micah: Isshiah;
    from the sons of Isshiah: Zechariah.
²⁶The sons of Merari:[b] Mahli and Mushi.

ᵃ23 Two Hebrew manuscripts and some Septuagint manuscripts (see also 1 Chron. 23:19); most Hebrew manuscripts *The sons of Jeriah:*

The son of Jaaziah: Beno.
27The sons of Merari:
  from Jaaziah: Beno, Shoham, Zaccur and Ibri.
28From Mahli: Eleazar, who had no sons.
29From Kish: the son of Kish:
  Jerahmeel.
30And the sons of Mushi: Mahli, Eder and Jerimoth.

These were the Levites, according to their families. 31They also cast lots,c just as their brothers the descendants of Aaron did, in the presence of King David and of Zadok, Ahimelech, and the heads of families of the priests and of the Levites. The families of the oldest brother were treated the same as those of the youngest.

The Singers

25 David, together with the commanders of the army, set apart some of the sons of Asaph,d Hemane and Jeduthunf for the ministry of prophesying,g accompanied by harps, lyres and cymbals.h Here is the list of the meni who performed this service:j

2From the sons of Asaph:
  Zaccur, Joseph, Nethaniah and Asarelah. The sons of Asaph were under the supervision of Asaph, who prophesied under the king's supervision.
3As for Jeduthun, from his sons:k
  Gedaliah, Zeri, Jeshaiah, Shimei,a Hashabiah and Mattithiah, six in all, under the supervision of their father Jeduthun, who prophesied, using the harpl in thanking and praising the LORD.
4As for Heman, from his sons:
  Bukkiah, Mattaniah, Uzziel, Shubael and Jerimoth; Hananiah, Hanani, Eliathah, Giddalti and Romamti-Ezer; Joshbekashah, Mallothi, Hothir and Mahazioth. 5All these were sons of Heman the king's seer. They were given him through the promises of God to exalt him.b God gave Heman fourteen sons and three daughters.

6All these men were under the supervision of their fathersm for the music of the temple of the LORD, with cymbals, lyres and harps, for the ministry at the house of God. Asaph, Jeduthun and Hemann were under the supervision of the king.o 7Along with their relatives—all of them trained and skilled in music for the LORD—they numbered 288. 8Young and old alike, teacher as well as student, cast lotsp for their duties.

9The first lot, which was for Asaph,q fell to
  Joseph,
    his sons and relatives,c   12d
  the second to Gedaliah,
    he and his relatives and sons,   12
10the third to Zaccur,

24:31
cver 5
25:1
d1Ch 6:39
e1Ch 6:33
f1Ch 16:41,42;
Ne 11:17
g1Sa 10:5;
2Ki 3:15
h1Ch 15:16
i1Ch 6:31
j2Ch 5:12;
8:14; 34:12;
35:15; Ezr 3:10
25:3
k1Ch 16:41-42
lGe 4:21;
Ps 33:2
25:6
m1Ch 15:16
n1Ch 15:19
o2Ch 23:18;
29:25
25:8
p1Ch 26:13
25:9
q1Ch 6:39

---

a3 One Hebrew manuscript and some Septuagint manuscripts (see also verse 17); most Hebrew manuscripts do not have *Shimei*.   b5 Hebrew *exalt the horn*   c9 See Septuagint; Hebrew does not have *his sons and relatives*.   d9 See the total in verse 7; Hebrew does not have *twelve*.

his sons and relatives, 12

11the fourth to Izri,[a]

his sons and relatives, 12

12the fifth to Nethaniah,

his sons and relatives, 12

13the sixth to Bukkiah,

his sons and relatives, 12

14the seventh to Jesarelah,[b]

his sons and relatives, 12

15the eighth to Jeshaiah,

his sons and relatives, 12

16the ninth to Mattaniah,

his sons and relatives, 12

17the tenth to Shimei,

his sons and relatives, 12

18the eleventh to Azarel,[c]

his sons and relatives, 12

19the twelfth to Hashabiah,

his sons and relatives, 12

20the thirteenth to Shubael,

his sons and relatives, 12

21the fourteenth to Mattithiah,

his sons and relatives, 12

22the fifteenth to Jerimoth,

his sons and relatives, 12

23the sixteenth to Hananiah,

his sons and relatives, 12

24the seventeenth to Joshbekashah,

his sons and relatives, 12

25the eighteenth to Hanani,

his sons and relatives, 12

26the nineteenth to Mallothi,

his sons and relatives, 12

27the twentieth to Eliathah,

his sons and relatives, 12

28the twenty-first to Hothir,

his sons and relatives, 12

29the twenty-second to Giddalti,

his sons and relatives, 12

30the twenty-third to Mahazioth,

his sons and relatives, 12

31the twenty-fourth to Romamti-Ezer,

his sons and relatives, 12[r]

25:31
r1Ch 9:33
26:1
s1Ch 9:17

The Gatekeepers

26 The divisions of the gatekeepers:[s]

From the Korahites: Meshelemiah son of Kore, one of the sons of Asaph.

2Meshelemiah had sons:

---

[a]11 A variant of *Zeri* [b]14 A variant of *Asarelah* [c]18 A variant of *Uzziel*

Zechariah[t] the firstborn,
Jediael the second,
Zebadiah the third,
Jathniel the fourth,
[3]Elam the fifth,
Jehohanan the sixth
and Eliehoenai the seventh.
[4]Obed-Edom also had sons:
Shemaiah the firstborn,
Jehozabad the second,
Joah the third,
Sacar the fourth,
Nethanel the fifth,
[5]Ammiel the sixth,
Issachar the seventh
and Peullethai the eighth.
(For God had blessed Obed-Edom.[u])

[6]His son Shemaiah also had sons, who were leaders in their father's family because they were very capable men. [7]The sons of Shemaiah: Othni, Rephael, Obed and Elzabad; his relatives Elihu and Semakiah were also able men. [8]All these were descendants of Obed-Edom; they and their sons and their relatives were capable men with the strength to do the work—descendants of Obed-Edom, 62 in all.
[9]Meshelemiah had sons and relatives, who were able men—18 in all.

[10]Hosah the Merarite had sons: Shimri the first (although he was not the firstborn, his father had appointed him the first),[v] [11]Hilkiah the second, Tabaliah the third and Zechariah the fourth. The sons and relatives of Hosah were 13 in all.

[12]These divisions of the gatekeepers, through their chief men, had duties for ministering[w] in the temple of the Lord, just as their relatives had. [13]Lots[x] were cast for each gate, according to their families, young and old alike.

[14]The lot for the East Gate[y] fell to Shelemiah.[a] Then lots were cast for his son Zechariah,[z] a wise counselor, and the lot for the North Gate fell to him. [15]The lot for the South Gate fell to Obed-Edom,[a] and the lot for the storehouse fell to his sons. [16]The lots for the West Gate and the Shalleketh Gate on the upper road fell to Shuppim and Hosah.

Guard was alongside of guard: [17]There were six Levites a day on the east, four a day on the north, four a day on the south and two at a time at the storehouse. [18]As for the court to the west, there were four at the road and two at the court itself.

[19]These were the divisions of the gatekeepers who were descendants of Korah and Merari.[b]

The Treasurers and Other Officials

[20]Their fellow Levites[c] were[b] in charge of the treasuries of the house of God and the treasuries for the dedicated things.[d]

26:2
t1Ch 9:21
26:5
u2Sa 6:10;
1Ch 13:13;
16:38
26:10
vDt 21:16;
1Ch 5:1
26:12
w1Ch 9:22
26:13
x1Ch 24:5,31;
25:8
26:14
y1Ch 9:18
z1Ch 9:21
26:15
a1Ch 13:13;
2Ch 25:24
26:19
b2Ch 35:15;
Ne 7:1;
Eze 44:11
26:20
c2Ch 24:5
d1Ch 28:12

[a]14 A variant of *Meshelemiah*   [b]20 Septuagint; Hebrew *As for the Levites, Ahijah was*

21The descendants of Ladan, who were Gershonites through Ladan and who were heads of families belonging to Ladan the Gershonite, e were Jehieli, 22the sons of Jehieli, Zetham and his brother Joel. They were in charge of the treasuries f of the temple of the LORD.

23From the Amramites, the Izharites, the Hebronites and the Uzzielites: g

24Shubael, h a descendant of Gershom son of Moses, was the officer in charge of the treasuries. 25His relatives through Eliezer: Rehabiah his son, Jeshaiah his son, Joram his son, Zicri his son and Shelomith i his son. 26Shelomith and his relatives were in charge of all the treasuries for the things dedicated j by King David, by the heads of families who were the commanders of thousands and commanders of hundreds, and by the other army commanders. 27Some of the plunder taken in battle they dedicated for the repair of the temple of the LORD. 28And everything dedicated by Samuel the seer k and by Saul son of Kish, Abner son of Ner and Joab son of Zeruiah, and all the other dedicated things were in the care of Shelomith and his relatives.

29From the Izharites: Kenaniah and his sons were assigned duties away from the temple, as officials and judges l over Israel.

30From the Hebronites: Hashabiah m and his relatives—seventeen hundred able men—were responsible in Israel west of the Jordan for all the work of the LORD and for the king's service. 31As for the Hebronites, n Jeriah was their chief according to the genealogical records of their families. In the fortieth o year of David's reign a search was made in the records, and capable men among the Hebronites were found at Jazer in Gilead. 32Jeriah had twenty-seven hundred relatives, who were able men and heads of families, and King David put them in charge of the Reubenites, the Gadites and the half-tribe of Manasseh for every matter pertaining to God and for the affairs of the king.

Army Divisions

27 This is the list of the Israelites—heads of families, commanders of thousands and commanders of hundreds, and their officers, who served the king in all that concerned the army divisions that were on duty month by month throughout the year. Each division consisted of 24,000 men.

2In charge of the first division, for the first month, was Jashobeam p son of Zabdiel. There were 24,000 men in his division. 3He was a descendant of Perez and chief of all the army officers for the first month.

4In charge of the division for the second month was Dodai q the Ahohite; Mikloth was the leader of his division. There were 24,000 men in his division.

5The third army commander, for the third month, was Benaiah r son of Jehoiada the priest. He was chief and there were 24,000 men in his division. 6This was the Benaiah who was a mighty man among

26:21
e1Ch 23:7; 29:8
26:22
f1Ch 9:26
26:23
gNu 3:27
26:24
h1Ch 23:16
26:25
i1Ch 23:18
26:26
j2Sa 8:11
26:28
k1Sa 9:9
26:29
lDt 17:8-13;
1Ch 23:4;
Ne 11:16
26:30
m1Ch 27:17
26:31
n1Ch 23:19
o2Sa 5:4
27:2
p2Sa 23:8;
1Ch 11:11
27:4
q2Sa 23:9
27:5
r2Sa 23:20

the Thirty and was over the Thirty. His son Ammizabad was in charge of his division.

7The fourth, for the fourth month, was Asahel[s] the brother of Joab; his son Zebadiah was his successor. There were 24,000 men in his division.

8The fifth, for the fifth month, was the commander Shamhuth[t] the Izrahite. There were 24,000 men in his division.

9The sixth, for the sixth month, was Ira[u] the son of Ikkesh the Tekoite. There were 24,000 men in his division.

10The seventh, for the seventh month, was Helez[v] the Pelonite, an Ephraimite. There were 24,000 men in his division.

11The eighth, for the eighth month, was Sibbecai[w] the Hushathite, a Zerahite. There were 24,000 men in his division.

12The ninth, for the ninth month, was Abiezer[x] the Anathothite, a Benjamite. There were 24,000 men in his division.

13The tenth, for the tenth month, was Maharai[y] the Netophathite, a Zerahite. There were 24,000 men in his division.

14The eleventh, for the eleventh month, was Benaiah[z] the Pirathonite, an Ephraimite. There were 24,000 men in his division.

15The twelfth, for the twelfth month, was Heldai[a] the Netophathite, from the family of Othniel.[b] There were 24,000 men in his division.

Officers of the Tribes

16The officers over the tribes of Israel:

over the Reubenites: Eliezer son of Zicri;
over the Simeonites: Shephatiah son of Maacah;
17over Levi: Hashabiah[c] son of Kemuel;
over Aaron: Zadok;[d]
18over Judah: Elihu, a brother of David;
over Issachar: Omri son of Michael;
19over Zebulun: Ishmaiah son of Obadiah;
over Naphtali: Jerimoth son of Azriel;
20over the Ephraimites: Hoshea son of Azaziah;
over half the tribe of Manasseh: Joel son of Pedaiah;
21over the half-tribe of Manasseh in Gilead: Iddo son of Zechariah;
over Benjamin: Jaasiel son of Abner;
22over Dan: Azarel son of Jeroham.

These were the officers over the tribes of Israel.

23David did not take the number of the men twenty years old or less,[e] because the LORD had promised to make Israel as numerous as the stars[f] in the sky. 24Joab son of Zeruiah began to count the men but did not finish. Wrath came on Israel on account of this numbering,[g] and the number was not entered in the book[a] of the annals of King David.

The King's Overseers

25Azmaveth son of Adiel was in charge of the royal storehouses. Jonathan son of Uzziah was in charge of the storehouses in the outlying districts, in the towns, the villages and the watchtowers.

27:7
s2Sa 2:18;
1Ch 11:26
27:8
t1Ch 11:27
27:9
u2Sa 23:26;
1Ch 11:28
27:10
v2Sa 23:26;
1Ch 11:27
27:11
w2Sa 21:18
27:12
x2Sa 23:27;
1Ch 11:28
27:13
y2Sa 23:28;
1Ch 11:30
27:14
z1Ch 11:31
27:15
a2Sa 23:29
bJos 15:17
27:17
c1Ch 26:30
d2Sa 8:17;
1Ch 12:28
27:23
e1Ch 21:2-5
fGe 15:5
27:24
g2Sa 24:15;
1Ch 21:7

a24 Septuagint; Hebrew number

26Ezri son of Kelub was in charge of the field workers who farmed the land.

27Shimei the Ramathite was in charge of the vineyards.

Zabdi the Shiphmite was in charge of the produce of the vineyards for the wine vats.

28Baal-Hanan the Gederite was in charge of the olive and sycamore-fig[h] trees in the western foothills.

Joash was in charge of the supplies of olive oil.

29Shitrai the Sharonite was in charge of the herds grazing in Sharon.

Shaphat son of Adlai was in charge of the herds in the valleys.

30Obil the Ishmaelite was in charge of the camels.

Jehdeiah the Meronothite was in charge of the donkeys.

31Jaziz the Hagrite[i] was in charge of the flocks.

All these were the officials in charge of King David's property.

32Jonathan, David's uncle, was a counselor, a man of insight and a scribe. Jehiel son of Hacmoni took care of the king's sons.

33Ahithophel[j] was the king's counselor.

Hushai[k] the Arkite was the king's friend. 34Ahithophel was succeeded by Jehoiada son of Benaiah and by Abiathar.[l]

Joab[m] was the commander of the royal army.

David's Plans for the Temple

28 David summoned all the officials[n] of Israel to assemble at Jerusalem: the officers over the tribes, the commanders of the divisions in the service of the king, the commanders of thousands and commanders of hundreds, and the officials in charge of all the property and livestock belonging to the king and his sons, together with the palace officials, the mighty men and all the brave warriors.

2King David rose to his feet and said: "Listen to me, my brothers and my people. I had it in my heart[o] to build a house as a place of rest for the ark of the covenant of the LORD, for the footstool[p] of our God, and I made plans to build it. 3But God said to me,[q] 'You are not to build a house for my Name,[r] because you are a warrior and have shed blood.'[s]

4"Yet the LORD, the God of Israel, chose me[t] from my whole family[u] to be king over Israel forever. He chose Judah[v] as leader, and from the house of Judah he chose my family, and from my father's sons he was pleased to make me king over all Israel. 5Of all my sons—and the LORD has given me many[w]—he has chosen my son Solomon[x] to sit on the throne of the kingdom of the LORD over Israel. 6He said to me: 'Solomon your son is the one who will build my house and my courts, for I have chosen him to be my son,[y] and I will be his father. 7I will establish his kingdom forever if he is unswerving in carrying out my commands and laws,[z] as is being done at this time.'

8"So now I charge you in the sight of all Israel and of the assembly of the LORD, and in the hearing of our God: Be careful to follow all the commands[a] of the LORD your God, that you may possess this good land and pass it on as an inheritance to your descendants forever.[b]

9"And you, my son Solomon, acknowledge the God of your father, and serve him with wholehearted devotion[c] and with a willing mind, for the LORD searches every heart[d] and understands every motive behind the thoughts. If you seek him,[e] he will be found by you; but if

27:28
h1Ki 10:27;
2Ch 1:15

27:31
i1Ch 5:10

27:33
j2Sa 15:12
k2Sa 15:37

27:34
l1Ki 1:7
m1Ch 11:6

28:1
n1Ch 11:10;
27:1-31

28:2
o1Ch 17:2
pPs 99:5; 132:7

28:3
q2Sa 7:5
r1Ch 22:8
s1Ki 5:3;
1Ch 17:4

28:4
t1Ch 17:23,27;
2Ch 6:6
u1Sa 16:1-13
vGe 49:10;
1Ch 5:2

28:5
w1Ch 3:1
x1Ch 22:9; 23:1

28:6
y2Sa 7:13;
1Ch 22:9-10

28:7
z1Ch 22:13

28:8
aDt 6:1 bDt 4:1

28:9
c1Ch 29:19
d1Sa 16:7;
Ps 7:9
ePs 40:16;
Jer 29:13

you forsake[f] him, he will reject[g] you forever. [10]Consider now, for the LORD has chosen you to build a temple as a sanctuary. Be strong and do the work."

[11]Then David gave his son Solomon the plans[h] for the portico of the temple, its buildings, its storerooms, its upper parts, its inner rooms and the place of atonement. [12]He gave him the plans of all that the Spirit[i] had put in his mind for the courts of the temple of the LORD and all the surrounding rooms, for the treasuries of the temple of God and for the treasuries for the dedicated things.[j] [13]He gave him instructions for the divisions[k] of the priests and Levites, and for all the work of serving in the temple of the LORD, as well as for all the articles to be used in its service. [14]He designated the weight of gold for all the gold articles to be used in various kinds of service, and the weight of silver for all the silver articles to be used in various kinds of service: [15]the weight of gold for the gold lampstands[l] and their lamps, with the weight for each lampstand and its lamps; and the weight of silver for each silver lampstand and its lamps, according to the use of each lampstand; [16]the weight of gold for each table[m] for consecrated bread; the weight of silver for the silver tables; [17]the weight of pure gold for the forks, sprinkling bowls[n] and pitchers; the weight of gold for each gold dish; the weight of silver for each silver dish; [18]and the weight of the refined gold for the altar of incense.[o] He also gave him the plan for the chariot,[p] that is, the cherubim of gold that spread their wings and shelter[q] the ark of the covenant of the LORD.

[19]"All this," David said, "I have in writing from the hand of the LORD upon me, and he gave me understanding in all the details[r] of the plan.[s]"

[20]David also said to Solomon his son, "Be strong and courageous,[t] and do the work. Do not be afraid or discouraged, for the LORD God, my God, is with you. He will not fail you or forsake[u] you until all the work for the service of the temple of the LORD is finished.[v] [21]The divisions of the priests and Levites are ready for all the work on the temple of God, and every willing man skilled[w] in any craft will help you in all the work. The officials and all the people will obey your every command."

Gifts for Building the Temple

29 Then King David said to the whole assembly: "My son Solomon, the one whom God has chosen, is young and inexperienced.[x] The task is great, because this palatial structure is not for man but for the LORD God. [2]With all my resources I have provided for the temple of my God—gold[y] for the gold work, silver for the silver, bronze for the bronze, iron for the iron and wood for the wood, as well as onyx for the settings, turquoise,[az] stones of various colors, and all kinds of fine stone and marble—all of these in large quantities.[a] [3]Besides, in my devotion to the temple of my God I now give my personal treasures of gold and silver for the temple of my God, over and above everything I have provided[b] for this holy temple: [4]three thousand talents[b] of gold (gold of Ophir)[c] and seven thousand talents[c] of refined silver,[d] for the

28:9
f Jos 24:20;
2Ch 15:2
g Ps 44:23
28:11
h Ex 25:9
28:12
i 1Ch 12:18
j 1Ch 26:20
28:13
k 1Ch 24:1
28:15
l Ex 25:31
28:16
m Ex 25:23
28:17
n Ex 27:3
28:18
o Ex 30:1-10
p Ex 25:18-22
q Ex 25:20
28:19
r 1Ki 6:38
s Ex 25:9
28:20
t Dt 31:6;
1Ch 22:13;
2Ch 19:11;
Hag 2:4
u Dt 4:31;
Jos 24:20
v 1Ki 6:14;
2Ch 7:11
28:21
w Ex 35:25-36:5
29:1
x 1Ki 3:7;
1Ch 22:5;
2Ch 13:7
29:2
y ver 7,14,16;
Ezr 1:4; 6:5;
Hag 2:8
z Isa 54:11
a 1Ch 22:2-5
29:3
b 2Ch 24:10;
31:3; 35:8
29:4
c Ge 10:29
d 1Ch 22:14

---

a2 The meaning of the Hebrew for this word is uncertain.   b4 That is, about 110 tons (about 100 metric tons)   c4 That is, about 260 tons (about 240 metric tons) overlaying of the walls of the buildings, [5]for the gold work and the silver work, and for all the work to be done by the craftsmen. Now, who is willing to consecrate himself today to the LORD?"

[6]Then the leaders of families, the officers of the tribes of Israel, the commanders of thousands and commanders of hundreds, and the officials[e] in charge of the king's work gave willingly.[f] [7]They[g] gave toward the work on the temple of God five thousand talents[a] and ten thousand darics[b] of gold, ten thousand talents[c] of silver, eighteen thousand talents[d] of bronze and a hundred thousand talents[e] of iron. [8]Any who had precious stones[h] gave them to the treasury of the temple of the LORD in the custody of Jehiel the Gershonite.[i] [9]The people rejoiced at the willing response of their leaders, for they had given freely and wholeheartedly[j] to the LORD. David the king also rejoiced greatly.

David's Prayer

[10]David praised the LORD in the presence of the whole assembly, saying,

"Praise be to you, O LORD,
    God of our father Israel,
    from everlasting to everlasting.
[11]Yours, O LORD, is the greatness and the power[k]
    and the glory and the majesty and the splendor,
    for everything in heaven and earth is yours.[l]
Yours, O LORD, is the kingdom;
    you are exalted as head over all.[m]
[12]Wealth and honor[n] come from you;
    you are the ruler[o] of all things.
In your hands are strength and power
    to exalt and give strength to all.
[13]Now, our God, we give you thanks,
    and praise your glorious name.

[14]"But who am I, and who are my people, that we should be able to give as generously as this? Everything comes from you, and we have given you only what comes from your hand. [15]We are aliens and strangers[p] in your sight, as were all our forefathers. Our days on earth are like a shadow,[q] without hope. [16]O LORD our God, as for all this abundance that we have provided for building you a temple for your Holy Name, it comes from your hand, and all of it belongs to you. [17]I know, my God, that you test the heart[r] and are pleased with integrity. All these things have I given willingly and with honest intent. And now I have seen with joy how willingly your people who are here have given to you.[s] [18]O LORD, God of our fathers Abraham, Isaac and Israel, keep this desire in the hearts of your people forever, and keep their hearts loyal to you. [19]And give my son Solomon the wholehearted devotion[t] to keep your commands, requirements and decrees[u] and to do everything to build the palatial structure for which I have provided."[v]

29:6
e1Ch 27:1; 28:1
fver 9;
Ex 25:1-8;
35:20-29; 36:2;
2Ch 24:10;
Ezr 7:15
29:7
gEx 25:2;
Ne 7:70-71
29:8
hEx 35:27
i1Ch 26:21
29:9
j1Ki 8:61;
2Co 9:7
29:11
kPs 24:8;
59:17; 62:11
lPs 89:11
mRev 5:12-13
29:12
n2Ch 1:12
o2Ch 20:6;
Ro 11:36
29:15
pPs 39:12;
Heb 11:13
qJob 14:2
29:17
rPs 139:23;
Pr 15:11; 17:3;
Jer 11:20; 17:10
s1Ch 28:9;
Ps 15:1-5
29:19
t1Ch 28:9
uPs 72:1
v1Ch 22:14

---

[a]7 That is, about 190 tons (about 170 metric tons)   [b]7 That is, about 185 pounds (about 84 kilograms)   [c]7 That is, about 375 tons (about 345 metric tons)   [d]7 That is, about 675 tons (about 610 metric tons)   [e]7 That is, about 3,750 tons (about 3,450 metric tons)

20Then David said to the whole assembly, "Praise the LORD your God." So they all praised the LORD, the God of their fathers; they bowed low and fell prostrate before the LORD and the king.

Solomon Acknowledged as King

29:21-25pp —1Ki 1:28-53

21The next day they made sacrifices to the LORD and presented burnt offerings to him:ʷ a thousand bulls, a thousand rams and a thousand male lambs, together with their drink offerings, and other sacrifices in abundance for all Israel. 22They ate and drank with great joyˣ in the presence of the LORD that day.

Then they acknowledged Solomon son of David as king a second time, anointing him before the LORD to be ruler and Zadokʸ to be priest. 23So Solomon sat on the throneᶻ of the LORD as king in place of his father David. He prospered and all Israel obeyed him. 24All the officers and mighty men, as well as all of King David's sons, pledged their submission to King Solomon.

25The LORD highly exalted Solomon in the sight of all Israel and bestowed on him royal splendorᵃ such as no king over Israel ever had before.ᵇ

The Death of David

29:26-28pp — 1Ki 2:10-12

26David son of Jesse was kingᶜ over all Israel. 27He ruled over Israel forty years—seven in Hebron and thirty-three in Jerusalem.ᵈ 28He diedᵉ at a good old age, having enjoyed long life, wealth and honor. His son Solomon succeeded him as king.ᶠ

29As for the events of King David's reign, from beginning to end, they are written in the records of Samuel the seer,ᵍ the records of Nathanʰ the prophet and the records of Gadⁱ the seer, 30together with the details of his reign and power, and the circumstances that surrounded him and Israel and the kingdoms of all the other lands.

29:21
w 1Ki 8:62
29:22
x 1Ch 23:1
y 1Ki 1:33-39
29:23
z 1Ki 2:12
29:25
a 2Ch 1:1,12
b 1Ki 3:13;
Ecc 2:9
29:26
c 1Ch 18:14
29:27
d 2Sa 5:4-5;
1Ki 2:11;
1Ch 3:4
29:28
e Ge 15:15;
Ac 13:36
f 1Ch 23:1
29:29
g 1Sa 9:9
h 2Sa 7:2
i 1Sa 22:5

2 Chronicles

Title and Background

See Introduction to 1 Chronicles.

Author and Date of Writing

See Introduction to 1 Chronicles.

Theme and Message

2 Chronicles continues the history of David's royal line. This book, like 1 Chronicles, shows that the people's relationship to God was most important. When the author wrote about the kings, he measured them on the basis of their faithfulness to God. The reigns of evil kings are reported by the author briefly, while the reigns of good kings are described in more detail.

Outline

Solomon Asks for Wisdom

1:2–13pp — 1Ki 3:4–15
1:14–17pp — 1Ki 10:26–29; 2Ch 9:25–28

1:1
a1Ki 2:12,26;
2Ch 12:1
bGe 21:22;
39:2; Nu 14:43
c1Ch 29:25

1:2
d1Ch 9:1; 28:1

1:3
eEx 36:8
fEx 40:18

1:4
g2Sa 6:2;
1Ch 15:25
h2Sa 6:17;
1Ch 15:1

1:5
iEx 38:2
jEx 31:2
k1Ch 13:3

1:7
l2Ch 7:12

1:8
m1Ch 23:1;
28:5

1:9
n2Sa 7:25;
1Ki 8:25
oGe 12:2

1:10
pNu 27:17;
2Sa 5:2;
Pr 8:15-16

1 Solomon son of David established[a] himself firmly over his kingdom, for the LORD his God was with[b] him and made him exceedingly great.[c]

²Then Solomon spoke to all Israel[d]—to the commanders of thousands and commanders of hundreds, to the judges and to all the leaders in Israel, the heads of families— ³and Solomon and the whole assembly went to the high place at Gibeon, for God's Tent of Meeting[e] was there, which Moses[f] the LORD's servant had made in the desert. ⁴Now David had brought up the ark[g] of God from Kiriath Jearim to the place he had prepared for it, because he had pitched a tent[h] for it in Jerusalem. ⁵But the bronze altar[i] that Bezalel[j] son of Uri, the son of Hur, had made was in Gibeon in front of the tabernacle of the LORD; so Solomon and the assembly inquired[k] of him there. ⁶Solomon went up to the bronze altar before the LORD in the Tent of Meeting and offered a thousand burnt offerings on it.

⁷That night God appeared[l] to Solomon and said to him, "Ask for whatever you want me to give you."

⁸Solomon answered God, "You have shown great kindness to David my father and have made me[m] king in his place. ⁹Now, LORD God, let your promise[n] to my father David be confirmed, for you have made me king over a people who are as numerous as the dust of the earth.[o] ¹⁰Give me wisdom and knowledge, that I may lead[p] this people, for who is able to govern this great people of yours?"

11God said to Solomon, "Since this is your heart's desire and you have not asked for wealth,q riches or honor, nor for the death of your enemies, and since you have not asked for a long life but for wisdom and knowledge to govern my people over whom I have made you king, 12therefore wisdom and knowledge will be given you. And I will also give you wealth, riches and honor,r such as no king who was before you ever had and none after you will have.s"

13Then Solomon went to Jerusalem from the high place at Gibeon, from before the Tent of Meeting. And he reigned over Israel.

14Solomon accumulated chariotst and horses; he had fourteen hundred chariots and twelve thousand horses,a which he kept in the chariot cities and also with him in Jerusalem. 15The king made silver and goldu as common in Jerusalem as stones, and cedar as plentiful as sycamore-fig trees in the foothills. 16Solomon's horses were imported from Egyptb and from Kuec—the royal merchants purchased them from Kue. 17They imported a chariotv from Egypt for six hundred shekelsd of silver, and a horse for a hundred and fifty.e They also exported them to all the kings of the Hittites and of the Arameans.

Preparations for Building the Temple

2:1–18pp — 1Ki 5:1–16

2 Solomon gave orders to build a templew for the Name of the LORD and a royal palace for himself.x 2He conscripted seventy thousand men as carriers and eighty thousand as stonecutters in the hills and thirty-six hundred as foremen over them.y

3Solomon sent this message to Hiramf/z king of Tyre:

"Send me cedar logsa as you did for my father David when you sent him cedar to build a palace to live in. 4Now I am about to build a templeb for the Name of the LORD my God and to dedicate it to him for burning fragrant incensec before him, for setting out the consecrated breadd regularly, and for making burnt offeringse every morning and evening and on Sabbathsf and New Moons and at the appointed feasts of the LORD our God. This is a lasting ordinance for Israel.

5"The temple I am going to build will be great,g because our God is greater than all other gods.h 6But who is able to build a temple for him, since the heavens, even the highest heavens, cannot contain him?i Who then am Ij to build a temple for him, except as a place to burn sacrifices before him?

7"Send me, therefore, a man skilled to work in gold and silver, bronze and iron, and in purple, crimson and blue yarn, and experienced in the art of engraving, to work in Judah and Jerusalem with my skilled craftsmen,k whom my father David provided.

8"Send me also cedar, pine and algumg logs from Lebanon, for I know that your men are skilled in cutting timber there. My men will work with yours 9to provide me with plenty of lumber, be-

1:11
qDt 17:17
1:12
r1Ch 29:12
s1Ch 29:25;
2Ch 9:22;
Ne 13:26
1:14
t1Sa 8:11;
1Ki 4:26; 9:19
1:15
u1Ki 9:28;
Isa 60:5
1:17
vSS 1:9
2:1
wDt 12:5
xEcc 2:4
2:2
yver 18;
2Ch 10:4
2:3
z2Sa 5:11
a1Ch 14:1
2:4
bver 1; Dt 12:5
cEx 30:7
dEx 25:30
eEx 29:42;
2Ch 13:11
fNu 28:9-10
2:5
g1Ch 22:5;
Ps 135:5
h1Ch 16:25
2:6
i1Ki 8:27;
2Ch 6:18;
Jer 23:24
jEx 3:11
2:7
kver 13-14;
Ex 35:31;
1Ch 22:16

---

a14 Or *charioteers*   b16 Or possibly *Muzur*, a region in Cilicia; also in verse 17   c16 Probably Cilicia   d17 That is, about 15 pounds (about 7 kilograms)   e17 That is, about 3 3/4 pounds (about 1.7 kilograms)   f3 Hebrew *Huram*, a variant of *Hiram*; also in verses 11 and 12   g8 Probably a variant of *almug*; possibly juniper cause the temple I build must be large and magnificent. [10]I will give your servants, the woodsmen who cut the timber, twenty thousand cors[a] of ground wheat, twenty thousand cors of barley, twenty thousand baths[b] of wine and twenty thousand baths of olive oil.[1]"

[11]Hiram king of Tyre replied by letter to Solomon:

"Because the LORD loves[m] his people, he has made you their king."

[12]And Hiram added:

"Praise be to the LORD, the God of Israel, who made heaven and earth![n] He has given King David a wise son, endowed with intelligence and discernment, who will build a temple for the LORD and a palace for himself.

[13]"I am sending you Huram-Abi,[o] a man of great skill, [14]whose mother was from Dan[p] and whose father was from Tyre. He is trained[q] to work in gold and silver, bronze and iron, stone and wood, and with purple and blue[r] and crimson yarn and fine linen. He is experienced in all kinds of engraving and can execute any design given to him. He will work with your craftsmen and with those of my lord, David your father.

[15]"Now let my lord send his servants the wheat and barley and the olive oil[s] and wine he promised, [16]and we will cut all the logs from Lebanon that you need and will float them in rafts by sea down to Joppa.[t] You can then take them up to Jerusalem."

[17]Solomon took a census of all the aliens[u] who were in Israel, after the census[v] his father David had taken; and they were found to be 153,600. [18]He assigned[w] 70,000 of them to be carriers and 80,000 to be stonecutters in the hills, with 3,600 foremen over them to keep the people working.

Solomon Builds the Temple

3:1–14pp — 1Ki 6:1–29

3 Then Solomon began to build[x] the temple of the LORD[y] in Jerusalem on Mount Moriah, where the LORD had appeared to his father David. It was on the threshing floor of Araunah[cz] the Jebusite, the place provided by David. [2]He began building on the second day of the second month in the fourth year of his reign.[a]

[3]The foundation Solomon laid for building the temple of God was sixty cubits long and twenty cubits wide[db] (using the cubit of the old standard). [4]The portico at the front of the temple was twenty cubits[e] long across the width of the building and twenty cubits[f] high.

He overlaid the inside with pure gold. [5]He paneled the main hall with pine and covered it with fine gold and decorated it with palm tree[c] and chain designs. [6]He adorned the temple with precious stones. And

### Cross references (margin)

2:10
lEzr 3:7
2:11
m1Ki 10:9;
2Ch 9:8
2:12
nNe 9:6;
Ps 8:3; 33:6;
102:25
2:13
o1Ki 7:13
2:14
pEx 31:6
qEx 35:31
rEx 35:35
2:15
sver 10; Ezr 3:7
2:16
tJos 19:46;
Jnh 1:3
2:17
u1Ch 22:2
v2Sa 24:2
2:18
wver 2;
1Ch 22:2;
2Ch 8:8
3:1
xAc 7:47
yGe 28:17
z2Sa 24:18;
1Ch 21:18
3:2
aEzr 5:11
3:3
bEze 41:2
3:5
cEze 40:16

---

[a]10 That is, probably about 125,000 bushels (about 4,400 kiloliters)   [b]10 That is, probably about 115,000 gallons (about 440 kiloliters)   [c]1 Hebrew *Ornan*, a variant of *Araunah*   [d]3 That is, about 90 feet (about 27 meters) long and 30 feet (about 9 meters) wide   [e]4 That is, about 30 feet (about 9 meters); also in verses 8, 11 and 13   [f]4 Some Septuagint and Syriac manuscripts; Hebrew *and a hundred and twenty*

the gold he used was gold of Parvaim. [7]He overlaid the ceiling beams, doorframes, walls and doors of the temple with gold, and he carved cherubim[d] on the walls.

[8]He built the Most Holy Place,[e] its length corresponding to the width of the temple—twenty cubits long and twenty cubits wide. He overlaid the inside with six hundred talents[a] of fine gold. [9]The gold nails[f] weighed fifty shekels.[b] He also overlaid the upper parts with gold.

[10]In the Most Holy Place he made a pair[g] of sculptured cherubim and overlaid them with gold. [11]The total wingspan of the cherubim was twenty cubits. One wing of the first cherub was five cubits[c] long and touched the temple wall, while its other wing, also five cubits long, touched the wing of the other cherub. [12]Similarly one wing of the second cherub was five cubits long and touched the other temple wall, and its other wing, also five cubits long, touched the wing of the first cherub. [13]The wings of these cherubim[h] extended twenty cubits. They stood on their feet, facing the main hall.[d]

[14]He made the curtain[i] of blue, purple and crimson yarn and fine linen, with cherubim[j] worked into it.

[15]In the front of the temple he made two pillars,[k] which together were thirty-five cubits[e] long, each with a capital[l] on top measuring five cubits. [16]He made interwoven chains[f][m] and put them on top of the pillars. He also made a hundred pomegranates[n] and attached them to the chains. [17]He erected the pillars in the front of the temple, one to the south and one to the north. The one to the south he named Jakin[g] and the one to the north Boaz.[h]

The Temple's Furnishings

4:2–6,10–5:1pp — 1Ki 7:23–26,38–51

4 He made a bronze altar[o] twenty cubits long, twenty cubits wide and ten cubits high.[i] [2]He made the Sea[p] of cast metal, circular in shape, measuring ten cubits from rim to rim and five cubits[j] high. It took a line of thirty cubits[k] to measure around it. [3]Below the rim, figures of bulls encircled it—ten to a cubit.[l] The bulls were cast in two rows in one piece with the Sea.

[4]The Sea stood on twelve bulls, three facing north, three facing west, three facing south and three facing east.[q] The Sea rested on top of them, and their hindquarters were toward the center. [5]It was a handbreadth[m] in thickness, and its rim was like the rim of a cup, like a lily blossom. It held three thousand baths.[n]

[6]He then made ten basins[r] for washing and placed five on the south side and five on the north. In them the things to be used for the burnt offerings[s] were rinsed, but the Sea was to be used by the priests for washing.

[7]He made ten gold lampstands[t] according to the specifications[u] for

---

3:7
d Ge 3:24;
1Ki 6:29-35;
Eze 41:18
3:8
e Ex 26:33
3:9
f Ex 26:32
3:10
g Ex 25:18
3:13
h Ex 25:18
3:14
i Ex 26:31,33;
Heb 9:3
j Ge 3:24
3:15
k 1Ki 7:15;
Rev 3:12
l 1Ki 7:22
3:16
m 1Ki 7:17
n 1Ki 7:20
4:1
o Ex 20:24;
27:1-2; 40:6;
1Ki 8:64;
2Ki 16:14
4:2
p Rev 4:6; 15:2
4:4
q Nu 2:3-25;
Eze 48:30-34;
Rev 21:13
4:6
r Ex 30:18
s Ne 13:5,9;
Eze 40:38
4:7
t Ex 25:31
u Ex 25:40

---

[a]8 That is, about 23 tons (about 21 metric tons)   [b]9 That is, about 1 1/4 pounds (about 0.6 kilogram)   [c]11 That is, about 7 1/2 feet (about 2.3 meters)   [d]13 Or *facing inward*   [e]15 That is, about 52 feet (about 16 meters)   [f]16 Or possibly *made chains in the inner sanctuary*; the meaning of the Hebrew for this phrase is uncertain.   [g]17 *Jakin* probably means *he establishes.*   [h]17 *Boaz* probably means *in him is strength.*   [i]1 That is, about 30 feet (about 9 meters) long and wide, and about 15 feet (about 4.5 meters) high   [j]2 That is, about 7 1/2 feet (about 2.3 meters)   [k]2 That is, about 45 feet (about 13.5 meters)   [l]3 That is, about 1 1/2 feet (about 0.5 meter)   [m]5 That is, about 3 inches (about 8 centimeters)   [n]5 That is, about 17,500 gallons (about 66 kiloliters)

them and placed them in the temple, five on the south side and five on the north.

⁸He made ten tables[v] and placed them in the temple, five on the south side and five on the north. He also made a hundred gold sprinkling bowls.[w]

⁹He made the courtyard[x] of the priests, and the large court and the doors for the court, and overlaid the doors with bronze. ¹⁰He placed the Sea on the south side, at the southeast corner.

¹¹He also made the pots and shovels and sprinkling bowls.

So Huram finished[y] the work he had undertaken for King Solomon in the temple of God:

¹²the two pillars;

the two bowl-shaped capitals on top of the pillars;

the two sets of network decorating the two bowl-shaped capitals on top of the pillars;

¹³the four hundred pomegranates for the two sets of network (two rows of pomegranates for each network, decorating the bowl-shaped capitals on top of the pillars);

¹⁴the stands[z] with their basins;

¹⁵the Sea and the twelve bulls under it;

¹⁶the pots, shovels, meat forks and all related articles.

All the objects that Huram-Abi[a] made for King Solomon for the temple of the LORD were of polished bronze. ¹⁷The king had them cast in clay molds in the plain of the Jordan between Succoth[b] and Zarethan.[a] ¹⁸All these things that Solomon made amounted to so much that the weight of the bronze[c] was not determined.

¹⁹Solomon also made all the furnishings that were in God's temple:

the golden altar;

the tables[d] on which was the bread of the Presence;

²⁰the lampstands[e] of pure gold with their lamps, to burn in front of the inner sanctuary as prescribed;

²¹the gold floral work and lamps and tongs (they were solid gold);

²²the pure gold wick trimmers, sprinkling bowls, dishes[f] and censers;[g] and the gold doors of the temple: the inner doors to the Most Holy Place and the doors of the main hall.

5 When all the work Solomon had done for the temple of the LORD was finished,[h] he brought in the things his father David had dedicated[i]—the silver and gold and all the furnishings—and he placed them in the treasuries of God's temple.

The Ark Brought to the Temple

5:2–6:11pp — 1Ki 8:1–21

²Then Solomon summoned to Jerusalem the elders of Israel, all the heads of the tribes and the chiefs of the Israelite families, to bring up the ark[j] of the LORD's covenant from Zion, the City of David. ³And all the men of Israel[k] came together to the king at the time of the festival in the seventh month.

⁴When all the elders of Israel had arrived, the Levites took up the ark,

---

4:8
v Ex 25:23
w Nu 4:14
4:9
x 1Ki 6:36;
2Ki 21:5;
2Ch 33:5
4:11
y 1Ki 7:14
4:14
z 1Ki 7:27-30
4:16
a 1Ki 7:13
4:17
b Ge 33:17
4:18
c 1Ki 7:23
4:19
d Ex 25:23,30
4:20
e Ex 25:31
4:22
f Nu 7:14
g Lev 10:1
5:1
h 1Ki 6:14
i 2Sa 8:11
5:2
j Nu 3:31;
2Sa 6:12;
1Ch 15:25
5:3
k 1Ch 9:1;
2Ch 7:8-10

---

[5]and they brought up the ark and the Tent of Meeting and all the sacred furnishings in it. The priests, who were Levites,[1] carried them up; [6]and King Solomon and the entire assembly of Israel that had gathered about him were before the ark, sacrificing so many sheep and cattle that they could not be recorded or counted.

[7]The priests then brought the ark[m] of the LORD's covenant to its place in the inner sanctuary of the temple, the Most Holy Place, and put it beneath the wings of the cherubim. [8]The cherubim[n] spread their wings over the place of the ark and covered the ark and its carrying poles. [9]These poles were so long that their ends, extending from the ark, could be seen from in front of the inner sanctuary, but not from outside the Holy Place; and they are still there today. [10]There was nothing in the ark except[o] the two tablets[p] that Moses had placed in it at Horeb, where the LORD made a covenant with the Israelites after they came out of Egypt.

[11]The priests then withdrew from the Holy Place. All the priests who were there had consecrated themselves, regardless of their divisions. [q] [12]All the Levites who were musicians[r]—Asaph, Heman, Jeduthun and their sons and relatives—stood on the east side of the altar, dressed in fine linen and playing cymbals, harps and lyres. They were accompanied by 120 priests sounding trumpets. [s] [13]The trumpeters and singers joined in unison, as with one voice, to give praise and thanks to the LORD. Accompanied by trumpets, cymbals and other instruments, they raised their voices in praise to the LORD and sang:

> "He is good;
>   his love endures forever."[t]

Then the temple of the LORD was filled with a cloud, [14]and the priests could not perform[u] their service because of the cloud,[v] for the glory[w] of the LORD filled the temple of God.

6 Then Solomon said, "The LORD has said that he would dwell in a dark cloud;[x] [2]I have built a magnificent temple for you, a place for you to dwell forever.[y]"

[3]While the whole assembly of Israel was standing there, the king turned around and blessed them. [4]Then he said:

"Praise be to the LORD, the God of Israel, who with his hands has fulfilled what he promised with his mouth to my father David. For he said, [5]'Since the day I brought my people out of Egypt, I have not chosen a city in any tribe of Israel to have a temple built for my Name to be there, nor have I chosen anyone to be the leader over my people Israel. [6]But now I have chosen Jerusalem[z] for my Name[a] to be there, and I have chosen David[b] to rule my people Israel.'

[7]"My father David had it in his heart[c] to build a temple for the Name of the LORD, the God of Israel. [8]But the LORD said to my father David, 'Because it was in your heart to build a temple for my Name, you did well to have this in your heart. [9]Nevertheless, you are not the one to build the temple, but your son, who is your own flesh and blood—he is the one who will build the temple for my Name.'

[10]"The LORD has kept the promise he made. I have succeeded

5:5
[1]Nu 3:31;
1Ch 15:2
5:7
mRev 11:19
5:8
nGe 3:24
5:10
oHeb 9:4
pEx 16:34;
Dt 10:2
5:11
q1Ch 24:1
5:12
r1Ki 10:12;
1Ch 25:1;
Ps 68:25
s1Ch 13:8;
15:24
5:13
t1Ch 16:34,41;
2Ch 7:3; 20:21;
Ezr 3:11;
Ps 100:5; 136:1;
Jer 33:11
5:14
uEx 40:35;
Rev 15:8
vEx 19:16
wEx 29:43;
2Ch 7:2
6:1
xEx 19:9;
1Ki 8:12-50
6:2
yEzr 6:12; 7:15;
Ps 135:21
6:6
zDt 12:5;
Isa 14:1
aEx 20:24;
2Ch 12:13
b1Ch 28:4
6:7
c1Sa 10:7;
1Ch 17:2; 28:2;
Ac 7:46

David my father and now I sit on the throne of Israel, just as the LORD promised, and I have built the temple for the Name of the LORD, the God of Israel. [11]There I have placed the ark, in which is the covenant[d] of the LORD that he made with the people of Israel."

Solomon's Prayer of Dedication

6:12–40pp — 1Ki 8:22–53
6:41–42pp — Ps 132:8–10

[12]Then Solomon stood before the altar of the LORD in front of the whole assembly of Israel and spread out his hands. [13]Now he had made a bronze platform,[e] five cubits[a] long, five cubits wide and three cubits[b] high, and had placed it in the center of the outer court. He stood on the platform and then knelt down[f] before the whole assembly of Israel and spread out his hands toward heaven. [14]He said:

"O LORD, God of Israel, there is no God like you[g] in heaven or on earth—you who keep your covenant of love[h] with your servants who continue wholeheartedly in your way. [15]You have kept your promise to your servant David my father; with your mouth you have promised[i] and with your hand you have fulfilled it—as it is today.

[16]"Now LORD, God of Israel, keep for your servant David my father the promises you made to him when you said, 'You shall never fail[j] to have a man to sit before me on the throne of Israel, if only your sons are careful in all they do to walk before me according to my law,[k] as you have done.' [17]And now, O LORD, God of Israel, let your word that you promised your servant David come true.

[18]"But will God really dwell[l] on earth with men? The heavens,[m] even the highest heavens, cannot contain you. How much less this temple I have built! [19]Yet give attention to your servant's prayer and his plea for mercy, O LORD my God. Hear the cry and the prayer that your servant is praying in your presence. [20]May your eyes[n] be open toward this temple day and night, this place of which you said you would put your Name[o] there. May you hear[p] the prayer your servant prays toward this place. [21]Hear the supplications of your servant and of your people Israel when they pray toward this place. Hear from heaven, your dwelling place; and when you hear, forgive. [q]

[22]"When a man wrongs his neighbor and is required to take an oath[r] and he comes and swears the oath before your altar in this temple, [23]then hear from heaven and act. Judge between your servants, repaying[s] the guilty by bringing down on his own head what he has done. Declare the innocent not guilty and so establish his innocence.

[24]"When your people Israel have been defeated[t] by an enemy because they have sinned against you and when they turn back and confess your name, praying and making supplication before you in this temple, [25]then hear from heaven and forgive the sin of

### Cross references (margin)

6:11
d Dt 10:2;
2Ch 5:10;
Ps 25:10; 50:5

6:13
e Ne 8:4
f Ps 95:6

6:14
g Ex 8:10; 15:11
h Dt 7:9

6:15
i 1Ch 22:10

6:16
j 2Sa 7:13,15;
1Ki 2:4;
2Ch 7:18; 23:3
k Ps 132:12

6:18
l Rev 21:3
m 2Ch 2:6;
Ps 11:4;
Isa 40:22; 66:1;
Ac 7:49

6:20
n Ex 3:16;
Ps 34:15
o Dt 12:11
p 2Ch 7:14;
30:20

6:21
q Ps 51:1;
Isa 33:24; 40:2;
43:25; 44:22;
55:7; Mic 7:18

6:22
r Ex 22:11

6:23
s Isa 3:11; 65:6;
Mt 16:27

6:24
t Lev 26:17

---

[a]13 That is, about 7 1/2 feet (about 2.3 meters)   [b]13 That is, about 4 1/2 feet (about 1.3 meters)

your people Israel and bring them back to the land you gave to them and their fathers.

26"When the heavens are shut up and there is no rain[u] because your people have sinned against you, and when they pray toward this place and confess your name and turn from their sin because you have afflicted them, 27then hear from heaven and forgive[v] the sin of your servants, your people Israel. Teach them the right way to live, and send rain on the land you gave your people for an inheritance.

28"When famine[w] or plague comes to the land, or blight or mildew, locusts or grasshoppers, or when enemies besiege them in any of their cities, whatever disaster or disease may come, 29and when a prayer or plea is made by any of your people Israel—each one aware of his afflictions and pains, and spreading out his hands toward this temple— 30then hear from heaven, your dwelling place. Forgive,[x] and deal with each man according to all he does, since you know his heart (for you alone know the hearts of men),[y] 31so that they will fear you[z] and walk in your ways all the time they live in the land you gave our fathers.

32"As for the foreigner who does not belong to your people Israel but has come[a] from a distant land because of your great name and your mighty hand[b] and your outstretched arm—when he comes and prays toward this temple, 33then hear from heaven, your dwelling place, and do whatever the foreigner[c] asks of you, so that all the peoples of the earth may know your name and fear you, as do your own people Israel, and may know that this house I have built bears your Name.

34"When your people go to war against their enemies,[d] wherever you send them, and when they pray[e] to you toward this city you have chosen and the temple I have built for your Name, 35then hear from heaven their prayer and their plea, and uphold their cause.

36"When they sin against you—for there is no one who does not sin[f]—and you become angry with them and give them over to the enemy, who takes them captive[g] to a land far away or near; 37and if they have a change of heart[h] in the land where they are held captive, and repent and plead with you in the land of their captivity and say, 'We have sinned, we have done wrong and acted wickedly'; 38and if they turn back to you with all their heart and soul in the land of their captivity where they were taken, and pray toward the land you gave their fathers, toward the city you have chosen and toward the temple I have built for your Name; 39then from heaven, your dwelling place, hear their prayer and their pleas, and uphold their cause. And forgive your people, who have sinned against you.

40"Now, my God, may your eyes be open and your ears attentive[i] to the prayers offered in this place.

> 41"Now arise,[j] O LORD God, and come to your
>   resting place,[k]
>   you and the ark of your might.

6:26
u Lev 26:19;
Dt 11:17;
28:24;
2Sa 1:21;
1Ki 17:1
6:27
v ver 30,39;
2Ch 7:14
6:28
w 2Ch 20:9
6:30
x ver 27
y 1Sa 16:7;
1Ch 28:9;
Ps 7:9; 44:21;
Pr 16:2; 17:3
6:31
z Ps 103:11,13;
Pr 8:13
6:32
a 2Ch 9:6;
Jn 12:20;
Ac 8:27
b Ex 3:19,20
6:33
c 2Ch 7:14
6:34
d Dt 28:7
e 1Ch 5:20
6:36
f Job 15:14;
Ps 143:2;
Ecc 7:20;
Jer 17:9;
Jas 3:1;
1Jn 1:8-10
g Lev 26:44
6:37
h 2Ch 7:14;
33:12,19,23;
Jer 29:13
6:40
i 2Ch 7:15;
Ne 1:6,11;
Ps 17:1,6
6:41
j Isa 33:10
k 1Ch 28:2

May your priests,[1] O Lord God, be clothed with
  salvation,
 may your saints rejoice in your goodness. [m]
 [42]O Lord God, do not reject your anointed one.
  Remember the great love[n] promised to David
  your servant."

The Dedication of the Temple
7:1–10pp — 1Ki 8:62–66

7 When Solomon finished praying, fire[o] came down from heaven
and consumed the burnt offering and the sacrifices, and the glory of
the Lord filled[p] the temple. [q] [2]The priests could not enter[r] the temple
of the Lord because the glory[s] of the Lord filled it. [3]When all the
Israelites saw the fire coming down and the glory of the Lord above the
temple, they knelt on the pavement with their faces to the ground, and
they worshiped and gave thanks to the Lord, saying,

"He is good;
  his love endures forever."[t]

[4]Then the king and all the people offered sacrifices before the Lord.
[5]And King Solomon offered a sacrifice of twenty-two thousand head of
cattle and a hundred and twenty thousand sheep and goats. So the
king and all the people dedicated the temple of God. [6]The priests took
their positions, as did the Levites[u] with the Lord's musical instruments, [v] which King David had made for praising the Lord and which
were used when he gave thanks, saying, "His love endures forever."
Opposite the Levites, the priests blew their trumpets, and all the Israelites were standing.

[7]Solomon consecrated the middle part of the courtyard in front of the
temple of the Lord, and there he offered burnt offerings and the fat of
the fellowship offerings, [a] because the bronze altar he had made could
not hold the burnt offerings, the grain offerings and the fat portions.

[8]So Solomon observed the festival[w] at that time for seven days, and
all Israel with him—a vast assembly, people from Lebo[b] Hamath to the
Wadi of Egypt. [x] [9]On the eighth day they held an assembly, for they
had celebrated the dedication of the altar for seven days and the festival[y] for seven days more. [10]On the twenty-third day of the seventh
month he sent the people to their homes, joyful and glad in heart for
the good things the Lord had done for David and Solomon and for his
people Israel.

The Lord Appears to Solomon
7:11–22pp — 1Ki 9:1–9

[11]When Solomon had finished the temple of the Lord and the royal
palace, and had succeeded in carrying out all he had in mind to do in
the temple of the Lord and in his own palace, [12]the Lord appeared to
him at night and said:

"I have heard your prayer and have chosen this place for myself[z] as a temple for sacrifices.

6:41
lPs 132:16
mPs 116:12
6:42
nPs 89:24,28;
Isa 55:3
7:1
oLev 9:24;
1Ki 18:38
pEx 16:10
qPs 26:8
7:2
r1Ki 8:11
sEx 29:43;
40:35; 2Ch 5:14
7:3
t1Ch 16:34;
2Ch 5:13; 20:21
7:6
u1Ch 15:16
v2Ch 5:12
7:8
w2Ch 30:26
xGe 15:18
7:9
yLev 23:36
7:12
zDt 12:5

---

[a]7 Traditionally *peace offerings*   [b]8 Or *from the entrance to*

[13]"When I shut up the heavens so that there is no rain,[a] or command locusts to devour the land or send a plague among my people, [14]if my people, who are called by my name, will humble[b] themselves and pray and seek my face[c] and turn[d] from their wicked ways, then will I hear from heaven and will forgive[e] their sin and will heal[f] their land. [15]Now my eyes will be open and my ears attentive to the prayers offered in this place.[g] [16]I have chosen[h] and consecrated this temple so that my Name may be there forever. My eyes and my heart will always be there.

[17]"As for you, if you walk before me[i] as David your father did, and do all I command, and observe my decrees and laws, [18]I will establish your royal throne, as I covenanted with David your father when I said, 'You shall never fail to have a man[j] to rule over Israel.'[k]

[19]"But if you[a] turn away[l] and forsake[m] the decrees and commands I have given you[a] and go off to serve other gods and worship them, [20]then I will uproot[n] Israel from my land,[o] which I have given them, and will reject this temple I have consecrated for my Name. I will make it a byword and an object of ridicule[p] among all peoples. [21]And though this temple is now so imposing, all who pass by will be appalled and say,[q] 'Why has the LORD done such a thing to this land and to this temple?' [22]People will answer, 'Because they have forsaken the LORD, the God of their fathers, who brought them out of Egypt, and have embraced other gods, worshiping and serving them—that is why he brought all this disaster on them.' "

Solomon's Other Activities

8:1–18pp — 1Ki 9:10–28

8 At the end of twenty years, during which Solomon built the temple of the LORD and his own palace, [2]Solomon rebuilt the villages that Hiram[b] had given him, and settled Israelites in them. [3]Solomon then went to Hamath Zobah and captured it. [4]He also built up Tadmor in the desert and all the store cities he had built in Hamath. [5]He rebuilt Upper Beth Horon[r] and Lower Beth Horon as fortified cities, with walls and with gates and bars, [6]as well as Baalath and all his store cities, and all the cities for his chariots and for his horses[c]—whatever he desired to build in Jerusalem, in Lebanon and throughout all the territory he ruled.

[7]All the people left from the Hittites, Amorites, Perizzites, Hivites and Jebusites[s] (these peoples were not Israelites), [8]that is, their descendants remaining in the land, whom the Israelites had not destroyed—these Solomon conscripted[t] for his slave labor force, as it is to this day. [9]But Solomon did not make slaves of the Israelites for his work; they were his fighting men, commanders of his captains, and commanders of his chariots and charioteers. [10]They were also King Solomon's chief officials—two hundred and fifty officials supervising the men.

[11]Solomon brought Pharaoh's daughter[u] up from the City of David to

---

7:13
[a]2Ch 6:26-28;
Am 4:7
7:14
[b]Lev 26:41;
2Ch 6:37;
Jas 4:10
[c]1Ch 16:11
[d]Isa 55:7;
Zec 1:4
[e]2Ch 6:27
[f]2Ch 30:20;
Isa 30:26; 57:18
7:15
[g]2Ch 6:40
7:16
[h]ver 12;
2Ch 6:6
7:17
[i]1Ki 9:4
7:18
[j]2Ch 6:16
[k]2Sa 7:13;
2Ch 13:5
7:19
[l]Dt 28:15
[m]Lev 26:14,33
7:20
[n]Dt 29:28
[o]1Ki 14:15
[p]Dt 28:37
7:21
[q]Dt 29:24
8:5
[r]1Ch 7:24;
2Ch 14:7
8:7
[s]Ge 10:16
8:8
[t]1Ki 4:6; 9:21
8:11
[u]1Ki 3:1; 7:8

---

a19 The Hebrew is plural.   *b2* Hebrew *Huram,* a variant of *Hiram;* also in verse 18   *c6* Or *charioteers* the palace he had built for her, for he said, "My wife must not live in the palace of David king of Israel, because the places the ark of the LORD has entered are holy."

12On the altar^v of the LORD that he had built in front of the portico, Solomon sacrificed burnt offerings to the LORD, 13according to the daily requirement^w for offerings commanded by Moses for Sabbaths,^x New Moons and the three^y annual feasts—the Feast of Unleavened Bread, the Feast of Weeks^z and the Feast of Tabernacles. 14In keeping with the ordinance of his father David, he appointed the divisions^a of the priests for their duties, and the Levites^b to lead the praise and to assist the priests according to each day's requirement. He also appointed the gatekeepers^c by divisions for the various gates, because this was what David the man of God^d had ordered.^e 15They did not deviate from the king's commands to the priests or to the Levites in any matter, including that of the treasuries.

16All Solomon's work was carried out, from the day the foundation of the temple of the LORD was laid until its completion. So the temple of the LORD was finished.

17Then Solomon went to Ezion Geber and Elath on the coast of Edom. 18And Hiram sent him ships commanded by his own officers, men who knew the sea. These, with Solomon's men, sailed to Ophir and brought back four hundred and fifty talents^a of gold,^f which they delivered to King Solomon.

The Queen of Sheba Visits Solomon

9:1–12pp — 1Ki 10:1–13

9 When the queen of Sheba^g heard of Solomon's fame, she came to Jerusalem to test him with hard questions. Arriving with a very great caravan—with camels carrying spices, large quantities of gold, and precious stones—she came to Solomon and talked with him about all she had on her mind. 2Solomon answered all her questions; nothing was too hard for him to explain to her. 3When the queen of Sheba saw the wisdom of Solomon,^h as well as the palace he had built, 4the food on his table, the seating of his officials, the attending servants in their robes, the cupbearers in their robes and the burnt offerings he made at^b the temple of the LORD, she was overwhelmed.

5She said to the king, "The report I heard in my own country about your achievements and your wisdom is true. 6But I did not believe what they said until I cameⁱ and saw with my own eyes. Indeed, not even half the greatness of your wisdom was told me; you have far exceeded the report I heard. 7How happy your men must be! How happy your officials, who continually stand before you and hear your wisdom! 8Praise be to the LORD your God, who has delighted in you and placed you on his throne^j as king to rule for the LORD your God. Because of the love of your God for Israel and his desire to uphold them forever, he has made you king^k over them, to maintain justice and righteousness."

9Then she gave the king 120 talents^c of gold,^l large quantities of spices, and precious stones. There had never been such spices as those the queen of Sheba gave to King Solomon.

8:12
v1Ki 8:64;
2Ch 4:1; 15:8
8:13
wEx 29:38;
Nu 28:3
xNu 28:9
yEx 23:14;
Dt 16:16
zEx 23:16
8:14
a1Ch 24:1
b1Ch 25:1
c1Ch 9:17; 26:1
dNe 12:24,36
e1Ch 23:6;
Ne 12:45
8:18
f2Ch 9:9
9:1
gGe 10:7;
Eze 23:42;
Mt 12:42;
Lk 11:31
9:3
h1Ki 5:12
9:6
i2Ch 6:32
9:8
j1Ki 2:12;
1Ch 17:14;
28:5; 29:23;
2Ch 13:8
k2Ch 2:11
9:9
l2Ch 8:18

---

^a18 That is, about 17 tons (about 16 metric tons)   ^b4 Or *the ascent by which he went up to*
^c9 That is, about 4 1/2 tons (about 4 metric tons)

¹⁰(The men of Hiram and the men of Solomon brought gold from Ophir;ᵐ they also brought algumwoodᵃ and precious stones. ¹¹The king used the algumwood to make steps for the temple of the LORD and for the royal palace, and to make harps and lyres for the musicians. Nothing like them had ever been seen in Judah.)

¹²King Solomon gave the queen of Sheba all she desired and asked for; he gave her more than she had brought to him. Then she left and returned with her retinue to her own country.

Solomon's Splendor
9:13–28pp — 1Ki 10:14–29; 2Ch 1:14–17

¹³The weight of the gold that Solomon received yearly was 666 talents,ᵇ ¹⁴not including the revenues brought in by merchants and traders. Also all the kings of Arabiaⁿ and the governors of the land brought gold and silver to Solomon.

¹⁵King Solomon made two hundred large shields of hammered gold; six hundred bekasᶜ of hammered gold went into each shield. ¹⁶He also made three hundred small shieldsᵒ of hammered gold, with three hundred bekasᵈ of gold in each shield. The king put them in the Palace of the Forest of Lebanon.ᴾ

¹⁷Then the king made a great throne inlaid with ivory�q and overlaid with pure gold. ¹⁸The throne had six steps, and a footstool of gold was attached to it. On both sides of the seat were armrests, with a lion standing beside each of them. ¹⁹Twelve lions stood on the six steps, one at either end of each step. Nothing like it had ever been made for any other kingdom. ²⁰All King Solomon's goblets were gold, and all the household articles in the Palace of the Forest of Lebanon were pure gold. Nothing was made of silver, because silver was considered of little value in Solomon's day. ²¹The king had a fleet of trading shipsᵉ manned by Hiram'sᶠ men. Once every three years it returned, carrying gold, silver and ivory, and apes and baboons.

²²King Solomon was greater in riches and wisdom than all the other kings of the earth.ʳ ²³All the kingsˢ of the earth sought audience with Solomon to hear the wisdom God had put in his heart. ²⁴Year after year, everyone who came brought a giftᵗ—articles of silver and gold, and robes, weapons and spices, and horses and mules.

²⁵Solomon had four thousand stalls for horses and chariots,ᵘ and twelve thousand horses,ᵍ which he kept in the chariot cities and also with him in Jerusalem. ²⁶He ruledᵛ over all the kings from the Riverʰ ʷ to the land of the Philistines, as far as the border of Egypt.ˣ ²⁷The king made silver as common in Jerusalem as stones, and cedar as plentiful as sycamore-fig trees in the foothills. ²⁸Solomon's horses were imported from Egyptⁱ and from all other countries.

Solomon's Death
9:29–31pp — 1Ki 11:41–43

²⁹As for the other events of Solomon's reign, from beginning to end,

---

9:10 m2Ch 8:18
9:14 n2Ch 17:11; Isa 21:13; Jer 25:24; Eze 27:21; 30:5
9:16 o2Ch 12:9 p1Ki 7:2
9:17 q1Ki 22:39
9:22 r1Ki 3:13; 2Ch 1:12
9:23 s1Ki 4:34
9:24 t2Ch 32:23; Ps 45:12; 68:29; 72:10; Isa 18:7
9:25 u1Sa 8:11; 1Ki 4:26
9:26 v1Ki 4:21 wPs 72:8-9 xGe 15:18-21

ᵃ10 Probably a variant of *almugwood*   ᵇ13 That is, about 25 tons (about 23 metric tons)   ᶜ15 That is, about 7 1/2 pounds (about 3.5 kilograms)   ᵈ16 That is, about 3 3/4 pounds (about 1.7 kilograms)   ᵉ21 Hebrew *of ships that could go to Tarshish*   ᶠ21 Hebrew *Huram*, a variant of *Hiram*   ᵍ25 Or *charioteers*   ʰ26 That is, the Euphrates   ⁱ28 Or possibly *Muzur*, a region in Cilicia are they not written in the records of Nathan[y] the prophet, in the prophecy of Ahijah[z] the Shilonite and in the visions of Iddo the seer concerning Jeroboam[a] son of Nebat? [30]Solomon reigned in Jerusalem over all Israel forty years. [31]Then he rested with his fathers and was buried in the city of David[b] his father. And Rehoboam his son succeeded him as king.

Israel Rebels Against Rehoboam

10:1–11:4pp — 1Ki 12:1–24

10 Rehoboam went to Shechem, for all the Israelites had gone there to make him king. [2]When Jeroboam[c] son of Nebat heard this (he was in Egypt, where he had fled[d] from King Solomon), he returned from Egypt. [3]So they sent for Jeroboam, and he and all Israel[e] went to Rehoboam and said to him: [4]"Your father put a heavy yoke on us,[f] but now lighten the harsh labor and the heavy yoke he put on us, and we will serve you."

[5]Rehoboam answered, "Come back to me in three days." So the people went away.

[6]Then King Rehoboam consulted the elders[g] who had served his father Solomon during his lifetime. "How would you advise me to answer these people?" he asked.

[7]They replied, "If you will be kind to these people and please them and give them a favorable answer,[h] they will always be your servants."

[8]But Rehoboam rejected[i] the advice the elders[j] gave him and consulted the young men who had grown up with him and were serving him. [9]He asked them, "What is your advice? How should we answer these people who say to me, 'Lighten the yoke your father put on us'?"

[10]The young men who had grown up with him replied, "Tell the people who have said to you, 'Your father put a heavy yoke on us, but make our yoke lighter'—tell them, 'My little finger is thicker than my father's waist. [11]My father laid on you a heavy yoke; I will make it even heavier. My father scourged you with whips; I will scourge you with scorpions.'"

[12]Three days later Jeroboam and all the people returned to Rehoboam, as the king had said, "Come back to me in three days." [13]The king answered them harshly. Rejecting the advice of the elders, [14]he followed the advice of the young men and said, "My father made your yoke heavy; I will make it even heavier. My father scourged you with whips; I will scourge you with scorpions." [15]So the king did not listen to the people, for this turn of events was from God,[k] to fulfill the word the Lord had spoken to Jeroboam son of Nebat through Ahijah the Shilonite.[l]

[16]When all Israel[m] saw that the king refused to listen to them, they answered the king:

> "What share do we have in David,[n]
>   what part in Jesse's son?
> To your tents, O Israel!
>   Look after your own house, O David!"

### Cross references (margin)

9:29
y 2Sa 7:2;
1Ch 29:29
z 1Ki 11:29
a 2Ch 10:2
9:31
b 1Ki 2:10
10:2
c 2Ch 9:29
d 1Ki 11:40
10:3
e 1Ch 9:1
10:4
f 2Ch 2:2
10:6
g Job 8:8-9;
12:12; 15:10;
32:7
10:7
h Pr 15:1
10:8
i 2Sa 17:14
j Pr 13:20
10:15
k 2Ch 11:4;
25:16-20
l 1Ki 11:29
10:16
m 1Ch 9:1
n ver 19;
2Sa 20:1

So all the Israelites went home. [17]But as for the Israelites who were living in the towns of Judah, Rehoboam still ruled over them.

[18]King Rehoboam sent out Adoniram,[ao] who was in charge of forced labor, but the Israelites stoned him to death. King Rehoboam, however, managed to get into his chariot and escape to Jerusalem. [19]So Israel has been in rebellion against the house of David to this day.

11 When Rehoboam arrived in Jerusalem,[p] he mustered the house of Judah and Benjamin—a hundred and eighty thousand fighting men—to make war against Israel and to regain the kingdom for Rehoboam.

[2]But this word of the LORD came to Shemaiah[q] the man of God: [3]"Say to Rehoboam son of Solomon king of Judah and to all the Israelites in Judah and Benjamin, [4]'This is what the LORD says: Do not go up to fight against your brothers.[r] Go home, every one of you, for this is my doing.' " So they obeyed the words of the LORD and turned back from marching against Jeroboam.

Rehoboam Fortifies Judah

[5]Rehoboam lived in Jerusalem and built up towns for defense in Judah: [6]Bethlehem, Etam, Tekoa, [7]Beth Zur, Soco, Adullam, [8]Gath, Mareshah, Ziph, [9]Adoraim, Lachish, Azekah, [10]Zorah, Aijalon and Hebron. These were fortified cities in Judah and Benjamin. [11]He strengthened their defenses and put commanders in them, with supplies of food, olive oil and wine. [12]He put shields and spears in all the cities, and made them very strong. So Judah and Benjamin were his.

[13]The priests and Levites from all their districts throughout Israel sided with him. [14]The Levites[s] even abandoned their pasturelands and property,[t] and came to Judah and Jerusalem because Jeroboam and his sons had rejected them as priests of the LORD. [15]And he appointed[u] his own priests[v] for the high places and for the goat[w] and calf[x] idols he had made. [16]Those from every tribe of Israel[y] who set their hearts on seeking the LORD, the God of Israel, followed the Levites to Jerusalem to offer sacrifices to the LORD, the God of their fathers. [17]They strengthened[z] the kingdom of Judah and supported Rehoboam son of Solomon three years, walking in the ways of David and Solomon during this time.

Rehoboam's Family

[18]Rehoboam married Mahalath, who was the daughter of David's son Jerimoth and of Abihail, the daughter of Jesse's son Eliab. [19]She bore him sons: Jeush, Shemariah and Zaham. [20]Then he married Maacah[a] daughter of Absalom, who bore him Abijah,[b] Attai, Ziza and Shelomith. [21]Rehoboam loved Maacah daughter of Absalom more than any of his other wives and concubines. In all, he had eighteen wives[c] and sixty concubines, twenty-eight sons and sixty daughters.

[22]Rehoboam appointed Abijah[d] son of Maacah to be the chief prince among his brothers, in order to make him king. [23]He acted wisely,

10:18
o1Ki 5:14
11:1
p1Ki 12:21
11:2
q2Ch 12:5-7,15
11:4
r2Ch 28:8-11
11:14
sNu 35:2-5
t2Ch 13:9
11:15
u1Ki 13:33
v1Ki 12:31
wLev 17:7
x1Ki 12:28;
2Ch 13:8
11:16
y2Ch 15:9
11:17
z2Ch 12:1
11:20
a1Ki 15:2
b2Ch 13:2
11:21
cDt 17:17
11:22
dDt 21:15-17

a18 Hebrew *Hadoram*, a variant of *Adoniram*

dispersing some of his sons throughout the districts of Judah and Benjamin, and to all the fortified cities. He gave them abundant provisions and took many wives for them.

Shishak Attacks Jerusalem

12:9–16pp — 1Ki 14:21, 25–31

12 After Rehoboam's position as king was established[e] and he had become strong,[f] he and all Israel[a] with him abandoned the law of the LORD. [2]Because they had been unfaithful[g] to the LORD, Shishak[h] king of Egypt attacked Jerusalem in the fifth year of King Rehoboam. [3]With twelve hundred chariots and sixty thousand horsemen and the innumerable troops of Libyans, Sukkites and Cushites[b][i] that came with him from Egypt, [4]he captured the fortified cities[j] of Judah and came as far as Jerusalem.

[5]Then the prophet Shemaiah[k] came to Rehoboam and to the leaders of Judah who had assembled in Jerusalem for fear of Shishak, and he said to them, "This is what the LORD says, 'You have abandoned me; therefore, I now abandon[l] you to Shishak.' "

[6]The leaders of Israel and the king humbled themselves and said, "The LORD is just."[m]

[7]When the LORD saw that they humbled themselves, this word of the LORD came to Shemaiah: "Since they have humbled themselves, I will not destroy them but will soon give them deliverance.[n] My wrath will not be poured out on Jerusalem through Shishak. [8]They will, however, become subject[o] to him, so that they may learn the difference between serving me and serving the kings of other lands."

[9]When Shishak king of Egypt attacked Jerusalem, he carried off the treasures of the temple of the LORD and the treasures of the royal palace. He took everything, including the gold shields[p] Solomon had made. [10]So King Rehoboam made bronze shields to replace them and assigned these to the commanders of the guard on duty at the entrance to the royal palace. [11]Whenever the king went to the LORD's temple, the guards went with him, bearing the shields, and afterward they returned them to the guardroom.

[12]Because Rehoboam humbled himself, the LORD's anger turned from him, and he was not totally destroyed. Indeed, there was some good[q] in Judah.

[13]King Rehoboam established himself firmly in Jerusalem and continued as king. He was forty-one years old when he became king, and he reigned seventeen years in Jerusalem, the city the LORD had chosen out of all the tribes of Israel in which to put his Name.[r] His mother's name was Naamah; she was an Ammonite. [14]He did evil because he had not set his heart on seeking the LORD.

[15]As for the events of Rehoboam's reign, from beginning to end, are they not written in the records of Shemaiah[s] the prophet and of Iddo the seer that deal with genealogies? There was continual warfare between Rehoboam and Jeroboam. [16]Rehoboam rested with his fathers and was buried in the City of David. And Abijah[t] his son succeeded him as king.

12:1
e ver 13
f 2Ch 11:17
12:2
g 1Ki 14:22-24
h 1Ki 11:40
12:3
i 2Ch 16:8;
Na 3:9
12:4
j 2Ch 11:10
12:5
k 2Ch 11:2
l Dt 28:15;
2Ch 15:2
12:6
m Ex 9:27;
Da 9:14
12:7
n 1Ki 21:29;
Ps 78:38
12:8
o Dt 28:48
12:9
p 2Ch 9:16
12:12
q 1Ki 14:13;
2Ch 19:3
12:13
r Dt 12:5;
2Ch 6:6
12:15
s 2Ch 9:29; 11:2
12:16
t 2Ch 11:20

---

a1 That is, Judah, as frequently in 2 Chronicles   *b3* That is, people from the upper Nile region

Abijah King of Judah

13:1–2,22–14:1pp — 1Ki 15:1–2,6–8

13 In the eighteenth year of the reign of Jeroboam, Abijah became king of Judah, [2]and he reigned in Jerusalem three years. His mother's name was Maacah,[a] a daughter[b] of Uriel of Gibeah.

There was war between Abijah[u] and Jeroboam.[v] [3]Abijah went into battle with a force of four hundred thousand able fighting men, and Jeroboam drew up a battle line against him with eight hundred thousand able troops.

[4]Abijah stood on Mount Zemaraim,[w] in the hill country of Ephraim, and said, "Jeroboam and all Israel,[x] listen to me! [5]Don't you know that the LORD, the God of Israel, has given the kingship of Israel to David and his descendants forever[y] by a covenant of salt?[z] [6]Yet Jeroboam son of Nebat, an official of Solomon son of David, rebelled[a] against his master. [7]Some worthless scoundrels[b] gathered around him and opposed Rehoboam son of Solomon when he was young and indecisive and not strong enough to resist them.

[8]"And now you plan to resist the kingdom of the LORD, which is in the hands of David's descendants. You are indeed a vast army and have with you the golden calves[c] that Jeroboam made to be your gods. [9]But didn't you drive out the priests of the LORD,[d] the sons of Aaron, and the Levites, and make priests of your own as the peoples of other lands do? Whoever comes to consecrate himself with a young bull[e] and seven rams may become a priest of what are not gods.[f]

[10]"As for us, the LORD is our God, and we have not forsaken him. The priests who serve the LORD are sons of Aaron, and the Levites assist them. [11]Every morning and evening[g] they present burnt offerings and fragrant incense to the LORD. They set out the bread on the ceremonially clean table[h] and light the lamps on the gold lampstand every evening. We are observing the requirements of the LORD our God. But you have forsaken him. [12]God is with us; he is our leader. His priests with their trumpets will sound the battle cry against you.[i] Men of Israel, do not fight against the LORD,[j] the God of your fathers, for you will not succeed."

[13]Now Jeroboam had sent troops around to the rear, so that while he was in front of Judah the ambush[k] was behind them. [14]Judah turned and saw that they were being attacked at both front and rear. Then they cried out[l] to the LORD. The priests blew their trumpets [15]and the men of Judah raised the battle cry. At the sound of their battle cry, God routed Jeroboam and all Israel[m] before Abijah and Judah. [16]The Israelites fled before Judah, and God delivered[n] them into their hands. [17]Abijah and his men inflicted heavy losses on them, so that there were five hundred thousand casualties among Israel's able men. [18]The men of Israel were subdued on that occasion, and the men of Judah were victorious because they relied[o] on the LORD, the God of their fathers.

[19]Abijah pursued Jeroboam and took from him the towns of Bethel, Jeshanah and Ephron, with their surrounding villages. [20]Jeroboam did not regain power during the time of Abijah. And the LORD struck him down and he died.

13:2
u 2Ch 11:20
v 1Ki 15:6
13:4
w Jos 18:22
x 1Ch 11:1
13:5
y 2Sa 7:13
z Lev 2:13;
Nu 18:19
13:6
a 1Ki 11:26
13:7
b Jdg 9:4
13:8
c 1Ki 12:28;
2Ch 11:15
13:9
d 2Ch 11:14-15
e Ex 29:35-36
f Jer 2:11
13:11
g Ex 29:39;
2Ch 2:4
h Lev 24:5-9
13:12
i Nu 10:8-9
j Ac 5:39
13:13
k Jos 8:9
13:14
l 2Ch 14:11
13:15
m 2Ch 14:12
13:16
n 2Ch 16:8
13:18
o 1Ch 5:20;
2Ch 14:11;
Ps 22:5

---

[a]2 Most Septuagint manuscripts and Syriac (see also 2 Chron. 11:20 and 1 Kings 15:2); Hebrew *Micaiah*   [b]2 Or *granddaughter*

21But Abijah grew in strength. He married fourteen wives and had twenty-two sons and sixteen daughters.

22The other events of Abijah's reign, what he did and what he said, are written in the annotations of the prophet Iddo.

14 And Abijah rested with his fathers and was buried in the City of David. Asa his son succeeded him as king, and in his days the country was at peace for ten years.

Asa King of Judah

14:2–3pp — 1Ki 15:11–12

2Asa did what was good and right in the eyes of the LORD his God. 3He removed the foreign altars and the high places, smashed the sacred stones and cut down the Asherah poles.*a*p 4He commanded Judah to seek the LORD, the God of their fathers, and to obey his laws and commands. 5He removed the high places and incense altarsq in every town in Judah, and the kingdom was at peace under him. 6He built up the fortified cities of Judah, since the land was at peace. No one was at war with him during those years, for the LORD gave him rest.r

7"Let us build up these towns," he said to Judah, "and put walls around them, with towers, gates and bars. The land is still ours, because we have sought the LORD our God; we sought him and he has given us rest on every side." So they built and prospered.

8Asa had an army of three hundred thousand men from Judah, equipped with large shields and with spears, and two hundred and eighty thousand from Benjamin, armed with small shields and with bows. All these were brave fighting men.

9Zerah the Cushites marched out against them with a vast armyb and three hundred chariots, and came as far as Mareshah.t 10Asa went out to meet him, and they took up battle positions in the Valley of Zephathah near Mareshah.

11Then Asa calledu to the LORD his God and said, "LORD, there is no one like you to help the powerless against the mighty. Help us, O LORD our God, for we relyv on you, and in your namew we have come against this vast army. O LORD, you are our God; do not let man prevailx against you."

12The LORD struck downy the Cushites before Asa and Judah. The Cushites fled, 13and Asa and his army pursued them as far as Gerar.z Such a great number of Cushites fell that they could not recover; they were crushed before the LORD and his forces. The men of Judah carried off a large amount of plunder. 14They destroyed all the villages around Gerar, for the terrora of the LORD had fallen upon them. They plundered all these villages, since there was much booty there. 15They also attacked the camps of the herdsmen and carried off droves of sheep and goats and camels. Then they returned to Jerusalem.

Asa's Reform

15:16–19pp — 1Ki 15:13–16

15 The Spirit of God came uponb Azariah son of Oded. 2He went out to meet Asa and said to him, "Listen to me, Asa and all Judah

14:3
pEx 34:13;
Dt 7:5;
1Ki 15:12-14
14:5
q2Ch 34:4,7
14:6
r1Ch 22:9;
2Ch 15:15
14:9
s2Ch 12:3; 16:8
t2Ch 11:8
14:11
u2Ch 13:14
v2Ch 13:18
w1Sa 17:45
x1Sa 14:6;
Ps 9:19
14:12
y2Ch 13:15
14:13
zGe 10:19
14:14
aGe 35:5;
2Ch 17:10
15:1
bNu 11:25,26;
24:2;
2Ch 20:14;
24:20

a3 That is, symbols of the goddess Asherah; here and elsewhere in 2 Chronicles   b9 Hebrew *with an army of a thousand thousands* or *with an army of thousands upon thousands* and Benjamin. The LORD is with you[c] when you are with him.[d] If you seek[e] him, he will be found by you, but if you forsake him, he will forsake you.[f] [3]For a long time Israel was without the true God, without a priest to teach[g] and without the law.[h] [4]But in their distress they turned to the LORD, the God of Israel, and sought him,[i] and he was found by them. [5]In those days it was not safe to travel about,[j] for all the inhabitants of the lands were in great turmoil. [6]One nation was being crushed by another and one city by another,[k] because God was troubling them with every kind of distress. [7]But as for you, be strong[l] and do not give up, for your work will be rewarded."[m]

[8]When Asa heard these words and the prophecy of Azariah son of[a] Oded the prophet, he took courage. He removed the detestable idols from the whole land of Judah and Benjamin and from the towns he had captured[n] in the hills of Ephraim. He repaired the altar[o] of the LORD that was in front of the portico of the LORD's temple.

[9]Then he assembled all Judah and Benjamin and the people from Ephraim, Manasseh and Simeon who had settled among them, for large numbers[p] had come over to him from Israel when they saw that the LORD his God was with him.

[10]They assembled at Jerusalem in the third month of the fifteenth year of Asa's reign. [11]At that time they sacrificed to the LORD seven hundred head of cattle and seven thousand sheep and goats from the plunder[q] they had brought back. [12]They entered into a covenant[r] to seek the LORD,[s] the God of their fathers, with all their heart and soul. [13]All who would not seek the LORD, the God of Israel, were to be put to death,[t] whether small or great, man or woman. [14]They took an oath to the LORD with loud acclamation, with shouting and with trumpets and horns. [15]All Judah rejoiced about the oath because they had sworn it wholeheartedly. They sought God[u] eagerly, and he was found by them. So the LORD gave them rest[v] on every side.

[16]King Asa also deposed his grandmother Maacah from her position as queen mother, because she had made a repulsive Asherah pole.[w] Asa cut the pole down, broke it up and burned it in the Kidron Valley. [17]Although he did not remove the high places from Israel, Asa's heart was fully committed ⸢to the LORD⸣ all his life. [18]He brought into the temple of God the silver and gold and the articles that he and his father had dedicated.

[19]There was no more war until the thirty-fifth year of Asa's reign.

Asa's Last Years

16:1–6pp — 1Ki 15:17–22
16:11–17:1pp — 1Ki 15:23–24

16 In the thirty-sixth year of Asa's reign Baasha[x] king of Israel went up against Judah and fortified Ramah to prevent anyone from leaving or entering the territory of Asa king of Judah.

[2]Asa then took the silver and gold out of the treasuries of the LORD's temple and of his own palace and sent it to Ben-Hadad king of Aram, who was ruling in Damascus. [3]"Let there be a treaty[y] between me and you," he said, "as there was between my father and your father. See, I

15:2
c ver 4,15;
2Ch 20:17
d Jas 4:8
e Jer 29:13
f 1Ch 28:9;
2Ch 24:20
15:3
g Lev 10:11
h 2Ch 17:9;
La 2:9
15:4
i Dt 4:29
15:5
j Jdg 5:6
15:6
k Mt 24:7
15:7
l Jos 1:7,9
m Ps 58:11
15:8
n 2Ch 13:19
o 2Ch 8:12
15:9
p 2Ch 11:16-17
15:11
q 2Ch 14:13
15:12
r 2Ki 11:17;
2Ch 23:16;
34:31
s 1Ch 16:11
15:13
t Ex 22:20;
Dt 13:9-16
15:15
u Dt 4:29
v 1Ch 22:9;
2Ch 14:7
15:16
w Ex 34:13;
2Ch 14:2-5
16:1
x Jer 41:9
16:3
y 2Ch 20:35

---

[a]8 Vulgate and Syriac (see also Septuagint and verse 1); Hebrew does not have *Azariah son of*.

am sending you silver and gold. Now break your treaty with Baasha king of Israel so he will withdraw from me."

[4]Ben-Hadad agreed with King Asa and sent the commanders of his forces against the towns of Israel. They conquered Ijon, Dan, Abel Maim[a] and all the store cities of Naphtali. [5]When Baasha heard this, he stopped building Ramah and abandoned his work. [6]Then King Asa brought all the men of Judah, and they carried away from Ramah the stones and timber Baasha had been using. With them he built up Geba and Mizpah.

[7]At that time Hanani[z] the seer came to Asa king of Judah and said to him: "Because you relied on the king of Aram and not on the LORD your God, the army of the king of Aram has escaped from your hand. [8]Were not the Cushites[ba] and Libyans a mighty army with great numbers of chariots and horsemen[c]? Yet when you relied on the LORD, he delivered[b] them into your hand. [9]For the eyes[c] of the LORD range throughout the earth to strengthen those whose hearts are fully committed to him. You have done a foolish[d] thing, and from now on you will be at war."

[10]Asa was angry with the seer because of this; he was so enraged that he put him in prison. At the same time Asa brutally oppressed some of the people.

[11]The events of Asa's reign, from beginning to end, are written in the book of the kings of Judah and Israel. [12]In the thirty-ninth year of his reign Asa was afflicted with a disease in his feet. Though his disease was severe, even in his illness he did not seek help from the LORD,[e] but only from the physicians. [13]Then in the forty-first year of his reign Asa died and rested with his fathers. [14]They buried him in the tomb that he had cut out for himself in the City of David. They laid him on a bier covered with spices and various blended perfumes,[f] and they made a huge fire[g] in his honor.

Jehoshaphat King of Judah

17 Jehoshaphat his son succeeded him as king and strengthened himself against Israel. [2]He stationed troops in all the fortified cities of Judah and put garrisons in Judah and in the towns of Ephraim that his father Asa had captured.[h]

[3]The LORD was with Jehoshaphat because in his early years he walked in the ways his father David[i] had followed. He did not consult the Baals [4]but sought[j] the God of his father and followed his commands rather than the practices of Israel. [5]The LORD established the kingdom under his control; and all Judah brought gifts[k] to Jehoshaphat, so that he had great wealth and honor.[l] [6]His heart was devoted[m] to the ways of the LORD; furthermore, he removed the high places[n] and the Asherah poles[o] from Judah.[p]

[7]In the third year of his reign he sent his officials Ben-Hail, Obadiah, Zechariah, Nethanel and Micaiah to teach[q] in the towns of Judah. [8]With them were certain Levites[r]—Shemaiah, Nethaniah, Zebadiah, Asahel, Shemiramoth, Jehonathan, Adonijah, Tobijah and Tob-Adonijah—and the priests Elishama and Jehoram. [9]They taught throughout

16:7
z 1Ki 16:1
16:8
a 2Ch 12:3; 14:9
b 2Ch 13:16
16:9
c Pr 15:3;
Jer 16:17;
Zec 4:10
d 1Sa 13:13
16:12
e Jer 17:5-6
16:14
f Ge 50:2;
Jn 19:39-40
g 2Ch 21:19;
Jer 34:5
17:2
h 2Ch 15:8
17:3
i 1Ki 22:43
17:4
j 1Ki 12:28;
2Ch 22:9
17:5
k 1Sa 10:27
l 2Ch 18:1
17:6
m 1Ki 8:61;
2Ch 15:17
n 1Ki 15:14;
2Ch 19:3; 20:33
o Ex 34:13
p 2Ch 21:12
17:7
q Lev 10:11;
Dt 6:4-9;
2Ch 15:3; 35:3
17:8
r 2Ch 19:8;
Ne 8:7-8

---

[a]4 Also known as *Abel Beth Maacah*   [b]8 That is, people from the upper Nile region   [c]8 Or *charioteers*

Judah, taking with them the Book of the Law^s of the LORD; they went around to all the towns of Judah and taught the people.

¹⁰The fear^t of the LORD fell on all the kingdoms of the lands surrounding Judah, so that they did not make war with Jehoshaphat. ¹¹Some Philistines brought Jehoshaphat gifts and silver as tribute, and the Arabs^u brought him flocks:^v seven thousand seven hundred rams and seven thousand seven hundred goats.

¹²Jehoshaphat became more and more powerful; he built forts and store cities in Judah ¹³and had large supplies in the towns of Judah. He also kept experienced fighting men in Jerusalem. ¹⁴Their enrollment^w by families was as follows:

> From Judah, commanders of units of 1,000:
>> Adnah the commander, with 300,000 fighting men;
> ¹⁵next, Jehohanan the commander, with 280,000;
> ¹⁶next, Amasiah son of Zicri, who volunteered^x himself for the service of the LORD, with 200,000.
> ¹⁷From Benjamin:^y
>> Eliada, a valiant soldier, with 200,000 men armed with bows and shields;
> ¹⁸next, Jehozabad, with 180,000 men armed for battle.

¹⁹These were the men who served the king, besides those he stationed in the fortified cities^z throughout Judah.^a

Micaiah Prophesies Against Ahab

18:1–27pp — 1Ki 22:1–28

18 Now Jehoshaphat had great wealth and honor,^b and he allied^c himself with Ahab^d by marriage. ²Some years later he went down to visit Ahab in Samaria. Ahab slaughtered many sheep and cattle for him and the people with him and urged him to attack Ramoth Gilead. ³Ahab king of Israel asked Jehoshaphat king of Judah, "Will you go with me against Ramoth Gilead?"

Jehoshaphat replied, "I am as you are, and my people as your people; we will join you in the war." ⁴But Jehoshaphat also said to the king of Israel, "First seek the counsel of the LORD."

⁵So the king of Israel brought together the prophets—four hundred men—and asked them, "Shall we go to war against Ramoth Gilead, or shall I refrain?"

"Go," they answered, "for God will give it into the king's hand."

⁶But Jehoshaphat asked, "Is there not a prophet of the LORD here whom we can inquire of?"

⁷The king of Israel answered Jehoshaphat, "There is still one man through whom we can inquire of the LORD, but I hate him because he never prophesies anything good about me, but always bad. He is Micaiah son of Imlah."

"The king should not say that," Jehoshaphat replied.

⁸So the king of Israel called one of his officials and said, "Bring Micaiah son of Imlah at once."

⁹Dressed in their royal robes, the king of Israel and Jehoshaphat king of Judah were sitting on their thrones at the threshing floor by the entrance to the gate of Samaria, with all the prophets prophesying before them. ¹⁰Now Zedekiah son of Kenaanah had made iron horns,

17:9
^sDt 6:4-9; 28:61
17:10
^tGe 35:5;
Dt 2:25;
2Ch 14:14
17:11
^u2Ch 9:14; 26:8
^v2Ch 21:16
17:14
^w2Sa 24:2
17:16
^xJdg 5:9;
1Ch 29:9
17:17
^yNu 1:36
17:19
^z2Ch 11:10
^a2Ch 25:5
18:1
^b2Ch 17:5
^c2Ch 19:1-3;
22:3 ^d2Ch 21:6

and he declared, "This is what the LORD says: 'With these you will gore the Arameans until they are destroyed.' "

[11]All the other prophets were prophesying the same thing. "Attack Ramoth Gilead[e] and be victorious," they said, "for the LORD will give it into the king's hand."

[12]The messenger who had gone to summon Micaiah said to him, "Look, as one man the other prophets are predicting success for the king. Let your word agree with theirs, and speak favorably."

[13]But Micaiah said, "As surely as the LORD lives, I can tell him only what my God says."[f]

[14]When he arrived, the king asked him, "Micaiah, shall we go to war against Ramoth Gilead, or shall I refrain?"

"Attack and be victorious," he answered, "for they will be given into your hand."

[15]The king said to him, "How many times must I make you swear to tell me nothing but the truth in the name of the LORD?"

[16]Then Micaiah answered, "I saw all Israel[g] scattered on the hills like sheep without a shepherd,[h] and the LORD said, 'These people have no master. Let each one go home in peace.' "

[17]The king of Israel said to Jehoshaphat, "Didn't I tell you that he never prophesies anything good about me, but only bad?"

[18]Micaiah continued, "Therefore hear the word of the LORD: I saw the LORD sitting on his throne[i] with all the host of heaven standing on his right and on his left. [19]And the LORD said, 'Who will lure Ahab king of Israel into attacking Ramoth Gilead and going to his death there?'

"One suggested this, and another that. [20]Finally, a spirit came forward, stood before the LORD and said, 'I will lure him.'

" 'By what means?' the LORD asked.

[21]" 'I will go and be a lying spirit[j] in the mouths of all his prophets,' he said.

" 'You will succeed in luring him,' said the LORD. 'Go and do it.'

[22]"So now the LORD has put a lying spirit in the mouths of these prophets of yours.[k] The LORD has decreed disaster for you."

[23]Then Zedekiah son of Kenaanah went up and slapped[l] Micaiah in the face. "Which way did the spirit from[a] the LORD go when he went from me to speak to you?" he asked.

[24]Micaiah replied, "You will find out on the day you go to hide in an inner room."

[25]The king of Israel then ordered, "Take Micaiah and send him back to Amon the ruler of the city and to Joash the king's son, [26]and say, 'This is what the king says: Put this fellow in prison[m] and give him nothing but bread and water until I return safely.' "

[27]Micaiah declared, "If you ever return safely, the LORD has not spoken through me." Then he added, "Mark my words, all you people!"

Ahab Killed at Ramoth Gilead

18:28-34pp — 1Ki 22:29-36

[28]So the king of Israel and Jehoshaphat king of Judah went up to Ramoth Gilead. [29]The king of Israel said to Jehoshaphat, "I will enter

18:11
e2Ch 22:5
18:13
fNu 22:18,20,35
18:16
g1Ch 9:1
hNu 27:17;
Eze 34:5-8
18:18
iDa 7:9
18:21
j1Ch 21:1;
Job 1:6;
Zec 3:1; Jn 8:44
18:22
kJob 12:16;
Isa 19:14;
Eze 14:9
18:23
lJer 20:2;
Mk 14:65;
Ac 23:2
18:26
m2Ch 16:10;
Heb 11:36

a23 Or *Spirit of*

the battle in disguise, but you wear your royal robes." So the king of Israel disguised[n] himself and went into battle.

[30]Now the king of Aram had ordered his chariot commanders, "Do not fight with anyone, small or great, except the king of Israel." [31]When the chariot commanders saw Jehoshaphat, they thought, "This is the king of Israel." So they turned to attack him, but Jehoshaphat cried out,[o] and the LORD helped him. God drew them away from him, [32]for when the chariot commanders saw that he was not the king of Israel, they stopped pursuing him.

[33]But someone drew his bow at random and hit the king of Israel between the sections of his armor. The king told the chariot driver, "Wheel around and get me out of the fighting. I've been wounded." [34]All day long the battle raged, and the king of Israel propped himself up in his chariot facing the Arameans until evening. Then at sunset he died.[p]

19 When Jehoshaphat king of Judah returned safely to his palace in Jerusalem, [2]Jehu[q] the seer, the son of Hanani, went out to meet him and said to the king, "Should you help the wicked[r] and love[s] those who hate the LORD?[s] Because of this, the wrath[t] of the LORD is upon you. [3]There is, however, some good[u] in you, for you have rid the land of the Asherah poles[v] and have set your heart on seeking God. [w]"

Jehoshaphat Appoints Judges

[4]Jehoshaphat lived in Jerusalem, and he went out again among the people from Beersheba to the hill country of Ephraim and turned them back to the LORD, the God of their fathers. [5]He appointed judges[x] in the land, in each of the fortified cities of Judah. [6]He told them, "Consider carefully what you do,[y] because you are not judging for man[z] but for the LORD, who is with you whenever you give a verdict. [7]Now let the fear of the LORD be upon you. Judge carefully, for with the LORD our God there is no injustice[a] or partiality[b] or bribery."

[8]In Jerusalem also, Jehoshaphat appointed some of the Levites, priests and heads of Israelite families to administer[c] the law of the LORD and to settle disputes. And they lived in Jerusalem. [9]He gave them these orders: "You must serve faithfully and wholeheartedly in the fear of the LORD. [10]In every case that comes before you from your fellow countrymen who live in the cities—whether bloodshed or other concerns of the law, commands, decrees or ordinances—you are to warn them not to sin against the LORD;[d] otherwise his wrath will come on you and your brothers. Do this, and you will not sin.

[11]"Amariah the chief priest will be over you in any matter concerning the LORD, and Zebadiah son of Ishmael, the leader of the tribe of Judah, will be over you in any matter concerning the king, and the Levites will serve as officials before you. Act with courage,[e] and may the LORD be with those who do well."

Jehoshaphat Defeats Moab and Ammon

20 After this, the Moabites and Ammonites with some of the Meunites[bf] came to make war on Jehoshaphat.

[2]Some men came and told Jehoshaphat, "A vast army is coming

---

18:29
n 1Sa 28:8
18:31
o 2Ch 13:14
18:34
p 2Ch 22:5
19:2
q 1Ki 16:1
r 2Ch 16:2-9
s Ps 139:21-22
t 2Ch 24:18;
32:25; Ps 7:11
19:3
u 1Ki 14:13;
2Ch 12:12
v 2Ch 17:6
w 2Ch 18:1;
20:35; 25:7;
Ezr 7:10
19:5
x Ge 47:6;
Ex 18:26
19:6
y Lev 19:15
z Dt 1:17;
16:18-20;
17:8-13
19:7
a Ge 18:25;
Dt 32:4
b Dt 10:17;
Job 34:19;
Ro 2:11;
Col 3:25
19:8
c 2Ch 17:8-9
19:10
d Dt 17:8-13
19:11
e 1Ch 28:20
20:1
f 1Ch 4:41

---

[a]2 Or *and make alliances with*   [b]1 Some Septuagint manuscripts; Hebrew *Ammonites*

against you from Edom,ᵃ from the other side of the Sea.ᵇ It is already in Hazazon Tamarᵍ" (that is, En Gedi). ³Alarmed, Jehoshaphat resolved to inquire of the LORD, and he proclaimed a fastʰ for all Judah. ⁴The people of Judah came together to seek help from the LORD; indeed, they came from every town in Judah to seek him.

⁵Then Jehoshaphat stood up in the assembly of Judah and Jerusalem at the temple of the LORD in the front of the new courtyard ⁶and said:

"O LORD, God of our fathers,ⁱ are you not the God who is in heaven?ʲ You rule over all the kingdomsᵏ of the nations. Power and might are in your hand, and no one can withstand you. ⁷O our God, did you not drive out the inhabitants of this land before your people Israel and give it forever to the descendants of Abraham your friend?ˡ ⁸They have lived in it and have built in it a sanctuaryᵐ for your Name, saying, ⁹'If calamity comes upon us, whether the sword of judgment, or plague or famine,ⁿ we will stand in your presence before this temple that bears your Name and will cry out to you in our distress, and you will hear us and save us.'

¹⁰"But now here are men from Ammon, Moab and Mount Seir, whose territory you would not allow Israel to invade when they came from Egypt;ᵒ so they turned away from them and did not destroy them. ¹¹See how they are repaying us by coming to drive us out of the possessionᵖ you gave us as an inheritance. ¹²O our God, will you not judge them?�q For we have no power to face this vast army that is attacking us. We do not know what to do, but our eyes are upon you.ʳ"

¹³All the men of Judah, with their wives and children and little ones, stood there before the LORD.

¹⁴Then the Spiritˢ of the LORD came upon Jahaziel son of Zechariah, the son of Benaiah, the son of Jeiel, the son of Mattaniah, a Levite and descendant of Asaph, as he stood in the assembly.

¹⁵He said: "Listen, King Jehoshaphat and all who live in Judah and Jerusalem! This is what the LORD says to you: 'Do not be afraid or discouragedᵗ because of this vast army. For the battleᵘ is not yours, but God's. ¹⁶Tomorrow march down against them. They will be climbing up by the Pass of Ziz, and you will find them at the end of the gorge in the Desert of Jeruel. ¹⁷You will not have to fight this battle. Take up your positions; stand firm and seeᵛ the deliverance the LORD will give you, O Judah and Jerusalem. Do not be afraid; do not be discouraged. Go out to face them tomorrow, and the LORD will be with you.'"

¹⁸Jehoshaphat bowedʷ with his face to the ground, and all the people of Judah and Jerusalem fell down in worship before the LORD. ¹⁹Then some Levites from the Kohathites and Korahites stood up and praised the LORD, the God of Israel, with very loud voice.

²⁰Early in the morning they left for the Desert of Tekoa. As they set out, Jehoshaphat stood and said, "Listen to me, Judah and people of Jerusalem! Have faithˣ in the LORD your God and you will be upheld; have faith in his prophets and you will be successful.ʸ" ²¹After consult-

20:2
ᵍGe 14:7
20:3
ʰ1Sa 7:6;
2Ch 19:3;
Ezr 8:21;
Jer 36:9;
Jnh 3:5,7
20:6
ⁱMt 6:9 ʲDt 4:39
ᵏ1Ch 29:11-12
20:7
ˡIsa 41:8;
Jas 2:23
20:8
ᵐ2Ch 6:20
20:9
ⁿ2Ch 6:28
20:10
ᵒNu 20:14-21;
Dt 2:4-6,9,18-19
20:11
ᵖPs 83:1-12
20:12
qJdg 11:27
ʳPs 25:15;
121:1-2
20:14
ˢ2Ch 15:1
20:15
ᵗ2Ch 32:7
ᵘEx 14:13-14;
1Sa 17:47
20:17
ᵛEx 14:13;
2Ch 15:2
20:18
ʷEx 4:31
20:20
ˣIsa 7:9
ʸGe 39:3;
Pr 16:3

ᵃ2 One Hebrew manuscript; most Hebrew manuscripts, Septuagint and Vulgate *Aram*   ᵇ2 That is, the Dead Sea ing the people, Jehoshaphat appointed men to sing to the LORD and to praise him for the splendor of his[a] holiness[z] as they went out at the head of the army, saying:

"Give thanks to the LORD,
   for his love endures forever."[a]

[22]As they began to sing and praise, the LORD set ambushes[b] against the men of Ammon and Moab and Mount Seir who were invading Judah, and they were defeated. [23]The men of Ammon[c] and Moab rose up against the men from Mount Seir[d] to destroy and annihilate them. After they finished slaughtering the men from Seir, they helped to destroy one another.[e]

[24]When the men of Judah came to the place that overlooks the desert and looked toward the vast army, they saw only dead bodies lying on the ground; no one had escaped. [25]So Jehoshaphat and his men went to carry off their plunder, and they found among them a great amount of equipment and clothing[b] and also articles of value—more than they could take away. There was so much plunder that it took three days to collect it. [26]On the fourth day they assembled in the Valley of Beracah, where they praised the LORD. This is why it is called the Valley of Beracah[c] to this day.

[27]Then, led by Jehoshaphat, all the men of Judah and Jerusalem returned joyfully to Jerusalem, for the LORD had given them cause to rejoice over their enemies. [28]They entered Jerusalem and went to the temple of the LORD with harps and lutes and trumpets.

[29]The fear[f] of God came upon all the kingdoms of the countries when they heard how the LORD had fought[g] against the enemies of Israel. [30]And the kingdom of Jehoshaphat was at peace, for his God had given him rest[h] on every side.

The End of Jehoshaphat's Reign
20:31–21:1pp — 1Ki 22:41–50

[31]So Jehoshaphat reigned over Judah. He was thirty-five years old when he became king of Judah, and he reigned in Jerusalem twenty-five years. His mother's name was Azubah daughter of Shilhi. [32]He walked in the ways of his father Asa and did not stray from them; he did what was right in the eyes of the LORD. [33]The high places,[i] however, were not removed, and the people still had not set their hearts on the God of their fathers.

[34]The other events of Jehoshaphat's reign, from beginning to end, are written in the annals of Jehu[j] son of Hanani, which are recorded in the book of the kings of Israel.

[35]Later, Jehoshaphat king of Judah made an alliance[k] with Ahaziah king of Israel, who was guilty of wickedness.[l] [36]He agreed with him to construct a fleet of trading ships.[d] After these were built at Ezion Geber, [37]Eliezer son of Dodavahu of Mareshah prophesied against Jehoshaphat, saying, "Because you have made an alliance with Ahazi-

20:21
z1Ch 16:29;
Ps 29:2
a2Ch 5:13;
Ps 136:1
20:22
bJdg 7:22;
2Ch 13:13
20:23
cGe 19:38
d2Ch 21:8
eJdg 7:22;
1Sa 14:20;
Eze 38:21
20:29
fGe 35:5;
Dt 2:25;
2Ch 14:14;
17:10 gEx 14:14
20:30
h1Ch 22:9;
2Ch 14:6-7;
15:15
20:33
i2Ch 17:6; 19:3
20:34
j1Ki 16:1
20:35
k2Ch 16:3
l2Ch 19:1-3

---

[a]21 Or *him with the splendor of*   [b]25 Some Hebrew manuscripts and Vulgate; most Hebrew manuscripts *corpses*   [c]26 *Beracah* means *praise.*   [d]36 Hebrew *of ships that could go to Tarshish*

ah, the LORD will destroy what you have made." The ships[m] were wrecked and were not able to set sail to trade.[a]

21 Then Jehoshaphat rested with his fathers and was buried with them in the City of David. And Jehoram[n] his son succeeded him as king. ²Jehoram's brothers, the sons of Jehoshaphat, were Azariah, Jehiel, Zechariah, Azariahu, Michael and Shephatiah. All these were sons of Jehoshaphat king of Israel.[b] ³Their father had given them many gifts[o] of silver and gold and articles of value, as well as fortified cities[p] in Judah, but he had given the kingdom to Jehoram because he was his firstborn son.

Jehoram King of Judah

21:5–10,20pp — 2Ki 8:16–24

⁴When Jehoram established[q] himself firmly over his father's kingdom, he put all his brothers[r] to the sword along with some of the princes of Israel. ⁵Jehoram was thirty-two years old when he became king, and he reigned in Jerusalem eight years. ⁶He walked in the ways of the kings of Israel,[s] as the house of Ahab had done, for he married a daughter of Ahab.[t] He did evil in the eyes of the LORD. ⁷Nevertheless, because of the covenant the LORD had made with David,[u] the LORD was not willing to destroy the house of David.[v] He had promised to maintain a lamp[w] for him and his descendants forever.

⁸In the time of Jehoram, Edom[x] rebelled against Judah and set up its own king. ⁹So Jehoram went there with his officers and all his chariots. The Edomites surrounded him and his chariot commanders, but he rose up and broke through by night. ¹⁰To this day Edom has been in rebellion against Judah.

Libnah[y] revolted at the same time, because Jehoram had forsaken the LORD, the God of his fathers. ¹¹He had also built high places on the hills of Judah and had caused the people of Jerusalem to prostitute themselves and had led Judah astray.

¹²Jehoram received a letter from Elijah[z] the prophet, which said:

"This is what the LORD, the God of your father[a] David, says: 'You have not walked in the ways of your father Jehoshaphat or of Asa[b] king of Judah. ¹³But you have walked in the ways of the kings of Israel, and you have led Judah and the people of Jerusalem to prostitute themselves, just as the house of Ahab did.[c] You have also murdered your own brothers, members of your father's house, men who were better[d] than you. ¹⁴So now the LORD is about to strike your people, your sons, your wives and everything that is yours, with a heavy blow. ¹⁵You yourself will be very ill with a lingering disease[e] of the bowels, until the disease causes your bowels to come out.' "

¹⁶The LORD aroused against Jehoram the hostility of the Philistines and of the Arabs[f] who lived near the Cushites. ¹⁷They attacked Judah, invaded it and carried off all the goods found in the king's palace, together with his sons and wives. Not a son was left to him except Ahaziah,[c] the youngest.[g]

20:37
m 1Ki 9:26;
2Ch 9:21
21:1
n 1Ch 3:11
21:3
o 2Ch 11:23
p 2Ch 11:10
21:4
q 1Ki 2:12
r Jdg 9:5
21:6
s 1Ki 12:28-30
t 2Ch 18:1; 22:3
21:7
u 2Sa 7:13
v 2Sa 7:15;
2Ch 23:3
w 2Sa 21:17;
1Ki 11:36
21:8
x 2Ch 20:22-23
21:10
y Nu 33:20
21:12
z 2Ki 1:16-17
a 2Ch 17:3-6
b 2Ch 14:2
21:13
c ver 6,11;
1Ki 16:29-33
d ver 4; 1Ki 2:32
21:15
e ver 18-19;
Nu 12:10
21:16
f 2Ch 17:10-11;
22:1; 26:7
21:17
g 2Ki 12:18;
2Ch 22:1;
25:23; Joel 3:5

---

*a*37 Hebrew *sail for Tarshish*   *b*2 That is, Judah, as frequently in 2 Chronicles   *c*17 Hebrew *Jehoahaz,* a variant of *Ahaziah*

¹⁸After all this, the LORD afflicted Jehoram with an incurable disease of the bowels. ¹⁹In the course of time, at the end of the second year, his bowels came out because of the disease, and he died in great pain. His people made no fire in his honor,^h as they had for his fathers.

²⁰Jehoram was thirty-two years old when he became king, and he reigned in Jerusalem eight years. He passed away, to no one's regret, and was buriedⁱ in the City of David, but not in the tombs of the kings.

Ahaziah King of Judah

22:1–6pp — 2Ki 8:25–29
22:7–9pp — 2Ki 9:21–29

22 The people^j of Jerusalem^k made Ahaziah, Jehoram's youngest son, king in his place, since the raiders,^l who came with the Arabs into the camp, had killed all the older sons. So Ahaziah son of Jehoram king of Judah began to reign.

²Ahaziah was twenty-two^a years old when he became king, and he reigned in Jerusalem one year. His mother's name was Athaliah, a granddaughter of Omri.

³He too walked^m in the ways of the house of Ahab,ⁿ for his mother encouraged him in doing wrong. ⁴He did evil in the eyes of the LORD, as the house of Ahab had done, for after his father's death they became his advisers, to his undoing. ⁵He also followed their counsel when he went with Joram^b son of Ahab king of Israel to war against Hazael king of Aram at Ramoth Gilead. ^o The Arameans wounded Joram; ⁶so he returned to Jezreel to recover from the wounds they had inflicted on him at Ramoth^c in his battle with Hazael^p king of Aram.

Then Ahaziah^d son of Jehoram king of Judah went down to Jezreel to see Joram son of Ahab because he had been wounded.

⁷Through Ahaziah's^q visit to Joram, God brought about Ahaziah's downfall. When Ahaziah arrived, he went out with Joram to meet Jehu son of Nimshi, whom the LORD had anointed to destroy the house of Ahab. ⁸While Jehu was executing judgment on the house of Ahab,^r he found the princes of Judah and the sons of Ahaziah's relatives, who had been attending Ahaziah, and he killed them. ⁹He then went in search of Ahaziah, and his men captured him while he was hiding^s in Samaria. He was brought to Jehu and put to death. They buried him, for they said, "He was a son of Jehoshaphat, who sought^t the LORD with all his heart." So there was no one in the house of Ahaziah powerful enough to retain the kingdom.

Athaliah and Joash

22:10–23:21pp — 2Ki 11:1–21

¹⁰When Athaliah the mother of Ahaziah saw that her son was dead, she proceeded to destroy the whole royal family of the house of Judah. ¹¹But Jehosheba,^e the daughter of King Jehoram, took Joash son of Ahaziah and stole him away from among the royal princes who were about to be murdered and put him and his nurse in a bedroom. Because

21:19
h2Ch 16:14
21:20
i2Ch 24:25;
28:27; 33:20;
Jer 22:18,28
22:1
j2Ch 33:25;
36:1
k2Ch 23:20-21;
26:1
l2Ch 21:16-17
22:3
m2Ch 18:1
n2Ch 21:6
22:5
o2Ch 18:11,34
22:6
p1Ki 19:15;
2Ki 8:13-15;
9:15
22:7
q2Ki 9:16;
2Ch 10:15
22:8
r2Ki 10:13
22:9
sJdg 9:5
t2Ch 17:4

---

^a2 Some Septuagint manuscripts and Syriac (see also 2 Kings 8:26); Hebrew *forty-two*
^b5 Hebrew *Jehoram*, a variant of *Joram*; also in verses 6 and 7   ^c6 Hebrew *Ramah*, a variant of *Ramoth*   ^d6 Some Hebrew manuscripts, Septuagint, Vulgate and Syriac (see also 2 Kings 8:29); most Hebrew manuscripts *Azariah*

Jehosheba,[a] the daughter of King Jehoram and wife of the priest Jehoiada, was Ahaziah's sister, she hid the child from Athaliah so she could not kill him. [12]He remained hidden with them at the temple of God for six years while Athaliah ruled the land.

23 In the seventh year Jehoiada showed his strength. He made a covenant with the commanders of units of a hundred: Azariah son of Jeroham, Ishmael son of Jehohanan, Azariah son of Obed, Maaseiah son of Adaiah, and Elishaphat son of Zicri. [2]They went throughout Judah and gathered the Levites[u] and the heads of Israelite families from all the towns. When they came to Jerusalem, [3]the whole assembly made a covenant[v] with the king at the temple of God.

Jehoiada said to them, "The king's son shall reign, as the LORD promised concerning the descendants of David.[w] [4]Now this is what you are to do: A third of you priests and Levites who are going on duty on the Sabbath are to keep watch at the doors, [5]a third of you at the royal palace and a third at the Foundation Gate, and all the other men are to be in the courtyards of the temple of the LORD. [6]No one is to enter the temple of the LORD except the priests and Levites on duty; they may enter because they are consecrated, but all the other men are to guard[x] what the LORD has assigned to them.[b] [7]The Levites are to station themselves around the king, each man with his weapons in his hand. Anyone who enters the temple must be put to death. Stay close to the king wherever he goes."

[8]The Levites and all the men of Judah did just as Jehoiada the priest ordered.[y] Each one took his men—those who were going on duty on the Sabbath and those who were going off duty—for Jehoiada the priest had not released any of the divisions.[z] [9]Then he gave the commanders of units of a hundred the spears and the large and small shields that had belonged to King David and that were in the temple of God. [10]He stationed all the men, each with his weapon in his hand, around the king—near the altar and the temple, from the south side to the north side of the temple.

[11]Jehoiada and his sons brought out the king's son and put the crown on him; they presented him with a copy[a] of the covenant and proclaimed him king. They anointed him and shouted, "Long live the king!"

[12]When Athaliah heard the noise of the people running and cheering the king, she went to them at the temple of the LORD. [13]She looked, and there was the king,[b] standing by his pillar[c] at the entrance. The officers and the trumpeters were beside the king, and all the people of the land were rejoicing and blowing trumpets, and singers with musical instruments were leading the praises. Then Athaliah tore her robes and shouted, "Treason! Treason!"

[14]Jehoiada the priest sent out the commanders of units of a hundred, who were in charge of the troops, and said to them: "Bring her out between the ranks[c] and put to the sword anyone who follows her." For the priest had said, "Do not put her to death at the temple of the LORD." [15]So they seized her as she reached the entrance of the Horse Gate[d] on the palace grounds, and there they put her to death.

23:2
u Nu 35:2-5
23:3
v 2Ki 11:17
w 2Sa 7:12;
1Ki 2:4;
2Ch 6:16; 7:18;
21:7
23:6
x 1Ch 23:28-29;
Zec 3:7
23:8
y 2Ki 11:9
z 1Ch 24:1
23:11
a Ex 25:16;
Dt 17:18;
1Sa 10:24
23:13
b 1Ki 1:41
c 1Ki 7:15
23:15
d Ne 3:28;
Jer 31:40

---

[a]11 Hebrew *Jehoshabeath*, a variant of *Jehosheba*   [b]6 Or *to observe the LORD's command not to enter*,
[c]14 Or *out from the precincts*

¹⁶Jehoiada then made a covenant ͤ that he and the people and the king ͣ would be the LORD's people. ¹⁷All the people went to the temple of Baal and tore it down. They smashed the altars and idols and killed ͤ Mattan the priest of Baal in front of the altars.

¹⁸Then Jehoiada placed the oversight of the temple of the LORD in the hands of the priests, who were Levites, ᵍ to whom David had made assignments in the temple, ͪ to present the burnt offerings of the LORD as written in the Law of Moses, with rejoicing and singing, as David had ordered. ¹⁹He also stationed doorkeepers ͥ at the gates of the LORD's temple so that no one who was in any way unclean might enter.

²⁰He took with him the commanders of hundreds, the nobles, the rulers of the people and all the people of the land and brought the king down from the temple of the LORD. They went into the palace through the Upper Gate ʲ and seated the king on the royal throne, ²¹and all the people of the land rejoiced. And the city was quiet, because Athaliah had been slain with the sword. ᵏ

Joash Repairs the Temple

24:1–14pp — 2Ki 12:1–16
24:23–27pp — 2Ki 12:17–21

24 Joash was seven years old when he became king, and he reigned in Jerusalem forty years. His mother's name was Zibiah; she was from Beersheba. ²Joash did what was right in the eyes of the LORD ͥ all the years of Jehoiada the priest. ³Jehoiada chose two wives for him, and he had sons and daughters.

⁴Some time later Joash decided to restore the temple of the LORD. ⁵He called together the priests and Levites and said to them, "Go to the towns of Judah and collect the money ͫ due annually from all Israel, ͫ to repair the temple of your God. Do it now." But the Levites ͦ did not act at once.

⁶Therefore the king summoned Jehoiada the chief priest and said to him, "Why haven't you required the Levites to bring in from Judah and Jerusalem the tax imposed by Moses the servant of the LORD and by the assembly of Israel for the Tent of the Testimony?" ᵖ

⁷Now the sons of that wicked woman Athaliah had broken into the temple of God and had used even its sacred objects for the Baals.

⁸At the king's command, a chest was made and placed outside, at the gate of the temple of the LORD. ⁹A proclamation was then issued in Judah and Jerusalem that they should bring to the LORD the tax that Moses the servant of God had required of Israel in the desert. ¹⁰All the officials and all the people brought their contributions gladly, �q dropping them into the chest until it was full. ¹¹Whenever the chest was brought in by the Levites to the king's officials and they saw that there was a large amount of money, the royal secretary and the officer of the chief priest would come and empty the chest and carry it back to its place. They did this regularly and collected a great amount of money. ¹²The king and Jehoiada gave it to the men who carried out the work

---

23:16
ᵉ2Ch 29:10;
34:31; Ne 9:38
23:17
ᶠDt 13:6-9
23:18
ᵍ1Ch 23:28-32;
2Ch 5:5
ͪ1Ch 23:6; 25:6
23:19
ͥ1Ch 9:22
23:20
ʲ2Ki 15:35
23:21
ᵏ2Ch 22:1
24:2
ˡ2Ch 25:2; 26:5
24:5
ͫEx 30:16;
Ne 10:32-33;
Mt 17:24
ͫ1Ch 11:1
ͦ1Ch 26:20
24:6
ᵖEx 30:12-16;
Nu 1:50
24:10
qEx 25:2;
1Ch 29:3,6,9

ᵃ16 Or *covenant between ˌthe LORDˌ and the people and the king that they* (see 2 Kings 11:17) required for the temple of the LORD. They hired[r] masons and carpenters to restore the LORD's temple, and also workers in iron and bronze to repair the temple.

13The men in charge of the work were diligent, and the repairs progressed under them. They rebuilt the temple of God according to its original design and reinforced it. 14When they had finished, they brought the rest of the money to the king and Jehoiada, and with it were made articles for the LORD's temple: articles for the service and for the burnt offerings, and also dishes and other objects of gold and silver. As long as Jehoiada lived, burnt offerings were presented continually in the temple of the LORD.

15Now Jehoiada was old and full of years, and he died at the age of a hundred and thirty. 16He was buried with the kings in the City of David, because of the good he had done in Israel for God and his temple.

The Wickedness of Joash

17After the death of Jehoiada, the officials of Judah came and paid homage to the king, and he listened to them. 18They abandoned[s] the temple of the LORD, the God of their fathers, and worshiped Asherah poles and idols.[t] Because of their guilt, God's anger[u] came upon Judah and Jerusalem. 19Although the LORD sent prophets to the people to bring them back to him, and though they testified against them, they would not listen.[v]

20Then the Spirit[w] of God came upon Zechariah[x] son of Jehoiada the priest. He stood before the people and said, "This is what God says: 'Why do you disobey the LORD's commands? You will not prosper.[y] Because you have forsaken the LORD, he has forsaken[z] you.'"

21But they plotted against him, and by order of the king they stoned[a] him to death[b] in the courtyard of the LORD's temple.[c] 22King Joash did not remember the kindness Zechariah's father Jehoiada had shown him but killed his son, who said as he lay dying, "May the LORD see this and call you to account."[d]

23At the turn of the year,[a] the army of Aram marched against Joash; it invaded Judah and Jerusalem and killed all the leaders of the people.[e] They sent all the plunder to their king in Damascus. 24Although the Aramean army had come with only a few men,[f] the LORD delivered into their hands a much larger army.[g] Because Judah had forsaken the LORD, the God of their fathers, judgment was executed on Joash. 25When the Arameans withdrew, they left Joash severely wounded. His officials conspired against him for murdering the son of Jehoiada the priest, and they killed him in his bed. So he died and was buried[h] in the City of David, but not in the tombs of the kings.

26Those who conspired against him were Zabad,[b] son of Shimeath an Ammonite woman, and Jehozabad, son of Shimrith[c]i a Moabite woman.[j] 27The account of his sons, the many prophecies about him, and the record of the restoration of the temple of God are written in the annotations on the book of the kings. And Amaziah his son succeeded him as king.

24:12
r2Ch 34:11
24:18
sver 4;
Jos 24:20;
2Ch 7:19
tEx 34:13;
1Ki 14:23;
2Ch 33:3;
Jer 17:2
uJos 22:20;
2Ch 19:2
24:19
vNu 11:29;
Jer 7:25;
Zec 1:4
24:20
wJdg 3:10;
1Ch 12:18;
2Ch 20:14
xMt 23:35;
Lk 11:51
yNu 14:41
zDt 31:17;
2Ch 15:2
24:21
aJos 7:25;
Ac 7:58-59
bNe 9:26;
Jer 26:21
cJer 20:2;
Mt 23:35
24:22
dGe 9:5
24:23
e2Ki 12:17-18
24:24
f2Ch 14:9;
16:8; 20:2,12
gLev 26:23-25;
Dt 28:25
24:25
h2Ch 21:20
24:26
i2Ki 12:21
jRu 1:4

a23 Probably in the spring   b26 A variant of *Jozabad*   c26 A variant of *Shomer*

Amaziah King of Judah

25:1–4pp — 2Ki 14:1–6
25:11–12pp — 2Ki 14:7
25:17–28pp — 2Ki 14:8–20

25 Amaziah was twenty-five years old when he became king, and he reigned in Jerusalem twenty-nine years. His mother's name was Jehoaddin[a]; she was from Jerusalem. [2]He did what was right in the eyes of the LORD, but not wholeheartedly.[k] [3]After the kingdom was firmly in his control, he executed the officials who had murdered his father the king. [4]Yet he did not put their sons to death, but acted in accordance with what is written in the Law, in the Book of Moses,[l] where the LORD commanded: "Fathers shall not be put to death for their children, nor children put to death for their fathers; each is to die for his own sins."[b] [m]

[5]Amaziah called the people of Judah together and assigned them according to their families to commanders of thousands and commanders of hundreds for all Judah and Benjamin. He then mustered[n] those twenty years old[o] or more and found that there were three hundred thousand men ready for military service,[p] able to handle the spear and shield. [6]He also hired a hundred thousand fighting men from Israel for a hundred talents[c] of silver.

[7]But a man of God came to him and said, "O king, these troops from Israel[q] must not march with you, for the LORD is not with Israel—not with any of the people of Ephraim. [8]Even if you go and fight courageously in battle, God will overthrow you before the enemy, for God has the power to help or to overthrow."[r]

[9]Amaziah asked the man of God, "But what about the hundred talents I paid for these Israelite troops?"

The man of God replied, "The LORD can give you much more than that."[s]

[10]So Amaziah dismissed the troops who had come to him from Ephraim and sent them home. They were furious with Judah and left for home in a great rage.[t]

[11]Amaziah then marshaled his strength and led his army to the Valley of Salt, where he killed ten thousand men of Seir. [12]The army of Judah also captured ten thousand men alive, took them to the top of a cliff and threw them down so that all were dashed to pieces.[u]

[13]Meanwhile the troops that Amaziah had sent back and had not allowed to take part in the war raided Judean towns from Samaria to Beth Horon. They killed three thousand people and carried off great quantities of plunder.

[14]When Amaziah returned from slaughtering the Edomites, he brought back the gods of the people of Seir. He set them up as his own gods,[v] bowed down to them and burned sacrifices to them. [15]The anger of the LORD burned against Amaziah, and he sent a prophet to him, who said, "Why do you consult this people's gods, which could not save[w] their own people from your hand?"

[16]While he was still speaking, the king said to him, "Have we appointed you an adviser to the king? Stop! Why be struck down?"

25:2
k ver 14;
1Ki 8:61;
2Ch 24:2
25:4
l Dt 28:61
m Nu 26:11;
Dt 24:16
25:5
n 2Sa 24:2
o Ex 30:14
p Nu 1:3;
1Ch 21:1;
2Ch 17:14-19
25:7
q 2Ch 16:2-9;
19:1-3
25:8
r 2Ch 14:11;
20:6
25:9
s Dt 8:18;
Pr 10:22
25:10
t ver 13
25:12
u Ps 141:6;
Ob 1:3
25:14
v Ex 20:3;
2Ch 28:23;
Isa 44:15
25:15
w Ps 96:5;
Isa 36:20

---

[a]1 Hebrew *Jehoaddan*, a variant of *Jehoaddin*   [b]4 Deut. 24:16   [c]6 That is, about 3 3/4 tons (about 3.4 metric tons); also in verse 9

So the prophet stopped but said, "I know that God has determined to destroy you, because you have done this and have not listened to my counsel."

[17]After Amaziah king of Judah consulted his advisers, he sent this challenge to Jehoash[a] son of Jehoahaz, the son of Jehu, king of Israel: "Come, meet me face to face."

[18]But Jehoash king of Israel replied to Amaziah king of Judah: "A thistle[x] in Lebanon sent a message to a cedar in Lebanon, 'Give your daughter to my son in marriage.' Then a wild beast in Lebanon came along and trampled the thistle underfoot. [19]You say to yourself that you have defeated Edom, and now you are arrogant and proud. But stay at home! Why ask for trouble and cause your own downfall and that of Judah also?"

[20]Amaziah, however, would not listen, for God so worked that he might hand them over to ˌJehoash, because they sought the gods of Edom.[y] [21]So Jehoash king of Israel attacked. He and Amaziah king of Judah faced each other at Beth Shemesh in Judah. [22]Judah was routed by Israel, and every man fled to his home. [23]Jehoash king of Israel captured Amaziah king of Judah, the son of Joash, the son of Ahaziah,[b] at Beth Shemesh. Then Jehoash brought him to Jerusalem and broke down the wall of Jerusalem from the Ephraim Gate[z] to the Corner Gate[a]—a section about six hundred feet[c] long. [24]He took all the gold and silver and all the articles found in the temple of God that had been in the care of Obed-Edom,[b] together with the palace treasures and the hostages, and returned to Samaria.

[25]Amaziah son of Joash king of Judah lived for fifteen years after the death of Jehoash son of Jehoahaz king of Israel. [26]As for the other events of Amaziah's reign, from beginning to end, are they not written in the book of the kings of Judah and Israel? [27]From the time that Amaziah turned away from following the Lord, they conspired against him in Jerusalem and he fled to Lachish[c], but they sent men after him to Lachish and killed him there. [28]He was brought back by horse and was buried with his fathers in the City of Judah.

Uzziah King of Judah

26:1-4pp — 2Ki 14:21-22; 15:1-3
26:21-23pp — 2Ki 15:5-7

26 Then all the people of Judah[d] took Uzziah,[d] who was sixteen years old, and made him king in place of his father Amaziah. [2]He was the one who rebuilt Elath and restored it to Judah after Amaziah rested with his fathers.

[3]Uzziah was sixteen years old when he became king, and he reigned in Jerusalem fifty-two years. His mother's name was Jecoliah; she was from Jerusalem. [4]He did what was right in the eyes of the Lord, just as his father Amaziah had done. [5]He sought God during the days of Zechariah, who instructed him in the fear[e] of God.[e] As long as he sought the Lord, God gave him success.[f]

25:18
xJdg 9:8-15
25:20
y1Ki 12:15;
2Ch 10:15; 22:7
25:23
z2Ki 14:13;
Ne 8:16; 12:39
a2Ch 26:9;
Jer 31:38
25:24
b1Ch 26:15
25:27
cJos 10:3
26:1
d2Ch 22:1
26:5
e2Ch 15:2;
24:2; Da 1:17
f2Ch 27:6

---

a17 Hebrew Joash, a variant of Jehoash; also in verses 18, 21, 23 and 25   *b23 Hebrew Jehoahaz, a variant of Ahaziah*   *c23 Hebrew four hundred cubits (about 180 meters)*   *d1 Also called Azariah*   *e5 Many Hebrew manuscripts, Septuagint and Syriac; other Hebrew manuscripts vision*

6He went to war against the Philistines8 and broke down the walls of Gath, Jabneh and Ashdod.h He then rebuilt towns near Ashdod and elsewhere among the Philistines. 7God helped him against the Philistines and against the Arabsi who lived in Gur Baal and against the Meunites.j 8The Ammonitesk brought tribute to Uzziah, and his fame spread as far as the border of Egypt, because he had become very powerful.

9Uzziah built towers in Jerusalem at the Corner Gate,l at the Valley Gatem and at the angle of the wall, and he fortified them. 10He also built towers in the desert and dug many cisterns, because he had much livestock in the foothills and in the plain. He had people working his fields and vineyards in the hills and in the fertile lands, for he loved the soil.

11Uzziah had a well-trained army, ready to go out by divisions according to their numbers as mustered by Jeiel the secretary and Maaseiah the officer under the direction of Hananiah, one of the royal officials. 12The total number of family leaders over the fighting men was 2,600. 13Under their command was an army of 307,500 men trained for war, a powerful force to support the king against his enemies. 14Uzziah provided shields, spears, helmets, coats of armor, bows and slingstones for the entire army.n 15In Jerusalem he made machines designed by skillful men for use on the towers and on the corner defenses to shoot arrows and hurl large stones. His fame spread far and wide, for he was greatly helped until he became powerful.

16But after Uzziah became powerful, his prideo led to his downfall.p He was unfaithfulq to the LORD his God, and entered the temple of the LORD to burn incenser on the altar of incense. 17Azariahs the priest with eighty other courageous priests of the LORD followed him in. 18They confronted him and said, "It is not right for you, Uzziah, to burn incense to the LORD. That is for the priests,t the descendantsu of Aaron,v who have been consecrated to burn incense.w Leave the sanctuary, for you have been unfaithful; and you will not be honored by the LORD God."

19Uzziah, who had a censer in his hand ready to burn incense, became angry. While he was raging at the priests in their presence before the incense altar in the LORD's temple, leprosyax broke out on his forehead. 20When Azariah the chief priest and all the other priests looked at him, they saw that he had leprosy on his forehead, so they hurried him out. Indeed, he himself was eager to leave, because the LORD had afflicted him.

21King Uzziah had leprosy until the day he died. He lived in a separate houseby —leprous, and excluded from the temple of the LORD. Jotham his son had charge of the palace and governed the people of the land.

22The other events of Uzziah's reign, from beginning to end, are recorded by the prophet Isaiahz son of Amoz. 23Uzziaha rested with his fathers and was buried near them in a field for burial that belonged to the kings, for people said, "He had leprosy." And Jotham his son succeeded him as king.b

26:6
8Isa 2:6; 11:14; 14:29; Jer 25:20
hAm 1:8; 3:9
26:7
i2Ch 21:16
j2Ch 20:1
26:8
kGe 19:38; 2Ch 17:11
26:9
l2Ki 14:13; 2Ch 25:23
mNe 2:13; 3:13
26:14
nJer 46:4
26:16
o2Ki 14:10
pDt 32:15; 2Ch 25:19
q1Ch 5:25
r2Ki 16:12
26:17
s1Ki 4:2; 1Ch 6:10
26:18
tNu 16:39
uNu 18:1-7
vEx 30:7
w1Ch 6:49
26:19
xNu 12:10; 2Ki 5:25-27
26:21
yEx 4:6; Lev 13:46; 14:8; Nu 5:2; 19:12
26:22
z2Ki 15:1; Isa 1:1; 6:1
26:23
aIsa 1:1; 6:1
b2Ki 14:21; 15:7; Am 1:1

---

a19 The Hebrew word was used for various diseases affecting the skin—not necessarily leprosy; also in verses 20, 21 and 23.   *b21* Or *in a house where he was relieved of responsibilities*

Jotham King of Judah

27:1-4,7-9pp — 2Ki 15:33-38

27 Jotham[c] was twenty-five years old when he became king, and he reigned in Jerusalem sixteen years. His mother's name was Jerusha daughter of Zadok. [2]He did what was right in the eyes of the Lord, just as his father Uzziah had done, but unlike him he did not enter the temple of the Lord. The people, however, continued their corrupt practices. [3]Jotham rebuilt the Upper Gate of the temple of the Lord and did extensive work on the wall at the hill of Ophel. [d] [4]He built towns in the Judean hills and forts and towers in the wooded areas.

[5]Jotham made war on the king of the Ammonites[e] and conquered them. That year the Ammonites paid him a hundred talents[a] of silver, ten thousand cors[b] of wheat and ten thousand cors of barley. The Ammonites brought him the same amount also in the second and third years.

[6]Jotham grew powerful[f] because he walked steadfastly before the Lord his God.

[7]The other events in Jotham's reign, including all his wars and the other things he did, are written in the book of the kings of Israel and Judah. [8]He was twenty-five years old when he became king, and he reigned in Jerusalem sixteen years. [9]Jotham rested with his fathers and was buried in the City of David. And Ahaz his son succeeded him as king.

Ahaz King of Judah

28:1-27pp — 2Ki 16:1-20

28 Ahaz[g] was twenty years old when he became king, and he reigned in Jerusalem sixteen years. Unlike David his father, he did not do what was right in the eyes of the Lord. [2]He walked in the ways of the kings of Israel and also made cast idols[h] for worshiping the Baals. [3]He burned sacrifices in the Valley of Ben Hinnom[i] and sacrificed his sons[j] in the fire, following the detestable[k] ways of the nations the Lord had driven out before the Israelites. [4]He offered sacrifices and burned incense at the high places, on the hilltops and under every spreading tree.

[5]Therefore the Lord his God handed him over to the king of Aram.[l] The Arameans defeated him and took many of his people as prisoners and brought them to Damascus.

He was also given into the hands of the king of Israel, who inflicted heavy casualties on him. [6]In one day Pekah[m] son of Remaliah killed a hundred and twenty thousand soldiers in Judah[n]—because Judah had forsaken the Lord, the God of their fathers. [7]Zicri, an Ephraimite warrior, killed Maaseiah the king's son, Azrikam the officer in charge of the palace, and Elkanah, second to the king. [8]The Israelites took captive from their kinsmen[o] two hundred thousand wives, sons and daughters. They also took a great deal of plunder, which they carried back to Samaria.[p]

[9]But a prophet of the Lord named Oded was there, and he went out

### Cross references (margin)

27:1 c2Ki 15:5,32; 1Ch 3:12
27:3 d2Ch 33:14; Ne 3:26
27:5 eGe 19:38
27:6 f2Ch 26:5
28:1 g1Ch 3:13; Isa 1:1
28:2 hEx 34:17; 2Ch 22:3
28:3 iJos 15:8; 2Ki 23:10 jLev 18:21; 2Ki 3:27; 2Ch 33:6; Eze 20:26 kDt 18:9; 2Ch 33:2
28:5 lIsa 7:1
28:6 m2Ki 15:25,27 nver 8; Isa 9:21; 11:13
28:8 oDt 28:25-41; 2Ch 11:4 p2Ch 29:9

---

a5 That is, about 3 3/4 tons (about 3.4 metric tons)   b5 That is, probably about 62,000 bushels (about 2,200 kiloliters) to meet the army when it returned to Samaria. He said to them, "Because the LORD, the God of your fathers, was angry[q] with Judah, he gave them into your hand. But you have slaughtered them in a rage that reaches to heaven.[r] [10]And now you intend to make the men and women of Judah and Jerusalem your slaves.[s] But aren't you also guilty of sins against the LORD your God? [11]Now listen to me! Send back your fellow countrymen you have taken as prisoners, for the LORD's fierce anger rests on you.[t] "

[12]Then some of the leaders in Ephraim—Azariah son of Jehohanan, Berekiah son of Meshillemoth, Jehizkiah son of Shallum, and Amasa son of Hadlai—confronted those who were arriving from the war. [13]"You must not bring those prisoners here," they said, "or we will be guilty before the LORD. Do you intend to add to our sin and guilt? For our guilt is already great, and his fierce anger rests on Israel."

[14]So the soldiers gave up the prisoners and plunder in the presence of the officials and all the assembly. [15]The men designated by name took the prisoners, and from the plunder they clothed all who were naked. They provided them with clothes and sandals, food and drink,[u] and healing balm. All those who were weak they put on donkeys. So they took them back to their fellow countrymen at Jericho, the City of Palms,[v] and returned to Samaria.

[16]At that time King Ahaz sent to the king[a] of Assyria[w] for help. [17]The Edomites[x] had again come and attacked Judah and carried away prisoners,[y] [18]while the Philistines[z] had raided towns in the foothills and in the Negev of Judah. They captured and occupied Beth Shemesh, Aijalon[a] and Gederoth, as well as Soco, Timnah and Gimzo, with their surrounding villages. [19]The LORD had humbled Judah because of Ahaz king of Israel,[b] for he had promoted wickedness in Judah and had been most unfaithful[b] to the LORD. [20]Tiglath-Pileser[cc] king of Assyria came to him, but he gave him trouble instead of help.[d] [21]Ahaz took some of the things from the temple of the LORD and from the royal palace and from the princes and presented them to the king of Assyria, but that did not help him.

[22]In his time of trouble King Ahaz became even more unfaithful[e] to the LORD. [23]He offered sacrifices to the gods[f] of Damascus, who had defeated him; for he thought, "Since the gods of the kings of Aram have helped them, I will sacrifice to them so they will help me."[g] But they were his downfall and the downfall of all Israel.

[24]Ahaz gathered together the furnishings from the temple of God[h] and took them away.[d] He shut the doors[i] of the LORD's temple and set up altars[j] at every street corner in Jerusalem. [25]In every town in Judah he built high places to burn sacrifices to other gods and provoked the LORD, the God of his fathers, to anger.

[26]The other events of his reign and all his ways, from beginning to end, are written in the book of the kings of Judah and Israel. [27]Ahaz rested[k] with his fathers and was buried[l] in the city of Jerusalem, but he was not placed in the tombs of the kings of Israel. And Hezekiah his son succeeded him as king.

28:9
q2Ch 25:15;
Isa 10:6; 47:6;
Zec 1:15
rEzr 9:6;
Rev 18:5
28:10
sLev 25:39-46
28:11
t2Ch 11:4;
Jas 2:13
28:15
u2Ki 6:22;
Pr 25:21-22
vDt 34:3;
Jdg 1:16
28:16
w2Ki 16:7
28:17
xPs 137:7;
Isa 34:5
y2Ch 29:9
28:18
zEze 16:27,57
aJos 10:12
28:19
b2Ch 21:2
28:20
c2Ki 15:29;
1Ch 5:6
d2Ki 16:7
28:22
eJer 5:3
28:23
f2Ch 25:14
gJer 44:17-18
28:24
h2Ki 16:18
i2Ch 29:7
j2Ch 30:14
28:27
kIsa 14:28-32
l2Ch 21:20;
24:25

a16 One Hebrew manuscript, Septuagint and Vulgate (see also 2 Kings 16:7); most Hebrew manuscripts *kings*   *b19* That is, Judah, as frequently in 2 Chronicles   *c20* Hebrew *Tilgath-Pilneser*, a variant of *Tiglath-Pileser*   *d24* Or *and cut them up*

Hezekiah Purifies the Temple
29:1–2pp — 2Ki 18:2–3

29 Hezekiah[m] was twenty-five years old when he became king, and he reigned in Jerusalem twenty-nine years. His mother's name was Abijah daughter of Zechariah. [2]He did what was right in the eyes of the LORD, just as his father David[n] had done.

[3]In the first month of the first year of his reign, he opened the doors of the temple of the LORD and repaired[o] them. [4]He brought in the priests and the Levites, assembled them in the square on the east side [5]and said: "Listen to me, Levites! Consecrate[p] yourselves now and consecrate the temple of the LORD, the God of your fathers. Remove all defilement from the sanctuary. [6]Our fathers[q] were unfaithful;[r] they did evil in the eyes of the LORD our God and forsook him. They turned their faces away from the LORD's dwelling place and turned their backs on him. [7]They also shut the doors of the portico and put out the lamps. They did not burn incense or present any burnt offerings at the sanctuary to the God of Israel. [8]Therefore, the anger of the LORD has fallen on Judah and Jerusalem; he has made them an object of dread and horror[s] and scorn,[t] as you can see with your own eyes. [9]This is why our fathers have fallen by the sword and why our sons and daughters and our wives are in captivity.[u] [10]Now I intend to make a covenant[v] with the LORD, the God of Israel, so that his fierce anger will turn away from us. [11]My sons, do not be negligent now, for the LORD has chosen you to stand before him and serve him,[w] to minister[x] before him and to burn incense."

[12]Then these Levites[y] set to work:

from the Kohathites,

Mahath son of Amasai and Joel son of Azariah;

from the Merarites,

Kish son of Abdi and Azariah son of Jehallelel;

from the Gershonites,

Joah son of Zimmah and Eden[z] son of Joah;

[13]from the descendants of Elizaphan,

Shimri and Jeiel;

from the descendants of Asaph,[a]

Zechariah and Mattaniah;

[14]from the descendants of Heman,

Jehiel and Shimei;

from the descendants of Jeduthun,

Shemaiah and Uzziel.

[15]When they had assembled their brothers and consecrated themselves, they went in to purify[b] the temple of the LORD, as the king had ordered, following the word of the LORD. [16]The priests went into the sanctuary of the LORD to purify it. They brought out to the courtyard of the LORD's temple everything unclean that they found in the temple of the LORD. The Levites took it and carried it out to the Kidron Valley.[c] [17]They began the consecration on the first day of the first month, and by the eighth day of the month they reached the portico of the LORD. For eight more days they consecrated the temple of the LORD itself, finishing on the sixteenth day of the first month.

[18]Then they went in to King Hezekiah and reported: "We have

29:1
m 1Ch 3:13
29:2
n 2Ch 28:1; 34:2
29:3
o 2Ch 28:24
29:5
p 2Ch 35:6
29:6
q Ps 106:6-47;
Jer 2:27
r 1Ch 5:25;
Eze 8:16
29:8
s Dt 28:25;
2Ch 24:18
t Jer 18:16;
19:8; 25:9,18
29:9
u 2Ch 28:5-8,17
29:10
v 2Ch 15:12;
23:16
29:11
w Nu 3:6; 8:6,
14 x 1Ch 15:2
29:12
y Nu 3:17-20
z 2Ch 31:15
29:13
a 1Ch 6:39
29:15
b ver 5;
1Ch 23:28;
2Ch 30:12
29:16
c 2Sa 15:23

purified the entire temple of the LORD, the altar of burnt offering with all its utensils, and the table for setting out the consecrated bread, with all its articles. [19]We have prepared and consecrated all the articles[d] that King Ahaz removed in his unfaithfulness while he was king. They are now in front of the LORD's altar."

[20]Early the next morning King Hezekiah gathered the city officials together and went up to the temple of the LORD. [21]They brought seven bulls, seven rams, seven male lambs and seven male goats as a sin offering[e] for the kingdom, for the sanctuary and for Judah. The king commanded the priests, the descendants of Aaron, to offer these on the altar of the LORD. [22]So they slaughtered the bulls, and the priests took the blood and sprinkled it on the altar; next they slaughtered the rams and sprinkled their blood on the altar; then they slaughtered the lambs and sprinkled their blood[f] on the altar. [23]The goats for the sin offering were brought before the king and the assembly, and they laid their hands[g] on them. [24]The priests then slaughtered the goats and presented their blood on the altar for a sin offering to atone[h] for all Israel, because the king had ordered the burnt offering and the sin offering for all Israel.

[25]He stationed the Levites in the temple of the LORD with cymbals, harps and lyres in the way prescribed by David[i] and Gad[j] the king's seer and Nathan the prophet; this was commanded by the LORD through his prophets. [26]So the Levites stood ready with David's instruments,[k] and the priests with their trumpets.[l]

[27]Hezekiah gave the order to sacrifice the burnt offering on the altar. As the offering began, singing to the LORD began also, accompanied by trumpets and the instruments[m] of David king of Israel. [28]The whole assembly bowed in worship, while the singers sang and the trumpeters played. All this continued until the sacrifice of the burnt offering was completed.

[29]When the offerings were finished, the king and everyone present with him knelt down and worshiped.[n] [30]King Hezekiah and his officials ordered the Levites to praise the LORD with the words of David and of Asaph the seer. So they sang praises with gladness and bowed their heads and worshiped.

[31]Then Hezekiah said, "You have now dedicated yourselves to the LORD. Come and bring sacrifices[o] and thank offerings to the temple of the LORD." So the assembly brought sacrifices and thank offerings, and all whose hearts were willing[p] brought burnt offerings.

[32]The number of burnt offerings the assembly brought was seventy bulls, a hundred rams and two hundred male lambs—all of them for burnt offerings to the LORD. [33]The animals consecrated as sacrifices amounted to six hundred bulls and three thousand sheep and goats. [34]The priests, however, were too few to skin all the burnt offerings;[q] so their kinsmen the Levites helped them until the task was finished and until other priests had been consecrated,[r] for the Levites had been more conscientious in consecrating themselves than the priests had been. [35]There were burnt offerings in abundance, together with the fat[s] of the fellowship offerings[at] and the drink offerings[u] that accompanied the burnt offerings.

29:19
d2Ch 28:24
29:21
eLev 4:13-14
29:22
fLev 4:18
29:23
gLev 4:15
29:24
hEx 29:36;
Lev 4:26
29:25
i1Ch 25:6;
2Ch 8:14
j1Sa 22:5;
2Sa 24:11
29:26
k1Ch 15:16
l1Ch 15:24;
23:5; 2Ch 5:12
29:27
m2Ch 23:18
29:29
n2Ch 20:18
29:31
oHeb 13:15-16
pEx 25:2; 35:22
29:34
q2Ch 35:11
r2Ch 30:3,15
29:35
sEx 29:13;
Lev 3:16
tLev 7:11-21
uNu 15:5-10

---

a35 Traditionally *peace offerings*

So the service of the temple of the LORD was reestablished. [36]Hezekiah and all the people rejoiced at what God had brought about for his people, because it was done so quickly.

Hezekiah Celebrates the Passover

30 Hezekiah sent word to all Israel and Judah and also wrote letters to Ephraim and Manasseh,[v] inviting them to come to the temple of the LORD in Jerusalem and celebrate the Passover[w] to the LORD, the God of Israel. [2]The king and his officials and the whole assembly in Jerusalem decided to celebrate[x] the Passover in the second month. [3]They had not been able to celebrate it at the regular time because not enough priests had consecrated[y] themselves and the people had not assembled in Jerusalem. [4]The plan seemed right both to the king and to the whole assembly. [5]They decided to send a proclamation throughout Israel, from Beersheba to Dan,[z] calling the people to come to Jerusalem and celebrate the Passover to the LORD, the God of Israel. It had not been celebrated in large numbers according to what was written.

[6]At the king's command, couriers went throughout Israel and Judah with letters from the king and from his officials, which read:

"People of Israel, return to the LORD, the God of Abraham, Isaac and Israel, that he may return to you who are left, who have escaped from the hand of the kings of Assyria. [7]Do not be like your fathers[a] and brothers, who were unfaithful to the LORD, the God of their fathers, so that he made them an object of horror,[b] as you see. [8]Do not be stiff-necked,[c] as your fathers were; submit to the LORD. Come to the sanctuary, which he has consecrated forever. Serve the LORD your God, so that his fierce anger[d] will turn away from you. [9]If you return[e] to the LORD, then your brothers and your children will be shown compassion[f] by their captors and will come back to this land, for the LORD your God is gracious and compassionate.[g] He will not turn his face from you if you return to him."

[10]The couriers went from town to town in Ephraim and Manasseh, as far as Zebulun, but the people scorned and ridiculed[h] them. [11]Nevertheless, some men of Asher, Manasseh and Zebulun humbled themselves and went to Jerusalem.[i] [12]Also in Judah the hand of God was on the people to give them unity[j] of mind to carry out what the king and his officials had ordered, following the word of the LORD.

[13]A very large crowd of people assembled in Jerusalem to celebrate the Feast of Unleavened Bread[k] in the second month. [14]They removed the altars[l] in Jerusalem and cleared away the incense altars and threw them into the Kidron Valley.[m]

[15]They slaughtered the Passover lamb on the fourteenth day of the second month. The priests and the Levites were ashamed and consecrated[n] themselves and brought burnt offerings to the temple of the LORD. [16]Then they took up their regular positions[o] as prescribed in the Law of Moses the man of God. The priests sprinkled the blood handed to them by the Levites. [17]Since many in the crowd had not consecrated themselves, the Levites had to kill[p] the Passover lambs for all those who were not ceremonially clean and could not consecrate their lambs to the LORD. [18]Although most of the many people who came from

Cross references

30:1
v Ge 41:52
w Ex 12:11;
Nu 28:16

30:2
x Nu 9:10

30:3
y 2Ch 29:34

30:5
z Jdg 20:1

30:7
a Ps 78:8,57;
106:6;
Eze 20:18
b 2Ch 29:8

30:8
c Ex 32:9
d Nu 25:4;
2Ch 29:10

30:9
e Dt 30:2-5;
Isa 1:16; 55:7
f 1Ki 8:50;
Ps 106:46
g Ex 34:6-7;
Dt 4:31;
Mic 7:18

30:10
h 2Ch 36:16

30:11
i ver 25

30:12
j Jer 32:39;
Eze 11:19;
Php 2:13

30:13
k Nu 28:16

30:14
l 2Ch 28:24
m 2Sa 15:23

30:15
n 2Ch 29:34

30:16
o 2Ch 35:10

30:17
p 2Ch 29:34

Ephraim, Manasseh, Issachar and Zebulun had not purified themselves, q yet they ate the Passover, contrary to what was written. But Hezekiah prayed for them, saying, "May the LORD, who is good, pardon everyone [19]who sets his heart on seeking God—the LORD, the God of his fathers—even if he is not clean according to the rules of the sanctuary." [20]And the LORD heard r Hezekiah and healed s the people. t

[21]The Israelites who were present in Jerusalem celebrated the Feast of Unleavened Bread u for seven days with great rejoicing, while the Levites and priests sang to the LORD every day, accompanied by the LORD's instruments of praise. a

[22]Hezekiah spoke encouragingly to all the Levites, who showed good understanding of the service of the LORD. For the seven days they ate their assigned portion and offered fellowship offerings b and praised the LORD, the God of their fathers.

[23]The whole assembly then agreed to celebrate v the festival seven more days; so for another seven days they celebrated joyfully. [24]Hezekiah king of Judah provided w a thousand bulls and seven thousand sheep and goats for the assembly, and the officials provided them with a thousand bulls and ten thousand sheep and goats. A great number of priests consecrated themselves. [25]The entire assembly of Judah rejoiced, along with the priests and Levites and all who had assembled from Israel x, including the aliens who had come from Israel and those who lived in Judah. [26]There was great joy in Jerusalem, for since the days of Solomon y son of David king of Israel there had been nothing like this in Jerusalem. [27]The priests and the Levites stood to bless z the people, and God heard them, for their prayer reached heaven, his holy dwelling place.

31 When all this had ended, the Israelites who were there went out to the towns of Judah, smashed the sacred stones and cut down a the Asherah poles. They destroyed the high places and the altars throughout Judah and Benjamin and in Ephraim and Manasseh. After they had destroyed all of them, the Israelites returned to their own towns and to their own property.

Contributions for Worship

31:20-21pp — 2Ki 18:5-7

[2]Hezekiah b assigned the priests and Levites to divisions c—each of them according to their duties as priests or Levites—to offer burnt offerings and fellowship offerings, b to minister, d to give thanks and to sing praises e at the gates of the LORD's dwelling. f [3]The king contributed g from his own possessions for the morning and evening burnt offerings and for the burnt offerings on the Sabbaths, New Moons and appointed feasts as written in the Law of the LORD. h [4]He ordered the people living in Jerusalem to give the portion i due the priests and Levites so they could devote themselves to the Law of the LORD. [5]As soon as the order went out, the Israelites generously gave the first-fruits j of their grain, new wine, k oil and honey and all that the fields produced. They brought a great amount, a tithe of everything. [6]The men of Israel and Judah who lived in the towns of Judah also brought

30:18
qEx 12:43-49;
Nu 9:6-10
30:20
r2Ch 6:20
s2Ch 7:14;
Mal 4:2
tJas 5:16
30:21
uEx 12:15,17;
13:6
30:23
v1Ki 8:65;
2Ch 7:9
30:24
w1Ki 8:5;
2Ch 29:34;
35:7; Ezr 6:17;
8:35
30:25
xver 11
30:26
y2Ch 7:8
30:27
zEx 39:43;
Nu 6:23;
Dt 26:15;
2Ch 23:18;
Ps 68:5
31:1
a2Ki 18:4;
2Ch 32:12;
Isa 36:7
31:2
b2Ch 29:9
c1Ch 24:1
d1Ch 15:2
ePs 7:17; 9:2;
47:6; 71:22
f1Ch 23:28-32
31:3
g1Ch 29:3;
2Ch 35:7;
Eze 45:17
hNu 28:1-29:40
31:4
iNu 18:8;
Dt 18:8;
Ne 13:10;
Mal 2:7
31:5
jNu 18:12,24;
Ne 13:12;
Eze 44:30
kDt 12:17

---

a21 Or *priests praised the* LORD *every day with resounding instruments belonging to the* LORD
b22,2 Traditionally *peace offerings*

a tithe[1] of their herds and flocks and a tithe of the holy things dedicated to the LORD their God, and they piled them in heaps. [m] [7]They began doing this in the third month and finished in the seventh month. [n] [8]When Hezekiah and his officials came and saw the heaps, they praised the LORD and blessed[o] his people Israel.

[9]Hezekiah asked the priests and Levites about the heaps; [10]and Azariah the chief priest, from the family of Zadok,[p] answered, "Since the people began to bring their contributions to the temple of the LORD, we have had enough to eat and plenty to spare, because the LORD has blessed his people, and this great amount is left over."[q]

[11]Hezekiah gave orders to prepare storerooms in the temple of the LORD, and this was done. [12]Then they faithfully brought in the contributions, tithes and dedicated gifts. Conaniah,[r] a Levite, was in charge of these things, and his brother Shimei was next in rank. [13]Jehiel, Azaziah, Nahath, Asahel, Jerimoth, Jozabad,[s] Eliel, Ismakiah, Mahath and Benaiah were supervisors under Conaniah and Shimei his brother, by appointment of King Hezekiah and Azariah the official in charge of the temple of God.

[14]Kore son of Imnah the Levite, keeper of the East Gate, was in charge of the freewill offerings given to God, distributing the contributions made to the LORD and also the consecrated gifts. [15]Eden,[t] Miniamin, Jeshua, Shemaiah, Amariah and Shecaniah assisted him faithfully in the towns[u] of the priests, distributing to their fellow priests according to their divisions, old and young alike.

[16]In addition, they distributed to the males three years old or more whose names were in the genealogical records[v]—all who would enter the temple of the LORD to perform the daily duties of their various tasks, according to their responsibilities and their divisions. [17]And they distributed to the priests enrolled by their families in the genealogical records and likewise to the Levites twenty years old or more, according to their responsibilities and their divisions. [18]They included all the little ones, the wives, and the sons and daughters of the whole community listed in these genealogical records. For they were faithful in consecrating themselves.

[19]As for the priests, the descendants of Aaron, who lived on the farm lands around their towns or in any other towns,[w] men were designated by name to distribute portions to every male among them and to all who were recorded in the genealogies of the Levites.

[20]This is what Hezekiah did throughout Judah, doing what was good and right and faithful[x] before the LORD his God. [21]In everything that he undertook in the service of God's temple and in obedience to the law and the commands, he sought his God and worked wholeheartedly. And so he prospered.[y]

Sennacherib Threatens Jerusalem

32:9–19pp — 2Ki 18:17–35; Isa 36:2–20
32:20–21pp — 2Ki 19:35–37; Isa 37:36–38

32 After all that Hezekiah had so faithfully done, Sennacherib[z] king of Assyria came and invaded Judah. He laid siege to the fortified cities, thinking to conquer them for himself. [2]When Hezekiah saw that Sennacherib had come and that he intended to make war on Jerusalem,[a] [3]he consulted with his officials and military staff about

---

31:6
l Lev 27:30;
Ne 13:10-12
m Dt 14:28;
Ru 3:7
31:7
n Ex 23:16
31:8
o Ps 144:13-15
31:10
p 2Sa 8:17
q Ex 36:5;
Eze 44:30;
Mal 3:10-12
31:12
r 2Ch 35:9
31:13
s 2Ch 35:9
31:15
t 2Ch 29:12
u Jos 21:9-19
31:16
v 1Ch 23:3;
Ezr 3:4
31:19
w ver 12-15;
Lev 25:34;
Nu 35:2-5
31:20
x 2Ki 20:3; 22:2
31:21
y Dt 29:9
32:1
z 2Ki 18:13-19;
Isa 36:1;
37:9,17,37
32:2
a Isa 22:7;
Jer 1:15

blocking off the water from the springs outside the city, and they helped him. ⁴A large force of men assembled, and they blocked all the springsᵇ and the stream that flowed through the land. "Why should the kingsᵃ of Assyria come and find plenty of water?" they said. ⁵Then he worked hard repairing all the broken sections of the wallᶜ and building towers on it. He built another wall outside that one and reinforced the supporting terracesᵇᵈ of the City of David. He also made large numbers of weaponsᵉ and shields.

⁶He appointed military officers over the people and assembled them before him in the square at the city gate and encouraged them with these words: ⁷"Be strong and courageous.ᶠ Do not be afraid or discouragedᵍ because of the king of Assyria and the vast army with him, for there is a greater power with us than with him. ʰ ⁸With him is only the arm of flesh,ⁱ but with usʲ is the LORD our God to help us and to fight our battles."ᵏ And the people gained confidence from what Hezekiah the king of Judah said.

⁹Later, when Sennacherib king of Assyria and all his forces were laying siege to Lachish,ˡ he sent his officers to Jerusalem with this message for Hezekiah king of Judah and for all the people of Judah who were there:

¹⁰"This is what Sennacherib king of Assyria says: On what are you basing your confidence,ᵐ that you remain in Jerusalem under siege? ¹¹When Hezekiah says, 'The LORD our God will save us from the hand of the king of Assyria,' he is misleadingⁿ you, to let you die of hunger and thirst. ¹²Did not Hezekiah himself remove this god's high places and altars, saying to Judah and Jerusalem, 'You must worship before one altarᵒ and burn sacrifices on it'?

¹³"Do you not know what I and my fathers have done to all the peoples of the other lands? Were the gods of those nations ever able to deliver their land from my hand?ᵖ ¹⁴Who of all the gods of these nations that my fathers destroyed has been able to save his people from me? How then can your god deliver you from my hand? ¹⁵Now do not let Hezekiah deceiveᑫ you and mislead you like this. Do not believe him, for no god of any nation or kingdom has been able to deliverʳ his people from my hand or the hand of my fathers. ˢ How much less will your god deliver you from my hand!"

¹⁶Sennacherib's officers spoke further against the LORD God and against his servant Hezekiah. ¹⁷The king also wrote lettersᵗ insultingᵘ the LORD, the God of Israel, and saying this against him: "Just as the godsᵛ of the peoples of the other lands did not rescue their people from my hand, so the god of Hezekiah will not rescue his people from my hand." ¹⁸Then they called out in Hebrew to the people of Jerusalem who were on the wall, to terrify them and make them afraid in order to capture the city. ¹⁹They spoke about the God of Jerusalem as they did about the gods of the other peoples of the world—the work of men's hands. ʷ

²⁰King Hezekiah and the prophet Isaiah son of Amoz cried out in prayer to heaven about this. ²¹And the LORD sent an angel,ˣ who

---

ᵃ4 Hebrew; Septuagint and Syriac *king*   ᵇ5 Or *the Millo*

32:4
ᵇ2Ki 18:17;
20:20; Isa 22:9,
11; Na 3:14
32:5
ᶜ2Ch 25:23;
Isa 22:10
ᵈ1Ki 9:24;
1Ch 11:8
ᵉIsa 22:8
32:7
ᶠDt 31:6;
1Ch 22:13
ᵍ2Ch 20:15
ʰNu 14:9;
2Ki 6:16
32:8
ⁱJob 40:9;
Isa 52:10;
Jer 17:5; 32:21
ʲDt 3:22;
1Sa 17:45;
2Ch 13:12
ᵏ1Ch 5:22;
2Ch 20:17;
Ps 20:7;
Isa 28:6
32:9
ˡJos 10:3,31
32:10
ᵐEze 29:16
32:11
ⁿIsa 37:10
32:12
ᵒ2Ch 31:1
32:13
ᵖver 15
32:15
ᑫIsa 37:10
ʳDa 3:15 ˢEx 5:2
32:17
ᵗIsa 37:14
ᵘPs 74:22;
Isa 37:4,17
ᵛ2Ki 19:12
32:19
ʷ2Ki 19:18;
Ps 115:4,4-8;
Isa 2:8; 17:8
32:21
ˣGe 19:13

annihilated all the fighting men and the leaders and officers in the camp of the Assyrian king. So he withdrew to his own land in disgrace. And when he went into the temple of his god, some of his sons cut him down with the sword. y

[22] So the LORD saved Hezekiah and the people of Jerusalem from the hand of Sennacherib king of Assyria and from the hand of all others. He took care of them[a] on every side. [23] Many brought offerings to Jerusalem for the LORD and valuable gifts[z] for Hezekiah king of Judah. From then on he was highly regarded by all the nations.

Hezekiah's Pride, Success and Death
32:24–33pp — 2Ki 20:1–21; Isa 37:21–38; 38:1–8

[24] In those days Hezekiah became ill and was at the point of death. He prayed to the LORD, who answered him and gave him a miraculous sign. [25] But Hezekiah's heart was proud[a] and he did not respond to the kindness shown him; therefore the LORD's wrath[b] was on him and on Judah and Jerusalem. [26] Then Hezekiah repented[c] of the pride of his heart, as did the people of Jerusalem; therefore the LORD's wrath did not come upon them during the days of Hezekiah. [d]

[27] Hezekiah had very great riches and honor, [e] and he made treasuries for his silver and gold and for his precious stones, spices, shields and all kinds of valuables. [28] He also made buildings to store the harvest of grain, new wine and oil; and he made stalls for various kinds of cattle, and pens for the flocks. [29] He built villages and acquired great numbers of flocks and herds, for God had given him very great riches. [f]

[30] It was Hezekiah who blocked[g] the upper outlet of the Gihon[h] spring and channeled the water down to the west side of the City of David. He succeeded in everything he undertook. [31] But when envoys were sent by the rulers of Babylon[i] to ask him about the miraculous sign[j] that had occurred in the land, God left him to test[k] him and to know everything that was in his heart.

[32] The other events of Hezekiah's reign and his acts of devotion are written in the vision of the prophet Isaiah son of Amoz in the book of the kings of Judah and Israel. [33] Hezekiah rested with his fathers and was buried on the hill where the tombs of David's descendants are. All Judah and the people of Jerusalem honored him when he died. And Manasseh his son succeeded him as king.

Manasseh King of Judah
33:1–10pp — 2Ki 21:1–10
33:18–20pp — 2Ki 21:17–18

33 Manasseh[l] was twelve years old when he became king, and he reigned in Jerusalem fifty-five years. [2] He did evil in the eyes of the LORD, [m] following the detestable[n] practices of the nations the LORD had driven out before the Israelites. [3] He rebuilt the high places his father Hezekiah had demolished; he also erected altars to the Baals and made Asherah poles. [o] He bowed down[p] to all the starry hosts and worshiped them. [4] He built altars in the temple of the LORD, of which the LORD had said, "My Name[q] will remain in Jerusalem forever." [5] In both courts of the temple of the LORD, [r] he built altars to all the starry

---

[a]22 Hebrew; Septuagint and Vulgate *He gave them rest*

**Cross references (margin):**

32:21
y 2Ki 19:7

32:23
z 2Ch 9:24; 17:5; Isa 45:14; Zec 14:16-17

32:25
a 2Ki 14:10; 2Ch 26:16
b 2Ch 19:2; 24:18

32:26
c Jer 26:18-19
d 2Ch 34:27,28; Isa 39:8

32:27
e 1Ch 29:12

32:29
f 1Ch 29:12

32:30
g 2Ki 18:17
h 1Ki 1:33

32:31
i Isa 39:1
j ver 24; Isa 38:7
k Ge 22:1; Dt 8:16

33:1
l 1Ch 3:13

33:2
m Jer 15:4
n Dt 18:9; 2Ch 28:3

33:3
o Dt 16:21-22
p Dt 17:3; 2Ch 31:1

33:4
q 2Ch 7:16

33:5
r 2Ch 4:9

hosts. [6]He sacrificed his sons[s] in[a] the fire in the Valley of Ben Hinnom, practiced sorcery, divination and witchcraft, and consulted mediums[t] and spiritists.[u] He did much evil in the eyes of the Lord, provoking him to anger.

[7]He took the carved image he had made and put it in God's temple,[v] of which God had said to David and to his son Solomon, "In this temple and in Jerusalem, which I have chosen out of all the tribes of Israel, I will put my Name forever. [8]I will not again make the feet of the Israelites leave the land[w] I assigned to your forefathers, if only they will be careful to do everything I commanded them concerning all the laws, decrees and ordinances given through Moses." [9]But Manasseh led Judah and the people of Jerusalem astray, so that they did more evil than the nations the Lord had destroyed before the Israelites.[x]

[10]The Lord spoke to Manasseh and his people, but they paid no attention. [11]So the Lord brought against them the army commanders of the king of Assyria, who took Manasseh prisoner,[y] put a hook in his nose, bound him with bronze shackles[z] and took him to Babylon. [12]In his distress he sought the favor of the Lord his God and humbled[a] himself greatly before the God of his fathers. [13]And when he prayed to him, the Lord was moved by his entreaty and listened to his plea; so he brought him back to Jerusalem and to his kingdom. Then Manasseh knew that the Lord is God.

[14]Afterward he rebuilt the outer wall of the City of David, west of the Gihon[b] spring in the valley, as far as the entrance of the Fish Gate[c] and encircling the hill of Ophel;[d] he also made it much higher. He stationed military commanders in all the fortified cities in Judah.

[15]He got rid of the foreign gods and removed[e] the image from the temple of the Lord, as well as all the altars he had built on the temple hill and in Jerusalem; and he threw them out of the city. [16]Then he restored the altar of the Lord and sacrificed fellowship offerings[b] and thank offerings[f] on it, and told Judah to serve the Lord, the God of Israel. [17]The people, however, continued to sacrifice at the high places, but only to the Lord their God.

[18]The other events of Manasseh's reign, including his prayer to his God and the words the seers spoke to him in the name of the Lord, the God of Israel, are written in the annals of the kings of Israel.[c] [19]His prayer and how God was moved by his entreaty, as well as all his sins and unfaithfulness, and the sites where he built high places and set up Asherah poles and idols before he humbled[g] himself—all are written in the records of the seers.[d][h] [20]Manasseh rested with his fathers and was buried[i] in his palace. And Amon his son succeeded him as king.

Amon King of Judah

33:21–25pp — 2Ki 21:19–24

[21]Amon[j] was twenty-two years old when he became king, and he reigned in Jerusalem two years. [22]He did evil in the eyes of the Lord, as his father Manasseh had done. Amon worshiped and offered sacrifices to all the idols Manasseh had made. [23]But unlike his father Manasseh,

---

33:6
s Lev 18:21;
Dt 18:10;
2Ch 28:3
t Lev 19:31
u 1Sa 28:13
33:7
v 2Ch 7:16
33:8
w 2Sa 7:10
33:9
x Jer 15:4
33:11
y Dt 28:36
z Ps 149:8
33:12
a 2Ch 6:37;
32:26; 1Pe 5:6
33:14
b 1Ki 1:33
c Ne 3:3; 12:39;
Zep 1:10
d 2Ch 27:3;
Ne 3:26
33:15
e ver 3-7;
2Ki 23:12
33:16
f Lev 7:11-18
33:19
g 2Ch 6:37
h 2Ki 21:17
33:20
i 2Ki 21:18;
2Ch 21:20
33:21
j 1Ch 3:14

---

a6 Or He made his sons pass through   *b16 Traditionally peace offerings*   *c18 That is, Judah, as frequently in 2 Chronicles*   *d19 One Hebrew manuscript and Septuagint; most Hebrew manuscripts of Hozai* he did not humble[k] himself before the LORD; Amon increased his guilt.

[24]Amon's officials conspired against him and assassinated him in his palace. [25]Then the people[l] of the land killed all who had plotted against King Amon, and they made Josiah his son king in his place.

Josiah's Reforms

34:1–2pp — 2Ki 22:1–2
34:3–7Ref — 2Ki 23:4–20
34:8–13pp — 2Ki 22:3–7

34 Josiah[m] was eight years old when he became king,[n] and he reigned in Jerusalem thirty-one years. [2]He did what was right in the eyes of the LORD and walked in the ways of his father David,[o] not turning aside to the right or to the left.

[3]In the eighth year of his reign, while he was still young, he began to seek the God[p] of his father David. In his twelfth year he began to purge Judah and Jerusalem of high places, Asherah poles, carved idols and cast images. [4]Under his direction the altars of the Baals were torn down; he cut to pieces the incense altars that were above them, and smashed the Asherah poles,[q] the idols and the images. These he broke to pieces and scattered over the graves of those who had sacrificed to them.[r] [5]He burned[s] the bones of the priests on their altars, and so he purged Judah and Jerusalem. [6]In the towns of Manasseh, Ephraim and Simeon, as far as Naphtali, and in the ruins around them, [7]he tore down the altars and the Asherah poles and crushed the idols to powder[t] and cut to pieces all the incense altars throughout Israel. Then he went back to Jerusalem.

[8]In the eighteenth year of Josiah's reign, to purify the land and the temple, he sent Shaphan son of Azaliah and Maaseiah the ruler of the city, with Joah son of Joahaz, the recorder, to repair the temple of the LORD his God.

[9]They went to Hilkiah[u] the high priest and gave him the money that had been brought into the temple of God, which the Levites who were the doorkeepers had collected from the people of Manasseh, Ephraim and the entire remnant of Israel and from all the people of Judah and Benjamin and the inhabitants of Jerusalem. [10]Then they entrusted it to the men appointed to supervise the work on the LORD's temple. These men paid the workers who repaired and restored the temple. [11]They also gave money[v] to the carpenters and builders to purchase dressed stone, and timber for joists and beams for the buildings that the kings of Judah had allowed to fall into ruin.[w]

[12]The men did the work faithfully.[x] Over them to direct them were Jahath and Obadiah, Levites descended from Merari, and Zechariah and Meshullam, descended from Kohath. The Levites—all who were skilled in playing musical instruments—[y] [13]had charge of the laborers[z] and supervised all the workers from job to job. Some of the Levites were secretaries, scribes and doorkeepers.

The Book of the Law Found

34:14–28pp — 2Ki 22:8–20
34:29–32pp — 2Ki 23:1–3

[14]While they were bringing out the money that had been taken into the temple of the LORD, Hilkiah the priest found the Book of the Law of

---

33:23
kver 12;
Ex 10:3;
2Ch 7:14;
Ps 18:27; 147:6;
Pr 3:34
33:25
l2Ch 22:1
34:1
m1Ch 3:14
nZep 1:1
34:2
o2Ch 29:2
34:3
p1Ki 13:2;
1Ch 16:11;
2Ch 15:2;
33:17,22
34:4
qEx 34:13
rEx 32:20;
Lev 26:30;
2Ki 23:11;
Mic 1:5
34:5
s1Ki 13:2
34:7
tEx 32:20;
2Ch 31:1
34:9
u1Ch 6:13;
2Ch 35:8
34:11
v2Ch 24:12
w2Ch 33:4-7
34:12
x2Ki 12:15
y1Ch 25:1
34:13
z1Ch 23:4

the LORD that had been given through Moses. [15]Hilkiah said to Shaphan the secretary, "I have found the Book of the Law[a] in the temple of the LORD." He gave it to Shaphan.

[16]Then Shaphan took the book to the king and reported to him: "Your officials are doing everything that has been committed to them. [17]They have paid out the money that was in the temple of the LORD and have entrusted it to the supervisors and workers." [18]Then Shaphan the secretary informed the king, "Hilkiah the priest has given me a book." And Shaphan read from it in the presence of the king.

[19]When the king heard the words of the Law,[b] he tore[c] his robes. [20]He gave these orders to Hilkiah, Ahikam son of Shaphan[d], Abdon son of Micah,[a] Shaphan the secretary and Asaiah the king's attendant: [21]"Go and inquire of the LORD for me and for the remnant in Israel and Judah about what is written in this book that has been found. Great is the LORD's anger that is poured out[e] on us because our fathers have not kept the word of the LORD; they have not acted in accordance with all that is written in this book."

[22]Hilkiah and those the king had sent with him[b] went to speak to the prophetess[f] Huldah, who was the wife of Shallum son of Tokhath,[c] the son of Hasrah,[d] keeper of the wardrobe. She lived in Jerusalem, in the Second District.

[23]She said to them, "This is what the LORD, the God of Israel, says: Tell the man who sent you to me, [24]'This is what the LORD says: I am going to bring disaster[g] on this place and its people[h]—all the curses[i] written in the book that has been read in the presence of the king of Judah. [25]Because they have forsaken me[j] and burned incense to other gods and provoked me to anger by all that their hands have made,[e] my anger will be poured out on this place and will not be quenched.' [26]Tell the king of Judah, who sent you to inquire of the LORD, 'This is what the LORD, the God of Israel, says concerning the words you heard: [27]Because your heart was responsive[k] and you humbled[l] yourself before God when you heard what he spoke against this place and its people, and because you humbled yourself before me and tore your robes and wept in my presence, I have heard you, declares the LORD. [28]Now I will gather you to your fathers,[m] and you will be buried in peace. Your eyes will not see all the disaster I am going to bring on this place and on those who live here.'"[n]

So they took her answer back to the king.

[29]Then the king called together all the elders of Judah and Jerusalem. [30]He went up to the temple of the LORD[o] with the men of Judah, the people of Jerusalem, the priests and the Levites—all the people from the least to the greatest. He read in their hearing all the words of the Book of the Covenant, which had been found in the temple of the LORD. [31]The king stood by his pillar[p] and renewed the covenant[q] in the presence of the LORD—to follow[r] the LORD and keep his commands, regulations and decrees with all his heart and all his soul, and to obey the words of the covenant written in this book.

[32]Then he had everyone in Jerusalem and Benjamin pledge them-

34:15
a2Ki 22:8;
Ezr 7:6; Ne 8:1
34:19
bDt 28:3-68
cJos 7:6;
Isa 36:22; 37:1
34:20
d2Ki 22:3
34:21
e2Ch 29:8;
La 2:4; 4:11;
Eze 36:18
34:22
fEx 15:20;
Ne 6:14
34:24
gPr 16:4;
Isa 3:9;
Jer 40:2; 42:10;
44:2,11
h2Ch 36:14-20
iDt 28:15-68
34:25
j2Ch 33:3-6;
Jer 22:9
34:27
k2Ch 12:7;
32:26 lEx 10:3;
2Ch 6:37
34:28
m2Ch 35:20-25
n2Ch 32:26
34:30
o2Ki 23:2;
Ne 8:1-3
34:31
p1Ki 7:15;
2Ki 11:14
q2Ki 11:17;
2Ch 23:16;
29:10 rDt 13:4

---

[a]20 Also called *Acbor son of Micaiah*   [b]22 One Hebrew manuscript, Vulgate and Syriac; most Hebrew manuscripts do not have *had sent with him.*   [c]22 Also called *Tikvah*   [d]22 Also called *Harhas*   [e]25 Or *by everything they have done*

selves to it; the people of Jerusalem did this in accordance with the covenant of God, the God of their fathers.

[33]Josiah removed all the detestable[s] idols from all the territory belonging to the Israelites, and he had all who were present in Israel serve the LORD their God. As long as he lived, they did not fail to follow the LORD, the God of their fathers.

Josiah Celebrates the Passover
35:1,18–19pp — 2Ki 23:21–23

34:33
[s]ver 3-7;
Dt 18:9

35:1
[t]Ex 12:1-30;
Nu 9:3; 28:16

35:3
[u]Dt 33:10;
1Ch 23:26;
2Ch 5:7; 17:7

35:4
[v]ver 10;
1Ch 9:10-13;
24:1; 2Ch 8:14;
Ezr 6:18

35:6
[w]Lev 11:44;
2Ch 29:5,15

35:7
[x]2Ch 30:24
[y]2Ch 31:3

35:8
[z]1Ch 29:3;
2Ch 29:31-36
[a]1Ch 6:13

35:9
[b]2Ch 31:12
[c]2Ch 31:13

35:10
[d]ver 4; Ezr 6:18
[e]2Ch 30:16

35:11
[f]2Ch 29:22,34;
30:17

35:13
[g]Ex 12:2-11;
Lev 6:25;
1Sa 2:13-15

35:14
[h]Ex 29:13

35:15
[i]1Ch 25:1;
26:12-19;
2Ch 29:30;
Ne 12:46;
Ps 68:25

35 Josiah celebrated the Passover[t] to the LORD in Jerusalem, and the Passover lamb was slaughtered on the fourteenth day of the first month. [2]He appointed the priests to their duties and encouraged them in the service of the LORD's temple. [3]He said to the Levites, who instructed[u] all Israel and who had been consecrated to the LORD: "Put the sacred ark in the temple that Solomon son of David king of Israel built. It is not to be carried about on your shoulders. Now serve the LORD your God and his people Israel. [4]Prepare yourselves by families in your divisions,[v] according to the directions written by David king of Israel and by his son Solomon.

[5]"Stand in the holy place with a group of Levites for each subdivision of the families of your fellow countrymen, the lay people. [6]Slaughter the Passover lambs, consecrate yourselves[w] and prepare ˌthe lambs, for your fellow countrymen, doing what the LORD commanded through Moses."

[7]Josiah provided for all the lay people who were there a total of thirty thousand sheep and goats for the Passover offerings,[x] and also three thousand cattle—all from the king's own possessions.[y]

[8]His officials also contributed[z] voluntarily to the people and the priests and Levites. Hilkiah,[a] Zechariah and Jehiel, the administrators of God's temple, gave the priests twenty-six hundred Passover offerings and three hundred cattle. [9]Also Conaniah[b] along with Shemaiah and Nethanel, his brothers, and Hashabiah, Jeiel and Jozabad,[c] the leaders of the Levites, provided five thousand Passover offerings and five hundred head of cattle for the Levites.

[10]The service was arranged and the priests stood in their places with the Levites in their divisions[d] as the king had ordered.[e] [11]The Passover lambs were slaughtered,[f] and the priests sprinkled the blood handed to them, while the Levites skinned the animals. [12]They set aside the burnt offerings to give them to the subdivisions of the families of the people to offer to the LORD, as is written in the Book of Moses. They did the same with the cattle. [13]They roasted the Passover animals over the fire as prescribed,[g] and boiled the holy offerings in pots, caldrons and pans and served them quickly to all the people. [14]After this, they made preparations for themselves and for the priests, because the priests, the descendants of Aaron, were sacrificing the burnt offerings and the fat portions[h] until nightfall. So the Levites made preparations for themselves and for the Aaronic priests.

[15]The musicians,[i] the descendants of Asaph, were in the places prescribed by David, Asaph, Heman and Jeduthun the king's seer. The gatekeepers at each gate did not need to leave their posts, because their fellow Levites made the preparations for them.

[16]So at that time the entire service of the LORD was carried out for the

celebration of the Passover and the offering of burnt offerings on the altar of the LORD, as King Josiah had ordered. [17]The Israelites who were present celebrated the Passover at that time and observed the Feast of Unleavened Bread for seven days. [18]The Passover had not been observed like this in Israel since the days of the prophet Samuel; and none of the kings of Israel had ever celebrated such a Passover as did Josiah, with the priests, the Levites and all Judah and Israel who were there with the people of Jerusalem. [19]This Passover was celebrated in the eighteenth year of Josiah's reign.

The Death of Josiah
35:20–36:1pp — 2Ki 23:28–30

[20]After all this, when Josiah had set the temple in order, Neco king of Egypt went up to fight at Carchemish[j] on the Euphrates,[k] and Josiah marched out to meet him in battle. [21]But Neco sent messengers to him, saying, "What quarrel is there between you and me, O king of Judah? It is not you I am attacking at this time, but the house with which I am at war. God has told[l] me to hurry; so stop opposing God, who is with me, or he will destroy you."

[22]Josiah, however, would not turn away from him, but disguised[m] himself to engage him in battle. He would not listen to what Neco had said at God's command but went to fight him on the plain of Megiddo.

[23]Archers[n] shot King Josiah, and he told his officers, "Take me away; I am badly wounded." [24]So they took him out of his chariot, put him in the other chariot he had and brought him to Jerusalem, where he died. He was buried in the tombs of his fathers, and all Judah and Jerusalem mourned for him.

[25]Jeremiah composed laments for Josiah, and to this day all the men and women singers commemorate Josiah in the laments.[o] These became a tradition in Israel and are written in the Laments.

[26]The other events of Josiah's reign and his acts of devotion, according to what is written in the Law of the LORD— [27]all the events, from beginning to end, are written in the book of the kings of Israel and

36 Judah. [1]And the people of the land took Jehoahaz son of Josiah and made him king in Jerusalem in place of his father.

Jehoahaz King of Judah
36:2–4pp — 2Ki 23:31–34

[2]Jehoahaz[a] was twenty-three years old when he became king, and he reigned in Jerusalem three months. [3]The king of Egypt dethroned him in Jerusalem and imposed on Judah a levy of a hundred talents[b] of silver and a talent[c] of gold. [4]The king of Egypt made Eliakim, a brother of Jehoahaz, king over Judah and Jerusalem and changed Eliakim's name to Jehoiakim. But Neco[p] took Eliakim's brother Jehoahaz and carried him off to Egypt.

Jehoiakim King of Judah
36:5–8pp — 2Ki 23:36–24:6

[5]Jehoiakim[q] was twenty-five years old when he became king, and he

35:20
j Isa 10:9;
Jer 46:2
k Ge 2:14
35:21
l 1Ki 13:18;
2Ki 18:25
35:22
m Jdg 5:19;
1Sa 28:8;
2Ch 18:29
35:23
n 1Ki 22:34
35:25
o Jer 22:10,15-16
36:4
p Jer 22:10-12
36:5
q Jer 22:18;
26:1; 35:1

a2 Hebrew *Joahaz*, a variant of *Jehoahaz*; also in verse 4   b3 That is, about 3 3/4 tons (about 3.4 metric tons)   c3 That is, about 75 pounds (about 34 kilograms) reigned in Jerusalem eleven years. He did evil in the eyes of the LORD his God. [6]Nebuchadnezzar[r] king of Babylon attacked him and bound him with bronze shackles to take him to Babylon.[s] [7]Nebuchadnezzar also took to Babylon articles from the temple of the LORD and put them in his temple[a] there.[t]

[8]The other events of Jehoiakim's reign, the detestable things he did and all that was found against him, are written in the book of the kings of Israel and Judah. And Jehoiachin his son succeeded him as king.

Jehoiachin King of Judah

36:9–10pp — 2Ki 24:8–17

[9]Jehoiachin[u] was eighteen[b] years old when he became king, and he reigned in Jerusalem three months and ten days. He did evil in the eyes of the LORD. [10]In the spring, King Nebuchadnezzar sent for him and brought him to Babylon,[v] together with articles of value from the temple of the LORD, and he made Jehoiachin's uncle,[c] Zedekiah, king over Judah and Jerusalem.

Zedekiah King of Judah

36:11–16pp — 2Ki 24:18–20; Jer 52:1–3

[11]Zedekiah[w] was twenty-one years old when he became king, and he reigned in Jerusalem eleven years. [12]He did evil in the eyes of the LORD[x] his God and did not humble[y] himself before Jeremiah the prophet, who spoke the word of the LORD. [13]He also rebelled against King Nebuchadnezzar, who had made him take an oath[z] in God's name. He became stiff-necked[a] and hardened his heart and would not turn to the LORD, the God of Israel. [14]Furthermore, all the leaders of the priests and the people became more and more unfaithful,[b] following all the detestable practices of the nations and defiling the temple of the LORD, which he had consecrated in Jerusalem.

The Fall of Jerusalem

36:17–20pp — 2Ki 25:1–21; Jer 52:4–27
36:22–23pp — Ezr 1:1–3

[15]The LORD, the God of their fathers, sent word to them through his messengers[c] again and again,[d] because he had pity on his people and on his dwelling place. [16]But they mocked God's messengers, despised his words and scoffed[e] at his prophets until the wrath[f] of the LORD was aroused against his people and there was no remedy.[g] [17]He brought up against them the king of the Babylonians,[d] who killed their young men with the sword in the sanctuary, and spared neither young man[h] nor young woman, old man or aged. God handed all of them over to Nebuchadnezzar.[i] [18]He carried to Babylon all the articles[j] from the temple of God, both large and small, and the treasures of the LORD's temple and the treasures of the king and his officials. [19]They set fire[k] to God's temple[l] and broke down the wall[m] of Jerusalem; they burned all the palaces and destroyed[n] everything of value there.[o]

[20]He carried into exile[p] to Babylon the remnant, who escaped from the sword, and they became servants[q] to him and his sons until the

36:6
r Jer 25:9; 27:6;
Eze 29:18
s 2Ch 33:11;
Eze 19:9;
Da 1:1
36:7
t 2Ki 24:13;
Ezr 1:7; Da 1:2
36:9
u Jer 22:24-28;
52:31
36:10
v ver 18;
2Ki 20:17;
Ezr 1:7;
Jer 22:25; 24:1;
29:1; 37:1;
Eze 17:12
36:11
w 2Ki 24:17;
Jer 27:1; 28:1
36:12
x Jer 37:1-39:18
y Dt 8:3;
2Ch 7:14;
2Ch 33:23;
Jer 21:3-7
36:13
z Eze 17:13
a 2Ki 17:14;
2Ch 30:8
36:14
b 1Ch 5:25
36:15
c Isa 5:4; 44:26;
Jer 7:25;
Hag 1:13;
Zec 1:4;
Mal 2:7; 3:1
d Jer 7:13,25;
25:3-4; 35:14,
15; 44:4-6
36:16
e 2Ki 2:23;
Pr 1:25; Jer 5:13
f Ezr 5:12;
Pr 1:30-31
g 2Ch 30:10;
Pr 29:1; Zec 1:2
36:17
h Jer 6:11
i Ezr 5:12;
Jer 32:28
36:18
j ver 7,10
36:19
k Jer 11:16;
17:27; 21:10,
14; 22:7; 32:29;
39:8; La 4:11;
Eze 20:47;
Am 2:5;
Zec 11:1
l 1Ki 9:8-9
m 2Ki 14:13
n La 2:6
o Ps 79:1-3
36:20
p Lev 26:44;
2Ki 24:14;
Ezr 2:1; Ne 7:6
q Jer 27:7

a7 Or *palace*　　b9 One Hebrew manuscript, some Septuagint manuscripts and Syriac (see also 2 Kings 24:8); most Hebrew manuscripts *eight*　　c10 Hebrew *brother*, that is, relative (see 2 Kings 24:17)　　d17 Or *Chaldeans* kingdom of Persia came to power. [21]The land enjoyed its sabbath rests;[r] all the time of its desolation it rested,[s] until the seventy years[t] were completed in fulfillment of the word of the LORD spoken by Jeremiah.

[22]In the first year of Cyrus[u] king of Persia, in order to fulfill the word of the LORD spoken by Jeremiah, the LORD moved the heart of Cyrus king of Persia to make a proclamation throughout his realm and to put it in writing:

[23]"This is what Cyrus king of Persia says:

" 'The LORD, the God of heaven, has given me all the kingdoms of the earth and he has appointed[v] me to build a temple for him at Jerusalem in Judah. Anyone of his people among you—may the LORD his God be with him, and let him go up.' "

36:21
rLev 25:4; 26:34
s1Ch 22:9
tJer 1:1; 25:11;
27:22; 29:10;
40:1; Da 9:2;
Zec 1:12; 7:5
36:22
uIsa 44:28;
45:1,13;
Jer 25:12;
29:10; Da 1:21;
6:28; 10:1
36:23
vJdg 4:10

Ezra

Title and Background

The books of Ezra and Nehemiah were one book in the earliest Hebrew manuscripts. Origen (A.D. 185-253) is the first writer known to distinguish between two books, which he called I Ezra and II Ezra. Although they were regarded as one book, the caption to Nehemiah 1:1 indicates they were two separate compositions.

Author and Date of Writing

Many scholars have assumed that the author/compiler of Ezra-Nehemiah was also the author of 1,2 Chronicles. This viewpoint is based on certain characteristics common to both. The verses at the end of Chronicles and at the beginning of Ezra are virtually identical, and both of these books exhibit a fondness for lists. But there are also striking differences, so the name of the author cannot be known for certain. Ezra can be dated about 440 B.C.

Theme and Message

Ezra tells of the return of the Jews from exile in Babylon and also of the rebuilding of the temple. The people completed and dedicated the temple in 516 B.C., after being delayed for eighteen years by their enemies from the north. A decree from Darius in 520 B.C. allowed them to finish. Ezra taught the people the law and reformed their religious life so the other nations around them could see they were God's chosen nation.

Outline

I. The First Exiles Return to the Land of Judah (1:1-2:70)
II. The Temple Is Rebuilt (3:1-6:22)
III. Ezra's Return and Ministry (7:1-10:44)

Cyrus Helps the Exiles to Return

1:1–3pp — 2Ch 36:22–23

1 In the first year of Cyrus king of Persia, in order to fulfill the word of the LORD spoken by Jeremiah,[a] the LORD moved the heart[b] of Cyrus king of Persia to make a proclamation throughout his realm and to put it in writing:

2"This is what Cyrus king of Persia says:

" 'The LORD, the God of heaven, has given me all the kingdoms of the earth and he has appointed[c] me to build[d] a temple for him at Jerusalem in Judah. 3Anyone of his people among you—may his God be with him, and let him go up to Jerusalem in Judah and build the temple of the LORD, the God of Israel, the God who is in Jerusalem. 4And the people of any place where survivors[e] may now be living are to provide him with silver and gold, with goods and livestock, and with freewill offerings[f] for the temple of God in Jerusalem.' "[g]

1:1
a Jer 25:11-12;
29:10-14
b 2Ch 36:22,23

1:2
c Isa 44:28;
45:13 d Ezr 5:13

1:4
e Isa 10:20-22
f Nu 15:3;
Ps 50:14; 54:6;
116:17 g Ezr 4:3;
5:13; 6:3,14

5Then the family heads of Judah and Benjamin, h and the priests and Levites—everyone whose heart God had moved i—prepared to go up and build the house j of the LORD in Jerusalem. 6All their neighbors assisted them with articles of silver and gold, with goods and livestock, and with valuable gifts, in addition to all the freewill offerings. 7Moreover, King Cyrus brought out the articles belonging to the temple of the LORD, which Nebuchadnezzar had carried away from Jerusalem and had placed in the temple of his god. *a* k 8Cyrus king of Persia had them brought by Mithredath the treasurer, who counted them out to Sheshbazzar l the prince of Judah. 9This was the inventory:

gold dishes	30
silver dishes	1,000
silver pans *b*	29
10gold bowls	30
matching silver bowls	410
other articles	1,000

11In all, there were 5,400 articles of gold and of silver. Sheshbazzar brought all these along when the exiles came up from Babylon to Jerusalem.

The List of the Exiles Who Returned

2:1–70pp — Ne 7:6–73

2 Now these are the people of the province who came up from the captivity of the exiles, m whom Nebuchadnezzar king of Babylon n had taken captive to Babylon (they returned to Jerusalem and Judah, each to his own town, o 2in company with Zerubbabel, p Jeshua, q Nehemiah, Seraiah, r Reelaiah, Mordecai, Bilshan, Mispar, Bigvai, Rehum and Baanah):

The list of the men of the people of Israel:

3the descendants of Parosh s	2,172
4of Shephatiah	372
5of Arah	775
6of Pahath-Moab	
(through the line of Jeshua and Joab)	2,812
7of Elam	1,254
8of Zattu	945
9of Zaccai	760
10of Bani	642
11of Bebai	623
12of Azgad	1,222
13of Adonikam t	666
14of Bigvai	2,056
15of Adin	454
16of Ater (through Hezekiah)	98
17of Bezai	323
18of Jorah	112
19of Hashum	223

a7 Or *gods*   *b9* The meaning of the Hebrew for this word is uncertain.

1:5
h Ezr 4:1;
Ne 11:4 i ver 1;
Ex 35:20-22;
2Ch 36:22;
Hag 1:14;
Php 2:13
j Ps 127:1
1:7
k 2Ki 24:13;
2Ch 36:7,10;
Ezr 5:14; 6:5
1:8
l Ezr 5:14
2:1
m 2Ch 36:20;
Ne 7:6
n 2Ki 24:16;
25:12 o Ne 7:73
2:2
p 1Ch 3:19
q Ezr 3:2
r Ne 10:2
2:3
s Ezr 8:3
2:13
t Ezr 8:13

²⁰of Gibbar   95

²¹the men of Bethlehemᵘ   123
²²of Netophah   56
²³of Anathoth   128
²⁴of Azmaveth   42
²⁵of Kiriath Jearim,ᵃ Kephirah and Beeroth   743
²⁶of Ramahᵛ and Geba   621
²⁷of Micmash   122
²⁸of Bethel and Aiʷ   223
²⁹of Nebo   52
³⁰of Magbish   156
³¹of the other Elam   1,254
³²of Harim   320
³³of Lod, Hadid and Ono   725
³⁴of Jerichoˣ   345
³⁵of Senaah   3,630

³⁶The priests:

the descendants of Jedaiahʸ
(through the family of Jeshua)   973
³⁷of Immerᶻ   1,052
³⁸of Pashhurᵃ   1,247
³⁹of Harimᵇ   1,017

⁴⁰The Levites:ᶜ

the descendants of Jeshuaᵈ and Kadmiel
(through the line of Hodaviah)   74

⁴¹The singers:ᵉ

the descendants of Asaph   128

⁴²The gatekeepersᶠ of the temple:

the descendants of
Shallum, Ater, Talmon,
Akkub, Hatita and Shobai   139

⁴³The temple servants:ᵍ

the descendants of
Ziha, Hasupha, Tabbaoth,
⁴⁴Keros, Siaha, Padon,
⁴⁵Lebanah, Hagabah, Akkub,
⁴⁶Hagab, Shalmai, Hanan,
⁴⁷Giddel, Gahar, Reaiah,
⁴⁸Rezin, Nekoda, Gazzam,
⁴⁹Uzza, Paseah, Besai,
⁵⁰Asnah, Meunim, Nephussim,
⁵¹Bakbuk, Hakupha, Harhur,
⁵²Bazluth, Mehida, Harsha,
⁵³Barkos, Sisera, Temah,

2:21
uMic 5:2
2:26
vJos 18:25
2:28
wGe 12:8
2:34
x1Ki 16:34;
2Ch 28:15
2:36
y1Ch 24:7
2:37
z1Ch 24:14
2:38
a1Ch 9:12
2:39
b1Ch 24:8
2:40
cGe 29:34;
Nu 3:9;
Dt 18:6-7;
1Ch 16:4;
Ezr 7:7; 8:15;
Ne 12:24
dEzr 3:9
2:41
e1Ch 15:16
2:42
f1Sa 3:15;
1Ch 9:17
2:43
g1Ch 9:2;
Ne 11:21

ᵃ25 See Septuagint (see also Neh. 7:29); Hebrew *Kiriath Arim.*

⁵⁴Neziah and Hatipha

⁵⁵The descendants of the servants of Solomon:

the descendants of
Sotai, Hassophereth, Peruda,
⁵⁶Jaala, Darkon, Giddel,
⁵⁷Shephatiah, Hattil,
Pokereth-Hazzebaim and Ami

⁵⁸The temple servants^h and the descendants
of the servants of Solomon   392

⁵⁹The following came up from the towns of Tel Melah, Tel Harsha, Kerub, Addon and Immer, but they could not show that their families were descendedⁱ from Israel:

⁶⁰The descendants of
Delaiah, Tobiah and Nekoda   652

⁶¹And from among the priests:

The descendants of
Hobaiah, Hakkoz and Barzillai (a man who had
married a daughter of Barzillai the Gileadite^j
and was called by that name).

⁶²These searched for their family records, but they could not find them and so were excluded from the priesthood^k as unclean. ⁶³The governor ordered them not to eat any of the most sacred food^l until there was a priest ministering with the Urim and Thummim. ^m

⁶⁴The whole company numbered 42,360, ⁶⁵besides their 7,337 menservants and maidservants; and they also had 200 men and women singers. ⁿ ⁶⁶They had 736 horses, ^o 245 mules, ⁶⁷435 camels and 6,720 donkeys.

⁶⁸When they arrived at the house of the Lord in Jerusalem, some of the heads of the families^p gave freewill offerings toward the rebuilding of the house of God on its site. ⁶⁹According to their ability they gave to the treasury for this work 61,000 drachmas^a of gold, 5,000 minas^b of silver and 100 priestly garments.

⁷⁰The priests, the Levites, the singers, the gatekeepers and the temple servants settled in their own towns, along with some of the other people, and the rest of the Israelites settled in their towns. ^q

Rebuilding the Altar

3 When the seventh month came and the Israelites had settled in their towns,^r the people assembled^s as one man in Jerusalem. ²Then Jeshua^t son of Jozadak^u and his fellow priests and Zerubbabel son of Shealtiel^v and his associates began to build the altar of the God of Israel to sacrifice burnt offerings on it, in accordance with what is written in the Law of Moses^w the man of God. ³Despite their fear^x of the

2:58
h1Ki 9:21;
1Ch 9:2
2:59
iNu 1:18
2:61
j2Sa 17:27
2:62
kNu 3:10;
16:39-40
2:63
lLev 2:3,10
mEx 28:30;
Nu 27:21
2:65
n2Sa 19:35
2:66
oIsa 66:20
2:68
pEx 25:2
2:70
qver 1;
1Ch 9:2;
Ne 11:3-4
3:1
rNe 7:73; 8:1
sLev 23:24
3:2
tEzr 2:2;
Ne 12:1,8;
Hag 2:2
uHag 1:1;
Zec 6:11
v1Ch 3:17
wEx 20:24;
Dt 12:5-6
3:3
xEzr 4:4;
Da 9:25

peoples around them, they built the altar on its foundation and sacrificed burnt offerings on it to the LORD, both the morning and evening sacrifices. [y] 4Then in accordance with what is written, they celebrated the Feast of Tabernacles[z] with the required number of burnt offerings prescribed for each day. 5After that, they presented the regular burnt offerings, the New Moon[a] sacrifices and the sacrifices for all the appointed sacred feasts of the LORD, [b] as well as those brought as freewill offerings to the LORD. 6On the first day of the seventh month they began to offer burnt offerings to the LORD, though the foundation of the LORD's temple had not yet been laid.

Rebuilding the Temple

7Then they gave money to the masons and carpenters, and gave food and drink and oil to the people of Sidon and Tyre, so that they would bring cedar logs[c] by sea from Lebanon[d] to Joppa, as authorized by Cyrus[e] king of Persia.

8In the second month of the second year after their arrival at the house of God in Jerusalem, Zerubbabel[f] son of Shealtiel, Jeshua son of Jozadak and the rest of their brothers (the priests and the Levites and all who had returned from the captivity to Jerusalem) began the work, appointing Levites twenty[g] years of age and older to supervise the building of the house of the LORD. 9Jeshua[h] and his sons and brothers and Kadmiel and his sons (descendants of Hodaviah[a]) and the sons of Henadad and their sons and brothers—all Levites—joined together in supervising those working on the house of God.

10When the builders laid[i] the foundation of the temple of the LORD, the priests in their vestments and with trumpets,[j] and the Levites (the sons of Asaph) with cymbals, took their places to praise[k] the LORD, as prescribed by David[l] king of Israel. [m] 11With praise and thanksgiving they sang to the LORD:

"He is good;
    his love to Israel endures forever."[n]

And all the people gave a great shout[o] of praise to the LORD, because the foundation of the house of the LORD was laid. 12But many of the older priests and Levites and family heads, who had seen the former temple,[p] wept aloud when they saw the foundation of this temple being laid, while many others shouted for joy. 13No one could distinguish the sound of the shouts of joy[q] from the sound of weeping, because the people made so much noise. And the sound was heard far away.

Opposition to the Rebuilding

4 When the enemies of Judah and Benjamin heard that the exiles were building a temple for the LORD, the God of Israel, 2they came to Zerubbabel and to the heads of the families and said, "Let us help you build because, like you, we seek your God and have been sacrificing to him since the time of Esarhaddon[r] king of Assyria, who brought us here."[s]

3But Zerubbabel, Jeshua and the rest of the heads of the families of

### Cross references (margin)

3:3
[y]Ex 29:39;
Nu 28:1-8
3:4
[z]Ex 23:16;
Nu 29:12-38;
Ne 8:14-18;
Zec 14:16-19
3:5
[a]Nu 28:3,11,14;
Col 2:16
[b]Lev 23:1-44;
Nu 29:39
3:7
[c]1Ch 14:1
[d]Isa 35:2
[e]Ezr 1:2-4; 6:3
3:8
[f]Zec 4:9
[g]1Ch 23:24
3:9
[h]Ezr 2:40
3:10
[i]Ezr 5:16
[j]Nu 10:2;
1Ch 16:6
[k]1Ch 25:1
[l]1Ch 6:31
[m]Zec 6:12
3:11
[n]1Ch 16:34,41;
2Ch 7:3;
Ps 107:1; 118:1
[o]Ne 12:24
3:12
[p]Hag 2:3,9
3:13
[q]Job 8:21;
Ps 27:6;
Isa 16:9
4:2
[r]2Ki 17:24;
19:37 [s]2Ki 17:41

---

[a]9 Hebrew *Yehudah*, probably a variant of *Hodaviah*

Israel answered, "You have no part with us in building a temple to our God. We alone will build it for the LORD, the God of Israel, as King Cyrus, the king of Persia, commanded us."[t]

[4]Then the peoples around them set out to discourage the people of Judah and make them afraid to go on building.[a][u] [5]They hired counselors to work against them and frustrate their plans during the entire reign of Cyrus king of Persia and down to the reign of Darius king of Persia.

Later Opposition Under Xerxes and Artaxerxes

[6]At the beginning of the reign of Xerxes,[b][v] they lodged an accusation against the people of Judah and Jerusalem.[w]

[7]And in the days of Artaxerxes[x] king of Persia, Bishlam, Mithredath, Tabeel and the rest of his associates wrote a letter to Artaxerxes. The letter was written in Aramaic script and in the Aramaic[y] language.[c,d]

[8]Rehum the commanding officer and Shimshai the secretary wrote a letter against Jerusalem to Artaxerxes the king as follows:

[9]Rehum the commanding officer and Shimshai the secretary, together with the rest of their associates[z]—the judges and officials over the men from Tripolis, Persia,[e] Erech and Babylon, the Elamites of Susa, [10]and the other people whom the great and honorable Ashurbanipal[f] deported and settled in the city of Samaria and elsewhere in Trans-Euphrates.[a]

[11](This is a copy of the letter they sent him.)

To King Artaxerxes,

From your servants, the men of Trans-Euphrates:

[12]The king should know that the Jews who came up to us from you have gone to Jerusalem and are rebuilding that rebellious and wicked city. They are restoring the walls and repairing the foundations.[b]

[13]Furthermore, the king should know that if this city is built and its walls are restored, no more taxes, tribute or duty[c] will be paid, and the royal revenues will suffer. [14]Now since we are under obligation to the palace and it is not proper for us to see the king dishonored, we are sending this message to inform the king, [15]so that a search may be made in the archives[d] of your predecessors. In these records you will find that this city is a rebellious city, troublesome to kings and provinces, a place of rebellion from ancient times. That is why this city was destroyed.[e] [16]We inform the king that if this city is built and its walls are restored, you will be left with nothing in Trans-Euphrates.

[17]The king sent this reply:

To Rehum the commanding officer, Shimshai the secretary and

4:3
tEzr 1:1-4;
Ne 2:20
4:4
uEzr 3:3
4:6
vEst 1:1; Da 9:1
wEst 3:13; 9:5
4:7
xEzr 7:1; Ne 2:1
y2Ki 18:26;
Isa 36:11;
Da 2:4
4:9
zEzr 5:6; 6:6,13
4:10
aver 17; Ne 4:2
4:12
bEzr 5:3,9
4:13
cEzr 7:24;
Ne 5:4
4:15
dEzr 5:17; 6:1
eEst 3:8

---

[a]4 Or *and troubled them as they built*   [b]6 Hebrew *Ahasuerus*, a variant of Xerxes' name   [c]7 Or *written in Aramaic and translated*   [d]7 The text of Ezra 4:8—6:18 is in Aramaic.   [e]9 Or *officials, magistrates and governors over the men from*   [f]10 Aramaic *Osnappar*, a variant of *Ashurbanipal*

the rest of their associates living in Samaria and elsewhere in Trans-Euphrates:f

Greetings.

18The letter you sent us has been read and translated in my presence. 19I issued an order and a search was made, and it was found that this city has a long history of revoltg against kings and has been a place of rebellion and sedition. 20Jerusalem has had powerful kings ruling over the whole of Trans-Euphrates,h and taxes, tribute and duty were paid to them. 21Now issue an order to these men to stop work, so that this city will not be rebuilt until I so order. 22Be careful not to neglect this matter. Why let this threat grow, to the detriment of the royal interests?i

23As soon as the copy of the letter of King Artaxerxes was read to Rehum and Shimshai the secretary and their associates,j they went immediately to the Jews in Jerusalem and compelled them by force to stop.

24Thus the work on the house of God in Jerusalem came to a standstill until the second year of the reign of Dariusk king of Persia.

Tattenai's Letter to Darius

5 Now Haggail the prophet and Zechariahm the prophet, a descendant of Iddo, prophesiedn to the Jews in Judah and Jerusalem in the name of the God of Israel, who was over them. 2Then Zerubbabelo son of Shealtiel and Jeshuap son of Jozadak set to workq to rebuild the house of God in Jerusalem. And the prophets of God were with them, helping them.

3At that time Tattenai,r governor of Trans-Euphrates, and Shethar-Bozenais and their associates went to them and asked, "Who authorized you to rebuild this temple and restore this structure?"t 4They also asked, "What are the names of the men constructing this building?"a 5But the eye of their Godu was watching over the elders of the Jews, and they were not stopped until a report could go to Darius and his written reply be received.

6This is a copy of the letter that Tattenai, governor of Trans-Euphrates, and Shethar-Bozenai and their associates, the officials of Trans-Euphrates, sent to King Darius. 7The report they sent him read as follows:

To King Darius:

Cordial greetings.

8The king should know that we went to the district of Judah, to the temple of the great God. The people are building it with large stones and placing the timbers in the walls. The workv is being carried on with diligence and is making rapid progress under their direction.

9We questioned the elders and asked them, "Who authorized you to rebuild this temple and restore this structure?"w 10We also

---

4:17
fver 10
4:19
g2Ki 18:7
4:20
hGe 15:18-21;
Ex 23:31;
Jos 1:4;
1Ki 4:21;
1Ch 18:3;
Ps 72:8-11
4:22
iDa 6:2
4:23
jver 9
4:24
kNe 2:1-8;
Da 9:25;
Hag 1:1,15;
Zec 1:1
5:1
lEzr 6:14;
Hag 1:1,3,12;
2:1,10,20
mZec 1:1; 7:1
nHag 1:14-2:9;
Zec 4:9-10; 8:9
5:2
o1Ch 3:19;
Hag 1:14; 2:21;
Zec 4:6-10
pEzr 2:2; 3:2
qver 8;
Hag 2:2-5
5:3
rEzr 6:6 sEzr 6:6
tver 9; Ezr 1:3;
4:12
5:5
u2Ki 25:28;
Ezr 7:6,9,28;
8:18,22,31;
Ne 2:8,18;
Ps 33:18;
Isa 66:14
5:8
vver 2
5:9
wEzr 4:12

---

a4 See Septuagint; Aramaic 4We told them the names of the men constructing this building.

asked them their names, so that we could write down the names of their leaders for your information.

¹¹This is the answer they gave us:

"We are the servants of the God of heaven and earth, and we are rebuilding the templeˣ that was built many years ago, one that a great king of Israel built and finished. ¹²But because our fathers angeredʸ the God of heaven, he handed them over to Nebuchadnezzar the Chaldean, king of Babylon, who destroyed this temple and deported the people to Babylon.ᶻ

¹³"However, in the first year of Cyrus king of Babylon, King Cyrus issued a decreeᵃ to rebuild this house of God. ¹⁴He even removed from the templeᵃ of Babylon the gold and silver articles of the house of God, which Nebuchadnezzar had taken from the temple in Jerusalem and brought to the templeᵃ in Babylon.ᵇ

"Then King Cyrus gave them to a man named Sheshbazzar,ᶜ whom he had appointed governor, ¹⁵and he told him, 'Take these articles and go and deposit them in the temple in Jerusalem. And rebuild the house of God on its site.' ¹⁶So this Sheshbazzar came and laid the foundations of the house of Godᵈ in Jerusalem. From that day to the present it has been under construction but is not yet finished."

¹⁷Now if it pleases the king, let a search be made in the royal archivesᵉ of Babylon to see if King Cyrus did in fact issue a decree to rebuild this house of God in Jerusalem. Then let the king send us his decision in this matter.

The Decree of Darius

6 King Darius then issued an order, and they searched in the archivesᶠ stored in the treasury at Babylon. ²A scroll was found in the citadel of Ecbatana in the province of Media, and this was written on it:

Memorandum:

³In the first year of King Cyrus, the king issued a decree concerning the temple of God in Jerusalem:

Let the temple be rebuilt as a place to present sacrifices, and let its foundations be laid.ᵍ It is to be ninety feetᵇ high and ninety feet wide, ⁴with three coursesʰ of large stones and one of timbers. The costs are to be paid by the royal treasury.ⁱ ⁵Also, the goldʲ and silver articles of the house of God, which Nebuchadnezzar took from the temple in Jerusalem and brought to Babylon, are to be returned to their places in the temple in Jerusalem; they are to be deposited in the house of God.ᵏ

⁶Now then, Tattenai,ˡ governor of Trans-Euphrates, and Shethar-Bozenaiᵐ and you, their fellow officials of that province, stay away from there. ⁷Do not interfere with the work on this temple of God. Let the governor of the Jews and the Jewish elders rebuild this house of God on its site.

5:11
ˣ1Ki 6:1;
2Ch 3:1-2
5:12
ʸ2Ch 36:16
ᶻDt 21:10;
28:36; 2Ki 24:1;
25:8,9,11;
Jer 1:3
5:13
ᵃEzr 1:1
5:14
ᵇEzr 1:7; 6:5;
Da 5:2
ᶜ1Ch 3:18
5:16
ᵈEzr 3:10; 6:15
5:17
ᵉEzr 4:15; 6:1,2
6:1
ᶠEzr 4:15; 5:17
6:3
ᵍEzr 3:10;
Hag 2:3
6:4
ʰ1Ki 6:36
ⁱver 8; Ezr 7:20
6:5
ʲ1Ch 29:2
ᵏEzr 1:7; 5:14
6:6
ˡEzr 5:3
ᵐEzr 5:3

ᵃ14 Or *palace*   ᵇ3 Aramaic *sixty cubits* (about 27 meters)

6:8
nver 4
o1Sa 9:20
6:9
pLev 1:3,10
6:10
qEzr 7:23;
1Ti 2:1-2
6:11
rDt 21:22-23;
Est 2:23; 5:14;
9:14 sEzr 7:26;
Da 2:5; 3:29
6:12
tEx 20:24;
Dt 12:5;
1Ki 9:3; 2Ch 6:2
uver 14
6:13
vEzr 4:9
6:14
wEzr 5:1
xEzr 1:1-4
yver 12
zEzr 7:1; Ne 2:1
6:15
aZec 1:1; 4:9
6:16
b1Ki 8:63;
2Ch 7:5
6:17
c2Sa 6:13;
2Ch 29:21;
30:24; Ezr 8:35
6:18
d1Ch 23:6;
2Ch 35:4;
Lk 1:5
e1Ch 24:1
fNu 3:6-9;
8:9-11; 18:1-32
6:19
gEx 12:11;
Nu 28:16
6:20
h2Ch 30:15,17;
35:11
6:21
iEzr 9:1; Ne 9:2
jDt 18:9;
Ezr 9:11;
Eze 36:25
k1Ch 22:19;
Ps 14:2
6:22
lEx 12:17
mEzr 1:1

[8]Moreover, I hereby decree what you are to do for these elders of the Jews in the construction of this house of God:

The expenses of these men are to be fully paid out of the royal treasury,[n] from the revenues[o] of Trans-Euphrates, so that the work will not stop. [9]Whatever is needed—young bulls, rams, male lambs for burnt offerings[p] to the God of heaven, and wheat, salt, wine and oil, as requested by the priests in Jerusalem—must be given them daily without fail, [10]so that they may offer sacrifices pleasing to the God of heaven and pray for the well-being of the king and his sons. [q]

[11]Furthermore, I decree that if anyone changes this edict, a beam is to be pulled from his house and he is to be lifted up and impaled[r] on it. And for this crime his house is to be made a pile of rubble. [s] [12]May God, who has caused his Name to dwell there,[t] overthrow any king or people who lifts a hand to change this decree or to destroy this temple in Jerusalem.

I Darius[u] have decreed it. Let it be carried out with diligence.

Completion and Dedication of the Temple

[13]Then, because of the decree King Darius had sent, Tattenai, governor of Trans-Euphrates, and Shethar-Bozenai and their associates[v] carried it out with diligence. [14]So the elders of the Jews continued to build and prosper under the preaching[w] of Haggai the prophet and Zechariah, a descendant of Iddo. They finished building the temple according to the command of the God of Israel and the decrees of Cyrus,[x] Darius[y] and Artaxerxes,[z] kings of Persia. [15]The temple was completed on the third day of the month Adar, in the sixth year of the reign of King Darius. [a]

[16]Then the people of Israel—the priests, the Levites and the rest of the exiles—celebrated the dedication[b] of the house of God with joy. [17]For the dedication of this house of God they offered[c] a hundred bulls, two hundred rams, four hundred male lambs and, as a sin offering for all Israel, twelve male goats, one for each of the tribes of Israel. [18]And they installed the priests in their divisions[d] and the Levites in their groups[e] for the service of God at Jerusalem, according to what is written in the Book of Moses. [f]

The Passover

[19]On the fourteenth day of the first month, the exiles celebrated the Passover. [g] [20]The priests and Levites had purified themselves and were all ceremonially clean. The Levites slaughtered[h] the Passover lamb for all the exiles, for their brothers the priests and for themselves. [21]So the Israelites who had returned from the exile ate it, together with all who had separated themselves[i] from the unclean practices[j] of their Gentile neighbors in order to seek the LORD,[k] the God of Israel. [22]For seven days they celebrated with joy the Feast of Unleavened Bread,[l] because the LORD had filled them with joy by changing the attitude[m] of the king of Assyria, so that he assisted them in the work on the house of God, the God of Israel.

Ezra Comes to Jerusalem

7 After these things, during the reign of Artaxerxes[n] king of Persia, Ezra son of Seraiah, the son of Azariah, the son of Hilkiah,[o] [2]the son of Shallum, the son of Zadok,[p] the son of Ahitub,[q] [3]the son of Amariah, the son of Azariah, the son of Meraioth, [4]the son of Zerahiah, the son of Uzzi, the son of Bukki, [5]the son of Abishua, the son of Phinehas, the son of Eleazar, the son of Aaron the chief priest— [6]this Ezra[r] came up from Babylon. He was a teacher well versed in the Law of Moses, which the LORD, the God of Israel, had given. The king had granted him everything he asked, for the hand of the LORD his God was on him.[s] [7]Some of the Israelites, including priests, Levites, singers, gatekeepers and temple servants, also came up to Jerusalem in the seventh year of King Artaxerxes.[t]

[8]Ezra arrived in Jerusalem in the fifth month of the seventh year of the king. [9]He had begun his journey from Babylon on the first day of the first month, and he arrived in Jerusalem on the first day of the fifth month, for the gracious hand of his God was on him.[u] [10]For Ezra had devoted himself to the study and observance of the Law of the LORD, and to teaching[v] its decrees and laws in Israel.

King Artaxerxes' Letter to Ezra

[11]This is a copy of the letter King Artaxerxes had given to Ezra the priest and teacher, a man learned in matters concerning the commands and decrees of the LORD for Israel:

[12][a]Artaxerxes, king of kings,[w]

To Ezra the priest, a teacher of the Law of the God of heaven:

Greetings.

[13]Now I decree that any of the Israelites in my kingdom, including priests and Levites, who wish to go to Jerusalem with you, may go. [14]You are sent by the king and his seven advisers[x] to inquire about Judah and Jerusalem with regard to the Law of your God, which is in your hand. [15]Moreover, you are to take with you the silver and gold that the king and his advisers have freely given[y] to the God of Israel, whose dwelling[z] is in Jerusalem, [16]together with all the silver and gold[a] you may obtain from the province of Babylon, as well as the freewill offerings of the people and priests for the temple of their God in Jerusalem.[b] [17]With this money be sure to buy bulls, rams and male lambs,[c] together with their grain offerings and drink offerings,[d] and sacrifice[e] them on the altar of the temple of your God in Jerusalem.

[18]You and your brother Jews may then do whatever seems best with the rest of the silver and gold, in accordance with the will of your God. [19]Deliver[f] to the God of Jerusalem all the articles entrusted to you for worship in the temple of your God. [20]And anything else needed for the temple of your God that you may have occasion to supply, you may provide from the royal treasury.[g]

---

[a]12 The text of Ezra 7:12-26 is in Aramaic.

7:1
nEzr 4:7; 6:14;
Ne 2:1
o2Ki 22:4
7:2
p1Ki 1:8;
1Ch 6:8
qNe 11:11
7:6
rNe 12:36
sEzr 5:5;
Isa 41:20
7:7
tEzr 8:1
7:9
uver 6
7:10
vver 25;
Dt 33:10;
Ne 8:1-8
7:12
wEze 26:7;
Da 2:37
7:14
xEst 1:14
7:15
y1Ch 29:6
z1Ch 29:6,9;
2Ch 6:2
7:16
aEzr 8:25
bZec 6:10
7:17
c2Ki 3:4
dNu 15:5-12
eDt 12:5-11
7:19
fEzr 5:14;
Jer 27:22
7:20
gEzr 6:4

[21]Now I, King Artaxerxes, order all the treasurers of Trans-Euphrates to provide with diligence whatever Ezra the priest, a teacher of the Law of the God of heaven, may ask of you— [22]up to a hundred talents[a] of silver, a hundred cors[b] of wheat, a hundred baths[c] of wine, a hundred baths[c] of olive oil, and salt without limit. [23]Whatever the God of heaven has prescribed, let it be done with diligence for the temple of the God of heaven. Why should there be wrath against the realm of the king and of his sons?[h] [24]You are also to know that you have no authority to impose taxes, tribute or duty[i] on any of the priests, Levites, singers, gatekeepers, temple servants or other workers at this house of God.[j]

[25]And you, Ezra, in accordance with the wisdom of your God, which you possess, appoint[k] magistrates and judges to administer justice to all the people of Trans-Euphrates—all who know the laws of your God. And you are to teach[l] any who do not know them. [26]Whoever does not obey the law of your God and the law of the king must surely be punished by death, banishment, confiscation of property, or imprisonment. [m]

[27]Praise be to the LORD, the God of our fathers, who has put it into the king's heart[n] to bring honor[o] to the house of the LORD in Jerusalem in this way [28]and who has extended his good favor[p] to me before the king and his advisers and all the king's powerful officials. Because the hand of the LORD my God was on me,[q] I took courage and gathered leading men from Israel to go up with me.

List of the Family Heads Returning With Ezra

8 These are the family heads and those registered with them who came up with me from Babylon during the reign of King Artaxerxes:[r]

[2]of the descendants of Phinehas, Gershom;
of the descendants of Ithamar, Daniel;
of the descendants of David, Hattush [3]of the descendants of Shecaniah;[s]

of the descendants of Parosh,[t] Zechariah, and with him were registered 150 men;
[4]of the descendants of Pahath-Moab,[u] Eliehoenai son of Zerahiah, and with him 200 men;
[5]of the descendants of Zattu,[d] Shecaniah son of Jahaziel, and with him 300 men;
[6]of the descendants of Adin,[v] Ebed son of Jonathan, and with him 50 men;
[7]of the descendants of Elam, Jeshaiah son of Athaliah, and with him 70 men;
[8]of the descendants of Shephatiah, Zebadiah son of Michael, and with him 80 men;
[9]of the descendants of Joab, Obadiah son of Jehiel, and with him 218 men;

### Cross references (margin)

7:23
h Ezr 6:10
7:24
i Ezr 4:13
j Ezr 8:36
7:25
k Ex 18:21,26;
Dt 16:18
l ver 10;
Lev 10:11
7:26
m Ezr 6:11
7:27
n Ezr 1:1; 6:22
o 1Ch 29:12
7:28
p 2Ki 25:28
q Ezr 5:5; 9:9
8:1
r Ezr 7:7
8:3
s 1Ch 3:22
t Ezr 2:3
8:4
u Ezr 2:6
8:6
v Ezr 2:15;
Ne 7:20; 10:16

---

[a]22 That is, about 3 3/4 tons (about 3.4 metric tons)   [b]22 That is, probably about 600 bushels (about 22 kiloliters)   [c]22 That is, probably about 600 gallons (about 2.2 kiloliters)   [d]5 Some Septuagint manuscripts (also 1 Esdras 8:32); Hebrew does not have *Zattu*.

¹⁰of the descendants of Bani,^a Shelomith son of Josiphiah, and with him 160 men;

¹¹of the descendants of Bebai, Zechariah son of Bebai, and with him 28 men;

¹²of the descendants of Azgad, Johanan son of Hakkatan, and with him 110 men;

¹³of the descendants of Adonikam,^w the last ones, whose names were Eliphelet, Jeuel and Shemaiah, and with them 60 men;

¹⁴of the descendants of Bigvai, Uthai and Zaccur, and with them 70 men.

The Return to Jerusalem

¹⁵I assembled them at the canal that flows toward Ahava,^x and we camped there three days. When I checked among the people and the priests, I found no Levites^y there. ¹⁶So I summoned Eliezer, Ariel, Shemaiah, Elnathan, Jarib, Elnathan, Nathan, Zechariah and Meshullam, who were leaders, and Joiarib and Elnathan, who were men of learning, ¹⁷and I sent them to Iddo, the leader in Casiphia. I told them what to say to Iddo and his kinsmen, the temple servants^z in Casiphia, so that they might bring attendants to us for the house of our God. ¹⁸Because the gracious hand of our God was on us,^a they brought us Sherebiah, a capable man, from the descendants of Mahli son of Levi, the son of Israel, and Sherebiah's sons and brothers, 18 men; ¹⁹and Hashabiah, together with Jeshaiah from the descendants of Merari, and his brothers and nephews, 20 men. ²⁰They also brought 220 of the temple servants^b—a body that David and the officials had established to assist the Levites. All were registered by name.

²¹There, by the Ahava Canal,^c I proclaimed a fast, so that we might humble ourselves before our God and ask him for a safe journey^d for us and our children, with all our possessions. ²²I was ashamed to ask the king for soldiers^e and horsemen to protect us from enemies on the road, because we had told the king, "The gracious hand of our God is on everyone^f who looks to him, but his great anger is against all who forsake him.^g" ²³So we fasted^h and petitioned our God about this, and he answered our prayer.

²⁴Then I set apart twelve of the leading priests, together with Sherebiah,ⁱ Hashabiah and ten of their brothers, ²⁵and I weighed out^j to them the offering of silver and gold and the articles that the king, his advisers, his officials and all Israel present there had donated for the house of our God. ²⁶I weighed out to them 650 talents^b of silver, silver articles weighing 100 talents,^c 100 talents^c of gold, ²⁷20 bowls of gold valued at 1,000 darics,^d and two fine articles of polished bronze, as precious as gold.

²⁸I said to them, "You as well as these articles are consecrated to the LORD.^k The silver and gold are a freewill offering to the LORD, the God of your fathers. ²⁹Guard them carefully until you weigh them out in the chambers of the house of the LORD in Jerusalem before the leading priests and the Levites and the family heads of Israel." ³⁰Then the

---

8:13
wEzr 2:13

8:15
xver 21,31
yEzr 2:40; 7:7

8:17
zEzr 2:43

8:18
aEzr 5:5

8:20
b1Ch 9:2;
Ezr 2:43

8:21
cver 15;
2Ch 20:3
dPs 5:8; 107:7

8:22
eNe 2:9;
Ezr 7:6,9,28
fEzr 5:5
gDt 31:17;
2Ch 15:2

8:23
h2Ch 20:3;
33:13

8:24
iver 18

8:25
jver 33;
Ezr 7:15,16

8:28
kLev 21:6;
22:2-3

---

^a10 Some Septuagint manuscripts (also 1 Esdras 8:36); Hebrew does not have *Bani*.   ^b26 That is, about 25 tons (about 22 metric tons)   ^c26 That is, about 3 3/4 tons (about 3.4 metric tons)   ^d27 That is, about 19 pounds (about 8.5 kilograms)

priests and Levites received the silver and gold and sacred articles that had been weighed out to be taken to the house of our God in Jerusalem.

31On the twelfth day of the first month we set out from the Ahava Canal[1] to go to Jerusalem. The hand of our God was on us, and he protected us from enemies and bandits along the way. 32So we arrived in Jerusalem, where we rested three days. m

33On the fourth day, in the house of our God, we weighed out the silver and gold and the sacred articles into the hands of Meremoth n son of Uriah, the priest. Eleazar son of Phinehas was with him, and so were the Levites Jozabad son of Jeshua and Noadiah son of Binnui. o 34Everything was accounted for by number and weight, and the entire weight was recorded at that time.

35Then the exiles who had returned from captivity sacrificed burnt offerings to the God of Israel: twelve bulls for all Israel, ninety-six rams, seventy-seven male lambs and, as a sin offering, twelve male goats. p All this was a burnt offering to the LORD. 36They also delivered the king's orders q to the royal satraps and to the governors of Trans-Euphrates, who then gave assistance to the people and to the house of God. r

Ezra's Prayer About Intermarriage

9 After these things had been done, the leaders came to me and said, "The people of Israel, including the priests and the Levites, have not kept themselves separate s from the neighboring peoples with their detestable practices, like those of the Canaanites, Hittites, Perizzites, Jebusites, Ammonites, t Moabites, Egyptians and Amorites. u 2They have taken some of their daughters v as wives for themselves and their sons, and have mingled the holy race w with the peoples around them. And the leaders and officials have led the way in this unfaithfulness." x

3When I heard this, I tore my tunic and cloak, pulled hair from my head and beard and sat down appalled. 4Then everyone who trembled y at the words of the God of Israel gathered around me because of this unfaithfulness of the exiles. And I sat there appalled until the evening sacrifice.

5Then, at the evening sacrifice, z I rose from my self-abasement, with my tunic and cloak torn, and fell on my knees with my hands spread out to the LORD my God 6and prayed:

"O my God, I am too ashamed and disgraced to lift up my face to you, my God, because our sins are higher than our heads and our guilt has reached to the heavens. a 7From the days of our forefathers b until now, our guilt has been great. Because of our sins, we and our kings and our priests have been subjected to the sword c and captivity, d to pillage and humiliation e at the hand of foreign kings, as it is today.

8"But now, for a brief moment, the LORD our God has been gracious f in leaving us a remnant g and giving us a firm place h in his sanctuary, and so our God gives light to our eyes i and a little relief in our bondage. 9Though we are slaves, j our God has not deserted us in our bondage. He has shown us kindness k in the sight of the kings of Persia: He has granted us new life to rebuild

---

8:31
lver 15
8:32
mGe 40:13;
Ne 2:11
8:33
nNe 3:4,21
oNe 3:24
8:35
p2Ch 29:21;
Ezr 6:17
8:36
qEzr 7:21-24
rEst 9:3
9:1
sEzr 6:21;
Ne 9:2
tGe 19:38
uEx 13:5
9:2
vEx 34:16
wEx 22:31
xEzr 10:2
9:4
yEzr 10:3
9:5
zEx 29:41
9:6
a2Ch 28:9;
Job 42:6;
Ps 38:4;
Rev 18:5
9:7
b2Ch 29:6
cEze 21:1-32
dDt 28:64
eDt 28:37
9:8
fPs 25:16;
Isa 33:2
gGe 45:7
hEcc 12:11;
Isa 22:23
iPs 13:3
9:9
jEx 1:14;
Ne 9:36
kEzr 7:28

the house of our God and repair its ruins,[1] and he has given us a wall of protection in Judah and Jerusalem.

[10]"But now, O our God, what can we say after this? For we have disregarded the commands[m] [11]you gave through your servants the prophets when you said: 'The land you are entering to possess is a land polluted[n] by the corruption of its peoples. By their detestable practices[o] they have filled it with their impurity from one end to the other. [12]Therefore, do not give your daughters in marriage to their sons or take their daughters for your sons. Do not seek a treaty of friendship with them[p] at any time, that you may be strong and eat the good things of the land and leave it to your children as an everlasting inheritance.'

[13]"What has happened to us is a result of our evil deeds and our great guilt, and yet, our God, you have punished us less than our sins have deserved[q] and have given us a remnant like this. [14]Shall we again break your commands and intermarry[r] with the peoples who commit such detestable practices? Would you not be angry enough with us to destroy us,[s] leaving us no remnant[t] or survivor? [15]O LORD, God of Israel, you are righteous![u] We are left this day as a remnant. Here we are before you in our guilt, though because of it not one of us can stand[v] in your presence.[w]"

The People's Confession of Sin

10 While Ezra was praying and confessing,[x] weeping and throwing himself down before the house of God, a large crowd of Israelites—men, women and children—gathered around him. They too wept bitterly. [2]Then Shecaniah son of Jehiel, one of the descendants of Elam, said to Ezra, "We have been unfaithful[y] to our God by marrying foreign women from the peoples around us. But in spite of this, there is still hope for Israel.[z] [3]Now let us make a covenant[a] before our God to send away[b] all these women and their children, in accordance with the counsel of my lord and of those who fear the commands of our God. Let it be done according to the Law. [4]Rise up; this matter is in your hands. We will support you, so take courage and do it."

[5]So Ezra rose up and put the leading priests and Levites and all Israel under oath[c] to do what had been suggested. And they took the oath. [6]Then Ezra withdrew from before the house of God and went to the room of Jehohanan son of Eliashib. While he was there, he ate no food and drank no water,[d] because he continued to mourn over the unfaithfulness of the exiles.

[7]A proclamation was then issued throughout Judah and Jerusalem for all the exiles to assemble in Jerusalem. [8]Anyone who failed to appear within three days would forfeit all his property, in accordance with the decision of the officials and elders, and would himself be expelled from the assembly of the exiles.

[9]Within the three days, all the men of Judah and Benjamin[e] had gathered in Jerusalem. And on the twentieth day of the ninth month, all the people were sitting in the square before the house of God, greatly distressed by the occasion and because of the rain. [10]Then Ezra the priest stood up and said to them, "You have been unfaithful; you have married foreign women, adding to Israel's guilt. [11]Now make

9:9
l Ps 69:35;
Isa 43:1;
Jer 32:44
9:10
m Dt 11:8;
Isa 1:19-20
9:11
n Lev 18:25-28
o Dt 9:4
9:12
p Ex 34:15;
Dt 7:3; 23:6
9:13
q Job 11:6;
Ps 103:10
9:14
r Ne 13:27
s Dt 9:8 t Dt 9:14
9:15
u Ge 18:25;
Ps 51:4;
Jer 12:1; Da 9:7
v Ne 9:33;
Ps 130:3;
Mal 3:2
w 1Ki 8:47
10:1
x 2Ch 20:9;
Da 9:20
10:2
y Ezr 9:2;
Ne 13:27
z Dt 30:8-10
10:3
a 2Ch 34:31
b Ex 34:16;
Dt 7:2-3;
Ezr 9:4
10:5
c Ne 5:12; 13:25
10:6
d Ex 34:28;
Dt 9:18
10:9
e Ezr 1:5

confession to the LORD, the God of your fathers, and do his will. Separate yourselves from the peoples around you and from your foreign wives."[f]

[12]The whole assembly responded with a loud voice:[g] "You are right! We must do as you say. [13]But there are many people here and it is the rainy season; so we cannot stand outside. Besides, this matter cannot be taken care of in a day or two, because we have sinned greatly in this thing. [14]Let our officials act for the whole assembly. Then let everyone in our towns who has married a foreign woman come at a set time, along with the elders and judges[h] of each town, until the fierce anger[i] of our God in this matter is turned away from us." [15]Only Jonathan son of Asahel and Jahzeiah son of Tikvah, supported by Meshullam and Shabbethai[j] the Levite, opposed this.

[16]So the exiles did as was proposed. Ezra the priest selected men who were family heads, one from each family division, and all of them designated by name. On the first day of the tenth month they sat down to investigate the cases, [17]and by the first day of the first month they finished dealing with all the men who had married foreign women.

Those Guilty of Intermarriage

[18]Among the descendants of the priests, the following had married foreign women:[k]

From the descendants of Jeshua[l] son of Jozadak, and his brothers: Maaseiah, Eliezer, Jarib and Gedaliah. [19](They all gave their hands[m] in pledge to put away their wives, and for their guilt they each presented a ram from the flock as a guilt offering.)[n]
[20]From the descendants of Immer:[o]
Hanani and Zebadiah.
[21]From the descendants of Harim:[p]
Maaseiah, Elijah, Shemaiah, Jehiel and Uzziah.
[22]From the descendants of Pashhur:[q]
Elioenai, Maaseiah, Ishmael, Nethanel, Jozabad and Elasah.

[23]Among the Levites:[r]

Jozabad, Shimei, Kelaiah (that is, Kelita), Pethahiah, Judah and Eliezer.
[24]From the singers:
Eliashib.[s]
From the gatekeepers:
Shallum, Telem and Uri.

[25]And among the other Israelites:

From the descendants of Parosh:[t]
Ramiah, Izziah, Malkijah, Mijamin, Eleazar, Malkijah and Benaiah.
[26]From the descendants of Elam:[u]
Mattaniah, Zechariah, Jehiel, Abdi, Jeremoth and Elijah.
[27]From the descendants of Zattu:
Elioenai, Eliashib, Mattaniah, Jeremoth, Zabad and Aziza.
[28]From the descendants of Bebai:
Jehohanan, Hananiah, Zabbai and Athlai.

10:11
fver 3; Dt 24:1;
Ne 9:2;
Mal 2:10-16
10:12
gJos 6:5
10:14
hDt 16:18
iNu 25:4;
2Ch 29:10; 30:8
10:15
jNe 11:16
10:18
kJdg 3:6
lEzr 2:2
10:19
m2Ki 10:15
nLev 5:15; 6:6
10:20
o1Ch 24:14
10:21
p1Ch 24:8
10:22
q1Ch 9:12
10:23
rNe 8:7; 9:4
10:24
sNe 3:1; 12:10;
13:7,28
10:25
tEzr 2:3
10:26
uver 2

[29]From the descendants of Bani:

Meshullam, Malluch, Adaiah, Jashub, Sheal and Jeremoth.

[30]From the descendants of Pahath-Moab:

Adna, Kelal, Benaiah, Maaseiah, Mattaniah, Bezalel, Binnui and Manasseh.

[31]From the descendants of Harim:

Eliezer, Ishijah, Malkijah, Shemaiah, Shimeon, [32]Benjamin, Malluch and Shemariah.

[33]From the descendants of Hashum:

Mattenai, Mattattah, Zabad, Eliphelet, Jeremai, Manasseh and Shimei.

[34]From the descendants of Bani:

Maadai, Amram, Uel, [35]Benaiah, Bedeiah, Keluhi, [36]Vaniah, Meremoth, Eliashib, [37]Mattaniah, Mattenai and Jaasu.

[38]From the descendants of Binnui:[a]

Shimei, [39]Shelemiah, Nathan, Adaiah, [40]Macnadebai, Shashai, Sharai, [41]Azarel, Shelemiah, Shemariah, [42]Shallum, Amariah and Joseph.

[43]From the descendants of Nebo:

Jeiel, Mattithiah, Zabad, Zebina, Jaddai, Joel and Benaiah.

[44]All these had married foreign women, and some of them had children by these wives. [b]

---

[a]37,38 See Septuagint (also 1 Esdras 9:34); Hebrew *Jaasu* [38]and Bani and Binnui,   [b]44 Or and they sent them away with their children

Nehemiah

Title and Background
See Introduction to Ezra.

Author and Date of Writing
See Introduction to Ezra. Nehemiah can be dated about 430 B.C.

Theme and Message
Nehemiah continues the history of the Jews upon their return from exile in Babylon. Nehemiah went to Jerusalem in 445 B.C. and led the people in repairing the walls. With Ezra, he provided leadership for the people. A recurring theme of this book is the description of the importance of prayer to Nehemiah.

Outline

Nehemiah's Prayer

1 The words of Nehemiah son of Hacaliah:

In the month of Kislev[a] in the twentieth year, while I was in the citadel of Susa, [2]Hanani,[b] one of my brothers, came from Judah with some other men, and I questioned them about the Jewish remnant[c] that survived the exile, and also about Jerusalem.

[3]They said to me, "Those who survived the exile and are back in the province are in great trouble and disgrace. The wall of Jerusalem is broken down, and its gates have been burned with fire.[d]"

[4]When I heard these things, I sat down and wept.[e] For some days I mourned and fasted[f] and prayed before the God of heaven. [5]Then I said:

"O LORD, God of heaven, the great and awesome God,[g] who keeps his covenant of love[h] with those who love him and obey his commands, [6]let your ear be attentive and your eyes open to hear[i] the prayer[j] your servant is praying before you day and night for your servants, the people of Israel. I confess the sins we Israelites, including myself and my father's house, have committed against you. [7]We have acted very wickedly[k] toward you. We have not obeyed the commands, decrees and laws you gave your servant Moses.

[8]"Remember[l] the instruction you gave your servant Moses, saying, 'If you are unfaithful, I will scatter[m] you among the nations, [9]but if you return to me and obey my commands, then even if your exiled people are at the farthest horizon, I will gather[n]

1:1
aNe 10:1;
Zec 7:1
1:2
bNe 7:2
cJer 52:28
1:3
d2Ki 25:10;
Ne 2:3,13,17
1:4
ePs 137:1
fEzr 9:4
1:5
gDt 7:21;
Ne 4:14
hEx 20:6;
Da 9:4
1:6
i1Ki 8:29
jDa 9:17
1:7
kDt 28:14-15;
Ps 106:6
1:8
l2Ki 20:3
mLev 26:33
1:9
nDt 30:4

them from there and bring them to the place I have chosen as a dwelling for my Name.' ᵒ

¹⁰"They are your servants and your people, whom you redeemed by your great strength and your mighty hand. ᵖ ¹¹O Lord, let your ear be attentive �q to the prayer of this your servant and to the prayer of your servants who delight in revering your name. Give your servant success today by granting him favor in the presence of this man."

I was cupbearer ʳ to the king.

Artaxerxes Sends Nehemiah to Jerusalem

2 In the month of Nisan in the twentieth year of King Artaxerxes, ˢ when wine was brought for him, I took the wine and gave it to the king. I had not been sad in his presence before; ²so the king asked me, "Why does your face look so sad when you are not ill? This can be nothing but sadness of heart."

I was very much afraid, ³but I said to the king, "May the king live forever! ᵗ Why should my face not look sad when the city ᵘ where my fathers are buried lies in ruins, and its gates have been destroyed by fire? ᵛ "

⁴The king said to me, "What is it you want?"

Then I prayed to the God of heaven, ⁵and I answered the king, "If it pleases the king and if your servant has found favor in his sight, let him send me to the city in Judah where my fathers are buried so that I can rebuild it."

⁶Then the king ʷ, with the queen sitting beside him, asked me, "How long will your journey take, and when will you get back?" It pleased the king to send me; so I set a time.

⁷I also said to him, "If it pleases the king, may I have letters to the governors of Trans-Euphrates, ˣ so that they will provide me safe-conduct until I arrive in Judah? ⁸And may I have a letter to Asaph, keeper of the king's forest, so he will give me timber to make beams for the gates of the citadel ʸ by the temple and for the city wall and for the residence I will occupy?" And because the gracious hand of my God was upon me, ᶻ the king granted my requests. ⁹So I went to the governors of Trans-Euphrates and gave them the king's letters. The king had also sent army officers and cavalry ᵃ with me.

¹⁰When Sanballat ᵇ the Horonite and Tobiah ᶜ the Ammonite official heard about this, they were very much disturbed that someone had come to promote the welfare of the Israelites. ᵈ

Nehemiah Inspects Jerusalem's Walls

¹¹I went to Jerusalem, and after staying there three days ᵉ ¹²I set out during the night with a few men. I had not told anyone what my God had put in my heart to do for Jerusalem. There were no mounts with me except the one I was riding on.

¹³By night I went out through the Valley Gate ᶠ toward the Jackal ᵃ Well and the Dung Gate, ᵍ examining the walls ʰ of Jerusalem, which had been broken down, and its gates, which had been destroyed by

1:9
ᵒ1Ki 8:48;
Jer 29:14
1:10
ᵖEx 32:11;
Dt 9:29
1:11
qver 6 ʳGe 40:1
2:1
ˢEzr 7:1
2:3
ᵗ1Ki 1:31;
Da 2:4; 5:10;
6:6,21 ᵘPs 137:6
ᵛNe 1:3
2:6
ʷNe 5:14; 13:6
2:7
ˣEzr 8:36
2:8
ʸNe 7:2
zver 18;
Ezr 5:5; 7:6
2:9
ᵃEzr 8:22
2:10
ᵇver 19;
Ne 4:1,7
ᶜNe 4:3; 13:4-7
ᵈEst 10:3
2:11
ᵉGe 40:13
2:13
ᶠ2Ch 26:9
ᵍNe 3:13
ʰNe 1:3

ᵃ13 Or *Serpent* or *Fig*

fire. [14]Then I moved on toward the Fountain Gate[i] and the King's Pool,[j] but there was not enough room for my mount to get through; [15]so I went up the valley by night, examining the wall. Finally, I turned back and reentered through the Valley Gate. [16]The officials did not know where I had gone or what I was doing, because as yet I had said nothing to the Jews or the priests or nobles or officials or any others who would be doing the work.

[17]Then I said to them, "You see the trouble we are in: Jerusalem lies in ruins, and its gates have been burned with fire.[k] Come, let us rebuild the wall[l] of Jerusalem, and we will no longer be in disgrace.[m]" [18]I also told them about the gracious hand of my God upon me[n] and what the king had said to me.

They replied, "Let us start rebuilding." So they began this good work.

[19]But when Sanballat the Horonite, Tobiah the Ammonite official and Geshem[o] the Arab heard about it, they mocked and ridiculed us.[p] "What is this you are doing?" they asked. "Are you rebelling against the king?"

[20]I answered them by saying, "The God of heaven will give us success. We his servants will start rebuilding, but as for you, you have no share[q] in Jerusalem or any claim or historic right to it."

Builders of the Wall

3 Eliashib[r] the high priest and his fellow priests went to work and rebuilt[s] the Sheep Gate.[t] They dedicated it and set its doors in place, building as far as the Tower of the Hundred, which they dedicated, and as far as the Tower of Hananel.[u] [2]The men of Jericho[v] built the adjoining section, and Zaccur son of Imri built next to them.

[3]The Fish Gate[w] was rebuilt by the sons of Hassenaah. They laid its beams and put its doors and bolts and bars in place. [4]Meremoth son of Uriah, the son of Hakkoz, repaired the next section. Next to him Meshullam son of Berekiah, the son of Meshezabel, made repairs, and next to him Zadok son of Baana also made repairs. [5]The next section was repaired by the men of Tekoa,[x] but their nobles would not put their shoulders to the work under their supervisors.[a]

[6]The Jeshanah[b] Gate[y] was repaired by Joiada son of Paseah and Meshullam son of Besodeiah. They laid its beams and put its doors and bolts and bars in place. [7]Next to them, repairs were made by men from Gibeon[z] and Mizpah—Melatiah of Gibeon and Jadon of Meronoth—places under the authority of the governor of Trans-Euphrates. [8]Uzziel son of Harhaiah, one of the goldsmiths, repaired the next section; and Hananiah, one of the perfume-makers, made repairs next to that. They restored[c] Jerusalem as far as the Broad Wall.[a] [9]Rephaiah son of Hur, ruler of a half-district of Jerusalem, repaired the next section. [10]Adjoining this, Jedaiah son of Harumaph made repairs opposite his house, and Hattush son of Hashabneiah made repairs next to him. [11]Malkijah son of Harim and Hasshub son of Pahath-Moab repaired another section and the Tower of the Ovens.[b] [12]Shallum son of Hallohesh, ruler of

2:14
iNe 3:15
j2Ki 18:17
2:17
kNe 1:3
lPs 102:16;
Isa 30:13; 58:12
mEze 5:14
2:18
n2Sa 2:7
2:19
oNe 6:1,2,6
pPs 44:13-16
2:20
qEzr 4:3
3:1
rEzr 10:24
sIsa 58:12
tver 32;
Ne 12:39
uNe 12:39;
Jer 31:38;
Zec 14:10
3:2
vNe 7:36
3:3
w2Ch 33:14;
Ne 12:39
3:5
x2Sa 14:2
3:6
yNe 12:39
3:7
zJos 9:3; Ne 2:7
3:8
aNe 12:38
3:11
bNe 12:38

---

a5 Or their Lord or the governor   b6 Or Old   c8 Or They left out part of a half-district of Jerusalem, repaired the next section with the help of his daughters.

[13]The Valley Gate[c] was repaired by Hanun and the residents of Zanoah.[d] They rebuilt it and put its doors and bolts and bars in place. They also repaired five hundred yards[a] of the wall as far as the Dung Gate.[e]

[14]The Dung Gate was repaired by Malkijah son of Recab, ruler of the district of Beth Hakkerem.[f] He rebuilt it and put its doors and bolts and bars in place.

[15]The Fountain Gate was repaired by Shallun son of Col-Hozeh, ruler of the district of Mizpah. He rebuilt it, roofing it over and putting its doors and bolts and bars in place. He also repaired the wall of the Pool of Siloam,[b][g] by the King's Garden, as far as the steps going down from the City of David. [16]Beyond him, Nehemiah son of Azbuk, ruler of a half-district of Beth Zur,[h] made repairs up to a point opposite the tombs[c][i] of David, as far as the artificial pool and the House of the Heroes.

[17]Next to him, the repairs were made by the Levites under Rehum son of Bani. Beside him, Hashabiah, ruler of half the district of Keilah,[j] carried out repairs for his district. [18]Next to him, the repairs were made by their countrymen under Binnui[d] son of Henadad, ruler of the other half-district of Keilah. [19]Next to him, Ezer son of Jeshua, ruler of Mizpah, repaired another section, from a point facing the ascent to the armory as far as the angle. [20]Next to him, Baruch son of Zabbai zealously repaired another section, from the angle to the entrance of the house of Eliashib the high priest. [21]Next to him, Meremoth[k] son of Uriah, the son of Hakkoz, repaired another section, from the entrance of Eliashib's house to the end of it.

[22]The repairs next to him were made by the priests from the surrounding region. [23]Beyond them, Benjamin and Hasshub made repairs in front of their house; and next to them, Azariah son of Maaseiah, the son of Ananiah, made repairs beside his house. [24]Next to him, Binnui[l] son of Henadad repaired another section, from Azariah's house to the angle and the corner, [25]and Palal son of Uzai worked opposite the angle and the tower projecting from the upper palace near the court of the guard.[m] Next to him, Pedaiah son of Parosh[n] [26]and the temple servants[o] living on the hill of Ophel[p] made repairs up to a point opposite the Water Gate[q] toward the east and the projecting tower. [27]Next to them, the men of Tekoa[r] repaired another section, from the great projecting tower[s] to the wall of Ophel.

[28]Above the Horse Gate,[t] the priests made repairs, each in front of his own house. [29]Next to them, Zadok son of Immer made repairs opposite his house. Next to him, Shemaiah son of Shecaniah, the guard at the East Gate, made repairs. [30]Next to him, Hananiah son of Shelemiah, and Hanun, the sixth son of Zalaph, repaired another section. Next to them, Meshullam son of Berekiah made repairs opposite his living

3:13
c2Ch 26:9
dJos 15:34
eNe 2:13
3:14
fJer 6:1
3:15
gIsa 8:6; Jn 9:7
3:16
hJos 15:58
iAc 2:29
3:17
jJos 15:44
3:21
kEzr 8:33
3:24
lEzr 8:33
3:25
mJer 32:2;
37:21; 39:14
nEzr 2:3
3:26
oNe 7:46; 11:21
p2Ch 33:14
qNe 8:1,3,16;
12:37
3:27
rver 5 sPs 48:12
3:28
t2Ki 11:16;
2Ch 23:15;
Jer 31:40

---

a13 Hebrew *a thousand cubits* (about 450 meters)   *b15* Hebrew *Shelah,* a variant of *Shiloah,* that is, Siloam   *c16* Hebrew; Septuagint, some Vulgate manuscripts and Syriac *tomb*   *d18* Two Hebrew manuscripts and Syriac (see also Septuagint and verse 24); most Hebrew manuscripts *Bavvai* quarters. [31]Next to him, Malkijah, one of the goldsmiths, made repairs as far as the house of the temple servants and the merchants, opposite the Inspection Gate, and as far as the room above the corner; [32]and between the room above the corner and the Sheep Gate[u] the goldsmiths and merchants made repairs.

Opposition to the Rebuilding

4 When Sanballat[v] heard that we were rebuilding the wall, he became angry and was greatly incensed. He ridiculed the Jews, [2]and in the presence of his associates[w] and the army of Samaria, he said, "What are those feeble Jews doing? Will they restore their wall? Will they offer sacrifices? Will they finish in a day? Can they bring the stones back to life from those heaps of rubble[x]—burned as they are?"

[3]Tobiah[y] the Ammonite, who was at his side, said, "What they are building—if even a fox climbed up on it, he would break down their wall of stones!"[z]

[4]Hear us, O our God, for we are despised.[a] Turn their insults back on their own heads. Give them over as plunder in a land of captivity. [5]Do not cover up their guilt[b] or blot out their sins from your sight,[c] for they have thrown insults in the face of[d] the builders.

[6]So we rebuilt the wall till all of it reached half its height, for the people worked with all their heart.

[7]But when Sanballat, Tobiah,[d] the Arabs, the Ammonites and the men of Ashdod heard that the repairs to Jerusalem's walls had gone ahead and that the gaps were being closed, they were very angry. [8]They all plotted together[e] to come and fight against Jerusalem and stir up trouble against it. [9]But we prayed to our God and posted a guard day and night to meet this threat.

[10]Meanwhile, the people in Judah said, "The strength of the laborers[f] is giving out, and there is so much rubble that we cannot rebuild the wall."

[11]Also our enemies said, "Before they know it or see us, we will be right there among them and will kill them and put an end to the work."

[12]Then the Jews who lived near them came and told us ten times over, "Wherever you turn, they will attack us."

[13]Therefore I stationed some of the people behind the lowest points of the wall at the exposed places, posting them by families, with their swords, spears and bows. [14]After I looked things over, I stood up and said to the nobles, the officials and the rest of the people, "Don't be afraid[g] of them. Remember[h] the Lord, who is great and awesome,[i] and fight[j] for your brothers, your sons and your daughters, your wives and your homes."

[15]When our enemies heard that we were aware of their plot and that God had frustrated it,[k] we all returned to the wall, each to his own work.

[16]From that day on, half of my men did the work, while the other half were equipped with spears, shields, bows and armor. The officers posted themselves behind all the people of Judah [17]who were building the wall. Those who carried materials did their work with one hand and

3:32
u ver 1; Jn 5:2
4:1
v Ne 2:10
4:2
w Ezr 4:9-10
x Ps 79:1;
Jer 26:18
4:3
y Ne 2:10
z Job 13:12;
15:3
4:4
a Ps 44:13;
79:12; 123:3-4;
Jer 33:24
4:5
b Isa 2:9;
La 1:22
c 2Ki 14:27;
Ps 51:1;
69:27-28;
109:14;
Jer 18:23
4:7
d Ne 2:10
4:8
e Ps 2:2; 83:1-18
4:10
f 1Ch 23:4
4:14
g Ge 28:15;
Nu 14:9;
Dt 1:29 h Ne 1:8
i Ne 1:5
j 2Sa 10:12
4:15
k 2Sa 17:14;
Job 5:12

---

[a]5 Or *have provoked you to anger before*

held a weapon[1] in the other, [18]and each of the builders wore his sword at his side as he worked. But the man who sounded the trumpet[m] stayed with me.

[19]Then I said to the nobles, the officials and the rest of the people, "The work is extensive and spread out, and we are widely separated from each other along the wall. [20]Wherever you hear the sound of the trumpet,[n] join us there. Our God will fight[o] for us!"

[21]So we continued the work with half the men holding spears, from the first light of dawn till the stars came out. [22]At that time I also said to the people, "Have every man and his helper stay inside Jerusalem at night, so they can serve us as guards by night and workmen by day." [23]Neither I nor my brothers nor my men nor the guards with me took off our clothes; each had his weapon, even when he went for water.[a]

Nehemiah Helps the Poor

5 Now the men and their wives raised a great outcry against their Jewish brothers. [2]Some were saying, "We and our sons and daughters are numerous; in order for us to eat and stay alive, we must get grain."

[3]Others were saying, "We are mortgaging our fields,[p] our vineyards and our homes to get grain during the famine."[q]

[4]Still others were saying, "We have had to borrow money to pay the king's tax[r] on our fields and vineyards. [5]Although we are of the same flesh and blood[s] as our countrymen and though our sons are as good as theirs, yet we have to subject our sons and daughters to slavery.[t] Some of our daughters have already been enslaved, but we are powerless, because our fields and our vineyards belong to others."[u]

[6]When I heard their outcry and these charges, I was very angry. [7]I pondered them in my mind and then accused the nobles and officials. I told them, "You are exacting usury[v] from your own countrymen!" So I called together a large meeting to deal with them [8]and said: "As far as possible, we have bought[w] back our Jewish brothers who were sold to the Gentiles. Now you are selling your brothers, only for them to be sold back to us!" They kept quiet, because they could find nothing to say.[x]

[9]So I continued, "What you are doing is not right. Shouldn't you walk in the fear of our God to avoid the reproach[y] of our Gentile enemies? [10]I and my brothers and my men are also lending the people money and grain. But let the exacting of usury stop![z] [11]Give back to them immediately their fields, vineyards, olive groves and houses, and also the usury[a] you are charging them—the hundredth part of the money, grain, new wine and oil."

[12]"We will give it back," they said. "And we will not demand anything more from them. We will do as you say."

Then I summoned the priests and made the nobles and officials take an oath[b] to do what they had promised. [13]I also shook[c] out the folds of my robe and said, "In this way may God shake out of his house and possessions every man who does not keep this promise. So may such a man be shaken out and emptied!"

---

[a]23 The meaning of the Hebrew for this clause is uncertain.

4:17
lPs 149:6
4:18
mNu 10:2
4:20
nEze 33:3
oEx 14:14;
Dt 1:30; 20:4;
Jos 10:14
5:3
pPs 109:11
qGe 47:23
5:4
rEzr 4:13
5:5
sGe 29:14
tLev 25:39-43,
47; 2Ki 4:1;
Isa 50:1
uDt 15:7-11;
2Ki 4:1
5:7
vEx 22:25-27;
Lev 25:35-37;
Dt 23:19-20;
24:10-13
5:8
wLev 25:47
xJer 34:8
5:9
yIsa 52:5
5:10
zEx 22:25
5:11
aIsa 58:6
5:12
bEzr 10:5
5:13
cMt 10:14;
Ac 18:6

At this the whole assembly said, "Amen,"[d] and praised the LORD. And the people did as they had promised.

[14]Moreover, from the twentieth year of King Artaxerxes,[e] when I was appointed to be their governor[f] in the land of Judah, until his thirty-second year—twelve years—neither I nor my brothers ate the food allotted to the governor. [15]But the earlier governors—those preceding me—placed a heavy burden on the people and took forty shekels[a] of silver from them in addition to food and wine. Their assistants also lorded it over the people. But out of reverence for God[g] I did not act like that. [16]Instead,[h] I devoted myself to the work on this wall. All my men were assembled there for the work; we[b] did not acquire any land.

[17]Furthermore, a hundred and fifty Jews and officials ate at my table, as well as those who came to us from the surrounding nations. [18]Each day one ox, six choice sheep and some poultry[i] were prepared for me, and every ten days an abundant supply of wine of all kinds. In spite of all this, I never demanded the food allotted to the governor, because the demands were heavy on these people.

[19]Remember[j] me with favor, O my God, for all I have done for these people.

Further Opposition to the Rebuilding

6 When word came to Sanballat, Tobiah,[k] Geshem[l] the Arab and the rest of our enemies that I had rebuilt the wall and not a gap was left in it—though up to that time I had not set the doors in the gates— [2]Sanballat and Geshem sent me this message: "Come, let us meet together in one of the villages[c] on the plain of Ono.[m]"

But they were scheming to harm me; [3]so I sent messengers to them with this reply: "I am carrying on a great project and cannot go down. Why should the work stop while I leave it and go down to you?" [4]Four times they sent me the same message, and each time I gave them the same answer.

[5]Then, the fifth time, Sanballat[n] sent his aide to me with the same message, and in his hand was an unsealed letter [6]in which was written:

"It is reported among the nations—and Geshem[d][o] says it is true—that you and the Jews are plotting to revolt, and therefore you are building the wall. Moreover, according to these reports you are about to become their king [7]and have even appointed prophets to make this proclamation about you in Jerusalem: 'There is a king in Judah!' Now this report will get back to the king; so come, let us confer together."

[8]I sent him this reply: "Nothing like what you are saying is happening; you are just making it up out of your head."

[9]They were all trying to frighten us, thinking, "Their hands will get too weak for the work, and it will not be completed."

But I prayed, "Now strengthen my hands."

[10]One day I went to the house of Shemaiah son of Delaiah, the son of Mehetabel, who was shut in at his home. He said, "Let us meet in the

---

5:13
d Dt 27:15-26
5:14
e Ne 2:6; 13:6
f Ge 42:6;
Ezr 6:7;
Jer 40:7;
Hag 1:1
5:15
g Ge 20:11
5:16
h 2Th 3:7-10
5:18
i 1Ki 4:23
5:19
j Ge 8:1;
2Ki 20:3;
Ne 1:8; 13:14,
22,31
6:1
k Ne 2:10
l Ne 2:19
6:2
m 1Ch 8:12
6:5
n Ne 2:10
6:6
o Ne 2:19

---

[a]15 That is, about 1 pound (about 0.5 kilogram)　　[b]16 Most Hebrew manuscripts; some Hebrew manuscripts, Septuagint, Vulgate and Syriac *I*　　[c]2 Or *in Kephirim*　　[d]6 Hebrew *Gashmu*, a variant of *Geshem*

house of God, inside the temple[p], and let us close the temple doors, because men are coming to kill you—by night they are coming to kill you."

[11]But I said, "Should a man like me run away? Or should one like me go into the temple to save his life? I will not go!" [12]I realized that God had not sent him, but that he had prophesied against me[q] because Tobiah and Sanballat[r] had hired him. [13]He had been hired to intimidate me so that I would commit a sin by doing this, and then they would give me a bad name to discredit me. [s]

[14]Remember[t] Tobiah and Sanballat, [u] O my God, because of what they have done; remember also the prophetess[v] Noadiah and the rest of the prophets[w] who have been trying to intimidate me.

The Completion of the Wall

[15]So the wall was completed on the twenty-fifth of Elul, in fifty-two days. [16]When all our enemies heard about this, all the surrounding nations were afraid and lost their self-confidence, because they realized that this work had been done with the help of our God.

[17]Also, in those days the nobles of Judah were sending many letters to Tobiah, and replies from Tobiah kept coming to them. [18]For many in Judah were under oath to him, since he was son-in-law to Shecaniah son of Arah, and his son Jehohanan had married the daughter of Meshullam son of Berekiah. [19]Moreover, they kept reporting to me his good deeds and then telling him what I said. And Tobiah sent letters to intimidate me.

7 After the wall had been rebuilt and I had set the doors in place, the gatekeepers[x] and the singers[y] and the Levites[z] were appointed. [2]I put in charge of Jerusalem my brother Hanani, [a] along with[a] Hananiah[b] the commander of the citadel, [c] because he was a man of integrity and feared[d] God more than most men do. [3]I said to them, "The gates of Jerusalem are not to be opened until the sun is hot. While the gatekeepers are still on duty, have them shut the doors and bar them. Also appoint residents of Jerusalem as guards, some at their posts and some near their own houses."

The List of the Exiles Who Returned

7:6-73pp — Ezr 2:1-70

[4]Now the city was large and spacious, but there were few people in it, [e] and the houses had not yet been rebuilt. [5]So my God put it into my heart to assemble the nobles, the officials and the common people for registration by families. I found the genealogical record of those who had been the first to return. This is what I found written there:

[6]These are the people of the province who came up from the captivity of the exiles[f] whom Nebuchadnezzar king of Babylon had taken captive (they returned to Jerusalem and Judah, each to his own town, [7]in company with Zerubbabel, [g] Jeshua, Nehemiah, Azariah, Raamiah, Nahamani, Mordecai, Bilshan, Mispereth, Bigvai, Nehum and Baanah):

a2 Or Hanani, that is,

6:10
pNu 18:7
6:12
qEze 13:22-23
rNe 2:10
6:13
sJer 20:10
6:14
tNe 1:8
uNe 2:10
vEx 15:20;
Eze 13:17-23;
Ac 21:9;
Rev 2:20
wNe 13:29;
Jer 23:9-40;
Zec 13:2-3
7:1
x1Ch 9:27;
26:12-19;
Ne 6:1,15
yPs 68:25
zNe 8:9
7:2
aNe 1:2
bNe 10:23
cNe 2:8
d1Ki 18:3
7:4
eNe 11:1
7:6
f2Ch 36:20;
Ezr 2:1-70;
Ne 1:2
7:7
g1Ch 3:19;
Ezr 2:2

The list of the men of Israel:

8the descendants of Parosh	2,172
9of Shephatiah	372
10of Arah	652
11of Pahath-Moab (through the line of Jeshua and Joab)	2,818
12of Elam	1,254
13of Zattu	845
14of Zaccai	760
15of Binnui	648
16of Bebai	628
17of Azgad	2,322
18of Adonikam	667
19of Bigvai	2,067
20of Adin[h]	655
21of Ater (through Hezekiah)	98
22of Hashum	328
23of Bezai	324
24of Hariph	112
25of Gibeon	95
26the men of Bethlehem and Netophah[i]	188
27of Anathoth[j]	128
28of Beth Azmaveth	42
29of Kiriath Jearim, Kephirah[k] and Beeroth[l]	743
30of Ramah and Geba	621
31of Micmash	122
32of Bethel and Ai[m]	123
33of the other Nebo	52
34of the other Elam	1,254
35of Harim	320
36of Jericho[n]	345
37of Lod, Hadid and Ono[o]	721
38of Senaah	3,930

39The priests:

the descendants of Jedaiah (through the family of Jeshua)	973
40of Immer	1,052
41of Pashhur	1,247
42of Harim	1,017

43The Levites:

the descendants of Jeshua (through Kadmiel through the line of Hodaviah)	74

44The singers:[p]

the descendants of Asaph	148

45The gatekeepers:[q]

the descendants of Shallum, Ater, Talmon, Akkub, Hatita and Shobai	138

⁴⁶The temple servants:ʳ

the descendants of
   Ziha, Hasupha, Tabbaoth,
⁴⁷Keros, Sia, Padon,
⁴⁸Lebana, Hagaba, Shalmai,
⁴⁹Hanan, Giddel, Gahar,
⁵⁰Reaiah, Rezin, Nekoda,
⁵¹Gazzam, Uzza, Paseah,
⁵²Besai, Meunim, Nephussim,
⁵³Bakbuk, Hakupha, Harhur,
⁵⁴Bazluth, Mehida, Harsha,
⁵⁵Barkos, Sisera, Temah,
⁵⁶Neziah and Hatipha

⁵⁷The descendants of the servants of Solomon:

the descendants of
   Sotai, Sophereth, Perida,
⁵⁸Jaala, Darkon, Giddel,
⁵⁹Shephatiah, Hattil,
   Pokereth-Hazzebaim and Amon

⁶⁰The temple servants and the descendants
   of the servants of Solomonˢ   392

⁶¹The following came up from the towns of Tel Melah, Tel Harsha, Kerub, Addon and Immer, but they could not show that their families were descended from Israel:

⁶²the descendants of
   Delaiah, Tobiah and Nekoda   642

⁶³And from among the priests:

the descendants of
   Hobaiah, Hakkoz and Barzillai (a man who had
   married a daughter of Barzillai the Gileadite
   and was called by that name).

⁶⁴These searched for their family records, but they could not find them and so were excluded from the priesthood as unclean. ⁶⁵The governor, therefore, ordered them not to eat any of the most sacred food until there should be a priest ministering with the Urim and Thummim.ᵗ

⁶⁶The whole company numbered 42,360, ⁶⁷besides their 7,337 menservants and maidservants; and they also had 245 men and women singers. ⁶⁸There were 736 horses, 245 mules,ᵃ ⁶⁹435 camels and 6,720 donkeys.

⁷⁰Some of the heads of the families contributed to the work. The governor gave to the treasury 1,000 drachmasᵇ of gold, 50 bowls

7:46
ʳNe 3:26
7:60
ˢ1Ch 9:2
7:65
ᵗEx 28:30;
Ne 8:9

ᵃ68 Some Hebrew manuscripts (see also Ezra 2:66); most Hebrew manuscripts do not have this verse.   ᵇ70 That is, about 19 pounds (about 8.5 kilograms) and 530 garments for priests. ⁷¹Some of the heads of the families ᵘ gave to the treasury for the work 20,000 drachmas ᵃ of gold and 2,200 minas ᵇ of silver. ⁷²The total given by the rest of the people was 20,000 drachmas of gold, 2,000 minas ᶜ of silver and 67 garments for priests. ᵛ

⁷³The priests, the Levites, the gatekeepers, the singers and the temple servants, ʷ along with certain of the people and the rest of the Israelites, settled in their own towns. ˣ

Ezra Reads the Law

When the seventh month came and the Israelites had settled in their towns, ʸ ¹all the people assembled as one man in the square before the Water Gate. ᶻ They told Ezra the scribe to bring out the Book of the Law of Moses, ᵃ which the LORD had commanded for Israel.

²So on the first day of the seventh month ᵇ Ezra the priest brought the Law ᶜ before the assembly, which was made up of men and women and all who were able to understand. ³He read it aloud from daybreak till noon as he faced the square before the Water Gate ᵈ in the presence of the men, women and others who could understand. And all the people listened attentively to the Book of the Law.

⁴Ezra the scribe stood on a high wooden platform ᵉ built for the occasion. Beside him on his right stood Mattithiah, Shema, Anaiah, Uriah, Hilkiah and Maaseiah; and on his left were Pedaiah, Mishael, Malkijah, Hashum, Hashbaddanah, Zechariah and Meshullam.

⁵Ezra opened the book. All the people could see him because he was standing ᶠ above them; and as he opened it, the people all stood up. ⁶Ezra praised the LORD, the great God; and all the people lifted their hands ᵍ and responded, "Amen! Amen!" Then they bowed down and worshiped the LORD with their faces to the ground.

⁷The Levites ʰ—Jeshua, Bani, Sherebiah, Jamin, Akkub, Shabbethai, Hodiah, Maaseiah, Kelita, Azariah, Jozabad, Hanan and Pelaiah—instructed ⁱ the people in the Law while the people were standing there. ⁸They read from the Book of the Law of God, making it clear ᵈ and giving the meaning so that the people could understand what was being read.

⁹Then Nehemiah the governor, Ezra the priest and scribe, and the Levites ʲ who were instructing the people said to them all, "This day is sacred to the LORD your God. Do not mourn or weep." ᵏ For all the people had been weeping as they listened to the words of the Law.

¹⁰Nehemiah said, "Go and enjoy choice food and sweet drinks, and send some to those who have nothing ˡ prepared. This day is sacred to our Lord. Do not grieve, for the joy ᵐ of the LORD is your strength."

¹¹The Levites calmed all the people, saying, "Be still, for this is a sacred day. Do not grieve."

¹²Then all the people went away to eat and drink, to send portions of food and to celebrate with great joy, ⁿ because they now understood the words that had been made known to them.

¹³On the second day of the month, the heads of all the families, along

### Cross references (margin)

7:71
u 1Ch 29:7

7:72
v Ex 25:2

7:73
w Ne 1:10; Ps 34:22; 103:21; 113:1; 135:1 x Ezr 3:1; Ne 11:1 y Ezr 3:1

8:1
z Ne 3:26; a Dt 28:61; 2Ch 34:15; Ezr 7:6

8:2
b Lev 23:23-25; Nu 29:1-6 c Dt 31:11

8:3
d Ne 3:26

8:4
e 2Ch 6:13

8:5
f Jdg 3:20

8:6
g Ex 4:31; Ezr 9:5; 1Ti 2:8

8:7
h Ezr 10:23 i Lev 10:11; 2Ch 17:7

8:9
j Ne 7:1,65,70 k Dt 12:7,12; 16:14-15

8:10
l 1Sa 25:8; Lk 14:12-14 m Lev 23:40; Dt 12:18; 16:11, 14-15

8:12
n Est 9:22

ᵃ71 That is, about 375 pounds (about 170 kilograms); also in verse 72   ᵇ71 That is, about 1 1/3 tons (about 1.2 metric tons)   ᶜ72 That is, about 1 1/4 tons (about 1.1 metric tons)   ᵈ8 Or *God, translating it* with the priests and the Levites, gathered around Ezra the scribe to give attention to the words of the Law. [14]They found written in the Law, which the LORD had commanded through Moses, that the Israelites were to live in booths during the feast of the seventh month [15]and that they should proclaim this word and spread it throughout their towns and in Jerusalem: "Go out into the hill country and bring back branches from olive and wild olive trees, and from myrtles, palms and shade trees, to make booths"—as it is written. [a]

[16]So the people went out and brought back branches and built themselves booths on their own roofs, in their courtyards, in the courts of the house of God and in the square by the Water Gate and the one by the Gate of Ephraim. [o] [17]The whole company that had returned from exile built booths and lived in them. From the days of Joshua son of Nun until that day, the Israelites had not celebrated[p] it like this. And their joy was very great.

[18]Day after day, from the first day to the last, Ezra read[q] from the Book of the Law of God. They celebrated the feast for seven days, and on the eighth day, in accordance with the regulation,[r] there was an assembly.

The Israelites Confess Their Sins

9 On the twenty-fourth day of the same month, the Israelites gathered together, fasting and wearing sackcloth and having dust on their heads. [s] [2]Those of Israelite descent had separated themselves from all foreigners. [t] They stood in their places and confessed their sins and the wickedness of their fathers. [u] [3]They stood where they were and read from the Book of the Law of the LORD their God for a quarter of the day, and spent another quarter in confession and in worshiping the LORD their God. [4]Standing on the stairs were the Levites[v]—Jeshua, Bani, Kadmiel, Shebaniah, Bunni, Sherebiah, Bani and Kenani—who called with loud voices to the LORD their God. [5]And the Levites—Jeshua, Kadmiel, Bani, Hashabneiah, Sherebiah, Hodiah, Shebaniah and Pethahiah—said: "Stand up and praise the LORD your God,[w] who is from everlasting to everlasting. [b] "

"Blessed be your glorious name, and may it be exalted above all blessing and praise. [6]You alone are the LORD. [x] You made the heavens,[y] even the highest heavens, and all their starry host, the earth[z] and all that is on it, the seas[a] and all that is in them. [b] You give life to everything, and the multitudes of heaven worship you.

[7]"You are the LORD God, who chose Abram and brought him out of Ur of the Chaldeans[c] and named him Abraham. [d] [8]You found his heart faithful to you, and you made a covenant with him to give to his descendants the land of the Canaanites, Hittites, Amorites, Perizzites, Jebusites and Girgashites. [e] You have kept your promise[f] because you are righteous. [g]

[9]"You saw the suffering of our forefathers in Egypt;[h] you heard their cry at the Red Sea. [ci] [10]You sent miraculous signs[j] and

8:16
o2Ki 14:13;
Ne 12:39
8:17
p2Ch 7:8; 8:13;
30:21
8:18
qDt 31:11
rLev 23:36,40;
Nu 29:35
9:1
sJos 7:6;
1Sa 4:12
9:2
tNe 13:3,30
uEzr 10:11;
Ps 106:6
9:4
vEzr 10:23
9:5
wPs 78:4
9:6
xDt 6:4
y2Ki 19:15
zGe 1:1;
Isa 37:16
aPs 95:5
bDt 10:14
9:7
cGe 11:31
dGe 17:5
9:8
eGe 15:18-21
fJos 21:45
gGe 15:6;
Ezr 9:15
9:9
hEx 3:7
iEx 14:10-30
9:10
jEx 10:1

wonders against Pharaoh, against all his officials and all the people of his land, for you knew how arrogantly the Egyptians treated them. You made a name[k] for yourself, which remains to this day. [11]You divided the sea before them,[l] so that they passed through it on dry ground, but you hurled their pursuers into the depths, like a stone into mighty waters.[m] [12]By day you led[n] them with a pillar of cloud,[o] and by night with a pillar of fire to give them light on the way they were to take.

[13]"You came down on Mount Sinai;[p] you spoke[q] to them from heaven. You gave them regulations and laws that are just[r] and right, and decrees and commands that are good.[s] [14]You made known to them your holy Sabbath[t] and gave them commands, decrees and laws through your servant Moses. [15]In their hunger you gave them bread from heaven[u] and in their thirst you brought them water from the rock;[v] you told them to go in and take possession of the land you had sworn with uplifted hand to give them.[w]

[16]"But they, our forefathers, became arrogant and stiff-necked, and did not obey your commands.[x] [17]They refused to listen and failed to remember[y] the miracles you performed among them. They became stiff-necked and in their rebellion appointed a leader in order to return to their slavery.[z] But you are a forgiving God, gracious and compassionate, slow to anger[a] and abounding in love.[b] Therefore you did not desert them,[c] [18]even when they cast for themselves an image of a calf[d] and said, 'This is your god, who brought you up out of Egypt,' or when they committed awful blasphemies.

[19]"Because of your great compassion you did not abandon them in the desert. By day the pillar of cloud did not cease to guide them on their path, nor the pillar of fire by night to shine on the way they were to take. [20]You gave your good Spirit[e] to instruct them. You did not withhold your manna[f] from their mouths, and you gave them water[g] for their thirst. [21]For forty years you sustained them in the desert; they lacked nothing,[h] their clothes did not wear out nor did their feet become swollen.[i]

[22]"You gave them kingdoms and nations, allotting to them even the remotest frontiers. They took over the country of Sihon[a][j] king of Heshbon and the country of Og king of Bashan.[k] [23]You made their sons as numerous as the stars in the sky, and you brought them into the land that you told their fathers to enter and possess. [24]Their sons went in and took possession of the land.[l] You subdued before them the Canaanites, who lived in the land; you handed the Canaanites over to them, along with their kings and the peoples of the land, to deal with them as they pleased. [25]They captured fortified cities and fertile land; they took possession of houses filled with all kinds of good things, wells already dug, vineyards, olive groves and fruit trees in abundance. They ate to the full and were well-nourished;[m] they reveled in your great goodness.[n]

9:10
k Jer 32:20;
Da 9:15
9:11
l Ex 14:21;
Ps 78:13
m Ex 15:4-5,10;
Heb 11:29
9:12
n Ex 15:13
o Ex 13:21
9:13
p Ex 19:11
q Ex 19:19
r Ps 119:137
s Ex 20:1
9:14
t Ge 2:3;
Ex 20:8-11
9:15
u Ex 16:4;
Jn 6:31
v Ex 17:6;
Nu 20:7-13
w Dt 1:8,21
9:16
x Dt 1:26-33;
31:29
9:17
y Ps 78:42
z Nu 14:1-4
a Ex 34:6
b Nu 14:17-19
c Ps 78:11
9:18
d Ex 32:4
9:20
e Nu 11:17;
Isa 63:11,14
f Ex 16:15
g Ex 17:6
9:21
h Dt 2:7 i Dt 8:4
9:22
j Nu 21:21
k Nu 21:33
9:24
l Jos 11:23
9:25
m Dt 6:10-12
n Nu 13:27;
Dt 32:12-15

---

[a]22 One Hebrew manuscript and Septuagint; most Hebrew manuscripts *Sihon, that is, the country of the*

26"But they were disobedient and rebelled against you; they put your law behind their backs.° They killed your prophets,ᵖ who had admonished them in order to turn them back to you; they committed awful blasphemies.�q 27So you handed them over to their enemies,ʳ who oppressed them. But when they were oppressed they cried out to you. From heaven you heard them, and in your great compassionˢ you gave them deliverers, who rescued them from the hand of their enemies.

28"But as soon as they were at rest, they again did what was evil in your sight. Then you abandoned them to the hand of their enemies so that they ruled over them. And when they cried out to you again, you heard from heaven, and in your compassion you delivered themᵗ time after time.

29"You warned them to return to your law, but they became arrogantᵘ and disobeyed your commands. They sinned against your ordinances, by which a man will live if he obeys them.ᵛ Stubbornly they turned their backs on you, became stiff-necked and refused to listen.ʷ 30For many years you were patient with them. By your Spirit you admonished them through your prophets.ˣ Yet they paid no attention, so you handed them over to the neighboring peoples. 31But in your great mercy you did not put an endʸ to them or abandon them, for you are a gracious and merciful God.

32"Now therefore, O our God, the great, mightyᶻ and awesome God, who keeps his covenant of love,ᵃ do not let all this hardship seem trifling in your eyes—the hardship that has come upon us, upon our kings and leaders, upon our priests and prophets, upon our fathers and all your people, from the days of the kings of Assyria until today. 33In all that has happened to us, you have been just;ᵇ you have acted faithfully, while we did wrong.ᶜ 34Our kings,ᵈ our leaders, our priests and our fathersᵉ did not follow your law; they did not pay attention to your commands or the warnings you gave them. 35Even while they were in their kingdom, enjoying your great goodnessᶠ to them in the spacious and fertile land you gave them, they did not serve youᵍ or turn from their evil ways.

36"But see, we are slavesʰ today, slaves in the land you gave our forefathers so they could eat its fruit and the other good things it produces. 37Because of our sins, its abundant harvest goes to the kings you have placed over us. They rule over our bodies and our cattle as they please. We are in great distress.ⁱ

The Agreement of the People

38"In view of all this, we are making a binding agreement,ʲ putting it in writing,ᵏ and our leaders, our Levites and our priests are affixing their seals to it."

10 Those who sealed it were:

Nehemiah the governor, the son of Hacaliah.

Zedekiah, 2Seraiah,ˡ Azariah, Jeremiah,
3Pashhur,ᵐ Amariah, Malkijah,

9:26
o1Ki 14:9
pMt 21:35-36
qJdg 2:12-13
9:27
rJdg 2:14
sPs 106:45
9:28
tPs 106:43
9:29
uPs 5:5;
Isa 2:11;
Jer 43:2
vDt 30:16
wZec 7:11-12
9:30
x2Ki 17:13-18;
2Ch 36:16
9:31
yIsa 48:9;
Jer 4:27
9:32
zPs 24:8 aDt 7:9
9:33
bGe 18:25
cJer 44:3;
Da 9:7-8,14
9:34
d2Ki 23:11
eJer 44:17
9:35
fIsa 63:7
gDt 28:45-48
9:36
hDt 28:48;
Ezr 9:9
9:37
iDt 28:33;
La 5:5
9:38
j2Ch 23:16
kIsa 44:5
10:2
lEzr 2:2
10:3
m1Ch 9:12

⁴Hattush, Shebaniah, Malluch,
⁵Harim,ⁿ Meremoth, Obadiah,
⁶Daniel, Ginnethon, Baruch,
⁷Meshullam, Abijah, Mijamin,
⁸Maaziah, Bilgai and Shemaiah.
These were the priests.

⁹The Levites:^o

Jeshua son of Azaniah, Binnui of the sons of Henadad, Kadmiel,
¹⁰and their associates: Shebaniah,
Hodiah, Kelita, Pelaiah, Hanan,
¹¹Mica, Rehob, Hashabiah,
¹²Zaccur, Sherebiah, Shebaniah,
¹³Hodiah, Bani and Beninu.

¹⁴The leaders of the people:

Parosh, Pahath-Moab, Elam, Zattu, Bani,
¹⁵Bunni, Azgad, Bebai,
¹⁶Adonijah, Bigvai, Adin,^p
¹⁷Ater, Hezekiah, Azzur,
¹⁸Hodiah, Hashum, Bezai,
¹⁹Hariph, Anathoth, Nebai,
²⁰Magpiash, Meshullam, Hezir,^q
²¹Meshezabel, Zadok, Jaddua,
²²Pelatiah, Hanan, Anaiah,
²³Hoshea, Hananiah,^r Hasshub,
²⁴Hallohesh, Pilha, Shobek,
²⁵Rehum, Hashabnah, Maaseiah,
²⁶Ahiah, Hanan, Anan,
²⁷Malluch, Harim and Baanah.

²⁸"The rest of the people—priests, Levites, gatekeepers, singers, temple servants^s and all who separated themselves from the neighboring peoples^t for the sake of the Law of God, together with their wives and all their sons and daughters who are able to understand— ²⁹all these now join their brothers the nobles, and bind themselves with a curse and an oath^u to follow the Law of God given through Moses the servant of God and to obey carefully all the commands, regulations and decrees of the LORD our Lord.

³⁰"We promise not to give our daughters in marriage to the peoples around us or take their daughters for our sons.^v

³¹"When the neighboring peoples bring merchandise or grain to sell on the Sabbath,^w we will not buy from them on the Sabbath or on any holy day. Every seventh year we will forgo working the land^x and will cancel all debts.^y

³²"We assume the responsibility for carrying out the commands to give a third of a shekel^a each year for the service of the house of our God: ³³for the bread set out on the table;^z for the regular grain offerings and burnt offerings; for the offerings on the Sabbaths,

---

10:5
ⁿ1Ch 24:8
10:9
^oNe 12:1
10:16
^pEzr 8:6
10:20
^q1Ch 24:15
10:23
^rNe 7:2
10:28
^sPs 135:1
^t2Ch 6:26;
Ne 9:2
10:29
^uNu 5:21;
Ps 119:106
10:30
^vEx 34:16;
Dt 7:3;
Ne 13:23
10:31
^wNe 13:16,18;
Jer 17:27;
Eze 23:38;
Am 8:5
^xEx 23:11;
Lev 25:1-7
^yDt 15:1
10:33
^zLev 24:6

---

^a32 That is, about 1/8 ounce (about 4 grams)

New Moon[a] festivals and appointed feasts; for the holy offerings; for sin offerings to make atonement for Israel; and for all the duties of the house of our God. [b]

34"We—the priests, the Levites and the people—have cast lots[c] to determine when each of our families is to bring to the house of our God at set times each year a contribution of wood[d] to burn on the altar of the LORD our God, as it is written in the Law.

35"We also assume responsibility for bringing to the house of the LORD each year the firstfruits[e] of our crops and of every fruit tree. [f]

36"As it is also written in the Law, we will bring the firstborn[g] of our sons and of our cattle, of our herds and of our flocks to the house of our God, to the priests ministering there. [h]

37"Moreover, we will bring to the storerooms of the house of our God, to the priests, the first of our ground meal, of our grain offerings, of the fruit of all our trees and of our new wine and oil. [i] And we will bring a tithe[j] of our crops to the Levites, [k] for it is the Levites who collect the tithes in all the towns where we work. [l] 38A priest descended from Aaron is to accompany the Levites when they receive the tithes, and the Levites are to bring a tenth of the tithes[m] up to the house of our God, to the storerooms of the treasury. 39The people of Israel, including the Levites, are to bring their contributions of grain, new wine and oil to the storerooms where the articles for the sanctuary are kept and where the ministering priests, the gatekeepers and the singers stay.

"We will not neglect the house of our God."[n]

The New Residents of Jerusalem

11:3–19pp — 1Ch 9:1–17

11 Now the leaders of the people settled in Jerusalem, and the rest of the people cast lots to bring one out of every ten to live in Jerusalem,[o] the holy city,[p] while the remaining nine were to stay in their own towns.[q] 2The people commended all the men who volunteered to live in Jerusalem.

3These are the provincial leaders who settled in Jerusalem (now some Israelites, priests, Levites, temple servants and descendants of Solomon's servants lived in the towns of Judah, each on his own property in the various towns,[r] 4while other people from both Judah and Benjamin[s] lived in Jerusalem):[t]

From the descendants of Judah:

Athaiah son of Uzziah, the son of Zechariah, the son of Amariah, the son of Shephatiah, the son of Mahalalel, a descendant of Perez; 5and Maaseiah son of Baruch, the son of Col-Hozeh, the son of Hazaiah, the son of Adaiah, the son of Joiarib, the son of Zechariah, a descendant of Shelah. 6The descendants of Perez who lived in Jerusalem totaled 468 able men.

7From the descendants of Benjamin:

Sallu son of Meshullam, the son of Joed, the son of Pedaiah, the son of Kolaiah, the son of Maaseiah, the son of Ithiel, the son of Jeshaiah, 8and his followers, Gabbai and Sallai—928 men.

10:33
a Nu 10:10;
Ps 81:3;
Isa 1:14
b 2Ch 24:5
10:34
c Lev 16:8
d Ne 13:31
10:35
e Ex 22:29;
23:19; Nu 18:12
f Dt 26:1-11
10:36
g Ex 13:2;
Nu 18:14-16
h Ne 13:31
10:37
i Lev 23:17;
Nu 18:12
j Lev 27:30;
Nu 18:21
k Dt 14:22-29
l Eze 44:30
10:38
m Nu 18:26
10:39
n Dt 12:6;
Ne 13:11,12
11:1
o Ne 7:4
p ver 18;
Isa 48:2; 52:1;
64:10;
Zec 14:20-21
q Ne 7:73
11:3
r 1Ch 9:2-3;
Ezr 2:1
11:4
s Ezr 1:5
t Ezr 2:70

⁹Joel son of Zicri was their chief officer, and Judah son of Hassenuah was over the Second District of the city.

¹⁰From the priests:

Jedaiah; the son of Joiarib; Jakin; ¹¹Seraiah[u] son of Hilkiah, the son of Meshullam, the son of Zadok, the son of Meraioth, the son of Ahitub,[v] supervisor in the house of God, ¹²and their associates, who carried on work for the temple—822 men; Adaiah son of Jeroham, the son of Pelaliah, the son of Amzi, the son of Zechariah, the son of Pashhur, the son of Malkijah, ¹³and his associates, who were heads of families—242 men; Amashsai son of Azarel, the son of Ahzai, the son of Meshillemoth, the son of Immer, ¹⁴and his[a] associates, who were able men—128. Their chief officer was Zabdiel son of Haggedolim.

¹⁵From the Levites:

Shemaiah son of Hasshub, the son of Azrikam, the son of Hashabiah, the son of Bunni; ¹⁶Shabbethai[w] and Jozabad,[x] two of the heads of the Levites, who had charge of the outside work of the house of God; ¹⁷Mattaniah[y] son of Mica, the son of Zabdi, the son of Asaph,[z] the director who led in thanksgiving and prayer; Bakbukiah, second among his associates; and Abda son of Shammua, the son of Galal, the son of Jeduthun.[a] ¹⁸The Levites in the holy city[b] totaled 284.

¹⁹The gatekeepers:

Akkub, Talmon and their associates, who kept watch at the gates—172 men.

²⁰The rest of the Israelites, with the priests and Levites, were in all the towns of Judah, each on his ancestral property.

²¹The temple servants[c] lived on the hill of Ophel, and Ziha and Gishpa were in charge of them.

²²The chief officer of the Levites in Jerusalem was Uzzi son of Bani, the son of Hashabiah, the son of Mattaniah,[d] the son of Mica. Uzzi was one of Asaph's descendants, who were the singers responsible for the service of the house of God. ²³The singers[e] were under the king's orders, which regulated their daily activity.

²⁴Pethahiah son of Meshezabel, one of the descendants of Zerah[f] son of Judah, was the king's agent in all affairs relating to the people.

²⁵As for the villages with their fields, some of the people of Judah lived in Kiriath Arba[g] and its surrounding settlements, in Dibon[h] and its settlements, in Jekabzeel and its villages, ²⁶in Jeshua, in Moladah, in Beth Pelet,[i] ²⁷in Hazar Shual, in Beersheba[j] and its settlements, ²⁸in Ziklag,[k] in Meconah and its settlements, ²⁹in En Rimmon, in Zorah,[l] in Jarmuth,[m] ³⁰Zanoah, Adullam[n] and their villages, in Lachish[o] and its fields, and in Azekah[p] and its settlements. So they were living all the way from Beersheba[q] to the Valley of Hinnom.

³¹The descendants of the Benjamites from Geba[r] lived in Micmash,[s] Aija, Bethel and its settlements, ³²in Anathoth,[t] Nob[u] and Ananiah,

11:11
u 2Ki 25:18;
Ezr 2:2 v Ezr 7:2
11:16
w Ezr 10:15
x Ezr 8:33
11:17
y 1Ch 9:15;
Ne 12:8
z 2Ch 5:12
a 1Ch 25:1
11:18
b Rev 21:2
11:21
c Ezr 2:43;
Ne 3:26
11:22
d 1Ch 9:15
11:23
e Ne 7:44
11:24
f Ge 38:30
11:25
g Ge 35:27;
Jos 14:15
h Nu 21:30
11:26
i Jos 15:27
11:27
j Ge 21:14
11:28
k 1Sa 27:6
11:29
l Jos 15:33
m Jos 10:3
11:30
n Jos 15:35
o Jos 10:3
p Jos 10:10
q Jos 15:28
11:31
r Jos 21:17;
Isa 10:29
s 1Sa 13:2
11:32
t Jos 21:18;
Isa 10:30
u 1Sa 21:1

a 14 Most Septuagint manuscripts; Hebrew their

³³in Hazor,ᵛ Ramah and Gittaim,ʷ ³⁴in Hadid, Zeboimˣ and Neballat, ³⁵in Lod and Ono,ʸ and in the Valley of the Craftsmen.

³⁶Some of the divisions of the Levites of Judah settled in Benjamin.

Priests and Levites

12 These were the priestsᶻ and Levites who returned with Zerubbabelᵃ son of Shealtiel and with Jeshua:ᵇ

Seraiah,ᶜ Jeremiah, Ezra,

²Amariah, Malluch, Hattush,

³Shecaniah, Rehum, Meremoth,

⁴Iddo,ᵈ Ginnethon,ᵃ Abijah,ᵉ

⁵Mijamin,ᵇ Moadiah, Bilgah,

⁶Shemaiah, Joiarib, Jedaiah,ᶠ

⁷Sallu, Amok, Hilkiah and Jedaiah.

These were the leaders of the priests and their associates in the days of Jeshua.

⁸The Levites were Jeshua, Binnui, Kadmiel, Sherebiah, Judah, and also Mattaniah,ᵍ who, together with his associates, was in charge of the songs of thanksgiving. ⁹Bakbukiah and Unni, their associates, stood opposite them in the services.

¹⁰Jeshua was the father of Joiakim, Joiakim the father of Eliashib,ʰ Eliashib the father of Joiada, ¹¹Joiada the father of Jonathan, and Jonathan the father of Jaddua.

¹²In the days of Joiakim, these were the heads of the priestly families:

of Seraiah's family, Meraiah;

of Jeremiah's, Hananiah;

¹³of Ezra's, Meshullam;

of Amariah's, Jehohanan;

¹⁴of Malluch's, Jonathan;

of Shecaniah's,ᶜ Joseph;

¹⁵of Harim's, Adna;

of Meremoth's,ᵈ Helkai;

¹⁶of Iddo's,ⁱ Zechariah;

of Ginnethon's, Meshullam;

¹⁷of Abijah's, Zicri;

of Miniamin's and of Moadiah's, Piltai;

¹⁸of Bilgah's, Shammua;

of Shemaiah's, Jehonathan;

¹⁹of Joiarib's, Mattenai;

of Jedaiah's, Uzzi;

²⁰of Sallu's, Kallai;

of Amok's, Eber;

²¹of Hilkiah's, Hashabiah;

of Jedaiah's, Nethanel.

²²The family heads of the Levites in the days of Eliashib, Joiada, Johanan and Jaddua, as well as those of the priests, were recorded in the reign of Darius the Persian. ²³The family heads among the descendants of Levi up to the time of Johanan son of Eliashib were recorded in

11:33
vJos 11:1
w2Sa 4:3
11:34
x1Sa 13:18
11:35
y1Ch 8:12
12:1
zNe 10:1-8
a1Ch 3:19
bEzr 2:2
cEzr 2:2
12:4
dZec 1:1
eLk 1:5
12:6
f1Ch 24:7
12:8
gNe 11:17
12:10
hEzr 10:24
12:16
iver 4

ᵃ4 Many Hebrew manuscripts and Vulgate (see also Neh. 12:16); most Hebrew manuscripts *Ginnethoi*　　ᵇ5 A variant of *Miniamin*　　ᶜ14 Very many Hebrew manuscripts, some Septuagint manuscripts and Syriac (see also Neh. 12:3); most Hebrew manuscripts *Shebaniah's*　　ᵈ15 Some Septuagint manuscripts (see also Neh. 12:3); Hebrew *Meraioth's* the book of the annals. 24And the leaders of the Levites[j] were Hashabiah, Sherebiah, Jeshua son of Kadmiel, and their associates, who stood opposite them to give praise and thanksgiving, one section responding to the other, as prescribed by David the man of God.

25Mattaniah, Bakbukiah, Obadiah, Meshullam, Talmon and Akkub were gatekeepers who guarded the storerooms at the gates. 26They served in the days of Joiakim son of Jeshua, the son of Jozadak, and in the days of Nehemiah the governor and of Ezra the priest and scribe.

Dedication of the Wall of Jerusalem

27At the dedication[k] of the wall of Jerusalem, the Levites were sought out from where they lived and were brought to Jerusalem to celebrate joyfully the dedication with songs of thanksgiving and with the music of cymbals,[l] harps and lyres. [m] 28The singers also were brought together from the region around Jerusalem—from the villages of the Netophathites,[n] 29from Beth Gilgal, and from the area of Geba and Azmaveth, for the singers had built villages for themselves around Jerusalem. 30When the priests and Levites had purified themselves ceremonially, they purified the people,[o] the gates and the wall.

31I had the leaders of Judah go up on top[a] of the wall. I also assigned two large choirs to give thanks. One was to proceed on top[b] of the wall to the right, toward the Dung Gate. [p] 32Hoshaiah and half the leaders of Judah followed them, 33along with Azariah, Ezra, Meshullam, 34Judah, Benjamin, [q] Shemaiah, Jeremiah, 35as well as some priests with trumpets,[r] and also Zechariah son of Jonathan, the son of Shemaiah, the son of Mattaniah, the son of Micaiah, the son of Zaccur, the son of Asaph, 36and his associates—Shemaiah, Azarel, Milalai, Gilalai, Maai, Nethanel, Judah and Hanani—with musical instruments[s] prescribed by David the man of God. [t] Ezra[u] the scribe led the procession. 37At the Fountain Gate[v] they continued directly up the steps of the City of David on the ascent to the wall and passed above the house of David to the Water Gate[w] on the east.

38The second choir proceeded in the opposite direction. I followed them on top[c] of the wall, together with half the people—past the Tower of the Ovens[x] to the Broad Wall,[y] 39over the Gate of Ephraim,[z] the Jeshanah[d] Gate,[a] the Fish Gate,[b] the Tower of Hananel[c] and the Tower of the Hundred,[d] as far as the Sheep Gate.[e] At the Gate of the Guard they stopped.

40The two choirs that gave thanks then took their places in the house of God; so did I, together with half the officials, 41as well as the priests—Eliakim, Maaseiah, Miniamin, Micaiah, Elioenai, Zechariah and Hananiah with their trumpets— 42and also Maaseiah, Shemaiah, Eleazar, Uzzi, Jehohanan, Malkijah, Elam and Ezer. The choirs sang under the direction of Jezrahiah. 43And on that day they offered great sacrifices, rejoicing because God had given them great joy. The women and children also rejoiced. The sound of rejoicing in Jerusalem could be heard far away.

44At that time men were appointed to be in charge of the storerooms[f] for the contributions, firstfruits and tithes.[g] From the fields around the towns they were to bring into the storerooms the portions required by

12:24
jEzr 2:40
12:27
kDt 20:5
l2Sa 6:5
m1Ch 15:16,28;
25:6; Ps 92:3
12:28
n1Ch 2:54; 9:16
12:30
oEx 19:10;
Job 1:5
12:31
pNe 2:13
12:34
qEzr 1:5
12:35
rEzr 3:10
12:36
s1Ch 15:16
t2Ch 8:14
uEzr 7:6
12:37
vNe 2:14; 3:15
wNe 3:26
12:38
xNe 3:11
yNe 3:8
12:39
z2Ki 14:13;
Ne 8:16 aNe 3:6
b2Ch 33:14;
Ne 3:3 cNe 3:1
dNe 3:1
eNe 3:1
12:44
fNe 13:4,13
gLev 27:30

---

[a]31 Or *go alongside*   [b]31 Or *proceed alongside*   [c]38 Or *them alongside*   [d]39 Or *Old*

the Law for the priests and the Levites, for Judah was pleased with the ministering priests and Levites.[h] [45]They performed the service of their God and the service of purification, as did also the singers and gatekeepers, according to the commands of David[i] and his son Solomon.[j] [46]For long ago, in the days of David and Asaph,[k] there had been directors for the singers and for the songs of praise[l] and thanksgiving to God. [47]So in the days of Zerubbabel and of Nehemiah, all Israel contributed the daily portions for the singers and gatekeepers. They also set aside the portion for the other Levites, and the Levites set aside the portion for the descendants of Aaron.[m]

Nehemiah's Final Reforms

13 On that day the Book of Moses was read aloud in the hearing of the people and there it was found written that no Ammonite or Moabite should ever be admitted into the assembly of God,[n] [2]because they had not met the Israelites with food and water but had hired Balaam[o] to call a curse down on them.[p] (Our God, however, turned the curse into a blessing.)[q] [3]When the people heard this law, they excluded from Israel all who were of foreign descent.[r]

[4]Before this, Eliashib the priest had been put in charge of the storerooms[s] of the house of our God. He was closely associated with Tobiah,[t] [5]and he had provided him with a large room formerly used to store the grain offerings and incense and temple articles, and also the tithes[u] of grain, new wine and oil prescribed for the Levites, singers and gatekeepers, as well as the contributions for the priests.

[6]But while all this was going on, I was not in Jerusalem, for in the thirty-second year of Artaxerxes[v] king of Babylon I had returned to the king. Some time later I asked his permission [7]and came back to Jerusalem. Here I learned about the evil thing Eliashib[w] had done in providing Tobiah a room in the courts of the house of God. [8]I was greatly displeased and threw all Tobiah's household goods out of the room.[x] [9]I gave orders to purify the rooms,[y] and then I put back into them the equipment of the house of God, with the grain offerings and the incense.

[10]I also learned that the portions assigned to the Levites had not been given to them,[z] and that all the Levites and singers responsible for the service had gone back to their own fields. [11]So I rebuked the officials and asked them, "Why is the house of God neglected?"[a] Then I called them together and stationed them at their posts.

[12]All Judah brought the tithes[b] of grain, new wine and oil into the storerooms.[c] [13]I put Shelemiah the priest, Zadok the scribe, and a Levite named Pedaiah in charge of the storerooms and made Hanan son of Zaccur, the son of Mattaniah, their assistant, because these men were considered trustworthy. They were made responsible for distributing the supplies to their brothers.[d]

[14]Remember[e] me for this, O my God, and do not blot out what I have so faithfully done for the house of my God and its services.

[15]In those days I saw men in Judah treading winepresses on the Sabbath and bringing in grain and loading it on donkeys, together with wine, grapes, figs and all other kinds of loads. And they were bringing all this into Jerusalem on the Sabbath.[f] Therefore I warned them

12:44
hDt 18:8
12:45
i1Ch 25:1;
2Ch 8:14
j1Ch 6:31; 23:5
12:46
k2Ch 35:15
l2Ch 29:27;
Ps 137:4
12:47
mNu 18:21;
Dt 18:8
13:1
nver 23; Dt 23:3
13:2
oNu 22:3-11
pNu 23:7;
Dt 23:3
qNu 23:11;
Dt 23:4-5
13:3
rver 23; Ne 9:2
13:4
sNe 12:44
tNe 2:10
13:5
uLev 27:30;
Nu 18:21
13:6
vNe 2:6; 5:14
13:7
wEzr 10:24
13:8
xMt 21:12-13;
Jn 2:13-16
13:9
y1Ch 23:28;
2Ch 29:5
13:10
zDt 12:19
13:11
aNe 10:37-39;
Hag 1:1-9
13:12
b2Ch 31:6
c1Ki 7:51;
Ne 10:37-39;
Mal 3:10
13:13
dNe 12:44;
Ac 6:1-5
13:14
eGe 8:1
13:15
fEx 20:8-11;
34:21;
Dt 5:12-15;
Ne 10:31

against selling food on that day. [16]Men from Tyre who lived in Jerusalem were bringing in fish and all kinds of merchandise and selling them in Jerusalem on the Sabbath[g] to the people of Judah. [17]I rebuked the nobles of Judah and said to them, "What is this wicked thing you are doing—desecrating the Sabbath day? [18]Didn't your forefathers do the same things, so that our God brought all this calamity upon us and upon this city? Now you are stirring up more wrath against Israel by desecrating the Sabbath."[h]

[19]When evening shadows fell on the gates of Jerusalem before the Sabbath,[i] I ordered the doors to be shut and not opened until the Sabbath was over. I stationed some of my own men at the gates so that no load could be brought in on the Sabbath day. [20]Once or twice the merchants and sellers of all kinds of goods spent the night outside Jerusalem. [21]But I warned them and said, "Why do you spend the night by the wall? If you do this again, I will lay hands on you." From that time on they no longer came on the Sabbath. [22]Then I commanded the Levites to purify themselves and go and guard the gates in order to keep the Sabbath day holy.

Remember[j] me for this also, O my God, and show mercy to me according to your great love.

[23]Moreover, in those days I saw men of Judah who had married[k] women from Ashdod, Ammon and Moab.[l] [24]Half of their children spoke the language of Ashdod or the language of one of the other peoples, and did not know how to speak the language of Judah. [25]I rebuked them and called curses down on them. I beat some of the men and pulled out their hair. I made them take an oath[m] in God's name and said: "You are not to give your daughters in marriage to their sons, nor are you to take their daughters in marriage for your sons or for yourselves. [26]Was it not because of marriages like these that Solomon king of Israel sinned? Among the many nations there was no king like him.[n] He was loved by his God,[o] and God made him king over all Israel, but even he was led into sin by foreign women.[p] [27]Must we hear now that you too are doing all this terrible wickedness and are being unfaithful to our God by marrying[q] foreign women?"

[28]One of the sons of Joiada son of Eliashib[r] the high priest was son-in-law to Sanballat[s] the Horonite. And I drove him away from me.

[29]Remember[t] them, O my God, because they defiled the priestly office and the covenant of the priesthood and of the Levites.

[30]So I purified the priests and the Levites of everything foreign,[u] and assigned them duties, each to his own task. [31]I also made provision for contributions of wood[v] at designated times, and for the firstfruits.

Remember[w] me with favor, O my God.

13:16
g Ne 10:31
13:18
h Ne 10:31;
Jer 17:21-23
13:19
i Lev 23:32
13:22
j Ge 8:1;
Ne 12:30
13:23
k Ezr 9:1-2;
Mal 2:11 l ver 1;
Ne 10:30
13:25
m Ezr 10:5
13:26
n 1Ki 3:13;
2Ch 1:12
o 2Sa 12:25
p 1Ki 11:3
13:27
q Ezr 9:14; 10:2
13:28
r Ezr 10:24
s Ne 2:10
13:29
t Ne 6:14
13:30
u Ne 10:30
13:31
v Ne 10:34
w ver 14,22;
Ge 8:1

Esther

Title and Background

This book has the name of its leading character, a beautiful Jewish girl whom King Xerxes of Persia chose to be his queen. The setting is in Susa, the Persian capital during Xerxes' rule (486-465 B.C.).

Author and Date of Writing

We do not know who wrote the book, but it is clear that the author was a Jew, both from the purpose of the book in accounting for the origin of a Jewish festival and from the Jewish nationalism that permeates the story. Many things point to the fact that he was a resident of a Persian city. The earliest date for the book would be shortly after the events narrated, that is, around 460 B.C.; the latest date would be before the Persian empire fell to Greece in 331.

Theme and Message

The central purpose of the author was to record the institution of the annual festival of Purim and to keep alive for later generations the memory of the great deliverance of the Jewish people during the reign of Xerxes. Although the name of God does not appear in the book, his care for his chosen people is clearly shown. Feasting is a prominent theme in Esther (see Outline).

Outline

I. The Feast of Xerxes (1:1-2:18)
II. The Feasts of Esther (2:19-7:10)
III. The Feasts of Purim (8:1-10:3)

Queen Vashti Deposed

1 This is what happened during the time of Xerxes,ᵃᵃ the Xerxes who ruled over 127 provincesᵇ stretching from India to Cushᵇːᶜ ²At that time King Xerxes reigned from his royal throne in the citadel of Susa,ᵈ ³and in the third year of his reign he gave a banquetᵉ for all his nobles and officials. The military leaders of Persia and Media, the princes, and the nobles of the provinces were present.

⁴For a full 180 days he displayed the vast wealth of his kingdom and the splendor and glory of his majesty. ⁵When these days were over, the king gave a banquet, lasting seven days,ᶠ in the enclosed gardenᵍ of the king's palace, for all the people from the least to the greatest, who were in the citadel of Susa. ⁶The garden had hangings of white and blue linen, fastened with cords of white linen and purple material to silver rings on marble pillars. There were couchesʰ of gold and silver on a mosaic pavement of porphyry, marble, mother-of-pearl and other costly stones. ⁷Wine was served in goblets of gold, each one different from

1:1
aEzr 4:6; Da 9:1
bEst 9:30;
Da 3:2; 6:1
cEst 8:9

1:2
dEzr 4:9;
Ne 1:1; Est 2:8

1:3
e1Ki 3:15;
Est 2:18

1:5
fJdg 14:17
g2Ki 21:18;
Est 7:7-8

1:6
hEst 7:8;
Eze 23:41;
Am 3:12; 6:4

ᵃ1 Hebrew Ahasuerus, a variant of Xerxes' name; here and throughout Esther   ᵇ1 That is, the upper Nile region the other, and the royal wine was abundant, in keeping with the king's liberality.[i] [8]By the king's command each guest was allowed to drink in his own way, for the king instructed all the wine stewards to serve each man what he wished.

[9]Queen Vashti also gave a banquet[j] for the women in the royal palace of King Xerxes.

[10]On the seventh day, when King Xerxes was in high spirits[k] from wine,[l] he commanded the seven eunuchs who served him—Mehuman, Biztha, Harbona,[m] Bigtha, Abagtha, Zethar and Carcas— [11]to bring[n] before him Queen Vashti, wearing her royal crown, in order to display her beauty[o] to the people and nobles, for she was lovely to look at. [12]But when the attendants delivered the king's command, Queen Vashti refused to come. Then the king became furious and burned with anger.[p]

[13]Since it was customary for the king to consult experts in matters of law and justice, he spoke with the wise men who understood the times[q] [14]and were closest to the king—Carshena, Shethar, Admatha, Tarshish, Meres, Marsena and Memucan, the seven nobles[r] of Persia and Media who had special access to the king and were highest in the kingdom.

[15]"According to law, what must be done to Queen Vashti?" he asked. "She has not obeyed the command of King Xerxes that the eunuchs have taken to her."

[16]Then Memucan replied in the presence of the king and the nobles, "Queen Vashti has done wrong, not only against the king but also against all the nobles and the peoples of all the provinces of King Xerxes. [17]For the queen's conduct will become known to all the women, and so they will despise their husbands and say, 'King Xerxes commanded Queen Vashti to be brought before him, but she would not come.' [18]This very day the Persian and Median women of the nobility who have heard about the queen's conduct will respond to all the king's nobles in the same way. There will be no end of disrespect and discord.[s]

[19]"Therefore, if it pleases the king,[t] let him issue a royal decree and let it be written in the laws of Persia and Media, which cannot be repealed,[u] that Vashti is never again to enter the presence of King Xerxes. Also let the king give her royal position to someone else who is better than she. [20]Then when the king's edict is proclaimed throughout all his vast realm, all the women will respect their husbands, from the least to the greatest."

[21]The king and his nobles were pleased with this advice, so the king did as Memucan proposed. [22]He sent dispatches to all parts of the kingdom, to each province in its own script and to each people in its own language,[v] proclaiming in each people's tongue that every man should be ruler over his own household.

Esther Made Queen

2 Later when the anger of King Xerxes had subsided,[w] he remembered Vashti and what she had done and what he had decreed about her. [2]Then the king's personal attendants proposed, "Let a search be made for beautiful young virgins for the king. [3]Let the king appoint commissioners in every province of his realm to bring all these

1:7
[i]Est 2:18;
Da 5:2

1:9
[j]1Ki 3:15

1:10
[k]Jdg 16:25;
Ru 3:7
[l]Ge 14:18;
Est 3:15; 5:6;
7:2; Pr 31:4-7;
Da 5:1-4
[m]Est 7:9

1:11
[n]SS 2:4
[o]Ps 45:11;
Eze 16:14

1:12
[p]Ge 39:19;
Est 2:21; 7:7;
Pr 19:12

1:13
[q]1Ch 12:32;
Jer 10:7;
Da 2:12

1:14
[r]2Ki 25:19;
Ezr 7:14

1:18
[s]Pr 19:13; 27:15

1:19
[t]Ecc 8:4
[u]Est 8:8;
Da 6:8,12

1:22
[v]Ne 13:24;
Est 8:9;
Eph 5:22-24;
1Ti 2:12

2:1
[w]Est 1:19-20;
7:10

beautiful girls into the harem at the citadel of Susa. Let them be placed under the care of Hegai, the king's eunuch, who is in charge of the women; and let beauty treatments be given to them. [4]Then let the girl who pleases the king be queen instead of Vashti." This advice appealed to the king, and he followed it.

[5]Now there was in the citadel of Susa a Jew of the tribe of Benjamin, named Mordecai son of Jair, the son of Shimei, the son of Kish,[x] [6]who had been carried into exile from Jerusalem by Nebuchadnezzar king of Babylon, among those taken captive with Jehoiachin[a][y] king of Judah.[z] [7]Mordecai had a cousin named Hadassah, whom he had brought up because she had neither father nor mother. This girl, who was also known as Esther,[a] was lovely[b] in form and features, and Mordecai had taken her as his own daughter when her father and mother died.

[8]When the king's order and edict had been proclaimed, many girls were brought to the citadel of Susa[c] and put under the care of Hegai. Esther also was taken to the king's palace and entrusted to Hegai, who had charge of the harem. [9]The girl pleased him and won his favor.[d] Immediately he provided her with her beauty treatments and special food.[e] He assigned to her seven maids selected from the king's palace and moved her and her maids into the best place in the harem.

[10]Esther had not revealed her nationality and family background, because Mordecai had forbidden her to do so.[f] [11]Every day he walked back and forth near the courtyard of the harem to find out how Esther was and what was happening to her.

[12]Before a girl's turn came to go in to King Xerxes, she had to complete twelve months of beauty treatments prescribed for the women, six months with oil of myrrh and six with perfumes[g] and cosmetics. [13]And this is how she would go to the king: Anything she wanted was given her to take with her from the harem to the king's palace. [14]In the evening she would go there and in the morning return to another part of the harem to the care of Shaashgaz, the king's eunuch who was in charge of the concubines.[h] She would not return to the king unless he was pleased with her and summoned her by name.[i]

[15]When the turn came for Esther (the girl Mordecai had adopted, the daughter of his uncle Abihail[j]) to go to the king,[k] she asked for nothing other than what Hegai, the king's eunuch who was in charge of the harem, suggested. And Esther won the favor[l] of everyone who saw her. [16]She was taken to King Xerxes in the royal residence in the tenth month, the month of Tebeth, in the seventh year of his reign.

[17]Now the king was attracted to Esther more than to any of the other women, and she won his favor and approval more than any of the other virgins. So he set a royal crown on her head and made her queen[m] instead of Vashti. [18]And the king gave a great banquet,[n] Esther's banquet, for all his nobles and officials.[o] He proclaimed a holiday throughout the provinces and distributed gifts with royal liberality.[p]

Mordecai Uncovers a Conspiracy

[19]When the virgins were assembled a second time, Mordecai was sitting at the king's gate.[q] [20]But Esther had kept secret her family background and nationality just as Mordecai had told her to do, for she

---

2:5
x1Sa 9:1;
Est 3:2

2:6
y2Ki 24:6,15;
2Ch 36:10,20
zDa 1:1-5; 5:13

2:7
aGe 41:45
bGe 39:6

2:8
cver 3,15;
Ne 1:1; Est 1:2;
Da 8:2

2:9
dGe 39:21
ever 3,12;
Ge 37:3;
1Sa 9:22-24;
2Ki 25:30;
Eze 16:9-13;
Da 1:5

2:10
fver 20

2:12
gPr 27:9;
SS 1:3; Isa 3:24

2:14
h1Ki 11:3;
SS 6:8; Da 5:2
iEst 4:11

2:15
jEst 9:29
kPs 45:14
lGe 18:3;
30:27; Est 5:8

2:17
mEst 1:11;
Eze 16:9-13

2:18
n1Ki 3:15;
Est 1:3
oGe 40:20
pEst 1:7

2:19
qver 21;
Est 3:2; 4:2;
5:13

---

[a]6 Hebrew *Jeconiah*, a variant of *Jehoiachin*

continued to follow Mordecai's instructions as she had done when he was bringing her up. [r]

[21]During the time Mordecai was sitting at the king's gate, Bigthana[a] and Teresh, two of the king's officers[s] who guarded the doorway, became angry[t] and conspired to assassinate King Xerxes. [22]But Mordecai found out about the plot and told Queen Esther, who in turn reported it to the king, giving credit to Mordecai. [23]And when the report was investigated and found to be true, the two officials were hanged[u] on a gallows. [b] All this was recorded in the book of the annals[v] in the presence of the king.

Haman's Plot to Destroy the Jews

3 After these events, King Xerxes honored Haman son of Hammedatha, the Agagite,[w] elevating him and giving him a seat of honor higher than that of all the other nobles. [2]All the royal officials at the king's gate knelt down and paid honor to Haman, for the king had commanded this concerning him. But Mordecai would not kneel down or pay him honor.

[3]Then the royal officials at the king's gate asked Mordecai, "Why do you disobey the king's command?"[x] [4]Day after day they spoke to him but he refused to comply. [y] Therefore they told Haman about it to see whether Mordecai's behavior would be tolerated, for he had told them he was a Jew.

[5]When Haman saw that Mordecai would not kneel down or pay him honor, he was enraged. [z] [6]Yet having learned who Mordecai's people were, he scorned the idea of killing only Mordecai. Instead Haman looked for a way[a] to destroy[b] all Mordecai's people, the Jews,[c] throughout the whole kingdom of Xerxes.

[7]In the twelfth year of King Xerxes, in the first month, the month of Nisan, they cast the *pur*[d] (that is, the lot[e]) in the presence of Haman to select a day and month. And the lot fell on[c] the twelfth month, the month of Adar. [f]

[8]Then Haman said to King Xerxes, "There is a certain people dispersed and scattered among the peoples in all the provinces of your kingdom whose customs[g] are different from those of all other people and who do not obey[h] the king's laws; it is not in the king's best interest to tolerate them. [i] [9]If it pleases the king, let a decree be issued to destroy them, and I will put ten thousand talents[d] of silver into the royal treasury for the men who carry out this business."[j]

[10]So the king took his signet ring[k] from his finger and gave it to Haman son of Hammedatha, the Agagite, the enemy of the Jews. [11]"Keep the money," the king said to Haman, "and do with the people as you please."

[12]Then on the thirteenth day of the first month the royal secretaries were summoned. They wrote out in the script of each province and in the language[l] of each people all Haman's orders to the king's satraps, the governors of the various provinces and the nobles of the various peoples. These were written in the name of King Xerxes himself and

2:20
rver 10
2:21
sGe 40:2;
Est 6:2
tEst 1:12; 3:5;
5:9; 7:7
2:23
uGe 40:19;
Ps 7:14-16;
Pr 26:27
vEst 6:1; 10:2
3:1
wver 10;
Ex 17:8-16;
Nu 24:7;
Dt 25:17-19;
1Sa 14:48;
Est 5:11
3:3
xEst 5:9;
Da 3:12
3:4
yGe 39:10
3:5
zEst 2:21; 5:9
3:6
aPr 16:25
bPs 74:8; 83:4
cEst 9:24
3:7
dEst 9:24,26
eLev 16:8;
1Sa 10:21
fver 13;
Ezr 6:15;
Est 9:19
3:8
gAc 16:20-21
hJer 29:7;
Da 6:13
iEzr 4:15
3:9
jEst 7:4
3:10
kGe 41:42;
Est 7:6; 8:2
3:12
lNe 13:24

---

[a]21 Hebrew *Bigthan*, a variant of *Bigthana*   [b]23 Or *were hung* (or *impaled*) *on poles*; similarly elsewhere in Esther   [c]7 Septuagint; Hebrew does not have *And the lot fell on.*   [d]9 That is, about 375 tons (about 345 metric tons)

sealed[m] with his own ring. [13]Dispatches were sent by couriers to all the king's provinces with the order to destroy, kill and annihilate all the Jews[n]—young and old, women and little children—on a single day, the thirteenth day of the twelfth month, the month of Adar,[o] and to plunder[p] their goods. [14]A copy of the text of the edict was to be issued as law in every province and made known to the people of every nationality so they would be ready for that day.[q]

[15]Spurred on by the king's command, the couriers went out, and the edict was issued in the citadel of Susa.[r] The king and Haman sat down to drink,[s] but the city of Susa was bewildered.[t]

Mordecai Persuades Esther to Help

4 When Mordecai learned of all that had been done, he tore his clothes,[u] put on sackcloth and ashes,[v] and went out into the city, wailing[w] loudly and bitterly. [2]But he went only as far as the king's gate,[x] because no one clothed in sackcloth was allowed to enter it. [3]In every province to which the edict and order of the king came, there was great mourning among the Jews, with fasting, weeping and wailing. Many lay in sackcloth and ashes.

[4]When Esther's maids and eunuchs came and told her about Mordecai, she was in great distress. She sent clothes for him to put on instead of his sackcloth, but he would not accept them. [5]Then Esther summoned Hathach, one of the king's eunuchs assigned to attend her, and ordered him to find out what was troubling Mordecai and why.

[6]So Hathach went out to Mordecai in the open square of the city in front of the king's gate. [7]Mordecai told him everything that had happened to him, including the exact amount of money Haman had promised to pay into the royal treasury for the destruction of the Jews.[y] [8]He also gave him a copy of the text of the edict for their annihilation, which had been published in Susa, to show to Esther and explain it to her, and he told him to urge her to go into the king's presence to beg for mercy and plead with him for her people.

[9]Hathach went back and reported to Esther what Mordecai had said. [10]Then she instructed him to say to Mordecai, [11]"All the king's officials and the people of the royal provinces know that for any man or woman who approaches the king in the inner court without being summoned[z] the king has but one law:[a] that he be put to death. The only exception to this is for the king to extend the gold scepter[b] to him and spare his life. But thirty days have passed since I was called to go to the king."

[12]When Esther's words were reported to Mordecai, [13]he sent back this answer: "Do not think that because you are in the king's house you alone of all the Jews will escape. [14]For if you remain silent[c] at this time, relief[d] and deliverance[e] for the Jews will arise from another place, but you and your father's family will perish. And who knows but that you have come to royal position for such a time as this?"[f]

[15]Then Esther sent this reply to Mordecai: [16]"Go, gather together all the Jews who are in Susa, and fast[g] for me. Do not eat or drink for three days, night or day. I and my maids will fast as you do. When this is done, I will go to the king, even though it is against the law. And if I perish, I perish."[h]

[17]So Mordecai went away and carried out all of Esther's instructions.

3:12
m Ge 38:18;
1Ki 21:8;
Est 8:8-10
3:13
n 1Sa 15:3;
Ezr 4:6;
Est 8:10-14
o ver 7
p Est 8:11; 9:10
3:14
q Est 8:8; 9:1
3:15
r Est 8:14
s Est 1:10
t Est 8:15
4:1
u Nu 14:6
v 2Sa 13:19;
Eze 27:30-31;
Jnh 3:5-6
w Ex 11:6;
Ps 30:11
4:2
x Est 2:19
4:7
y Est 3:9; 7:4
4:11
z Est 2:14
a Da 2:9
b Est 5:1,2; 8:4
4:14
c Ecc 3:7;
Isa 62:1;
Am 5:13
d Est 9:16,22
e Ge 45:7;
Dt 28:29
f Ge 50:20
4:16
g 2Ch 20:3;
Est 9:31
h Ge 43:14

Esther's Request to the King

5 On the third day Esther put on her royal robes[i] and stood in the inner court of the palace, in front of the king's[j] hall. The king was sitting on his royal throne in the hall, facing the entrance. [2]When he saw Queen Esther standing in the court, he was pleased with her and held out to her the gold scepter that was in his hand. So Esther approached and touched the tip of the scepter.[k]

[3]Then the king asked, "What is it, Queen Esther? What is your request? Even up to half the kingdom,[l] it will be given you."

[4]"If it pleases the king," replied Esther, "let the king, together with Haman, come today to a banquet I have prepared for him."

[5]"Bring Haman at once," the king said, "so that we may do what Esther asks."

So the king and Haman went to the banquet Esther had prepared. [6]As they were drinking wine,[m] the king again asked Esther, "Now what is your petition? It will be given you. And what is your request? Even up to half the kingdom,[n] it will be granted."[o]

[7]Esther replied, "My petition and my request is this: [8]If the king regards me with favor[p] and if it pleases the king to grant my petition and fulfill my request, let the king and Haman come tomorrow to the banquet[q] I will prepare for them. Then I will answer the king's question."

Haman's Rage Against Mordecai

[9]Haman went out that day happy and in high spirits. But when he saw Mordecai at the king's gate and observed that he neither rose nor showed fear in his presence, he was filled with rage[r] against Mordecai.[s] [10]Nevertheless, Haman restrained himself and went home.

Calling together his friends and Zeresh,[t] his wife, [11]Haman boasted[u] to them about his vast wealth, his many sons,[v] and all the ways the king had honored him and how he had elevated him above the other nobles and officials. [12]"And that's not all," Haman added. "I'm the only person[w] Queen Esther invited to accompany the king to the banquet she gave. And she has invited me along with the king tomorrow. [13]But all this gives me no satisfaction as long as I see that Jew Mordecai sitting at the king's gate.[x]"

[14]His wife Zeresh and all his friends said to him, "Have a gallows built, seventy-five feet[a] high,[y] and ask the king in the morning to have Mordecai hanged[z] on it. Then go with the king to the dinner and be happy." This suggestion delighted Haman, and he had the gallows built.

Mordecai Honored

6 That night the king could not sleep;[a] so he ordered the book of the chronicles,[b] the record of his reign, to be brought in and read to him. [2]It was found recorded there that Mordecai had exposed Bigthana and Teresh, two of the king's officers who guarded the doorway, who had conspired to assassinate King Xerxes.

---

[a]14 Hebrew *fifty cubits* (about 23 meters)

5:1
iEst 4:16;
Eze 16:13
jEst 6:4; Pr 21:1
5:2
kEst 4:11; 8:4;
Pr 21:1
5:3
lEst 7:2;
Da 5:16;
Mk 6:23
5:6
mEst 1:10
nMk 6:23
oEst 7:2; 9:12
5:8
pEst 2:15; 7:3;
8:5 q1Ki 3:15;
Est 6:14
5:9
rEst 2:21;
Pr 14:17
sEst 3:3,5
5:10
tEst 6:13
5:11
uPr 13:16
vEst 9:7-10,13
5:12
wJob 22:29;
Pr 16:18; 29:23
5:13
xEst 2:19
5:14
yEst 7:9
zEzr 6:11;
Est 6:4
6:1
aDa 2:1; 6:18
bEst 2:23; 10:2

³"What honor and recognition has Mordecai received for this?" the king asked.

"Nothing has been done for him,"ᶜ his attendants answered.

⁴The king said, "Who is in the court?" Now Haman had just entered the outer court of the palace to speak to the king about hanging Mordecai on the gallows he had erected for him.

⁵His attendants answered, "Haman is standing in the court."

"Bring him in," the king ordered.

⁶When Haman entered, the king asked him, "What should be done for the man the king delights to honor?"

Now Haman thought to himself, "Who is there that the king would rather honor than me?" ⁷So he answered the king, "For the man the king delights to honor, ⁸have them bring a royal robeᵈ the king has worn and a horseᵉ the king has ridden, one with a royal crest placed on its head. ⁹Then let the robe and horse be entrusted to one of the king's most noble princes. Let them robe the man the king delights to honor, and lead him on the horse through the city streets, proclaiming before him, 'This is what is done for the man the king delights to honor!'"

¹⁰"Go at once," the king commanded Haman. "Get the robe and the horse and do just as you have suggested for Mordecai the Jew, who sits at the king's gate. Do not neglect anything you have recommended."

¹¹So Haman gotᵍ the robe and the horse. He robed Mordecai, and led him on horseback through the city streets, proclaiming before him, "This is what is done for the man the king delights to honor!"

¹²Afterward Mordecai returned to the king's gate. But Haman rushed home, with his head coveredʰ in grief, ¹³and told Zereshⁱ his wife and all his friends everything that had happened to him.

His advisers and his wife Zeresh said to him, "Since Mordecai, before whom your downfallʲ has started, is of Jewish origin, you cannot stand against him—you will surely come to ruin!" ¹⁴While they were still talking with him, the king's eunuchs arrived and hurried Haman away to the banquetᵏ Esther had prepared.

Haman Hanged

7 So the king and Haman went to dineˡ with Queen Esther, ²and as they were drinking wineᵐ on that second day, the king again asked, "Queen Esther, what is your petition? It will be given you. What is your request? Even up to half the kingdom,ⁿ it will be granted.ᵒ"

³Then Queen Esther answered, "If I have found favorᵖ with you, O king, and if it pleases your majesty, grant me my life—this is my petition. And spare my people—this is my request. ⁴For I and my people have been sold for destruction and slaughter and annihilation.�q If we had merely been sold as male and female slaves, I would have kept quiet, because no such distress would justify disturbing the king.ᵃ"

⁵King Xerxes asked Queen Esther, "Who is he? Where is the man who has dared to do such a thing?"

⁶Esther said, "The adversary and enemy is this vile Haman."

Then Haman was terrified before the king and queen. ⁷The king got

6:3
c Ecc 9:13-16
6:8
d Ge 41:42;
Isa 52:1
e 1Ki 1:33
6:9
f Ge 41:43
6:11
g Ge 41:42
6:12
h 2Sa 15:30;
Jer 14:3,4;
Mic 3:7
6:13
i Est 5:10
j Ps 57:6;
Pr 26:27; 28:18
6:14
k 1Ki 3:15;
Est 5:8
7:1
l Ge 40:20-22;
Mt 22:1-14
7:2
m Est 1:10
n Est 5:3
o Est 9:12
7:3
p Est 2:15
7:4
q Est 3:9

ᵃ4 Or *quiet, but the compensation our adversary offers cannot be compared with the loss the king would suffer* up in a rage,[r] left his wine and went out into the palace garden.[s] But Haman, realizing that the king had already decided his fate,[t] stayed behind to beg Queen Esther for his life.

8Just as the king returned from the palace garden to the banquet hall, Haman was falling on the couch[u] where Esther was reclining.[v]

The king exclaimed, "Will he even molest the queen while she is with me in the house?"[w]

As soon as the word left the king's mouth, they covered Haman's face.[x] 9Then Harbona,[y] one of the eunuchs attending the king, said, "A gallows seventy-five feet[a] high[z] stands by Haman's house. He had it made for Mordecai, who spoke up to help the king."

The king said, "Hang him on it!"[a] 10So they hanged Haman[b] on the gallows[c] he had prepared for Mordecai.[d] Then the king's fury subsided.[e]

The King's Edict in Behalf of the Jews

8 That same day King Xerxes gave Queen Esther the estate of Haman,[f] the enemy of the Jews. And Mordecai came into the presence of the king, for Esther had told how he was related to her. 2The king took off his signet ring,[g] which he had reclaimed from Haman, and presented it to Mordecai. And Esther appointed him over Haman's estate.[h]

3Esther again pleaded with the king, falling at his feet and weeping. She begged him to put an end to the evil plan of Haman the Agagite, which he had devised against the Jews. 4Then the king extended the gold scepter[i] to Esther and she arose and stood before him.

5"If it pleases the king," she said, "and if he regards me with favor and thinks it the right thing to do, and if he is pleased with me, let an order be written overruling the dispatches that Haman son of Hammedatha, the Agagite, devised and wrote to destroy the Jews in all the king's provinces. 6For how can I bear to see disaster fall on my people? How can I bear to see the destruction of my family?"[j]

7King Xerxes replied to Queen Esther and to Mordecai the Jew, "Because Haman attacked the Jews, I have given his estate to Esther, and they have hanged him on the gallows. 8Now write another decree[k] in the king's name in behalf of the Jews as seems best to you, and seal it with the king's signet ring[l]—for no document written in the king's name and sealed with his ring can be revoked."[m]

9At once the royal secretaries were summoned—on the twenty-third day of the third month, the month of Sivan. They wrote out all Mordecai's orders to the Jews, and to the satraps, governors and nobles of the 127 provinces stretching from India to Cush.[bn] These orders were written in the script of each province and the language of each people and also to the Jews in their own script and language.[o] 10Mordecai wrote in the name of King Xerxes, sealed the dispatches with the king's signet ring, and sent them by mounted couriers, who rode fast horses especially bred for the king.

11The king's edict granted the Jews in every city the right to assemble and protect themselves; to destroy, kill and annihilate any armed force of any nationality or province that might attack them and their women

---

7:7
rGe 34:7;
Est 1:12;
Pr 19:12; 20:1-2
s2Ki 21:18
tEst 6:13

7:8
uEst 1:6
vGe 39:14
wGe 34:7
xEst 6:12

7:9
yEst 1:10
zEst 5:14
aPs 7:14-16;
9:16; Pr 11:5-6;
26:27; Mt 7:2

7:10
bPr 10:28
cEst 9:25
dDa 6:24
eEst 2:1

8:1
fEst 2:7; 7:6;
Pr 22:22-23

8:2
gGe 41:42;
Est 3:10
hPr 13:22;
Da 2:48

8:4
iEst 4:11; 5:2

8:6
jEst 7:4; 9:1

8:8
kEst 3:12-14
lGe 41:42
mEst 1:19;
Da 6:15

8:9
nEst 1:1
oEst 1:22

---

[a]9 Hebrew *fifty cubits* (about 23 meters)   [b]9 That is, the upper Nile region

and children; and to plunder[p] the property of their enemies. [12]The day appointed for the Jews to do this in all the provinces of King Xerxes was the thirteenth day of the twelfth month, the month of Adar. [q] [13]A copy of the text of the edict was to be issued as law in every province and made known to the people of every nationality so that the Jews would be ready on that day[r] to avenge themselves on their enemies.

[14]The couriers, riding the royal horses, raced out, spurred on by the king's command. And the edict was also issued in the citadel of Susa.

[15]Mordecai[s] left the king's presence wearing royal garments of blue and white, a large crown of gold and a purple robe of fine linen. [t] And the city of Susa held a joyous celebration. [u] [16]For the Jews it was a time of happiness and joy, [v] gladness and honor. [w] [17]In every province and in every city, wherever the edict of the king went, there was joy[x] and gladness among the Jews, with feasting and celebrating. And many people of other nationalities became Jews because fear[y] of the Jews had seized them. [z]

Triumph of the Jews

9 On the thirteenth day of the twelfth month, the month of Adar, [a] the edict commanded by the king was to be carried out. On this day the enemies of the Jews had hoped to overpower them, but now the tables were turned and the Jews got the upper hand[b] over those who hated them. [c] [2]The Jews assembled in their cities[d] in all the provinces of King Xerxes to attack those seeking their destruction. No one could stand against them, [e] because the people of all the other nationalities were afraid of them. [3]And all the nobles of the provinces, the satraps, the governors and the king's administrators helped the Jews, [f] because fear of Mordecai had seized them. [4]Mordecai was prominent[g] in the palace; his reputation spread throughout the provinces, and he became more and more powerful. [h]

[5]The Jews struck down all their enemies with the sword, killing and destroying them, [i] and they did what they pleased to those who hated them. [6]In the citadel of Susa, the Jews killed and destroyed five hundred men. [7]They also killed Parshandatha, Dalphon, Aspatha, [8]Poratha, Adalia, Aridatha, [9]Parmashta, Arisai, Aridai and Vaizatha, [10]the ten sons[j] of Haman son of Hammedatha, the enemy of the Jews. But they did not lay their hands on the plunder. [k]

[11]The number of those slain in the citadel of Susa was reported to the king that same day. [12]The king said to Queen Esther, "The Jews have killed and destroyed five hundred men and the ten sons of Haman in the citadel of Susa. What have they done in the rest of the king's provinces? Now what is your petition? It will be given you. What is your request? It will also be granted."[l]

[13]"If it pleases the king," Esther answered, "give the Jews in Susa permission to carry out this day's edict tomorrow also, and let Haman's ten sons[m] be hanged[n] on gallows."

[14]So the king commanded that this be done. An edict was issued in Susa, and they hanged[o] the ten sons of Haman. [15]The Jews in Susa came together on the fourteenth day of the month of Adar, and they put to death in Susa three hundred men, but they did not lay their hands on the plunder. [p]

8:11
pEst 9:10,15,16
8:12
qEst 3:13; 9:1
8:13
rEst 3:14
8:15
sEst 9:4
tGe 41:42
uEst 3:15
8:16
vPs 97:10-12
wPs 112:4
8:17
xEst 9:19,27;
Ps 35:27;
Pr 11:10
yEx 15:14,16;
Dt 11:25
zEst 9:3
9:1
aEst 8:12
bJer 29:4-7
cEst 3:12-14;
Pr 22:22-23
9:2
dver 15-18
eEst 8:11,17;
Ps 71:13,24
9:3
fEzr 8:36
9:4
gEx 11:3
h2Sa 3:1;
1Ch 11:9
9:5
iEzr 4:6
9:10
jEst 5:11
kGe 14:23;
1Sa 14:32;
Est 3:13; 8:11
9:12
lEst 5:6; 7:2
9:13
mEst 5:11
nDt 21:22-23
9:14
oEzr 6:11
9:15
pGe 14:23;
Est 8:11

[16]Meanwhile, the remainder of the Jews who were in the king's provinces also assembled to protect themselves and get relief[q] from their enemies.[r] They killed seventy-five thousand of them[s] but did not lay their hands on the plunder. [17]This happened on the thirteenth day of the month of Adar, and on the fourteenth they rested and made it a day of feasting[t] and joy.

Purim Celebrated

[18]The Jews in Susa, however, had assembled on the thirteenth and fourteenth, and then on the fifteenth they rested and made it a day of feasting and joy.

[19]That is why rural Jews—those living in villages—observe the fourteenth of the month of Adar[u] as a day of joy and feasting, a day for giving presents to each other.[v]

[20]Mordecai recorded these events, and he sent letters to all the Jews throughout the provinces of King Xerxes, near and far, [21]to have them celebrate annually the fourteenth and fifteenth days of the month of Adar [22]as the time when the Jews got relief[w] from their enemies, and as the month when their sorrow was turned into joy and their mourning into a day of celebration.[x] He wrote them to observe the days as days of feasting and joy and giving presents of food[y] to one another and gifts to the poor.

[23]So the Jews agreed to continue the celebration they had begun, doing what Mordecai had written to them. [24]For Haman son of Hammedatha, the Agagite,[z] the enemy of all the Jews, had plotted against the Jews to destroy them and had cast the *pur*[a] (that is, the lot[b]) for their ruin and destruction. [25]But when the plot came to the king's attention,[a] he issued written orders that the evil scheme Haman had devised against the Jews should come back onto his own head,[c] and that he and his sons should be hanged[d] on the gallows.[e] [26](Therefore these days were called Purim, from the word *pur.*[f]) Because of everything written in this letter and because of what they had seen and what had happened to them, [27]the Jews took it upon themselves to establish the custom that they and their descendants and all who join them should without fail observe these two days every year, in the way prescribed and at the time appointed. [28]These days should be remembered and observed in every generation by every family, and in every province and in every city. And these days of Purim should never cease to be celebrated by the Jews, nor should the memory of them die out among their descendants.

[29]So Queen Esther, daughter of Abihail,[g] along with Mordecai the Jew, wrote with full authority to confirm this second letter concerning Purim. [30]And Mordecai sent letters to all the Jews in the 127 provinces[h] of the kingdom of Xerxes—words of goodwill and assurance— [31]to establish these days of Purim at their designated times, as Mordecai the Jew and Queen Esther had decreed for them, and as they had established for themselves and their descendants in regard to their times of fasting[i] and lamentation.[j] [32]Esther's decree confirmed these regulations about Purim, and it was written down in the records.

9:16
q Est 4:14
r Dt 25:19
s 1Ch 4:43
9:17
t 1Ki 3:15
9:19
u Est 3:7
v ver 22;
Dt 16:11,14;
Ne 8:10,12;
Est 2:9;
Rev 11:10
9:22
w Est 4:14
x Ne 8:12;
Ps 30:11-12
y 2Ki 25:30
9:24
z Ex 17:8-16
a Est 3:7
b Lev 16:8
9:25
c Ps 7:16
d Dt 21:22-23
e Est 7:10
9:26
f ver 20; Est 3:7
9:29
g Est 2:15
9:30
h Est 1:1
9:31
i Est 4:16
j Est 4:1-3

---

[a]25 Or *when Esther came before the king*

The Greatness of Mordecai

10 King Xerxes imposed tribute throughout the empire, to its distant shores. [k] [2]And all his acts of power and might, together with a full account of the greatness of Mordecai[1] to which the king had raised him, [m] are they not written in the book of the annals[n] of the kings of Media and Persia? [3]Mordecai the Jew was second[o] in rank[p] to King Xerxes,[q] preeminent among the Jews, and held in high esteem by his many fellow Jews, because he worked for the good of his people and spoke up for the welfare of all the Jews.[r]

10:1
k Ps 72:10;
97:1; Isa 24:15
10:2
l Est 8:15; 9:4
m Ge 41:44
n Est 2:23
10:3
o Da 5:7
p Ge 41:43
q Ge 41:40
r Ne 2:10;
Jer 29:4-7;
Da 6:3

Job

Title and Background

The book of Job is named for its main character, a righteous man who was very rich. Even after losing everything he owned and suffering from a terrible sickness, Job still confessed his trust in God.

Author and Date of Writing

Although most of the book consists of the words of Job and his counselors, Job himself was not the author. We can be sure the author was an Israelite who probably had access to oral and/or written sources from which he composed the book.

Two dates are involved: (1) the date of the man Job and his historical setting, and (2) the date of the inspired writer of the book. The latter could be dated anytime from the reign of Solomon to the exile. The date of the actual events described in this book was most likely between 2000 and 1000 B.C., and probably late in that millennium.

Theme and Message

The book provides a profound statement on the justice of God in light of human suffering. How can the justice of an almighty God be defended in the face of evil, especially human suffering, and even more particularly, the suffering of the innocent? The suffering of the righteous has a meaning and value commensurate with the titanic spiritual struggle of the ages.

Outline

I. Prologue (1:1-2:13)
II. Dialogue—Dispute: Job and His Friends (3:1-27:23)
III. Interlude on Wisdom (28:1-28)
IV. Monologues: Job, Elihu and God (29:1-42:6)
V. Epilogue (42:7-17)

Prologue

1 In the land of Uz[a] there lived a man whose name was Job.[b] This man was blameless[c] and upright; he feared God[d] and shunned evil. ²He had seven sons and three daughters,[e] ³and he owned seven thousand sheep, three thousand camels, five hundred yoke of oxen and five hundred donkeys, and had a large number of servants. He was the greatest man[f] among all the people of the East.

⁴His sons used to take turns holding feasts in their homes, and they would invite their three sisters to eat and drink with them. ⁵When a period of feasting had run its course, Job would send and have them purified. Early in the morning he would sacrifice a burnt offering[g] for each of them, thinking, "Perhaps my children have sinned[h] and cursed God[i] in their hearts." This was Job's regular custom.

1:1
a Jer 25:20
b Eze 14:14,20; Jas 5:11
c Ge 6:9; 17:1
d Ge 22:12; Ex 18:21
1:2
e Job 42:13
1:3
f Job 29:25
1:5
g Ge 8:20; Job 42:8
h Job 8:4
i 1Ki 21:10,13

Job's First Test

[6]One day the angels[aj] came to present themselves before the Lᴏʀᴅ, and Satan[b] also came with them.[k] [7]The Lᴏʀᴅ said to Satan, "Where have you come from?"

Satan answered the Lᴏʀᴅ, "From roaming through the earth and going back and forth in it."[l]

[8]Then the Lᴏʀᴅ said to Satan, "Have you considered my servant Job?[m] There is no one on earth like him; he is blameless and upright, a man who fears God and shuns evil."[n]

[9]"Does Job fear God for nothing?"[o] Satan replied. [10]"Have you not put a hedge around him and his household and everything he has?[p] You have blessed the work of his hands, so that his flocks and herds are spread throughout the land.[q] [11]But stretch out your hand and strike everything he has,[r] and he will surely curse you to your face."[s]

[12]The Lᴏʀᴅ said to Satan, "Very well, then, everything he has is in your hands, but on the man himself do not lay a finger."

Then Satan went out from the presence of the Lᴏʀᴅ.

[13]One day when Job's sons and daughters were feasting and drinking wine at the oldest brother's house, [14]a messenger came to Job and said, "The oxen were plowing and the donkeys were grazing nearby, [15]and the Sabeans[t] attacked and carried them off. They put the servants to the sword, and I am the only one who has escaped to tell you!"

[16]While he was still speaking, another messenger came and said, "The fire of God fell from the sky[u] and burned up the sheep and the servants,[v] and I am the only one who has escaped to tell you!"

[17]While he was still speaking, another messenger came and said, "The Chaldeans[w] formed three raiding parties and swept down on your camels and carried them off. They put the servants to the sword, and I am the only one who has escaped to tell you!"

[18]While he was still speaking, yet another messenger came and said, "Your sons and daughters were feasting and drinking wine at the oldest brother's house, [19]when suddenly a mighty wind[x] swept in from the desert and struck the four corners of the house. It collapsed on them and they are dead, and I am the only one who has escaped to tell you!"

[20]At this, Job got up and tore his robe[y] and shaved his head. Then he fell to the ground in worship[z] [21]and said:

> "Naked I came from my mother's womb,
>   and naked I will depart.[c][a]
> The Lᴏʀᴅ gave and the Lᴏʀᴅ has taken away;[b]
>   may the name of the Lᴏʀᴅ be praised."[c]

[22]In all this, Job did not sin by charging God with wrongdoing.[d]

Job's Second Test

2 On another day the angels[a] came to present themselves before the Lᴏʀᴅ, and Satan also came with them[e] to present himself before him. [2]And the Lᴏʀᴅ said to Satan, "Where have you come from?"

Satan answered the Lᴏʀᴅ, "From roaming through the earth and going back and forth in it."

1:6
j Job 38:7
k Job 2:1
1:7
l 1Pe 5:8
1:8
m Jos 1:7; Job 42:7-8
n ver 1
1:9
o 1Ti 6:5
1:10
p Ps 34:7 q ver 3; Job 29:6; 31:25; Ps 128:1-2
1:11
r Job 19:21
s Job 2:5
1:15
t Ge 10:7; Job 6:19
1:16
u Ge 19:24
v Lev 10:2; Nu 11:1-3
1:17
w Ge 11:28,31
1:19
x Jer 4:11; 13:24
1:20
y Ge 37:29
z 1Pe 5:6
1:21
a Ecc 5:15; 1Ti 6:7 b 1Sa 2:7
c Job 2:10; Eph 5:20; 1Th 5:18
1:22
d Job 2:10
2:1
e Job 1:6

---

³Then the LORD said to Satan, "Have you considered my servant Job? There is no one on earth like him; he is blameless and upright, a man who fears God and shuns evil.ᶠ And he still maintains his integrity,ᵍ though you incited me against him to ruin him without any reason."ʰ

⁴"Skin for skin!" Satan replied. "A man will give all he has for his own life. ⁵But stretch out your hand and strike his flesh and bones,ⁱ and he will surely curse you to your face."ʲ

⁶The LORD said to Satan, "Very well, then, he is in your hands; but you must spare his life."ᵏ

⁷So Satan went out from the presence of the LORD and afflicted Job with painful sores from the soles of his feet to the top of his head.ˡ ⁸Then Job took a piece of broken pottery and scraped himself with it as he sat among the ashes.ᵐ

⁹His wife said to him, "Are you still holding on to your integrity? Curse God and die!"

¹⁰He replied, "You are talking like a foolishᵃ woman. Shall we accept good from God, and not trouble?"ⁿ

In all this, Job did not sin in what he said.ᵒ

Job's Three Friends

¹¹When Job's three friends, Eliphaz the Temanite,ᵖ Bildad the Shuhite�q and Zophar the Naamathite, heard about all the troubles that had come upon him, they set out from their homes and met together by agreement to go and sympathize with him and comfort him.ʳ ¹²When they saw him from a distance, they could hardly recognize him; they began to weep aloud, and they tore their robes and sprinkled dust on their heads.ˢ ¹³Then they sat on the ground with him for seven days and seven nights.ᵗ No one said a word to him, because they saw how great his suffering was.

Job Speaks

3 After this, Job opened his mouth and cursed the day of his birth. ²He said:

> ³"May the day of my birth perish,
> and the night it was said, 'A boy is born!'ᵘ
> ⁴That day—may it turn to darkness;
> may God above not care about it;
> may no light shine upon it.
> ⁵May darkness and deep shadowᵇᵛ claim it once more;
> may a cloud settle over it;
> may blackness overwhelm its light.
> ⁶That night—may thick darknessʷ seize it;
> may it not be included among the days of the year
> nor be entered in any of the months.
> ⁷May that night be barren;
> may no shout of joy be heard in it.
> ⁸May those who curse daysᶜ curse that day,
> those who are ready to rouse Leviathan.ˣ

ᵃ10 The Hebrew word rendered *foolish* denotes moral deficiency.   ᵇ5 Or *and the shadow of death*
ᶜ8 Or *the sea*

2:3
fJob 1:1,8
gJob 27:6
hJob 9:17
2:5
iJob 19:20
jJob 1:11
2:6
kJob 1:12
2:7
lDt 28:35;
Job 7:5
2:8
mJob 42:6;
Jer 6:26;
Eze 27:30;
Mt 11:21
2:10
nJob 1:21
oJob 1:22;
Ps 39:1;
Jas 1:12; 5:11
2:11
pGe 36:11;
Jer 49:7
qGe 25:2
rJob 42:11;
Ro 12:15
2:12
sJos 7:6;
Ne 9:1;
La 2:10;
Eze 27:30
2:13
tGe 50:10;
Eze 3:15
3:3
uJob 10:18-19;
Jer 20:14-18
3:5
vJob 10:21,22;
Ps 23:4; Jer 2:6;
13:16
3:6
wJob 23:17
3:8
xJob 41:1,8,
10,25

[9]May its morning stars become dark;
    may it wait for daylight in vain
    and not see the first rays of dawn,[y]
[10]for it did not shut the doors of the womb on me
    to hide trouble from my eyes.

[11]"Why did I not perish at birth,
    and die as I came from the womb?[z]
[12]Why were there knees to receive me[a]
    and breasts that I might be nursed?
[13]For now I would be lying down[b] in peace;
    I would be asleep and at rest[c]
[14]with kings and counselors of the earth,[d]
    who built for themselves places now lying in ruins,[e]
[15]with rulers[f] who had gold,
    who filled their houses with silver.[g]
[16]Or why was I not hidden in the ground like a stillborn
      child,[h]
    like an infant who never saw the light of day?
[17]There the wicked cease from turmoil,
    and there the weary are at rest.[i]
[18]Captives also enjoy their ease;
    they no longer hear the slave driver's shout.[j]
[19]The small and the great are there,
    and the slave is freed from his master.

[20]"Why is light given to those in misery,
    and life to the bitter of soul,[k]
[21]to those who long for death that does not come,[l]
    who search for it more than for hidden treasure,[m]
[22]who are filled with gladness
    and rejoice when they reach the grave?
[23]Why is life given to a man
    whose way is hidden,
    whom God has hedged in?[n]
[24]For sighing comes to me instead of food;[o]
    my groans pour out like water.[p]
[25]What I feared has come upon me;
    what I dreaded[q] has happened to me.
[26]I have no peace, no quietness;
    I have no rest,[r] but only turmoil."

Eliphaz

4 Then Eliphaz the Temanite replied:

[2]"If someone ventures a word with you, will you be
      impatient?
    But who can keep from speaking?[s]
[3]Think how you have instructed many,
    how you have strengthened feeble hands.[t]
[4]Your words have supported those who stumbled;
    you have strengthened faltering knees.[u]

3:9
y Job 41:18
3:11
z Job 10:18
3:12
a Ge 30:3;
Isa 66:12
3:13
b Job 17:13
c Job 7:8-10,21;
10:22;
14:10-12;
19:27; 21:13,23
3:14
d Job 12:17
e Job 15:28
3:15
f Job 12:21
g Job 27:17
3:16
h Ps 58:8;
Ecc 6:3
3:17
i Job 17:16
3:18
j Job 39:7
3:20
k 1Sa 1:10;
Jer 20:18;
Eze 27:30-31
3:21
l Rev 9:6
m Pr 2:4
3:23
n Job 19:6,8,12;
Ps 88:8; La 3:7
3:24
o Job 6:7; 33:20
p Ps 42:3,4
3:25
q Job 30:15
3:26
r Job 7:4,14
4:2
s Job 32:20
4:3
t Isa 35:3;
Heb 12:12
4:4
u Isa 35:3;
Heb 12:12

4:5
vJob 19:21
wJob 6:14
4:6
xPr 3:26
yJob 1:1
4:7
zJob 36:7
aJob 8:20;
Ps 37:25
4:8
bJob 15:35
cPr 22:8;
Hos 10:13;
Gal 6:7-8
4:9
dJob 15:30;
Isa 30:33;
2Th 2:8
eJob 40:13
4:10
fJob 5:15;
Ps 58:6
4:11
gJob 27:14;
Ps 34:10
4:12
hJob 26:14
iJob 33:14
4:13
jJob 33:15
4:14
kJer 23:9;
Hab 3:16
4:17
lJob 9:2
mJob 35:10
4:18
nJob 15:15
4:19
oJob 10:9
pJob 22:16
qGe 2:7
4:20
rJob 14:2,20;
20:7; Ps 90:5-6
4:21
sJob 8:22
tJob 18:21;
36:12
5:1
uJob 15:15
5:2
vPr 12:16
5:3
wPs 37:35;
Jer 12:2
xJob 24:18
5:4
yJob 4:11
zAm 5:12
5:5
aJob 18:8-10

⁵But now trouble comes to you, and you are discouraged;
  it strikesᵛ you, and you are dismayed.ʷ
⁶Should not your piety be your confidenceˣ
  and your blamelessʸ ways your hope?

⁷"Consider now: Who, being innocent, has
      ever perished?ᶻ
  Where were the upright ever destroyed?ᵃ
⁸As I have observed, those who plow evilᵇ
  and those who sow trouble reap it.ᶜ
⁹At the breath of Godᵈ they are destroyed;
  at the blast of his anger they perish.ᵉ
¹⁰The lions may roar and growl,
  yet the teeth of the great lions are broken.ᶠ
¹¹The lion perishes for lack of prey,ᵍ
  and the cubs of the lioness are scattered.

¹²"A word was secretly brought to me,
  my ears caught a whisperʰ of it.ⁱ
¹³Amid disquieting dreams in the night,
  when deep sleep falls on men,ʲ
¹⁴fear and trembling seized me
  and made all my bones shake.ᵏ
¹⁵A spirit glided past my face,
  and the hair on my body stood on end.
¹⁶It stopped,
  but I could not tell what it was.
  A form stood before my eyes,
  and I heard a hushed voice:
¹⁷'Can a mortal be more righteous than God?ˡ
  Can a man be more pure than his Maker?ᵐ
¹⁸If God places no trust in his servants,
  if he charges his angels with error,ⁿ
¹⁹how much more those who live in houses of clay,°
  whose foundationsᵖ are in the dust,ᑫ
  who are crushed more readily than a moth!
²⁰Between dawn and dusk they are broken to pieces;
  unnoticed, they perish forever.ʳ
²¹Are not the cords of their tent pulled up,ˢ
  so that they die without wisdom?'ᵃ ᵗ

5 "Call if you will, but who will answer you?
  To which of the holy onesᵘ will you turn?
²Resentment kills a fool,
  and envy slays the simple.ᵛ
³I myself have seen a fool taking root,ʷ
  but suddenly his house was cursed.ˣ
⁴His children are far from safety,ʸ
  crushed in courtᶻ without a defender.
⁵The hungry consume his harvest,ᵃ

ᵃ21 Some interpreters end the quotation after verse 17.

taking it even from among thorns,
and the thirsty pant after his wealth.
⁶For hardship does not spring from the soil,
nor does trouble sprout from the ground.
⁷Yet man is born to trouble[b]
as surely as sparks fly upward.

⁸"But if it were I, I would appeal to God;
I would lay my cause before him.[c]
⁹He performs wonders that cannot be fathomed,[d]
miracles that cannot be counted.
¹⁰He bestows rain on the earth;
he sends water upon the countryside.[e]
¹¹The lowly he sets on high,[f]
and those who mourn are lifted to safety.
¹²He thwarts the plans[g] of the crafty,
so that their hands achieve no success.
¹³He catches the wise in their craftiness,[h]
and the schemes of the wily are swept away.
¹⁴Darkness[i] comes upon them in the daytime;
at noon they grope as in the night.[j]
¹⁵He saves the needy[k] from the sword in their mouth;
he saves them from the clutches of the powerful.[l]
¹⁶So the poor have hope,
and injustice shuts its mouth.[m]

¹⁷"Blessed is the man whom God corrects;[n]
so do not despise the discipline[o] of the Almighty.[a][p]
¹⁸For he wounds, but he also binds up;[q]
he injures, but his hands also heal.[r]
¹⁹From six calamities he will rescue you;
in seven no harm will befall you.[s]
²⁰In famine[t] he will ransom you from death,
and in battle from the stroke of the sword.[u]
²¹You will be protected from the lash of the tongue,[v]
and need not fear[w] when destruction comes.
²²You will laugh at destruction and famine,
and need not fear the beasts of the earth.[x]
²³For you will have a covenant with the stones[y] of the
field,
and the wild animals will be at peace with you.[z]
²⁴You will know that your tent is secure;
you will take stock of your property and find nothing
missing.[a]
²⁵You will know that your children will be many,[b]
and your descendants like the grass of the earth.[c]
²⁶You will come to the grave in full vigor,[d]
like sheaves gathered in season.

²⁷"We have examined this, and it is true.
So hear it and apply it to yourself."

5:7
b Job 14:1
5:8
c Ps 35:23; 50:15
5:9
d Job 42:3;
Ps 40:5
5:10
e Job 36:28
5:11
f Ps 113:7-8
5:12
g Ne 4:15;
Ps 33:10
5:13
h 1Co 3:19*
5:14
i Job 12:25
j Dt 28:29
5:15
k Ps 35:10
l Job 4:10
5:16
m Ps 107:42
5:17
n Jas 1:12
o Ps 94:12;
Pr 3:11
p Heb 12:5-11
5:18
q Isa 30:26
r 1Sa 2:6
5:19
s Ps 34:19; 91:10
5:20
t Ps 33:19
u Ps 144:10
5:21
v Ps 31:20
w Ps 91:5
5:22
x Ps 91:13;
Eze 34:25
5:23
y Ps 91:12
z Isa 11:6-9
5:24
a Job 8:6
5:25
b Ps 112:2
c Ps 72:16;
Isa 44:3-4
5:26
d Ge 15:15

a17 Hebrew *Shaddai*; here and throughout Job

Job

6

Then Job replied:

2"If only my anguish could be weighed
   and all my misery be placed on the scales!e
3It would surely outweigh the sandf of the seas—
   no wonder my words have been impetuous. g
4The arrowsh of the Almighty are in me,i
   my spirit drinksj in their poison;
   God's terrorsk are marshaled against me.l
5Does a wild donkey bray when it has grass,
   or an ox bellow when it has fodder?
6Is tasteless food eaten without salt,
   or is there flavor in the white of an egga?
7I refuse to touch it;
   such food makes me ill. m

8"Oh, that I might have my request,
   that God would grant what I hope for, n
9that God would be willing to crush me,
   to let loose his hand and cut me off!o
10Then I would still have this consolation—
   my joy in unrelenting pain—
   that I had not denied the wordsp of the Holy One. q

11"What strength do I have, that I should still hope?
   What prospects, that I should be patient?r
12Do I have the strength of stone?
   Is my flesh bronze?
13Do I have any power to help myself,s
   now that success has been driven from me?

14"A despairing mant should have the devotionu of his
     friends,
   even though he forsakes the fear of the Almighty.
15But my brothers are as undependable as intermittent
     streams,v
   as the streams that overflow
16when darkened by thawing ice
   and swollen with melting snow,
17but that cease to flow in the dry season,
   and in the heatw vanish from their channels.
18Caravans turn aside from their routes;
   they go up into the wasteland and perish.
19The caravans of Temax look for water,
   the traveling merchants of Sheba look in hope.
20They are distressed, because they had been confident;
   they arrive there, only to be disappointed. y
21Now you too have proved to be of no help;
   you see something dreadful and are afraid. z
22Have I ever said, 'Give something on my behalf,

6:2
eJob 31:6
6:3
fPr 27:3
gJob 23:2
6:4
hPs 38:2
iJob 16:12,13
jJob 21:20
kJob 30:15
lPs 88:15-18
6:7
mJob 3:24
6:8
nGe 14:13
6:9
oNu 11:15;
1Ki 19:4
6:10
pJob 22:22;
23:12
qLev 19:2;
Isa 57:15
6:11
rJob 21:4
6:13
sJob 26:2
6:14
tJob 4:5
uJob 15:4
6:15
vPs 38:11;
Jer 15:18
6:17
wJob 24:19
6:19
xGe 25:15;
Isa 21:14
6:20
yJer 14:3
6:21
zPs 38:11

---

a6 The meaning of the Hebrew for this phrase is uncertain.

pay a ransom for me from your wealth,
²³deliver me from the hand of the enemy,
ransom me from the clutches of the ruthless'?

²⁴"Teach me, and I will be quiet;[a]
show me where I have been wrong.
²⁵How painful are honest words![b]
But what do your arguments prove?
²⁶Do you mean to correct what I say,
and treat the words of a despairing man as wind?[c]
²⁷You would even cast lots[d] for the fatherless
and barter away your friend.

²⁸"But now be so kind as to look at me.
Would I lie to your face?[e]
²⁹Relent, do not be unjust;
reconsider, for my integrity is at stake.[a][f]
³⁰Is there any wickedness on my lips?[g]
Can my mouth not discern[h] malice?

7 "Does not man have hard service[i] on earth?[j]
Are not his days like those of a hired man?[k]
²Like a slave longing for the evening shadows,
or a hired man waiting eagerly for his wages,[l]
³so I have been allotted months of futility,
and nights of misery have been assigned to me.[m]
⁴When I lie down I think, 'How long before I get up?'[n]
The night drags on, and I toss till dawn.
⁵My body is clothed with worms[o] and scabs,
my skin is broken and festering.

⁶"My days are swifter than a weaver's shuttle,[p]
and they come to an end without hope.[q]
⁷Remember, O God, that my life is but a breath;[r]
my eyes will never see happiness again.[s]
⁸The eye that now sees me will see me no longer;
you will look for me, but I will be no more.[t]
⁹As a cloud vanishes and is gone,
so he who goes down to the grave[b][u] does not
return.[v]
¹⁰He will never come to his house again;
his place[w] will know him no more.[x]

¹¹"Therefore I will not keep silent;[y]
I will speak out in the anguish of my spirit,
I will complain in the bitterness of my soul.[z]
¹²Am I the sea, or the monster of the deep,[a]
that you put me under guard?
¹³When I think my bed will comfort me
and my couch will ease my complaint,[b]
¹⁴even then you frighten me with dreams
and terrify[c] me with visions,

6:24
[a]Ps 39:1
6:25
[b]Ecc 12:11
6:26
[c]Job 8:2; 15:3
6:27
[d]Joel 3:3;
Na 3:10;
2Pe 2:3
6:28
[e]Job 27:4;
33:1,3; 36:3,4
6:29
[f]Job 23:7,10;
34:5,36; 42:6
6:30
[g]Job 27:4
[h]Job 12:11
7:1
[i]Job 14:14;
Isa 40:2
[j]Job 5:7
[k]Job 14:6
7:2
[l]Lev 19:13
7:3
[m]Job 16:7;
Ps 6:6
7:4
[n]Dt 28:67
7:5
[o]Job 17:14;
Isa 14:11
7:6
[p]Job 9:25
[q]Job 13:15;
17:11,15
7:7
[r]Ps 78:39;
Jas 4:14
[s]Job 9:25
7:8
[t]Job 20:7,9,21
7:9
[u]Job 11:8
[v]2Sa 12:23;
Job 30:15
7:10
[w]Job 27:21,23
[x]Job 8:18
7:11
[y]Ps 40:9
[z]1Sa 1:10
7:12
[a]Eze 32:2-3
7:13
[b]Job 9:27
7:14
[c]Job 9:34

---

[a]29 Or *my righteousness still stands*   [b]9 Hebrew *Sheol*

[15]so that I prefer strangling and death, [d]
    rather than this body of mine.
[16]I despise my life;[e] I would not live forever.
    Let me alone; my days have no meaning.

[17]"What is man that you make so much of him,
    that you give him so much attention,[f]
[18]that you examine him every morning
    and test him every moment?[g]
[19]Will you never look away from me,
    or let me alone even for an instant?[h]
[20]If I have sinned, what have I done to you,[i]
    O watcher of men?
  Why have you made me your target?[j]
    Have I become a burden to you?[a]
[21]Why do you not pardon my offenses
    and forgive my sins?[k]
  For I will soon lie down in the dust;[l]
    you will search for me, but I will be no more."

Bildad

8 Then Bildad the Shuhite replied:

[2]"How long will you say such things?
    Your words are a blustering wind.[m]
[3]Does God pervert justice?[n]
    Does the Almighty pervert what is right?[o]
[4]When your children sinned against him,
    he gave them over to the penalty of their sin.[p]
[5]But if you will look to God
    and plead[q] with the Almighty,
[6]if you are pure and upright,
    even now he will rouse himself on your behalf[r]
    and restore you to your rightful place.[s]
[7]Your beginnings will seem humble,
    so prosperous[t] will your future be.

[8]"Ask the former generations[u]
    and find out what their fathers learned,
[9]for we were born only yesterday and know nothing,[v]
    and our days on earth are but a shadow.[w]
[10]Will they not instruct you and tell you?
    Will they not bring forth words from their
        understanding?
[11]Can papyrus grow tall where there is no marsh?
    Can reeds thrive without water?
[12]While still growing and uncut,
    they wither more quickly than grass.[x]
[13]Such is the destiny of all who forget God;[y]
    so perishes the hope of the godless.[z]

---

[a]20 A few manuscripts of the Masoretic Text, an ancient Hebrew scribal tradition and Septuagint; most manuscripts of the Masoretic Text *I have become a burden to myself.*

7:15
d1Ki 19:4
7:16
eJob 9:21; 10:1
7:17
fPs 8:4; 144:3;
Heb 2:6
7:18
gJob 14:3
7:19
hJob 9:18
7:20
iJob 35:6
jJob 16:12
7:21
kJob 10:14
lJob 10:9;
Ps 104:29
8:2
mJob 6:26
8:3
nDt 32:4;
2Ch 19:7;
Ro 3:5
oGe 18:25
8:4
pJob 1:19
8:5
qJob 11:13
8:6
rPs 7:6
sJob 5:24
8:7
tJob 42:12
8:8
uDt 4:32; 32:7;
Job 15:18
8:9
vGe 47:9
w1Ch 29:15;
Job 7:6
8:12
xPs 129:6;
Jer 17:6
8:13
yPs 9:17
zJob 11:20;
13:16; 15:34;
Pr 10:28

¹⁴What he trusts in is fragile^a;
　　what he relies on is a spider's web.^a
¹⁵He leans on his web,^b but it gives way;
　　he clings to it, but it does not hold.^c
¹⁶He is like a well-watered plant in the sunshine,
　　spreading its shoots^d over the garden;^e
¹⁷it entwines its roots around a pile of rocks
　　and looks for a place among the stones.
¹⁸But when it is torn from its spot,
　　that place disowns it and says, 'I never saw you.'^f
¹⁹Surely its life withers^g away,
　　and^b from the soil other plants grow.^h

²⁰"Surely God does not reject a blamelessⁱ man
　　or strengthen the hands of evildoers.^j
²¹He will yet fill your mouth with laughter^k
　　and your lips with shouts of joy.^l
²²Your enemies will be clothed in shame,^m
　　and the tents of the wicked will be no more."ⁿ

Job

9 Then Job replied:

²"Indeed, I know that this is true.
　　But how can a mortal be righteous before God?^o
³Though one wished to dispute with him,
　　he could not answer him one time out of a thousand.^p
⁴His wisdom^q is profound, his power is vast.^r
　　Who has resisted him and come out unscathed?^s
⁵He moves mountains without their knowing it
　　and overturns them in his anger.^t
⁶He shakes the earth^u from its place
　　and makes its pillars tremble.^v
⁷He speaks to the sun and it does not shine;
　　he seals off the light of the stars.^w
⁸He alone stretches out the heavens^x
　　and treads on the waves of the sea.^y
⁹He is the Maker of the Bear and Orion,
　　the Pleiades and the constellations of the south.^z
¹⁰He performs wonders^a that cannot be fathomed,
　　miracles that cannot be counted.^b
¹¹When he passes me, I cannot see him;
　　when he goes by, I cannot perceive him.^c
¹²If he snatches away, who can stop him?^d
　　Who can say to him, 'What are you doing?'^e
¹³God does not restrain his anger;
　　even the cohorts of Rahab^f cowered at his feet.

¹⁴"How then can I dispute with him?
　　How can I find words to argue with him?

---

^a14 The meaning of the Hebrew for this word is uncertain.　　^b19 Or *Surely all the joy it has / is that*

8:14
aIsa 59:5
8:15
bJob 27:18
cPs 49:11
8:16
dPs 80:11
ePs 37:35;
Jer 11:16
8:18
fJob 7:8;
Ps 37:36
8:19
gJob 20:5
hEcc 1:4
8:20
iJob 1:1
jJob 21:30
8:21
kJob 5:22
lPs 126:2;
132:16
8:22
mPs 35:26;
109:29; 132:18
nJob 18:6,14,21
9:2
oJob 4:17;
Ps 143:2;
Ro 3:20
9:3
pJob 10:2; 40:2
9:4
qJob 11:6
rJob 36:5
s2Ch 13:12
9:5
tMic 1:4
9:6
uIsa 2:21;
Hag 2:6;
Heb 12:26
vJob 26:11
9:7
wIsa 13:10;
Eze 32:8
9:8
xGe 1:6;
Ps 104:2-3
yJob 38:16;
Ps 77:19
9:9
zGe 1:16;
Job 38:31;
Am 5:8
9:10
aPs 71:15
bJob 5:9
9:11
cJob 23:8-9;
35:14
9:12
dJob 11:10
eIsa 45:9;
Ro 9:20
9:13
fJob 26:12;
Ps 89:10;
Isa 30:7; 51:9

9:15
g Job 10:15
h Job 8:5
9:17
i Job 16:12
j Job 30:22
k Job 16:14
l Job 2:3
9:18
m Job 7:19; 27:2
9:21
n Job 1:1
o Job 7:16
9:22
p Job 10:8;
Ecc 9:2,3;
Eze 21:3
9:23
q Heb 11:36
r Job 24:1,12
9:24
s Job 10:3;
16:11 t Job 12:6
9:25
u Job 7:6
9:26
v Isa 18:2
w Hab 1:8
9:27
x Job 7:11
9:28
y Job 3:25;
Ps 119:120
z Job 7:21
9:29
a Ps 37:33
9:30
b Job 31:7
c Jer 2:22
9:32
d Ro 9:20
e Ps 143:2;
Ecc 6:10
9:33
f 1Sa 2:25
9:34
g Job 13:21;
Ps 39:10
9:35
h Job 13:21
10:1
i 1Ki 19:4
j Job 7:11

[15]Though I were innocent, I could not answer him;[g]
　　I could only plead[h] with my Judge for mercy.
[16]Even if I summoned him and he responded,
　　I do not believe he would give me a hearing.
[17]He would crush me[i] with a storm[j]
　　and multiply[k] my wounds for no reason.[l]
[18]He would not let me regain my breath
　　but would overwhelm me with misery.[m]
[19]If it is a matter of strength, he is mighty!
　　And if it is a matter of justice, who will summon
　　　him[a]?
[20]Even if I were innocent, my mouth would condemn me;
　　if I were blameless, it would pronounce me guilty.

[21]"Although I am blameless,[n]
　　I have no concern for myself;
　　I despise my own life.[o]
[22]It is all the same; that is why I say,
　　'He destroys both the blameless and the wicked.'[p]
[23]When a scourge[q] brings sudden death,
　　he mocks the despair of the innocent.[r]
[24]When a land falls into the hands of the wicked,[s]
　　he blindfolds its judges.[t]
　　If it is not he, then who is it?

[25]"My days are swifter than a runner;[u]
　　they fly away without a glimpse of joy.
[26]They skim past like boats of papyrus,[v]
　　like eagles swooping down on their prey.[w]
[27]If I say, 'I will forget my complaint,[x]
　　I will change my expression, and smile,'
[28]I still dread[y] all my sufferings,
　　for I know you will not hold me innocent.[z]
[29]Since I am already found guilty,
　　why should I struggle in vain?[a]
[30]Even if I washed myself with soap[b]
　　and my hands[b] with washing soda,[c]
[31]you would plunge me into a slime pit
　　so that even my clothes would detest me.

[32]"He is not a man like me that I might answer him,[d]
　　that we might confront each other in court.[e]
[33]If only there were someone to arbitrate between us,[f]
　　to lay his hand upon us both,
[34]someone to remove God's rod from me,[g]
　　so that his terror would frighten me no more.
[35]Then I would speak up without fear of him,
　　but as it now stands with me, I cannot.[h]

10 　"I loathe my very life;[i]
　　therefore I will give free rein to my complaint
　　and speak out in the bitterness of my soul.[j]

---

[a]19 See Septuagint; Hebrew *me*.　　[b]30 Or *snow*

²I will say to God: Do not condemn me,
  but tell me what charges[k] you have against me.
³Does it please you to oppress me,[l]
  to spurn the work of your hands,[m]
  while you smile on the schemes of the wicked?[n]
⁴Do you have eyes of flesh?
  Do you see as a mortal sees?[o]
⁵Are your days like those of a mortal
  or your years like those of a man,[p]
⁶that you must search out my faults
  and probe after my sin[q]—
⁷though you know that I am not guilty
  and that no one can rescue me from your hand?

⁸"Your hands shaped[r] me and made me.
  Will you now turn and destroy me?
⁹Remember that you molded me like clay.[s]
  Will you now turn me to dust again?[t]
¹⁰Did you not pour me out like milk
  and curdle me like cheese,
¹¹clothe me with skin and flesh
  and knit me together[u] with bones and sinews?
¹²You gave me life[v] and showed me kindness,
  and in your providence watched over my spirit.

¹³"But this is what you concealed in your heart,
  and I know that this was in your mind:[w]
¹⁴If I sinned, you would be watching me
  and would not let my offense go unpunished.[x]
¹⁵If I am guilty—woe to me![y]
  Even if I am innocent, I cannot lift my head,[z]
 for I am full of shame
  and drowned in[a] my affliction.
¹⁶If I hold my head high, you stalk me like a lion[a]
  and again display your awesome power against me.[b]
¹⁷You bring new witnesses against me[c]
  and increase your anger toward me;[d]
  your forces come against me wave upon wave.

¹⁸"Why then did you bring me out of the womb?[e]
  I wish I had died before any eye saw me.
¹⁹If only I had never come into being,
  or had been carried straight from the womb to the
    grave!
²⁰Are not my few days[f] almost over?[g]
  Turn away from me[h] so I can have a moment's joy
²¹before I go to the place of no return,[i]
  to the land of gloom and deep shadow,[b][j]
²²to the land of deepest night,
  of deep shadow and disorder,
  where even the light is like darkness."

10:2
k Job 9:29
10:3
l Job 9:22
m Job 14:15;
Ps 138:8;
Isa 64:8
n Job 21:16;
22:18
10:4
o 1Sa 16:7
10:5
p Ps 90:2,4;
2Pe 3:8
10:6
q Job 14:16
10:8
r Ps 119:73
10:9
s Isa 64:8
t Ge 2:7
10:11
u Ps 139:13,15
10:12
v Job 33:4
10:13
w Job 23:13
10:14
x Job 7:21
10:15
y Job 9:13;
Isa 3:11
z Job 9:15
10:16
a Isa 38:13;
La 3:10 b Job 5:9
10:17
c Job 16:8
d Ru 1:21
10:18
e Job 3:11
10:20
f Job 14:1
g Job 7:19
h Job 7:16
10:21
i 2Sa 12:23;
Job 3:13; 16:22
j Ps 23:4; 88:12

---

a15 Or *and aware of*   b21 Or *and the shadow of death*; also in verse 22

Zophar

11 Then Zophar the Naamathite replied:

²"Are all these words to go unanswered?ᵏ
  Is this talker to be vindicated?
³Will your idle talk reduce men to silence?
  Will no one rebuke you when you mock?ˡ
⁴You say to God, 'My beliefs are flawlessᵐ
  and I am pureⁿ in your sight.'
⁵Oh, how I wish that God would speak,
  that he would open his lips against you
⁶and disclose to you the secrets of wisdom,ᵒ
  for true wisdom has two sides.
  Know this: God has even forgotten some of your sin.ᵖ

⁷"Can you fathom�q the mysteries of God?
  Can you probe the limits of the Almighty?
⁸They are higher than the heavensʳ—what can you do?
  They are deeper than the depths of the graveᵃ—what
    can you know?
⁹Their measure is longer than the earth
  and wider than the sea.

¹⁰"If he comes along and confines you in prison
  and convenes a court, who can oppose him?ˢ
¹¹Surely he recognizes deceitful men;
  and when he sees evil, does he not take note?ᵗ
¹²But a witless man can no more become wise
  than a wild donkey's colt can be born a man. ᵇ

¹³"Yet if you devote your heartᵘ to him
  and stretch out your hands to him,ᵛ
¹⁴if you put away the sin that is in your hand
  and allow no evilʷ to dwell in your tent,ˣ
¹⁵then you will lift up your faceʸ without shame;
  you will stand firm and without fear.
¹⁶You will surely forget your trouble,ᶻ
  recalling it only as waters gone by. ᵃ
¹⁷Life will be brighter than noonday,ᵇ
  and darkness will become like morning.
¹⁸You will be secure, because there is hope;
  you will look about you and take your restᶜ in safety. ᵈ
¹⁹You will lie down, with no one to make you afraid,ᵉ
  and many will court your favor. ᶠ
²⁰But the eyes of the wicked will fail,ᵍ
  and escape will elude them;ʰ
  their hope will become a dying gasp."ⁱ

Job

12 Then Job replied:

²"Doubtless you are the people,

11:2
k Job 8:2
11:3
l Job 17:2; 21:3
11:4
m Job 6:10
n Job 10:7
11:6
o Job 9:4
p Ezr 9:13;
Job 15:5
11:7
q Ecc 3:11;
Ro 11:33
11:8
r Job 22:12
11:10
s Job 9:12;
Rev 3:7
11:11
t Job 34:21-25;
Ps 10:14
11:13
u 1Sa 7:3;
Ps 78:8 v Ps 88:9
11:14
w Ps 101:4
x Job 22:23
11:15
y Job 22:26;
1Jn 3:21
11:16
z Isa 65:16
a Job 22:11
11:17
b Job 22:28;
Ps 37:6;
Isa 58:8,10
11:18
c Ps 3:5
d Lev 26:6;
Pr 3:24
11:19
e Lev 26:6
f Isa 45:14
11:20
g Dt 28:65;
Job 17:5
h Job 27:22;
34:22 i Job 8:13

ᵃ8 Hebrew *than Sheol*   ᵇ12 Or *wild donkey can be born tame*

and wisdom will die with you!^j
³But I have a mind as well as you;
    I am not inferior to you.
    Who does not know all these things?^k

⁴"I have become a laughingstock^l to my friends,
    though I called upon God and he answered^m—
    a mere laughingstock, though righteous and
        blameless!ⁿ
⁵Men at ease have contempt for misfortune
    as the fate of those whose feet are slipping.
⁶The tents of marauders are undisturbed,^o
    and those who provoke God are secure^p—
    those who carry their god in their hands.^a

⁷"But ask the animals, and they will teach you,
    or the birds of the air, and they will tell you;
⁸or speak to the earth, and it will teach you,
    or let the fish of the sea inform you.
⁹Which of all these does not know
    that the hand of the LORD has done this?^q
¹⁰In his hand is the life of every creature
    and the breath of all mankind.^r
¹¹Does not the ear test words
    as the tongue tastes food?^s
¹²Is not wisdom found among the aged?^t
    Does not long life bring understanding?^u

¹³"To God belong wisdom^v and power;^w
    counsel and understanding are his.^x
¹⁴What he tears down^y cannot be rebuilt;^z
    the man he imprisons cannot be released.
¹⁵If he holds back the waters,^a there is drought;^b
    if he lets them loose, they devastate the land.^c
¹⁶To him belong strength and victory;
    both deceived and deceiver are his.^d
¹⁷He leads counselors away stripped^e
    and makes fools of judges.^f
¹⁸He takes off the shackles^g put on by kings
    and ties a loincloth^b around their waist.
¹⁹He leads priests away stripped
    and overthrows men long established.^h
²⁰He silences the lips of trusted advisers
    and takes away the discernment of elders.ⁱ
²¹He pours contempt on nobles
    and disarms the mighty.
²²He reveals the deep things of darkness^j
    and brings deep shadows^k into the light.^l
²³He makes nations great, and destroys them;^m
    he enlarges nations,ⁿ and disperses them.
²⁴He deprives the leaders of the earth of their reason;

12:2
j Job 17:10
12:3
k Job 13:2
12:4
l Job 21:3
m Ps 91:15
n Job 6:29
12:6
o Job 22:18
p Job 9:24;
21:9
12:9
q Isa 41:20
12:10
r Job 27:3; 33:4;
Ac 17:28
12:11
s Job 34:3
12:12
t Job 15:10
u Job 32:7,9
12:13
v Job 11:6
w Job 9:4
x Job 32:8;
38:36
12:14
y Job 19:10
z Job 37:7;
Isa 25:2
12:15
a 1Ki 8:35
b 1Ki 17:1
c Ge 7:11
12:16
d Job 13:7,9
12:17
e Job 19:9
f Job 3:14
12:18
g Ps 116:16
12:19
h Job 24:12,22;
34:20,28; 35:9
12:20
i Job 32:9
12:22
j 1Co 4:5
k Job 3:5
l Da 2:22
12:23
m Jer 25:9
n Ps 107:38;
Isa 9:3; 26:15

---

a6 Or secure / in what God's hand brings them   *b18 Or shackles of kings / and ties a belt*

he sends them wandering through a trackless waste. °
25They grope in darkness with no light; p
   he makes them stagger like drunkards. q

13   "My eyes have seen all this,
   my ears have heard and understood it.
2What you know, I also know;
   I am not inferior to you. r
3But I desire to speak to the Almighty
   and to argue my case with God. s
4You, however, smear me with lies; t
   you are worthless physicians, all of you!
5If only you would be altogether silent!
   For you, that would be wisdom. u
6Hear now my argument;
   listen to the plea of my lips.
7Will you speak wickedly on God's behalf?
   Will you speak deceitfully for him? v
8Will you show him partiality? w
   Will you argue the case for God?
9Would it turn out well if he examined you?
   Could you deceive him as you might deceive men? x
10He would surely rebuke you
   if you secretly showed partiality.
11Would not his splendor y terrify you?
   Would not the dread of him fall on you?
12Your maxims are proverbs of ashes;
   your defenses are defenses of clay.

13"Keep silent and let me speak;
   then let come to me what may.
14Why do I put myself in jeopardy
   and take my life in my hands?
15Though he slay me, yet will I hope z in him; a
   I will surely a defend my ways to his face. b
16Indeed, this will turn out for my deliverance, c
   for no godless man would dare come before him!
17Listen carefully to my words; d
   let your ears take in what I say.
18Now that I have prepared my case, e
   I know I will be vindicated.
19Can anyone bring charges against me? f
   If so, I will be silent and die. g

20"Only grant me these two things, O God,
   and then I will not hide from you:
21Withdraw your hand h far from me,
   and stop frightening me with your terrors.
22Then summon me and I will answer, i
   or let me speak, and you reply. j
23How many wrongs and sins have I committed? k

12:24
oPs 107:40
12:25
pJob 5:14
qPs 107:27;
Isa 24:20
13:2
rJob 12:3
13:3
sJob 23:3-4
13:4
tPs 119:69;
Jer 23:32
13:5
uPr 17:28
13:7
vJob 36:4
13:8
wLev 19:15
13:9
xJob 12:16;
Gal 6:7
13:11
yJob 31:23
13:15
zJob 7:6
aPs 23:4;
Pr 14:32
bJob 27:5
13:16
cIsa 12:1
13:17
dJob 21:2
13:18
eJob 23:4
13:19
fJob 40:4;
Isa 50:8
gJob 10:8
13:21
hPs 39:10
13:22
iJob 14:15
jJob 9:16
13:23
k1Sa 26:18

---

a15 Or *He will surely slay me; I have no hope — / yet I will*

Show me my offense and my sin.
24Why do you hide your face[l]
 and consider me your enemy?[m]
25Will you torment a windblown leaf?[n]
 Will you chase after dry chaff?[o]
26For you write down bitter things against me
 and make me inherit the sins of my youth.[p]
27You fasten my feet in shackles;[q]
 you keep close watch on all my paths
 by putting marks on the soles of my feet.

28"So man wastes away like something rotten,
 like a garment eaten by moths.[r]

14

"Man born of woman
 is of few days and full of trouble.[s]
2He springs up like a flower[t] and withers away;[u]
 like a fleeting shadow,[v] he does not endure.
3Do you fix your eye on such a one?[w]
 Will you bring him[a] before you for judgment?[x]
4Who can bring what is pure[y] from the impure?[z]
 No one![a]
5Man's days are determined;
 you have decreed the number of his months[b]
 and have set limits he cannot exceed.
6So look away from him and let him alone,[c]
 till he has put in his time like a hired man.[d]

7"At least there is hope for a tree:
 If it is cut down, it will sprout again,
 and its new shoots will not fail.
8Its roots may grow old in the ground
 and its stump die in the soil,
9yet at the scent of water it will bud
 and put forth shoots like a plant.
10But man dies and is laid low;
 he breathes his last and is no more.[e]
11As water disappears from the sea
 or a riverbed becomes parched and dry,[f]
12so man lies down and does not rise;
 till the heavens are no more,[g] men will not awake
 or be roused from their sleep.[h]

13"If only you would hide me in the grave[b]
 and conceal me till your anger has passed![i]
If only you would set me a time
 and then remember me!
14If a man dies, will he live again?
 All the days of my hard service
 I will wait for my renewal[c] to come.
15You will call and I will answer you;[j]
 you will long for the creature your hands have made.

13:24
[l]Dt 32:20;
Ps 13:1;
Isa 8:17
[m]Job 19:11;
La 2:5
13:25
[n]Lev 26:36
[o]Job 21:18;
Isa 42:3
13:26
[p]Ps 25:7
13:27
[q]Job 33:11
13:28
[r]Isa 50:9;
Jas 5:2
14:1
[s]Job 5:7;
Ecc 2:23
14:2
[t]Jas 1:10
[u]Ps 90:5-6
[v]Job 8:9
14:3
[w]Ps 8:4; 144:3
[x]Ps 143:2
14:4
[y]Ps 51:10
[z]Eph 2:1-3
[a]Jn 3:6; Ro 5:12
14:5
[b]Job 21:21
14:6
[c]Job 7:19
[d]Job 7:1,2;
Ps 39:13
14:10
[e]Job 13:19
14:11
[f]Isa 19:5
14:12
[g]Rev 20:11;
21:1 [h]Ac 3:21
14:13
[i]Isa 26:20
14:15
[j]Job 13:22

---

[a]3 Septuagint, Vulgate and Syriac; Hebrew *me* [b]13 Hebrew *Sheol* [c]14 Or *release*

16Surely then you will count my steps[k]
    but not keep track of my sin.[l]
17My offenses will be sealed up in a bag;[m]
    you will cover over my sin.[n]

18"But as a mountain erodes and crumbles
    and as a rock is moved from its place,
19as water wears away stones
    and torrents wash away the soil,
    so you destroy man's hope.[o]
20You overpower him once for all, and he is gone;
    you change his countenance and send him away.
21If his sons are honored, he does not know it;
    if they are brought low, he does not see it.[p]
22He feels but the pain of his own body
    and mourns only for himself."

Eliphaz

15 Then Eliphaz the Temanite replied:

2"Would a wise man answer with empty notions
    or fill his belly with the hot east wind?[q]
3Would he argue with useless words,
    with speeches that have no value?
4But you even undermine piety
    and hinder devotion to God.
5Your sin prompts your mouth;
    you adopt the tongue of the crafty.[r]
6Your own mouth condemns you, not mine;
    your own lips testify against you.[s]

7"Are you the first man ever born?[t]
    Were you brought forth before the hills?[u]
8Do you listen in on God's council?[v]
    Do you limit wisdom to yourself?
9What do you know that we do not know?
    What insights do you have that we do not have?[w]
10The gray-haired and the aged[x] are on our side,
    men even older than your father.
11Are God's consolations[y] not enough for you,
    words[z] spoken gently to you?[a]
12Why has your heart[b] carried you away,
    and why do your eyes flash,
13so that you vent your rage against God
    and pour out such words from your mouth?

14"What is man, that he could be pure,
    or one born of woman,[c] that he could be righteous?[d]
15If God places no trust in his holy ones,
    if even the heavens are not pure in his eyes,[e]
16how much less man, who is vile and corrupt,[f]
    who drinks up evil like water![g]

17"Listen to me and I will explain to you;

14:16
k Ps 139:1-3;
Pr 5:21;
Jer 32:19
l Job 10:6
14:17
m Dt 32:34
n Hos 13:12
14:19
o Job 7:6
14:21
p Ecc 9:5;
Isa 63:16
15:2
q Job 6:26
15:5
r Job 5:13
15:6
s Lk 19:22
15:7
t Job 38:21
u Ps 90:2;
Pr 8:25
15:8
v Ro 11:34;
1Co 2:11
15:9
w Job 13:2
15:10
x Job 32:6-7
15:11
y 2Co 1:3-4
z Zec 1:13
a Job 36:16
15:12
b Job 11:13
15:14
c Job 14:4; 25:4
d Pr 20:9;
Ecc 7:20
15:15
e Job 4:18; 25:5
15:16
f Ps 14:1
g Job 34:7;
Pr 19:28

let me tell you what I have seen,
18what wise men have declared,
  hiding nothing received from their fathers[h]
19(to whom alone the land was given
  when no alien passed among them):
20All his days the wicked man suffers torment,
  the ruthless through all the years stored up for him. [i]
21Terrifying sounds fill his ears;[j]
  when all seems well, marauders attack him. [k]
22He despairs of escaping the darkness;
  he is marked for the sword. [l]
23He wanders about[m]—food for vultures[a];
  he knows the day of darkness is at hand. [n]
24Distress and anguish fill him with terror;
  they overwhelm him, like a king poised to attack,
25because he shakes his fist at God
  and vaunts himself against the Almighty, [o]
26defiantly charging against him
  with a thick, strong shield.

27"Though his face is covered with fat
  and his waist bulges with flesh, [p]
28he will inhabit ruined towns
  and houses where no one lives, [q]
  houses crumbling to rubble. [r]
29He will no longer be rich and his wealth will not
      endure, [s]
  nor will his possessions spread over the land.
30He will not escape the darkness;[t]
  a flame[u] will wither his shoots,
  and the breath of God's mouth[v] will carry him away.
31Let him not deceive himself by trusting what is
      worthless, [w]
  for he will get nothing in return.
32Before his time[x] he will be paid in full, [y]
  and his branches will not flourish. [z]
33He will be like a vine stripped of its unripe grapes, [a]
  like an olive tree shedding its blossoms.
34For the company of the godless will be barren,
  and fire will consume the tents of those who love
      bribes. [b]
35They conceive trouble and give birth to evil;[c]
  their womb fashions deceit."

Job

16 Then Job replied:

2"I have heard many things like these;
  miserable comforters are you all![d]
3Will your long-winded speeches never end?
  What ails you that you keep on arguing?[e]

15:18
h Job 8:8
15:20
i Job 24:1;
27:13-23
15:21
j Job 18:11;
20:25
k Job 27:20;
1Th 5:3
15:22
l Job 19:29;
27:14
15:23
m Ps 59:15;
109:10
n Job 18:12
15:25
o Job 36:9
15:27
p Ps 17:10
15:28
q Isa 5:9
r Job 3:14
15:29
s Job 27:16-17
15:30
t Job 5:14
u Job 22:20
v Job 4:9
15:31
w Isa 59:4
15:32
x Ecc 7:17
y Job 22:16;
Ps 55:23
z Job 18:16
15:33
a Hab 3:17
15:34
b Job 8:22
15:35
c Ps 7:14;
Isa 59:4;
Hos 10:13
16:2
d Job 13:4
16:3
e Job 6:26

---

a23 Or about, looking for food

⁴I also could speak like you,
    if you were in my place;
I could make fine speeches against you
    and shake my head[f] at you.
⁵But my mouth would encourage you;
    comfort from my lips would bring you relief.

⁶"Yet if I speak, my pain is not relieved;
    and if I refrain, it does not go away.
⁷Surely, O God, you have worn me out;[g]
    you have devastated my entire household.
⁸You have bound me—and it has become a witness;
    my gauntness[h] rises up and testifies against me.[i]
⁹God assails me and tears[j] me in his anger
    and gnashes his teeth at me;[k]
    my opponent fastens on me his piercing eyes.[l]
¹⁰Men open their mouths[m] to jeer at me;
    they strike my cheek[n] in scorn
    and unite together against me.[o]
¹¹God has turned me over to evil men
    and thrown me into the clutches of the wicked.[p]
¹²All was well with me, but he shattered me;
    he seized me by the neck and crushed me.[q]
He has made me his target;[r]
¹³ his archers surround me.
Without pity, he pierces[s] my kidneys
    and spills my gall on the ground.
¹⁴Again and again[t] he bursts upon me;
    he rushes at me like a warrior.[u]

¹⁵"I have sewed sackcloth[v] over my skin
    and buried my brow in the dust.
¹⁶My face is red with weeping,
    deep shadows ring my eyes;
¹⁷yet my hands have been free of violence[w]
    and my prayer is pure.

¹⁸"O earth, do not cover my blood;[x]
    may my cry never be laid to rest![y]
¹⁹Even now my witness[z] is in heaven;
    my advocate is on high.
²⁰My intercessor is my friend[a]
    as my eyes pour out[a] tears to God;
²¹on behalf of a man he pleads[b] with God
    as a man pleads for his friend.

²²"Only a few years will pass
    before I go on the journey of no return.[c]

17

¹My spirit is broken,
    my days are cut short,
    the grave awaits me.[d]
²Surely mockers[e] surround me;

16:4
f Ps 22:7;
109:25; La 2:15;
Zep 2:15;
Mt 27:39
16:7
g Job 7:3
16:8
h Job 19:20
i Job 10:17
16:9
j Hos 6:1
k Ps 35:16;
La 2:16; Ac 7:54
l Job 13:24
16:10
m Ps 22:13
n Isa 50:6;
La 3:30;
Mic 5:1;
Ac 23:2
o Ps 35:15
16:11
p Job 1:15,17
16:12
q Job 9:17
r La 3:12
16:13
s Job 20:24
16:14
t Job 9:17
u Joel 2:7
16:15
v Ge 37:34
16:17
w Isa 59:6;
Jnh 3:8
16:18
x Isa 26:21
y Ps 66:18-19
16:19
z Ge 31:50;
Ro 1:9; 1Th 2:5
16:20
a La 2:19
16:21
b Ps 9:4
16:22
c Ecc 12:5
17:1
d Ps 88:3-4
17:2
e 1Sa 1:6-7

---

a20 Or My friends treat me with scorn

my eyes must dwell on their hostility.

[3]"Give me, O God, the pledge you demand. [f]
Who else will put up security[g] for me?[h]
[4]You have closed their minds to understanding;
therefore you will not let them triumph.
[5]If a man denounces his friends for reward,
the eyes of his children will fail. [i]

[6]"God has made me a byword[j] to everyone,
a man in whose face people spit.
[7]My eyes have grown dim with grief;[k]
my whole frame is but a shadow.
[8]Upright men are appalled at this;
the innocent are aroused[l] against the ungodly.
[9]Nevertheless, the righteous[m] will hold to their ways,
and those with clean hands[n] will grow stronger.

[10]"But come on, all of you, try again!
I will not find a wise man among you. [o]
[11]My days have passed, my plans are shattered,
and so are the desires of my heart. [p]
[12]These men turn night into day;
in the face of darkness they say, 'Light is near.'
[13]If the only home I hope for is the grave,[a][q]
if I spread out my bed in darkness,
[14]if I say to corruption,[r] 'You are my father,'
and to the worm,[s] 'My mother' or 'My sister,'
[15]where then is my hope?[t]
Who can see any hope for me?
[16]Will it go down to the gates of death[a]?[u]
Will we descend together into the dust?"

Bildad

18 Then Bildad the Shuhite replied:

[2]"When will you end these speeches?
Be sensible, and then we can talk.
[3]Why are we regarded as cattle
and considered stupid in your sight?[v]
[4]You who tear yourself[w] to pieces in your anger,
is the earth to be abandoned for your sake?
Or must the rocks be moved from their place?

[5]"The lamp of the wicked is snuffed out;[x]
the flame of his fire stops burning.
[6]The light in his tent becomes dark;
the lamp beside him goes out.
[7]The vigor of his step is weakened;[y]
his own schemes[z] throw him down. [a]
[8]His feet thrust him into a net[b]
and he wanders into its mesh.

[a]13,16 Hebrew *Sheol*

17:3
f Ps 119:122
g Pr 6:1
h Isa 38:14
17:5
i Job 11:20
17:6
j Job 30:9
17:7
k Job 16:8
17:8
l Job 22:19
17:9
m Pr 4:18
n Job 22:30
17:10
o Job 12:2
17:11
p Job 7:6
17:13
q Job 3:13
17:14
r Job 13:28;
30:28,30;
Ps 16:10
s Job 21:26
17:15
t Job 7:6
17:16
u Job 3:17-19;
Jnh 2:6
18:3
v Ps 73:22
18:4
w Job 13:14
18:5
x Job 21:17;
Pr 13:9; 20:20;
24:20
18:7
y Pr 4:12
z Job 5:13
a Job 15:6
18:8
b Job 22:10;
Ps 9:15; 35:7

⁹A trap seizes him by the heel;
a snare holds him fast.
¹⁰A noose is hidden for him on the ground;
a trap lies in his path.
¹¹Terrors startle him on every side[c]
and dog[d] his every step.
¹²Calamity is hungry[e] for him;
disaster is ready for him when he falls.
¹³It eats away parts of his skin;
death's firstborn devours his limbs.[f]
¹⁴He is torn from the security of his tent[g]
and marched off to the king of terrors.
¹⁵Fire resides[a] in his tent;
burning sulfur[h] is scattered over his dwelling.
¹⁶His roots dry up below[i]
and his branches wither above.[j]
¹⁷The memory of him perishes from the earth;
he has no name in the land.[k]
¹⁸He is driven from light into darkness[l]
and is banished from the world.
¹⁹He has no offspring[m] or descendants[n] among his
people,
no survivor where once he lived.[o]
²⁰Men of the west are appalled at his fate;[p]
men of the east are seized with horror.
²¹Surely such is the dwelling[q] of an evil man;
such is the place of one who knows not God."[r]

Job

19 Then Job replied:

²"How long will you torment me
and crush me with words?
³Ten times now you have reproached me;
shamelessly you attack me.
⁴If it is true that I have gone astray,
my error[s] remains my concern alone.
⁵If indeed you would exalt yourselves above me[t]
and use my humiliation against me,
⁶then know that God has wronged me[u]
and drawn his net[v] around me.

⁷"Though I cry, 'I've been wronged!' I get no response;[w]
though I call for help, there is no justice.[x]
⁸He has blocked my way so I cannot pass;[y]
he has shrouded my paths in darkness.[z]
⁹He has stripped[a] me of my honor
and removed the crown from my head.[b]
¹⁰He tears me down[c] on every side till I am gone;
he uproots my hope[d] like a tree.[e]
¹¹His anger[f] burns against me;

18:11
c Job 15:21;
Jer 6:25; 20:3
d Job 20:8
18:12
e Isa 8:21
18:13
f Zec 14:12
18:14
g Job 8:22
18:15
h Ps 11:6
18:16
i Isa 5:24;
Hos 9:1-16;
Am 2:9
j Job 15:30;
Mal 4:1
18:17
k Ps 34:16;
Pr 2:22; 10:7
18:18
l Job 5:14
18:19
m Jer 22:30
n Isa 14:22
o Job 27:14-15
18:20
p Ps 37:13;
Jer 50:27,31
18:21
q Job 21:28
r Jer 9:3;
1Th 4:5
19:4
s Job 6:24
19:5
t Ps 35:26;
38:16; 55:12
19:6
u Job 27:2
v Job 18:8
19:7
w Job 30:20
x Job 9:24;
Hab 1:2-4
19:8
y Job 3:23;
La 3:7
z Job 30:26
19:9
a Job 12:17
b Ps 89:39,44;
La 5:16
19:10
c Job 12:14
d Job 7:6
e Job 24:20
19:11
f Job 16:9

a15 Or *Nothing he had remains*

he counts me among his enemies.[g]

[12]His troops advance in force;[h]
they build a siege ramp[i] against me
and encamp around my tent.

[13]"He has alienated my brothers[j] from me;
my acquaintances are completely estranged from me.[k]
[14]My kinsmen have gone away;
my friends have forgotten me.
[15]My guests and my maidservants count me a stranger;
they look upon me as an alien.
[16]I summon my servant, but he does not answer,
though I beg him with my own mouth.
[17]My breath is offensive to my wife;
I am loathsome to my own brothers.
[18]Even the little boys[l] scorn me;
when I appear, they ridicule me.
[19]All my intimate friends[m] detest me;[n]
those I love have turned against me.
[20]I am nothing but skin and bones;[o]
I have escaped with only the skin of my teeth.[a]

[21]"Have pity on me, my friends, have pity,
for the hand of God has struck me.
[22]Why do you pursue[p] me as God does?
Will you never get enough of my flesh?[q]

[23]"Oh, that my words were recorded,
that they were written on a scroll,[r]
[24]that they were inscribed with an iron tool on[b] lead,
or engraved in rock forever!
[25]I know that my Redeemer[cs] lives,[t]
and that in the end he will stand upon the earth.[d]
[26]And after my skin has been destroyed,
yet[e] in[f] my flesh I will see God;[u]
[27]I myself will see him
with my own eyes—I, and not another.
How my heart yearns[v] within me!

[28]"If you say, 'How we will hound him,
since the root of the trouble lies in him,[g]'
[29]you should fear the sword yourselves;
for wrath will bring punishment by the sword,[w]
and then you will know that there is judgment.[h] "[x]

Zophar

20 Then Zophar the Naamathite replied:

[2]"My troubled thoughts prompt me to answer
because I am greatly disturbed.

19:11
g Job 13:24
19:12
h Job 16:13
i Job 30:12
19:13
j Ps 69:8
k Job 16:7;
Ps 88:8
19:18
l 2Ki 2:23
19:19
m Ps 55:12-13
n Ps 38:11
19:20
o Job 33:21;
Ps 102:5
19:22
p Job 13:25;
16:11 q Ps 69:26
19:23
r Isa 30:8
19:25
s Ps 78:35;
Pr 23:11;
Isa 43:14;
Jer 50:34
t Job 16:19
19:26
u Ps 17:15;
Mt 5:8;
1Co 13:12;
1Jn 3:2
19:27
v Ps 73:26
19:29
w Job 15:22
x Job 22:4;
Ps 1:5; 9:7

---

[a]20 Or *only my gums*   [b]24 Or *and*   [c]25 Or *defender*   [d]25 Or *upon my grave*   [e]26 Or
And after I awake, / though this body, has been destroyed, / then   [f]26 Or */ apart from*   [g]28 **Many**
Hebrew manuscripts, Septuagint and Vulgate; most Hebrew manuscripts *me*   [h]29 Or / *that you*
may come to know the Almighty

³I hear a rebukeʸ that dishonors me,
and my understanding inspires me to reply.

⁴"Surely you know how it has been from of old,
ever since manᵃ was placed on the earth,
⁵that the mirth of the wicked is brief,
the joy of the godless lasts but a moment. ᶻ
⁶Though his pride reaches to the heavens
and his head touches the clouds, ᵃ
⁷he will perish forever, ᵇ like his own dung;
those who have seen him will say, 'Where is he?'ᶜ
⁸Like a dreamᵈ he flies away, ᵉ no more to be found,
bannishedᶠ like a vision of the night. ᵍ
⁹The eye that saw him will not see him again;
his place will look on him no more. ʰ
¹⁰His childrenⁱ must make amends to the poor;
his own hands must give back his wealth. ʲ
¹¹The youthful vigorᵏ that fills his bones
will lie with him in the dust. ˡ

¹²"Though evil is sweet in his mouth
and he hides it under his tongue,
¹³though he cannot bear to let it go
and keeps it in his mouth, ᵐ
¹⁴yet his food will turn sour in his stomach;
it will become the venom of serpents within him.
¹⁵He will spit out the riches he swallowed;
God will make his stomach vomit them up.
¹⁶He will suck the poisonⁿ of serpents;
the fangs of an adder will kill him. ᵒ
¹⁷He will not enjoy the streams,
the rivers flowing with honeyᵖ and cream. �q
¹⁸What he toiled for he must give back uneaten;
he will not enjoy the profit from his trading.
¹⁹For he has oppressed the poor and left them destitute;ʳ
he has seized houses he did not build.

²⁰"Surely he will have no respite from his craving;ˢ
he cannot save himself by his treasure.
²¹Nothing is left for him to devour;
his prosperity will not endure. ᵗ
²²In the midst of his plenty, distress will overtake him;
the full force of misery will come upon him.
²³When he has filled his belly,
God will vent his burning anger against him
and rain down his blows upon him. ᵘ
²⁴Though he fleesᵛ from an iron weapon,
a bronze-tipped arrow pierces him.
²⁵He pulls it out of his back,
the gleaming point out of his liver.
Terrorsʷ will come over him;ˣ

20:3
y Job 19:3
20:5
z Job 8:12;
Ps 37:35-36;
73:19
20:6
a Isa 14:13-14;
Ob 1:3-4
20:7
b Job 4:20
c Job 7:10; 8:18
20:8
d Ps 73:20
e Job 27:21-23
f Job 18:18
g Ps 90:5
20:9
h Job 7:8
20:10
i Job 5:4
j Job 27:16-17
20:11
k Job 13:26
l Job 21:26
20:13
m Nu 11:18-20
20:16
n Dt 32:32
o Dt 32:24
20:17
p Dt 32:13
q Job 29:6
20:19
r Job 24:4,14;
35:9
20:20
s Ecc 5:12-14
20:21
t Job 15:29
20:23
u Ps 78:30-31
20:24
v Isa 24:18;
Am 5:19
20:25
w Job 18:11
x Job 16:13

ᵃ4 Or *Adam*

²⁶ total darkness^y lies in wait for his treasures.
  A fire unfanned will consume him^z
  and devour what is left in his tent.
²⁷The heavens will expose his guilt;
  the earth will rise up against him.^a
²⁸A flood will carry off his house,^b
  rushing waters^a on the day of God's wrath.^c
²⁹Such is the fate God allots the wicked,
  the heritage appointed for them by God."^d

Job
21

Then Job replied:

²"Listen carefully to my words;
  let this be the consolation you give me.
³Bear with me while I speak,
  and after I have spoken, mock on.^e

⁴"Is my complaint directed to man?
  Why should I not be impatient?^f
⁵Look at me and be astonished;
  clap your hand over your mouth.^g
⁶When I think about this, I am terrified;
  trembling seizes my body.
⁷Why do the wicked live on,
  growing old and increasing in power?^h
⁸They see their children established around them,
  their offspring before their eyes.ⁱ
⁹Their homes are safe and free from fear;^j
  the rod of God is not upon them.
¹⁰Their bulls never fail to breed;
  their cows calve and do not miscarry.^k
¹¹They send forth their children as a flock;
  their little ones dance about.
¹²They sing to the music of tambourine and harp;
  they make merry to the sound of the flute.^l
¹³They spend their years in prosperity^m
  and go down to the grave^b in peace.^c
¹⁴Yet they say to God, 'Leave us alone!ⁿ
  We have no desire to know your ways.^o
¹⁵Who is the Almighty, that we should serve him?
  What would we gain by praying to him?'^p
¹⁶But their prosperity is not in their own hands,
  so I stand aloof from the counsel of the wicked.

¹⁷"Yet how often is the lamp of the wicked snuffed out?^q
  How often does calamity come upon them,
  the fate God allots in his anger?
¹⁸How often are they like straw before the wind,
  like chaff^r swept away by a gale?

20:26
y Job 18:18
z Ps 21:9
20:27
a Dt 31:28
20:28
b Dt 28:31
c Job 21:17, 20,30
20:29
d Job 27:13
21:3
e Job 16:10
21:4
f Job 6:11
21:5
g Jdg 18:19; Job 29:9; 40:4
21:7
h Job 12:6; Ps 73:3; Jer 12:1; Hab 1:13
21:8
i Ps 17:14
21:9
j Ps 73:5
21:10
k Ex 23:26
21:12
l Ps 81:2
21:13
m Job 36:11
21:14
n Job 22:17
o Pr 1:29
21:15
p Ex 5:2; Job 34:9; Mal 3:14
21:17
q Job 18:5
21:18
r Job 13:25; Ps 1:4

---

^a28 Or *The possessions in his house will be carried off, / washed away*   ^b13 Hebrew *Sheol*   ^c13 Or
in an instant

19It is said, 'God stores up a man's punishment for his
    sons.'s
Let him repay the man himself, so that he will know
    it!
20Let his own eyes see his destruction;
    let him drinkᵗ of the wrath of the Almighty.ᵃ ᵘ
21For what does he care about the family he leaves behind
    when his allotted monthsᵛ come to an end?

22"Can anyone teach knowledge to God,ʷ
    since he judges even the highest?ˣ
23One man dies in full vigor,
    completely secure and at ease,
24his bodyᵇ well nourished,
    his bones rich with marrow.ʸ
25Another man dies in bitterness of soul,
    never having enjoyed anything good.
26Side by side they lie in the dust,
    and worms cover them both.ᶻ

27"I know full well what you are thinking,
    the schemes by which you would wrong me.
28You say, 'Where now is the great man'sᵃ house,
    the tents where wicked men lived?'ᵇ
29Have you never questioned those who travel?
    Have you paid no regard to their accounts—
30that the evil man is spared from the day of calamity,ᶜ
    that he is delivered fromᶜ the day of wrath?ᵈ
31Who denounces his conduct to his face?
    Who repays him for what he has done?
32He is carried to the grave,
    and watch is kept over his tomb.
33The soil in the valley is sweet to him;ᵉ
    all men follow after him,
    and a countless throng goesᵈ before him.ᶠ

34"So how can you console meᵍ with your nonsense?
    Nothing is left of your answers but falsehood!"

Eliphaz

22 Then Eliphaz the Temanite replied:

2"Can a man be of benefit to God?ʰ
    Can even a wise man benefit him?
3What pleasure would it give the Almighty if you were
    righteous?
    What would he gain if your ways were blameless?

4"Is it for your piety that he rebukes you
    and brings charges against you?ⁱ
5Is not your wickedness great?

21:19
sEx 20:5;
Jer 31:29;
Eze 18:2
21:20
tPs 75:8;
Isa 51:17
uJer 25:15;
Rev 14:10
21:21
vJob 14:5
21:22
wJob 35:11;
36:22;
Isa 40:13-14;
Ro 11:34
xPs 82:1
21:24
yPr 3:8
21:26
zJob 24:20;
Ecc 9:2-3;
Isa 14:11
21:28
aJob 1:3;
12:21; 31:37
bJob 8:22
21:30
cPr 16:4
dJob 20:22,28;
2Pe 2:9
21:33
eJob 3:22;
17:16; 24:24
fJob 3:19
21:34
gJob 16:2
22:2
hLk 17:10
22:4
iJob 14:3;
19:29; Ps 143:2

ᵃ17-20 Verses 17 and 18 may be taken as exclamations and 19 and 20 as declarations.   ᵇ24 The
meaning of the Hebrew for this word is uncertain.   ᶜ30 Or *man is reserved for the day of calamity,*
/ that he is brought forth to   ᵈ33 Or */ as a countless throng went*

Are not your sins[j] endless?
6You demanded security[k] from your brothers for no
  reason;
  you stripped men of their clothing, leaving them
  naked.
7You gave no water to the weary
  and you withheld food from the hungry,[l]
8though you were a powerful man, owning land—
  an honored man,[m] living on it.
9And you sent widows away empty-handed[n]
  and broke the strength of the fatherless.
10That is why snares are all around you,
  why sudden peril terrifies you,
11why it is so dark[o] you cannot see,
  and why a flood of water covers you.[p]

12"Is not God in the heights of heaven?[q]
  And see how lofty are the highest stars!
13Yet you say, 'What does God know?[r]
  Does he judge through such darkness?[s]
14Thick clouds[t] veil him, so he does not see us
  as he goes about in the vaulted heavens.'
15Will you keep to the old path
  that evil men have trod?
16They were carried off before their time,[u]
  their foundations washed away by a flood.[v]
17They said to God, 'Leave us alone!
  What can the Almighty do to us?'[w]
18Yet it was he who filled their houses with good things,[x]
  so I stand aloof from the counsel of the wicked.[y]

19"The righteous see their ruin and rejoice;[z]
  the innocent mock[a] them, saying,
20'Surely our foes are destroyed,
  and fire[b] devours their wealth.'

21"Submit to God and be at peace with him;
  in this way prosperity will come to you.[c]
22Accept instruction from his mouth
  and lay up his words in your heart.
23If you return[d] to the Almighty, you will be restored:[e]
  If you remove wickedness far from your tent[f]
24and assign your nuggets to the dust,
  your gold of Ophir to the rocks in the ravines,[g]
25then the Almighty will be your gold,
  the choicest silver for you.[h]
26Surely then you will find delight in the Almighty[i]
  and will lift up your face to God.
27You will pray to him,[j] and he will hear you,
  and you will fulfill your vows.
28What you decide on will be done,
  and light will shine on your ways.
29When men are brought low and you say, 'Lift them up!'

22:5
jJob 11:6; 15:5
22:6
kEx 22:26;
Dt 24:6,17;
Eze 18:12,16
22:7
lJob 31:17,21,31
22:8
mIsa 3:3; 9:15
22:9
nJob 24:3,21
22:11
oJob 5:14
pPs 69:1-2;
124:4-5; La 3:54
22:12
qJob 11:8
22:13
rPs 10:11;
Isa 29:15
sEze 8:12
22:14
tJob 26:9
22:16
uJob 15:32
vJob 14:19;
Mt 7:26-27
22:17
wJob 21:15
22:18
xJob 12:6
yJob 21:16
22:19
zPs 58:10;
107:42 aPs 52:6
22:20
bJob 15:30
22:21
cPs 34:8-10
22:23
dJob 8:5;
Isa 31:6;
Zec 1:3
eIsa 19:22;
Ac 20:32
fJob 11:14
22:24
gJob 31:25
22:25
hIsa 33:6
22:26
iJob 27:10;
Isa 58:14
22:27
jJob 33:26;
34:28; Isa 58:9

then he will save the downcast. [k]

[30]He will deliver even one who is not innocent,
    who will be delivered through the cleanness of your
      hands."[l]

Job

23

Then Job replied:

[2]"Even today my complaint[m] is bitter;[n]
    his hand[a] is heavy in spite of[b] my groaning.
[3]If only I knew where to find him;
    if only I could go to his dwelling!
[4]I would state my case[o] before him
    and fill my mouth with arguments.
[5]I would find out what he would answer me,
    and consider what he would say.
[6]Would he oppose me with great power?[p]
    No, he would not press charges against me.
[7]There an upright man could present his case before
      him,[q]
    and I would be delivered forever from my judge.

[8]"But if I go to the east, he is not there;
    if I go to the west, I do not find him.
[9]When he is at work in the north, I do not see him;
    when he turns to the south, I catch no glimpse of
      him.[r]
[10]But he knows the way that I take;
    when he has tested me,[s] I will come forth as gold.[t]
[11]My feet have closely followed his steps;[u]
    I have kept to his way without turning aside.[v]
[12]I have not departed from the commands of his lips;[w]
    I have treasured the words of his mouth more than
      my daily bread.[x]

[13]"But he stands alone, and who can oppose him?
    He does whatever he pleases.[y]
[14]He carries out his decree against me,
    and many such plans he still has in store.[z]
[15]That is why I am terrified before him;
    when I think of all this, I fear him.
[16]God has made my heart faint;[a]
    the Almighty[b] has terrified me.
[17]Yet I am not silenced by the darkness,[c]
    by the thick darkness that covers my face.

24

"Why does the Almighty not set times for judgment?[d]
    Why must those who know him look in vain for such
      days?[e]
[2]Men move boundary stones;[f]
    they pasture flocks they have stolen.
[3]They drive away the orphan's donkey

22:29
k Mt 23:12;
1Pe 5:5
22:30
l Job 42:7-8
23:2
m Job 7:11
n Job 6:3
23:4
o Job 13:18
23:6
p Job 9:4
23:7
q Job 13:3
23:9
r Job 9:11
23:10
s Ps 66:10;
139:1-3 t 1Pe 1:7
23:11
u Ps 17:5
v Ps 44:18
23:12
w Job 6:10
x Jn 4:32,34
23:13
y Ps 115:3
23:14
z 1Th 3:3
23:16
a Dt 20:3;
Ps 22:14;
Jer 51:46
b Job 27:2
23:17
c Job 19:8
24:1
d Jer 46:10
e Ac 1:7
24:2
f Dt 19:14;
27:17; Pr 23:10

---

[a]2 Septuagint and Syriac; Hebrew / *the hand on me*   [b]2 Or *heavy on me in*

and take the widow's ox in pledge. g
⁴They thrust the needy from the path
   and force all the poorʰ of the land into hiding. i
⁵Like wild donkeys in the desert,
   the poor go about their laborʲ of foraging food;
   the wasteland provides food for their children.
⁶They gather fodder in the fields
   and glean in the vineyards of the wicked.
⁷Lacking clothes, they spend the night naked;
   they have nothing to cover themselves in the cold. k
⁸They are drenched by mountain rains
   and hugˡ the rocks for lack of shelter.
⁹The fatherlessᵐ child is snatched from the breast;
   the infant of the poor is seized for a debt.
¹⁰Lacking clothes, they go about naked;
   they carry the sheaves, but still go hungry.
¹¹They crush olives among the terracesᵃ;
   they tread the winepresses, yet suffer thirst.
¹²The groans of the dying rise from the city,
   and the souls of the wounded cry out for help. n
   But God charges no one with wrongdoing. o

¹³"There are those who rebel against the light,ᵖ
   who do not know its ways
   or stay in its paths. q
¹⁴When daylight is gone, the murderer rises up
   and kills the poor and needy;
   in the night he steals forth like a thief. r
¹⁵The eye of the adulterer watches for dusk;ˢ
   he thinks, 'No eye will see me,'ᵗ
   and he keeps his face concealed.
¹⁶In the dark, men break into houses,ᵘ
   but by day they shut themselves in;
   they want nothing to do with the light. v
¹⁷For all of them, deep darkness is their morningᵇ;
   they make friends with the terrors of darkness. c

¹⁸"Yet they are foamʷ on the surface of the water;ˣ
   their portion of the land is cursed,
   so that no one goes to the vineyards.
¹⁹As heat and drought snatch away the melted snow,ʸ
   so the graveᵈᶻ snatches away those who have sinned.
²⁰The womb forgets them,
   the worm feasts on them;
  evil men are no longer rememberedᵃ
   but are broken like a tree. b
²¹They prey on the barren and childless woman,
   and to the widow show no kindness. c
²²But God drags away the mighty by his power;

24:3
gDt 24:6,10,12,
17; Job 22:6
24:4
hJob 29:12;
30:25; Ps 41:1
iPr 28:28
24:5
jPs 104:23
24:7
kEx 22:27;
Job 22:6
24:8
lLa 4:5
24:9
mDt 24:17
24:12
nEze 26:15
oJob 9:23
24:13
pJn 3:19-20
qIsa 5:20
24:14
rPs 10:9
24:15
sPr 7:8-9
tPs 10:11
24:16
uEx 22:2;
Mt 6:19
vJn 3:20
24:18
wJob 9:26
xJob 22:16
24:19
yJob 6:17
zJob 21:13
24:20
aJob 18:17;
Pr 10:7
bPs 31:12;
Da 4:14
24:21
cJob 22:9

ᵃ11 Or *olives between the millstones; the meaning of the Hebrew for this word is uncertain.*
ᵇ17 Or *them, their morning is like the shadow of death*   ᶜ17 Or *of the shadow of death*
ᵈ19 Hebrew *Sheol*

though they become established, they have no
 assurance of life. d
23He may let them rest in a feeling of security, e
 but his eyes are on their ways. f
24For a little while they are exalted, and then they are
 gone; g
 they are brought low and gathered up like all others;
 they are cut off like heads of grain. h

25"If this is not so, who can prove me false
 and reduce my words to nothing?" i

Bildad

25 Then Bildad the Shuhite replied:

2"Dominion and awe belong to God; j
 he establishes order in the heights of heaven.
3Can his forces be numbered?
 Upon whom does his light not rise? k
4How then can a man be righteous before God?
 How can one born of woman be pure? l
5If even the moon m is not bright
 and the stars are not pure in his eyes, n
6how much less man, who is but a maggot—
 a son of man, o who is only a worm!" p

Job

26 Then Job replied:

2"How you have helped the powerless! q
 How you have saved the arm that is feeble! r
3What advice you have offered to one without wisdom!
 And what great insight you have displayed!
4Who has helped you utter these words?
 And whose spirit spoke from your mouth?

5"The dead are in deep anguish, s
 those beneath the waters and all that live in them.
6Death a t is naked before God;
 Destruction b lies uncovered. u
7He spreads out the northern skies v over empty space;
 he suspends the earth over nothing.
8He wraps up the waters w in his clouds, x
 yet the clouds do not burst under their weight.
9He covers the face of the full moon,
 spreading his clouds y over it.
10He marks out the horizon on the face of the waters z
 for a boundary between light and darkness. a
11The pillars of the heavens quake,
 aghast at his rebuke.
12By his power he churned up the sea; b
 by his wisdom c he cut Rahab to pieces.

a6 Hebrew *Sheol*   b6 Hebrew *Abaddon*

24:22
d Dt 28:66
24:23
e Job 12:6
f Job 11:11
24:24
g Job 14:21;
Ps 37:10
h Isa 17:5
24:25
i Job 6:28; 27:4
25:2
j Job 9:4;
Rev 1:6
25:3
k Jas 1:17
25:4
l Job 4:17; 14:4
25:5
m Job 31:26
n Job 15:15
25:6
o Job 7:17
p Ps 22:6
26:2
q Job 6:12
r Ps 71:9
26:5
s Ps 88:10
26:6
t Ps 139:8
u Job 41:11;
Pr 15:11;
Heb 4:13
26:7
v Job 9:8
26:8
w Pr 30:4
x Job 37:11
26:9
y Job 22:14;
Ps 97:2
26:10
z Pr 8:27,29
a Job 38:8-11
26:12
b Ex 14:21;
Isa 51:15;
Jer 31:35
c Job 12:13

¹³By his breath the skies became fair;
  his hand pierced the gliding serpent. ᵈ
¹⁴And these are but the outer fringe of his works;
  how faint the whisper we hear of him!
  Who then can understand the thunder of his
    power?" ᵉ

27

And Job continued his discourse: ᶠ

²"As surely as God lives, who has denied me
    justice, ᵍ
  the Almighty, who has made me taste bitterness of
    soul, ʰ
³as long as I have life within me,
  the breath of Godⁱ in my nostrils,
⁴my lips will not speak wickedness,
  and my tongue will utter no deceit. ʲ
⁵I will never admit you are in the right;
  till I die, I will not deny my integrity. ᵏ
⁶I will maintain my righteousness and never let go of it;
  my conscience will not reproach me as long as I live. ˡ

⁷"May my enemies be like the wicked,
  my adversaries like the unjust!
⁸For what hope has the godlessᵐ when he is cut off,
  when God takes away his life?ⁿ
⁹Does God listen to his cry
  when distress comes upon him?ᵒ
¹⁰Will he find delight in the Almighty?ᵖ
  Will he call upon God at all times?

¹¹"I will teach you about the power of God;
  the ways of the Almighty I will not conceal.
¹²You have all seen this yourselves.
  Why then this meaningless talk?

¹³"Here is the fate God allots to the wicked,
  the heritage a ruthless man receives from the
    Almighty:ᑫ
¹⁴However many his children, their fate is the sword;ʳ
  his offspring will never have enough to eat. ˢ
¹⁵The plague will bury those who survive him,
  and their widows will not weep for them. ᵗ
¹⁶Though he heaps up silver like dust
  and clothes like piles of clay, ᵘ
¹⁷what he lays up the righteous will wear, ᵛ
  and the innocent will divide his silver.
¹⁸The house he builds is like a moth's cocoon, ʷ
  like a hutˣ made by a watchman.
¹⁹He lies down wealthy, but will do so no more;ʸ
  when he opens his eyes, all is gone.
²⁰Terrors overtake him like a flood;ᶻ
  a tempest snatches him away in the night. ᵃ
²¹The east wind carries him off, and he is gone;

26:13
d Isa 27:1
26:14
e Job 36:29
27:1
f Job 29:1
27:2
g Job 34:5
h Job 9:18
27:3
i Job 32:8; 33:4
27:4
j Job 6:28
27:5
k Job 2:9; 13:15
27:6
l Job 2:3
27:8
m Job 8:13
n Job 11:20;
  Lk 12:20
27:9
o Job 35:12;
  Pr 1:28;
  Isa 1:15;
  Jer 14:12;
  Mic 3:4
27:10
p Job 22:26
27:13
q Job 15:20;
  20:29
27:14
r Dt 28:41;
  Job 15:22;
  Hos 9:13
s Job 20:10
27:15
t Ps 78:64
27:16
u Zec 9:3
27:17
v Pr 28:8;
  Ecc 2:26
27:18
w Job 8:14
x Isa 1:8
27:19
y Job 7:8
27:20
z Job 15:21
a Job 20:8

it sweeps him out of his place. [b]
²²It hurls itself against him without mercy[c]
  as he flees headlong from its power. [d]
²³It claps its hands in derision
  and hisses him out of his place. [e]

28

"There is a mine for silver
  and a place where gold is refined.
²Iron is taken from the earth,
  and copper is smelted from ore. [f]
³Man puts an end to the darkness;[g]
  he searches the farthest recesses
  for ore in the blackest darkness.
⁴Far from where people dwell he cuts a shaft,
  in places forgotten by the foot of man;
  far from men he dangles and sways.
⁵The earth, from which food comes, [h]
  is transformed below as by fire;
⁶sapphires[a] come from its rocks,
  and its dust contains nuggets of gold.
⁷No bird of prey knows that hidden path,
  no falcon's eye has seen it.
⁸Proud beasts do not set foot on it,
  and no lion prowls there.
⁹Man's hand assaults the flinty rock
  and lays bare the roots of the mountains.
¹⁰He tunnels through the rock;
  his eyes see all its treasures.
¹¹He searches[b] the sources of the rivers
  and brings hidden things to light.

¹²"But where can wisdom be found?[i]
  Where does understanding dwell?
¹³Man does not comprehend its worth;[j]
  it cannot be found in the land of the living.
¹⁴The deep says, 'It is not in me';
  the sea says, 'It is not with me.'
¹⁵It cannot be bought with the finest gold,
  nor can its price be weighed in silver. [k]
¹⁶It cannot be bought with the gold of Ophir,
  with precious onyx or sapphires.
¹⁷Neither gold nor crystal can compare with it,
  nor can it be had for jewels of gold. [l]
¹⁸Coral and jasper are not worthy of mention;
  the price of wisdom is beyond rubies. [m]
¹⁹The topaz of Cush cannot compare with it;
  it cannot be bought with pure gold. [n]

²⁰"Where then does wisdom come from?
  Where does understanding dwell?[o]
²¹It is hidden from the eyes of every living thing,

27:21
b Job 7:10;
21:18
27:22
c Jer 13:14;
Eze 5:11; 24:14
d Job 11:20
27:23
e Job 18:18
28:2
f Dt 8:9
28:3
g Ecc 1:13
28:5
h Ps 104:14
28:12
i Ecc 7:24
28:13
j Pr 3:15;
Mt 13:44-46
28:15
k Pr 3:13-14;
8:10-11; 16:16
28:17
l Pr 16:16
28:18
m Pr 3:15
28:19
n Pr 8:19
28:20
o ver 23,28

---

a 6 Or *lapis lazuli;* also in verse 16   b 11 Septuagint, Aquila and Vulgate; Hebrew *He dams up* concealed even from the birds of the air.

²²Destruction[a][p] and Death say,
    'Only a rumor of it has reached our ears.'
²³God understands the way to it
    and he alone knows where it dwells,[q]
²⁴for he views the ends of the earth[r]
    and sees everything under the heavens.[s]
²⁵When he established the force of the wind
    and measured out the waters,[t]
²⁶when he made a decree for the rain
    and a path for the thunderstorm,[u]
²⁷then he looked at wisdom and appraised it;
    he confirmed it and tested it.
²⁸And he said to man,
    'The fear of the Lord—that is wisdom,
    and to shun evil is understanding.[v] '"

29

Job continued his discourse:[w]

²"How I long for the months gone by,
    for the days when God watched over me,[x]
³when his lamp shone upon my head
    and by his light I walked through darkness![y]
⁴Oh, for the days when I was in my prime,
    when God's intimate friendship blessed my house,[z]
⁵when the Almighty was still with me
    and my children were around me,
⁶when my path was drenched with cream[a]
    and the rock[b] poured out for me streams of olive oil.[c]

⁷"When I went to the gate[d] of the city
    and took my seat in the public square,
⁸the young men saw me and stepped aside
    and the old men rose to their feet;
⁹the chief men refrained from speaking
    and covered their mouths with their hands;[e]
¹⁰the voices of the nobles were hushed,
    and their tongues stuck to the roof of their mouths.[f]
¹¹Whoever heard me spoke well of me,
    and those who saw me commended me,
¹²because I rescued the poor[g] who cried for help,
    and the fatherless[h] who had none to assist him.[i]
¹³The man who was dying blessed me;[j]
    I made the widow's[k] heart sing.
¹⁴I put on righteousness[l] as my clothing;
    justice was my robe and my turban.
¹⁵I was eyes[m] to the blind
    and feet to the lame.
¹⁶I was a father to the needy;[n]
    I took up the case of the stranger.
¹⁷I broke the fangs of the wicked

28:22
p Job 26:6
28:23
q Pr 8:22-31
28:24
r Ps 33:13-14
s Pr 15:3
28:25
t Job 12:15;
Ps 135:7
28:26
u Job 37:3,8,11;
38:25,27
28:28
v Dt 4:6;
Ps 111:10;
Pr 1:7; 9:10
29:1
w Job 13:12;
27:1
29:2
x Jer 31:28
29:3
y Job 11:17
29:4
z Ps 25:14;
Pr 3:32
29:6
a Job 20:17
b Ps 81:16
c Dt 32:13
29:7
d Job 31:21
29:9
e Job 21:5
29:10
f Ps 137:6
29:12
g Job 24:4
h Job 31:17,21
i Ps 72:12;
Pr 21:13
29:13
j Job 31:20
k Job 22:9
29:14
l Job 27:6;
Ps 132:9;
Isa 59:17;
61:10; Eph 6:14
29:15
m Nu 10:31
29:16
n Job 24:4;
Pr 29:7

ᵃ22 Hebrew *Abaddon*

and snatched the victims from their teeth. °

18"I thought, 'I will die in my own house,
　　my days as numerous as the grains of sand. ᵖ
19My roots will reach to the water, �۾
　　and the dew will lie all night on my branches.
20My glory will remain fresh in me,
　　the bowʳ ever new in my hand.'ˢ

21"Men listened to me expectantly,
　　waiting in silence for my counsel.
22After I had spoken, they spoke no more;
　　my words fell gently on their ears. ᵗ
23They waited for me as for showers
　　and drank in my words as the spring rain.
24When I smiled at them, they scarcely believed it;
　　the light of my face was precious to them. ᵃ
25I chose the way for them and sat as their chief;
　　I dwelt as a kingᵘ among his troops;
　　I was like one who comforts mourners. ᵛ

30

"But now they mock me, ʷ
　　men younger than I,
whose fathers I would have disdained
　　to put with my sheep dogs.
2Of what use was the strength of their hands to me,
　　since their vigor had gone from them?
3Haggard from want and hunger,
　　they roamedᵇ the parched land
　　in desolate wastelands at night.
4In the brush they gathered salt herbs,
　　and their foodᶜ was the root of the broom tree.
5They were banished from their fellow men,
　　shouted at as if they were thieves.
6They were forced to live in the dry stream beds,
　　among the rocks and in holes in the ground.
7They brayed among the bushes
　　and huddled in the undergrowth.
8A base and nameless brood,
　　they were driven out of the land.

9"And now their sons mock meˣ in song;ʸ
　　I have become a bywordᶻ among them.
10They detest me and keep their distance;
　　they do not hesitate to spit in my face. ᵃ
11Now that God has unstrung my bow and afflicted me, ᵇ
　　they throw off restraintᶜ in my presence.
12On my right the tribeᵈ attacks;
　　they lay snares for my feet, ᵈ
　　they build their siege ramps against me. ᵉ
13They break up my road;ᶠ

29:17
ºPs 3:7
29:18
ᵖPs 30:6
29:19
ᵠJob 18:16;
Jer 17:8
29:20
ʳPs 18:34
ˢGe 49:24
29:22
ᵗDt 32:2
29:25
ᵘJob 1:3; 31:37
ᵛJob 4:4
30:1
ʷJob 12:4
30:9
ˣPs 69:11
ʸJob 12:4;
La 3:14,63
ᶻJob 17:6
30:10
ᵃNu 12:14;
Dt 25:9;
Isa 50:6;
Mt 26:67
30:11
ᵇRu 1:21
ᶜPs 32:9
30:12
ᵈPs 140:4-5
ᵉJob 19:12
30:13
ᶠIsa 3:12

they succeed in destroying me—
without anyone's helping them. *ᵃ*

¹⁴They advance as through a gaping breach;
amid the ruins they come rolling in.

¹⁵Terrors overwhelm me;ᵍ
my dignity is driven away as by the wind,
my safety vanishes like a cloud. ʰ

¹⁶"And now my life ebbs away;ⁱ
days of suffering grip me.

¹⁷Night pierces my bones;
my gnawing pains never rest.

¹⁸In his great power ⸤God⸥ becomes like clothing to me*ᵇ* ;
he binds me like the neck of my garment.

¹⁹He throws me into the mud,ʲ
and I am reduced to dust and ashes.

²⁰"I cry out to you, O God, but you do not answer;ᵏ
I stand up, but you merely look at me.

²¹You turn on me ruthlessly;ˡ
with the might of your handᵐ you attack me. ⁿ

²²You snatch me up and drive me before the wind;ᵒ
you toss me about in the storm. ᵖ

²³I know you will bring me down to death,�q
to the place appointed for all the living. ʳ

²⁴"Surely no one lays a hand on a broken man
when he cries for help in his distress. ˢ

²⁵Have I not wept for those in trouble?
Has not my soul grieved for the poor?ᵗ

²⁶Yet when I hoped for good, evil came;
when I looked for light, then came darkness. ᵘ

²⁷The churning inside me never stops;ᵛ
days of suffering confront me.

²⁸I go about blackened, ʷ but not by the sun;
I stand up in the assembly and cry for help. ˣ

²⁹I have become a brother of jackals,ʸ
a companion of owls. ᶻ

³⁰My skin grows black and peels;ᵃ
my body burns with fever. ᵇ

³¹My harp is tuned to mourning, ᶜ
and my flute to the sound of wailing.

31 "I made a covenant with my eyes
not to look lustfully at a girl. ᵈ

²For what is man's lot from God above,
his heritage from the Almighty on high?ᵉ

³Is it not ruinᶠ for the wicked,
disaster for those who do wrong?ᵍ

⁴Does he not see my waysʰ
and count my every step?ⁱ

30:15
gJob 31:23;
Ps 55:4-5
hJob 3:25;
Hos 13:3
30:16
iJob 3:24;
Ps 22:14; 42:4
30:19
jPs 69:2,14
30:20
kJob 19:7
30:21
lJob 19:6,22
mJob 16:9,14
nJob 10:3
30:22
oJob 27:21
pJob 9:17
30:23
qJob 9:22; 10:8
rJob 3:19
30:24
sJob 19:7
30:25
tJob 24:4;
Ps 35:13-14;
Ro 12:15
30:26
uJob 3:25-26;
19:8; Jer 8:15
30:27
vLa 2:11
30:28
wPs 38:6; 42:9;
43:2 xJob 19:7
30:29
yPs 44:19
zPs 102:6;
Mic 1:8
30:30
aLa 4:8
bPs 102:3
30:31
cIsa 24:8
31:1
dMt 5:28
31:2
eJob 20:29
31:3
fJob 21:30
gJob 34:22
31:4
h2Ch 16:9
iPr 5:21

---

*ᵃ*13 Or *me.* / 'No one can help him,' ⸤they say⸥.   *ᵇ*18 Hebrew; Septuagint ⸤God⸥ grasps my clothing

31:5
jMic 2:11
31:6
kJob 6:2; 27:5-6
31:7
lJob 23:11
mJob 9:30
31:8
nLev 26:16;
Job 20:18
oMic 6:15
31:9
pJob 24:15
31:10
qDt 28:30;
Jer 8:10
31:11
rGe 38:24;
Lev 20:10;
Dt 22:22-24
31:12
sJob 15:30
tJob 26:6
uJob 20:28
31:13
vDt 24:14-15
31:15
wJob 10:3
31:16
xJob 5:16;
20:19 yJob 22:9
31:17
zJob 22:7;
29:12
31:19
aJob 22:6
bJob 24:4
31:21
cJob 22:9
31:22
dJob 38:15
31:23
eJob 13:11
31:24
fJob 22:25
gMt 6:24;
Mk 10:24
31:25
hPs 62:10
31:26
iEze 8:16

[5]"If I have walked in falsehood
  or my foot has hurried after deceit[j] —
[6]let God weigh me in honest scales[k]
  and he will know that I am blameless—
[7]if my steps have turned from the path,[l]
  if my heart has been led by my eyes,
  or if my hands[m] have been defiled,
[8]then may others eat what I have sown,[n]
  and may my crops be uprooted.[o]

[9]"If my heart has been enticed[p] by a woman,
  or if I have lurked at my neighbor's door,
[10]then may my wife grind another man's grain,
  and may other men sleep with her.[q]
[11]For that would have been shameful,
  a sin to be judged.[r]
[12]It is a fire[s] that burns to Destruction[a];[t]
  it would have uprooted my harvest.[u]

[13]"If I have denied justice to my menservants and
      maidservants
  when they had a grievance against me,[v]
[14]what will I do when God confronts me?
  What will I answer when called to account?
[15]Did not he who made me in the womb make them?
  Did not the same one form us both within our
      mothers?[w]

[16]"If I have denied the desires of the poor[x]
  or let the eyes of the widow[y] grow weary,
[17]if I have kept my bread to myself,
  not sharing it with the fatherless[z] —
[18]but from my youth I reared him as would a father,
  and from my birth I guided the widow—
[19]if I have seen anyone perishing for lack of clothing,[a]
  or a needy[b] man without a garment,
[20]and his heart did not bless me
  for warming him with the fleece from my sheep,
[21]if I have raised my hand against the fatherless,[c]
  knowing that I had influence in court,
[22]then let my arm fall from the shoulder,
  let it be broken off at the joint.[d]
[23]For I dreaded destruction from God,
  and for fear of his splendor[e] I could not do such
      things.

[24]"If I have put my trust in gold[f]
  or said to pure gold, 'You are my security,'[g]
[25]if I have rejoiced over my great wealth,[h]
  the fortune my hands had gained,
[26]if I have regarded the sun[i] in its radiance
  or the moon moving in splendor,

---

a12 Hebrew *Abaddon*

²⁷so that my heart was secretly enticed
   and my hand offered them a kiss of homage,
²⁸then these also would be sins to be judged,[j]
   for I would have been unfaithful to God on high.

²⁹"If I have rejoiced at my enemy's misfortune[k]
   or gloated over the trouble that came to him[l] —
³⁰I have not allowed my mouth to sin
   by invoking a curse against his life—
³¹if the men of my household have never said,
   'Who has not had his fill of Job's meat?'[m]—
³²but no stranger had to spend the night in the street,
   for my door was always open to the traveler[n]—
³³if I have concealed[o] my sin as men do,[a]
   by hiding[p] my guilt in my heart
³⁴because I so feared the crowd[q]
   and so dreaded the contempt of the clans
   that I kept silent and would not go outside

³⁵("Oh, that I had someone to hear me![r]
   I sign now my defense—let the Almighty answer me;
   let my accuser[s] put his indictment in writing.
³⁶Surely I would wear it on my shoulder,
   I would put it on like a crown.
³⁷I would give him an account of my every step;
   like a prince[t] I would approach him.)—

³⁸"if my land cries out against me[u]
   and all its furrows are wet with tears,
³⁹if I have devoured its yield without payment[v]
   or broken the spirit of its tenants,[w]
⁴⁰then let briers[x] come up instead of wheat
   and weeds instead of barley."

The words of Job are ended.

Elihu

32 So these three men stopped answering Job, because he was righteous in his own eyes.[y] ²But Elihu son of Barakel the Buzite,[z] of the family of Ram, became very angry with Job for justifying himself rather than God.[a] ³He was also angry with the three friends, because they had found no way to refute Job, and yet had condemned him.[b] ⁴Now Elihu had waited before speaking to Job because they were older than he. ⁵But when he saw that the three men had nothing more to say, his anger was aroused.
⁶So Elihu son of Barakel the Buzite said:

   "I am young in years,
      and you are old;[b]
   that is why I was fearful,
      not daring to tell you what I know.

---

^a33 Or *as Adam did*   ^b3 Masoretic Text; an ancient Hebrew scribal tradition *Job, and so had condemned God*

31:28
j Dt 17:2-7
31:29
k Ob 1:12
l Pr 17:5;
24:17-18
31:31
m Job 22:7
31:32
n Ge 19:2-3;
Ro 12:13
31:33
o Pr 28:13
p Ge 3:8
31:34
q Ex 23:2
31:35
r Job 19:7; 30:28
s Job 27:7;
35:14
31:37
t Job 1:3; 29:25
31:38
u Ge 4:10
31:39
v 1Ki 21:19
w Lev 19:13;
Jas 5:4
31:40
x Ge 3:18
32:1
y Job 10:7; 33:9
32:2
z Ge 22:21
a Job 27:5;
30:21
32:6
b Job 15:10

7I thought, 'Age should speak;
　　advanced years should teach wisdom.'
8But it is the spirit[a] in a man,
　　the breath of the Almighty,[c] that gives him
　　　　understanding.[d]
9It is not only the old[b] who are wise,[e]
　　not only the aged who understand what is right.

10"Therefore I say: Listen to me;
　　I too will tell you what I know.
11I waited while you spoke,
　　I listened to your reasoning;
　　while you were searching for words,
12　　I gave you my full attention.
　　But not one of you has proved Job wrong;
　　none of you has answered his arguments.
13Do not say, 'We have found wisdom;[f]
　　let God refute him, not man.'
14But Job has not marshaled his words against me,
　　and I will not answer him with your arguments.

15"They are dismayed and have no more to say;
　　words have failed them.
16Must I wait, now that they are silent,
　　now that they stand there with no reply?
17I too will have my say;
　　I too will tell what I know.
18For I am full of words,
　　and the spirit within me compels me;
19inside I am like bottled-up wine,
　　like new wineskins ready to burst.
20I must speak and find relief;
　　I must open my lips and reply.
21I will show partiality[g] to no one,[h]
　　nor will I flatter any man;
22for if I were skilled in flattery,
　　my Maker would soon take me away.

33 "But now, Job, listen to my words;
　　pay attention to everything I say.[i]
2I am about to open my mouth;
　　my words are on the tip of my tongue.
3My words come from an upright heart;
　　my lips sincerely speak what I know.[j]
4The Spirit of God has made me;[k]
　　the breath of the Almighty[l] gives me life.
5Answer me[m] then, if you can;
　　prepare[n] yourself and confront me.
6I am just like you before God;
　　I too have been taken from clay.[o]
7No fear of me should alarm you,

32:8
c Job 27:3; 33:4
d Pr 2:6
32:9
e 1Co 1:26
32:13
f Jer 9:23
32:21
g Lev 19:15;
Job 13:10
h Mt 22:16
33:1
i Job 13:6
33:3
j Job 6:28; 27:4;
36:4
33:4
k Ge 2:7;
Job 10:3
l Job 27:3
33:5
m ver 32
n Job 13:18
33:6
o Job 4:19

---

a8 Or *Spirit*; also in verse 18　　　b9 Or *many*; or *great*

nor should my hand be heavy upon you. [p]

8"But you have said in my hearing—
  I heard the very words—
9'I am pure [q] and without sin; [r]
  I am clean and free from guilt.
10Yet God has found fault with me;
  he considers me his enemy. [s]
11He fastens my feet in shackles; [t]
  he keeps close watch on all my paths.' [u]

12"But I tell you, in this you are not right,
  for God is greater than man. [v]
13Why do you complain to him [w]
  that he answers none of man's words[a]?
14For God does speak [x]—now one way, now another—
  though man may not perceive it.
15In a dream, [y] in a vision of the night,
  when deep sleep falls on men
  as they slumber in their beds,
16he may speak [z] in their ears
  and terrify them with warnings,
17to turn man from wrongdoing
  and keep him from pride,
18to preserve his soul from the pit, [b] [a]
  his life from perishing by the sword. [c] [b]
19Or a man may be chastened on a bed of pain
  with constant distress in his bones, [c]
20so that his very being finds food [d] repulsive
  and his soul loathes the choicest meal. [e]
21His flesh wastes away to nothing,
  and his bones, once hidden, now stick out. [f]
22His soul draws near to the pit, [d]
  and his life to the messengers of death. [e] [g]

23"Yet if there is an angel on his side
  as a mediator, one out of a thousand,
  to tell a man what is right for him, [h]
24to be gracious to him and say,
  'Spare him from going down to the pit [f]; [i]
  I have found a ransom for him'—
25then his flesh is renewed like a child's;
  it is restored as in the days of his youth. [j]
26He prays to God and finds favor with him, [k]
  he sees God's face and shouts for joy; [l]
  he is restored by God to his righteous state. [m]
27Then he comes to men and says,
  'I sinned, [n] and perverted what was right, [o]
  but I did not get what I deserved. [p]
28He redeemed my soul from going down to the pit, [g]

33:7
p Job 9:34;
13:21; 2Co 2:4
33:9
q Job 10:7
r Job 13:23;
16:17
33:10
s Job 13:24
33:11
t Job 13:27
u Job 14:16
33:12
v Ecc 7:20
33:13
w Job 40:2;
Isa 45:9
33:14
x Ps 62:11
33:15
y Job 4:13
33:16
z Job 36:10,15
33:18
a ver 22,24,28,30
b Job 15:22
33:19
c Job 30:17
33:20
d Ps 107:18
e Job 3:24; 6:6
33:21
f Job 16:8; 19:20
33:22
g Ps 88:3
33:23
h Mic 6:8
33:24
i Isa 38:17
33:25
j 2Ki 5:14
33:26
k Job 34:28
l Job 22:26
m Ps 50:15;
51:12
33:27
n 2Sa 12:13
o Lk 15:21
p Ro 6:21

---

[a]13 Or *that he does not answer for any of his actions*   [b]18 Or *preserve him from the grave*   [c]18 Or
from crossing the River   [d]22 Or *He draws near to the grave*   [e]22 Or *to the dead*   [f]24 Or *grave*
[g]28 Or *redeemed me from going down to the grave*

and I will live to enjoy the light.'�q

29"God does all these things to a manʳ —
　　twice, even three times—
30to turn back his soul from the pit,ᵃ
　　that the light of lifeˢ may shine on him.

31"Pay attention, Job, and listen to me;
　　be silent, and I will speak.
32If you have anything to say, answer me;
　　speak up, for I want you to be cleared.
33But if not, then listen to me;
　　be silent, and I will teach you wisdom.ᵗ "

34 Then Elihu said:

2"Hear my words, you wise men;
　　listen to me, you men of learning.
3For the ear tests words
　　as the tongue tastes food.ᵘ
4Let us discern for ourselves what is right;
　　let us learn together what is good.ᵛ

5"Job says, 'I am innocent,ʷ
　　but God denies me justice.ˣ
6Although I am right,
　　I am considered a liar;
although I am guiltless,
　　his arrow inflicts an incurable wound.'ʸ
7What man is like Job,
　　who drinks scorn like water?ᶻ
8He keeps company with evildoers;
　　he associates with wicked men.ᵃ
9For he says, 'It profits a man nothing
　　when he tries to please God.'ᵇ

10"So listen to me, you men of understanding.
　　Far be it from God to do evil,ᶜ
　　from the Almighty to do wrong.ᵈ
11He repays a man for what he has done;ᵉ
　　he brings upon him what his conduct deserves.ᶠ
12It is unthinkable that God would do wrong,
　　that the Almighty would pervert justice.ᵍ
13Who appointed him over the earth?
　　Who put him in charge of the whole world?ʰ
14If it were his intention
　　and he withdrew his spiritᵇ and breath,ⁱ
15all mankind would perish together
　　and man would return to the dust.ʲ

16"If you have understanding, hear this;
　　listen to what I say.
17Can he who hates justice govern?ᵏ

33:28
qJob 22:28
33:29
r1Co 12:6;
Eph 1:11;
Php 2:13
33:30
sPs 56:13
33:33
tPs 34:11
34:3
uJob 12:11
34:4
v1Th 5:21
34:5
wJob 33:9
xJob 27:2
34:6
yJob 6:4
34:7
zJob 15:16
34:8
aJob 22:15;
Ps 50:18
34:9
bJob 21:15;
35:3
34:10
cGe 18:25
dDt 32:4;
Job 8:3;
Ro 9:14
34:11
ePs 62:12;
Mt 16:27;
Ro 2:6;
2Co 5:10
fJer 32:19;
Eze 33:20
34:12
gJob 8:3
34:13
hJob 38:4,6
34:14
iPs 104:29
34:15
jGe 3:19;
Job 9:22
34:17
k2Sa 23:3-4

ᵃ30 Or *turn him back from the grave*　　ᵇ14 Or *Spirit*

Will you condemn the just and mighty One?[l]
18Is he not the One who says to kings, 'You are
      worthless,'
  and to nobles, 'You are wicked,'[m]
19who shows no partiality[n] to princes
  and does not favor the rich over the poor,[o]
  for they are all the work of his hands?[p]
20They die in an instant, in the middle of the night;[q]
  the people are shaken and they pass away;
  the mighty are removed without human hand.[r]

21"His eyes are on the ways of men;
  he sees their every step.[s]
22There is no dark place,[t] no deep shadow,[u]
  where evildoers can hide.
23God has no need to examine men further,
  that they should come before him for judgment.[v]
24Without inquiry he shatters the mighty[w]
  and sets up others in their place.[x]
25Because he takes note of their deeds,
  he overthrows them in the night and they are
      crushed.
26He punishes them for their wickedness
  where everyone can see them,
27because they turned from following him[y]
  and had no regard for any of his ways.[z]
28They caused the cry of the poor to come before him,
  so that he heard the cry of the needy.[a]
29But if he remains silent, who can condemn him?
  If he hides his face, who can see him?
  Yet he is over man and nation alike,
30   to keep a godless man from ruling,
  from laying snares for the people.[b]

31"Suppose a man says to God,
  'I am guilty but will offend no more.
32Teach me what I cannot see;[c]
  if I have done wrong, I will not do so again.'[d]
33Should God then reward you on your terms,
  when you refuse to repent?[e]
  You must decide, not I;
  so tell me what you know.

34"Men of understanding declare,
  wise men who hear me say to me,
35'Job speaks without knowledge;[f]
  his words lack insight.'
36Oh, that Job might be tested to the utmost
  for answering like a wicked man![g]
37To his sin he adds rebellion;
  scornfully he claps his hands[h] among us
  and multiplies his words against God."[i]

34:17
l Job 40:8
34:18
m Ex 22:28
34:19
n Dt 10:17;
Ac 10:34
o Lev 19:15
p Job 10:3
34:20
q Ex 12:29
r Job 12:19
34:21
s Job 31:4;
Pr 15:3
34:22
t Ps 139:12
u Am 9:2-3
34:23
v Job 11:11
34:24
w Job 12:19
x Da 2:21
34:27
y Ps 28:5;
Isa 5:12
z 1Sa 15:11
34:28
a Ex 22:23;
Job 35:9;
Jas 5:4
34:30
b Pr 29:2-12
34:32
c Job 35:11;
Ps 25:4
d Job 33:27
34:33
e Job 41:11
34:35
f Job 35:16; 38:2
34:36
g Job 22:15
34:37
h Job 27:23
i Job 23:2

35 Then Elihu said:

2"Do you think this is just?
    You say, 'I will be cleared by God.[a]'
3Yet you ask him, 'What profit is it to me,[b]
    and what do I gain by not sinning?'[j]

4"I would like to reply to you
    and to your friends with you.
5Look up at the heavens[k] and see;
    gaze at the clouds so high above you.[l]
6If you sin, how does that affect him?
    If your sins are many, what does that do to him?[m]
7If you are righteous, what do you give to him,[n]
    or what does he receive[o] from your hand?[p]
8Your wickedness affects only a man like yourself,
    and your righteousness only the sons of men.

9"Men cry out[q] under a load of oppression;
    they plead for relief from the arm of the powerful.[r]
10But no one says, 'Where is God my Maker,[s]
    who gives songs in the night,[t]
11who teaches[u] more to us than to[c] the beasts of the earth
    and makes us wiser than[d] the birds of the air?'
12He does not answer[v] when men cry out
    because of the arrogance of the wicked.
13Indeed, God does not listen to their empty plea;
    the Almighty pays no attention to it.[w]
14How much less, then, will he listen
    when you say that you do not see him,[x]
that your case[y] is before him
    and you must wait for him,
15and further, that his anger never punishes
    and he does not take the least notice of wickedness.[e]
16So Job opens his mouth with empty talk;
    without knowledge he multiplies words."[z]

36 Elihu continued:

2"Bear with me a little longer and I will show you
    that there is more to be said in God's behalf.
3I get my knowledge from afar;
    I will ascribe justice to my Maker.[a]
4Be assured that my words are not false;[b]
    one perfect in knowledge[c] is with you.

5"God is mighty, but does not despise men;[d]
    he is mighty, and firm in his purpose.[e]
6He does not keep the wicked alive[f]
    but gives the afflicted their rights.[g]
7He does not take his eyes off the righteous;[h]

35:3
jJob 9:29-31;
  34:9
35:5
kGe 15:5
lJob 22:12
35:6
mPr 8:36
35:7
nRo 11:35
oPr 9:12
pJob 22:2-3;
  Lk 17:10
35:9
qEx 2:23
rJob 12:19
35:10
sJob 27:10;
  Isa 51:13
tPs 42:8; 149:5;
  Ac 16:25
35:11
uPs 94:12
35:12
vPr 1:28
35:13
wJob 27:9;
  Pr 15:29;
  Isa 1:15;
  Jer 11:11
35:14
xJob 9:11
yPs 37:6
35:16
zJob 34:35,37
36:3
aJob 8:3; 37:23
36:4
bJob 33:3
cJob 37:5,16,23
36:5
dPs 22:24
eJob 12:13
36:6
fJob 8:22
gJob 5:15
36:7
hPs 33:18

---

[a]2 Or *My righteousness is more than God's*   [b]3 Or *you*   [c]11 Or *teaches us by*   [d]11 Or *us wise by*   [e]15 Symmachus, Theodotion and Vulgate; the meaning of the Hebrew for this word is uncertain.

he enthrones them with kings[i]
and exalts them forever.
[8]But if men are bound in chains,[j]
held fast by cords of affliction,
[9]he tells them what they have done—
that they have sinned arrogantly.[k]
[10]He makes them listen[l] to correction
and commands them to repent of their evil.[m]
[11]If they obey and serve him,[n]
they will spend the rest of their days in prosperity
and their years in contentment.
[12]But if they do not listen,
they will perish by the sword[a][o]
and die without knowledge.[p]

[13]"The godless in heart[q] harbor resentment;
even when he fetters them, they do not cry for help.
[14]They die in their youth,
among male prostitutes of the shrines.[r]
[15]But those who suffer he delivers in their suffering;
he speaks to them in their affliction.

[16]"He is wooing[s] you from the jaws of distress
to a spacious place free from restriction,
to the comfort of your table[t] laden with choice food.
[17]But now you are laden with the judgment due the
wicked;
judgment and justice have taken hold of you.[u]
[18]Be careful that no one entices you by riches;
do not let a large bribe turn you aside.[v]
[19]Would your wealth
or even all your mighty efforts
sustain you so you would not be in distress?
[20]Do not long for the night,[w]
to drag people away from their homes.[b]
[21]Beware of turning to evil,[x]
which you seem to prefer to affliction.[y]

[22]"God is exalted in his power.
Who is a teacher like him?[z]
[23]Who has prescribed his ways for him,[a]
or said to him, 'You have done wrong'?[b]
[24]Remember to extol his work,[c]
which men have praised in song.[d]
[25]All mankind has seen it;
men gaze on it from afar.
[26]How great is God—beyond our understanding![e]
The number of his years is past finding out.[f]

[27]"He draws up the drops of water,
which distill as rain to the streams[c];[g]

36:7
iPs 113:8
36:8
jPs 107:10,14
36:9
kJob 15:25
36:10
lJob 33:16
m2Ki 17:13
36:11
nIsa 1:19
36:12
oJob 15:22
pJob 4:21
36:13
qRo 2:5
36:14
rDt 23:17
36:16
sHos 2:14
tPs 23:5
36:17
uJob 22:11
36:18
vJob 34:33
36:20
wJob 34:20,25
36:21
xPs 66:18
yHeb 11:25
36:22
zIsa 40:13;
1Co 2:16
36:23
aJob 34:13
bJob 8:3
36:24
cPs 92:5; 138:5
dPs 59:16;
Rev 15:3
36:26
e1Co 13: 12
fJob 10:5;
Ps 90:2; 102:24;
Heb 1:12
36:27
gJob 38:28;
Ps 147:8

---

[a]12 Or *will cross the River*   [b]20 The meaning of the Hebrew for verses 18-20 is uncertain.
[c]27 Or *distill from the mist as rain*

²⁸the clouds pour down their moisture
　　and abundant showers fall on mankind. ʰ
²⁹Who can understand how he spreads out the clouds,
　　how he thunders from his pavilion?ⁱ
³⁰See how he scatters his lightning about him,
　　bathing the depths of the sea.
³¹This is the way he governsᵃ the nationsʲ
　　and provides food in abundance. ᵏ
³²He fills his hands with lightning
　　and commands it to strike its mark. ˡ
³³His thunder announces the coming storm;
　　even the cattle make known its approach. ᵇ

37 "At this my heart pounds
　　and leaps from its place.
²Listen! Listen to the roar of his voice,
　　to the rumbling that comes from his mouth. ᵐ
³He unleashes his lightning beneath the whole heaven
　　and sends it to the ends of the earth.
⁴After that comes the sound of his roar;
　　he thunders with his majestic voice.
　When his voice resounds,
　　he holds nothing back.
⁵God's voice thunders in marvelous ways;
　　he does great things beyond our understanding. ⁿ
⁶He says to the snow, ᵒ 'Fall on the earth,'
　　and to the rain shower, 'Be a mighty downpour.'ᴾ
⁷So that all men he has made may know his work,
　　he stops every man from his labor. ᶜ �q
⁸The animals take cover;
　　they remain in their dens. ʳ
⁹The tempest comes out from its chamber,
　　the cold from the driving winds.
¹⁰The breath of God produces ice,
　　and the broad waters become frozen. ˢ
¹¹He loads the clouds with moisture;
　　he scatters his lightning through them. ᵗ
¹²At his direction they swirl around
　　over the face of the whole earth
　　to do whatever he commands them. ᵘ
¹³He brings the clouds to punish men, ᵛ
　　or to water his earthᵈ and show his love. ʷ

¹⁴"Listen to this, Job;
　　stop and consider God's wonders.
¹⁵Do you know how God controls the clouds
　　and makes his lightning flash?
¹⁶Do you know how the clouds hang poised,
　　those wonders of him who is perfect in knowledge?ˣ
¹⁷You who swelter in your clothes

36:28
h Job 5:10
36:29
i Job 26:14;
37:16
36:31
j Job 37:13
k Ps 136:25;
Ac 14:17
36:32
l Job 37:12,15
37:2
m Ps 29:3-9
37:5
n Job 5:9
37:6
o Job 38:22
p Job 36:27
37:7
q Job 12:14
37:8
r Job 38:40;
Ps 104:22
37:10
s Job 38:29-30;
Ps 147:17
37:11
t Job 36:27,29
37:12
u Ps 148:8
37:13
v 1Sa 12:17
w Ex 9:18;
1Ki 18:45;
Job 38:27
37:16
x Job 36:4

ᵃ31 Or *nourishes*　　ᵇ33 Or *announces his coming—* / *the One zealous against evil*　　ᶜ7 Or / *he fills
all men with fear by his power*　　ᵈ13 Or *to favor them*

when the land lies hushed under the south wind,
18can you join him in spreading out the skies,y
   hard as a mirror of cast bronze?

19"Tell us what we should say to him;
   we cannot draw up our case because of our darkness.
20Should he be told that I want to speak?
   Would any man ask to be swallowed up?
21Now no one can look at the sun,
   bright as it is in the skies
   after the wind has swept them clean.
22Out of the north he comes in golden splendor;
   God comes in awesome majesty.
23The Almighty is beyond our reach and exalted in
      power;z
   in his justicea and great righteousness, he does not
      oppress. b
24Therefore, men revere him, c
   for does he not have regard for all the wised in
      heart?a "

The Lord Speaks

38 Then the Lord answered Job out of the storm. e He said:

2"Who is this that darkens my counsel
   with words without knowledge?f
3Brace yourself like a man;
   I will question you,
   and you shall answer me. g

4"Where were you when I laid the earth's foundation?h
   Tell me, if you understand.
5Who marked off its dimensions?i Surely you know!
   Who stretched a measuring line across it?
6On what were its footings set,
   or who laid its cornerstonej —
7while the morning stars sang together
   and all the angelsb shouted for joy?

8"Who shut up the sea behind doorsk
   when it burst forth from the womb, l
9when I made the clouds its garment
   and wrapped it in thick darkness,
10when I fixed limits for itm
   and set its doors and bars in place, n
11when I said, 'This far you may come and no farther;
   here is where your proud waves halt'?o

12"Have you ever given orders to the morning,
   or shown the dawn its place,
13that it might take the earth by the edges
   and shake the wickedp out of it?

37:18
yJob 9:8;
Ps 104:2;
Isa 44:24
37:23
zJob 9:4; 36:4;
1Ti 6:16
aJob 8:3
bIsa 63:9;
Eze 18:23,32
37:24
cMt 10:28
dMt 11:25
38:1
eJob 40:6
38:2
fJob 35:16;
42:3; 1Ti 1:7
38:3
gJob 40:7
38:4
hPs 104:5;
Pr 8:29
38:5
iPr 8:29;
Isa 40:12
38:6
jJob 26:7
38:8
kJer 5:22
lGe 1:9-10
38:10
mPs 33:7; 104:9
nJob 26:10
38:11
oPs 89:9
38:13
pPs 104:35

---

a24 Or *for he does not have regard for any who think they are wise.*   b7 Hebrew *the sons of God*

¹⁴The earth takes shape like clay under a seal;
    its features stand out like those of a garment.
¹⁵The wicked are denied their light,�q
    and their upraised arm is broken.ʳ

¹⁶"Have you journeyed to the springs of the sea
    or walked in the recesses of the deep?ˢ
¹⁷Have the gates of deathᵗ been shown to you?
    Have you seen the gates of the shadow of deathᵃ?
¹⁸Have you comprehended the vast expanses of the
        earth?ᵘ
    Tell me, if you know all this.

¹⁹"What is the way to the abode of light?
    And where does darkness reside?
²⁰Can you take them to their places?
    Do you know the pathsᵛ to their dwellings?
²¹Surely you know, for you were already born!ʷ
    You have lived so many years!

²²"Have you entered the storehouses of the snowˣ
    or seen the storehouses of the hail,
²³which I reserve for times of trouble,ʸ
    for days of war and battle?ᶻ
²⁴What is the way to the place where the lightning is
        dispersed,
    or the place where the east winds are scattered
        over the earth?
²⁵Who cuts a channel for the torrents of rain,
    and a path for the thunderstorm,ᵃ
²⁶to waterᵇ a land where no man lives,
    a desert with no one in it,
²⁷to satisfy a desolate wasteland
    and make it sprout with grass?ᶜ
²⁸Does the rain have a father?ᵈ
    Who fathers the drops of dew?
²⁹From whose womb comes the ice?
    Who gives birth to the frost from the heavensᵉ
³⁰when the waters become hard as stone,
    when the surface of the deep is frozen?ᶠ

³¹"Can you bind the beautifulᵇ Pleiades?
    Can you loose the cords of Orion?ᵍ
³²Can you bring forth the constellations in their seasonsᶜ
    or lead out the Bearᵈ with its cubs?
³³Do you know the lawsʰ of the heavens?
    Can you set up ⌊God's⌋ dominion over the earth?

³⁴"Can you raise your voice to the clouds
    and cover yourself with a flood of water?ⁱ
³⁵Do you send the lightning bolts on their way?ʲ

38:15
qJob 18:5
rPs 10:15
38:16
sPs 77:19
38:17
tPs 9:13
38:18
uJob 28:24
38:20
vJob 26:10
38:21
wJob 15:7
38:22
xJob 37:6
38:23
yIsa 30:30;
Eze 13:11
zEx 9:18;
Jos 10:11;
Rev 16:21
38:25
aJob 28:26
38:26
bJob 36:27
38:27
cPs 104:14;
107:35
38:28
dPs 147:8;
Jer 14:22
38:29
ePs 147:16-17
38:30
fJob 37:10
38:31
gJob 9:9;
Am 5:8
38:33
hPs 148:6;
Jer 31:36
38:34
iJob 22:11;
36:27-28
38:35
jJob 36:32; 37:3

ᵃ17 Or *gates of deep shadows*   ᵇ31 Or *the twinkling*; or *the chains of the*   ᶜ32 Or *the morning star*
in its season   ᵈ32 Or *out Leo*   ᵉ33 Or *his*; or *their*

Do they report to you, 'Here we are'?
36Who endowed the heart^a with wisdom^k
    or gave understanding^l to the mind^a?
37Who has the wisdom to count the clouds?
    Who can tip over the water jars of the heavens
38when the dust becomes hard
    and the clods of earth stick together?

39"Do you hunt the prey for the lioness
    and satisfy the hunger of the lions^m
40when they crouch in their densⁿ
    or lie in wait in a thicket?
41Who provides food for the raven^o
    when its young cry out to God
    and wander about for lack of food?^p

39   "Do you know when the mountain goats^q give birth?
    Do you watch when the doe bears her fawn?
2Do you count the months till they bear?
    Do you know the time they give birth?
3They crouch down and bring forth their young;
    their labor pains are ended.
4Their young thrive and grow strong in the wilds;
    they leave and do not return.

5"Who let the wild donkey^r go free?
    Who untied his ropes?
6I gave him the wasteland^s as his home,
    the salt flats as his habitat.^t
7He laughs at the commotion in the town;
    he does not hear a driver's shout.^u
8He ranges the hills for his pasture
    and searches for any green thing.

9"Will the wild ox^v consent to serve you?
    Will he stay by your manger at night?
10Can you hold him to the furrow with a harness?
    Will he till the valleys behind you?
11Will you rely on him for his great strength?
    Will you leave your heavy work to him?
12Can you trust him to bring in your grain
    and gather it to your threshing floor?

13"The wings of the ostrich flap joyfully,
    but they cannot compare with the pinions and
        feathers of the stork.
14She lays her eggs on the ground
    and lets them warm in the sand,
15unmindful that a foot may crush them,
    that some wild animal may trample them.
16She treats her young harshly,^w as if they were not hers;
    she cares not that her labor was in vain,

38:36
k Job 9:4
l Job 32:8;
Ps 51:6;
Ecc 2:26
38:39
m Ps 104:21
38:40
n Job 37:8
38:41
o Lk 12:24
p Ps 147:9;
Mt 6:26
39:1
q Dt 14:5
39:5
r Job 6:5; 11:12;
24:5
39:6
s Job 24:5;
Ps 107:34;
Jer 2:24
t Hos 8:9
39:7
u Job 3:18
39:9
v Nu 23:22;
Dt 33:17
39:16
w La 4:3

---

^a36 The meaning of the Hebrew for this word is uncertain.

17for God did not endow her with wisdom
>   or give her a share of good sense.ˣ
18Yet when she spreads her feathers to run,
>   she laughs at horse and rider.

19"Do you give the horse his strength
>   or clothe his neck with a flowing mane?
20Do you make him leap like a locust,ʸ
>   striking terror with his proud snorting?ᶻ
21He paws fiercely, rejoicing in his strength,
>   and charges into the fray.ᵃ
22He laughs at fear, afraid of nothing;
>   he does not shy away from the sword.
23The quiver rattles against his side,
>   along with the flashing spear and lance.
24In frenzied excitement he eats up the ground;
>   he cannot stand still when the trumpet sounds.ᵇ
25At the blast of the trumpetᶜ he snorts, 'Aha!'
>   He catches the scent of battle from afar,
>   the shout of commanders and the battle cry.ᵈ

26"Does the hawk take flight by your wisdom
>   and spread his wings toward the south?
27Does the eagle soar at your command
>   and build his nest on high?ᵉ
28He dwells on a cliff and stays there at night;
>   a rocky crag is his stronghold.
29From there he seeks out his food;ᶠ
>   his eyes detect it from afar.
30His young ones feast on blood,
>   and where the slain are, there is he."ᵍ

40

The LORD said to Job:ʰ

2"Will the one who contends with the Almighty
>   correct him?
>   Let him who accuses God answer him!"

3Then Job answered the LORD:

4"I am unworthyⁱ—how can I reply to you?
>   I put my hand over my mouth.ʲ
5I spoke once, but I have no answerᵏ—
>   twice, but I will say no more."ˡ

6Then the LORD spoke to Job out of the storm:ᵐ

7"Brace yourself like a man;
>   I will question you,
>   and you shall answer me.ⁿ

8"Would you discredit my justice?ᵒ
>   Would you condemn me to justify yourself?
9Do you have an arm like God's,ᵖ
>   and can your voice thunder like his?ᑫ
10Then adorn yourself with glory and splendor,

39:17
xJob 35:11
39:20
yJoel 2:4-5
zJer 8:16
39:21
aJer 8:6
39:24
bJer 4:5,19;
Eze 7:14;
Am 3:6
39:25
cJos 6:5
dAm 1:14; 2:2
39:27
eJer 49:16;
Ob 1:4
39:29
fJob 9:26
39:30
gMt 24:28;
Lk 17:37
40:1
hJob 10:2;
13:3; 23:4;
31:35; 33:13
40:4
iJob 42:6
jJob 29:9
40:5
kJob 9:3
lJob 9:15
40:6
mJob 38:1
40:7
nJob 38:3; 42:4
40:8
oJob 27:2;
Ro 3:3
40:9
p2Ch 32:8
qJob 37:5;
Ps 29:3-4

and clothe yourself in honor and majesty. ʳ
¹¹Unleash the fury of your wrath, ˢ
  look at every proud man and bring him low, ᵗ
¹²look at every proud man and humble him, ᵘ
  crushᵛ the wicked where they stand.
¹³Bury them all in the dust together;
  shroud their faces in the grave.
¹⁴Then I myself will admit to you
  that your own right hand can save you. ʷ

¹⁵"Look at the behemoth, ᵃ
  which I made along with you
  and which feeds on grass like an ox.
¹⁶What strength he has in his loins,
  what power in the muscles of his belly!
¹⁷His tailᵇ sways like a cedar;
  the sinews of his thighs are close-knit.
¹⁸His bones are tubes of bronze,
  his limbs like rods of iron.
¹⁹He ranks first among the works of God, ˣ
  yet his Maker can approach him with his sword.
²⁰The hills bring him their produce, ʸ
  and all the wild animals playᶻ nearby.
²¹Under the lotus plants he lies,
  hidden among the reeds in the marsh.
²²The lotuses conceal him in their shadow;
  the poplars by the streamᵃ surround him.
²³When the river rages, he is not alarmed;
  he is secure, though the Jordan should surge against
    his mouth.
²⁴Can anyone capture him by the eyes, ᶜ
  or trap him and pierce his nose?ᵇ

41 "Can you pull in the leviathanᵈᶜ with a fishhook
  or tie down his tongue with a rope?
²Can you put a cord through his nose
  or pierce his jaw with a hook?ᵈ
³Will he keep begging you for mercy?
  Will he speak to you with gentle words?
⁴Will he make an agreement with you
  for you to take him as your slave for life?ᵉ
⁵Can you make a pet of him like a bird
  or put him on a leash for your girls?
⁶Will traders barter for him?
  Will they divide him up among the merchants?
⁷Can you fill his hide with harpoons
  or his head with fishing spears?
⁸If you lay a hand on him,
  you will remember the struggle and never do it again!
⁹Any hope of subduing him is false;

40:10
ʳPs 93:1; 104:1
40:11
ˢIsa 42:25;
Na 1:6
ᵗIsa 2:11,12,17;
Da 4:37
40:12
ᵘ1Sa 2:7
ᵛIsa 13:11;
63:2-3,6
40:14
ʷPs 20:6; 60:5;
108:6
40:19
ˣJob 41:33
40:20
ʸPs 104:14
ᶻPs 104:26
40:22
ᵃIsa 44:4
40:24
ᵇJob 41:2,7,26
41:1
ᶜJob 3:8;
Ps 104:26;
Isa 27:1
41:2
ᵈIsa 37:29
41:4
ᵉEx 21:6

ᵃ15 Possibly the hippopotamus or the elephant   ᵇ17 Possibly trunk   ᶜ24 Or *by a water hole*
ᵈ1 Possibly the crocodile

the mere sight of him is overpowering.
[10]No one is fierce enough to rouse him.[f]
Who then is able to stand against me?[g]
[11]Who has a claim against me that I must pay?[h]
Everything under heaven belongs to me.[i]

[12]"I will not fail to speak of his limbs,
his strength and his graceful form.
[13]Who can strip off his outer coat?
Who would approach him with a bridle?
[14]Who dares open the doors of his mouth,
ringed about with his fearsome teeth?
[15]His back has[a] rows of shields
tightly sealed together;
[16]each is so close to the next
that no air can pass between.
[17]They are joined fast to one another;
they cling together and cannot be parted.
[18]His snorting throws out flashes of light;
his eyes are like the rays of dawn.[j]
[19]Firebrands stream from his mouth;
sparks of fire shoot out.
[20]Smoke pours from his nostrils
as from a boiling pot over a fire of reeds.
[21]His breath[k] sets coals ablaze,
and flames dart from his mouth.[l]
[22]Strength resides in his neck;
dismay goes before him.
[23]The folds of his flesh are tightly joined;
they are firm and immovable.
[24]His chest is hard as rock,
hard as a lower millstone.
[25]When he rises up, the mighty are terrified;
they retreat before his thrashing.
[26]The sword that reaches him has no effect,
nor does the spear or the dart or the javelin.
[27]Iron he treats like straw
and bronze like rotten wood.
[28]Arrows do not make him flee;
slingstones are like chaff to him.
[29]A club seems to him but a piece of straw;
he laughs at the rattling of the lance.
[30]His undersides are jagged potsherds,
leaving a trail in the mud like a threshing sledge.[m]
[31]He makes the depths churn like a boiling caldron
and stirs up the sea like a pot of ointment.
[32]Behind him he leaves a glistening wake;
one would think the deep had white hair.
[33]Nothing on earth is his equal[n]—
a creature without fear.

41:10
f Job 3:8
g Jer 50:44
41:11
h Ro 11:35
i Ex 19:5;
Dt 10:14;
Ps 24:1; 50:12;
1Co 10:26
41:18
j Job 3:9
41:21
k Isa 40:7
l Ps 18:8
41:30
m Isa 41:15
41:33
n Job 40:19

---

a15 Or His pride is his

³⁴He looks down on all that are haughty;
    he is king over all that are proud. °"

Job

42

Then Job replied to the Lᴏʀᴅ:

²"I know that you can do all things;ᴾ
    no plan of yours can be thwarted. �q
³You asked, 'Who is this that obscures my counsel
      without knowledge?'ʳ
Surely I spoke of things I did not understand,
    things too wonderful for me to know. ˢ

⁴"You said, 'Listen now, and I will speak;
I will question you,
    and you shall answer me.'ᵗ
⁵My ears had heard of youᵘ
    but now my eyes have seen you. ᵛ
⁶Therefore I despise myselfʷ
    and repent in dust and ashes."ˣ

Epilogue

⁷After the Lᴏʀᴅ had said these things to Job, he said to Eliphaz the Temanite, "I am angry with you and your two friends,ʸ because you have not spoken of me what is right, as my servant Job has. ⁸So now take seven bulls and seven ramsᶻ and go to my servant Job and sacrifice a burnt offeringª for yourselves. My servant Job will pray for you, and I will accept his prayerᵇ and not deal with you according to your folly. ᶜ You have not spoken of me what is right, as my servant Job has." ⁹So Eliphaz the Temanite, Bildad the Shuhite and Zophar the Naamathite did what the Lᴏʀᴅ told them; and the Lᴏʀᴅ accepted Job's prayer.

¹⁰After Job had prayed for his friends, the Lᴏʀᴅ made him prosperous againᵈ and gave him twice as much as he had before. ᵉ ¹¹All his brothers and sisters and everyone who had known him beforeᶠ came and ate with him in his house. They comforted and consoled him over all the trouble the Lᴏʀᴅ had brought upon him, and each one gave him a piece of silverª and a gold ring.

¹²The Lᴏʀᴅ blessed the latter part of Job's life more than the first. He had fourteen thousand sheep, six thousand camels, a thousand yoke of oxen and a thousand donkeys. ¹³And he also had seven sons and three daughters. ¹⁴The first daughter he named Jemimah, the second Keziah and the third Keren-Happuch. ¹⁵Nowhere in all the land were there found women as beautiful as Job's daughters, and their father granted them an inheritance along with their brothers.

¹⁶After this, Job lived a hundred and forty years; he saw his children and their children to the fourth generation. ¹⁷And so he died, old and full of years. ᵍ

ª11 Hebrew *him a kesitah*; a kesitah was a unit of money of unknown weight and value.

41:34
o Job 28:8
42:2
p Ge 18:14;
Mt 19:26
q 2Ch 20:6
42:3
r Job 38:2
s Ps 40:5; 131:1;
139:6
42:4
t Job 38:3; 40:7
42:5
u Job 26:14;
Ro 10:17
v Jdg 13:22;
Isa 6:5;
Eph 1:17-18
42:6
w Job 40:4
x Ezr 9:6
42:7
y Job 32:3
42:8
z Nu 23:1,29
a Job 1:5
b Ge 20:17;
Jas 5:15-16;
1Jn 5:16
c Job 22:30
42:10
d Dt 30:3;
Ps 14:7
e Job 1:3;
Ps 85:1-3;
126:5-6
42:11
f Job 19:13
42:17
g Ge 15:15; 25:8

Psalms

Title and Background

The names "Psalms" and "Psalter" come from the Septuagint (the Greek translation of the Old Testament). Both originally referred to stringed instruments (e.g., harp, lyre, lute), then to songs sung with their accompaniment. The traditional Hebrew title means "praises," even though many of the psalms are prayers.

Author and Date of Writing

Of the 150 Psalms, 100 of them are thought to be written by the following authors: David—73; Asaph—12; Sons of Korah—10; Moses—1; Heman the Ezrahite—1; Ethan the Ezrahite—1; and one or two by Solomon. The rest of the Psalms have no recorded author. The final collection and arrangement of the Psalter was the work of postexilic temple personnel, completed probably in the third century B.C. By the first century A.D. it could be referred to as the "Book of Psalms" (Lk 20:42; Ac 1:20).

Theme and Message

The Psalter is not a book of catechism or doctrine. It is rather for the most part a book of prayer and praise. It speaks to God in prayer and of God in praise and in professions of faith and trust. At the core of the theology of the Psalter is the conviction that the gravitational center of life, but also of history and the whole creation, is God. He is the great King over all, and the One to whom all things are subject.

Outline

Book I.   Psalms 1-41
Book II.   Psalms 42-72
Book III. Psalms 73-89
Book IV.   Psalms 90-106
Book V.   Psalms 107-150

BOOK I

Psalms 1–41

Psalm 1

¹Blessed is the man
  who does not walk[a] in the counsel of the wicked
or stand in the way of sinners
  or sit[b] in the seat of mockers.
²But his delight[c] is in the law of the LORD,[d]
  and on his law he meditates[e] day and night.
³He is like a tree[f] planted by streams of water,[g]
  which yields its fruit[h] in season

1:1
aPr 4:14
bPs 26:4;
Jer 15:17
1:2
cPs 119:16,35
dPs 119:1
eJos 1:8
1:3
fPs 128:3
gJer 17:8
hEze 47:12

and whose leaf does not wither.
    Whatever he does prospers. [i]

[4]Not so the wicked!
    They are like chaff[j]
    that the wind blows away.
[5]Therefore the wicked will not stand[k] in the judgment,[l]
    nor sinners in the assembly of the righteous.

[6]For the LORD watches over[m] the way of the righteous,
    but the way of the wicked will perish. [n]

Psalm 2

[1]Why do the nations conspire[a]
    and the peoples plot[o] in vain?
[2]The kings[p] of the earth take their stand
    and the rulers gather together
  against the LORD
    and against his Anointed[q] One. [b] [r]
[3]"Let us break their chains," they say,
    "and throw off their fetters."[s]

[4]The One enthroned in heaven laughs;[t]
    the Lord scoffs at them.
[5]Then he rebukes them in his anger
    and terrifies them in his wrath, [u] saying,
[6]"I have installed my King[c]
    on Zion, my holy hill."

[7]I will proclaim the decree of the LORD:

    He said to me, "You are my Son[d];
    today I have become your Father.[e] [v]
[8]Ask of me,
    and I will make the nations your inheritance,
    the ends of the earth[w] your possession.
[9]You will rule them with an iron scepter[f] ;[x]
    you will dash them to pieces[y] like pottery.[z] "

[10]Therefore, you kings, be wise;
    be warned, you rulers of the earth.
[11]Serve the LORD with fear
    and rejoice[a] with trembling. [b]
[12]Kiss the Son, [c] lest he be angry
    and you be destroyed in your way,
    for his wrath[d] can flare up in a moment.
    Blessed are all who take refuge[e] in him.

1:3
iGe 39:3
1:4
jJob 21:18;
Isa 17:13
1:5
kPs 5:5
lPs 9:7-8,16
1:6
mPs 37:18;
2Ti 2:19 nPs 9:6
2:1
oPs 21:11
2:2
pPs 48:4
qJn 1:41
rPs 74:18,23;
Ac 4:25-26*
2:3
sJer 5:5
2:4
tPs 37:13; 59:8;
Pr 1:26
2:5
uPs 21:9;
78:49-50
2:7
vAc 13:33*;
Heb 1:5*
2:8
wPs 22:27
2:9
xRev 12:5
yPs 89:23
zRev 2:27*
2:11
aHeb 12:28
bPs 119:119-120
2:12
cJn 5:23
dRev 6:16
ePs 34:8;
Ro 9:33

---

a1 Hebrew; Septuagint *rage*   *b2* Or *anointed one*   *c6* Or *king*   *d7* Or *son;* also in verse 12
e7 Or *have begotten you*   *f9* Or *will break them with a rod of iron*

Psalm 3

A psalm of David. When he fled from his son Absalom. [f]

[1]O LORD, how many are my foes!
How many rise up against me!
[2]Many are saying of me,
"God will not deliver him. [g]"   *Selah*[a]

[3]But you are a shield[h] around me, O LORD;
you bestow glory on me and lift[b] up my head. [i]
[4]To the LORD I cry aloud,
and he answers me from his holy hill. [j]   *Selah*

[5]I lie down and sleep;[k]
I wake again, because the LORD sustains me.
[6]I will not fear[l] the tens of thousands
drawn up against me on every side.

[7]Arise, [m] O LORD!
Deliver me, [n] O my God!
Strike[o] all my enemies on the jaw;
break the teeth[p] of the wicked.

[8]From the LORD comes deliverance. [q]
May your blessing be on your people.   *Selah*

Psalm 4

For the director of music. With stringed instruments. A psalm of David.

[1]Answer me when I call to you,
O my righteous God.
Give me relief from my distress;
be merciful[r] to me and hear my prayer. [s]

[2]How long, O men, will you turn my glory into shame[c]?
How long will you love delusions and seek false
gods[d]?[t]   *Selah*
[3]Know that the LORD has set apart the godly[u] for himself;
the LORD will hear[v] when I call to him.

[4]In your anger do not sin;[w]
when you are on your beds, [x]
search your hearts and be silent.   *Selah*
[5]Offer right sacrifices
and trust in the LORD. [y]

[6]Many are asking, "Who can show us any good?"
Let the light of your face shine upon us, [z] O LORD.

3:Title
f2Sa 15:14
3:2
gPs 71:11
3:3
hGe 15:1;
Ps 28:7 iPs 27:6
3:4
jPs 2:6
3:5
kLev 26:6;
Pr 3:24
3:6
lPs 27:3
3:7
mPs 7:6 nPs 6:4
oJob 16:10
pPs 58:6
3:8
qIsa 43:3,11
4:1
rPs 25:16
sPs 17:6
4:2
tPs 31:6
4:3
uPs 31:23
vPs 6:8
4:4
wEph 4:26*
xPs 77:6
4:5
yDt 33:19;
Ps 37:3
4:6
zNu 6:25

---

[a]2 A word of uncertain meaning, occurring frequently in the Psalms; possibly a musical term
[b]3 Or LORD, / my Glorious One, who lifts   [c]2 Or you dishonor my Glorious One   [d]2 Or seek lies

7You have filled my heart[a] with greater joy[b]
    than when their grain and new wine abound.
8I will lie down and sleep[c] in peace,
    for you alone, O LORD,
    make me dwell in safety.[d]

Psalm 5

For the director of music. For flutes. A psalm of David.

1Give ear to my words, O LORD,
    consider my sighing.
2Listen to my cry for help,[e]
    my King and my God,[f]
    for to you I pray.
3In the morning,[g] O LORD, you hear my voice;
    in the morning I lay my requests before you
    and wait in expectation.

4You are not a God who takes pleasure in evil;
    with you the wicked[h] cannot dwell.
5The arrogant[i] cannot stand[j] in your presence;
    you hate[k] all who do wrong.
6You destroy those who tell lies;[l]
    bloodthirsty and deceitful men
    the LORD abhors.

7But I, by your great mercy,
    will come into your house;
in reverence will I bow down[m]
    toward your holy temple.
8Lead me, O LORD, in your righteousness[n]
    because of my enemies—
    make straight your way[o] before me.

9Not a word from their mouth can be trusted;
    their heart is filled with destruction.
Their throat is an open grave;[p]
    with their tongue they speak deceit.[q]
10Declare them guilty, O God!
    Let their intrigues be their downfall.
Banish them for their many sins,[r]
    for they have rebelled[s] against you.

11But let all who take refuge in you be glad;
    let them ever sing for joy.[t]
Spread your protection over them,
    that those who love your name[u] may rejoice in you.[v]
12For surely, O LORD, you bless the righteous;
    you surround them[w] with your favor as with a shield.

4:7
aAc 14:17
bIsa 9:3
4:8
cPs 3:5
dLev 25:18
5:2
ePs 3:4 fPs 84:3
5:3
gPs 88:13
5:4
hPs 11:5; 92:15
5:5
iPs 73:3 jPs 1:5
kPs 11:5
5:6
lPs 55:23;
Rev 21:8
5:7
mPs 138:2
5:8
nPs 31:1
oPs 27:11
5:9
pLk 11:44
qRo 3:13*
5:10
rPs 9:16
sPs 107:11
5:11
tPs 2:12
uPs 69:36
vIsa 65:13
5:12
wPs 32:7

Psalm 6

For the director of music. With stringed instruments. According to
sheminith.[a] A psalm of David.

[1]O LORD, do not rebuke me in your anger[x]
or discipline me in your wrath.
[2]Be merciful to me, LORD, for I am faint;
O LORD, heal me,[y] for my bones are in agony.[z]
[3]My soul is in anguish.[a]
How long,[b] O LORD, how long?

[4]Turn, O LORD, and deliver me;
save me because of your unfailing love.[c]
[5]No one remembers you when he is dead.
Who praises you from the grave[b]?[d]

[6]I am worn out[e] from groaning;
all night long I flood my bed with weeping
and drench my couch with tears.[f]
[7]My eyes grow weak[g] with sorrow;
they fail because of all my foes.

[8]Away from me,[h] all you who do evil,[i]
for the LORD has heard my weeping.
[9]The LORD has heard my cry for mercy;[j]
the LORD accepts my prayer.
[10]All my enemies will be ashamed and dismayed;
they will turn back in sudden disgrace.[k]

Psalm 7

A *shiggaion*[c] of David, which he sang to the LORD concerning Cush, a
Benjamite.

[1]O LORD my God, I take refuge in you;
save and deliver me from all who pursue me,[l]
[2]or they will tear me like a lion[m]
and rip me to pieces with no one to rescue[n] me.

[3]O LORD my God, if I have done this
and there is guilt on my hands[o]—
[4]if I have done evil to him who is at peace with me
or without cause have robbed my foe—
[5]then let my enemy pursue and overtake me;
let him trample my life to the ground
and make me sleep in the dust.   *Selah*

[6]Arise,[p] O LORD, in your anger;
rise up against the rage of my enemies.[q]

6:1
x Ps 38:1
6:2
y Hos 6:1
z Ps 22:14;
31:10
6:3
a Jn 12:27
b Ps 90:13
6:4
c Ps 17:13
6:5
d Ps 30:9;
88:10-12;
Ecc 9:10;
Isa 38:18
6:6
e Ps 69:3
f Ps 42:3
6:7
g Ps 31:9
6:8
h Ps 119:115
i Mt 7:23;
Lk 13:27
6:9
j Ps 116:1
6:10
k Ps 71:24;
73:19
7:1
l Ps 31:15
7:2
m Isa 38:13
n Ps 50:22
7:3
o 1Sa 24:11;
Isa 59:3
7:6
p Ps 94:2
q Ps 138:7

---

[a] Title: Probably a musical term   [b] 5 Hebrew *Sheol*   [c] Title: Probably a literary or musical term

Awake,[r] my God; decree justice.
7Let the assembled peoples gather around you.
    Rule over them from on high;
8   let the LORD judge the peoples.
Judge me, O LORD, according to my righteousness,[s]
    according to my integrity, O Most High.
9O righteous God,[t]
    who searches minds and hearts,[u]
bring to an end the violence of the wicked
    and make the righteous secure.[v]

10My shield[a] is God Most High,
    who saves the upright in heart.[w]
11God is a righteous judge,[x]
    a God who expresses his wrath every day.
12If he does not relent,
    he[b] will sharpen his sword;[y]
    he will bend and string his bow.
13He has prepared his deadly weapons;
    he makes ready his flaming arrows.

14He who is pregnant with evil
    and conceives trouble gives birth[z] to disillusionment.
15He who digs a hole and scoops it out
    falls into the pit he has made.[a]
16The trouble he causes recoils on himself;
    his violence comes down on his own head.

17I will give thanks to the LORD because of his
        righteousness[b]
    and will sing praise[c] to the name of the LORD Most
        High.

Psalm 8

For the director of music. According to *gittith*.[c] A psalm of David.

1O LORD, our Lord,
    how majestic is your name in all the earth!

You have set your glory
    above the heavens.[d]
2From the lips of children and infants
    you have ordained praise[d] [e]
because of your enemies,
    to silence the foe[f] and the avenger.

3When I consider your heavens,[g]
    the work of your fingers,
    the moon and the stars,[h]

7:6
rPs 44:23
7:8
sPs 18:20; 96:13
7:9
tJer 11:20
u1Ch 28:9;
Ps 26:2;
Rev 2:23
vPs 37:23
7:10
wPs 125:4
7:11
xPs 50:6
7:12
yDt 32:41
7:14
zJob 15:35;
Isa 59:4;
Jas 1:15
7:15
aJob 4:8
7:17
bPs 71:15-16
cPs 9:2
8:1
dPs 57:5;
113:4; 148:13
8:2
eMt 21:16*
fPs 44:16;
1Co 1:27
8:3
gPs 89:11
hPs 136:9

---

a10 Or *sovereign*   b12 Or *If a man does not repent, / God*   cTitle: Probably a musical term
d2 Or *strength*

which you have set in place,
[4]what is man that you are mindful of him,
the son of man that you care for him?[i]
[5]You made him a little lower than the heavenly beings[a]
and crowned him with glory and honor.[j]

[6]You made him ruler[k] over the works of your hands;
you put everything under his feet:[l] [m]
[7]all flocks and herds,
and the beasts of the field,
[8]the birds of the air,
and the fish of the sea,
all that swim the paths of the seas.

[9]O LORD, our Lord,
how majestic is your name in all the earth![n]

Psalm 9[b]

For the director of music. To the tune of, "The Death of the Son."
A psalm of David.

[1]I will praise you, O LORD, with all my heart;[o]
I will tell of all your wonders.[p]
[2]I will be glad and rejoice[q] in you;
I will sing praise to your name,[r] O Most High.

[3]My enemies turn back;
they stumble and perish before you.
[4]For you have upheld my right and my cause;[s]
you have sat on your throne, judging righteously.[t]
[5]You have rebuked the nations and destroyed the
wicked;
you have blotted out their name[u] for ever and ever.
[6]Endless ruin has overtaken the enemy,
you have uprooted their cities;
even the memory of them[v] has perished.

[7]The LORD reigns forever;
he has established his throne[w] for judgment.
[8]He will judge the world in righteousness;[x]
he will govern the peoples with justice.
[9]The LORD is a refuge for the oppressed,
a stronghold in times of trouble.[y]
[10]Those who know your name[z] will trust in you,
for you, LORD, have never forsaken[a] those who seek
you.

[11]Sing praises to the LORD, enthroned in Zion;[b]
proclaim among the nations[c] what he has done.[d]

8:4
iJob 7:17;
Ps 144:3;
Heb 2:6
8:5
jPs 21:5; 103:4
8:6
kGe 1:28
lHeb 2:6-8*
m1Co 15:25,27;
Eph 1:22
8:9
nver 1
9:1
oPs 86:12
pPs 26:7
9:2
qPs 5:11
rPs 92:1; 83:18
9:4
sPs 140:12
t1Pe 2:23
9:5
uPr 10:7
9:6
vPs 34:16
9:7
wPs 89:14
9:8
xPs 96:13
9:9
yPs 32:7
9:10
zPs 91:14
aPs 37:28
9:11
bPs 76:2
cPs 107:22
dPs 105:1

---

[a]5 Or *than God*   [b]Psalms 9 and 10 may have been originally a single acrostic poem, the stanzas of which begin with the successive letters of the Hebrew alphabet. In the Septuagint they constitute one psalm.

¹²For he who avenges blood⁽ᵉ⁾ remembers;
  he does not ignore the cry of the afflicted.

¹³O LORD, see how my enemies⁽ᶠ⁾ persecute me!
  Have mercy and lift me up from the gates of death,
¹⁴that I may declare your praises⁽ᵍ⁾
  in the gates of the Daughter of Zion
  and there rejoice in your salvation. ⁽ʰ⁾
¹⁵The nations have fallen into the pit they have dug;⁽ⁱ⁾
  their feet are caught in the net they have hidden. ⁽ʲ⁾
¹⁶The LORD is known by his justice;
  the wicked are ensnared by the work of their hands.
                              Higgaion. ⁽ᵃ⁾ *Selah*

¹⁷The wicked return to the grave,⁽ᵇ⁾ ⁽ᵏ⁾
  all the nations that forget God. ⁽ˡ⁾
¹⁸But the needy will not always be forgotten,
  nor the hope⁽ᵐ⁾ of the afflicted⁽ⁿ⁾ ever perish.

¹⁹Arise, O LORD, let not man triumph;
  let the nations be judged in your presence.
²⁰Strike them with terror, O LORD;
  let the nations know they are but men. ⁽ᵒ⁾   *Selah*

Psalm 10⁽ᶜ⁾

¹Why, O LORD, do you stand far off?⁽ᵖ⁾
  Why do you hide yourself⁽�q⁾ in times of trouble?

²In his arrogance the wicked man hunts down the weak,
  who are caught in the schemes he devises.
³He boasts⁽ʳ⁾ of the cravings of his heart;
  he blesses the greedy and reviles the LORD.
⁴In his pride the wicked does not seek him;
  in all his thoughts there is no room for God. ⁽ˢ⁾
⁵His ways are always prosperous;
  he is haughty and your laws are far from him;
  he sneers at all his enemies.
⁶He says to himself, "Nothing will shake me;
  I'll always be happy⁽ᵗ⁾ and never have trouble."
⁷His mouth is full of curses⁽ᵘ⁾ and lies and threats;⁽ᵛ⁾
  trouble and evil are under his tongue. ⁽ʷ⁾
⁸He lies in wait near the villages;
  from ambush he murders the innocent, ⁽ˣ⁾
  watching in secret for his victims.
⁹He lies in wait like a lion in cover;
  he lies in wait to catch the helpless;⁽ʸ⁾
  he catches the helpless and drags them off in his net.
¹⁰His victims are crushed, they collapse;

9:12
eGe 9:5
9:13
fPs 38:19
9:14
gPs 106:2
hPs 13:5; 51:12
9:15
iPs 7:15-16
jPs 35:8; 57:6
9:17
kPs 49:14
lJob 8:13;
Ps 50:22
9:18
mPs 71:5;
Pr 23:18
nPs 12:5
9:20
oPs 62:9;
Isa 31:3
10:1
pPs 22:1,11
qPs 13:1
10:3
rPs 94:4
10:4
sPs 14:1; 36:1
10:6
tRev 18:7
10:7
uRo 3:14*
vPs 73:8
wPs 140:3
10:8
xPs 94:6
10:9
yPs 17:12;
59:3; 140:5

ᵃ16 Or *Meditation;* possibly a musical notation   ᵇ17 Hebrew *Sheol*   ᶜPsalms 9 and 10 may
have been originally a single acrostic poem, the stanzas of which begin with the successive letters
of the Hebrew alphabet. In the Septuagint they constitute one psalm.

they fall under his strength.
[11]He says to himself, "God has forgotten;[z]
  he covers his face and never sees."

[12]Arise, LORD! Lift up your hand,[a] O God.
  Do not forget the helpless.[b]
[13]Why does the wicked man revile God?
  Why does he say to himself,
  "He won't call me to account"?
[14]But you, O God, do see trouble[c] and grief;
  you consider it to take it in hand.
The victim commits himself to you;[d]
  you are the helper[e] of the fatherless.
[15]Break the arm of the wicked and evil man;[f]
  call him to account for his wickedness
  that would not be found out.

[16]The LORD is King for ever and ever;[g]
  the nations[h] will perish from his land.
[17]You hear, O LORD, the desire of the afflicted;[i]
  you encourage them, and you listen to their cry,
[18]defending the fatherless[j] and the oppressed,[k]
  in order that man, who is of the earth, may terrify no
  more.

Psalm 11

For the director of music. Of David.

[1]In the LORD I take refuge.[l]
  How then can you say to me:
  "Flee like a bird to your mountain.
[2]For look, the wicked bend their bows;
  they set their arrows[m] against the strings
to shoot from the shadows
  at the upright in heart.[n]
[3]When the foundations[o] are being destroyed,
  what can the righteous do[a]?"

[4]The LORD is in his holy temple;[p]
  the LORD is on his heavenly throne.[q]
He observes the sons of men;[r]
  his eyes examine[s] them.
[5]The LORD examines the righteous,[t]
  but the wicked[b] and those who love violence
  his soul hates.[u]
[6]On the wicked he will rain
  fiery coals and burning sulfur;[v]
  a scorching wind[w] will be their lot.

---

[a]3 Or *what is the Righteous One doing*   [b]5 Or *The LORD, the Righteous One, examines the wicked,* /

7For the LORD is righteous, [x]
   he loves justice; [y]
   upright men will see his face. [z]

Psalm 12

For the director of music. According to *sheminith*. [a] A psalm of David.

1Help, LORD, for the godly are no more; [a]
   the faithful have vanished from among men.
2Everyone lies to his neighbor;
   their flattering lips speak with deception. [b]

3May the LORD cut off all flattering lips
   and every boastful tongue [c]
4that says, "We will triumph with our tongues;
   we own our lips [b]—who is our master?"

5"Because of the oppression of the weak
   and the groaning of the needy,
I will now arise," says the LORD.
   "I will protect them [d] from those who malign them."
6And the words of the LORD are flawless, [e]
   like silver refined in a furnace of clay,
   purified seven times.

7O LORD, you will keep us safe
   and protect us from such people forever. [f]
8The wicked freely strut [g] about
   when what is vile is honored among men.

Psalm 13

For the director of music. A psalm of David.

1How long, O LORD? Will you forget me forever?
   How long will you hide your face [h] from me?
2How long must I wrestle with my thoughts [i]
   and every day have sorrow in my heart?
   How long will my enemy triumph over me? [j]

3Look on me and answer, [k] O LORD my God.
   Give light to my eyes, [l] or I will sleep in death; [m]
4my enemy will say, "I have overcome him, [n]"
   and my foes will rejoice when I fall.

5But I trust in your unfailing love; [o]
   my heart rejoices in your salvation. [p]
6I will sing [q] to the LORD,
   for he has been good to me.

11:7
x Ps 7:9,11; 45:7
y Ps 33:5
z Ps 17:15
12:1
a Isa 57:1
12:2
b Ps 10:7; 41:6;
55:21; Ro 16:18
12:3
c Da 7:8;
Rev 13:5
12:5
d Ps 10:18; 34:6
12:6
e 2Sa 22:31;
Ps 18:30;
Pr 30:5
12:7
f Ps 37:28
12:8
g Ps 55:10-11
13:1
h Job 13:24;
Ps 44:24
13:2
i Ps 42:4
j Ps 42:9
13:3
k Ps 5:1 l Ezr 9:8
m Jer 51:39
13:4
n Ps 25:2
13:5
o Ps 52:8
p Ps 9:14
13:6
q Ps 116:7

---

a Title: Probably a musical term   b 4 Or / *our lips are our plowshares*

Psalm 14

14:1–7pp — Ps 53:1–6

For the director of music. Of David.

¹The fool*ᵃ* says in his heart,
    "There is no God."*ʳ*
They are corrupt, their deeds are vile;
    there is no one who does good.

²The LORD looks down from heaven*ˢ*
    on the sons of men
to see if there are any who understand,*ᵗ*
    any who seek God.
³All have turned aside,
    they have together become corrupt;*ᵘ*
there is no one who does good,*ᵛ*
    not even one.*ʷ*

⁴Will evildoers never learn—*ˣ*
    those who devour my people*ʸ* as men eat bread
    and who do not call on the LORD?*ᶻ*
⁵There they are, overwhelmed with dread,
    for God is present in the company of the righteous.
⁶You evildoers frustrate the plans of the poor,
    but the LORD is their refuge.*ᵃ*

⁷Oh, that salvation for Israel would come out of Zion!
    When the LORD restores the fortunes*ᵇ* of his people,
    let Jacob rejoice and Israel be glad!

Psalm 15

A psalm of David.

¹LORD, who may dwell in your sanctuary?*ᶜ*
    Who may live on your holy hill?*ᵈ*

²He whose walk is blameless
    and who does what is righteous,
who speaks the truth*ᵉ* from his heart
³   and has no slander*ᶠ* on his tongue,
who does his neighbor no wrong
    and casts no slur on his fellowman,
⁴who despises a vile man
    but honors*ᵍ* those who fear the LORD,
who keeps his oath*ʰ*
    even when it hurts,
⁵who lends his money without usury*ⁱ*
    and does not accept a bribe*ʲ* against the innocent.

ᵃ1 The Hebrew words rendered fool *in Psalms denote one who is morally deficient.*

14:1
rPs 10:4
14:2
sPs 33:13
tPs 92:6
14:3
uPs 58:3
vPs 143:2
wRo 3:10-12*
14:4
xPs 82:5
yPs 27:2
zPs 79:6;
Isa 64:7
14:6
aPs 9:9; 40:17
14:7
bPs 53:6
15:1
cPs 27:5-6
dPs 24:3-5
15:2
ePs 24:4;
Zec 8:3,16;
Eph 4:25
15:3
fEx 23:1
15:4
gAc 28:10
hJdg 11:35
15:5
iEx 22:25
jEx 23:8;
Dt 16:19

He who does these things
will never be shaken. [k]

Psalm 16

A *miktam* [a] of David.

[1]Keep me safe, [1] O God,
for in you I take refuge. [m]

[2]I said to the Lord, "You are my Lord;
apart from you I have no good thing." [n]
[3]As for the saints who are in the land, [o]
they are the glorious ones in whom is all my delight. [b]
[4]The sorrows [p] of those will increase
who run after other gods. [q]
I will not pour out their libations of blood
or take up their names [r] on my lips.

[5]Lord, you have assigned me my portion [s] and my cup; [t]
you have made my lot secure.
[6]The boundary lines have fallen for me in pleasant places;
surely I have a delightful inheritance. [u]

[7]I will praise the Lord, who counsels me; [v]
even at night [w] my heart instructs me.
[8]I have set the Lord always before me.
Because he is at my right hand, [x]
I will not be shaken.

[9]Therefore my heart is glad [y] and my tongue rejoices;
my body also will rest secure, [z]
[10]because you will not abandon me to the grave, [c]
nor will you let your Holy One [d] see decay. [a]
[11]You have made [e] known to me the path of life; [b]
you will fill me with joy in your presence, [c]
with eternal pleasures [d] at your right hand.

Psalm 17

A prayer of David.

[1]Hear, O Lord, my righteous plea;
listen to my cry. [e]
Give ear to my prayer—
it does not rise from deceitful lips. [f]
[2]May my vindication come from you;
may your eyes see what is right.

15:5
k 2Pe 1:10
16:1
l Ps 17:8 m Ps 7:1
16:2
n Ps 73:25
16:3
o Ps 101:6
16:4
p Ps 32:10
q Ps 106:37-38
r Ex 23:13
16:5
s Ps 73:26
t Ps 23:5
16:6
u Ps 78:55;
Jer 3:19
16:7
v Ps 73:24
w Ps 77:6
16:8
x Ps 73:23
16:9
y Ps 4:7; 30:11
z Ps 4:8
16:10
a Ac 13:35*
16:11
b Mt 7:14
c Ac 2:25-28*
d Ps 36:7-8
17:1
e Ps 61:1
f Isa 29:13

---

a Title: Probably a literary or musical term   b 3 Or *As for the pagan priests who are in the land / and
the nobles in whom all delight, I said:*   c 10 Hebrew *Sheol*   d 10 Or *your faithful one*   e 11 Or
You will make

17:3
g Ps 26:2; 66:10
h Job 23:10;
Jer 50:20
i Ps 39:1
17:5
j Ps 44:18;
119:133
k Ps 18:36
17:6
l Ps 86:7
m Ps 116:2
n Ps 88:2
17:7
o Ps 31:21
p Ps 20:6
17:8
q Dt 32:10
17:9
r Ps 31:20; 109:3
17:10
s Ps 73:7
t 1Sa 2:3
17:11
u Ps 37:14;
88:17
17:12
v Ps 7:2; 10:9
17:13
w Ps 7:12;
22:20; 73:18
17:14
x Lk 16:8
y Ps 73:3-7
17:15
z Nu 12:8;
Ps 4:6-7; 16:11;
1Jn 3:2
18:2
a Ps 19:14

³Though you probe my heart and examine me at night,
    though you test me, g you will find nothing; h
    I have resolved that my mouth will not sin. i
⁴As for the deeds of men—
    by the word of your lips
  I have kept myself
    from the ways of the violent.
⁵My steps have held to your paths; j
    my feet have not slipped. k

⁶I call on you, O God, for you will answer me; l
    give ear to me m and hear my prayer. n
⁷Show the wonder of your great love, o
    you who save by your right hand p
    those who take refuge in you from their foes.
⁸Keep me as the apple of your eye; q
    hide me in the shadow of your wings
⁹from the wicked who assail me,
    from my mortal enemies who surround me. r

¹⁰They close up their callous hearts, s
    and their mouths speak with arrogance. t
¹¹They have tracked me down, they now surround me, u
    with eyes alert, to throw me to the ground.
¹²They are like a lion v hungry for prey,
    like a great lion crouching in cover.

¹³Rise up, O LORD, confront them, bring them down; w
    rescue me from the wicked by your sword.
¹⁴O LORD, by your hand save me from such men,
    from men of this world x whose reward is in this life.

  You still the hunger of those you cherish;
    their sons have plenty,
    and they store up wealth y for their children.
¹⁵And I—in righteousness I will see your face;
    when I awake, I will be satisfied with seeing your
      likeness. z

Psalm 18

18:Title–50pp — 2Sa 22:1-51

For the director of music. Of David the servant of the LORD. He sang to
the LORD the words of this song when the LORD delivered him from the
hand of all his enemies and from the hand of Saul. He said:

¹I love you, O LORD, my strength.

²The LORD is my rock, a my fortress and my deliverer;
    my God is my rock, in whom I take refuge.

He is my shield[b] and the horn[a] of my salvation,[c] my
  stronghold.
[3]I call to the LORD, who is worthy of praise,[d]
  and I am saved from my enemies.

[4]The cords of death[e] entangled me;
  the torrents[f] of destruction overwhelmed me.
[5]The cords of the grave[b] coiled around me;
  the snares of death[g] confronted me.
[6]In my distress I called to the LORD;
  I cried to my God for help.
From his temple he heard my voice;[h]
  my cry came before him, into his ears.

[7]The earth trembled and quaked,[i]
  and the foundations of the mountains shook;
  they trembled because he was angry.[j]
[8]Smoke rose from his nostrils;
  consuming fire[k] came from his mouth,
  burning coals blazed out of it.
[9]He parted the heavens and came down;[l]
  dark clouds were under his feet.
[10]He mounted the cherubim[m] and flew;
  he soared on the wings of the wind.[n]
[11]He made darkness his covering,[o] his canopy around
    him—
  the dark rain clouds of the sky.
[12]Out of the brightness of his presence[p] clouds advanced,
  with hailstones and bolts of lightning.[q]
[13]The LORD thundered[r] from heaven;
  the voice of the Most High resounded.[c]
[14]He shot his arrows and scattered the enemies,
  great bolts of lightning and routed them.[s]
[15]The valleys of the sea were exposed
  and the foundations of the earth laid bare
at your rebuke,[t] O LORD,
  at the blast of breath from your nostrils.

[16]He reached down from on high and took hold of me;
  he drew me out of deep waters.[u]
[17]He rescued me from my powerful enemy,
  from my foes, who were too strong for me.[v]
[18]They confronted me in the day of my disaster,
  but the LORD was my support.[w]
[19]He brought me out into a spacious place;[x]
  he rescued me because he delighted in me.[y]

[20]The LORD has dealt with me according to my
  righteousness;

18:2
b Ps 59:11
c Ps 75:10
18:3
d Ps 48:1
18:4
e Ps 116:3
f Ps 124:4
18:5
g Ps 116:3
18:6
h Ps 34:15
18:7
i Jdg 5:4
j Ps 68:7-8
18:8
k Ps 50:3
18:9
l Ps 144:5
18:10
m Ps 80:1
n Ps 104:3
18:11
o Dt 4:11;
Ps 97:2
18:12
p Ps 104:2
q Ps 97:3
18:13
r Ps 29:3; 104:7
18:14
s Ps 144:6
18:15
t Ps 76:6; 106:9
18:16
u Ps 144:7
18:17
v Ps 35:10
18:18
w Ps 59:16
18:19
x Ps 31:8
y Ps 118:5

---

[a]2 *Horn* here symbolizes strength.   [b]5 Hebrew *Sheol*   [c]13 Some Hebrew manuscripts and
Septuagint (see also 2 Samuel 22:14); most Hebrew manuscripts *resounded, / amid hailstones and bolts
of lightning*

according to the cleanness of my hands[z] he has
    rewarded me.
21For I have kept the ways of the LORD;[a]
    I have not done evil by turning[b] from my God.
22All his laws are before me;[c]
    I have not turned away from his decrees.
23I have been blameless before him
    and have kept myself from sin.
24The LORD has rewarded me according to my
    righteousness,[d]
according to the cleanness of my hands in his sight.

25To the faithful[e] you show yourself faithful,
    to the blameless you show yourself blameless,
26to the pure you show yourself pure,
    but to the crooked you show yourself shrewd.[f]
27You save the humble
    but bring low those whose eyes are haughty.[g]
28You, O LORD, keep my lamp burning;
    my God turns my darkness into light.[h]
29With your help[i] I can advance against a troop[a];
    with my God I can scale a wall.

30As for God, his way is perfect;[j]
    the word of the LORD is flawless.[k]
He is a shield
    for all who take refuge[l] in him.
31For who is God besides the LORD?[m]
    And who is the Rock[n] except our God?
32It is God who arms me with strength[o]
    and makes my way perfect.
33He makes my feet like the feet of a deer;[p]
    he enables me to stand on the heights.[q]
34He trains my hands for battle;[r]
    my arms can bend a bow of bronze.
35You give me your shield of victory,
    and your right hand sustains[s] me;
    you stoop down to make me great.
36You broaden the path beneath me,
    so that my ankles do not turn.

37I pursued my enemies[t] and overtook them;
    I did not turn back till they were destroyed.
38I crushed them so that they could not rise;[u]
    they fell beneath my feet.[v]
39You armed me with strength for battle;
    you made my adversaries bow at my feet.
40You made my enemies turn their backs[w] in flight,
    and I destroyed[x] my foes.
41They cried for help, but there was no one to save
    them[y]—

18:20
zPs 24:4
18:21
a2Ch 34:33
bPs 119:102
18:22
cPs 119:30
18:24
d1Sa 26:23
18:25
e1Ki 8:32;
Ps 62:12;
Mt 5:7
18:26
fPr 3:34
18:27
gPr 6:17
18:28
hJob 18:6; 29:3
18:29
iHeb 11:34
18:30
jDt 32:4;
Rev 15:3
kPs 12:6
lPs 17:7
18:31
mDt 32:39;
86:8; Isa 45:5,6,
14,18,21
nDt 32:31;
1Sa 2:2
18:32
oIsa 45:5
18:33
pHab 3:19
qDt 32:13
18:34
rPs 144:1
18:35
sPs 119:116
18:37
tPs 37:20; 44:5
18:38
uPs 36:12
vPs 47:3
18:40
wPs 21:12
xPs 94:23
18:41
yPs 50:22

a29 Or can run through a barricade

to the LORD, but he did not answer. [z]
42I beat them as fine as dust borne on the wind;
　　I poured them out like mud in the streets.

43You have delivered me from the attacks of the people;
　　you have made me the head of nations;[a]
　　people I did not know[b] are subject to me.
44As soon as they hear me, they obey me;
　　foreigners[c] cringe before me.
45They all lose heart;
　　they come trembling from their strongholds. [d]

46The LORD lives! Praise be to my Rock!
　　Exalted be God my Savior![e]
47He is the God who avenges me,
　　who subdues nations[f] under me,
48　who saves[g] me from my enemies.
　You exalted me above my foes;
　　from violent men you rescued me.
49Therefore I will praise you among the nations, O LORD;
　　I will sing[h] praises to your name. [i]
50He gives his king great victories;
　　he shows unfailing kindness to his anointed,
　　to David[j] and his descendants forever. [k]

Psalm 19

For the director of music. A psalm of David.

1The heavens[l] declare[m] the glory of God;
　　the skies proclaim the work of his hands.
2Day after day they pour forth speech;
　　night after night they display knowledge. [n]
3There is no speech or language
　　where their voice is not heard. [a]
4Their voice[b] goes out into all the earth,
　　their words to the ends of the world. [o]

　In the heavens he has pitched a tent[p] for the sun,
5　which is like a bridegroom coming forth from his
　　　pavilion,
　like a champion rejoicing to run his course.
6It rises at one end of the heavens
　　and makes its circuit to the other;[q]
　　nothing is hidden from its heat.

7The law of the LORD is perfect,
　　reviving the soul. [r]
　The statutes of the LORD are trustworthy,[s]
　　making wise the simple. [t]

18:41
zJob 27:9;
Pr 1:28
18:43
a2Sa 8:1-14
bIsa 52:15; 55:5
18:44
cPs 66:3
18:45
dMic 7:17
18:46
ePs 51:14
18:47
fPs 47:3
18:48
gPs 59:1
18:49
hPs 108:1
iRo 15:9*
18:50
jPs 144:10
kPs 89:4
19:1
lIsa 40:22
mPs 50:6;
Ro 1:19
19:2
nPs 74:16
19:4
oRo 10:18*
pPs 104:2
19:6
qPs 113:3;
Ecc 1:5
19:7
rPs 23:3
sPs 93:5; 111:7
tPs 119:98-100

---

[a]3 Or *They have no speech, there are no words; / no sound is heard from them*　　[b]4 Septuagint, Jerome and Syriac; Hebrew *line*

[8]The precepts of the LORD are right,[u]
    giving joy to the heart.
The commands of the LORD are radiant,
    giving light to the eyes.
[9]The fear of the LORD is pure,
    enduring forever.
The ordinances of the LORD are sure
    and altogether righteous.[v]
[10]They are more precious than gold,[w]
    than much pure gold;
they are sweeter than honey,
    than honey from the comb.
[11]By them is your servant warned;
    in keeping them there is great reward.

[12]Who can discern his errors?
    Forgive my hidden faults.[x]
[13]Keep your servant also from willful sins;
    may they not rule over me.
Then will I be blameless,
    innocent of great transgression.

[14]May the words of my mouth and the meditation of my
    heart
be pleasing[y] in your sight,
O LORD, my Rock[z] and my Redeemer.[a]

Psalm 20

For the director of music. A psalm of David.

[1]May the LORD answer you when you are in distress;
    may the name of the God of Jacob[b] protect you.[c]
[2]May he send you help from the sanctuary[d]
    and grant you support from Zion.
[3]May he remember[e] all your sacrifices
    and accept your burnt offerings.[f]   *Selah*
[4]May he give you the desire of your heart[g]
    and make all your plans succeed.
[5]We will shout for joy when you are victorious
    and will lift up our banners[h] in the name of our God.
May the LORD grant all your requests.[i]

[6]Now I know that the LORD saves his anointed;[j]
    he answers him from his holy heaven
    with the saving power of his right hand.
[7]Some trust in chariots and some in horses,[k]
    but we trust in the name of the LORD our God.[l]
[8]They are brought to their knees and fall,
    but we rise up[m] and stand firm.[n]

19:8
uPs 12:6;
119:128
19:9
vPs 119:138,142
19:10
wPr 8:10
19:12
xPs 51:2; 90:8;
139:6
19:14
yPs 104:34
zPs 18:2
aIsa 47:4
20:1
bPs 46:7,11
cPs 91:14
20:2
dPs 3:4
20:3
eAc 10:4
fPs 51:19
20:4
gPs 21:2;
145:16,19
20:5
hPs 9:14; 60:4
i1Sa 1:17
20:6
jPs 28:8; 41:11;
Isa 58:9
20:7
kPs 33:17;
Isa 31:1
l2Ch 32:8
20:8
mMic 7:8
nPs 37:23

⁹O LORD, save the king!
    Answer[a] us° when we call!

Psalm 21

For the director of music. A psalm of David.

¹O LORD, the king rejoices in your strength.
    How great is his joy in the victories you give![p]
²You have granted him the desire of his heart[q]
    and have not withheld the request of his lips.   *Selah*
³You welcomed him with rich blessings
    and placed a crown of pure gold[r] on his head.
⁴He asked you for life, and you gave it to him—
    length of days, for ever and ever.[s]
⁵Through the victories[t] you gave, his glory is great;
    you have bestowed on him splendor and majesty.
⁶Surely you have granted him eternal blessings
    and made him glad with the joy[u] of your presence.[v]
⁷For the king trusts in the LORD;
    through the unfailing love of the Most High
    he will not be shaken.

⁸Your hand will lay hold[w] on all your enemies;
    your right hand will seize your foes.
⁹At the time of your appearing
    you will make them like a fiery furnace.
In his wrath the LORD will swallow them up,
    and his fire will consume them.[x]
¹⁰You will destroy their descendants from the earth,
    their posterity from mankind.[y]
¹¹Though they plot evil[z] against you
    and devise wicked schemes,[a] they cannot succeed;
¹²for you will make them turn their backs[b]
    when you aim at them with drawn bow.

¹³Be exalted, O LORD, in your strength;
    we will sing and praise your might.

Psalm 22

*For the director of music. To ˌthe tune ofˌ "The Doe of the Morning."
A psalm of David.*

¹My God, my God, why have you forsaken me?[c]
    Why are you so far[d] from saving me,
    so far from the words of my groaning?
²O my God, I cry out by day, but you do not answer,
    by night,[e] and am not silent.

20:9
o Ps 3:7; 17:6
21:1
p Ps 59:16-17
21:2
q Ps 37:4
21:3
r 2Sa 12:30
21:4
s Ps 61:5-6;
91:16; 133:3
21:5
t Ps 18:50
21:6
u Ps 43:4
v 1Ch 17:27
21:8
w Isa 10:10
21:9
x Ps 50:3;
La 2:2; Mal 4:1
21:10
y Dt 28:18;
Ps 37:28
21:11
z Ps 2:1 a Ps 10:2
21:12
b Ps 7:12-13;
18:40
22:1
c Mt 27:46*;
Mk 15:34*
d Ps 10:1
22:2
e Ps 42:3

---

[a]9 Or *save! / O King, answer*

3Yet you are enthroned as the Holy One;f
   you are the praiseg of Israel.a
4In you our fathers put their trust;
   they trusted and you delivered them.
5They cried to you and were saved;
   in you they trusted and were not disappointed.h

6But I am a wormi and not a man,
   scorned by menj and despisedk by the people.
7All who see me mock me;
   they hurl insults,l shaking their heads:m
8"He trusts in the Lord;
   let the Lord rescue him.n
Let him deliver him,
   since he delightso in him."

9Yet you brought me out of the womb;p
   you made me trust in you
   even at my mother's breast.
10From birthq I was cast upon you;
   from my mother's womb you have been my God.
11Do not be far from me,
   for trouble is near
   and there is no one to help.r

12Many bullss surround me;
   strong bulls of Bashant encircle me.
13Roaring lionsu tearing their prey
   open their mouths widev against me.
14I am poured out like water,
   and all my bones are out of joint.w
My heart has turned to wax;
   it has melted awayx within me.
15My strength is dried up like a potsherd,
   and my tongue sticks to the roof of my mouth;y
   you lay meb in the dustz of death.
16Dogsa have surrounded me;
   a band of evil men has encircled me,
   they have piercedcb my hands and my feet.
17I can count all my bones;
   people starec and gloat over me.d
18They divide my garments among them
   and cast lotse for my clothing.

19But you, O Lord, be not far off;
   O my Strength, come quicklyf to help me.
20Deliver my life from the sword,
   my precious lifeg from the power of the dogs.
21Rescue me from the mouth of the lions;
   saved me from the horns of the wild oxen.

22:3
fPs 99:9
gDt 10:21
22:5
hIsa 49:23
22:6
iJob 25:6;
Isa 41:14
jPs 31:11
kIsa 49:7; 53:3
22:7
lMt 27:39,44
mMk 15:29
22:8
nPs 91:14
oMt 27:43
22:9
pPs 71:6
22:10
qIsa 46:3
22:11
rPs 72:12
22:12
sPs 68:30
tDt 32:14
22:13
uPs 17:12
vPs 35:21
22:14
wPs 31:10
xJob 30:16;
Da 5:6
22:15
yPs 38:10;
Jn 19:28
zPs 104:29
22:16
aPs 59:6
bIsa 53:5;
Zec 12:10;
Jn 19:34
22:17
cLk 23:35
dLk 23:27
22:18
eMt 27:35*;
Lk 23:34;
Jn 19:24*
22:19
fPs 70:5
22:20
gPs 35:17

---

a3 Or *Yet you are holy, / enthroned on the praises of Israel*   b15 Or /*I am laid*   c16 Some Hebrew manuscripts, Septuagint and Syriac; most Hebrew manuscripts /*like the lion,*   d21 Or /*you have heard*

22I will declare your name to my brothers;
  in the congregation I will praise you. h
23You who fear the LORD, praise him! i
  All you descendants of Jacob, honor him!
  Revere him, j all you descendants of Israel!
24For he has not despised or disdained
  the suffering of the afflicted one;
he has not hidden his face k from him
  but has listened to his cry for help. l

25From you comes the theme of my praise in the great
    assembly; m
  before those who fear you a will I fulfill my vows. n
26The poor will eat o and be satisfied;
  they who seek the LORD will praise him— p
  may your hearts live forever!
27All the ends of the earth q
  will remember and turn to the LORD,
and all the families of the nations
  will bow down before him, r
28for dominion belongs to the LORD s
  and he rules over the nations.

29All the rich t of the earth will feast and worship;
  all who go down to the dust u will kneel before
    him—
  those who cannot keep themselves alive.
30Posterity v will serve him;
  future generations will be told about the Lord.
31They will proclaim his righteousness
  to a people yet unborn w—
  for he has done it.

Psalm 23

A psalm of David.

1The LORD is my shepherd, x I shall not be in want. y
2 He makes me lie down in green pastures,
he leads me beside quiet waters, z
3 he restores my soul. a
He guides me in paths of righteousness b
  for his name's sake.
4Even though I walk
  through the valley of the shadow of death, b c
I will fear no evil, d
  for you are with me; e
your rod and your staff,
  they comfort me.

22:22
h Heb 2:12*
22:23
i Ps 86:12;
135:19 j Ps 33:8
22:24
k Ps 69:17
l Heb 5:7
22:25
m Ps 35:18
n Ecc 5:4
22:26
o Ps 107:9
p Ps 40:16
22:27
q Ps 2:8 r Ps 86:9
22:28
s Ps 47:7-8
22:29
t Ps 45:12
u Isa 26:19
22:30
v Ps 102:28
22:31
w Ps 78:6
23:1
x Isa 40:11;
Jn 10:11;
1Pe 2:25
y Php 4:19
23:2
z Eze 34:14;
Rev 7:17
23:3
a Ps 19:7
b Ps 5:8; 85:13
23:4
c Job 10:21-22
d Ps 3:6; 27:1
e Isa 43:2

a25 Hebrew him   b4 Or through the darkest valley

⁵You prepare a table before me
   in the presence of my enemies.
You anoint my head with oil;ᶠ
   my cupᵍ overflows.
⁶Surely goodness and love will follow me
   all the days of my life,
and I will dwell in the house of the LORD
   forever.

Psalm 24

Of David. A psalm.

¹The earth is the LORD's,ʰ and everything in it,
   the world, and all who live in it;ⁱ
²for he founded it upon the seas
   and established it upon the waters.

³Who may ascend the hillʲ of the LORD?
   Who may stand in his holy place?ᵏ
⁴He who has clean handsˡ and a pure heart,ᵐ
   who does not lift up his soul to an idol
   or swear by what is false.ᵃ
⁵He will receive blessing from the LORD
   and vindication from God his Savior.
⁶Such is the generation of those who seek him,
   who seek your face,ⁿ O God of Jacob.ᵇ   *Selah*

⁷Lift up your heads, O you gates;ᵒ
   be lifted up, you ancient doors,
   that the King of gloryᵖ may come in.
⁸Who is this King of glory?
   The LORD strong and mighty,
   the LORD mighty in battle.�q
⁹Lift up your heads, O you gates;
   lift them up, you ancient doors,
   that the King of glory may come in.
¹⁰Who is he, this King of glory?
   The LORD Almighty—
   he is the King of glory.   *Selah*

Psalm 25ᶜ

Of David.

¹To you, O LORD, I lift up my soul;ʳ
²   in you I trust,ˢ O my God.

23:5
fPs 92:10
gPs 16:5
24:1
hEx 9:29;
Job 41:11;
Ps 89:11
i1Co 10:26*
24:3
jPs 2:6
kPs 15:1; 65:4
24:4
lJob 17:9
mMt 5:8
24:6
nPs 27:8
24:7
oIsa 26:2
pPs 97:6;
1Co 2:8
24:8
qPs 76:3-6
25:1
rPs 86:4
25:2
sPs 41:11

ᵃ4 Or *swear falsely*   ᵇ6 Two Hebrew manuscripts and Syriac (see also Septuagint); most Hebrew manuscripts *face, Jacob*   ᶜThis psalm is an acrostic poem, the verses of which begin with the successive letters of the Hebrew alphabet.

Do not let me be put to shame,
    nor let my enemies triumph over me.
3No one whose hope is in you
    will ever be put to shame,t
but they will be put to shame
    who are treacherous without excuse.

4Show me your ways, O Lord,
    teach me your paths;u
5guide me in your truth and teach me,
    for you are God my Savior,
    and my hope is in you all day long.
6Remember, O Lord, your great mercy and
      love,v
    for they are from of old.
7Remember not the sins of my youthw
    and my rebellious ways;
according to your lovex remember me,
    for you are good, O Lord.

8Good and uprighty is the Lord;
    therefore he instructsz sinners in his ways.
9He guidesa the humble in what is right
    and teaches themb his way.
10All the ways of the Lord are loving and faithfulc
    for those who keep the demands of his covenant. d
11For the sake of your name,e O Lord,
    forgive my iniquity, though it is great.
12Who, then, is the man that fears the Lord?
    He will instruct him in the wayf chosen for him.
13He will spend his days in prosperity,g
    and his descendants will inherit the land. h
14The Lord confidesi in those who fear him;
    he makes his covenant knownj to them.
15My eyes are ever on the Lord,k
    for only he will release my feet from the snare.

16Turn to mel and be gracious to me,
    for I am lonely and afflicted.
17The troubles of my heart have multiplied;
    free me from my anguish. m
18Look upon my affliction and my distressn
    and take away all my sins.
19See how my enemieso have increased
    and how fiercely they hate me!
20Guard my lifep and rescue me;
    let me not be put to shame,
    for I take refuge in you.
21May integrityq and uprightness protect me,
    because my hope is in you.

22Redeem Israel,r O God,
    from all their troubles!

25:3
t Isa 49:23
25:4
u Ex 33:13
25:6
v Ps 103:17;
Isa 63:7,15
25:7
w Job 13:26;
Jer 3:25
x Ps 51:1
25:8
y Ps 92:15
z Ps 32:8
25:9
a Ps 23:3
b Ps 27:11
25:10
c Ps 40:11
d Ps 103:18
25:11
e Ps 31:3; 79:9
25:12
f Ps 37:23
25:13
g Pr 19:23
h Ps 37:11
25:14
i Pr 3:32 j Jn 7:17
25:15
k Ps 141:8
25:16
l Ps 69:16
25:17
m Ps 107:6
25:18
n 2Sa 16:12
25:19
o Ps 3:1
25:20
p Ps 86:2
25:21
q Ps 41:12
25:22
r Ps 130:8

Psalm 26

Of David.

¹Vindicate me, O LORD,
  for I have led a blameless life;[s]
I have trusted[t] in the LORD
  without wavering.[u]
²Test me,[v] O LORD, and try me,
  examine my heart and my mind;[w]
³for your love is ever before me,
  and I walk continually[x] in your truth.
⁴I do not sit[y] with deceitful men,
  nor do I consort with hypocrites;
⁵I abhor[z] the assembly of evildoers
  and refuse to sit with the wicked.
⁶I wash my hands in innocence,[a]
  and go about your altar, O LORD,
⁷proclaiming aloud your praise
  and telling of all your wonderful deeds.[b]
⁸I love[c] the house where you live, O LORD,
  the place where your glory dwells.

⁹Do not take away my soul along with sinners,
  my life with bloodthirsty men,[d]
¹⁰in whose hands are wicked schemes,
  whose right hands are full of bribes.[e]
¹¹But I lead a blameless life;
  redeem me[f] and be merciful to me.

¹²My feet stand on level ground;[g]
  in the great assembly[h] I will praise the LORD.

Psalm 27

Of David.

¹The LORD is my light[i] and my salvation[j] —
  whom shall I fear?
The LORD is the stronghold of my life—
  of whom shall I be afraid?[k]
²When evil men advance against me
  to devour my flesh,[a]
when my enemies and my foes attack me,
  they will stumble and fall.[l]
³Though an army besiege me,
  my heart will not fear;[m]
though war break out against me,
  even then will I be confident.[n]

26:1
s Ps 7:8; Pr 20:7
t Ps 28:7
u 2Ki 20:3;
Heb 10:23
26:2
v Ps 17:3
w Ps 7:9
26:3
x 2Ki 20:3
26:4
y Ps 1:1
26:5
z Ps 31:6;
139:21
26:6
a Ps 73:13
26:7
b Ps 9:1
26:8
c Ps 27:4
26:9
d Ps 28:3
26:10
e 1Sa 8:3
26:11
f Ps 69:18
26:12
g Ps 27:11; 40:2
h Ps 22:22
27:1
i Isa 60:19
j Ex 15:2
k Ps 118:6
27:2
l Ps 9:3; 14:4
27:3
m Ps 3:6
n Job 4:6

---

a2 Or *to slander me*

⁴One thing° I ask of the Lord,
   this is what I seek:
that I may dwell in the house of the Lord
   all the days of my life, ᴾ
to gaze upon the beauty of the Lord
   and to seek him in his temple.
⁵For in the day of trouble
   he will keep me safe in his dwelling;
he will hide me�q in the shelter of his tabernacle
   and set me high upon a rock. ʳ
⁶Then my head will be exaltedˢ
   above the enemies who surround me;
at his tabernacle will I sacrificeᵗ with shouts of joy;
   I will sing and make music to the Lord.

⁷Hear my voice when I call, O Lord;
   be merciful to me and answer me. ᵘ
⁸My heart says of you, "Seek hisᵃ face!"
   Your face, Lord, I will seek.
⁹Do not hide your faceᵛ from me,
   do not turn your servant away in anger;
   you have been my helper.
Do not reject me or forsake me,
   O God my Savior.
¹⁰Though my father and mother forsake me,
   the Lord will receive me.
¹¹Teach me your way, O Lord;
   lead me in a straight pathʷ
   because of my oppressors.
¹²Do not turn me over to the desire of my foes,
   for false witnessesˣ rise up against me,
   breathing out violence.

¹³I am still confident of this:
   I will see the goodness of the Lordʸ
   in the land of the living. ᶻ
¹⁴Waitᵃ for the Lord;
   be strong and take heart
   and wait for the Lord.

Psalm 28

Of David.

¹To you I call, O Lord my Rock;
   do not turn a deaf ear to me.
For if you remain silent, ᵇ
   I will be like those who have gone down to the pit. ᶜ
²Hear my cry for mercyᵈ

27:4
ᵒPs 90:17
ᵖPs 23:6; 26:8
27:5
qPs 17:8; 31:20
ʳPs 40:2
27:6
ˢPs 3:3
ᵗPs 107:22
27:7
ᵘPs 13:3
27:9
ᵛPs 69:17
27:11
ʷPs 5:8; 25:4;
86:11
27:12
ˣMt 26:60;
Ac 9:1
27:13
ʸPs 31:19
ᶻJer 11:19;
Eze 26:20
27:14
ᵃPs 40:1
28:1
ᵇPs 83:1
ᶜPs 88:4
28:2
ᵈPs 138:2;
140:6

ᵃ8 Or *To you, O my heart, he has said, "Seek my*

as I call to you for help,
as I lift up my hands
　　toward your Most Holy Place. e

³Do not drag me away with the wicked,
　　with those who do evil,
who speak cordially with their neighbors
　　but harbor malice in their hearts. f
⁴Repay them for their deeds
　　and for their evil work;
repay them for what their hands have done g
　　and bring back upon them what they deserve. h
⁵Since they show no regard for the works of the LORD
　　and what his hands have done, i
he will tear them down
　　and never build them up again.

⁶Praise be to the LORD,
　　for he has heard my cry for mercy.
⁷The LORD is my strength j and my shield;
　　my heart trusts k in him, and I am helped.
My heart leaps for joy
　　and I will give thanks to him in song. l

⁸The LORD is the strength of his people,
　　a fortress of salvation for his anointed one. m
⁹Save your people and bless your inheritance; n
　　be their shepherd o and carry them p forever.

Psalm 29

A psalm of David.

¹Ascribe to the LORD, q O mighty ones,
　　ascribe to the LORD glory r and strength.
²Ascribe to the LORD the glory due his name;
　　worship the LORD in the splendor of his a holiness. s

³The voice t of the LORD is over the waters;
　　the God of glory thunders, u
　　the LORD thunders over the mighty waters.
⁴The voice of the LORD is powerful; v
　　the voice of the LORD is majestic.
⁵The voice of the LORD breaks the cedars;
　　the LORD breaks in pieces the cedars of Lebanon. w
⁶He makes Lebanon skip x like a calf,
　　Sirion b y like a young wild ox.
⁷The voice of the LORD strikes
　　with flashes of lightning.
⁸The voice of the LORD shakes the desert;

28:2
e Ps 5:7
28:3
f Ps 12:2;
Ps 26:9; Jer 9:8
28:4
g 2Ti 4:14;
Rev 22:12
h Rev 18:6
28:5
i Isa 5:12
28:7
j Ps 18:1
k Ps 13:5
l Ps 40:3; 69:30
28:8
m Ps 20:6
28:9
n Dt 9:29;
Ezr 1:4
o Isa 40:11
p Dt 1:31; 32:11
29:1
q 1Ch 16:28
r Ps 96:7-9
29:2
s 2Ch 20:21
29:3
t Job 37:5
u Ps 18:13
29:4
v Ps 68:33
29:5
w Jdg 9:15
29:6
x Ps 114:4
y Dt 3:9

a2 Or LORD *with the splendor of*　　b6 That is, Mount Hermon

the Lord shakes the Desert of Kadesh. [z]
9The voice of the Lord twists the oaks[a]
and strips the forests bare.
And in his temple all cry, "Glory!"[a]

10The Lord sits[b] enthroned over the flood;[b]
the Lord is enthroned as King forever.[c]
11The Lord gives strength to his people;[d]
the Lord blesses his people with peace.[e]

Psalm 30

A psalm. A song. For the dedication of the temple.[c] Of David.

1I will exalt you, O Lord,
for you lifted me out of the depths
and did not let my enemies gloat over me.[f]
2O Lord my God, I called to you for help[g]
and you healed me.[h]
3O Lord, you brought me up from the grave[d];
you spared me from going down into the pit.[i]

4Sing to the Lord, you saints[j] of his;
praise his holy name.[k]
5For his anger[l] lasts only a moment,
but his favor lasts a lifetime;
weeping may remain for a night,
but rejoicing comes in the morning.[m]

6When I felt secure, I said,
"I will never be shaken."
7O Lord, when you favored me,
you made my mountain[e] stand firm;
but when you hid your face,[n]
I was dismayed.

8To you, O Lord, I called;
to the Lord I cried for mercy:
9"What gain is there in my destruction,[f]
in my going down into the pit?
Will the dust praise you?
Will it proclaim your faithfulness?[o]
10Hear, O Lord, and be merciful to me;
O Lord, be my help."

11You turned my wailing into dancing;
you removed my sackcloth and clothed me with joy,[p]
12that my heart may sing to you and not be silent.
O Lord my God, I will give you thanks[q] forever.[r]

29:8
zNu 13:26
29:9
aPs 26:8
29:10
bGe 6:17
cPs 10:16
29:11
dPs 28:8
ePs 37:11
30:1
fPs 25:2; 28:9
30:2
gPs 88:13
hPs 6:2
30:3
iPs 28:1; 86:13
30:4
jPs 149:1
kPs 97:12
30:5
lPs 103:9
m2Co 4:17
30:7
nDt 31:17;
Ps 104:29
30:9
oPs 6:5
30:11
pPs 4:7;
Jer 31:4,13
30:12
qPs 16:9
rPs 44:8

---

a9 Or Lord *makes the deer give birth*   b10 Or *sat*   cTitle: Or *palace*   d3 Hebrew *Sheol*
e7 Or *hill country*   f9 Or *there if I am silenced*

Psalm 31

31:1–4pp — Ps 71:1–3

For the director of music. A psalm of David.

¹In you, O Lord, I have taken refuge;
    let me never be put to shame;
    deliver me in your righteousness.
²Turn your ear to me,
    come quickly to my rescue;ˢ
 be my rock of refuge,ᵗ
    a strong fortress to save me.
³Since you are my rock and my fortress,ᵘ
    for the sake of your nameᵛ lead and guide me.
⁴Free me from the trap that is set for me,
    for you are my refuge.ʷ
⁵Into your hands I commit my spirit;ˣ
    redeem me, O Lord, the God of truth.

⁶I hate those who cling to worthless idols;
    I trust in the Lord.ʸ
⁷I will be glad and rejoice in your love,
    for you saw my afflictionᶻ
    and knew the anguishᵃ of my soul.
⁸You have not handed me overᵇ to the enemy
    but have set my feet in a spacious place.

⁹Be merciful to me, O Lord, for I am in distress;
    my eyes grow weak with sorrow,ᶜ
    my soul and my body with grief.
¹⁰My life is consumed by anguish
    and my years by groaning;ᵈ
 my strength fails because of my affliction,ᵃ
    and my bones grow weak.ᵉ
¹¹Because of all my enemies,
    I am the utter contempt of my neighbors;ᶠ
 I am a dread to my friends—
    those who see me on the street flee from me.
¹²I am forgotten by them as though I were dead;ᵍ
    I have become like broken pottery.
¹³For I hear the slander of many;
    there is terror on every side;ʰ
 they conspire against me
    and plot to take my life.ⁱ

¹⁴But I trustʲ in you, O Lord;
    I say, "You are my God."
¹⁵My timesᵏ are in your hands;
    deliver me from my enemies
    and from those who pursue me.

31:2
ˢPs 71:2
ᵗPs 18:2
31:3
ᵘPs 18:2
ᵛPs 23:3
31:4
ʷPs 25:15
31:5
ˣLk 23:46;
 Ac 7:59
31:6
ʸJnh 2:8
31:7
ᶻPs 90:14
ᵃPs 10:14;
Jn 10:27
31:8
ᵇDt 32:30
31:9
ᶜPs 6:7
31:10
ᵈPs 13:2
ᵉPs 38:3; 39:11
31:11
ᶠJob 19:13;
Ps 38:11; 64:8;
Isa 53:4
31:12
ᵍPs 88:4
31:13
ʰJer 20:3,10;
La 2:22 ⁱMt 27:1
31:14
ʲPs 140:6
31:15
ᵏJob 24:1;
Ps 143:9

ᵃ10 Or *guilt*

16Let your face shine[1] on your servant;
    save me in your unfailing love.
17Let me not be put to shame, [m] O LORD,
    for I have cried out to you;
but let the wicked be put to shame
    and lie silent[n] in the grave.[a]
18Let their lying lips[o] be silenced,
    for with pride and contempt
    they speak arrogantly[p] against the righteous.

19How great is your goodness, [q]
    which you have stored up for those who fear you,
which you bestow in the sight of men[r]
    on those who take refuge in you.
20In the shelter of your presence you hide[s] them
    from the intrigues of men;[t]
in your dwelling you keep them safe
    from accusing tongues.

21Praise be to the LORD,
    for he showed his wonderful love[u] to me
    when I was in a besieged city. [v]
22In my alarm[w] I said,
    "I am cut off from your sight!"
Yet you heard my cry[x] for mercy
    when I called to you for help.

23Love the LORD, all his saints![y]
    The LORD preserves the faithful, [z]
    but the proud he pays back[a] in full.
24Be strong and take heart, [b]
    all you who hope in the LORD.

Psalm 32

Of David. A *maskil.* [b]

1Blessed is he
    whose transgressions are forgiven,
    whose sins are covered. [c]
2Blessed is the man
    whose sin the LORD does not count against him[d]
    and in whose spirit is no deceit. [e]

3When I kept silent,
    my bones wasted away[f]
    through my groaning all day long.
4For day and night
    your hand was heavy[g] upon me;
my strength was sapped

31:16
lNu 6:25;
Ps 4:6
31:17
mPs 25:2-3
nPs 115:17
31:18
oPs 120:2
pPs 94:4
31:19
qRo 11:22
rIsa 64:4
31:20
sPs 27:5
tJob 5:21
31:21
uPs 17:7
v1Sa 23:7
31:22
wPs 116:11
xLa 3:54
31:23
yPs 34:9
zPs 145:20
aPs 94:2
31:24
bPs 27:14
32:1
cPs 85:2
32:2
dRo 4:7-8*;
2Co 5:19
eJn 1:47
32:3
fPs 31:10
32:4
gJob 33:7

[a]17 Hebrew *Sheol*   [b]Title: Probably a literary or musical term

as in the heat of summer.   *Selah*
5Then I acknowledged my sin to you
    and did not cover up my iniquity.
I said, "I will confess[h]
    my transgressions[i] to the LORD"—
and you forgave
    the guilt of my sin.[j]   *Selah*

6Therefore let everyone who is godly pray to you
    while you may be found;[k]
surely when the mighty waters rise,
    they will not reach him.[l]
7You are my hiding place;
    you will protect me from trouble[m]
    and surround me with songs of deliverance.[n]   *Selah*

8I will instruct[o] you and teach you in the way you should
    go;
    I will counsel you and watch over[p] you.
9Do not be like the horse or the mule,
    which have no understanding
but must be controlled by bit and bridle[q]
    or they will not come to you.
10Many are the woes of the wicked,[r]
    but the LORD's unfailing love
    surrounds the man who trusts[s] in him.

11Rejoice in the LORD[t] and be glad, you righteous;
    sing, all you who are upright in heart!

Psalm 33

1Sing joyfully to the LORD, you righteous;
    it is fitting[u] for the upright[v] to praise him.
2Praise the LORD with the harp;
    make music to him on the ten-stringed lyre.[w]
3Sing to him a new song;[x]
    play skillfully, and shout for joy.

4For the word of the LORD is right[y] and true;
    he is faithful in all he does.
5The LORD loves righteousness and justice;[z]
    the earth is full of his unfailing love.[a]

6By the word[b] of the LORD were the heavens made,
    their starry host by the breath of his mouth.
7He gathers the waters of the sea into jars[a];
    he puts the deep into storehouses.
8Let all the earth fear the LORD;
    let all the people of the world revere him.[c]
9For he spoke, and it came to be;

32:5
h Pr 28:13
i Ps 103:12
j Lev 26:40
32:6
k Ps 69:13;
  Isa 55:6
l Isa 43:2
32:7
m Ps 9:9
n Ex 15:1
32:8
o Ps 25:8
p Ps 33:18
32:9
q Pr 26:3
32:10
r Ro 2:9
s Pr 16:20
32:11
t Ps 64:10
33:1
u Ps 147:1
v Ps 32:11
33:2
w Ps 92:3
33:3
x Ps 96:1
33:4
y Ps 19:8
33:5
z Ps 11:7
a Ps 119:64
33:6
b Heb 11:3
33:8
c Ps 67:7; 96:9

a 7 Or sea as into a heap

he commanded, [d] and it stood firm.
10The LORD foils the plans of the nations; [e]
he thwarts the purposes of the peoples.
11But the plans of the LORD stand firm forever,
the purposes [f] of his heart through all generations.

12Blessed is the nation whose God is the LORD, [g]
the people he chose [h] for his inheritance.
13From heaven the LORD looks down
and sees all mankind; [i]
14from his dwelling place [j] he watches
all who live on earth—
15he who forms [k] the hearts of all,
who considers everything they do. [l]
16No king is saved by the size of his army; [m]
no warrior escapes by his great strength.
17A horse [n] is a vain hope for deliverance;
despite all its great strength it cannot save.
18But the eyes [o] of the LORD are on those who fear him,
on those whose hope is in his unfailing love, [p]
19to deliver them from death
and keep them alive in famine. [q]

20We wait [r] in hope for the LORD;
he is our help and our shield.
21In him our hearts rejoice, [s]
for we trust in his holy name.
22May your unfailing love rest upon us, O LORD,
even as we put our hope in you.

Psalm 34

Of David. When he pretended to be insane before Abimelech,
who drove him away, and he left.

1I [a] will extol the LORD at all times; [t]
his praise will always be on my lips.
2My soul will boast [u] in the LORD;
let the afflicted hear and rejoice. [v]
3Glorify the LORD with me;
let us exalt [w] his name together.

4I sought the LORD, [x] and he answered me;
he delivered me from all my fears.
5Those who look to him are radiant; [y]
their faces are never covered with shame. [z]
6This poor man called, and the LORD heard him;
he saved him out of all his troubles.

[a]This psalm is an acrostic poem, the verses of which begin with the successive letters of the
Hebrew alphabet.

33:9
dGe 1:3;
Ps 148:5
33:10
eIsa 8:10
33:11
fJob 23:13
33:12
gPs 144:15
hEx 19:5; Dt 7:6
33:13
iJob 28:24;
Ps 11:4
33:14
j1Ki 8:39
33:15
kJob 10:8
lJer 32:19
33:16
mPs 44:6
33:17
nPs 20:7;
Pr 21:31
33:18
oJob 36:7;
Ps 34:15
pPs 147:11
33:19
qJob 5:20
33:20
rPs 130:6
33:21
sZec 10:7;
Jn 16:22
34:1
tPs 71:6;
Eph 5:20
34:2
uJer 9:24;
1Co 1:31
vPs 119:74
34:3
wLk 1:46
34:4
xMt 7:7
34:5
yPs 36:9
zPs 25:3

[7]The angel of the Lord[a] encamps around those who fear
him,
and he delivers them.

[8]Taste and see that the Lord is good;[b]
blessed is the man who takes refuge[c] in him.
[9]Fear the Lord, you his saints,
for those who fear him lack nothing. [d]
[10]The lions may grow weak and hungry,
but those who seek the Lord lack no good thing. [e]

[11]Come, my children, listen to me;
I will teach you[f] the fear of the Lord.
[12]Whoever of you loves life[g]
and desires to see many good days,
[13]keep your tongue from evil
and your lips from speaking lies. [h]
[14]Turn from evil and do good;[i]
seek peace[j] and pursue it.

[15]The eyes of the Lord[k] are on the righteous[l]
and his ears are attentive to their cry;
[16]the face of the Lord is against[m] those who do evil, [n]
to cut off the memory[o] of them from the earth.

[17]The righteous cry out, and the Lord hears[p] them;
he delivers them from all their troubles.
[18]The Lord is close[q] to the brokenhearted[r]
and saves those who are crushed in spirit.

[19]A righteous man may have many troubles, [s]
but the Lord delivers him from them all;[t]
[20]he protects all his bones,
not one of them will be broken. [u]

[21]Evil will slay the wicked;[v]
the foes of the righteous will be condemned.
[22]The Lord redeems[w] his servants;
no one will be condemned who takes refuge in him.

Psalm 35

Of David.

[1]Contend, O Lord, with those who contend with me;
fight[x] against those who fight against me.
[2]Take up shield and buckler;
arise[y] and come to my aid.
[3]Brandish spear and javelin[a]
against those who pursue me.
Say to my soul,
"I am your salvation."

a3 Or *and block the way*

⁴May those who seek my life
  be disgraced[z] and put to shame;
 may those who plot my ruin
  be turned back in dismay.
⁵May they be like chaff[a] before the wind,
  with the angel of the LORD driving them away;
⁶may their path be dark and slippery,
  with the angel of the LORD pursuing them.
⁷Since they hid their net for me without cause
  and without cause dug a pit for me,
⁸may ruin overtake them by surprise—[b]
 may the net they hid entangle them,
 may they fall into the pit,[c] to their ruin.
⁹Then my soul will rejoice[d] in the LORD
  and delight in his salvation.[e]
¹⁰My whole being will exclaim,
  "Who is like you,[f] O LORD?
 You rescue the poor from those too strong[g] for
   them,
  the poor and needy[h] from those who rob them."

¹¹Ruthless witnesses[i] come forward;
  they question me on things I know nothing about.
¹²They repay me evil for good[j]
  and leave my soul forlorn.
¹³Yet when they were ill, I put on sackcloth
  and humbled myself with fasting.[k]
 When my prayers returned to me unanswered,
¹⁴ I went about mourning
  as though for my friend or brother.
 I bowed my head in grief
  as though weeping for my mother.
¹⁵But when I stumbled, they gathered in glee;
  attackers gathered against me when I was unaware.
  They slandered[l] me without ceasing.
¹⁶Like the ungodly they maliciously mocked[a];
  they gnashed their teeth[m] at me.
¹⁷O Lord, how long[n] will you look on?
  Rescue my life from their ravages,
  my precious life[o] from these lions.
¹⁸I will give you thanks in the great assembly;[p]
  among throngs of people I will praise you.[q]

¹⁹Let not those gloat over me
  who are my enemies without cause;
 let not those who hate me without reason[r]
  maliciously wink the eye.[s]
²⁰They do not speak peaceably,
  but devise false accusations
  against those who live quietly in the land.

35:4
zPs 70:2
35:5
aJob 21:18;
Ps 1:4; Isa 29:5
35:8
b1Th 5:3
cPs 9:15
35:9
dLk 1:47
eIsa 61:10
35:10
fEx 15:11
gPs 18:17
hPs 37:14
35:11
iPs 27:12
35:12
jJn 10:32
35:13
kJob 30:25;
Ps 69:10
35:15
lJob 30:1,8
35:16
mJob 16:9;
La 2:16
35:17
nHab 1:13
oPs 22:20
35:18
pPs 22:25
qPs 22:22
35:19
rPs 38:19; 69:4;
Jn 15:25*
sPs 13:4;
Pr 6:13

---

[a]16 Septuagint; Hebrew may mean *ungodly circle of mockers.*

²¹They gape[t] at me and say, "Aha! Aha![u]
  With our own eyes we have seen it."

²²O LORD, you have seen[v] this; be not silent.
  Do not be far[w] from me, O Lord.
²³Awake,[x] and rise to my defense!
  Contend for me, my God and Lord.
²⁴Vindicate me in your righteousness, O LORD my God;
  do not let them gloat over me.
²⁵Do not let them think, "Aha, just what we wanted!"
  or say, "We have swallowed him up."[y]

²⁶May all who gloat over my distress
  be put to shame[z] and confusion;
 may all who exalt themselves over me[a]
  be clothed with shame and disgrace.
²⁷May those who delight in my vindication[b]
  shout for joy[c] and gladness;
 may they always say, "The LORD be exalted,
  who delights[d] in the well-being of his servant."
²⁸My tongue will speak of your righteousness[e]
  and of your praises all day long.

Psalm 36

For the director of music. Of David the servant of the LORD.

¹An oracle is within my heart
  concerning the sinfulness of the wicked:[a]
 There is no fear of God
  before his eyes.[f]
²For in his own eyes he flatters himself
  too much to detect or hate his sin.
³The words of his mouth[g] are wicked and deceitful;
  he has ceased to be wise[h] and to do good.[i]
⁴Even on his bed he plots evil;[j]
  he commits himself to a sinful course[k]
  and does not reject what is wrong.[l]

⁵Your love, O LORD, reaches to the heavens,
  your faithfulness to the skies.
⁶Your righteousness is like the mighty mountains,
  your justice like the great deep.[m]
 O LORD, you preserve both man and beast.
⁷ How priceless is your unfailing love!
 Both high and low among men
  find[b] refuge in the shadow of your wings.[n]
⁸They feast on the abundance of your house;[o]
  you give them drink from your river[p] of delights.

---

[a]1 Or *heart: / Sin proceeds from the wicked.*   [b]7 Or *love, O God! / Men find; or love! / Both heavenly beings and men / find*

**Cross references (margin):**

35:21
t Ps 22:13
u Ps 40:15
35:22
v Ex 3:7
w Ps 10:1; 28:1
35:23
x Ps 44:23
35:25
y La 2:16
35:26
z Ps 40:14; 109:29
a Ps 38:16
35:27
b Ps 9:4
c Ps 32:11
d Ps 40:16; 147:11
35:28
e Ps 51:14
36:1
f Ro 3:18*
36:3
g Ps 10:7
h Ps 94:8
i Jer 4:22
36:4
j Pr 4:16; Mic 2:1
k Isa 65:2
l Ps 52:3; Ro 12:9
36:6
m Job 11:8; Ps 77:19; Ro 11:33
36:7
n Ru 2:12; Ps 17:8
36:8
o Ps 65:4
p Job 20:17; Rev 22:1

⁹For with you is the fountain of life;�q
  in your lightʳ we see light.

¹⁰Continue your love to those who know you,
  your righteousness to the upright in heart.
¹¹May the foot of the proud not come against me,
  nor the hand of the wicked drive me away.
¹²See how the evildoers lie fallen—
  thrown down, not able to rise!ˢ

Psalm 37ᵃ

Of David.

¹Do not fret because of evil men
  or be enviousᵗ of those who do wrong;ᵘ
²for like the grass they will soon wither,
  like green plants they will soon die away.ᵛ

³Trust in the LORD and do good;
  dwell in the landʷ and enjoy safe pasture.ˣ
⁴Delightʸ yourself in the LORD
  and he will give you the desires of your heart.

⁵Commit your way to the LORD;
  trust in himᶻ and he will do this:
⁶He will make your righteousnessᵃ shine like the dawn,ᵇ
  the justice of your cause like the noonday sun.

⁷Be stillᶜ before the LORD and wait patientlyᵈ for him;
  do not fret when men succeed in their ways,
  when they carry out their wicked schemes.

⁸Refrain from angerᵉ and turn from wrath;
  do not fret—it leads only to evil.
⁹For evil men will be cut off,
  but those who hope in the LORD will inherit the land.ᶠ

¹⁰A little while, and the wicked will be no more;ᵍ
  though you look for them, they will not be found.
¹¹But the meek will inherit the landʰ
  and enjoy great peace.

¹²The wicked plot against the righteous
  and gnash their teethⁱ at them;
¹³but the Lord laughs at the wicked,
  for he knows their day is coming.ʲ

¹⁴The wicked draw the sword
  and bend the bowᵏ
to bring down the poor and needy,ˡ
  to slay those whose ways are upright.

ᵃThis psalm is an acrostic poem, the stanzas of which begin with the successive letters of the Hebrew alphabet.

36:9
qJer 2:13
r1Pe 2:9
36:12
sPs 140:10
37:1
tPr 23:17-18
uPs 73:3
37:2
vPs 90:6
37:3
wDt 30:20
xIsa 40:11;
Jn 10:9
37:4
yIsa 58:14
37:5
zPs 4:5;
Ps 55:22;
Pr 16:3; 1Pe 5:7
37:6
aMic 7:9
bJob 11:17
37:7
cPs 62:5;
La 3:26 dPs 40:1
37:8
eEph 4:31;
Col 3:8
37:9
fIsa 57:13;
60:21
37:10
gJob 7:10;
24:24
37:11
hMt 5:5
37:12
iPs 35:16
37:13
j1Sa 26:10;
Ps 2:4
37:14
kPs 11:2
lPs 35:10

[15]But their swords will pierce their own hearts, [m]
    and their bows will be broken.

[16]Better the little that the righteous have
    than the wealth[n] of many wicked;
[17]for the power of the wicked will be broken, [o]
    but the LORD upholds the righteous.

[18]The days of the blameless are known to the LORD, [p]
    and their inheritance will endure forever.
[19]In times of disaster they will not wither;
    in days of famine they will enjoy plenty.

[20]But the wicked will perish:
    The LORD's enemies will be like the beauty of the
        fields,
    they will vanish—vanish like smoke. [q]

[21]The wicked borrow and do not repay,
    but the righteous give generously; [r]
[22]those the LORD blesses will inherit the land,
    but those he curses[s] will be cut off.

[23]If the LORD delights[t] in a man's way,
    he makes his steps firm; [u]
[24]though he stumble, he will not fall, [v]
    for the LORD upholds[w] him with his hand.

[25]I was young and now I am old,
    yet I have never seen the righteous forsaken[x]
    or their children begging bread.
[26]They are always generous and lend freely;
    their children will be blessed. [y]

[27]Turn from evil and do good; [z]
    then you will dwell in the land forever.
[28]For the LORD loves the just
    and will not forsake his faithful ones.

    They will be protected forever,
    but the offspring of the wicked will be cut off; [a]
[29]the righteous will inherit the land[b]
    and dwell in it forever.

[30]The mouth of the righteous man utters wisdom,
    and his tongue speaks what is just.
[31]The law of his God is in his heart; [c]
    his feet do not slip. [d]

[32]The wicked lie in wait[e] for the righteous,
    seeking their very lives;
[33]but the LORD will not leave them in their power
    or let them be condemned when brought to trial. [f]

[34]Wait for the LORD[g]
    and keep his way.
    He will exalt you to inherit the land;

37:15
mPs 9:16
37:16
nPr 15:16
37:17
oJob 38:15;
Ps 10:15
37:18
pPs 1:6
37:20
qPs 102:3
37:21
rPs 112:5
37:22
sJob 5:3;
Pr 3:33
37:23
tPs 147:11
u1Sa 2:9
37:24
vPr 24:16
wPs 145:14;
147:6
37:25
xHeb 13:5
37:26
yPs 147:13
37:27
zPs 34:14
37:28
aPs 21:10;
Isa 14:20
37:29
bver 9; Pr 2:21
37:31
cDt 6:6;
Ps 40:8;
Isa 51:7 dver 23
37:32
ePs 10:8
37:33
fPs 109:31;
2Pe 2:9
37:34
gPs 27:14

when the wicked are cut off, you will see[h] it.

35I have seen a wicked and ruthless man
　　flourishing[i] like a green tree in its native soil,
36but he soon passed away and was no more;
　　though I looked for him, he could not be found.[j]

37Consider the blameless, observe the upright;
　　there is a future[a] for the man of peace.[k]
38But all sinners will be destroyed;
　　the future[b] of the wicked will be cut off.[l]

39The salvation[m] of the righteous comes from the LORD;
　　he is their stronghold in time of trouble.[n]
40The LORD helps[o] them and delivers[p] them;
　　he delivers them from the wicked and saves them,
　　because they take refuge in him.

Psalm 38

A psalm of David. A petition.

1O LORD, do not rebuke me in your anger
　　or discipline me in your wrath.[q]
2For your arrows[r] have pierced me,
　　and your hand has come down upon me.
3Because of your wrath there is no health in my body;
　　my bones[s] have no soundness because of my sin.
4My guilt has overwhelmed me
　　like a burden too heavy to bear.[t]

5My wounds fester and are loathsome
　　because of my sinful folly.[u]
6I am bowed down and brought very low;
　　all day long I go about mourning.[v]
7My back is filled with searing pain;[w]
　　there is no health in my body.
8I am feeble and utterly crushed;
　　I groan[x] in anguish of heart.

9All my longings lie open before you, O Lord;
　　my sighing[y] is not hidden from you.
10My heart pounds, my strength fails[z] me;
　　even the light has gone from my eyes.[a]
11My friends and companions avoid me because of my
　　　　wounds;[b]
　　my neighbors stay far away.
12Those who seek my life set their traps,[c]
　　those who would harm me talk of my ruin;[d]
　　all day long they plot deception.[e]

37:34
h Ps 52:6
37:35
i Job 5:3
37:36
j Job 20:5
37:37
k Isa 57:1-2
37:38
l Ps 1:4
37:39
m Ps 3:8 n Ps 9:9
37:40
o 1Ch 5:20
p Isa 31:5
38:1
q Ps 6:1
38:2
r Job 6:4;
Ps 32:4
38:3
s Ps 6:2; Isa 1:6
38:4
t Ezr 9:6
38:5
u Ps 69:5
38:6
v Job 30:28;
Ps 35:14; 42:9
38:7
w Ps 102:3
38:8
x Ps 22:1
38:9
y Job 3:24;
Ps 6:6; 10:17
38:10
z Ps 31:10
a Ps 6:7
38:11
b Ps 31:11
38:12
c Ps 140:5
d Ps 35:4; 54:3
e Ps 35:20

---

a37 Or *there will be posterity*　　b38 Or *posterity*

[13]I am like a deaf man, who cannot hear,
    like a mute, who cannot open his mouth;
[14]I have become like a man who does not hear,
    whose mouth can offer no reply.
[15]I wait[f] for you, O LORD;
    you will answer,[g] O Lord my God.
[16]For I said, "Do not let them gloat[h]
    or exalt themselves over me when my foot slips."[i]

[17]For I am about to fall,
    and my pain is ever with me.
[18]I confess my iniquity;[j]
    I am troubled by my sin.
[19]Many are those who are my vigorous enemies;[k]
    those who hate me without reason[l] are numerous.
[20]Those who repay my good with evil[m]
    slander me when I pursue what is good.

[21]O LORD, do not forsake me;
    be not far[n] from me, O my God.
[22]Come quickly to help me,[o]
    O Lord my Savior.[p]

Psalm 39

For the director of music. For Jeduthun. A psalm of David.

[1]I said, "I will watch my ways[q]
    and keep my tongue from sin;[r]
 I will put a muzzle on my mouth
    as long as the wicked are in my presence."
[2]But when I was silent[s] and still,
    not even saying anything good,
    my anguish increased.
[3]My heart grew hot within me,
    and as I meditated, the fire burned;
    then I spoke with my tongue:

[4]"Show me, O LORD, my life's end
    and the number of my days;[t]
    let me know how fleeting is my life.[u]
[5]You have made my days[v] a mere handbreadth;
    the span of my years is as nothing before you.
    Each man's life is but a breath.[w]   *Selah*
[6]Man is a mere phantom[x] as he goes to and fro:
    He bustles about, but only in vain;[y]
    he heaps up wealth, not knowing who will get it.[z]

[7]"But now, Lord, what do I look for?
    My hope is in you.[a]
[8]Save me[b] from all my transgressions;[c]
    do not make me the scorn of fools.

38:15
f Ps 39:7
g Ps 17:6
38:16
h Ps 35:26
i Ps 13:4
38:18
j Ps 32:5
38:19
k Ps 18:17
l Ps 35:19
38:20
m Ps 35:12;
1Jn 3:12
38:21
n Ps 35:22
38:22
o Ps 40:13
p Ps 27:1
39:1
q 1Ki 2:4
r Job 2:10;
Jas 3:2
39:2
s Ps 38:13
39:4
t Ps 90:12
u Ps 103:14
39:5
v Ps 89:45
w Ps 62:9
39:6
x 1Pe 1:24
y Ps 127:2
z Lk 12:20
39:7
a Ps 38:15
39:8
b Ps 51:9
c Ps 44:13

[9]I was silent; I would not open my mouth,[d]
    for you are the one who has done this.
[10]Remove your scourge from me;
    I am overcome by the blow of your hand.[e]
[11]You rebuke[f] and discipline men for their sin;
    you consume their wealth like a moth[g]—
    each man is but a breath.   *Selah*

[12]"Hear my prayer, O LORD,
    listen to my cry for help;
    be not deaf to my weeping.
For I dwell with you as an alien,[h]
    a stranger,[i] as all my fathers were.
[13]Look away from me, that I may rejoice again
    before I depart and am no more."[j]

Psalm 40

40:13–17pp — Ps 70:1–5

For the director of music. Of David. A psalm.

[1]I waited patiently[k] for the LORD;
    he turned to me and heard my cry.[l]
[2]He lifted me out of the slimy pit,
    out of the mud and mire;[m]
he set my feet on a rock[n]
    and gave me a firm place to stand.
[3]He put a new song[o] in my mouth,
    a hymn of praise to our God.
Many will see and fear
    and put their trust in the LORD.

[4]Blessed is the man[p]
    who makes the LORD his trust,[q]
who does not look to the proud,
    to those who turn aside to false gods.[a]
[5]Many, O LORD my God,
    are the wonders[r] you have done.
The things you planned for us
    no one can recount[s] to you;
were I to speak and tell of them,
    they would be too many to declare.

[6]Sacrifice and offering you did not desire,[t]
    but my ears you have pierced[b,c];
burnt offerings[u] and sin offerings
    you did not require.
[7]Then I said, "Here I am, I have come—
    it is written about me in the scroll.[d]

39:9
d Job 2:10
39:10
e Job 9:34;
Ps 32:4
39:11
f 2Pe 2:16
g Job 13:28
39:12
h 1Pe 2:11
i Heb 11:13
39:13
j Job 10:21;
14:10
40:1
k Ps 27:14
l Ps 34:15
40:2
m Ps 69:14
n Ps 27:5
40:3
o Ps 33:3
40:4
p Ps 34:8
q Ps 84:12
40:5
r Ps 136:4
s Ps 139:18;
Isa 55:8
40:6
t 1Sa 15:22;
Am 5:22
u Isa 1:11

---

a 4 Or *to falsehood*   b 6 Hebrew; Septuagint *but a body you have prepared for me* (see also Symmachus and Theodotion)   c 6 Or *opened*   d 7 Or *come / with the scroll written for me*

[8]I desire to do your will,[v] O my God;
    your law is within my heart."[w]

[9]I proclaim righteousness in the great assembly;[x]
    I do not seal my lips,
    as you know,[y] O LORD.
[10]I do not hide your righteousness in my heart;
    I speak of your faithfulness[z] and salvation.
I do not conceal your love and your truth
    from the great assembly.[a]

[11]Do not withhold your mercy from me, O LORD;
    may your love[b] and your truth[c] always protect me.
[12]For troubles[d] without number surround me;
    my sins have overtaken me, and I cannot see.[e]
They are more than the hairs of my head,[f]
    and my heart fails[g] within me.

[13]Be pleased, O LORD, to save me;
    O LORD, come quickly to help me.[h]
[14]May all who seek to take my life
    be put to shame and confusion;
may all who desire my ruin[i]
    be turned back in disgrace.
[15]May those who say to me, "Aha! Aha!"
    be appalled at their own shame.
[16]But may all who seek you
    rejoice and be glad in you;
may those who love your salvation always say,
    "The LORD be exalted!"[j]

[17]Yet I am poor and needy;
    may the Lord think of me.
You are my help and my deliverer;
    O my God, do not delay.[k]

Psalm 41

For the director of music. A psalm of David.

[1]Blessed is he who has regard for the weak;[1]
    the LORD delivers him in times of trouble.
[2]The LORD will protect him and preserve his life;
    he will bless him in the land[m]
    and not surrender him to the desire of his foes.[n]
[3]The LORD will sustain him on his sickbed
    and restore him from his bed of illness.

[4]I said, "O LORD, have mercy[o] on me;
    heal me, for I have sinned[p] against you."
[5]My enemies say of me in malice,
    "When will he die and his name perish?[q]"
[6]Whenever one comes to see me,

Margin notes

40:8
v Jn 4:34
w Ps 37:31
40:9
x Ps 22:25
y Jos 22:22;
Ps 119:13
40:10
z Ps 89:1
a Ac 20:20
40:11
b Pr 20:28
c Ps 43:3
40:12
d Ps 116:3
e Ps 38:4
f Ps 69:4
g Ps 73:26
40:13
h Ps 70:1
40:14
i Ps 35:4
40:16
j Ps 35:27
40:17
k Ps 70:5
41:1
l Ps 82:3-4;
Pr 14:21
41:2
m Ps 37:22
n Ps 27:12
41:4
o Ps 6:2 p Ps 51:4
41:5
q Ps 38:12

he speaks falsely,ʳ while his heart gathers slander;ˢ
then he goes out and spreads it abroad.

⁷All my enemies whisper togetherᵗ against me;
they imagine the worst for me, saying,
⁸"A vile disease has beset him;
he will never get up from the place where he lies."
⁹Even my close friend,ᵘ whom I trusted,
he who shared my bread,
has lifted up his heel against me.ᵛ

¹⁰But you, O Lᴏʀᴅ, have mercy on me;
raise me up,ʷ that I may repay them.
¹¹I know that you are pleased with me,ˣ
for my enemy does not triumph over me.ʸ
¹²In my integrity you uphold meᶻ
and set me in your presence forever.ᵃ

¹³Praise be to the Lᴏʀᴅ, the God of Israel,ᵇ
from everlasting to everlasting.
Amen and Amen.ᶜ

BOOK II

Psalms 42–72

Psalm 42ᵃ

For the director of music. A *maskil*ᵇ of the Sons of Korah.

¹As the deer pants for streams of water,
so my soul pantsᵈ for you, O God.
²My soul thirstsᵉ for God, for the living God.ᶠ
When can I goᵍ and meet with God?
³My tearsʰ have been my food
day and night,
while men say to me all day long,
"Where is your God?"ⁱ
⁴These things I remember
as I pour out my soul:
how I used to go with the multitude,
leading the procession to the house of God,ʲ
with shouts of joy and thanksgivingᵏ
among the festive throng.

⁵Why are you downcast,ˡ O my soul?
Why so disturbed within me?
Put your hope in God,ᵐ

41:6
ʳPs 12:2
ˢPr 26:24
41:7
ᵗPs 56:5;
71:10-11
41:9
ᵘ2Sa 15:12;
Ps 55:12
ᵛJob 19:19;
Ps 55:20;
Mt 26:23;
Jn 13:18*
41:10
ʷPs 3:3
41:11
ˣPs 147:11
ʸPs 25:2
41:12
ᶻPs 37:17
ᵃJob 36:7
41:13
ᵇPs 72:18
ᶜPs 89:52;
106:48
42:1
ᵈPs 119:131
42:2
ᵉPs 63:1
ᶠJer 10:10
ᵍPs 43:4
42:3
ʰPs 80:5
ⁱPs 79:10
42:4
ʲIsa 30:29
ᵏPs 100:4
42:5
ˡPs 38:6; 77:3
ᵐLa 3:24

ᵃIn many Hebrew manuscripts Psalms 42 and 43 constitute one psalm.   ᵇTitle: Probably a literary or musical term

for I will yet praise him,
   my Savior[n] and [6]my God.

My[a] soul is downcast within me;
   therefore I will remember you
from the land of the Jordan,
   the heights of Hermon—from Mount Mizar.
[7]Deep calls to deep
   in the roar of your waterfalls;
all your waves and breakers
   have swept over me. [o]

[8]By day the LORD directs his love,[p]
   at night[q] his song[r] is with me—
   a prayer to the God of my life.

[9]I say to God my Rock,
   "Why have you forgotten me?
Why must I go about mourning,[s]
   oppressed by the enemy?"
[10]My bones suffer mortal agony
   as my foes taunt me,
saying to me all day long,
   "Where is your God?"

[11]Why are you downcast, O my soul?
   Why so disturbed within me?
Put your hope in God,
   for I will yet praise him,
   my Savior and my God. [t]

Psalm 43[b]

[1]Vindicate me, O God,
   and plead my cause[u] against an ungodly nation;
   rescue me from deceitful and wicked men. [v]
[2]You are God my stronghold.
   Why have you rejected[w] me?
Why must I go about mourning,
   oppressed by the enemy?[x]
[3]Send forth your light[y] and your truth,
   let them guide me;
let them bring me to your holy mountain,[z]
   to the place where you dwell. [a]
[4]Then will I go to the altar[b] of God,
   to God, my joy and my delight.
I will praise you with the harp,[c]
   O God, my God.

42:5
n Ps 44:3
42:7
o Ps 88:7;
Jnh 2:3
42:8
p Ps 57:3
q Job 35:10
r Ps 63:6; 149:5
42:9
s Ps 38:6
42:11
t Ps 43:5
43:1
u 1Sa 24:15;
Ps 26:1; 35:1
v Ps 5:6
43:2
w Ps 44:9
x Ps 42:9
43:3
y Ps 36:9
z Ps 42:4
a Ps 84:1
43:4
b Ps 26:6
c Ps 33:2

---

[a]5,6 A few Hebrew manuscripts, Septuagint and Syriac; most Hebrew manuscripts *praise him for his saving help. /* [6]*O my God, my*   [b]In many Hebrew manuscripts Psalms 42 and 43 constitute one psalm.

⁵Why are you downcast, O my soul?
    Why so disturbed within me?
Put your hope in God,
    for I will yet praise him,
    my Savior and my God. [d]

Psalm 44

For the director of music. Of the Sons of Korah. A *maskil*. [a]

¹We have heard with our ears, O God;
    our fathers have told us [e]
what you did in their days,
    in days long ago.
²With your hand you drove out [f] the nations
    and planted [g] our fathers;
you crushed the peoples
    and made our fathers flourish. [h]
³It was not by their sword [i] that they won the land,
    nor did their arm bring them victory;
it was your right hand, your arm, [j]
    and the light of your face, for you loved [k] them.

⁴You are my King [l] and my God,
    who decrees [b] victories for Jacob.
⁵Through you we push back our enemies;
    through your name we trample [m] our foes.
⁶I do not trust in my bow, [n]
    my sword does not bring me victory;
⁷but you give us victory [o] over our enemies,
    you put our adversaries to shame. [p]
⁸In God we make our boast [q] all day long,
    and we will praise your name forever. [r]   *Selah*

⁹But now you have rejected [s] and humbled us;
    you no longer go out with our armies. [t]
¹⁰You made us retreat [u] before the enemy,
    and our adversaries have plundered us.
¹¹You gave us up to be devoured like sheep [v]
    and have scattered us among the nations. [w]
¹²You sold your people for a pittance, [x]
    gaining nothing from their sale.

¹³You have made us a reproach to our neighbors, [y]
    the scorn [z] and derision of those around us.
¹⁴You have made us a byword among the nations;
    the peoples shake their heads [a] at us.
¹⁵My disgrace is before me all day long,
    and my face is covered with shame

---

[a] Title: Probably a literary or musical term   [b] 4 Septuagint, Aquila and Syriac; Hebrew *King, O God; / command*

43:5
d Ps 42:6
44:1
e Ex 12:26;
Ps 78:3
44:2
f Ps 78:55
g Ex 15:17
h Ps 80:9
44:3
i Dt 8:17;
Jos 24:12
j Ps 77:15
k Dt 4:37; 7:7-8
44:4
l Ps 74:12
44:5
m Ps 108:13
44:6
n Ps 33:16
44:7
o Ps 136:24
p Ps 53:5
44:8
q Ps 34:2
r Ps 30:12
44:9
s Ps 74:1
t Ps 60:1,10
44:10
u Lev 26:17;
Jos 7:8;
Ps 89:41
44:11
v Ro 8:36
w Dt 4:27;
28:64;
Ps 106:27
44:12
x Isa 52:3;
Jer 15:13
44:13
y Ps 79:4; 80:6
z Dt 28:37
44:14
a Ps 109:25;
Jer 24:9

16at the taunts of those who reproach and revile[b] me,
    because of the enemy, who is bent on revenge.

17All this happened to us,
    though we had not forgotten[c] you
    or been false to your covenant.
18Our hearts had not turned[d] back;
    our feet had not strayed from your path.
19But you crushed[e] us and made us a haunt for jackals
    and covered us over with deep darkness. [f]

20If we had forgotten[g] the name of our God
    or spread out our hands to a foreign god, [h]
21would not God have discovered it,
    since he knows the secrets of the heart?[i]
22Yet for your sake we face death all day long;
    we are considered as sheep to be slaughtered.[j]

23Awake, [k] O Lord! Why do you sleep?[l]
    Rouse yourself! Do not reject us forever. [m]
24Why do you hide your face[n]
    and forget our misery and oppression?[o]

25We are brought down to the dust;[p]
    our bodies cling to the ground.
26Rise up[q] and help us;
    redeem[r] us because of your unfailing love.

Psalm 45

For the director of music. To the tune of "Lilies." Of the Sons of Korah.
A *maskil.* [a] A wedding song.

1My heart is stirred by a noble theme
    as I recite my verses for the king;
    my tongue is the pen of a skillful writer.

2You are the most excellent of men
    and your lips have been anointed with grace, [s]
    since God has blessed you forever.
3Gird your sword[t] upon your side, O mighty one;[u]
    clothe yourself with splendor and majesty.
4In your majesty ride forth victoriously[v]
    in behalf of truth, humility and righteousness;
    let your right hand display awesome deeds.
5Let your sharp arrows pierce the hearts of the king's
        enemies;
    let the nations fall beneath your feet.
6Your throne, O God, will last for ever and ever;[w]
    a scepter of justice will be the scepter of your
        kingdom.

44:16
bPs 74:10
44:17
cPs 78:7,57;
Da 9:13
44:18
dJob 23:11
44:19
ePs 51:8
fJob 3:5
44:20
gPs 78:11
hDt 6:14;
Ps 81:9
44:21
iPs 139:1-2;
Jer 17:10
44:22
jIsa 53:7;
Ro 8:36*
44:23
kPs 7:6
lPs 78:65
mPs 77:7
44:24
nJob 13:24
oPs 42:9
44:25
pPs 119:25
44:26
qPs 35:2
rPs 25:22
45:2
sLk 4:22
45:3
tHeb 4:12;
Rev 1:16
uIsa 9:6
45:4
vRev 6:2
45:6
wPs 93:2; 98:9

aTitle: Probably a literary or musical term

⁷You love righteousnessˣ and hate wickedness;
    therefore God, your God, has set you above your
        companions
    by anointingʸ you with the oil of joy.ᶻ
⁸All your robes are fragrantᵃ with myrrh and aloes and
        cassia;
    from palaces adorned with ivory
    the music of the strings makes you glad.
⁹Daughters of kingsᵇ are among your honored women;
    at your right handᶜ is the royal bride in gold of Ophir.

¹⁰Listen, O daughter, consider and give ear:
    Forget your peopleᵈ and your father's house.
¹¹The king is enthralled by your beauty;
    honorᵉ him, for he is your lord.ᶠ
¹²The Daughter of Tyre will come with a gift,ᵃ ᵍ
    men of wealth will seek your favor.

¹³All gloriousʰ is the princess within her chamber;
    her gown is interwoven with gold.
¹⁴In embroidered garments she is led to the king;ⁱ
    her virgin companions follow her
    and are brought to you.
¹⁵They are led in with joy and gladness;
    they enter the palace of the king.

¹⁶Your sons will take the place of your fathers;
    you will make them princes throughout the land.
¹⁷I will perpetuate your memory through all generations;ʲ
    therefore the nations will praise youᵏ for ever and
        ever.

Psalm 46

For the director of music. Of the Sons of Korah. According to *alamoth*.ᵇ
A song.

¹God is our refugeˡ and strength,
    an ever-presentᵐ help in trouble.
²Therefore we will not fear,ⁿ though the earth give wayᵒ
    and the mountains fallᵖ into the heart of the sea,
³though its waters roar�q and foam
    and the mountains quake with their surging.   *Selah*

⁴There is a river whose streams make glad the city of
        God,ʳ
    the holy place where the Most High dwells.
⁵God is within her,ˢ she will not fall;
    God will helpᵗ her at break of day.
⁶Nationsᵘ are in uproar, kingdomsᵛ fall;
    he lifts his voice, the earth melts.ʷ

ᵃ12 Or *A Tyrian robe is among the gifts*   ᵇTitle: Probably a musical term

45:7
ˣPs 33:5
ʸIsa 61:1
ᶻPs 21:6;
Heb 1:8-9*
45:8
ᵃSS 1:3
45:9
ᵇSS 6:8
ᶜ1Ki 2:19
45:10
ᵈDt 21:13
45:11
ᵉPs 95:6
ᶠIsa 54:5
45:12
ᵍPs 22:29;
Isa 49:23
45:13
ʰIsa 61:10
45:14
ⁱSS 1:4
45:17
ʲMal 1:11
ᵏPs 138:4
46:1
ˡPs 9:9; 14:6
ᵐDt 4:7
46:2
ⁿPs 23:4
ᵒPs 82:5
ᵖPs 18:7
46:3
qPs 93:3
46:4
ʳPs 48:1,8;
Isa 60:14
46:5
ˢIsa 12:6;
Eze 43:7
ᵗPs 37:40
46:6
ᵘPs 2:1
ᵛPs 68:32
ʷMic 1:4

⁷The LORD Almighty is with us;^x
  the God of Jacob is our fortress.^y   *Selah*

⁸Come and see the works of the LORD,^z
  the desolations^a he has brought on the earth.
⁹He makes wars^b cease to the ends of the earth;
  he breaks the bow^c and shatters the spear,
  he burns the shields^a with fire.^d
¹⁰"Be still, and know that I am God;^e
  I will be exalted^f among the nations,
  I will be exalted in the earth."

¹¹The LORD Almighty is with us;
  the God of Jacob is our fortress.   *Selah*

Psalm 47

For the director of music. Of the Sons of Korah. A psalm.

¹Clap your hands,^g all you nations;
  shout to God with cries of joy.^h
²How awesomeⁱ is the LORD Most High,
  the great King^j over all the earth!
³He subdued^k nations under us,
  peoples under our feet.
⁴He chose our inheritance^l for us,
  the pride of Jacob, whom he loved.   *Selah*

⁵God has ascended amid shouts of joy,
  the LORD amid the sounding of trumpets.^m
⁶Sing praisesⁿ to God, sing praises;
  sing praises to our King, sing praises.

⁷For God is the King of all the earth;^o
  sing to him a psalm^{b p} of praise.
⁸God reigns^q over the nations;
  God is seated on his holy throne.
⁹The nobles of the nations assemble
  as the people of the God of Abraham,
  for the kings^c of the earth belong to God;^r
  he is greatly exalted.^s

Psalm 48

A song. A psalm of the Sons of Korah.

¹Great is the LORD,^t and most worthy of praise,
  in the city of our God,^u his holy mountain.^v

---

^a9 Or *chariots*   ^b7 Or *a maskil* (probably a literary or musical term)   ^c9 Or *shields*

46:7
x2Ch 13:12
yPs 9:9
46:8
zPs 66:5
aIsa 61:4
46:9
bIsa 2:4
cPs 76:3
dEze 39:9
46:10
ePs 100:3
fIsa 2:11
47:1
gPs 98:8;
Isa 55:12
hPs 106:47
47:2
iDt 7:21
jMal 1:14
47:3
kPs 18:39,47
47:4
l1Pe 1:4
47:5
mPs 68:33; 98:6
47:6
nPs 68:4; 89:18
47:7
oZec 14:9
pCol 3:16
47:8
q1Ch 16:31
47:9
rPs 72:11; 89:18
sPs 97:9
48:1
tPs 96:4
uPs 46:4
vIsa 2:2-3;
Mic 4:1;
Zec 8:3

²It is beautiful^w in its loftiness,
    the joy of the whole earth.
Like the utmost heights of Zaphon^a is Mount Zion,
    the^b city of the Great King.^x
³God is in her citadels;
    he has shown himself to be her fortress.^y

⁴When the kings joined forces,
    when they advanced together,^z
⁵they saw ˌherˌ and were astounded;
    they fled in terror.^a
⁶Trembling seized them there,
    pain like that of a woman in labor.
⁷You destroyed them like ships of Tarshish
    shattered by an east wind.^b

⁸As we have heard,
    so have we seen
in the city of the LORD Almighty,
    in the city of our God:
God makes her secure forever.^c   *Selah*

⁹Within your temple, O God,
    we meditate on your unfailing love.^d
¹⁰Like your name,^e O God,
    your praise reaches to the ends of the earth;^f
    your right hand is filled with righteousness.
¹¹Mount Zion rejoices,
    the villages of Judah are glad
    because of your judgments.^g

¹²Walk about Zion, go around her,
    count her towers,
¹³consider well her ramparts,
    view her citadels,^h
    that you may tell of them to the next generation.ⁱ
¹⁴For this God is our God for ever and ever;
    he will be our guide^j even to the end.

Psalm 49

For the director of music. Of the Sons of Korah. A psalm.

¹Hear this, all you peoples;^k
    listen, all who live in this world,^l
²both low and high,
    rich and poor alike:
³My mouth will speak words of wisdom;^m

48:2
wPs 50:2;
La 2:15
48:3
yPs 46:7
48:4
z2Sa 10:1-19
48:5
aEx 15:16
48:7
bJer 18:17;
Eze 27:26
48:8
cPs 87:5
48:9
dPs 26:3
48:10
eDt 28:58;
Jos 7:9
fIsa 41:10
48:11
gPs 97:8
48:13
hver 3; Ps 122:7
iPs 78:6
48:14
jPs 23:4
49:1
kPs 78:1
lPs 33:8
49:3
mPs 37:30

---

^a2 *Zaphon* can refer to a sacred mountain or the direction north.   ^b2 Or *earth, / Mount Zion, on the northern side / of the*

the utterance from my heart will give understanding. [n]
[4]I will turn my ear to a proverb; [o]
    with the harp I will expound my riddle: [p]
[5]Why should I fear [q] when evil days come,
    when wicked deceivers surround me—
[6]those who trust in their wealth [r]
    and boast of their great riches?
[7]No man can redeem the life of another
    or give to God a ransom for him—
[8]the ransom for a life is costly,
    no payment is ever enough— [s]
[9]that he should live on [t] forever
    and not see decay.

[10]For all can see that wise men die; [u]
    the foolish and the senseless alike perish
    and leave their wealth to others. [v]
[11]Their tombs will remain their houses [a] forever,
    their dwellings for endless generations,
    though they had [b] named [w] lands after
        themselves.

[12]But man, despite his riches, does not endure;
    he is [c] like the beasts that perish.

[13]This is the fate of those who trust in themselves, [x]
    and of their followers, who approve their sayings.
                              Selah

[14]Like sheep they are destined for the grave, [d] [y]
    and death will feed on them.
  The upright will rule [z] over them in the morning;
    their forms will decay in the grave, [d]
    far from their princely mansions.
[15]But God will redeem my life [e] from the grave; [a]
    he will surely take me to himself. [b]   *Selah*

[16]Do not be overawed when a man grows rich,
    when the splendor of his house increases;
[17]for he will take nothing with him when he dies,
    his splendor will not descend with him. [c]
[18]Though while he lived he counted himself
        blessed— [d]
    and men praise you when you prosper—
[19]he will join the generation of his fathers, [e]
    who will never see the light [f] of life.

[20]A man who has riches without understanding
    is like the beasts that perish. [g]

49:3
[n] Ps 119:130
49:4
[o] Ps 78:2
[p] Nu 12:8
49:5
[q] Ps 23:4
49:6
[r] Job 31:24
49:8
[s] Mt 16:26
49:9
[t] Ps 22:29; 89:48
49:10
[u] Ecc 2:16
[v] Ecc 2:18,21
49:11
[w] Ge 4:17;
Dt 3:14
49:13
[x] Lk 12:20
49:14
[y] Job 24:19;
Ps 9:17
[z] Da 7:18;
Mal 4:3;
1Co 6:2;
Rev 2:26
49:15
[a] Ps 56:13;
Hos 13:14
[b] Ps 73:24
49:17
[c] Ps 17:14;
1Tim 6:7
49:18
[d] Dt 29:19;
Lk 12:19
49:19
[e] Ge 15:15
[f] Job 33:30
49:20
[g] Ecc 3:19

[a]11 Septuagint and Syriac; Hebrew *In their thoughts their houses will remain*   [b]11 Or */ for they have*   [c]12 Hebrew; Septuagint and Syriac read verse 12 the same as verse 20.   [d]14 Hebrew *Sheol*; also in verse 15   [e]15 Or *soul*

Psalm 50

A psalm of Asaph.

[1]The Mighty One, God, the LORD,[h]
  speaks and summons the earth
  from the rising of the sun to the place where it sets.[i]
[2]From Zion, perfect in beauty,[j]
  God shines forth.[k]
[3]Our God comes[1] and will not be silent;
  a fire devours before him,[m]
  and around him a tempest rages.
[4]He summons the heavens above,
  and the earth,[n] that he may judge his people:
[5]"Gather to me my consecrated ones,[o]
  who made a covenant[p] with me by sacrifice."
[6]And the heavens proclaim[q] his righteousness,
  for God himself is judge.[r]   *Selah*

[7]"Hear, O my people, and I will speak,
  O Israel, and I will testify[s] against you:
  I am God, your God.[t]
[8]I do not rebuke you for your sacrifices
  or your burnt offerings,[u] which are ever before me.
[9]I have no need of a bull[v] from your stall
  or of goats from your pens,
[10]for every animal of the forest is mine,
  and the cattle on a thousand hills.[w]
[11]I know every bird in the mountains,
  and the creatures of the field are mine.
[12]If I were hungry I would not tell you,
  for the world[x] is mine, and all that is in it.
[13]Do I eat the flesh of bulls
  or drink the blood of goats?
[14]Sacrifice thank offerings[y] to God,
  fulfill your vows[z] to the Most High,
[15]and call[a] upon me in the day of trouble;
  I will deliver you, and you will honor[b] me."

[16]But to the wicked, God says:

  "What right have you to recite my laws
  or take my covenant on your lips?[c]
[17]You hate my instruction
  and cast my words behind[d] you.
[18]When you see a thief, you join[e] with him;
  you throw in your lot with adulterers.
[19]You use your mouth for evil
  and harness your tongue to deceit.[f]
[20]You speak continually against your brother[g]
  and slander your own mother's son.
[21]These things you have done and I kept silent;[h]

50:1
h Jos 22:22
i Ps 113:3
50:2
j Ps 48:2
k Dt 33:2;
Ps 80:1
50:3
l Ps 96:13
m Ps 97:3;
Da 7:10
50:4
n Dt 4:26;
Isa 1:2
50:5
o Ps 30:4
p Ex 24:7
50:6
q Ps 89:5
r Ps 75:7
50:7
s Ps 81:8
t Ex 20:2
50:8
u Ps 40:6;
Hos 6:6
50:9
v Ps 69:31
50:10
w Ps 104:24
50:12
x Ex 19:5
50:14
y Heb 13:15
z Dt 23:21
50:15
a Ps 81:7
b Ps 22:23
50:16
c Isa 29:13
50:17
d Ne 9:26;
Ro 2:21-22
50:18
e Ro 1:32;
1Ti 5:22
50:19
f Ps 10:7; 52:2
50:20
g Mt 10:21
50:21
h Ecc 8:11;
Isa 42:14

you thought I was altogether[a] like you.
But I will rebuke you
    and accuse[i] you to your face.

22"Consider this, you who forget God,[j]
    or I will tear you to pieces, with none to rescue:[k]
23He who sacrifices thank offerings honors me,
    and he prepares the way[l]
    so that I may show him[b] the salvation of God.[m]'

Psalm 51

For the director of music. A psalm of David. When the prophet Nathan came to him after David had committed adultery with Bathsheba.

1Have mercy on me, O God,
    according to your unfailing love;
according to your great compassion
    blot out[n] my transgressions.[o]
2Wash away[p] all my iniquity
    and cleanse[q] me from my sin.

3For I know my transgressions,
    and my sin is always before me.[r]
4Against you, you only, have I sinned
    and done what is evil in your sight,[s]
so that you are proved right when you speak
    and justified when you judge.[t]
5Surely I was sinful[u] at birth,
    sinful from the time my mother conceived me.
6Surely you desire truth in the inner parts[c];
    you teach[d] me wisdom[v] in the inmost place.[w]

7Cleanse me with hyssop,[x] and I will be clean;
    wash me, and I will be whiter than snow.[y]
8Let me hear joy and gladness;[z]
    let the bones you have crushed rejoice.
9Hide your face from my sins[a]
    and blot out all my iniquity.

10Create in me a pure heart,[b] O God,
    and renew a steadfast spirit within me.[c]
11Do not cast me from your presence
    or take your Holy Spirit[d] from me.
12Restore to me the joy of your salvation[e]
    and grant me a willing spirit, to sustain me.

13Then I will teach transgressors your ways,[f]
    and sinners will turn back to you.[g]
14Save me from bloodguilt,[h] O God,

50:21
iPs 90:8
50:22
jJob 8:13;
Ps 9:17 kPs 7:2
50:23
lPs 85:13
mPs 91:16
51:1
nAc 3:19
oIsa 43:25;
Col 2:14
51:2
p1Jn 1:9
qHeb 9:14
51:3
rIsa 59:12
51:4
sGe 20:6;
Lk 15:21
tRo 3:4*
51:5
uJob 14:4
51:6
vPr 2:6
wPs 15:2
51:7
xLev 14:4;
Heb 9:19
yIsa 1:18
51:8
zIsa 35:10
51:9
aJer 16:17
51:10
bPs 78:37;
Ac 15:9
cEze 18:31
51:11
dEph 4:30
51:12
ePs 13:5
51:13
fAc 9:21-22
gPs 22:27
51:14
h2Sa 12:9

a21 Or *thought the 'I AM' was*   b23 Or *and to him who considers his way / I will show*   c6 The meaning of the Hebrew for this phrase is uncertain.   d6 Or *you desired . . . ; / you taught*

the God who saves me, [i]
and my tongue will sing of your righteousness. [j]
15O Lord, open my lips, [k]
and my mouth will declare your praise.
16You do not delight in sacrifice, [l] or I would bring it;
you do not take pleasure in burnt offerings.
17The sacrifices of God are[a] a broken spirit;
a broken and contrite heart, [m]
O God, you will not despise.

18In your good pleasure make Zion[n] prosper;
build up the walls of Jerusalem.
19Then there will be righteous sacrifices, [o]
whole burnt offerings[p] to delight you;
then bulls[q] will be offered on your altar.

Psalm 52

For the director of music. A *maskil*[b] of David. When Doeg the Edomite[r]
had gone to Saul and told him: "David has gone
to the house of Ahimelech."

1Why do you boast of evil, you mighty man?
Why do you boast[s] all day long,
you who are a disgrace in the eyes of God?
2Your tongue plots destruction;
it is like a sharpened razor, [t]
you who practice deceit. [u]
3You love evil rather than good,
falsehood[v] rather than speaking the truth.　　　*Selah*
4You love every harmful word,
O you deceitful tongue![w]

5Surely God will bring you down to everlasting ruin:
He will snatch you up and tear[x] you from your tent;
he will uproot[y] you from the land of the living. [z]　*Selah*
6The righteous will see and fear;
they will laugh[a] at him, saying,
7"Here now is the man
who did not make God his stronghold
but trusted in his great wealth[b]
and grew strong by destroying others!"

8But I am like an olive tree[c]
flourishing in the house of God;
I trust[d] in God's unfailing love
for ever and ever.
9I will praise you forever[e] for what you have done;
in your name I will hope, for your name is good. [f]
I will praise you in the presence of your saints.

---

a17 Or My sacrifice, O God, is　　*bTitle: Probably a literary or musical term*

51:14
iPs 25:5
jPs 35:28
51:15
kPs 9:14
51:16
l1Sa 15:22;
Ps 40:6
51:17
mPs 34:18
51:18
nPs 102:16;
Isa 51:3
51:19
oPs 4:5
pPs 66:13
qPs 66:15
52:Title
r1Sa 22:9
52:1
sPs 94:4
52:2
tPs 57:4
uPs 50:19
52:3
vJer 9:5
52:4
wPs 120:2,3
52:5
xIsa 22:19
yPr 2:22
zPs 27:13
52:6
aJob 22:19;
Ps 37:34; 40:3
52:7
bPs 49:6
52:8
cJer 11:16
dPs 13:5
52:9
ePs 30:12
fPs 54:6

Psalm 53

53:1–6pp — Ps 14:1–7

For the director of music. According to *mahalath.*[a] A *maskil*[b] of David.

¹The fool[g] says in his heart,
"There is no God."[h]
They are corrupt, and their ways are vile;
there is no one who does good.

²God looks down from heaven[i]
on the sons of men
to see if there are any who understand,
any who seek God.[j]
³Everyone has turned away,
they have together become corrupt;
there is no one who does good,
not even one.[k]

⁴Will the evildoers never learn—
those who devour my people as men eat bread
and who do not call on God?
⁵There they were, overwhelmed with dread,
where there was nothing to dread.[l]
God scattered the bones[m] of those who attacked you;
you put them to shame, for God despised them.

⁶Oh, that salvation for Israel would come out of Zion!
When God restores the fortunes of his people,
let Jacob rejoice and Israel be glad!

Psalm 54

For the director of music. With stringed instruments. A *maskil*[b] of David. When the Ziphites had gone to Saul and said, "Is not David hiding among us?"

¹Save me, O God, by your name;[n]
vindicate me by your might.[o]
²Hear my prayer, O God;[p]
listen to the words of my mouth.

³Strangers are attacking me;[q]
ruthless men seek my life[r]—
men without regard for God.[s]   *Selah*

⁴Surely God is my help;[t]
the Lord is the one who sustains me.[u]

⁵Let evil recoil[v] on those who slander me;
in your faithfulness[w] destroy them.

[a]Title: Probably a musical term   [b]Title: Probably a literary or musical term

⁶I will sacrifice a freewill offeringˣ to you;
  I will praise your name, O Lᴏʀᴅ,
  for it is good.ʸ
⁷For he has delivered meᶻ from all my troubles,
  and my eyes have looked in triumph on my foes.ᵃ

Psalm 55

For the director of music. With stringed instruments. A *maskil*ᵃ of David.

¹Listen to my prayer, O God,
  do not ignore my plea;ᵇ
² hear me and answer me.ᶜ
My thoughts trouble me and I am distraughtᵈ
³ at the voice of the enemy,
  at the stares of the wicked;
for they bring down suffering upon meᵉ
  and revile me in their anger.ᶠ

⁴My heart is in anguish within me;
  the terrorsᵍ of death assail me.
⁵Fear and tremblingʰ have beset me;
  horror has overwhelmed me.
⁶I said, "Oh, that I had the wings of a dove!
  I would fly away and be at rest—
⁷I would flee far away
  and stay in the desert;   *Selah*
⁸I would hurry to my place of shelter,
  far from the tempest and storm.ⁱ "

⁹Confuse the wicked, O Lord, confound their speech,
  for I see violence and strifeʲ in the city.
¹⁰Day and night they prowl about on its walls;
  malice and abuse are within it.
¹¹Destructive forcesᵏ are at work in the city;
  threats and liesˡ never leave its streets.

¹²If an enemy were insulting me,
  I could endure it;
if a foe were raising himself against me,
  I could hide from him.
¹³But it is you, a man like myself,
  my companion, my close friend,ᵐ
¹⁴with whom I once enjoyed sweet fellowship
  as we walked with the throng at the house of God.ⁿ

¹⁵Let death take my enemies by surprise;ᵒ
  let them go down alive to the grave,ᵇ ᵖ
  for evil finds lodging among them.

¹⁶But I call to God,

54:6
ˣPs 50:14
ʸPs 52:9
54:7
ᶻPs 34:6
ᵃPs 59:10
55:1
ᵇPs 27:9; 61:1
55:2
ᶜPs 66:19
ᵈPs 77:3;
Isa 38:14
55:3
ᵉ2Sa 16:6-8;
Ps 17:9
ᶠPs 71:11
55:4
ᵍPs 116:3
55:5
ʰJob 21:6;
Ps 119:120
55:8
ⁱIsa 4:6
55:9
ʲJer 6:7
55:11
ᵏPs 5:9 lPs 10:7
55:13
ᵐ2Sa 15:12;
Ps 41:9
55:14
ⁿPs 42:4
55:15
ᵒPs 64:7
ᵖNu 16:30,33

ᵃTitle: Probably a literary or musical term   ᵇ15 Hebrew *Sheol*

and the LORD saves me.
[17]Evening,[q] morning[r] and noon
   I cry out in distress,
   and he hears my voice.
[18]He ransoms me unharmed
   from the battle waged against me,
   even though many oppose me.
[19]God, who is enthroned forever,[s]
   will hear[t] them and afflict them—   *Selah*
men who never change their ways
   and have no fear of God.

[20]My companion attacks his friends;[u]
   he violates his covenant.[v]
[21]His speech is smooth as butter,
   yet war is in his heart;
his words are more soothing than oil,[w]
   yet they are drawn swords.[x]

[22]Cast your cares on the LORD
   and he will sustain you;[y]
   he will never let the righteous fall.[z]
[23]But you, O God, will bring down the wicked
   into the pit[a] of corruption;
bloodthirsty and deceitful men[b]
   will not live out half their days.[c]

But as for me, I trust in you.[d]

Psalm 56

For the director of music. To the tune of, "A Dove on Distant Oaks." Of David. A *miktam*.[a] When the Philistines had seized him in Gath.

[1]Be merciful to me, O God, for men hotly pursue me;[e]
   all day long they press their attack.
[2]My slanderers pursue me all day long;[f]
   many are attacking me in their pride.[g]

[3]When I am afraid,[h]
   I will trust in you.
[4]In God, whose word I praise,
   in God I trust; I will not be afraid.
   What can mortal man do to me?[i]

[5]All day long they twist my words;[j]
   they are always plotting to harm me.
[6]They conspire,[k] they lurk,
   they watch my steps,
   eager to take my life.[l]

[7]On no account let them escape;

55:17
qPs 141:2;
Ac 3:1 rPs 5:3
55:19
sDt 33:27
tPs 78:59
55:20
uPs 7:4
vPs 89:34
55:21
wPr 5:3
xPs 28:3;
Ps 57:4; 59:7
55:22
yPs 37:5;
Mt 6:25-34;
1Pe 5:7
zPs 37:24
55:23
aPs 73:18
bPs 5:6
cJob 15:32;
Pr 10:27
dPs 25:2
56:1
ePs 57:1-3
56:2
fPs 57:3
gPs 35:1
56:3
hPs 55:4-5
56:4
iPs 118:6;
Heb 13:6
56:5
jPs 41:7
56:6
kPs 59:3
lPs 71:10

*a*Title: Probably a literary or musical term

in your anger, O God, bring down the nations. ᵐ
⁸Record my lament;
  list my tears on your scrollᵃ—
  are they not in your record?ⁿ

⁹Then my enemies will turn backᵒ
  when I call for help. ᵖ
By this I will know that God is for me. ۹
¹⁰In God, whose word I praise,
  in the Lᴏʀᴅ, whose word I praise—
¹¹in God I trust; I will not be afraid.
  What can man do to me?

¹²I am under vowsʳ to you, O God;
  I will present my thank offerings to you.
¹³For you have delivered meᵇ from deathˢ
  and my feet from stumbling,
that I may walk before God
  in the light of life. ᶜ ᵗ

Psalm 57

57:7–11pp — Ps 108:1–5

For the director of music. To the tune of, "Do Not Destroy." Of David.
A *miktam.*ᵈ When he had fled from Saul into the cave.

¹Have mercy on me, O God, have mercy on me,
  for in you my soul takes refuge. ᵘ
I will take refuge in the shadow of your wingsᵛ
  until the disaster has passed. ʷ

²I cry out to God Most High,
  to God, who fulfills his purpose for me. ˣ
³He sends from heaven and saves me, ʸ
  rebuking those who hotly pursue me;ᶻ   *Selah*
God sends his love and his faithfulness. ᵃ

⁴I am in the midst of lions;ᵇ
  I lie among ravenous beasts—
men whose teeth are spears and arrows,
  whose tongues are sharp swords. ᶜ

⁵Be exalted, O God, above the heavens;
  let your glory be over all the earth. ᵈ

⁶They spread a net for my feet—
  I was bowed downᵉ in distress.
They dug a pitᶠ in my path—
  but they have fallen into it themselves. ᵍ   *Selah*

⁷My heart is steadfast, O God,

56:7
ᵐPs 36:12;
55:23
56:8
ⁿMal 3:16
56:9
ᵒPs 9:3
ᵖPs 102:2
۹Ro 8:31
56:12
ʳPs 50:14
56:13
ˢPs 116:8
ᵗJob 33:30
57:1
ᵘPs 2:12
ᵛPs 17:8
ʷIsa 26:20
57:2
ˣPs 138:8
57:3
ʸPs 18:9,16
ᶻPs 56:1
ᵃPs 40:11
57:4
ᵇPs 35:17
ᶜPs 55:21;
Pr 30:14
57:5
ᵈPs 108:5
57:6
ᵉPs 145:14
ᶠPs 35:7
ᵍPs 7:15;
Pr 28:10

ᵃ8 Or *I put my tears in your wineskin*   ᵇ13 Or *my soul*   ᶜ13 Or *the land of the living*   ᵈTitle:
Probably a literary or musical term

my heart is steadfast;[h]
I will sing and make music.
8Awake, my soul!
    Awake, harp and lyre![i]
    I will awaken the dawn.

9I will praise you, O Lord, among the nations;
    I will sing of you among the peoples.
10For great is your love, reaching to the heavens;
    your faithfulness reaches to the skies.[j]

11Be exalted, O God, above the heavens;
    let your glory be over all the earth.[k]

Psalm 58

For the director of music. ⌊To the tune of⌋ "Do Not Destroy." Of David.
A *miktam.*[a]

1Do you rulers indeed speak justly?[1]
    Do you judge uprightly among men?
2No, in your heart you devise injustice,
    and your hands mete out violence on the earth.[m]
3Even from birth the wicked go astray;
    from the womb they are wayward and speak lies.
4Their venom is like the venom of a snake,[n]
    like that of a cobra that has stopped its ears,
5that will not heed the tune of the charmer,
    however skillful the enchanter may be.

6Break the teeth in their mouths, O God;[o]
    tear out, O LORD, the fangs of the lions![p]
7Let them vanish like water that flows away;[q]
    when they draw the bow, let their arrows be
        blunted.[r]
8Like a slug melting away as it moves along,
    like a stillborn child,[s] may they not see the sun.

9Before your pots can feel ⌊the heat of⌋ the thorns[t] —
    whether they be green or dry—the wicked will be
        swept away.[b][u]
10The righteous will be glad when they are avenged,[v]
    when they bathe their feet in the blood of the
        wicked.[w]
11Then men will say,
    "Surely the righteous still are rewarded;
    surely there is a God who judges the earth."[x]

57:7
hPs 108:1
57:8
iPs 16:9; 30:12;
  150:3
57:10
jPs 36:5; 103:11
57:11
kver 5
58:1
lPs 82:2
58:2
mPs 94:20;
Mal 3:15
58:4
nPs 140:3;
Ecc 10:11
58:6
oPs 3:7
pJob 4:10
58:7
qJos 7:5;
Ps 112:10
rPs 64:3
58:8
sJob 3:16
58:9
tPs 118:12
uPr 10:25
58:10
vPs 64:10; 91:8
wPs 68:23
58:11
xPs 9:8; 18:20

---

[a]Title: Probably a literary or musical term   [b]9 The meaning of the Hebrew for this verse is
uncertain.

Psalm 59

For the director of music. To the tune of "Do Not Destroy." Of David.
A *miktam.*[a] When Saul had sent men to watch David's house
in order to kill him.

[1]Deliver me from my enemies, O God;[y]
  protect me from those who rise up against me.
[2]Deliver me from evildoers
  and save me from bloodthirsty men.[z]

[3]See how they lie in wait for me!
  Fierce men conspire[a] against me
  for no offense or sin of mine, O Lord.
[4]I have done no wrong, yet they are ready to
      attack me.[b]
  Arise to help me; look on my plight!
[5]O Lord God Almighty, the God of Israel,
  rouse yourself to punish all the nations;
  show no mercy to wicked traitors.[c]   *Selah*

[6]They return at evening,
  snarling like dogs,[d]
  and prowl about the city.
[7]See what they spew from their mouths—
  they spew out swords[e] from their lips,
  and they say, "Who can hear us?"[f]
[8]But you, O Lord, laugh at them;[g]
  you scoff at all those nations.[h]

[9]O my Strength, I watch for you;
  you, O God, are my fortress,[i] [10]my loving God.

 God will go before me
  and will let me gloat over those who slander me.
[11]But do not kill them, O Lord our shield,[b][j]
  or my people will forget.[k]
 In your might make them wander about,
  and bring them down.[l]
[12]For the sins of their mouths,[m]
  for the words of their lips,[n]
  let them be caught in their pride.[o]
 For the curses and lies they utter,
[13] consume them in wrath,
  consume them till they are no more.[p]
 Then it will be known to the ends of the earth
  that God rules over Jacob.[q]   *Selah*

[14]They return at evening,
  snarling like dogs,
  and prowl about the city.

59:1
y Ps 143:9
59:2
z Ps 139:19
59:3
a Ps 56:6
59:4
b Ps 35:19,23
59:5
c Jer 18:23
59:6
d ver 14
59:7
e Ps 57:4
f Ps 10:11
59:8
g Ps 37:13;
Pr 1:26 h Ps 2:4
59:9
i Ps 9:9; 62:2
59:11
j Ps 84:9 k Dt 4:9
l Ps 106:27
59:12
m Ps 10:7
n Pr 12:13
o Zep 3:11
59:13
p Ps 104:35
q Ps 83:18

---

[a]Title: Probably a literary or musical term   [b]11 Or *sovereign*

¹⁵They wander about for food^r
   and howl if not satisfied.
¹⁶But I will sing of your strength,^s
   in the morning^t I will sing of your love;^u
for you are my fortress,
   my refuge in times of trouble.^v

¹⁷O my Strength, I sing praise to you;
   you, O God, are my fortress, my loving God.

Psalm 60

60:5–12pp — Ps 108:6–13

For the director of music. To the tune of "The Lily of the Covenant." A *miktam*^a of David. For teaching. When he fought Aram Naharaim^b and Aram Zobah,^c and when Joab returned and struck down twelve thousand Edomites in the Valley of Salt.

¹You have rejected us,^w O God, and burst forth
     upon us;
  you have been angry^x—now restore us!^y
²You have shaken the land^z and torn it open;
  mend its fractures,^a for it is quaking.
³You have shown your people desperate times;^b
  you have given us wine that makes us stagger.^c

⁴But for those who fear you, you have raised a banner
  to be unfurled against the bow.   *Selah*

⁵Save us and help us with your right hand,^d
  that those you love^e may be delivered.
⁶God has spoken from his sanctuary:
  "In triumph I will parcel out Shechem^f
  and measure off the Valley of Succoth.
⁷Gilead^g is mine, and Manasseh is mine;
  Ephraim is my helmet,
  Judah^h my scepter.ⁱ
⁸Moab is my washbasin,
  upon Edom I toss my sandal;
  over Philistia I shout in triumph.^j"

⁹Who will bring me to the fortified city?
  Who will lead me to Edom?
¹⁰Is it not you, O God, you who have rejected us
  and no longer go out with our armies?^k
¹¹Give us aid against the enemy,
  for the help of man is worthless.^l
¹²With God we will gain the victory,
  and he will trample down our enemies.^m

59:15
^rJob 15:23
59:16
^sPs 21:13
^tPs 88:13
^uPs 101:1
^vPs 46:1
60:1
^w2Sa 5:20;
Ps 44:9 ^xPs 79:5
^yPs 80:3
60:2
^zPs 18:7
^a2Ch 7:14
60:3
^bPs 71:20
^cIsa 51:17;
Jer 25:16
60:5
^dPs 17:7; 108:6
^ePs 127:2
60:6
^fGe 12:6
60:7
^gJos 13:31
^hDt 33:17
ⁱGe 49:10
60:8
^j2Sa 8:1
60:10
^kJos 7:12;
Ps 44:9; 108:11
60:11
^lPs 146:3
60:12
^mNu 24:18;
Ps 44:5

^aTitle: Probably a literary or musical term   ^bTitle: That is, Arameans of Northwest Mesopotamia
^cTitle: That is, Arameans of central Syria

Psalm 61

For the director of music. With stringed instruments. Of David.

¹Hear my cry, O God;[n]
  listen to my prayer.[o]

²From the ends of the earth I call to you,
  I call as my heart grows faint;[p]
  lead me to the rock[q] that is higher than I.
³For you have been my refuge,[r]
  a strong tower against the foe.[s]

⁴I long to dwell[t] in your tent forever
  and take refuge in the shelter of your wings.[u]   *Selah*
⁵For you have heard my vows,[v] O God;
  you have given me the heritage of those who fear
    your name.[w]

⁶Increase the days of the king's life,
  his years for many generations.[x]
⁷May he be enthroned in God's presence forever;[y]
  appoint your love and faithfulness to protect him.[z]

⁸Then will I ever sing praise to your name[a]
  and fulfill my vows day after day.

Psalm 62

For the director of music. For Jeduthun. A psalm of David.

¹My soul finds rest[b] in God alone;
  my salvation comes from him.
²He alone is my rock[c] and my salvation;
  he is my fortress, I will never be shaken.

³How long will you assault a man?
  Would all of you throw him down—
  this leaning wall,[d] this tottering fence?
⁴They fully intend to topple him
  from his lofty place;
  they take delight in lies.
  With their mouths they bless,
  but in their hearts they curse.[e]   *Selah*

⁵Find rest, O my soul, in God alone;
  my hope comes from him.
⁶He alone is my rock and my salvation;
  he is my fortress, I will not be shaken.
⁷My salvation and my honor depend on God[a];
  he is my mighty rock, my refuge.[f]

---

[a]7 Or / God Most High is my salvation and my honor

61:1
n Ps 64:1
o Ps 86:6
61:2
p Ps 77:3
q Ps 18:2
61:3
r Ps 62:7
s Pr 18:10
61:4
t Ps 23:6
u Ps 91:4
61:5
v Ps 56:12
w Ps 86:11
61:6
x Ps 21:4
61:7
y Ps 41:12
z Ps 40:11
61:8
a Ps 65:1; 71:22
62:1
b Ps 33:20
62:2
c Ps 89:26
62:3
d Isa 30:13
62:4
e Ps 28:3
62:7
f Ps 46:1; 85:9;
Jer 3:23

⁸Trust in him at all times, O people;
  pour out your hearts to him, [g]
  for God is our refuge.   *Selah*

⁹Lowborn men are but a breath, [h]
  the highborn are but a lie;
if weighed on a balance, [i] they are nothing;
  together they are only a breath.
¹⁰Do not trust in extortion
  or take pride in stolen goods; [j]
though your riches increase,
  do not set your heart on them. [k]

¹¹One thing God has spoken,
  two things have I heard:
that you, O God, are strong,
12 and that you, O Lord, are loving.
  Surely you will reward each person
    according to what he has done. [l]

Psalm 63

A psalm of David. When he was in the Desert of Judah.

¹O God, you are my God,
  earnestly I seek you;
my soul thirsts for you, [m]
  my body longs for you,
in a dry and weary land
  where there is no water.

²I have seen you in the sanctuary [n]
  and beheld your power and your glory.
³Because your love is better than life, [o]
  my lips will glorify you.
⁴I will praise you as long as I live, [p]
  and in your name I will lift up my hands. [q]
⁵My soul will be satisfied as with the richest of foods; [r]
  with singing lips my mouth will praise you.

⁶On my bed I remember you;
  I think of you through the watches of the night. [s]
⁷Because you are my help, [t]
  I sing in the shadow of your wings.
⁸My soul clings to you;
  your right hand upholds me. [u]

⁹They who seek my life will be destroyed; [v]
  they will go down to the depths of the earth. [w]
¹⁰They will be given over to the sword
  and become food for jackals.

¹¹But the king will rejoice in God;

62:8
g 1Sa 1:15;
Ps 42:4; La 2:19
62:9
h Ps 39:5,11
i Isa 40:15
62:10
j Isa 61:8
k Job 31:25;
1Ti 6:6-10
62:12
l Job 34:11;
Mt 16:27
63:1
m Ps 42:2; 84:2
63:2
n Ps 27:4
63:3
o Ps 69:16
63:4
p Ps 104:33
q Ps 28:2
63:5
r Ps 36:8
63:6
s Ps 42:8
63:7
t Ps 27:9
63:8
u Ps 18:35
63:9
v Ps 40:14
w Ps 55:15

all who swear by God's name will praise him, [x]
while the mouths of liars will be silenced.

Psalm 64

For the director of music. A psalm of David.

[1]Hear me, O God, as I voice my complaint; [y]
protect my life from the threat of the enemy. [z]
[2]Hide me from the conspiracy of the wicked, [a]
from that noisy crowd of evildoers.

[3]They sharpen their tongues like swords
and aim their words like deadly arrows. [b]
[4]They shoot from ambush at the innocent man; [c]
they shoot at him suddenly, without fear. [d]

[5]They encourage each other in evil plans,
they talk about hiding their snares;
they say, "Who will see them[a]?" [e]
[6]They plot injustice and say,
"We have devised a perfect plan!"
Surely the mind and heart of man are cunning.

[7]But God will shoot them with arrows;
suddenly they will be struck down.
[8]He will turn their own tongues against them [f]
and bring them to ruin;
all who see them will shake their heads [g] in scorn.

[9]All mankind will fear;
they will proclaim the works of God
and ponder what he has done. [h]
[10]Let the righteous rejoice in the LORD
and take refuge in him; [i]
let all the upright in heart praise him! [j]

Psalm 65

For the director of music. A psalm of David. A song.

[1]Praise awaits[b] you, O God, in Zion;
to you our vows will be fulfilled. [k]
[2]O you who hear prayer,
to you all men will come. [l]
[3]When we were overwhelmed by sins, [m]
you forgave[c] our transgressions. [n]
[4]Blessed are those you choose[o]

63:11
x Dt 6:13;
Ps 21:1;
Isa 45:23
64:1
y Ps 55:2
z Ps 140:1
64:2
a Ps 56:6; 59:2
64:3
b Ps 58:7
64:4
c Ps 11:2
d Ps 55:19
64:5
e Ps 10:11
64:8
f Ps 9:3; Pr 18:7
g Ps 22:7
64:9
h Jer 51:10
64:10
i Ps 25:20
j Ps 32:11
65:1
k Ps 116:18
65:2
l Isa 66:23
65:3
m Ps 38:4
n Heb 9:14
65:4
o Ps 4:3; 33:12

---

[a]5 *Or us atonement for*   [b]1 *Or befits*; the meaning of the Hebrew for this word is uncertain.   [c]3 *Or made*

and bring near to live in your courts!
We are filled with the good things of your house, ᴾ
   of your holy temple.

⁵You answer us with awesome deeds of righteousness,
   O God our Savior, �q
the hope of all the ends of the earth
   and of the farthest seas, ʳ
⁶who formed the mountains by your power,
   having armed yourself with strength, ˢ
⁷who stilled the roaring of the seas, ᵗ
   the roaring of their waves,
   and the turmoil of the nations. ᵘ
⁸Those living far away fear your wonders;
   where morning dawns and evening fades
   you call forth songs of joy.

⁹You care for the land and water it; ᵛ
   you enrich it abundantly.
The streams of God are filled with water
   to provide the people with grain, ʷ
   for so you have ordained it. ᵃ
¹⁰You drench its furrows
   and level its ridges;
you soften it with showers
   and bless its crops.
¹¹You crown the year with your bounty,
   and your carts overflow with abundance.
¹²The grasslands of the desert overflow; ˣ
   the hills are clothed with gladness.
¹³The meadows are covered with flocksʸ
   and the valleys are mantled with grain; ᶻ
   they shout for joy and sing. ᵃ

Psalm 66

For the director of music. A song. A psalm.

¹Shout with joy to God, all the earth! ᵇ
² Sing the glory of his name; ᶜ
   make his praise glorious!
³Say to God, "How awesome are your deeds! ᵈ
   So great is your power
   that your enemies cringeᵉ before you.
⁴All the earth bows downᶠ to you;
   they sing praiseᵍ to you,
   they sing praise to your name."   *Selah*

⁵Come and see what God has done,
   how awesome his worksʰ in man's behalf!

65:4
pPs 36:8
65:5
qPs 85:4
rPs 107:23
65:6
sPs 93:1
65:7
tMt 8:26
uIsa 17:12-13
65:9
vPs 68:9-10
wPs 46:4;
104:14
65:12
xJob 28:26
65:13
yPs 144:13
zPs 72:16
aPs 98:8;
Isa 55:12
66:1
bPs 100:1
66:2
cPs 79:9
66:3
dPs 65:5
ePs 18:44
66:4
fPs 22:27
gPs 67:3
66:5
hPs 106:22

ᵃ9 Or *for that is how you prepare the land*

⁶He turned the sea into dry land,ⁱ
  they passed through the waters on foot—
  come, let us rejoice in him.
⁷He rules foreverʲ by his power,
  his eyes watchᵏ the nations—
  let not the rebelliousˡ rise up against him.   *Selah*

⁸Praiseᵐ our God, O peoples,
  let the sound of his praise be heard;
⁹he has preserved our lives
  and kept our feet from slipping.ⁿ
¹⁰For you, O God, tested us;
  you refined us like silver.ᵒ
¹¹You brought us into prison
  and laid burdensᵖ on our backs.
¹²You let men ride over our heads;�q
  we went through fire and water,
  but you brought us to a place of abundance.ʳ

¹³I will come to your temple with burnt offerings
  and fulfill my vowsˢ to you—
¹⁴vows my lips promised and my mouth spoke
  when I was in trouble.
¹⁵I will sacrifice fat animals to you
  and an offering of rams;
  I will offer bulls and goats.ᵗ   *Selah*

¹⁶Come and listen,ᵘ all you who fear God;
  let me tellᵛ you what he has done for me.
¹⁷I cried out to him with my mouth;
  his praise was on my tongue.
¹⁸If I had cherished sin in my heart,
  the Lord would not have listened;ʷ
¹⁹but God has surely listened
  and heard my voiceˣ in prayer.
²⁰Praise be to God,
  who has not rejectedʸ my prayer
  or withheld his love from me!

Psalm 67

For the director of music. With stringed instruments. A psalm. A song.

¹May God be gracious to us and bless us
  and make his face shine upon us,ᶻ   *Selah*
²that your ways may be known on earth,
  your salvationᵃ among all nations.ᵇ

³May the peoples praise you, O God;
  may all the peoples praise you.
⁴May the nations be glad and sing for joy,
  for you rule the peoples justlyᶜ

66:6
i Ex 14:22
66:7
j Ps 145:13
k Ps 11:4
l Ps 140:8
66:8
m Ps 98:4
66:9
n Ps 121:3
66:10
o Ps 17:3;
Isa 48:10;
Zec 13:9;
1Pe 1:6-7
66:11
p La 1:13
66:12
q Isa 51:23
r Isa 43:2
66:13
s Ecc 5:4
66:15
t Nu 6:14;
Ps 51:19
66:16
u Ps 34:11
v Ps 71:15,24
66:18
w Job 36:21;
Isa 1:15; Jas 4:3
66:19
x Ps 116:1-2
66:20
y Ps 22:24;
68:35
67:1
z Nu 6:24-26;
Ps 4:6
67:2
a Isa 52:10
b Tit 2:11
67:4
c Ps 96:10-13

and guide the nations of the earth.   *Selah*
5May the peoples praise you, O God;
  may all the peoples praise you.

6Then the land will yield its harvest, d
  and God, our God, will bless us.
7God will bless us,
  and all the ends of the earth will fear him. e

Psalm 68

For the director of music. Of David. A psalm. A song.

1May God arise, may his enemies be scattered;
  may his foes flee f before him.
2As smoke g is blown away by the wind,
  may you blow them away;
as wax melts h before the fire,
  may the wicked perish before God.
3But may the righteous be glad
  and rejoice i before God;
  may they be happy and joyful.

4Sing to God, sing praise to his name, j
  extol him who rides on the clouds a k—
his name is the LORD l —
  and rejoice before him.
5A father to the fatherless, m a defender of widows, n
  is God in his holy dwelling. o
6God sets the lonely in families, b p
  he leads forth the prisoners q with singing;
  but the rebellious live in a sun-scorched land. r

7When you went out s before your people, O God,
  when you marched through the wasteland,   *Selah*
8the earth shook,
  the heavens poured down rain, t
before God, the One of Sinai, u
  before God, the God of Israel.
9You gave abundant showers, v O God;
  you refreshed your weary inheritance.
10Your people settled in it,
  and from your bounty, O God, you provided w for the
    poor.

11The Lord announced the word,
  and great was the company of those who proclaimed
    it:
12"Kings and armies flee x in haste;
  in the camps men divide the plunder.

67:6
dLev 26:4;
Ps 85:12;
Eze 34:27
67:7
ePs 33:8
68:1
fNu 10:35;
Isa 33:3
68:2
gHos 13:3
hIsa 9:18;
Mic 1:4
68:3
iPs 32:11
68:4
jPs 66:2
kDt 33:26
lEx 6:3;
Ps 83:18
68:5
mPs 10:14
nDt 10:18
oDt 26:15
68:6
pPs 113:9
qAc 12:6
rPs 107:34
68:7
sEx 13:21;
Jdg 4:14
68:8
tJdg 5:4
uEx 19:16,18
68:9
vDt 11:11
68:10
wPs 74:19
68:12
xJos 10:16

a4 Or *prepare the way for him who rides through the deserts*   b6 Or *the desolate in a homeland*

13Even while you sleep among the campfires,[a] [y]
   the wings of ˎmyˏ dove are sheathed with silver,
   its feathers with shining gold."
14When the Almighty[b] scattered[z] the kings in the land,
   it was like snow fallen on Zalmon.

15The mountains of Bashan are majestic mountains;
   rugged are the mountains of Bashan.
16Why gaze in envy, O rugged mountains,
   at the mountain where God chooses[a] to reign,
   where the LORD himself will dwell forever?
17The chariots of God are tens of thousands
   and thousands of thousands;[b]
   the Lord ˎhas comeˏ from Sinai into his sanctuary.
18When you ascended on high,
   you led captives[c] in your train;
   you received gifts from men,[d]
even from[c] the rebellious—
   that you,[d] O LORD God, might dwell there.

19Praise be to the Lord, to God our Savior,[e]
   who daily bears our burdens.[f]   *Selah*
20Our God is a God who saves;
   from the Sovereign LORD comes escape from death.[g]

21Surely God will crush the heads[h] of his enemies,
   the hairy crowns of those who go on in their sins.
22The Lord says, "I will bring them from Bashan;
   I will bring them from the depths of the sea,[i]
23that you may plunge your feet in the blood of your
      foes,[j]
   while the tongues of your dogs[k] have their share."

24Your procession has come into view, O God,
   the procession of my God and King into the
      sanctuary.[l]
25In front are the singers, after them the musicians;
   with them are the maidens playing tambourines.[m]
26Praise God in the great congregation;
   praise the LORD in the assembly of Israel.[n]
27There is the little tribe[o] of Benjamin, leading them,
   there the great throng of Judah's princes,
   and there the princes of Zebulun and of Naphtali.

28Summon your power, O God[e];
   show us your strength, O God, as you have done
      before.
29Because of your temple at Jerusalem
   kings will bring you gifts.[p]
30Rebuke the beast among the reeds,
   the herd of bulls[q] among the calves of the nations.

68:13
y Ge 49:14
68:14
z Jos 10:10
68:16
a Dt 12:5
68:17
b Dt 33:2;
Da 7:10
68:18
c Jdg 5:12
d Eph 4:8*
68:19
e Ps 65:5
f Ps 55:22
68:20
g Ps 56:13
68:21
h Ps 110:5;
Hab 3:13
68:22
i Nu 21:33
68:23
j Ps 58:10
k 1Ki 21:19
68:24
l Ps 63:2
68:25
m Jdg 11:34;
1Ch 13:8
68:26
n Ps 26:12;
Isa 48:1
68:27
o 1Sa 9:21
68:29
p Ps 72:10
68:30
q Ps 22:12

---

[a]13 Or *saddlebags*   [b]14 Hebrew *Shaddai*   [c]18 Or *gifts for men, / even*   [d]18 Or *they*
[e]28 Many Hebrew manuscripts, Septuagint and Syriac; most Hebrew manuscripts *Your God has summoned power for you*

Humbled, may it bring bars of silver.
Scatter the nations[r] who delight in war.
[31]Envoys will come from Egypt;[s]
Cush[a] will submit herself to God.

[32]Sing to God, O kingdoms of the earth,
sing praise to the Lord,   *Selah*
[33]to him who rides[t] the ancient skies above,
who thunders with mighty voice.[u]
[34]Proclaim the power[v] of God,
whose majesty is over Israel,
whose power is in the skies.
[35]You are awesome, O God, in your sanctuary;
the God of Israel gives power and strength to his
people.[w]

Praise be to God![x]

Psalm 69

For the director of music. To ˻the tune of˼ "Lilies." Of David.

[1]Save me, O God,
for the waters have come up to my neck.[y]
[2]I sink in the miry depths,[z]
where there is no foothold.
I have come into the deep waters;
the floods engulf me.
[3]I am worn out calling for help;[a]
my throat is parched.
My eyes fail,[b]
looking for my God.
[4]Those who hate me without reason[c]
outnumber the hairs of my head;
many are my enemies without cause,[d]
those who seek to destroy me.
I am forced to restore
what I did not steal.

[5]You know my folly,[e] O God;
my guilt is not hidden from you.[f]

[6]May those who hope in you
not be disgraced because of me,
O Lord, the LORD Almighty;
may those who seek you
not be put to shame because of me,
O God of Israel.
[7]For I endure scorn for your sake,[g]
and shame covers my face.[h]

68:30
rPs 89:10
68:31
sIsa 19:19;
45:14
68:33
tPs 18:10
uPs 29:4
68:34
vPs 29:1
68:35
wPs 29:11
xPs 66:20
69:1
yJnh 2:5
69:2
zPs 40:2
69:3
aPs 6:6
bPs 119:82;
Isa 38:14
69:4
cJn 15:25*
dPs 35:19;
38:19
69:5
ePs 38:5
fPs 44:21
69:7
gJer 15:15
hPs 44:15

---

a31 That is, the upper Nile region

⁸I am a stranger to my brothers,
    an alien to my own mother's sons;ⁱ
⁹for zeal for your house consumes me,ʲ
    and the insults of those who insult you fall on me.ᵏ
¹⁰When I weep and fast,ˡ
    I must endure scorn;
¹¹when I put on sackcloth,ᵐ
    people make sport of me.
¹²Those who sit at the gate mock me,
    and I am the song of the drunkards.ⁿ

¹³But I pray to you, O Lᴏʀᴅ,
    in the time of your favor;ᵒ
in your great love,ᵖ O God,
    answer me with your sure salvation.
¹⁴Rescue me from the mire,
    do not let me sink;
deliver me from those who hate me,
    from the deep waters.�q
¹⁵Do not let the floodwatersʳ engulf me
    or the depths swallow me upˢ
    or the pit close its mouth over me.
¹⁶Answer me, O Lᴏʀᴅ, out of the goodness of your love;ᵗ
    in your great mercy turn to me.
¹⁷Do not hide your faceᵘ from your servant;
    answer me quickly, for I am in trouble.ᵛ
¹⁸Come near and rescue me;
    redeemʷ me because of my foes.

¹⁹You know how I am scorned,ˣ disgraced and shamed;
    all my enemies are before you.
²⁰Scorn has broken my heart
    and has left me helpless;
I looked for sympathy, but there was none,
    for comforters,ʸ but I found none.ᶻ
²¹They put gall in my food
    and gave me vinegar for my thirst.ᵃ

²²May the table set before them become a snare;
    may it become retribution andᵃ a trap.
²³May their eyes be darkened so they cannot see,
    and their backs be bent forever.ᵇ
²⁴Pour out your wrathᶜ on them;
    let your fierce anger overtake them.
²⁵May their place be deserted;ᵈ
    let there be no one to dwell in their tents.ᵉ
²⁶For they persecute those you wound
    and talk about the pain of those you hurt.ᶠ
²⁷Charge them with crime upon crime;ᵍ
    do not let them share in your salvation.ʰ
²⁸May they be blotted out of the book of lifeⁱ

ᵃ22 Or *snare / and their fellowship become*

69:8
iPs 31:11;
Isa 53:3
69:9
jJn 2:17*
kPs 89:50-51;
Ro 15:3
69:10
lPs 35:13
69:11
mPs 35:13
69:12
nJob 30:9
69:13
oIsa 49:8;
2Co 6:2
pPs 51:1
69:14
qver 2; Ps 144:7
69:15
rPs 124:4-5
sNu 16:33
69:16
tPs 63:3
69:17
uPs 27:9
vPs 66:14
69:18
wPs 49:15
69:19
xPs 22:6
69:20
yJob 16:2
zIsa 63:5
69:21
aMt 27:34;
Mk 15:23;
Jn 19:28-30
69:23
bIsa 6:9-10;
Ro 11:9-10*
69:24
cPs 79:6
69:25
dMt 23:38
eAc 1:20*
69:26
fIsa 53:4;
Zec 1:15
69:27
gNe 4:5
hPs 109:14;
Isa 26:10
69:28
iEx 32:32-33;
Lk 10:20;
Php 4:3

and not be listed with the righteous.ʲ

²⁹I am in pain and distress;
    may your salvation, O God, protect me.ᵏ

³⁰I will praise God's name in songˡ
    and glorify himᵐ with thanksgiving.
³¹This will please the LORD more than an ox,
    more than a bull with its horns and hoofs.ⁿ
³²The poor will see and be gladᵒ—
    you who seek God, may your hearts live!ᵖ
³³The LORD hears the needy�q
    and does not despise his captive people.

³⁴Let heaven and earth praise him,
    the seas and all that move in them,ʳ
³⁵for God will save Zionˢ
    and rebuild the cities of Judah.ᵗ
Then people will settle there and possess it;
³⁶   the children of his servants will inherit it,
    and those who love his name will dwell there.ᵘ

Psalm 70

70:1–5pp — Ps 40:13–17

For the director of music. Of David. A petition.

¹Hasten, O God, to save me;
    O LORD, come quickly to help me.ᵛ
²May those who seek my lifeʷ
    be put to shame and confusion;
may all who desire my ruin
    be turned back in disgrace.ˣ
³May those who say to me, "Aha! Aha!"
    turn back because of their shame.
⁴But may all who seek you
    rejoice and be glad in you;
may those who love your salvation always say,
    "Let God be exalted!"

⁵Yet I am poor and needy;ʸ
    come quickly to me,ᶻ O God.
You are my help and my deliverer;
    O LORD, do not delay.

Psalm 71

71:1–3pp — Ps 31:1–4

¹In you, O LORD, I have taken refuge;
    let me never be put to shame.ᵃ
²Rescue me and deliver me in your righteousness;

69:28
jEze 13:9
69:29
kPs 59:1; 70:5
69:30
lPs 28:7
mPs 34:3
69:31
nPs 50:9-13
69:32
oPs 34:2
pPs 22:26
69:33
qPs 12:5; 68:6
69:34
rPs 96:11;
148:1;
Isa 44:23;
49:13; 55:12
69:35
sOb 1:17
tPs 51:18;
Isa 44:26
69:36
uPs 37:29;
102:28
70:1
vPs 40:13
70:2
wPs 35:4
xPs 35:26
70:5
yPs 40:17
zPs 141:1
71:1
aPs 25:2-3; 31:1

turn your ear[b] to me and save me.
³Be my rock of refuge,
  to which I can always go;
 give the command to save me,
  for you are my rock and my fortress.[c]
⁴Deliver me, O my God, from the hand of the wicked,[d]
  from the grasp of evil and cruel men.

⁵For you have been my hope, O Sovereign LORD,
  my confidence[e] since my youth.
⁶From birth[f] I have relied on you;
  you brought me forth from my mother's womb.[g]
  I will ever praise[h] you.
⁷I have become like a portent[i] to many,
  but you are my strong refuge.[j]
⁸My mouth[k] is filled with your praise,
  declaring your splendor[l] all day long.

⁹Do not cast[m] me away when I am old;[n]
  do not forsake me when my strength is gone.
¹⁰For my enemies speak against me;
  those who wait to kill[o] me conspire[p] together.
¹¹They say, "God has forsaken him;
  pursue him and seize him,
  for no one will rescue[q] him."
¹²Be not far[r] from me, O God;
  come quickly, O my God, to help[s] me.
¹³May my accusers perish in shame;
  may those who want to harm me
  be covered with scorn and disgrace.[t]

¹⁴But as for me, I will always have hope;[u]
  I will praise you more and more.
¹⁵My mouth will tell[v] of your righteousness,
  of your salvation all day long,
  though I know not its measure.
¹⁶I will come and proclaim your mighty acts,[w]
    O Sovereign LORD;
  I will proclaim your righteousness, yours alone.
¹⁷Since my youth, O God, you have taught[x] me,
  and to this day I declare your marvelous deeds.[y]
¹⁸Even when I am old and gray,[z]
  do not forsake me, O God,
 till I declare your power to the next generation,
  your might to all who are to come.[a]

¹⁹Your righteousness reaches to the skies,[b] O God,
  you who have done great things.[c]
  Who, O God, is like you?[d]
²⁰Though you have made me see troubles,[e] many and
    bitter,
  you will restore[f] my life again;
 from the depths of the earth
  you will again bring me up.

71:2
[b]Ps 17:6
71:3
[c]Ps 18:2;
31:2-3; 44:4
71:4
[d]Ps 140:4
71:5
[e]Job 4:6;
Jer 17:7
71:6
[f]Ps 22:10
[g]Ps 22:9;
Isa 46:3
[h]Ps 9:1; 34:1;
52:9; 119:164;
145:2
71:7
[i]Isa 8:18;
1Co 4:9
[j]2Sa 22:3;
Ps 61:3
71:8
[k]Ps 51:15; 63:5
[l]Ps 35:28; 96:6;
104:1
71:9
[m]Ps 51:11
[n]ver 18;
Ps 92:14;
Isa 46:4
71:10
[o]Ps 10:8; 59:3;
Pr 1:18
[p]Ps 31:13;
56:6; Mt 12:14
71:11
[q]Ps 7:2
71:12
[r]Ps 35:22; 38:21
[s]Ps 38:22; 70:1
71:13
[t]ver 24
71:14
[u]Ps 130:7
71:15
[v]Ps 35:28; 40:5
71:16
[w]Ps 106:2
71:17
[x]Dt 4:5 [y]Ps 26:7
71:18
[z]ver 9
[a]Ps 22:30,31;
78:4
71:19
[b]Ps 36:5; 57:10
[c]Ps 126:2;
Lk 1:49
[d]Ps 35:10
71:20
[e]Ps 60:3
[f]Hos 6:2

21You will increase my honor[g]
and comfort[h] me once again.

22I will praise you with the harp[i]
for your faithfulness, O my God;
I will sing praise to you with the lyre,[j]
O Holy One of Israel.[k]
23My lips will shout for joy
when I sing praise to you—
I, whom you have redeemed.[l]
24My tongue will tell of your righteous acts
all day long,[m]
for those who wanted to harm me[n]
have been put to shame and confusion.

Psalm 72

Of Solomon.

1Endow the king with your justice, O God,
the royal son with your righteousness.
2He will[a] judge your people in righteousness,[o]
your afflicted ones with justice.
3The mountains will bring prosperity to the people,
the hills the fruit of righteousness.
4He will defend the afflicted among the people
and save the children of the needy;[p]
he will crush the oppressor.

5He will endure[b] as long as the sun,
as long as the moon, through all generations.
6He will be like rain[q] falling on a mown field,
like showers watering the earth.
7In his days the righteous will flourish;[r]
prosperity will abound till the moon is no more.

8He will rule from sea to sea
and from the River[c][s] to the ends of the earth.[d][t]
9The desert tribes will bow before him
and his enemies will lick the dust.
10The kings of Tarshish and of distant shores
will bring tribute to him;
the kings of Sheba[u] and Seba
will present him gifts.[v]
11All kings will bow down to him
and all nations will serve him.

12For he will deliver the needy who cry out,
the afflicted who have no one to help.
13He will take pity on the weak and the needy

71:21
gPs 18:35
hPs 23:4;
86:17; Isa 12:1;
49:13
71:22
iPs 33:2
jPs 92:3; 144:9
k2Ki 19:22
71:23
lPs 103:4
71:24
mPs 35:28
nver 13
72:2
oIsa 9:7;
11:4-5; 32:1
72:4
pIsa 11:4
72:6
qDt 32:2;
Hos 6:3
72:7
rPs 92:12;
Isa 2:4
72:8
sEx 23:31
tZec 9:10
72:10
uGe 10:7
v2Ch 9:24

---

a2 Or *May he; similarly in verses 3-11 and 17*   *b5* Septuagint; Hebrew *You will be feared*
c8 That is, the Euphrates   *d8* Or *the end of the land*

and save the needy from death.
14He will rescue[w] them from oppression and violence,
    for precious[x] is their blood in his sight.

15Long may he live!
    May gold from Sheba[y] be given him.
May people ever pray for him
    and bless him all day long.
16Let grain abound throughout the land;
    on the tops of the hills may it sway.
Let its fruit flourish like Lebanon;[z]
    let it thrive like the grass of the field.
17May his name endure forever;[a]
    may it continue as long as the sun.[b]

All nations will be blessed through him,
    and they will call him blessed.[c]

18Praise be to the LORD God, the God of Israel,[d]
    who alone does marvelous deeds.[e]
19Praise be to his glorious name forever;
    may the whole earth be filled with his glory.[f]
           Amen and Amen.[g]

20This concludes the prayers of David son of Jesse.

BOOK III

Psalms 73–89

Psalm 73

A psalm of Asaph.

1Surely God is good to Israel,
    to those who are pure in heart.[h]

2But as for me, my feet had almost slipped;
    I had nearly lost my foothold.
3For I envied[i] the arrogant
    when I saw the prosperity of the wicked.[j]

4They have no struggles;
    their bodies are healthy and strong.[a]
5They are free[k] from the burdens common to man;
    they are not plagued by human ills.
6Therefore pride is their necklace;[l]
    they clothe themselves with violence.[m]
7From their callous hearts[n] comes iniquity[b];

72:14
wPs 69:18
x1Sa 26:21;
Ps 116:15
72:15
yIsa 60:6
72:16
zPs 104:16
72:17
aEx 3:15
bPs 89:36
cGe 12:3;
Lk 1:48
72:18
d1Ch 29:10;
Ps 41:13;
106:48 eJob 5:9
72:19
fNu 14:21;
Ne 9:5
gPs 41:13
73:1
hMt 5:8
73:3
iPs 37:1;
Pr 23:17
jJob 21:7;
Jer 12:1
73:5
kJob 21:9
73:6
lGe 41:42
mPs 109:18
73:7
nPs 17:10

---

a4 With a different word division of the Hebrew; Masoretic Text *struggles at their death;* / *their bodies are healthy*   b7 Syriac (see also Septuagint); Hebrew *Their eyes bulge with fat*

the evil conceits of their minds know no limits.
8They scoff, and speak with malice;
in their arrogance° they threaten oppression.
9Their mouths lay claim to heaven,
and their tongues take possession of the earth.
10Therefore their people turn to them
and drink up waters in abundance. *a*
11They say, "How can God know?
Does the Most High have knowledge?"

12This is what the wicked are like—
always carefree, they increase in wealth. P

13Surely in vainq have I kept my heart pure;
in vain have I washed my hands in innocence. r
14All day long I have been plagued;
I have been punished every morning.

15If I had said, "I will speak thus,"
I would have betrayed your children.
16When I tried to understands all this,
it was oppressive to me
17till I entered the sanctuaryt of God;
then I understood their final destiny. u

18Surely you place them on slippery ground;v
you cast them down to ruin.
19How suddenlyw are they destroyed,
completely swept away by terrors!
20As a dreamx when one awakes,y
so when you arise, O Lord,
you will despise them as fantasies.

21When my heart was grieved
and my spirit embittered,
22I was senselessz and ignorant;
I was a brute beasta before you.

23Yet I am always with you;
you hold me by my right hand.
24You guideb me with your counsel,c
and afterward you will take me into glory.
25Whom have I in heaven but you?
And earth has nothing I desire besides you. d
26My flesh and my hearte may fail, f
but God is the strength of my heart
and my portion forever.

27Those who are far from you will perish;g
you destroy all who are unfaithful to you.
28But as for me, it is good to be near God. h
I have made the Sovereign Lord my refuge;
I will tell of all your deeds. i

73:8
oPs 17:10;
Jude 16
73:12
pPs 49:6
73:13
qJob 21:15;
34:9 rPs 26:6
73:16
sEcc 8:17
73:17
tPs 77:13
uPs 37:38
73:18
vPs 35:6
73:19
wIsa 47:11
73:20
xJob 20:8
yPs 78:65
73:22
zPs 49:10; 92:6
aEcc 3:18
73:24
bPs 48:14
cPs 32:8
73:25
dPhp 3:8
73:26
ePs 84:2
fPs 40:12
73:27
gPs 119:155
73:28
hHeb 10:22;
Jas 4:8 iPs 40:5

---

a10 The meaning of the Hebrew for this verse is uncertain.

Psalm 74

A *maskil*[a] of Asaph.

[1]Why have you rejected us forever,[j] O God?
    Why does your anger smolder against the sheep of
        your pasture?[k]
[2]Remember the people you purchased[l] of old,[m]
    the tribe of your inheritance, whom you redeemed[n]—
    Mount Zion, where you dwelt.[o]
[3]Turn your steps toward these everlasting ruins,
    all this destruction the enemy has brought on the
        sanctuary.

[4]Your foes roared[p] in the place where you met with
        us;
    they set up their standards[q] as signs.
[5]They behaved like men wielding axes
    to cut through a thicket of trees.[r]
[6]They smashed all the carved[s] paneling
    with their axes and hatchets.
[7]They burned your sanctuary to the ground;
    they defiled the dwelling place of your Name.
[8]They said in their hearts, "We will crush[t] them
        completely!"
    They burned every place where God was worshiped
        in the land.
[9]We are given no miraculous signs;
    no prophets[u] are left,
    and none of us knows how long this will be.

[10]How long will the enemy mock you, O God?
    Will the foe revile[v] your name forever?
[11]Why do you hold back your hand, your right hand?[w]
    Take it from the folds of your garment and destroy
        them!

[12]But you, O God, are my king[x] from of old;
    you bring salvation upon the earth.
[13]It was you who split open the sea[y] by your power;
    you broke the heads of the monster[z] in the waters.
[14]It was you who crushed the heads of Leviathan
    and gave him as food to the creatures of the desert.
[15]It was you who opened up springs[a] and streams;
    you dried up[b] the ever flowing rivers.
[16]The day is yours, and yours also the night;
    you established the sun and moon.[c]
[17]It was you who set all the boundaries[d] of the earth;
    you made both summer and winter.[e]

74:1
[j] Dt 29:20;
Ps 44:23
[k] Ps 79:13;
95:7; 100:3
74:2
[l] Ex 15:16
[m] Dt 32:7
[n] Ex 15:13
[o] Ps 68:16
74:4
[p] La 2:7 [q] Nu 2:2
74:5
[r] Jer 46:22
74:6
[s] 1Ki 6:18
74:8
[t] Ps 83:4
74:9
[u] 1Sa 3:1
74:10
[v] Ps 44:16
74:11
[w] La 2:3
74:12
[x] Ps 44:4
74:13
[y] Ex 14:21
[z] Isa 51:9;
Eze 29:3
74:15
[a] Ex 17:6;
Nu 20:11
[b] Jos 2:10; 3:13
74:16
[c] Ge 1:16;
Ps 136:7-9
74:17
[d] Dt 32:8;
Ac 17:26
[e] Ge 8:22

---

[a] Title: Probably a literary or musical term

[18]Remember how the enemy has mocked you, O Lord,
  how foolish people[f] have reviled your name.
[19]Do not hand over the life of your dove to wild beasts;
  do not forget the lives of your afflicted[g] people
    forever.
[20]Have regard for your covenant,[h]
  because haunts of violence fill the dark places of the
    land.
[21]Do not let the oppressed[i] retreat in disgrace;
  may the poor and needy[j] praise your name.

[22]Rise up, O God, and defend your cause;
  remember how fools[k] mock you all day long.
[23]Do not ignore the clamor of your adversaries,[l]
  the uproar of your enemies, which rises
    continually.

Psalm 75

For the director of music. To the tune of, "Do Not Destroy."
A psalm of Asaph. A song.

[1]We give thanks to you, O God,
  we give thanks, for your Name is near;[m]
  men tell of your wonderful deeds.[n]

[2]You say, "I choose the appointed time;
  it is I who judge uprightly.
[3]When the earth and all its people quake,[o]
  it is I who hold its pillars[p] firm.   *Selah*
[4]To the arrogant I say, 'Boast no more,'
  and to the wicked, 'Do not lift up your horns.[q]
[5]Do not lift your horns against heaven;
  do not speak with outstretched neck.' "

[6]No one from the east or the west
  or from the desert can exalt a man.
[7]But it is God who judges:[r]
  He brings one down, he exalts another.[s]
[8]In the hand of the Lord is a cup
  full of foaming wine mixed[t] with spices;
  he pours it out, and all the wicked of the earth
  drink it down to its very dregs.[u]

[9]As for me, I will declare[v] this forever;
  I will sing praise to the God of Jacob.
[10]I will cut off the horns of all the wicked,
  but the horns of the righteous will be lifted up.[w]

74:18
f Dt 32:6;
Ps 39:8
74:19
g Ps 9:18
74:20
h Ge 17:7;
Ps 106:45
74:21
i Ps 103:6
j Ps 35:10
74:22
k Ps 53:1
74:23
l Ps 65:7
75:1
m Ps 145:18
n Ps 44:1; 71:16
75:3
o Isa 24:19
p 1Sa 2:8
75:4
q Zec 1:21
75:7
r Ps 50:6
s 1Sa 2:7;
Ps 147:6;
Da 2:21
75:8
t Pr 23:30
u Job 21:20;
Jer 25:15
75:9
v Ps 40:10
75:10
w Ps 89:17;
92:10; 148:14

Psalm 76

For the director of music. With stringed instruments.
A psalm of Asaph. A song.

[1]In Judah God is known;
    his name is great in Israel.
[2]His tent is in Salem,[x]
    his dwelling place in Zion.
[3]There he broke the flashing arrows,
    the shields and the swords, the weapons of war.[y]

                                                        Selah

[4]You are resplendent with light,
    more majestic than mountains rich with game.
[5]Valiant men lie plundered,
    they sleep their last sleep;[z]
not one of the warriors
    can lift his hands.
[6]At your rebuke, O God of Jacob,
    both horse and chariot[a] lie still.
[7]You alone are to be feared.[b]
    Who can stand[c] before you when you are angry?[d]
[8]From heaven you pronounced judgment,
    and the land feared[e] and was quiet—
[9]when you, O God, rose up to judge,[f]
    to save all the afflicted of the land.   *Selah*
[10]Surely your wrath against men brings you praise,[g]
    and the survivors of your wrath are restrained.[a]

[11]Make vows to the LORD your God and fulfill them;[h]
    let all the neighboring lands
    bring gifts[i] to the One to be feared.
[12]He breaks the spirit of rulers;
    he is feared by the kings of the earth.

Psalm 77

For the director of music. For Jeduthun. Of Asaph. A psalm.

[1]I cried out to God[j] for help;
    I cried out to God to hear me.
[2]When I was in distress,[k] I sought the Lord;
    at night I stretched out untiring hands[l]
    and my soul refused to be comforted.[m]

[3]I remembered you, O God, and I groaned;
    I mused, and my spirit grew faint.[n]   *Selah*
[4]You kept my eyes from closing;

76:2
xGe 14:18
76:3
yPs 46:9
76:5
zPs 13:3
76:6
aEx 15:1
76:7
b1Ch 16:25
cEzr 9:15;
Rev 6:17
dPs 2:5; Na 1:6
76:8
e1Ch 16:30;
2Ch 20:29-30
76:9
fPs 9:8
76:10
gEx 9:16;
Ro 9:17
76:11
hPs 50:14;
Ecc 5:4-5
i2Ch 32:23;
Ps 68:29
77:1
jPs 3:4
77:2
kPs 50:15;
Isa 26:9,16
lJob 11:13
mGe 37:35
77:3
nPs 143:4

---

[a]10 Or *Surely the wrath of men brings you praise, / and with the remainder of wrath you arm yourself*

I was too troubled to speak.
⁵I thought about the former days, °
  the years of long ago;
⁶I remembered my songs in the night.
  My heart mused and my spirit inquired:

⁷"Will the Lord reject forever?
  Will he never show his favor ᵖ again?
⁸Has his unfailing love vanished forever?
  Has his promise �q failed for all time?
⁹Has God forgotten to be merciful? ʳ
  Has he in anger withheld his compassion? ˢ"   *Selah*

¹⁰Then I thought, "To this I will appeal:
  the years of the right hand ᵗ of the Most High."
¹¹I will remember the deeds of the LORD;
  yes, I will remember your miracles ᵘ of long ago.
¹²I will meditate on all your works
  and consider all your mighty deeds.

¹³Your ways, O God, are holy.
  What god is so great as our God? ᵛ
¹⁴You are the God who performs miracles;
  you display your power among the peoples.
¹⁵With your mighty arm you redeemed your people, ʷ
  the descendants of Jacob and Joseph.   *Selah*

¹⁶The waters ˣ saw you, O God,
  the waters saw you and writhed; ʸ
  the very depths were convulsed.
¹⁷The clouds poured down water, ᶻ
  the skies resounded with thunder;
  your arrows flashed back and forth.
¹⁸Your thunder was heard in the whirlwind,
  your lightning lit up the world;
  the earth trembled and quaked. ᵃ
¹⁹Your path led through the sea, ᵇ
  your way through the mighty waters,
  though your footprints were not seen.

²⁰You led your people ᶜ like a flock ᵈ
  by the hand of Moses and Aaron.

Psalm 78

A maskil ᵃ of Asaph.

¹O my people, hear my teaching; ᵉ
  listen to the words of my mouth.
²I will open my mouth in parables, ᶠ
  I will utter hidden things, things from of old—

ᵃTitle: Probably a literary or musical term

77:5
oDt 32:7;
Ps 44:1; 143:5;
Isa 51:9
77:7
pPs 85:1
77:8
q2Pe 3:9
77:9
rPs 25:6; 40:11;
51:1 sIsa 49:15
77:10
tPs 31:22
77:11
uPs 143:5
77:13
vEx 15:11;
Ps 71:19; 86:8
77:15
wEx 6:6;
Dt 9:29
77:16
xEx 14:21,28;
Hab 3:8
yPs 114:4;
Hab 3:10
77:17
zJdg 5:4
77:18
aJdg 5:4
77:19
bHab 3:15
77:20
cEx 13:21
dPs 78:52;
Isa 63:11
78:1
eIsa 51:4; 55:3
78:2
fPs 49:4;
Mt 13:35*

³what we have heard and known,
  what our fathers have told us. g
⁴We will not hide them from their children; h
  we will tell the next generation
the praiseworthy deeds i of the LORD,
  his power, and the wonders he has done.
⁵He decreed statutes j for Jacob k
  and established the law in Israel,
which he commanded our forefathers
  to teach their children,
⁶so the next generation would know them,
  even the children yet to be born, l
  and they in turn would tell their children.
⁷Then they would put their trust in God
  and would not forget m his deeds
  but would keep his commands. n
⁸They would not be like their forefathers o—
  a stubborn p and rebellious q generation,
whose hearts were not loyal to God,
  whose spirits were not faithful to him.

⁹The men of Ephraim, though armed with bows, r
  turned back on the day of battle; s
¹⁰they did not keep God's covenant t
  and refused to live by his law.
¹¹They forgot what he had done, u
  the wonders he had shown them.
¹²He did miracles v in the sight of their fathers
  in the land of Egypt, w in the region of Zoan. x
¹³He divided the sea y and led them through;
  he made the water stand firm like a wall. z
¹⁴He guided them with the cloud by day
  and with light from the fire all night. a
¹⁵He split the rocks b in the desert
  and gave them water as abundant as the seas;
¹⁶he brought streams out of a rocky crag
  and made water flow down like rivers.

¹⁷But they continued to sin c against him,
  rebelling in the desert against the Most High.
¹⁸They willfully put God to the test d
  by demanding the food they craved. e
¹⁹They spoke against God, f saying,
  "Can God spread a table in the desert?
²⁰When he struck the rock, water gushed out, g
  and streams flowed abundantly.
But can he also give us food?
  Can he supply meat h for his people?"
²¹When the LORD heard them, he was very angry;
  his fire broke out i against Jacob,
  and his wrath rose against Israel,
²²for they did not believe in God
  or trust j in his deliverance.

78:3
g Ps 44:1
78:4
h Dt 11:19
i Ps 26:7; 71:17
78:5
j Ps 19:7; 81:5
k Ps 147:19
78:6
l Ps 22:31;
102:18
78:7
m Dt 6:12
n Dt 5:29
78:8
o 2Ch 30:7
p Ex 32:9
q ver 37;
Isa 30:9
78:9
r ver 57;
1Ch 12:2
s Jdg 20:39
78:10
t 2Ki 17:15
78:11
u Ps 106:13
78:12
v Ps 106:22
w Ex 7-12
x Nu 13:22
78:13
y Ex 14:21;
Ps 136:13
z Ex 15:8
78:14
a Ex 13:21;
Ps 105:39
78:15
b Nu 20:11;
1Co 10:4
78:17
c Dt 9:22;
Isa 63:10;
Heb 3:16
78:18
d 1Co 10:9
e Ex 16:2;
Nu 11:4
78:19
f Nu 21:5
78:20
g Nu 20:11
h Nu 11:18
78:21
i Nu 11:1
78:22
j Dt 1:32;
Heb 3:19

78:23
k Ge 7:11;
Mal 3:10
78:24
l Ex 16:4;
Jn 6:31*
78:26
m Nu 11:31
78:29
n Nu 11:20
78:30
o Nu 11:33
78:31
p Isa 10:16
78:32
q ver 11 r ver 22
78:33
s Nu 14:29,35
78:34
t Hos 5:15
78:35
u Dt 32:4
v Dt 9:26
78:36
w Eze 33:31
78:37
x ver 8; Ac 8:21
78:38
y Ex 34:6
z Isa 48:10
a Nu 14:18,20
78:39
b Ge 6:3;
Ps 103:14
c Job 7:7;
Jas 4:14
78:40
d Heb 3:16
e Ps 95:8;
106:14
f Eph 4:30
78:41
g Nu 14:22
h 2Ki 19:22;
Ps 89:18
78:44
i Ex 7:20-21;
Ps 105:29
78:45
j Ex 8:24;
Ps 105:31
k Ex 8:2,6

23 Yet he gave a command to the skies above
   and opened the doors of the heavens;[k]
24 he rained down manna[l] for the people to eat,
   he gave them the grain of heaven.
25 Men ate the bread of angels;
   he sent them all the food they could eat.
26 He let loose the east wind[m] from the heavens
   and led forth the south wind by his power.
27 He rained meat down on them like dust,
   flying birds like sand on the seashore.
28 He made them come down inside their camp,
   all around their tents.
29 They ate till they had more than enough,[n]
   for he had given them what they craved.
30 But before they turned from the food they craved,
   even while it was still in their mouths,[o]
31 God's anger rose against them;
   he put to death the sturdiest[p] among them,
   cutting down the young men of Israel.

32 In spite of all this, they kept on sinning;
   in spite of his wonders,[q] they did not believe.[r]
33 So he ended their days in futility[s]
   and their years in terror.
34 Whenever God slew them, they would seek[t] him;
   they eagerly turned to him again.
35 They remembered that God was their Rock,[u]
   that God Most High was their Redeemer.[v]
36 But then they would flatter him with their mouths,[w]
   lying to him with their tongues;
37 their hearts were not loyal[x] to him,
   they were not faithful to his covenant.
38 Yet he was merciful;[y]
   he forgave[z] their iniquities[a]
   and did not destroy them.
   Time after time he restrained his anger
   and did not stir up his full wrath.
39 He remembered that they were but flesh,[b]
   a passing breeze[c] that does not return.

40 How often they rebelled[d] against him in the desert[e]
   and grieved him[f] in the wasteland!
41 Again and again they put God to the test;[g]
   they vexed the Holy One of Israel.[h]
42 They did not remember his power—
   the day he redeemed them from the oppressor,
43 the day he displayed his miraculous signs in Egypt,
   his wonders in the region of Zoan.
44 He turned their rivers to blood;[i]
   they could not drink from their streams.
45 He sent swarms of flies[j] that devoured them,
   and frogs[k] that devastated them.
46 He gave their crops to the grasshopper,

their produce to the locust.[1]
[47]He destroyed their vines with hail[m]
and their sycamore-figs with sleet.
[48]He gave over their cattle to the hail,
their livestock[n] to bolts of lightning.
[49]He unleashed against them his hot anger,[o]
his wrath, indignation and hostility—
a band of destroying angels.
[50]He prepared a path for his anger;
he did not spare them from death
but gave them over to the plague.
[51]He struck down all the firstborn of Egypt,[p]
the firstfruits of manhood in the tents of Ham.[q]
[52]But he brought his people out like a flock;[r]
he led them like sheep through the desert.
[53]He guided them safely, so they were unafraid;
but the sea engulfed[s] their enemies.[t]
[54]Thus he brought them to the border of his holy land,
to the hill country his right hand[u] had taken.
[55]He drove out nations[v] before them
and allotted their lands to them as an inheritance;[w]
he settled the tribes of Israel in their homes.

[56]But they put God to the test
and rebelled against the Most High;
they did not keep his statutes.
[57]Like their fathers[x] they were disloyal and faithless,
as unreliable as a faulty bow.[y]
[58]They angered him[z] with their high places;[a]
they aroused his jealousy with their idols.[b]
[59]When God heard them, he was very angry;
he rejected Israel[c] completely.
[60]He abandoned the tabernacle of Shiloh,[d]
the tent he had set up among men.
[61]He sent the ark of his might[e] into captivity,[f]
his splendor into the hands of the enemy.
[62]He gave his people over to the sword;
he was very angry with his inheritance.
[63]Fire consumed[g] their young men,
and their maidens had no wedding songs;[h]
[64]their priests were put to the sword,[i]
and their widows could not weep.

[65]Then the Lord awoke as from sleep,[j]
as a man wakes from the stupor of wine.
[66]He beat back his enemies;
he put them to everlasting shame.[k]
[67]Then he rejected the tents of Joseph,
he did not choose the tribe of Ephraim;
[68]but he chose the tribe of Judah,
Mount Zion,[l] which he loved.
[69]He built his sanctuary like the heights,
like the earth that he established forever.

78:46
l Ex 10:13
78:47
m Ex 9:23;
Ps 105:32
78:48
n Ex 9:25
78:49
o Ex 15:7
78:51
p Ex 12:29;
Ps 135:8
q Ps 105:23;
106:22
78:52
r Ps 77:20
78:53
s Ex 14:28
t Ps 106:10
78:54
u Ex 15:17;
Ps 44:3
78:55
v Ps 44:2
w Jos 13:7
78:57
x Eze 20:27
y Hos 7:16
78:58
z Jdg 2:12
a Lev 26:30
b Ex 20:4;
Dt 32:21
78:59
c Dt 32:19
78:60
d Jos 18:1
78:61
e Ps 132:8
f 1Sa 4:17
78:63
g Nu 11:1
h Jer 7:34; 16:9
78:64
i 1Sa 4:17; 22:18
78:65
j Ps 44:23
78:66
k 1Sa 5:6
78:68
l Ps 87:2

70He chose David[m] his servant
  and took him from the sheep pens;
71from tending the sheep he brought him
  to be the shepherd[n] of his people Jacob,
  of Israel his inheritance.
72And David shepherded them with integrity of heart;[o]
  with skillful hands he led them.

Psalm 79

A psalm of Asaph.

1O God, the nations have invaded your inheritance;[p]
  they have defiled your holy temple,
  they have reduced Jerusalem to rubble.[q]
2They have given the dead bodies of your servants
  as food to the birds of the air,
  the flesh of your saints to the beasts of the earth.[r]
3They have poured out blood like water
  all around Jerusalem,
  and there is no one to bury the dead.[s]
4We are objects of reproach to our neighbors,
  of scorn and derision to those around us.[t]

5How long,[u] O Lord? Will you be angry[v] forever?
  How long will your jealousy burn like fire?[w]
6Pour out your wrath[x] on the nations
  that do not acknowledge[y] you,
on the kingdoms
  that do not call on your name;[z]
7for they have devoured Jacob
  and destroyed his homeland.
8Do not hold against us the sins of the fathers;[a]
  may your mercy come quickly to meet us,
  for we are in desperate need.[b]

9Help us,[c] O God our Savior,
  for the glory of your name;
deliver us and forgive our sins
  for your name's sake.[d]
10Why should the nations say,
  "Where is their God?"[e]
Before our eyes, make known among the nations
  that you avenge[f] the outpoured blood of your
  servants.
11May the groans of the prisoners come before you;
  by the strength of your arm
  preserve those condemned to die.

12Pay back into the laps[g] of our neighbors seven times[h]
  the reproach they have hurled at you, O Lord.
13Then we your people, the sheep of your pasture,[i]

will praise you forever;[j]
from generation to generation
we will recount your praise.

Psalm 80

For the director of music. To the tune of, "The Lilies of the Covenant."
Of Asaph. A psalm.

[1]Hear us, O Shepherd of Israel,
    you who lead Joseph like a flock;[k]
you who sit enthroned between the cherubim,[l] shine
        forth
[2]   before Ephraim, Benjamin and Manasseh.[m]
Awaken[n] your might;
    come and save us.

[3]Restore[o] us,[p] O God;
    make your face shine upon us,
    that we may be saved.

[4]O LORD God Almighty,
    how long will your anger smolder
    against the prayers of your people?
[5]You have fed them with the bread of tears;
    you have made them drink tears by the bowlful.[q]
[6]You have made us a source of contention to our
        neighbors,
    and our enemies mock us.[r]

[7]Restore us, O God Almighty;
    make your face shine upon us,
    that we may be saved.

[8]You brought a vine[s] out of Egypt;
    you drove out[t] the nations and planted it.
[9]You cleared the ground for it,
    and it took root and filled the land.
[10]The mountains were covered with its shade,
    the mighty cedars with its branches.
[11]It sent out its boughs to the Sea,[a]
    its shoots as far as the River.[b][u]

[12]Why have you broken down its walls[v]
    so that all who pass by pick its grapes?
[13]Boars from the forest ravage[w] it
    and the creatures of the field feed on it.
[14]Return to us, O God Almighty!
    Look down from heaven and see![x]
    Watch over this vine,
[15]   the root your right hand has planted,

79:13
jPs 44:8
80:1
kPs 77:20
lEx 25:22
80:2
mNu 2:18-24
nPs 35:23
80:3
oPs 85:4;
La 5:21
pNu 6:25
80:5
qPs 42:3;
Isa 30:20
80:6
rPs 79:4
80:8
sIsa 5:1-2;
Jer 2:21
tJos 13:6;
Ac 7:45
80:11
uPs 72:8
80:12
vPs 89:40;
Isa 5:5
80:13
wJer 5:6
80:14
xIsa 63:15

---

[a]11 Probably the Mediterranean   [b]11 That is, the Euphrates

the son[a] you have raised up for yourself.

16Your vine is cut down, it is burned with fire;
　　at your rebuke[y] your people perish.
17Let your hand rest on the man at your right hand,
　　the son of man you have raised up for yourself.
18Then we will not turn away from you;
　　revive us, and we will call on your name.

19Restore us, O LORD God Almighty;
　　make your face shine upon us,
　　that we may be saved.

Psalm 81

For the director of music. According to *gittith.*[b] Of Asaph.

1Sing for joy to God our strength;
　　shout aloud to the God of Jacob![z]
2Begin the music, strike the tambourine,[a]
　　play the melodious harp[b] and lyre.

3Sound the ram's horn at the New Moon,
　　and when the moon is full, on the day of our Feast;
4this is a decree for Israel,
　　an ordinance of the God of Jacob.
5He established it as a statute for Joseph
　　when he went out against Egypt,[c]
　　where we heard a language we did not understand.[c] [d]

6He says, "I removed the burden from their shoulders;[e]
　　their hands were set free from the basket.
7In your distress you called[f] and I rescued you,
　　I answered[g] you out of a thundercloud;
　　I tested you at the waters of Meribah.[h]　　　　　*Selah*

8"Hear, O my people,[i] and I will warn you—
　　if you would but listen to me, O Israel!
9You shall have no foreign god[j] among you;
　　you shall not bow down to an alien god.
10I am the LORD your God,
　　who brought you up out of Egypt.[k]
　　Open wide your mouth and I will fill[l] it.

11"But my people would not listen to me;
　　Israel would not submit to me.[m]
12So I gave them over[n] to their stubborn hearts
　　to follow their own devices.

13"If my people would but listen to me,[o]
　　if Israel would follow my ways,
14how quickly would I subdue[p] their enemies

a15 Or branch　　　*bTitle: Probably a musical term*　　　*c5 Or / and we heard a voice we had not known*

and turn my hand against^q their foes!
¹⁵Those who hate the LORD would cringe before him,
    and their punishment would last forever.
¹⁶But you would be fed with the finest of wheat;^r
    with honey from the rock I would satisfy you.''

Psalm 82

A psalm of Asaph.

¹God presides in the great assembly;
    he gives judgment^s among the ''gods'':

²''How long will you^a defend the unjust
    and show partiality^t to the wicked?^u   *Selah*
³Defend the cause of the weak and fatherless;^v
    maintain the rights of the poor^w and oppressed.
⁴Rescue the weak and needy;
    deliver them from the hand of the wicked.

⁵''They know nothing, they understand nothing.^x
    They walk about in darkness;^y
    all the foundations^z of the earth are shaken.

⁶''I said, 'You are ''gods'';^a
    you are all sons of the Most High.'
⁷But you will die^b like mere men;
    you will fall like every other ruler.''

⁸Rise up,^c O God, judge the earth,
    for all the nations are your inheritance.^d

Psalm 83

A song. A psalm of Asaph.

¹O God, do not keep silent;^e
    be not quiet, O God, be not still.
²See how your enemies are astir,^f
    how your foes rear their heads.^g
³With cunning they conspire^h against your people;
    they plot against those you cherish.
⁴''Come,'' they say, ''let us destroyⁱ them as a nation,
    that the name of Israel be remembered^j no more.''

⁵With one mind they plot together;^k
    they form an alliance against you—
⁶the tents of Edom^l and the Ishmaelites,
    of Moab^m and the Hagrites,ⁿ
⁷Gebal,^{b o} Ammon and Amalek,

---

^a2 The Hebrew is plural.   ^b7 That is, Byblos

81:14
qAm 1:8
81:16
rDt 32:14
82:1
sPs 58:11;
Isa 3:13
82:2
tDt 1:17
uPs 58:1-2;
Pr 18:5
82:3
vDt 24:17
wJer 22:16
82:5
xPs 14:4;
Mic 3:1
yIsa 59:9
zPs 11:3
82:6
aJn 10:34*
82:7
bPs 49:12;
Eze 31:14
82:8
cPs 12:5
dPs 2:8;
Rev 11:15
83:1
ePs 28:1; 35:22
83:2
fPs 2:1;
Isa 17:12
gJdg 8:28;
Ps 81:15
83:3
hPs 31:13
83:4
iEst 3:6
jJer 11:19
83:5
kPs 2:2
83:6
lPs 137:7
m2Ch 20:1
nGe 25:16
83:7
oJos 13:5

Philistia, with the people of Tyre. P
8Even Assyria has joined them
　to lend strength to the descendants of Lot. q   *Selah*

9Do to them as you did to Midian, r
　as you did to Sisera and Jabin at the river Kishon, s
10who perished at Endor
　and became like refuse t on the ground.
11Make their nobles like Oreb and Zeeb, u
　all their princes like Zebah and Zalmunna, v
12who said, "Let us take possession w
　of the pasturelands of God."

13Make them like tumbleweed, O my God,
　like chaff x before the wind.
14As fire consumes the forest
　or a flame sets the mountains ablaze, y
15so pursue them with your tempest
　and terrify them with your storm. z
16Cover their faces with shame a
　so that men will seek your name, O LORD.

17May they ever be ashamed and dismayed;
　may they perish in disgrace. b
18Let them know that you, whose name is the LORD—
　that you alone are the Most High over all the earth. c

Psalm 84

For the director of music. According to *gittith*. a Of the Sons of Korah.
A psalm.

1How lovely is your dwelling place, d
　O LORD Almighty!
2My soul yearns, e even faints,
　for the courts of the LORD;
my heart and my flesh cry out
　for the living God.

3Even the sparrow has found a home,
　and the swallow a nest for herself,
　where she may have her young—
a place near your altar, f
　O LORD Almighty, my King and my God. g
4Blessed are those who dwell in your house;
　they are ever praising you.   *Selah*

5Blessed are those whose strength h is in you,
　who have set their hearts on pilgrimage. i
6As they pass through the Valley of Baca,
　they make it a place of springs;

83:7
pEze 27:3
83:8
qDt 2:9
83:9
rJdg 7:1-23
sJdg 4:23-24
83:10
tZep 1:17
83:11
uJdg 7:25
vJdg 8:12,21
83:12
w2Ch 20:11
83:13
xPs 35:5;
Isa 17:13
83:14
yDt 32:22;
Isa 9:18
83:15
zJob 9:17
83:16
aPs 109:29;
132:18
83:17
bPs 35:4
83:18
cPs 59:13
84:1
dPs 27:4; 43:3;
132:5
84:2
ePs 42:1-2
84:3
fPs 43:4 gPs 5:2
84:5
hPs 81:1
iJer 31:6

aTitle: Probably a musical term

the autumn[j] rains also cover it with pools.[a]
[7]They go from strength to strength,[k]
    till each appears[l] before God in Zion.

[8]Hear my prayer, O LORD God Almighty;
    listen to me, O God of Jacob.   *Selah*
[9]Look upon our shield,[bm] O God;
    look with favor on your anointed one.[n]

[10]Better is one day in your courts
    than a thousand elsewhere;
I would rather be a doorkeeper[o] in the house of my God
    than dwell in the tents of the wicked.
[11]For the LORD God is a sun[p] and shield;[q]
    the LORD bestows favor and honor;
no good thing does he withhold[r]
    from those whose walk is blameless.

[12]O LORD Almighty,
    blessed[s] is the man who trusts in you.

Psalm 85

For the director of music. Of the Sons of Korah. A psalm.

[1]You showed favor to your land, O LORD;
    you restored the fortunes[t] of Jacob.
[2]You forgave[u] the iniquity[v] of your people
    and covered all their sins.   *Selah*
[3]You set aside all your wrath[w]
    and turned from your fierce anger.[x]

[4]Restore[y] us again, O God our Savior,
    and put away your displeasure toward us.
[5]Will you be angry with us forever?[z]
    Will you prolong your anger through all generations?
[6]Will you not revive[a] us again,
    that your people may rejoice in you?
[7]Show us your unfailing love, O LORD,
    and grant us your salvation.

[8]I will listen to what God the LORD will say;
    he promises peace[b] to his people, his saints—
    but let them not return to folly.
[9]Surely his salvation[c] is near those who fear him,
    that his glory[d] may dwell in our land.

[10]Love and faithfulness[e] meet together;
    righteousness[f] and peace kiss each other.
[11]Faithfulness springs forth from the earth,
    and righteousness[g] looks down from heaven.

[a]6 Or *blessings*   [b]9 Or *sovereign*

84:6
jJoel 2:23
84:7
kPr 4:18
lDt 16:16
84:9
mPs 59:11
n1Sa 16:6;
Ps 2:2; 132:17
84:10
o1Ch 23:5
84:11
pIsa 60:19;
Rev 21:23
qGe 15:1
rPs 34:10
84:12
sPs 2:12
85:1
tPs 14:7;
Jer 30:18;
Eze 39:25
85:2
uNu 14:19
vPs 78:38
85:3
wPs 106:23
xEx 32:12;
Dt 13:17;
Ps 78:38;
Jnh 3:9
85:4
yPs 80:3,7
85:5
zPs 79:5
85:6
aPs 80:18;
Hab 3:2
85:8
bZec 9:10
85:9
cIsa 46:13
dZec 2:5
85:10
ePs 89:14;
Pr 3:3
fPs 72:2-3;
Isa 32:17
85:11
gIsa 45:8

¹²The LORD will indeed give what is good,ʰ
    and our land will yieldⁱ its harvest.
¹³Righteousness goes before him
    and prepares the way for his steps.

Psalm 86

A prayer of David.

¹Hear, O LORD, and answerʲ me,
    for I am poor and needy.
²Guard my life, for I am devoted to you.
    You are my God; save your servant
    who trusts in you.ᵏ
³Have mercyˡ on me, O Lord,
    for I callᵐ to you all day long.
⁴Bring joy to your servant,
    for to you, O Lord,
    I liftⁿ up my soul.

⁵You are forgiving and good, O Lord,
    abounding in loveᵒ to all who call to you.
⁶Hear my prayer, O LORD;
    listen to my cry for mercy.
⁷In the day of my troubleᵖ I will call to you,
    for you will answer me.

⁸Among the gods there is none like you,�q O Lord;
    no deeds can compare with yours.
⁹All the nations you have made
    will come and worshipʳ before you, O Lord;
    they will bring gloryˢ to your name.
¹⁰For you are great and do marvelous deeds;ᵗ
    you aloneᵘ are God.

¹¹Teach me your way,ᵛ O LORD,
    and I will walk in your truth;
give me an undividedʷ heart,
    that I may fear your name.
¹²I will praise you, O Lord my God, with all my heart;
    I will glorify your name forever.
¹³For great is your love toward me;
    you have delivered me from the depths of the grave.ᵃ

¹⁴The arrogant are attacking me, O God;
    a band of ruthless men seeks my life—
    men without regard for you.ˣ
¹⁵But you, O Lord, are a compassionate and graciousʸ
        God,
    slow to anger, abounding in love and faithfulness.ᶻ

85:12
hPs 84:11;
Jas 1:17
iLev 26:4;
Ps 67:6;
Zec 8:12
86:1
jPs 17:6
86:2
kPs 25:2; 31:14
86:3
lPs 4:1; 57:1
mPs 88:9
86:4
nPs 25:1; 143:8
86:5
oEx 34:6;
Ne 9:17;
Ps 103:8; 145:8;
Joel 2:13;
Jnh 4:2
86:7
pPs 50:15
86:8
qEx 15:11;
Dt 3:24; Ps 89:6
86:9
rPs 66:4;
Rev 15:4
sIsa 43:7
86:10
tPs 72:18
uDt 6:4;
Mk 12:29;
1Co 8:4
86:11
vPs 25:5
wJer 32:39
86:14
xPs 54:3
86:15
yPs 103:8
zEx 34:6;
Ne 9:17;
Joel 2:13

ᵃ13 Hebrew *Sheol*

16Turn to me and have mercy on me;
  grant your strength to your servant
  and save the son of your maidservant.ᵃ ᵃ
17Give me a sign of your goodness,
  that my enemies may see it and be put to shame,
  for you, O Lord, have helped me and comforted me.

Psalm 87

Of the Sons of Korah. A psalm. A song.

1He has set his foundation on the holy mountain;
2 the Lord loves the gates of Zionᵇ
  more than all the dwellings of Jacob.
3Glorious things are said of you,
  O city of God:ᶜ   *Selah*
4"I will record Rahabᵇᵈ and Babylon
  among those who acknowledge me—
Philistia too, and Tyreᵉ, along with Cushᶜ —
  and will say, 'Thisᵈ one was born in Zion.ᶠ '"

5Indeed, of Zion it will be said,
  "This one and that one were born in her,
  and the Most High himself will establish her."
6The Lord will write in the registerᵍ of the peoples:
  "This one was born in Zion."   *Selah*
7As they make musicʰ they will sing,
  "All my fountainsⁱ are in you."

Psalm 88

A song. A psalm of the Sons of Korah. For the director of music.
According to mahalath leannoth.ᵉ A maskilᶠ of Heman the Ezrahite.

1O Lord, the God who saves me,ʲ
  day and night I cry outᵏ before you.
2May my prayer come before you;
  turn your ear to my cry.

3For my soul is full of trouble
  and my life draws near the grave.ᵍ ˡ
4I am counted among those who go down to the pit;ᵐ
  I am like a man without strength.
5I am set apart with the dead,
  like the slain who lie in the grave,
  whom you remember no more,

86:16
ᵃPs 116:16
87:2
ᵇPs 78:68
87:3
ᶜPs 46:4;
Isa 60:1
87:4
ᵈJob 9:13
ᵉPs 45:12
ᶠIsa 19:25
87:6
ᵍPs 69:28;
Isa 4:3;
Eze 13:9
87:7
ʰPs 149:3
ⁱPs 36:9
88:1
ʲPs 51:14
ᵏPs 22:2; 27:9;
Lk 18:7
88:3
ˡPs 107:18,26
88:4
ᵐPs 28:1

ᵃ16 Or *save your faithful son*   ᵇ4 A poetic name for Egypt   ᶜ4 That is, the upper Nile region
ᵈ4 Or "*O Rahab and Babylon, / Philistia, Tyre and Cush, / I will record concerning those who acknowledge
me: / This*   ᵉTitle: Possibly a tune, "The Suffering of Affliction"   ᶠTitle: Probably a literary or
musical term   ᵍ3 Hebrew *Sheol*

who are cut off[n] from your care.

⁶You have put me in the lowest pit,
    in the darkest depths.[o]
⁷Your wrath lies heavily upon me;
    you have overwhelmed me with all your waves.[p]

                                             Selah

⁸You have taken from me my closest friends[q]
    and have made me repulsive to them.
  I am confined[r] and cannot escape;
⁹ my eyes[s] are dim with grief.

I call[t] to you, O Lᴏʀᴅ, every day;
    I spread out my hands[u] to you.
¹⁰Do you show your wonders to the dead?
    Do those who are dead rise up and praise you?[v] *Selah*
¹¹Is your love declared in the grave,
    your faithfulness[w] in Destruction[a]?
¹²Are your wonders known in the place of darkness,
    or your righteous deeds in the land of oblivion?

¹³But I cry to you for help,[x] O Lᴏʀᴅ;
    in the morning[y] my prayer comes before you.[z]
¹⁴Why, O Lᴏʀᴅ, do you reject[a] me
    and hide your face[b] from me?

¹⁵From my youth I have been afflicted and close to death;
    I have suffered your terrors[c] and am in despair.
¹⁶Your wrath has swept over me;
    your terrors have destroyed me.
¹⁷All day long they surround me like a flood;[d]
    they have completely engulfed me.
¹⁸You have taken my companions[e] and loved ones from
         me;
    the darkness is my closest friend.

Psalm 89

A maskil[b] of Ethan the Ezrahite.

¹I will sing[f] of the Lᴏʀᴅ's great love forever;
    with my mouth I will make your faithfulness known[g]
        through all generations.
²I will declare that your love stands firm forever,
    that you established your faithfulness in heaven
        itself.[h]

³You said, "I have made a covenant with my chosen one,
    I have sworn to David my servant,
⁴'I will establish your line forever

88:5
nPs 31:22;
Isa 53:8
88:6
oPs 69:15;
La 3:55
88:7
pPs 42:7
88:8
qJob 19:13;
Ps 31:11
rJer 32:2
88:9
sPs 38:10
tPs 86:3
uJob 11:13;
Ps 143:6
88:10
vPs 6:5
88:11
wPs 30:9
88:13
xPs 30:2 yPs 5:3
zPs 119:147
88:14
aPs 43:2
bJob 13:24;
Ps 13:1
88:15
cJob 6:4
88:17
dPs 22:16;
124:4
88:18
ever 8;
Job 19:13;
Ps 38:11
89:1
fPs 59:16;
Ps 101:1
gPs 36:5; 40:10
89:2
hPs 36:5

---

a11 Hebrew *Abaddon*   *b*Title: Probably a literary or musical term

and make your throne firm through all
    generations.' "[i]   *Selah*

[5]The heavens[j] praise your wonders, O LORD,
    your faithfulness too, in the assembly of the holy
    ones.
[6]For who in the skies above can compare with the LORD?
    Who is like the LORD among the heavenly beings?[k]
[7]In the council of the holy ones God is greatly feared;
    he is more awesome than all who surround him.[l]
[8]O LORD God Almighty, who is like you?[m]
    You are mighty, O LORD, and your faithfulness
    surrounds you.

[9]You rule over the surging sea;
    when its waves mount up, you still them.[n]
[10]You crushed Rahab[o] like one of the slain;
    with your strong arm you scattered[p] your enemies.
[11]The heavens are yours, and yours also the earth;[q]
    you founded the world and all that is in it.[r]
[12]You created the north and the south;
    Tabor[s] and Hermon[t] sing for joy[u] at your name.
[13]Your arm is endued with power;
    your hand is strong, your right hand exalted.

[14]Righteousness and justice are the foundation of your
    throne;[v]
    love and faithfulness go before you.
[15]Blessed are those who have learned to acclaim you,
    who walk in the light[w] of your presence, O LORD.
[16]They rejoice in your name[x] all day long;
    they exult in your righteousness.
[17]For you are their glory and strength,
    and by your favor you exalt our horn.[a] [y]
[18]Indeed, our shield[b] belongs to the LORD,
    our king[z] to the Holy One of Israel.

[19]Once you spoke in a vision,
    to your faithful people you said:
"I have bestowed strength on a warrior;
    I have exalted a young man from among the people.
[20]I have found David[a] my servant;[b]
    with my sacred oil I have anointed[c] him.
[21]My hand will sustain him;
    surely my arm will strengthen him.[d]
[22]No enemy will subject him to tribute;
    no wicked man will oppress[e] him.
[23]I will crush his foes before him[f]
    and strike down his adversaries.[g]
[24]My faithful love will be with him,[h]
    and through my name his horn[c] will be exalted.

89:4
i2Sa 7:12-16;
1Ki 8:16;
Ps 132:11-12;
Isa 9:7; Lk 1:33
89:5
jPs 19:1
89:6
kPs 113:5
89:7
lPs 47:2
89:8
mPs 71:19
89:9
nPs 65:7
89:10
oPs 87:4
pPs 68:1
89:11
q1Ch 29:11;
Ps 24:1 rGe 1:1
89:12
sJos 19:22
tDt 3:8;
Jos 12:1
uPs 98:8
89:14
vPs 97:2
89:15
wPs 44:3
89:16
xPs 105:3
89:17
yPs 75:10;
92:10; 148:14
89:18
zPs 47:9
89:20
aAc 13:22
bPs 78:70
c1Sa 16:1,12
89:21
dPs 18:35
89:22
e2Sa 7:10
89:23
fPs 18:40
g2Sa 7:9
89:24
h2Sa 7:15

---

[a]17 *Horn* here symbolizes strong one.   [b]18 Or *sovereign*   [c]24 *Horn* here symbolizes
strength.

25I will set his hand over the sea,
   his right hand over the rivers. i
26He will call out to me, 'You are my Father, j
   my God, the Rock my Savior.' k
27I will also appoint him my firstborn, l
   the most exalted m of the kings n of the earth.
28I will maintain my love to him forever,
   and my covenant with him will never fail. o
29I will establish his line forever,
   his throne as long as the heavens endure. P

30"If his sons forsake my law
   and do not follow my statutes,
31if they violate my decrees
   and fail to keep my commands,
32I will punish their sin with the rod,
   their iniquity with flogging; q
33but I will not take my love from him, r
   nor will I ever betray my faithfulness.
34I will not violate my covenant
   or alter what my lips have uttered. s
35Once for all, I have sworn by my holiness—
   and I will not lie to David—
36that his line will continue forever
   and his throne endure before me like the sun;
37it will be established forever like the moon,
   the faithful witness in the sky."   *Selah*

38But you have rejected, t you have spurned,
   you have been very angry with your anointed one.
39You have renounced the covenant with your servant
   and have defiled his crown in the dust. u
40You have broken through all his walls v
   and reduced his strongholds w to ruins.
41All who pass by have plundered him;
   he has become the scorn of his neighbors. x
42You have exalted the right hand of his foes;
   you have made all his enemies rejoice. y
43You have turned back the edge of his sword
   and have not supported him in battle. z
44You have put an end to his splendor
   and cast his throne to the ground.
45You have cut short the days of his youth;
   you have covered him with a mantle of shame. a   *Selah*

46How long, O LORD? Will you hide yourself forever?
   How long will your wrath burn like fire? b
47Remember how fleeting is my life. c
   For what futility you have created all men!
48What man can live and not see death,
   or save himself from the power of the grave a ?d   *Selah*

a48 Hebrew *Sheol*

⁴⁹O Lord, where is your former great love,
　　which in your faithfulness you swore to David?
⁵⁰Remember, Lord, how your servant has*ᵃ* been
　　　mocked,ᵉ
　how I bear in my heart the taunts of all the nations,
⁵¹the taunts with which your enemies have mocked,
　　O Lᴏʀᴅ,
　with which they have mocked every step of your
　　anointed one. ᶠ

⁵²Praise be to the Lᴏʀᴅ forever!
　　Amen and Amen. ᵍ

BOOK IV

Psalms 90–106

Psalm 90

A prayer of Moses the man of God.

¹Lord, you have been our dwelling placeʰ
　throughout all generations.
²Before the mountains were bornⁱ
　or you brought forth the earth and the world,
　from everlasting to everlasting you are God. ʲ

³You turn men back to dust,
　saying, "Return to dust, O sons of men."ᵏ
⁴For a thousand years in your sight
　are like a day that has just gone by,
　or like a watch in the night. ˡ
⁵You sweep men awayᵐ in the sleep of death;
　they are like the new grass of the morning—
⁶though in the morning it springs up new,
　by evening it is dry and withered. ⁿ

⁷We are consumed by your anger
　and terrified by your indignation.
⁸You have set our iniquities before you,
　our secret sinsᵒ in the light of your presence.
⁹All our days pass away under your wrath;
　we finish our years with a moan. ᵖ
¹⁰The length of our days is seventy years—
　or eighty, if we have the strength;
　yet their spanᵇ is but trouble and sorrow,
　for they quickly pass, and we fly away. �q

¹¹Who knows the power of your anger?

89:50
ePs 69:19
89:51
fPs 74:10
89:52
gPs 41:13;
72:19
90:1
hDt 33:27;
Eze 11:16
90:2
iJob 15:7;
Pr 8:25
jPs 102:24-27
90:3
kGe 3:19;
Job 34:15
90:4
l2Pe 3:8
90:5
mPs 73:20;
Isa 40:6
90:6
nMt 6:30;
Jas 1:10
90:8
oPs 19:12
90:9
pPs 78:33
90:10
qJob 20:8

ᵃ50 Or your servants have　　　*ᵇ10 Or yet the best of them*

For your wrath is as great as the fear that is due you. [r]
[12]Teach us to number our days[s] aright,
    that we may gain a heart of wisdom. [t]

[13]Relent, O LORD! How long[u] will it be?
    Have compassion on your servants. [v]
[14]Satisfy[w] us in the morning with your unfailing love,
    that we may sing for joy[x] and be glad all our days. [y]
[15]Make us glad for as many days as you have afflicted us,
    for as many years as we have seen trouble.
[16]May your deeds be shown to your servants,
    your splendor to their children. [z]

[17]May the favor[a] of the Lord our God rest upon us;
    establish the work of our hands for us—
    yes, establish the work of our hands. [a]

Psalm 91

[1]He who dwells in the shelter[b] of the Most High
    will rest in the shadow[c] of the Almighty. [b]
[2]I will say[c] of the LORD, "He is my refuge[d] and my
        fortress,
    my God, in whom I trust."

[3]Surely he will save you from the fowler's snare[e]
    and from the deadly pestilence. [f]
[4]He will cover you with his feathers,
    and under his wings you will find refuge;[g]
    his faithfulness will be your shield[h] and rampart.
[5]You will not fear[i] the terror of night,
    nor the arrow that flies by day,
[6]nor the pestilence that stalks in the darkness,
    nor the plague that destroys at midday.
[7]A thousand may fall at your side,
    ten thousand at your right hand,
    but it will not come near you.
[8]You will only observe with your eyes
    and see the punishment of the wicked. [j]

[9]If you make the Most High your dwelling—
    even the LORD, who is my refuge—
[10]then no harm[k] will befall you,
    no disaster will come near your tent.
[11]For he will command his angels[l] concerning you
    to guard you in all your ways;[m]
[12]they will lift you up in their hands,
    so that you will not strike your foot against a stone. [n]
[13]You will tread upon the lion and the cobra;
    you will trample the great lion and the serpent. [o]

90:11
rPs 76:7
90:12
sPs 39:4
tDt 32:29
90:13
uPs 6:3
vDt 32:36;
Ps 135:14
90:14
wPs 103:5
xPs 85:6
yPs 31:7
90:16
zPs 44:1;
Hab 3:2
90:17
aIsa 26:12
91:1
bPs 31:20
cPs 17:8
91:2
dPs 142:5
91:3
ePs 124:7;
Pr 6:5 f1Ki 8:37
91:4
gPs 17:8
hPs 35:2
91:5
iJob 5:21
91:8
jPs 37:34;
58:10; Mal 1:5
91:10
kPr 12:21
91:11
lHeb 1:14
mPs 34:7
91:12
nMt 4:6*;
Lk 4:10-11*
91:13
oDa 6:22;
Lk 10:19

a17 Or *beauty*   b1 Hebrew *Shaddai*   c2 Or *He says*

14"Because he loves me," says the LORD, "I will rescue
  him;
  I will protect him, for he acknowledges my name.
15He will call upon me, and I will answer him;
  I will be with him in trouble,
  I will deliver him and honor him. ᴾ
16With long life �q will I satisfy him
  and show him my salvation. ʳ "

Psalm 92

A psalm. A song. For the Sabbath day.

1It is good to praise the LORD
  and make music to your name, ˢ O Most High, ᵗ
2to proclaim your love in the morning ᵘ
  and your faithfulness at night,
3to the music of the ten-stringed lyre
  and the melody of the harp. ᵛ

4For you make me glad by your deeds, O LORD;
  I sing for joy at the works of your hands. ʷ
5How great are your works, ˣ O LORD,
  how profound your thoughts! ʸ
6The senseless man ᶻ does not know,
  fools do not understand,
7that though the wicked spring up like grass
  and all evildoers flourish,
they will be forever destroyed.

8But you, O LORD, are exalted forever.

9For surely your enemies, O LORD,
  surely your enemies will perish;
  all evildoers will be scattered. ᵃ
10You have exalted my horn ᵃ ᵇ like that of a wild ox;
  fine oils ᶜ have been poured upon me.
11My eyes have seen the defeat of my adversaries;
  my ears have heard the rout of my wicked foes. ᵈ

12The righteous will flourish like a palm tree,
  they will grow like a cedar of Lebanon; ᵉ
13planted in the house of the LORD,
  they will flourish in the courts of our God. ᶠ
14They will still bear fruit ᵍ in old age,
  they will stay fresh and green,
15proclaiming, "The LORD is upright;
  he is my Rock, and there is no wickedness in him. ʰ "

ᵃ10 *Horn* here symbolizes strength.

91:15
p 1Sa 2:30;
Ps 50:15;
Jn 12:26
91:16
q Dt 6:2; Ps 21:4
r Ps 50:23
92:1
s Ps 147:1
t Ps 135:3
92:2
u Ps 89:1
92:3
v 1Sa 10:5;
Ne 12:27;
Ps 33:2
92:4
w Ps 8:6; 143:5
92:5
x Rev 15:3
y Ps 40:5;
139:17;
Isa 28:29;
Ro 11:33
92:6
z Ps 73:22
92:9
a Ps 68:1; 89:10
92:10
b Ps 89:17
c Ps 23:5
92:11
d Ps 54:7; 91:8
92:12
e Ps 1:3; 52:8;
Jer 17:8;
Hos 14:6
92:13
f Ps 100:4
92:14
g Jn 15:2
92:15
h Job 34:10

Psalm 93

¹The LORD reigns,ⁱ he is robed in majesty;^j
    the LORD is robed in majesty
    and is armed with strength.^k
The world is firmly established;
    it cannot be moved.^l
²Your throne was established long ago;
    you are from all eternity.^m

³The seasⁿ have lifted up, O LORD,
    the seas have lifted up their voice;
    the seas have lifted up their pounding waves.
⁴Mightier than the thunder^o of the great waters,
    mightier than the breakers of the sea—
    the LORD on high is mighty.

⁵Your statutes stand firm;
    holiness^p adorns your house
    for endless days, O LORD.

Psalm 94

¹O LORD, the God who avenges,^q
    O God who avenges, shine forth.^r
²Rise up, O Judge^s of the earth;
    pay back^t to the proud what they deserve.
³How long will the wicked, O LORD,
    how long will the wicked be jubilant?

⁴They pour out arrogant^u words;
    all the evildoers are full of boasting.^v
⁵They crush your people,^w O LORD;
    they oppress your inheritance.
⁶They slay the widow and the alien;
    they murder the fatherless.
⁷They say, "The LORD does not see;^x
    the God of Jacob pays no heed."

⁸Take heed, you senseless ones^y among the people;
    you fools, when will you become wise?
⁹Does he who implanted the ear not hear?
    Does he who formed the eye not see?^z
¹⁰Does he who disciplines nations not punish?
    Does he who teaches^a man lack knowledge?
¹¹The LORD knows the thoughts of man;
    he knows that they are futile.^b

¹²Blessed is the man you discipline,^c O LORD,
    the man you teach^d from your law;
¹³you grant him relief from days of trouble,
    till a pit^e is dug for the wicked.

93:1
iPs 97:1
jPs 104:1
kPs 65:6
lPs 96:10
93:2
mPs 45:6
93:3
nPs 96:11
93:4
oPs 65:7
93:5
pPs 29:2
94:1
qNa 1:2;
Ro 12:19
rPs 80:1
94:2
sGe 18:25
tPs 31:23
94:4
uPs 31:18
vPs 52:1
94:5
wIsa 3:15
94:7
xJob 22:14;
Ps 10:11
94:8
yPs 92:6
94:9
zEx 4:11;
Pr 20:12
94:10
aJob 35:11;
Isa 28:26
94:11
b1Co 3:20*
94:12
cJob 5:17;
Heb 12:5
dDt 8:3
94:13
ePs 55:23

¹⁴For the LORD will not reject his people;[f]
    he will never forsake his inheritance.
¹⁵Judgment will again be founded on righteousness,[g]
    and all the upright in heart will follow it.

¹⁶Who will rise up[h] for me against the wicked?
    Who will take a stand for me against evildoers?[i]
¹⁷Unless the LORD had given me help,[j]
    I would soon have dwelt in the silence of death.
¹⁸When I said, "My foot is slipping,[k]"
    your love, O LORD, supported me.
¹⁹When anxiety was great within me,
    your consolation brought joy to my soul.

²⁰Can a corrupt throne be allied with you—
    one that brings on misery by its decrees?[l]
²¹They band together[m] against the righteous
    and condemn the innocent[n] to death.
²²But the LORD has become my fortress,
    and my God the rock in whom I take refuge.[o]
²³He will repay[p] them for their sins
    and destroy them for their wickedness;
    the LORD our God will destroy them.

Psalm 95

¹Come, let us sing for joy to the LORD;
    let us shout aloud[q] to the Rock[r] of our salvation.
²Let us come before him[s] with thanksgiving
    and extol him with music[t] and song.

³For the LORD is the great God,[u]
    the great King above all gods.[v]
⁴In his hand are the depths of the earth,
    and the mountain peaks belong to him.
⁵The sea is his, for he made it,
    and his hands formed the dry land.[w]

⁶Come, let us bow down[x] in worship,
    let us kneel[y] before the LORD our Maker;[z]
⁷for he is our God
    and we are the people of his pasture,[a]
    the flock under his care.

Today, if you hear his voice,
⁸ do not harden your hearts as you did at Meribah,[a] [b]
    as you did that day at Massah[b] in the desert,
⁹where your fathers tested[c] and tried me,
    though they had seen what I did.
¹⁰For forty years[d] I was angry with that generation;
    I said, "They are a people whose hearts go astray,

94:14
f1Sa 12:22;
Ps 37:28;
Ro 11:2
94:15
gPs 97:2
94:16
hNu 10:35;
Ps 17:13
iPs 59:2
94:17
jPs 124:2
94:18
kPs 38:16
94:20
lPs 58:2
94:21
mPs 56:6
nPs 106:38;
Pr 17:15,26
94:22
oPs 18:2; 59:9
94:23
pPs 7:16
95:1
qPs 81:1
r2Sa 22:47
95:2
sMic 6:6
tPs 81:2;
Eph 5:19
95:3
uPs 48:1; 145:3
vPs 96:4; 97:9
95:5
wGe 1:9;
Ps 146:6
95:6
xPhp 2:10
y2Ch 6:13
zPs 100:3;
149:2; Isa 17:7;
Da 6:10-11;
Hos 8:14
95:7
aPs 74:1; 79:13
95:8
bEx 17:7
95:9
cNu 14:22;
Ps 78:18;
1Co 10:9
95:10
dAc 7:36;
Heb 3:17

ᵃ8 Meribah means quarreling.   *ᵇ8 Massah means testing.*

and they have not known my ways."
[11]So I declared on oath[e] in my anger,
    "They shall never enter my rest."[f]

Psalm 96

96:1–13pp — 1Ch 16:23–33

[1]Sing to the LORD[g] a new song;
    sing to the LORD, all the earth.
[2]Sing to the LORD, praise his name;
    proclaim his salvation[h] day after day.
[3]Declare his glory among the nations,
    his marvelous deeds among all peoples.

[4]For great is the LORD and most worthy of praise;[i]
    he is to be feared[j] above all gods.[k]
[5]For all the gods of the nations are idols,
    but the LORD made the heavens.[l]
[6]Splendor and majesty are before him;
    strength and glory[m] are in his sanctuary.

[7]Ascribe to the LORD,[n] O families of nations,[o]
    ascribe to the LORD glory and strength.
[8]Ascribe to the LORD the glory due his name;
    bring an offering[p] and come into his courts.
[9]Worship the LORD in the splendor of his[a] holiness;[q]
    tremble[r] before him, all the earth.[s]

[10]Say among the nations, "The LORD reigns.[t]"
    The world is firmly established, it cannot be moved;[u]
    he will judge the peoples with equity.[v]
[11]Let the heavens rejoice, let the earth be glad;[w]
    let the sea resound, and all that is in it;
[12]   let the fields be jubilant, and everything in them.
    Then all the trees of the forest[x] will sing for joy;[y]
[13]   they will sing before the LORD, for he comes,
    he comes to judge[z] the earth.
He will judge the world in righteousness
    and the peoples in his truth.

Psalm 97

[1]The LORD reigns,[a] let the earth be glad;[b]
    let the distant shores rejoice.

[2]Clouds and thick darkness[c] surround him;
    righteousness and justice are the foundation of his
        throne.[d]
[3]Fire[e] goes before[f] him

Cross references (left margin):

95:11
eNu 14:23
fDt 1:35;
Heb 4:3*
96:1
g1Ch 16:23
96:2
hPs 71:15
96:4
iPs 18:3; 145:3
jPs 89:7
kPs 95:3
96:5
lPs 115:15
96:6
mPs 29:1
96:7
nPs 29:1
oPs 22:27
96:8
pPs 45:12;
72:10
96:9
qPs 29:2
rPs 114:7
sPs 33:8
96:10
tPs 97:1
uPs 93:1
vPs 67:4
96:11
wPs 97:1; 98:7;
Isa 49:13
96:12
xIsa 44:23
yPs 65:13
96:13
zRev 19:11
97:1
aPs 96:10
bPs 96:11
97:2
cEx 19:9;
Ps 18:11
dPs 89:14
97:3
eDa 7:10
fHab 3:5

[a]9 Or LORD *with the splendor of*

and consumes[g] his foes on every side.
4His lightning lights up the world;
    the earth sees and trembles.[h]
5The mountains melt[i] like wax before the Lord,
    before the Lord of all the earth.[j]
6The heavens proclaim his righteousness,[k]
    and all the peoples see his glory.[l]

7All who worship images[m] are put to shame,[n]
    those who boast in idols—
    worship him,[o] all you gods!

8Zion hears and rejoices
    and the villages of Judah are glad
    because of your judgments,[p] O Lord.
9For you, O Lord, are the Most High over all the earth;[q]
    you are exalted[r] far above all gods.

10Let those who love the Lord hate evil,[s]
    for he guards the lives of his faithful ones[t]
    and delivers[u] them from the hand of the wicked.[v]
11Light is shed[w] upon the righteous
    and joy on the upright in heart.
12Rejoice in the Lord, you who are righteous,
    and praise his holy name.[x]

Psalm 98

A psalm.

1Sing to the Lord a new song,[y]
    for he has done marvelous things;[z]
his right hand[a] and his holy arm[b]
    have worked salvation for him.
2The Lord has made his salvation known[c]
    and revealed his righteousness to the nations.
3He has remembered[d] his love
    and his faithfulness to the house of Israel;
all the ends of the earth have seen
    the salvation of our God.

4Shout for joy[e] to the Lord, all the earth,
    burst into jubilant song with music;
5make music to the Lord with the harp,[f]
    with the harp and the sound of singing,[g]
6with trumpets[h] and the blast of the ram's horn—
    shout for joy before the Lord, the King.[i]

7Let the sea resound, and everything in it,
    the world, and all who live in it.[j]
8Let the rivers clap their hands,
    let the mountains[k] sing together for joy;
9let them sing before the Lord,

97:3
g Ps 18:8
97:4
h Ps 104:32
97:5
i Ps 46:2,6;
Mic 1:4
j Jos 3:11
97:6
k Ps 50:6
l Ps 19:1
97:7
m Lev 26:1
n Jer 10:14
o Heb 1:6
97:8
p Ps 48:11
97:9
q Ps 83:18; 95:3
r Ex 18:11
97:10
s Ps 34:14;
Am 5:15;
Ro 12:9 t Pr 2:8
u Da 3:28
v Ps 37:40;
Jer 15:21
97:11
w Job 22:28
97:12
x Ps 30:4
98:1
y Ps 96:1
z Ps 96:3
a Ex 15:6
b Isa 52:10
98:2
c Isa 52:10
98:3
d Lk 1:54
98:4
e Isa 44:23
98:5
f Ps 92:3
g Isa 51:3
98:6
h Nu 10:10
i Ps 47:7
98:7
j Ps 24:1
98:8
k Isa 55:12

for he comes to judge the earth.
He will judge the world in righteousness
   and the peoples with equity. [1]

Psalm 99

[1]The LORD reigns, [m]
   let the nations tremble;
he sits enthroned between the cherubim, [n]
   let the earth shake.
[2]Great is the LORD [o] in Zion;
   he is exalted [p] over all the nations.
[3]Let them praise your great and awesome name [q]—
   he is holy.

[4]The King is mighty, he loves justice [r]—
   you have established equity; [s]
in Jacob you have done
   what is just and right.
[5]Exalt [t] the LORD our God
   and worship at his footstool;
   he is holy.

[6]Moses [u] and Aaron were among his priests,
   Samuel [v] was among those who called on his name;
they called on the LORD
   and he answered [w] them.
[7]He spoke to them from the pillar of cloud; [x]
   they kept his statutes and the decrees he gave them.

[8]O LORD our God,
   you answered them;
you were to Israel [a] a forgiving God, [y]
   though you punished their misdeeds. [b]
[9]Exalt the LORD our God
   and worship at his holy mountain,
   for the LORD our God is holy.

Psalm 100

A psalm. For giving thanks.

[1]Shout for joy [z] to the LORD, all the earth.
[2] Worship the LORD with gladness;
   come before him [a] with joyful songs.
[3]Know that the LORD is God. [b]
   It is he who made us, [c] and we are his [c];
   we are his people, the sheep of his pasture. [d]

98:9
lPs 96:10
99:1
mPs 97:1
nEx 25:22
99:2
oPs 48:1
pPs 97:9; 113:4
99:3
qPs 76:1
99:4
rPs 11:7
sPs 98:9
99:5
tPs 132:7
99:6
uEx 24:6
vJer 15:1
w1Sa 7:9
99:7
xEx 33:9
99:8
yNu 14:20
100:1
zPs 98:4
100:2
aPs 95:2
100:3
bPs 46:10
cJob 10:3
dPs 74:1;
Eze 34:31

a8 Hebrew *them*   b8 Or *I an avenger of the wrongs done to them*   c3 Or *and not we ourselves*

⁴Enter his gates with thanksgiving
and his courts with praise;
give thanks to him and praise his name.^e
⁵For the LORD is good^f and his love endures forever;^g
his faithfulness^h continues through all generations.

Psalm 101

Of David. A psalm.

¹I will sing of your loveⁱ and justice;
to you, O LORD, I will sing praise.
²I will be careful to lead a blameless life—
when will you come to me?

I will walk in my house
with blameless heart.
³I will set before my eyes
no vile thing.^j

The deeds of faithless men I hate;^k
they will not cling to me.
⁴Men of perverse heart^l shall be far from me;
I will have nothing to do with evil.

⁵Whoever slanders his neighbor^m in secret,
him will I put to silence;
whoever has haughty eyesⁿ and a proud heart,
him will I not endure.

⁶My eyes will be on the faithful in the land,
that they may dwell with me;
he whose walk is blameless^o
will minister to me.

⁷No one who practices deceit
will dwell in my house;
no one who speaks falsely
will stand in my presence.

⁸Every morning^p I will put to silence
all the wicked^q in the land;
I will cut off every evildoer^r
from the city of the LORD.^s

Psalm 102

A prayer of an afflicted man. When he is faint and pours out his lament
before the LORD.

¹Hear my prayer, O LORD;
let my cry for help^t come to you.

100:4
ePs 116:17
100:5
f1Ch 16:34;
Ps 25:8
gEzr 3:11;
Ps 106:1
hPs 119:90
101:1
iPs 51:14; 89:1;
145:7
101:3
jDt 15:9
kPs 40:4
101:4
lPr 11:20
101:5
mPs 50:20
nPs 10:5;
Pr 6:17
101:6
oPs 119:1
101:8
pJer 21:12
qPs 75:10
rPs 118:10-12
sPs 46:4
102:1
tEx 2:23

2Do not hide your face[u] from me
  when I am in distress.
Turn your ear to me;
  when I call, answer me quickly.

3For my days vanish like smoke;[v]
  my bones burn like glowing embers.
4My heart is blighted and withered like grass;[w]
  I forget to eat my food.
5Because of my loud groaning
  I am reduced to skin and bones.
6I am like a desert owl,[x]
  like an owl among the ruins.
7I lie awake;[y] I have become
  like a bird alone[z] on a roof.
8All day long my enemies taunt me;
  those who rail against me use my name as a curse.
9For I eat ashes as my food
  and mingle my drink with tears[a]
10because of your great wrath,[b]
  for you have taken me up and thrown me aside.
11My days are like the evening shadow;[c]
  I wither away like grass.

12But you, O LORD, sit enthroned forever;[d]
  your renown endures[e] through all generations.
13You will arise and have compassion[f] on Zion,
  for it is time to show favor to her;
  the appointed time has come.
14For her stones are dear to your servants;
  her very dust moves them to pity.
15The nations will fear[g] the name of the LORD,
  all the kings[h] of the earth will revere your glory.
16For the LORD will rebuild Zion
  and appear in his glory.[i]
17He will respond to the prayer[j] of the destitute;
  he will not despise their plea.

18Let this be written[k] for a future generation,
  that a people not yet created[l] may praise the LORD:
19"The LORD looked down[m] from his sanctuary on high,
  from heaven he viewed the earth,
20to hear the groans of the prisoners[n]
  and release those condemned to death."
21So the name of the LORD will be declared[o] in Zion
  and his praise in Jerusalem
22when the peoples and the kingdoms
  assemble to worship the LORD.

23In the course of my life[a] he broke my strength;
  he cut short my days.
24So I said:

102:2
u Ps 69:17
102:3
v Jas 4:14
102:4
w Ps 37:2
102:6
x Job 30:29;
Isa 34:11
102:7
y Ps 77:4
z Ps 38:11
102:9
a Ps 42:3
102:10
b Ps 38:3
102:11
c Job 14:2
102:12
d Ps 9:7
e Ps 135:13
102:13
f Isa 60:10
102:15
g 1Ki 8:43
h Ps 138:4
102:16
i Isa 60:1-2
102:17
j Ne 1:6
102:18
k Ro 15:4
l Ps 22:31
102:19
m Dt 26:15
102:20
n Ps 79:11
102:21
o Ps 22:22

a23 Or By his power

"Do not take me away, O my God, in the midst of my
     days;
your years go on[p] through all generations.
25In the beginning[q] you laid the foundations of the earth,
     and the heavens are the work of your hands.
26They will perish,[r] but you remain;
     they will all wear out like a garment.
Like clothing you will change them
     and they will be discarded.
27But you remain the same,[s]
     and your years will never end.
28The children of your servants[t] will live in your
     presence;
     their descendants[u] will be established before you."

Psalm 103

Of David.

1Praise the LORD, O my soul;[v]
     all my inmost being, praise his holy name.
2Praise the LORD, O my soul,
     and forget not all his benefits—
3who forgives all your sins[w]
     and heals[x] all your diseases,
4who redeems your life from the pit
     and crowns you with love and compassion,
5who satisfies your desires with good things
     so that your youth is renewed like the eagle's.[y]

6The LORD works righteousness
     and justice for all the oppressed.

7He made known[z] his ways[a] to Moses,
     his deeds[b] to the people of Israel:
8The LORD is compassionate and gracious,[c]
     slow to anger, abounding in love.
9He will not always accuse,
     nor will he harbor his anger forever;[d]
10he does not treat us as our sins deserve[e]
     or repay us according to our iniquities.
11For as high as the heavens are above the earth,
     so great is his love[f] for those who fear him;
12as far as the east is from the west,
     so far has he removed our transgressions[g] from us.
13As a father has compassion[h] on his children,
     so the LORD has compassion on those who fear him;
14for he knows how we are formed,[i]
     he remembers that we are dust.
15As for man, his days are like grass,[j]
     he flourishes like a flower[k] of the field;

102:24
pPs 90:2;
Isa 38:10
102:25
qGe 1:1;
Heb 1:10-12*
102:26
rIsa 34:4;
Mt 24:35;
2Pe 3:7-10;
Rev 20:11
102:27
sMal 3:6;
Heb 13:8;
Jas 1:17
102:28
tPs 69:36
uPs 89:4
103:1
vPs 104:1
103:3
wPs 130:8
xEx 15:26
103:5
yIsa 40:31
103:7
zPs 99:7;
147:19
aEx 33:13
bPs 106:22
103:8
cEx 34:6;
Ps 86:15;
Jas 5:11
103:9
dPs 30:5;
Isa 57:16;
Jer 3:5,12;
Mic 7:18
103:10
eEzr 9:13
103:11
fPs 57:10
103:12
g2Sa 12:13
103:13
hMal 3:17
103:14
iIsa 29:16
103:15
jPs 90:5
kJob 14:2;
Jas 1:10;
1Pe 1:24

¹⁶the wind blows^l over it and it is gone,
    and its place^m remembers it no more.
¹⁷But from everlasting to everlasting
    the LORD's love is with those who fear him,
    and his righteousness with their children's children—
¹⁸with those who keep his covenant
    and remember to obey his precepts.ⁿ

¹⁹The LORD has established his throne in heaven,
    and his kingdom rules^o over all.

²⁰Praise the LORD, you his angels,^p
    you mighty ones^q who do his bidding,
    who obey his word.
²¹Praise the LORD, all his heavenly hosts,^r
    you his servants who do his will.
²²Praise the LORD, all his works^s
    everywhere in his dominion.

Praise the LORD, O my soul.

Psalm 104

¹Praise the LORD, O my soul.^t

O LORD my God, you are very great;
    you are clothed with splendor and majesty.
²He wraps^u himself in light as with a garment;
    he stretches out the heavens^v like a tent
³ and lays the beams^w of his upper chambers on their
      waters.
He makes the clouds^x his chariot
    and rides on the wings of the wind.^y
⁴He makes winds his messengers,^{a z}
    flames of fire^a his servants.

⁵He set the earth^b on its foundations;
    it can never be moved.
⁶You covered it^c with the deep^d as with a garment;
    the waters stood above the mountains.
⁷But at your rebuke^e the waters fled,
    at the sound of your thunder they took to flight;
⁸they flowed over the mountains,
    they went down into the valleys,
    to the place you assigned^f for them.
⁹You set a boundary they cannot cross;
    never again will they cover the earth.

¹⁰He makes springs^g pour water into the ravines;
    it flows between the mountains.
¹¹They give water to all the beasts of the field;

103:16
l Isa 40:7
m Job 7:10
103:18
n Dt 7:9
103:19
o Ps 47:2
103:20
p Ps 148:2;
Heb 1:14
q Ps 29:1
103:21
r 1Ki 22:19
103:22
s Ps 145:10
104:1
t Ps 103:22
104:2
u Da 7:9
v Isa 40:22
104:3
w Am 9:6
x Isa 19:1
y Ps 18:10
104:4
z Ps 148:8;
Heb 1:7*
a 2Ki 2:11
104:5
b Job 26:7;
Ps 24:1-2
104:6
c Ge 7:19
d Ge 1:2
104:7
e Ps 18:15
104:8
f Ps 33:7
104:10
g Ps 107:33;
Isa 41:18

^a4 Or *angels*

the wild donkeys quench their thirst.
12The birds of the air[h] nest by the waters;
    they sing among the branches.
13He waters the mountains[i] from his upper chambers;
    the earth is satisfied by the fruit of his work.
14He makes grass grow[j] for the cattle,
    and plants for man to cultivate—
    bringing forth food[k] from the earth:
15wine[l] that gladdens the heart of man,
    oil[m] to make his face shine,
    and bread that sustains his heart.
16The trees of the LORD are well watered,
    the cedars of Lebanon that he planted.
17There the birds[n] make their nests;
    the stork has its home in the pine trees.
18The high mountains belong to the wild goats;
    the crags are a refuge for the coneys.[a] [o]

19The moon marks off the seasons,[p]
    and the sun[q] knows when to go down.
20You bring darkness,[r] it becomes night,[s]
    and all the beasts of the forest[t] prowl.
21The lions roar for their prey
    and seek their food from God.[u]
22The sun rises, and they steal away;
    they return and lie down in their dens.[v]
23Then man goes out to his work,[w]
    to his labor until evening.

24How many are your works,[x] O LORD!
    In wisdom you made[y] them all;
    the earth is full of your creatures.
25There is the sea,[z] vast and spacious,
    teeming with creatures beyond number—
    living things both large and small.
26There the ships[a] go to and fro,
    and the leviathan,[b] which you formed to frolic there.

27These all look to you
    to give them their food[c] at the proper time.
28When you give it to them,
    they gather it up;
  when you open your hand,
    they are satisfied[d] with good things.
29When you hide your face,[e]
    they are terrified;
  when you take away their breath,
    they die and return to the dust.[f]
30When you send your Spirit,
    they are created,
    and you renew the face of the earth.

---

[a]18 That is, the hyrax or rock badger

104:12
hMt 8:20
104:13
iPs 147:8;
Jer 10:13
104:14
jJob 38:27;
Ps 147:8
kGe 1:30;
Job 28:5
104:15
lJdg 9:13
mPs 23:5;
92:10; Lk 7:46
104:17
nver 12
104:18
oPr 30:26
104:19
pGe 1:14
qPs 19:6
104:20
rIsa 45:7
sPs 74:16
tPs 50:10
104:21
uJob 38:39;
Ps 145:15;
Joel 1:20
104:22
vJob 37:8
104:23
wGe 3:19
104:24
xPs 40:5
yPr 3:19
104:25
zPs 69:34
104:26
aPs 107:23;
Eze 27:9
bJob 41:1
104:27
cJob 36:31;
Ps 136:25;
145:15; 147:9
104:28
dPs 145:16
104:29
eDt 31:17
fJob 34:14;
Ecc 12:7

³¹May the glory of the LORD endure forever;
    may the LORD rejoice in his works⁸—
³²he who looks at the earth, and it trembles, ʰ
    who touches the mountains, ⁱ and they smoke. ʲ

³³I will sing ᵏ to the LORD all my life;
    I will sing praise to my God as long as I live.
³⁴May my meditation be pleasing to him,
    as I rejoice ˡ in the LORD.
³⁵But may sinners vanish ᵐ from the earth
    and the wicked be no more.

Praise the LORD, O my soul.

Praise the LORD. ᵃ ⁿ

Psalm 105

105:1–15pp — 1Ch 16:8–22

¹Give thanks to the LORD, ᵒ call on his name; ᵖ
    make known among the nations what he has done.
²Sing to him, �q sing praise to him;
    tell of all his wonderful acts.
³Glory in his holy name;
    let the hearts of those who seek the LORD rejoice.
⁴Look to the LORD and his strength;
    seek his face ʳ always.

⁵Remember the wonders ˢ he has done,
    his miracles, and the judgments he pronounced, ᵗ
⁶O descendants of Abraham his servant, ᵘ
    O sons of Jacob, his chosen ᵛ ones.
⁷He is the LORD our God;
    his judgments are in all the earth.

⁸He remembers his covenant ʷ forever,
    the word he commanded, for a thousand generations,
⁹the covenant he made with Abraham, ˣ
    the oath he swore to Isaac.
¹⁰He confirmed it ʸ to Jacob as a decree,
    to Israel as an everlasting covenant:
¹¹"To you I will give the land of Canaan ᶻ
    as the portion you will inherit."

¹²When they were but few in number, ᵃ
    few indeed, and strangers in it, ᵇ
¹³they wandered from nation to nation,
    from one kingdom to another.
¹⁴He allowed no one to oppress ᶜ them;
    for their sake he rebuked kings: ᵈ
¹⁵"Do not touch ᵉ my anointed ones;

104:31
g Ge 1:31
104:32
h Ps 97:4
i Ex 19:18
j Ps 144:5
104:33
k Ps 63:4
104:34
l Ps 9:2
104:35
m Ps 37:38
n Ps 105:45;
106:48
105:1
o 1Ch 16:34
p Ps 99:6
105:2
q Ps 96:1
105:4
r Ps 27:8
105:5
s Ps 40:5
t Ps 77:11
105:6
u ver 42
v Ps 106:5
105:8
w Ps 106:45;
Lk 1:72
105:9
x Ge 12:7; 17:2;
22:16-18;
Gal 3:15-18
105:10
y Ge 28:13-15
105:11
z Ge 13:15;
15:18
105:12
a Ge 34:30;
Dt 7:7
b Ge 23:4;
Heb 11:9
105:14
c Ge 35:5
d Ge 12:17-20
105:15
e Ge 26:11

ᵃ35 Hebrew *Hallelu Yah*; in the Septuagint this line stands at the beginning of Psalm 105.

do my prophets no harm.''

[16]He called down famine[f] on the land
   and destroyed all their supplies of food;
[17]and he sent a man before them—
   Joseph, sold as a slave. [g]
[18]They bruised his feet with shackles, [h]
   his neck was put in irons,
[19]till what he foretold[i] came to pass,
   till the word of the Lord proved him true.
[20]The king sent and released him,
   the ruler of peoples set him free. [j]
[21]He made him master of his household,
   ruler over all he possessed,
[22]to instruct his princes[k] as he pleased
   and teach his elders wisdom.

[23]Then Israel entered Egypt;[l]
   Jacob lived as an alien in the land of Ham.
[24]The Lord made his people very fruitful;
   he made them too numerous[m] for their foes,
[25]whose hearts he turned[n] to hate his people,
   to conspire[o] against his servants.
[26]He sent Moses[p] his servant,
   and Aaron, whom he had chosen. [q]
[27]They performed[r] his miraculous signs among them,
   his wonders in the land of Ham.
[28]He sent darkness[s] and made the land dark—
   for had they not rebelled against his words?
[29]He turned their waters into blood, [t]
   causing their fish to die. [u]
[30]Their land teemed with frogs, [v]
   which went up into the bedrooms of their rulers.
[31]He spoke, and there came swarms of flies, [w]
   and gnats[x] throughout their country.
[32]He turned their rain into hail, [y]
   with lightning throughout their land;
[33]he struck down their vines[z] and fig trees
   and shattered the trees of their country.
[34]He spoke, and the locusts came, [a]
   grasshoppers without number;
[35]they ate up every green thing in their land,
   ate up the produce of their soil.
[36]Then he struck down all the firstborn[b] in their land,
   the firstfruits of all their manhood.

[37]He brought out Israel, laden with silver and gold, [c]
   and from among their tribes no one faltered.
[38]Egypt was glad when they left,
   because dread of Israel[d] had fallen on them.
[39]He spread out a cloud[e] as a covering,
   and a fire to give light at night. [f]
[40]They asked, [g] and he brought them quail[h]

105:16
fGe 41:54;
Lev 26:26;
Isa 3:1;
Eze 4:16
105:17
gGe 37:28;
45:5; Ac 7:9
105:18
hGe 40:15
105:19
iGe 40:20-22
105:20
jGe 41:14
105:22
kGe 41:43-44
105:23
lGe 46:6;
Ac 13:17
105:24
mEx 1:7,9
105:25
nEx 4:21
oEx 1:6-10;
Ac 7:19
105:26
pEx 3:10
qNu 16:5;
17:5-8
105:27
rEx 7:8-12:51
105:28
sEx 10:22
105:29
tPs 78:44
uEx 7:21
105:30
vEx 8:2,6
105:31
wEx 8:21-24
xEx 8:16-18
105:32
yEx 9:22-25
105:33
zPs 78:47
105:34
aEx 10:4,12-15
105:36
bEx 12:29
105:37
cEx 12:35
105:38
dEx 12:33;
15:16
105:39
eEx 13:21
fNe 9:12;
Ps 78:14
105:40
gPs 78:18,24
hEx 16:13

and satisfied them with the bread of heaven. [i]
[41]He opened the rock, [j] and water gushed out;
  like a river it flowed in the desert.

[42]For he remembered his holy promise [k]
  given to his servant Abraham.
[43]He brought out his people with rejoicing, [l]
  his chosen ones with shouts of joy;
[44]he gave them the lands of the nations, [m]
  and they fell heir to what others had toiled for—
[45]that they might keep his precepts
  and observe his laws. [n]

Praise the LORD. [a]

Psalm 106

106:1,47–48pp — 1Ch 16:34-36

[1]Praise the LORD. [b]

Give thanks to the LORD, for he is good; [o]
  his love endures forever.
[2]Who can proclaim the mighty acts [p] of the LORD
  or fully declare his praise?
[3]Blessed are they who maintain justice,
  who constantly do what is right. [q]
[4]Remember me, [r] O LORD, when you show favor to your
    people,
  come to my aid when you save them,
[5]that I may enjoy the prosperity [s] of your chosen ones,
  that I may share in the joy [t] of your nation
  and join your inheritance in giving praise.

[6]We have sinned, [u] even as our fathers did;
  we have done wrong and acted wickedly.
[7]When our fathers were in Egypt,
  they gave no thought to your miracles;
they did not remember [v] your many kindnesses,
  and they rebelled by the sea, [w] the Red Sea. [c]
[8]Yet he saved them for his name's sake, [x]
  to make his mighty power known.
[9]He rebuked [y] the Red Sea, and it dried up; [z]
  he led them through [a] the depths as through a desert.
[10]He saved them [b] from the hand of the foe;
  from the hand of the enemy he redeemed them. [c]
[11]The waters covered [d] their adversaries;
  not one of them survived.
[12]Then they believed his promises
  and sang his praise. [e]

105:40
i Jn 6:31
105:41
j Ex 17:6;
Nu 20:11;
Ps 78:15-16;
1Co 10:4
105:42
k Ge 15:13-16
105:43
l Ex 15:1-18;
Ps 106:12
105:44
m Jos 13:6-7
105:45
n Dt 4:40;
6:21-24
106:1
o Ps 100:5;
105:1
106:2
p Ps 145:4,12
106:3
q Ps 15:2
106:4
r Ps 119:132
106:5
s Ps 1:3
t Ps 118:15
106:6
u Da 9:5
106:7
v Ps 78:11,42
w Ex 14:11-12
106:8
x Ex 9:16
106:9
y Ps 18:15
z Ex 14:21;
Na 1:4
a Isa 63:11-14
106:10
b Ex 14:30
c Ps 107:2
106:11
d Ex 14:28; 15:5
106:12
e Ex 15:1-21

---

[a]45 Hebrew *Hallelu Yah*   [b]1 Hebrew *Hallelu Yah;* also in verse 48   [c]7 Hebrew *Yam Suph;*
that is, Sea of Reeds; also in verses 9 and 22

[13]But they soon forgot[f] what he had done
and did not wait for his counsel.
[14]In the desert they gave in to their craving;
in the wasteland they put God to the test. [g]
[15]So he gave them[h] what they asked for,
but sent a wasting disease[i] upon them.

[16]In the camp they grew envious[j] of Moses
and of Aaron, who was consecrated to the LORD.
[17]The earth opened[k] up and swallowed Dathan;
it buried the company of Abiram.
[18]Fire blazed[l] among their followers;
a flame consumed the wicked.

[19]At Horeb they made a calf[m]
and worshiped an idol cast from metal.
[20]They exchanged their Glory[n]
for an image of a bull, which eats grass.
[21]They forgot the God[o] who saved them,
who had done great things[p] in Egypt,
[22]miracles in the land of Ham[q]
and awesome deeds by the Red Sea.
[23]So he said he would destroy[r] them—
had not Moses, his chosen one,
stood in the breach[s] before him
to keep his wrath from destroying them.

[24]Then they despised the pleasant land;[t]
they did not believe[u] his promise.
[25]They grumbled[v] in their tents
and did not obey the LORD.
[26]So he swore[w] to them with uplifted hand
that he would make them fall in the desert, [x]
[27]make their descendants fall among the nations
and scatter[y] them throughout the lands.

[28]They yoked themselves to the Baal of Peor[z]
and ate sacrifices offered to lifeless gods;
[29]they provoked the LORD to anger by their wicked deeds,
and a plague broke out among them.
[30]But Phinehas stood up and intervened,
and the plague was checked. [a]
[31]This was credited to him[b] as righteousness
for endless generations to come.

[32]By the waters of Meribah[c] they angered the LORD,
and trouble came to Moses because of them;
[33]for they rebelled against the Spirit of God,
and rash words came from Moses' lips. [a] [d]

[34]They did not destroy[e] the peoples
as the LORD had commanded[f] them,
[35]but they mingled[g] with the nations

106:13
f Ex 15:24
106:14
g 1Co 10:9
106:15
h Nu 11:31
i Isa 10:16
106:16
j Nu 16:1-3
106:17
k Dt 11:6
106:18
l Nu 16:35
106:19
m Ex 32:4
106:20
n Jer 2:11;
Ro 1:23
106:21
o Ps 78:11
p Dt 10:21
106:22
q Ps 105:27
106:23
r Ex 32:10
s Ex 32:11-14
106:24
t Dt 8:7;
Eze 20:6
u Heb 3:18-19
106:25
v Nu 14:2
106:26
w Eze 20:15;
Heb 3:11
x Nu 14:28-35
106:27
y Lev 26:33;
Ps 44:11
106:28
z Nu 25:2-3;
Hos 9:10
106:30
a Nu 25:8
106:31
b Nu 25:11-13
106:32
c Nu 20:2-13;
Ps 81:7
106:33
d Nu 20:8-12
106:34
e Jdg 1:21
f Dt 7:16
106:35
g Jdg 3:5-6

---

a33 Or against his spirit, / and rash words came from his lips

and adopted their customs.
36They worshiped their idols, h
  which became a snare to them.
37They sacrificed their sonsi
  and their daughters to demons.
38They shed innocent blood,
  the blood of their sonsj and daughters,
 whom they sacrificed to the idols of Canaan,
  and the land was desecrated by their blood.
39They defiled themselvesk by what they did;
  by their deeds they prostituted1 themselves.

40Therefore the Lord was angrym with his people
  and abhorred his inheritance. n
41He handed them overo to the nations,
  and their foes ruled over them.
42Their enemies oppressed them
  and subjected them to their power.
43Many times he delivered them,
  but they were bent on rebellionp
  and they wasted away in their sin.

44But he took note of their distress
  when he heard their cry;q
45for their sake he remembered his covenantr
  and out of his great loves he relented.
46He caused them to be pitiedt
  by all who held them captive.

47Save us, O Lord our God,
  and gather usu from the nations,
 that we may give thanks to your holy name
  and glory in your praise.

48Praise be to the Lord, the God of Israel,
  from everlasting to everlasting.
 Let all the people say, "Amen!"v

Praise the Lord.

BOOK V

Psalms 107–150

Psalm 107

1Give thanks to the Lord, w for he is good;
  his love endures forever.
2Let the redeemedx of the Lord say this—
  those he redeemed from the hand of the foe,
3those he gatheredy from the lands,

106:36
h Jdg 2:12
106:37
i 2Ki 16:3; 17:17
106:38
j Nu 35:33
106:39
k Eze 20:18
l Lev 17:7;
Nu 15:39
106:40
m Jdg 2:14;
Ps 78:59
n Dt 9:29
106:41
o Jdg 2:14;
Ne 9:27
106:43
p Jdg 2:16-19
106:44
q Jdg 3:9; 10:10
106:45
r Lev 26:42;
Ps 105:8
s Jdg 2:18
106:46
t Ezr 9:9;
Jer 42:12
106:47
u Ps 147:2
106:48
v Ps 41:13
107:1
w Ps 106:1
107:2
x Ps 106:10
107:3
y Ps 106:47;
Isa 43:5-6

from east and west, from north and south.[a]

4Some wandered in desert[z] wastelands,
    finding no way to a city where they could settle.
5They were hungry and thirsty,
    and their lives ebbed away.
6Then they cried out[a] to the LORD in their trouble,
    and he delivered them from their distress.
7He led them by a straight way[b]
    to a city where they could settle.
8Let them give thanks to the LORD for his unfailing love
    and his wonderful deeds for men,
9for he satisfies[c] the thirsty
    and fills the hungry with good things.[d]

10Some sat in darkness[e] and the deepest gloom,
    prisoners suffering in iron chains,[f]
11for they had rebelled[g] against the words of God
    and despised the counsel[h] of the Most High.
12So he subjected them to bitter labor;
    they stumbled, and there was no one to help.[i]
13Then they cried to the LORD in their trouble,
    and he saved them from their distress.
14He brought them out of darkness and the deepest gloom
    and broke away their chains.[j]
15Let them give thanks to the LORD for his unfailing love
    and his wonderful deeds for men,
16for he breaks down gates of bronze
    and cuts through bars of iron.

17Some became fools through their rebellious ways
    and suffered affliction[k] because of their iniquities.
18They loathed all food[l]
    and drew near the gates of death.[m]
19Then they cried to the LORD in their trouble,
    and he saved them from their distress.
20He sent forth his word[n] and healed them;[o]
    he rescued[p] them from the grave.[q]
21Let them give thanks to the LORD for his unfailing love
    and his wonderful deeds for men.
22Let them sacrifice thank offerings[r]
    and tell of his works[s] with songs of joy.

23Others went out on the sea in ships;
    they were merchants on the mighty waters.
24They saw the works of the LORD,
    his wonderful deeds in the deep.
25For he spoke[t] and stirred up a tempest[u]
    that lifted high the waves.[v]
26They mounted up to the heavens and went down to the
        depths;
    in their peril their courage melted[w] away.

---

a3 Hebrew north and the sea

107:4
zNu 14:33;
32:13
107:6
aPs 50:15
107:7
bEzr 8:21
107:9
cPs 22:26;
Lk 1:53
dPs 34:10
107:10
eLk 1:79
fJob 36:8
107:11
gPs 106:7;
La 3:42
h2Ch 36:16
107:12
iPs 22:11
107:14
jPs 116:16;
Lk 13:16;
Ac 12:7
107:17
kIsa 65:6-7;
La 3:39
107:18
lJob 33:20
mJob 33:22;
Ps 9:13; 88:3
107:20
nMt 8:8
oPs 103:3
pJob 33:28
qPs 30:3; 49:15
107:22
rLev 7:12;
Ps 50:14;
116:17 sPs 9:11;
73:28; 118:17
107:25
tPs 105:31
uJnh 1:4
vPs 93:3
107:26
wPs 22:14

²⁷They reeled and staggered like drunken men;
  they were at their wits' end.
²⁸Then they cried out to the LORD in their trouble,
  and he brought them out of their distress.
²⁹He stilled the storm˟ to a whisper;
  the waves˅ of the sea were hushed.
³⁰They were glad when it grew calm,
  and he guided them to their desired haven.
³¹Let them give thanks to the LORD for his unfailing love
  and his wonderful deeds for men.
³²Let them exalt him in the assembly�misc of the people
  and praise him in the council of the elders.

³³He turned rivers into a desert,ᵃ
  flowing springs into thirsty ground,
³⁴and fruitful land into a salt waste,ᵇ
  because of the wickedness of those who lived there.
³⁵He turned the desert into pools of waterᶜ
  and the parched ground into flowing springs;
³⁶there he brought the hungry to live,
  and they founded a city where they could settle.
³⁷They sowed fields and planted vineyardsᵈ
  that yielded a fruitful harvest;
³⁸he blessed them, and their numbers greatly increased,ᵉ
  and he did not let their herds diminish.

³⁹Then their numbers decreased,ᶠ and they were humbled
  by oppression, calamity and sorrow;
⁴⁰he who pours contempt on noblesᵍ
  made them wander in a trackless waste.ʰ
⁴¹But he lifted the needyⁱ out of their affliction
  and increased their families like flocks.
⁴²The upright see and rejoice,ʲ
  but all the wicked shut their mouths.ᵏ

⁴³Whoever is wise,ˡ let him heed these things
  and consider the great loveᵐ of the LORD.

Psalm 108

108:1–5pp — Ps 57:7–11
108:6–13pp — Ps 60:5–12

A song. A psalm of David.

¹My heart is steadfast, O God;
  I will sing and make music with all my soul.
²Awake, harp and lyre!
  I will awaken the dawn.
³I will praise you, O LORD, among the nations;
  I will sing of you among the peoples.
⁴For great is your love, higher than the heavens;
  your faithfulness reaches to the skies.

107:29
˟Mt 8:26
˅Ps 89:9
107:32
ᶻPs 22:22,25;
35:18
107:33
ᵃ1Ki 17:1;
Ps 74:15
107:34
ᵇGe 13:10;
14:3; 19:25
107:35
ᶜPs 114:8;
Isa 41:18
107:37
ᵈIsa 65:21
107:38
ᵉGe 12:2;
17:16,20; Ex 1:7
107:39
ᶠ2Ki 10:32;
Eze 5:12
107:40
ᵍJob 12:21
ʰJob 12:24
107:41
ⁱ1Sa 2:8;
Ps 113:7-9
107:42
ʲJob 22:19
ᵏJob 5:16;
Ps 63:11;
Ro 3:19
107:43
ˡJer 9:12;
Hos 14:9
ᵐPs 64:9

[5]Be exalted, O God, above the heavens,
  and let your glory be over all the earth.[n]

[6]Save us and help us with your right hand,
  that those you love may be delivered.
[7]God has spoken from his sanctuary:
  "In triumph I will parcel out Shechem
  and measure off the Valley of Succoth.
[8]Gilead is mine, Manasseh is mine;
  Ephraim is my helmet,
  Judah[o] my scepter.
[9]Moab is my washbasin,
  upon Edom I toss my sandal;
  over Philistia I shout in triumph."

[10]Who will bring me to the fortified city?
  Who will lead me to Edom?
[11]Is it not you, O God, you who have rejected us
  and no longer go out with our armies?[p]
[12]Give us aid against the enemy,
  for the help of man is worthless.
[13]With God we will gain the victory,
  and he will trample down our enemies.

Psalm 109

For the director of music. Of David. A psalm.

[1]O God, whom I praise,
  do not remain silent,[q]
[2]for wicked and deceitful men
  have opened their mouths against me;
  they have spoken against me with lying tongues.[r]
[3]With words of hatred[s] they surround me;
  they attack me without cause.[t]
[4]In return for my friendship they accuse me,
  but I am a man of prayer.[u]
[5]They repay me evil for good,[v]
  and hatred for my friendship.

[6]Appoint[a] an evil man[b] to oppose him;
  let an accuser[c][w] stand at his right hand.
[7]When he is tried, let him be found guilty,
  and may his prayers condemn[x] him.
[8]May his days be few;
  may another take his place[y] of leadership.
[9]May his children be fatherless
  and his wife a widow.[z]
[10]May his children be wandering beggars;

108:5
nPs 57:5
108:8
oGe 49:10
108:11
pPs 44:9
109:1
qPs 83:1
109:2
rPs 52:4; 120:2
109:3
sPs 69:4
tPs 35:7;
Jn 15:25
109:4
uPs 69:13
109:5
vPs 35:12;
38:20
109:6
wZec 3:1
109:7
xPr 28:9
109:8
yAc 1:20*
109:9
zEx 22:24

---

[a]6 Or *They say:* "*Appoint* (with quotation marks at the end of verse 19)   [b]6 Or *the Evil One*
[c]6 Or *let Satan*

may they be driven[a] from their ruined homes.
[11]May a creditor seize all he has;
    may strangers plunder the fruits of his labor. [a]
[12]May no one extend kindness to him
    or take pity[b] on his fatherless children.
[13]May his descendants be cut off,[c]
    their names blotted out[d] from the next generation.
[14]May the iniquity of his fathers[e] be remembered before
      the LORD;
    may the sin of his mother never be blotted out.
[15]May their sins always remain before the LORD,
    that he may cut off the memory[f] of them from the
      earth.

[16]For he never thought of doing a kindness,
    but hounded to death the poor
    and the needy[g] and the brokenhearted. [h]
[17]He loved to pronounce a curse—
    may it[b] come on him;[i]
he found no pleasure in blessing—
    may it be[c] far from him.
[18]He wore cursing[j] as his garment;
    it entered into his body like water,[k]
    into his bones like oil.
[19]May it be like a cloak wrapped about him,
    like a belt tied forever around him.
[20]May this be the LORD's payment[l] to my accusers,
    to those who speak evil[m] of me.

[21]But you, O Sovereign LORD,
    deal well with me for your name's sake;[n]
    out of the goodness of your love,[o] deliver me.
[22]For I am poor and needy,
    and my heart is wounded within me.
[23]I fade away like an evening shadow;[p]
    I am shaken off like a locust.
[24]My knees give[q] way from fasting;
    my body is thin and gaunt.
[25]I am an object of scorn[r] to my accusers;
    when they see me, they shake their heads. [s]

[26]Help me, [t] O LORD my God;
    save me in accordance with your love.
[27]Let them know[u] that it is your hand,
    that you, O LORD, have done it.
[28]They may curse,[v] but you will bless;
    when they attack they will be put to shame,
    but your servant will rejoice. [w]
[29]My accusers will be clothed with disgrace
    and wrapped in shame[x] as in a cloak.

[30]With my mouth I will greatly extol the LORD;

109:11
a Job 5:5
109:12
b Isa 9:17
109:13
c Job 18:19;
Ps 37:28
d Pr 10:7
109:14
e Ex 20:5;
Ne 4:5;
Jer 18:23
109:15
f Job 18:17;
Ps 34:16
109:16
g Ps 37:14,32
h Ps 34:18
109:17
i Pr 14:14;
Eze 35:6
109:18
j Ps 73:6
k Nu 5:22
109:20
l Ps 94:23;
2Ti 4:14
m Ps 71:10
109:21
n Ps 79:9
o Ps 69:16
109:23
p Ps 102:11
109:24
q Heb 12:12
109:25
r Ps 22:6
s Mt 27:39;
Mk 15:29
109:26
t Ps 119:86
109:27
u Job 37:7
109:28
v 2Sa 16:12
w Isa 65:14
109:29
x Ps 35:26;
132:18

---

a10 Septuagint; Hebrew *sought*   b17 Or *curse, / and it has*   c17 Or *blessing, / and it is*

in the great throng[y] I will praise him.
[31]For he stands at the right hand[z] of the needy one,
to save his life from those who condemn him.

Psalm 110

Of David. A psalm.

[1]The LORD says[a] to my Lord:
"Sit at my right hand
until I make your enemies
a footstool for your feet."[b]

[2]The LORD will extend your mighty scepter[c] from Zion;
you will rule in the midst of your enemies.
[3]Your troops will be willing
on your day of battle.
Arrayed in holy majesty,[d]
from the womb of the dawn
you will receive the dew of your youth.[a]

[4]The LORD has sworn
and will not change his mind:[e]
"You are a priest forever,[f]
in the order of Melchizedek.[g]"

[5]The Lord is at your right hand;[h]
he will crush kings[i] on the day of his wrath.[j]
[6]He will judge the nations,[k] heaping up the dead[l]
and crushing the rulers[m] of the whole earth.
[7]He will drink from a brook beside the way[b];
therefore he will lift up his head.[n]

Psalm 111[c]

[1]Praise the LORD.[d]

I will extol the LORD with all my heart
in the council of the upright and in the assembly.

[2]Great are the works[o] of the LORD;
they are pondered by all who delight in them.
[3]Glorious and majestic are his deeds,
and his righteousness endures forever.
[4]He has caused his wonders to be remembered;
the LORD is gracious and compassionate.[p]
[5]He provides food[q] for those who fear him;

109:30
yPs 35:18;
111:1
109:31
zPs 16:8; 73:23;
121:5
110:1
aMt 22:44*;
Mk 12:36*;
Lk 20:42*;
Ac 2:34*
b1Co 15:25
110:2
cPs 45:6
110:3
dJdg 5:2;
Ps 96:9
110:4
eNu 23:19
fHeb 5:6*;
7:21*
gHeb 7:15-17*
110:5
hPs 16:8
iPs 2:12 jPs 2:5;
Ro 2:5
110:6
kIsa 2:4
lIsa 66:24
mPs 68:21
110:7
nPs 27:6
111:2
oPs 92:5; 143:5
111:4
pPs 103:8
111:5
qMt 6:26,31-33

---

[a]3 Or / *your young men will come to you like the dew*   [b]7 Or / *The One who grants succession will set him in authority*   [c]This psalm is an acrostic poem, the lines of which begin with the successive letters of the Hebrew alphabet.   [d]1 Hebrew *Hallelu Yah*

he remembers his covenant forever.
[6]He has shown his people the power of his works,
giving them the lands of other nations.
[7]The works of his hands are faithful and just;
all his precepts are trustworthy.[r]
[8]They are steadfast for ever[s] and ever,
done in faithfulness and uprightness.
[9]He provided redemption[t] for his people;
he ordained his covenant forever—
holy and awesome[u] is his name.

[10]The fear of the LORD is the beginning of wisdom;[v]
all who follow his precepts have good
understanding.[w]
To him belongs eternal praise.[x]

Psalm 112[a]

[1]Praise the LORD.[b]

Blessed is the man who fears the LORD,[y]
who finds great delight[z] in his commands.

[2]His children will be mighty in the land;
the generation of the upright will be blessed.
[3]Wealth and riches are in his house,
and his righteousness endures forever.
[4]Even in darkness light dawns[a] for the upright,
for the gracious and compassionate and righteous[b]
man.[c]
[5]Good will come to him who is generous and lends
freely,[c]
who conducts his affairs with justice.
[6]Surely he will never be shaken;
a righteous man will be remembered[d] forever.
[7]He will have no fear of bad news;
his heart is steadfast,[e] trusting in the LORD.
[8]His heart is secure, he will have no fear;
in the end he will look in triumph on his foes.[f]
[9]He has scattered abroad his gifts to the poor,[g]
his righteousness endures forever;
his horn[d] will be lifted[h] high in honor.

[10]The wicked man will see[i] and be vexed,
he will gnash his teeth[j] and waste away;[k]
the longings of the wicked will come to nothing.[l]

111:7
r Ps 19:7;
Rev 15:3
111:8
s Isa 40:8;
Mt 5:18
111:9
t Lk 1:68
u Ps 99:3;
Lk 1:49
111:10
v Pr 9:10
w Ecc 12:13
x Ps 145:2
112:1
y Ps 128:1
z Ps 119:14,16,
47,92
112:4
a Job 11:17
b Ps 97:11
112:5
c Ps 37:21,26
112:6
d Pr 10:7
112:7
e Ps 57:7;
Pr 1:33
112:8
f Ps 59:10
112:9
g 2Co 9:9*
h Ps 75:10
112:10
i Ps 86:17
j Ps 37:12
k Ps 58:7-8
l Pr 11:7

---

[a]This psalm is an acrostic poem, the lines of which begin with the successive letters of the Hebrew alphabet.   [b]1 Hebrew *Hallelu Yah*   [c]4 Or / *for the* LORD *is gracious and compassionate and righteous*   [d]9 *Horn* here symbolizes dignity.

Psalm 113

[1]Praise the LORD.[a]

Praise, O servants of the LORD,[m]
    praise the name of the LORD.
[2]Let the name of the LORD be praised,
    both now and forevermore.[n]
[3]From the rising of the sun[o] to the place where it sets,
    the name of the LORD is to be praised.

[4]The LORD is exalted[p] over all the nations,
    his glory above the heavens.[q]
[5]Who is like the LORD our God,[r]
    the One who sits enthroned[s] on high,
[6]who stoops down to look[t]
    on the heavens and the earth?

[7]He raises the poor[u] from the dust
    and lifts the needy[v] from the ash heap;
[8]he seats them[w] with princes,
    with the princes of their people.
[9]He settles the barren[x] woman in her home
    as a happy mother of children.

Praise the LORD.

Psalm 114

[1]When Israel came out of Egypt,[y]
    the house of Jacob from a people of foreign tongue,
[2]Judah became God's sanctuary,
    Israel his dominion.

[3]The sea looked and fled,[z]
    the Jordan turned back;[a]
[4]the mountains skipped like rams,
    the hills like lambs.

[5]Why was it, O sea, that you fled,
    O Jordan, that you turned back,
[6]you mountains, that you skipped like rams,
    you hills, like lambs?

[7]Tremble, O earth,[b] at the presence of the Lord,
    at the presence of the God of Jacob,
[8]who turned the rock into a pool,
    the hard rock into springs of water.[c]

[a]1 Hebrew *Hallelu Yah*; also in verse 9

113:1
m Ps 135:1
113:2
n Da 2:20
113:3
o Isa 59:19;
Mal 1:11
113:4
p Ps 99:2
q Ps 8:1; 97:9
113:5
r Ps 89:6
s Ps 103:19
113:6
t Ps 11:4; 138:6;
Isa 57:15
113:7
u 1Sa 2:8
v Ps 107:41
113:8
w Job 36:7
113:9
x 1Sa 2:5;
Ps 68:6;
Isa 54:1
114:1
y Ex 13:3
114:3
z Ex 14:21;
Ps 77:16
a Jos 3:16
114:7
b Ps 96:9
114:8
c Ex 17:6;
Nu 20:11;
Ps 107:35

Psalm 115

115:4–11pp — Ps 135:15–20

¹Not to us, O Lᴏʀᴅ, not to us
    but to your name be the glory, ᵈ
    because of your love and faithfulness.

²Why do the nations say,
    "Where is their God?" ᵉ
³Our God is in heaven; ᶠ
    he does whatever pleases him. ᵍ
⁴But their idols are silver and gold,
    made by the hands of men. ʰ
⁵They have mouths, but cannot speak, ⁱ
    eyes, but they cannot see;
⁶they have ears, but cannot hear,
    noses, but they cannot smell;
⁷they have hands, but cannot feel,
    feet, but they cannot walk;
    nor can they utter a sound with their throats.
⁸Those who make them will be like them,
    and so will all who trust in them.

⁹O house of Israel, trust in the Lᴏʀᴅ—
    he is their help and shield.
¹⁰O house of Aaron, ʲ trust in the Lᴏʀᴅ—
    he is their help and shield.
¹¹You who fear him, trust in the Lᴏʀᴅ—
    he is their help and shield.

¹²The Lᴏʀᴅ remembers us and will bless us:
    He will bless the house of Israel,
    he will bless the house of Aaron,
¹³he will bless those who fear ᵏ the Lᴏʀᴅ—
    small and great alike.

¹⁴May the Lᴏʀᴅ make you increase, ˡ
    both you and your children.
¹⁵May you be blessed by the Lᴏʀᴅ,
    the Maker of heaven ᵐ and earth.

¹⁶The highest heavens belong to the Lᴏʀᴅ, ⁿ
    but the earth he has given ᵒ to man.
¹⁷It is not the dead ᵖ who praise the Lᴏʀᴅ,
    those who go down to silence;
¹⁸it is we who extol the Lᴏʀᴅ,
    both now and forevermore. �q

Praise the Lᴏʀᴅ. ᵃ

115:1
dPs 96:8;
Isa 48:11;
Eze 36:32
115:2
ePs 42:3; 79:10
115:3
fPs 103:19
gPs 135:6;
Da 4:35
115:4
hDt 4:28;
Jer 10:3-5
115:5
iJer 10:5
115:10
jPs 118:3
115:13
kPs 128:1,4
115:14
lDt 1:11
115:15
mGe 1:1;
14:19; Ps 96:5
115:16
nPs 89:11
oPs 8:6-8
115:17
pPs 6:5;
88:10-12;
Isa 38:18
115:18
qPs 113:2;
Da 2:20

ᵃ18 Hebrew *Hallelu Yah*

Psalm 116

¹I love the LORD,ʳ for he heard my voice;
　he heard my cryˢ for mercy.
²Because he turned his earᵗ to me,
　I will call on him as long as I live.

³The cords of deathᵘ entangled me,
　the anguish of the graveᵃ came upon me;
　I was overcome by trouble and sorrow.
⁴Then I called on the nameᵛ of the LORD:
　"O LORD, save me!ʷ"

⁵The LORD is gracious and righteous;ˣ
　our God is full of compassion.
⁶The LORD protects the simplehearted;
　when I was in great need,ʸ he saved me.

⁷Be at restᶻ once more, O my soul,
　for the LORD has been goodᵃ to you.

⁸For you, O LORD, have delivered my soulᵇ from death,
　my eyes from tears,
　my feet from stumbling,
⁹that I may walk before the LORD
　in the land of the living.ᶜ
¹⁰I believed;ᵈ thereforeᵇ I said,
　"I am greatly afflicted."
¹¹And in my dismay I said,
　"All men are liars."ᵉ

¹²How can I repay the LORD
　for all his goodness to me?
¹³I will lift up the cup of salvation
　and call on the nameᶠ of the LORD.
¹⁴I will fulfill my vowsᵍ to the LORD
　in the presence of all his people.

¹⁵Precious in the sightʰ of the LORD
　is the death of his saints.
¹⁶O LORD, truly I am your servant;ⁱ
　I am your servant, the son of your maidservantᶜ ;ʲ
　you have freed me from my chains.

¹⁷I will sacrifice a thank offeringᵏ to you
　and call on the name of the LORD.
¹⁸I will fulfill my vows to the LORD
　in the presence of all his people,
¹⁹in the courtsˡ of the house of the LORD—
　in your midst, O Jerusalem.

Praise the LORD. ᵈ

116:1
rPs 18:1
sPs 66:19
116:2
tPs 40:1
116:3
uPs 18:4-5
116:4
vPs 118:5
wPs 22:20
116:5
xEzr 9:15;
Ne 9:8;
Ps 103:8;
145:17
116:6
yPs 19:7; 79:8
116:7
zJer 6:16;
Mt 11:29
aPs 13:6
116:8
bPs 56:13
116:9
cPs 27:13
116:10
d2Co 4:13*
116:11
eRo 3:4
116:13
fPs 16:5; 80:18
116:14
gPs 22:25;
Jnh 2:9
116:15
hPs 72:14
116:16
iPs 119:125;
143:12 jPs 86:16
116:17
kLev 7:12;
Ps 50:14
116:19
lPs 96:8; 135:2

ᵃ3 Hebrew *Sheol*　　ᵇ10 Or *believed even when*　　ᶜ16 Or *servant, your faithful son*
ᵈ19 Hebrew *Hallelu Yah*

Psalm 117

[1]Praise the LORD, all you nations;[m]
　　extol him, all you peoples.
[2]For great is his love toward us,
　　and the faithfulness of the LORD[n] endures forever.

Praise the LORD.[a]

Psalm 118

[1]Give thanks to the LORD,[o] for he is good;
　　his love endures forever.[p]

[2]Let Israel say:[q]
　　"His love endures forever."
[3]Let the house of Aaron say:
　　"His love endures forever."
[4]Let those who fear the LORD say:
　　"His love endures forever."

[5]In my anguish[r] I cried to the LORD,
　　and he answered[s] by setting me free.
[6]The LORD is with me;[t] I will not be afraid.
　　What can man do to me?[u]
[7]The LORD is with me; he is my helper.[v]
　　I will look in triumph on my enemies.[w]

[8]It is better to take refuge in the LORD[x]
　　than to trust in man.[y]
[9]It is better to take refuge in the LORD
　　than to trust in princes.[z]

[10]All the nations surrounded me,
　　but in the name of the LORD I cut them off.[a]
[11]They surrounded me[b] on every side,[c]
　　but in the name of the LORD I cut them off.
[12]They swarmed around me like bees,[d]
　　but they died out as quickly as burning thorns;[e]
　　in the name of the LORD I cut them off.

[13]I was pushed back and about to fall,
　　but the LORD helped me.[f]
[14]The LORD is my strength[g] and my song;
　　he has become my salvation.[h]

[15]Shouts of joy[i] and victory
　　resound in the tents of the righteous:
　　"The LORD's right hand[j] has done mighty things!
[16]　The LORD's right hand is lifted high;
　　the LORD's right hand has done mighty things!"

117:1
mRo 15:11*
117:2
nPs 100:5
118:1
o1Ch 16:8
pPs 106:1;
　136:1
118:2
qPs 115:9
118:5
rPs 120:1
sPs 18:19
118:6
tHeb 13:6*
uPs 27:1; 56:4
118:7
vPs 54:4
wPs 59:10
118:8
xPs 40:4
yJer 17:5
118:9
zPs 146:3
118:10
aPs 18:40
118:11
bPs 88:17
cPs 3:6
118:12
dDt 1:44
ePs 58:9
118:13
fPs 86:17; 140:4
118:14
gEx 15:2
hIsa 12:2
118:15
iPs 68:3
jPs 89:13

a2 Hebrew *Hallelu Yah*

¹⁷I will not die[k] but live,
and will proclaim[l] what the LORD has done.
¹⁸The LORD has chastened me severely,
but he has not given me over to death. [m]

¹⁹Open for me the gates[n] of righteousness;
I will enter and give thanks to the LORD.
²⁰This is the gate of the LORD
through which the righteous may enter. [o]
²¹I will give you thanks, for you answered me;[p]
you have become my salvation.

²²The stone the builders rejected
has become the capstone;[q]
²³the LORD has done this,
and it is marvelous in our eyes.
²⁴This is the day the LORD has made;
let us rejoice and be glad in it.

²⁵O LORD, save us;
O LORD, grant us success.
²⁶Blessed is he who comes[r] in the name of the LORD.
From the house of the LORD we bless you. [a]
²⁷The LORD is God,
and he has made his light shine[s] upon us.
With boughs in hand, join in the festal procession
up[b] to the horns of the altar.

²⁸You are my God, and I will give you thanks;
you are my God,[t] and I will exalt[u] you.

²⁹Give thanks to the LORD, for he is good;
his love endures forever.

Psalm 119[c]

א Aleph

¹Blessed are they whose ways are blameless,
who walk[v] according to the law of the LORD.
²Blessed are they who keep his statutes
and seek him with all their heart. [w]
³They do nothing wrong;[x]
they walk in his ways.
⁴You have laid down precepts
that are to be fully obeyed.
⁵Oh, that my ways were steadfast
in obeying your decrees!
⁶Then I would not be put to shame
when I consider all your commands.

118:17
k Ps 6:5;
Hab 1:12
l Ex 15:6;
Ps 73:28
118:18
m 2Co 6:9
118:19
n Isa 26:2
118:20
o Ps 24:7;
Isa 35:8;
Rev 22:14
118:21
p Ps 116:1
118:22
q Mt 21:42;
Mk 12:10;
Lk 20:17*;
Ac 4:11*;
1Pe 2:7
118:26
r Mt 21:9*;
Mk 11:9*;
Lk 13:35*;
19:38; Jn 12:13*
118:27
s 1Pe 2:9
118:28
t Isa 25:1
u Ex 15:2
119:1
v Ps 128:1
119:2
w Dt 6:5
119:3
x 1Jn 3:9; 5:18

---

a26 The Hebrew is plural.   b27 Or *Bind the festal sacrifice with ropes / and take it*   cThis psalm
is an acrostic poem; the verses of each stanza begin with the same letter of the Hebrew alphabet.

⁷I will praise you with an upright heart
  as I learn your righteous laws.
⁸I will obey your decrees;
  do not utterly forsake me.

‎ב‎ Beth

⁹How can a young man keep his way pure?
  By living according to your word.ʸ
¹⁰I seek you with all my heart;ᶻ
  do not let me stray from your commands.ᵃ
¹¹I have hidden your word in my heartᵇ
  that I might not sin against you.
¹²Praise be to you, O Lᴏʀᴅ;
  teach me your decrees.ᶜ
¹³With my lips I recount
  all the laws that come from your mouth.ᵈ
¹⁴I rejoice in following your statutes
  as one rejoices in great riches.
¹⁵I meditate on your preceptsᵉ
  and consider your ways.
¹⁶I delightᶠ in your decrees;
  I will not neglect your word.

‎ג‎ Gimel

¹⁷Do good to your servant,ᵍ and I will live;
  I will obey your word.
¹⁸Open my eyes that I may see
  wonderful things in your law.
¹⁹I am a stranger on earth;ʰ
  do not hide your commands from me.
²⁰My soul is consumedⁱ with longing
  for your lawsʲ at all times.
²¹You rebuke the arrogant, who are cursed
  and who strayᵏ from your commands.
²²Remove from me scornˡ and contempt,
  for I keep your statutes.
²³Though rulers sit together and slander me,
  your servant will meditate on your decrees.
²⁴Your statutes are my delight;
  they are my counselors.

‎ד‎ Daleth

²⁵I am laid low in the dust;ᵐ
  preserve my lifeⁿ according to your word.
²⁶I recounted my ways and you answered me;
  teach me your decrees.ᵒ
²⁷Let me understand the teaching of your precepts;
  then I will meditate on your wonders.ᵖ
²⁸My soul is weary with sorrow;�q
  strengthen meʳ according to your word.

119:9
y2Ch 6:16
119:10
z2Ch 15:15
ᵃver 21,118
119:11
bPs 37:31;
Lk 2:19,51
119:12
cver 26
119:13
dPs 40:9
119:15
ePs 1:2
119:16
fPs 1:2
119:17
gPs 13:6; 116:7
119:19
h1Ch 29:15;
Ps 39:12;
2Co 5:6;
Heb 11:13
119:20
iPs 42:2; 84:2
jPs 63:1
119:21
kver 10
119:22
lPs 39:8
119:25
mPs 44:25
nPs 143:11
119:26
oPs 25:4;
27:11; 86:11
119:27
pPs 145:5
119:28
qPs 107:26
rPs 20:2;
1Pe 5:10

²⁹Keep me from deceitful ways;
  be gracious to me through your law.
³⁰I have chosen the way of truth;
  I have set my heart on your laws.
³¹I hold fast[s] to your statutes, O Lᴏʀᴅ;
  do not let me be put to shame.
³²I run in the path of your commands,
  for you have set my heart free.

ה   He

³³Teach me,[t] O Lᴏʀᴅ, to follow your decrees;
  then I will keep them to the end.
³⁴Give me understanding, and I will keep your law
  and obey it with all my heart.
³⁵Direct me in the path of your commands,
  for there I find delight.
³⁶Turn my heart[u] toward your statutes
  and not toward selfish gain.[v]
³⁷Turn my eyes away from worthless things;
  preserve my life[w] according to your word.[a]
³⁸Fulfill your promise[x] to your servant,
  so that you may be feared.
³⁹Take away the disgrace I dread,
  for your laws are good.
⁴⁰How I long[y] for your precepts!
  Preserve my life in your righteousness.

ו   Waw

⁴¹May your unfailing love come to me, O Lᴏʀᴅ,
  your salvation according to your promise;
⁴²then I will answer[z] the one who taunts me,
  for I trust in your word.
⁴³Do not snatch the word of truth from my mouth,
  for I have put my hope in your laws.
⁴⁴I will always obey your law,
  for ever and ever.
⁴⁵I will walk about in freedom,
  for I have sought out your precepts.
⁴⁶I will speak of your statutes before kings[a]
  and will not be put to shame,
⁴⁷for I delight in your commands
  because I love them.
⁴⁸I lift up my hands to[b] your commands, which I love,
  and I meditate on your decrees.

ז   Zayin

⁴⁹Remember your word to your servant,
  for you have given me hope.

119:31
sDt 11:22
119:33
tver 12
119:36
u1Ki 8:58
vEze 33:31;
Mk 7:21-22;
Lk 12:15;
Heb 13:5
119:37
wPs 71:20;
Isa 33:15
119:38
x2Sa 7:25
119:40
yver 20
119:42
zPr 27:11
119:46
aMt 10:18;
Ac 26:1-2

*a37 Two manuscripts of the Masoretic Text and Dead Sea Scrolls; most manuscripts of the
Masoretic Text* life in your way   *b48 Or* for

⁵⁰My comfort in my suffering is this:
  Your promise preserves my life. ^b
⁵¹The arrogant mock me^c without restraint,
  but I do not turn^d from your law.
⁵²I remember^e your ancient laws, O LORD,
  and I find comfort in them.
⁵³Indignation grips me^f because of the wicked,
  who have forsaken your law.^g
⁵⁴Your decrees are the theme of my song
  wherever I lodge.
⁵⁵In the night I remember^h your name, O LORD,
  and I will keep your law.
⁵⁶This has been my practice:
  I obey your precepts.

ח   Heth

⁵⁷You are my portion,ⁱ O LORD;
  I have promised to obey your words.
⁵⁸I have sought your face with all my heart;
  be gracious to me^j according to your promise. ^k
⁵⁹I have considered my ways^l
  and have turned my steps to your statutes.
⁶⁰I will hasten and not delay
  to obey your commands.
⁶¹Though the wicked bind me with ropes,
  I will not forget^m your law.
⁶²At midnightⁿ I rise to give you thanks
  for your righteous laws.
⁶³I am a friend to all who fear you,^o
  to all who follow your precepts.
⁶⁴The earth is filled with your love,^p O LORD;
  teach me your decrees.

ט   Teth

⁶⁵Do good to your servant
  according to your word, O LORD.
⁶⁶Teach me knowledge and good judgment,
  for I believe in your commands.
⁶⁷Before I was afflicted I went astray,^q
  but now I obey your word.
⁶⁸You are good,^r and what you do is good;
  teach me your decrees. ^s
⁶⁹Though the arrogant have smeared me with lies,^t
  I keep your precepts with all my heart.
⁷⁰Their hearts are callous^u and unfeeling,
  but I delight in your law.
⁷¹It was good for me to be afflicted
  so that I might learn your decrees.
⁷²The law from your mouth is more precious to me
  than thousands of pieces of silver and gold. ^v

119:50
bRo 15:4
119:51
cJer 20:7
dver 157;
Job 23:11;
Ps 44:18
119:52
ePs 103:18
119:53
fEzr 9:3
gPs 89:30
119:55
hPs 63:6
119:57
iPs 16:5;
La 3:24
119:58
j1Ki 13:6
kver 41
119:59
lLk 15:17-18
119:61
mPs 140:5
119:62
nAc 16:25
119:63
oPs 101:6-7
119:64
pPs 33:5
119:67
qJer 31:18-19;
Heb 12:11
119:68
rPs 106:1;
107:1; Mt 19:17
sver 12
119:69
tJob 13:4;
Ps 109:2
119:70
uPs 17:10;
Isa 6:10;
Ac 28:27
119:72
vPs 19:10;
Pr 8:10-11,19

' Yodh

73Your hands made me[w] and formed me;
    give me understanding to learn your commands.
74May those who fear you rejoice[x] when they see me,
    for I have put my hope in your word.
75I know, O Lord, that your laws are righteous,
    and in faithfulness[y] you have afflicted me.
76May your unfailing love be my comfort,
    according to your promise to your servant.
77Let your compassion[z] come to me that I may live,
    for your law is my delight.
78May the arrogant[a] be put to shame for wronging me
       without cause;[b]
    but I will meditate on your precepts.
79May those who fear you turn to me,
    those who understand your statutes.
80May my heart be blameless toward your decrees,
    that I may not be put to shame.

כ Kaph

81My soul faints[c] with longing for your salvation,
    but I have put my hope in your word.
82My eyes fail,[d] looking for your promise;
    I say, "When will you comfort me?"
83Though I am like a wineskin in the smoke,
    I do not forget your decrees.
84How long[e] must your servant wait?
    When will you punish my persecutors?
85The arrogant dig pitfalls[f] for me,
    contrary to your law.
86All your commands are trustworthy;[g]
    help me,[h] for men persecute me without cause.[i]
87They almost wiped me from the earth,
    but I have not forsaken[j] your precepts.
88Preserve my life according to your love,
    and I will obey the statutes of your mouth.

ל Lamedh

89Your word, O Lord, is eternal;[k]
    it stands firm in the heavens.
90Your faithfulness[l] continues through all generations;
    you established the earth, and it endures.[m]
91Your laws endure[n] to this day,
    for all things serve you.
92If your law had not been my delight,
    I would have perished in my affliction.
93I will never forget your precepts,
    for by them you have preserved my life.
94Save me, for I am yours;
    I have sought out your precepts.

119:73
wJob 10:8;
Ps 100:3; 138:8;
139:13-16
119:74
xPs 34:2
119:75
yHeb 12:5-11
119:77
zver 41
119:78
aJer 50:32
bver 86,161
119:81
cPs 84:2
119:82
dPs 69:3;
La 2:11
119:84
ePs 39:4;
Rev 6:10
119:85
fPs 35:7;
Jer 18:20,22
119:86
gPs 35:19
hPs 109:26
iver 78
119:87
jIsa 58:2
119:89
kMt 24:34-35;
1Pe 1:25
119:90
lPs 36:5
mPs 148:6;
Ecc 1:4
119:91
nJer 33:25

119:97
oPs 1:2
119:98
pDt 4:6
119:100
qJob 32:7-9
119:101
rPr 1:15
119:103
sPs 19:10;
Pr 8:11
tPr 24:13-14
119:104
uver 128
119:105
vPr 6:23
119:106
wNe 10:29
119:108
xHos 14:2;
Heb 13:15
119:109
yJdg 12:3;
Job 13:14
119:110
zPs 140:5;
141:9 aver 10
119:112
bver 33
119:113
cJas 1:8
119:114
dPs 32:7; 91:1
ever 74
119:115
fPs 6:8; 139:19;
Mt 7:23
119:116
gPs 54:4
hPs 25:2;
Ro 5:5; 9:33

⁹⁵The wicked are waiting to destroy me,
but I will ponder your statutes.
⁹⁶To all perfection I see a limit;
but your commands are boundless.

‫מ‬ Mem

⁹⁷Oh, how I love your law!
I meditate° on it all day long.
⁹⁸Your commands make me wiserᵖ than my enemies,
for they are ever with me.
⁹⁹I have more insight than all my teachers,
for I meditate on your statutes.
¹⁰⁰I have more understanding than the elders,
for I obey your precepts. ᑫ
¹⁰¹I have kept my feetʳ from every evil path
so that I might obey your word.
¹⁰²I have not departed from your laws,
for you yourself have taught me.
¹⁰³How sweet are your words to my taste,
sweeter than honeyˢ to my mouth!ᵗ
¹⁰⁴I gain understanding from your precepts;
therefore I hate every wrong path. ᵘ

‫נ‬ Nun

¹⁰⁵Your word is a lamp to my feet
and a lightᵛ for my path.
¹⁰⁶I have taken an oathʷ and confirmed it,
that I will follow your righteous laws.
¹⁰⁷I have suffered much;
preserve my life, O LORD, according to your word.
¹⁰⁸Accept, O LORD, the willing praise of my mouth,ˣ
and teach me your laws.
¹⁰⁹Though I constantly take my life in my hands,ʸ
I will not forget your law.
¹¹⁰The wicked have set a snareᶻ for me,
but I have not strayedᵃ from your precepts.
¹¹¹Your statutes are my heritage forever;
they are the joy of my heart.
¹¹²My heart is set on keeping your decrees
to the very end. ᵇ

‫ס‬ Samekh

¹¹³I hate double-minded men,ᶜ
but I love your law.
¹¹⁴You are my refuge and my shield;ᵈ
I have put my hopeᵉ in your word.
¹¹⁵Away from me, ᶠ you evildoers,
that I may keep the commands of my God!
¹¹⁶Sustain meᵍ according to your promise, and I will live;
do not let my hopes be dashed. ʰ

117Uphold me, and I will be delivered;
  I will always have regard for your decrees.
118You reject all who stray from your decrees,
  for their deceitfulness is in vain.
119All the wicked of the earth you discard like dross;i
  therefore I love your statutes.
120My flesh tremblesj in fear of you;
  I stand in awe of your laws.

ע Ayin

121I have done what is righteous and just;
  do not leave me to my oppressors.
122Ensure your servant's well-being;k
  let not the arrogant oppress me.
123My eyes fail, looking for your salvation,
  looking for your righteous promise.l
124Deal with your servant according to your love
  and teach me your decrees.m
125I am your servant;n give me discernment
  that I may understand your statutes.
126It is time for you to act, O Lord;
  your law is being broken.
127Because I love your commands
  more than gold,o more than pure gold,
128and because I consider all your precepts right,
  I hate every wrong path.p

פ Pe

129Your statutes are wonderful;
  therefore I obey them.
130The unfolding of your words gives light;q
  it gives understanding to the simple.r
131I open my mouth and pant,s
  longing for your commands.t
132Turn to me and have mercyu on me,
  as you always do to those who love your name.
133Direct my footsteps according to your word;v
  let no sin rulew over me.
134Redeem me from the oppression of men,x
  that I may obey your precepts.
135Make your face shiney upon your servant
  and teach me your decrees.
136Streams of tearsz flow from my eyes,
  for your law is not obeyed.a

צ Tsadhe

137Righteous are you,b O Lord,
  and your laws are right.c
138The statutes you have laid down are righteous;d
  they are fully trustworthy.

119:119
iEze 22:18,19
119:120
jHab 3:16
119:122
kJob 17:3
119:123
lver 82
119:124
mver 12
119:125
nPs 116:16
119:127
oPs 19:10
119:128
pver 104,163
119:130
qPr 6:23
rPs 19:7
119:131
sPs 42:1 tver 20
119:132
uPs 25:16;
106:4
119:133
vPs 17:5
wPs 19:13;
Ro 6:12
119:134
xPs 142:6;
Lk 1:74
119:135
yNu 6:25;
Ps 4:6
119:136
zJer 9:1,18
aEze 9:4
119:137
bEzr 9:15;
Jer 12:1
cNe 9:13
119:138
dPs 19:7

139My zeal wears me out,[e]
    for my enemies ignore your words.
140Your promises have been thoroughly tested,[f]
    and your servant loves them.
141Though I am lowly and despised,[g]
    I do not forget your precepts.
142Your righteousness is everlasting
    and your law is true.[h]
143Trouble and distress have come upon me,
    but your commands are my delight.
144Your statutes are forever right;
    give me understanding[i] that I may live.

ק Qoph

145I call with all my heart; answer me, O Lᴏʀᴅ,
    and I will obey your decrees.
146I call out to you; save me
    and I will keep your statutes.
147I rise before dawn[j] and cry for help;
    I have put my hope in your word.
148My eyes stay open through the watches of the
        night,[k]
    that I may meditate on your promises.
149Hear my voice in accordance with your love;
    preserve my life, O Lᴏʀᴅ, according to your
        laws.
150Those who devise wicked schemes are near,
    but they are far from your law.
151Yet you are near,[l] O Lᴏʀᴅ,
    and all your commands are true.[m]
152Long ago I learned from your statutes
    that you established them to last forever.[n]

ר Resh

153Look upon my suffering[o] and deliver me,
    for I have not forgotten[p] your law.
154Defend my cause[q] and redeem me;[r]
    preserve my life according to your promise.
155Salvation is far from the wicked,
    for they do not seek out[s] your decrees.
156Your compassion is great, O Lᴏʀᴅ;
    preserve my life[t] according to your laws.
157Many are the foes who persecute me,[u]
    but I have not turned from your statutes.
158I look on the faithless with loathing,[v]
    for they do not obey your word.
159See how I love your precepts;
    preserve my life, O Lᴏʀᴅ, according to your
        love.
160All your words are true;
    all your righteous laws are eternal.

119:139
[e] Ps 69:9;
  Jn 2:17
119:140
[f] Ps 12:6
119:141
[g] Ps 22:6
119:142
[h] Ps 19:7
119:144
[i] Ps 19:9
119:147
[j] Ps 5:3; 57:8;
  108:2
119:148
[k] Ps 63:6
119:151
[l] Ps 34:18;
145:18 [m] ver 142
119:152
[n] Lk 21:33
119:153
[o] La 5:1 [p] Pr 3:1
119:154
[q] Mic 7:9
[r] 1Sa 24:15
119:155
[s] Job 5:4
119:156
[t] 2Sa 24:14
119:157
[u] Ps 7:1
119:158
[v] Ps 139:21

שׂ   Sin and Shin

161Rulers persecute me[w] without cause,
    but my heart trembles at your word.
162I rejoice in your promise
    like one who finds great spoil.[x]
163I hate and abhor falsehood
    but I love your law.
164Seven times a day I praise you
    for your righteous laws.
165Great peace[y] have they who love your law,
    and nothing can make them stumble.
166I wait for your salvation,[z] O LORD,
    and I follow your commands.
167I obey your statutes,
    for I love them greatly.
168I obey your precepts and your statutes,
    for all my ways are known[a] to you.

ת   Taw

169May my cry come[b] before you, O LORD;
    give me understanding according to your word.
170May my supplication come[c] before you;
    deliver me[d] according to your promise.
171May my lips overflow with praise,[e]
    for you teach me[f] your decrees.
172May my tongue sing of your word,
    for all your commands are righteous.
173May your hand be ready to help[g] me,
    for I have chosen[h] your precepts.
174I long for your salvation,[i] O LORD,
    and your law is my delight.
175Let me live[j] that I may praise you,
    and may your laws sustain me.
176I have strayed like a lost sheep.[k]
    Seek your servant,
    for I have not forgotten your commands.

Psalm 120

A song of ascents.

1I call on the LORD in my distress,[l]
    and he answers me.
2Save me, O LORD, from lying lips[m]
    and from deceitful tongues.[n]

3What will he do to you,
    and what more besides, O deceitful tongue?
4He will punish you with a warrior's sharp arrows,[o]
    with burning coals of the broom tree.

119:161
w 1Sa 24:11
119:162
x 1Sa 30:16
119:165
y Pr 3:2;
Isa 26:3,12;
32:17
119:166
z Ge 49:18
119:168
a Pr 5:21
119:169
b Ps 18:6
119:170
c Ps 28:2
d Ps 31:2
119:171
e Ps 51:15
f Ps 94:12
119:173
g Ps 37:24
h Jos 24:22
119:174
i ver 166
119:175
j Isa 55:3
119:176
k Isa 53:6
120:1
l Ps 102:2;
Jnh 2:2
120:2
m Pr 12:22
n Ps 52:4
120:4
o Ps 45:5

⁵Woe to me that I dwell in Meshech,
    that I live among the tents of Kedar!ᴾ
⁶Too long have I lived
    among those who hate peace.
⁷I am a man of peace;
    but when I speak, they are for war.

Psalm 121

A song of ascents.

¹I lift up my eyes to the hills—
    where does my help come from?
²My help comes from the LORD,
    the Maker of heaven and earth. �q

³He will not let your foot slip—
    he who watches over you will not slumber;
⁴indeed, he who watches over Israel
    will neither slumber nor sleep.

⁵The LORD watches overʳ you—
    the LORD is your shade at your right hand;
⁶the sunˢ will not harm you by day,
    nor the moon by night.

⁷The LORD will keep you from all harmᵗ —
    he will watch over your life;
⁸the LORD will watch over your coming and going
    both now and forevermore. ᵘ

Psalm 122

A song of ascents. Of David.

¹I rejoiced with those who said to me,
    "Let us go to the house of the LORD."
²Our feet are standing
    in your gates, O Jerusalem.

³Jerusalem is built like a city
    that is closely compacted together.
⁴That is where the tribes go up,
    the tribes of the LORD,
 to praise the name of the LORD
    according to the statute given to Israel.
⁵There the thrones for judgment stand,
    the thrones of the house of David.

120:5
ᵖGe 25:13;
Jer 49:28
121:2
qPs 115:15;
124:8
121:5
rIsa 25:4
121:6
sPs 91:5;
Isa 49:10;
Rev 7:16
121:7
tPs 41:2;
91:10-12
121:8
uDt 28:6

⁶Pray for the peace of Jerusalem:
　　"May those who love[v] you be secure.
⁷May there be peace within your walls
　　and security within your citadels."
⁸For the sake of my brothers and friends,
　　I will say, "Peace be within you."
⁹For the sake of the house of the LORD our God,
　　I will seek your prosperity.[w]

Psalm 123

A song of ascents.

¹I lift up my eyes to you,
　　to you whose throne[x] is in heaven.
²As the eyes of slaves look to the hand of their master,
　　as the eyes of a maid look to the hand of her mistress,
so our eyes look to the LORD[y] our God,
　　till he shows us his mercy.

³Have mercy on us, O LORD, have mercy on us,
　　for we have endured much contempt.
⁴We have endured much ridicule from the proud,
　　much contempt from the arrogant.

Psalm 124

A song of ascents. Of David.

¹If the LORD had not been on our side—
　　let Israel say[z]—
²if the LORD had not been on our side
　　when men attacked us,
³when their anger flared against us,
　　they would have swallowed us alive;
⁴the flood would have engulfed us,
　　the torrent would have swept over us,
⁵the raging waters
　　would have swept us away.

⁶Praise be to the LORD,
　　who has not let us be torn by their teeth.
⁷We have escaped like a bird
　　out of the fowler's snare;[a]
the snare has been broken,
　　and we have escaped.
⁸Our help is in the name of the LORD,
　　the Maker of heaven[b] and earth.

122:6
vPs 51:18
122:9
wNe 2:10
123:1
xPs 11:4; 121:1;
141:8
123:2
yPs 25:15
124:1
zPs 129:1
124:7
aPs 91:3; Pr 6:5
124:8
bGe 1:1;
Ps 121:2; 134:3

Psalm 125

A song of ascents.

[1]Those who trust in the LORD are like Mount Zion,
   which cannot be shaken[c] but endures forever.
[2]As the mountains surround Jerusalem,
   so the LORD surrounds[d] his people
   both now and forevermore.

[3]The scepter of the wicked will not remain[e]
   over the land allotted to the righteous,
for then the righteous might use
   their hands to do evil. [f]

[4]Do good, O LORD,[g] to those who are good,
   to those who are upright in heart. [h]
[5]But those who turn[i] to crooked ways[j]
   the LORD will banish with the evildoers.

Peace be upon Israel. [k]

Psalm 126

A song of ascents.

[1]When the LORD brought back[1] the captives to[a] Zion,
   we were like men who dreamed. [b]
[2]Our mouths were filled with laughter,
   our tongues with songs of joy. [m]
Then it was said among the nations,
   "The LORD has done great things[n] for them."
[3]The LORD has done great things for us,
   and we are filled with joy. [o]

[4]Restore our fortunes,[c] O LORD,
   like streams in the Negev. [p]
[5]Those who sow in tears
   will reap with songs of joy. [q]
[6]He who goes out weeping,
   carrying seed to sow,
will return with songs of joy,
   carrying sheaves with him.

125:1
c Ps 46:5
125:2
d Ps 121:8;
Zec 2:4-5
125:3
e Ps 89:22;
Pr 22:8; Isa 14:5
f 1Sa 24:10;
Ps 55:20
125:4
g Ps 119:68
h Ps 7:10;
36:10; 94:15
125:5
i Job 23:11
j Pr 2:15;
Isa 59:8
k Ps 128:6
126:1
l Ps 85:1;
Hos 6:11
126:2
m Job 8:21;
Ps 51:14
n Ps 71:19
126:3
o Isa 25:9
126:4
p Isa 35:6; 43:19
126:5
q Isa 35:10

Psalm 127

A song of ascents. Of Solomon.

1Unless the Lord builds^r the house,
    its builders labor in vain.
Unless the Lord watches^s over the city,
    the watchmen stand guard in vain.
2In vain you rise early
    and stay up late,
toiling for food^t to eat—
    for he grants sleep^u to^a those he loves.

3Sons are a heritage from the Lord,
    children a reward^v from him.
4Like arrows in the hands of a warrior
    are sons born in one's youth.
5Blessed is the man
    whose quiver is full of them.
They will not be put to shame
    when they contend with their enemies^w in the gate.

Psalm 128

A song of ascents.

1Blessed are all who fear the Lord,^x
    who walk in his ways.^y
2You will eat the fruit of your labor;^z
    blessings and prosperity^a will be yours.
3Your wife will be like a fruitful vine^b
    within your house;
your sons will be like olive shoots^c
    around your table.
4Thus is the man blessed
    who fears the Lord.

5May the Lord bless you from Zion^d
    all the days of your life;
may you see the prosperity of Jerusalem,
6   and may you live to see your children's children.^e

Peace be upon Israel.^f

127:1
rPs 78:69
sPs 121:4
127:2
tGe 3:17
uJob 11:18
127:3
vGe 33:5
127:5
wPr 27:11
128:1
xPs 112:1
yPs 119:1-3
128:2
zIsa 3:10
aEcc 8:12
128:3
bEze 19:10
cPs 52:8; 144:12
128:5
dPs 20:2; 134:3
128:6
eGe 50:23;
Job 42:16
fPs 125:5

^a2 Or *eat—* / *for while they sleep he provides for*

Psalm 129

A song of ascents.

[1]They have greatly oppressed me from my youth[g]—
　　let Israel say[h]—
[2]they have greatly oppressed me from my youth,
　　büt they have not gained the victory[i] over me.
[3]Plowmen have plowed my back
　　and made their furrows long.
[4]But the Lord is righteous;[j]
　　he has cut me free from the cords of the wicked.

[5]May all who hate Zion[k]
　　be turned back in shame.[l]
[6]May they be like grass on the roof,
　　which withers[m] before it can grow;
[7]with it the reaper cannot fill his hands,
　　nor the one who gathers fill his arms.
[8]May those who pass by not say,
　　"The blessing of the Lord be upon you;
　　we bless you[n] in the name of the Lord."

Psalm 130

A song of ascents.

[1]Out of the depths[o] I cry to you, O Lord;
[2]　O Lord, hear my voice.[p]
Let your ears be attentive[q]
　　to my cry for mercy.

[3]If you, O Lord, kept a record of sins,
　　O Lord, who could stand?[r]
[4]But with you there is forgiveness;[s]
　　therefore you are feared.[t]

[5]I wait for the Lord,[u] my soul waits,
　　and in his word[v] I put my hope.
[6]My soul waits for the Lord
　　more than watchmen[w] wait for the morning,
　　more than watchmen wait for the morning.[x]

[7]O Israel, put your hope[y] in the Lord,
　　for with the Lord is unfailing love
　　and with him is full redemption.
[8]He himself will redeem[z] Israel
　　from all their sins.

129:1
g Ps 88:15;
Hos 2:15
h Ps 124:1
129:2
i Mt 16:18
129:4
j Ps 119:137
129:5
k Mic 4:11
l Ps 71:13
129:6
m Ps 37:2
129:8
n Ru 2:4;
Ps 118:26
130:1
o Ps 42:7; 69:2;
La 3:55
130:2
p Ps 28:2
q 2Ch 6:40;
Ps 64:1
130:3
r Ps 76:7; 143:2
130:4
s Ex 34:7;
Isa 55:7;
Jer 33:8
t 1Ki 8:40
130:5
u Ps 27:14;
33:20; Isa 8:17
v Ps 119:81
130:6
w Ps 63:6
x Ps 119:147
130:7
y Ps 131:3
130:8
z Lk 1:68

Psalm 131

A song of ascents. Of David.

¹My heart is not proud,ᵃ O L<small>ORD</small>,
  my eyes are not haughty;
I do not concern myself with great matters
  or things too wonderful for me.
²But I have stilled and quieted my soul;
  like a weaned child with its mother,
  like a weaned child is my soulᵇ within me.

³O Israel, put your hopeᶜ in the L<small>ORD</small>
  both now and forevermore.

Psalm 132

132:8–10pp — 2Ch 6:41–42

A song of ascents.

¹O L<small>ORD</small>, remember David
  and all the hardships he endured.

²He swore an oath to the L<small>ORD</small>
  and made a vow to the Mighty One of Jacob:ᵈ
³"I will not enter my house
  or go to my bed—
⁴I will allow no sleep to my eyes,
  no slumber to my eyelids,
⁵till I find a placeᵉ for the L<small>ORD</small>,
  a dwelling for the Mighty One of Jacob."

⁶We heard it in Ephrathah,ᶠ
  we came upon it in the fields of Jaarᵃ :ᵇ ᵍ
⁷"Let us go to his dwelling place;ʰ
  let us worship at his footstoolⁱ —
⁸arise, O L<small>ORD</small>,ʲ and come to your resting place,
  you and the ark of your might.
⁹May your priests be clothed with righteousness;ᵏ
  may your saints sing for joy."

¹⁰For the sake of David your servant,
  do not reject your anointed one.

¹¹The L<small>ORD</small> swore an oath to David,ˡ
  a sure oath that he will not revoke:
"One of your own descendantsᵐ

131:1
ᵃPs 101:5;
Ro 12:16
131:2
ᵇMt 18:3;
1Co 14:20
131:3
ᶜPs 130:7
132:2
ᵈGe 49:24
132:5
ᵉAc 7:46
132:6
ᶠ1Sa 17:12
ᵍ1Sa 7:2
132:7
ʰPs 5:7 ⁱPs 99:5
132:8
ʲNu 10:35;
Ps 78:61
132:9
ᵏJob 29:14;
Isa 61:3,10
132:11
ˡPs 89:3-4,35
ᵐ2Sa 7:12

ᵃ6 That is, Kiriath Jearim   ᵇ6 Or *heard of it in Ephrathah, / we found it in the fields of Jaar.* (And no
quotes around verses 7-9)

I will place on your throne—
[12]if your sons keep my covenant
 and the statutes I teach them,
then their sons will sit
 on your throne[n] for ever and ever.''

[13]For the LORD has chosen Zion,[o]
 he has desired it for his dwelling:
[14]''This is my resting place for ever and ever;[p]
 here I will sit enthroned, for I have desired it—
[15]I will bless her with abundant provisions;
 her poor will I satisfy with food.[q]
[16]I will clothe her priests[r] with salvation,
 and her saints will ever sing for joy.

[17]''Here I will make a horn[a] grow[s] for David
 and set up a lamp[t] for my anointed one.
[18]I will clothe his enemies with shame,[u]
 but the crown on his head will be resplendent.''

Psalm 133

A song of ascents. Of David.

[1]How good and pleasant it is
 when brothers live together[v] in unity!
[2]It is like precious oil poured on the head,[w]
 running down on the beard,
running down on Aaron's beard,
 down upon the collar of his robes.
[3]It is as if the dew of Hermon[x]
 were falling on Mount Zion.
For there the LORD bestows his blessing,[y]
 even life forevermore.[z]

Psalm 134

A song of ascents.

[1]Praise the LORD, all you servants[a] of the LORD
 who minister by night[b] in the house of the
  LORD.
[2]Lift up your hands[c] in the sanctuary
 and praise the LORD.

[3]May the LORD, the Maker of heaven[d] and earth,
 bless you from Zion.[e]

132:12
[n]Lk 1:32;
Ac 2:30
132:13
[o]Ps 48:1-2
132:14
[p]Ps 68:16
132:15
[q]Ps 107:9;
147:14
132:16
[r]2Ch 6:41
132:17
[s]Eze 29:21;
Lk 1:69
[t]1Ki 11:36;
2Ch 21:7
132:18
[u]Ps 35:26;
109:29
133:1
[v]Ge 13:8;
Heb 13:1
133:2
[w]Ex 30:25
133:3
[x]Dt 4:48
[y]Lev 25:21;
Dt 28:8 [z]Ps 42:8
134:1
[a]Ps 135:1-2
[b]1Ch 9:33
134:2
[c]Ps 28:2;
1Ti 2:8
134:3
[d]Ps 124:8
[e]Ps 128:5

---

[a]17 *Horn* here symbolizes strong one, that is, king.

Psalm 135

135:15-20pp — Ps 115:4-11

¹Praise the Lord. ᵃ

Praise the name of the Lord;
　praise him, you servantsᶠ of the Lord,
²you who minister in the houseᵍ of the Lord,
　in the courtsʰ of the house of our God.

³Praise the Lord, for the Lord is good;ⁱ
　sing praise to his name, for that is pleasant. ʲ
⁴For the Lord has chosen Jacobᵏ to be his own,
　Israel to be his treasured possession. ˡ

⁵I know that the Lord is great, ᵐ
　that our Lord is greater than all gods. ⁿ
⁶The Lord does whatever pleases him, ᵒ
　in the heavens and on the earth,
　in the seas and all their depths.
⁷He makes clouds rise from the ends of the earth;
　he sends lightning with the rainᵖ
　and brings out the wind�q from his storehouses. ʳ

⁸He struck down the firstbornˢ of Egypt,
　the firstborn of men and animals.
⁹He sent his signsᵗ and wonders into your midst,
　　O Egypt,
　against Pharaoh and all his servants. ᵘ
¹⁰He struck down manyᵛ nations
　and killed mighty kings—
¹¹Sihonʷ king of the Amorites,
　Og king of Bashan
　and all the kings of Canaanˣ—
¹²and he gave their land as an inheritance,ʸ
　an inheritance to his people Israel.

¹³Your name, O Lord, endures forever,ᶻ
　your renown, ᵃ O Lord, through all generations.
¹⁴For the Lord will vindicate his people
　and have compassion on his servants. ᵇ

¹⁵The idols of the nations are silver and gold,
　made by the hands of men.
¹⁶They have mouths, but cannot speak,
　eyes, but they cannot see;
¹⁷they have ears, but cannot hear,
　nor is there breath in their mouths.
¹⁸Those who make them will be like them,
　and so will all who trust in them.

¹⁹O house of Israel, praise the Lord;

ᵃ1 Hebrew *Hallelu Yah*; also in verses 3 and 21

135:1
fPs 113:1; 134:1
135:2
gLk 2:37
hPs 116:19
135:3
iPs 119:68
jPs 147:1
135:4
kDt 10:15;
1Pe 2:9
lEx 19:5; Dt 7:6
135:5
mPs 48:1
nPs 97:9
135:6
oPs 115:3
135:7
pJer 10:13;
Zec 10:1
qJob 28:25
rJob 38:22
135:8
sEx 12:12;
Ps 78:51
135:9
tDt 6:22
uPs 136:10-15
135:10
vNu 21:21-25;
Ps 136:17-21
135:11
wNu 21:21
xJos 12:7-24
135:12
yPs 78:55
135:13
zEx 3:15
aPs 102:12
135:14
bDt 32:36

O house of Aaron, praise the LORD;
20O house of Levi, praise the LORD;
   you who fear him, praise the LORD.
21Praise be to the LORD from Zion,c
   to him who dwells in Jerusalem.

Praise the LORD.

Psalm 136

1Give thanks to the LORD, for he is good. d
                    His love endures forever. e
2Give thanks to the God of gods. f
                    His love endures forever.
3Give thanks to the Lord of lords:
                    His love endures forever.

4to him who alone does great wonders, g
                    His love endures forever.
5who by his understanding h made the heavens, i
                    His love endures forever.
6who spread out the earth j upon the waters, k
                    His love endures forever.
7who made the great lights l —
                    His love endures forever.
8the sun to govern m the day,
                    His love endures forever.
9the moon and stars to govern the night;
                    His love endures forever.

10to him who struck down the firstborn n of Egypt
                    His love endures forever.
11and brought Israel out o from among them
                    His love endures forever.
12with a mighty hand and outstretched arm; p
                    His love endures forever.

13to him who divided the Red Sea a q asunder
                    His love endures forever.
14and brought Israel through r the midst of it,
                    His love endures forever.
15but swept Pharaoh and his army into the Red Sea; s
                    His love endures forever.

16to him who led his people through the desert, t
                    His love endures forever.
17who struck down great kings, u
                    His love endures forever.
18and killed mighty kings v —
                    His love endures forever.

a13 Hebrew *Yam Suph*; that is, Sea of Reeds; also in verse 15

¹⁹Sihon king of the Amorites^w

His love endures forever.

²⁰and Og king of Bashan—

His love endures forever.

²¹and gave their land^x as an inheritance,

His love endures forever.

²²an inheritance to his servant Israel;

His love endures forever.

²³to the One who remembered us^y in our low estate

His love endures forever.

²⁴and freed us from our enemies,^z

His love endures forever.

²⁵and who gives food^a to every creature.

His love endures forever.

²⁶Give thanks to the God of heaven.

His love endures forever.

Psalm 137

¹By the rivers of Babylon^b we sat and wept^c
  when we remembered Zion.
²There on the poplars
  we hung our harps,
³for there our captors asked us for songs,
  our tormentors demanded^d songs of joy;
  they said, "Sing us one of the songs of Zion!"

⁴How can we sing the songs of the LORD
  while in a foreign land?
⁵If I forget you, O Jerusalem,
  may my right hand forget its skill.
⁶May my tongue cling to the roof^e of my
    mouth
  if I do not remember you,
if I do not consider Jerusalem
  my highest joy.

⁷Remember, O LORD, what the Edomites^f did
  on the day Jerusalem fell.^g
"Tear it down," they cried,
  "tear it down to its foundations!"

⁸O Daughter of Babylon, doomed to destruction,^h
  happy is he who repays you
  for what you have done to us—
⁹he who seizes your infants
  and dashes themⁱ against the rocks.

136:19
wNu 21:21-25
136:21
xJos 12:1
136:23
yPs 113:7
136:24
zPs 107:2
136:25
aPs 104:27;
145:15
137:1
bEze 1:1,3
cNe 1:4
137:3
dPs 80:6
137:6
eEze 3:26
137:7
fJer 49:7;
La 4:21-22;
Eze 25:12
gOb 1:11
137:8
hIsa 13:1,19;
Jer 25:12,26;
Jer 50:15;
Rev 18:6
137:9
i2Ki 8:12;
Isa 13:16

Psalm 138

Of David.

[1]I will praise you, O LORD, with all my heart;
    before the "gods"[j] I will sing your praise.
[2]I will bow down toward your holy temple[k]
    and will praise your name
    for your love and your faithfulness,
  for you have exalted above all things
    your name and your word.[l]
[3]When I called, you answered me;
    you made me bold and stouthearted.[m]

[4]May all the kings of the earth[n] praise you, O LORD,
    when they hear the words of your mouth.
[5]May they sing of the ways of the LORD,
    for the glory of the LORD is great.

[6]Though the LORD is on high, he looks upon the lowly,[o]
    but the proud[p] he knows from afar.
[7]Though I walk[q] in the midst of trouble,
    you preserve my life;
  you stretch out your hand against the anger of my foes,[r]
    with your right hand[s] you save me.[t]
[8]The LORD will fulfill ˌhis purposeˌ[u] for me;
    your love, O LORD, endures forever—
    do not abandon the works of your hands.[v]

Psalm 139

For the director of music. Of David. A psalm.

[1]O LORD, you have searched me[w]
    and you know[x] me.
[2]You know when I sit and when I rise;[y]
    you perceive my thoughts[z] from afar.
[3]You discern my going out and my lying down;
    you are familiar with all my ways.[a]
[4]Before a word is on my tongue
    you know it completely,[b] O LORD.

[5]You hem me in[c]—behind and before;
    you have laid your hand upon me.
[6]Such knowledge is too wonderful for me,
    too lofty[d] for me to attain.

138:1
jPs 95:3; 96:4
138:2
k1Ki 8:29;
Ps 5:7; 28:2
lIsa 42:21
138:3
mPs 28:7
138:4
nPs 102:15
138:6
oPs 113:6;
Isa 57:15
pPr 3:34;
Jas 4:6
138:7
qPs 23:4
rJer 51:25
sPs 20:6
tPs 71:20
138:8
uPs 57:2;
Php 1:6
vJob 10:3,8;
14:15
139:1
wPs 17:3
xJer 12:3
139:2
y2Ki 19:27
zMt 9:4; Jn 2:24
139:3
aJob 31:4
139:4
bHeb 4:13
139:5
cPs 34:7
139:6
dJob 42:3;
Ro 11:33

⁷Where can I go from your Spirit?
    Where can I flee[e] from your presence?
⁸If I go up to the heavens,[f] you are there;
    if I make my bed[g] in the depths,[a] you are there.
⁹If I rise on the wings of the dawn,
    if I settle on the far side of the sea,
¹⁰even there your hand will guide me,[h]
    your right hand will hold me fast.

¹¹If I say, "Surely the darkness will hide me
    and the light become night around me,"
¹²even the darkness will not be dark[i] to you;
    the night will shine like the day,
    for darkness is as light to you.

¹³For you created my inmost being;[j]
    you knit me together[k] in my mother's womb.
¹⁴I praise you because I am fearfully and wonderfully
        made;
    your works are wonderful,[l]
    I know that full well.
¹⁵My frame was not hidden from you
    when I was made in the secret place.
When I was woven together[m] in the depths of the
        earth,[n]
16   your eyes saw my unformed body.
    All the days ordained for me
    were written in your book
    before one of them came to be.

¹⁷How precious to[b] me are your thoughts, O God![o]
    How vast is the sum of them!
¹⁸Were I to count them,
    they would outnumber the grains of sand.
    When I awake,
    I am still with you.

¹⁹If only you would slay the wicked,[p] O God!
    Away from me,[q] you bloodthirsty men!
²⁰They speak of you with evil intent;
    your adversaries misuse your name.[r]
²¹Do I not hate those[s] who hate you, O Lᴏʀᴅ,
    and abhor those who rise up against you?
²²I have nothing but hatred for them;
    I count them my enemies.

²³Search me,[t] O God, and know my heart;[u]
    test me and know my anxious thoughts.
²⁴See if there is any offensive way in me,
    and lead me[v] in the way everlasting.

139:7
e Jer 23:24;
Jnh 1:3
139:8
f Am 9:2-3
g Pr 15:11
139:10
h Ps 23:3
139:12
i Job 34:22;
Da 2:22
139:13
j Ps 119:73
k Job 10:11
139:14
l Ps 40:5
139:15
m Job 10:11
n Ps 63:9
139:17
o Ps 40:5
139:19
p Isa 11:4
q Ps 119:115
139:20
r Jude 15
139:21
s 2Ch 19:2;
Ps 31:6;
119:113;
Ps 119:158
139:23
t Job 31:6;
Ps 26:2
u Jer 11:20
139:24
v Ps 5:8;
143:10; Pr 15:9

---

a8 Hebrew Sheol   *b17 Or concerning*

Psalm 140

For the director of music. A psalm of David.

[1]Rescue me,[w] O Lord, from evil men;
  protect me from men of violence,[x]
[2]who devise evil plans[y] in their hearts
  and stir up war every day.
[3]They make their tongues as sharp as[z] a serpent's;
  the poison of vipers[a] is on their lips.   *Selah*

[4]Keep me,[b] O Lord, from the hands of the wicked;[c]
  protect me from men of violence
  who plan to trip my feet.
[5]Proud men have hidden a snare for me;
  they have spread out the cords of their net
  and have set traps[d] for me along my path.   *Selah*

[6]O Lord, I say to you, "You are my God."[e]
  Hear, O Lord, my cry for mercy.[f]
[7]O Sovereign Lord,[g] my strong deliverer,
  who shields my head in the day of battle—
[8]do not grant the wicked[h] their desires, O Lord;
  do not let their plans succeed,
  or they will become proud.   *Selah*

[9]Let the heads of those who surround me
  be covered with the trouble their lips have caused.[i]
[10]Let burning coals fall upon them;
  may they be thrown into the fire,[j]
  into miry pits, never to rise.
[11]Let slanderers not be established in the land;
  may disaster hunt down men of violence.[k]

[12]I know that the Lord secures justice for the poor
  and upholds the cause[l] of the needy.[m]
[13]Surely the righteous will praise your name[n]
  and the upright will live[o] before you.

Psalm 141

A psalm of David.

[1]O Lord, I call to you; come quickly[p] to me.
  Hear my voice[q] when I call to you.
[2]May my prayer be set before you like incense;[r]
  may the lifting up of my hands[s] be like the evening
    sacrifice.[t]

[3]Set a guard over my mouth, O Lord;
  keep watch over the door of my lips.
[4]Let not my heart be drawn to what is evil,

140:1
w Ps 17:13
x Ps 18:48
140:2
y Ps 36:4; 56:6
140:3
z Ps 57:4
a Ps 58:4;
Jas 3:8
140:4
b Ps 141:9
c Ps 71:4
140:5
d Ps 31:4; 35:7
140:6
e Ps 16:2
f Ps 116:1; 143:1
140:7
g Ps 28:8
140:8
h Ps 10:2-3
140:9
i Ps 7:16
140:10
j Ps 11:6; 21:9
140:11
k Ps 34:21
140:12
l Ps 9:4
m Ps 35:10
140:13
n Ps 97:12
o Ps 11:7
141:1
p Ps 22:19; 70:5
q Ps 143:1
141:2
r Rev 5:8; 8:3
s 1Ti 2:8
t Ex 29:39,41

to take part in wicked deeds
with men who are evildoers;
   let me not eat of their delicacies. [u]

5Let a righteous man[a] strike me—it is a kindness;
   let him rebuke me[v]—it is oil on my head. [w]
My head will not refuse it.

Yet my prayer is ever against the deeds of evildoers;
6   their rulers will be thrown down from the cliffs,
   and the wicked will learn that my words were well
      spoken.
7They will say, "As one plows and breaks up the earth,
   so our bones have been scattered at the mouth[x] of the
      grave. [b] "

8But my eyes are fixed[y] on you, O Sovereign Lord;
   in you I take refuge[z]—do not give me over to death.
9Keep me[a] from the snares they have laid for me,
   from the traps set[b] by evildoers.
10Let the wicked fall[c] into their own nets,
   while I pass by in safety.

Psalm 142

A *maskil*[c] of David. When he was in the cave. A prayer.

1I cry aloud to the Lord;
   I lift up my voice to the Lord for mercy. [d]
2I pour out my complaint[e] before him;
   before him I tell my trouble.

3When my spirit grows faint[f] within me,
   it is you who know my way.
In the path where I walk
   men have hidden a snare for me.
4Look to my right and see;
   no one is concerned for me.
I have no refuge;
   no one cares[g] for my life.

5I cry to you, O Lord;
   I say, "You are my refuge, [h]
   my portion[i] in the land of the living."[j]
6Listen to my cry, [k]
   for I am in desperate need;[l]
rescue me from those who pursue me,
   for they are too strong for me.
7Set me free from my prison, [m]
   that I may praise your name.

141:4
uPr 23:6
141:5
vPr 9:8
wPs 23:5
141:7
xPs 53:5
141:8
yPs 25:15
zPs 2:12
141:9
aPs 140:4
bPs 38:12
141:10
cPs 35:8
142:1
dPs 30:8
142:2
eIsa 26:16
142:3
fPs 140:5;
143:4,7
142:4
gPs 31:11;
Jer 30:17
142:5
hPs 46:1
iPs 16:5
jPs 27:13
142:6
kPs 17:1
lPs 79:8; 116:6
142:7
mPs 146:7

---

a5 Or *Let the Righteous One*   b7 Hebrew *Sheol*   cTitle: Probably a literary or musical term

Then the righteous will gather about me
    because of your goodness to me. [n]

Psalm 143

A psalm of David.

[1] O LORD, hear my prayer,
    listen to my cry for mercy; [o]
in your faithfulness [p] and righteousness [q]
    come to my relief.
[2] Do not bring your servant into judgment,
    for no one living is righteous [r] before you.

[3] The enemy pursues me,
    he crushes me to the ground;
he makes me dwell in darkness
    like those long dead.
[4] So my spirit grows faint within me;
    my heart within me is dismayed. [s]

[5] I remember [t] the days of long ago;
    I meditate on all your works
    and consider what your hands have done.
[6] I spread out my hands [u] to you;
    my soul thirsts for you like a parched land.   *Selah*

[7] Answer me quickly, [v] O LORD;
    my spirit fails.
Do not hide your face [w] from me
    or I will be like those who go down to the pit.
[8] Let the morning bring me word of your unfailing
        love, [x]
    for I have put my trust in you.
Show me the way [y] I should go,
    for to you I lift up my soul. [z]
[9] Rescue me from my enemies, [a] O LORD,
    for I hide myself in you.
[10] Teach me to do your will,
    for you are my God;
may your good Spirit
    lead [b] me on level ground.

[11] For your name's sake, O LORD, preserve my
        life; [c]
    in your righteousness, [d] bring me out of
        trouble.
[12] In your unfailing love, silence my enemies;
    destroy all my foes, [e]
    for I am your servant. [f]

142:7
n Ps 13:6
143:1
o Ps 140:6
p Ps 89:1-2
q Ps 71:2
143:2
r Ps 14:3;
Ecc 7:20;
Ro 3:20
143:4
s Ps 142:3
143:5
t Ps 77:6
143:6
u Ps 63:1; 88:9
143:7
v Ps 69:17
w Ps 27:9; 28:1
143:8
x Ps 46:5; 90:14
y Ps 27:11
z Ps 25:1-2
143:9
a Ps 31:15
143:10
b Ne 9:20;
Ps 23:3; 25:4-5
143:11
c Ps 119:25
d Ps 31:1
143:12
e Ps 52:5; 54:5
f Ps 116:16

Psalm 144

Of David.

¹Praise be to the LORD my Rock,[g]
  who trains my hands for war,
  my fingers for battle.
²He is my loving God and my fortress,[h]
  my stronghold and my deliverer,
 my shield,[i] in whom I take refuge,
  who subdues peoples[a] under me.

³O LORD, what is man[j] that you care for him,
  the son of man that you think of him?
⁴Man is like a breath;
  his days are like a fleeting shadow.[k]

⁵Part your heavens,[l] O LORD, and come down;
  touch the mountains, so that they smoke.[m]
⁶Send forth lightning and scatter the enemies;
  shoot your arrows[n] and rout them.
⁷Reach down your hand from on high;
  deliver me and rescue me
 from the mighty waters,[o]
  from the hands of foreigners[p]
⁸whose mouths are full of lies,[q]
  whose right hands are deceitful.

⁹I will sing a new song to you, O God;
  on the ten-stringed lyre[r] I will make music to you,
¹⁰to the One who gives victory to kings,
  who delivers his servant David[s] from the deadly
   sword.

¹¹Deliver me and rescue me
  from the hands of foreigners
 whose mouths are full of lies,
  whose right hands are deceitful.[t]

¹²Then our sons in their youth
  will be like well-nurtured plants,[u]
 and our daughters will be like pillars
  carved to adorn a palace.
¹³Our barns will be filled
  with every kind of provision.
 Our sheep will increase by thousands,
  by tens of thousands in our fields;
¹⁴ our oxen will draw heavy loads.[b]
 There will be no breaching of walls,
  no going into captivity,
  no cry of distress in our streets.

144:1
g Ps 18:2,34
144:2
h Ps 59:9; 91:2
i Ps 84:9
144:3
j Ps 8:4;
Heb 2:6
144:4
k Ps 39:11;
102:11
144:5
l Ps 18:9;
Isa 64:1
m Ps 104:32
144:6
n Ps 7:12-13;
18:14
144:7
o Ps 69:2
p Ps 18:44
144:8
q Ps 12:2
144:9
r Ps 33:2-3
144:10
s Ps 18:50
144:11
t Ps 12:2;
Isa 44:20
144:12
u Ps 128:3

---

a2 Many manuscripts of the Masoretic Text, Dead Sea Scrolls, Aquila, Jerome and Syriac; most
manuscripts of the Masoretic Text *subdues my people*   *b14 Or our chieftains will be firmly established*

[15]Blessed are the people[v] of whom this is true;
  blessed are the people whose God is the Lord.

Psalm 145[a]

A psalm of praise. Of David.

[1]I will exalt you,[w] my God the King;[x]
  I will praise your name for ever and ever.
[2]Every day I will praise[y] you
  and extol your name for ever and ever.

[3]Great is the Lord and most worthy of praise;
  his greatness no one can fathom.[z]
[4]One generation[a] will commend your works to another;
  they will tell of your mighty acts.
[5]They will speak of the glorious splendor of your
      majesty,
  and I will meditate on your wonderful works.[b][b]
[6]They will tell of the power of your awesome works,[c]
  and I will proclaim[d] your great deeds.
[7]They will celebrate your abundant goodness[e]
  and joyfully sing of your righteousness.[f]

[8]The Lord is gracious and compassionate,[g]
  slow to anger and rich in love.[h]
[9]The Lord is good[i] to all;
  he has compassion on all he has made.
[10]All you have made will praise you,[j] O Lord;
  your saints will extol you.[k]
[11]They will tell of the glory of your kingdom
  and speak of your might,
[12]so that all men may know of your mighty acts[l]
  and the glorious splendor of your kingdom.
[13]Your kingdom is an everlasting kingdom,[m]
  and your dominion endures through all generations.

  The Lord is faithful to all his promises
  and loving toward all he has made.[c]
[14]The Lord upholds[n] all those who fall
  and lifts up all[o] who are bowed down.
[15]The eyes of all look to you,
  and you give them their food[p] at the proper time.
[16]You open your hand
  and satisfy the desires[q] of every living thing.

[17]The Lord is righteous in all his ways
  and loving toward all he has made.

### Cross-references (margin)

144:15
vPs 33:12
145:1
wPs 30:1; 34:1
xPs 5:2
145:2
yPs 71:6
145:3
zJob 5:9;
Ps 147:5;
Ro 11:33
145:4
aIsa 38:19
145:5
bPs 119:27
145:6
cPs 66:3
dDt 32:3
145:7
eIsa 63:7
fPs 51:14
145:8
gPs 86:15
hEx 34:6;
Nu 14:18
145:9
iPs 100:5
145:10
jPs 19:1
kPs 68:26
145:12
lPs 105:1
145:13
m1Ti 1:17;
2Pe 1:11
145:14
nPs 37:24
oPs 146:8
145:15
pPs 104:27;
136:25
145:16
qPs 104:28

---

[a]This psalm is an acrostic poem, the verses of which (including verse 13b) begin with the successive letters of the Hebrew alphabet.   [b]5 Dead Sea Scrolls and Syriac (see also Septuagint); Masoretic Text *On the glorious splendor of your majesty / and on your wonderful works I will meditate*   [c]13 One manuscript of the Masoretic Text, Dead Sea Scrolls and Syriac (see also Septuagint); most manuscripts of the Masoretic Text do not have the last two lines of verse 13.

¹⁸The Lord is near ʳ to all who call on him, ˢ
  to all who call on him in truth.
¹⁹He fulfills the desires ᵗ of those who fear him;
  he hears their cry ᵘ and saves them.
²⁰The Lord watches over all who love him, ᵛ
  but all the wicked he will destroy. ʷ

²¹My mouth will speak ˣ in praise of the Lord.
  Let every creature ʸ praise his holy name
  for ever and ever.

Psalm 146

¹Praise the Lord. ᵃ

Praise the Lord, ᶻ O my soul.
2   I will praise the Lord all my life; ᵃ
  I will sing praise to my God as long as I live.

³Do not put your trust in princes, ᵇ
  in mortal men, ᶜ who cannot save.
⁴When their spirit departs, they return to the ground; ᵈ
  on that very day their plans come to nothing. ᵉ

⁵Blessed is he ᶠ whose help ᵍ is the God of Jacob,
  whose hope is in the Lord his God,
⁶the Maker of heaven ʰ and earth,
  the sea, and everything in them—
  the Lord, who remains faithful ⁱ forever.
⁷He upholds the cause of the oppressed ʲ
  and gives food to the hungry. ᵏ
  The Lord sets prisoners free, ˡ
8   the Lord gives sight to the blind, ᵐ
  the Lord lifts up those who are bowed down,
  the Lord loves the righteous.
⁹The Lord watches over the alien
  and sustains the fatherless and the widow, ⁿ
  but he frustrates the ways of the wicked.

¹⁰The Lord reigns ᵒ forever,
  your God, O Zion, for all generations.

Praise the Lord.

Psalm 147

¹Praise the Lord. ᵇ

How good it is to sing praises to our God,
  how pleasant ᵖ and fitting to praise him! �q

ᵃ1 Hebrew *Hallelu Yah*; also in verse 10   ᵇ1 Hebrew *Hallelu Yah*; also in verse 20

145:18
r Dt 4:7 s Jn 4:24
145:19
t Ps 37:4
u Pr 15:29
145:20
v Ps 31:23;
97:10 w Ps 9:5
145:21
x Ps 71:8
y Ps 65:2
146:1
z Ps 103:1
146:2
a Ps 104:33
146:3
b Ps 118:9
c Isa 2:22
146:4
d Ps 104:29;
Ecc 12:7
e Ps 33:10;
1Co 2:6
146:5
f Ps 144:15;
Jer 17:7
g Ps 71:5
146:6
h Ps 115:15;
Ac 14:15;
Rev 14:7
i Ps 117:2
146:7
j Ps 103:6
k Ps 107:9
l Ps 68:6
146:8
m Mt 9:30
146:9
n Ex 22:22;
Dt 10:18;
Ps 68:5
146:10
o Ex 15:18;
Ps 10:16
147:1
p Ps 135:3
q Ps 33:1

²The Lord builds up Jerusalem;ʳ
  he gathers the exilesˢ of Israel.
³He heals the brokenhearted
  and binds up their wounds.

⁴He determines the number of the starsᵗ
  and calls them each by name.
⁵Great is our Lordᵘ and mighty in power;
  his understanding has no limit. ᵛ
⁶The Lord sustains the humbleʷ
  but casts the wicked to the ground.

⁷Sing to the Lordˣ with thanksgiving;
  make music to our God on the harp.
⁸He covers the sky with clouds;
  he supplies the earth with rainʸ
  and makes grass growᶻ on the hills.
⁹He provides foodᵃ for the cattle
  and for the young ravensᵇ when they call.

¹⁰His pleasure is not in the strengthᶜ of the
  horse, ᵈ
  nor his delight in the legs of a man;
¹¹the Lord delights in those who fear him,
  who put their hope in his unfailing love.

¹²Extol the Lord, O Jerusalem;
  praise your God, O Zion,
¹³for he strengthens the bars of your gates
  and blesses your people within you.
¹⁴He grants peaceᵉ to your borders
  and satisfies youᶠ with the finest of
  wheat.

¹⁵He sends his commandᵍ to the earth;
  his word runs swiftly.
¹⁶He spreads the snowʰ like wool
  and scatters the frostⁱ like ashes.
¹⁷He hurls down his hail like pebbles.
  Who can withstand his icy blast?
¹⁸He sends his wordʲ and melts them;
  he stirs up his breezes, and the waters
  flow.

¹⁹He has revealed his word to Jacob,
  his laws and decreesᵏ to Israel.
²⁰He has done this for no other nation;ˡ
  they do not know his laws.

Praise the Lord.

147:2
ʳPs 102:16
ˢDt 30:3
147:4
ᵗIsa 40:26
147:5
ᵘPs 48:1
ᵛIsa 40:28
147:6
ʷPs 146:8-9
147:7
ˣPs 33:3
147:8
ʸJob 38:26
ᶻPs 104:14
147:9
ᵃPs 104:27-28;
Mt 6:26
ᵇJob 38:41
147:10
ᶜ1Sa 16:7
ᵈPs 33:16-17
147:14
ᵉIsa 60:17-18
ᶠPs 132:15
147:15
ᵍJob 37:12
147:16
ʰJob 37:6
ⁱJob 38:29
147:18
ʲPs 33:9
147:19
ᵏDt 33:4;
Mal 4:4
147:20
ˡDt 4:7-8,32-34

Psalm 148

[1]Praise the Lord.[a]

Praise the Lord from the heavens,
    praise him in the heights above.
[2]Praise him, all his angels,[m]
    praise him, all his heavenly hosts.
[3]Praise him, sun and moon,
    praise him, all you shining stars.
[4]Praise him, you highest heavens
    and you waters above the skies.[n]
[5]Let them praise the name of the Lord,
    for he commanded[o] and they were created.
[6]He set them in place for ever and ever;
    he gave a decree[p] that will never pass away.

[7]Praise the Lord from the earth,
    you great sea creatures[q] and all ocean depths,
[8]lightning and hail, snow and clouds,
    stormy winds that do his bidding,[r]
[9]you mountains and all hills,[s]
    fruit trees and all cedars,
[10]wild animals and all cattle,
    small creatures and flying birds,
[11]kings of the earth and all nations,
    you princes and all rulers on earth,
[12]young men and maidens,
    old men and children.

[13]Let them praise the name of the Lord,[t]
    for his name alone is exalted;
    his splendor is above the earth and the heavens.[u]
[14]He has raised up for his people a horn,[b][v]
    the praise of all his saints,
    of Israel, the people close to his heart.

    Praise the Lord.

Psalm 149

[1]Praise the Lord.[c][w]

Sing to the Lord a new song,
    his praise in the assembly[x] of the saints.

[2]Let Israel rejoice in their Maker;[y]
    let the people of Zion be glad in their King.[z]
[3]Let them praise his name with dancing
    and make music to him with tambourine and harp.[a]

148:2
m Ps 103:20
148:4
n Ge 1:7;
1Ki 8:27
148:5
o Ge 1:1,6;
Ps 33:6,9
148:6
p Job 38:33;
Ps 89:37;
Jer 33:25
148:7
q Ps 74:13-14
148:8
r Ps 147:15-18
148:9
s Isa 44:23;
49:13; 55:12
148:13
t Isa 12:4
u Ps 8:1; 113:4
148:14
v Ps 75:10
149:1
w Ps 33:2
x Ps 35:18
149:2
y Ps 95:6
z Ps 47:6;
Zec 9:9
149:3
a Ps 81:2; 150:4

---

a1 Hebrew *Hallelu Yah*; also in verse 14   b14 *Horn* here symbolizes strong one, that is, king.
c1 Hebrew *Hallelu Yah*; also in verse 9

4For the LORD takes delight[b] in his people;
  he crowns the humble with salvation.[c]
5Let the saints rejoice[d] in this honor
  and sing for joy on their beds.[e]

6May the praise of God be in their mouths[f]
  and a double-edged[g] sword in their hands,
7to inflict vengeance on the nations
  and punishment on the peoples,
8to bind their kings with fetters,
  their nobles with shackles of iron,
9to carry out the sentence written against them.[h]
  This is the glory of all his saints.[i]

Praise the LORD.

Psalm 150

1Praise the LORD.[a]

Praise God in his sanctuary;[j]
  praise him in his mighty heavens.[k]
2Praise him for his acts of power;[l]
  praise him for his surpassing greatness.[m]
3Praise him with the sounding of the trumpet,
  praise him with the harp and lyre,[n]
4praise him with tambourine and dancing,[o]
  praise him with the strings[p] and flute,
5praise him with the clash of cymbals,[q]
  praise him with resounding cymbals.

6Let everything[r] that has breath praise the LORD.

Praise the LORD.

---

[a]1 Hebrew *Hallelu Yah*; also in verse 6

Proverbs

Title and Background

The Hebrew word translated "proverb" is also translated "taunt" (Isa 14:4), "oracle" (Nu 23:7,18) and "parable" (Eze 17:2), so its meaning is considerably broader than the English term. Most proverbs are short, compact statements that express a truth about human behavior. A common feature of the proverbs is the use of figurative language.

Author and Date of Writing

Although the book begins with a title ascribing the proverbs to Solomon, it is clear from later chapters that he was not the only author of the book (see Outline). Since Solomon has a prominent role in the book, most of Proverbs would stem from the tenth century B.C. and Israel's united kingdom.

Theme and Message

According to the prologue (1:1-7), Proverbs was written to give "prudence to the simple, knowledge and discretion to the young" (1:4), and to make wise men wiser (1:5). Acquiring wisdom and knowing how to avoid the pitfalls of folly will lead to health and success. Although Proverbs is a practical book dealing with the art of living, it bases wisdom solidly on the fear of the Lord (1:7).

Outline

Prologue: Purpose and Theme

1 The proverbs of Solomon[a] son of David, king of Israel:[b]

>²for attaining wisdom and discipline;
>for understanding words of insight;
>³for acquiring a disciplined and prudent life,
>doing what is right and just and fair;
>⁴for giving prudence to the simple,[c]
>knowledge and discretion[d] to the young—
>⁵let the wise listen and add to their learning,[e]
>and let the discerning get guidance—
>⁶for understanding proverbs and parables,[f]
>the sayings and riddles[g] of the wise.

1:1
a 1Ki 4:29-34
b Pr 10:1; 25:1;
Ecc 1:1

1:4
c Pr 8:5
d Pr 2:10-11;
8:12

1:5
e Pr 9:9

1:6
f Ps 49:4; 78:2
g Nu 12:8

7The fear of the LORD[h] is the beginning of knowledge,
　　but fools[a] despise wisdom and discipline.

Exhortations to Embrace Wisdom

Warning Against Enticement

8Listen, my son,[i] to your father's instruction
　　and do not forsake your mother's teaching.[j]
9They will be a garland to grace your head
　　and a chain to adorn your neck.[k]

10My son, if sinners entice[l] you,
　　do not give in[m] to them.[n]
11If they say, "Come along with us;
　　let's lie in wait[o] for someone's blood,
　　let's waylay some harmless soul;
12let's swallow them alive, like the grave,[b]
　　and whole, like those who go down to the pit;[p]
13we will get all sorts of valuable things
　　and fill our houses with plunder;
14throw in your lot with us,
　　and we will share a common purse"—
15my son, do not go along with them,
　　do not set foot[q] on their paths;[r]
16for their feet rush into sin,
　　they are swift to shed blood.[s]
17How useless to spread a net
　　in full view of all the birds!
18These men lie in wait for their own blood;
　　they waylay only themselves!
19Such is the end of all who go after ill-gotten gain;
　　it takes away the lives of those who get it.[t]

Warning Against Rejecting Wisdom

20Wisdom calls aloud[u] in the street,
　　she raises her voice in the public squares;
21at the head of the noisy streets[c] she cries out,
　　in the gateways of the city she makes her speech:

22"How long will you simple ones[d][v] love your simple
　　　　ways?
　　How long will mockers delight in mockery
　　and fools hate knowledge?
23If you had responded to my rebuke,
　　I would have poured out my heart to you
　　and made my thoughts known to you.
24But since you rejected me when I called[w]
　　and no one gave heed when I stretched out my hand,

1:7
hJob 28:28;
Ps 111:10;
Pr 9:10; 15:33;
Ecc 12:13
1:8
iPr 4:1 jPr 6:20
1:9
kPr 4:1-9
1:10
lGe 39:7
mDt 13:8
nPr 16:29;
Eph 5:11
1:11
oPs 10:8
1:12
pPs 28:1
1:15
qPs 119:101
rPs 1:1; Pr 4:14
1:16
sPr 6:18;
Isa 59:7
1:19
tPr 15:27
1:20
uPr 8:1; 9:1-3,
13-15
1:22
vPr 8:5; 9:4,16
1:24
wIsa 65:12;
66:4; Jer 7:13;
Zec 7:11

---

a7 The Hebrew words rendered *fool* in Proverbs, and often elsewhere in the Old Testament, denote one who is morally deficient.   *b12* Hebrew *Sheol*   *c21* Hebrew; Septuagint / *on the tops of the walls*   *d22* The Hebrew word rendered *simple* in Proverbs generally denotes one without moral direction and inclined to evil.

[25]since you ignored all my advice
    and would not accept my rebuke,
[26]I in turn will laugh[x] at your disaster;
    I will mock when calamity overtakes you[y]—
[27]when calamity overtakes you like a storm,
    when disaster sweeps over you like a whirlwind,
    when distress and trouble overwhelm you.

[28]"Then they will call to me but I will not answer;[z]
    they will look for me but will not find me.[a]
[29]Since they hated knowledge
    and did not choose to fear the LORD,[b]
[30]since they would not accept my advice
    and spurned my rebuke,[c]
[31]they will eat the fruit of their ways
    and be filled with the fruit of their schemes.[d]
[32]For the waywardness of the simple will kill them,
    and the complacency of fools will destroy them;[e]
[33]but whoever listens to me will live in safety[f]
    and be at ease, without fear of harm."[g]

Moral Benefits of Wisdom

2   My son, if you accept my words
      and store up my commands within you,
[2]turning your ear to wisdom
    and applying your heart to understanding,[h]
[3]and if you call out for insight
    and cry aloud for understanding,
[4]and if you look for it as for silver
    and search for it as for hidden treasure,[i]
[5]then you will understand the fear of the LORD
    and find the knowledge of God.[j]
[6]For the LORD gives wisdom,[k]
    and from his mouth come knowledge and
      understanding.
[7]He holds victory in store for the upright,
    he is a shield[l] to those whose walk is blameless,[m]
[8]for he guards the course of the just
    and protects the way of his faithful ones.[n]

[9]Then you will understand what is right and just
    and fair—every good path.
[10]For wisdom will enter your heart,[o]
    and knowledge will be pleasant to your soul.
[11]Discretion will protect you,
    and understanding will guard you.[p]

[12]Wisdom will save you from the ways of wicked men,
    from men whose words are perverse,
[13]who leave the straight paths
    to walk in dark ways,[q]
[14]who delight in doing wrong
    and rejoice in the perverseness of evil,[r]

1:26
x Ps 2:4
y Pr 6:15; 10:24

1:28
z 1Sa 8:18;
Isa 1:15;
Jer 11:11;
Mic 3:4
a Job 27:9;
Pr 8:17;
Eze 8:18;
Zec 7:13

1:29
b Job 21:14

1:30
c ver 25;
Ps 81:11

1:31
d Job 4:8;
Pr 14:14;
Isa 3:11;
Jer 6:19

1:32
e Jer 2:19

1:33
f Ps 25:12;
Pr 3:23
g Ps 112:8

2:2
h Pr 22:17

2:4
i Job 3:21;
Pr 3:14;
Mt 13:44

2:5
j Pr 1:7

2:6
k 1Ki 3:9,12;
Jas 1:5

2:7
l Pr 30:5-6
m Ps 84:11

2:8
n 1Sa 2:9;
Ps 66:9

2:10
o Pr 14:33

2:11
p Pr 4:6; 6:22

2:13
q Pr 4:19;
Jn 3:19

2:14
r Pr 10:23;
Jer 11:15

¹⁵whose paths are crooked^s
and who are devious in their ways.^t

¹⁶It will save you also from the adulteress,^u
from the wayward wife with her seductive words,
¹⁷who has left the partner of her youth
and ignored the covenant she made before God.^{a v}
¹⁸For her house leads down to death
and her paths to the spirits of the dead.^w
¹⁹None who go to her return
or attain the paths of life.^x

²⁰Thus you will walk in the ways of good men
and keep to the paths of the righteous.
²¹For the upright will live in the land,^y
and the blameless will remain in it;
²²but the wicked will be cut off from the land,^z
and the unfaithful will be torn from it.^a

Further Benefits of Wisdom

3 My son, do not forget my teaching,^b
but keep my commands in your heart,
²for they will prolong your life many years^c
and bring you prosperity.

³Let love and faithfulness never leave you;
bind them around your neck,
write them on the tablet of your heart.^d
⁴Then you will win favor and a good name
in the sight of God and man.^e

⁵Trust in the Lord^f with all your heart
and lean not on your own understanding;
⁶in all your ways acknowledge him,
and he will make your paths^g straight.^{b h}

⁷Do not be wise in your own eyes;ⁱ
fear the Lord and shun evil.^j
⁸This will bring health to your body^k
and nourishment to your bones.^l

⁹Honor the Lord with your wealth,
with the firstfruits^m of all your crops;
¹⁰then your barns will be filledⁿ to overflowing,
and your vats will brim over with new wine.^o

¹¹My son, do not despise the Lord's discipline^p
and do not resent his rebuke,
¹²because the Lord disciplines those he loves,^q
as a father^c the son he delights in.^r

¹³Blessed is the man who finds wisdom,
the man who gains understanding,

2:15
sPs 125:5
tPr 21:8
2:16
uPr 5:1-6;
6:20-29; 7:5-27
2:17
vMal 2:14
2:18
wPr 7:27
2:19
xEcc 7:26
2:21
yPs 37:29
2:22
zJob 18:17;
Ps 37:38
aDt 28:63;
Pr 10:30
3:1
bPr 4:5
3:2
cPr 4:10
3:3
dEx 13:9;
Pr 6:21; 7:3;
2Co 3:3
3:4
e1Sa 2:26;
Lk 2:52
3:5
fPs 37:3,5
3:6
g1Ch 28:9
hPr 16:3;
Isa 45:13
3:7
iRo 12:16
jJob 1:1;
Pr 16:6
3:8
kPr 4:22
lJob 21:24
3:9
mEx 22:29;
23:19;
Dt 26:1-15
3:10
nDt 28:8
oJoel 2:24
3:11
pJob 5:17
3:12
qPr 13:24;
Rev 3:19
rDt 8:5;
Heb 12:5-6*

---

a17 Or covenant of her God *b6 Or will direct your paths* *c12 Hebrew; Septuagint / and he punishes*

[14]for she is more profitable than silver
  and yields better returns than gold. [s]
[15]She is more precious than rubies; [t]
  nothing you desire can compare with her. [u]
[16]Long life is in her right hand;
  in her left hand are riches and honor. [v]
[17]Her ways are pleasant ways,
  and all her paths are peace. [w]
[18]She is a tree of life [x] to those who embrace her;
  those who lay hold of her will be blessed.

[19]By wisdom the LORD laid the earth's foundations, [y]
  by understanding he set the heavens [z] in place;
[20]by his knowledge the deeps were divided,
  and the clouds let drop the dew.

[21]My son, preserve sound judgment and discernment,
  do not let them out of your sight; [a]
[22]they will be life for you,
  an ornament to grace your neck. [b]
[23]Then you will go on your way in safety,
  and your foot will not stumble; [c]
[24]when you lie down, [d] you will not be afraid;
  when you lie down, your sleep [e] will be sweet.
[25]Have no fear of sudden disaster
  or of the ruin that overtakes the wicked,
[26]for the LORD will be your confidence
  and will keep your foot [f] from being snared.

[27]Do not withhold good from those who deserve it,
  when it is in your power to act.
[28]Do not say to your neighbor,
  "Come back later; I'll give it tomorrow"—
  when you now have it with you. [g]

[29]Do not plot harm against your neighbor,
  who lives trustfully near you.
[30]Do not accuse a man for no reason—
  when he has done you no harm.

[31]Do not envy [h] a violent man
  or choose any of his ways,
[32]for the LORD detests a perverse man [i]
  but takes the upright into his confidence. [j]

[33]The LORD's curse [k] is on the house of the wicked, [l]
  but he blesses the home of the righteous. [m]
[34]He mocks proud mockers
  but gives grace to the humble. [n]
[35]The wise inherit honor,
  but fools he holds up to shame.

3:14
s Job 28:15;
Pr 8:19; 16:16
3:15
t Job 28:18
u Pr 8:11
3:16
v Pr 8:18
3:17
w Pr 16:7;
Mt 11:28-30
3:18
x Ge 2:9;
Pr 11:30;
Rev 2:7
3:19
y Ps 104:24
z Pr 8:27-29
3:21
a Pr 4:20-22
3:22
b Pr 1:8-9
3:23
c Ps 37:24;
Pr 4:12
3:24
d Lev 26:6;
Ps 3:5
e Job 11:18
3:26
f 1Sa 2:9
3:28
g Lev 19:13;
Dt 24:15
3:31
h Ps 37:1;
Pr 24:1-2
3:32
i Pr 11:20
j Job 29:4;
Ps 25:14
3:33
k Dt 11:28;
Mal 2:2
l Zec 5:4
m Ps 1:3
3:34
n Jas 4:6*;
1Pe 5:5*

Wisdom Is Supreme

4 Listen, my sons,[o] to a father's instruction;
    pay attention and gain understanding.
[2]I give you sound learning,
    so do not forsake my teaching.
[3]When I was a boy in my father's house,
    still tender, and an only child of my mother,
[4]he taught me and said,
    "Lay hold of my words with all your heart;
    keep my commands and you will live.[p]
[5]Get wisdom,[q] get understanding;
    do not forget my words or swerve from them.
[6]Do not forsake wisdom, and she will protect you;[r]
    love her, and she will watch over you.
[7]Wisdom is supreme; therefore get wisdom.
    Though it cost all[s] you have,[a] get understanding.[t]
[8]Esteem her, and she will exalt you;
    embrace her, and she will honor you.[u]
[9]She will set a garland of grace on your head
    and present you with a crown of splendor.[v]"

[10]Listen, my son, accept what I say,
    and the years of your life will be many.[w]
[11]I guide[x] you in the way of wisdom
    and lead you along straight paths.
[12]When you walk, your steps will not be hampered;
    when you run, you will not stumble.[y]
[13]Hold on to instruction, do not let it go;
    guard it well, for it is your life.[z]
[14]Do not set foot on the path of the wicked
    or walk in the way of evil men.[a]
[15]Avoid it, do not travel on it;
    turn from it and go on your way.
[16]For they cannot sleep till they do evil;[b]
    they are robbed of slumber till they make someone
      fall.
[17]They eat the bread of wickedness
    and drink the wine of violence.

[18]The path of the righteous[c] is like the first gleam of
      dawn,
    shining ever brighter till the full light of day.[d]
[19]But the way of the wicked is like deep darkness;[e]
    they do not know what makes them stumble.

[20]My son, pay attention to what I say;
    listen closely to my words.[f]
[21]Do not let them out of your sight,[g]
    keep them within your heart;
[22]for they are life to those who find them
    and health to a man's whole body.[h]

4:1
oPr 1:8
4:4
pPr 7:2
4:5
qPr 16:16
4:6
r2Th 2:10
4:7
sMt 13:44-46
tPr 23:23
4:8
u1Sa 2:30;
Pr 3:18
4:9
vPr 1:8-9
4:10
wPr 3:2
4:11
x1Sa 12:23
4:12
yJob 18:7;
Pr 3:23
4:13
zPr 3:22
4:14
aPs 1:1; Pr 1:15
4:16
bPs 36:4;
Mic 2:1
4:18
cIsa 26:7
d2Sa 23:4;
Da 12:3;
Mt 5:14;
Php 2:15
4:19
eJob 18:5;
Pr 2:13;
Isa 59:9-10;
Jn 12:35
4:20
fPr 5:1
4:21
gPr 3:21; 7:1-2
4:22
hPr 3:8; 12:18

---

[a]7 Or *Whatever else you get*

²³Above all else, guard your heart,
  for it is the wellspring of life. ⁱ
²⁴Put away perversity from your mouth;
  keep corrupt talk far from your lips.
²⁵Let your eyes look straight ahead,
  fix your gaze directly before you.
²⁶Make level ᵃ paths for your feet ʲ
  and take only ways that are firm.
²⁷Do not swerve to the right or the left; ᵏ
  keep your foot from evil.

Warning Against Adultery

5 My son, pay attention to my wisdom,
  listen well to my words ˡ of insight,
²that you may maintain discretion
  and your lips may preserve knowledge.
³For the lips of an adulteress drip honey,
  and her speech is smoother than oil; ᵐ
⁴but in the end she is bitter as gall, ⁿ
  sharp as a double-edged sword.
⁵Her feet go down to death;
  her steps lead straight to the grave. ᵇ ᵒ
⁶She gives no thought to the way of life;
  her paths are crooked, but she knows it not. ᵖ

⁷Now then, my sons, listen �q to me;
  do not turn aside from what I say.
⁸Keep to a path far from her, ʳ
  do not go near the door of her house,
⁹lest you give your best strength to others
  and your years to one who is cruel,
¹⁰lest strangers feast on your wealth
  and your toil enrich another man's house.
¹¹At the end of your life you will groan,
  when your flesh and body are spent.
¹²You will say, "How I hated discipline!
  How my heart spurned correction! ˢ
¹³I would not obey my teachers
  or listen to my instructors.
¹⁴I have come to the brink of utter ruin
  in the midst of the whole assembly."

¹⁵Drink water from your own cistern,
  running water from your own well.
¹⁶Should your springs overflow in the streets,
  your streams of water in the public squares?
¹⁷Let them be yours alone,
  never to be shared with strangers.
¹⁸May your fountain ᵗ be blessed,
  and may you rejoice in the wife of your youth. ᵘ
¹⁹A loving doe, a graceful deer ᵛ —

4:23
ⁱMt 12:34;
Lk 6:45
4:26
ʲHeb 12:13*
4:27
ᵏDt 5:32; 28:14
5:1
ˡPr 4:20; 22:17
5:3
ᵐPs 55:21;
Pr 2:16; 7:5
5:4
ⁿEcc 7:26
5:5
ᵒPr 7:26-27
5:6
ᵖPr 30:20
5:7
qPr 7:24
5:8
ʳPr 7:1-27
5:12
ˢPr 1:29; 12:1
5:18
ᵗSS 4:12-15
ᵘEcc 9:9;
Mal 2:14
5:19
ᵛSS 2:9; 4:5

ᵃ26 Or *Consider the*   ᵇ5 Hebrew *Sheol*

may her breasts satisfy you always,
    may you ever be captivated by her love.
20Why be captivated, my son, by an adulteress?
    Why embrace the bosom of another man's wife?

21For a man's ways are in full view[w] of the LORD,
    and he examines all his paths.[x]
22The evil deeds of a wicked man ensnare him;[y]
    the cords of his sin hold him fast.[z]
23He will die for lack of discipline,[a]
    led astray by his own great folly.

Warnings Against Folly

6 My son, if you have put up security for your neighbor,[b]
    if you have struck hands in pledge[c] for another,
2if you have been trapped by what you said,
    ensnared by the words of your mouth,
3then do this, my son, to free yourself,
    since you have fallen into your neighbor's hands:
Go and humble yourself;
    press your plea with your neighbor!
4Allow no sleep to your eyes,
    no slumber to your eyelids.[d]
5Free yourself, like a gazelle from the hand of the hunter,
    like a bird from the snare of the fowler.[e]

6Go to the ant, you sluggard;[f]
    consider its ways and be wise!
7It has no commander,
    no overseer or ruler,
8yet it stores its provisions in summer
    and gathers its food at harvest.[g]

9How long will you lie there, you sluggard?[h]
    When will you get up from your sleep?
10A little sleep, a little slumber,
    a little folding of the hands to rest[i] —
11and poverty[j] will come on you like a bandit
    and scarcity like an armed man.[a]

12A scoundrel and villain,
    who goes about with a corrupt mouth,
13 who winks with his eye,[k]
signals with his feet
and motions with his fingers,
14 who plots evil[l] with deceit in his heart—
    he always stirs up dissension.[m]
15Therefore disaster will overtake him in an instant;
    he will suddenly be destroyed—without remedy.[n]

16There are six things the LORD hates,
    seven that are detestable to him:

<hr>

a11 Or *like a vagrant / and scarcity like a beggar*

5:21
w Ps 119:168;
  Hos 7:2
x Job 14:16;
  Job 31:4;
  34:21; Pr 15:3;
  Jer 16:17;
  32:19; Heb 4:13
5:22
y Ps 9:16
z Nu 32:23;
  Ps 7:15-16;
  Pr 1:31-32
5:23
a Job 4:21;
  36:12
6:1
b Pr 17:18
c Pr 11:15;
  22:26-27
6:4
d Ps 132:4
6:5
e Ps 91:3
6:6
f Pr 20:4
6:8
g Pr 10:4
6:9
h Pr 24:30-34
6:10
i Pr 24:33
6:11
j Pr 24:30-34
6:13
k Ps 35:19
6:14
l Mic 2:1
m ver 16-19
6:15
n 2Ch 36:16

17   haughty eyes,
      a lying tongue,°
      hands that shed innocent blood,ᵖ
18   a heart that devises wicked schemes,
      feet that are quick to rush into evil,�q
19   a false witnessʳ who pours out lies
      and a man who stirs up dissension among
            brothers.ˢ

Warning Against Adultery

²⁰My son, keep your father's commands
      and do not forsake your mother's teaching.ᵗ
²¹Bind them upon your heart forever;
      fasten them around your neck.ᵘ
²²When you walk, they will guide you;
      when you sleep, they will watch over you;
      when you awake, they will speak to you.
²³For these commands are a lamp,
      this teaching is a light,ᵛ
   and the corrections of discipline
      are the way to life,
²⁴keeping you from the immoral woman,
      from the smooth tongue of the wayward wife.ʷ
²⁵Do not lust in your heart after her beauty
      or let her captivate you with her eyes,
²⁶for the prostitute reduces you to a loaf of bread,
      and the adulteress preys upon your very life.ˣ
²⁷Can a man scoop fire into his lap
      without his clothes being burned?
²⁸Can a man walk on hot coals
      without his feet being scorched?
²⁹So is he who sleepsʸ with another man's wife;ᶻ
      no one who touches her will go unpunished.

³⁰Men do not despise a thief if he steals
      to satisfy his hunger when he is starving.
³¹Yet if he is caught, he must pay sevenfold,ᵃ
      though it costs him all the wealth of his house.
³²But a man who commits adulteryᵇ lacks judgment;ᶜ
      whoever does so destroys himself.
³³Blows and disgrace are his lot,
      and his shame will neverᵈ be wiped away;
³⁴for jealousyᵉ arouses a husband's fury,ᶠ
      and he will show no mercy when he takes revenge.
³⁵He will not accept any compensation;
      he will refuse the bribe, however great it is.ᵍ

Warning Against the Adulteress

7   My son,ʰ keep my words
      and store up my commands within you.
   ²Keep my commands and you will live;ⁱ
      guard my teachings as the apple of your eye.

6:17
oPs 120:2;
Pr 12:22
pDt 19:10;
Isa 1:15; 59:7
6:18
qGe 6:5
6:19
rPs 27:12
sver 12-15
6:20
tPr 1:8
6:21
uPr 3:3; 7:1-3
6:23
vPs 19:8;
119:105
6:24
wPr 2:16; 7:5
6:26
xPr 7:22-23;
29:3
6:29
yEx 20:14
zPr 2:16-19; 5:8
6:31
aEx 22:1-14
6:32
bEx 20:14
cPr 7:7; 9:4,16
6:33
dPr 5:9-14
6:34
eNu 5:14
fGe 34:7
6:35
gJob 31:9-11;
SS 8:7
7:1
hPr 1:8; 2:1
7:2
iPr 4:4

³Bind them on your fingers;
 write them on the tablet of your heart.[j]
⁴Say to wisdom, "You are my sister,"
 and call understanding your kinsman;
⁵they will keep you from the adulteress,
 from the wayward wife with her seductive words.[k]

⁶At the window of my house
 I looked out through the lattice.
⁷I saw among the simple,
 I noticed among the young men,
 a youth who lacked judgment.[l]
⁸He was going down the street near her corner,
 walking along in the direction of her house
⁹at twilight,[m] as the day was fading,
 as the dark of night set in.

¹⁰Then out came a woman to meet him,
 dressed like a prostitute and with crafty intent.
¹¹(She is loud[n] and defiant,
 her feet never stay at home;
¹²now in the street, now in the squares,
 at every corner she lurks.)[o]
¹³She took hold of him[p] and kissed him
 and with a brazen face she said:[q]

¹⁴"I have fellowship offerings[a][r] at home;
 today I fulfilled my vows.
¹⁵So I came out to meet you;
 I looked for you and have found you!
¹⁶I have covered my bed
 with colored linens from Egypt.
¹⁷I have perfumed my bed[s]
 with myrrh,[t] aloes and cinnamon.
¹⁸Come, let's drink deep of love till morning;
 let's enjoy ourselves with love![u]
¹⁹My husband is not at home;
 he has gone on a long journey.
²⁰He took his purse filled with money
 and will not be home till full moon."

²¹With persuasive words she led him astray;
 she seduced him with her smooth talk.[v]
²²All at once he followed her
 like an ox going to the slaughter,
 like a deer[b] stepping into a noose[c][w]
²³ till an arrow pierces[x] his liver,
 like a bird darting into a snare,
 little knowing it will cost him his life.[y]

²⁴Now then, my sons, listen[z] to me;

7:3
jDt 6:8; Pr 3:3
7:5
kver 21;
Job 31:9;
Pr 2:16; 6:24
7:7
lPr 1:22; 6:32
7:9
mJob 24:15
7:11
nPr 9:13;
1Ti 5:13
7:12
oPr 8:1-36;
23:26-28
7:13
pGe 39:12
qPr 1:20
7:14
rLev 7:11-18
7:17
sEst 1:6;
Isa 57:7;
Eze 23:41;
Am 6:4
tGe 37:25
7:18
uGe 39:7
7:21
vPr 5:3
7:22
wJob 18:10
7:23
xJob 15:22;
16:13 yPr 6:26;
Ecc 7:26; 9:12
7:24
zPr 1:8-9; 5:7;
8:32

---

[a]14 Traditionally *peace offerings* [b]22 Syriac (see also Septuagint); Hebrew *fool* [c]22 The meaning of the Hebrew for this line is uncertain.

      pay attention to what I say.

25Do not let your heart turn to her ways
    or stray into her paths. [a]
26Many are the victims she has brought down;
    her slain are a mighty throng.
27Her house is a highway to the grave, [a]
    leading down to the chambers of death. [b]

Wisdom's Call

8   Does not wisdom call out? [c]
    Does not understanding raise her voice?
2On the heights along the way,
    where the paths meet, she takes her stand;
3beside the gates leading into the city,
    at the entrances, she cries aloud: [d]
4"To you, O men, I call out;
    I raise my voice to all mankind.
5You who are simple, [e] gain prudence; [f]
    you who are foolish, gain understanding.
6Listen, for I have worthy things to say;
    I open my lips to speak what is right.
7My mouth speaks what is true, [g]
    for my lips detest wickedness.
8All the words of my mouth are just;
    none of them is crooked or perverse.
9To the discerning all of them are right;
    they are faultless to those who have knowledge.
10Choose my instruction instead of silver,
    knowledge rather than choice gold, [h]
11for wisdom is more precious [i] than rubies,
    and nothing you desire can compare with her. [j]

12"I, wisdom, dwell together with prudence;
    I possess knowledge and discretion. [k]
13To fear the LORD is to hate evil; [l]
    I hate [m] pride and arrogance,
    evil behavior and perverse speech.
14Counsel and sound judgment are mine;
    I have understanding and power. [n]
15By me kings reign
    and rulers [o] make laws that are just;
16by me princes govern,
    and all nobles who rule on earth. [b]
17I love those who love me, [p]
    and those who seek me find me. [q]
18With me are riches and honor, [r]
    enduring wealth and prosperity. [s]
19My fruit is better than fine gold;
    what I yield surpasses choice silver. [t]

7:25
a Pr 5:7-8
7:27
b Pr 2:18; 5:5;
9:18; Rev 22:15
8:1
c Pr 1:20; 9:3
8:3
d Job 29:7
8:5
e Pr 1:22 f Pr 1:4
8:7
g Ps 37:30;
Jn 8:14
8:10
h Pr 3:14-15
8:11
i Job 28:17-19
j Pr 3:13-15
8:12
k Pr 1:4
8:13
l Pr 16:6
m Jer 44:4
8:14
n Pr 21:22;
Ecc 7:19
8:15
o Da 2:21;
Ro 13:1
8:17
p 1Sa 2:30;
Ps 91:14;
Jn 14:21-24
q Pr 1:28;
Jas 1:5
8:18
r Pr 3:16
s Dt 8:18;
Mt 6:33
8:19
t Pr 3:13-14;
10:20

---

a27 Hebrew *Sheol*   b16 Many Hebrew manuscripts and Septuagint; most Hebrew manuscripts
and nobles—all righteous rulers

²⁰I walk in the way of righteousness,
　along the paths of justice,
²¹bestowing wealth on those who love me
　and making their treasuries full. ᵘ

²²"The LORD brought me forth as the first of his works, ᵃ ᵇ
　before his deeds of old;
²³I was appointedᶜ from eternity,
　from the beginning, before the world began.
²⁴When there were no oceans, I was given birth,
　when there were no springs abounding with water;ᵛ
²⁵before the mountains were settled in place,
　before the hills, I was given birth, ʷ
²⁶before he made the earth or its fields
　or any of the dust of the world. ˣ
²⁷I was there when he set the heavens in place, ʸ
　when he marked out the horizon on the face of the
　　deep,
²⁸when he established the clouds above
　and fixed securely the fountains of the deep,
²⁹when he gave the sea its boundaryᶻ
　so the waters would not overstep his command, ᵃ
　and when he marked out the foundations of the earth. ᵇ
30　Then I was the craftsman at his side. ᶜ
　I was filled with delight day after day,
　　rejoicing always in his presence,
³¹rejoicing in his whole world
　and delighting in mankind. ᵈ

³²"Now then, my sons, listen to me;
　blessed areᵉ those who keep my ways. ᶠ
³³Listen to my instruction and be wise;
　do not ignore it.
³⁴Blessed is the man who listensᵍ to me,
　watching daily at my doors,
　　waiting at my doorway.
³⁵For whoever finds meʰ finds life
　and receives favor from the LORD. ⁱ
³⁶But whoever fails to find me harms himself;ʲ
　all who hate me love death."

Invitations of Wisdom and of Folly

9　Wisdom has builtᵏ her house;
　she has hewn out its seven pillars.
²She has prepared her meat and mixed her wine;
　she has also set her table. ˡ
³She has sent out her maids, and she callsᵐ
　from the highest point of the city. ⁿ
⁴"Let all who are simple come in here!"
　she says to those who lack judgment. ᵒ

8:21
uPr 24:4
8:24
vGe 7:11
8:25
wJob 15:7
8:26
xPs 90:2
8:27
yPr 3:19
8:29
zGe 1:9;
Job 38:10;
Ps 16:6
aPs 104:9
bJob 38:5
8:30
cJn 1:1-3
8:31
dPs 16:3;
104:1-30
8:32
eLk 11:28
fPs 119:1-2
8:34
gPr 3:13,18
8:35
hPr 3:13-18
iPr 12:2
8:36
jPr 15:32
9:1
kEph 2:20-22;
1Pe 2:5
9:2
lLk 14:16-23
9:3
mPr 8:1-3
nver 14
9:4
oPr 6:32

ᵃ22 Or *way*; or *dominion*　　ᵇ22 Or *The* LORD *possessed me at the beginning of his work*; or *The* LORD
brought me forth at the beginning of his work　　ᶜ23 Or *fashioned*

⁵"Come, eat my food
    and drink the wine I have mixed. ᵖ
⁶Leave your simple ways and you will live;�q
    walk in the way of understanding.

⁷"Whoever corrects a mocker invites insult;
    whoever rebukes a wicked man incurs abuse. ʳ
⁸Do not rebuke a mockerˢ or he will hate you;
    rebuke a wise man and he will love you. ᵗ
⁹Instruct a wise man and he will be wiser still;
    teach a righteous man and he will add to his
        learning. ᵘ

¹⁰"The fear of the LORDᵛ is the beginning of wisdom,
    and knowledge of the Holy One is understanding.
¹¹For through me your days will be many,
    and years will be added to your life. ʷ
¹²If you are wise, your wisdom will reward you;
    if you are a mocker, you alone will suffer."

¹³The woman Folly is loud;ˣ
    she is undisciplined and without knowledge. ʸ
¹⁴She sits at the door of her house,
    on a seat at the highest point of the city, ᶻ
¹⁵calling out to those who pass by,
    who go straight on their way.
¹⁶"Let all who are simple come in here!"
    she says to those who lack judgment.
¹⁷"Stolen water is sweet;
    food eaten in secret is delicious!ᵃ"
¹⁸But little do they know that the dead are there,
    that her guests are in the depths of the grave. ᵃ ᵇ

Proverbs of Solomon

10 The proverbs of Solomon:ᶜ

A wise son brings joy to his father, ᵈ
    but a foolish son grief to his mother.

²Ill-gotten treasures are of no value, ᵉ
    but righteousness delivers from death. ᶠ

³The LORD does not let the righteous go hungryᵍ
    but he thwarts the craving of the wicked.

⁴Lazy hands make a man poor, ʰ
    but diligent hands bring wealth. ⁱ

⁵He who gathers crops in summer is a wise son,
    but he who sleeps during harvest is a disgraceful son.

⁶Blessings crown the head of the righteous,

9:5
pIsa 55:1
9:6
qPr 8:35
9:7
rPr 23:9
9:8
sPr 15:12
tPs 141:5
9:9
uPr 1:5,7
9:10
vJob 28:28;
Pr 1:7
9:11
wPr 3:16; 10:27
9:13
xPr 7:11 yPr 5:6
9:14
zver 3
9:17
aPr 20:17
9:18
bPr 2:18;
7:26-27
10:1
cPr 1:1
dPr 15:20; 29:3
10:2
ePr 21:6
fPr 11:4,19
10:3
gMt 6:25-34
10:4
hPr 19:15
iPr 12:24; 13:4;
21:5

ᵃ18 Hebrew *Sheol*

but violence overwhelms the mouth of the wicked. [a] [j]

7The memory of the righteous [k] will be a blessing,
    but the name of the wicked [l] will rot. [m]

8The wise in heart accept commands,
    but a chattering fool comes to ruin. [n]

9The man of integrity [o] walks securely, [p]
    but he who takes crooked paths will be found out. [q]

10He who winks maliciously [r] causes grief,
    and a chattering fool comes to ruin.

11The mouth of the righteous is a fountain of life, [s]
    but violence overwhelms the mouth of the wicked. [t]

12Hatred stirs up dissension,
    but love covers over all wrongs. [u]

13Wisdom is found on the lips of the discerning, [v]
    but a rod is for the back of him who lacks judgment. [w]

14Wise men store up knowledge,
    but the mouth of a fool invites ruin. [x]

15The wealth of the rich is their fortified city, [y]
    but poverty is the ruin of the poor. [z]

16The wages of the righteous bring them life,
    but the income of the wicked brings them
        punishment. [a]

17He who heeds discipline shows the way to life, [b]
    but whoever ignores correction leads others astray.

18He who conceals his hatred has lying lips,
    and whoever spreads slander is a fool.

19When words are many, sin is not absent,
    but he who holds his tongue is wise. [c]

20The tongue of the righteous is choice silver,
    but the heart of the wicked is of little value.

21The lips of the righteous nourish many,
    but fools die for lack of judgment. [d]

22The blessing of the LORD brings wealth, [e]
    and he adds no trouble to it.

23A fool finds pleasure in evil conduct, [f]
    but a man of understanding delights in wisdom.

24What the wicked dreads [g] will overtake him;
    what the righteous desire will be granted. [h]

25When the storm has swept by, the wicked are gone,
    but the righteous stand firm [i] forever. [j]

---

[a] 6 Or *but the mouth of the wicked conceals violence*; also in verse 11

10:6
j ver 8,11,14
10:7
k Ps 112:6
l Ps 109:13
m Ps 9:6
10:8
n Mt 7:24-27
10:9
o Isa 33:15
p Ps 23:4
q Pr 28:18
10:10
r Ps 35:19
10:11
s Ps 37:30;
Pr 13:12,14,19
t ver 6
10:12
u Pr 17:9;
1Co 13:4-7;
1Pe 4:8
10:13
v ver 31
w Pr 26:3
10:14
x Pr 18:6,7
10:15
y Pr 18:11
z Pr 19:7
10:16
a Pr 11:18-19
10:17
b Pr 6:23
10:19
c Pr 17:28;
Ecc 5:3;
Jas 1:19; 3:2-12
10:21
d Pr 5:22-23;
Hos 4:1,6,14
10:22
e Ge 24:35;
Ps 37:22
10:23
f Pr 2:14; 15:21
10:24
g Isa 66:4
h Ps 145:17-19;
Mt 5:6;
1Jn 5:14-15
10:25
i Ps 15:5
j Pr 12:3,7;
Mt 7:24-27

²⁶As vinegar to the teeth and smoke to the eyes,
  so is a sluggard to those who send him.ᵏ

²⁷The fear of the LORD adds length to life,ˡ
  but the years of the wicked are cut short.ᵐ

²⁸The prospect of the righteous is joy,
  but the hopes of the wicked come to nothing.ⁿ

²⁹The way of the LORD is a refuge for the righteous,
  but it is the ruin of those who do evil.ᵒ

³⁰The righteous will never be uprooted,
  but the wicked will not remain in the land.ᵖ

³¹The mouth of the righteous brings forth wisdom,�q
  but a perverse tongue will be cut out.

³²The lips of the righteous know what is fitting,ʳ
  but the mouth of the wicked only what is perverse.

11
The LORD abhors dishonest scales,ˢ
  but accurate weights are his delight.ᵗ

²When pride comes, then comes disgrace,ᵘ
  but with humility comes wisdom.ᵛ

³The integrity of the upright guides them,
  but the unfaithful are destroyed by their duplicity.ʷ

⁴Wealth is worthless in the day of wrath,ˣ
  but righteousness delivers from death.ʸ

⁵The righteousness of the blameless makes a straight way
    for them,
  but the wicked are brought down by their own
    wickedness.ᶻ

⁶The righteousness of the upright delivers them,
  but the unfaithful are trapped by evil desires.

⁷When a wicked man dies, his hope perishes;
  all he expected from his power comes to nothing.ᵃ

⁸The righteous man is rescued from trouble,
  and it comes on the wicked instead.ᵇ

⁹With his mouth the godless destroys his neighbor,
  but through knowledge the righteous escape.

¹⁰When the righteous prosper, the city rejoices;ᶜ
  when the wicked perish, there are shouts of joy.

¹¹Through the blessing of the upright a city is exalted,
  but by the mouth of the wicked it is destroyed.ᵈ

¹²A man who lacks judgment derides his neighbor,ᵉ
  but a man of understanding holds his tongue.

¹³A gossip betrays a confidence,ᶠ
  but a trustworthy man keeps a secret.

10:26
k Pr 26:6
10:27
l Pr 9:10-11
m Job 15:32
10:28
n Job 8:13;
Pr 11:7
10:29
o Pr 21:15
10:30
p Ps 37:9,28-29;
Pr 2:20-22
10:31
q Ps 37:30
10:32
r Ecc 10:12
11:1
s Lev 19:36;
Dt 25:13-16;
Pr 20:10,23
t Pr 16:11
11:2
u Pr 16:18
v Pr 18:12;
29:23
11:3
w Pr 13:6
11:4
x Eze 7:19;
Zep 1:18
y Ge 7:1;
Pr 10:2
11:5
z Pr 5:21-23
11:7
a Pr 10:28
11:8
b Pr 21:18
11:10
c Pr 28:12
11:11
d Pr 29:8
11:12
e Pr 14:21
11:13
f Lev 19:16;
Pr 20:19;
1Ti 5:13

¹⁴For lack of guidance a nation falls, ^g
   but many advisers make victory sure. ^h

¹⁵He who puts up securityⁱ for another will surely suffer,
   but whoever refuses to strike hands in pledge is safe.

¹⁶A kindhearted woman gains respect, ^j
   but ruthless men gain only wealth.

¹⁷A kind man benefits himself,
   but a cruel man brings trouble on himself.

¹⁸The wicked man earns deceptive wages,
   but he who sows righteousness reaps a sure reward. ^k

¹⁹The truly righteous man attains life,
   but he who pursues evil goes to his death.

²⁰The LORD detests men of perverse heart
   but he delights in those whose ways are blameless. ^l

²¹Be sure of this: The wicked will not go unpunished,
   but those who are righteous will go free. ^m

²²Like a gold ring in a pig's snout
   is a beautiful woman who shows no discretion.

²³The desire of the righteous ends only in good,
   but the hope of the wicked only in wrath.

²⁴One man gives freely, yet gains even more;
   another withholds unduly, but comes to poverty.

²⁵A generous man will prosper;
   he who refreshes others will himself be refreshed. ⁿ

²⁶People curse the man who hoards grain,
   but blessing crowns him who is willing to sell.

²⁷He who seeks good finds goodwill,
   but evil comes to him who searches for it. ^o

²⁸Whoever trusts in his riches will fall, ^p
   but the righteous will thrive like a green leaf. ^q

²⁹He who brings trouble on his family will inherit only
      wind,
   and the fool will be servant to the wise. ^r

³⁰The fruit of the righteous is a tree of life, ^s
   and he who wins souls is wise.

³¹If the righteous receive their due^t on earth,
   how much more the ungodly and the sinner!

12

Whoever loves discipline loves knowledge,
   but he who hates correction is stupid. ^u

²A good man obtains favor from the LORD,
   but the LORD condemns a crafty man.

³A man cannot be established through wickedness,

11:14
gPr 20:18
hPr 15:22; 24:6
11:15
iPr 6:1
11:16
jPr 31:31
11:18
kHos 10:12-13
11:20
lCh 29:17;
Ps 119:1;
Pr 12:2,22
11:21
mPr 16:5
11:25
nMt 5:7;
2Co 9:6-9
11:27
oEst 7:10;
Ps 7:15-16
11:28
pJob 31:24-28;
Ps 49:6; 52:7;
Mk 10:25;
1Ti 6:17
qPs 1:3;
92:12-14;
Jer 17:8
11:29
rPr 14:19
11:30
sJas 5:20
11:31
tPr 13:21;
Jer 25:29;
1Pe 4:18
12:1
uPr 9:7-9; 15:5,
10,12,32

but the righteous cannot be uprooted. ᵛ

⁴A wife of noble character is her husband's crown,
but a disgraceful wife is like decay in his bones. ʷ

⁵The plans of the righteous are just,
but the advice of the wicked is deceitful.

⁶The words of the wicked lie in wait for blood,
but the speech of the upright rescues them. ˣ

⁷Wicked men are overthrown and are no more, ʸ
but the house of the righteous stands firm. ᶻ

⁸A man is praised according to his wisdom,
but men with warped minds are despised.

⁹Better to be a nobody and yet have a servant
than pretend to be somebody and have no food.

¹⁰A righteous man cares for the needs of his animal,
but the kindest acts of the wicked are cruel.

¹¹He who works his land will have abundant food,
but he who chases fantasies lacks judgment. ᵃ

¹²The wicked desire the plunder of evil men,
but the root of the righteous flourishes.

¹³An evil man is trapped by his sinful talk, ᵇ
but a righteous man escapes trouble. ᶜ

¹⁴From the fruit of his lips a man is filled with good
things ᵈ
as surely as the work of his hands rewards him. ᵉ

¹⁵The way of a fool seems right to him, ᶠ
but a wise man listens to advice.

¹⁶A fool shows his annoyance at once,
but a prudent man overlooks an insult. ᵍ

¹⁷A truthful witness gives honest testimony,
but a false witness tells lies. ʰ

¹⁸Reckless words pierce like a sword, ⁱ
but the tongue of the wise brings healing. ʲ

¹⁹Truthful lips endure forever,
but a lying tongue lasts only a moment.

²⁰There is deceit in the hearts of those who plot evil,
but joy for those who promote peace.

²¹No harm befalls the righteous, ᵏ
but the wicked have their fill of trouble.

²²The LORD detests lying lips, ˡ
but he delights in men who are truthful. ᵐ

²³A prudent man keeps his knowledge to himself, ⁿ
but the heart of fools blurts out folly.

12:3
vPr 10:25
12:4
wPr 14:30
12:6
xPr 14:3
12:7
yPs 37:36
zPr 10:25
12:11
aPr 28:19
12:13
bPr 18:7
cPr 21:23;
2Pe 2:9
12:14
dPr 13:2; 15:23;
18:20
eIsa 3:10-11
12:15
fPr 14:12; 16:2,
25; Lk 18:11
12:16
gPr 29:11
12:17
hPr 14:5,25
12:18
iPs 57:4 jPr 15:4
12:21
kPs 91:10
12:22
lPr 6:17;
Rev 22:15
mPr 11:20
12:23
nPr 10:14;
13:16

24Diligent hands will rule,
    but laziness ends in slave labor. o

25An anxious heart weighs a man down, p
    but a kind word cheers him up.

26A righteous man is cautious in friendship, a
    but the way of the wicked leads them astray.

27The lazy man does not roast b his game,
    but the diligent man prizes his possessions.

28In the way of righteousness there is life; q
    along that path is immortality.

13 A wise son heeds his father's instruction,
    but a mocker does not listen to rebuke. r

2From the fruit of his lips a man enjoys good things, s
    but the unfaithful have a craving for violence.

3He who guards his lips t guards his life, u
    but he who speaks rashly will come to ruin. v

4The sluggard craves and gets nothing,
    but the desires of the diligent are fully satisfied.

5The righteous hate what is false,
    but the wicked bring shame and disgrace.

6Righteousness guards the man of integrity,
    but wickedness overthrows the sinner. w

7One man pretends to be rich, yet has nothing;
    another pretends to be poor, yet has great wealth. x

8A man's riches may ransom his life,
    but a poor man hears no threat.

9The light of the righteous shines brightly,
    but the lamp of the wicked is snuffed out. y

10Pride only breeds quarrels,
    but wisdom is found in those who take advice.

11Dishonest money dwindles away, z
    but he who gathers money little by little makes it
        grow.

12Hope deferred makes the heart sick,
    but a longing fulfilled is a tree of life.

13He who scorns instruction will pay for it, a
    but he who respects a command is rewarded.

14The teaching of the wise is a fountain of life, b
    turning a man from the snares of death. c

15Good understanding wins favor,

12:24
o Pr 10:4
12:25
p Pr 15:13;
Isa 50:4
12:28
q Dt 30:15
13:1
r Pr 10:1
13:2
s Pr 12:14
13:3
t Jas 3:2
u Pr 21:23
v Pr 18:7,20-21
13:6
w Pr 11:3,5
13:7
x 2Co 6:10
13:9
y Job 18:5;
Pr 4:18-19;
24:20
13:11
z Pr 10:2
13:13
a Nu 15:31;
2Ch 36:16
13:14
b Pr 10:11
c Pr 14:27

a26 Or *man is a guide to his neighbor*   b27 The meaning of the Hebrew for this word is uncertain.

but the way of the unfaithful is hard. [a]

[16]Every prudent man acts out of knowledge,
but a fool exposes his folly. [d]

[17]A wicked messenger falls into trouble,
but a trustworthy envoy brings healing. [e]

[18]He who ignores discipline comes to poverty and shame,
but whoever heeds correction is honored. [f]

[19]A longing fulfilled is sweet to the soul,
but fools detest turning from evil.

[20]He who walks with the wise grows wise,
but a companion of fools suffers harm. [g]

[21]Misfortune pursues the sinner,
but prosperity is the reward of the righteous. [h]

[22]A good man leaves an inheritance for his children's
children,
but a sinner's wealth is stored up for the righteous. [i]

[23]A poor man's field may produce abundant food,
but injustice sweeps it away.

[24]He who spares the rod hates his son,
but he who loves him is careful to discipline him. [j]

[25]The righteous eat to their hearts' content,
but the stomach of the wicked goes hungry. [k]

14

The wise woman builds her house, [l]
but with her own hands the foolish one tears hers
down.

[2]He whose walk is upright fears the LORD,
but he whose ways are devious despises him.

[3]A fool's talk brings a rod to his back,
but the lips of the wise protect them. [m]

[4]Where there are no oxen, the manger is empty,
but from the strength of an ox comes an abundant
harvest.

[5]A truthful witness does not deceive,
but a false witness pours out lies. [n]

[6]The mocker seeks wisdom and finds none,
but knowledge comes easily to the discerning.

[7]Stay away from a foolish man,
for you will not find knowledge on his lips.

[8]The wisdom of the prudent is to give thought to their
ways,
but the folly of fools is deception. [o]

13:16
d Pr 12:23
13:17
e Pr 25:13
13:18
f Pr 15:5,31-32
13:20
g Pr 15:31
13:21
h Ps 32:10
13:22
i Job 27:17;
Ecc 2:26
13:24
j Pr 19:18;
22:15;
23:13-14; 29:15,
17; Heb 12:7
13:25
k Ps 34:10;
Pr 10:3
14:1
l Pr 24:3
14:3
m Pr 12:6
14:5
n Pr 6:19; 12:17
14:8
o ver 24

---

a 15 Or *unfaithful does not endure*

⁹Fools mock at making amends for sin,
  but goodwill is found among the upright.

¹⁰Each heart knows its own bitterness,
  and no one else can share its joy.

¹¹The house of the wicked will be destroyed,
  but the tent of the upright will flourish. ᵖ

¹²There is a way that seems right to a man, ᑫ
  but in the end it leads to death. ʳ

¹³Even in laughterˢ the heart may ache,
  and joy may end in grief.

¹⁴The faithless will be fully repaid for their ways, ᵗ
  and the good man rewarded for his. ᵘ

¹⁵A simple man believes anything,
  but a prudent man gives thought to his steps.

¹⁶A wise man fears the LORD and shuns evil, ᵛ
  but a fool is hotheaded and reckless.

¹⁷A quick-tempered man does foolish things, ʷ
  and a crafty man is hated.

¹⁸The simple inherit folly,
  but the prudent are crowned with knowledge.

¹⁹Evil men will bow down in the presence of the good,
  and the wicked at the gates of the righteous. ˣ

²⁰The poor are shunned even by their neighbors,
  but the rich have many friends. ʸ

²¹He who despises his neighbor sins, ᶻ
  but blessed is he who is kind to the needy. ᵃ

²²Do not those who plot evil go astray?
  But those who plan what is good findᵃ love and
    faithfulness.

²³All hard work brings a profit,
  but mere talk leads only to poverty.

²⁴The wealth of the wise is their crown,
  but the folly of fools yields folly.

²⁵A truthful witness saves lives,
  but a false witness is deceitful. ᵇ

²⁶He who fears the LORD has a secure fortress, ᶜ
  and for his children it will be a refuge.

²⁷The fear of the LORD is a fountain of life,
  turning a man from the snares of death. ᵈ

²⁸A large population is a king's glory,

14:11
pPr 3:33; 12:7
14:12
qPr 12:15
rPr 16:25
14:13
sEcc 2:2
14:14
tPr 1:31
uPr 12:14
14:16
vPr 22:3
14:17
wver 29
14:19
xPr 11:29
14:20
yPr 19:4,7
14:21
zPr 11:12
aPs 41:1;
Pr 19:17
14:25
bver 5
14:26
cPr 18:10;
19:23; Isa 33:6
14:27
dPr 13:14

ᵃ22 Or *show*

but without subjects a prince is ruined.

²⁹A patient man has great understanding,
but a quick-tempered man displays folly. ᵉ

³⁰A heart at peace gives life to the body,
but envy rots the bones. ᶠ

³¹He who oppresses the poor shows contempt for their
Maker, ᵍ
but whoever is kind to the needy honors God.

³²When calamity comes, the wicked are brought down, ʰ
but even in death the righteous have a refuge. ⁱ

³³Wisdom reposes in the heart of the discerningʲ
and even among fools she lets herself be known. ᵃ

³⁴Righteousness exalts a nation, ᵏ
but sin is a disgrace to any people.

³⁵A king delights in a wise servant,
but a shameful servant incurs his wrath. ˡ

15 A gentle answer turns away wrath, ᵐ
but a harsh word stirs up anger.

²The tongue of the wise commends knowledge,
but the mouth of the fool gushes folly. ⁿ

³The eyesᵒ of the LORD are everywhere, ᵖ
keeping watch on the wicked and the good. �q

⁴The tongue that brings healing is a tree of life,
but a deceitful tongue crushes the spirit.

⁵A fool spurns his father's discipline,
but whoever heeds correction shows prudence. ʳ

⁶The house of the righteous contains great treasure, ˢ
but the income of the wicked brings them trouble.

⁷The lips of the wise spread knowledge;
not so the hearts of fools.

⁸The LORD detests the sacrifice of the wicked, ᵗ
but the prayer of the upright pleases him. ᵘ

⁹The LORD detests the way of the wicked
but he loves those who pursue righteousness. ᵛ

¹⁰Stern discipline awaits him who leaves the path;
he who hates correction will die. ʷ

¹¹Death and Destructionᵇ lie open before the LORDˣ—
how much more the hearts of men!ʸ

¹²A mocker resents correction;ᶻ

14:29
eEcc 7:8-9;
Jas 1:19
14:30
fPr 12:4
14:31
gPr 17:5
14:32
hPr 6:15
iJob 13:15;
2Ti 4:18
14:33
jPr 2:6-10
14:34
kPr 11:11
14:35
lMt 24:45-51;
25:14-30
15:1
mPr 25:15
15:2
nPr 12:23
15:3
o2Ch 16:9
pJob 31:4;
Heb 4:13
qJob 34:21;
Jer 16:17
15:5
rPr 13:1
15:6
sPr 8:21
15:8
tPr 21:27;
Isa 1:11;
Jer 6:20 uver 29
15:9
vPr 21:21;
1Ti 6:11
15:10
wPr 1:31-32;
5:12
15:11
xJob 26:6;
Ps 139:8
y2Ch 6:30;
Ps 44:21
15:12
zAm 5:10

ᵃ33 Hebrew; Septuagint and Syriac / *but in the heart of fools she is not known*   ᵇ11 Hebrew *Sheol and Abaddon* he will not consult the wise.

13A happy heart makes the face cheerful,
　　but heartache crushes the spirit. [a]

14The discerning heart seeks knowledge, [b]
　　but the mouth of a fool feeds on folly.

15All the days of the oppressed are wretched,
　　but the cheerful heart has a continual feast. [c]

16Better a little with the fear of the LORD
　　than great wealth with turmoil. [d]

17Better a meal of vegetables where there is love
　　than a fattened calf with hatred. [e]

18A hot-tempered man stirs up dissension, [f]
　　but a patient man calms a quarrel. [g]

19The way of the sluggard is blocked with thorns, [h]
　　but the path of the upright is a highway.

20A wise son brings joy to his father, [i]
　　but a foolish man despises his mother.

21Folly delights a man who lacks judgment, [j]
　　but a man of understanding keeps a straight course.

22Plans fail for lack of counsel,
　　but with many advisers they succeed. [k]

23A man finds joy in giving an apt reply[l] —
　　and how good is a timely word![m]

24The path of life leads upward for the wise
　　to keep him from going down to the grave. [a]

25The LORD tears down the proud man's house[n]
　　but he keeps the widow's boundaries intact. [o]

26The LORD detests the thoughts of the wicked, [p]
　　but those of the pure are pleasing to him.

27A greedy man brings trouble to his family,
　　but he who hates bribes will live. [q]

28The heart of the righteous weighs its answers, [r]
　　but the mouth of the wicked gushes evil.

29The LORD is far from the wicked
　　but he hears the prayer of the righteous. [s]

30A cheerful look brings joy to the heart,
　　and good news gives health to the bones.

31He who listens to a life-giving rebuke
　　will be at home among the wise. [t]

32He who ignores discipline despises himself, [u]

15:13
aPr 12:25;
17:22; 18:14
15:14
bPr 18:15
15:15
cver 13
15:16
dPs 37:16-17;
Pr 16:8; 1Ti 6:6
15:17
ePr 17:1
15:18
fPr 26:21
gGe 13:8
15:19
hPr 22:5
15:20
iPr 10:1
15:21
jPr 10:23
15:22
kPr 11:14
15:23
lPr 12:14
mPr 25:11
15:25
nPr 12:7
oDt 19:14;
Ps 68:5-6;
Pr 23:10-11
15:26
pPr 6:16
15:27
qEx 23:8;
Isa 33:15
15:28
r1Pe 3:15
15:29
sPs 145:18-19
15:31
tver 5
15:32
uPr 1:7

a24 Hebrew *Sheol*

but whoever heeds correction gains understanding.

[33]The fear of the LORD[v] teaches a man wisdom,[a]
and humility comes before honor.[w]

16

To man belong the plans of the heart,
but from the LORD comes the reply of the tongue.[x]

[2]All a man's ways seem innocent to him,
but motives are weighed by the LORD.[y]

[3]Commit to the LORD whatever you do,
and your plans will succeed.[z]

[4]The LORD works out everything for his own ends[a]—
even the wicked for a day of disaster.[b]

[5]The LORD detests all the proud of heart.[c]
Be sure of this: They will not go unpunished.[d]

[6]Through love and faithfulness sin is atoned for;
through the fear of the LORD a man avoids evil.[e]

[7]When a man's ways are pleasing to the LORD,
he makes even his enemies live at peace with him.

[8]Better a little with righteousness
than much gain[f] with injustice.

[9]In his heart a man plans his course,
but the LORD determines his steps.[g]

[10]The lips of a king speak as an oracle,
and his mouth should not betray justice.

[11]Honest scales and balances are from the LORD;
all the weights in the bag are of his making.[h]

[12]Kings detest wrongdoing,
for a throne is established through righteousness.[i]

[13]Kings take pleasure in honest lips;
they value a man who speaks the truth.[j]

[14]A king's wrath is a messenger of death,[k]
but a wise man will appease it.

[15]When a king's face brightens, it means life;[l]
his favor is like a rain cloud in spring.

[16]How much better to get wisdom than gold,
to choose understanding rather than silver![m]

[17]The highway of the upright avoids evil;
he who guards his way guards his life.

[18]Pride goes before destruction,
a haughty spirit before a fall.[n]

[19]Better to be lowly in spirit and among the oppressed

15:33
v Pr 1:7
w Pr 18:12
16:1
x Pr 19:21
16:2
y Pr 21:2
16:3
z Ps 37:5-6;
Pr 3:5-6
16:4
a Isa 43:7
b Ro 9:22
16:5
c Pr 6:16
d Pr 11:20-21
16:6
e Pr 14:16
16:8
f Ps 37:16
16:9
g Jer 10:23
16:11
h Pr 11:1
16:12
i Pr 25:5
16:13
j Pr 14:35
16:14
k Pr 19:12
16:15
l Job 29:24
16:16
m Pr 8:10,19
16:18
n Pr 11:2; 18:12

---

a33 Or *Wisdom teaches the fear of the* LORD

than to share plunder with the proud.

20Whoever gives heed to instruction prospers,
    and blessed is he who trusts in the LORD. º

21The wise in heart are called discerning,
    and pleasant words promote instruction. ᵃ ᴾ

22Understanding is a fountain of life to those who have
        it, �q
    but folly brings punishment to fools.

23A wise man's heart guides his mouth,
    and his lips promote instruction. ᵇ

24Pleasant words are a honeycomb,
    sweet to the soul and healing to the bones. ʳ

25There is a way that seems right to a man, ˢ
    but in the end it leads to death. ᵗ

26The laborer's appetite works for him;
    his hunger drives him on.

27A scoundrel plots evil,
    and his speech is like a scorching fire. ᵘ

28A perverse man stirs up dissension, ᵛ
    and a gossip separates close friends. ʷ

29A violent man entices his neighbor
    and leads him down a path that is not good. ˣ

30He who winks with his eye is plotting perversity;
    he who purses his lips is bent on evil.

31Gray hair is a crown of splendor; ʸ
    it is attained by a righteous life.

32Better a patient man than a warrior,
    a man who controls his temper than one who takes a
        city.

33The lot is cast into the lap,
    but its every decision is from the LORD. ᶻ

17   Better a dry crust with peace and quiet
    than a house full of feasting, ᶜ with strife. ᵃ

2A wise servant will rule over a disgraceful son,
    and will share the inheritance as one of the brothers.

3The crucible for silver and the furnace for gold, ᵇ
    but the LORD tests the heart. ᶜ

4A wicked man listens to evil lips;
    a liar pays attention to a malicious tongue.

16:20
ºPs 2:12; 34:8;
Pr 19:8; Jer 17:7
16:21
ᵖver 23
16:22
qPr 13:14
16:24
ʳPr 24:13-14
16:25
ˢPr 12:15
ᵗPr 14:12
16:27
ᵘJas 3:6
16:28
ᵛPr 15:18
ʷPr 17:9
16:29
ˣPr 1:10; 12:26
16:31
ʸPr 20:29
16:33
ᶻPr 18:18; 29:26
17:1
ᵃPr 15:16,17
17:3
ᵇPr 27:21
ᶜ1Ch 29:17;
Ps 26:2;
Jer 17:10

ᵃ21 Or *words make a man persuasive*   ᵇ23 Or *mouth / and makes his lips persuasive*   ᶜ1 Hebrew
sacrifices

[5]He who mocks the poor shows contempt for their
    Maker;[d]
  whoever gloats over disaster[e] will not go
    unpunished.[f]

[6]Children's children[g] are a crown to the aged,
  and parents are the pride of their children.

[7]Arrogant[a] lips are unsuited to a fool—
  how much worse lying lips to a ruler!

[8]A bribe is a charm to the one who gives it;
  wherever he turns, he succeeds.

[9]He who covers over an offense promotes love,[h]
  but whoever repeats the matter separates close
    friends.[i]

[10]A rebuke impresses a man of discernment
  more than a hundred lashes a fool.

[11]An evil man is bent only on rebellion;
  a merciless official will be sent against him.

[12]Better to meet a bear robbed of her cubs
  than a fool in his folly.

[13]If a man pays back evil[j] for good,
  evil will never leave his house.

[14]Starting a quarrel is like breaching a dam;
  so drop the matter before a dispute breaks out.[k]

[15]Acquitting the guilty and condemning the innocent[l]—
  the LORD detests them both.[m]

[16]Of what use is money in the hand of a fool,
  since he has no desire to get wisdom?[n]

[17]A friend loves at all times,
  and a brother is born for adversity.

[18]A man lacking in judgment strikes hands in pledge
  and puts up security for his neighbor.[o]

[19]He who loves a quarrel loves sin;
  he who builds a high gate invites destruction.

[20]A man of perverse heart does not prosper;
  he whose tongue is deceitful falls into trouble.

[21]To have a fool for a son brings grief;
  there is no joy for the father of a fool.[p]

[22]A cheerful heart is good medicine,
  but a crushed spirit dries up the bones.[q]

[23]A wicked man accepts a bribe[r] in secret
  to pervert the course of justice.

17:5
d Pr 14:31
e Job 31:29
f Ob 1:12
17:6
g Pr 13:22
17:9
h Pr 10:12
i Pr 16:28
17:13
j Ps 109:4-5;
Jer 18:20
17:14
k Pr 20:3
17:15
l Pr 18:5
m Ex 23:6-7;
Isa 5:23
17:16
n Pr 23:23
17:18
o Pr 6:1-5;
11:15; 22:26-27
17:21
p Pr 10:1
17:22
q Ps 22:15;
Pr 15:13
17:23
r Ex 23:8

---

[a]7 Or *Eloquent*

24A discerning man keeps wisdom in view,
but a fool's eyes[s] wander to the ends of the earth.

25A foolish son brings grief to his father
and bitterness to the one who bore him.[t]

26It is not good to punish an innocent man,[u]
or to flog officials for their integrity.

27A man of knowledge uses words with restraint,
and a man of understanding is even-tempered.[v]

28Even a fool is thought wise if he keeps silent,
and discerning if he holds his tongue.[w]

18

An unfriendly man pursues selfish ends;
he defies all sound judgment.

2A fool finds no pleasure in understanding
but delights in airing his own opinions.[x]

3When wickedness comes, so does contempt,
and with shame comes disgrace.

4The words of a man's mouth are deep waters,
but the fountain of wisdom is a bubbling brook.

5It is not good to be partial to the wicked[y]
or to deprive the innocent of justice.[z]

6A fool's lips bring him strife,
and his mouth invites a beating.

7A fool's mouth is his undoing,
and his lips are a snare[a] to his soul.[b]

8The words of a gossip are like choice morsels;
they go down to a man's inmost parts.[c]

9One who is slack in his work
is brother to one who destroys.[d]

10The name of the Lord is a strong tower;[e]
the righteous run to it and are safe.

11The wealth of the rich is their fortified city;[f]
they imagine it an unscalable wall.

12Before his downfall a man's heart is proud,
but humility comes before honor.[g]

13He who answers before listening—
that is his folly and his shame.[h]

14A man's spirit sustains him in sickness,
but a crushed spirit who can bear?[i]

15The heart of the discerning acquires knowledge;[j]
the ears of the wise seek it out.

16A gift[k] opens the way for the giver
and ushers him into the presence of the great.

17:24
s Ecc 2:14
17:25
t Pr 10:1
17:26
u Pr 18:5
17:27
v Pr 14:29;
Jas 1:19
17:28
w Job 13:5
18:2
x Pr 12:23
18:5
y Lev 19:15;
Pr 24:23-25;
28:21 z Ps 82:2;
Pr 17:15
18:7
a Ps 140:9
b Ps 64:8;
Pr 10:14; 12:13;
13:3; Ecc 10:12
18:8
c Pr 26:22
18:9
d Pr 28:24
18:10
e 2Sa 22:3;
Ps 61:3
18:11
f Pr 10:15
18:12
g Pr 11:2; 15:33;
16:18
18:13
h Pr 20:25;
Jn 7:51
18:14
i Pr 15:13; 17:22
18:15
j Pr 15:14
18:16
k Ge 32:20

¹⁷The first to present his case seems right,
    till another comes forward and questions him.

¹⁸Casting the lot settles disputes¹
    and keeps strong opponents apart.

¹⁹An offended brother is more unyielding than a fortified
        city,
    and disputes are like the barred gates of a citadel.

²⁰From the fruit of his mouth a man's stomach is filled;
    with the harvest from his lips he is satisfied. ᵐ

²¹The tongue has the power of life and death,
    and those who love it will eat its fruit. ⁿ

²²He who finds a wife finds what is good ᵒ
    and receives favor from the LORD. ᵖ

²³A poor man pleads for mercy,
    but a rich man answers harshly.

²⁴A man of many companions may come to ruin,
    but there is a friend who sticks closer than a brother. ᑫ

19 Better a poor man whose walk is blameless
    than a fool whose lips are perverse. ʳ

²It is not good to have zeal without knowledge,
    nor to be hasty and miss the way. ˢ

³A man's own folly ruins his life,
    yet his heart rages against the LORD.

⁴Wealth brings many friends,
    but a poor man's friend deserts him. ᵗ

⁵A false witness ᵘ will not go unpunished,
    and he who pours out lies will not go free. ᵛ

⁶Many curry favor with a ruler, ʷ
    and everyone is the friend of a man who gives gifts. ˣ

⁷A poor man is shunned by all his relatives—
    how much more do his friends avoid him!
Though he pursues them with pleading,
    they are nowhere to be found. ᵃ ʸ

⁸He who gets wisdom loves his own soul;
    he who cherishes understanding prospers. ᶻ

⁹A false witness will not go unpunished,
    and he who pours out lies will perish. ᵃ

¹⁰It is not fitting for a fool ᵇ to live in luxury—
    how much worse for a slave to rule over princes! ᶜ

¹¹A man's wisdom gives him patience; ᵈ
    it is to his glory to overlook an offense.

18:18
lPr 16:33
18:20
mPr 12:14
18:21
nPr 13:2-3;
Mt 12:37
18:22
oPr 12:4
pPr 19:14;
31:10
18:24
qPr 17:17;
Jn 15:13-15
19:1
rPr 28:6
19:2
sPr 29:20
19:4
tPr 14:20
19:5
uEx 23:1
vDt 19:19;
Pr 21:28
19:6
wPr 29:26
xPr 17:8; 18:16
19:7
yver 4; Ps 38:11
19:8
zPr 16:20
19:9
aver 5
19:10
bPr 26:1
cPr 30:21-23;
Ecc 10:5-7
19:11
dPr 16:32

ᵃ7 The meaning of the Hebrew for this sentence is uncertain.

¹²A king's rage is like the roar of a lion,
　　but his favor is like dew^e on the grass. ^f

¹³A foolish son is his father's ruin,^g
　　and a quarrelsome wife is like a constant dripping. ^h

¹⁴Houses and wealth are inherited from parents, ⁱ
　　but a prudent wife is from the Lord. ^j

¹⁵Laziness brings on deep sleep,
　　and the shiftless man goes hungry. ^k

¹⁶He who obeys instructions guards his life,
　　but he who is contemptuous of his ways will die. ^l

¹⁷He who is kind to the poor lends to the Lord,
　　and he will reward him for what he has done. ^m

¹⁸Discipline your son, for in that there is hope;
　　do not be a willing party to his death. ⁿ

¹⁹A hot-tempered man must pay the penalty;
　　if you rescue him, you will have to do it again.

²⁰Listen to advice and accept instruction, ^o
　　and in the end you will be wise. ^p

²¹Many are the plans in a man's heart,
　　but it is the Lord's purpose that prevails. ^q

²²What a man desires is unfailing love^a;
　　better to be poor than a liar.

²³The fear of the Lord leads to life:
　　Then one rests content, untouched by trouble. ^r

²⁴The sluggard buries his hand in the dish;
　　he will not even bring it back to his mouth!^s

²⁵Flog a mocker, and the simple will learn prudence;
　　rebuke a discerning man, and he will gain
　　　　knowledge. ^t

²⁶He who robs his father and drives out his mother^u
　　is a son who brings shame and disgrace.

²⁷Stop listening to instruction, my son,
　　and you will stray from the words of knowledge.

²⁸A corrupt witness mocks at justice,
　　and the mouth of the wicked gulps down evil. ^v

²⁹Penalties are prepared for mockers,
　　and beatings for the backs of fools. ^w

20

Wine is a mocker and beer a brawler;
　　whoever is led astray by them is not wise. ^x

²A king's wrath is like the roar of a lion;^y

19:12
ePs 133:3
fPr 16:14-15
19:13
gPr 10:1
hPr 21:9
19:14
i2Co 12:14
jPr 18:22
19:15
kPr 6:9; 10:4
19:16
lPr 16:17;
Lk 10:28
19:17
mMt 10:42;
2Co 9:6-8
19:18
nPr 13:24;
23:13-14
19:20
oPr 4:1
pPr 12:15
19:21
qPs 33:11;
Pr 16:9;
Isa 14:24,27
19:23
rPs 25:13;
Pr 12:21;
1Ti 4:8
19:24
sPr 26:15
19:25
tPr 9:9; 21:11
19:26
uPr 28:24
19:28
vJob 15:16
19:29
wPr 26:3
20:1
xPr 31:4
20:2
yPr 19:12

^a22 Or *A man's greed is his shame*

he who angers him forfeits his life. z

3It is to a man's honor to avoid strife,
but every fool is quick to quarrel. a

4A sluggard does not plow in season;
so at harvest time he looks but finds nothing.

5The purposes of a man's heart are deep waters,
but a man of understanding draws them out.

6Many a man claims to have unfailing love,
but a faithful man who can find? b

7The righteous man leads a blameless life;
blessed are his children after him. c

8When a king sits on his throne to judge,
he winnows out all evil with his eyes. d

9Who can say, "I have kept my heart pure;
I am clean and without sin"? e

10Differing weights and differing measures—
the LORD detests them both. f

11Even a child is known by his actions,
by whether his conduct is pure g and right.

12Ears that hear and eyes that see—
the LORD has made them both. h

13Do not love sleep or you will grow poor; i
stay awake and you will have food to spare.

14"It's no good, it's no good!" says the buyer;
then off he goes and boasts about his purchase.

15Gold there is, and rubies in abundance,
but lips that speak knowledge are a rare jewel.

16Take the garment of one who puts up security for a
stranger;
hold it in pledge j if he does it for a wayward
woman. k

17Food gained by fraud tastes sweet to a man, l
but he ends up with a mouth full of gravel.

18Make plans by seeking advice;
if you wage war, obtain guidance. m

19A gossip betrays a confidence; n
so avoid a man who talks too much.

20If a man curses his father or mother, o
his lamp will be snuffed out in pitch darkness. p

21An inheritance quickly gained at the beginning
will not be blessed at the end.

22Do not say, "I'll pay you back for this wrong!" q

20:2
z Pr 8:36
20:3
a Pr 17:14
20:6
b Ps 12:1
20:7
c Ps 37:25-26;
112:2
20:8
d ver 26;
Pr 25:4-5
20:9
e 1Ki 8:46;
Ecc 7:20;
1Jn 1:8
20:10
f ver 23; Pr 11:1
20:11
g Mt 7:16
20:12
h Ps 94:9
20:13
i Pr 6:11; 19:15
20:16
j Ex 22:26
k Pr 27:13
20:17
l Pr 9:17
20:18
m Pr 11:14; 24:6
20:19
n Pr 11:13
20:20
o Pr 30:11
p Ex 21:17;
Job 18:5
20:22
q Pr 24:29

Wait for the Lord, and he will deliver you. [r]

23The Lord detests differing weights,
and dishonest scales do not please him. [s]

24A man's steps are directed by the Lord.
How then can anyone understand his own way? [t]

25It is a trap for a man to dedicate something rashly
and only later to consider his vows. [u]

26A wise king winnows out the wicked;
he drives the threshing wheel over them. [v]

27The lamp of the Lord searches the spirit of a man[a];
it searches out his inmost being.

28Love and faithfulness keep a king safe;
through love his throne is made secure. [w]

29The glory of young men is their strength,
gray hair the splendor of the old. [x]

30Blows and wounds cleanse[y] away evil,
and beatings purge the inmost being.

21 The king's heart is in the hand of the Lord;
he directs it like a watercourse wherever he pleases.

2All a man's ways seem right to him,
but the Lord weighs the heart. [z]

3To do what is right and just
is more acceptable to the Lord than sacrifice. [a]

4Haughty eyes[b] and a proud heart,
the lamp of the wicked, are sin!

5The plans of the diligent lead to profit[c]
as surely as haste leads to poverty.

6A fortune made by a lying tongue
is a fleeting vapor and a deadly snare. [b] [d]

7The violence of the wicked will drag them away,
for they refuse to do what is right.

8The way of the guilty is devious, [e]
but the conduct of the innocent is upright.

9Better to live on a corner of the roof
than share a house with a quarrelsome wife. [f]

10The wicked man craves evil;
his neighbor gets no mercy from him.

11When a mocker is punished, the simple gain wisdom;
when a wise man is instructed, he gets knowledge. [g]

20:22
rRo 12:19
20:23
sver 10
20:24
tJer 10:23
20:25
uEcc 5:2,4-5
20:26
vver 8
20:28
wPr 29:14
20:29
xPr 16:31
20:30
yPr 22:15
21:2
zPr 16:2; 24:12;
Lk 16:15
21:3
a1Sa 15:22;
Pr 15:8;
Isa 1:11;
Hos 6:6;
Mic 6:6-8
21:4
bPr 6:17
21:5
cPr 10:4; 28:22
21:6
d2Pe 2:3
21:8
ePr 2:15
21:9
fPr 25:24
21:11
gPr 19:25

[a]27 Or *The spirit of man is the* Lord*'s lamp*   [b]6 Some Hebrew manuscripts, Septuagint and Vulgate; most Hebrew manuscripts *vapor for those who seek death*

¹²The Righteous One[a] takes note of the house of the
  wicked
and brings the wicked to ruin. [h]

¹³If a man shuts his ears to the cry of the poor,
  he too will cry out and not be answered. [i]

¹⁴A gift given in secret soothes anger,
  and a bribe concealed in the cloak pacifies great
  wrath. [j]

¹⁵When justice is done, it brings joy to the righteous
  but terror to evildoers. [k]

¹⁶A man who strays from the path of understanding
  comes to rest in the company of the dead. [l]

¹⁷He who loves pleasure will become poor;
  whoever loves wine and oil will never be rich. [m]

¹⁸The wicked become a ransom[n] for the righteous,
  and the unfaithful for the upright.

¹⁹Better to live in a desert
  than with a quarrelsome and ill-tempered wife. [o]

²⁰In the house of the wise are stores of choice food and
  oil,
  but a foolish man devours all he has.

²¹He who pursues righteousness and love
  finds life, prosperity[b] and honor. [p]

²²A wise man attacks the city of the mighty[q]
  and pulls down the stronghold in which they trust.

²³He who guards his mouth[r] and his tongue
  keeps himself from calamity. [s]

²⁴The proud and arrogant[t] man—"Mocker" is his name;
  he behaves with overweening pride.

²⁵The sluggard's craving will be the death of him, [u]
  because his hands refuse to work.

²⁶All day long he craves for more,
  but the righteous give without sparing. [v]

²⁷The sacrifice of the wicked is detestable[w]—
  how much more so when brought with evil intent![x]

²⁸A false witness will perish, [y]
  and whoever listens to him will be destroyed forever. [c]

²⁹A wicked man puts up a bold front,
  but an upright man gives thought to his ways.

³⁰There is no wisdom, [z] no insight, no plan

21:12
h Pr 14:11
21:13
i Mt 18:30-34;
Jas 2:13
21:14
j Pr 18:16; 19:6
21:15
k Pr 10:29
21:16
l Ps 49:14
21:17
m Pr 23:20-21,
29-35
21:18
n Pr 11:8;
Isa 43:3
21:19
o ver 9
21:21
p Mt 5:6
21:22
q Ecc 9:15-16
21:23
r Jas 3:2
s Pr 12:13; 13:3
21:24
t Ps 1:1;
Pr 1:22;
Isa 16:6;
Jer 48:29
21:25
u Pr 13:4
21:26
v Ps 37:26;
Mt 5:42;
Eph 4:28
21:27
w Isa 66:3;
Jer 6:20;
Am 5:22
x Pr 15:8
21:28
y Pr 19:5
21:30
z Jer 9:23

---

a12 Or The righteous man   *b21 Or righteousness*   *c28 Or / but the words of an obedient man will*
live on

that can succeed against the LORD. [a]

31The horse is made ready for the day of battle,
    but victory rests with the LORD. [b]

22 A good name is more desirable than great riches;
    to be esteemed is better than silver or gold. [c]

2Rich and poor have this in common:
    The LORD is the Maker of them all. [d]

3A prudent man sees danger and takes refuge, [e]
    but the simple keep going and suffer for it. [f]

4Humility and the fear of the LORD
    bring wealth and honor and life.

5In the paths of the wicked lie thorns and snares, [g]
    but he who guards his soul stays far from them.

6Train[a] a child in the way he should go, [h]
    and when he is old he will not turn from it.

7The rich rule over the poor,
    and the borrower is servant to the lender.

8He who sows wickedness reaps trouble, [i]
    and the rod of his fury will be destroyed. [j]

9A generous man will himself be blessed, [k]
    for he shares his food with the poor. [l]

10Drive out the mocker, and out goes strife;
    quarrels and insults are ended. [m]

11He who loves a pure heart and whose speech is gracious
    will have the king for his friend. [n]

12The eyes of the LORD keep watch over knowledge,
    but he frustrates the words of the unfaithful.

13The sluggard says, "There is a lion outside!"[o]
    or, "I will be murdered in the streets!"

14The mouth of an adulteress is a deep pit;[p]
    he who is under the LORD's wrath will fall into it. [q]

15Folly is bound up in the heart of a child,
    but the rod of discipline will drive it far from him. [r]

16He who oppresses the poor to increase his wealth
    and he who gives gifts to the rich—both come to
        poverty.

Sayings of the Wise

17Pay attention and listen to the sayings of the wise;[s]

21:30
[a] Isa 8:10;
Ac 5:39
21:31
[b] Ps 3:8;
33:12-19;
Isa 31:1
22:1
[c] Ecc 7:1
22:2
[d] Job 31:15
22:3
[e] Pr 14:16
[f] Pr 27:12
22:5
[g] Pr 15:19
22:6
[h] Eph 6:4
22:8
[i] Job 4:8
[j] Ps 125:3
22:9
[k] 2Co 9:6
[l] Pr 19:17
22:10
[m] Pr 18:6; 26:20
22:11
[n] Pr 16:13;
Mt 5:8
22:13
[o] Pr 26:13
22:14
[p] Pr 2:16; 5:3-5;
7:5; 23:27
[q] Ecc 7:26
22:15
[r] Pr 13:24; 23:14
22:17
[s] Pr 5:1

a6 Or Start

apply your heart to what I teach,
18for it is pleasing when you keep them in your heart
and have all of them ready on your lips.
19So that your trust may be in the LORD,
I teach you today, even you.
20Have I not written thirty[a] sayings for you,
sayings of counsel and knowledge,
21teaching you true and reliable words,[t]
so that you can give sound answers
to him who sent you?

22Do not exploit the poor[u] because they are poor
and do not crush the needy in court,[v]
23for the LORD will take up their case[w]
and will plunder those who plunder them.[x]

24Do not make friends with a hot-tempered man,
do not associate with one easily angered,
25or you may learn his ways
and get yourself ensnared.[y]

26Do not be a man who strikes hands in pledge[z]
or puts up security for debts;
27if you lack the means to pay,
your very bed will be snatched from under you.[a]

28Do not move an ancient boundary stone[b]
set up by your forefathers.

29Do you see a man skilled in his work?
He will serve[c] before kings;
he will not serve before obscure men.

23

When you sit to dine with a ruler,
note well what[b] is before you,
2and put a knife to your throat
if you are given to gluttony.
3Do not crave his delicacies,[d]
for that food is deceptive.

4Do not wear yourself out to get rich;
have the wisdom to show restraint.
5Cast but a glance at riches, and they are gone,
for they will surely sprout wings
and fly off to the sky like an eagle.[e]

6Do not eat the food of a stingy man,
do not crave his delicacies;[f]
7for he is the kind of man
who is always thinking about the cost.[c]
"Eat and drink," he says to you,
but his heart is not with you.
8You will vomit up the little you have eaten

22:21
tLk 1:3-4;
1Pe 3:15
22:22
uZec 7:10
vEx 23:6;
Mal 3:5
22:23
wPs 12:5
x1Sa 25:39;
Pr 23:10-11
22:25
y1Co 15:33
22:26
zPr 11:15
22:27
aPr 17:18
22:28
bDt 19:14;
Pr 23:10
22:29
cGe 41:46
23:3
dver 6-8
23:5
ePr 27:24
23:6
fPs 141:4

---

a20 Or not formerly written; or not written excellent   *b1 Or who*   *c7 Or for as he thinks within*
himself, / so he is; or for as he puts on a feast, / so he is

and will have wasted your compliments.

[9]Do not speak to a fool,
for he will scorn the wisdom of your words. [g]

[10]Do not move an ancient boundary stone[h]
or encroach on the fields of the fatherless,
[11]for their Defender[i] is strong;
he will take up their case against you. [j]

[12]Apply your heart to instruction
and your ears to words of knowledge.

[13]Do not withhold discipline from a child;
if you punish him with the rod, he will not die.
[14]Punish him with the rod
and save his soul from death. [a]

[15]My son, if your heart is wise,
then my heart will be glad;
[16]my inmost being will rejoice
when your lips speak what is right. [k]

[17]Do not let your heart envy[l] sinners,
but always be zealous for the fear of the LORD.
[18]There is surely a future hope for you,
and your hope will not be cut off. [m]

[19]Listen, my son, and be wise,
and keep your heart on the right path.
[20]Do not join those who drink too much wine[n]
or gorge themselves on meat,
[21]for drunkards and gluttons become poor, [o]
and drowsiness clothes them in rags.

[22]Listen to your father, who gave you life,
and do not despise your mother when she is old. [p]
[23]Buy the truth and do not sell it;
get wisdom, discipline and understanding. [q]
[24]The father of a righteous man has great joy;
he who has a wise son delights in him. [r]
[25]May your father and mother be glad;
may she who gave you birth rejoice!

[26]My son, [s] give me your heart
and let your eyes keep to my ways, [t]
[27]for a prostitute is a deep pit[u]
and a wayward wife is a narrow well.
[28]Like a bandit she lies in wait, [v]
and multiplies the unfaithful among men.

[29]Who has woe? Who has sorrow?
Who has strife? Who has complaints?
Who has needless bruises? Who has bloodshot eyes?
[30]Those who linger over wine, [w]

23:9
g Pr 1:7; 9:7;
Mt 7:6
23:10
h Dt 19:14;
Pr 22:28
23:11
i Job 19:25
j Pr 22:22-23
23:16
k ver 24;
Pr 27:11
23:17
l Ps 37:1;
Pr 28:14
23:18
m Ps 9:18;
Pr 24:14,19-20
23:20
n Isa 5:11,22;
Ro 13:13;
Eph 5:18
23:21
o Pr 21:17
23:22
p Lev 19:32;
Pr 1:8; 30:17;
Eph 6:1-2
23:23
q Pr 4:7
23:24
r ver 15-16;
Pr 10:1; 15:20
23:26
s Pr 3:1; 5:1-6
t Ps 18:21;
Pr 4:4
23:27
u Pr 22:14
23:28
v Pr 7:11-12;
Ecc 7:26
23:30
w Ps 75:8;
Isa 5:11;
Eph 5:18

---

[a]14 Hebrew *Sheol*

who go to sample bowls of mixed wine.
³¹Do not gaze at wine when it is red,
  when it sparkles in the cup,
  when it goes down smoothly!
³²In the end it bites like a snake
  and poisons like a viper.
³³Your eyes will see strange sights
  and your mind imagine confusing things.
³⁴You will be like one sleeping on the high seas,
  lying on top of the rigging.
³⁵"They hit me," you will say, "but I'm not hurt!
  They beat me, but I don't feel it!
  When will I wake up
  so I can find another drink?"

24

Do not envyˣ wicked men,
  do not desire their company;
²for their hearts plot violence,
  and their lips talk about making trouble.ʸ

³By wisdom a house is built,ᶻ
  and through understanding it is established;
⁴through knowledge its rooms are filled
  with rare and beautiful treasures.ª

⁵A wise man has great power,
  and a man of knowledge increases strength;
⁶for waging war you need guidance,
  and for victory many advisers.ᵇ

⁷Wisdom is too high for a fool;
  in the assembly at the gate he has nothing to say.

⁸He who plots evil
  will be known as a schemer.
⁹The schemes of folly are sin,
  and men detest a mocker.

¹⁰If you falter in times of trouble,
  how small is your strength!ᶜ

¹¹Rescue those being led away to death;
  hold back those staggering toward slaughter.ᵈ
¹²If you say, "But we knew nothing about this,"
  does not he who weighsᵉ the heart perceive it?
  Does not he who guards your life know it?
  Will he not repay each person according to what he
  has done?ᶠ

¹³Eat honey, my son, for it is good;
  honey from the comb is sweet to your taste.
¹⁴Know also that wisdom is sweet to your soul;
  if you find it, there is a future hope for you,
  and your hope will not be cut off.ᵍ ʰ

24:1
ˣPs 37:1; 73:3;
Pr 3:31-32;
23:17-18
24:2
ʸPs 10:7
24:3
ᶻPr 14:1
24:4
ªPr 8:21
24:6
ᵇPr 11:14;
20:18; Lk 14:31
24:10
ᶜJob 4:5;
Jer 51:46;
Heb 12:3
24:11
ᵈPs 82:4;
Isa 58:6-7
24:12
ᵉPr 21:2
ᶠJob 34:11;
Ps 62:12;
Ro 2:6*
24:14
ᵍPs 119:103;
Pr 16:24
ʰPr 23:18

¹⁵Do not lie in wait like an outlaw against a righteous
man's house,
do not raid his dwelling place;
¹⁶for though a righteous man falls seven times, he rises
again,
but the wicked are brought down by calamity. ⁱ

¹⁷Do not gloat^j when your enemy falls;
when he stumbles, do not let your heart rejoice, ^k
¹⁸or the LORD will see and disapprove
and turn his wrath away from him.

¹⁹Do not fret^l because of evil men
or be envious of the wicked,
²⁰for the evil man has no future hope,
and the lamp of the wicked will be snuffed out. ^m

²¹Fear the LORD and the king, ⁿ my son,
and do not join with the rebellious,
²²for those two will send sudden destruction upon them,
and who knows what calamities they can bring?

Further Sayings of the Wise

²³These also are sayings of the wise: ^o

To show partiality^p in judging is not good: ^q
²⁴Whoever says to the guilty, "You are innocent"^r —
peoples will curse him and nations denounce him.
²⁵But it will go well with those who convict the guilty,
and rich blessing will come upon them.

²⁶An honest answer
is like a kiss on the lips.

²⁷Finish your outdoor work
and get your fields ready;
after that, build your house.

²⁸Do not testify against your neighbor without cause, ^s
or use your lips to deceive.
²⁹Do not say, "I'll do to him as he has done to me;
I'll pay that man back for what he did."^t

³⁰I went past the field of the sluggard, ^u
past the vineyard of the man who lacks judgment;
³¹thorns had come up everywhere,
the ground was covered with weeds,
and the stone wall was in ruins.
³²I applied my heart to what I observed
and learned a lesson from what I saw:
³³A little sleep, a little slumber,
a little folding of the hands to rest^v—

24:16
i Job 5:19;
Ps 34:19;
Mic 7:8
24:17
j Job 1:12
k Job 31:29
24:19
l Ps 37:1
24:20
m Job 18:5;
Pr 13:9;
23:17-18
24:21
n Ro 13:1-5;
1Pe 2:17
24:23
o Pr 1:6
p Lev 19:15
q Pr 28:21
24:24
r Pr 17:15
24:28
s Ps 7:4;
Pr 25:18;
Eph 4:25
24:29
t Pr 20:22;
Mt 5:38-41;
Ro 12:17
24:30
u Pr 6:6-11;
26:13-16
24:33
v Pr 6:10

³⁴and poverty will come on you like a bandit
  and scarcity like an armed man. *ᵃ ʷ*

More Proverbs of Solomon

25 These are more proverbsˣ of Solomon, copied by the men of
Hezekiah king of Judah:ʸ

²It is the glory of God to conceal a matter;
  to search out a matter is the glory of kings. ᶻ

³As the heavens are high and the earth is deep,
  so the hearts of kings are unsearchable.

⁴Remove the dross from the silver,
  and out comes material forᵇ the silversmith;
⁵remove the wicked from the king's presence, ᵃ
  and his throne will be establishedᵇ through
    righteousness. ᶜ

⁶Do not exalt yourself in the king's presence,
  and do not claim a place among great men;
⁷it is better for him to say to you, "Come up here," ᵈ
  than for him to humiliate you before a nobleman.

  What you have seen with your eyes
⁸ do not bringᶜ hastily to court,
  for what will you do in the end
    if your neighbor puts you to shame?ᵉ

⁹If you argue your case with a neighbor,
  do not betray another man's confidence,
¹⁰or he who hears it may shame you
  and you will never lose your bad reputation.

¹¹A word aptly spoken
  is like apples of gold in settings of silver. ᶠ

¹²Like an earring of gold or an ornament of fine gold
  is a wise man's rebuke to a listening ear. ᵍ

¹³Like the coolness of snow at harvest time
  is a trustworthy messenger to those who send him;
  he refreshes the spirit of his masters. ʰ

¹⁴Like clouds and wind without rain
  is a man who boasts of gifts he does not give.

¹⁵Through patience a ruler can be persuaded, ⁱ
  and a gentle tongue can break a bone. ʲ

¹⁶If you find honey, eat just enough—
  too much of it, and you will vomit. ᵏ
¹⁷Seldom set foot in your neighbor's house—
  too much of you, and he will hate you.

24:34
wPr 10:4;
Ecc 10:18
25:1
x1Ki 4:32
yPr 1:1
25:2
zPr 16:10-15
25:5
aPr 20:8
b2Sa 7:13
cPr 16:12; 29:14
25:7
dLk 14:7-10
25:8
eMt 5:25-26
25:11
fver 12;
Pr 15:23
25:12
gver 11;
Ps 141:5;
Pr 13:18; 15:31
25:13
hPr 10:26;
13:17
25:15
iEcc 10:4
jPr 15:1
25:16
kver 27

ᵃ34 Or *like a vagrant / and scarcity like a beggar*   ᵇ4 Or *comes a vessel from*   ᶜ7,8 Or *nobleman /*
on whom you had set your eyes. / ⁸Do not go

[18]Like a club or a sword or a sharp arrow
    is the man who gives false testimony against his
        neighbor.[l]

[19]Like a bad tooth or a lame foot
    is reliance on the unfaithful in times of trouble.

[20]Like one who takes away a garment on a cold day,
    or like vinegar poured on soda,
    is one who sings songs to a heavy heart.

[21]If your enemy is hungry, give him food to eat;
    if he is thirsty, give him water to drink.
[22]In doing this, you will heap burning coals[m] on his head,
    and the LORD will reward you.[n]

[23]As a north wind brings rain,
    so a sly tongue brings angry looks.

[24]Better to live on a corner of the roof
    than share a house with a quarrelsome wife.[o]

[25]Like cold water to a weary soul
    is good news from a distant land.[p]

[26]Like a muddied spring or a polluted well
    is a righteous man who gives way to the wicked.

[27]It is not good to eat too much honey,[q]
    nor is it honorable to seek one's own honor.[r]

[28]Like a city whose walls are broken down
    is a man who lacks self-control.

26 Like snow in summer or rain[s] in harvest,
    honor is not fitting for a fool.[t]

[2]Like a fluttering sparrow or a darting swallow,
    an undeserved curse does not come to rest.[u]

[3]A whip for the horse, a halter for the donkey,[v]
    and a rod for the backs of fools![w]

[4]Do not answer a fool according to his folly,
    or you will be like him yourself.[x]

[5]Answer a fool according to his folly,
    or he will be wise in his own eyes.[y]

[6]Like cutting off one's feet or drinking violence
    is the sending of a message by the hand of a fool.[z]

[7]Like a lame man's legs that hang limp
    is a proverb in the mouth of a fool.[a]

[8]Like tying a stone in a sling
    is the giving of honor to a fool.[b]

[9]Like a thornbush in a drunkard's hand
    is a proverb in the mouth of a fool.[c]

25:18
lPs 57:4;
Pr 12:18
25:22
mPs 18:8
n2Sa 16:12;
2Ch 28:15;
Mt 5:44;
Ro 12:20*
25:24
oPr 21:9
25:25
pPr 15:30
25:27
qver 16
rPr 27:2;
Mt 23:12
26:1
s1Sa 12:17
tver 8; Pr 19:10
26:2
uNu 23:8;
Dt 23:5
26:3
vPs 32:9
wPr 10:13
26:4
xver 5;
Isa 36:21
26:5
yver 4; Pr 3:7
26:6
zPr 10:26
26:7
aver 9
26:8
bver 1
26:9
cver 7

[10] Like an archer who wounds at random
is he who hires a fool or any passer-by.

[11] As a dog returns to its vomit, [d]
so a fool repeats his folly. [e]

[12] Do you see a man wise in his own eyes? [f]
There is more hope for a fool than for him. [g]

[13] The sluggard says, [h] "There is a lion in the road,
a fierce lion roaming the streets!" [i]

[14] As a door turns on its hinges,
so a sluggard turns on his bed. [j]

[15] The sluggard buries his hand in the dish;
he is too lazy to bring it back to his mouth. [k]

[16] The sluggard is wiser in his own eyes
than seven men who answer discreetly.

[17] Like one who seizes a dog by the ears
is a passer-by who meddles in a quarrel not his own.

[18] Like a madman shooting
firebrands or deadly arrows
[19] is a man who deceives his neighbor
and says, "I was only joking!"

[20] Without wood a fire goes out;
without gossip a quarrel dies down. [l]

[21] As charcoal to embers and as wood to fire,
so is a quarrelsome man for kindling strife. [m]

[22] The words of a gossip are like choice morsels;
they go down to a man's inmost parts. [n]

[23] Like a coating of glaze[a] over earthenware
are fervent lips with an evil heart.

[24] A malicious man disguises himself with his lips, [o]
but in his heart he harbors deceit. [p]
[25] Though his speech is charming, [q] do not believe him,
for seven abominations fill his heart. [r]
[26] His malice may be concealed by deception,
but his wickedness will be exposed in the assembly.

[27] If a man digs a pit, [s] he will fall into it; [t]
if a man rolls a stone, it will roll back on him. [u]

[28] A lying tongue hates those it hurts,
and a flattering mouth [v] works ruin.

27

Do not boast [w] about tomorrow,
for you do not know what a day may bring forth. [x]

[2] Let another praise you, and not your own mouth;

26:11
d 2Pe 2:22*
e Ex 8:15;
Ps 85:8
26:12
f Pr 3:7
g Pr 29:20
26:13
h Pr 6:6-11;
24:30-34
i Pr 22:13
26:14
j Pr 6:9
26:15
k Pr 19:24
26:20
l Pr 22:10
26:21
m Pr 14:17;
15:18
26:22
n Pr 18:8
26:24
o Ps 31:18
p Ps 41:6;
Pr 10:18; 12:20
26:25
q Ps 28:3
r Jer 9:4-8
26:27
s Ps 7:15
t Est 6:13
u Est 2:23; 7:9;
Ps 35:8; 141:10;
Pr 28:10; 29:6;
Isa 50:11
26:28
v Ps 12:3;
Pr 29:5
27:1
w 1Ki 20:11
x Mt 6:34;
Lk 12:19-20;
Jas 4:13-16

---

[a] 23 With a different word division of the Hebrew; Masoretic Text *of silver dross*

someone else, and not your own lips. y

3Stone is heavy and sandz a burden,
  but provocation by a fool is heavier than both.

4Anger is cruel and fury overwhelming,
  but who can stand before jealousy?a

5Better is open rebuke
  than hidden love.

6Wounds from a friend can be trusted,
  but an enemy multiplies kisses. b

7He who is full loathes honey,
  but to the hungry even what is bitter tastes sweet.

8Like a bird that strays from its nestc
  is a man who strays from his home.

9Perfumed and incense bring joy to the heart,
  and the pleasantness of one's friend springs from his
      earnest counsel.

10Do not forsake your friend and the friend of your father,
  and do not go to your brother's house when disastere
      strikes you—
  better a neighbor nearby than a brother far away.

11Be wise, my son, and bring joy to my heart;f
  then I can answer anyone who treats me with
      contempt. g

12The prudent see danger and take refuge,
  but the simple keep going and suffer for it. h

13Take the garment of one who puts up security for a
      stranger;
  hold it in pledge if he does it for a wayward woman. i

14If a man loudly blesses his neighbor early in the
      morning,
  it will be taken as a curse.

15A quarrelsome wife is like
  a constant drippingj on a rainy day;
16restraining her is like restraining the wind
  or grasping oil with the hand.

17As iron sharpens iron,
  so one man sharpens another.

18He who tends a fig tree will eat its fruit,k
  and he who looks after his master will be honored. l

19As water reflects a face,
  so a man's heart reflects the man.

27:2
yPr 25:27
27:3
zJob 6:3
27:4
aNu 5:14
27:6
bPs 141:5;
Pr 28:23
27:8
cIsa 16:2
27:9
dEst 2:12;
Ps 45:8
27:10
ePr 17:17; 18:24
27:11
fPr 10:1;
23:15-16
gGe 24:60
27:12
hPr 22:3
27:13
iPr 20:16
27:15
jEst 1:18;
Pr 19:13
27:18
k1Co 9:7
lLk 19:12-27

20Death and Destruction[a] are never satisfied,[m]
and neither are the eyes of man.[n]

21The crucible for silver and the furnace for gold,[o]
but man is tested by the praise he receives.

22Though you grind a fool in a mortar,
grinding him like grain with a pestle,
you will not remove his folly from him.

23Be sure you know the condition of your flocks,[p]
give careful attention to your herds;
24for riches do not endure forever,[q]
and a crown is not secure for all generations.
25When the hay is removed and new growth appears
and the grass from the hills is gathered in,
26the lambs will provide you with clothing,
and the goats with the price of a field.
27You will have plenty of goats' milk
to feed you and your family
and to nourish your servant girls.

28

The wicked man flees[r] though no one pursues,[s]
but the righteous are as bold as a lion.[t]

2When a country is rebellious, it has many rulers,
but a man of understanding and knowledge maintains
order.

3A ruler[b] who oppresses the poor
is like a driving rain that leaves no crops.

4Those who forsake the law praise the wicked,
but those who keep the law resist them.

5Evil men do not understand justice,
but those who seek the LORD understand it fully.

6Better a poor man whose walk is blameless
than a rich man whose ways are perverse.[u]

7He who keeps the law is a discerning son,
but a companion of gluttons disgraces his father.[v]

8He who increases his wealth by exorbitant interest[w]
amasses it for another,[x] who will be kind to the
poor.[y]

9If anyone turns a deaf ear to the law,
even his prayers are detestable.[z]

10He who leads the upright along an evil path
will fall into his own trap,[a]
but the blameless will receive a good inheritance.

11A rich man may be wise in his own eyes,

27:20
m Pr 30:15-16;
Hab 2:5
n Ecc 1:8; 6:7
27:21
o Pr 17:3
27:23
p Pr 12:10
27:24
q Pr 23:5
28:1
r 2Ki 7:7
s Lev 26:17;
Ps 53:5
t Ps 138:3
28:6
u Pr 19:1
28:7
v Pr 23:19-21
28:8
w Ex 18:21
x Job 27:17;
Pr 13:22
y Ps 112:9;
Pr 14:31;
Lk 14:12-14
28:9
z Ps 66:18;
109:7; Pr 15:8;
Isa 1:13
28:10
a Pr 26:27

a20 Hebrew *Sheol and Abaddon*   b3 Or *A poor man*

but a poor man who has discernment sees through
him.

¹²When the righteous triumph, there is great elation;[b]
but when the wicked rise to power, men go into
hiding.[c]

¹³He who conceals his sins[d] does not prosper,
but whoever confesses and renounces them finds
mercy.[e]

¹⁴Blessed is the man who always fears the LORD,
but he who hardens his heart falls into trouble.

¹⁵Like a roaring lion or a charging bear
is a wicked man ruling over a helpless people.

¹⁶A tyrannical ruler lacks judgment,
but he who hates ill-gotten gain will enjoy a long life.

¹⁷A man tormented by the guilt of murder
will be a fugitive[f] till death;
let no one support him.

¹⁸He whose walk is blameless is kept safe,
but he whose ways are perverse will suddenly fall.[g]

¹⁹He who works his land will have abundant food,
but the one who chases fantasies will have his fill of
poverty.[h]

²⁰A faithful man will be richly blessed,
but one eager to get rich will not go unpunished.[i]

²¹To show partiality is not good[j] —
yet a man will do wrong for a piece of bread.[k]

²²A stingy man is eager to get rich
and is unaware that poverty awaits him.[l]

²³He who rebukes a man will in the end gain more favor
than he who has a flattering tongue.[m]

²⁴He who robs his father or mother[n]
and says, "It's not wrong"—
he is partner to him who destroys.[o]

²⁵A greedy man stirs up dissension,
but he who trusts in the LORD[p] will prosper.

²⁶He who trusts in himself is a fool,[q]
but he who walks in wisdom is kept safe.

²⁷He who gives to the poor will lack nothing,[r]
but he who closes his eyes to them receives many
curses.

²⁸When the wicked rise to power, people go into hiding;[s]
but when the wicked perish, the righteous thrive.

28:12
b 2Ki 11:20
c Pr 11:10; 29:2
28:13
d Job 31:33
e Ps 32:1-5;
1Jn 1:9
28:17
f Ge 9:6
28:18
g Pr 10:9
28:19
h Pr 12:11
28:20
i ver 22;
Pr 10:6; 1Ti 6:9
28:21
j Pr 18:5
k Eze 13:19
28:22
l ver 20; Pr 23:6
28:23
m Pr 27:5-6
28:24
n Pr 19:26
o Pr 18:9
28:25
p Pr 29:25
28:26
q Ps 4:5; Pr 3:5
28:27
r Dt 15:7; 24:19;
Pr 19:17; 22:9
28:28
s ver 12

29

A man who remains stiff-necked after many rebukes
will suddenly be destroyed—without remedy. [t]

[2]When the righteous thrive, the people rejoice; [u]
when the wicked rule, the people groan. [v]

[3]A man who loves wisdom brings joy to his father, [w]
but a companion of prostitutes squanders his wealth. [x]

[4]By justice a king gives a country stability, [y]
but one who is greedy for bribes tears it down.

[5]Whoever flatters his neighbor
is spreading a net for his feet.

[6]An evil man is snared by his own sin, [z]
but a righteous one can sing and be glad.

[7]The righteous care about justice for the poor, [a]
but the wicked have no such concern.

[8]Mockers stir up a city,
but wise men turn away anger. [b]

[9]If a wise man goes to court with a fool,
the fool rages and scoffs, and there is no peace.

[10]Bloodthirsty men hate a man of integrity
and seek to kill the upright. [c]

[11]A fool gives full vent to his anger,
but a wise man keeps himself under control. [d]

[12]If a ruler listens to lies,
all his officials become wicked.

[13]The poor man and the oppressor have this in common:
The LORD gives sight to the eyes of both. [e]

[14]If a king judges the poor with fairness,
his throne will always be secure. [f]

[15]The rod of correction imparts wisdom,
but a child left to himself disgraces his mother. [g]

[16]When the wicked thrive, so does sin,
but the righteous will see their downfall. [h]

[17]Discipline your son, and he will give you peace;
he will bring delight to your soul. [i]

[18]Where there is no revelation, the people cast off
restraint;
but blessed is he who keeps the law. [j]

[19]A servant cannot be corrected by mere words;
though he understands, he will not respond.

[20]Do you see a man who speaks in haste?
There is more hope for a fool than for him. [k]

[21]If a man pampers his servant from youth,

29:1
t2Ch 36:16;
Pr 6:15
29:2
uEst 8:15
vPr 28:12
29:3
wPr 10:1
xPr 5:8-10;
Lk 15:11-32
29:4
yPr 8:15-16
29:6
zEcc 9:12
29:7
aJob 29:16;
Ps 41:1;
Pr 31:8-9
29:8
bPr 11:11;
16:14
29:10
c1Jn 3:12
29:11
dPr 12:16;
19:11
29:13
ePr 22:2;
Mt 5:45
29:14
fPs 72:1-5;
Pr 16:12
29:15
gPr 10:1; 13:24;
17:21,25
29:16
hPs 37:35-36;
58:10; 91:8;
92:11
29:17
iver 15; Pr 10:1
29:18
jPs 1:1-2;
119:1-2;
Jn 13:17
29:20
kPr 26:12;
Jas 1:19

he will bring grief[a] in the end.

22An angry man stirs up dissension,
and a hot-tempered one commits many sins.[1]

23A man's pride brings him low,
but a man of lowly spirit gains honor.[m]

24The accomplice of a thief is his own enemy;
he is put under oath and dare not testify.[n]

25Fear of man will prove to be a snare,
but whoever trusts in the LORD[o] is kept safe.

26Many seek an audience with a ruler,[p]
but it is from the LORD that man gets justice.

27The righteous detest the dishonest;
the wicked detest the upright.[q]

Sayings of Agur

30 The sayings of Agur son of Jakeh—an oracle[b]:

This man declared to Ithiel,
to Ithiel and to Ucal:[c]

2"I am the most ignorant of men;
I do not have a man's understanding.
3I have not learned wisdom,
nor have I knowledge of the Holy One.[r]
4Who has gone up[s] to heaven and come down?
Who has gathered up the wind in the hollow[t] of his
hands?
Who has wrapped up the waters[u] in his cloak?[v]
Who has established all the ends of the earth?
What is his name,[w] and the name of his son?
Tell me if you know!

5"Every word of God is flawless;[x]
he is a shield[y] to those who take refuge in him.
6Do not add[z] to his words,
or he will rebuke you and prove you a liar.

7"Two things I ask of you, O LORD;
do not refuse me before I die:
8Keep falsehood and lies far from me;
give me neither poverty nor riches,
but give me only my daily bread.[a]
9Otherwise, I may have too much and disown[b] you
and say, 'Who is the LORD?'[c]
Or I may become poor and steal,

29:22
1Pr 14:17;
15:18; 26:21
29:23
mPr 11:2;
15:33; 16:18;
Isa 66:2;
Mt 23:12
29:24
nLev 5:1
29:25
oPr 28:25
29:26
pPr 19:6
29:27
qver 10
30:3
rPr 9:10
30:4
sPs 24:1-2;
Jn 3:13;
Eph 4:7-10
tPs 104:3;
Isa 40:12
uJob 26:8;
38:8-9 vGe 1:2
wRev 19:12
30:5
xPs 12:6; 18:30
yGe 15:1;
Ps 84:11
30:6
zDt 4:2; 12:32;
Rev 22:18
30:8
aMt 6:11
30:9
bJos 24:27;
Isa 1:4; 59:13
cDt 6:12;
8:10-14;
Hos 13:6

a21 The meaning of the Hebrew for this word is uncertain.   b1 Or *Jakeh of Massa*
c1 Masoretic Text; with a different word division of the Hebrew *declared, "I am weary, O God; / I am*
weary, O God, and faint.

and so dishonor the name of my God. [d]

[10]"Do not slander a servant to his master,
 or he will curse you, and you will pay for it.

[11]"There are those who curse their fathers
 and do not bless their mothers; [e]
[12]those who are pure in their own eyes [f]
 and yet are not cleansed of their filth; [g]
[13]those whose eyes are ever so haughty, [h]
 whose glances are so disdainful;
[14]those whose teeth [i] are swords
 and whose jaws are set with knives [j]
to devour [k] the poor [l] from the earth,
 the needy from among mankind. [m]

[15]"The leech has two daughters.
 'Give! Give!' they cry.

"There are three things that are never satisfied, [n]
 four that never say, 'Enough!':
[16]the grave, [a][o] the barren womb,
 land, which is never satisfied with water,
 and fire, which never says, 'Enough!'

[17]"The eye that mocks [p] a father,
 that scorns obedience to a mother,
will be pecked out by the ravens of the valley,
 will be eaten by the vultures. [q]

[18]"There are three things that are too amazing for me,
 four that I do not understand:
[19]the way of an eagle in the sky,
 the way of a snake on a rock,
the way of a ship on the high seas,
 and the way of a man with a maiden.

[20]"This is the way of an adulteress:
 She eats and wipes her mouth
 and says, 'I've done nothing wrong.' [r]

[21]"Under three things the earth trembles,
 under four it cannot bear up:
[22]a servant who becomes king, [s]
 a fool who is full of food,
[23]an unloved woman who is married,
 and a maidservant who displaces her mistress.

[24]"Four things on earth are small,
 yet they are extremely wise:
[25]Ants are creatures of little strength,
 yet they store up their food in the summer; [t]
[26]coneys [b][u] are creatures of little power,
 yet they make their home in the crags;

30:9
[d] Dt 8:12
30:11
[e] Pr 20:20
30:12
[f] Pr 16:2;
Lk 18:11
[g] Jer 2:23,35
30:13
[h] 2Sa 22:28;
Job 41:34;
Ps 131:1;
Pr 6:17
30:14
[i] Job 4:11;
29:17; Ps 3:7
[j] Ps 57:4
[k] Job 24:9;
Ps 14:4
[l] Am 8:4;
Mic 2:2
[m] Job 19:22
30:15
[n] Pr 27:20
30:16
[o] Pr 27:20;
Isa 5:14; 14:9,
11; Hab 2:5
30:17
[p] Dt 21:18-21;
Pr 23:22
[q] Job 15:23
30:20
[r] Pr 5:6
30:22
[s] Pr 19:10; 29:2
30:25
[t] Pr 6:6-8
30:26
[u] Ps 104:18

---

[a]16 Hebrew *Sheol*   [b]26 That is, the hyrax or rock badger

²⁷locusts^v have no king,
>   yet they advance together in ranks;
²⁸a lizard can be caught with the hand,
>   yet it is found in kings' palaces.

²⁹"There are three things that are stately in their stride,
>   four that move with stately bearing:
³⁰a lion, mighty among beasts,
>   who retreats before nothing;
³¹a strutting rooster, a he-goat,
>   and a king with his army around him. ^a

³²"If you have played the fool and exalted yourself,
>   or if you have planned evil,
>   clap your hand over your mouth!^w
³³For as churning the milk produces butter,
>   and as twisting the nose produces blood,
>   so stirring up anger produces strife."

Sayings of King Lemuel

31 The sayings^x of King Lemuel—an oracle^b his mother taught him:

²"O my son, O son of my womb,
>   O son of my vows,^{c y}
³do not spend your strength on women,
>   your vigor on those who ruin kings. ^z

⁴"It is not for kings, O Lemuel—
>   not for kings to drink wine,^a
>   not for rulers to crave beer,
⁵lest they drink^b and forget what the law decrees,^c
>   and deprive all the oppressed of their rights.
⁶Give beer to those who are perishing,
>   wine^d to those who are in anguish;
⁷let them drink^e and forget their poverty
>   and remember their misery no more.

⁸"Speak^f up for those who cannot speak for themselves,
>   for the rights of all who are destitute.
⁹Speak up and judge fairly;
>   defend the rights of the poor and needy."^g

Epilogue: The Wife of Noble Character

¹⁰^dA wife of noble character^h who can find?ⁱ
>   She is worth far more than rubies.
¹¹Her husband^j has full confidence in her

30:27
v Ex 10:4
30:32
w Job 21:5; 29:9
31:1
x Pr 22:17
31:2
y Jdg 11:30;
Isa 49:15
31:3
z Dt 17:17;
1Ki 11:3;
Ne 13:26;
Pr 5:1-14
31:4
a Pr 20:1;
Ecc 10:16-17;
Isa 5:22
31:5
b 1Ki 16:9
c Pr 16:12;
Hos 4:11
31:6
d Ge 14:18
31:7
e Est 1:10
31:8
f 1Sa 19:4;
Job 29:12-17
31:9
g Lev 19:15;
Dt 1:16;
Pr 24:23; 29:7;
Isa 1:17;
Jer 22:16
31:10
h Ru 3:11;
Pr 12:4; 18:22
i Pr 8:35; 19:14
31:11
j Ge 2:18

---

^a31 Or *king secure against revolt*   ^b1 Or *of Lemuel king of Massa, which*   ^c2 Or / *the answer to my prayers*   ^d10 Verses 10-31 are an acrostic, each verse beginning with a successive letter of the Hebrew alphabet.

and lacks nothing of value. [k]

[12] She brings him good, not harm,
all the days of her life.
[13] She selects wool and flax
and works with eager hands. [l]
[14] She is like the merchant ships,
bringing her food from afar.
[15] She gets up while it is still dark;
she provides food for her family
and portions for her servant girls.
[16] She considers a field and buys it;
out of her earnings she plants a vineyard.
[17] She sets about her work vigorously;
her arms are strong for her tasks.
[18] She sees that her trading is profitable,
and her lamp does not go out at night.
[19] In her hand she holds the distaff
and grasps the spindle with her fingers.
[20] She opens her arms to the poor
and extends her hands to the needy. [m]
[21] When it snows, she has no fear for her household;
for all of them are clothed in scarlet.
[22] She makes coverings for her bed;
she is clothed in fine linen and purple.
[23] Her husband is respected at the city gate,
where he takes his seat among the elders [n] of the land.
[24] She makes linen garments and sells them,
and supplies the merchants with sashes.
[25] She is clothed with strength and dignity;
she can laugh at the days to come.
[26] She speaks with wisdom,
and faithful instruction is on her tongue. [o]
[27] She watches over the affairs of her household
and does not eat the bread of idleness.
[28] Her children arise and call her blessed;
her husband also, and he praises her:
[29] "Many women do noble things,
but you surpass them all."
[30] Charm is deceptive, and beauty is fleeting;
but a woman who fears the LORD is to be praised.
[31] Give her the reward she has earned,
and let her works bring her praise [p] at the city gate.

31:11
k Pr 12:4
31:13
l 1Ti 2:9-10
31:20
m Dt 15:11;
Eph 4:28;
Heb 13:16
31:23
n Ex 3:16;
Ru 4:1,11;
Pr 12:4
31:26
o Pr 10:31
31:31
p Pr 11:16

Ecclesiastes

Title and Background

The writer's title ("Teacher") comes from a Hebrew root word related to "assembly" or "congregation." Perhaps the Teacher also held an office in the assembly. The Septuagint word for "Teacher" is *ecclesiastes,* from which most English titles of the book are taken.

Author and Date of Writing

No time period or writer's name is mentioned in the book, but several passages strongly suggest that Solomon is the author. Though some date the book as late as the third century B.C., Solomonic authorship would demand a date of the tenth century B.C.

Theme and Message

Life not centered on God is purposeless and meaningless. Without him, nothing else can satisfy (2:25). With him, all of life and his other good gifts are to be gratefully received and used and enjoyed to the full (2:26; 11:8). The book contains the philosophical and theological reflections of an old man, most of whose life was meaningless because he had not himself relied on God.

Outline

Everything Is Meaningless

1 The words of the Teacher,ᵃᵃ son of David, king in Jerusalem:ᵇ

> ²"Meaningless! Meaningless!"
>   says the Teacher.
>   "Utterly meaningless!
>   Everything is meaningless."ᶜ
>
> ³What does man gain from all his labor
>   at which he toils under the sun?ᵈ
> ⁴Generations come and generations go,
>   but the earth remains forever.ᵉ
> ⁵The sun rises and the sun sets,
>   and hurries back to where it rises.ᶠ
> ⁶The wind blows to the south
>   and turns to the north;

1:1
ᵃver 12;
Ecc 7:27; 12:10
ᵇPr 1:1
1:2
ᶜPs 39:5-6;
62:9; 144:4;
Ecc 12:8;
Ro 8:20-21
1:3
ᵈEcc 2:11,22;
3:9; 5:15-16
1:4
ᵉPs 104:5;
119:90
1:5
ᶠPs 19:5-6

ᵃ1 Or *leader of the assembly;* also in verses 2 and 12

round and round it goes,
　　ever returning on its course.
[7]All streams flow into the sea,
　　yet the sea is never full.
To the place the streams come from,
　　there they return again. [g]
[8]All things are wearisome,
　　more than one can say.
The eye never has enough of seeing, [h]
　　nor the ear its fill of hearing.
[9]What has been will be again,
　　what has been done will be done again;[i]
　　there is nothing new under the sun.
[10]Is there anything of which one can say,
　　"Look! This is something new"?
It was here already, long ago;
　　it was here before our time.
[11]There is no remembrance of men of old,
　　and even those who are yet to come
will not be remembered
　　by those who follow.[j]

Wisdom Is Meaningless

[12]I, the Teacher,[k] was king over Israel in Jerusalem. [13]I devoted myself to study and to explore by wisdom all that is done under heaven. What a heavy burden God has laid on men![l] [14]I have seen all the things that are done under the sun; all of them are meaningless, a chasing after the wind. [m]

[15]What is twisted cannot be straightened;[n]
　　what is lacking cannot be counted.

[16]I thought to myself, "Look, I have grown and increased in wisdom more than anyone who has ruled over Jerusalem before me;[o] I have experienced much of wisdom and knowledge." [17]Then I applied myself to the understanding of wisdom,[p] and also of madness and folly,[q] but I learned that this, too, is a chasing after the wind.

[18]For with much wisdom comes much sorrow;
　　the more knowledge, the more grief.[r]

Pleasures Are Meaningless

2 I thought in my heart, "Come now, I will test you with pleasure[s] to find out what is good." But that also proved to be meaningless. [2]"Laughter,"[t] I said, "is foolish. And what does pleasure accomplish?" [3]I tried cheering myself with wine,[u] and embracing folly[v]—my mind still guiding me with wisdom. I wanted to see what was worthwhile for men to do under heaven during the few days of their lives.

[4]I undertook great projects: I built houses for myself[w] and planted vineyards.[x] [5]I made gardens and parks and planted all kinds of fruit trees in them. [6]I made reservoirs to water groves of flourishing trees. [7]I bought male and female slaves and had other slaves who were born in my house. I also owned more herds and flocks than anyone in Jerusa-

1:7
gJob 36:28
1:8
hPr 27:20
1:9
iEcc 2:12; 3:15
1:11
jEcc 2:16
1:12
kver 1
1:13
lGe 3:17;
Ecc 3:10
1:14
mEcc 2:11,17
1:15
nEcc 7:13
1:16
o1Ki 3:12; 4:30;
Ecc 2:9
1:17
pEcc 7:23
qEcc 2:3,12;
7:25
1:18
rEcc 2:23; 12:12
2:1
sEcc 7:4; 8:15;
Lk 12:19
2:2
tPr 14:13;
Ecc 7:6
2:3
uver 24-25;
Ecc 3:12-13
vEcc 1:17
2:4
w1Ki 7:1-12
xSS 8:11

lem before me. [8]I amassed silver and gold[y] for myself, and the treasure of kings and provinces. I acquired men and women singers,[z] and a harem[a] as well—the delights of the heart of man. [9]I became greater by far than anyone in Jerusalem before me.[a] In all this my wisdom stayed with me.

> [10]I denied myself nothing my eyes desired;
> I refused my heart no pleasure.
> My heart took delight in all my work,
> and this was the reward for all my labor.
> [11]Yet when I surveyed all that my hands had done
> and what I had toiled to achieve,
> everything was meaningless, a chasing after the wind;[b]
> nothing was gained under the sun.[c]

Wisdom and Folly Are Meaningless

> [12]Then I turned my thoughts to consider wisdom,
> and also madness and folly.[d]
> What more can the king's successor do
> than what has already been done?[e]
> [13]I saw that wisdom[f] is better than folly,[g]
> just as light is better than darkness.
> [14]The wise man has eyes in his head,
> while the fool walks in the darkness;
> but I came to realize
> that the same fate overtakes them both.[h]

> [15]Then I thought in my heart,

> "The fate of the fool will overtake me also.
> What then do I gain by being wise?"[i]
> I said in my heart,
> "This too is meaningless."
> [16]For the wise man, like the fool, will not be long
> remembered;
> in days to come both will be forgotten.[j]
> Like the fool, the wise man too must die!

Toil Is Meaningless

[17]So I hated life, because the work that is done under the sun was grievous to me. All of it is meaningless, a chasing after the wind.[k] [18]I hated all the things I had toiled for under the sun, because I must leave them to the one who comes after me.[l] [19]And who knows whether he will be a wise man or a fool? Yet he will have control over all the work into which I have poured my effort and skill under the sun. This too is meaningless. [20]So my heart began to despair over all my toilsome labor under the sun. [21]For a man may do his work with wisdom, knowledge and skill, and then he must leave all he owns to someone who has not worked for it. This too is meaningless and a great misfortune. [22]What does a man get for all the toil and anxious striving with which he labors

2:8
y 1Ki 9:28;
10:10,14,21
z 2Sa 19:35
2:9
a 1Ch 29:25;
Ecc 1:16
2:11
b Ecc 1:14
c Ecc 1:3
2:12
d Ecc 1:17
e Ecc 1:9; 7:25
2:13
f Ecc 7:19; 9:18
g Ecc 7:11-12
2:14
h Ps 49:10;
Pr 17:24;
Ecc 3:19; 6:6;
7:2; 9:3,11-12
2:15
i Ecc 6:8
2:16
j Ecc 1:11; 9:5
2:17
k Ecc 4:2
2:18
l Ps 39:6; 49:10

---

[a]8 The meaning of the Hebrew for this phrase is uncertain.

under the sun?ᵐ ²³All his days his work is pain and grief;ⁿ even at night his mind does not rest. This too is meaningless.

²⁴A man can do nothing better than to eat and drinkᵒ and find satisfaction in his work. ᵖ This too, I see, is from the hand of God, ᑫ ²⁵for without him, who can eat or find enjoyment? ²⁶To the man who pleases him, God gives wisdom, knowledge and happiness, but to the sinner he gives the task of gathering and storing up wealthʳ to hand it over to the one who pleases God. ˢ This too is meaningless, a chasing after the wind.

A Time for Everything

3 There is a timeᵗ for everything,
　　and a season for every activity under heaven:

² 　a time to be born and a time to die,
　　a time to plant and a time to uproot,
³ 　a time to kill and a time to heal,
　　a time to tear down and a time to build,
⁴ 　a time to weep and a time to laugh,
　　a time to mourn and a time to dance,
⁵ 　a time to scatter stones and a time to gather
　　　them,
　　a time to embrace and a time to refrain,
⁶ 　a time to search and a time to give up,
　　a time to keep and a time to throw away,
⁷ 　a time to tear and a time to mend,
　　a time to be silentᵘ and a time to speak,
⁸ 　a time to love and a time to hate,
　　a time for war and a time for peace.

⁹What does the worker gain from his toil?ᵛ ¹⁰I have seen the burden God has laid on men. ʷ ¹¹He has made everything beautiful in its time. ˣ He has also set eternity in the hearts of men; yet they cannot fathomʸ what God has done from beginning to end. ᶻ ¹²I know that there is nothing better for men than to be happy and do good while they live. ¹³That everyone may eat and drink, ᵃ and find satisfactionᵇ in all his toil—this is the gift of God. ᶜ ¹⁴I know that everything God does will endure forever; nothing can be added to it and nothing taken from it. God does it so that men will revere him. ᵈ

¹⁵Whatever is has already been, ᵉ
　　and what will be has been before;ᶠ
　　and God will call the past to account. ᵃ

¹⁶And I saw something else under the sun:

　　In the place of judgment—wickedness was there,
　　in the place of justice—wickedness was there.

¹⁷I thought in my heart,

　　"God will bring to judgmentᵍ
　　both the righteous and the wicked,

ᵃ15 Or *God calls back the past*

> for there will be a time for every activity,
> a time for every deed." [h]

[18]I also thought, "As for men, God tests them so that they may see that they are like the animals. [i] [19]Man's fate [j] is like that of the animals; the same fate awaits them both: As one dies, so dies the other. All have the same breath [a]; man has no advantage over the animal. Everything is meaningless. [20]All go to the same place; all come from dust, and to dust all return. [k] [21]Who knows if the spirit of man rises upward [l] and if the spirit of the animal [b] goes down into the earth?"

[22]So I saw that there is nothing better for a man than to enjoy his work, [m] because that is his lot. [n] For who can bring him to see what will happen after him?

Oppression, Toil, Friendlessness

4 Again I looked and saw all the oppression [o] that was taking place under the sun:

> I saw the tears of the oppressed—
> and they have no comforter;
> power was on the side of their oppressors—
> and they have no comforter. [p]
> [2]And I declared that the dead, [q]
> who had already died,
> are happier than the living,
> who are still alive. [r]
> [3]But better than both
> is he who has not yet been, [s]
> who has not seen the evil
> that is done under the sun. [t]

[4]And I saw that all labor and all achievement spring from man's envy of his neighbor. This too is meaningless, a chasing after the wind. [u]

> [5]The fool folds his hands [v]
> and ruins himself.
> [6]Better one handful with tranquillity
> than two handfuls with toil [w]
> and chasing after the wind.

[7]Again I saw something meaningless under the sun:

> [8]There was a man all alone;
> he had neither son nor brother.
> There was no end to his toil,
> yet his eyes were not content [x] with his wealth.
> "For whom am I toiling," he asked,
> "and why am I depriving myself of enjoyment?"
> This too is meaningless—
> a miserable business!

> [9]Two are better than one,
> because they have a good return for their work:

3:17
h ver 1
3:18
i Ps 73:22
3:19
j Ecc 2:14
3:20
k Ge 2:7; 3:19;
Job 34:15
3:21
l Ecc 12:7
3:22
m Ecc 2:24; 5:18
n Job 31:2
4:1
o Ps 12:5;
Ecc 3:16
p La 1:16
4:2
q Jer 20:17-18;
22:10 r Job 3:17;
10:18
4:3
s Job 3:16;
Ecc 6:3
t Job 3:22
4:4
u Ecc 1:14
4:5
v Pr 6:10
4:6
w Pr 15:16-17;
16:8
4:8
x Pr 27:20

[a]19 Or *spirit which*   [b]21 Or *Who knows the spirit of man, which rises upward, or the spirit of the animal,*

¹⁰If one falls down,
   his friend can help him up.
But pity the man who falls
   and has no one to help him up!
¹¹Also, if two lie down together, they will keep warm.
   But how can one keep warm alone?
¹²Though one may be overpowered,
   two can defend themselves.
A cord of three strands is not quickly broken.

Advancement Is Meaningless

¹³Better a poor but wise youth than an old but foolish king who no longer knows how to take warning. ¹⁴The youth may have come from prison to the kingship, or he may have been born in poverty within his kingdom. ¹⁵I saw that all who lived and walked under the sun followed the youth, the king's successor. ¹⁶There was no end to all the people who were before them. But those who came later were not pleased with the successor. This too is meaningless, a chasing after the wind.

Stand in Awe of God

5 Guard your steps when you go to the house of God. Go near to listen rather than to offer the sacrifice of fools, who do not know that they do wrong.

²Do not be quick with your mouth,
   do not be hasty in your heart
   to utter anything before God.ʸ
God is in heaven
   and you are on earth,
   so let your words be few.ᶻ
³As a dreamᵃ comes when there are many cares,
   so the speech of a fool when there are many words.ᵇ

⁴When you make a vow to God, do not delay in fulfilling it.ᶜ He has no pleasure in fools; fulfill your vow.ᵈ ⁵It is better not to vow than to make a vow and not fulfill it.ᵉ ⁶Do not let your mouth lead you into sin. And do not protest to the ˌtempleˌ messenger, "My vow was a mistake." Why should God be angry at what you say and destroy the work of your hands? ⁷Much dreaming and many words are meaningless. Therefore stand in awe of God.ᶠ

Riches Are Meaningless

⁸If you see the poor oppressedᵍ in a district, and justice and rights denied, do not be surprised at such things; for one official is eyed by a higher one, and over them both are others higher still. ⁹The increase from the land is taken by all; the king himself profits from the fields.

¹⁰Whoever loves money never has money enough;
   whoever loves wealth is never satisfied with his
      income.
This too is meaningless.

¹¹As goods increase,
   so do those who consume them.

5:2
yJdg 11:35
zJob 6:24;
Pr 10:19; 20:25
5:3
aJob 20:8
bEcc 10:14
5:4
cDt 23:21;
Jdg 11:35;
Ps 119:60
dNu 30:2;
Ps 66:13-14;
76:11
5:5
eNu 30:2-4;
Pr 20:25;
Jnh 2:9; Ac 5:4
5:7
fEcc 3:14; 12:13
5:8
gPs 12:5;
Ecc 4:1

And what benefit are they to the owner
except to feast his eyes on them?

¹²The sleep of a laborer is sweet,
whether he eats little or much,
but the abundance of a rich man
permits him no sleep. ^h

¹³I have seen a grievous evil under the sun:ⁱ

wealth hoarded to the harm of its owner,
¹⁴   or wealth lost through some misfortune,
so that when he has a son
there is nothing left for him.
¹⁵Naked a man comes from his mother's womb,
and as he comes, so he departs.^j
He takes nothing from his labor^k
that he can carry in his hand. ^l

¹⁶This too is a grievous evil:

As a man comes, so he departs,
and what does he gain,
since he toils for the wind?^m
¹⁷All his days he eats in darkness,
with great frustration, affliction and anger.

¹⁸Then I realized that it is good and proper for a man to eat and
drink, ⁿ and to find satisfaction in his toilsome labor^o under the sun
during the few days of life God has given him—for this is his lot.
¹⁹Moreover, when God gives any man wealth and possessions,^p and
enables him to enjoy them, ^q to accept his lot^r and be happy in his
work—this is a gift of God. ^s ²⁰He seldom reflects on the days of his life,
because God keeps him occupied with gladness of heart. ^t

6 I have seen another evil under the sun, and it weighs heavily on
men: ²God gives a man wealth, possessions and honor, so that he
lacks nothing his heart desires, but God does not enable him to enjoy
them, ^u and a stranger enjoys them instead. This is meaningless, a
grievous evil. ^v

³A man may have a hundred children and live many years; yet no
matter how long he lives, if he cannot enjoy his prosperity and does not
receive proper burial, I say that a stillborn^w child is better off than he.^x
⁴It comes without meaning, it departs in darkness, and in darkness its
name is shrouded. ⁵Though it never saw the sun or knew anything, it
has more rest than does that man— ⁶even if he lives a thousand years
twice over but fails to enjoy his prosperity. Do not all go to the same
place?

⁷All man's efforts are for his mouth,
yet his appetite is never satisfied. ^y
⁸What advantage has a wise man
over a fool?^z
What does a poor man gain
by knowing how to conduct himself before others?
⁹Better what the eye sees

5:12
h Job 20:20
5:13
i Ecc 6:1-2
5:15
j Job 1:21
k Ps 49:17;
1Ti 6:7 l Ecc 1:3
5:16
m Pr 11:29;
Ecc 1:3
5:18
n Ecc 2:3
o Ecc 2:10,24
5:19
p 1Ch 29:12;
2Ch 1:12
q Ecc 6:2
r Job 31:2
s Ecc 2:24; 3:13
5:20
t Dt 12:7,18
6:2
u Ps 17:14;
Ecc 5:19
v Ecc 5:13
6:3
w Job 3:16;
Ecc 4:3 x Job 3:3
6:7
y Pr 16:26;
27:20
6:8
z Ecc 2:15

than the roving of the appetite.
This too is meaningless,
     a chasing after the wind. [a]

[10]Whatever exists has already been named,
     and what man is has been known;
no man can contend
     with one who is stronger than he.
[11]The more the words,
     the less the meaning,
     and how does that profit anyone?

[12]For who knows what is good for a man in life, during the few and
meaningless days[b] he passes through like a shadow?[c] Who can tell him
what will happen under the sun after he is gone?

Wisdom

7

A good name is better than fine perfume, [d]
     and the day of death better than the day of birth.
[2]It is better to go to a house of mourning
     than to go to a house of feasting,
for death[e] is the destiny[f] of every man;
     the living should take this to heart.
[3]Sorrow is better than laughter, [g]
     because a sad face is good for the heart.
[4]The heart of the wise is in the house of mourning,
     but the heart of fools is in the house of pleasure. [h]
[5]It is better to heed a wise man's rebuke[i]
     than to listen to the song of fools.
[6]Like the crackling of thorns[j] under the pot,
     so is the laughter[k] of fools.
     This too is meaningless.

[7]Extortion turns a wise man into a fool,
     and a bribe[l] corrupts the heart.

[8]The end of a matter is better than its beginning,
     and patience[m] is better than pride.
[9]Do not be quickly provoked[n] in your spirit,
     for anger resides in the lap of fools.

[10]Do not say, "Why were the old days better than these?"
     For it is not wise to ask such questions.

[11]Wisdom, like an inheritance, is a good thing[o]
     and benefits those who see the sun. [p]
[12]Wisdom is a shelter
     as money is a shelter,
but the advantage of knowledge is this:
     that wisdom preserves the life of its possessor.

[13]Consider what God has done:[q]

Who can straighten
     what he has made crooked?[r]

6:9
aEcc 1:14
6:12
bJob 10:20
cJob 14:2;
Ps 39:6;
Jas 4:14
7:1
dPr 22:1; SS 1:3
7:2
ePr 11:19
fPs 90:12
7:3
gPr 14:13
7:4
hEcc 2:1;
Jer 16:8
7:5
iPs 141:5;
Pr 13:18;
15:31-32
7:6
jPs 58:9; 118:12
kEcc 2:2
7:7
lEx 18:21; 23:8;
Dt 16:19
7:8
mPr 14:29;
Gal 5:22;
Eph 4:2
7:9
nMt 5:22;
Pr 14:17;
Jas 1:19
7:11
oPr 8:10-11;
Ecc 2:13
pEcc 11:7
7:13
qEcc 2:24
rEcc 1:15

¹⁴When times are good, be happy;
    but when times are bad, consider:
God has made the one
    as well as the other.
Therefore, a man cannot discover
    anything about his future.

¹⁵In this meaningless life^s of mine I have seen both of these:

a righteous man perishing in his righteousness,
    and a wicked man living long in his wickedness.^t
¹⁶Do not be overrighteous,
    neither be overwise—
    why destroy yourself?
¹⁷Do not be overwicked,
    and do not be a fool—
    why die before your time?^u
¹⁸It is good to grasp the one
    and not let go of the other.
The man who fears God^v will avoid all ⌊extremes⌋.^a

¹⁹Wisdom^w makes one wise man more powerful^x
    than ten rulers in a city.

²⁰There is not a righteous man^y on earth
    who does what is right and never sins.^z

²¹Do not pay attention to every word people say,
    or you^a may hear your servant cursing you—
²²for you know in your heart
    that many times you yourself have cursed others.

²³All this I tested by wisdom and I said,

"I am determined to be wise"^b—
    but this was beyond me.
²⁴Whatever wisdom may be,
    it is far off and most profound—
    who can discover it?^c
²⁵So I turned my mind to understand,
    to investigate and to search out wisdom and the
        scheme of things^d
and to understand the stupidity of wickedness
    and the madness of folly.^e

²⁶I find more bitter than death
    the woman who is a snare,^f
whose heart is a trap
    and whose hands are chains.
The man who pleases God will escape her,
    but the sinner she will ensnare.^g

²⁷"Look," says the Teacher,^{b h} "this is what I have discovered:

7:15
s Job 7:7
t Ecc 8:12-14;
Jer 12:1
7:17
u Job 15:32;
Ps 55:23
7:18
v Ecc 3:14
7:19
w Ecc 2:13
x Ecc 9:13-18
7:20
y Ps 14:3
z 1Ki 8:46;
2Ch 6:36;
Pr 20:9; Ro 3:23
7:21
a Pr 30:10
7:23
b Ecc 1:17;
Ro 1:22
7:24
c Job 28:12
7:25
d Job 28:3
e Ecc 1:17
7:26
f Ex 10:7;
Jdg 14:15
g Pr 2:16-19;
5:3-5; 7:23;
22:14
7:27
h Ecc 1:1

^a18 Or *will follow them both*   ^b27 Or *leader of the assembly*

"Adding one thing to another to discover the scheme of
    things—
  28 while I was still searching
    but not finding—
  I found one ˻upright˼ man among a thousand,
    but not one ˻upright˼ woman[i] among them all.
  29This only have I found:
    God made mankind upright,
    but men have gone in search of many schemes."

8

Who is like the wise man?
  Who knows the explanation of things?
  Wisdom brightens a man's face
  and changes its hard appearance.

Obey the King

2Obey the king's command, I say, because you took an oath before
God. 3Do not be in a hurry to leave the king's presence.[j] Do not stand
up for a bad cause, for he will do whatever he pleases. 4Since a king's
word is supreme, who can say to him, "What are you doing?[k]"

  5Whoever obeys his command will come to no harm,
    and the wise heart will know the proper time and
      procedure.
  6For there is a proper time and procedure for every
      matter,[l]
    though a man's misery weighs heavily upon him.

  7Since no man knows the future,
    who can tell him what is to come?
  8No man has power over the wind to contain it[a];
    so no one has power over the day of his death.
  As no one is discharged in time of war,
    so wickedness will not release those who practice it.

9All this I saw, as I applied my mind to everything done under the
sun. There is a time when a man lords it over others to his own[b] hurt.
10Then too, I saw the wicked buried[m]—those who used to come and go
from the holy place and receive praise[c] in the city where they did this.
This too is meaningless.

11When the sentence for a crime is not quickly carried out, the hearts
of the people are filled with schemes to do wrong. 12Although a wicked
man commits a hundred crimes and still lives a long time, I know that
it will go better[n] with God-fearing men,[o] who are reverent before
God.[p] 13Yet because the wicked do not fear God,[q] it will not go well
with them, and their days[r] will not lengthen like a shadow.

14There is something else meaningless that occurs on earth: righteous
men who get what the wicked deserve, and wicked men who get what
the righteous deserve.[s] This too, I say, is meaningless.[t] 15So I commend the enjoyment of life[u], because nothing is better for a man under
the sun than to eat and drink[v] and be glad.[w] Then joy will accompany

7:28
i 1Ki 11:3
8:3
j Ecc 10:4
8:4
k Job 9:12;
Est 1:19;
Da 4:35
8:6
l Ecc 3:1
8:10
m Ecc 1:11
8:12
n Dt 12:28;
Ps 37:11,18-19;
Pr 1:32-33;
Isa 3:10-11
o Ex 1:20
p Ecc 3:14
8:13
q Ecc 3:14;
Isa 3:11
r Dt 4:40;
Job 5:26;
Ps 34:12;
Isa 65:20
8:14
s Job 21:7;
Ps 73:14;
Mal 3:15
t Ecc 7:15
8:15
u Ps 42:8
v Ex 32:6;
Ecc 2:3
w Ecc 2:24;
3:12-13; 5:18;
9:7

---

a8 Or *over his spirit to retain it*   b9 Or *to their*   c10 Some Hebrew manuscripts and
Septuagint (Aquila); most Hebrew manuscripts *and are forgotten*

him in his work all the days of the life God has given him under the sun.

[16]When I applied my mind to know wisdom[x] and to observe man's labor on earth[y]—his eyes not seeing sleep day or night— [17]then I saw all that God has done.[z] No one can comprehend what goes on under the sun. Despite all his efforts to search it out, man cannot discover its meaning. Even if a wise man claims he knows, he cannot really comprehend it.[a]

A Common Destiny for All

9 So I reflected on all this and concluded that the righteous and the wise and what they do are in God's hands, but no man knows whether love or hate awaits him.[b] [2]All share a common destiny—the righteous and the wicked, the good and the bad,[a] the clean and the unclean, those who offer sacrifices and those who do not.

> As it is with the good man,
>> so with the sinner;
> as it is with those who take oaths,
>> so with those who are afraid to take them.[c]

[3]This is the evil in everything that happens under the sun: The same destiny overtakes all.[d] The hearts of men, moreover, are full of evil and there is madness in their hearts while they live,[e] and afterward they join the dead.[f] [4]Anyone who is among the living has hope[b]—even a live dog is better off than a dead lion!

> [5]For the living know that they will die,
>> but the dead know nothing;[g]
> they have no further reward,
>> and even the memory of them[h] is forgotten.[i]
> [6]Their love, their hate
>> and their jealousy have long since vanished;
> never again will they have a part
>> in anything that happens under the sun.[j]

[7]Go, eat your food with gladness, and drink your wine[k] with a joyful heart,[l] for it is now that God favors what you do. [8]Always be clothed in white,[m] and always anoint your head with oil. [9]Enjoy life with your wife,[n] whom you love, all the days of this meaningless life that God has given you under the sun— all your meaningless days. For this is your lot[o] in life and in your toilsome labor under the sun. [10]Whatever[p] your hand finds to do, do it with all your might,[q] for in the grave,[cr] where you are going, there is neither working nor planning nor knowledge nor wisdom.[s]

[11]I have seen something else under the sun:

> The race is not to the swift
>> or the battle to the strong,[t]
> nor does food come to the wise[u]
> or wealth to the brilliant
> or favor to the learned;

8:16
xEcc 1:17
yEcc 1:13
8:17
zJob 28:3
aJob 5:9;
28:23; Ecc 3:11;
Ro 11:33
9:1
bDt 33:3;
Job 12:10;
Ecc 10:14
9:2
cJob 9:22;
Ecc 2:14; 6:6;
7:2
9:3
dJob 9:22;
Ecc 2:14
eJer 11:8;
13:10; 16:12;
17:9 fJob 21:26
9:5
gJob 14:21
hPs 9:6
iEcc 1:11; 2:16;
Isa 26:14
9:6
jJob 21:21
9:7
kNu 6:20
lEcc 2:24; 8:15
9:8
mPs 23:5;
Rev 3:4
9:9
nPr 5:18
oJob 31:2
9:10
p1Sa 10:7
qEcc 11:6;
Ro 12:11;
Col 3:23
rNu 16:33
sEcc 2:24
9:11
tAm 2:14-15
uJob 32:13;
Isa 47:10;
Jer 9:23

---

[a]2 Septuagint (Aquila), Vulgate and Syriac; Hebrew does not have *and the bad.*   [b]4 Or *What then is to be chosen? With all who live, there is hope*   [c]10 Hebrew *Sheol*

but time and chance[v] happen to them all. [w]

[12]Moreover, no man knows when his hour will come:

As fish are caught in a cruel net,
    or birds are taken in a snare,
so men are trapped by evil times[x]
    that fall unexpectedly upon them. [y]

Wisdom Better Than Folly

[13]I also saw under the sun this example of wisdom[z] that greatly impressed me: [14]There was once a small city with only a few people in it. And a powerful king came against it, surrounded it and built huge siegeworks against it. [15]Now there lived in that city a man poor but wise, and he saved the city by his wisdom. But nobody remembered that poor man. [a] [16]So I said, "Wisdom is better than strength." But the poor man's wisdom is despised, and his words are no longer heeded. [b]

[17]The quiet words of the wise are more to be heeded
    than the shouts of a ruler of fools.
[18]Wisdom[c] is better than weapons of war,
    but one sinner destroys much good.

10 As dead flies give perfume a bad smell,
    so a little folly[d] outweighs wisdom and honor.
[2]The heart of the wise inclines to the right,
    but the heart of the fool to the left.
[3]Even as he walks along the road,
    the fool lacks sense
    and shows everyone[e] how stupid he is.
[4]If a ruler's anger rises against you,
    do not leave your post;[f]
    calmness can lay great errors to rest. [g]

[5]There is an evil I have seen under the sun,
    the sort of error that arises from a ruler:
[6]Fools are put in many high positions, [h]
    while the rich occupy the low ones.
[7]I have seen slaves on horseback,
    while princes go on foot like slaves. [i]

[8]Whoever digs a pit may fall into it;[j]
    whoever breaks through a wall may be bitten by a
    snake. [k]
[9]Whoever quarries stones may be injured by them;
    whoever splits logs may be endangered by them. [l]

[10]If the ax is dull
    and its edge unsharpened,
more strength is needed
    but skill will bring success.

[11]If a snake bites before it is charmed,
    there is no profit for the charmer. [m]

[12]Words from a wise man's mouth are gracious, [n]

9:11
v Ecc 2:14
w Dt 8:18
9:12
x Pr 29:6
y Ps 73:22;
Ecc 2:14; 8:7
9:13
z 2Sa 20:22
9:15
a Ge 40:14;
Ecc 1:11; 2:16;
4:13
9:16
b Pr 21:22;
Ecc 7:19
9:18
c ver 16
10:1
d Pr 13:16; 18:2
10:3
e Pr 13:16; 18:2
10:4
f Ecc 8:3
g Pr 16:14;
25:15
10:6
h Pr 29:2
10:7
i Pr 19:10
10:8
j Ps 7:15; 57:6;
Pr 26:27
k Est 2:23;
Ps 9:16;
Am 5:19
10:9
l Pr 26:27
10:11
m Ps 58:5;
Isa 3:3
10:12
n Pr 10:32

but a fool is consumed by his own lips. °

13At the beginning his words are folly;
    at the end they are wicked madness—
14 and the fool multiplies words. ᵖ

No one knows what is coming—
    who can tell him what will happen after him? �q

15A fool's work wearies him;
    he does not know the way to town.

16Woe to you, O land whose king was a servantᵃ ʳ
    and whose princes feast in the morning.
17Blessed are you, O land whose king is of noble birth
    and whose princes eat at a proper time—
    for strength and not for drunkenness. ˢ

18If a man is lazy, the rafters sag;
    if his hands are idle, the house leaks. ᵗ

19A feast is made for laughter,
    and wineᵘ makes life merry,
    but money is the answer for everything.

20Do not revile the kingᵛ even in your thoughts,
    or curse the rich in your bedroom,
because a bird of the air may carry your words,
    and a bird on the wing may report what you say.

Bread Upon the Waters

11

Castʷ your bread upon the waters,
    for after many days you will find it again. ˣ
2Give portions to seven, yes to eight,
    for you do not know what disaster may come upon
        the land.

3If clouds are full of water,
    they pour rain upon the earth.
Whether a tree falls to the south or to the north,
    in the place where it falls, there will it lie.
4Whoever watches the wind will not plant;
    whoever looks at the clouds will not reap.

5As you do not know the path of the wind, ʸ
    or how the body is formedᵇ in a mother's womb, ᶻ
so you cannot understand the work of God,
    the Maker of all things.

6Sow your seed in the morning,
    and at evening let not your hands be idle, ᵃ
for you do not know which will succeed,
    whether this or that,
    or whether both will do equally well.

10:12
oPr 10:14; 14:3;
15:2; 18:7
10:14
pPr 15:2;
Ecc 5:3; 6:12;
8:7 qEcc 9:1
10:16
rIsa 3:4-5,12
10:17
sDt 14:26;
1Sa 25:36;
Pr 31:4
10:18
tPr 20:4;
24:30-34
10:19
uGe 14:18;
Jdg 9:13
10:20
vEx 22:28
11:1
wver 6;
Isa 32:20;
Hos 10:12
xDt 24:19;
Pr 19:17;
Mt 10:42
11:5
yJn 3:8-10
zPs 139:14-16
11:6
aEcc 9:10

ᵃ16 Or *king is a child*   ᵇ5 Or *know how life (or the spirit) / enters the body being formed*

Remember Your Creator While Young

⁷Light is sweet,
    and it pleases the eyes to see the sun.ᵇ
⁸However many years a man may live,
    let him enjoy them all.
But let him rememberᶜ the days of darkness,
    for they will be many.
Everything to come is meaningless.

⁹Be happy, young man, while you are young,
    and let your heart give you joy in the days of your
        youth.
Follow the ways of your heart
    and whatever your eyes see,
but know that for all these things
    God will bring you to judgment.ᵈ
¹⁰So then, banish anxietyᵉ from your heart
    and cast off the troubles of your body,
    for youth and vigor are meaningless.ᶠ

12 Rememberᵍ your Creator
        in the days of your youth,
    before the days of troubleʰ come
        and the years approach when you will say,
        "I find no pleasure in them"—
²before the sun and the light
        and the moon and the stars grow dark,
        and the clouds return after the rain;
³when the keepers of the house tremble,
        and the strong men stoop,
    when the grinders cease because they are few,
        and those looking through the windows grow
            dim;
⁴when the doors to the street are closed
        and the sound of grinding fades;
    when men rise up at the sound of birds,
        but all their songs grow faint;ⁱ
⁵when men are afraid of heights
        and of dangers in the streets;
    when the almond tree blossoms
        and the grasshopper drags himself along
        and desire no longer is stirred.
    Then man goes to his eternal homeʲ
        and mournersᵏ go about the streets.

⁶Remember him—before the silver cord is severed,
        or the golden bowl is broken;
    before the pitcher is shattered at the spring,
        or the wheel broken at the well,
⁷and the dust returnsˡ to the ground it came from,
        and the spirit returns to Godᵐ who gave it.ⁿ

11:7
ᵇEcc 7:11
11:8
ᶜEcc 12:1
11:9
ᵈJob 19:29;
Ecc 2:24; 3:17;
12:14; Ro 14:10
11:10
ᵉPs 94:19
ᶠEcc 2:24
12:1
ᵍEcc 11:8
ʰ2Sa 19:35
12:4
ⁱJer 25:10
12:5
ʲJob 17:13;
10:21 ᵏJer 9:17;
Am 5:16
12:7
ˡGe 3:19;
Job 34:15;
Ps 146:4
ᵐEcc 3:21
ⁿJob 20:8;
Zec 12:1

8"Meaningless! Meaningless!" says the Teacher.ᵃ
"Everything is meaningless!ᵒ"

The Conclusion of the Matter

⁹Not only was the Teacher wise, but also he imparted knowledge to the people. He pondered and searched out and set in order many proverbs.ᵖ ¹⁰The Teacher searched to find just the right words, and what he wrote was upright and true.�q

¹¹The words of the wise are like goads, their collected sayings like firmly embedded nailsʳ—given by one Shepherd. ¹²Be warned, my son, of anything in addition to them.

Of making many books there is no end, and much study wearies the body.ˢ

¹³Now all has been heard;
　here is the conclusion of the matter:
Fear God and keep his commandments,ᵗ
　for this is the whole ͺduty ͺof man.ᵘ
¹⁴For God will bring every deed into judgment,ᵛ
　including every hidden thing,ʷ
　whether it is good or evil.

12:8
ᵒEcc 1:2
12:9
ᵖ1Ki 4:32
12:10
qPr 22:20-21
12:11
ʳEzr 9:8
12:12
ˢEcc 1:18
12:13
ᵗDt 4:2; 10:12
ᵘMic 6:8
12:14
ᵛEcc 3:17
ʷMt 10:26;
1Co 4:5

Song of Songs

Title and Background

The title in the Hebrew text is "Solomon's Song of Songs," meaning a song either by, for or about Solomon. The phrase "Song of Songs" means the greatest of songs.

Author and Date of Writing

Verse 1 seems to ascribe authorship to Solomon. He is referred to seven times in the book, but whether he was the author remains an open question. Consistency of language, style, tone, perspective and recurring refrains seems to argue for a single author. If Solomon is the author, the Song can be dated in the tenth century B.C.

Theme and Message

In ancient Israel everything human came to expression in words. In the Song, love finds words—inspired words that disclose its exquisite charm and beauty as one of God's choicest gifts. The woman's voice of love in the Song suggests that love and wisdom draw men powerfully with the subtlety and mystery of a woman's allurements. God intends that such love be a normal part of marital life in his good creation.

Outline

1

Solomon's Song of Songs. [a]

Beloved [a]

> [2]Let him kiss me with the kisses of his mouth—
> for your love [b] is more delightful than wine.
> [3]Pleasing is the fragrance of your perfumes; [c]
> your name [d] is like perfume poured out.
> No wonder the maidens [e] love you!
> [4]Take me away with you—let us hurry!
> Let the king bring me into his chambers. [f]

Friends

> We rejoice and delight in you [b];
> we will praise your love more than wine.

1:1
a 1Ki 4:32
1:2
b SS 4:10
1:3
c SS 4:10
d Ecc 7:1
e Ps 45:14
1:4
f Ps 45:15

---

aPrimarily on the basis of the gender of the Hebrew pronouns used, male and female speakers are indicated in the margins by the captions *Lover* and *Beloved* respectively. The words of others are marked *Friends*. In some instances the divisions and their captions are debatable.   b4 The Hebrew is masculine singular.

Beloved

How right they are to adore you!

5Dark am I, yet lovely, g
　O daughters of Jerusalem, h
　dark like the tents of Kedar,
　like the tent curtains of Solomon. a
6Do not stare at me because I am dark,
　because I am darkened by the sun.
My mother's sons were angry with me
　and made me take care of the vineyards; i
　my own vineyard I have neglected.
7Tell me, you whom I love, where you graze your flock
　and where you rest your sheep j at midday.
Why should I be like a veiled woman
　beside the flocks of your friends?

Friends

8If you do not know, most beautiful of women, k
　follow the tracks of the sheep
and graze your young goats
　by the tents of the shepherds.

Lover

9I liken you, my darling, to a mare
　harnessed to one of the chariots l of Pharaoh.
10Your cheeks m are beautiful with earrings,
　your neck with strings of jewels. n
11We will make you earrings of gold,
　studded with silver.

Beloved

12While the king was at his table,
　my perfume spread its fragrance. o
13My lover is to me a sachet of myrrh
　resting between my breasts.
14My lover is to me a cluster of henna p blossoms
　from the vineyards of En Gedi. q

Lover

15How beautiful r you are, my darling!
　Oh, how beautiful!
　Your eyes are doves. s

Beloved

16How handsome you are, my lover!
　Oh, how charming!
　And our bed is verdant.

1:5
gSS 2:14; 4:3
hSS 2:7; 5:8;
　5:16
1:6
iPs 69:8;
　SS 8:12
1:7
jSS 3:1-4;
　Isa 13:20
1:8
kSS 5:9; 6:1
1:9
l2Ch 1:17
1:10
mSS 5:13
nIsa 61:10
1:12
oSS 4:11-14
1:14
pSS 4:13
q1Sa 23:29
1:15
rSS 4:7
sSS 2:14; 4:1;
　5:2,12; 6:9

a5 Or *Salma*

Lover

> [17]The beams of our house are cedars;[t]
>   our rafters are firs.

Beloved[a]

2

> I am a rose[bu] of Sharon,[v]
>   a lily[w] of the valleys.

Lover

> [2]Like a lily among thorns
>   is my darling among the maidens.

Beloved

> [3]Like an apple tree among the trees of the forest
>   is my lover[x] among the young men.
> I delight[y] to sit in his shade,
>   and his fruit is sweet to my taste.[z]
> [4]He has taken me to the banquet hall,[a]
>   and his banner[b] over me is love.
> [5]Strengthen me with raisins,
>   refresh me with apples,[c]
>   for I am faint with love.[d]
> [6]His left arm is under my head,
>   and his right arm embraces me.[e]
> [7]Daughters of Jerusalem, I charge you[f]
>   by the gazelles and by the does of the field:
> Do not arouse or awaken love
>   until it so desires.[g]
>
> [8]Listen! My lover!
>   Look! Here he comes,
> leaping across the mountains,
>   bounding over the hills.[h]
> [9]My lover is like a gazelle[i] or a young stag.[j]
>   Look! There he stands behind our wall,
> gazing through the windows,
>   peering through the lattice.
> [10]My lover spoke and said to me,
>   "Arise, my darling,
>   my beautiful one, and come with me.
> [11]See! The winter is past;
>   the rains are over and gone.
> [12]Flowers appear on the earth;
>   the season of singing has come,
> the cooing of doves
>   is heard in our land.
> [13]The fig tree forms its early fruit;[k]
>   the blossoming[l] vines spread their fragrance.

1:17
t1Ki 6:9
2:1
uIsa 35:1
vS 1Ch 27:29
wSS 5:13;
Hos 14:5
2:3
xSS 1:14
ySS 1:4
zSS 4:16
2:4
aEst 1:11
bNu 1:52
2:5
cSS 7:8 dSS 5:8
2:6
eSS 8:3
2:7
fSS 5:8 gSS 3:5;
8:4
2:8
hver 17; SS 8:14
2:9
i2Sa 2:18
jver 17; SS 8:14
2:13
kIsa 28:4;
Jer 24:2;
Hos 9:10;
Mic 7:1;
Na 3:12
lSS 7:12

Arise, come, my darling;
  my beautiful one, come with me."

Lover

[14]My dove[m] in the clefts of the rock,
  in the hiding places on the mountainside,
show me your face,
  let me hear your voice;
for your voice is sweet,
  and your face is lovely.[n]
[15]Catch for us the foxes,[o]
  the little foxes
that ruin the vineyards,[p]
  our vineyards that are in bloom.[q]

Beloved

2:14
mGe 8:8;
SS 1:15
nSS 1:5; 8:13
2:15
oJdg 15:4
pSS 1:6
qSS 7:12
2:16
rSS 7:10
sSS 4:5; 6:3
2:17
tSS 4:6 uSS 1:14
vver 9 wver 8
3:1
xSS 5:6;
Isa 26:9
3:3
ySS 5:7
3:4
zSS 8:2 aSS 6:9
3:5
bSS 2:7 cSS 8:4
3:6
dSS 8:5
eSS 1:13; 4:6,14
fEx 30:34
3:7
g1Sa 8:11

[16]My lover is mine and I am his;[r]
  he browses among the lilies.[s]
[17]Until the day breaks
  and the shadows flee,[t]
turn, my lover,[u]
  and be like a gazelle
or like a young stag[v]
  on the rugged hills.[a][w]

3 All night long on my bed
  I looked[x] for the one my heart loves;
  I looked for him but did not find him.
[2]I will get up now and go about the city,
  through its streets and squares;
I will search for the one my heart loves.
  So I looked for him but did not find him.
[3]The watchmen found me
  as they made their rounds in the city.[y]
  "Have you seen the one my heart loves?"
[4]Scarcely had I passed them
  when I found the one my heart loves.
I held him and would not let him go
  till I had brought him to my mother's house,[z]
  to the room of the one who conceived me.[a]
[5]Daughters of Jerusalem, I charge you[b]
  by the gazelles and by the does of the field:
Do not arouse or awaken love
  until it so desires.[c]

[6]Who is this coming up from the desert[d]
  like a column of smoke,
perfumed with myrrh[e] and incense
  made from all the spices[f] of the merchant?
[7]Look! It is Solomon's carriage,
  escorted by sixty warriors,[g]

---

[a]17 Or *the hills of Bether*

the noblest of Israel,
[8]all of them wearing the sword,
　all experienced in battle,
each with his sword at his side,
　prepared for the terrors of the night. [h]
[9]King Solomon made for himself the carriage;
　he made it of wood from Lebanon.
[10]Its posts he made of silver,
　its base of gold.
Its seat was upholstered with purple,
　its interior lovingly inlaid
by[a] the daughters of Jerusalem.
[11]Come out, you daughters of Zion, [i]
　and look at King Solomon wearing the crown,
　the crown with which his mother crowned him
on the day of his wedding,
　the day his heart rejoiced. [j]

Lover

4

How beautiful you are, my darling!
　Oh, how beautiful!
　Your eyes behind your veil are doves. [k]
Your hair is like a flock of goats
　descending from Mount Gilead. [l]
[2]Your teeth are like a flock of sheep just shorn,
　coming up from the washing.
Each has its twin;
　not one of them is alone. [m]
[3]Your lips are like a scarlet ribbon;
　your mouth[n] is lovely.
Your temples behind your veil
　are like the halves of a pomegranate. [o]
[4]Your neck is like the tower[p] of David,
　built with elegance[b];
on it hang a thousand shields, [q]
　all of them shields of warriors.
[5]Your two breasts[r] are like two fawns,
　like twin fawns of a gazelle[s]
　that browse among the lilies. [t]
[6]Until the day breaks
　and the shadows flee, [u]
I will go to the mountain of myrrh[v]
　and to the hill of incense.
[7]All beautiful[w] you are, my darling;
　there is no flaw in you.

[8]Come with me from Lebanon, my bride, [x]
　come with me from Lebanon.
Descend from the crest of Amana,

3:8
hJob 15:22;
Ps 91:5
3:11
iIsa 4:4
jIsa 62:5
4:1
kSS 1:15; 5:12
lSS 6:5;
Mic 7:14
4:2
mSS 6:6
4:3
nSS 5:16
oSS 6:7
4:4
pSS 7:4
qEze 27:10
4:5
rSS 7:3 sPr 5:19
tSS 2:16; 6:2-3
4:6
uSS 2:17
vver 14
4:7
wSS 1:15
4:8
xSS 5:1

---

a10 Or *its inlaid interior a gift of love / from*　　b4 The meaning of the Hebrew for this word is
uncertain.

from the top of Senir, y the summit of Hermon, z
from the lions' dens
    and the mountain haunts of the leopards.
⁹You have stolen my heart, my sister, my bride;
    you have stolen my heart
with one glance of your eyes,
    with one jewel of your necklace. a
¹⁰How delightful b is your love c, my sister, my bride!
    How much more pleasing is your love than wine,
    and the fragrance of your perfume than any spice!
¹¹Your lips drop sweetness as the honeycomb, my bride;
    milk and honey are under your tongue. d
    The fragrance of your garments is like that of
        Lebanon. e
¹²You are a garden locked up, my sister, my bride;
    you are a spring enclosed, a sealed fountain. f
¹³Your plants are an orchard of pomegranates g
    with choice fruits,
    with henna h and nard,
¹⁴   nard and saffron,
    calamus and cinnamon, i
    with every kind of incense tree,
    with myrrh j and aloes
    and all the finest spices. k
¹⁵You are a a garden fountain,
    a well of flowing water
    streaming down from Lebanon.

Beloved

¹⁶Awake, north wind,
    and come, south wind!
Blow on my garden,
    that its fragrance may spread abroad.
Let my lover come into his garden
    and taste its choice fruits. l

Lover

5

I have come into my garden, my sister, my bride; m
    I have gathered my myrrh with my spice.
I have eaten my honeycomb and my honey;
    I have drunk my wine and my milk. n

Friends

Eat, O friends, and drink;
    drink your fill, O lovers.

Beloved

²I slept but my heart was awake.
    Listen! My lover is knocking:

4:8
y Dt 3:9
z 1Ch 5:23
4:9
a Ge 41:42
4:10
b SS 7:6 c SS 1:2
4:11
d Ps 19:10;
SS 5:1
e Hos 14:6
4:12
f Pr 5:15-18
4:13
g SS 6:11; 7:12
h SS 1:14
4:14
i Ex 30:23
j SS 3:6 k SS 1:12
4:16
l SS 2:3; 5:1
5:1
m SS 4:8
n SS 4:11;
Isa 55:1

a15 Or *I am* (spoken by the *Beloved*)

"Open to me, my sister, my darling,
  my dove, my flawless[o] one.[p]
My head is drenched with dew,
  my hair with the dampness of the night."
[3]I have taken off my robe—
  must I put it on again?
I have washed my feet—
  must I soil them again?
[4]My lover thrust his hand through the latch-opening;
  my heart began to pound for him.
[5]I arose to open for my lover,
  and my hands dripped with myrrh,[q]
my fingers with flowing myrrh,
  on the handles of the lock.
[6]I opened for my lover,[r]
  but my lover had left; he was gone.[s]
  My heart sank at his departure.[a]
I looked[t] for him but did not find him.
  I called him but he did not answer.
[7]The watchmen found me
  as they made their rounds in the city.[u]
They beat me, they bruised me;
  they took away my cloak,
  those watchmen of the walls!
[8]O daughters of Jerusalem, I charge you[v]—
  if you find my lover,
what will you tell him?
  Tell him I am faint with love.[w]

Friends

[9]How is your beloved better than others,
  most beautiful of women?[x]
How is your beloved better than others,
  that you charge us so?

Beloved

[10]My lover is radiant and ruddy,
  outstanding among ten thousand.[y]
[11]His head is purest gold;
  his hair is wavy
  and black as a raven.
[12]His eyes are like doves[z]
  by the water streams,
washed in milk,[a]
  mounted like jewels.
[13]His cheeks[b] are like beds of spice[c]
  yielding perfume.
His lips are like lilies[d]
  dripping with myrrh.

5:2
o SS 4:7 p SS 6:9
5:5
q ver 13
5:6
r SS 6:1 s SS 6:2
t SS 3:1
5:7
u SS 3:3
5:8
v SS 2:7; 3:5
w SS 2:5
5:9
x SS 1:8; 6:1
5:10
y Ps 45:2
5:12
z SS 1:15; 4:1
a Ge 49:12
5:13
b SS 1:10
c SS 6:2 d SS 2:1

---

[a]6 Or *heart had gone out to him when he spoke*

¹⁴His arms are rods of gold
    set with chrysolite.
His body is like polished ivory
    decorated with sapphires. ^{a e}
¹⁵His legs are pillars of marble
    set on bases of pure gold.
His appearance is like Lebanon, ^f
    choice as its cedars.
¹⁶His mouth^g is sweetness itself;
    he is altogether lovely.
This is my lover, ^h this my friend,
    O daughters of Jerusalem. ⁱ

Friends

6 Where has your lover^j gone,
    most beautiful of women?^k
Which way did your lover turn,
    that we may look for him with you?

Beloved

²My lover has gone^l down to his garden, ^m
    to the beds of spices, ⁿ
to browse in the gardens
    and to gather lilies.
³I am my lover's and my lover is mine;^o
    he browses among the lilies. ^p

Lover

⁴You are beautiful, my darling, as Tirzah, ^q
    lovely as Jerusalem, ^r
    majestic as troops with banners. ^s
⁵Turn your eyes from me;
    they overwhelm me.
Your hair is like a flock of goats
    descending from Gilead. ^t
⁶Your teeth are like a flock of sheep
    coming up from the washing.
Each has its twin,
    not one of them is alone. ^u
⁷Your temples behind your veil^v
    are like the halves of a pomegranate. ^w
⁸Sixty queens^x there may be,
    and eighty concubines, ^y
    and virgins beyond number;
⁹but my dove, ^z my perfect one, ^a is unique,
    the only daughter of her mother,
    the favorite of the one who bore her. ^b
The maidens saw her and called her blessed;
    the queens and concubines praised her.

5:14
^eJob 28:6
5:15
^f1Ki 4:33;
SS 7:4
5:16
^gSS 4:3 ^hSS 7:9
ⁱSS 1:5
6:1
^jSS 5:6 ^kSS 1:8
6:2
^lSS 5:6
^mSS 4:12
ⁿSS 5:13
6:3
^oSS 7:10
^pSS 2:16
6:4
^qJos 12:24
^rPs 48:2; 50:2
^sver 10
6:5
^tSS 4:1
6:6
^uSS 4:2
6:7
^vGe 24:65
^wSS 4:3
6:8
^xPs 45:9
^yGe 22:24
6:9
^zSS 1:15
^aSS 5:2 ^bSS 3:4

^a14 Or *lapis lazuli*

Friends

10Who is this that appears like the dawn,
    fair as the moon, bright as the sun,
    majestic as the stars in procession?

Lover

11I went down to the grove of nut trees
    to look at the new growth in the valley,
to see if the vines had budded
    or the pomegranates were in bloom. [c]
12Before I realized it,
    my desire set me among the royal chariots of my
      people. [a]

Friends

13Come back, come back, O Shulammite;
    come back, come back, that we may gaze on you!

Lover

Why would you gaze on the Shulammite
    as on the dance [d] of Mahanaim?

7 How beautiful your sandaled feet,
    O prince's [e] daughter!
Your graceful legs are like jewels,
    the work of a craftsman's hands.
2Your navel is a rounded goblet
    that never lacks blended wine.
Your waist is a mound of wheat
    encircled by lilies.
3Your breasts [f] are like two fawns,
    twins of a gazelle.
4Your neck is like an ivory tower. [g]
Your eyes are the pools of Heshbon [h]
    by the gate of Bath Rabbim.
Your nose is like the tower of Lebanon [i]
    looking toward Damascus.
5Your head crowns you like Mount Carmel. [j]
    Your hair is like royal tapestry;
    the king is held captive by its tresses.
6How beautiful [k] you are and how pleasing,
    O love, with your delights! [l]
7Your stature is like that of the palm,
    and your breasts [m] like clusters of fruit.
8I said, "I will climb the palm tree;
    I will take hold of its fruit."
May your breasts be like the clusters of the vine,
    the fragrance of your breath like apples, [n]
9 and your mouth like the best wine.

6:11
c SS 7:12
6:13
d Ex 15:20
7:1
e Ps 45:13
7:3
f SS 4:5
7:4
g Ps 144:12;
SS 4:4
h Nu 21:26
i SS 5:15
7:5
j Isa 35:2
7:6
k SS 1:15
l SS 4:10
7:7
m SS 4:5
7:8
n SS 2:5

---

a12 Or among the chariots of Amminadab; or among the chariots of the people of the prince

Beloved

　　　May the wine go straight to my lover,[o]
　　　　　flowing gently over lips and teeth.[a]
　　　[10]I belong to my lover,
　　　　　and his desire[p] is for me.[q]
　　　[11]Come, my lover, let us go to the countryside,
　　　　　let us spend the night in the villages.[b]
　　　[12]Let us go early to the vineyards[r]
　　　　　to see if the vines have budded,[s]
　　　if their blossoms[t] have opened,
　　　　　and if the pomegranates[u] are in bloom[v]—
　　　　　there I will give you my love.
　　　[13]The mandrakes[w] send out their fragrance,
　　　　　and at our door is every delicacy,
　　　both new and old,
　　　　　that I have stored up for you, my lover.[x]

8　　If only you were to me like a brother,
　　　　　who was nursed at my mother's breasts!
　　　Then, if I found you outside,
　　　　　I would kiss you,
　　　　　and no one would despise me.
　　　[2]I would lead you
　　　　　and bring you to my mother's house[y]—
　　　　　she who has taught me.
　　　I would give you spiced wine to drink,
　　　　　the nectar of my pomegranates.
　　　[3]His left arm is under my head
　　　　　and his right arm embraces me.[z]
　　　[4]Daughters of Jerusalem, I charge you:
　　　　　Do not arouse or awaken love
　　　　　until it so desires.[a]

Friends

　　　[5]Who is this coming up from the desert[b]
　　　　　leaning on her lover?

Beloved

　　　Under the apple tree I roused you;
　　　　　there your mother conceived[c] you,
　　　　　there she who was in labor gave you birth.
　　　[6]Place me like a seal over your heart,
　　　　　like a seal on your arm;
　　　for love[d] is as strong as death,
　　　　　its jealousy[ce] unyielding as the grave.[d]
　　　It burns like blazing fire,
　　　　　like a mighty flame.[e]
　　　[7]Many waters cannot quench love;
　　　　　rivers cannot wash it away.

7:9
[o] S S 5:16
7:10
[p] Ps 45:11
[q] SS 2:16; 6:3
7:12
[r] SS 1:6 [s] SS 2:15
[t] SS 2:13
[u] SS 4:13
[v] SS 6:11
7:13
[w] Ge 30:14
[x] SS 4:16
8:2
[y] SS 3:4
8:3
[z] SS 2:6
8:4
[a] SS 2:7; 3:5
8:5
[b] SS 3:6 [c] SS 3:4
8:6
[d] SS 1:2
[e] Nu 5:14

---

[a]9 Septuagint, Aquila, Vulgate and Syriac; Hebrew *lips of sleepers*　　　[b]11 Or *henna bushes*
[c] Or *ardor*　　　[d]6 Hebrew *Sheol*　　　[e]6 Or / *like the very flame of the* LORD

> If one were to give
>   all the wealth of his house for love,
>   it*ᵃ* would be utterly scorned. *ᶠ*

Friends

> ⁸We have a young sister,
>   and her breasts are not yet grown.
> What shall we do for our sister
>   for the day she is spoken for?
> ⁹If she is a wall,
>   we will build towers of silver on her.
> If she is a door,
>   we will enclose her with panels of cedar.

Beloved

> ¹⁰I am a wall,
>   and my breasts are like towers.
> Thus I have become in his eyes
>   like one bringing contentment.
> ¹¹Solomon had a vineyard*ᵍ* in Baal Hamon;
>   he let out his vineyard to tenants.
> Each was to bring for its fruit
>   a thousand shekels*ᵇʰ* of silver.
> ¹²But my own vineyard*ⁱ* is mine to give;
>   the thousand shekels are for you, O Solomon,
>   and two hundred*ᶜ* are for those who tend its fruit.

Lover

> ¹³You who dwell in the gardens
>   with friends in attendance,
>   let me hear your voice!

Beloved

> ¹⁴Come away, my lover,
>   and be like a gazelle*ʲ*
> or like a young stag*ᵏ*
>   on the spice-laden mountains. *ˡ*

8:7
f Pr 6:35
8:11
g Ecc 2:4
h Isa 7:23
8:12
i SS 1:6
8:14
j Pr 5:19 k SS 2:9
l SS 2:8,17

---

*ᵃ*7 Or *he*   *ᵇ*11 That is, about 25 pounds (about 11.5 kilograms); also in verse 12   *ᶜ*12 That is, about 5 pounds (about 2.3 kilograms)

Isaiah

Title and Background

The book is named after the prophet whose message it records. Isaiah wrote during the stormy period marking the expansion of the Assyrian empire and the decline of Israel. He warned Judah that her sin would bring captivity at the hands of Babylon. Although the fall of Jerusalem would not take place until 586 B.C., Isaiah assumes its demise and proceeds to predict the restoration of the people from captivity. The decree of Cyrus would allow the Jews to return home, a deliverance that prefigured the greater salvation from sin through Jesus Christ. Significantly, Isaiah's name means "The LORD saves."

Author and Date of Writing

Isaiah son of Amoz was the greatest of the writing prophets and a contemporary of Amos, Hosea and Micah. Most of the events discussed in chapters 1-39 occurred during Isaiah's ministry, so it is likely they were completed around 700 B.C. He lived until at least 681 and may have written chapters 40-66 during his later years.

Theme and Message

Isaiah unveils the full dimensions of God's judgment and salvation. The awful judgment to be unleashed on Israel and all who defy God is called "the day of the LORD." The Lord's kingdom on earth, with its righteous Ruler and his righteous subjects, is the goal toward which the book of Isaiah steadily moves. The restored earth and the restored people will then conform to the divine ideal, and all will result in the praise and glory of the Holy One of Israel.

Outline

- I. Rebuke and Promise (1:1-6:13)
- II. Immanuel and His Kingdom (7:1-12:6)
- III. Judgment Against the Nations (13:1-23:18)
- IV. Judgment and Promise (24:1-27:13)
- V. Six Woes on Israel and Assyria (28:1-33:24)
- VI. Judgment and Promise (34:1-35:10)
- VII. From the Assyrian Threat to the Babylonian Exile (36:1-39:8)
- VIII. Deliverance and Restoration of Israel (40:1-48:22)
- IX. The Servant's Ministry and Israel's Restoration (49:1-57:21)
- X. Everlasting Deliverance and Judgment (58:1-66:24)

1:1
aNu 12:6
bIsa 40:9
cIsa 2:1
d2Ch 26:22
e2Ki 16:1

1 The vision[a] concerning Judah and Jerusalem[b] that Isaiah son of Amoz saw[c] during the reigns of Uzziah,[d] Jotham, Ahaz[e] and Hezekiah, kings of Judah.

A Rebellious Nation

1:2
fMic 1:2

²Hear, O heavens! Listen, O earth!
For the LORD has spoken:[f]
"I reared children and brought them up,

but they have rebelled[g] against me.
[3]The ox knows his master,
the donkey his owner's manger,
but Israel does not know,[h]
my people do not understand."

[4]Ah, sinful nation,
a people loaded with guilt,
a brood of evildoers,[i]
children given to corruption!
They have forsaken the LORD;
they have spurned the Holy One[j] of Israel
and turned their backs on him.

[5]Why should you be beaten anymore?
Why do you persist in rebellion?[k]
Your whole head is injured,
your whole heart afflicted.[l]
[6]From the sole of your foot to the top of your head
there is no soundness[m]—
only wounds and welts
and open sores,
not cleansed or bandaged[n]
or soothed with oil.[o]

[7]Your country is desolate,[p]
your cities burned with fire;
your fields are being stripped by foreigners
right before you,
laid waste as when overthrown by strangers.
[8]The Daughter of Zion is left
like a shelter in a vineyard,
like a hut[q] in a field of melons,
like a city under siege.
[9]Unless the LORD Almighty
had left us some survivors,[r]
we would have become like Sodom,
we would have been like Gomorrah.[s]

[10]Hear the word of the LORD,[t]
you rulers of Sodom;[u]
listen to the law[v] of our God,
you people of Gomorrah!
[11]"The multitude of your sacrifices—
what are they to me?" says the LORD.
"I have more than enough of burnt offerings,
of rams and the fat of fattened animals;[w]
I have no pleasure
in the blood of bulls[x] and lambs and goats.[y]
[12]When you come to appear before me,
who has asked this of you,[z]
this trampling of my courts?
[13]Stop bringing meaningless offerings![a]
Your incense[b] is detestable to me.

1:2
g Isa 30:1,9;
65:2
1:3
h Jer 8:7; 9:3,6
1:4
i Isa 14:20
j Isa 5:19,24
1:5
k Isa 31:6
l Isa 33:6,24
1:6
m Ps 38:3
n Isa 30:26;
Jer 8:22
o Lk 10:34
1:7
p Lev 26:34
1:8
q Job 27:18
1:9
r Isa 10:20-22;
37:4,31-32
s Ge 19:24;
Ro 9:29*
1:10
t Isa 28:14
u Isa 3:9;
Eze 16:49;
Ro 9:29;
Rev 11:8
v Isa 8:20
1:11
w Ps 50:8
x Jer 6:20
y 1Sa 15:22;
Mal 1:10
1:12
z Ex 23:17
1:13
a Isa 66:3
b Jer 7:9

New Moons, Sabbaths and convocations[c]—
I cannot bear your evil assemblies.
[14]Your New Moon festivals and your appointed feasts[d]
my soul hates.
They have become a burden to me;
I am weary[e] of bearing them.
[15]When you spread out your hands in prayer,
I will hide[f] my eyes from you;
even if you offer many prayers,
I will not listen.
Your hands are full of blood;[g]
[16]   wash and make yourselves clean.
Take your evil deeds
out of my sight![h]
Stop doing wrong,[i]
[17]   learn to do right!
Seek justice,[j]
encourage the oppressed.[a]
Defend the cause of the fatherless,[k]
plead the case of the widow.

[18]"Come now, let us reason together,"[l]
says the LORD.
"Though your sins are like scarlet,
they shall be as white as snow;[m]
though they are red as crimson,
they shall be like wool.
[19]If you are willing and obedient,
you will eat the best from the land;[n]
[20]but if you resist and rebel,
you will be devoured by the sword."[o]
For the mouth of the LORD has spoken.[p]

[21]See how the faithful city
has become a harlot![q]
She once was full of justice;
righteousness used to dwell in her—
but now murderers!
[22]Your silver has become dross,
your choice wine is diluted with water.
[23]Your rulers are rebels,
companions of thieves;
they all love bribes[r]
and chase after gifts.
They do not defend the cause of the fatherless;
the widow's case does not come before them.[s]
[24]Therefore the Lord, the LORD Almighty,
the Mighty One of Israel, declares:
"Ah, I will get relief from my foes
and avenge[t] myself on my enemies.
[25]I will turn my hand against you;

1:13
c1Ch 23:31
1:14
dLev 23:1-44;
Nu 28:11-29:39;
Isa 29:1
eIsa 7:13;
43:22,24
1:15
fIsa 8:17; 59:2;
Mic 3:4
gIsa 59:3
1:16
hIsa 52:11
iIsa 55:7;
Jer 25:5
1:17
jZep 2:3
kPs 82:3
1:18
lIsa 41:1; 43:9,
26 mPs 51:7;
Rev 7:14
1:19
nDt 30:15-16;
Isa 55:2
1:20
oIsa 3:25; 65:12
pIsa 34:16;
40:5; 58:14;
Mic 4:4
1:21
qIsa 57:3-9;
Jer 2:20
1:23
rEx 23:8
sIsa 10:2;
Jer 5:28;
Eze 22:6-7;
Zec 7:10
1:24
tIsa 35:4;
59:17; 61:2;
63:4

---

[a]17 Or / *rebuke the oppressor*

> I will thoroughly purge away your dross
> and remove all your impurities. ᵘ
> ²⁶I will restore your judges as in days of old, ᵛ
> your counselors as at the beginning.
> Afterward you will be called
> the City of Righteousness, ʷ
> the Faithful City. ˣ"
>
> ²⁷Zion will be redeemed with justice,
> her penitent ones with righteousness. ʸ
> ²⁸But rebels and sinners will both be broken,
> and those who forsake the Lord will perish. ᶻ
>
> ²⁹"You will be ashamed because of the sacred oaksᵃ
> in which you have delighted;
> you will be disgraced because of the gardensᵇ
> that you have chosen.
> ³⁰You will be like an oak with fading leaves,
> like a garden without water.
> ³¹The mighty man will become tinder
> and his work a spark;
> both will burn together,
> with no one to quench the fire. ᶜ"

The Mountain of the Lord

2:1–4pp — Mic 4:1–3

2 This is what Isaiah son of Amoz saw concerning Judah and Jerusalem:ᵈ

> ²In the last days
>
> the mountainᵉ of the Lord's temple will be established
> as chief among the mountains;
> it will be raised above the hills,
> and all nations will stream to it.
>
> ³Many peoples will come and say,
>
> "Come, let us go up to the mountain of the Lord,
> to the house of the God of Jacob.
> He will teach us his ways,
> so that we may walk in his paths."
> The lawᶠ will go out from Zion,
> the word of the Lord from Jerusalem. ᵍ
> ⁴He will judge between the nations
> and will settle disputes for many peoples.
> They will beat their swords into plowshares
> and their spears into pruning hooks. ʰ
> Nation will not take up sword against nation, ⁱ
> nor will they train for war anymore.
>
> ⁵Come, O house of Jacob, ʲ
> let us walk in the lightᵏ of the Lord.

1:25
uEze 22:22;
Mal 3:3
1:26
vJer 33:7,11
wIsa 33:5;
62:1; Zec 8:3
xIsa 60:14; 62:2
1:27
yIsa 35:10;
62:12; 63:4
1:28
zPs 9:5;
Isa 24:20;
66:24;
2Th 1:8-9
1:29
aIsa 57:5
bIsa 65:3; 66:17
1:31
cIsa 5:24;
9:18-19; 26:11;
33:14; 66:15-16,
24
2:1
dIsa 1:1
2:2
eIsa 27:13;
56:7; 66:20;
Mic 4:7
2:3
fIsa 51:4,7
gLk 24:47
2:4
hJoel 3:10
iPs 46:9;
Isa 9:5; 11:6-9;
32:18;
Hos 2:18;
Zec 9:10
2:5
jIsa 58:1
kIsa 60:1,19-20;
1Jn 1:5,7

The Day of the LORD

6You have abandoned[1] your people,
    the house of Jacob.
They are full of superstitions from the East;
    they practice divination like the Philistines[m]
    and clasp hands[n] with pagans.[o]
7Their land is full of silver and gold;
    there is no end to their treasures.
Their land is full of horses;[p]
    there is no end to their chariots.[q]
8Their land is full of idols;[r]
    they bow down to the work of their hands,
    to what their fingers[s] have made.
9So man will be brought low[t]
    and mankind humbled[u]—
    do not forgive them.[a] [v]

10Go into the rocks,
    hide in the ground
from dread of the LORD
    and the splendor of his majesty![w]
11The eyes of the arrogant man will be humbled
    and the pride[x] of men brought low;
the LORD alone will be exalted in that day.

12The LORD Almighty has a day in store
    for all the proud and lofty,
    for all that is exalted[y]
    (and they will be humbled),[z]
13for all the cedars of Lebanon, tall and lofty,
    and all the oaks of Bashan,[a]
14for all the towering mountains
    and all the high hills,[b]
15for every lofty tower
    and every fortified wall,[c]
16for every trading ship[b] [d]
    and every stately vessel.
17The arrogance of man will be brought low
    and the pride of men humbled;
the LORD alone will be exalted in that day,[e]
18 and the idols will totally disappear.[f]

19Men will flee to caves in the rocks
    and to holes in the ground
from dread of the LORD
    and the splendor of his majesty,
    when he rises to shake the earth.[g]
20In that day men will throw away
    to the rodents and bats[h]
their idols of silver and idols of gold,
    which they made to worship.

2:6
l Dt 31:17
m 2Ki 1:2
n Pr 6:1
o 2Ki 16:7
2:7
p Dt 17:16
q Isa 31:1;
Mic 5:10
2:8
r Isa 10:9-11
s Isa 17:8
2:9
t Ps 62:9
u Isa 5:15
v Ne 4:5
2:10
w 2Th 1:9;
Rev 6:15-16
2:11
x Isa 5:15; 37:23
2:12
y Isa 24:4,21;
Mal 4:1
z Job 40:11
2:13
a Zec 11:2
2:14
b Isa 30:25; 40:4
2:15
c Isa 25:2,12
2:16
d 1Ki 10:22
2:17
e ver 11
2:18
f Isa 21:9
2:19
g Heb 12:26
2:20
h Lev 11:19

a9 Or not raise them up   *b16 Hebrew every ship of Tarshish*

²¹They will flee to caverns in the rocks
     and to the overhanging crags
from dread of the LORD
     and the splendor of his majesty,
     when he rises to shake the earth. ⁱ

²²Stop trusting in man, ʲ
     who has but a breath in his nostrils.
Of what account is he? ᵏ

Judgment on Jerusalem and Judah

3 See now, the Lord,
     the LORD Almighty,
is about to take from Jerusalem and Judah
     both supply and support:
all supplies of food¹ and all supplies of water, ᵐ
² the hero and warrior, ⁿ
the judge and prophet,
     the soothsayer and elder, ᵒ
³the captain of fifty and man of rank,
     the counselor, skilled craftsman and clever enchanter.

⁴I will make boys their officials;
     mere children will govern them. ᵖ
⁵People will oppress each other—
     man against man, neighbor against neighbor. �q
The young will rise up against the old,
     the base against the honorable.

⁶A man will seize one of his brothers
     at his father's home, and say,
"You have a cloak, you be our leader;
     take charge of this heap of ruins!"
⁷But in that day he will cry out,
     "I have no remedy. ʳ
I have no food or clothing in my house;
     do not make me the leader of the people."

⁸Jerusalem staggers,
     Judah is falling; ˢ
their words ᵗ and deeds are against the LORD,
     defying ᵘ his glorious presence.
⁹The look on their faces testifies against them;
     they parade their sin like Sodom; ᵛ
     they do not hide it.
Woe to them!
     They have brought disaster ʷ upon themselves.

¹⁰Tell the righteous it will be well ˣ with them,
     for they will enjoy the fruit of their deeds. ʸ
¹¹Woe to the wicked! Disaster ᶻ is upon them!
     They will be paid back for what their hands have done.

¹²Youths ᵃ oppress my people,

2:21
ⁱver 19
2:22
ʲPs 146:3;
Jer 17:5
ᵏPs 8:4; 144:3;
Isa 40:15;
Jas 4:14
3:1
ˡLev 26:26
ᵐIsa 5:13;
Eze 4:16
3:2
ⁿEze 17:13
ᵒ2Ki 24:14;
Isa 9:14-15
3:4
ᵖEcc 10:16 *fn*
3:5
qIsa 9:19;
Jer 9:8;
Mic 7:2,6
3:7
ʳEze 34:4;
Hos 5:13
3:8
ˢIsa 1:7
ᵗIsa 9:15,17
ᵘPs 73:9,11
3:9
ᵛGe 13:13
ʷPr 8:36;
Ro 6:23
3:10
ˣDt 28:1-14
ʸPs 128:2
3:11
ᶻDt 28:15-68
3:12
ᵃver 4

women rule over them.
O my people, your guides lead you astray;[b]
they turn you from the path.

[13]The LORD takes his place in court;
he rises to judge[c] the people.
[14]The LORD enters into judgment[d]
against the elders and leaders of his people:
"It is you who have ruined my vineyard;
the plunder[e] from the poor is in your houses.
[15]What do you mean by crushing my people[f]
and grinding the faces of the poor?"
declares the Lord, the LORD Almighty.

[16]The LORD says,
"The women of Zion[g] are haughty,
walking along with outstretched necks,
flirting with their eyes,
tripping along with mincing steps,
with ornaments jingling on their ankles.
[17]Therefore the Lord will bring sores on the heads of the
women of Zion;
the LORD will make their scalps bald."

[18]In that day the Lord will snatch away their finery: the bangles and headbands and crescent necklaces,[h] [19]the earrings and bracelets and veils, [20]the headdresses[i] and ankle chains and sashes, the perfume bottles and charms, [21]the signet rings and nose rings, [22]the fine robes and the capes and cloaks, the purses [23]and mirrors, and the linen garments and tiaras and shawls.

[24]Instead of fragrance[j] there will be a stench;
instead of a sash,[k] a rope;
instead of well-dressed hair, baldness;[l]
instead of fine clothing, sackcloth;[m]
instead of beauty,[n] branding.
[25]Your men will fall by the sword,[o]
your warriors in battle.
[26]The gates of Zion will lament and mourn;[p]
destitute, she will sit on the ground.[q]

4 In that day seven women
will take hold of one man[r]
and say, "We will eat our own food[s]
and provide our own clothes;
only let us be called by your name.
Take away our disgrace!"[t]

The Branch of the LORD

[2]In that day the Branch of the LORD[u] will be beautiful and glorious, and the fruit[v] of the land will be the pride and glory of the survivors in Israel. [3]Those who are left in Zion, who remain[w] in Jerusalem, will be called holy,[x] all who are recorded[y] among the living in Jerusalem. [4]The Lord will wash away the filth[z] of the women of Zion; he will cleanse the

3:12
bIsa 9:16
3:13
cMic 6:2
3:14
dJob 22:4
eJob 24:9;
Jas 2:6
3:15
fPs 94:5
3:16
gSS 3:11
3:18
hJdg 8:21
3:20
iEx 39:28
3:24
jEst 2:12
kPr 31:24
lIsa 22:12
mLa 2:10;
Eze 27:30-31
n1Pe 3:3
3:25
oIsa 1:20
3:26
pJer 14:2
qLa 2:10
4:1
rIsa 13:12
s2Th 3:12
tGe 30:23
4:2
uIsa 11:1-5;
53:2;
Jer 23:5-6;
Zec 3:8; 6:12
vPs 72:16
4:3
wRo 11:5
xIsa 52:1; 60:21
yLk 10:20
4:4
zIsa 3:24

bloodstains[a] from Jerusalem by a spirit[a] of judgment[b] and a spirit[a] of fire.[c] [5]Then the LORD will create over all of Mount Zion and over those who assemble there a cloud of smoke by day and a glow of flaming fire by night;[d] over all the glory[e] will be a canopy. [6]It will be a shelter[f] and shade from the heat of the day, and a refuge[g] and hiding place from the storm and rain.

The Song of the Vineyard

5　　I will sing for the one I love
　　　　a song about his vineyard:[h]
　　My loved one had a vineyard
　　　　on a fertile hillside.
　　[2]He dug it up and cleared it of stones
　　　　and planted it with the choicest vines.[i]
　　He built a watchtower in it
　　　　and cut out a winepress as well.
　　Then he looked for a crop of good grapes,
　　　　but it yielded only bad fruit.[j]

　　[3]"Now you dwellers in Jerusalem and men of Judah,
　　　　judge between me and my vineyard.[k]
　　[4]What more could have been done for my vineyard
　　　　than I have done for it?[l]
　　When I looked for good grapes,
　　　　why did it yield only bad?
　　[5]Now I will tell you
　　　　what I am going to do to my vineyard:
　　I will take away its hedge,
　　　　and it will be destroyed;
　　I will break down its wall,[m]
　　　　and it will be trampled.[n]
　　[6]I will make it a wasteland,
　　　　neither pruned nor cultivated,
　　　　and briers and thorns[o] will grow there.
　　I will command the clouds
　　　　not to rain on it."

　　[7]The vineyard[p] of the LORD Almighty
　　　　is the house of Israel,
　　and the men of Judah
　　　　are the garden of his delight.
　　And he looked for justice,[q] but saw bloodshed;
　　　　for righteousness, but heard cries of distress.

Woes and Judgments

　　[8]Woe[r] to you who add house to house
　　　　and join field to field[s]
　　till no space is left
　　　　and you live alone in the land.

　　[9]The LORD Almighty has declared in my hearing:[t]

4:4
a Isa 1:15
b Isa 28:6
c Isa 1:31;
Mt 3:11
4:5
d Ex 13:21
e Isa 60:1
4:6
f Ps 27:5
g Isa 25:4
5:1
h Ps 80:8-9
5:2
i Jer 2:21
j Mt 21:19;
Mk 11:13;
Lk 13:6
5:3
k Mt 21:40
5:4
l 2Ch 36:15;
Jer 2:5-7;
Mic 6:3-4;
Mt 23:37
5:5
m Ps 80:12
n Isa 28:3,18;
La 1:15;
Lk 21:24
5:6
o Isa 7:23,24;
Heb 6:8
5:7
p Ps 80:8
q Isa 59:15
5:8
r Jer 22:13
s Mic 2:2;
Hab 2:9-12
5:9
t Isa 22:14

a4 Or *the Spirit*

"Surely the great houses will become desolate,[u]
    the fine mansions left without occupants.
[10]A ten-acre[a] vineyard will produce only a bath[b] of wine,
    a homer[c] of seed only an ephah[d] of grain."[v]

[11]Woe to those who rise early in the morning
    to run after their drinks,
who stay up late at night
    till they are inflamed with wine.[w]
[12]They have harps and lyres at their banquets,
    tambourines and flutes and wine,
but they have no regard[x] for the deeds of the LORD,
    no respect for the work of his hands.[y]
[13]Therefore my people will go into exile
    for lack of understanding;[z]
their men of rank will die of hunger
    and their masses will be parched with thirst.
[14]Therefore the grave[ea] enlarges its appetite
    and opens its mouth[b] without limit;
into it will descend their nobles and masses
    with all their brawlers and revelers.
[15]So man will be brought low[c]
    and mankind humbled,[d]
    the eyes of the arrogant[e] humbled.
[16]But the LORD Almighty will be exalted by his justice,[f]
    and the holy God will show himself holy[g] by his
        righteousness.
[17]Then sheep will graze as in their own pasture;[h]
    lambs will feed[f] among the ruins of the rich.

[18]Woe to those who draw sin along with cords of deceit,
    and wickedness[i] as with cart ropes,
[19]to those who say, "Let God hurry,
    let him hasten his work
    so we may see it.
Let it approach,
    let the plan of the Holy One of Israel come,
    so we may know it."[j]

[20]Woe to those who call evil good
    and good evil,
who put darkness for light
    and light for darkness,[k]
who put bitter for sweet
    and sweet for bitter.[l]

[21]Woe to those who are wise in their own eyes[m]
    and clever in their own sight.

[22]Woe to those who are heroes at drinking wine[n]

5:9
u Isa 6:11-12;
Mt 23:38
5:10
v Lev 26:26
5:11
w Pr 23:29-30
5:12
x Job 34:27
y Ps 28:5;
Am 6:5-6
5:13
z Isa 1:3;
Hos 4:6
5:14
a Pr 30:16
b Nu 16:30
5:15
c Isa 10:33
d Isa 2:9
e Isa 2:11
5:16
f Isa 28:17;
30:18; 33:5;
61:8 g Isa 29:23
5:17
h Isa 7:25;
Zep 2:6,14
5:18
i Isa 59:4-8;
Jer 23:14
5:19
j Jer 17:15;
Eze 12:22;
2Pe 3:4
5:20
k Mt 6:22-23;
Lk 11:34-35
l Am 5:7
5:21
m Pr 3:7;
Ro 12:16;
1Co 3:18-20
5:22
n Pr 23:20

---

*a*10 Hebrew *ten-yoke*, that is, the land plowed by 10 yoke of oxen in one day   *b*10 That is,
probably about 6 gallons (about 22 liters)   *c*10 That is, probably about 6 bushels (about 220
liters)   *d*10 That is, probably about 3/5 bushel (about 22 liters)   *e*14 Hebrew *Sheol*
*f*17 Septuagint; Hebrew / *strangers will eat*

and champions at mixing drinks,
²³who acquit the guilty for a bribe, º
    but deny justiceᴾ to the innocent. ۹
²⁴Therefore, as tongues of fire lick up straw
    and as dry grass sinks down in the flames,
so their roots will decayʳ
    and their flowers blow away like dust;
for they have rejected the law of the Lᴏʀᴅ Almighty
    and spurned the wordˢ of the Holy One of Israel.
²⁵Therefore the Lᴏʀᴅ's angerᵗ burns against his people;
    his hand is raised and he strikes them down.
The mountains shake,
    and the dead bodies are like refuseᵘ in the streets.

Yet for all this, his anger is not turned away, ᵛ
    his hand is still upraised. ʷ

²⁶He lifts up a banner for the distant nations,
    he whistlesˣ for those at the ends of the earth. ʸ
Here they come,
    swiftly and speedily!
²⁷Not one of them grows tired or stumbles,
    not one slumbers or sleeps;
not a belt is loosened at the waist, ᶻ
    not a sandal thong is broken. ᵃ
²⁸Their arrows are sharp, ᵇ
    all their bowsᶜ are strung;
their horses' hoofs seem like flint,
    their chariot wheels like a whirlwind.
²⁹Their roar is like that of the lion, ᵈ
    they roar like young lions;
they growl as they seizeᵉ their prey
    and carry it off with no one to rescue. ᶠ
³⁰In that day they will roar over it
    like the roaring of the sea. ᵍ
And if one looks at the land,
    he will see darkness and distress;ʰ
    even the light will be darkenedⁱ by the clouds.

Isaiah's Commission

6 In the year that King Uzziahʲ died,ᵏ I saw the Lordˡ seated on a throne,ᵐ high and exalted, and the train of his robe filled the temple. ²Above him were seraphs,ⁿ each with six wings: With two wings they covered their faces, with two they covered their feet,º and with two they were flying. ³And they were calling to one another:

"Holy, holy, holy is the Lᴏʀᴅ Almighty;
    the whole earth is full of his glory."ᵖ

⁴At the sound of their voices the doorposts and thresholds shook and the temple was filled with smoke.

⁵"Woe to me!" I cried. "I am ruined! For I am a man of unclean lips, and I live among a people of unclean lips, ۹ and my eyes have seen the King,ʳ the Lᴏʀᴅ Almighty."

5:23
ºEx 23:8
ᵖIsa 10:2
۹Ps 94:21;
Jas 5:6
5:24
ʳJob 18:16
ˢIsa 8:6; 30:9,
12
5:25
ᵗ2Ki 22:13
ᵘ2Ki 9:37
ᵛJer 4:8;
Da 9:16
ʷIsa 9:12,17,
21; 10:4
5:26
ˣIsa 7:18;
Zec 10:8
ʸDt 28:49;
Isa 13:5; 18:3
5:27
ᶻJob 12:18
ᵃJoel 2:7-8
5:28
ᵇPs 45:5
ᶜPs 7:12
5:29
ᵈJer 51:38;
Zep 3:3;
Zec 11:3
ᵉIsa 10:6;
49:24-25
ᶠIsa 42:22;
Mic 5:8
5:30
ᵍLk 21:25
ʰIsa 8:22;
Jer 4:23-28
ⁱJoel 2:10
6:1
ʲ2Ch 26:22,23
ᵏ2Ki 15:7
ˡJn 12:41
ᵐRev 4:2
6:2
ⁿRev 4:8
ºEze 1:11
6:3
ᵖPs 72:19;
Rev 4:8
6:5
۹Jer 9:3-8
ʳJer 51:57

⁶Then one of the seraphs flew to me with a live coal in his hand, which he had taken with tongs from the altar. ⁷With it he touched my mouth and said, "See, this has touched your lips;ˢ your guilt is taken away and your sin atoned for.ᵗ "

⁸Then I heard the voiceᵘ of the Lord saying, "Whom shall I send? And who will go for us?"

And I said, "Here am I. Send me!"

⁹He said, "Goᵛ and tell this people:

" 'Be ever hearing, but never understanding;
　be ever seeing, but never perceiving.'ʷ
¹⁰Make the heart of this people calloused;ˣ
　make their ears dull
　and close their eyes.ᵃ
Otherwise they might see with their eyes,
　hear with their ears,ʸ
　understand with their hearts,
and turn and be healed."ᶻ

¹¹Then I said, "For how long, O Lord?"ᵃ
And he answered:

"Until the cities lie ruinedᵇ
　and without inhabitant,
until the houses are left deserted
　and the fields ruined and ravaged,
¹²until the Lᴏʀᴅ has sent everyone far awayᶜ
　and the land is utterly forsaken.ᵈ
¹³And though a tenth remainsᵉ in the land,
　it will again be laid waste.
But as the terebinth and oak
　leave stumps when they are cut down,
　so the holy seed will be the stump in the land."ᶠ

The Sign of Immanuel

7 When Ahaz son of Jotham, the son of Uzziah, was king of Judah, King Rezinᵍ of Aramʰ and Pekahⁱ son of Remaliah king of Israel marched up to fight against Jerusalem, but they could not overpower it. ²Now the house of Davidʲ was told, "Aram has allied itself withᵇ Ephraimᵏ"; so the hearts of Ahaz and his people were shaken, as the trees of the forest are shaken by the wind.

³Then the Lᴏʀᴅ said to Isaiah, "Go out, you and your son Shear-Jashub,ᶜ to meet Ahaz at the end of the aqueduct of the Upper Pool, on the road to the Washerman's Field.ˡ ⁴Say to him, 'Be careful, keep calmᵐ and don't be afraid.ⁿ Do not lose heartᵒ because of these two smoldering stubsᵖ of firewood—because of the fierce angerᵠ of Rezin and Aram and of the son of Remaliah. ⁵Aram, Ephraim and Remaliah's son have plotted your ruin, saying, ⁶"Let us invade Judah; let us tear it apart and divide it among ourselves, and make the son of Tabeel king over it." ⁷Yet this is what the Sovereign Lᴏʀᴅ says:

6:7
ˢJer 1:9 ᵗJn 1:7
6:8
ᵘAc 9:4
6:9
ᵛEze 3:11
ʷMt 13:15*;
Lk 8:10*
6:10
ˣDt 32:15;
Ps 119:70
ʸJer 5:21
ᶻMt 13:13-15;
Mk 4:12*;
Ac 28:26-27*
6:11
ᵃPs 79:5
ᵇLev 26:31
6:12
ᶜDt 28:64
ᵈJer 4:29
6:13
ᵉIsa 1:9
ᶠJob 14:7
7:1
ᵍ2Ki 15:37
ʰ2Ch 28:5
ⁱ2Ki 15:25
7:2
ʲver 13;
Isa 22:22
ᵏIsa 9:9
7:3
ˡ2Ki 18:17;
Isa 36:2
7:4
ᵐIsa 30:15
ⁿIsa 35:4
ᵒDt 20:3
ᵖZec 3:2
ᵠIsa 10:24

ᵃ9,10 Hebrew; Septuagint *'You will be ever hearing, but never understanding; / you will be ever seeing, but never perceiving.' / ¹⁰This people's heart has become calloused; / they hardly hear with their ears, / and they have closed their eyes*   ᵇ2 Or *has set up camp in*   ᶜ3 *Shear-Jashub* means *a remnant will return.*

" 'It will not take place,
    it will not happen,[r]
8for the head of Aram is Damascus,[s]
    and the head of Damascus is only Rezin.
Within sixty-five years
    Ephraim will be too shattered[t] to be a people.
9The head of Ephraim is Samaria,
    and the head of Samaria is only Remaliah's son.
If you do not stand firm in your faith,[u]
    you will not stand at all.' "[v]

10Again the LORD spoke to Ahaz, 11"Ask the LORD your God for a sign, whether in the deepest depths or in the highest heights."

12But Ahaz said, "I will not ask; I will not put the LORD to the test."

13Then Isaiah said, "Hear now, you house of David! Is it not enough to try the patience of men? Will you try the patience of my God[w] also? 14Therefore the Lord himself will give you[a] a sign: The virgin will be with child and will give birth to a son,[x] and[b] will call him Immanuel.[c] [y] 15He will eat curds and honey[z] when he knows enough to reject the wrong and choose the right. 16But before the boy knows[a] enough to reject the wrong and choose the right, the land of the two kings you dread will be laid waste.[b] 17The LORD will bring on you and on your people and on the house of your father a time unlike any since Ephraim broke away[c] from Judah—he will bring the king of Assyria.[d]"

18In that day the LORD will whistle[e] for flies from the distant streams of Egypt and for bees from the land of Assyria.[f] 19They will all come and settle in the steep ravines and in the crevices[g] in the rocks, on all the thornbushes and at all the water holes. 20In that day the Lord will use[h] a razor hired from beyond the River[d]—the king of Assyria[i]—to shave your head and the hair of your legs, and to take off your beards also. 21In that day, a man will keep alive a young cow and two goats. 22And because of the abundance of the milk they give, he will have curds to eat. All who remain in the land will eat curds and honey. 23In that day, in every place where there were a thousand vines worth a thousand silver shekels,[e] there will be only briers and thorns.[j] 24Men will go there with bow and arrow, for the land will be covered with briers and thorns. 25As for all the hills once cultivated by the hoe, you will no longer go there for fear of the briers and thorns; they will become places where cattle are turned loose and where sheep run.[k]

Assyria, the LORD's Instrument

8 The LORD said to me, "Take a large scroll[l] and write on it with an ordinary pen: Maher-Shalal-Hash-Baz.[f] [m] 2And I will call in Uriah[n] the priest and Zechariah son of Jeberekiah as reliable witnesses for me."

3Then I went to the prophetess, and she conceived and gave birth to a son. And the LORD said to me, "Name him Maher-Shalal-Hash-Baz. 4Before the boy knows[o] how to say 'My father' or 'My mother,' the

7:7
r Isa 8:10;
Ac 4:25
7:8
s Ge 14:15
t Isa 17:1-3
7:9
u 2Ch 20:20
v Isa 8:6-8;
30:12-14
7:13
w Isa 25:1
7:14
x Lk 1:31
y Isa 8:8,10;
Mt 1:23*
7:15
z ver 22
7:16
a Isa 8:4
b Isa 17:3;
Hos 5:9,13;
Am 1:3-5
7:17
c 1Ki 12:16
d 2Ch 28:20
7:18
e Isa 5:26
f Isa 13:5
7:19
g Isa 2:19
7:20
h Isa 10:15
i Isa 8:7; 10:5
7:23
j Isa 5:6
7:25
k Isa 5:17
8:1
l Isa 30:8 m ver 3;
Hab 2:2
8:2
n 2Ki 16:10
8:4
o Isa 7:16

---

*a14 The Hebrew is plural.   b14 Masoretic Text; Dead Sea Scrolls and he or and they
c14 Immanuel means God with us.   d20 That is, the Euphrates   e23 That is, about 25 pounds
(about 11.5 kilograms)   f1 Maher-Shalal-Hash-Baz means quick to the plunder, swift to the spoil;
also in verse 3.*

wealth of Damascus and the plunder of Samaria will be carried off by the king of Assyria. P"

⁵The LORD spoke to me again:

⁶"Because this people has rejected �q
    the gently flowing waters of Shiloah ʳ
and rejoices over Rezin
    and the son of Remaliah, ˢ
⁷therefore the Lord is about to bring against them
    the mighty floodwaters ᵗ of the River ᵃ—
the king of Assyria ᵘ with all his pomp.
It will overflow all its channels,
    run over all its banks
⁸and sweep on into Judah, swirling over it,
    passing through it and reaching up to the neck.
Its outspread wings will cover the breadth of your land,
    O Immanuel ᵇ!" ᵛ

⁹Raise the war cry, ᶜʷ you nations, and be shattered!
    Listen, all you distant lands.
Prepare ˣ for battle, and be shattered!
    Prepare for battle, and be shattered!
¹⁰Devise your strategy, but it will be thwarted; ʸ
    propose your plan, but it will not stand, ᶻ
for God is with us. ᵈ ᵃ

Fear God

¹¹The LORD spoke to me with his strong hand upon me, ᵇ warning me not to follow ᶜ the way of this people. He said:

¹²"Do not call conspiracy ᵈ
    everything that these people call conspiracy ᵉ;
do not fear what they fear,
    and do not dread it. ᵉ
¹³The LORD Almighty is the one you are to regard as
    holy, ᶠ
he is the one you are to fear,
    he is the one you are to dread, ᵍ
¹⁴and he will be a sanctuary; ʰ
    but for both houses of Israel he will be
a stone that causes men to stumble
    and a rock that makes them fall. ⁱ
And for the people of Jerusalem he will be
    a trap and a snare. ʲ
¹⁵Many of them will stumble; ᵏ
    they will fall and be broken,
they will be snared and captured."

¹⁶Bind up the testimony
    and seal ˡ up the law among my disciples.
¹⁷I will wait ᵐ for the LORD,

8:4
pIsa 7:8
8:6
qIsa 5:24
rJn 9:7 sIsa 7:1
8:7
tIsa 17:12-13
uIsa 7:20
8:8
vIsa 7:14
8:9
wIsa 17:12-13
xJoel 3:9
8:10
yJob 5:12
zIsa 7:7
aIsa 7:14;
Ro 8:31
8:11
bEze 3:14
cEze 2:8
8:12
dIsa 7:2; 30:1
e1Pe 3:14*
8:13
fNu 20:12
gIsa 29:23
8:14
hIsa 4:6;
Eze 11:16
iLk 2:34;
Ro 9:33*;
1Pe 2:8*
jIsa 24:17-18
8:15
kIsa 28:13;
59:10;
Lk 20:18;
Ro 9:32
8:16
lIsa 29:11-12
8:17
mHab 2:3

ᵃ7 That is, the Euphrates   ᵇ8 *Immanuel* means *God with us.*   ᶜ9 Or *Do your worst*
ᵈ10 Hebrew *Immanuel*   ᵉ12 Or *Do not call for a treaty / every time these people call for a treaty*

who is hiding[n] his face from the house of Jacob.
I will put my trust in him.

[18]Here am I, and the children the LORD has given me.[o] We are signs[p] and symbols in Israel from the LORD Almighty, who dwells on Mount Zion.[q]

[19]When men tell you to consult[r] mediums and spiritists, who whisper and mutter,[s] should not a people inquire of their God? Why consult the dead on behalf of the living? [20]To the law[t] and to the testimony! If they do not speak according to this word, they have no light[u] of dawn. [21]Distressed and hungry, they will roam through the land; when they are famished, they will become enraged and, looking upward, will curse[v] their king and their God. [22]Then they will look toward the earth and see only distress and darkness and fearful gloom, and they will be thrust into utter darkness.[w]

To Us a Child Is Born

9 Nevertheless, there will be no more gloom for those who were in distress. In the past he humbled the land of Zebulun and the land of Naphtali,[x] but in the future he will honor Galilee of the Gentiles, by the way of the sea, along the Jordan—

[2]The people walking in darkness
        have seen a great light;[y]
on those living in the land of the shadow of death[a][z]
        a light has dawned.[a]
[3]You have enlarged the nation
        and increased their joy;
they rejoice before you
        as people rejoice at the harvest,
as men rejoice
        when dividing the plunder.
[4]For as in the day of Midian's defeat,[b]
        you have shattered
the yoke[c] that burdens them,
        the bar across their shoulders,[d]
        the rod of their oppressor.[e]
[5]Every warrior's boot used in battle
        and every garment rolled in blood
will be destined for burning,[f]
        will be fuel for the fire.
[6]For to us a child is born,[g]
        to us a son is given,[h]
and the government[i] will be on his shoulders.
And he will be called
        Wonderful Counselor,[bj] Mighty God,[k]
        Everlasting Father, Prince of Peace.[l]
[7]Of the increase of his government and peace
        there will be no end.[m]
He will reign on David's throne
        and over his kingdom,

8:17
nDt 31:17;
Isa 54:8
8:18
oHeb 2:13*
pLk 2:34
qPs 9:11
8:19
r1Sa 28:8
sIsa 29:4
8:20
tIsa 1:10;
Lk 16:29
uMic 3:6
8:21
vRev 16:11
8:22
wver 20;
Isa 5:30
9:1
x2Ki 15:29
9:2
yEph 5:8
zLk 1:79
aMt 4:15-16*
9:4
bJdg 7:25
cIsa 14:25
dIsa 10:27
eIsa 14:4;
49:26; 51:13;
54:14
9:5
fIsa 2:4
9:6
gIsa 53:2;
Lk 2:11 hJn 3:16
iMt 28:18
jIsa 28:29
kIsa 10:21; 11:2
lIsa 26:3,12;
66:12
9:7
mDa 2:44;
Lk 1:33

---

[a]2 Or *land of darkness*   [b]6 Or *Wonderful, Counselor*

establishing and upholding it
  with justice[n] and righteousness
  from that time on and forever.
The zeal[o] of the Lord Almighty
  will accomplish this.

The Lord's Anger Against Israel

[8]The Lord has sent a message against Jacob;
  it will fall on Israel.
[9]All the people will know it—
  Ephraim and the inhabitants of Samaria[p]—
who say with pride
  and arrogance[q] of heart,
[10]"The bricks have fallen down,
  but we will rebuild with dressed stone;
the fig trees have been felled,
  but we will replace them with cedars."
[11]But the Lord has strengthened Rezin's[r] foes against
    them
  and has spurred their enemies on.
[12]Arameans[s] from the east and Philistines[t] from the west
  have devoured[u] Israel with open mouth.

Yet for all this, his anger is not turned away,
  his hand is still upraised.[v]

[13]But the people have not returned to him who struck[w]
    them,
  nor have they sought[x] the Lord Almighty.
[14]So the Lord will cut off from Israel both head and tail,
  both palm branch and reed[y] in a single day;[z]
[15]the elders[a] and prominent men are the head,
  the prophets who teach lies are the tail.
[16]Those who guide[b] this people mislead them,
  and those who are guided are led astray.[c]
[17]Therefore the Lord will take no pleasure in the young
    men,[d]
  nor will he pity[e] the fatherless and widows,
for everyone is ungodly[f] and wicked,[g]
  every mouth speaks vileness.[h]

Yet for all this, his anger is not turned away,
  his hand is still upraised.[i]

[18]Surely wickedness burns like a fire;[j]
  it consumes briers and thorns,
it sets the forest thickets ablaze,[k]
  so that it rolls upward in a column of smoke.
[19]By the wrath[l] of the Lord Almighty
  the land will be scorched
and the people will be fuel for the fire;[m]
  no one will spare his brother.[n]
[20]On the right they will devour,

9:7
n Isa 11:4; 16:5;
  32:1,16
o Isa 37:32;
  59:17
9:9
p Isa 7:9
q Isa 46:12
9:11
r Isa 7:8
9:12
s 2Ki 16:6
t 2Ch 28:18
u Ps 79:7
v Isa 5:25
9:13
w Jer 5:3
x Isa 31:1;
  Hos 7:7,10
9:14
y Isa 19:15
z Rev 18:8
9:15
a Isa 3:2-3
9:16
b Mt 15:14;
  23:16,24
c Isa 3:12
9:17
d Jer 18:21
e Isa 27:11
f Isa 10:6
g Isa 1:4
h Mt 12:34
i Isa 5:25
9:18
j Mal 4:1
k Ps 83:14
9:19
l Isa 13:9,13
m Isa 1:31
n Mic 7:2,6

but still be hungry;[o]
on the left they will eat,[p]
but not be satisfied.
Each will feed on the flesh of his own offspring[a]:
21 Manasseh will feed on Ephraim, and Ephraim on
Manasseh;
together they will turn against Judah.[q]

Yet for all this, his anger is not turned away,
his hand is still upraised.[r]

10 Woe to those who make unjust laws,
to those who issue oppressive decrees,[s]
²to deprive[t] the poor of their rights
and withhold justice from the oppressed of my
people,[u]
making widows their prey
and robbing the fatherless.
³What will you do on the day of reckoning,[v]
when disaster[w] comes from afar?
To whom will you run for help?[x]
Where will you leave your riches?
⁴Nothing will remain but to cringe among the captives[y]
or fall among the slain.[z]

Yet for all this, his anger is not turned away,[a]
his hand is still upraised.

God's Judgment on Assyria

⁵"Woe to the Assyrian,[b] the rod of my anger,
in whose hand is the club[c] of my wrath![d]
⁶I send him against a godless[e] nation,
I dispatch him against a people who anger me,[f]
to seize loot and snatch plunder,[g]
and to trample them down like mud in the streets.
⁷But this is not what he intends,[h]
this is not what he has in mind;
his purpose is to destroy,
to put an end to many nations.
⁸'Are not my commanders[i] all kings?' he says.
9 'Has not Calno[j] fared like Carchemish?[k]
Is not Hamath like Arpad,
and Samaria[l] like Damascus?[m]
¹⁰As my hand seized the kingdoms of the idols,[n]
kingdoms whose images excelled those of Jerusalem
and Samaria—
¹¹shall I not deal with Jerusalem and her images
as I dealt with Samaria and her idols?' "

¹²When the Lord has finished all his work[o] against Mount Zion[p] and
Jerusalem, he will say, "I will punish the king of Assyria[q] for the willful

---

9:20
oLev 26:26
pIsa 49:26
9:21
q2Ch 28:6
rIsa 5:25
10:1
sPs 58:2
10:2
tIsa 3:14
uIsa 5:23
10:3
vJob 31:14;
Hos 9:7
wLk 19:44
xIsa 20:6
10:4
yIsa 24:22
zIsa 22:2; 34:3;
66:16 aIsa 5:25
10:5
bIsa 14:25;
Zep 2:13
cJer 51:20
dIsa 13:3,5,13;
30:30; 66:14
10:6
eIsa 9:17
fIsa 9:19
gIsa 5:29
10:7
hGe 50:20;
Ac 4:23-28
10:8
i2Ki 18:24
10:9
jGe 10:10
k2Ch 35:20
l2Ki 17:6
m2Ki 16:9
10:10
n2Ki 19:18
10:12
oIsa 28:21-22;
65:7 p2Ki 19:31
qJer 50:18

---

a20 Or arm

pride of his heart and the haughty look in his eyes. [13]For he says:

" 'By the strength of my hand I have done this,[r]
   and by my wisdom, because I have understanding.
I removed the boundaries of nations,
   I plundered their treasures;[s]
   like a mighty one I subdued[a] their kings.
[14]As one reaches into a nest,[t]
   so my hand reached for the wealth[u] of the nations;
as men gather abandoned eggs,
   so I gathered all the countries;
not one flapped a wing,
   or opened its mouth to chirp.' "

[15]Does the ax raise itself above him who swings it,
   or the saw boast against him who uses it?[v]
As if a rod were to wield him who lifts it up,
   or a club[w] brandish him who is not wood!
[16]Therefore, the Lord, the LORD Almighty,
   will send a wasting disease[x] upon his sturdy warriors;
under his pomp[y] a fire will be kindled
   like a blazing flame.
[17]The Light of Israel will become a fire,[z]
   their Holy One[a] a flame;
in a single day it will burn and consume
   his thorns[b] and his briers.[c]
[18]The splendor of his forests[d] and fertile fields
   it will completely destroy,
   as when a sick man wastes away.
[19]And the remaining trees of his forests will be so few[e]
   that a child could write them down.

The Remnant of Israel

[20]In that day[f] the remnant of Israel,
   the survivors of the house of Jacob,
will no longer rely[g] on him
   who struck them down[h]
but will truly rely[i] on the LORD,
   the Holy One of Israel.
[21]A remnant[j] will return,[b] a remnant of Jacob
   will return to the Mighty God.[k]
[22]Though your people, O Israel, be like the sand by the sea,
   only a remnant will return.[l]
Destruction has been decreed,[m]
   overwhelming and righteous.
[23]The Lord, the LORD Almighty, will carry out
   the destruction decreed upon the whole land.[n]

[24]Therefore, this is what the Lord, the LORD Almighty, says:

"O my people who live in Zion,[o]

10:13
r Isa 37:24;
Da 4:30
s Eze 28:4
10:14
t Jer 49:16;
Ob 1:4
u Job 31:25
10:15
v Isa 45:9;
Ro 9:20-21
w ver 5
10:16
x ver 18;
Isa 17:4 y Isa 8:7
10:17
z Isa 31:9
a Isa 37:23
b Nu 11:1-3
c Isa 9:18
10:18
d 2Ki 19:23
10:19
e Isa 21:17
10:20
f Isa 11:10,11
g 2Ki 16:7
h 2Ch 28:20
i Isa 17:7
10:21
j Isa 6:13
k Isa 9:6
10:22
l Ro 9:27-28
m Isa 28:22;
Da 9:27
10:23
n Isa 28:22;
Ro 9:27-28*
10:24
o Ps 87:5-6

---

a13 Or / *I subdued the mighty,*   *b21* Hebrew *shear-jashub*; also in verse 22

do not be afraid of the Assyrians,
who beat[p] you with a rod
and lift up a club against you, as Egypt did.
25Very soon[q] my anger against you will end
and my wrath[r] will be directed to their destruction."

26The Lord Almighty will lash[s] them with a whip,
as when he struck down Midian[t] at the rock of Oreb;
and he will raise his staff over the waters,[u]
as he did in Egypt.
27In that day their burden will be lifted from your
shoulders,
their yoke[v] from your neck;[w]
the yoke will be broken
because you have grown so fat.[a]

28They enter Aiath;
they pass through Migron;[x]
they store supplies at Micmash.[y]
29They go over the pass, and say,
"We will camp overnight at Geba."
Ramah[z] trembles;
Gibeah of Saul flees.
30Cry out, O Daughter of Gallim![a]
Listen, O Laishah!
Poor Anathoth![b]
31Madmenah is in flight;
the people of Gebim take cover.
32This day they will halt at Nob;[c]
they will shake their fist
at the mount of the Daughter of Zion,[d]
at the hill of Jerusalem.

33See, the Lord, the Lord Almighty,
will lop off the boughs with great power.
The lofty trees will be felled,
the tall[e] ones will be brought low.
34He will cut down the forest thickets with an ax;
Lebanon will fall before the Mighty One.

The Branch From Jesse

11 A shoot will come up from the stump of Jesse;[f]
from his roots a Branch[g] will bear fruit.
2The Spirit[h] of the Lord will rest on him—
the Spirit of wisdom[i] and of understanding,
the Spirit of counsel and of power,[j]
the Spirit of knowledge and of the fear of the Lord—
3and he will delight in the fear of the Lord.

He will not judge by what he sees with his eyes,[k]
or decide by what he hears with his ears;[l]
4but with righteousness[m] he will judge the needy,

10:24
pEx 5:14
10:25
qIsa 17:14
rver 5; Da 11:36
10:26
sIsa 37:36-38
tIsa 9:4
uEx 14:16
10:27
vIsa 9:4
wIsa 14:25
10:28
xISa 14:2
yISa 13:2
10:29
zJos 18:25
10:30
aISa 25:44
bNe 11:32
10:32
cISa 21:1
dJer 6:23
10:33
eAm 2:9
11:1
fver 10; Isa 9:7;
Rev 5:5 gIsa 4:2
11:2
hIsa 42:1;
48:16; 61:1;
Mt 3:16;
Jn 1:32-33
iEph 1:17
j2Ti 1:7
11:3
kJn 7:24
lJn 2:25
11:4
mPs 72:2

a27 Hebrew; Septuagint *broken / from your shoulders*

with justice[n] he will give decisions for the poor[o] of
    the earth.
He will strike[p] the earth with the rod of his mouth;
    with the breath[q] of his lips he will slay the wicked.
[5]Righteousness will be his belt
    and faithfulness[r] the sash around his waist.[s]

[6]The wolf will live with the lamb,[t]
    the leopard will lie down with the goat,
the calf and the lion and the yearling[a] together;
    and a little child will lead them.
[7]The cow will feed with the bear,
    their young will lie down together,
    and the lion will eat straw like the ox.
[8]The infant will play near the hole of the cobra,
    and the young child put his hand into the viper's
      nest.
[9]They will neither harm nor destroy[u]
    on all my holy mountain,
for the earth[v] will be full of the knowledge[w] of the LORD
    as the waters cover the sea.

[10]In that day the Root of Jesse will stand as a banner[x] for the peoples;
the nations[y] will rally to him,[z] and his place of rest[a] will be glorious.
[11]In that day[b] the Lord will reach out his hand a second time to reclaim
the remnant that is left of his people from Assyria,[c] from Lower Egypt,
from Upper Egypt,[b] from Cush,[c] from Elam,[d] from Babylonia,[d] from
Hamath and from the islands[e] of the sea.

[12]He will raise a banner for the nations
    and gather the exiles of Israel;
he will assemble the scattered people[f] of Judah
    from the four quarters of the earth.
[13]Ephraim's jealousy will vanish,
    and Judah's enemies[e] will be cut off;
Ephraim will not be jealous of Judah,
    nor Judah hostile toward Ephraim.[g]
[14]They will swoop down on the slopes of Philistia to the
    west;
    together they will plunder the people to the east.
They will lay hands on Edom[h] and Moab,[i]
    and the Ammonites will be subject to them.
[15]The LORD will dry up
    the gulf of the Egyptian sea;
with a scorching wind he will sweep his hand[j]
    over the Euphrates River.[f] [k]
He will break it up into seven streams
    so that men can cross over in sandals.
[16]There will be a highway[l] for the remnant of his people
    that is left from Assyria,

11:4
[n]Isa 9:7
[o]Isa 3:14
[p]Mal 4:6
[q]Job 4:9;
2Th 2:8
11:5
[r]Isa 25:1
[s]Eph 6:14
11:6
[t]Isa 65:25
11:9
[u]Job 5:23
[v]Ps 98:2-3;
Isa 52:10
[w]Isa 45:6,14;
Hab 2:14
11:10
[x]Jn 12:32
[y]Isa 49:23;
Lk 2:32
[z]Ro 15:12*
[a]Isa 14:3;
28:12; 32:17-18
11:11
[b]Isa 10:20
[c]Isa 19:24;
Hos 11:11;
Mic 7:12;
Zec 10:10
[d]Ge 10:22
[e]Isa 42:4,10,12;
66:19
11:12
[f]Zep 3:10
11:13
[g]Jer 3:18;
Eze 37:16-17,
22; Hos 1:11
11:14
[h]Da 11:41;
Joel 3:19
[i]Isa 16:14;
25:10
11:15
[j]Isa 19:16
[k]Isa 7:20
11:16
[l]Isa 19:23;
62:10

---

[a]6 Hebrew; Septuagint *lion will feed*   [b]11 Hebrew *from Pathros*   [c]11 That is, the upper Nile
region   [d]11 Hebrew *Shinar*   [e]13 Or *hostility*   [f]15 Hebrew *the River*

as there was for Israel
  when they came up from Egypt. ᵐ

Songs of Praise

12 In that day you will say:

"I will praiseⁿ you, O Lᴏʀᴅ.
  Although you were angry with me,
your anger has turned away
  and you have comforted me.
²Surely God is my salvation;
  I will trustᵒ and not be afraid.
The Lᴏʀᴅ, the Lᴏʀᴅ, is my strength and my song;
  he has become my salvation. ᵖ"
³With joy you will draw waterq
  from the wells of salvation.

⁴In that day you will say:

"Give thanks to the Lᴏʀᴅ, call on his name;ʳ
  make known among the nations what he has done,
  and proclaim that his name is exalted.
⁵Sings to the Lᴏʀᴅ, for he has done glorious things;ᵗ
  let this be known to all the world.
⁶Shout aloud and sing for joy, people of Zion,
  for great is the Holy One of Israelᵘ among you. ᵛ"

A Prophecy Against Babylon

13 An oracle concerning Babylon that Isaiah son of Amoz saw:

²Raise a bannerʷ on a bare hilltop,
  shout to them;
beckon to them
  to enter the gates of the nobles.
³I have commanded my holy ones;
  I have summoned my warriorsˣ to carry out my
    wrath—
those who rejoiceʸ in my triumph.

⁴Listen, a noise on the mountains,
  like that of a great multitude!ᶻ
Listen, an uproar among the kingdoms,
  like nations massing together!
The Lᴏʀᴅ Almighty is mustering
  an army for war.
⁵They come from faraway lands,
  from the ends of the heavensᵃ—
the Lᴏʀᴅ and the weapons of his wrath—
  to destroyᵇ the whole country.

⁶Wail,ᶜ for the dayᵈ of the Lᴏʀᴅ is near;
  it will come like destruction from the Almighty. ᵃ
⁷Because of this, all hands will go limp,
  every man's heart will melt. ᵉ

ᵃ6 Hebrew *Shaddai*

11:16
mEx 14:26-31
12:1
nIsa 25:1
12:2
oIsa 26:3
pEx 15:2;
Ps 118:14
12:3
qJn 4:10,14
12:4
rPs 105:1;
Isa 24:15
12:5
sEx 15:1
tPs 98:1
12:6
uIsa 49:26
vZep 3:14-17
13:2
wJer 50:2;
51:27
13:3
xJoel 3:11
yPs 149:2
13:4
zJoel 3:14
13:5
aIsa 5:26
bIsa 24:1
13:6
cEze 30:2
dIsa 2:12;
Joel 1:15
13:7
eEze 21:7

⁸Terror^f will seize them,
　　pain and anguish will grip them;
　　they will writhe like a woman in labor.
They will look aghast at each other,
　　their faces aflame. ^{g}

⁹See, the day of the LORD is coming
　　—a cruel day, with wrath and fierce anger—
to make the land desolate
　　and destroy the sinners within it.
¹⁰The stars of heaven and their constellations
　　will not show their light.
The rising sun^h will be darkened^i
　　and the moon will not give its light. ^{j}
¹¹I will punish^k the world for its evil,
　　the wicked for their sins.
I will put an end to the arrogance of the haughty
　　and will humble the pride of the ruthless.
¹²I will make man^l scarcer than pure gold,
　　more rare than the gold of Ophir.
¹³Therefore I will make the heavens tremble;^{m}
　　and the earth will shake from its place
at the wrath of the LORD Almighty,
　　in the day of his burning anger.

¹⁴Like a hunted gazelle,
　　like sheep without a shepherd, ^{n}
each will return to his own people,
　　each will flee to his native land. ^{o}
¹⁵Whoever is captured will be thrust through;
　　all who are caught will fall^p by the sword. ^{q}
¹⁶Their infants^r will be dashed to pieces before their eyes;
　　their houses will be looted and their wives ravished.

¹⁷See, I will stir up^s against them the Medes,
　　who do not care for silver
　　and have no delight in gold. ^{t}
¹⁸Their bows will strike down the young men;
　　they will have no mercy on infants
　　nor will they look with compassion on children.
¹⁹Babylon, the jewel of kingdoms,
　　the glory^u of the Babylonians'^{a} pride,
will be overthrown^v by God
　　like Sodom and Gomorrah. ^{w}
²⁰She will never be inhabited^x
　　or lived in through all generations;
no Arab^y will pitch his tent there,
　　no shepherd will rest his flocks there.
²¹But desert creatures^z will lie there,
　　jackals will fill her houses;
there the owls will dwell,

13:8
f Isa 21:4
g Na 2:10
13:10
h Isa 24:23
i Isa 5:30;
Rev 8:12
j Eze 32:7;
Mt 24:29*;
Mk 13:24*
13:11
k Isa 3:11; 11:4;
26:21
13:12
l Isa 4:1
13:13
m Isa 34:4;
51:6; Hag 2:6
13:14
n 1Ki 22:17
o Jer 50:16
13:15
p Jer 51:4
q Isa 14:19;
Jer 50:25
13:16
r Ps 137:9
13:17
s Jer 51:1
t Pr 6:34-35
13:19
u Da 4:30
v Rev 14:8
w Ge 19:24
13:20
x Isa 14:23;
34:10-15
y 2Ch 17:11
13:21
z Rev 18:2

^{a}19 Or *Chaldeans'*

and there the wild goats will leap about.
[22]Hyenas will howl in her strongholds,[a]
  jackals[b] in her luxurious palaces.
Her time is at hand,[c]
  and her days will not be prolonged.

14 The Lord will have compassion[d] on Jacob;
  once again he will choose[e] Israel
  and will settle them in their own land.
Aliens[f] will join them
  and unite with the house of Jacob.
[2]Nations will take them
  and bring[g] them to their own place.
And the house of Israel will possess the nations[h]
  as menservants and maidservants in the Lord's land.
They will make captives of their captors
  and rule over their oppressors.[i]

[3]On the day the Lord gives you relief[j] from suffering and turmoil and cruel bondage, [4]you will take up this taunt[k] against the king of Babylon:

How the oppressor[l] has come to an end!
  How his fury[a] has ended!
[5]The Lord has broken the rod of the wicked,[m]
  the scepter of the rulers,
[6]which in anger struck down peoples[n]
  with unceasing blows,
  and in fury subdued nations
  with relentless aggression.[o]
[7]All the lands are at rest and at peace;
  they break into singing.[p]
[8]Even the pine trees[q] and the cedars of Lebanon
  exult over you and say,
"Now that you have been laid low,
  no woodsman comes to cut us down."

[9]The grave[br] below is all astir
  to meet you at your coming;
it rouses the spirits of the departed to greet you—
  all those who were leaders in the world;
it makes them rise from their thrones—
  all those who were kings over the nations.
[10]They will all respond,
  they will say to you,
"You also have become weak, as we are;
  you have become like us."[s]
[11]All your pomp has been brought down to the grave,
  along with the noise of your harps;
  maggots are spread out beneath you

13:22
[a]Isa 25:2
[b]Isa 34:13
[c]Jer 51:33
14:1
[d]Ps 102:13;
Isa 49:10,13;
54:7-8,10
[e]Isa 41:8; 44:1;
49:7; Zec 1:17;
2:12
[f]Eph 2:12-19
14:2
[g]Isa 60:9
[h]Isa 49:7,23
[i]Isa 60:14; 61:5
14:3
[j]Isa 11:10
14:4
[k]Hab 2:6
[l]Isa 9:4
14:5
[m]Ps 125:3
14:6
[n]Isa 10:14
[o]Isa 47:6
14:7
[p]Ps 98:1;
126:1-3
14:8
[q]Eze 31:16
14:9
[r]Eze 32:21
14:10
[s]Eze 32:21

---

[a]4 Dead Sea Scrolls, Septuagint and Syriac; the meaning of the word in the Masoretic Text is uncertain.   [b]9 Hebrew *Sheol*; also in verses 11 and 15

and worms[t] cover you.

¹²How you have fallen[u] from heaven,
    O morning star,[v] son of the dawn!
You have been cast down to the earth,
    you who once laid low the nations!
¹³You said in your heart,
    "I will ascend[w] to heaven;
I will raise my throne[x]
    above the stars of God;
I will sit enthroned on the mount of assembly,
    on the utmost heights of the sacred mountain.[a]
¹⁴I will ascend above the tops of the clouds;
    I will make myself like the Most High."[y]
¹⁵But you are brought down to the grave,
    to the depths[z] of the pit.

¹⁶Those who see you stare at you,
    they ponder your fate:[a]
"Is this the man who shook the earth
    and made kingdoms tremble,
¹⁷the man who made the world a desert,[b]
    who overthrew its cities
    and would not let his captives go home?"

¹⁸All the kings of the nations lie in state,
    each in his own tomb.
¹⁹But you are cast out[c] of your tomb
    like a rejected branch;
you are covered with the slain,
    with those pierced by the sword,
    those who descend to the stones of the pit.[d]
Like a corpse trampled underfoot,
²⁰ you will not join them in burial,
for you have destroyed your land
    and killed your people.

The offspring[e] of the wicked[f]
    will never be mentioned[g] again.
²¹Prepare a place to slaughter his sons
    for the sins of their forefathers;[h]
they are not to rise to inherit the land
    and cover the earth with their cities.

²²"I will rise up against them,"
    declares the Lord Almighty.
"I will cut off from Babylon her name and survivors,
    her offspring and descendants,[i] "
                   declares the Lord.
²³"I will turn her into a place for owls[j]
    and into swampland;

14:11
t Isa 51:8
14:12
u Isa 34:4;
Lk 10:18
v 2Pe 1:19;
Rev 2:28; 8:10;
9:1
14:13
w Da 5:23;
8:10; Mt 11:23
x Eze 28:2;
2Th 2:4
14:14
y Isa 47:8;
2Th 2:4
14:15
z Mt 11:23;
Lk 10:15
14:16
a Jer 50:23
14:17
b Joel 2:3
14:19
c Isa 22:16-18
d Jer 41:7-9
14:20
e Job 18:19
f Isa 1:4
g Ps 21:10
14:21
h Ex 20:5;
Lev 26:39
14:22
i 1Ki 14:10;
Job 18:19
14:23
j Isa 34:11-15;
Zep 2:14

a13 Or *the north;* Hebrew *Zaphon*

I will sweep her with the broom of destruction,"
　　declares the LORD Almighty.

A Prophecy Against Assyria

24The LORD Almighty has sworn,[k]

"Surely, as I have planned, so it will be,
　　and as I have purposed, so it will stand.[l]
25I will crush the Assyrian[m] in my land;
　　on my mountains I will trample him down.
His yoke[n] will be taken from my people,
　　and his burden removed from their shoulders.[o]"

26This is the plan[p] determined for the whole world;
　　this is the hand[q] stretched out over all nations.
27For the LORD Almighty has purposed, and who can
　　thwart him?
His hand is stretched out, and who can turn it back?[r]

A Prophecy Against the Philistines

28This oracle[s] came in the year King Ahaz[t] died:

29Do not rejoice, all you Philistines,[u]
　　that the rod that struck you is broken;
from the root of that snake will spring up a viper,[v]
　　its fruit will be a darting, venomous serpent.
30The poorest of the poor will find pasture,
　　and the needy[w] will lie down in safety.[x]
But your root I will destroy by famine;[y]
　　it will slay[z] your survivors.

31Wail, O gate![a] Howl, O city!
　　Melt away, all you Philistines!
A cloud of smoke comes from the north,[b]
　　and there is not a straggler in its ranks.
32What answer shall be given
　　to the envoys[c] of that nation?
"The LORD has established Zion,[d]
　　and in her his afflicted people will find refuge.[e]"

A Prophecy Against Moab

16:6–12pp — Jer 48:29–36

15 An oracle concerning Moab:[f]

Ar in Moab is ruined,[g]
　　destroyed in a night!
Kir in Moab is ruined,
　　destroyed in a night!
2Dibon goes up to its temple,
　　to its high places[h] to weep;
Moab wails over Nebo and Medeba.
Every head is shaved[i]
　　and every beard cut off.
3In the streets they wear sackcloth;
　　on the roofs and in the public squares[j]

14:24
k Isa 45:23
l Ac 4:28
14:25
m Isa 10:5,12
n Isa 9:4
o Isa 10:27
14:26
p Isa 23:9
q Ex 15:12
14:27
r 2Ch 20:6;
Isa 43:13;
Da 4:35
14:28
s Isa 13:1
t 2Ki 16:20
14:29
u 2Ch 26:6
v Isa 11:8
14:30
w Isa 3:15
x Isa 7:21-22
y Isa 8:21; 9:20;
51:19 z Jer 25:16
14:31
a Isa 3:26
b Jer 1:14
14:32
c Isa 37:9
d Ps 87:2,5;
Isa 44:28; 54:11
e Isa 4:6; Jas 2:5
15:1
f Isa 11:14
g Jer 48:24,41
15:2
h Jer 48:35
i Lev 21:5
15:3
j Jer 48:38

they all wail,
    prostrate with weeping. [k]
[4]Heshbon and Elealeh[l] cry out,
    their voices are heard all the way to Jahaz.
Therefore the armed men of Moab cry out,
    and their hearts are faint.

[5]My heart cries out over Moab;[m]
    her fugitives flee as far as Zoar,
    as far as Eglath Shelishiyah.
They go up the way to Luhith,
    weeping as they go;
on the road to Horonaim[n]
    they lament their destruction. [o]
[6]The waters of Nimrim are dried up[p]
    and the grass is withered;[q]
the vegetation is gone
    and nothing green is left.
[7]So the wealth they have acquired[r] and stored up
    they carry away over the Ravine of the Poplars.
[8]Their outcry echoes along the border of Moab;
    their wailing reaches as far as Eglaim,
    their lamentation as far as Beer Elim.
[9]Dimon's[a] waters are full of blood,
    but I will bring still more upon Dimon[a] —
a lion[s] upon the fugitives of Moab
    and upon those who remain in the land.

16

Send lambs[t] as tribute
    to the ruler of the land,
from Sela, [u] across the desert,
    to the mount of the Daughter of Zion. [v]
[2]Like fluttering birds
    pushed from the nest, [w]
so are the women of Moab
    at the fords of the Arnon. [x]

[3]"Give us counsel,
    render a decision.
Make your shadow like night—
    at high noon.
Hide the fugitives, [y]
    do not betray the refugees.
[4]Let the Moabite fugitives stay with you;
    be their shelter from the destroyer."

The oppressor[z] will come to an end,
    and destruction will cease;
    the aggressor will vanish from the land.
[5]In love a throne[a] will be established;
    in faithfulness a man will sit on it—

15:3
k Isa 22:4
15:4
l Nu 32:3
15:5
m Jer 48:31
n Jer 48:3,34
o Jer 4:20; 48:5
15:6
p Isa 19:5-7;
Jer 48:34
q Joel 1:12
15:7
r Isa 30:6;
Jer 48:36
15:9
s 2Ki 17:25
16:1
t 2Ki 3:4
u 2Ki 14:7
v Isa 10:32
16:2
w Pr 27:8
x Nu 21:13-14;
Jer 48:20
16:3
y 1Ki 18:4
16:4
z Isa 9:4
16:5
a Da 7:14;
Mic 4:7

---

[a]9 Masoretic Text; Dead Sea Scrolls, some Septuagint manuscripts and Vulgate *Dibon*

    one from the house[a] of David[b]—
    one who in judging seeks justice[c]
      and speeds the cause of righteousness.

6We have heard of Moab's[d] pride[e]—
    her overweening pride and conceit,
    her pride and her insolence—
      but her boasts are empty.
7Therefore the Moabites wail,[f]
    they wail together for Moab.
    Lament and grieve
      for the men[b][g] of Kir Hareseth.[h]
8The fields of Heshbon wither,
    the vines of Sibmah also.
    The rulers of the nations
      have trampled down the choicest vines,
    which once reached Jazer
      and spread toward the desert.
    Their shoots spread out
      and went as far as the sea.
9So I weep,[i] as Jazer weeps,
    for the vines of Sibmah.
    O Heshbon, O Elealeh,
      I drench you with tears!
    The shouts of joy over your ripened fruit
      and over your harvests[j] have been stilled.
10Joy and gladness are taken away from the orchards;[k]
    no one sings or shouts in the vineyards;
    no one treads[l] out wine at the presses,[m]
      for I have put an end to the shouting.
11My heart laments for Moab[n] like a harp,
    my inmost being[o] for Kir Hareseth.
12When Moab appears at her high place,
    she only wears herself out;
    when she goes to her shrine[p] to pray,
      it is to no avail.[q]

13This is the word the Lord has already spoken concerning Moab. 14But now the Lord says: "Within three years, as a servant bound by contract would count them, Moab's splendor and all her many people will be despised,[r] and her survivors will be very few and feeble."[s]

An Oracle Against Damascus

17 An oracle concerning Damascus:[t]

    "See, Damascus will no longer be a city
      but will become a heap of ruins.[u]
2The cities of Aroer will be deserted
    and left to flocks,[v] which will lie down,
      with no one to make them afraid.[w]
3The fortified city will disappear from Ephraim,

16:5
bLk 1:32
cIsa 9:7
16:6
dAm 2:1;
Zep 2:8
eOb 1:3;
Zep 2:10
16:7
fJer 48:20
g1Ch 16:3
h2Ki 3:25
16:9
iIsa 15:3
jJer 40:12
16:10
kIsa 24:7-8
lJdg 9:27
mJob 24:11
16:11
nIsa 15:5
oIsa 63:15;
Hos 11:8;
Php 2:1
16:12
pIsa 15:2
q1Ki 18:29
16:14
rIsa 25:10;
Jer 48:42
sIsa 21:17
17:1
tGe 14:15;
Jer 49:23;
Ac 9:2
uIsa 25:2;
Am 1:3; Zec 9:1
17:2
vIsa 7:21;
Eze 25:5
wJer 7:33;
Mic 4:4

a5 Hebrew *tent*   b7 Or *"raisin cakes,"* a wordplay

and royal power from Damascus;
the remnant of Aram will be
like the glory[x] of the Israelites,"[y]

declares the LORD Almighty.

4"In that day the glory of Jacob will fade;
the fat of his body will waste[z] away.
5It will be as when a reaper gathers the standing grain
and harvests[a] the grain with his arm—
as when a man gleans heads of grain
in the Valley of Rephaim.
6Yet some gleanings will remain,[b]
as when an olive tree is beaten,[c]
leaving two or three olives on the topmost branches,
four or five on the fruitful boughs,"

declares the LORD, the God of Israel.

7In that day men will look[d] to their Maker
and turn their eyes to the Holy One[e] of Israel.
8They will not look to the altars,
the work of their hands,[f]
and they will have no regard for the Asherah poles[a]
and the incense altars their fingers have made.

9In that day their strong cities, which they left because of the Israelites, will be like places abandoned to thickets and undergrowth. And all will be desolation.

10You have forgotten[g] God your Savior;[h]
you have not remembered the Rock, your fortress.
Therefore, though you set out the finest plants
and plant imported vines,
11though on the day you set them out, you make them grow,
and on the morning[i] when you plant them, you bring them to bud,
yet the harvest will be as nothing[j]
in the day of disease and incurable pain.[k]

12Oh, the raging of many nations—
they rage like the raging sea![l]
Oh, the uproar of the peoples—
they roar like the roaring of great waters!
13Although the peoples roar like the roar of surging waters,
when he rebukes[m] them they flee[n] far away,
driven before the wind like chaff[o] on the hills,
like tumbleweed before a gale.[p]
14In the evening, sudden terror!
Before the morning, they are gone![q]
This is the portion of those who loot us,
the lot of those who plunder us.

17:3
xver 4;
Hos 9:11
yIsa 7:8,16; 8:4
17:4
zIsa 10:16
17:5
aver 11;
Jer 51:33;
Joel 3:13;
Mt 13:30
17:6
bDt 4:27;
Isa 24:13
cIsa 27:12
17:7
dIsa 10:20
eMic 7:7
17:8
fIsa 2:18,20;
30:22
17:10
gIsa 51:13
hPs 68:19;
Isa 12:2
17:11
iPs 90:6
jHos 8:7
kJob 4:8
17:12
lPs 18:4;
Jer 6:23;
Lk 21:25
17:13
mPs 9:5
nIsa 13:14
oIsa 41:2,15-16
pJob 21:18
17:14
q2Ki 19:35

---

[a]8 That is, symbols of the goddess Asherah

A Prophecy Against Cush

18 Woe to the land of whirring wings[a]
along the rivers of Cush,[b][r]
[2]which sends envoys by sea
in papyrus[s] boats over the water.

Go, swift messengers,
to a people tall and smooth-skinned,
to a people feared far and wide,
an aggressive[t] nation of strange speech,
whose land is divided by rivers.[u]

[3]All you people of the world,
you who live on the earth,
when a banner[v] is raised on the mountains,
you will see it,
and when a trumpet sounds,
you will hear it.
[4]This is what the LORD says to me:
"I will remain quiet and will look on from my
dwelling place,[w]
like shimmering heat in the sunshine,
like a cloud of dew[x] in the heat of harvest."
[5]For, before the harvest, when the blossom is gone
and the flower becomes a ripening grape,
he will cut off the shoots with pruning knives,
and cut down and take away the spreading
branches.[y]
[6]They will all be left to the mountain birds of prey
and to the wild animals;[z]
the birds will feed on them all summer,
the wild animals all winter.

[7]At that time gifts will be brought to the LORD Almighty

from a people tall and smooth-skinned,
from a people feared far and wide,
an aggressive nation of strange speech,
whose land is divided by rivers—

the gifts will be brought to Mount Zion, the place of the Name of the
LORD Almighty.[a]

A Prophecy About Egypt

19 An oracle[b] concerning Egypt:[c][d]

See, the LORD rides on a swift cloud[e]
and is coming to Egypt.
The idols of Egypt tremble before him,
and the hearts of the Egyptians melt[f] within them.

[2]"I will stir up Egyptian against Egyptian—
brother will fight against brother,[g]

18:1
[r]Isa 20:3-5;
Eze 30:4-5,9;
Zep 2:12; 3:10
18:2
[s]Ex 2:3
[t]Ge 10:8-9;
2Ch 12:3 [u]ver 7
18:3
[v]Isa 5:26
18:4
[w]Isa 26:21;
Hos 5:15
[x]Isa 26:19;
Hos 14:5
18:5
[y]Isa 17:10-11;
Eze 17:6
18:6
[z]Isa 56:9;
Jer 7:33;
Eze 32:4; 39:17
18:7
[a]Ps 68:31
19:1
[b]Isa 13:1;
Jer 43:12
[c]Joel 3:19
[d]Ex 12:12
[e]Ps 18:10;
104:3; Rev 1:7
[f]Jos 2:11
19:2
[g]Jdg 7:22;
Mt 10:21,36

neighbor against neighbor,
city against city,
kingdom against kingdom. [h]
[3] The Egyptians will lose heart,
and I will bring their plans to nothing;
they will consult the idols and the spirits of the dead,
the mediums and the spiritists. [i]
[4] I will hand the Egyptians over
to the power of a cruel master,
and a fierce king [j] will rule over them,"
declares the Lord, the LORD Almighty.

[5] The waters of the river will dry up, [k]
and the riverbed will be parched and dry.
[6] The canals will stink; [l]
the streams of Egypt will dwindle and dry up. [m]
The reeds and rushes will wither, [n]
[7] also the plants along the Nile,
at the mouth of the river.
Every sown field [o] along the Nile
will become parched, will blow away and be no more.
[8] The fishermen [p] will groan and lament,
all who cast hooks [q] into the Nile;
those who throw nets on the water
will pine away.
[9] Those who work with combed flax will despair,
the weavers of fine linen [r] will lose hope.
[10] The workers in cloth will be dejected,
and all the wage earners will be sick at heart.

[11] The officials of Zoan [s] are nothing but fools;
the wise counselors of Pharaoh give senseless advice.
How can you say to Pharaoh,
"I am one of the wise men, [t]
a disciple of the ancient kings"?

[12] Where are your wise men [u] now?
Let them show you and make known
what the LORD Almighty
has planned [v] against Egypt.
[13] The officials of Zoan have become fools,
the leaders of Memphis [a][w] are deceived;
the cornerstones of her peoples
have led Egypt astray.
[14] The LORD has poured into them
a spirit of dizziness; [x]
they make Egypt stagger in all that she does,
as a drunkard staggers around in his vomit.
[15] There is nothing Egypt can do—
head or tail, palm branch or reed. [y]

[16] In that day the Egyptians will be like women. [z] They will shudder

---

19:2
h 2Ch 20:23
19:3
i Isa 8:19;
47:13; Da 2:2,
10
19:4
j Isa 20:4;
Jer 46:26;
Eze 29:19
19:5
k Jer 51:36
19:6
l Ex 7:18
m Isa 37:25;
Eze 30:12
n Isa 15:6
19:7
o Isa 23:3
19:8
p Eze 47:10
q Hab 1:15
19:9
r Pr 7:16;
Eze 27:7
19:11
s Nu 13:22
t 1Ki 4:30;
Ac 7:22
19:12
u 1Co 1:20
v Isa 14:24;
Ro 9:17
19:13
w Jer 2:16;
Eze 30:13,16
19:14
x Mt 17:17
19:15
y Isa 9:14
19:16
z 51:30; Na 3:13

---

[a] 13 Hebrew *Noph*

with fear[a] at the uplifted hand[b] that the Lord Almighty raises against them. [17]And the land of Judah will bring terror to the Egyptians; everyone to whom Judah is mentioned will be terrified, because of what the Lord Almighty is planning[c] against them.

[18]In that day five cities in Egypt will speak the language of Canaan and swear allegiance[d] to the Lord Almighty. One of them will be called the City of Destruction. [a]

[19]In that day there will be an altar[e] to the Lord in the heart of Egypt, and a monument[f] to the Lord at its border. [20]It will be a sign and witness to the Lord Almighty in the land of Egypt. When they cry out to the Lord because of their oppressors, he will send them a savior and defender, and he will rescue[g] them. [21]So the Lord will make himself known to the Egyptians, and in that day they will acknowledge[h] the Lord. They will worship[i] with sacrifices and grain offerings; they will make vows to the Lord and keep them. [22]The Lord will strike[j] Egypt with a plague; he will strike them and heal them. They will turn[k] to the Lord, and he will respond to their pleas and heal[l] them.

[23]In that day there will be a highway[m] from Egypt to Assyria. The Assyrians will go to Egypt and the Egyptians to Assyria. The Egyptians and Assyrians will worship[n] together. [24]In that day Israel will be the third, along with Egypt and Assyria, a blessing on the earth. [25]The Lord Almighty will bless them, saying, "Blessed be Egypt my people, [o] Assyria my handiwork, [p] and Israel my inheritance. [q]"

A Prophecy Against Egypt and Cush

20 In the year that the supreme commander, [r] sent by Sargon king of Assyria, came to Ashdod and attacked and captured it— [2]at that time the Lord spoke through Isaiah son of Amoz. [s] He said to him, "Take off the sackcloth[t] from your body and the sandals[u] from your feet." And he did so, going around stripped[v] and barefoot. [w]

[3]Then the Lord said, "Just as my servant Isaiah has gone stripped and barefoot for three years, as a sign[x] and portent against Egypt and Cush, [b][y] [4]so the king[z] of Assyria will lead away stripped and barefoot the Egyptian captives and Cushite exiles, young and old, with buttocks bared—to Egypt's shame. [a] [5]Those who trusted in Cush and boasted in Egypt[b] will be afraid and put to shame. [6]In that day the people who live on this coast will say, 'See what has happened to those we relied on, those we fled to for help[c] and deliverance from the king of Assyria! How then can we escape?[d]'"

A Prophecy Against Babylon

21 An oracle concerning the Desert[e] by the Sea:

Like whirlwinds sweeping through the southland, [f]
    an invader comes from the desert,
    from a land of terror.

[2]A dire[g] vision has been shown to me:
    The traitor betrays, [h] the looter takes loot.

---

[a]18 Most manuscripts of the Masoretic Text; some manuscripts of the Masoretic Text, Dead Sea Scrolls and Vulgate *City of the Sun* (that is, Heliopolis)   [b]3 That is, the upper Nile region; also in verse 5

19:16
a Heb 10:31
b Isa 11:15
19:17
c Isa 14:24
19:18
d Zep 3:9
19:19
e Jos 22:10
f Ge 28:18
19:20
g Isa 49:24-26
19:21
h Isa 11:9
i Isa 56:7;
Mal 1:11
19:22
j Heb 12:11
k Isa 45:14;
Hos 14:1
l Dt 32:39
19:23
m Isa 11:16
n Isa 27:13
19:25
o Ps 100:3
p Isa 29:23;
45:11; 60:21;
64:8; Eph 2:10
q Hos 2:23
20:1
r 2Ki 18:17
20:2
s Isa 13:1
t Zec 13:4;
Mt 3:4
u Eze 24:17,23
v 1Sa 19:24
w Mic 1:8
20:3
x Isa 8:18
y Isa 37:9; 43:3
20:4
z Isa 19:4
a Isa 47:3;
Jer 13:22,26
20:5
b 2Ki 18:21;
Isa 30:5
20:6
c Isa 10:3
d Jer 30:15-17;
Mt 23:33;
1Th 5:3;
Heb 2:3
21:1
e Isa 13:21;
Jer 51:43
f Zec 9:14
21:2
g Ps 60:3
h Isa 33:1

Elam,[i] attack! Media, lay siege!
    I will bring to an end all the groaning she caused.

[3]At this my body is racked with pain,
    pangs seize me, like those of a woman in labor;[j]
I am staggered by what I hear,
    I am bewildered by what I see.
[4]My heart falters,
    fear makes me tremble;
the twilight I longed for
    has become a horror to me.

[5]They set the tables,
    they spread the rugs,
    they eat, they drink![k]
Get up, you officers,
    oil the shields!

[6]This is what the Lord says to me:

"Go, post a lookout
    and have him report what he sees.
[7]When he sees chariots[l]
    with teams of horses,
riders on donkeys
    or riders on camels,
let him be alert,
    fully alert."

[8]And the lookout[a][m] shouted,

"Day after day, my lord, I stand on the watchtower;
    every night I stay at my post.
[9]Look, here comes a man in a chariot
    with a team of horses.
And he gives back the answer:
    'Babylon[n] has fallen,[o] has fallen!
All the images of its gods[p]
    lie shattered on the ground!' "

[10]O my people, crushed on the threshing floor,[q]
    I tell you what I have heard
from the LORD Almighty,
    from the God of Israel.

A Prophecy Against Edom

[11]An oracle concerning Dumah[b]:[r]

Someone calls to me from Seir,[s]
    "Watchman, what is left of the night?
    Watchman, what is left of the night?"
[12]The watchman replies,
    "Morning is coming, but also the night.

21:2
[i]Isa 22:6;
Jer 49:34
21:3
[j]Ps 48:6;
Isa 26:17
21:5
[k]Jer 51:39,57;
Da 5:2
21:7
[l]ver 9
21:8
[m]Hab 2:1
21:9
[n]Rev 14:8
[o]Jer 51:8;
Rev 18:2
[p]Isa 46:1;
Jer 50:2; 51:44
21:10
[q]Jer 51:33
21:11
[r]Ge 25:14
[s]Ge 32:3

---

[a]8 Dead Sea Scrolls and Syriac; Masoretic Text *A lion*   [b]11 *Dumah* means *silence* or *stillness,* a wordplay on *Edom.*

If you would ask, then ask;
    and come back yet again.''

A Prophecy Against Arabia

[13]An oracle[t] concerning Arabia:

You caravans of Dedanites,
    who camp in the thickets of Arabia,
[14] bring water for the thirsty;
    you who live in Tema,[u]
    bring food for the fugitives.
[15]They flee[v] from the sword,
    from the drawn sword,
from the bent bow
    and from the heat of battle.

[16]This is what the Lord says to me: "Within one year, as a servant bound by contract[w] would count it, all the pomp[x] of Kedar[y] will come to an end. [17]The survivors of the bowmen, the warriors of Kedar, will be few.[z]'' The LORD, the God of Israel, has spoken.

A Prophecy About Jerusalem

22 An oracle[a] concerning the Valley[b] of Vision:

What troubles you now,
    that you have all gone up on the roofs,
[2]O town full of commotion,
    O city of tumult and revelry?[c]
Your slain were not killed by the sword,
    nor did they die in battle.
[3]All your leaders have fled together;
    they have been captured without using the bow.
All you who were caught were taken prisoner together,
    having fled while the enemy was still far away.
[4]Therefore I said, "Turn away from me;
    let me weep[d] bitterly.
Do not try to console me
    over the destruction of my people."[e]

[5]The Lord, the LORD Almighty, has a day
    of tumult and trampling and terror[f]
    in the Valley of Vision,
a day of battering down walls
    and of crying out to the mountains.
[6]Elam[g] takes up the quiver,[h]
    with her charioteers and horses;
    Kir[i] uncovers the shield.
[7]Your choicest valleys are full of chariots,
    and horsemen are posted at the city gates;[j]
[8] the defenses of Judah are stripped away.

And you looked in that day
    to the weapons[k] in the Palace of the Forest;[l]
[9]you saw that the City of David

21:13
tIsa 13:1
21:14
uGe 25:15
21:15
vIsa 13:14
21:16
wIsa 16:14
xIsa 17:3
yPs 120:5;
Isa 60:7
21:17
zIsa 10:19
22:1
aIsa 13:1
bPs 125:2;
Jer 21:13;
Joel 3:2,12,14
22:2
cIsa 32:13
22:4
dIsa 15:3;
Lk 19:41
eJer 9:1
22:5
fLa 1:5
22:6
gIsa 21:2
hJer 49:35
i2Ki 16:9
22:7
j2Ch 32:1-2
22:8
k2Ch 32:5
l1Ki 7:2

had many breaches in its defenses;
you stored up water
in the Lower Pool. [m]
[10]You counted the buildings in Jerusalem
and tore down houses to strengthen the wall.
[11]You built a reservoir between the two walls[n]
for the water of the Old Pool, [o]
but you did not look to the One who made it,
or have regard for the One who planned it long ago.

[12]The Lord, the LORD Almighty,
called you on that day
to weep[p] and to wail,
to tear out your hair[q] and put on sackcloth. [r]
[13]But see, there is joy and revelry,
slaughtering of cattle and killing of sheep,
eating of meat and drinking of wine![s]
"Let us eat and drink," you say,
"for tomorrow we die!"[t]

[14]The LORD Almighty has revealed this in my hearing:[u] "Till your dying day this sin will not be atoned[v] for," says the Lord, the LORD Almighty.

[15]This is what the Lord, the LORD Almighty, says:

"Go, say to this steward,
to Shebna, [w] who is in charge of the palace:
[16]What are you doing here and who gave you permission
to cut out a grave[x] for yourself here,
hewing your grave on the height
and chiseling your resting place in the rock?

[17]"Beware, the LORD is about to take firm hold of you
and hurl you away, O you mighty man.
[18]He will roll you up tightly like a ball
and throw[y] you into a large country.
There you will die
and there your splendid chariots will remain—
you disgrace to your master's house!
[19]I will depose you from your office,
and you will be ousted from your position.

[20]"In that day I will summon my servant, Eliakim[z] son of Hilkiah. [21]I will clothe him with your robe and fasten your sash around him and hand your authority over to him. He will be a father to those who live in Jerusalem and to the house of Judah. [22]I will place on his shoulder the key[a] to the house of David;[b] what he opens no one can shut, and what he shuts no one can open. [c] [23]I will drive him like a peg[d] into a firm place;[e] he will be a seat[a] of honor[f] for the house of his father. [24]All the glory of his family will hang on him: its offspring and offshoots—all its lesser vessels, from the bowls to all the jars.

[a]23 Or *throne*

22:9
m2Ch 32:4
22:11
n2Ki 25:4;
Jer 39:4
o2Ch 32:4
22:12
pJoel 2:17
qMic 1:16
rJoel 1:13
22:13
sIsa 5:22;
28:7-8; 56:12;
Lk 17:26-29
t1Co 15:32*
22:14
uIsa 5:9
vIsa 13:11;
26:21;
30:13-14;
Eze 24:13
22:15
w2Ki 18:18;
Isa 36:3
22:16
xMt 27:60
22:18
yIsa 17:13
22:20
z2Ki 18:18;
Isa 36:3
22:22
aRev 3:7
bIsa 7:2
cJob 12:14
22:23
dZec 10:4
eEzr 9:8
f1Sa 2:7-8;
Job 36:7

²⁵"In that day," declares the LORD Almighty, "the peg^g driven into the firm place will give way; it will be sheared off and will fall, and the load hanging on it will be cut down." The LORD has spoken. ^h

A Prophecy About Tyre

23 An oracle concerning Tyre:ⁱ

> Wail, O ships^j of Tarshish!^k
> For Tyre is destroyed
> and left without house or harbor.
> From the land of Cyprus^a
> word has come to them.

²Be silent, you people of the island
and you merchants of Sidon,
whom the seafarers have enriched.
³On the great waters
came the grain of the Shihor;
the harvest of the Nile^{b1} was the revenue of Tyre, ^m
and she became the marketplace of the nations.

⁴Be ashamed, O Sidon, ⁿ and you, O fortress of the sea,
for the sea has spoken:
"I have neither been in labor nor given birth;
I have neither reared sons nor brought up daughters."
⁵When word comes to Egypt,
they will be in anguish at the report from Tyre.

⁶Cross over to Tarshish;
wail, you people of the island.
⁷Is this your city of revelry, ^o
the old, old city,
whose feet have taken her
to settle in far-off lands?
⁸Who planned this against Tyre,
the bestower of crowns,
whose merchants are princes,
whose traders are renowned in the earth?
⁹The LORD Almighty planned it,
to bring low^p the pride of all glory
and to humble^q all who are renowned^r on the earth.

¹⁰Till^c your land as along the Nile,
O Daughter of Tarshish,
for you no longer have a harbor.
¹¹The LORD has stretched out his hand^s over the sea
and made its kingdoms tremble.
He has given an order concerning Phoenicia^d
that her fortresses be destroyed. ^t
¹²He said, "No more of your reveling, ^u
O Virgin Daughter^v of Sidon, now crushed!

22:25
gver 23
hIsa 46:11;
Mic 4:4
23:1
iJos 19:29;
1Ki 5:1;
Jer 47:4; Eze 26,
27,28;
Joel 3:4-8;
Am 1:9-10;
Zec 9:2-4
j1Ki 10:22
kGe 10:4;
Isa 2:16 *fn*
23:3
lIsa 19:7
mEze 27:3
23:4
nGe 10:15,19
23:7
oIsa 22:2; 32:13
23:9
pJob 40:11
qIsa 13:11
rIsa 5:13; 9:15
23:11
sEx 14:21
tIsa 25:2;
Zec 9:3-4
23:12
uRev 18:22
vIsa 47:1

---

^a1,12 Hebrew *Kittim*   ^b2,3 Masoretic Text; one Dead Sea Scroll *Sidon, / who cross over the sea; / your envoys* ³*are on the great waters. / The grain of the Shihor, / the harvest of the Nile,*   ^c10 Dead Sea Scrolls and some Septuagint manuscripts; Masoretic Text *Go through*   ^d11 Hebrew *Canaan*

"Up, cross over to Cyprus[a];
    even there you will find no rest."
[13]Look at the land of the Babylonians,[b]
    this people that is now of no account!
The Assyrians[w] have made it
    a place for desert creatures;
they raised up their siege towers,
        they stripped its fortresses bare
        and turned it into a ruin.[x]

[14]Wail, you ships of Tarshish;[y]
    your fortress is destroyed!

[15]At that time Tyre[z] will be forgotten for seventy years, the span of a king's life. But at the end of these seventy years, it will happen to Tyre as in the song of the prostitute:

[16]"Take up a harp, walk through the city,
    O prostitute forgotten;
play the harp well, sing many a song,
    so that you will be remembered."

[17]At the end of seventy years, the Lord will deal with Tyre. She will return to her hire as a prostitute[a] and will ply her trade with all the kingdoms on the face of the earth. [18]Yet her profit and her earnings will be set apart for the Lord;[b] they will not be stored up or hoarded. Her profits will go to those who live before the Lord,[c] for abundant food and fine clothes.

The Lord's Devastation of the Earth

24 See, the Lord is going to lay waste the earth[d]
        and devastate it;
    he will ruin its face
        and scatter its inhabitants—
[2]it will be the same
        for priest as for people,[e]
        for master as for servant,
        for mistress as for maid,
        for seller as for buyer,[f]
        for borrower as for lender,
        for debtor as for creditor.[g]
[3]The earth will be completely laid waste
        and totally plundered.[h]
                    The Lord has spoken this word.

[4]The earth dries up and withers,
        the world languishes and withers,
        the exalted[i] of the earth languish.
[5]The earth is defiled[j] by its people;
        they have disobeyed[k] the laws,
    violated the statutes
        and broken the everlasting covenant.

23:13
wIsa 10:5
xIsa 10:7
23:14
yIsa 2:16 *fn*
23:15
zJer 25:22
23:17
aEze 16:26;
Na 3:4;
Rev 17:1
23:18
bEx 28:36;
Ps 72:10
cIsa 60:5-9;
Mic 4:13
24:1
dver 20;
Isa 2:19-21;
33:9
24:2
eHos 4:9
fEze 7:12
gLev 25:35-37;
Dt 23:19-20
24:3
hIsa 6:11-12
24:4
iIsa 2:12
24:5
jGe 3:17;
Nu 35:33
kIsa 10:6; 59:12

[a]1,12 Hebrew *Kittim*   [b]13 Or *Chaldeans*

⁶Therefore a curse consumes the earth;
    its people must bear their guilt.
Therefore earth's inhabitants are burned up,[l]
    and very few are left.
⁷The new wine dries up and the vine withers;[m]
    all the merrymakers groan.[n]
⁸The gaiety of the tambourines[o] is stilled,
    the noise[p] of the revelers has stopped,
    the joyful harp[q] is silent.[r]
⁹No longer do they drink wine[s] with a song;
    the beer is bitter[t] to its drinkers.
¹⁰The ruined city lies desolate;
    the entrance to every house is barred.
¹¹In the streets they cry out for wine;
    all joy turns to gloom,[u]
    all gaiety is banished from the earth.
¹²The city is left in ruins,
    its gate is battered to pieces.
¹³So will it be on the earth
    and among the nations,
as when an olive tree is beaten,[v]
    or as when gleanings are left after the grape harvest.

¹⁴They raise their voices, they shout for joy;[w]
    from the west they acclaim the LORD's majesty.
¹⁵Therefore in the east give glory[x] to the LORD;
    exalt[y] the name of the LORD, the God of Israel,
    in the islands of the sea.
¹⁶From the ends of the earth we hear singing:
    "Glory[z] to the Righteous One."

But I said, "I waste away, I waste away!
    Woe to me!
The treacherous betray!
    With treachery the treacherous betray![a]"
¹⁷Terror and pit and snare[b] await you,
    O people of the earth.
¹⁸Whoever flees at the sound of terror
    will fall into a pit;
whoever climbs out of the pit
    will be caught in a snare.

The floodgates of the heavens[c] are opened,
    the foundations of the earth shake.[d]
¹⁹The earth is broken up,
    the earth is split asunder,[e]
    the earth is thoroughly shaken.
²⁰The earth reels like a drunkard,[f]
    it sways like a hut in the wind;
so heavy upon it is the guilt of its rebellion[g]
    that it falls—never to rise again.

²¹In that day the LORD will punish[h]
    the powers in the heavens above

24:6
l Isa 1:31
24:7
m Joel 1:10-12
n Isa 16:8-10
24:8
o Isa 5:12
p Jer 7:34; 16:9;
25:10; Hos 2:11
q Rev 18:22
r Eze 26:13
24:9
s Isa 5:11,22
t Isa 5:20
24:11
u Isa 16:10;
32:13; Jer 14:3
24:13
v Isa 17:6
24:14
w Isa 12:6
24:15
x Isa 66:19
y Isa 25:3;
Mal 1:11
24:16
z Isa 28:5
a Isa 21:2;
Jer 5:11
24:17
b Jer 48:43
24:18
c Ge 7:11
d Ps 18:7
24:19
e Dt 11:6
24:20
f Isa 19:14
g Isa 1:2,28;
43:27
24:21
h Isa 10:12

and the kings on the earth below.
²²They will be herded together
    like prisoners[i] bound in a dungeon;[j]
they will be shut up in prison
    and be punished[a] after many days.[k]
²³The moon will be abashed, the sun[l] ashamed;
    for the LORD Almighty will reign[m]
on Mount Zion[n] and in Jerusalem,
    and before its elders, gloriously.[o]

Praise to the LORD

25

O LORD, you are my God;
    I will exalt you and praise your name,
for in perfect faithfulness
    you have done marvelous things,[p]
    things planned[q] long ago.
²You have made the city a heap of rubble,[r]
    the fortified[s] town a ruin,
the foreigners' stronghold[t] a city no more;
    it will never be rebuilt.
³Therefore strong peoples will honor you;
    cities of ruthless[u] nations will revere you.
⁴You have been a refuge[v] for the poor,
    a refuge for the needy in his distress,
a shelter from the storm
    and a shade from the heat.
For the breath of the ruthless[w]
    is like a storm driving against a wall
⁵ and like the heat of the desert.
You silence[x] the uproar of foreigners;
    as heat is reduced by the shadow of a cloud,
    so the song of the ruthless is stilled.

⁶On this mountain[y] the LORD Almighty will prepare
    a feast[z] of rich food for all peoples,
a banquet of aged wine—
    the best of meats and the finest of wines.[a]
⁷On this mountain he will destroy
    the shroud[b] that enfolds all peoples,
the sheet that covers all nations;
⁸ he will swallow up death[c] forever.
The Sovereign LORD will wipe away the tears[d]
    from all faces;
he will remove the disgrace[e] of his people
    from all the earth.

                The LORD has spoken.

⁹In that day they will say,

    "Surely this is our God;[f]
    we trusted in him, and he saved[g] us.

24:22
[i] Isa 10:4
[j] Isa 42:7,22
[k] Eze 38:8
24:23
[l] Isa 13:10
[m] Rev 22:5
[n] Heb 12:22
[o] Isa 60:19
25:1
[p] Ps 98:1
[q] Nu 23:19
25:2
[r] Isa 17:1
[s] Isa 17:3
[t] Isa 13:22
25:3
[u] Isa 13:11
25:4
[v] Isa 4:6; 17:10; 27:5; 33:16
[w] Isa 29:5; 49:25
25:5
[x] Jer 51:55
25:6
[y] Isa 2:2
[z] Isa 1:19; Mt 8:11; 22:4
[a] Pr 9:2
25:7
[b] 2Co 3:15-16; Eph 4:18
25:8
[c] Hos 13:14; 1Co 15:54-55*
[d] Isa 30:19; 35:10; 51:11; 65:19; Rev 7:17; 21:4
[e] Mt 5:11; 1Pe 4:14
25:9
[f] Isa 40:9
[g] Ps 20:5; Isa 33:22; 35:4; 49:25-26,26; 60:16

---

[a]22 Or *released*

This is the Lord, we trusted in him;
    let us rejoice[h] and be glad in his salvation."

[10]The hand of the Lord will rest on this mountain;
    but Moab[i] will be trampled under him
    as straw is trampled down in the manure.
[11]They will spread out their hands in it,
    as a swimmer spreads out his hands to swim.
God will bring down[j] their pride[k]
    despite the cleverness[a] of their hands.
[12]He will bring down your high fortified walls
    and lay them low;[l]
he will bring them down to the ground,
    to the very dust.

A Song of Praise

26 In that day this song will be sung in the land of Judah:

  We have a strong city;[m]
    God makes salvation
    its walls[n] and ramparts.
[2]Open the gates
    that the righteous[o] nation may enter,
    the nation that keeps faith.
[3]You will keep in perfect peace
    him whose mind is steadfast,
    because he trusts in you.
[4]Trust[p] in the Lord forever,
    for the Lord, the Lord, is the Rock eternal.
[5]He humbles those who dwell on high,
    he lays the lofty city low;
he levels it to the ground[q]
    and casts it down to the dust.
[6]Feet trample it down—
    the feet of the oppressed,
    the footsteps of the poor.[r]

[7]The path of the righteous is level;
    O upright One, you make the way of the righteous
      smooth.[s]
[8]Yes, Lord, walking in the way of your laws,[b][t]
    we wait for you;
your name[u] and renown
    are the desire of our hearts.
[9]My soul yearns for you in the night;
    in the morning my spirit longs[v] for you.
When your judgments come upon the earth,
    the people of the world learn righteousness.[w]
[10]Though grace is shown to the wicked,
    they do not learn righteousness;
even in a land of uprightness they go on doing evil[x]

25:9
h Isa 35:2,10
25:10
i Am 2:1-3
25:11
j Isa 5:25;
14:26; 16:14
k Job 40:12
25:12
l Isa 15:1
26:1
m Isa 14:32
n Isa 60:18
26:2
o Isa 54:14;
58:8; 62:2
26:4
p Isa 12:2; 50:10
26:5
q Isa 25:12
26:6
r Isa 3:15
26:7
s Isa 42:16
26:8
t Isa 56:1
u Isa 12:4
26:9
v Ps 63:1;
78:34; Isa 55:6
w Mt 6:33
26:10
x Isa 32:6

---

[a]11 The meaning of the Hebrew for this word is uncertain.　　　[b]8 Or *judgments*

and regard[y] not the majesty of the LORD.
11O LORD, your hand is lifted high,
but they do not see[z] it.
Let them see your zeal for your people and be put to
shame;
let the fire[a] reserved for your enemies consume them.

12LORD, you establish peace for us;
all that we have accomplished you have done for us.
13O LORD, our God, other lords[b] besides you have ruled
over us,
but your name alone do we honor.[c]
14They are now dead,[d] they live no more;
those departed spirits do not rise.
You punished them and brought them to ruin;[e]
you wiped out all memory of them.
15You have enlarged the nation, O LORD;
you have enlarged the nation.
You have gained glory for yourself;
you have extended all the borders[f] of the land.

16LORD, they came to you in their distress;[g]
when you disciplined them,
they could barely whisper a prayer.[a]
17As a woman with child and about to give birth[h]
writhes and cries out in her pain,
so were we in your presence, O LORD.
18We were with child, we writhed in pain,
but we gave birth[i] to wind.
We have not brought salvation[j] to the earth;
we have not given birth to people of the world.

19But your dead[k] will live;
their bodies will rise.
You who dwell in the dust,
wake up and shout for joy.
Your dew is like the dew of the morning;
the earth will give birth to her dead.[l]

20Go, my people, enter your rooms
and shut the doors[m] behind you;
hide[n] yourselves for a little while
until his wrath has passed by.[o]
21See, the LORD is coming[p] out of his dwelling[q]
to punish[r] the people of the earth for their sins.
The earth will disclose the blood[s] shed upon her;
she will conceal her slain no longer.

Deliverance of Israel

27 In that day,

the LORD will punish with his sword,[t]

a16 The meaning of the Hebrew for this clause is uncertain.

26:10
y Isa 22:12-13;
Hos 11:7;
Jn 5:37-38;
Ro 2:4
26:11
z Isa 44:9,18
a Heb 10:27
26:13
b Isa 2:8; 10:5,
11 c Isa 63:7
26:14
d Dt 4:28
e Isa 10:3
26:15
f Isa 33:17
26:16
g Hos 5:15
26:17
h Jn 16:21
26:18
i Isa 33:11; 59:4
j Ps 17:14
26:19
k Isa 25:8;
Eph 5:14
l Eze 37:1-14;
Da 12:2
26:20
m Ex 12:23
n Ps 91:1,4
o Ps 30:5;
Isa 54:7-8
26:21
p Jude 1:14
q Mic 1:3
r Isa 13:9,11;
30:12-14
s Job 16:18;
Lk 11:50-51
27:1
t Isa 34:6; 66:16

his fierce, great and powerful sword,
Leviathan[u] the gliding serpent,
Leviathan the coiling serpent;
he will slay the monster[v] of the sea.

²In that day—

"Sing about a fruitful vineyard:[w]
³ I, the LORD, watch over it;
I water[x] it continually.
I guard it day and night
so that no one may harm it.
⁴ I am not angry.
If only there were briers and thorns confronting me!
I would march against them in battle;
I would set them all on fire.[y]
⁵Or else let them come to me for refuge;[z]
let them make peace[a] with me,
yes, let them make peace with me."

⁶In days to come Jacob will take root,
Israel will bud and blossom[b]
and fill all the world with fruit.[c]

⁷Has the LORD struck her
as he struck[d] down those who struck her?
Has she been killed
as those were killed who killed her?
⁸By warfare[a] and exile[e] you contend with her—
with his fierce blast he drives her out,
as on a day the east wind blows.
⁹By this, then, will Jacob's guilt be atoned for,
and this will be the full fruitage of the removal of his
sin:[f]
When he makes all the altar stones
to be like chalk stones crushed to pieces,
no Asherah poles[b][g] or incense altars
will be left standing.
¹⁰The fortified city stands desolate,[h]
an abandoned settlement, forsaken like the desert;
there the calves graze,
there they lie down;[i]
they strip its branches bare.
¹¹When its twigs are dry, they are broken off
and women come and make fires with them.
For this is a people without understanding;[j]
so their Maker has no compassion on them,
and their Creator[k] shows them no favor.[l]

¹²In that day the LORD will thresh from the flowing Euphrates[c] to the
Wadi of Egypt,[m] and you, O Israelites, will be gathered[n] up one by one.

---

[a]8 See Septuagint; the meaning of the Hebrew for this word is uncertain.   [b]9 That is, symbols
of the goddess Asherah   [c]12 Hebrew *River*

27:1
u Job 3:8
v Ps 74:13
27:2
w Jer 2:21
27:3
x Isa 58:11
27:4
y Isa 10:17;
Mt 3:12;
Heb 6:8
27:5
z Isa 25:4
a Job 22:21;
Ro 5:1;
2Co 5:20
27:6
b Hos 14:5-6
c Isa 37:31
27:7
d Isa 37:36-38
27:8
e Isa 50:1; 54:7
27:9
f Ro 11:27*
g Ex 34:13
27:10
h Isa 32:14;
Jer 26:6
i Isa 17:2
27:11
j Dt 32:28;
Isa 1:3; Jer 8:7
k Dt 32:18;
Isa 43:1,7,15;
44:1-2,21,24
l Isa 9:17
27:12
m Ge 15:18
n Dt 30:4;
Isa 11:12; 17:6

[13]And in that day a great trumpet[o] will sound. Those who were perishing in Assyria and those who were exiled in Egypt[p] will come and worship the LORD on the holy mountain in Jerusalem.

Woe to Ephraim

28 Woe to that wreath, the pride of Ephraim's[q] drunkards,
　　to the fading flower, his glorious beauty,
set on the head of a fertile valley[r] —
　　to that city, the pride of those laid low by wine![s]
[2]See, the Lord has one who is powerful[t] and strong.
　　Like a hailstorm[u] and a destructive wind,[v]
like a driving rain and a flooding[w] downpour,
　　he will throw it forcefully to the ground.
[3]That wreath, the pride of Ephraim's[x] drunkards,
　　will be trampled underfoot.
[4]That fading flower, his glorious beauty,
　　set on the head of a fertile valley,[y]
will be like a fig[z] ripe before harvest—
　　as soon as someone sees it and takes it in his hand,
　　he swallows it.

[5]In that day the LORD Almighty
　　will be a glorious crown,[a]
a beautiful wreath
　　for the remnant of his people.
[6]He will be a spirit of justice[b]
　　to him who sits in judgment,[c]
a source of strength
　　to those who turn back the battle[d] at the gate.

[7]And these also stagger from wine[e]
　　and reel[f] from beer:
Priests[g] and prophets[h] stagger from beer
　　and are befuddled with wine;
they reel from beer,
　　they stagger when seeing visions,[i]
　　they stumble when rendering decisions.
[8]All the tables are covered with vomit[j]
　　and there is not a spot without filth.

[9]"Who is it he is trying to teach?[k]
　　To whom is he explaining his message?
To children weaned[l] from their milk,[m]
　　to those just taken from the breast?
[10]For it is:
　　Do and do, do and do,
　　rule on rule, rule on rule[a];
　　a little here, a little there.''

[11]Very well then, with foreign lips and strange tongues[n]
　　God will speak to this people,[o]

27:13
oLev 25:9;
Mt 24:31
pIsa 19:21,25
28:1
qver 3; Isa 9:9
rver 4 sHos 7:5
28:2
tIsa 40:10
uIsa 30:30;
Eze 13:11
vIsa 29:6
wIsa 8:7
28:3
xver 1
28:4
yver 1
zHos 9:10;
Na 3:12
28:5
aIsa 62:3
28:6
bIsa 11:2-4;
32:1,16 cJn 5:30
d2Ch 32:8
28:7
eIsa 22:13
fIsa 56:10-12
gIsa 24:2
hIsa 9:15
iIsa 29:11;
Hos 4:11
28:8
jJer 48:26
28:9
kver 26;
Isa 30:20;
48:17; 50:4;
54:13 lPs 131:2
mHeb 5:12-13
28:11
nIsa 33:19
o1Co 14:21*

---

[a]10 Hebrew / *sav lasav sav lasav* / *kav lakav kav lakav* (possibly meaningless sounds; perhaps a mimicking of the prophet's words); also in verse 13

¹²to whom he said,
"This is the resting place, let the weary rest";ᴾ
and, "This is the place of repose"—
but they would not listen.
¹³So then, the word of the Lᴏʀᴅ to them will become:
Do and do, do and do,
rule on rule, rule on rule;
a little here, a little there—
so that they will go and fall backward,
be injured�q and snared and captured.ʳ

¹⁴Therefore hear the word of the Lᴏʀᴅ,ˢ you scoffers
who rule this people in Jerusalem.
¹⁵You boast, "We have entered into a covenant with death,
with the graveᵃ we have made an agreement.
When an overwhelming scourge sweeps by,ᵗ
it cannot touch us,
for we have made a lieᵘ our refuge
and falsehoodᵇ our hiding place.ᵛ"

¹⁶So this is what the Sovereign Lᴏʀᴅ says:

"See, I lay a stone in Zion,
a tested stone,ʷ
a precious cornerstone for a sure foundation;
the one who trusts will never be dismayed.ˣ
¹⁷I will make justiceʸ the measuring line
and righteousness the plumb line;ᶻ
hail will sweep away your refuge, the lie,
and water will overflow your hiding place.
¹⁸Your covenant with death will be annulled;
your agreement with the grave will not stand.ᵃ
When the overwhelming scourge sweeps by,ᵇ
you will be beaten downᶜ by it.
¹⁹As often as it comes it will carry you away;ᵈ
morning after morning, by day and by night,
it will sweep through."

The understanding of this message
will bring sheer terror.ᵉ
²⁰The bed is too short to stretch out on,
the blanket too narrow to wrap around you.ᶠ
²¹The Lᴏʀᴅ will rise up as he did at Mount Perazim,ᵍ
he will rouse himself as in the Valley of Gibeonʰ—
to do his work,ⁱ his strange work,
and perform his task, his alien task.
²²Now stop your mocking,
or your chains will become heavier;
the Lord, the Lᴏʀᴅ Almighty, has told me
of the destruction decreedʲ against the whole land.ᵏ

28:12
ᵖIsa 11:10;
Mt 11:28-29
28:13
qMt 21:44
rIsa 8:15
28:14
ˢIsa 1:10
28:15
tver 2,18;
Isa 8:7-8;
30:28; Da 11:22
uIsa 9:15
vIsa 29:15
28:16
wPs 118:22;
Isa 8:14-15;
Mt 21:42;
Ac 4:11;
Eph 2:20
xRo 9:33*;
10:11*;
1Pe 2:6*
28:17
yIsa 5:16
zZKi 21:13
28:18
aIsa 7:7 bver 15
cDa 8:13
28:19
d2Ki 24:2
eJob 18:11
28:20
fIsa 59:6
28:21
g1Ch 14:11
hJos 10:10,12;
1Ch 14:16
iIsa 10:12;
Lk 19:41-44
28:22
jIsa 10:22
kIsa 10:23

ᵃ15 Hebrew *Sheol*; also in verse 18   ᵇ15 Or *false gods*

23Listen and hear my voice;
pay attention and hear what I say.
24When a farmer plows for planting, does he plow
continually?
Does he keep on breaking up and harrowing the soil?
25When he has leveled the surface,
does he not sow caraway and scatter cummin?[1]
Does he not plant wheat in its place,[a]
barley in its plot,[a]
and spelt[m] in its field?
26His God instructs him
and teaches him the right way.

27Caraway is not threshed with a sledge,
nor is a cartwheel rolled over cummin;
caraway is beaten out with a rod,
and cummin with a stick.
28Grain must be ground to make bread;
so one does not go on threshing it forever.
Though he drives the wheels of his threshing cart
over it,
his horses do not grind it.
29All this also comes from the LORD Almighty,
wonderful in counsel[n] and magnificent in wisdom. [o]

Woe to David's City

29

Woe[p] to you, Ariel, Ariel,[q]
the city where David settled!
Add year to year
and let your cycle of festivals[r] go on.
2Yet I will besiege Ariel;
she will mourn and lament,[s]
she will be to me like an altar hearth. [b]
3I will encamp against you all around;
I will encircle[t] you with towers
and set up my siege works against you.
4Brought low, you will speak from the ground;
your speech will mumble[u] out of the dust.
Your voice will come ghostlike from the earth;
out of the dust your speech will whisper.

5But your many enemies will become like fine dust,
the ruthless hordes like blown chaff. [v]
Suddenly,[w] in an instant,
6 the LORD Almighty will come
with thunder and earthquake[x] and great noise,
with windstorm and tempest and flames of a
devouring fire.
7Then the hordes of all the nations[y] that fight against
Ariel,

28:25
lMt 23:23
mEx 9:32
28:29
nIsa 9:6
oRo 11:33
29:1
pIsa 22:12-13
q2Sa 5:9
rIsa 1:14
29:2
sIsa 3:26; La 2:5
29:3
tLk 19:43-44
29:4
uIsa 8:19
29:5
vIsa 17:13
wIsa 17:14;
1Th 5:3
29:6
xMt 24:7;
Mk 13:8;
Lk 21:11;
Rev 11:19
29:7
yMic 4:11-12;
Zec 12:9

[a]25 The meaning of the Hebrew for this word is uncertain.   [b]2 The Hebrew for *altar hearth* sounds like the Hebrew for *Ariel*.

that attack her and her fortress and besiege her,
will be as it is with a dream, z
with a vision in the night—
8as when a hungry man dreams that he is eating,
but he awakens, a and his hunger remains;
as when a thirsty man dreams that he is drinking,
but he awakens faint, with his thirst unquenched.
So will it be with the hordes of all the nations
that fight against Mount Zion.

9Be stunned and amazed,
blind yourselves and be sightless;
be drunk, b but not from wine, c
stagger, but not from beer.
10The Lord has brought over you a deep sleep:
He has sealed your eyesd (the prophets);e
he has covered your heads (the seers). f

11For you this whole vision is nothing but words sealedg in a scroll.
And if you give the scroll to someone who can read, and say to him,
"Read this, please," he will answer, "I can't; it is sealed." 12Or if you
give the scroll to someone who cannot read, and say, "Read this,
please," he will answer, "I don't know how to read."

13The Lord says:

"These people come near to me with their mouth
and honor me with their lips,
but their hearts are far from me. h
Their worship of me
is made up only of rules taught by men.a i
14Therefore once more I will astound these people
with wonder upon wonder;j
the wisdom of the wisek will perish,
the intelligence of the intelligent will vanish.l "
15Woe to those who go to great depths
to hide their plans from the Lord,
who do their work in darkness and think,
"Who sees us?m Who will know?"n
16You turn things upside down,
as if the potter were thought to be like the clay!
Shall what is formed say to him who formed it,
"He did not make me"?
Can the pot say of the potter, o
"He knows nothing"?

17In a very short time, will not Lebanon be turned into a
fertile fieldp
and the fertile field seem like a forest?q
18In that day the deafr will hear the words of the scroll,
and out of gloom and darkness
the eyes of the blind will see. s

29:7
zJob 20:8
29:8
aPs 73:20
29:9
bIsa 51:17
cIsa 51:21-22
29:10
dPs 69:23;
Isa 6:9-10;
Ro 11:8*
eMic 3:6
fISa 9:9
29:11
gIsa 8:16;
Mt 13:11;
Rev 5:1-2
29:13
hEze 33:31
iMt 15:8-9*;
Mk 7:6-7*;
Col 2:22
29:14
jHab 1:5
kJer 8:9; 49:7
lIsa 6:9-10;
1Co 1:19*
29:15
mPs 10:11-13;
94:7; Isa 57:12
nJob 22:13
29:16
oIsa 45:9; 64:8;
Ro 9:20-21*
29:17
pPs 84:6
qIsa 32:15
29:18
rMk 7:37
sIsa 32:3; 35:5;
Mt 11:5

a13 Hebrew; Septuagint *They worship me in vain; / their teachings are but rules taught by men*

¹⁹Once more the humble[t] will rejoice in the LORD;
    the needy[u] will rejoice in the Holy One of Israel.
²⁰The ruthless will vanish,
    the mockers[v] will disappear,
    and all who have an eye for evil[w] will be cut down—
²¹those who with a word make a man out to be guilty,
    who ensnare the defender in court[x]
    and with false testimony deprive the innocent of
        justice.[y]

²²Therefore this is what the LORD, who redeemed Abraham,[z] says to
the house of Jacob:

    "No longer will Jacob be ashamed;[a]
        no longer will their faces grow pale.
    ²³When they see among them their children,[b]
        the work of my hands,[c]
    they will keep my name holy;
        they will acknowledge the holiness of the Holy One of
            Jacob,
        and will stand in awe of the God of Israel.
    ²⁴Those who are wayward[d] in spirit will gain
            understanding;[e]
        those who complain will accept instruction."[f]

Woe to the Obstinate Nation

30   "Woe[g] to the obstinate children,"[h]
        declares the LORD,
    "to those who carry out plans that are not mine,
        forming an alliance,[i] but not by my Spirit,
        heaping sin upon sin;
    ²who go down to Egypt[j]
        without consulting[k] me;
    who look for help to Pharaoh's protection,[l]
        to Egypt's shade for refuge.
    ³But Pharaoh's protection will be to your shame,
        Egypt's shade will bring you disgrace.[m]
    ⁴Though they have officials in Zoan[n]
        and their envoys have arrived in Hanes,
    ⁵everyone will be put to shame
        because of a people[o] useless to them,
    who bring neither help nor advantage,
        but only shame and disgrace."

⁶An oracle concerning the animals of the Negev:

    Through a land of hardship and distress,[p]
        of lions and lionesses,
        of adders and darting snakes,[q]
    the envoys carry their riches on donkeys' backs,
        their treasures[r] on the humps of camels,
    to that unprofitable nation,
    ⁷   to Egypt, whose help is utterly useless.

29:19
t Isa 61:1;
Mt 5:5; 11:29
u Isa 14:30;
Mt 11:5;
Jas 1:9; 2:5
29:20
v Isa 28:22
w Isa 59:4;
Mic 2:1
29:21
x Am 5:10,15
y Isa 32:7
29:22
z Isa 41:8; 63:16
a Isa 49:23
29:23
b Isa 49:20-26
c Isa 19:25
29:24
d Isa 28:7;
Heb 5:2
e Isa 41:20;
60:16 f Isa 30:21
30:1
g Isa 29:15
h Isa 1:2
i Isa 8:12
30:2
j Isa 31:1
k Nu 27:21
l Isa 36:9
30:3
m Isa 20:4-5;
36:6
30:4
n Isa 19:11
30:5
o ver 7
30:6
p Ex 5:10,21;
Isa 8:22;
Jer 11:4
q Dt 8:15
r Isa 15:7

Therefore I call her
 Rahab the Do-Nothing.

[8]Go now, write it on a tablet for them,
 inscribe it on a scroll, [s]
that for the days to come
 it may be an everlasting witness.
[9]These are rebellious people, deceitful[t] children,
 children unwilling to listen to the LORD's instruction. [u]
[10]They say to the seers,
 "See no more visions[v]!"
and to the prophets,
 "Give us no more visions of what is right!
Tell us pleasant things, [w]
 prophesy illusions. [x]
[11]Leave this way,
 get off this path,
and stop confronting[y] us
 with the Holy One of Israel!"

[12]Therefore, this is what the Holy One of Israel says:

 "Because you have rejected this message, [z]
  relied on oppression[a]
  and depended on deceit,
[13]this sin will become for you
  like a high wall, [b] cracked and bulging,
  that collapses[c] suddenly, [d] in an instant.
[14]It will break in pieces like pottery, [e]
  shattered so mercilessly
 that among its pieces not a fragment will be found
  for taking coals from a hearth
  or scooping water out of a cistern."

[15]This is what the Sovereign LORD, the Holy One of Israel, says:

 "In repentance and rest is your salvation,
  in quietness and trust[f] is your strength,
  but you would have none of it.
[16]You said, 'No, we will flee on horses.'[g]
  Therefore you will flee!
You said, 'We will ride off on swift horses.'
  Therefore your pursuers will be swift!
[17]A thousand will flee
  at the threat of one;
at the threat of five[h]
  you will all flee[i] away,
till you are left
  like a flagstaff on a mountaintop,
  like a banner on a hill."

[18]Yet the LORD longs[j] to be gracious to you;
 he rises to show you compassion.
For the LORD is a God of justice. [k]
 Blessed are all who wait for him![l]

30:8
[s]Isa 8:1;
Hab 2:2
30:9
[t]Isa 28:15;
59:3-4 [u]Isa 1:10
30:10
[v]Jer 11:21;
Am 7:13
[w]1Ki 22:8
[x]Eze 13:7;
Ro 16:18
30:11
[y]Job 21:14
30:12
[z]Isa 5:24
[a]Isa 5:7
30:13
[b]Ps 62:3
[c]1Ki 20:30
[d]Isa 29:5
30:14
[e]Ps 2:9;
Jer 19:10-11
30:15
[f]Isa 32:17
30:16
[g]Isa 31:1,3
30:17
[h]Lev 26:8;
Jos 23:10
[i]Lev 26:36;
Dt 28:25
30:18
[j]Isa 42:14;
2Pe 3:9,15
[k]Isa 5:16
[l]Isa 25:9

[19]O people of Zion, who live in Jerusalem, you will weep no more. [m] How gracious he will be when you cry for help! As soon as he hears, he will answer[n] you. [20]Although the Lord gives you the bread[o] of adversity and the water of affliction, your teachers will be hidden[p] no more; with your own eyes you will see them. [21]Whether you turn to the right or to the left, your ears will hear a voice[q] behind you, saying, "This is the way; walk in it." [22]Then you will defile your idols[r] overlaid with silver and your images covered with gold; you will throw them away like a menstrual cloth and say to them, "Away with you!"

[23]He will also send you rain[s] for the seed you sow in the ground, and the food that comes from the land will be rich and plentiful. In that day your cattle will graze in broad meadows.[t] [24]The oxen and donkeys that work the soil will eat fodder and mash, spread out with fork[u] and shovel. [25]In the day of great slaughter, when the towers[v] fall, streams of water will flow[w] on every high mountain and every lofty hill. [26]The moon will shine like the sun,[x] and the sunlight will be seven times brighter, like the light of seven full days, when the Lord binds up the bruises of his people and heals[y] the wounds he inflicted.

> [27]See, the Name[z] of the Lord comes from afar,
>   with burning anger[a] and dense clouds of smoke;
> his lips are full of wrath,[b]
>   and his tongue is a consuming fire.
> [28]His breath[c] is like a rushing torrent,
>   rising up to the neck.[d]
> He shakes the nations in the sieve[e] of destruction;
>   he places in the jaws of the peoples
>   a bit[f] that leads them astray.
> [29]And you will sing
>   as on the night you celebrate a holy festival;
> your hearts will rejoice
>   as when people go up with flutes
> to the mountain[g] of the Lord,
>   to the Rock of Israel.
> [30]The Lord will cause men to hear his majestic voice
>   and will make them see his arm coming down
> with raging anger and consuming fire,
>   with cloudburst, thunderstorm and hail.
> [31]The voice of the Lord will shatter Assyria;[h]
>   with his scepter he will strike[i] them down.
> [32]Every stroke the Lord lays on them
>   with his punishing rod
> will be to the music of tambourines and harps,
>   as he fights them in battle with the blows of
>   his arm.[j]
> [33]Topheth[k] has long been prepared;
>   it has been made ready for the king.
> Its fire pit has been made deep and wide,
>   with an abundance of fire and wood;
> the breath of the Lord,
>   like a stream of burning sulfur,[l]
>   sets it ablaze.

30:19
m Isa 60:20;
61:3 n Ps 50:15;
Isa 58:9; 65:24;
Mt 7:7-11
30:20
o 1Ki 22:27
p Ps 74:9;
Am 8:11
30:21
q Isa 29:24
30:22
r Ex 32:4
30:23
s Isa 65:21-22
t Ps 65:13
30:24
u Mt 3:12;
Lk 3:17
30:25
v Isa 2:15
w Isa 41:18
30:26
x Isa 24:23;
60:19-20;
Rev 21:23; 22:5
y Dt 32:39;
Isa 1:5
30:27
z Isa 59:19
a Isa 66:14
b Isa 10:5
30:28
c Isa 11:4
d Isa 8:8
e Am 9:9
f 2Ki 19:28;
Isa 37:29
30:29
g Ps 42:4
30:31
h Isa 10:5,12
i Isa 11:4
30:32
j Isa 11:15;
Eze 32:10
30:33
k 2Ki 23:10
l Ge 19:24

Woe to Those Who Rely on Egypt

31 Woe to those who go down to Egypt[m] for help,
    who rely on horses,
who trust in the multitude of their chariots[n]
    and in the great strength of their horsemen,
but do not look to the Holy One of Israel,
    or seek help from the LORD.[o]
[2]Yet he too is wise[p] and can bring disaster;[q]
    he does not take back his words.[r]
He will rise up against the house of the wicked,[s]
    against those who help evildoers.
[3]But the Egyptians[t] are men and not God;[u]
    their horses are flesh and not spirit.
When the LORD stretches out his hand,[v]
    he who helps will stumble,
    he who is helped[w] will fall;
    both will perish together.

[4]This is what the LORD says to me:

  "As a lion[x] growls,
    a great lion over his prey—
and though a whole band of shepherds
    is called together against him,
he is not frightened by their shouts
    or disturbed by their clamor—
so the LORD Almighty will come down[y]
    to do battle on Mount Zion and on its heights.
[5]Like birds hovering overhead,
    the LORD Almighty will shield[z] Jerusalem;
he will shield it and deliver[a] it,
    he will 'pass over' it and will rescue it."

[6]Return to him you have so greatly revolted against, O Israelites. [7]For in that day every one of you will reject the idols of silver and gold[b] your sinful hands have made.

  [8]"Assyria[c] will fall by a sword that is not of man;
    a sword, not of mortals, will devour[d] them.
They will flee before the sword
    and their young men will be put to forced labor. [e]
[9]Their stronghold[f] will fall because of terror;
    at sight of the battle standard their commanders will
        panic,"
declares the LORD,
    whose fire[g] is in Zion,
    whose furnace is in Jerusalem.

The Kingdom of Righteousness

32 See, a king[h] will reign in righteousness
    and rulers will rule with justice.[i]
[2]Each man will be like a shelter[j] from the wind
    and a refuge from the storm,

31:1
m Dt 17:16;
Isa 30:2,5
n Isa 2:7
o Ps 20:7;
Da 9:13
31:2
p Ro 16:27
q Isa 45:7
r Nu 23:19
s Isa 32:6
31:3
t Isa 36:9
u Eze 28:9;
2Th 2:4
v Isa 9:17,21
w Isa 30:5-7
31:4
x Nu 24:9;
Hos 11:10;
Am 3:8
y Isa 42:13
31:5
z Ps 91:4
a Isa 37:35; 38:6
31:7
b Isa 2:20; 30:22
31:8
c Isa 10:12
d Isa 14:25; 37:7
e Ge 49:15
31:9
f Dt 32:31,37
g Isa 10:17
32:1
h Eze 37:24
i Ps 72:1-4;
Isa 9:7
32:2
j Isa 4:6

like streams of water in the desert
　　and the shadow of a great rock in a thirsty land.

3Then the eyes of those who see will no longer be
　　closed,k
　　and the ears of those who hear will listen.
4The mind of the rash will know and understand,l
　　and the stammering tongue will be fluent and clear.
5No longer will the foolm be called noble
　　nor the scoundrel be highly respected.
6For the fool speaks folly,n
　　his mind is busy with evil:
He practices ungodlinesso
　　and spreads errorp concerning the LORD;
the hungry he leaves emptyq
　　and from the thirsty he withholds water.
7The scoundrel's methods are wicked,r
　　he makes up evil schemess
to destroy the poor with lies,
　　even when the plea of the needyt is just.
8But the noble man makes noble plans,
　　and by noble deedsu he stands.

The Women of Jerusalem

9You women who are so complacent,
　　rise up and listenv to me;
you daughters who feel secure,w
　　hear what I have to say!
10In little more than a year
　　you who feel secure will tremble;
the grape harvest will fail,x
　　and the harvest of fruit will not come.
11Tremble, you complacent women;
　　shudder, you daughters who feel secure!
Strip off your clothes,y
　　put sackcloth around your waists.
12Beat your breastsz for the pleasant fields,
　　for the fruitful vines
13and for the land of my people,
　　a land overgrown with thorns and briersa —
yes, mourn for all houses of merriment
　　and for this city of revelry.b
14The fortressc will be abandoned,
　　the noisy city deserted;d
citadel and watchtowere will become a wasteland
　　forever,
　　the delight of donkeys,f a pasture for flocks,
15till the Spiritg is poured upon us from on high,
　　and the desert becomes a fertile field,h
　　and the fertile field seems like a forest.i
16Justice will dwell in the desert
　　and righteousness live in the fertile field.

32:3
klsa 29:18
32:4
llsa 29:24
32:5
m1Sa 25:25
32:6
nPr 19:3
olsa 9:17
plsa 9:16
qlsa 3:15
32:7
rJer 5:26-28
sMic 7:3
tlsa 61:1
32:8
uPr 11:25
32:9
vlsa 28:23
wlsa 47:8;
Am 6:1;
Zep 2:15
32:10
xlsa 5:5-6; 24:7
32:11
ylsa 47:2
32:12
zNa 2:7
32:13
alsa 5:6
blsa 22:2
32:14
clsa 13:22
dlsa 6:11; 27:10
elsa 34:13
fPs 104:11
32:15
glsa 11:2;
Joel 2:28
hPs 107:35;
Isa 35:1-2
ilsa 29:17

[17]The fruit of righteousness will be peace;[j]
    the effect of righteousness will be quietness and
        confidence[k] forever.
[18]My people will live in peaceful dwelling places,
    in secure homes,
    in undisturbed places of rest.[l]
[19]Though hail[m] flattens the forest[n]
    and the city is leveled[o] completely,
[20]how blessed you will be,
    sowing[p] your seed by every stream,
    and letting your cattle and donkeys range free.[q]

Distress and Help

33 Woe to you, O destroyer,
        you who have not been destroyed!
    Woe to you, O traitor,
        you who have not been betrayed!
    When you stop destroying,
        you will be destroyed;[r]
    when you stop betraying,
        you will be betrayed.[s]

[2]O LORD, be gracious to us;
    we long for you.
Be our strength[t] every morning,
    our salvation[u] in time of distress.
[3]At the thunder of your voice, the peoples flee;
    when you rise up,[v] the nations scatter.
[4]Your plunder, O nations, is harvested as by young
        locusts;
    like a swarm of locusts men pounce on it.

[5]The LORD is exalted,[w] for he dwells on high;
    he will fill Zion with justice[x] and righteousness.[y]
[6]He will be the sure foundation for your times,
    a rich store of salvation[z] and wisdom and knowledge;
    the fear[a] of the LORD is the key to this treasure.[a]

[7]Look, their brave men cry aloud in the streets;
    the envoys[b] of peace weep bitterly.
[8]The highways are deserted,
    no travelers are on the roads.[c]
The treaty is broken,
    its witnesses[b] are despised,
    no one is respected.
[9]The land mourns[cd] and wastes away,
    Lebanon[e] is ashamed and withers;[f]
Sharon is like the Arabah,
    and Bashan and Carmel drop their leaves.

[10]"Now will I arise,[g]" says the LORD.
    "Now will I be exalted;

32:17
jPs 119:165;
Ro 14:17;
Jas 3:18
kIsa 30:15
32:18
lHos 2:18-23
32:19
mIsa 28:17;
30:30
nIsa 10:19;
Zec 11:2
oIsa 24:10;
27:10
32:20
pEcc 11:1
qIsa 30:24
33:1
rHab 2:8;
Mt 7:2 sIsa 21:2
33:2
tIsa 40:10;
51:9; 59:16
uIsa 25:9
33:3
vIsa 59:16-18
33:5
wPs 97:9
xIsa 28:6
yIsa 1:26
33:6
zIsa 51:6
aIsa 11:2-3;
Mt 6:33
33:7
b2Ki 18:37
33:8
cJdg 5:6;
Isa 35:8
33:9
dIsa 3:26
eIsa 2:13; 35:2
fIsa 24:4
33:10
gPs 12:5;
Isa 2:21

---

a6 Or is a treasure from him   *b8 Dead Sea Scrolls; Masoretic Text / the cities*   *c9 Or dries up*

now will I be lifted up.
[11] You conceive[h] chaff,
    you give birth[i] to straw;
    your breath is a fire[j] that consumes you.
[12] The peoples will be burned as if to lime;
    like cut thornbushes they will be set ablaze.[k]"

[13] You who are far away,[l] hear[m] what I have done;
    you who are near, acknowledge my power!
[14] The sinners in Zion are terrified;
    trembling[n] grips the godless:
"Who of us can dwell with the consuming fire?[o]
    Who of us can dwell with everlasting burning?"
[15] He who walks righteously[p]
    and speaks what is right,[q]
who rejects gain from extortion
    and keeps his hand from accepting bribes,
who stops his ears against plots of murder
    and shuts his eyes[r] against contemplating evil—
[16] this is the man who will dwell on the heights,
    whose refuge[s] will be the mountain fortress.[t]
His bread will be supplied,
    and water will not fail[u] him.

[17] Your eyes will see the king[v] in his beauty
    and view a land that stretches afar.[w]
[18] In your thoughts you will ponder the former terror:[x]
    "Where is that chief officer?
Where is the one who took the revenue?
    Where is the officer in charge of the towers?"
[19] You will see those arrogant people no more,
    those people of an obscure speech,
    with their strange, incomprehensible tongue.[y]

[20] Look upon Zion, the city of our festivals;
    your eyes will see Jerusalem,
    a peaceful abode,[z] a tent that will not be moved;[a]
its stakes will never be pulled up,
    nor any of its ropes broken.
[21] There the LORD will be our Mighty One.
    It will be like a place of broad rivers and streams.[b]
No galley with oars will ride them,
    no mighty ship will sail them.
[22] For the LORD is our judge,[c]
    the LORD is our lawgiver,[d]
the LORD is our king;[e]
    it is he who will save[f] us.

[23] Your rigging hangs loose:
    The mast is not held secure,
    the sail is not spread.
Then an abundance of spoils will be divided
    and even the lame[g] will carry off plunder.[h]
[24] No one living in Zion will say, "I am ill";[i]

33:11
h Ps 7:14;
Isa 59:4;
Jas 1:15
i Isa 26:18
j Isa 1:31
33:12
k Isa 10:17
33:13
l Ps 48:10; 49:1
m Isa 49:1
33:14
n Isa 32:11
o Isa 30:30;
Heb 12:29
33:15
p Isa 58:8
q Ps 15:2; 24:4
r Ps 119:37
33:16
s Isa 25:4
t Isa 26:1
u Isa 49:10
33:17
v Isa 6:5
w Isa 26:15
33:18
x Isa 17:14
33:19
y Isa 28:11;
Jer 5:15
33:20
z Isa 32:18
a Ps 46:5;
125:1-2
33:21
b Isa 41:18;
48:18; 66:12
33:22
c Isa 11:4
d Isa 2:3;
Jas 4:12
e Ps 89:18
f Isa 25:9
33:23
g 2Ki 7:8
h 2Ki 7:16
33:24
i Isa 30:26

and the sins of those who dwell there will be
   forgiven.[j]

Judgment Against the Nations

34 Come near, you nations, and listen;
   pay attention, you peoples![k]
Let the earth[l] hear, and all that is in it,
   the world, and all that comes out of it![m]
[2]The Lord is angry with all nations;
   his wrath is upon all their armies.
He will totally destroy[an] them,
   he will give them over to slaughter.[o]
[3]Their slain will be thrown out,
   their dead bodies will send up a stench;[p]
   the mountains will be soaked with their blood.[q]
[4]All the stars of the heavens will be dissolved[r]
   and the sky rolled up[s] like a scroll;
all the starry host will fall[t]
   like withered leaves from the vine,
   like shriveled figs from the fig tree.

[5]My sword[u] has drunk its fill in the heavens;
   see, it descends in judgment on Edom,[v]
   the people I have totally destroyed.[w]
[6]The sword of the Lord is bathed in blood,
   it is covered with fat—
the blood of lambs and goats,
   fat from the kidneys of rams.
For the Lord has a sacrifice in Bozrah
   and a great slaughter in Edom.
[7]And the wild oxen will fall with them,
   the bull calves and the great bulls.[x]
Their land will be drenched with blood,
   and the dust will be soaked with fat.

[8]For the Lord has a day of vengeance,[y]
   a year of retribution, to uphold Zion's cause.
[9]Edom's streams will be turned into pitch,
   her dust into burning sulfur;
   her land will become blazing pitch!
[10]It will not be quenched night and day;
   its smoke will rise forever.[z]
From generation to generation it will lie desolate;[a]
   no one will ever pass through it again.
[11]The desert owl[bb] and screech owl[b] will possess it;
   the great owl[b] and the raven will nest there.
God will stretch out over Edom
   the measuring line of chaos
   and the plumb line[c] of desolation.

---

[a]2 The Hebrew term refers to the irrevocable giving over of things or persons to the Lord, often by totally destroying them; also in verse 5.   [b]11 The precise identification of these birds is uncertain.

33:24
j Jer 50:20;
1Jn 1:7-9
34:1
k Isa 41:1; 43:9
l Ps 49:1
m Dt 32:1
34:2
n Isa 13:5
o Isa 30:25
34:3
p Joel 2:20;
Am 4:10 q ver 7;
Eze 14:19;
35:6; 38:22
34:4
r Isa 13:13;
2Pe 3:10
s Eze 32:7-8
t Joel 2:31;
Mt 24:29*;
Rev 6:13
34:5
u Dt 32:41-42;
Jer 46:10;
Eze 21:5
v Am 1:11-12
w Isa 24:6;
Mal 1:4
34:7
x Ps 68:30
34:8
y Isa 63:4
34:10
z Rev 14:10-11;
19:3 a Isa 13:20;
24:1;
Eze 29:12;
Mal 1:3
34:11
b Zep 2:14;
Rev 18:2
c 2Ki 21:13;
La 2:8

¹²Her nobles will have nothing there to be called a
        kingdom,
    all her princes[d] will vanish[e] away.
¹³Thorns will overrun her citadels,
    nettles and brambles her strongholds.[f]
She will become a haunt for jackals,[g]
    a home for owls.
¹⁴Desert creatures will meet with hyenas,[h]
    and wild goats will bleat to each other;
there the night creatures will also repose
    and find for themselves places of rest.
¹⁵The owl will nest there and lay eggs,
    she will hatch them, and care for her young under the
        shadow of her wings;
there also the falcons[i] will gather,
    each with its mate.

¹⁶Look in the scroll[j] of the LORD and read:

    None of these will be missing,
        not one will lack her mate.
    For it is his mouth[k] that has given the order,
        and his Spirit will gather them together.
    ¹⁷He allots their portions;[l]
        his hand distributes them by measure.
    They will possess it forever
        and dwell there from generation to generation.[m]

Joy of the Redeemed

35 The desert[n] and the parched land will be glad;
        the wilderness will rejoice and blossom.[o]
    Like the crocus, ²it will burst into bloom;
        it will rejoice greatly and shout for joy.[p]
    The glory of Lebanon[q] will be given to it,
        the splendor of Carmel[r] and Sharon;
    they will see the glory of the LORD,
        the splendor of our God.[s]

³Strengthen the feeble hands,
    steady the knees[t] that give way;
⁴say to those with fearful hearts,
    "Be strong, do not fear;
your God will come,
    he will come with vengeance;[u]
with divine retribution
    he will come to save you."

⁵Then will the eyes of the blind be opened[v]
    and the ears of the deaf[w] unstopped.
⁶Then will the lame[x] leap like a deer,
    and the mute tongue[y] shout for joy.
Water will gush forth in the wilderness
    and streams[z] in the desert.

34:12
d Jer 27:20; 39:6
e Isa 41:11-12
34:13
f Isa 13:22;
  32:13
g Ps 44:19;
Jer 9:11; 10:22
34:14
h Isa 13:22
34:15
i Dt 14:13
34:16
j Isa 30:8
k Isa 1:20; 58:14
34:17
l Isa 17:14;
Jer 13:25
m ver 10
35:1
n Isa 27:10;
41:18-19
o Isa 51:3
35:2
p Isa 25:9; 55:12
q Isa 32:15
r SS 7:5
s Isa 25:9
35:3
t Job 4:4;
Heb 12:12
35:4
u Isa 1:24; 34:8
35:5
v Mt 11:5;
Jn 9:6-7
w Isa 29:18;
50:4
35:6
x Mt 15:30;
Jn 5:8-9; Ac 3:8
y Isa 32:4;
Mt 9:32-33;
12:22; Lk 11:14
z Isa 41:18;
Jn 7:38

[7]The burning sand will become a pool,
    the thirsty ground bubbling springs. [a]
In the haunts where jackals[b] once lay,
    grass and reeds and papyrus will grow.

[8]And a highway[c] will be there;
    it will be called the Way of Holiness. [d]
The unclean[e] will not journey on it;
    it will be for those who walk in that Way;
    wicked fools will not go about on it. [a]
[9]No lion[f] will be there,
    nor will any ferocious beast[g] get up on it;
    they will not be found there.
But only the redeemed[h] will walk there,
[10]   and the ransomed of the LORD will return.
They will enter Zion with singing;
    everlasting joy[i] will crown their heads.
Gladness and joy will overtake them,
    and sorrow and sighing will flee away.[j]

Sennacherib Threatens Jerusalem

36:1–22pp — 2Ki 18:13,17–37; 2Ch 32:9–19

36 In the fourteenth year of King Hezekiah's reign, Sennacherib[k] king of Assyria attacked all the fortified cities of Judah and captured them. [2]Then the king of Assyria sent his field commander with a large army from Lachish to King Hezekiah at Jerusalem. When the commander stopped at the aqueduct of the Upper Pool, on the road to the Washerman's Field,[l] [3]Eliakim[m] son of Hilkiah the palace administrator, Shebna[n] the secretary, and Joah son of Asaph the recorder went out to him.

[4]The field commander said to them, "Tell Hezekiah,

" 'This is what the great king, the king of Assyria, says: On what are you basing this confidence of yours? [5]You say you have strategy and military strength—but you speak only empty words. On whom are you depending, that you rebel[o] against me? [6]Look now, you are depending on Egypt,[p] that splintered reed[q] of a staff, which pierces a man's hand and wounds him if he leans on it! Such is Pharaoh king of Egypt to all who depend on him. [7]And if you say to me, "We are depending on the LORD our God"—isn't he the one whose high places and altars Hezekiah removed,[r] saying to Judah and Jerusalem, "You must worship before this altar"?[s]

[8]" 'Come now, make a bargain with my master, the king of Assyria: I will give you two thousand horses—if you can put riders on them! [9]How then can you repulse one officer of the least of my master's officials, even though you are depending on Egypt[t] for chariots and horsemen?[u] [10]Furthermore, have I come to attack and destroy this land without the LORD? The LORD himself told[v] me to march against this country and destroy it.' "

[a]8 Or / *the simple will not stray from it*

35:7
[a]Isa 49:10
[b]Isa 13:22
35:8
[c]Isa 11:16;
33:8;
Mt 7:13-14
[d]Isa 4:3;
1Pe 1:15
[e]Isa 52:1
35:9
[f]Isa 30:6
[g]Isa 34:14
[h]Isa 51:11;
62:12; 63:4
35:10
[i]Isa 25:9
[j]Isa 30:19;
51:11;
Rev 7:17; 21:4
36:1
[k]2Ch 32:1
36:2
[l]Isa 7:3
36:3
[m]Isa 22:20-21
[n]2Ki 18:18
36:5
[o]2Ki 18:7
36:6
[p]Isa 30:2,5
[q]Eze 29:6-7
36:7
[r]2Ki 18:4
[s]Dt 12:2-5
36:9
[t]Isa 31:3
[u]Isa 30:2-5
36:10
[v]1Ki 13:18

¹¹Then Eliakim, Shebna and Joah said to the field commander, "Please speak to your servants in Aramaic,ʷ since we understand it. Don't speak to us in Hebrew in the hearing of the people on the wall."

¹²But the commander replied, "Was it only to your master and you that my master sent me to say these things, and not to the men sitting on the wall—who, like you, will have to eat their own filth and drink their own urine?"

¹³Then the commander stood and called out in Hebrew,ˣ "Hear the words of the great king, the king of Assyria! ¹⁴This is what the king says: Do not let Hezekiah deceive you. He cannot deliver you! ¹⁵Do not let Hezekiah persuade you to trust in the LORD when he says, 'The LORD will surely deliver us; this city will not be given into the hand of the king of Assyria.'ʸ

¹⁶"Do not listen to Hezekiah. This is what the king of Assyria says: Make peace with me and come out to me. Then every one of you will eat from his own vine and fig treeᶻ and drink water from his own cistern,ᵃ ¹⁷until I come and take you to a land like your own—a land of grain and new wine, a land of bread and vineyards.

¹⁸"Do not let Hezekiah mislead you when he says, 'The LORD will deliver us.' Has the god of any nation ever delivered his land from the hand of the king of Assyria? ¹⁹Where are the gods of Hamath and Arpad? Where are the gods of Sepharvaim? Have they rescued Samaria from my hand? ²⁰Who of all the godsᵇ of these countries has been able to save his land from me? How then can the LORD deliver Jerusalem from my hand?"

²¹But the people remained silent and said nothing in reply, because the king had commanded, "Do not answer him."ᶜ

²²Then Eliakim son of Hilkiah the palace administrator, Shebna the secretary, and Joah son of Asaph the recorder went to Hezekiah, with their clothes torn, and told him what the field commander had said.

Jerusalem's Deliverance Foretold

37:1–13pp — 2Ki 19:1–13

37 When King Hezekiah heard this, he tore his clothes and put on sackcloth and went into the temple of the LORD. ²He sent Eliakim the palace administrator, Shebna the secretary, and the leading priests, all wearing sackcloth, to the prophet Isaiah son of Amoz.ᵈ ³They told him, "This is what Hezekiah says: This day is a day of distress and rebuke and disgrace, as when children come to the point of birthᵉ and there is no strength to deliver them. ⁴It may be that the LORD your God will hear the words of the field commander, whom his master, the king of Assyria, has sent to ridicule the living God, and that he will rebuke him for the words the LORD your God has heard.ᶠ Therefore pray for the remnantᵍ that still survives."

⁵When King Hezekiah's officials came to Isaiah, ⁶Isaiah said to them, "Tell your master, 'This is what the LORD says: Do not be afraidʰ of what you have heard—those words with which the underlings of the king of Assyria have blasphemed me. ⁷Listen! I am going to put a spirit in him so that when he hears a certain report,ⁱ he will return to his own country, and there I will have him cut down with the sword.'"

⁸When the field commander heard that the king of Assyria had left Lachish, he withdrew and found the king fighting against Libnah.ʲ

36:11
wEzr 4:7
36:13
x2Ch 32:18
36:15
yIsa 37:10
36:16
z1Ki 4:25;
Zec 3:10
aPr 5:15
36:20
b1Ki 20:23
36:21
cPr 9:7-8; 26:4
37:2
dIsa 1:1
37:3
eIsa 26:18;
66:9; Hos 13:13
37:4
fIsa 36:13,18-20
gIsa 1:9
37:6
hIsa 7:4
37:7
iver 9
37:8
jNu 33:20

[9] Now Sennacherib received a report[k] that Tirhakah, the Cushite[a] king ͺof Egyptͺ, was marching out to fight against him. When he heard it, he sent messengers to Hezekiah with this word: [10]"Say to Hezekiah king of Judah: Do not let the god you depend on deceive you when he says, 'Jerusalem will not be handed over to the king of Assyria.'[l] [11]Surely you have heard what the kings of Assyria have done to all the countries, destroying them completely. And will you be delivered?[m] [12]Did the gods of the nations that were destroyed by my forefathers[n] deliver them—the gods of Gozan, Haran,[o] Rezeph and the people of Eden who were in Tel Assar? [13]Where is the king of Hamath, the king of Arpad, the king of the city of Sepharvaim, or of Hena or Ivvah?"

Hezekiah's Prayer
37:14–20pp — 2Ki 19:14–19

[14]Hezekiah received the letter from the messengers and read it. Then he went up to the temple of the LORD and spread it out before the LORD. [15]And Hezekiah prayed to the LORD: [16]"O LORD Almighty, God of Israel, enthroned between the cherubim, you alone are God[p] over all the kingdoms of the earth. You have made heaven and earth. [17]Give ear, O LORD, and hear;[q] open your eyes, O LORD, and see;[r] listen to all the words Sennacherib has sent to insult the living God.

[18]"It is true, O LORD, that the Assyrian kings have laid waste all these peoples and their lands.[s] [19]They have thrown their gods into the fire and destroyed them,[t] for they were not gods[u] but only wood and stone, fashioned by human hands. [20]Now, O LORD our God, deliver us from his hand, so that all kingdoms on earth may know that you alone, O LORD, are God.[b][v]"

Sennacherib's Fall
37:21–38pp — 2Ki 19:20–37; 2Ch 32:20–21

[21]Then Isaiah son of Amoz[w] sent a message to Hezekiah: "This is what the LORD, the God of Israel, says: Because you have prayed to me concerning Sennacherib king of Assyria, [22]this is the word the LORD has spoken against him:

"The Virgin Daughter of Zion
  despises and mocks you.
The Daughter of Jerusalem
  tosses her head[x] as you flee.
[23]Who is it you have insulted and blasphemed?[y]
  Against whom have you raised your voice
and lifted your eyes in pride?[z]
  Against the Holy One of Israel!
[24]By your messengers
  you have heaped insults on the Lord.
And you have said,
  'With my many chariots
I have ascended the heights of the mountains,
  the utmost heights of Lebanon.[a]

37:9
kver 7
37:10
lIsa 36:15
37:11
mIsa 36:18-20
37:12
n2Ki 18:11
oGe 11:31;
12:1-4; Ac 7:2
37:16
pDt 10:17;
Ps 86:10;
136:2-3
37:17
q2Ch 6:40
rDa 9:18
37:18
s2Ki 15:29;
Na 2:11-12
37:19
tIsa 26:14
uIsa 41:24,29
37:20
vPs 46:10
37:21
wver 2
37:22
xJob 16:4
37:23
yver 4 zIsa 2:11
37:24
aIsa 14:8

---

[a]9 That is, from the upper Nile region   [b]20 Dead Sea Scrolls (see also 2 Kings 19:19); Masoretic Text *alone are the* LORD

I have cut down its tallest cedars,
    the choicest of its pines.
I have reached its remotest heights,
    the finest of its forests.
²⁵I have dug wells in foreign lands[a]
    and drunk the water there.
With the soles of my feet
    I have dried up all the streams of Egypt.[b]'

²⁶"Have you not heard?
    Long ago I ordained[c] it.
In days of old I planned[d] it;
    now I have brought it to pass,
that you have turned fortified cities
    into piles of stone.[e]
²⁷Their people, drained of power,
    are dismayed and put to shame.
They are like plants in the field,
    like tender green shoots,
like grass sprouting on the roof,[f]
    scorched[b] before it grows up.

²⁸"But I know where you stay
    and when you come and go[g]
    and how you rage[h] against me.
²⁹Because you rage against me
    and because your insolence[i] has reached my ears,
I will put my hook in your nose[j]
    and my bit in your mouth,
and I will make you return
    by the way you came.[k]

³⁰"This will be the sign for you, O Hezekiah:

"This year you will eat what grows by itself,
    and the second year what springs from that.
But in the third year sow and reap,
    plant vineyards and eat their fruit.
³¹Once more a remnant of the house of Judah
    will take root below and bear fruit[l] above.
³²For out of Jerusalem will come a remnant,
    and out of Mount Zion a band of survivors.
The zeal[m] of the LORD Almighty
    will accomplish this.

³³"Therefore this is what the LORD says concerning the king of Assyria:

"He will not enter this city
    or shoot an arrow here.
He will not come before it with shield

37:25
b Dt 11:10
37:26
c Ac 2:23;
4:27-28; 1Pe 2:8
d Isa 10:6; 25:1
e Isa 25:2
37:27
f Ps 129:6
37:28
g Ps 139:1-3
h Ps 2:1
37:29
i Isa 10:12
j Isa 30:28;
Eze 38:4 k ver 34
37:31
l Isa 27:6
37:32
m Isa 9:7

---

a25 Dead Sea Scrolls (see also 2 Kings 19:24); Masoretic Text does not have *in foreign lands.*
b27 Some manuscripts of the Masoretic Text, Dead Sea Scrolls and some Septuagint manuscripts (see also 2 Kings 19:26); most manuscripts of the Masoretic Text *roof / and terraced fields*

or build a siege ramp against it.
34By the way that he came he will return;[n]
   he will not enter this city,"
                                    declares the LORD.
35"I will defend[o] this city and save it,
   for my sake[p] and for the sake of David[q] my servant!"

36Then the angel of the LORD went out and put to death a hundred and eighty-five thousand men in the Assyrian[r] camp. When the people got up the next morning—there were all the dead bodies! 37So Sennacherib king of Assyria broke camp and withdrew. He returned to Nineveh[s] and stayed there.

38One day, while he was worshiping in the temple of his god Nisroch, his sons Adrammelech and Sharezer cut him down with the sword, and they escaped to the land of Ararat.[t] And Esarhaddon his son succeeded him as king.

Hezekiah's Illness
38:1–8pp — 2Ki 20:1–11; 2Ch 32:24–26

38 In those days Hezekiah became ill and was at the point of death. The prophet Isaiah son of Amoz[u] went to him and said, "This is what the LORD says: Put your house in order,[v] because you are going to die; you will not recover."

2Hezekiah turned his face to the wall and prayed to the LORD, 3"Remember, O LORD, how I have walked[w] before you faithfully and with wholehearted devotion[x] and have done what is good in your eyes.[y]" And Hezekiah wept[z] bitterly.

4Then the word of the LORD came to Isaiah: 5"Go and tell Hezekiah, 'This is what the LORD, the God of your father David, says: I have heard your prayer and seen your tears; I will add fifteen years[a] to your life. 6And I will deliver you and this city from the hand of the king of Assyria. I will defend[b] this city.

7" 'This is the LORD's sign[c] to you that the LORD will do what he has promised: 8I will make the shadow cast by the sun go back the ten steps it has gone down on the stairway of Ahaz.' " So the sunlight went back the ten steps it had gone down.[d]

9A writing of Hezekiah king of Judah after his illness and recovery:

10I said, "In the prime of my life[e]
   must I go through the gates of death[a][f]
   and be robbed of the rest of my years?[g]"
11I said, "I will not again see the LORD,
   the LORD, in the land of the living;[h]
no longer will I look on mankind,
   or be with those who now dwell in this world.[b]
12Like a shepherd's tent[i] my house
   has been pulled down[j] and taken from me.
Like a weaver I have rolled[k] up my life,
   and he has cut me off from the loom;[l]

37:34
nver 29
37:35
oIsa 31:5; 38:6
pIsa 43:25;
48:9,11
q2Ki 20:6
37:36
rIsa 10:12
37:37
sGe 10:11
37:38
tGe 8:4;
Jer 51:27
38:1
uIsa 37:2
v2Sa 17:23
38:3
wNe 13:14;
Ps 26:3
x1Ch 29:19
yDt 6:18 zPs 6:8
38:5
a2Ki 18:2
38:6
bIsa 31:5; 37:35
38:7
cIsa 7:11,14
38:8
dJos 10:13
38:10
ePs 102:24
fPs 107:18;
2Co 1:9
gJob 17:11
38:11
hPs 27:13;
116:9
38:12
i2Co 5:1,4;
2Pe 1:13-14
jJob 4:21
kHeb 1:12
lJob 7:6

day and night[m] you made an end of me.

¹³I waited patiently till dawn,
    but like a lion he broke[n] all my bones;[o]
    day and night you made an end of me.
¹⁴I cried like a swift or thrush,
    I moaned like a mourning dove.[p]
My eyes grew weak as I looked to the heavens.
    I am troubled; O Lord, come to my aid!"[q]

¹⁵But what can I say?
    He has spoken to me, and he himself has done this.[r]
I will walk humbly[s] all my years
    because of this anguish of my soul.[t]
¹⁶Lord, by such things men live;
    and my spirit finds life in them too.
You restored me to health
    and let me live.[u]
¹⁷Surely it was for my benefit
    that I suffered such anguish.
In your love you kept me
    from the pit[v] of destruction;
you have put all my sins[w]
    behind your back.[x]
¹⁸For the grave[a][y] cannot praise you,
    death cannot sing your praise;[z]
those who go down to the pit[a]
    cannot hope for your faithfulness.
¹⁹The living, the living—they praise[b] you,
    as I am doing today;
fathers tell their children[c]
    about your faithfulness.

²⁰The LORD will save me,
    and we will sing[d] with stringed instruments[e]
all the days of our lives[f]
    in the temple[g] of the LORD.

²¹Isaiah had said, "Prepare a poultice of figs and apply it to the boil, and he will recover."

²²Hezekiah had asked, "What will be the sign that I will go up to the temple of the LORD?"

Envoys From Babylon

39:1–8pp — 2Ki 20:12–19

39 At that time Merodach-Baladan son of Baladan king of Babylon[h] sent Hezekiah letters and a gift, because he had heard of his illness and recovery. ²Hezekiah received the envoys[i] gladly and showed them what was in his storehouses—the silver, the gold,[j] the spices, the fine oil, his entire armory and everything found among his treasures. There was nothing in his palace or in all his kingdom that Hezekiah did not show them.

---

a18 Hebrew Sheol

38:12
m Ps 73:14
38:13
n Ps 51:8
o Job 10:16;
Da 6:24
38:14
p Isa 59:11
q Job 17:3
38:15
r Ps 39:9
s 1Ki 21:27
t Job 7:11
38:16
u Ps 119:25
38:17
v Ps 30:3
w Jer 31:34
x Isa 43:25;
Mic 7:19
38:18
y Ecc 9:10
z Ps 6:5;
88:10-11;
115:17 a Ps 30:9
38:19
b Dt 6:7;
Ps 118:17;
119:175
c Dt 11:19
38:20
d Ps 68:25
e Ps 33:2
f Ps 116:2
g Ps 116:17-19
39:1
h 2Ch 32:31
39:2
i 2Ch 32:31
j 2Ki 18:15

³Then Isaiah the prophet went to King Hezekiah and asked, "What did those men say, and where did they come from?"

"From a distant land,ᵏ" Hezekiah replied. "They came to me from Babylon."

⁴The prophet asked, "What did they see in your palace?"

"They saw everything in my palace," Hezekiah said. "There is nothing among my treasures that I did not show them."

⁵Then Isaiah said to Hezekiah, "Hear the word of the Lᴏʀᴅ Almighty: ⁶The time will surely come when everything in your palace, and all that your fathers have stored up until this day, will be carried off to Babylon.ˡ Nothing will be left, says the Lᴏʀᴅ. ⁷And some of your descendants, your own flesh and blood who will be born to you, will be taken away, and they will become eunuchs in the palace of the king of Babylon.ᵐ"

⁸"The word of the Lᴏʀᴅ you have spoken is good," Hezekiah replied. For he thought, "There will be peace and security in my lifetime.ⁿ"

Comfort for God's People

40 Comfort, comfortᵒ my people,
    says your God.
²Speak tenderlyᵖ to Jerusalem,
    and proclaim to her
that her hard service has been completed,�q
    that her sin has been paid for,
that she has received from the Lᴏʀᴅ's hand
    doubleʳ for all her sins.

³A voice of one calling:
"In the desert prepare
    the wayˢ for the Lᴏʀᴅᵃ;
make straight in the wilderness
    a highway for our God.ᵇ ᵗ
⁴Every valley shall be raised up,
    every mountain and hill made low;
the rough ground shall become level,ᵘ
    the rugged places a plain.
⁵And the glory of the Lᴏʀᴅ will be revealed,
    and all mankind together will see it.ᵛ
        For the mouth of the Lᴏʀᴅ has spoken."ʷ

⁶A voice says, "Cry out."
    And I said, "What shall I cry?"

"All men are like grass,ˣ
    and all their glory is like the flowers of the field.
⁷The grass withers and the flowers fall,
    because the breathʸ of the Lᴏʀᴅ blows on them.
    Surely the people are grass.
⁸The grass withers and the flowers fall,
    but the wordᶻ of our God stands forever.ᵃ"

ᵃ3 Or *A voice of one calling in the desert:* / *"Prepare the way for the* Lᴏʀᴅ   ᵇ3 Hebrew; Septuagint *make straight the paths of our God*

39:3
ᵏDt 28:49
39:6
ˡ2Ki 24:13;
Jer 20:5
39:7
ᵐ2Ki 24:15;
Da 1:1-7
39:8
ⁿ2Ch 32:26
40:1
ᵒIsa 12:1;
49:13; 51:3,12;
52:9; 61:2;
66:13;
Jer 31:13;
Zep 3:14-17;
2Co 1:3
40:2
ᵖIsa 35:4
qIsa 41:11-13;
49:25 ʳIsa 61:7;
Jer 16:18;
Zec 9:12;
Rev 18:6
40:3
ˢMal 3:1
ᵗMt 3:3*;
Mk 1:3*;
Jn 1:23*
40:4
ᵘIsa 45:2,13
40:5
ᵛIsa 52:10;
Lk 3:4-6*
ʷIsa 1:20;
58:14
40:6
ˣJob 14:2
40:7
ʸJob 41:21
40:8
ᶻIsa 55:11;
59:21 ᵃMt 5:18;
1Pe 1:24-25*

⁹You who bring good tidings^b to Zion,
   go up on a high mountain.
You who bring good tidings to Jerusalem,^a
   lift up your voice with a shout,
lift it up, do not be afraid;
   say to the towns of Judah,
   "Here is your God!"^c
¹⁰See, the Sovereign LORD comes^d with power,
   and his arm^e rules^f for him.
See, his reward^g is with him,
   and his recompense accompanies him.
¹¹He tends his flock like a shepherd:^h
   He gathers the lambs in his arms
and carries them close to his heart;
   he gently leads those that have young.

¹²Who has measured the watersⁱ in the hollow of his
      hand,^j
   or with the breadth of his hand marked off the
      heavens?^k
Who has held the dust of the earth in a basket,
   or weighed the mountains on the scales
   and the hills in a balance?
¹³Who has understood the mind^b of the LORD,
   or instructed him as his counselor?^l
¹⁴Whom did the LORD consult to enlighten him,
   and who taught him the right way?
Who was it that taught him knowledge^m
   or showed him the path of understanding?

¹⁵Surely the nations are like a drop in a bucket;
   they are regarded as dust on the scales;
   he weighs the islands as though they were fine dust.
¹⁶Lebanon is not sufficient for altar fires,
   nor its animalsⁿ enough for burnt offerings.
¹⁷Before him all the nations^o are as nothing;^p
   they are regarded by him as worthless
   and less than nothing.^q

¹⁸To whom, then, will you compare God?^r
   What image^s will you compare him to?
¹⁹As for an idol,^t a craftsman casts it,
   and a goldsmith^u overlays it with gold^v
   and fashions silver chains for it.
²⁰A man too poor to present such an offering
   selects wood that will not rot.
He looks for a skilled craftsman
   to set up an idol that will not topple.^w

²¹Do you not know?
   Have you not heard?

40:9
b Isa 52:7-10;
61:1; Ro 10:15
c Isa 25:9
40:10
d Rev 22:7
e Isa 59:16
f Isa 9:6-7
g Isa 62:11;
Rev 22:12
40:11
h Eze 34:23;
Mic 5:4;
Jn 10:11
40:12
i Job 38:10
j Pr 30:4
k Heb 1:10-12
40:13
l Ro 11:34*;
1Co 2:16*
40:14
m Job 21:22;
Col 2:3
40:16
n Ps 50:9-11;
Mic 6:7;
Heb 10:5-9
40:17
o Isa 30:28
p Isa 29:7
q Da 4:35
40:18
r Ex 8:10;
1Sa 2:2;
Isa 46:5
s Ac 17:29
40:19
t Ps 115:4
u Isa 41:7;
Jer 10:3
v Isa 2:20
40:20
w 1Sa 5:3

---

a 9 Or *O Zion, bringer of good tidings, / go up on a high mountain. / O Jerusalem, bringer of good tidings*
b 13 Or *Spirit; or spirit*

Has it not been told[x] you from the beginning?
　Have you not understood[y] since the earth was
　　founded?[z]
22He sits enthroned above the circle of the earth,
　and its people are like grasshoppers. [a]
He stretches out the heavens like a canopy,[b]
　and spreads them out like a tent[c] to live in.
23He brings princes[d] to naught
　and reduces the rulers of this world to nothing. [e]
24No sooner are they planted,
　no sooner are they sown,
　no sooner do they take root in the ground,
than he blows[f] on them and they wither,
　and a whirlwind sweeps them away like chaff.

25"To whom will you compare me?[g]
　Or who is my equal?" says the Holy One.
26Lift your eyes and look to the heavens:[h]
　Who created[i] all these?
He who brings out the starry host[j] one by one,
　and calls them each by name.
Because of his great power and mighty strength,
　not one of them is missing. [k]

27Why do you say, O Jacob,
　and complain, O Israel,
"My way is hidden from the LORD;
　my cause is disregarded by my God"?[l]
28Do you not know?
　Have you not heard?[m]
The LORD is the everlasting[n] God,
　the Creator of the ends of the earth.
He will not grow tired or weary,
　and his understanding no one can fathom. [o]
29He gives strength to the weary[p]
　and increases the power of the weak.
30Even youths grow tired and weary,
　and young men[q] stumble and fall;
31but those who hope[r] in the LORD
　will renew their strength. [s]
They will soar on wings like eagles;[t]
　they will run and not grow weary,
　they will walk and not be faint. [u]

The Helper of Israel

41 "Be silent[v] before me, you islands![w]
　　Let the nations renew their strength!
　Let them come forward[x] and speak;
　　let us meet together[y] at the place of judgment.

2"Who has stirred[z] up one from the east,[a]

40:21
xPs 19:1; 50:6;
Ac 14:17
yRo 1:19
zIsa 48:13;
51:13
40:22
aNu 13:33;
Ps 104:2;
Isa 42:5
bJob 22:14
cJob 36:29
40:23
dIsa 34:12
eJob 12:21;
Ps 107:40
40:24
fIsa 41:16
40:25
gver 18
40:26
hIsa 51:6
iPs 89:11-13;
Isa 42:5
jPs 147:4
kIsa 34:16
40:27
lJob 27:2;
Lk 18:7-8
40:28
mver 21
nPs 90:2
oPs 147:5;
Ro 11:33
40:29
pIsa 50:4;
Jer 31:25
40:30
qIsa 9:17;
Jer 6:11; 9:21
40:31
rLk 18:1
s2Co 4:16
tEx 19:4;
Ps 103:5
u2Co 4:1;
Heb 12:1-3
41:1
vHab 2:20;
Zec 2:13
wIsa 11:11
xIsa 48:16
yIsa 1:18; 34:1;
50:8
41:2
zEzr 1:2
aver 25;
Isa 45:1,13

calling him in righteousness to his service[a]?
He hands nations over to him
    and subdues kings before him.
He turns them to dust[b] with his sword,
    to windblown chaff[c] with his bow.
[3]He pursues them and moves on unscathed,
    by a path his feet have not traveled before.
[4]Who has done this and carried it through,
    calling forth the generations from the beginning?[d]
I, the LORD—with the first of them
    and with the last[e]—I am he."

[5]The islands[f] have seen it and fear;
    the ends of the earth tremble.
They approach and come forward;
6   each helps the other
    and says to his brother, "Be strong!"
[7]The craftsman encourages the goldsmith,[g]
    and he who smooths with the hammer
    spurs on him who strikes the anvil.
He says of the welding, "It is good."
    He nails down the idol so it will not topple.

[8]"But you, O Israel, my servant,
    Jacob, whom I have chosen,
    you descendants of Abraham[h] my friend,[i]
[9]I took you from the ends of the earth,[j]
    from its farthest corners I called you.
I said, 'You are my servant';
    I have chosen[k] you and have not rejected you.
[10]So do not fear, for I am with you;[l]
    do not be dismayed, for I am your God.
I will strengthen you and help[m] you;
    I will uphold you with my righteous right hand.

[11]"All who rage[n] against you
    will surely be ashamed and disgraced;[o]
those who oppose[p] you
    will be as nothing and perish.[q]
[12]Though you search for your enemies,
    you will not find them.[r]
Those who wage war against you
    will be as nothing[s] at all.
[13]For I am the LORD, your God,
    who takes hold of your right hand[t]
and says to you, Do not fear;
    I will help[u] you.
[14]Do not be afraid, O worm Jacob,
    O little Israel,
for I myself will help you," declares the LORD,
    your Redeemer, the Holy One of Israel.

41:2
b2Sa 22:43
cIsa 40:24
41:4
dver 26;
Isa 46:10
eIsa 44:6;
48:12; Rev 1:8,
17; 22:13
41:5
fEze 26:17-18
41:7
gIsa 40:19
41:8
hIsa 29:22;
51:2; 63:16
i2Ch 20:7;
Jas 2:23
41:9
jIsa 11:12
kDt 7:6
41:10
lJos 1:9;
Isa 43:2,5;
Ro 8:31
mver 13-14;
Isa 44:2; 49:8
41:11
nIsa 17:12
oIsa 45:24
pEx 23:22
qIsa 29:8
41:12
rPs 37:35-36
sIsa 17:14
41:13
tIsa 42:6; 45:1
uver 10

[a]2 Or / *whom victory meets at every step*

15"See, I will make you into a threshing sledge,ᵛ
    new and sharp, with many teeth.
You will thresh the mountains and crush them,
    and reduce the hills to chaff.
16You will winnowʷ them, the wind will pick them up,
    and a gale will blow them away.
But you will rejoice in the Lᴏʀᴅ
    and gloryˣ in the Holy One of Israel.

17"The poor and needy search for water,ʸ
    but there is none;
    their tongues are parched with thirst.
But I the Lᴏʀᴅ will answerᶻ them;
    I, the God of Israel, will not forsake them.
18I will make rivers flowᵃ on barren heights,
    and springs within the valleys.
I will turn the desertᵇ into pools of water,
    and the parched ground into springs.ᶜ
19I will put in the desert
    the cedar and the acacia, the myrtle and the olive.
I will set pines in the wasteland,
    the fir and the cypress together,ᵈ
20so that people may see and know,
    may consider and understand,
that the hand of the Lᴏʀᴅ has done this,
    that the Holy One of Israel has createdᵉ it.

21"Present your case," says the Lᴏʀᴅ.
    "Set forth your arguments," says Jacob's King.ᶠ
22"Bring in ˌyour idolsˌ to tell us
    what is going to happen.ᵍ
Tell us what the former things were,
    so that we may consider them
    and know their final outcome.
Or declare to us the things to come,ʰ
23   tell us what the future holds,
    so we may knowⁱ that you are gods.
Do something, whether good or bad,ʲ
    so that we will be dismayed and filled with fear.
24But you are less than nothingᵏ
    and your works are utterly worthless;
    he who chooses you is detestable.ˡ

25"I have stirred up one from the north,ᵐ and he comes—
    one from the rising sun who calls on my name.
He treadsⁿ on rulers as if they were mortar,
    as if he were a potter treading the clay.
26Who told of this from the beginning, so we could know,
    or beforehand, so we could say, 'He was right'?
No one told of this,
    no one foretold it,
    no one heard any wordsᵒ from you.
27I was the first to tellᵖ Zion, 'Look, here they are!'

41:15
ᵛMic 4:13
41:16
ʷJer 51:2
ˣIsa 45:25
41:17
ʸIsa 43:20
ᶻIsa 30:19
41:18
ᵃIsa 30:25
ᵇIsa 43:19
ᶜIsa 35:7
41:19
ᵈIsa 60:13
41:20
ᵉJob 12:9
41:21
ᶠIsa 43:15
41:22
ᵍIsa 43:9; 45:21
ʰIsa 46:10
41:23
ⁱIsa 42:9;
44:7-8; 45:3
ʲJer 10:5
41:24
ᵏIsa 37:19;
44:9; 1Co 8:4
ˡPs 115:8
41:25
ᵐver 2
ⁿ2Sa 22:43
41:26
ᵒHab 2:18-19
41:27
ᵖIsa 48:3,16

I gave to Jerusalem a messenger of good tidings. q
28I look but there is no one r —
        no one among them to give counsel, s
        no one to give answer when I ask them.
29See, they are all false!
        Their deeds amount to nothing; t
        their images are but wind u and confusion.

The Servant of the LORD

41:27
q Isa 40:9
41:28
r Isa 50:2;
59:16; 63:5
s Isa 40:13-14
41:29
t ver 24
u Jer 5:13
42:1
v Isa 43:10;
Lk 9:35;
1Pe 2:4,6
w Isa 11:2;
Mt 3:16-17;
Jn 3:34
42:3
x Ps 72:2
42:4
y Ge 49:10;
Mt 12:18-21*
42:5
z Ps 24:2
a Ac 17:25
42:6
b Isa 43:1
c Jer 23:6
d Isa 26:3
e Isa 49:8
f Lk 2:32;
Ac 13:47
42:7
g Isa 35:5
h Isa 49:9; 61:1
i Lk 4:19;
2Ti 2:26;
Heb 2:14-15
42:8
j Ex 3:15
k Isa 48:11
42:10
l Ps 33:3; 40:3;
98:1 m Isa 49:6
n 1Ch 16:32;
Ps 96:11
42:11
o Isa 32:16
p Isa 60:7

42

"Here is my servant, whom I uphold,
        my chosen one v in whom I delight;
I will put my Spirit w on him
        and he will bring justice to the nations.
2He will not shout or cry out,
        or raise his voice in the streets.
3A bruised reed he will not break,
        and a smoldering wick he will not snuff out.
In faithfulness he will bring forth justice; x
4 he will not falter or be discouraged
till he establishes justice on earth.
        In his law the islands will put their hope." y

5This is what God the LORD says—
he who created the heavens and stretched them out,
        who spread out the earth and all that comes out of it, z
who gives breath a to its people,
        and life to those who walk on it:
6"I, the LORD, have called b you in righteousness; c
        I will take hold of your hand.
I will keep d you and will make you
        to be a covenant e for the people
        and a light for the Gentiles, f
7to open eyes that are blind, g
        to free h captives from prison i
        and to release from the dungeon those who sit in
                darkness.

8"I am the LORD; that is my name! j
        I will not give my glory to another k
        or my praise to idols.
9See, the former things have taken place,
        and new things I declare;
before they spring into being
        I announce them to you."

Song of Praise to the LORD

10Sing to the LORD a new song, l
        his praise from the ends of the earth; m
you who go down to the sea, and all that is in it, n
        you islands, and all who live in them.
11Let the desert o and its towns raise their voices;
        let the settlements where Kedar p lives rejoice.

Let the people of Sela sing for joy;
   let them shout from the mountaintops. q
12Let them give glory r to the Lord
   and proclaim his praise in the islands.
13The Lord will march out like a mighty s man,
   like a warrior he will stir up his zeal; t
with a shout u he will raise the battle cry
   and will triumph over his enemies. v

14"For a long time I have kept silent,
   I have been quiet and held myself back.
But now, like a woman in childbirth,
   I cry out, I gasp and pant.
15I will lay waste w the mountains and hills
   and dry up all their vegetation;
I will turn rivers into islands
   and dry up x the pools.
16I will lead y the blind z by ways they have not known,
   along unfamiliar paths I will guide them;
I will turn the darkness into light before them
   and make the rough places smooth. a
These are the things I will do;
   I will not forsake b them.
17But those who trust in idols,
   who say to images, 'You are our gods,'
will be turned back in utter shame. c

Israel Blind and Deaf

18"Hear, you deaf; d
   look, you blind, and see!
19Who is blind e but my servant, f
   and deaf like the messenger g I send?
Who is blind like the one committed h to me,
   blind like the servant of the Lord?
20You have seen many things, but have paid no attention;
   your ears are open, but you hear nothing." i
21It pleased the Lord
   for the sake of his righteousness
   to make his law j great and glorious.
22But this is a people plundered and looted,
   all of them trapped in pits k
   or hidden away in prisons. l
They have become plunder,
   with no one to rescue them;
they have been made loot,
   with no one to say, "Send them back."

23Which of you will listen to this
   or pay close attention m in time to come?
24Who handed Jacob over to become loot,
   and Israel to the plunderers?
Was it not the Lord,

42:11
qIsa 52:7;
Na 1:15
42:12
rIsa 24:15
42:13
sIsa 9:6
tIsa 26:11
uHos 11:10
vIsa 66:14
42:15
wEze 38:20
xIsa 50:2;
Na 1:4-6
42:16
yLk 1:78-79
zIsa 32:3
aLk 3:5
bHeb 13:5
42:17
cPs 97:7;
Isa 1:29; 44:11;
45:16
42:18
dIsa 35:5
42:19
eIsa 43:8;
Eze 12:2
fIsa 41:8-9
gIsa 44:26
hIsa 26:3
42:20
iJer 6:10
42:21
jver 4
42:22
kIsa 24:18
lIsa 24:22
42:23
mIsa 48:18

against whom we have sinned?
For they would not follow[n] his ways;
    they did not obey his law.
25So he poured out on them his burning anger,
    the violence of war.
It enveloped them in flames,[o] yet they did not
    understand;
    it consumed them, but they did not take it to heart.[p]

Israel's Only Savior

43 But now, this is what the LORD says—
    he who created you, O Jacob,
    he who formed[q] you, O Israel:[r]
"Fear not, for I have redeemed[s] you;
    I have summoned you by name;[t] you are mine.
2When you pass through the waters,[u]
    I will be with you;[v]
and when you pass through the rivers,
    they will not sweep over you.
When you walk through the fire,[w]
    you will not be burned;
    the flames will not set you ablaze.[x]
3For I am the LORD, your God,[y]
    the Holy One of Israel, your Savior;
I give Egypt for your ransom,
    Cush[a][z] and Seba in your stead.[a]
4Since you are precious and honored in my sight,
    and because I love[b] you,
I will give men in exchange for you,
    and people in exchange for your life.
5Do not be afraid,[c] for I am with you;[d]
    I will bring your children[e] from the east
    and gather you from the west.
6I will say to the north, 'Give them up!'
    and to the south,[f] 'Do not hold them back.'
Bring my sons from afar
    and my daughters[g] from the ends of the earth—
7everyone who is called by my name,[h]
    whom I created for my glory,
    whom I formed and made.[i] "

8Lead out those who have eyes but are blind,[j]
    who have ears but are deaf.[k]
9All the nations gather together[l]
    and the peoples assemble.
Which of them foretold[m] this
    and proclaimed to us the former things?
Let them bring in their witnesses to prove they were
    right,
    so that others may hear and say, "It is true."

42:24
n Isa 30:15
42:25
o 2Ki 25:9
p Isa 29:13;
47:7; 57:1,11;
Hos 7:9
43:1
q ver 7
r Ge 32:28;
Isa 44:21
s Isa 44:2,6
t Isa 42:6; 45:3-4
43:2
u Isa 8:7
v Dt 31:6,8
w Isa 29:6;
30:27
x Ps 66:12;
Da 3:25-27
43:3
y Ex 20:2
z Isa 20:3
a Pr 21:18
43:4
b Isa 63:9
43:5
c Isa 44:2
d Jer 30:10-11
e Isa 41:8
43:6
f Ps 107:3
g 2Co 6:18
43:7
h Isa 56:5;
63:19; Jas 2:7
i ver 1,21;
Ps 100:3;
Eph 2:10
43:8
j Isa 6:9-10
k Isa 42:20;
Eze 12:2
43:9
l Isa 41:1
m Isa 41:26

a3 That is, the upper Nile region

¹⁰"You are my witnesses," declares the LORD,
    "and my servant[n] whom I have chosen,
so that you may know and believe me
    and understand that I am he.
Before me no god[o] was formed,
    nor will there be one after me.
¹¹I, even I, am the LORD,
    and apart from me there is no savior.[p]
¹²I have revealed and saved and proclaimed—
    I, and not some foreign god[q] among you.
You are my witnesses,[r]" declares the LORD, "that I am
        God.
¹³ Yes, and from ancient days[s] I am he.
No one can deliver out of my hand.
    When I act, who can reverse it?"[t]

God's Mercy and Israel's Unfaithfulness

¹⁴This is what the LORD says—
    your Redeemer, the Holy One of Israel:
"For your sake I will send to Babylon
    and bring down as fugitives[u] all the Babylonians,[a] [v]
    in the ships in which they took pride.
¹⁵I am the LORD, your Holy One,
    Israel's Creator, your King."

¹⁶This is what the LORD says—
    he who made a way through the sea,
    a path through the mighty waters,[w]
¹⁷who drew out[x] the chariots and horses,
    the army and reinforcements together,[y]
and they lay there, never to rise again,
    extinguished, snuffed out like a wick:
¹⁸"Forget the former things;
    do not dwell on the past.
¹⁹See, I am doing a new thing![z]
    Now it springs up; do you not perceive it?
I am making a way in the desert[a]
    and streams in the wasteland.
²⁰The wild animals honor me,
    the jackals[b] and the owls,
because I provide water[c] in the desert
    and streams in the wasteland,
to give drink to my people, my chosen,
²¹ the people I formed for myself
    that they may proclaim my praise.[d]

²²"Yet you have not called upon me, O Jacob,
    you have not wearied yourselves for me, O Israel.[e]
²³You have not brought me sheep for burnt offerings,
    nor honored[f] me with your sacrifices.[g]
I have not burdened you with grain offerings

43:10
n Isa 41:8-9
o Isa 44:6,8
43:11
p Isa 45:21
43:12
q Dt 32:12;
Ps 81:9 r Isa 44:8
43:13
s Ps 90:2
t Job 9:12;
Isa 14:27
43:14
u Isa 13:14-15
v Isa 23:13
43:16
w Ps 77:19;
Isa 11:15; 51:10
43:17
x Ps 118:12;
Isa 1:31
y Ex 14:9
43:19
z 2Co 5:17;
Rev 21:5
a Ex 17:6;
Nu 20:11
43:20
b Isa 13:22
c Isa 48:21
43:21
d Ps 102:18;
1Pe 2:9
43:22
e Isa 30:11
43:23
f Zec 7:5-6;
Mal 1:6-8
g Am 5:25

nor wearied you with demands[h] for incense. [i]
24You have not bought any fragrant calamus[j] for me,
    or lavished on me the fat of your sacrifices.
But you have burdened me with your sins
    and wearied[k] me with your offenses. [l]

25"I, even I, am he who blots out
    your transgressions, [m] for my own sake, [n]
    and remembers your sins no more. [o]
26Review the past for me,
    let us argue the matter together;[p]
    state the case[q] for your innocence.
27Your first father sinned;
    your spokesmen[r] rebelled against me.
28So I will disgrace the dignitaries of your temple,
    and I will consign Jacob to destruction[a]
    and Israel to scorn. [s]

Israel the Chosen

44 "But now listen, O Jacob, my servant,[t]
    Israel, whom I have chosen.
2This is what the LORD says—
    he who made you, who formed you in the womb,
    and who will help[u] you:
Do not be afraid, O Jacob, my servant,
    Jeshurun, [v] whom I have chosen.
3For I will pour water[w] on the thirsty land,
    and streams on the dry ground;
I will pour out my Spirit[x] on your offspring,
    and my blessing on your descendants. [y]
4They will spring up like grass in a meadow,
    like poplar trees[z] by flowing streams. [a]
5One will say, 'I belong to the LORD';
    another will call himself by the name of Jacob;
still another will write on his hand, [b] 'The LORD's,'[c]
    and will take the name Israel.

The LORD, Not Idols

6"This is what the LORD says—
    Israel's King[d] and Redeemer, [e] the LORD Almighty:
I am the first and I am the last;[f]
    apart from me there is no God.
7Who then is like me? Let him proclaim it.
    Let him declare and lay out before me
what has happened since I established my ancient
        people,
    and what is yet to come—
    yes, let him foretell[g] what will come.
8Do not tremble, do not be afraid.

---

[a]28 The Hebrew term refers to the irrevocable giving over of things or persons to the LORD, often by totally destroying them.

### Cross references (margin)

43:23
h Jer 7:22
i Ex 30:35;
  Lev 2:1
43:24
j Ex 30:23
k Isa 1:14; 7:13
l Mal 2:17
43:25
m Ac 3:19
n Isa 37:35;
  Eze 36:22
o Isa 38:17;
  Jer 31:34
43:26
p Isa 1:18
q Isa 41:1; 50:8
43:27
r Isa 9:15; 28:7;
  Jer 5:31
43:28
s Jer 24:9;
  Eze 5:15
44:1
t ver 21;
  Jer 30:10;
  46:27-28
44:2
u Isa 41:10
v Dt 32:15
44:3
w Joel 3:18
x Joel 2:28;
  Ac 2:17
y Isa 61:9; 65:23
44:4
z Lev 23:40
a Job 40:22
44:5
b Ex 13:9
c Zec 8:20-22
44:6
d Isa 41:21
e Isa 43:1
f Isa 41:4;
  Rev 1:8,17;
  22:13
44:7
g Isa 41:22,26

Did I not proclaim this and foretell it long ago?
You are my witnesses. Is there any God[h] besides me?
No, there is no other Rock;[i] I know not one."

9All who make idols are nothing,
    and the things they treasure are worthless.[j]
Those who would speak up for them are blind;
    they are ignorant, to their own shame.
10Who shapes a god and casts an idol,
    which can profit him nothing?[k]
11He and his kind will be put to shame;[l]
    craftsmen are nothing but men.
Let them all come together and take their stand;
    they will be brought down to terror and infamy.[m]

12The blacksmith[n] takes a tool
    and works with it in the coals;
he shapes an idol with hammers,
    he forges it with the might of his arm.[o]
He gets hungry and loses his strength;
    he drinks no water and grows faint.
13The carpenter[p] measures with a line
    and makes an outline with a marker;
he roughs it out with chisels
    and marks it with compasses.
He shapes it in the form of man,[q]
    of man in all his glory,
    that it may dwell in a shrine.[r]
14He cut down cedars,
    or perhaps took a cypress or oak.
He let it grow among the trees of the forest,
    or planted a pine, and the rain made it grow.
15It is man's fuel[s] for burning;
    some of it he takes and warms himself,
    he kindles a fire and bakes bread.
But he also fashions a god and worships it;
    he makes an idol and bows[t] down to it.
16Half of the wood he burns in the fire;
    over it he prepares his meal,
    he roasts his meat and eats his fill.
He also warms himself and says,
    "Ah! I am warm; I see the fire."
17From the rest he makes a god, his idol;
    he bows down to it and worships.
He prays[u] to it and says,
    "Save[v] me; you are my god."
18They know nothing, they understand[w] nothing;
    their eyes[x] are plastered over so they cannot see,
    and their minds closed so they cannot understand.
19No one stops to think,
    no one has the knowledge or understanding[y] to say,
    "Half of it I used for fuel;
    I even baked bread over its coals,

44:8
h Isa 43:10
i Dt 4:35;
1Sa 2:2
44:9
j Isa 41:24
44:10
k Isa 41:29;
Jer 10:5;
Ac 19:26
44:11
l Isa 1:29
m Isa 42:17
44:12
n Isa 40:19;
41:6-7
o Jer 10:3-5;
Ac 17:29
44:13
p Isa 41:7
q Ps 115:4-7
r Jdg 17:4-5
44:15
s ver 19
t 2Ch 25:14
44:17
u 1Ki 18:26
v Isa 45:20
44:18
w Isa 1:3
x Isa 6:9-10
44:19
y Isa 5:13;
27:11; 45:20

I roasted meat and I ate.
Shall I make a detestable[z] thing from what is left?
  Shall I bow down to a block of wood?"
20He feeds on ashes,[a] a deluded[b] heart misleads him;
  he cannot save himself, or say,
  "Is not this thing in my right hand a lie?[c]"

21"Remember[d] these things, O Jacob,
  for you are my servant, O Israel.
I have made you, you are my servant;[e]
  O Israel, I will not forget you.[f]
22I have swept away[g] your offenses like a cloud,
  your sins like the morning mist.
Return[h] to me,
  for I have redeemed[i] you."

23Sing for joy,[j] O heavens, for the LORD has done this;
  shout aloud, O earth[k] beneath.
Burst into song, you mountains,[l]
  you forests and all your trees,
for the LORD has redeemed Jacob,
  he displays his glory[m] in Israel.

Jerusalem to Be Inhabited

24"This is what the LORD says—
  your Redeemer,[n] who formed you in the womb:

I am the LORD,
who has made all things,
who alone stretched out the heavens,[o]
who spread out the earth by myself,

25who foils[p] the signs of false prophets
  and makes fools of diviners,[q]
who overthrows the learning of the wise[r]
  and turns it into nonsense,[s]
26who carries out the words[t] of his servants
  and fulfills[u] the predictions of his messengers,

who says of Jerusalem, 'It shall be inhabited,'
  of the towns of Judah, 'They shall be built,'
  and of their ruins, 'I will restore them,'[v]
27who says to the watery deep, 'Be dry,
  and I will dry up your streams,'
28who says of Cyrus,[w] 'He is my shepherd
  and will accomplish all that I please;
he will say of Jerusalem,[x] "Let it be rebuilt,"
  and of the temple,[y] "Let its foundations be laid." '

45

"This is what the LORD says to his anointed,
  to Cyrus, whose right hand I take hold[z] of
to subdue nations[a] before him
  and to strip kings of their armor,
to open doors before him

44:19
zDt 27:15
44:20
aPs 102:9
bJob 15:31;
Ro 1:21-23,28;
2Th 2:11;
2Ti 3:13
cIsa 59:3,4,13;
Ro 1:25
44:21
dIsa 46:8;
Zec 10:9
ever 1-2
fIsa 49:15
44:22
gIsa 43:25;
Ac 3:19
hIsa 55:7
i1Co 6:20
44:23
jIsa 42:10
kPs 148:7
lPs 98:8
mIsa 61:3
44:24
nIsa 43:14
oIsa 42:5
44:25
pPs 33:10
qIsa 47:13
r1Co 1:27
s2Sa 15:31;
1Co 1:19-20
44:26
tZec 1:6
uIsa 55:11;
Mt 5:18
vIsa 49:8-21
44:28
w2Ch 36:22
xIsa 14:32
yEzr 1:2-4
45:1
zPs 73:23;
Isa 41:13; 42:6
aJer 50:35

so that gates will not be shut:
²I will go before you
   and will level^b the mountains^a;
I will break down gates of bronze
   and cut through bars of iron.^c
³I will give you the treasures^d of darkness,
   riches stored in secret places,^e
so that you may know^f that I am the Lord,
   the God of Israel, who summons you by name.^g
⁴For the sake of Jacob my servant,^h
   of Israel my chosen,
I summon you by name
   and bestow on you a title of honor,
   though you do not acknowledgeⁱ me.
⁵I am the Lord, and there is no other;^j
   apart from me there is no God.^k
I will strengthen you,^l
   though you have not acknowledged me,
⁶so that from the rising of the sun
   to the place of its setting^m
men may know there is none besides me.ⁿ
   I am the Lord, and there is no other.
⁷I form the light and create darkness,
   I bring prosperity and create disaster;^o
   I, the Lord, do all these things.

⁸"You heavens above, rain^p down righteousness;^q
   let the clouds shower it down.
Let the earth open wide,
   let salvation^r spring up,
let righteousness grow with it;
   I, the Lord, have created it.

⁹"Woe to him who quarrels^s with his Maker,
   to him who is but a potsherd among the potsherds on
      the ground.
Does the clay say to the potter,^t
   'What are you making?'
Does your work say,
   'He has no hands'?
¹⁰Woe to him who says to his father,
   'What have you begotten?'
or to his mother,
   'What have you brought to birth?'

¹¹"This is what the Lord says—
   the Holy One of Israel, and its Maker:
Concerning things to come,
   do you question me about my children,
   or give me orders about the work of my hands?^u
¹²It is I who made the earth

45:2
b Isa 40:4
c Ps 107:16;
Jer 51:30
45:3
d Jer 50:37
e Jer 41:8
f Isa 41:23
g Ex 33:12;
Isa 43:1
45:4
h Isa 41:8-9
i Ac 17:23
45:5
j Isa 44:8
k Ps 18:31
l Ps 18:39
45:6
m Isa 43:5;
Mal 1:11 n ver 5,
18
45:7
o Isa 31:2;
Am 3:6
45:8
p Ps 72:6;
Joel 3:18
q Ps 85:11;
Isa 60:21;
61:10,11;
Hos 10:12
r Isa 12:3
45:9
s Job 15:25
t Isa 29:16;
Ro 9:20-21*
45:11
u Isa 19:25

---

^a2 Dead Sea Scrolls and Septuagint; the meaning of the word in the Masoretic Text is uncertain.

and created mankind upon it.
My own hands stretched out the heavens;[v]
I marshaled their starry hosts. [w]
13I will raise up Cyrus[ax] in my righteousness:
I will make all his ways straight.
He will rebuild my city
and set my exiles free,
but not for a price or reward, [y]
says the LORD Almighty."

14This is what the LORD says:

"The products of Egypt and the merchandise of Cush, [b]
and those tall Sabeans—
they will come over to you
and will be yours;
they will trudge behind you,
coming over to you in chains. [z]
They will bow down before you
and plead[a] with you, saying,
'Surely God is with you, [b] and there is no other;
there is no other god.' "

15Truly you are a God who hides[c] himself,
O God and Savior of Israel.
16All the makers of idols will be put to shame and
disgraced;[d]
they will go off into disgrace together.
17But Israel will be saved[e] by the LORD
with an everlasting salvation;[f]
you will never be put to shame or disgraced,
to ages everlasting.

18For this is what the LORD says—
he who created the heavens,
he is God;
he who fashioned and made the earth,
he founded it;
he did not create it to be empty, [g]
but formed it to be inhabited[h]—
he says:
"I am the LORD,
and there is no other. [i]
19I have not spoken in secret, [j]
from somewhere in a land of darkness;
I have not said to Jacob's descendants, [k]
'Seek me in vain.'
I, the LORD, speak the truth;
I declare what is right. [l]

20"Gather together[m] and come;
assemble, you fugitives from the nations.

45:12
vGe 2:1;
Isa 42:5
wNe 9:6
45:13
x2Ch 36:22;
Isa 41:2
yIsa 52:3
45:14
zIsa 14:1-2
aJer 16:19;
Zec 8:20-23
b1Co 14:25
45:15
cPs 44:24
45:16
dIsa 44:9,11
45:17
eRo 11:26
fIsa 26:4
45:18
gGe 1:2
hGe 1:26;
Isa 42:5 iver 5
45:19
jIsa 48:16
kIsa 41:8
lDt 30:11
45:20
mIsa 43:9

a13 Hebrew *him*　　　b14 That is, the upper Nile region

Ignorant[n] are those who carry[o] about idols of wood,
who pray to gods that cannot save.[p]
21Declare what is to be, present it—
let them take counsel together.
Who foretold[q] this long ago,
who declared it from the distant past?
Was it not I, the LORD?
And there is no God apart from me,[r]
a righteous God and a Savior;
there is none but me.

22"Turn[s] to me and be saved,[t]
all you ends of the earth;[u]
for I am God, and there is no other.
23By myself I have sworn,[v]
my mouth has uttered in all integrity[w]
a word that will not be revoked:[x]
Before me every knee will bow;
by me every tongue will swear.[y]
24They will say of me, 'In the LORD alone
are righteousness[z] and strength.'"
All who have raged against him
will come to him and be put to shame.[a]
25But in the LORD all the descendants of Israel
will be found righteous and will exult.[b]

Gods of Babylon

46 Bel[c] bows down, Nebo stoops low;
their idols are borne by beasts of burden.[a]
The images that are carried[d] about are burdensome,
a burden for the weary.
2They stoop and bow down together;
unable to rescue the burden,
they themselves go off into captivity.[e]

3"Listen[f] to me, O house of Jacob,
all you who remain of the house of Israel,
you whom I have upheld since you were conceived,
an have carried since your birth.
4Even to your old age and gray hairs[g]
I am he,[h] I am he who will sustain you.
I have made you and I will carry you;
I will sustain you and I will rescue you.

5"To whom will you compare me or count me equal?
To whom will you liken me that we may be
compared?[i]
6Some pour out gold from their bags
and weigh out silver on the scales;
they hire a goldsmith[j] to make it into a god,
and they bow down and worship it.[k]

---

[a]1 Or *are but beasts and cattle*

45:20
n Isa 44:19
o Isa 46:1;
Jer 10:5
p Isa 44:17;
46:6-7
45:21
q Isa 41:22
r ver 5
45:22
s Zec 12:10
t Nu 21:8-9;
2Ch 20:12
u Isa 49:6,12
45:23
v Ge 22:16
w Heb 6:13
x Isa 55:11
y Ps 63:11;
Isa 19:18;
Ro 14:11*;
Php 2:10-11
45:24
z Jer 33:16
a Isa 41:11
45:25
b Isa 41:16
46:1
c Isa 21:9;
Jer 50:2; 51:44
d Isa 45:20
46:2
e Jdg 18:17-18;
2Sa 5:21
46:3
f ver 12
46:4
g Ps 71:18
h Isa 43:13
46:5
i Isa 40:18,25
46:6
j Isa 40:19
k Isa 44:17

[7]They lift it to their shoulders and carry[1] it;
    they set it up in its place, and there it stands.
From that spot it cannot move.
Though one cries out to it, it does not answer;
    it cannot save[m] him from his troubles.

[8]"Remember[n] this, fix it in mind,
    take it to heart, you rebels.
[9]Remember the former things, those of long ago;[o]
    I am God, and there is no other;
    I am God, and there is none like me. [p]
[10]I make known the end from the beginning,
    from ancient times,[q] what is still to come.
I say: My purpose will stand,[r]
    and I will do all that I please.
[11]From the east I summon a bird of prey;
    from a far-off land, a man to fulfill my purpose.
What I have said, that will I bring about;
    what I have planned, that will I do.
[12]Listen[s] to me, you stubborn-hearted,
    you who are far from righteousness.[t]
[13]I am bringing my righteousness near,
    it is not far away;
    and my salvation will not be delayed.
I will grant salvation to Zion,
    my splendor[u] to Israel.

The Fall of Babylon

47 "Go down, sit in the dust,
    Virgin Daughter[v] of Babylon;
sit on the ground without a throne,
    Daughter of the Babylonians. [a] [w]
No more will you be called
    tender or delicate.[x]
[2]Take millstones[y] and grind[z] flour;
    take off your veil. [a]
Lift up your skirts, [b] bare your legs,
    and wade through the streams.
[3]Your nakedness[c] will be exposed
    and your shame[d] uncovered.
I will take vengeance;[e]
    I will spare no one."

[4]Our Redeemer—the Lord Almighty is his name[f]—
    is the Holy One of Israel.

[5]"Sit in silence, go into darkness,[g]
    Daughter of the Babylonians;
no more will you be called
    queen of kingdoms. [h]
[6]I was angry[i] with my people

[a]1 Or *Chaldeans*; also in verse 5

and desecrated my inheritance;
I gave them into your hand,[j]
    and you showed them no mercy.
Even on the aged
    you laid a very heavy yoke.
[7]You said, 'I will continue forever—
    the eternal queen!'[k]
But you did not consider these things
    or reflect[l] on what might happen.[m]

[8]"Now then, listen, you wanton creature,
    lounging in your security[n]
and saying to yourself,
    'I am, and there is none besides me.[o]
I will never be a widow[p]
    or suffer the loss of children.'
[9]Both of these will overtake you
    in a moment,[q] on a single day:
    loss of children[r] and widowhood.
They will come upon you in full measure,
    in spite of your many sorceries[s]
    and all your potent spells.[t]
[10]You have trusted[u] in your wickedness
    and have said, 'No one sees me.'[v]
Your wisdom[w] and knowledge mislead[x] you
    when you say to yourself,
    'I am, and there is none besides me.'
[11]Disaster will come upon you,
    and you will not know how to conjure it away.
A calamity will fall upon you
    that you cannot ward off with a ransom;
a catastrophe you cannot foresee
    will suddenly[y] come upon you.

[12]"Keep on, then, with your magic spells
    and with your many sorceries,[z]
    which you have labored at since childhood.
Perhaps you will succeed,
    perhaps you will cause terror.
[13]All the counsel you have received has only worn you
        out![a]
Let your astrologers[b] come forward,
those stargazers who make predictions month by
        month,
    let them save[c] you from what is coming upon you.
[14]Surely they are like stubble;[d]
    the fire will burn them up.
They cannot even save themselves
    from the power of the flame.[e]
Here are no coals to warm anyone;
    here is no fire to sit by.
[15]That is all they can do for you—
    these you have labored with

47:6
j Isa 10:13
47:7
k ver 5;
Rev 18:7
l Isa 42:23,25
m Dt 32:29
47:8
n Isa 32:9
o Isa 45:6;
Zep 2:15
p Rev 18:7
47:9
q Ps 73:19;
1Th 5:3;
Rev 18:8-10
r Isa 13:18
s Na 3:4
t Rev 18:23
47:10
u Ps 52:7; 62:10
v Isa 29:15
w Isa 5:21
x Isa 44:20
47:11
y 1Th 5:3
47:12
z ver 9
47:13
a Isa 57:10;
Jer 51:58
b Isa 44:25
c ver 15
47:14
d Isa 5:24;
Na 1:10
e Isa 10:17;
Jer 51:30,32,58

and trafficked[f] with since childhood.
Each of them goes on in his error;
    there is not one that can save you.

Stubborn Israel

48 "Listen to this, O house of Jacob,
    you who are called by the name of Israel
    and come from the line of Judah,
you who take oaths in the name of the Lord
    and invoke[g] the God of Israel—
    but not in truth[h] or righteousness—
[2]you who call yourselves citizens of the holy city[i]
    and rely[j] on the God of Israel—
    the Lord Almighty is his name:
[3]I foretold the former things[k] long ago,
    my mouth announced[l] them and I made them
        known;
    then suddenly I acted, and they came to pass.
[4]For I knew how stubborn[m] you were;
    the sinews of your neck[n] were iron,
    your forehead[o] was bronze.
[5]Therefore I told you these things long ago;
    before they happened I announced them to you
so that you could not say,
    'My idols did them;[p]
    my wooden image and metal god ordained them.'
[6]You have heard these things; look at them all.
    Will you not admit them?

"From now on I will tell you of new things,
    of hidden things unknown to you.
[7]They are created now, and not long ago;
    you have not heard of them before today.
So you cannot say,
    'Yes, I knew of them.'
[8]You have neither heard nor understood;
    from of old your ear has not been open.
Well do I know how treacherous you are;
    you were called a rebel[q] from birth.
[9]For my own name's sake I delay my wrath;[r]
    for the sake of my praise I hold it back from you,
    so as not to cut you off.[s]
[10]See, I have refined you, though not as silver;
    I have tested you in the furnace[t] of affliction.
[11]For my own sake,[u] for my own sake, I do this.
    How can I let myself be defamed?[v]
    I will not yield my glory to another.[w]

Israel Freed

[12]"Listen[x] to me, O Jacob,
    Israel, whom I have called:
    I am he;

47:15
f Rev 18:11
48:1
g Isa 58:2
h Jer 4:2
48:2
i Isa 52:1
j Isa 10:20;
Mic 3:11;
Ro 2:17
48:3
k Isa 41:22
l Isa 45:21
48:4
m Dt 31:27
n Ex 32:9;
Ac 7:51
o Eze 3:9
48:5
p Jer 44:15-18
48:8
q Dt 9:7,24;
Ps 58:3
48:9
r Ps 78:38;
Isa 30:18
s Ne 9:31
48:10
t 1Ki 8:51
48:11
u 1Sa 12:22;
Isa 37:35
v Dt 32:27;
Jer 14:7,21;
Eze 20:9,14,22,
44 w Isa 42:8
48:12
x Isa 46:3

I am the first and I am the last.[y]
13My own hand laid the foundations of the earth,[z]
  and my right hand spread out the heavens;[a]
when I summon them,
  they all stand up together.[b]

14"Come together,[c] all of you, and listen:
  Which of the idols has foretold these things?
The Lord's chosen ally
  will carry out his purpose[d] against Babylon;
  his arm will be against the Babylonians.[a]
15I, even I, have spoken;
  yes, I have called[e] him.
I will bring him,
  and he will succeed in his mission.

16"Come near[f] me and listen to this:

"From the first announcement I have not spoken in
    secret;[g]
  at the time it happens, I am there."

And now the Sovereign Lord has sent[h] me,
  with his Spirit.

17This is what the Lord says—
  your Redeemer,[i] the Holy One[j] of Israel:
"I am the Lord your God,
  who teaches you what is best for you,
  who directs[k] you in the way[l] you should go.
18If only you had paid attention[m] to my commands,
  your peace[n] would have been like a river,
  your righteousness[o] like the waves of the sea.
19Your descendants would have been like the sand,
  your children like its numberless grains;[p]
their name would never be cut off[q]
  nor destroyed from before me."

20Leave Babylon,
  flee[r] from the Babylonians!
Announce this with shouts of joy[s]
  and proclaim it.
Send it out to the ends of the earth;
  say, "The Lord has redeemed[t] his servant Jacob."
21They did not thirst[u] when he led them through the
    deserts;
  he made water flow[v] for them from the rock;
he split the rock
  and water gushed out.[w]

22"There is no peace," says the Lord, "for the wicked."[x]

48:12
y Isa 41:4;
Rev 1:17; 22:13
48:13
z Heb 1:10-12
a Ex 20:11
b Isa 40:26
48:14
c Isa 43:9
d Isa 46:10-11
48:15
e Isa 45:1
48:16
f Isa 41:1
g Isa 45:19
h Zec 2:9,11
48:17
i Isa 49:7
j Isa 43:14
k Isa 49:10
l Ps 32:8
48:18
m Dt 32:29
n Ps 119:165;
Isa 66:12
o Isa 45:8
48:19
p Ge 22:17
q Isa 56:5; 66:22
48:20
r Jer 50:8; 51:6,
45; Zec 2:6-7;
Rev 18:4
s Isa 49:13
t Isa 52:9; 63:9
48:21
u Isa 41:17
v Isa 30:25
w Ex 17:6;
Nu 20:11;
Ps 105:41;
Isa 35:6
48:22
x Isa 57:21

---

a14 Or *Chaldeans*; also in verse 20

The Servant of the Lord

49

Listen to me, you islands;
  hear this, you distant nations:
Before I was born[y] the Lord called[z] me;
  from my birth he has made mention of my name.
[2]He made my mouth like a sharpened sword,[a]
  in the shadow of his hand he hid me;
he made me into a polished arrow
  and concealed me in his quiver.
[3]He said to me, "You are my servant,[b]
  Israel, in whom I will display my splendor.[c]"
[4]But I said, "I have labored to no purpose;
  I have spent my strength in vain[d] and for nothing.
Yet what is due me is in the Lord's hand,
  and my reward[e] is with my God."

[5]And now the Lord says—
  he who formed me in the womb to be his servant
to bring Jacob back to him
  and gather Israel[f] to himself,
for I am honored[g] in the eyes of the Lord
  and my God has been my strength—
[6]he says:
"It is too small a thing for you to be my servant
  to restore the tribes of Jacob
  and bring back those of Israel I have kept.
I will also make you a light for the Gentiles,[h]
  that you may bring my salvation to the ends of the
    earth."[i]

[7]This is what the Lord says—
  the Redeemer and Holy One of Israel[j]—
to him who was despised[k] and abhorred by the nation,
  to the servant of rulers:
"Kings[l] will see you and rise up,
  princes will see and bow down,
because of the Lord, who is faithful,
  the Holy One of Israel, who has chosen you."

Restoration of Israel

[8]This is what the Lord says:

"In the time of my favor[m] I will answer you,
  and in the day of salvation I will help you;[n]
I will keep[o] you and will make you
  to be a covenant for the people,[p]
to restore the land[q]
  and to reassign its desolate inheritances,
[9]to say to the captives,[r] 'Come out,'
  and to those in darkness, 'Be free!'

"They will feed beside the roads
  and find pasture on every barren hill.[s]

49:1
y Isa 44:24;
46:3; Mt 1:20
z Isa 7:14; 9:6;
44:2; Jer 1:5;
Gal 1:15
49:2
a Isa 11:4;
Rev 1:16
49:3
b Zec 3:8
c Isa 44:23
49:4
d Isa 65:23
e Isa 35:4
49:5
f Isa 11:12
g Isa 43:4
49:6
h Lk 2:32
i Ac 13:47*
49:7
j Isa 48:17
k Ps 22:6; 69:7-9
l Isa 52:15
49:8
m Ps 69:13
n 2Co 6:2*
o Isa 26:3
p Isa 42:6
q Isa 44:26
49:9
r Isa 42:7; 61:1;
Lk 4:19
s Isa 41:18

¹⁰They will neither hunger nor thirst,ᵗ
    nor will the desert heat or the sun beat upon them.ᵘ
He who has compassionᵛ on them will guide them
    and lead them beside springsʷ of water.
¹¹I will turn all my mountains into roads,
    and my highwaysˣ will be raised up.ʸ
¹²See, they will come from afarᶻ—
    some from the north, some from the west,
    some from the region of Aswan.ᵃ "

¹³Shout for joy, O heavens;
    rejoice, O earth;
    burst into song, O mountains!ᵃ
For the LORD comfortsᵇ his people
    and will have compassion on his afflicted ones.

¹⁴But Zion said, "The LORD has forsaken me,
    the Lord has forgotten me."

¹⁵"Can a mother forget the baby at her breast
    and have no compassion on the child she has borne?
Though she may forget,
    I will not forget you!ᶜ
¹⁶See, I have engravedᵈ you on the palms of my hands;
    your wallsᵉ are ever before me.
¹⁷Your sons hasten back,
    and those who laid you wasteᶠ depart from you.
¹⁸Lift up your eyes and look around;
    all your sons gatherᵍ and come to you.
As surely as I live,ʰ" declares the LORD,
    "you will wearⁱ them all as ornaments;
    you will put them on, like a bride.

¹⁹"Though you were ruined and made desolateʲ
    and your land laid waste,ᵏ
now you will be too small for your people,ˡ
    and those who devoured you will be far away.
²⁰The children born during your bereavement
    will yet say in your hearing,
'This place is too small for us;
    give us more space to live in.'ᵐ
²¹Then you will say in your heart,
    'Who bore me these?
I was bereaved and barren;
    I was exiled and rejected.ⁿ
Who brought these up?
I was leftᵒ all alone,
    but these—where have they come from?' "

²²This is what the Sovereign LORD says:

    "See, I will beckon to the Gentiles,

49:10
ᵗ Isa 33:16
ᵘ Ps 121:6;
Rev 7:16
ᵛ Isa 14:1
ʷ Isa 35:7
49:11
ˣ Isa 11:16
ʸ Isa 40:4
49:12
ᶻ Isa 43:5-6
49:13
ᵃ Isa 44:23
ᵇ Isa 40:1
49:15
ᶜ Isa 44:21
49:16
ᵈ SS 8:6
ᵉ Ps 48:12-13;
Isa 62:6
49:17
ᶠ Isa 10:6
49:18
ᵍ Isa 43:5; 54:7;
Isa 60:4
ʰ Isa 45:23
ⁱ Isa 52:1
49:19
ʲ Isa 54:1,3
ᵏ Isa 5:6
ˡ Zec 10:10
49:20
ᵐ Isa 54:1-3
49:21
ⁿ Isa 5:13
ᵒ Isa 1:8

ᵃ12 Dead Sea Scrolls; Masoretic Text *Sinim*

I will lift up my banner[p] to the peoples;
  they will bring your sons in their arms
    and carry your daughters on their shoulders. [q]
[23]Kings[r] will be your foster fathers,
  and their queens your nursing mothers. [s]
They will bow down before you with their faces to the
    ground;
  they will lick the dust[t] at your feet.
Then you will know that I am the LORD;[u]
  those who hope in me will not be disappointed."

[24]Can plunder be taken from warriors, [v]
  or captives rescued from the fierce[a]?

[25]But this is what the LORD says:

"Yes, captives[w] will be taken from warriors, [x]
  and plunder retrieved from the fierce;
I will contend with those who contend with you,
  and your children I will save. [y]
[26]I will make your oppressors[z] eat[a] their own flesh;
  they will be drunk on their own blood, [b] as with wine.
Then all mankind will know[c]
  that I, the LORD, am your Savior,
  your Redeemer, the Mighty One of Jacob."

Israel's Sin and the Servant's Obedience

50 This is what the LORD says:

"Where is your mother's certificate of divorce[d]
  with which I sent her away?
Or to which of my creditors
  did I sell[e] you?
Because of your sins you were sold;[f]
  because of your transgressions your mother was sent
    away.
[2]When I came, why was there no one?
  When I called, why was there no one to answer?[g]
Was my arm too short[h] to ransom you?
  Do I lack the strength[i] to rescue you?
By a mere rebuke I dry up the sea,[j]
  I turn rivers into a desert;
their fish rot for lack of water
  and die of thirst.
[3]I clothe the sky with darkness
  and make sackcloth[k] its covering."

[4]The Sovereign LORD has given me an instructed
    tongue, [l]
  to know the word that sustains the weary. [m]
He wakens me morning by morning, [n]

49:22
p Isa 11:10
q Isa 60:4

49:23
r Isa 60:3,10-11
s Isa 60:16
t Ps 72:9
u Mic 7:17

49:24
v Mt 12:29;
Lk 11:21

49:25
w Isa 14:2
x Jer 50:33-34
y Isa 25:9; 35:4

49:26
z Isa 9:4
a Isa 9:20
b Rev 16:6
c Eze 39:7

50:1
d Dt 24:1;
Jer 3:8; Hos 2:2
e Ne 5:5;
Mt 18:25
f Dt 32:30;
Isa 52:3

50:2
g Isa 41:28
h Nu 11:23;
Isa 59:1
i Ge 18:14
j Ex 14:22;
Jos 3:16

50:3
k Rev 6:12

50:4
l Ex 4:12
m Mt 11:28
n Ps 5:3;
119:147; 143:8

---

[a]24 Dead Sea Scrolls, Vulgate and Syriac (see also Septuagint and verse 25); Masoretic Text
righteous

wakens my ear to listen like one being taught.
⁵The Sovereign LORD has opened my ears, °
    and I have not been rebellious;ᴾ
I have not drawn back.
⁶I offered my back to those who beatᑫ me,
    my cheeks to those who pulled out my beard;
I did not hide my face
    from mocking and spitting. ʳ
⁷Because the Sovereign LORD helpsˢ me,
    I will not be disgraced.
Therefore have I set my face like flint, ᵗ
    and I know I will not be put to shame.
⁸He who vindicates me is near.
    Who then will bring charges against me?ᵘ
    Let us face each other!ᵛ
Who is my accuser?
    Let him confront me!
⁹It is the Sovereign LORD who helpsʷ me.
    Who is he that will condemn me?
They will all wear out like a garment;
    the mothsˣ will eat them up.

¹⁰Who among you fears the LORD
    and obeys the word of his servant?ʸ
Let him who walks in the dark,
    who has no light,
trustᶻ in the name of the LORD
    and rely on his God.
¹¹But now, all you who light fires
    and provide yourselves with flaming torches, ᵃ
go, walk in the light of your firesᵇ
    and of the torches you have set ablaze.
This is what you shall receive from my hand:
    You will lie down in torment. ᶜ

Everlasting Salvation for Zion

51 "Listenᵈ to me, you who pursue righteousnessᵉ
    and who seek the LORD:
Look to the rock from which you were cut
    and to the quarry from which you were hewn;
²look to Abraham,ᶠ your father,
    and to Sarah, who gave you birth.
When I called him he was but one,
    and I blessed him and made him many. ᵍ
³The LORD *will* surely comfortʰ Zion
    and will look with compassion on all her ruins;ⁱ
he will make her deserts like Eden, ʲ
    her wastelands like the garden of the LORD.
Joy and gladnessᵏ will be found in her,
    thanksgiving and the sound of singing.

⁴"Listen to me, my people;ˡ

50:5
oIsa 35:5
pMt 26:39;
Jn 8:29; 14:31;
15:10;
Ac 26:19;
Heb 5:8
50:6
qIsa 53:5;
Mt 27:30;
Mk 14:65;
15:19; Lk 22:63
rLa 3:30;
Mt 26:67
50:7
sIsa 42:1
tEze 3:8-9
50:8
uIsa 43:26;
Ro 8:32-34
vIsa 41:1
50:9
wIsa 41:10
xJob 13:28;
Isa 51:8
50:10
yIsa 49:3
zIsa 26:4
50:11
aPr 26:18
bJas 3:6
cIsa 65:13-15
51:1
dIsa 46:3
ever 7;
Ps 94:15;
Ro 9:30-31
51:2
fIsa 29:22;
Ro 4:16;
Heb 11:11
gGe 12:2
51:3
hIsa 40:1
iIsa 52:9
jGe 2:8
kIsa 25:9; 66:10
51:4
lPs 50:7

hear me, my nation:
The law will go out from me;
my justice^m will become a light to the nations.ⁿ

5My righteousness draws near speedily,
my salvation is on the way,^o
and my arm^p will bring justice to the nations.
The islands will look to me
and wait in hope for my arm.

6Lift up your eyes to the heavens,
look at the earth beneath;
the heavens will vanish like smoke,^q
the earth will wear out like a garment^r
and its inhabitants die like flies.
But my salvation will last forever,
my righteousness will never fail.

7"Hear me, you who know what is right,^s
you people who have my law in your hearts:^t
Do not fear the reproach of men
or be terrified by their insults.^u

8For the moth will eat them up like a garment;^v
the worm will devour them like wool.
But my righteousness will last forever,^w
my salvation through all generations."

9Awake, awake! Clothe yourself with strength,^x
O arm of the Lord;
awake, as in days gone by,
as in generations of old.^y
Was it not you who cut Rahab to pieces,
who pierced that monster^z through?

10Was it not you who dried up the sea,^a
the waters of the great deep,
who made a road in the depths of the sea
so that the redeemed might cross over?

11The ransomed^b of the Lord will return.
They will enter Zion with singing;
everlasting joy will crown their heads.
Gladness and joy^c will overtake them,
and sorrow and sighing will flee away.^d

12"I, even I, am he who comforts^e you.
Who are you that you fear mortal men,^f
the sons of men, who are but grass,^g

13that you forget^h the Lord your Maker,ⁱ
who stretched out the heavens^j
and laid the foundations of the earth,
that you live in constant terror^k every day
because of the wrath of the oppressor,
who *is bent on destruction?*
For where is the wrath of the oppressor?

14   The cowering prisoners will soon be set free;
they will not die in their dungeon,

51:4
m Isa 2:4
n Isa 42:4,6
51:5
o Isa 46:13
p Isa 40:10;
63:1,5
51:6
q Mt 24:35;
2Pe 3:10
r Ps 102:25-26
51:7
s ver 1 t Ps 37:31
u Mt 5:11;
Ac 5:41
51:8
v Isa 50:9 w ver 6
51:9
x Isa 52:1
y Dt 4:34
z Ps 74:13
51:10
a Ex 14:22
51:11
b Isa 35:9
c Jer 33:11
d Rev 7:17
51:12
e 2Co 1:4
f Ps 118:6;
Isa 2:22
g Isa 40:6-7;
1Pe 1:24
51:13
h Isa 17:10
i Isa 45:11
j Ps 104:2;
Isa 48:13
k Isa 7:4

nor will they lack bread. [1]
¹⁵For I am the Lord your God,
  who churns up the sea^m so that its waves roar—
  the Lord Almighty is his name.
¹⁶I have put my words in your mouthⁿ
  and covered you with the shadow of my hand^o—
I who set the heavens in place,
  who laid the foundations of the earth,
  and who say to Zion, 'You are my people.' "

The Cup of the Lord's Wrath

¹⁷Awake, awake!^p
  Rise up, O Jerusalem,
you who have drunk from the hand of the Lord
  the cup of his wrath, ^q
you who have drained to its dregs
  the goblet that makes men stagger. ^r
¹⁸Of all the sons^s she bore
  there was none to guide her;^t
of all the sons she reared
  there was none to take her by the hand.
¹⁹These double calamities^u have come upon you—
  who can comfort you?—
ruin and destruction, famine^v and sword—
  who can^a console you?
²⁰Your sons have fainted;
  they lie at the head of every street, ^w
  like antelope caught in a net.
They are filled with the wrath of the Lord
  and the rebuke of your God.

²¹Therefore hear this, you afflicted one,
  made drunk, ^x but not with wine.
²²This is what your Sovereign Lord says,
  your God, who defends^y his people:
"See, I have taken out of your hand
  the cup^z that made you stagger;
from that cup, the goblet of my wrath,
  you will never drink again.
²³I will put it into the hands of your tormentors, ^a
  who said to you,
  'Fall prostrate^b that we may walk^c over you.'
And you made your back like the ground,
  like a street to be walked over."

52 Awake, awake, ^d O Zion,
  clothe yourself with strength. ^e
Put on your garments of splendor, ^f
  O Jerusalem, the holy city. ^g
The uncircumcised and defiled

51:14
l Isa 49:10
51:15
m Jer 31:35
51:16
n Dt 18:18;
Isa 59:21
o Ex 33:22
51:17
p Isa 52:1
q Job 21:20;
Rev 14:10;
16:19 r Ps 60:3
51:18
s Ps 88:18
t Isa 49:21
51:19
u Isa 47:9
v Isa 14:30
51:20
w Isa 5:25;
Jer 14:16
51:21
x ver 17;
Isa 29:9
51:22
y Isa 49:25
z ver 17
51:23
a Isa 49:26;
Jer 25:15-17,26,
28; 49:12
b Zec 12:2
c Jos 10:24
52:1
d Isa 51:17
e Isa 51:9
f Ex 28:2,40;
Ps 110:3;
Zec 3:4
g Ne 11:1;
Mt 4:5;
Rev 21:2

^a19 Dead Sea Scrolls, Septuagint, Vulgate and Syriac; Masoretic Text / *how can I*

will not enter you again. [h]
2Shake off your dust; [i]
  rise up, sit enthroned, O Jerusalem.
Free yourself from the chains on your neck,
  O captive Daughter of Zion.

3For this is what the LORD says:

  "You were sold for nothing, [j]
    and without money [k] you will be redeemed."

4For this is what the Sovereign LORD says:

  "At first my people went down to Egypt [l] to live;
    lately, Assyria has oppressed them.

5"And now what do I have here?" declares the LORD.

  "For my people have been taken away for nothing,
    and those who rule them mock, [a] "
                                        declares the LORD.

  "And all day long
    my name is constantly blasphemed. [m]
6Therefore my people will know [n] my name;
    therefore in that day they will know
  that it is I who foretold it.
    Yes, it is I."

7How beautiful on the mountains
  are the feet of those who bring good news, [o]
who proclaim peace, [p]
  who bring good tidings,
  who proclaim salvation,
who say to Zion,
  "Your God reigns!" [q]
8Listen! Your watchmen [r] lift up their voices;
  together they shout for joy.
When the LORD returns to Zion,
  they will see it with their own eyes.
9Burst into songs of joy [s] together,
  you ruins [t] of Jerusalem,
for the LORD has comforted his people,
  he has redeemed Jerusalem. [u]
10The LORD will lay bare his holy arm
  in the sight of all the nations, [v]
and all the ends of the earth will see
  the salvation [w] of our God.

11Depart, [x] depart, go out from there!
  Touch no unclean thing! [y]
Come out from it and be pure, [z]
  you who carry the vessels of the LORD.
12But you will not leave in haste [a]
  or go in flight;

52:1
hNa 1:15;
Rev 21:27
52:2
iIsa 29:4
52:3
jPs 44:12
kIsa 45:13
52:4
lGe 46:6
52:5
mEze 36:20;
Ro 2:24*
52:6
nIsa 49:23
52:7
oIsa 40:9;
Ro 10:15*
pNa 1:15;
Eph 6:15
qPs 93:1
52:8
rIsa 62:6
52:9
sPs 98:4
tIsa 51:3
uIsa 48:20
52:10
vIsa 66:18
wPs 98:2-3;
Lk 3:6
52:11
xIsa 48:20
yIsa 1:16;
2Co 6:17*
z2Ti 2:19
52:12
aEx 12:11

---

a5 Dead Sea Scrolls and Vulgate; Masoretic Text *wail*

for the Lord will go before you,[b]
the God of Israel will be your rear guard.[c]

The Suffering and Glory of the Servant

[13]See, my servant[d] will act wisely[a];
he will be raised and lifted up and highly exalted.[e]
[14]Just as there were many who were appalled at him[b]—
his appearance was so disfigured beyond that of any
man
and his form marred beyond human likeness—
[15]so will he sprinkle many nations,[c]
and kings will shut their mouths because of him.
For what they were not told, they will see,
and what they have not heard, they will understand.[f]

53 Who has believed our message[g]
and to whom has the arm of the Lord been revealed?[h]
[2]He grew up before him like a tender shoot,
and like a root out of dry ground.
He had no beauty or majesty to attract us to him,
nothing in his appearance[i] that we should desire him.
[3]He was despised and rejected by men,
a man of sorrows, and familiar with suffering.[j]
Like one from whom men hide their faces
he was despised,[k] and we esteemed him not.

[4]Surely he took up our infirmities
and carried our sorrows,[l]
yet we considered him stricken by God,[m]
smitten by him, and afflicted.
[5]But he was pierced for our transgressions,[n]
he was crushed for our iniquities;
the punishment that brought us peace was upon him,
and by his wounds we are healed.[o]
[6]We all, like sheep, have gone astray,
each of us has turned to his own way;
and the Lord has laid on him
the iniquity of us all.

[7]He was oppressed and afflicted,
yet he did not open his mouth;[p]
he was led like a lamb to the slaughter,
and as a sheep before her shearers is silent,
so he did not open his mouth.
[8]By oppression[d] and judgment he was taken away.
And who can speak of his descendants?
For he was cut off from the land of the living;[q]
for the transgression[r] of my people he was stricken.[e]
[9]He was assigned a grave with the wicked,
and with the rich[s] in his death,

52:12
b Mic 2:13
c Ex 14:19
52:13
d Isa 42:1
e Isa 57:15;
Php 2:9
52:15
f Ro 15:21*;
Eph 3:4-5
53:1
g Ro 10:16*
h Jn 12:38*
53:2
i Isa 52:14
53:3
j ver 4,10;
Lk 18:31-33
k Ps 22:6;
Jn 1:10-11
53:4
l Mt 8:17*
m Jn 19:7
53:5
n Ro 4:25;
1Co 15:3;
Heb 9:28
o 1Pe 2:24-25
53:7
p Mk 14:61
53:8
q Da 9:26;
Ac 8:32-33*
r ver 12
53:9
s Mt 27:57-60

---

a13 Or will prosper   b14 Hebrew you   c15 Hebrew; Septuagint so will many nations marvel at
him   d8 Or From arrest   e8 Or away. / Yet who of his generation considered / that he was cut off
from the land of the living / for the transgression of my people, / to whom the blow was due?

though he had done no violence, [t]
   nor was any deceit in his mouth. [u]

[10]Yet it was the LORD's will [v] to crush [w] him and cause him
     to suffer, [x]
   and though the LORD makes [a] his life a guilt offering,
he will see his offspring [y] and prolong his days,
   and the will of the LORD will prosper in his hand.
[11]After the suffering [z] of his soul,
   he will see the light ₎of life₎ [b] and be satisfied [c];
by his knowledge [d] my righteous servant will justify [a]
     many,
   and he will bear their iniquities.
[12]Therefore I will give him a portion among the great, [e] [b]
   and he will divide the spoils with the strong, [f]
because he poured out his life unto death, [c]
   and was numbered with the transgressors. [d]
For he bore the sin of many,
   and made intercession for the transgressors.

The Future Glory of Zion

54 "Sing, O barren woman,
   you who never bore a child;
burst into song, shout for joy,
   you who were never in labor;
because more are the children [e] of the desolate woman
   than of her who has a husband, [f] "
                    says the LORD.

[2]"Enlarge the place of your tent, [g]
   stretch your tent curtains wide,
   do not hold back;
lengthen your cords,
   strengthen your stakes. [h]
[3]For you will spread out to the right and to the left;
   your descendants will dispossess nations
   and settle in their desolate [i] cities.

[4]"Do not be afraid; you will not suffer shame.
   Do not fear disgrace; you will not be humiliated.
You will forget the shame of your youth
   and remember no more the reproach [j] of your
         widowhood.
[5]For your Maker is your husband [k]—
   the LORD Almighty is his name—
the Holy One of Israel is your Redeemer; [l]
   he is called the God of all the earth. [m]
[6]The LORD will call you back [n]

53:9
t Isa 42:1-3
u 1Pe 2:22*
53:10
v Isa 46:10
w ver 5 x ver 3
y Ps 22:30
53:11
z Jn 10:14-18
a Ro 5:18-19
53:12
b Php 2:9
c Mt 26:28,38,
39,42
d Mk 15:27*;
Lk 22:37*;
23:32
54:1
e Isa 49:20
f 1Sa 2:5;
Gal 4:27*
54:2
g Isa 49:19-20
h Ex 35:18;
39:40
54:3
i Isa 49:19
54:4
j Isa 51:7
54:5
k Jer 3:14
l Isa 48:17
m Isa 6:3
54:6
n Isa 49:14-21

*a10 Hebrew though you make   b11 Dead Sea Scrolls (see also Septuagint); Masoretic Text does
not have the light ₎of life₎.   c11 Or (with Masoretic Text) 11He will see the result of the suffering of his
soul / and be satisfied   d11 Or by knowledge of him   e12 Or many   f12 Or numerous*

as if you were a wife deserted° and distressed in
    spirit—
a wife who married young,
    only to be rejected," says your God.
7"For a brief moment^p I abandoned you,
    but with deep compassion I will bring you back.^q
8In a surge of anger^r
    I hid my face from you for a moment,
but with everlasting kindness^s
    I will have compassion on you,"
    says the LORD your Redeemer.

9"To me this is like the days of Noah,
    when I swore that the waters of Noah would
        never again cover the earth.^t
So now I have sworn not to be angry^u with you,
    never to rebuke you again.
10Though the mountains be shaken^v
    and the hills be removed,
yet my unfailing love for you will not be shaken^w
    nor my covenant^x of peace be removed,"
    says the LORD, who has compassion^y on you.

11"O afflicted^z city, lashed by storms^a and not
        comforted,^b
I will build you with stones of turquoise,^{a c}
    your foundations^d with sapphires.^b
12I will make your battlements of rubies,
    your gates of sparkling jewels,
    and all your walls of precious stones.
13All your sons will be taught by the LORD,^e
    and great will be your children's peace.^f
14In righteousness you will be established:
Tyranny^g will be far from you;
    you will have nothing to fear.
Terror will be far removed;
    it will not come near you.
15If anyone does attack you, it will not be my doing;
    whoever attacks you will surrender^h to you.

16"See, it is I who created the blacksmith
    who fans the coals into flame
    and forges a weapon fit for its work.
And it is I who have created the destroyer to work
        havoc;
17   no weapon forged against you will prevail,ⁱ
    and you will refute^j every tongue that accuses you.
This is the heritage of the servants of the LORD,
    and this is their vindication from me,"
                   declares the LORD.

54:6
°Isa 50:1-2;
62:4,12
54:7
pIsa 26:20
qIsa 49:18
54:8
rIsa 60:10
sver 10
54:9
tGe 8:21
uIsa 12:1
54:10
vPs 46:2
wIsa 51:6
xPs 89:34 yver 8
54:11
zIsa 14:32
aIsa 28:2; 29:6
bIsa 51:19
c1Ch 29:2;
Rev 21:18
dIsa 28:16;
Rev 21:19-20
54:13
eJn 6:45*
fIsa 48:18
54:14
gIsa 9:4
54:15
hIsa 41:11-16
54:17
iIsa 29:8
jIsa 45:24-25

---

^a11 The meaning of the Hebrew for this word is uncertain.   ^b11 Or *lapis lazuli*

Invitation to the Thirsty

55 "Come, all you who are thirsty,[k]
　　come to the waters;
and you who have no money,
　　come, buy[1] and eat!
Come, buy wine and milk[m]
　　without money and without cost.[n]
[2]Why spend money on what is not bread,
　　and your labor on what does not satisfy?[o]
Listen, listen to me, and eat what is good,[p]
　　and your soul will delight in the richest of fare.
[3]Give ear and come to me;
　　hear me, that your soul may live.[q]
I will make an everlasting covenant[r] with you,
　　my faithful love[s] promised to David.[t]
[4]See, I have made him a witness to the peoples,
　　a leader and commander[u] of the peoples.
[5]Surely you will summon nations[v] you know not,
　　and nations that do not know you will hasten to you,
because of the LORD your God,
　　the Holy One of Israel,
　　for he has endowed you with splendor."[w]

[6]Seek the LORD while he may be found;[x]
　　call[y] on him while he is near.
[7]Let the wicked forsake his way
　　and the evil man his thoughts.[z]
Let him turn[a] to the LORD, and he will have mercy[b] on
　　him,
　　and to our God, for he will freely pardon.[c]

[8]"For my thoughts are not your thoughts,
　　neither are your ways my ways,"[d]
　　　　　　　　　　　　　　　　　　declares the LORD.
[9]"As the heavens are higher than the earth,[e]
　　so are my ways higher than your ways
　　and my thoughts than your thoughts.
[10]As the rain[f] and the snow
　　come down from heaven,
and do not return to it
　　without watering the earth
and making it bud and flourish,
　　so that it yields seed for the sower and bread for the
　　　　eater,[g]
[11]so is my word that goes out from my mouth:
　　It will not return to me empty,[h]
but will accomplish what I desire
　　and achieve the purpose[i] for which I sent it.
[12]You will go out in joy
　　and be led forth in peace;[j]
the mountains and hills
　　will burst into song before you,

55:1
k Jn 4:14; 7:37
1 La 5:4;
Mt 13:44;
Rev 3:18
m SS 5:1
n Hos 14:4;
Mt 10:8;
Rev 21:6
55:2
o Ps 22:26;
Ecc 6:2;
Hos 8:7
p Isa 1:19
55:3
q Lev 18:5;
Ro 10:5
r Isa 61:8
s Isa 54:8
t Ac 13:34*
55:4
u Jer 30:9;
Eze 34:23-24
55:5
v Isa 49:6
w Isa 60:9
55:6
x Ps 32:6;
Isa 49:8;
2Co 6:1-2
y Isa 65:24
55:7
z Isa 32:7; 59:7
a Isa 44:22
b Isa 54:10
c Isa 1:18; 40:2
55:8
d Isa 53:6
55:9
e Ps 103:11
55:10
f Isa 30:23
g 2Co 9:10
55:11
h Isa 45:23
i Isa 44:26
55:12
j Isa 54:10,13

and all the trees[k] of the field
    will clap their hands.[l]
[13]Instead of the thornbush will grow the pine tree,
    and instead of briers[m] the myrtle[n] will grow.
This will be for the LORD's renown,[o]
    for an everlasting sign,
    which will not be destroyed."

Salvation for Others

56 This is what the LORD says:

    "Maintain justice[p]
      and do what is right,
for my salvation[q] is close at hand
    and my righteousness will soon be revealed.
[2]Blessed[r] is the man who does this,
    the man who holds it fast,
who keeps the Sabbath[s] without desecrating it,
    and keeps his hand from doing any evil."

[3]Let no foreigner who has bound himself to the LORD
    say,
    "The LORD will surely exclude me from his people."
And let not any eunuch[t] complain,
    "I am only a dry tree."

[4]For this is what the LORD says:

    "To the eunuchs who keep my Sabbaths,
    who choose what pleases me
    and hold fast to my covenant—
[5]to them I will give within my temple and its walls[u]
    a memorial and a name
    better than sons and daughters;
I will give them an everlasting name
    that will not be cut off.[v]
[6]And foreigners who bind themselves to the LORD
    to serve[w] him,
to love the name of the LORD,
    and to worship him,
all who keep the Sabbath[x] without desecrating it
    and who hold fast to my covenant—
[7]these I will bring to my holy mountain[y]
    and give them joy in my house of prayer.
Their burnt offerings and sacrifices[z]
    will be accepted on my altar;
for my house will be called
    a house of prayer for all nations.[a]"[b]
[8]The Sovereign LORD declares—
    he who gathers the exiles of Israel:
"I will gather[c] still others to them
    besides those already gathered."

55:12
k 1Ch 16:33
l Ps 98:8
55:13
m Isa 5:6
n Isa 41:19
o Isa 63:12
56:1
p Isa 1:17
q Ps 85:9
56:2
r Ps 119:2
s Ex 20:8,10;
Isa 58:13
56:3
t Jer 38:7 *fn*;
Ac 8:27
56:5
u Isa 26:1; 60:18
v Isa 48:19;
55:13
56:6
w Isa 60:7,10;
61:5 x ver 2,4
56:7
y Isa 2:2
z Ro 12:1;
Heb 13:15
a Mt 21:13*;
Lk 19:46*
b Mk 11:17*
56:8
c Isa 11:12;
60:3-11;
Jn 10:16

God's Accusation Against the Wicked

⁹Come, all you beasts of the field, ᵈ
    come and devour, all you beasts of the forest!
¹⁰Israel's watchmenᵉ are blind,
    they all lack knowledge;
they are all mute dogs,
    they cannot bark;
they lie around and dream,
    they love to sleep. ᶠ
¹¹They are dogs with mighty appetites;
    they never have enough.
They are shepherdsᵍ who lack understanding;ʰ
    they all turn to their own way,
    each seeks his own gain. ⁱ
¹²"Come," each one cries, "let me get wine!
    Let us drink our fill of beer!
And tomorrow will be like today,
    or even far better."ʲ

57

The righteous perish, ᵏ
    and no one ponders it in his heart;ˡ
devout men are taken away,
    and no one understands
that the righteous are taken away
    to be spared from evil. ᵐ
²Those who walk uprightlyⁿ
    enter into peace;
    they find rest as they lie in death.

³"But you—come here, you sons of a sorceress,
    you offspring of adulterersᵒ and prostitutes!ᵖ
⁴Whom are you mocking?
    At whom do you sneer
    and stick out your tongue?
Are you not a brood of rebels,
    the offspring of liars?
⁵You burn with lust among the oaks
    and under every spreading tree;�q
you sacrifice your childrenʳ in the ravines
    and under the overhanging crags.
⁶⌊The idols⌋ˢ among the smooth stones of the ravines are
        your portion;
    they, they are your lot.
Yes, to them you have poured out drink offeringsᵗ
    and offered grain offerings.
    In the light of these things, should I relent?ᵘ
⁷You have made your bed on a high and lofty hill;ᵛ
    there you went up to offer your sacrifices.
⁸Behind your doors and your doorposts
    you have put your pagan symbols.
Forsaking me, you uncovered your bed,
    you climbed into it and opened it wide;

56:9
dIsa 18:6;
Jer 12:9
56:10
eEze 3:17
fNa 3:18
56:11
gEze 34:2
hIsa 1:3
iIsa 57:17;
Eze 13:19;
Mic 3:11
56:12
jPs 10:6;
Lk 12:18-19
57:1
kPs 12:1
lIsa 42:25
m2Ki 22:20
57:2
nIsa 26:7
57:3
oMt 16:4
pIsa 1:21
57:5
q2Ki 16:4
rLev 18:21;
Ps 106:37-38;
Eze 16:20
57:6
sJer 3:9
tJer 7:18
uJer 5:9,29; 9:9
57:7
vJer 3:6;
Eze 16:16

you made a pact with those whose beds you love,ʷ
   and you looked on their nakedness.ˣ
⁹You went to Molechᵃ with olive oil
   and increased your perfumes.
You sent your ambassadorsᵇʸ far away;
   you descended to the graveᶜ itself!
¹⁰You were wearied by all your ways,
   but you would not say, 'It is hopeless.'ᶻ
You found renewal of your strength,
   and so you did not faint.

¹¹"Whom have you so dreaded and fearedᵃ
   that you have been false to me,
and have neither rememberedᵇ me
   nor pondered this in your hearts?
Is it not because I have long been silentᶜ
   that you do not fear me?
¹²I will expose your righteousness and your works,ᵈ
   and they will not benefit you.
¹³When you cry outᵉ for help,
   let your collection of idols save you!
The wind will carry all of them off,
   a mere breath will blow them away.
But the man who makes me his refuge
   will inherit the landᶠ
   and possess my holy mountain."ᵍ

Comfort for the Contrite

¹⁴And it will be said:

   "Build up, build up, prepare the road!
   Remove the obstacles out of the way of my people."ʰ
¹⁵For this is what the high and loftyⁱ One says—
   he who lives forever,ʲ whose name is holy:
"I live in a high and holy place,
   but also with him who is contriteᵏ and lowly in
      spirit,ˡ
to revive the spirit of the lowly
   and to revive the heart of the contrite.ᵐ
¹⁶I will not accuse forever,
   nor will I always be angry,ⁿ
for then the spirit of man would grow faint before me—
   the breath of man that I have created.
¹⁷I was enraged by his sinful greed;ᵒ
   I punished him, and hid my face in anger,
   yet he kept on in his willful ways.ᵖ
¹⁸I have seen his ways, but I will heal�q him;
   I will guide him and restore comfortʳ to him,
¹⁹   creating praise on the lipsˢ of the mourners in Israel.
Peace, peace,ᵗ to those far and near,"ᵘ
   says the Lᴏʀᴅ. "And I will heal them."

57:8
wEze 16:26;
23:7 xEze 23:18
57:9
yEze 23:16,40
57:10
zJer 2:25; 18:12
57:11
aPr 29:25
bJer 2:32; 3:21
cPs 50:21
57:12
dIsa 29:15;
Mic 3:2-4,8
57:13
eJer 22:20;
30:15 fPs 37:9
gIsa 65:9-11
57:14
hIsa 62:10;
Jer 18:15
57:15
iIsa 52:13
jDt 33:27
kPs 147:3
lPs 34:18;
51:17; Isa 66:2
mIsa 61:1
57:16
nPs 85:5;
103:9; Mic 7:18
57:17
oIsa 56:11
pIsa 1:4
57:18
qIsa 30:26
rIsa 61:1-3
57:19
sIsa 6:7;
Heb 13:15
tEph 2:17
uAc 2:39

ᵃ9 Or *to the king*   ᵇ9 Or *idols*   ᶜ9 Hebrew *Sheol*

²⁰But the wicked^v are like the tossing sea,
    which cannot rest,
    whose waves cast up mire and mud.
²¹"There is no peace,"^w says my God, "for the wicked."^x

True Fasting

58 "Shout it aloud,^y do not hold back.
    Raise your voice like a trumpet.
Declare to my people their rebellion^z
    and to the house of Jacob their sins.
²For day after day they seek^a me out;
    they seem eager to know my ways,
as if they were a nation that does what is right
    and has not forsaken the commands of its God.
They ask me for just decisions
    and seem eager for God to come near^b them.
³'Why have we fasted,'^c they say,
    'and you have not seen it?
Why have we humbled ourselves,
    and you have not noticed?'^d

"Yet on the day of your fasting, you do as you please^e
    and exploit all your workers.
⁴Your fasting ends in quarreling and strife,^f
    and in striking each other with wicked fists.
You cannot fast as you do today
    and expect your voice to be heard^g on high.
⁵Is this the kind of fast^h I have chosen,
    only a day for a man to humbleⁱ himself?
Is it only for bowing one's head like a reed
    and for lying on sackcloth and ashes?^j
Is that what you call a fast,
    a day acceptable to the LORD?

⁶"Is not this the kind of fasting I have chosen:
to loose the chains of injustice^k
    and untie the cords of the yoke,
to set the oppressed^l free
    and break every yoke?
⁷Is it not to share your food with the hungry^m
    and to provide the poor wanderer with shelterⁿ—
when you see the naked, to clothe^o him,
    and not to turn away from your own flesh and
        blood?^p
⁸Then your light will break forth like the dawn,^q
    and your healing^r will quickly appear;
then your righteousness^a will go before you,
    and the glory of the LORD will be your rear guard.^s
⁹Then you will call,^t and the LORD will answer;
    you will cry for help, and he will say: Here am I.

57:20
vJob 18:5-21
57:21
wIsa 59:8
xIsa 48:22
58:1
yIsa 40:6
zIsa 48:8
58:2
aIsa 48:1;
Tit 1:16; Jas 4:8
bIsa 29:13
58:3
cLev 16:29
dMal 3:14
eIsa 22:13;
Zec 7:5-6
58:4
f1Ki 21:9-13;
Isa 59:6
gIsa 59:2
58:5
hZec 7:5
i1Ki 21:27
jJob 2:8
58:6
kNe 5:10-11
lJer 34:9
58:7
mEze 18:16;
Lk 3:11
nIsa 16:4;
Heb 13:2
oJob 31:19-20;
Mt 25:36
pGe 29:14;
Lk 10:31-32
58:8
qJob 11:17
rIsa 30:26
sEx 14:19
58:9
tPs 50:15

---

^a8 Or *your righteous One*

"If you do away with the yoke of oppression,
  with the pointing finger[u] and malicious talk,[v]
[10]and if you spend yourselves in behalf of the hungry
  and satisfy the needs of the oppressed,[w]
then your light[x] will rise in the darkness,
  and your night will become like the noonday.[y]
[11]The LORD will guide you always;
  he will satisfy your needs[z] in a sun-scorched land
  and will strengthen your frame.
You will be like a well-watered garden,[a]
  like a spring[b] whose waters never fail.
[12]Your people will rebuild the ancient ruins[c]
  and will raise up the age-old foundations;[d]
you will be called Repairer of Broken Walls,
  Restorer of Streets with Dwellings.

[13]"If you keep your feet from breaking the Sabbath[e]
  and from doing as you please on my holy day,
if you call the Sabbath a delight[f]
  and the LORD's holy day honorable,
and if you honor it by not going your own way
  and not doing as you please or speaking idle words,
[14]then you will find your joy[g] in the LORD,
  and I will cause you to ride on the heights[h] of the land
  and to feast on the inheritance of your father Jacob."
          The mouth of the LORD has spoken.[i]

Sin, Confession and Redemption

59 Surely the arm of the LORD is not too short[j] to save,
  nor his ear too dull to hear.[k]
[2]But your iniquities have separated
  you from your God;
your sins have hidden his face from you,
  so that he will not hear.[l]
[3]For your hands are stained with blood,[m]
  your fingers with guilt.
Your lips have spoken lies,
  and your tongue mutters wicked things.
[4]No one calls for justice;
  no one pleads his case with integrity.
They rely on empty arguments and speak lies;
  they conceive trouble and give birth to evil.[n]
[5]They hatch the eggs of vipers
  and spin a spider's web.[o]
Whoever eats their eggs will die,
  and when one is broken, an adder is hatched.
[6]Their cobwebs are useless for clothing;
  they cannot cover themselves with what they make.[p]
Their deeds are evil deeds,
  and acts of violence[q] are in their hands.
[7]Their feet rush into sin;
  they are swift to shed innocent blood.[r]

58:9
u Pr 6:13
v Ps 12:2;
  Isa 59:13
58:10
w Dt 15:7-8
x Isa 42:16
y Job 11:17
58:11
z Ps 107:9
a SS 4:15
b Jn 4:14
58:12
c Isa 49:8
d Isa 44:28
58:13
e Isa 56:2
f Ps 84:2,10
58:14
g Job 22:26
h Dt 32:13
i Isa 1:20
59:1
j Nu 11:23;
  Isa 50:2
k Isa 58:9; 65:24
59:2
l Isa 1:15; 58:4
59:3
m Isa 1:15
59:4
n Job 15:35;
  Ps 7:14
59:5
o Job 8:14
59:6
p Isa 28:20
q Isa 58:4
59:7
r Pr 6:17

Their thoughts are evil thoughts;[s]
 ruin and destruction mark their ways.[t]
[8]The way of peace they do not know;
 there is no justice in their paths.
They have turned them into crooked roads;
 no one who walks in them will know peace.[u]

[9]So justice is far from us,
 and righteousness does not reach us.
We look for light, but all is darkness;[v]
 for brightness, but we walk in deep shadows.
[10]Like the blind[w] we grope along the wall,
 feeling our way like men without eyes.
At midday we stumble[x] as if it were twilight;
 among the strong, we are like the dead.[y]
[11]We all growl like bears;
 we moan mournfully like doves.[z]
We look for justice, but find none;
 for deliverance, but it is far away.

[12]For our offenses[a] are many in your sight,
 and our sins testify[b] against us.
Our offenses are ever with us,
 and we acknowledge our iniquities:
[13]rebellion and treachery against the LORD,
 turning our backs[c] on our God,
fomenting oppression[d] and revolt,
 uttering lies[e] our hearts have conceived.
[14]So justice is driven back,
 and righteousness[f] stands at a distance;
truth[g] has stumbled in the streets,
 honesty cannot enter.
[15]Truth is nowhere to be found,
 and whoever shuns evil becomes a prey.

The LORD looked and was displeased
 that there was no justice.
[16]He saw that there was no one,[h]
 he was appalled that there was no one to intervene;
so his own arm worked salvation[i] for him,
 and his own righteousness sustained him.
[17]He put on righteousness as his breastplate,[j]
 and the helmet[k] of salvation on his head;
he put on the garments[l] of vengeance
 and wrapped himself in zeal[m] as in a cloak.
[18]According to what they have done,
 so will he repay
wrath to his enemies
 and retribution to his foes;
 he will repay the islands their due.
[19]From the west,[n] men will fear the name of the LORD,
 and from the rising of the sun,[o] they will revere his
 glory.

59:7
sMk 7:21-22
tRo 3:15-17*
59:8
uIsa 57:21;
 Lk 1:79
59:9
vIsa 5:30; 8:20
59:10
wDt 28:29
xIsa 8:15
yLa 3:6
59:11
zIsa 38:14;
 Eze 7:16
59:12
aEzr 9:6
bIsa 3:9
59:13
cPr 30:9;
 Mt 10:33;
Tit 1:16 dIsa 5:7
eMk 7:21-22
59:14
fIsa 1:21
gIsa 48:1
59:16
hIsa 41:28
iPs 98:1;
 Isa 63:5
59:17
jEph 6:14
kEph 6:17;
 1Th 5:8
lIsa 63:3
mIsa 9:7
59:19
nIsa 49:12
oPs 113:3

For he will come like a pent-up flood
    that the breath of the LORD drives along. *a*

20"The Redeemer will come to Zion,
    to those in Jacob who repent of their sins," *p*
                               declares the LORD.

21"As for me, this is my covenant with them," says the LORD. "My Spirit, *q* who is on you, and my words that I have put in your mouth will not depart from your mouth, or from the mouths of your children, or from the mouths of their descendants from this time on and forever," says the LORD.

The Glory of Zion

60   "Arise, *r* shine, for your light *s* has come,
    and the glory of the LORD rises upon you.
2See, darkness covers the earth
    and thick darkness *t* is over the peoples,
but the LORD rises upon you
    and his glory appears over you.
3Nations *u* will come to your light,
    and kings *v* to the brightness of your dawn.

4"Lift up your eyes and look about you:
    All assemble *w* and come to you;
your sons come from afar,
    and your daughters *x* are carried on the arm. *y*
5Then you will look and be radiant,
    your heart will throb and swell with joy;
the wealth on the seas will be brought to you,
    to you the riches of the nations will come.
6Herds of camels will cover your land,
    young camels of Midian *z* and Ephah. *a*
And all from Sheba *b* will come,
    bearing gold and incense *c*
    and proclaiming the praise *d* of the LORD.
7All Kedar's *e* flocks will be gathered to you,
    the rams of Nebaioth will serve you;
they will be accepted as offerings on my altar,
    and I will adorn my glorious temple. *f*

8"Who are these *g* that fly along like clouds,
    like doves to their nests?
9Surely the islands *h* look to me;
    in the lead are the ships of Tarshish, *b i*
bringing *j* your sons from afar,
    with their silver and gold,
to the honor of the LORD your God,
    the Holy One of Israel,
    for he has endowed you with splendor. *k*

---

a19 Or When the enemy comes in like a flood, / the Spirit of the LORD will put him to flight   *b9 Or the trading ships*

59:20
pAc 2:38-39;
Ro 11:26-27*
59:21
qIsa 11:2; 44:3
60:1
rIsa 52:2
sEph 5:14
60:2
tJer 13:16;
Col 1:13
60:3
uIsa 45:14;
Rev 21:24
vIsa 49:23
60:4
wIsa 11:12
xIsa 43:6
yIsa 49:20-22
60:6
zGe 25:2
aGe 25:4
bPs 72:10
cIsa 43:23;
Mt 2:11
dIsa 42:10
60:7
eGe 25:13
fver 13;
Hag 2:3,7,9
60:8
gIsa 49:21
60:9
hIsa 11:11
iIsa 2:16 *fn*
jIsa 14:2; 43:6
kIsa 55:5

10"Foreigners[l] will rebuild your walls,
  and their kings[m] will serve you.
Though in anger I struck you,
  in favor I will show you compassion.[n]
11Your gates[o] will always stand open,
  they will never be shut, day or night,
so that men may bring you the wealth of the nations[p]—
  their kings[q] led in triumphal procession.
12For the nation or kingdom that will not serve[r] you will
        perish;
  it will be utterly ruined.

13"The glory of Lebanon[s] will come to you,
  the pine, the fir and the cypress together,[t]
to adorn the place of my sanctuary;
  and I will glorify the place of my feet.[u]
14The sons of your oppressors[v] will come bowing before
        you;
  all who despise you will bow down[w] at your feet
and will call you the City of the LORD,
  Zion[x] of the Holy One of Israel.

15"Although you have been forsaken[y] and hated,
  with no one traveling[z] through,
I will make you the everlasting pride[a]
  and the joy[b] of all generations.
16You will drink the milk of nations
  and be nursed[c] at royal breasts.
Then you will know that I, the LORD, am your Savior,
  your Redeemer,[d] the Mighty One of Jacob.
17Instead of bronze I will bring you gold,
  and silver in place of iron.
Instead of wood I will bring you bronze,
  and iron in place of stones.
I will make peace your governor
  and righteousness your ruler.
18No longer will violence be heard in your land,
  nor ruin or destruction within your borders,
but you will call your walls Salvation[e]
  and your gates Praise.
19The sun will no more be your light by day,
  nor will the brightness of the moon shine on you,
for the LORD will be your everlasting light,[f]
  and your God will be your glory.[g]
20Your sun[h] will never set again,
  and your moon will wane no more;
the LORD will be your everlasting light,
  and your days of sorrow[i] will end.
21Then will all your people be righteous[j]
  and they will possess[k] the land forever.
They are the shoot I have planted,[l]
  the work of my hands,[m]
  for the display of my splendor.[n]

60:10
l Isa 14:1-2
m Isa 49:23;
  Rev 21:24
n Isa 54:8
60:11
o ver 18;
  Isa 62:10;
  Rev 21:25
p ver 5;
  Rev 21:26
q Ps 149:8
60:12
r Isa 14:2
60:13
s Isa 35:2
t Isa 41:19
u 1Ch 28:2;
  Ps 132:7
60:14
v Isa 14:2
w Isa 49:23;
  Rev 3:9
x Heb 12:22
60:15
y Isa 1:7-9; 6:12
z Isa 33:8
a Isa 4:2
b Isa 65:18
60:16
c Isa 49:23;
  66:11,12
d Isa 59:20
60:18
e Isa 26:1
60:19
f Rev 22:5
g Zec 2:5;
  Rev 21:23
60:20
h Isa 30:26
i Isa 35:10
60:21
j Rev 21:27
k Ps 37:11,22;
  Isa 57:13; 61:7
l Mt 15:13
m Isa 19:25;
  29:23; Eph 2:10
n Isa 52:1

22The least of you will become a thousand,
    the smallest a mighty nation.
I am the Lord;
    in its time I will do this swiftly."

The Year of the Lord's Favor

61 The Spirit° of the Sovereign Lord is on me,
    because the Lord has anointedᴾ me
    to preach good news to the poor.�q
He has sent me to bind upʳ the brokenhearted,
    to proclaim freedom for the captivesˢ
    and release from darkness for the prisoners,ᵃ
²to proclaim the year of the Lord's favorᵗ
    and the day of vengeanceᵘ of our God,
to comfortᵛ all who mourn,
³ and provide for those who grieve in Zion—
    to bestow on them a crown of beauty
    instead of ashes,
the oil of gladness
    instead of mourning,
and a garment of praise
    instead of a spirit of despair.
They will be called oaks of righteousness,
    a planting of the Lord
    for the display of his splendor.ʷ

⁴They will rebuild the ancient ruinsˣ
    and restore the places long devastated;
they will renew the ruined cities
    that have been devastated for generations.
⁵Aliensʸ will shepherd your flocks;
    foreigners will work your fields and vineyards.
⁶And you will be called priestsᶻ of the Lord,
    you will be named ministers of our God.
You will feed on the wealthᵃ of nations,
    and in their riches you will boast.

⁷Instead of their shame
    my people will receive a doubleᵇ portion,
and instead of disgrace
    they will rejoice in their inheritance;
and so they will inherit a double portion in their land,
    and everlasting joy will be theirs.

⁸"For I, the Lord, love justice;ᶜ
    I hate robbery and iniquity.
In my faithfulness I will reward them
    and make an everlasting covenantᵈ with them.
⁹Their descendants will be known among the nations
    and their offspring among the peoples.
All who see them will acknowledge

61:1
oIsa 11:2
pPs 45:7
qMt 11:5;
Lk 7:22
rIsa 57:15
sIsa 42:7; 49:9
61:2
tIsa 49:8;
Lk 4:18-19*
uIsa 34:8
vIsa 57:18;
Mt 5:4
61:3
wIsa 60:20-21
61:4
xIsa 49:8;
Eze 36:33;
Am 9:14
61:5
yIsa 14:1-2
61:6
zEx 19:6;
1Pe 2:5
aIsa 60:11
61:7
bIsa 40:2;
Zec 9:12
61:8
cPs 11:7;
Isa 5:16
dIsa 55:3

ᵃ1 Hebrew; Septuagint *the blind*

that they are a people the LORD has blessed."

[10]I delight greatly in the LORD;
  my soul rejoices[e] in my God.
For he has clothed me with garments of salvation
  and arrayed me in a robe of righteousness,[f]
as a bridegroom adorns his head like a priest,
  and as a bride[g] adorns herself with her jewels.
[11]For as the soil makes the sprout come up
  and a garden causes seeds to grow,
so the Sovereign LORD will make righteousness[h] and praise
  spring up before all nations.

Zion's New Name

62 For Zion's sake I will not keep silent,
  for Jerusalem's sake I will not remain quiet,
till her righteousness[i] shines out like the dawn,
  her salvation like a blazing torch.
[2]The nations[j] will see your righteousness,
  and all kings your glory;
you will be called by a new name[k]
  that the mouth of the LORD will bestow.
[3]You will be a crown[l] of splendor in the LORD's hand,
  a royal diadem in the hand of your God.
[4]No longer will they call you Deserted,[m]
  or name your land Desolate.
But you will be called Hephzibah,[a]
  and your land Beulah[b];
for the LORD will take delight[n] in you,
  and your land will be married.[o]
[5]As a young man marries a maiden,
  so will your sons[c] marry you;
as a bridegroom rejoices over his bride,
  so will your God rejoice[p] over you.

[6]I have posted watchmen[q] on your walls, O Jerusalem;
  they will never be silent day or night.
You who call on the LORD,
  give yourselves no rest,
[7]and give him no rest[r] till he establishes Jerusalem
  and makes her the praise of the earth.

[8]The LORD has sworn by his right hand
  and by his mighty arm:
"Never again will I give your grain[s]
  as food for your enemies,
and never again will foreigners drink the new wine
  for which you have toiled;
[9]but those who harvest it will eat it
  and praise the LORD,

61:10
eIsa 25:9;
Hab 3:18
fPs 132:9;
Isa 52:1
gIsa 49:18;
Rev 21:2
61:11
hPs 85:11
62:1
iIsa 1:26
62:2
jIsa 52:10; 60:3
kver 4,12
62:3
lIsa 28:5;
Zec 9:16;
1Th 2:19
62:4
mIsa 54:6
nJer 32:41;
Zep 3:17
oJer 3:14;
Hos 2:19
62:5
pIsa 65:19
62:6
qIsa 52:8;
Eze 3:17
62:7
rMt 15:21-28;
Lk 18:1-8
62:8
sDt 28:30-33;
Isa 1:7; Jer 5:17

---

[a]4 *Hephzibah* means *my delight is in her.*   [b]4 *Beulah* means *married.*   [c]5 Or *Builder*

and those who gather the grapes will drink it
  in the courts of my sanctuary."

¹⁰Pass through, pass through the gates!ᵗ
  Prepare the way for the people.
Build up, build up the highway!ᵘ ᵛ
  Remove the stones.
Raise a bannerʷ for the nations.

¹¹The LORD has made proclamation
  to the ends of the earth:
"Say to the Daughter of Zion,ˣ
  'See, your Savior comes!ʸ
See, his reward is with him,
  and his recompense accompanies him.' "ᶻ
¹²They will be calledᵃ the Holy People,ᵇ
  the Redeemedᶜ of the LORD;
and you will be called Sought After,
  the City No Longer Deserted. ᵈ

God's Day of Vengeance and Redemption

63 Who is this coming from Edom,
  from Bozrah,ᵉ with his garments stained crimson?
Who is this, robed in splendor,
  striding forward in the greatness of his strength?

"It is I, speaking in righteousness,
  mighty to save."ᶠ

²Why are your garments red,
  like those of one treading the winepress?

³"I have trodden the winepressᵍ alone;
  from the nations no one was with me.
I trampled them in my anger
  and trod them down in my wrath;ʰ
their blood spattered my garments,ⁱ
  and I stained all my clothing.
⁴For the day of vengeance was in my heart,
  and the year of my redemption has come.
⁵I looked, but there was no oneʲ to help,
  I was appalled that no one gave support;
so my own armᵏ worked salvation for me,
  and my own wrath sustained me.ˡ
⁶I trampled the nations in my anger;
  in my wrath I made them drunkᵐ
and poured their bloodⁿ on the ground."

Praise and Prayer

⁷I will tell of the kindnessesᵒ of the LORD,
  the deeds for which he is to be praised,
according to all the LORD has done for us—
  yes, the many good things he has done
  for the house of Israel,

62:10
t Isa 60:11
u Isa 57:14
v Isa 11:16
w Isa 11:10
62:11
x Zec 9:9;
Mt 21:5
y Rev 22:12
z Isa 40:10
62:12
a ver 4 b 1Pe 2:9
c Isa 35:9
d Isa 42:16
63:1
e Am 1:12
f Zep 3:17
63:3
g Rev 14:20;
19:15 h Isa 22:5
i Rev 19:13
63:5
j Isa 41:28
k Ps 44:3; 98:1
l Isa 59:16
63:6
m Isa 29:9
n Isa 34:3
63:7
o Isa 54:8

according to his compassion[p] and many kindnesses.

[8]He said, "Surely they are my people,[q]
  sons who will not be false to me";
  and so he became their Savior.
[9]In all their distress he too was distressed,
  and the angel of his presence[r] saved them.
In his love and mercy he redeemed[s] them;
  he lifted them up and carried[t] them
  all the days of old.
[10]Yet they rebelled[u]
  and grieved his Holy Spirit.[v]
So he turned and became their enemy[w]
  and he himself fought against them.

[11]Then his people recalled[a] the days of old,
  the days of Moses and his people—
where is he who brought them through the sea,[x]
  with the shepherd of his flock?
Where is he who set
  his Holy Spirit[y] among them,
[12]who sent his glorious arm of power
  to be at Moses' right hand,
who divided the waters[z] before them,
  to gain for himself everlasting renown,
[13]who led[a] them through the depths?
Like a horse in open country,
  they did not stumble;[b]
[14]like cattle that go down to the plain,
  they were given rest by the Spirit of the LORD.
This is how you guided your people
  to make for yourself a glorious name.

[15]Look down from heaven[c] and see
  from your lofty throne,[d] holy and glorious.
Where are your zeal[e] and your might?
  Your tenderness and compassion[f] are withheld from
    us.
[16]But you are our Father,
  though Abraham does not know us
  or Israel acknowledge[g] us;
you, O LORD, are our Father,
  our Redeemer[h] from of old is your name.
[17]Why, O LORD, do you make us wander from your
    ways
  and harden our hearts so we do not revere[i] you?
Return[j] for the sake of your servants,
  the tribes that are your inheritance.
[18]For a little while your people possessed your holy place,
  but now our enemies have trampled down your
    sanctuary.[k]
[19]We are yours from of old;

63:7
pPs 51:1;
 Eph 2:4
63:8
qIsa 51:4
63:9
rEx 33:14
sDt 7:7-8
tDt 1:31
63:10
uPs 78:40
vPs 51:11;
 Ac 7:51;
 Eph 4:30
wPs 106:40
63:11
xEx 14:22,30
yNu 11:17
63:12
zEx 14:21-22;
 Isa 11:15
63:13
aDt 32:12
bJer 31:9
63:15
cDt 26:15;
 Ps 80:14
dPs 123:1
eIsa 9:7; 26:11
fJer 31:20;
 Hos 11:8
63:16
gJob 14:21
hIsa 41:14; 44:6
63:17
iIsa 29:13
jNu 10:36
63:18
kPs 74:3-8

a11 Or *But may he recall*

but you have not ruled over them,
   they have not been called by your name.ᵃ

64

Oh, that you would rend the heavens¹ and come down,ᵐ
   that the mountainsⁿ would tremble before you!
²As when fire sets twigs ablaze
   and causes water to boil,
come down to make your name known to your enemies
   and cause the nations to quakeᵒ before you!
³For when you did awesomeᵖ things that we did not
      expect,
   you came down, and the mountains trembled before
      you.
⁴Since ancient times no one has heard,
   no ear has perceived,
no eye has seen any God besides you,
   who acts on behalf of those who wait for him.�q
⁵You come to the help of those who gladly do right,ʳ
   who remember your ways.
But when we continued to sin against them,
   you were angry.
   How then can we be saved?
⁶All of us have become like one who is unclean,
   and all our righteousˢ acts are like filthy rags;
we all shrivel up like a leaf,ᵗ
   and like the wind our sins sweep us away.
⁷No oneᵘ calls on your name
   or strives to lay hold of you;
for you have hidden�v your face from us
   and made us waste awayʷ because of our sins.

⁸Yet, O Lᴏʀᴅ, you are our Father.ˣ
   We are the clay, you are the potter;ʸ
   we are all the work of your hand.
⁹Do not be angryᶻ beyond measure, O Lᴏʀᴅ;
   do not remember our sinsᵃ forever.
   Oh, look upon us, we pray,
   for we are all your people.
¹⁰Your sacred cities have become a desert;
   even Zion is a desert, Jerusalem a desolation.
¹¹Our holy and glorious temple,ᵇ where our fathers
      praised you,
   has been burned with fire,
   and all that we treasuredᶜ lies in ruins.
¹²After all this, O Lᴏʀᴅ, will you hold yourself back?ᵈ
   Will you keep silentᵉ and punish us beyond measure?

Judgment and Salvation

65

"I revealed myself to those who did not ask for me;
   I was found by those who did not seek me.ᶠ
To a nationᵍ that did not call on my name,

64:1
lPs 18:9; 144:5
mMic 1:3
nEx 19:18
64:2
oPs 99:1;
Jer 5:22; 33:9
64:3
pPs 65:5
64:4
qIsa 30:18;
1Co 2:9*
64:5
rIsa 26:8
64:6
sIsa 46:12; 48:1
tPs 90:5-6
64:7
uIsa 59:4
vDt 31:18;
Isa 1:15; 54:8
wIsa 9:18
64:8
xIsa 63:16
yIsa 29:16
64:9
zIsa 57:17;
60:10 aIsa 43:25
64:11
bPs 74:3-7
cLa 1:7,10
64:12
dPs 74:10-11;
Isa 42:14
ePs 83:1
65:1
fHos 1:10;
Ro 9:24-26;
10:20*
gEph 2:12

ᵃ19 Or *We are like those you have never ruled, / like those never called by your name*

I said, 'Here am I, here am I.'
²All day long I have held out my hands
    to an obstinate people, ʰ
who walk in ways not good,
    pursuing their own imaginations ⁱ —
³a people who continually provoke me
    to my very face, ʲ
offering sacrifices in gardens ᵏ
    and burning incense on altars of brick;
⁴who sit among the graves
    and spend their nights keeping secret vigil;
who eat the flesh of pigs, ˡ
    and whose pots hold broth of unclean meat;
⁵who say, 'Keep away; don't come near me,
    for I am too sacred ᵐ for you!'
Such people are smoke in my nostrils,
    a fire that keeps burning all day.

⁶"See, it stands written before me:
    I will not keep silent ⁿ but will pay back ᵒ in full;
    I will pay it back into their laps ᵖ—
⁷both your sins ᑫ and the sins of your fathers," ʳ
    says the LORD.
"Because they burned sacrifices on the mountains
    and defied me on the hills, ˢ
I will measure into their laps
    the full payment for their former deeds."

⁸This is what the LORD says:

"As when juice is still found in a cluster of grapes
    and men say, 'Don't destroy it,
    there is yet some good in it,'
so will I do in behalf of my servants;
    I will not destroy them all.
⁹I will bring forth descendants ᵗ from Jacob,
    and from Judah those who will possess ᵘ my
        mountains;
my chosen people will inherit them,
    and there will my servants live. ᵛ
¹⁰Sharon ʷ will become a pasture for flocks,
    and the Valley of Achor ˣ a resting place for herds,
    for my people who seek ʸ me.

¹¹"But as for you who forsake ᶻ the LORD
    and forget my holy mountain,
who spread a table for Fortune
    and fill bowls of mixed wine for Destiny,
¹²I will destine you for the sword, ᵃ
    and you will all bend down for the slaughter;
for I called but you did not answer, ᵇ
    I spoke but you did not listen. ᶜ
You did evil in my sight
    and chose what displeases me."

65:2
h Isa 1:2,23;
Ro 10:21*
i Ps 81:11-12;
Isa 66:18
65:3
j Job 1:11
k Isa 1:29
65:4
l Lev 11:7
65:5
m Mt 9:11;
Lk 7:39; 18:9-12
65:6
n Ps 50:3
o Jer 16:18
p Ps 79:12
65:7
q Isa 22:14
r Ex 20:5
s Isa 57:7
65:9
t Isa 45:19
u Am 9:11-15
v Isa 32:18
65:10
w Isa 35:2
x Jos 7:26
y Isa 51:1
65:11
z Dt 29:24-25;
Isa 1:28
65:12
a Isa 27:1
b Pr 1:24-25;
Isa 41:28; 66:4
c 2Ch 36:15-16;
Jer 7:13

¹³Therefore this is what the Sovereign Lᴏʀᴅ says:

> "My servants will eat, [d]
> but you will go hungry;
> my servants will drink,
> but you will go thirsty; [e]
> my servants will rejoice,
> but you will be put to shame. [f]
> ¹⁴My servants will sing
> out of the joy of their hearts,
> but you will cry out [g]
> from anguish of heart
> and wail in brokenness of spirit.
> ¹⁵You will leave your name
> to my chosen ones as a curse; [h]
> the Sovereign Lᴏʀᴅ will put you to death,
> but to his servants he will give another name.
> ¹⁶Whoever invokes a blessing in the land
> will do so by the God of truth; [i]
> he who takes an oath in the land
> will swear [j] by the God of truth.
> For the past troubles will be forgotten
> and hidden from my eyes.

New Heavens and a New Earth

> ¹⁷"Behold, I will create
> new heavens and a new earth. [k]
> The former things will not be remembered, [l]
> nor will they come to mind.
> ¹⁸But be glad and rejoice [m] forever
> in what I will create,
> for I will create Jerusalem to be a delight
> and its people a joy.
> ¹⁹I will rejoice [n] over Jerusalem
> and take delight in my people;
> the sound of weeping and of crying [o]
> will be heard in it no more.
>
> ²⁰"Never again will there be in it
> an infant who lives but a few days,
> or an old man who does not live out his years; [p]
> he who dies at a hundred
> will be thought a mere youth;
> he who fails to reach [a] a hundred
> will be considered accursed.
> ²¹They will build houses [q] and dwell in them;
> they will plant vineyards and eat their fruit. [r]
> ²²No longer will they build houses and others live in
> them,
> or plant and others eat.
> For as the days of a tree, [s]

[a] 20 Or / *the sinner who reaches*

65:13
[d] Isa 1:19
[e] Isa 41:17
[f] Isa 44:9
65:14
[g] Mt 8:12;
Lk 13:28
65:15
[h] Zec 8:13
65:16
[i] Ps 31:5
[j] Isa 19:18
65:17
[k] Isa 66:22;
2Pe 3:13
[l] Isa 43:18;
Jer 3:16
65:18
[m] Ps 98:1-9;
Isa 25:9
65:19
[n] Isa 35:10; 62:5
[o] Isa 25:8;
Rev 7:17
65:20
[p] Ecc 8:13
65:21
[q] Isa 32:18
[r] Isa 37:30;
Am 9:14
65:22
[s] Ps 92:12-14

so will be the days[t] of my people;
my chosen ones will long enjoy
    the works of their hands.
23They will not toil in vain
    or bear children doomed to misfortune;
for they will be a people blessed[u] by the LORD,
    they and their descendants[v] with them.
24Before they call[w] I will answer;
    while they are still speaking[x] I will hear.
25The wolf and the lamb[y] will feed together,
    and the lion will eat straw like the ox,
    but dust will be the serpent's[z] food.
They will neither harm nor destroy
    on all my holy mountain,"

            says the LORD.

Judgment and Hope

66 This is what the LORD says:

"Heaven is my throne,[a]
    and the earth is my footstool.[b]
Where is the house[c] you will build for me?
    Where will my resting place be?
2Has not my hand made all these things,[d]
    and so they came into being?"

            declares the LORD.

"This is the one I esteem:
    he who is humble and contrite in spirit,[e]
    and trembles at my word.[f]
3But whoever sacrifices a bull[g]
    is like one who kills a man,
and whoever offers a lamb,
    like one who breaks a dog's neck;
whoever makes a grain offering
    is like one who presents pig's blood,
and whoever burns memorial incense,[h]
    like one who worships an idol.
They have chosen their own ways,[i]
    and their souls delight in their abominations;
4so I also will choose harsh treatment for them
    and will bring upon them what they dread.[j]
For when I called, no one answered,[k]
    when I spoke, no one listened.
They did evil[l] in my sight
    and chose what displeases me."[m]

5Hear the word of the LORD,
    you who tremble at his word:
"Your brothers who hate[n] you,
    and exclude you because of my name, have said,
'Let the LORD be glorified,
    that we may see your joy!'

65:22
tPs 21:4; 91:16
65:23
uDt 28:3-12;
Isa 61:9
vAc 2:39
65:24
wIsa 55:6
xDa 9:20-23;
10:12
65:25
yIsa 11:6
zGe 3:14;
Mic 7:17
66:1
aMt 23:22
b1Ki 8:27;
Mt 5:34-35
c2Sa 7:7;
Jn 4:20-21;
Ac 7:48; 17:24
66:2
dIsa 40:26;
Ac 7:50*
eIsa 57:15;
Mt 5:3-4;
Lk 18:13-14
fEzr 9:4
66:3
gIsa 1:11
hLev 2:2
iIsa 57:17
66:4
jPr 10:24
kPr 1:24;
Jer 7:13
l2Ki 21:2,4,6
mIsa 65:12
66:5
nPs 38:20;
Isa 60:15

Yet they will be put to shame. °
⁶Hear that uproar from the city,
    hear that noise from the temple!
It is the sound of the LORD
    repaying ᵖ his enemies all they deserve.

⁷"Before she goes into labor, �q
    she gives birth;
before the pains come upon her,
    she delivers a son. ʳ
⁸Who has ever heard of such a thing?
    Who has ever seen ˢ such things?
Can a country be born in a day
    or a nation be brought forth in a moment?
Yet no sooner is Zion in labor
    than she gives birth to her children.
⁹Do I bring to the moment of birth ᵗ
    and not give delivery?" says the LORD.
"Do I close up the womb
    when I bring to delivery?" says your God.
¹⁰"Rejoice ᵘ with Jerusalem and be glad for her,
    all you who love ᵛ her;
rejoice greatly with her,
    all you who mourn over her.
¹¹For you will nurse ʷ and be satisfied
    at her comforting breasts;
you will drink deeply
    and delight in her overflowing abundance."

¹²For this is what the LORD says:

"I will extend peace to her like a river, ˣ
    and the wealth ʸ of nations like a flooding stream;
you will nurse and be carried ᶻ on her arm
    and dandled on her knees.
¹³As a mother comforts her child,
    so will I comfort ᵃ you;
and you will be comforted over Jerusalem."

¹⁴When you see this, your heart will rejoice
    and you will flourish like grass;
the hand of the LORD will be made known to his
        servants,
but his fury ᵇ will be shown to his foes.
¹⁵See, the LORD is coming with fire,
    and his chariots ᶜ are like a whirlwind;
he will bring down his anger with fury,
    and his rebuke ᵈ with flames of fire.
¹⁶For with fire ᵉ and with his sword ᶠ
    the LORD will execute judgment upon all men,
    and many will be those slain by the LORD.

¹⁷"Those who consecrate and purify themselves to go into the gar-

66:5
o Lk 13:17
66:6
p Isa 65:6;
Joel 3:7
66:7
q Isa 54:1
r Rev 12:5
66:8
s Isa 64:4
66:9
t Isa 37:3
66:10
u Dt 32:43;
Ro 15:10
v Ps 26:8
66:11
w Isa 60:16
66:12
x Isa 48:18
y Ps 72:3;
Isa 60:5; 61:6
z Isa 60:4
66:13
a Isa 40:1;
2Co 1:4
66:14
b Isa 10:5
66:15
c Ps 68:17
d Ps 9:5
66:16
e Isa 30:30
f Isa 27:1

66:17
g Isa 1:29
h Lev 11:7
i Ps 37:20;
Isa 1:28
66:19
j Isa 11:10;
49:22 k Isa 2:16
l Eze 27:10
m Ge 10:2
n Isa 11:11
o 1Ch 16:24;
Isa 24:15
66:20
p Isa 52:11
66:21
q Ex 19:6;
Isa 61:6;
1Pe 2:5,9
66:22
r Isa 65:17;
Heb 12:26-27;
2Pe 3:13;
Rev 21:1
s Jn 10:27-29;
1Pe 1:4-5
66:23
t Eze 46:1-3
u Isa 19:21
66:24
v Isa 14:11
w Isa 1:31;
Mk 9:48*

dens,ᵍ following the one in the midst ofᵃ those who eat the flesh of pigsʰ and rats and other abominable things—they will meet their endⁱ together," declares the Lᴏʀᴅ.

¹⁸"And I, because of their actions and their imaginations, am about to comeᵇ and gather all nations and tongues, and they will come and see my glory.

¹⁹"I will set a signʲ among them, and I will send some of those who survive to the nations—to Tarshish,ᵏ to the Libyansᶜ and Lydiansˡ (famous as archers), to Tubalᵐ and Greece, and to the distant islandsⁿ that have not heard of my fame or seen my glory.ᵒ They will proclaim my glory among the nations. ²⁰And they will bring all your brothers, from all the nations, to my holy mountain in Jerusalem as an offering to the Lᴏʀᴅ—on horses, in chariots and wagons, and on mules and camels," says the Lᴏʀᴅ. "They will bring them, as the Israelites bring their grain offerings, to the temple of the Lᴏʀᴅ in ceremonially clean vessels.ᵖ ²¹And I will select some of them also to be priests�q and Levites," says the Lᴏʀᴅ.

²²"As the new heavens and the new earthʳ that I make will endure before me," declares the Lᴏʀᴅ, "so will your name and descendants endure.ˢ ²³From one New Moon to another and from one Sabbathᵗ to another, all mankind will come and bow downᵘ before me," says the Lᴏʀᴅ. ²⁴"And they will go out and look upon the dead bodies of those who rebelled against me; their wormᵛ will not die, nor will their fire be quenched,ʷ and they will be loathsome to all mankind."

ᵃ17 Or *gardens behind one of your temples, and*   ᵇ18 The meaning of the Hebrew for this clause is uncertain.   ᶜ19 Some Septuagint manuscripts *Put* (Libyans); Hebrew *Pul*

Jeremiah

Title and Background

The book is named after the prophet whose ministry it records. Jeremiah prophesied in Judah during the reigns of Josiah and succeeding kings up to the Babylonian exile. It was a period of storm and stress when the doom of entire nations—including Judah itself—was being sealed. After Josiah's reign, Jeremiah was often in danger from political and religious leaders who were angry because of his messages. Through all this, God protected Jeremiah so he could continue to warn the wicked and comfort those who trusted in God.

Author and Date of Writing

The book preserves an account of the prophetic ministry of Jeremiah, whose personal life and struggles are known to us in greater depth and detail than those of any other Old Testament prophet. His prophetic ministry began in 626 B.C. and ended sometime after 586.

Theme and Message

Jeremiah was always conscious of his call from the Lord to be a prophet, and as such proclaimed words that were spoken first by God himself and were therefore certain of fulfillment. Judgment is one of the all-pervasive themes in his writings, though he was careful to point out that repentance, if sincere, would postpone the inevitable. For Jeremiah, God was ultimate. His theology conceived of the Lord as the Creator of all that exists, as all-powerful and as everywhere present. At the same time, God is very much concerned about individual people and their accountability to him.

Outline

I. The Call of Jeremiah (1:1-19)
II. Warnings and Exhortations to Judah (2:1-29:32)
III. Promises of Restoration (30:1-33:26)
IV. Historical Insertion (34:1-35:19)
V. The Sufferings of Jeremiah (36:1-38:28)
VI. The Fall of Jerusalem and Its Aftermath (39:1-45:5)
VII. Judgment Against the Nations (46:1-51:64)
VIII. Historical Appendix (52:1-34)

---

1 The words of Jeremiah son of Hilkiah, one of the priests at Anathoth[a] in the territory of Benjamin. ²The word of the LORD came to him in the thirteenth year of the reign of Josiah son of Amon king of Judah, ³and through the reign of Jehoiakim[b] son of Josiah king of Judah, down to the fifth month of the eleventh year of Zedekiah[c] son of Josiah king of Judah, when the people of Jerusalem went into exile. [d]

The Call of Jeremiah

⁴The word of the LORD came to me, saying,

1:1
a Jos 21:18;
1Ch 6:60;
Jer 32:7-9
1:3
b 2Ki 23:34
c 2Ki 24:17;
Jer 39:2
d Jer 52:15

[5]"Before I formed you in the womb I knew[ae] you,
   before you were born[f] I set you apart;
   I appointed you as a prophet to the nations.[g]"

[6]"Ah, Sovereign LORD," I said, "I do not know how to speak;[h] I am only a child."[i]

[7]But the LORD said to me, "Do not say, 'I am only a child.' You must go to everyone I send you to and say whatever I command you. [8]Do not be afraid[j] of them, for I am with you[k] and will rescue you," declares the LORD.

[9]Then the LORD reached out his hand and touched[l] my mouth and said to me, "Now, I have put my words in your mouth. [m] [10]See, today I appoint you over nations and kingdoms to uproot and tear down, to destroy and overthrow, to build and to plant."[n]

[11]The word of the LORD came to me: "What do you see, Jeremiah?"[o]

"I see the branch of an almond tree," I replied.

[12]The LORD said to me, "You have seen correctly, for I am watching[b] to see that my word is fulfilled."

[13]The word of the LORD came to me again: "What do you see?"[p]

"I see a boiling pot, tilting away from the north," I answered.

[14]The LORD said to me, "From the north disaster will be poured out on all who live in the land. [15]I am about to summon all the peoples of the northern kingdoms," declares the LORD.

"Their kings will come and set up their thrones
   in the entrance of the gates of Jerusalem;
they will come against all her surrounding walls
   and against all the towns of Judah.[q]
[16]I will pronounce my judgments on my people
   because of their wickedness[r] in forsaking me,[s]
in burning incense to other gods[t]
   and in worshiping what their hands have made.

[17]"Get yourself ready! Stand up and say to them whatever I command you. Do not be terrified[u] by them, or I will terrify you before them. [18]Today I have made you[v] a fortified city, an iron pillar and a bronze wall to stand against the whole land—against the kings of Judah, its officials, its priests and the people of the land. [19]They will fight against you but will not overcome you, for I am with you[w] and will rescue[x] you," declares the LORD.

Israel Forsakes God

2 The word of the LORD came to me: [2]"Go and proclaim in the hearing of Jerusalem:

" 'I remember the devotion of your youth,[y]
   how as a bride you loved me
and followed me through the desert,[z]
   through a land not sown.
[3]Israel was holy[a] to the LORD,[b]
   the firstfruits[c] of his harvest;
all who devoured[d] her were held guilty,[e]

1:5
ePs 139:16
fIsa 49:1
gver 10;
Jer 25:15-26
1:6
hEx 4:10; 6:12
i1Ki 3:7
1:8
jEze 2:6
kJos 1:5;
Jer 15:20
1:9
lIsa 6:7
mEx 4:12
1:10
nJer 18:7-10;
24:6; 31:4,28
1:11
oJer 24:3;
Am 7:8
1:13
pZec 4:2
1:15
qJer 4:16; 9:11
1:16
rDt 28:20
sJer 17:13
tJer 7:9; 19:4
1:17
uEze 2:6
1:18
vIsa 50:7
1:19
wJer 20:11
xver 8
2:2
yEze 16:8-14,
60; Hos 2:15
zDt 2:7
2:3
aDt 7:6
bEx 19:6
cJas 1:18;
Rev 14:4
dIsa 41:11;
Jer 30:16
eJer 50:7

---

[a]5 Or *chose*   [b]12 The Hebrew for *watching* sounds like the Hebrew for *almond tree*.

and disaster overtook them,' "

declares the Lord.

⁴Hear the word of the Lord, O house of Jacob,
  all you clans of the house of Israel.

⁵This is what the Lord says:

"What fault did your fathers find in me,
  that they strayed so far from me?
They followed worthless idols
  and became worthless ᶠ themselves.
⁶They did not ask, 'Where is the Lord,
  who brought us up out of Egypt ᵍ
and led us through the barren wilderness,
  through a land of deserts ʰ and rifts, ⁱ
a land of drought and darkness, ᵃ
  a land where no one travels and no one lives?'
⁷I brought you into a fertile land
  to eat its fruit and rich produce. ʲ
But you came and defiled my land
  and made my inheritance detestable. ᵏ
⁸The priests did not ask,
  'Where is the Lord?'
Those who deal with the law did not know me;ˡ
  the leaders rebelled against me.
The prophets prophesied by Baal, ᵐ
  following worthless idols. ⁿ

⁹"Therefore I bring charges ᵒ against you again,"

declares the Lord.

"And I will bring charges against your children's
  children.
¹⁰Cross over to the coasts of Kittim ᵇ and look,
  send to Kedar ᶜ and observe closely;
  see if there has ever been anything like this:
¹¹Has a nation ever changed its gods?
  (Yet they are not gods ᵖ at all.)
But my people have exchanged their ᵈ Glory �q
  for worthless idols.
¹²Be appalled at this, O heavens,
  and shudder with great horror,"

declares the Lord.

¹³"My people have committed two sins:
They have forsaken me,
  the spring of living water, ʳ
and have dug their own cisterns,
  broken cisterns that cannot hold water.
¹⁴Is Israel a servant, a slave ˢ by birth?
  Why then has he become plunder?

2:5
f 2Ki 17:15
2:6
g Hos 13:4
h Dt 8:15
i Dt 32:10
2:7
j Nu 13:27;
Dt 8:7-9;
11:10-12
k Ps 106:34-39;
Jer 16:18
2:8
l Jer 4:22
m Jer 23:13
n Jer 16:19
2:9
o Eze 20:35-36;
Mic 6:2
2:11
p Isa 37:19;
Jer 16:20
q Ps 106:20;
Ro 1:23
2:13
r Ps 36:9;
Jn 4:14
2:14
s Ex 4:22

ᵃ6 Or *and the shadow of death*   ᵇ10 That is, Cyprus and western coastlands   ᶜ10 The home of
Bedouin tribes in the Syro-Arabian desert   ᵈ11 Masoretic Text; an ancient Hebrew scribal
tradition *my*

¹⁵Lions^t have roared;
    they have growled at him.
They have laid waste^u his land;
    his towns are burned and deserted.
¹⁶Also, the men of Memphis^{a v} and Tahpanhes^w
    have shaved the crown of your head. ^b
¹⁷Have you not brought this on yourselves^x
    by forsaking the LORD your God
    when he led you in the way?
¹⁸Now why go to Egypt^y
    to drink water from the Shihor^c?^z
And why go to Assyria
    to drink water from the River^d?
¹⁹Your wickedness will punish you;
    your backsliding^a will rebuke^b you.
Consider then and realize
    how evil and bitter^c it is for you
when you forsake the LORD your God
    and have no awe^d of me,"
                declares the Lord, the LORD Almighty.

²⁰"Long ago you broke off your yoke^e
    and tore off your bonds;
    you said, 'I will not serve you!'
Indeed, on every high hill^f
    and under every spreading tree^g
    you lay down as a prostitute.
²¹I had planted^h you like a choice vineⁱ
    of sound and reliable stock.
How then did you turn against me
    into a corrupt,^j wild vine?
²²Although you wash yourself with soda
    and use an abundance of soap,
    the stain of your guilt is still before me,"
                declares the Sovereign LORD.
²³"How can you say, 'I am not defiled;^k
    I have not run after the Baals'?^l
See how you behaved in the valley;^m
    consider what you have done.
You are a swift she-camel
    runningⁿ here and there,
²⁴a wild donkey^o accustomed to the desert,
    sniffing the wind in her craving—
    in her heat who can restrain her?
Any males that pursue her need not tire themselves;
    at mating time they will find her.
²⁵Do not run until your feet are bare
    and your throat is dry.
But you said, 'It's no use!

2:15
t Jer 4:7; 50:17
u Isa 1:7
2:16
v Isa 19:13
w Jer 43:7-9
2:17
x Jer 4:18
2:18
y Isa 30:2
z Jos 13:3
2:19
a Jer 3:11,22
b Isa 3:9;
Hos 5:5
c Job 20:14;
Am 8:10
d Ps 36:1
2:20
e Lev 26:13
f Isa 57:7;
Jer 17:2
g Dt 12:2
2:21
h Ex 15:17
i Ps 80:8 j Isa 5:4
2:23
k Pr 30:12
l Jer 9:14
m Jer 7:31
n ver 33;
Jer 31:22
2:24
o Jer 14:6

^a16 Hebrew *Noph*   ^b16 Or *have cracked your skull*   ^c18 That is, a branch of the Nile
^d18 That is, the Euphrates

I love foreign gods, ᴾ
and I must go after them.'

²⁶"As a thief is disgraced �q when he is caught,
so the house of Israel is disgraced—
they, their kings and their officials,
their priests and their prophets.
²⁷They say to wood, 'You are my father,'
and to stone, ʳ 'You gave me birth.'
They have turned their backs to me
and not their faces; ˢ
yet when they are in trouble, ᵗ they say,
'Come and save us!'
²⁸Where then are the gods ᵘ you made for yourselves?
Let them come if they can save you
when you are in trouble! ᵛ
For you have as many gods
as you have towns, ʷ O Judah.

²⁹"Why do you bring charges against me?
You have all ˣ rebelled against me,"
declares the Lᴏʀᴅ.
³⁰"In vain I punished your people;
they did not respond to correction.
Your sword has devoured your prophets ʸ
like a ravening lion.

³¹"You of this generation, consider the word of the Lᴏʀᴅ:

"Have I been a desert to Israel
or a land of great darkness? ᶻ
Why do my people say, 'We are free to roam;
we will come to you no more'?
³²Does a maiden forget her jewelry,
a bride her wedding ornaments?
Yet my people have forgotten me,
days without number.
³³How skilled you are at pursuing love!
Even the worst of women can learn from your
ways.
³⁴On your clothes men find
the lifeblood ᵃ of the innocent poor,
though you did not catch them breaking in. ᵇ
Yet in spite of all this
³⁵ you say, 'I am innocent;
he is not angry with me.'
But I will pass judgment ᶜ on you
because you say, 'I have not sinned.' ᵈ
³⁶Why do you go about so much,
changing ᵉ your ways?
You will be disappointed by Egypt ᶠ
as you were by Assyria.
³⁷You will also leave that place
with your hands on your head, ᵍ

2:25
pDt 32:16;
Jer 3:13; 14:10
2:26
qJer 48:27
2:27
rJer 3:9
sJer 18:17;
32:33
tJdg 10:10;
Isa 26:16
2:28
uIsa 45:20
vDt 32:37
w2Ki 17:29;
Jer 11:13
2:29
xJer 5:1; 6:13;
Da 9:11
2:30
yNe 9:26;
Ac 7:52;
1Th 2:15
2:31
zIsa 45:19
2:34
a2Ki 21:16
bEx 22:2
2:35
cJer 25:31
d1Jn 1:8,10
2:36
eJer 31:22
fIsa 30:2,3,7
2:37
g2Sa 13:19

for the LORD has rejected those you trust;
    you will not be helped[h] by them.

3   "If a man divorces[i] his wife
        and she leaves him and marries another man,
    should he return to her again?
        Would not the land be completely defiled?
    But you have lived as a prostitute with many lovers[j] —
        would you now return to me?"

                                        declares the LORD.

²"Look up to the barren heights and see.
    Is there any place where you have not been
        ravished?
By the roadside[k] you sat waiting for lovers,
    sat like a nomad[a] in the desert.
You have defiled the land[l]
    with your prostitution and wickedness.
³Therefore the showers have been withheld,[m]
    and no spring rains[n] have fallen.
Yet you have the brazen look of a prostitute;
    you refuse to blush with shame.[o]
⁴Have you not just called to me:
    'My Father,[p] my friend from my youth,[q]
⁵will you always be angry?[r]
    Will your wrath continue forever?'
This is how you talk,
    but you do all the evil you can."

Unfaithful Israel

⁶During the reign of King Josiah, the LORD said to me, "Have you seen what faithless Israel has done? She has gone up on every high hill and under every spreading tree[s] and has committed adultery[t] there. ⁷I thought that after she had done all this she would return to me but she did not, and her unfaithful sister[u] Judah saw it. ⁸I gave faithless Israel her certificate of divorce and sent her away because of all her adulteries. Yet I saw that her unfaithful sister Judah had no fear;[v] she also went out and committed adultery. ⁹Because Israel's immorality mattered so little to her, she defiled the land[w] and committed adultery with stone[x] and wood.[y] ¹⁰In spite of all this, her unfaithful sister Judah did not return to me with all her heart, but only in pretense,[z]" declares the LORD.

¹¹The LORD said to me, "Faithless Israel is more righteous[a] than unfaithful[b] Judah. ¹²Go, proclaim this message toward the north:[c]

    " 'Return,[d] faithless Israel,' declares the LORD,
        'I will frown on you no longer,
    for I am merciful,' declares the LORD,
        'I will not be angry[e] forever.
¹³Only acknowledge[f] your guilt—
    you have rebelled against the LORD your God,

Cross references

2:37
h Jer 37:7
3:1
i Dt 24:1-4
j Jer 2:20,25;
Eze 16:26,29
3:2
k Ge 38:14;
Eze 16:25
l Jer 2:7
3:3
m Lev 26:19
n Jer 14:4
o Jer 6:15; 8:12;
Zep 3:5
3:4
p ver 19 q Jer 2:2
3:5
r Ps 103:9;
Isa 57:16
3:6
s Jer 17:2
t Jer 2:20
3:7
u Eze 16:46
3:8
v Eze 16:47;
23:11
3:9
w ver 2 x Isa 57:6
y Jer 2:27
3:10
z Jer 12:2
3:11
a Eze 16:52;
23:11 b ver 7
3:12
c 2Ki 17:3-6
d ver 14;
Jer 31:21,22;
Eze 33:11
e Ps 86:15
3:13
f Dt 30:1-3;
Jer 14:20;
1Jn 1:9

---

a 2 Or *an Arab*

you have scattered your favors to foreign gods[g]
    under every spreading tree,[h]
    and have not obeyed[i] me,' "

declares the LORD.

14"Return,[j] faithless people," declares the LORD, "for I am your husband. I will choose you—one from a town and two from a clan—and bring you to Zion. 15Then I will give you shepherds[k] after my own heart, who will lead you with knowledge and understanding. 16In those days, when your numbers have increased greatly in the land," declares the LORD, "men will no longer say, 'The ark of the covenant of the LORD.' It will never enter their minds or be remembered;[l] it will not be missed, nor will another one be made. 17At that time they will call Jerusalem The Throne[m] of the LORD, and all nations will gather in Jerusalem to honor[n] the name of the LORD. No longer will they follow the stubbornness of their evil hearts.[o] 18In those days the house of Judah will join the house of Israel,[p] and together[q] they will come from a northern[r] land to the land[s] I gave your forefathers as an inheritance.

19"I myself said,

    " 'How gladly would I treat you like sons
        and give you a desirable land,
        the most beautiful inheritance of any nation.'
    I thought you would call me 'Father'[t]
        and not turn away from following me.
20But like a woman unfaithful to her husband,
    so you have been unfaithful to me, O house of Israel,"

declares the LORD.

21A cry is heard on the barren heights,[u]
    the weeping and pleading of the people of Israel,
because they have perverted their ways
    and have forgotten the LORD their God.

22"Return,[v] faithless people;
    I will cure[w] you of backsliding."

"Yes, we will come to you,
    for you are the LORD our God.
23Surely the idolatrous commotion on the hills
    and mountains is a deception;
surely in the LORD our God
    is the salvation[x] of Israel.
24From our youth shameful[y] gods have consumed
    the fruits of our fathers' labor—
their flocks and herds,
    their sons and daughters.
25Let us lie down in our shame,[z]
    and let our disgrace cover us.
We have sinned against the LORD our God,
    both we and our fathers;
from our youth[a] till this day
    we have not obeyed the LORD our God."

3:13
gJer 2:25
hDt 12:2
iver 25
3:14
jHos 2:19
3:15
kAc 20:28
3:16
lIsa 65:17
3:17
mJer 17:12;
Eze 43:7
nIsa 60:9
oJer 11:8
3:18
pHos 1:11
qIsa 11:13;
Jer 50:4
rJer 16:15; 31:8
sAm 9:15
3:19
tver 4; Isa 63:16
3:21
uver 2
3:22
vHos 14:4
wJer 33:6;
Hos 6:1
3:23
xPs 3:8;
Jer 17:14
3:24
yHos 9:10
3:25
zEzr 9:6
aJer 22:21

4 "If you will return[b], O Israel,
        return to me,"

                                          declares the LORD.
"If you put your detestable idols[c] out of my sight
        and no longer go astray,
²and if in a truthful, just and righteous way
        you swear,[d] 'As surely as the LORD lives,'[e]
then the nations will be blessed[f] by him
        and in him they will glory."

³This is what the LORD says to the men of Judah and to Jerusalem:

    "Break up your unplowed ground[g]
        and do not sow among thorns.[h]
    ⁴Circumcise yourselves to the LORD,
        circumcise your hearts,[i]
        you men of Judah and people of Jerusalem,
    or my wrath[j] will break out and burn like fire
        because of the evil you have done—
        burn with no one to quench[k] it.

Disaster From the North

    ⁵"Announce in Judah and proclaim in Jerusalem and say:
        'Sound the trumpet throughout the land!'
    Cry aloud and say:
        'Gather together!
    Let us flee to the fortified cities!'[l]
    ⁶Raise the signal to go to Zion!
        Flee for safety without delay!
    For I am bringing disaster from the north,[m]
        even terrible destruction."

    ⁷A lion[n] has come out of his lair;
        a destroyer of nations has set out.
    He has left his place
        to lay waste[o] your land.
    Your towns will lie in ruins[p]
        without inhabitant.
    ⁸So put on sackcloth,[q]
        lament and wail,
    for the fierce anger[r] of the LORD
        has not turned away from us.

    ⁹"In that day," declares the LORD,
        "the king and the officials will lose heart,
    the priests will be horrified,
        and the prophets will be appalled."[s]

¹⁰Then I said, "Ah, Sovereign LORD, how completely you have deceived[t] this people and Jerusalem by saying, 'You will have peace,'[u] when the sword is at our throats."

¹¹At that time this people and Jerusalem will be told, "A scorching wind[v] from the barren heights in the desert blows toward my people,

4:1
b Jer 3:1,22;
Joel 2:12
c Jer 35:15

4:2
d Dt 10:20;
Isa 65:16
e Jer 12:16
f Ge 22:18;
Gal 3:8

4:3
g Hos 10:12
h Mk 4:18

4:4
i Dt 10:16;
Jer 9:26;
Ro 2:28-29
j Zep 2:2
k Am 5:6

4:5
l Jos 10:20;
Jer 8:14

4:6
m Jer 1:13-15;
50:3

4:7
n 2Ki 24:1;
Jer 2:15 o Isa 1:7
p Jer 25:9

4:8
q Isa 22:12;
Jer 6:26
r Jer 30:24

4:9
s Isa 29:9

4:10
t 2Th 2:11
u Jer 14:13

4:11
v Eze 17:10;
Hos 13:15

but not to winnow or cleanse; [12]a wind too strong for that comes from me.[a] Now I pronounce my judgments[w] against them."

13Look! He advances like the clouds,[x]
   his chariots[y] come like a whirlwind,[z]
his horses are swifter than eagles.[a]
   Woe to us! We are ruined!
14O Jerusalem, wash[b] the evil from your heart and be
    saved.
   How long will you harbor wicked thoughts?
15A voice is announcing from Dan,[c]
   proclaiming disaster from the hills of Ephraim.
16"Tell this to the nations,
   proclaim it to Jerusalem:
'A besieging army is coming from a distant land,
   raising a war cry[d] against the cities of Judah.
17They surround[e] her like men guarding a field,
   because she has rebelled[f] against me,' "
                        declares the LORD.
18"Your own conduct and actions[g]
   have brought this upon you.[h]
This is your punishment.
   How bitter[i] it is!
   How it pierces to the heart!"

19Oh, my anguish, my anguish![j]
   I writhe in pain.
Oh, the agony of my heart!
   My heart pounds within me,
   I cannot keep silent.[k]
For I have heard the sound of the trumpet;
   I have heard the battle cry.[l]
20Disaster follows disaster;[m]
   the whole land lies in ruins.
In an instant my tents[n] are destroyed,
   my shelter in a moment.
21How long must I see the battle standard
   and hear the sound of the trumpet?

22"My people are fools;[o]
   they do not know me.[p]
They are senseless children;
   they have no understanding.
They are skilled in doing evil;[q]
   they know not how to do good."[r]

23I looked at the earth,
   and it was formless and empty;[s]
and at the heavens,
   and their light was gone.
24I looked at the mountains,
   and they were quaking;[t]

4:12
w Jer 1:16
4:13
x Isa 19:1
y Isa 66:15
z Isa 5:28
a Dt 28:49;
Hab 1:8
4:14
b Jas 4:8
4:15
c Jer 8:16
4:16
d Eze 21:22
4:17
e 2Ki 25:1,4
f Jer 5:23
4:18
g Ps 107:17;
Isa 50:1
h Jer 2:17
i Jer 2:19
4:19
j Isa 16:11;
22:4; Jer 9:10
k Jer 20:9
l Nu 10:9
4:20
m Ps 42:7;
Eze 7:26
n Jer 10:20
4:22
o Jer 10:8
p Jer 2:8
q Jer 13:23;
1Co 14:20
r Ro 16:19
4:23
s Ge 1:2
4:24
t Isa 5:25;
Eze 38:20

all the hills were swaying.
25I looked, and there were no people;
    every bird in the sky had flown away. u
26I looked, and the fruitful land was a desert;
    all its towns lay in ruins
    before the LORD, before his fierce anger.

27This is what the LORD says:

    "The whole land will be ruined,
        though I will not destroyv it completely.
28Therefore the earth will mournw
    and the heavens above grow dark, x
    because I have spoken and will not relent, y
    I have decided and will not turn back. z"

29At the sound of horsemen and archersa
    every town takes to flight. b
Some go into the thickets;
    some climb up among the rocks.
All the towns are deserted;c
    no one lives in them.

30What are you doing, d O devastated one?
    Why dress yourself in scarlet
    and put on jewelse of gold?
Why shade your eyes with paint?f
    You adorn yourself in vain.
Your loversg despise you;
    they seek your life.

31I hear a cry as of a woman in labor, h
    a groan as of one bearing her first child—
the cry of the Daughter of Zion gasping for breath, i
    stretching out her handsj and saying,
"Alas! I am fainting;
    my life is given over to murderers."

Not One Is Upright

5   "Go up and downk the streets of Jerusalem,
        look around and consider,
        search through her squares.
    If you can find but one person1
        who deals honestly and seeks the truth,
        I will forgivem this city.
    2Although they say, 'As surely as the LORD lives,'n
        still they are swearing falsely."

    3O LORD, do not your eyeso look for truth?
        You struckp them, but they felt no pain;
        you crushed them, but they refused correction. q
    They made their faces harder than stoner
        and refused to repent.
    4I thought, "These are only the poor;

4:25
uJer 9:10; 12:4;
    Zep 1:3
4:27
vJer 5:10,18;
12:12; 30:11;
    46:28
4:28
wJer 12:4,11;
14:2; Hos 4:3
xIsa 5:30; 50:3
yNu 23:19
zJer 23:20;
    30:24
4:29
aJer 6:23
b2Ki 25:4 cver 7
4:30
dIsa 10:3-4
eEze 23:40
f2Ki 9:30
gLa 1:2;
Eze 23:9,22
4:31
hJer 13:21
iIsa 42:14
jIsa 1:15;
    La 1:17
5:1
k2Ch 16:9;
Eze 22:30
lGe 18:32
mGe 18:24
5:2
nJer 4:2
5:3
o2Ch 16:9
pIsa 9:13
qJer 2:30;
    Zep 3:2
rJer 7:26;
19:15; Eze 3:8-9

they are foolish,
for they do not know[s] the way of the LORD,
the requirements of their God.
[5]So I will go to the leaders[t]
and speak to them;
surely they know the way of the LORD,
the requirements of their God."
But with one accord they too had broken off the yoke
and torn off the bonds. [u]
[6]Therefore a lion from the forest will attack them,
a wolf from the desert will ravage them,
a leopard[v] will lie in wait near their towns
to tear to pieces any who venture out,
for their rebellion is great
and their backslidings many. [w]

[7]"Why should I forgive you?
Your children have forsaken me
and sworn[x] by gods that are not gods.[y]
I supplied all their needs,
yet they committed adultery[z]
and thronged to the houses of prostitutes.
[8]They are well-fed, lusty stallions,
each neighing for another man's wife. [a]
[9]Should I not punish them for this?"[b]
declares the LORD.
"Should I not avenge myself
on such a nation as this?

[10]"Go through her vineyards and ravage them,
but do not destroy them completely. [c]
Strip off her branches,
for these people do not belong to the LORD.
[11]The house of Israel and the house of Judah
have been utterly unfaithful[d] to me,"
declares the LORD.

[12]They have lied about the LORD;
they said, "He will do nothing!
No harm will come to us;[e]
we will never see sword or famine. [f]
[13]The prophets[g] are but wind
and the word is not in them;
so let what they say be done to them."

[14]Therefore this is what the LORD God Almighty says:

"Because the people have spoken these words,
I will make my words in your mouth[h] a fire[i]
and these people the wood it consumes.
[15]O house of Israel," declares the LORD,
"I am bringing a distant nation[j] against you—
an ancient and enduring nation,
a people whose language[k] you do not know,

5:4
[s] Jer 8:7
5:5
[t] Mic 3:1,9
[u] Ps 2:3;
Jer 2:20
5:6
[v] Hos 13:7
[w] Jer 30:14
5:7
[x] Jos 23:7;
Zep 1:5
[y] Dt 32:21;
Jer 2:11;
Gal 4:8
[z] Nu 25:1
5:8
[a] Jer 29:23;
Eze 22:11
5:9
[b] ver 29; Jer 9:9
5:10
[c] Jer 4:27
5:11
[d] Jer 3:20
5:12
[e] Jer 23:17
[f] 2Ch 36:16;
Jer 14:13
5:13
[g] Jer 14:15
5:14
[h] Jer 1:9;
Hos 6:5
[i] Jer 23:29
5:15
[j] Dt 28:49;
Isa 5:26;
Jer 4:16
[k] Isa 28:11

whose speech you do not understand.
¹⁶Their quivers are like an open grave;
all of them are mighty warriors.
¹⁷They will devour[l][m] your harvests and food,
devour[n][o] your sons and daughters;
they will devour[p] your flocks and herds,
devour your vines and fig trees.
With the sword they will destroy
the fortified cities in which you trust. [q]

¹⁸"Yet even in those days," declares the LORD, "I will not destroy[r] you completely. ¹⁹And when the people ask,[s] 'Why has the LORD our God done all this to us?' you will tell them, 'As you have forsaken me and served foreign gods[t] in your own land, so now you will serve foreigners[u] in a land not your own.'

²⁰"Announce this to the house of Jacob
and proclaim it in Judah:
²¹Hear this, you foolish and senseless people,
who have eyes[v] but do not see,
who have ears but do not hear:[w]
²²Should you not fear[x] me?" declares the LORD.
"Should you not tremble in my presence?
I made the sand a boundary for the sea,
an everlasting barrier it cannot cross.
The waves may roll, but they cannot prevail;
they may roar, but they cannot cross it.
²³But these people have stubborn and rebellious[y] hearts;
they have turned aside and gone away.
²⁴They do not say to themselves,
'Let us fear the LORD our God,
who gives autumn and spring rains[z] in season,
who assures us of the regular weeks of harvest.'[a]
²⁵Your wrongdoings have kept these away;
your sins have deprived you of good.

²⁶"Among my people are wicked men
who lie in wait[b] like men who snare birds
and like those who set traps to catch men.
²⁷Like cages full of birds,
their houses are full of deceit;[c]
they have become rich[d] and powerful
²⁸ and have grown fat[e] and sleek.
Their evil deeds have no limit;
they do not plead the case of the fatherless[f] to win it,
they do not defend the rights of the poor.[g]
²⁹Should I not punish them for this?"
declares the LORD.
"Should I not avenge myself
on such a nation as this?

³⁰"A horrible[h] and shocking thing
has happened in the land:
³¹The prophets prophesy lies,[i]

5:17
l Jer 8:16
m Lev 26:16
n Jer 50:7,17
o Dt 28:32
p Dt 28:31
q Dt 28:33
5:18
r Jer 4:27
5:19
s Dt 29:24-26;
1Ki 9:9
t Jer 16:13
u Dt 28:48
5:21
v Isa 6:10;
Eze 12:2
w Mt 13:15;
Mk 8:18
5:22
x Dt 28:58
5:23
y Dt 21:18
5:24
z Ps 147:8;
Joel 2:23
a Ge 8:22;
Ac 14:17
5:26
b Ps 10:8;
Pr 1:11
5:27
c Jer 9:6
d Jer 12:1
5:28
e Dt 32:15
f Zec 7:10
g Isa 1:23;
Jer 7:6
5:30
h Jer 23:14;
Hos 6:10
5:31
i Eze 13:6;
Mic 2:11

the priests rule by their own authority,
and my people love it this way.
But what will you do in the end?

Jerusalem Under Siege

6 "Flee for safety, people of Benjamin!
Flee from Jerusalem!
Sound the trumpet in Tekoa!ʲ
Raise the signal over Beth Hakkerem!ᵏ
For disaster looms out of the north,ˡ
even terrible destruction.
²I will destroy the Daughter of Zion,
so beautiful and delicate.
³Shepherdsᵐ with their flocks will come against her;
they will pitch their tents aroundⁿ her,
each tending his own portion."

⁴"Prepare for battle against her!
Arise, let us attack at noon!ᵒ
But, alas, the daylight is fading,
and the shadows of evening grow long.
⁵So arise, let us attack at night
and destroy her fortresses!"

⁶This is what the LORD Almighty says:

"Cut down the treesᵖ
and build siege ramps�q against Jerusalem.
This city must be punished;
it is filled with oppression.
⁷As a well pours out its water,
so she pours out her wickedness.
Violenceʳ and destructionˢ resound in her;
her sickness and wounds are ever before me.
⁸Take warning, O Jerusalem,
or I will turn awayᵗ from you
and make your land desolate
so no one can live in it."

⁹This is what the LORD Almighty says:

"Let them glean the remnant of Israel
as thoroughly as a vine;
pass your hand over the branches again,
like one gathering grapes."

¹⁰To whom can I speak and give warning?
Who will listen to me?
Their ears are closedᵃ ᵘ
so they cannot hear.
The wordᵛ of the LORD is offensive to them;
they find no pleasure in it.
¹¹But I am full of the wrathʷ of the LORD,

6:1
j2Ch 11:6
kNe 3:14
lJer 4:6
6:3
mJer 12:10
n2Ki 25:4;
Lk 19:43
6:4
oJer 15:8
6:6
pDt 20:19-20
qJer 32:24
6:7
rPs 55:9;
Eze 7:11,23
sJer 20:8
6:8
tEze 23:18;
Hos 9:12
6:10
uAc 7:51
vJer 20:8
6:11
wJer 7:20

ᵃ10 Hebrew *uncircumcised*

and I cannot hold it in.ˣ

"Pour it out on the children in the street
    and on the young menʸ gathered together;
both husband and wife will be caught in it,
    and the old, those weighed down with years.
¹²Their houses will be turned over to others,ᶻ
    together with their fields and their wives,ᵃ
when I stretch out my handᵇ
    against those who live in the land,"
                                    declares the Lᴏʀᴅ.

¹³"From the least to the greatest,
    all are greedy for gain;ᶜ
prophets and priests alike,
    all practice deceit. ᵈ
¹⁴They dress the wound of my people
    as though it were not serious.
'Peace, peace,' they say,
    when there is no peace. ᵉ
¹⁵Are they ashamed of their loathsome conduct?
    No, they have no shame at all;
    they do not even know how to blush. ᶠ
So they will fall among the fallen;
    they will be brought down when I punish them,"
                                    says the Lᴏʀᴅ.

¹⁶This is what the Lᴏʀᴅ says:

"Stand at the crossroads and look;
    ask for the ancient paths,ᵍ
ask where the good wayʰ is, and walk in it,
    and you will find restⁱ for your souls.
    But you said, 'We will not walk in it.'
¹⁷I appointed watchmenʲ over you and said,
    'Listen to the sound of the trumpet!'
    But you said, 'We will not listen.'ᵏ
¹⁸Therefore hear, O nations;
    observe, O witnesses,
    what will happen to them.
¹⁹Hear, O earth:ˡ
I am bringing disaster on this people,
    the fruit of their schemes, ᵐ
because they have not listened to my words
    and have rejected my law. ⁿ
²⁰What do I care about incense from Sheba
    or sweet calamusᵒ from a distant land?
Your burnt offerings are not acceptable;ᵖ
    your sacrifices�q do not please me."ʳ

²¹Therefore this is what the Lᴏʀᴅ says:

"I will put obstacles before this people.
    Fathers and sons alike will stumbleˢ over them;
    neighbors and friends will perish."

6:11
xJob 32:20;
Jer 20:9
yJer 9:21
6:12
zDt 28:30
aJer 8:10; 38:22
bIsa 5:25
6:13
cIsa 56:11
dJer 8:10
6:14
eJer 4:10; 8:11;
Eze 13:10
6:15
fJer 3:3;
8:10-12
6:16
gJer 18:15
hPs 119:3
iMt 11:29
6:17
jEze 3:17
kJer 11:7-8;
25:4
6:19
lIsa 1:2;
Jer 22:29
mPr 1:31
nJer 8:9
6:20
oEx 30:23
pAm 5:22
qPs 50:8-10;
Jer 7:21;
Mic 6:7-8
rIsa 1:11
6:21
sIsa 8:14

²²This is what the LORD says:

"Look, an army is coming
   from the land of the north;ᵗ
a great nation is being stirred up
   from the ends of the earth.
²³They are armed with bow and spear;
   they are cruel and show no mercy. ᵘ
They sound like the roaring sea
   as they ride on their horses;ᵛ
they come like men in battle formation
   to attack you, O Daughter of Zion."

²⁴We have heard reports about them,
   and our hands hang limp.
Anguishʷ has gripped us,
   pain like that of a woman in labor. ˣ
²⁵Do not go out to the fields
   or walk on the roads,
for the enemy has a sword,
   and there is terror on every side. ʸ
²⁶O my people, put on sackclothᶻ
   and roll in ashes;ᵃ
mourn with bitter wailing
   as for an only son, ᵇ
for suddenly the destroyer
   will come upon us.

²⁷"I have made you a testerᶜ of metals
   and my people the ore,
that you may observe
   and test their ways.
²⁸They are all hardened rebels, ᵈ
   going about to slander. ᵉ
They are bronze and iron;ᶠ
   they all act corruptly.
²⁹The bellows blow fiercely
   to burn away the lead with fire,
but the refining goes on in vain;
   the wicked are not purged out.
³⁰They are called rejected silver,
   because the LORD has rejected them."ᵍ

False Religion Worthless

7 This is the word that came to Jeremiah from the LORD: ²"Standʰ at
the gate of the LORD's house and there proclaim this message:
" 'Hear the word of the LORD, all you people of Judah who come
through these gates to worship the LORD. ³This is what the LORD
Almighty, the God of Israel, says: Reform your waysⁱ and your actions,
and I will let you live in this place. ⁴Do not trust in deceptiveʲ words
and say, "This is the temple of the LORD, the temple of the LORD, the
temple of the LORD!" ⁵If you really change your ways and your actions
and deal with each other justly,ᵏ ⁶if you do not oppress the alien, the

6:22
ᵗJer 1:15; 10:22
6:23
ᵘIsa 13:18
ᵛJer 4:29
6:24
ʷJer 4:19
ˣJer 4:31;
50:41-43
6:25
ʸJer 49:29
6:26
ᶻJer 4:8
ᵃJer 25:34;
Mic 1:10
ᵇZec 12:10
6:27
ᶜJer 9:7
6:28
ᵈJer 5:23
ᵉJer 9:4
ᶠEze 22:18
6:30
ᵍPs 119:119;
Jer 7:29;
Hos 9:17
7:2
ʰJer 17:19
7:3
ⁱJer 18:11;
26:13
7:4
ʲMic 3:11
7:5
ᵏJer 22:3

7:6
1Jer 2:34; 19:4
mDt 8:19
7:7
nDt 4:40
7:8
over 4
7:9
pJer 11:13,17
qEx 20:3
7:10
rver 30;
Jer 32:34;
Eze 23:38-39
7:11
sIsa 56:7
tMt 21:13*;
Mk 11:17*;
Lk 19:46
uJer 29:23
7:12
vJos 18:1
w1Sa 4:10-11,
22; Ps 78:60-64
7:13
x2Ch 36:15
yIsa 65:12
zPr 1:24
aJer 35:17
7:14
b1Ki 9:7 cver 4
7:15
dPs 78:67
7:16
eEx 32:10;
Dt 9:14;
Jer 15:1
7:18
fJer 44:17-19
gJer 19:13
h1Ki 14:9
7:19
iDt 32:21
jJer 9:19
7:20
kJer 42:18;
La 2:3-5
1Jer 6:11-12
mJer 11:16
7:21
nIsa 1:11;
Am 5:21-22
oHos 8:13
7:22
p1Sa 15:22;
Ps 51:16;
Hos 6:6
7:23
qEx 19:5
rLev 26:12
sEx 15:26
7:24
tPs 81:11-12;
Jer 11:8
7:25
u2Ch 36:15
vJer 25:4
7:26
wJer 16:12
7:27
xEze 2:7
yEze 3:7
7:29
zJob 1:20;
Isa 15:2;
Mic 1:16

fatherless or the widow and do not shed innocent blood[1] in this place, and if you do not follow other gods[m] to your own harm, [7]then I will let you live in this place, in the land[n] I gave your forefathers for ever and ever. [8]But look, you are trusting in deceptive[o] words that are worthless.

[9]" 'Will you steal and murder, commit adultery and perjury,[a] burn incense to Baal[p] and follow other gods[q] you have not known, [10]and then come and stand before me in this house,[r] which bears my Name, and say, "We are safe"—safe to do all these detestable things? [11]Has this house,[s] which bears my Name, become a den of robbers[t] to you? But I have been watching![u] declares the LORD.

[12]" 'Go now to the place in Shiloh[v] where I first made a dwelling for my Name, and see what I did[w] to it because of the wickedness of my people Israel. [13]While you were doing all these things, declares the LORD, I spoke to you again and again,[x] but you did not listen;[y] I called[z] you, but you did not answer.[a] [14]Therefore, what I did to Shiloh I will now do to the house that bears my Name,[b] the temple[c] you trust in, the place I gave to you and your fathers. [15]I will thrust you from my presence, just as I did all your brothers, the people of Ephraim.'[d]

[16]"So do not pray for this people nor offer any plea[e] or petition for them; do not plead with me, for I will not listen to you. [17]Do you not see what they are doing in the towns of Judah and in the streets of Jerusalem? [18]The children gather wood, the fathers light the fire, and the women knead the dough and make cakes of bread for the Queen of Heaven.[f] They pour out drink offerings[g] to other gods to provoke[h] me to anger. [19]But am I the one they are provoking?[i] declares the LORD. Are they not rather harming themselves, to their own shame?[j]

[20]" 'Therefore this is what the Sovereign LORD says: My anger[k] and my wrath will be poured[l] out on this place, on man and beast, on the trees of the field and on the fruit of the ground, and it will burn and not be quenched.[m]

[21]" 'This is what the LORD Almighty, the God of Israel, says: Go ahead, add your burnt offerings to your other sacrifices[n] and eat[o] the meat yourselves! [22]For when I brought your forefathers out of Egypt and spoke to them, I did not just give them commands about burnt offerings and sacrifices,[p] [23]but I gave them this command: Obey[q] me, and I will be your God and you will be my people.[r] Walk in all the ways I command you, that it may go well[s] with you. [24]But they did not listen or pay attention;[t] instead, they followed the stubborn inclinations of their evil hearts. They went backward and not forward. [25]From the time your forefathers left Egypt until now, day after day, again and again[u] I sent you my servants the prophets.[v] [26]But they did not listen to me or pay attention. They were stiff-necked and did more evil than their forefathers.'[w]

[27]"When you tell[x] them all this, they will not listen[y] to you; when you call to them, they will not answer. [28]Therefore say to them, 'This is the nation that has not obeyed the LORD its God or responded to correction. Truth has perished; it has vanished from their lips. [29]Cut off[z] your hair and throw it away; take up a lament on the barren

a9 Or *and swear by false gods*

heights, for the LORD has rejected and abandoned[a] this generation that is under his wrath.

The Valley of Slaughter

30" 'The people of Judah have done evil in my eyes, declares the LORD. They have set up their detestable idols[b] in the house that bears my Name and have defiled[c] it. 31They have built the high places of Topheth[d] in the Valley of Ben Hinnom to burn their sons and daughters[e] in the fire—something I did not command, nor did it enter my mind.[f] 32So beware, the days are coming, declares the LORD, when people will no longer call it Topheth or the Valley of Ben Hinnom, but the Valley of Slaughter,[g] for they will bury[h] the dead in Topheth until there is no more room. 33Then the carcasses of this people will become food[i] for the birds of the air and the beasts of the earth, and there will be no one to frighten them away. 34I will bring an end to the sounds[j] of joy and gladness and to the voices of bride and bridegroom[k] in the towns of Judah and the streets of Jerusalem, for the land will become desolate.[l]

8 " 'At that time, declares the LORD, the bones of the kings and officials of Judah, the bones of the priests and prophets, and the bones of the people of Jerusalem will be removed from their graves. 2They will be exposed to the sun and the moon and all the stars of the heavens, which they have loved and served[m] and which they have followed and consulted and worshiped. They will not be gathered up or buried, but will be like refuse lying on the ground. 3Wherever I banish them, all the survivors of this evil nation will prefer death to life,[n] declares the LORD Almighty.'

Sin and Punishment

4"Say to them, 'This is what the LORD says:

" 'When men fall down, do they not get up?[o]
When a man turns away, does he not return?
5Why then have these people turned away?
Why does Jerusalem always turn away?
They cling to deceit;[p]
they refuse to return.[q]
6I have listened attentively,
but they do not say what is right.
No one repents[r] of his wickedness,
saying, "What have I done?"
Each pursues his own course[s]
like a horse charging into battle.
7Even the stork in the sky
knows her appointed seasons,
and the dove, the swift and the thrush
observe the time of their migration.
But my people do not know[t]
the requirements of the LORD.

8" 'How can you say, "We are wise,
for we have the law[u] of the LORD,"
when actually the lying pen of the scribes

7:29
aJer 6:30
7:30
bEze 7:20-22
cJer 32:34
7:31
d2Ki 23:10
ePs 106:38
fJer 19:5
7:32
gJer 19:6
hJer 19:11
7:33
iDt 28:26
7:34
jIsa 24:8;
Eze 26:13
kRev 18:23
lLev 26:34
8:2
m2Ki 23:5;
Ac 7:42
8:3
nJob 3:22;
Rev 9:6
8:4
oPr 24:16
8:5
pJer 5:27
qJer 7:24; 9:6
8:6
rRev 9:20
sPs 14:1-3
8:7
tIsa 1:3;
Jer 5:4-5
8:8
uRo 2:17

has handled it falsely?
⁹The wise[v] will be put to shame;
   they will be dismayed and trapped.
Since they have rejected the word[w] of the Lord,
   what kind of wisdom do they have?
¹⁰Therefore I will give their wives to other men
   and their fields to new owners.[x]
From the least to the greatest,
   all are greedy for gain;[y]
prophets and priests alike,
   all practice deceit.
¹¹They dress the wound of my people
   as though it were not serious.
"Peace, peace," they say,
   when there is no peace.[z]
¹²Are they ashamed of their loathsome conduct?
   No, they have no shame[a] at all;
   they do not even know how to blush.
So they will fall among the fallen;
   they will be brought down when they are punished,[b]
                says the Lord.[c]

¹³ 'I will take away their harvest,
             declares the Lord.
There will be no grapes on the vine.[d]
There will be no figs[e] on the tree,
   and their leaves will wither.[f]
What I have given them
   will be taken[g] from them.[a] ' "

¹⁴"Why are we sitting here?
   Gather together!
Let us flee to the fortified cities[h]
   and perish there!
For the Lord our God has doomed us to perish
   and given us poisoned water[i] to drink,
   because we have sinned[j] against him.
¹⁵We hoped for peace[k]
   but no good has come,
for a time of healing
   but there was only terror.[l]
¹⁶The snorting of the enemy's horses
   is heard from Dan;[m]
at the neighing of their stallions
   the whole land trembles.
They have come to devour
   the land and everything in it,
   the city and all who live there."

¹⁷"See, I will send venomous snakes[n] among you,
   vipers that cannot be charmed,[o]

8:9
v Jer 6:15
w Jer 6:19
8:10
x Jer 6:12
y Isa 56:11
8:11
z Jer 6:14
8:12
a Jer 3:3
b Ps 52:5-7;
Isa 3:9 c Jer 6:15
8:13
d Joel 1:7
e Lk 13:6
f Mt 21:19
g Jer 5:17
8:14
h Jer 4:5;
Jer 35:11
i Dt 29:18;
Jer 9:15; 23:15
j Jer 14:7,20
8:15
k ver 11
l Jer 14:19
8:16
m Jer 4:15
8:17
n Nu 21:6;
Dt 32:24
o Ps 58:5

ᵃ13 The meaning of the Hebrew for this sentence is uncertain.

and they will bite you,"

declares the LORD.

[18]O my Comforter[a] in sorrow,
    my heart is faint[p] within me.
[19]Listen to the cry of my people
    from a land far away:[q]
"Is the LORD not in Zion?
    Is her King no longer there?"

"Why have they provoked me to anger with their
        images,
    with their worthless foreign idols?"[r]

[20]"The harvest is past,
    the summer has ended,
    and we are not saved."

[21]Since my people are crushed, I am crushed;
    I mourn,[s] and horror grips me.
[22]Is there no balm in Gilead?[t]
    Is there no physician there?
Why then is there no healing[u]
    for the wound of my people?

9 [1]Oh, that my head were a spring of water
    and my eyes a fountain of tears!
I would weep[v] day and night
    for the slain of my people.[w]
[2]Oh, that I had in the desert
    a lodging place for travelers,
so that I might leave my people
    and go away from them;
for they are all adulterers,[x]
    a crowd of unfaithful people.

[3]"They make ready their tongue
    like a bow, to shoot lies;[y]
it is not by truth
    that they triumph[b] in the land.
They go from one sin to another;
    they do not acknowledge me,"

declares the LORD.

[4]"Beware of your friends;
    do not trust your brothers.[z]
For every brother is a deceiver,[c][a]
    and every friend a slanderer.
[5]Friend deceives friend,
    and no one speaks the truth.
They have taught their tongues to lie;
    they weary themselves with sinning.
[6]You[d] live in the midst of deception;[b]

8:18
pLa 5:17
8:19
qJer 9:16
rDt 32:21
8:21
sJer 14:17
8:22
tGe 37:25
uJer 30:12
9:1
vJer 13:17;
La 2:11,18
wIsa 22:4
9:2
xJer 5:7-8;
23:10; Hos 4:2
9:3
yPs 64:3
9:4
zMic 7:5-6
aGe 27:35
9:6
bJer 5:27

---

*a18 The meaning of the Hebrew for this word is uncertain.   b3 Or lies; / they are not valiant for
truth   c4 Or a deceiving Jacob   d6 That is, Jeremiah (the Hebrew is singular)*

in their deceit they refuse to acknowledge me,"
                                   declares the LORD.

7Therefore this is what the LORD Almighty says:

"See, I will refine[c] and test[d] them,
     for what else can I do
     because of the sin of my people?
8Their tongue[e] is a deadly arrow;
     it speaks with deceit.
With his mouth each speaks cordially to his neighbor,
     but in his heart he sets a trap[f] for him.
9Should I not punish them for this?"
     declares the LORD.
"Should I not avenge[g] myself
     on such a nation as this?"

10I will weep and wail for the mountains
     and take up a lament concerning the desert pastures.
They are desolate and untraveled,
     and the lowing of cattle is not heard.
The birds of the air[h] have fled
     and the animals are gone.

11"I will make Jerusalem a heap of ruins,
     a haunt of jackals;[i]
and I will lay waste the towns of Judah
     so no one can live there."[j]

12What man is wise[k] enough to understand this? Who has been instructed by the LORD and can explain it? Why has the land been ruined and laid waste like a desert that no one can cross?

13The LORD said, "It is because they have forsaken my law, which I set before them; they have not obeyed me or followed my law.[l] 14Instead, they have followed[m] the stubbornness of their hearts;[n] they have followed the Baals, as their fathers taught them." 15Therefore, this is what the LORD Almighty, the God of Israel, says: "See, I will make this people eat bitter food[o] and drink poisoned water.[p] 16I will scatter them among nations[q] that neither they nor their fathers have known,[r] and I will pursue them with the sword[s] until I have destroyed them."[t]

17This is what the LORD Almighty says:

"Consider now! Call for the wailing women[u] to come;
     send for the most skillful of them.
18Let them come quickly
     and wail over us
till our eyes overflow with tears
     and water streams from our eyelids.[v]
19The sound of wailing is heard from Zion:
     'How ruined[w] we are!
     How great is our shame!
We must leave our land
     because our houses are in ruins.' "

20Now, O women, hear the word of the LORD;

9:7
c Isa 1:25
d Jer 6:27
9:8
e ver 3 f Jer 5:26
9:9
g Jer 5:9,29
9:10
h Jer 4:25; 12:4;
Hos 4:3
9:11
i Isa 34:13
j Isa 25:2;
Jer 26:9
9:12
k Ps 107:43;
Hos 14:9
9:13
l 2Ch 7:19;
Ps 89:30-32
9:14
m Jer 2:8,23
n Jer 7:24
9:15
o La 3:15
p Jer 8:14
9:16
q Lev 26:33
r Dt 28:64
s Eze 5:2
t Jer 44:27;
Eze 5:12
9:17
u 2Ch 35:25;
Ecc 12:5;
Am 5:16
9:18
v Jer 14:17
9:19
w Jer 4:13

open your ears to the words of his mouth.
Teach your daughters how to wail;
   teach one another a lament. ˣ
²¹Death has climbed in through our windows
   and has entered our fortresses;
it has cut off the children from the streets
   and the young menʸ from the public squares.

²²Say, "This is what the LORD declares:

" 'The dead bodies of men will lie
   like refuseᶻ on the open field,
like cut grain behind the reaper,
   with no one to gather them.' "

²³This is what the LORD says:

"Let not the wise man boast of his wisdomᵃ
   or the strong man boast of his strengthᵇ
   or the rich man boast of his riches,ᶜ
²⁴but let him who boasts boastᵈ about this:
   that he understands and knows me,
that I am the LORD,ᵉ who exercises kindness,ᶠ
   justice and righteousnessᵍ on earth,
   for in these I delight,"

declares the LORD.

²⁵"The days are coming," declares the LORD, "when I will punish all who are circumcised only in the fleshʰ— ²⁶Egypt, Judah, Edom, Ammon, Moab and all who live in the desert in distant places.ᵃⁱ   For all these nations are really uncircumcised, and even the whole house of Israel is uncircumcised in heart.ʲ "

God and Idols

10:12–16pp — Jer 51:15–19

10 Hear what the LORD says to you, O house of Israel. ²This is what the LORD says:

"Do not learn the ways of the nationsᵏ
   or be terrified by signs in the sky,
   though the nations are terrified by them.
³For the customs of the peoples are worthless;
   they cut a tree out of the forest,
   and a craftsmanˡ shapes it with his chisel.
⁴They adorn it with silver and gold;
   they fasten it with hammer and nails
   so it will not totter. ᵐ
⁵Like a scarecrow in a melon patch,
   their idols cannot speak;ⁿ
they must be carried
   because they cannot walk.ᵒ
Do not fear them;
   they can do no harm

ᵃ26 Or *desert and who clip the hair by their foreheads*

9:20
xIsa 32:9-13
9:21
y2Ch 36:17
9:22
zJer 8:2
9:23
aEcc 9:11
b1Ki 20:11
cEze 28:4-5
9:24
d1Co 1:31*;
Gal 6:14
e2Co 10:17*
fPs 51:1;
Mic 7:18
gPs 36:6
9:25
hRo 2:8-9
9:26
iJer 25:23
jLev 26:41;
Ac 7:51;
Ro 2:28
10:2
kLev 20:23
10:3
lIsa 40:19
10:4
mIsa 41:7
10:5
n1Co 12:2
oPs 115:5,7

nor can they do any good."ᵖ

⁶No one is like you, O Lᴏʀᴅ;
    you are great,�q
    and your name is mighty in power.
⁷Who should not revere you,
    O King of the nations?ʳ
    This is your due.
  Among all the wise men of the nations
    and in all their kingdoms,
    there is no one like you.
  ⁸They are all senseless and foolish;ˢ
    they are taught by worthless wooden idols.
  ⁹Hammered silver is brought from Tarshish
    and gold from Uphaz.
  What the craftsman and goldsmith have madeᵗ
    is then dressed in blue and purple—
    all made by skilled workers.
  ¹⁰But the Lᴏʀᴅ is the true God;
    he is the living God, the eternal King.
  When he is angry, the earth trembles;
    the nations cannot endure his wrath. ᵘ

¹¹"Tell them this: 'These gods, who did not make the heavens and the
earth, will perishᵛ from the earth and from under the heavens.' "ᵃ

  ¹²But God made the earth by his power;
    he founded the world by his wisdom
    and stretched out the heavensʷ by his understanding.
  ¹³When he thunders,ˣ the waters in the heavens roar;
    he makes clouds rise from the ends of the earth.
  He sends lightning with the rainʸ
    and brings out the wind from his storehouses.

  ¹⁴Everyone is senseless and without knowledge;
    every goldsmith is shamed by his idols.
  His images are a fraud;
    they have no breath in them.
  ¹⁵They are worthless,ᶻ the objects of mockery;
    when their judgment comes, they will perish.
  ¹⁶He who is the Portionᵃ of Jacob is not like these,
    for he is the Maker of all things,ᵇ
  including Israel, the tribe of his inheritanceᶜ—
    the Lᴏʀᴅ Almighty is his name.ᵈ

Coming Destruction

  ¹⁷Gather up your belongingsᵉ to leave the land,
    you who live under siege.
  ¹⁸For this is what the Lᴏʀᴅ says:
    "At this time I will hurlᶠ out
    those who live in this land;
    I will bring distress on them

10:5
p Isa 41:24; 46:7
10:6
q Ps 48:1
10:7
r Ps 22:28;
Rev 15:4
10:8
s Isa 40:19;
Jer 4:22
10:9
t Ps 115:4;
Isa 40:19
10:10
u Ps 76:7
10:11
v Ps 96:5;
Isa 2:18
10:12
w Ge 1:1,8;
Job 9:8;
Isa 40:22
10:13
x Job 36:29
y Ps 135:7
10:15
z Isa 41:24;
Jer 14:22
10:16
a Dt 32:9;
Ps 119:57
b ver 12 c Ps 74:2
d Jer 31:35;
32:18
10:17
e Eze 12:3-12
10:18
f 1Sa 25:29

ᵃ11 The text of this verse is in Aramaic.

so that they may be captured."

19Woe to me because of my injury!
　　My wound[g] is incurable!
Yet I said to myself,
　　"This is my sickness, and I must endure[h] it."
20My tent[i] is destroyed;
　　all its ropes are snapped.
My sons are gone from me and are no more;[j]
　　no one is left now to pitch my tent
　　or to set up my shelter.
21The shepherds are senseless
　　and do not inquire of the LORD;
so they do not prosper
　　and all their flock is scattered.[k]
22Listen! The report is coming—
　　a great commotion from the land of the north!
It will make the towns of Judah desolate,
　　a haunt of jackals.[l]

Jeremiah's Prayer

23I know, O LORD, that a man's life is not his own;
　　it is not for man to direct his steps.[m]
24Correct me, LORD, but only with justice—
　　not in your anger,[n]
　　lest you reduce me to nothing.[o]
25Pour out your wrath on the nations[p]
　　that do not acknowledge you,
　　on the peoples who do not call on your name.[q]
For they have devoured[r] Jacob;
　　they have devoured him completely
　　and destroyed his homeland.[s]

The Covenant Is Broken

11 This is the word that came to Jeremiah from the LORD: 2"Listen to the terms of this covenant and tell them to the people of Judah and to those who live in Jerusalem. 3Tell them that this is what the LORD, the God of Israel, says: 'Cursed[t] is the man who does not obey the terms of this covenant— 4the terms I commanded your forefathers when I brought them out of Egypt, out of the iron-smelting furnace.[u]' I said, 'Obey[v] me and do everything I command you, and you will be my people,[w] and I will be your God. 5Then I will fulfill the oath I swore[x] to your forefathers, to give them a land flowing with milk and honey'—the land you possess today."

I answered, "Amen, LORD."

6The LORD said to me, "Proclaim all these words in the towns of Judah and in the streets of Jerusalem: 'Listen to the terms of this covenant and follow[y] them. 7From the time I brought your forefathers up from Egypt until today, I warned them again and again,[z] saying, "Obey me." 8But they did not listen or pay attention;[a] instead, they followed the stubbornness of their evil hearts. So I brought on them all

10:19
g Jer 14:17
h Mic 7:9
10:20
i Jer 4:20
j Jer 31:15;
La 1:5
10:21
k Jer 23:2
10:22
l Jer 9:11
10:23
m Pr 20:24
10:24
n Ps 6:1; 38:1
o Jer 30:11
10:25
p Zep 3:8
q Job 18:21;
Ps 14:4
r Ps 79:7;
Jer 8:16
s Ps 79:6-7
11:3
t Dt 27:26;
Gal 3:10
11:4
u Dt 4:20;
1Ki 8:51
v Ex 24:8
w Jer 7:23;
31:33
11:5
x Ex 13:5;
Dt 7:12;
Ps 105:8-11
11:6
y Dt 15:5;
Ro 2:13;
Jas 1:22
11:7
z 2Ch 36:15
11:8
a Jer 7:26

the curses [b] of the covenant I had commanded them to follow but that they did not keep.' "

[9]Then the LORD said to me, "There is a conspiracy [c] among the people of Judah and those who live in Jerusalem. [10]They have returned to the sins of their forefathers, [d] who refused to listen to my words. They have followed other gods [e] to serve them. Both the house of Israel and the house of Judah have broken the covenant I made with their forefathers. [11]Therefore this is what the LORD says: 'I will bring on them a disaster [f] they cannot escape. Although they cry [g] out to me, I will not listen [h] to them. [12]The towns of Judah and the people of Jerusalem will go and cry out to the gods to whom they burn incense, [i] but they will not help them at all when disaster [j] strikes. [13]You have as many gods as you have towns, O Judah; and the altars you have set up to burn incense [k] to that shameful [l] god Baal are as many as the streets of Jerusalem.'

[14]"Do not pray [m] for this people nor offer any plea or petition for them, because I will not listen [n] when they call to me in the time of their distress.

> [15]"What is my beloved doing in my temple
>   as she works out her evil schemes with many?
>   Can consecrated meat avert ˌyour punishmentˌ?
> When you engage in your wickedness,
>   then you rejoice. [a] "

> [16]The LORD called you a thriving olive tree
>   with fruit beautiful in form.
> But with the roar of a mighty storm
>   he will set it on fire, [o]
>   and its branches will be broken. [p]

[17]The LORD Almighty, who planted [q] you, has decreed disaster for you, because the house of Israel and the house of Judah have done evil and provoked me to anger by burning incense to Baal. [r]

Plot Against Jeremiah

[18]Because the LORD revealed their plot to me, I knew it, for at that time he showed me what they were doing. [19]I had been like a gentle lamb led to the slaughter; I did not realize that they had plotted [s] against me, saying,

> "Let us destroy the tree and its fruit;
>   let us cut him off from the land of the living, [t]
>   that his name be remembered [u] no more."
> [20]But, O LORD Almighty, you who judge righteously
>   and test the heart and mind, [v]
> let me see your vengeance upon them,
>   for to you I have committed my cause.

[21]"Therefore this is what the LORD says about the men of Anathoth who are seeking your life [w] and saying, 'Do not prophesy in the name of the LORD or you will die [x] by our hands'— [22]therefore this is what the LORD Almighty says: 'I will punish them. Their young men [y] will die by

11:8
b Lev 26:14-43
11:9
c Eze 22:25
11:10
d Dt 9:7
e Jdg 2:12-13
11:11
f 2Ki 22:16
g Jer 14:12;
Eze 8:18
h ver 14;
Pr 1:28;
Isa 1:15;
Zec 7:13
11:12
i Jer 44:17
j Dt 32:37
11:13
k Jer 7:9
l Jer 3:24
11:14
m Ex 32:10
n ver 11
11:16
o Jer 21:14
p Isa 27:11;
Ro 11:17-24
11:17
q Isa 5:2;
Jer 12:2 r Jer 7:9
11:19
s Jer 18:18;
20:10
t Job 28:13;
Isa 53:8
u Ps 83:4
11:20
v Ps 7:9
11:21
w Jer 12:6
x Jer 26:8,11;
38:4
11:22
y Jer 18:21

---

a 15 Or *Could consecrated meat avert your punishment? | Then you would rejoice* the sword, their sons and daughters by famine. [23]Not even a remnant[z] will be left to them, because I will bring disaster on the men of Anathoth in the year of their punishment.[a]' "

Jeremiah's Complaint

12 You are always righteous,[b] O LORD,
　　　when I bring a case before you.
　Yet I would speak with you about your justice:
　　　Why does the way of the wicked prosper?[c]
　　　Why do all the faithless live at ease?
　[2]You have planted[d] them, and they have taken root;
　　　they grow and bear fruit.
　You are always on their lips
　　　but far from their hearts.[e]
　[3]Yet you know me, O LORD;
　　　you see me and test[f] my thoughts about you.
　Drag them off like sheep to be butchered!
　　　Set them apart for the day of slaughter![g]
　[4]How long will the land lie parched[a][h]
　　　and the grass in every field be withered?[i]
　Because those who live in it are wicked,
　　　the animals and birds have perished.[j]
　Moreover, the people are saying,
　　　"He will not see what happens to us."

God's Answer

　[5]"If you have raced with men on foot
　　　and they have worn you out,
　　　how can you compete with horses?
　If you stumble in safe country,[b]
　　　how will you manage in the thickets[k] by[c] the Jordan?
　[6]Your brothers, your own family—
　　　even they have betrayed you;
　　　they have raised a loud cry against you.[l]
　Do not trust them,
　　　though they speak well of you.[m]

　[7]"I will forsake my house,
　　　abandon[n] my inheritance;
　I will give the one I love
　　　into the hands of her enemies.
　[8]My inheritance has become to me
　　　like a lion in the forest.
　She roars at me;
　　　therefore I hate her.[o]
　[9]Has not my inheritance become to me
　　　like a speckled bird of prey
　　　that other birds of prey surround and attack?
　Go and gather all the wild beasts;
　　　bring them to devour.[p]

11:23
z Jer 6:9
a Jer 23:12
12:1
b Ezr 9:15
c Jer 5:27-28
12:2
d Jer 11:17
e Isa 29:13;
Jer 3:10;
Mt 15:8;
Tit 1:16
12:3
f Ps 7:9; 11:5;
139:1-4;
Jer 11:20
g Jer 17:18
12:4
h Jer 4:28
i Joel 1:10-12
j Jer 4:25; 9:10
12:5
k Jer 49:19;
50:44
12:6
l Pr 26:24-25;
Jer 9:4 m Ps 12:2
12:7
n Jer 7:29
12:8
o Hos 9:15;
Am 6:8
12:9
p Isa 56:9;
Jer 15:3;
Eze 23:25

---

[a]4 Or *land mourn*　　　[b]5 Or *If you put your trust in a land of safety*　　　[c]5 Or *the flooding of*

¹⁰Many shepherds^q will ruin my vineyard
  and trample down my field;
they will turn my pleasant field
  into a desolate wasteland.^r
¹¹It will be made a wasteland,
  parched and desolate before me;^s
the whole land will be laid waste
  because there is no one who cares.
¹²Over all the barren heights in the desert
  destroyers will swarm,
for the sword of the LORD^t will devour
  from one end of the land to the other;^u
  no one will be safe.
¹³They will sow wheat but reap thorns;
  they will wear themselves out but gain nothing.^v
So bear the shame of your harvest
  because of the LORD's fierce anger."^w

¹⁴This is what the LORD says: "As for all my wicked neighbors who seize the inheritance I gave my people Israel, I will uproot^x them from their lands and I will uproot the house of Judah from among them. ¹⁵But after I uproot them, I will again have compassion and will bring^y each of them back to his own inheritance and his own country. ¹⁶And if they learn well the ways of my people and swear by my name, saying, 'As surely as the LORD lives'^z—even as they once taught my people to swear by Baal^a—then they will be established among my people.^b ¹⁷But if any nation does not listen, I will completely uproot and destroy^c it," declares the LORD.

A Linen Belt

13 This is what the LORD said to me: "Go and buy a linen belt and put it around your waist, but do not let it touch water." ²So I bought a belt, as the LORD directed, and put it around my waist.

³Then the word of the LORD came to me a second time: ⁴"Take the belt you bought and are wearing around your waist, and go now to Perath^a and hide it there in a crevice in the rocks." ⁵So I went and hid it at Perath, as the LORD told me. ^d

⁶Many days later the LORD said to me, "Go now to Perath and get the belt I told you to hide there." ⁷So I went to Perath and dug up the belt and took it from the place where I had hidden it, but now it was ruined and completely useless.

⁸Then the word of the LORD came to me: ⁹"This is what the LORD says: 'In the same way I will ruin the pride of Judah and the great pride^e of Jerusalem. ¹⁰These wicked people, who refuse to listen to my words, who follow the stubbornness of their hearts^f and go after other gods^g to serve and worship them, will be like this belt—completely useless! ¹¹For as a belt is bound around a man's waist, so I bound the whole house of Israel and the whole house of Judah to me,' declares the LORD, 'to be my people for my renown^h and praise and honor.ⁱ But they have not listened.'^j

^a4 Or possibly *the Euphrates*; also in verses 5-7

12:10
q Jer 23:1
r Isa 5:1-7
12:11
s ver 4;
Isa 42:25;
Jer 23:10
12:12
t Jer 47:6
u Jer 3:2
12:13
v Lev 26:20;
Dt 28:38;
Mic 6:15;
Hag 1:6
w Jer 4:26
12:14
x Zec 2:7-9
12:15
y Am 9:14-15
12:16
z Jer 4:2
a Jos 23:7
b Isa 49:6;
Jer 3:17
12:17
c Isa 60:12
13:5
d Ex 40:16
13:9
e Lev 26:19
13:10
f Jer 11:8; 16:12
g Jer 9:14
13:11
h Jer 32:20; 33:9
i Ex 19:5-6
j Jer 7:26

Wineskins

12"Say to them: 'This is what the Lord, the God of Israel, says: Every wineskin should be filled with wine.' And if they say to you, 'Don't we know that every wineskin should be filled with wine?' 13then tell them, 'This is what the Lord says: I am going to fill with drunkenness[k] all who live in this land, including the kings who sit on David's throne, the priests, the prophets and all those living in Jerusalem. 14I will smash them one against the other, fathers and sons alike, declares the Lord. I will allow no pity or mercy or compassion[l] to keep me from destroying[m] them.' "

Threat of Captivity

15Hear and pay attention,
    do not be arrogant,
        for the Lord has spoken.
16Give glory[n] to the Lord your God
    before he brings the darkness,
    before your feet stumble[o]
        on the darkening hills.
You hope for light,
    but he will turn it to thick darkness
    and change it to deep gloom.[p]
17But if you do not listen,[q]
    I will weep in secret
    because of your pride;
my eyes will weep bitterly,
    overflowing with tears,[r]
    because the Lord's flock[s] will be taken captive.[t]

18Say to the king and to the queen mother,
    "Come down from your thrones,
for your glorious crowns
    will fall from your heads."
19The cities in the Negev will be shut up,
    and there will be no one to open them.
All Judah[u] will be carried into exile,
    carried completely away.

20Lift up your eyes and see
    those who are coming from the north.[v]
Where is the flock[w] that was entrusted to you,
    the sheep of which you boasted?
21What will you say when ⌊the Lord⌋ sets over you
    those you cultivated as your special allies?[x]
Will not pain grip you
    like that of a woman in labor?[y]
22And if you ask yourself,
    "Why has this happened to me?"—
it is because of your many sins[z]
    that your skirts have been torn off
    and your body mistreated.[a]

13:13
k Ps 60:3; 75:8;
Isa 51:17; 63:6;
Jer 51:57
13:14
l Jer 16:5
m Dt 29:20;
Eze 5:10
13:16
n Jos 7:19
o Jer 23:12
p Isa 59:9
13:17
q Mal 2:2
r Jer 9:1
s Ps 80:1;
Jer 23:1
t Jer 14:18
13:19
u Jer 20:4; 52:30
13:20
v Jer 6:22;
Hab 1:6
w Jer 23:2
13:21
x Jer 38:22
y Jer 4:31
13:22
z Jer 9:2-6;
16:10-12
a Eze 16:37;
Na 3:5-6

²³Can the Ethiopian^a change his skin
    or the leopard its spots?
Neither can you do good
    who are accustomed to doing evil.

²⁴"I will scatter you like chaff^b
    driven by the desert wind. ^c
²⁵This is your lot,
    the portion^d I have decreed for you,"

                    declares the LORD,

"because you have forgotten me
    and trusted in false gods.
²⁶I will pull up your skirts over your face
    that your shame may be seen^e—
²⁷your adulteries and lustful neighings,
    your shameless prostitution!^f
I have seen your detestable acts
    on the hills and in the fields. ^g
Woe to you, O Jerusalem!
    How long will you be unclean?"^h

Drought, Famine, Sword

14 This is the word of the LORD to Jeremiah concerning the drought:

²"Judah mourns, ⁱ
    her cities languish;
they wail for the land,
    and a cry goes up from Jerusalem.
³The nobles send their servants for water;
    they go to the cisterns
    but find no water. ^j
They return with their jars unfilled;
    dismayed and despairing,
    they cover their heads. ^k
⁴The ground is cracked
    because there is no rain in the land;^l
the farmers are dismayed
    and cover their heads.
⁵Even the doe in the field
    deserts her newborn fawn
    because there is no grass. ^m
⁶Wild donkeys stand on the barren heightsⁿ
    and pant like jackals;
their eyesight fails
    for lack of pasture."

⁷Although our sins testify^o against us,
    O LORD, do something for the sake of your name.
For our backsliding^p is great;
    we have sinned^q against you.
⁸O Hope^r of Israel,

---

^a23 Hebrew *Cushite* (probably a person from the upper Nile region)

13:24
bPs 1:4
cLev 26:33
13:25
dJob 20:29;
Mt 24:51
13:26
eLa 1:8;
Eze 16:37;
Hos 2:10
13:27
fJer 2:20
gEze 6:13
hHos 8:5
14:2
iIsa 3:26;
Jer 8:21
14:3
j2Ki 18:31;
Job 6:19-20
k2Sa 15:30
14:4
lJer 3:3
14:5
mIsa 15:6
14:6
nJob 39:5-6;
Jer 2:24
14:7
oHos 5:5
pJer 5:6
qJer 8:14
14:8
rJer 17:13

its Savior in times of distress,
why are you like a stranger in the land,
like a traveler who stays only a night?
⁹Why are you like a man taken by surprise,
like a warrior powerless to save?ˢ
You are amongᵗ us, O Lᴏʀᴅ,
and we bear your name;ᵘ
do not forsake us!

¹⁰This is what the Lᴏʀᴅ says about this people:

"They greatly love to wander;
they do not restrain their feet.ᵛ
So the Lᴏʀᴅ does not acceptʷ them;
he will now rememberˣ their wickedness
and punish them for their sins."ʸ

¹¹Then the Lᴏʀᴅ said to me, "Do not prayᶻ for the well-being of this people. ¹²Although they fast, I will not listen to their cry;ᵃ though they offer burnt offeringsᵇ and grain offerings, I will not acceptᶜ them. Instead, I will destroy them with the sword, famine and plague."

¹³But I said, "Ah, Sovereign Lᴏʀᴅ, the prophets keep telling them, 'You will not see the sword or suffer famine.ᵈ Indeed, I will give you lasting peace in this place.'"

¹⁴Then the Lᴏʀᴅ said to me, "The prophets are prophesying liesᵉ in my name. I have not sentᶠ them or appointed them or spoken to them. They are prophesying to you false visions,ᵍ divinations,ʰ idolatriesᵃ and the delusions of their own minds. ¹⁵Therefore, this is what the Lᴏʀᴅ says about the prophets who are prophesying in my name: I did not send them, yet they are saying, 'No sword or famine will touch this land.' Those same prophets will perishⁱ by sword and famine.ʲ ¹⁶And the people they are prophesying to will be thrown out into the streets of Jerusalem because of the famine and sword. There will be no one to buryᵏ them or their wives, their sons or their daughters.ˡ I will pour out on them the calamity they deserve.ᵐ

¹⁷"Speak this word to them:

" 'Let my eyes overflow with tearsⁿ
night and day without ceasing;
for my virgin daughter—my people—
has suffered a grievous wound,
a crushing blow.ᵒ
¹⁸If I go into the country,
I see those slain by the sword;
if I go into the city,
I see the ravages of famine.ᵖ
Both prophet and priest
have gone to a land they know not.'"

¹⁹Have you rejected Judah completely?ᵠ
Do you despise Zion?
Why have you afflicted us

14:9
ˢIsa 50:2
ᵗJer 8:19
ᵘIsa 63:19;
Jer 15:16
14:10
ᵛPs 119:101;
Jer 2:25
ʷJer 6:20;
Am 5:22
ˣHos 9:9
ʸJer 44:21-23;
Hos 8:13
14:11
ᶻEx 32:10
14:12
ᵃIsa 1:15;
Jer 11:11
ᵇJer 7:21
ᶜJer 6:20
14:13
ᵈJer 5:12
14:14
ᵉJer 27:14
ᶠJer 23:21,32
ᵍJer 23:16
ʰEze 12:24
14:15
ⁱEze 14:9
ʲJer 5:12-13
14:16
ᵏPs 79:3
ˡJer 7:33
ᵐPr 1:31
14:17
ⁿJer 9:1
ᵒJer 8:21
14:18
ᵖEze 7:15
14:19
ᵠJer 7:29

ᵃ14 Or *visions, worthless divinations*

so that we cannot be healed?^r
We hoped for peace
    but no good has come,
for a time of healing
    but there is only terror.^s
²⁰O LORD, we acknowledge our wickedness
    and the guilt of our fathers;
    we have indeed sinned^t against you.
²¹For the sake of your name^u do not despise us;
    do not dishonor your glorious throne.^v
Remember your covenant with us
    and do not break it.
²²Do any of the worthless idols of the nations bring rain?^w
    Do the skies themselves send down showers?
No, it is you, O LORD our God.
    Therefore our hope is in you,
    for you are the one who does all this.

15 Then the LORD said to me: "Even if Moses^x and Samuel^y were to stand before me, my heart would not go out to this people.^z Send them away from my presence!^a Let them go! ²And if they ask you, 'Where shall we go?' tell them, 'This is what the LORD says:

" 'Those destined for death, to death;
    those for the sword, to the sword;^b
    those for starvation, to starvation;^c
    those for captivity, to captivity.'^d

³"I will send four kinds of destroyers^e against them," declares the LORD, "the sword to kill and the dogs to drag away and the birds^f of the air and the beasts of the earth to devour and destroy.^g ⁴I will make them abhorrent^h to all the kingdoms of the earthⁱ because of what Manasseh^j son of Hezekiah king of Judah did in Jerusalem.

⁵"Who will have pity^k on you, O Jerusalem?
    Who will mourn for you?
    Who will stop to ask how you are?
⁶You have rejected^l me," declares the LORD.
    "You keep on backsliding.
So I will lay hands^m on you and destroy you;
    I can no longer show compassion.
⁷I will winnow them with a winnowing fork
    at the city gates of the land.
I will bring bereavement and destruction on my
        people,ⁿ
    for they have not changed their ways.
⁸I will make their widows more numerous
    than the sand of the sea.
At midday I will bring a destroyer^o
    against the mothers of their young men;
suddenly I will bring down on them
    anguish and terror.
⁹The mother of seven will grow faint^p
    and breathe her last.

14:19
r Jer 30:12-13
s Jer 8:15
14:20
t Da 9:7-8
14:21
u ver 7 v Jer 3:17
14:22
w Ps 135:7
15:1
x Ex 32:11;
Nu 14:13-20
y 1Sa 7:9
z Jer 7:16;
Eze 14:14,20
a 2Ki 17:20
15:2
b Jer 43:11
c Jer 14:12
d Rev 13:10
15:3
e Lev 26:16
f Dt 28:26
g Lev 26:22;
Eze 14:21
15:4
h Jer 24:9; 29:18
i Dt 28:25
j 2Ki 21:2;
23:26-27
15:5
k Isa 51:19;
Jer 13:14; 21:7;
Na 3:7
15:6
l Jer 6:19; 7:24
m Zep 1:4
15:7
n Jer 18:21
15:8
o Jer 6:4
15:9
p 1Sa 2:5

Her sun will set while it is still day;
she will be disgraced and humiliated.
I will put the survivors to the sword[q]
before their enemies,"

declares the LORD.

[10]Alas, my mother, that you gave me birth,[r]
a man with whom the whole land strives and
contends![s]
I have neither lent[t] nor borrowed,
yet everyone curses me.

[11]The LORD said,

"Surely I will deliver you[u] for a good purpose;
surely I will make your enemies plead[v] with you
in times of disaster and times of distress.

[12]"Can a man break iron—
iron from the north[w]—or bronze?
[13]Your wealth and your treasures
I will give as plunder, without charge,[x]
because of all your sins
throughout your country.[y]
[14]I will enslave you to your enemies
in[a] a land you do not know,[z]
for my anger will kindle a fire[a]
that will burn against you."

[15]You understand, O LORD;
remember me and care for me.
Avenge me on my persecutors.[b]
You are long-suffering—do not take me away;
think of how I suffer reproach for your sake.[c]
[16]When your words came, I ate[d] them;
they were my joy and my heart's delight,[e]
for I bear your name,[f]
O LORD God Almighty.
[17]I never sat[g] in the company of revelers,
never made merry with them;
I sat alone because your hand was on me
and you had filled me with indignation.
[18]Why is my pain unending
and my wound grievous and incurable?[h]
Will you be to me like a deceptive brook,
like a spring that fails?[i]

[19]Therefore this is what the LORD says:

"If you repent, I will restore you
that you may serve[j] me;
if you utter worthy, not worthless, words,

---

[a]14 Some Hebrew manuscripts, Septuagint and Syriac (see also Jer. 17:4); most Hebrew
manuscripts *I will cause your enemies to bring you* / *into*

15:9
q Jer 21:7
15:10
r Job 3:1
s Jer 1:19
t Lev 25:36
15:11
u Jer 40:4
v Jer 21:1-2;
37:3; 42:1-3
15:12
w Jer 28:14
15:13
x Ps 44:12
y Jer 17:3
15:14
z Dt 28:36;
Jer 16:13
a Dt 32:22;
Ps 21:9
15:15
b Jer 12:3
c Ps 69:7-9
15:16
d Eze 3:3;
Rev 10:10
e Ps 119:72,103
f Jer 14:9
15:17
g Ps 1:1; 26:4-5;
Jer 16:8
15:18
h Jer 30:15;
Mic 1:9
i Job 6:15
15:19
j Zec 3:7

you will be my spokesman.
Let this people turn to you,
    but you must not turn to them.
[20]I will make you a wall to this people,
    a fortified wall of bronze;
they will fight against you
    but will not overcome you,
for I am with you
    to rescue and save you,"[k]

                      declares the LORD.
[21]"I will save you from the hands of the wicked
    and redeem[l] you from the grasp of the cruel."[m]

Day of Disaster

16 Then the word of the LORD came to me: [2]"You must not marry[n] and have sons or daughters in this place." [3]For this is what the LORD says about the sons and daughters born in this land and about the women who are their mothers and the men who are their fathers:[o] [4]"They will die of deadly diseases. They will not be mourned or buried[p] but will be like refuse lying on the ground. [q] They will perish by sword and famine, and their dead bodies will become food for the birds of the air and the beasts of the earth."[r]

[5]For this is what the LORD says: "Do not enter a house where there is a funeral meal; do not go to mourn or show sympathy, because I have withdrawn my blessing, my love and my pity from this people," declares the LORD. [6]"Both high and low will die in this land.[s] They will not be buried or mourned, and no one will cut[t] himself or shave[u] his head for them. [7]No one will offer food to comfort those who mourn[v] for the dead—not even for a father or a mother—nor will anyone give them a drink to console them.

[8]"And do not enter a house where there is feasting and sit down to eat and drink.[w] [9]For this is what the LORD Almighty, the God of Israel, says: Before your eyes and in your days I will bring an end to the sounds[x] of joy and gladness and to the voices of bride and bridegroom in this place.[y]

[10]"When you tell these people all this and they ask you, 'Why has the LORD decreed such a great disaster against us? What wrong have we done? What sin have we committed against the LORD our God?'[z] [11]then say to them, 'It is because your fathers forsook me,' declares the LORD, 'and followed other gods and served and worshiped them. They forsook me and did not keep my law.[a] [12]But you have behaved more wickedly than your fathers.[b] See how each of you is following the stubbornness of his evil heart[c] instead of obeying me. [13]So I will throw you out of this land into a land neither you nor your fathers have known,[d] and there you will serve other gods[e] day and night, for I will show you no favor.'[f]

[14]"However, the days are coming," declares the LORD, "when men will no longer say, 'As surely as the LORD lives, who brought the Israelites up out of Egypt,'[g] [15]but they will say, 'As surely as the LORD lives, who brought the Israelites up out of the land of the north and out of all the countries where he had banished them.'[h] For I will restore[i] them to the land I gave their forefathers.

15:20
k Jer 20:11;
Eze 3:8
15:21
l Jer 50:34
m Ge 48:16
16:2
n 1Co 7:26-27
16:3
o Jer 6:21
16:4
p Jer 25:33
q Ps 83:10;
Jer 9:22
r Ps 79:1-3;
Jer 15:3; 34:20
16:6
s Eze 9:5-6
t Lev 19:28
u Jer 41:5; 47:5
16:7
v Eze 24:17;
Hos 9:4
16:8
w Ecc 7:2-4;
Jer 15:17
16:9
x Isa 24:8;
Eze 26:13;
Hos 2:11
y Rev 18:23
16:10
z Dt 29:24;
Jer 5:19
16:11
a Dt 29:25-26;
1Ki 9:9;
Ps 106:35-43;
Jer 22:9
16:12
b Jer 7:26
c Ecc 9:3;
Jer 13:10
16:13
d Dt 28:36;
Jer 5:19
e Dt 4:28
f Jer 15:5
16:14
g Dt 15:15;
Jer 23:7-8
16:15
h Isa 11:11;
Jer 23:8
i Jer 24:6

[16]"But now I will send for many fishermen," declares the LORD, "and they will catch them.[j] After that I will send for many hunters, and they will hunt[k] them down on every mountain and hill and from the crevices of the rocks.[l] [17]My eyes are on all their ways; they are not hidden[m] from me, nor is their sin concealed from my eyes.[n] [18]I will repay them double[o] for their wickedness and their sin, because they have defiled my land[p] with the lifeless forms of their vile images and have filled my inheritance with their detestable idols."

[19]O LORD, my strength and my fortress,
　　my refuge in time of distress,
to you the nations will come[q]
　　from the ends of the earth and say,
"Our fathers possessed nothing but false gods,[r]
　　worthless idols that did them no good.
[20]Do men make their own gods?
　　Yes, but they are not gods!"[s]

[21]"Therefore I will teach them—
　　this time I will teach them
　　my power and might.
Then they will know
　　that my name is the LORD.

17 "Judah's sin is engraved with an iron tool,[t]
　　inscribed with a flint point,
on the tablets of their hearts[u]
　　and on the horns of their altars.
[2]Even their children remember
　　their altars and Asherah poles[a][v]
beside the spreading trees
　　and on the high hills.[w]
[3]My mountain in the land
　　and your[b] wealth and all your treasures
I will give away as plunder,[x]
　　together with your high places,[y]
　　because of sin throughout your country.[z]
[4]Through your own fault you will lose
　　the inheritance[a] I gave you.
I will enslave you to your enemies[b]
　　in a land[c] you do not know,
for you have kindled my anger,
　　and it will burn[d] forever."

[5]This is what the LORD says:

"Cursed is the one who trusts in man,[e]
　　who depends on flesh for his strength
　　and whose heart turns away from the LORD.
[6]He will be like a bush in the wastelands;
　　he will not see prosperity when it comes.
He will dwell in the parched places of the desert,

16:16
jAm 4:2;
Hab 1:14-15
kAm 9:3;
Mic 7:2
l1Sa 26:20
16:17
m1Co 4:5;
Heb 4:13
nPr 15:3
16:18
oIsa 40:2;
Rev 18:6
pNu 35:34;
Jer 2:7
16:19
qIsa 2:2;
Jer 3:17 rPs 4:2
16:20
sPs 115:4-7;
Isa 37:19;
Jer 2:11
17:1
tJob 19:24
uPr 3:3;
2Co 3:3
17:2
v 2Ch 24:18
wJer 2:20
17:3
x2Ki 24:13
yJer 26:18;
Mic 3:12
zJer 15:13
17:4
aLa 5:2
bDt 28:48;
Jer 12:7
cJer 16:13
dJer 7:20; 15:14
17:5
eIsa 2:22;
30:1-3

---

a2 That is, symbols of the goddess Asherah　　b2,3 Or hills / ³and the mountains of the land. / Your in a salt[f] land where no one lives.

7"But blessed is the man who trusts[g] in the LORD,
    whose confidence is in him.
8He will be like a tree planted by the water
    that sends out its roots by the stream.
It does not fear when heat comes;
    its leaves are always green.
It has no worries in a year of drought[h]
    and never fails to bear fruit."[i]

9The heart[j] is deceitful above all things
    and beyond cure.
    Who can understand it?

10"I the LORD search the heart[k]
    and examine the mind,[l]
to reward[m] a man according to his conduct,
    according to what his deeds deserve."[n]

11Like a partridge that hatches eggs it did not lay
    is the man who gains riches by unjust means.
When his life is half gone, they will desert him,
    and in the end he will prove to be a fool.[o]

12A glorious throne,[p] exalted from the beginning,
    is the place of our sanctuary.
13O LORD, the hope[q] of Israel,
    all who forsake[r] you will be put to shame.
Those who turn away from you will be written in the
      dust
    because they have forsaken the LORD,
    the spring of living water.

14Heal me, O LORD, and I will be healed;
    save me and I will be saved,
    for you are the one I praise.[s]
15They keep saying to me,
    "Where is the word of the LORD?
    Let it now be fulfilled!"[t]
16I have not run away from being your shepherd;
    you know I have not desired the day of despair.
    What passes my lips is open before you.
17Do not be a terror[u] to me;
    you are my refuge[v] in the day of disaster.
18Let my persecutors be put to shame,
    but keep me from shame;
let them be terrified,
    but keep me from terror.
Bring on them the day of disaster;
    destroy them with double destruction.[w]

Keeping the Sabbath Holy

19This is what the LORD said to me: "Go and stand at the gate of the people, through which the kings of Judah go in and out; stand also at all

17:6
fDt 29:23;
Job 39:6
17:7
gPs 34:8; 40:4;
Pr 16:20
17:8
hJer 14:1-6
iPs 1:3;
92:12-14
17:9
jEcc 9:3;
Mt 13:15;
Mk 7:21-22
17:10
k1Sa 16:7;
Rev 2:23
lPs 17:3;
139:23;
Jer 11:20;
20:12; Ro 8:27
mPs 62:12;
Jer 32:19
nRo 2:6
17:11
oLk 12:20
17:12
pJer 3:17
17:13
qJer 14:8
rIsa 1:28;
Jer 2:17
17:14
sPs 109:1
17:15
tIsa 5:19;
2Pe 3:4
17:17
uPs 88:15-16
vJer 16:19;
Na 1:7
17:18
wPs 35:1-8

the other gates of Jerusalem.ˣ ²⁰Say to them, 'Hear the word of the LORD, O kings of Judah and all people of Judah and everyone living in Jerusalemʸ who come through these gates.ᶻ ²¹This is what the LORD says: Be careful not to carry a load on the Sabbathᵃ day or bring it through the gates of Jerusalem. ²²Do not bring a load out of your houses or do any work on the Sabbath, but keep the Sabbath day holy, as I commanded your forefathers.ᵇ ²³Yet they did not listen or pay attention;ᶜ they were stiff-neckedᵈ and would not listen or respond to discipline.ᵉ ²⁴But if you are careful to obey me, declares the LORD, and bring no load through the gates of this city on the Sabbath, but keep the Sabbath day holy by not doing any work on it, ²⁵then kings who sit on David's throneᶠ will come through the gates of this city with their officials. They and their officials will come riding in chariots and on horses, accompanied by the men of Judah and those living in Jerusalem, and this city will be inhabited forever. ²⁶People will come from the towns of Judah and the villages around Jerusalem, from the territory of Benjamin and the western foothills, from the hill country and the Negev,ᵍ bringing burnt offerings and sacrifices, grain offerings, incense and thank offerings to the house of the LORD. ²⁷But if you do not obeyʰ me to keep the Sabbath day holy by not carrying any load as you come through the gates of Jerusalem on the Sabbath day, then I will kindle an unquenchable fireⁱ in the gates of Jerusalem that will consume her fortresses.' "ʲ

At the Potter's House

18 This is the word that came to Jeremiah from the LORD: ²"Go down to the potter's house, and there I will give you my message." ³So I went down to the potter's house, and I saw him working at the wheel. ⁴But the pot he was shaping from the clay was marred in his hands; so the potter formed it into another pot, shaping it as seemed best to him.

⁵Then the word of the LORD came to me: ⁶"O house of Israel, can I not do with you as this potter does?" declares the LORD. "Like clayᵏ in the hand of the potter, so are you in my hand, O house of Israel. ⁷If at any time I announce that a nation or kingdom is to be uprooted,ˡ torn down and destroyed, ⁸and if that nation I warned repents of its evil, then I will relentᵐ and not inflict on it the disasterⁿ I had planned. ⁹And if at another time I announce that a nation or kingdom is to be builtᵒ up and planted, ¹⁰and if it does evilᵖ in my sight and does not obey me, then I will reconsider�q the good I had intended to do for it.

¹¹"Now therefore say to the people of Judah and those living in Jerusalem, 'This is what the LORD says: Look! I am preparing a disasterʳ for you and devising a plan against you. So turnˢ from your evil ways,ᵗ each one of you, and reform your ways and your actions.' ¹²But they will reply, 'It's no use.ᵘ We will continue with our own plans; each of us will follow the stubbornness of his evil heart.' "

¹³Therefore this is what the LORD says:

"Inquire among the nations:
    Who has ever heard anything like this?ᵛ
A most horribleʷ thing has been done
    by Virgin Israel.

17:19
xJer 7:2; 26:2
17:20
yJer 19:3
zJer 22:2
17:21
aNu 15:32-36;
Ne 13:15-21;
Jn 5:10
17:22
bEx 20:8;
31:13;
Isa 56:2-6;
Eze 20:12
17:23
cJer 7:26
dJer 19:15
eJer 7:28
17:25
f2Sa 7:13;
Isa 9:7;
Jer 22:2,4;
Lk 1:32
17:26
gJer 32:44;
33:13; Zec 7:7
17:27
hJer 22:5
iJer 7:20
j2Ki 25:9;
Am 2:5
18:6
kIsa 45:9;
Ro 9:20-21
18:7
lJer 1:10
18:8
mJer 26:13;
Jnh 3:8-10
nEze 18:21;
Hos 11:8-9
18:9
oJer 1:10; 31:28
18:10
pEze 33:18
q1Sa 2:29-30
18:11
rJer 4:6
s2Ki 17:13;
Isa 1:16-19
tJer 7:3
18:12
uIsa 57:10;
Jer 2:25
18:13
vIsa 66:8;
Jer 2:10
wJer 5:30

¹⁴Does the snow of Lebanon
      ever vanish from its rocky slopes?
  Do its cool waters from distant sources
      ever cease to flow?^a
¹⁵Yet my people have forgotten me;
      they burn incense to worthless idols,^x
  which made them stumble in their ways
      and in the ancient paths.^y
  They made them walk in bypaths
      and on roads not built up.^z
¹⁶Their land will be laid waste,^a
      an object of lasting scorn;^b
  all who pass by will be appalled
      and will shake their heads.^c
¹⁷Like a wind^d from the east,
      I will scatter them before their enemies;
  I will show them my back and not my face^e
      in the day of their disaster."

¹⁸They said, "Come, let's make plans^f against Jeremiah; for the teaching of the law by the priest^g will not be lost, nor will counsel from the wise, nor the word from the prophets.^h So come, let's attack him with our tonguesⁱ and pay no attention to anything he says."

¹⁹Listen to me, O LORD;
      hear what my accusers are saying!
²⁰Should good be repaid with evil?
      Yet they have dug a pit^j for me.
  Remember that I stood before you
      and spoke in their behalf^k
      to turn your wrath away from them.
²¹So give their children over to famine;^l
      hand them over to the power of the sword.
  Let their wives be made childless and widows;^m
      let their men be put to death,
      their young men slain by the sword in battle.
²²Let a cryⁿ be heard from their houses
      when you suddenly bring invaders against them,
  for they have dug a pit to capture me
      and have hidden snares^o for my feet.
²³But you know, O LORD,
      all their plots to kill^p me.
  Do not forgive^q their crimes
      or blot out their sins from your sight.
  Let them be overthrown before you;
      deal with them in the time of your anger.

19

This is what the LORD says: "Go and buy a clay jar from a potter.^r Take along some of the elders^s of the people and of the priests ²and go out to the Valley of Ben Hinnom,^t near the entrance of the Potsherd Gate. There proclaim the words I tell you, ³and say, 'Hear

18:15
xJer 10:15
yJer 6:16
zIsa 57:14;
    62:10
18:16
aJer 25:9
bJer 19:8
cPs 22:7
18:17
dJer 13:24
eJer 2:27
18:18
fJer 11:19
gMal 2:7
hJer 5:13
iPs 52:2
18:20
jPs 35:7; 57:6
kPs 106:23
18:21
lJer 11:22
mPs 109:9
18:22
nJer 6:26
oPs 140:5
18:23
pJer 11:21
qPs 109:14
19:1
rJer 18:2
sNu 11:17
19:2
tJos 15:8

^a14 The meaning of the Hebrew for this sentence is uncertain.

the word of the LORD, O kings^u of Judah and people of Jerusalem. This is what the LORD Almighty, the God of Israel, says: Listen! I am going to bring a disaster^v on this place that will make the ears of everyone who hears of it tingle. ^{w 4}For they have forsaken^x me and made this a place of foreign gods; they have burned sacrifices^y in it to gods that neither they nor their fathers nor the kings of Judah ever knew, and they have filled this place with the blood of the innocent. ^{z 5}They have built the high places of Baal to burn their sons^a in the fire as offerings to Baal—something I did not command or mention, nor did it enter my mind. ^{b 6}So beware, the days are coming, declares the LORD, when people will no longer call this place Topheth or the Valley of Ben Hinnom, ^c but the Valley of Slaughter. ^d

7" 'In this place I will ruin^a the plans of Judah and Jerusalem. I will make them fall by the sword before their enemies,^e at the hands of those who seek their lives, and I will give their carcasses^f as food^g to the birds of the air and the beasts of the earth. ⁸I will devastate this city and make it an object of scorn;^h all who pass by will be appalled and will scoff because of all its wounds. ⁹I will make them eatⁱ the flesh of their sons and daughters, and they will eat one another's flesh during the stress of the siege imposed on them by the enemies^j who seek their lives.'

10"Then break the jar^k while those who go with you are watching, ¹¹and say to them, 'This is what the LORD Almighty says: I will smash^l this nation and this city just as this potter's jar is smashed and cannot be repaired. They will bury^m the dead in Topheth until there is no more room. ¹²This is what I will do to this place and to those who live here, declares the LORD. I will make this city like Topheth. ¹³The housesⁿ in Jerusalem and those of the kings of Judah will be defiled like this place, Topheth—all the houses where they burned incense on the roofs to all the starry hosts^o and poured out drink offerings^p to other gods.' "

14Jeremiah then returned from Topheth, where the LORD had sent him to prophesy, and stood in the court^q of the LORD's temple and said to all the people, ¹⁵"This is what the LORD Almighty, the God of Israel, says: 'Listen! I am going to bring on this city and the villages around it every disaster I pronounced against them, because they were stiff-necked^r and would not listen to my words.'"

Jeremiah and Pashhur

20 When the priest Pashhur son of Immer,^s the chief officer^t in the temple of the LORD, heard Jeremiah prophesying these things, ²he had Jeremiah the prophet beaten^u and put in the stocks^v at the Upper Gate of Benjamin^w at the LORD's temple. ³The next day, when Pashhur released him from the stocks, Jeremiah said to him, "The LORD's name for you is not Pashhur, but Magor-Missabib.^{bx 4}For this is what the LORD says: 'I will make you a terror to yourself and to all your friends; with your own eyes^y you will see them fall by the sword of their enemies. I will hand^z all Judah over to the king of Babylon, who will carry^a them away to Babylon or put them to the sword. ⁵I will hand over to their enemies all the wealth^b of this city—all its products, all its

---

19:3
u Jer 17:20
v Jer 6:19
w 1Sa 3:11
19:4
x Dt 28:20;
Isa 65:11
y Lev 18:21
z 2Ki 21:16;
Jer 2:34
19:5
a Lev 18:21;
Ps 106:37-38
b Jer 7:31; 32:35
19:6
c Jos 15:8
d Jer 7:32
19:7
e Lev 26:17;
Dt 28:25
f Jer 16:4; 34:20
g Ps 79:2
19:8
h Jer 18:16
19:9
i Lev 26:29;
Dt 28:49-57;
La 4:10 j Isa 9:20
19:10
k ver 1
19:11
l Ps 2:9;
Isa 30:14
m Jer 7:32
19:13
n Jer 32:29;
52:13 o Dt 4:19;
Ac 7:42
p Jer 7:18;
Eze 20:28
19:14
q 2Ch 20:5;
Jer 26:2
19:15
r Ne 9:16;
Jer 7:26; 17:23
20:1
s 1Ch 24:14
t 2Ki 25:18
20:2
u Jer 1:19
v Job 13:27
w Jer 37:13;
38:7; Zec 14:10
20:3
x ver 10
20:4
y Jer 29:21
z Jer 21:10
a Jer 52:27
20:5
b Jer 17:3

---

^a7 The Hebrew for *ruin* sounds like the Hebrew for *jar* (see verses 1 and 10).   ^b3 *Magor-Missabib* means *terror on every side.*

valuables and all the treasures of the kings of Judah. They will take it away[c] as plunder and carry it off to Babylon. [6]And you, Pashhur, and all who live in your house will go into exile to Babylon. There you will die and be buried, you and all your friends to whom you have prophesied[d] lies.'"

Jeremiah's Complaint

[7]O Lord, you deceived[a] me, and I was deceived[a];
    you overpowered me and prevailed.
I am ridiculed all day long;
    everyone mocks me.
[8]Whenever I speak, I cry out
    proclaiming violence and destruction.[e]
So the word of the Lord has brought me
    insult and reproach[f] all day long.
[9]But if I say, "I will not mention him
    or speak any more in his name,"
his word is in my heart like a fire,[g]
    a fire shut up in my bones.
I am weary of holding it in;[h]
    indeed, I cannot.
[10]I hear many whispering,
    "Terror[i] on every side!
    Report[j] him! Let's report him!"
All my friends[k]
    are waiting for me to slip,[l] saying,
"Perhaps he will be deceived;
    then we will prevail[m] over him
    and take our revenge on him."

[11]But the Lord[n] is with me like a mighty warrior;
    so my persecutors[o] will stumble and not prevail.[p]
They will fail and be thoroughly disgraced;[q]
    their dishonor will never be forgotten.
[12]O Lord Almighty, you who examine the righteous
    and probe the heart and mind,[r]
let me see your vengeance[s] upon them,
    for to you I have committed[t] my cause.

[13]Sing to the Lord!
    Give praise to the Lord!
He rescues[u] the life of the needy
    from the hands of the wicked.

[14]Cursed be the day I was born![v]
    May the day my mother bore me not be blessed!
[15]Cursed be the man who brought my father the news,
    who made him very glad, saying,
    "A child is born to you—a son!"
[16]May that man be like the towns[w]
    the Lord overthrew without pity.

20:5
c 2Ki 20:17
20:6
d Jer 14:15;
La 2:14
20:8
e Jer 6:7
f 2Ch 36:16;
Jer 6:10
20:9
g Ps 39:3
h Job 32:18-20;
Ac 4:20
20:10
i Ps 31:13;
Jer 6:25
j Isa 29:21
k Ps 41:9
l Lk 11:53-54
m 1Ki 19:2
20:11
n Jer 1:8;
Ro 8:31
o Jer 17:18
p Jer 15:20
q Jer 23:40
20:12
r Jer 17:10
s Ps 54:7; 59:10
t Ps 62:8;
Jer 11:20
20:13
u Ps 35:10
20:14
v Job 3:3;
Jer 15:10
20:16
w Ge 19:25

---

a 7 Or persuaded

May he hear wailing in the morning,
 a battle cry at noon.
[17]For he did not kill me in the womb,[x]
 with my mother as my grave,
 her womb enlarged forever.
[18]Why did I ever come out of the womb
 to see trouble and sorrow
 and to end my days in shame?[y]

God Rejects Zedekiah's Request

21 The word came to Jeremiah from the Lord when King Zedekiah[z] sent to him Pashhur[a] son of Malkijah and the priest Zephaniah[b] son of Maaseiah. They said: [2]"Inquire[c] now of the Lord for us because Nebuchadnezzar[a d] king of Babylon is attacking us. Perhaps the Lord will perform wonders[e] for us as in times past so that he will withdraw from us."

[3]But Jeremiah answered them, "Tell Zedekiah, [4]'This is what the Lord, the God of Israel, says: I am about to turn[f] against you the weapons of war that are in your hands, which you are using to fight the king of Babylon and the Babylonians[b] who are outside the wall besieging[g] you. And I will gather them inside this city. [5]I myself will fight against you with an outstretched hand[h] and a mighty arm in anger and fury and great wrath. [6]I will strike down those who live in this city—both men and animals—and they will die of a terrible plague.[i] [7]After that, declares the Lord, I will hand over Zedekiah[j] king of Judah, his officials and the people in this city who survive the plague, sword and famine, to Nebuchadnezzar king of Babylon[k] and to their enemies who seek their lives. He will put them to the sword; he will show them no mercy or pity or compassion.'[l]

[8]"Furthermore, tell the people, 'This is what the Lord says: See, I am setting before you the way of life and the way of death. [9]Whoever stays in this city will die by the sword, famine or plague.[m] But whoever goes out and surrenders to the Babylonians who are besieging you will live; he will escape with his life.[n] [10]I have determined to do this city harm[o] and not good, declares the Lord. It will be given into the hands[p] of the king of Babylon, and he will destroy it with fire.'[q]

[11]"Moreover, say to the royal house[r] of Judah, 'Hear the word of the Lord; [12]O house of David, this is what the Lord says:

" 'Administer justice[s] every morning;
 rescue from the hand of his oppressor
 the one who has been robbed,
 or my wrath will break out and burn like fire
 because of the evil you have done—
 burn with no one to quench[t] it.
[13]I am against[u] you, ⌊Jerusalem,⌋
 you who live above this valley[v]
 on the rocky plateau,
              declares the Lord—

20:17
xJob 10:18-19
20:18
yPs 90:9
21:1
z2Ki 24:18;
 Jer 52:1
aJer 38:1
b2Ki 25:18;
Jer 29:25; 37:3
21:2
cJer 37:3,7
d2Ki 25:1
ePs 44:1-4;
 Jer 32:17
21:4
fJer 32:5
gJer 37:8-10
21:5
hJer 6:12
21:6
iJer 14:12
21:7
j2Ki 25:7;
 Jer 52:9
kJer 37:17; 39:5
 lCh 36:17;
 Eze 7:9;
 Hab 1:6
21:9
mJer 14:12
nJer 38:2,17;
39:18; 45:5
21:10
oJer 44:11,27;
 Am 9:4
pJer 32:28;
38:2-3
qJer 52:13
21:11
rJer 13:18
21:12
sJer 22:3
tIsa 1:31
21:13
uEze 13:8
vPs 125:2

---

[a]2 Hebrew *Nebuchadrezzar*, of which *Nebuchadnezzar* is a variant; here and often in Jeremiah and Ezekiel   [b]4 Or *Chaldeans*; also in verse 9

you who say, "Who can come against us?
　　Who can enter our refuge?"[w]
[14]I will punish you as your deeds[x] deserve,
　　　　　　　　declares the LORD.
I will kindle a fire[y] in your forests[z]
　　that will consume everything around you.' "

Judgment Against Evil Kings

22 This is what the LORD says: "Go down to the palace of the king of Judah and proclaim this message there: [2]'Hear the word of the LORD, O king of Judah, you who sit on David's throne[a]—you, your officials and your people who come through these gates. [b] [3]This is what the LORD says: Do what is just[c] and right. Rescue from the hand of his oppressor[d] the one who has been robbed. Do no wrong or violence to the alien, the fatherless or the widow, [e] and do not shed innocent blood in this place. [4]For if you are careful to carry out these commands, then kings[f] who sit on David's throne will come through the gates of this palace, riding in chariots and on horses, accompanied by their officials and their people. [5]But if you do not obey[g] these commands, declares the LORD, I swear[h] by myself that this palace will become a ruin.' "

[6]For this is what the LORD says about the palace of the king of Judah:

"Though you are like Gilead to me,
　　like the summit of Lebanon,
I will surely make you like a desert,[i]
　　like towns not inhabited.
[7]I will send destroyers[j] against you,
　　each man with his weapons,
and they will cut[k] up your fine cedar beams
　　and throw them into the fire.

[8]"People from many nations will pass by this city and will ask one another, 'Why has the LORD done such a thing to this great city?'[l] [9]And the answer will be: 'Because they have forsaken the covenant of the LORD their God and have worshiped and served other gods. [m] ' "

[10]Do not weep for the dead[n] king, or mourn[o] his loss;
　　rather, weep bitterly for him who is exiled,
because he will never return
　　nor see his native land again.

[11]For this is what the LORD says about Shallum[a][p] son of Josiah, who succeeded his father as king of Judah but has gone from this place: "He will never return. [12]He will die[q] in the place where they have led him captive; he will not see this land again."

[13]"Woe to him who builds[r] his palace by
　　unrighteousness,
　　his upper rooms by injustice,
making his countrymen work for nothing,
　　not paying[s] them for their labor.
[14]He says, 'I will build myself a great palace[t]

---

[a]11 Also called *Jehoahaz*

with spacious upper rooms.'
So he makes large windows in it,
   panels it with cedar[u]
   and decorates it in red.

15"Does it make you a king
   to have more and more cedar?
Did not your father have food and drink?
   He did what was right and just,[v]
   so all went well[w] with him.
16He defended the cause of the poor and needy,[x]
   and so all went well.
Is that not what it means to know me?"
   declares the LORD.
17"But your eyes and your heart
   are set only on dishonest gain,
on shedding innocent blood[y]
   and on oppression and extortion."

18Therefore this is what the LORD says about Jehoiakim son of Josiah king of Judah:

"They will not mourn for him:
   'Alas, my brother! Alas, my sister!'
They will not mourn for him:
   'Alas, my master! Alas, his splendor!'
19He will have the burial of a donkey—
   dragged away and thrown[z]
   outside the gates of Jerusalem."

20"Go up to Lebanon and cry out,
   let your voice be heard in Bashan,
cry out from Abarim,[a]
   for all your allies are crushed.
21I warned you when you felt secure,
   but you said, 'I will not listen!'
This has been your way from your youth;[b]
   you have not obeyed[c] me.
22The wind will drive all your shepherds away,
   and your allies will go into exile.
Then you will be ashamed and disgraced
   because of all your wickedness.
23You who live in 'Lebanon,[a]'
   who are nestled in cedar buildings,
how you will groan when pangs come upon you,
   pain[d] like that of a woman in labor!

24"As surely as I live," declares the LORD, "even if you, Jehoiachin[b][e] son of Jehoiakim king of Judah, were a signet ring on my right hand, I would still pull you off. 25I will hand you over[f] to those who seek your life, those you fear—to Nebuchadnezzar king of Babylon and to the

22:14
[u]2Sa 7:2
22:15
[v]2Ki 23:25
[w]Ps 128:2;
Isa 3:10
22:16
[x]Ps 72:1-4,12-13
22:17
[y]2Ki 24:4
22:19
[z]Jer 36:30
22:20
[a]Nu 27:12
22:21
[b]Jer 3:25; 32:30
[c]Jer 7:23-28
22:23
[d]Jer 4:31
22:24
[e]2Ki 24:6,8;
Jer 37:1
22:25
[f]2Ki 24:16;
Jer 34:20

---

[a]23 That is, the palace in Jerusalem (see 1 Kings 7:2)   [b]24 Hebrew *Coniah*, a variant of *Jehoiachin*; also in verse 28

Babylonians.ᵃ ²⁶I will hurlᵍ you and the mother who gave you birth into another country, where neither of you was born, and there you both will die. ²⁷You will never come back to the land you long to return to."

²⁸Is this man Jehoiachin a despised, broken pot,ʰ
  an object no one wants?
Why will he and his children be hurledⁱ out,
  cast into a landʲ they do not know?
²⁹O land,ᵏ land, land,
  hear the word of the LORD!
³⁰This is what the LORD says:
"Record this man as if childless,ˡ
  a man who will not prosperᵐ in his lifetime,
for none of his offspring will prosper,
  none will sit on the throneⁿ of David
  or rule anymore in Judah."

The Righteous Branch

23 "Woe to the shepherdsᵒ who are destroying and scatteringᵖ the sheep of my pasture!"�q declares the LORD. ²Therefore this is what the LORD, the God of Israel, says to the shepherds who tend my people: "Because you have scattered my flock and driven them away and have not bestowed care on them, I will bestow punishment on you for the evilʳ you have done," declares the LORD. ³"I myself will gather the remnantˢ of my flock out of all the countries where I have driven them and will bring them back to their pasture, where they will be fruitful and increase in number. ⁴I will place shepherdsᵗ over them who will tend them, and they will no longer be afraidᵘ or terrified, nor will any be missing,ᵛ" declares the LORD.

⁵"The days are coming," declares the LORD,
  "when I will raise up to Davidᵇ a righteous Branch,ʷ
a King who will reignˣ wisely
  and do what is just and rightʸ in the land.
⁶In his days Judah will be saved
  and Israel will live in safety.
This is the nameᶻ by which he will be called:
  The LORD Our Righteousness. ᵃ

⁷"So then, the days are coming," declares the LORD, "when people will no longer say, 'As surely as the LORD lives, who brought the Israelites up out of Egypt,'ᵇ ⁸but they will say, 'As surely as the LORD lives, who brought the descendants of Israel up out of the land of the north and out of all the countries where he had banished them.' Then they will live in their own land."ᶜ

Lying Prophets

⁹Concerning the prophets:

My heart is broken within me;
  all my bones tremble.

22:26
g2Ki 24:8;
2Ch 36:10
22:28
hPs 31:12;
Jer 48:38;
Hos 8:8
iJer 15:1
jJer 17:4
22:29
kJer 6:19;
Mic 1:2
22:30
l1Ch 3:18;
Mt 1:12
mJer 10:21
nPs 94:20
23:1
oJer 10:21;
Eze 34:1-10;
Zec 11:15-17
pIsa 56:11
qEze 34:31
23:2
rJer 21:12
23:3
sIsa 11:10-12;
Jer 32:37;
Eze 34:11-16
23:4
tJer 3:15;
31:10;
Eze 34:23
uJer 30:10;
46:27-28
vJn 6:39
23:5
wIsa 4:2
xIsa 9:7
yIsa 11:1;
Zec 6:12
23:6
zJer 33:16;
Mt 1:21-23
aRo 3:21-22;
1Co 1:30
23:7
bJer 16:14
23:8
cIsa 43:5-6;
Am 9:14-15

ᵃ25 Or *Chaldeans*   ᵇ5 Or *up from David's line*

I am like a drunken man,
   like a man overcome by wine,
because of the LORD
   and his holy words. [d]
[10]The land is full of adulterers; [e]
   because of the curse [a] the land lies parched [b]
   and the pastures [f] in the desert are withered. [g]
The ˌprophetsˌ follow an evil course
   and use their power unjustly.

[11]"Both prophet and priest are godless; [h]
   even in my temple [i] I find their wickedness,"
                    declares the LORD.
[12]"Therefore their path will become slippery; [j]
   they will be banished to darkness
   and there they will fall.
I will bring disaster on them
   in the year they are punished, [k]"
                    declares the LORD.

[13]"Among the prophets of Samaria
   I saw this repulsive thing:
They prophesied by Baal [l]
   and led my people Israel astray.
[14]And among the prophets of Jerusalem
   I have seen something horrible: [m]
   They commit adultery and live a lie. [n]
They strengthen the hands of evildoers, [o]
   so that no one turns from his wickedness.
They are all like Sodom [p] to me;
   the people of Jerusalem are like Gomorrah." [q]

[15]Therefore, this is what the LORD Almighty says concerning the prophets:

   "I will make them eat bitter food
      and drink poisoned water, [r]
   because from the prophets of Jerusalem
      ungodliness has spread throughout the land."

[16]This is what the LORD Almighty says:

   "Do not listen [s] to what the prophets are prophesying to
         you;
      they fill you with false hopes.
   They speak visions [t] from their own minds,
      not from the mouth [u] of the LORD.
[17]They keep saying to those who despise me,
   'The LORD says: You will have peace.' [v]
And to all who follow the stubbornness [w] of their hearts
   they say, 'No harm [x] will come to you.'
[18]But which of them has stood in the council of the LORD
   to see or to hear his word?

23:9
d Jer 20:8-9
23:10
e Jer 9:2
f Ps 107:34;
Jer 9:10
g Hos 4:2-3
23:11
h Jer 6:13; 8:10;
Zep 3:4
i Jer 7:10
23:12
j Ps 35:6;
Jer 13:16
k Jer 11:23
23:13
l Jer 2:8
23:14
m Jer 5:30
n Jer 29:23
o Eze 13:22
p Ge 18:20
q Isa 1:9-10;
Jer 20:16
23:15
r Jer 8:14; 9:15
23:16
s Jer 27:9-10,14;
Mt 7:15
t Jer 14:14
u Jer 9:20
23:17
v Jer 8:11
w Jer 13:10
x Jer 5:12;
Am 9:10;
Mic 3:11

---

a10 Or *because of these things*   b10 Or *land mourns*

Who has listened and heard his word?
¹⁹See, the stormʸ of the LORD
　　will burst out in wrath,
a whirlwind swirling down
　　on the heads of the wicked.
²⁰The angerᶻ of the LORD will not turn backᵃ
　　until he fully accomplishes
　　the purposes of his heart.
In days to come
　　you will understand it clearly.
²¹I did not sendᵇ these prophets,
　　yet they have run with their message;
I did not speak to them,
　　yet they have prophesied.
²²But if they had stood in my council,
　　they would have proclaimed my words to my people
and would have turnedᶜ them from their evil ways
　　and from their evil deeds.

²³"Am I only a God nearby,ᵈ"

declares the LORD,

"and not a God far away?
²⁴Can anyone hideᵉ in secret places
　　so that I cannot see him?"

declares the LORD.

"Do not I fill heaven and earth?"ᶠ

declares the LORD.

²⁵"I have heard what the prophets say who prophesy liesᵍ in my name. They say, 'I had a dream!ʰ I had a dream!' ²⁶How long will this continue in the hearts of these lying prophets, who prophesy the delusionsⁱ of their own minds? ²⁷They think the dreams they tell one another will make my people forgetʲ my name, just as their fathers forgotᵏ my name through Baal worship. ²⁸Let the prophet who has a dream tell his dream, but let the one who has my word speak it faithfully. For what has straw to do with grain?" declares the LORD. ²⁹"Is not my word like fire,"ˡ declares the LORD, "and like a hammer that breaks a rock in pieces?

³⁰"Therefore," declares the LORD, "I am againstᵐ the prophetsⁿ who steal from one another words supposedly from me. ³¹Yes," declares the LORD, "I am against the prophets who wag their own tongues and yet declare, 'The LORD declares.'ᵒ ³²Indeed, I am against those who prophesy false dreams,ᵖ" declares the LORD. "They tell them and lead my people astray with their reckless lies, yet I did not send or appoint them. They do not benefitᵠ these people in the least," declares the LORD.

False Oracles and False Prophets

³³"When these people, or a prophet or a priest, ask you, 'What is the oracleᵃʳ of the LORD?' say to them, 'What oracle?ᵇ I will forsakeˢ you,

---

23:19
y Jer 25:32;
　30:23
23:20
z 2Ki 23:26
a Jer 30:24
23:21
b Jer 14:14;
　27:15
23:22
c Jer 25:5;
　Zec 1:4
23:23
d Ps 139:1-10
23:24
e Job 22:12-14
f 1Ki 8:27
23:25
g Jer 14:14
h ver 28,32;
　Jer 29:8
23:26
i 1Ti 4:1-2
23:27
j Dt 13:1-3;
　Jer 29:8
k Jdg 3:7;
　8:33-34
23:29
l Jer 5:14
23:30
m Ps 34:16
n Dt 18:20;
　Jer 14:15
23:31
o ver 17
23:32
p ver 25
q Jer 7:8;
　La 2:14
23:33
r Mal 1:1 s ver 39

ᵃ33 Or *burden* (see Septuagint and Vulgate)　ᵇ33 Hebrew; Septuagint and Vulgate *'You are the burden.* (The Hebrew for *oracle* and *burden* is the same.)

declares the LORD.' ³⁴If a prophet or a priest or anyone else claims, 'This is the oracle[t] of the LORD,' I will punish[u] that man and his household. ³⁵This is what each of you keeps on saying to his friend or relative: 'What is the LORD's answer?'[v] or 'What has the LORD spoken?' ³⁶But you must not mention 'the oracle of the LORD' again, because every man's own word becomes his oracle and so you distort[w] the words of the living God, the LORD Almighty, our God. ³⁷This is what you keep saying to a prophet: 'What is the LORD's answer to you?' or 'What has the LORD spoken?' ³⁸Although you claim, 'This is the oracle of the LORD,' this is what the LORD says: You used the words, 'This is the oracle of the LORD,' even though I told you that you must not claim, 'This is the oracle of the LORD.' ³⁹Therefore, I will surely forget you and cast[x] you out of my presence along with the city I gave to you and your fathers. ⁴⁰I will bring upon you everlasting disgrace[y]—everlasting shame that will not be forgotten."

Two Baskets of Figs

24 After Jehoiachin[az] son of Jehoiakim king of Judah and the officials, the craftsmen and the artisans of Judah were carried into exile from Jerusalem to Babylon by Nebuchadnezzar king of Babylon, the LORD showed me two baskets of figs[a] placed in front of the temple of the LORD. ²One basket had very good figs, like those that ripen early; the other basket had very poor[b] figs, so bad they could not be eaten.

³Then the LORD asked me, "What do you see,[c] Jeremiah?"

"Figs," I answered. "The good ones are very good, but the poor ones are so bad they cannot be eaten."

⁴Then the word of the LORD came to me: ⁵"This is what the LORD, the God of Israel, says: 'Like these good figs, I regard as good the exiles from Judah, whom I sent away from this place to the land of the Babylonians.[b] ⁶My eyes will watch over them for their good, and I will bring them back[d] to this land. I will build[e] them up and not tear them down; I will plant them and not uproot them. ⁷I will give them a heart to know me, that I am the LORD. They will be my people,[f] and I will be their God, for they will return[g] to me with all their heart.[h]

⁸'But like the poor[i] figs, which are so bad they cannot be eaten,' says the LORD, 'so will I deal with Zedekiah king of Judah, his officials[j] and the survivors[k] from Jerusalem, whether they remain in this land or live in Egypt.[l] ⁹I will make them abhorrent[m] and an offense to all the kingdoms of the earth, a reproach and a byword,[n] an object of ridicule and cursing,[o] wherever I banish[p] them. ¹⁰I will send the sword,[q] famine and plague[r] against them until they are destroyed from the land I gave to them and their fathers.' "

Seventy Years of Captivity

25 The word came to Jeremiah concerning all the people of Judah in the fourth year of Jehoiakim[s] son of Josiah king of Judah, which was the first year of Nebuchadnezzar[t] king of Babylon. ²So Jeremiah the prophet said to all the people of Judah[u] and to all those living in Jerusalem: ³For twenty-three years—from the thirteenth year of Josiah[v]

23:34
tLa 2:14
uZec 13:3
23:35
vJer 33:3; 42:4
23:36
wGal 1:7-8;
2Pe 3:16
23:39
xJer 7:15
23:40
yJer 20:11;
Eze 5:14-15
24:1
z2Ki 24:16;
2Ch 36:9;
Jer 29:2
aAm 8:1-2
24:2
bIsa 5:4
24:3
cJer 1:11;
Am 8:2
24:6
dJer 29:10;
Eze 11:17
eJer 33:7; 42:10
24:7
fIsa 51:16;
Jer 31:33;
Heb 8:10
gJer 32:40
hEze 11:19
24:8
iJer 29:17
jJer 39:6
kJer 39:9
lJer 44:1,26
24:9
mJer 15:4;
34:17
nDt 28:25;
1Ki 9:7
oJer 29:18
pDt 28:37
24:10
qIsa 51:19
rJer 27:8
25:1
s2Ki 24:2;
Jer 36:1
t2Ki 24:1
25:2
uJer 18:11
25:3
vJer 1:2

---

[a]1 Hebrew *Jeconiah,* a variant of *Jehoiachin*   [b]5 Or *Chaldeans*

son of Amon king of Judah until this very day—the word of the LORD has come to me and I have spoken to you again and again, ^w but you have not listened. ^x

⁴And though the LORD has sent all his servants the prophets^y to you again and again, you have not listened or paid any attention. ⁵They said, "Turn now, each of you, from your evil ways and your evil practices, and you can stay in the land the LORD gave to you and your fathers for ever and ever. ⁶Do not follow other gods^z to serve and worship them; do not provoke me to anger with what your hands have made. Then I will not harm you."

⁷"But you did not listen to me," declares the LORD, "and you have provoked me with what your hands have made, ^a and you have brought harm^b to yourselves."

⁸Therefore the LORD Almighty says this: "Because you have not listened to my words, ⁹I will summon^c all the peoples of the north^d and my servant^e Nebuchadnezzar king of Babylon," declares the LORD, "and I will bring them against this land and its inhabitants and against all the surrounding nations. I will completely destroy^a them and make them an object of horror and scorn, ^f and an everlasting ruin. ¹⁰I will banish from them the sounds^g of joy and gladness, the voices of bride and bridegroom, ^h the sound of millstonesⁱ and the light of the lamp.^j ¹¹This whole country will become a desolate wasteland, ^k and these nations will serve the king of Babylon seventy years. ^l

¹²"But when the seventy years^m are fulfilled, I will punish the king of Babylon and his nation, the land of the Babylonians, ^b for their guilt," declares the LORD, "and will make it desolateⁿ forever. ¹³I will bring upon that land all the things I have spoken against it, all that are written in this book and prophesied by Jeremiah against all the nations. ¹⁴They themselves will be enslaved^o by many nations^p and great kings; I will repay^q them according to their deeds and the work of their hands."

The Cup of God's Wrath

¹⁵This is what the LORD, the God of Israel, said to me: "Take from my hand this cup^r filled with the wine of my wrath and make all the nations to whom I send you drink it. ¹⁶When they drink it, they will stagger^s and go mad^t because of the sword I will send among them."

¹⁷So I took the cup from the LORD's hand and made all the nations to whom he sent^u me drink it: ¹⁸Jerusalem and the towns of Judah, its kings and officials, to make them a ruin and an object of horror and scorn and cursing, ^v as they are today; ^w ¹⁹Pharaoh king of Egypt, his attendants, his officials and all his people, ²⁰and all the foreign people there; all the kings of Uz; ^x all the kings of the Philistines (those of Ashkelon, ^y Gaza, Ekron, and the people left at Ashdod); ²¹Edom, Moab and Ammon; ^z ²²all the kings of Tyre and Sidon; ^a the kings of the coastlands^b across the sea; ²³Dedan, Tema, Buz and all who are in distant places^c; ^c ²⁴all the kings of Arabia^d and all the kings of the foreign people who live in the desert; ²⁵all the kings of Zimri, Elam^e and Media; ²⁶and all the kings of the north, ^f near and far, one after the

25:3
wJer 11:7; 26:5
xJer 7:26
25:4
yJer 7:25
25:6
zDt 8:19
25:7
aDt 32:21
b2Ki 21:15
25:9
cIsa 13:3-5
dJer 1:15
eJer 27:6
fJer 18:16
25:10
gIsa 24:8;
Eze 26:13
hJer 7:34
iEcc 12:3-4
jRev 18:22-23
25:11
kJer 4:26-27;
12:11-12
l2Ch 36:21
25:12
mJer 29:10
nIsa 13:19-22;
14:22-23
25:14
oJer 27:7
pJer 50:9;
51:27-28
qJer 51:6
25:15
rIsa 51:17;
Ps 75:8;
Rev 14:10
25:16
sNa 3:11
tJer 51:7
25:17
uJer 1:10
25:18
vJer 24:9
wJer 44:22
25:20
xJob 1:1
yJer 47:5
25:21
zJer 49:1
25:22
aJer 47:4
bJer 31:10
25:23
cJer 9:26; 49:32
25:24
d2Ch 9:14
25:25
eGe 10:22
25:26
fJer 50:3,9

^a9 The Hebrew term refers to the irrevocable giving over of things or persons to the LORD, often by totally destroying them.   ^b12 Or *Chaldeans*   ^c23 Or *who clip the hair by their foreheads*

other—all the kingdoms on the face of the earth. And after all of them, the king of Sheshach[a] [g] will drink it too.

27"Then tell them, 'This is what the LORD Almighty, the God of Israel, says: Drink, get drunk[h] and vomit, and fall to rise no more because of the sword[i] I will send among you.' 28But if they refuse to take the cup from your hand and drink, tell them, 'This is what the LORD Almighty says: You must drink it! 29See, I am beginning to bring disaster[j] on the city that bears my Name,[k] and will you indeed go unpunished?[l] You will not go unpunished, for I am calling down a sword upon all[m] who live on the earth, declares the LORD Almighty.'

30"Now prophesy all these words against them and say to them:

" 'The LORD will roar[n] from on high;
    he will thunder[o] from his holy dwelling
    and roar mightily against his land.
He will shout like those who tread the grapes,
    shout against all who live on the earth.
31The tumult will resound to the ends of the earth,
    for the LORD will bring charges[p] against the
        nations;
    he will bring judgment on all mankind
    and put the wicked to the sword,' "
                                    declares the LORD.

32This is what the LORD Almighty says:

"Look! Disaster is spreading
    from nation to nation;[q]
a mighty storm[r] is rising
    from the ends of the earth."

33At that time those slain[s] by the LORD will be everywhere—from one end of the earth to the other. They will not be mourned or gathered[t] up or buried,[u] but will be like refuse lying on the ground.

34Weep and wail, you shepherds;
    roll[v] in the dust, you leaders of the flock.
For your time to be slaughtered[w] has come;
    you will fall and be shattered like fine pottery.
35The shepherds will have nowhere to flee,
    the leaders of the flock no place to escape.[x]
36Hear the cry of the shepherds,
    the wailing of the leaders of the flock,
    for the LORD is destroying their pasture.
37The peaceful meadows will be laid waste
    because of the fierce anger of the LORD.
38Like a lion[y] he will leave his lair,
    and their land will become desolate
because of the sword[b] of the oppressor
    and because of the LORD's fierce anger.

25:26
gJer 51:41
25:27
hver 16,28;
Hab 2:16
iEze 21:4
25:29
jJer 13:12-14
k1Pe 4:17
lPr 11:31
mver 30-31
25:30
nIsa 16:10;
42:13
oJoel 3:16;
Am 1:2
25:31
pHos 4:1;
Joel 3:2;
Mic 6:2
25:32
qIsa 34:2
rJer 23:19
25:33
sIsa 66:16;
Eze 39:17-20
tJer 16:4
uPs 79:3
25:34
vJer 6:26
wIsa 34:6;
Jer 50:27
25:35
xJob 11:20
25:38
yJer 4:7

---

a26 Sheshach is a cryptogram for Babylon.   *b38* Some Hebrew manuscripts and Septuagint (see also Jer. 46:16 and 50:16); most Hebrew manuscripts *anger*

Jeremiah Threatened With Death

26 Early in the reign of Jehoiakim[z] son of Josiah king of Judah, this word came from the Lord: [2]"This is what the Lord says: Stand in the courtyard[a] of the Lord's house and speak to all the people of the towns of Judah who come to worship in the house of the Lord. Tell[b] them everything I command you; do not omit[c] a word. [3]Perhaps they will listen and each will turn[d] from his evil way. Then I will relent[e] and not bring on them the disaster I was planning because of the evil they have done. [4]Say to them, 'This is what the Lord says: If you do not listen[f] to me and follow my law,[g] which I have set before you, [5]and if you do not listen to the words of my servants the prophets, whom I have sent to you again and again (though you have not listened[h]), [6]then I will make this house like Shiloh[i] and this city an object of cursing[j] among all the nations of the earth.'"

[7]The priests, the prophets and all the people heard Jeremiah speak these words in the house of the Lord. [8]But as soon as Jeremiah finished telling all the people everything the Lord had commanded him to say, the priests, the prophets and all the people seized him and said, "You must die! [9]Why do you prophesy in the Lord's name that this house will be like Shiloh and this city will be desolate and deserted?"[k] And all the people crowded around Jeremiah in the house of the Lord.

[10]When the officials of Judah heard about these things, they went up from the royal palace to the house of the Lord and took their places at the entrance of the New Gate of the Lord's house. [11]Then the priests and the prophets said to the officials and all the people, "This man should be sentenced to death[l] because he has prophesied against this city. You have heard it with your own ears!"

[12]Then Jeremiah said to all the officials[m] and all the people: "The Lord sent me to prophesy[n] against this house and this city all the things you have heard. [13]Now reform[p] your ways and your actions and obey the Lord your God. Then the Lord will relent and not bring the disaster he has pronounced against you. [14]As for me, I am in your hands;[q] do with me whatever you think is good and right. [15]Be assured, however, that if you put me to death, you will bring the guilt of innocent blood on yourselves and on this city and on those who live in it, for in truth the Lord has sent me to you to speak all these words in your hearing."

[16]Then the officials[r] and all the people said to the priests and the prophets, "This man should not be sentenced to death![s] He has spoken to us in the name of the Lord our God."

[17]Some of the elders of the land stepped forward and said to the entire assembly of people, [18]"Micah[t] of Moresheth prophesied in the days of Hezekiah king of Judah. He told all the people of Judah, 'This is what the Lord Almighty says:

" 'Zion[u] will be plowed like a field,
    Jerusalem will become a heap of rubble,[v]
    the temple hill[w] a mound overgrown with thickets.'[a][x]

[19]"Did Hezekiah king of Judah or anyone else in Judah put him to

---

26:1
z2Ki 23:36
26:2
aJer 19:14
bJer 1:17;
Mt 28:20;
Ac 20:27
cDt 4:2
26:3
dJer 36:7
eJer 18:8
26:4
fLev 26:14
g1Ki 9:6
26:5
hJer 25:4
26:6
iJos 18:1
j2Ki 22:19
26:9
kJer 9:11
26:11
lDt 18:20;
Jer 18:23; 38:4;
Mt 26:66;
Ac 6:11
26:12
mJer 1:18
nAm 7:15;
Ac 4:18-20;
5:29 over 2,15
26:13
pJer 7:5;
Joel 2:12-14
26:14
qJer 38:5
26:16
rAc 23:9
sAc 5:34-39;
23:29
26:18
tMic 1:1
uIsa 2:3
vNe 4:2;
Jer 9:11
wMic 4:1;
Zec 8:3
xJer 17:3

---

[a]18 Micah 3:12

death? Did not Hezekiah[y] fear the LORD and seek his favor? And did not the LORD relent,[z] so that he did not bring the disaster[a] he pronounced against them? We are about to bring a terrible disaster[b] on ourselves!"

20(Now Uriah son of Shemaiah from Kiriath Jearim[c] was another man who prophesied in the name of the LORD; he prophesied the same things against this city and this land as Jeremiah did. 21When King Jehoiakim[d] and all his officers and officials heard his words, the king sought to put him to death. But Uriah heard of it and fled[e] in fear to Egypt. 22King Jehoiakim, however, sent Elnathan[f] son of Acbor to Egypt, along with some other men. 23They brought Uriah out of Egypt and took him to King Jehoiakim, who had him struck down with a sword and his body thrown into the burial place of the common people.)

24Furthermore, Ahikam[g] son of Shaphan supported Jeremiah, and so he was not handed over to the people to be put to death.

Judah to Serve Nebuchadnezzar

27 Early in the reign of Zedekiah[a][h] son of Josiah king of Judah, this word came to Jeremiah from the LORD: 2This is what the LORD said to me: "Make a yoke[i] out of straps and crossbars and put it on your neck. 3Then send word to the kings of Edom, Moab, Ammon,[j] Tyre and Sidon through the envoys who have come to Jerusalem to Zedekiah king of Judah. 4Give them a message for their masters and say, 'This is what the LORD Almighty, the God of Israel, says: "Tell this to your masters: 5With my great power and outstretched arm[k] I made the earth and its people and the animals that are on it, and I give[l] it to anyone I please. 6Now I will hand all your countries over to my servant[m] Nebuchadnezzar[n] king of Babylon; I will make even the wild animals subject to him.[o] 7All nations will serve[p] him and his son and his grandson until the time[q] for his land comes; then many nations and great kings will subjugate[r] him.

8" ' "If, however, any nation or kingdom will not serve Nebuchadnezzar king of Babylon or bow its neck under his yoke, I will punish that nation with the sword, famine and plague, declares the LORD, until I destroy it by his hand. 9So do not listen to your prophets, your diviners, your interpreters of dreams, your mediums[s] or your sorcerers who tell you, 'You will not serve the king of Babylon.' 10They prophesy lies[t] to you that will only serve to remove you far from your lands; I will banish you and you will perish. 11But if any nation will bow its neck under the yoke[u] of the king of Babylon and serve him, I will let that nation remain in its own land to till it and to live there, declares the LORD." ' "

12I gave the same message to Zedekiah king of Judah. I said, "Bow your neck under the yoke of the king of Babylon; serve him and his people, and you will live. 13Why will you and your people die[v] by the sword, famine and plague with which the LORD has threatened any nation that will not serve the king of Babylon? 14Do not listen to the words of the prophets who say to you, 'You will not serve the king of

26:19
y2Ch 32:24-26;
Isa 37:14-20
zEx 32:14;
2Sa 24:16
aJer 44:7
bHab 2:10
26:20
cJos 9:17
26:21
d1Ki 19:2
eMt 10:23
26:22
fJer 36:12,25
26:24
g2Ki 22:12
27:1
h2Ch 36:11
27:2
iJer 28:10,13
27:3
jJer 25:21
27:5
kDt 9:29
lPs 115:16
27:6
mJer 25:9
nJer 21:7;
Eze 29:18-20
oJer 28:14;
Da 2:37-38
27:7
p2Ch 36:20
qJer 25:12
rJer 25:14;
Da 5:28
27:9
sDt 18:11
27:10
tJer 23:25
27:11
uJer 21:9
27:13
vEze 18:31

a1 A few Hebrew manuscripts and Syriac (see also Jer. 27:3, 12 and 28:1); most Hebrew manuscripts *Jehoiakim* (Most Septuagint manuscripts do not have this verse.)

Babylon,' for they are prophesying lies[w] to you. [15]'I have not sent[x] them,' declares the LORD. 'They are prophesying lies in my name.[y] Therefore, I will banish you and you will perish,[z] both you and the prophets who prophesy to you.' "

[16]Then I said to the priests and all these people, "This is what the LORD says: Do not listen to the prophets who say, 'Very soon now the articles[a] from the LORD's house will be brought back from Babylon.' They are prophesying lies to you. [17]Do not listen to them. Serve the king of Babylon, and you will live. Why should this city become a ruin? [18]If they are prophets and have the word of the LORD, let them plead[b] with the LORD Almighty that the furnishings remaining in the house of the LORD and in the palace of the king of Judah and in Jerusalem not be taken to Babylon. [19]For this is what the LORD Almighty says about the pillars, the Sea,[c] the movable stands and the other furnishings[d] that are left in this city, [20]which Nebuchadnezzar king of Babylon did not take away when he carried[e] Jehoiachin[a][f] son of Jehoiakim king of Judah into exile from Jerusalem to Babylon, along with all the nobles of Judah and Jerusalem— [21]yes, this is what the LORD Almighty, the God of Israel, says about the things that are left in the house of the LORD and in the palace of the king of Judah and in Jerusalem: [22]'They will be taken[g] to Babylon and there they will remain until the day[h] I come for them,' declares the LORD. 'Then I will bring[i] them back and restore them to this place.' "

The False Prophet Hananiah

28 In the fifth month of that same year, the fourth year, early in the reign of Zedekiah[j] king of Judah, the prophet Hananiah son of Azzur, who was from Gibeon,[k] said to me in the house of the LORD in the presence of the priests and all the people: [2]"This is what the LORD Almighty, the God of Israel, says: 'I will break the yoke[l] of the king of Babylon. [3]Within two years I will bring back to this place all the articles[m] of the LORD's house that Nebuchadnezzar king of Babylon removed from here and took to Babylon. [4]I will also bring back to this place Jehoiachin[a][n] son of Jehoiakim king of Judah and all the other exiles from Judah who went to Babylon,' declares the LORD, 'for I will break the yoke of the king of Babylon.' "

[5]Then the prophet Jeremiah replied to the prophet Hananiah before the priests and all the people who were standing in the house of the LORD. [6]He said, "Amen! May the LORD do so! May the LORD fulfill the words you have prophesied by bringing the articles of the LORD's house and all the exiles back to this place from Babylon. [7]Nevertheless, listen to what I have to say in your hearing and in the hearing of all the people: [8]From early times the prophets who preceded you and me have prophesied war, disaster and plague[o] against many countries and great kingdoms. [9]But the prophet who prophesies peace will be recognized as one truly sent by the LORD only if his prediction comes true.[p]"

[10]Then the prophet Hananiah took the yoke[q] off the neck of the prophet Jeremiah and broke it, [11]and he said[r] before all the people, "This is what the LORD says: 'In the same way will I break the yoke of

*Cross references (margin):*

27:14
w Jer 14:14
27:15
x Jer 23:21
y Jer 29:9
z Jer 6:15
27:16
a 2Ki 24:13;
2Ch 36:7,10;
Jer 28:3; Da 1:2
27:18
b 1Sa 7:8
27:19
c 2Ki 25:13
d Jer 52:17-23
27:20
e 2Ch 36:10;
Jer 24:1
f Jer 22:24
27:22
g 2Ki 25:13
h 2Ch 36:21
i Ezr 1:7; 7:19
28:1
j Jer 27:1,3
k Jos 9:3
28:2
l Jer 27:12
28:3
m 2Ki 24:13
28:4
n Jer 22:24-27
28:8
o Lev 26:14-17;
Isa 5:5-7
28:9
p Dt 18:22
28:10
q Jer 27:2
28:11
r Jer 14:14;
27:10

---

[a]20,4 Hebrew *Jeconiah*, a variant of *Jehoiachin*

Nebuchadnezzar king of Babylon off the neck of all the nations within two years.'" At this, the prophet Jeremiah went on his way.

[12] Shortly after the prophet Hananiah had broken the yoke off the neck of the prophet Jeremiah, the word of the LORD came to Jeremiah: [13] "Go and tell Hananiah, 'This is what the LORD says: You have broken a wooden yoke, but in its place you will get a yoke of iron. [14] This is what the LORD Almighty, the God of Israel, says: I will put an iron yoke[s] on the necks of all these nations to make them serve[t] Nebuchadnezzar king of Babylon, and they will serve him. I will even give him control over the wild animals.[u]'"

[15] Then the prophet Jeremiah said to Hananiah the prophet, "Listen, Hananiah! The LORD has not sent[v] you, yet you have persuaded this nation to trust in lies.[w] [16] Therefore, this is what the LORD says: 'I am about to remove you from the face of the earth.[x] This very year you are going to die, because you have preached rebellion[y] against the LORD.'"

[17] In the seventh month of that same year, Hananiah the prophet died.

A Letter to the Exiles

29 This is the text of the letter that the prophet Jeremiah sent from Jerusalem to the surviving elders among the exiles and to the priests, the prophets and all the other people Nebuchadnezzar had carried into exile from Jerusalem to Babylon.[z] [2](This was after King Jehoiachin[aa] and the queen mother, the court officials and the leaders of Judah and Jerusalem, the craftsmen and the artisans had gone into exile from Jerusalem.) [3] He entrusted the letter to Elasah son of Shaphan and to Gemariah son of Hilkiah, whom Zedekiah king of Judah sent to King Nebuchadnezzar in Babylon. It said:

[4] This is what the LORD Almighty, the God of Israel, says to all those I carried[b] into exile from Jerusalem to Babylon: [5] "Build[c] houses and settle down; plant gardens and eat what they produce. [6] Marry and have sons and daughters; find wives for your sons and give your daughters in marriage, so that they too may have sons and daughters. Increase in number there; do not decrease. [7] Also, seek the peace and prosperity of the city to which I have carried you into exile. Pray[d] to the LORD for it, because if it prospers, you too will prosper." [8] Yes, this is what the LORD Almighty, the God of Israel, says: "Do not let the prophets and diviners among you deceive[e] you. Do not listen to the dreams you encourage them to have.[f] [9] They are prophesying lies[g] to you in my name. I have not sent them," declares the LORD.

[10] This is what the LORD says: "When seventy years[h] are completed for Babylon, I will come to you and fulfill my gracious promise to bring you back[i] to this place. [11] For I know the plans[j] I have for you," declares the LORD, "plans to prosper you and not to harm you, plans to give you hope and a future. [12] Then you will call upon me and come and pray to me, and I will listen[k] to you. [13] You will seek[l] me and find me when you seek me with all your heart.[m] [14] I will be found by you," declares the LORD, "and will

Cross references

28:14
s Dt 28:48
t Jer 25:11
u Jer 27:6

28:15
v Jer 29:31
w Jer 20:6; 29:21; La 2:14; Eze 13:6

28:16
x Ge 7:4
y Dt 13:5; Jer 29:32

29:1
z 2Ch 36:10

29:2
a 2Ki 24:12; Jer 22:24-28

29:4
b Jer 24:5

29:5
c ver 28

29:7
d Ezr 6:10; 1Ti 2:1-2

29:8
e Jer 37:9
f Jer 23:27

29:9
g Jer 14:14; 27:15

29:10
h 2Ch 36:21; Jer 25:12; Da 9:2
i Jer 21:22

29:11
j Ps 40:5

29:12
k Ps 145:19

29:13
l Mt 7:7
m Dt 4:29; Jer 24:7

---

[a]2 Hebrew *Jeconiah*, a variant of *Jehoiachin*

bring you back[n] from captivity.[o] I will gather you from all the nations and places where I have banished you," declares the LORD, "and will bring you back to the place from which I carried you into exile."[o]

[15]You may say, "The LORD has raised up prophets for us in Babylon," [16]but this is what the LORD says about the king who sits on David's throne and all the people who remain in this city, your countrymen who did not go with you into exile— [17]yes, this is what the LORD Almighty says: "I will send the sword, famine and plague[p] against them and I will make them like poor figs[q] that are so bad they cannot be eaten. [18]I will pursue them with the sword, famine and plague and will make them abhorrent[r] to all the kingdoms of the earth and an object of cursing and horror,[s] of scorn and reproach, among all the nations where I drive them. [19]For they have not listened to my words,"[t] declares the LORD, "words that I sent to them again and again by my servants the prophets.[u] And you exiles have not listened either," declares the LORD.

[20]Therefore, hear the word of the LORD, all you exiles whom I have sent[v] away from Jerusalem to Babylon. [21]This is what the LORD Almighty, the God of Israel, says about Ahab son of Kolaiah and Zedekiah son of Maaseiah, who are prophesying lies[w] to you in my name: "I will hand them over to Nebuchadnezzar king of Babylon, and he will put them to death before your very eyes. [22]Because of them, all the exiles from Judah who are in Babylon will use this curse: 'The LORD treat you like Zedekiah and Ahab, whom the king of Babylon burned[x] in the fire.' [23]For they have done outrageous things in Israel; they have committed adultery[y] with their neighbors' wives and in my name have spoken lies, which I did not tell them to do. I know[z] it and am a witness to it," declares the LORD.

Message to Shemaiah

[24]Tell Shemaiah the Nehelamite, [25]"This is what the LORD Almighty, the God of Israel, says: You sent letters in your own name to all the people in Jerusalem, to Zephaniah[a] son of Maaseiah the priest, and to all the other priests. You said to Zephaniah, [26]'The LORD has appointed you priest in place of Jehoiada to be in charge of the house of the LORD; you should put any madman[b] who acts like a prophet into the stocks[c] and neck-irons. [27]So why have you not reprimanded Jeremiah from Anathoth, who poses as a prophet among you? [28]He has sent this message[d] to us in Babylon: It will be a long time.[e] Therefore build[f] houses and settle down; plant gardens and eat what they produce.' "

[29]Zephaniah the priest, however, read the letter to Jeremiah the prophet. [30]Then the word of the LORD came to Jeremiah: [31]"Send this message to all the exiles: 'This is what the LORD says about Shemaiah[g] the Nehelamite: Because Shemaiah has prophesied to you, even though I did not send[h] him, and has led you to believe a lie, [32]this is what the LORD says: I will surely punish Shemaiah the Nehelamite and his descendants.[i] He will have no one left among this people, nor will

29:14
n Dt 30:3;
Jer 30:3
o Jer 23:3-4
29:17
p Jer 27:8
q Jer 24:8-10
29:18
r Jer 15:4
s Dt 28:25;
Jer 42:18
29:19
t Jer 6:19
u Jer 25:4
29:20
v Jer 24:5
29:21
w ver 9;
Jer 14:14
29:22
x Da 3:6
29:23
y Jer 23:14
z Heb 4:13
29:25
a 2Ki 25:18;
Jer 21:1
29:26
b 2Ki 9:11;
Hos 9:7;
Jn 10:20
c Jer 20:2
29:28
d ver 1 e ver 10
f ver 5
29:31
g ver 24
h Jer 14:14;
28:15
29:32
i 1Sa 2:30-33

a14 Or will restore your fortunes

he see the good[j] things I will do for my people, declares the LORD, because he has preached rebellion[k] against me.' "

Restoration of Israel

30 This is the word that came to Jeremiah from the LORD: [2]"This is what the LORD, the God of Israel, says: 'Write[l] in a book all the words I have spoken to you. [3]The days are coming,' declares the LORD, 'when I will bring[m] my people Israel and Judah back from captivity[a] and restore[n] them to the land I gave their forefathers to possess,' says the LORD."

[4]These are the words the LORD spoke concerning Israel and Judah: [5]"This is what the LORD says:

> " 'Cries of fear[o] are heard—
>   terror, not peace.
> [6]Ask and see:
>   Can a man bear children?
> Then why do I see every strong man
>   with his hands on his stomach like a woman in labor,[p]
>   every face turned deathly pale?
> [7]How awful that day[q] will be!
>   None will be like it.
> It will be a time of trouble[r] for Jacob,
>   but he will be saved[s] out of it.

> [8]" ' In that day,' declares the LORD Almighty,
>   'I will break the yoke[t] off their necks
> and will tear off their bonds;
>   no longer will foreigners enslave them. [u]
> [9]Instead, they will serve the LORD their God
>   and David[v] their king, [w]
>   whom I will raise up for them.

> [10]" 'So do not fear,[x] O Jacob my servant;[y]
>   do not be dismayed, O Israel,'
>   declares the LORD.
> 'I will surely save[z] you out of a distant place,
>   your descendants from the land of their exile.
> Jacob will again have peace and security, [a]
>   and no one will make him afraid.
> [11]I am with you and will save you,'
>   declares the LORD.
> 'Though I completely destroy all the nations
>   among which I scatter you,
>   I will not completely destroy[b] you.
> I will discipline[c] you but only with justice;
>   I will not let you go entirely unpunished.'[d]

[12]"This is what the LORD says:

> " 'Your wound is incurable,
>   your injury beyond healing.[e]

---

[a]3 Or *will restore the fortunes of my people Israel and Judah*

29:32
[j]ver 10
[k]Jer 28:16
30:2
[l]Isa 30:8
30:3
[m]Jer 29:14
[n]Jer 16:15
30:5
[o]Jer 6:25
30:6
[p]Jer 4:31
30:7
[q]Isa 2:12;
Joel 2:11
[r]Zep 1:15
[s]ver 10
30:8
[t]Isa 9:4
[u]Eze 34:27
30:9
[v]Isa 55:3-4;
Lk 1:69;
Ac 2:30; 13:23
[w]Eze 34:23-24;
37:24; Hos 3:5
30:10
[x]Isa 43:5;
Jer 46:27-28
[y]Isa 44:2
[z]Jer 29:14
[a]Isa 35:9
30:11
[b]Jer 4:27; 46:28
[c]Jer 10:24
[d]Am 9:8
30:12
[e]Jer 15:18

¹³There is no one to plead your cause,
no remedy for your sore,
no healing^f for you.
¹⁴All your allies^g have forgotten you;
they care nothing for you.
I have struck you as an enemy^h would
and punished you as would the cruel,ⁱ
because your guilt is so great
and your sins^j so many.
¹⁵Why do you cry out over your wound,
your pain that has no cure?
Because of your great guilt and many sins
I have done these things to you.

¹⁶" 'But all who devour^k you will be devoured;
all your enemies will go into exile.^l
Those who plunder^m you will be plundered;
all who make spoil of you I will despoil.
¹⁷But I will restore you to health
and heal your wounds,'

declares the LORD,

'because you are called an outcast,ⁿ
Zion for whom no one cares.'

¹⁸"This is what the LORD says:

" 'I will restore the fortunes^o of Jacob's tents
and have compassion^p on his dwellings;
the city will be rebuilt^q on her ruins,
and the palace will stand in its proper place.
¹⁹From them will come songs^r of thanksgiving^s
and the sound of rejoicing.^t
I will add to their numbers,^u
and they will not be decreased;
I will bring them honor,^v
and they will not be disdained.
²⁰Their children^w will be as in days of old,
and their community will be established^x before me;
I will punish all who oppress them.
²¹Their leader^y will be one of their own;
their ruler will arise from among them.
I will bring him near^z and he will come close to me,
for who is he who will devote himself
to be close to me?'

declares the LORD.

²²" 'So you will be my people,
and I will be your God.' "

²³See, the storm^a of the LORD
will burst out in wrath,
a driving wind swirling down
on the heads of the wicked.
²⁴The fierce anger^b of the LORD will not turn back^c
until he fully accomplishes

30:13
f Jer 8:22;
14:19; 46:11
30:14
g Jer 22:20;
La 1:2
h Job 13:24
i Job 30:21
j Jer 5:6
30:16
k Isa 33:1;
Jer 2:3; 10:25
l Isa 14:2;
Joel 3:4-8
m Jer 50:10
30:17
n Jer 33:24
30:18
over 3;
Jer 31:23
p Ps 102:13
q Jer 31:4,24,38
30:19
r Isa 35:10;
51:11 s Isa 51:3
t Ps 126:1-2;
Jer 31:4
u Jer 33:22
v Isa 60:9
30:20
w Isa 54:13;
Jer 31:17
x Isa 54:14
30:21
y ver 9 z Nu 16:5
30:23
a Jer 23:19
30:24
b Jer 4:8
c Jer 4:28

the purposes of his heart.
In days to come
you will understand[d] this.

31 "At that time," declares the LORD, "I will be the God[e] of all the clans of Israel, and they will be my people."
[2]This is what the LORD says:

"The people who survive the sword
will find favor[f] in the desert;
I will come to give rest[g] to Israel."

[3]The LORD appeared to us in the past,[a] saying:

"I have loved[h] you with an everlasting love;
I have drawn[i] you with loving-kindness.
[4]I will build you up again
and you will be rebuilt, O Virgin Israel.
Again you will take up your tambourines
and go out to dance with the joyful.[j]
[5]Again you will plant vineyards
on the hills of Samaria;[k]
the farmers will plant them
and enjoy their fruit.[l]
[6]There will be a day when watchmen cry out
on the hills of Ephraim,
'Come, let us go up to Zion,
to the LORD our God.' "[m]

[7]This is what the LORD says:

"Sing with joy for Jacob;
shout for the foremost[n] of the nations.
Make your praises heard, and say,
'O LORD, save[o] your people,
the remnant[p] of Israel.'
[8]See, I will bring them from the land of the north[q]
and gather[r] them from the ends of the earth.
Among them will be the blind[s] and the lame,[t]
expectant mothers and women in labor;
a great throng will return.
[9]They will come with weeping;[u]
they will pray as I bring them back.
I will lead[v] them beside streams of water
on a level[w] path where they will not stumble,
because I am Israel's father,[x]
and Ephraim is my firstborn son.

[10]"Hear the word of the LORD, O nations;
proclaim it in distant coastlands:[y]
'He who scattered Israel will gather[z] them
and will watch over his flock like a shepherd.'[a]
[11]For the LORD will ransom Jacob

---

a3 Or LORD *has appeared to us from afar*

30:24
d Jer 23:19-20
31:1
e Jer 30:22
31:2
f Nu 14:20
g Ex 33:14
31:3
h Dt 4:37
i Hos 11:4
31:4
j Jer 30:19
31:5
k Jer 50:19
l Isa 65:21;
Am 9:14
31:6
m Isa 2:3;
Jer 50:4-5;
Mic 4:2
31:7
n Dt 28:13;
Isa 61:9
o Ps 14:7; 28:9
p Isa 37:31
31:8
q Jer 3:18; 23:8
r Dt 30:4;
Eze 34:12-14
s Isa 42:16
t Eze 34:16;
Mic 4:6
31:9
u Ps 126:5
v Isa 63:13
w Isa 49:11
x Ex 4:22;
Jer 3:4
31:10
y Isa 66:19;
Jer 25:22
z Jer 50:19
a Isa 40:11;
Eze 34:12

and redeem[b] them from the hand of those stronger[c]
　　than they.
[12]They will come and shout for joy on the heights[d] of
　　Zion;
　　they will rejoice in the bounty[e] of the LORD—
the grain, the new wine and the oil,[f]
　　the young of the flocks and herds.
They will be like a well-watered garden,[g]
　　and they will sorrow[h] no more.
[13]Then maidens will dance and be glad,
　　young men and old as well.
I will turn their mourning[i] into gladness;
　　I will give them comfort and joy[j] instead of sorrow.
[14]I will satisfy[k] the priests with abundance,
　　and my people will be filled with my bounty,"
　　　　　　　　　　　　　　　　　　　declares the LORD.

[15]This is what the LORD says:

　　"A voice is heard in Ramah,[l]
　　　mourning and great weeping,
　　Rachel weeping for her children
　　　and refusing to be comforted,[m]
　　　because her children are no more."[n]

[16]This is what the LORD says:

　　"Restrain your voice from weeping
　　　and your eyes from tears,[o]
　　for your work will be rewarded,[p]"
　　　　　　　　　　　　　　　　　　　declares the LORD.
　　"They will return[q] from the land of the enemy.
[17]So there is hope for your future,"
　　　　　　　　　　　　　　　　　　　declares the LORD.
　　"Your children will return to their own land.

[18]"I have surely heard Ephraim's moaning:
　　'You disciplined[r] me like an unruly calf,[s]
　　and I have been disciplined.
Restore[t] me, and I will return,
　　because you are the LORD my God.
[19]After I strayed,[u]
　　I repented;
after I came to understand,
　　I beat[v] my breast.
I was ashamed and humiliated
　　because I bore the disgrace of my youth.'
[20]Is not Ephraim my dear son,
　　the child in whom I delight?
Though I often speak against him,
　　I still remember[w] him.
Therefore my heart yearns for him;
　　I have great compassion[x] for him,"
　　　　　　　　　　　　　　　　　　　declares the LORD.

31:11
b Isa 44:23;
48:20 c Ps 142:6
31:12
d Eze 17:23;
Mic 4:1
e Joel 3:18
f Hos 2:21-22
g Isa 58:11
h Isa 65:19;
Jn 16:22;
Rev 7:17
31:13
i Isa 61:3
j Ps 30:11;
Isa 51:11
31:14
k ver 25
31:15
l Jos 18:25
m Ge 37:35
n Jer 10:20;
Mt 2:17-18*
31:16
o Isa 25:8; 30:19
p Ru 2:12
q Jer 30:3;
Eze 11:17
31:18
r Job 5:17
s Hos 4:16
t Ps 80:3
31:19
u Eze 36:31
v Eze 21:12;
Lk 18:13
31:20
w Hos 4:4; 11:8
x Isa 55:7;
63:15; Mic 7:18

²¹"Set up road signs;
    put up guideposts.
Take note of the highway,^y
    the road that you take.
Return,^z O Virgin^a Israel,
    return to your towns.
²²How long will you wander,^b
    O unfaithful^c daughter?
The LORD will create a new thing on earth—
    a woman will surround^a a man."

²³This is what the LORD Almighty, the God of Israel, says: "When I bring them back from captivity,^{bd} the people in the land of Judah and in its towns will once again use these words: 'The LORD bless you, O righteous dwelling,^e O sacred mountain.'^f ²⁴People will live^g together in Judah and all its towns—farmers and those who move about with their flocks. ²⁵I will refresh the weary and satisfy the faint."^h

²⁶At this I awokeⁱ and looked around. My sleep had been pleasant to me.

²⁷"The days are coming," declares the LORD, "when I will plant^j the house of Israel and the house of Judah with the offspring of men and of animals. ²⁸Just as I watched over them to uproot and tear down, and to overthrow, destroy and bring disaster,^k so I will watch over them to build and to plant,"^l declares the LORD. ²⁹"In those days people will no longer say,

'The fathers^m have eaten sour grapes,
    and the children's teeth are set on edge.'ⁿ

³⁰Instead, everyone will die for his own sin;^o whoever eats sour grapes—his own teeth will be set on edge.

³¹"The time is coming," declares the LORD,
    "when I will make a new covenant^p
with the house of Israel
    and with the house of Judah.
³²It will not be like the covenant^q
    I made with their forefathers^r
when I took them by the hand
    to lead them out of Egypt,
because they broke my covenant,
    though I was a husband to^c them,^d "
                    declares the LORD.
³³"This is the covenant I will make with the house of
    Israel
    after that time," declares the LORD.
"I will put my law in their minds
    and write it on their hearts.^s
I will be their God,
    and they will be my people.^t
³⁴No longer will a man teach^u his neighbor,

31:21
y Jer 50:5
z Isa 52:11
a ver 4
31:22
b Jer 2:23
c Jer 3:6
31:23
d Jer 30:18
e Isa 1:26
f Ps 48:1;
Zec 8:3
31:24
g Zec 8:4-8
31:25
h Jn 4:14
31:26
i Zec 4:1
31:27
j Eze 36:9-11;
Hos 2:23
31:28
k Jer 18:8; 44:27
l Jer 1:10
31:29
m La 5:7
n Eze 18:2
31:30
o Isa 3:11;
Gal 6:7
31:31
p Jer 32:40;
Eze 37:26;
Lk 22:20;
Heb 8:8-12*;
10:16-17
31:32
q Ex 24:8 r Dt 5:3
31:33
s 2Co 3:3
t Jer 24:7;
Heb 10:16
31:34
u 1Jn 2:27

---

^a22 Or *will go about seeking;* or *will protect*   ^b23 Or *I restore their fortunes*   ^c32 Hebrew;
Septuagint and Syriac / *and I turned away from*   ^d32 Or *was their master*

or a man his brother, saying, 'Know the LORD,'
because they will all know[v] me,
 from the least of them to the greatest,"
                                    declares the LORD.
"For I will forgive[w] their wickedness
 and will remember their sins[x] no more."

35This is what the LORD says,

he who appoints[y] the sun
 to shine by day,
who decrees the moon and stars
 to shine by night,[z]
who stirs up the sea
 so that its waves roar—
 the LORD Almighty is his name:[a]
36"Only if these decrees[b] vanish from my sight,"
 declares the LORD,
"will the descendants[c] of Israel ever cease
 to be a nation before me."

37This is what the LORD says:

"Only if the heavens above can be measured[d]
 and the foundations of the earth below be searched
   out
will I reject[e] all the descendants of Israel
 because of all they have done,"
                                    declares the LORD.

38"The days are coming," declares the LORD, "when this city will be
rebuilt[f] for me from the Tower of Hananel[g] to the Corner Gate.[h] 39The
measuring line will stretch from there straight to the hill of Gareb and
then turn to Goah. 40The whole valley[i] where dead bodies[j] and ashes
are thrown, and all the terraces out to the Kidron Valley[k] on the east as
far as the corner of the Horse Gate,[l] will be holy[m] to the LORD. The city
will never again be uprooted or demolished."

Jeremiah Buys a Field

32 This is the word that came to Jeremiah from the LORD in the
tenth[n] year of Zedekiah king of Judah, which was the eighteenth[o] year of Nebuchadnezzar. 2The army of the king of Babylon was
then besieging Jerusalem, and Jeremiah the prophet was confined in
the courtyard of the guard[p] in the royal palace of Judah.

3Now Zedekiah king of Judah had imprisoned him there, saying,
"Why do you prophesy[q] as you do? You say, 'This is what the LORD
says: I am about to hand this city over to the king of Babylon, and he
will capture[r] it. 4Zedekiah king of Judah will not escape[s] out of the
hands of the Babylonians[a] but will certainly be handed over to the king
of Babylon, and will speak with him face to face and see him with his

31:34
vJn 6:45
wIsa 54:13;
Jer 33:8; 50:20
xRo 11:27;
Mic 7:19;
Heb 10:17*

31:35
yPs 136:7-9
zGe 1:16
aJer 10:16

31:36
bIsa 54:9-10;
Jer 33:20-26
cPs 89:36-37

31:37
dJer 33:22
eJer 33:24-26;
Ro 11:1-5

31:38
fJer 30:18
gNe 3:1
h2Ki 14:13;
Zec 14:10

31:40
iJer 7:31-32
jJer 8:2
k2Sa 15:23;
Jn 18:1
lJer 11:16
mJoel 3:17;
Zec 14:21

32:1
n2Ki 25:1
oJer 25:1; 39:1

32:2
pNe 3:25;
Jer 37:21

32:3
qJer 26:8-9
rver 28;
Jer 34:2-3

32:4
sJer 38:18,23;
39:5-7; 52:9

a4 Or *Chaldeans*; also in verses 5, 24, 25, 28, 29 and 43

own eyes. [5]He will take[t] Zedekiah to Babylon, where he will remain until I deal with him, declares the LORD. If you fight against the Babylonians, you will not succeed.'"[u]

[6]Jeremiah said, "The word of the LORD came to me: [7]Hanamel son of Shallum your uncle is going to come to you and say, 'Buy my field at Anathoth, because as nearest relative it is your right and duty[v] to buy it.'

[8]"Then, just as the LORD had said, my cousin Hanamel came to me in the courtyard of the guard and said, 'Buy my field at Anathoth in the territory of Benjamin. Since it is your right to redeem it and possess it, buy it for yourself.'

"I knew that this was the word of the LORD; [9]so I bought the field at Anathoth from my cousin Hanamel and weighed out for him seventeen shekels[a] of silver. [w] [10]I signed and sealed the deed, had it witnessed, [x] and weighed out the silver on the scales. [11]I took the deed of purchase—the sealed copy containing the terms and conditions, as well as the unsealed copy— [12]and I gave this deed to Baruch[y] son of Neriah, [z] the son of Mahseiah, in the presence of my cousin Hanamel and of the witnesses who had signed the deed and of all the Jews sitting in the courtyard of the guard.

[13]"In their presence I gave Baruch these instructions: [14]'This is what the LORD Almighty, the God of Israel, says: Take these documents, both the sealed and unsealed copies of the deed of purchase, and put them in a clay jar so they will last a long time. [15]For this is what the LORD Almighty, the God of Israel, says: Houses, fields and vineyards will again be bought in this land.'[a]

[16]"After I had given the deed of purchase to Baruch son of Neriah, I prayed to the LORD:

[17]"Ah, Sovereign LORD,[b] you have made the heavens and the earth by your great power and outstretched arm. [c] Nothing is too hard[d] for you. [18]You show love[e] to thousands but bring the punishment for the fathers' sins into the laps of their children[f] after them. O great and powerful God, whose name is the LORD Almighty,[g] [19]great are your purposes and mighty are your deeds. [h] Your eyes are open to all the ways of men;[i] you reward everyone according to his conduct and as his deeds deserve.[j] [20]You performed miraculous signs and wonders in Egypt[k] and have continued them to this day, both in Israel and among all mankind, and have gained the renown that is still yours. [21]You brought your people Israel out of Egypt with signs and wonders, by a mighty hand[l] and an outstretched arm and with great terror. [m] [22]You gave them this land you had sworn to give their forefathers, a land flowing with milk and honey. [n] [23]They came in and took possession[o] of it, but they did not obey you or follow your law;[p] they did not do what you commanded them to do. So you brought all this disaster[q] upon them.

[24]"See how the siege ramps are built up to take the city. Because of the sword, famine and plague, [r] the city will be handed over to

---

32:5
t Jer 39:7;
Eze 12:13
u Jer 21:4
32:7
v Lev 25:24-25;
Ru 4:3-4;
Mt 27:10*
32:9
w Ge 23:16
32:10
x Ru 4:9
32:12
y ver 16;
Jer 36:4;
43:3,6; 45:1
z Jer 51:59
32:15
a ver 43-44;
Jer 30:18;
Am 9:14-15
32:17
b Jer 1:6
c 2Ki 19:15;
Ps 102:25
d Mt 19:26
32:18
e Dt 5:10
f Ex 20:5
g Jer 10:16
32:19
h Isa 28:29
i Pr 5:21;
Jer 16:17
j Jer 17:10;
Mt 16:27
32:20
k Ex 9:16
32:21
l Ex 6:6;
1Ch 17:21;
Da 9:15
m Dt 26:8
32:22
n Ex 3:8;
Jer 11:5
32:23
o Ps 44:2;
78:54-55
p Ne 9:26;
Jer 11:8
q Da 9:14
32:24
r Jer 14:12

---

[a]9 That is, about 7 ounces (about 200 grams)

the Babylonians who are attacking it. What you said[s] has happened, as you now see. 25And though the city will be handed over to the Babylonians, you, O Sovereign LORD, say to me, 'Buy the field with silver and have the transaction witnessed.' "

26Then the word of the LORD came to Jeremiah: 27"I am the LORD, the God of all mankind.[t] Is anything too hard for me? 28Therefore, this is what the LORD says: I am about to hand this city over to the Babylonians and to Nebuchadnezzar[u] king of Babylon, who will capture it.[v] 29The Babylonians who are attacking this city will come in and set it on fire; they will burn it down,[w] along with the houses[x] where the people provoked me to anger by burning incense on the roofs to Baal and by pouring out drink offerings[y] to other gods.

30"The people of Israel and Judah have done nothing but evil in my sight from their youth;[z] indeed, the people of Israel have done nothing but provoke[a] me with what their hands have made,[b] declares the LORD. 31From the day it was built until now, this city has so aroused my anger and wrath that I must remove[c] it from my sight. 32The people of Israel and Judah have provoked me by all the evil[d] they have done— they, their kings and officials, their priests and prophets, the men of Judah and the people of Jerusalem. 33They turned their backs[e] to me and not their faces; though I taught[f] them again and again, they would not listen or respond to discipline. 34They set up their abominable idols in the house that bears my Name and defiled[g] it. 35They built high places for Baal in the Valley of Ben Hinnom to sacrifice their sons and daughters[a] to Molech,[h] though I never commanded, nor did it enter my mind,[i] that they should do such a detestable thing and so make Judah sin.

36"You are saying about this city, 'By the sword, famine and plague[j] it will be handed over to the king of Babylon'; but this is what the LORD, the God of Israel, says: 37I will surely gather[k] them from all the lands where I banish them in my furious anger and great wrath; I will bring them back to this place and let them live in safety.[l] 38They will be my people,[m] and I will be their God. 39I will give them singleness[n] of heart and action, so that they will always fear me for their own good and the good of their children after them. 40I will make an everlasting covenant[o] with them: I will never stop doing good to them, and I will inspire them to fear me, so that they will never turn away from me.[p] 41I will rejoice in doing them good[q] and will assuredly plant[r] them in this land with all my heart and soul.

42"This is what the LORD says: As I have brought all this great calamity on this people, so I will give them all the prosperity I have promised[s] them. 43Once more fields will be bought[t] in this land of which you say, 'It is a desolate waste, without men or animals, for it has been handed over to the Babylonians.' 44Fields will be bought for silver, and deeds[u] will be signed, sealed and witnessed in the territory of Benjamin, in the villages around Jerusalem, in the towns of Judah and in the towns of the hill country, of the western foothills and of the Negev,[v] because I will restore[w] their fortunes,[b] declares the LORD."

32:24
sDt 4:25-26;
Jos 23:15-16
32:27
tNu 16:22
32:28
u2Ch 36:17
vver 3
32:29
w2Ch 36:19;
Jer 21:10;
37:8,10; 52:13
xJer 19:13
yJer 44:18
32:30
zJer 22:21
aJer 8:19
bJer 25:7
32:31
c2Ki 23:27; 24:3
32:32
dIsa 1:4-6;
Da 9:8
32:33
eJer 2:27;
Eze 8:16
fJer 7:13
32:34
gJer 7:30
32:35
hLev 18:21
iJer 7:31; 19:5
32:36
jver 24
32:37
kJer 23:3,6
lDt 30:3;
Eze 34:28
32:38
mJer 24:7;
2Co 6:16*
32:39
nEze 11:19
32:40
oIsa 55:3
pJer 24:7
32:41
qDt 30:9
rJer 24:6;
31:28; Am 9:15
32:42
sJer 31:28
32:43
tver 15
32:44
uver 10
vJer 17:26
wJer 33:7,11,26

a35 Or *to make their sons and daughters pass through the fire*   b44 Or *will bring them back from captivity*

Promise of Restoration

33 While Jeremiah was still confined in the courtyard[x] of the guard, the word of the LORD came to him a second time: [2]"This is what the LORD says, he who made the earth,[y] the LORD who formed it and established it—the LORD is his name:[z] [3]'Call[a] to me and I will answer you and tell you great and unsearchable things you do not know.' [4]For this is what the LORD, the God of Israel, says about the houses in this city and the royal palaces of Judah that have been torn down to be used against the siege[b] ramps[c] and the sword [5]in the fight with the Babylonians[a]: 'They will be filled with the dead bodies of the men I will slay in my anger and wrath.[d] I will hide my face[e] from this city because of all its wickedness.

[6]" 'Nevertheless, I will bring health and healing to it; I will heal my people and will let them enjoy abundant peace and security. [7]I will bring Judah[f] and Israel back from captivity[b][g] and will rebuild them as they were before.[h] [8]I will cleanse[i] them from all the sin they have committed against me and will forgive[j] all their sins of rebellion against me. [9]Then this city will bring me renown, joy, praise[k] and honor[l] before all nations on earth that hear of all the good things I do for it; and they will be in awe and will tremble at the abundant prosperity and peace I provide for it.'

[10]"This is what the LORD says: 'You say about this place, "It is a desolate waste, without men or animals."[m] Yet in the towns of Judah and the streets of Jerusalem that are deserted, inhabited by neither men nor animals, there will be heard once more [11]the sounds of joy and gladness,[n] the voices of bride and bridegroom, and the voices of those who bring thank offerings[o] to the house of the LORD, saying,

"Give thanks to the LORD Almighty,
  for the LORD is good;[p]
  his love endures forever."[q]

For I will restore the fortunes of the land as they were before,' says the LORD.

[12]"This is what the LORD Almighty says: 'In this place, desolate[r] and without men or animals—in all its towns there will again be pastures for shepherds to rest their flocks.[s] [13]In the towns of the hill country, of the western foothills and of the Negev,[t] in the territory of Benjamin, in the villages around Jerusalem and in the towns of Judah, flocks will again pass under the hand[u] of the one who counts them,' says the LORD.

[14]" 'The days are coming,' declares the LORD, 'when I will fulfill the gracious promise[v] I made to the house of Israel and to the house of Judah.

[15]" 'In those days and at that time
  I will make a righteous[w] Branch[x] sprout from David's
    line;
  he will do what is just and right in the land.
[16]In those days Judah will be saved[y]
  and Jerusalem will live in safety.

33:1
xJer 32:2-3;
37:21; 38:28
33:2
yJer 10:16
zEx 3:15; 15:3
33:3
aIsa 55:6;
Jer 29:12
33:4
bEze 4:2
cJer 32:24;
Hab 1:10
33:5
dJer 21:4-7
eIsa 8:17
33:7
fJer 32:44
gJer 30:3;
Am 9:14
hIsa 1:26
33:8
iHeb 9:13-14
jJer 31:34;
Mic 7:18;
Zec 13:1
33:9
kJer 13:11
lIsa 62:7;
Jer 3:17
33:10
mJer 32:43
33:11
nIsa 51:3
oLev 7:12
p1Ch 16:8;
Ps 136:1
q1Ch 16:34;
2Ch 5:13;
Ps 100:4-5
33:12
rJer 32:43
sIsa 65:10;
Eze 34:11-15
33:13
tJer 17:26
uLev 27:32
33:14
vJer 29:10
33:15
wPs 72:2
xIsa 4:2; 11:1;
Jer 23:5
33:16
yIsa 45:17

---

[a]5 Or *Chaldeans*   [b]7 Or *will restore the fortunes of Judah and Israel*

This is the name by which it[a] will be called:
The Lord Our Righteousness.'[z]

[17]For this is what the Lord says: 'David will never fail[a] to have a man to sit on the throne of the house of Israel, [18]nor will the priests, who are Levites,[b] ever fail to have a man to stand before me continually to offer burnt offerings, to burn grain offerings and to present sacrifices.[c]' "

[19]The word of the Lord came to Jeremiah: [20]"This is what the Lord says: 'If you can break my covenant with the day[d] and my covenant with the night, so that day and night no longer come at their appointed time, [21]then my covenant[e] with David my servant—and my covenant with the Levites who are priests ministering before me—can be broken and David will no longer have a descendant to reign on his throne.[f] [22]I will make the descendants of David my servant and the Levites who minister before me as countless[g] as the stars of the sky and as measureless as the sand on the seashore.' "

[23]The word of the Lord came to Jeremiah: [24]"Have you not noticed that these people are saying, 'The Lord has rejected the two kingdoms[b][h] he chose'? So they despise[i] my people and no longer regard them as a nation.[j] [25]This is what the Lord says: 'If I have not established my covenant with day and night[k] and the fixed laws of heaven and earth,[l] [26]then I will reject[m] the descendants of Jacob[n] and David my servant and will not choose one of his sons to rule over the descendants of Abraham, Isaac and Jacob. For I will restore their fortunes[c][o] and have compassion on them.' "

Warning to Zedekiah

34 While Nebuchadnezzar king of Babylon and all his army and all the kingdoms and peoples[p] in the empire he ruled were fighting against Jerusalem[q] and all its surrounding towns, this word came to Jeremiah from the Lord: [2]"This is what the Lord, the God of Israel, says: Go to Zedekiah[r] king of Judah and tell him, 'This is what the Lord says: I am about to hand this city over to the king of Babylon, and he will burn it down.[s] [3]You will not escape from his grasp but will surely be captured and handed over[t] to him. You will see the king of Babylon with your own eyes, and he will speak with you face to face. And you will go to Babylon.

[4]" 'Yet hear the promise of the Lord, O Zedekiah king of Judah. This is what the Lord says concerning you: You will not die by the sword; [5]you will die peacefully. As people made a funeral fire[u] in honor of your fathers, the former kings who preceded you, so they will make a fire in your honor and lament, "Alas,[v] O master!" I myself make this promise, declares the Lord.' "

[6]Then Jeremiah the prophet told all this to Zedekiah king of Judah, in Jerusalem, [7]while the army of the king of Babylon was fighting against Jerusalem and the other cities of Judah that were still holding out—Lachish[w] and Azekah.[x] These were the only fortified cities left in Judah.

Freedom for Slaves

[8]The word came to Jeremiah from the Lord after King Zedekiah had

33:16
z1Co 1:30
33:17
a2Sa 7:13;
1Ki 2:4;
Ps 89:29-37;
Lk 1:33
33:18
bDt 18:1
cHeb 13:15
33:20
dPs 89:36
33:21
ePs 89:34
f2Ch 7:18
33:22
gGe 15:5
33:24
hEze 37:22
iNe 4:4
jJer 30:17
33:25
kJer 31:35-36
lPs 74:16-17
33:26
mJer 31:37
nIsa 14:1 over 7
34:1
pJer 27:7
q2Ki 25:1;
Jer 39:1
34:2
r2Ch 36:11
sver 22;
Jer 32:29; 37:8
34:3
t2Ki 25:7;
Jer 21:7; 32:4
34:5
u2Ch 16:14;
21:19 vJer 22:18
34:7
wJos 10:3
xJos 10:10;
2Ch 11:9

[a]16 Or *he*   [b]24 Or *families*   [c]26 Or *will bring them back from captivity*

made a covenant with all the people[y] in Jerusalem to proclaim freedom[z] for the slaves. [9]Everyone was to free his Hebrew slaves, both male and female; no one was to hold a fellow Jew in bondage.[a] [10]So all the officials and people who entered into this covenant agreed that they would free their male and female slaves and no longer hold them in bondage. They agreed, and set them free. [11]But afterward they changed their minds and took back the slaves they had freed and enslaved them again.

[12]Then the word of the LORD came to Jeremiah: [13]"This is what the LORD, the God of Israel, says: I made a covenant with your forefathers[b] when I brought them out of Egypt, out of the land of slavery. I said, [14]'Every seventh year each of you must free any fellow Hebrew who has sold himself to you. After he has served you six years, you must let him go free.'[ac] Your fathers, however, did not listen to me or pay attention[d] to me. [15]Recently you repented and did what is right in my sight: Each of you proclaimed freedom to his countrymen.[e] You even made a covenant before me in the house that bears my Name.[f] [16]But now you have turned around[g] and profaned[h] my name; each of you has taken back the male and female slaves you had set free to go where they wished. You have forced them to become your slaves again.

[17]"Therefore, this is what the LORD says: You have not obeyed me; you have not proclaimed freedom for your fellow countrymen. So I now proclaim 'freedom' for you,[i] declares the LORD—'freedom' to fall by the sword, plague and famine. I will make you abhorrent to all the kingdoms of the earth.[j] [18]The men who have violated my covenant and have not fulfilled the terms of the covenant they made before me, I will treat like the calf they cut in two and then walked between its pieces.[k] [19]The leaders of Judah and Jerusalem, the court officials,[l] the priests and all the people of the land who walked between the pieces of the calf, [20]I will hand over[m] to their enemies who seek their lives.[n] Their dead bodies will become food for the birds of the air and the beasts of the earth.[o]

[21]"I will hand Zedekiah[p] king of Judah and his officials[q] over to their enemies who seek their lives, to the army of the king of Babylon, which has withdrawn[r] from you. [22]I am going to give the order, declares the LORD, and I will bring them back to this city. They will fight against it, take[s] it and burn[t] it down. And I will lay waste the towns of Judah so no one can live there."

The Recabites

35 This is the word that came to Jeremiah from the LORD during the reign of Jehoiakim[u] son of Josiah king of Judah: [2]"Go to the Recabite[v] family and invite them to come to one of the side rooms[w] of the house of the LORD and give them wine to drink."

[3]So I went to get Jaazaniah son of Jeremiah, the son of Habazziniah, and his brothers and all his sons—the whole family of the Recabites. [4]I brought them into the house of the LORD, into the room of the sons of Hanan son of Igdaliah the man of God.[x] It was next to the room of the officials, which was over that of Maaseiah son of Shallum[y] the door-

a14 Deut. 15:12

34:8
y2Ki 11:17
zEx 21:2;
Lev 25:10,
39-41; Ne 5:5-8
34:9
aLev 25:39-46
34:13
bEx 24:8
34:14
cEx 21:2
dDt 15:12;
2Ki 17:14
34:15
ever 8
fJer 7:10-11;
32:34
34:16
gEze 3:20;
18:24 hEx 20:7;
Lev 19:12
34:17
iMt 7:2; Gal 6:7
jDt 28:25,64;
Jer 29:18
34:18
kGe 15:10
34:19
lZep 3:3-4
34:20
mJer 21:7
nJer 11:21
oDt 28:26;
Jer 7:33; 19:7
34:21
pJer 32:4
qJer 39:6;
52:24-27
rJer 37:5
34:22
sJer 39:1-2
tJer 39:8
35:1
u2Ch 36:5
35:2
v2Ki 10:15;
1Ch 2:55
w1Ki 6:5
35:4
xDt 33:1
y1Ch 9:19

keeper.ᶻ ⁵Then I set bowls full of wine and some cups before the men of the Recabite family and said to them, "Drink some wine."

⁶But they replied, "We do not drink wine, because our forefather Jonadabᵃ son of Recab gave us this command: 'Neither you nor your descendants must ever drink wine.ᵇ ⁷Also you must never build houses, sow seed or plant vineyards; you must never have any of these things, but must always live in tents.ᶜ Then you will live a long time in the landᵈ where you are nomads.' ⁸We have obeyed everything our forefatherᵉ Jonadab son of Recab commanded us. Neither we nor our wives nor our sons and daughters have ever drunk wine ⁹or built houses to live in or had vineyards, fields or crops.ᶠ ¹⁰We have lived in tents and have fully obeyed everything our forefather Jonadab commanded us. ¹¹But when Nebuchadnezzar king of Babylon invadedᵍ this land, we said, 'Come, we must go to Jerusalemʰ to escape the Babylonianᵃ and Aramean armies.' So we have remained in Jerusalem."

¹²Then the word of the LORD came to Jeremiah, saying: ¹³"This is what the LORD Almighty, the God of Israel, says: Go and tell the men of Judah and the people of Jerusalem, 'Will you not learn a lessonⁱ and obey my words?' declares the LORD. ¹⁴'Jonadab son of Recab ordered his sons not to drink wine and this command has been kept. To this day they do not drink wine, because they obey their forefather's command. But I have spoken to you again and again,ʲ yet you have not obeyedᵏ me. ¹⁵Again and again I sent all my servants the prophetsˡ to you. They said, "Each of you must turnᵐ from your wicked ways and reformⁿ your actions; do not follow other gods to serve them. Then you will live in the landᵒ I have given to you and your fathers." But you have not paid attention or listenedᵖ to me. ¹⁶The descendants of Jonadab son of Recab have carried out the command their forefatherq gave them, but these people have not obeyed me.'

¹⁷"Therefore, this is what the LORD God Almighty, the God of Israel, says: 'Listen! I am going to bring on Judah and on everyone living in Jerusalem every disasterʳ I pronounced against them. I spoke to them, but they did not listen;ˢ I called to them, but they did not answer.' "ᵗ

¹⁸Then Jeremiah said to the family of the Recabites, "This is what the LORD Almighty, the God of Israel, says: 'You have obeyed the command of your forefather Jonadab and have followed all his instructions and have done everything he ordered.' ¹⁹Therefore, this is what the LORD Almighty, the God of Israel, says: 'Jonadab son of Recab will never failᵘ to have a man to serveᵛ me.' "

Jehoiakim Burns Jeremiah's Scroll

36 In the fourth year of Jehoiakimʷ son of Josiah king of Judah, this word came to Jeremiah from the LORD: ²"Take a scrollˣ and write on it all the words I have spoken to you concerning Israel, Judah and all the other nations from the time I began speaking to you in the reign of Josiahʸ till now. ³Perhapsᶻ when the people of Judah hearᵃ about every disaster I plan to inflict on them, each of them will turnᵇ from his wicked way; then I will forgiveᶜ their wickedness and their sin."

⁴So Jeremiah called Baruchᵈ son of Neriah, and while Jeremiah dic-

35:4
z2Ki 12:9
35:6
a2Ki 10:15
bLev 10:9;
Nu 6:2-4;
Lk 1:15
35:7
cHeb 11:9
dEx 20:12;
Eph 6:2-3
35:8
ePr 1:8;
Col 3:20
35:9
f1Ti 6:6
35:11
g2Ki 24:1
hJer 8:14
35:13
iJer 6:10; 32:33
35:14
jJer 7:13; 25:3
kIsa 30:9
35:15
lJer 7:25
mJer 26:3
nIsa 1:16-17;
Jer 4:1; 18:11;
Eze 18:30
oJer 25:5
pJer 7:26
35:16
qMal 1:6
35:17
rJos 23:15;
Jer 21:4-7
sPr 1:24;
Ro 10:21
tIsa 65:12;
66:4; Jer 7:13
35:19
uJer 33:17
vJer 15:19
36:1
w2Ch 36:5
36:2
xEx 17:14;
Jer 30:2;
Hab 2:2
yJer 1:2; 25:3
36:3
zver 7; Eze 12:3
aMk 4:12
bJer 26:3;
Jnh 3:8; Ac 3:19
cJer 18:8
36:4
dJer 32:12

ᵃ11 Or *Chaldean*

tated[e] all the words the Lord had spoken to him, Baruch wrote them on the scroll. [f] 5Then Jeremiah told Baruch, "I am restricted; I cannot go to the Lord's temple. 6So you go to the house of the Lord on a day of fasting[g] and read to the people from the scroll the words of the Lord that you wrote as I dictated. Read them to all the people of Judah who come in from their towns. 7Perhaps they will bring their petition before the Lord, and each will turn[h] from his wicked ways, for the anger[i] and wrath pronounced against this people by the Lord are great."

8Baruch son of Neriah did everything Jeremiah the prophet told him to do; at the Lord's temple he read the words of the Lord from the scroll. 9In the ninth month[j] of the fifth year of Jehoiakim son of Josiah king of Judah, a time of fasting[k] before the Lord was proclaimed for all the people in Jerusalem and those who had come from the towns of Judah. 10From the room of Gemariah son of Shaphan the secretary,[l] which was in the upper courtyard at the entrance of the New Gate[m] of the temple, Baruch read to all the people at the Lord's temple the words of Jeremiah from the scroll.

11When Micaiah son of Gemariah, the son of Shaphan, heard all the words of the Lord from the scroll, 12he went down to the secretary's room in the royal palace, where all the officials were sitting: Elishama the secretary, Delaiah son of Shemaiah, Elnathan[n] son of Acbor, Gemariah son of Shaphan, Zedekiah son of Hananiah, and all the other officials. 13After Micaiah told them everything he had heard Baruch read to the people from the scroll, 14all the officials sent Jehudi[o] son of Nethaniah, the son of Shelemiah, the son of Cushi, to say to Baruch, "Bring the scroll from which you have read to the people and come." So Baruch son of Neriah went to them with the scroll in his hand. 15They said to him, "Sit down, please, and read it to us."

So Baruch read it to them. 16When they heard all these words, they looked at each other in fear and said to Baruch, "We must report all these words to the king." 17Then they asked Baruch, "Tell us, how did you come to write all this? Did Jeremiah dictate it?"

18"Yes," Baruch replied, "he dictated[p] all these words to me, and I wrote them in ink on the scroll."

19Then the officials said to Baruch, "You and Jeremiah, go and hide. [q] Don't let anyone know where you are."

20After they put the scroll in the room of Elishama the secretary, they went to the king in the courtyard and reported everything to him. 21The king sent Jehudi[r] to get the scroll, and Jehudi brought it from the room of Elishama the secretary and read it to the king[s] and all the officials standing beside him. 22It was the ninth month and the king was sitting in the winter apartment,[t] with a fire burning in the firepot in front of him. 23Whenever Jehudi had read three or four columns of the scroll, the king cut them off with a scribe's knife and threw them into the firepot, until the entire scroll was burned in the fire. [u] 24The king and all his attendants who heard all these words showed no fear, [v] nor did they tear their clothes. [w] 25Even though Elnathan, Delaiah and Gemariah urged the king not to burn the scroll, he would not listen to them. 26Instead, the king commanded Jerahmeel, a son of the king, Seraiah son of Azriel and Shelemiah son of Abdeel to arrest[x] Baruch the scribe and Jeremiah the prophet. But the Lord had hidden[y] them.

27After the king burned the scroll containing the words that Baruch

36:4
e ver 18 f Eze 2:9
36:6
g ver 9
36:7
h Jer 26:3
i Dt 31:17
36:9
j ver 22
k 2Ch 20:3
36:10
l Jer 52:25
m Jer 26:10
36:12
n Jer 26:22
36:14
o ver 21
36:18
p ver 4
36:19
q 1Ki 17:3
36:21
r ver 14
s 2Ki 22:10
36:22
t Am 3:15
36:23
u 1Ki 22:8
36:24
v Ps 36:1
w Ge 37:29;
2Ki 22:11;
Isa 37:1
36:26
x Mt 23:34
y Jer 15:21

had written at Jeremiah's dictation,[z] the word of the LORD came to Jeremiah: [28]"Take another scroll and write on it all the words that were on the first scroll, which Jehoiakim king of Judah burned up. [29]Also tell Jehoiakim king of Judah, 'This is what the LORD says: You burned that scroll and said, "Why did you write on it that the king of Babylon would certainly come and destroy this land and cut off both men and animals from it?"[a] [30]Therefore, this is what the LORD says about Jehoiakim king of Judah: He will have no one to sit on the throne of David; his body will be thrown out[b] and exposed to the heat by day and the frost by night. [31]I will punish him and his children and his attendants for their wickedness; I will bring on them and those living in Jerusalem and the people of Judah every disaster[c] I pronounced against them, because they have not listened.'"

[32]So Jeremiah took another scroll and gave it to the scribe Baruch son of Neriah, and as Jeremiah dictated, [d] Baruch wrote[e] on it all the words of the scroll that Jehoiakim king of Judah had burned[f] in the fire. And many similar words were added to them.

Jeremiah in Prison

37 Zedekiah[g] son of Josiah was made king[h] of Judah by Nebuchadnezzar king of Babylon; he reigned in place of Jehoiachin[a][i] son of Jehoiakim. [2]Neither he nor his attendants nor the people of the land paid any attention[j] to the words the LORD had spoken through Jeremiah the prophet.

[3]King Zedekiah, however, sent Jehucal son of Shelemiah with the priest Zephaniah[k] son of Maaseiah to Jeremiah the prophet with this message: "Please pray[l] to the LORD our God for us."

[4]Now Jeremiah was free to come and go among the people, for he had not yet been put in prison. [m] [5]Pharaoh's army had marched out of Egypt,[n] and when the Babylonians[b] who were besieging Jerusalem heard the report about them, they withdrew[o] from Jerusalem. [p]

[6]Then the word of the LORD came to Jeremiah the prophet: [7]"This is what the LORD, the God of Israel, says: Tell the king of Judah, who sent you to inquire[q] of me, 'Pharaoh's army, which has marched out to support you, will go back to its own land, to Egypt.[r] [8]Then the Babylonians will return and attack this city; they will capture it and burn[s] it down.'

[9]"This is what the LORD says: Do not deceive[t] yourselves, thinking, 'The Babylonians will surely leave us.' They will not! [10]Even if you were to defeat the entire Babylonian[c] army that is attacking you and only wounded men were left in their tents, they would come out and burn this city down."

[11]After the Babylonian army had withdrawn[u] from Jerusalem because of Pharaoh's army, [12]Jeremiah started to leave the city to go to the territory of Benjamin to get his share of the property[v] among the people there. [13]But when he reached the Benjamin Gate, the captain of the guard, whose name was Irijah son of Shelemiah, the son of Hananiah, arrested him and said, "You are deserting to the Babylonians!"

[14]"That's not true!" Jeremiah said. "I am not deserting to the Babylo-

36:27
z ver 4
36:29
a Isa 30:10
36:30
b Jer 22:19
36:31
c Pr 29:1
36:32
d ver 4 e Ex 34:1
f ver 23
37:1
g 2Ki 24:17
h Eze 17:13
i 2Ki 24:8,12;
2Ch 36:10;
Jer 22:24
37:2
j 2Ki 24:19;
2Ch 36:12,14
37:3
k Jer 29:25;
52:24 l 1Ki 13:6;
Jer 21:1-2; 42:2
37:4
m ver 15;
Jer 32:2
37:5
n Eze 17:15
o Jer 34:21
p 2Ki 24:7
37:7
q 2Ki 22:18
r Jer 2:36;
La 4:17
37:8
s Jer 34:22; 39:8
37:9
t Jer 29:8
37:11
u ver 5
37:12
v Jer 32:9

[a]1 Hebrew *Coniah*, a variant of *Jehoiachin*   [b]5 Or *Chaldeans*; also in verses 8, 9, 13 and 14
[c]10 Or *Chaldean*; also in verse 11

nians." But Irijah would not listen to him; instead, he arrested^w Jeremiah and brought him to the officials. ¹⁵They were angry with Jeremiah and had him beaten^x and imprisoned in the house^y of Jonathan the secretary, which they had made into a prison.

¹⁶Jeremiah was put into a vaulted cell in a dungeon, where he remained a long time. ¹⁷Then King Zedekiah sent for him and had him brought to the palace, where he asked^z him privately,^a "Is there any word from the LORD?"

"Yes," Jeremiah replied, "you will be handed over^b to the king of Babylon."

¹⁸Then Jeremiah said to King Zedekiah, "What crime^c have I committed against you or your officials or this people, that you have put me in prison? ¹⁹Where are your prophets who prophesied to you, 'The king of Babylon will not attack you or this land'? ²⁰But now, my lord the king, please listen. Let me bring my petition before you: Do not send me back to the house of Jonathan the secretary, or I will die there."

²¹King Zedekiah then gave orders for Jeremiah to be placed in the courtyard of the guard and given bread from the street of the bakers each day until all the bread^d in the city was gone.^e So Jeremiah remained in the courtyard of the guard.^f

Jeremiah Thrown Into a Cistern

38 Shephatiah son of Mattan, Gedaliah son of Pashhur, Jehucal^{a g} son of Shelemiah, and Pashhur son of Malkijah heard what Jeremiah was telling all the people when he said, ²"This is what the LORD says: 'Whoever stays in this city will die by the sword, famine or plague,^h but whoever goes over to the Babylonians^b will live. He will escape with his life; he will live.'ⁱ ³And this is what the LORD says: 'This city will certainly be handed over to the army of the king of Babylon, who will capture it.'"^j

⁴Then the officials^k said to the king, "This man should be put to death.^l He is discouraging the soldiers who are left in this city, as well as all the people, by the things he is saying to them. This man is not seeking the good of these people but their ruin."

⁵"He is in your hands," King Zedekiah answered. "The king can do nothing to oppose you."

⁶So they took Jeremiah and put him into the cistern of Malkijah, the king's son, which was in the courtyard of the guard.^m They lowered Jeremiah by ropes into the cistern; it had no water in it, only mud, and Jeremiah sank down into the mud.

⁷But Ebed-Melech,ⁿ a Cushite,^c an official^{d o} in the royal palace, heard that they had put Jeremiah into the cistern. While the king was sitting in the Benjamin Gate,^p ⁸Ebed-Melech went out of the palace and said to him, ⁹"My lord the king, these men have acted wickedly in all they have done to Jeremiah the prophet. They have thrown him into a cistern, where he will starve to death when there is no longer any bread^q in the city."

¹⁰Then the king commanded Ebed-Melech the Cushite, "Take thirty

37:14
w Jer 40:4
37:15
x Jer 20:2
y Jer 38:26
37:17
z Jer 15:11
a Jer 38:16
b Jer 21:7
37:18
c 1Sa 26:18;
Jn 10:32;
Ac 25:8
37:21
d Isa 33:16;
Jer 38:9
e 2Ki 25:3;
Jer 52:6
f Jer 32:2;
38:6,13,28
38:1
g Jer 37:3
38:2
h Jer 34:17
i Jer 21:9;
39:18; 45:5
38:3
j Jer 21:4,10;
32:3
38:4
k Jer 36:12
l Jer 26:11
38:6
m Jer 37:21
38:7
n Jer 39:16
o Ac 8:27
p Job 29:7
38:9
q Jer 37:21

---

^a1 Hebrew *Jucal*, a variant of *Jehucal*   ^b2 Or *Chaldeans*; also in verses 18, 19 and 23
^c7 Probably from the upper Nile region   ^d7 Or *a eunuch*

men from here with you and lift Jeremiah the prophet out of the cistern before he dies."

[11]So Ebed-Melech took the men with him and went to a room under the treasury in the palace. He took some old rags and worn-out clothes from there and let them down with ropes to Jeremiah in the cistern. [12]Ebed-Melech the Cushite said to Jeremiah, "Put these old rags and worn-out clothes under your arms to pad the ropes." Jeremiah did so, [13]and they pulled him up with the ropes and lifted him out of the cistern. And Jeremiah remained in the courtyard of the guard. [r]

Zedekiah Questions Jeremiah Again

[14]Then King Zedekiah sent for Jeremiah the prophet and had him brought to the third entrance to the temple of the LORD. "I am going to ask you something," the king said to Jeremiah. "Do not hide[s] anything from me."

[15]Jeremiah said to Zedekiah, "If I give you an answer, will you not kill me? Even if I did give you counsel, you would not listen to me."

[16]But King Zedekiah swore this oath secretly[t] to Jeremiah: "As surely as the LORD lives, who has given us breath,[u] I will neither kill you nor hand you over to those who are seeking your life."[v]

[17]Then Jeremiah said to Zedekiah, "This is what the LORD God Almighty, the God of Israel, says: 'If you surrender to the officers of the king of Babylon, your life will be spared and this city will not be burned down; you and your family will live. [w] [18]But if you will not surrender to the officers of the king of Babylon, this city will be handed over[x] to the Babylonians and they will burn[y] it down; you yourself will not escape[z] from their hands.' "

[19]King Zedekiah said to Jeremiah, "I am afraid[a] of the Jews who have gone over[b] to the Babylonians, for the Babylonians may hand me over to them and they will mistreat me."

[20]"They will not hand you over," Jeremiah replied. "Obey[c] the LORD by doing what I tell you. Then it will go well with you, and your life[d] will be spared. [21]But if you refuse to surrender, this is what the LORD has revealed to me: [22]All the women[e] left in the palace of the king of Judah will be brought out to the officials of the king of Babylon. Those women will say to you:

> " 'They misled you and overcame you—
> those trusted friends of yours.
> Your feet are sunk in the mud;
> your friends have deserted you.'

[23]"All your wives and children[f] will be brought out to the Babylonians. You yourself will not escape from their hands but will be captured[g] by the king of Babylon; and this city will[a] be burned down."

[24]Then Zedekiah said to Jeremiah, "Do not let anyone know about this conversation, or you may die. [25]If the officials hear that I talked with you, and they come to you and say, 'Tell us what you said to the king and what the king said to you; do not hide it from us or we will kill you,' [26]then tell them, 'I was pleading with the king not to send me back to Jonathan's house[h] to die there.' "

Side reference column

38:13
r Jer 37:21
38:14
s 1Sa 3:17
38:16
t Jer 37:17
u Isa 42:5; 57:16
v ver 4
38:17
w 2Ki 24:12;
Jer 21:9
38:18
x ver 3; Jer 34:3
y Jer 37:8
z Jer 24:8; 32:4
38:19
a Isa 51:12;
Jn 12:42
b Jer 39:9
38:20
c Jer 11:4
d Isa 55:3
38:22
e Jer 6:12
38:23
f 2Ki 25:6
g Jer 41:10
38:26
h Jer 37:15

---

[a] 23 Or *and you will cause this city to*

²⁷All the officials did come to Jeremiah and question him, and he told them everything the king had ordered him to say. So they said no more to him, for no one had heard his conversation with the king.

²⁸And Jeremiah remained in the courtyard of the guard[i] until the day Jerusalem was captured.

The Fall of Jerusalem

39:1–10pp — 2Ki 25:1–12; Jer 52:4–16

39 This is how Jerusalem was taken: ¹In the ninth year of Zedekiah king of Judah, in the tenth month, Nebuchadnezzar king of Babylon marched against Jerusalem with his whole army and laid siege[j] to it. ²And on the ninth day of the fourth month of Zedekiah's eleventh year, the city wall was broken through. ³Then all the officials[k] of the king of Babylon came and took seats in the Middle Gate: Nergal-Sharezer of Samgar, Nebo-Sarsekim[a] a chief officer, Nergal-Sharezer a high official and all the other officials of the king of Babylon. ⁴When Zedekiah king of Judah and all the soldiers saw them, they fled; they left the city at night by way of the king's garden, through the gate between the two walls, and headed toward the Arabah.[b]

⁵But the Babylonian[c] army pursued them and overtook Zedekiah[l] in the plains of Jericho. They captured him and took him to Nebuchadnezzar king of Babylon at Riblah[m] in the land of Hamath, where he pronounced sentence on him. ⁶There at Riblah the king of Babylon slaughtered the sons of Zedekiah before his eyes and also killed all the nobles of Judah. ⁷Then he put out Zedekiah's eyes[n] and bound him with bronze shackles to take him to Babylon.[o]

⁸The Babylonians[d] set fire[p] to the royal palace and the houses of the people and broke down the walls[q] of Jerusalem. ⁹Nebuzaradan commander of the imperial guard carried into exile to Babylon the people who remained in the city, along with those who had gone over to him, and the rest of the people.[r] ¹⁰But Nebuzaradan the commander of the guard left behind in the land of Judah some of the poor people, who owned nothing; and at that time he gave them vineyards and fields.

¹¹Now Nebuchadnezzar king of Babylon had given these orders about Jeremiah through Nebuzaradan commander of the imperial guard: ¹²"Take him and look after him; don't harm[s] him but do for him whatever he asks." ¹³So Nebuzaradan the commander of the guard, Nebushazban a chief officer, Nergal-Sharezer a high official and all the other officers of the king of Babylon ¹⁴sent and had Jeremiah taken out of the courtyard of the guard.[t] They turned him over to Gedaliah son of Ahikam,[u] the son of Shaphan, to take him back to his home. So he remained among his own people.[v]

¹⁵While Jeremiah had been confined in the courtyard of the guard, the word of the LORD came to him: ¹⁶"Go and tell Ebed-Melech[w] the Cushite, 'This is what the LORD Almighty, the God of Israel, says: I am about to fulfill my words against this city through disaster,[x] not prosperity. At that time they will be fulfilled before your eyes. ¹⁷But I will rescue[y] you on that day, declares the LORD; you will not be handed over to those you fear. ¹⁸I will save you; you will not fall by the sword[z]

38:28
i Jer 37:21;
39:14
39:1
j 2Ki 25:1;
Jer 52:4;
Eze 24:2
39:3
k Jer 21:4
39:5
l Jer 32:4
m 2Ki 23:33
39:7
n Eze 12:13
o Jer 32:5
39:8
p Jer 38:18
q Ne 1:3
39:9
r Jer 40:1
39:12
s Pr 16:7;
1Pe 3:13
39:14
t Jer 38:28
u 2Ki 22:12
v Jer 40:5
39:16
w Jer 38:7
x Jer 21:10;
Da 9:12
39:17
y Ps 41:1-2
39:18
z Jer 45:5

---

a3 Or *Nergal-Sharezer, Samgar-Nebo, Sarsekim*   *b4* Or *the Jordan Valley*   *c5* Or *Chaldean*
d8 Or *Chaldeans*

but will escape with your life,[a] because you trust[b] in me, declares the LORD.' "

Jeremiah Freed

40 The word came to Jeremiah from the LORD after Nebuzaradan commander of the imperial guard had released him at Ramah. He had found Jeremiah bound in chains among all the captives from Jerusalem and Judah who were being carried into exile to Babylon. [2]When the commander of the guard found Jeremiah, he said to him, "The LORD your God decreed this disaster for this place.[c] [3]And now the LORD has brought it about; he has done just as he said he would. All this happened because you people sinned[d] against the LORD and did not obey[e] him. [4]But today I am freeing you from the chains on your wrists. Come with me to Babylon, if you like, and I will look after you; but if you do not want to, then don't come. Look, the whole country lies before you; go wherever you please."[f] [5]However, before Jeremiah turned to go,[a] Nebuzaradan added, "Go back to Gedaliah[g] son of Ahikam, the son of Shaphan, whom the king of Babylon has appointed over the towns of Judah, and live with him among the people, or go anywhere else you please."[h]

Then the commander gave him provisions and a present and let him go. [6]So Jeremiah went to Gedaliah son of Ahikam at Mizpah[i] and stayed with him among the people who were left behind in the land.

Gedaliah Assassinated

40:7–9; 41:1–3pp — 2Ki 25:22–26

[7]When all the army officers and their men who were still in the open country heard that the king of Babylon had appointed Gedaliah son of Ahikam as governor over the land and had put him in charge of the men, women and children who were the poorest[j] in the land and who had not been carried into exile to Babylon, [8]they came to Gedaliah at Mizpah[k]—Ishmael[l] son of Nethaniah, Johanan and Jonathan the sons of Kareah, Seraiah son of Tanhumeth, the sons of Ephai the Netophathite,[m] and Jaazaniah[b] the son of the Maacathite,[n] and their men. [9]Gedaliah son of Ahikam, the son of Shaphan, took an oath to reassure them and their men. "Do not be afraid to serve[o] the Babylonians,[c]" he said. "Settle down in the land and serve the king of Babylon, and it will go well with you.[p] [10]I myself will stay at Mizpah[q] to represent you before the Babylonians who come to us, but you are to harvest the wine, summer fruit and oil, and put them in your storage jars, and live in the towns you have taken over."[r]

[11]When all the Jews in Moab,[s] Ammon, Edom and all the other countries heard that the king of Babylon had left a remnant in Judah and had appointed Gedaliah son of Ahikam, the son of Shaphan, as governor over them, [12]they all came back to the land of Judah, to Gedaliah at Mizpah, from all the countries where they had been scattered.[t] And they harvested an abundance of wine and summer fruit.

[13]Johanan son of Kareah and all the army officers still in the open country came to Gedaliah at Mizpah[u] [14]and said to him, "Don't you

39:18
a Jer 21:9; 38:2
b Jer 17:7
40:2
c Jer 50:7
40:3
d Da 9:11
e Dt 29:24-28;
Ro 2:5-9
40:4
f Ge 13:9;
Jer 39:11-12
40:5
g 2Ki 25:22
h Jer 39:14
40:6
i Jdg 20:1;
1Sa 7:5-17
40:7
j Jer 39:10
40:8
k ver 13 l ver 14;
Jer 41:1,2
m 2Sa 23:28
n Dt 3:14
40:9
o Jer 27:11
p Jer 38:20
40:10
q ver 6 r Dt 1:39
40:11
s Nu 25:1
40:12
t Jer 43:5
40:13
u ver 8

a5 Or *Jeremiah answered*   b8 Hebrew *Jezaniah*, a variant of *Jaazaniah*   c9 Or *Chaldeans*; also in verse 10 know that Baalis king of the Ammonites[v] has sent Ishmael son of Nethaniah to take your life?" But Gedaliah son of Ahikam did not believe them.

[15]Then Johanan son of Kareah said privately to Gedaliah in Mizpah, "Let me go and kill Ishmael son of Nethaniah, and no one will know it. Why should he take your life and cause all the Jews who are gathered around you to be scattered and the remnant of Judah to perish?"

[16]But Gedaliah son of Ahikam said to Johanan son of Kareah, "Don't do such a thing! What you are saying about Ishmael is not true."

41 In the seventh month Ishmael[w] son of Nethaniah, the son of Elishama, who was of royal blood and had been one of the king's officers, came with ten men to Gedaliah son of Ahikam at Mizpah. While they were eating together there, [2]Ishmael[x] son of Nethaniah and the ten men who were with him got up and struck down Gedaliah son of Ahikam, the son of Shaphan, with the sword, killing the one whom the king of Babylon had appointed[y] as governor over the land.[z] [3]Ishmael also killed all the Jews who were with Gedaliah at Mizpah, as well as the Babylonian[a] soldiers who were there.

[4]The day after Gedaliah's assassination, before anyone knew about it, [5]eighty men who had shaved off their beards,[a] torn their clothes and cut themselves came from Shechem,[b] Shiloh[c] and Samaria,[d] bringing grain offerings and incense with them to the house of the LORD.[e] [6]Ishmael son of Nethaniah went out from Mizpah to meet them, weeping[f] as he went. When he met them, he said, "Come to Gedaliah son of Ahikam." [7]When they went into the city, Ishmael son of Nethaniah and the men who were with him slaughtered them and threw them into a cistern. [8]But ten of them said to Ishmael, "Don't kill us! We have wheat and barley, oil and honey, hidden in a field."[g] So he let them alone and did not kill them with the others. [9]Now the cistern where he threw all the bodies of the men he had killed along with Gedaliah was the one King Asa[h] had made as part of his defense[i] against Baasha[j] king of Israel. Ishmael son of Nethaniah filled it with the dead.

[10]Ishmael made captives of all the rest of the people[k] who were in Mizpah—the king's daughters along with all the others who were left there, over whom Nebuzaradan commander of the imperial guard had appointed Gedaliah son of Ahikam. Ishmael son of Nethaniah took them captive and set out to cross over to the Ammonites.[l]

[11]When Johanan[m] son of Kareah and all the army officers who were with him heard about all the crimes Ishmael son of Nethaniah had committed, [12]they took all their men and went to fight Ishmael son of Nethaniah. They caught up with him near the great pool[n] in Gibeon. [13]When all the people[o] Ishmael had with him saw Johanan son of Kareah and the army officers who were with him, they were glad. [14]All the people Ishmael had taken captive at Mizpah turned and went over to Johanan son of Kareah. [15]But Ishmael son of Nethaniah and eight of his men escaped[p] from Johanan and fled to the Ammonites.

Flight to Egypt

[16]Then Johanan son of Kareah and all the army officers who were with him led away all the survivors[q] from Mizpah whom he had

a3 Or Chaldean

40:14
v2Sa 10:1-19;
Jer 25:21; 41:10
41:1
wJer 40:8
41:2
xPs 41:9; 109:5
yJer 40:5
z2Sa 3:27;
20:9-10
41:5
aLev 19:27
bGe 33:18;
Jdg 9:1-57;
1Ki 12:1
cJos 18:1
d1Ki 16:24
e2Ki 25:9
41:6
f2Sa 3:16
41:8
gIsa 45:3
41:9
h1Ki 15:22;
2Ch 16:6
iJdg 6:2
j2Ch 16:1
41:10
kJer 40:7,12
lJer 40:14
41:11
mJer 40:8
41:12
n2Sa 2:13
41:13
over 10
41:15
pJob 21:30;
Pr 28:17
41:16
qJer 43:4

recovered from Ishmael son of Nethaniah after he had assassinated Gedaliah son of Ahikam: the soldiers, women, children and court officials he had brought from Gibeon. ¹⁷And they went on, stopping at Geruth Kimham‌ʳ near Bethlehem on their way to Egypt‌ˢ ¹⁸to escape the Babylonians.‌ᵃ They were afraid‌ᵗ of them because Ishmael son of Nethaniah had killed Gedaliah‌ᵘ son of Ahikam, whom the king of Babylon had appointed as governor over the land.

42 Then all the army officers, including Johanan‌ᵛ son of Kareah and Jezaniah‌ᵇ son of Hoshaiah, and all the people from the least to the greatest‌ʷ approached ²Jeremiah the prophet and said to him, "Please hear our petition and pray‌ˣ to the Lᴏʀᴅ your God for this entire remnant.‌ʸ For as you now see, though we were once many, now only a few‌ᶻ are left. ³Pray that the Lᴏʀᴅ your God will tell us where we should go and what we should do."‌ᵃ

⁴"I have heard you," replied Jeremiah the prophet. "I will certainly pray‌ᵇ to the Lᴏʀᴅ your God as you have requested; I will tell you everything the Lᴏʀᴅ says and will keep nothing back from you."‌ᶜ

⁵Then they said to Jeremiah, "May the Lᴏʀᴅ be a true and faithful witness‌ᵈ against us if we do not act in accordance with everything the Lᴏʀᴅ your God sends you to tell us. ⁶Whether it is favorable or unfavorable, we will obey the Lᴏʀᴅ our God, to whom we are sending you, so that it will go well‌ᵉ with us, for we will obey‌ᶠ the Lᴏʀᴅ our God."

⁷Ten days later the word of the Lᴏʀᴅ came to Jeremiah. ⁸So he called together Johanan son of Kareah and all the army officers‌ᵍ who were with him and all the people from the least to the greatest. ⁹He said to them, "This is what the Lᴏʀᴅ, the God of Israel, to whom you sent me to present your petition, says:‌ʰ ¹⁰'If you stay in this land, I will build‌ⁱ you up and not tear you down; I will plant‌ʲ you and not uproot you,‌ᵏ for I am grieved over the disaster I have inflicted on you.‌ˡ ¹¹Do not be afraid of the king of Babylon,‌ᵐ whom you now fear.‌ⁿ Do not be afraid of him, declares the Lᴏʀᴅ, for I am with you and will save‌ᵒ you and deliver you from his hands.‌ᵖ ¹²I will show you compassion so that he will have compassion on you and restore you to your land.'‌�q

¹³"However, if you say, 'We will not stay in this land,' and so disobey‌ʳ the Lᴏʀᴅ your God, ¹⁴and if you say, 'No, we will go and live in Egypt,‌ˢ where we will not see war or hear the trumpet or be hungry for bread,' ¹⁵then hear the word of the Lᴏʀᴅ, O remnant of Judah. This is what the Lᴏʀᴅ Almighty, the God of Israel, says: 'If you are determined to go to Egypt and you do go to settle there, ¹⁶then the sword‌ᵗ you fear will overtake you there, and the famine you dread will follow you into Egypt, and there you will die. ¹⁷Indeed, all who are determined to go to Egypt to settle there will die by the sword, famine and plague;‌ᵘ not one of them will survive or escape the disaster I will bring on them.' ¹⁸This is what the Lᴏʀᴅ Almighty, the God of Israel, says: 'As my anger and wrath‌ᵛ have been poured out on those who lived in Jerusalem,‌ʷ so will my wrath be poured out on you when you go to Egypt. You will be an object of cursing and horror,‌ˣ of condemnation and reproach; you will never see this place again.'‌ʸ

¹⁹"O remnant of Judah, the Lᴏʀᴅ has told you, 'Do not go to Egypt.'‌ᶻ

41:17
r 2Sa 19:37
s Jer 42:14
41:18
t Isa 51:12;
Jer 42:16;
Lk 12:4-5
u Jer 40:5
42:1
v Jer 40:13;
41:11
w Jer 6:13;
44:12
42:2
x Jer 36:7;
Ac 8:24;
Jas 5:16 y Isa 1:9
z Lev 26:22;
La 1:1
42:3
a Ps 86:11;
Pr 3:6
42:4
b Ex 8:29;
1Sa 12:23
c 1Ki 22:14;
1Sa 3:17
42:5
d Ge 31:50
42:6
e Dt 5:29; 6:3;
Jer 7:23
f Ex 24:7;
Jos 24:24
42:8
g ver 1
42:9
h 2Ki 22:15
42:10
i Jer 24:6
j Jer 31:28
k Eze 36:36
l Jer 18:8
42:11
m Jer 27:11
n Nu 14:9
o Isa 43:5
p Jer 1:8;
Ro 8:31
42:12
q Ps 106:44-46
42:13
r Jer 44:16
42:14
s Nu 11:4-5
42:16
t Eze 11:8
42:17
u ver 22;
Jer 44:13
42:18
v Dt 29:18-20;
Jer 7:20
w 2Ch 36:19;
Jer 39:1-9
x Jer 29:18
y Jer 22:10
42:19
z Dt 17:16;
Isa 30:7

ᵃ18 Or *Chaldeans*   ᵇ1 Hebrew; Septuagint (see also 43:2) *Azariah*

Be sure of this: I warn you today [20]that you made a fatal mistake[a] when you sent me to the LORD your God and said, 'Pray to the LORD our God for us; tell us everything he says and we will do it.'[a] [21]I have told you today, but you still have not obeyed the LORD your God in all he sent me to tell you. [b] [22]So now, be sure of this: You will die by the sword, famine and plague[c] in the place where you want to go to settle."[d]

43 When Jeremiah finished telling the people all the words of the LORD their God—everything the LORD had sent him to tell them[e]— [2]Azariah son of Hoshaiah and Johanan[f] son of Kareah and all the arrogant men said to Jeremiah, "You are lying! The LORD our God has not sent you to say, 'You must not go to Egypt to settle there.' [3]But Baruch son of Neriah is inciting you against us to hand us over to the Babylonians,[b] so they may kill us or carry us into exile to Babylon."[g]

[4]So Johanan son of Kareah and all the army officers and all the people disobeyed the LORD's command[h] to stay in the land of Judah.[i] [5]Instead, Johanan son of Kareah and all the army officers led away all the remnant of Judah who had come back to live in the land of Judah from all the nations where they had been scattered.[j] [6]They also led away all the men, women and children and the king's daughters whom Nebuzaradan commander of the imperial guard had left with Gedaliah son of Ahikam, the son of Shaphan, and Jeremiah the prophet and Baruch son of Neriah. [7]So they entered Egypt in disobedience to the LORD and went as far as Tahpanhes.[k]

[8]In Tahpanhes[l] the word of the LORD came to Jeremiah: [9]"While the Jews are watching, take some large stones with you and bury them in clay in the brick pavement at the entrance to Pharaoh's palace in Tahpanhes. [10]Then say to them, 'This is what the LORD Almighty, the God of Israel, says: I will send for my servant[m] Nebuchadnezzar king of Babylon, and I will set his throne over these stones I have buried here; he will spread his royal canopy above them. [11]He will come and attack Egypt,[n] bringing death to those destined for death, captivity to those destined for captivity, and the sword to those destined for the sword.[o] [12]He[c] will set fire to the temples of the gods[p] of Egypt; he will burn their temples and take their gods captive. As a shepherd wraps[q] his garment around him, so will he wrap Egypt around himself and depart from there unscathed. [13]There in the temple of the sun[d] in Egypt he will demolish the sacred pillars and will burn down the temples of the gods of Egypt.' "

Disaster Because of Idolatry

44 This word came to Jeremiah concerning all the Jews living in Lower Egypt—in Migdol,[r] Tahpanhes[s] and Memphis[e] [t]—and in Upper Egypt[f]:[u] [2]"This is what the LORD Almighty, the God of Israel, says: You saw the great disaster I brought on Jerusalem and on all the towns of Judah. Today they lie deserted and in ruins[v] [3]because of the evil they have done. They provoked me to anger by burning incense and by worshiping other gods[w] that neither they nor you nor your fathers[x] ever knew. [4]Again and again[y] I sent my servants the prophets,[z] who said, 'Do not do this detestable thing that I hate!' [5]But they

42:20
[a] ver 2
42:21
[b] Eze 2:7;
Zec 7:11-12
42:22
[c] ver 17;
Eze 6:11
[d] Hos 9:6
43:1
[e] Jer 26:8;
42:9-22
43:2
[f] Jer 42:1
43:3
[g] Jer 38:4
43:4
[h] Jer 42:5-6
[i] Jer 42:10
43:5
[j] Jer 40:12
43:7
[k] Jer 2:16; 44:1
43:8
[l] Jer 2:16
43:10
[m] Isa 44:28;
Jer 25:9; 27:6
43:11
[n] Jer 46:13-26;
Eze 29:19-20
[o] Jer 15:2;
44:13; Zec 11:9
43:12
[p] Jer 46:25;
Eze 30:13
[q] Ps 104:2;
109:18-19
44:1
[r] Ex 14:2
[s] Jer 43:7,8
[t] Isa 19:13
[u] Isa 11:11;
Jer 46:14
44:2
[v] Isa 6:11;
Jer 9:11; 34:22
44:3
[w] ver 8;
Dt 13:6-11;
29:26
[x] Dt 32:17;
Jer 19:4
44:4
[y] Jer 7:13
[z] Jer 7:25; 25:4;
26:5

did not listen or pay attention; they did not turn from their wickedness or stop burning incense to other gods. ^a 6Therefore, my fierce anger was poured out; it raged against the towns of Judah and the streets of Jerusalem and made them the desolate ruins they are today.

7"Now this is what the LORD God Almighty, the God of Israel, says: Why bring such great disaster^b on yourselves by cutting off from Judah the men and women,^c the children and infants, and so leave yourselves without a remnant? 8Why provoke me to anger with what your hands have made,^d burning incense to other gods in Egypt, where you have come to live?^e You will destroy yourselves and make yourselves an object of cursing and reproach^f among all the nations on earth. 9Have you forgotten the wickedness committed by your fathers and by the kings and queens of Judah and the wickedness committed by you and your wives in the land of Judah and the streets of Jerusalem?^g 10To this day they have not humbled themselves or shown reverence, nor have they followed my law^h and the decrees I set before you and your fathers.ⁱ

11"Therefore, this is what the LORD Almighty, the God of Israel, says: I am determined to bring disaster^j on you and to destroy all Judah. 12I will take away the remnant^k of Judah who were determined to go to Egypt to settle there. They will all perish in Egypt; they will fall by the sword or die from famine. From the least to the greatest, they will die by sword or famine.^l They will become an object of cursing and horror, of condemnation and reproach.^m 13I will punish those who live in Egypt with the sword, famine and plague,ⁿ as I punished Jerusalem. 14None of the remnant of Judah who have gone to live in Egypt will escape or survive to return to the land of Judah, to which they long to return and live; none will return except a few fugitives."^o

15Then all the men who knew that their wives were burning incense to other gods, along with all the women who were present—a large assembly—and all the people living in Lower and Upper Egypt,^a said to Jeremiah, 16"We will not listen^p to the message you have spoken to us in the name of the LORD! 17We will certainly do everything we said we would:^q We will burn incense to the Queen of Heaven^r and will pour out drink offerings to her just as we and our fathers, our kings and our officials did in the towns of Judah and in the streets of Jerusalem. At that time we had plenty of food and were well off and suffered no harm.^s 18But ever since we stopped burning incense to the Queen of Heaven and pouring out drink offerings to her, we have had nothing and have been perishing by sword and famine.^t"

19The women added, "When we burned incense to the Queen of Heaven^u and poured out drink offerings to her, did not our husbands know that we were making cakes like her image and pouring out drink offerings to her?"

20Then Jeremiah said to all the people, both men and women, who were answering him, 21"Did not the LORD remember^v and think about the incense^w burned in the towns of Judah and the streets of Jerusalem^x by you and your fathers,^y your kings and your officials and the people of the land? 22When the LORD could no longer endure your wicked actions and the detestable things you did, your land became an object

^a15 Hebrew *in Egypt and Pathros*

of cursing[z] and a desolate waste without inhabitants, as it is today.[a]
[23]Because you have burned incense and have sinned against the LORD
and have not obeyed him or followed his law or his decrees or his
stipulations, this disaster[b] has come upon you, as you now see."[c]

[24]Then Jeremiah said to all the people, including the women,[d] "Hear
the word of the LORD, all you people of Judah in Egypt.[e] [25]This is what
the LORD Almighty, the God of Israel, says: You and your wives have
shown by your actions what you promised when you said, 'We will
certainly carry out the vows we made to burn incense and pour out
drink offerings to the Queen of Heaven.'[f]

"Go ahead then, do what you promised! Keep your vows![g] [26]But
hear the word of the LORD, all Jews living in Egypt: 'I swear[h] by my
great name,' says the LORD, 'that no one from Judah living anywhere in
Egypt will ever again invoke my name or swear, "As surely as the
Sovereign LORD lives."[i] [27]For I am watching over them for harm,[j] not
for good; the Jews in Egypt will perish by sword and famine until they
are all destroyed. [28]Those who escape the sword and return to the land
of Judah from Egypt will be very few.[k] Then the whole remnant of
Judah who came to live in Egypt will know whose word will stand—
mine or theirs.[l]

[29]" 'This will be the sign to you that I will punish you in this place,'
declares the LORD, 'so that you will know that my threats of harm
against you will surely stand.'[m] [30]This is what the LORD says: 'I am
going to hand Pharaoh[n] Hophra king of Egypt over to his enemies who
seek his life, just as I handed Zedekiah[o] king of Judah over to Nebuchadnezzar king of Babylon, the enemy who was seeking his life.' "[p]

A Message to Baruch

45 This is what Jeremiah the prophet told Baruch[q] son of Neriah in
the fourth year of Jehoiakim[r] son of Josiah king of Judah, after
Baruch had written on a scroll the words Jeremiah was then dictating:
[2]"This is what the LORD, the God of Israel, says to you, Baruch: [3]You
said, 'Woe to me! The LORD has added sorrow to my pain; I am worn
out with groaning[s] and find no rest.' "

[4]The LORD said, "Say this to him: 'This is what the LORD says: I will
overthrow what I have built and uproot what I have planted,[t] throughout the land.[u] [5]Should you then seek great things for yourself? Seek
them not.[v] For I will bring disaster on all people, declares the LORD, but
wherever you go I will let you escape with your life.' "[w]

A Message About Egypt

46 This is the word of the LORD that came to Jeremiah the prophet
concerning the nations:[x]

[2]Concerning Egypt:

This is the message against the army of Pharaoh Neco[y] king of
Egypt, which was defeated at Carchemish[z] on the Euphrates River by
Nebuchadnezzar king of Babylon in the fourth year of Jehoiakim[a] son
of Josiah king of Judah:

> [3]"Prepare your shields,[b] both large and small,
> and march out for battle!

44:22
z Jer 25:18
a Ge 19:13;
Ps 107:33-34
44:23
b Jer 40:2
c 1Ki 9:9;
Jer 7:13-15;
Da 9:11-12
44:24
d ver 15
e Jer 43:7
44:25
f ver 17
g Eze 20:39
44:26
h Ge 22:16;
Isa 48:1;
Heb 5:13-17
i Dt 32:40;
Ps 50:16
44:27
j Jer 31:28
44:28
k ver 13-14;
Isa 10:19
l ver 17,25-26
44:29
m Pr 19:21
44:30
n Jer 46:26;
Eze 30:21
o 2Ki 25:1-7
p Jer 39:5
45:1
q Jer 32:12;
36:4,18,32
r 2Ch 36:5
45:3
s Ps 69:3
45:4
t Jer 11:17
u Isa 5:5-7;
Jer 18:7-10
45:5
v Mt 6:25-27,33
w Jer 21:9;
38:2; 39:18
46:1
x Jer 1:10;
25:15-38
46:2
y 2Ki 23:29
z 2Ch 35:20
a Jer 45:1
46:3
b Isa 21:5;
Jer 51:11-12

[4]Harness the horses,
    mount the steeds!
Take your positions
    with helmets on!
Polish[c] your spears,
    put on your armor![d]
[5]What do I see?
    They are terrified,
they are retreating,
    their warriors are defeated.
They flee[e] in haste
    without looking back,
and there is terror[f] on every side,"

                  declares the LORD.

[6]"The swift cannot flee[g]
    nor the strong escape.
In the north by the River Euphrates
    they stumble and fall.[h]

[7]"Who is this that rises like the Nile,
    like rivers of surging waters?[i]
[8]Egypt rises like the Nile,
    like rivers of surging waters.
She says, 'I will rise and cover the earth;
    I will destroy cities and their people.'
[9]Charge, O horses!
    Drive furiously, O charioteers![j]
March on, O warriors—
    men of Cush[a] and Put who carry shields,
    men of Lydia[k] who draw the bow.
[10]But that day[l] belongs to the Lord, the LORD Almighty—
    a day of vengeance, for vengeance on his foes.
The sword will devour[m] till it is satisfied,
    till it has quenched its thirst with blood.
For the Lord, the LORD Almighty, will offer sacrifice[n]
    in the land of the north by the River Euphrates.

[11]"Go up to Gilead and get balm,[o]
    O Virgin[p] Daughter of Egypt.
But you multiply remedies in vain;
    there is no healing[q] for you.
[12]The nations will hear of your shame;
    your cries will fill the earth.
One warrior will stumble over another;
    both will fall[r] down together."

[13]This is the message the LORD spoke to Jeremiah the prophet about the coming of Nebuchadnezzar king of Babylon to attack Egypt:[s]

    [14]"Announce this in Egypt, and proclaim it in Migdol;
        proclaim it also in Memphis[b] and Tahpanhes:[t]
    'Take your positions and get ready,

46:4
c Eze 21:9-11
d 1Sa 17:5,38;
2Ch 26:14;
Ne 4:16
46:5
e ver 21
f Jer 49:29
46:6
g Isa 30:16
h ver 12,16;
Da 11:19
46:7
i Jer 47:2
46:9
j Jer 47:3
k Isa 66:19
46:10
l Joel 1:15
m Dt 32:42
n Zep 1:7
46:11
o Jer 8:22
p Isa 47:1
q Jer 30:13;
Mic 1:9
46:12
r Isa 19:4;
Na 3:8-10
46:13
s Isa 19:1
46:14
t Jer 43:8

---

a9 That is, the upper Nile region   *b14* Hebrew *Noph;* also in verse 19

for the sword devours those around you.'
15Why will your warriors be laid low?
  They cannot stand, for the LORD will push them
    down. u
16They will stumblev repeatedly;
  they will fallw over each other.
They will say, 'Get up, let us go back
  to our own people and our native lands,
  away from the sword of the oppressor.'
17There they will exclaim,
  'Pharaoh king of Egypt is only a loud noise;
  he has missed his opportunity. x'

18"As surely as I live," declares the King, y
  whose name is the LORD Almighty,
  "one will come who is like Taborz among the
    mountains,
  like Carmela by the sea.
19Pack your belongings for exile, b
  you who live in Egypt,
for Memphis will be laid waste
  and lie in ruins without inhabitant.

20"Egypt is a beautiful heifer,
  but a gadfly is coming
  against her from the north. c
21The mercenariesd in her ranks
  are like fattened calves.
They too will turn and fleee together,
  they will not stand their ground,
for the dayf of disaster is coming upon them,
  the time for them to be punished.
22Egypt will hiss like a fleeing serpent
  as the enemy advances in force;
they will come against her with axes,
  like men who cut down trees.
23They will chop down her forest,"
                     declares the LORD,
  "dense though it be.
They are more numerous than locusts, g
  they cannot be counted.
24The Daughter of Egypt will be put to shame,
  handed over to the people of the north. h"

25The LORD Almighty, the God of Israel, says: "I am about to bring punishment on Amon god of Thebes, ai on Pharaoh, on Egypt and her godsj and her kings, and on those who relyk on Pharaoh. 26I will hand them overl to those who seek their lives, to Nebuchadnezzar kingm of Babylon and his officers. Later, however, Egypt will be inhabitedn as in times past," declares the LORD.

---

a25 Hebrew *No*

46:15
ulsa 66:15-16
46:16
vLev 26:37
wver 6
46:17
xlsa 19:11-16
46:18
yJer 48:15
zJos 19:22
a1Ki 18:42
46:19
blsa 20:4
46:20
cver 24; Jer 47:2
46:21
d2Ki 7:6 ever 5
fPs 37:13
46:23
gJdg 7:12
46:24
hJer 1:15
46:25
iEze 30:14; Na 3:8
jJer 43:12
klsa 20:6
46:26
lJer 44:30
mEze 32:11
nEze 29:11-16

27"Do not fear,° O Jacob my servant;
  do not be dismayed, O Israel.
I will surely save you out of a distant place,
  your descendants from the land of their exile.ᵖ
Jacob will again have peace and security,
  and no one will make him afraid.
28Do not fear, O Jacob my servant,
  for I am with you,"�q declares the LORD.
"Though I completely destroyʳ all the nations
  among which I scatter you,
  I will not completely destroy you.
I will discipline you but only with justice;
  I will not let you go entirely unpunished."

A Message About the Philistines

47 This is the word of the LORD that came to Jeremiah the prophet concerning the Philistines before Pharaoh attacked Gaza:ˢ

2This is what the LORD says:

"See how the waters are rising in the north;ᵗ
  they will become an overflowing torrent.
They will overflow the land and everything in it,
  the towns and those who live in them.
The people will cry out;
  all who dwell in the land will wail
3at the sound of the hoofs of galloping steeds,
  at the noise of enemy chariots
  and the rumble of their wheels.
Fathers will not turn to help their children;
  their hands will hang limp.
4For the day has come
  to destroy all the Philistines
and to cut off all survivors
  who could help Tyreᵘ and Sidon.ᵛ
The LORD is about to destroy the Philistines,ʷ
  the remnant from the coasts of Caphtor.ᵃ ˣ
5Gaza will shaveʸ her head in mourning;
  Ashkelonᶻ will be silenced.
O remnant on the plain,
  how long will you cut yourselves?

6" 'Ah, swordᵃ of the LORD,' ⌊you cry,⌋
  'how long till you rest?
Return to your scabbard;
  cease and be still.'
7But how can it rest
  when the LORD has commanded it,
when he has ordered it
  to attack Ashkelon and the coast?"

46:27
olsa 41:43; 43:5
plsa 11:11;
Jer 50:19
46:28
qlsa 8:9-10
rJer 4:27
47:1
sGe 10:19;
Am 1:6;
Zec 9:5-7
47:2
tlsa 8:7; 14:31
47:4
uAm 1:9-10;
Zec 9:2-4
vJer 25:22
wGe 10:14;
Joel 3:4
xDt 2:23
47:5
yJer 41:5;
Mic 1:16
zJer 25:20
47:6
aJer 12:12

ᵃ4 That is, Crete

A Message About Moab

48:29–36pp — Isa 16:6–12

48 Concerning Moab:

This is what the Lord Almighty, the God of Israel, says:

"Woe to Nebo, [b] for it will be ruined.
　　Kiriathaim [c] will be disgraced and captured;
　　the stronghold [a] will be disgraced and shattered.
[2]Moab will be praised [d] no more;
　　in Heshbon [b][e] men will plot her downfall:
　　'Come, let us put an end to that nation.'
You too, O Madmen, [c] will be silenced;
　　the sword will pursue you.
[3]Listen to the cries from Horonaim, [f]
　　cries of great havoc and destruction.
[4]Moab will be broken;
　　her little ones will cry out. [d]
[5]They go up the way to Luhith, [g]
　　weeping bitterly as they go;
on the road down to Horonaim
　　anguished cries over the destruction are heard.
[6]Flee! Run for your lives;
　　become like a bush [e] in the desert. [h]
[7]Since you trust in your deeds and riches,
　　you too will be taken captive,
and Chemosh [i] will go into exile, [j]
　　together with his priests and officials.
[8]The destroyer will come against every town,
　　and not a town will escape.
The valley will be ruined
　　and the plateau destroyed,
　　because the Lord has spoken.
[9]Put salt on Moab,
　　for she will be laid waste [f] ;
her towns will become desolate,
　　with no one to live in them.

[10]"A curse on him who is lax in doing the Lord's work!
　　A curse on him who keeps his sword [k] from
　　　　bloodshed! [l]

[11]"Moab has been at rest [m] from youth,
　　like wine left on its dregs, [n]
not poured from one jar to another—
　　she has not gone into exile.
So she tastes as she did,
　　and her aroma is unchanged.
[12]But days are coming,"
　　declares the Lord,

48:1
b Nu 32:38
c Nu 32:37
48:2
d Isa 16:14
e Nu 21:25
48:3
f Isa 15:5
48:5
g Isa 15:5
48:6
h Jer 17:6
48:7
i Nu 21:29
j Isa 46:1-2;
Jer 49:3
48:10
k Jer 47:6
l 1Ki 20:42;
2Ki 13:15-19
48:11
m Zec 1:15
n Zep 1:12

---

a1 Or / *Misgab*　　　*b2* The Hebrew for *Heshbon* sounds like the Hebrew for *plot*.　　　*c2* The name of the Moabite town Madmen sounds like the Hebrew for *be silenced*.　　　*d4* Hebrew; Septuagint / *proclaim it to Zoar*　　　*e6* Or *like Aroer*　　　*f9* Or *Give wings to Moab, / for she will fly away*

"when I will send men who pour from jars,
  and they will pour her out;
they will empty her jars
  and smash her jugs.
13Then Moab will be ashamed[o] of Chemosh,
  as the house of Israel was ashamed
  when they trusted in Bethel.

14"How can you say, 'We are warriors,[p]
  men valiant in battle'?
15Moab will be destroyed and her towns invaded;
  her finest young men will go down in the slaughter,[q]"
  declares the King,[r] whose name is the LORD
    Almighty.[s]
16"The fall of Moab is at hand;[t]
  her calamity will come quickly.
17Mourn for her, all who live around her,
  all who know her fame;
say, 'How broken is the mighty scepter,
  how broken the glorious staff!'

18"Come down from your glory
  and sit on the parched ground,[u]
  O inhabitants of the Daughter of Dibon,[v]
for he who destroys Moab
  will come up against you
  and ruin your fortified cities.[w]
19Stand by the road and watch,
  you who live in Aroer.[x]
Ask the man fleeing and the woman escaping,
  ask them, 'What has happened?'
20Moab is disgraced, for she is shattered.
  Wail[y] and cry out!
Announce by the Arnon[z]
  that Moab is destroyed.
21Judgment has come to the plateau—
  to Holon, Jahzah[a] and Mephaath,[b]
22 to Dibon,[c] Nebo and Beth Diblathaim,
23 to Kiriathaim, Beth Gamul and Beth Meon,[d]
24 to Kerioth[e] and Bozrah—
  to all the towns of Moab, far and near.
25Moab's horn[af] is cut off;
  her arm[g] is broken,"

declares the LORD.

26"Make her drunk,[h]
  for she has defied the LORD.
Let Moab wallow in her vomit;
  let her be an object of ridicule.
27Was not Israel the object of your ridicule?[i]
  Was she caught among thieves,

48:13
oHos 10:6
48:14
pPs 33:16
48:15
qJer 50:27
rJer 46:18
sJer 51:57
48:16
tIsa 13:22
48:18
uIsa 47:1
vNu 21:30;
Jos 13:9 wver 8
48:19
xDt 2:36
48:20
yIsa 16:7
zNu 21:13
48:21
aNu 21:23;
Isa 15:4
bJos 13:18
48:22
cJos 13:9,17
48:23
dJos 13:17
48:24
eAm 2:2
48:25
fPs 75:10
gPs 10:15;
Eze 30:21
48:26
hJer 25:16,27
48:27
iJer 2:26

a25 Horn here symbolizes strength.

that you shake your head[j] in scorn[k]
  whenever you speak of her?
[28] Abandon your towns and dwell among the rocks,
  you who live in Moab.
Be like a dove[l] that makes its nest
  at the mouth of a cave.[m]

[29] "We have heard of Moab's pride[n]—
  her overweening pride and conceit,
her pride and arrogance
  and the haughtiness of her heart.
[30] I know her insolence but it is futile,"

                    declares the LORD,

  "and her boasts accomplish nothing.
[31] Therefore I wail[o] over Moab,
  for all Moab I cry out,
  I moan for the men of Kir Hareseth.[p]
[32] I weep for you, as Jazer weeps,
  O vines of Sibmah.[q]
Your branches spread as far as the sea;
  they reached as far as the sea of Jazer.
The destroyer has fallen
  on your ripened fruit and grapes.
[33] Joy and gladness are gone
  from the orchards and fields of Moab.
I have stopped the flow of wine[r] from the presses;
  no one treads them with shouts of joy.[s]
Although there are shouts,
  they are not shouts of joy.

[34] "The sound of their cry rises
  from Heshbon to Elealeh[t] and Jahaz,[u]
from Zoar[v] as far as Horonaim[w] and Eglath Shelishiyah,
  for even the waters of Nimrim are dried up.[x]
[35] In Moab I will put an end
  to those who make offerings on the high places[y]
  and burn incense[z] to their gods,"

                    declares the LORD.

[36] "So my heart laments[a] for Moab like a flute;
  it laments like a flute for the men of Kir Hareseth.
The wealth they acquired[b] is gone.
[37] Every head is shaved[c]
  and every beard cut off;
every hand is slashed
  and every waist is covered with sackcloth.[d]
[38] On all the roofs in Moab
  and in the public squares
there is nothing but mourning,
  for I have broken Moab
  like a jar[e] that no one wants,"

                    declares the LORD.

[39] "How shattered she is! How they wail!
  How Moab turns her back in shame!

48:27
j Job 16:4;
Jer 18:16
k Mic 7:8-10
48:28
l Ps 55:6-7
m Jdg 6:2
48:29
n Job 40:12;
Isa 16:6
48:31
o Isa 15:5-8
p 2Ki 3:25
48:32
q Isa 16:8-9
48:33
r Isa 16:10
s Joel 1:12
48:34
t Nu 32:3
u Isa 15:4
v Ge 13:10
w Isa 15:5
x Isa 15:6
48:35
y Isa 15:2; 16:12
z Jer 11:13
48:36
a Isa 16:11
b Isa 15:7
48:37
c Isa 15:2;
Jer 41:5
d Ge 37:34
48:38
e Jer 22:28

Moab has become an object of ridicule,
    an object of horror to all those around her."

⁴⁰This is what the LORD says:

"Look! An eagle is swooping^f down,
    spreading its wings^g over Moab.
⁴¹Kerioth^a will be captured
    and the strongholds taken.
In that day the hearts of Moab's warriors
    will be like the heart of a woman in labor. ^h
⁴²Moab will be destroyed^i as a nation^j
    because she defied^k the LORD.
⁴³Terror and pit and snare^l await you,
    O people of Moab,"
                                declares the LORD.

⁴⁴"Whoever flees^m from the terror
    will fall into a pit,
whoever climbs out of the pit
    will be caught in a snare;
for I will bring upon Moab
    the year^n of her punishment,"
                                declares the LORD.

⁴⁵"In the shadow of Heshbon
    the fugitives stand helpless,
for a fire has gone out from Heshbon,
    a blaze from the midst of Sihon;^o
it burns the foreheads of Moab,
    the skulls^p of the noisy boasters.
⁴⁶Woe to you, O Moab!^q
    The people of Chemosh are destroyed;
your sons are taken into exile
    and your daughters into captivity.

⁴⁷"Yet I will restore^r the fortunes of Moab
    in days to come,"
                                declares the LORD.

Here ends the judgment on Moab.

A Message About Ammon

49 Concerning the Ammonites:^s

This is what the LORD says:

"Has Israel no sons?
    Has she no heirs?
Why then has Molech^b taken possession of Gad?
    Why do his people live in its towns?
²But the days are coming,"
    declares the LORD,
"when I will sound the battle cry^t

48:40
fDt 28:49;
Hab 1:8
gIsa 8:8
48:41
hIsa 21:3
48:42
iPs 83:4;
Isa 16:14 jver 2
kver 26
48:43
lIsa 24:17
48:44
m1Ki 19:17;
Isa 24:18
nJer 11:23
48:45
oNu 21:21,26-28
pNu 24:17
48:46
qNu 21:29
48:47
rJer 12:15;
49:6,39
49:1
sAm 1:13;
Zep 2:8-9
49:2
tJer 4:19

ᵃ41 Or *The cities*   ᵇ1 Or *their king*; Hebrew *malcam*; also in verse 3

against Rabbah[u] of the Ammonites;
  it will become a mound of ruins,
  and its surrounding villages will be set on fire.
Then Israel will drive out
  those who drove her out,[v]"

says the LORD.

3"Wail, O Heshbon, for Ai[w] is destroyed!
  Cry out, O inhabitants of Rabbah!
Put on sackcloth and mourn;
  rush here and there inside the walls,
for Molech will go into exile,[x]
  together with his priests and officials.
4Why do you boast of your valleys,
  boast of your valleys so fruitful?
O unfaithful daughter,
  you trust in your riches[y] and say,
  'Who will attack me?'[z]
5I will bring terror on you
  from all those around you,"

declares the Lord, the LORD Almighty.

"Every one of you will be driven away,
  and no one will gather the fugitives.

6"Yet afterward, I will restore[a] the fortunes of the
  Ammonites,"

declares the LORD.

A Message About Edom

49:9-10pp — Ob 5-6
49:14-16pp — Ob 1-4

7Concerning Edom:[b]

This is what the LORD Almighty says:

"Is there no longer wisdom in Teman?[c]
  Has counsel perished from the prudent?
  Has their wisdom decayed?
8Turn and flee, hide in deep caves,
  you who live in Dedan,[d]
for I will bring disaster on Esau
  at the time I punish him.
9If grape pickers came to you,
  would they not leave a few grapes?
If thieves came during the night,
  would they not steal only as much as they wanted?
10But I will strip Esau bare;
  I will uncover his hiding places,
  so that he cannot conceal himself.
His children, relatives and neighbors will perish,
  and he will be no more.[e]
11Leave your orphans;[f] I will protect their lives.
  Your widows too can trust in me."

12This is what the LORD says: "If those who do not deserve to drink

49:2
uDt 3:11
vIsa 14:2;
Eze 21:28-32;
25:2-11
49:3
wJos 8:28
xJer 48:7
49:4
yJer 9:23;
1Ti 6:17
zJer 21:13
49:6
aver 39;
Jer 48:47
49:7
bGe 25:30;
Eze 25:12
cGe 36:11,15,34
49:8
dJer 25:23
49:10
eMal 1:2-5
49:11
fHos 14:3

the cup[g] must drink it, why should you go unpunished?[h] You will not go unpunished, but must drink it. [13]I swear[i] by myself," declares the LORD, "that Bozrah[j] will become a ruin and an object of horror, of reproach and of cursing; and all its towns will be in ruins forever."

[14]I have heard a message from the LORD:
    An envoy was sent to the nations to say,
"Assemble yourselves to attack it!
    Rise up for battle!"

[15]"Now I will make you small among the nations,
    despised among men.
[16]The terror you inspire
    and the pride of your heart have deceived you,
you who live in the clefts of the rocks,
    who occupy the heights of the hill.
Though you build your nest[k] as high as the eagle's,
    from there I will bring you down,"
                    declares the LORD.

[17]"Edom will become an object of horror;[l]
    all who pass by will be appalled and will scoff
    because of all its wounds.[m]
[18]As Sodom and Gomorrah[n] were overthrown,
    along with their neighboring towns,"
                    says the LORD,
"so no one will live there;
    no man will dwell[o] in it.

[19]"Like a lion coming up from Jordan's thickets[p]
    to a rich pastureland,
I will chase Edom from its land in an instant.
    Who is the chosen one I will appoint for this?
Who is like me and who can challenge me?[q]
    And what shepherd can stand against me?"
[20]Therefore, hear what the LORD has planned against Edom,
    what he has purposed[r] against those who live in Teman:
The young of the flock[s] will be dragged away;
    he will completely destroy[t] their pasture because of them.
[21]At the sound of their fall the earth will tremble;[u]
    their cry[v] will resound to the Red Sea.[a]
[22]Look! An eagle will soar and swoop[w] down,
    spreading its wings over Bozrah.
In that day the hearts of Edom's warriors
    will be like the heart of a woman in labor.[x]

A Message About Damascus

[23]Concerning Damascus:[y]

"Hamath[z] and Arpad[a] are dismayed,

49:12
g Jer 25:15
h Jer 25:28-29
49:13
i Ge 22:16
j Ge 36:33;
Isa 34:6
49:16
k Job 39:27;
Am 9:2
49:17
l ver 13
m Jer 50:13;
Eze 35:7
49:18
n Ge 19:24;
Dt 29:23 o ver 33
49:19
p Jer 12:5
q Jer 50:44
49:20
r Isa 14:27
s Jer 50:45
t Mal 1:3-4
49:21
u Eze 26:15
v Jer 50:46;
Eze 26:18
49:22
w Hos 8:1
x Isa 13:8;
Jer 48:40-41
49:23
y Ge 14:15;
2Ch 16:2;
Ac 9:2
z Isa 10:9;
Am 6:2; Zec 9:2
a 2Ki 18:34

---

a 21 Hebrew Yam Suph; that is, Sea of Reeds

for they have heard bad news.
They are disheartened,
   troubled like^a the restless sea.^b
24Damascus has become feeble,
   she has turned to flee
   and panic has gripped her;
anguish and pain have seized her,
   pain like that of a woman in labor.
25Why has the city of renown not been abandoned,
   the town in which I delight?
26Surely, her young men will fall in the streets;
   all her soldiers will be silenced^c in that day,"
                declares the LORD Almighty.
27"I will set fire^d to the walls of Damascus;
   it will consume the fortresses of Ben-Hadad.^e"

A Message About Kedar and Hazor

28Concerning Kedar^f and the kingdoms of Hazor, which Nebuchadnezzar king of Babylon attacked:

This is what the LORD says:

"Arise, and attack Kedar
   and destroy the people of the East.^g
29Their tents and their flocks will be taken;
   their shelters will be carried off
   with all their goods and camels.
Men will shout to them,
   'Terror^h on every side!'

30"Flee quickly away!
   Stay in deep caves, you who live in Hazor,"
                declares the LORD.
"Nebuchadnezzar king of Babylon has plotted against
     you;
   he has devised a plan against you.

31"Arise and attack a nation at ease,
   which lives in confidence,"
                declares the LORD,
"a nation that has neither gates nor bars;ⁱ
   its people live alone.
32Their camels will become plunder,
   and their large herds will be booty.
I will scatter to the winds those who are in distant
     places^b ^j
   and will bring disaster on them from every side,"
                declares the LORD.
33"Hazor will become a haunt of jackals,
   a desolate^k place forever.
No one will live there;
   no man will dwell^l in it."

49:23
b Ge 49:4;
Isa 57:20
49:26
c Jer 50:30
49:27
d Jer 43:12;
Am 1:4
e 1Ki 15:18
49:28
f Ge 25:13
g Jdg 6:3
49:29
h Jer 6:25; 46:5
49:31
i Eze 38:11
49:32
j Jer 9:26
49:33
k Jer 10:22
l ver 18;
Jer 51:37

^a23 Hebrew *on* or *by*   ^b32 Or *who clip the hair by their foreheads*

A Message About Elam

³⁴This is the word of the LORD that came to Jeremiah the prophet concerning Elam, ᵐ early in the reign of Zedekiahⁿ king of Judah:

³⁵This is what the LORD Almighty says:

"See, I will break the bowᵒ of Elam,
  the mainstay of their might.
³⁶I will bring against Elam the four windsᵖ
  from the four quarters of the heavens;
I will scatter them to the four winds,
  and there will not be a nation
  where Elam's exiles do not go.
³⁷I will shatter Elam before their foes,
  before those who seek their lives;
I will bring disaster upon them,
  even my fierce anger,"�q

declares the LORD.

"I will pursue them with the swordʳ
  until I have made an end of them.
³⁸I will set my throne in Elam
  and destroy her king and officials,"

declares the LORD.

³⁹"Yet I will restoreˢ the fortunes of Elam
  in days to come,"

declares the LORD.

A Message About Babylon

51:15–19pp — Jer 10:12–16

50 This is the word the LORD spoke through Jeremiah the prophet concerning Babylonᵗ and the land of the Babyloniansᵃ:

²"Announce and proclaimᵘ among the nations,
  lift up a banner and proclaim it;
  keep nothing back, but say,
'Babylon will be captured;ᵛ
  Belʷ will be put to shame,
  Mardukˣ filled with terror.
Her images will be put to shame
  and her idols filled with terror.'
³A nation from the north will attack her
  and lay waste her land.
No one will liveʸ in it;
  both men and animalsᶻ will flee away.

⁴"In those days, at that time,"
  declares the LORD,
"the people of Israel and the people of Judah togetherᵃ
  will go in tearsᵇ to seekᶜ the LORD their God.
⁵They will ask the way to Zion
  and turn their faces toward it.

ᵃ1 Or *Chaldeans*; also in verses 8, 25, 35 and 45

49:34
mGe 10:22
n2Ki 24:18
49:35
oIsa 22:6
49:36
pver 32
49:37
qJer 30:24
rJer 9:16
49:39
sJer 48:47
50:1
tGe 10:10;
Isa 13:1
50:2
uJer 4:16
vJer 51:31
wIsa 46:1
xJer 51:47
50:3
yver 13;
Isa 14:22-23
zZep 1:3
50:4
aJer 3:18;
Hos 1:11
bEzr 3:12;
Jer 31:9
cHos 3:5

They will come[d] and bind themselves to the LORD
　　in an everlasting covenant[e]
　　that will not be forgotten.

[6]"My people have been lost sheep;[f]
　　their shepherds have led them astray
　　and caused them to roam on the mountains.
They wandered over mountain and hill[g]
　　and forgot their own resting place. [h]
[7]Whoever found them devoured them;
　　their enemies said, 'We are not guilty,[i]
for they sinned against the LORD, their true pasture,
　　the LORD, the hope[j] of their fathers.'

[8]"Flee[k] out of Babylon;
　　leave the land of the Babylonians,
　　and be like the goats that lead the flock.
[9]For I will stir up and bring against Babylon
　　an alliance of great nations from the land of the north.
They will take up their positions against her,
　　and from the north she will be captured.
Their arrows will be like skilled warriors
　　who do not return empty-handed.
[10]So Babylonia[a] will be plundered;
　　all who plunder her will have their fill,"

　　　　　　　　　　　　　　　declares the LORD.

[11]"Because you rejoice and are glad,
　　you who pillage my inheritance,[l]
because you frolic like a heifer threshing grain
　　and neigh like stallions,
[12]your mother will be greatly ashamed;
　　she who gave you birth will be disgraced.
She will be the least of the nations—
　　a wilderness, a dry land, a desert.
[13]Because of the LORD's anger she will not be inhabited
　　but will be completely desolate.
All who pass Babylon will be horrified and scoff[m]
　　because of all her wounds. [n]

[14]"Take up your positions around Babylon,
　　all you who draw the bow. [o]
Shoot at her! Spare no arrows,
　　for she has sinned against the LORD.
[15]Shout[p] against her on every side!
　　She surrenders, her towers fall,
　　her walls[q] are torn down.
Since this is the vengeance[r] of the LORD,
　　take vengeance on her;
　　do to her[s] as she has done to others.
[16]Cut off from Babylon the sower,
　　and the reaper with his sickle at harvest.

50:5
d Jer 33:7
e Isa 55:3;
Jer 32:40;
Heb 8:6-10
50:6
f Isa 53:6;
Mt 9:36; 10:6
g Jer 3:6;
Eze 34:6 h ver 19
50:7
i Jer 2:3
j Jer 14:8
50:8
k Isa 48:20;
Jer 51:6;
Rev 18:4
50:11
l Isa 47:6
50:13
m Jer 18:16
n Jer 49:17
50:14
o ver 29,42
50:15
p Jer 51:14
q Jer 51:44,58
r Jer 51:6
s Ps 137:8;
Rev 18:6

a10 Or *Chaldea*

Because of the sword[t] of the oppressor
　　let everyone return to his own people,[u]
　　let everyone flee to his own land.[v]

17"Israel is a scattered flock
　　that lions[w] have chased away.
The first to devour him
　　was the king[x] of Assyria;
the last to crush his bones
　　was Nebuchadnezzar[y] king[z] of Babylon."

18Therefore this is what the LORD Almighty, the God of Israel, says:

"I will punish the king of Babylon and his land
　　as I punished the king[a] of Assyria.[b]
19But I will bring[c] Israel back to his own pasture
　　and he will graze on Carmel and Bashan;
his appetite will be satisfied
　　on the hills[d] of Ephraim and Gilead.
20In those days, at that time,"
　　declares the LORD,
"search will be made for Israel's guilt,
　　but there will be none,
and for the sins[e] of Judah,
　　but none will be found,
for I will forgive[f] the remnant[g] I spare.

21"Attack the land of Merathaim
　　and those who live in Pekod.[h]
Pursue, kill and completely destroy[a] them,"
　　　　　　　　　　　　　　　declares the LORD.
"Do everything I have commanded you.
22The noise[i] of battle is in the land,
　　the noise of great destruction!
23How broken and shattered
　　is the hammer of the whole earth!
How desolate[j] is Babylon
　　among the nations!
24I set a trap[k] for you, O Babylon,
　　and you were caught before you knew it;
you were found and captured[l]
　　because you opposed[m] the LORD.
25The LORD has opened his arsenal
　　and brought out the weapons[n] of his wrath,
for the Sovereign LORD Almighty has work to do
　　in the land of the Babylonians.[o]
26Come against her from afar.
　　Break open her granaries;
　　pile her up like heaps of grain.
Completely destroy[p] her
　　and leave her no remnant.

50:16
t Jer 25:38
u Isa 13:14
v Jer 51:9
50:17
w Jer 2:15
x 2Ki 17:6
y 2Ki 24:10,14
z 2Ki 25:7
50:18
a Isa 10:12
b Eze 31:3
50:19
c Jer 31:10;
Eze 34:13
d Jer 31:5; 33:12
50:20
e Mic 7:18,19
f Jer 31:34
g Isa 1:9
50:21
h Eze 23:23
50:22
i Jer 4:19-21;
51:54
50:23
j Isa 14:16
50:24
k Da 5:30-31
l Jer 51:31
m Job 9:4
50:25
n Isa 13:5
o Jer 51:25,55
50:26
p Isa 14:22-23

---

a21 The Hebrew term refers to the irrevocable giving over of things or persons to the LORD, often by totally destroying them; also in verse 26.

²⁷Kill all her young bulls;
    let them go down to the slaughter!
Woe to them! For their day has come,
    the time for them to be punished.
²⁸Listen to the fugitives and refugees from Babylon
    declaring in Zion^q
how the LORD our God has taken vengeance,^r
    vengeance for his temple.

²⁹"Summon archers against Babylon,
    all those who draw the bow.^s
Encamp all around her;
    let no one escape.
Repay^t her for her deeds;^u
    do to her as she has done.
For she has defied^v the LORD,
    the Holy One of Israel.
³⁰Therefore, her young men^w will fall in the streets;
    all her soldiers will be silenced in that day,"
                      declares the LORD.

³¹"See, I am against^x you, O arrogant one,"
    declares the Lord, the LORD Almighty,
"for your day has come,
    the time for you to be punished.
³²The arrogant one will stumble and fall
    and no one will help her up;
I will kindle a fire^y in her towns
    that will consume all who are around her."

³³This is what the LORD Almighty says:

"The people of Israel are oppressed,^z
    and the people of Judah as well.
All their captors hold them fast,
    refusing to let them go.^a
³⁴Yet their Redeemer is strong;
    the LORD Almighty^b is his name.
He will vigorously defend their cause^c
    so that he may bring rest^d to their land,
    but unrest to those who live in Babylon.

³⁵"A sword^e against the Babylonians!"
    declares the LORD—
"against those who live in Babylon
    and against her officials and wise^f men!
³⁶A sword against her false prophets!
    They will become fools.
A sword against her warriors!^g
    They will be filled with terror.
³⁷A sword against her horses and chariots^h
    and all the foreigners in her ranks!
    They will become women.ⁱ
A sword against her treasures!
    They will be plundered.

50:28
q Isa 48:20;
Jer 51:10 r ver 15
50:29
s ver 14
t Rev 18:6
u Jer 51:56
v Isa 47:10
50:30
w Isa 13:18;
Jer 49:26
50:31
x Jer 21:13
50:32
y Jer 21:14;
49:27
50:33
z Isa 58:6
a Isa 14:17
50:34
b Jer 51:19
c Jer 15:21;
51:36 d Isa 14:7
50:35
e Jer 47:6
f Da 5:7
50:36
g Jer 49:22
50:37
h Jer 51:21
i Jer 51:30;
Na 3:13

[38]A drought on[a] her waters!
 They will dry[j] up.
For it is a land of idols,[k]
 idols that will go mad with terror.

[39]"So desert creatures and hyenas will live there,
 and there the owl will dwell.
It will never again be inhabited
 or lived in from generation to generation.[l]
[40]As God overthrew Sodom and Gomorrah[m]
 along with their neighboring towns,"

declares the LORD,

"so no one will live there;
 no man will dwell in it.

[41]"Look! An army is coming from the north;[n]
 a great nation and many kings
 are being stirred up from the ends of the earth.[o]
[42]They are armed with bows[p] and spears;
 they are cruel and without mercy.[q]
They sound like the roaring sea[r]
 as they ride on their horses;
they come like men in battle formation
 to attack you, O Daughter of Babylon.[s]
[43]The king of Babylon has heard reports about them,
 and his hands hang limp.
Anguish has gripped him,
 pain like that of a woman in labor.
[44]Like a lion coming up from Jordan's thickets
 to a rich pastureland,
I will chase Babylon from its land in an instant.
 Who is the chosen[t] one I will appoint for this?
Who is like me and who can challenge me?[u]
 And what shepherd can stand against me?"
[45]Therefore, hear what the LORD has planned against
  Babylon,
 what he has purposed[v] against the land of the
  Babylonians:
The young of the flock will be dragged away;
 he will completely destroy their pasture because of
  them.
[46]At the sound of Babylon's capture the earth will tremble;
 its cry[w] will resound among the nations.

51

This is what the LORD says:

"See, I will stir up the spirit of a destroyer
 against Babylon and the people of Leb Kamai.[b]
[2]I will send foreigners to Babylon
 to winnow[x] her and to devastate her land;
they will oppose her on every side

50:38
j Jer 51:36
k ver 2
50:39
l Isa 13:19-22;
34:13-15;
Jer 51:37;
Rev 18:2
50:40
m Ge 19:24
50:41
n Jer 6:22
o Isa 13:4;
Jer 51:22-28
50:42
p ver 14
q Isa 13:18
r Isa 5:30
s Jer 6:23
50:44
t Nu 16:5
u Job 41:10;
Isa 46:9;
Jer 49:19
50:45
v Ps 33:11;
Isa 14:24;
Jer 51:11
50:46
w Rev 18:9-10
51:2
x Isa 41:16;
Jer 15:7;
Mt 3:12

---

[a]38 Or *A sword against* [b]1 *Leb Kamai* is a cryptogram for Chaldea, that is, Babylonia.

in the day of her disaster.
[3]Let not the archer string his bow, [y]
nor let him put on his armor. [z]
Do not spare her young men;
completely destroy[a] her army.
[4]They will fall[a] down slain in Babylon, [b]
fatally wounded in her streets. [b]
[5]For Israel and Judah have not been forsaken[c]
by their God, the LORD Almighty,
though their land[c] is full of guilt[d]
before the Holy One of Israel.

[6]"Flee[e] from Babylon!
Run for your lives!
Do not be destroyed because of her sins. [f]
It is time for the LORD's vengeance;[g]
he will pay[h] her what she deserves.
[7]Babylon was a gold cup[i] in the LORD's hand;
she made the whole earth drunk.
The nations drank her wine;
therefore they have now gone mad.
[8]Babylon will suddenly fall[j] and be broken.
Wail over her!
Get balm[k] for her pain;
perhaps she can be healed.

[9]" 'We would have healed Babylon,
but she cannot be healed;
let us leave[l] her and each go to his own land,
for her judgment[m] reaches to the skies,
it rises as high as the clouds.'

[10]" 'The LORD has vindicated[n] us;
come, let us tell in Zion
what the LORD our God has done.'[o]

[11]"Sharpen the arrows, [p]
take up the shields![q]
The LORD has stirred up the kings of the Medes, [r]
because his purpose[s] is to destroy Babylon.
The LORD will take vengeance,
vengeance for his temple. [t]
[12]Lift up a banner against the walls of Babylon!
Reinforce the guard,
station the watchmen,
prepare an ambush!
The LORD will carry out his purpose,
his decree against the people of Babylon.
[13]You who live by many waters[u]
and are rich in treasures, [v]
your end has come,

51:3
y Jer 50:29
z Jer 46:4
51:4
a Isa 13:15
b Jer 49:26;
50:30
51:5
c Isa 54:6-8
d Hos 4:1
51:6
e Jer 50:8
f Nu 16:26;
Rev 18:4
g Jer 50:15
h Jer 25:14
51:7
i Jer 25:15-16;
Rev 14:8-10;
17:4
51:8
j Isa 21:9;
Rev 14:8
k Jer 46:11
51:9
l Isa 13:14;
Jer 50:16
m Rev 18:4-5
51:10
n Mic 7:9
o Jer 50:28
51:11
p Jer 50:9
q Jer 46:4
r ver 28
s Jer 50:45
t Jer 50:28
51:13
u Rev 17:1,15
v Isa 45:3;
Hab 2:9

---

[a]3 The Hebrew term refers to the irrevocable giving over of things or persons to the LORD, often by totally destroying them.   [b]4 Or *Chaldea*   [c]5 Or / *and the land of the Babylonians*

the time for you to be cut off.
¹⁴The LORD Almighty has sworn by himself:ʷ
I will surely fill you with men, as with a swarm of
    locusts,ˣ
and they will shoutʸ in triumph over you.

¹⁵"He made the earth by his power;
he founded the world by his wisdom
and stretchedᶻ out the heavens by his understanding.
¹⁶When he thunders,ᵃ the waters in the heavens roar;
he makes clouds rise from the ends of the earth.
He sends lightning with the rain
and brings out the wind from his storehouses.ᵇ

¹⁷"Every man is senseless and without knowledge;
every goldsmith is shamed by his idols.
His images are a fraud;ᶜ
they have no breath in them.
¹⁸They are worthless,ᵈ the objects of mockery;
when their judgment comes, they will perish.
¹⁹He who is the Portion of Jacob is not like these,
for he is the Maker of all things,
including the tribe of his inheritance—
the LORD Almighty is his name.

²⁰"You are my war club,ᵉ
my weapon for battle—
with you I shatterᶠ nations,
with you I destroy kingdoms,
²¹with you I shatter horse and rider,ᵍ
with you I shatter chariot and driver,
²²with you I shatter man and woman,
with you I shatter old man and youth,
with you I shatter young man and maiden,ʰ
²³with you I shatter shepherd and flock,
with you I shatter farmer and oxen,
with you I shatter governors and officials.ⁱ

²⁴"Before your eyes I will repayʲ Babylon and all who live in Babylo-
niaᵃ for all the wrong they have done in Zion," declares the LORD.

²⁵"I am against you, O destroying mountain,
you who destroy the whole earth,"
                                            declares the LORD.
"I will stretch out my hand against you,
roll you off the cliffs,
and make you a burned-out mountain.ᵏ
²⁶No rock will be taken from you for a cornerstone,
nor any stone for a foundation,
for you will be desolateˡ forever,"
                                            declares the LORD.

²⁷"Lift up a bannerᵐ in the land!

51:14
w Am 6:8
x ver 27;
Na 3:15
y Jer 50:15
51:15
z Ge 1:1;
Job 9:8;
Ps 104:2
51:16
a Ps 18:11-13
b Ps 135:7;
Jnh 1:4
51:17
c Isa 44:20;
Hab 2:18-19
51:18
d Jer 18:15
51:20
e Isa 10:5
f Mic 4:13
51:21
g Ex 15:1
51:22
h 2Ch 36:17;
Isa 13:17-18
51:23
i ver 57
51:24
j Jer 50:15
51:25
k Zec 4:7
51:26
l ver 29;
Isa 13:19-22;
Jer 50:12
51:27
m Isa 13:2;
Jer 50:2

ᵃ24 Or *Chaldea*; also in verse 35

Blow the trumpet among the nations!
Prepare the nations for battle against her;
   summon against her these kingdoms:[n]
   Ararat,[o] Minni and Ashkenaz.[p]
Appoint a commander against her;
   send up horses like a swarm of locusts.
[28]Prepare the nations for battle against her—
   the kings of the Medes,[q]
their governors and all their officials,
   and all the countries they rule.
[29]The land trembles and writhes,
   for the LORD's purposes against Babylon stand—
to lay waste the land of Babylon
   so that no one will live there.[r]
[30]Babylon's warriors[s] have stopped fighting;
   they remain in their strongholds.
Their strength is exhausted;
   they have become like women.[t]
Her dwellings are set on fire;
   the bars[u] of her gates are broken.
[31]One courier[v] follows another
   and messenger follows messenger
to announce to the king of Babylon
   that his entire city is captured,
[32]the river crossings seized,
   the marshes set on fire,
   and the soldiers terrified.[w]"

[33]This is what the LORD Almighty, the God of Israel, says:

   "The Daughter of Babylon is like a threshing floor[x]
      at the time it is trampled;
      the time to harvest[y] her will soon come."

[34]"Nebuchadnezzar[z] king of Babylon has devoured us,
   he has thrown us into confusion,
   he has made us an empty jar.
Like a serpent he has swallowed us
   and filled his stomach with our delicacies,
   and then has spewed us out.
[35]May the violence done to our flesh[a] be upon Babylon,"
   say the inhabitants of Zion.
"May our blood be on those who live in Babylonia,"
   says Jerusalem.[a]

[36]Therefore, this is what the LORD says:

   "See, I will defend your cause[b]
      and avenge[c] you;
   I will dry up[d] her sea
      and make her springs dry.
[37]Babylon will be a heap of ruins,

51:27
n Jer 25:14
o Ge 8:4
p Ge 10:3
51:28
q ver 11
51:29
r ver 43;
Isa 13:20
51:30
s Jer 50:36
t Isa 19:16
u Isa 45:2;
La 2:9; Na 3:13
51:31
v 2Sa 18:19-31
51:32
w Jer 50:36
51:33
x Isa 21:10
y Isa 17:5;
Hos 6:11
51:34
z Jer 50:17
51:35
a ver 24;
Ps 137:8
51:36
b Ps 140:12;
Jer 50:34;
La 3:58 c ver 6;
Ro 12:19
d Jer 50:38

---

a 35 Or *done to us and to our children*

a haunt[e] of jackals,
an object of horror and scorn,
a place where no one lives.[f]
38Her people all roar like young lions,
they growl like lion cubs.
39But while they are aroused,
I will set out a feast for them
and make them drunk,
so that they shout with laughter—
then sleep forever and not awake,"
declares the LORD.[g]
40"I will bring them down
like lambs to the slaughter,
like rams and goats.

41"How Sheshach[a][h] will be captured,[i]
the boast of the whole earth seized!
What a horror Babylon will be
among the nations!
42The sea will rise over Babylon;
its roaring waves[j] will cover her.
43Her towns will be desolate,
a dry and desert land,
a land where no one lives,
through which no man travels.[k]
44I will punish Bel[l] in Babylon
and make him spew out[m] what he has swallowed.
The nations will no longer stream to him.
And the wall[n] of Babylon will fall.

45"Come out[o] of her, my people!
Run[p] for your lives!
Run from the fierce anger of the LORD.
46Do not lose heart or be afraid[q]
when rumors[r] are heard in the land;
one rumor comes this year, another the next,
rumors of violence in the land
and of ruler against ruler.
47For the time will surely come
when I will punish the idols[s] of Babylon;
her whole land will be disgraced[t]
and her slain will all lie fallen within her.
48Then heaven and earth and all that is in them
will shout[u] for joy over Babylon,
for out of the north[v]
destroyers will attack her,"
declares the LORD.

49"Babylon must fall because of Israel's slain,
just as the slain in all the earth
have fallen because of Babylon.[w]

51:37
e Isa 13:22;
Rev 18:2
f Jer 50:13,39
51:39
g ver 57
51:41
h Jer 25:26
i Isa 13:19
51:42
j Isa 8:7
51:43
k ver 29,62;
Isa 13:20;
Jer 2:6
51:44
l Isa 46:1
m ver 34
n ver 58;
Jer 50:15
51:45
o Rev 18:4
p ver 6;
Isa 48:20;
Jer 50:8
51:46
q Jer 46:27
r 2Ki 19:7
51:47
s ver 52;
Isa 46:1-2;
Jer 50:2
t Jer 50:12
51:48
u Isa 44:23;
Rev 18:20
v ver 11
51:49
w Ps 137:8;
Jer 50:29

---

a41 *Sheshach* is a cryptogram for Babylon.

⁵⁰You who have escaped the sword,
  leaveˣ and do not linger!
Rememberʸ the LORD in a distant land,
  and think on Jerusalem."

⁵¹"We are disgraced,ᶻ
  for we have been insulted
  and shame covers our faces,
because foreigners have entered
  the holy places of the LORD's house."ᵃ

⁵²"But days are coming," declares the LORD,
  "when I will punish her idols,ᵇ
and throughout her land
  the wounded will groan.
⁵³Even if Babylon reaches the skyᶜ
  and fortifies her lofty stronghold,
I will send destroyersᵈ against her,"
                    declares the LORD.

⁵⁴"The sound of a cry comes from Babylon,
  the sound of great destructionᵉ
  from the land of the Babylonians.ᵃ
⁵⁵The LORD will destroy Babylon;
  he will silence her noisy din.
Wavesᶠ of enemies will rage like great waters;
  the roar of their voices will resound.
⁵⁶A destroyerᵍ will come against Babylon;
  her warriors will be captured,
  and their bows will be broken.ʰ
For the LORD is a God of retribution;
  he will repayⁱ in full.
⁵⁷I will make her officials and wise men drunk,
  her governors, officers and warriors as well;
they will sleepʲ forever and not awake,"
  declares the King,ᵏ whose name is the LORD
    Almighty.

⁵⁸This is what the LORD Almighty says:

"Babylon's thick wallˡ will be leveled
  and her high gates set on fire;
the peoplesᵐ exhaust themselves for nothing,
  the nations' labor is only fuel for the flames."ⁿ

⁵⁹This is the message Jeremiah gave to the staff officer Seraiah son of
Neriah,ᵒ the son of Mahseiah, when he went to Babylon with Zedeki-
ahᵖ king of Judah in the fourth�ۋ year of his reign. ⁶⁰Jeremiah had
written on a scrollʳ about all the disasters that would come upon
Babylon—all that had been recorded concerning Babylon. ⁶¹He said to
Seraiah, "When you get to Babylon, see that you read all these words
aloud. ⁶²Then say, 'O LORD, you have said you will destroy this place,
so that neither man nor animal will live in it; it will be desolateˢ

51:50
xver 45
yPs 137:6
51:51
zPs 44:13-16;
79:4 aLa 1:10
51:52
bver 47
51:53
cGe 11:4;
Isa 14:13-14
dJer 49:16
51:54
eJer 50:22
51:55
fPs 18:4
51:56
gver 48 hPs 46:9
iver 6;
Ps 94:1-2;
Hab 2:8
51:57
jPs 76:5;
Jer 25:27
kJer 46:18;
48:15
51:58
lver 44 mver 64
nHab 2:13
51:59
oJer 36:4
pJer 52:1
qJer 28:1
51:60
rJer 30:2; 36:2
51:62
sIsa 13:20;
Jer 50:13,39

ᵃ54 Or *Chaldeans*

forever.' [63]When you finish reading this scroll, tie a stone to it and throw it into the Euphrates. [64]Then say, 'So will Babylon sink to rise no more because of the disaster I will bring upon her. And her people[t] will fall.' "

The words of Jeremiah end[u] here.

The Fall of Jerusalem

52:1–3pp — 2Ki 24:18–20; 2Ch 36:11–16
52:4–16pp — Jer 39:1–10
52:4–21pp — 2Ki 25:1–21; 2Ch 36:17–20

51:64
t ver 58
u Job 31:40
52:1
v 2Ki 24:17
w Jos 10:29;
2Ki 8:22
52:2
x Jer 36:30
52:3
y Isa 3:1
z Eze 17:12-16
52:4
a Zec 8:19
b 2Ki 25:1-7;
Jer 39:1
c Eze 24:1-2
52:6
d Isa 3:1
52:9
e Jer 32:4
f Nu 34:11
g Nu 13:21
52:10
h Jer 22:30
52:11
i Eze 12:13
52:12
j Zec 7:5; 8:19
k Jer 39:9
52:13
l 2Ch 36:19;
Ps 74:8; La 2:6
m Ps 79:1;
Mic 3:12
52:14
n Ne 1:3
52:16
o Jer 40:6
52:17
p 1Ki 7:15
q 1Ki 7:27-37

52 Zedekiah[v] was twenty-one years old when he became king, and he reigned in Jerusalem eleven years. His mother's name was Hamutal daughter of Jeremiah; she was from Libnah.[w] [2]He did evil in the eyes of the LORD, just as Jehoiakim[x] had done. [3]It was because of the LORD's anger that all this happened to Jerusalem and Judah,[y] and in the end he thrust them from his presence.

Now Zedekiah rebelled[z] against the king of Babylon.

[4]So in the ninth year of Zedekiah's reign, on the tenth[a] day of the tenth month, Nebuchadnezzar king of Babylon marched against Jerusalem[b] with his whole army. They camped outside the city and built siege works all around it.[c] [5]The city was kept under siege until the eleventh year of King Zedekiah.

[6]By the ninth day of the fourth month the famine in the city had become so severe that there was no food for the people to eat.[d] [7]Then the city wall was broken through, and the whole army fled. They left the city at night through the gate between the two walls near the king's garden, though the Babylonians[a] were surrounding the city. They fled toward the Arabah,[b] [8]but the Babylonian[c] army pursued King Zedekiah and overtook him in the plains of Jericho. All his soldiers were separated from him and scattered, [9]and he was captured.[e]

He was taken to the king of Babylon at Riblah[f] in the land of Hamath,[g] where he pronounced sentence on him. [10]There at Riblah the king of Babylon slaughtered the sons[h] of Zedekiah before his eyes; he also killed all the officials of Judah. [11]Then he put out Zedekiah's eyes, bound him with bronze shackles and took him to Babylon, where he put him in prison till the day of his death.[i]

[12]On the tenth day of the fifth[j] month, in the nineteenth year of Nebuchadnezzar king of Babylon, Nebuzaradan[k] commander of the imperial guard, who served the king of Babylon, came to Jerusalem. [13]He set fire[l] to the temple[m] of the LORD, the royal palace and all the houses of Jerusalem. Every important building he burned down. [14]The whole Babylonian army under the commander of the imperial guard broke down all the walls[n] around Jerusalem. [15]Nebuzaradan the commander of the guard carried into exile some of the poorest people and those who remained in the city, along with the rest of the craftsmen[d] and those who had gone over to the king of Babylon. [16]But Nebuzaradan left behind[o] the rest of the poorest people of the land to work the vineyards and fields.

[17]The Babylonians broke up the bronze pillars,[p] the movable stands[q]

---

[a]7 Or *Chaldeans*; also in verse 17   [b]7 Or *the Jordan Valley*   [c]8 Or *Chaldean*; also in verse 14
[d]15 Or *populace*

and the bronze Sea[r] that were at the temple of the LORD and they carried all the bronze to Babylon.[s] [18]They also took away the pots, shovels, wick trimmers, sprinkling bowls, dishes and all the bronze articles used in the temple service.[t] [19]The commander of the imperial guard took away the basins, censers,[u] sprinkling bowls, pots, lampstands, dishes and bowls used for drink offerings—all that were made of pure gold or silver.

[20]The bronze from the two pillars, the Sea and the twelve bronze bulls under it, and the movable stands, which King Solomon had made for the temple of the LORD, was more than could be weighed.[v] [21]Each of the pillars was eighteen cubits high and twelve cubits in circumference[a]; each was four fingers thick, and hollow.[w] [22]The bronze capital[x] on top of the one pillar was five cubits[b] high and was decorated with a network and pomegranates of bronze all around. The other pillar, with its pomegranates, was similar. [23]There were ninety-six pomegranates on the sides; the total number of pomegranates[y] above the surrounding network was a hundred.

[24]The commander of the guard took as prisoners Seraiah[z] the chief priest, Zephaniah[a] the priest next in rank and the three doorkeepers. [25]Of those still in the city, he took the officer in charge of the fighting men, and seven royal advisers. He also took the secretary who was chief officer in charge of conscripting the people of the land and sixty of his men who were found in the city. [26]Nebuzaradan[b] the commander took them all and brought them to the king of Babylon at Riblah. [27]There at Riblah, in the land of Hamath, the king had them executed.

So Judah went into captivity, away[c] from her land. [28]This is the number of the people Nebuchadnezzar carried into exile:[d]

in the seventh year, 3,023 Jews;
[29]in Nebuchadnezzar's eighteenth year,
832 people from Jerusalem;
[30]in his twenty-third year,
745 Jews taken into exile by Nebuzaradan the commander of the imperial guard.
There were 4,600 people in all.

Jehoiachin Released

52:31–34pp — 2Ki 25:27–30

[31]In the thirty-seventh year of the exile of Jehoiachin king of Judah, in the year Evil-Merodach[c] became king of Babylon, he released Jehoiachin king of Judah and freed him from prison on the twenty-fifth day of the twelfth month. [32]He spoke kindly to him and gave him a seat of honor higher than those of the other kings who were with him in Babylon. [33]So Jehoiachin put aside his prison clothes and for the rest of his life ate regularly at the king's table.[e] [34]Day by day the king of Babylon gave Jehoiachin a regular allowance[f] as long as he lived, till the day of his death.

[a]21 That is, about 27 feet (about 8.1 meters) high and 18 feet (about 5.4 meters) in circumference
[b]22 That is, about 7 1/2 feet (about 2.3 meters)   [c]31 Also called *Amel-Marduk*

52:17
r1Ki 7:23
sJer 27:19-22
52:18
tEx 27:3;
1Ki 7:45
52:19
u1Ki 7:50
52:20
v1Ki 7:47
52:21
w1Ki 7:15
52:22
x1Ki 7:16
52:23
y1Ki 7:20
52:24
z2Ki 25:18
aJer 21:1; 37:3
52:26
bver 12
52:27
cJer 20:4
52:28
d2Ki 24:14-16;
2Ch 36:20
52:33
e2Sa 9:7
52:34
f2Sa 9:10

Lamentations

Title and Background

Because of its subject matter, the book is referred to in Jewish tradition as "Lamentations." It was written as a reminder of the fall of Jerusalem and of the burning of the temple.

Author and Date of Writing

Although the writer of Lamentations is anonymous, ancient Jewish and Christian tradition ascribes it to Jeremiah. Since he was an eyewitness to the divine judgment on Jerusalem in 586 B.C., it is reasonable to assume he was the author. The book was probably written shortly after 586.

Theme and Message

Lamentations is the only Old Testament book that consists solely of laments. Jeremiah recognizes that the judgment on Jerusalem and the temple is the judgment of a righteous God. The book that begins with a lament (1:1-2) rightly ends in repentance (5:21-22). Knowing that God is merciful, the author appeals for mercy in prayer to God. In the middle of the book, the theology of Lamentations reaches its apex as it focuses on the goodness of God. In spite of all evidence to the contrary, "his compassions never fail."

Outline

I. Jerusalem's Misery and Desolation (1:1-22)
II. The Lord's Anger Against His People (2:1-22)
III. Judah's Complaint and the Basis for Consolation (3:1-66)
IV. The Contrast Between Zion's Past and Present (4:1-22)
V. Judah's Appeal for God's Forgiveness (5:1-22)

1[a]

How deserted lies the city,
  once so full of people!
How like a widow[a] is she,
  who once was great[b] among the nations!
She who was queen among the provinces
  has now become a slave.[c]

²Bitterly she weeps[d] at night,
  tears are upon her cheeks.
Among all her lovers[e]
  there is none to comfort her.
All her friends have betrayed[f] her;
  they have become her enemies.[g]

³After affliction and harsh labor,

1:1
a Isa 47:8
b 1Ki 4:21
c Isa 3:26;
  Jer 40:9

1:2
d Ps 6:6 e Jer 3:1
f Jer 4:30;
Mic 7:5 g ver 16

[a]This chapter is an acrostic poem, the verses of which begin with the successive letters of the Hebrew alphabet.

Judah has gone into exile. [h]
She dwells among the nations;
    she finds no resting place. [i]
All who pursue her have overtaken her
    in the midst of her distress.

4The roads to Zion mourn,
    for no one comes to her appointed feasts.
All her gateways are desolate, [j]
    her priests groan,
her maidens grieve,
    and she is in bitter anguish. [k]

5Her foes have become her masters;
    her enemies are at ease.
The LORD has brought her grief [l]
    because of her many sins.
Her children have gone into exile, [m]
    captive before the foe.

6All the splendor has departed
    from the Daughter of Zion. [n]
Her princes are like deer
    that find no pasture;
in weakness they have fled
    before the pursuer.

7In the days of her affliction and wandering
    Jerusalem remembers all the treasures
    that were hers in days of old.
When her people fell into enemy hands,
    there was no one to help her. [o]
Her enemies looked at her
    and laughed at her destruction.

8Jerusalem has sinned [p] greatly
    and so has become unclean.
All who honored her despise her,
    for they have seen her nakedness; [q]
she herself groans [r]
    and turns away.

9Her filthiness clung to her skirts;
    she did not consider her future. [s]
Her fall [t] was astounding;
    there was none to comfort [u] her.
"Look, O LORD, on my affliction, [v]
    for the enemy has triumphed."

10The enemy laid hands
    on all her treasures; [w]
she saw pagan nations
    enter her sanctuary [x]—
those you had forbidden [y]
    to enter your assembly.

1:3
h Jer 13:19
i Dt 28:65
1:4
j Jer 9:11
k Joel 1:8-13
1:5
l Jer 30:15
m Jer 39:9;
52:28-30
1:6
n Jer 13:18
1:7
o Jer 37:7;
La 4:17
1:8
p ver 20;
Isa 59:2-13
q Jer 13:22,26
r ver 21,22
1:9
s Dt 32:28-29;
Isa 47:7;
Eze 24:13
t Jer 13:18
u Ecc 4:1;
Jer 16:7
v Ps 25:18
1:10
w Isa 64:11
x Ps 74:7-8;
Jer 51:51
y Dt 23:3

¹¹All her people groan[z]
    as they search for bread;[a]
they barter their treasures for food
    to keep themselves alive.
"Look, O LORD, and consider,
    for I am despised."

¹²"Is it nothing to you, all you who pass by?[b]
    Look around and see.
Is any suffering like my suffering[c]
    that was inflicted on me,
that the LORD brought on me
    in the day of his fierce anger?[d]

¹³"From on high he sent fire,
    sent it down into my bones.[e]
He spread a net for my feet
    and turned me back.
He made me desolate,[f]
    faint[g] all the day long.

¹⁴"My sins have been bound into a yoke[a];[h]
    by his hands they were woven together.
They have come upon my neck
    and the Lord has sapped my strength.
He has handed me over[i]
    to those I cannot withstand.

¹⁵"The Lord has rejected
    all the warriors in my midst;[j]
he has summoned an army[k] against me
    to[b] crush my young men.[l]
In his winepress the Lord has trampled
    the Virgin Daughter of Judah.

¹⁶"This is why I weep
    and my eyes overflow with tears.[m]
No one is near to comfort[n] me,
    no one to restore my spirit.
My children are destitute
    because the enemy has prevailed."[o]

¹⁷Zion stretches out her hands,[p]
    but there is no one to comfort her.
The LORD has decreed for Jacob
    that his neighbors become his foes;
Jerusalem has become
    an unclean thing among them.

¹⁸"The LORD is righteous,
    yet I rebelled[q] against his command.
Listen, all you peoples;

1:11
z Ps 38:8
a Jer 52:6
1:12
b Jer 18:16
c ver 18
d Isa 13:13;
Jer 30:24
1:13
e Job 30:30
f Jer 44:6
g Hab 3:16
1:14
h Dt 28:48;
Isa 47:6
i Jer 32:5
1:15
j Jer 37:10
k Isa 41:2
l Isa 28:18;
Jer 18:21
1:16
m La 2:11,18;
3:48-49
n Ps 69:20;
Ecc 4:1 over 2;
Jer 13:17; 14:17
1:17
p Jer 4:31
1:18
q 1Sa 12:14

---

[a]14 Most Hebrew manuscripts; Septuagint *He kept watch over my sins*   [b]15 Or *has set a time for me*
/ *when he will*

look upon my suffering. [r]
My young men and maidens
  have gone into exile. [s]

19"I called to my allies
  but they betrayed me.
My priests and my elders
  perished[t] in the city
while they searched for food
  to keep themselves alive.

20"See, O LORD, how distressed[u] I am!
  I am in torment[v] within,
and in my heart I am disturbed,
  for I have been most rebellious.
Outside, the sword bereaves;
  inside, there is only death. [w]

21"People have heard my groaning, [x]
  but there is no one to comfort me. [y]
All my enemies have heard of my distress;
  they rejoice[z] at what you have done.
May you bring the day[a] you have announced
  so they may become like me.

22"Let all their wickedness come before you;
  deal with them
as you have dealt with me
  because of all my sins. [b]
My groans are many
  and my heart is faint."

2[a]　How the Lord has covered the Daughter of Zion
  with the cloud of his anger[b]![c]
He has hurled down the splendor of Israel
  from heaven to earth;
he has not remembered his footstool[d]
  in the day of his anger.

2Without pity[e] the Lord has swallowed[f] up
  all the dwellings of Jacob;
in his wrath he has torn down
  the strongholds[g] of the Daughter of Judah.
He has brought her kingdom and its princes
  down to the ground[h] in dishonor.

3In fierce anger he has cut off
  every horn[c][i] of Israel.
He has withdrawn his right hand[j]
  at the approach of the enemy.
He has burned in Jacob like a flaming fire

1:18
r ver 12
s Dt 28:32,41
1:19
t Jer 14:15;
La 2:20
1:20
u Jer 4:19
v La 2:11
w Dt 32:25;
Eze 7:15
1:21
x ver 8
y ver 4
z La 2:15
a Isa 47:11;
Jer 30:16
1:22
b Ne 4:5
2:1
c La 3:44
d Ps 99:5; 132:7
2:2
e La 3:43
f Ps 21:9
g Ps 89:39-40;
Mic 5:11
h Isa 25:12
2:3
i Ps 75:5,10
j Ps 74:11

---

[a]This chapter is an acrostic poem, the verses of which begin with the successive letters of the Hebrew alphabet.　[b]1 Or *How the Lord in his anger / has treated the Daughter of Zion with contempt*　[c]3 Or / *all the strength;* or *every king; horn* here symbolizes strength.

that consumes everything around it. [k]

[4]Like an enemy he has strung his bow;[l]
　　his right hand is ready.
Like a foe he has slain
　　all who were pleasing to the eye;[m]
he has poured out his wrath like fire[n]
　　on the tent of the Daughter of Zion.

[5]The Lord is like an enemy;[o]
　　he has swallowed up Israel.
He has swallowed up all her palaces
　　and destroyed her strongholds. [p]
He has multiplied mourning and lamentation
　　for the Daughter of Judah. [q]

[6]He has laid waste his dwelling like a garden;
　　he has destroyed his place of meeting. [r]
The Lord has made Zion forget
　　her appointed feasts and her Sabbaths;[s]
in his fierce anger he has spurned
　　both king and priest. [t]

[7]The Lord has rejected his altar
　　and abandoned his sanctuary.
He has handed over to the enemy
　　the walls of her palaces;[u]
they have raised a shout in the house of the Lord
　　as on the day of an appointed feast. [v]

[8]The Lord determined to tear down
　　the wall around the Daughter of Zion.
He stretched out a measuring line[w]
　　and did not withhold his hand from destroying.
He made ramparts and walls lament;
　　together they wasted away. [x]

[9]Her gates[y] have sunk into the ground;
　　their bars he has broken and destroyed.
Her king and her princes are exiled[z] among the nations,
　　the law[a] is no more,
and her prophets no longer find
　　visions[b] from the Lord.

[10]The elders of the Daughter of Zion
　　sit on the ground in silence;
they have sprinkled dust on their heads[c]
　　and put on sackcloth. [d]
The young women of Jerusalem
　　have bowed their heads to the ground. [e]

[11]My eyes fail from weeping, [f]
　　I am in torment within, [g]
my heart is poured out[h] on the ground
　　because my people are destroyed,
because children and infants faint[i]

2:3
k Isa 42:25;
Jer 21:4-5,14
2:4
l Job 16:13;
La 3:12-13
m Eze 24:16,25
n Isa 42:25;
Jer 7:20
2:5
o Jer 30:14
p ver 2
q Jer 9:17-20
2:6
r Jer 52:13
s La 1:4;
Zep 3:18
t La 4:16
2:7
u Ps 74:7-8;
Isa 64:11;
Jer 33:4-5
v Jer 52:13
2:8
w 2Ki 21:13;
Isa 34:11
x Isa 3:26
2:9
y Ne 1:3
z Dt 28:36;
2Ki 24:15
a 2Ch 15:3
b Jer 14:14
2:10
c Job 2:12
d Isa 15:3
e Job 2:13;
Isa 3:26
2:11
f La 1:16;
3:48-51 g La 1:20
h ver 19;
Ps 22:14 i La 4:4

in the streets of the city.

12They say to their mothers,
    "Where is bread and wine?"
as they faint like wounded men
    in the streets of the city,
as their lives ebb away
    in their mothers' arms. j

13What can I say for you?
    With what can I compare you,
    O Daughter of Jerusalem?
To what can I liken you,
    that I may comfort you,
    O Virgin Daughter of Zion? k
Your wound is as deep as the sea. l
    Who can heal you?

14The visions of your prophets
    were false and worthless;
they did not expose your sin
    to ward off your captivity. m
The oracles they gave you
    were false and misleading. n

15All who pass your way
    clap their hands at you; o
they scoff p and shake their heads
    at the Daughter of Jerusalem:
"Is this the city that was called
    the perfection of beauty, q
    the joy of the whole earth?" r

16All your enemies open their mouths
    wide against you; s
they scoff and gnash their teeth t
    and say, "We have swallowed her up. u
This is the day we have waited for;
    we have lived to see it."

17The LORD has done what he planned;
    he has fulfilled his word,
    which he decreed long ago. v
He has overthrown you without pity, w
    he has let the enemy gloat over you,
    he has exalted the horn*a* of your foes. x

18The hearts of the people
    cry out to the Lord. y
O wall of the Daughter of Zion,
    let your tears z flow like a river
    day and night; a
give yourself no relief,

---

a17 Horn here symbolizes strength.

2:12
jLa 4:4
2:13
kIsa 37:22
lJer 14:17;
La 1:12
2:14
mIsa 58:1
nJer 2:8;
23:25-32,33-40;
29:9; Eze 13:3;
22:28
2:15
oEze 25:6
pJer 19:8
qPs 50:2
rPs 48:2
2:16
sPs 56:2;
La 3:46
tJob 16:9
uPs 35:25
2:17
vDt 28:15-45
wver 2;
Eze 5:11
xPs 89:42
2:18
yPs 119:145
zLa 1:16
aJer 9:1

your eyes no rest. ᵇ

¹⁹Arise, cry out in the night,
   as the watches of the night begin;
pour out your heartᶜ like water
   in the presence of the Lord. ᵈ
Lift up your hands to him
   for the lives of your children,
who faintᵉ from hunger
   at the head of every street.

²⁰"Look, O LORD, and consider:
   Whom have you ever treated like this?
Should women eat their offspring, ᶠ
   the children they have cared for?�g
Should priest and prophet be killedʰ
   in the sanctuary of the Lord?

²¹"Young and old lie together
   in the dust of the streets;
my young men and maidens
   have fallen by the sword.ⁱ
You have slain them in the day of your anger;
   you have slaughtered them without pity. ʲ

²²"As you summon to a feast day,
   so you summoned against me terrorsᵏ on every side.
In the day of the LORD's anger
   no one escaped or survived;
those I cared for and reared,ˡ
   my enemy has destroyed."

3 ᵃ   I am the man who has seen affliction
   by the rod of his wrath. ᵐ
²He has driven me away and made me walk
   in darknessⁿ rather than light;
³indeed, he has turned his hand against meᵒ
   again and again, all day long.

⁴He has made my skin and my flesh grow old
   and has broken my bones. ᵖ
⁵He has besieged me and surrounded me
   with bitterness�q and hardship. ʳ
⁶He has made me dwell in darkness
   like those long dead. ˢ

⁷He has walled me in so I cannot escape;ᵗ
   he has weighed me down with chains. ᵘ
⁸Even when I call out or cry for help,
   he shuts out my prayer. ᵛ
⁹He has barred my way with blocks of stone;
   he has made my paths crooked. ʷ

ᵃThis chapter is an acrostic poem; the verses of each stanza begin with the successive letters of the Hebrew alphabet, and the verses within each stanza begin with the same letter.

2:18
ᵇLa 3:49
2:19
ᶜ1Sa 1:15;
Ps 62:8
ᵈIsa 26:9
ᵉIsa 51:20
2:20
ᶠDt 28:53;
Jer 19:9
gLa 4:10
ʰPs 78:64;
Jer 14:15
2:21
ⁱ2Ch 36:17;
Ps 78:62-63;
Jer 6:11
ʲJer 13:14;
La 3:43;
Zec 11:6
2:22
ᵏPs 31:13;
Jer 6:25
ˡHos 9:13
3:1
ᵐJob 19:21;
Ps 88:7
3:2
ⁿJer 4:23
3:3
ᵒIsa 5:25
3:4
ᵖPs 51:8;
Isa 38:13;
Jer 50:17
3:5
qver 19
ʳJer 23:15
3:6
ˢPs 88:5-6
3:7
ᵗJob 3:23
ᵘJer 40:4
3:8
ᵛJob 30:20;
Ps 22:2
3:9
ʷIsa 63:17;
Hos 2:6

¹⁰Like a bear lying in wait,
  like a lion in hiding,
¹¹he dragged me from the path and mangled[x] me
  and left me without help.
¹²He drew his bow[y]
  and made me the target[z] for his arrows.[a]

¹³He pierced my heart
  with arrows from his quiver.[b]
¹⁴I became the laughingstock[c] of all my people;
  they mock me in song[d] all day long.
¹⁵He has filled me with bitter herbs
  and sated me with gall.[e]

¹⁶He has broken my teeth with gravel;[f]
  he has trampled me in the dust.
¹⁷I have been deprived of peace;
  I have forgotten what prosperity is.
¹⁸So I say, "My splendor is gone
  and all that I had hoped from the Lord."[g]

¹⁹I remember my affliction and my wandering,
  the bitterness and the gall.
²⁰I well remember them,
  and my soul is downcast[h] within me.[i]
²¹Yet this I call to mind
  and therefore I have hope:

²²Because of the Lord's great love we are not consumed,
  for his compassions never fail.[j]
²³They are new every morning;
  great is your faithfulness.[k]
²⁴I say to myself, "The Lord is my portion;[l]
  therefore I will wait for him."

²⁵The Lord is good to those whose hope is in him,
  to the one who seeks him;[m]
²⁶it is good to wait quietly
  for the salvation of the Lord.[n]
²⁷It is good for a man to bear the yoke
  while he is young.

²⁸Let him sit alone in silence,[o]
  for the Lord has laid it on him.
²⁹Let him bury his face in the dust—
  there may yet be hope.[p]
³⁰Let him offer his cheek to one who would strike him,[q]
  and let him be filled with disgrace.

³¹For men are not cast off
  by the Lord forever.[r]
³²Though he brings grief, he will show compassion,
  so great is his unfailing love.[s]
³³For he does not willingly bring affliction
  or grief to the children of men.[t]

3:11
xHos 6:1

3:12
yLa 2:4
zJob 7:20
aPs 7:12-13;
38:2

3:13
bJob 6:4

3:14
cJer 20:7
dJob 30:9

3:15
eJer 9:15

3:16
fPr 20:17

3:18
gJob 17:15

3:20
hPs 42:5
iPs 42:11

3:22
jPs 78:38;
Mal 3:6

3:23
kZep 3:5

3:24
lPs 16:5

3:25
mIsa 25:9;
30:18

3:26
nPs 37:7; 40:1

3:28
oJer 15:17

3:29
pJer 31:17

3:30
qJob 16:10;
Isa 50:6

3:31
rPs 94:14;
Isa 54:7

3:32
sPs 78:38;
Hos 11:8

3:33
tEze 33:11

³⁴To crush underfoot
   all prisoners in the land,
³⁵to deny a man his rights
   before the Most High,
³⁶to deprive a man of justice—
   would not the Lord see such things?ᵘ

³⁷Who can speak and have it happen
   if the Lord has not decreed it?ᵛ
³⁸Is it not from the mouth of the Most High
   that both calamities and good things come?ʷ
³⁹Why should any living man complain
   when punished for his sins?ˣ

⁴⁰Let us examine our ways and test them,ʸ
   and let us return to the Lᴏʀᴅ.ᶻ
⁴¹Let us lift up our hearts and our hands
   to God in heaven,ᵃ and say:
⁴²"We have sinned and rebelledᵇ
   and you have not forgiven.ᶜ

⁴³"You have covered yourself with anger and pursued us;
   you have slain without pity.ᵈ
⁴⁴You have covered yourself with a cloudᵉ
   so that no prayerᶠ can get through.
⁴⁵You have made us scumᵍ and refuse
   among the nations.

⁴⁶"All our enemies have opened their mouths
   wide against us.ʰ
⁴⁷We have suffered terror and pitfalls,ⁱ
   ruin and destruction.ʲ "
⁴⁸Streams of tears flow from my eyesᵏ
   because my people are destroyed.ˡ

⁴⁹My eyes will flow unceasingly,
   without relief,ᵐ
⁵⁰until the Lᴏʀᴅ looks down
   from heaven and sees.ⁿ
⁵¹What I see brings grief to my soul
   because of all the women of my city.

⁵²Those who were my enemies without cause
   hunted me like a bird.ᵒ
⁵³They tried to end my life in a pitᵖ
   and threw stones at me;
⁵⁴the waters closed over my head,�q
   and I thought I was about to be cut off.

⁵⁵I called on your name, O Lᴏʀᴅ,
   from the depths of the pit.ʳ
⁵⁶You heard my plea:ˢ "Do not close your ears
   to my cry for relief."
⁵⁷You came near when I called you,
   and you said, "Do not fear."ᵗ

3:36
u Jer 22:3;
Hab 1:13
3:37
v Ps 33:9-11
3:38
w Job 2:10;
Isa 45:7;
Jer 32:42
3:39
x Jer 30:15;
Mic 7:9
3:40
y 2Co 13:5
z Ps 119:59;
139:23-24
3:41
a Ps 25:1; 28:2
3:42
b Da 9:5
c Jer 5:7-9
3:43
d La 2:2,17,21
3:44
e Ps 97:2 f ver 8
3:45
g 1Co 4:13
3:46
h La 2:16
3:47
i Jer 48:43
j Isa 24:17-18;
51:19
3:48
k La 1:16
l La 2:11
3:49
m Jer 14:17
3:50
n Isa 63:15
3:52
o Ps 35:7
3:53
p Jer 37:16
3:54
q Ps 69:2;
Jnh 2:3-5
3:55
r Ps 130:1;
Jnh 2:2
3:56
s Ps 55:1
3:57
t Isa 41:10

⁵⁸O Lord, you took up my case;ᵘ
  you redeemed my life.ᵛ
⁵⁹You have seen, O Lᴏʀᴅ, the wrong done to me.ʷ
  Uphold my cause!
⁶⁰You have seen the depth of their vengeance,
  all their plots against me.ˣ

⁶¹O Lᴏʀᴅ, you have heard their insults,
  all their plots against me—
⁶²what my enemies whisper and mutter
  against me all day long.ʸ
⁶³Look at them! Sitting or standing,
  they mock me in their songs.

⁶⁴Pay them back what they deserve, O Lᴏʀᴅ,
  for what their hands have done.ᶻ
⁶⁵Put a veil over their hearts,ᵃ
  and may your curse be on them!
⁶⁶Pursue them in anger and destroy them
  from under the heavens of the Lᴏʀᴅ.

4ᵃ How the gold has lost its luster,
  the fine gold become dull!
The sacred gems are scattered
  at the head of every street.ᵇ

²How the precious sons of Zion,
  once worth their weight in gold,
are now considered as pots of clay,
  the work of a potter's hands!

³Even jackals offer their breasts
  to nurse their young,
but my people have become heartless
  like ostriches in the desert.ᶜ

⁴Because of thirst the infant's tongue
  sticks to the roof of its mouth;ᵈ
the children beg for bread,
  but no one gives it to them.ᵉ

⁵Those who once ate delicacies
  are destitute in the streets.
Those nurtured in purpleᶠ
  now lie on ash heaps.ᵍ

⁶The punishment of my people
  is greater than that of Sodom,ʰ
which was overthrown in a moment
  without a hand turned to help her.

⁷Their princes were brighter than snow
  and whiter than milk,

3:58
uJer 51:36
3:59
vPs 34:22;
Jer 50:34
wJer 18:19-20
3:60
xJer 11:20;
18:18
3:62
yEze 36:3
3:64
zPs 28:4
3:65
aIsa 6:10
4:1
bEze 7:19
4:3
cJob 39:16
4:4
dPs 22:15
eLa 2:11,12
4:5
fJer 6:2
gAm 6:3-7
4:6
hGe 19:25

ᵃThis chapter is an acrostic poem, the verses of which begin with the successive letters of the Hebrew alphabet.

their bodies more ruddy than rubies,
  their appearance like sapphires. [a]

[8]But now they are blacker[i] than soot;
  they are not recognized in the streets.
Their skin has shriveled on their bones;[j]
  it has become as dry as a stick.

[9]Those killed by the sword are better off
  than those who die of famine;
racked with hunger, they waste away
  for lack of food from the field. [k]

[10]With their own hands compassionate women
  have cooked their own children, [l]
who became their food
  when my people were destroyed.

[11]The LORD has given full vent to his wrath;
  he has poured out his fierce anger.
He kindled a fire[m] in Zion
  that consumed her foundations. [n]

[12]The kings of the earth did not believe,
  nor did any of the world's people,
that enemies and foes could enter
  the gates of Jerusalem. [o]

[13]But it happened because of the sins of her prophets
  and the iniquities of her priests, [p]
who shed within her
  the blood of the righteous.

[14]Now they grope through the streets
  like men who are blind. [q]
They are so defiled with blood[r]
  that no one dares to touch their garments.

[15]"Go away! You are unclean!" men cry to them.
  "Away! Away! Don't touch us!"
When they flee and wander about,
  people among the nations say,
  "They can stay here no longer."[s]

[16]The LORD himself has scattered them;
  he no longer watches over them. [t]
The priests are shown no honor,
  the elders[u] no favor.

[17]Moreover, our eyes failed,
  looking in vain[v] for help;[w]
from our towers we watched
  for a nation[x] that could not save us.

[18]Men stalked us at every step,

4:8
i Job 30:28
j Ps 102:3-5
4:9
k Jer 15:2; 16:4
4:10
l Lev 26:29;
Dt 28:53-57;
Jer 19:9;
La 2:20;
Eze 5:10
4:11
m Jer 17:27
n Dt 32:22;
Jer 7:20;
Eze 22:31
4:12
o 1Ki 9:9;
Jer 21:13
4:13
p Jer 5:31; 6:13;
Eze 22:28;
Mic 3:11
4:14
q Isa 59:10
r Jer 2:34; 19:4
4:15
s Lev 13:46
4:16
t Isa 9:14-16
u La 5:12
4:17
v Isa 20:5;
Eze 29:16
w La 1:7
x Jer 37:7

a 7 Or *lapis lazuli*

so we could not walk in our streets.
Our end was near, our days were numbered,
for our end had come. ᵛ

¹⁹Our pursuers were swifter
than eagles ᶻ in the sky;
they chased us ᵃ over the mountains
and lay in wait for us in the desert.

²⁰The Lᴏʀᴅ's anointed, ᵇ our very life breath,
was caught in their traps. ᶜ
We thought that under his shadow
we would live among the nations.

²¹Rejoice and be glad, O Daughter of Edom,
you who live in the land of Uz.
But to you also the cup ᵈ will be passed;
you will be drunk and stripped naked. ᵉ

²²O Daughter of Zion, your punishment will end; ᶠ
he will not prolong your exile.
But, O Daughter of Edom, he will punish your sin
and expose your wickedness. ᵍ

5 Remember, O Lᴏʀᴅ, what has happened to us;
look, and see our disgrace. ʰ
²Our inheritance ⁱ has been turned over to aliens,
our homes ʲ to foreigners.
³We have become orphans and fatherless,
our mothers like widows. ᵏ
⁴We must buy the water we drink;
our wood can be had only at a price. ˡ
⁵Those who pursue us are at our heels;
we are weary ᵐ and find no rest.
⁶We submitted to Egypt and Assyria ⁿ
to get enough bread.
⁷Our fathers sinned and are no more,
and we bear their punishment. ᵒ
⁸Slaves ᵖ rule over us,
and there is none to free us from their hands. �q
⁹We get our bread at the risk of our lives
because of the sword in the desert.
¹⁰Our skin is hot as an oven,
feverish from hunger. ʳ
¹¹Women have been ravished ˢ in Zion,
and virgins in the towns of Judah.
¹²Princes have been hung up by their hands;
elders are shown no respect. ᵗ
¹³Young men toil at the millstones;
boys stagger under loads of wood.
¹⁴The elders are gone from the city gate;
the young men have stopped their music. ᵘ
¹⁵Joy is gone from our hearts;
our dancing has turned to mourning. ᵛ

4:18
y Eze 7:2-12;
Am 8:2
4:19
z Dt 28:49
a Isa 5:26-28
4:20
b 2Sa 19:21
c Jer 39:5;
Eze 12:12-13;
19:4,8
4:21
d Jer 25:15
e Isa 34:6-10;
Am 1:11-12;
Ob 1:16
4:22
f Isa 40:2;
Jer 33:8
g Ps 137:7;
Mal 1:4
5:1
h Ps 44:13-16;
89:50
5:2
i Ps 79:1
j Zep 1:13
5:3
k Jer 15:8; 18:21
5:4
l Isa 3:1
5:5
m Ne 9:37
5:6
n Hos 9:3
5:7
o Jer 14:20;
16:12
5:8
p Ne 5:15
q Zec 11:6
5:10
r La 4:8-9
5:11
s Zec 14:2
5:12
t La 4:16
5:14
u Isa 24:8;
Jer 7:34
5:15
v Jer 25:10

5:16
wPs 89:39
xIsa 3:11
5:17
yIsa 1:5 zPs 6:7
5:18
aMic 3:12
5:19
bPs 45:6;
102:12,24-27
5:20
cPs 13:1; 44:24
5:21
dPs 80:3
5:22
eIsa 64:9

16The crown[w] has fallen from our head.
    Woe to us, for we have sinned![x]
17Because of this our hearts[y] are faint,
    because of these things our eyes[z] grow dim
18for Mount Zion, which lies desolate,[a]
    with jackals prowling over it.

19You, O LORD, reign forever;
    your throne endures[b] from generation to generation.
20Why do you always forget us?[c]
    Why do you forsake us so long?
21Restore[d] us to yourself, O LORD, that we may return;
    renew our days as of old
22unless you have utterly rejected us
    and are angry with us beyond measure.[e]

Ezekiel

Title and Background

This book is named after the prophet Ezekiel, whose name means "God is strong." The Babylonians laid siege to Jerusalem in 588 B.C., and in 586 the city and temple were burned. Israel's monarchy was ended; the City of David and the Lord's temple were no more.

Author and Date of Writing

Ezekiel was among the more than 3,000 Jews exiled to Babylon by Nebuchadnezzar in 597 B.C., and there among the exiles he received his call to become a prophet. As a priest-prophet called to minister to the exiles, his message had much to do with the temple and its ritual. Since the book of Ezekiel contains more dates than any other Biblical book, its prophecies can be dated with considerable precision. Ezekiel's period of activity coincides with Jerusalem's darkest hour. His messages are dated between 593 and 571 B.C.

Theme and Message

Nowhere in the Bible are God's initiative and control over all creation expressed more clearly and pervasively than in Ezekiel. This sovereign God resolved that he would be known and acknowledged, for at least 65 times we read the clause (or variations): "Then they will know that I am the Lord." God's total sovereignty is also evident in his mobility. He was not limited to the temple; he can respond to his people under any circumstance.

Outline

The Living Creatures and the Glory of the Lord

1 In the[a] thirtieth year, in the fourth month on the fifth day, while I was among the exiles[a] by the Kebar River, the heavens were opened[b] and I saw visions[c] of God.

2On the fifth of the month—it was the fifth year of the exile of King Jehoiachin[d]— 3the word of the Lord came to Ezekiel the priest, the son of Buzi,[b] by the Kebar River in the land of the Babylonians.[c] There the hand of the Lord was upon him. [e]

4I looked, and I saw a windstorm coming out of the north[f]—an immense cloud with flashing lightning and surrounded by brilliant light. The center of the fire looked like glowing metal,[g] 5and in the fire was what looked like four living creatures. [h] In appearance their form

1:1
a Eze 11:24-25
b Mt 3:16;
Ac 7:56
c Ex 24:10
1:2
d 2Ki 24:15
1:3
e 2Ki 3:15;
Eze 3:14,22
1:4
f Jer 1:14
g Eze 8:2
1:5
h Rev 4:6

---

a1 Or my;   b3 Or Ezekiel son of Buzi the priest   c3 Or Chaldeans was that of a man,[i] [6]but each of them had four faces[j] and four wings. [7]Their legs were straight; their feet were like those of a calf and gleamed like burnished bronze.[k] [8]Under their wings on their four sides they had the hands of a man.[l] All four of them had faces and wings, [9]and their wings touched one another. Each one went straight ahead; they did not turn as they moved.[m]

[10]Their faces looked like this: Each of the four had the face of a man, and on the right side each had the face of a lion, and on the left the face of an ox; each also had the face of an eagle.[n] [11]Such were their faces. Their wings[o] were spread out upward; each had two wings, one touching the wing of another creature on either side, and two wings covering its body. [12]Each one went straight ahead. Wherever the spirit would go, they would go, without turning as they went. [13]The appearance of the living creatures was like burning coals of fire or like torches. Fire moved back and forth among the creatures; it was bright, and lightning[p] flashed out of it. [14]The creatures sped back and forth like flashes of lightning.[q]

[15]As I looked at the living creatures, I saw a wheel on the ground beside each creature with its four faces. [16]This was the appearance and structure of the wheels: They sparkled like chrysolite,[r] and all four looked alike. Each appeared to be made like a wheel intersecting a wheel. [17]As they moved, they would go in any one of the four directions the creatures faced; the wheels did not turn[s] about[a] as the creatures went. [18]Their rims were high and awesome, and all four rims were full of eyes[t] all around.

[19]When the living creatures moved, the wheels beside them moved; and when the living creatures rose from the ground, the wheels also rose. [20]Wherever the spirit would go, they would go,[u] and the wheels would rise along with them, because the spirit of the living creatures was in the wheels. [21]When the creatures moved, they also moved; when the creatures stood still, they also stood still; and when the creatures rose from the ground, the wheels rose along with them, because the spirit of the living creatures was in the wheels.[v]

[22]Spread out above the heads of the living creatures was what looked like an expanse,[w] sparkling like ice, and awesome. [23]Under the expanse their wings were stretched out one toward the other, and each had two wings covering its body. [24]When the creatures moved, I heard the sound of their wings, like the roar of rushing waters, like the voice[x] of the Almighty,[b] like the tumult of an army.[y] When they stood still, they lowered their wings.

[25]Then there came a voice from above the expanse over their heads as they stood with lowered wings. [26]Above the expanse over their heads was what looked like a throne of sapphire,[c][z] and high above on the throne was a figure like that of a man.[a] [27]I saw that from what appeared to be his waist up he looked like glowing metal, as if full of fire, and that from there down he looked like fire; and brilliant light surrounded him.[b] [28]Like the appearance of a rainbow[c] in the clouds on a rainy day, so was the radiance around him.[d]

This was the appearance of the likeness of the glory[e] of the LORD. When I saw it, I fell facedown,[f] and I heard the voice of one speaking.

1:5
i ver 26
1:6
j Eze 10:14
1:7
k Da 10:6;
Rev 1:15
1:8
l Eze 10:8
1:9
m Eze 10:22
1:10
n Eze 10:14;
Rev 4:7
1:11
o Isa 6:2
1:13
p Rev 4:5
1:14
q Ps 29:7
1:16
r Eze 10:9-11;
Da 10:6
1:17
s ver 9
1:18
t Eze 10:12;
Rev 4:6
1:20
u ver 12
1:21
v Eze 10:17
1:22
w Eze 10:1
1:24
x Eze 10:5;
43:2; Da 10:6;
Rev 1:15; 19:6
y 2Ki 7:6
1:26
z Ex 24:10;
Eze 10:1
a Rev 1:13
1:27
b Eze 8:2
1:28
c Ge 9:13;
Rev 10:1
d Rev 4:2
e Eze 8:4
f Eze 3:23;
Da 8:17;
Rev 1:17

---

[a]17 Or *aside*   [b]24 Hebrew *Shaddai*   [c]26 Or *lapis lazuli*

Ezekiel's Call

2 He said to me, "Son of man, stand[g] up on your feet and I will speak to you." [2]As he spoke, the Spirit came into me and raised me[h] to my feet, and I heard him speaking to me.

[3]He said: "Son of man, I am sending you to the Israelites, to a rebellious nation that has rebelled against me; they and their fathers have been in revolt against me to this very day.[i] [4]The people to whom I am sending you are obstinate and stubborn.[j] Say to them, 'This is what the Sovereign LORD says.' [5]And whether they listen or fail to listen[k]—for they are a rebellious house[l]—they will know that a prophet has been among them.[m] [6]And you, son of man, do not be afraid[n] of them or their words. Do not be afraid, though briers and thorns[o] are all around you and you live among scorpions. Do not be afraid of what they say or terrified by them, though they are a rebellious house.[p] [7]You must speak my words to them, whether they listen or fail to listen, for they are rebellious.[q] [8]But you, son of man, listen to what I say to you. Do not rebel like that rebellious house;[r] open your mouth and eat[s] what I give you."

[9]Then I looked, and I saw a hand[t] stretched out to me. In it was a scroll, [10]which he unrolled before me. On both sides of it were written words of lament and mourning and woe.[u]

3 And he said to me, "Son of man, eat what is before you, eat this scroll; then go and speak to the house of Israel." [2]So I opened my mouth, and he gave me the scroll to eat.

[3]Then he said to me, "Son of man, eat this scroll I am giving you and fill your stomach with it." So I ate[v] it, and it tasted as sweet as honey[w] in my mouth.

[4]He then said to me: "Son of man, go now to the house of Israel and speak my words to them. [5]You are not being sent to a people of obscure speech and difficult language,[x] but to the house of Israel— [6]not to many peoples of obscure speech and difficult language, whose words you cannot understand. Surely if I had sent you to them, they would have listened to you.[y] [7]But the house of Israel is not willing to listen to you because they are not willing to listen to me, for the whole house of Israel is hardened and obstinate.[z] [8]But I will make you as unyielding and hardened as they are.[a] [9]I will make your forehead like the hardest stone, harder than flint. Do not be afraid of them or terrified by them, though they are a rebellious house.[b]"

[10]And he said to me, "Son of man, listen carefully and take to heart all the words I speak to you. [11]Go now to your countrymen in exile and speak to them. Say to them, 'This is what the Sovereign LORD says,' whether they listen or fail to listen.[c]"

[12]Then the Spirit lifted me up,[d] and I heard behind me a loud rumbling sound—May the glory of the LORD be praised in his dwelling place!— [13]the sound of the wings of the living creatures brushing against each other and the sound of the wheels beside them, a loud rumbling sound.[e] [14]The Spirit then lifted me up and took me away, and I went in bitterness and in the anger of my spirit, with the strong hand of the LORD upon me. [15]I came to the exiles who lived at Tel Abib near the Kebar River.[f] And there, where they were living, I sat among them for seven days[g]—overwhelmed.

2:1
gDa 10:11
2:2
hEze 3:24;
Da 8:18
2:3
iJer 3:25;
Eze 20:8-24
2:4
jEze 3:7
2:5
kEze 3:11
lEze 3:27
mEze 33:33
2:6
nJer 1:8,17
oIsa 9:18;
Mic 7:4
pEze 3:9
2:7
qJer 1:7;
Eze 3:10-11
2:8
rIsa 50:5
sJer 15:16;
Rev 10:9
2:9
tEze 8:3
2:10
uRev 8:13
3:3
vJer 15:16
wPs 19:10;
Ps 119:103;
Rev 10:9-10
3:5
xIsa 28:11;
Jnh 1:2
3:6
yMt 11:21-23
3:7
zEze 2:4;
Jn 15:20-23
3:8
aJer 1:18
3:9
bIsa 50:7;
Eze 2:6;
Mic 3:8
3:11
cEze 2:4-5,7
3:12
dEze 8:3;
Ac 8:39
3:13
eEze 1:24;
10:5,16-17
3:15
fPs 137:1
gJob 2:13

Warning to Israel

¹⁶At the end of seven days the word of the LORD came to me:^h ¹⁷"Son of man, I have made you a watchmanⁱ for the house of Israel; so hear the word I speak and give them warning from me. ¹⁸When I say to a wicked man, 'You will surely die,' and you do not warn him or speak out to dissuade him from his evil ways in order to save his life, that wicked man will die for^a his sin, and I will hold you accountable for his blood.^j ¹⁹But if you do warn the wicked man and he does not turn from his wickedness or from his evil ways, he will die for his sin; but you will have saved yourself.^k

²⁰"Again, when a righteous man turns from his righteousness and does evil, and I put a stumbling block before him, he will die. Since you did not warn him, he will die for his sin. The righteous things he did will not be remembered, and I will hold you accountable for his blood.^l ²¹But if you do warn the righteous man not to sin and he does not sin, he will surely live because he took warning, and you will have saved yourself.^m"

²²The hand of the LORDⁿ was upon me there, and he said to me, "Get up and go^o out to the plain,^p and there I will speak to you." ²³So I got up and went out to the plain. And the glory of the LORD was standing there, like the glory I had seen by the Kebar River,^q and I fell face-down.^r

²⁴Then the Spirit came into me and raised me^s to my feet. He spoke to me and said: "Go, shut yourself inside your house. ²⁵And you, son of man, they will tie with ropes; you will be bound so that you cannot go out among the people.^t ²⁶I will make your tongue stick to the roof of your mouth so that you will be silent and unable to rebuke them, though they are a rebellious house.^u ²⁷But when I speak to you, I will open your mouth and you shall say to them, 'This is what the Sovereign LORD says.'^v Whoever will listen let him listen, and whoever will refuse let him refuse; for they are a rebellious house.^w

Siege of Jerusalem Symbolized

4 "Now, son of man, take a clay tablet, put it in front of you and draw the city of Jerusalem on it. ²Then lay siege to it: Erect siege works against it, build a ramp^x up to it, set up camps against it and put battering rams around it.^y ³Then take an iron pan, place it as an iron wall between you and the city and turn your face toward it. It will be under siege, and you shall besiege it. This will be a sign^z to the house of Israel.^a

⁴"Then lie on your left side and put the sin of the house of Israel upon yourself.^b You are to bear their sin for the number of days you lie on your side. ⁵I have assigned you the same number of days as the years of their sin. So for 390 days you will bear the sin of the house of Israel.

⁶"After you have finished this, lie down again, this time on your right side, and bear the sin of the house of Judah. I have assigned you 40 days, a day for each year.^b ⁷Turn your face toward the siege of Jerusalem and with bared arm prophesy against her. ⁸I will tie you up with

### Cross references (margin)

3:16
h Jer 42:7
3:17
i Isa 52:8;
Jer 6:17;
Eze 33:7-9
3:18
j ver 20;
Eze 33:6
3:19
k 2Ki 17:13;
Eze 14:14,20;
Ac 18:6; 20:26;
1Ti 4:14-16
3:20
l Ps 125:5;
Eze 18:24;
33:12,18
3:21
m Ac 20:31
3:22
n Eze 1:3
o Ac 9:6
p Eze 8:4
3:23
q Eze 1:1
r Eze 1:28
3:24
s Eze 2:2
3:25
t Eze 4:8
3:26
u Eze 2:5;
24:27; 33:22
3:27
v ver 11
w Eze 12:3;
24:27; 33:22
4:2
x Jer 6:6
y Eze 21:22
4:3
z Isa 8:18; 20:3;
Eze 12:3-6;
24:24,27
a Jer 39:1
4:6
b Nu 14:34;
Da 9:24-26;
12:11-12

---

^a18 Or *in*; also in verses 19 and 20   ^b4 Or *your side*

ropes so that you cannot turn from one side to the other until you have finished the days of your siege. [c]

[9]"Take wheat and barley, beans and lentils, millet and spelt;[d] put them in a storage jar and use them to make bread for yourself. You are to eat it during the 390 days you lie on your side. [10]Weigh out twenty shekels[a] of food to eat each day and eat it at set times. [11]Also measure out a sixth of a hin[b] of water and drink it at set times. [12]Eat the food as you would a barley cake; bake it in the sight of the people, using human excrement[e] for fuel." [13]The LORD said, "In this way the people of Israel will eat defiled food among the nations where I will drive them."[f]

[14]Then I said, "Not so, Sovereign LORD![g] I have never defiled myself. From my youth until now I have never eaten anything found dead[h] or torn by wild animals. No unclean meat has ever entered my mouth.[i]"

[15]"Very well," he said, "I will let you bake your bread over cow manure instead of human excrement."

[16]He then said to me: "Son of man, I will cut off[j] the supply of food in Jerusalem. The people will eat rationed food in anxiety and drink rationed water in despair,[k] [17]for food and water will be scarce. They will be appalled at the sight of each other and will waste away because of[c] their sin.[l]

5 "Now, son of man, take a sharp sword and use it as a barber's razor[m] to shave[n] your head and your beard.[o] Then take a set of scales and divide up the hair. [2]When the days of your siege come to an end, burn a third of the hair with fire inside the city. Take a third and strike it with the sword all around the city. And scatter a third to the wind. For I will pursue them with drawn sword.[p] [3]But take a few strands of hair and tuck them away in the folds of your garment.[q] [4]Again, take a few of these and throw them into the fire and burn them up. A fire will spread from there to the whole house of Israel.

[5]"This is what the Sovereign LORD says: This is Jerusalem, which I have set in the center of the nations, with countries all around her. [6]Yet in her wickedness she has rebelled against my laws and decrees more than the nations and countries around her. She has rejected my laws and has not followed my decrees.[r]

[7]"Therefore this is what the Sovereign LORD says: You have been more unruly than the nations around you and have not followed my decrees or kept my laws. You have not even[d] conformed to the standards of the nations around you.[s]

[8]"Therefore this is what the Sovereign LORD says: I myself am against you, Jerusalem, and I will inflict punishment on you in the sight of the nations.[t] [9]Because of all your detestable idols, I will do to you what I have never done before and will never do again.[u] [10]Therefore in your midst fathers will eat their children, and children will eat their fathers.[v] I will inflict punishment on you and will scatter all your survivors to the winds.[w] [11]Therefore as surely as I live, declares the Sovereign LORD, because you have defiled my sanctuary with all your vile images[x] and detestable practices,[y] I myself will withdraw my favor; I will not look on you with pity or spare you.[z] [12]A third of your people will die of the plague or perish by famine inside you; a third will fall by the sword

Cross references

4:8
c Eze 3:25
4:9
d Isa 28:25
4:12
e Isa 36:12
4:13
f Hos 9:3
4:14
g Jer 1:6;
Eze 9:8; 20:49
h Lev 11:39
i Ex 22:31;
Dt 14:3;
Ac 10:14
4:16
j Ps 105:16;
Eze 5:16
k ver 10-11;
Lev 26:26;
Isa 3:1;
Eze 12:19
4:17
l Lev 26:39;
Eze 24:23;
33:10
5:1
m Isa 7:20
n Eze 44:20
o Lev 21:5
5:2
p ver 12;
Lev 26:33
5:3
q Jer 39:10
5:6
r Jer 11:10;
Eze 16:47-51;
Zec 7:11
5:7
s 2Ch 33:9;
Jer 2:10-11;
Eze 16:47
5:8
t Eze 15:7
5:9
u Da 9:12;
Mt 24:21
5:10
v Lev 26:29;
La 2:20
w Lev 26:33;
Ps 44:11;
Eze 12:14;
Zec 2:6
5:11
x Eze 7:20
y 2Ch 36:14;
Eze 8:6
z Eze 7:4,9

---

[a]10 That is, about 8 ounces (about 0.2 kilogram)   [b]11 That is, about 2/3 quart (about 0.6 liter)
[c]17 Or *away in*   [d]7 Most Hebrew manuscripts; some Hebrew manuscripts and Syriac *You have*

outside your walls; and a third I will scatter to the winds and pursue with drawn sword. ª

13"Then my anger will cease and my wrath ᵇ against them will subside, and I will be avenged. ᶜ And when I have spent my wrath upon them, they will know that I the LORD have spoken in my zeal.

14"I will make you a ruin and a reproach among the nations around you, in the sight of all who pass by. ᵈ 15You will be a reproach and a taunt, a warning and an object of horror to the nations around you when I inflict punishment on you in anger and in wrath and with stinging rebuke. ᵉ I the LORD have spoken. ᶠ 16When I shoot at you with my deadly and destructive arrows of famine, I will shoot to destroy you. I will bring more and more famine upon you and cut off your supply of food. ᵍ 17I will send famine and wild beasts against you, and they will leave you childless. Plague and bloodshed ʰ will sweep through you, and I will bring the sword against you. I the LORD have spoken. ⁱ "

A Prophecy Against the Mountains of Israel

6 The word of the LORD came to me: 2"Son of man, set your face against the mountains ʲ of Israel; prophesy against them 3and say: 'O mountains of Israel, hear the word of the Sovereign LORD. This is what the Sovereign LORD says to the mountains and hills, to the ravines and valleys: ᵏ I am about to bring a sword against you, and I will destroy your high places. ˡ 4Your altars will be demolished and your incense altars ᵐ will be smashed; and I will slay your people in front of your idols. 5I will lay the dead bodies of the Israelites in front of their idols, and I will scatter your bones ⁿ around your altars. 6Wherever you live, the towns will be laid waste and the high places demolished, so that your altars will be laid waste and devastated, your idols ᵒ smashed and ruined, your incense altars ᵖ broken down, and what you have made wiped out. �q 7Your people will fall slain among you, and you will know that I am the LORD.

8" 'But I will spare some, for some of you will escape ʳ the sword when you are scattered among the lands and nations. ˢ 9Then in the nations where they have been carried captive, those who escape will remember me—how I have been grieved ᵗ by their adulterous hearts, which have turned away from me, and by their eyes, which have lusted after their idols. ᵘ They will loathe themselves for the evil they have done and for all their detestable practices. ᵛ 10And they will know that I am the LORD; I did not threaten in vain to bring this calamity on them.

11" 'This is what the Sovereign LORD says: Strike your hands together and stamp your feet and cry out "Alas!" because of all the wicked and detestable practices of the house of Israel, for they will fall by the sword, famine and plague. ʷ 12He that is far away will die of the plague, and he that is near will fall by the sword, and he that survives and is spared will die of famine. So will I spend my wrath upon them. ˣ 13And they will know that I am the LORD, when their people lie slain among their idols around their altars, on every high hill and on all the mountaintops, under every spreading tree and every leafy oak ʸ—places where they offered fragrant incense to all their idols. ᶻ 14And I will

5:12
ªver 2,17;
Jer 15:2; 21:9;
Eze 6:11-12;
12:14
5:13
ᵇEze 21:17;
36:6
ᶜIsa 1:24
5:14
ᵈLev 26:32;
Ne 2:17;
Ps 74:3-10;
79:1-4
5:15
ᵉ1Ki 9:7;
Jer 22:8-9; 24:9
ᶠEze 25:17
5:16
ᵍDt 32:24
5:17
ʰEze 38:22
ⁱEze 14:21
6:2
ʲEze 36:1
6:3
ᵏEze 36:4
ˡLev 26:30
6:4
ᵐ2Ch 14:5
6:5
ⁿJer 8:1-2
6:6
ᵒMic 1:7;
Zec 13:2
ᵖLev 26:30
qIsa 6:11;
Eze 5:14
6:8
ʳJer 44:28
ˢIsa 6:13;
Jer 44:14;
Eze 12:16;
14:22
6:9
ᵗPs 78:40;
Isa 7:13
ᵘEze 20:7,24
ᵛEze 20:43;
36:31
6:11
ʷEze 5:12;
21:14,17; 25:6
6:12
ˣEze 5:12
6:13
ʸIsa 57:5
ᶻ1Ki 14:23;
Jer 2:20;
Eze 20:28;
Hos 4:13

stretch out my hand[a] against them and make the land a desolate waste from the desert to Diblah[a]—wherever they live. Then they will know that I am the Lord. [b]' "

The End Has Come

7 The word of the Lord came to me: [2]"Son of man, this is what the Sovereign Lord says to the land of Israel: The end![c] The end has come upon the four corners[d] of the land. [3]The end is now upon you and I will unleash my anger against you. I will judge you according to your conduct and repay you for all your detestable practices. [4]I will not look on you with pity[e] or spare you; I will surely repay you for your conduct and the detestable practices among you. Then you will know that I am the Lord.

[5]"This is what the Sovereign Lord says: Disaster![f] An unheard-of[b] disaster is coming. [6]The end has come! The end has come! It has roused itself against you. It has come! [7]Doom has come upon you—you who dwell in the land. The time has come, the day is near;[g] there is panic, not joy, upon the mountains. [8]I am about to pour out my wrath[h] on you and spend my anger against you; I will judge you according to your conduct and repay you for all your detestable practices. [i] [9]I will not look on you with pity or spare you; I will repay you in accordance with your conduct and the detestable practices among you. Then you will know that it is I the Lord who strikes the blow.

[10]"The day is here! It has come! Doom has burst forth, the rod[j] has budded, arrogance has blossomed! [11]Violence has grown into[c] a rod to punish wickedness; none of the people will be left, none of that crowd—no wealth, nothing of value. [k] [12]The time has come, the day has arrived. Let not the buyer rejoice nor the seller grieve, for wrath is upon the whole crowd. [l] [13]The seller will not recover the land he has sold as long as both of them live, for the vision concerning the whole crowd will not be reversed. Because of their sins, not one of them will preserve his life. [m] [14]Though they blow the trumpet and get everything ready, no one will go into battle, for my wrath is upon the whole crowd.

[15]"Outside is the sword, inside are plague and famine; those in the country will die by the sword, and those in the city will be devoured by famine and plague. [n] [16]All who survive and escape will be in the mountains, moaning like doves[o] of the valleys, each because of his sins.[p] [17]Every hand will go limp, [q] and every knee will become as weak as water. [18]They will put on sackcloth and be clothed with terror. [r] Their faces will be covered with shame and their heads will be shaved. [s] [19]They will throw their silver into the streets, and their gold will be an unclean thing. Their silver and gold will not be able to save them in the day of the Lord's wrath. [t] They will not satisfy their hunger or fill their stomachs with it, for it has made them stumble[u] into sin. [v] [20]They were proud of their beautiful jewelry and used it to make their detestable idols and vile images. [w] Therefore I will turn these into an unclean thing for them. [21]I will hand it all over as plunder to foreigners and as loot to the wicked of the earth, and they will defile it. [x] [22]I will turn my face[y]

6:14
a Isa 5:25
b Eze 14:13
7:2
c Am 8:2,10
d Rev 7:1; 20:8
7:4
e Eze 5:11
7:5
f 2Ki 21:12
7:7
g Eze 12:23;
Zep 1:14
7:8
h Isa 42:25;
Eze 9:8; 14:19;
Na 1:6
i Eze 20:8,21;
36:19
7:10
j Ps 89:32;
Isa 10:5
7:11
k Jer 16:6;
Zep 1:18
7:12
l ver 7;
Isa 5:13-14;
Eze 30:3
7:13
m Lev 25:24-28
7:15
n Dt 32:25;
Jer 14:18;
La 1:20;
Eze 5:12
7:16
o Isa 59:11
p Ezr 9:15;
Eze 6:8
7:17
q Isa 13:7;
Eze 21:7; 22:14
7:18
r Ps 55:5
s Isa 15:2-3;
Eze 27:31;
Am 8:10
7:19
t Eze 13:5;
Zep 1:7,18
u Eze 14:3
v Pr 11:4
7:20
w Jer 7:30
7:21
x 2Ki 24:13
7:22
y Eze 39:23-24

---

[a]14 Most Hebrew manuscripts; a few Hebrew manuscripts *Riblah*   [b]5 Most Hebrew manuscripts; some Hebrew manuscripts and Syriac *Disaster after*   [c]11 Or *The violent one has become*

away from them, and they will desecrate my treasured place; robbers will enter it and desecrate it.

23"Prepare chains, because the land is full of bloodshed^z and the city is full of violence. 24I will bring the most wicked of the nations to take possession of their houses; I will put an end to the pride of the mighty, and their sanctuaries^a will be desecrated.^b 25When terror comes, they will seek peace, but there will be none.^c 26Calamity upon calamity^d will come, and rumor upon rumor. They will try to get a vision from the prophet; the teaching of the law by the priest will be lost, as will the counsel of the elders.^e 27The king will mourn, the prince will be clothed with despair,^f and the hands of the people of the land will tremble. I will deal with them according to their conduct,^g and by their own standards I will judge them. Then they will know that I am the Lord.^h"

Idolatry in the Temple

8 In the sixth year, in the sixth month on the fifth day, while I was sitting in my house and the eldersⁱ of Judah were sitting before^j me, the hand of the Sovereign Lord came upon me there.^k 2I looked, and I saw a figure like that of a man.^a From what appeared to be his waist down he was like fire, and from there up his appearance was as bright as glowing metal.^l 3He stretched out what looked like a hand and took me by the hair of my head. The Spirit lifted me up^m between earth and heaven and in visions of God he took me to Jerusalem, to the entrance to the north gate of the inner court, where the idol that provokes to jealousyⁿ stood. 4And there before me was the glory^o of the God of Israel, as in the vision I had seen in the plain.^p

5Then he said to me, "Son of man, look toward the north." So I looked, and in the entrance north of the gate of the altar I saw this idol^q of jealousy.

6And he said to me, "Son of man, do you see what they are doing —the utterly detestable^r things the house of Israel is doing here, things that will drive me far from my sanctuary? But you will see things that are even more detestable."

7Then he brought me to the entrance to the court. I looked, and I saw a hole in the wall. 8He said to me, "Son of man, now dig into the wall." So I dug into the wall and saw a doorway there.

9And he said to me, "Go in and see the wicked and detestable things they are doing here." 10So I went in and looked, and I saw portrayed all over the walls all kinds of crawling things and detestable animals and all the idols of the house of Israel.^s 11In front of them stood seventy elders of the house of Israel, and Jaazaniah son of Shaphan was standing among them. Each had a censer^t in his hand, and a fragrant cloud of incense^u was rising.

12He said to me, "Son of man, have you seen what the elders of the house of Israel are doing in the darkness, each at the shrine of his own idol? They say, 'The Lord does not see^v us; the Lord has forsaken the land.'" 13Again, he said, "You will see them doing things that are even more detestable."

14Then he brought me to the entrance to the north gate of the house of the Lord, and I saw women sitting there, mourning for Tammuz.

7:23
z2Ki 21:16
7:24
aEze 24:21
b2Ch 7:20;
Eze 28:7
7:25
cEze 13:10,16
7:26
dJer 4:20
eIsa 47:11;
Eze 20:1-3;
Mic 3:6
7:27
fPs 109:19;
Eze 26:16
gEze 18:20
hver 4
8:1
iEze 14:1
jEze 33:31
kEze 1:1-3
8:2
lEze 1:4,26-27
8:3
mEze 3:12; 11:1
nEx 20:5;
Dt 32:16
8:4
oEze 1:28
pEze 3:22
8:5
qPs 78:58;
Jer 32:34
8:6
rEze 5:11
8:10
sEx 20:4
8:11
tNu 16:17
uNu 16:35
8:12
vPs 10:11;
Isa 29:15;
Eze 9:9

^a2 Or *saw a fiery figure*

[15]He said to me, "Do you see this, son of man? You will see things that are even more detestable than this."

[16]He then brought me into the inner court of the house of the LORD, and there at the entrance to the temple, between the portico and the altar,[w] were about twenty-five men. With their backs toward the temple of the LORD and their faces toward the east, they were bowing down to the sun in the east.[x]

[17]He said to me, "Have you seen this, son of man? Is it a trivial matter for the house of Judah to do the detestable things they are doing here? Must they also fill the land with violence[y] and continually provoke me to anger?[z] Look at them putting the branch to their nose! [18]Therefore I will deal with them in anger; I will not look on them with pity[a] or spare them. Although they shout in my ears, I will not listen[b] to them."

Idolaters Killed

9 Then I heard him call out in a loud voice, "Bring the guards of the city here, each with a weapon in his hand." [2]And I saw six men coming from the direction of the upper gate, which faces north, each with a deadly weapon in his hand. With them was a man clothed in linen[c] who had a writing kit at his side. They came in and stood beside the bronze altar.

[3]Now the glory[d] of the God of Israel went up from above the cherubim,[e] where it had been, and moved to the threshold of the temple. Then the LORD called to the man clothed in linen who had the writing kit at his side [4]and said to him, "Go throughout the city of Jerusalem and put a mark[f] on the foreheads of those who grieve and lament[g] over all the detestable things that are done in it.[h]"

[5]As I listened, he said to the others, "Follow him through the city and kill, without showing pity[i] or compassion. [6]Slaughter old men, young men and maidens, women and children, but do not touch anyone who has the mark. Begin at my sanctuary." So they began with the elders[j] who were in front of the temple.[k]

[7]Then he said to them, "Defile the temple and fill the courts with the slain. Go!" So they went out and began killing throughout the city. [8]While they were killing and I was left alone, I fell facedown,[l] crying out, "Ah, Sovereign LORD! Are you going to destroy the entire remnant of Israel in this outpouring of your wrath on Jerusalem?[m]"

[9]He answered me, "The sin of the house of Israel and Judah is exceedingly great; the land is full of bloodshed and the city is full of injustice.[n] They say, 'The LORD has forsaken the land; the LORD does not see.'[o] [10]So I will not look on them with pity[p] or spare them, but I will bring down on their own heads what they have done.[q]"

[11]Then the man in linen with the writing kit at his side brought back word, saying, "I have done as you commanded."

The Glory Departs From the Temple

10 I looked, and I saw the likeness of a throne[r] of sapphire[a s] above the expanse[t] that was over the heads of the cherubim. [2]The LORD said to the man clothed in linen,[u] "Go in among the wheels[v] beneath the cherubim. Fill[w] your hands with burning coals from among

[a]1 Or *lapis lazuli*

8:16
w Joel 2:17
x Dt 4:19; 17:3;
Job 31:28;
Jer 2:27;
Eze 11:1,12
8:17
y Eze 9:9
z Eze 16:26
8:18
a Eze 9:10;
24:14 b Isa 1:15;
Jer 11:11;
Mic 3:4;
Zec 7:13
9:2
c Lev 16:4;
Eze 10:2;
Rev 15:6
9:3
d Eze 10:4
e Eze 11:22
9:4
f Ex 12:7;
2Co 1:22;
Rev 7:3; 9:4
g Ps 119:136;
Jer 13:17;
Eze 21:6
h Ps 119:53
9:5
i Eze 5:11
9:6
j Eze 8:11-13,16
k 2Ch 36:17;
Jer 25:29;
1Pe 4:17
9:8
l Jos 7:6
m Eze 11:13;
Am 7:1-6
9:9
n Eze 22:29
o Job 22:13;
Eze 8:12
9:10
p Eze 7:4; 8:18
q Isa 65:6;
Eze 11:21
10:1
r Rev 4:2
s Ex 24:10
t Eze 1:22
10:2
u Eze 9:2
v Eze 1:15
w Rev 8:5

the cherubim and scatter them over the city." And as I watched, he went in.

[3]Now the cherubim were standing on the south side of the temple when the man went in, and a cloud filled the inner court. [4]Then the glory of the LORD[x] rose from above the cherubim and moved to the threshold of the temple. The cloud filled the temple, and the court was full of the radiance of the glory of the LORD. [5]The sound of the wings of the cherubim could be heard as far away as the outer court, like the voice[y] of God Almighty[a] when he speaks.

[6]When the LORD commanded the man in linen, "Take fire from among the wheels, from among the cherubim," the man went in and stood beside a wheel. [7]Then one of the cherubim reached out his hand to the fire that was among them. He took up some of it and put it into the hands of the man in linen, who took it and went out. [8](Under the wings of the cherubim could be seen what looked like the hands of a man.)[z]

[9]I looked, and I saw beside the cherubim four wheels, one beside each of the cherubim; the wheels sparkled like chrysolite.[a] [10]As for their appearance, the four of them looked alike; each was like a wheel intersecting a wheel. [11]As they moved, they would go in any one of the four directions the cherubim faced; the wheels did not turn about[b] as the cherubim went. The cherubim went in whatever direction the head faced, without turning as they went. [12]Their entire bodies, including their backs, their hands and their wings, were completely full of eyes,[b] as were their four wheels.[c] [13]I heard the wheels being called "the whirling wheels." [14]Each of the cherubim[d] had four faces:[e] One face was that of a cherub, the second the face of a man, the third the face of a lion, and the fourth the face of an eagle.[f]

[15]Then the cherubim rose upward. These were the living creatures[g] I had seen by the Kebar River. [16]When the cherubim moved, the wheels beside them moved; and when the cherubim spread their wings to rise from the ground, the wheels did not leave their side. [17]When the cherubim stood still, they also stood still; and when the cherubim rose, they rose with them, because the spirit of the living creatures was in them.[h]

[18]Then the glory of the LORD departed from over the threshold of the temple and stopped above the cherubim.[i] [19]While I watched, the cherubim spread their wings and rose from the ground, and as they went, the wheels went with them.[j] They stopped at the entrance to the east gate of the LORD's house, and the glory of the God of Israel was above them.

[20]These were the living creatures I had seen beneath the God of Israel by the Kebar River,[k] and I realized that they were cherubim. [21]Each had four faces[l] and four wings,[m] and under their wings was what looked like the hands of a man. [22]Their faces had the same appearance as those I had seen by the Kebar River. Each one went straight ahead.

Judgment on Israel's Leaders

11 Then the Spirit lifted me up and brought me to the gate of the house of the LORD that faces east. There at the entrance to the

---

10:4
xEze 1:28; 9:3
10:5
yJob 40:9;
Eze 1:24
10:8
zEze 1:8
10:9
aEze 1:15-16;
Rev 21:20
10:12
bRev 4:6-8
cEze 1:15-21
10:14
d1Ki 7:36
eEze 1:6
fEze 1:10;
Rev 4:7
10:15
gEze 1:3,5
10:17
hEze 1:20-21
10:18
iPs 18:10
10:19
jEze 11:1,22
10:20
kEze 1:1
10:21
lEze 41:18
mEze 1:6

---

[a]5 Hebrew *El-Shaddai*   [b]11 Or *aside*

gate were twenty-five men, and I saw among them Jaazaniah son of Azzur and Pelatiah son of Benaiah, leaders of the people.[n] [2]The LORD said to me, "Son of man, these are the men who are plotting evil and giving wicked advice in this city. [3]They say, 'Will it not soon be time to build houses?[a] This city is a cooking pot,[o] and we are the meat.'[p] [4]Therefore prophesy[q] against them; prophesy, son of man.''

[5]Then the Spirit of the LORD came upon me, and he told me to say: "This is what the LORD says: That is what you are saying, O house of Israel, but I know what is going through your mind.[r] [6]You have killed many people in this city and filled its streets with the dead.[s]

[7]"Therefore this is what the Sovereign LORD says: The bodies you have thrown there are the meat and this city is the pot, but I will drive you out of it.[t] [8]You fear the sword, and the sword is what I will bring against you, declares the Sovereign LORD.[u] [9]I will drive you out of the city and hand you over[v] to foreigners and inflict punishment on you.[w] [10]You will fall by the sword, and I will execute judgment on you at the borders of Israel.[x] Then you will know that I am the LORD. [11]This city will not be a pot[y] for you, nor will you be the meat in it; I will execute judgment on you at the borders of Israel. [12]And you will know that I am the LORD, for you have not followed my decrees[z] or kept my laws but have conformed to the standards of the nations around you.[a]''

[13]Now as I was prophesying, Pelatiah[b] son of Benaiah died. Then I fell facedown and cried out in a loud voice, "Ah, Sovereign LORD! Will you completely destroy the remnant of Israel?[c]''

[14]The word of the LORD came to me: [15]"Son of man, your brothers —your brothers who are your blood relatives[b] and the whole house of Israel—are those of whom the people of Jerusalem have said, 'They are[c] far away from the LORD; this land was given to us as our possession.'[d]

Promised Return of Israel

[16]"Therefore say: 'This is what the Sovereign LORD says: Although I sent them far away among the nations and scattered them among the countries, yet for a little while I have been a sanctuary[e] for them in the countries where they have gone.'

[17]"Therefore say: 'This is what the Sovereign LORD says: I will gather you from the nations and bring you back from the countries where you have been scattered, and I will give you back the land of Israel again.'[f]

[18]"They will return to it and remove all its vile images[g] and detestable idols.[h] [19]I will give them an undivided heart[i] and put a new spirit in them; I will remove from them their heart of stone[j] and give them a heart of flesh.[k] [20]Then they will follow my decrees and be careful to keep my laws.[l] They will be my people, and I will be their God.[m] [21]But as for those whose hearts are devoted to their vile images and detestable idols, I will bring down on their own heads what they have done, declares the Sovereign LORD.[n]''

[22]Then the cherubim, with the wheels beside them, spread their wings, and the glory of the God of Israel was above them.[o] [23]The glory[p] of the LORD went up from within the city and stopped above the

11:1
nEze 8:16;
10:19; 43:4-5
11:3
oJer 1:13;
Eze 24:3
pver 7,11
11:4
qEze 3:4,17
11:5
rJer 17:10
11:6
sEze 7:23; 22:6
11:7
tEze 24:3-13;
Mic 3:2-3
11:8
uPr 10:24
11:9
vPs 106:41
wDt 28:36;
Eze 5:8
11:10
x2Ki 14:25
11:11
yver 3
11:12
zLev 18:4;
Eze 18:9
aEze 8:10
11:13
bver 1 cEze 9:8
11:15
dEze 33:24
11:16
ePs 90:1; 91:9;
Isa 8:14
11:17
fJer 3:18;
24:5-6;
Eze 28:25;
34:13
11:18
gEze 5:11
hEze 37:23
11:19
iJer 32:39
jZec 7:12
kEze 18:31;
36:26; 2Co 3:3
11:20
lPs 105:45
mEze 14:11;
36:26-28
11:21
nEze 9:10;
16:43
11:22
oEze 10:19
11:23
pEze 8:4; 10:4

---

[a]3 Or *This is not the time to build houses.*   [b]15 Or *are in exile with you* (see Septuagint and Syriac)
[c]15 Or *those to whom the people of Jerusalem have said, 'Stay*

mountain⁹ east of it. ²⁴The Spirit ʳ lifted me up and brought me to the exiles in Babylonia ᵃ in the vision ˢ given by the Spirit of God.

Then the vision I had seen went up from me, ²⁵and I told the exiles everything the Lᴏʀᴅ had shown me. ᵗ

The Exile Symbolized

12 The word of the Lᴏʀᴅ came to me: ²"Son of man, you are living among a rebellious people. They have eyes to see but do not see and ears to hear but do not hear, for they are a rebellious people. ᵘ

³"Therefore, son of man, pack your belongings for exile and in the daytime, as they watch, set out and go from where you are to another place. Perhaps ᵛ they will understand, ʷ though they are a rebellious house. ˣ ⁴During the daytime, while they watch, bring out your belongings packed for exile. Then in the evening, while they are watching, go out like those who go into exile. ʸ ⁵While they watch, dig through the wall and take your belongings out through it. ⁶Put them on your shoulder as they are watching and carry them out at dusk. Cover your face so that you cannot see the land, for I have made you a sign ᶻ to the house of Israel."

⁷So I did as I was commanded. ᵃ During the day I brought out my things packed for exile. Then in the evening I dug through the wall with my hands. I took my belongings out at dusk, carrying them on my shoulders while they watched.

⁸In the morning the word of the Lᴏʀᴅ came to me: ⁹"Son of man, did not that rebellious house of Israel ask you, 'What are you doing?' ᵇ

¹⁰"Say to them, 'This is what the Sovereign Lᴏʀᴅ says: This oracle concerns the prince in Jerusalem and the whole house of Israel who are there.' ¹¹Say to them, 'I am a sign to you.'

"As I have done, so it will be done to them. They will go into exile as captives. ᶜ

¹²"The prince among them will put his things on his shoulder at dusk ᵈ and leave, and a hole will be dug in the wall for him to go through. He will cover his face so that he cannot see the land. ᵉ ¹³I will spread my net ᶠ for him, and he will be caught in my snare; ᵍ I will bring him to Babylonia, the land of the Chaldeans, but he will not see ʰ it, and there he will die. ⁱ ¹⁴I will scatter to the winds all those around him—his staff and all his troops—and I will pursue them with drawn sword. ʲ

¹⁵"They will know that I am the Lᴏʀᴅ, when I disperse them among the nations and scatter them through the countries. ¹⁶But I will spare a few of them from the sword, famine and plague, so that in the nations where they go they may acknowledge all their detestable practices. Then they will know that I am the Lᴏʀᴅ. ᵏ"

¹⁷The word of the Lᴏʀᴅ came to me: ¹⁸"Son of man, tremble as you eat your food, ˡ and shudder in fear as you drink your water. ¹⁹Say to the people of the land: 'This is what the Sovereign Lᴏʀᴅ says about those living in Jerusalem and in the land of Israel: They will eat their food in anxiety and drink their water in despair, for their land will be stripped of everything ᵐ in it because of the violence of all who live there. ⁿ ²⁰The inhabited towns will be laid waste and the land will be desolate. Then you will know that I am the Lᴏʀᴅ. ᵒ'"

11:23
qZec 14:4
11:24
rEze 8:3
s2Co 12:2-4
11:25
tEze 3:4,11
12:2
uIsa 6:10;
Eze 2:6-8;
Mt 13:15
12:3
vJer 36:3
wJer 26:3
x2Ti 2:25-26
12:4
yver 12;
Jer 39:4
12:6
zver 12;
Isa 8:18; 20:3;
Eze 4:3; 24:24
12:7
aEze 24:18;
37:10
12:9
bEze 17:12;
20:49; 24:19
12:11
c2Ki 25:7;
Jer 15:2; 52:15
12:12
dJer 39:4
eJer 52:7
12:13
fEze 17:20;
19:8; Hos 7:12
gIsa 24:17-18
hJer 39:7
iJer 52:11;
Eze 17:16
12:14
j2Ki 25:5;
Eze 5:10,12
12:16
kJer 22:8-9;
Eze 6:8-10;
14:22
12:18
lLa 5:9;
Eze 4:16
12:19
mEze 6:6-14;
Mic 7:13;
Zec 7:14
nEze 4:16;
23:33
12:20
oIsa 7:23-24;
Jer 4:7

ᵃ24 Or *Chaldea*

21The word of the Lord came to me: 22"Son of man, what is this proverb you have in the land of Israel: 'The days go by and every vision comes to nothing'?ᴾ 23Say to them, 'This is what the Sovereign Lord says: I am going to put an end to this proverb, and they will no longer quote it in Israel.' Say to them, 'The days are near when every vision will be fulfilled.�q 24For there will be no more false visions or flattering divinationsʳ among the people of Israel. 25But I the Lord will speak what I will, and it shall be fulfilled without delay. For in your days, you rebellious house, I will fulfill whatever I say, declares the Sovereign Lord.ˢ'"

26The word of the Lord came to me: 27"Son of man, the house of Israel is saying, 'The vision he sees is for many years from now, and he prophesies about the distant future.'ᵗ

28"Therefore say to them, 'This is what the Sovereign Lord says: None of my words will be delayed any longer; whatever I say will be fulfilled, declares the Sovereign Lord.'"

False Prophets Condemned

13 The word of the Lord came to me: 2"Son of man, prophesy against the prophets of Israel who are now prophesying. Say to those who prophesy out of their own imagination: 'Hear the word of the Lord!ᵘ 3This is what the Sovereign Lord says: Woe to the foolishᵃ prophetsᵛ who follow their own spirit and have seen nothing!ʷ 4Your prophets, O Israel, are like jackals among ruins. 5You have not gone up to the breaks in the wall to repairˣ it for the house of Israel so that it will stand firm in the battle on the day of the Lord.ʸ 6Their visions are false and their divinations a lie. They say, "The Lord declares," when the Lord has not sent them; yet they expect their words to be fulfilled.ᶻ 7Have you not seen false visions and uttered lying divinations when you say, "The Lord declares," though I have not spoken?

8"'Therefore this is what the Sovereign Lord says: Because of your false words and lying visions, I am against you, declares the Sovereign Lord. 9My hand will be against the prophets who see false visions and utter lying divinations. They will not belong to the council of my people or be listed in the recordsᵃ of the house of Israel, nor will they enter the land of Israel. Then you will know that I am the Sovereign Lord.ᵇ

10"'Because they lead my people astray,ᶜ saying, "Peace," when there is no peace, and because, when a flimsy wall is built, they cover it with whitewash,ᵈ 11therefore tell those who cover it with whitewash that it is going to fall. Rain will come in torrents, and I will send hailstones hurtling down, and violent winds will burst forth.ᵉ 12When the wall collapses, will people not ask you, "Where is the whitewash you covered it with?"

13"'Therefore this is what the Sovereign Lord says: In my wrath I will unleash a violent wind, and in my anger hailstonesᶠ and torrents of rain will fall with destructive fury.ᵍ 14I will tear down the wall you have covered with whitewash and will level it to the ground so that its foundationʰ will be laid bare. When itᵇ falls,ⁱ you will be destroyed in it; and you will know that I am the Lord. 15So I will spend my wrath against the wall and against those who covered it with whitewash. I

12:22
pEze 11:3;
Am 6:3; 2Pe 3:4
12:23
qPs 37:13;
Joel 2:1;
Zep 1:14
12:24
rJer 14:14;
Eze 13:23;
Zec 13:2-4
12:25
sIsa 14:24;
Hab 1:5
12:27
tDa 10:14
13:2
uver 17;
Jer 23:16; 37:19
13:3
vLa 2:14
wJer 23:25-32
13:5
xIsa 58:12;
Eze 22:30
yEze 7:19
13:6
zJer 28:15;
Eze 22:28
13:9
aJer 17:13
bEze 20:38
13:10
cJer 50:6
dEze 7:25;
22:28
13:11
eEze 38:22
13:13
fRev 11:19;
16:21 gEx 9:25;
Isa 30:30
13:14
hMic 1:6
iJer 6:15

will say to you, "The wall is gone and so are those who whitewashed it, [16]those prophets of Israel who prophesied to Jerusalem and saw visions of peace for her when there was no peace, declares the Sovereign Lord.j"'

[17]"Now, son of man, set your face against the daughtersk of your people who prophesy out of their own imagination. Prophesy against theml [18]and say, 'This is what the Sovereign Lord says: Woe to the women who sew magic charms on all their wrists and make veils of various lengths for their heads in order to ensnare people. Will you ensnare the lives of my people but preserve your own? [19]You have profanedm me among my people for a few handfuls of barley and scraps of bread. By lying to my people, who listen to lies, you have killed those who should not have died and have spared those who should not live. n

[20]"'Therefore this is what the Sovereign Lord says: I am against your magic charms with which you ensnare people like birds and I will tear them from your arms; I will set free the people that you ensnare like birds. [21]I will tear off your veils and save my people from your hands, and they will no longer fall prey to your power. Then you will know that I am the Lord.o [22]Because you disheartened the righteous with your lies, when I had brought them no grief, and because you encouraged the wicked not to turn from their evil ways and so save their lives,p [23]therefore you will no longer see false visions or practice divination.q I will save my people from your hands. And then you will know that I am the Lord.r'"

Idolaters Condemned

14 Some of the elders of Israel came to me and sat down in front of me.s [2]Then the word of the Lord came to me: [3]"Son of man, these men have set up idols in their hearts and put wicked stumbling blockst before their faces. Should I let them inquire of me at all?u [4]Therefore speak to them and tell them, 'This is what the Sovereign Lord says: When any Israelite sets up idols in his heart and puts a wicked stumbling block before his face and then goes to a prophet, I the Lord will answer him myself in keeping with his great idolatry. [5]I will do this to recapture the hearts of the people of Israel, who have all desertedv me for their idols.'w

[6]"Therefore say to the house of Israel, 'This is what the Sovereign Lord says: Repent! Turn from your idols and renounce all your detestable practices!x

[7]"'When any Israelite or any alieny living in Israel separates himself from me and sets up idols in his heart and puts a wicked stumbling block before his face and then goes to a prophet to inquire of me, I the Lord will answer him myself. [8]I will set my face againstz that man and make him an example and a byword.a I will cut him off from my people. Then you will know that I am the Lord.

[9]"'And if the prophetb is enticedc to utter a prophecy, I the Lord have enticed that prophet, and I will stretch out my hand against him and destroy him from among my people Israel.d [10]They will bear their guilt—the prophet will be as guilty as the one who consults him. [11]Then the people of Israel will no longer straye from me, nor will they defile themselves anymore with all their sins. They will be my people, and I will be their God, declares the Sovereign Lord.f'"

13:16
jIsa 57:21;
Jer 6:14
13:17
kRev 2:20 lver 2
13:19
mEze 20:39;
22:26 nPr 28:21
13:21
oPs 91:3
13:22
pJer 23:14;
Eze 33:14-16
13:23
qver 6;
Eze 12:24
rMic 3:6
14:1
sEze 8:1; 20:1
14:3
tver 7; Eze 7:19
uIsa 1:15;
Eze 20:31
14:5
vZec 11:8
wJer 2:11
14:6
xIsa 2:20; 30:22
14:7
yEx 12:48;
20:10
14:8
zEze 15:7
aEze 5:15
14:9
bJer 14:15
cJer 4:10
d1Ki 22:23
14:11
eEze 48:11
fEze 11:19-20;
37:23

Judgment Inescapable

12The word of the LORD came to me: 13"Son of man, if a country sins against me by being unfaithful and I stretch out my hand against it to cut off its food supply[g] and send famine upon it and kill its men and their animals,[h] 14even if these three men—Noah,[i] Daniel[a][j] and Job[k] —were in it, they could save only themselves by their righteousness,[l] declares the Sovereign LORD.

15"Or if I send wild beasts[m] through that country and they leave it childless and it becomes desolate so that no one can pass through it because of the beasts,[n] 16as surely as I live, declares the Sovereign LORD, even if these three men were in it, they could not save their own sons or daughters. They alone would be saved, but the land would be desolate.[o]

17"Or if I bring a sword[p] against that country and say, 'Let the sword pass throughout the land,' and I kill its men and their animals,[q] 18as surely as I live, declares the Sovereign LORD, even if these three men were in it, they could not save their own sons or daughters. They alone would be saved.

19"Or if I send a plague into that land and pour out my wrath[r] upon it through bloodshed, killing its men and their animals,[s] 20as surely as I live, declares the Sovereign LORD, even if Noah, Daniel and Job were in it, they could save neither son nor daughter. They would save only themselves by their righteousness.[t]

21"For this is what the Sovereign LORD says: How much worse will it be when I send against Jerusalem my four dreadful judgments—sword and famine and wild beasts and plague—to kill its men and their animals![u] 22Yet there will be some survivors—sons and daughters who will be brought out of it.[v] They will come to you, and when you see their conduct[w] and their actions, you will be consoled regarding the disaster I have brought upon Jerusalem—every disaster I have brought upon it. 23You will be consoled when you see their conduct and their actions, for you will know that I have done nothing in it without cause, declares the Sovereign LORD.[x]"

Jerusalem, A Useless Vine

15 The word of the LORD came to me: 2"Son of man, how is the wood of a vine[y] better than that of a branch on any of the trees in the forest? 3Is wood ever taken from it to make anything useful? Do they make pegs from it to hang things on? 4And after it is thrown on the fire as fuel and the fire burns both ends and chars the middle, is it then useful for anything?[z] 5If it was not useful for anything when it was whole, how much less can it be made into something useful when the fire has burned it and it is charred?

6"Therefore this is what the Sovereign LORD says: As I have given the wood of the vine among the trees of the forest as fuel for the fire, so will I treat the people living in Jerusalem. 7I will set my face against[a] them. Although they have come out of the fire, the fire will yet consume them. And when I set my face against them, you will know that I am

14:13
gLev 26:26
hEze 5:16;
6:14; 15:8
14:14
iGe 6:8 jver 20;
Eze 28:3;
Da 1:6; 6:13
kJob 1:1
lJob 42:9;
Jer 15:1;
Eze 18:20
14:15
mEze 5:17
nLev 26:22
14:16
oEze 18:20
14:17
pLev 26:25;
Eze 5:12; 21:3-4
qEze 25:13;
Zep 1:3
14:19
rEze 7:8
sEze 38:22
14:20
tver 14
14:21
uJer 15:3;
Eze 5:17;
33:27;
Am 4:6-10;
Rev 6:8
14:22
vEze 12:16
wEze 20:43
14:23
xJer 22:8-9
15:2
yIsa 5:1-7;
Jer 2:21;
Hos 10:1
15:4
zEze 19:14;
Jn 15:6
15:7
aPs 34:16;
Eze 14:8

---

a14 Or *Danel*; the Hebrew spelling may suggest a person other than the prophet Daniel; also in verse 20.

the Lord.ᵇ ⁸I will make the land desolateᶜ because they have been unfaithful,ᵈ declares the Sovereign Lord.''

An Allegory of Unfaithful Jerusalem

16 The word of the Lord came to me: ²''Son of man, confront Jerusalem with her detestable practicesᵉ ³and say, 'This is what the Sovereign Lord says to Jerusalem: Your ancestryᶠ and birth were in the land of the Canaanites; your father was an Amorite and your mother a Hittite.ᵍ ⁴On the day you were bornʰ your cord was not cut, nor were you washed with water to make you clean, nor were you rubbed with salt or wrapped in cloths. ⁵No one looked on you with pity or had compassion enough to do any of these things for you. Rather, you were thrown out into the open field, for on the day you were born you were despised.

⁶'' 'Then I passed by and saw you kicking about in your blood, and as you lay there in your blood I said to you, ''Live!''ᵃⁱ ⁷I made you growʲ like a plant of the field. You grew up and developed and became the most beautiful of jewels.ᵇ Your breasts were formed and your hair grew, you who were naked and bare.ᵏ

⁸'' 'Later I passed by, and when I looked at you and saw that you were old enough for love, I spread the corner of my garmentˡ over you and covered your nakedness. I gave you my solemn oath and entered into a covenant with you, declares the Sovereign Lord, and you became mine.ᵐ

⁹'' 'I bathedᶜ you with water and washedⁿ the blood from you and put ointments on you. ¹⁰I clothed you with an embroideredᵒ dress and put leather sandals on you. I dressed you in fine linenᵖ and covered you with costly garments.�q ¹¹I adorned you with jewelry:ʳ I put braceletsˢ on your arms and a necklaceᵗ around your neck, ¹²and I put a ring on your nose,ᵘ earrings on your ears and a beautiful crownᵛ on your head. ¹³So you were adorned with gold and silver; your clothes were of fine linen and costly fabric and embroidered cloth. Your food was fine flour, honey and olive oil.ʷ You became very beautiful and rose to be a queen.ˣ ¹⁴And your fameʸ spread among the nations on account of your beauty,ᶻ because the splendor I had given you made your beauty perfect, declares the Sovereign Lord.

¹⁵'' 'But you trusted in your beauty and used your fame to become a prostitute. You lavished your favors on anyone who passed byᵃ and your beauty became his.ᵈᵇ ¹⁶You took some of your garments to make gaudy high places, where you carried on your prostitution.ᶜ Such things should not happen, nor should they ever occur. ¹⁷You also took the fine jewelry I gave you, the jewelry made of my gold and silver, and you made for yourself male idols and engaged in prostitution with them.ᵈ ¹⁸And you took your embroidered clothes to put on them, and you offered my oil and incense before them. ¹⁹Also the food I provided for you—the fine flour, olive oil and honey I gave you to eat—you offered as fragrant incense before them. That is what happened, declares the Sovereign Lord.ᵉ

15:7
ᵇIsa 24:18;
Am 9:1-4
15:8
ᶜEze 14:13
ᵈEze 17:20
16:2
ᵉEze 20:4; 22:2
16:3
ᶠEze 21:30
ᵍver 45
16:4
ʰHos 2:3
16:6
ⁱEx 19:4
16:7
ʲDt 1:10 ᵏEx 1:7
16:8
ˡRu 3:9
ᵐJer 2:2;
Hos 2:7,19-20
16:9
ⁿRu 3:3
16:10
ᵒEx 26:36
ᵖEze 27:16
qver 18
16:11
ʳEze 23:40
ˢIsa 3:19;
Eze 23:42
ᵗGe 41:42
16:12
ᵘIsa 3:21
ᵛIsa 28:5;
Jer 13:18
16:13
ʷ1Sa 10:1
ˣDt 32:13-14;
1Ki 4:21
16:14
ʸ1Ki 10:24
ᶻLa 2:15
16:15
ᵃver 25
ᵇIsa 57:8;
Jer 2:20;
Eze 23:3; 27:3
16:16
ᶜ2Ki 23:7
16:17
ᵈEze 7:20
16:19
ᵉHos 2:8

ᵃ6 A few Hebrew manuscripts, Septuagint and Syriac; most Hebrew manuscripts *''Live!'' And as you lay there in your blood I said to you, ''Live!''*   ᵇ7 Or *became mature*   ᶜ9 Or *I had bathed*
ᵈ15 Most Hebrew manuscripts; one Hebrew manuscript (see some Septuagint manuscripts) *by. Such a thing should not happen*

20" 'And you took your sons and daughters[f] whom you bore to me[g] and sacrificed them as food to the idols. Was your prostitution not enough?[h] 21You slaughtered my children and sacrificed them[a] to the idols.[i] 22In all your detestable practices and your prostitution you did not remember the days of your youth,[j] when you were naked and bare, kicking about in your blood.[k]

23" 'Woe! Woe to you, declares the Sovereign LORD. In addition to all your other wickedness, 24you built a mound for yourself and made a lofty shrine[l] in every public square.[m] 25At the head of every street you built your lofty shrines and degraded your beauty, offering your body with increasing promiscuity to anyone who passed by.[n] 26You engaged in prostitution with the Egyptians, your lustful neighbors, and provoked[o] me to anger with your increasing promiscuity.[p] 27So I stretched out my hand[q] against you and reduced your territory; I gave you over to the greed of your enemies, the daughters of the Philistines,[r] who were shocked by your lewd conduct. 28You engaged in prostitution with the Assyrians[s] too, because you were insatiable; and even after that, you still were not satisfied. 29Then you increased your promiscuity to include Babylonia,[b][t] a land of merchants, but even with this you were not satisfied.

30" 'How weak-willed you are, declares the Sovereign LORD, when you do all these things, acting like a brazen prostitute![u] 31When you built your mounds at the head of every street and made your lofty shrines[v] in every public square, you were unlike a prostitute, because you scorned payment.

32" 'You adulterous wife! You prefer strangers to your own husband! 33Every prostitute receives a fee, but you give gifts[w] to all your lovers, bribing them to come to you from everywhere for your illicit favors.[x] 34So in your prostitution you are the opposite of others; no one runs after you for your favors. You are the very opposite, for you give payment and none is given to you.

35" 'Therefore, you prostitute, hear the word of the LORD! 36This is what the Sovereign LORD says: Because you poured out your wealth[c] and exposed your nakedness in your promiscuity with your lovers, and because of all your detestable idols, and because you gave them your children's blood,[y] 37therefore I am going to gather all your lovers, with whom you found pleasure, those you loved as well as those you hated. I will gather them against you from all around and will strip you in front of them, and they will see all your nakedness.[z] 38I will sentence you to the punishment of women who commit adultery and who shed blood;[a] I will bring upon you the blood vengeance of my wrath and jealous anger.[b] 39Then I will hand you over to your lovers, and they will tear down your mounds and destroy your lofty shrines. They will strip you of your clothes and take your fine jewelry and leave you naked and bare.[c] 40They will bring a mob against you, who will stone[d] you and hack you to pieces with their swords. 41They will burn down[e] your houses and inflict punishment on you in the sight of many women.[f] I will put a stop[g] to your prostitution, and you will no longer pay your lovers. 42Then my wrath against you will subside and my jealous anger will turn away from you; I will be calm and no longer angry.[h]

16:20
f Jer 7:31
g Ex 13:2
h Ps 106:37-38;
Isa 57:5;
Eze 23:37
16:21
i 2Ki 17:17;
Jer 19:5
16:22
j Jer 2:2;
Hos 11:1 k ver 6
16:24
l ver 31; Isa 57:7
m Ps 78:58;
Jer 2:20; 3:2;
Eze 20:28
16:25
n ver 15; Pr 9:14
16:26
o Eze 8:17
p Eze 20:8;
23:19-21
16:27
q Eze 20:33
r 2Ch 28:18
16:28
s 2Ki 16:7
16:29
t Eze 23:14-17
16:30
u Jer 3:3
16:31
v ver 24
16:33
w Isa 30:6; 57:9
x Hos 8:9-10
16:36
y Jer 19:5;
Eze 23:10
16:37
z Jer 13:22
16:38
a Eze 23:45
b Lev 20:10;
Eze 23:25
16:39
c Eze 23:26;
Hos 2:3
16:40
d Jn 8:5,7
16:41
e Dt 13:16
f Eze 23:10
g Eze 23:27,48
16:42
h Isa 54:9;
Eze 5:13; 39:29

---

a21 Or *and made them pass through the fire*   b29 Or *Chaldea*   c36 Or *lust*

16:43
iPs 78:42
jEze 22:31
kver 22;
Eze 11:21
16:45
lEze 23:2
16:46
mGe 13:10-13;
Eze 23:4
16:47
n2Ki 21:9;
Eze 5:7
16:48
oMt 10:15;
11:23-24
16:49
pGe 13:13
qPs 138:6
rEze 18:7,12,16;
Lk 12:16-20
16:50
sGe 18:20-21;
19:5
16:51
tJer 3:8-11
16:53
uIsa 19:24-25
16:54
vJer 2:26;
Eze 14:22
16:55
wMal 3:4
16:57
x2Ki 16:6
16:58
yEze 23:49
16:59
zEze 17:19
16:60
aJer 32:40;
Eze 37:26
16:61
bEze 20:43
16:62
cJer 24:7;
Eze 20:37,
43-44;
Hos 2:19-20
16:63
dPs 65:3; 79:9

43" 'Because you did not remember[i] the days of your youth but enraged me with all these things, I will surely bring down[j] on your head what you have done, declares the Sovereign Lord. Did you not add lewdness to all your other detestable practices?[k]

44" 'Everyone who quotes proverbs will quote this proverb about you: "Like mother, like daughter." 45You are a true daughter of your mother, who despised her husband and her children; and you are a true sister of your sisters, who despised their husbands and their children. Your mother was a Hittite and your father an Amorite.[l] 46Your older sister was Samaria, who lived to the north of you with her daughters; and your younger sister, who lived to the south of you with her daughters, was Sodom.[m] 47You not only walked in their ways and copied their detestable practices, but in all your ways you soon became more depraved than they.[n] 48As surely as I live, declares the Sovereign Lord, your sister Sodom and her daughters never did what you and your daughters have done.[o]

49" 'Now this was the sin of your sister Sodom:[p] She and her daughters were arrogant,[q] overfed and unconcerned; they did not help the poor and needy.[r] 50They were haughty and did detestable things before me. Therefore I did away with them as you have seen.[s] 51Samaria did not commit half the sins you did. You have done more detestable things than they, and have made your sisters seem righteous by all these things you have done.[t] 52Bear your disgrace, for you have furnished some justification for your sisters. Because your sins were more vile than theirs, they appear more righteous than you. So then, be ashamed and bear your disgrace, for you have made your sisters appear righteous.

53" 'However, I will restore[u] the fortunes of Sodom and her daughters and of Samaria and her daughters, and your fortunes along with them, 54so that you may bear your disgrace[v] and be ashamed of all you have done in giving them comfort. 55And your sisters, Sodom with her daughters and Samaria with her daughters, will return to what they were before; and you and your daughters will return to what you were before.[w] 56You would not even mention your sister Sodom in the day of your pride, 57before your wickedness was uncovered. Even so, you are now scorned by the daughters of Edom[a][x] and all her neighbors and the daughters of the Philistines—all those around you who despise you. 58You will bear the consequences of your lewdness and your detestable practices, declares the Lord.[y]

59" 'This is what the Sovereign Lord says: I will deal with you as you deserve, because you have despised my oath by breaking the covenant.[z] 60Yet I will remember the covenant I made with you in the days of your youth, and I will establish an everlasting covenant[a] with you. 61Then you will remember your ways and be ashamed[b] when you receive your sisters, both those who are older than you and those who are younger. I will give them to you as daughters, but not on the basis of my covenant with you. 62So I will establish my covenant with you, and you will know that I am the Lord.[c] 63Then, when I make atonement[d] for you for all you have done, you will remember and be

---

a57 Many Hebrew manuscripts and Syriac; most Hebrew manuscripts, Septuagint and Vulgate Aram ashamed and never again open your mouth[e] because of your humiliation, declares the Sovereign LORD.[f] ' "

Two Eagles and a Vine

17 The word of the LORD came to me: [2]"Son of man, set forth an allegory and tell the house of Israel a parable.[g] [3]Say to them, 'This is what the Sovereign LORD says: A great eagle[h] with powerful wings, long feathers and full plumage of varied colors came to Lebanon.[i] Taking hold of the top of a cedar, [4]he broke off its topmost shoot and carried it away to a land of merchants, where he planted it in a city of traders.

[5]' 'He took some of the seed of your land and put it in fertile soil. He planted it like a willow by abundant water.[j] [6]and it sprouted and became a low, spreading vine. Its branches turned toward him, but its roots remained under it. So it became a vine and produced branches and put out leafy boughs.

[7]' 'But there was another great eagle with powerful wings and full plumage. The vine now sent out its roots toward him from the plot where it was planted and stretched out its branches to him for water.[k] [8]It had been planted in good soil by abundant water so that it would produce branches, bear fruit and become a splendid vine.'

[9]"Say to them, 'This is what the Sovereign LORD says: Will it thrive? Will it not be uprooted and stripped of its fruit so that it withers? All its new growth will wither. It will not take a strong arm or many people to pull it up by the roots. [10]Even if it[l] is transplanted, will it thrive? Will it not wither completely when the east wind strikes it—wither away in the plot where it grew?' "

[11]Then the word of the LORD came to me: [12]"Say to this rebellious house, 'Do you not know what these things mean?[m]' Say to them: 'The king of Babylon went to Jerusalem and carried off her king and her nobles,[n] bringing them back with him to Babylon.[o] [13]Then he took a member of the royal family and made a treaty with him, putting him under oath.[p] He also carried away the leading men of the land, [14]so that the kingdom would be brought low,[q] unable to rise again, surviving only by keeping his treaty. [15]But the king rebelled[r] against him by sending his envoys to Egypt to get horses and a large army.[s] Will he succeed? Will he who does such things escape? Will he break the treaty and yet escape?[t]

[16]' 'As surely as I live, declares the Sovereign LORD, he shall die[u] in Babylon, in the land of the king who put him on the throne, whose oath he despised and whose treaty he broke.[v] [17]Pharaoh[w] with his mighty army and great horde will be of no help to him in war, when ramps[x] are built and siege works erected to destroy many lives.[y] [18]He despised the oath by breaking the covenant. Because he had given his hand in pledge[z] and yet did all these things, he shall not escape.

[19]' 'Therefore this is what the Sovereign LORD says: As surely as I live, I will bring down on his head my oath that he despised and my covenant that he broke.[a] [20]I will spread my net[b] for him, and he will be caught in my snare. I will bring him to Babylon and execute judgment[c] upon him there because he was unfaithful to me. [21]All his fleeing troops will fall by the sword,[d] and the survivors[e] will be scattered to the winds.[f] Then you will know that I the LORD have spoken.

16:63
e Ro 3:19
f Ps 39:9;
Da 9:7-8
17:2
g Eze 20:49
17:3
h Hos 8:1
i Jer 22:23
17:5
j Dt 8:7-9;
Isa 44:4
17:7
k Eze 31:4
17:10
l Hos 13:15
17:12
m Eze 12:9
n 2Ki 24:15
o Eze 24:19
17:13
p 2Ch 36:13
17:14
q Eze 29:14
17:15
r Jer 52:3
s Dt 17:16
t Jer 34:3; 38:18
17:16
u Jer 52:11;
Eze 12:13
v 2Ki 24:17
17:17
w Jer 37:7
x Eze 4:2
y Isa 36:6;
Jer 37:5;
Eze 29:6-7
17:18
z 1Ch 29:24
17:19
a Eze 16:59
17:20
b Eze 12:13;
32:3 c Jer 2:35;
Eze 20:36
17:21
d Eze 12:14
e 2Ki 25:11
f 2Ki 25:5

22" 'This is what the Sovereign Lord says: I myself will take a shoot from the very top of a cedar and plant it; I will break off a tender sprig from its topmost shoots and plant it on a high and lofty mountain. ^g ²³On the mountain heights of Israel I will plant it; it will produce branches and bear fruit and become a splendid cedar. Birds of every kind will nest in it; they will find shelter in the shade of its branches. ^h ²⁴All the trees of the fieldⁱ will know that I the Lord bring down the tall tree and make the low tree grow tall. I dry up the green tree and make the dry tree flourish.

" 'I the Lord have spoken, and I will do it.^j '"

The Soul Who Sins Will Die

18 The word of the Lord came to me: ²"What do you people mean by quoting this proverb about the land of Israel:

" 'The fathers eat sour grapes,
    and the children's teeth are set on edge'?^k

³"As surely as I live, declares the Sovereign Lord, you will no longer quote this proverb in Israel. ⁴For every living soul belongs to me, the father as well as the son—both alike belong to me. The soul who sins is the one who will die.^l

⁵"Suppose there is a righteous man
    who does what is just and right.
⁶He does not eat at the mountain^m shrines
    or look to the idolsⁿ of the house of Israel.
He does not defile his neighbor's wife
    or lie with a woman during her period.
⁷He does not oppress^o anyone,
    but returns what he took in pledge^p for a loan.
He does not commit robbery
    but gives his food to the hungry
    and provides clothing for the naked.^q
⁸He does not lend at usury
    or take excessive interest.^a ^r
He withholds his hand from doing wrong
    and judges fairly^s between man and man.
⁹He follows my decrees
    and faithfully keeps my laws.
That man is righteous;^t
    he will surely live,^u

declares the Sovereign Lord.

¹⁰"Suppose he has a violent son, who sheds blood^v or does any of these other things^b ¹¹(though the father has done none of them):

"He eats at the mountain shrines.
He defiles his neighbor's wife.
¹²He oppresses the poor^w and needy.
He commits robbery.
He does not return what he took in pledge.

^a8 Or *take interest; similarly in verses 13 and 17*   ^b10 Or *things to a brother*

17:22
gJer 23:5;
Eze 20:40;
36:1,36; 37:22
17:23
hPs 92:12;
Isa 2:2;
Eze 31:6;
Da 4:12;
Hos 14:5-7;
Mt 13:32
17:24
iPs 96:12
jEze 19:12;
21:26; 22:14;
Am 9:11
18:2
kIsa 3:15;
Jer 31:29;
La 5:7
18:4
lver 20;
Isa 42:5;
Ro 6:23
18:6
mEze 22:9
nDt 4:19;
Eze 6:13; 20:24
18:7
oEx 22:21
pEx 22:26;
Dt 24:12
qDt 15:11;
Mt 25:36
18:8
rEx 22:25;
Lev 25:35-37;
Dt 23:19-20
sZec 8:16
18:9
tHab 2:4
uLev 18:5;
Eze 20:11;
Am 5:4
18:10
vEx 21:12
18:12
wAm 4:1

He looks to the idols.
He does detestable things. ˣ
¹³He lends at usury and takes excessive interest. ʸ

Will such a man live? He will not! Because he has done all these detestable things, he will surely be put to death and his blood will be on his own head. ᶻ

¹⁴"But suppose this son has a son who sees all the sins his father commits, and though he sees them, he does not do such things:ᵃ

¹⁵"He does not eat at the mountain shrines
or look to the idols of the house of Israel.
He does not defile his neighbor's wife.
¹⁶He does not oppress anyone
or require a pledge for a loan.
He does not commit robbery
but gives his food to the hungry
and provides clothing for the naked. ᵇ
¹⁷He withholds his hand from sinᵃ
and takes no usury or excessive interest.
He keeps my laws and follows my decrees.

He will not die for his father's sin; he will surely live. ¹⁸But his father will die for his own sin, because he practiced extortion, robbed his brother and did what was wrong among his people.

¹⁹"Yet you ask, 'Why does the son not share the guilt of his father?' Since the son has done what is just and right and has been careful to keep all my decrees, he will surely live. ᶜ ²⁰The soul who sins is the one who will die. The son will not share the guilt of the father, nor will the father share the guilt of the son. The righteousness of the righteous man will be credited to him, and the wickedness of the wicked will be charged against him. ᵈ

²¹"But if a wicked man turns away from all the sins he has committed and keeps all my decrees and does what is just and right, he will surely live; he will not die. ᵉ ²²None of the offenses he has committed will be remembered against him. Because of the righteous things he has done, he will live. ᶠ ²³Do I take any pleasure in the death of the wicked? declares the Sovereign LORD. Rather, am I not pleasedᵍ when they turn from their ways and live?ʰ

²⁴"But if a righteous man turns from his righteousness and commits sin and does the same detestable things the wicked man does, will he live? None of the righteous things he has done will be remembered. Because of the unfaithfulness he is guilty of and because of the sins he has committed, he will die. ⁱ

²⁵"Yet you say, 'The way of the Lord is not just.' Hear, O house of Israel: Is my way unjust?ʲ Is it not your ways that are unjust? ²⁶If a righteous man turns from his righteousness and commits sin, he will die for it; because of the sin he has committed he will die. ²⁷But if a wicked man turns away from the wickedness he has committed and does what is just and right, he will save his life. ᵏ ²⁸Because he considers all the offenses he has committed and turns away from them, he will

18:12
ˣ2Ki 21:11;
Isa 59:6-7;
Jer 22:17;
Eze 8:6,17
18:13
ʸEx 22:25
ᶻEze 33:4-5
18:14
ᵃ2Ch 34:21;
Pr 23:24
18:16
ᵇPs 41:1;
Isa 58:10
18:19
ᶜEx 20:5;
Dt 5:9;
Jer 15:4;
Zec 1:3-6
18:20
ᵈDt 24:16;
1Ki 8:32;
2Ki 14:6;
Isa 3:11;
Mt 16:27;
Ro 2:9
18:21
ᵉEze 33:12,19
18:22
ᶠPs 18:20-24;
Isa 43:25;
Mic 7:19
18:23
ᵍPs 147:11
ʰEze 33:11;
1Ti 2:4
18:24
ⁱ1Sa 15:11;
2Ch 24:17-20;
Eze 3:20;
20:27;
2Pe 2:20-22
18:25
ʲGe 18:25;
Jer 12:1;
Eze 33:17;
Zep 3:5;
Mal 2:17;
3:13-15
18:27
ᵏIsa 1:18

ᵃ17 Septuagint (see also verse 8); Hebrew *from the poor*

surely live; he will not die. [29]Yet the house of Israel says, 'The way of the Lord is not just.' Are my ways unjust, O house of Israel? Is it not your ways that are unjust?

[30]"Therefore, O house of Israel, I will judge you, each one according to his ways, declares the Sovereign LORD. Repent![l] Turn away from all your offenses; then sin will not be your downfall. [m] [31]Rid yourselves of all the offenses you have committed, and get a new heart[n] and a new spirit. Why will you die, O house of Israel?[o] [32]For I take no pleasure in the death of anyone, declares the Sovereign LORD. Repent and live![p]

A Lament for Israel's Princes

19

"Take up a lament[q] concerning the princes[r] of Israel [2]and say:

" 'What a lioness was your mother
    among the lions!
She lay down among the young lions
    and reared her cubs.
[3]She brought up one of her cubs,
    and he became a strong lion.
He learned to tear the prey
    and he devoured men.
[4]The nations heard about him,
    and he was trapped in their pit.
They led him with hooks
    to the land of Egypt. [s]

[5]" 'When she saw her hope unfulfilled,
    her expectation gone,
she took another of her cubs
    and made him a strong lion. [t]
[6]He prowled among the lions,
    for he was now a strong lion.
He learned to tear the prey
    and he devoured men. [u]
[7]He broke down[a] their strongholds
    and devastated[v] their towns.
The land and all who were in it
    were terrified by his roaring.
[8]Then the nations[w] came against him,
    those from regions round about.
They spread their net for him,
    and he was trapped in their pit. [x]
[9]With hooks they pulled him into a cage
    and brought him to the king of Babylon. [y]
They put him in prison,
    so his roar was heard no longer
    on the mountains of Israel. [z]

[10]" 'Your mother was like a vine in your vineyard[b]
    planted by the water;

18:30
lMt 3:2
mEze 7:3;
33:20; Hos 12:6
18:31
nPs 51:10
oIsa 1:16-17;
Eze 11:19;
36:26
18:32
pEze 33:11
19:1
qEze 26:17;
27:2,32
r2Ki 24:6
19:4
s2Ki 23:33-34;
2Ch 36:4
19:5
t2Ki 23:34
19:6
u2Ki 24:9;
2Ch 36:9
19:7
vEze 30:12
19:8
w2Ki 24:2
x2Ki 24:11
19:9
y2Ch 36:6
z2Ki 24:15

---

[a]7 Targum (see Septuagint); Hebrew *He knew*   [b]10 Two Hebrew manuscripts; most Hebrew manuscripts *your blood*

it was fruitful and full of branches
　　because of abundant water. ᵃ
¹¹Its branches were strong,
　　fit for a ruler's scepter.
It towered high
　　above the thick foliage,
conspicuous for its height
　　and for its many branches. ᵇ
¹²But it was uprootedᶜ in fury
　　and thrown to the ground.
The east wind made it shrivel,
　　it was stripped of its fruit;
its strong branches withered
　　and fire consumed them. ᵈ
¹³Now it is planted in the desert, ᵉ
　　in a dry and thirsty land. ᶠ
¹⁴Fire spread from one of its mainᵃ branches
　　and consumedᵍ its fruit.
No strong branch is left on it
　　fit for a ruler's scepter.' ʰ

This is a lament and is to be used as a lament."

Rebellious Israel

20 In the seventh year, in the fifth month on the tenth day, some of the elders of Israel came to inquire of the LORD, and they sat down in front of me. ⁱ

²Then the word of the LORD came to me: ³"Son of man, speak to the elders of Israel and say to them, 'This is what the Sovereign LORD says: Have you come to inquireʲ of me? As surely as I live, I will not let you inquire of me, declares the Sovereign LORD. ᵏ'

⁴"Will you judge them? Will you judge them, son of man? Then confront them with the detestable practices of their fathersˡ ⁵and say to them: 'This is what the Sovereign LORD says: On the day I choseᵐ Israel, I swore with uplifted hand to the descendants of the house of Jacob and revealed myself to them in Egypt. With uplifted hand I said to them, "I am the LORD your God. ⁿ" ⁶On that day I swore to them that I would bring them out of Egypt into a land I had searched out for them, a land flowing with milk and honey, ᵒ the most beautiful of all lands. ᵖ ⁷And I said to them, "Each of you, get rid of the vile images�q you have set your eyes on, and do not defile yourselves with the idols of Egypt. I am the LORD your God. ʳ"

⁸" 'But they rebelled against me and would not listen to me; they did not get rid of the vile images they had set their eyes on, nor did they forsake the idols of Egypt. ˢ So I said I would pour out my wrath on them and spend my anger against them in Egypt. ᵗ ⁹But for the sake of my name I did what would keep it from being profaned in the eyes of the nations they lived among and in whose sight I had revealed myself to the Israelites by bringing them out of Egypt. ᵘ ¹⁰Therefore I led them out of Egypt and brought them into the desert. ᵛ ¹¹I gave them my

ᵃ14 Or *from under its*

19:10
aPs 80:8-11
19:11
bEze 31:3;
Da 4:11
19:12
cEze 17:10
dIsa 27:11;
Eze 28:17;
Hos 13:15
19:13
eEze 20:35
fHos 2:3
19:14
gEze 20:47
hEze 15:4
20:1
iEze 8:1
20:3
jEze 14:3
kMic 3:7
20:4
lEze 16:2; 22:2;
Mt 23:32
20:5
mDt 7:6 nEx 6:7
20:6
oEx 3:8;
Jer 32:22
pDt 8:7;
Ps 48:2; Da 8:9
20:7
qEx 20:4
rEx 20:2;
Lev 18:3;
Dt 29:18
20:8
sEze 7:8
tIsa 63:10
20:9
uEze 36:22;
39:7
20:10
vEx 13:18

decrees and made known to them my laws, for the man who obeys them will live by them. ʷ ¹²Also I gave them my Sabbaths as a sign ˣ between us, so they would know that I the LORD made them holy.

¹³" 'Yet the people of Israel rebelled ʸ against me in the desert. They did not follow my decrees but rejected my laws—although the man who obeys them will live by them—and they utterly desecrated my Sabbaths. So I said I would pour out my wrath ᶻ on them and destroy them in the desert. ᵃ ¹⁴But for the sake of my name I did what would keep it from being profaned in the eyes of the nations in whose sight I had brought them out. ᵇ ¹⁵Also with uplifted hand I swore to them in the desert that I would not bring them into the land I had given them—a land flowing with milk and honey, most beautiful of all lands ᶜ— ¹⁶because they rejected my laws and did not follow my decrees and desecrated my Sabbaths. For their hearts ᵈ were devoted to their idols. ᵉ ¹⁷Yet I looked on them with pity and did not destroy them or put an end to them in the desert. ¹⁸I said to their children in the desert, "Do not follow the statutes of your fathers ᶠ or keep their laws or defile yourselves with their idols. ¹⁹I am the LORD your God; ᵍ follow my decrees and be careful to keep my laws. ʰ ²⁰Keep my Sabbaths holy, that they may be a sign between us. Then you will know that I am the LORD your God. ⁱ "

²¹" 'But the children rebelled against me: They did not follow my decrees, they were not careful to keep my laws—although the man who obeys them will live by them—and they desecrated my Sabbaths. So I said I would pour out my wrath on them and spend my anger against them in the desert. ²²But I withheld ʲ my hand, and for the sake of my name I did what would keep it from being profaned in the eyes of the nations in whose sight I had brought them out. ²³Also with uplifted hand I swore to them in the desert that I would disperse them among the nations and scatter ᵏ them through the countries, ²⁴because they had not obeyed my laws but had rejected my decrees and desecrated my Sabbaths, ˡ and their eyes lusted after ᵐ their fathers' idols. ⁿ ²⁵I also gave them over ᵒ to statutes that were not good and laws they could not live by; ᵖ ²⁶I let them become defiled through their gifts—the sacrifice of every firstborn ᵃ—that I might fill them with horror so they would know that I am the LORD. �q '

²⁷"Therefore, son of man, speak to the people of Israel and say to them, 'This is what the Sovereign LORD says: In this also your fathers blasphemed ʳ me by forsaking me: ˢ ²⁸When I brought them into the land ᵗ I had sworn to give them and they saw any high hill or any leafy tree, there they offered their sacrifices, made offerings that provoked me to anger, presented their fragrant incense and poured out their drink offerings. ᵘ ²⁹Then I said to them: What is this high place you go to?' " (It is called Bamah ᵇ to this day.)

Judgment and Restoration

³⁰"Therefore say to the house of Israel: 'This is what the Sovereign LORD says: Will you defile yourselves ᵛ the way your fathers did and lust after their vile images? ʷ ³¹When you offer your gifts—the sacrifice

20:11
ʷLev 18:5;
Dt 4:7-8;
Ro 10:5
20:12
ˣEx 31:13
20:13
ʸPs 78:40
ᶻDt 9:8
ᵃNu 14:29;
Ps 95:8-10;
Isa 56:6
20:14
ᵇEze 36:23
20:15
ᶜPs 95:11;
106:26
20:16
ᵈNu 15:39
ᵉAm 5:26
20:18
ᶠZec 1:4
20:19
ᵍEx 20:2
ʰDt 5:32-33;
6:1-2; 8:1;
11:1; 12:1
20:20
ⁱJer 17:22
20:22
ʲPs 78:38
20:23
ᵏLev 26:33;
Dt 28:64
20:24
ˡver 13
ᵐEze 6:9
ⁿver 16
20:25
ᵒPs 81:12
ᵖ2Th 2:11
20:26
qᵉ2Ki 17:17
20:27
ʳRo 2:24
ˢEze 18:24
20:28
ᵗPs 78:55,58
ᵘEze 6:13
20:30
ᵛver 43
ʷJer 16:12

ᵃ26 Or —*making every firstborn pass through the fire*   ᵇ29 *Bamah* means *high place.*

of your sons^x in^a the fire—you continue to defile yourselves with all your idols to this day. Am I to let you inquire of me, O house of Israel? As surely as I live, declares the Sovereign Lord, I will not let you inquire of me.^y

³²" 'You say, "We want to be like the nations, like the peoples of the world, who serve wood and stone." But what you have in mind will never happen. ³³As surely as I live, declares the Sovereign Lord, I will rule over you with a mighty hand and an outstretched arm and with outpoured wrath.^z ³⁴I will bring you from the nations^a and gather you from the countries where you have been scattered—with a mighty hand and an outstretched arm and with outpoured wrath.^b ³⁵I will bring you into the desert of the nations and there, face to face, I will execute judgment^c upon you. ³⁶As I judged your fathers in the desert of the land of Egypt, so I will judge you, declares the Sovereign Lord.^d ³⁷I will take note of you as you pass under my rod,^e and I will bring you into the bond of the covenant.^f ³⁸I will purge^g you of those who revolt and rebel against me. Although I will bring them out of the land where they are living, yet they will not enter the land of Israel. Then you will know that I am the Lord.^h

³⁹" 'As for you, O house of Israel, this is what the Sovereign Lord says: Go and serve your idols,ⁱ every one of you! But afterward you will surely listen to me and no longer profane my holy name with your gifts and idols.^j ⁴⁰For on my holy mountain, the high mountain of Israel, declares the Sovereign Lord, there in the land the entire house of Israel will serve me, and there I will accept them. There I will require your offerings^k and your choice gifts,^b along with all your holy sacrifices.^l ⁴¹I will accept you as fragrant incense when I bring you out from the nations and gather you from the countries where you have been scattered, and I will show myself holy^m among you in the sight of the nations.ⁿ ⁴²Then you will know that I am the Lord,^o when I bring you into the land of Israel,^p the land I had sworn with uplifted hand to give to your fathers. ⁴³There you will remember your conduct and all the actions by which you have defiled yourselves, and you will loathe yourselves for all the evil you have done.^q ⁴⁴You will know that I am the Lord, when I deal with you for my name's sake^r and not according to your evil ways and your corrupt practices, O house of Israel, declares the Sovereign Lord.^s '"

Prophecy Against the South

⁴⁵The word of the Lord came to me: ⁴⁶"Son of man, set your face toward the south; preach against the south and prophesy against^t the forest of the southland.^u ⁴⁷Say to the southern forest: 'Hear the word of the Lord. This is what the Sovereign Lord says: I am about to set fire to you, and it will consume all your trees, both green and dry. The blazing flame will not be quenched, and every face from south to north will be scorched by it.^v ⁴⁸Everyone will see that I the Lord have kindled it; it will not be quenched.^w '"

⁴⁹Then I said, "Ah, Sovereign Lord! They are saying of me, 'Isn't he just telling parables?^x '"

20:31
xEze 16:20
yPs 106:37-39;
Jer 7:31
20:33
zJer 21:5
20:34
a2Co 6:17*
bIsa 27:12-13;
S Jer 44:6;
La 2:4
20:35
cJer 2:35
20:36
dNu 11:1-35;
1Co 10:5-10
20:37
eLev 27:32;
Jer 33:13
fEze 16:62
20:38
gEze 34:17-22;
Am 9:9-10
hPs 95:11;
Jer 44:14;
Eze 13:9;
Mal 3:3;
Heb 4:3
20:39
iJer 44:25
jIsa 1:13;
Eze 43:7;
Am 4:4
20:40
kIsa 60:7
lIsa 56:7;
Mal 3:4
20:41
mEze 28:25;
36:23
nEze 11:17
20:42
oEze 38:23
pEze 34:13;
36:24
20:43
qEze 6:9;
16:61; Hos 5:15
20:44
rEze 36:22
sEze 24:24
20:46
tEze 21:2;
Am 7:16
uIsa 30:6;
Jer 13:19
20:47
vIsa 9:18-19;
13:8; Jer 21:14
20:48
wJer 7:20
20:49
xMt 13:13;
Jn 16:25

---

^a31 Or —*making your sons pass through*   ^b40 Or *and the gifts of your firstfruits*

Babylon, God's Sword of Judgment

21

The word of the LORD came to me: [2]"Son of man, set your face against Jerusalem and preach against the sanctuary. Prophesy against[y] the land of Israel [3]and say to her: 'This is what the LORD says: I am against you.[z] I will draw my sword from its scabbard and cut off from you both the righteous and the wicked.[a] [4]Because I am going to cut off the righteous and the wicked, my sword will be unsheathed against everyone from south to north.[b] [5]Then all people will know that I the LORD have drawn my sword from its scabbard; it will not return[c] again.'[d]

[6]"Therefore groan, son of man! Groan before them with broken heart and bitter grief.[e] [7]And when they ask you, 'Why are you groaning?' you shall say, 'Because of the news that is coming. Every heart will melt and every hand go limp;[f] every spirit will become faint and every knee become as weak as water.' It is coming! It will surely take place, declares the Sovereign LORD."

[8]The word of the LORD came to me: [9]"Son of man, prophesy and say, 'This is what the Lord says:

" 'A sword, a sword,
    sharpened and polished—
[10]sharpened for the slaughter,[g]
    polished to flash like lightning!

" 'Shall we rejoice in the scepter of my son ⌞Judah⌟? The sword despises every such stick.

[11]" 'The sword is appointed to be polished,[h]
    to be grasped with the hand;
it is sharpened and polished,
    made ready for the hand of the slayer.
[12]Cry out and wail, son of man,
    for it is against my people;
    it is against all the princes of Israel.
They are thrown to the sword
    along with my people.
Therefore beat your breast.[i]

[13]" 'Testing will surely come. And what if the scepter ⌞of Judah⌟, which the sword despises, does not continue? declares the Sovereign LORD.'

[14]"So then, son of man, prophesy
    and strike your hands[j] together.
Let the sword strike twice,
    even three times.
It is a sword for slaughter—
    a sword for great slaughter,
    closing in on them from every side.[k]
[15]So that hearts may melt[l]
    and the fallen be many,
I have stationed the sword for slaughter[a]

21:2
yEze 20:46
21:3
zJer 21:13
aver 9-11;
Job 9:22
21:4
bEze 20:47
21:5
cver 30 dNa 1:9
21:6
eIsa 22:4
21:7
fEze 22:14; 7:17
21:10
gPs 110:5-6;
Isa 34:5-6
21:11
hJer 46:4
21:12
iJer 31:19
21:14
jNu 24:10
kEze 6:11;
30:24
21:15
lSa 17:10

---

[a]15 Septuagint; the meaning of the Hebrew for this word is uncertain.

at all their gates.
Oh! It is made to flash like lightning,
it is grasped for slaughter. [m]
[16]O sword, slash to the right,
then to the left,
wherever your blade is turned.
[17]I too will strike my hands[n] together,
and my wrath[o] will subside.
I the LORD have spoken."

[18]The word of the LORD came to me: [19]"Son of man, mark out two roads for the sword of the king of Babylon to take, both starting from the same country. Make a signpost where the road branches off to the city. [20]Mark out one road for the sword to come against Rabbah of the Ammonites[p] and another against Judah and fortified Jerusalem. [21]For the king of Babylon will stop at the fork in the road, at the junction of the two roads, to seek an omen: He will cast lots[q] with arrows, he will consult his idols, he will examine the liver. [r] [22]Into his right hand will come the lot for Jerusalem, where he is to set up battering rams, to give the command to slaughter, to sound the battle cry, to set battering rams against the gates, to build a ramp and to erect siege works. [s] [23]It will seem like a false omen to those who have sworn allegiance to him, but he will remind[t] them of their guilt and take them captive.

[24]"Therefore this is what the Sovereign LORD says: 'Because you people have brought to mind your guilt by your open rebellion, revealing your sins in all that you do—because you have done this, you will be taken captive.

[25]" 'O profane and wicked prince of Israel, whose day has come, whose time of punishment has reached its climax, [u] [26]this is what the Sovereign LORD says: Take off the turban, remove the crown. [v] It will not be as it was: The lowly will be exalted and the exalted will be brought low. [w] [27]A ruin! A ruin! I will make it a ruin! It will not be restored until he comes to whom it rightfully belongs; to him I will give it.' [x]

[28]"And you, son of man, prophesy and say, 'This is what the Sovereign LORD says about the Ammonites[y] and their insults:

" 'A sword, [z] a sword,
drawn for the slaughter,
polished to consume
and to flash like lightning!
[29]Despite false visions concerning you
and lying divinations about you,
it will be laid on the necks
of the wicked who are to be slain,
whose day has come,
whose time of punishment has reached its climax. [a]
[30]Return the sword to its scabbard. [b]
In the place where you were created,
in the land of your ancestry, [c]
I will judge you.
[31]I will pour out my wrath upon you
and breathe out my fiery anger[d] against you;

21:15
m Ps 22:14
21:17
n ver 14;
Eze 22:13
o Eze 5:13
21:20
p Dt 3:11;
Jer 49:2;
Am 1:14
21:21
q Pr 16:33
r Nu 22:7; 23:23
21:22
s Eze 4:2; 26:9
21:23
t Nu 5:15
21:25
u Eze 35:5
21:26
v Jer 13:18
w Ps 75:7;
Eze 17:24
21:27
x Ps 2:6;
Jer 23:5-6;
Eze 37:24;
Hag 2:21-22
21:28
y Zep 2:8
z Jer 12:12
21:29
a ver 25;
Eze 22:28; 35:5
21:30
b Jer 47:6
c Eze 16:3
21:31
d Eze 22:20-21

I will hand you over to brutal men,
    men skilled in destruction. ^e
³²You will be fuel for the fire, ^f
    your blood will be shed in your land,
    you will be remembered^g no more;
    for I the LORD have spoken.' "

Jerusalem's Sins

21:31
eJer 51:20-23
21:32
fMal 4:1
gEze 25:10
22:2
hEze 24:6,9;
Na 3:1
iEze 16:2
22:3
jver 6,13,27;
Eze 23:37,45
22:4
k2Ki 21:16
lEze 21:25
mEze 5:14
22:6
nIsa 1:23
22:7
oDt 5:16; 27:16
pEx 22:21-22
22:8
qEze 23:38-39
22:9
rLev 19:16
sEze 18:11
tHos 4:10,14
22:10
uLev 18:8,19
22:11
vLev 18:15
wLev 18:9;
2Sa 13:14
22:12
xDt 27:25;
Mic 7:3
yLev 19:13
22:13
zEze 21:17
aIsa 33:15
bver 3
22:14
cEze 24:14
dEze 17:24;
21:7
22:15
eDt 4:27;
Zec 7:14
fEze 23:27
22:18
gPs 119:119;
Isa 1:22
hJer 6:28-30
22:20
iMal 3:2
22:22
jIsa 1:25

22 The word of the LORD came to me: ²"Son of man, will you judge her? Will you judge this city of bloodshed?^h Then confront her with all her detestable practicesⁱ ³and say: 'This is what the Sovereign LORD says: O city that brings on herself doom by shedding blood^j in her midst and defiles herself by making idols, ⁴you have become guilty because of the blood you have shed^k and have become defiled by the idols you have made. You have brought your days to a close, and the end of your years has come.^l Therefore I will make you an object of scorn to the nations and a laughingstock to all the countries. ^m ⁵Those who are near and those who are far away will mock you, O infamous city, full of turmoil.

⁶" 'See how each of the princes of Israel who are in you uses his power to shed blood.ⁿ ⁷In you they have treated father and mother with contempt;^o in you they have oppressed the alien and mistreated the fatherless and the widow.^p ⁸You have despised my holy things and desecrated my Sabbaths. ^q ⁹In you are slanderous men^r bent on shedding blood; in you are those who eat at the mountain shrines^s and commit lewd acts. ^t ¹⁰In you are those who dishonor their fathers' bed; in you are those who violate women during their period, when they are ceremonially unclean. ^u ¹¹In you one man commits a detestable offense with his neighbor's wife, another shamefully defiles his daughter-in-law,^v and another violates his sister,^w his own father's daughter. ¹²In you men accept bribes^x to shed blood; you take usury and excessive interest^a and make unjust gain from your neighbors^y by extortion. And you have forgotten me, declares the Sovereign LORD.

¹³" 'I will surely strike my hands^z together at the unjust gain^a you have made and at the blood^b you have shed in your midst. ¹⁴Will your courage endure or your hands be strong in the day I deal with you? I the LORD have spoken,^c and I will do it. ^d ¹⁵I will disperse you among the nations and scatter^e you through the countries; and I will put an end to your uncleanness. ^f ¹⁶When you have been defiled^b in the eyes of the nations, you will know that I am the LORD.' "

¹⁷Then the word of the LORD came to me: ¹⁸"Son of man, the house of Israel has become dross^g to me; all of them are the copper, tin, iron and lead left inside a furnace. They are but the dross of silver. ^h ¹⁹Therefore this is what the Sovereign LORD says: 'Because you have all become dross, I will gather you into Jerusalem. ²⁰As men gather silver, copper, iron, lead and tin into a furnace to melt it with a fiery blast, so will I gather you in my anger and my wrath and put you inside the city and melt you. ⁱ ²¹I will gather you and I will blow on you with my fiery wrath, and you will be melted inside her. ²²As silver is melted^j in a

---

^a12 Or *usury and interest*   ^b16 Or *When I have allotted you your inheritance*

furnace, so you will be melted inside her, and you will know that I the LORD have poured out my wrath upon you.'"[k]

[23]Again the word of the LORD came to me: [24]"Son of man, say to the land, 'You are a land that has had no rain or showers[a] in the day of wrath.'[l] [25]There is a conspiracy[m] of her princes[b] within her like a roaring lion tearing its prey; they devour people,[n] take treasures and precious things and make many widows[o] within her. [26]Her priests do violence to my law[p] and profane my holy things; they do not distinguish between the holy and the common;[q] they teach that there is no difference between the unclean and the clean;[r] and they shut their eyes to the keeping of my Sabbaths, so that I am profaned among them.[s] [27]Her officials within her are like wolves tearing their prey; they shed blood and kill people to make unjust gain.[t] [28]Her prophets whitewash[u] these deeds for them by false visions and lying divinations. They say, 'This is what the Sovereign LORD says'—when the LORD has not spoken.[v] [29]The people of the land practice extortion and commit robbery; they oppress the poor and needy and mistreat the alien,[w] denying them justice.[x]

[30]"I looked for a man among them who would build up the wall[y] and stand before me in the gap on behalf of the land so I would not have to destroy it, but I found none.[z] [31]So I will pour out my wrath on them and consume them with my fiery anger, bringing down[a] on their own heads all they have done, declares the Sovereign LORD.[b]"

Two Adulterous Sisters

23 The word of the LORD came to me: [2]"Son of man, there were two women, daughters of the same mother.[c] [3]They became prostitutes in Egypt,[d] engaging in prostitution[e] from their youth. In that land their breasts were fondled and their virgin bosoms caressed. [4]The older was named Oholah, and her sister was Oholibah. They were mine and gave birth to sons and daughters. Oholah is Samaria, and Oholibah is Jerusalem.

[5]"Oholah engaged in prostitution while she was still mine; and she lusted after her lovers, the Assyrians[f]—warriors[g] [6]clothed in blue, governors and commanders, all of them handsome young men, and mounted horsemen. [7]She gave herself as a prostitute to all the elite of the Assyrians and defiled herself with all the idols of everyone she lusted after.[h] [8]She did not give up the prostitution she began in Egypt,[i] when during her youth men slept with her, caressed her virgin bosom and poured out their lust upon her.[j]

[9]"Therefore I handed her over[k] to her lovers, the Assyrians, for whom she lusted.[l] [10]They stripped[m] her naked, took away her sons and daughters and killed her with the sword. She became a byword among women,[n] and punishment was inflicted on her.[o]

[11]"Her sister Oholibah saw this, yet in her lust and prostitution she was more depraved than her sister.[p] [12]She too lusted after the Assyrians—governors and commanders, warriors in full dress, mounted horsemen, all handsome young men.[q] [13]I saw that she too defiled herself; both of them went the same way.

[14]"But she carried her prostitution still further. She saw men por-

22:22
kEze 20:8,33
22:24
lEze 24:13
22:25
mJer 11:9
nHos 6:9
oJer 15:8
22:26
pMal 2:7-8
qEze 44:23
rLev 10:10
sISa 2:12-17;
Jer 2:8,26;
Hag 2:11-14
22:27
tIsa 1:23
22:28
uEze 13:10
vEze 13:2,6-7
22:29
wEze 22:21; 23:9
xIsa 5:7
22:30
yEze 13:5
zPs 106:23;
Jer 5:1
22:31
aEze 16:43
bEze 7:8-9;
9:10; Ro 2:8
23:2
cJer 3:7;
Eze 16:45
23:3
dJos 24:14
eLev 17:7
23:5
f2Ki 16:7;
Hos 5:13
gHos 8:9
23:7
hHos 5:3; 6:10
23:8
iEx 32:4
jEze 16:15
23:9
k2Ki 18:11
lHos 11:5
23:10
mHos 2:10
nEze 16:41
oEze 16:36
23:11
pJer 3:8-11;
Eze 16:51
23:12
q2Ki 16:7-15;
2Ch 28:16

trayed on a wall,ʳ figures of Chaldeansª portrayed in red,ˢ ¹⁵with belts around their waists and flowing turbans on their heads; all of them looked like Babylonian chariot officers, natives of Chaldea.ᵇ ¹⁶As soon as she saw them, she lusted after them and sent messengers to them in Chaldea. ¹⁷Then the Babylonians came to her, to the bed of love, and in their lust they defiled her. After she had been defiled by them, she turned away from them in disgust. ¹⁸When she carried on her prostitution openly and exposed her nakedness, I turned awayᵗ from her in disgust, just as I had turned away from her sister.ᵘ ¹⁹Yet she became more and more promiscuous as she recalled the days of her youth, when she was a prostitute in Egypt. ²⁰There she lusted after her lovers, whose genitals were like those of donkeys and whose emission was like that of horses. ²¹So you longed for the lewdness of your youth, when in Egypt your bosom was caressed and your young breasts fondled.ᶜ ᵛ

²²"Therefore, Oholibah, this is what the Sovereign Lᴏʀᴅ says: I will stir up your lovers against you, those you turned away from in disgust, and I will bring them against you from every sideʷ— ²³the Babyloniansˣ and all the Chaldeans, the men of Pekodʸ and Shoa and Koa, and all the Assyrians with them, handsome young men, all of them governors and commanders, chariot officers and men of high rank, all mounted on horses.ᶻ ²⁴They will come against you with weapons,ᵈ chariots and wagonsª and with a throng of people; they will take up positions against you on every side with large and small shields and with helmets. I will turn you over to them for punishment,ᵇ and they will punish you according to their standards. ²⁵I will direct my jealous anger against you, and they will deal with you in fury. They will cut off your noses and your ears, and those of you who are left will fall by the sword. They will take away your sons and daughters,ᶜ and those of you who are left will be consumed by fire.ᵈ ²⁶They will also stripᵉ you of your clothes and take your fine jewelry.ᶠ ²⁷So I will put a stopᵍ to the lewdness and prostitution you began in Egypt. You will not look on these things with longing or remember Egypt anymore.

²⁸"For this is what the Sovereign Lᴏʀᴅ says: I am about to hand you overʰ to those you hate, to those you turned away from in disgust. ²⁹They will deal with you in hatred and take away everything you have worked for. They will leave you naked and bare, and the shame of your prostitution will be exposed. Your lewdness and promiscuityⁱ ³⁰have brought this upon you, because you lusted after the nations and defiled yourself with their idols.ʲ ³¹You have gone the way of your sister; so I will put her cupᵏ into your hand.ˡ

³²"This is what the Sovereign Lᴏʀᴅ says:

"You will drink your sister's cup,
    a cup large and deep;
it will bring scorn and derision,
    for it holds so much.ᵐ
³³You will be filled with drunkenness and sorrow,
    the cup of ruin and desolation,
    the cup of your sister Samaria.ⁿ

23:14
rEze 8:10
sJer 22:14
23:18
tPs 78:59;
106:40; Jer 6:8
uJer 12:8;
Am 5:21
23:21
vEze 16:26
23:22
wEze 16:37
23:23
x2Ki 20:14-18
yJer 50:21
z2Ki 24:2
23:24
aJer 47:3;
Eze 26:7,10;
Na 2:4
bJer 39:5-6
23:25
cver 47
dEze 20:47-48
23:26
eJer 13:22
fIsa 3:18-23;
Eze 16:39
23:27
gEze 16:41
23:28
hJer 34:20
23:29
iDt 28:48
23:30
jEze 6:9
23:31
kJer 25:15
l2Ki 21:13
23:32
mPs 60:3;
Isa 51:17;
Jer 25:15
23:33
nJer 25:15-16

ª14 Or *Babylonians*   ᵇ15 Or *Babylonia*; also in verse 16   ᶜ21 Syriac (see also verse 3); Hebrew *caressed because of your young breasts*   ᵈ24 The meaning of the Hebrew for this word is uncertain.

³⁴You will drink it° and drain it dry;
    you will dash it to pieces
    and tear your breasts.

I have spoken, declares the Sovereign LORD.

³⁵"Therefore this is what the Sovereign LORD says: Since you have forgotten ᵖ me and thrust me behind your back,�q you must bear the consequences of your lewdness and prostitution."

³⁶The LORD said to me: "Son of man, will you judge Oholah and Oholibah? Then confrontʳ them with their detestable practices,ˢ ³⁷for they have committed adultery and blood is on their hands. They committed adultery with their idols; they even sacrificed their children, whom they bore to me,ᵃ as food for them.ᵗ ³⁸They have also done this to me: At that same time they defiled my sanctuary and desecrated my Sabbaths. ³⁹On the very day they sacrificed their children to their idols, they entered my sanctuary and desecratedᵘ it. That is what they did in my house.ᵛ

⁴⁰"They even sent messengers for men who came from far away,ʷ and when they arrived you bathed yourself for them, painted your eyesˣ and put on your jewelry.ʸ ⁴¹You sat on an elegant couch,ᶻ with a tableᵃ spread before it on which you had placed the incense and oil that belonged to me.

⁴²"The noise of a carefree crowd was around her; Sabeansᵇ were brought from the desert along with men from the rabble, and they put braceletsᵇ on the arms of the woman and her sister and beautiful crowns on their heads.ᶜ ⁴³Then I said about the one worn out by adultery, 'Now let them use her as a prostitute,ᵈ for that is all she is.' ⁴⁴And they slept with her. As men sleep with a prostitute, so they slept with those lewd women, Oholah and Oholibah. ⁴⁵But righteous men will sentence them to the punishment of women who commit adultery and shed blood, because they are adulterous and blood is on their hands.ᵉ

⁴⁶"This is what the Sovereign LORD says: Bring a mobᶠ against them and give them over to terror and plunder. ⁴⁷The mob will stone them and cut them down with their swords; they will kill their sons and daughters and burn�g down their houses.ʰ

⁴⁸"So I will put an end to lewdness in the land, that all women may take warning and not imitate you.ⁱ ⁴⁹You will suffer the penalty for your lewdness and bear the consequences of your sins of idolatry. Then you will know that I am the Sovereign LORD.ʲ "

The Cooking Pot

24 In the ninth year, in the tenth month on the tenth day, the word of the LORD came to me:ᵏ ²"Son of man, record this date, this very date, because the king of Babylon has laid siege to Jerusalem this very day.ˡ ³Tell this rebellious houseᵐ a parableⁿ and say to them: 'This is what the Sovereign LORD says:

" 'Put on the cooking pot;° put it on
    and pour water into it.

ᵃ37 Or *even made the children they bore to me pass through the fire;*   ᵇ42 Or *drunkards*

23:34
°Ps 75:8;
Isa 51:17
23:35
ᵖIsa 17:10;
Jer 3:21
q1Ki 14:9
23:36
rEze 16:2
sIsa 58:1;
Eze 22:2;
Mic 3:8
23:37
tEze 16:36
23:39
u2Ki 21:4
vJer 7:10
23:40
wIsa 57:9
x2Ki 9:30
yJer 4:30;
Eze 16:13-19
23:41
zEst 1:6;
Pr 7:17; Am 6:4
aIsa 65:11;
Eze 44:16
23:42
bGe 24:30
cEze 16:11-12
23:43
dver 3
23:45
eLev 20:10;
Eze 16:38;
Hos 6:5
23:46
fEze 16:40
23:47
g2Ch 36:19
h2Ch 36:17;
Eze 16:40-41
23:48
i2Pe 2:6
23:49
jEze 7:4; 9:10;
20:38
24:1
kEze 8:1
24:2
l2Ki 25:1;
Jer 39:1; 52:4
24:3
mIsa 1:2;
Eze 2:3,6
nEze 17:2;
20:49 oJer 1:13;
Eze 11:3

⁴Put into it the pieces of meat,
    all the choice pieces—the leg and the shoulder.
Fill it with the best of these bones;
⁵   take the pick of the flock. ᵖ
Pile wood beneath it for the bones;
    bring it to a boil
    and cook the bones in it. �q

⁶" 'For this is what the Sovereign LORD says:

  " 'Woe to the city of bloodshed, ʳ
    to the pot now encrusted,
    whose deposit will not go away!
Empty it piece by piece
    without casting lots ˢ for them.

⁷" 'For the blood she shed is in her midst:
    She poured it on the bare rock;
she did not pour it on the ground,
    where the dust would cover it. ᵗ
⁸To stir up wrath and take revenge
    I put her blood on the bare rock,
    so that it would not be covered.

⁹" 'Therefore this is what the Sovereign LORD says:

  " 'Woe to the city of bloodshed!
    I, too, will pile the wood high.
¹⁰So heap on the wood
    and kindle the fire.
Cook the meat well,
    mixing in the spices;
    and let the bones be charred.
¹¹Then set the empty pot on the coals
    till it becomes hot and its copper glows
so its impurities may be melted
    and its deposit burned away. ᵘ
¹²It has frustrated all efforts;
    its heavy deposit has not been removed,
    not even by fire.

¹³" 'Now your impurity is lewdness. Because I tried to cleanse you but you would not be cleansed from your impurity, you will not be clean again until my wrath against you has subsided. ᵛ

¹⁴" 'I the LORD have spoken. The time has come for me to act. I will not hold back; I will not have pity, nor will I relent. You will be judged according to your conduct and your actions, ʷ declares the Sovereign LORD. ˣ' "

Ezekiel's Wife Dies

¹⁵The word of the LORD came to me: ¹⁶"Son of man, with one blow I am about to take away from you the delight of your eyes. Yet do not lament or weep or shed any tears. ʸ ¹⁷Groan quietly; do not mourn for the dead. Keep your turban fastened and your sandals on your feet; do

24:5
p Jer 52:10
q Jer 52:24-27
24:6
r Eze 22:2
s Ob 1:11;
  Na 3:10
24:7
t Lev 17:13
24:11
u Jer 21:10;
  Eze 22:15
24:13
v Jer 6:28-30;
  Eze 16:42;
  22:24
24:14
w Eze 36:19
x Eze 18:30
24:16
y Jer 13:17;
  16:5; 22:10

not cover the lower part of your face or eat the customary food ⌊of mourners⌋. ᶻ"

18So I spoke to the people in the morning, and in the evening my wife died. The next morning I did as I had been commanded.

19Then the people asked me, "Won't you tell us what these things have to do with us?ᵃ"

20So I said to them, "The word of the LORD came to me: 21Say to the house of Israel, 'This is what the Sovereign LORD says: I am about to desecrate my sanctuary—the stronghold in which you take pride, the delight of your eyes, ᵇ the object of your affection. The sons and daughtersᶜ you left behind will fall by the sword. ᵈ 22And you will do as I have done. You will not cover the lower part of your face or eat the customary food ⌊of mourners⌋. ᵉ 23You will keep your turbans on your heads and your sandals on your feet. You will not mournᶠ or weep but will waste away because ofᵃ your sins and groan among yourselves. ᵍ 24Ezekiel will be a signʰ to you; you will do just as he has done. When this happens, you will know that I am the Sovereign LORD.'

25"And you, son of man, on the day I take away their stronghold, their joy and glory, the delight of their eyes, their heart's desire, and their sons and daughtersⁱ as well— 26on that day a fugitive will come to tell youʲ the news. 27At that time your mouth will be opened; you will speak with him and will no longer be silent. So you will be a sign to them, and they will know that I am the LORD.ᵏ"

A Prophecy Against Ammon

25 The word of the LORD came to me: 2"Son of man, set your face against the Ammonitesˡ and prophesy against them.ᵐ 3Say to them, 'Hear the word of the Sovereign LORD. This is what the Sovereign LORD says: Because you said "Aha!ⁿ" over my sanctuary when it was desecrated and over the land of Israel when it was laid waste and over the people of Judah when they went into exile,ᵒ 4therefore I am going to give you to the people of the Eastᵖ as a possession. They will set up their camps and pitch their tents among you; they will eat your fruit and drink your milk.�q 5I will turn Rabbahʳ into a pasture for camels and Ammon into a resting place for sheep. ˢ Then you will know that I am the LORD. 6For this is what the Sovereign LORD says: Because you have clapped your hands and stamped your feet, rejoicing with all the malice of your heart against the land of Israel,ᵗ 7therefore I will stretch out my handᵘ against you and give you as plunder to the nations. I will cut you off from the nations and exterminate you from the countries. I will destroyᵛ you, and you will know that I am the LORD.ʷ"

A Prophecy Against Moab

8"This is what the Sovereign LORD says: 'Because Moabˣ and Seir said, "Look, the house of Judah has become like all the other nations," 9therefore I will expose the flank of Moab, beginning at its frontier towns—Beth Jeshimothʸ, Baal Meonᶻ and Kiriathaimᵃ—the glory of that land. 10I will give Moab along with the Ammonites to the people of the East as a possession, so that the Ammonites will not be remem-

---

24:17
z Jer 16:7
24:19
a Eze 12:9;
37:18
24:21
b Ps 27:4
c Eze 23:25
d Jer 7:14,15;
Eze 23:47
24:22
e Jer 16:7
24:23
f Job 27:15
g Ps 78:64
24:24
h Isa 20:3;
Eze 4:3; 12:11
24:25
i Jer 11:22
24:26
j 1Sa 4:12;
Job 1:15-19
24:27
k Eze 3:26;
33:22
25:2
l Eze 21:28;
Zep 2:8-9
m Jer 49:1-6
25:3
n Eze 26:2; 36:2
o Pr 17:5
25:4
p Jdg 6:3
q Dt 28:33,51;
Jdg 6:33
25:5
r Dt 3:11;
Eze 21:20
s Isa 17:2
25:6
t Ob 1:12;
Zep 2:8
25:7
u Zep 1:4
v Eze 21:31
w Am 1:14-15
25:8
x Jer 48:1;
Am 2:1
25:9
y Nu 33:49
z Nu 32:3;
Jos 13:17
a Nu 32:37;
Jos 13:19

ᵃ23 Or *away in*

bered[b] among the nations; [11]and I will inflict punishment on Moab. Then they will know that I am the LORD.' "

A Prophecy Against Edom

[12]"This is what the Sovereign LORD says: 'Because Edom[c] took revenge on the house of Judah and became very guilty by doing so, [13]therefore this is what the Sovereign LORD says: I will stretch out my hand against Edom and kill its men and their animals.[d] I will lay it waste, and from Teman to Dedan[e] they will fall by the sword. [14]I will take vengeance on Edom by the hand of my people Israel, and they will deal with Edom in accordance with my anger[f] and my wrath; they will know my vengeance, declares the Sovereign LORD.' "

A Prophecy Against Philistia

[15]"This is what the Sovereign LORD says: 'Because the Philistines[g] acted in vengeance and took revenge with malice in their hearts, and with ancient hostility sought to destroy Judah, [16]therefore this is what the Sovereign LORD says: I am about to stretch out my hand against the Philistines,[h] and I will cut off the Kerethites[i] and destroy those remaining along the coast. [17]I will carry out great vengeance on them and punish them in my wrath. Then they will know that I am the LORD, when I take vengeance on them.' "

A Prophecy Against Tyre

26 In the eleventh year, on the first day of the month, the word of the LORD came to me: [2]"Son of man, because Tyre[j] has said of Jerusalem, 'Aha![k] The gate to the nations is broken, and its doors have swung open to me; now that she lies in ruins I will prosper,' [3]therefore this is what the Sovereign LORD says: I am against you, O Tyre, and I will bring many nations against you, like the sea[l] casting up its waves. [4]They will destroy[m] the walls of Tyre[n] and pull down her towers; I will scrape away her rubble and make her a bare rock. [5]Out in the sea[o] she will become a place to spread fishnets, for I have spoken, declares the Sovereign LORD. She will become plunder[p] for the nations, [6]and her settlements on the mainland will be ravaged by the sword. Then they will know that I am the LORD.

[7]"For this is what the Sovereign LORD says: From the north I am going to bring against Tyre Nebuchadnezzar[a][q] king of Babylon, king of kings,[r] with horses and chariots,[s] with horsemen and a great army. [8]He will ravage your settlements on the mainland with the sword; he will set up siege works[t] against you, build a ramp[u] up to your walls and raise his shields against you. [9]He will direct the blows of his battering rams against your walls and demolish your towers with his weapons. [10]His horses will be so many that they will cover you with dust. Your walls will tremble at the noise of the war horses, wagons and chariots[v] when he enters your gates as men enter a city whose walls have been broken through. [11]The hoofs[w] of his horses will trample all your streets; he will kill your people with the sword, and your strong pillars[x] will fall to the ground.[y] [12]They will plunder your wealth

25:10
b Eze 21:32
25:12
c 2Ch 28:17
25:13
d Eze 29:8
e Jer 25:23
25:14
f Eze 35:11
25:15
g 2Ch 28:18
25:16
h Jer 47:1-7
i 1Sa 30:14;
Zep 2:4-5
26:2
j 2Sa 5:11;
Isa 23 k Eze 25:3
26:3
l Isa 5:30;
Jer 50:42; 51:42
26:4
m Isa 23:1,11
n Am 1:10
26:5
o Eze 27:32
p Eze 29:19
26:7
q Jer 27:6
r Ezr 7:12;
Da 2:37
s Eze 23:24;
Na 2:3-4
26:8
t Jer 6:6
u Eze 21:22
26:10
v Jer 4:13
26:11
w Isa 5:28
x Jer 43:13
y Isa 26:5

[a]7 Hebrew *Nebuchadrezzar*, of which *Nebuchadnezzar* is a variant; here and often in Ezekiel and Jeremiah

and loot your merchandise; they will break down your walls and demolish your fine houses and throw your stones, timber and rubble into the sea.ᶻ ¹³I will put an endᵃ to your noisy songs, and the music of your harpsᵇ will be heard no more.ᶜ ¹⁴I will make you a bare rock, and you will become a place to spread fishnets. You will never be rebuilt,ᵈ for I the LORD have spoken, declares the Sovereign LORD.

¹⁵"This is what the Sovereign LORD says to Tyre: Will not the coastlandsᵉ trembleᶠ at the sound of your fall, when the wounded groan and the slaughter takes place in you? ¹⁶Then all the princes of the coast will step down from their thrones and lay aside their robes and take off their embroidered garments. Clothedᵍ with terror, they will sit on the ground, tremblingʰ every moment, appalledⁱ at you. ¹⁷Then they will take up a lamentʲ concerning you and say to you:

" 'How you are destroyed, O city of renown,
    peopled by men of the sea!
You were a power on the seas,
    you and your citizens;
you put your terror
    on all who lived there.ᵏ
¹⁸Now the coastlands tremble
    on the day of your fall;
the islands in the sea
    are terrified at your collapse.'ˡ

¹⁹"This is what the Sovereign LORD says: When I make you a desolate city, like cities no longer inhabited, and when I bring the ocean depths over you and its vast waters cover you,ᵐ ²⁰then I will bring you down with those who go down to the pit,ⁿ to the people of long ago. I will make you dwell in the earth below, as in ancient ruins, with those who go down to the pit, and you will not return or take your placeᵃ in the land of the living.ᵒ ²¹I will bring you to a horrible end and you will be no more. You will be sought, but you will never again be found, declares the Sovereign LORD."ᵖ

A Lament for Tyre

27 The word of the LORD came to me: ²"Son of man, take up a lament concerning Tyre. ³Say to Tyre, situated at the gateway to the sea,�q merchant of peoples on many coasts, 'This is what the Sovereign LORD says:

" 'You say, O Tyre,
    "I am perfect in beauty.ʳ"
⁴Your domain was on the high seas;
    your builders brought your beauty to perfection.
⁵They made all your timbers
    of pine trees from Senirᵇ;ˢ
they took a cedar from Lebanon
    to make a mast for you.
⁶Of oaksᵗ from Bashan
    they made your oars;

ᵃ20 Septuagint; Hebrew *return, and I will give glory*   ᵇ5 That is, Hermon

26:12
zIsa 23:8;
Eze 27:3-27;
28:8
26:13
aJer 7:34
bIsa 14:11
cJer 25:10;
Rev 18:22
26:14
dJob 12:14;
Mal 1:4
26:15
eEze 27:35
fJer 49:21
26:16
gJob 8:22
hHos 11:10
iEze 32:10
26:17
jEze 19:1; 27:32
kIsa 14:12
26:18
lIsa 23:5; 41:5;
Eze 27:35
26:19
mIsa 8:7-8
26:20
nEze 32:18;
Am 9:2;
Jnh 2:2,6
oEze 32:24,30
26:21
pEze 27:36;
28:19;
Rev 18:21
27:3
qver 33
rEze 28:2
27:5
sDt 3:9
27:6
tNu 21:33;
Jer 22:20;
Zec 11:2

of cypress wood[a] from the coasts of Cyprus[b] [u]
   they made your deck, inlaid with ivory.
[7]Fine embroidered linen from Egypt was your sail
   and served as your banner;
your awnings were of blue and purple[v]
   from the coasts of Elishah.
[8]Men of Sidon and Arvad[w] were your oarsmen;
   your skilled men, O Tyre, were aboard as your
      seamen.[x]
[9]Veteran craftsmen of Gebal[cy] were on board
   as shipwrights to caulk your seams.
All the ships of the sea and their sailors
   came alongside to trade for your wares.

[10]" 'Men of Persia,[z] Lydia and Put[a]
   served as soldiers in your army.
They hung their shields and helmets on your walls,
   bringing you splendor.
[11]Men of Arvad and Helech
   manned your walls on every side;
men of Gammad
   were in your towers.
They hung their shields around your walls;
   they brought your beauty to perfection.

[12]" 'Tarshish[b] did business with you because of your great wealth of goods;[c] they exchanged silver, iron, tin and lead for your merchandise.
[13]" 'Greece, Tubal and Meshech[d] traded with you; they exchanged slaves[e] and articles of bronze for your wares.
[14]" 'Men of Beth Togarmah[f] exchanged work horses, war horses and mules for your merchandise.
[15]" 'The men of Rhodes[dg] traded with you, and many coastlands[h] were your customers; they paid you with ivory[i] tusks and ebony.
[16]" 'Aram[ej] did business with you because of your many products; they exchanged turquoise,[k] purple fabric, embroidered work, fine linen, coral and rubies for your merchandise.
[17]" 'Judah and Israel traded with you; they exchanged wheat from Minnith[l] and confections,[f] honey, oil and balm for your wares.
[18]" 'Damascus,[m] because of your many products and great wealth of goods, did business with you in wine from Helbon and wool from Zahar.
[19]" 'Danites and Greeks from Uzal bought your merchandise; they exchanged wrought iron, cassia and calamus for your wares.
[20]" 'Dedan traded in saddle blankets with you.
[21]" 'Arabia and all the princes of Kedar[n] were your customers; they did business with you in lambs, rams and goats.
[22]" 'The merchants of Sheba[o] and Raamah traded with you; for your merchandise they exchanged the finest of all kinds of spices[p] and precious stones, and gold.

27:6
uGe 10:4;
Isa 23:12
27:7
vEx 25:4;
Jer 10:9
27:8
wGe 10:18
x1Ki 9:27
27:9
yJos 13:5;
1Ki 5:18
27:10
zEze 38:5
aEze 30:5
27:12
bGe 10:4
cver 18,33
27:13
dGe 10:2;
Isa 66:19;
Eze 38:2
eRev 18:13
27:14
fGe 10:3;
Eze 38:6
27:15
gGe 10:7
hJer 25:22
i1Ki 10:22;
Rev 18:12
27:16
jJdg 10:6;
Isa 7:1-8
kEze 28:13
27:17
lJdg 11:33
27:18
mGe 14:15;
Eze 47:16-18
27:21
nGe 25:13;
Isa 60:7
27:22
oGe 10:7,28;
1Ki 10:1-2;
Isa 60:6
pGe 43:11

---

[a]6 Targum; the Masoretic Text has a different division of the consonants.   [b]6 Hebrew *Kittim*   [c]9 That is, Byblos   [d]15 Septuagint; Hebrew *Dedan*   [e]16 Most Hebrew manuscripts; some Hebrew manuscripts and Syriac *Edom*   [f]17 The meaning of the Hebrew for this word is uncertain.

23" 'Haran,q Canneh and Edenr and merchants of Sheba, Asshur and Kilmad traded with you. 24In your marketplace they traded with you beautiful garments, blue fabric, embroidered work and multicolored rugs with cords twisted and tightly knotted.

25" 'The ships of Tarshishs serve
    as carriers for your wares.
You are filled with heavy cargo
    in the heart of the sea.
26Your oarsmen take you
    out to the high seas.
But the east windt will break you to pieces
    in the heart of the sea.
27Your wealth,u merchandise and wares,
    your mariners, seamen and shipwrights,
your merchants and all your soldiers,
    and everyone else on board
will sink into the heart of the sea
    on the day of your shipwreck.
28The shorelands will quakev
    when your seamen cry out.
29All who handle the oars
    will abandon their ships;
the mariners and all the seamen
    will stand on the shore.
30They will raise their voice
    and cry bitterly over you;
they will sprinkle dustw on their heads
    and rollx in ashes.y
31They will shave their heads because of you
    and will put on sackcloth.
They will weepz over you with anguish of soul
    and with bitter mourning.a
32As they wail and mourn over you,
    they will take up a lamentb concerning you:
"Who was ever silenced like Tyre,
    surrounded by the sea?"
33When your merchandise went out on the seas,
    you satisfied many nations;
with your great wealthc and your wares
    you enriched the kings of the earth.
34Now you are shattered by the sea
    in the depths of the waters;
your wares and all your company
    have gone down with you.d
35All who live in the coastlandse
    are appalled at you;
their kings shudder with horror
    and their faces are distorted with fear.
36The merchants among the nations hiss at you;f
    you have come to a horrible end
    and will be no more.g' "

27:23
q2Ki 19:12
rIsa 37:12
27:25
sIsa 2:16 fn
27:26
tPs 48:7;
Jer 18:17
27:27
uPr 11:4
27:28
vEze 26:15
27:30
w2Sa 1:2
xJer 6:26
yRev 18:18-19
27:31
zIsa 16:9
aIsa 22:12;
Eze 7:18
27:32
bEze 26:17
27:33
cver 12;
Eze 28:4-5
27:34
dZec 9:4
27:35
eEze 26:15
27:36
fJer 18:16;
19:8; 49:17;
50:13; Zep 2:15
gPs 37:10,36;
Eze 26:21

A Prophecy Against the King of Tyre

28 The word of the LORD came to me: [2]"Son of man, say to the ruler of Tyre, 'This is what the Sovereign LORD says:

> " 'In the pride of your heart
>   you say, "I am a god;
> I sit on the throne[h] of a god
>   in the heart of the seas."
> But you are a man and not a god,
>   though you think you are as wise as a god.[i]
> [3]Are you wiser than Daniel[a]?[j]
>   Is no secret hidden from you?
> [4]By your wisdom and understanding
>   you have gained wealth for yourself
> and amassed gold and silver
>   in your treasuries.[k]
> [5]By your great skill in trading
>   you have increased your wealth,
> and because of your wealth
>   your heart has grown proud.[l]

[6]" 'Therefore this is what the Sovereign LORD says:

> " 'Because you think you are wise,
>   as wise as a god,
> [7]I am going to bring foreigners against you,
>   the most ruthless of nations;[m]
> they will draw their swords against your beauty and
>   wisdom
>   and pierce your shining splendor.
> [8]They will bring you down to the pit,[n]
>   and you will die a violent death
>   in the heart of the seas.[o]
> [9]Will you then say, "I am a god,"
>   in the presence of those who kill you?
> You will be but a man, not a god,
>   in the hands of those who slay you.
> [10]You will die the death of the uncircumcised[p]
>   at the hands of foreigners.

I have spoken, declares the Sovereign LORD.' "

[11]The word of the LORD came to me: [12]"Son of man, take up a lament[q] concerning the king of Tyre and say to him: 'This is what the Sovereign LORD says:

> " 'You were the model of perfection,
>   full of wisdom and perfect in beauty.[r]
> [13]You were in Eden,[s]
>   the garden of God;[t]
> every precious stone adorned you:
>   ruby, topaz and emerald,

---

[a]3 Or *Danel*; the Hebrew spelling may suggest a person other than the prophet Daniel.

28:2
h Isa 14:13
i Ps 9:20;
82:6-7;
Isa 31:3;
2Th 2:4
28:3
j Da 1:20;
5:11-12
28:4
k Zec 9:3
28:5
l Job 31:25;
Ps 52:7; 62:10;
Hos 12:8; 13:6
28:7
m Eze 30:11;
31:12; 32:12;
Hab 1:6
28:8
n Eze 32:30
o Eze 27:27
28:10
p Eze 31:18;
32:19,24
28:12
q Eze 19:1
r Eze 27:2-4
28:13
s Ge 2:8
t Eze 31:8-9

chrysolite, onyx and jasper,
sapphire,ᵃ turquoiseᵘ and beryl.ᵇ
Your settings and mountingsᶜ were made of gold;
on the day you were created they were prepared.
¹⁴You were anointedᵛ as a guardian cherub,ʷ
for so I ordained you.
You were on the holy mount of God;
you walked among the fiery stones.
¹⁵You were blameless in your ways
from the day you were created
till wickedness was found in you.
¹⁶Through your widespread trade
you were filled with violence,ˣ
and you sinned.
So I drove you in disgrace from the mount of God,
and I expelled you, O guardian cherub,ʸ
from among the fiery stones.
¹⁷Your heart became proudᶻ
on account of your beauty,
and you corrupted your wisdom
because of your splendor.
So I threw you to the earth;
I made a spectacle of you before kings.
¹⁸By your many sins and dishonest trade
you have desecrated your sanctuaries.
So I made a fire come out from you,
and it consumed you,
and I reduced you to ashesᵃ on the ground
in the sight of all who were watching.
¹⁹All the nations who knew you
are appalled at you;
you have come to a horrible end
and will be no more.ᵇ' "

A Prophecy Against Sidon

²⁰The word of the LORD came to me: ²¹"Son of man, set your face
againstᶜ Sidon;ᵈ prophesy against her ²²and say: 'This is what the
Sovereign LORD says:

" 'I am against you, O Sidon,
and I will gain gloryᵉ within you.
They will know that I am the LORD,
when I inflict punishmentᶠ on her
and show myself holy within her.
²³I will send a plague upon her
and make blood flow in her streets.
The slain will fall within her,
with the sword against her on every side.
Then they will know that I am the LORD.ᵍ

ᵃ13 Or *lapis lazuli*   ᵇ13 The precise identification of some of these precious stones is uncertain.
ᶜ13 The meaning of the Hebrew for this phrase is uncertain.

28:13
ᵘEze 27:16
28:14
ᵛEx 30:26; 40:9
ʷEx 25:17-20
28:16
ˣHab 2:17
ʸGe 3:24
28:17
ᶻEze 31:10
28:18
ᵃMal 4:3
28:19
ᵇJer 51:64;
Eze 26:21;
27:36
28:21
ᶜEze 6:2
ᵈGe 10:15;
Jer 25:22
28:22
ᵉEze 39:13
ᶠEze 30:19
28:23
ᵍEze 38:22

24" 'No longer will the people of Israel have malicious neighbors who are painful briers and sharp thorns.ʰ Then they will know that I am the Sovereign Lᴏʀᴅ.

25" 'This is what the Sovereign Lᴏʀᴅ says: When I gatherⁱ the people of Israel from the nations where they have been scattered,ʲ I will show myself holyᵏ among them in the sight of the nations. Then they will live in their own land, which I gave to my servant Jacob.ˡ 26They will live there in safetyᵐ and will build houses and plant vineyards; they will live in safety when I inflict punishment on all their neighbors who maligned them. Then they will know that I am the Lᴏʀᴅ their God.ⁿ' "

A Prophecy Against Egypt

29 In the tenth year, in the tenth month on the twelfth day, the word of the Lᴏʀᴅ came to me:ᵒ 2"Son of man, set your face against Pharaoh king of Egyptᵖ and prophesy against him and against all Egypt.�q 3Speak to him and say: 'This is what the Sovereign Lᴏʀᴅ says:

" 'I am against you, Pharaohʳ king of Egypt,
    you great monsterˢ lying among your streams.
You say, "The Nile is mine;
    I made it for myself."
4But I will put hooksᵗ in your jaws
    and make the fish of your streams stick to your scales.
I will pull you out from among your streams,
    with all the fish sticking to your scales.ᵘ
5I will leave you in the desert,
    you and all the fish of your streams.
You will fall on the open field
    and not be gathered or picked up.
I will give you as food
    to the beasts of the earth and the birds of the air.ᵛ

6Then all who live in Egypt will know that I am the Lᴏʀᴅ.

" 'You have been a staff of reedʷ for the house of Israel. 7When they grasped you with their hands, you splinteredˣ and you tore open their shoulders; when they leaned on you, you broke and their backs were wrenched.ᵃ ʸ

8" 'Therefore this is what the Sovereign Lᴏʀᴅ says: I will bring a sword against you and kill your men and their animals.ᶻ 9Egypt will become a desolate wasteland. Then they will know that I am the Lᴏʀᴅ.

" 'Because you said, "The Nile is mine; I made it,ᵃ" 10therefore I am against you and against your streams, and I will make the land of Egypt a ruin and a desolate waste from Migdol to Aswan,ᵇ as far as the border of Cush.ᵇ 11No foot of man or animal will pass through it; no one will live there for forty years.ᶜ 12I will make the land of Egypt desolate among devastated lands, and her cities will lie desolate forty years among ruined cities. And I will disperse the Egyptians among the nations and scatter them through the countries.ᵈ

ᵃ7 Syriac (see also Septuagint and Vulgate); Hebrew *and you caused their backs to stand*   ᵇ10 That is, the upper Nile region

28:24
ʰNu 33:55;
Jos 23:13;
Eze 2:6
28:25
ⁱPs 106:47;
Jer 32:37
ʲIsa 11:12
ᵏEze 20:41
ˡJer 23:8;
Eze 11:17;
34:27; 37:25
28:26
ᵐJer 23:6
ⁿIsa 65:21;
Jer 32:15;
Eze 38:8;
Am 9:14-15
29:1
ᵒver 17;
Eze 26:1
29:2
ᵖJer 25:19
qIsa 19:1-17;
Jer 46:2;
Eze 30:1-26;
31:1-18; 32:1-32
29:3
ʳJer 44:30
ˢPs 74:13;
Isa 27:1;
Eze 32:2
29:4
ᵗ2Ki 19:28
ᵘEze 38:4
29:5
ᵛJer 7:33;
34:20;
Eze 32:4-6; 39:4
29:6
ʷ2Ki 18:21;
Isa 36:6
29:7
ˣIsa 36:6
ʸEze 17:15-17
29:8
ᶻEze 14:17;
32:11-13
29:9
ᵃEze 30:7-8,
13-19
29:10
ᵇEze 30:6
29:11
ᶜEze 32:13
29:12
ᵈJer 46:19;
Eze 30:7,23,26

13'' 'Yet this is what the Sovereign LORD says: At the end of forty years I will gather the Egyptians from the nations where they were scattered. 14I will bring them back from captivity and return them to Upper Egypt,*ᵃᵉ* the land of their ancestry. There they will be a lowly*ᶠ* kingdom. 15It will be the lowliest of kingdoms and will never again exalt itself above the other nations.*ᵍ* I will make it so weak that it will never again rule over the nations. 16Egypt will no longer be a source of confidence*ʰ* for the people of Israel but will be a reminder of their sin in turning to her for help. Then they will know that I am the Sovereign LORD.*ⁱ* ' ''

17In the twenty-seventh year, in the first month on the first day, the word of the LORD came to me:*ʲ* 18''Son of man, Nebuchadnezzar*ᵏ* king of Babylon drove his army in a hard campaign against Tyre; every head was rubbed bare*ˡ* and every shoulder made raw. Yet he and his army got no reward from the campaign he led against Tyre. 19Therefore this is what the Sovereign LORD says: I am going to give Egypt to Nebuchadnezzar king of Babylon, and he will carry off its wealth. He will loot and plunder the land as pay for his army.*ᵐ* 20I have given him Egypt as a reward for his efforts because he and his army did it for me, declares the Sovereign LORD.*ⁿ*

21''On that day I will make a horn*ᵇᵒ* grow for the house of Israel, and I will open your mouth*ᵖ* among them. Then they will know that I am the LORD.*�q*''

A Lament for Egypt

30 The word of the LORD came to me: 2''Son of man, prophesy and say: 'This is what the Sovereign LORD says:

" 'Wail*ʳ* and say,
  "Alas for that day!"
3For the day is near,*ˢ*
  the day of the LORD*ᵗ* is near—
a day of clouds,
  a time of doom for the nations.
4A sword will come against Egypt,
  and anguish will come upon Cush.*ᶜ*
When the slain fall in Egypt,
  her wealth will be carried away
  and her foundations torn down.*ᵘ*

5Cush and Put,*ᵛ* Lydia and all Arabia, Libya*ᵈ* and the people*ʷ* of the covenant land will fall by the sword along with Egypt.

6'' 'This is what the LORD says:

" 'The allies of Egypt will fall
  and her proud strength will fail.
From Migdol to Aswan*ˣ*
  they will fall by the sword within her,
                declares the Sovereign LORD.
  7'' 'They will be desolate

29:14
eEze 30:14
fEze 17:14
29:15
gZec 10:11
29:16
hIsa 36:4,6
iIsa 30:2;
Hos 8:13
29:17
jEze 24:1
29:18
kJer 27:6;
Eze 26:7-8
lJer 48:37
29:19
mJer 43:10-13;
Eze 30:4,10,
24-25
29:20
nIsa 10:6-7;
45:1; Jer 25:9
29:21
oPs 132:17
pEze 33:22
qEze 24:27
30:2
rIsa 13:6
30:3
sEze 7:7;
Joel 2:1,11;
Ob 1:15
tver 18;
Eze 7:12,19
30:4
uEze 29:19
30:5
vEze 27:10
wJer 25:20
30:6
xEze 29:10

ᵃ14 Hebrew *to Pathros*   ᵇ21 *Horn* here symbolizes strength.   ᶜ4 That is, the upper Nile region; also in verses 5 and 9   ᵈ5 Hebrew *Cub*

among desolate lands,
  and their cities will lie
    among ruined cities. [y]
     [8]Then they will know that I am the LORD,
  when I set fire to Egypt
  and all her helpers are crushed.

    [9]" 'On that day messengers will go out from me in ships to frighten Cush[z] out of her complacency. Anguish[a] will take hold of them on the day of Egypt's doom, for it is sure to come. [b]

    [10]" 'This is what the Sovereign LORD says:

" 'I will put an end to the hordes of Egypt
  by the hand of Nebuchadnezzar king of Babylon. [c]
[11]He and his army—the most ruthless of nations[d]—
  will be brought in to destroy the land.
They will draw their swords against Egypt
  and fill the land with the slain.
[12]I will dry up[e] the streams of the Nile[f]
  and sell the land to evil men;
by the hand of foreigners
  I will lay waste the land and everything in it.

I the LORD have spoken.

    [13]" 'This is what the Sovereign LORD says:

" 'I will destroy the idols[g]
  and put an end to the images in Memphis. [a] [h]
No longer will there be a prince in Egypt, [i]
  and I will spread fear throughout the land.
[14]I will lay[j] waste Upper Egypt, [b]
  set fire to Zoan[k]
  and inflict punishment on Thebes. [c] [l]
[15]I will pour out my wrath on Pelusium, [d]
  the stronghold of Egypt,
  and cut off the hordes of Thebes.
[16]I will set fire to Egypt;
  Pelusium will writhe in agony.
Thebes will be taken by storm;
  Memphis will be in constant distress.
[17]The young men of Heliopolis[e] [m] and Bubastis[f]
  will fall by the sword,
  and the cities themselves will go into captivity.
[18]Dark will be the day at Tahpanhes
  when I break the yoke of Egypt;[n]
  there her proud strength will come to an end.
She will be covered with clouds,
  and her villages will go into captivity. [o]
[19]So I will inflict punishment on Egypt,

30:7
y Eze 29:12
30:9
z Isa 18:1-2
a Isa 23:5
b Eze 32:9-10
30:10
c Eze 29:19
30:11
d Eze 28:7
30:12
e Isa 19:6
f Eze 29:9
30:13
g Jer 43:12
h Isa 19:13
i Zec 10:11
30:14
j Eze 29:14
k Ps 78:12,43
l Jer 46:25
30:17
m Ge 41:45
30:18
n Lev 26:13
o ver 3

---

a13 Hebrew *Noph;* also in verse 16   *b14* Hebrew *waste Pathros*   *c14* Hebrew *No;* also in verses 15 and 16   *d15* Hebrew *Sin;* also in verse 16   *e17* Hebrew *Awen* (or *On*) *f17* Hebrew *Pi Beseth* and they will know that I am the Lord.' "

20In the eleventh year, in the first month on the seventh day, the word of the Lord came to me:ᴾ 21"Son of man, I have broken the arm�q of Pharaoh king of Egypt. It has not been bound up for healingʳ or put in a splint so as to become strong enough to hold a sword. 22Therefore this is what the Sovereign Lord says: I am against Pharaoh king of Egypt.ˢ I will break both his arms, the good arm as well as the broken one, and make the sword fall from his hand.ᵗ 23I will disperse the Egyptians among the nations and scatter them through the countries.ᵘ 24I will strengthen�v the arms of the king of Babylon and put my swordʷ in his hand, but I will break the arms of Pharaoh, and he will groan before him like a mortally wounded man. 25I will strengthen the arms of the king of Babylon, but the arms of Pharaoh will fall limp. Then they will know that I am the Lord, when I put my sword into the hand of the king of Babylon and he brandishes it against Egypt. 26I will disperse the Egyptians among the nations and scatter them through the countries. Then they will know that I am the Lord.ˣ "

A Cedar in Lebanon

31 In the eleventh year,ʸ in the third month on the first day, the word of the Lord came to me:ᶻ 2"Son of man, say to Pharaoh king of Egypt and to his hordes:

" 'Who can be compared with you in majesty?
3Consider Assyria, once a cedar in Lebanon,
　　with beautiful branches overshadowing the forest;
it towered on high,
　　its top above the thick foliage.ᵃ
4The waters nourished it,
　　deep springs made it grow tall;
their streams flowed
　　all around its base
and sent their channels
　　to all the trees of the field.
5So it towered higher
　　than all the trees of the field;
its boughs increased
　　and its branches grew long,
　　spreading because of abundant waters.ᵇ
6All the birds of the air
　　nested in its boughs,
all the beasts of the field
　　gave birth under its branches;
all the great nations
　　lived in its shade.ᶜ
7It was majestic in beauty,
　　with its spreading boughs,
for its roots went down
　　to abundant waters.
8The cedarsᵈ in the garden of God
　　could not rival it,
　　nor could the pine trees

30:20
pEze 26:1;
29:17; 31:1
30:21
qJer 48:25
rJer 30:13;
46:11
30:22
sJer 46:25
tPs 37:17
30:23
uEze 29:12
30:24
vZec 10:6,12
wEze 21:14;
Zep 2:12
30:26
xEze 29:12
31:1
yJer 52:5
zEze 30:20
31:3
aIsa 10:34
31:5
bEze 17:5
31:6
cEze 17:23;
Mt 13:32
31:8
dPs 80:10

equal its boughs,
nor could the plane trees
  compare with its branches—
no tree in the garden of God
  could match its beauty. e
⁹I made it beautiful
  with abundant branches,
the envy of all the trees of Eden f
  in the garden of God. g

10″ 'Therefore this is what the Sovereign Lord says: Because it towered on high, lifting its top above the thick foliage, and because it was proud h of its height, 11I handed it over to the ruler of the nations, for him to deal with according to its wickedness. I cast it aside, i 12and the most ruthless of foreign nations j cut it down and left it. Its boughs fell on the mountains and in all the valleys; k its branches lay broken in all the ravines of the land. All the nations of the earth came out from under its shade and left it. l 13All the birds of the air settled on the fallen tree, and all the beasts of the field were among its branches. m 14Therefore no other trees by the waters are ever to tower proudly on high, lifting their tops above the thick foliage. No other trees so well-watered are ever to reach such a height; they are all destined for death, n for the earth below, among mortal men, with those who go down to the pit. o

15″ 'This is what the Sovereign Lord says: On the day it was brought down to the grave a I covered the deep springs with mourning for it; I held back its streams, and its abundant waters were restrained. Because of it I clothed Lebanon with gloom, and all the trees of the field withered away. 16I made the nations tremble p at the sound of its fall when I brought it down to the grave with those who go down to the pit. Then all the trees q of Eden, the choicest and best of Lebanon, all the trees that were well-watered, were consoled r in the earth below. s 17Those who lived in its shade, its allies among the nations, had also gone down to the grave with it, joining those killed by the sword. t

18″ 'Which of the trees of Eden can be compared with you in splendor and majesty? Yet you, too, will be brought down with the trees of Eden to the earth below; you will lie among the uncircumcised, u with those killed by the sword.

″ 'This is Pharaoh and all his hordes, declares the Sovereign Lord.' ″

A Lament for Pharaoh

32 In the twelfth year, in the twelfth month on the first day, the word of the Lord came to me: v 2″Son of man, take up a lament w concerning Pharaoh king of Egypt and say to him:

″ 'You are like a lion x among the nations;
  you are like a monster in the seas
thrashing about in your streams,
  churning the water with your feet
  and muddying the streams. y

3″ 'This is what the Sovereign Lord says:

31:8
eGe 2:8-9
31:9
fGe 2:8
gGe 13:10;
Eze 28:13
31:10
hIsa 14:13-14;
Eze 28:17
31:11
iDa 5:20
31:12
jEze 28:7
kEze 32:5; 35:8
lEze 32:11-12;
Da 4:14
31:13
mIsa 18:6;
Eze 29:5; 32:4
31:14
nPs 82:7
oPs 63:9;
Eze 26:20;
32:24
31:16
pEze 26:15
qIsa 14:8
rEze 14:22;
32:31
sIsa 14:15;
Eze 32:18
31:17
tPs 9:17
31:18
uJer 9:26;
Eze 32:19,21
32:1
vEze 31:1;
33:21
32:2
wEze 19:1; 27:2
xEze 19:3,6;
Na 2:11-13
yEze 29:3;
34:18

---

a15 Hebrew *Sheol*; also in verses 16 and 17

'' 'With a great throng of people
    I will cast my net over you,
    and they will haul you up in my net. [z]
  ⁴I will throw you on the land
    and hurl you on the open field.
I will let all the birds of the air settle on you
    and all the beasts of the earth gorge themselves on
        you. [a]
  ⁵I will spread your flesh on the mountains
    and fill the valleys[b] with your remains.
  ⁶I will drench the land with your flowing blood[c]
    all the way to the mountains,
    and the ravines will be filled with your flesh.
⁷When I snuff you out, I will cover the heavens
    and darken their stars;
I will cover the sun with a cloud,
    and the moon will not give its light. [d]
  ⁸All the shining lights in the heavens
    I will darken over you;
    I will bring darkness over your land,
          declares the Sovereign Lord.
  ⁹I will trouble the hearts of many peoples
    when I bring about your destruction among the
        nations,
    among[a] lands you have not known.
¹⁰I will cause many peoples to be appalled at you,
    and their kings will shudder with horror because of
        you
    when I brandish my sword before them.
On the day[e] of your downfall
    each of them will tremble
    every moment for his life. [f]

¹¹'' 'For this is what the Sovereign Lord says:

  '' 'The sword of the king of Babylon[g]
    will come against you.
¹²I will cause your hordes to fall
    by the swords of mighty men—
    the most ruthless of all nations. [h]
They will shatter the pride of Egypt,
    and all her hordes will be overthrown. [i]
¹³I will destroy all her cattle
    from beside abundant waters
no longer to be stirred by the foot of man
    or muddied by the hoofs of cattle. [j]
¹⁴Then I will let her waters settle
    and make her streams flow like oil,
          declares the Sovereign Lord.
¹⁵When I make Egypt desolate
    and strip the land of everything in it,

32:3
z Eze 12:13
32:4
a Isa 18:6;
Eze 31:12-13
32:5
b Eze 31:12
32:6
c Isa 34:3
32:7
d Isa 13:10;
34:4; Eze 30:3;
Joel 2:2,31;
3:15; Mt 24:29;
Rev 8:12
32:10
e Jer 46:10
f Eze 26:16;
27:35
32:11
g Jer 46:26
32:12
h Eze 28:7
i Eze 31:11-12
32:13
j Eze 29:8,11

---

a9 Hebrew; Septuagint *bring you into captivity among the nations, / to*

> when I strike down all who live there,
> then they will know that I am the LORD. k'

16"This is the lament[l] they will chant for her. The daughters of the nations will chant it; for Egypt and all her hordes they will chant it, declares the Sovereign LORD."

17In the twelfth year, on the fifteenth day of the month, the word of the LORD came to me:[m] 18"Son of man, wail for the hordes of Egypt and consign[n] to the earth below both her and the daughters of mighty nations, with those who go down to the pit.[o] 19Say to them, 'Are you more favored than others? Go down and be laid among the uncircumcised.'[p] 20They will fall among those killed by the sword. The sword is drawn; let her be dragged[q] off with all her hordes. 21From within the grave[ar] the mighty leaders will say of Egypt and her allies, 'They have come down and they lie with the uncircumcised, with those killed by the sword.'

22"Assyria is there with her whole army; she is surrounded by the graves of all her slain, all who have fallen by the sword. 23Their graves are in the depths of the pit[s] and her army lies around her grave. All who had spread terror in the land of the living are slain, fallen by the sword.

24"Elam[t] is there, with all her hordes around her grave. All of them are slain, fallen by the sword.[u] All who had spread terror in the land of the living[v] went down uncircumcised to the earth below. They bear their shame with those who go down to the pit.[w] 25A bed is made for her among the slain, with all her hordes around her grave. All of them are uncircumcised, killed by the sword. Because their terror had spread in the land of the living, they bear their shame with those who go down to the pit; they are laid among the slain.

26"Meshech and Tubal[x] are there, with all their hordes around their graves. All of them are uncircumcised, killed by the sword because they spread their terror in the land of the living. 27Do they not lie with the other uncircumcised warriors who have fallen, who went down to the grave with their weapons of war, whose swords were placed under their heads? The punishment for their sins rested on their bones, though the terror of these warriors had stalked through the land of the living.

28"You too, O Pharaoh, will be broken and will lie among the uncircumcised, with those killed by the sword.

29"Edom[y] is there, her kings and all her princes; despite their power, they are laid with those killed by the sword. They lie with the uncircumcised, with those who go down to the pit.[z]

30"All the princes of the north[a] and all the Sidonians[b] are there; they went down with the slain in disgrace despite the terror caused by their power. They lie uncircumcised with those killed by the sword and bear their shame with those who go down to the pit.

31"Pharaoh—he and all his army—will see them and he will be consoled[c] for all his hordes that were killed by the sword, declares the Sovereign LORD. 32Although I had him spread terror in the land of the living, Pharaoh and all his hordes will be laid among the uncircum-

32:15
kEx 7:5; 14:4,
18;
Ps 107:33-34;
Eze 6:7
32:16
l2Sa 1:17;
2Ch 35:25;
Eze 26:17
32:17
mver 1
32:18
nJer 1:10
oEze 31:14,16;
Mic 1:8
32:19
pver 29-30;
Eze 28:10;
31:18
32:20
qPs 28:3
32:21
rIsa 14:9
32:23
sIsa 14:15
32:24
tGe 10:22
uJer 49:37
vJob 28:13
wEze 26:20
32:26
xGe 10:2;
Eze 27:13
32:29
yIsa 34:5-15;
Jer 49:7;
Eze 35:15;
Ob 1:1
zEze 25:12-14
32:30
aJer 25:26;
Eze 38:6; 39:2
bJer 25:22;
Eze 28:21
32:31
cEze 14:22;
31:16

a21 Hebrew *Sheol*; also in verse 27

cised, with those killed by the sword, declares the Sovereign LORD."

Ezekiel a Watchman

33 The word of the LORD came to me: [2]"Son of man, speak to your countrymen and say to them: 'When I bring the sword[d] against a land, and the people of the land choose one of their men and make him their watchman,[e] [3]and he sees the sword coming against the land and blows the trumpet[f] to warn the people, [4]then if anyone hears the trumpet but does not take warning[g] and the sword comes and takes his life, his blood will be on his own head.[h] [5]Since he heard the sound of the trumpet but did not take warning, his blood will be on his own head. If he had taken warning, he would have saved himself. [6]But if the watchman sees the sword coming and does not blow the trumpet to warn the people and the sword comes and takes the life of one of them, that man will be taken away because of his sin, but I will hold the watchman accountable for his blood.'[i]

[7]"Son of man, I have made you a watchman for the house of Israel; so hear the word I speak and give them warning from me.[j] [8]When I say to the wicked, 'O wicked man, you will surely die,[k]' and you do not speak out to dissuade him from his ways, that wicked man will die for[a] his sin, and I will hold you accountable for his blood.[l] [9]But if you do warn the wicked man to turn from his ways and he does not do so, he will die for his sin, but you will have saved yourself.[m]

[10]"Son of man, say to the house of Israel, 'This is what you are saying: "Our offenses and sins weigh us down, and we are wasting away[n] because of[b] them. How then can we live?[o]"' [11]Say to them, 'As surely as I live, declares the Sovereign LORD, I take no pleasure in the death of the wicked, but rather that they turn from their ways and live.[p] Turn! Turn from your evil ways! Why will you die, O house of Israel?'[q]

[12]"Therefore, son of man, say to your countrymen, 'The righteousness of the righteous man will not save him when he disobeys, and the wickedness of the wicked man will not cause him to fall when he turns from it. The righteous man, if he sins, will not be allowed to live because of his former righteousness.'[r] [13]If I tell the righteous man that he will surely live, but then he trusts in his righteousness and does evil, none of the righteous things he has done will be remembered; he will die for the evil he has done.[s] [14]And if I say to the wicked man, 'You will surely die,' but he then turns away from his sin and does what is just[t] and right— [15]if he gives back what he took in pledge for a loan, returns what he has stolen,[u] follows the decrees that give life, and does no evil, he will surely live; he will not die.[v] [16]None of the sins he has committed will be remembered against him. He has done what is just and right; he will surely live.[w]

[17]"Yet your countrymen say, 'The way of the Lord is not just.' But it is their way that is not just. [18]If a righteous man turns from his righteousness and does evil, he will die for it.[x] [19]And if a wicked man turns away from his wickedness and does what is just and right, he will live by doing so. [20]Yet, O house of Israel, you say, 'The way of the Lord is not just.' But I will judge each of you according to his own ways."

33:2
d Jer 12:12
e Eze 3:11
33:3
f Hos 8:1
33:4
g 2Ch 25:16
h Jer 6:17;
Eze 18:13;
Zec 1:4;
Ac 18:6
33:6
i Eze 3:18
33:7
j Jer 26:2;
Eze 3:17
33:8
k ver 14
l Eze 18:4
33:9
m Eze 3:17-19
33:10
n Eze 24:23
o Lev 26:39;
Eze 4:17
33:11
p Eze 18:32;
2Pe 3:9
q Eze 18:23
33:12
r 2Ch 7:14;
Eze 3:20
33:13
s Eze 18:24;
Heb 10:38;
2Pe 2:20-21
33:14
t Eze 18:27
33:15
u Ex 22:1-4;
Lev 6:2-5
v Eze 20:11;
Lk 19:8
33:16
w Isa 43:25;
Eze 18:22
33:18
x Eze 3:20;
Eze 18:26

[a]8 Or in; also in verse 9   [b]10 Or away in

Jerusalem's Fall Explained

21In the twelfth year of our exile, in the tenth month on the fifth day, a man who had escaped[y] from Jerusalem came to me and said, "The city has fallen![z]" 22Now the evening before the man arrived, the hand of the LORD was upon me,[a] and he opened my mouth[b] before the man came to me in the morning. So my mouth was opened and I was no longer silent.[c]

23Then the word of the LORD came to me: 24"Son of man, the people living in those ruins[d] in the land of Israel are saying, 'Abraham was only one man, yet he possessed the land. But we are many; surely the land has been given to us as our possession.'[e] 25Therefore say to them, 'This is what the Sovereign LORD says: Since you eat meat with the blood[f] still in it and look to your idols and shed blood, should you then possess the land?[g] 26You rely on your sword, you do detestable things, and each of you defiles his neighbor's wife.[h] Should you then possess the land?'

27"Say this to them: 'This is what the Sovereign LORD says: As surely as I live, those who are left in the ruins will fall by the sword, those out in the country I will give to the wild animals to be devoured, and those in strongholds and caves will die of a plague.[i] 28I will make the land a desolate waste, and her proud strength will come to an end, and the mountains of Israel will become desolate so that no one will cross them. 29Then they will know that I am the LORD, when I have made the land a desolate waste because of all the detestable things they have done.'

30"As for you, son of man, your countrymen are talking together about you by the walls and at the doors of the houses, saying to each other, 'Come and hear the message that has come from the LORD.' 31My people come to you, as they usually do, and sit before[j] you to listen to your words, but they do not put them into practice. With their mouths they express devotion, but their hearts are greedy for unjust gain.[k] 32Indeed, to them you are nothing more than one who sings love songs with a beautiful voice and plays an instrument well, for they hear your words but do not put them into practice.[l]

33"When all this comes true—and it surely will—then they will know that a prophet has been among them.[m]"

Shepherds and Sheep

34 The word of the LORD came to me: 2"Son of man, prophesy against the shepherds of Israel; prophesy and say to them: 'This is what the Sovereign LORD says: Woe to the shepherds of Israel who only take care of themselves! Should not shepherds take care of the flock?[n] 3You eat the curds, clothe yourselves with the wool and slaughter the choice animals, but you do not take care of the flock.[o] 4You have not strengthened the weak or healed the sick or bound up the injured. You have not brought back the strays or searched for the lost. You have ruled them harshly and brutally.[p] 5So they were scattered because there was no shepherd,[q] and when they were scattered they became food for all the wild animals.[r] 6My sheep wandered over all the mountains and on every high hill. They were scattered over the whole earth, and no one searched or looked for them.[s]

7" 'Therefore, you shepherds, hear the word of the LORD: 8As surely

33:21
y Eze 24:26
z 2Ki 25:4,10;
Jer 39:1-2;
Eze 32:1
33:22
a Eze 1:3
b Lk 1:64
c Eze 3:26-27;
24:27
33:24
d Eze 36:4
e Isa 51:2;
Jer 40:7;
Eze 11:15;
Ac 7:5
33:25
f Ge 9:4;
Dt 12:16
g Jer 7:9-10;
Eze 22:6,27
33:26
h Eze 22:11
33:27
i 1Sa 13:6;
Isa 2:19;
Jer 42:22;
Eze 39:4
33:31
j Eze 8:1
k Ps 78:36-37;
Isa 29:13;
Eze 22:27;
Mt 13:22;
1Jn 3:18
33:32
l Mk 6:20
33:33
m 1Sa 3:20;
Jer 28:9;
Eze 2:5
34:2
n Ps 78:70-72;
Isa 40:11;
Jer 3:15; 23:1;
Mic 3:11;
Jn 10:11;
21:15-17
34:3
o Isa 56:11;
Eze 22:27;
Zec 11:16
34:4
p Zec 11:15-17
34:5
q Nu 27:17
r ver 28; Isa 56:9
34:6
s Ps 142:4;
1Pe 2:25

as I live, declares the Sovereign LORD, because my flock lacks a shepherd and so has been plundered and has become food for all the wild animals, and because my shepherds did not search for my flock but cared for themselves rather than for my flock, ⁹therefore, O shepherds, hear the word of the LORD: ¹⁰This is what the Sovereign LORD says: I am against ᵗ the shepherds and will hold them accountable for my flock. I will remove them from tending the flock so that the shepherds can no longer feed themselves. I will rescue ᵘ my flock from their mouths, and it will no longer be food for them. ᵛ

¹¹' 'For this is what the Sovereign LORD says: I myself will search for my sheep and look after them. ¹²As a shepherd ʷ looks after his scattered flock when he is with them, so will I look after my sheep. I will rescue them from all the places where they were scattered on a day of clouds and darkness. ˣ ¹³I will bring them out from the nations and gather them from the countries, and I will bring them into their own land. I will pasture them on the mountains of Israel, in the ravines and in all the settlements in the land. ʸ ¹⁴I will tend them in a good pasture, and the mountain heights of Israel ᶻ will be their grazing land. There they will lie down in good grazing land, and there they will feed in a rich pasture ª on the mountains of Israel. ᵇ ¹⁵I myself will tend my sheep and have them lie down, declares the Sovereign LORD. ᶜ ¹⁶I will search for the lost and bring back the strays. I will bind up the injured and strengthen the weak, ᵈ but the sleek and the strong I will destroy. I will shepherd the flock with justice. ᵉ

¹⁷' 'As for you, my flock, this is what the Sovereign LORD says: I will judge between one sheep and another, and between rams and goats. ᶠ ¹⁸Is it not enough for you to feed on the good pasture? Must you also trample the rest of your pasture with your feet? Is it not enough for you to drink clear water? Must you also muddy the rest with your feet? ¹⁹Must my flock feed on what you have trampled and drink what you have muddied with your feet?

²⁰' 'Therefore this is what the Sovereign LORD says to them: See, I myself will judge between the fat sheep and the lean sheep. ²¹Because you shove with flank and shoulder, butting all the weak sheep with your horns ᵍ until you have driven them away, ²²I will save my flock, and they will no longer be plundered. I will judge between one sheep and another. ʰ ²³I will place over them one shepherd, my servant David, and he will tend ⁱ them; he will tend them and be their shepherd. ²⁴I the LORD will be their God, ʲ and my servant David will be prince among them. I the LORD have spoken. ᵏ

²⁵' 'I will make a covenant of peace with them and rid the land of wild beasts ˡ so that they may live in the desert and sleep in the forests in safety. ᵐ ²⁶I will bless ⁿ them and the places surrounding my hill. ª I will send down showers in season; ° there will be showers of blessing. ᵖ ²⁷The trees of the field will yield their fruit and the ground will yield its crops; the people will be secure in their land. They will know that I am the LORD, when I break the bars of their yoke �q and rescue them from the hands of those who enslaved them. ʳ ²⁸They will no longer be plundered by the nations, nor will wild animals devour them. They will live in safety, and no one will make them afraid. ˢ ²⁹I will provide for

ª26 Or *I will make them and the places surrounding my hill a blessing*

34:10
ᵗJer 21:13
ᵘPs 72:14
ᵛ1Sa 2:29-30;
Zec 10:3
34:12
ʷIsa 40:11;
Jer 31:10;
Lk 19:10
ˣEze 30:3
34:13
ʸJer 23:3
34:14
ᶻEze 20:40
ªPs 23:2
ᵇEze 36:29-30
34:15
ᶜPs 23:1-2
34:16
ᵈMic 4:6
ᵉIsa 10:16;
Lk 5:32
34:17
ᶠMt 25:32-33
34:21
ᵍDt 33:17
34:22
ʰPs 72:12-14;
Jer 23:2-3
34:23
ⁱIsa 40:11
34:24
ʲEze 36:28
ᵏJer 30:9
34:25
ˡLev 26:6
ᵐIsa 11:6-9;
Hos 2:18
34:26
ⁿGe 12:2
°Ps 68:9
ᵖDt 11:13-15;
Isa 44:3
34:27
qLev 26:13
ʳJer 30:8
34:28
ˢJer 30:10;
Eze 39:26

them a land renowned[t] for its crops, and they will no longer be victims of famine[u] in the land or bear the scorn[v] of the nations.[w] 30Then they will know that I, the LORD their God, am with them and that they, the house of Israel, are my people, declares the Sovereign LORD.[x] 31You my sheep, the sheep of my pasture,[y] are people, and I am your God, declares the Sovereign LORD.' "

A Prophecy Against Edom

35 The word of the LORD came to me: 2"Son of man, set your face against Mount Seir; prophesy against it 3and say: 'This is what the Sovereign LORD says: I am against you, Mount Seir, and I will stretch out my hand[z] against you and make you a desolate waste.[a] 4I will turn your towns into ruins and you will be desolate. Then you will know that I am the LORD.[b]

5" 'Because you harbored an ancient hostility and delivered the Israelites over to the sword at the time of their calamity, the time their punishment reached its climax,[c] 6therefore as surely as I live, declares the Sovereign LORD, I will give you over to bloodshed and it will pursue you.[d] Since you did not hate bloodshed, bloodshed will pursue you. 7I will make Mount Seir a desolate waste and cut off from it all who come and go. 8I will fill your mountains with the slain; those killed by the sword will fall on your hills and in your valleys and in all your ravines.[e] 9I will make you desolate forever; your towns will not be inhabited. Then you will know that I am the LORD.[f]

10" 'Because you have said, "These two nations and countries will be ours and we will take possession[g] of them," even though I the LORD was there, 11therefore as surely as I live, declares the Sovereign LORD, I will treat you in accordance with the anger[h] and jealousy you showed in your hatred of them and I will make myself known among them when I judge you.[i] 12Then you will know that I the LORD have heard all the contemptible things you have said against the mountains of Israel. You said, "They have been laid waste and have been given over to us to devour.[j]" 13You boasted against me and spoke against me without restraint, and I heard it.[k] 14This is what the Sovereign LORD says: While the whole earth rejoices, I will make you desolate.[l] 15Because you rejoiced[m] when the inheritance of the house of Israel became desolate, that is how I will treat you. You will be desolate, O Mount Seir,[n] you and all of Edom.[o] Then they will know that I am the LORD.' "

A Prophecy to the Mountains of Israel

36 "Son of man, prophesy to the mountains of Israel and say, 'O mountains of Israel, hear the word of the LORD. 2This is what the Sovereign LORD says: The enemy said of you, "Aha![p] The ancient heights[q] have become our possession."[r] ' 3Therefore prophesy and say, 'This is what the Sovereign LORD says: Because they ravaged and hounded you from every side so that you became the possession of the rest of the nations and the object of people's malicious talk and slander,[s] 4therefore, O mountains of Israel, hear the word of the Sovereign LORD: This is what the Sovereign LORD says to the mountains and hills, to the ravines and valleys,[t] to the desolate ruins and the deserted towns that have been plundered and ridiculed by the rest of the nations around you[u]— 5this is what the Sovereign LORD says: In my burning

34:29
t Isa 4:2
u Eze 36:29
v Eze 36:6
w Eze 36:15
34:30
x Eze 14:11;
37:27
34:31
y Ps 100:3;
Jer 23:1
35:3
z Jer 6:12
a Eze 25:12-14
35:4
b ver 9
35:5
c Ps 137:7;
Eze 21:29
35:6
d Isa 63:2-6
35:8
e Eze 31:12
35:9
f Jer 49:13
35:10
g Ps 83:12;
Eze 36:2,5
35:11
h Eze 25:14
i Ps 9:16; Mt 7:2
35:12
j Jer 50:7
35:13
k Da 11:36
35:14
l Jer 51:48
35:15
m Ob 1:12
n ver 3
o Isa 34:5-6,11;
Jer 50:11-13;
La 4:21
36:2
p Eze 25:3
q Dt 32:13
r Eze 35:10
36:3
s Ps 44:13-14
36:4
t Eze 6:3
u Dt 11:11;
Ps 79:4;
Eze 34:28

zeal I have spoken against the rest of the nations, and against all Edom, for with glee and with malice in their hearts they made my land their own possession so that they might plunder its pastureland.'[v] [6]Therefore prophesy concerning the land of Israel and say to the mountains and hills, to the ravines and valleys: 'This is what the Sovereign LORD says: I speak in my jealous wrath because you have suffered the scorn of the nations.[w] [7]Therefore this is what the Sovereign LORD says: I swear with uplifted hand that the nations around you will also suffer scorn.

[8]" 'But you, O mountains of Israel, will produce branches and fruit[x] for my people Israel, for they will soon come home. [9]I am concerned for you and will look on you with favor; you will be plowed and sown, [10]and I will multiply the number of people upon you, even the whole house of Israel. The towns will be inhabited and the ruins rebuilt.[y] [11]I will increase the number of men and animals upon you, and they will be fruitful and become numerous. I will settle people on you as in the past[z] and will make you prosper more than before.[a] Then you will know that I am the LORD. [12]I will cause people, my people Israel, to walk upon you. They will possess you, and you will be their inheritance;[b] you will never again deprive them of their children.

[13]" 'This is what the Sovereign LORD says: Because people say to you, "You devour men[c] and deprive your nation of its children," [14]therefore you will no longer devour men or make your nation childless, declares the Sovereign LORD. [15]No longer will I make you hear the taunts of the nations, and no longer will you suffer the scorn of the peoples or cause your nation to fall, declares the Sovereign LORD.[d] ' "

[16]Again the word of the LORD came to me: [17]"Son of man, when the people of Israel were living in their own land, they defiled it by their conduct and their actions. Their conduct was like a woman's monthly uncleanness in my sight.[e] [18]So I poured out[f] my wrath on them because they had shed blood in the land and because they had defiled it with their idols. [19]I dispersed them among the nations, and they were scattered[g] through the countries; I judged them according to their conduct and their actions.[h] [20]And wherever they went among the nations they profaned[i] my holy name, for it was said of them, 'These are the LORD's people, and yet they had to leave his land.'[j] [21]I had concern for my holy name, which the house of Israel profaned among the nations where they had gone.[k]

[22]"Therefore say to the house of Israel, 'This is what the Sovereign LORD says: It is not for your sake, O house of Israel, that I am going to do these things, but for the sake of my holy name, which you have profaned[l] among the nations where you have gone.[m] [23]I will show the holiness of my great name, which has been profaned among the nations, the name you have profaned among them. Then the nations will know that I am the LORD, declares the Sovereign LORD, when I show myself holy[n] through you before their eyes.[o]

[24]" 'For I will take you out of the nations; I will gather you from all the countries and bring you back into your own land.[p] [25]I will sprinkle[q] clean water on you, and you will be clean; I will cleanse[r] you from all your impurities and from all your idols.[s] [26]I will give you a new heart[t] and put a new spirit in you; I will remove from you your heart of stone and give you a heart of flesh.[u] [27]And I will put my Spirit[v] in you and

36:5
v Jer 50:11;
Eze 25:12-14;
35:10,15
36:6
w Ps 123:3-4;
Eze 34:29
36:8
x Isa 27:6
36:10
y ver 33;
Isa 49:17-23
36:11
z Mic 7:14
a Jer 31:28;
Eze 16:55
36:12
b Eze 47:14,22
36:13
c Nu 13:32
36:15
d Ps 89:50-51;
Eze 34:29
36:17
e Jer 2:7
36:18
f 2Ch 34:21
36:19
g Dt 28:64
h Eze 39:24
36:20
i Ro 2:24
j Isa 52:5;
Jer 33:24;
Eze 12:16
36:21
k Ps 74:18;
Isa 48:9
36:22
l Ro 2:24*
m Ps 106:8
36:23
n Eze 20:41
o Ps 126:2;
Isa 5:16
36:24
p Eze 34:13;
37:21
36:25
q Heb 9:13;
10:22 r Ps 51:2,7
s Zec 13:2
36:26
t Jer 24:7
u Ps 51:10;
Eze 11:19
36:27
v Eze 37:14

move you to follow my decrees and be careful to keep my laws. [28]You will live in the land I gave your forefathers; you will be my people, [w] and I will be your God. [x] [29]I will save you from all your uncleanness. I will call for the grain and make it plentiful and will not bring famine [y] upon you. [30]I will increase the fruit of the trees and the crops of the field, so that you will no longer suffer disgrace among the nations because of famine. [z] [31]Then you will remember your evil ways and wicked deeds, and you will loathe yourselves for your sins and detestable practices. [a] [32]I want you to know that I am not doing this for your sake, declares the Sovereign Lord. Be ashamed and disgraced for your conduct, O house of Israel! [b]

[33]" 'This is what the Sovereign Lord says: On the day I cleanse you from all your sins, I will resettle your towns, and the ruins will be rebuilt. [34]The desolate land will be cultivated instead of lying desolate in the sight of all who pass through it. [35]They will say, "This land that was laid waste has become like the garden of Eden; [c] the cities that were lying in ruins, desolate and destroyed, are now fortified and inhabited. [d]" [36]Then the nations around you that remain will know that I the Lord have rebuilt what was destroyed and have replanted what was desolate. I the Lord have spoken, and I will do it.' [e]

[37]"This is what the Sovereign Lord says: Once again I will yield to the plea of the house of Israel and do this for them: I will make their people as numerous as sheep, [38]as numerous as the flocks for offerings [f] at Jerusalem during her appointed feasts. So will the ruined cities be filled with flocks of people. Then they will know that I am the Lord."

The Valley of Dry Bones

37 The hand of the Lord was upon me, [g] and he brought me out by the Spirit [h] of the Lord and set me in the middle of a valley; [i] it was full of bones. [j] [2]He led me back and forth among them, and I saw a great many bones on the floor of the valley, bones that were very dry. [3]He asked me, "Son of man, can these bones live?"

I said, "O Sovereign Lord, you alone know. [k]"

[4]Then he said to me, "Prophesy to these bones and say to them, 'Dry bones, hear the word of the Lord! [l] [5]This is what the Sovereign Lord says to these bones: I will make breath [a] enter you, and you will come to life. [m] [6]I will attach tendons to you and make flesh come upon you and cover you with skin; I will put breath in you, and you will come to life. Then you will know that I am the Lord. [n]' "

[7]So I prophesied as I was commanded. And as I was prophesying, there was a noise, a rattling sound, and the bones came together, bone to bone. [8]I looked, and tendons and flesh appeared on them and skin covered them, but there was no breath in them.

[9]Then he said to me, "Prophesy to the breath; [o] prophesy, son of man, and say to it, 'This is what the Sovereign Lord says: Come from the four winds, O breath, and breathe into these slain, that they may live.' " [10]So I prophesied as he commanded me, and breath entered them; they came to life and stood up on their feet—a vast army. [p]

[11]Then he said to me: "Son of man, these bones are the whole house of Israel. They say, 'Our bones are dried up and our hope is gone; we

---

Cross References

36:28
w Jer 30:22
x Eze 14:11;
37:14,27

36:29
y Eze 34:29

36:30
z Lev 26:4-5;
Eze 34:27;
Hos 2:21-22

36:31
a Eze 6:9; 20:43

36:32
b Dt 9:5

36:35
c Joel 2:3
d Isa 51:3

36:36
e Eze 17:22;
22:14; 37:14;
39:27-28

36:38
f 1Ki 8:63;
2Ch 35:7-9

37:1
g Eze 1:3; 8:3
h Eze 11:24;
Lk 4:1; Ac 8:39
i Jer 7:32
j Jer 8:2;
Eze 40:1

37:3
k Dt 32:39;
1Sa 2:6;
Isa 26:19

37:4
l Jer 22:29

37:5
m Ge 2:7;
Ps 104:29-30

37:6
n Eze 38:23;
Joel 2:27; 3:17

37:9
o Ps 104:30

37:10
p Rev 11:11

---

[a]5 The Hebrew for this word can also mean *wind* or *spirit* (see verses 6-14).

are cut off.'�q 12Therefore prophesy and say to them: 'This is what the Sovereign LORD says: O my people, I am going to open your graves and bring you up from them; I will bring you back to the land of Israel.ʳ 13Then you, my people, will know that I am the LORD, when I open your graves and bring you up from them. 14I will put my Spiritˢ in you and you will live, and I will settle you in your own land. Then you will know that I the LORD have spoken, and I have done it, declares the LORD.ᵗ ' "

One Nation Under One King

15The word of the LORD came to me: 16"Son of man, take a stick of wood and write on it, 'Belonging to Judah and the Israelitesᵘ associated with him.ᵛ' Then take another stick of wood, and write on it, 'Ephraim's stick, belonging to Joseph and all the house of Israel associated with him.' 17Join them together into one stick so that they will become one in your hand.ʷ

18"When your countrymen ask you, 'Won't you tell us what you mean by this?'ˣ 19say to them, 'This is what the Sovereign LORD says: I am going to take the stick of Joseph—which is in Ephraim's hand—and of the Israelite tribes associated with him, and join it to Judah's stick, making them a single stick of wood, and they will become one in my hand.'ʸ 20Hold before their eyes the sticks you have written on 21and say to them, 'This is what the Sovereign LORD says: I will take the Israelites out of the nations where they have gone. I will gather them from all around and bring them back into their own land.ᶻ 22I will make them one nation in the land, on the mountains of Israel. There will be one king over all of them and they will never again be two nations or be divided into two kingdoms.ᵃ 23They will no longer defileᵇ themselves with their idols and vile images or with any of their offenses, for I will save them from all their sinful backsliding,ᵈ and I will cleanse them. They will be my people, and I will be their God.ᶜ

24" 'My servant Davidᵈ will be king over them, and they will all have one shepherd.ᵉ They will follow my laws and be careful to keep my decrees.ᶠ 25They will live in the land I gave to my servant Jacob, the land where your fathers lived.ᵍ They and their children and their children's children will live there forever,ʰ and David my servant will be their prince forever.ⁱ 26I will make a covenant of peaceʲ with them; it will be an everlasting covenant. I will establish them and increase their numbers,ᵏ and I will put my sanctuary among them forever.ˡ 27My dwelling placeᵐ will be with them; I will be their God, and they will be my people.ⁿ 28Then the nations will know that I the LORD make Israel holy,ᵒ when my sanctuary is among them forever.' "

A Prophecy Against Gog

38 The word of the LORD came to me: 2"Son of man, set your face against Gog, of the land of Magog,ᵖ the chief prince ofᵇ Meshech and Tubal;�q prophesy against him 3and say: 'This is what the Sovereign LORD says: I am against you, O Gog, chief prince ofᶜ Me-

---

ᵃ23 Many Hebrew manuscripts (see also Septuagint); most Hebrew manuscripts *all their dwelling places where they sinned*   ᵇ2 *Or the prince of Rosh,*   ᶜ3 *Or Gog, prince of Rosh,*

37:11
qLa 3:54
37:12
rDt 32:39;
1Sa 2:6;
Isa 26:19;
Hos 13:14;
Am 9:14-15
37:14
sJoel 2:28-29
tEze 36:27-28,36
37:16
u1Ki 12:20;
2Ch 10:17-19
vNu 17:2-3;
2Ch 15:9
37:17
wver 24;
Isa 11:13;
Jer 50:4;
Hos 1:11
37:18
xEze 24:19
37:19
yZec 10:6
37:21
zIsa 43:5-6;
Eze 36:24;
39:27
37:22
aIsa 11:13;
Jer 3:18;
Hos 1:11
37:23
bEze 36:25;
43:7
cEze 11:18;
36:28
37:24
dHos 3:5
eIsa 40:11;
Eze 34:23
fPs 78:70-71
37:25
gEze 28:25
hAm 9:15
iIsa 11:1
37:26
jIsa 55:3
kJer 30:19
lEze 16:62
37:27
mLev 26:11;
Jn 1:14
n2Co 6:16*
37:28
oEx 31:13;
Eze 20:12
38:2
pGe 10:2
qRev 20:8

shech and Tubal.ʳ ⁴I will turn you around, put hooksˢ in your jaws and bring you out with your whole army—your horses, your horsemen fully armed, and a great horde with large and small shields, all of them brandishing their swords.ᵗ ⁵Persia, Cushᵃ ᵘ and Putᵛ will be with them, all with shields and helmets, ⁶also Gomerʷ with all its troops, and Beth Togarmahˣ from the far north with all its troops—the many nations with you.

⁷" 'Get ready; be prepared,ʸ you and all the hordes gathered about you, and take command of them. ⁸After many daysᶻ you will be called to arms. In future years you will invade a land that has recovered from war, whose people were gathered from many nationsᵃ to the mountains of Israel, which had long been desolate. They had been brought out from the nations, and now all of them live in safety.ᵇ ⁹You and all your troops and the many nations with you will go up, advancing like a storm;ᶜ you will be like a cloudᵈ covering the land.

¹⁰" 'This is what the Sovereign LORD says: On that day thoughts will come into your mind and you will devise an evil scheme.ᵉ ¹¹You will say, "I will invade a land of unwalled villages; I will attack a peaceful and unsuspecting people—all of them living without walls and without gates and bars.ᶠ ¹²I will plunder and loot and turn my hand against the resettled ruins and the people gathered from the nations, rich in livestock and goods, living at the center of the land." ¹³Shebaᵍ and Dedan and the merchants of Tarshish and all her villagesᵇ will say to you, "Have you come to plunder? Have you gathered your hordes to loot, to carry off silver and gold, to take away livestock and goods and to seize much plunder?ʰ" '

¹⁴"Therefore, son of man, prophesy and say to Gog: 'This is what the Sovereign LORD says: In that day, when my people Israel are living in safety,ᶦ will you not take notice of it? ¹⁵You will come from your place in the far north, you and many nations with you, all of them riding on horses, a great horde, a mighty army.ʲ ¹⁶You will advance against my people Israel like a cloudᵏ that covers the land. In days to come, O Gog, I will bring you against my land, so that the nations may know me when I show myself holy through you before their eyes.ˡ

¹⁷" 'This is what the Sovereign LORD says: Are you not the one I spoke of in former days by my servants the prophets of Israel? At that time they prophesied for years that I would bring you against them. ¹⁸This is what will happen in that day: When Gog attacks the land of Israel, my hot anger will be aroused, declares the Sovereign LORD. ¹⁹In my zeal and fiery wrath I declare that at that time there shall be a great earthquake in the land of Israel.ᵐ ²⁰The fish of the sea, the birds of the air, the beasts of the field, every creature that moves along the ground, and all the people on the face of the earth will tremble at my presence. The mountains will be overturned, the cliffs will crumble and every wall will fall to the ground.ⁿ ²¹I will summon a swordᵒ against Gog on all my mountains, declares the Sovereign LORD. Every man's sword will be against his brother.ᵖ ²²I will execute judgmentᵠ upon him with plague and bloodshed; I will pour down torrents of rain, hailstonesʳ and burning sulfur on him and on his troops and on the many nations with him. ²³And so I will show my greatness and my holiness, and I will

38:3
rEze 39:1
38:4
s2Ki 19:28
tEze 29:4;
Da 11:40
38:5
uGe 10:6
vEze 27:10
38:6
wGe 10:2
xEze 27:14
38:7
yIsa 8:9
38:8
zIsa 24:22
aIsa 11:11
bJer 23:6
38:9
cIsa 28:2
dJer 4:13;
Joel 2:2
38:10
ePs 36:4;
Mic 2:1
38:11
fJer 49:31;
Zec 2:4
38:13
gEze 27:22
hIsa 10:6;
Jer 15:13
38:14
iver 8; Zec 2:5
38:15
jEze 39:2
38:16
kver 9
lIsa 29:23;
Eze 39:21
38:19
mPs 18:7;
Eze 5:13;
Hag 2:6,21
38:20
nHos 4:3;
Na 1:5
38:21
oEze 14:17
p1Sa 14:20;
2Ch 20:23;
Hag 2:22
38:22
qIsa 66:16;
Jer 25:31
rPs 18:12;
Rev 16:21

ᵃ5 That is, the upper Nile region   ᵇ13 Or *her strong lions* make myself known in the sight of many nations. Then they will know that I am the LORD.ˢ'

39 "Son of man, prophesy against Gog and say: 'This is what the Sovereign LORD says: I am against you, O Gog, chief prince ofᵃ Meshech and Tubal.ᵗ ²I will turn you around and drag you along. I will bring you from the far north and send you against the mountains of Israel. ³Then I will strike your bowᵘ from your left hand and make your arrowsᵛ drop from your right hand. ⁴On the mountains of Israel you will fall, you and all your troops and the nations with you. I will give you as food to all kinds of carrion birds and to the wild animals.ʷ ⁵You will fall in the open field, for I have spoken, declares the Sovereign LORD. ⁶I will send fireˣ on Magog and on those who live in safety in the coastlands,ʸ and they will know that I am the LORD.

⁷'' 'I will make known my holy name among my people Israel. I will no longer let my holy name be profaned,ᶻ and the nations will know that I the LORD am the Holy One in Israel.ᵃ ⁸It is coming! It will surely take place, declares the Sovereign LORD. This is the day I have spoken of.

⁹'' 'Then those who live in the towns of Israel will go out and use the weapons for fuel and burn them up—the small and large shields, the bows and arrows, the war clubs and spears. For seven years they will use them for fuel.ᵇ ¹⁰They will not need to gather wood from the fields or cut it from the forests, because they will use the weapons for fuel. And they will plunder those who plundered them and loot those who looted them, declares the Sovereign LORD.ᶜ

¹¹'' 'On that day I will give Gog a burial place in Israel, in the valley of those who travel east towardᵇ the Sea.ᶜ It will block the way of travelers, because Gog and all his hordes will be buried there. So it will be called the Valley of Hamon Gog.ᵈ ᵈ

¹²'' 'For seven months the house of Israel will be burying them in order to cleanse the land.ᵉ ¹³All the people of the land will bury them, and the day I am glorifiedᶠ will be a memorable day for them, declares the Sovereign LORD.

¹⁴'' 'Men will be regularly employed to cleanse the land. Some will go throughout the land and, in addition to them, others will bury those that remain on the ground. At the end of the seven months they will begin their search. ¹⁵As they go through the land and one of them sees a human bone, he will set up a marker beside it until the gravediggers have buried it in the Valley of Hamon Gog. ¹⁶(Also a town called Hamonahᵉ will be there.) And so they will cleanse the land.'

¹⁷"Son of man, this is what the Sovereign LORD says: Call out to every kind of birdᵍ and all the wild animals: 'Assemble and come together from all around to the sacrifice I am preparing for you, the great sacrifice on the mountains of Israel. There you will eat flesh and drink blood. ¹⁸You will eat the flesh of mighty men and drink the blood of the princes of the earth as if they were rams and lambs, goats and bulls—all of them fattened animals from Bashan.ʰ ¹⁹At the sacrifice I am preparing for you, you will eat fat till you are glutted and drink blood till you are drunk. ²⁰At my table you will eat your fill of horses and riders,

38:23
ˢEze 36:23
39:1
ᵗEze 38:2,3
39:3
ᵘHos 1:5
ᵛPs 76:3
39:4
ʷver 17-20;
Eze 29:5; 33:27
39:6
ˣEze 30:8;
Am 1:4
ʸJer 25:22
39:7
ᶻEx 20:7
ᵃIsa 12:6;
Eze 36:16,23
39:9
ᵇPs 46:9
39:10
ᶜIsa 14:2; 33:1;
Hab 2:8
39:11
ᵈEze 38:2
39:12
ᵉDt 21:23
39:13
ᶠEze 28:22
39:17
ᵍRev 19:17
39:18
ʰPs 22:12;
Jer 51:40

ᵃ1 Or *Gog, prince of Rosh*,　　ᵇ11 Or *of*　　ᶜ11 That is, the Dead Sea　　ᵈ11 *Hamon Gog* means *hordes of Gog*.　　ᵉ16 *Hamonah* means *horde*.

mighty men and soldiers of every kind,' declares the Sovereign Lord. [i]

21"I will display my glory among the nations, and all the nations will see the punishment I inflict and the hand I lay upon them. [j] 22From that day forward the house of Israel will know that I am the Lord their God. 23And the nations will know that the people of Israel went into exile for their sin, because they were unfaithful to me. So I hid my face from them and handed them over to their enemies, and they all fell by the sword. [k] 24I dealt with them according to their uncleanness and their offenses, and I hid my face from them. [l]

25"Therefore this is what the Sovereign Lord says: I will now bring Jacob back from captivity [a][m] and will have compassion [n] on all the people of Israel, and I will be zealous for my holy name. [o] 26They will forget their shame and all the unfaithfulness they showed toward me when they lived in safety [p] in their land with no one to make them afraid. [q] 27When I have brought them back from the nations and have gathered them from the countries of their enemies, I will show myself holy through them in the sight of many nations. [r] 28Then they will know that I am the Lord their God, for though I sent them into exile among the nations, I will gather them to their own land, not leaving any behind. 29I will no longer hide my face from them, for I will pour out my Spirit [s] on the house of Israel, declares the Sovereign Lord."

The New Temple Area

40 In the twenty-fifth year of our exile, at the beginning of the year, on the tenth of the month, in the fourteenth year after the fall of the city [t]—on that very day the hand of the Lord was upon me [u] and he took me there. 2In visions [v] of God he took me to the land of Israel and set me on a very high mountain, [w] on whose south side were some buildings that looked like a city. 3He took me there, and I saw a man whose appearance was like bronze; [x] he was standing in the gateway with a linen cord and a measuring rod [y] in his hand. 4The man said to me, "Son of man, look with your eyes and hear with your ears and pay attention to everything I am going to show you, for that is why you have been brought here. Tell [z] the house of Israel everything you see. [a]"

The East Gate to the Outer Court

5I saw a wall completely surrounding the temple area. The length of the measuring rod in the man's hand was six long cubits, each of which was a cubit [b] and a handbreadth. [c] He measured [b] the wall; it was one measuring rod thick and one rod high.

6Then he went to the gate facing east. [c] He climbed its steps and measured the threshold of the gate; it was one rod deep. [d] 7The alcoves [d] for the guards were one rod long and one rod wide, and the projecting walls between the alcoves were five cubits thick. And the threshold of the gate next to the portico facing the temple was one rod deep.

8Then he measured the portico of the gateway; 9it [e] was eight cubits

39:20
i Rev 19:17-18

39:21
j Ex 9:16;
Isa 37:20;
Eze 38:16

39:23
k Isa 1:15; 59:2;
Jer 22:8-9;
44:23

39:24
l Jer 2:17,19;
4:18; Eze 36:19

39:25
m Jer 33:7;
Eze 34:13
n Jer 30:18
o Isa 27:12-13

39:26
p 1Ki 4:25
q Isa 17:2;
Eze 34:28;
Mic 4:4

39:27
r Eze 36:23-24;
37:21; 38:16

39:29
s Joel 2:28;
Ac 2:17

40:1
t 2Ki 25:7;
Jer 39:1-10;
52:4-11;
Eze 33:21
u Eze 1:3

40:2
v Da 7:1,7
w Eze 17:22;
Rev 21:10

40:3
x Eze 1:7;
Da 10:6;
Rev 1:15
y Eze 47:3;
Zec 2:1-2;
Rev 11:1; 21:15

40:4
z Jer 26:2
a Eze 44:5

40:5
b Eze 42:20

40:6
c Eze 8:16

40:7
d ver 36

deep and its jambs were two cubits thick. The portico of the gateway faced the temple.

¹⁰Inside the east gate were three alcoves on each side; the three had the same measurements, and the faces of the projecting walls on each side had the same measurements. ¹¹Then he measured the width of the entrance to the gateway; it was ten cubits and its length was thirteen cubits. ¹²In front of each alcove was a wall one cubit high, and the alcoves were six cubits square. ¹³Then he measured the gateway from the top of the rear wall of one alcove to the top of the opposite one; the distance was twenty-five cubits from one parapet opening to the opposite one. ¹⁴He measured along the faces of the projecting walls all around the inside of the gateway—sixty cubits. The measurement was up to the portico*ᵃ* facing the courtyard.*ᵇᵉ* ¹⁵The distance from the entrance of the gateway to the far end of its portico was fifty cubits. ¹⁶The alcoves and the projecting walls inside the gateway were surmounted by narrow parapet openings all around, as was the portico; the openings all around faced inward. The faces of the projecting walls were decorated with palm trees.*ᶠ*

The Outer Court

¹⁷Then he brought me into the outer court.*ᵍ* There I saw some rooms and a pavement that had been constructed all around the court; there were thirty rooms*ʰ* along the pavement.*ⁱ* ¹⁸It abutted the sides of the gateways and was as wide as they were long; this was the lower pavement. ¹⁹Then he measured the distance from the inside of the lower gateway to the outside of the inner court;*ʲ* it was a hundred cubits*ᵏ* on the east side as well as on the north.

The North Gate

²⁰Then he measured the length and width of the gate facing north, leading into the outer court. ²¹Its alcoves*ˡ*—three on each side—its projecting walls and its portico had the same measurements as those of the first gateway. It was fifty cubits long and twenty-five cubits wide. ²²Its openings, its portico*ᵐ* and its palm tree decorations had the same measurements as those of the gate facing east. Seven steps led up to it, with its portico opposite them. ²³There was a gate to the inner court facing the north gate, just as there was on the east. He measured from one gate to the opposite one; it was a hundred cubits.*ⁿ*

The South Gate

²⁴Then he led me to the south side and I saw a gate facing south. He measured its jambs and its portico, and they had the same measurements as the others. ²⁵The gateway and its portico had narrow openings all around, like the openings of the others. It was fifty cubits long and twenty-five cubits wide.*ᵒ* ²⁶Seven steps led up to it, with its portico opposite them; it had palm tree decorations on the faces of the projecting walls on each side.*ᵖ* ²⁷The inner court*�q* also had a gate facing south, and he measured from this gate to the outer gate on the south side; it was a hundred cubits.

ᵃ14 Septuagint; Hebrew projecting wall   *ᵇ14 The meaning of the Hebrew for this verse is uncertain.*

40:14
eEx 27:9

40:16
fver 21-22;
2Ch 3:5;
Eze 41:26

40:17
gRev 11:2
hEze 41:6
iEze 42:1

40:19
jEze 46:1
kver 23,27

40:21
lver 7

40:22
mver 49

40:23
nver 19

40:25
over 33

40:26
pver 22

40:27
qver 32

Gates to the Inner Court

28Then he brought me into the inner court through the south gate, and he measured the south gate; it had the same measurements[r] as the others. 29Its alcoves, its projecting walls and its portico had the same measurements as the others. The gateway and its portico had openings all around. It was fifty cubits long and twenty-five cubits wide. 30(The porticoes[s] of the gateways around the inner court were twenty-five cubits wide and five cubits deep.) 31Its portico[t] faced the outer court; palm trees decorated its jambs, and eight steps led up to it.

32Then he brought me to the inner court on the east side, and he measured the gateway; it had the same measurements as the others. 33Its alcoves, its projecting walls and its portico had the same measurements as the others. The gateway and its portico had openings all around. It was fifty cubits long and twenty-five cubits wide. 34Its portico[u] faced the outer court; palm trees decorated the jambs on either side, and eight steps led up to it.

35Then he brought me to the north gate[v] and measured it. It had the same measurements as the others, 36as did its alcoves,[w] its projecting walls and its portico, and it had openings all around. It was fifty cubits long and twenty-five cubits wide. 37Its portico[a] faced the outer court; palm trees decorated the jambs on either side, and eight steps led up to it.

The Rooms for Preparing Sacrifices

38A room with a doorway was by the portico in each of the inner gateways, where the burnt offerings[x] were washed. 39In the portico of the gateway were two tables on each side, on which the burnt offerings,[y] sin offerings[z] and guilt offerings[a] were slaughtered. 40By the outside wall of the portico of the gateway, near the steps at the entrance to the north gateway were two tables, and on the other side of the steps were two tables. 41So there were four tables on one side of the gateway and four on the other—eight tables in all—on which the sacrifices were slaughtered. 42There were also four tables of dressed stone[b] for the burnt offerings, each a cubit and a half long, a cubit and a half wide and a cubit high. On them were placed the utensils for slaughtering the burnt offerings and the other sacrifices. [c] 43And double-pronged hooks, each a handbreadth long, were attached to the wall all around. The tables were for the flesh of the offerings.

Rooms for the Priests

44Outside the inner gate, within the inner court, were two rooms, one[b] at the side of the north gate and facing south, and another at the side of the south[c] gate and facing north. 45He said to me, "The room facing south is for the priests who have charge of the temple, [d] 46and the room facing north[e] is for the priests who have charge of the altar.[f] These are the sons of Zadok,[g] who are the only Levites who may draw near to the LORD to minister before him. [h]"

47Then he measured the court: It was square—a hundred cubits long and a hundred cubits wide. And the altar was in front of the temple.

40:28
rver 35
40:30
sver 21
40:31
tver 22
40:34
uver 22
40:35
vEze 44:4; 47:2
40:36
wver 7
40:38
x2Ch 4:6;
Eze 42:13
40:39
yEze 46:2
zLev 4:3,28
aLev 7:1
40:42
bEx 20:25
cver 39
40:45
d1Ch 9:23
40:46
eEze 42:13
fNu 18:5
g1Ki 2:35
hNu 16:5;
Eze 43:19;
44:15; 45:4;
48:11

---

a37 Septuagint (see also verses 31 and 34); Hebrew *jambs for singers, which were*   c44 Septuagint; Hebrew *east*   b44 Septuagint; Hebrew *were rooms*

The Temple

48He brought me to the portico of the temple[i] and measured the jambs of the portico; they were five cubits wide on either side. The width of the entrance was fourteen cubits and its projecting walls were[a] three cubits wide on either side. 49The portico[j] was twenty cubits wide, and twelve[b] cubits from front to back. It was reached by a flight of stairs,[c] and there were pillars[k] on each side of the jambs.

41 Then the man brought me to the outer sanctuary[l] and measured the jambs; the width of the jambs was six cubits[d] on each side.[e] 2The entrance was ten cubits wide, and the projecting walls on each side of it were five cubits wide. He also measured the outer sanctuary; it was forty cubits long and twenty cubits wide.[m]

3Then he went into the inner sanctuary and measured the jambs of the entrance; each was two cubits wide. The entrance was six cubits wide, and the projecting walls on each side of it were seven cubits wide. 4And he measured the length of the inner sanctuary; it was twenty cubits, and its width was twenty cubits across the end of the outer sanctuary.[n] He said to me, "This is the Most Holy Place.[o]"

5Then he measured the wall of the temple; it was six cubits thick, and each side room around the temple was four cubits wide. 6The side rooms were on three levels, one above another, thirty[p] on each level. There were ledges all around the wall of the temple to serve as supports for the side rooms, so that the supports were not inserted into the wall of the temple.[q] 7The side rooms all around the temple were wider at each successive level. The structure surrounding the temple was built in ascending stages, so that the rooms widened as one went upward. A stairway[r] went up from the lowest floor to the top floor through the middle floor.

8I saw that the temple had a raised base all around it, forming the foundation of the side rooms. It was the length of the rod, six long cubits. 9The outer wall of the side rooms was five cubits thick. The open area between the side rooms of the temple 10and the ⌊priests'⌋ rooms was twenty cubits wide all around the temple. 11There were entrances to the side rooms from the open area, one on the north and another on the south; and the base adjoining the open area was five cubits wide all around.

12The building facing the temple courtyard on the west side was seventy cubits wide. The wall of the building was five cubits thick all around, and its length was ninety cubits.

13Then he measured the temple; it was a hundred cubits long, and the temple courtyard and the building with its walls were also a hundred cubits long. 14The width of the temple courtyard on the east, including the front of the temple, was a hundred cubits.[s]

15Then he measured the length of the building facing the courtyard at the rear of the temple, including its galleries[t] on each side; it was a hundred cubits.

The outer sanctuary, the inner sanctuary and the portico facing the court, 16as well as the thresholds and the narrow windows[u] and galler-

40:48
[i]1Ki 6:2
40:49
[j]ver 22; 1Ki 6:3
[k]1Ki 7:15
41:1
[l]ver 23
41:2
[m]2Ch 3:3
41:4
[n]1Ki 6:20
[o]Ex 26:33;
Heb 9:3-8
41:6
[p]Eze 40:17
[q]1Ki 6:5
41:7
[r]1Ki 6:8
41:14
[s]Eze 40:47
41:15
[t]Eze 42:3
41:16
[u]1Ki 6:4

ies around the three of them—everything beyond and including the threshold was covered with wood. The floor, the wall up to the windows, and the windows were covered. [v] 17In the space above the outside of the entrance to the inner sanctuary and on the walls at regular intervals all around the inner and outer sanctuary 18were carved [w] cherubim [x] and palm trees. [y] Palm trees alternated with cherubim. Each cherub had two faces: [z] 19the face of a man toward the palm tree on one side and the face of a lion toward the palm tree on the other. They were carved all around the whole temple. [a] 20From the floor to the area above the entrance, cherubim and palm trees were carved on the wall of the outer sanctuary.

21The outer sanctuary [b] had a rectangular doorframe, and the one at the front of the Most Holy Place was similar. 22There was a wooden altar [c] three cubits high and two cubits square [a]; its corners, its base [b] and its sides were of wood. The man said to me, "This is the table [d] that is before the LORD." 23Both the outer sanctuary [e] and the Most Holy Place had double doors. [f] 24Each door had two leaves—two hinged leaves [g] for each door. 25And on the doors of the outer sanctuary were carved cherubim and palm trees like those carved on the walls, and there was a wooden overhang on the front of the portico. 26On the sidewalls of the portico were narrow windows with palm trees carved on each side. The side rooms of the temple also had overhangs. [h]

Rooms for the Priests

42 Then the man led me northward into the outer court and brought me to the rooms [i] opposite the temple courtyard [j] and opposite the outer wall on the north side. [k] 2The building whose door faced north was a hundred cubits [c] long and fifty cubits wide. 3Both in the section twenty cubits from the inner court and in the section opposite the pavement of the outer court, gallery [l] faced gallery at the three levels. [m] 4In front of the rooms was an inner passageway ten cubits wide and a hundred cubits [d] long. Their doors were on the north. [n] 5Now the upper rooms were narrower, for the galleries took more space from them than from the rooms on the lower and middle floors of the building. 6The rooms on the third floor had no pillars, as the courts had; so they were smaller in floor space than those on the lower and middle floors. 7There was an outer wall parallel to the rooms and the outer court; it extended in front of the rooms for fifty cubits. 8While the row of rooms on the side next to the outer court was fifty cubits long, the row on the side nearest the sanctuary was a hundred cubits long. 9The lower rooms had an entrance [o] on the east side as one enters them from the outer court.

10On the south side [e] along the length of the wall of the outer court, adjoining the temple courtyard and opposite the outer wall, were rooms [p] 11with a passageway in front of them. These were like the rooms on the north; they had the same length and width, with similar exits and dimensions. Similar to the doorways on the north 12were the doorways of the rooms on the south. There was a doorway at the

41:16
vver 25-26;
1Ki 6:15;
Eze 42:3
41:18
wki 6:18
xEx 37:7;
2Ch 3:7
y1Ki 6:29; 7:36
zEze 10:21
41:19
aEze 10:14
41:21
bver 1
41:22
cEx 30:1
dEx 25:23;
Eze 23:41;
44:16;
Mal 1:7,12
41:23
ever 1 f1Ki 6:32
41:24
g1Ki 6:34
41:26
hver 15-16;
Eze 40:16
42:1
iver 13
jEze 41:12-14
kEze 40:17
42:3
lEze 41:15
mEze 41:16
42:4
nEze 46:19
42:9
oEze 44:5;
46:19
42:10
pver 1

a22 Septuagint; Hebrew *long*   b22 Septuagint; Hebrew *length*   c2 The common cubit was about 1 1/2 feet (about 0.5 meter).   d4 Septuagint and Syriac; Hebrew *and one cubit*
e10 Septuagint; Hebrew *Eastward*

beginning of the passageway that was parallel to the corresponding wall extending eastward, by which one enters the rooms.

[13]Then he said to me, "The north[q] and south rooms facing the temple courtyard are the priests' rooms, where the priests who approach the LORD will eat the most holy offerings. There they will put the most holy offerings—the grain offerings, the sin offerings[r] and the guilt offerings[s]—for the place is holy.[t] [14]Once the priests enter the holy precincts, they are not to go into the outer court until they leave behind the garments[u] in which they minister, for these are holy. They are to put on other clothes before they go near the places that are for the people.[v]"

[15]When he had finished measuring what was inside the temple area, he led me out by the east gate[w] and measured the area all around: [16]He measured the east side with the measuring rod; it was five hundred cubits.[a] [17]He measured the north side; it was five hundred cubits[b] by the measuring rod. [18]He measured the south side; it was five hundred cubits by the measuring rod. [19]Then he turned to the west side and measured; it was five hundred cubits by the measuring rod. [20]So he measured[x] the area on all four sides. It had a wall around it,[y] five hundred cubits long and five hundred cubits wide,[z] to separate the holy from the common.[a]

The Glory Returns to the Temple

43 Then the man brought me to the gate facing east,[b] [2]and I saw the glory of the God of Israel coming from the east. His voice was like the roar of rushing waters,[c] and the land was radiant with his glory.[d] [3]The vision I saw was like the vision I had seen when he[c] came to destroy the city and like the visions I had seen by the Kebar River, and I fell facedown. [4]The glory[e] of the LORD entered the temple through the gate facing east.[f] [5]Then the Spirit[g] lifted me up[h] and brought me into the inner court, and the glory of the LORD filled the temple.

[6]While the man was standing beside me, I heard someone speaking to me from inside the temple. [7]He said: "Son of man, this is the place of my throne and the place for the soles of my feet. This is where I will live among the Israelites forever. The house of Israel will never again defile my holy name—neither they nor their kings—by their prostitution[d] and the lifeless idols[e] of their kings at their high places.[i] [8]When they placed their threshold next to my threshold and their doorposts beside my doorposts, with only a wall between me and them, they defiled my holy name by their detestable practices. So I destroyed them in my anger. [9]Now let them put away from me their prostitution and the lifeless idols of their kings, and I will live among them forever.[j]

[10]"Son of man, describe the temple to the people of Israel, that they may be ashamed[k] of their sins. Let them consider the plan, [11]and if they are ashamed of all they have done, make known to them the design of the temple—its arrangement, its exits and entrances—its whole design and all its regulations[f] and laws. Write these down before them so that they may be faithful to its design and follow all its regulations.[l]

42:13
qEze 40:46
rLev 10:17; 6:25
sLev 14:13
tEx 29:31;
Lev 6:29; 7:6;
10:12-13;
Nu 18:9-10
42:14
uEze 44:19
vEx 29:9;
Lev 8:7-9
42:15
wEze 43:1
42:20
xEze 40:5
yZec 2:5
zEze 45:2;
Rev 21:16
aEze 22:26
43:1
bEze 10:19;
42:15; 44:1;
46:1
43:2
cRev 1:15
dIsa 6:3;
Eze 11:23;
Rev 18:1
43:4
eEze 1:28
fEze 10:19
43:5
gEze 11:24
hEze 3:12; 8:3
43:7
iLev 26:30
43:9
jEze 37:26-28
43:10
kEze 16:61
43:11
lEze 44:5

---

[a]16 See Septuagint of verse 17; Hebrew *rods*; also in verses 18 and 19.   [b]17 Septuagint; Hebrew *rods*   [c]3 Some Hebrew manuscripts and Vulgate; most Hebrew manuscripts *I*   [d]7 Or *their spiritual adultery*; also in verse 9   [e]7 Or *the corpses*; also in verse 9   [f]11 Some Hebrew manuscripts and Septuagint; most Hebrew manuscripts *regulations and its whole design*

¹²"This is the law of the temple: All the surrounding area ᵐ on top of the mountain will be most holy. Such is the law of the temple.

The Altar

¹³"These are the measurements of the altar ⁿ in long cubits, that cubit being a cubit ᵃ and a handbreadth ᵇ: Its gutter is a cubit deep and a cubit wide, with a rim of one span ᶜ around the edge. And this is the height of the altar: ¹⁴From the gutter on the ground up to the lower ledge it is two cubits high and a cubit wide, and from the smaller ledge up to the larger ledge it is four cubits high and a cubit wide. ¹⁵The altar hearth is four cubits high, and four horns ᵒ project upward from the hearth. ¹⁶The altar hearth is square, twelve cubits long and twelve cubits wide. ¹⁷The upper ledge also is square, fourteen cubits long and fourteen cubits wide, with a rim of half a cubit and a gutter of a cubit all around. The steps ᵖ of the altar face east."

¹⁸Then he said to me, "Son of man, this is what the Sovereign LORD says: These will be the regulations for sacrificing burnt offerings �q and sprinkling blood ʳ upon the altar when it is built: ¹⁹You are to give a young bull ˢ as a sin offering to the priests, who are Levites, of the family of Zadok, ᵗ who come near ᵘ to minister before me, declares the Sovereign LORD. ²⁰You are to take some of its blood and put it on the four horns of the altar and on the four corners of the upper ledge ᵛ and all around the rim, and so purify the altar ʷ and make atonement for it. ²¹You are to take the bull for the sin offering and burn it in the designated part of the temple area outside the sanctuary. ˣ

²²"On the second day you are to offer a male goat without defect for a sin offering, and the altar is to be purified as it was purified with the bull. ²³When you have finished purifying it, you are to offer a young bull and a ram from the flock, both without defect. ʸ ²⁴You are to offer them before the LORD, and the priests are to sprinkle salt ᶻ on them and sacrifice them as a burnt offering to the LORD.

²⁵"For seven days ᵃ you are to provide a male goat daily for a sin offering; you are also to provide a young bull and a ram from the flock, both without defect. ᵇ ²⁶For seven days they are to make atonement for the altar and cleanse it; thus they will dedicate it. ²⁷At the end of these days, from the eighth day ᶜ on, the priests are to present your burnt offerings and fellowship offerings ᵈᵈ on the altar. Then I will accept you, declares the Sovereign LORD."

The Prince, the Levites, the Priests

44 Then the man brought me back to the outer gate of the sanctuary, the one facing east, ᵉ and it was shut. ²The LORD said to me, "This gate is to remain shut. It must not be opened; no one may enter through it. ᶠ It is to remain shut because the LORD, the God of Israel, has entered through it. ³The prince himself is the only one who may sit inside the gateway to eat in the presence ᵍ of the LORD. He is to enter by way of the portico of the gateway and go out the same way. ʰ"

⁴Then the man brought me by way of the north gate to the front of the

43:12
ᵐEze 40:2
43:13
ⁿ2Ch 4:1
43:15
ᵒEx 27:2
43:17
ᵖEx 20:26
43:18
qEx 40:29
rLev 1:5,11;
Heb 9:21-22
43:19
sLev 4:3;
Eze 45:18-19
tEze 44:15
uNu 16:40;
Eze 40:46
43:20
vver 17
wLev 16:19
43:21
xEx 29:14;
Heb 13:11
43:23
yEx 29:1
43:24
zLev 2:13;
Mk 9:49-50
43:25
aLev 8:33
bEx 29:37
43:27
cLev 9:1
dLev 17:5
44:1
eEze 43:1
44:2
fEze 43:4-5
44:3
gEx 24:9-11
hEze 46:2,8

ᵃ13 The common cubit was about 1 1/2 feet (about 0.5 meter).   ᵇ13 That is, about 3 inches (about 8 centimeters)   ᶜ13 That is, about 9 inches (about 22 centimeters)   ᵈ27 Traditionally *peace offerings* temple. I looked and saw the glory of the LORD filling the temple[i] of the LORD, and I fell facedown.[j]

[5]The LORD said to me, "Son of man, look carefully, listen closely and give attention to everything I tell you concerning all the regulations regarding the temple of the LORD. Give attention to the entrance of the temple and all the exits of the sanctuary.[k] [6]Say to the rebellious house[l] of Israel, 'This is what the Sovereign LORD says: Enough of your detestable practices, O house of Israel! [7]In addition to all your other detestable practices, you brought foreigners uncircumcised in heart[m] and flesh into my sanctuary, desecrating my temple while you offered me food, fat and blood, and you broke my covenant.[n] [8]Instead of carrying out your duty in regard to my holy things, you put others in charge of my sanctuary.[o] [9]This is what the Sovereign LORD says: No foreigner uncircumcised in heart and flesh is to enter my sanctuary, not even the foreigners who live among the Israelites.[p]

[10]" 'The Levites who went far from me when Israel went astray[q] and who wandered from me after their idols must bear the consequences of their sin.[r] [11]They may serve in my sanctuary, having charge of the gates of the temple and serving in it; they may slaughter the burnt offerings[s] and sacrifices for the people and stand before the people and serve them.[t] [12]But because they served them in the presence of their idols and made the house of Israel fall into sin, therefore I have sworn with uplifted hand[u] that they must bear the consequences of their sin, declares the Sovereign LORD.[v] [13]They are not to come near to serve me as priests or come near any of my holy things or my most holy offerings; they must bear the shame[w] of their detestable practices.[x] [14]Yet I will put them in charge of the duties of the temple and all the work that is to be done in it.[y]

[15]" 'But the priests, who are Levites and descendants of Zadok and who faithfully carried out the duties of my sanctuary when the Israelites went astray from me, are to come near to minister before me; they are to stand before me to offer sacrifices of fat and blood, declares the Sovereign LORD.[z] [16]They alone are to enter my sanctuary; they alone are to come near my table[a] to minister before me and perform my service.[b]

[17]" 'When they enter the gates of the inner court, they are to wear linen clothes;[c] they must not wear any woolen garment while ministering at the gates of the inner court or inside the temple. [18]They are to wear linen turbans[d] on their heads and linen undergarments[e] around their waists. They must not wear anything that makes them perspire.[f] [19]When they go out into the outer court where the people are, they are to take off the clothes they have been ministering in and are to leave them in the sacred rooms, and put on other clothes, so that they do not consecrate[g] the people by means of their garments.[h]

[20]" 'They must not shave their heads or let their hair grow long, but they are to keep the hair of their heads trimmed.[i] [21]No priest is to drink wine when he enters the inner court.[j] [22]They must not marry widows or divorced women; they may marry only virgins of Israelite descent or widows of priests.[k] [23]They are to teach my people the difference between the holy and the common[l] and show them how to distinguish between the unclean and the clean.[m]

[24]" 'In any dispute, the priests are to serve as judges[n] and decide it

44:4
i Isa 6:4;
Rev 15:8
j Eze 1:28; 3:23
44:5
k Eze 40:4;
43:10-11
44:6
l Eze 3:9
44:7
m Lev 26:41
n Ge 17:14;
Ex 12:48;
Lev 22:25
44:8
o Lev 22:2;
Nu 18:7
44:9
p Joel 3:17;
Zec 14:21
44:10
q 2Ki 23:8
r Nu 18:23
44:11
s 2Ch 29:34
t Nu 3:5-37;
16:9;
1Ch 26:12-19
44:12
u Ps 106:26
v 2Ki 16:10-16
44:13
w Eze 16:61
x Nu 18:3
44:14
y Nu 18:4;
1Ch 23:28-32
44:15
z Jer 33:18;
Eze 40:46;
Zec 3:7
44:16
a Eze 41:22
b Nu 18:5
44:17
c Ex 39:27-28;
Rev 19:8
44:18
d Ex 28:39;
Isa 3:20
e Ex 28:42
f Lev 16:4
44:19
g Lev 6:27;
Eze 46:20
h Lev 6:10-11;
Eze 42:14
44:20
i Lev 21:5;
Nu 6:5
44:21
j Lev 10:9
44:22
k Lev 21:7
44:23
l Eze 22:26
m Mal 2:7
44:24
n Dt 17:8-9;
1Ch 23:4

according to my ordinances. They are to keep my laws and my decrees for all my appointed feasts, and they are to keep my Sabbaths holy. °

25" 'A priest must not defile himself by going near a dead person; however, if the dead person was his father or mother, son or daughter, brother or unmarried sister, then he may defile himself. ᵖ ²⁶After he is cleansed, he must wait seven days. ۹ ²⁷On the day he goes into the inner court of the sanctuary to minister in the sanctuary, he is to offer a sin offering for himself, declares the Sovereign LORD.

28" 'I am to be the only inheritance ʳ the priests have. You are to give them no possession in Israel; I will be their possession. ²⁹They will eat the grain offerings, the sin offerings and the guilt offerings; and everything in Israel devoted ᵃ to the LORD ˢ will belong to them. ᵗ ³⁰The best of all the firstfruits ᵘ and of all your special gifts will belong to the priests. You are to give them the first portion of your ground meal ᵛ so that a blessing ʷ may rest on your household. ˣ ³¹The priests must not eat anything, bird or animal, found dead or torn by wild animals. ʸ

Division of the Land

45 " 'When you allot the land as an inheritance, ᶻ you are to present to the LORD a portion of the land as a sacred district, 25,000 cubits long and 20,000 ᵇ cubits wide; the entire area will be holy. ᵃ ²Of this, a section 500 cubits square ᵇ is to be for the sanctuary, with 50 cubits around it for open land. ³In the sacred district, measure off a section 25,000 cubits ᶜ long and 10,000 cubits ᵈ wide. In it will be the sanctuary, the Most Holy Place. ⁴It will be the sacred portion of the land for the priests, ᶜ who minister in the sanctuary and who draw near to minister before the LORD. It will be a place for their houses as well as a holy place for the sanctuary. ᵈ ⁵An area 25,000 cubits long and 10,000 cubits wide will belong to the Levites, who serve in the temple, as their possession for towns to live in. ᵉ ᵉ

6" 'You are to give the city as its property an area 5,000 cubits wide and 25,000 cubits long, adjoining the sacred portion; it will belong to the whole house of Israel. ᶠ

7" 'The prince will have the land bordering each side of the area formed by the sacred district and the property of the city. It will extend westward from the west side and eastward from the east side, running lengthwise from the western to the eastern border parallel to one of the tribal portions. ᵍ ⁸This land will be his possession in Israel. And my princes will no longer oppress my people but will allow the house of Israel to possess the land according to their tribes. ʰ

9" 'This is what the Sovereign LORD says: You have gone far enough, O princes of Israel! Give up your violence and oppression and do what is just and right. ⁱ Stop dispossessing my people, declares the Sovereign LORD. ¹⁰You are to use accurate scales, ʲ an accurate ephah ᶠᵏ and an accurate bath. ᵍ ¹¹The ephah ˡ and the bath are to be the same size, the bath containing a tenth of a homer ʰ and the ephah a tenth of a

44:24
o2Ch 19:8
44:25
pLev 21:1-4
44:26
qNu 19:14
44:28
rNu 18:20;
Dt 10:9; 18:1-2;
Jos 13:33
44:29
sLev 27:21
tNu 18:9,14
44:30
uNu 18:12-13
vNu 15:18-21
wMal 3:10
xNe 10:35-37
44:31
yEx 22:31;
Lev 22:8
45:1
zEze 47:21-22
aEze 48:8-9,29
45:2
bEze 42:20
45:4
cEze 40:46
dEze 48:10-11
45:5
eEze 48:13
45:6
fEze 48:15-18
45:7
gEze 48:21
45:8
hNu 26:53;
Eze 46:18
45:9
iJer 22:3;
Zec 7:9-10;
8:16
45:10
jDt 25:15;
Pr 11:1;
Am 8:4-6;
Mic 6:10-11
kLev 19:36
45:11
lIsa 5:10

ᵃ29 The Hebrew term refers to the irrevocable giving over of things or persons to the LORD.
ᵇ1 Septuagint (see also verses 3 and 5 and 48:9); Hebrew 10,000   ᶜ3 That is, about 7 miles (about 12 kilometers)   ᵈ3 That is, about 3 miles (about 5 kilometers)   ᵉ5 Septuagint; Hebrew *temple; they will have as their possession 20 rooms*   ᶠ10 An ephah was a dry measure.
ᵍ10 A bath was a liquid measure.   ʰ11 A homer was a dry measure.

homer; the homer is to be the standard measure for both. [12]The shekel[a] is to consist of twenty gerahs. [m]Twenty shekels plus twenty-five shekels plus fifteen shekels equal one mina. [b]

Offerings and Holy Days

[13]" 'This is the special gift you are to offer: a sixth of an ephah from each homer of wheat and a sixth of an ephah from each homer of barley. [14]The prescribed portion of oil, measured by the bath, is a tenth of a bath from each cor (which consists of ten baths or one homer, for ten baths are equivalent to a homer). [15]Also one sheep is to be taken from every flock of two hundred from the well-watered pastures of Israel. These will be used for the grain offerings, burnt offerings[n] and fellowship offerings[c] to make atonement[o] for the people, declares the Sovereign LORD. [16]All the people of the land will participate in this special gift for the use of the prince in Israel. [17]It will be the duty of the prince to provide the burnt offerings, grain offerings and drink offerings at the festivals, the New Moons and the Sabbaths[p]—at all the appointed feasts of the house of Israel. He will provide the sin offerings, grain offerings, burnt offerings and fellowship offerings to make atonement for the house of Israel. [q]

[18]" 'This is what the Sovereign LORD says: In the first month[r] on the first day you are to take a young bull without defect[s] and purify the sanctuary. [t] [19]The priest is to take some of the blood of the sin offering and put it on the doorposts of the temple, on the four corners of the upper ledge[u] of the altar[v] and on the gateposts of the inner court. [20]You are to do the same on the seventh day of the month for anyone who sins unintentionally[w] or through ignorance; so you are to make atonement for the temple.

[21]" 'In the first month on the fourteenth day you are to observe the Passover,[x] a feast lasting seven days, during which you shall eat bread made without yeast. [22]On that day the prince is to provide a bull as a sin offering for himself and for all the people of the land. [y] [23]Every day during the seven days of the Feast he is to provide seven bulls and seven rams[z] without defect as a burnt offering to the LORD, and a male goat for a sin offering. [a] [24]He is to provide as a grain offering[b] an ephah for each bull and an ephah for each ram, along with a hin[d] of oil for each ephah. [c]

[25]" 'During the seven days of the Feast,[d] which begins in the seventh month on the fifteenth day, he is to make the same provision for sin offerings, burnt offerings, grain offerings and oil. [e]

46 " 'This is what the Sovereign LORD says: The gate of the inner court[f] facing east[g] is to be shut on the six working days, but on the Sabbath day and on the day of the New Moon[h] it is to be opened. [2]The prince is to enter from the outside through the portico[i] of the gateway and stand by the gatepost. The priests are to sacrifice his burnt offering and his fellowship offerings. [e] He is to worship at the threshold of the gateway and then go out, but the gate will not be shut until evening. [j] [3]On the Sabbaths and New Moons the people of the land are

45:12
m Ex 30:13;
Lev 27:25;
Nu 3:47
45:15
n Lev 1:4
o Lev 6:30
45:17
p Lev 23:38;
Isa 66:23
q 1Ki 8:62;
2Ch 31:3;
Eze 46:4-12
45:18
r Ex 12:2;
s Lev 22:20;
Heb 9:14
t Lev 16:16,33
45:19
u Eze 43:17
v Lev 16:18-19;
Eze 43:20
45:20
w Lev 4:27
45:21
x Ex 12:11;
Lev 23:5-6
45:22
y Lev 4:14
45:23
z Job 42:8
a Nu 28:16-25
45:24
b Nu 28:12-13
c Eze 46:5-7
45:25
d Dt 16:13
e Lev 23:34-43;
Nu 29:12-38
46:1
f Eze 40:19
g 1Ch 9:18
h ver 6;
Isa 66:23
46:2
i ver 8
j ver 12; Eze 44:3

a[12] A shekel weighed about 2/5 ounce (about 11.5 grams). b[12] That is, 60 shekels; the common mina was 50 shekels. c[15] Traditionally *peace offerings*; also in verse 17 d[24] That is, probably about 4 quarts (about 4 liters) e[2] Traditionally *peace offerings*; also in verse 12 to worship in the presence of the Lord at the entrance to that gateway. k 4The burnt offering the prince brings to the Lord on the Sabbath day is to be six male lambs and a ram, all without defect. 5The grain offering given with the ram is to be an ephah, *a* and the grain offering with the lambs is to be as much as he pleases, along with a hin*b* of oil for each ephah.1 6On the day of the New Moonm he is to offer a young bull, six lambs and a ram, all without defect. 7He is to provide as a grain offering one ephah with the bull, one ephah with the ram, and with the lambs as much as he wants to give, along with a hin of oil with each ephah. n 8When the prince enters, he is to go in through the porticoᵒ of the gateway, and he is to come out the same way. P

9'' 'When the people of the land come before the Lord at the appointed feasts, q whoever enters by the north gate to worship is to go out the south gate; and whoever enters by the south gate is to go out the north gate. No one is to return through the gate by which he entered, but each is to go out the opposite gate. 10The prince is to be among them, going in when they go in and going out when they go out. r

11'' 'At the festivals and the appointed feasts, the grain offering is to be an ephah with a bull, an ephah with a ram, and with the lambs as much as one pleases, along with a hin of oil for each ephah. s 12When the prince providest a freewill offeringu to the Lord—whether a burnt offering or fellowship offerings—the gate facing east is to be opened for him. He shall offer his burnt offering or his fellowship offerings as he does on the Sabbath day. Then he shall go out, and after he has gone out, the gate will be shut. v

13'' 'Every day you are to provide a year-old lamb without defect for a burnt offering to the Lord; morning by morning you shall provide it. w 14You are also to provide with it morning by morning a grain offering, consisting of a sixth of an ephah with a third of a hin of oil to moisten the flour. The presenting of this grain offering to the Lord is a lasting ordinance. x 15So the lamb and the grain offering and the oil shall be provided morning by morning for a regulary burnt offering. z

16'' 'This is what the Sovereign Lord says: If the prince makes a gift from his inheritance to one of his sons, it will also belong to his descendants; it is to be their property by inheritance. a 17If, however, he makes a gift from his inheritance to one of his servants, the servant may keep it until the year of freedom;b then it will revert to the prince. His inheritance belongs to his sons only; it is theirs. 18The prince must not take any of the inheritancec of the people, driving them off their property. He is to give his sons their inheritance out of his own property, so that none of my people will be separated from his property.' "

19Then the man brought me through the entranced at the side of the gate to the sacred rooms facing north, which belonged to the priests, and showed me a place at the western end. 20He said to me, "This is the place where the priests will cook the guilt offering and the sin offering and bake the grain offering, to avoid bringing them into the outer court and consecratinge the people."f

21He then brought me to the outer court and led me around to its four corners, and I saw in each corner another court. 22In the four corners of

46:3
kLk 1:10
46:5
lver 11;
Eze 45:24
46:6
mver 1;
Nu 10:10
46:7
nEze 45:24
46:8
over 2
pEze 44:3
46:9
qEx 23:14;
34:20
46:10
r2Sa 6:14-15;
Ps 42:4
46:11
sver 5
46:12
tEze 45:17
uLev 7:16
vver 2
46:13
wEx 29:38;
Nu 28:3
46:14
xDa 8:11
46:15
yEx 29:42
zEx 29:38;
Nu 28:5-6
46:16
a2Ch 21:3
46:17
bLev 25:10
46:18
cLev 25:23;
Eze 45:8;
Mic 2:1-2
46:19
dEze 42:9
46:20
eLev 6:27
fZec 14:20

---

*a5 That is, probably about 3/5 bushel (about 22 liters)   *b5 That is, probably about 4 quarts (about 4 liters) the outer court were enclosed[a] courts, forty cubits long and thirty cubits wide; each of the courts in the four corners was the same size. 23Around the inside of each of the four courts was a ledge of stone, with places for fire built all around under the ledge. 24He said to me, "These are the kitchens where those who minister at the temple will cook the sacrifices of the people."

The River From the Temple

47 The man brought me back to the entrance of the temple, and I saw water[g] coming out from under the threshold of the temple toward the east (for the temple faced east). The water was coming down from under the south side of the temple, south of the altar.[h] 2He then brought me out through the north gate and led me around the outside to the outer gate facing east, and the water was flowing from the south side.

3As the man went eastward with a measuring line[i] in his hand, he measured off a thousand cubits[b] and then led me through water that was ankle-deep. 4He measured off another thousand cubits and led me through water that was knee-deep. He measured off another thousand and led me through water that was up to the waist. 5He measured off another thousand, but now it was a river that I could not cross, because the water had risen and was deep enough to swim in—a river that no one could cross.[j] 6He asked me, "Son of man, do you see this?"

Then he led me back to the bank of the river. 7When I arrived there, I saw a great number of trees on each side of the river.[k] 8He said to me, "This water flows toward the eastern region and goes down into the Arabah,[c1] where it enters the Sea.[d] When it empties into the Sea,[d] the water there becomes fresh.[m] 9Swarms of living creatures will live wherever the river flows. There will be large numbers of fish, because this water flows there and makes the salt water fresh; so where the river flows everything will live.[n] 10Fishermen[o] will stand along the shore; from En Gedi[p] to En Eglaim there will be places for spreading nets.[q] The fish will be of many kinds[r]—like the fish of the Great Sea.[es] 11But the swamps and marshes will not become fresh; they will be left for salt.[t] 12Fruit trees of all kinds will grow on both banks of the river.[u] Their leaves will not wither, nor will their fruit[v] fail. Every month they will bear, because the water from the sanctuary flows to them. Their fruit will serve for food and their leaves for healing.[w]"

The Boundaries of the Land

13This is what the Sovereign Lord says: "These are the boundaries[x] by which you are to divide the land for an inheritance among the twelve tribes of Israel, with two portions for Joseph.[y] 14You are to divide it equally among them. Because I swore with uplifted hand to give it to your forefathers, this land will become your inheritance.[z]

15"This is to be the boundary of the land:

"On the north side it will run from the Great Sea by the Hethlon road[a]

47:1
g Isa 55:1
h Ps 46:4;
Joel 3:18;
Rev 22:1
47:3
i Eze 40:3
47:5
j Isa 11:9;
Hab 2:14
47:7
k ver 12;
Rev 22:2
47:8
l Dt 3:17;
Jos 3:16
m Isa 41:18
47:9
n Isa 12:3; 55:1;
Jn 4:14; 7:37-38
47:10
o Mt 4:19
p Jos 15:62
q Eze 26:5
r Ps 104:25;
Mt 13:47
s Nu 34:6
47:11
t Dt 29:23
47:12
u ver 7;
Rev 22:2
v Ps 1:3
w Ge 2:9;
Jer 17:8
47:13
x Nu 34:2-12
y Ge 48:5
47:14
z Ge 12:7;
Dt 1:8;
Eze 20:5-6
47:15
a Eze 48:1

---

a22 The meaning of the Hebrew for this word is uncertain.   *b3* That is, about 1,500 feet (about 450 meters)   *c8* Or *the Jordan Valley*   *d8* That is, the Dead Sea   *e10* That is, the Mediterranean; also in verses 15, 19 and 20 past Lebo[a] Hamath to Zedad, [16]Berothah[b b] and Sibraim (which lies on the border between Damascus and Hamath),[c] as far as Hazer Hatticon, which is on the border of Hauran. [17]The boundary will extend from the sea to Hazar Enan,[c] along the northern border of Damascus, with the border of Hamath to the north. This will be the north boundary.[d]

[18]"On the east side the boundary will run between Hauran and Damascus, along the Jordan between Gilead and the land of Israel, to the eastern sea and as far as Tamar.[d] This will be the east boundary.

[19]"On the south side it will run from Tamar as far as the waters of Meribah Kadesh,[e] then along the Wadi ⌊of Egypt⌋[f] to the Great Sea.[g] This will be the south boundary.

[20]"On the west side, the Great Sea will be the boundary to a point opposite Lebo[e] Hamath.[h] This will be the west boundary.[i]

[21]"You are to distribute this land among yourselves according to the tribes of Israel. [22]You are to allot it as an inheritance for yourselves and for the aliens[j] who have settled among you and who have children. You are to consider them as native-born Israelites; along with you they are to be allotted an inheritance among the tribes of Israel.[k] [23]In whatever tribe the alien settles, there you are to give him his inheritance," declares the Sovereign LORD.

The Division of the Land

48 "These are the tribes, listed by name: At the northern frontier, Dan[l] will have one portion; it will follow the Hethlon road[m] to Lebo[f] Hamath;[n] Hazar Enan and the northern border of Damascus next to Hamath will be part of its border from the east side to the west side.

[2]"Asher[o] will have one portion; it will border the territory of Dan from east to west.

[3]"Naphtali[p] will have one portion; it will border the territory of Asher from east to west.

[4]"Manasseh[q] will have one portion; it will border the territory of Naphtali from east to west.

[5]"Ephraim[r] will have one portion; it will border the territory of Manasseh[s] from east to west.[t]

[6]"Reuben[u] will have one portion; it will border the territory of Ephraim from east to west.

[7]"Judah[v] will have one portion; it will border the territory of Reuben from east to west.

[8]"Bordering the territory of Judah from east to west will be the portion you are to present as a special gift. It will be 25,000 cubits[g] wide, and its length from east to west will equal one of the tribal portions; the sanctuary will be in the center of it.[w]

[9]"The special portion you are to offer to the LORD will be 25,000 cubits

47:16
b 2Sa 8:8
c Nu 13:21;
Eze 48:1

47:17
d Eze 48:1

47:19
e Dt 32:51
f Isa 27:12
g Eze 48:28

47:20
h Eze 48:1
i Nu 34:6

47:22
j Isa 14:1
k Nu 26:55-56;
Isa 56:6-7;
Ro 10:12;
Eph 2:12-16;
3:6; Col 3:11

48:1
l Ge 30:6
m Eze 47:15-17
n Eze 47:20

48:2
o Jos 19:24-31

48:3
p Jos 19:32-39

48:4
q Jos 17:1-11

48:5
r Jos 16:5-9
s Jos 17:7-10
t Jos 17:17

48:6
u Jos 13:15-21

48:7
v Jos 15:1-63

48:8
w ver 21

a15 Or past the entrance to *b15,16 See Septuagint and Ezekiel 48:1; Hebrew road to go into Zedad,* *16Hamath, Berothah* *c17 Hebrew Enon, a variant of Enan* *d18 Septuagint and Syriac; Hebrew Israel. You will measure to the eastern sea* *e20 Or opposite the entrance to* *f1 Or to the entrance to* *g8 That is, about 7 miles (about 12 kilometers)* long and 10,000 cubits[a] wide.[x] [10]This will be the sacred portion for the priests. It will be 25,000 cubits long on the north side, 10,000 cubits wide on the west side, 10,000 cubits wide on the east side and 25,000 cubits long on the south side. In the center of it will be the sanctuary of the LORD.[y] [11]This will be for the consecrated priests, the Zadokites,[z] who were faithful in serving me[a] and did not go astray as the Levites did when the Israelites went astray.[b] [12]It will be a special gift to them from the sacred portion of the land, a most holy portion, bordering the territory of the Levites.

[13]"Alongside the territory of the priests, the Levites will have an allotment 25,000 cubits long and 10,000 cubits wide. Its total length will be 25,000 cubits and its width 10,000 cubits.[c] [14]They must not sell or exchange any of it. This is the best of the land and must not pass into other hands, because it is holy to the LORD.[d]

[15]"The remaining area, 5,000 cubits wide and 25,000 cubits long, will be for the common use of the city, for houses and for pastureland. The city will be in the center of it [16]and will have these measurements: the north side 4,500 cubits, the south side 4,500 cubits, the east side 4,500 cubits, and the west side 4,500 cubits.[e] [17]The pastureland for the city will be 250 cubits on the north, 250 cubits on the south, 250 cubits on the east, and 250 cubits on the west. [18]What remains of the area, bordering on the sacred portion and running the length of it, will be 10,000 cubits on the east side and 10,000 cubits on the west side. Its produce will supply food for the workers of the city.[f] [19]The workers from the city who farm it will come from all the tribes of Israel. [20]The entire portion will be a square, 25,000 cubits on each side. As a special gift you will set aside the sacred portion, along with the property of the city.

[21]"What remains on both sides of the area formed by the sacred portion and the city property will belong to the prince. It will extend eastward from the 25,000 cubits of the sacred portion to the eastern border, and westward from the 25,000 cubits to the western border. Both these areas running the length of the tribal portions will belong to the prince, and the sacred portion with the temple sanctuary will be in the center of them.[g] [22]So the property of the Levites and the property of the city will lie in the center of the area that belongs to the prince. The area belonging to the prince will lie between the border of Judah and the border of Benjamin.

[23]"As for the rest of the tribes: Benjamin[h] will have one portion; it will extend from the east side to the west side.

[24]"Simeon[i] will have one portion; it will border the territory of Benjamin from east to west.

[25]"Issachar[j] will have one portion; it will border the territory of Simeon from east to west.

[26]"Zebulun[k] will have one portion; it will border the territory of Issachar from east to west.

[27]"Gad[l] will have one portion; it will border the territory of Zebulun from east to west.

[28]"The southern boundary of Gad will run south from Tamar[m] to the waters of Meribah Kadesh, then along the Wadi ˌof Egyptˌ to the Great Sea.[b][n]

48:9
x Eze 45:1
48:10
y ver 21;
Eze 45:3-4
48:11
z 2Sa 8:17
a Lev 8:35
b Eze 14:11;
44:15
48:13
c Eze 45:5
48:14
d Lev 25:34;
27:10,28
48:16
e Rev 21:16
48:18
f Eze 45:6
48:21
g ver 8,10;
Eze 45:7
48:23
h Jos 18:11-28
48:24
i Ge 29:33;
Jos 19:1-9
48:25
j Jos 19:17-23
48:26
k Jos 19:10-16
48:27
l Jos 13:24-28
48:28
m Ge 14:7
n Eze 47:19

---

[a]9 That is, about 3 miles (about 5 kilometers)   [b]28 That is, the Mediterranean

²⁹"This is the land you are to allot as an inheritance to the tribes of Israel, and these will be their portions," declares the Sovereign LORD.

The Gates of the City

48:35
o Isa 12:6;
24:23; Jer 3:17;
14:9; Jer 33:16;
Joel 3:21;
Zec 2:10;
Rev 21:3

³⁰"These will be the exits of the city: Beginning on the north side, which is 4,500 cubits long, ³¹the gates of the city will be named after the tribes of Israel. The three gates on the north side will be the gate of Reuben, the gate of Judah and the gate of Levi.

³²"On the east side, which is 4,500 cubits long, will be three gates: the gate of Joseph, the gate of Benjamin and the gate of Dan.

³³"On the south side, which measures 4,500 cubits, will be three gates: the gate of Simeon, the gate of Issachar and the gate of Zebulun.

³⁴"On the west side, which is 4,500 cubits long, will be three gates: the gate of Gad, the gate of Asher and the gate of Naphtali.

³⁵"The distance all around will be 18,000 cubits.

"And the name of the city from that time on will be:

THE LORD IS THERE. ᵒ"

Daniel

Title and Background

Daniel records events that took place during Israel's captivity and encourages the people to trust in the God who controls all history.

Author and Date of Writing

In several passages, such as 9:2 and 10:2, the book itself mentions Daniel as the author. Jesus himself referred to Daniel as the author (Mt 24:15). Objective evidence indicates that the book was written about 530 B.C., shortly after the capture of Babylon by Cyrus in 539.

Theme and Message

The theological theme of the book is God's sovereignty: "The Most High God is sovereign over the kingdoms of men" (5:21). Daniel's visions always show God as triumphant. The climax of his sovereignty is described in Revelation 11:15 (compare Da 2:44; 7:27).

Outline

Daniel's Training in Babylon

1 In the third year of the reign of Jehoiakim king of Judah, Nebuchadnezzar[a] king of Babylon came to Jerusalem and besieged it.[b] [2]And the Lord delivered Jehoiakim king of Judah into his hand, along with some of the articles from the temple of God. These he carried off to the temple of his god in Babylonia[a] and put in the treasure house of his god.[c]

[3]Then the king ordered Ashpenaz, chief of his court officials, to bring in some of the Israelites from the royal family and the nobility[d]— [4]young men without any physical defect, handsome, showing aptitude for every kind of learning, well informed, quick to understand, and qualified to serve in the king's palace. He was to teach them the language and literature of the Babylonians.[b] [5]The king assigned them a daily amount of food and wine[e] from the king's table. They were to be

1:1
a 2Ki 24:1
b 2Ch 36:6
1:2
c 2Ch 36:7;
Jer 27:19-20;
Zec 5:5-11
1:3
d 2Ki 20:18;
24:15; Isa 39:7
1:5
e ver 8,10

a 2 Hebrew *Shinar*   b 4 Or *Chaldeans*

trained for three years, and after that they were to enter the king's service. [f]

[6]Among these were some from Judah: Daniel,[g] Hananiah, Mishael and Azariah. [7]The chief official gave them new names: to Daniel, the name Belteshazzar;[h] to Hananiah, Shadrach; to Mishael, Meshach; and to Azariah, Abednego.[i]

[8]But Daniel resolved not to defile[j] himself with the royal food and wine, and he asked the chief official for permission not to defile himself this way. [9]Now God had caused the official to show favor[k] and sympathy[l] to Daniel, [10]but the official told Daniel, "I am afraid of my lord the king, who has assigned your[a] food and drink. Why should he see you looking worse than the other young men your age? The king would then have my head because of you."

[11]Daniel then said to the guard whom the chief official had appointed over Daniel, Hananiah, Mishael and Azariah, [12]"Please test your servants for ten days: Give us nothing but vegetables to eat and water to drink. [13]Then compare our appearance with that of the young men who eat the royal food, and treat your servants in accordance with what you see." [14]So he agreed to this and tested them for ten days.

[15]At the end of the ten days they looked healthier and better nourished than any of the young men who ate the royal food.[m] [16]So the guard took away their choice food and the wine they were to drink and gave them vegetables instead.[n]

[17]To these four young men God gave knowledge and understanding[o] of all kinds of literature and learning.[p] And Daniel could understand visions and dreams of all kinds.[q]

[18]At the end of the time[r] set by the king to bring them in, the chief official presented them to Nebuchadnezzar. [19]The king talked with them, and he found none equal to Daniel, Hananiah, Mishael and Azariah; so they entered the king's service.[s] [20]In every matter of wisdom and understanding about which the king questioned them, he found them ten times better than all the magicians and enchanters in his whole kingdom.[t]

[21]And Daniel remained there until the first year of King Cyrus.[u]

Nebuchadnezzar's Dream

2 In the second year of his reign, Nebuchadnezzar had dreams;[v] his mind was troubled[w] and he could not sleep.[x] [2]So the king summoned the magicians,[y] enchanters, sorcerers[z] and astrologers[ba] to tell him what he had dreamed.[b] When they came in and stood before the king, [3]he said to them, "I have had a dream that troubles[c] me and I want to know what it means.[c] "

[4]Then the astrologers answered the king in Aramaic,[dd] "O king, live forever![e] Tell your servants the dream, and we will interpret it."

[5]The king replied to the astrologers, "This is what I have firmly decided: If you do not tell me what my dream was and interpret it, I will have you cut into pieces[f] and your houses turned into piles of rubble.[g] [6]But if you tell me the dream and explain it, you will receive from me

1:5
f ver 19
1:6
g Eze 14:14
1:7
h Da 4:8; 5:12
i Da 2:49; 3:12
1:8
j Eze 4:13-14
1:9
k Ge 39:21;
Pr 16:7
l 1Ki 8:50;
Ps 106:46
1:15
m Ex 23:25
1:16
n ver 12-13
1:17
o 1Ki 3:12
p Da 2:23;
Jas 1:5
q Da 2:19,30;
7:1; 8:1
1:18
r ver 5
1:19
s Ge 41:46
1:20
t 1Ki 4:30;
Da 2:13,28
1:21
u Da 6:28; 10:1
2:1
v Job 33:15,18;
Da 4:5
w Ge 41:8
x Est 6:1;
Da 6:18
2:2
y Ge 41:8
z Ex 7:11
a ver 10; Da 5:7
b Da 4:6
2:3
c Da 4:5
2:4
d Ezr 4:7
e Da 3:9; 5:10
2:5
f ver 12
g Ezr 6:11;
Da 3:29

---

[a]10 The Hebrew for *your* and *you* in this verse is plural.   [b]2 Or *Chaldeans*; also in verses 4, 5 and 10   [c]3 Or *was*   [d]4 The text from here through chapter 7 is in Aramaic.

gifts and rewards and great honor.[h] So tell me the dream and interpret it for me.''

[7]Once more they replied, ''Let the king tell his servants the dream, and we will interpret it.''

[8]Then the king answered, ''I am certain that you are trying to gain time, because you realize that this is what I have firmly decided: [9]If you do not tell me the dream, there is just one penalty[i] for you. You have conspired to tell me misleading and wicked things, hoping the situation will change. So then, tell me the dream, and I will know that you can interpret it for me.''[j]

[10]The astrologers answered the king, ''There is not a man on earth who can do what the king asks! No king, however great and mighty, has ever asked such a thing of any magician or enchanter or astrologer.[k] [11]What the king asks is too difficult. No one can reveal it to the king except the gods,[l] and they do not live among men.''

[12]This made the king so angry and furious[m] that he ordered the execution[n] of all the wise men of Babylon. [13]So the decree was issued to put the wise men to death, and men were sent to look for Daniel and his friends to put them to death.[o]

[14]When Arioch, the commander of the king's guard, had gone out to put to death the wise men of Babylon, Daniel spoke to him with wisdom and tact. [15]He asked the king's officer, ''Why did the king issue such a harsh decree?'' Arioch then explained the matter to Daniel. [16]At this, Daniel went in to the king and asked for time, so that he might interpret the dream for him.

[17]Then Daniel returned to his house and explained the matter to his friends Hananiah, Mishael and Azariah.[p] [18]He urged them to plead for mercy[q] from the God of heaven concerning this mystery,[r] so that he and his friends might not be executed with the rest of the wise men of Babylon. [19]During the night the mystery[s] was revealed to Daniel in a vision.[t] Then Daniel praised the God of heaven [20]and said:

> ''Praise be to the name of God for ever and ever;[u]
>   wisdom and power[v] are his.
> [21]He changes times and seasons;[w]
>   he sets up kings and deposes[x] them.
> He gives wisdom[y] to the wise
>   and knowledge to the discerning.
> [22]He reveals deep and hidden things;[z]
>   he knows what lies in darkness,[a]
>   and light[b] dwells with him.
> [23]I thank and praise you, O God of my fathers:[c]
>   You have given me wisdom[d] and power,
> you have made known to me what we asked of you,
>   you have made known to us the dream of the king.''

Daniel Interprets the Dream

[24]Then Daniel went to Arioch,[e] whom the king had appointed to execute the wise men of Babylon, and said to him, ''Do not execute the wise men of Babylon. Take me to the king, and I will interpret his dream for him.''

[25]Arioch took Daniel to the king at once and said, ''I have found a

2:6
h ver 48;
Da 5:7,16
2:9
i Est 4:11
j Isa 41:22-24
2:10
k ver 27
2:11
l Da 5:11
2:12
m Da 3:13,19
n ver 5
2:13
o Da 1:20
2:17
p Da 1:6
2:18
q Isa 37:4
r Jer 33:3
2:19
s ver 28
t Job 33:15;
Da 1:17
2:20
u Ps 113:2;
145:1-2
v Jer 32:19
2:21
w Da 7:25
x Job 12:19;
Ps 75:6-7
y Jas 1:5
2:22
z Job 12:22;
Ps 25:14;
Da 5:11
a Ps 139:11-12;
Jer 23:24;
Heb 4:13
b Isa 45:7;
Jas 1:17
2:23
c Ex 3:15
d Da 1:17
2:24
e ver 14

man among the exiles from Judah[f] who can tell the king what his dream means."

[26]The king asked Daniel (also called Belteshazzar),[g] "Are you able to tell me what I saw in my dream and interpret it?"

[27]Daniel replied, "No wise man, enchanter, magician or diviner can explain to the king the mystery he has asked about,[h] [28]but there is a God in heaven who reveals mysteries.[i] He has shown King Nebuchadnezzar what will happen in days to come.[j] Your dream and the visions that passed through your mind[k] as you lay on your bed are these:

[29]"As you were lying there, O king, your mind turned to things to come, and the revealer of mysteries showed you what is going to happen. [30]As for me, this mystery has been revealed[l] to me, not because I have greater wisdom than other living men, but so that you, O king, may know the interpretation and that you may understand what went through your mind.

[31]"You looked, O king, and there before you stood a large statue—an enormous, dazzling statue,[m] awesome in appearance. [32]The head of the statue was made of pure gold, its chest and arms of silver, its belly and thighs of bronze, [33]its legs of iron, its feet partly of iron and partly of baked clay. [34]While you were watching, a rock was cut out, but not by human hands.[n] It struck the statue on its feet of iron and clay and smashed them.[o] [35]Then the iron, the clay, the bronze, the silver and the gold were broken to pieces at the same time and became like chaff on a threshing floor in the summer. The wind swept them away[p] without leaving a trace. But the rock that struck the statue became a huge mountain[q] and filled the whole earth.

[36]"This was the dream, and now we will interpret it to the king. [37]You, O king, are the king of kings.[r] The God of heaven has given you dominion[s] and power and might and glory; [38]in your hands he has placed mankind and the beasts of the field and the birds of the air. Wherever they live, he has made you ruler over them all.[t] You are that head of gold.

[39]"After you, another kingdom will rise, inferior to yours. Next, a third kingdom, one of bronze, will rule over the whole earth. [40]Finally, there will be a fourth kingdom, strong as iron—for iron breaks and smashes everything—and as iron breaks things to pieces, so it will crush and break all the others.[u] [41]Just as you saw that the feet and toes were partly of baked clay and partly of iron, so this will be a divided kingdom; yet it will have some of the strength of iron in it, even as you saw iron mixed with clay. [42]As the toes were partly iron and partly clay, so this kingdom will be partly strong and partly brittle. [43]And just as you saw the iron mixed with baked clay, so the people will be a mixture and will not remain united, any more than iron mixes with clay.

[44]"In the time of those kings, the God of heaven will set up a kingdom that will never be destroyed, nor will it be left to another people. It will crush[v] all those kingdoms[w] and bring them to an end, but it will itself endure forever.[x] [45]This is the meaning of the vision of the rock[y] cut out of a mountain, but not by human hands[z]—a rock that broke the iron, the bronze, the clay, the silver and the gold to pieces.

"The great God has shown the king what will take place in the future. The dream is true and the interpretation is trustworthy."

[46]Then King Nebuchadnezzar fell prostrate[a] before Daniel and paid

him honor and ordered that an offering[b] and incense be presented to him. [47]The king said to Daniel, "Surely your God is the God of gods[c] and the Lord of kings[d] and a revealer of mysteries,[e] for you were able to reveal this mystery."

[48]Then the king placed Daniel in a high position and lavished many gifts on him. He made him ruler over the entire province of Babylon and placed him in charge of all its wise men.[f] [49]Moreover, at Daniel's request the king appointed Shadrach, Meshach and Abednego administrators over the province of Babylon,[g] while Daniel himself remained at the royal court.

The Image of Gold and the Fiery Furnace

3 King Nebuchadnezzar made an image[h] of gold, ninety feet high and nine feet[a] wide, and set it up on the plain of Dura in the province of Babylon. [2]He then summoned the satraps, prefects, governors, advisers, treasurers, judges, magistrates and all the other provincial officials[i] to come to the dedication of the image he had set up. [3]So the satraps, prefects, governors, advisers, treasurers, judges, magistrates and all the other provincial officials assembled for the dedication of the image that King Nebuchadnezzar had set up, and they stood before it.

[4]Then the herald loudly proclaimed, "This is what you are commanded to do, O peoples, nations and men of every language:[j] [5]As soon as you hear the sound of the horn, flute, zither, lyre, harp, pipes and all kinds of music, you must fall down and worship the image of gold that King Nebuchadnezzar has set up.[k] [6]Whoever does not fall down and worship will immediately be thrown into a blazing furnace."[l]

[7]Therefore, as soon as they heard the sound of the horn, flute, zither, lyre, harp and all kinds of music, all the peoples, nations and men of every language fell down and worshiped the image of gold that King Nebuchadnezzar had set up.[m]

[8]At this time some astrologers[bn] came forward and denounced the Jews. [9]They said to King Nebuchadnezzar, "O king, live forever![o] [10]You have issued a decree,[p] O king, that everyone who hears the sound of the horn, flute, zither, lyre, harp, pipes and all kinds of music must fall down and worship the image of gold,[q] [11]and that whoever does not fall down and worship will be thrown into a blazing furnace. [12]But there are some Jews whom you have set over the affairs of the province of Babylon—Shadrach, Meshach and Abednego[r]—who pay no attention[s] to you, O king. They neither serve your gods nor worship the image of gold you have set up."[t]

[13]Furious[u] with rage, Nebuchadnezzar summoned Shadrach, Meshach and Abednego. So these men were brought before the king, [14]and Nebuchadnezzar said to them, "Is it true, Shadrach, Meshach and Abednego, that you do not serve my gods[v] or worship the image[w] of gold I have set up? [15]Now when you hear the sound of the horn, flute, zither, lyre, harp, pipes and all kinds of music, if you are ready to fall down and worship the image I made, very good. But if you do not

---

2:46
bAc 14:13
2:47
cDa 11:36
dDa 4:25
ever 22,28
2:48
fver 6; Da 4:9;
5:11
2:49
gDa 1:7
3:1
hIsa 46:6;
Jer 16:20;
Hab 2:19
3:2
iver 27; Da 6:7
3:4
jDa 4:1; 6:25
3:5
kver 10,15
3:6
lver 11,15,21;
Jer 29:22;
Da 6:7;
Mt 13:42,50;
Rev 13:15
3:7
mver 5
3:8
nDa 2:10
3:9
oNe 2:3;
Da 5:10; 6:6
3:10
pDa 6:12
qver 4-6
3:12
rDa 2:49
sDa 6:13
tEst 3:3
3:13
uDa 2:12
3:14
vIsa 46:1;
Jer 50:2
wver 1

---

[a]1 Aramaic *sixty cubits high and six cubits wide* (about 27 meters high and 2.7 meters wide)
[b]8 Or *Chaldeans*

worship it, you will be thrown immediately into a blazing furnace. Then what god[x] will be able to rescue[y] you from my hand?"

[16]Shadrach, Meshach and Abednego[z] replied to the king, "O Nebuchadnezzar, we do not need to defend ourselves before you in this matter. [17]If we are thrown into the blazing furnace, the God we serve is able to save[a] us from it, and he will rescue[b] us from your hand, O king. [18]But even if he does not, we want you to know, O king, that we will not serve your gods or worship the image of gold you have set up.[c]"

[19]Then Nebuchadnezzar was furious with Shadrach, Meshach and Abednego, and his attitude toward them changed. He ordered the furnace heated seven[d] times hotter than usual [20]and commanded some of the strongest soldiers in his army to tie up Shadrach, Meshach and Abednego and throw them into the blazing furnace. [21]So these men, wearing their robes, trousers, turbans and other clothes, were bound and thrown into the blazing furnace. [22]The king's command was so urgent and the furnace so hot that the flames of the fire killed the soldiers who took up Shadrach, Meshach and Abednego,[e] [23]and these three men, firmly tied, fell into the blazing furnace.

[24]Then King Nebuchadnezzar leaped to his feet in amazement and asked his advisers, "Weren't there three men that we tied up and threw into the fire?"

They replied, "Certainly, O king."

[25]He said, "Look! I see four men walking around in the fire, unbound and unharmed, and the fourth looks like a son of the gods."

[26]Nebuchadnezzar then approached the opening of the blazing furnace and shouted, "Shadrach, Meshach and Abednego, servants of the Most High God,[f] come out! Come here!"

So Shadrach, Meshach and Abednego came out of the fire, [27]and the satraps, prefects, governors and royal advisers[g] crowded around them.[h] They saw that the fire[i] had not harmed their bodies, nor was a hair of their heads singed; their robes were not scorched, and there was no smell of fire on them.

[28]Then Nebuchadnezzar said, "Praise be to the God of Shadrach, Meshach and Abednego, who has sent his angel[j] and rescued his servants! They trusted[k] in him and defied the king's command and were willing to give up their lives rather than serve or worship any god except their own God.[l] [29]Therefore I decree[m] that the people of any nation or language who say anything against the God of Shadrach, Meshach and Abednego be cut into pieces and their houses be turned into piles of rubble,[n] for no other god can save[o] in this way."

[30]Then the king promoted Shadrach, Meshach and Abednego in the province of Babylon.[p]

Nebuchadnezzar's Dream of a Tree

4 King Nebuchadnezzar,

To the peoples, nations and men of every language,[q] who live in all the world:

May you prosper greatly![r]

[2]It is my pleasure to tell you about the miraculous signs[s] and wonders that the Most High God[t] has performed for me.

**Margin cross-references (left column):**

3:15
[x]Isa 36:18-20
[y]Ex 5:2;
2Ch 32:15

3:16
[z]Da 1:7

3:17
[a]Ps 27:1-2
[b]Job 5:19;
Jer 1:8

3:18
[c]ver 28;
Jos 24:15

3:19
[d]Lev 26:18-28

3:22
[e]Da 1:7

3:26
[f]Da 4:2,34

3:27
[g]ver 2
[h]Isa 43:2;
Heb 11:32-34
[i]Da 6:23

3:28
[j]Ps 34:7;
Da 6:22;
Ac 5:19
[k]Job 13:15;
Ps 26:1; 84:12;
Jer 17:7 [l]ver 18

3:29
[m]Da 6:26
[n]Ezr 6:11
[o]Da 6:27

3:30
[p]Da 2:49

4:1
[q]Da 3:4
[r]Da 6:25

4:2
[s]Ps 74:9
[t]Da 3:26

[3]How great are his signs,
    how mighty his wonders![u]
His kingdom is an eternal kingdom;
    his dominion endures[v] from generation to
        generation.

[4]I, Nebuchadnezzar, was at home in my palace, contented[w] and prosperous. [5]I had a dream[x] that made me afraid. As I was lying in my bed, the images and visions that passed through my mind[y] terrified me. [6]So I commanded that all the wise men of Babylon be brought before me to interpret[z] the dream for me. [7]When the magicians,[a] enchanters, astrologers[a] and diviners[b] came, I told them the dream, but they could not interpret it for me.[c] [8]Finally, Daniel came into my presence and I told him the dream. (He is called Belteshazzar,[d] after the name of my god, and the spirit of the holy gods[e] is in him.)

[9]I said, "Belteshazzar, chief[f] of the magicians, I know that the spirit of the holy gods[g] is in you, and no mystery is too difficult for you. Here is my dream; interpret it for me. [10]These are the visions I saw while lying in my bed:[h] I looked, and there before me stood a tree in the middle of the land. Its height was enormous.[i] [11]The tree grew large and strong and its top touched the sky; it was visible to the ends of the earth. [12]Its leaves were beautiful, its fruit abundant, and on it was food for all. Under it the beasts of the field found shelter, and the birds of the air lived in its branches;[j] from it every creature was fed.

[13]"In the visions I saw while lying in my bed,[k] I looked, and there before me was a messenger,[b] a holy one,[l] coming down from heaven. [14]He called in a loud voice: 'Cut down the tree and trim off its branches; strip off its leaves and scatter its fruit. Let the animals flee from under it and the birds from its branches.[m] [15]But let the stump and its roots, bound with iron and bronze, remain in the ground, in the grass of the field.

" 'Let him be drenched with the dew of heaven, and let him live with the animals among the plants of the earth. [16]Let his mind be changed from that of a man and let him be given the mind of an animal, till seven times[c] pass by for him.[n]

[17]" 'The decision is announced by messengers, the holy ones declare the verdict, so that the living may know that the Most High[o] is sovereign[p] over the kingdoms of men and gives them to anyone he wishes and sets over them the lowliest[q] of men.'

[18]"This is the dream that I, King Nebuchadnezzar, had. Now, Belteshazzar, tell me what it means, for none of the wise men in my kingdom can interpret it for me.[r] But you can,[s] because the spirit of the holy gods is in you."[t]

Daniel Interprets the Dream

[19]Then Daniel (also called Belteshazzar) was greatly perplexed for a time, and his thoughts terrified[u] him. So the king said,

4:3
u Ps 105:27;
Da 6:27
v Da 2:44
4:4
w Ps 30:6
4:5
x Da 2:1
y Da 2:28
4:6
z Da 2:2
4:7
a Ge 41:8
b Isa 44:25;
Da 2:2 c Da 2:10
4:8
d Da 1:7
e Da 5:11,14
4:9
f Da 2:48
g Da 5:11-12
4:10
h ver 5
i Eze 31:3-4
4:12
j Eze 17:23;
Mt 13:32
4:13
k Da 7:1 l ver 23;
Dt 33:2;
Da 8:13
4:14
m Eze 31:12;
Mt 3:10
4:16
n ver 23,32
4:17
o ver 2,25;
Ps 83:18
p Jer 27:5-7;
Da 2:21;
5:18-21
q Da 11:21
4:18
r Ge 41:8;
Da 5:8,15
s Ge 41:15
t ver 7-9
4:19
u Da 7:15,28;
8:27; 10:16-17

---

a7 Or Chaldeans   *b13 Or watchman; also in verses 17 and 23*   *c16 Or years; also in verses 23, 25 and 32*

"Belteshazzar, do not let the dream or its meaning alarm you."

Belteshazzar answered, "My lord, if only the dream applied to your enemies and its meaning to your adversaries! 20The tree you saw, which grew large and strong, with its top touching the sky, visible to the whole earth, 21with beautiful leaves and abundant fruit, providing food for all, giving shelter to the beasts of the field, and having nesting places in its branches for the birds of the air— 22you, O king, are that tree!ᵛ You have become great and strong; your greatness has grown until it reaches the sky, and your dominion extends to distant parts of the earth.ʷ

23"You, O king, saw a messenger, a holy one,ˣ coming down from heaven and saying, 'Cut down the tree and destroy it, but leave the stump, bound with iron and bronze, in the grass of the field, while its roots remain in the ground. Let him be drenched with the dew of heaven; let him live like the wild animals, until seven times pass by for him.'ʸ

24"This is the interpretation, O king, and this is the decreeᶻ the Most High has issued against my lord the king: 25You will be driven away from people and will live with the wild animals; you will eat grass like cattle and be drenched with the dew of heaven. Seven times will pass by for you until you acknowledge that the Most Highᵃ is sovereign over the kingdoms of men and gives them to anyone he wishes.ᵇ 26The command to leave the stump of the tree with its rootsᶜ means that your kingdom will be restored to you when you acknowledge that Heaven rules.ᵈ 27Therefore, O king, be pleased to accept my advice: Renounce your sins by doing what is right, and your wickedness by being kind to the oppressed.ᵉ It may be that then your prosperity will continue.ᶠ"

The Dream Is Fulfilled

28All this happenedᵍ to King Nebuchadnezzar. 29Twelve months later, as the king was walking on the roof of the royal palace of Babylon, 30he said, "Is not this the great Babylon I have built as the royal residence, by my mighty power and for the glory of my majesty?"ʰ

31The words were still on his lips when a voice came from heaven, "This is what is decreed for you, King Nebuchadnezzar: Your royal authority has been taken from you. 32You will be driven away from people and will live with the wild animals; you will eat grass like cattle. Seven times will pass by for you until you acknowledge that the Most High is sovereign over the kingdoms of men and gives them to anyone he wishes."

33Immediately what had been said about Nebuchadnezzar was fulfilled. He was driven away from people and ate grass like cattle. His body was drenched with the dew of heaven until his hair grew like the feathers of an eagle and his nails like the claws of a bird.ⁱ

34At the end of that time, I, Nebuchadnezzar, raised my eyes toward heaven, and my sanity was restored. Then I praised the Most High; I honored and glorified him who lives forever.ʲ

His dominion is an eternal dominion;

4:22
v2Sa 12:7
wJer 27:7;
Da 2:37-38;
5:18-19
4:23
xver 13
yDa 5:21
4:24
zJob 40:12;
Ps 107:40
4:25
aver 17;
Ps 83:18
bJer 27:5;
Da 5:21
4:26
cver 15
dDa 2:37
4:27
eIsa 55:6-7
f1Ki 21:29;
Ps 41:3;
Eze 18:22
4:28
gNu 23:19
4:30
hIsa 37:24-25;
Da 5:20;
Hab 2:4
4:33
iDa 5:20-21
4:34
jDa 12:7;
Rev 4:10

his kingdom endures from generation to generation.[k]
35All the peoples of the earth
    are regarded as nothing.[l]
He does as he pleases[m]
    with the powers of heaven
    and the peoples of the earth.
No one can hold back his hand
    or say to him: "What have you done?"[n]

36At the same time that my sanity was restored, my honor and splendor were returned to me for the glory of my kingdom.[o] My advisers and nobles sought me out, and I was restored to my throne and became even greater than before. 37Now I, Nebuchadnezzar, praise and exalt and glorify the King of heaven, because everything he does is right and all his ways are just.[p] And those who walk in pride he is able to humble.[q]

The Writing on the Wall

5 King Belshazzar gave a great banquet[r] for a thousand of his nobles and drank wine with them. 2While Belshazzar was drinking his wine, he gave orders to bring in the gold and silver goblets[s] that Nebuchadnezzar his father[a] had taken from the temple in Jerusalem, so that the king and his nobles, his wives and his concubines might drink from them.[t] 3So they brought in the gold goblets that had been taken from the temple of God in Jerusalem, and the king and his nobles, his wives and his concubines drank from them. 4As they drank the wine, they praised the gods of gold and silver, of bronze, iron, wood and stone.[u]

5Suddenly the fingers of a human hand appeared and wrote on the plaster of the wall, near the lampstand in the royal palace. The king watched the hand as it wrote. 6His face turned pale and he was so frightened[v] that his knees knocked together and his legs gave way.[w]

7The king called out for the enchanters, astrologers[b] and diviners[x] to be brought and said to these wise[y] men of Babylon, "Whoever reads this writing and tells me what it means will be clothed in purple and have a gold chain placed around his neck,[z] and he will be made the third highest ruler in the kingdom."[a]

8Then all the king's wise men came in, but they could not read the writing or tell the king what it meant.[b] 9So King Belshazzar became even more terrified[c] and his face grew more pale. His nobles were baffled.

10The queen,[c] hearing the voices of the king and his nobles, came into the banquet hall. "O king, live forever!"[d] she said. "Don't be alarmed! Don't look so pale! 11There is a man in your kingdom who has the spirit of the holy gods[e] in him. In the time of your father he was found to have insight and intelligence and wisdom[f] like that of the gods. King Nebuchadnezzar your father—your father the king, I say —appointed him chief of the magicians, enchanters, astrologers and diviners.[g] 12This man Daniel, whom the king called Belteshazzar,[h] was

---

[a]2 Or *ancestor;* or *predecessor;* also in verses 11, 13 and 18   [b]7 Or *Chaldeans;* also in verse 11
[c]10 Or *queen mother*

4:34
kPs 145:13;
Da 2:44; 5:21;
6:26; Lk 1:33
4:35
lIsa 40:17
mPs 115:3;
135:6 nIsa 45:9;
Ro 9:20
4:36
oPr 22:4
4:37
pDt 32:4;
Ps 33:4-5
qEx 18:11;
Job 40:11-12;
Da 5:20,23
5:1
rEst 1:3
5:2
s2Ki 24:13;
Jer 52:19
tEst 1:7; Da 1:2
5:4
uPs 135:15-18;
Hab 2:19;
Rev 9:20
5:6
vDa 4:5
wEze 7:17
5:7
xIsa 44:25
yDa 4:6-7
zGe 41:42
aDa 2:5-6,48;
6:2-3
5:8
bDa 2:10,27
5:9
cIsa 21:4
5:10
dDa 3:9
5:11
eDa 4:8-9,19
fver 14; Da 1:17
gDa 2:47-48
5:12
hDa 1:7

found to have a keen mind and knowledge and understanding, and also the ability to interpret dreams, explain riddles and solve difficult problems.[i] Call for Daniel, and he will tell you what the writing means."

[13]So Daniel was brought before the king, and the king said to him, "Are you Daniel, one of the exiles my father the king brought from Judah?[j] [14]I have heard that the spirit of the gods is in you and that you have insight, intelligence and outstanding wisdom. [15]The wise men and enchanters were brought before me to read this writing and tell me what it means, but they could not explain it. [16]Now I have heard that you are able to give interpretations and to solve difficult problems. If you can read this writing and tell me what it means, you will be clothed in purple and have a gold chain placed around your neck, and you will be made the third highest ruler in the kingdom."

[17]Then Daniel answered the king, "You may keep your gifts for yourself and give your rewards to someone else.[k] Nevertheless, I will read the writing for the king and tell him what it means.

[18]"O king, the Most High God gave your father Nebuchadnezzar sovereignty and greatness and glory and splendor.[l] [19]Because of the high position he gave him, all the peoples and nations and men of every language dreaded and feared him. Those the king wanted to put to death, he put to death;[m] those he wanted to spare, he spared; those he wanted to promote, he promoted; and those he wanted to humble, he humbled. [20]But when his heart became arrogant and hardened with pride,[n] he was deposed from his royal throne and stripped[o] of his glory.[p] [21]He was driven away from people and given the mind of an animal; he lived with the wild donkeys and ate grass like cattle; and his body was drenched with the dew of heaven, until he acknowledged that the Most High God is sovereign[q] over the kingdoms of men and sets over them anyone he wishes.[r]

[22]"But you his son,[a] O Belshazzar, have not humbled[s] yourself, though you knew all this. [23]Instead, you have set yourself up against[t] the Lord of heaven. You had the goblets from his temple brought to you, and you and your nobles, your wives and your concubines drank wine from them. You praised the gods of silver and gold, of bronze, iron, wood and stone, which cannot see or hear or understand.[u] But you did not honor the God who holds in his hand your life[v] and all your ways.[w] [24]Therefore he sent the hand that wrote the inscription.

[25]"This is the inscription that was written:

MENE, MENE, TEKEL, PARSIN[b]

[26]"This is what these words mean:

> *Mene*[c]: God has numbered the days[x] of your reign and brought it to an end.[y]
> [27]*Tekel*[d]: You have been weighed on the scales and found wanting.[z]
> [28]*Peres*[e]: Your kingdom is divided and given to the Medes[a] and Persians."[b]

5:12
iver 14-16;
Da 6:3
5:13
jDa 6:13
5:17
k2Ki 5:16
5:18
lJer 27:7;
Da 2:37-38
5:19
mDa 2:12-13;
3:6
5:20
nDa 4:30
oJer 13:18
pJob 40:12;
Isa 14:13-15
5:21
qEze 17:24
rDa 4:16-17,35
5:22
sEx 10:3;
2Ch 33:23
5:23
tJer 50:29
uPs 115:4-8;
Hab 2:19
vJob 12:10
wJob 31:4;
Jer 10:23
5:26
xJer 27:7
yIsa 13:6
5:27
zPs 62:9
5:28
aIsa 13:17
bDa 6:28

---

[a]22 Or *descendant*; or *successor*   [b]25 Aramaic UPARSIN (that is, AND PARSIN)   [c]26 *Mene* can mean *numbered* or *mina* (a unit of money).   [d]27 *Tekel* can mean *weighed* or *shekel*.   [e]28 *Peres* (the singular of *Parsin*) can mean *divided* or *Persia* or *a half mina* or *a half shekel*.

²⁹Then at Belshazzar's command, Daniel was clothed in purple, a gold chain was placed around his neck, and he was proclaimed the third highest ruler in the kingdom.

³⁰That very night Belshazzar,ᶜ king of the Babylonians,ᵃ was slain,ᵈ ³¹and Dariusᵉ the Mede took over the kingdom, at the age of sixty-two.

Daniel in the Den of Lions

6 It pleased Dariusᶠ to appoint 120 satrapsᵍ to rule throughout the kingdom, ²with three administrators over them, one of whom was Daniel.ʰ The satraps were made accountableⁱ to them so that the king might not suffer loss. ³Now Daniel so distinguished himself among the administrators and the satraps by his exceptional qualities that the king planned to set him over the whole kingdom.ʲ ⁴At this, the administrators and the satraps tried to find grounds for charges against Daniel in his conduct of government affairs, but they were unable to do so. They could find no corruption in him, because he was trustworthy and neither corrupt nor negligent. ⁵Finally these men said, "We will never find any basis for charges against this man Daniel unless it has something to do with the law of his God."ᵏ

⁶So the administrators and the satraps went as a group to the king and said: "O King Darius, live forever!ˡ ⁷The royal administrators, prefects, satraps, advisers and governorsᵐ have all agreed that the king should issue an edict and enforce the decree that anyone who prays to any god or man during the next thirty days, except to you, O king, shall be thrown into the lions' den.ⁿ ⁸Now, O king, issue the decree and put it in writing so that it cannot be altered—in accordance with the laws of the Medes and Persians, which cannot be repealed."ᵒ ⁹So King Darius put the decree in writing.

¹⁰Now when Daniel learned that the decree had been published, he went home to his upstairs room where the windows opened towardᵖ Jerusalem. Three times a day he got down on his knees�q and prayed, giving thanks to his God, just as he had done before.ʳ ¹¹Then these men went as a group and found Daniel praying and asking God for help. ¹²So they went to the king and spoke to him about his royal decree: "Did you not publish a decree that during the next thirty days anyone who prays to any god or man except to you, O king, would be thrown into the lions' den?"

The king answered, "The decree stands—in accordance with the laws of the Medes and Persians, which cannot be repealed."ˢ

¹³Then they said to the king, "Daniel, who is one of the exiles from Judah,ᵗ pays no attentionᵘ to you, O king, or to the decree you put in writing. He still prays three times a day." ¹⁴When the king heard this, he was greatly distressed;ᵛ he was determined to rescue Daniel and made every effort until sundown to save him.

¹⁵Then the men went as a group to the king and said to him, "Remember, O king, that according to the law of the Medes and Persians no decree or edict that the king issues can be changed."ʷ

¹⁶So the king gave the order, and they brought Daniel and threw him into the lions' den.ˣ The king said to Daniel, "May your God, whom you serve continually, rescueʸ you!"

ᵃ30 Or *Chaldeans*

5:30
ᶜver 1
ᵈIsa 21:9;
Jer 51:31
5:31
ᵉDa 6:1; 9:1
6:1
ᶠDa 5:31
ᵍEst 1:1
6:2
ʰDa 2:48-49
ⁱEzr 4:22
6:3
ʲGe 41:41;
Est 10:3;
Da 5:12-14
6:5
ᵏAc 24:13-16
6:6
ˡNe 2:3; Da 2:4
6:7
ᵐDa 3:2
ⁿPs 59:3;
64:2-6; Da 3:6
6:8
ᵒEst 1:19
6:10
ᵖ1Ki 8:48-49
qPs 95:6
ʳAc 5:29
6:12
ˢEst 1:19;
Da 3:8-12
6:13
ᵗDa 2:25; 5:13
ᵘEst 3:8;
Da 3:12
6:14
ᵛMk 6:26
6:15
ʷEst 8:8
6:16
ˣver 7
ʸJob 5:19;
Ps 37:39-40

[17]A stone was brought and placed over the mouth of the den, and the king sealed[z] it with his own signet ring and with the rings of his nobles, so that Daniel's situation might not be changed. [18]Then the king returned to his palace and spent the night without eating[a] and without any entertainment being brought to him. And he could not sleep.[b]

[19]At the first light of dawn, the king got up and hurried to the lions' den. [20]When he came near the den, he called to Daniel in an anguished voice, "Daniel, servant of the living God, has your God, whom you serve continually, been able to rescue you from the lions?"[c]

[21]Daniel answered, "O king, live forever![d] [22]My God sent his angel,[e] and he shut the mouths of the lions.[f] They have not hurt me, because I was found innocent in his sight.[g] Nor have I ever done any wrong before you, O king."

[23]The king was overjoyed and gave orders to lift Daniel out of the den. And when Daniel was lifted from the den, no wound[h] was found on him, because he had trusted[i] in his God.

[24]At the king's command, the men who had falsely accused Daniel were brought in and thrown into the lions' den,[j] along with their wives and children.[k] And before they reached the floor of the den, the lions overpowered them and crushed all their bones.[l]

[25]Then King Darius wrote to all the peoples, nations and men of every language throughout the land:

"May you prosper greatly![m]

[26]"I issue a decree that in every part of my kingdom people must fear and reverence the God of Daniel.[n]

"For he is the living God
    and he endures forever;
his kingdom will not be destroyed,
    his dominion will never end.[o]
[27]He rescues and he saves;
    he performs signs and wonders[p]
    in the heavens and on the earth.
He has rescued Daniel
    from the power of the lions."[q]

[28]So Daniel prospered during the reign of Darius and the reign of Cyrus[a r] the Persian.

Daniel's Dream of Four Beasts

7 In the first year of Belshazzar[s] king of Babylon, Daniel had a dream, and visions passed through his mind[t] as he was lying on his bed. He wrote[u] down the substance of his dream.

[2]Daniel said: "In my vision at night I looked, and there before me were the four winds of heaven[v] churning up the great sea. [3]Four great beasts,[w] each different from the others, came up out of the sea.

[4]"The first was like a lion,[x] and it had the wings of an eagle.[y] I watched until its wings were torn off and it was lifted from the ground so that it stood on two feet like a man, and the heart of a man was given to it.

---

[a]28 Or *Darius, that is, the reign of Cyrus*

6:17
z Mt 27:66
6:18
a 2Sa 12:17
b Est 6:1; Da 2:1
6:20
c Da 3:17
6:21
d Da 2:4
6:22
e Da 3:28
f Ps 91:11-13;
Heb 11:33
g Ac 12:11;
2Ti 4:17
6:23
h Da 3:27
i 1Ch 5:20
6:24
j Dt 19:18-19;
Est 7:9-10;
Ps 54:5
k Dt 24:16;
2Ki 14:6
l Isa 38:13
6:25
m Da 4:1
6:26
n Ps 99:1-3;
Da 3:29
o Da 2:44; 4:34
6:27
p Da 4:3 q ver 22
6:28
r 2Ch 36:22;
Da 1:21
7:1
s Da 5:1
t Da 1:17
u Jer 36:4
7:2
v Rev 7:1
7:3
w Rev 13:1
7:4
x Jer 4:7
y Eze 17:3

⁵"And there before me was a second beast, which looked like a bear. It was raised up on one of its sides, and it had three ribs in its mouth between its teeth. It was told, 'Get up and eat your fill of flesh!'ᶻ

⁶"After that, I looked, and there before me was another beast, one that looked like a leopard.ᵃ And on its back it had four wings like those of a bird. This beast had four heads, and it was given authority to rule.

⁷"After that, in my vision at night I looked, and there before me was a fourth beast—terrifying and frightening and very powerful. It had large ironᵇ teeth; it crushed and devoured its victims and trampled underfoot whatever was left. It was different from all the former beasts, and it had ten horns.ᶜ

⁸"While I was thinking about the horns, there before me was another horn, a littleᵈ one, which came up among them; and three of the first horns were uprooted before it. This horn had eyes like the eyes of a manᵉ and a mouth that spoke boastfully.ᶠ

⁹"As I looked,

"thrones were set in place,
    and the Ancient of Days took his seat.
His clothing was as white as snow;
    the hair of his head was white like wool.ᵍ
His throne was flaming with fire,
    and its wheelsʰ were all ablaze.
¹⁰A river of fireⁱ was flowing,
    coming out from before him.ʲ
Thousands upon thousands attended him;
    ten thousand times ten thousand stood before him.
The court was seated,
    and the booksᵏ were opened.

¹¹"Then I continued to watch because of the boastful words the horn was speaking. I kept looking until the beast was slain and its body destroyed and thrown into the blazing fire.ˡ ¹²(The other beasts had been stripped of their authority, but were allowed to live for a period of time.)

¹³"In my vision at night I looked, and there before me was one like a son of man,ᵐ coming with the clouds of heaven.ⁿ He approached the Ancient of Days and was led into his presence. ¹⁴He was given authority,ᵒ glory and sovereign power; all peoples, nations and men of every language worshiped him.ᵖ His dominion is an everlasting dominion that will not pass away, and his kingdom is one that will never be destroyed.�q

The Interpretation of the Dream

¹⁵"I, Daniel, was troubled in spirit, and the visions that passed through my mind disturbed me.ʳ ¹⁶I approached one of those standing there and asked him the true meaning of all this.

"So he told me and gave me the interpretationˢ of these things: ¹⁷'The four great beasts are four kingdoms that will rise from the earth. ¹⁸But the saints of the Most High will receive the kingdom and will possess it forever—yes, for ever and ever.'ᵗ

¹⁹"Then I wanted to know the true meaning of the fourth beast, which was different from all the others and most terrifying, with its

7:5
zDa 2:39
7:6
aRev 13:2
7:7
bDa 2:40
cRev 12:3
7:8
dDa 8:9
eRev 9:7
fPs 12:3;
Rev 13:5-6
7:9
gRev 1:14
hEze 1:15; 10:6
7:10
iPs 50:3; 97:3;
Isa 30:27
jDt 33:2;
Ps 68:17;
Rev 5:11
kRev 20:11-15
7:11
lRev 19:20
7:13
mMt 8:20*;
Rev 1:13*
nMt 24:30;
Rev 1:7
7:14
oMt 28:18
pPs 72:11;
102:22;
1Co 15:27;
Eph 1:22
qDa 2:44;
Heb 12:28;
Rev 11:15
7:15
rDa 4:19
7:16
sDa 8:16; 9:22;
Zec 1:9
7:18
tIsa 60:12-14;
Rev 2:26; 20:4

iron teeth and bronze claws—the beast that crushed and devoured its victims and trampled underfoot whatever was left. ²⁰I also wanted to know about the ten horns on its head and about the other horn that came up, before which three of them fell—the horn that looked more imposing than the others and that had eyes and a mouth that spoke boastfully. ²¹As I watched, this horn was waging war against the saints and defeating them, ^u ²²until the Ancient of Days came and pronounced judgment in favor of the saints of the Most High, and the time came when they possessed the kingdom.

²³"He gave me this explanation: 'The fourth beast is a fourth kingdom that will appear on earth. It will be different from all the other kingdoms and will devour the whole earth, trampling it down and crushing it. ^v ²⁴The ten horns ^w are ten kings who will come from this kingdom. After them another king will arise, different from the earlier ones; he will subdue three kings. ²⁵He will speak against the Most High ^x and oppress his saints and try to change the set times ^y and the laws. The saints will be handed over to him for a time, times and half a time. ^a ^z

²⁶" 'But the court will sit, and his power will be taken away and completely destroyed forever. ²⁷Then the sovereignty, power and greatness of the kingdoms under the whole heaven will be handed over to the saints, the people of the Most High. His kingdom will be an everlasting ^a kingdom, and all rulers will worship ^b and obey him.'

²⁸"This is the end of the matter. I, Daniel, was deeply troubled ^c by my thoughts, and my face turned pale, but I kept the matter to myself."

Daniel's Vision of a Ram and a Goat

8 In the third year of King Belshazzar's reign, I, Daniel, had a vision, after the one that had already appeared to me. ²In my vision I saw myself in the citadel of Susa ^d in the province of Elam; ^e in the vision I was beside the Ulai Canal. ³I looked up, ^f and there before me was a ram with two horns, standing beside the canal, and the horns were long. One of the horns was longer than the other but grew up later. ⁴I watched the ram as he charged toward the west and the north and the south. No animal could stand against him, and none could rescue from his power. He did as he pleased ^g and became great.

⁵As I was thinking about this, suddenly a goat with a prominent horn between his eyes came from the west, crossing the whole earth without touching the ground. ⁶He came toward the two-horned ram I had seen standing beside the canal and charged at him in great rage. ⁷I saw him attack the ram furiously, striking the ram and shattering his two horns. The ram was powerless to stand against him; the goat knocked him to the ground and trampled on him, ^h and none could rescue the ram from his power. ⁸The goat became very great, but at the height of his power his large horn was broken off, ⁱ and in its place four prominent horns grew up toward the four winds of heaven. ^j

⁹Out of one of them came another horn, which started small but grew in power to the south and to the east and toward the Beautiful Land. ^k ¹⁰It grew until it reached ^l the host of the heavens, and it threw some of the starry host down to the earth ^m and trampled ⁿ on them. ¹¹It set itself up to be as great as the Prince of the host; ^o it took away the daily

^a25 Or *for a year, two years and half a year*

sacrifice[p] from him, and the place of his sanctuary was brought low.[q] [12]Because of rebellion, the host of the saints,[a] and the daily sacrifice were given over to it. It prospered in everything it did, and truth was thrown to the ground.

[13]Then I heard a holy one[r] speaking, and another holy one said to him, "How long will it take for the vision to be fulfilled[s]—the vision concerning the daily sacrifice, the rebellion that causes desolation, and the surrender of the sanctuary and of the host that will be trampled[t] underfoot?"

[14]He said to me, "It will take 2,300 evenings and mornings; then the sanctuary will be reconsecrated."[u]

The Interpretation of the Vision

[15]While I, Daniel, was watching the vision[v] and trying to understand it, there before me stood one who looked like a man.[w] [16]And I heard a man's voice from the Ulai calling, "Gabriel,[x] tell this man the meaning of the vision."

[17]As he came near the place where I was standing, I was terrified and fell prostrate.[y] "Son of man," he said to me, "understand that the vision concerns the time of the end."[z]

[18]While he was speaking to me, I was in a deep sleep, with my face to the ground.[a] Then he touched me and raised me to my feet.[b]

[19]He said: "I am going to tell you what will happen later in the time of wrath, because the vision concerns the appointed time of the end.[b c] [20]The two-horned ram that you saw represents the kings of Media and Persia. [21]The shaggy goat is the king of Greece,[d] and the large horn between his eyes is the first king.[e] [22]The four horns that replaced the one that was broken off represent four kingdoms that will emerge from his nation but will not have the same power.

[23]"In the latter part of their reign, when rebels have become completely wicked, a stern-faced king, a master of intrigue, will arise. [24]He will become very strong, but not by his own power. He will cause astounding devastation and will succeed in whatever he does. He will destroy the mighty men and the holy people.[f] [25]He will cause deceit to prosper, and he will consider himself superior. When they feel secure, he will destroy many and take his stand against the Prince of princes.[g] Yet he will be destroyed, but not by human power.[h]

[26]"The vision of the evenings and mornings that has been given you is true,[i] but seal[j] up the vision, for it concerns the distant future."[k]

[27]I, Daniel, was exhausted and lay ill for several days. Then I got up and went about the king's business.[l] I was appalled[m] by the vision; it was beyond understanding.

Daniel's Prayer

9 In the first year of Darius[n] son of Xerxes[c] (a Mede by descent), who was made ruler over the Babylonian[d] kingdom— [2]in the first year of his reign, I, Daniel, understood from the Scriptures, according to the word of the LORD given to Jeremiah the prophet, that the desolation of Jerusalem would last seventy[o] years. [3]So I turned to the Lord God and

---

8:11
p Eze 46:13-14
q Da 11:31; 12:11
8:13
r Da 4:23
s Da 12:6
t Lk 21:24; Rev 11:2
8:14
u Da 12:11-12
8:15
v ver 1
w Da 10:16-18
8:16
x Da 9:21; Lk 1:19
8:17
y Eze 1:28; Da 2:46; Rev 1:17
z Hab 2:3
8:18
a Da 10:9
b Eze 2:2; Da 10:16-18
8:19
c Hab 2:3
8:21
d Da 10:20
e Da 11:3
8:24
f Da 7:25; 11:36
8:25
g Da 11:36
h Da 2:34; 11:21
8:26
i Da 10:1
j Rev 22:10
k Da 10:14
8:27
l Da 2:48
m Da 7:28
9:1
n Da 5:31
9:2
o 2Ch 36:21; Jer 29:10; Zec 7:5

---

a 12 Or *rebellion, the armies*   b 19 Or *because the end will be at the appointed time*   c 1 Hebrew *Ahasuerus*   d 1 Or *Chaldean* pleaded with him in prayer and petition, in fasting, and in sackcloth and ashes. ᴾ

⁴I prayed to the Lᴏʀᴅ my God and confessed:

"O Lord, the great and awesome God, �q who keeps his covenant of love ʳ with all who love him and obey his commands, ⁵we have sinned and done wrong. ˢ We have been wicked and have rebelled; we have turned away ᵗ from your commands and laws. ᵘ ⁶We have not listened to your servants the prophets, ᵛ who spoke in your name to our kings, our princes and our fathers, and to all the people of the land.

⁷"Lord, you are righteous, but this day we are covered with shame ʷ—the men of Judah and people of Jerusalem and all Israel, both near and far, in all the countries where you have scattered ˣ us because of our unfaithfulness to you. ʸ ⁸O Lᴏʀᴅ, we and our kings, our princes and our fathers are covered with shame because we have sinned against you. ⁹The Lord our God is merciful and forgiving, ᶻ even though we have rebelled against him; ᵃ ¹⁰we have not obeyed the Lᴏʀᴅ our God or kept the laws he gave us through his servants the prophets. ᵇ ¹¹All Israel has transgressed your law and turned away, refusing to obey you.

"Therefore the curses and sworn judgments written in the Law of Moses, the servant of God, have been poured out on us, because we have sinned ᶜ against you. ¹²You have fulfilled ᵈ the words spoken against us and against our rulers by bringing upon us great disaster. Under the whole heaven nothing has ever been done like what has been done to Jerusalem. ᵉ ¹³Just as it is written in the Law of Moses, all this disaster has come upon us, yet we have not sought the favor of the Lᴏʀᴅ our God by turning from our sins and giving attention to your truth. ᶠ ¹⁴The Lᴏʀᴅ did not hesitate to bring the disaster ᵍ upon us, for the Lᴏʀᴅ our God is righteous in everything he does; yet we have not obeyed him. ʰ

¹⁵"Now, O Lord our God, who brought your people out of Egypt with a mighty hand ⁱ and who made for yourself a name ʲ that endures to this day, we have sinned, we have done wrong. ¹⁶O Lord, in keeping with all your righteous acts, ᵏ turn away your anger and your wrath from Jerusalem, ˡ your city, your holy hill. ᵐ Our sins and the iniquities of our fathers have made Jerusalem and your people an object of scorn ⁿ to all those around us.

¹⁷"Now, our God, hear the prayers and petitions of your servant. For your sake, O Lord, look with favor ᵒ on your desolate sanctuary. ¹⁸Give ear, O God, and hear; open your eyes and see ᵖ the desolation of the city that bears your Name. q We do not make requests of you because we are righteous, but because of your great mercy. ¹⁹O Lord, listen! O Lord, forgive! ʳ O Lord, hear and act! For your sake, O my God, do not delay, because your city and your people bear your Name."

The Seventy "Sevens"

²⁰While I was speaking and praying, confessing my sin and the sin of my people Israel and making my request to the Lᴏʀᴅ my God for his holy hill ˢ— ²¹while I was still in prayer, Gabriel, ᵗ the man I had seen in

9:3
ᵖNe 1:4;
Jer 29:12
9:4
qDt 7:21
rDt 7:9
9:5
sPs 106:6
tIsa 53:6
uver 11; La 1:20
9:6
v2Ch 36:16;
Jer 44:5
9:7
wPs 44:15
xDt 4:27;
Am 9:9
yJer 3:25
9:9
zPs 130:4
aNe 9:17;
Jer 14:7
9:10
b2Ki 17:13-15;
18:12
9:11
cIsa 1:4-6;
Jer 8:5-10
9:12
dIsa 44:26;
Zec 1:6
eJer 44:2-6;
Eze 5:9
9:13
fIsa 9:13;
Jer 2:30
9:14
gJer 44:27
hNe 9:33
9:15
iJer 32:21
jNe 9:10
9:16
kPs 31:1
lJer 32:32
mZec 8:3
nEze 5:14
9:17
oNu 6:24-26;
Ps 80:19
9:18
pPs 80:14
qIsa 37:17;
Jer 7:10-12;
25:29
9:19
rPs 44:23
9:20
sver 3;
Ps 145:18;
Isa 58:9
9:21
tDa 8:16;
Lk 1:19

the earlier vision, came to me in swift flight about the time of the evening sacrifice. [u] [22]He instructed me and said to me, "Daniel, I have now come to give you insight and understanding. [23]As soon as you began to pray, an answer was given, which I have come to tell you, for you are highly esteemed. [v] Therefore, consider the message and understand the vision: [w]

[24]"Seventy 'sevens' [a] are decreed for your people and your holy city to finish [b] transgression, to put an end to sin, to atone [x] for wickedness, to bring in everlasting righteousness, [y] to seal up vision and prophecy and to anoint the most holy. [c]

[25]"Know and understand this: From the issuing of the decree [d] to restore and rebuild [z] Jerusalem until the Anointed One, [e a] the ruler, comes, there will be seven 'sevens,' and sixty-two 'sevens.' It will be rebuilt with streets and a trench, but in times of trouble. [26]After the sixty-two 'sevens,' the Anointed One will be cut off [b] and will have nothing. [f] The people of the ruler who will come will destroy the city and the sanctuary. The end will come like a flood: [c] War will continue until the end, and desolations have been decreed. [27]He will confirm a covenant with many for one 'seven.' [g] In the middle of the 'seven' [g] he will put an end to sacrifice and offering. And on a wing ,of the temple, he will set up an abomination that causes desolation, until the end that is decreed [d] is poured out on him. [h ''i]

Daniel's Vision of a Man

10 In the third year of Cyrus [e] king of Persia, a revelation was given to Daniel (who was called Belteshazzar). [f] Its message was true [g] and it concerned a great war. [j] The understanding of the message came to him in a vision.

[2]At that time I, Daniel, mourned [h] for three weeks. [3]I ate no choice food; no meat or wine touched my lips; and I used no lotions at all until the three weeks were over.

[4]On the twenty-fourth day of the first month, as I was standing on the bank of the great river, the Tigris, [i] [5]I looked up and there before me was a man dressed in linen, [j] with a belt of the finest gold [k] around his waist. [6]His body was like chrysolite, his face like lightning, [l] his eyes like flaming torches, [m] his arms and legs like the gleam of burnished bronze, [n] and his voice like the sound of a multitude.

[7]I, Daniel, was the only one who saw the vision; the men with me did not see it, [o] but such terror overwhelmed them that they fled and hid themselves. [8]So I was left alone, [p] gazing at this great vision; I had no strength left, [q] my face turned deathly pale and I was helpless. [r] [9]Then I heard him speaking, and as I listened to him, I fell into a deep sleep, my face to the ground. [s]

[10]A hand touched me [t] and set me trembling on my hands and knees. [u] [11]He said, "Daniel, you who are highly esteemed, [v] consider carefully the words I am about to speak to you, and stand up, [w] for I

9:21
u Ex 29:39
9:23
v Da 10:19;
Lk 1:28
w Da 10:11-12;
Mt 24:15
9:24
x Isa 53:10
y Isa 56:1
9:25
z Ezr 4:24
a Jn 4:25
9:26
b Isa 53:8
c Na 1:8
9:27
d Isa 10:22
10:1
e Da 1:21
f Da 1:7
g Da 8:26
10:2
h Ezr 9:4
10:4
i Ge 2:14
10:5
j Eze 9:2;
Rev 15:6
k Jer 10:9
10:6
l Mt 17:2
m Rev 19:12
n Rev 1:15
10:7
o 2Ki 6:17-20;
Ac 9:7
10:8
p Ge 32:24
q Da 8:27
r Hab 3:16
10:9
s Da 8:18
10:10
t Jer 1:9
u Rev 1:17
10:11
v Da 9:23
w Eze 2:1

---

[a]24 Or *'weeks'*; also in verses 25 and 26　　[b]24 Or *restrain*　　[c]24 Or *Most Holy Place; or most holy One*　　[d]25 Or *word*　　[e]25 Or *an anointed one*; also in verse 26　　[f]26 Or *off and will have no one; or off, but not for himself*　　[g]27 Or *'week'*　　[h]27 Or *it*　　[i]27 Or *And one who causes desolation will come upon the pinnacle of the abominable ,temple, until the end that is decreed is poured out on the desolated ,city,*　　[j]1 Or *true and burdensome*

have now been sent to you." And when he said this to me, I stood up trembling.

12Then he continued, "Do not be afraid, Daniel. Since the first day that you set your mind to gain understanding and to humble[x] yourself before your God, your words were heard, and I have come in response to them.[y] 13But the prince of the Persian kingdom resisted me twenty-one days. Then Michael,[z] one of the chief princes, came to help me, because I was detained there with the king of Persia. 14Now I have come to explain[a] to you what will happen to your people in the future, for the vision concerns a time yet to come.[b]"

15While he was saying this to me, I bowed with my face toward the ground and was speechless.[c] 16Then one who looked like a man[a] touched my lips, and I opened my mouth and began to speak.[d] I said to the one standing before me, "I am overcome with anguish[e] because of the vision, my lord, and I am helpless. 17How can I, your servant, talk with you, my lord? My strength is gone and I can hardly breathe."[f]

18Again the one who looked like a man touched[g] me and gave me strength. 19"Do not be afraid, O man highly esteemed," he said. "Peace![h] Be strong now; be strong."[i]

When he spoke to me, I was strengthened and said, "Speak, my lord, since you have given me strength."[j]

20So he said, "Do you know why I have come to you? Soon I will return to fight against the prince of Persia, and when I go, the prince of Greece[k] will come; 21but first I will tell you what is written in the Book of Truth.[l] (No one supports me against them except Michael,[m] your prince. 1And in the first year of Darius[n] the Mede, I took my stand to support and protect him.)

The Kings of the South and the North

2"Now then, I tell you the truth:[o] Three more kings will appear in Persia, and then a fourth, who will be far richer than all the others. When he has gained power by his wealth, he will stir up everyone against the kingdom of Greece.[p] 3Then a mighty king will appear, who will rule with great power and do as he pleases.[q] 4After he has appeared, his empire will be broken up and parceled out toward the four winds of heaven.[r] It will not go to his descendants, nor will it have the power he exercised, because his empire will be uprooted and given to others.

5"The king of the South will become strong, but one of his commanders will become even stronger than he and will rule his own kingdom with great power. 6After some years, they will become allies. The daughter of the king of the South will go to the king of the North to make an alliance, but she will not retain her power, and he and his power[b] will not last. In those days she will be handed over, together with her royal escort and her father[c] and the one who supported her.

7"One from her family line will arise to take her place. He will attack the forces of the king of the North[s] and enter his fortress; he will fight against them and be victorious. 8He will also seize their gods,[t] their

10:12
xDa 9:3
yDa 9:20
10:13
zver 21;
Da 12:1;
Jude 1:9
10:14
aDa 9:22
bDa 2:28; 8:26;
Hab 2:3
10:15
cEze 24:27;
Lk 1:20
10:16
dIsa 6:7;
Jer 1:9;
Da 8:15-18
eIsa 21:3
10:17
fDa 4:19
10:18
gver 16
10:19
hJdg 6:23;
Isa 35:4 iJos 1:9
jIsa 6:1-8
10:20
kDa 8:21; 11:2
10:21
lDa 11:2
mver 12;
Jude 1:9
11:1
nDa 5:31
11:2
oDa 10:21
pDa 10:20
11:3
qDa 8:4,21
11:4
rDa 7:2; 8:22
11:7
sver 6
11:8
tIsa 37:19;
46:1-2

---

[a]16 Most manuscripts of the Masoretic Text; one manuscript of the Masoretic Text, Dead Sea Scrolls and Septuagint *Then something that looked like a man's hand*   [b]6 Or *offspring*   [c]6 Or *child* (see Vulgate and Syriac)

metal images and their valuable articles of silver and gold and carry them off to Egypt. [u] For some years he will leave the king of the North alone. [9]Then the king of the North will invade the realm of the king of the South but will retreat to his own country. [10]His sons will prepare for war and assemble a great army, which will sweep on like an irresistible flood[v] and carry the battle as far as his fortress.

[11]"Then the king of the South will march out in a rage and fight against the king of the North, who will raise a large army, but it will be defeated. [w] [12]When the army is carried off, the king of the South will be filled with pride and will slaughter many thousands, yet he will not remain triumphant. [13]For the king of the North will muster another army, larger than the first; and after several years, he will advance with a huge army fully equipped.

[14]"In those times many will rise against the king of the South. The violent men among your own people will rebel in fulfillment of the vision, but without success. [15]Then the king of the North will come and build up siege ramps[x] and will capture a fortified city. The forces of the South will be powerless to resist; even their best troops will not have the strength to stand. [16]The invader will do as he pleases;[y] no one will be able to stand against him. [z] He will establish himself in the Beautiful Land and will have the power to destroy it.[a] [17]He will determine to come with the might of his entire kingdom and will make an alliance with the king of the South. And he will give him a daughter in marriage in order to overthrow the kingdom, but his plans[a] will not succeed[b] or help him. [18]Then he will turn his attention to the coastlands[c] and will take many of them, but a commander will put an end to his insolence and will turn his insolence back upon him. [d] [19]After this, he will turn back toward the fortresses of his own country but will stumble and fall,[e] to be seen no more. [f]

[20]"His successor will send out a tax collector to maintain the royal splendor. [g] In a few years, however, he will be destroyed, yet not in anger or in battle.

[21]"He will be succeeded by a contemptible[h] person who has not been given the honor of royalty. [i] He will invade the kingdom when its people feel secure, and he will seize it through intrigue. [22]Then an overwhelming army will be swept away before him; both it and a prince of the covenant will be destroyed.[j] [23]After coming to an agreement with him, he will act deceitfully,[k] and with only a few people he will rise to power. [24]When the richest provinces feel secure, he will invade them and will achieve what neither his fathers nor his forefathers did. He will distribute plunder, loot and wealth among his followers.[l] He will plot the overthrow of fortresses—but only for a time.

[25]"With a large army he will stir up his strength and courage against the king of the South. The king of the South will wage war with a large and very powerful army, but he will not be able to stand because of the plots devised against him. [26]Those who eat from the king's provisions will try to destroy him; his army will be swept away, and many will fall in battle. [27]The two kings, with their hearts bent on evil, [m] will sit at the same table and lie[n] to each other, but to no avail, because an end will still come at the appointed time. [o] [28]The king of the North will return to

---

11:8
uJer 43:12
11:10
vIsa 8:8;
Jer 46:8;
Da 9:26
11:11
wDa 8:7-8
11:15
xEze 4:2
11:16
yDa 8:4
zJos 1:5; Da 8:7
aDa 8:9
11:17
bPs 20:4
11:18
cIsa 66:19;
Jer 25:22
dHos 12:14
11:19
ePs 27:2
fPs 37:36;
Eze 26:21
11:20
gIsa 60:17
11:21
hDa 4:17
iDa 8:25
11:22
jDa 8:10-11
11:23
kDa 8:25
11:24
lNe 9:25
11:27
mPs 64:6
nPs 12:2;
Jer 9:5
oHab 2:3

---

a17 Or *but she*

his own country with great wealth, but his heart will be set against the holy covenant. He will take action against it and then return to his own country.

29"At the appointed time he will invade the South again, but this time the outcome will be different from what it was before. 30Ships of the western coastlands[a][p] will oppose him, and he will lose heart. Then he will turn back and vent his fury against the holy covenant. He will return and show favor to those who forsake the holy covenant.

31"His armed forces will rise up to desecrate the temple fortress and will abolish the daily sacrifice. Then they will set up the abomination that causes desolation. [q] 32With flattery he will corrupt those who have violated the covenant, but the people who know their God will firmly resist[r] him.

33"Those who are wise will instruct[s] many, though for a time they will fall by the sword or be burned or captured or plundered.[t] 34When they fall, they will receive a little help, and many who are not sincere[u] will join them. 35Some of the wise will stumble, so that they may be refined,[v] purified and made spotless until the time of the end, for it will still come at the appointed time.

The King Who Exalts Himself

36"The king will do as he pleases. He will exalt and magnify himself above every god and will say unheard-of things[w] against the God of gods.[x] He will be successful until the time of wrath[y] is completed, for what has been determined must take place. 37He will show no regard for the gods of his fathers or for the one desired by women, nor will he regard any god, but will exalt himself above them all. 38Instead of them, he will honor a god of fortresses; a god unknown to his fathers he will honor with gold and silver, with precious stones and costly gifts. 39He will attack the mightiest fortresses with the help of a foreign god and will greatly honor those who acknowledge him. He will make them rulers over many people and will distribute the land at a price.[b]

40"At the time of the end the king of the South[z] will engage him in battle, and the king of the North will storm[a] out against him with chariots and cavalry and a great fleet of ships. He will invade many countries and sweep through them like a flood.[b] 41He will also invade the Beautiful Land. Many countries will fall, but Edom,[c] Moab[d] and the leaders of Ammon will be delivered from his hand. 42He will extend his power over many countries; Egypt will not escape. 43He will gain control of the treasures of gold and silver and all the riches of Egypt,[e] with the Libyans[f] and Nubians in submission. 44But reports from the east and the north will alarm him, and he will set out in a great rage to destroy and annihilate many. 45He will pitch his royal tents between the seas at[c] the beautiful holy mountain. Yet he will come to his end, and no one will help him.

The End Times

12 "At that time Michael,[g] the great prince who protects your people, will arise. There will be a time of distress[h] such as has not happened from the beginning of nations until then. But at that time

---

11:30
pGe 10:4
11:31
qDa 8:11-13;
9:27;
Mt 24:15*;
Mk 13:14*
11:32
rMic 5:7-9
11:33
sMal 2:7
tMt 24:9;
Jn 16:2;
Heb 11:32-38
11:34
uMt 7:15;
Ro 16:18
11:35
vPs 78:38;
Da 12:10;
Zec 13:9;
Jn 15:2
11:36
wRev 13:5-6
xDt 10:17;
Isa 14:13-14;
Da 7:25;
8:11-12,25;
2Th 2:4
yIsa 10:25;
26:20
11:40
zIsa 21:1
aIsa 5:28
bEze 38:4
11:41
cIsa 11:14
dJer 48:47
11:43
eEze 30:4
f2Ch 12:3;
Na 3:9
12:1
gDa 10:13
hDa 9:12;
Mt 24:21;
Mk 13:19;
Rev 16:18

---

[a]30 Hebrew *of Kittim*   [b]39 Or *land for a reward*   [c]45 Or *the sea and*

your people—everyone whose name is found written in the book[i] — will be delivered.[j] [2]Multitudes who sleep in the dust of the earth will awake: some to everlasting life, others to shame and everlasting contempt.[k] [3]Those who are wise[a1] will shine[m] like the brightness of the heavens, and those who lead many to righteousness, like the stars for ever and ever.[n] [4]But you, Daniel, close up and seal[o] the words of the scroll until the time of the end.[p] Many will go here and there to increase knowledge."

[5]Then I, Daniel, looked, and there before me stood two others, one on this bank of the river and one on the opposite bank.[q] [6]One of them said to the man clothed in linen,[r] who was above the waters of the river, "How long will it be before these astonishing things are fulfilled?"[s]

[7]The man clothed in linen, who was above the waters of the river, lifted his right hand and his left hand toward heaven, and I heard him swear by him who lives forever,[t] saying, "It will be for a time, times and half a time.[b][u] When the power of the holy people[v] has been finally broken, all these things will be completed.[w]"

[8]I heard, but I did not understand. So I asked, "My lord, what will the outcome of all this be?"

[9]He replied, "Go your way, Daniel, because the words are closed up and sealed until the time of the end.[x] [10]Many will be purified, made spotless and refined,[y] but the wicked will continue to be wicked.[z] None of the wicked will understand, but those who are wise will understand.[a]

[11]"From the time that the daily sacrifice is abolished and the abomination that causes desolation[b] is set up, there will be 1,290 days. [12]Blessed is the one who waits[c] for and reaches the end of the 1,335 days.[d]

[13]"As for you, go your way till the end. You will rest,[e] and then at the end of the days you will rise to receive your allotted inheritance.[f]"

12:1
iEx 32:32;
Ps 56:8 jJer 30:7
12:2
kIsa 26:19;
Mt 25:46;
Jn 5:28-29
12:3
lDa 11:33
mMt 13:43;
Jn 5:35
n1Co 15:42
12:4
oIsa 8:16
pver 9,13;
Rev 22:10
12:5
qDa 10:4
12:6
rEze 9:2
sDa 8:13
12:7
tRev 10:5-6
uDa 7:25
vDa 8:24
wLk 21:24;
Rev 10:7
12:9
xver 4
12:10
yDa 11:35
zIsa 32:7;
Rev 22:11
aHos 14:9
12:11
bDa 8:11; 9:27;
Mt 24:15*;
Mk 13:14*
12:12
cIsa 30:18
dDa 8:14
12:13
eIsa 57:2
fPs 16:5;
Rev 14:13

---

[a]3 Or *who impart wisdom*   [b]7 Or *a year, two years and half a year*

Hosea

Title and Background

The book is named after the prophet whose message it preserves. Hosea's time encompasses the tragic last days of the northern kingdom (Israel), during which six kings reigned within twenty-five years. Assyria was expanding westward, and in about 733 B.C. they dismembered Israel. Then in 722-721 B.C. Samaria was captured and its people exiled. The northern kingdom was at an end.

Author and Date of Writing

Hosea prophesied about the middle of the eighth century B.C., shortly after the ministry of Amos. Amos threatened God's judgment on Israel at the hands of an unnamed enemy; Hosea identifies that enemy as Assyria. Hosea stands first in the division of the Bible called the Minor Prophets (Hosea-Malachi).

Theme and Message

In the first half of the book, Hosea's family life is made a symbolic action to convey the message Hosea had from the Lord for his people. The Lord loved his covenant people and would take them back, however often they would wander. The second half of the book gives the details of Israel's involvement in Canaanite religion. Like other prophetic books, Hosea carried a call to repentance. The alternative to destruction is to forsake idols and return to the Lord.

Outline

I. The Unfaithful Wife and the Faithful Husband (1:1-3:5)
II. The Unfaithful Nation and the Faithful God (4:1-14:9)
   A. Israel's Unfaithfulness (4:1-6:3)
   B. Israel's Punishment (6:4-10:15)
   C. The Lord's Faithful Love (11:1-14:9)

---

1 The word of the LORD that came to Hosea son of Beeri during the reigns of Uzziah, Jotham, Ahaz and Hezekiah, kings of Judah,ᵃ and during the reign of Jeroboamᵇ son of Jehoashᵃ king of Israel:ᶜ

Hosea's Wife and Children

²When the LORD began to speak through Hosea, the LORD said to him, "Go, take to yourself an adulterousᵈ wife and children of unfaithfulness, because the land is guilty of the vilest adulteryᵉ in departing from the LORD." ³So he married Gomer daughter of Diblaim, and she conceived and bore him a son.

⁴Then the LORD said to Hosea, "Call him Jezreel,ᶠ because I will soon punish the house of Jehu for the massacre at Jezreel, and I will put an end to the kingdom of Israel. ⁵In that day I will break Israel's bow in the Valley of Jezreel.ᵍ"

1:1
ᵃIsa 1:1;
Mic 1:1
ᵇ2Ki 13:13
ᶜAm 1:1
1:2
ᵈJer 3:1;
Hos 2:2,5; 3:1
ᵉDt 31:16;
Jer 3:14;
Eze 23:3-21;
Hos 5:3
1:4
ᶠ2Ki 10:1-14;
Hos 2:22
1:5
ᵍ2Ki 15:29

ᵃ1 Hebrew *Joash*, a variant of *Jehoash*

[6]Gomer[h] conceived again and gave birth to a daughter. Then the LORD said to Hosea, "Call her Lo-Ruhamah,[a] for I will no longer show love to the house of Israel,[i] that I should at all forgive them. [7]Yet I will show love to the house of Judah; and I will save them—not by bow,[j] sword or battle, or by horses and horsemen, but by the LORD their God.[k]"

[8]After she had weaned Lo-Ruhamah, Gomer had another son. [9]Then the LORD said, "Call him Lo-Ammi,[b] for you are not my people, and I am not your God.

[10]"Yet the Israelites will be like the sand on the seashore, which cannot be measured or counted.[l] In the place where it was said to them, 'You are not my people,' they will be called 'sons of the living God.'[m] [11]The people of Judah and the people of Israel will be reunited,[n] and they will appoint one leader[o] and will come up out of the land,[p] for great will be the day of Jezreel.

2 "Say of your brothers, 'My people,' and of your sisters, 'My loved one.'[q]

Israel Punished and Restored

[2]"Rebuke your mother,[r] rebuke her,
   for she is not my wife,
   and I am not her husband.
Let her remove the adulterous[s] look from her face
   and the unfaithfulness from between her breasts.
[3]Otherwise I will strip her naked
   and make her as bare as on the day she was born;[t]
I will make her like a desert,[u]
   turn her into a parched land,
   and slay her with thirst.
[4]I will not show my love to her children,[v]
   because they are the children of adultery.
[5]Their mother has been unfaithful
   and has conceived them in disgrace.
She said, 'I will go after my lovers,[w]
   who give me my food and my water,
   my wool and my linen, my oil and my drink.'[x]
[6]Therefore I will block her path with thornbushes;
   I will wall her in so that she cannot find her way.[y]
[7]She will chase after her lovers but not catch them;
   she will look for them but not find them.[z]
Then she will say,
   'I will go back to my husband as at first,[a]
   for then I was better off[b] than now.'
[8]She has not acknowledged[c] that I was the one
   who gave her the grain, the new wine and oil,
   who lavished on her the silver and gold—
   which they used for Baal.[d]

[9]"Therefore I will take away my grain[e] when it ripens,
   and my new wine[f] when it is ready.

---

[a]6 *Lo-Ruhamah* means *not loved.*   [b]9 *Lo-Ammi* means *not my people.*

1:6
h ver 3; i Hos 2:4
1:7
j Ps 44:6
k Zec 4:6
1:10
l Ge 22:17;
Jer 33:22
m ver 9;
Ro 9:26*
1:11
n Isa 11:12,13
o Jer 23:5-8
p Eze 37:15-28
2:1
q ver 23
2:2
r ver 5; Isa 50:1;
Hos 1:2
s Eze 23:45
2:3
t Eze 16:4,22
u Isa 32:13-14
2:4
v Eze 8:18
2:5
w Jer 3:6
x Jer 44:17-18
2:6
y Job 3:23;
19:8; La 3:9
2:7
z Hos 5:13
a Jer 2:2; 3:1
b Eze 16:8
2:8
c Isa 1:3
d Eze 16:15-19;
Hos 8:4
2:9
e Hos 8:7
f Hos 9:2

I will take back my wool and my linen,
    intended to cover her nakedness.
¹⁰So now I will expose her lewdness
    before the eyes of her lovers;
    no one will take her out of my hands. ᵍ
¹¹I will stop ʰ all her celebrations:
    her yearly festivals, her New Moons,
    her Sabbath days—all her appointed feasts. ⁱ
¹²I will ruin her vinesʲ and her fig trees,
    which she said were her pay from her lovers;
I will make them a thicket, ᵏ
    and wild animals will devour them. ˡ
¹³I will punish her for the days
    she burned incense to the Baals;ᵐ
she decked herself with rings and jewelry, ⁿ
    and went after her lovers, ᵒ
    but me she forgot, ᵖ"

            declares the LORD.

¹⁴"Therefore I am now going to allure her;
    I will lead her into the desert
    and speak tenderly to her.
¹⁵There I will give her back her vineyards,
    and will make the Valley of Achorᵃ�q a door of hope.
There she will singᵇʳ as in the days of her youth, ˢ
    as in the day she came up out of Egypt. ᵗ

¹⁶"In that day," declares the LORD,
    "you will call me 'my husband';
    you will no longer call me 'my master.ᶜ'
¹⁷I will remove the names of the Baals from her lips;ᵘ
    no longer will their names be invoked. ᵛ
¹⁸In that day I will make a covenant for them
    with the beasts of the field and the birds of the air
    and the creatures that move along the ground. ʷ
Bow and sword and battle
    I will abolishˣ from the land,
    so that all may lie down in safety. ʸ
¹⁹I will betrothᶻ you to me forever;
    I will betroth you inᵈ righteousness and justice, ᵃ
    inᵉ love and compassion.
²⁰I will betroth you in faithfulness,
    and you will acknowledgeᵇ the LORD.

²¹"In that day I will respond,"
    declares the LORD—
    "I will respondᶜ to the skies,
    and they will respond to the earth;
²²and the earth will respond to the grain,
    the new wine and oil, ᵈ

2:10
gEze 16:37
2:11
hJer 7:34
iIsa 1:14;
Jer 16:9;
Hos 3:4;
Am 8:10
2:12
jIsa 7:23;
Jer 8:13 kIsa 5:6
lHos 13:8
2:13
mHos 11:2
nEze 16:17
oHos 4:13
pHos 4:6; 8:14;
13:6
2:15
qJos 7:24,26
rEx 15:1-18
sJer 2:2
tHos 12:9
2:17
uEx 23:13;
Ps 16:4
vJos 23:7
2:18
wJob 5:22
xIsa 2:4
yJer 23:6;
Eze 34:25
2:19
zIsa 62:4
aIsa 1:27
2:20
bJer 31:34;
Hos 6:6; 13:4
2:21
cIsa 55:10;
Zec 8:12
2:22
dJer 31:12;
Joel 2:19

ᵃ15 *Achor* means *trouble.*   ᵇ15 Or *respond*   ᶜ16 Hebrew *baal*   ᵈ19 Or *with*; also in verse
20   ᵉ19 Or *with*

and they will respond to Jezreel. [a]
[23]I will plant[e] her for myself in the land;
    I will show my love to the one I called 'Not my loved
        one.[b][f]'
    I will say to those called 'Not my people,[c]' 'You are my
        people';[g]
    and they will say, 'You are my God.[h]' "

Hosea's Reconciliation With His Wife

3 The LORD said to me, "Go, show your love to your wife again,
though she is loved by another and is an adulteress.[i] Love her as
the LORD loves the Israelites, though they turn to other gods and love
the sacred raisin cakes.[j] "

[2]So I bought her for fifteen shekels[d] of silver and about a homer and
a lethek[e] of barley. [3]Then I told her, "You are to live with[f] me many
days; you must not be a prostitute or be intimate with any man, and I
will live with[f] you."

[4]For the Israelites will live many days without king or prince,[k] without sacrifice[l] or sacred stones, without ephod or idol.[m] [5]Afterward the
Israelites will return and seek the LORD their God and David their
king.[n] They will come trembling to the LORD and to his blessings in the
last days.[o]

The Charge Against Israel

4
Hear the word of the LORD, you Israelites,
    because the LORD has a charge to bring
    against you who live in the land:
"There is no faithfulness, no love,
    no acknowledgment[p] of God in the land.
[2]There is only cursing,[g] lying[q] and murder,[r]
    stealing[s] and adultery;
they break all bounds,
    and bloodshed follows bloodshed.
[3]Because of this the land mourns,[h][t]
    and all who live in it waste away;[u]
the beasts of the field and the birds of the air
    and the fish of the sea are dying.[v]

[4]"But let no man bring a charge,
    let no man accuse another,
for your people are like those
    who bring charges against a priest.[w]
[5]You stumble[x] day and night,
    and the prophets stumble with you.
So I will destroy your mother[y]—
[6]   my people are destroyed from lack of knowledge.[z]

"Because you have rejected knowledge,
    I also reject you as my priests;

2:23
e Jer 31:27
f Hos 1:6
g Hos 1:10
h Ro 9:25*;
1Pe 2:10
3:1
i Hos 1:2
j 2Sa 6:19
3:4
k Hos 13:11
l Da 11:31;
Hos 2:11
m Jdg 17:5-6;
Zec 10:2
3:5
n Eze 34:23-24
o Jer 50:4-5
4:1
p Jer 7:28
4:2
q Hos 7:3; 10:4
r Hos 6:9
s Hos 7:1
4:3
t Jer 4:28
u Isa 33:9
v Jer 4:25;
Zep 1:3
4:4
w Dt 17:12;
Eze 3:26
4:5
x Eze 14:7
y Hos 2:2
4:6
z Hos 2:13;
Mal 2:7-8

---

[a]22 *Jezreel* means *God plants.*   [b]23 Hebrew *Lo-Ruhamah*   [c]23 Hebrew *Lo-Ammi*   [d]2 That
is, about 6 ounces (about 170 grams)   [e]2 That is, probably about 10 bushels (about 330 liters)
[f]3 Or *wait for*   [g]2 That is, to pronounce a curse upon   [h]3 Or *dries up*

because you have ignored the law[a] of your God,
    I also will ignore your children.
[7]The more the priests increased,
    the more they sinned against me;
    they exchanged[a] their[b] Glory[b] for something
      disgraceful.[c]
[8]They feed on the sins of my people
    and relish their wickedness.[d]
[9]And it will be: Like people, like priests.[e]
    I will punish both of them for their ways
    and repay them for their deeds.[f]

[10]"They will eat but not have enough;[g]
    they will engage in prostitution but not increase,
because they have deserted[h] the LORD
    to give themselves [11]to prostitution,[i]
to old wine and new,
    which take away the understanding[j] [12]of my people.
They consult a wooden idol[k]
    and are answered by a stick of wood.[l]
A spirit of prostitution leads them astray;[m]
    they are unfaithful to their God.
[13]They sacrifice on the mountaintops
    and burn offerings on the hills,
under oak,[n] poplar and terebinth,
    where the shade is pleasant.[o]
Therefore your daughters turn to prostitution[p]
    and your daughters-in-law to adultery.[q]

[14]"I will not punish your daughters
    when they turn to prostitution,
nor your daughters-in-law
    when they commit adultery,
because the men themselves consort with harlots[r]
    and sacrifice with shrine prostitutes—
a people without understanding will come to ruin!

[15]"Though you commit adultery, O Israel,
    let not Judah become guilty.

"Do not go to Gilgal;[s]
    do not go up to Beth Aven.[c]
    And do not swear, 'As surely as the LORD lives!'
[16]The Israelites are stubborn,
    like a stubborn heifer.
How then can the LORD pasture them
    like lambs[t] in a meadow?
[17]Ephraim is joined to idols;
    leave him alone!
[18]Even when their drinks are gone,

4:6
a Hos 8:1,12
4:7
b Hab 2:16
c Hos 10:1,6;
13:6
4:8
d Isa 56:11;
Mic 3:11
4:9
e Isa 24:2
f Jer 5:31;
Hos 8:13; 9:9,
15
4:10
g Lev 26:26;
Mic 6:14
h Hos 7:14; 9:17
4:11
i Hos 5:4
j Pr 20:1
4:12
k Jer 2:27
l Hab 2:19
m Isa 44:20
4:13
n Isa 1:29
o Jer 3:6;
Hos 11:2
p Jer 2:20;
Am 7:17
q Hos 2:13
4:14
r ver 11
4:15
s Hos 9:15;
12:11; Am 4:4
4:16
t Isa 5:17; 7:25

---

[a]7 Syriac and an ancient Hebrew scribal tradition; Masoretic Text *I will exchange*   [b]7 Masoretic Text; an ancient Hebrew scribal tradition *my*   [c]15 *Beth Aven* means *house of wickedness* (a name for Bethel, which means *house of God*).

they continue their prostitution;
their rulers dearly love shameful ways.
[19] A whirlwind[u] will sweep them away,
and their sacrifices will bring them shame.[v]

Judgment Against Israel

5 "Hear this, you priests!
Pay attention, you Israelites!
Listen, O royal house!
This judgment is against you:
You have been a snare[w] at Mizpah,
a net spread out on Tabor.
[2] The rebels are deep in slaughter.[x]
I will discipline all of them.[y]
[3] I know all about Ephraim;
Israel is not hidden from me.
Ephraim, you have now turned to prostitution;
Israel is corrupt.[z]

[4] "Their deeds do not permit them
to return to their God.
A spirit of prostitution[a] is in their heart;
they do not acknowledge[b] the LORD.
[5] Israel's arrogance testifies[c] against them;
the Israelites, even Ephraim, stumble in their sin;
Judah also stumbles with them.
[6] When they go with their flocks and herds
to seek the LORD,[d]
they will not find him;
he has withdrawn[e] himself from them.
[7] They are unfaithful[f] to the LORD;
they give birth to illegitimate[g] children.
Now their New Moon festivals
will devour[h] them and their fields.

[8] "Sound the trumpet in Gibeah,[i]
the horn in Ramah.[j]
Raise the battle cry in Beth Aven[a];[k]
lead on, O Benjamin.
[9] Ephraim will be laid waste
on the day of reckoning.[l]
Among the tribes of Israel
I proclaim what is certain.[m]
[10] Judah's leaders are like those
who move boundary stones.[n]
I will pour out my wrath[o] on them
like a flood of water.
[11] Ephraim is oppressed,
trampled in judgment,
intent on pursuing idols.[b][p]

4:19
uHos 12:1;
13:15 vIsa 1:29
5:1
wHos 6:9; 9:8
5:2
xHos 4:2
yHos 9:15
5:3
zHos 6:10
5:4
aHos 4:11
bHos 4:6
5:5
cHos 7:10
5:6
dMic 6:6-7
ePr 1:28;
Isa 1:15;
Eze 8:6
5:7
fHos 6:7
gHos 2:4
hHos 2:11-12
5:8
iHos 9:9; 10:9
jIsa 10:29
kHos 4:15
5:9
lIsa 37:3;
Hos 9:11-17
mIsa 46:10;
Zec 1:6
5:10
nDt 19:14
oEze 7:8
5:11
pHos 9:16;
Mic 6:16

---

a8 Beth Aven means *house of wickedness* (a name for Bethel, which means *house of God*).   *b11* The
meaning of the Hebrew for this word is uncertain.

¹²I am like a moth⁹ to Ephraim,
like rot to the people of Judah.

¹³"When Ephraim saw his sickness,
and Judah his sores,
then Ephraim turned to Assyria,ʳ
and sent to the great king for help.ˢ
But he is not able to cureᵗ you,
not able to heal your sores.ᵘ
¹⁴For I will be like a lionᵛ to Ephraim,
like a great lion to Judah.
I will tear them to pieces and go away;
I will carry them off, with no one to rescue them.ʷ
¹⁵Then I will go back to my place
until they admit their guilt.
And they will seek my face;ˣ
in their miseryʸ they will earnestly seek me.ᶻ"

Israel Unrepentant

6 "Come, let us return to the LORD.
He has torn us to pieasᵃ
but he will heal us;
he has injured us
but he will bind up our wounds.ᵇ
²After two days he will revive us;ᶜ
on the third day he will restore us,
that we may live in his presence.
³Let us acknowledge the LORD;
let us press on to acknowledge him.
As surely as the sun rises,
he will appear;
he will come to us like the winter rains,ᵈ
like the spring rains that water the earth.ᵉ"

⁴"What can I do with you, Ephraim?ᶠ
What can I do with you, Judah?
Your love is like the morning mist,
like the early dew that disappears.ᵍ
⁵Therefore I cut you in pieces with my prophets,
I killed you with the words of my mouth;ʰ
my judgments flashed like lightning upon you.ⁱ
⁶For I desire mercy, not sacrifice,ʲ
and acknowledgmentᵏ of God rather than burnt
offerings.
⁷Like Adam,ᵃ they have broken the covenantˡ—
they were unfaithfulᵐ to me there.
⁸Gilead is a city of wicked men,
stained with footprints of blood.
⁹As marauders lie in ambush for a man,
so do bands of priests;
they murder on the road to Shechem,

5:12
qIsa 51:8
5:13
rHos 7:11; 8:9
sHos 10:6
tHos 14:3
uJer 30:12
5:14
vAm 3:4
wMic 5:8
5:15
xHos 3:5
yJer 2:27
zIsa 64:9
6:1
aHos 5:14
bDt 32:39;
Jer 30:17;
Hos 14:4
6:2
cPs 30:5
6:3
dJoel 2:23
ePs 72:6
6:4
fHos 11:8
gHos 7:1; 13:3
6:5
hJer 1:9-10;
23:29 iHeb 4:12
6:6
jIsa 1:11;
Mt 9:13*; 12:7*
kHos 2:20
6:7
lHos 8:1
mHos 5:7

ᵃ7 Or *As at Adam;* or *Like men*

committing shameful crimes. ⁿ

¹⁰I have seen a horribleº thing
in the house of Israel.
There Ephraim is given to prostitution
and Israel is defiled. ᵖ

¹¹"Also for you, Judah,
a harvest�q is appointed.

"Whenever I would restore the fortunes of my people,
¹whenever I would heal Israel,
the sins of Ephraim are exposed
and the crimes of Samaria revealed. ʳ
They practice deceit, ˢ
thieves break into houses, ᵗ
bandits rob in the streets;
²but they do not realize
that I rememberᵘ all their evil deeds.
Their sins engulf them; ᵛ
they are always before me.

³"They delight the king with their wickedness,
the princes with their lies. ʷ
⁴They are all adulterers, ˣ
burning like an oven
whose fire the baker need not stir
from the kneading of the dough till it rises.
⁵On the day of the festival of our king
the princes become inflamed with wine, ʸ
and he joins hands with the mockers.
⁶Their hearts are like an oven; ᶻ
they approach him with intrigue.
Their passion smolders all night;
in the morning it blazes like a flaming fire.
⁷All of them are hot as an oven;
they devour their rulers.
All their kings fall,
and none of them callsª on me.

⁸"Ephraim mixesᵇ with the nations;
Ephraim is a flat cake not turned over.
⁹Foreigners sap his strength, ᶜ
but he does not realize it.
His hair is sprinkled with gray,
but he does not notice.
¹⁰Israel's arrogance testifies against him, ᵈ
but despite all this
he does not return to the LORD his God
or searchᵉ for him.

¹¹"Ephraim is like a dove, ᶠ
easily deceived and senseless—
now calling to Egypt,
now turning to Assyria. ᵍ

6:9
n Jer 7:9-10;
Eze 22:9;
Hos 7:1
6:10
o Jer 5:30
p Hos 5:3
6:11
q Jer 51:33;
Joel 3:13
7:1
r Hos 6:4
s ver 13 t Hos 4:2
7:2
u Jer 14:10;
Hos 8:13
v Jer 2:19
7:3
w Hos 4:2;
Mic 7:3
7:4
x Jer 9:2
7:5
y Isa 28:1,7
7:6
z Ps 21:9
7:7
a ver 16
7:8
b ver 11;
Ps 106:35;
Hos 5:13
7:9
c Isa 1:7;
Hos 8:7
7:10
d Hos 5:5
e Isa 9:13
7:11
f Hos 11:11
g Hos 5:13; 12:1

[12] When they go, I will throw my net[h] over them;
  I will pull them down like birds of the air.
 When I hear them flocking together,
  I will catch them.
[13] Woe[i] to them,
  because they have strayed[j] from me!
 Destruction to them,
  because they have rebelled against me!
 I long to redeem them
  but they speak lies against me.[k]
[14] They do not cry out to me from their hearts[l]
  but wail upon their beds.
 They gather together[a] for grain and new wine[m]
  but turn away from me.[n]
[15] I trained them and strengthened them,
  but they plot evil[o] against me.
[16] They do not turn to the Most High;
  they are like a faulty bow.[p]
 Their leaders will fall by the sword
  because of their insolent words.
 For this they will be ridiculed[q]
  in the land of Egypt.[r]

Israel to Reap the Whirlwind

8 "Put the trumpet to your lips!
  An eagle[s] is over the house of the LORD
 because the people have broken my covenant
  and rebelled against my law.[t]
[2] Israel cries out to me,
  'O our God, we acknowledge you!'
[3] But Israel has rejected what is good;
  an enemy will pursue him.
[4] They set up kings without my consent;
  they choose princes without my approval.[u]
 With their silver and gold
  they make idols[v] for themselves
  to their own destruction.
[5] Throw out your calf-idol, O Samaria![w]
  My anger burns against them.
 How long will they be incapable of purity?[x]
[6] They are from Israel!
 This calf—a craftsman has made it;
  it is not God.
 It will be broken in pieces,
  that calf of Samaria.

[7] "They sow the wind
  and reap the whirlwind.[y]
 The stalk has no head;
  it will produce no flour.

7:12
hEze 12:13
7:13
iHos 9:12
jJer 14:10;
Eze 34:4-6;
Hos 9:17
kver 1;
Mt 23:37
7:14
lJer 3:10
mAm 2:8
nHos 13:16
7:15
oNa 1:9,11
7:16
pPs 78:9,57
qEze 23:32
rHos 9:3
8:1
sDt 28:49;
Jer 4:13
tHos 4:6; 6:7
8:4
uHos 13:10
vHos 2:8
8:5
wHos 10:5
xJer 13:27
8:7
yPr 22:8;
Isa 66:15;
Hos 10:12-13;
Na 1:3

a14 Most Hebrew manuscripts; some Hebrew manuscripts and Septuagint They slash themselves

Were it to yield grain,
    foreigners would swallow it up. [z]
[8]Israel is swallowed up; [a]
    now she is among the nations
    like a worthless [b] thing.
[9]For they have gone up to Assyria
    like a wild donkey wandering alone.
    Ephraim has sold herself to lovers.
[10]Although they have sold themselves among the nations,
    I will now gather them together. [c]
They will begin to waste away [d]
    under the oppression of the mighty king.

[11]"Though Ephraim built many altars for sin offerings,
    these have become altars for sinning. [e]
[12]I wrote for them the many things of my law,
    but they regarded them as something alien.
[13]They offer sacrifices given to me
    and they eat [f] the meat,
    but the LORD is not pleased with them.
Now he will remember [g] their wickedness
    and punish their sins: [h]
    They will return to Egypt. [i]
[14]Israel has forgotten [j] his Maker
    and built palaces;
    Judah has fortified many towns.
But I will send fire upon their cities
    that will consume their fortresses." [k]

Punishment for Israel

9 Do not rejoice, O Israel;
    do not be jubilant [l] like the other nations.
For you have been unfaithful [m] to your God;
    you love the wages of a prostitute
    at every threshing floor.
[2]Threshing floors and winepresses will not feed the
      people;
    the new wine [n] will fail them.
[3]They will not remain [o] in the LORD's land;
    Ephraim will return to Egypt [p]
    and eat unclean [a] food in Assyria. [q]
[4]They will not pour out wine offerings to the LORD,
    nor will their sacrifices please [r] him.
Such sacrifices will be to them like the bread of
      mourners;
    all who eat them will be unclean. [s]
This food will be for themselves;
    it will not come into the temple of the LORD.

[5]What will you do [t] on the day of your appointed feasts, [u]
    on the festival days of the LORD?

---

[a]3 That is, ceremonially unclean

8:7
z Hos 2:9
8:8
a Jer 51:34
b Jer 22:28
8:10
c Eze 16:37;
22:20 d Jer 42:2
8:11
e Hos 10:1;
12:11
8:13
f Jer 7:21
g Hos 7:2
h Hos 4:9
i Hos 9:3,6
8:14
j Dt 32:18;
Hos 2:13
k Jer 17:27
9:1
l Isa 22:12-13
m Hos 10:5
9:2
n Hos 2:9
9:3
o Lev 25:23
p Hos 8:13
q Eze 4:13;
Hos 7:11
9:4
r Jer 6:20;
Hos 8:13
s Hag 2:13-14
9:5
t Isa 10:3;
Jer 5:31
u Hos 2:11

⁶Even if they escape from destruction,
  Egypt will gather them,
  and Memphisᵛ will bury them.
Their treasures of silver will be taken over by briers,
  and thornsʷ will overrun their tents.
⁷The days of punishmentˣ are coming,
  the days of reckoning are at hand.
  Let Israel know this.
Because your sinsʸ are so many
  and your hostility so great,
the prophet is considered a fool,ᶻ
  the inspired man a maniac.
⁸The prophet, along with my God,
  is the watchman over Ephraim,ᵃ
yet snaresᵃ await him on all his paths,
  and hostility in the house of his God.
⁹They have sunk deep into corruption,
  as in the days of Gibeah.ᵇ
God will rememberᶜ their wickedness
  and punish them for their sins.

¹⁰"When I found Israel,
  it was like finding grapes in the desert;
when I saw your fathers,
  it was like seeing the early fruit on the fig tree.
But when they came to Baal Peor,ᵈ
  they consecrated themselves to that shameful idolᵉ
  and became as vile as the thing they loved.
¹¹Ephraim's glory will fly away like a birdᶠ —
  no birth, no pregnancy, no conception.ᵍ
¹²Even if they rear children,
  I will bereave them of every one.
Woeʰ to them
  when I turn away from them!ⁱ
¹³I have seen Ephraim, like Tyre,
  planted in a pleasant place.ʲ
But Ephraim will bring out
  their children to the slayer."

¹⁴Give them, O LORD—
  what will you give them?
Give them wombs that miscarry
  and breasts that are dry.ᵏ

¹⁵"Because of all their wickedness in Gilgal,ˡ
  I hated them there.
Because of their sinful deeds,ᵐ
  I will drive them out of my house.
I will no longer love them;
  all their leaders are rebellious.ⁿ
¹⁶Ephraimᵒ is blighted,

9:6
vIsa 19:13
wIsa 5:6;
Hos 10:8
9:7
xIsa 34:8;
Jer 10:15;
Mic 7:4
yJer 16:18
zIsa 44:25;
La 2:14;
Eze 14:9-10
9:8
aHos 5:1
9:9
bJdg 19:16-30;
Hos 5:8; 10:9
cHos 8:13
9:10
dNu 25:1-5;
Ps 106:28-29
eJer 11:13;
Hos 4:14
9:11
fHos 4:7; 10:5
gver 14
9:12
hHos 7:13
iDt 31:17
9:13
jEze 27:3
9:14
kver 11;
Lk 23:29
9:15
lHos 4:15
mHos 7:2
nIsa 1:23;
Hos 4:9; 5:2
9:16
oHos 5:11

ᵃ8 Or *The prophet is the watchman over Ephraim, / the people of my God*

their root is withered,
they yield no fruit. p
Even if they bear children,
I will slay q their cherished offspring."

[17]My God will reject them
because they have not obeyed r him;
they will be wanderers among the nations. s

10 Israel was a spreading vine; t
he brought forth fruit for himself.
As his fruit increased,
he built more altars; u
as his land prospered,
he adorned his sacred stones. v
[2]Their heart is deceitful, w
and now they must bear their guilt. x
The LORD will demolish their altars y
and destroy their sacred stones. z

[3]Then they will say, "We have no king
because we did not revere the LORD.
But even if we had a king,
what could he do for us?"
[4]They make many promises,
take false oaths a
and make agreements; b
therefore lawsuits spring up
like poisonous weeds in a plowed field.
[5]The people who live in Samaria fear
for the calf-idol of Beth Aven. a c
Its people will mourn over it,
and so will its idolatrous priests, d
those who had rejoiced over its splendor,
because it is taken from them into exile. e
[6]It will be carried to Assyria f
as tribute for the great king. g
Ephraim will be disgraced; h
Israel will be ashamed of its wooden idols. b
[7]Samaria and its king will float away i
like a twig on the surface of the waters.
[8]The high places of wickedness c i will be destroyed—
it is the sin of Israel.
Thorns k and thistles will grow up
and cover their altars. l
Then they will say to the mountains, "Cover us!"
and to the hills, "Fall on us!" m

[9]"Since the days of Gibeah, n you have sinned, O Israel,
and there you have remained. d

9:16
pHos 8:7
qver 12
9:17
rHos 4:10
sDt 28:65;
Hos 7:13
10:1
tEze 15:2
u1Ki 14:23
vHos 8:11;
12:11
10:2
w1Ki 18:21
xHos 13:16
yver 8
zMic 5:13
10:4
aHos 4:2
bEze 17:19;
Am 5:7
10:5
cHos 5:8
d2Ki 23:5
eHos 8:5;
9:1,3,11
10:6
fHos 11:5
gHos 5:13
hIsa 30:3;
Hos 4:7
10:7
iHos 13:11
10:8
j1Ki 12:28-30;
Hos 4:13
kHos 9:6
lver 2; Isa 32:13
mLk 23:30*;
Rev 6:16
10:9
nHos 5:8

---

a5 Beth Aven means *house of wickedness* (a name for Bethel, which means *house of God*).   b6 Or *its*
counsel   c8 Hebrew *aven*, a reference to Beth Aven (a derogatory name for Bethel)   d9 Or
there a stand was taken

Did not war overtake
  the evildoers in Gibeah?
¹⁰When I please, I will punish° them;
  nations will be gathered against them
  to put them in bonds for their double sin.
¹¹Ephraim is a trained heifer
  that loves to thresh;
so I will put a yoke
  on her fair neck.
I will drive Ephraim,
  Judah must plow,
  and Jacob must break up the ground.
¹²Sow for yourselves righteousness, ᵖ
  reap the fruit of unfailing love,
and break up your unplowed ground; q
  for it is time to seekʳ the LORD,
until he comes
  and showers righteousnessˢ on you.
¹³But you have planted wickedness,
  you have reaped evil, ᵗ
  you have eaten the fruit of deception.
Because you have depended on your own strength
  and on your many warriors, ᵘ
¹⁴the roar of battle will rise against your people,
  so that all your fortresses will be devastatedᵛ—
as Shalman devastated Beth Arbel on the day of battle,
  when mothers were dashed to the ground with their
    children. ʷ
¹⁵Thus will it happen to you, O Bethel,
  because your wickedness is great.
When that day dawns,
  the king of Israel will be completely destroyed. ˣ

God's Love for Israel

11

¹"When Israel was a child, I loved him,
  and out of Egypt I called my son. ʸ
²But the more Iᵃ called Israel,
  the further they went from me. ᵇ
They sacrificed to the Baalsᶻ
  and they burned incense to images. ᵃ
³It was I who taught Ephraim to walk,
  taking them by the arms; ᵇ
but they did not realize
  it was I who healedᶜ them.
⁴I led them with cords of human kindness,
  with ties of love; ᵈ
I lifted the yokeᵉ from their neck
  and bent down to feedᶠ them.

⁵"Will they not return to Egyptᵍ

10:10
°Eze 5:13;
Hos 4:9
10:12
ᵖPr 11:18
qJer 4:3
rHos 12:6
ˢIsa 45:8
10:13
tJob 4:8;
Hos 7:3; 11:12;
Gal 6:7-8
uPs 33:16
10:14
vIsa 17:3
wHos 13:16
10:15
xver 7
11:1
yEx 4:22;
Hos 12:9,13;
13:4; Mt 2:15*
11:2
zHos 2:13
a2Ki 17:15;
Isa 65:7;
Jer 18:15
11:3
bDt 1:31;
Hos 7:15
cJer 30:17
11:4
dJer 31:2-3
eLev 26:13
fEx 16:32;
Ps 78:2⁷
11:5
gHos 7:16

ᵃ2 Some Septuagint manuscripts; Hebrew *they*   ᵇ2 Septuagint; Hebrew *them*

and will not Assyria[h] rule over them
   because they refuse to repent?
[6]Swords[i] will flash in their cities,
   will destroy the bars of their gates
   and put an end to their plans.
[7]My people are determined to turn from me.[j]
   Even if they call to the Most High,
   he will by no means exalt them.

[8]"How can I give you up, Ephraim?[k]
   How can I hand you over, Israel?
How can I treat you like Admah?
   How can I make you like Zeboiim?[l]
My heart is changed within me;
   all my compassion is aroused.
[9]I will not carry out my fierce anger,[m]
   nor will I turn and devastate[n] Ephraim.
For I am God, and not man[o]—
   the Holy One among you.
I will not come in wrath.[a]
[10]They will follow the LORD;
   he will roar like a lion.
When he roars,
   his children will come trembling from the west.[p]
[11]They will come trembling
   like birds from Egypt,
   like doves from Assyria.[q]
I will settle them in their homes,"[r]
   declares the LORD.

Israel's Sin

[12]Ephraim has surrounded me with lies,[s]
   the house of Israel with deceit.
And Judah is unruly against God,
   even against the faithful Holy One.

12 [1]Ephraim feeds on the wind;[t]
   he pursues the east wind all day
   and multiplies lies and violence.
He makes a treaty with Assyria
   and sends olive oil to Egypt.[u]
[2]The LORD has a charge[v] to bring against Judah;
   he will punish Jacob[b] according to his ways
   and repay him according to his deeds.[w]
[3]In the womb he grasped his brother's heel;[x]
   as a man he struggled[y] with God.
[4]He struggled with the angel and overcame him;
   he wept and begged for his favor.
He found him at Bethel[z]
   and talked with him there—
[5]the LORD God Almighty,

11:5
h Hos 10:6
11:6
i Hos 13:16
11:7
j Jer 3:6-7; 8:5
11:8
k Hos 6:4
l Ge 14:8
11:9
m Dt 13:17;
Jer 30:11
n Mal 3:6
o Nu 23:19
11:10
p Hos 6:1-3
11:11
q Isa 11:11
r Eze 28:26
11:12
s Hos 4:2
12:1
t Eze 17:10
u 2Ki 17:4
12:2
v Mic 6:2
w Hos 4:9
12:3
x Ge 25:26
y Ge 32:24-29
12:4
z Ge 28:12-15;
35:15

---

[a]9 Or *come against any city*   [b]2 *Jacob* means *he grasps the heel* (figuratively, *he deceives*).

the Lord is his name[a] of renown!
6But you must return to your God;
    maintain love and justice,[b]
    and wait for your God always.[c]

7The merchant uses dishonest scales;[d]
    he loves to defraud.
8Ephraim boasts,
    "I am very rich; I have become wealthy.[e]
With all my wealth they will not find in me
    any iniquity or sin."

9"I am the Lord your God,
    who brought you out of[a] Egypt;[f]
I will make you live in tents[g] again,
    as in the days of your appointed feasts.
10I spoke to the prophets,
    gave them many visions
    and told parables[h] through them."[i]

11Is Gilead wicked?[j]
    Its people are worthless!
Do they sacrifice bulls in Gilgal?[k]
    Their altars will be like piles of stones
    on a plowed field.[l]
12Jacob fled to the country of Aram[b];[m]
    Israel served to get a wife,
    and to pay for her he tended sheep.[n]
13The Lord used a prophet to bring Israel up from Egypt,
    by a prophet he cared for him.[o]
14But Ephraim has bitterly provoked him to anger;
    his Lord will leave upon him the guilt of his
        bloodshed[p]
    and will repay him for his contempt.[q]

The Lord's Anger Against Israel

13 When Ephraim spoke, men trembled;[r]
    he was exalted[s] in Israel.
But he became guilty of Baal worship[t] and died.
2Now they sin more and more;
    they make idols for themselves from their silver,[u]
cleverly fashioned images,
    all of them the work of craftsmen.
It is said of these people,
    "They offer human sacrifice
    and kiss[c] the calf-idols.[v]"
3Therefore they will be like the morning mist,
    like the early dew that disappears,[w]
    like chaff[x] swirling from a threshing floor,[y]

Cross-references

12:5
a Ex 3:15
12:6
b Mic 6:8
c Hos 6:1-3;
10:12; Mic 7:7
12:7
d Am 8:5
12:8
e Ps 62:10;
Rev 3:17
12:9
f Lev 23:43;
Hos 11:1
g Ne 8:17
12:10
h Eze 20:49
i 2Ki 17:13;
Jer 7:25
12:11
j Hos 6:8
k Hos 4:15
l Hos 8:11
12:12
m Ge 28:5
n Ge 29:18
12:13
o Ex 13:3;
Isa 63:11-14
12:14
p Eze 18:13
q Da 11:18
13:1
r Jdg 12:1
s Jdg 8:1
t Hos 11:2
13:2
u Isa 46:6;
Jer 10:4
v Isa 44:17-20
13:3
w Hos 6:4
x Isa 17:13
y Da 2:35

---

[a]9 Or God / ever since you were in   [b]12 That is, Northwest Mesopotamia   [c]2 Or "Men who
sacrifice / kiss

like smoke[z] escaping through a window.
4"But I am the LORD your God,
⌊who brought you⌋ out of[a] Egypt.[a]
You shall acknowledge no God but me,[b]
no Savior[c] except me.
5I cared for you in the desert,
in the land of burning heat.
6When I fed them, they were satisfied;
when they were satisfied, they became proud;
then they forgot me.[d]
7So I will come upon them like a lion,
like a leopard I will lurk by the path.
8Like a bear robbed of her cubs,[e]
I will attack them and rip them open.
Like a lion I will devour them;
a wild animal will tear them apart.[f]

9"You are destroyed, O Israel,
because you are against me,[g] against your helper.[h]
10Where is your king,[i] that he may save you?
Where are your rulers in all your towns,
of whom you said,
'Give me a king and princes'?[j]
11So in my anger I gave you a king,
and in my wrath I took him away.[k]
12The guilt of Ephraim is stored up,
his sins are kept on record.[l]
13Pains as of a woman in childbirth[m] come to him,
but he is a child without wisdom;
when the time arrives,
he does not come to the opening of the womb.[n]

14"I will ransom them from the power of the grave[b];[o]
I will redeem them from death.
Where, O death, are your plagues?
Where, O grave,[b] is your destruction?[p]

"I will have no compassion,
15   even though he thrives[q] among his brothers.
An east wind[r] from the LORD will come,
blowing in from the desert;
his spring will fail
and his well dry up.[s]
His storehouse will be plundered[t]
of all its treasures.
16The people of Samaria must bear their guilt,[u]
because they have rebelled[v] against their God.
They will fall by the sword;[w]
their little ones will be dashed[x] to the ground,
their pregnant women[y] ripped open."

13:3
zPs 68:2
13:4
aHos 12:9
bEx 20:3
cIsa 43:11;
45:21-22
13:6
dDt 32:12-15;
Hos 2:13
13:8
e2Sa 17:8
fPs 50:22
13:9
gJer 2:17-19
hDt 33:29
13:10
i2Ki 17:4
j1Sa 8:6;
Hos 8:4
13:11
k1Ki 14:10;
Hos 10:7
13:12
lDt 32:34
13:13
mIsa 13:8;
Mic 4:9-10
nIsa 66:9
13:14
oPs 49:15;
Eze 37:12-13
p1Co 15:55*
13:15
qHos 10:1
rEze 19:12
sJer 51:36
tJer 20:5
13:16
uHos 10:2
vHos 7:14
wHos 11:6
x2Ki 8:12;
Hos 10:14
y2Ki 15:16;
Isa 13:16

---

a4 Or God / *ever since you were in*   b14 Hebrew *Sheol*

Repentance to Bring Blessing

14 Return, O Israel, to the LORD your God.
　　Your sins have been your downfall![z]
²Take words with you
　　and return to the LORD.
Say to him:
　　"Forgive all our sins
and receive us graciously,[a]
　　that we may offer the fruit of our lips.[a][b]
³Assyria cannot save us;
　　we will not mount war-horses.[c]
We will never again say 'Our gods'[d]
　　to what our own hands have made,
　　for in you the fatherless[e] find compassion."

⁴"I will heal[f] their waywardness
　　and love them freely,[g]
　　for my anger has turned away from them.
⁵I will be like the dew to Israel;
　　he will blossom like a lily.[h]
Like a cedar of Lebanon[i]
　　he will send down his roots;[j]
⁶　his young shoots will grow.
His splendor will be like an olive tree,[k]
　　his fragrance like a cedar of Lebanon.[l]
⁷Men will dwell again in his shade.[m]
　　He will flourish like the grain.
He will blossom like a vine,
　　and his fame will be like the wine[n] from Lebanon.[o]
⁸O Ephraim, what more have I[b] to do with idols?[p]
　　I will answer him and care for him.
I am like a green pine tree;
　　your fruitfulness comes from me."

⁹Who is wise?[q] He will realize these things.
　　Who is discerning? He will understand them.[r]
The ways of the LORD are right;[s]
　　the righteous walk[t] in them,
　　but the rebellious stumble in them.

14:1
zHos 5:5
14:2
aMic 7:18-19
bHeb 13:15
14:3
cPs 33:17;
Isa 31:1
dHos 8:6
ePs 10:14; 68:5
14:4
fHos 6:1
gZep 3:17
14:5
hSS 2:1
iIsa 35:2
jJob 29:19
14:6
kPs 52:8;
Jer 11:16
lSS 4:11
14:7
mPs 91:1-4
nHos 2:22
oEze 17:23
14:8
pver 3
14:9
qPs 107:43
rPr 10:29;
Isa 1:28
sPs 111:7-8;
Zep 3:5;
Ac 13:10
tIsa 26:7

---

[a]2 Or *offer our lips as sacrifices of bulls*   [b]8 Or *What more has Ephraim*

Joel

Title and Background

Joel was a common Old Testament name meaning "The LORD is God." Locust plagues were frequent occurrences in the Near East for millennia, and Joel envisions one coming on Israel as a judgment from God.

Author and Date of Writing

The book contains no references to datable historical events, but a good case can be made for its being written about 830 B.C., during the reign of King Joash and at a time when Jehoiada the high priest was regent in Judah.

Theme and Message

Joel sees in the massive locust plague and severe drought devastating Judah a harbinger of the "great and dreadful day of the LORD" (2:31). Confronted with this crisis, he calls on everyone to repent. He sees this day as a day of punishment for unfaithful Israel as well as for her neighbors. Restoration and blessing will come only after judgment and repentance.

Outline

---

1 The word of the LORD that came^a to Joel^b son of Pethuel.

An Invasion of Locusts

²Hear this,^c you elders;
   listen, all who live in the land. ^d
Has anything like this ever happened in your days
   or in the days of your forefathers?^e
³Tell it to your children, ^f
   and let your children tell it to their children,
   and their children to the next generation.
⁴What the locust swarm has left
   the great locusts have eaten;
what the great locusts have left
   the young locusts have eaten;
what the young locusts have left

1:1
a Jer 1:2
b Ac 2:16
1:2
c Hos 5:1
d Hos 4:1
e Joel 2:2
1:3
f Ex 10:2;
Ps 78:4

other locusts^a have eaten.^g

⁵Wake up, you drunkards, and weep!
    Wail, all you drinkers of wine;^h
wail because of the new wine,
    for it has been snatched from your lips.
⁶A nation has invaded my land,
    powerful and without number;ⁱ
it has the teeth^j of a lion,
    the fangs of a lioness.
⁷It has laid waste^k my vines
    and ruined my fig trees.^l
It has stripped off their bark
    and thrown it away,
    leaving their branches white.

⁸Mourn like a virgin^b in sackcloth^m
    grieving for the husband^c of her youth.
⁹Grain offerings and drink offeringsⁿ
    are cut off from the house of the LORD.
The priests are in mourning,
    those who minister before the LORD.
¹⁰The fields are ruined,
    the ground is dried up^d;^o
the grain is destroyed,
    the new wine^p is dried up,
    the oil fails.
¹¹Despair, you farmers,^q
    wail, you vine growers;
grieve for the wheat and the barley,
    because the harvest of the field is destroyed.^r
¹²The vine is dried up
    and the fig tree is withered;
the pomegranate, the palm and the apple tree—
    all the trees of the field—are dried up.^s
Surely the joy of mankind
    is withered away.

A Call to Repentance

¹³Put on sackcloth,^t O priests, and mourn;
    wail, you who minister^u before the altar.
Come, spend the night in sackcloth,
    you who minister before my God;
for the grain offerings and drink offerings^v
    are withheld from the house of your God.
¹⁴Declare a holy fast;^w
    call a sacred assembly.
Summon the elders
    and all who live in the land
to the house of the LORD your God,

^a4 The precise meaning of the four Hebrew words used here for locusts is uncertain.   ^b8 Or
young woman   ^c8 Or *betrothed*   ^d10 Or *ground mourns*

and cry out[x] to the LORD.

15Alas for that[y] day!
  For the day of the LORD[z] is near;
  it will come like destruction from the Almighty.[a]

16Has not the food been cut off[a]
    before our very eyes—
  joy and gladness
    from the house of our God?[b]
17The seeds are shriveled
    beneath the clods.[b][c]
  The storehouses are in ruins,
    the granaries have been broken down,
    for the grain has dried up.
18How the cattle moan!
    The herds mill about
  because they have no pasture;
    even the flocks of sheep are suffering.

19To you, O LORD, I call,[d]
  for fire[e] has devoured the open pastures[f]
  and flames have burned up all the trees of the field.
20Even the wild animals pant for you;[g]
  the streams of water have dried up[h]
  and fire has devoured the open pastures.

An Army of Locusts

2 Blow the trumpet[i] in Zion;[j]
    sound the alarm on my holy hill.
  Let all who live in the land tremble,
    for the day of the LORD[k] is coming.
  It is close at hand[l]—
  2 a day of darkness[m] and gloom,[n]
    a day of clouds and blackness.
  Like dawn spreading across the mountains
    a large and mighty army[o] comes,
  such as never was of old[p]
    nor ever will be in ages to come.

3Before them fire devours,
    behind them a flame blazes.
  Before them the land is like the garden of Eden,[q]
    behind them, a desert waste[r]—
    nothing escapes them.
4They have the appearance of horses;[s]
    they gallop along like cavalry.
5With a noise like that of chariots[t]
    they leap over the mountaintops,
  like a crackling fire[u] consuming stubble,
    like a mighty army drawn up for battle.

---

a15 Hebrew *Shaddai*   *b17* The meaning of the Hebrew for this word is uncertain.

1:14
xJnh 3:8
1:15
yJer 30:7
zIsa 13:6,9;
Joel 2:1,11,31
1:16
aIsa 3:7
bDt 12:7
1:17
cIsa 17:10-11
1:19
dPs 50:15
eAm 7:4
fJer 9:10
1:20
gPs 104:21
h1Ki 17:7
2:1
iJer 4:5 jver 15
kJoel 1:15;
Zep 1:14-16
lOb 1:15
2:2
mAm 5:18
nDa 9:12
oJoel 1:6
pJoel 1:2
2:3
qGe 2:8
rPs 105:34-35
2:4
sRev 9:7
2:5
tRev 9:9
uIsa 5:24; 30:30

6At the sight of them, nations are in anguish;v
    every face turns pale. w
7They charge like warriors;
    they scale walls like soldiers.
They all march in line,
    not swervingx from their course.
8They do not jostle each other;
    each marches straight ahead.
They plunge through defenses
    without breaking ranks.
9They rush upon the city;
    they run along the wall.
They climb into the houses;
    like thieves they enter through the windows. y

10Before them the earth shakes,z
    the sky trembles,
the sun and moon are darkened,a
    and the stars no longer shine. b
11The Lordc thunders
    at the head of his army;
his forces are beyond number,
    and mighty are those who obey his command.
The day of the Lord is great;d
    it is dreadful.
    Who can endure it?e

Rend Your Heart

12"Even now," declares the Lord,
    "returnf to me with all your heart,
    with fasting and weeping and mourning."

13Rend your heartg
    and not your garments. h
Return to the Lord your God,
    for he is gracious and compassionate,
slow to anger and abounding in love,i
    and he relents from sending calamity.j
14Who knows? He may turnk and have pity
    and leave behind a blessingl —
grain offerings and drink offeringsm
    for the Lord your God.

15Blow the trumpetn in Zion,
    declare a holy fast,o
    call a sacred assembly. p
16Gather the people,
    consecrateq the assembly;
bring together the elders,
    gather the children,
    those nursing at the breast.
Let the bridegroomr leave his room
    and the bride her chamber.

2:6
vIsa 13:8
wNa 2:10
2:7
xIsa 5:27
2:9
yJer 9:21
2:10
zPs 18:7
aMt 24:29
bIsa 13:10;
Eze 32:8
2:11
cJoel 1:15
dZep 1:14;
Rev 18:8
eEze 22:14
2:12
fJer 4:1;
Hos 12:6
2:13
gPs 34:18;
Isa 57:15
hJob 1:20
iEx 34:6
jJer 18:8
2:14
kJer 26:3
lHag 2:19
mJoel 1:13
2:15
nNu 10:2
oJer 36:9
pJoel 1:14
2:16
qEx 19:10,22
rPs 19:5

¹⁷Let the priests, who minister before the Lord,
 weep between the temple porch and the altar. ˢ
Let them say, "Spare your people, O Lord.
 Do not make your inheritance an object of scorn, ᵗ
 a byword among the nations.
Why should they say among the peoples,
 'Where is their God?ᵘ' "

The Lord's Answer

¹⁸Then the Lord will be jealousᵛ for his land
 and take pity on his people.

¹⁹The Lord will replyᵃ to them:

 "I am sending you grain, new wine and oil, ʷ
  enough to satisfy you fully;
 never again will I make you
  an object of scornˣ to the nations.

²⁰"I will drive the northern armyʸ far from you,
 pushing it into a parched and barren land,
with its front columns going into the easternᶻ seaᵇ
 and those in the rear into the western sea. ᶜ
And its stenchᵃ will go up;
 its smell will rise."

Surely he has done great things. ᵈ
²¹ Be not afraid, ᵇ O land;
 be glad and rejoice.
Surely the Lord has done great things. ᶜ
²² Be not afraid, O wild animals,
 for the open pastures are becoming green. ᵈ
The trees are bearing their fruit;
 the fig tree and the vine yield their riches. ᵉ
²³Be glad, O people of Zion,
 rejoiceᶠ in the Lord your God,
for he has given you
 the autumn rains in righteousness. ᵉ
He sends you abundant showers,
 both autumn and spring rains, ᵍ as before.
²⁴The threshing floors will be filled with grain;
 the vats will overflowʰ with new wineⁱ and oil.

²⁵"I will repay you for the years the locusts have eaten—
 the great locust and the young locust,
 the other locusts and the locust swarmᶠ —
 my great army that I sent among you.
²⁶You will have plenty to eat, until you are full, ʲ
 and you will praiseᵏ the name of the Lord your God,
 who has worked wondersˡ for you;

ᵃ18,19 Or *Lord was jealous . . . / and took pity . . . / ¹⁹The Lord replied* ᵇ20 That is, the Dead Sea
ᶜ20 That is, the Mediterranean ᵈ20 Or *rise. / Surely it has done great things."* ᵉ23 Or / *the
teacher for righteousness:* ᶠ25 The precise meaning of the four Hebrew words used here for
locusts is uncertain.

2:17
ˢEze 8:16;
Mt 23:35
ᵗDt 9:26-29;
Ps 44:13
ᵘPs 42:3
2:18
ᵛZec 1:14
2:19
ʷJer 31:12
ˣEze 34:29
2:20
ʸJer 1:14-15
ᶻZec 14:8
ᵃIsa 34:3
2:21
ᵇIsa 54:4;
Zep 3:16-17
ᶜPs 126:3
2:22
ᵈPs 65:12
ᵉJoel 1:18-20
2:23
ᶠPs 149:2;
Isa 12:6; 41:16;
Hab 3:18;
Zec 10:7
ᵍLev 26:4
2:24
ʰLev 26:10;
Mal 3:10
ⁱAm 9:13
2:26
ʲLev 26:5
ᵏIsa 62:9
ˡPs 126:3;
Isa 25:1

never again will my people be shamed.
²⁷Then you will know that I am in Israel,
　　that I am the LORD^m your God,
　　and that there is no other;
never again will my people be shamed.

The Day of the LORD

²⁸"And afterward,
　　I will pour out my Spiritⁿ on all people.
Your sons and daughters will prophesy,
　　your old men will dream dreams,
　　your young men will see visions.
²⁹Even on my servants,^o both men and women,
　　I will pour out my Spirit in those days.
³⁰I will show wonders in the heavens^p
　　and on the earth,^q
　　blood and fire and billows of smoke.
³¹The sun will be turned to darkness^r
　　and the moon to blood
　　before the coming of the great and dreadful day of the
　　　　LORD.^s
³²And everyone who calls
　　on the name of the LORD will be saved;^t
for on Mount Zion^u and in Jerusalem
　　there will be deliverance,^v
　　as the LORD has said,
among the survivors^w
　　whom the LORD calls.

The Nations Judged

3 "In those days and at that time,
　　when I restore the fortunes^x of Judah and Jerusalem,
²I will gather all nations
　　and bring them down to the Valley of Jehoshaphat.^a
There I will enter into judgment^y against them
　　concerning my inheritance, my people Israel,
for they scattered my people among the nations
　　and divided up my land.
³They cast lots for my people
　　and traded boys for prostitutes;
they sold girls for wine^z
　　that they might drink.

⁴"Now what have you against me, O Tyre and Sidon^a and all you regions of Philistia? Are you repaying me for something I have done? If you are paying me back, I will swiftly and speedily return on your own heads what you have done.^b ⁵For you took my silver and my gold and carried off my finest treasures to your temples.^c ⁶You sold the people of Judah and Jerusalem to the Greeks, that you might send them far from their homeland.

---

^a2 *Jehoshaphat* means *the LORD judges;* also in verse 12.

2:27
m Joel 3:17
2:28
n Eze 39:29
2:29
o 1Co 12:13;
Gal 3:28
2:30
p Lk 21:11
q Mk 13:24-25
2:31
r Mt 24:29
s Isa 13:9-10;
Mal 4:1,5
2:32
t Ac 2:17-21*;
Ro 10:13*
u Isa 46:13
v Ob 1:17
w Isa 11:11;
Mic 4:7;
Ro 9:27
3:1
x Jer 16:15
3:2
y Eze 36:5
3:3
z Am 2:6
3:4
a Mt 11:21
b Isa 34:8
3:5
c 2Ch 21:16-17

7"See, I am going to rouse them out of the places to which you sold them, d and I will return on your own heads what you have done. 8I will sell your sons e and daughters to the people of Judah, f and they will sell them to the Sabeans, a nation far away." The LORD has spoken.

9Proclaim this among the nations:
  Prepare for war! g
Rouse the warriors! h
  Let all the fighting men draw near and attack.
10Beat your plowshares into swords
  and your pruning hooks i into spears.
Let the weakling j say,
  "I am strong!"
11Come quickly, all you nations from every side,
  and assemble k there.

Bring down your warriors, l O LORD!

12"Let the nations be roused;
  let them advance into the Valley of Jehoshaphat,
for there I will sit
  to judge m all the nations on every side.
13Swing the sickle,
  for the harvest n is ripe.
Come, trample the grapes,
  for the winepress o is full
  and the vats overflow—
so great is their wickedness!"

14Multitudes, multitudes
  in the valley of decision!
For the day of the LORD p is near
  in the valley of decision.
15The sun and moon will be darkened,
  and the stars no longer shine.
16The LORD will roar from Zion
  and thunder from Jerusalem; q
  the earth and the sky will tremble. r
But the LORD will be a refuge for his people,
  a stronghold s for the people of Israel.

Blessings for God's People

17"Then you will know that I, the LORD your God, t
  dwell in Zion, u my holy hill.
Jerusalem will be holy;
  never again will foreigners invade her.

18"In that day the mountains will drip new wine,
  and the hills will flow with milk; v
all the ravines of Judah will run with water. w
A fountain will flow out of the LORD's house x
  and will water the valley of acacias. a y

a18 Or *Valley of Shittim*

3:7
d Isa 43:5-6;
Jer 23:8
3:8
e Isa 60:14
f Isa 14:2
3:9
g Isa 8:9
h Jer 46:4
3:10
i Isa 2:4;
Mic 4:3
j Zec 12:8
3:11
k Eze 38:15-16;
Zep 3:8
l Isa 13:3
3:12
m Isa 2:4
3:13
n Hos 6:11;
Mt 13:39;
Rev 14:15-19
o Rev 14:20
3:14
p Isa 34:2-8;
Joel 1:15
3:16
q Am 1:2
r Eze 38:19
s Jer 16:19
3:17
t Joel 2:27
u Isa 4:3
3:18
v Ex 3:8
w Isa 30:25;
35:6
x Rev 22:1-2
y Eze 47:1;
Am 9:13

3:19
zOb 1:10
3:20
aAm 9:15
3:21
bEze 36:25

¹⁹But Egypt will be desolate,
  Edom a desert waste,
because of violenceᶻ done to the people of Judah,
  in whose land they shed innocent blood.
²⁰Judah will be inhabited foreverᵃ
  and Jerusalem through all generations.
²¹Their bloodguilt, which I have not pardoned,
  I will pardon.ᵇ"

        The LORD dwells in Zion!

Amos

Title and Background

The concurrent reigns of Uzziah of Judah and Jeroboam II of Israel were marked by a period of peace and prosperity. Prosperity was accompanied by an almost unprecedented degree of social corruption, and it is to this that the book of Amos is addressed.

Author and Date of Writing

Amos was a herdsman from the small town of Tekoa; he was not a man of the court like Isaiah, or a priest like Jeremiah. Though he lived in Judah, he was sent to announce God's judgment on the northern kingdom (Israel). Amos prophesied during the reigns of Uzziah and Jeroboam II. The main part of his ministry was probably carried out about 760-750 B.C., and this book can be dated during that time.

Theme and Message

The dominant theme is clearly stated in 5:24, which calls for social justice as the indispensable expression of true piety. Amos was a vigorous spokesman for God's justice and righteousness. He condemns all who make themselves powerful or rich at the expense of others.

Outline

    I. Judgments on Israel's Neighbors (1:1-2:5)
   II. Judgment on Israel (2:6-16)
  III. Oracles Against Israel (3:1-5:17)
  IV. Announcements of Exile (5:18-6:14)
   V. Visions of Divine Retribution (7:1-9:10)
  VI. Restoration of Israel (9:11-15)

---

1 The words of Amos, one of the shepherds of Tekoa[a]—what he saw concerning Israel two years before the earthquake,[b] when Uzziah[c] was king of Judah and Jeroboam[d] son of Jehoash[a] was king of Israel.[e] ²He said:

> "The LORD roars[f] from Zion
>   and thunders from Jerusalem;[g]
> the pastures of the shepherds dry up,[b]
>   and the top of Carmel[h] withers."[i]

Judgment on Israel's Neighbors

³This is what the LORD says:

> "For three sins of Damascus,[j]
>   even for four, I will not turn back ⌊my wrath⌋.[k]
> Because she threshed Gilead

1:1
a2Sa 14:2
bZec 14:5
c2Ch 26:23
d2Ki 14:23
eHos 1:1
1:2
fIsa 42:13
gJoel 3:16
hAm 9:3
iJer 12:4
1:3
jIsa 8:4; 17:1-3
kAm 2:6

---

a1 Hebrew Joash, a variant of Jehoash   b2 Or shepherds mourn

with sledges having iron teeth,
4I will send fire[1] upon the house of Hazael
    that will consume the fortresses[m] of Ben-Hadad.[n]
5I will break down the gate[o] of Damascus;
    I will destroy the king who is in[a] the Valley of Aven[b]
and the one who holds the scepter in Beth Eden.
    The people of Aram will go into exile to Kir,[p]"
                says the LORD.

6This is what the LORD says:

    "For three sins of Gaza,[q]
       even for four, I will not turn back ⌞my wrath⌟.
    Because she took captive whole communities
       and sold them to Edom,[r]
7I will send fire upon the walls of Gaza
    that will consume her fortresses.
8I will destroy the king[c] of Ashdod[s]
    and the one who holds the scepter in Ashkelon.
I will turn my hand[t] against Ekron,
    till the last of the Philistines[u] is dead,"
            says the Sovereign LORD.[v]

9This is what the LORD says:

    "For three sins of Tyre,[w]
       even for four, I will not turn back ⌞my wrath⌟.
    Because she sold whole communities of captives to
       Edom,
       disregarding a treaty of brotherhood,
10I will send fire upon the walls of Tyre
    that will consume her fortresses.[x]"

11This is what the LORD says:

    "For three sins of Edom,[y]
       even for four, I will not turn back ⌞my wrath⌟.
    Because he pursued his brother with a sword,
       stifling all compassion,[d]
    because his anger raged continually
       and his fury flamed unchecked,[z]
12I will send fire upon Teman[a]
    that will consume the fortresses of Bozrah."

13This is what the LORD says:

    "For three sins of Ammon,[b]
       even for four, I will not turn back ⌞my wrath⌟.
    Because he ripped open the pregnant women[c] of Gilead
       in order to extend his borders,
14I will set fire to the walls of Rabbah[d]
    that will consume her fortresses
    amid war cries[e] on the day of battle,

1:4
l Jer 49:27
m Jer 17:27
n 1Ki 20:1;
2Ki 6:24
1:5
o Jer 51:30
p 2Ki 16:9
1:6
q 1Sa 6:17;
Zep 2:4
r Ob 1:11
1:8
s 2Ch 26:6
t Ps 81:14
u Eze 25:16
v Isa 14:28-32;
Zep 2:4-7
1:9
w 1Ki 5:1;
9:11-14;
Isa 23:1-18;
Jer 25:22;
Joel 3:4;
Mt 11:21
1:10
x Zec 9:1-4
1:11
y Nu 20:14-21;
2Ch 28:17;
Jer 49:7-22
z Eze 25:12-14
1:12
a Ob 1:9-10
1:13
b Jer 49:1-6;
Eze 21:28;
25:2-7
c Hos 13:16
1:14
d Dt 3:11
e Am 2:2

---

[a]5 Or *the inhabitants of*   [b]5 *Aven* means *wickedness.*   [c]8 Or *inhabitants*   [d]11 Or *sword / and*
destroyed his allies

amid violent winds on a stormy day.
    [15] Her king[a] will go into exile,
        he and his officials together,"

                                    says the LORD.

2 This is what the LORD says:

    "For three sins of Moab,
        even for four, I will not turn back ⌊my wrath⌋.
    Because he burned, as if to lime,
        the bones of Edom's king,
    [2] I will send fire upon Moab
        that will consume the fortresses of Kerioth. [b]
    Moab will go down in great tumult
        amid war cries and the blast of the trumpet.
    [3] I will destroy her ruler[f]
        and kill all her officials with him,"[g]

                                    says the LORD.

[4] This is what the LORD says:

    "For three sins of Judah, [h]
        even for four, I will not turn back ⌊my wrath⌋.
    Because they have rejected the law[i] of the LORD
        and have not kept his decrees,[j]
    because they have been led astray[k] by false gods, [c][l]
        the gods[d] their ancestors followed,[m]
    [5] I will send fire upon Judah
        that will consume the fortresses of Jerusalem. [n]"

Judgment on Israel

[6] This is what the LORD says:

    "For three sins of Israel,
        even for four, I will not turn back ⌊my wrath⌋.
    They sell the righteous for silver,
        and the needy for a pair of sandals. [o]
    [7] They trample on the heads of the poor
        as upon the dust of the ground
        and deny justice to the oppressed.
    Father and son use the same girl
        and so profane my holy name. [p]
    [8] They lie down beside every altar
        on garments taken in pledge. [q]
    In the house of their god
        they drink wine[r] taken as fines.

    [9] "I destroyed the Amorite[s] before them,
        though he was tall as the cedars
        and strong as the oaks.
    I destroyed his fruit above
        and his roots[t] below.

2:3	
fPs 2:10	
gIsa 40:23	
2:4	
h2Ki 17:19;	
Hos 12:2	
iJer 6:19	
jEze 20:24	
kIsa 9:16	
lIsa 28:15	
m2Ki 22:13;	
Jer 16:12	
2:5	
nJer 17:27;	
Hos 8:14	
2:6	
oJoel 3:3;	
Am 8:6	
2:7	
pAm 5:11-12;	
8:4	
2:8	
qEx 22:26	
rAm 4:1; 6:6	
2:9	
sNu 21:23-26;	
Jos 10:12	
tEze 17:9;	
Mal 4:1	

[a]15 Or / Molech; Hebrew *malcam*   [b]2 Or *of her cities*   [c]4 Or *by lies*   [d]4 Or *lies*

[10]"I brought you up out of Egypt, [u]
    and I led you forty years in the desert[v]
    to give you the land of the Amorites. [w]
[11]I also raised up prophets[x] from among your sons
    and Nazirites[y] from among your young men.
    Is this not true, people of Israel?"

                     declares the LORD.

[12]"But you made the Nazirites drink wine
    and commanded the prophets not to prophesy. [z]

[13]"Now then, I will crush you
    as a cart crushes when loaded with grain.
[14]The swift will not escape,
    the strong[a] will not muster their strength,
    and the warrior will not save his life. [b]
[15]The archer[c] will not stand his ground,
    the fleet-footed soldier will not get away,
    and the horseman will not save his life.
[16]Even the bravest warriors[d]
    will flee naked on that day,"

                     declares the LORD.

Witnesses Summoned Against Israel

3 Hear this word the LORD has spoken against you, O people of Israel—against the whole family I brought up out of Egypt:[e]

[2]"You only have I chosen[f]
    of all the families of the earth;
therefore I will punish you
    for all your sins.[g]"

[3]Do two walk together
    unless they have agreed to do so?
[4]Does a lion roar in the thicket
    when he has no prey?[h]
Does he growl in his den
    when he has caught nothing?
[5]Does a bird fall into a trap on the ground
    where no snare has been set?
Does a trap spring up from the earth
    when there is nothing to catch?
[6]When a trumpet sounds in a city,
    do not the people tremble?
When disaster comes to a city,
    has not the LORD caused it?[i]

[7]Surely the Sovereign LORD does nothing
    without revealing his plan[j]
    to his servants the prophets. [k]

[8]The lion has roared—
    who will not fear?
The Sovereign LORD has spoken—
    who can but prophesy?[l]

2:10
[u]Ex 20:2;
Am 3:1 [v]Dt 2:7
[w]Ex 3:8;
Am 9:7
2:11
[x]Dt 18:18;
Jer 7:25
[y]Nu 6:2-3;
Jdg 13:5
2:12
[z]Isa 30:10;
Jer 11:21;
Am 7:12-13;
Mic 2:6
2:14
[a]Jer 9:23
[b]Ps 33:16;
Isa 30:16-17
2:15
[c]Eze 39:3
2:16
[d]Jer 48:41
3:1
[e]Am 2:10
3:2
[f]Dt 7:6;
Lk 12:47
[g]Jer 14:10
3:4
[h]Ps 104:21;
Hos 5:14
3:6
[i]Isa 14:24-27;
45:7
3:7
[j]Ge 18:17;
Da 9:22;
Jn 15:15;
Rev 10:7
[k]Jer 23:22
3:8
[l]Jer 20:9;
Jnh 1:1-3;
3:1-3; Ac 4:20

[9]Proclaim to the fortresses of Ashdod
  and to the fortresses of Egypt:
"Assemble yourselves on the mountains of Samaria;[m]
  see the great unrest within her
  and the oppression among her people."

[10]"They do not know how to do right,[n]" declares the
    Lord,
"who hoard plunder[o] and loot in their fortresses."[p]

[11]Therefore this is what the Sovereign Lord says:

"An enemy will overrun the land;
  he will pull down your strongholds
  and plunder your fortresses.[q]"

[12]This is what the Lord says:

"As a shepherd saves from the lion's[r] mouth
  only two leg bones or a piece of an ear,
  so will the Israelites be saved,
those who sit in Samaria
  on the edge of their beds
  and in Damascus on their couches.[a][s]"

[13]"Hear this and testify[t] against the house of Jacob," declares the
Lord, the Lord God Almighty.

[14]"On the day I punish Israel for her sins,
  I will destroy the altars of Bethel;[u]
the horns of the altar will be cut off
  and fall to the ground.
[15]I will tear down the winter house[v]
  along with the summer house;[w]
the houses adorned with ivory[x] will be destroyed
  and the mansions will be demolished,"
                declares the Lord.

Israel Has Not Returned to God

4   Hear this word, you cows of Bashan[y] on Mount Samaria,[z]
    you women who oppress the poor and crush the
      needy
    and say to your husbands, "Bring us some drinks![a]"
[2]The Sovereign Lord has sworn by his holiness:
  "The time will surely come
when you will be taken away[b] with hooks,
  the last of you with fishhooks.
[3]You will each go straight out
  through breaks in the wall,[c]
  and you will be cast out toward Harmon,[b]"
                declares the Lord.

[4]"Go to Bethel and sin;

---

[a]12 The meaning of the Hebrew for this line is uncertain.   [b]3 Masoretic Text; with a different
word division of the Hebrew (see Septuagint) *out, O mountain of oppression*

3:9
m Am 4:1; 6:1
3:10
n Jer 4:22;
Am 5:7; 6:12
o Hab 2:8
p Zep 1:9
3:11
q Am 2:5; 6:14
3:12
r 1Sa 17:34
s Am 6:4
3:13
t Eze 2:7
3:14
u Am 5:5-6
3:15
v Jer 36:22
w Jdg 3:20
x 1Ki 22:39
4:1
y Ps 22:12;
Eze 39:18
z Am 3:9
a Am 2:8; 5:11;
8:6
4:2
b Am 6:8
4:3
c Eze 12:5

go to Gilgal[d] and sin yet more.
Bring your sacrifices every morning,[e]
    your tithes[f] every three years.[a 8]
[5]Burn leavened bread[h] as a thank offering
    and brag about your freewill offerings[i] —
boast about them, you Israelites,
    for this is what you love to do,"

                      declares the Sovereign LORD.

[6]"I gave you empty stomachs[b] in every city
    and lack of bread in every town,
yet you have not returned to me,"

                          declares the LORD.[j]

[7]"I also withheld rain from you
    when the harvest was still three months away.
I sent rain on one town,
    but withheld it from another.[k]
One field had rain;
    another had none and dried up.
[8]People staggered from town to town for water[l]
    but did not get enough to drink,
yet you have not returned[m] to me,"

                          declares the LORD.[n]

[9]"Many times I struck your gardens and vineyards,
    I struck them with blight and mildew.[o]
Locusts devoured your fig and olive trees,[p]
    yet you have not returned[q] to me,"

                          declares the LORD.

[10]"I sent plagues[r] among you
    as I did to Egypt.
I killed your young men with the sword,
    along with your captured horses.
I filled your nostrils with the stench of your camps,
    yet you have not returned to me,"

                          declares the LORD.[s]

[11]"I overthrew some of you
    as I[c] overthrew Sodom and Gomorrah.[t]
You were like a burning stick snatched from the fire,
    yet you have not returned to me,"

                          declares the LORD.

[12]"Therefore this is what I will do to you, Israel,
    and because I will do this to you,
prepare to meet your God, O Israel."

[13]He who forms the mountains,[u]
    creates the wind,
    and reveals his thoughts[v] to man,
he who turns dawn to darkness,

4:4
d Hos 4:15
e Nu 28:3
f Dt 14:28
g Eze 20:39;
Am 5:21-22
4:5
h Lev 7:13
i Lev 22:18-21
4:6
j Isa 3:1;
Jer 5:3;
Hag 2:17
4:7
k Ex 9:4,26;
Dt 11:17;
2Ch 7:13
4:8
l Eze 4:16-17
m Jer 3:7
n Jer 14:4
4:9
o Dt 28:22
p Joel 1:7
q Jer 3:10;
Hag 2:17
4:10
r Ex 9:3;
Dt 28:27
s Isa 9:13
4:11
t Ge 19:24;
Jer 23:14
4:13
u Ps 65:6
v Da 2:28

---

[a]4 Or *tithes on the third day*   [b]6 Hebrew *you cleanness of teeth*   [c]11 Hebrew *God*

and treads the high places of the earth[w]—
the LORD God Almighty is his name.[x]

A Lament and Call to Repentance

5 Hear this word, O house of Israel, this lament[y] I take up concerning you:

2"Fallen is Virgin[z] Israel,
    never to rise again,
deserted in her own land,
    with no one to lift her up.[a]"

3This is what the Sovereign LORD says:

"The city that marches out a thousand strong for Israel
    will have only a hundred left;
the town that marches out a hundred strong
    will have only ten left.[b]"

4This is what the LORD says to the house of Israel:

"Seek me and live;[c]
5 do not seek Bethel,
do not go to Gilgal,[d]
    do not journey to Beersheba.[e]
For Gilgal will surely go into exile,
    and Bethel will be reduced to nothing.[a][f]"
6Seek[g] the LORD and live,[h]
    or he will sweep through the house of Joseph like a
        fire;[i]
it will devour,
    and Bethel[j] will have no one to quench it.

7You who turn justice into bitterness[k]
    and cast righteousness to the ground
8(he who made the Pleiades and Orion,[l]
    who turns blackness into dawn[m]
    and darkens day into night,[n]
who calls for the waters of the sea
    and pours them out over the face of the land—
    the LORD is his name[o]—
9he flashes destruction on the stronghold
    and brings the fortified city to ruin),[p]
10you hate the one who reproves in court[q]
    and despise him who tells the truth.[r]

11You trample on the poor[s]
    and force him to give you grain.
Therefore, though you have built stone mansions,[t]
    you will not live in them;
though you have planted lush vineyards,
    you will not drink their wine.[u]
12For I know how many are your offenses

4:13
wMic 1:3
xIsa 47:4;
Am 5:8,27; 9:6
5:1
yEze 19:1
5:2
zJer 14:17
aJer 50:32;
Am 8:14
5:3
bIsa 6:13;
Am 6:9
5:4
cIsa 55:3;
Jer 29:13
5:5
d1Sa 11:14;
Am 4:4
eAm 8:14
f1Sa 7:16
5:6
gIsa 55:6
hver 14 iDt 4:24
jAm 3:14
5:7
kAm 6:12
5:8
lJob 9:9
mIsa 42:16
nPs 104:20;
Am 8:9
oPs 104:6-9;
Am 4:13
5:9
pMic 5:11
5:10
qIsa 29:21
r1Ki 22:8
5:11
sAm 8:6
tAm 3:15
uMic 6:15

---

a5 Or *grief*; or *wickedness*; Hebrew *aven*, a reference to Beth Aven (a derogatory name for Bethel) and how great your sins.

You oppress the righteous and take bribes
and you deprive the poor of justice in the courts.[v]
¹³Therefore the prudent man keeps quiet in such times,
for the times are evil.

¹⁴Seek good, not evil,
that you may live.
Then the LORD God Almighty will be with you,
just as you say he is.
¹⁵Hate evil,[w] love good;
maintain justice in the courts.
Perhaps the LORD God Almighty will have mercy[x]
on the remnant[y] of Joseph.

¹⁶Therefore this is what the Lord, the LORD God Almighty, says:

"There will be wailing[z] in all the streets
and cries of anguish in every public square.
The farmers[a] will be summoned to weep
and the mourners to wail.
¹⁷There will be wailing in all the vineyards,
for I will pass through[b] your midst,"

says the LORD.[c]

The Day of the LORD

¹⁸Woe to you who long
for the day of the LORD![d]
Why do you long for the day of the LORD?
That day will be darkness,[e] not light.[f]
¹⁹It will be as though a man fled from a lion
only to meet a bear,
as though he entered his house
and rested his hand on the wall
only to have a snake bite him.[g]
²⁰Will not the day of the LORD be darkness, not light—
pitch-dark, without a ray of brightness?[h]

²¹"I hate, I despise your religious feasts;[i]
I cannot stand your assemblies.[j]
²²Even though you bring me burnt offerings and grain offerings,
I will not accept them.
Though you bring choice fellowship offerings,[a]
I will have no regard for them.[k][l]
²³Away with the noise of your songs!
I will not listen to the music of your harps.[m]
²⁴But let justice[n] roll on like a river,
righteousness like a never-failing stream![o]

²⁵"Did you bring me sacrifices[p] and offerings
forty years[q] in the desert, O house of Israel?

5:12
v Isa 5:23;
Am 2:6-7
5:15
w Ps 97:10;
Ro 12:9
x Joel 2:14
y Mic 5:7,8
5:16
z Jer 9:17
a Joel 1:11
5:17
b Ex 12:12
c Isa 16:10;
Jer 48:33
5:18
d Joel 1:15
e Joel 2:2
f Isa 5:19,30;
Jer 30:7
5:19
g Job 20:24;
Isa 24:17-18;
Jer 15:2-3;
48:44
5:20
h Isa 13:10;
Zep 1:15
5:21
i Lev 26:31
j Isa 1:11-16
5:22
k Am 4:4;
Mic 6:6-7
l Isa 66:3
5:23
m Am 6:5
5:24
n Jer 22:3
o Mic 6:8
5:25
p Isa 43:23
q Dt 32:17

a22 Traditionally peace offerings

26You have lifted up the shrine of your king,
    the pedestal of your idols,
    the star of your god[a] —
    which you made for yourselves.
27Therefore I will send you into exile beyond Damascus,"
    says the Lord, whose name is God Almighty.[r]

Woe to the Complacent

6 Woe to you[s] who are complacent in Zion,
    and to you who feel secure on Mount Samaria,
you notable men of the foremost nation,
    to whom the people of Israel come![t]
2Go to Calneh[u] and look at it;
    go from there to great Hamath,[v]
    and then go down to Gath[w] in Philistia.
Are they better off than[x] your two kingdoms?
    Is their land larger than yours?
3You put off the evil day
    and bring near a reign of terror.[y]
4You lie on beds inlaid with ivory
    and lounge on your couches.
You dine on choice lambs
    and fattened calves.[z]
5You strum away on your harps[a] like David
    and improvise on musical instruments.[b]
6You drink wine[c] by the bowlful
    and use the finest lotions,
    but you do not grieve[d] over the ruin of Joseph.
7Therefore you will be among the first to go into exile;
    your feasting and lounging will end.

The Lord Abhors the Pride of Israel

8The Sovereign Lord has sworn by himself[e]—the Lord God Almighty declares:

"I abhor[f] the pride of Jacob[g]
    and detest his fortresses;
I will deliver up[h] the city
    and everything in it.[i] "

9If ten[j] men are left in one house, they too will die. 10And if a relative who is to burn the bodies[k] comes to carry them out of the house and asks anyone still hiding there, "Is anyone with you?" and he says, "No," then he will say, "Hush![l] We must not mention the name of the Lord."

11For the Lord has given the command,
    and he will smash the great house[m] into pieces
    and the small house into bits.[n]

12Do horses run on the rocky crags?

---

[a]26 Or lifted up Sakkuth your king / and Kaiwan your idols, / your star-gods; Septuagint lifted up the shrine of Molech / and the star of your god Rephan, / their idols

5:27
[r]Am 4:13;
Ac 7:42-43*
6:1
[s]Lk 6:24
[t]Isa 32:9-11
6:2
[u]Ge 10:10
[v]2Ki 18:34
[w]2Ch 26:6
[x]Na 3:8
6:3
[y]Isa 56:12;
Am 9:10
6:4
[z]Eze 34:2-3;
Am 3:12
6:5
[a]Isa 5:12;
Am 5:23
[b]1Ch 15:16
6:6
[c]Am 2:8
[d]Eze 9:4
6:8
[e]Ge 22:16;
Heb 6:13
[f]Lev 26:30
[g]Ps 47:4
[h]Am 4:2
[i]Dt 32:19
6:9
[j]Am 5:3
6:10
[k]1Sa 31:12
[l]Am 8:3
6:11
[m]Am 3:15
[n]Isa 55:11

> Does one plow there with oxen?
> But you have turned justice into poison[o]
>   and the fruit of righteousness into bitterness[p]—
> [13]you who rejoice in the conquest of Lo Debar[a]
>   and say, "Did we not take Karnaim[b] by our own
>   strength?[q]"

> [14]For the LORD God Almighty declares,
>   "I will stir up a nation[r] against you, O house of Israel,
> that will oppress you all the way
>   from Lebo[c] Hamath[s] to the valley of the Arabah.[t] "

Locusts, Fire and a Plumb Line

7 This is what the Sovereign LORD showed me:[u] He was preparing swarms of locusts[v] after the king's share had been harvested and just as the second crop was coming up. [2]When they had stripped the land clean,[w] I cried out, "Sovereign LORD, forgive! How can Jacob survive?[x] He is so small![y]"

[3]So the LORD relented.[z]

"This will not happen," the LORD said.[a]

[4]This is what the Sovereign LORD showed me: The Sovereign LORD was calling for judgment by fire;[b] it dried up the great deep and devoured[c] the land. [5]Then I cried out, "Sovereign LORD, I beg you, stop! How can Jacob survive? He is so small![d]"

[6]So the LORD relented.[e]

"This will not happen either," the Sovereign LORD said.

[7]This is what he showed me: The Lord was standing by a wall that had been built true to plumb, with a plumb line in his hand. [8]And the LORD asked me, "What do you see,[f] Amos?[g]"

"A plumb line,[h]" I replied.

Then the Lord said, "Look, I am setting a plumb line among my people Israel; I will spare them no longer.[i]

> [9]"The high places of Isaac will be destroyed
>   and the sanctuaries[j] of Israel will be ruined;
> with my sword I will rise against the house of
>   Jeroboam.[k]"

Amos and Amaziah

[10]Then Amaziah the priest of Bethel[l] sent a message to Jeroboam[m] king of Israel: "Amos is raising a conspiracy[n] against you in the very heart of Israel. The land cannot bear all his words.[o] [11]For this is what Amos is saying:

> " 'Jeroboam will die by the sword,
>   and Israel will surely go into exile,
> away from their native land.' "

[12]Then Amaziah said to Amos, "Get out, you seer! Go back to the land of Judah. Earn your bread there and do your prophesying there.[p]

### Cross references (margin)

6:12
o Hos 10:4
p Am 5:7
6:13
q Job 8:15;
Isa 28:14-15
6:14
r Jer 5:15
s 1Ki 8:65
t Am 3:11
7:1
u Am 8:1
v Joel 1:4
7:2
w Ex 10:15
x Isa 37:4
y Eze 11:13
7:3
z Dt 32:36;
Jer 26:19;
Jnh 3:10
a Hos 11:8
7:4
b Isa 66:16
c Dt 32:22
7:5
d ver 1-2;
Joel 2:17
7:6
e Jnh 3:10
7:8
f Jer 1:11,13
g Isa 28:17;
La 2:8; Am 8:2
h 2Ki 21:13
i Jer 15:6;
Eze 7:2-9
7:9
j Lev 26:31
k 2Ki 15:9;
Isa 63:18;
Hos 10:8
7:10
l 1Ki 12:32
m 2Ki 14:23
n Jer 38:4
o Jer 26:8-11
7:12
p Mt 8:34

---

[a]13 *Lo Debar* means *nothing.*   [b]13 *Karnaim* means *horns; horn* here symbolizes strength.
[c]14 Or *from the entrance to*

¹³Don't prophesy anymore at Bethel, because this is the king's sanctuary and the temple of the kingdom.�q"

¹⁴Amos answered Amaziah, "I was neither a prophetʳ nor a prophet's son, but I was a shepherd, and I also took care of sycamore-fig trees. ¹⁵But the LORD took me from tending the flockˢ and said to me, 'Go, prophesy to my people Israel.'ᵗ ¹⁶Now then, hear the word of the LORD. You say,

> " 'Do not prophesy againstᵘ Israel,
> and stop preaching against the house of Isaac.'

¹⁷"Therefore this is what the LORD says:

> " 'Your wife will become a prostituteᵛ in the city,
> and your sons and daughters will fall by the sword.
> Your land will be measured and divided up,
> and you yourself will die in a paganᵃ country.
> And Israel will certainly go into exile,
> away from their native land.ʷ ' "

A Basket of Ripe Fruit

8 This is what the Sovereign LORD showed me: a basket of ripe fruit. ²"What do you see,ˣ Amos?ʸ" he asked.

"A basket of ripe fruit," I answered.

Then the LORD said to me, "The time is ripe for my people Israel; I will spare them no longer.ᶻ

³"In that day," declares the Sovereign LORD, "the songs in the temple will turn to wailing.ᵇᵃ Many, many bodies—flung everywhere! Silence!ᵇ"

> ⁴Hear this, you who trample the needy
> and do away with the poorᶜ of the land,ᵈ

⁵saying,

> "When will the New Moon be over
> that we may sell grain,
> and the Sabbath be ended
> that we may market wheat?"—
> skimping the measure,
> boosting the price
> and cheating with dishonest scales,ᵉ
> ⁶buying the poor with silver
> and the needy for a pair of sandals,
> selling even the sweepings with the wheat.ᶠ

⁷The LORD has sworn by the Pride of Jacob:ᵍ "I will never forgetʰ anything they have done.

> ⁸"Will not the land trembleⁱ for this,
> and all who live in it mourn?
> The whole land will rise like the Nile;
> it will be stirred up and then sink
> like the river of Egypt.ʲ

7:13
qAm 2:12;
Ac 4:18
7:14
r2Ki 2:5; 4:38
7:15
s2Sa 7:8
tJer 7:1-2;
Eze 2:3-4
7:16
uEze 20:46;
Mic 2:6
7:17
vHos 4:13
w2Ki 17:6;
Eze 4:13;
Hos 9:3
8:2
xJer 24:3
yAm 7:8
zEze 7:2-9
8:3
aAm 5:16
bAm 5:23; 6:10
8:4
cPr 30:14
dPs 14:4;
Am 2:7
8:5
e2Ki 4:23;
Ne 13:15-16;
Hos 12:7;
Mic 6:10-11
8:6
fAm 2:6
8:7
gAm 6:8
hHos 8:13
8:8
iHos 4:3
jPs 18:7;
Jer 46:8;
Am 9:5

ᵃ17 Hebrew *an unclean*   ᵇ3 Or *"the temple singers will wail"*

9"In that day," declares the Sovereign LORD,

> "I will make the sun go down at noon
> and darken the earth in broad daylight. k
> 10I will turn your religious feasts into mourning
> and all your singing into weeping.
> I will make all of you wear sackclothl
> and shave your heads.
> I will make that time like mourning for an only sonm
> and the end of it like a bitter day. n

11"The days are coming," declares the Sovereign LORD,
> "when I will send a famine through the land—
> not a famine of food or a thirst for water,
> but a famine of hearing the words of the LORD. o
> 12Men will stagger from sea to sea
> and wander from north to east,
> searching for the word of the LORD,
> but they will not find it. p

13"In that day

> "the lovely young women and strong young men
> will faint because of thirst. q
> 14They who swear by the shamea of Samaria,
> or say, 'As surely as your god lives, O Dan,'r
> or, 'As surely as the godb of Beershebas lives'—
> they will fall,
> never to rise again. t "

Israel to Be Destroyed

9 I saw the Lord standing by the altar, and he said:

> "Strike the tops of the pillars
> so that the thresholds shake.
> Bring them down on the headsu of all the people;
> those who are left I will kill with the sword.
> Not one will get away,
> none will escape.
> 2Though they dig down to the depths of the grave,c v
> from there my hand will take them.
> Though they climb up to the heavens,w
> from there I will bring them down. x
> 3Though they hide themselves on the top of Carmel,y
> there I will hunt them down and seize them. z
> Though they hide from me at the bottom of the sea,
> there I will command the serpent to bite them. a
> 4Though they are driven into exile by their enemies,
> there I will command the swordb to slay them.
> I will fix my eyes upon them
> for evilc and not for good. d "e

5The Lord, the LORD Almighty,

8:9
kJob 5:14;
Isa 59:9-10;
Jer 15:9;
Am 5:8;
Mic 3:6
8:10
lJer 48:37
mJer 6:26;
Zec 12:10
nEze 7:18
8:11
o1Sa 3:1;
2Ch 15:3;
Eze 7:26
8:12
pEze 20:3,31
8:13
qIsa 41:17;
Hos 2:3
8:14
r1Ki 12:29
sAm 5:5
tAm 5:2
9:1
uPs 68:21
9:2
vPs 139:8
wJer 51:53
xOb 1:4
9:3
yAm 1:2
zPs 139:8-10
aJer 16:16-17
9:4
bLev 26:33;
Eze 5:12
cJer 21:10
dJer 39:16
eJer 44:11

---

a14 Or *by Ashima; or by the idol*   b14 Or *power*   c2 Hebrew *to Sheol*

he who touches the earth and it melts, [f]
and all who live in it mourn—
the whole land rises like the Nile,
then sinks like the river of Egypt [g]—
[6]he who builds his lofty palace [a] in the heavens
and sets its foundation [b] on the earth,
who calls for the waters of the sea
and pours them out over the face of the land—
the Lord is his name. [h]

[7]"Are not you Israelites
the same to me as the Cushites [c] ?" [i]

                 declares the Lord.

"Did I not bring Israel up from Egypt,
the Philistines from Caphtor [d] [j]
and the Arameans from Kir? [k]

[8]"Surely the eyes of the Sovereign Lord
are on the sinful kingdom.
I will destroy it
from the face of the earth—
yet I will not totally destroy
the house of Jacob,"

                 declares the Lord. [l]

[9]"For I will give the command,
and I will shake the house of Israel
among all the nations
as grain [m] is shaken in a sieve, [n]
and not a pebble will reach the ground.
[10]All the sinners among my people
will die by the sword,
all those who say,
'Disaster will not overtake or meet us.' [o]

Israel's Restoration

[11]"In that day I will restore
David's fallen tent.
I will repair its broken places,
restore its ruins,
and build it as it used to be, [p]
[12]so that they may possess the remnant of Edom [q]
and all the nations that bear my name, [e] [r] "
         declares the Lord, who will do these things. [s]

[13]"The days are coming," declares the Lord,

"when the reaper will be overtaken by the plowman [t]
and the planter by the one treading grapes.
New wine will drip from the mountains

9:5
fPs 46:2;
Mic 1:4
gAm 8:8
9:6
hPs 104:1-3,5-6,
13; Am 5:8
9:7
iIsa 20:4; 43:3
jDt 2:23;
Jer 47:4
k2Ki 16:9;
Isa 22:6;
Am 1:5; 2:10
9:8
lJer 44:27
9:9
mLk 22:31
nIsa 30:28
9:10
oAm 6:3
9:11
pPs 80:12
9:12
qNu 24:18
rIsa 43:7
sAc 15:16-17*
9:13
tLev 26:5

---

[a]6 The meaning of the Hebrew for this phrase is uncertain.   [b]6 The meaning of the Hebrew for this word is uncertain.   [c]7 That is, people from the upper Nile region   [d]7 That is, Crete
[e]12 Hebrew; Septuagint *so that the remnant of men / and all the nations that bear my name may seek the Lord.*

9:13
u Joel 3:18
9:14
v Isa 61:4
w Jer 30:18;
31:28;
Eze 28:25-26
9:15
x Isa 60:21
y Jer 24:6;
Eze 34:25-28;
37:12,25

and flow from all the hills. u

¹⁴I will bring back my exiled[a] people Israel;
　　they will rebuild the ruined cities v and live in them.
　They will plant vineyards and drink their wine;
　　they will make gardens and eat their fruit. w
¹⁵I will plant x Israel in their own land,
　never again to be uprooted
　from the land I have given them,"

　　　　　　　says the LORD your God. y

---

[a] 14 Or *will restore the fortunes of my*

Obadiah

Title and Background

Obadiah's name means "servant of the Lord." The prophecy centers around an ancient feud between Edom and Israel. The Edomites were descendants of Esau, who carried a grudge against Israel because Jacob had cheated their ancestor out of his birthright.

Author and Date of Writing

The author is Obadiah. The date and place of composition are uncertain. A date between 853 and 841 B.C. is suggested by relating verses 11-14 to the invasion of Jerusalem by Philistines and Arabians during Jehoram's reign (2 Kings 8:20-22). An exilic date is arrived at by relating those verses to the Babylonian attacks on Jerusalem (605-586 B.C.).

Theme and Message

Its theme is that Edom is proud of her own security and has gloated over God's people when Israel was devastated by foreign powers, but her participation in that disaster will bring on God's wrath. Edom herself will be destroyed, but Mount Zion and Israel will be delivered, and God's kingdom will triumph.

Outline

---

¹The vision of Obadiah.

1-4pp — Jer 49:14-16
5-6pp — Jer 49:9-10

This is what the Sovereign Lord says about Edom[a] —

> We have heard a message from the Lord:
> An envoy[b] was sent to the nations to say,
> "Rise, and let us go against her for battle"[c] —
>
> ²"See, I will make you small among the nations;
> you will be utterly despised.
> ³The pride[d] of your heart has deceived you,
> you who live in the clefts of the rocks[a]
> and make your home on the heights,
> you who say to yourself,
> 'Who can bring me down to the ground?'[e]
> ⁴Though you soar like the eagle
> and make your nest[f] among the stars,
> from there I will bring you down,"[g]
> declares the Lord.[h]

1:1
a Isa 63:1-6;
Jer 49:7-22;
Eze 25:12-14;
Am 1:11-12
b Isa 18:2
c Jer 6:4-5
1:3
d Isa 16:6
e Isa 14:13-15;
Rev 18:7
1:4
f Hab 2:9
g Isa 14:13
h Job 20:6

a3 Or of Sela

⁵"If thieves came to you,
  if robbers in the night—
Oh, what a disaster awaits you—
  would they not steal only as much as they wanted?
If grape pickers came to you,
  would they not leave a few grapes?[i]
⁶But how Esau will be ransacked,
  his hidden treasures pillaged!
⁷All your allies[j] will force you to the border;
  your friends will deceive and overpower you;
those who eat your bread[k] will set a trap for you,[a]
  but you will not detect it.

⁸"In that day," declares the Lord,
  "will I not destroy[l] the wise men of Edom,
  men of understanding in the mountains of Esau?
⁹Your warriors, O Teman,[m] will be terrified,
  and everyone in Esau's mountains
  will be cut down in the slaughter.
¹⁰Because of the violence[n] against your brother Jacob,[o]
  you will be covered with shame;
  you will be destroyed forever.[p]
¹¹On the day you stood aloof
  while strangers carried off his wealth
and foreigners entered his gates
  and cast lots[q] for Jerusalem,
  you were like one of them.
¹²You should not look down on your brother
  in the day of his misfortune,
nor rejoice[r] over the people of Judah
  in the day of their destruction,[s]
nor boast so much
  in the day of their trouble.[t]
¹³You should not march through the gates of my people
  in the day of their disaster,
nor look down on them in their calamity[u]
  in the day of their disaster,
nor seize their wealth
  in the day of their disaster.
¹⁴You should not wait at the crossroads
  to cut down their fugitives,
nor hand over their survivors
  in the day of their trouble.

¹⁵"The day of the Lord is near[v]
  for all nations.
As you have done, it will be done to you;
  your deeds[w] will return upon your own head.
¹⁶Just as you drank on my holy hill,
  so all the nations will drink[x] continually;
  they will drink and drink

1:5	iDt 24:21
1:7	jJer 30:14
	kPs 41:9
1:8	lJob 5:12;
	Isa 29:14
1:9	mGe 36:11,34
1:10	nJoel 3:19
	oPs 137:7;
	Am 1:11-12
	pEze 35:9
1:11	qNa 3:10
1:12	rEze 35:15
	sPr 17:5
	tMic 4:11
1:13	uEze 35:5
1:15	vEze 30:3
	wJer 50:29;
	Hab 2:8
1:16	xJer 25:15;
	49:12

---

[a]7 The meaning of the Hebrew for this clause is uncertain.

and be as if they had never been.
17But on Mount Zion will be deliverance;y
    it will be holy,z
and the house of Jacob
    will possess its inheritance.
18The house of Jacob will be a fire
    and the house of Joseph a flame;
the house of Esau will be stubble,
    and they will set it on fire and consumea it.
There will be no survivors
    from the house of Esau.''

The LORD has spoken.

19People from the Negev will occupy
    the mountains of Esau,
and people from the foothills will possess
    the land of the Philistines. b
They will occupy the fields of Ephraim and Samaria, c
    and Benjamin will possess Gilead.
20This company of Israelite exiles who are in Canaan
    will possess the land as far as Zarephath;d
the exiles from Jerusalem who are in Sepharad
    will possess the towns of the Negev. e
21Deliverers will go up ona Mount Zion
    to govern the mountains of Esau.
    And the kingdom will be the LORD's. f

1:17
yAm 9:11-15
zIsa 4:3
1:18
aZec 12:6
1:19
bIsa 11:14
cJer 31:5
1:20
d1Ki 17:9-10
eJer 33:13
1:21
fPs 22:28;
Zec 14:9,16;
Rev 11:15

a21 Or *from*

Jonah

Title and Background

The book is named after its principal character, whose name means "dove." The events in the book took place probably during the eighth century, when the Assyrians were a feared and despised enemy.

Author and Date of Writing

Traditionally, the book has been ascribed to Jonah son of Amittai, though nowhere in the book is it plainly stated. To accept that the book is authored by Jonah would necessitate a date no later than the third quarter of the eighth century B.C.

Theme and Message

The theme that runs throughout the four chapters of the book is God's great mercy to Gentile nations through repentance. The book also depicts the larger scope of God's purpose for Israel: that she might rediscover the truth of his concern for the whole creation and that she might better understand her own role in carrying out that concern.

Outline

Jonah Flees From the LORD

1 The word of the LORD came to Jonah[a] son of Amittai:[b] 2"Go to the great city of Nineveh[c] and preach against it, because its wickedness has come up before me."

3But Jonah ran[d] away from the LORD and headed for Tarshish. He went down to Joppa,[e] where he found a ship bound for that port. After paying the fare, he went aboard and sailed for Tarshish to flee from the LORD.

4Then the LORD sent a great wind on the sea, and such a violent storm arose that the ship threatened to break up.[f] 5All the sailors were afraid and each cried out to his own god. And they threw the cargo into the sea to lighten the ship.[g]

But Jonah had gone below deck, where he lay down and fell into a deep sleep. 6The captain went to him and said, "How can you sleep?

1:1
a Mt 12:39-41
b 2Ki 14:25
1:2
c Ge 10:11
1:3
d Ps 139:7
e Jos 19:46;
Ac 9:36,43
1:4
f Ps 107:23-26
1:5
g Ac 27:18-19

Get up and call[h] on your god! Maybe he will take notice of us, and we will not perish."[i]

[7]Then the sailors said to each other, "Come, let us cast lots to find out who is responsible for this calamity."[j] They cast lots and the lot fell on Jonah.

[8]So they asked him, "Tell us, who is responsible for making all this trouble for us? What do you do? Where do you come from? What is your country? From what people are you?"

[9]He answered, "I am a Hebrew and I worship the LORD, the God of heaven,[k] who made the sea and the land.[l]"

[10]This terrified them and they asked, "What have you done?" (They knew he was running away from the LORD, because he had already told them so.)

[11]The sea was getting rougher and rougher. So they asked him, "What should we do to you to make the sea calm down for us?"

[12]"Pick me up and throw me into the sea," he replied, "and it will become calm. I know that it is my fault that this great storm has come upon you."[m]

[13]Instead, the men did their best to row back to land. But they could not, for the sea grew even wilder than before.[n] [14]Then they cried to the LORD, "O LORD, please do not let us die for taking this man's life. Do not hold us accountable for killing an innocent man,[o] for you, O LORD, have done as you pleased."[p] [15]Then they took Jonah and threw him overboard, and the raging sea grew calm.[q] [16]At this the men greatly feared[r] the LORD, and they offered a sacrifice to the LORD and made vows to him.

[17]But the LORD provided a great fish to swallow Jonah,[s] and Jonah was inside the fish three days and three nights.

Jonah's Prayer

2 From inside the fish Jonah prayed to the LORD his God. [2]He said:

"In my distress I called to the LORD,[t]
    and he answered me.
From the depths of the grave[a] I called for help,
    and you listened to my cry.
[3]You hurled me into the deep,[u]
    into the very heart of the seas,
    and the currents swirled about me;
all your waves and breakers
    swept over me.[v]
[4]I said, 'I have been banished
    from your sight;[w]
yet I will look again
    toward your holy temple.'
[5]The engulfing waters threatened me,[b]
    the deep surrounded me;
    seaweed was wrapped around my head.[x]
[6]To the roots of the mountains I sank down;
    the earth beneath barred me in forever.

1:6
h Jnh 3:8
i Ps 107:28
1:7
j Jos 7:10-18;
1Sa 14:42
1:9
k Ac 17:24
l Ps 146:6
1:12
m 2Sa 24:17;
1Ch 21:17
1:13
n Pr 21:30
1:14
o Dt 21:8
p Ps 115:3
1:15
q Ps 107:29;
Lk 8:24
1:16
r Mk 4:41
1:17
s Mt 12:40;
16:4; Lk 11:30
2:2
t Ps 18:6; 120:1
2:3
u Ps 88:6
v Ps 42:7
2:4
w Ps 31:22
2:5
x Ps 69:1-2

a 2 Hebrew *Sheol*   b 5 Or *waters were at my throat*

But you brought my life up from the pit,
   O LORD my God.

7"When my life was ebbing away,
   I remembered[y] you, LORD,
and my prayer[z] rose to you,
   to your holy temple.[a]

8"Those who cling to worthless idols[b]
   forfeit the grace that could be theirs.
9But I, with a song of thanksgiving,
   will sacrifice[c] to you.
What I have vowed[d] I will make good.
   Salvation[e] comes from the LORD."

10And the LORD commanded the fish, and it vomited Jonah onto dry land.

Jonah Goes to Nineveh

3 Then the word of the LORD came to Jonah[f] a second time: 2"Go to the great city of Nineveh and proclaim to it the message I give you."

3Jonah obeyed the word of the LORD and went to Nineveh. Now Nineveh was a very important city—a visit required three days. 4On the first day, Jonah started into the city. He proclaimed: "Forty more days and Nineveh will be overturned." 5The Ninevites believed God. They declared a fast, and all of them, from the greatest to the least, put on sackcloth.[g]

6When the news reached the king of Nineveh, he rose from his throne, took off his royal robes, covered himself with sackcloth and sat down in the dust.[h] 7Then he issued a proclamation in Nineveh:

"By the decree of the king and his nobles:

Do not let any man or beast, herd or flock, taste anything; do not let them eat or drink.[i] 8But let man and beast be covered with sackcloth. Let everyone call[j] urgently on God. Let them give up their evil ways and their violence. 9Who knows?[k] God may yet relent and with compassion turn[l] from his fierce anger so that we will not perish."

10When God saw what they did and how they turned from their evil ways, he had compassion[m] and did not bring upon them the destruction[n] he had threatened.[o]

Jonah's Anger at the LORD's Compassion

4 But Jonah was greatly displeased and became angry.[p] 2He prayed to the LORD, "O LORD, is this not what I said when I was still at home? That is why I was so quick to flee to Tarshish. I knew[q] that you are a gracious and compassionate God, slow to anger and abounding in love,[r] a God who relents from sending calamity.[s] 3Now, O LORD, take away my life,[t] for it is better for me to die[u] than to live."

4But the LORD replied, "Have you any right to be angry?"[v]

5Jonah went out and sat down at a place east of the city. There he made himself a shelter, sat in its shade and waited to see what would happen to the city. 6Then the LORD God provided a vine and made it grow up over Jonah to give shade for his head to ease his discomfort, and Jonah was very happy about the vine. [7]But at dawn the next day God provided a worm, which chewed the vine so that it withered. [w] [8]When the sun rose, God provided a scorching east wind, and the sun blazed on Jonah's head so that he grew faint. He wanted to die, and said, "It would be better for me to die than to live."

[9]But God said to Jonah, "Do you have a right to be angry about the vine?"

"I do," he said. "I am angry enough to die."

[10]But the Lord said, "You have been concerned about this vine, though you did not tend it or make it grow. It sprang up overnight and died overnight. [11]But Nineveh[x] has more than a hundred and twenty thousand people who cannot tell their right hand from their left, and many cattle as well. Should I not be concerned[y] about that great city?"

4:7
w Joel 1:12
4:11
x Jnh 1:2; 3:2
y Jnh 3:10

Micah

Title and Background

The book is named after Micah, a shortened form of Micaiah, meaning "Who is like the LORD?" Judah had enjoyed comparative economic prosperity when Micah came on the scene. This prosperity placed wealth and power in the hands of a few and brought with it social injustice.

Author and Date of Writing

Little is known about Micah beyond what can be learned from the book itself. He was deeply sensitive to the social ills of his day, especially as they affected the small towns and villages of his homeland. Micah prophesied sometime between 750 and 686 B.C., and his book was written prior to 686.

Theme and Message

Micah's message alternated between oracles of doom and oracles of hope. The theme is judgment and deliverance by God. Micah also stresses that God hates idolatry, injustice, rebellion and empty ritualism, but he delights in pardoning the penitent.

Outline

I. Judgment Against Israel and Judah (1:1-3:12)
II. Hope for Israel and Judah (4:1-5:15)
III. The Lord's Case Against Israel (6:1-16)
IV. Gloom Turns to Triumph (7:1-20)

---

1 The word of the LORD that came to Micah of Moresheth[a] during the reigns of Jotham,[b] Ahaz[c] and Hezekiah, kings of Judah[d]—the vision[e] he saw concerning Samaria and Jerusalem.

1:1
a Jer 26:18
b 1Ch 3:12
c 1Ch 3:13
d Hos 1:1
e Isa 1:1

²Hear, O peoples, all of you,[f]
    listen, O earth[g] and all who are in it,
that the Sovereign LORD may witness[h] against you,
    the Lord from his holy temple.[i]

1:2
f Ps 50:7
g Jer 6:19
h Ge 31:50;
Dt 4:26; Isa 1:2
i Ps 11:4

Judgment Against Samaria and Jerusalem

³Look! The LORD is coming from his dwelling[j] place;
    he comes down and treads the high places of the
        earth.[k]

1:3
j Isa 18:4
k Am 4:13

⁴The mountains melt[l] beneath him
    and the valleys split apart,[m]
like wax before the fire,
    like water rushing down a slope.
⁵All this is because of Jacob's transgression,
    because of the sins of the house of Israel.
What is Jacob's transgression?

1:4
l Ps 46:2,6
m Nu 16:31;
Na 1:5

Is it not Samaria?ⁿ
What is Judah's high place?
Is it not Jerusalem?

⁶"Therefore I will make Samaria a heap of rubble,
a place for planting vineyards.
I will pour her stonesᵒ into the valley
and lay bare her foundations. ᵖ
⁷All her idols�q will be broken to pieces;
all her temple gifts will be burned with fire;
I will destroy all her images. ʳ
Since she gathered her gifts from the wages of
prostitutes,ˢ
as the wages of prostitutes they will again be used."

Weeping and Mourning

⁸Because of this I will weepᵗ and wail;
I will go about barefoot and naked.
I will howl like a jackal
and moan like an owl.
⁹For her woundᵘ is incurable;
it has come to Judah. ᵛ
Itᵃ has reached the very gateʷ of my people,
even to Jerusalem itself.
¹⁰Tell it not in Gathᵇ;
weep not at all. ᶜ
In Beth Ophrahᵈ
roll in the dust.
¹¹Pass on in nakednessˣ and shame,
you who live in Shaphir. ᵉ
Those who live in Zaananᶠ
will not come out.
Beth Ezel is in mourning;
its protection is taken from you.
¹²Those who live in Marothᵍ writhe in pain,
waiting for relief,ʸ
because disaster has come from the LORD,
even to the gate of Jerusalem.
¹³You who live in Lachish,ʰ ᶻ
harness the team to the chariot.
You were the beginning of sin
to the Daughter of Zion,
for the transgressions of Israel
were found in you.
¹⁴Therefore you will give parting giftsᵃ
to Moresheth Gath.
The town of Aczibⁱᵇ will prove deceptiveᶜ

1:5
ⁿAm 8:14
1:6
ᵒAm 5:11
ᵖEze 13:14
1:7
qEze 6:6
ʳDt 9:21
ˢDt 23:17-18
1:8
ᵗIsa 15:3
1:9
ᵘJer 46:11
ᵛ2Ki 18:13
ʷIsa 3:26
1:11
ˣEze 23:29
1:12
ʸJer 14:19
1:13
ᶻJos 10:3
1:14
ᵃ2Ki 16:8
ᵇJos 15:44
ᶜJer 15:18

ᵃ9 Or *He*   ᵇ10 *Gath* sounds like the Hebrew for *tell*.   ᶜ10 Hebrew; Septuagint may suggest
not in Acco. The Hebrew for *in Acco* sounds like the Hebrew for *weep.*   ᵈ10 *Beth Ophrah* means
house of dust.   ᵉ11 *Shaphir* means *pleasant.*   ᶠ11 *Zaanan* sounds like the Hebrew for *come out.*
ᵍ12 *Maroth* sounds like the Hebrew for *bitter.*   ʰ13 *Lachish* sounds like the Hebrew for *team.*
ⁱ14 *Aczib* means *deception.*

to the kings of Israel.
¹⁵I will bring a conqueror against you
    who live in Mareshah.^{a d}
He who is the glory of Israel
    will come to Adullam.^e
¹⁶Shave^f your heads in mourning
    for the children in whom you delight;
make yourselves as bald as the vulture,
    for they will go from you into exile.

Man's Plans and God's

2 Woe to those who plan iniquity,
    to those who plot evil on their beds!^g
At morning's light they carry it out
    because it is in their power to do it.
²They covet fields^h and seize them,
    and houses, and take them.
They defraudⁱ a man of his home,
    a fellowman of his inheritance.

³Therefore, the LORD says:

    "I am planning disaster^j against this people,
        from which you cannot save yourselves.
You will no longer walk proudly,^k
    for it will be a time of calamity.
⁴In that day men will ridicule you;
    they will taunt you with this mournful song:
'We are utterly ruined;^l
    my people's possession is divided up.
He takes it from me!
    He assigns our fields to traitors.' "

⁵Therefore you will have no one in the assembly of the
    LORD
    to divide the land^m by lot.

False Prophets

⁶"Do not prophesy," their prophets say.
    "Do not prophesy about these things;
    disgraceⁿ will not overtake us.^o"
⁷Should it be said, O house of Jacob:
    "Is the Spirit of the LORD angry?
    Does he do such things?"

    "Do not my words do good^p
    to him whose ways are upright?^q
⁸Lately my people have risen up
    like an enemy.
You strip off the rich robe
    from those who pass by without a care,

1:15
d Jos 15:44
e Jos 12:15
1:16
f Job 1:20
2:1
g Ps 36:4
2:2
h Isa 5:8
i Jer 22:17
2:3
j Jer 18:11;
Am 3:1-2
k Isa 2:12
2:4
l Jer 4:13
2:5
m Jos 18:4
2:6
n Mic 6:16
o Am 2:12
2:7
p Ps 119:65
q Ps 15:2; 84:11

---

^a15 *Mareshah* sounds like the Hebrew for *conqueror*.

    like men returning from battle.
⁹You drive the women of my people
    from their pleasant homes.ʳ
You take away my blessing
    from their children forever.
¹⁰Get up, go away!
    For this is not your resting place,ˢ
because it is defiled,ᵗ
    it is ruined, beyond all remedy.
¹¹If a liar and deceiverᵘ comes and says,
    'I will prophesy for you plenty of wine and beer,'
    he would be just the prophet for this people!ᵛ

Deliverance Promised

¹²"I will surely gather all of you, O Jacob;
    I will surely bring together the remnantʷ of Israel.
I will bring them together like sheep in a pen,
    like a flock in its pasture;
    the place will throng with people.
¹³One who breaks open the way will go up beforeˣ them;
    they will break through the gate and go out.
Their king will pass through before them,
    the LORD at their head."

Leaders and Prophets Rebuked

3 Then I said,

    "Listen, you leadersʸ of Jacob,
    you rulers of the house of Israel.
Should you not know justice,
²   you who hate good and love evil;
who tear the skin from my people
    and the flesh from their bones;ᶻ
³who eat my people's flesh,ᵃ
    strip off their skin
    and break their bones in pieces;ᵇ
who chop them up like meat for the pan,
    like flesh for the pot?ᶜ"

⁴Then they will cry out to the LORD,
    but he will not answer them.ᵈ
At that time he will hide his faceᵉ from them
    because of the evil they have done.

⁵This is what the LORD says:

    "As for the prophets
    who lead my people astray,ᶠ
if one feeds them,
    they proclaim 'peace';
if he does not,
    they prepare to wage war against him.
⁶Therefore night will come over you, without visions,

2:9
rJer 10:20
2:10
sDt 12:9
tLev 18:25-29;
Ps 106:38-39
2:11
uJer 5:31
vIsa 30:10
2:12
wMic 4:7; 5:7;
7:18
2:13
xIsa 52:12
3:1
yJer 5:5
3:2
zPs 53:4;
Eze 22:27
3:3
aPs 14:4
bZep 3:3
cEze 11:7
3:4
dPs 18:41;
Isa 1:15
eDt 31:17
3:5
fIsa 3:12; 9:16

and darkness, without divination. [g]
The sun will set for the prophets, [h]
and the day will go dark for them.
[7]The seers will be ashamed [i]
and the diviners disgraced. [j]
They will all cover their faces
because there is no answer from God."

[8]But as for me, I am filled with power,
with the Spirit of the LORD,
and with justice and might,
to declare to Jacob his transgression,
to Israel his sin. [k]
[9]Hear this, you leaders of the house of Jacob,
you rulers of the house of Israel,
who despise justice
and distort all that is right; [l]
[10]who build [m] Zion with bloodshed, [n]
and Jerusalem with wickedness. [o]
[11]Her leaders judge for a bribe,
her priests teach for a price,
and her prophets tell fortunes for money. [p]
Yet they lean upon the LORD and say,
"Is not the LORD among us?
No disaster will come upon us." [q]
[12]Therefore because of you,
Zion will be plowed like a field,
Jerusalem will become a heap of rubble, [r]
the temple hill a mound overgrown with thickets.

The Mountain of the LORD

4:1–3pp — Isa 2:1-4

4 In the last days

the mountain [s] of the LORD's temple will be established
as chief among the mountains;
it will be raised above the hills, [t]
and peoples will stream to it. [u]
[2]Many nations will come and say,

"Come, let us go up to the mountain of the LORD, [v]
to the house of the God of Jacob. [w]
He will teach us his ways, [x]
so that we may walk in his paths."
The law will go out from Zion,
the word of the LORD from Jerusalem.
[3]He will judge between many peoples
and will settle disputes for strong nations far and
wide. [y]
They will beat their swords into plowshares
and their spears into pruning hooks. [z]
Nation will not take up sword against nation,
nor will they train for war anymore. [a]

3:6
g Isa 8:19-22
h Isa 29:10
3:7
i Mic 7:16
j Isa 44:25
3:8
k Isa 58:1
3:9
l Ps 58:1-2;
Isa 1:23
3:10
m Jer 22:13
n Hab 2:12
o Eze 22:27
3:11
p Isa 1:23;
Jer 6:13;
Hos 4:8,18
q Jer 7:4
3:12
r Jer 26:18
4:1
s Zec 8:3
t Eze 17:22
u Ps 22:27;
86:9; Jer 3:17
4:2
v Jer 31:6
w Zec 2:11;
14:16
x Ps 25:8-9;
Isa 54:13
4:3
y Isa 11:4
z Joel 3:10
a Isa 2:4

4Every man will sit under his own vine
    and under his own fig tree,[b]
and no one will make them afraid,[c]
    for the Lord Almighty has spoken.[d]
5All the nations may walk
    in the name of their gods;[e]
we will walk in the name of the Lord
    our God for ever and ever.[f]

The Lord's Plan

6"In that day," declares the Lord,

    "I will gather the lame;
      I will assemble the exiles[g]
    and those I have brought to grief.[h]
7I will make the lame a remnant,[i]
    those driven away a strong nation.
The Lord will rule over them in Mount Zion
    from that day and forever.[j]
8As for you, O watchtower of the flock,
    O stronghold[a] of the Daughter of Zion,
the former dominion will be restored[k] to you;
    kingship will come to the Daughter of Jerusalem."

9Why do you now cry aloud—
    have you no king?[l]
Has your counselor perished,
    that pain seizes you like that of a woman in labor?[m]
10Writhe in agony, O Daughter of Zion,
    like a woman in labor,
for now you must leave the city
    to camp in the open field.
You will go to Babylon;[n]
    there you will be rescued.
There the Lord will redeem[o] you
    out of the hand of your enemies.

11But now many nations
    are gathered against you.
They say, "Let her be defiled,
    let our eyes gloat[p] over Zion!"
12But they do not know
    the thoughts of the Lord;
they do not understand his plan,[q]
    he who gathers them like sheaves to the threshing
      floor.

13"Rise and thresh, O Daughter of Zion,
    for I will give you horns of iron;
I will give you hoofs of bronze
    and you will break to pieces many nations."[r]

a8 Or hill

4:4
b1Ki 4:25
cLev 26:6
dIsa 1:20;
Zec 3:10
4:5
e2Ki 17:29
fJos 24:14-15;
Isa 26:8;
Zec 10:12
4:6
gPs 147:2
hEze 34:13,16;
37:21; Zep 3:19
4:7
iMic 2:12
jDa 7:14;
Lk 1:33;
Rev 11:15
4:8
kIsa 1:26
4:9
lJer 8:19
mJer 30:6
4:10
n2Ki 20:18;
Isa 43:14
oIsa 48:20
4:11
pLa 2:16;
Ob 1:12
4:12
qIsa 55:8;
Ro 11:33-34
4:13
rDa 2:44

You will devote their ill-gotten gains to the LORD,
their wealth to the Lord of all the earth.

A Promised Ruler From Bethlehem

5 Marshal your troops, O city of troops, [a]
for a siege is laid against us.
They will strike Israel's ruler
on the cheek [s] with a rod.

2"But you, Bethlehem [t] Ephrathah, [u]
though you are small among the clans [b] of Judah,
out of you will come for me
one who will be ruler over Israel,
whose origins [c] are from of old, [v]
from ancient times. [d] " [w]

3Therefore Israel will be abandoned
until the time when she who is in labor gives birth
and the rest of his brothers return
to join the Israelites.

4He will stand and shepherd his flock [x]
in the strength of the LORD,
in the majesty of the name of the LORD his God.
And they will live securely, for then his greatness [y]
will reach to the ends of the earth.
5 And he will be their peace. [z]

Deliverance and Destruction

When the Assyrian invades [a] our land
and marches through our fortresses,
we will raise against him seven shepherds,
even eight leaders of men. [b]
6They will rule [e] the land of Assyria with the sword,
the land of Nimrod [c] with drawn sword. [f] [d]
He will deliver us from the Assyrian
when he invades our land
and marches into our borders. [e]

7The remnant [f] of Jacob will be
in the midst of many peoples
like dew from the LORD,
like showers on the grass, [g]
which do not wait for man
or linger for mankind.
8The remnant of Jacob will be among the nations,
in the midst of many peoples,
like a lion among the beasts of the forest, [h]
like a young lion among flocks of sheep,
which mauls and mangles [i] as it goes,
and no one can rescue. [j]

5:1
sLa 3:30
5:2
tJn 7:42
uGe 48:7
vPs 102:25
wMt 2:6*
5:4
xIsa 40:11;
49:9;
Eze 34:11-15,
23; Mic 7:14
yIsa 52:13;
Lk 1:32
5:5
zIsa 9:6;
Lk 2:14;
Col 1:19-20
aIsa 8:7
bIsa 10:24-27
5:6
cGe 10:8
dZep 2:13
eNa 2:11-13
5:7
fMic 2:12
gIsa 44:4
5:8
hGe 49:9
iMic 4:13;
Zec 10:5
jPs 50:22;
Hos 5:14

---

[a]1 Or *Strengthen your walls, O walled city*   [b]2 Or *rulers*   [c]2 Hebrew *goings out*   [d]2 Or
from days of eternity   [e]6 Or *crush*   [f]6 Or *Nimrod in its gates*

⁹Your hand will be lifted up[k] in triumph over your
    enemies,
    and all your foes will be destroyed.

¹⁰"In that day," declares the Lord,

    "I will destroy your horses from among you
       and demolish your chariots.[l]
¹¹I will destroy the cities[m] of your land
       and tear down all your strongholds.[n]
¹²I will destroy your witchcraft
       and you will no longer cast spells.[o]
¹³I will destroy your carved images
       and your sacred stones from among you;
    you will no longer bow down
       to the work of your hands.[p]
¹⁴I will uproot from among you your Asherah poles[a] [q]
       and demolish your cities.
¹⁵I will take vengeance[r] in anger and wrath
       upon the nations that have not obeyed me."

The Lord's Case Against Israel

6 Listen to what the Lord says:

    "Stand up, plead your case before the mountains;[s]
       let the hills hear what you have to say.
²Hear,[t] O mountains, the Lord's accusation;[u]
       listen, you everlasting foundations of the earth.
For the Lord has a case against his people;
       he is lodging a charge[v] against Israel.

³"My people, what have I done to you?
       How have I burdened[w] you? Answer me.
⁴I brought you up out of Egypt
       and redeemed you from the land of slavery.[x]
I sent Moses[y] to lead you,
       also Aaron[z] and Miriam.[a]
⁵My people, remember
       what Balak[b] king of Moab counseled
       and what Balaam son of Beor answered.
Remember ˪your journey˩ from Shittim[c] to Gilgal,[d]
       that you may know the righteous acts[e] of the Lord."

⁶With what shall I come before the Lord
       and bow down before the exalted God?
Shall I come before him with burnt offerings,
       with calves a year old?[f]
⁷Will the Lord be pleased with thousands of rams,[g]
       with ten thousand rivers of oil?[h]
Shall I offer my firstborn[i] for my transgression,
       the fruit of my body for the sin of my soul?[j]
⁸He has showed you, O man, what is good.

5:9
k Ps 10:12
5:10
l Hos 14:3;
Zec 9:10
5:11
m Isa 6:11
n Hos 10:14;
Am 5:9
5:12
o Dt 18:10-12;
Isa 2:6; 8:19
5:13
p Eze 6:9;
Zec 13:2
5:14
q Ex 34:13
5:15
r Isa 65:12
6:1
s Ps 50:1;
Eze 6:2
6:2
t Dt 32:1
u Hos 12:2
v Ps 50:7
6:3
w Jer 2:5
6:4
x Dt 7:8 y Ex 4:16
z Ps 77:20
a Ex 15:20
6:5
b Nu 22:5-6
c Nu 25:1
d Jos 5:9-10
e Jdg 5:11;
1Sa 12:7
6:6
f Ps 40:6-8;
51:16-17
6:7
g Isa 40:16
h Ps 50:8-10
i Lev 18:21
j 2Ki 16:3

---

a14 That is, symbols of the goddess Asherah

And what does the LORD require of you?
To act justly[k] and to love mercy
and to walk humbly[l] with your God.[m]

Israel's Guilt and Punishment

[9]Listen! The LORD is calling to the city—
and to fear your name is wisdom—
"Heed the rod and the One who appointed it.[a]
[10]Am I still to forget, O wicked house,
your ill-gotten treasures
and the short ephah,[b] which is accursed?[n]
[11]Shall I acquit a man with dishonest scales,[o]
with a bag of false weights?
[12]Her rich men are violent;[p]
her people are liars[q]
and their tongues speak deceitfully.[r]
[13]Therefore, I have begun to destroy[s] you,
to ruin you because of your sins.
[14]You will eat but not be satisfied;[t]
your stomach will still be empty.[c]
You will store up but save nothing,[u]
because what you save I will give to the sword.
[15]You will plant but not harvest;[v]
you will press olives but not use the oil on yourselves,
you will crush grapes but not drink the wine.[w]
[16]You have observed the statutes of Omri[x]
and all the practices of Ahab's[y] house,
and you have followed their traditions.[z]
Therefore I will give you over to ruin[a]
and your people to derision;
you will bear the scorn[b] of the nations.[d] "

Israel's Misery

7 What misery is mine!
I am like one who gathers summer fruit
at the gleaning of the vineyard;
there is no cluster of grapes to eat,
none of the early figs that I crave.
[2]The godly have been swept from the land;[c]
not one upright man remains.
All men lie in wait to shed blood;[d]
each hunts his brother with a net.[e]
[3]Both hands are skilled in doing evil;[f]
the ruler demands gifts,
the judge accepts bribes,
the powerful dictate what they desire—
they all conspire together.
[4]The best of them is like a brier,[g]

---

[a]9 The meaning of the Hebrew for this line is uncertain.   [b]10 An ephah was a dry measure.
[c]14 The meaning of the Hebrew for this word is uncertain.   [d]16 Septuagint; Hebrew *scorn due my people*

the most upright worse than a thorn hedge.
The day of your watchmen has come,
  the day God visits you.
Now is the time of their confusion. [h]
[5]Do not trust a neighbor;
  put no confidence in a friend. [i]
Even with her who lies in your embrace
  be careful of your words.
[6]For a son dishonors his father,
  a daughter rises up against her mother, [j]
a daughter-in-law against her mother-in-law—
  a man's enemies are the members of his own
      household. [k]

[7]But as for me, I watch in hope[l] for the LORD,
  I wait for God my Savior;
  my God will hear[m] me.

Israel Will Rise

[8]Do not gloat over me, [n] my enemy!
  Though I have fallen, I will rise. [o]
Though I sit in darkness,
  the LORD will be my light.[p]
[9]Because I have sinned against him,
  I will bear the LORD's wrath, [q]
until he pleads my case
  and establishes my right.
He will bring me out into the light;
  I will see his righteousness. [r]
[10]Then my enemy will see it
  and will be covered with shame, [s]
she who said to me,
  "Where is the LORD your God?"
My eyes will see her downfall;[t]
  even now she will be trampled[u] underfoot
  like mire in the streets.

[11]The day for building your walls[v] will come,
  the day for extending your boundaries.
[12]In that day people will come to you
  from Assyria and the cities of Egypt,
even from Egypt to the Euphrates
  and from sea to sea
  and from mountain to mountain. [w]
[13]The earth will become desolate because of its
      inhabitants,
  as the result of their deeds. [x]

Prayer and Praise

[14]Shepherd[y] your people with your staff,[z]
  the flock of your inheritance,
which lives by itself in a forest,

7:4
h Isa 22:5;
Hos 9:7
7:5
i Jer 9:4
7:6
j Eze 22:7
k Mt 10:35-36*
7:7
l Ps 130:5;
Isa 25:9 m Ps 4:3
7:8
n Pr 24:17
o Ps 37:24;
Am 9:11
p Isa 9:2
7:9
q La 3:39-40
r Isa 46:13
7:10
s Ps 35:26
t Isa 51:23
u Zec 10:5
7:11
v Isa 54:11
7:12
w Isa 19:23-25
7:13
x Isa 3:10-11
7:14
y Mic 5:4
z Ps 23:4

in fertile pasturelands. *a*
Let them feed in Bashan and Gilead *a*
as in days long ago.

¹⁵"As in the days when you came out of Egypt,
I will show them my wonders. *b*"

¹⁶Nations will see and be ashamed, *c*
deprived of all their power.
They will lay their hands on their mouths
and their ears will become deaf.
¹⁷They will lick dust like a snake,
like creatures that crawl on the ground.
They will come trembling out of their dens;
they will turn in fear *d* to the LORD our God
and will be afraid of you.
¹⁸Who is a God like you,
who pardons sin *e* and forgives *f* the transgression
of the remnant *g* of his inheritance? *h*
You do not stay angry *i* forever
but delight to show mercy. *j*
¹⁹You will again have compassion on us;
you will tread our sins underfoot
and hurl all our iniquities *k* into the depths of the sea. *l*
²⁰You will be true to Jacob,
and show mercy to Abraham,
as you pledged on oath to our fathers *m*
in days long ago.

7:14
a Jer 50:19
7:15
b Ex 3:20;
Ps 78:12
7:16
c Isa 26:11
7:17
d Isa 25:3;
49:23; 59:19
7:18
e Isa 43:25;
Jer 50:20
f Ps 103:8-13
g Mic 2:12
h Ex 34:9
i Ps 103:9
j Jer 32:41
7:19
k Isa 43:25
l Jer 31:34
7:20
m Dt 7:8;
Lk 1:72

a14 Or in the middle of Carmel

Nahum

Title and Background

The name Nahum means "comfort" or "consolation." During Jonah's time, Nineveh repented and their destruction was temporarily averted. Not long after that, however, Nineveh reverted to its extreme wickedness, brutality and pride.

Author and Date of Writing

Nothing is known about Nahum except his hometown (Elkosh), but even its precise location is uncertain. In all three chapters Nahum prophesied Nineveh's fall, which was fulfilled in 612 B.C. Nahum therefore probably uttered this oracle between 663 and 612, perhaps near the end of this period.

Theme and Message

The focal point of the whole book is the Lord's judgment on Nineveh for her oppression, cruelty, idolatry and wickedness. God's righteous and just kingdom will ultimately triumph, for kingdoms built on wickedness and tyranny must eventually fall, as Assyria did.

Finally, Nahum declares the universal sovereignty of God. God is Lord of history and of all nations; as such he controls their destinies.

Outline

---

1 An oracle[a] concerning Nineveh. [b] The book of the vision of Nahum the Elkoshite.

The Lord's Anger Against Nineveh

²The Lord is a jealous[c] and avenging God;
  the Lord takes vengeance[d] and is filled with wrath.
The Lord takes vengeance on his foes
  and maintains his wrath against his enemies.
³The Lord is slow to anger[e] and great in power;
  the Lord will not leave the guilty unpunished. [f]
His way is in the whirlwind and the storm,
  and clouds[g] are the dust of his feet.
⁴He rebukes the sea and dries it up;
  he makes all the rivers run dry.
Bashan and Carmel[h] wither
  and the blossoms of Lebanon fade.
⁵The mountains quake[i] before him
  and the hills melt away. [j]
The earth trembles at his presence,

1:1
[a] Isa 13:1; 19:1;
Jer 23:33-34
[b] Jnh 1:2;
Na 2:8;
Zep 2:13
1:2
[c] Ex 20:5
[d] Dt 32:41;
Ps 94:1
1:3
[e] Ne 9:17
[f] Ex 34:7
[g] Ps 104:3
1:4
[h] Isa 33:9
1:5
[i] Ex 19:18
[j] Mic 1:4

the world and all who live in it.
[6]Who can withstand his indignation?
Who can endure[k] his fierce anger?
His wrath is poured out like fire;[l]
the rocks are shattered[m] before him.

[7]The LORD is good,[n]
a refuge in times of trouble.
He cares for[o] those who trust in him,
[8] but with an overwhelming flood
he will make an end of ͺNinevehͺ;
he will pursue his foes into darkness.

[9]Whatever they plot against the LORD
he[a] will bring to an end;
trouble will not come a second time.
[10]They will be entangled among thorns[p]
and drunk from their wine;
they will be consumed like dry stubble.[b] [q]
[11]From you, ͺO Ninevehͺ, has one come forth
who plots evil against the LORD
and counsels wickedness.

[12]This is what the LORD says:

"Although they have allies and are numerous,
they will be cut off[r] and pass away.
Although I have afflicted you, ͺO Judah,ͺ
I will afflict you no more.[s]
[13]Now I will break their yoke[t] from your neck
and tear your shackles away."

[14]The LORD has given a command concerning you,
ͺNineveh,ͺ:
"You will have no descendants to bear your name.[u]
I will destroy the carved images[v] and cast idols
that are in the temple of your gods.
I will prepare your grave,[w]
for you are vile."

[15]Look, there on the mountains,
the feet of one who brings good news,[x]
who proclaims peace![y]
Celebrate your festivals,[z] O Judah,
and fulfill your vows.
No more will the wicked invade you;[a]
they will be completely destroyed.

Nineveh to Fall

2 An attacker[b] advances against you, ͺNineveh,ͺ.
Guard the fortress,
watch the road,

1:6
k Mal 3:2
l Jer 10:10
m 1Ki 19:11
1:7
n Jer 33:11
o Ps 1:6
1:10
p 2Sa 23:6
q Isa 5:24;
Mal 4:1
1:12
r Isa 10:34
s Isa 54:6-8;
La 3:31-32
1:13
t Isa 9:4
1:14
u Isa 14:22
v Mic 5:13
w Eze 32:22-23
1:15
x Isa 40:9;
Ro 10:15
y Isa 52:7
z Lev 23:2-4
a Isa 52:1
2:1
b Jer 51:20

---

[a]9 Or *What do you foes plot against the LORD? / He*   [b]10 The meaning of the Hebrew for this verse is uncertain.

brace yourselves,
marshal all your strength!

²The LORD will restore[c] the splendor[d] of Jacob
like the splendor of Israel,
though destroyers have laid them waste
and have ruined their vines.

³The shields of his soldiers are red;
the warriors are clad in scarlet. [e]
The metal on the chariots flashes
on the day they are made ready;
the spears of pine are brandished. [a]
⁴The chariots[f] storm through the streets,
rushing back and forth through the squares.
They look like flaming torches;
they dart about like lightning.

⁵He summons his picked troops,
yet they stumble[g] on their way.
They dash to the city wall;
the protective shield is put in place.
⁶The river gates[h] are thrown open
and the palace collapses.
⁷It is decreed[b] that the city
be exiled and carried away.
Its slave girls moan[i] like doves
and beat upon their breasts. [j]
⁸Nineveh is like a pool,
and its water is draining away.
"Stop! Stop!" they cry,
but no one turns back.
⁹Plunder the silver!
Plunder the gold!
The supply is endless,
the wealth from all its treasures!
¹⁰She is pillaged, plundered, stripped!
Hearts melt, knees give way,
bodies tremble, every face grows pale. [k]

¹¹Where now is the lions' den, [l]
the place where they fed their young,
where the lion and lioness went,
and the cubs, with nothing to fear?
¹²The lion killed[m] enough for his cubs
and strangled the prey for his mate,
filling his lairs with the kill
and his dens with the prey.

¹³"I am against[n] you,"
declares the LORD Almighty.

2:2
c Eze 37:23
d Isa 60:15
2:3
e Eze 23:14-15
2:4
f Jer 4:13
2:5
g Jer 46:12
2:6
h Na 3:13
2:7
i Isa 59:11
j Isa 32:12
2:10
k Isa 29:22
2:11
l Isa 5:29
2:12
m Jer 51:34
2:13
n Jer 21:13;
Na 3:5

---

a 3 Hebrew; Septuagint and Syriac / *the horsemen rush to and fro*   *b* 7 The meaning of the Hebrew
for this word is uncertain.

"I will burn up your chariots in smoke,°
    and the sword will devour your young lions.
I will leave you no prey on the earth.
The voices of your messengers
    will no longer be heard."

Woe to Nineveh

3 Woe to the city of blood,ᴾ
        full of lies,
    full of plunder,
        never without victims!
²The crack of whips,
    the clatter of wheels,
galloping horses
    and jolting chariots!
³Charging cavalry,
    flashing swords
    and glittering spears!
Many casualties,
    piles of dead,
bodies without number,
    people stumbling over the corpses�q—
⁴all because of the wanton lust of a harlot,
    alluring, the mistress of sorceries,ʳ
who enslaved nations by her prostitutionˢ
    and peoples by her witchcraft.

⁵"I am againstᵗ you," declares the Lord Almighty.
    "I will lift your skirtsᵘ over your face.
I will show the nations your nakednessᵛ
    and the kingdoms your shame.
⁶I will pelt you with filth,ʷ
    I will treat you with contemptˣ
    and make you a spectacle.ʸ
⁷All who see you will flee from you and say,
    'Ninevehᶻ is in ruins—who will mourn for her?'ᵃ
Where can I find anyone to comfortᵇ you?"

⁸Are you better thanᶜ Thebes,ᵃ ᵈ
    situated on the Nile,ᵉ
    with water around her?
The river was her defense,
    the waters her wall.
⁹Cushᵇᶠ and Egypt were her boundless strength;
    Putᵍ and Libyaʰ were among her allies.
¹⁰Yet she was taken captiveⁱ
    and went into exile.
Her infants were dashedʲ to pieces
    at the head of every street.
Lots were cast for her nobles,
    and all her great men were put in chains.

2:13
oPs 46:9
3:1
pEze 22:2;
Mic 3:10
3:3
q2Ki 19:35;
Isa 34:3
3:4
rIsa 47:9
sIsa 23:17;
Eze 16:25-29
3:5
tNa 2:13
uJer 13:22
vIsa 47:3
3:6
wJob 9:31
x1Sa 2:30;
Jer 51:37
yIsa 14:16
3:7
zNa 1:1
aJer 15:5
bIsa 51:19
3:8
cAm 6:2
dJer 46:25
eIsa 19:6-9
3:9
f2Ch 12:3
gEze 27:10
hEze 30:5
3:10
iIsa 20:4
jIsa 13:16;
Hos 13:16

ᵃ8 Hebrew *No Amon*   ᵇ9 That is, the upper Nile region

[11]You too will become drunk;[k]
   you will go into hiding[l]
   and seek refuge from the enemy.

[12]All your fortresses are like fig trees
   with their first ripe fruit;
when they are shaken,
   the figs[m] fall into the mouth of the eater.
[13]Look at your troops—
   they are all women![n]
The gates[o] of your land
   are wide open to your enemies;
   fire has consumed their bars.[p]

[14]Draw water for the siege,[q]
   strengthen your defenses![r]
Work the clay,
   tread the mortar,
   repair the brickwork!
[15]There the fire will devour you;
   the sword will cut you down
   and, like grasshoppers, consume you.
Multiply like grasshoppers,
   multiply like locusts![s]
[16]You have increased the number of your merchants
   till they are more than the stars of the sky,
but like locusts they strip the land
   and then fly away.
[17]Your guards are like locusts,[t]
   your officials like swarms of locusts
   that settle in the walls on a cold day—
but when the sun appears they fly away,
   and no one knows where.

[18]O king of Assyria, your shepherds[a] slumber;[u]
   your nobles lie down to rest.[v]
Your people are scattered[w] on the mountains
   with no one to gather them.
[19]Nothing can heal your wound;[x]
   your injury is fatal.
Everyone who hears the news about you
   claps his hands[y] at your fall,
for who has not felt
   your endless cruelty?

3:11
k Isa 49:26
l Isa 2:10
3:12
m Isa 28:4
3:13
n Isa 19:16;
Jer 50:37
o Na 2:6
p Isa 45:2
3:14
q 2Ch 32:4
r Na 2:1
3:15
s Joel 1:4
3:17
t Jer 51:27
3:18
u Ps 76:5-6
v Isa 56:10
w 1Ki 22:17
3:19
x Jer 30:13;
Mic 1:9
y Job 27:23;
La 2:15;
Zep 2:15

[a]18 Or *rulers*

Habakkuk

Title and Background

The title of the book is the author's name and apparently comes from a Hebrew root meaning "to clasp" or "to embrace." Habakkuk prayed and prophesied in times of crisis. The international scene was shocked by events of far-reaching import. Internally the people of God were caught up in a crisis of religious and moral bewilderment.

Author and Date of Writing

Little is known about the author except his name and that he was a contemporary of Jeremiah. He was a man of vigorous faith, a faith rooted deeply in the religious traditions of Israel. The prophecy is generally dated a little before or after the battle of Carchemish (605 B.C.).

Theme and Message

Habakkuk was written as a dialogue or conversation between God and the prophet. He saw that the leaders were oppressing the poor, so he asked why God allowed the wicked to prosper. Having received replies, he responds with a beautiful confession of faith. His confession became a public expression and appears to have been used as a psalm.

Outline

I. Habakkuk's First Question and God's Answer (1:1-11)
II. Habakkuk's Second Question and God's Answer (1:12-2:20)
III. Habakkuk's Prayer (3:1-19)

1

The oracle[a] that Habakkuk the prophet received.

Habakkuk's Complaint

> [2]How long, O Lord, must I call for help,
>   but you do not listen?[b]
> Or cry out to you, "Violence!"
>   but you do not save?[c]
> [3]Why do you make me look at injustice?
>   Why do you tolerate[d] wrong?
> Destruction and violence[e] are before me;
>   there is strife,[f] and conflict abounds.
> [4]Therefore the law[g] is paralyzed,
>   and justice never prevails.
> The wicked hem in the righteous,
>   so that justice is perverted.[h]

The Lord's Answer

> [5]"Look at the nations and watch—
>   and be utterly amazed.[i]

1:1
a Na 1:1
1:2
b Ps 13:1-2;
22:1-2 c Jer 14:9
1:3
d ver 13
e Jer 20:8
f Ps 55:9
1:4
g Ps 119:126
h Job 19:7;
Isa 1:23; 5:20;
Eze 9:9
1:5
i Isa 29:9

For I am going to do something in your days
    that you would not believe,
    even if you were told.[j]
  6I am raising up the Babylonians,[a][k]
    that ruthless and impetuous people,
  who sweep across the whole earth
    to seize dwelling places not their own.[l]
  7They are a feared and dreaded people;[m]
    they are a law to themselves
    and promote their own honor.
  8Their horses are swifter[n] than leopards,
    fiercer than wolves at dusk.
  Their cavalry gallops headlong;
    their horsemen come from afar.
  They fly like a vulture swooping to devour;
  9   they all come bent on violence.
    Their hordes[b] advance like a desert wind
    and gather prisoners[o] like sand.
  10They deride kings
    and scoff at rulers.[p]
  They laugh at all fortified cities;
    they build earthen ramps and capture them.
  11Then they sweep past like the wind[q] and go on—
    guilty men, whose own strength is their god."[r]

Habakkuk's Second Complaint

  12O LORD, are you not from everlasting?
    My God, my Holy One,[s] we will not die.
  O LORD, you have appointed[t] them to execute
        judgment;
    O Rock, you have ordained them to punish.
  13Your eyes are too pure to look on evil;
    you cannot tolerate wrong.[u]
  Why then do you tolerate the treacherous?
  Why are you silent while the wicked
    swallow up those more righteous than
        themselves?
  14You have made men like fish in the sea,
    like sea creatures that have no ruler.
  15The wicked foe pulls all of them up with hooks,[v]
    he catches them in his net,[w]
  he gathers them up in his dragnet;
    and so he rejoices and is glad.
  16Therefore he sacrifices to his net
    and burns incense[x] to his dragnet,
  for by his net he lives in luxury
    and enjoys the choicest food.
  17Is he to keep on emptying his net,
    destroying nations without mercy?[y]

1:5
jAc 13:41*
1:6
k2Ki 24:2
lJer 13:20
1:7
mIsa 18:7;
Jer 39:5-9
1:8
nJer 4:13
1:9
oHab 2:5
1:10
p2Ch 36:6
1:11
qJer 4:11-12
rDa 4:30
1:12
sIsa 31:1
tIsa 10:6
1:13
uLa 3:34-36
1:15
vIsa 19:8
wJer 16:16
1:16
xJer 44:8
1:17
yIsa 14:6; 19:8

---

a6 Or *Chaldeans*   b9 The meaning of the Hebrew for this word is uncertain.

2
I will stand at my watch[z]
　and station myself on the ramparts;[a]
I will look to see what he will say[b] to me,
　and what answer I am to give to this complaint.[a][c]

The Lord's Answer

[2]Then the Lord replied:

"Write[d] down the revelation
　and make it plain on tablets
　so that a herald[b] may run with it.
[3]For the revelation awaits an appointed time;
　it speaks of the end[e]
　and will not prove false.
Though it linger, wait[f] for it;
　it[c] will certainly come and will not delay.[g]

[4]"See, he is puffed up;
　his desires are not upright—
　but the righteous will live by his faith[d][h]—
[5]indeed, wine[i] betrays him;
　he is arrogant and never at rest.
Because he is as greedy as the grave[e]
　and like death is never satisfied,[j]
he gathers to himself all the nations
　and takes captive all the peoples.

[6]"Will not all of them taunt[k] him with ridicule and scorn, saying,

" 'Woe to him who piles up stolen goods
　and makes himself wealthy by extortion![l]
　How long must this go on?'
[7]Will not your debtors[f] suddenly arise?
　Will they not wake up and make you tremble?
　Then you will become their victim.[m]
[8]Because you have plundered many nations,
　the peoples who are left will plunder you.[n]
For you have shed man's blood;[o]
　you have destroyed lands and cities and everyone in
　　them.

[9]"Woe to him who builds[p] his realm by unjust gain
　to set his nest on high,
　to escape the clutches of ruin!
[10]You have plotted the ruin[q] of many peoples,
　shaming[r] your own house and forfeiting your life.
[11]The stones[s] of the wall will cry out,
　and the beams of the woodwork will echo it.

[12]"Woe to him who builds a city with bloodshed[t]
　and establishes a town by crime!

2:1
z Isa 21:8
a Ps 48:13
b Ps 85:8 c Ps 5:3
2:2
d Rev 1:19
2:3
e Da 8:17; 10:14
f Ps 27:14
g Eze 12:25;
Heb 10:37-38
2:4
h Ro 1:17*;
Gal 3:11*;
Heb 10:37-38*
2:5
i Pr 20:1
j Pr 27:20;
30:15-16
2:6
k Isa 14:4
l Am 2:8
2:7
m Pr 29:1
2:8
n Isa 33:1;
Zec 2:8-9
over 17
2:9
p Jer 22:13
2:10
q Jer 26:19
r ver 16
2:11
s Jos 24:27;
Lk 19:40
2:12
t Mic 3:10

---

[a]1 Or *and what to answer when I am rebuked*　　[b]2 Or *so that whoever reads it*　　[c]3 Or *Though he linger, wait for him; / he*　　[d]4 Or *faithfulness*　　[e]5 Hebrew *Sheol*　　[f]7 Or *creditors*

¹³Has not the LORD Almighty determined
  that the people's labor is only fuel for the fire, ᵘ
  that the nations exhaust themselves for nothing?ᵛ
¹⁴For the earth will be filled with the knowledge of the
    gloryʷ of the LORD,
  as the waters cover the sea.ˣ

¹⁵"Woe to him who gives drink to his neighbors,
  pouring it from the wineskin till they are drunk,
  so that he can gaze on their naked bodies.
¹⁶You will be filled with shameʸ instead of glory.
  Now it is your turn! Drink and be exposedᵃ!ᶻ
The cupᵃ from the LORD's right hand is coming around
    to you,
  and disgrace will cover your glory.
¹⁷The violenceᵇ you have done to Lebanon will
    overwhelm you,
  and your destruction of animals will terrify you. ᶜ
For you have shed man's blood;ᵈ
  you have destroyed lands and cities and everyone in
    them.

¹⁸"Of what value is an idol,ᵉ since a man has carved it?
  Or an image that teaches lies?
For he who makes it trusts in his own creation;
  he makes idols that cannot speak. ᶠ
¹⁹Woe to him who says to wood, 'Come to life!'
  Or to lifeless stone, 'Wake up!'ᵍ
Can it give guidance?
  It is covered with gold and silver;ʰ
  there is no breath in it.
²⁰But the LORD is in his holy temple;ⁱ
  let all the earth be silentʲ before him."

Habakkuk's Prayer

3 A prayer of Habakkuk the prophet. On *shigionoth.* ᵇ

  ²LORD, I have heardᵏ of your fame;
    I stand in aweˡ of your deeds, O LORD.
  Renewᵐ them in our day,
    in our time make them known;
    in wrath remember mercy. ⁿ

  ³God came from Teman,
    the Holy One from Mount Paran.   *Selah*ᶜ
  His glory covered the heavens
    and his praise filled the earth. ᵒ
  ⁴His splendor was like the sunrise;
    rays flashed from his hand,
    where his power was hidden.

2:13
u Isa 50:11
v Isa 47:13
2:14
w Nu 14:21
x Isa 11:9
2:16
y ver 10 z La 4:21
a Isa 51:22
2:17
b Jer 51:35
c Jer 50:15
d ver 8
2:18
e Jer 5:21
f Ps 115:4-5;
Jer 10:14
2:19
g 1Ki 18:27
h Jer 10:4
2:20
i Ps 11:4
j Isa 41:1
3:2
k Ps 44:1
l Ps 119:120
m Ps 85:6
n Isa 54:8
3:3
o Ps 48:10

ᵃ16 Masoretic Text; Dead Sea Scrolls, Aquila, Vulgate and Syriac (see also Septuagint) *and stagger*
ᵇ1 Probably a literary or musical term   *ᶜ3* A word of uncertain meaning; possibly a musical
term; also in verses 9 and 13

⁵Plague went before him;
  pestilence followed his steps.
⁶He stood, and shook the earth;
  he looked, and made the nations tremble.
The ancient mountains crumbled
  and the age-old hills collapsed. ᴾ
  His ways are eternal.
⁷I saw the tents of Cushan in distress,
  the dwellings of Midian �q in anguish. ʳ

⁸Were you angry with the rivers, ˢ O Lᴏʀᴅ?
  Was your wrath against the streams?
Did you rage against the sea
  when you rode with your horses
  and your victorious chariots? ᵗ
⁹You uncovered your bow,
  you called for many arrows. ᵘ   *Selah*
You split the earth with rivers;
¹⁰ the mountains saw you and writhed.
Torrents of water swept by;
  the deep roared ᵛ
  and lifted its waves ʷ on high.

¹¹Sun and moon stood still ˣ in the heavens
  at the glint of your flying arrows, ʸ
  at the lightning of your flashing spear.
¹²In wrath you strode through the earth
  and in anger you threshed ᶻ the nations.
¹³You came out to deliver ᵃ your people,
  to save your anointed one.
You crushed ᵇ the leader of the land of wickedness,
  you stripped him from head to foot.   *Selah*
¹⁴With his own spear you pierced his head
  when his warriors stormed out to scatter us, ᶜ
gloating as though about to devour
  the wretched ᵈ who were in hiding.
¹⁵You trampled the sea with your horses,
  churning the great waters. ᵉ

¹⁶I heard and my heart pounded,
  my lips quivered at the sound;
decay crept into my bones,
  and my legs trembled.
Yet I will wait patiently for the day of calamity
  to come on the nation invading us.
¹⁷Though the fig tree does not bud
  and there are no grapes on the vines,
though the olive crop fails
  and the fields produce no food, ᶠ
though there are no sheep in the pen
  and no cattle in the stalls, ᵍ
¹⁸yet I will rejoice in the Lᴏʀᴅ, ʰ

3:6
pPs 114:1-6
3:7
qJdg 7:24-25
rEx 15:14
3:8
sEx 7:20
tPs 68:17
3:9
uPs 7:12-13
3:10
vPs 98:7
wPs 93:3
3:11
xJos 10:13
yPs 18:14
3:12
zIsa 41:15
3:13
aPs 20:6; 28:8
bPs 68:21;
110:6
3:14
cJdg 7:22
dPs 64:2-5
3:15
eEx 15:8;
Ps 77:19
3:17
fJoel 1:10-12,18
gJer 5:17
3:18
hIsa 61:10;
Php 4:4

I will be joyful in God my Savior.

¹⁹The Sovereign Lord is my strength;ⁱ

he makes my feet like the feet of a deer,

he enables me to go on the heights.^j

For the director of music. On my stringed instruments.

3:19
i Dt 33:29;
Ps 46:1-5
j Dt 32:13;
2Sa 22:34;
Ps 18:33

Zephaniah

Title and Background

The name Zephaniah means "The LORD hides (or protects)."

The religious state of Judah declined markedly following the death of Hezekiah, but Josiah launched a sweeping reform. He was backed by Jeremiah and Nahum, but their calls for repentance fell on deaf ears. Judah became ripe for judgment.

Author and Date of Writing

The prophet was evidently a person of considerable social standing in Judah. He was a fourth-generation descendant of King Hezekiah. Zephaniah shows great familiarity with court circles and current political issues. According to 1:1, Zephaniah prophesied during the reign of King Josiah (640-609 B.C.), so this prophecy could have been written about 630 B.C.

Theme and Message

The intent of the author was to announce to Judah God's approaching judgment. His main theme was the coming of the day of the Lord, when God would severely punish the nations. He portrays the stark horror of that ordeal, but also makes it clear that God will yet be merciful toward his people.

Outline

---

1 The word of the LORD that came to Zephaniah son of Cushi, the son of Gedaliah, the son of Amariah, the son of Hezekiah, during the reign of Josiah[a] son of Amon king of Judah:

Warning of Coming Destruction

2"I will sweep away everything
    from the face of the earth,"[b]

                    declares the LORD.
3"I will sweep away both men and animals;
    I will sweep away the birds of the air[c]
    and the fish of the sea.
The wicked will have only heaps of rubble[a]
    when I cut off man from the face of the earth,"[d]

                    declares the LORD.

Against Judah

4"I will stretch out my hand[e] against Judah

1:1
a 2Ki 22:1;
2Ch 34:1-35:25
1:2
b Ge 6:7
1:3
c Jer 4:25
d Hos 4:3
1:4
e Jer 6:12

---

a3 The meaning of the Hebrew for this line is uncertain.

and against all who live in Jerusalem.
I will cut off from this place every remnant of Baal,[f]
     the names of the pagan and the idolatrous priests[g]—
[5]those who bow down on the roofs
     to worship the starry host,
those who bow down and swear by the Lord
     and who also swear by Molech,[a][h]
[6]those who turn back from following[i] the Lord
     and neither seek[j] the Lord nor inquire[k] of him.
[7]Be silent[l] before the Sovereign Lord,
     for the day of the Lord[m] is near.
The Lord has prepared a sacrifice;[n]
     he has consecrated those he has invited.
[8]On the day of the Lord's sacrifice
     I will punish[o] the princes
     and the king's sons[p]
and all those clad
     in foreign clothes.
[9]On that day I will punish
     all who avoid stepping on the threshold,[b]
who fill the temple of their gods
     with violence and deceit.[q]

[10]"On that day," declares the Lord,
     "a cry will go up from the Fish Gate,[r]
wailing from the New Quarter,
     and a loud crash from the hills.
[11]Wail,[s] you who live in the market district[c];
     all your merchants will be wiped out,
     all who trade with[d] silver will be ruined.[t]
[12]At that time I will search Jerusalem with lamps
     and punish those who are complacent,[u]
     who are like wine left on its dregs,[v]
who think, 'The Lord will do nothing,[w]
     either good or bad.'
[13]Their wealth will be plundered,[x]
     their houses demolished.
They will build houses
     but not live in them;
they will plant vineyards
     but not drink the wine.[y]

The Great Day of the Lord

[14]"The great day of the Lord[z] is near[a]—
     near and coming quickly.
Listen! The cry on the day of the Lord will be bitter,
     the shouting of the warrior there.
[15]That day will be a day of wrath,
     a day of distress and anguish,
     a day of trouble and ruin,

1:4
fMic 5:13
gHos 10:5
1:5
hJer 5:7
1:6
iIsa 1:4;
Jer 2:13
jIsa 9:13
kHos 7:7
1:7
lHab 2:20;
Zec 2:13
mver 14;
Isa 13:6
nIsa 34:6;
Jer 46:10
1:8
oIsa 24:21
pJer 39:6
1:9
qAm 3:10
1:10
r2Ch 33:14
1:11
sJas 5:1
tHos 9:6
1:12
uAm 6:1
vJer 48:11
wEze 8:12
1:13
xJer 15:13
yDt 28:30,39;
Am 5:11;
Mic 6:15
1:14
zver 7;
Joel 1:15
aEze 7:7

---

a5 Hebrew *Malcam,* that is, Milcom   b9 See 1 Samuel 5:5.   c11 Or *the Mortar*   d11 Or *in*

a day of darkness and gloom,
    a day of clouds and blackness, [b]
[16]a day of trumpet and battle cry[c]
    against the fortified cities
    and against the corner towers. [d]
[17]I will bring distress on the people
    and they will walk like blind[e] men,
    because they have sinned against the LORD.
Their blood will be poured out[f] like dust
    and their entrails like filth. [g]
[18]Neither their silver nor their gold
    will be able to save them
    on the day of the LORD's wrath. [h]
In the fire of his jealousy
    the whole world will be consumed, [i]
for he will make a sudden end
    of all who live in the earth. [j] "

2

Gather together, [k] gather together,
    O shameful[l] nation,
[2]before the appointed time arrives
    and that day sweeps on like chaff, [m]
before the fierce anger[n] of the LORD comes upon you,
    before the day of the LORD's wrath comes upon you.
[3]Seek[o] the LORD, all you humble of the land,
    you who do what he commands.
Seek righteousness, seek humility;[p]
    perhaps you will be sheltered[q]
    on the day of the LORD's anger.

Against Philistia

[4]Gaza[r] will be abandoned
    and Ashkelon left in ruins.
At midday Ashdod will be emptied
    and Ekron uprooted.
[5]Woe to you who live by the sea,
    O Kerethite[s] people;
the word of the LORD is against you, [t]
    O Canaan, land of the Philistines.

"I will destroy you,
    and none will be left."[u]

[6]The land by the sea, where the Kerethites[a] dwell,
    will be a place for shepherds and sheep pens. [v]
[7]It will belong to the remnant of the house of Judah;
    there they will find pasture.
In the evening they will lie down
    in the houses of Ashkelon.

1:15
b Isa 22:5;
Joel 2:2
1:16
c Jer 4:19
d Isa 2:15
1:17
e Isa 59:10
f Ps 79:3
g Jer 9:22
1:18
h Eze 7:19
i ver 2-3;
Zep 3:8 jGe 6:7
2:1
k 2Ch 20:4;
Joel 1:14
l Jer 3:3; 6:15
2:2
m Isa 17:13;
Hos 13:3
n La 4:11
2:3
o Am 5:6
p Ps 45:4;
Am 5:14-15
q Ps 57:1
2:4
r Am 1:6,7-8)
Zec 9:5-7
2:5
s Eze 25:16
t Am 3:1
u Isa 14:30
2:6
v Isa 5:17

---

[a]6 The meaning of the Hebrew for this word is uncertain.

The LORD their God will care for them;
    he will restore their fortunes.[a][w]

Against Moab and Ammon

[8]"I have heard the insults[x] of Moab
    and the taunts of the Ammonites,
who insulted[y] my people
    and made threats against their land.
[9]Therefore, as surely as I live,"
    declares the LORD Almighty, the God of Israel,
"surely Moab[z] will become like Sodom,[a]
    the Ammonites[b] like Gomorrah—
a place of weeds and salt pits,
    a wasteland forever.
The remnant of my people will plunder[c] them;
    the survivors of my nation will inherit their land.[d]"

[10]This is what they will get in return for their pride,[e]
    for insulting[f] and mocking the people of the LORD
        Almighty.
[11]The LORD will be awesome[g] to them
    when he destroys all the gods[h] of the land.
The nations on every shore will worship him,[i]
    every one in its own land.

Against Cush

[12]"You too, O Cushites,[b][j]
    will be slain by my sword.[k]"

Against Assyria

[13]He will stretch out his hand against the north
    and destroy Assyria,
leaving Nineveh[l] utterly desolate
    and dry as the desert.[m]
[14]Flocks and herds will lie down there,
    creatures of every kind.
The desert owl[n] and the screech owl
    will roost on her columns.
Their calls will echo through the windows,
    rubble will be in the doorways,
    the beams of cedar will be exposed.
[15]This is the carefree[o] city
    that lived in safety.[p]
She said to herself,
    "I am, and there is none besides me."[q]
What a ruin she has become,
    a lair for wild beasts!
All who pass by her scoff[r]
    and shake their fists.

2:7
wPs 126:4;
Jer 32:44
2:8
xJer 48:27
yEze 25:3
2:9
zIsa 15:1-16:14;
Jer 48:1-47
aDt 29:23
bJer 49:1-6;
Eze 25:1-7
cIsa 11:14
dAm 2:1-3
2:10
eIsa 16:6
fJer 48:27
2:11
gJoel 2:11
hZep 1:4
iZep 3:9
2:12
jIsa 18:1; 20:4
kJer 46:10
2:13
lNa 1:1
mMic 5:6
2:14
nIsa 14:23
2:15
oIsa 32:9
pIsa 47:8
qEze 28:2
rNa 3:19

---

[a]7 Or *will bring back their captives*   [b]12 That is, people from the upper Nile region

The Future of Jerusalem

3

Woe to the city of oppressors, ^s
   rebellious and defiled! ^t
²She obeys ^u no one,
   she accepts no correction. ^v
She does not trust in the LORD,
   she does not draw near ^w to her God.
³Her officials are roaring lions,
   her rulers are evening wolves, ^x
   who leave nothing for the morning.
⁴Her prophets are arrogant;
   they are treacherous ^y men.
Her priests profane the sanctuary
   and do violence to the law. ^z
⁵The LORD within her is righteous;
   he does no wrong. ^a
Morning by morning he dispenses his justice,
   and every new day he does not fail,
   yet the unrighteous know no shame.

⁶"I have cut off nations;
   their strongholds are demolished.
I have left their streets deserted,
   with no one passing through.
Their cities are destroyed; ^b
   no one will be left—no one at all.
⁷I said to the city,
   'Surely you will fear me
   and accept correction!'
Then her dwelling would not be cut off,
   nor all my punishments come upon her.
But they were still eager
   to act corruptly ^c in all they did.
⁸Therefore wait ^d for me," declares the LORD,
   "for the day I will stand up to testify. ^a
I have decided to assemble the nations, ^e
   to gather the kingdoms
and to pour out my wrath on them—
   all my fierce anger.
The whole world will be consumed ^f
   by the fire of my jealous anger.

⁹"Then will I purify the lips of the peoples,
   that all of them may call ^g on the name of the LORD
   and serve ^h him shoulder to shoulder.
¹⁰From beyond the rivers of Cush ^{b i}
   my worshipers, my scattered people,
   will bring me offerings. ^j
¹¹On that day you will not be put to shame ^k
   for all the wrongs you have done to me,

3:1
s Jer 6:6
t Eze 23:30
3:2
u Jer 22:21
v Jer 7:28
w Ps 73:28;
   Jer 5:3
3:3
x Eze 22:27
3:4
y Jer 9:4
z Eze 22:26
3:5
a Dt 32:4
3:6
b Lev 26:31
3:7
c Hos 9:9
3:8
d Ps 27:14
e Joel 3:2
f Zep 1:18
3:9
g Zep 2:11
h Isa 19:18
3:10
i Ps 68:31
j Isa 60:7
3:11
k Joel 2:26-27

a8 Septuagint and Syriac; Hebrew *will rise up to plunder*   *b10* That is, the upper Nile region

because I will remove from this city
    those who rejoice in their pride.
Never again will you be haughty
    on my holy hill.
[12]But I will leave within you
    the meek[l] and humble,
who trust[m] in the name of the LORD.
[13]The remnant[n] of Israel will do no wrong;[o]
    they will speak no lies,[p]
nor will deceit be found in their mouths.
They will eat and lie down[q]
    and no one will make them afraid.[r] "

[14]Sing, O Daughter of Zion;[s]
    shout aloud,[t] O Israel!
Be glad and rejoice with all your heart,
    O Daughter of Jerusalem!
[15]The LORD has taken away your punishment,
    he has turned back your enemy.
The LORD, the King of Israel, is with you;[u]
    never again will you fear[v] any harm.
[16]On that day they will say to Jerusalem,
    "Do not fear, O Zion;
do not let your hands hang limp.[w]
[17]The LORD your God is with you,
    he is mighty to save.[x]
He will take great delight[y] in you,
    he will quiet you with his love,
    he will rejoice over you with singing."

[18]"The sorrows for the appointed feasts
    I will remove from you;
they are a burden and a reproach to you.[a]
[19]At that time I will deal
    with all who oppressed you;
I will rescue the lame
    and gather those who have been scattered.[z]
I will give them praise[a] and honor
    in every land where they were put to shame.
[20]At that time I will gather you;
    at that time I will bring[b] you home.
I will give you honor[c] and praise
    among all the peoples of the earth
when I restore your fortunes[b] [d]
    before your very eyes,"
                    says the LORD.

3:12
l Isa 14:32
m Na 1:7
3:13
n Isa 10:21;
Mic 4:7
o Ps 119:3
p Rev 14:5
q Eze 34:15;
Zep 2:7
r Eze 34:25-28
3:14
s Zec 2:10
t Isa 12:6
3:15
u Eze 37:26-28
v Isa 54:14
3:16
w Job 4:3;
Isa 35:3-4;
Heb 12:12
3:17
x Isa 63:1
y Isa 62:4
3:19
z Eze 34:16;
Mic 4:6
a Isa 60:18
3:20
b Jer 29:14;
Eze 37:12
c Isa 56:5; 66:22
d Joel 3:1

---

a 18 Or "I will gather you who mourn for the appointed feasts; / your reproach is a burden to you
b 20 Or I bring back your captives

Haggai

Title and Background

The book is named for its author, and the name means "festal" or "festival."

In 538 B.C. Cyrus issued a decree allowing the Jews to return to Jerusalem and rebuild the temple. The Samaritans and other neighbors opposed the project vigorously and managed to halt work until Darius the Great became king. Haggai began to preach in Darius's second year.

Author and Date of Writing

Haggai was a prophet who, along with Zechariah, encouraged the returned exiles to rebuild the temple. Based on 2:3, Haggai may have witnessed the destruction of Solomon's temple. If so, he was about 80 years old during his ministry recorded in this book. The messages of Haggai were given during a four-month period in 520 B.C.

Theme and Message

Haggai clearly shows the consequences of disobedience and the blessings of obedience. When the people give priority to God and his house, they are blessed. Obedience brings the encouragement and strength of the Spirit of God.

Outline

A Call to Build the House of the LORD

1 In the second year of King Darius,[a] on the first day of the sixth month, the word of the LORD came through the prophet Haggai[b] to Zerubbabel[c] son of Shealtiel, governor[d] of Judah, and to Joshua[ae] son of Jehozadak,[f] the high priest:

²This is what the LORD Almighty says: "These people say, 'The time has not yet come for the LORD's house to be built.' "

³Then the word of the LORD came through the prophet Haggai:[g] ⁴"Is it a time for you yourselves to be living in your paneled houses,[h] while this house remains a ruin?[i] "

⁵Now this is what the LORD Almighty says: "Give careful thought[j] to your ways. ⁶You have planted much, but have harvested little.[k] You eat, but never have enough. You drink, but never have your fill. You put on clothes, but are not warm. You earn wages,[l] only to put them in a purse with holes in it."

⁷This is what the LORD Almighty says: "Give careful thought to your ways. ⁸Go up into the mountains and bring down timber and build the

1:1
aEzr 4:24
bEzr 5:1
cMt 1:12-13
dEzr 5:3
eEzr 2:2
f1Ch 6:15;
Ezr 3:2
1:3
gEzr 5:1
1:4
h2Sa 7:2 iver 9;
Jer 33:12
1:5
jLa 3:40
1:6
kDt 28:38
lHag 2:16;
Zec 8:10

---

[a]1 A variant of *Jeshua*; here and elsewhere in Haggai

house, so that I may take pleasure[m] in it and be honored," says the LORD. [9]"You expected much, but see, it turned out to be little. What you brought home, I blew away. Why?" declares the LORD Almighty. "Because of my house, which remains a ruin,[n] while each of you is busy with his own house. [10]Therefore, because of you the heavens have withheld their dew and the earth its crops.[o] [11]I called for a drought[p] on the fields and the mountains, on the grain, the new wine, the oil and whatever the ground produces, on men and cattle, and on the labor of your hands.[q]"

[12]Then Zerubbabel[r] son of Shealtiel, Joshua son of Jehozadak, the high priest, and the whole remnant[s] of the people obeyed[t] the voice of the LORD their God and the message of the prophet Haggai, because the LORD their God had sent him. And the people feared[u] the LORD.

[13]Then Haggai, the LORD's messenger, gave this message of the LORD to the people: "I am with[v] you," declares the LORD. [14]So the LORD stirred up the spirit of Zerubbabel[w] son of Shealtiel, governor of Judah, and the spirit of Joshua son of Jehozadak, the high priest, and the spirit of the whole remnant[x] of the people. They came and began to work on the house of the LORD Almighty, their God, [15]on the twenty-fourth day of the sixth month[y] in the second year of King Darius.

The Promised Glory of the New House

2 On the twenty-first day of the seventh month, the word of the LORD came through the prophet Haggai: [2]"Speak to Zerubbabel son of Shealtiel, governor of Judah, to Joshua son of Jehozadak, the high priest, and to the remnant of the people. Ask them, [3]'Who of you is left who saw this house[z] in its former glory? How does it look to you now? Does it not seem to you like nothing?[a] [4]But now be strong, O Zerubbabel,' declares the LORD. 'Be strong,[b] O Joshua son of Jehozadak, the high priest. Be strong, all you people of the land,' declares the LORD, 'and work. For I am with[c] you,' declares the LORD Almighty. [5]'This is what I covenanted with you when you came out of Egypt.[d] And my Spirit[e] remains among you. Do not fear.'

[6]"This is what the LORD Almighty says: 'In a little while[f] I will once more shake the heavens and the earth,[g] the sea and the dry land. [7]I will shake all nations, and the desired of all nations will come, and I will fill this house[h] with glory,' says the LORD Almighty. [8]'The silver is mine and the gold is mine,' declares the LORD Almighty. [9]'The glory[i] of this present house will be greater than the glory of the former house,' says the LORD Almighty. 'And in this place I will grant peace,' declares the LORD Almighty."

Blessings for a Defiled People

[10]On the twenty-fourth day of the ninth month,[j] in the second year of Darius, the word of the LORD came to the prophet Haggai: [11]"This is what the LORD Almighty says: 'Ask the priests[k] what the law says: [12]If a person carries consecrated meat in the fold of his garment, and that fold touches some bread or stew, some wine, oil or other food, does it become consecrated?[l]'"

The priests answered, "No."

1:8
m Ps 132:13-14
1:9
n ver 4
1:10
o Lev 26:19;
Dt 28:23
1:11
p Dt 28:22;
1Ki 17:1
q Hag 2:17
1:12
r ver 1 s ver 14;
Isa 1:9; Hag 2:2
t Isa 50:10
u Dt 31:12
1:13
v Mt 28:20;
Ro 8:31
1:14
w Ezr 5:2 x ver 12
1:15
y ver 1
2:3
z Ezr 3:12
a Zec 4:10
2:4
b 1Ch 28:20;
Zec 8:9;
Eph 6:10
c 2Sa 5:10;
Ac 7:9
2:5
d Ex 29:46
e Ne 9:20;
Isa 63:11
2:6
f Isa 10:25
g Heb 12:26*
2:7
h Isa 60:7
2:9
i Ps 85:9
2:10
j ver 1
2:11
k Lev 10:10-11;
Dt 17:8-11;
Mal 2:7
2:12
l Lev 6:27;
Mt 23:19

[13]Then Haggai said, "If a person defiled by contact with a dead body touches one of these things, does it become defiled?"

"Yes," the priests replied, "it becomes defiled. [m]"

[14]Then Haggai said, " 'So it is with this people and this nation in my sight,' declares the Lord. 'Whatever they do and whatever they offer[n] there is defiled.

[15]" 'Now give careful thought[o] to this from this day on[a]—consider how things were before one stone was laid[p] on another in the Lord's temple. [q] [16]When anyone came to a heap of twenty measures, there were only ten. When anyone went to a wine vat to draw fifty measures, there were only twenty.[r] [17]I struck all the work of your hands[s] with blight,[t] mildew and hail, yet you did not turn to me,' declares the Lord. [u] [18]'From this day on, from this twenty-fourth day of the ninth month, give careful thought to the day when the foundation[v] of the Lord's temple was laid. Give careful thought: [19]Is there yet any seed left in the barn? Until now, the vine and the fig tree, the pomegranate and the olive tree have not borne fruit.

" 'From this day on I will bless you.' "

Zerubbabel the Lord's Signet Ring

[20]The word of the Lord came to Haggai a second time on the twenty-fourth day of the month: [21]"Tell Zerubbabel[w] governor of Judah that I will shake the heavens and the earth. [22]I will overturn royal thrones and shatter the power of the foreign kingdoms.[x] I will overthrow chariots[y] and their drivers; horses and their riders will fall, each by the sword of his brother.[z]

[23]" 'On that day,' declares the Lord Almighty, 'I will take you, my servant[a] Zerubbabel son of Shealtiel,' declares the Lord, 'and I will make you like my signet ring, for I have chosen you,' declares the Lord Almighty."

2:13
m Lev 22:4-6
2:14
n Isa 1:13
2:15
o Hag 1:5
p Ezr 3:10
q Ezr 4:24
2:16
r Hag 1:6
2:17
s Hag 1:11
t Dt 28:22;
1Ki 8:37;
Am 4:9
u Am 4:6
2:18
v Zec 8:9
2:21
w Ezr 5:2
2:22
x Da 2:44
y Mic 5:10
z Jdg 7:22
2:23
a Isa 43:10

a15 Or *to the days past*

Zechariah

Title and Background

The book is named after its author, and the title means "The LORD remembers." Zechariah's prophetic ministry took place in the postexilic period, the time of the Jewish restoration from Babylonian captivity. His prophecies began two months after Haggai's first message.

Author and Date of Writing

Zechariah was not only a prophet but also a priest. He was among those who returned to Judah in 538 B.C. He was a contemporary of Haggai but continued his ministry long after him. The book of Zechariah was probably written sometime before 480 B.C.

Theme and Message

Zechariah was concerned about the rebuilding of the temple, and in his first message he warned the people they were to listen to God's message through the prophets. He was also interested in their spiritual renewal. Zechariah also contains many Messianic passages: he predicted Christ's coming in lowliness (6:12), his humanity (6:12; 13:7), his rejection and betrayal for thirty pieces of silver (11:12-13), his being struck by the sword of the Lord (13:7), his priesthood (6:13), his kingship (6:13; 9:9; 14:9,16), his coming in glory (14:4), his building of the Lord's temple (6:12-13), his reign (9:10,14) and his establishment of enduring peace and prosperity (3:10; 9:9-10).

Outline

I.   A Call to Repentance (1:1-6)
II.   Eight Visions (1:7-6:8)
III. The Crowning of Joshua the High Priest (6:9-15)
IV.   Fasting and the Future (7:1-8:23)
V.   The Advent and Rejection of the Messiah (9:I-11:17)
VI.   The Advent and Redemption of the Messiah (12:1-14:21)

A Call to Return to the LORD

1 In the eighth month of the second year of Darius,[a] the word of the LORD came to the prophet Zechariah[b] son of Berekiah,[c] the son of Iddo:[d]

2 "The LORD was very angry[e] with your forefathers. 3 Therefore tell the people: This is what the LORD Almighty says: 'Return to me,' declares the LORD Almighty, 'and I will return to you,'[f] says the LORD Almighty. 4 Do not be like your forefathers,[g] to whom the earlier prophets proclaimed: This is what the LORD Almighty says: 'Turn from your evil ways[h] and your evil practices.' But they would not listen or pay attention to me,[i] declares the LORD. 5 Where are your forefathers now? And the prophets, do they live forever? 6 But did not my words and my decrees, which I commanded my servants the prophets, overtake your forefathers?

1:1
a Ezr 4:24; 6:15
b Ezr 5:1
c Mt 23:35;
Lk 11:51 d ver 7;
Ne 12:4
1:2
e 2Ch 36:16
1:3
f Mal 3:7;
Jas 4:8
1:4
g 2Ch 36:15
h Ps 106:6
i 2Ch 24:19;
Ps 78:8;
Jer 6:17

"Then they repented and said, 'The LORD Almighty has done to us what our ways and practices deserve,[j] just as he determined to do.' "

The Man Among the Myrtle Trees

[7]On the twenty-fourth day of the eleventh month, the month of Shebat, in the second year of Darius, the word of the LORD came to the prophet Zechariah son of Berekiah, the son of Iddo.

[8]During the night I had a vision—and there before me was a man riding a red[k] horse! He was standing among the myrtle trees in a ravine. Behind him were red, brown and white horses.[l]

[9]I asked, "What are these, my lord?"

The angel[m] who was talking with me answered, "I will show you what they are."

[10]Then the man standing among the myrtle trees explained, "They are the ones the LORD has sent to go throughout the earth."[n]

[11]And they reported to the angel of the LORD, who was standing among the myrtle trees, "We have gone throughout the earth and found the whole world at rest and in peace."[o]

[12]Then the angel of the LORD said, "LORD Almighty, how long will you withhold mercy from Jerusalem and from the towns of Judah, which you have been angry with these seventy[p] years?" [13]So the LORD spoke kind and comforting words to the angel who talked with me.[q]

[14]Then the angel who was speaking to me said, "Proclaim this word: This is what the LORD Almighty says: 'I am very jealous[r] for Jerusalem and Zion, [15]but I am very angry with the nations that feel secure.[s] I was only a little angry, but they added to the calamity.'[t]

[16]"Therefore, this is what the LORD says: 'I will return[u] to Jerusalem with mercy, and there my house will be rebuilt. And the measuring line[v] will be stretched out over Jerusalem,' declares the LORD Almighty.

[17]"Proclaim further: This is what the LORD Almighty says: 'My towns will again overflow with prosperity, and the LORD will again comfort[w] Zion and choose[x] Jerusalem.' "[y]

Four Horns and Four Craftsmen

[18]Then I looked up—and there before me were four horns! [19]I asked the angel who was speaking to me, "What are these?"

He answered me, "These are the horns[z] that scattered Judah, Israel and Jerusalem."

[20]Then the LORD showed me four craftsmen. [21]I asked, "What are these coming to do?"

He answered, "These are the horns that scattered Judah so that no one could raise his head, but the craftsmen have come to terrify them and throw down these horns of the nations who lifted up their horns[a] against the land of Judah to scatter its people."[b]

A Man With a Measuring Line

2 Then I looked up—and there before me was a man with a measuring line in his hand! [2]I asked, "Where are you going?"

He answered me, "To measure Jerusalem, to find out how wide and how long it is."[c]

[3]Then the angel who was speaking to me left, and another angel

came to meet him ⁴and said to him: "Run, tell that young man, 'Jerusalem will be a city without walls ᵈ because of the great number ᵉ of men and livestock in it. ⁵And I myself will be a wall ᶠ of fire around it,' declares the LORD, 'and I will be its glory ᵍ within.'

⁶"Come! Come! Flee from the land of the north," declares the LORD, "for I have scattered you to the four winds of heaven," ʰ declares the LORD.

⁷"Come, O Zion! Escape, you who live in the Daughter of Babylon!" ⁱ ⁸For this is what the LORD Almighty says: "After he has honored me and has sent me against the nations that have plundered you—for whoever touches you touches the apple of his eye ʲ— ⁹I will surely raise my hand against them so that their slaves will plunder them. ᵃᵏ Then you will know that the LORD Almighty has sent me. ˡ

¹⁰"Shout and be glad, O Daughter of Zion. ᵐ For I am coming, ⁿ and I will live among you," ᵒ declares the LORD. ¹¹"Many nations will be joined with the LORD in that day and will become my people. I will live among you and you will know that the LORD Almighty has sent me to you. ¹²The LORD will inherit ᵖ Judah as his portion in the holy land and will again choose ᑫ Jerusalem. ¹³Be still ʳ before the LORD, all mankind, because he has roused himself from his holy dwelling."

Clean Garments for the High Priest

3 Then he showed me Joshua ᵇˢ the high priest standing before the angel of the LORD, and Satan ᶜᵗ standing at his right side to accuse him. ²The LORD said to Satan, "The LORD rebuke you, ᵘ Satan! The LORD, who has chosen ᵛ Jerusalem, rebuke you! Is not this man a burning stick snatched from the fire?" ʷ

³Now Joshua was dressed in filthy clothes as he stood before the angel. ⁴The angel said to those who were standing before him, "Take off his filthy clothes."

Then he said to Joshua, "See, I have taken away your sin, ˣ and I will put rich garments ʸ on you."

⁵Then I said, "Put a clean turban ᶻ on his head." So they put a clean turban on his head and clothed him, while the angel of the LORD stood by.

⁶The angel of the LORD gave this charge to Joshua: ⁷"This is what the LORD Almighty says: 'If you will walk in my ways and keep my requirements, then you will govern my house ᵃ and have charge of my courts, and I will give you a place among these standing here.

⁸" 'Listen, O high priest Joshua and your associates seated before you, who are men symbolic ᵇ of things to come: I am going to bring my servant, the Branch. ᶜ ⁹See, the stone I have set in front of Joshua! There are seven eyes ᵈ on that one stone, ᵈ and I will engrave an inscription on it,' says the LORD Almighty, 'and I will remove the sin ᵉ of this land in a single day.

¹⁰" 'In that day each of you will invite his neighbor to sit under his vine and fig tree, ᶠ' declares the LORD Almighty."

2:4
dEze 38:11
eIsa 49:20;
Jer 30:19; 33:22
2:5
fIsa 26:1
gRev 21:23
2:6
hEze 17:21
2:7
iIsa 48:20
2:8
jDt 32:10
2:9
kIsa 14:2
lZec 4:9
2:10
mZep 3:14
nZec 9:9
oLev 26:12;
Zec 8:3
2:12
pDt 32:9;
Ps 33:12;
Jer 10:16
qZec 1:17
2:13
rHab 2:20
3:1
sHag 1:1;
Zec 6:11
tPs 109:6
3:2
uJude 1:9
vIsa 14:1
wAm 4:11;
Jude 1:23
3:4
xEze 36:25;
Mic 7:18
yIsa 52:1;
Rev 19:8
3:5
zEx 29:6
3:7
aDt 17:8-11;
Eze 44:15-16
3:8
bEze 12:11
cIsa 4:2
3:9
dIsa 28:16
eJer 50:20
3:10
f1Ki 4:25;
Mic 4:4

ᵃ8,9 Or *says after . . . eye:* ⁹"*I . . . plunder them."*   ᵇ1 A variant of *Jeshua;* here and elsewhere in Zechariah   ᶜ1 *Satan* means *accuser.*   ᵈ9 Or *facets*

The Gold Lampstand and the Two Olive Trees

4 Then the angel who talked with me returned and wakened[g] me, as a man is wakened from his sleep.[h] [2]He asked me, "What do you see?"[i]

I answered, "I see a solid gold lampstand[j] with a bowl at the top and seven lights[k] on it, with seven channels to the lights. [3]Also there are two olive trees[l] by it, one on the right of the bowl and the other on its left."

[4]I asked the angel who talked with me, "What are these, my lord?"
[5]He answered, "Do you not know what these are?"
"No, my lord," I replied.[m]

[6]So he said to me, "This is the word of the LORD to Zerubbabel:[n] 'Not by might nor by power, but by my Spirit,'[o] says the LORD Almighty.

[7]"What[a] are you, O mighty mountain? Before Zerubbabel you will become level ground.[p] Then he will bring out the capstone[q] to shouts of 'God bless it! God bless it!'"

[8]Then the word of the LORD came to me: [9]"The hands of Zerubbabel have laid the foundation[r] of this temple; his hands will also complete it.[s] Then you will know that the LORD Almighty has sent me[t] to you.

[10]"Who despises the day of small things?[u] Men will rejoice when they see the plumb line in the hand of Zerubbabel.

"(These seven are the eyes[v] of the LORD, which range throughout the earth.)"

[11]Then I asked the angel, "What are these two olive trees[w] on the right and the left of the lampstand?"

[12]Again I asked him, "What are these two olive branches beside the two gold pipes that pour out golden oil?"

[13]He replied, "Do you not know what these are?"
"No, my lord," I said.

[14]So he said, "These are the two who are anointed[x] to[b] serve the Lord of all the earth."

The Flying Scroll

5 I looked again—and there before me was a flying scroll![y] [2]He asked me, "What do you see?"

I answered, "I see a flying scroll, thirty feet long and fifteen feet wide.[c]"

[3]And he said to me, "This is the curse[z] that is going out over the whole land; for according to what it says on one side, every thief[a] will be banished, and according to what it says on the other, everyone who swears falsely[b] will be banished. [4]The LORD Almighty declares, 'I will send it out, and it will enter the house of the thief and the house of him who swears falsely by my name. It will remain in his house and destroy it, both its timbers and its stones.[c]'"

The Woman in a Basket

[5]Then the angel who was speaking to me came forward and said to me, "Look up and see what this is that is appearing."

[6]I asked, "What is it?"

4:1
gDa 8:18
hJer 31:26
4:2
iJer 1:13
jEx 25:31;
Rev 1:12
kRev 4:5
4:3
lver 11;
Rev 11:4
4:5
mZec 1:9
4:6
nEzr 5:2
oIsa 11:2-4;
Hos 1:7
4:7
pJer 51:25
qPs 118:22
4:9
rEzr 3:11
sEzr 3:8; 6:15;
Zec 6:12
tZec 2:9
4:10
uHag 2:3
vZec 3:9;
Rev 5:6
4:11
wver 3;
Rev 11:4
4:14
xEx 29:7; 40:15;
Da 9:24-26;
Zec 3:1-7
5:1
yEze 2:9;
Rev 5:1
5:3
zIsa 24:6;
43:28; Mal 3:9;
4:6 aEx 20:15;
Mal 3:8
bIsa 48:1
5:4
cLev 14:34-45;
Hab 2:9-11;
Mal 3:5

---

[a]7 Or *Who*   [b]14 Or *two who bring oil and*   [c]2 Hebrew *twenty cubits long and ten cubits wide* (about 9 meters long and 4.5 meters wide)

He replied, "It is a measuring basket.[a]" And he added, "This is the iniquity[b] of the people throughout the land."

[7]Then the cover of lead was raised, and there in the basket sat a woman! [8]He said, "This is wickedness," and he pushed her back into the basket and pushed the lead cover down over its mouth. [d]

[9]Then I looked up—and there before me were two women, with the wind in their wings! They had wings like those of a stork,[e] and they lifted up the basket between heaven and earth.

[10]"Where are they taking the basket?" I asked the angel who was speaking to me.

[11]He replied, "To the country of Babylonia[c][f] to build a house[g] for it. When it is ready, the basket will be set there in its place."[h]

Four Chariots

6 I looked up again—and there before me were four chariots[i] coming out from between two mountains—mountains of bronze! [2]The first chariot had red horses, the second black,[j] [3]the third white,[k] and the fourth dappled—all of them powerful. [4]I asked the angel who was speaking to me, "What are these, my lord?"

[5]The angel answered me, "These are the four spirits[d][1] of heaven, going out from standing in the presence of the Lord of the whole world. [6]The one with the black horses is going toward the north country, the one with the white horses toward the west,[e] and the one with the dappled horses toward the south."

[7]When the powerful horses went out, they were straining to go throughout the earth. [m] And he said, "Go throughout the earth!" So they went throughout the earth.

[8]Then he called to me, "Look, those going toward the north country have given my Spirit[f] rest[n] in the land of the north."

A Crown for Joshua

[9]The word of the LORD came to me: [10]"Take silver and gold from the exiles Heldai, Tobijah and Jedaiah, who have arrived from Babylon. [o] Go the same day to the house of Josiah son of Zephaniah. [11]Take the silver and gold and make a crown,[p] and set it on the head of the high priest, Joshua[q] son of Jehozadak.[r] [12]Tell him this is what the LORD Almighty says: 'Here is the man whose name is the Branch,[s] and he will branch out from his place and build the temple of the LORD. [t] [13]It is he who will build the temple of the LORD, and he will be clothed with majesty and will sit and rule on his throne. And he will be a priest[u] on his throne. And there will be harmony between the two.' [14]The crown will be given to Heldai,[g] Tobijah, Jedaiah and Hen[h] son of Zephaniah as a memorial in the temple of the LORD. [15]Those who are far away will come and help to build the temple of the LORD,[v] and you will know that the LORD Almighty has sent me to you.[w] This will happen if you diligently obey[x] the LORD your God."

---

[a]6 Hebrew *an ephah*; also in verses 7-11   [b]6 Or *appearance*   [c]11 Hebrew *Shinar*   [d]5 Or *winds*   [e]6 Or *horses after them*   [f]8 Or *spirit*   [g]14 Syriac; Hebrew *Helem*   [h]14 Or *and the gracious one, the*

5:8 dMic 6:11
5:9 eLev 11:19
5:11 fGe 10:10; gJer 29:5,28; hDa 1:2
6:1 iver 5
6:2 jRev 6:5
6:3 kRev 6:2
6:5 lEze 37:9; Mt 24:31; Rev 7:1
6:7 mZec 1:10
6:8 nEze 5:13; 24:13
6:10 oEzr 7:14-16; Jer 28:6
6:11 pPs 21:3; qZec 3:1; rEzr 3:2
6:12 sIsa 4:2; Zec 3:8; tEzr 3:8-10; Zec 4:6-9
6:13 uPs 110:4
6:15 vIsa 60:10; wZec 2:9-11; xIsa 58:12; Jer 7:23; Zec 3:7

Justice and Mercy, Not Fasting

7 In the fourth year of King Darius, the word of the Lord came to Zechariah on the fourth day of the ninth month, the month of Kislev.[y] [2]The people of Bethel had sent Sharezer and Regem-Melech, together with their men, to entreat[z] the Lord [3]by asking the priests of the house of the Lord Almighty and the prophets, "Should I mourn[a] and fast in the fifth[b] month, as I have done for so many years?"

[4]Then the word of the Lord Almighty came to me: [5]"Ask all the people of the land and the priests, 'When you fasted[c] and mourned in the fifth and seventh months for the past seventy years, was it really for me that you fasted? [6]And when you were eating and drinking, were you not just feasting for yourselves? [7]Are these not the words the Lord proclaimed through the earlier prophets[d] when Jerusalem and its surrounding towns were at rest[e] and prosperous, and the Negev and the western foothills[f] were settled?' "

[8]And the word of the Lord came again to Zechariah: [9]"This is what the Lord Almighty says: 'Administer true justice;[g] show mercy and compassion to one another. [10]Do not oppress the widow or the fatherless, the alien[h] or the poor. In your hearts do not think evil of each other.'[i]

[11]"But they refused to pay attention; stubbornly they turned their backs and stopped up their ears.[j] [12]They made their hearts as hard as flint[k] and would not listen to the law or to the words that the Lord Almighty had sent by his Spirit through the earlier prophets.[l] So the Lord Almighty was very angry.[m]

[13]" 'When I called, they did not listen;[n] so when they called, I would not listen,'[o] says the Lord Almighty.[p] [14]'I scattered[q] them with a whirlwind[r] among all the nations, where they were strangers. The land was left so desolate behind them that no one could come or go. This is how they made the pleasant land desolate.[s]' "

The Lord Promises to Bless Jerusalem

8 Again the word of the Lord Almighty came to me. [2]This is what the Lord Almighty says: "I am very jealous for Zion; I am burning with jealousy for her."

[3]This is what the Lord says: "I will return[t] to Zion and dwell in Jerusalem.[u] Then Jerusalem will be called the City of Truth, and the mountain of the Lord Almighty will be called the Holy Mountain."

[4]This is what the Lord Almighty says: "Once again men and women of ripe old age will sit in the streets of Jerusalem,[v] each with cane in hand because of his age. [5]The city streets will be filled with boys and girls playing there.[w]"

[6]This is what the Lord Almighty says: "It may seem marvelous to the remnant of this people at that time,[x] but will it seem marvelous to me?[y]" declares the Lord Almighty.

[7]This is what the Lord Almighty says: "I will save my people from the countries of the east and the west.[z] [8]I will bring them back[a] to live in Jerusalem; they will be my people,[b] and I will be faithful and righteous to them as their God."

[9]This is what the Lord Almighty says: "You who now hear these words spoken by the prophets[c] who were there when the foundation

was laid for the house of the Lord Almighty, let your hands be strong[d] so that the temple may be built. [10]Before that time there were no wages[e] for man or beast. No one could go about his business safely because of his enemy, for I had turned every man against his neighbor. [11]But now I will not deal with the remnant of this people as I did in the past,"[f] declares the Lord Almighty.

[12]"The seed will grow well, the vine will yield its fruit,[g] the ground will produce its crops,[h] and the heavens will drop their dew.[i] I will give all these things as an inheritance[j] to the remnant of this people. [13]As you have been an object of cursing[k] among the nations, O Judah and Israel, so will I save you, and you will be a blessing.[l] Do not be afraid, but let your hands be strong."

[14]This is what the Lord Almighty says: "Just as I had determined to bring disaster[m] upon you and showed no pity when your fathers angered me," says the Lord Almighty, [15]"so now I have determined to do good[n] again to Jerusalem and Judah. Do not be afraid. [16]These are the things you are to do: Speak the truth[o] to each other, and render true and sound judgment in your courts;[p] [17]do not plot evil[q] against your neighbor, and do not love to swear falsely.[r] I hate all this," declares the Lord.

[18]Again the word of the Lord Almighty came to me. [19]This is what the Lord Almighty says: "The fasts of the fourth,[s] fifth,[t] seventh[u] and tenth[v] months will become joyful[w] and glad occasions and happy festivals for Judah. Therefore love truth[x] and peace."

[20]This is what the Lord Almighty says: "Many peoples and the inhabitants of many cities will yet come, [21]and the inhabitants of one city will go to another and say, 'Let us go at once to entreat[y] the Lord and seek the Lord Almighty. I myself am going.' [22]And many peoples and powerful nations will come to Jerusalem to seek the Lord Almighty and to entreat him."[z]

[23]This is what the Lord Almighty says: "In those days ten men from all languages and nations will take firm hold of one Jew by the hem of his robe and say, 'Let us go with you, because we have heard that God is with you.' "[a]

Judgment on Israel's Enemies

An Oracle

9 The word of the Lord is against the land of Hadrach
　　and will rest upon Damascus[b]—
for the eyes of men and all the tribes of Israel
　　are on the Lord—[a]
[2]and upon Hamath[c] too, which borders on it,
　　and upon Tyre[d] and Sidon, though they are very
　　　skillful.
[3]Tyre has built herself a stronghold;
　　she has heaped up silver like dust,
　　and gold like the dirt of the streets.[e]
[4]But the Lord will take away her possessions
　　and destroy her power on the sea,

---

a1 Or *Damascus. / For the eye of the Lord is on all mankind, / as well as on the tribes of Israel,*

8:9
d Hag 2:4
8:10
e Hag 1:6
8:11
f Isa 12:1
8:12
g Joel 2:22
h Ps 67:6
i Ge 27:28
j Ob 1:17
8:13
k Jer 42:18
l Ge 12:2
8:14
m Jer 31:28;
Eze 24:14
8:15
n ver 13;
Jer 29:11;
Mic 7:18-20
8:16
o Ps 15:2;
Eph 4:25
p Zec 7:9
8:17
q Pr 3:29
r Pr 6:16-19
8:19
s Jer 39:2
t Jer 52:12
u 2Ki 25:25
v Jer 52:4
w Ps 30:11
x ver 16
8:21
y Zec 7:2
8:22
z Ps 117:1;
Isa 60:3;
Zec 2:11
8:23
a Isa 45:14;
1Co 14:25
9:1
b Isa 17:1
9:2
c Jer 49:23
d Eze 28:1-19
9:3
e Job 27:16;
Eze 28:4

and she will be consumed by fire. [f]

[5]Ashkelon will see it and fear;
  Gaza will writhe in agony,
    and Ekron too, for her hope will wither.
  Gaza will lose her king
    and Ashkelon will be deserted.
[6]Foreigners will occupy Ashdod,
    and I will cut off the pride of the Philistines.
[7]I will take the blood from their mouths,
    the forbidden food from between their teeth.
  Those who are left will belong to our God
    and become leaders in Judah,
    and Ekron will be like the Jebusites.
[8]But I will defend my house
    against marauding forces.
  Never again will an oppressor overrun my people,
    for now I am keeping watch. [g]

The Coming of Zion's King

[9]Rejoice greatly, O Daughter of Zion!
    Shout, Daughter of Jerusalem!
  See, your king[a] comes to you,
    righteous and having salvation, [h]
    gentle and riding on a donkey,
    on a colt, the foal of a donkey. [i]
[10]I will take away the chariots from Ephraim
    and the war-horses from Jerusalem,
    and the battle bow will be broken. [j]
  He will proclaim peace to the nations.
    His rule will extend from sea to sea
    and from the River[b] to the ends of the earth. [c] [k]
[11]As for you, because of the blood of my covenant[l] with
      you,
  I will free your prisoners[m] from the waterless pit.
[12]Return to your fortress, [n] O prisoners of hope;
    even now I announce that I will restore twice as much
      to you.
[13]I will bend Judah as I bend my bow
    and fill it with Ephraim. [o]
  I will rouse your sons, O Zion,
    against your sons, O Greece, [p]
    and make you like a warrior's sword. [q]

The Lord Will Appear

[14]Then the Lord will appear over them; [r]
    his arrow will flash like lightning. [s]
  The Sovereign Lord will sound the trumpet;
    he will march in the storms[t] of the south,
[15] and the Lord Almighty will shield[u] them.

9:4
f Isa 23:1;
Eze 26:3-5;
28:18
9:8
g Isa 52:1; 54:14
9:9
h Isa 9:6-7;
43:3-11;
Jer 23:5-6;
Zep 3:14-15;
Zec 2:10
i Mt 21:5*;
Jn 12:15*
9:10
j Hos 1:7; 2:18;
Mic 4:3; 5:10;
Zec 10:4
k Ps 72:8
9:11
l Ex 24:8
m Isa 42:7
9:12
n Joel 3:16
9:13
o Isa 49:2
p Joel 3:6
q Jer 51:20
9:14
r Isa 31:5
s Ps 18:14;
Hab 3:11
t Isa 21:1; 66:15
9:15
u Isa 37:35;
Zec 12:8

a9 Or *King*   *b10* That is, the Euphrates   *c10* Or *the end of the land*

They will destroy
and overcome with slingstones.
They will drink and roar as with wine;
they will be full like a bowl
used for sprinkling[a] the corners[v] of the altar.
16The Lord their God will save them on that day
as the flock of his people.
They will sparkle in his land
like jewels in a crown.[w]
17How attractive and beautiful they will be!
Grain will make the young men thrive,
and new wine the young women.

The Lord Will Care for Judah

10 Ask the Lord for rain in the springtime;
it is the Lord who makes the storm clouds.
He gives showers of rain to men,
and plants of the field to everyone.
2The idols[x] speak deceit,
diviners see visions that lie;
they tell dreams that are false,
they give comfort in vain.
Therefore the people wander like sheep
oppressed for lack of a shepherd.[y]

3"My anger burns against the shepherds,
and I will punish the leaders;[z]
for the Lord Almighty will care
for his flock, the house of Judah,
and make them like a proud horse in battle.
4From Judah will come the cornerstone,
from him the tent peg,[a]
from him the battle bow,[b]
from him every ruler.
5Together they[b] will be like mighty men
trampling the muddy streets in battle.[c]
Because the Lord is with them,
they will fight and overthrow the horsemen.[d]

6"I will strengthen the house of Judah
and save the house of Joseph.
I will restore them
because I have compassion on them.[e]
They will be as though
I had not rejected them,
for I am the Lord their God
and I will answer[f] them.
7The Ephraimites will become like mighty men,
and their hearts will be glad as with wine.[g]
Their children will see it and be joyful;
their hearts will rejoice in the Lord.

9:15
vEx 27:2
9:16
wIsa 62:3;
Jer 31:11
10:2
xEze 21:21
yEze 34:5;
Hos 3:4;
Mt 9:36
10:3
zJer 25:34
10:4
aIsa 22:23
bZec 9:10
10:5
c2Sa 22:43
dAm 2:15;
Hag 2:22
10:6
eZec 8:7-8
fZec 13:9
10:7
gZec 9:15

a15 Or bowl, / like   b4,5 Or ruler, all of them together. / 5They

⁸I will signal[h] for them
    and gather them in.
Surely I will redeem them;
    they will be as numerous[i] as before.
⁹Though I scatter them among the peoples,
    yet in distant lands they will remember me.[j]
They and their children will survive,
    and they will return.
¹⁰I will bring them back from Egypt
    and gather them from Assyria.[k]
I will bring them to Gilead[l] and Lebanon,
    and there will not be room[m] enough for them.
¹¹They will pass through the sea of trouble;
    the surging sea will be subdued
    and all the depths of the Nile will dry up.[n]
Assyria's pride[o] will be brought down
    and Egypt's scepter[p] will pass away.
¹²I will strengthen them in the LORD
    and in his name they will walk,[q]"

                    declares the LORD.

11   Open your doors, O Lebanon,[r]
    so that fire may devour your cedars!
²Wail, O pine tree, for the cedar has fallen;
    the stately trees are ruined!
Wail, oaks of Bashan;
    the dense forest[s] has been cut down!
³Listen to the wail of the shepherds;
    their rich pastures are destroyed!
Listen to the roar of the lions;
    the lush thicket of the Jordan is ruined![t]

Two Shepherds

⁴This is what the LORD my God says: "Pasture the flock marked for slaughter. ⁵Their buyers slaughter them and go unpunished. Those who sell them say, 'Praise the LORD, I am rich!' Their own shepherds do not spare them.[u] ⁶For I will no longer have pity on the people of the land," declares the LORD. "I will hand everyone over to his neighbor[v] and his king. They will oppress the land, and I will not rescue them from their hands."[w]

⁷So I pastured the flock marked for slaughter, particularly the oppressed of the flock. Then I took two staffs and called one Favor and the other Union, and I pastured the flock. ⁸In one month I got rid of the three shepherds.

The flock detested me, and I grew weary of them ⁹and said, "I will not be your shepherd. Let the dying die, and the perishing perish.[x] Let those who are left eat one another's flesh."

¹⁰Then I took my staff called Favor[y] and broke it, revoking[z] the covenant I had made with all the nations. ¹¹It was revoked on that day, and so the afflicted of the flock who were watching me knew it was the word of the LORD.

10:8
h Isa 5:26
i Jer 33:22;
Eze 36:11
10:9
j Eze 6:9
10:10
k Isa 11:11
l Jer 50:19
m Isa 49:19
10:11
n Isa 19:5-7;
51:10 o Zep 2:13
p Eze 30:13
10:12
q Mic 4:5
11:1
r Eze 31:3
11:2
s Isa 32:19
11:3
t Jer 2:15; 50:44
11:5
u Jer 50:7;
Eze 34:2-3
11:6
v Zec 14:13
w Isa 9:19-21;
Jer 13:14;
Mic 5:8; 7:2-6
11:9
x Jer 15:2; 43:11
11:10
y ver 7
z Ps 89:39;
Jer 14:21

¹²I told them, "If you think it best, give me my pay; but if not, keep it." So they paid me thirty pieces of silver. ª

¹³And the LORD said to me, "Throw it to the potter"—the handsome price at which they priced me! So I took the thirty pieces of silver and threw them into the house of the LORD to the potter. ᵇ

¹⁴Then I broke my second staff called Union, breaking the brotherhood between Judah and Israel.

¹⁵Then the LORD said to me, "Take again the equipment of a foolish shepherd. ¹⁶For I am going to raise up a shepherd over the land who will not care for the lost, or seek the young, or heal the injured, or feed the healthy, but will eat the meat of the choice sheep, tearing off their hoofs.

> ¹⁷"Woe to the worthless shepherd, ᶜ
> who deserts the flock!
> May the sword strike his arm ᵈ and his right eye!
> May his arm be completely withered,
> his right eye totally blinded!" ᵉ

Jerusalem's Enemies to Be Destroyed

An Oracle

12 This is the word of the LORD concerning Israel. The LORD, who stretches out the heavens, ᶠ who lays the foundation of the earth, ᵍ and who forms the spirit of man ʰ within him, declares: ²"I am going to make Jerusalem a cup ⁱ that sends all the surrounding peoples reeling. ʲ Judah ᵏ will be besieged as well as Jerusalem. ³On that day, when all the nations ˡ of the earth are gathered against her, I will make Jerusalem an immovable rock ᵐ for all the nations. All who try to move it will injure ⁿ themselves. ⁴On that day I will strike every horse with panic and its rider with madness," declares the LORD. "I will keep a watchful eye over the house of Judah, but I will blind all the horses of the nations. ᵒ ⁵Then the leaders of Judah will say in their hearts, 'The people of Jerusalem are strong, because the LORD Almighty is their God.'

⁶"On that day I will make the leaders of Judah like a firepot ᵖ in a woodpile, like a flaming torch among sheaves. They will consume �q right and left all the surrounding peoples, but Jerusalem will remain intact in her place.

⁷"The LORD will save the dwellings of Judah first, so that the honor of the house of David and of Jerusalem's inhabitants may not be greater than that of Judah. ʳ ⁸On that day the LORD will shield ˢ those who live in Jerusalem, so that the feeblest among them will be like David, and the house of David will be like God, ᵗ like the Angel of the LORD going before ᵘ them. ⁹On that day I will set out to destroy all the nations that attack Jerusalem. ᵛ

Mourning for the One They Pierced

¹⁰"And I will pour out on the house of David and the inhabitants of Jerusalem a spirit ª of grace and supplication. ʷ They will look on ᵇ me, the one they have pierced, ˣ and they will mourn for him as one mourns

---

ª10 Or *the Spirit*   ᵇ10 Or *to*

11:12
ªEx 21:32;
Mt 26:15
11:13
ᵇMt 27:9-10*;
Ac 1:18-19
11:17
ᶜJer 23:1
ᵈEze 30:21-22
ᵉJer 23:1
12:1
ᶠIsa 42:5;
Jer 51:15
ᵍPs 102:25;
Heb 1:10
ʰIsa 57:16
12:2
ⁱPs 75:8
ʲIsa 51:23
ᵏZec 14:14
12:3
ˡZec 14:2
ᵐDa 2:34-35
ⁿMt 21:44
12:4
ᵒPs 76:6
12:6
ᵖIsa 10:17-18;
Zec 11:1
qOb 1:18
12:7
ʳJer 30:18;
Am 9:11
12:8
ˢJoel 3:16;
Zec 9:15
ᵗPs 82:6
ᵘMic 7:8
12:9
ᵛZec 14:2-3
12:10
ʷIsa 44:3;
Eze 39:29;
Joel 2:28-29
ˣJn 19:34,37*;
Rev 1:7

for an only child, and grieve bitterly for him as one grieves for a firstborn son. ¹¹On that day the weeping in Jerusalem will be great, like the weeping of Hadad Rimmon in the plain of Megiddo. ʸ ¹²The land will mourn, ᶻ each clan by itself, with their wives by themselves: the clan of the house of David and their wives, the clan of the house of Nathan and their wives, ¹³the clan of the house of Levi and their wives, the clan of Shimei and their wives, ¹⁴and all the rest of the clans and their wives.

Cleansing From Sin

13 "On that day a fountainᵃ will be opened to the house of David and the inhabitants of Jerusalem, to cleanseᵇ them from sin and impurity.

²"On that day, I will banish the names of the idolsᶜ from the land, and they will be remembered no more," declares the Lord Almighty. "I will remove both the prophetsᵈ and the spirit of impurity from the land. ³And if anyone still prophesies, his father and mother, to whom he was born, will say to him, 'You must die, because you have told lies in the Lord's name.' When he prophesies, his own parents will stab him. ᵉ

⁴"On that day every prophet will be ashamedᶠ of his prophetic vision. He will not put on a prophet's garmentᵍ of hairʰ in order to deceive. ⁵He will say, 'I am not a prophet. I am a farmer; the land has been my livelihood since my youth. ᵃ'ⁱ ⁶If someone asks him, 'What are these wounds on your bodyᵇ?' he will answer, 'The wounds I was given at the house of my friends.'

The Shepherd Struck, the Sheep Scattered

⁷"Awake, O sword,ʲ against my shepherd,ᵏ
  against the man who is close to me!"
  declares the Lord Almighty.
"Strike the shepherd,
  and the sheep will be scattered,ˡ
  and I will turn my hand against the little ones.
⁸In the whole land," declares the Lord,
  "two-thirds will be struck down and perish;
  yet one-third will be left in it. ᵐ
⁹This third I will bring into the fire;ⁿ
  I will refine them like silverᵒ
  and test them like gold.
They will callᵖ on my name
  and I will answer�q them;
I will say, 'They are my people,'ʳ
  and they will say, 'The Lord is our God.ˢ'"

The Lord Comes and Reigns

14 A day of the Lordᵗ is coming when your plunder will be divided among you.

12:11
y 2Ki 23:29
12:12
z Mt 24:30;
Rev 1:7
13:1
a Jer 17:13
b Ps 51:2;
Heb 9:14
13:2
c Ex 23:13;
Eze 36:25;
Hos 2:17
d 1Ki 22:22;
Jer 23:14-15
13:3
e Dt 13:6-11;
18:20;
Jer 23:34;
Eze 14:9
13:4
f Jer 6:15;
Mic 3:6-7
g Mt 3:4
h 2Ki 1:8;
Isa 20:2
13:5
i Am 7:14
13:7
j Jer 47:6
k Isa 40:11;
53:4; Eze 37:24
l Mt 26:31*;
Mk 14:27*
13:8
m Eze 5:2-4,12
13:9
n Mal 3:2
o Isa 48:10;
1Pe 1:6-7
p Ps 50:15
q Zec 10:6
r Jer 30:22
s Jer 29:12
14:1
t Isa 13:9;
Mal 4:1

ᵃ5 Or *farmer; a man sold me in my youth*   ᵇ6 Or *wounds between your hands*

²I will gather all the nations to Jerusalem to fight against it; the city will be captured, the houses ransacked, and the women raped. Half of the city will go into exile, but the rest of the people will not be taken from the city. ᵘ

³Then the Lord will go out and fightᵛ against those nations, as he fights in the day of battle. ⁴On that day his feet will stand on the Mount of Olives, ʷ east of Jerusalem, and the Mount of Olives will be split in two from east to west, forming a great valley, with half of the mountain moving north and half moving south. ⁵You will flee by my mountain valley, for it will extend to Azel. You will flee as you fled from the earthquakeᵃˣ in the days of Uzziah king of Judah. Then the Lord my God will come, ʸ and all the holy ones with him. ᶻ

⁶On that day there will be no light, ᵃ no cold or frost. ⁷It will be a uniqueᵇ day, without daytime or nighttimeᶜ—a day known to the Lord. When evening comes, there will be light. ᵈ

⁸On that day living waterᵉ will flow out from Jerusalem, half to the easternᶠ seaᵇ and half to the western sea, ᶜ in summer and in winter.

⁹The Lord will be king over the whole earth. ᵍ On that day there will be one Lord, and his name the only name. ʰ

¹⁰The whole land, from Gebaⁱ to Rimmon, south of Jerusalem, will become like the Arabah. But Jerusalem will be raised upʲ and remain in its place, ᵏ from the Benjamin Gate to the site of the First Gate, to the Corner Gate, and from the Tower of Hananel to the royal winepresses. ¹¹It will be inhabited; never again will it be destroyed. Jerusalem will be secure. ˡ

¹²This is the plague with which the Lord will strike all the nations that fought against Jerusalem: Their flesh will rot while they are still standing on their feet, their eyes will rot in their sockets, and their tongues will rot in their mouths. ᵐ ¹³On that day men will be stricken by the Lord with great panic. Each man will seize the hand of another, and they will attack each other. ⁿ ¹⁴Judahᵒ too will fight at Jerusalem. The wealth of all the surrounding nations will be collectedᵖ—great quantities of gold and silver and clothing. ¹⁵A similar plagueᑫ will strike the horses and mules, the camels and donkeys, and all the animals in those camps.

¹⁶Then the survivors from all the nations that have attacked Jerusalem will go up year after year to worship the King, the Lord Almighty, and to celebrate the Feast of Tabernacles. ʳ ¹⁷If any of the peoples of the earth do not go up to Jerusalem to worship the King, the Lord Almighty, they will have no rain. ˢ ¹⁸If the Egyptian people do not go up and take part, they will have no rain. The Lordᵈ will bring on them the plague he inflicts on the nations that do not go up to celebrate the Feast of Tabernacles. ᵗ ¹⁹This will be the punishment of Egypt and the punishment of all the nations that do not go up to celebrate the Feast of Tabernacles.

²⁰On that day HOLY TO THE LORD will be inscribed on the bells of the

---

ᵃ5 Or ⁵*My mountain valley will be blocked and will extend to Azel. It will be blocked as it was blocked because of the earthquake*   ᵇ8 That is, the Dead Sea   ᶜ8 That is, the Mediterranean   ᵈ18 Or *part, then the Lord*

14:2
ᵘ Isa 13:6;
Zec 13:8
14:3
ᵛ Zec 9:14-15
14:4
ʷ Eze 11:23
14:5
ˣ Am 1:1
ʸ Isa 29:6;
66:15-16
ᶻ Mt 16:27;
25:31
14:6
ᵃ Isa 13:10;
Jer 4:23
14:7
ᵇ Jer 30:7
ᶜ Rev 21:23-25;
22:5 ᵈ Isa 30:26
14:8
ᵉ Eze 47:1-12;
Jn 7:38;
Rev 22:1-2
ᶠ Joel 2:20
14:9
ᵍ Dt 6:4;
Isa 45:24;
Rev 11:15
ʰ Eph 4:5-6
14:10
ⁱ 1Ki 15:22
ʲ Jer 30:18;
Am 9:11
ᵏ Zec 12:6
14:11
ˡ Eze 34:25-28
14:12
ᵐ Lev 26:16;
Dt 28:22
14:13
ⁿ Zec 11:6
14:14
ᵒ Zec 12:2
ᵖ Isa 23:18
14:15
ᑫ ver 12
14:16
ʳ Isa 60:6-9
14:17
ˢ Jer 14:4;
Am 4:7
14:18
ᵗ ver 12

14:20
uEze 46:20
vZec 9:15
14:21
wRo 14:6-7
xNe 8:10
yZec 9:8
zEze 44:9

horses, and the cooking pots[u] in the Lord's house will be like the sacred bowls[v] in front of the altar. [21]Every pot in Jerusalem and Judah will be holy[w] to the Lord Almighty, and all who come to sacrifice will take some of the pots and cook in them. And on that day[x] there will no longer be a Canaanite[a][y] in the house of the Lord Almighty. [z]

Malachi

Title and Background

The temple had been rebuilt, but times of prosperity had not come. The people were suffering drought, famine and blighted crops, and they met these conditions with indifference and spiritual lethargy. They had forgotten God and treated him with dishonor. They had also married foreign women. Against such a background Malachi, meaning "my messenger," was written.

Author and Date of Writing

Since the term "my messenger" occurs in 3:1, and since both prophets and priests were called messengers of the Lord, some have thought "Malachi" only a title that tradition has given the author. There is no certainty about this, however, and it seems likely that Malachi was in fact the author's name. The book was written probably 433-430 B.C.

Theme and Message

Malachi's message is filled with indictments and warnings. He rebukes the Jews for doubting God's love (1:2-5) and for the faithlessness of both priests (1:6-2:9) and people (2:10-16). How quickly the nation had forgotten! Only through repentance and reformation will the people again experience God's blessing (3:6-12). That "great and dreadful day of the LORD" (4:5) was coming, and Malachi both reassures and warns his people.

Outline

   I. God's Covenant Love for Israel (1:1-5)
  II. Israel's Unfaithfulness (1:6-2:16)
     A. The Unfaithfulness of the Priests (1:6-2:9)
     B. The Unfaithfulness of the People (2:10-16)
 III. The Lord's Coming (2:17-4:6)

---

1 An oracle:^a The word^b of the LORD to Israel through Malachi.^a

Jacob Loved, Esau Hated

²"I have loved^c you," says the LORD.

"But you ask, 'How have you loved us?'

"Was not Esau Jacob's brother?" the LORD says. "Yet I have loved Jacob,^d ³but Esau I have hated, and I have turned his mountains into a wasteland^e and left his inheritance to the desert jackals.^f"

⁴Edom may say, "Though we have been crushed, we will rebuild^g the ruins."

But this is what the LORD Almighty says: "They may build, but I will demolish. They will be called the Wicked Land, a people always under

^a1 Malachi means my messenger.

1:1
^aNa 1:1
^b1Pe 4:11
1:2
^cDt 4:37
^dRo 9:13*
1:3
^eIsa 34:10
^fEze 35:3-9
1:4
^gIsa 9:10

the wrath of the LORD. ʰ ⁵You will see it with your own eyes and say, 'Greatⁱ is the LORD—even beyond the borders of Israel!'ʲ

Blemished Sacrifices

⁶"A son honors his father, and a servant his master. If I am a father, where is the honor due me? If I am a master, where is the respectᵏ due me?" says the LORD Almighty.ˡ "It is you, O priests, who show contempt for my name.

"But you ask, 'How have we shown contempt for your name?' ⁷"You place defiled foodᵐ on my altar.

"But you ask, 'How have we defiled you?'

"By saying that the LORD's table is contemptible. ⁸When you bring blind animals for sacrifice, is that not wrong? When you sacrifice crippled or diseased animals,ⁿ is that not wrong? Try offering them to your governor! Would he be pleased with you? Would he accept you?" says the LORD Almighty.ᵒ

⁹"Now implore God to be gracious to us. With such offeringsᵖ from your hands, will he accept you?"—says the LORD Almighty.

¹⁰"Oh, that one of you would shut the temple doors, so that you would not light useless fires on my altar! I am not pleased�q with you," says the LORD Almighty, "and I will accept no offeringʳ from your hands. ¹¹My name will be great among the nations, from the rising to the setting of the sun. In every place incenseˢ and pure offerings will be brought to my name, because my name will be great among the nations," says the LORD Almighty.

¹²"But you profane it by saying of the Lord's table, 'It is defiled,' and of its food,ᵗ 'It is contemptible.' ¹³And you say, 'What a burden!'ᵘ and you sniff at it contemptuously," says the LORD Almighty.

"When you bring injured, crippled or diseased animals and offer them as sacrifices, should I accept them from your hands?" says the LORD. ¹⁴"Cursed is the cheat who has an acceptable male in his flock and vows to give it, but then sacrifices a blemished animalᵛ to the Lord. For I am a great king,ʷ" says the LORD Almighty, "and my name is to be feared among the nations.

Admonition for the Priests

2 "And now this admonition is for you, O priests.ˣ ²If you do not listen, and if you do not set your heart to honor my name," says the LORD Almighty, "I will send a curseʸ upon you, and I will curse your blessings. Yes, I have already cursed them, because you have not set your heart to honor me.

³"Because of you I will rebukeᵃ your descendantsᵇ; I will spread on your faces the offalᶻ from your festival sacrifices, and you will be carried off with it.ᵃ ⁴And you will know that I have sent you this admonition so that my covenant with Leviᵇ may continue," says the LORD Almighty. ⁵"My covenant was with him, a covenantᶜ of life and peace,ᵈ and I gave them to him; this called for reverence and he revered me and stood in awe of my name. ⁶True instructionᵉ was in his mouth and nothing false was found on his lips. He walked with me in peace and uprightness, and turned many from sin.ᶠ

ᵃ3 Or *cut off* (see Septuagint)   ᵇ3 Or *will blight your grain*

1:4
hEze 25:12-14
1:5
iPs 35:27;
Mic 5:4
jAm 1:11-12
1:6
kIsa 1:2
lJob 5:17
1:7
mver 12;
Lev 21:6
1:8
nLev 22:22;
Dt 15:21
oIsa 43:23
1:9
pLev 23:33-44
1:10
qHos 5:6
rIsa 1:11-14;
Jer 14:12
1:11
sIsa 60:6-7;
Rev 8:3
1:12
tver 7
1:13
uIsa 43:22-24
1:14
vLev 22:18-21
w1Ti 6:15
2:1
xver 7
2:2
yDt 28:20
2:3
zEx 29:14
a1Ki 14:10
2:4
bNu 3:12
2:5
cDt 33:9
dNu 25:12
2:6
eDt 33:10
fJer 23:22;
Jas 5:19-20

7"For the lips of a priestᵍ ought to preserve knowledge, and from his mouth men should seek instruction ʰ—because he is the messenger ⁱ of the Lᴏʀᴅ Almighty. ⁸But you have turned from the way and by your teaching have caused many to stumble;ʲ you have violated the covenant with Levi," says the Lᴏʀᴅ Almighty. ⁹"So I have caused you to be despised ᵏ and humiliated before all the people, because you have not followed my ways but have shown partiality in matters of the law."

Judah Unfaithful

¹⁰Have we not all one Father ᵃ?¹ Did not one God create us? Why do we profane the covenant ᵐ of our fathers by breaking faith with one another?

¹¹Judah has broken faith. A detestable thing has been committed in Israel and in Jerusalem: Judah has desecrated the sanctuary the Lᴏʀᴅ loves, by marrying ⁿ the daughter of a foreign god.ᵒ ¹²As for the man who does this, whoever he may be, may the Lᴏʀᴅ cut him off ᵖ from the tents of Jacob ᵇ—even though he brings offerings �q to the Lᴏʀᴅ Almighty.

¹³Another thing you do: You flood the Lᴏʀᴅ's altar with tears. You weep and wail because he no longer pays attention ʳ to your offerings or accepts them with pleasure from your hands. ¹⁴You ask, "Why?" It is because the Lᴏʀᴅ is acting as the witness between you and the wife of your youth, ˢ because you have broken faith with her, though she is your partner, the wife of your marriage covenant.

¹⁵Has not ͺthe Lᴏʀᴅͺ made them one? ᵗ In flesh and spirit they are his. And why one? Because he was seeking godly offspring.ᶜ ᵘ So guard yourself in your spirit, and do not break faith with the wife of your youth.

¹⁶"I hate divorce,ᵛ" says the Lᴏʀᴅ God of Israel, "and I hate a man's covering himself ᵈ with violence as well as with his garment," says the Lᴏʀᴅ Almighty.

So guard yourself in your spirit, and do not break faith.

The Day of Judgment

¹⁷You have wearied ʷ the Lᴏʀᴅ with your words.

"How have we wearied him?" you ask.

By saying, "All who do evil are good in the eyes of the Lᴏʀᴅ, and he is pleased with them" or "Where is the God of justice?"

3 "See, I will send my messenger, who will prepare the way before me.ˣ Then suddenly the Lord you are seeking will come to his temple; the messenger of the covenant, whom you desire, will come," says the Lᴏʀᴅ Almighty.

²But who can endure ʸ the day of his coming? Who can stand when he appears? For he will be like a refiner's fire ᶻ or a launderer's soap. ³He will sit as a refiner and purifier of silver;ᵃ he will purify ᵇ the Levites and refine them like gold and silver. Then the Lᴏʀᴅ will have men who will bring offerings in righteousness, ⁴and the offerings ᶜ of Judah and

---

2:7
gJer 18:18
hLev 10:11
iNu 27:21
2:8
jJer 18:15
2:9
k1Sa 2:30
2:10
l1Co 8:6
mEx 19:5
2:11
nNe 13:23
oEzr 9:1;
Jer 3:7-9
2:12
pEze 24:21
qMal 1:10
2:13
rJer 14:12
2:14
sPr 5:18
2:15
tGe 2:24;
Mt 19:4-6
u1Co 7:14
2:16
vDt 24:1;
Mt 5:31-32;
19:4-9
2:17
wIsa 43:24
3:1
xIsa 40:3;
Mt 11:10*;
Mk 1:2*;
Lk 7:27*
3:2
yEze 22:14;
Rev 6:17
zZec 13:9;
Mt 3:10-12
3:3
aDa 12:10
bIsa 1:25
3:4
c2Ch 7:12;
Ps 51:19;
Mal 1:11

ᵃ10 Or *father*   ᵇ12 Or ¹²May the Lᴏʀᴅ *cut off from the tents of Jacob anyone who gives testimony in behalf of the man who does this*   ᶜ15 Or ¹⁵But *the one ͺwho is our father ͺ did not do this, not as long as life remained in him. And what was he seeking? An offspring from God*   ᵈ16 Or *his wife*

Jerusalem will be acceptable to the LORD, as in days gone by, as in former years. [d]

[5]"So I will come near to you for judgment. I will be quick to testify against sorcerers, adulterers and perjurers, [e] against those who defraud laborers of their wages, [f] who oppress the widows[g] and the fatherless, and deprive aliens of justice, but do not fear me," says the LORD Almighty.

Robbing God

[6]"I the LORD do not change. [h] So you, O descendants of Jacob, are not destroyed. [7]Ever since the time of your forefathers you have turned away[i] from my decrees and have not kept them. Return to me, and I will return to you," [j] says the LORD Almighty.

"But you ask, 'How are we to return?'

[8]"Will a man rob God? Yet you rob me.

"But you ask, 'How do we rob you?'

"In tithes[k] and offerings. [9]You are under a curse—the whole nation of you—because you are robbing me. [10]Bring the whole tithe into the storehouse, [l] that there may be food in my house. Test me in this," says the LORD Almighty, "and see if I will not throw open the floodgates[m] of heaven and pour out so much blessing that you will not have room enough for it. [11]I will prevent pests from devouring your crops, and the vines in your fields will not cast their fruit," says the LORD Almighty. [12]"Then all the nations will call you blessed, [n] for yours will be a delightful land," [o] says the LORD Almighty.

[13]"You have said harsh things[p] against me," says the LORD.

"Yet you ask, 'What have we said against you?'

[14]"You have said, 'It is futile[q] to serve God. What did we gain by carrying out his requirements and going about like mourners[r] before the LORD Almighty? [15]But now we call the arrogant blessed. Certainly the evildoers[s] prosper, and even those who challenge God escape.' "

[16]Then those who feared the LORD talked with each other, and the LORD listened and heard. [t] A scroll[u] of remembrance was written in his presence concerning those who feared the LORD and honored his name.

[17]"They will be mine," says the LORD Almighty, "in the day when I make up my treasured possession. [a]v I will spare[w] them, just as in compassion a man spares his son who serves him. [18]And you will again see the distinction between the righteous[x] and the wicked, between those who serve God and those who do not.

The Day of the LORD

4 "Surely the day is coming;[y] it will burn like a furnace. All the arrogant and every evildoer will be stubble, [z] and that day that is coming will set them on fire," says the LORD Almighty. "Not a root or a branch will be left to them. [2]But for you who revere my name, the sun of righteousness[a] will rise with healing[b] in its wings. And you will go out and leap[c] like calves released from the stall. [3]Then you will trample[d] down the wicked; they will be ashes[e] under the soles of your feet on the day when I do these things," says the LORD Almighty.

---

[a]17 Or *Almighty, "my treasured possession, in the day when I act*

3:4
d 2Ch 7:3
3:5
e Jer 7:9
f Lev 19:13;
Jas 5:4
g Ex 22:22
3:6
h Nu 23:19;
Jas 1:17
3:7
i Jer 7:26;
Ac 7:51
j Zec 1:3
3:8
k Ne 13:10-12
3:10
l Ne 13:12
m 2Ki 7:2
3:12
n Isa 61:9
o Isa 62:4
3:13
p Mal 2:17
3:14
q Ps 73:13
r Isa 58:3
3:15
s Jer 7:10
3:16
t Ps 34:15
u Ps 56:8
3:17
v Dt 7:6
w Ps 103:13;
Isa 26:20
3:18
x Ge 18:25
4:1
y Joel 2:31
z Isa 5:24;
Ob 1:18
4:2
a Lk 1:78;
Eph 5:14
b Isa 30:26
c Isa 35:6
4:3
d Job 40:12
e Eze 28:18

4"Remember the law[f] of my servant Moses, the decrees and laws I gave him at Horeb for all Israel.

5"See, I will send you the prophet Elijah[g] before that great and dreadful day of the Lord comes.[h] 6He will turn the hearts of the fathers to their children,[i] and the hearts of the children to their fathers; or else I will come and strike[j] the land with a curse."[k]

4:4
f Ps 147:19
4:5
g Mt 11:14;
h Joel 2:31
4:6
i Lk 1:17
j Isa 11:4;
Rev 19:15
k Zec 5:3

The New Testament

Matthew

Title and Background

The Gospel of Matthew was so named to distinguish it from the other Gospel accounts. There is only one gospel, but four accounts of it. So we have here Matthew's version of the "good news" from God. Matthew's name means "gift of the LORD."

Author and Date of Writing

All four of the canonical Gospels are anonymous, but the early church fathers were unanimous in holding that Matthew was the author of this Gospel. He was a tax collector and was also known as Levi. The gospel was most likely written before the destruction of Jerusalem in A.D. 70.

Theme and Message

Matthew's main purpose is to prove to his Jewish readers that Jesus is their Messiah. He quotes the Old Testament often and uses the phrase "kingdom of heaven" frequently. The whole Gospel is woven around five great discourses: (1) chapters 5-7; (2) chapter 10; (3) chapter 13; (4) chapter 18; (5) chapters 24-25.

Outline

   I. The Birth and Early Years of Jesus (1:1-2:23)
  II. The Beginnings of Jesus' Ministry (3:1-4:11)
 III. Jesus' Ministry in Galilee (4:12-14:12)
 IV. Jesus' Withdrawals From Galilee (14:13-17:20)
  V. Jesus' Last Ministry in Galilee (17:22-18:35)
 VI. Jesus' Ministry in Judea and Perea (19:1-20:34)
VII. Passion Week (2l:1-27:66)
VIII. The Resurrection (28:1-20)

The Genealogy of Jesus

1:1–17pp — Lk 3:23–38
1:3–6pp — Ru 4:18–22
1:7–11pp — 1Ch 3:10–17

1 A record of the genealogy of Jesus Christ the son of David,[a] the son of Abraham:[b]

²Abraham was the father of Isaac,[c]
  Isaac the father of Jacob,[d]
  Jacob the father of Judah and his brothers,[e]
  ³Judah the father of Perez and Zerah, whose mother was Tamar,[f]
  Perez the father of Hezron,
  Hezron the father of Ram,
  ⁴Ram the father of Amminadab,
  Amminadab the father of Nahshon,
  Nahshon the father of Salmon,
  ⁵Salmon the father of Boaz, whose mother was Rahab,
  Boaz the father of Obed, whose mother was Ruth,

1:1
a 2Sa 7:12-16;
Isa 9:6,7; 11:1;
Jer 23:5,6;
Mt 9:27;
Lk 1:32,69;
Ro 1:3;
Rev 22:16
b Ge 22:18;
Gal 3:16
1:2
c Ge 21:3,12
d Ge 25:26
e Ge 29:35
1:3
f Ge 38:27-30

Obed the father of Jesse,
⁶and Jesse the father of King David. ᵍ

David was the father of Solomon, whose mother had been Uriah's
     wife, ʰ
⁷Solomon the father of Rehoboam,
Rehoboam the father of Abijah,
Abijah the father of Asa,
⁸Asa the father of Jehoshaphat,
Jehoshaphat the father of Jehoram,
Jehoram the father of Uzziah,
⁹Uzziah the father of Jotham,
Jotham the father of Ahaz,
Ahaz the father of Hezekiah,
¹⁰Hezekiah the father of Manasseh, ⁱ
Manasseh the father of Amon,
Amon the father of Josiah,
¹¹and Josiah the father of Jeconiahᵃ and his brothers at the time of
     the exile to Babylon. ʲ

¹²After the exile to Babylon:
Jeconiah was the father of Shealtiel, ᵏ
Shealtiel the father of Zerubbabel, ˡ
¹³Zerubbabel the father of Abiud,
Abiud the father of Eliakim,
Eliakim the father of Azor,
¹⁴Azor the father of Zadok,
Zadok the father of Akim,
Akim the father of Eliud,
¹⁵Eliud the father of Eleazar,
Eleazar the father of Matthan,
Matthan the father of Jacob,
¹⁶and Jacob the father of Joseph, the husband of Mary, ᵐ of whom
     was born Jesus, who is called Christ. ⁿ

¹⁷Thus there were fourteen generations in all from Abraham to David, fourteen from David to the exile to Babylon, and fourteen from the exile to the Christ. ᵇ

The Birth of Jesus Christ

¹⁸This is how the birth of Jesus Christ came about: His mother Mary was pledged to be married to Joseph, but before they came together, she was found to be with child through the Holy Spirit. ᵒ ¹⁹Because Joseph her husband was a righteous man and did not want to expose her to public disgrace, he had in mind to divorceᵖ her quietly.

²⁰But after he had considered this, an angel of the Lord appeared to him in a dream and said, "Joseph son of David, do not be afraid to take Mary home as your wife, because what is conceived in her is from the Holy Spirit. ²¹She will give birth to a son, and you are to give him the name Jesus, ᶜ�q because he will save his people from their sins." ʳ

1:6
g 1Sa 16:1;
17:12
h 2Sa 12:24
1:10
i 2Ki 20:21
1:11
j 2Ki 24:14-16;
Jer 27:20;
Da 1:1,2
1:12
k 1Ch 3:17
l 1Ch 3:19;
Ezr 3:2
1:16
m Lk 1:27
n Mt 27:17
1:18
o Lk 1:35
1:19
p Dt 24:1
1:21
q Lk 1:31
r Lk 2:11;
Ac 5:31; 13:23,
28

ᵃ11 That is, Jehoiachin; also in verse 12   ᵇ17 Or *Messiah.* "The Christ" (Greek) and "the Messiah" (Hebrew) both mean "the Anointed One."   ᶜ21 *Jesus* is the Greek form of *Joshua,* which means *the* Lᴏʀᴅ *saves.*

22All this took place to fulfill what the Lord had said through the prophet: 23"The virgin will be with child and will give birth to a son, and they will call him Immanuel"ᵃˢ—which means, "God with us."

24When Joseph woke up, he did what the angel of the Lord had commanded him and took Mary home as his wife. 25But he had no union with her until she gave birth to a son. And he gave him the name Jesus.ᵗ

The Visit of the Magi

2 After Jesus was born in Bethlehem in Judea,ᵘ during the time of King Herod,ᵛ Magiᵇ from the east came to Jerusalem 2and asked, "Where is the one who has been born king of the Jews?ʷ We saw his starˣ in the eastᶜ and have come to worship him."

3When King Herod heard this he was disturbed, and all Jerusalem with him. 4When he had called together all the people's chief priests and teachers of the law, he asked them where the Christᵈ was to be born. 5"In Bethlehemʸ in Judea," they replied, "for this is what the prophet has written:

6" 'But you, Bethlehem, in the land of Judah,
    are by no means least among the rulers of Judah;
for out of you will come a ruler
    who will be the shepherd of my people Israel.'ᵉ "ᶻ

7Then Herod called the Magi secretly and found out from them the exact time the star had appeared. 8He sent them to Bethlehem and said, "Go and make a careful search for the child. As soon as you find him, report to me, so that I too may go and worship him."

9After they had heard the king, they went on their way, and the star they had seen in the eastᶠ went ahead of them until it stopped over the place where the child was. 10When they saw the star, they were overjoyed. 11On coming to the house, they saw the child with his mother Mary, and they bowed down and worshiped him.ᵃ Then they opened their treasures and presented him with giftsᵇ of gold and of incense and of myrrh. 12And having been warnedᶜ in a dreamᵈ not to go back to Herod, they returned to their country by another route.

The Escape to Egypt

13When they had gone, an angelᵉ of the Lord appeared to Joseph in a dream.ᶠ "Get up," he said, "take the child and his mother and escape to Egypt. Stay there until I tell you, for Herod is going to search for the child to kill him."

14So he got up, took the child and his mother during the night and left for Egypt, 15where he stayed until the death of Herod. And so was fulfilled what the Lord had said through the prophet: "Out of Egypt I called my son."ᵍ ᵍ

16When Herod realized that he had been outwitted by the Magi, he was furious, and he gave orders to kill all the boys in Bethlehem and its vicinity who were two years old and under, in accordance with the time

1:23
sIsa 7:14; 8:8, 10

1:25
tver 21

2:1
uLk 2:4-7
vLk 1:5

2:2
wJer 23:5;
Mt 27:11;
Mk 15:2;
Jn 1:49;
18:33-37
xNu 24:17

2:5
yJn 7:42

2:6
zMic 5:2;
2Sa 5:2

2:11
aIsa 60:3
bPs 72:10

2:12
cHeb 11:7
dver 13,19,22;
Mt 27:19

2:13
eAc 5:19
fver 12,19,22

2:15
gHos 11:1;
Ex 4:22,23

ᵃ23 Isaiah 7:14   ᵇ1 Traditionally *Wise Men*   ᶜ2 Or *star when it rose*   ᵈ4 Or *Messiah*
ᵉ6 Micah 5:2   ᶠ9 Or *seen when it rose*   ᵍ15 Hosea 11:1

he had learned from the Magi. [17]Then what was said through the prophet Jeremiah was fulfilled:

> [18]"A voice is heard in Ramah,
>   weeping and great mourning,
> Rachel weeping for her children
>   and refusing to be comforted,
> because they are no more."[a] [h]

The Return to Nazareth

[19]After Herod died, an angel of the Lord appeared in a dream[i] to Joseph in Egypt [20]and said, "Get up, take the child and his mother and go to the land of Israel, for those who were trying to take the child's life are dead."

[21]So he got up, took the child and his mother and went to the land of Israel. [22]But when he heard that Archelaus was reigning in Judea in place of his father Herod, he was afraid to go there. Having been warned in a dream,[j] he withdrew to the district of Galilee,[k] [23]and he went and lived in a town called Nazareth.[l] So was fulfilled[m] what was said through the prophets: "He will be called a Nazarene."[n]

John the Baptist Prepares the Way

3:1–12pp — Mk 1:3–8; Lk 3:2–17

3 In those days John the Baptist[o] came, preaching in the Desert of Judea [2]and saying, "Repent, for the kingdom of heaven[p] is near." [3]This is he who was spoken of through the prophet Isaiah:

> "A voice of one calling in the desert,
> 'Prepare the way for the Lord,
>   make straight paths for him.' "[b] [q]

[4]John's clothes were made of camel's hair, and he had a leather belt around his waist.[r] His food was locusts[s] and wild honey. [5]People went out to him from Jerusalem and all Judea and the whole region of the Jordan. [6]Confessing their sins, they were baptized by him in the Jordan River.

[7]But when he saw many of the Pharisees and Sadducees coming to where he was baptizing, he said to them: "You brood of vipers![t] Who warned you to flee from the coming wrath?[u] [8]Produce fruit in keeping with repentance.[v] [9]And do not think you can say to yourselves, 'We have Abraham as our father.' I tell you that out of these stones God can raise up children for Abraham. [10]The ax is already at the root of the trees, and every tree that does not produce good fruit will be cut down and thrown into the fire.[w]

[11]"I baptize you with[c] water for repentance. But after me will come one who is more powerful than I, whose sandals I am not fit to carry. He will baptize you with the Holy Spirit[x] and with fire.[y] [12]His winnowing fork is in his hand, and he will clear his threshing floor, gathering his wheat into the barn and burning up the chaff with unquenchable fire."[z]

[a]18 Jer. 31:15   [b]3 Isaiah 40:3   [c]11 Or *in*

**Marginal references:**

2:18
h Jer 31:15
2:19
i ver 12,13,22
2:22
j ver 12,13,19;
Mt 27:19;
k Lk 2:39
2:23
l Lk 1:26;
Jn 1:45,46
m Mt 1:22
n Mk 1:24
3:1
o Lk 1:13,57-66;
3:2-19
3:2
p Da 2:44;
Mt 4:17; 6:10;
Lk 11:20;
21:31; Jn 3:3,5;
Ac 1:3,6
3:3
q Isa 40:3;
Mal 3:1;
Lk 1:76; Jn 1:23
3:4
r 2Ki 1:8
s Lev 11:22
3:7
t Mt 12:34;
23:33 u Ro 1:18;
1Th 1:10
3:8
v Ac 26:20
3:10
w Mt 7:19;
Lk 13:6-9;
Jn 15:2,6
3:11
x Mk 1:8
y Isa 4:4;
Ac 2:3,4
3:12
z Mt 13:30

The Baptism of Jesus
3:13–17pp — Mk 1:9–11; Lk 3:21,22; Jn 1:31–34

¹³Then Jesus came from Galilee to the Jordan to be baptized by John. ª ¹⁴But John tried to deter him, saying, "I need to be baptized by you, and do you come to me?"

¹⁵Jesus replied, "Let it be so now; it is proper for us to do this to fulfill all righteousness." Then John consented.

¹⁶As soon as Jesus was baptized, he went up out of the water. At that moment heaven was opened, and he saw the Spirit of God ᵇ descending like a dove and lighting on him. ¹⁷And a voice from heaven ᶜ said, "This is my Son, ᵈ whom I love; with him I am well pleased." ᵉ

The Temptation of Jesus
4:1–11pp — Mk 1:12,13; Lk 4:1–13

4 Then Jesus was led by the Spirit into the desert to be tempted by the devil. ²After fasting forty days and forty nights, ᶠ he was hungry. ³The tempter ᵍ came to him and said, "If you are the Son of God, ʰ tell these stones to become bread."

⁴Jesus answered, "It is written: 'Man does not live on bread alone, but on every word that comes from the mouth of God.'ᵃ "ⁱ

⁵Then the devil took him to the holy city ʲ and had him stand on the highest point of the temple. ⁶"If you are the Son of God," he said, "throw yourself down. For it is written:

" 'He will command his angels concerning you,
    and they will lift you up in their hands,
  so that you will not strike your foot against a stone.'ᵇ "ᵏ

⁷Jesus answered him, "It is also written: 'Do not put the Lord your God to the test.'ᶜ "ˡ

⁸Again, the devil took him to a very high mountain and showed him all the kingdoms of the world and their splendor. ⁹"All this I will give you," he said, "if you will bow down and worship me."

¹⁰Jesus said to him, "Away from me, Satan! ᵐ For it is written: 'Worship the Lord your God, and serve him only.'ᵈ "ⁿ

¹¹Then the devil left him, and angels came and attended him. ᵒ

Jesus Begins to Preach
¹²When Jesus heard that John had been put in prison, ᵖ he returned to Galilee. �q ¹³Leaving Nazareth, he went and lived in Capernaum, ʳ which was by the lake in the area of Zebulun and Naphtali— ¹⁴to fulfill what was said through the prophet Isaiah:

¹⁵"Land of Zebulun and land of Naphtali,
    the way to the sea, along the Jordan,
    Galilee of the Gentiles—
¹⁶the people living in darkness
    have seen a great light;
  on those living in the land of the shadow of death
    a light has dawned." ᵉ ˢ

3:13
ªMk 1:4
3:16
ᵇIsa 11:2; 42:1
3:17
ᶜMt 17:5;
Jn 12:28
ᵈPs 2:7;
2Pe 1:17,18
ᵉIsa 42:1;
Mt 12:18; 17:5;
Mk 1:11; 9:7;
Lk 9:35
4:2
ᶠEx 34:28;
1Ki 19:8
4:3
ᵍ1Th 3:5
ʰMt 3:17;
Jn 5:25; Ac 9:20
4:4
ⁱDt 8:3
4:5
ʲNe 11:1;
Da 9:24;
Mt 27:53
4:6
ᵏPs 91:11,12
4:7
ˡDt 6:16
4:10
ᵐ1Ch 21:1
ⁿDt 6:13
4:11
ᵒMt 26:53;
Lk 22:43;
Heb 1:14
4:12
ᵖMt 14:3
qMk 1:14
4:13
ʳMk 1:21;
Lk 4:23,31;
Jn 2:12; 4:46,47
4:16
ˢIsa 9:1,2;
Lk 2:32

ᵃ4 Deut. 8:3   ᵇ6 Psalm 91:11,12   ᶜ7 Deut. 6:16   ᵈ10 Deut. 6:13   ᵉ16 Isaiah 9:1,2

[17]From that time on Jesus began to preach, "Repent, for the kingdom of heaven[t] is near."

The Calling of the First Disciples

4:18–22pp — Mk 1:16–20; Lk 5:2–11; Jn 1:35–42

[18]As Jesus was walking beside the Sea of Galilee,[u] he saw two brothers, Simon called Peter[v] and his brother Andrew. They were casting a net into the lake, for they were fishermen. [19]"Come, follow me,"[w] Jesus said, "and I will make you fishers of men." [20]At once they left their nets and followed him.

[21]Going on from there, he saw two other brothers, James son of Zebedee and his brother John.[x] They were in a boat with their father Zebedee, preparing their nets. Jesus called them, [22]and immediately they left the boat and their father and followed him.

Jesus Heals the Sick

[23]Jesus went throughout Galilee,[y] teaching in their synagogues,[z] preaching the good news[a] of the kingdom,[b] and healing every disease and sickness among the people.[c] [24]News about him spread all over Syria,[d] and people brought to him all who were ill with various diseases, those suffering severe pain, the demon-possessed,[e] those having seizures,[f] and the paralyzed,[g] and he healed them. [25]Large crowds from Galilee, the Decapolis,[a] Jerusalem, Judea and the region across the Jordan followed him.[h]

The Beatitudes

5:3–12pp — Lk 6:20–23

5 Now when he saw the crowds, he went up on a mountainside and sat down. His disciples came to him, [2]and he began to teach them, saying:

[3]"Blessed are the poor in spirit,
   for theirs is the kingdom of heaven.[i]
[4]Blessed are those who mourn,
   for they will be comforted.[j]
[5]Blessed are the meek,
   for they will inherit the earth.[k]
[6]Blessed are those who hunger and thirst for
      righteousness,
   for they will be filled.[l]
[7]Blessed are the merciful,
   for they will be shown mercy.
[8]Blessed are the pure in heart,[m]
   for they will see God.[n]
[9]Blessed are the peacemakers,
   for they will be called sons of God.[o]
[10]Blessed are those who are persecuted because of
      righteousness,[p]
   for theirs is the kingdom of heaven.

[11]"Blessed are you when people insult you,[q] persecute you and

*Cross references (left margin):*

4:17
[t] Mt 3:2
4:18
[u] Mt 15:29;
Mk 7:31; Jn 6:1
[v] Mt 16:17,18
4:19
[w] Mk 10:21,28,
52
4:21
[x] Mt 20:20
4:23
[y] Mk 1:39;
Lk 4:15,44
[z] Mt 9:35;
13:54; Mk 1:21;
Lk 4:15; Jn 6:59
[a] Mk 1:14
[b] Mt 3:2;
Ac 20:25
[c] Mt 8:16;
15:30; Ac 10:38
4:24
[d] Lk 2:2
[e] Mt 8:16,28;
9:32; 15:22;
Mk 1:32; 5:15,
16,18 [f] Mt 17:15
[g] Mt 8:6; 9:2;
Mk 2:3
4:25
[h] Mk 3:7,8;
Lk 6:17
5:3
[i] ver 10,19;
Mt 25:34
5:4
[j] Isa 61:2,3;
Rev 7:17
5:5
[k] Ps 37:11;
Ro 4:13
5:6
[l] Isa 55:1,2
5:8
[m] Ps 24:3,4
[n] Heb 12:14;
Rev 22:4
5:9
[o] ver 44,45;
Ro 8:14
5:10
[p] 1Pe 3:14
5:11
[q] 1Pe 4:14

[a]25 That is, the Ten Cities

falsely say all kinds of evil against you because of me. [12]Rejoice and be glad,[r] because great is your reward in heaven, for in the same way they persecuted the prophets who were before you.[s]

Salt and Light

[13]"You are the salt of the earth. But if the salt loses its saltiness, how can it be made salty again? It is no longer good for anything, except to be thrown out and trampled by men.[t]

[14]"You are the light of the world.[u] A city on a hill cannot be hidden. [15]Neither do people light a lamp and put it under a bowl. Instead they put it on its stand, and it gives light to everyone in the house.[v] [16]In the same way, let your light shine before men, that they may see your good deeds and praise[w] your Father in heaven.

The Fulfillment of the Law

[17]"Do not think that I have come to abolish the Law or the Prophets; I have not come to abolish them but to fulfill them.[x] [18]I tell you the truth, until heaven and earth disappear, not the smallest letter, not the least stroke of a pen, will by any means disappear from the Law until everything is accomplished.[y] [19]Anyone who breaks one of the least of these commandments[z] and teaches others to do the same will be called least in the kingdom of heaven, but whoever practices and teaches these commands will be called great in the kingdom of heaven. [20]For I tell you that unless your righteousness surpasses that of the Pharisees and the teachers of the law, you will certainly not enter the kingdom of heaven.

Murder

5:25,26pp — Lk 12:58,59

[21]"You have heard that it was said to the people long ago, 'Do not murder,[aa] and anyone who murders will be subject to judgment.' [22]But I tell you that anyone who is angry with his brother[b] will be subject to judgment.[b] Again, anyone who says to his brother, 'Raca,[c]' is answerable to the Sanhedrin.[c] But anyone who says, 'You fool!' will be in danger of the fire of hell.[d]

[23]"Therefore, if you are offering your gift at the altar and there remember that your brother has something against you, [24]leave your gift there in front of the altar. First go and be reconciled to your brother; then come and offer your gift.

[25]"Settle matters quickly with your adversary who is taking you to court. Do it while you are still with him on the way, or he may hand you over to the judge, and the judge may hand you over to the officer, and you may be thrown into prison. [26]I tell you the truth, you will not get out until you have paid the last penny.[d]

Adultery

[27]"You have heard that it was said, 'Do not commit adultery.'[ee] [28]But I tell you that anyone who looks at a woman lustfully has already committed adultery with her in his heart.[f] [29]If your right eye causes

5:12	rAc 5:41; 1Pe 4:13,16
	sMt 23:31,37; Ac 7:52; 1Th 2:15
5:13	tMk 9:50; Lk 14:34,35
5:14	uJn 8:12
5:15	vMk 4:21; Lk 8:16
5:16	wMt 9:8
5:17	xRo 3:31
5:18	yLk 16:17
5:19	zJas 2:10
5:21	aEx 20:13; Dt 5:17
5:22	b1Jn 3:15
	cMt 26:59
	dJas 3:6
5:27	eEx 20:14; Dt 5:18
5:28	fPr 6:25

---

[a]21 Exodus 20:13   [b]22 Some manuscripts *brother without cause*   [c]22 An Aramaic term of contempt   [d]26 Greek *kodrantes*   [e]27 Exodus 20:14

you to sin,⁸ gouge it out and throw it away. It is better for you to lose one part of your body than for your whole body to be thrown into hell. ³⁰And if your right hand causes you to sin, cut it off and throw it away. It is better for you to lose one part of your body than for your whole body to go into hell.

Divorce

³¹"It has been said, 'Anyone who divorces his wife must give her a certificate of divorce.'ᵃʰ ³²But I tell you that anyone who divorces his wife, except for marital unfaithfulness, causes her to become an adulteress, and anyone who marries the divorced woman commits adultery.ⁱ

Oaths

³³"Again, you have heard that it was said to the people long ago, 'Do not break your oath,ʲ but keep the oaths you have made to the Lord.'ᵏ ³⁴But I tell you, Do not swear at all:¹ either by heaven, for it is God's throne;ᵐ ³⁵or by the earth, for it is his footstool; or by Jerusalem, for it is the city of the Great King.ⁿ ³⁶And do not swear by your head, for you cannot make even one hair white or black. ³⁷Simply let your 'Yes' be 'Yes,' and your 'No,' 'No';ᵒ anything beyond this comes from the evil one.ᵖ

An Eye for an Eye

³⁸"You have heard that it was said, 'Eye for eye, and tooth for tooth.'ᵇq ³⁹But I tell you, Do not resist an evil person. If someone strikes you on the right cheek, turn to him the other also.ʳ ⁴⁰And if someone wants to sue you and take your tunic, let him have your cloak as well. ⁴¹If someone forces you to go one mile, go with him two miles. ⁴²Give to the one who asks you, and do not turn away from the one who wants to borrow from you.ˢ

Love for Enemies

⁴³"You have heard that it was said, 'Love your neighborᶜt and hate your enemy.'ᵘ ⁴⁴But I tell you: Love your enemiesᵈ and pray for those who persecute you,ᵛ ⁴⁵that you may be sonsʷ of your Father in heaven. He causes his sun to rise on the evil and the good, and sends rain on the righteous and the unrighteous.ˣ ⁴⁶If you love those who love you, what reward will you get?ʸ Are not even the tax collectors doing that? ⁴⁷And if you greet only your brothers, what are you doing more than others? Do not even pagans do that? ⁴⁸Be perfect, therefore, as your heavenly Father is perfect.ᶻ

Giving to the Needy

6 "Be careful not to do your 'acts of righteousness' before men, to be seen by them.ᵃ If you do, you will have no reward from your Father in heaven.

²"So when you give to the needy, do not announce it with trumpets, as the hypocrites do in the synagogues and on the streets, to be hon-

### Cross references (margin)

5:29
ᵍMt 18:6,8,9;
Mk 9:42-47
5:31
ʰDt 24:1-4
5:32
ⁱLk 16:18
5:33
ʲLev 19:12
ᵏNu 30:2;
Dt 23:21;
Mt 23:16-22
5:34
lJas 5:12
ᵐIsa 66:1;
Mt 23:22
5:35
ⁿPs 48:2
5:37
ᵒJas 5:12
ᵖMt 6:13;
13:19,38;
Jn 17:15;
2Th 3:3;
1Jn 2:13,14;
3:12; 5:18,19
5:38
qEx 21:24;
Lev 24:20;
Dt 19:21
5:39
rLk 6:29;
Ro 12:17,19;
1Co 6:7;
1Pe 3:9
5:42
sDt 15:8;
Lk 6:30
5:43
tLev 19:18
uDt 23:6
5:44
vLk 6:27,28;
23:34; Ac 7:60;
Ro 12:14;
1Co 4:12;
1Pe 2:23
5:45
wver 9
xJob 25:3
5:46
yLk 6:32
5:48
zLev 19:2;
1Pe 1:16
6:1
aMt 23:5

ᵃ31 Deut. 24:1   ᵇ38 Exodus 21:24; Lev. 24:20; Deut. 19:21   ᶜ43 Lev. 19:18   ᵈ44 Some late manuscripts *enemies, bless those who curse you, do good to those who hate you* ored by men. I tell you the truth, they have received their reward in full. [3]But when you give to the needy, do not let your left hand know what your right hand is doing, [4]so that your giving may be in secret. Then your Father, who sees what is done in secret, will reward you. [b]

Prayer

6:9–13pp — Lk 11:2-4

[5]"And when you pray, do not be like the hypocrites, for they love to pray standing[c] in the synagogues and on the street corners to be seen by men. I tell you the truth, they have received their reward in full. [6]But when you pray, go into your room, close the door and pray to your Father,[d] who is unseen. Then your Father, who sees what is done in secret, will reward you. [7]And when you pray, do not keep on babbling[e] like pagans, for they think they will be heard because of their many words.[f] [8]Do not be like them, for your Father knows what you need[g] before you ask him.

[9]"This, then, is how you should pray:

" 'Our Father in heaven,
    hallowed be your name,
[10]your kingdom[h] come,
    your will be done[i]
      on earth as it is in heaven.
[11]Give us today our daily bread.[j]
[12]Forgive us our debts,
    as we also have forgiven our debtors.[k]
[13]And lead us not into temptation,[l]
    but deliver us from the evil one.[a] '[m]

[14]For if you forgive men when they sin against you, your heavenly Father will also forgive you.[n] [15]But if you do not forgive men their sins, your Father will not forgive your sins.[o]

Fasting

[16]"When you fast, do not look somber[p] as the hypocrites do, for they disfigure their faces to show men they are fasting. I tell you the truth, they have received their reward in full. [17]But when you fast, put oil on your head and wash your face, [18]so that it will not be obvious to men that you are fasting, but only to your Father, who is unseen; and your Father, who sees what is done in secret, will reward you.[q]

Treasures in Heaven

6:22,23pp — Lk 11:34-36

[19]"Do not store up for yourselves treasures on earth,[r] where moth and rust destroy,[s] and where thieves break in and steal. [20]But store up for yourselves treasures in heaven,[t] where moth and rust do not destroy, and where thieves do not break in and steal. [u] [21]For where your treasure is, there your heart will be also.[v]

[22]"The eye is the lamp of the body. If your eyes are good, your whole body will be full of light. [23]But if your eyes are bad, your whole body

---

6:4
[b]ver 6,18;
Col 3:23,24
6:5
[c]Mk 11:25;
Lk 18:10-14
6:6
[d]2Ki 4:33
6:7
[e]Ecc 5:2
[f]1Ki 18:26-29
6:8
[g]ver 32
6:10
[h]Mt 3:2
[i]Mt 26:39
6:11
[j]Pr 30:8
6:12
[k]Mt 18:21-35
6:13
[l]Jas 1:13
[m]Mt 5:37
6:14
[n]Mt 18:21-35;
Mk 11:25,26;
Eph 4:32;
Col 3:13
6:15
[o]Mt 18:35
6:16
[p]Isa 58:5
6:18
[q]ver 4,6
6:19
[r]Pr 23:4;
Heb 13:5
[s]Jas 5:2,3
6:20
[t]Mt 19:21;
Lk 12:33;
18:22; 1Ti 6:19
[u]Lk 12:33
6:21
[v]Lk 12:34

---

[a]13 Or *from evil*; some late manuscripts *one,* / *for yours is the kingdom and the power and the glory forever. Amen.*

will be full of darkness. If then the light within you is darkness, how great is that darkness!

24"No one can serve two masters. Either he will hate the one and love the other, or he will be devoted to the one and despise the other. You cannot serve both God and Money. [w]

Do Not Worry

6:25–33pp — Lk 12:22–31

25"Therefore I tell you, do not worry [x] about your life, what you will eat or drink; or about your body, what you will wear. Is not life more important than food, and the body more important than clothes? 26Look at the birds of the air; they do not sow or reap or store away in barns, and yet your heavenly Father feeds them. [y] Are you not much more valuable than they? [z] 27Who of you by worrying can add a single hour to his life [a] ? [a]

28"And why do you worry about clothes? See how the lilies of the field grow. They do not labor or spin. 29Yet I tell you that not even Solomon in all his splendor [b] was dressed like one of these. 30If that is how God clothes the grass of the field, which is here today and tomorrow is thrown into the fire, will he not much more clothe you, O you of little faith? [c] 31So do not worry, saying, 'What shall we eat?' or 'What shall we drink?' or 'What shall we wear?' 32For the pagans run after all these things, and your heavenly Father knows that you need them. [d] 33But seek first his kingdom and his righteousness, and all these things will be given to you as well. [e] 34Therefore do not worry about tomorrow, for tomorrow will worry about itself. Each day has enough trouble of its own.

Judging Others

7:3–5pp — Lk 6:41,42

7 "Do not judge, or you too will be judged. [f] 2For in the same way you judge others, you will be judged, and with the measure you use, it will be measured to you. [g]

3"Why do you look at the speck of sawdust in your brother's eye and pay no attention to the plank in your own eye? 4How can you say to your brother, 'Let me take the speck out of your eye,' when all the time there is a plank in your own eye? 5You hypocrite, first take the plank out of your own eye, and then you will see clearly to remove the speck from your brother's eye.

6"Do not give dogs what is sacred; do not throw your pearls to pigs. If you do, they may trample them under their feet, and then turn and tear you to pieces.

Ask, Seek, Knock

7:7–11pp — Lk 11:9–13

7"Ask and it will be given to you; [h] seek and you will find; knock and the door will be opened to you. 8For everyone who asks receives; he who seeks finds; [i] and to him who knocks, the door will be opened.

9"Which of you, if his son asks for bread, will give him a stone? 10Or if he asks for a fish, will give him a snake? 11If you, then, though you are

---

6:24
w Lk 16:13
6:25
x ver 27,28,31, 34; Lk 10:41; 12:11,22; Php 4:6; 1Pe 5:7
6:26
y Job 38:41; Ps 147:9
z Mt 10:29-31
6:27
a Ps 39:5
6:29
b 1Ki 10:4-7
6:30
c Mt 8:26; 14:31; 16:8
6:32
d ver 8
6:33
e Mt 19:29; Mk 10:29-30
7:1
f Lk 6:37; Ro 14:4,10,13; 1Co 4:5; Jas 4:11,12
7:2
g Mk 4:24; Lk 6:38
7:7
h Mt 21:22; Mk 11:24; Jn 14:13,14; 15:7,16; 16:23, 24; Jas 1:5-8; 4:2,3; 1Jn 3:22; 5:14,15
7:8
i Pr 8:17; Jer 29:12,13

---

[a]27 Or *single cubit to his height*

evil, know how to give good gifts to your children, how much more will your Father in heaven give good gifts to those who ask him! [12]So in everything, do to others what you would have them do to you, [j] for this sums up the Law and the Prophets. [k]

The Narrow and Wide Gates

[13]"Enter through the narrow gate. [l] For wide is the gate and broad is the road that leads to destruction, and many enter through it. [14]But small is the gate and narrow the road that leads to life, and only a few find it.

A Tree and Its Fruit

[15]"Watch out for false prophets. [m] They come to you in sheep's clothing, but inwardly they are ferocious wolves. [n] [16]By their fruit you will recognize them. [o] Do people pick grapes from thornbushes, or figs from thistles? [p] [17]Likewise every good tree bears good fruit, but a bad tree bears bad fruit. [18]A good tree cannot bear bad fruit, and a bad tree cannot bear good fruit. [19]Every tree that does not bear good fruit is cut down and thrown into the fire. [q] [20]Thus, by their fruit you will recognize them.

[21]"Not everyone who says to me, 'Lord, Lord,' [r] will enter the kingdom of heaven, but only he who does the will of my Father who is in heaven. [s] [22]Many will say to me on that day, [t] 'Lord, Lord, did we not prophesy in your name, and in your name drive out demons and perform many miracles?' [u] [23]Then I will tell them plainly, 'I never knew you. Away from me, you evildoers!' [v]

The Wise and Foolish Builders

7:24–27pp — Lk 6:47–49

[24]"Therefore everyone who hears these words of mine and puts them into practice [w] is like a wise man who built his house on the rock. [25]The rain came down, the streams rose, and the winds blew and beat against that house; yet it did not fall, because it had its foundation on the rock. [26]But everyone who hears these words of mine and does not put them into practice is like a foolish man who built his house on sand. [27]The rain came down, the streams rose, and the winds blew and beat against that house, and it fell with a great crash."

[28]When Jesus had finished saying these things, [x] the crowds were amazed at his teaching, [y] [29]because he taught as one who had authority, and not as their teachers of the law.

The Man With Leprosy

8:2–4pp — Mk 1:40–44; Lk 5:12–14

8 When he came down from the mountainside, large crowds followed him. [2]A man with leprosy [a] [z] came and knelt before him [a] and said, "Lord, if you are willing, you can make me clean."

[3]Jesus reached out his hand and touched the man. "I am willing," he said. "Be clean!" Immediately he was cured [b] of his leprosy. [4]Then Jesus

---

[a]2 The Greek word was used for various diseases affecting the skin—not necessarily leprosy.
[b]3 Greek *made clean*

7:12
j Lk 6:31
k Ro 13:8-10;
Gal 5:14
7:13
l Lk 13:24
7:15
m Jer 23:16;
Mt 24:24;
Mk 13:22;
Lk 6:26;
2Pe 2:1;
1Jn 4:1;
Rev 16:13
n Ac 20:29
7:16
o Mt 12:33;
Lk 6:44
p Jas 3:12
7:19
q Mt 3:10
7:21
r Hos 8:2;
Mt 25:11
s Ro 2:13;
Jas 1:22
7:22
t Mt 10:15
u 1Co 13:1-3
7:23
v Ps 6:8;
Mt 25:12,41;
Lk 13:25-27
7:24
w Jas 1:22-25
7:28
x Mt 11:1;
13:53; 19:1;
26:1 y Mt 13:54;
Mk 1:22; 6:2;
Lk 4:32; Jn 7:46
8:2
z Lk 5:12
a Mt 9:18;
15:25; 18:26;
20:20

said to him, "See that you don't tell anyone. [b] But go, show yourself to the priest and offer the gift Moses commanded, [c] as a testimony to them."

The Faith of the Centurion

8:5–13pp — Lk 7:1–10

[5]When Jesus had entered Capernaum, a centurion came to him, asking for help. [6]"Lord," he said, "my servant lies at home paralyzed and in terrible suffering."

[7]Jesus said to him, "I will go and heal him."

[8]The centurion replied, "Lord, I do not deserve to have you come under my roof. But just say the word, and my servant will be healed. [d] [9]For I myself am a man under authority, with soldiers under me. I tell this one, 'Go,' and he goes; and that one, 'Come,' and he comes. I say to my servant, 'Do this,' and he does it."

[10]When Jesus heard this, he was astonished and said to those following him, "I tell you the truth, I have not found anyone in Israel with such great faith. [e] [11]I say to you that many will come from the east and the west, [f] and will take their places at the feast with Abraham, Isaac and Jacob in the kingdom of heaven. [g] [12]But the subjects of the kingdom [h] will be thrown outside, into the darkness, where there will be weeping and gnashing of teeth." [i]

[13]Then Jesus said to the centurion, "Go! It will be done just as you believed it would." [j] And his servant was healed at that very hour.

Jesus Heals Many

8:14–16pp — Mk 1:29–34; Lk 4:38–41

[14]When Jesus came into Peter's house, he saw Peter's mother-in-law lying in bed with a fever. [15]He touched her hand and the fever left her, and she got up and began to wait on him.

[16]When evening came, many who were demon-possessed were brought to him, and he drove out the spirits with a word and healed all the sick. [k] [17]This was to fulfill[l] what was spoken through the prophet Isaiah:

"He took up our infirmities
and carried our diseases." [a] [m]

The Cost of Following Jesus

8:19–22pp — Lk 9:57–60

[18]When Jesus saw the crowd around him, he gave orders to cross to the other side of the lake. [n] [19]Then a teacher of the law came to him and said, "Teacher, I will follow you wherever you go."

[20]Jesus replied, "Foxes have holes and birds of the air have nests, but the Son of Man[o] has no place to lay his head."

[21]Another disciple said to him, "Lord, first let me go and bury my father."

[22]But Jesus told him, "Follow me, [p] and let the dead bury their own dead."

a17 Isaiah 53:4

8:4
bMt 9:30;
Mk 5:43; 7:36;
8:30
cLev 14:2-32
8:8
dPs 107:20
8:10
eMt 15:28
8:11
fPs 107:3;
Isa 49:12;
59:19; Mal 1:11
gLk 13:29
8:12
hMt 13:38
iMt 13:42,50;
22:13; 24:51;
25:30; Lk 13:28
8:13
jMt 9:22
8:16
kMt 4:23,24
8:17
lMt 1:22
mIsa 53:4
8:18
nMk 4:35
8:20
oDa 7:13;
Mt 12:8,32,40;
16:13,27,28;
17:9; 19:28;
Mk 2:10; 8:31
8:22
pMt 4:19

Jesus Calms the Storm

8:23–27pp — Mk 4:36–41; Lk 8:22–25
8:23–27Ref — Mt 14:22–33

23Then he got into the boat and his disciples followed him. 24Without warning, a furious storm came up on the lake, so that the waves swept over the boat. But Jesus was sleeping. 25The disciples went and woke him, saying, "Lord, save us! We're going to drown!"

26He replied, "You of little faith,�q why are you so afraid?" Then he got up and rebuked the winds and the waves, and it was completely calm.ʳ

27The men were amazed and asked, "What kind of man is this? Even the winds and the waves obey him!"

The Healing of Two Demon-possessed Men

8:28–34pp — Mk 5:1–17; Lk 8:26–37

28When he arrived at the other side in the region of the Gadarenes,ᵃ two demon-possessedˢ men coming from the tombs met him. They were so violent that no one could pass that way. 29"What do you want with us,ᵗ Son of God?" they shouted. "Have you come here to torture us before the appointed time?"ᵘ

30Some distance from them a large herd of pigs was feeding. 31The demons begged Jesus, "If you drive us out, send us into the herd of pigs."

32He said to them, "Go!" So they came out and went into the pigs, and the whole herd rushed down the steep bank into the lake and died in the water. 33Those tending the pigs ran off, went into the town and reported all this, including what had happened to the demon-possessed men. 34Then the whole town went out to meet Jesus. And when they saw him, they pleaded with him to leave their region.ᵛ

Jesus Heals a Paralytic

9:2–8pp — Mk 2:3–12; Lk 5:18–26

9 Jesus stepped into a boat, crossed over and came to his own town.ʷ 2Some men brought to him a paralytic,ˣ lying on a mat. When Jesus saw their faith,ʸ he said to the paralytic, "Take heart,ᶻ son; your sins are forgiven."ᵃ

3At this, some of the teachers of the law said to themselves, "This fellow is blaspheming!"ᵇ

4Knowing their thoughts,ᶜ Jesus said, "Why do you entertain evil thoughts in your hearts? 5Which is easier: to say, 'Your sins are forgiven,' or to say, 'Get up and walk'? 6But so that you may know that the Son of Manᵈ has authority on earth to forgive sins. . . ." Then he said to the paralytic, "Get up, take your mat and go home." 7And the man got up and went home. 8When the crowd saw this, they were filled with awe; and they praised God,ᵉ who had given such authority to men.

The Calling of Matthew

9:9–13pp — Mk 2:14–17; Lk 5:27–32

9As Jesus went on from there, he saw a man named Matthew sitting

8:26
qMt 6:30
rPs 65:7; 89:9;
107:29
8:28
sMt 4:24
8:29
tJdg 11:12;
2Sa 16:10;
1Ki 17:18;
Mk 1:24;
Lk 4:34; Jn 2:4
u2Pe 2:4
8:34
vLk 5:8;
Ac 16:39
9:1
wMt 4:13
9:2
xMt 4:24
yver 22
zJn 16:33
aLk 7:48
9:3
bMt 26:65;
Jn 10:33
9:4
cPs 94:11;
Mt 12:25;
Lk 6:8; 9:47;
11:17
9:6
dMt 8:20
9:8
eMt 5:16;
15:31; Lk 7:16;
13:13; 17:15;
23:47; Jn 15:8;
Ac 4:21; 11:18;
21:20

ᵃ28 Some manuscripts *Gergesenes*; others *Gerasenes*

at the tax collector's booth. "Follow me," he told him, and Matthew got up and followed him.

[10]While Jesus was having dinner at Matthew's house, many tax collectors and "sinners" came and ate with him and his disciples. [11]When the Pharisees saw this, they asked his disciples, "Why does your teacher eat with tax collectors and 'sinners'?"[f]

[12]On hearing this, Jesus said, "It is not the healthy who need a doctor, but the sick. [13]But go and learn what this means: 'I desire mercy, not sacrifice.'[a][g] For I have not come to call the righteous, but sinners."[h]

Jesus Questioned About Fasting

9:14-17pp — Mk 2:18-22; Lk 5:33-39

[14]Then John's disciples came and asked him, "How is it that we and the Pharisees fast,[i] but your disciples do not fast?"

[15]Jesus answered, "How can the guests of the bridegroom mourn while he is with them?[j] The time will come when the bridegroom will be taken from them; then they will fast.[k]

[16]"No one sews a patch of unshrunk cloth on an old garment, for the patch will pull away from the garment, making the tear worse. [17]Neither do men pour new wine into old wineskins. If they do, the skins will burst, the wine will run out and the wineskins will be ruined. No, they pour new wine into new wineskins, and both are preserved."

A Dead Girl and a Sick Woman

9:18-26pp — Mk 5:22-43; Lk 8:41-56

[18]While he was saying this, a ruler came and knelt before him[l] and said, "My daughter has just died. But come and put your hand on her,[m] and she will live." [19]Jesus got up and went with him, and so did his disciples.

[20]Just then a woman who had been subject to bleeding for twelve years came up behind him and touched the edge of his cloak.[n] [21]She said to herself, "If I only touch his cloak, I will be healed."

[22]Jesus turned and saw her. "Take heart, daughter," he said, "your faith has healed you."[o] And the woman was healed from that moment.[p]

[23]When Jesus entered the ruler's house and saw the flute players and the noisy crowd,[q] [24]he said, "Go away. The girl is not dead[r] but asleep."[s] But they laughed at him. [25]After the crowd had been put outside, he went in and took the girl by the hand, and she got up. [26]News of this spread through all that region.[t]

Jesus Heals the Blind and Mute

[27]As Jesus went on from there, two blind men followed him, calling out, "Have mercy on us, Son of David!"[u]

[28]When he had gone indoors, the blind men came to him, and he asked them, "Do you believe that I am able to do this?"

"Yes, Lord," they replied.

[29]Then he touched their eyes and said, "According to your faith will it be done to you";[v] [30]and their sight was restored. Jesus warned them

---

9:11
f Mt 11:19;
Lk 5:30; 15:2;
Gal 2:15
9:13
g Hos 6:6;
Mic 6:6-8;
Mt 12:7
h 1Ti 1:15
9:14
i Lk 18:12
9:15
j Jn 3:29
k Ac 13:2,3;
14:23
9:18
l Mt 8:2
m Mk 5:23
9:20
n Mt 14:36;
Mk 3:10
9:22
o Mk 10:52;
Lk 7:50; 17:19;
18:42 p Mt 15:28
9:23
q 2Ch 35:25;
Jer 9:17,18
9:24
r Ac 20:10
s Jn 11:11-14
9:26
t Mt 4:24
9:27
u Mt 15:22;
Mk 10:47;
Lk 18:38-39
9:29
v ver 22

---

[a]13 Hosea 6:6

sternly, "See that no one knows about this."ʷ ³¹But they went out and spread the news about him all over that region.ˣ

³²While they were going out, a man who was demon-possessedʸ and could not talkᶻ was brought to Jesus. ³³And when the demon was driven out, the man who had been mute spoke. The crowd was amazed and said, "Nothing like this has ever been seen in Israel."ᵃ

³⁴But the Pharisees said, "It is by the prince of demons that he drives out demons."ᵇ

The Workers Are Few

³⁵Jesus went through all the towns and villages, teaching in their synagogues, preaching the good news of the kingdom and healing every disease and sickness.ᶜ ³⁶When he saw the crowds, he had compassion on them,ᵈ because they were harassed and helpless, like sheep without a shepherd.ᵉ ³⁷Then he said to his disciples, "The harvestᶠ is plentiful but the workers are few.ᵍ ³⁸Ask the Lord of the harvest, therefore, to send out workers into his harvest field."

Jesus Sends Out the Twelve

10:2–4pp — Mk 3:16–19; Lk 6:14–16; Ac 1:13
10:9–15pp — Mk 6:8–11; Lk 9:3–5; 10:4–12
10:19–22pp — Mk 13:11–13; Lk 21:12–17
10:26–33pp — Lk 12:2–9
10:34,35pp — Lk 12:51–53

10 He called his twelve disciples to him and gave them authority to drive out evilᵃ spiritsʰ and to heal every disease and sickness.

²These are the names of the twelve apostles: first, Simon (who is called Peter) and his brother Andrew; James son of Zebedee, and his brother John; ³Philip and Bartholomew; Thomas and Matthew the tax collector; James son of Alphaeus, and Thaddaeus; ⁴Simon the Zealot and Judas Iscariot, who betrayed him.ⁱ

⁵These twelve Jesus sent out with the following instructions: "Do not go among the Gentiles or enter any town of the Samaritans.ʲ ⁶Go rather to the lost sheep of Israel.ᵏ ⁷As you go, preach this message: 'The kingdom of heavenˡ is near.' ⁸Heal the sick, raise the dead, cleanse those who have leprosy,ᵇ drive out demons. Freely you have received, freely give. ⁹Do not take along any gold or silver or copper in your belts;ᵐ ¹⁰take no bag for the journey, or extra tunic, or sandals or a staff; for the worker is worth his keep.ⁿ

¹¹"Whatever town or village you enter, search for some worthy person there and stay at his house until you leave. ¹²As you enter the home, give it your greeting.ᵒ ¹³If the home is deserving, let your peace rest on it; if it is not, let your peace return to you. ¹⁴If anyone will not welcome you or listen to your words, shake the dust off your feetᵖ when you leave that home or town. ¹⁵I tell you the truth, it will be more bearable for Sodom and Gomorrah�q on the day of judgmentʳ than for that town.ˢ ¹⁶I am sending you out like sheep among wolves.ᵗ Therefore be as shrewd as snakes and as innocent as doves.ᵘ

ᵃ1 Greek *unclean*   ᵇ8 The Greek word was used for various diseases affecting the skin—not necessarily leprosy.

9:30
ʷMt 8:4
9:31
ˣver 26;
Mk 7:36
9:32
ʸMt 4:24
ᶻMt 12:22-24
9:33
ᵃMk 2:12
9:34
ᵇMt 12:24;
Lk 11:15
9:35
ᶜMt 4:23
9:36
ᵈMt 14:14
ᵉNu 27:17;
Eze 34:5,6;
Zec 10:2;
Mk 6:34
9:37
ᶠJn 4:35
ᵍLk 10:2
10:1
ʰMk 3:13-15;
Lk 9:1
10:4
ⁱMt 26:14-16,25,
47; Jn 13:2,26,
27
10:5
ʲ2Ki 17:24;
Lk 9:52;
Jn 4:4-26,39,40;
Ac 8:5,25
10:6
ᵏJer 50:6;
Mt 15:24
10:7
ˡMt 3:2
10:9
ᵐLk 22:35
10:10
ⁿ1Ti 5:18
10:12
ᵒ1Sa 25:6
10:14
ᵖNe 5:13;
Lk 10:11;
Ac 13:51
10:15
qZPe 2:6
ʳMt 12:36;
2Pe 2:9;
1Jn 4:17
ˢMt 11:22,24
10:16
ᵗLk 10:3
ᵘRo 16:19

17"Be on your guard against men; they will hand you over to the local councils[v] and flog you in their synagogues. [w] 18On my account you will be brought before governors and kings[x] as witnesses to them and to the Gentiles. 19But when they arrest you, do not worry about what to say or how to say it. [y] At that time you will be given what to say, 20for it will not be you speaking, but the Spirit of your Father[z] speaking through you.

21"Brother will betray brother to death, and a father his child; children will rebel against their parents[a] and have them put to death. 22All men will hate you because of me, but he who stands firm to the end will be saved. [b] 23When you are persecuted in one place, flee to another. I tell you the truth, you will not finish going through the cities of Israel before the Son of Man comes.

24"A student is not above his teacher, nor a servant above his master. [c] 25It is enough for the student to be like his teacher, and the servant like his master. If the head of the house has been called Beelzebub,[a] [d] how much more the members of his household!

26"So do not be afraid of them. There is nothing concealed that will not be disclosed, or hidden that will not be made known. [e] 27What I tell you in the dark, speak in the daylight; what is whispered in your ear, proclaim from the roofs. 28Do not be afraid of those who kill the body but cannot kill the soul. Rather, be afraid of the One[f] who can destroy both soul and body in hell. 29Are not two sparrows sold for a penny[b]? Yet not one of them will fall to the ground apart from the will of your Father. 30And even the very hairs of your head are all numbered. [g] 31So don't be afraid; you are worth more than many sparrows. [h]

32"Whoever acknowledges me before men, [i] I will also acknowledge him before my Father in heaven. 33But whoever disowns me before men, I will disown him before my Father in heaven.[j]

34"Do not suppose that I have come to bring peace to the earth. I did not come to bring peace, but a sword. 35For I have come to turn

> " 'a man against his father,
> a daughter against her mother,
> a daughter-in-law against her mother-in-law[k]—
> 36   a man's enemies will be the members of his own
>   household.'[c] [l]

37"Anyone who loves his father or mother more than me is not worthy of me; anyone who loves his son or daughter more than me is not worthy of me;[m] 38and anyone who does not take his cross and follow me is not worthy of me. [n] 39Whoever finds his life will lose it, and whoever loses his life for my sake will find it. [o]

40"He who receives you receives me,[p] and he who receives me receives the one who sent me. [q] 41Anyone who receives a prophet because he is a prophet will receive a prophet's reward, and anyone who receives a righteous man because he is a righteous man will receive a righteous man's reward. 42And if anyone gives even a cup of cold water to one of these little ones because he is my disciple, I tell you the truth, he will certainly not lose his reward."[r]

**Cross references (left margin):**

10:17
vMt 5:22
wMt 23:34;
Mk 13:9;
Ac 5:40; 26:11
10:18
xAc 25:24-26
10:19
yEx 4:12
10:20
zAc 4:8
10:21
aver 35,36;
Mic 7:6
10:22
bMt 24:13;
Mk 13:13
10:24
cLk 6:40;
Jn 13:16; 15:20
10:25
dMk 3:22
10:26
eMk 4:22;
Lk 8:17
10:28
fIsa 8:12,13;
Heb 10:31
10:30
g1Sa 14:45;
2Sa 14:11;
Lk 21:18;
Ac 27:34
10:31
hMt 12:12
10:32
iRo 10:9
10:33
jMk 8:38;
2Ti 2:12
10:35
kver 21
10:36
lMic 7:6
10:37
mLk 14:26
10:38
nMt 16:24;
Lk 14:27
10:39
oLk 17:33;
Jn 12:25
10:40
pMt 18:5;
Gal 4:14
qLk 9:48;
Jn 12:44; 13:20
10:42
rMt 25:40;
Mk 9:41;
Heb 6:10

---

[a]25 Greek *Beezeboul* or *Beelzeboul*   [b]29 Greek *an assarion*   [c]36 Micah 7:6

Jesus and John the Baptist

11:2–19pp — Lk 7:18–35

11 After Jesus had finished instructing his twelve disciples,[s] he went on from there to teach and preach in the towns of Galilee.[a]

2When John heard in prison[t] what Christ was doing, he sent his disciples 3to ask him, "Are you the one who was to come,[u] or should we expect someone else?"

4Jesus replied, "Go back and report to John what you hear and see: 5The blind receive sight, the lame walk, those who have leprosy[b] are cured, the deaf hear, the dead are raised, and the good news is preached to the poor.[v] 6Blessed is the man who does not fall away on account of me."[w]

7As John's[x] disciples were leaving, Jesus began to speak to the crowd about John: "What did you go out into the desert to see? A reed swayed by the wind? 8If not, what did you go out to see? A man dressed in fine clothes? No, those who wear fine clothes are in kings' palaces. 9Then what did you go out to see? A prophet?[y] Yes, I tell you, and more than a prophet. 10This is the one about whom it is written:

> " 'I will send my messenger ahead of you,
>   who will prepare your way before you.'[c][z]

11I tell you the truth: Among those born of women there has not risen anyone greater than John the Baptist; yet he who is least in the kingdom of heaven is greater than he. 12From the days of John the Baptist until now, the kingdom of heaven has been forcefully advancing, and forceful men lay hold of it. 13For all the Prophets and the Law prophesied until John. 14And if you are willing to accept it, he is the Elijah who was to come.[a] 15He who has ears, let him hear.[b]

16"To what can I compare this generation? They are like children sitting in the marketplaces and calling out to others:

> 17" 'We played the flute for you,
>   and you did not dance;
> we sang a dirge,
>   and you did not mourn.'

18For John came neither eating[c] nor drinking,[d] and they say, 'He has a demon.' 19The Son of Man came eating and drinking, and they say, 'Here is a glutton and a drunkard, a friend of tax collectors and "sinners." '[e] But wisdom is proved right by her actions."

Woe on Unrepentant Cities

11:21–23pp — Lk 10:13–15

20Then Jesus began to denounce the cities in which most of his miracles had been performed, because they did not repent. 21"Woe to you, Korazin! Woe to you, Bethsaida![f] If the miracles that were performed in you had been performed in Tyre and Sidon,[g] they would have repented long ago in sackcloth and ashes.[h] 22But I tell you, it will be more bearable for Tyre and Sidon on the day of judgment than for you.[i] 23And you, Capernaum,[j] will you be lifted up to the skies? No,

11:1
sMt 7:28
11:2
tMt 14:3
11:3
uPs 118:26;
Jn 11:27;
Heb 10:37
11:5
vIsa 35:4-6;
61:1; Lk 4:18,19
11:6
wMt 13:21
11:7
xMt 3:1
11:9
yMt 21:26;
Lk 1:76
11:10
zMal 3:1;
Mk 1:2
11:14
aMal 4:5;
Mt 17:10-13;
Mk 9:11-13;
Lk 1:17; Jn 1:21
11:15
bMt 13:9,43;
Mk 4:23;
Lk 14:35;
Rev 2:7
11:18
cMt 3:4
dLk 1:15
11:19
eMt 9:11
11:21
fMk 6:45;
Lk 9:10;
Jn 12:21
gMt 15:21;
Lk 6:17;
Ac 12:20
hJnh 3:5-9
11:22
iver 24;
Mt 10:15
11:23
jMt 4:13

---

*a*1 Greek *in their towns*   *b*5 The Greek word was used for various diseases affecting the skin—not necessarily leprosy.   *c*10 Mal. 3:1

you will go down to the depths.[a][k] If the miracles that were performed in you had been performed in Sodom, it would have remained to this day. [24]But I tell you that it will be more bearable for Sodom on the day of judgment than for you."[l]

Rest for the Weary

11:25–27pp — Lk 10:21,22

[25]At that time Jesus said, "I praise you, Father, [m] Lord of heaven and earth, because you have hidden these things from the wise and learned, and revealed them to little children.[n] [26]Yes, Father, for this was your good pleasure.

[27]"All things have been committed to me[o] by my Father.[p] No one knows the Son except the Father, and no one knows the Father except the Son and those to whom the Son chooses to reveal him. [q]

[28]"Come to me,[r] all you who are weary and burdened, and I will give you rest. [29]Take my yoke upon you and learn from me,[s] for I am gentle and humble in heart, and you will find rest for your souls.[t] [30]For my yoke is easy and my burden is light."[u]

Lord of the Sabbath

12:1–8pp — Mk 2:23–28; Lk 6:1–5
12:9–14pp — Mk 3:1–6; Lk 6:6–11

12 At that time Jesus went through the grainfields on the Sabbath. His disciples were hungry and began to pick some heads of grain[v] and eat them. [2]When the Pharisees saw this, they said to him, "Look! Your disciples are doing what is unlawful on the Sabbath."[w]

[3]He answered, "Haven't you read what David did when he and his companions were hungry?[x] [4]He entered the house of God, and he and his companions ate the consecrated bread—which was not lawful for them to do, but only for the priests. [y] [5]Or haven't you read in the Law that on the Sabbath the priests in the temple desecrate the day[z] and yet are innocent? [6]I tell you that one[b] greater than the temple is here. [a] [7]If you had known what these words mean, 'I desire mercy, not sacrifice,'[c][b] you would not have condemned the innocent. [8]For the Son of Man[c] is Lord of the Sabbath."

[9]Going on from that place, he went into their synagogue, [10]and a man with a shriveled hand was there. Looking for a reason to accuse Jesus, they asked him, "Is it lawful to heal on the Sabbath?"[d]

[11]He said to them, "If any of you has a sheep and it falls into a pit on the Sabbath, will you not take hold of it and lift it out?[e] [12]How much more valuable is a man than a sheep![f] Therefore it is lawful to do good on the Sabbath."

[13]Then he said to the man, "Stretch out your hand." So he stretched it out and it was completely restored, just as sound as the other. [14]But the Pharisees went out and plotted how they might kill Jesus. [g]

God's Chosen Servant

[15]Aware of this, Jesus withdrew from that place. Many followed him, and he healed all their sick, [h] [16]warning them not to tell who he was. [i] [17]This was to fulfill what was spoken through the prophet Isaiah:

---

[a]23 Greek *Hades*   [b]6 Or *something*; also in verses 41 and 42   [c]7 Hosea 6:6

18"Here is my servant whom I have chosen,
    the one I love, in whom I delight;[j]
I will put my Spirit on him,
    and he will proclaim justice to the nations.
19He will not quarrel or cry out;
    no one will hear his voice in the streets.
20A bruised reed he will not break,
    and a smoldering wick he will not snuff out,
    till he leads justice to victory.
21   In his name the nations will put their hope."[a] [k]

Jesus and Beelzebub

12:25–29pp — Mk 3:23–27; Lk 11:17–22

22Then they brought him a demon-possessed man who was blind and mute, and Jesus healed him, so that he could both talk and see.[l] 23All the people were astonished and said, "Could this be the Son of David?"[m]

24But when the Pharisees heard this, they said, "It is only by Beelzebub,[b] [n] the prince of demons, that this fellow drives out demons."[o]

25Jesus knew their thoughts[p] and said to them, "Every kingdom divided against itself will be ruined, and every city or household divided against itself will not stand. 26If Satan[q] drives out Satan, he is divided against himself. How then can his kingdom stand? 27And if I drive out demons by Beelzebub, by whom do your people[r] drive them out? So then, they will be your judges. 28But if I drive out demons by the Spirit of God, then the kingdom of God has come upon you.

29"Or again, how can anyone enter a strong man's house and carry off his possessions unless he first ties up the strong man? Then he can rob his house.

30"He who is not with me is against me, and he who does not gather with me scatters.[s] 31And so I tell you, every sin and blasphemy will be forgiven men, but the blasphemy against the Spirit will not be forgiven.[t] 32Anyone who speaks a word against the Son of Man will be forgiven, but anyone who speaks against the Holy Spirit will not be forgiven, either in this age[u] or in the age to come.[v]

33"Make a tree good and its fruit will be good, or make a tree bad and its fruit will be bad, for a tree is recognized by its fruit.[w] 34You brood of vipers,[x] how can you who are evil say anything good? For out of the overflow of the heart the mouth speaks.[y] 35The good man brings good things out of the good stored up in him, and the evil man brings evil things out of the evil stored up in him. 36But I tell you that men will have to give account on the day of judgment for every careless word they have spoken. 37For by your words you will be acquitted, and by your words you will be condemned."

The Sign of Jonah

12:39–42pp — Lk 11:29–32
12:43–45pp — Lk 11:24–26

38Then some of the Pharisees and teachers of the law said to him, "Teacher, we want to see a miraculous sign from you."[z]

---

[a]21 Isaiah 42:1-4   [b]24 Greek *Beezeboul* or *Beelzeboul*; also in verse 27

12:18
[j]Mt 3:17
12:21
[k]Isa 42:1-4
12:22
[l]Mt 4:24;
9:32-33
12:23
[m]Mt 9:27
12:24
[n]Mk 3:22
[o]Mt 9:34
12:25
[p]Mt 9:4
12:26
[q]Mt 4:10
12:27
[r]Ac 19:13
12:30
[s]Mk 9:40;
Lk 11:23
12:31
[t]Mk 3:28,29;
Lk 12:10
12:32
[u]Tit 2:12
[v]Mk 10:30;
Lk 20:34,35;
Eph 1:21;
Heb 6:5
12:33
[w]Mt 7:16,17;
Lk 6:43,44
12:34
[x]Mt 3:7; 23:33
[y]Mt 15:18;
Lk 6:45
12:38
[z]Mt 16:1;
Mk 8:11,12;
Lk 11:16;
Jn 2:18; 6:30;
1Co 1:22

[39]He answered, "A wicked and adulterous generation asks for a miraculous sign! But none will be given it except the sign of the prophet Jonah. [a] [40]For as Jonah was three days and three nights in the belly of a huge fish, [b] so the Son of Man[c] will be three days and three nights in the heart of the earth. [d] [41]The men of Nineveh[e] will stand up at the judgment with this generation and condemn it; for they repented at the preaching of Jonah, [f] and now one[a] greater than Jonah is here. [42]The Queen of the South will rise at the judgment with this generation and condemn it; for she came[g] from the ends of the earth to listen to Solomon's wisdom, and now one greater than Solomon is here.

[43]"When an evil[b] spirit comes out of a man, it goes through arid places seeking rest and does not find it. [44]Then it says, 'I will return to the house I left.' When it arrives, it finds the house unoccupied, swept clean and put in order. [45]Then it goes and takes with it seven other spirits more wicked than itself, and they go in and live there. And the final condition of that man is worse than the first. [h] That is how it will be with this wicked generation."

Jesus' Mother and Brothers

12:46–50pp — Mk 3:31–35; Lk 8:19–21

[46]While Jesus was still talking to the crowd, his mother[i] and brothers[j] stood outside, wanting to speak to him. [47]Someone told him, "Your mother and brothers are standing outside, wanting to speak to you."[c]

[48]He replied to him, "Who is my mother, and who are my brothers?" [49]Pointing to his disciples, he said, "Here are my mother and my brothers. [50]For whoever does the will of my Father in heaven[k] is my brother and sister and mother."

The Parable of the Sower

13:1–15pp — Mk 4:1–12; Lk 8:4–10
13:16,17pp — Lk 10:23,24
13:18–23pp — Mk 4:13–20; Lk 8:11–15

13 That same day Jesus went out of the house[l] and sat by the lake. [2]Such large crowds gathered around him that he got into a boat[m] and sat in it, while all the people stood on the shore. [3]Then he told them many things in parables, saying: "A farmer went out to sow his seed. [4]As he was scattering the seed, some fell along the path, and the birds came and ate it up. [5]Some fell on rocky places, where it did not have much soil. It sprang up quickly, because the soil was shallow. [6]But when the sun came up, the plants were scorched, and they withered because they had no root. [7]Other seed fell among thorns, which grew up and choked the plants. [8]Still other seed fell on good soil, where it produced a crop—a hundred, [n] sixty or thirty times what was sown. [9]He who has ears, let him hear."[o]

[10]The disciples came to him and asked, "Why do you speak to the people in parables?"

[11]He replied, "The knowledge of the secrets of the kingdom of heaven has been given to you, [p] but not to them. [12]Whoever has will be given more, and he will have an abundance. Whoever does not have, even

---

12:39
aMt 16:4;
Lk 11:29
12:40
bJnh 1:17
cMt 8:20
dMt 16:21
12:41
eJnh 1:2
fJnh 3:5
12:42
g1Ki 10:1;
2Ch 9:1
12:45
h2Pe 2:20
12:46
iMt 1:18; 2:11,
13,14,20;
Lk 1:43; 2:33,
34,48,51;
Jn 2:1,5; 19:25,
26 jMt 13:55;
Jn 2:12; 7:3,5;
Ac 1:14;
1Co 9:5;
Gal 1:19
12:50
kJn 15:14
13:1
lver 36; Mt 9:28
13:2
mLk 5:3
13:8
nGe 26:12
13:9
oMt 11:15
13:11
pMt 11:25;
16:17; 19:11;
Jn 6:65;
1Co 2:10,14;
Col 1:27;
1Jn 2:20,27

---

[a]41 Or *something*; also in verse 42   [b]43 Greek *unclean*   [c]47 Some manuscripts do not have verse 47.

what he has will be taken from him. q 13This is why I speak to them in parables:

> "Though seeing, they do not see;
>> though hearing, they do not hear or understand. r

14In them is fulfilled the prophecy of Isaiah:

> " 'You will be ever hearing but never understanding;
>> you will be ever seeing but never perceiving.
> 15For this people's heart has become calloused;
>> they hardly hear with their ears,
>> and they have closed their eyes.
> Otherwise they might see with their eyes,
>> hear with their ears,
>> understand with their hearts
> and turn, and I would heal them.' a s

16But blessed are your eyes because they see, and your ears because they hear. t 17For I tell you the truth, many prophets and righteous men longed to see what you see u but did not see it, and to hear what you hear but did not hear it.

18"Listen then to what the parable of the sower means: 19When anyone hears the message about the kingdom v and does not understand it, the evil one w comes and snatches away what was sown in his heart. This is the seed sown along the path. 20The one who received the seed that fell on rocky places is the man who hears the word and at once receives it with joy. 21But since he has no root, he lasts only a short time. When trouble or persecution comes because of the word, he quickly falls away. x 22The one who received the seed that fell among the thorns is the man who hears the word, but the worries of this life and the deceitfulness of wealth y choke it, making it unfruitful. 23But the one who received the seed that fell on good soil is the man who hears the word and understands it. He produces a crop, yielding a hundred, sixty or thirty times what was sown." z

The Parable of the Weeds

24Jesus told them another parable: "The kingdom of heaven is like a a man who sowed good seed in his field. 25But while everyone was sleeping, his enemy came and sowed weeds among the wheat, and went away. 26When the wheat sprouted and formed heads, then the weeds also appeared.

27"The owner's servants came to him and said, 'Sir, didn't you sow good seed in your field? Where then did the weeds come from?'

28" 'An enemy did this,' he replied.

"The servants asked him, 'Do you want us to go and pull them up?'

29" 'No,' he answered, 'because while you are pulling the weeds, you may root up the wheat with them. 30Let both grow together until the harvest. At that time I will tell the harvesters: First collect the weeds and tie them in bundles to be burned; then gather the wheat and bring it into my barn.' " b

a15 Isaiah 6:9,10

13:12
qMt 25:29;
Lk 19:26
13:13
rDt 29:4;
Jer 5:21;
Eze 12:2
13:15
sIsa 6:9,10;
Jn 12:40;
Ac 28:26,27;
Ro 11:8
13:16
tMt 16:17
13:17
uJn 8:56;
Heb 11:13;
1Pe 1:10-12
13:19
vMt 4:23
wMt 5:37
13:21
xMt 11:6
13:22
yMt 19:23;
1Ti 6:9,10,17
13:23
zver 8
13:24
aver 31,33,45,
47; Mt 18:23;
20:1; 22:2;
25:1; Mk 4:26,
30
13:30
bMt 3:12

The Parables of the Mustard Seed and the Yeast

13:31,32pp — Mk 4:30–32
13:31–33pp — Lk 13:18–21

13:31
c ver 24
d Mt 17:20;
Lk 17:6
13:32
e Ps 104:12;
Eze 17:23;
31:6; Da 4:12
13:33
f ver 24
g Ge 18:6
h Gal 5:9
13:34
i Mk 4:33;
Jn 16:25
13:35
j Ps 78:2;
Ro 16:25,26;
1Co 2:7;
Eph 3:9;
Col 1:26
13:36
k Mt 15:15
13:37
l Mt 8:20
13:38
m Jn 8:44,45;
1Jn 3:10
13:39
n Joel 3:13
o Mt 24:3; 28:20
p Rev 14:15
13:41
q Mt 8:20
r Mt 24:31
13:42
s ver 50; Mt 8:12
13:43
t Da 12:3
u Mt 11:15
13:44
v ver 24
w Isa 55:1;
Php 3:7,8
13:45
x ver 24
13:47
y ver 24
z Mt 22:10

31He told them another parable: "The kingdom of heaven is like[c] a mustard seed,[d] which a man took and planted in his field. 32Though it is the smallest of all your seeds, yet when it grows, it is the largest of garden plants and becomes a tree, so that the birds of the air come and perch in its branches."[e]

33He told them still another parable: "The kingdom of heaven is like[f] yeast that a woman took and mixed into a large amount[a] of flour[g] until it worked all through the dough."[h]

34Jesus spoke all these things to the crowd in parables; he did not say anything to them without using a parable.[i] 35So was fulfilled what was spoken through the prophet:

"I will open my mouth in parables,
    I will utter things hidden since the creation of the
        world."[b] [j]

The Parable of the Weeds Explained

36Then he left the crowd and went into the house. His disciples came to him and said, "Explain to us the parable[k] of the weeds in the field."

37He answered, "The one who sowed the good seed is the Son of Man.[l] 38The field is the world, and the good seed stands for the sons of the kingdom. The weeds are the sons of the evil one,[m] 39and the enemy who sows them is the devil. The harvest[n] is the end of the age,[o] and the harvesters are angels.[p]

40"As the weeds are pulled up and burned in the fire, so it will be at the end of the age. 41The Son of Man[q] will send out his angels,[r] and they will weed out of his kingdom everything that causes sin and all who do evil. 42They will throw them into the fiery furnace, where there will be weeping and gnashing of teeth.[s] 43Then the righteous will shine like the sun[t] in the kingdom of their Father. He who has ears, let him hear.[u]

The Parables of the Hidden Treasure and the Pearl

44"The kingdom of heaven is like[v] treasure hidden in a field. When a man found it, he hid it again, and then in his joy went and sold all he had and bought that field.[w]

45"Again, the kingdom of heaven is like[x] a merchant looking for fine pearls. 46When he found one of great value, he went away and sold everything he had and bought it.

The Parable of the Net

47"Once again, the kingdom of heaven is like[y] a net that was let down into the lake and caught all kinds[z] of fish. 48When it was full, the fishermen pulled it up on the shore. Then they sat down and collected the good fish in baskets, but threw the bad away. 49This is how it will be at the end of the age. The angels will come and separate the wicked

---

a33 Greek *three satas* (probably about 1/2 bushel or 22 liters)   b35 Psalm 78:2

from the righteous[a] 50and throw them into the fiery furnace, where there will be weeping and gnashing of teeth.[b]

51"Have you understood all these things?" Jesus asked.

"Yes," they replied.

52He said to them, "Therefore every teacher of the law who has been instructed about the kingdom of heaven is like the owner of a house who brings out of his storeroom new treasures as well as old."

A Prophet Without Honor
13:54-58pp — Mk 6:1-6

53When Jesus had finished these parables,[c] he moved on from there. 54Coming to his hometown, he began teaching the people in their synagogue,[d] and they were amazed.[e] "Where did this man get this wisdom and these miraculous powers?" they asked. 55"Isn't this the carpenter's son?[f] Isn't his mother's[g] name Mary, and aren't his brothers James, Joseph, Simon and Judas? 56Aren't all his sisters with us? Where then did this man get all these things?" 57And they took offense[h] at him.

But Jesus said to them, "Only in his hometown and in his own house is a prophet without honor."[i]

58And he did not do many miracles there because of their lack of faith.

John the Baptist Beheaded
14:1-12pp — Mk 6:14-29

14 At that time Herod[j] the tetrarch heard the reports about Jesus,[k] 2and he said to his attendants, "This is John the Baptist;[l] he has risen from the dead! That is why miraculous powers are at work in him."

3Now Herod had arrested John and bound him and put him in prison[m] because of Herodias, his brother Philip's wife,[n] 4for John had been saying to him: "It is not lawful for you to have her."[o] 5Herod wanted to kill John, but he was afraid of the people, because they considered him a prophet.[p]

6On Herod's birthday the daughter of Herodias danced for them and pleased Herod so much 7that he promised with an oath to give her whatever she asked. 8Prompted by her mother, she said, "Give me here on a platter the head of John the Baptist." 9The king was distressed, but because of his oaths and his dinner guests, he ordered that her request be granted 10and had John beheaded[q] in the prison. 11His head was brought in on a platter and given to the girl, who carried it to her mother. 12John's disciples came and took his body and buried it.[r] Then they went and told Jesus.

Jesus Feeds the Five Thousand
14:13-21pp — Mk 6:32-44; Lk 9:10-17; Jn 6:1-13
14:13-21Ref — Mt 15:32-38

13When Jesus heard what had happened, he withdrew by boat privately to a solitary place. Hearing of this, the crowds followed him on foot from the towns. 14When Jesus landed and saw a large crowd, he had compassion on them[s] and healed their sick.[t]

15As evening approached, the disciples came to him and said, "This

13:49
a Mt 25:32
13:50
b Mt 8:12
13:53
c Mt 7:28
13:54
d Mt 4:23
e Mt 7:28
13:55
f Lk 3:23;
Jn 6:42
g Mt 12:46
13:57
h Jn 6:61
i Lk 4:24;
Jn 4:44
14:1
j Mk 8:15;
Lk 3:1,19;
13:31; 23:7,8;
Ac 4:27; 12:1
k Lk 9:7-9
14:2
l Mt 3:1
14:3
m Mt 4:12; 11:2
n Lk 3:19,20
14:4
o Lev 18:16;
20:21
14:5
p Mt 11:9
14:10
q Mt 17:12
14:12
r Ac 8:2
14:14
s Mt 9:36
t Mt 4:23

is a remote place, and it's already getting late. Send the crowds away, so they can go to the villages and buy themselves some food."

[16]Jesus replied, "They do not need to go away. You give them something to eat."

[17]"We have here only five loaves[u] of bread and two fish," they answered.

[18]"Bring them here to me," he said. [19]And he directed the people to sit down on the grass. Taking the five loaves and the two fish and looking up to heaven, he gave thanks and broke the loaves. [v]Then he gave them to the disciples, and the disciples gave them to the people. [20]They all ate and were satisfied, and the disciples picked up twelve basketfuls of broken pieces that were left over. [21]The number of those who ate was about five thousand men, besides women and children.

Jesus Walks on the Water

14:22–33pp — Mk 6:45–51; Jn 6:15–21
14:34–36pp — Mk 6:53–56

[22]Immediately Jesus made the disciples get into the boat and go on ahead of him to the other side, while he dismissed the crowd. [23]After he had dismissed them, he went up on a mountainside by himself to pray.[w] When evening came, he was there alone, [24]but the boat was already a considerable distance[a] from land, buffeted by the waves because the wind was against it.

[25]During the fourth watch of the night Jesus went out to them, walking on the lake. [26]When the disciples saw him walking on the lake, they were terrified. "It's a ghost,"[x] they said, and cried out in fear.

[27]But Jesus immediately said to them: "Take courage![y] It is I. Don't be afraid."[z]

[28]"Lord, if it's you," Peter replied, "tell me to come to you on the water."

[29]"Come," he said.

Then Peter got down out of the boat, walked on the water and came toward Jesus. [30]But when he saw the wind, he was afraid and, beginning to sink, cried out, "Lord, save me!"

[31]Immediately Jesus reached out his hand and caught him. "You of little faith,"[a] he said, "why did you doubt?"

[32]And when they climbed into the boat, the wind died down. [33]Then those who were in the boat worshiped him, saying, "Truly you are the Son of God."[b]

[34]When they had crossed over, they landed at Gennesaret. [35]And when the men of that place recognized Jesus, they sent word to all the surrounding country. People brought all their sick to him [36]and begged him to let the sick just touch the edge of his cloak,[c] and all who touched him were healed.

Clean and Unclean

15:1–20pp — Mk 7:1–23

15 Then some Pharisees and teachers of the law came to Jesus from Jerusalem and asked, [2]"Why do your disciples break the tradition of the elders? They don't wash their hands before they eat!"[d]

14:17
u Mt 16:9
14:19
v 1Sa 9:13;
Mt 26:26;
Mk 8:6;
Lk 24:30;
Ac 2:42; 27:35;
1Ti 4:4
14:23
w Lk 3:21
14:26
x Lk 24:37
14:27
y Mt 9:2;
Ac 23:11
z Da 10:12;
Mt 17:7; 28:10;
Lk 1:13,30;
2:10; Ac 18:9;
23:11; Rev 1:17
14:31
a Mt 6:30
14:33
b Ps 2:7; Mt 4:3
14:36
c Mt 9:20
15:2
d Lk 11:38

---

a24 Greek *many stadia*

³Jesus replied, "And why do you break the command of God for the sake of your tradition? ⁴For God said, 'Honor your father and mother'ᵃᵉ and 'Anyone who curses his father or mother must be put to death.'ᵇᶠ ⁵But you say that if a man says to his father or mother, 'Whatever help you might otherwise have received from me is a gift devoted to God,' ⁶he is not to 'honor his fatherᶜ' with it. Thus you nullify the word of God for the sake of your tradition. ⁷You hypocrites! Isaiah was right when he prophesied about you:

⁸" 'These people honor me with their lips,
    but their hearts are far from me.
⁹They worship me in vain;
    their teachings are but rules taught by men.ᵍ'ᵈ ʰ"

¹⁰Jesus called the crowd to him and said, "Listen and understand. ¹¹What goes into a man's mouth does not make him 'unclean,'ⁱ but what comes out of his mouth, that is what makes him 'unclean.' "ʲ

¹²Then the disciples came to him and asked, "Do you know that the Pharisees were offended when they heard this?"

¹³He replied, "Every plant that my heavenly Father has not plantedᵏ will be pulled up by the roots. ¹⁴Leave them; they are blind guides.ᵉˡ If a blind man leads a blind man, both will fall into a pit."ᵐ

¹⁵Peter said, "Explain the parable to us."ⁿ

¹⁶"Are you still so dull?"ᵒ Jesus asked them. ¹⁷"Don't you see that whatever enters the mouth goes into the stomach and then out of the body? ¹⁸But the things that come out of the mouth come from the heart,ᵖ and these make a man 'unclean.' ¹⁹For out of the heart come evil thoughts, murder, adultery, sexual immorality, theft, false testimony, slander.�q ²⁰These are what make a man 'unclean';ʳ but eating with unwashed hands does not make him 'unclean.' "

The Faith of the Canaanite Woman

15:21–28pp — Mk 7:24–30

²¹Leaving that place, Jesus withdrew to the region of Tyre and Sidon.ˢ ²²A Canaanite woman from that vicinity came to him, crying out, "Lord, Son of David,ᵗ have mercy on me! My daughter is suffering terribly from demon-possession."ᵘ

²³Jesus did not answer a word. So his disciples came to him and urged him, "Send her away, for she keeps crying out after us."

²⁴He answered, "I was sent only to the lost sheep of Israel."ᵛ

²⁵The woman came and knelt before him.ʷ "Lord, help me!" she said.

²⁶He replied, "It is not right to take the children's bread and toss it to their dogs."

²⁷"Yes, Lord," she said, "but even the dogs eat the crumbs that fall from their masters' table."

²⁸Then Jesus answered, "Woman, you have great faith!ˣ Your request is granted." And her daughter was healed from that very hour.

15:4
eEx 20:12;
Dt 5:16;
Eph 6:2
fEx 21:17;
Lev 20:9
15:9
gCol 2:20-22
hIsa 29:13;
Mal 2:2
15:11
iAc 10:14,15
jver 18
15:13
kIsa 60:21;
61:3; Jn 15:2
15:14
lMt 23:16,24;
Ro 2:19
mLk 6:39
15:15
nMt 13:36
15:16
oMt 16:9
15:18
pMt 12:34;
Lk 6:45; Jas 3:6
15:19
qGal 5:19-21
15:20
rRo 14:14
15:21
sMt 11:21
15:22
tMt 9:27
uMt 4:24
15:24
vMt 10:6,23;
Ro 15:8
15:25
wMt 8:2
15:28
xMt 9:22

ᵃ4 Exodus 20:12; Deut. 5:16   ᵇ4 Exodus 21:17; Lev. 20:9   ᶜ6 Some manuscripts *father or his mother*   ᵈ9 Isaiah 29:13   ᵉ14 Some manuscripts *guides of the blind*

Jesus Feeds the Four Thousand

15:29–31pp — Mk 7:31–37
15:32–39pp — Mk 8:1–10
15:32–39Ref — Mt 14:13–21

²⁹Jesus left there and went along the Sea of Galilee. Then he went up on a mountainside and sat down. ³⁰Great crowds came to him, bringing the lame, the blind, the crippled, the mute and many others, and laid them at his feet; and he healed them. ^y ³¹The people were amazed when they saw the mute speaking, the crippled made well, the lame walking and the blind seeing. And they praised the God of Israel. ^z

³²Jesus called his disciples to him and said, "I have compassion for these people; ^a they have already been with me three days and have nothing to eat. I do not want to send them away hungry, or they may collapse on the way."

³³His disciples answered, "Where could we get enough bread in this remote place to feed such a crowd?"

³⁴"How many loaves do you have?" Jesus asked.

"Seven," they replied, "and a few small fish."

³⁵He told the crowd to sit down on the ground. ³⁶Then he took the seven loaves and the fish, and when he had given thanks, he broke them ^b and gave them to the disciples, and they in turn to the people. ³⁷They all ate and were satisfied. Afterward the disciples picked up seven basketfuls of broken pieces that were left over. ^c ³⁸The number of those who ate was four thousand, besides women and children. ³⁹After Jesus had sent the crowd away, he got into the boat and went to the vicinity of Magadan.

The Demand for a Sign

16:1–12pp — Mk 8:11–21

16 The Pharisees and Sadducees ^d came to Jesus and tested him by asking him to show them a sign from heaven. ^e

²He replied, ^a "When evening comes, you say, 'It will be fair weather, for the sky is red,' ³and in the morning, 'Today it will be stormy, for the sky is red and overcast.' You know how to interpret the appearance of the sky, but you cannot interpret the signs of the times. ^f ⁴A wicked and adulterous generation looks for a miraculous sign, but none will be given it except the sign of Jonah." ^g Jesus then left them and went away.

The Yeast of the Pharisees and Sadducees

⁵When they went across the lake, the disciples forgot to take bread. ⁶"Be careful," Jesus said to them. "Be on your guard against the yeast of the Pharisees and Sadducees." ^h

⁷They discussed this among themselves and said, "It is because we didn't bring any bread."

⁸Aware of their discussion, Jesus asked, "You of little faith, ⁱ why are you talking among yourselves about having no bread? ⁹Do you still not understand? Don't you remember the five loaves for the five thousand, and how many basketfuls you gathered? ^j ¹⁰Or the seven loaves for the four thousand, and how many basketfuls you gathered? ^k ¹¹How is it you don't understand that I was not talking to you about bread? But be

15:30
yMt 4:23
15:31
zMt 9:8
15:32
aMt 9:36
15:36
bMt 14:19
15:37
cMt 16:10
16:1
dAc 4:1
eMt 12:38
16:3
fLk 12:54-56
16:4
gMt 12:39
16:6
hLk 12:1
16:8
iMt 6:30
16:9
jMt 14:17-21
16:10
kMt 15:34-38

---

^a2 Some early manuscripts do not have the rest of verse 2 and all of verse 3.

on your guard against the yeast of the Pharisees and Sadducees." ¹²Then they understood that he was not telling them to guard against the yeast used in bread, but against the teaching of the Pharisees and Sadducees.[l]

Peter's Confession of Christ

16:13–16pp — Mk 8:27–29; Lk 9:18–20

¹³When Jesus came to the region of Caesarea Philippi, he asked his disciples, "Who do people say the Son of Man is?"

¹⁴They replied, "Some say John the Baptist;[m] others say Elijah; and still others, Jeremiah or one of the prophets."[n]

¹⁵"But what about you?" he asked. "Who do you say I am?"

¹⁶Simon Peter answered, "You are the Christ,[a] the Son of the living God."[o]

¹⁷Jesus replied, "Blessed are you, Simon son of Jonah, for this was not revealed to you by man,[p] but by my Father in heaven. ¹⁸And I tell you that you are Peter,[b][q] and on this rock I will build my church,[r] and the gates of Hades[c] will not overcome it.[d] ¹⁹I will give you the keys[s] of the kingdom of heaven; whatever you bind on earth will be[e] bound in heaven, and whatever you loose on earth will be[e] loosed in heaven."[t] ²⁰Then he warned his disciples not to tell anyone[u] that he was the Christ.

Jesus Predicts His Death

16:21–28pp — Mk 8:31 — 9:1; Lk 9:22–27

²¹From that time on Jesus began to explain to his disciples that he must go to Jerusalem and suffer many things[v] at the hands of the elders, chief priests and teachers of the law, and that he must be killed and on the third day[w] be raised to life.[x]

²²Peter took him aside and began to rebuke him. "Never, Lord!" he said. "This shall never happen to you!"

²³Jesus turned and said to Peter, "Get behind me, Satan![y] You are a stumbling block to me; you do not have in mind the things of God, but the things of men."

²⁴Then Jesus said to his disciples, "If anyone would come after me, he must deny himself and take up his cross and follow me.[z] ²⁵For whoever wants to save his life[f] will lose it, but whoever loses his life for me will find it.[a] ²⁶What good will it be for a man if he gains the whole world, yet forfeits his soul? Or what can a man give in exchange for his soul? ²⁷For the Son of Man[b] is going to come[c] in his Father's glory with his angels, and then he will reward each person according to what he has done.[d] ²⁸I tell you the truth, some who are standing here will not taste death before they see the Son of Man coming in his kingdom."

The Transfiguration

17:1–8pp — Lk 9:28–36
17:1–13pp — Mk 9:2–13

17 After six days Jesus took with him Peter, James and John the brother of James, and led them up a high mountain by them-

16:12
lAc 4:1
16:14
mMt 3:1; 14:2
nMk 6:15;
Jn 1:21
16:16
oMt 4:3;
Ps 42:2;
Jn 11:27;
Ac 14:15;
2Co 6:16;
1Th 1:9;
1Ti 3:15;
Heb 10:31;
12:22
16:17
pLCo 15:50;
Gal 1:16;
Eph 6:12;
Heb 2:14
16:18
qJn 1:42
rEph 2:20
16:19
sIsa 22:22;
Rev 3:7
tMt 18:18;
Jn 20:23
16:20
uMk 8:30
16:21
vMk 10:34;
Lk 17:25
wJn 2:19
xMt 17:22,23;
Mk 9:31;
Lk 9:22;
18:31-33; 24:6,7
16:23
yMt 4:10
16:24
zMt 10:38;
Lk 14:27
16:25
aJn 12:25
16:27
bMt 8:20
cAc 1:11
dJob 34:11;
Ps 62:12;
Jer 17:10;
Ro 2:6;
2Co 5:10;
Rev 22:12

---

[a]16 Or *Messiah*; also in verse 20   [b]18 *Peter* means *rock*.   [c]18 Or *hell*   [d]18 Or *not prove stronger than it*   [e]19 Or *have been*   [f]25 The Greek word means either *life* or *soul*; also in verse 26.

selves. 2There he was transfigured before them. His face shone like the sun, and his clothes became as white as the light. 3Just then there appeared before them Moses and Elijah, talking with Jesus.

4Peter said to Jesus, "Lord, it is good for us to be here. If you wish, I will put up three shelters—one for you, one for Moses and one for Elijah."

5While he was still speaking, a bright cloud enveloped them, and a voice from the cloud said, "This is my Son, whom I love; with him I am well pleased. e Listen to him!" f

6When the disciples heard this, they fell facedown to the ground, terrified. 7But Jesus came and touched them. "Get up," he said. "Don't be afraid." g 8When they looked up, they saw no one except Jesus.

9As they were coming down the mountain, Jesus instructed them, "Don't tell anyoneh what you have seen, until the Son of Mani has been raised from the dead." j

10The disciples asked him, "Why then do the teachers of the law say that Elijah must come first?"

11Jesus replied, "To be sure, Elijah comes and will restore all things. k 12But I tell you, Elijah has already come, l and they did not recognize him, but have done to him everything they wished. m In the same way the Son of Man is going to suffern at their hands." 13Then the disciples understood that he was talking to them about John the Baptist.

The Healing of a Boy With a Demon

17:14–19pp — Mk 9:14–28; Lk 9:37–42

14When they came to the crowd, a man approached Jesus and knelt before him. 15"Lord, have mercy on my son," he said. "He has seizureso and is suffering greatly. He often falls into the fire or into the water. 16I brought him to your disciples, but they could not heal him."

17"O unbelieving and perverse generation," Jesus replied, "how long shall I stay with you? How long shall I put up with you? Bring the boy here to me." 18Jesus rebuked the demon, and it came out of the boy, and he was healed from that moment.

19Then the disciples came to Jesus in private and asked, "Why couldn't we drive it out?"

20He replied, "Because you have so little faith. I tell you the truth, if you have faithp as small as a mustard seed,q you can say to this mountain, 'Move from here to there' and it will move. r Nothing will be impossible for you. a "

22When they came together in Galilee, he said to them, "The Son of Mans is going to be betrayed into the hands of men. 23They will kill him, t and on the third dayu he will be raised to life." v And the disciples were filled with grief.

The Temple Tax

24After Jesus and his disciples arrived in Capernaum, the collectors of the two-drachma taxw came to Peter and asked, "Doesn't your teacher pay the temple taxb ?"

25"Yes, he does," he replied.

17:5
eMt 3:17;
2Pe 1:17
fAc 3:22,23
17:7
gMt 14:27
17:9
hMk 8:30
iMt 8:20
jMt 16:21
17:11
kMal 4:6;
Lk 1:16,17
17:12
lMt 11:14
mMt 14:3,10
nMt 16:21
17:15
oMt 4:24
17:20
pMt 21:21
qMt 13:31;
Mk 11:23;
Lk 17:6
r1Co 13:2
17:22
sMt 8:20
17:23
tAc 2:23; 3:13
uMt 16:21
vMt 16:21
17:24
wEx 30:13

---

a20 Some manuscripts you. 21But this kind does not go out except by prayer and fasting.   b24 Greek the two drachmas

When Peter came into the house, Jesus was the first to speak. "What do you think, Simon?" he asked. "From whom do the kings of the earth collect duty and taxes×—from their own sons or from others?"

²⁶"From others," Peter answered.

"Then the sons are exempt," Jesus said to him. ²⁷"But so that we may not offendʸ them, go to the lake and throw out your line. Take the first fish you catch; open its mouth and you will find a four-drachma coin. Take it and give it to them for my tax and yours."

The Greatest in the Kingdom of Heaven
18:1–5pp — Mk 9:33–37; Lk 9:46–48

18 At that time the disciples came to Jesus and asked, "Who is the greatest in the kingdom of heaven?"

²He called a little child and had him stand among them. ³And he said: "I tell you the truth, unless you change and become like little children,ᶻ you will never enter the kingdom of heaven.ᵃ ⁴Therefore, whoever humbles himself like this child is the greatest in the kingdom of heaven.ᵇ

⁵"And whoever welcomes a little child like this in my name welcomes me.ᶜ ⁶But if anyone causes one of these little ones who believe in me to sin,ᵈ it would be better for him to have a large millstone hung around his neck and to be drowned in the depths of the sea.ᵉ

⁷"Woe to the world because of the things that cause people to sin! Such things must come, but woe to the man through whom they come!ᶠ ⁸If your hand or your foot causes you to sinᵍ cut it off and throw it away. It is better for you to enter life maimed or crippled than to have two hands or two feet and be thrown into eternal fire. ⁹And if your eye causes you to sin,ʰ gouge it out and throw it away. It is better for you to enter life with one eye than to have two eyes and be thrown into the fire of hell.ⁱ

The Parable of the Lost Sheep
18:12–14pp — Lk 15:4–7

¹⁰"See that you do not look down on one of these little ones. For I tell you that their angelsʲ in heaven always see the face of my Father in heaven.ᵃ

¹²"What do you think? If a man owns a hundred sheep, and one of them wanders away, will he not leave the ninety-nine on the hills and go to look for the one that wandered off? ¹³And if he finds it, I tell you the truth, he is happier about that one sheep than about the ninety-nine that did not wander off. ¹⁴In the same way your Father in heaven is not willing that any of these little ones should be lost.

A Brother Who Sins Against You

¹⁵"If your brother sins against you,ᵇ go and show him his fault,ᵏ just between the two of you. If he listens to you, you have won your brother over. ¹⁶But if he will not listen, take one or two others along, so that 'every matter may be established by the testimony of two or three witnesses.'ᶜˡ ¹⁷If he refuses to listen to them, tell it to the church;ᵐ and

---

17:25
×Mt 22:17-21;
Ro 13:7
17:27
ʸJn 6:61
18:3
ᶻMt 19:14;
1Pe 2:2 ᵃMt 3:2
18:4
ᵇMk 9:35
18:5
ᶜMt 10:40
18:6
ᵈMt 5:29
ᵉMk 9:42;
Lk 17:2
18:7
ᶠLk 17:1
18:8
ᵍMt 5:29;
Mk 9:43,45
18:9
ʰMt 5:29
ⁱMt 5:22
18:10
ʲGe 48:16;
Ps 34:7;
Ac 12:11,15;
Heb 1:14
18:15
ᵏLev 19:17;
Lk 17:3;
Gal 6:1;
Jas 5:19,20
18:16
ˡNu 35:30;
Dt 17:6; 19:15;
Jn 8:17;
2Co 13:1;
1Ti 5:19;
Heb 10:28
18:17
ᵐ1Co 6:1-6

ᵃ10 Some manuscripts *heaven.* ¹¹*The Son of Man came to save what was lost.*   ᵇ15 Some
manuscripts do not have *against you.*   ᶜ16 Deut. 19:15

if he refuses to listen even to the church, treat him as you would a pagan or a tax collector. [n]

[18]"I tell you the truth, whatever you bind on earth will be[a] bound in heaven, and whatever you loose on earth will be[a] loosed in heaven. [o]

[19]"Again, I tell you that if two of you on earth agree about anything you ask for, it will be done for you[p] by my Father in heaven. [20]For where two or three come together in my name, there am I with them."

The Parable of the Unmerciful Servant

[21]Then Peter came to Jesus and asked, "Lord, how many times shall I forgive my brother when he sins against me?[q] Up to seven times?"[r]

[22]Jesus answered, "I tell you, not seven times, but seventy-seven times.[b] [s]

[23]"Therefore, the kingdom of heaven is like[t] a king who wanted to settle accounts[u] with his servants. [24]As he began the settlement, a man who owed him ten thousand talents[c] was brought to him. [25]Since he was not able to pay,[v] the master ordered that he and his wife and his children and all that he had be sold[w] to repay the debt.

[26]"The servant fell on his knees before him.[x] 'Be patient with me,' he begged, 'and I will pay back everything.' [27]The servant's master took pity on him, canceled the debt and let him go.

[28]"But when that servant went out, he found one of his fellow servants who owed him a hundred denarii.[d] He grabbed him and began to choke him. 'Pay back what you owe me!' he demanded.

[29]"His fellow servant fell to his knees and begged him, 'Be patient with me, and I will pay you back.'

[30]"But he refused. Instead, he went off and had the man thrown into prison until he could pay the debt. [31]When the other servants saw what had happened, they were greatly distressed and went and told their master everything that had happened.

[32]"Then the master called the servant in. 'You wicked servant,' he said, 'I canceled all that debt of yours because you begged me to. [33]Shouldn't you have had mercy on your fellow servant just as I had on you?' [34]In anger his master turned him over to the jailers to be tortured, until he should pay back all he owed.

[35]"This is how my heavenly Father will treat each of you unless you forgive your brother from your heart."[y]

Divorce

19:1-9pp — Mk 10:1-12

19 When Jesus had finished saying these things,[z] he left Galilee and went into the region of Judea to the other side of the Jordan. [2]Large crowds followed him, and he healed them[a] there.

[3]Some Pharisees came to him to test him. They asked, "Is it lawful for a man to divorce his wife[b] for any and every reason?"

[4]"Haven't you read," he replied, "that at the beginning the Creator 'made them male and female,'[e c] [5]and said, 'For this reason a man will leave his father and mother and be united to his wife, and the two will

### Cross references (margin)

18:17
n Ro 16:17; 2Th 3:6,14
18:18
o Mt 16:19; Jn 20:23
18:19
p Mt 7:7
18:21
q Mt 6:14
r Lk 17:4
18:22
s Ge 4:24
18:23
t Mt 13:24
u Mt 25:19
18:25
v Lk 7:42
w Lev 25:39; 2Ki 4:1; Ne 5:5, 8
18:26
x Mt 8:2
18:35
y Mt 6:14; Jas 2:13
19:1
z Mt 7:28
19:2
a Mt 4:23
19:3
b Mt 5:31
19:4
c Ge 1:27; 5:2

---

[a]18 Or *have been is, a few dollars*   [b]22 Or *seventy times seven*   [c]24 That is, millions of dollars   [d]28 That

[e]4 Gen. 1:27

become one flesh'*a*?*d* 6So they are no longer two, but one. Therefore what God has joined together, let man not separate."

7"Why then," they asked, "did Moses command that a man give his wife a certificate of divorce and send her away?"*e*

8Jesus replied, "Moses permitted you to divorce your wives because your hearts were hard. But it was not this way from the beginning. 9I tell you that anyone who divorces his wife, except for marital unfaithfulness, and marries another woman commits adultery."*f*

10The disciples said to him, "If this is the situation between a husband and wife, it is better not to marry."

11Jesus replied, "Not everyone can accept this word, but only those to whom it has been given. *g* 12For some are eunuchs because they were born that way; others were made that way by men; and others have renounced marriage*b* because of the kingdom of heaven. The one who can accept this should accept it."

The Little Children and Jesus

19:13–15pp — Mk 10:13–16; Lk 18:15–17

13Then little children were brought to Jesus for him to place his hands on them*h* and pray for them. But the disciples rebuked those who brought them.

14Jesus said, "Let the little children come to me, and do not hinder them, for the kingdom of heaven belongs*i* to such as these."*j* 15When he had placed his hands on them, he went on from there.

The Rich Young Man

19:16–29pp — Mk 10:17–30; Lk 18:18–30

16Now a man came up to Jesus and asked, "Teacher, what good thing must I do to get eternal life*k*?"*l*

17"Why do you ask me about what is good?" Jesus replied. "There is only One who is good. If you want to enter life, obey the commandments."*m*

18"Which ones?" the man inquired.

Jesus replied, " 'Do not murder, do not commit adultery,*n* do not steal, do not give false testimony, 19honor your father and mother,'*c* *o* and 'love your neighbor as yourself.'*d* "*p*

20"All these I have kept," the young man said. "What do I still lack?"

21Jesus answered, "If you want to be perfect,*q* go, sell your possessions and give to the poor,*r* and you will have treasure in heaven.*s* Then come, follow me."

22When the young man heard this, he went away sad, because he had great wealth.

23Then Jesus said to his disciples, "I tell you the truth, it is hard for a rich man*t* to enter the kingdom of heaven. 24Again I tell you, it is easier for a camel to go through the eye of a needle than for a rich man to enter the kingdom of God."

25When the disciples heard this, they were greatly astonished and asked, "Who then can be saved?"

19:5
dGe 2:24;
1Co 6:16;
Eph 5:31

19:7
eDt 24:1-4;
Mt 5:31

19:9
fMt 5:32;
Lk 16:18

19:11
gMt 13:11;
1Co 7:7-9,17

19:13
hMk 5:23

19:14
iMt 25:34
jMt 18:3;
1Pe 2:2

19:16
kMt 25:46
lLk 10:25

19:17
mLev 18:5

19:18
nJas 2:11

19:19
oEx 20:12-16;
Dt 5:16-20
pLev 19:18;
Mt 5:43

19:21
qMt 5:48
rLk 12:33;
Ac 2:45;
4:34-35
sMt 6:20

19:23
tMt 13:22;
1Ti 6:9,10

---

a5 Gen. 2:24   *b12* Or *have made themselves eunuchs*   *c19* Exodus 20:12-16; Deut. 5:16-20
d19 Lev. 19:18

26Jesus looked at them and said, "With man this is impossible, but with God all things are possible."u

27Peter answered him, "We have left everything to follow you!v What then will there be for us?"

28Jesus said to them, "I tell you the truth, at the renewal of all things, when the Son of Man sits on his glorious throne,w you who have followed me will also sit on twelve thrones, judging the twelve tribes of Israel.x 29And everyone who has left houses or brothers or sisters or father or mothera or children or fields for my sake will receive a hundred times as much and will inherit eternal life.y 30But many who are first will be last, and many who are last will be first.z

The Parable of the Workers in the Vineyard

20 "For the kingdom of heaven is likea a landowner who went out early in the morning to hire men to work in his vineyard.b 2He agreed to pay them a denarius for the day and sent them into his vineyard.

3"About the third hour he went out and saw others standing in the marketplace doing nothing. 4He told them, 'You also go and work in my vineyard, and I will pay you whatever is right.' 5So they went.

"He went out again about the sixth hour and the ninth hour and did the same thing. 6About the eleventh hour he went out and found still others standing around. He asked them, 'Why have you been standing here all day long doing nothing?'

7" 'Because no one has hired us,' they answered.

"He said to them, 'You also go and work in my vineyard.'

8"When evening came,c the owner of the vineyard said to his foreman, 'Call the workers and pay them their wages, beginning with the last ones hired and going on to the first.'

9"The workers who were hired about the eleventh hour came and each received a denarius. 10So when those came who were hired first, they expected to receive more. But each one of them also received a denarius. 11When they received it, they began to grumbled against the landowner. 12'These men who were hired last worked only one hour,' they said, 'and you have made them equal to us who have borne the burden of the work and the heate of the day.'

13"But he answered one of them, 'Friend,f I am not being unfair to you. Didn't you agree to work for a denarius? 14Take your pay and go. I want to give the man who was hired last the same as I gave you. 15Don't I have the right to do what I want with my own money? Or are you envious because I am generous?'g

16"So the last will be first, and the first will be last."h

Jesus Again Predicts His Death

20:17–19pp — Mk 10:32–34; Lk 18:31–33

17Now as Jesus was going up to Jerusalem, he took the twelve disciples aside and said to them, 18"We are going up to Jerusalem,i and the Son of Manj will be betrayed to the chief priests and the teachers of the law.k They will condemn him to death 19and will turn him over to the

19:26
uGe 18:14;
Job 42:2;
Jer 32:17;
Zec 8:6;
Lk 1:37; 18:27;
Ro 4:21
19:27
vMt 4:19
19:28
wMt 20:21;
25:31
xLk 22:28-30;
Rev 3:21; 4:4;
20:4
19:29
yMt 6:33; 25:46
19:30
zMt 20:16;
Mk 10:31;
Lk 13:30
20:1
aMt 13:24
bMt 21:28,33
20:8
cLev 19:13;
Dt 24:15
20:11
dJnh 4:1
20:12
eJnh 4:8;
Lk 12:55;
Jas 1:11
20:13
fMt 22:12;
26:50
20:15
gDt 15:9;
Mk 7:22
20:16
hMt 19:30
20:18
iLk 9:51
jMt 8:20
kMt 16:21;
27:1,2

a29 Some manuscripts *mother or wife*

Gentiles to be mocked and flogged[l] and crucified. [m] On the third day[n] he will be raised to life!" [o]

A Mother's Request

20:20–28pp — Mk 10:35–45

[20]Then the mother of Zebedee's sons[p] came to Jesus with her sons and, kneeling down, [q] asked a favor of him.

[21]"What is it you want?" he asked.

She said, "Grant that one of these two sons of mine may sit at your right and the other at your left in your kingdom." [r]

[22]"You don't know what you are asking," Jesus said to them. "Can you drink the cup[s] I am going to drink?"

"We can," they answered.

[23]Jesus said to them, "You will indeed drink from my cup, [t] but to sit at my right or left is not for me to grant. These places belong to those for whom they have been prepared by my Father."

[24]When the ten heard about this, they were indignant[u] with the two brothers. [25]Jesus called them together and said, "You know that the rulers of the Gentiles lord it over them, and their high officials exercise authority over them. [26]Not so with you. Instead, whoever wants to become great among you must be your servant, [v] [27]and whoever wants to be first must be your slave— [28]just as the Son of Man[w] did not come to be served, but to serve, [x] and to give his life as a ransom[y] for many."

Two Blind Men Receive Sight

20:29–34pp — Mk 10:46–52; Lk 18:35–43

[29]As Jesus and his disciples were leaving Jericho, a large crowd followed him. [30]Two blind men were sitting by the roadside, and when they heard that Jesus was going by, they shouted, "Lord, Son of David, [z] have mercy on us!"

[31]The crowd rebuked them and told them to be quiet, but they shouted all the louder, "Lord, Son of David, have mercy on us!"

[32]Jesus stopped and called them. "What do you want me to do for you?" he asked.

[33]"Lord," they answered, "we want our sight."

[34]Jesus had compassion on them and touched their eyes. Immediately they received their sight and followed him.

The Triumphal Entry

21:1–9pp — Mk 11:1–10; Lk 19:29–38
21:4–9pp — Jn 12:12–15

21 As they approached Jerusalem and came to Bethphage on the Mount of Olives, [a] Jesus sent two disciples, [2]saying to them, "Go to the village ahead of you, and at once you will find a donkey tied there, with her colt by her. Untie them and bring them to me. [3]If anyone says anything to you, tell him that the Lord needs them, and he will send them right away."

[4]This took place to fulfill what was spoken through the prophet:

[5]"Say to the Daughter of Zion,
'See, your king comes to you,

20:19
l Mt 16:21
m Ac 2:23
n Mt 16:21
o Mt 16:21
20:20
p Mt 4:21
q Mt 8:2
20:21
r Mt 19:28
20:22
s Isa 51:17,22;
Jer 49:12;
Mt 26:39,42;
Mk 14:36;
Lk 22:42;
Jn 18:11
20:23
t Ac 12:2;
Rev 1:9
20:24
u Lk 22:24,25
20:26
v Mt 23:11;
Mk 9:35
20:28
w Mt 8:20
x Lk 22:27;
Jn 13:13-16;
2Co 8:9;
Php 2:7
y Isa 53:10;
Mt 26:28;
1Ti 2:6;
Tit 2:14;
Heb 9:28;
1Pe 1:18,19
20:30
z Mt 9:27
21:1
a Mt 24:3;
26:30;
Mk 14:26;
Lk 19:37;
21:37; 22:39;
Jn 8:1; Ac 1:12

> gentle and riding on a donkey,
> on a colt, the foal of a donkey.' "ᵃ ᵇ

⁶The disciples went and did as Jesus had instructed them. ⁷They brought the donkey and the colt, placed their cloaks on them, and Jesus sat on them. ⁸A very large crowd spread their cloaksᶜ on the road, while others cut branches from the trees and spread them on the road. ⁹The crowds that went ahead of him and those that followed shouted,

> "Hosannaᵇ to the Son of David!"ᵈ

> "Blessed is he who comes in the name of the Lord!"ᶜ ᵉ

> "Hosannaᵇ in the highest!"ᶠ

¹⁰When Jesus entered Jerusalem, the whole city was stirred and asked, "Who is this?"

¹¹The crowds answered, "This is Jesus, the prophetᵍ from Nazareth in Galilee."

Jesus at the Temple

21:12–16pp — Mk 11:15–18; Lk 19:45–47

¹²Jesus entered the temple area and drove out all who were buyingʰ and selling there. He overturned the tables of the money changersⁱ and the benches of those selling doves. ʲ ¹³"It is written," he said to them, " 'My house will be called a house of prayer,'ᵈᵏ but you are making it a 'den of robbers.'ᵉ "ˡ

¹⁴The blind and the lame came to him at the temple, and he healed them. ᵐ ¹⁵But when the chief priests and the teachers of the law saw the wonderful things he did and the children shouting in the temple area, "Hosanna to the Son of David,"ⁿ they were indignant. ᵒ

¹⁶"Do you hear what these children are saying?" they asked him.

"Yes," replied Jesus, "have you never read,

> " 'From the lips of children and infants
> you have ordained praise'ᶠ ?"ᵖ

¹⁷And he left them and went out of the city to Bethany, �q where he spent the night.

The Fig Tree Withers

21:18–22pp — Mk 11:12–14,20–24

¹⁸Early in the morning, as he was on his way back to the city, he was hungry. ¹⁹Seeing a fig tree by the road, he went up to it but found nothing on it except leaves. Then he said to it, "May you never bear fruit again!" Immediately the tree withered. ʳ

²⁰When the disciples saw this, they were amazed. "How did the fig tree wither so quickly?" they asked.

²¹Jesus replied, "I tell you the truth, if you have faith and do not doubt, ˢ not only can you do what was done to the fig tree, but also you can say to this mountain, 'Go, throw yourself into the sea,' and it will be done. ²²If you believe, you will receive whatever you ask forᵗ in prayer."

ᵃ5 Zech. 9:9   ᵇ9 A Hebrew expression meaning "Save!" which became an exclamation of praise; also in verse 15   ᶜ9 Psalm 118:26   ᵈ13 Isaiah 56:7   ᵉ13 Jer. 7:11   ᶠ16 Psalm 8:2

**Cross references (margin):**

21:5
ᵇZec 9:9;
Isa 62:11

21:8
ᶜ2Ki 9:13

21:9
ᵈver 15;
Mt 9:27
ᵉPs 118:26;
Mt 23:39
ᶠLk 2:14

21:11
ᵍLk 7:16,39;
24:19; Jn 1:21,
25; 6:14; 7:40

21:12
ʰDt 14:26
ⁱEx 30:13
ʲLev 1:14

21:13
ᵏIsa 56:7
ˡJer 7:11

21:14
ᵐMt 4:23

21:15
ⁿver 9; Mt 9:27
ᵒLk 19:39

21:16
ᵖPs 8:2

21:17
qMt 26:6;
Mk 11:1;
Lk 24:50;
Jn 11:1,18; 12:1

21:19
ʳIsa 34:4;
Jer 8:13

21:21
ˢMt 17:20;
Lk 17:6;
1Co 13:2;
Jas 1:6

21:22
ᵗMt 7:7

The Authority of Jesus Questioned

21:23–27pp — Mk 11:27–33; Lk 20:1–8

²³Jesus entered the temple courts, and, while he was teaching, the chief priests and the elders of the people came to him. "By what authority^u are you doing these things?" they asked. "And who gave you this authority?"

²⁴Jesus replied, "I will also ask you one question. If you answer me, I will tell you by what authority I am doing these things. ²⁵John's baptism—where did it come from? Was it from heaven, or from men?"

They discussed it among themselves and said, "If we say, 'From heaven,' he will ask, 'Then why didn't you believe him?' ²⁶But if we say, 'From men'—we are afraid of the people, for they all hold that John was a prophet."^v

²⁷So they answered Jesus, "We don't know."

Then he said, "Neither will I tell you by what authority I am doing these things.

The Parable of the Two Sons

²⁸"What do you think? There was a man who had two sons. He went to the first and said, 'Son, go and work today in the vineyard.'^w

²⁹" 'I will not,' he answered, but later he changed his mind and went.

³⁰"Then the father went to the other son and said the same thing. He answered, 'I will, sir,' but he did not go.

³¹"Which of the two did what his father wanted?"

"The first," they answered.

Jesus said to them, "I tell you the truth, the tax collectors^x and the prostitutes^y are entering the kingdom of God ahead of you. ³²For John came to you to show you the way of righteousness,^z and you did not believe him, but the tax collectors^a and the prostitutes^b did. And even after you saw this, you did not repent^c and believe him.

The Parable of the Tenants

21:33–46pp — Mk 12:1–12; Lk 20:9–19

³³"Listen to another parable: There was a landowner who planted^d a vineyard. He put a wall around it, dug a winepress in it and built a watchtower.^e Then he rented the vineyard to some farmers and went away on a journey.^f ³⁴When the harvest time approached, he sent his servants^g to the tenants to collect his fruit.

³⁵"The tenants seized his servants; they beat one, killed another, and stoned a third.^h ³⁶Then he sent other servantsⁱ to them, more than the first time, and the tenants treated them the same way. ³⁷Last of all, he sent his son to them. 'They will respect my son,' he said.

³⁸"But when the tenants saw the son, they said to each other, 'This is the heir.^j Come, let's kill him^k and take his inheritance.'^l ³⁹So they took him and threw him out of the vineyard and killed him.

⁴⁰"Therefore, when the owner of the vineyard comes, what will he do to those tenants?"

⁴¹"He will bring those wretches to a wretched end,"^m they replied, "and he will rent the vineyard to other tenants,ⁿ who will give him his share of the crop at harvest time."

⁴²Jesus said to them, "Have you never read in the Scriptures:

21:23
u Ac 4:7; 7:27
21:26
v Mt 11:9;
Mk 6:20
21:28
w ver 33;
Mt 20:1
21:31
x Lk 7:29
y Lk 7:50
21:32
z Mt 3:1-12
a Lk 3:12,13;
7:29
b Lk 7:36-50
c Lk 7:30
21:33
d Ps 80:8
e Isa 5:1-7
f Mt 25:14,15
21:34
g Mt 22:3
21:35
h 2Ch 24:21;
Mt 23:34,37;
Heb 11:36,37
21:36
i Mt 22:4
21:38
j Heb 1:2
k Mt 12:14
l Ps 2:8
21:41
m Mt 8:11,12
n Ac 13:46;
18:6; 28:28

" 'The stone the builders rejected
    has become the capstone[a];
the Lord has done this,
    and it is marvelous in our eyes'[b]?[o]

43"Therefore I tell you that the kingdom of God will be taken away from you[p] and given to a people who will produce its fruit. 44He who falls on this stone will be broken to pieces, but he on whom it falls will be crushed."[c][q]

45When the chief priests and the Pharisees heard Jesus' parables, they knew he was talking about them. 46They looked for a way to arrest him, but they were afraid of the crowd because the people held that he was a prophet.[r]

The Parable of the Wedding Banquet

22:2–14Ref — Lk 14:16–24

22 Jesus spoke to them again in parables, saying:2"The kingdom of heaven is like[s] a king who prepared a wedding banquet for his son. 3He sent his servants[t] to those who had been invited to the banquet to tell them to come, but they refused to come.

4"Then he sent some more servants[u] and said, 'Tell those who have been invited that I have prepared my dinner: My oxen and fattened cattle have been butchered, and everything is ready. Come to the wedding banquet.'

5"But they paid no attention and went off—one to his field, another to his business. 6The rest seized his servants, mistreated them and killed them. 7The king was enraged. He sent his army and destroyed those murderers[v] and burned their city.

8"Then he said to his servants, 'The wedding banquet is ready, but those I invited did not deserve to come. 9Go to the street corners[w] and invite to the banquet anyone you find.' 10So the servants went out into the streets and gathered all the people they could find, both good and bad,[x] and the wedding hall was filled with guests.

11"But when the king came in to see the guests, he noticed a man there who was not wearing wedding clothes. 12'Friend,'[y] he asked, 'how did you get in here without wedding clothes?' The man was speechless.

13"Then the king told the attendants, 'Tie him hand and foot, and throw him outside, into the darkness, where there will be weeping and gnashing of teeth.'[z]

14"For many are invited, but few are chosen."[a]

Paying Taxes to Caesar

22:15–22pp — Mk 12:13–17; Lk 20:20–26

15Then the Pharisees went out and laid plans to trap him in his words. 16They sent their disciples to him along with the Herodians.[b] "Teacher," they said, "we know you are a man of integrity and that you teach the way of God in accordance with the truth. You aren't swayed by men, because you pay no attention to who they are. 17Tell us then, what is your opinion? Is it right to pay taxes[c] to Caesar or not?"

21:42
oPs 118:22,23;
   Ac 4:11;
   1Pe 2:7
21:43
pMt 8:12
21:44
qLk 2:34
21:46
rver 11,26
22:2
sMt 13:24
22:3
tMt 21:34
22:4
uMt 21:36
22:7
vLk 19:27
22:9
wEze 21:21
22:10
xMt 13:47,48
22:12
yMt 20:13;
   26:50
22:13
zMt 8:12
22:14
aRev 17:14
22:16
bMk 3:6
22:17
cMt 17:25

---

[a]42 Or *cornerstone*   [b]42 Psalm 118:22,23   [c]44 Some manuscripts do not have verse 44.

18But Jesus, knowing their evil intent, said, "You hypocrites, why are you trying to trap me? 19Show me the coin used for paying the tax." They brought him a denarius, 20and he asked them, "Whose portrait is this? And whose inscription?"

21"Caesar's," they replied.

Then he said to them, "Give to Caesar what is Caesar's, d and to God what is God's."

22When they heard this, they were amazed. So they left him and went away. e

Marriage at the Resurrection
22:23–33pp — Mk 12:18–27; Lk 20:27–40

23That same day the Sadducees, f who say there is no resurrection, g came to him with a question. 24"Teacher," they said, "Moses told us that if a man dies without having children, his brother must marry the widow and have children for him. h 25Now there were seven brothers among us. The first one married and died, and since he had no children, he left his wife to his brother. 26The same thing happened to the second and third brother, right on down to the seventh. 27Finally, the woman died. 28Now then, at the resurrection, whose wife will she be of the seven, since all of them were married to her?"

29Jesus replied, "You are in error because you do not know the Scriptures i or the power of God. 30At the resurrection people will neither marry nor be given in marriage; j they will be like the angels in heaven. 31But about the resurrection of the dead—have you not read what God said to you, 32'I am the God of Abraham, the God of Isaac, and the God of Jacob' a? k He is not the God of the dead but of the living."

33When the crowds heard this, they were astonished at his teaching. l

The Greatest Commandment
22:34–40pp — Mk 12:28–31

34Hearing that Jesus had silenced the Sadducees, m the Pharisees got together. 35One of them, an expert in the law, n tested him with this question: 36"Teacher, which is the greatest commandment in the Law?"

37Jesus replied: " 'Love the Lord your God with all your heart and with all your soul and with all your mind.' b o 38This is the first and greatest commandment. 39And the second is like it: 'Love your neighbor as yourself.' c p 40All the Law and the Prophets hang on these two commandments." q

Whose Son Is the Christ?
22:41–46pp — Mk 12:35–37; Lk 20:41–44

41While the Pharisees were gathered together, Jesus asked them, 42"What do you think about the Christ d? Whose son is he?"

"The son of David," r they replied.

43He said to them, "How is it then that David, speaking by the Spirit, calls him 'Lord'? For he says,

44" 'The Lord said to my Lord:

22:21
dRo 13:7
22:22
eMk 12:12
22:23
fAc 4:1
gAc 23:8;
1Co 15:12
22:24
hDt 25:5,6
22:29
iJn 20:9
22:30
jMt 24:38
22:32
kEx 3:6;
Ac 7:32
22:33
lMt 7:28
22:34
mAc 4:1
22:35
nLk 7:30;
10:25; 11:45;
14:3
22:37
oDt 6:5
22:39
pLev 19:18;
Mt 5:43; 19:19;
Gal 5:14
22:40
qMt 7:12
22:42
rMt 9:27

---

a32 Exodus 3:6   b37 Deut. 6:5   c39 Lev. 19:18   d42 Or *Messiah*

"Sit at my right hand
until I put your enemies
under your feet." ' ª ˢ

45If then David calls him 'Lord,' how can he be his son?" 46No one could say a word in reply, and from that day on no one dared to ask him any more questions. ᵗ

Seven Woes

23:1–7pp — Mk 12:38,39; Lk 20:45,46
23:37–39pp — Lk 13:34,35

23 Then Jesus said to the crowds and to his disciples: 2"The teachers of the lawᵘ and the Pharisees sit in Moses' seat. 3So you must obey them and do everything they tell you. But do not do what they do, for they do not practice what they preach. 4They tie up heavy loads and put them on men's shoulders, but they themselves are not willing to lift a finger to move them. ᵛ

5"Everything they do is done for men to see:ʷ They make their phylacteriesᵇˣ wide and the tassels on their garmentsʸ long; 6they love the place of honor at banquets and the most important seats in the synagogues;ᶻ 7they love to be greeted in the marketplaces and to have men call them 'Rabbi.'ª

8"But you are not to be called 'Rabbi,' for you have only one Master and you are all brothers. 9And do not call anyone on earth 'father,' for you have one Father,ᵇ and he is in heaven. 10Nor are you to be called 'teacher,' for you have one Teacher, the Christ.ᶜ 11The greatest among you will be your servant.ᶜ 12For whoever exalts himself will be humbled, and whoever humbles himself will be exalted. ᵈ

13"Woe to you, teachers of the law and Pharisees, you hypocrites!ᵉ You shut the kingdom of heaven in men's faces. You yourselves do not enter, nor will you let those enter who are trying to.ᵈ ᶠ

15"Woe to you, teachers of the law and Pharisees, you hypocrites! You travel over land and sea to win a single convert,ᵍ and when he becomes one, you make him twice as much a son of hellʰ as you are.

16"Woe to you, blind guides!ⁱ You say, 'If anyone swears by the temple, it means nothing; but if anyone swears by the gold of the temple, he is bound by his oath.'ʲ 17You blind fools! Which is greater: the gold, or the temple that makes the gold sacred?ᵏ 18You also say, 'If anyone swears by the altar, it means nothing; but if anyone swears by the gift on it, he is bound by his oath.' 19You blind men! Which is greater: the gift, or the altar that makes the gift sacred?ˡ 20Therefore, he who swears by the altar swears by it and by everything on it. 21And he who swears by the temple swears by it and by the one who dwellsᵐ in it. 22And he who swears by heaven swears by God's throne and by the one who sits on it. ⁿ

23"Woe to you, teachers of the law and Pharisees, you hypocrites! You give a tenthᵒ of your spices—mint, dill and cummin. But you have neglected the more important matters of the law—justice, mercy and

---

22:44
ˢPs 110:1;
Ac 2:34,35;
1Co 15:25;
Heb 1:13; 10:13
22:46
ᵗMk 12:34;
Lk 20:40
23:2
ᵘEzr 7:6,25;
Ne 8:4
23:4
ᵛLk 11:46;
Ac 15:10;
Gal 6:13
23:5
ʷMt 6:1,2,5,16
ˣEx 13:9; Dt 6:8
ʸNu 15:38;
Dt 22:12
23:6
ᶻLk 11:43;
14:7; 20:46
23:7
ªver 8; Mk 9:5;
10:51; Jn 1:38,
49
23:9
ᵇMal 1:6;
Mt 7:11
23:11
ᶜMt 20:26;
Mk 9:35
23:12
ᵈLk 14:11
23:13
ᵉver 15,23,25,
27,29 ᶠLk 11:52
23:15
ᵍAc 2:11; 6:5;
13:43 ʰMt 5:22
23:16
ⁱver 24;
Mt 15:14
ʲMt 5:33-35
23:17
ᵏEx 30:29
23:19
ˡEx 29:37
23:21
ᵐ1Ki 8:13;
Ps 26:8
23:22
ⁿPs 11:4;
Mt 5:34
23:23
ᵒLev 27:30

ª44 Psalm 110:1   ᵇ5 That is, boxes containing Scripture verses, worn on forehead and arm
ᶜ10 Or Messiah   ᵈ13 Some manuscripts to. 14Woe to you, teachers of the law and Pharisees, you hypocrites! You devour widows' houses and for a show make lengthy prayers. Therefore you will be punished more severely.

faithfulness. ᴾ You should have practiced the latter, without neglecting the former. 24You blind guides!ᑫ You strain out a gnat but swallow a camel.

25"Woe to you, teachers of the law and Pharisees, you hypocrites! You clean the outside of the cup and dish,ʳ but inside they are full of greed and self-indulgence. ˢ 26Blind Pharisee! First clean the inside of the cup and dish, and then the outside also will be clean.

27"Woe to you, teachers of the law and Pharisees, you hypocrites! You are like whitewashed tombs,ᵗ which look beautiful on the outside but on the inside are full of dead men's bones and everything unclean. 28In the same way, on the outside you appear to people as righteous but on the inside you are full of hypocrisy and wickedness.

29"Woe to you, teachers of the law and Pharisees, you hypocrites! You build tombs for the prophetsᵘ and decorate the graves of the righteous. 30And you say, 'If we had lived in the days of our forefathers, we would not have taken part with them in shedding the blood of the prophets.' 31So you testify against yourselves that you are the descendants of those who murdered the prophets.ᵛ 32Fill up, then, the measureʷ of the sin of your forefathers!

33"You snakes! You brood of vipers!ˣ How will you escape being condemned to hell?ʸ 34Therefore I am sending you prophets and wise men and teachers. Some of them you will kill and crucify;ᶻ others you will flog in your synagoguesᵃ and pursue from town to town. ᵇ 35And so upon you will come all the righteous blood that has been shed on earth, from the blood of righteous Abelᶜ to the blood of Zechariah son of Berekiah, ᵈ whom you murdered between the temple and the altar. ᵉ 36I tell you the truth, all this will come upon this generation. ᶠ

37"O Jerusalem, Jerusalem, you who kill the prophets and stone those sent to you, ᵍ how often I have longed to gather your children together, as a hen gathers her chicks under her wings, but you were not willing. 38Look, your house is left to you desolate. ʰ 39For I tell you, you will not see me again until you say, 'Blessed is he who comes in the name of the Lord.'ᵃ "ⁱ

Signs of the End of the Age

24:1–51pp — Mk 13:1–37; Lk 21:5–36

24 Jesus left the temple and was walking away when his disciples came up to him to call his attention to its buildings. 2"Do you see all these things?" he asked. "I tell you the truth, not one stone here will be left on another;ⱼ every one will be thrown down."

3As Jesus was sitting on the Mount of Olives,ᵏ the disciples came to him privately. "Tell us," they said, "when will this happen, and what will be the sign of your coming and of the end of the age?"

4Jesus answered: "Watch out that no one deceives you. 5For many will come in my name, claiming, 'I am the Christ,ᵇ' and will deceive many.ˡ 6You will hear of wars and rumors of wars, but see to it that you are not alarmed. Such things must happen, but the end is still to come. 7Nation will rise against nation, and kingdom against kingdom.ᵐ There will be faminesⁿ and earthquakes in various places. 8All these are the beginning of birth pains.

ᵃ39 Psalm 118:26   ᵇ5 Or *Messiah*; also in verse 23

23:23
pMic 6:8;
Lk 11:42
23:24
qver 16
23:25
rMk 7:4
sLk 11:39
23:27
tLk 11:44;
Ac 23:3
23:29
uLk 11:47,48
23:31
vAc 7:51-52
23:32
w1Th 2:16
23:33
xMt 3:7; 12:34
yMt 5:22
23:34
z2Ch 36:15,16;
Lk 11:49
aMt 10:17
bMt 10:23
23:35
cGe 4:8;
Heb 11:4
dZec 1:1
e2Ch 24:21
23:36
fMt 10:23;
24:34
23:37
g2Ch 24:21;
Mt 5:12
23:38
h1Ki 9:7,8;
Jer 22:5
23:39
iPs 118:26;
Mt 21:9
24:2
jLk 19:44
24:3
kMt 21:1
24:5
lver 11,23,24;
1Jn 2:18
24:7
mIsa 19:2
nAc 11:28

9"Then you will be handed over to be persecuted[o] and put to death,[p] and you will be hated by all nations because of me. 10At that time many will turn away from the faith and will betray and hate each other, 11and many false prophets[q] will appear and deceive many people. 12Because of the increase of wickedness, the love of most will grow cold, 13but he who stands firm to the end will be saved.[r] 14And this gospel of the kingdom[s] will be preached in the whole world[t] as a testimony to all nations, and then the end will come.

15"So when you see standing in the holy place[u] 'the abomination that causes desolation,'[a v] spoken of through the prophet Daniel—let the reader understand— 16then let those who are in Judea flee to the mountains. 17Let no one on the roof of his house[w] go down to take anything out of the house. 18Let no one in the field go back to get his cloak. 19How dreadful it will be in those days for pregnant women and nursing mothers![x] 20Pray that your flight will not take place in winter or on the Sabbath. 21For then there will be great distress, unequaled from the beginning of the world until now—and never to be equaled again.[y] 22If those days had not been cut short, no one would survive, but for the sake of the elect[z] those days will be shortened. 23At that time if anyone says to you, 'Look, here is the Christ!' or, 'There he is!' do not believe it.[a] 24For false Christs and false prophets will appear and perform great signs and miracles[b] to deceive even the elect—if that were possible. 25See, I have told you ahead of time.

26"So if anyone tells you, 'There he is, out in the desert,' do not go out; or, 'Here he is, in the inner rooms,' do not believe it. 27For as lightning[c] that comes from the east is visible even in the west, so will be the coming of the Son of Man.[d] 28Wherever there is a carcass, there the vultures will gather.[e]

29"Immediately after the distress of those days

" 'the sun will be darkened,
     and the moon will not give its light;
the stars will fall from the sky,
     and the heavenly bodies will be shaken.'[b f]

30"At that time the sign of the Son of Man will appear in the sky, and all the nations of the earth will mourn. They will see the Son of Man coming on the clouds of the sky,[g] with power and great glory. 31And he will send his angels[h] with a loud trumpet call,[i] and they will gather his elect from the four winds, from one end of the heavens to the other.

32"Now learn this lesson from the fig tree: As soon as its twigs get tender and its leaves come out, you know that summer is near. 33Even so, when you see all these things, you know that it[c] is near, right at the door.[j] 34I tell you the truth, this generation[d] will certainly not pass away until all these things have happened.[k] 35Heaven and earth will pass away, but my words will never pass away.[l]

The Day and Hour Unknown

24:37–39pp — Lk 17:26,27
24:45–51pp — Lk 12:42–46

36"No one knows about that day or hour, not even the angels in

---

*Cross references (left margin):*

24:9
o Mt 10:17
p Jn 16:2
24:11
q Mt 7:15
24:13
r Mt 10:22
24:14
s Mt 4:23
t Ro 10:18;
Col 1:6,23;
Lk 2:1; 4:5;
Ac 11:28; 17:6;
Rev 3:10; 16:14
24:15
u Ac 6:13
v Da 9:27;
11:31; 12:11
24:17
w 1Sa 9:25;
Mt 10:27;
Lk 12:3; Ac 10:9
24:19
x Lk 23:29
24:21
y Da 12:1;
Joel 2:2
24:22
z ver 24,31
24:23
a Lk 17:23;
21:8
24:24
b 2Th 2:9–11;
Rev 13:13
24:27
c Lk 17:24
d Mt 8:20
24:28
e Lk 17:37
24:29
f Isa 13:10;
34:4; Eze 32:7;
Joel 2:10,31;
Zep 1:15;
Rev 6:12,13;
8:12
24:30
g Da 7:13;
Rev 1:7
24:31
h Mt 13:41
i Isa 27:13;
Zec 9:14;
1Co 15:52;
1Th 4:16;
Rev 8:2; 10:7;
11:15
24:33
i Jas 5:9
24:34
k Mt 16:28;
23:36
24:35
l Mt 5:18

---

a15 Daniel 9:27; 11:31; 12:11   b29 Isaiah 13:10; 34:4   c33 Or *he*   d34 Or *race* heaven, nor the Son,ᵃ but only the Father.ᵐ ³⁷As it was in the days of Noah,ⁿ so it will be at the coming of the Son of Man. ³⁸For in the days before the flood, people were eating and drinking, marrying and giving in marriage,ᵒ up to the day Noah entered the ark; ³⁹and they knew nothing about what would happen until the flood came and took them all away. That is how it will be at the coming of the Son of Man. ⁴⁰Two men will be in the field; one will be taken and the other left.ᵖ ⁴¹Two women will be grinding with a hand mill; one will be taken and the other left.�q

⁴²"Therefore keep watch, because you do not know on what day your Lord will come.ʳ ⁴³But understand this: If the owner of the house had known at what time of night the thief was coming,ˢ he would have kept watch and would not have let his house be broken into. ⁴⁴So you also must be ready,ᵗ because the Son of Man will come at an hour when you do not expect him.

⁴⁵"Who then is the faithful and wise servant,ᵘ whom the master has put in charge of the servants in his household to give them their food at the proper time? ⁴⁶It will be good for that servant whose master finds him doing so when he returns.ᵛ ⁴⁷I tell you the truth, he will put him in charge of all his possessions.ʷ ⁴⁸But suppose that servant is wicked and says to himself, 'My master is staying away a long time,' ⁴⁹and he then begins to beat his fellow servants and to eat and drink with drunkards.ˣ ⁵⁰The master of that servant will come on a day when he does not expect him and at an hour he is not aware of. ⁵¹He will cut him to pieces and assign him a place with the hypocrites, where there will be weeping and gnashing of teeth.ʸ

The Parable of the Ten Virgins

25 "At that time the kingdom of heaven will be likeᶻ ten virgins who took their lampsᵃ and went out to meet the bridegroom.ᵇ ²Five of them were foolish and five were wise.ᶜ ³The foolish ones took their lamps but did not take any oil with them. ⁴The wise, however, took oil in jars along with their lamps. ⁵The bridegroom was a long time in coming, and they all became drowsy and fell asleep.ᵈ

⁶"At midnight the cry rang out: 'Here's the bridegroom! Come out to meet him!'

⁷"Then all the virgins woke up and trimmed their lamps. ⁸The foolish ones said to the wise, 'Give us some of your oil; our lamps are going out.'ᵉ

⁹"'No,' they replied, 'there may not be enough for both us and you. Instead, go to those who sell oil and buy some for yourselves.'

¹⁰"But while they were on their way to buy the oil, the bridegroom arrived. The virgins who were ready went in with him to the wedding banquet.ᶠ And the door was shut.

¹¹"Later the others also came. 'Sir! Sir!' they said. 'Open the door for us!'

¹²"But he replied, 'I tell you the truth, I don't know you.'

¹³"Therefore keep watch, because you do not know the day or the hour.ᵍ

24:36
mAc 1:7
24:37
nGe 6:5; 7:6-23
24:38
oMt 22:30
24:40
pLk 17:34
24:41
qLk 17:35
24:42
rMt 25:13;
Lk 12:40
24:43
sLk 12:39
24:44
t1Th 5:6
24:45
uMt 25:21,23
24:46
vRev 16:15
24:47
wMt 25:21,23
24:49
xLk 21:34
24:51
yMt 8:12
25:1
zMt 13:24
aLk 12:35-38;
Ac 20:8;
Rev 4:5
bRev 19:7; 21:2
25:2
cMt 24:45
25:5
d1Th 5:6
25:8
eLk 12:35
25:10
fRev 19:9
25:13
gMt 24:42,44;
Mk 13:35;
Lk 12:40

ᵃ36 Some manuscripts do not have *nor the Son.*

The Parable of the Talents

25:14–30Ref — Lk 19:12–27

14"Again, it will be like a man going on a journey,[h] who called his servants and entrusted his property to them. 15To one he gave five talents[a] of money, to another two talents, and to another one talent, each according to his ability.[i] Then he went on his journey. 16The man who had received the five talents went at once and put his money to work and gained five more. 17So also, the one with the two talents gained two more. 18But the man who had received the one talent went off, dug a hole in the ground and hid his master's money.

19"After a long time the master of those servants returned and settled accounts with them.[j] 20The man who had received the five talents brought the other five. 'Master,' he said, 'you entrusted me with five talents. See, I have gained five more.'

21"His master replied, 'Well done, good and faithful servant! You have been faithful with a few things; I will put you in charge of many things.[k] Come and share your master's happiness!'

22"The man with the two talents also came. 'Master,' he said, 'you entrusted me with two talents; see, I have gained two more.'

23"His master replied, 'Well done, good and faithful servant! You have been faithful with a few things; I will put you in charge of many things.[l] Come and share your master's happiness!'

24"Then the man who had received the one talent came. 'Master,' he said, 'I knew that you are a hard man, harvesting where you have not sown and gathering where you have not scattered seed. 25So I was afraid and went out and hid your talent in the ground. See, here is what belongs to you.'

26"His master replied, 'You wicked, lazy servant! So you knew that I harvest where I have not sown and gather where I have not scattered seed? 27Well then, you should have put my money on deposit with the bankers, so that when I returned I would have received it back with interest.

28"'Take the talent from him and give it to the one who has the ten talents. 29For everyone who has will be given more, and he will have an abundance. Whoever does not have, even what he has will be taken from him.[m] 30And throw that worthless servant outside, into the darkness, where there will be weeping and gnashing of teeth.'[n]

The Sheep and the Goats

31"When the Son of Man comes[o] in his glory, and all the angels with him, he will sit on his throne[p] in heavenly glory. 32All the nations will be gathered before him, and he will separate[q] the people one from another as a shepherd separates the sheep from the goats.[r] 33He will put the sheep on his right and the goats on his left.

34"Then the King will say to those on his right, 'Come, you who are blessed by my Father; take your inheritance, the kingdom[s] prepared for you since the creation of the world.[t] 35For I was hungry and you gave me something to eat, I was thirsty and you gave me something to drink, I was a stranger and you invited me in,[u] 36I needed clothes and

---

a15 A talent was worth more than a thousand dollars.

25:14
hMt 21:33;
Lk 19:12

25:15
iMt 18:24,25

25:19
jMt 18:23

25:21
kver 23;
Mt 24:45,47;
Lk 16:10

25:23
lver 21

25:29
mMt 13:12;
Mk 4:25;
Lk 8:18; 19:26

25:30
nMt 8:12

25:31
oMt 16:27;
Lk 17:30
pMt 19:28

25:32
qMal 3:18
rEze 34:17,20

25:34
sMt 3:2; 5:3,10,
19; 19:14;
Ac 20:32;
1Co 15:50;
Gal 5:21;
Jas 2:5
tHeb 4:3; 9:26;
Rev 13:8; 17:8

25:35
uJob 31:32;
Isa 58:7;
Eze 18:7;
Heb 13:2

you clothed me,ᵛ I was sick and you looked after me,ʷ I was in prison and you came to visit me.'ˣ

³⁷"Then the righteous will answer him, 'Lord, when did we see you hungry and feed you, or thirsty and give you something to drink? ³⁸When did we see you a stranger and invite you in, or needing clothes and clothe you? ³⁹When did we see you sick or in prison and go to visit you?'

⁴⁰"The King will reply, 'I tell you the truth, whatever you did for one of the least of these brothers of mine, you did for me.'ʸ

⁴¹"Then he will say to those on his left, 'Depart from me,ᶻ you who are cursed, into the eternal fireᵃ prepared for the devil and his angels.ᵇ ⁴²For I was hungry and you gave me nothing to eat, I was thirsty and you gave me nothing to drink, ⁴³I was a stranger and you did not invite me in, I needed clothes and you did not clothe me, I was sick and in prison and you did not look after me.'

⁴⁴"They also will answer, 'Lord, when did we see you hungry or thirsty or a stranger or needing clothes or sick or in prison, and did not help you?'

⁴⁵"He will reply, 'I tell you the truth, whatever you did not do for one of the least of these, you did not do for me.'ᶜ

⁴⁶"Then they will go away to eternal punishment, but the righteous to eternal life.ᵈ"ᵉ

The Plot Against Jesus

26:2–5pp — Mk 14:1,2; Lk 22:1,2

26 When Jesus had finished saying all these things,ᶠ he said to his disciples, ²"As you know, the Passoverᵍ is two days away—and the Son of Man will be handed over to be crucified."

³Then the chief priests and the elders of the people assembledʰ in the palace of the high priest, whose name was Caiaphas,ⁱ ⁴and they plotted to arrest Jesus in some sly way and kill him.ʲ ⁵"But not during the Feast," they said, "or there may be a riotᵏ among the people."

Jesus Anointed at Bethany

26:6–13pp — Mk 14:3–9
26:6–13Ref — Lk 7:37,38; Jn 12:1–8

⁶While Jesus was in Bethany¹ in the home of a man known as Simon the Leper, ⁷a woman came to him with an alabaster jar of very expensive perfume, which she poured on his head as he was reclining at the table.

⁸When the disciples saw this, they were indignant. "Why this waste?" they asked. ⁹"This perfume could have been sold at a high price and the money given to the poor."

¹⁰Aware of this, Jesus said to them, "Why are you bothering this woman? She has done a beautiful thing to me. ¹¹The poor you will always have with you,ᵐ but you will not always have me. ¹²When she poured this perfume on my body, she did it to prepare me for burial.ⁿ ¹³I tell you the truth, wherever this gospel is preached throughout the world, what she has done will also be told, in memory of her."

25:36
ᵛIsa 58:7;
Eze 18:7;
Jas 2:15,16
ʷJas 1:27
ˣ2Ti 1:16
25:40
ʸPr 19:17;
Mt 10:40,42;
Heb 6:10; 13:2
25:41
ᶻMt 7:23
ᵃIsa 66:24;
Mt 3:12;
5:22;
Mk 9:43,48;
Lk 3:17; Jude 7
ᵇ2Pe 2:4
25:45
ᶜPr 14:31; 17:5
25:46
ᵈMt 19:29;
Jn 3:15,16,36;
17:2,3; Ro 2:7;
Gal 6:8; 5:11,
13,20 ᵉDa 12:2;
Jn 5:29;
Ac 24:15;
Ro 2:7,8;
Gal 6:8
26:1
ᶠMt 7:28
26:2
ᵍJn 11:55; 13:1
26:3
ʰPs 2:2 ⁱver 57;
Jn 11:47-53;
18:13,14,24,28
26:4
ʲMt 12:14
26:5
ᵏMt 27:24
26:6
ˡMt 21:17
26:11
ᵐDt 15:11
26:12
ⁿJn 19:40

Judas Agrees to Betray Jesus

26:14–16pp — Mk 14:10,11; Lk 22:3–6

[14]Then one of the Twelve—the one called Judas Iscariot[o]—went to the chief priests [15]and asked, "What are you willing to give me if I hand him over to you?" So they counted out for him thirty silver coins.[p] [16]From then on Judas watched for an opportunity to hand him over.

The Lord's Supper

26:17–19pp — Mk 14:12–16; Lk 22:7–13
26:20–24pp — Mk 14:17–21
26:26–29pp — Mk 14:22–25; Lk 22:17–20; 1Co 11:23–25

[17]On the first day of the Feast of Unleavened Bread,[q] the disciples came to Jesus and asked, "Where do you want us to make preparations for you to eat the Passover?"

[18]He replied, "Go into the city to a certain man and tell him, 'The Teacher says: My appointed time[r] is near. I am going to celebrate the Passover with my disciples at your house.' " [19]So the disciples did as Jesus had directed them and prepared the Passover.

[20]When evening came, Jesus was reclining at the table with the Twelve. [21]And while they were eating, he said, "I tell you the truth, one of you will betray me."[s]

[22]They were very sad and began to say to him one after the other, "Surely not I, Lord?"

[23]Jesus replied, "The one who has dipped his hand into the bowl with me will betray me.[t] [24]The Son of Man will go just as it is written about him.[u] But woe to that man who betrays the Son of Man! It would be better for him if he had not been born."

[25]Then Judas, the one who would betray him, said, "Surely not I, Rabbi?"[v]

Jesus answered, "Yes, it is you."[a]

[26]While they were eating, Jesus took bread, gave thanks and broke it,[w] and gave it to his disciples, saying, "Take and eat; this is my body."

[27]Then he took the cup, gave thanks and offered it to them, saying, "Drink from it, all of you. [28]This is my blood of the[b] covenant,[x] which is poured out for many for the forgiveness of sins.[y] [29]I tell you, I will not drink of this fruit of the vine from now on until that day when I drink it anew with you[z] in my Father's kingdom."

[30]When they had sung a hymn, they went out to the Mount of Olives.[a]

Jesus Predicts Peter's Denial

26:31–35pp — Mk 14:27–31; Lk 22:31–34

[31]Then Jesus told them, "This very night you will all fall away on account of me,[b] for it is written:

" 'I will strike the shepherd,
    and the sheep of the flock will be scattered.'[c] [c]

[32]But after I have risen, I will go ahead of you into Galilee."[d]

[33]Peter replied, "Even if all fall away on account of you, I never will."

26:14
over 25,47;
Mt 10:4
26:15
pEx 21:32;
Zec 11:12
26:17
qEx 12:18-20
26:18
rJn 7:6,8,30;
12:23; 13:1;
17:1
26:21
sLk 22:21-23;
Jn 13:21
26:23
tPs 41:9;
Jn 13:18
26:24
uIsa 53;
Da 9:26;
Mk 9:12;
Lk 24:25-27,46;
Ac 17:2,3;
26:22,23
26:25
vMt 23:7
26:26
wMt 14:19;
1Co 10:16
26:28
xEx 24:6-8;
Heb 9:20
yMt 20:28;
Mk 1:4
26:29
zAc 10:41
26:30
aMt 21:1;
Mk 14:26
26:31
bMt 11:6
cZec 13:7;
Jn 16:32
26:32
dMt 28:7,10,16

---

[a]25 Or "You yourself have said it"   [b]28 Some manuscripts the new   [c]31 Zech. 13:7

34"I tell you the truth," Jesus answered, "this very night, before the rooster crows, you will disown me three times."ᵉ

35But Peter declared, "Even if I have to die with you,ᶠ I will never disown you." And all the other disciples said the same.

Gethsemane

26:36–46pp — Mk 14:32–42; Lk 22:40–46

36Then Jesus went with his disciples to a place called Gethsemane, and he said to them, "Sit here while I go over there and pray." 37He took Peter and the two sons of Zebedeeᵍ along with him, and he began to be sorrowful and troubled. 38Then he said to them, "My soul is overwhelmed with sorrowʰ to the point of death. Stay here and keep watch with me."ⁱ

39Going a little farther, he fell with his face to the ground and prayed, "My Father, if it is possible, may this cupʲ be taken from me. Yet not as I will, but as you will."ᵏ

40Then he returned to his disciples and found them sleeping. "Could you men not keep watch with meˡ for one hour?" he asked Peter. 41"Watch and pray so that you will not fall into temptation.ᵐ The spirit is willing, but the body is weak."

42He went away a second time and prayed, "My Father, if it is not possible for this cup to be taken away unless I drink it, may your will be done."

43When he came back, he again found them sleeping, because their eyes were heavy. 44So he left them and went away once more and prayed the third time, saying the same thing.

45Then he returned to the disciples and said to them, "Are you still sleeping and resting? Look, the hourⁿ is near, and the Son of Man is betrayed into the hands of sinners. 46Rise, let us go! Here comes my betrayer!"

Jesus Arrested

26:47–56pp — Mk 14:43–50; Lk 22:47–53

47While he was still speaking, Judas, one of the Twelve, arrived. With him was a large crowd armed with swords and clubs, sent from the chief priests and the elders of the people. 48Now the betrayer had arranged a signal with them: "The one I kiss is the man; arrest him." 49Going at once to Jesus, Judas said, "Greetings, Rabbi!"ᵒ and kissed him.

50Jesus replied, "Friend,ᵖ do what you came for."ᵃ

Then the men stepped forward, seized Jesus and arrested him. 51With that, one of Jesus' companions reached for his sword,�q drew it out and struck the servant of the high priest, cutting off his ear.ʳ

52"Put your sword back in its place," Jesus said to him, "for all who draw the sword will die by the sword.ˢ 53Do you think I cannot call on my Father, and he will at once put at my disposal more than twelve legions of angels?ᵗ 54But how then would the Scriptures be fulfilledᵘ that say it must happen in this way?"

55At that time Jesus said to the crowd, "Am I leading a rebellion, that you have come out with swords and clubs to capture me? Every day I

26:34
ever 75;
Jn 13:38
26:35
fJn 13:37
26:37
gMt 4:21
26:38
hJn 12:27
iver 40,41
26:39
jMt 20:22
kver 42;
Ps 40:6-8;
Isa 50:5;
Jn 5:30; 6:38
26:40
lver 38
26:41
mMt 6:13
26:45
nver 18
26:49
over 25
26:50
pMt 20:13;
22:12
26:51
qLk 22:36,38
rJn 18:10
26:52
sGe 9:6;
Rev 13:10
26:53
t2Ki 6:17;
Da 7:10;
Mt 4:11
26:54
uver 24

ᵃ50 Or "Friend, why have you come?"

sat in the temple courts teaching,ᵛ and you did not arrest me. ⁵⁶But this has all taken place that the writings of the prophets might be fulfilled."ʷ Then all the disciples deserted him and fled.

Before the Sanhedrin

26:57–68pp — Mk 14:53–65; Jn 18:12,13,19–24

⁵⁷Those who had arrested Jesus took him to Caiaphas,ˣ the high priest, where the teachers of the law and the elders had assembled. ⁵⁸But Peter followed him at a distance, right up to the courtyard of the high priest.ʸ He entered and sat down with the guardsᶻ to see the outcome.

⁵⁹The chief priests and the whole Sanhedrinᵃ were looking for false evidence against Jesus so that they could put him to death. ⁶⁰But they did not find any, though many false witnessesᵇ came forward.

Finally twoᶜ came forward ⁶¹and declared, "This fellow said, 'I am able to destroy the temple of God and rebuild it in three days.'"ᵈ

⁶²Then the high priest stood up and said to Jesus, "Are you not going to answer? What is this testimony that these men are bringing against you?" ⁶³But Jesus remained silent.ᵉ

The high priest said to him, "I charge you under oathᶠ by the living God:ᵍ Tell us if you are the Christ,ᵃ the Son of God."

⁶⁴"Yes, it is as you say," Jesus replied. "But I say to all of you: In the future you will see the Son of Man sitting at the right hand of the Mighty Oneʰ and coming on the clouds of heaven."ⁱ

⁶⁵Then the high priest tore his clothesʲ and said, "He has spoken blasphemy! Why do we need any more witnesses? Look, now you have heard the blasphemy. ⁶⁶What do you think?"

"He is worthy of death,"ᵏ they answered.

⁶⁷Then they spit in his face and struck him with their fists.ˡ Others slapped him ⁶⁸and said, "Prophesy to us, Christ. Who hit you?"ᵐ

Peter Disowns Jesus

26:69–75pp — Mk 14:66–72; Lk 22:55–62; Jn 18:16–18,25–27

⁶⁹Now Peter was sitting out in the courtyard, and a servant girl came to him. "You also were with Jesus of Galilee," she said.

⁷⁰But he denied it before them all. "I don't know what you're talking about," he said.

⁷¹Then he went out to the gateway, where another girl saw him and said to the people there, "This fellow was with Jesus of Nazareth."

⁷²He denied it again, with an oath: "I don't know the man!"

⁷³After a little while, those standing there went up to Peter and said, "Surely you are one of them, for your accent gives you away."

⁷⁴Then he began to call down curses on himself and he swore to them, "I don't know the man!"

Immediately a rooster crowed. ⁷⁵Then Peter remembered the word Jesus had spoken: "Before the rooster crows, you will disown me three times."ⁿ And he went outside and wept bitterly.

ᵃ63 Or *Messiah*; also in verse 68

**Cross references (margin):**

26:55
vMk 12:35;
Lk 21:37;
Jn 7:14,28;
18:20

26:56
wver 24

26:57
xver 3

26:58
yJn 18:15
zJn 7:32,45,46

26:59
aMt 5:22

26:60
bPs 27:12;
35:11; Ac 6:13
cDt 19:15

26:61
dJn 2:19

26:63
eMt 27:12,14
fLev 5:1
gMt 16:16

26:64
hPs 110:1
iDa 7:13;
Rev 1:7

26:65
jMk 14:63

26:66
kLev 24:16;
Jn 19:7

26:67
lMt 16:21;
27:30

26:68
mLk 22:63–65

26:75
nver 34;
Jn 13:38

Judas Hangs Himself

27 Early in the morning, all the chief priests and the elders of the people came to the decision to put Jesus to death.° ²They bound him, led him away and handed him overᵖ to Pilate, the governor.�q

³When Judas, who had betrayed him,ʳ saw that Jesus was condemned, he was seized with remorse and returned the thirty silver coinsˢ to the chief priests and the elders. ⁴"I have sinned," he said, "for I have betrayed innocent blood."

"What is that to us?" they replied. "That's your responsibility."ᵗ

⁵So Judas threw the money into the templeᵘ and left. Then he went away and hanged himself.ᵛ

⁶The chief priests picked up the coins and said, "It is against the law to put this into the treasury, since it is blood money." ⁷So they decided to use the money to buy the potter's field as a burial place for foreigners. ⁸That is why it has been called the Field of Bloodʷ to this day. ⁹Then what was spoken by Jeremiah the prophet was fulfilled:ˣ "They took the thirty silver coins, the price set on him by the people of Israel, ¹⁰and they used them to buy the potter's field, as the Lord commanded me."ᵃ ʸ

Jesus Before Pilate

27:11-26pp — Mk 15:2-15; Lk 23:2,3; 18-25; Jn 18:29-19:16

¹¹Meanwhile Jesus stood before the governor, and the governor asked him, "Are you the king of the Jews?"ᶻ

"Yes, it is as you say," Jesus replied.

¹²When he was accused by the chief priests and the elders, he gave no answer.ᵃ ¹³Then Pilate asked him, "Don't you hear the testimony they are bringing against you?"ᵇ ¹⁴But Jesus made no reply,ᶜ not even to a single charge—to the great amazement of the governor.

¹⁵Now it was the governor's custom at the Feast to release a prisonerᵈ chosen by the crowd. ¹⁶At that time they had a notorious prisoner, called Barabbas. ¹⁷So when the crowd had gathered, Pilate asked them, "Which one do you want me to release to you: Barabbas, or Jesus who is called Christ?"ᵉ ¹⁸For he knew it was out of envy that they had handed Jesus over to him.

¹⁹While Pilate was sitting on the judge's seat,ᶠ his wife sent him this message: "Don't have anything to do with that innocentᵍ man, for I have suffered a great deal today in a dreamʰ because of him."

²⁰But the chief priests and the elders persuaded the crowd to ask for Barabbas and to have Jesus executed.ⁱ

²¹"Which of the two do you want me to release to you?" asked the governor.

"Barabbas," they answered.

²²"What shall I do, then, with Jesus who is called Christ?"ʲ Pilate asked.

They all answered, "Crucify him!"

²³"Why? What crime has he committed?" asked Pilate.

But they shouted all the louder, "Crucify him!"

²⁴When Pilate saw that he was getting nowhere, but that instead an

a10 See Zech. 11:12,13; Jer. 19:1-13; 32:6-9.

27:1
oMt 12:14;
Mk 15:1;
Lk 22:66

27:2
pMt 20:19
qMk 15:1;
Lk 13:1;
Ac 3:13;
1Ti 6:13

27:3
rMt 10:4
sMt 26:14,15

27:4
tver 24

27:5
uLk 1:9,21
vAc 1:18

27:8
wAc 1:19

27:9
xMt 1:22

27:10
yZec 11:12,13;
Jer 32:6-9

27:11
zMt 2:2

27:12
aMt 26:63;
Mk 14:61;
Jn 19:9

27:13
bMt 26:62

27:14
cMk 14:61

27:15
dJn 18:39

27:17
ever 22;
Mt 1:16

27:19
fJn 19:13
gver 24
hGe 20:6;
Nu 12:6;
1Ki 3:5;
Job 33:14-16;
Mt 1:20; 2:12,
13,19,22

27:20
iAc 3:14

27:22
jMt 1:16

uproar[k] was starting, he took water and washed his hands[l] in front of the crowd. "I am innocent of this man's blood,"[m] he said. "It is your responsibility!"[n]

[25]All the people answered, "Let his blood be on us and on our children!"[o]

[26]Then he released Barabbas to them. But he had Jesus flogged,[p] and handed him over to be crucified.

The Soldiers Mock Jesus

27:27–31pp — Mk 15:16–20

[27]Then the governor's soldiers took Jesus into the Praetorium[q] and gathered the whole company of soldiers around him. [28]They stripped him and put a scarlet robe on him,[r] [29]and then twisted together a crown of thorns and set it on his head. They put a staff in his right hand and knelt in front of him and mocked him. "Hail, king of the Jews!" they said.[s] [30]They spit on him, and took the staff and struck him on the head again and again.[t] [31]After they had mocked him, they took off the robe and put his own clothes on him. Then they led him away to crucify him.[u]

The Crucifixion

27:33–44pp — Mk 15:22–32; Lk 23:33–43; Jn 19:17–24

[32]As they were going out,[v] they met a man from Cyrene,[w] named Simon, and they forced him to carry the cross.[x] [33]They came to a place called Golgotha (which means The Place of the Skull).[y] [34]There they offered Jesus wine to drink, mixed with gall;[z] but after tasting it, he refused to drink it. [35]When they had crucified him, they divided up his clothes by casting lots.[aa] [36]And sitting down, they kept watch[b] over him there. [37]Above his head they placed the written charge against him: THIS IS JESUS, THE KING OF THE JEWS. [38]Two robbers were crucified with him,[c] one on his right and one on his left. [39]Those who passed by hurled insults at him, shaking their heads[d] [40]and saying, "You who are going to destroy the temple and build it in three days,[e] save yourself![f] Come down from the cross, if you are the Son of God!"[g]

[41]In the same way the chief priests, the teachers of the law and the elders mocked him. [42]"He saved others," they said, "but he can't save himself! He's the King of Israel![h] Let him come down now from the cross, and we will believe[i] in him. [43]He trusts in God. Let God rescue him[j] now if he wants him, for he said, 'I am the Son of God.' " [44]In the same way the robbers who were crucified with him also heaped insults on him.

The Death of Jesus

27:45–56pp — Mk 15:33–41; Lk 23:44–49

[45]From the sixth hour until the ninth hour darkness[k] came over all the land. [46]About the ninth hour Jesus cried out in a loud voice, "*Eloi, Eloi,[b] lama sabachthani?*"—which means, "My God, my God, why have you forsaken me?"[c] [l]

27:24
kMt 26:5
lPs 26:6
mDt 21:6-8
nver 4
27:25
oJos 2:19;
Ac 5:28
27:26
pIsa 53:5;
Jn 19:1
27:27
qJn 18:28,33;
19:9
27:28
rJn 19:2
27:29
sIsa 53:3;
Jn 19:2,3
27:30
tMt 16:21;
26:67
27:31
uIsa 53:7
27:32
vHeb 13:12
wAc 2:10; 6:9;
11:20; 13:1
xMk 15:21;
Lk 23:26
27:33
yJn 19:17
27:34
zver 48;
Ps 69:21
27:35
aPs 22:18
27:36
bver 54
27:38
cIsa 53:12
27:39
dPs 22:7;
109:25; La 2:15
27:40
eMt 26:61;
Jn 2:19 fver 42
gMt 4:3,6
27:42
hJn 1:49; 12:13
iJn 3:15
27:43
jPs 22:8
27:45
kAm 8:9
27:46
lPs 22:1

[a]35 A few late manuscripts *lots that the word spoken by the prophet might be fulfilled: "They divided my garments among themselves and cast lots for my clothing"* (Psalm 22:18)   [b]46 Some manuscripts *Eli, Eli*   [c]46 Psalm 22:1

⁴⁷When some of those standing there heard this, they said, "He's calling Elijah."

⁴⁸Immediately one of them ran and got a sponge. He filled it with wine vinegar,ᵐ put it on a stick, and offered it to Jesus to drink. ⁴⁹The rest said, "Now leave him alone. Let's see if Elijah comes to save him."

⁵⁰And when Jesus had cried out again in a loud voice, he gave up his spirit.ⁿ

⁵¹At that moment the curtain of the templeᵒ was torn in two from top to bottom. The earth shook and the rocks split.ᵖ ⁵²The tombs broke open and the bodies of many holy people who had died were raised to life. ⁵³They came out of the tombs, and after Jesus' resurrection they went into the holy city�q and appeared to many people.

⁵⁴When the centurion and those with him who were guardingʳ Jesus saw the earthquake and all that had happened, they were terrified, and exclaimed, "Surely he was the Sonᵃ of God!"ˢ

⁵⁵Many women were there, watching from a distance. They had followed Jesus from Galilee to care for his needs.ᵗ ⁵⁶Among them were Mary Magdalene, Mary the mother of James and Joses, and the mother of Zebedee's sons.ᵘ

The Burial of Jesus

27:57–61pp — Mk 15:42–47; Lk 23:50–56; Jn 19:38–42

⁵⁷As evening approached, there came a rich man from Arimathea, named Joseph, who had himself become a disciple of Jesus. ⁵⁸Going to Pilate, he asked for Jesus' body, and Pilate ordered that it be given to him. ⁵⁹Joseph took the body, wrapped it in a clean linen cloth, ⁶⁰and placed it in his own new tombᵛ that he had cut out of the rock. He rolled a big stone in front of the entrance to the tomb and went away. ⁶¹Mary Magdalene and the other Mary were sitting there opposite the tomb.

The Guard at the Tomb

⁶²The next day, the one after Preparation Day, the chief priests and the Pharisees went to Pilate. ⁶³"Sir," they said, "we remember that while he was still alive that deceiver said, 'After three days I will rise again.'ʷ ⁶⁴So give the order for the tomb to be made secure until the third day. Otherwise, his disciples may come and steal the body and tell the people that he has been raised from the dead. This last deception will be worse than the first."

⁶⁵"Take a guard,"ˣ Pilate answered. "Go, make the tomb as secure as you know how." ⁶⁶So they went and made the tomb secure by putting a sealʸ on the stoneᶻ and posting the guard.ᵃ

The Resurrection

28:1–8pp — Mk 16:1–8; Lk 24:1–10

28 After the Sabbath, at dawn on the first day of the week, Mary Magdalene and the other Maryᵇ went to look at the tomb.

²There was a violent earthquake,ᶜ for an angelᵈ of the Lord came down from heaven and, going to the tomb, rolled back the stone and sat on it. ³His appearance was like lightning, and his clothes were white

ᵃ54 Or *a son*

27:48
mver 34;
Ps 69:21

27:50
nJn 19:30

27:51
oEx 26:31-33;
Heb 9:3,8
pver 54

27:53
qMt 4:5

27:54
rver 36 sMt 4:3;
17:5

27:55
tLk 8:2,3

27:56
uMk 15:47;
Lk 24:10;
Jn 19:25

27:60
vMt 27:66;
28:2; Mk 16:4

27:63
wMt 16:21

27:65
xver 66;
Mt 28:11

27:66
yDa 6:17
zver 60;
Mt 28:2
aMt 28:11

28:1
bMt 27:56

28:2
cMt 27:51
dJn 20:12

as snow.[e] [4]The guards were so afraid of him that they shook and became like dead men.

[5]The angel said to the women, "Do not be afraid,[f] for I know that you are looking for Jesus, who was crucified. [6]He is not here; he has risen, just as he said.[g] Come and see the place where he lay. [7]Then go quickly and tell his disciples: 'He has risen from the dead and is going ahead of you into Galilee.[h] There you will see him.' Now I have told you."

[8]So the women hurried away from the tomb, afraid yet filled with joy, and ran to tell his disciples. [9]Suddenly Jesus met them.[i] "Greetings," he said. They came to him, clasped his feet and worshiped him. [10]Then Jesus said to them, "Do not be afraid. Go and tell my brothers[j] to go to Galilee; there they will see me."

The Guards' Report

[11]While the women were on their way, some of the guards[k] went into the city and reported to the chief priests everything that had happened. [12]When the chief priests had met with the elders and devised a plan, they gave the soldiers a large sum of money, [13]telling them, "You are to say, 'His disciples came during the night and stole him away while we were asleep.' [14]If this report gets to the governor,[l] we will satisfy him and keep you out of trouble." [15]So the soldiers took the money and did as they were instructed. And this story has been widely circulated among the Jews to this very day.

The Great Commission

[16]Then the eleven disciples went to Galilee, to the mountain where Jesus had told them to go.[m] [17]When they saw him, they worshiped him; but some doubted. [18]Then Jesus came to them and said, "All authority in heaven and on earth has been given to me.[n] [19]Therefore go and make disciples of all nations,[o] baptizing them in[a] the name of the Father and of the Son and of the Holy Spirit,[p] [20]and teaching[q] them to obey everything I have commanded you. And surely I am with you[r] always, to the very end of the age."[s]

---

a19 Or *into*; see Acts 8:16; 19:5; Romans 6:3; 1 Cor. 1:13; 10:2 and Gal. 3:27.

28:3
eDa 10:6;
Mk 9:3;
Jn 20:12
28:5
fver 10;
Mt 14:27
28:6
gMt 16:21
28:7
hver 10,16;
Mt 26:32
28:9
iJn 20:14-18
28:10
jJn 20:17;
Ro 8:29;
Heb 2:11-13,17
28:11
kMt 27:65,66
28:14
lMt 27:2
28:16
mver 7,10;
Mt 26:32
28:18
nDa 7:13,14;
Lk 10:22;
Jn 3:35; 17:2;
1Co 15:27;
Eph 1:20-22;
Php 2:9,10
28:19
oMk 16:15,16;
Lk 24:47;
Ac 1:8; 14:21
pAc 2:38; 8:16;
Ro 6:3,4
28:20
qAc 2:42
rMt 18:20;
Ac 18:10
sMt 13:39

Mark

Title and Background

The early church fathers agreed that Mark's Gospel reproduces the preaching of Peter. Peter's personality can be found on almost every page, and the main characteristic of this Gospel is action.

Author and Date of Writing

Mark was the son of Mary (Ac 12:12) and the cousin of Barnabas (Col 4:10). He accompanied Paul and Barnabas on their first missionary journey. Paul speaks of him as his companion in Rome and pays high tribute to his service. It is believed that Mark is the first of the Gospels, and therefore it can be dated about A.D. 55.

Theme and Message

The book of Mark stresses facts and actions rather than themes or topics. Although it is the shortest of the four Gospels, it is often the most detailed. Jewish customs are carefully explained for Roman readers, and one of Mark's purposes was to demonstrate the deity of Christ. He tells the stories of Christ's ministry, especially his miracles. Mark spends one-third of the book telling the events of Christ's last week on earth, ending with his death and resurrection.

Outline

- I. The Beginnings of Jesus' Ministry (1:1-13)
- II. Jesus' Ministry in Galilee (1:14-6:29)
- III. Withdrawals From Galilee (6:30-9:32)
- IV. Final Ministry in Galilee (9:33-50)
- V. Jesus' Ministry in Judea and Perea (10:1-52)
- VI. The Passion of Jesus (11:1-15:47)
- VII. The Resurrection of Jesus (16:1-20)

John the Baptist Prepares the Way

1:2-8pp — Mt 3:1-11; Lk 3:2-16

1 The beginning of the gospel about Jesus Christ, the Son of God.*ᵃ*

²It is written in Isaiah the prophet:

"I will send my messenger ahead of you,
who will prepare your way"ᵇ ᵇ—
³"a voice of one calling in the desert,
'Prepare the way for the Lord,
make straight paths for him.' "ᶜ ᶜ

⁴And so Johnᵈ came, baptizing in the desert region and preaching a baptism of repentanceᵉ for the forgiveness of sins.ᶠ ⁵The whole Judean countryside and all the people of Jerusalem went out to him. Confess-

1:1
aMt 4:3
1:2
bMal 3:1;
Mt 11:10;
Lk 7:27
1:3
cIsa 40:3;
Jn 1:23
1:4
dMt 3:1
eAc 13:24
fLk 1:77

ᵃ1 Some manuscripts do not have *the Son of God.*   ᵇ2 Mal. 3:1   ᶜ3 Isaiah 40:3

ing their sins, they were baptized by him in the Jordan River. 6John wore clothing made of camel's hair, with a leather belt around his waist, and he ate locusts[g] and wild honey. 7And this was his message: "After me will come one more powerful than I, the thongs of whose sandals I am not worthy to stoop down and untie.[h] 8I baptize you with[a] water, but he will baptize you with the Holy Spirit."[i]

The Baptism and Temptation of Jesus

1:9–11pp — Mt 3:13–17; Lk 3:21,22
1:12,13pp — Mt 4:1–11; Lk 4:1–13

9At that time Jesus came from Nazareth[j] in Galilee and was baptized by John in the Jordan. 10As Jesus was coming up out of the water, he saw heaven being torn open and the Spirit descending on him like a dove.[k] 11And a voice came from heaven: "You are my Son,[l] whom I love; with you I am well pleased."

12At once the Spirit sent him out into the desert, 13and he was in the desert forty days, being tempted by Satan.[m] He was with the wild animals, and angels attended him.

The Calling of the First Disciples

1:16–20pp — Mt 4:18–22; Lk 5:2–11; Jn 1:35–42

14After John was put in prison, Jesus went into Galilee,[n] proclaiming the good news of God.[o] 15"The time has come," he said. "The kingdom of God is near. Repent and believe the good news!"[q]

16As Jesus walked beside the Sea of Galilee, he saw Simon and his brother Andrew casting a net into the lake, for they were fishermen. 17"Come, follow me," Jesus said, "and I will make you fishers of men." 18At once they left their nets and followed him.

19When he had gone a little farther, he saw James son of Zebedee and his brother John in a boat, preparing their nets. 20Without delay he called them, and they left their father Zebedee in the boat with the hired men and followed him.

Jesus Drives Out an Evil Spirit

1:21–28pp — Lk 4:31–37

21They went to Capernaum, and when the Sabbath came, Jesus went into the synagogue and began to teach.[r] 22The people were amazed at his teaching, because he taught them as one who had authority, not as the teachers of the law.[s] 23Just then a man in their synagogue who was possessed by an evil[b] spirit cried out, 24"What do you want with us,[t] Jesus of Nazareth?[u] Have you come to destroy us? I know who you are—the Holy One of God!"[v]

25"Be quiet!" said Jesus sternly. "Come out of him!"[w] 26The evil spirit shook the man violently and came out of him with a shriek.[x]

27The people were all so amazed[y] that they asked each other, "What is this? A new teaching—and with authority! He even gives orders to evil spirits and they obey him." 28News about him spread quickly over the whole region[z] of Galilee.

---

[a]8 Or *in*   [b]23 Greek *unclean*; also in verses 26 and 27

1:6
gLev 11:22
1:7
hAc 13:25
1:8
iIsa 44:3;
Joel 2:28;
Ac 1:5; 2:4;
11:16; 19:4-6
1:9
jMt 2:23
1:10
kJn 1:32
1:11
lMt 3:17
1:13
mMt 4:10
1:14
nMt 4:12
oMt 4:23
1:15
pGal 4:4;
Eph 1:10
qAc 20:21
1:21
rMt 4:23;
Mk 10:1
1:22
sMt 7:28,29
1:24
tMt 8:29
uMt 2:23;
Lk 24:19;
Ac 24:5
vLk 1:35;
Jn 6:69; Ac 3:14
1:25
wver 34
1:26
xMk 9:20
1:27
yMk 10:24,32
1:28
zMt 9:26

Jesus Heals Many

1:29–31pp — Mt 8:14,15; Lk 4:38,39
1:32–34pp — Mt 8:16,17; Lk 4:40,41

29As soon as they left the synagogue,[a] they went with James and John to the home of Simon and Andrew. 30Simon's mother-in-law was in bed with a fever, and they told Jesus about her. 31So he went to her, took her hand and helped her up.[b] The fever left her and she began to wait on them.

32That evening after sunset the people brought to Jesus all the sick and demon-possessed.[c] 33The whole town gathered at the door, 34and Jesus healed many who had various diseases.[d] He also drove out many demons, but he would not let the demons speak because they knew who he was.[e]

Jesus Prays in a Solitary Place

1:35–38pp — Lk 4:42,43

35Very early in the morning, while it was still dark, Jesus got up, left the house and went off to a solitary place, where he prayed.[f] 36Simon and his companions went to look for him, 37and when they found him, they exclaimed: "Everyone is looking for you!"

38Jesus replied, "Let us go somewhere else—to the nearby villages —so I can preach there also. That is why I have come."[g] 39So he traveled throughout Galilee, preaching in their synagogues[h] and driving out demons.[i]

A Man With Leprosy

1:40–44pp — Mt 8:2–4; Lk 5:12–14

40A man with leprosy[a] came to him and begged him on his knees,[j] "If you are willing, you can make me clean."

41Filled with compassion, Jesus reached out his hand and touched the man. "I am willing," he said. "Be clean!"[42] 42Immediately the leprosy left him and he was cured.

43Jesus sent him away at once with a strong warning: 44"See that you don't tell this to anyone.[k] But go, show yourself to the priest[l] and offer the sacrifices that Moses commanded for your cleansing,[m] as a testimony to them." 45Instead he went out and began to talk freely, spreading the news. As a result, Jesus could no longer enter a town openly but stayed outside in lonely places.[n] Yet the people still came to him from everywhere.[o]

Jesus Heals a Paralytic

2:3–12pp — Mt 9:2–8; Lk 5:18–26

2 A few days later, when Jesus again entered Capernaum, the people heard that he had come home. 2So many[p] gathered that there was no room left, not even outside the door, and he preached the word to them. 3Some men came, bringing to him a paralytic,[q] carried by four of them. 4Since they could not get him to Jesus because of the crowd, they made an opening in the roof above Jesus and, after digging through it, lowered the mat the paralyzed man was lying on. 5When Jesus saw their faith, he said to the paralytic, "Son, your sins are forgiven."[r]

---

[a]40 The Greek word was used for various diseases affecting the skin—not necessarily leprosy.

1:29
[a]ver 21,23
1:31
[b]Lk 7:14
1:32
[c]Mt 4:24
1:34
[d]Mt 4:23
[e]Mk 3:12;
Ac 16:17,18
1:35
[f]Lk 3:21
1:38
[g]Isa 61:1
1:39
[h]Mt 4:23
[i]Mt 4:24
1:40
[j]Mk 10:17
1:44
[k]Mt 8:4
[l]Lev 13:49
[m]Lev 14:1-32
1:45
[n]Lk 5:15,16
[o]Mk 2:13;
Lk 5:17; Jn 6:2
2:2
[p]ver 13;
Mk 1:45
2:3
[q]Mt 4:24
2:5
[r]Lk 7:48

6Now some teachers of the law were sitting there, thinking to themselves, 7"Why does this fellow talk like that? He's blaspheming! Who can forgive sins but God alone?"ˢ

8Immediately Jesus knew in his spirit that this was what they were thinking in their hearts, and he said to them, "Why are you thinking these things? 9Which is easier: to say to the paralytic, 'Your sins are forgiven,' or to say, 'Get up, take your mat and walk'? 10But that you may know that the Son of Manᵗ has authority on earth to forgive sins . . . ." He said to the paralytic, 11"I tell you, get up, take your mat and go home." 12He got up, took his mat and walked out in full view of them all. This amazed everyone and they praised God,ᵘ saying, "We have never seen anything like this!"ᵛ

The Calling of Levi

2:14–17pp — Mt 9:9–13; Lk 5:27–32

13Once again Jesus went out beside the lake. A large crowd came to him,ʷ and he began to teach them. 14As he walked along, he saw Levi son of Alphaeus sitting at the tax collector's booth. "Follow me,"ˣ Jesus told him, and Levi got up and followed him.

15While Jesus was having dinner at Levi's house, many tax collectors and "sinners" were eating with him and his disciples, for there were many who followed him. 16When the teachers of the law who were Phariseesʸ saw him eating with the "sinners" and tax collectors, they asked his disciples: "Why does he eat with tax collectors and 'sinners'?"ᶻ

17On hearing this, Jesus said to them, "It is not the healthy who need a doctor, but the sick. I have not come to call the righteous, but sinners."ᵃ

Jesus Questioned About Fasting

2:18–22pp — Mt 9:14–17; Lk 5:33–38

18Now John's disciples and the Pharisees were fasting.ᵇ Some people came and asked Jesus, "How is it that John's disciples and the disciples of the Pharisees are fasting, but yours are not?"

19Jesus answered, "How can the guests of the bridegroom fast while he is with them? They cannot, so long as they have him with them. 20But the time will come when the bridegroom will be taken from them,ᶜ and on that day they will fast.

21"No one sews a patch of unshrunk cloth on an old garment. If he does, the new piece will pull away from the old, making the tear worse. 22And no one pours new wine into old wineskins. If he does, the wine will burst the skins, and both the wine and the wineskins will be ruined. No, he pours new wine into new wineskins."

Lord of the Sabbath

2:23–28pp — Mt 12:1–8; Lk 6:1–5
3:1–6pp — Mt 12:9–14; Lk 6:6–11

23One Sabbath Jesus was going through the grainfields, and as his disciples walked along, they began to pick some heads of grain.ᵈ 24The Pharisees said to him, "Look, why are they doing what is unlawful on the Sabbath?"ᵉ

25He answered, "Have you never read what David did when he and

---

2:7
ˢIsa 43:25
2:10
ᵗMt 8:20
2:12
ᵘMt 9:8
ᵛMt 9:33
2:13
ʷMk 1:45;
Lk 5:15; Jn 6:2
2:14
ˣMt 4:19
2:16
ʸAc 23:9
ᶻMt 9:11
2:17
ᵃLk 19:10;
1Ti 1:15
2:18
ᵇMt 6:16–18;
Ac 13:2
2:20
ᶜLk 17:22
2:23
ᵈDt 23:25
2:24
ᵉMt 12:2

his companions were hungry and in need? [26]In the days of Abiathar the high priest, [f] he entered the house of God and ate the consecrated bread, which is lawful only for priests to eat. [g] And he also gave some to his companions."[h]

[27]Then he said to them, "The Sabbath was made for man, [i] not man for the Sabbath. [j] [28]So the Son of Man[k] is Lord even of the Sabbath."

3 Another time he went into the synagogue, [l] and a man with a shriveled hand was there. [2]Some of them were looking for a reason to accuse Jesus, so they watched him closely[m] to see if he would heal him on the Sabbath. [n] [3]Jesus said to the man with the shriveled hand, "Stand up in front of everyone."

[4]Then Jesus asked them, "Which is lawful on the Sabbath: to do good or to do evil, to save life or to kill?" But they remained silent.

[5]He looked around at them in anger and, deeply distressed at their stubborn hearts, said to the man, "Stretch out your hand." He stretched it out, and his hand was completely restored. [6]Then the Pharisees went out and began to plot with the Herodians[o] how they might kill Jesus. [p]

Crowds Follow Jesus

3:7–12pp — Mt 12:15,16; Lk 6:17–19

[7]Jesus withdrew with his disciples to the lake, and a large crowd from Galilee followed. [q] [8]When they heard all he was doing, many people came to him from Judea, Jerusalem, Idumea, and the regions across the Jordan and around Tyre and Sidon. [r] [9]Because of the crowd he told his disciples to have a small boat ready for him, to keep the people from crowding him. [10]For he had healed many, [s] so that those with diseases were pushing forward to touch him. [t] [11]Whenever the evil[a] spirits saw him, they fell down before him and cried out, "You are the Son of God."[u] [12]But he gave them strict orders not to tell who he was. [v]

The Appointing of the Twelve Apostles

3:16–19pp — Mt 10:2–4; Lk 6:14–16; Ac 1:13

[13]Jesus went up on a mountainside and called to him those he wanted, and they came to him. [w] [14]He appointed twelve—designating them apostles[b]—that they might be with him and that he might send them out to preach [15]and to have authority to drive out demons. [y] [16]These are the twelve he appointed: Simon (to whom he gave the name Peter);[z] [17]James son of Zebedee and his brother John (to them he gave the name Boanerges, which means Sons of Thunder); [18]Andrew, Philip, Bartholomew, Matthew, Thomas, James son of Alphaeus, Thaddaeus, Simon the Zealot [19]and Judas Iscariot, who betrayed him.

Jesus and Beelzebub

3:23–27pp — Mt 12:25–29; Lk 11:17–22

[20]Then Jesus entered a house, and again a crowd gathered, [a] so that he and his disciples were not even able to eat. [b] [21]When his family heard about this, they went to take charge of him, for they said, "He is out of his mind."[c]

[22]And the teachers of the law who came down from Jerusalem[d] said,

---

[a]11 Greek *unclean*; also in verse 30   [b]14 Some manuscripts do not have *designating them apostles.*

2:26
f1Ch 24:6;
2Sa 8:17
gLev 24:5-9
h1Sa 21:1-6
2:27
iEx 23:12;
Dt 5:14
jCol 2:16
2:28
kMt 8:20
3:1
lMt 4:23;
Mk 1:21
3:2
mMt 12:10
nLk 14:1
3:6
oMt 22:16;
Mk 12:13
pMt 12:14
3:7
qMt 4:25
3:8
rMt 11:21
3:10
sMt 4:23
tMt 9:20
3:11
uMt 4:3;
Mk 1:23,24
3:12
vMt 8:4;
Mk 1:24,25,34;
Ac 16:17,18
3:13
wMt 5:1
3:14
xMk 6:30
3:15
yMt 10:1
3:16
zJn 1:42
3:20
aver 7 bMk 6:31
3:21
cJn 10:20;
Ac 26:24
3:22
dMt 15:1

"He is possessed by Beelzebub![a]![e] By the prince of demons he is driving out demons."[f]

[23]So Jesus called them and spoke to them in parables:[g] "How can Satan[h] drive out Satan? [24]If a kingdom is divided against itself, that kingdom cannot stand. [25]If a house is divided against itself, that house cannot stand. [26]And if Satan opposes himself and is divided, he cannot stand; his end has come. [27]In fact, no one can enter a strong man's house and carry off his possessions unless he first ties up the strong man. Then he can rob his house.[i] [28]I tell you the truth, all the sins and blasphemies of men will be forgiven them. [29]But whoever blasphemes against the Holy Spirit will never be forgiven; he is guilty of an eternal sin."[j]

[30]He said this because they were saying, "He has an evil spirit."

Jesus' Mother and Brothers

3:31–35pp — Mt 12:46–50; Lk 8:19–21

[31]Then Jesus' mother and brothers arrived.[k] Standing outside, they sent someone in to call him. [32]A crowd was sitting around him, and they told him, "Your mother and brothers are outside looking for you."

[33]"Who are my mother and my brothers?" he asked.

[34]Then he looked at those seated in a circle around him and said, "Here are my mother and my brothers! [35]Whoever does God's will is my brother and sister and mother."

The Parable of the Sower

4:1–12pp — Mt 13:1–15; Lk 8:4–10
4:13–20pp — Mt 13:18–23; Lk 8:11–15

4 Again Jesus began to teach by the lake.[l] The crowd that gathered around him was so large that he got into a boat and sat in it out on the lake, while all the people were along the shore at the water's edge. [2]He taught them many things by parables,[m] and in his teaching said: [3]"Listen! A farmer went out to sow his seed.[n] [4]As he was scattering the seed, some fell along the path, and the birds came and ate it up. [5]Some fell on rocky places, where it did not have much soil. It sprang up quickly, because the soil was shallow. [6]But when the sun came up, the plants were scorched, and they withered because they had no root. [7]Other seed fell among thorns, which grew up and choked the plants, so that they did not bear grain. [8]Still other seed fell on good soil. It came up, grew and produced a crop, multiplying thirty, sixty, or even a hundred times."[o]

[9]Then Jesus said, "He who has ears to hear, let him hear."[p]

[10]When he was alone, the Twelve and the others around him asked him about the parables. [11]He told them, "The secret of the kingdom of God[q] has been given to you. But to those on the outside[r] everything is said in parables [12]so that,

" 'they may be ever seeing but never perceiving,
    and ever hearing but never understanding;
    otherwise they might turn and be forgiven!'[b] "[s]

[13]Then Jesus said to them, "Don't you understand this parable? How

3:22
[e]Mt 10:25;
11:18; 12:24;
Jn 7:20; 8:48,
52; 10:20
[f]Mt 9:34
3:23
[g]Mk 4:2
[h]Mt 4:10
3:27
[i]Isa 49:24,25
3:29
[j]Mt 12:31,32;
Lk 12:10
3:31
[k]ver 21
4:1
[l]Mk 2:13; 3:7
4:2
[m]ver 11;
Mk 3:23
4:3
[n]ver 26
4:8
[o]Jn 15:5;
Col 1:6
4:9
[p]ver 23;
Mt 11:15
4:11
[q]Mt 3:2
[r]1Co 5:12,13;
Col 4:5;
1Th 4:12;
1Ti 3:7
4:12
[s]Isa 6:9,10;
Mt 13:13-15

---

[a]22 Greek *Beezeboul* or *Beelzeboul*   [b]12 Isaiah 6:9,10

then will you understand any parable? [14]The farmer sows the word. [t]
[15]Some people are like seed along the path, where the word is sown. As
soon as they hear it, Satan[u] comes and takes away the word that was
sown in them. [16]Others, like seed sown on rocky places, hear the word
and at once receive it with joy. [17]But since they have no root, they last
only a short time. When trouble or persecution comes because of the
word, they quickly fall away. [18]Still others, like seed sown among
thorns, hear the word; [19]but the worries of this life, the deceitfulness of
wealth[v] and the desires for other things come in and choke the word,
making it unfruitful. [20]Others, like seed sown on good soil, hear the
word, accept it, and produce a crop—thirty, sixty or even a hundred
times what was sown."

A Lamp on a Stand

[21]He said to them, "Do you bring in a lamp to put it under a bowl or
a bed? Instead, don't you put it on its stand?[w] [22]For whatever is hidden
is meant to be disclosed, and whatever is concealed is meant to be
brought out into the open. [x] [23]If anyone has ears to hear, let him hear."[y]

[24]"Consider carefully what you hear," he continued. "With the measure you use, it will be measured to you—and even more. [z] [25]Whoev-
er has will be given more; whoever does not have, even what he has
will be taken from him." [a]

The Parable of the Growing Seed

[26]He also said, "This is what the kingdom of God is like. [b] A man
scatters seed on the ground. [27]Night and day, whether he sleeps or gets
up, the seed sprouts and grows, though he does not know how. [28]All
by itself the soil produces grain—first the stalk, then the head, then the
full kernel in the head. [29]As soon as the grain is ripe, he puts the sickle
to it, because the harvest has come."[c]

The Parable of the Mustard Seed

4:30–32pp — Mt 13:31,32; Lk 13:18,19

[30]Again he said, "What shall we say the kingdom of God is like, [d] or
what parable shall we use to describe it? [31]It is like a mustard seed,
which is the smallest seed you plant in the ground. [32]Yet when planted,
it grows and becomes the largest of all garden plants, with such big
branches that the birds of the air can perch in its shade."

[33]With many similar parables Jesus spoke the word to them, as much
as they could understand. [e] [34]He did not say anything to them without
using a parable. [f] But when he was alone with his own disciples, he
explained everything.

Jesus Calms the Storm

4:35–41pp — Mt 8:18,23–27; Lk 8:22–25

[35]That day when evening came, he said to his disciples, "Let us go
over to the other side." [36]Leaving the crowd behind, they took him
along, just as he was, in the boat. [g] There were also other boats with
him. [37]A furious squall came up, and the waves broke over the boat, so
that it was nearly swamped. [38]Jesus was in the stern, sleeping on a
cushion. The disciples woke him and said to him, "Teacher, don't you
care if we drown?"

4:14
tMk 16:20;
Lk 1:2; Ac 4:31;
8:4; 16:6;
17:11; Php 1:14
4:15
uMt 4:10
4:19
vMt 19:23;
1Ti 6:9,10,17;
1Jn 2:15-17
4:21
wMt 5:15
4:22
xJer 16:17;
Mt 10:26;
Lk 8:17; 12:2
4:23
yver 9;
Mt 11:15
4:24
zMt 7:2;
Lk 6:38
4:25
aMt 13:12;
25:29
4:26
bMt 13:24
4:29
cRev 14:15
4:30
dMt 13:24
4:33
eJn 16:12
4:34
fJn 16:25
4:36
gver 1; Mk 3:9;
5:2,21; 6:32,45

[39]He got up, rebuked the wind and said to the waves, "Quiet! Be still!" Then the wind died down and it was completely calm.

[40]He said to his disciples, "Why are you so afraid? Do you still have no faith?"[h]

[41]They were terrified and asked each other, "Who is this? Even the wind and the waves obey him!"

The Healing of a Demon-possessed Man

5:1–17pp — Mt 8:28–34; Lk 8:26–37
5:18–20pp — Lk 8:38,39

5 They went across the lake to the region of the Gerasenes.[a] [2]When Jesus got out of the boat,[i] a man with an evil[b] spirit[j] came from the tombs to meet him. [3]This man lived in the tombs, and no one could bind him any more, not even with a chain. [4]For he had often been chained hand and foot, but he tore the chains apart and broke the irons on his feet. No one was strong enough to subdue him. [5]Night and day among the tombs and in the hills he would cry out and cut himself with stones.

[6]When he saw Jesus from a distance, he ran and fell on his knees in front of him. [7]He shouted at the top of his voice, "What do you want with me,[k] Jesus, Son of the Most High God?[l] Swear to God that you won't torture me!" [8]For Jesus had said to him, "Come out of this man, you evil spirit!"

[9]Then Jesus asked him, "What is your name?"

"My name is Legion,"[m] he replied, "for we are many." [10]And he begged Jesus again and again not to send them out of the area.

[11]A large herd of pigs was feeding on the nearby hillside. [12]The demons begged Jesus, "Send us among the pigs; allow us to go into them." [13]He gave them permission, and the evil spirits came out and went into the pigs. The herd, about two thousand in number, rushed down the steep bank into the lake and were drowned.

[14]Those tending the pigs ran off and reported this in the town and countryside, and the people went out to see what had happened. [15]When they came to Jesus, they saw the man who had been possessed by the legion[n] of demons,[o] sitting there, dressed and in his right mind; and they were afraid. [16]Those who had seen it told the people what had happened to the demon-possessed man—and told about the pigs as well. [17]Then the people began to plead with Jesus to leave their region.

[18]As Jesus was getting into the boat, the man who had been demon-possessed begged to go with him. [19]Jesus did not let him, but said, "Go home to your family and tell them[p] how much the Lord has done for you, and how he has had mercy on you." [20]So the man went away and began to tell in the Decapolis[c][q] how much Jesus had done for him. And all the people were amazed.

A Dead Girl and a Sick Woman

5:22–43pp — Mt 9:18–26; Lk 8:41–56

[21]When Jesus had again crossed over by boat to the other side of the lake,[r] a large crowd gathered around him while he was by the lake.[s]

4:40 hMt 14:31; Mk 16:14
5:2 iMk 4:1 jMk 1:23
5:7 kMt 8:29 lMt 4:3; Lk 1:32; 6:35; Ac 16:17; Heb 7:1
5:9 mver 15
5:15 nver 9 over 16, 18; Mt 4:24
5:19 pMt 8:4
5:20 qMt 4:25; Mk 7:31
5:21 rMt 9:1 sMk 4:1

---

[a]1 Some manuscripts *Gadarenes*; other manuscripts *Gergesenes*   [b]2 Greek *unclean*; also in verses 8 and 13   [c]20 That is, the Ten Cities

²²Then one of the synagogue rulers,ᵗ named Jairus, came there. Seeing Jesus, he fell at his feet ²³and pleaded earnestly with him, "My little daughter is dying. Please come and put your hands onᵘ her so that she will be healed and live." ²⁴So Jesus went with him.

A large crowd followed and pressed around him. ²⁵And a woman was there who had been subject to bleedingᵛ for twelve years. ²⁶She had suffered a great deal under the care of many doctors and had spent all she had, yet instead of getting better she grew worse. ²⁷When she heard about Jesus, she came up behind him in the crowd and touched his cloak, ²⁸because she thought, "If I just touch his clothes,ʷ I will be healed." ²⁹Immediately her bleeding stopped and she felt in her body that she was freed from her suffering.ˣ

³⁰At once Jesus realized that powerʸ had gone out from him. He turned around in the crowd and asked, "Who touched my clothes?"

³¹"You see the people crowding against you," his disciples answered, "and yet you can ask, 'Who touched me?' "

³²But Jesus kept looking around to see who had done it. ³³Then the woman, knowing what had happened to her, came and fell at his feet and, trembling with fear, told him the whole truth. ³⁴He said to her, "Daughter, your faith has healed you.ᶻ Go in peaceᵃ and be freed from your suffering."

³⁵While Jesus was still speaking, some men came from the house of Jairus, the synagogue ruler.ᵇ "Your daughter is dead," they said. "Why bother the teacher any more?"

³⁶Ignoring what they said, Jesus told the synagogue ruler, "Don't be afraid; just believe."

³⁷He did not let anyone follow him except Peter, James and John the brother of James.ᶜ ³⁸When they came to the home of the synagogue ruler,ᵈ Jesus saw a commotion, with people crying and wailing loudly. ³⁹He went in and said to them, "Why all this commotion and wailing? The child is not dead but asleep."ᵉ ⁴⁰But they laughed at him.

After he put them all out, he took the child's father and mother and the disciples who were with him, and went in where the child was. ⁴¹He took her by the handᶠ and said to her, *"Talitha koum!"* (which means, "Little girl, I say to you, get up!").ᵍ ⁴²Immediately the girl stood up and walked around (she was twelve years old). At this they were completely astonished. ⁴³He gave strict orders not to let anyone know about this,ʰ and told them to give her something to eat.

A Prophet Without Honor

6:1-6pp — Mt 13:54-58

6 Jesus left there and went to his hometown,ⁱ accompanied by his disciples. ²When the Sabbath came,ʲ he began to teach in the synagogue,ᵏ and many who heard him were amazed.ˡ

"Where did this man get these things?" they asked. "What's this wisdom that has been given him, that he even does miracles! ³Isn't this the carpenter? Isn't this Mary's son and the brother of James, Joseph,ᵃ Judas and Simon?ᵐ Aren't his sisters here with us?" And they took offense at him.ⁿ

⁴Jesus said to them, "Only in his hometown, among his relatives and

---

ᵃ3 Greek *Joses*, a variant of *Joseph*

5:22
tver 35,36,38;
Lk 13:14;
Ac 13:15; 18:8,
17

5:23
uMt 19:13;
Mk 6:5; 7:32;
8:23; 16:18;
Lk 4:40; 13:13;
Ac 6:6

5:25
vLev 15:25-30

5:28
wMt 9:20

5:29
xver 34

5:30
yLk 5:17; 6:19

5:34
zMt 9:22
aAc 15:33

5:35
bver 22

5:37
cMt 4:21

5:38
dver 22

5:39
eMt 9:24

5:41
fMk 1:31
gLk 7:14;
Ac 9:40

5:43
hMt 8:4

6:1
iMt 2:23

6:2
jMk 1:21
kMt 4:23
lMt 7:28

6:3
mMt 12:46
nMt 11:6;
Jn 6:61

in his own house is a prophet without honor."° ⁵He could not do any miracles there, except lay his hands onᵖ a few sick people and heal them. ⁶And he was amazed at their lack of faith.

Jesus Sends Out the Twelve

6:7–11pp — Mt 10:1,9–14; Lk 9:1,3–5

Then Jesus went around teaching from village to village.�q ⁷Calling the Twelve to him,ʳ he sent them out two by twosˢ and gave them authority over evilᵃ spirits.ᵗ

⁸These were his instructions: "Take nothing for the journey except a staff—no bread, no bag, no money in your belts. ⁹Wear sandals but not an extra tunic. ¹⁰Whenever you enter a house, stay there until you leave that town. ¹¹And if any place will not welcome you or listen to you, shake the dust off your feetᵘ when you leave, as a testimony against them."

¹²They went out and preached that people should repent.ᵛ ¹³They drove out many demons and anointed many sick people with oilʷ and healed them.

John the Baptist Beheaded

6:14–29pp — Mt 14:1–12
6:14–16pp — Lk 9:7–9

¹⁴King Herod heard about this, for Jesus' name had become well known. Some were saying,ᵇ "John the Baptistˣ has been raised from the dead, and that is why miraculous powers are at work in him."

¹⁵Others said, "He is Elijah."ʸ

And still others claimed, "He is a prophet,ᶻ like one of the prophets of long ago."ᵃ

¹⁶But when Herod heard this, he said, "John, the man I beheaded, has been raised from the dead!"

¹⁷For Herod himself had given orders to have John arrested, and he had him bound and put in prison.ᵇ He did this because of Herodias, his brother Philip's wife, whom he had married. ¹⁸For John had been saying to Herod, "It is not lawful for you to have your brother's wife."ᶜ ¹⁹So Herodias nursed a grudge against John and wanted to kill him. But she was not able to, ²⁰because Herod feared John and protected him, knowing him to be a righteous and holy man.ᵈ When Herod heard John, he was greatly puzzledᶜ; yet he liked to listen to him.

²¹Finally the opportune time came. On his birthday Herod gave a banquetᵉ for his high officials and military commanders and the leading men of Galilee.ᶠ ²²When the daughter of Herodias came in and danced, she pleased Herod and his dinner guests.

The king said to the girl, "Ask me for anything you want, and I'll give it to you." ²³And he promised her with an oath, "Whatever you ask I will give you, up to half my kingdom."ᵍ

²⁴She went out and said to her mother, "What shall I ask for?"

"The head of John the Baptist," she answered.

²⁵At once the girl hurried in to the king with the request: "I want you to give me right now the head of John the Baptist on a platter."

6:4
oLk 4:24;
Jn 4:44
6:5
pMk 5:23
6:6
qMt 9:35;
Mk 1:39;
Lk 13:22
6:7
rMk 3:13
sDt 17:6;
Lk 10:1
tMt 10:1
6:11
uMt 10:14
6:12
vLk 9:6
6:13
wJas 5:14
6:14
xMt 3:1
6:15
yMal 4:5
zMt 21:11
aMt 16:14;
Mk 8:28
6:17
bMt 4:12; 11:2;
Lk 3:19,20
6:18
cLev 18:16;
20:21
6:20
dMt 11:9; 21:26
6:21
eEst 1:3; 2:18
fLk 3:1
6:23
gEst 5:3,6; 7:2

ᵃ7 Greek unclean   ᵇ14 Some early manuscripts He was saying   ᶜ20 Some early manuscripts
he did many things

26The king was greatly distressed, but because of his oaths and his dinner guests, he did not want to refuse her. 27So he immediately sent an executioner with orders to bring John's head. The man went, beheaded John in the prison, 28and brought back his head on a platter. He presented it to the girl, and she gave it to her mother. 29On hearing of this, John's disciples came and took his body and laid it in a tomb.

Jesus Feeds the Five Thousand

6:32–44pp — Mt 14:13–21; Lk 9:10–17; Jn 6:5–13
6:32–44Ref — Mk 8:2–9

30The apostles[h] gathered around Jesus and reported to him all they had done and taught.[i] 31Then, because so many people were coming and going that they did not even have a chance to eat,[j] he said to them, "Come with me by yourselves to a quiet place and get some rest."

32So they went away by themselves in a boat[k] to a solitary place. 33But many who saw them leaving recognized them and ran on foot from all the towns and got there ahead of them. 34When Jesus landed and saw a large crowd, he had compassion on them, because they were like sheep without a shepherd.[l] So he began teaching them many things.

35By this time it was late in the day, so his disciples came to him. "This is a remote place," they said, "and it's already very late. 36Send the people away so they can go to the surrounding countryside and villages and buy themselves something to eat."

37But he answered, "You give them something to eat."[m]

They said to him, "That would take eight months of a man's wages[a]! Are we to go and spend that much on bread and give it to them to eat?"

38"How many loaves do you have?" he asked. "Go and see."

When they found out, they said, "Five—and two fish."[n]

39Then Jesus directed them to have all the people sit down in groups on the green grass. 40So they sat down in groups of hundreds and fifties. 41Taking the five loaves and the two fish and looking up to heaven, he gave thanks and broke the loaves.[o] Then he gave them to his disciples to set before the people. He also divided the two fish among them all. 42They all ate and were satisfied, 43and the disciples picked up twelve basketfuls of broken pieces of bread and fish. 44The number of the men who had eaten was five thousand.

Jesus Walks on the Water

6:45–51pp — Mt 14:22–32; Jn 6:15–21
6:53–56pp — Mt 14:34–36

45Immediately Jesus made his disciples get into the boat[p] and go on ahead of him to Bethsaida,[q] while he dismissed the crowd. 46After leaving them, he went up on a mountainside to pray.[r]

47When evening came, the boat was in the middle of the lake, and he was alone on land. 48He saw the disciples straining at the oars, because the wind was against them. About the fourth watch of the night he went out to them, walking on the lake. He was about to pass by them, 49but when they saw him walking on the lake, they thought he was a ghost.[s] They cried out, 50because they all saw him and were terrified.

Immediately he spoke to them and said, "Take courage! It is I. Don't

6:30
hMt 10:2;
Lk 9:10; 17:5;
22:14; 24:10;
Ac 1:2,26
iLk 9:10

6:31
jMk 3:20

6:32
kver 45;
Mk 4:36

6:34
lMt 9:36

6:37
m2Ki 4:42-44

6:38
nMt 15:34;
Mk 8:5

6:41
oMt 14:19

6:45
pver 32
qMt 11:21

6:46
rLk 3:21

6:49
sLk 24:37

a37 Greek *take two hundred denarii*

be afraid."[t] 51Then he climbed into the boat[u] with them, and the wind died down.[v] They were completely amazed, 52for they had not understood about the loaves; their hearts were hardened.[w]

53When they had crossed over, they landed at Gennesaret and anchored there.[x] 54As soon as they got out of the boat, people recognized Jesus. 55They ran throughout that whole region and carried the sick on mats to wherever they heard he was. 56And wherever he went—into villages, towns or countryside—they placed the sick in the marketplaces. They begged him to let them touch even the edge of his cloak,[y] and all who touched him were healed.

Clean and Unclean

7:1–23pp — Mt 15:1–20

7 The Pharisees and some of the teachers of the law who had come from Jerusalem gathered around Jesus and 2saw some of his disciples eating food with hands that were "unclean,"[z] that is, unwashed. 3(The Pharisees and all the Jews do not eat unless they give their hands a ceremonial washing, holding to the tradition of the elders.[a] 4When they come from the marketplace they do not eat unless they wash. And they observe many other traditions, such as the washing of cups, pitchers and kettles.[a])[b]

5So the Pharisees and teachers of the law asked Jesus, "Why don't your disciples live according to the tradition of the elders[c] instead of eating their food with 'unclean' hands?"

6He replied, "Isaiah was right when he prophesied about you hypocrites; as it is written:

" 'These people honor me with their lips,
    but their hearts are far from me.
7They worship me in vain;
    their teachings are but rules taught by men.'[b] [d]

8You have let go of the commands of God and are holding on to the traditions of men."[e]

9And he said to them: "You have a fine way of setting aside the commands of God in order to observe[c] your own traditions![f] 10For Moses said, 'Honor your father and your mother,'[d][g] and, 'Anyone who curses his father or mother must be put to death.'[e][h] 11But you say[i] that if a man says to his father or mother: 'Whatever help you might otherwise have received from me is Corban' (that is, a gift devoted to God), 12then you no longer let him do anything for his father or mother. 13Thus you nullify the word of God[j] by your tradition[k] that you have handed down. And you do many things like that."

14Again Jesus called the crowd to him and said, "Listen to me, everyone, and understand this. 15Nothing outside a man can make him 'unclean' by going into him. Rather, it is what comes out of a man that makes him 'unclean.'[f] "

17After he had left the crowd and entered the house, his disciples asked him[l] about this parable. 18"Are you so dull?" he asked. "Don't

---

6:50
[t]Mt 14:27
6:51
[u]ver 32
[v]Mk 4:39
6:52
[w]Mk 8:17-21
6:53
[x]Jn 6:24,25
6:56
[y]Mt 9:20
7:2
[z]Ac 10:14,28;
11:8; Ro 14:14
7:3
[a]ver 5,8,9,13;
Lk 11:38
7:4
[b]Mt 23:25;
Lk 11:39
7:5
[c]ver 3;
Gal 1:14;
Col 2:8
7:7
[d]Isa 29:13
7:8
[e]ver 3
7:9
[f]ver 3
7:10
[g]Ex 20:12;
Dt 5:16
[h]Ex 21:17;
Lev 20:9
7:11
[i]Mt 23:16,18
7:13
[j]Heb 4:12
[k]ver 3
7:17
[l]Mk 9:28

---

[a]4 Some early manuscripts *pitchers, kettles and dining couches*   [b]6,7 Isaiah 29:13   [c]9 Some manuscripts *set up*   [d]10 Exodus 20:12; Deut. 5:16   [e]10 Exodus 21:17; Lev. 20:9   [f]15 Some early manuscripts *'unclean.'* [16]*If anyone has ears to hear, let him hear.*

you see that nothing that enters a man from the outside can make him 'unclean'? [19]For it doesn't go into his heart but into his stomach, and then out of his body." (In saying this, Jesus declared all foods[m] "clean.")[n]

[20]He went on: "What comes out of a man is what makes him 'unclean.' [21]For from within, out of men's hearts, come evil thoughts, sexual immorality, theft, murder, adultery, [22]greed,[o] malice, deceit, lewdness, envy, slander, arrogance and folly. [23]All these evils come from inside and make a man 'unclean.' "

The Faith of a Syrophoenician Woman

7:24–30pp — Mt 15:21–28

[24]Jesus left that place and went to the vicinity of Tyre.[a][p] He entered a house and did not want anyone to know it; yet he could not keep his presence secret. [25]In fact, as soon as she heard about him, a woman whose little daughter was possessed by an evil[b] spirit[q] came and fell at his feet. [26]The woman was a Greek, born in Syrian Phoenicia. She begged Jesus to drive the demon out of her daughter.

[27]"First let the children eat all they want," he told her, "for it is not right to take the children's bread and toss it to their dogs."

[28]"Yes, Lord," she replied, "but even the dogs under the table eat the children's crumbs."

[29]Then he told her, "For such a reply, you may go; the demon has left your daughter."

[30]She went home and found her child lying on the bed, and the demon gone.

The Healing of a Deaf and Mute Man

7:31–37pp — Mt 15:29–31

[31]Then Jesus left the vicinity of Tyre[r] and went through Sidon, down to the Sea of Galilee[s] and into the region of the Decapolis.[c][t] [32]There some people brought to him a man who was deaf and could hardly talk,[u] and they begged him to place his hand on[v] the man.

[33]After he took him aside, away from the crowd, Jesus put his fingers into the man's ears. Then he spit[w] and touched the man's tongue. [34]He looked up to heaven[x] and with a deep sigh[y] said to him, "*Ephphatha!*" (which means, "Be opened!"). [35]At this, the man's ears were opened, his tongue was loosened and he began to speak plainly.[z]

[36]Jesus commanded them not to tell anyone.[a] But the more he did so, the more they kept talking about it. [37]People were overwhelmed with amazement. "He has done everything well," they said. "He even makes the deaf hear and the mute speak."

Jesus Feeds the Four Thousand

8:1–9pp — Mt 15:32–39
8:1–9Ref — Mk 6:32–44
8:11–21pp — Mt 16:1–12

8 During those days another large crowd gathered. Since they had nothing to eat, Jesus called his disciples to him and said, [2]"I have compassion for these people;[b] they have already been with me three

7:19
m Ro 14:1-12;
Col 2:16;
1Ti 4:3-5
n Ac 10:15
7:22
o Mt 20:15
7:24
p Mt 11:21
7:25
q Mt 4:24
7:31
r ver 24;
Mt 11:21
s Mt 4:18
t Mt 4:25;
Mk 5:20
7:32
u Mt 9:32;
Lk 11:14
v Mk 5:23
7:33
w Mk 8:23
7:34
x Mk 6:41;
Jn 11:41
y Mk 8:12
7:35
z Isa 35:5,6
7:36
a Mt 8:4
8:2
b Mt 9:36

---

[a]24 Many early manuscripts *Tyre and Sidon*   [b]25 Greek *unclean*   [c]31 That is, the Ten Cities

days and have nothing to eat. ³If I send them home hungry, they will collapse on the way, because some of them have come a long distance.''

⁴His disciples answered, ''But where in this remote place can anyone get enough bread to feed them?''

⁵''How many loaves do you have?'' Jesus asked.

''Seven,'' they replied.

⁶He told the crowd to sit down on the ground. When he had taken the seven loaves and given thanks, he broke them and gave them to his disciples to set before the people, and they did so. ⁷They had a few small fish as well; he gave thanks for them also and told the disciples to distribute them.ᶜ ⁸The people ate and were satisfied. Afterward the disciples picked up seven basketfuls of broken pieces that were left over.ᵈ ⁹About four thousand men were present. And having sent them away, ¹⁰he got into the boat with his disciples and went to the region of Dalmanutha.

¹¹The Pharisees came and began to question Jesus. To test him, they asked him for a sign from heaven.ᵉ ¹²He sighed deeplyᶠ and said, ''Why does this generation ask for a miraculous sign? I tell you the truth, no sign will be given to it.'' ¹³Then he left them, got back into the boat and crossed to the other side.

The Yeast of the Pharisees and Herod

¹⁴The disciples had forgotten to bring bread, except for one loaf they had with them in the boat. ¹⁵''Be careful,'' Jesus warned them. ''Watch out for the yeastᵍ of the Phariseesʰ and that of Herod.''ⁱ

¹⁶They discussed this with one another and said, ''It is because we have no bread.''

¹⁷Aware of their discussion, Jesus asked them: ''Why are you talking about having no bread? Do you still not see or understand? Are your hearts hardened?ʲ ¹⁸Do you have eyes but fail to see, and ears but fail to hear? And don't you remember? ¹⁹When I broke the five loaves for the five thousand, how many basketfuls of pieces did you pick up?''

''Twelve,''ᵏ they replied.

²⁰''And when I broke the seven loaves for the four thousand, how many basketfuls of pieces did you pick up?''

They answered, ''Seven.''ˡ

²¹He said to them, ''Do you still not understand?''ᵐ

The Healing of a Blind Man at Bethsaida

²²They came to Bethsaida,ⁿ and some people brought a blind manᵒ and begged Jesus to touch him. ²³He took the blind man by the hand and led him outside the village. When he had spitᵖ on the man's eyes and put his hands on�q him, Jesus asked, ''Do you see anything?''

²⁴He looked up and said, ''I see people; they look like trees walking around.''

²⁵Once more Jesus put his hands on the man's eyes. Then his eyes were opened, his sight was restored, and he saw everything clearly. ²⁶Jesus sent him home, saying, ''Don't go into the village.ᵃ ''

ᵃ26 Some manuscripts *Don't go and tell anyone in the village*

8:7
cMt 14:19
8:8
dver 20
8:11
eMt 12:38
8:12
fMk 7:34
8:15
g1Co 5:6-8
hLk 12:1
iMt 14:1;
Mk 12:13
8:17
jIsa 6:9,10;
Mk 6:52
8:19
kMt 14:20;
Mk 6:41-44;
Lk 9:17; Jn 6:13
8:20
lver 6-9;
Mt 15:37
8:21
mMk 6:52
8:22
nMt 11:21
oMk 10:46;
Jn 9:1
8:23
pMk 7:33
qMk 5:23

Peter's Confession of Christ

8:27–29pp — Mt 16:13–16; Lk 9:18–20

27Jesus and his disciples went on to the villages around Caesarea Philippi. On the way he asked them, "Who do people say I am?"

28They replied, "Some say John the Baptist;[r] others say Elijah;[s] and still others, one of the prophets."

29"But what about you?" he asked. "Who do you say I am?"

Peter answered, "You are the Christ.[a] "[t]

30Jesus warned them not to tell anyone about him. [u]

Jesus Predicts His Death

8:31 — 9:1pp — Mt 16:21–28; Lk 9:22–27

31He then began to teach them that the Son of Man[v] must suffer many things[w] and be rejected by the elders, chief priests and teachers of the law,[x] and that he must be killed[y] and after three days[z] rise again.[a] 32He spoke plainly[b] about this, and Peter took him aside and began to rebuke him.

33But when Jesus turned and looked at his disciples, he rebuked Peter. "Get behind me, Satan!"[c] he said. "You do not have in mind the things of God, but the things of men."

34Then he called the crowd to him along with his disciples and said: "If anyone would come after me, he must deny himself and take up his cross and follow me. [d] 35For whoever wants to save his life[b] will lose it, but whoever loses his life for me and for the gospel will save it. [e] 36What good is it for a man to gain the whole world, yet forfeit his soul? 37Or what can a man give in exchange for his soul? 38If anyone is ashamed of me and my words in this adulterous and sinful generation, the Son of Man[f] will be ashamed of him[g] when he comes[h] in his Father's glory with the holy angels."

9 And he said to them, "I tell you the truth, some who are standing here will not taste death before they see the kingdom of God come[i] with power."[j]

The Transfiguration

9:2–8pp — Lk 9:28–36
9:2–13pp — Mt 17:1–13

2After six days Jesus took Peter, James and John[k] with him and led them up a high mountain, where they were all alone. There he was transfigured before them. 3His clothes became dazzling white,[l] whiter than anyone in the world could bleach them. 4And there appeared before them Elijah and Moses, who were talking with Jesus.

5Peter said to Jesus, "Rabbi, [m] it is good for us to be here. Let us put up three shelters—one for you, one for Moses and one for Elijah." 6(He did not know what to say, they were so frightened.)

7Then a cloud appeared and enveloped them, and a voice came from the cloud:[n] "This is my Son, whom I love. Listen to him!"[o]

8Suddenly, when they looked around, they no longer saw anyone with them except Jesus.

9As they were coming down the mountain, Jesus gave them orders

8:28
r Mt 3:1
s Mal 4:5
8:29
t Jn 6:69; 11:27
8:30
u Mt 8:4; 16:20; 17:9; Mk 9:9; Lk 9:21
8:31
v Mt 8:20
w Mt 16:21
x Mt 27:1,2
y Ac 2:23; 3:13
z Mt 16:21
a Mt 16:21
8:32
b Jn 18:20
8:33
c Mt 4:10
8:34
d Mt 10:38; Lk 14:27
8:35
e Jn 12:25
8:38
f Mt 8:20
g Mt 10:33; Lk 12:9
h 1Th 2:19
9:1
i Mk 13:30; Lk 22:18
j Mt 24:30; 25:31
9:2
k Mt 4:21
9:3
l Mt 28:3
9:5
m Mt 23:7
9:7
n Ex 24:16
o Mt 3:17

---

a29 Or Messiah. "The Christ" (Greek) and "the Messiah" (Hebrew) both mean "the Anointed One."   b35 The Greek word means either life or soul; also in verse 36.

not to tell anyone[p] what they had seen until the Son of Man[q] had risen from the dead. [10]They kept the matter to themselves, discussing what "rising from the dead" meant.

[11]And they asked him, "Why do the teachers of the law say that Elijah must come first?"

[12]Jesus replied, "To be sure, Elijah does come first, and restores all things. Why then is it written that the Son of Man[r] must suffer much[s] and be rejected?[t] [13]But I tell you, Elijah has come,[u] and they have done to him everything they wished, just as it is written about him."

The Healing of a Boy With an Evil Spirit
9:14–28; 30–32pp — Mt 17:14–19; 22,23; Lk 9:37–45

[14]When they came to the other disciples, they saw a large crowd around them and the teachers of the law arguing with them. [15]As soon as all the people saw Jesus, they were overwhelmed with wonder and ran to greet him.

[16]"What are you arguing with them about?" he asked.

[17]A man in the crowd answered, "Teacher, I brought you my son, who is possessed by a spirit that has robbed him of speech. [18]Whenever it seizes him, it throws him to the ground. He foams at the mouth, gnashes his teeth and becomes rigid. I asked your disciples to drive out the spirit, but they could not."

[19]"O unbelieving generation," Jesus replied, "how long shall I stay with you? How long shall I put up with you? Bring the boy to me."

[20]So they brought him. When the spirit saw Jesus, it immediately threw the boy into a convulsion. He fell to the ground and rolled around, foaming at the mouth.[v]

[21]Jesus asked the boy's father, "How long has he been like this?"

"From childhood," he answered. [22]"It has often thrown him into fire or water to kill him. But if you can do anything, take pity on us and help us."

[23]" 'If you can'?" said Jesus. "Everything is possible for him who believes."[w]

[24]Immediately the boy's father exclaimed, "I do believe; help me overcome my unbelief!"

[25]When Jesus saw that a crowd was running to the scene,[x] he rebuked the evil[a] spirit. "You deaf and mute spirit," he said, "I command you, come out of him and never enter him again."

[26]The spirit shrieked, convulsed him violently and came out. The boy looked so much like a corpse that many said, "He's dead." [27]But Jesus took him by the hand and lifted him to his feet, and he stood up.

[28]After Jesus had gone indoors, his disciples asked him privately,[y] "Why couldn't we drive it out?"

[29]He replied, "This kind can come out only by prayer.[b] "

[30]They left that place and passed through Galilee. Jesus did not want anyone to know where they were, [31]because he was teaching his disciples. He said to them, "The Son of Man[z] is going to be betrayed into the hands of men. They will kill him,[a] and after three days[b] he will rise."[c] [32]But they did not understand what he meant[d] and were afraid to ask him about it.

9:9
p Mk 8:30
q Mt 8:20
9:12
r Mt 8:20
s Mt 16:21
t Lk 23:11
9:13
u Mt 11:14
9:20
v Mk 1:26
9:23
w Mt 21:21;
Mk 11:23;
Jn 11:40
9:25
x ver 15
9:28
y Mk 7:17
9:31
z Mt 8:20
a ver 12;
Ac 2:23; 3:13
b Mt 16:21
c Mt 16:21
9:32
d Lk 2:50; 9:45;
18:34; Jn 12:16

---

[a]25 Greek *unclean*   [b]29 Some manuscripts *prayer and fasting*

Who Is the Greatest?

9:33–37pp — Mt 18:1–5; Lk 9:46–48

³³They came to Capernaum.ᵉ When he was in the house,ᶠ he asked them, "What were you arguing about on the road?" ³⁴But they kept quiet because on the way they had argued about who was the greatest.ᵍ

³⁵Sitting down, Jesus called the Twelve and said, "If anyone wants to be first, he must be the very last, and the servant of all."ʰ

³⁶He took a little child and had him stand among them. Taking him in his arms,ⁱ he said to them, ³⁷"Whoever welcomes one of these little children in my name welcomes me; and whoever welcomes me does not welcome me but the one who sent me."ʲ

Whoever Is Not Against Us Is for Us

9:38–40pp — Lk 9:49,50

³⁸"Teacher," said John, "we saw a man driving out demons in your name and we told him to stop, because he was not one of us."ᵏ

³⁹"Do not stop him," Jesus said. "No one who does a miracle in my name can in the next moment say anything bad about me, ⁴⁰for whoever is not against us is for us.ˡ ⁴¹I tell you the truth, anyone who gives you a cup of water in my name because you belong to Christ will certainly not lose his reward.ᵐ

Causing to Sin

⁴²"And if anyone causes one of these little ones who believe in me to sin,ⁿ it would be better for him to be thrown into the sea with a large millstone tied around his neck.ᵒ ⁴³If your hand causes you to sin,ᵖ cut it off. It is better for you to enter life maimed than with two hands to go into hell,ᑫ where the fire never goes out.ᵃʳ ⁴⁵And if your foot causes you to sin,ˢ cut it off. It is better for you to enter life crippled than to have two feet and be thrown into hell.ᵇᵗ ⁴⁷And if your eye causes you to sin,ᵘ pluck it out. It is better for you to enter the kingdom of God with one eye than to have two eyes and be thrown into hell,ᵛ ⁴⁸where

> " 'their worm does not die,
> and the fire is not quenched.'ᶜ ʷ

⁴⁹Everyone will be saltedˣ with fire.

⁵⁰"Salt is good, but if it loses its saltiness, how can you make it salty again?ʸ Have salt in yourselves,ᶻ and be at peace with each other."ᵃ

Divorce

10:1–12pp — Mt 19:1–9

10 Jesus then left that place and went into the region of Judea and across the Jordan.ᵇ Again crowds of people came to him, and as was his custom, he taught them.ᶜ

²Some Phariseesᵈ came and tested him by asking, "Is it lawful for a man to divorce his wife?"

³"What did Moses command you?" he replied.

ᵃ43 Some manuscripts *out,* ⁴⁴*where* / " *'their worm does not die,* / *and the fire is not quenched.'*
ᵇ45 Some manuscripts *hell,* ⁴⁶*where* / " *'their worm does not die,* / *and the fire is not quenched.'*
ᶜ48 Isaiah 66:24

9:33
eMt 4:13
fMk 1:29
9:34
gLk 22:24
9:35
hMt 18:4;
20:26;
Mk 10:43;
Lk 22:26
9:36
iMk 10:16
9:37
jMt 10:40
9:38
kNu 11:27-29
9:40
lMt 12:30;
Lk 11:23
9:41
mMt 10:42
9:42
nMt 5:29
oMt 18:6;
Lk 17:2
9:43
pMt 5:29
qMt 5:30; 18:8
rMt 25:41
9:45
sMt 5:29
tMt 18:8
9:47
uMt 5:29
vMt 5:29; 18:9
9:48
wIsa 66:24;
Mt 25:41
9:49
xLev 2:13
9:50
yMt 5:13;
Lk 14:34,35
zCol 4:6
aRo 12:18;
2Co 13:11;
1Th 5:13
10:1
bMk 1:5;
Jn 10:40; 11:7
cMt 4:23;
Mk 2:13; 4:2;
6:6,34
10:2
dMk 2:16

[4]They said, "Moses permitted a man to write a certificate of divorce and send her away."[e]

[5]"It was because your hearts were hard[f] that Moses wrote you this law," Jesus replied. [6]"But at the beginning of creation God 'made them male and female.'[a][g] [7]For this reason a man will leave his father and mother and be united to his wife,[b] [8]and the two will become one flesh.'[c][h] So they are no longer two, but one. [9]Therefore what God has joined together, let man not separate."

[10]When they were in the house again, the disciples asked Jesus about this. [11]He answered, "Anyone who divorces his wife and marries another woman commits adultery against her. [i] [12]And if she divorces her husband and marries another man, she commits adultery."[j]

The Little Children and Jesus

10:13–16pp — Mt 19:13–15; Lk 18:15–17

[13]People were bringing little children to Jesus to have him touch them, but the disciples rebuked them. [14]When Jesus saw this, he was indignant. He said to them, "Let the little children come to me, and do not hinder them, for the kingdom of God belongs to such as these. [k] [15]I tell you the truth, anyone who will not receive the kingdom of God like a little child will never enter it."[l] [16]And he took the children in his arms, [m] put his hands on them and blessed them.

The Rich Young Man

10:17–31pp — Mt 19:16–30; Lk 18:18–30

[17]As Jesus started on his way, a man ran up to him and fell on his knees[n] before him. "Good teacher," he asked, "what must I do to inherit eternal life?"[o]

[18]"Why do you call me good?" Jesus answered. "No one is good—except God alone. [19]You know the commandments: 'Do not murder, do not commit adultery, do not steal, do not give false testimony, do not defraud, honor your father and mother.'[d] "[p]

[20]"Teacher," he declared, "all these I have kept since I was a boy."

[21]Jesus looked at him and loved him. "One thing you lack," he said. "Go, sell everything you have and give to the poor,[q] and you will have treasure in heaven.[r] Then come, follow me."[s]

[22]At this the man's face fell. He went away sad, because he had great wealth.

[23]Jesus looked around and said to his disciples, "How hard it is for the rich[t] to enter the kingdom of God!"

[24]The disciples were amazed at his words. But Jesus said again, "Children, how hard it is[e] to enter the kingdom of God! [25]It is easier for a camel to go through the eye of a needle than for a rich man to enter the kingdom of God."[v]

[26]The disciples were even more amazed, and said to each other, "Who then can be saved?"

[27]Jesus looked at them and said, "With man this is impossible, but not with God; all things are possible with God."[w]

[28]Peter said to him, "We have left everything to follow you!"[x]

10:4
[e]Dt 24:1-4; Mt 5:31

10:5
[f]Ps 95:8; Heb 3:15

10:6
[g]Ge 1:27; 5:2

10:8
[h]Ge 2:24; 1Co 6:16

10:11
[i]Mt 5:32; Lk 16:18

10:12
[j]Ro 7:3; 1Co 7:10,11

10:14
[k]Mt 25:34

10:15
[l]Mt 18:3

10:16
[m]Mk 9:36

10:17
[n]Mk 1:40; [o]Lk 10:25; Ac 20:32

10:19
[p]Ex 20:12-16; Dt 5:16-20

10:21
[q]Ac 2:45; [r]Mt 6:20; Lk 12:33; [s]Mt 4:19

10:23
[t]Ps 52:7; 62:10; 1Ti 6:9,10,17

10:24
[u]Mt 7:13,14

10:25
[v]Lk 12:16-20

10:27
[w]Mt 19:26

10:28
[x]Mt 4:19

---

[a]6 Gen. 1:27   [b]7 Some early manuscripts do not have *and be united to his wife.*   [c]8 Gen. 2:24
[d]19 Exodus 20:12-16; Deut. 5:16-20   [e]24 Some manuscripts *is for those who trust in riches*

[29]"I tell you the truth," Jesus replied, "no one who has left home or brothers or sisters or mother or father or children or fields for me and the gospel [30]will fail to receive a hundred times as much[y] in this present age (homes, brothers, sisters, mothers, children and fields—and with them, persecutions) and in the age to come,[z] eternal life.[a] [31]But many who are first will be last, and the last first."[b]

Jesus Again Predicts His Death

10:32–34pp — Mt 20:17–19; Lk 18:31–33

[32]They were on their way up to Jerusalem, with Jesus leading the way, and the disciples were astonished, while those who followed were afraid. Again he took the Twelve[c] aside and told them what was going to happen to him. [33]"We are going up to Jerusalem,"[d] he said, "and the Son of Man[e] will be betrayed to the chief priests and teachers of the law.[f] They will condemn him to death and will hand him over to the Gentiles, [34]who will mock him and spit on him, flog him[g] and kill him.[h] Three days later[i] he will rise."[j]

The Request of James and John

10:35–45pp — Mt 20:20–28

[35]Then James and John, the sons of Zebedee, came to him. "Teacher," they said, "we want you to do for us whatever we ask."

[36]"What do you want me to do for you?" he asked.

[37]They replied, "Let one of us sit at your right and the other at your left in your glory."[k]

[38]"You don't know what you are asking,"[l] Jesus said. "Can you drink the cup[m] I drink or be baptized with the baptism I am baptized with?"[n]

[39]"We can," they answered.

Jesus said to them, "You will drink the cup I drink and be baptized with the baptism I am baptized with,[o] [40]but to sit at my right or left is not for me to grant. These places belong to those for whom they have been prepared."

[41]When the ten heard about this, they became indignant with James and John. [42]Jesus called them together and said, "You know that those who are regarded as rulers of the Gentiles lord it over them, and their high officials exercise authority over them. [43]Not so with you. Instead, whoever wants to become great among you must be your servant,[p] [44]and whoever wants to be first must be slave of all. [45]For even the Son of Man did not come to be served, but to serve,[q] and to give his life as a ransom for many."[r]

Blind Bartimaeus Receives His Sight

10:46–52pp — Mt 20:29–34; Lk 18:35–43

[46]Then they came to Jericho. As Jesus and his disciples, together with a large crowd, were leaving the city, a blind man, Bartimaeus (that is, the Son of Timaeus), was sitting by the roadside begging. [47]When he heard that it was Jesus of Nazareth,[s] he began to shout, "Jesus, Son of David,[t] have mercy on me!"

[48]Many rebuked him and told him to be quiet, but he shouted all the more, "Son of David, have mercy on me!"

[49]Jesus stopped and said, "Call him."

10:30
y Mt 6:33
z Mt 12:32
a Mt 25:46
10:31
b Mt 19:30
10:32
c Mk 3:16-19
10:33
d Lk 9:51
e Mt 8:20
f Mt 27:1,2
10:34
g Mt 16:21
h Ac 2:23; 3:13
i Mt 16:21
j Mt 16:21
10:37
k Mt 19:28
10:38
l Job 38:2
m Mt 20:22
n Lk 12:50
10:39
o Ac 12:2; Rev 1:9
10:43
p Mk 9:35
10:45
q Mt 20:28
r Mt 20:28
10:47
s Mk 1:24
t Mt 9:27

So they called to the blind man, "Cheer up! On your feet! He's calling you." [50]Throwing his cloak aside, he jumped to his feet and came to Jesus.

[51]"What do you want me to do for you?" Jesus asked him.

The blind man said, "Rabbi, [u] I want to see."

[52]"Go," said Jesus, "your faith has healed you."[v] Immediately he received his sight and followed[w] Jesus along the road.

The Triumphal Entry

11:1–10pp — Mt 21:1–9; Lk 19:29–38
11:7–10pp — Jn 12:12–15

11 As they approached Jerusalem and came to Bethphage and Bethany[x] at the Mount of Olives,[y] Jesus sent two of his disciples, [2]saying to them, "Go to the village ahead of you, and just as you enter it, you will find a colt tied there, which no one has ever ridden.[z] Untie it and bring it here. [3]If anyone asks you, 'Why are you doing this?' tell him, 'The Lord needs it and will send it back here shortly.' "

[4]They went and found a colt outside in the street, tied at a doorway.[a] As they untied it, [5]some people standing there asked, "What are you doing, untying that colt?" [6]They answered as Jesus had told them to, and the people let them go. [7]When they brought the colt to Jesus and threw their cloaks over it, he sat on it. [8]Many people spread their cloaks on the road, while others spread branches they had cut in the fields. [9]Those who went ahead and those who followed shouted,

> "Hosanna![a] "
>
> "Blessed is he who comes in the name of the Lord!"[b] [b]
>
> [10]"Blessed is the coming kingdom of our father David!"
>
> "Hosanna in the highest!"[c]

[11]Jesus entered Jerusalem and went to the temple. He looked around at everything, but since it was already late, he went out to Bethany with the Twelve.[d]

Jesus Clears the Temple

11:12–14pp — Mt 21:18–22
11:15–18pp — Mt 21:12–16; Lk 19:45–47; Jn 2:13–16

[12]The next day as they were leaving Bethany, Jesus was hungry. [13]Seeing in the distance a fig tree in leaf, he went to find out if it had any fruit. When he reached it, he found nothing but leaves, because it was not the season for figs.[e] [14]Then he said to the tree, "May no one ever eat fruit from you again." And his disciples heard him say it.

[15]On reaching Jerusalem, Jesus entered the temple area and began driving out those who were buying and selling there. He overturned the tables of the money changers and the benches of those selling doves, [16]and would not allow anyone to carry merchandise through the temple courts. [17]And as he taught them, he said, "Is it not written:

> " 'My house will be called
> a house of prayer for all nations'[c]?[f]

10:51
uMt 23:7
10:52
vMt 9:22
wMt 4:19
11:1
xMt 21:17
yMt 21:1
11:2
zNu 19:2;
Dt 21:3; 1Sa 6:7
11:4
aMk 14:16
11:9
bPs 118:25,26;
Mt 23:39
11:10
cLk 2:14
11:11
dMt 21:12,17
11:13
eLk 13:6-9
11:17
fIsa 56:7

---

[a]9 A Hebrew expression meaning "Save!" which became an exclamation of praise; also in verse 10
[b]9 Psalm 118:25,26   [c]17 Isaiah 56:7

But you have made it 'a den of robbers.'[a] "[g]

[18]The chief priests and the teachers of the law heard this and began looking for a way to kill him,[h] because the whole crowd was amazed at his teaching.[i]

[19]When evening came, they[b] went out of the city.[j]

The Withered Fig Tree
11:20–24pp — Mt 21:19–22

[20]In the morning, as they went along, they saw the fig tree withered from the roots. [21]Peter remembered and said to Jesus, "Rabbi,[k] look! The fig tree you cursed has withered!"

[22]"Have[c] faith in God," Jesus answered. [23]"I tell you the truth, if anyone says to this mountain, 'Go, throw yourself into the sea,' and does not doubt in his heart but believes that what he says will happen, it will be done for him.[l] [24]Therefore I tell you, whatever you ask for in prayer, believe that you have received it, and it will be yours.[m] [25]And when you stand praying, if you hold anything against anyone, forgive him, so that your Father in heaven may forgive you your sins.[d] "[n]

The Authority of Jesus Questioned
11:27–33pp — Mt 21:23–27; Lk 20:1–8

[27]They arrived again in Jerusalem, and while Jesus was walking in the temple courts, the chief priests, the teachers of the law and the elders came to him. [28]"By what authority are you doing these things?" they asked. "And who gave you authority to do this?"

[29]Jesus replied, "I will ask you one question. Answer me, and I will tell you by what authority I am doing these things. [30]John's baptism —was it from heaven, or from men? Tell me!"

[31]They discussed it among themselves and said, "If we say, 'From heaven,' he will ask, 'Then why didn't you believe him?' [32]But if we say, 'From men' . . . ." (They feared the people, for everyone held that John really was a prophet.)[o]

[33]So they answered Jesus, "We don't know."

Jesus said, "Neither will I tell you by what authority I am doing these things."

The Parable of the Tenants
12:1–12pp — Mt 21:33–46; Lk 20:9–19

12 He then began to speak to them in parables: "A man planted a vineyard.[p] He put a wall around it, dug a pit for the winepress and built a watchtower. Then he rented the vineyard to some farmers and went away on a journey. [2]At harvest time he sent a servant to the tenants to collect from them some of the fruit of the vineyard. [3]But they seized him, beat him and sent him away empty-handed. [4]Then he sent another servant to them; they struck this man on the head and treated him shamefully. [5]He sent still another, and that one they killed. He sent many others; some of them they beat, others they killed.

11:17
g Jer 7:11
11:18
h Mt 21:46;
Mk 12:12;
Lk 20:19
i Mt 7:28
11:19
j Lk 21:37
11:21
k Mt 23:7
11:23
l Mt 21:21
11:24
m Mt 7:7
11:25
n Mt 6:14
11:32
o Mt 11:9
12:1
p Isa 5:1-7

---

[a]17 Jer. 7:11   [b]19 Some early manuscripts he   [c]22 Some early manuscripts If you have
[d]25 Some manuscripts sins. [26]But if you do not forgive, neither will your Father who is in heaven forgive your sins.

[6]"He had one left to send, a son, whom he loved. He sent him last of all,[q] saying, 'They will respect my son.'

[7]"But the tenants said to one another, 'This is the heir. Come, let's kill him, and the inheritance will be ours.' [8]So they took him and killed him, and threw him out of the vineyard.

[9]"What then will the owner of the vineyard do? He will come and kill those tenants and give the vineyard to others. [10]Haven't you read this scripture:

> " 'The stone the builders rejected
>   has become the capstone[a];[r]
> [11]the Lord has done this,
>   and it is marvelous in our eyes'[b]?"[s]

[12]Then they looked for a way to arrest him because they knew he had spoken the parable against them. But they were afraid of the crowd;[t] so they left him and went away.[u]

Paying Taxes to Caesar

12:13–17pp — Mt 22:15–22; Lk 20:20–26

[13]Later they sent some of the Pharisees and Herodians[v] to Jesus to catch him[w] in his words. [14]They came to him and said, "Teacher, we know you are a man of integrity. You aren't swayed by men, because you pay no attention to who they are; but you teach the way of God in accordance with the truth. Is it right to pay taxes to Caesar or not? [15]Should we pay or shouldn't we?"

But Jesus knew their hypocrisy. "Why are you trying to trap me?" he asked. "Bring me a denarius and let me look at it." [16]They brought the coin, and he asked them, "Whose portrait is this? And whose inscription?"

"Caesar's," they replied.

[17]Then Jesus said to them, "Give to Caesar what is Caesar's and to God what is God's."[x]

And they were amazed at him.

Marriage at the Resurrection

12:18–27pp — Mt 22:23–33; Lk 20:27–38

[18]Then the Sadducees,[y] who say there is no resurrection,[z] came to him with a question. [19]"Teacher," they said, "Moses wrote for us that if a man's brother dies and leaves a wife but no children, the man must marry the widow and have children for his brother.[a] [20]Now there were seven brothers. The first one married and died without leaving any children. [21]The second one married the widow, but he also died, leaving no child. It was the same with the third. [22]In fact, none of the seven left any children. Last of all, the woman died too. [23]At the resurrection[c] whose wife will she be, since the seven were married to her?"

[24]Jesus replied, "Are you not in error because you do not know the Scriptures[b] or the power of God? [25]When the dead rise, they will neither marry nor be given in marriage; they will be like the angels in heaven.[c] [26]Now about the dead rising—have you not read in the book

---

12:6
q Heb 1:1-3
12:10
r Ac 4:11
12:11
s Ps 118:22,23
12:12
t Mk 11:18
u Mt 22:22
12:13
v Mt 22:16;
Mk 3:6
w Mt 12:10
12:17
x Ro 13:7
12:18
y Ac 4:1
z Ac 23:8;
1Co 15:12
12:19
a Dt 25:5
12:24
b 2Ti 3:15-17
12:25
c 1Co 15:42,49,
52

---

[a]10 Or *cornerstone*   [b]11 Psalm 118:22,23   [c]23 Some manuscripts *resurrection, when men rise from the dead,*

of Moses, in the account of the bush, how God said to him, 'I am the God of Abraham, the God of Isaac, and the God of Jacob'*a*?*d* 27He is not the God of the dead, but of the living. You are badly mistaken!"

The Greatest Commandment
12:28-34pp — Mt 22:34-40

28One of the teachers of the law*e* came and heard them debating. Noticing that Jesus had given them a good answer, he asked him, "Of all the commandments, which is the most important?"

29"The most important one," answered Jesus, "is this: 'Hear, O Israel, the Lord our God, the Lord is one.*b* 30Love the Lord your God with all your heart and with all your soul and with all your mind and with all your strength.'*cf* 31The second is this: 'Love your neighbor as yourself.'*dg* There is no commandment greater than these."

32"Well said, teacher," the man replied. "You are right in saying that God is one and there is no other but him.*h* 33To love him with all your heart, with all your understanding and with all your strength, and to love your neighbor as yourself is more important than all burnt offerings and sacrifices."*i*

34When Jesus saw that he had answered wisely, he said to him, "You are not far from the kingdom of God."*j* And from then on no one dared ask him any more questions.*k*

Whose Son Is the Christ?
12:35-37pp — Mt 22:41-46; Lk 20:41-44
12:38-40pp — Mt 23:1-7; Lk 20:45-47

35While Jesus was teaching in the temple courts,*l* he asked, "How is it that the teachers of the law say that the Christ*e* is the son of David?*m* 36David himself, speaking by the Holy Spirit,*n* declared:

" 'The Lord said to my Lord:
"Sit at my right hand
until I put your enemies
under your feet." '*f,o*

37David himself calls him 'Lord.' How then can he be his son?"

The large crowd*p* listened to him with delight.

38As he taught, Jesus said, "Watch out for the teachers of the law. They like to walk around in flowing robes and be greeted in the marketplaces, 39and have the most important seats in the synagogues and the places of honor at banquets.*q* 40They devour widows' houses and for a show make lengthy prayers. Such men will be punished most severely."

The Widow's Offering
12:41-44pp — Lk 21:1-4

41Jesus sat down opposite the place where the offerings were put*r* and watched the crowd putting their money into the temple treasury. Many rich people threw in large amounts. 42But a poor widow came

12:26
dEx 3:6
12:28
eLk 10:25-28;
20:39
12:30
fDt 6:4,5
12:31
gLev 19:18;
Mt 5:43
12:32
hDt 4:35,39;
Isa 45:6,14;
46:9
12:33
i1Sa 15:22;
Hos 6:6;
Mic 6:6-8;
Heb 10:8
12:34
jMt 3:2
kMt 22:46;
Lk 20:40
12:35
lMt 26:55
mMt 9:27
12:36
n2Sa 23:2
oPs 110:1;
Mt 22:44
12:37
pJn 12:9
12:39
qLk 11:43
12:41
r2Ki 12:9;
Jn 8:20

---

*a*26 Exodus 3:6   *b*29 Or *the Lord our God is one Lord*   *c*30 Deut. 6:4,5   *d*31 Lev. 19:18
*e*35 Or *Messiah*   *f*36 Psalm 110:1

and put in two very small copper coins,[a] worth only a fraction of a penny.[b]

43Calling his disciples to him, Jesus said, "I tell you the truth, this poor widow has put more into the treasury than all the others. 44They all gave out of their wealth; but she, out of her poverty, put in everything—all she had to live on."[s]

Signs of the End of the Age

13:1–37pp — Mt 24:1–51; Lk 21:5–36

13 As he was leaving the temple, one of his disciples said to him, "Look, Teacher! What massive stones! What magnificent buildings!"

2"Do you see all these great buildings?" replied Jesus. "Not one stone here will be left on another; every one will be thrown down."[t]

3As Jesus was sitting on the Mount of Olives[u] opposite the temple, Peter, James, John[v] and Andrew asked him privately, 4"Tell us, when will these things happen? And what will be the sign that they are all about to be fulfilled?"

5Jesus said to them: "Watch out that no one deceives you.[w] 6Many will come in my name, claiming, 'I am he,' and will deceive many. 7When you hear of wars and rumors of wars, do not be alarmed. Such things must happen, but the end is still to come. 8Nation will rise against nation, and kingdom against kingdom. There will be earthquakes in various places, and famines. These are the beginning of birth pains.

9"You must be on your guard. You will be handed over to the local councils and flogged in the synagogues.[x] On account of me you will stand before governors and kings as witnesses to them. 10And the gospel must first be preached to all nations. 11Whenever you are arrested and brought to trial, do not worry beforehand about what to say. Just say whatever is given you at the time, for it is not you speaking, but the Holy Spirit.[y]

12"Brother will betray brother to death, and a father his child. Children will rebel against their parents and have them put to death.[z] 13All men will hate you because of me,[a] but he who stands firm to the end will be saved.[b]

14"When you see 'the abomination that causes desolation'[cc] standing where it[d] does not belong—let the reader understand—then let those who are in Judea flee to the mountains. 15Let no one on the roof of his house go down or enter the house to take anything out. 16Let no one in the field go back to get his cloak. 17How dreadful it will be in those days for pregnant women and nursing mothers![d] 18Pray that this will not take place in winter, 19because those will be days of distress unequaled from the beginning, when God created the world,[e] until now—and never to be equaled again.[f] 20If the Lord had not cut short those days, no one would survive. But for the sake of the elect, whom he has chosen, he has shortened them. 21At that time if anyone says to you, 'Look, here is the Christ[e]!' or, 'Look, there he is!' do not believe it.[g] 22For false Christs and false prophets[h] will appear and perform

12:44
s2Co 8:12
13:2
tLk 19:44
13:3
uMt 21:1
vMt 4:21
13:5
wver 22;
Jer 29:8;
Eph 5:6;
2Th 2:3,10-12;
1Ti 4:1;
2Ti 3:13;
1Jn 4:6
13:9
xMt 10:17
13:11
yMt 10:19,20;
Lk 12:11,12
13:12
zMic 7:6;
Mt 10:21;
Lk 12:51-53
13:13
aJn 15:21
bMt 10:22
13:14
cDa 9:27;
11:31; 12:11
13:17
dLk 23:29
13:19
eMk 10:6
fDa 9:26; 12:1;
Joel 2:2
13:21
gLk 17:23; 21:8
13:22
hMt 7:15

---

a42 Greek *two lepta*   b42 Greek *kodrantes*   c14 Daniel 9:27; 11:31; 12:11   d14 Or *he;* also in verse 29   e21 Or *Messiah* signs and miracles[i] to deceive the elect—if that were possible. 23So be on your guard;[j] I have told you everything ahead of time. 24"But in those days, following that distress,

> " 'the sun will be darkened,
> and the moon will not give its light;
> 25the stars will fall from the sky,
> and the heavenly bodies will be shaken.'[a] [k]

26"At that time men will see the Son of Man coming in clouds[l] with great power and glory. 27And he will send his angels and gather his elect from the four winds, from the ends of the earth to the ends of the heavens. [m]

28"Now learn this lesson from the fig tree: As soon as its twigs get tender and its leaves come out, you know that summer is near. 29Even so, when you see these things happening, you know that it is near, right at the door. 30I tell you the truth, this generation[b] [n] will certainly not pass away until all these things have happened. [o] 31Heaven and earth will pass away, but my words will never pass away. [p]

The Day and Hour Unknown

32"No one knows about that day or hour, not even the angels in heaven, nor the Son, but only the Father. [q] 33Be on guard! Be alert[c] ![r] You do not know when that time will come. 34It's like a man going away: He leaves his house and puts his servants[s] in charge, each with his assigned task, and tells the one at the door to keep watch.

35"Therefore keep watch because you do not know when the owner of the house will come back—whether in the evening, or at midnight, or when the rooster crows, or at dawn. 36If he comes suddenly, do not let him find you sleeping. 37What I say to you, I say to everyone: 'Watch!' "[t]

Jesus Anointed at Bethany

14:1–11pp — Mt 26:2–16
14:1,2,10,11pp — Lk 22:1–6
14:3–8Ref — Jn 12:1–8

14 Now the Passover[u] and the Feast of Unleavened Bread were only two days away, and the chief priests and the teachers of the law were looking for some sly way to arrest Jesus and kill him. [v] 2"But not during the Feast," they said, "or the people may riot."

3While he was in Bethany, [w] reclining at the table in the home of a man known as Simon the Leper, a woman came with an alabaster jar of very expensive perfume, made of pure nard. She broke the jar and poured the perfume on his head. [x]

4Some of those present were saying indignantly to one another, "Why this waste of perfume? 5It could have been sold for more than a year's wages[d] and the money given to the poor." And they rebuked her harshly.

6"Leave her alone," said Jesus. "Why are you bothering her? She has done a beautiful thing to me. 7The poor you will always have with you, and you can help them any time you want. [y] But you will not always

13:22
i Jn 4:48;
2Th 2:9,10
13:23
j 2Pe 3:17
13:25
k Isa 13:10;
34:4; Mt 24:29
13:26
l Da 7:13;
Mt 16:27;
Rev 1:7
13:27
m Zec 2:6
13:30
n Mk 9:1
o Lk 17:25
13:31
p Mt 5:18
13:32
q Ac 1:7;
1Th 5:1,2
13:33
r 1Th 5:6
13:34
s Mt 25:14
13:37
t Lk 12:35-40
14:1
u Jn 11:55; 13:1
v Mt 12:14
14:3
w Mt 21:17
x Lk 7:37-39
14:7
y Dt 15:11

---

[a]25 Isaiah 13:10; 34:4   [b]30 Or *race*   [c]33 Some manuscripts *alert and pray*   [d]5 Greek *than three hundred denarii*

have me. [8]She did what she could. She poured perfume on my body beforehand to prepare for my burial.[z] [9]I tell you the truth, wherever the gospel is preached throughout the world,[a] what she has done will also be told, in memory of her."

[10]Then Judas Iscariot, one of the Twelve,[b] went to the chief priests to betray Jesus to them.[c] [11]They were delighted to hear this and promised to give him money. So he watched for an opportunity to hand him over.

The Lord's Supper

14:12–26pp — Mt 26:17–30; Lk 22:7–23
14:22–25pp — 1Co 11:23–25

[12]On the first day of the Feast of Unleavened Bread, when it was customary to sacrifice the Passover lamb,[d] Jesus' disciples asked him, "Where do you want us to go and make preparations for you to eat the Passover?"

[13]So he sent two of his disciples, telling them, "Go into the city, and a man carrying a jar of water will meet you. Follow him. [14]Say to the owner of the house he enters, 'The Teacher asks: Where is my guest room, where I may eat the Passover with my disciples?' [15]He will show you a large upper room,[e] furnished and ready. Make preparations for us there."

[16]The disciples left, went into the city and found things just as Jesus had told them. So they prepared the Passover.

[17]When evening came, Jesus arrived with the Twelve. [18]While they were reclining at the table eating, he said, "I tell you the truth, one of you will betray me—one who is eating with me."

[19]They were saddened, and one by one they said to him, "Surely not I?"

[20]"It is one of the Twelve," he replied, "one who dips bread into the bowl with me.[f] [21]The Son of Man[g] will go just as it is written about him. But woe to that man who betrays the Son of Man! It would be better for him if he had not been born."

[22]While they were eating, Jesus took bread, gave thanks and broke it,[h] and gave it to his disciples, saying, "Take it; this is my body."

[23]Then he took the cup, gave thanks and offered it to them, and they all drank from it.[i]

[24]"This is my blood of the[a] covenant,[j] which is poured out for many," he said to them. [25]"I tell you the truth, I will not drink again of the fruit of the vine until that day when I drink it anew in the kingdom of God."[k]

[26]When they had sung a hymn, they went out to the Mount of Olives.[l]

Jesus Predicts Peter's Denial

14:27–31pp — Mt 26:31–35

[27]"You will all fall away," Jesus told them, "for it is written:

" 'I will strike the shepherd,
and the sheep will be scattered.'[b] [m]

14:8
z Jn 19:40
14:9
a Mt 24:14;
Mk 16:15
14:10
b Mk 3:16-19
c Mt 10:4
14:12
d Ex 12:1-11;
Dt 16:1-4;
1Co 5:7
14:15
e Ac 1:13
14:20
f Jn 13:18-27
14:21
g Mt 8:20
14:22
h Mt 14:19
14:23
i 1Co 10:16
14:24
j Mt 26:28
14:25
k Mk 3:2
14:26
l Mt 21:1
14:27
m Zec 13:7

---

[a]24 Some manuscripts *the new*   [b]27 Zech. 13:7

[28]But after I have risen, I will go ahead of you into Galilee."[n]

[29]Peter declared, "Even if all fall away, I will not."

[30]"I tell you the truth," Jesus answered, "today—yes, tonight—before the rooster crows twice[a] you yourself will disown me three times."[o]

[31]But Peter insisted emphatically, "Even if I have to die with you,[p] I will never disown you." And all the others said the same.

Gethsemane

14:32-42pp — Mt 26:36-46; Lk 22:40-46

[32]They went to a place called Gethsemane, and Jesus said to his disciples, "Sit here while I pray." [33]He took Peter, James and John[q] along with him, and he began to be deeply distressed and troubled. [34]"My soul is overwhelmed with sorrow to the point of death,"[r] he said to them. "Stay here and keep watch."

[35]Going a little farther, he fell to the ground and prayed that if possible the hour[s] might pass from him. [36]"Abba,[b] Father,"[t] he said, "everything is possible for you. Take this cup[u] from me. Yet not what I will, but what you will."[v]

[37]Then he returned to his disciples and found them sleeping. "Simon," he said to Peter, "are you asleep? Could you not keep watch for one hour? [38]Watch and pray so that you will not fall into temptation.[w] The spirit is willing, but the body is weak."[x]

[39]Once more he went away and prayed the same thing. [40]When he came back, he again found them sleeping, because their eyes were heavy. They did not know what to say to him.

[41]Returning the third time, he said to them, "Are you still sleeping and resting? Enough! The hour[y] has come. Look, the Son of Man is betrayed into the hands of sinners. [42]Rise! Let us go! Here comes my betrayer!"

Jesus Arrested

14:43-50pp — Mt 26:47-56; Lk 22:47-50; Jn 18:3-11

[43]Just as he was speaking, Judas,[z] one of the Twelve, appeared. With him was a crowd armed with swords and clubs, sent from the chief priests, the teachers of the law, and the elders.

[44]Now the betrayer had arranged a signal with them: "The one I kiss is the man; arrest him and lead him away under guard." [45]Going at once to Jesus, Judas said, "Rabbi!"[a] and kissed him. [46]The men seized Jesus and arrested him. [47]Then one of those standing near drew his sword and struck the servant of the high priest, cutting off his ear.

[48]"Am I leading a rebellion," said Jesus, "that you have come out with swords and clubs to capture me? [49]Every day I was with you, teaching in the temple courts,[b] and you did not arrest me. But the Scriptures must be fulfilled."[c] [50]Then everyone deserted him and fled.[d]

[51]A young man, wearing nothing but a linen garment, was following Jesus. When they seized him, [52]he fled naked, leaving his garment behind.

---

a30 Some early manuscripts do not have *twice*.   b36 Aramaic for *Father*

14:28
nMk 16:7
14:30
over 66-72;
Lk 22:34;
Jn 13:38
14:31
pLk 22:33;
Jn 13:37
14:33
qMt 4:21
14:34
rJn 12:27
14:35
sver 41;
Mt 26:18
14:36
tRo 8:15;
Gal 4:6
uMt 20:22
vMt 26:39
14:38
wMt 6:13
xRo 7:22,23
14:41
yver 35;
Mt 26:18
14:43
zMt 10:4
14:45
aMt 23:7
14:49
bMt 26:55
cIsa 53:7-12;
Mt 1:22
14:50
dver 27

Before the Sanhedrin

14:53–65pp — Mt 26:57–68; Jn 18:12,13,19–24
14:61–63pp — Lk 22:67–71

⁵³They took Jesus to the high priest, and all the chief priests, elders and teachers of the law came together. ⁵⁴Peter followed him at a distance, right into the courtyard of the high priest. ᵉ There he sat with the guards and warmed himself at the fire. ᶠ

⁵⁵The chief priests and the whole Sanhedrinᵍ were looking for evidence against Jesus so that they could put him to death, but they did not find any. ⁵⁶Many testified falsely against him, but their statements did not agree.

⁵⁷Then some stood up and gave this false testimony against him: ⁵⁸"We heard him say, 'I will destroy this man-made temple and in three days will build another, ʰ not made by man.'" ⁵⁹Yet even then their testimony did not agree.

⁶⁰Then the high priest stood up before them and asked Jesus, "Are you not going to answer? What is this testimony that these men are bringing against you?" ⁶¹But Jesus remained silent and gave no answer. ⁱ

Again the high priest asked him, "Are you the Christ,ᵃ the Son of the Blessed One?"ʲ

⁶²"I am," said Jesus. "And you will see the Son of Man sitting at the right hand of the Mighty One and coming on the clouds of heaven."ᵏ

⁶³The high priest tore his clothes.ˡ "Why do we need any more witnesses?" he asked. ⁶⁴"You have heard the blasphemy. What do you think?"

They all condemned him as worthy of death. ᵐ ⁶⁵Then some began to spit at him; they blindfolded him, struck him with their fists, and said, "Prophesy!" And the guards took him and beat him. ⁿ

Peter Disowns Jesus

14:66–72pp — Mt 26:69–75; Lk 22:56–62; Jn 18:16–18,25–27

⁶⁶While Peter was below in the courtyard, ᵒ one of the servant girls of the high priest came by. ⁶⁷When she saw Peter warming himself, ᵖ she looked closely at him.

"You also were with that Nazarene, Jesus,"�q she said.

⁶⁸But he denied it. "I don't know or understand what you're talking about,"ʳ he said, and went out into the entryway. ᵇ

⁶⁹When the servant girl saw him there, she said again to those standing around, "This fellow is one of them." ⁷⁰Again he denied it. ˢ

After a little while, those standing near said to Peter, "Surely you are one of them, for you are a Galilean."ᵗ

⁷¹He began to call down curses on himself, and he swore to them, "I don't know this man you're talking about."ᵘ

⁷²Immediately the rooster crowed the second time. ᶜ Then Peter remembered the word Jesus had spoken to him: "Before the rooster crows twiceᵈ you will disown me three times."ᵛ And he broke down and wept.

14:54
eMt 26:3
fJn 18:18
14:55
gMt 5:22
14:58
hMk 15:29;
Jn 2:19
14:61
iIsa 53:7;
Mt 27:12,14;
Mk 15:5;
Lk 23:9; Jn 19:9
jMt 16:16;
Jn 4:25,26
14:62
kRev 1:7
14:63
lLev 10:6;
21:10; Nu 14:6;
Ac 14:14
14:64
mLev 24:16
14:65
nMt 16:21
14:66
over 54
14:67
pver 54
qMk 1:24
14:68
rver 30,72
14:70
sver 30,68,72
tAc 2:7
14:71
uver 30,72
14:72
vver 30,68

ᵃ61 Or *Messiah*   ᵇ68 Some early manuscripts *entryway and the rooster crowed*   ᶜ72 Some early manuscripts do not have *the second time.*   ᵈ72 Some early manuscripts do not have *twice.*

Jesus Before Pilate

15:2–15pp — Mt 27:11–26; Lk 23:2,3,18–25; Jn 18:29–19:16

15 Very early in the morning, the chief priests, with the elders, the teachers of the law[w] and the whole Sanhedrin,[x] reached a decision. They bound Jesus, led him away and handed him over to Pilate.[y]

2"Are you the king of the Jews?"[z] asked Pilate.

"Yes, it is as you say," Jesus replied.

3The chief priests accused him of many things. 4So again Pilate asked him, "Aren't you going to answer? See how many things they are accusing you of."

5But Jesus still made no reply,[a] and Pilate was amazed.

6Now it was the custom at the Feast to release a prisoner whom the people requested. 7A man called Barabbas was in prison with the insurrectionists who had committed murder in the uprising. 8The crowd came up and asked Pilate to do for them what he usually did.

9"Do you want me to release to you the king of the Jews?"[b] asked Pilate, 10knowing it was out of envy that the chief priests had handed Jesus over to him. 11But the chief priests stirred up the crowd to have Pilate release Barabbas[c] instead.

12"What shall I do, then, with the one you call the king of the Jews?" Pilate asked them.

13"Crucify him!" they shouted.

14"Why? What crime has he committed?" asked Pilate.

But they shouted all the louder, "Crucify him!"

15Wanting to satisfy the crowd, Pilate released Barabbas to them. He had Jesus flogged,[d] and handed him over to be crucified.

The Soldiers Mock Jesus

15:16–20pp — Mt 27:27–31

16The soldiers led Jesus away into the palace[e] (that is, the Praetorium) and called together the whole company of soldiers. 17They put a purple robe on him, then twisted together a crown of thorns and set it on him. 18And they began to call out to him, "Hail, king of the Jews!"[f] 19Again and again they struck him on the head with a staff and spit on him. Falling on their knees, they paid homage to him. 20And when they had mocked him, they took off the purple robe and put his own clothes on him. Then they led him out[g] to crucify him.

The Crucifixion

15:22–32pp — Mt 27:33–44; Lk 23:33–43; Jn 19:17–24

21A certain man from Cyrene,[h] Simon, the father of Alexander and Rufus,[i] was passing by on his way in from the country, and they forced him to carry the cross.[j] 22They brought Jesus to the place called Golgotha (which means The Place of the Skull). 23Then they offered him wine mixed with myrrh,[k] but he did not take it. 24And they crucified him. Dividing up his clothes, they cast lots[l] to see what each would get.

25It was the third hour when they crucified him. 26The written notice of the charge against him read: THE KING OF THE JEWS.[m] 27They crucified two robbers with him, one on his right and one on his left.[a] 29Those

---

15:1
wMt 27:1;
Lk 22:66
xMt 5:22
yMt 27:2
15:2
zver 9,12,18,26;
Mt 2:2
15:5
aMk 14:61
15:9
bver 2
15:11
cAc 3:14
15:15
dIsa 53:6
15:16
eJn 18:28,33;
19:9
15:18
fver 2
15:20
gHeb 13:12
15:21
hMt 27:32
iRo 16:13
jMt 27:32;
Lk 23:26
15:23
kver 36;
Ps 69:21;
Pr 31:6
15:24
lPs 22:18
15:26
mver 2

---

a27 Some manuscripts *left,* 28*and the scripture was fulfilled which says, "He was counted with the lawless ones"* (Isaiah 53:12) who passed by hurled insults at him, shaking their heads[n] and saying, "So! You who are going to destroy the temple and build it in three days,[o] 30come down from the cross and save yourself!"

31In the same way the chief priests and the teachers of the law mocked him[p] among themselves. "He saved others," they said, "but he can't save himself! 32Let this Christ,[a][q] this King of Israel,[r] come down now from the cross, that we may see and believe." Those crucified with him also heaped insults on him.

The Death of Jesus

15:33–41pp — Mt 27:45–56; Lk 23:44–49

33At the sixth hour darkness came over the whole land until the ninth hour.[s] 34And at the ninth hour Jesus cried out in a loud voice, *"Eloi, Eloi, lama sabachthani?"*—which means, "My God, my God, why have you forsaken me?"[b][t]

35When some of those standing near heard this, they said, "Listen, he's calling Elijah."

36One man ran, filled a sponge with wine vinegar,[u] put it on a stick, and offered it to Jesus to drink. "Now leave him alone. Let's see if Elijah comes to take him down," he said.

37With a loud cry, Jesus breathed his last.[v]

38The curtain of the temple was torn in two from top to bottom.[w] 39And when the centurion,[x] who stood there in front of Jesus, heard his cry and[c] saw how he died, he said, "Surely this man was the Son[d] of God!"[y]

40Some women were watching from a distance.[z] Among them were Mary Magdalene, Mary the mother of James the younger and of Joses, and Salome.[a] 41In Galilee these women had followed him and cared for his needs. Many other women who had come up with him to Jerusalem were also there.[b]

The Burial of Jesus

15:42–47pp — Mt 27:57–61; Lk 23:50–56; Jn 19:38–42

42It was Preparation Day (that is, the day before the Sabbath).[c] So as evening approached, 43Joseph of Arimathea, a prominent member of the Council,[d] who was himself waiting for the kingdom of God,[e] went boldly to Pilate and asked for Jesus' body. 44Pilate was surprised to hear that he was already dead. Summoning the centurion, he asked him if Jesus had already died. 45When he learned from the centurion[f] that it was so, he gave the body to Joseph. 46So Joseph bought some linen cloth, took down the body, wrapped it in the linen, and placed it in a tomb cut out of rock. Then he rolled a stone against the entrance of the tomb.[g] 47Mary Magdalene and Mary the mother of Joses[h] saw where he was laid.

The Resurrection

16:1–8pp — Mt 28:1–8; Lk 24:1–10

16 When the Sabbath was over, Mary Magdalene, Mary the mother of James, and Salome bought spices[i] so that they might go to

### Cross references (margin)

15:29
n Ps 22:7; 109:25
o Mk 14:58; Jn 2:19
15:31
p Ps 22:7
15:32
q Mk 14:61
r ver 2
15:33
s Am 8:9
15:34
t Ps 22:1
15:36
u ver 23; Ps 69:21
15:37
v Jn 19:30
15:38
w Heb 10:19,20
15:39
x ver 45
y Mk 1:1,11; 9:7; Mt 4:3
15:40
z Ps 38:11
a Mk 16:1; Lk 24:10; Jn 19:25
15:41
b Mt 27:55,56; Lk 8:2,3
15:42
c Mt 27:62; Jn 19:31
15:43
d Mt 5:22
e Mt 3:2; Lk 2:25,38
15:45
f ver 39
15:46
g Mk 16:3
15:47
h ver 40
16:1
i Lk 23:56; Jn 19:39,40

---

a32 Or *Messiah*   b34 Psalm 22:1   c39 Some manuscripts do not have *heard his cry and.*
d39 Or *a son*

anoint Jesus' body. ²Very early on the first day of the week, just after sunrise, they were on their way to the tomb ³and they asked each other, "Who will roll the stone away from the entrance of the tomb?"ʲ

⁴But when they looked up, they saw that the stone, which was very large, had been rolled away. ⁵As they entered the tomb, they saw a young man dressed in a white robeᵏ sitting on the right side, and they were alarmed.

⁶"Don't be alarmed," he said. "You are looking for Jesus the Nazarene,ˡ who was crucified. He has risen! He is not here. See the place where they laid him. ⁷But go, tell his disciples and Peter, 'He is going ahead of you into Galilee. There you will see him,ᵐ just as he told you.'"ⁿ

⁸Trembling and bewildered, the women went out and fled from the tomb. They said nothing to anyone, because they were afraid.

[The most reliable early manuscripts and other ancient witnesses do not have Mark 16:9–20.]

⁹When Jesus rose early on the first day of the week, he appeared first to Mary Magdalene,ᵒ out of whom he had driven seven demons. ¹⁰She went and told those who had been with him and who were mourning and weeping. ¹¹When they heard that Jesus was alive and that she had seen him, they did not believe it.ᵖ

¹²Afterward Jesus appeared in a different form to two of them while they were walking in the country.�q ¹³These returned and reported it to the rest; but they did not believe them either.

¹⁴Later Jesus appeared to the Eleven as they were eating; he rebuked them for their lack of faith and their stubborn refusal to believe those who had seen him after he had risen.ʳ

¹⁵He said to them, "Go into all the world and preach the good news to all creation.ˢ ¹⁶Whoever believes and is baptized will be saved, but whoever does not believe will be condemned.ᵗ ¹⁷And these signs will accompany those who believe: In my name they will drive out demons;ᵘ they will speak in new tongues;ᵛ ¹⁸they will pick up snakesʷ with their hands; and when they drink deadly poison, it will not hurt them at all; they will place their hands onˣ sick people, and they will get well."

¹⁹After the Lord Jesus had spoken to them, he was taken up into heavenʸ and he sat at the right hand of God.ᶻ ²⁰Then the disciples went out and preached everywhere, and the Lord worked with them and confirmed his word by the signs that accompanied it.

16:3
ʲMk 15:46
16:5
ᵏJn 20:12
16:6
ˡMk 1:24
16:7
ᵐJn 21:1-23
ⁿMk 14:28
16:9
ᵒJn 20:11-18
16:11
ᵖver 13,14;
Lk 24:11
16:12
qLk 24:13-32
16:14
ʳLk 24:36-43
16:15
ˢMt 28:18-20;
Lk 24:47,48
16:16
ᵗJn 3:16,18,36;
Ac 16:31
16:17
ᵘMk 9:38;
Lk 10:17;
Ac 5:16; 8:7;
16:18; 19:13-16
ᵛAc 2:4; 10:46;
19:6;
1Co 12:10,28,30
16:18
ʷLk 10:19;
Ac 28:3-5
ˣAc 6:6
16:19
ʸLk 24:50,51;
Jn 6:62;
Ac 1:9-11;
1Ti 3:16
ᶻPs 110:1;
Ro 8:34;
Col 3:1;
Heb 1:3; 12:2

Luke

Title and Background

The Gospel of Luke has been called the most beautiful book ever written. Luke's writing shows him to be a highly educated man, one who wrote from a Greek background and viewpoint. He wrote especially with Gentiles in mind, for he explained Jewish customs and traced the genealogy of Jesus back to Adam.

Author and Date of Writing

The author's name does not appear in the book, but much unmistakable evidence points to Luke. This Gospel is a companion volume to the book of Acts, and the language and structure of these books indicate that both were written by the same person. Luke was probably a Gentile by birth, well educated in Greek culture, a physician by profession and a companion of Paul at various times. The book was probably written between A.D. 59 and 63.

Theme and Message

Luke tells us in the first four verses of his book that he wrote this Gospel to give the true and complete story of Jesus' life. He wrote the fullest and most orderly story of his life. One of Luke's interests in writing this book was to show that Jesus loved all kinds of people. In the parables especially, he wrote about the poor and oppressed. The theme of joy is felt throughout the book, as Christ's coming brought joy as well as hope and salvation to a sinful world.

Outline

1:2
aMk 1:1;
Jn 15:27;
Ac 1:21,22
bHeb 2:3;
1Pe 5:1;
2Pe 1:16;
1Jn 1:1
cMk 4:14
1:3
dAc 11:4
eAc 24:3; 26:25
fAc 1:1
1:4
gJn 20:31

Introduction

1:1–4Ref — Ac 1:1

1 Many have undertaken to draw up an account of the things that have been fulfilled[a] among us, ²just as they were handed down to us by those who from the first[a] were eyewitnesses[b] and servants of the word.[c] ³Therefore, since I myself have carefully investigated everything from the beginning, it seemed good also to me to write an orderly account[d] for you, most excellent[e] Theophilus,[f] ⁴so that you may know the certainty of the things you have been taught.[g]

a1 Or been surely believed

The Birth of John the Baptist Foretold

⁵In the time of Herod king of Judea[h] there was a priest named Zechariah, who belonged to the priestly division of Abijah;[i] his wife Elizabeth was also a descendant of Aaron. ⁶Both of them were upright in the sight of God, observing all the Lord's commandments and regulations blamelessly.[j] ⁷But they had no children, because Elizabeth was barren; and they were both well along in years.

⁸Once when Zechariah's division was on duty and he was serving as priest before God,[k] ⁹he was chosen by lot, according to the custom of the priesthood, to go into the temple of the Lord and burn incense.[l] ¹⁰And when the time for the burning of incense came, all the assembled worshipers were praying outside.[m]

¹¹Then an angel[n] of the Lord appeared to him, standing at the right side of the altar of incense.[o] ¹²When Zechariah saw him, he was startled and was gripped with fear.[p] ¹³But the angel said to him: "Do not be afraid,[q] Zechariah; your prayer has been heard. Your wife Elizabeth will bear you a son, and you are to give him the name John.[r] ¹⁴He will be a joy and delight to you, and many will rejoice because of his birth,[s] ¹⁵for he will be great in the sight of the Lord. He is never to take wine or other fermented drink,[t] and he will be filled with the Holy Spirit even from birth.[a][u] ¹⁶Many of the people of Israel will he bring back to the Lord their God. ¹⁷And he will go on before the Lord,[v] in the spirit and power of Elijah,[w] to turn the hearts of the fathers to their children[x] and the disobedient to the wisdom of the righteous—to make ready a people prepared for the Lord."

¹⁸Zechariah asked the angel, "How can I be sure of this? I am an old man and my wife is well along in years."[y]

¹⁹The angel answered, "I am Gabriel.[z] I stand in the presence of God, and I have been sent to speak to you and to tell you this good news. ²⁰And now you will be silent and not able to speak[a] until the day this happens, because you did not believe my words, which will come true at their proper time."

²¹Meanwhile, the people were waiting for Zechariah and wondering why he stayed so long in the temple. ²²When he came out, he could not speak to them. They realized he had seen a vision in the temple, for he kept making signs[b] to them but remained unable to speak.

²³When his time of service was completed, he returned home. ²⁴After this his wife Elizabeth became pregnant and for five months remained in seclusion. ²⁵"The Lord has done this for me," she said. "In these days he has shown his favor and taken away my disgrace[c] among the people."

The Birth of Jesus Foretold

²⁶In the sixth month, God sent the angel Gabriel[d] to Nazareth,[e] a town in Galilee, ²⁷to a virgin pledged to be married to a man named Joseph,[f] a descendant of David. The virgin's name was Mary. ²⁸The angel went to her and said, "Greetings, you who are highly favored! The Lord is with you."

²⁹Mary was greatly troubled at his words and wondered what kind of

---

1:5
h Mt 2:1
i 1Ch 24:10
1:6
j Ge 7:1; 1Ki 9:4
1:8
k 1Ch 24:19;
2Ch 8:14
1:9
l Ex 30:7,8;
1Ch 23:13;
2Ch 29:11
1:10
m Lev 16:17
1:11
n Ac 5:19
o Ex 30:1-10
1:12
p Jdg 6:22,23;
13:22
1:13
q ver 30;
Mt 14:27
r ver 60,63
1:14
s ver 58
1:15
t Nu 6:3;
Jdg 13:4;
Lk 7:33
u Jer 1:5;
Gal 1:15
1:17
v ver 76
w Mt 11:14
x Mal 4:5,6
1:18
y ver 34;
Ge 17:17
1:19
z ver 26;
Mt 18:10;
Da 8:16; 9:21
1:20
a Eze 3:26
1:22
b ver 62
1:25
c Ge 30:23;
Isa 4:1
1:26
d ver 19
e Mt 2:23
1:27
f Mt 1:16,18,20;
Lk 2:4

---

[a]15 Or *from his mother's womb*

greeting this might be. [30]But the angel said to her, "Do not be afraid, [g] Mary, you have found favor with God. [31]You will be with child and give birth to a son, and you are to give him the name Jesus. [h] [32]He will be great and will be called the Son of the Most High. [i] The Lord God will give him the throne of his father David, [33]and he will reign over the house of Jacob forever; his kingdom[j] will never end."[k]

[34]"How will this be," Mary asked the angel, "since I am a virgin?"

[35]The angel answered, "The Holy Spirit will come upon you,[l] and the power of the Most High[m] will overshadow you. So the holy one[n] to be born will be called[a] the Son of God. [o] [36]Even Elizabeth your relative is going to have a child in her old age, and she who was said to be barren is in her sixth month. [37]For nothing is impossible with God."[p]

[38]"I am the Lord's servant," Mary answered. "May it be to me as you have said." Then the angel left her.

Mary Visits Elizabeth

[39]At that time Mary got ready and hurried to a town in the hill country of Judea,[q] [40]where she entered Zechariah's home and greeted Elizabeth. [41]When Elizabeth heard Mary's greeting, the baby leaped in her womb, and Elizabeth was filled with the Holy Spirit. [42]In a loud voice she exclaimed: "Blessed are you among women,[r] and blessed is the child you will bear! [43]But why am I so favored, that the mother of my Lord should come to me? [44]As soon as the sound of your greeting reached my ears, the baby in my womb leaped for joy. [45]Blessed is she who has believed that what the Lord has said to her will be accomplished!"

Mary's Song

1:46–53pp — 1Sa 2:1–10

[46]And Mary said:

> "My soul glorifies the Lord[s]
> [47]   and my spirit rejoices in God my Savior,[t]
> [48]for he has been mindful
>   of the humble state of his servant. [u]
> From now on all generations will call me blessed,[v]
> [49]   for the Mighty One has done great things[w] for me—
>   holy is his name. [x]
> [50]His mercy extends to those who fear him,
>   from generation to generation.[y]
> [51]He has performed mighty deeds with his arm;[z]
>   he has scattered those who are proud in their inmost
>   thoughts.
> [52]He has brought down rulers from their thrones
>   but has lifted up the humble.
> [53]He has filled the hungry with good things[a]
>   but has sent the rich away empty.
> [54]He has helped his servant Israel,
>   remembering to be merciful[b]

---

[a]35 Or *So the child to be born will be called holy,*

1:30
gver 13;
Mt 14:27
1:31
hIsa 7:14;
Mt 1:21,25;
Lk 2:21
1:32
iver 35,76;
Mk 5:7
1:33
jMt 28:18
kDa 2:44; 7:14,
27; Mic 4:7;
Heb 1:8
1:35
lMt 1:18
mver 32,76
nMk 1:24
oMt 4:3
1:37
pMt 19:26
1:39
qver 65
1:42
rJdg 5:24
1:46
sPs 34:2,3
1:47
t1Ti 1:1; 2:3
1:48
uPs 138:6
vLk 11:27
1:49
wPs 71:19
xPs 111:9
1:50
yEx 20:6;
Ps 103:17
1:51
zPs 98:1;
Isa 40:10
1:53
aPs 107:9
1:54
bPs 98:3

⁵⁵to Abraham and his descendants ͨ forever,
      even as he said to our fathers."

⁵⁶Mary stayed with Elizabeth for about three months and then returned home.

The Birth of John the Baptist

⁵⁷When it was time for Elizabeth to have her baby, she gave birth to a son. ⁵⁸Her neighbors and relatives heard that the Lord had shown her great mercy, and they shared her joy.

⁵⁹On the eighth day they came to circumcise ͩ the child, and they were going to name him after his father Zechariah, ⁶⁰but his mother spoke up and said, "No! He is to be called John." ͤ

⁶¹They said to her, "There is no one among your relatives who has that name."

⁶²Then they made signs ͛ to his father, to find out what he would like to name the child. ⁶³He asked for a writing tablet, and to everyone's astonishment he wrote, "His name is John." ͢ ⁶⁴Immediately his mouth was opened and his tongue was loosed, and he began to speak, ͪ praising God. ⁶⁵The neighbors were all filled with awe, and throughout the hill country of Judea ͥ people were talking about all these things. ⁶⁶Everyone who heard this wondered about it, asking, "What then is this child going to be?" For the Lord's hand was with him. ͪ

Zechariah's Song

⁶⁷His father Zechariah was filled with the Holy Spirit and prophesied: ͫ

⁶⁸"Praise be to the Lord, the God of Israel, ͥ
      because he has come and has redeemed his people. ͫ
⁶⁹He has raised up a horn ͣͫ of salvation for us
      in the house of his servant David ͦ
⁷⁰(as he said through his holy prophets of long ago), ͬ
⁷¹salvation from our enemies
      and from the hand of all who hate us—
⁷²to show mercy to our fathers ͨ
      and to remember his holy covenant, ͬ
⁷³   the oath he swore to our father Abraham: ˢ
⁷⁴to rescue us from the hand of our enemies,
      and to enable us to serve him ͭ without fear
⁷⁵   in holiness and righteousness ͩ before him all our days.

⁷⁶And you, my child, will be called a prophet ͮ of the Most
         High; ͫ
      for you will go on before the Lord to prepare the way
         for him, ͯ
⁷⁷to give his people the knowledge of salvation
      through the forgiveness of their sins, ͤ
⁷⁸because of the tender mercy of our God,
      by which the rising sun ͱ will come to us from heaven
⁷⁹to shine on those living in darkness

ͣ69 *Horn* here symbolizes strength.

1:55
cGe 17:19;
Ps 132:11;
Gal 3:16
1:59
dGe 17:12;
Lev 12:3;
Lk 2:21;
Php 3:5
1:60
ever 13,63
1:62
fver 22
1:63
gver 13,60
1:64
hver 20
1:65
iver 39
1:66
jGe 39:2;
Ac 11:21
1:67
kJoel 2:28
1:68
lPs 72:18
mPs 111:9;
Lk 7:16
1:69
n1Sa 2:1,10;
Ps 18:2; 89:17;
132:17;
Eze 29:21
oMt 1:1
1:70
pJer 23:5
1:72
qMic 7:20
rPs 105:8,9;
106:45;
Eze 16:60
1:73
sGe 22:16-18
1:74
tHeb 9:14
1:75
uEph 4:24
1:76
vMt 11:9
wver 32,35
xver 17; Mal 3:1
1:77
yJer 31:34;
Mk 1:4
1:78
zMal 4:2

and in the shadow of death,[a]
to guide our feet into the path of peace.''

80And the child grew and became strong in spirit;[b] and he lived in the desert until he appeared publicly to Israel.

The Birth of Jesus

2 In those days Caesar Augustus[c] issued a decree that a census should be taken of the entire Roman world.[d] 2(This was the first census that took place while Quirinius was governor of Syria.)[e] 3And everyone went to his own town to register.

4So Joseph also went up from the town of Nazareth in Galilee to Judea, to Bethlehem[f] the town of David, because he belonged to the house and line of David. 5He went there to register with Mary, who was pledged to be married to him and was expecting a child. 6While they were there, the time came for the baby to be born, 7and she gave birth to her firstborn, a son. She wrapped him in cloths and placed him in a manger, because there was no room for them in the inn.

The Shepherds and the Angels

8And there were shepherds living out in the fields nearby, keeping watch over their flocks at night. 9An angel[g] of the Lord appeared to them, and the glory of the Lord shone around them, and they were terrified. 10But the angel said to them, ''Do not be afraid.[h] I bring you good news of great joy that will be for all the people. 11Today in the town of David a Savior[i] has been born to you; he is Christ[a][j] the Lord. 12This will be a sign[k] to you: You will find a baby wrapped in cloths and lying in a manger.''

13Suddenly a great company of the heavenly host appeared with the angel, praising God and saying,

14''Glory to God in the highest,
and on earth peace[l] to men on whom his favor rests.''

15When the angels had left them and gone into heaven, the shepherds said to one another, ''Let's go to Bethlehem and see this thing that has happened, which the Lord has told us about.''

16So they hurried off and found Mary and Joseph, and the baby, who was lying in the manger. 17When they had seen him, they spread the word concerning what had been told them about this child, 18and all who heard it were amazed at what the shepherds said to them. 19But Mary treasured up all these things and pondered them in her heart.[m] 20The shepherds returned, glorifying and praising God[n] for all the things they had heard and seen, which were just as they had been told.

Jesus Presented in the Temple

21On the eighth day, when it was time to circumcise him,[o] he was named Jesus, the name the angel had given him before he had been conceived.[p]

22When the time of their purification according to the Law of Moses[q]

1:79
a Isa 9:2; 59:9;
Mt 4:16;
Ac 26:18
1:80
b Lk 2:40,52
2:1
c Lk 3:1;
Mt 22:17
d Mt 24:14
2:2
e Mt 4:24
2:4
f Jn 7:42
2:9
g Lk 1:11;
Ac 5:19
2:10
h Mt 14:27
2:11
i Mt 1:21;
Jn 4:42; Ac 5:31
j Mt 1:16; 16:16,
20; Jn 11:27;
Ac 2:36
2:12
k 1Sa 2:34;
2Ki 19:29;
Isa 7:14
2:14
l Lk 1:79;
Ro 5:1;
Eph 2:14,17
2:19
m ver 51
2:20
n Mt 9:8
2:21
o Lk 1:59
p Lk 1:31
2:22
q Lev 12:2-8

---

[a]11 Or *Messiah*. ''The Christ'' (Greek) and ''the Messiah'' (Hebrew) both mean ''the Anointed One''; also in verse 26.

had been completed, Joseph and Mary took him to Jerusalem to present him to the Lord [23](as it is written in the Law of the Lord, "Every firstborn male is to be consecrated to the Lord"[a]),[r] [24]and to offer a sacrifice in keeping with what is said in the Law of the Lord: "a pair of doves or two young pigeons."[b] [s]

[25]Now there was a man in Jerusalem called Simeon, who was righteous and devout.[t] He was waiting for the consolation of Israel,[u] and the Holy Spirit was upon him. [26]It had been revealed to him by the Holy Spirit that he would not die before he had seen the Lord's Christ. [27]Moved by the Spirit, he went into the temple courts. When the parents brought in the child Jesus to do for him what the custom of the Law required,[v] [28]Simeon took him in his arms and praised God, saying:

> [29]"Sovereign Lord, as you have promised,[w]
>   you now dismiss[c] your servant in peace.[x]
> [30]For my eyes have seen your salvation,[y]
> [31]   which you have prepared in the sight of all people,
> [32]a light for revelation to the Gentiles
>   and for glory to your people Israel."[z]

[33]The child's father and mother marveled at what was said about him. [34]Then Simeon blessed them and said to Mary, his mother:[a] "This child is destined to cause the falling[b] and rising of many in Israel, and to be a sign that will be spoken against, [35]so that the thoughts of many hearts will be revealed. And a sword will pierce your own soul too."

[36]There was also a prophetess,[c] Anna, the daughter of Phanuel, of the tribe of Asher. She was very old; she had lived with her husband seven years after her marriage, [37]and then was a widow until she was eighty-four.[d] [d] She never left the temple but worshiped night and day, fasting and praying.[e] [38]Coming up to them at that very moment, she gave thanks to God and spoke about the child to all who were looking forward to the redemption of Jerusalem.[f]

[39]When Joseph and Mary had done everything required by the Law of the Lord, they returned to Galilee to their own town of Nazareth.[g] [40]And the child grew and became strong; he was filled with wisdom, and the grace of God was upon him.[h]

The Boy Jesus at the Temple

[41]Every year his parents went to Jerusalem for the Feast of the Passover.[i] [42]When he was twelve years old, they went up to the Feast, according to the custom. [43]After the Feast was over, while his parents were returning home, the boy Jesus stayed behind in Jerusalem, but they were unaware of it. [44]Thinking he was in their company, they traveled on for a day. Then they began looking for him among their relatives and friends. [45]When they did not find him, they went back to Jerusalem to look for him. [46]After three days they found him in the temple courts, sitting among the teachers, listening to them and asking them questions. [47]Everyone who heard him was amazed[j] at his understanding and his answers. [48]When his parents saw him, they were astonished. His mother[k] said to him, "Son, why have you treated us

2:23
rEx 13:2,12,15;
Nu 3:13

2:24
sLev 12:8

2:25
tLk 1:6 uver 38;
Isa 52:9;
Lk 23:51

2:27
vver 22

2:29
wver 26
xAc 2:24

2:30
yIsa 52:10;
Lk 3:6

2:32
zIsa 42:6; 49:6;
Ac 13:47; 26:23

2:34
aMt 12:46
bIsa 8:14;
Mt 21:44;
1Co 1:23;
2Co 2:16;
1Pe 2:7,8

2:36
cAc 21:9

2:37
d1Ti 5:9
eAc 13:3;
14:23; 1Ti 5:5

2:38
fver 25;
Isa 40:2;
Lk 1:68; 24:21

2:39
gver 51;
Mt 2:23

2:40
hver 52; Lk 1:80

2:41
iEx 23:15;
Dt 16:1-8

2:47
jMt 7:28

2:48
kMt 12:46

---

[a]23 Exodus 13:2,12   [b]24 Lev. 12:8   [c]29 Or *promised, / now dismiss*   [d]37 Or *widow for eighty-four years*

like this? Your father[1] and I have been anxiously searching for you."

[49]"Why were you searching for me?" he asked. "Didn't you know I had to be in my Father's house?"[m] [50]But they did not understand what he was saying to them.[n]

[51]Then he went down to Nazareth with them[o] and was obedient to them. But his mother treasured all these things in her heart.[p] [52]And Jesus grew in wisdom and stature, and in favor with God and men.[q]

John the Baptist Prepares the Way

3 In the fifteenth year of the reign of Tiberius Caesar—when Pontius Pilate[r] was governor of Judea, Herod[s] tetrarch of Galilee, his brother Philip tetrarch of Iturea and Traconitis, and Lysanias tetrarch of Abilene— [2]during the high priesthood of Annas and Caiaphas,[t] the word of God came to John[u] son of Zechariah[v] in the desert. [3]He went into all the country around the Jordan, preaching a baptism of repentance for the forgiveness of sins.[w] [4]As is written in the book of the words of Isaiah the prophet:

> "A voice of one calling in the desert,
>   'Prepare the way for the Lord,
>   make straight paths for him.
> [5]Every valley shall be filled in,
>   every mountain and hill made low.
> The crooked roads shall become straight,
>   the rough ways smooth.
> [6]And all mankind will see God's salvation.' "[a] [x]

[7]John said to the crowds coming out to be baptized by him, "You brood of vipers![y] Who warned you to flee from the coming wrath?[z] [8]Produce fruit in keeping with repentance. And do not begin to say to yourselves, 'We have Abraham as our father.'[a] For I tell you that out of these stones God can raise up children for Abraham. [9]The ax is already at the root of the trees, and every tree that does not produce good fruit will be cut down and thrown into the fire."[b]

[10]"What should we do then?"[c] the crowd asked.

[11]John answered, "The man with two tunics should share with him who has none, and the one who has food should do the same."[d]

[12]Tax collectors also came to be baptized.[e] "Teacher," they asked, "what should we do?"

[13]"Don't collect any more than you are required to,"[f] he told them.

[14]Then some soldiers asked him, "And what should we do?"

He replied, "Don't extort money and don't accuse people falsely[g]—be content with your pay."

[15]The people were waiting expectantly and were all wondering in their hearts if John[h] might possibly be the Christ.[b] [i] [16]John answered them all, "I baptize you with[c] water.[j] But one more powerful than I will come, the thongs of whose sandals I am not worthy to untie. He will baptize you with the Holy Spirit and with fire.[k] [17]His winnowing fork[l] is in his hand to clear his threshing floor and to gather the wheat

---

2:48
lLk 3:23; 4:22
2:49
mJn 2:16
2:50
nMk 9:32
2:51
over 39;
Mt 2:23 pver 19
2:52
qver 40;
1Sa 2:26;
Lk 1:80
3:1
rMt 27:2
sMt 14:1
3:2
tMt 26:3;
Jn 18:13; Ac 4:6
uMt 3:1
vLk 1:13
3:3
wver 16;
Mk 1:4
3:6
xIsa 40:3-5;
Ps 98:2;
Isa 42:16;
52:10; Lk 2:30
3:7
yMt 12:34;
23:33 zRo 1:18
3:8
aIsa 51:2;
Lk 19:9;
Jn 8:33,39;
Ac 13:26;
Ro 4:1,11,12,16,
17; Gal 3:7
3:9
bMt 3:10
3:10
cver 12,14;
Ac 2:37; 16:30
3:11
dIsa 58:7
3:12
eLk 7:29
3:13
fLk 19:8
3:14
gEx 23:1;
Lev 19:11
3:15
hMt 3:1
iJn 1:19,20;
Ac 13:25
3:16
jver 3; Mk 1:4
kJn 1:26,33;
Ac 1:5; 11:16;
19:4
3:17
lIsa 30:24

---

into his barn, but he will burn up the chaff with unquenchable fire."ᵐ
¹⁸And with many other words John exhorted the people and preached the good news to them.

¹⁹But when John rebuked Herodⁿ the tetrarch because of Herodias, his brother's wife, and all the other evil things he had done, ²⁰Herod added this to them all: He locked John up in prison.ᵒ

The Baptism and Genealogy of Jesus

3:21,22pp — Mt 3:13–17; Mk 1:9–11
3:23–38pp — Mt 1:1–17

²¹When all the people were being baptized, Jesus was baptized too. And as he was praying,ᵖ heaven was opened ²²and the Holy Spirit descended on him�q in bodily form like a dove. And a voice came from heaven: "You are my Son,ʳ whom I love; with you I am well pleased."ˢ

²³Now Jesus himself was about thirty years old when he began his ministry.ᵗ He was the son, so it was thought, of Joseph,ᵘ

the son of Heli, ²⁴the son of Matthat,
the son of Levi, the son of Melki,
the son of Jannai, the son of Joseph,
²⁵the son of Mattathias, the son of Amos,
the son of Nahum, the son of Esli,
the son of Naggai, ²⁶the son of Maath,
the son of Mattathias, the son of Semein,
the son of Josech, the son of Joda,
²⁷the son of Joanan, the son of Rhesa,
the son of Zerubbabel,ᵛ the son of Shealtiel,
the son of Neri, ²⁸the son of Melki,
the son of Addi, the son of Cosam,
the son of Elmadam, the son of Er,
²⁹the son of Joshua, the son of Eliezer,
the son of Jorim, the son of Matthat,
the son of Levi, ³⁰the son of Simeon,
the son of Judah, the son of Joseph,
the son of Jonam, the son of Eliakim,
³¹the son of Melea, the son of Menna,
the son of Mattatha, the son of Nathan,ʷ
the son of David, ³²the son of Jesse,
the son of Obed, the son of Boaz,
the son of Salmon,ᵃ the son of Nahshon,
³³the son of Amminadab, the son of Ram,ᵇ
the son of Hezron, the son of Perez,ˣ
the son of Judah, ³⁴the son of Jacob,
the son of Isaac, the son of Abraham,
the son of Terah, the son of Nahor,ʸ
³⁵the son of Serug, the son of Reu,
the son of Peleg, the son of Eber,
the son of Shelah, ³⁶the son of Cainan,
the son of Arphaxad,ᶻ the son of Shem,
the son of Noah, the son of Lamech,ᵃ

3:17
mMt 13:30;
25:41
3:19
nver 1
3:20
oMt 14:3,4;
Mk 6:17-18
3:21
pMt 14:23;
Mk 1:35; 6:46;
Lk 5:16; 6:12;
9:18,28; 11:1
3:22
qIsa 42:1;
Jn 1:32,33;
Ac 10:38
rMt 3:17
sMt 3:17
3:23
tMt 4:17;
Ac 1:1 uLk 1:27
3:27
vMt 1:12
3:31
w2Sa 5:14;
1Ch 3:5
3:33
xRu 4:18-22;
1Ch 2:10-12
3:34
yGe 11:24,26
3:36
zGe 11:12
aGe 5:28-32

ᵃ32 Some early manuscripts *Sala*   ᵇ33 Some manuscripts *Amminadab, the son of Admin, the son of Arni*; other manuscripts vary widely.

37the son of Methuselah, the son of Enoch,
    the son of Jared, the son of Mahalalel,
    the son of Kenan, 38the son of Enosh,
    the son of Seth, the son of Adam,
    the son of God. b

The Temptation of Jesus

4:1–13pp — Mt 4:1–11; Mk 1:12,13

4 Jesus, full of the Holy Spirit, c returned from the Jordan d and was led by the Spirit e in the desert, 2where for forty days f he was tempted by the devil. He ate nothing during those days, and at the end of them he was hungry.

3The devil said to him, "If you are the Son of God, tell this stone to become bread."

4Jesus answered, "It is written: 'Man does not live on bread alone.'a "g

5The devil led him up to a high place and showed him in an instant all the kingdoms of the world. h 6And he said to him, "I will give you all their authority and splendor, for it has been given to me,i and I can give it to anyone I want to. 7So if you worship me, it will all be yours."

8Jesus answered, "It is written: 'Worship the Lord your God and serve him only.'b "j

9The devil led him to Jerusalem and had him stand on the highest point of the temple. "If you are the Son of God," he said, "throw yourself down from here. 10For it is written:

" 'He will command his angels concerning you
        to guard you carefully;
11they will lift you up in their hands,
        so that you will not strike your foot against a
            stone.'c "k

12Jesus answered, "It says: 'Do not put the Lord your God to the test.'d "l

13When the devil had finished all this tempting, m he left him n until an opportune time.

Jesus Rejected at Nazareth

14Jesus returned to Galilee o in the power of the Spirit, and news about him spread through the whole countryside. p 15He taught in their synagogues, q and everyone praised him.

16He went to Nazareth, r where he had been brought up, and on the Sabbath day he went into the synagogue, s as was his custom. And he stood up to read. 17The scroll of the prophet Isaiah was handed to him. Unrolling it, he found the place where it is written:

18"The Spirit of the Lord is on me,t
        because he has anointed me
        to preach good news to the poor.
    He has sent me to proclaim freedom for the prisoners
        and recovery of sight for the blind,

3:38
bGe 5:1,2,6-9
4:1
cver 14,18
dLk 3:3,21
eLk 2:27
4:2
fEx 34:28;
1Ki 19:8
4:4
gDt 8:3
4:5
hMt 24:14
4:6
iJn 12:31;
14:30; 1Jn 5:19
4:8
jDt 6:13
4:11
kPs 91:11,12
4:12
lDt 6:16
4:13
mHeb 4:15
nJn 14:30
4:14
oMt 4:12
pMt 9:26
4:15
qMt 4:23
4:16
rMt 2:23
sMt 13:54
4:18
tJn 3:34

a4 Deut. 8:3   b8 Deut. 6:13   c11 Psalm 91:11,12   d12 Deut. 6:16

> to release the oppressed,
> 19   to proclaim the year of the Lord's favor."[a][u]

20Then he rolled up the scroll, gave it back to the attendant and sat down.[v] The eyes of everyone in the synagogue were fastened on him, 21and he began by saying to them, "Today this scripture is fulfilled in your hearing."

22All spoke well of him and were amazed at the gracious words that came from his lips. "Isn't this Joseph's son?" they asked.[w]

23Jesus said to them, "Surely you will quote this proverb to me: 'Physician, heal yourself! Do here in your hometown[x] what we have heard that you did in Capernaum.' "[y]

24"I tell you the truth," he continued, "no prophet is accepted in his hometown.[z] 25I assure you that there were many widows in Israel in Elijah's time, when the sky was shut for three and a half years and there was a severe famine throughout the land.[a] 26Yet Elijah was not sent to any of them, but to a widow in Zarephath in the region of Sidon.[b] 27And there were many in Israel with leprosy[b] in the time of Elisha the prophet, yet not one of them was cleansed—only Naaman the Syrian."[c]

28All the people in the synagogue were furious when they heard this. 29They got up, drove him out of the town,[d] and took him to the brow of the hill on which the town was built, in order to throw him down the cliff. 30But he walked right through the crowd and went on his way.[e]

Jesus Drives Out an Evil Spirit

4:31-37pp — Mk 1:21-28

31Then he went down to Capernaum,[f] a town in Galilee, and on the Sabbath began to teach the people. 32They were amazed at his teaching,[g] because his message had authority.[h]

33In the synagogue there was a man possessed by a demon, an evil[c] spirit. He cried out at the top of his voice, 34"Ha! What do you want with us,[i] Jesus of Nazareth?[j] Have you come to destroy us? I know who you are[k]—the Holy One of God!"[l]

35"Be quiet!" Jesus said sternly.[m] "Come out of him!" Then the demon threw the man down before them all and came out without injuring him.

36All the people were amazed[n] and said to each other, "What is this teaching? With authority[o] and power he gives orders to evil spirits and they come out!" 37And the news about him spread throughout the surrounding area.[p]

Jesus Heals Many

4:38-41pp — Mt 8:14-17
4:38-43pp — Mk 1:29-38

38Jesus left the synagogue and went to the home of Simon. Now Simon's mother-in-law was suffering from a high fever, and they asked Jesus to help her. 39So he bent over her and rebuked[q] the fever, and it left her. She got up at once and began to wait on them.

40When the sun was setting, the people brought to Jesus all who had

4:19
u Isa 61:1,2;
Lev 25:10
4:20
v ver 17;
Mt 26:55
4:22
w Mt 13:54,55;
Jn 6:42; 7:15
4:23
x ver 16
y Mk 1:21-28;
2:1-12
4:24
z Mt 13:57;
Jn 4:44
4:25
a 1Ki 17:1; 18:1;
Jas 5:17,18
4:26
b 1Ki 17:8-16;
Mt 11:21
4:27
c 2Ki 5:1-14
4:29
d Nu 15:35;
Ac 7:58;
Heb 13:12
4:30
e Jn 8:59; 10:39
4:31
f ver 23; Mt 4:13
4:32
g Mt 7:28
h ver 36;
Mt 7:29
4:34
i Mt 8:29
j Mk 1:24
k Jas 2:19
l ver 41;
Mk 1:24
4:35
m ver 39,41;
Mt 8:26;
Lk 8:24
4:36
n Mt 7:28
o ver 32;
Mt 7:29;
Mt 10:1
4:37
p ver 14;
Mt 9:26
4:39
q ver 35,41

---

[a]19 Isaiah 61:1,2   [b]27 The Greek word was used for various diseases affecting the skin—not necessarily leprosy.   [c]33 Greek *unclean*; also in verse 36

various kinds of sickness, and laying his hands on each one,[r] he healed them.[s] [41]Moreover, demons came out of many people, shouting, "You are the Son of God!"[t] But he rebuked[u] them and would not allow them to speak,[v] because they knew he was the Christ.[a]

[42]At daybreak Jesus went out to a solitary place. The people were looking for him and when they came to where he was, they tried to keep him from leaving them. [43]But he said, "I must preach the good news of the kingdom of God[w] to the other towns also, because that is why I was sent." [44]And he kept on preaching in the synagogues of Judea.[b][x]

The Calling of the First Disciples

5:1–11pp — Mt 4:18–22; Mk 1:16–20; Jn 1:40–42

5 One day as Jesus was standing by the Lake of Gennesaret,[c] with the people crowding around him and listening to the word of God,[y] [2]he saw at the water's edge two boats, left there by the fishermen, who were washing their nets. [3]He got into one of the boats, the one belonging to Simon, and asked him to put out a little from shore. Then he sat down and taught the people from the boat.[z]

[4]When he had finished speaking, he said to Simon, "Put out into deep water, and let down[d] the nets for a catch."[a]

[5]Simon answered, "Master,[b] we've worked hard all night and haven't caught anything.[c] But because you say so, I will let down the nets."

[6]When they had done so, they caught such a large number of fish that their nets began to break.[d] [7]So they signaled their partners in the other boat to come and help them, and they came and filled both boats so full that they began to sink.

[8]When Simon Peter saw this, he fell at Jesus' knees and said, "Go away from me, Lord; I am a sinful man!"[e] [9]For he and all his companions were astonished at the catch of fish they had taken, [10]and so were James and John, the sons of Zebedee, Simon's partners.

Then Jesus said to Simon, "Don't be afraid;[f] from now on you will catch men." [11]So they pulled their boats up on shore, left everything and followed him.[g]

The Man With Leprosy

5:12–14pp — Mt 8:2–4; Mk 1:40–44

[12]While Jesus was in one of the towns, a man came along who was covered with leprosy.[e][h] When he saw Jesus, he fell with his face to the ground and begged him, "Lord, if you are willing, you can make me clean."

[13]Jesus reached out his hand and touched the man. "I am willing," he said. "Be clean!" And immediately the leprosy left him.

[14]Then Jesus ordered him, "Don't tell anyone,[i] but go, show yourself to the priest and offer the sacrifices that Moses commanded[j] for your cleansing, as a testimony to them."

[15]Yet the news about him spread all the more,[k] so that crowds of

---

4:40
r Mk 5:23
s Mt 4:23
4:41
t Mt 4:3 u ver 35
v Mt 8:4
4:43
w Mt 3:2
4:44
x Mt 4:23
5:1
y Mk 4:14;
Heb 4:12
5:3
z Mt 13:2
5:4
a Jn 21:6
5:5
b Lk 8:24,45;
9:33,49; 17:13
c Jn 21:3
5:6
d Jn 21:11
5:8
e Ge 18:27;
Job 42:6;
Isa 6:5
5:10
f Mt 14:27
5:11
g ver 28;
Mt 4:19
5:12
h Mt 8:2
5:14
i Mt 8:4
j Lev 14:2-32
5:15
k Mt 9:26

---

[a]41 Or *Messiah*   [b]44 Or *the land of the Jews*; some manuscripts *Galilee*   [c]1 That is, Sea of Galilee   [d]4 The Greek verb is plural.   [e]12 The Greek word was used for various diseases affecting the skin—not necessarily leprosy.

people came to hear him and to be healed of their sicknesses. [16]But Jesus often withdrew to lonely places and prayed.[l]

Jesus Heals a Paralytic
5:18–26pp — Mt 9:2–8; Mk 2:3–12

[17]One day as he was teaching, Pharisees and teachers of the law,[m] who had come from every village of Galilee and from Judea and Jerusalem, were sitting there. And the power of the Lord was present for him to heal the sick.[n] [18]Some men came carrying a paralytic on a mat and tried to take him into the house to lay him before Jesus. [19]When they could not find a way to do this because of the crowd, they went up on the roof and lowered him on his mat through the tiles into the middle of the crowd, right in front of Jesus.

[20]When Jesus saw their faith, he said, "Friend, your sins are forgiven."[o]

[21]The Pharisees and the teachers of the law began thinking to themselves, "Who is this fellow who speaks blasphemy? Who can forgive sins but God alone?"[p]

[22]Jesus knew what they were thinking and asked, "Why are you thinking these things in your hearts? [23]Which is easier: to say, 'Your sins are forgiven,' or to say, 'Get up and walk'? [24]But that you may know that the Son of Man[q] has authority on earth to forgive sins. . . ." He said to the paralyzed man, "I tell you, get up, take your mat and go home." [25]Immediately he stood up in front of them, took what he had been lying on and went home praising God. [26]Everyone was amazed and gave praise to God.[r] They were filled with awe and said, "We have seen remarkable things today."

The Calling of Levi
5:27–32pp — Mt 9:9–13; Mk 2:14–17

[27]After this, Jesus went out and saw a tax collector by the name of Levi sitting at his tax booth. "Follow me,"[s] Jesus said to him, [28]and Levi got up, left everything and followed him.[t]

[29]Then Levi held a great banquet for Jesus at his house, and a large crowd of tax collectors[u] and others were eating with them. [30]But the Pharisees and the teachers of the law who belonged to their sect[v] complained to his disciples, "Why do you eat and drink with tax collectors and 'sinners'?"[w]

[31]Jesus answered them, "It is not the healthy who need a doctor, but the sick. [32]I have not come to call the righteous, but sinners to repentance."[x]

Jesus Questioned About Fasting
5:33–39pp — Mt 9:14–17; Mk 2:18–22

[33]They said to him, "John's disciples[y] often fast and pray, and so do the disciples of the Pharisees, but yours go on eating and drinking."

[34]Jesus answered, "Can you make the guests of the bridegroom[z] fast while he is with them? [35]But the time will come when the bridegroom will be taken from them;[a] in those days they will fast."

[36]He told them this parable: "No one tears a patch from a new garment and sews it on an old one. If he does, he will have torn the new garment, and the patch from the new will not match the old. [37]And no

5:16
lMt 14:23;
Lk 3:21
5:17
mMt 15:1;
Lk 2:46
nMk 5:30;
Lk 6:19
5:20
oLk 7:48,49
5:21
pIsa 43:25
5:24
qMt 8:20
5:26
rMt 9:8
5:27
sMt 4:19
5:28
tver 11; Mt 4:19
5:29
uLk 15:1
5:30
vAc 23:9
wMt 9:11
5:32
xJn 3:17
5:33
yLk 7:18;
Jn 1:35; 3:25,26
5:34
zJn 3:29
5:35
aLk 9:22;
17:22; Jn 16:5-7

one pours new wine into old wineskins. If he does, the new wine will burst the skins, the wine will run out and the wineskins will be ruined. 38No, new wine must be poured into new wineskins. 39And no one after drinking old wine wants the new, for he says, 'The old is better.' "

Lord of the Sabbath

6:1–11pp — Mt 12:1–14; Mk 2:23–3:6

6 One Sabbath Jesus was going through the grainfields, and his disciples began to pick some heads of grain, rub them in their hands and eat the kernels.b 2Some of the Pharisees asked, "Why are you doing what is unlawful on the Sabbath?"c

3Jesus answered them, "Have you never read what David did when he and his companions were hungry?d 4He entered the house of God, and taking the consecrated bread, he ate what is lawful only for priests to eat.e And he also gave some to his companions." 5Then Jesus said to them, "The Son of Manf is Lord of the Sabbath."

6On another Sabbathg he went into the synagogue and was teaching, and a man was there whose right hand was shriveled. 7The Pharisees and the teachers of the law were looking for a reason to accuse Jesus, so they watched him closelyh to see if he would heal on the Sabbath.i 8But Jesus knew what they were thinkingj and said to the man with the shriveled hand, "Get up and stand in front of everyone." So he got up and stood there.

9Then Jesus said to them, "I ask you, which is lawful on the Sabbath: to do good or to do evil, to save life or to destroy it?"

10He looked around at them all, and then said to the man, "Stretch out your hand." He did so, and his hand was completely restored. 11But they were furiousk and began to discuss with one another what they might do to Jesus.

The Twelve Apostles

6:13–16pp — Mt 10:2–4; Mk 3:16–19; Ac 1:13

12One of those days Jesus went out to a mountainside to pray, and spent the night praying to God.l 13When morning came, he called his disciples to him and chose twelve of them, whom he also designated apostles:m 14Simon (whom he named Peter), his brother Andrew, James, John, Philip, Bartholomew, 15Matthew,n Thomas, James son of Alphaeus, Simon who was called the Zealot, 16Judas son of James, and Judas Iscariot, who became a traitor.

Blessings and Woes

6:20–23pp — Mt 5:3–12

17He went down with them and stood on a level place. A large crowd of his disciples was there and a great number of people from all over Judea, from Jerusalem, and from the coast of Tyre and Sidon,o 18who had come to hear him and to be healed of their diseases. Those troubled by evila spirits were cured, 19and the people all tried to touch him,p because power was coming from him and healing them all.q 20Looking at his disciples, he said:

a18 Greek unclean

6:1
bDt 23:25
6:2
cMt 12:2
6:3
d1Sa 21:6
6:4
eLev 24:5,9
6:5
fMt 8:20
6:6
gver 1
6:7
hMt 12:10
iMt 12:2
6:8
jMt 9:4
6:11
kJn 5:18
6:12
lLk 3:21
6:13
mMk 6:30
6:15
nMt 9:9
6:17
oMt 4:25;
Mt 11:21;
Mk 3:7,8
6:19
pMt 9:20
qMt 14:36;
Mk 5:30;
Lk 5:17

"Blessed are you who are poor,
for yours is the kingdom of God. r
21Blessed are you who hunger now,
for you will be satisfied. s
Blessed are you who weep now,
for you will laugh. t
22Blessed are you when men hate you,
when they exclude you u and insult you v
and reject your name as evil,
because of the Son of Man. w

23"Rejoice in that day and leap for joy, x because great is your reward in heaven. For that is how their fathers treated the prophets. y

24"But woe to you who are rich, z
for you have already received your comfort. a
25Woe to you who are well fed now,
for you will go hungry. b
Woe to you who laugh now,
for you will mourn and weep. c
26Woe to you when all men speak well of you,
for that is how their fathers treated the false
prophets. d

Love for Enemies
6:29,30pp — Mt 5:39–42

27"But I tell you who hear me: Love your enemies, do good to those who hate you, e 28bless those who curse you, pray for those who mistreat you. f 29If someone strikes you on one cheek, turn to him the other also. If someone takes your cloak, do not stop him from taking your tunic. 30Give to everyone who asks you, and if anyone takes what belongs to you, do not demand it back. g 31Do to others as you would have them do to you. h

32"If you love those who love you, what credit is that to you? i Even 'sinners' love those who love them. 33And if you do good to those who are good to you, what credit is that to you? Even 'sinners' do that. 34And if you lend to those from whom you expect repayment, what credit is that to you? j Even 'sinners' lend to 'sinners,' expecting to be repaid in full. 35But love your enemies, do good to them, k and lend to them without expecting to get anything back. Then your reward will be great, and you will be sons l of the Most High, m because he is kind to the ungrateful and wicked. 36Be merciful, n just as your Father o is merciful.

Judging Others
6:37–42pp — Mt 7:1–5

37"Do not judge, and you will not be judged. p Do not condemn, and you will not be condemned. Forgive, and you will be forgiven. q 38Give, and it will be given to you. A good measure, pressed down, shaken together and running over, will be poured into your lap. r For with the measure you use, it will be measured to you." s

39He also told them this parable: "Can a blind man lead a blind man?

6:20
r Mt 25:34
6:21
s Isa 55:1,2;
Mt 5:6
t Isa 61:2,3;
Mt 5:4;
Rev 7:17
6:22
u Jn 9:22; 16:2
v Isa 51:7
w Jn 15:21
6:23
x Mt 5:12
y Mt 5:12
6:24
z Jas 5:1
a Lk 16:25
6:25
b Isa 65:13
c Pr 14:13
6:26
d Mt 7:15
6:27
e ver 35;
Mt 5:44;
Ro 12:20
6:28
f Mt 5:44
6:30
g Dt 15:7,8,10;
Pr 21:26
6:31
h Mt 7:12
6:32
i Mt 5:46
6:34
j Mt 5:42
6:35
k ver 27 l Ro 8:14
m Mk 5:7
6:36
n Jas 2:13
o Mt 5:48; 6:1;
Lk 11:2; 12:32;
Ro 8:15;
Eph 4:6;
1Pe 1:17;
1Jn 1:3; 3:1
6:37
p Mt 7:1
q Mt 6:14
6:38
r Ps 79:12;
Isa 65:6,7
s Mt 7:2;
Mk 4:24

Will they not both fall into a pit?ᵗ ⁴⁰A student is not above his teacher, but everyone who is fully trained will be like his teacher.ᵘ

⁴¹"Why do you look at the speck of sawdust in your brother's eye and pay no attention to the plank in your own eye? ⁴²How can you say to your brother, 'Brother, let me take the speck out of your eye,' when you yourself fail to see the plank in your own eye? You hypocrite, first take the plank out of your eye, and then you will see clearly to remove the speck from your brother's eye.

A Tree and Its Fruit

6:43,44pp — Mt 7:16,18,20

⁴³"No good tree bears bad fruit, nor does a bad tree bear good fruit. ⁴⁴Each tree is recognized by its own fruit.ᵛ People do not pick figs from thornbushes, or grapes from briers. ⁴⁵The good man brings good things out of the good stored up in his heart, and the evil man brings evil things out of the evil stored up in his heart. For out of the overflow of his heart his mouth speaks.ʷ

The Wise and Foolish Builders

6:47–49pp — Mt 7:24–27

⁴⁶"Why do you call me, 'Lord, Lord,'ˣ and do not do what I say?ʸ ⁴⁷I will show you what he is like who comes to me and hears my words and puts them into practice.ᶻ ⁴⁸He is like a man building a house, who dug down deep and laid the foundation on rock. When a flood came, the torrent struck that house but could not shake it, because it was well built. ⁴⁹But the one who hears my words and does not put them into practice is like a man who built a house on the ground without a foundation. The moment the torrent struck that house, it collapsed and its destruction was complete."

The Faith of the Centurion

7:1–10pp — Mt 8:5–13

7 When Jesus had finished saying all thisᵃ in the hearing of the people, he entered Capernaum. ²There a centurion's servant, whom his master valued highly, was sick and about to die. ³The centurion heard of Jesus and sent some elders of the Jews to him, asking him to come and heal his servant. ⁴When they came to Jesus, they pleaded earnestly with him, "This man deserves to have you do this, ⁵because he loves our nation and has built our synagogue." ⁶So Jesus went with them.

He was not far from the house when the centurion sent friends to say to him: "Lord, don't trouble yourself, for I do not deserve to have you come under my roof. ⁷That is why I did not even consider myself worthy to come to you. But say the word, and my servant will be healed.ᵇ ⁸For I myself am a man under authority, with soldiers under me. I tell this one, 'Go,' and he goes; and that one, 'Come,' and he comes. I say to my servant, 'Do this,' and he does it."

⁹When Jesus heard this, he was amazed at him, and turning to the crowd following him, he said, "I tell you, I have not found such great faith even in Israel." ¹⁰Then the men who had been sent returned to the house and found the servant well.

6:39
ᵗMt 15:14
6:40
ᵘMt 10:24;
Jn 13:16
6:44
ᵛMt 12:33
6:45
ʷPr 4:23;
Mt 12:34,35;
Mk 7:20
6:46
ˣJn 13:13
ʸMal 1:6;
Mt 7:21
6:47
ᶻLk 8:21;
11:28;
Jas 1:22-25
7:1
ᵃMt 7:28
7:7
ᵇPs 107:20

Jesus Raises a Widow's Son

7:11–16Ref — 1Ki 17:17–24; 2Ki 4:32–37; Mk 5:21–24,35–43; Jn 11:1–44

[11]Soon afterward, Jesus went to a town called Nain, and his disciples and a large crowd went along with him. [12]As he approached the town gate, a dead person was being carried out—the only son of his mother, and she was a widow. And a large crowd from the town was with her. [13]When the Lord[c] saw her, his heart went out to her and he said, "Don't cry."

[14]Then he went up and touched the coffin, and those carrying it stood still. He said, "Young man, I say to you, get up!"[d] [15]The dead man sat up and began to talk, and Jesus gave him back to his mother.

[16]They were all filled with awe[e] and praised God.[f] "A great prophet[g] has appeared among us," they said. "God has come to help his people."[h] [17]This news about Jesus spread throughout Judea[a] and the surrounding country.[i]

Jesus and John the Baptist

7:18–35pp — Mt 11:2–19

[18]John's[j] disciples[k] told him about all these things. Calling two of them, [19]he sent them to the Lord to ask, "Are you the one who was to come, or should we expect someone else?"

[20]When the men came to Jesus, they said, "John the Baptist sent us to you to ask, 'Are you the one who was to come, or should we expect someone else?' "

[21]At that very time Jesus cured many who had diseases, sicknesses[l] and evil spirits, and gave sight to many who were blind. [22]So he replied to the messengers, "Go back and report to John what you have seen and heard: The blind receive sight, the lame walk, those who have leprosy[b] are cured, the deaf hear, the dead are raised, and the good news is preached to the poor.[m] [23]Blessed is the man who does not fall away on account of me."

[24]After John's messengers left, Jesus began to speak to the crowd about John: "What did you go out into the desert to see? A reed swayed by the wind? [25]If not, what did you go out to see? A man dressed in fine clothes? No, those who wear expensive clothes and indulge in luxury are in palaces. [26]But what did you go out to see? A prophet?[n] Yes, I tell you, and more than a prophet. [27]This is the one about whom it is written:

" 'I will send my messenger ahead of you,
    who will prepare your way before you.'[c] [o]

[28]I tell you, among those born of women there is no one greater than John; yet the one who is least in the kingdom of God[p] is greater than he."

[29](All the people, even the tax collectors, when they heard Jesus' words, acknowledged that God's way was right, because they had been baptized by John.[q] [30]But the Pharisees and experts in the law[r] rejected God's purpose for themselves, because they had not been baptized by John.)

---

[a]17 Or *the land of the Jews*   [b]22 The Greek word was used for various diseases affecting the skin—not necessarily leprosy.   [c]27 Mal. 3:1

7:13
cver 19;
Lk 10:1; 13:15;
17:5; 22:61;
24:34; Jn 11:2

7:14
dMt 9:25;
Mk 1:31;
Lk 8:54;
Jn 11:43;
Ac 9:40

7:16
eLk 1:65
fMt 9:8 gver 39;
Mt 21:11
hLk 1:68

7:17
iMt 9:26

7:18
jMt 3:1
kLk 5:33

7:21
lMt 4:23

7:22
mIsa 29:18,19;
35:5,6; 61:1,2;
Lk 4:18

7:26
nMt 11:9

7:27
oMal 3:1;
Mt 11:10;
Mk 1:2

7:28
pMt 3:2

7:29
qMt 21:32;
Mk 1:5; Lk 3:12

7:30
rMt 22:35

31"To what, then, can I compare the people of this generation? What are they like? 32They are like children sitting in the marketplace and calling out to each other:

" 'We played the flute for you,
    and you did not dance;
we sang a dirge,
    and you did not cry.'

33For John the Baptist came neither eating bread nor drinking wine,s and you say, 'He has a demon.' 34The Son of Man came eating and drinking, and you say, 'Here is a glutton and a drunkard, a friend of tax collectors and "sinners." 't 35But wisdom is proved right by all her children."

Jesus Anointed by a Sinful Woman

7:37–39Ref — Mt 26:6–13; Mk 14:3–9; Jn 12:1–8
7:41,42Ref — Mt 18:23–34

36Now one of the Pharisees invited Jesus to have dinner with him, so he went to the Pharisee's house and reclined at the table. 37When a woman who had lived a sinful life in that town learned that Jesus was eating at the Pharisee's house, she brought an alabaster jar of perfume, 38and as she stood behind him at his feet weeping, she began to wet his feet with her tears. Then she wiped them with her hair, kissed them and poured perfume on them.

39When the Pharisee who had invited him saw this, he said to himself, "If this man were a prophet,u he would know who is touching him and what kind of woman she is—that she is a sinner."

40Jesus answered him, "Simon, I have something to tell you."

"Tell me, teacher," he said.

41"Two men owed money to a certain moneylender. One owed him five hundred denarii,a and the other fifty. 42Neither of them had the money to pay him back, so he canceled the debts of both. Now which of them will love him more?"

43Simon replied, "I suppose the one who had the bigger debt canceled."

"You have judged correctly," Jesus said.

44Then he turned toward the woman and said to Simon, "Do you see this woman? I came into your house. You did not give me any water for my feet,v but she wet my feet with her tears and wiped them with her hair. 45You did not give me a kiss,w but this woman, from the time I entered, has not stopped kissing my feet. 46You did not put oil on my head,x but she has poured perfume on my feet. 47Therefore, I tell you, her many sins have been forgiven—for she loved much. But he who has been forgiven little loves little."

48Then Jesus said to her, "Your sins are forgiven."y

49The other guests began to say among themselves, "Who is this who even forgives sins?"

50Jesus said to the woman, "Your faith has saved you;z go in peace."a

---

a41 A denarius was a coin worth about a day's wages.

### Cross references (margin)

7:33
sLk 1:15
7:34
tLk 5:29,30;
15:1,2
7:39
uver 16;
Mt 21:11
7:44
vGe 18:4; 19:2;
43:24;
Jdg 19:21;
Jn 13:4-14;
1Ti 5:10
7:45
wLk 22:47,48;
Ro 16:16
7:46
xPs 23:5;
Ecc 9:8
7:48
yMt 9:2
7:50
zMt 9:22;
Mk 5:34;
Lk 8:48
aAc 15:33

The Parable of the Sower

8:4–15pp — Mt 13:2–23; Mk 4:1–20

8 After this, Jesus traveled about from one town and village to another, proclaiming the good news of the kingdom of God. [b] The Twelve were with him, [2]and also some women who had been cured of evil spirits and diseases: Mary (called Magdalene)[c] from whom seven demons had come out; [3]Joanna the wife of Cuza, the manager of Herod's[d] household; Susanna; and many others. These women were helping to support them out of their own means.

[4]While a large crowd was gathering and people were coming to Jesus from town after town, he told this parable:[5]"A farmer went out to sow his seed. As he was scattering the seed, some fell along the path; it was trampled on, and the birds of the air ate it up. [6]Some fell on rock, and when it came up, the plants withered because they had no moisture. [7]Other seed fell among thorns, which grew up with it and choked the plants. [8]Still other seed fell on good soil. It came up and yielded a crop, a hundred times more than was sown."

When he said this, he called out, "He who has ears to hear, let him hear."[e]

[9]His disciples asked him what this parable meant. [10]He said, "The knowledge of the secrets of the kingdom of God has been given to you,[f] but to others I speak in parables, so that,

" 'though seeing, they may not see;
though hearing, they may not understand.'[a] [g]

[11]"This is the meaning of the parable: The seed is the word of God. [h] [12]Those along the path are the ones who hear, and then the devil comes and takes away the word from their hearts, so that they may not believe and be saved. [13]Those on the rock are the ones who receive the word with joy when they hear it, but they have no root. They believe for a while, but in the time of testing they fall away. [i] [14]The seed that fell among thorns stands for those who hear, but as they go on their way they are choked by life's worries, riches[j] and pleasures, and they do not mature. [15]But the seed on good soil stands for those with a noble and good heart, who hear the word, retain it, and by persevering produce a crop.

A Lamp on a Stand

[16]"No one lights a lamp and hides it in a jar or puts it under a bed. Instead, he puts it on a stand, so that those who come in can see the light. [k] [17]For there is nothing hidden that will not be disclosed, and nothing concealed that will not be known or brought out into the open. [l] [18]Therefore consider carefully how you listen. Whoever has will be given more; whoever does not have, even what he thinks he has will be taken from him."[m]

Jesus' Mother and Brothers

8:19–21pp — Mt 12:46–50; Mk 3:31–35

[19]Now Jesus' mother and brothers came to see him, but they were not

8:1
b Mt 4:23
8:2
c Mt 27:55,56
8:3
d Mt 14:1
8:8
e Mt 11:15
8:10
f Mt 13:11
g Isa 6:9;
Mt 13:13,14
8:11
h Heb 4:12
8:13
i Mt 11:6
8:14
j Mt 19:23;
1Ti 6:9,10,17
8:16
k Mt 5:15;
Mk 4:21;
Lk 11:33
8:17
l Mt 10:26;
Mk 4:22;
Lk 12:2
8:18
m Mt 13:12;
25:29; Lk 19:26

[a]10 Isaiah 6:9

able to get near him because of the crowd. [20]Someone told him, "Your mother and brothers[n] are standing outside, wanting to see you."

[21]He replied, "My mother and brothers are those who hear God's word and put it into practice."[o]

Jesus Calms the Storm

8:22–25pp — Mt 8:23–27; Mk 4:36–41
8:22–25Ref — Mk 6:47–52; Jn 6:16–21

[22]One day Jesus said to his disciples, "Let's go over to the other side of the lake." So they got into a boat and set out. [23]As they sailed, he fell asleep. A squall came down on the lake, so that the boat was being swamped, and they were in great danger.

[24]The disciples went and woke him, saying, "Master, Master,[p] we're going to drown!"

He got up and rebuked[q] the wind and the raging waters; the storm subsided, and all was calm.[r] [25]"Where is your faith?" he asked his disciples.

In fear and amazement they asked one another, "Who is this? He commands even the winds and the water, and they obey him."

The Healing of a Demon-possessed Man

8:26–37pp — Mt 8:28–34
8:26–39pp — Mk 5:1–20

[26]They sailed to the region of the Gerasenes,[a] which is across the lake from Galilee. [27]When Jesus stepped ashore, he was met by a demon-possessed man from the town. For a long time this man had not worn clothes or lived in a house, but had lived in the tombs. [28]When he saw Jesus, he cried out and fell at his feet, shouting at the top of his voice, "What do you want with me,[s] Jesus, Son of the Most High God?[t] I beg you, don't torture me!" [29]For Jesus had commanded the evil[b] spirit to come out of the man. Many times it had seized him, and though he was chained hand and foot and kept under guard, he had broken his chains and had been driven by the demon into solitary places.

[30]Jesus asked him, "What is your name?"

"Legion," he replied, because many demons had gone into him. [31]And they begged him repeatedly not to order them to go into the Abyss.[u]

[32]A large herd of pigs was feeding there on the hillside. The demons begged Jesus to let them go into them, and he gave them permission. [33]When the demons came out of the man, they went into the pigs, and the herd rushed down the steep bank into the lake[v] and was drowned.

[34]When those tending the pigs saw what had happened, they ran off and reported this in the town and countryside, [35]and the people went out to see what had happened. When they came to Jesus, they found the man from whom the demons had gone out, sitting at Jesus' feet,[w] dressed and in his right mind; and they were afraid. [36]Those who had seen it told the people how the demon-possessed[x] man had been cured. [37]Then all the people of the region of the Gerasenes asked Jesus to leave them,[y] because they were overcome with fear. So he got into the boat and left.

---

[a]26 Some manuscripts *Gadarenes*; other manuscripts *Gergesenes*; also in verse 37   [b]29 Greek *unclean*

³⁸The man from whom the demons had gone out begged to go with him, but Jesus sent him away, saying, ³⁹"Return home and tell how much God has done for you." So the man went away and told all over town how much Jesus had done for him.

A Dead Girl and a Sick Woman

8:40–56pp — Mt 9:18–26; Mk 5:22–43

⁴⁰Now when Jesus returned, a crowd welcomed him, for they were all expecting him. ⁴¹Then a man named Jairus, a ruler of the synagogue,^z came and fell at Jesus' feet, pleading with him to come to his house ⁴²because his only daughter, a girl of about twelve, was dying.

As Jesus was on his way, the crowds almost crushed him. ⁴³And a woman was there who had been subject to bleeding^a for twelve years,^a but no one could heal her. ⁴⁴She came up behind him and touched the edge of his cloak,^b and immediately her bleeding stopped.

⁴⁵"Who touched me?" Jesus asked.

When they all denied it, Peter said, "Master,^c the people are crowding and pressing against you."

⁴⁶But Jesus said, "Someone touched me;^d I know that power has gone out from me."^e

⁴⁷Then the woman, seeing that she could not go unnoticed, came trembling and fell at his feet. In the presence of all the people, she told why she had touched him and how she had been instantly healed. ⁴⁸Then he said to her, "Daughter, your faith has healed you.^f Go in peace."^g

⁴⁹While Jesus was still speaking, someone came from the house of Jairus, the synagogue ruler.^h "Your daughter is dead," he said. "Don't bother the teacher any more."

⁵⁰Hearing this, Jesus said to Jairus, "Don't be afraid; just believe, and she will be healed."

⁵¹When he arrived at the house of Jairus, he did not let anyone go in with him except Peter, John and James,ⁱ and the child's father and mother. ⁵²Meanwhile, all the people were wailing and mourning^j for her. "Stop wailing," Jesus said. "She is not dead but asleep."^k

⁵³They laughed at him, knowing that she was dead. ⁵⁴But he took her by the hand and said, "My child, get up!"^l ⁵⁵Her spirit returned, and at once she stood up. Then Jesus told them to give her something to eat. ⁵⁶Her parents were astonished, but he ordered them not to tell anyone what had happened.^m

Jesus Sends Out the Twelve

9:3–5pp — Mt 10:9–15; Mk 6:8–11
9:7–9pp — Mt 14:1,2; Mk 6:14–16

9 When Jesus had called the Twelve together, he gave them power and authority to drive out all demonsⁿ and to cure diseases,^o ²and he sent them out to preach the kingdom of God^p and to heal the sick. ³He told them: "Take nothing for the journey—no staff, no bag, no bread, no money, no extra tunic.^q ⁴Whatever house you enter, stay there until you leave that town. ⁵If people do not welcome you, shake the dust off your feet when you leave their town, as a testimony against

---

8:41
zver 49;
Mk 5:22
8:43
aLev 15:25-30
8:44
bMt 9:20
8:45
cLk 5:5
8:46
dMt 14:36;
Mk 3:10
eLk 5:17; 6:19
8:48
fMt 9:22
gAc 15:33
8:49
hver 41
8:51
iMt 4:21
8:52
jLk 23:27
kMt 9:24;
Jn 11:11,13
8:54
lLk 7:14
8:56
mMt 8:4
9:1
nMt 10:1
oMt 4:23;
Lk 5:17
9:2
pMt 3:2
9:3
qLk 10:4; 22:35

---

^a43 Many manuscripts *years, and she had spent all she had on doctors*

them.'' r 6So they set out and went from village to village, preaching the gospel and healing people everywhere.

7Now Herod s the tetrarch heard about all that was going on. And he was perplexed, because some were saying that John t had been raised from the dead, u 8others that Elijah had appeared, v and still others that one of the prophets of long ago had come back to life. w 9But Herod said, ''I beheaded John. Who, then, is this I hear such things about?'' And he tried to see him. x

Jesus Feeds the Five Thousand

9:10–17pp — Mt 14:13–21; Mk 6:32–44; Jn 6:5–13
9:13–17Ref — 2Ki 4:42–44

10When the apostles y returned, they reported to Jesus what they had done. Then he took them with him and they withdrew by themselves to a town called Bethsaida, z 11but the crowds learned about it and followed him. He welcomed them and spoke to them about the kingdom of God, a and healed those who needed healing.

12Late in the afternoon the Twelve came to him and said, ''Send the crowd away so they can go to the surrounding villages and countryside and find food and lodging, because we are in a remote place here.''

13He replied, ''You give them something to eat.''

They answered, ''We have only five loaves of bread and two fish— unless we go and buy food for all this crowd.'' 14(About five thousand men were there.)

But he said to his disciples, ''Have them sit down in groups of about fifty each.'' 15The disciples did so, and everybody sat down. 16Taking the five loaves and the two fish and looking up to heaven, he gave thanks and broke them. b Then he gave them to the disciples to set before the people. 17They all ate and were satisfied, and the disciples picked up twelve basketfuls of broken pieces that were left over.

Peter's Confession of Christ

9:18–20pp — Mt 16:13–16; Mk 8:27–29
9:22–27pp — Mt 16:21–28; Mk 8:31 — 9:1

18Once when Jesus was praying c in private and his disciples were with him, he asked them, ''Who do the crowds say I am?''

19They replied, ''Some say John the Baptist; d others say Elijah; and still others, that one of the prophets of long ago has come back to life.'' e

20''But what about you?'' he asked. ''Who do you say I am?''

Peter answered, ''The Christ a of God.'' f

21Jesus strictly warned them not to tell this to anyone. g 22And he said, ''The Son of Man h must suffer many things i and be rejected by the elders, chief priests and teachers of the law, j and he must be killed k and on the third day l be raised to life.'' m

23Then he said to them all: ''If anyone would come after me, he must deny himself and take up his cross daily and follow me. n 24For whoever wants to save his life will lose it, but whoever loses his life for me will save it. o 25What good is it for a man to gain the whole world, and yet lose or forfeit his very self? 26If anyone is ashamed of me and my words, the Son of Man will be ashamed of him p when he comes in his glory

Cross-references (margin):

9:5 r Mt 10:14
9:7 s Mt 14:1 t Mt 3:1 u ver 19
9:8 v Mt 11:14 w ver 19; Jn 1:21
9:9 x Lk 23:8
9:10 y Mk 6:30 z Mt 11:21
9:11 a ver 2; Mt 3:2
9:16 b Mt 14:19
9:18 c Lk 3:21
9:19 d Mt 3:1 e ver 7, 8
9:20 f Jn 1:49; 6:66-69; 11:27
9:21 g Mt 16:20; Mk 8:30
9:22 h Mt 8:20 i Mt 16:21 j Mt 27:1,2 k Ac 2:23; 3:13 l Mt 16:21 m Mt 16:21
9:23 n Mt 10:38; Lk 14:27
9:24 o Jn 12:25
9:26 p Mt 10:33; Lk 12:9; 2Ti 2:12

a20 Or Messiah

and in the glory of the Father and of the holy angels. q 27I tell you the truth, some who are standing here will not taste death before they see the kingdom of God."

The Transfiguration

9:28–36pp — Mt 17:1–8; Mk 9:2–8

28About eight days after Jesus said this, he took Peter, John and James r with him and went up onto a mountain to pray. s 29As he was praying, the appearance of his face changed, and his clothes became as bright as a flash of lightning. 30Two men, Moses and Elijah, 31appeared in glorious splendor, talking with Jesus. They spoke about his departure, t which he was about to bring to fulfillment at Jerusalem. 32Peter and his companions were very sleepy, u but when they became fully awake, they saw his glory and the two men standing with him. 33As the men were leaving Jesus, Peter said to him, "Master, v it is good for us to be here. Let us put up three shelters—one for you, one for Moses and one for Elijah." (He did not know what he was saying.)

34While he was speaking, a cloud appeared and enveloped them, and they were afraid as they entered the cloud. 35A voice came from the cloud, saying, "This is my Son, whom I have chosen; w listen to him." x 36When the voice had spoken, they found that Jesus was alone. The disciples kept this to themselves, and told no one at that time what they had seen. y

The Healing of a Boy With an Evil Spirit

9:37–42,43–45pp — Mt 17:14–18; 22,23; Mk 9:14–27; 30–32

37The next day, when they came down from the mountain, a large crowd met him. 38A man in the crowd called out, "Teacher, I beg you to look at my son, for he is my only child. 39A spirit seizes him and he suddenly screams; it throws him into convulsions so that he foams at the mouth. It scarcely ever leaves him and is destroying him. 40I begged your disciples to drive it out, but they could not."

41"O unbelieving and perverse generation," z Jesus replied, "how long shall I stay with you and put up with you? Bring your son here."

42Even while the boy was coming, the demon threw him to the ground in a convulsion. But Jesus rebuked the evil a spirit, healed the boy and gave him back to his father. 43And they were all amazed at the greatness of God.

While everyone was marveling at all that Jesus did, he said to his disciples, 44"Listen carefully to what I am about to tell you: The Son of Man is going to be betrayed into the hands of men." a 45But they did not understand what this meant. It was hidden from them, so that they did not grasp it, b and they were afraid to ask him about it.

Who Will Be the Greatest?

9:46–48pp — Mt 18:1–5
9:46–50pp — Mk 9:33–40

46An argument started among the disciples as to which of them would be the greatest. c 47Jesus, knowing their thoughts, d took a little child and had him stand beside him. 48Then he said to them, "Whoev-

---

a42 Greek *unclean*

er welcomes this little child in my name welcomes me; and whoever welcomes me welcomes the one who sent me.[e] For he who is least among you all—he is the greatest."[f]

49"Master,"[g] said John, "we saw a man driving out demons in your name and we tried to stop him, because he is not one of us."

50"Do not stop him," Jesus said, "for whoever is not against you is for you."[h]

Samaritan Opposition

51As the time approached for him to be taken up to heaven,[i] Jesus resolutely set out for Jerusalem.[j] 52And he sent messengers on ahead, who went into a Samaritan[k] village to get things ready for him; 53but the people there did not welcome him, because he was heading for Jerusalem. 54When the disciples James and John[l] saw this, they asked, "Lord, do you want us to call fire down from heaven to destroy them[a]?"[m] 55But Jesus turned and rebuked them, 56and[b] they went to another village.

The Cost of Following Jesus

9:57–60pp — Mt 8:19–22

57As they were walking along the road,[n] a man said to him, "I will follow you wherever you go."

58Jesus replied, "Foxes have holes and birds of the air have nests, but the Son of Man[o] has no place to lay his head."

59He said to another man, "Follow me."[p]

But the man replied, "Lord, first let me go and bury my father."

60Jesus said to him, "Let the dead bury their own dead, but you go and proclaim the kingdom of God."[q]

61Still another said, "I will follow you, Lord; but first let me go back and say good-by to my family."[r]

62Jesus replied, "No one who puts his hand to the plow and looks back is fit for service in the kingdom of God."

Jesus Sends Out the Seventy-two

10:4–12pp — Lk 9:3–5
10:13–15,21,22pp — Mt 11:21–23,25–27
10:23,24pp — Mt 13:16,17

10 After this the Lord[s] appointed seventy-two[c] others[t] and sent them two by two[u] ahead of him to every town and place where he was about to go.[v] 2He told them, "The harvest is plentiful, but the workers are few. Ask the Lord of the harvest, therefore, to send out workers into his harvest field.[w] 3Go! I am sending you out like lambs among wolves.[x] 4Do not take a purse or bag or sandals; and do not greet anyone on the road.

5"When you enter a house, first say, 'Peace to this house.' 6If a man of peace is there, your peace will rest on him; if not, it will return to you. 7Stay in that house, eating and drinking whatever they give you, for the worker deserves his wages.[y] Do not move around from house to house.

9:48
eMt 10:40
fMk 9:35
9:49
gLk 5:5
9:50
hMt 12:30;
Lk 11:23
9:51
iMk 16:19
jLk 13:22;
17:11; 18:31;
19:28
9:52
kMt 10:5
9:54
lMt 4:21
m2Ki 1:10,12
9:57
nver 51
9:58
oMt 8:20
9:59
pMt 4:19
9:60
qMt 3:2
9:61
r1Ki 19:20
10:1
sLk 7:13
tLk 9:1,2,51,52
uMk 6:7
vMt 10:1
10:2
wMt 9:37,38;
Jn 4:35
10:3
xMt 10:16
10:7
yMt 10:10;
1Co 9:14;
1Ti 5:18

---

[a]54 Some manuscripts *them, even as Elijah did*   [b]55,56 Some manuscripts *them. And he said, "You do not know what kind of spirit you are of, for the Son of Man did not come to destroy men's lives, but to save them." 56And*   [c]1 Some manuscripts *seventy; also in verse 17*

8"When you enter a town and are welcomed, eat what is set before you. [z] 9Heal the sick who are there and tell them, 'The kingdom of God [a] is near you.' 10But when you enter a town and are not welcomed, go into its streets and say, 11'Even the dust of your town that sticks to our feet we wipe off against you. [b] Yet be sure of this: The kingdom of God is near.' [c] 12I tell you, it will be more bearable on that day for Sodom [d] than for that town. [e]

13"Woe to you, [f] Korazin! Woe to you, Bethsaida! For if the miracles that were performed in you had been performed in Tyre and Sidon, they would have repented long ago, sitting in sackcloth [g] and ashes. 14But it will be more bearable for Tyre and Sidon at the judgment than for you. 15And you, Capernaum, [h] will you be lifted up to the skies? No, you will go down to the depths. [a]

16"He who listens to you listens to me; he who rejects you rejects me; but he who rejects me rejects him who sent me." [i]

17The seventy-two [j] returned with joy and said, "Lord, even the demons submit to us in your name." [k]

18He replied, "I saw Satan [l] fall like lightning from heaven. [m] 19I have given you authority to trample on snakes [n] and scorpions and to overcome all the power of the enemy; nothing will harm you. 20However, do not rejoice that the spirits submit to you, but rejoice that your names are written in heaven." [o]

21At that time Jesus, full of joy through the Holy Spirit, said, "I praise you, Father, Lord of heaven and earth, because you have hidden these things from the wise and learned, and revealed them to little children. [p] Yes, Father, for this was your good pleasure.

22"All things have been committed to me by my Father. [q] No one knows who the Son is except the Father, and no one knows who the Father is except the Son and those to whom the Son chooses to reveal him." [r]

23Then he turned to his disciples and said privately, "Blessed are the eyes that see what you see. 24For I tell you that many prophets and kings wanted to see what you see but did not see it, and to hear what you hear but did not hear it." [s]

The Parable of the Good Samaritan

10:25–28pp — Mt 22:34–40; Mk 12:28–31

25On one occasion an expert in the law stood up to test Jesus. "Teacher," he asked, "what must I do to inherit eternal life?" [t]

26"What is written in the Law?" he replied. "How do you read it?"

27He answered: " 'Love the Lord your God with all your heart and with all your soul and with all your strength and with all your mind' [b] ; [u] and, 'Love your neighbor as yourself.' [c] " [v]

28"You have answered correctly," Jesus replied. "Do this and you will live." [w]

29But he wanted to justify himself, [x] so he asked Jesus, "And who is my neighbor?"

30In reply Jesus said: "A man was going down from Jerusalem to Jericho, when he fell into the hands of robbers. They stripped him of his clothes, beat him and went away, leaving him half dead. 31A priest

10:8
z 1Co 10:27
10:9
a Mt 3:2; 10:7
10:11
b Mt 10:14;
Mk 6:11 c ver 9
10:12
d Mt 10:15
e Mt 11:24
10:13
f Lk 6:24-26
g Rev 11:3
10:15
h Mt 4:13
10:16
i Mt 10:40;
Jn 13:20
10:17
j ver 1
k Mk 16:17
10:18
l Mt 4:10
m Isa 14:12;
Rev 9:1; 12:8,9
10:19
n Mk 16:18;
Ac 28:3-5
10:20
o Ex 32:32;
Ps 69:28;
Da 12:1;
Php 4:3;
Heb 12:23;
Rev 13:8;
20:12; 21:27
10:21
p 1Co 1:26-29
10:22
q Mt 28:18
r Jn 1:18
10:24
s 1Pe 1:10-12
10:25
t Mt 19:16;
Lk 18:18
10:27
u Dt 6:5
v Lev 19:18;
Mt 5:43
10:28
w Lev 18:5;
Ro 7:10
10:29
x Lk 16:15

---

a15 Greek *Hades*   b27 Deut. 6:5   c27 Lev. 19:18

happened to be going down the same road, and when he saw the man, he passed by on the other side. [y] ³²So too, a Levite, when he came to the place and saw him, passed by on the other side. ³³But a Samaritan, [z] as he traveled, came where the man was; and when he saw him, he took pity on him. ³⁴He went to him and bandaged his wounds, pouring on oil and wine. Then he put the man on his own donkey, took him to an inn and took care of him. ³⁵The next day he took out two silver coins[a] and gave them to the innkeeper. 'Look after him,' he said, 'and when I return, I will reimburse you for any extra expense you may have.'

³⁶"Which of these three do you think was a neighbor to the man who fell into the hands of robbers?"

³⁷The expert in the law replied, "The one who had mercy on him." Jesus told him, "Go and do likewise."

At the Home of Martha and Mary

³⁸As Jesus and his disciples were on their way, he came to a village where a woman named Martha[a] opened her home to him. ³⁹She had a sister called Mary, [b] who sat at the Lord's feet[c] listening to what he said. ⁴⁰But Martha was distracted by all the preparations that had to be made. She came to him and asked, "Lord, don't you care[d] that my sister has left me to do the work by myself? Tell her to help me!"

⁴¹"Martha, Martha," the Lord answered, "you are worried[e] and upset about many things, ⁴²but only one thing is needed.[bf] Mary has chosen what is better, and it will not be taken away from her."

Jesus' Teaching on Prayer

11:2–4pp — Mt 6:9–13
11:9–13pp — Mt 7:7–11

11 One day Jesus was praying[g] in a certain place. When he finished, one of his disciples said to him, "Lord,[h] teach us to pray, just as John taught his disciples."

²He said to them, "When you pray, say:

> " 'Father,[c]
> hallowed be your name,
> your kingdom[i] come. [d]
> ³Give us each day our daily bread.
> ⁴Forgive us our sins,
>   for we also forgive everyone who sins against us. [e j]
> And lead us not into temptation. [f] ' "[k]

⁵Then he said to them, "Suppose one of you has a friend, and he goes to him at midnight and says, 'Friend, lend me three loaves of bread, ⁶because a friend of mine on a journey has come to me, and I have nothing to set before him.'

⁷"Then the one inside answers, 'Don't bother me. The door is already locked, and my children are with me in bed. I can't get up and give you anything.' ⁸I tell you, though he will not get up and give him the bread

---

10:31
y Lev 21:1-3
10:33
z Mt 10:5
10:38
a Jn 11:1; 12:2
10:39
b Jn 11:1; 12:3
c Lk 8:35
10:40
d Mk 4:38
10:41
e Mt 6:25-34;
Lk 12:11,22
10:42
f Ps 27:4
11:1
g Lk 3:21
h Jn 13:13
11:2
i Mt 3:2
11:4
j Mt 18:35;
Mk 11:25
k Mt 26:41;
Jas 1:13

---

a35 Greek two denarii   *b42 Some manuscripts but few things are needed—or only one*   *c2 Some manuscripts Our Father in heaven*   *d2 Some manuscripts come. May your will be done on earth as it is in heaven.*   *e4 Greek everyone who is indebted to us*   *f4 Some manuscripts temptation but deliver us from the evil one* because he is his friend, yet because of the man's boldness[a] he will get up and give him as much as he needs.[1]

9"So I say to you: Ask and it will be given to you;[m] seek and you will find; knock and the door will be opened to you. 10For everyone who asks receives; he who seeks finds; and to him who knocks, the door will be opened.

11"Which of you fathers, if your son asks for[b] a fish, will give him a snake instead? 12Or if he asks for an egg, will give him a scorpion? 13If you then, though you are evil, know how to give good gifts to your children, how much more will your Father in heaven give the Holy Spirit to those who ask him!"

Jesus and Beelzebub

11:14,15; 17–22; 24–26pp — Mt 12:22,24–29; 43–45
11:17–22pp — Mk 3:23–27

14Jesus was driving out a demon that was mute. When the demon left, the man who had been mute spoke, and the crowd was amazed.[n] 15But some of them said, "By Beelzebub,[c][o] the prince of demons, he is driving out demons."[p] 16Others tested him by asking for a sign from heaven.[q]

17Jesus knew their thoughts[r] and said to them: "Any kingdom divided against itself will be ruined, and a house divided against itself will fall. 18If Satan[s] is divided against himself, how can his kingdom stand? I say this because you claim that I drive out demons by Beelzebub. 19Now if I drive out demons by Beelzebub, by whom do your followers drive them out? So then, they will be your judges. 20But if I drive out demons by the finger of God,[t] then the kingdom of God[u] has come to you.

21"When a strong man, fully armed, guards his own house, his possessions are safe. 22But when someone stronger attacks and overpowers him, he takes away the armor in which the man trusted and divides up the spoils.

23"He who is not with me is against me, and he who does not gather with me, scatters.[v]

24"When an evil[d] spirit comes out of a man, it goes through arid places seeking rest and does not find it. Then it says, 'I will return to the house I left.' 25When it arrives, it finds the house swept clean and put in order. 26Then it goes and takes seven other spirits more wicked than itself, and they go in and live there. And the final condition of that man is worse than the first."[w]

27As Jesus was saying these things, a woman in the crowd called out, "Blessed is the mother who gave you birth and nursed you."[x]

28He replied, "Blessed rather are those who hear the word of God[y] and obey it."[z]

The Sign of Jonah

11:29–32pp — Mt 12:39–42

29As the crowds increased, Jesus said, "This is a wicked generation. It asks for a miraculous sign,[a] but none will be given it except the sign of

11:8
lLk 18:1-6
11:9
mMt 7:7
11:14
nMt 9:32,33
11:15
oMk 3:22
pMt 9:34
11:16
qMt 12:38
11:17
rMt 9:4
11:18
sMt 4:10
11:20
tEx 8:19
uMt 3:2
11:23
vMt 12:30;
Mk 9:40;
Lk 9:50
11:26
w2Pe 2:20
11:27
xLk 23:29
11:28
yHeb 4:12
zPr 8:32;
Lk 6:47; 8:21;
Jn 14:21
11:29
aver 16;
Mt 12:38

---

a8 Or *persistence*   b11 Some manuscripts *for bread, will give him a stone; or if he asks for*
c15 Greek *Beezeboul* or *Beelzeboul*; also in verses 18 and 19   d24 Greek *unclean*

Jonah.^b ³⁰For as Jonah was a sign to the Ninevites, so also will the Son of Man be to this generation. ³¹The Queen of the South will rise at the judgment with the men of this generation and condemn them; for she came from the ends of the earth to listen to Solomon's wisdom,^c and now one^a greater than Solomon is here. ³²The men of Nineveh will stand up at the judgment with this generation and condemn it; for they repented at the preaching of Jonah,^d and now one greater than Jonah is here.

The Lamp of the Body

11:34,35pp — Mt 6:22,23

³³"No one lights a lamp and puts it in a place where it will be hidden, or under a bowl. Instead he puts it on its stand, so that those who come in may see the light.^e ³⁴Your eye is the lamp of your body. When your eyes are good, your whole body also is full of light. But when they are bad, your body also is full of darkness. ³⁵See to it, then, that the light within you is not darkness. ³⁶Therefore, if your whole body is full of light, and no part of it dark, it will be completely lighted, as when the light of a lamp shines on you."

Six Woes

³⁷When Jesus had finished speaking, a Pharisee invited him to eat with him; so he went in and reclined at the table.^f ³⁸But the Pharisee, noticing that Jesus did not first wash before the meal,^g was surprised.

³⁹Then the Lord^h said to him, "Now then, you Pharisees clean the outside of the cup and dish, but inside you are full of greed and wickedness.ⁱ ⁴⁰You foolish people!^j Did not the one who made the outside make the inside also? ⁴¹But give what is inside ͺthe dishͺ^b to the poor,^k and everything will be clean for you.^l

⁴²"Woe to you Pharisees, because you give God a tenth^m of your mint, rue and all other kinds of garden herbs, but you neglect justice and the love of God.ⁿ You should have practiced the latter without leaving the former undone.^o

⁴³"Woe to you Pharisees, because you love the most important seats in the synagogues and greetings in the marketplaces.^p

⁴⁴"Woe to you, because you are like unmarked graves,^q which men walk over without knowing it."

⁴⁵One of the experts in the law^r answered him, "Teacher, when you say these things, you insult us also."

⁴⁶Jesus replied, "And you experts in the law, woe to you, because you load people down with burdens they can hardly carry, and you yourselves will not lift one finger to help them.^s

⁴⁷"Woe to you, because you build tombs for the prophets, and it was your forefathers who killed them. ⁴⁸So you testify that you approve of what your forefathers did; they killed the prophets, and you build their tombs.^t ⁴⁹Because of this, God in his wisdom^u said, 'I will send them prophets and apostles, some of whom they will kill and others they will persecute.'^v ⁵⁰Therefore this generation will be held responsible for the blood of all the prophets that has been shed since the beginning of the world, ⁵¹from the blood of Abel^w to the blood of Zechariah,^x who was

^a31 Or *something*; also in verse 32   ^b41 Or *what you have*

killed between the altar and the sanctuary. Yes, I tell you, this generation will be held responsible for it all. y

52"Woe to you experts in the law, because you have taken away the key to knowledge. You yourselves have not entered, and you have hindered those who were entering." z

53When Jesus left there, the Pharisees and the teachers of the law began to oppose him fiercely and to besiege him with questions, 54waiting to catch him in something he might say. a

Warnings and Encouragements
12:2–9pp — Mt 10:26–33

12 Meanwhile, when a crowd of many thousands had gathered, so that they were trampling on one another, Jesus began to speak first to his disciples, saying: "Be on your guard against the yeast of the Pharisees, which is hypocrisy. b 2There is nothing concealed that will not be disclosed, or hidden that will not be made known. c 3What you have said in the dark will be heard in the daylight, and what you have whispered in the ear in the inner rooms will be proclaimed from the roofs.

4"I tell you, my friends, d do not be afraid of those who kill the body and after that can do no more. 5But I will show you whom you should fear: Fear him who, after the killing of the body, has power to throw you into hell. Yes, I tell you, fear him. e 6Are not five sparrows sold for two penniesª? Yet not one of them is forgotten by God. 7Indeed, the very hairs of your head are all numbered. f Don't be afraid; you are worth more than many sparrows. g

8"I tell you, whoever acknowledges me before men, the Son of Man will also acknowledge him before the angels of God. h 9But he who disowns me before men will be disowned i before the angels of God. 10And everyone who speaks a word against the Son of Manʲ will be forgiven, but anyone who blasphemes against the Holy Spirit will not be forgiven. k

11"When you are brought before synagogues, rulers and authorities, do not worry about how you will defend yourselves or what you will say, 1 12for the Holy Spirit will teach you at that time what you should say." m

The Parable of the Rich Fool

13Someone in the crowd said to him, "Teacher, tell my brother to divide the inheritance with me."

14Jesus replied, "Man, who appointed me a judge or an arbiter between you?" 15Then he said to them, "Watch out! Be on your guard against all kinds of greed; a man's life does not consist in the abundance of his possessions." n

16And he told them this parable: "The ground of a certain rich man produced a good crop. 17He thought to himself, 'What shall I do? I have no place to store my crops.'

18"Then he said, 'This is what I'll do. I will tear down my barns and build bigger ones, and there I will store all my grain and my goods.

ª6 Greek *two assaria*

11:51
y Mt 23:35,36
11:52
z Mt 23:13
11:54
a Mt 12:10;
Mk 12:13
12:1
b Mt 16:6,11,12;
Mk 8:15
12:2
c Mk 4:22;
Lk 8:17
12:4
d Jn 15:14,15
12:5
e Heb 10:31
12:7
f Mt 10:30
g Mt 12:12
12:8
h Lk 15:10
12:9
i Mk 8:38;
2Ti 2:12
12:10
j Mt 8:20
k Mt 12:31,32;
Mk 3:28-29;
1Jn 5:16
12:11
l Mt 10:17,19;
Mk 13:11;
Lk 21:12,14
12:12
m Ex 4:12;
Mt 10:20;
Mk 13:11;
Lk 21:15
12:15
n Job 20:20;
31:24; Ps 62:10

19And I'll say to myself, "You have plenty of good things laid up for many years. Take life easy; eat, drink and be merry." '

20"But God said to him, 'You fool!ᵒ This very night your life will be demanded from you.ᵖ Then who will get what you have prepared for yourself?'�q

21"This is how it will be with anyone who stores up things for himself but is not rich toward God."ʳ

Do Not Worry

12:22–31pp — Mt 6:25–33

22Then Jesus said to his disciples: "Therefore I tell you, do not worry about your life, what you will eat; or about your body, what you will wear. 23Life is more than food, and the body more than clothes. 24Consider the ravens: They do not sow or reap, they have no storeroom or barn; yet God feeds them.ˢ And how much more valuable you are than birds! 25Who of you by worrying can add a single hour to his lifeᵃ? 26Since you cannot do this very little thing, why do you worry about the rest?

27"Consider how the lilies grow. They do not labor or spin. Yet I tell you, not even Solomon in all his splendorᵗ was dressed like one of these. 28If that is how God clothes the grass of the field, which is here today, and tomorrow is thrown into the fire, how much more will he clothe you, O you of little faith!ᵘ 29And do not set your heart on what you will eat or drink; do not worry about it. 30For the pagan world runs after all such things, and your Fatherᵛ knows that you need them.ʷ 31But seek his kingdom,ˣ and these things will be given to you as well.ʸ

32"Do not be afraid,ᶻ little flock, for your Father has been pleased to give you the kingdom.ᵃ 33Sell your possessions and give to the poor.ᵇ Provide purses for yourselves that will not wear out, a treasure in heavenᶜ that will not be exhausted, where no thief comes near and no moth destroys.ᵈ 34For where your treasure is, there your heart will be also.ᵉ

Watchfulness

12:35,36pp — Mt 25:1–13; Mk 13:33–37
12:39,40; 42–46pp — Mt 24:43–51

35"Be dressed ready for service and keep your lamps burning, 36like men waiting for their master to return from a wedding banquet, so that when he comes and knocks they can immediately open the door for him. 37It will be good for those servants whose master finds them watching when he comes.ᶠ I tell you the truth, he will dress himself to serve, will have them recline at the table and will come and wait on them.ᵍ 38It will be good for those servants whose master finds them ready, even if he comes in the second or third watch of the night. 39But understand this: If the owner of the house had known at what hour the thiefʰ was coming, he would not have let his house be broken into. 40You also must be ready,ⁱ because the Son of Man will come at an hour when you do not expect him."

41Peter asked, "Lord, are you telling this parable to us, or to everyone?"

12:20
ᵒJer 17:11;
Lk 11:40
ᵖJob 27:8
qPs 39:6; 49:10
12:21
ʳver 33
12:24
ˢJob 38:41;
Ps 147:9
12:27
ᵗ1Ki 10:4-7
12:28
ᵘMt 6:30
12:30
ᵛLk 6:36
ʷMt 6:8
12:31
ˣMt 3:2
ʸMt 19:29
12:32
ᶻMt 14:27
ᵃMt 25:34
12:33
ᵇMt 19:21;
Ac 2:45
ᶜMt 6:20
ᵈJas 5:2
12:34
ᵉMt 6:21
12:37
ᶠMt 24:42,46;
25:13 ᵍMt 20:28
12:39
ʰMt 6:19;
1Th 5:2;
2Pe 3:10;
Rev 3:3; 16:15
12:40
ⁱMk 13:33;
Lk 21:36

42The Lord[j] answered, "Who then is the faithful and wise manager, whom the master puts in charge of his servants to give them their food allowance at the proper time? 43It will be good for that servant whom the master finds doing so when he returns. 44I tell you the truth, he will put him in charge of all his possessions. 45But suppose the servant says to himself, 'My master is taking a long time in coming,' and he then begins to beat the menservants and maidservants and to eat and drink and get drunk. 46The master of that servant will come on a day when he does not expect him and at an hour he is not aware of.[k] He will cut him to pieces and assign him a place with the unbelievers.

47"That servant who knows his master's will and does not get ready or does not do what his master wants will be beaten with many blows.[l] 48But the one who does not know and does things deserving punishment will be beaten with few blows.[m] From everyone who has been given much, much will be demanded; and from the one who has been entrusted with much, much more will be asked.

Not Peace but Division

12:51–53pp — Mt 10:34–36

49"I have come to bring fire on the earth, and how I wish it were already kindled! 50But I have a baptism[n] to undergo, and how distressed I am until it is completed![o] 51Do you think I came to bring peace on earth? No, I tell you, but division. 52From now on there will be five in one family divided against each other, three against two and two against three. 53They will be divided, father against son and son against father, mother against daughter and daughter against mother, mother-in-law against daughter-in-law and daughter-in-law against mother-in-law."[p]

Interpreting the Times

54He said to the crowd: "When you see a cloud rising in the west, immediately you say, 'It's going to rain,' and it does.[q] 55And when the south wind blows, you say, 'It's going to be hot,' and it is. 56Hypocrites! You know how to interpret the appearance of the earth and the sky. How is it that you don't know how to interpret this present time?[r]

57"Why don't you judge for yourselves what is right? 58As you are going with your adversary to the magistrate, try hard to be reconciled to him on the way, or he may drag you off to the judge, and the judge turn you over to the officer, and the officer throw you into prison.[s] 59I tell you, you will not get out until you have paid the last penny.[a]"[t]

Repent or Perish

13 Now there were some present at that time who told Jesus about the Galileans whose blood Pilate[u] had mixed with their sacrifices. 2Jesus answered, "Do you think that these Galileans were worse sinners than all the other Galileans because they suffered this way?[v] 3I tell you, no! But unless you repent, you too will all perish. 4Or those eighteen who died when the tower in Siloam[w] fell on them—do you think they were more guilty than all the others living in Jerusalem? 5I tell you, no! But unless you repent,[x] you too will all perish."

a59 Greek *lepton*

12:42
jLk 7:13
12:46
kver 40
12:47
lDt 25:2
12:48
mLev 5:17;
Nu 15:27-30
12:50
nMk 10:38
oJn 19:30
12:53
pMic 7:6;
Mt 10:21
12:54
qMt 16:2
12:56
rMt 16:3
12:58
sMt 5:25
12:59
tMt 5:26;
Mk 12:42
13:1
uMt 27:2
13:2
vJn 9:2,3
13:4
wJn 9:7,11
13:5
xMt 3:2;
Ac 2:38

6Then he told this parable: "A man had a fig tree, planted in his vineyard, and he went to look for fruit on it, but did not find any.y 7So he said to the man who took care of the vineyard, 'For three years now I've been coming to look for fruit on this fig tree and haven't found any. Cut it down!z Why should it use up the soil?'

8" 'Sir,' the man replied, 'leave it alone for one more year, and I'll dig around it and fertilize it. 9If it bears fruit next year, fine! If not, then cut it down.' "

A Crippled Woman Healed on the Sabbath

10On a Sabbath Jesus was teaching in one of the synagogues,a 11and a woman was there who had been crippled by a spirit for eighteen years.b She was bent over and could not straighten up at all. 12When Jesus saw her, he called her forward and said to her, "Woman, you are set free from your infirmity." 13Then he put his hands on her,c and immediately she straightened up and praised God.

14Indignant because Jesus had healed on the Sabbath,d the synagogue rulere said to the people, "There are six days for work.f So come and be healed on those days, not on the Sabbath."

15The Lord answered him, "You hypocrites! Doesn't each of you on the Sabbath untie his ox or donkey from the stall and lead it out to give it water?g 16Then should not this woman, a daughter of Abraham,h whom Satani has kept bound for eighteen long years, be set free on the Sabbath day from what bound her?"

17When he said this, all his opponents were humiliated,j but the people were delighted with all the wonderful things he was doing.

The Parables of the Mustard Seed and the Yeast

13:18,19pp — Mk 4:30–32
13:18–21pp — Mt 13:31–33

18Then Jesus asked, "What is the kingdom of Godk like?l What shall I compare it to? 19It is like a mustard seed, which a man took and planted in his garden. It grew and became a tree,m and the birds of the air perched in its branches."n

20Again he asked, "What shall I compare the kingdom of God to? 21It is like yeast that a woman took and mixed into a large amounta of flour until it worked all through the dough."o

The Narrow Door

22Then Jesus went through the towns and villages, teaching as he made his way to Jerusalem.p 23Someone asked him, "Lord, are only a few people going to be saved?"

He said to them, 24"Make every effort to enter through the narrow door,q because many, I tell you, will try to enter and will not be able to. 25Once the owner of the house gets up and closes the door, you will stand outside knocking and pleading, 'Sir, open the door for us.'

"But he will answer, 'I don't know you or where you come from.'r

26"Then you will say, 'We ate and drank with you, and you taught in our streets.'

a21 Greek three satas (probably about 1/2 bushel or 22 liters)

13:6
yIsa 5:2;
Jer 8:13;
Mt 21:19
13:7
zMt 3:10
13:10
aMt 4:23
13:11
bver 16
13:13
cMk 5:23
13:14
dMt 12:2;
Lk 14:3
eMk 5:22
fEx 20:9
13:15
gLk 14:5
13:16
hLk 3:8; 19:9
iMt 4:10
13:17
jIsa 66:5
13:18
kMt 3:2
lMt 13:24
13:19
mLk 17:6
nMt 13:32
13:21
o1Co 5:6
13:22
pLk 9:51
13:24
qMt 7:13
13:25
rMt 7:23;
25:10-12

27"But he will reply, 'I don't know you or where you come from. Away from me, all you evildoers!'ˢ

28"There will be weeping there, and gnashing of teeth,ᵗ when you see Abraham, Isaac and Jacob and all the prophets in the kingdom of God, but you yourselves thrown out. 29People will come from east and westᵘ and north and south, and will take their places at the feast in the kingdom of God. 30Indeed there are those who are last who will be first, and first who will be last."ᵛ

Jesus' Sorrow for Jerusalem

13:34,35pp — Mt 23:37–39
13:34,35Ref — Lk 19:41

31At that time some Pharisees came to Jesus and said to him, "Leave this place and go somewhere else. Herodʷ wants to kill you."

32He replied, "Go tell that fox, 'I will drive out demons and heal people today and tomorrow, and on the third day I will reach my goal.'ˣ 33In any case, I must keep going today and tomorrow and the next day—for surely no prophetʸ can die outside Jerusalem!

34"O Jerusalem, Jerusalem, you who kill the prophets and stone those sent to you, how often I have longed to gather your children together, as a hen gathers her chicks under her wings,ᶻ but you were not willing! 35Look, your house is left to you desolate.ᵃ I tell you, you will not see me again until you say, 'Blessed is he who comes in the name of the Lord.'ᵃ "ᵇ

Jesus at a Pharisee's House

14:8–10Ref — Pr 25:6,7

14 One Sabbath, when Jesus went to eat in the house of a prominent Pharisee,ᶜ he was being carefully watched.ᵈ 2There in front of him was a man suffering from dropsy. 3Jesus asked the Pharisees and experts in the law,ᵉ "Is it lawful to heal on the Sabbath or not?"ᶠ 4But they remained silent. So taking hold of the man, he healed him and sent him away.

5Then he asked them, "If one of you has a sonᵇ or an ox that falls into a well on the Sabbath day, will you not immediately pull him out?"ᵍ 6And they had nothing to say.

7When he noticed how the guests picked the places of honor at the table,ʰ he told them this parable: 8"When someone invites you to a wedding feast, do not take the place of honor, for a person more distinguished than you may have been invited. 9If so, the host who invited both of you will come and say to you, 'Give this man your seat.' Then, humiliated, you will have to take the least important place. 10But when you are invited, take the lowest place, so that when your host comes, he will say to you, 'Friend, move up to a better place.' Then you will be honored in the presence of all your fellow guests. 11For everyone who exalts himself will be humbled, and he who humbles himself will be exalted."ⁱ

12Then Jesus said to his host, "When you give a luncheon or dinner, do not invite your friends, your brothers or relatives, or your rich neighbors; if you do, they may invite you back and so you will be

13:27
ˢMt 7:23; 25:41
13:28
ᵗMt 8:12
13:29
ᵘMt 8:11
13:30
ᵛMt 19:30
13:31
ʷMt 14:1
13:32
ˣHeb 2:10
13:33
ʸMt 21:11
13:34
ᶻMt 23:37
13:35
ᵃJer 12:17; 22:5
ᵇPs 118:26;
Mt 21:9;
Lk 19:38
14:1
ᶜLk 7:36; 11:37
ᵈMt 12:10
14:3
ᵉMt 22:35
ᶠMt 12:2
14:5
ᵍLk 13:15
14:7
ʰLk 11:43
14:11
ⁱMt 23:12;
Lk 18:14

ᵃ35 Psalm 118:26   ᵇ5 Some manuscripts *donkey*

repaid. [13]But when you give a banquet, invite the poor, the crippled, the lame, the blind,[i] [14]and you will be blessed. Although they cannot repay you, you will be repaid at the resurrection of the righteous."[k]

The Parable of the Great Banquet

14:16–24Ref — Mt 22:2–14

[15]When one of those at the table with him heard this, he said to Jesus, "Blessed is the man who will eat at the feast[l] in the kingdom of God."[m]

[16]Jesus replied: "A certain man was preparing a great banquet and invited many guests. [17]At the time of the banquet he sent his servant to tell those who had been invited, 'Come, for everything is now ready.'

[18]"But they all alike began to make excuses. The first said, 'I have just bought a field, and I must go and see it. Please excuse me.'

[19]"Another said, 'I have just bought five yoke of oxen, and I'm on my way to try them out. Please excuse me.'

[20]"Still another said, 'I just got married, so I can't come.'

[21]"The servant came back and reported this to his master. Then the owner of the house became angry and ordered his servant, 'Go out quickly into the streets and alleys of the town and bring in the poor, the crippled, the blind and the lame.'[n]

[22]"'Sir,' the servant said, 'what you ordered has been done, but there is still room.'

[23]"Then the master told his servant, 'Go out to the roads and country lanes and make them come in, so that my house will be full. [24]I tell you, not one of those men who were invited will get a taste of my banquet.'"[o]

The Cost of Being a Disciple

[25]Large crowds were traveling with Jesus, and turning to them he said: [26]"If anyone comes to me and does not hate his father and mother, his wife and children, his brothers and sisters—yes, even his own life—he cannot be my disciple.[p] [27]And anyone who does not carry his cross and follow me cannot be my disciple.[q]

[28]"Suppose one of you wants to build a tower. Will he not first sit down and estimate the cost to see if he has enough money to complete it? [29]For if he lays the foundation and is not able to finish it, everyone who sees it will ridicule him, [30]saying, 'This fellow began to build and was not able to finish.'

[31]"Or suppose a king is about to go to war against another king. Will he not first sit down and consider whether he is able with ten thousand men to oppose the one coming against him with twenty thousand? [32]If he is not able, he will send a delegation while the other is still a long way off and will ask for terms of peace. [33]In the same way, any of you who does not give up everything he has cannot be my disciple.[r]

[34]"Salt is good, but if it loses its saltiness, how can it be made salty again?[s] [35]It is fit neither for the soil nor for the manure pile; it is thrown out.[t]

"He who has ears to hear, let him hear."[u]

14:13
i ver 21
14:14
k Ac 24:15
14:15
l Isa 25:6;
Mt 26:29;
Lk 13:29;
Rev 19:9
m Mt 3:2
14:21
n ver 13
14:24
o Mt 21:43;
Ac 13:46
14:26
p Mt 10:37;
Jn 12:25
14:27
q Mt 10:38;
Lk 9:23
14:33
r Php 3:7,8
14:34
s Mk 9:50
14:35
t Mt 5:13
u Mt 11:15

The Parable of the Lost Sheep

15:4–7pp — Mt 18:12–14

15 Now the tax collectors[v] and "sinners" were all gathering around to hear him. [2]But the Pharisees and the teachers of the law muttered, "This man welcomes sinners and eats with them."[w]

[3]Then Jesus told them this parable:[x] [4]"Suppose one of you has a hundred sheep and loses one of them. Does he not leave the ninety-nine in the open country and go after the lost sheep until he finds it?[y] [5]And when he finds it, he joyfully puts it on his shoulders [6]and goes home. Then he calls his friends and neighbors together and says, 'Rejoice with me; I have found my lost sheep.'[z] [7]I tell you that in the same way there will be more rejoicing in heaven over one sinner who repents than over ninety-nine righteous persons who do not need to repent.[a]

The Parable of the Lost Coin

[8]"Or suppose a woman has ten silver coins[a] and loses one. Does she not light a lamp, sweep the house and search carefully until she finds it? [9]And when she finds it, she calls her friends and neighbors together and says, 'Rejoice with me; I have found my lost coin.'[b] [10]In the same way, I tell you, there is rejoicing in the presence of the angels of God over one sinner who repents."[c]

The Parable of the Lost Son

[11]Jesus continued: "There was a man who had two sons.[d] [12]The younger one said to his father, 'Father, give me my share of the estate.'[e] So he divided his property[f] between them.

[13]"Not long after that, the younger son got together all he had, set off for a distant country and there squandered his wealth[g] in wild living. [14]After he had spent everything, there was a severe famine in that whole country, and he began to be in need. [15]So he went and hired himself out to a citizen of that country, who sent him to his fields to feed pigs.[h] [16]He longed to fill his stomach with the pods that the pigs were eating, but no one gave him anything.

[17]"When he came to his senses, he said, 'How many of my father's hired men have food to spare, and here I am starving to death! [18]I will set out and go back to my father and say to him: Father, I have sinned[i] against heaven and against you. [19]I am no longer worthy to be called your son; make me like one of your hired men.' [20]So he got up and went to his father.

"But while he was still a long way off, his father saw him and was filled with compassion for him; he ran to his son, threw his arms around him and kissed him.[j]

[21]"The son said to him, 'Father, I have sinned against heaven and against you.[k] I am no longer worthy to be called your son.[b] '

[22]"But the father said to his servants, 'Quick! Bring the best robe[l] and put it on him. Put a ring on his finger[m] and sandals on his feet. [23]Bring the fattened calf and kill it. Let's have a feast and celebrate. [24]For this

---

a8 Greek ten drachmas, each worth about a day's wages   *b21 Some early manuscripts son. Make me like one of your hired men.*

15:1
vLk 5:29
15:2
wMt 9:11
15:3
xMt 13:3
15:4
yPs 23;
119:176;
Jer 31:10;
Eze 34:11-16;
Lk 5:32; 19:10
15:6
zver 9
15:7
aver 10
15:9
bver 6
15:10
cver 7
15:11
dMt 21:28
15:12
eDt 21:17
fver 30
15:13
gver 30; Lk 16:1
15:15
hLev 11:7
15:18
iLev 26:40;
Mt 3:2
15:20
jGe 45:14,15;
46:29; Ac 20:37
15:21
kPs 51:4
15:22
lZec 3:4;
Rev 6:11
mGe 41:42

son of mine was dead and is alive again;[n] he was lost and is found.' So they began to celebrate.[o]

25"Meanwhile, the older son was in the field. When he came near the house, he heard music and dancing. 26So he called one of the servants and asked him what was going on. 27'Your brother has come,' he replied, 'and your father has killed the fattened calf because he has him back safe and sound.'

28"The older brother became angry[p] and refused to go in. So his father went out and pleaded with him. 29But he answered his father, 'Look! All these years I've been slaving for you and never disobeyed your orders. Yet you never gave me even a young goat so I could celebrate with my friends. 30But when this son of yours who has squandered your property[q] with prostitutes[r] comes home, you kill the fattened calf for him!'

31"'My son,' the father said, 'you are always with me, and everything I have is yours. 32But we had to celebrate and be glad, because this brother of yours was dead and is alive again; he was lost and is found.'"[s]

The Parable of the Shrewd Manager

16 Jesus told his disciples: "There was a rich man whose manager was accused of wasting his possessions.[t] 2So he called him in and asked him, 'What is this I hear about you? Give an account of your management, because you cannot be manager any longer.'

3"The manager said to himself, 'What shall I do now? My master is taking away my job. I'm not strong enough to dig, and I'm ashamed to beg— 4I know what I'll do so that, when I lose my job here, people will welcome me into their houses.'

5"So he called in each one of his master's debtors. He asked the first, 'How much do you owe my master?'

6"'Eight hundred gallons[a] of olive oil,' he replied.

"The manager told him, 'Take your bill, sit down quickly, and make it four hundred.'

7"Then he asked the second, 'And how much do you owe?'

"'A thousand bushels[b] of wheat,' he replied.

"He told him, 'Take your bill and make it eight hundred.'

8"The master commended the dishonest manager because he had acted shrewdly. For the people of this world[u] are more shrewd[v] in dealing with their own kind than are the people of the light.[w] 9I tell you, use worldly wealth[x] to gain friends for yourselves, so that when it is gone, you will be welcomed into eternal dwellings.[y]

10"Whoever can be trusted with very little can also be trusted with much,[z] and whoever is dishonest with very little will also be dishonest with much. 11So if you have not been trustworthy in handling worldly wealth,[a] who will trust you with true riches? 12And if you have not been trustworthy with someone else's property, who will give you property of your own?

13"No servant can serve two masters. Either he will hate the one and

15:24
nEph 2:1,5;
5:14; 1Ti 5:6
over 32
15:28
pJnh 4:1
15:30
qver 12,13
rPr 29:3
15:32
sver 24;
Mal 3:17
16:1
tLk 15:13,30
16:8
uPs 17:14
vPs 18:26
wJn 12:36;
Eph 5:8;
1Th 5:5
16:9
xver 11,13
yMt 19:21;
Lk 12:33
16:10
zMt 25:21,23;
Lk 19:17
16:11
aver 9,13

---

a6 Greek one hundred batous (probably about 3 kiloliters)   b7 Greek one hundred korous (probably about 35 kiloliters) love the other, or he will be devoted to the one and despise the other. You cannot serve both God and Money."[b]

[14]The Pharisees, who loved money,[c] heard all this and were sneering at Jesus.[d] [15]He said to them, "You are the ones who justify yourselves[e] in the eyes of men, but God knows your hearts.[f] What is highly valued among men is detestable in God's sight.

Additional Teachings

[16]"The Law and the Prophets were proclaimed until John.[g] Since that time, the good news of the kingdom of God is being preached,[h] and everyone is forcing his way into it. [17]It is easier for heaven and earth to disappear than for the least stroke of a pen to drop out of the Law.[i]

[18]"Anyone who divorces his wife and marries another woman commits adultery, and the man who marries a divorced woman commits adultery.[j]

The Rich Man and Lazarus

[19]"There was a rich man who was dressed in purple and fine linen and lived in luxury every day.[k] [20]At his gate was laid a beggar[l] named Lazarus, covered with sores [21]and longing to eat what fell from the rich man's table.[m] Even the dogs came and licked his sores.

[22]"The time came when the beggar died and the angels carried him to Abraham's side. The rich man also died and was buried. [23]In hell,[a] where he was in torment, he looked up and saw Abraham far away, with Lazarus by his side. [24]So he called to him, 'Father Abraham,[n] have pity on me and send Lazarus to dip the tip of his finger in water and cool my tongue, because I am in agony in this fire.'[o]

[25]"But Abraham replied, 'Son, remember that in your lifetime you received your good things, while Lazarus received bad things,[p] but now he is comforted here and you are in agony.[q] [26]And besides all this, between us and you a great chasm has been fixed, so that those who want to go from here to you cannot, nor can anyone cross over from there to us.'

[27]"He answered, 'Then I beg you, father, send Lazarus to my father's house, [28]for I have five brothers. Let him warn them,[r] so that they will not also come to this place of torment.'

[29]"Abraham replied, 'They have Moses[s] and the Prophets;[t] let them listen to them.'

[30]" 'No, father Abraham,'[u] he said, 'but if someone from the dead goes to them, they will repent.'

[31]"He said to him, 'If they do not listen to Moses and the Prophets, they will not be convinced even if someone rises from the dead.' "

Sin, Faith, Duty

17 Jesus said to his disciples: "Things that cause people to sin[v] are bound to come, but woe to that person through whom they come.[w] [2]It would be better for him to be thrown into the sea with a millstone tied around his neck than for him to cause one of these little ones[x] to sin.[y] [3]So watch yourselves.

"If your brother sins, rebuke him,[z] and if he repents, forgive him.[a]

[a]23 Greek *Hades*

16:13
bver 9,11;
Mt 6:24
16:14
c1Ti 3:3
dLk 23:35
16:15
eLk 10:29
f1Sa 16:7;
Rev 2:23
16:16
gMt 11:12,13
hMt 4:23
16:17
iMt 5:18
16:18
jMt 5:31,32;
19:9; Mk 10:11;
Ro 7:2,3;
1Co 7:10,11
16:19
kEze 16:49
16:20
lAc 3:2
16:21
mMt 15:27
16:24
nver 30; Lk 3:8
oMt 5:22
16:25
pPs 17:14
qLk 6:21,24,25
16:28
rAc 2:40;
20:23; 1Th 4:6
16:29
sLk 24:27,44;
Jn 5:45-47;
Ac 15:21
tLk 4:17;
Jn 1:45
16:30
uver 24; Lk 3:8
17:1
vMt 5:29
wMt 18:7
17:2
xMk 10:24;
Lk 10:21
yMt 5:29
17:3
zMt 18:15
aEph 4:32;
Col 3:13

4If he sins against you seven times in a day, and seven times comes back to you and says, 'I repent,' forgive him."[b]

5The apostles[c] said to the Lord,[d] "Increase our faith!"

6He replied, "If you have faith as small as a mustard seed,[e] you can say to this mulberry tree, 'Be uprooted and planted in the sea,' and it will obey you.[f]

7"Suppose one of you had a servant plowing or looking after the sheep. Would he say to the servant when he comes in from the field, 'Come along now and sit down to eat'? 8Would he not rather say, 'Prepare my supper, get yourself ready and wait on me[g] while I eat and drink; after that you may eat and drink'? 9Would he thank the servant because he did what he was told to do? 10So you also, when you have done everything you were told to do, should say, 'We are unworthy servants; we have only done our duty.' "[h]

Ten Healed of Leprosy

11Now on his way to Jerusalem,[i] Jesus traveled along the border between Samaria and Galilee.[j] 12As he was going into a village, ten men who had leprosy[a][k] met him. They stood at a distance[l] 13and called out in a loud voice, "Jesus, Master,[m] have pity on us!"

14When he saw them, he said, "Go, show yourselves to the priests."[n] And as they went, they were cleansed.

15One of them, when he saw he was healed, came back, praising God[o] in a loud voice. 16He threw himself at Jesus' feet and thanked him—and he was a Samaritan.[p]

17Jesus asked, "Were not all ten cleansed? Where are the other nine? 18Was no one found to return and give praise to God except this foreigner?" 19Then he said to him, "Rise and go; your faith has made you well."[q]

The Coming of the Kingdom of God

17:26,27pp — Mt 24:37-39

20Once, having been asked by the Pharisees when the kingdom of God would come,[r] Jesus replied, "The kingdom of God does not come with your careful observation, 21nor will people say, 'Here it is,' or 'There it is,'[s] because the kingdom of God is within[b] you."

22Then he said to his disciples, "The time is coming when you will long to see one of the days of the Son of Man,[t] but you will not see it.[u] 23Men will tell you, 'There he is!' or 'Here he is!' Do not go running off after them.[v] 24For the Son of Man in his day[c] will be like the lightning,[w] which flashes and lights up the sky from one end to the other. 25But first he must suffer many things[x] and be rejected[y] by this generation.[z]

26"Just as it was in the days of Noah,[a] so also will it be in the days of the Son of Man. 27People were eating, drinking, marrying and being given in marriage up to the day Noah entered the ark. Then the flood came and destroyed them all.

28"It was the same in the days of Lot.[b] People were eating and drinking, buying and selling, planting and building. 29But the day Lot

---

17:4
bMt 18:21,22
17:5
cMk 6:30
dLk 7:13
17:6
eMt 13:31;
17:20; Lk 13:19
fMt 21:21;
Mk 9:23
17:8
gLk 12:37
17:10
h1Co 9:16
17:11
iLk 9:51
jLk 9:51,52;
Jn 4:3,4
17:12
kMt 8:2
lLev 13:45,46
17:13
mLk 5:5
17:14
nLev 14:2;
Mt 8:4
17:15
oMt 9:8
17:16
pMt 10:5
17:19
qMt 9:22
17:20
rMt 3:2
17:21
sver 23
17:22
tMt 8:20
uMt 9:15;
Lk 5:35
17:23
vMt 24:23;
Mk 13:21;
Lk 21:8
17:24
wMt 24:27
17:25
xMt 16:21
yLk 9:22; 18:32
zMk 13:30;
Lk 21:32
17:26
aGe 7:6-24
17:28
bGe 19:1-28

---

a12 The Greek word was used for various diseases affecting the skin—not necessarily leprosy.
b21 Or *among*   c24 Some manuscripts do not have *in his day*.

left Sodom, fire and sulfur rained down from heaven and destroyed them all.

30"It will be just like this on the day the Son of Man is revealed. c 31On that day no one who is on the roof of his house, with his goods inside, should go down to get them. Likewise, no one in the field should go back for anything. d 32Remember Lot's wife!e 33Whoever tries to keep his life will lose it, and whoever loses his life will preserve it. f 34I tell you, on that night two people will be in one bed; one will be taken and the other left. 35Two women will be grinding grain together; one will be taken and the other left. a "g

37"Where, Lord?" they asked.

He replied, "Where there is a dead body, there the vultures will gather."h

The Parable of the Persistent Widow

18 Then Jesus told his disciples a parable to show them that they should always pray and not give up. i 2He said: "In a certain town there was a judge who neither feared God nor cared about men. 3And there was a widow in that town who kept coming to him with the plea, 'Grant me justicej against my adversary.'

4"For some time he refused. But finally he said to himself, 'Even though I don't fear God or care about men, 5yet because this widow keeps bothering me, I will see that she gets justice, so that she won't eventually wear me out with her coming!' "k

6And the Lordl said, "Listen to what the unjust judge says. 7And will not God bring about justice for his chosen ones, who cry outm to him day and night? Will he keep putting them off? 8I tell you, he will see that they get justice, and quickly. However, when the Son of Man n comes, o will he find faith on the earth?"

The Parable of the Pharisee and the Tax Collector

9To some who were confident of their own righteousnessp and looked down on everybody else, q Jesus told this parable: 10"Two men went up to the temple to pray,r one a Pharisee and the other a tax collector. 11The Pharisee stood ups and prayed aboutb himself: 'God, I thank you that I am not like other men—robbers, evildoers, adulterers—or even like this tax collector. 12I fastt twice a week and give a tenthu of all I get.'

13"But the tax collector stood at a distance. He would not even look up to heaven, but beat his breastv and said, 'God, have mercy on me, a sinner.'w

14"I tell you that this man, rather than the other, went home justified before God. For everyone who exalts himself will be humbled, and he who humbles himself will be exalted."x

The Little Children and Jesus

18:15–17pp — Mt 19:13–15; Mk 10:13–16

15People were also bringing babies to Jesus to have him touch them. When the disciples saw this, they rebuked them. 16But Jesus called the

---

a35 Some manuscripts *left.* 36*Two men will be in the field; one will be taken and the other left.*
b11 Or *to*

17:30
cMt 10:23;
16:27; 24:3,27,
37,39; 25:31;
1Co 1:7;
1Th 2:19;
2Th 1:7; 2:8;
2Pe 3:4;
Rev 1:7
17:31
dMt 24:17,18;
Mk 13:15-16
17:32
eGe 19:26
17:33
fJn 12:25
17:35
gMt 24:41
17:37
hMt 24:28
18:1
iIsa 40:31;
Lk 11:5-8;
Ac 1:14;
Ro 12:12;
Eph 6:18;
Col 4:2;
1Th 5:17
18:3
jIsa 1:17
18:5
kLk 11:8
18:6
lLk 7:13
18:7
mEx 22:23;
Ps 88:1;
Rev 6:10
18:8
nMt 8:20
oMt 16:27
18:9
pLk 16:15
qIsa 65:5
18:10
rAc 3:1
18:11
sMt 6:5;
Mk 11:25
18:12
tIsa 58:3;
Mt 9:14
uMal 3:8;
Lk 11:42
18:13
vIsa 66:2;
Jer 31:19;
Lk 23:48
wLk 5:32;
1Ti 1:15
18:14
xMt 23:12;
Lk 14:11

children to him and said, "Let the little children come to me, and do not hinder them, for the kingdom of God belongs to such as these. 17I tell you the truth, anyone who will not receive the kingdom of God like a little child[y] will never enter it."

The Rich Ruler

18:18–30pp — Mt 19:16–29; Mk 10:17–30

18A certain ruler asked him, "Good teacher, what must I do to inherit eternal life?"[z]

19"Why do you call me good?" Jesus answered. "No one is good—except God alone. 20You know the commandments: 'Do not commit adultery, do not murder, do not steal, do not give false testimony, honor your father and mother.'[a] "[a]

21"All these I have kept since I was a boy," he said.

22When Jesus heard this, he said to him, "You still lack one thing. Sell everything you have and give to the poor,[b] and you will have treasure in heaven.[c] Then come, follow me."

23When he heard this, he became very sad, because he was a man of great wealth. 24Jesus looked at him and said, "How hard it is for the rich to enter the kingdom of God![d] 25Indeed, it is easier for a camel to go through the eye of a needle than for a rich man to enter the kingdom of God."

26Those who heard this asked, "Who then can be saved?"

27Jesus replied, "What is impossible with men is possible with God."[e]

28Peter said to him, "We have left all we had to follow you!"[f]

29"I tell you the truth," Jesus said to them, "no one who has left home or wife or brothers or parents or children for the sake of the kingdom of God 30will fail to receive many times as much in this age and, in the age to come,[g] eternal life."[h]

Jesus Again Predicts His Death

18:31–33pp — Mt 20:17–19; Mk 10:32–34

31Jesus took the Twelve aside and told them, "We are going up to Jerusalem,[i] and everything that is written by the prophets[j] about the Son of Man[k] will be fulfilled. 32He will be handed over to the Gentiles.[l] They will mock him, insult him, spit on him, flog him[m] and kill him.[n] 33On the third day[o] he will rise again."[p]

34The disciples did not understand any of this. Its meaning was hidden from them, and they did not know what he was talking about.[q]

A Blind Beggar Receives His Sight

18:35–43pp — Mt 20:29–34; Mk 10:46–52

35As Jesus approached Jericho,[r] a blind man was sitting by the roadside begging. 36When he heard the crowd going by, he asked what was happening. 37They told him, "Jesus of Nazareth is passing by."[s]

38He called out, "Jesus, Son of David,[t] have mercy[u] on me!"

39Those who led the way rebuked him and told him to be quiet, but he shouted all the more, "Son of David, have mercy on me!"[v]

40Jesus stopped and ordered the man to be brought to him. When he

18:17
yMt 11:25; 18:3
18:18
zLk 10:25
18:20
aEx 20:12-16;
Dt 5:16-20;
Ro 13:9
18:22
bAc 2:45
cMt 6:20
18:24
dPr 11:28
18:27
eMt 19:26
18:28
fMt 4:19
18:30
gMt 12:32
hMt 25:46
18:31
iLk 9:51 jPs 22;
Isa 53 kMt 8:20
18:32
lLk 23:1
mMt 16:21
nAc 2:23
18:33
oMt 16:21
pMt 16:21
18:34
qMk 9:32;
Lk 9:45
18:35
rLk 19:1
18:37
sLk 19:4
18:38
tver 39; Mt 9:27
uMt 17:15;
Lk 18:13
18:39
vver 38

a20 Exodus 20:12-16; Deut. 5:16-20

came near, Jesus asked him, [41]"What do you want me to do for you?" "Lord, I want to see," he replied.

[42]Jesus said to him, "Receive your sight; your faith has healed you." [w]
[43]Immediately he received his sight and followed Jesus, praising God. When all the people saw it, they also praised God. [x]

Zacchaeus the Tax Collector

19 Jesus entered Jericho [y] and was passing through. [2]A man was there by the name of Zacchaeus; he was a chief tax collector and was wealthy. [3]He wanted to see who Jesus was, but being a short man he could not, because of the crowd. [4]So he ran ahead and climbed a sycamore-fig [z] tree to see him, since Jesus was coming that way. [a]

[5]When Jesus reached the spot, he looked up and said to him, "Zacchaeus, come down immediately. I must stay at your house today." [6]So he came down at once and welcomed him gladly.

[7]All the people saw this and began to mutter, "He has gone to be the guest of a 'sinner.' " [b]

[8]But Zacchaeus stood up and said to the Lord, [c] "Look, Lord! Here and now I give half of my possessions to the poor, and if I have cheated anybody out of anything, [d] I will pay back four times the amount." [e]

[9]Jesus said to him, "Today salvation has come to this house, because this man, too, is a son of Abraham. [f] [10]For the Son of Man came to seek and to save what was lost." [g]

The Parable of the Ten Minas

19:12–27Ref — Mt 25:14–30

[11]While they were listening to this, he went on to tell them a parable, because he was near Jerusalem and the people thought that the kingdom of God [h] was going to appear at once. [i] [12]He said: "A man of noble birth went to a distant country to have himself appointed king and then to return. [13]So he called ten of his servants [j] and gave them ten minas. [a] 'Put this money to work,' he said, 'until I come back.'

[14]"But his subjects hated him and sent a delegation after him to say, 'We don't want this man to be our king.'

[15]"He was made king, however, and returned home. Then he sent for the servants to whom he had given the money, in order to find out what they had gained with it.

[16]"The first one came and said, 'Sir, your mina has earned ten more.'

[17]" 'Well done, my good servant!' [k] his master replied. 'Because you have been trustworthy in a very small matter, take charge of ten cities.' [l]

[18]"The second came and said, 'Sir, your mina has earned five more.'

[19]"His master answered, 'You take charge of five cities.'

[20]"Then another servant came and said, 'Sir, here is your mina; I have kept it laid away in a piece of cloth. [21]I was afraid of you, because you are a hard man. You take out what you did not put in and reap what you did not sow.' [m]

[22]"His master replied, 'I will judge you by your own words, [n] you wicked servant! You knew, did you, that I am a hard man, taking out what I did not put in, and reaping what I did not sow? [o] [23]Why then

---

a13 A mina was about three months' wages.

18:42
w Mt 9:22
18:43
x Mt 9:8;
Lk 13:17
19:1
y Lk 18:35
19:4
z 1Ki 10:27;
1Ch 27:28;
Isa 9:10
a Lk 18:37
19:7
b Mt 9:11
19:8
c Lk 7:13
d Lk 3:12,13
e Ex 22:1;
Lev 6:4,5;
Nu 5:7;
2Sa 12:6
19:9
f Lk 3:8; 13:16;
Ro 4:16;
Gal 3:7
19:10
g Eze 34:12,16;
Jn 3:17
19:11
h Mt 3:2
i Lk 17:20;
Ac 1:6
19:13
j Mk 13:34
19:17
k Pr 27:18
l Lk 16:10
19:21
m Mt 25:24
19:22
n 2Sa 1:16;
Job 15:6
o Mt 25:26

didn't you put my money on deposit, so that when I came back, I could have collected it with interest?'

²⁴"Then he said to those standing by, 'Take his mina away from him and give it to the one who has ten minas.'

²⁵" 'Sir,' they said, 'he already has ten!'

²⁶"He replied, 'I tell you that to everyone who has, more will be given, but as for the one who has nothing, even what he has will be taken away. ᴾ ²⁷But those enemies of mine who did not want me to be king over them—bring them here and kill them in front of me.' "

The Triumphal Entry

19:29–38pp — Mt 21:1–9; Mk 11:1–10
19:35–38pp — Jn 12:12–15

²⁸After Jesus had said this, he went on ahead, going up to Jerusalem. �q ²⁹As he approached Bethphage and Bethany ʳ at the hill called the Mount of Olives, ˢ he sent two of his disciples, saying to them, ³⁰"Go to the village ahead of you, and as you enter it, you will find a colt tied there, which no one has ever ridden. Untie it and bring it here. ³¹If anyone asks you, 'Why are you untying it?' tell him, 'The Lord needs it.' "

³²Those who were sent ahead went and found it just as he had told them. ᵗ ³³As they were untying the colt, its owners asked them, "Why are you untying the colt?"

³⁴They replied, "The Lord needs it."

³⁵They brought it to Jesus, threw their cloaks on the colt and put Jesus on it. ³⁶As he went along, people spread their cloaksᵘ on the road.

³⁷When he came near the place where the road goes down the Mount of Olives, ᵛ the whole crowd of disciples began joyfully to praise God in loud voices for all the miracles they had seen:

³⁸"Blessed is the king who comes in the name of the
    Lord!" ᵃ ʷ

"Peace in heaven and glory in the highest!" ˣ

³⁹Some of the Pharisees in the crowd said to Jesus, "Teacher, rebuke your disciples!" ʸ

⁴⁰"I tell you," he replied, "if they keep quiet, the stones will cry out." ᶻ

⁴¹As he approached Jerusalem and saw the city, he wept over itᵃ ⁴²and said, "If you, even you, had only known on this day what would bring you peace—but now it is hidden from your eyes. ⁴³The days will come upon you when your enemies will build an embankment against you and encircle you and hem you in on every side. ᵇ ⁴⁴They will dash you to the ground, you and the children within your walls. ᶜ They will not leave one stone on another, ᵈ because you did not recognize the time of God's coming ᵉ to you."

Jesus at the Temple

19:45,46pp — Mt 21:12–16; Mk 11:15–18; Jn 2:13–16

⁴⁵Then he entered the temple area and began driving out those who

19:26
pMt 13:12;
25:29; Lk 8:18
19:28
qMk 10:32;
Lk 9:51
19:29
rMt 21:17
sMt 21:1
19:32
tLk 22:13
19:36
u2Ki 9:13
19:37
vMt 21:1
19:38
wPs 118:26;
Lk 13:35
xLk 2:14
19:39
yMt 21:15,16
19:40
zHab 2:11
19:41
aIsa 22:4;
Lk 13:34,35
19:43
bIsa 29:3;
Jer 6:6;
Eze 4:2; 26:8;
Lk 21:20
19:44
cPs 137:9
dMt 24:2;
Mk 13:2;
Lk 21:6
e1Pe 2:12

were selling. ⁴⁶"It is written," he said to them, " 'My house will be a house of prayer'ᵃ;ᶠ but you have made it 'a den of robbers.'ᵇ"ᵍ

⁴⁷Every day he was teaching at the temple.ʰ But the chief priests, the teachers of the law and the leaders among the people were trying to kill him.ⁱ ⁴⁸Yet they could not find any way to do it, because all the people hung on his words.

The Authority of Jesus Questioned
20:1–8pp — Mt 21:23–27; Mk 11:27–33

20 One day as he was teaching the people in the temple courtsʲ and preaching the gospel,ᵏ the chief priests and the teachers of the law, together with the elders, came up to him. ²"Tell us by what authority you are doing these things," they said. "Who gave you this authority?"ˡ

³He replied, "I will also ask you a question. Tell me, ⁴John's baptismᵐ—was it from heaven, or from men?"

⁵They discussed it among themselves and said, "If we say, 'From heaven,' he will ask, 'Why didn't you believe him?' ⁶But if we say, 'From men,' all the peopleⁿ will stone us, because they are persuaded that John was a prophet."ᵒ

⁷So they answered, "We don't know where it was from."

⁸Jesus said, "Neither will I tell you by what authority I am doing these things."

The Parable of the Tenants
20:9–19pp — Mt 21:33–46; Mk 12:1–12

⁹He went on to tell the people this parable: "A man planted a vineyard,ᵖ rented it to some farmers and went away for a long time.�q ¹⁰At harvest time he sent a servant to the tenants so they would give him some of the fruit of the vineyard. But the tenants beat him and sent him away empty-handed. ¹¹He sent another servant, but that one also they beat and treated shamefully and sent away empty-handed. ¹²He sent still a third, and they wounded him and threw him out.

¹³"Then the owner of the vineyard said, 'What shall I do? I will send my son, whom I love;ʳ perhaps they will respect him.'

¹⁴"But when the tenants saw him, they talked the matter over. 'This is the heir,' they said. 'Let's kill him, and the inheritance will be ours.' ¹⁵So they threw him out of the vineyard and killed him.

"What then will the owner of the vineyard do to them? ¹⁶He will come and kill those tenantsˢ and give the vineyard to others."

When the people heard this, they said, "May this never be!"

¹⁷Jesus looked directly at them and asked, "Then what is the meaning of that which is written:

" 'The stone the builders rejected
has become the capstoneᶜ'ᵈ?ᵗ

¹⁸Everyone who falls on that stone will be broken to pieces, but he on whom it falls will be crushed."ᵘ

¹⁹The teachers of the law and the chief priests looked for a way to

19:46
fIsa 56:7
gJer 7:11
19:47
hMt 26:55
iMt 12:14;
Mk 11:18
20:1
jMt 26:55
kLk 8:1
20:2
lJn 2:18;
Ac 4:7; 7:27
20:4
mMk 1:4
20:6
nLk 7:29
oMt 11:9
20:9
pIsa 5:1-7
qMt 25:14
20:13
rMt 3:17
20:16
sLk 19:27
20:17
tPs 118:22;
Ac 4:11
20:18
uIsa 8:14,15

ᵃ46 Isaiah 56:7   ᵇ46 Jer. 7:11   ᶜ17 Or *cornerstone*   ᵈ17 Psalm 118:22

arrest him[v] immediately, because they knew he had spoken this parable against them. But they were afraid of the people.[w]

Paying Taxes to Caesar

20:20–26pp — Mt 22:15–22; Mk 12:13–17

20Keeping a close watch on him, they sent spies, who pretended to be honest. They hoped to catch Jesus in something he said[x] so that they might hand him over to the power and authority of the governor.[y] 21So the spies questioned him: "Teacher, we know that you speak and teach what is right, and that you do not show partiality but teach the way of God in accordance with the truth.[z] 22Is it right for us to pay taxes to Caesar or not?"

23He saw through their duplicity and said to them, 24"Show me a denarius. Whose portrait and inscription are on it?"

25"Caesar's," they replied.

He said to them, "Then give to Caesar what is Caesar's,[a] and to God what is God's."

26They were unable to trap him in what he had said there in public. And astonished by his answer, they became silent.

The Resurrection and Marriage

20:27–40pp — Mt 22:23–33; Mk 12:18–27

27Some of the Sadducees,[b] who say there is no resurrection,[c] came to Jesus with a question. 28"Teacher," they said, "Moses wrote for us that if a man's brother dies and leaves a wife but no children, the man must marry the widow and have children for his brother.[d] 29Now there were seven brothers. The first one married a woman and died childless. 30The second 31and then the third married her, and in the same way the seven died, leaving no children. 32Finally, the woman died too. 33Now then, at the resurrection whose wife will she be, since the seven were married to her?"

34Jesus replied, "The people of this age marry and are given in marriage. 35But those who are considered worthy of taking part in that age[e] and in the resurrection from the dead will neither marry nor be given in marriage, 36and they can no longer die; for they are like the angels. They are God's children,[f] since they are children of the resurrection. 37But in the account of the bush, even Moses showed that the dead rise, for he calls the Lord 'the God of Abraham, and the God of Isaac, and the God of Jacob.'[a][g] 38He is not the God of the dead, but of the living, for to him all are alive."

39Some of the teachers of the law responded, "Well said, teacher!" 40And no one dared to ask him any more questions.[h]

Whose Son Is the Christ?

20:41–47pp — Mt 22:41–23:7; Mk 12:35–40

41Then Jesus said to them, "How is it that they say the Christ[b] is the Son of David?[i] 42David himself declares in the Book of Psalms:

" 'The Lord said to my Lord:
  "Sit at my right hand

20:19
vLk 19:47
wMk 11:18
20:20
xMt 12:10
yMt 27:2
20:21
zJn 3:2
20:25
aLk 23:2;
Ro 13:7
20:27
bAc 4:1
cAc 23:8;
1Co 15:12
20:28
dDt 25:5
20:35
eMt 12:32
20:36
fJn 1:12;
1Jn 3:1-2
20:37
gEx 3:6
20:40
hMt 22:46;
Mk 12:34
20:41
iMt 1:1

---

a37 Exodus 3:6   b41 Or *Messiah*

⁴³until I make your enemies
    a footstool for your feet.'' '^{a j}

⁴⁴David calls him 'Lord.' How then can he be his son?''

⁴⁵While all the people were listening, Jesus said to his disciples,
⁴⁶''Beware of the teachers of the law. They like to walk around in
flowing robes and love to be greeted in the marketplaces and have the
most important seats in the synagogues and the places of honor at
banquets.^k ⁴⁷They devour widows' houses and for a show make
lengthy prayers. Such men will be punished most severely.''

The Widow's Offering

21:1–4pp — Mk 12:41–44

21 As he looked up, Jesus saw the rich putting their gifts into the
temple treasury.^l ²He also saw a poor widow put in two very
small copper coins.^b ³''I tell you the truth,'' he said, ''this poor widow
has put in more than all the others. ⁴All these people gave their gifts out
of their wealth; but she out of her poverty put in all she had to live
on.''^m

Signs of the End of the Age

21:5–36pp — Mt 24; Mk 13
21:12–17pp — Mt 10:17–22

⁵Some of his disciples were remarking about how the temple was
adorned with beautiful stones and with gifts dedicated to God. But
Jesus said, ⁶''As for what you see here, the time will come when not one
stone will be left on another;ⁿ every one of them will be thrown down.''

⁷''Teacher,'' they asked, ''when will these things happen? And what
will be the sign that they are about to take place?''

⁸He replied: ''Watch out that you are not deceived. For many will
come in my name, claiming, 'I am he,' and, 'The time is near.' Do not
follow them.^o ⁹When you hear of wars and revolutions, do not be
frightened. These things must happen first, but the end will not come
right away.''

¹⁰Then he said to them: ''Nation will rise against nation, and king-
dom against kingdom.^p ¹¹There will be great earthquakes, famines and
pestilences in various places, and fearful events and great signs from
heaven.^q

¹²''But before all this, they will lay hands on you and persecute you.
They will deliver you to synagogues and prisons, and you will be
brought before kings and governors, and all on account of my name.
¹³This will result in your being witnesses to them.^r ¹⁴But make up your
mind not to worry beforehand how you will defend yourselves.^s ¹⁵For
I will give you^t words and wisdom that none of your adversaries will
be able to resist or contradict. ¹⁶You will be betrayed even by parents,
brothers, relatives and friends,^u and they will put some of you to
death. ¹⁷All men will hate you because of me.^v ¹⁸But not a hair of your
head will perish.^w ¹⁹By standing firm you will gain life.^x

²⁰''When you see Jerusalem being surrounded by armies,^y you will
know that its desolation is near. ²¹Then let those who are in Judea flee
to the mountains, let those in the city get out, and let those in the

20:43
jPs 110:1;
Mt 22:44
20:46
kLk 11:43
21:1
lMt 27:6;
Jn 8:20
21:4
m2Co 8:12
21:6
nLk 19:44
21:8
oLk 17:23
21:10
p2Ch 15:6;
Isa 19:2
21:11
qIsa 29:6;
Joel 2:30
21:13
rPhp 1:12
21:14
sLk 12:11
21:15
tLk 12:12
21:16
uLk 12:52,53
21:17
vJn 15:21
21:18
wMt 10:30
21:19
xMt 10:22
21:20
yLk 19:43

*a*43 Psalm 110:1   *b*2 Greek *two lepta*

country not enter the city.ᶻ ²²For this is the time of punishmentᵃ in fulfillmentᵇ of all that has been written. ²³How dreadful it will be in those days for pregnant women and nursing mothers! There will be great distress in the land and wrath against this people. ²⁴They will fall by the sword and will be taken as prisoners to all the nations. Jerusalem will be trampledᶜ on by the Gentiles until the times of the Gentiles are fulfilled.

²⁵"There will be signs in the sun, moon and stars. On the earth, nations will be in anguish and perplexity at the roaring and tossing of the sea.ᵈ ²⁶Men will faint from terror, apprehensive of what is coming on the world, for the heavenly bodies will be shaken.ᵉ ²⁷At that time they will see the Son of Manᶠ coming in a cloudᵍ with power and great glory. ²⁸When these things begin to take place, stand up and lift up your heads, because your redemption is drawing near."ʰ

²⁹He told them this parable: "Look at the fig tree and all the trees. ³⁰When they sprout leaves, you can see for yourselves and know that summer is near. ³¹Even so, when you see these things happening, you know that the kingdom of Godⁱ is near.

³²"I tell you the truth, this generationᵃʲ will certainly not pass away until all these things have happened. ³³Heaven and earth will pass away, but my words will never pass away.ᵏ

³⁴"Be careful, or your hearts will be weighed down with dissipation, drunkenness and the anxieties of life,ˡ and that day will close on you unexpectedlyᵐ like a trap. ³⁵For it will come upon all those who live on the face of the whole earth. ³⁶Be always on the watch, and prayⁿ that you may be able to escape all that is about to happen, and that you may be able to stand before the Son of Man."

³⁷Each day Jesus was teaching at the temple,ᵒ and each evening he went outᵖ to spend the night on the hill called the Mount of Olives,�q ³⁸and all the people came early in the morning to hear him at the temple.ʳ

Judas Agrees to Betray Jesus

22:1,2pp — Mt 26:2-5; Mk 14:1,2,10,11

22 Now the Feast of Unleavened Bread, called the Passover, was approaching,ˢ ²and the chief priests and the teachers of the law were looking for some way to get rid of Jesus,ᵗ for they were afraid of the people. ³Then Satanᵘ entered Judas, called Iscariot,ᵛ one of the Twelve. ⁴And Judas went to the chief priests and the officers of the temple guardʷ and discussed with them how he might betray Jesus. ⁵They were delighted and agreed to give him money.ˣ ⁶He consented, and watched for an opportunity to hand Jesus over to them when no crowd was present.

The Last Supper

22:7-13pp — Mt 26:17-19; Mk 14:12-16
22:17-20pp — Mt 26:26-29; Mk 14:22-25; 1Co 11:23-25
22:21-23pp — Mt 26:21-24; Mk 14:18-21; Jn 13:21-30
22:25-27pp — Mt 20:25-28; Mk 10:42-45
22:33,34pp — Mt 26:33-35; Mk 14:29-31; Jn 13:37,38

⁷Then came the day of Unleavened Bread on which the Pass-

21:21
zLk 17:31
21:22
aIsa 63:4;
Da 9:24-27;
Hos 9:7
bMt 1:22
21:24
cIsa 5:5; 63:18;
Da 8:13;
Rev 11:2
21:25
d2Pe 3:10,12
21:26
eMt 24:29
21:27
fMt 8:20
gRev 1:7
21:28
hLk 18:7
21:31
iMt 3:2
21:32
jLk 11:50; 17:25
21:33
kMt 5:18
21:34
lMk 4:19
mLk 12:40,46;
1Th 5:2-7
21:36
nMt 26:41
21:37
oMt 26:55
pMk 11:19
qMt 21:1
21:38
rJn 8:2
22:1
sJn 11:55
22:2
tMt 12:14
22:3
uMt 4:10;
Jn 13:2
vMt 10:4
22:4
wver 52;
Ac 4:1; 5:24
22:5
xZec 11:12

ᵃ32 Or *race*

over lamb had to be sacrificed.[y] [8]Jesus sent Peter and John,[z] saying, "Go and make preparations for us to eat the Passover."

[9]"Where do you want us to prepare for it?" they asked.

[10]He replied, "As you enter the city, a man carrying a jar of water will meet you. Follow him to the house that he enters, [11]and say to the owner of the house, 'The Teacher asks: Where is the guest room, where I may eat the Passover with my disciples?' [12]He will show you a large upper room, all furnished. Make preparations there."

[13]They left and found things just as Jesus had told them.[a] So they prepared the Passover.

[14]When the hour came, Jesus and his apostles[b] reclined at the table.[c] [15]And he said to them, "I have eagerly desired to eat this Passover with you before I suffer.[d] [16]For I tell you, I will not eat it again until it finds fulfillment in the kingdom of God."[e]

[17]After taking the cup, he gave thanks and said, "Take this and divide it among you. [18]For I tell you I will not drink again of the fruit of the vine until the kingdom of God comes."

[19]And he took bread, gave thanks and broke it,[f] and gave it to them, saying, "This is my body given for you; do this in remembrance of me."

[20]In the same way, after the supper he took the cup, saying, "This cup is the new covenant[g] in my blood, which is poured out for you. [21]But the hand of him who is going to betray me is with mine on the table.[h] [22]The Son of Man[i] will go as it has been decreed,[j] but woe to that man who betrays him." [23]They began to question among themselves which of them it might be who would do this.

[24]Also a dispute arose among them as to which of them was considered to be greatest.[k] [25]Jesus said to them, "The kings of the Gentiles lord it over them; and those who exercise authority over them call themselves Benefactors. [26]But you are not to be like that. Instead, the greatest among you should be like the youngest,[l] and the one who rules like the one who serves.[m] [27]For who is greater, the one who is at the table or the one who serves? Is it not the one who is at the table? But I am among you as one who serves.[n] [28]You are those who have stood by me in my trials. [29]And I confer on you a kingdom,[o] just as my Father conferred one on me, [30]so that you may eat and drink at my table in my kingdom[p] and sit on thrones, judging the twelve tribes of Israel.[q]

[31]"Simon, Simon, Satan has asked[r] to sift you[a] as wheat.[s] [32]But I have prayed for you,[t] Simon, that your faith may not fail. And when you have turned back, strengthen your brothers."[u]

[33]But he replied, "Lord, I am ready to go with you to prison and to death."[v]

[34]Jesus answered, "I tell you, Peter, before the rooster crows today, you will deny three times that you know me."

[35]Then Jesus asked them, "When I sent you without purse, bag or sandals,[w] did you lack anything?"

"Nothing," they answered.

[36]He said to them, "But now if you have a purse, take it, and also a bag; and if you don't have a sword, sell your cloak and buy one. [37]It is written: 'And he was numbered with the transgressors'[b];[x] and I tell

---

[a]31 The Greek is plural.   [b]37 Isaiah 53:12

22:7
yEx 12:18-20;
Dt 16:5-8;
Mk 14:12

22:8
zAc 3:1,11;
4:13,19; 8:14

22:13
aLk 19:32

22:14
bMk 6:30
cMt 26:20;
Mk 14:17,18

22:15
dMt 16:21

22:16
eLk 14:15;
Rev 19:9

22:19
fMt 14:19

22:20
gEx 24:8;
Isa 42:6;
Jer 31:31-34;
Zec 9:11;
2Co 3:6;
Heb 8:6; 9:15

22:21
hPs 41:9

22:22
iMt 8:20
jAc 2:23; 4:28

22:24
kMk 9:34;
Lk 9:46

22:26
l1Pe 5:5
mMk 9:35;
Lk 9:48

22:27
nMt 20:28;
Lk 12:37

22:29
oMt 25:34;
2Ti 2:12

22:30
pLk 14:15
qMt 19:28

22:31
rJob 1:6-12
sAm 9:9

22:32
tJn 17:9,15;
Ro 8:34
uJn 21:15-17

22:33
vJn 11:16

22:35
wMt 10:9,10;
Lk 9:3; 10:4

22:37
xIsa 53:12

you that this must be fulfilled in me. Yes, what is written about me is reaching its fulfillment."

38The disciples said, "See, Lord, here are two swords."

"That is enough," he replied.

Jesus Prays on the Mount of Olives

22:40–46pp — Mt 26:36–46; Mk 14:32–42

39Jesus went out as usual[y] to the Mount of Olives,[z] and his disciples followed him. 40On reaching the place, he said to them, "Pray that you will not fall into temptation."[a] 41He withdrew about a stone's throw beyond them, knelt down[b] and prayed, 42"Father, if you are willing, take this cup[c] from me; yet not my will, but yours be done."[d] 43An angel from heaven appeared to him and strengthened him.[e] 44And being in anguish, he prayed more earnestly, and his sweat was like drops of blood falling to the ground.[a]

45When he rose from prayer and went back to the disciples, he found them asleep, exhausted from sorrow. 46"Why are you sleeping?" he asked them. "Get up and pray so that you will not fall into temptation."[f]

Jesus Arrested

22:47–53pp — Mt 26:47–56; Mk 14:43–50; Jn 18:3–11

47While he was still speaking a crowd came up, and the man who was called Judas, one of the Twelve, was leading them. He approached Jesus to kiss him, 48but Jesus asked him, "Judas, are you betraying the Son of Man with a kiss?"

49When Jesus' followers saw what was going to happen, they said, "Lord, should we strike with our swords?"[g] 50And one of them struck the servant of the high priest, cutting off his right ear.

51But Jesus answered, "No more of this!" And he touched the man's ear and healed him.

52Then Jesus said to the chief priests, the officers of the temple guard,[h] and the elders, who had come for him, "Am I leading a rebellion, that you have come with swords and clubs? 53Every day I was with you in the temple courts,[i] and you did not lay a hand on me. But this is your hour[j]—when darkness reigns."[k]

Peter Disowns Jesus

22:55–62pp — Mt 26:69–75; Mk 14:66–72; Jn 18:16–18,25–27

54Then seizing him, they led him away and took him into the house of the high priest.[l] Peter followed at a distance.[m] 55But when they had kindled a fire in the middle of the courtyard and had sat down together, Peter sat down with them. 56A servant girl saw him seated there in the firelight. She looked closely at him and said, "This man was with him."

57But he denied it. "Woman, I don't know him," he said.

58A little later someone else saw him and said, "You also are one of them."

"Man, I am not!" Peter replied.

59About an hour later another asserted, "Certainly this fellow was with him, for he is a Galilean."[n]

22:39
yLk 21:37
zMt 21:1
22:40
aMt 6:13
22:41
bLk 18:11
22:42
cMt 20:22
dMt 26:39
22:43
eMt 4:11;
Mk 1:13
22:46
fver 40
22:49
gver 38
22:52
hver 4
22:53
iMt 26:55
jJn 12:27
kMt 8:12;
Jn 1:5; 3:20
22:54
lMt 26:57;
Mk 14:53
mMt 26:58;
Mk 14:54;
Jn 18:15
22:59
nLk 23:6

---

[a]44 Some early manuscripts do not have verses 43 and 44.

⁶⁰Peter replied, "Man, I don't know what you're talking about!" Just as he was speaking, the rooster crowed. ⁶¹The Lord° turned and looked straight at Peter. Then Peter remembered the word the Lord had spoken to him: "Before the rooster crows today, you will disown me three times."ᴾ ⁶²And he went outside and wept bitterly.

The Soldiers Mock Jesus

22:63–65pp — Mt 26:67,68; Mk 14:65; Jn 18:22,23

⁶³The men who were guarding Jesus began mocking and beating him. ⁶⁴They blindfolded him and demanded, "Prophesy! Who hit you?" ⁶⁵And they said many other insulting things to him. ۹

Jesus Before Pilate and Herod

22:67–71pp — Mt 26:63–66; Mk 14:61–63; Jn 18:19–21
23:2,3pp — Mt 27:11–14; Mk 15:2–5; Jn 18:29–37
23:18–25pp — Mt 27:15–26; Mk 15:6–15; Jn 18:39 — 19:16

⁶⁶At daybreak the councilʳ of the elders of the people, both the chief priests and teachers of the law, met together,ˢ and Jesus was led before them. ⁶⁷"If you are the Christ,ᵃ" they said, "tell us."

Jesus answered, "If I tell you, you will not believe me, ⁶⁸and if I asked you, you would not answer.ᵗ ⁶⁹But from now on, the Son of Man will be seated at the right hand of the mighty God."ᵘ

⁷⁰They all asked, "Are you then the Son of God?"ᵛ

He replied, "You are right in saying I am."ʷ

⁷¹Then they said, "Why do we need any more testimony? We have heard it from his own lips."

23 Then the whole assembly rose and led him off to Pilate.ˣ ²And they began to accuse him, saying, "We have found this man subverting our nation.ʸ He opposes payment of taxes to Caesarᶻ and claims to be Christ,ᵇ a king."ᵃ

³So Pilate asked Jesus, "Are you the king of the Jews?"

"Yes, it is as you say," Jesus replied.

⁴Then Pilate announced to the chief priests and the crowd, "I find no basis for a charge against this man."ᵇ

⁵But they insisted, "He stirs up the people all over Judeaᶜ by his teaching. He started in Galileeᶜ and has come all the way here."

⁶On hearing this, Pilate asked if the man was a Galilean.ᵈ ⁷When he learned that Jesus was under Herod's jurisdiction, he sent him to Herod,ᵉ who was also in Jerusalem at that time.

⁸When Herod saw Jesus, he was greatly pleased, because for a long time he had been wanting to see him.ᶠ From what he had heard about him, he hoped to see him perform some miracle. ⁹He plied him with many questions, but Jesus gave him no answer.ᵍ ¹⁰The chief priests and the teachers of the law were standing there, vehemently accusing him. ¹¹Then Herod and his soldiers ridiculed and mocked him. Dressing him in an elegant robe,ʰ they sent him back to Pilate. ¹²That day Herod and Pilate became friendsⁱ—before this they had been enemies.

¹³Pilate called together the chief priests, the rulers and the people, ¹⁴and said to them, "You brought me this man as one who was inciting the people to rebellion. I have examined him in your presence and have

22:61
oLk 7:13
pver 34
22:65
qMt 16:21
22:66
rMt 5:22
sMt 27:1;
Mk 15:1
22:68
tLk 20:3-8
22:69
uMk 16:19
22:70
vMt 4:3
wMt 27:11;
Lk 23:3
23:1
xMt 27:2;
Mk 15:1;
Jn 18:28
23:2
yver 14
zLk 20:22
aJn 19:12
23:4
bver 14,22,41;
Mt 27:23;
Jn 18:38;
1Ti 6:13;
2Cor 5:21
23:5
cMk 1:14
23:6
dLk 22:59
23:7
eMt 14:1;
Lk 3:1
23:8
fLk 9:9
23:9
gMk 14:61
23:11
hMk 15:17-19;
Jn 19:2,3
23:12
iAc 4:27

ᵃ67 Or *Messiah*   ᵇ2 Or *Messiah; also in verses 35 and 39*   ᶜ5 Or *over the land of the Jews* found no basis for your charges against him.ʲ ¹⁵Neither has Herod, for he sent him back to us; as you can see, he has done nothing to deserve death. ¹⁶Therefore, I will punish himᵏ and then release him.ᵃ "

¹⁸With one voice they cried out, "Away with this man! Release Barabbas to us!"ˡ ¹⁹(Barabbas had been thrown into prison for an insurrection in the city, and for murder.)

²⁰Wanting to release Jesus, Pilate appealed to them again. ²¹But they kept shouting, "Crucify him! Crucify him!"

²²For the third time he spoke to them: "Why? What crime has this man committed? I have found in him no grounds for the death penalty. Therefore I will have him punished and then release him."ᵐ

²³But with loud shouts they insistently demanded that he be crucified, and their shouts prevailed. ²⁴So Pilate decided to grant their demand. ²⁵He released the man who had been thrown into prison for insurrection and murder, the one they asked for, and surrendered Jesus to their will.

The Crucifixion

23:33–43pp — Mt 27:33–44; Mk 15:22–32; Jn 19:17–24

²⁶As they led him away, they seized Simon from Cyrene,ⁿ who was on his way in from the country, and put the cross on him and made him carry it behind Jesus.ᵒ ²⁷A large number of people followed him, including women who mourned and wailedᵖ for him. ²⁸Jesus turned and said to them, "Daughters of Jerusalem, do not weep for me; weep for yourselves and for your children.�q ²⁹For the time will come when you will say, 'Blessed are the barren women, the wombs that never bore and the breasts that never nursed!'ʳ ³⁰Then

" 'they will say to the mountains, "Fall on us!"
and to the hills, "Cover us!" 'ᵇ ˢ

³¹For if men do these things when the tree is green, what will happen when it is dry?"ᵗ

³²Two other men, both criminals, were also led out with him to be executed.ᵘ ³³When they came to the place called the Skull, there they crucified him, along with the criminals—one on his right, the other on his left. ³⁴Jesus said, "Father,ᵛ forgive them, for they do not know what they are doing."ᶜʷ And they divided up his clothes by casting lots.ˣ

³⁵The people stood watching, and the rulers even sneered at him.ʸ They said, "He saved others; let him save himself if he is the Christ of God, the Chosen One."ᶻ

³⁶The soldiers also came up and mocked him.ᵃ They offered him wine vinegarᵇ ³⁷and said, "If you are the king of the Jews,ᶜ save yourself."

³⁸There was a written notice above him, which read: THIS IS THE KING OF THE JEWS.ᵈ

³⁹One of the criminals who hung there hurled insults at him: "Aren't you the Christ? Save yourself and us!"ᵉ

⁴⁰But the other criminal rebuked him. "Don't you fear God," he said, "since you are under the same sentence? ⁴¹We are punished justly, for

23:14
jver 4
23:16
kver 22;
Mt 27:26;
Jn 19:1;
Ac 16:37;
2Co 11:23,24
23:18
lAc 3:13,14
23:22
mver 16
23:26
nMt 27:32
oMk 15:21;
Jn 19:17
23:27
pLk 8:52
23:28
qLk 19:41-44;
21:23,24
23:29
rMt 24:19
23:30
sHos 10:8;
Isa 2:19;
Rev 6:16
23:31
tEze 20:47
23:32
uIsa 53:12;
Mt 27:38;
Mk 15:27;
Jn 19:18
23:34
vMt 11:25
wMt 5:44
xPs 22:18
23:35
yPs 22:17
zIsa 42:1
23:36
aPs 22:7
bPs 69:21;
Mt 27:48
23:37
cLk 4:3,9
23:38
dMt 2:2
23:39
ever 35,37

ᵃ16 Some manuscripts him." ¹⁷Now he was obliged to release one man to them at the Feast.
ᵇ30 Hosea 10:8   ᶜ34 Some early manuscripts do not have this sentence.

we are getting what our deeds deserve. But this man has done nothing wrong."[f]

[42]Then he said, "Jesus, remember me when you come into your kingdom.[a] "[g]

[43]Jesus answered him, "I tell you the truth, today you will be with me in paradise."[h]

Jesus' Death

23:44-49pp — Mt 27:45-56; Mk 15:33-41

[44]It was now about the sixth hour, and darkness came over the whole land until the ninth hour,[i] [45]for the sun stopped shining. And the curtain of the temple[j] was torn in two.[k] [46]Jesus called out with a loud voice,[l] "Father, into your hands I commit my spirit."[m] When he had said this, he breathed his last.[n]

[47]The centurion, seeing what had happened, praised God[o] and said, "Surely this was a righteous man." [48]When all the people who had gathered to witness this sight saw what took place, they beat their breasts[p] and went away. [49]But all those who knew him, including the women who had followed him from Galilee,[q] stood at a distance,[r] watching these things.

Jesus' Burial

23:50-56pp — Mt 27:57-61; Mk 15:42-47; Jn 19:38-42

[50]Now there was a man named Joseph, a member of the Council, a good and upright man, [51]who had not consented to their decision and action. He came from the Judean town of Arimathea and he was waiting for the kingdom of God.[s] [52]Going to Pilate, he asked for Jesus' body. [53]Then he took it down, wrapped it in linen cloth and placed it in a tomb cut in the rock, one in which no one had yet been laid. [54]It was Preparation Day,[t] and the Sabbath was about to begin.

[55]The women who had come with Jesus from Galilee[u] followed Joseph and saw the tomb and how his body was laid in it. [56]Then they went home and prepared spices and perfumes.[v] But they rested on the Sabbath in obedience to the commandment.[w]

The Resurrection

24:1-10pp — Mt 28:1-8; Mk 16:1-8; Jn 20:1-8

24 On the first day of the week, very early in the morning, the women took the spices they had prepared[x] and went to the tomb. [2]They found the stone rolled away from the tomb, [3]but when they entered, they did not find the body of the Lord Jesus.[y] [4]While they were wondering about this, suddenly two men in clothes that gleamed like lightning[z] stood beside them. [5]In their fright the women bowed down with their faces to the ground, but the men said to them, "Why do you look for the living among the dead? [6]He is not here; he has risen! Remember how he told you, while he was still with you in Galilee:[a] [7]'The Son of Man[b] must be delivered into the hands of sinful men, be crucified and on the third day be raised again.' "[c] [8]Then they remembered his words.[d]

[9]When they came back from the tomb, they told all these things to the

23:41
f ver 4
23:42
g Mt 16:27
23:43
h 2Co 12:3,4;
Rev 2:7
23:44
i Am 8:9
23:45
j Ex 26:31-33;
Heb 9:3,8
k Heb 10:19,20
23:46
l Mt 27:50
m Ps 31:5;
1Pe 2:23
n Jn 19:30
23:47
o Mt 9:8
23:48
p Lk 18:13
23:49
q Lk 8:2
r Ps 38:11
23:51
s Lk 2:25,38
23:54
t Mt 27:62
23:55
u ver 49
23:56
v Mk 16:1;
Lk 24:1
w Ex 12:16;
20:10
24:1
x Lk 23:56
24:3
y ver 23,24
24:4
z Jn 20:12
24:6
a Mt 17:22,23;
Mk 9:30-31;
Lk 9:22; 24:44
24:7
b Mt 8:20
c Mt 16:21
24:8
d Jn 2:22

a42 Some manuscripts *come with your kingly power*

Eleven and to all the others. [10]It was Mary Magdalene, Joanna, Mary the mother of James, and the others with them[e] who told this to the apostles.[f] [11]But they did not believe[g] the women, because their words seemed to them like nonsense. [12]Peter, however, got up and ran to the tomb. Bending over, he saw the strips of linen lying by themselves,[h] and he went away,[i] wondering to himself what had happened.

On the Road to Emmaus

[13]Now that same day two of them were going to a village called Emmaus, about seven miles[a] from Jerusalem.[j] [14]They were talking with each other about everything that had happened. [15]As they talked and discussed these things with each other, Jesus himself came up and walked along with them;[k] [16]but they were kept from recognizing him.[l]

[17]He asked them, "What are you discussing together as you walk along?"

They stood still, their faces downcast. [18]One of them, named Cleopas,[m] asked him, "Are you only a visitor to Jerusalem and do not know the things that have happened there in these days?"

[19]"What things?" he asked.

"About Jesus of Nazareth,"[n] they replied. "He was a prophet,[o] powerful in word and deed before God and all the people. [20]The chief priests and our rulers[p] handed him over to be sentenced to death, and they crucified him; [21]but we had hoped that he was the one who was going to redeem Israel.[q] And what is more, it is the third day[r] since all this took place. [22]In addition, some of our women amazed us.[s] They went to the tomb early this morning [23]but didn't find his body. They came and told us that they had seen a vision of angels, who said he was alive. [24]Then some of our companions went to the tomb and found it just as the women had said, but him they did not see."[t]

[25]He said to them, "How foolish you are, and how slow of heart to believe all that the prophets have spoken! [26]Did not the Christ[b] have to suffer these things and then enter his glory?"[u] [27]And beginning with Moses[v] and all the Prophets,[w] he explained to them what was said in all the Scriptures concerning himself.[x]

[28]As they approached the village to which they were going, Jesus acted as if he were going farther. [29]But they urged him strongly, "Stay with us, for it is nearly evening; the day is almost over." So he went in to stay with them.

[30]When he was at the table with them, he took bread, gave thanks, broke it[y] and began to give it to them. [31]Then their eyes were opened and they recognized him,[z] and he disappeared from their sight. [32]They asked each other, "Were not our hearts burning within us[a] while he talked with us on the road and opened the Scriptures[b] to us?"

[33]They got up and returned at once to Jerusalem. There they found the Eleven and those with them, assembled together [34]and saying, "It is true! The Lord has risen and has appeared to Simon."[c] [35]Then the two told what had happened on the way, and how Jesus was recognized by them when he broke the bread.[d]

Margin references:

24:10 eLk 8:1-3 fMk 6:30
24:11 gMk 16:11
24:12 hJn 20:3-7 iJn 20:10
24:13 jMk 16:12
24:15 kver 36
24:16 lJn 20:14; 21:4
24:18 mJn 19:25
24:19 nMk 1:24 oMt 21:11
24:20 pLk 23:13
24:21 qLk 1:68; 2:38; 21:28 rMt 16:21
24:22 sver 1-10
24:24 tver 12
24:26 uHeb 2:10; 1Pe 1:11
24:27 vGe 3:15; Nu 21:9; Dt 18:15 wIsa 7:14; 9:6; 40:10,11; 53; Eze 34:23; Da 9:24; Mic 7:20; Mal 3:1 xJn 1:45
24:30 yMt 14:19
24:31 zver 16
24:32 aPs 39:3 bver 27,45
24:34 c1Co 15:5
24:35 dver 30,31

---

[a]13 Greek *sixty stadia* (about 11 kilometers)   [b]26 Or *Messiah;* also in verse 46

Jesus Appears to the Disciples

³⁶While they were still talking about this, Jesus himself stood among them and said to them, "Peace be with you."ᵉ

³⁷They were startled and frightened, thinking they saw a ghost.ᶠ ³⁸He said to them, "Why are you troubled, and why do doubts rise in your minds? ³⁹Look at my hands and my feet. It is I myself! Touch me and see;ᵍ a ghost does not have flesh and bones, as you see I have."

⁴⁰When he had said this, he showed them his hands and feet. ⁴¹And while they still did not believe it because of joy and amazement, he asked them, "Do you have anything here to eat?" ⁴²They gave him a piece of broiled fish, ⁴³and he took it and ate it in their presence.ʰ

⁴⁴He said to them, "This is what I told you while I was still with you:ⁱ Everything must be fulfilledʲ that is written about me in the Law of Moses,ᵏ the Prophets and the Psalms."ˡ

⁴⁵Then he opened their minds so they could understand the Scriptures. ⁴⁶He told them, "This is what is written: The Christ will suffer and rise from the dead on the third day, ⁴⁷and repentance and forgiveness of sins will be preached in his nameᵐ to all nations,ⁿ beginning at Jerusalem. ⁴⁸You are witnessesᵒ of these things. ⁴⁹I am going to send you what my Father has promised;ᵖ but stay in the city until you have been clothed with power from on high."

The Ascension

⁵⁰When he had led them out to the vicinity of Bethany,�q he lifted up his hands and blessed them. ⁵¹While he was blessing them, he left them and was taken up into heaven.ʳ ⁵²Then they worshiped him and returned to Jerusalem with great joy. ⁵³And they stayed continually at the temple,ˢ praising God.

24:36
eJn 20:19,21,26;
14:27
24:37
fMk 6:49
24:39
gJn 20:27;
1Jn 1:1
24:43
hAc 10:41
24:44
iLk 9:45; 18:34
jMt 16:21;
Lk 9:22,44;
18:31-33; 22:37
kver 27 lPs 2;
16; 22; 69; 72;
110; 118
24:47
mAc 5:31;
10:43; 13:38
nMt 28:19
24:48
oAc 1:8; 2:32;
5:32; 13:31;
1Pe 5:1
24:49
pJn 14:16;
Ac 1:4
24:50
qMt 21:17
24:51
r2Ki 2:11
24:53
sAc 2:46

John

Title and Background

The Gospel of John was greatly influenced by the Old Testament. The prologue, with its account of the origin of light and life, is evocative of the Genesis account of creation. Reminders of the Passover also occur frequently in John. His name means "The LORD is gracious."

Author and Date of Writing

The author is the apostle John, "the disciple whom Jesus loved." He knew Jewish life well and referred often to Jewish customs. John's account has many touches that were obviously based on the recollections of an eyewitness. The date of writing was probably about A.D. 85 or a little later.

Theme and Message

The writer states his main purpose clearly in 20:31. He may have had Greek readers mainly in mind, and his primary intention was evangelism. John's purpose is not so much to present new evidence as it is to clarify issues on which the evidence will be either accepted or rejected. He writes not so much to inform the reader as to confront him with the necessity to "believe."

Outline

The Word Became Flesh

1 In the beginning was the Word,[a] and the Word was with God,[b] and the Word was God.[c] [2]He was with God in the beginning.[d]

[3]Through him all things were made; without him nothing was made that has been made.[e] [4]In him was life,[f] and that life was the light[g] of men. [5]The light shines in the darkness, but the darkness has not understood[a] it.[h]

[6]There came a man who was sent from God; his name was John.[i] [7]He came as a witness to testify[j] concerning that light, so that through him all men might believe.[k] [8]He himself was not the light; he came only as a witness to the light. [9]The true light[l] that gives light to every man[m] was coming into the world.[b]

[10]He was in the world, and though the world was made through

1:1
a Rev 19:13
b Jn 17:5;
1Jn 1:2 c Php 2:6
1:2
d Ge 1:1
1:3
e 1Co 8:6;
Col 1:16;
Heb 1:2
1:4
f Jn 5:26; 11:25;
14:6 g Jn 8:12
1:5
h Jn 3:19
1:6
i Mt 3:1
1:7
j ver 15,19,32
k ver 12
1:9
l 1Jn 2:8
m Isa 49:6

[a]5 Or *darkness, and the darkness has not overcome*   [b]9 Or *This was the true light that gives light to* *every man who comes into the world*

him,[n] the world did not recognize him. [11]He came to that which was his own, but his own did not receive him. [12]Yet to all who received him, to those who believed[o] in his name,[p] he gave the right to become children of God[q]— [13]children born not of natural descent,[a] nor of human decision or a husband's will, but born of God.[r]

[14]The Word became flesh[s] and made his dwelling among us. We have seen his glory, the glory of the One and Only,[b] who came from the Father, full of grace and truth.[t]

[15]John testifies[u] concerning him. He cries out, saying, "This was he of whom I said, 'He who comes after me has surpassed me because he was before me.'"[v] [16]From the fullness[w] of his grace we have all received one blessing after another. [17]For the law was given through Moses;[x] grace and truth came through Jesus Christ.[y] [18]No one has ever seen God,[z] but God the One and Only,[b,c] [a] who is at the Father's side, has made him known.

John the Baptist Denies Being the Christ

[19]Now this was John's testimony when the Jews[b] of Jerusalem sent priests and Levites to ask him who he was. [20]He did not fail to confess, but confessed freely, "I am not the Christ.[d] "[c]

[21]They asked him, "Then who are you? Are you Elijah?"[d]

He said, "I am not."

"Are you the Prophet?"[e]

He answered, "No."

[22]Finally they said, "Who are you? Give us an answer to take back to those who sent us. What do you say about yourself?"

[23]John replied in the words of Isaiah the prophet, "I am the voice of one calling in the desert,[f] 'Make straight the way for the Lord.'"[e] [g]

[24]Now some Pharisees who had been sent [25]questioned him, "Why then do you baptize if you are not the Christ, nor Elijah, nor the Prophet?"

[26]"I baptize with[f] water," John replied, "but among you stands one you do not know. [27]He is the one who comes after me,[h] the thongs of whose sandals I am not worthy to untie."

[28]This all happened at Bethany on the other side of the Jordan,[i] where John was baptizing.

Jesus the Lamb of God

[29]The next day John saw Jesus coming toward him and said, "Look, the Lamb of God,[j] who takes away the sin of the world! [30]This is the one I meant when I said, 'A man who comes after me has surpassed me because he was before me.'[k] [31]I myself did not know him, but the reason I came baptizing with water was that he might be revealed to Israel."

[32]Then John gave this testimony: "I saw the Spirit come down from heaven as a dove and remain on him.[l] [33]I would not have known him, except that the one who sent me to baptize with water[m] told me, 'The man on whom you see the Spirit come down and remain is he who will

1:10
nHeb 1:2
1:12
over 7 p1Jn 3:23
qGal 3:26
1:13
rJn 3:6;
Jas 1:18;
1Pe 1:23;
1Jn 3:9
1:14
sGal 4:4;
Php 2:7,8;
1Ti 3:16;
Heb 2:14
tJn 14:6
1:15
uver 7 vver 30;
Mt 3:11
1:16
wEph 1:23;
Col 1:19
1:17
xJn 7:19 yver 14
1:18
zEx 33:20;
Jn 6:46;
Col 1:15;
1Ti 6:16
aJn 3:16,18;
1Jn 4:9
1:19
bJn 2:18; 5:10,
16; 6:41,52
1:20
cJn 3:28;
Lk 3:15,16
1:21
dMt 11:14
eDt 18:15
1:23
fMt 3:1
gIsa 40:3
1:27
hver 15,30
1:28
iJn 3:26; 10:40
1:29
jver 36;
Isa 53:7;
1Pe 1:19;
Rev 5:6
1:30
kver 15,27
1:32
lMt 3:16;
Mk 1:10
1:33
mMk 1:4

---

[a]13 Greek *of bloods*   [b]14,18 Or *the Only Begotten*   [c]18 Some manuscripts *but the only (or only begotten) Son*   [d]20 Or *Messiah.* "The Christ" (Greek) and "the Messiah" (Hebrew) both mean "the Anointed One"; also in verse 25.   [e]23 Isaiah 40:3   [f]26 Or *in;* also in verses 31 and 33

baptize with the Holy Spirit.'ⁿ ³⁴I have seen and I testify that this is the Son of God."ᵒ

Jesus' First Disciples

1:40–42pp — Mt 4:18–22; Mk 1:16–20; Lk 5:2–11

³⁵The next day Johnᵖ was there again with two of his disciples. ³⁶When he saw Jesus passing by, he said, "Look, the Lamb of God!"�q

³⁷When the two disciples heard him say this, they followed Jesus. ³⁸Turning around, Jesus saw them following and asked, "What do you want?"

They said, "Rabbi"ʳ (which means Teacher), "where are you staying?"

³⁹"Come," he replied, "and you will see."

So they went and saw where he was staying, and spent that day with him. It was about the tenth hour.

⁴⁰Andrew, Simon Peter's brother, was one of the two who heard what John had said and who had followed Jesus. ⁴¹The first thing Andrew did was to find his brother Simon and tell him, "We have found the Messiah" (that is, the Christ).ˢ ⁴²And he brought him to Jesus.

Jesus looked at him and said, "You are Simon son of John. You will be calledᵗ Cephas" (which, when translated, is Peterᵃ).ᵘ

Jesus Calls Philip and Nathanael

⁴³The next day Jesus decided to leave for Galilee. Finding Philip,ᵛ he said to him, "Follow me."ʷ

⁴⁴Philip, like Andrew and Peter, was from the town of Bethsaida.ˣ ⁴⁵Philip found Nathanaelʸ and told him, "We have found the one Moses wrote about in the Law,ᶻ and about whom the prophets also wroteᵃ—Jesus of Nazareth,ᵇ the son of Joseph."ᶜ

⁴⁶"Nazareth! Can anything good come from there?"ᵈ Nathanael asked.

"Come and see," said Philip.

⁴⁷When Jesus saw Nathanael approaching, he said of him, "Here is a true Israelite,ᵉ in whom there is nothing false."ᶠ

⁴⁸"How do you know me?" Nathanael asked.

Jesus answered, "I saw you while you were still under the fig tree before Philip called you."

⁴⁹Then Nathanael declared, "Rabbi,ᵍ you are the Son of God;ʰ you are the King of Israel."ⁱ

⁵⁰Jesus said, "You believeᵇ because I told you I saw you under the fig tree. You shall see greater things than that." ⁵¹He then added, "I tell youᶜ the truth, youᶜ shall see heaven open,ʲ and the angels of God ascending and descendingᵏ on the Son of Man."ˡ

Jesus Changes Water to Wine

2 On the third day a wedding took place at Cana in Galilee.ᵐ Jesus' motherⁿ was there, ²and Jesus and his disciples had also been

---

1:33
nMt 3:11;
Mk 1:8
1:34
over 49; Mt 4:3
1:35
pMt 3:1
1:36
qver 29
1:38
rver 49; Mt 23:7
1:41
sJn 4:25
1:42
tGe 17:5,15
uMt 16:18
1:43
vMt 10:3;
Jn 6:5-7; 12:21,
22; 14:8,9
wMt 4:19
1:44
xMt 11:21;
Jn 12:21
1:45
yJn 21:2
zLk 24:27
aLk 24:27
bMt 2:23;
Mk 1:24
cLk 3:23
1:46
dJn 7:41,42,52
1:47
eRo 9:4,6
fPs 32:2
1:49
gver 38;
Mt 23:7
hver 34; Mt 4:3
iMt 2:2; 27:42;
Jn 12:13
1:51
jMt 3:16
kGe 28:12
lMt 8:20
2:1
mJn 4:46; 21:2
nMt 12:46

ᵃ42 Both *Cephas* (Aramaic) and *Peter* (Greek) mean *rock*.   ᵇ50 Or *Do you believe . . . ?*
ᶜ51 The Greek is plural.

invited to the wedding. ³When the wine was gone, Jesus' mother said to him, "They have no more wine."

⁴"Dear woman,° why do you involve me?"ᵖ Jesus replied. "My time�q has not yet come."

⁵His mother said to the servants, "Do whatever he tells you."ʳ

⁶Nearby stood six stone water jars, the kind used by the Jews for ceremonial washing,ˢ each holding from twenty to thirty gallons.ᵃ

⁷Jesus said to the servants, "Fill the jars with water"; so they filled them to the brim.

⁸Then he told them, "Now draw some out and take it to the master of the banquet."

They did so, ⁹and the master of the banquet tasted the water that had been turned into wine.ᵗ He did not realize where it had come from, though the servants who had drawn the water knew. Then he called the bridegroom aside ¹⁰and said, "Everyone brings out the choice wine first and then the cheaper wine after the guests have had too much to drink; but you have saved the best till now."

¹¹This, the first of his miraculous signs,ᵘ Jesus performed in Cana of Galilee. He thus revealed his glory,ᵛ and his disciples put their faith in him.ʷ

Jesus Clears the Temple

2:14–16pp — Mt 21:12,13; Mk 11:15–17; Lk 19:45,46

¹²After this he went down to Capernaumˣ with his mother and brothersʸ and his disciples. There they stayed for a few days.

¹³When it was almost time for the Jewish Passover,ᶻ Jesus went up to Jerusalem.ᵃ ¹⁴In the temple courts he found men selling cattle, sheep and doves, and others sitting at tables exchanging money. ¹⁵So he made a whip out of cords, and drove all from the temple area, both sheep and cattle; he scattered the coins of the money changers and overturned their tables. ¹⁶To those who sold doves he said, "Get these out of here! How dare you turn my Father's houseᵇ into a market!"

¹⁷His disciples remembered that it is written: "Zeal for your house will consume me."ᵇ ᶜ

¹⁸Then the Jews demanded of him, "What miraculous sign can you show us to prove your authority to do all this?"ᵈ

¹⁹Jesus answered them, "Destroy this temple, and I will raise it again in three days."ᵉ

²⁰The Jews replied, "It has taken forty-six years to build this temple, and you are going to raise it in three days?" ²¹But the temple he had spoken of was his body.ᶠ ²²After he was raised from the dead, his disciples recalled what he had said.ᵍ Then they believed the Scripture and the words that Jesus had spoken.

²³Now while he was in Jerusalem at the Passover Feast,ʰ many people saw the miraculous signs he was doing and believed in his name.ᶜ ²⁴But Jesus would not entrust himself to them, for he knew all men. ²⁵He did not need man's testimony about man, for he knew what was in a man.ⁱ

2:4
oJn 19:26
pMt 8:29
qMt 26:18;
Jn 7:6
2:5
rGe 41:55
2:6
sMk 7:3,4;
Jn 3:25
2:9
tJn 4:46
2:11
uver 23; Jn 3:2;
4:48; 6:2,14,26,
30; 12:37; 20:30
vJn 1:14
wEx 14:31
2:12
xMt 4:13
yMt 12:46
2:13
zJn 11:55
aDt 16:1-6;
Lk 2:41
2:16
bLk 2:49
2:17
cPs 69:9
2:18
dMt 12:38
2:19
eMt 26:61;
27:40;
Mk 14:58;
15:29
2:21
f1Co 6:19
2:22
gLk 24:5-8;
Jn 12:16; 14:26
2:23
hver 13
2:25
iMt 9:4;
Jn 6:61,64;
13:11

ᵃ6 Greek *two to three metretes* (probably about 75 to 115 liters)   ᵇ17 Psalm 69:9   ᶜ23 Or *and believed in him*

Jesus Teaches Nicodemus

3 Now there was a man of the Pharisees named Nicodemus,[j] a member of the Jewish ruling council.[k] [2]He came to Jesus at night and said, "Rabbi, we know you are a teacher who has come from God. For no one could perform the miraculous signs[l] you are doing if God were not with him."[m]

[3]In reply Jesus declared, "I tell you the truth, no one can see the kingdom of God unless he is born again.[a] "[n]

[4]"How can a man be born when he is old?" Nicodemus asked. "Surely he cannot enter a second time into his mother's womb to be born!"

[5]Jesus answered, "I tell you the truth, no one can enter the kingdom of God unless he is born of water and the Spirit.[o] [6]Flesh gives birth to flesh, but the Spirit[b] gives birth to spirit.[p] [7]You should not be surprised at my saying, 'You[c] must be born again.' [8]The wind blows wherever it pleases. You hear its sound, but you cannot tell where it comes from or where it is going. So it is with everyone born of the Spirit."

[9]"How can this be?"[q] Nicodemus asked.

[10]"You are Israel's teacher,"[r] said Jesus, "and do you not understand these things? [11]I tell you the truth, we speak of what we know,[s] and we testify to what we have seen, but still you people do not accept our testimony.[t] [12]I have spoken to you of earthly things and you do not believe; how then will you believe if I speak of heavenly things? [13]No one has ever gone into heaven[u] except the one who came from heaven[v]—the Son of Man.[d] [14]Just as Moses lifted up the snake in the desert,[w] so the Son of Man must be lifted up,[x] [15]that everyone who believes[y] in him may have eternal life.[e]

[16]"For God so loved[z] the world that he gave his one and only Son,[f] that whoever believes in him shall not perish but have eternal life.[a] [17]For God did not send his Son into the world[b] to condemn the world, but to save the world through him.[c] [18]Whoever believes in him is not condemned,[d] but whoever does not believe stands condemned already because he has not believed in the name of God's one and only Son.[g] [e] [19]This is the verdict: Light[f] has come into the world, but men loved darkness instead of light because their deeds were evil. [20]Everyone who does evil hates the light, and will not come into the light for fear that his deeds will be exposed.[g] [21]But whoever lives by the truth comes into the light, so that it may be seen plainly that what he has done has been done through God."[h]

John the Baptist's Testimony About Jesus

[22]After this, Jesus and his disciples went out into the Judean countryside, where he spent some time with them, and baptized.[h] [23]Now John also was baptizing at Aenon near Salim, because there was plenty of water, and people were constantly coming to be baptized. [24](This was before John was put in prison.)[i] [25]An argument developed between some of John's disciples and a certain Jew[j] over the matter of ceremoni-

3:1 jJn 7:50; 19:39 kLk 23:13
3:2 lJn 9:16,33 mAc 2:22; 10:38
3:3 nJn 1:13; 1Pe 1:23
3:5 oTit 3:5
3:6 pJn 1:13; 1Co 15:50
3:9 qJn 6:52,60
3:10 rLk 2:46
3:11 sJn 1:18; 7:16, 17 tver 32
3:13 uPr 30:4; Ac 2:34; Eph 4:8-10 vJn 6:38,42
3:14 wNu 21:8,9 xJn 8:28; 12:32
3:15 yver 16,36
3:16 zRo 5:8; Eph 2:4; 1Jn 4:9,10 aver 36; Jn 6:29,40; 11:25,26
3:17 bJn 6:29,57; 10:36; 11:42; 17:8,21; 20:21 cJn 12:47; 1Jn 4:14
3:18 dJn 5:24 e1Jn 4:9
3:19 fJn 1:4; 8:12
3:20 gEph 5:11,13
3:22 hJn 4:2
3:24 iMt 4:12; 14:3

a3 Or born from above; also in verse 7   b6 Or but spirit   c7 The Greek is plural.
d13 Some manuscripts Man, who is in heaven   e15 Or believes may have eternal life in him
f16 Or his only begotten Son   g18 Or God's only begotten Son   h21 Some interpreters end the
quotation after verse 15.   i25 Some manuscripts and certain Jews

al washing.ⁱ ²⁶They came to John and said to him, "Rabbi,ᵏ that man who was with you on the other side of the Jordan—the one you testified¹ about—well, he is baptizing, and everyone is going to him."

²⁷To this John replied, "A man can receive only what is given him from heaven. ²⁸You yourselves can testify that I said, 'I am not the Christᵃ but am sent ahead of him.'ᵐ ²⁹The bride belongs to the bridegroom.ⁿ The friend who attends the bridegroom waits and listens for him, and is full of joy when he hears the bridegroom's voice. That joy is mine, and it is now complete.ᵒ ³⁰He must become greater; I must become less.

³¹"The one who comes from aboveᵖ is above all; the one who is from the earth belongs to the earth, and speaks as one from the earth.�q The one who comes from heaven is above all. ³²He testifies to what he has seen and heard,ʳ but no one accepts his testimony.ˢ ³³The man who has accepted it has certified that God is truthful. ³⁴For the one whom God has sentᵗ speaks the words of God, for Godᵇ gives the Spiritᵘ without limit. ³⁵The Father loves the Son and has placed everything in his hands.ᵛ ³⁶Whoever believes in the Son has eternal life,ʷ but whoever rejects the Son will not see life, for God's wrath remains on him."ᶜ

Jesus Talks With a Samaritan Woman

4 The Pharisees heard that Jesus was gaining and baptizing more disciples than John,ˣ ²although in fact it was not Jesus who baptized, but his disciples. ³When the Lord learned of this, he left Judeaʸ and went back once more to Galilee.

⁴Now he had to go through Samaria. ⁵So he came to a town in Samaria called Sychar, near the plot of ground Jacob had given to his son Joseph.ᶻ ⁶Jacob's well was there, and Jesus, tired as he was from the journey, sat down by the well. It was about the sixth hour.

⁷When a Samaritan woman came to draw water, Jesus said to her, "Will you give me a drink?" ⁸(His disciples had gone into the townᵃ to buy food.)

⁹The Samaritan woman said to him, "You are a Jew and I am a Samaritanᵇ woman. How can you ask me for a drink?" (For Jews do not associate with Samaritans.ᵈ)

¹⁰Jesus answered her, "If you knew the gift of God and who it is that asks you for a drink, you would have asked him and he would have given you living water."ᶜ

¹¹"Sir," the woman said, "you have nothing to draw with and the well is deep. Where can you get this living water? ¹²Are you greater than our father Jacob, who gave us the wellᵈ and drank from it himself, as did also his sons and his flocks and herds?"

¹³Jesus answered, "Everyone who drinks this water will be thirsty again, ¹⁴but whoever drinks the water I give him will never thirst.ᵉ Indeed, the water I give him will become in him a spring of waterᶠ welling up to eternal life."ᵍ

¹⁵The woman said to him, "Sir, give me this water so that I won't get thirstyʰ and have to keep coming here to draw water."

¹⁶He told her, "Go, call your husband and come back."

3:25
iJn 2:6
3:26
kMt 23:7 1Jn 1:7
3:28
mJn 1:20,23
3:29
nMt 9:15
oJn 16:24;
17:13; Php 2:2;
1Jn 1:4; 2Jn 12
3:31
pver 13
qJn 8:23;
1Jn 4:5
3:32
rJn 8:26; 15:15
sver 11
3:34
tver 17
uMt 12:18;
Lk 4:18;
Ac 10:38
3:35
vMt 28:18;
Jn 5:20,22; 17:2
3:36
wver 15;
Jn 5:24; 6:47
4:1
xJn 3:22,26
4:3
yJn 3:22
4:5
zGe 33:19;
48:22; Jos 24:32
4:8
aver 5,39
4:9
bMt 10:5;
Lk 9:52,53
4:10
cIsa 44:3;
Jer 2:13;
Zec 14:8;
Jn 7:37,38;
Rev 21:6; 22:1,
17
4:12
dver 6
4:14
eJn 6:35
fJn 7:38
gMt 25:46
4:15
hJn 6:34

ᵃ28 Or *Messiah*   ᵇ34 Greek *he*   ᶜ36 Some interpreters end the quotation after verse 30.
ᵈ9 Or *do not use dishes Samaritans have used*

¹⁷"I have no husband," she replied.

Jesus said to her, "You are right when you say you have no husband. ¹⁸The fact is, you have had five husbands, and the man you now have is not your husband. What you have just said is quite true."

¹⁹"Sir," the woman said, "I can see that you are a prophet.[i] ²⁰Our fathers worshiped on this mountain,[j] but you Jews claim that the place where we must worship is in Jerusalem."[k]

²¹Jesus declared, "Believe me, woman, a time is coming[l] when you will worship the Father neither on this mountain nor in Jerusalem.[m] ²²You Samaritans worship what you do not know;[n] we worship what we do know, for salvation is from the Jews.[o] ²³Yet a time is coming and has now come[p] when the true worshipers will worship the Father in spirit[q] and truth, for they are the kind of worshipers the Father seeks. ²⁴God is spirit,[r] and his worshipers must worship in spirit and in truth."

²⁵The woman said, "I know that Messiah" (called Christ)[s] "is coming. When he comes, he will explain everything to us."

²⁶Then Jesus declared, "I who speak to you am he."[t]

The Disciples Rejoin Jesus

²⁷Just then his disciples returned[u] and were surprised to find him talking with a woman. But no one asked, "What do you want?" or "Why are you talking with her?"

²⁸Then, leaving her water jar, the woman went back to the town and said to the people, ²⁹"Come, see a man who told me everything I ever did.[v] Could this be the Christ[a]?"[w] ³⁰They came out of the town and made their way toward him.

³¹Meanwhile his disciples urged him, "Rabbi,[x] eat something."

³²But he said to them, "I have food to eat[y] that you know nothing about."

³³Then his disciples said to each other, "Could someone have brought him food?"

³⁴"My food," said Jesus, "is to do the will[z] of him who sent me and to finish his work.[a] ³⁵Do you not say, 'Four months more and then the harvest'? I tell you, open your eyes and look at the fields! They are ripe for harvest.[b] ³⁶Even now the reaper draws his wages, even now he harvests[c] the crop for eternal life,[d] so that the sower and the reaper may be glad together. ³⁷Thus the saying 'One sows and another reaps'[e] is true. ³⁸I sent you to reap what you have not worked for. Others have done the hard work, and you have reaped the benefits of their labor."

Many Samaritans Believe

³⁹Many of the Samaritans from that town[f] believed in him because of the woman's testimony, "He told me everything I ever did."[g] ⁴⁰So when the Samaritans came to him, they urged him to stay with them, and he stayed two days. ⁴¹And because of his words many more became believers.

⁴²They said to the woman, "We no longer believe just because of what you said; now we have heard for ourselves, and we know that this man really is the Savior of the world."[h]

^a29 Or *Messiah*

4:19
i Mt 21:11
4:20
j Dt 11:29;
Jos 8:33
k Lk 9:53
4:21
l Jn 5:28; 16:2
m Mal 1:11;
1Ti 2:8
4:22
n 2Ki 17:28-41
o Isa 2:3;
Ro 3:1,2; 9:4,5
4:23
p Jn 5:25; 16:32
q Php 3:3
4:24
r Php 3:3
4:25
s Mt 1:16
4:26
t Jn 8:24;
9:35-37
4:27
u ver 8
4:29
v ver 17,18
w Mt 12:23;
Jn 7:26,31
4:31
x Mt 23:7
4:32
y Job 23:12;
Mt 4:4; Jn 6:27
4:34
z Mt 26:39;
Jn 6:38; 17:4;
19:30 a Jn 19:30
4:35
b Mt 9:37;
Lk 10:2
4:36
c Ro 1:13
d Mt 25:46
4:37
e Job 31:8;
Mic 6:15
4:39
f ver 5 g ver 29
4:42
h Lk 2:11;
1Jn 4:14

Jesus Heals the Official's Son

⁴³After the two days[i] he left for Galilee. ⁴⁴(Now Jesus himself had pointed out that a prophet has no honor in his own country.)[j] ⁴⁵When he arrived in Galilee, the Galileans welcomed him. They had seen all that he had done in Jerusalem at the Passover Feast,[k] for they also had been there.

⁴⁶Once more he visited Cana in Galilee, where he had turned the water into wine.[l] And there was a certain royal official whose son lay sick at Capernaum. ⁴⁷When this man heard that Jesus had arrived in Galilee from Judea,[m] he went to him and begged him to come and heal his son, who was close to death.

⁴⁸"Unless you people see miraculous signs and wonders,"[n] Jesus told him, "you will never believe."

⁴⁹The royal official said, "Sir, come down before my child dies."

⁵⁰Jesus replied, "You may go. Your son will live."

The man took Jesus at his word and departed. ⁵¹While he was still on the way, his servants met him with the news that his boy was living. ⁵²When he inquired as to the time when his son got better, they said to him, "The fever left him yesterday at the seventh hour."

⁵³Then the father realized that this was the exact time at which Jesus had said to him, "Your son will live." So he and all his household[o] believed.

⁵⁴This was the second miraculous sign[p] that Jesus performed, having come from Judea to Galilee.

The Healing at the Pool

5 Some time later, Jesus went up to Jerusalem for a feast of the Jews. ²Now there is in Jerusalem near the Sheep Gate[q] a pool, which in Aramaic[r] is called Bethesda[a] and which is surrounded by five covered colonnades. ³Here a great number of disabled people used to lie—the blind, the lame, the paralyzed.[b] ⁵One who was there had been an invalid for thirty-eight years. ⁶When Jesus saw him lying there and learned that he had been in this condition for a long time, he asked him, "Do you want to get well?"

⁷"Sir," the invalid replied, "I have no one to help me into the pool when the water is stirred. While I am trying to get in, someone else goes down ahead of me."

⁸Then Jesus said to him, "Get up! Pick up your mat and walk."[s] ⁹At once the man was cured; he picked up his mat and walked.

The day on which this took place was a Sabbath,[t] ¹⁰and so the Jews[u] said to the man who had been healed, "It is the Sabbath; the law forbids you to carry your mat."[v]

¹¹But he replied, "The man who made me well said to me, 'Pick up your mat and walk.'"

¹²So they asked him, "Who is this fellow who told you to pick it up and walk?"

4:43
iver 40
4:44
jMt 13:57;
Lk 4:24
4:45
kJn 2:23
4:46
lJn 2:1-11
4:47
mver 3,54
4:48
nDa 4:2,3;
Jn 2:11;
Ac 2:43; 14:3;
Ro 15:19;
2Co 12:12;
Heb 2:4
4:53
oAc 11:14
4:54
pver 48; Jn 2:11
5:2
qNe 3:1; 12:39
rJn 19:13,17,20;
20:16;
Ac 21:40; 22:2;
26:14
5:8
sMt 9:5,6;
Mk 2:11;
Lk 5:24
5:9
tJn 9:14
5:10
uver 16
vNe 13:15-22;
Jer 17:21;
Mt 12:2

ᵃ2 Some manuscripts *Bethzatha*; other manuscripts *Bethsaida*   ᵇ3 Some less important manuscripts *paralyzed—and they waited for the moving of the waters. ⁴From time to time an angel of the Lord would come down and stir up the waters. The first one into the pool after each such disturbance would be cured of whatever disease he had.*

13The man who was healed had no idea who it was, for Jesus had slipped away into the crowd that was there.

14Later Jesus found him at the temple and said to him, "See, you are well again. Stop sinningʷ or something worse may happen to you." 15The man went away and told the Jewsˣ that it was Jesus who had made him well.

Life Through the Son

16So, because Jesus was doing these things on the Sabbath, the Jews persecuted him. 17Jesus said to them, "My Father is always at his workʸ to this very day, and I, too, am working." 18For this reason the Jews tried all the harder to kill him;ᶻ not only was he breaking the Sabbath, but he was even calling God his own Father, making himself equal with God.ᵃ

19Jesus gave them this answer: "I tell you the truth, the Son can do nothing by himself;ᵇ he can do only what he sees his Father doing, because whatever the Father does the Son also does. 20For the Father loves the Sonᶜ and shows him all he does. Yes, to your amazement he will show him even greater things than these.ᵈ 21For just as the Father raises the dead and gives them life,ᵉ even so the Son gives lifeᶠ to whom he is pleased to give it. 22Moreover, the Father judges no one, but has entrusted all judgment to the Son,ᵍ 23that all may honor the Son just as they honor the Father. He who does not honor the Son does not honor the Father, who sent him.ʰ

24"I tell you the truth, whoever hears my word and believes him who sent me has eternal life and will not be condemned;ⁱ he has crossed over from death to life.ʲ 25I tell you the truth, a time is coming and has now comeᵏ when the dead will hearˡ the voice of the Son of God and those who hear will live. 26For as the Father has life in himself, so he has granted the Son to have life in himself. 27And he has given him authority to judgeᵐ because he is the Son of Man.

28"Do not be amazed at this, for a time is comingⁿ when all who are in their graves will hear his voice 29and come out—those who have done good will rise to live, and those who have done evil will rise to be condemned.ᵒ 30By myself I can do nothing;ᵖ I judge only as I hear, and my judgment is just, q for I seek not to please myself but him who sent me.ʳ

Testimonies About Jesus

31"If I testify about myself, my testimony is not valid.ˢ 32There is another who testifies in my favor,ᵗ and I know that his testimony about me is valid.

33"You have sent to John and he has testifiedᵘ to the truth. 34Not that I accept human testimony;ᵛ but I mention it that you may be saved. 35John was a lamp that burned and gave light,ʷ and you chose for a time to enjoy his light.

36"I have testimony weightier than that of John.ˣ For the very work that the Father has given me to finish, and which I am doing,ʸ testifies that the Father has sent me.ᶻ 37And the Father who sent me has himself testified concerning me.ᵃ You have never heard his voice nor seen his form,ᵇ 38nor does his word dwell in you,ᶜ for you do not believe the

5:14
wMk 2:5;
Jn 8:11
5:15
xJn 1:19
5:17
yJn 9:4; 14:10
5:18
zJn 7:1
aJn 10:30,33;
19:7
5:19
bver 30; Jn 8:28
5:20
cJn 3:35
dJn 14:12
5:21
eRo 4:17; 8:11
fJn 11:25
5:22
gver 27;
Jn 9:39;
Ac 10:42; 17:31
5:23
hLk 10:16;
1Jn 2:23
5:24
iJn 3:18
j1Jn 3:14
5:25
kJn 4:23
1Jn 8:43,47
5:27
mver 22;
Ac 10:42; 17:31
5:28
nJn 4:21
5:29
oDa 12:2;
Mt 25:46
5:30
pver 19 qJn 8:16
rMt 26:39;
Jn 4:34; 6:38
5:31
sJn 8:14
5:32
tver 37; Jn 8:18
5:33
uJn 1:7
5:34
v1Jn 5:9
5:35
w2Pe 1:19
5:36
x1Jn 5:9
yJn 14:11;
15:24 zJn 3:17;
10:25
5:37
aJn 8:18
bDt 4:12;
1Ti 1:17;
Jn 1:18
5:38
c1Jn 2:14

one he sent. [d] [39]You diligently study[a] the Scriptures[e] because you think that by them you possess eternal life. These are the Scriptures that testify about me, [f] [40]yet you refuse to come to me to have life.

[41]"I do not accept praise from men, [g] [42]but I know you. I know that you do not have the love of God in your hearts. [43]I have come in my Father's name, and you do not accept me; but if someone else comes in his own name, you will accept him. [44]How can you believe if you accept praise from one another, yet make no effort to obtain the praise that comes from the only God[b]?[h]

[45]"But do not think I will accuse you before the Father. Your accuser is Moses, [i] on whom your hopes are set.[j] [46]If you believed Moses, you would believe me, for he wrote about me.[k] [47]But since you do not believe what he wrote, how are you going to believe what I say?"[l]

Jesus Feeds the Five Thousand

6:1–13pp — Mt 14:13–21; Mk 6:32–44; Lk 9:10–17

6 Some time after this, Jesus crossed to the far shore of the Sea of Galilee (that is, the Sea of Tiberias), [2]and a great crowd of people followed him because they saw the miraculous signs[m] he had performed on the sick. [3]Then Jesus went up on a mountainside[n] and sat down with his disciples. [4]The Jewish Passover Feast[o] was near.

[5]When Jesus looked up and saw a great crowd coming toward him, he said to Philip, [p] "Where shall we buy bread for these people to eat?" [6]He asked this only to test him, for he already had in mind what he was going to do.

[7]Philip answered him, "Eight months' wages[c] would not buy enough bread for each one to have a bite!"

[8]Another of his disciples, Andrew, Simon Peter's brother, [q] spoke up, [9]"Here is a boy with five small barley loaves and two small fish, but how far will they go among so many?"[r]

[10]Jesus said, "Have the people sit down." There was plenty of grass in that place, and the men sat down, about five thousand of them. [11]Jesus then took the loaves, gave thanks, [s] and distributed to those who were seated as much as they wanted. He did the same with the fish.

[12]When they had all had enough to eat, he said to his disciples, "Gather the pieces that are left over. Let nothing be wasted." [13]So they gathered them and filled twelve baskets with the pieces of the five barley loaves left over by those who had eaten.

[14]After the people saw the miraculous sign[t] that Jesus did, they began to say, "Surely this is the Prophet who is to come into the world."[u] [15]Jesus, knowing that they intended to come and make him king[v] by force, withdrew again to a mountain by himself.[w]

Jesus Walks on the Water

6:16–21pp — Mt 14:22–33; Mk 6:47–51

[16]When evening came, his disciples went down to the lake, [17]where they got into a boat and set off across the lake for Capernaum. By now it was dark, and Jesus had not yet joined them. [18]A strong wind was

---

5:38
d Jn 3:17
5:39
e Ro 2:17,18
f Lk 24:27,44;
Ac 13:27
5:41
g ver 44
5:44
h Ro 2:29
5:45
i Jn 9:28
j Ro 2:17
5:46
k Ge 3:15;
Lk 24:27,44;
Ac 26:22
5:47
l Lk 16:29,31
6:2
m Jn 2:11
6:3
n ver 15
6:4
o Jn 2:13; 11:55
6:5
p Jn 1:43
6:8
q Jn 1:40
6:9
r 2Ki 4:43
6:11
s ver 23;
Mt 14:19
6:14
t Jn 2:11
u Dt 18:15,18;
Mt 11:3; 21:11
6:15
v Jn 18:36
w Mt 14:23;
Mk 6:46

---

[a]39 Or *Study diligently* (the imperative)   [b]44 Some early manuscripts *the Only One*
[c]7 Greek *two hundred denarii*

blowing and the waters grew rough. ¹⁹When they had rowed three or three and a half miles,ᵃ they saw Jesus approaching the boat, walking on the water;ˣ and they were terrified. ²⁰But he said to them, "It is I; don't be afraid."ʸ ²¹Then they were willing to take him into the boat, and immediately the boat reached the shore where they were heading.

²²The next day the crowd that had stayed on the opposite shore of the lakeᶻ realized that only one boat had been there, and that Jesus had not entered it with his disciples, but that they had gone away alone.ᵃ ²³Then some boats from Tiberiasᵇ landed near the place where the people had eaten the bread after the Lord had given thanks.ᶜ ²⁴Once the crowd realized that neither Jesus nor his disciples were there, they got into the boats and went to Capernaum in search of Jesus.

Jesus the Bread of Life

²⁵When they found him on the other side of the lake, they asked him, "Rabbi,ᵈ when did you get here?"

²⁶Jesus answered, "I tell you the truth, you are looking for me,ᵉ not because you saw miraculous signsᶠ but because you ate the loaves and had your fill. ²⁷Do not work for food that spoils, but for food that enduresᵍ to eternal life,ʰ which the Son of Manⁱ will give you. On him God the Father has placed his sealʲ of approval."

²⁸Then they asked him, "What must we do to do the works God requires?"

²⁹Jesus answered, "The work of God is this: to believeᵏ in the one he has sent."¹

³⁰So they asked him, "What miraculous signᵐ then will you give that we may see it and believe you?ⁿ What will you do? ³¹Our forefathers ate the mannaᵒ in the desert; as it is written: 'He gave them bread from heaven to eat.'ᵇ "ᵖ

³²Jesus said to them, "I tell you the truth, it is not Moses who has given you the bread from heaven, but it is my Father who gives you the true bread from heaven. ³³For the bread of God is he who comes down from heaven�q and gives life to the world."

³⁴"Sir," they said, "from now on give us this bread."ʳ

³⁵Then Jesus declared, "I am the bread of life.ˢ He who comes to me will never go hungry, and he who believes in me will never be thirsty.ᵗ ³⁶But as I told you, you have seen me and still you do not believe. ³⁷All that the Father gives meᵘ will come to me, and whoever comes to me I will never drive away. ³⁸For I have come down from heaven not to do my will but to do the will of him who sent me.ᵛ ³⁹And this is the will of him who sent me, that I shall lose none of all that he has given me,ʷ but raise them up at the last day.ˣ ⁴⁰For my Father's will is that everyone who looks to the Son and believes in him shall have eternal life,ʸ and I will raise him up at the last day."

⁴¹At this the Jews began to grumble about him because he said, "I am the bread that came down from heaven." ⁴²They said, "Is this not Jesus, the son of Joseph,ᶻ whose father and mother we know?ᵃ How can he now say, 'I came down from heaven'?"ᵇ

⁴³"Stop grumbling among yourselves," Jesus answered. ⁴⁴"No one

---

6:19
xJob 9:8
6:20
yMt 14:27
6:22
zver 2
aver 15-21
6:23
bver 1 cver 11
6:25
dMt 23:7
6:26
ever 24 fver 30;
Jn 2:11
6:27
gIsa 55:2
hver 54;
Mt 25:46;
Jn 4:14 iMt 8:20
jRo 4:11;
1Co 9:2;
2Co 1:22;
Eph 1:13; 4:30;
2Ti 2:19;
Rev 7:3
6:29
k1Jn 3:23
1Jn 3:17
6:30
mJn 2:11
nMt 12:38
6:31
oNu 11:7-9
pEx 16:4,15;
Ne 9:15;
Ps 78:24;
105:40
6:33
qver 50
6:34
rJn 4:15
6:35
sver 48,51
tJn 4:14
6:37
uver 39;
Jn 17:2,6,9,24
6:38
vJn 4:34; 5:30
6:39
wJn 10:28;
17:12; 18:9
xver 40,44,54
6:40
yJn 3:15,16
6:42
zLk 4:22
aJn 7:27,28
bver 38,62

ᵃ19 Greek *rowed twenty-five or thirty stadia* (about 5 or 6 kilometers)   ᵇ31 Exodus 16:4; Neh. 9:15; Psalm 78:24,25 can come to me unless the Father who sent me draws him,^c and I will raise him up at the last day. ⁴⁵It is written in the Prophets: 'They will all be taught by God.'^{a d} Everyone who listens to the Father and learns from him comes to me. ⁴⁶No one has seen the Father except the one who is from God;^e only he has seen the Father. ⁴⁷I tell you the truth, he who believes has everlasting life.^f ⁴⁸I am the bread of life.^f ⁴⁹Your forefathers ate the manna in the desert, yet they died. ^g ⁵⁰But here is the bread that comes down from heaven,^h which a man may eat and not die. ⁵¹I am the living bread that came down from heaven. If anyone eats of this bread, he will live forever. This bread is my flesh, which I will give for the life of the world."ⁱ

⁵²Then the Jews began to argue sharply among themselves,^j "How can this man give us his flesh to eat?"

⁵³Jesus said to them, "I tell you the truth, unless you eat the flesh of the Son of Man^k and drink his blood, you have no life in you. ⁵⁴Whoever eats my flesh and drinks my blood has eternal life, and I will raise him up at the last day.^l ⁵⁵For my flesh is real food and my blood is real drink. ⁵⁶Whoever eats my flesh and drinks my blood remains in me, and I in him. ^m ⁵⁷Just as the living Father sent meⁿ and I live because of the Father, so the one who feeds on me will live because of me. ⁵⁸This is the bread that came down from heaven. Your forefathers ate manna and died, but he who feeds on this bread will live forever."^o ⁵⁹He said this while teaching in the synagogue in Capernaum.

Many Disciples Desert Jesus

⁶⁰On hearing it, many of his disciples^p said, "This is a hard teaching. Who can accept it?"

⁶¹Aware that his disciples were grumbling about this, Jesus said to them, "Does this offend you?^q ⁶²What if you see the Son of Man ascend to where he was before!^r ⁶³The Spirit gives life;^s the flesh counts for nothing. The words I have spoken to you are spirit^b and they are life. ⁶⁴Yet there are some of you who do not believe." For Jesus had known^t from the beginning which of them did not believe and who would betray him. ⁶⁵He went on to say, "This is why I told you that no one can come to me unless the Father has enabled him."^u

⁶⁶From this time many of his disciples^v turned back and no longer followed him.

⁶⁷"You do not want to leave too, do you?" Jesus asked the Twelve. ^w

⁶⁸Simon Peter answered him,^x "Lord, to whom shall we go? You have the words of eternal life. ⁶⁹We believe and know that you are the Holy One of God."^y

⁷⁰Then Jesus replied, "Have I not chosen you,^z the Twelve? Yet one of you is a devil!"^a ⁷¹(He meant Judas, the son of Simon Iscariot, who, though one of the Twelve, was later to betray him.)

Jesus Goes to the Feast of Tabernacles

7 After this, Jesus went around in Galilee, purposely staying away from Judea because the Jews^b there were waiting to take his life.^c ²But when the Jewish Feast of Tabernacles^d was near, ³Jesus' brothers^e said to him, "You ought to leave here and go to Judea, so that your

---

^a45 Isaiah 54:13   ^b63 Or *Spirit*

6:44
^cver 65;
Jer 31:3;
Jn 12:32
6:45
^dIsa 54:13;
Jer 31:33,34;
Heb 8:10,11;
10:16
6:46
^eJn 1:18; 5:37;
7:29
6:48
^fver 35,51
6:49
^gver 31,58
6:50
^hver 33
6:51
ⁱHeb 10:10
6:52
^jJn 7:43; 9:16;
10:19
6:53
^kMt 8:20
6:54
^lver 39
6:56
^mJn 15:4-7;
1Jn 3:24; 4:15
6:57
ⁿJn 3:17
6:58
^over 49-51;
Jn 3:36
6:60
^pver 66
6:61
^qMt 11:6
6:62
^rMk 16:19;
Jn 3:13; 17:5
6:63
^s2Co 3:6
6:64
^tJn 2:25
6:65
^uver 37,44
6:66
^vver 60
6:67
^wMt 10:2
6:68
^xMt 16:16
6:69
^yMk 8:29;
Lk 9:20
6:70
^zJn 15:16,19
^aJn 13:27
7:1
^bJn 1:19
^cJn 5:18
7:2
^dLev 23:34;
Dt 16:16
7:3
^eMt 12:46

disciples may see the miracles you do. [4]No one who wants to become a public figure acts in secret. Since you are doing these things, show yourself to the world." [5]For even his own brothers did not believe in him. [f]

[6]Therefore Jesus told them, "The right time[g] for me has not yet come; for you any time is right. [7]The world cannot hate you, but it hates me[h] because I testify that what it does is evil. [i] [8]You go to the Feast. I am not yet[a] going up to this Feast, because for me the right time[j] has not yet come." [9]Having said this, he stayed in Galilee.

[10]However, after his brothers had left for the Feast, he went also, not publicly, but in secret. [11]Now at the Feast the Jews were watching for him[k] and asking, "Where is that man?"

[12]Among the crowds there was widespread whispering about him. Some said, "He is a good man."

Others replied, "No, he deceives the people."[l] [13]But no one would say anything publicly about him for fear of the Jews. [m]

Jesus Teaches at the Feast

[14]Not until halfway through the Feast did Jesus go up to the temple courts and begin to teach. [n] [15]The Jews[o] were amazed and asked, "How did this man get such learning[p] without having studied?"[q]

[16]Jesus answered, "My teaching is not my own. It comes from him who sent me. [r] [17]If anyone chooses to do God's will, he will find out[s] whether my teaching comes from God or whether I speak on my own. [18]He who speaks on his own does so to gain honor for himself, [t] but he who works for the honor of the one who sent him is a man of truth; there is nothing false about him. [19]Has not Moses given you the law?[u] Yet not one of you keeps the law. Why are you trying to kill me?"[v]

[20]"You are demon-possessed," [w] the crowd answered. "Who is trying to kill you?"

[21]Jesus said to them, "I did one miracle, and you are all astonished. [22]Yet, because Moses gave you circumcision[x] (though actually it did not come from Moses, but from the patriarchs), [y] you circumcise a child on the Sabbath. [23]Now if a child can be circumcised on the Sabbath so that the law of Moses may not be broken, why are you angry with me for healing the whole man on the Sabbath? [24]Stop judging by mere appearances, and make a right judgment."[z]

Is Jesus the Christ?

[25]At that point some of the people of Jerusalem began to ask, "Isn't this the man they are trying to kill? [26]Here he is, speaking publicly, and they are not saying a word to him. Have the authorities[a] really concluded that he is the Christ[b]? [27]But we know where this man is from;[b] when the Christ comes, no one will know where he is from."

[28]Then Jesus, still teaching in the temple courts, [c] cried out, "Yes, you know me, and you know where I am from. [d] I am not here on my own, but he who sent me is true. [e] You do not know him, [29]but I know him[f] because I am from him and he sent me."

[30]At this they tried to seize him, but no one laid a hand on him, [g] because his time had not yet come. [31]Still, many in the crowd put their

7:5 f Mk 3:21
7:6 g Mt 26:18
7:7 h Jn 15:18,19 i Jn 3:19,20
7:8 j ver 6
7:11 k Jn 11:56
7:12 l ver 40,43
7:13 m Jn 9:22; 12:42; 19:38
7:14 n ver 28; Mt 26:55
7:15 o Jn 1:19 p Ac 26:24 q Mt 13:54
7:16 r Jn 3:11; 14:24
7:17 s Ps 25:14; Jn 8:43
7:18 t Jn 5:41; 8:50, 54
7:19 u Jn 1:17 v ver 1; Mt 12:14
7:20 w Jn 8:48; 10:20
7:22 x Lev 12:3 y Ge 17:10-14
7:24 z Isa 11:3,4; Jn 8:15
7:26 a ver 48
7:27 b Mt 13:55; Lk 4:22
7:28 c ver 14 d Jn 8:14 e Jn 8:26,42
7:29 f Mt 11:27
7:30 g ver 32,44; Jn 10:39

---

[a]8 Some early manuscripts do not have *yet*.   [b]26 Or *Messiah*; also in verses 27, 31, 41 and 42

faith in him. [h] They said, "When the Christ comes, will he do more miraculous signs [i] than this man?"

[32] The Pharisees heard the crowd whispering such things about him. Then the chief priests and the Pharisees sent temple guards to arrest him.

[33] Jesus said, "I am with you for only a short time, [j] and then I go to the one who sent me. [k] [34] You will look for me, but you will not find me; and where I am, you cannot come." [l]

[35] The Jews said to one another, "Where does this man intend to go that we cannot find him? Will he go where our people live scattered [m] among the Greeks, [n] and teach the Greeks? [36] What did he mean when he said, 'You will look for me, but you will not find me,' and 'Where I am, you cannot come'?"

[37] On the last and greatest day of the Feast, [o] Jesus stood and said in a loud voice, "If anyone is thirsty, let him come to me and drink. [p] [38] Whoever believes in me, as [a] the Scripture has said, [q] streams of living water [r] will flow from within him." [s] [39] By this he meant the Spirit, [t] whom those who believed in him were later to receive. [u] Up to that time the Spirit had not been given, since Jesus had not yet been glorified. [v]

[40] On hearing his words, some of the people said, "Surely this man is the Prophet." [w]

[41] Others said, "He is the Christ."

Still others asked, "How can the Christ come from Galilee? [x] [42] Does not the Scripture say that the Christ will come from David's family [b] [y] and from Bethlehem, [z] the town where David lived?" [43] Thus the people were divided [a] because of Jesus. [44] Some wanted to seize him, but no one laid a hand on him. [b]

Unbelief of the Jewish Leaders

[45] Finally the temple guards went back to the chief priests and Pharisees, who asked them, "Why didn't you bring him in?"

[46] "No one ever spoke the way this man does," [c] the guards declared.

[47] "You mean he has deceived you also?" [d] the Pharisees retorted. [48] "Has any of the rulers or of the Pharisees believed in him? [e] [49] No! But this mob that knows nothing of the law—there is a curse on them."

[50] Nicodemus, [f] who had gone to Jesus earlier and who was one of their own number, asked, [51] "Does our law condemn anyone without first hearing him to find out what he is doing?"

[52] They replied, "Are you from Galilee, too? Look into it, and you will find that a prophet [c] does not come out of Galilee." [g]

[The earliest and most reliable manuscripts and other ancient witnesses do not have John 7:53—8:11.]

[53] Then each went to his own home.

8 But Jesus went to the Mount of Olives. [h] [2] At dawn he appeared again in the temple courts, where all the people gathered around

---

7:31
h Jn 8:30
i Jn 2:11

7:33
j Jn 13:33; 16:16
k Jn 16:5,10,17, 28

7:34
l Jn 8:21; 13:33

7:35
m Jas 1:1
n Jn 12:20; 1Pe 1:1

7:37
o Lev 23:36
p Isa 55:1; Rev 22:17

7:38
q Isa 58:11
r Jn 4:10
s Jn 4:14

7:39
t Joel 2:28; Ac 2:17,33
u Jn 20:22
v Jn 12:23; 13:31,32

7:40
w Mt 21:11; Jn 1:21

7:41
x ver 52; Jn 1:46

7:42
y Mt 1:1
z Mic 5:2; Mt 2:5,6; Lk 2:4

7:43
a Jn 9:16; 10:19

7:44
b ver 30

7:46
c Mt 7:28

7:47
d ver 12

7:48
e Jn 12:42

7:50
f Jn 3:1; 19:39

7:52
g ver 41

8:1
h Mt 21:1

---

[a] 37,38 Or / *If anyone is thirsty, let him come to me.* / *And let him drink,* [38] *who believes in me.* / *As*
[b] 42 Greek *seed*   [c] 52 Two early manuscripts *the Prophet*

him, and he sat down to teach them. [i] 3The teachers of the law and the Pharisees brought in a woman caught in adultery. They made her stand before the group 4and said to Jesus, "Teacher, this woman was caught in the act of adultery. 5In the Law Moses commanded us to stone such women. [j] Now what do you say?" 6They were using this question as a trap, [k] in order to have a basis for accusing him. [l]

But Jesus bent down and started to write on the ground with his finger. 7When they kept on questioning him, he straightened up and said to them, "If any one of you is without sin, let him be the first to throw a stone [m] at her." [n] 8Again he stooped down and wrote on the ground.

9At this, those who heard began to go away one at a time, the older ones first, until only Jesus was left, with the woman still standing there. 10Jesus straightened up and asked her, "Woman, where are they? Has no one condemned you?"

11"No one, sir," she said.

"Then neither do I condemn you," [o] Jesus declared. "Go now and leave your life of sin." [p]

The Validity of Jesus' Testimony

12When Jesus spoke again to the people, he said, "I am [q] the light of the world. [r] Whoever follows me will never walk in darkness, but will have the light of life." [s]

13The Pharisees challenged him, "Here you are, appearing as your own witness; your testimony is not valid." [t]

14Jesus answered, "Even if I testify on my own behalf, my testimony is valid, for I know where I came from and where I am going. [u] But you have no idea where I come from [v] or where I am going. 15You judge by human standards; [w] I pass judgment on no one. [x] 16But if I do judge, my decisions are right, because I am not alone. I stand with the Father, who sent me. [y] 17In your own Law it is written that the testimony of two men is valid. [z] 18I am one who testifies for myself; my other witness is the Father, who sent me." [a]

19Then they asked him, "Where is your father?"

"You do not know me or my Father," [b] Jesus replied. "If you knew me, you would know my Father also." [c] 20He spoke these words while teaching [d] in the temple area near the place where the offerings were put. [e] Yet no one seized him, because his time had not yet come. [f]

21Once more Jesus said to them, "I am going away, and you will look for me, and you will die [g] in your sin. Where I go, you cannot come." [h]

22This made the Jews ask, "Will he kill himself? Is that why he says, 'Where I go, you cannot come'?"

23But he continued, "You are from below; I am from above. You are of this world; I am not of this world. [i] 24I told you that you would die in your sins; if you do not believe that I am the one I claim to be, [a] [j] you will indeed die in your sins."

25"Who are you?" they asked.

[a]24 Or *I am he*; also in verse 28

8:2
iver 20;
Mt 26:55
8:5
jLev 20:10;
Dt 22:22
8:6
kMt 22:15,18
lMt 12:10
8:7
mDt 17:7
nRo 2:1,22
8:11
oJn 3:17
pJn 5:14
8:12
qJn 6:35
rJn 1:4; 12:35
sPr 4:18;
Mt 5:14
8:13
tJn 5:31
8:14
uJn 13:3; 16:28
vJn 7:28; 9:29
8:15
wJn 7:24
xJn 3:17
8:16
yJn 5:30
8:17
zDt 17:6;
Mt 18:16
8:18
aJn 5:37
8:19
bJn 16:3
cJn 14:7;
1Jn 2:23
8:20
dMt 26:55
eMk 12:41
fMt 26:18;
Jn 7:30
8:21
gEze 3:18
hJn 7:34; 13:33
8:23
iJn 3:31; 17:14
8:24
jJn 4:26; 13:19

"Just what I have been claiming all along," Jesus replied. 26"I have much to say in judgment of you. But he who sent me is reliable,ᵏ and what I have heard from him I tell the world."ˡ

27They did not understand that he was telling them about his Father. 28So Jesus said, "When you have lifted up the Son of Man,ᵐ then you will know that I am ¸the one I claim to be¸ and that I do nothing on my own but speak just what the Father has taught me. 29The one who sent me is with me; he has not left me alone,ⁿ for I always do what pleases him."ᵒ 30Even as he spoke, many put their faith in him.ᵖ

The Children of Abraham

31To the Jews who had believed him, Jesus said, "If you hold to my teaching,�q you are really my disciples. 32Then you will know the truth, and the truth will set you free."ʳ

33They answered him, "We are Abraham's descendantsᵃˢ and have never been slaves of anyone. How can you say that we shall be set free?"

34Jesus replied, "I tell you the truth, everyone who sins is a slave to sin.ᵗ 35Now a slave has no permanent place in the family, but a son belongs to it forever.ᵘ 36So if the Son sets you free, you will be free indeed. 37I know you are Abraham's descendants. Yet you are ready to kill me,ᵛ because you have no room for my word. 38I am telling you what I have seen in the Father's presence,ʷ and you do what you have heard from your father.ᵇ"

39"Abraham is our father," they answered.

"If you were Abraham's children,"ˣ said Jesus, "then you wouldᶜ do the things Abraham did. 40As it is, you are determined to kill me, a man who has told you the truth that I heard from God.ʸ Abraham did not do such things. 41You are doing the things your own father does."ᶻ

"We are not illegitimate children," they protested. "The only Father we have is God himself."ᵃ

The Children of the Devil

42Jesus said to them, "If God were your Father, you would love me,ᵇ for I came from Godᶜ and now am here. I have not come on my own;ᵈ but he sent me.ᵉ 43Why is my language not clear to you? Because you are unable to hear what I say. 44You belong to your father, the devil,ᶠ and you want to carry out your father's desire.ᵍ He was a murderer from the beginning, not holding to the truth, for there is no truth in him. When he lies, he speaks his native language, for he is a liar and the father of lies.ʰ 45Yet because I tell the truth,ⁱ you do not believe me! 46Can any of you prove me guilty of sin? If I am telling the truth, why don't you believe me? 47He who belongs to God hears what God says.ʲ The reason you do not hear is that you do not belong to God."

The Claims of Jesus About Himself

48The Jews answered him, "Aren't we right in saying that you are a Samaritanᵏ and demon-possessed?"ˡ

49"I am not possessed by a demon," said Jesus, "but I honor my

---

8:26
kJn 7:28
lJn 3:32; 15:15
8:28
mJn 3:14; 5:19; 12:32
8:29
nver 16;
Jn 16:32
oJn 4:34; 5:30; 6:38
8:30
pJn 7:31
8:31
qJn 15:7; 2Jn 9
8:32
rRo 8:2;
Jas 2:12
8:33
sver 37,39;
Mt 3:9
8:34
tRo 6:16;
2Pe 2:19
8:35
uGal 4:30
8:37
vver 39,40
8:38
wJn 5:19,30; 14:10,24
8:39
xver 37; Ro 9:7; Gal 3:7
8:40
yver 26
8:41
zver 38,44
aIsa 63:16; 64:8
8:42
b1Jn 5:1
cJn 16:27; 17:8
dJn 7:28
eJn 3:17
8:44
f1Jn 3:8
gver 38,41
hGe 3:4
8:45
iJn 18:37
8:47
jJn 18:37; 1Jn 4:6
8:48
kMt 10:5
lver 52; Jn 7:20

ᵃ33 Greek *seed*; also in verse 37   ᵇ38 Or *presence. Therefore do what you have heard from the Father.*
ᶜ39 Some early manuscripts "If you are Abraham's children," said Jesus, "then

Father and you dishonor me. ⁵⁰I am not seeking glory for myself;ᵐ but there is one who seeks it, and he is the judge. ⁵¹I tell you the truth, if anyone keeps my word, he will never see death."ⁿ

⁵²At this the Jews exclaimed, "Now we know that you are demon-possessed! Abraham died and so did the prophets, yet you say that if anyone keeps your word, he will never taste death. ⁵³Are you greater than our father Abraham?ᵒ He died, and so did the prophets. Who do you think you are?"

⁵⁴Jesus replied, "If I glorify myself,ᵖ my glory means nothing. My Father, whom you claim as your God, is the one who glorifies me.�q ⁵⁵Though you do not know him,ʳ I know him.ˢ If I said I did not, I would be a liar like you, but I do know him and keep his word.ᵗ ⁵⁶Your father Abrahamᵘ rejoiced at the thought of seeing my day; he saw itᵛ and was glad."

⁵⁷"You are not yet fifty years old," the Jews said to him, "and you have seen Abraham!"

⁵⁸"I tell you the truth," Jesus answered, "before Abraham was born,ʷ I am!"ˣ ⁵⁹At this, they picked up stones to stone him,ʸ but Jesus hid himself,ᶻ slipping away from the temple grounds.

Jesus Heals a Man Born Blind

9 As he went along, he saw a man blind from birth. ²His disciples asked him, "Rabbi,ᵃ who sinned,ᵇ this manᶜ or his parents,ᵈ that he was born blind?"

³"Neither this man nor his parents sinned," said Jesus, "but this happened so that the work of God might be displayed in his life.ᵉ ⁴As long as it is day,ᶠ we must do the work of him who sent me. Night is coming, when no one can work. ⁵While I am in the world, I am the light of the world."ᵍ

⁶Having said this, he spitʰ on the ground, made some mud with the saliva, and put it on the man's eyes. ⁷"Go," he told him, "wash in the Pool of Siloam"ⁱ (this word means Sent). So the man went and washed, and came home seeing.ʲ

⁸His neighbors and those who had formerly seen him begging asked, "Isn't this the same man who used to sit and beg?"ᵏ ⁹Some claimed that he was.

Others said, "No, he only looks like him."

But he himself insisted, "I am the man."

¹⁰"How then were your eyes opened?" they demanded.

¹¹He replied, "The man they call Jesus made some mud and put it on my eyes. He told me to go to Siloam and wash. So I went and washed, and then I could see."ˡ

¹²"Where is this man?" they asked him.

"I don't know," he said.

The Pharisees Investigate the Healing

¹³They brought to the Pharisees the man who had been blind. ¹⁴Now the day on which Jesus had made the mud and opened the man's eyes was a Sabbath.ᵐ ¹⁵Therefore the Pharisees also asked him how he had received his sight.ⁿ "He put mud on my eyes," the man replied, "and I washed, and now I see."

8:50
mver 54;
Jn 5:41
8:51
nJn 11:26
8:53
oJn 4:12
8:54
pver 50
qJn 16:14; 17:1,
5
8:55
rver 19 sJn 7:28,
29 tJn 15:10
8:56
uver 37,39
vMt 13:17;
Heb 11:13
8:58
wJn 1:2; 17:5,
24 xEx 3:14
8:59
yLev 24:16;
Jn 10:31; 11:8
zJn 12:36
9:2
aMt 23:7
bver 34;
Lk 13:2; Ac 28:4
cEze 18:20
dEx 20:5;
Job 21:19
9:3
eJn 11:4
9:4
fJn 11:9; 12:35
9:5
gJn 1:4; 8:12;
12:46
9:6
hMk 7:33; 8:23
9:7
iver 11;
2Ki 5:10;
Lk 13:4
jIsa 35:5;
Jn 11:37
9:8
kAc 3:2,10
9:11
lver 7
9:14
mJn 5:9
9:15
nver 10

16Some of the Pharisees said, "This man is not from God, for he does not keep the Sabbath." °

But others asked, "How can a sinner do such miraculous signs?" So they were divided. ᴾ

17Finally they turned again to the blind man, "What have you to say about him? It was your eyes he opened."

The man replied, "He is a prophet." �q

18The Jews ʳ still did not believe that he had been blind and had received his sight until they sent for the man's parents. 19"Is this your son?" they asked. "Is this the one you say was born blind? How is it that now he can see?"

20"We know he is our son," the parents answered, "and we know he was born blind. 21But how he can see now, or who opened his eyes, we don't know. Ask him. He is of age; he will speak for himself." 22His parents said this because they were afraid of the Jews, ˢ for already the Jews had decided that anyone who acknowledged that Jesus was the Christ ᵃ would be put out ᵗ of the synagogue. ᵘ 23That was why his parents said, "He is of age; ask him." ᵛ

24A second time they summoned the man who had been blind. "Give glory to God, ᵇ" ʷ they said. "We know this man is a sinner." ˣ

25He replied, "Whether he is a sinner or not, I don't know. One thing I do know. I was blind but now I see!"

26Then they asked him, "What did he do to you? How did he open your eyes?"

27He answered, "I have told you already ʸ and you did not listen. Why do you want to hear it again? Do you want to become his disciples, too?"

28Then they hurled insults at him and said, "You are this fellow's disciple! We are disciples of Moses! ᶻ 29We know that God spoke to Moses, but as for this fellow, we don't even know where he comes from." ᵃ

30The man answered, "Now that is remarkable! You don't know where he comes from, yet he opened my eyes. 31We know that God does not listen to sinners. He listens to the godly man who does his will. ᵇ 32Nobody has ever heard of opening the eyes of a man born blind. 33If this man were not from God, ᶜ he could do nothing."

34To this they replied, "You were steeped in sin at birth; ᵈ how dare you lecture us!" And they threw him out. ᵉ

Spiritual Blindness

35Jesus heard that they had thrown him out, and when he found him, he said, "Do you believe in the Son of Man?"

36"Who is he, sir?" the man asked. "Tell me so that I may believe in him." ᶠ

37Jesus said, "You have now seen him; in fact, he is the one speaking with you." ᵍ

38Then the man said, "Lord, I believe," and he worshiped him. ʰ

39Jesus said, "For judgment ⁱ I have come into this world, ʲ so that the blind will see ᵏ and those who see will become blind." ˡ

a22 Or *Messiah*   b24 A solemn charge to tell the truth (see Joshua 7:19)

9:16
o Mt 12:2
p Jn 6:52; 7:43;
10:19
9:17
q Mt 21:11
9:18
r Jn 1:19
9:22
s Jn 7:13
t ver 34; Lk 6:22
u Jn 12:42; 16:2
9:23
v ver 21
9:24
w Jos 7:19
x ver 16
9:27
y ver 15
9:28
z Jn 5:45
9:29
a Jn 8:14
9:31
b Ge 18:23-32;
Ps 34:15,16;
66:18; 145:19,
20; Pr 15:29;
Isa 1:15; 59:1,
2; Jn 15:7;
Jas 5:16-18;
1Jn 5:14,15
9:33
c ver 16; Jn 3:2
9:34
d ver 2 e ver 22,
35; Isa 66:5
9:36
f Ro 10:14
9:37
g Jn 4:26
9:38
h Mt 28:9
9:39
i Jn 5:22 j 1Jn 3:19
k Lk 4:18
l Mt 13:13

[40]Some Pharisees who were with him heard him say this and asked, "What? Are we blind too?"[m]

[41]Jesus said, "If you were blind, you would not be guilty of sin; but now that you claim you can see, your guilt remains.[n]

The Shepherd and His Flock

10 "I tell you the truth, the man who does not enter the sheep pen by the gate, but climbs in by some other way, is a thief and a robber. [2]The man who enters by the gate is the shepherd of his sheep.[o] [3]The watchman opens the gate for him, and the sheep listen to his voice.[p] He calls his own sheep by name and leads them out. [4]When he has brought out all his own, he goes on ahead of them, and his sheep follow him because they know his voice. [5]But they will never follow a stranger; in fact, they will run away from him because they do not recognize a stranger's voice." [6]Jesus used this figure of speech,[q] but they did not understand what he was telling them.

[7]Therefore Jesus said again, "I tell you the truth, I am the gate for the sheep. [8]All who ever came before me[r] were thieves and robbers, but the sheep did not listen to them. [9]I am the gate; whoever enters through me will be saved.[a] He will come in and go out, and find pasture. [10]The thief comes only to steal and kill and destroy; I have come that they may have life, and have it to the full.

[11]"I am the good shepherd.[s] The good shepherd lays down his life for the sheep.[t] [12]The hired hand is not the shepherd who owns the sheep. So when he sees the wolf coming, he abandons the sheep and runs away.[u] Then the wolf attacks the flock and scatters it. [13]The man runs away because he is a hired hand and cares nothing for the sheep.

[14]"I am the good shepherd;[v] I know my sheep[w] and my sheep know me— [15]just as the Father knows me and I know the Father[x]—and I lay down my life for the sheep. [16]I have other sheep[y] that are not of this sheep pen. I must bring them also. They too will listen to my voice, and there shall be one flock[z] and one shepherd.[a] [17]The reason my Father loves me is that I lay down my life[b]—only to take it up again. [18]No one takes it from me, but I lay it down of my own accord.[c] I have authority to lay it down and authority to take it up again. This command I received from my Father."[d]

[19]At these words the Jews were again divided.[e] [20]Many of them said, "He is demon-possessed[f] and raving mad.[g] Why listen to him?"

[21]But others said, "These are not the sayings of a man possessed by a demon.[h] Can a demon open the eyes of the blind?"[i]

The Unbelief of the Jews

[22]Then came the Feast of Dedication[b] at Jerusalem. It was winter, [23]and Jesus was in the temple area walking in Solomon's Colonnade.[j] [24]The Jews[k] gathered around him, saying, "How long will you keep us in suspense? If you are the Christ,[c] tell us plainly."[l]

[25]Jesus answered, "I did tell you,[m] but you do not believe. The miracles I do in my Father's name speak for me,[n] [26]but you do not believe because you are not my sheep.[o] [27]My sheep listen to my voice; I know them,[p] and they follow me.[q] [28]I give them eternal life, and they

---

**Cross-references (margin):**

9:40
m Ro 2:19
9:41
n Jn 15:22,24
10:2
o ver 11,14
10:3
p ver 4,5,14,16, 27
10:6
q Jn 16:25
10:8
r Jer 23:1,2
10:11
s ver 14;
Isa 40:11;
Eze 34:11-16, 23; Heb 13:20;
1Pe 5:4;
Rev 7:17
t Jn 15:13;
1Jn 3:16
10:12
u Zec 11:16,17
10:14
v ver 11 w ver 27
10:15
x Mt 11:27
10:16
y Isa 56:8
z Jn 11:52;
Eph 2:11-19
a Eze 37:24;
1Pe 2:25
10:17
b ver 11,15,18
10:18
c Mt 26:53
d Jn 15:10;
Php 2:8;
Heb 5:8
10:19
e Jn 7:43; 9:16
10:20
f Jn 7:20
g Mk 3:21
10:21
h Mt 4:24
i Ex 4:11;
Jn 9:32,33
10:23
j Ac 3:11; 5:12
10:24
k Jn 1:19
l Jn 16:25,29
10:25
m Jn 8:58
n Jn 5:36
10:26
o Jn 8:47
10:27
p ver 14 q ver 4

---

a9 Or *kept safe*   b22 That is, Hanukkah   c24 Or *Messiah* shall never perish; no one can snatch them out of my hand. ʳ ²⁹My Father, who has given them to me,ˢ is greater than all*ᵃ*;ᵗ no one can snatch them out of my Father's hand. ³⁰I and the Father are one."ᵘ

³¹Again the Jews picked up stones to stone him, ᵛ ³²but Jesus said to them, "I have shown you many great miracles from the Father. For which of these do you stone me?"

³³"We are not stoning you for any of these," replied the Jews, "but for blasphemy, because you, a mere man, claim to be God."ʷ

³⁴Jesus answered them, "Is it not written in your Law,ˣ 'I have said you are gods'*ᵇ*?ʸ ³⁵If he called them 'gods,' to whom the word of God came—and the Scripture cannot be broken— ³⁶what about the one whom the Father set apartᶻ as his very ownᵃ and sent into the world?ᵇ Why then do you accuse me of blasphemy because I said, 'I am God's Son'?ᶜ ³⁷Do not believe me unless I do what my Father does. ᵈ ³⁸But if I do it, even though you do not believe me, believe the miracles, that you may know and understand that the Father is in me, and I in the Father."ᵉ ³⁹Again they tried to seize him, ᶠ but he escaped their grasp. ᵍ

⁴⁰Then Jesus went back across the Jordanʰ to the place where John had been baptizing in the early days. Here he stayed ⁴¹and many people came to him. They said, "Though John never performed a miraculous sign, ⁱ all that John said about this man was true."ʲ ⁴²And in that place many believed in Jesus. ᵏ

The Death of Lazarus

11 Now a man named Lazarus was sick. He was from Bethany,ˡ the village of Mary and her sister Martha. ᵐ ²This Mary, whose brother Lazarus now lay sick, was the same one who poured perfume on the Lord and wiped his feet with her hair.ⁿ ³So the sisters sent word to Jesus, "Lord, the one you loveᵒ is sick."

⁴When he heard this, Jesus said, "This sickness will not end in death. No, it is for God's gloryᵖ so that God's Son may be glorified through it." ⁵Jesus loved Martha and her sister and Lazarus. ⁶Yet when he heard that Lazarus was sick, he stayed where he was two more days.

⁷Then he said to his disciples, "Let us go back to Judea."�q

⁸"But Rabbi,"ʳ they said, "a short while ago the Jews tried to stone you,ˢ and yet you are going back there?"

⁹Jesus answered, "Are there not twelve hours of daylight? A man who walks by day will not stumble, for he sees by this world's light.ᵗ ¹⁰It is when he walks by night that he stumbles, for he has no light."

¹¹After he had said this, he went on to tell them, "Our friendᵘ Lazarus has fallen asleep;ᵛ but I am going there to wake him up."

¹²His disciples replied, "Lord, if he sleeps, he will get better." ¹³Jesus had been speaking of his death, but his disciples thought he meant natural sleep.ʷ

¹⁴So then he told them plainly, "Lazarus is dead, ¹⁵and for your sake I am glad I was not there, so that you may believe. But let us go to him."

¹⁶Then Thomasˣ (called Didymus) said to the rest of the disciples, "Let us also go, that we may die with him."

10:28
ʳJn 6:39
10:29
ˢJn 17:2,6,24
ᵗJn 14:28
10:30
ᵘJn 17:21-23
10:31
ᵛJn 8:59
10:33
ʷLev 24:16;
Jn 5:18
10:34
ˣJn 8:17;
Ro 3:19
ʸPs 82:6
10:36
ᶻJer 1:5
ᵃJn 6:69
ᵇJn 3:17
ᶜJn 5:17,18
10:37
ᵈver 25;
Jn 15:24
10:38
ᵉJn 14:10,11,20;
17:21
10:39
ᶠJn 7:30
ᵍLk 4:30;
Jn 8:59
10:40
ʰJn 1:28
10:41
ⁱJn 2:11; 3:30
ʲJn 1:26,27,30,
34
10:42
ᵏJn 7:31
11:1
ˡMt 21:17
ᵐLk 10:38
11:2
ⁿMk 14:3;
Lk 7:38; Jn 12:3
11:3
ᵒver 5,36
11:4
ᵖver 40; Jn 9:3
11:7
qJn 10:40
11:8
ʳMt 23:7
ˢJn 8:59; 10:31
11:9
ᵗJn 9:4; 12:35
11:11
ᵘver 3 ᵛAc 7:60
11:13
ʷMt 9:24
11:16
ˣMt 10:3;
Jn 14:5;
20:24-28; 21:2;
Ac 1:13

ᵃ29 Many early manuscripts *What my Father has given me is greater than all*   *ᵇ34* Psalm 82:6

Jesus Comforts the Sisters

17On his arrival, Jesus found that Lazarus had already been in the tomb for four days. y **18**Bethany z was less than two miles a from Jerusalem, **19**and many Jews had come to Martha and Mary to comfort them in the loss of their brother. a **20**When Martha heard that Jesus was coming, she went out to meet him, but Mary stayed at home. b

21"Lord," Martha said to Jesus, "if you had been here, my brother would not have died. c **22**But I know that even now God will give you whatever you ask." d

23Jesus said to her, "Your brother will rise again."

24Martha answered, "I know he will rise again in the resurrection e at the last day."

25Jesus said to her, "I am the resurrection and the life. f He who believes in me will live, even though he dies; **26**and whoever lives and believes in me will never die. Do you believe this?"

27"Yes, Lord," she told him, "I believe that you are the Christ, b g the Son of God, h who was to come into the world." i

28And after she had said this, she went back and called her sister Mary aside. "The Teacher j is here," she said, "and is asking for you." **29**When Mary heard this, she got up quickly and went to him. **30**Now Jesus had not yet entered the village, but was still at the place where Martha had met him. k **31**When the Jews who had been with Mary in the house, comforting her, l noticed how quickly she got up and went out, they followed her, supposing she was going to the tomb to mourn there.

32When Mary reached the place where Jesus was and saw him, she fell at his feet and said, "Lord, if you had been here, my brother would not have died." m

33When Jesus saw her weeping, and the Jews who had come along with her also weeping, he was deeply moved n in spirit and troubled. o **34**"Where have you laid him?" he asked.

"Come and see, Lord," they replied.

35Jesus wept. p

36Then the Jews said, "See how he loved him!" q

37But some of them said, "Could not he who opened the eyes of the blind man r have kept this man from dying?" s

Jesus Raises Lazarus From the Dead

38Jesus, once more deeply moved, t came to the tomb. It was a cave with a stone laid across the entrance. u **39**"Take away the stone," he said.

"But, Lord," said Martha, the sister of the dead man, "by this time there is a bad odor, for he has been there four days." v

40Then Jesus said, "Did I not tell you that if you believed, w you would see the glory of God?" x

41So they took away the stone. Then Jesus looked up y and said, "Father, z I thank you that you have heard me. **42**I knew that you always hear me, but I said this for the benefit of the people standing here, a that they may believe that you sent me." b

---

11:17
yver 6,39
11:18
zver 1
11:19
aver 31;
Job 2:11
11:20
bLk 10:38-42
11:21
cver 32,37
11:22
dver 41,42;
Jn 9:31
11:24
eDa 12:2;
Jn 5:28,29;
Ac 24:15
11:25
fJn 1:4
11:27
gLk 2:11
hMt 16:16
iJn 6:14
11:28
jMt 26:18;
Jn 13:13
11:30
kver 20
11:31
lver 19
11:32
mver 21
11:33
nver 38
oJn 12:27
11:35
pLk 19:41
11:36
qver 3
11:37
rJn 9:6,7
sver 21,32
11:38
tver 33
uMt 27:60;
Lk 24:2; Jn 20:1
11:39
vver 17
11:40
wver 23-25
xver 4
11:41
yJn 17:1
zMt 11:25
11:42
aJn 12:30
bJn 3:17

---

a18 Greek *fifteen stadia* (about 3 kilometers)   b27 Or *Messiah*

43When he had said this, Jesus called in a loud voice, "Lazarus, come out!"c 44The dead man came out, his hands and feet wrapped with strips of linen,d and a cloth around his face.e

Jesus said to them, "Take off the grave clothes and let him go."

The Plot to Kill Jesus

45Therefore many of the Jews who had come to visit Mary,f and had seen what Jesus did,g put their faith in him.h 46But some of them went to the Pharisees and told them what Jesus had done. 47Then the chief priests and the Phariseesi called a meetingj of the Sanhedrin.k

"What are we accomplishing?" they asked. "Here is this man performing many miraculous signs.l 48If we let him go on like this, everyone will believe in him, and then the Romans will come and take away both our placea and our nation."

49Then one of them, named Caiaphas,m who was high priest that year,n spoke up, "You know nothing at all! 50You do not realize that it is better for you that one man die for the people than that the whole nation perish."o

51He did not say this on his own, but as high priest that year he prophesied that Jesus would die for the Jewish nation, 52and not only for that nation but also for the scattered children of God, to bring them together and make them one.p 53So from that day on they plotted to take his life.q

54Therefore Jesus no longer moved about publicly among the Jews.r Instead he withdrew to a region near the desert, to a village called Ephraim, where he stayed with his disciples.

55When it was almost time for the Jewish Passover,s many went up from the country to Jerusalem for their ceremonial cleansingt before the Passover. 56They kept looking for Jesus,u and as they stood in the temple area they asked one another, "What do you think? Isn't he coming to the Feast at all?" 57But the chief priests and Pharisees had given orders that if anyone found out where Jesus was, he should report it so that they might arrest him.

Jesus Anointed at Bethany

12:1–8Ref — Mt 26:6–13; Mk 14:3–9; Lk 7:37–39

12 Six days before the Passover,v Jesus arrived at Bethany,w where Lazarus lived, whom Jesus had raised from the dead. 2Here a dinner was given in Jesus' honor. Martha served,x while Lazarus was among those reclining at the table with him. 3Then Mary took about a pintb of pure nard, an expensive perfume;y she poured it on Jesus' feet and wiped his feet with her hair.z And the house was filled with the fragrance of the perfume.

4But one of his disciples, Judas Iscariot, who was later to betray him,a objected, 5"Why wasn't this perfume sold and the money given to the poor? It was worth a year's wages.c" 6He did not say this because he cared about the poor but because he was a thief; as keeper of the money bag,b he used to help himself to what was put into it.

7"Leave her alone," Jesus replied. "It was intended that she should

11:43
cLk 7:14
11:44
dJn 19:40
eJn 20:7
11:45
fver 19 gJn 2:23
hEx 14:31;
Jn 7:31
11:47
iver 57 jMt 26:3
kMt 5:22
lJn 2:11
11:49
mMt 26:3
nver 51;
Jn 18:13,14
11:50
oJn 18:14
11:52
pIsa 49:6;
Jn 10:16
11:53
qMt 12:14
11:54
rJn 7:1
11:55
sEx 12:13,23,27;
Mt 26:1,2;
Mk 14:1;
Jn 13:1
t2Ch 30:17,18
11:56
uJn 7:11
12:1
vJn 11:55
wMt 21:17
12:2
xLk 10:38-42
12:3
yMk 14:3
zJn 11:2
12:4
aMt 10:4
12:6
bJn 13:29

save this perfume for the day of my burial.[c] [8]You will always have the poor among you,[d] but you will not always have me."

[9]Meanwhile a large crowd of Jews found out that Jesus was there and came, not only because of him but also to see Lazarus, whom he had raised from the dead.[e] [10]So the chief priests made plans to kill Lazarus as well, [11]for on account of him[f] many of the Jews were going over to Jesus and putting their faith in him.[g]

The Triumphal Entry

12:12–15pp — Mt 21:4–9; Mk 11:7–10; Lk 19:35–38

[12]The next day the great crowd that had come for the Feast heard that Jesus was on his way to Jerusalem. [13]They took palm branches and went out to meet him, shouting,

> "Hosanna![a]"

> "Blessed is he who comes in the name of the Lord!"[b] [h]

> "Blessed is the King of Israel!"[i]

[14]Jesus found a young donkey and sat upon it, as it is written,

> [15]"Do not be afraid, O Daughter of Zion;
> see, your king is coming,
> seated on a donkey's colt."[c] [j]

[16]At first his disciples did not understand all this.[k] Only after Jesus was glorified[l] did they realize that these things had been written about him and that they had done these things to him.

[17]Now the crowd that was with him[m] when he called Lazarus from the tomb and raised him from the dead continued to spread the word. [18]Many people, because they had heard that he had given this miraculous sign,[n] went out to meet him. [19]So the Pharisees said to one another, "See, this is getting us nowhere. Look how the whole world has gone after him!"[o]

Jesus Predicts His Death

[20]Now there were some Greeks[p] among those who went up to worship at the Feast. [21]They came to Philip, who was from Bethsaida[q] in Galilee, with a request. "Sir," they said, "we would like to see Jesus." [22]Philip went to tell Andrew; Andrew and Philip in turn told Jesus.

[23]Jesus replied, "The hour has come for the Son of Man to be glorified.[r] [24]I tell you the truth, unless a kernel of wheat falls to the ground and dies,[s] it remains only a single seed. But if it dies, it produces many seeds. [25]The man who loves his life will lose it, while the man who hates his life in this world will keep it[t] for eternal life. [26]Whoever serves me must follow me; and where I am, my servant also will be.[u] My Father will honor the one who serves me.

[27]"Now my heart is troubled,[v] and what shall I say? 'Father,[w] save me from this hour'?[x] No, it was for this very reason I came to this hour. [28]Father, glorify your name!"

Then a voice came from heaven,[y] "I have glorified it, and will glorify

12:7
c Jn 19:40
12:8
d Dt 15:11
12:9
e Jn 11:43,44
12:11
f ver 17,18;
Jn 11:45
g Jn 7:31
12:13
h Ps 118:25,26
i Jn 1:49
12:15
j Zec 9:9
12:16
k Mk 9:32
l Jn 2:22; 7:39;
14:26
12:17
m Jn 11:42
12:18
n ver 11
12:19
o Jn 11:47,48
12:20
p Jn 7:35;
Ac 11:20
12:21
q Mt 11:21;
Jn 1:44
12:23
r Jn 13:32; 17:1
12:24
s 1Co 15:36
12:25
t Mt 10:39;
Mk 8:35;
Lk 14:26
12:26
u Jn 14:3; 17:24;
2Co 5:8;
1Th 4:17
12:27
v Mt 26:38,39;
Jn 11:33,38;
13:21
w Mt 11:25
x ver 23
12:28
y Mt 3:17

---

[a]13 A Hebrew expression meaning "Save!" which became an exclamation of praise   [b]13 Psalm 118:25, 26   [c]15 Zech. 9:9

it again." 29The crowd that was there and heard it said it had thundered; others said an angel had spoken to him.

30Jesus said, "This voice was for your benefit,z not mine. 31Now is the time for judgment on this world;a now the prince of this worldb will be driven out. 32But I, when I am lifted up from the earth,c will draw all men to myself."d 33He said this to show the kind of death he was going to die.e

34The crowd spoke up, "We have heard from the Law that the Christa will remain forever,f so how can you say, 'The Son of Mang must be lifted up'?h Who is this 'Son of Man'?"

35Then Jesus told them, "You are going to have the lighti just a little while longer. Walk while you have the light,j before darkness overtakes you.k The man who walks in the dark does not know where he is going. 36Put your trust in the light while you have it, so that you may become sons of light."l When he had finished speaking, Jesus left and hid himself from them.m

The Jews Continue in Their Unbelief

37Even after Jesus had done all these miraculous signsn in their presence, they still would not believe in him. 38This was to fulfill the word of Isaiah the prophet:

> "Lord, who has believed our message
> and to whom has the arm of the Lord been
> revealed?"b o

39For this reason they could not believe, because, as Isaiah says elsewhere:

> 40"He has blinded their eyes
> and deadened their hearts,
> so they can neither see with their eyes,
> nor understand with their hearts,
> nor turn—and I would heal them."c p

41Isaiah said this because he saw Jesus' gloryq and spoke about him.r

42Yet at the same time many even among the leaders believed in him.s But because of the Phariseest they would not confess their faith for fear they would be put out of the synagogue;u 43for they loved praise from men more than praise from God.v

44Then Jesus cried out, "When a man believes in me, he does not believe in me only, but in the one who sent me.w 45When he looks at me, he sees the one who sent me.x 46I have come into the world as a light,y so that no one who believes in me should stay in darkness.

47"As for the person who hears my words but does not keep them, I do not judge him. For I did not come to judge the world, but to save it.z 48There is a judge for the one who rejects me and does not accept my words; that very word which I spoke will condemn hima at the last day. 49For I did not speak of my own accord, but the Father who sent me commanded meb what to say and how to say it. 50I know that his command leads to eternal life. So whatever I say is just what the Father has told me to say."

12:30
z Jn 11:42
12:31
a Jn 16:11
b Jn 14:30;
16:11; 2Co 4:4;
Eph 2:2; 1Jn 4:4
12:32
c ver 34;
Jn 3:14; 8:28
d Jn 6:44
12:33
e Jn 18:32
12:34
f Ps 110:4;
Isa 9:7;
Eze 37:25;
Da 7:14
g Mt 8:20
h Jn 3:14
12:35
i ver 46 j Eph 5:8
k 1Jn 2:11
12:36
l Lk 16:8
m Jn 8:59
12:37
n Jn 2:11
12:38
o Isa 53:1;
Ro 10:16
12:40
p Isa 6:10;
Mt 13:13,15
12:41
q Isa 6:1-4
r Lk 24:27
12:42
s ver 11; Jn 7:48
t Jn 7:13
u Jn 9:22
12:43
v Jn 5:44
12:44
w Mt 10:40;
Jn 5:24
12:45
x Jn 14:9
12:46
y Jn 1:4; 3:19;
8:12; 9:5
12:47
z Jn 3:17
12:48
a Jn 5:45
12:49
b Jn 14:31

---

a34 Or *Messiah*   b38 Isaiah 53:1   c40 Isaiah 6:10

Jesus Washes His Disciples' Feet

13 It was just before the Passover Feast.[c] Jesus knew that the time had come[d] for him to leave this world and go to the Father.[e] Having loved his own who were in the world, he now showed them the full extent of his love.[a]

[2]The evening meal was being served, and the devil had already prompted Judas Iscariot, son of Simon, to betray Jesus. [3]Jesus knew that the Father had put all things under his power,[f] and that he had come from God[g] and was returning to God; [4]so he got up from the meal, took off his outer clothing, and wrapped a towel around his waist. [5]After that, he poured water into a basin and began to wash his disciples' feet,[h] drying them with the towel that was wrapped around him.

[6]He came to Simon Peter, who said to him, "Lord, are you going to wash my feet?"

[7]Jesus replied, "You do not realize now what I am doing, but later you will understand."[i]

[8]"No," said Peter, "you shall never wash my feet."

Jesus answered, "Unless I wash you, you have no part with me."

[9]"Then, Lord," Simon Peter replied, "not just my feet but my hands and my head as well!"

[10]Jesus answered, "A person who has had a bath needs only to wash his feet; his whole body is clean. And you are clean,[j] though not every one of you." [11]For he knew who was going to betray him, and that was why he said not every one was clean.

[12]When he had finished washing their feet, he put on his clothes and returned to his place. "Do you understand what I have done for you?" he asked them. [13]"You call me 'Teacher'[k] and 'Lord,'[l] and rightly so, for that is what I am. [14]Now that I, your Lord and Teacher, have washed your feet, you also should wash one another's feet. [m] [15]I have set you an example that you should do as I have done for you.[n] [16]I tell you the truth, no servant is greater than his master,[o] nor is a messenger greater than the one who sent him. [17]Now that you know these things, you will be blessed if you do them.[p]

Jesus Predicts His Betrayal

[18]"I am not referring to all of you;[q] I know those I have chosen.[r] But this is to fulfill the scripture: 'He who shares my bread[s] has lifted up his heel[t] against me.'[b][u]

[19]"I am telling you now before it happens, so that when it does happen you will believe[v] that I am He.[w] [20]I tell you the truth, whoever accepts anyone I send accepts me; and whoever accepts me accepts the one who sent me."[x]

[21]After he had said this, Jesus was troubled in spirit[y] and testified, "I tell you the truth, one of you is going to betray me."[z]

[22]His disciples stared at one another, at a loss to know which of them he meant. [23]One of them, the disciple whom Jesus loved,[a] was reclining next to him. [24]Simon Peter motioned to this disciple and said, "Ask him which one he means."

13:1
c Jn 11:55
d Jn 12:23
e Jn 16:28
13:3
f Mt 28:18
g Jn 8:42; 16:27, 28,30
13:5
h Lk 7:44
13:7
i ver 12
13:10
j Jn 15:3
13:13
k Jn 11:28
l Lk 6:46; 1Co 12:3; Php 2:11
13:14
m 1Pe 5:5
13:15
n Mt 11:29
13:16
o Mt 10:24; Lk 6:40; Jn 15:20
13:17
p Mt 7:24,25; Lk 11:28; Jas 1:25
13:18
q ver 10
r Jn 15:16,19
s Mt 26:23
t Jn 6:70
u Ps 41:9
13:19
v Jn 14:29; 16:4
w Jn 8:24
13:20
x Mt 10:40; Lk 10:16
13:21
y Jn 12:27
z Mt 26:21
13:23
a Jn 19:26; 20:2; 21:7,20

---

[a]1 Or *he loved them to the last*   [b]18 Psalm 41:9

25Leaning back against Jesus, he asked him, "Lord, who is it?"[b]
26Jesus answered, "It is the one to whom I will give this piece of bread when I have dipped it in the dish." Then, dipping the piece of bread, he gave it to Judas Iscariot, son of Simon. 27As soon as Judas took the bread, Satan entered into him.[c]

"What you are about to do, do quickly," Jesus told him, 28but no one at the meal understood why Jesus said this to him. 29Since Judas had charge of the money,[d] some thought Jesus was telling him to buy what was needed for the Feast, or to give something to the poor. 30As soon as Judas had taken the bread, he went out. And it was night.[e]

Jesus Predicts Peter's Denial

13:37,38pp — Mt 26:33–35; Mk 14:29–31; Lk 22:33,34

31When he was gone, Jesus said, "Now is the Son of Man glorified[f] and God is glorified in him.[g] 32If God is glorified in him,[a] God will glorify the Son in himself,[h] and will glorify him at once.

33"My children, I will be with you only a little longer. You will look for me, and just as I told the Jews, so I tell you now: Where I am going, you cannot come.[i]

34"A new command[j] I give you: Love one another.[k] As I have loved you, so you must love one another.[l] 35By this all men will know that you are my disciples, if you love one another."[m]

36Simon Peter asked him, "Lord, where are you going?"

Jesus replied, "Where I am going, you cannot follow now,[n] but you will follow later."[o]

37Peter asked, "Lord, why can't I follow you now? I will lay down my life for you."

38Then Jesus answered, "Will you really lay down your life for me? I tell you the truth, before the rooster crows, you will disown me three times![p]

Jesus Comforts His Disciples

14 "Do not let your hearts be troubled.[q] Trust in God[b]; trust also in me. 2In my Father's house are many rooms; if it were not so, I would have told you. I am going there[r] to prepare a place for you. 3And if I go and prepare a place for you, I will come back and take you to be with me that you also may be where I am.[s] 4You know the way to the place where I am going."

Jesus the Way to the Father

5Thomas[t] said to him, "Lord, we don't know where you are going, so how can we know the way?"

6Jesus answered, "I am the way[u] and the truth and the life.[v] No one comes to the Father except through me. 7If you really knew me, you would know[c] my Father as well.[w] From now on, you do know him and have seen him."

8Philip said, "Lord, show us the Father and that will be enough for us."

9Jesus answered: "Don't you know me, Philip, even after I have been

13:25
b Jn 21:20
13:27
c Lk 22:3
13:29
d Jn 12:6
13:30
e Lk 22:53
13:31
f Jn 7:39
g Jn 14:13; 17:4; 1Pe 4:11
13:32
h Jn 17:1
13:33
i Jn 7:33,34
13:34
j 1Jn 2:7-11; 3:11
k Lev 19:18; 1Th 4:9; 1Pe 1:22
l Jn 15:12; Eph 5:2; 1Jn 4:10,11
13:35
m 1Jn 3:14; 4:20
13:36
n ver 33; Jn 14:2
o Jn 21:18,19; 2Pe 1:14
13:38
p Jn 18:27
14:1
q ver 27
14:2
r Jn 13:33,36
14:3
s Jn 12:26
14:5
t Jn 11:16
14:6
u Jn 10:9
v Jn 11:25
14:7
w Jn 8:19

---

a32 Many early manuscripts do not have *If God is glorified in him.*   b1 Or *You trust in God*
c7 Some early manuscripts *If you really have known me, you will know*

among you such a long time? Anyone who has seen me has seen the Father.[x] How can you say, 'Show us the Father'? [10]Don't you believe that I am in the Father, and that the Father is in me?[y] The words I say to you are not just my own.[z] Rather, it is the Father, living in me, who is doing his work. [11]Believe me when I say that I am in the Father and the Father is in me; or at least believe on the evidence of the miracles themselves.[a] [12]I tell you the truth, anyone who has faith[b] in me will do what I have been doing.[c] He will do even greater things than these, because I am going to the Father. [13]And I will do whatever you ask[d] in my name, so that the Son may bring glory to the Father. [14]You may ask me for anything in my name, and I will do it.

Jesus Promises the Holy Spirit

[15]"If you love me, you will obey what I command.[e] [16]And I will ask the Father, and he will give you another Counselor[f] to be with you forever— [17]the Spirit of truth.[g] The world cannot accept him,[h] because it neither sees him nor knows him. But you know him, for he lives with you and will be[a] in you. [18]I will not leave you as orphans; I will come to you.[i] [19]Before long, the world will not see me anymore, but you will see me.[j] Because I live, you also will live.[k] [20]On that day you will realize that I am in my Father,[l] and you are in me, and I am in you. [21]Whoever has my commands and obeys them, he is the one who loves me.[m] He who loves me will be loved by my Father,[n] and I too will love him and show myself to him."

[22]Then Judas[o] (not Judas Iscariot) said, "But, Lord, why do you intend to show yourself to us and not to the world?"[p]

[23]Jesus replied, "If anyone loves me, he will obey my teaching.[q] My Father will love him, and we will come to him and make our home with him.[r] [24]He who does not love me will not obey my teaching. These words you hear are not my own; they belong to the Father who sent me.[s]

[25]"All this I have spoken while still with you. [26]But the Counselor,[t] the Holy Spirit, whom the Father will send in my name,[u] will teach you all things[v] and will remind you of everything I have said to you.[w] [27]Peace I leave with you; my peace I give you.[x] I do not give to you as the world gives. Do not let your hearts be troubled and do not be afraid.

[28]"You heard me say, 'I am going away and I am coming back to you.'[y] If you loved me, you would be glad that I am going to the Father,[z] for the Father is greater than I.[a] [29]I have told you now before it happens, so that when it does happen you will believe.[b] [30]I will not speak with you much longer, for the prince of this world[c] is coming. He has no hold on me, [31]but the world must learn that I love the Father and that I do exactly what my Father has commanded me.[d]

"Come now; let us leave.

The Vine and the Branches

15 "I am the true vine,[e] and my Father is the gardener. [2]He cuts off every branch in me that bears no fruit, while every branch that does bear fruit he prunes[b] so that it will be even more fruitful. [3]You are already clean because of the word I have spoken to you.[f] [4]Remain in

---

[a]17 Some early manuscripts *and is*   [b]2 The Greek for *prunes* also means *cleans*.

me, and I will remain in you.ᵍ No branch can bear fruit by itself; it must remain in the vine. Neither can you bear fruit unless you remain in me.

⁵"I am the vine; you are the branches. If a man remains in me and I in him, he will bear much fruit;ʰ apart from me you can do nothing. ⁶If anyone does not remain in me, he is like a branch that is thrown away and withers; such branches are picked up, thrown into the fire and burned.ⁱ ⁷If you remain in me and my words remain in you, ask whatever you wish, and it will be given you.ʲ ⁸This is to my Father's glory,ᵏ that you bear much fruit, showing yourselves to be my disciples.ˡ

⁹"As the Father has loved me,ᵐ so have I loved you. Now remain in my love. ¹⁰If you obey my commands,ⁿ you will remain in my love, just as I have obeyed my Father's commands and remain in his love. ¹¹I have told you this so that my joy may be in you and that your joy may be complete.ᵒ ¹²My command is this: Love each other as I have loved you.ᵖ ¹³Greater love has no one than this, that he lay down his life for his friends.�q ¹⁴You are my friendsʳ if you do what I command.ˢ ¹⁵I no longer call you servants, because a servant does not know his master's business. Instead, I have called you friends, for everything that I learned from my Father I have made known to you.ᵗ ¹⁶You did not choose me, but I chose you and appointed youᵘ to go and bear fruit—fruit that will last. Then the Father will give you whatever you ask in my name. ¹⁷This is my command: Love each other.ᵛ

The World Hates the Disciples

¹⁸"If the world hates you,ʷ keep in mind that it hated me first. ¹⁹If you belonged to the world, it would love you as its own. As it is, you do not belong to the world, but I have chosen youˣ out of the world. That is why the world hates you.ʸ ²⁰Remember the words I spoke to you: 'No servant is greater than his master.'ᵃᶻ If they persecuted me, they will persecute you also.ᵃ If they obeyed my teaching, they will obey yours also. ²¹They will treat you this way because of my name,ᵇ for they do not know the One who sent me.ᶜ ²²If I had not come and spoken to them, they would not be guilty of sin. Now, however, they have no excuse for their sin.ᵈ ²³He who hates me hates my Father as well. ²⁴If I had not done among them what no one else did,ᵉ they would not be guilty of sin. But now they have seen these miracles, and yet they have hated both me and my Father. ²⁵But this is to fulfill what is written in their Law: 'They hated me without reason.'ᵇ ᶠ

²⁶"When the Counselorᵍ comes, whom I will send to you from the Father,ʰ the Spirit of truthⁱ who goes out from the Father, he will testify about me.ʲ ²⁷And you also must testify,ᵏ for you have been with me from the beginning.ˡ

16 "All thisᵐ I have told you so that you will not go astray.ⁿ ²They will put you out of the synagogue;ᵒ in fact, a time is coming when anyone who kills you will think he is offering a service to God.ᵖ ³They will do such things because they have not known the Father or me.q ⁴I have told you this, so that when the time comes you will rememberʳ that I warned you. I did not tell you this at first because I was with you.

ᵃ20 John 13:16   ᵇ25 Psalms 35:19; 69:4

15:4
gJn 6:56;
1Jn 2:6
15:5
hver 16
15:6
iver 2
15:7
jMt 7:7
15:8
kMt 5:16
lJn 8:31
15:9
mJn 17:23,24,26
15:10
nJn 14:15
15:11
oJn 17:13
15:12
pJn 13:34
15:13
qJn 10:11;
Ro 5:7,8
15:14
rLk 12:4
sMt 12:50
15:15
tJn 8:26
15:16
uJn 6:70; 13:18
15:17
vver 12
15:18
w1Jn 3:13
15:19
xver 16
yJn 17:14
15:20
zJn 13:16
a2Ti 3:12
15:21
bMt 10:22
cJn 16:3
15:22
dJn 9:41;
Ro 1:20
15:24
eJn 5:36
15:25
fPs 35:19; 69:4
15:26
gJn 14:16
hJn 14:26
iJn 14:17
j1Jn 5:7
15:27
kLk 24:48;
1Jn 1:2; 4:14
lLk 1:2
16:1
mJn 15:18-27
nMt 11:6
16:2
oJn 9:22
pIsa 66:5;
Ac 26:9,10;
Rev 6:9
16:3
qJn 15:21;
17:25; 1Jn 3:1
16:4
rJn 13:19

The Work of the Holy Spirit

5"Now I am going to him who sent me,[s] yet none of you asks me, 'Where are you going?'[t] 6Because I have said these things, you are filled with grief. 7But I tell you the truth: It is for your good that I am going away. Unless I go away, the Counselor[u] will not come to you; but if I go, I will send him to you.[v] 8When he comes, he will convict the world of guilt[a] in regard to sin and righteousness and judgment: 9in regard to sin,[w] because men do not believe in me; 10in regard to right-eousness,[x] because I am going to the Father, where you can see me no longer; 11and in regard to judgment, because the prince of this world[y] now stands condemned.

12"I have much more to say to you, more than you can now bear.[z] 13But when he, the Spirit of truth,[a] comes, he will guide you into all truth.[b] He will not speak on his own; he will speak only what he hears, and he will tell you what is yet to come. 14He will bring glory to me by taking from what is mine and making it known to you. 15All that belongs to the Father is mine.[c] That is why I said the Spirit will take from what is mine and make it known to you.

16"In a little while[d] you will see me no more, and then after a little while you will see me."[e]

The Disciples' Grief Will Turn to Joy

17Some of his disciples said to one another, "What does he mean by saying, 'In a little while you will see me no more, and then after a little while you will see me,'[f] and 'Because I am going to the Father'?"[g] 18They kept asking, "What does he mean by 'a little while'? We don't understand what he is saying."

19Jesus saw that they wanted to ask him about this, so he said to them, "Are you asking one another what I meant when I said, 'In a little while you will see me no more, and then after a little while you will see me'? 20I tell you the truth, you will weep and mourn[h] while the world rejoices. You will grieve, but your grief will turn to joy.[i] 21A woman giving birth to a child has pain[j] because her time has come; but when her baby is born she forgets the anguish because of her joy that a child is born into the world. 22So with you: Now is your time of grief,[k] but I will see you again[l] and you will rejoice, and no one will take away your joy. 23In that day you will no longer ask me anything. I tell you the truth, my Father will give you whatever you ask in my name.[m] 24Until now you have not asked for anything in my name. Ask and you will receive, and your joy will be complete.[n]

25"Though I have been speaking figuratively,[o] a time is coming[p] when I will no longer use this kind of language but will tell you plainly about my Father. 26In that day you will ask in my name.[q] I am not saying that I will ask the Father on your behalf. 27No, the Father himself loves you because you have loved me[r] and have believed that I came from God. 28I came from the Father and entered the world; now I am leaving the world and going back to the Father."[s]

29Then Jesus' disciples said, "Now you are speaking clearly and without figures of speech.[t] 30Now we can see that you know all things

---

16:5
s Jn 7:33
t Jn 13:36; 14:5
16:7
u Jn 14:16,26;
15:26 v Jn 7:39
16:9
w Jn 15:22
16:10
x Ac 3:14; 7:52;
1Pe 3:18
16:11
y Jn 12:31
16:12
z Mk 4:33
16:13
a Jn 14:17
b Jn 14:26
16:15
c Jn 17:10
16:16
d Jn 7:33
e Jn 14:18-24
16:17
f ver 16 g ver 5
16:20
h Lk 23:27
i Jn 20:20
16:21
j Isa 26:17;
1Th 5:3
16:22
k ver 6 l ver 16
16:23
m Mt 7:7;
Jn 15:16
16:24
n Jn 3:29; 15:11
16:25
o Mt 13:34;
Jn 10:6 p ver 2
16:26
q ver 23,24
16:27
r Jn 14:21,23
16:28
s Jn 13:3
16:29
t ver 25

---

a8 Or will expose the guilt of the world

and that you do not even need to have anyone ask you questions. This makes us believe that you came from God."

31"You believe at last!"ᵃ Jesus answered. 32"But a time is coming,ᵘ and has come, when you will be scattered,ᵛ each to his own home. You will leave me all alone. Yet I am not alone, for my Father is with me.ʷ

33"I have told you these things, so that in me you may have peace.ˣ In this world you will have trouble.ʸ But take heart! I have overcomeᶻ the world."

Jesus Prays for Himself

17 After Jesus said this, he looked toward heavenᵃ and prayed: "Father, the time has come. Glorify your Son, that your Son may glorify you.ᵇ 2For you granted him authority over all people that he might give eternal life to all those you have given him.ᶜ 3Now this is eternal life: that they may know you, the only true God, and Jesus Christ, whom you have sent.ᵈ 4I have brought you gloryᵉ on earth by completing the work you gave me to do.ᶠ 5And now, Father, glorify me in your presence with the glory I had with youᵍ before the world began.ʰ

Jesus Prays for His Disciples

6"I have revealed youᵇⁱ to those whom you gave meʲ out of the world. They were yours; you gave them to me and they have obeyed your word. 7Now they know that everything you have given me comes from you. 8For I gave them the words you gave meᵏ and they accepted them. They knew with certainty that I came from you,ˡ and they believed that you sent me.ᵐ 9I pray for them.ⁿ I am not praying for the world, but for those you have given me, for they are yours. 10All I have is yours, and all you have is mine.ᵒ And glory has come to me through them. 11I will remain in the world no longer, but they are still in the world,ᵖ and I am coming to you. �q Holy Father, protect them by the power of your name—the name you gave me—so that they may be oneʳ as we are one.ˢ 12While I was with them, I protected them and kept them safe by that name you gave me. None has been lostᵗ except the one doomed to destructionᵘ so that Scripture would be fulfilled.

13"I am coming to you now, but I say these things while I am still in the world, so that they may have the full measure of my joyᵛ within them. 14I have given them your word and the world has hated them,ʷ for they are not of the world any more than I am of the world.ˣ 15My prayer is not that you take them out of the world but that you protect them from the evil one.ʸ 16They are not of the world, even as I am not of it.ᶻ 17Sanctifyᶜ them by the truth; your word is truth.ᵃ 18As you sent me into the world,ᵇ I have sent them into the world.ᶜ 19For them I sanctify myself, that they too may be truly sanctified.

ᵃ31 Or *"Do you now believe?"*   ᵇ6 Greek *your name*; also in verse 26   ᶜ17 Greek *hagiazo* (*set apart for sacred use* or *make holy*); also in verse 19

16:32
u ver 2,25
v Mt 26:31
w Jn 8:16,29
16:33
x Jn 14:27
y Jn 15:18-21
z Ro 8:37;
1Jn 4:4
17:1
a Jn 11:41
b Jn 12:23;
13:31,32
17:2
c ver 6,9,24;
Da 7:14;
Jn 6:37,39
17:3
d ver 8,18,21,23,
25; Jn 3:17
17:4
e Jn 13:31
f Jn 4:34
17:5
g Php 2:6
h Jn 1:2
17:6
i ver 26 j ver 2;
Jn 6:37,39
17:8
k ver 14,26
l Jn 16:27
m ver 3,18,21,
23,25; Jn 3:17
17:9
n Lk 22:32
17:10
o Jn 16:15
17:11
p Jn 13:1
q Jn 7:33
r ver 21-23
s Jn 10:30
17:12
t Jn 6:39
u Jn 6:70
17:13
v Jn 3:29
17:14
w Jn 15:19
x Jn 8:23
17:15
y Mt 5:37
17:16
z ver 14
17:17
a Jn 15:3
17:18
b ver 3,8,21,23,
25 c Jn 20:21

Jesus Prays for All Believers

20"My prayer is not for them alone. I pray also for those who will believe in me through their message, 21that all of them may be one, Father, just as you are in me and I am in you. ^d May they also be in us so that the world may believe that you have sent me. ^e 22I have given them the glory that you gave me, that they may be one as we are one: ^f 23I in them and you in me. May they be brought to complete unity to let the world know that you sent me ^g and have loved them ^h even as you have loved me.

24"Father, I want those you have given me to be with me where I am, ^i and to see my glory, ^j the glory you have given me because you loved me before the creation of the world. ^k

25"Righteous Father, though the world does not know you, ^l I know you, and they know that you have sent me. ^m 26I have made you known to them, ^n and will continue to make you known in order that the love you have for me may be in them ^o and that I myself may be in them."

Jesus Arrested

18:3–11pp — Mt 26:47–56; Mk 14:43–50; Lk 22:47–53

18 When he had finished praying, Jesus left with his disciples and crossed the Kidron Valley. ^p On the other side there was an olive grove, ^q and he and his disciples went into it. ^r

2Now Judas, who betrayed him, knew the place, because Jesus had often met there with his disciples. ^s 3So Judas came to the grove, guiding ^t a detachment of soldiers and some officials from the chief priests and Pharisees. ^u They were carrying torches, lanterns and weapons.

4Jesus, knowing all that was going to happen to him, ^v went out and asked them, "Who is it you want?" ^w

5"Jesus of Nazareth," they replied.

"I am he," Jesus said. (And Judas the traitor was standing there with them.) 6When Jesus said, "I am he," they drew back and fell to the ground.

7Again he asked them, "Who is it you want?" ^x

And they said, "Jesus of Nazareth."

8"I told you that I am he," Jesus answered. "If you are looking for me, then let these men go." 9This happened so that the words he had spoken would be fulfilled: "I have not lost one of those you gave me." ^a ^y

10Then Simon Peter, who had a sword, drew it and struck the high priest's servant, cutting off his right ear. (The servant's name was Malchus.)

11Jesus commanded Peter, "Put your sword away! Shall I not drink the cup ^z the Father has given me?"

Jesus Taken to Annas

18:12,13pp — Mt 26:57

12Then the detachment of soldiers with its commander and the Jewish officials ^a arrested Jesus. They bound him 13and brought him first to

17:21
d Jn 10:38
e ver 3,8,18,23,
25; Jn 3:17
17:22
f Jn 14:20
17:23
g Jn 3:17
h Jn 16:27
17:24
i Jn 12:26
j Jn 1:14 k ver 5;
Mt 25:34
17:25
l Jn 15:21; 16:3
m ver 3,8,18,21,
23; Jn 3:17;
7:29; 16:27
17:26
n ver 6 o Jn 15:9
18:1
p 2Sa 15:23
q ver 26
r Mt 26:36
18:2
s Lk 21:37;
22:39
18:3
t Ac 1:16 u ver 12
18:4
v Jn 6:64; 13:1,
11 w ver 7
18:7
x ver 4
18:9
y Jn 17:12
18:11
z Mt 20:22
18:12
a ver 3

a 9 John 6:39

Annas, who was the father-in-law of Caiaphas,[b] the high priest that year. [14]Caiaphas was the one who had advised the Jews that it would be good if one man died for the people.[c]

Peter's First Denial

18:16–18pp — Mt 26:69,70; Mk 14:66–68; Lk 22:55–57

[15]Simon Peter and another disciple were following Jesus. Because this disciple was known to the high priest,[d] he went with Jesus into the high priest's courtyard,[e] [16]but Peter had to wait outside at the door. The other disciple, who was known to the high priest, came back, spoke to the girl on duty there and brought Peter in.

[17]"You are not one of his disciples, are you?" the girl at the door asked Peter.

He replied, "I am not."[f]

[18]It was cold, and the servants and officials stood around a fire[g] they had made to keep warm. Peter also was standing with them, warming himself.[h]

The High Priest Questions Jesus

18:19–24pp — Mt 26:59–68; Mk 14:55–65; Lk 22:63–71

[19]Meanwhile, the high priest questioned Jesus about his disciples and his teaching.

[20]"I have spoken openly to the world," Jesus replied. "I always taught in synagogues[i] or at the temple,[j] where all the Jews come together. I said nothing in secret.[k] [21]Why question me? Ask those who heard me. Surely they know what I said."

[22]When Jesus said this, one of the officials[l] nearby struck him in the face.[m] "Is this the way you answer the high priest?" he demanded.

[23]"If I said something wrong," Jesus replied, "testify as to what is wrong. But if I spoke the truth, why did you strike me?"[n] [24]Then Annas sent him, still bound, to Caiaphas[o] the high priest.[a]

Peter's Second and Third Denials

18:25–27pp — Mt 26:71–75; Mk 14:69–72; Lk 22:58–62

[25]As Simon Peter stood warming himself,[p] he was asked, "You are not one of his disciples, are you?"

He denied it, saying, "I am not."[q]

[26]One of the high priest's servants, a relative of the man whose ear Peter had cut off,[r] challenged him, "Didn't I see you with him in the olive grove?"[s] [27]Again Peter denied it, and at that moment a rooster began to crow.[t]

Jesus Before Pilate

18:29–40pp — Mt 27:11–18,20–23; Mk 15:2–15; Lk 23:2,3,18–25

[28]Then the Jews led Jesus from Caiaphas to the palace of the Roman governor.[u] By now it was early morning, and to avoid ceremonial uncleanness the Jews did not enter the palace;[v] they wanted to be able to eat the Passover.[w] [29]So Pilate came out to them and asked, "What charges are you bringing against this man?"

---

[a]24 Or *(Now Annas had sent him, still bound, to Caiaphas the high priest.)*

18:13
[b]ver 24;
Mt 26:3
18:14
[c]Jn 11:49-51
18:15
[d]Mt 26:3
[e]Mt 26:58;
Mk 14:54;
Lk 22:54
18:17
[f]ver 25
18:18
[g]Jn 21:9
[h]Mk 14:54,67
18:20
[i]Mt 4:23
[j]Mt 26:55
[k]Jn 7:26
18:22
[l]ver 3
[m]Mt 16:21;
Jn 19:3
18:23
[n]Mt 5:39;
Ac 23:2-5
18:24
[o]ver 13;
Mt 26:3
18:25
[p]ver 18 [q]ver 17
18:26
[r]ver 10 [s]ver 1
18:27
[t]Jn 13:38
18:28
[u]Mt 27:2;
Mk 15:1;
Lk 23:1 [v]ver 33;
Jn 19:9
[w]Jn 11:55

³⁰"If he were not a criminal," they replied, "we would not have handed him over to you."

³¹Pilate said, "Take him yourselves and judge him by your own law."

"But we have no right to execute anyone," the Jews objected. ³²This happened so that the words Jesus had spoken indicating the kind of death he was going to die˟ would be fulfilled.

³³Pilate then went back inside the palace,ʸ summoned Jesus and asked him, "Are you the king of the Jews?"ᶻ

³⁴"Is that your own idea," Jesus asked, "or did others talk to you about me?"

³⁵"Am I a Jew?" Pilate replied. "It was your people and your chief priests who handed you over to me. What is it you have done?"

³⁶Jesus said, "My kingdomᵃ is not of this world. If it were, my servants would fight to prevent my arrest by the Jews.ᵇ But now my kingdom is from another place."ᶜ

³⁷"You are a king, then!" said Pilate.

Jesus answered, "You are right in saying I am a king. In fact, for this reason I was born, and for this I came into the world, to testify to the truth.ᵈ Everyone on the side of truth listens to me."ᵉ

³⁸"What is truth?" Pilate asked. With this he went out again to the Jews and said, "I find no basis for a charge against him.ᶠ ³⁹But it is your custom for me to release to you one prisoner at the time of the Passover. Do you want me to release 'the king of the Jews'?"

⁴⁰They shouted back, "No, not him! Give us Barabbas!" Now Barabbas had taken part in a rebellion.ᵍ

Jesus Sentenced to be Crucified

19:1–16pp — Mt 27:27–31; Mk 15:16–20

19 Then Pilate took Jesus and had him flogged.ʰ ²The soldiers twisted together a crown of thorns and put it on his head. They clothed him in a purple robe ³and went up to him again and again, saying, "Hail, king of the Jews!"ⁱ And they struck him in the face.ʲ

⁴Once more Pilate came out and said to the Jews, "Look, I am bringing him outᵏ to you to let you know that I find no basis for a charge against him."ˡ ⁵When Jesus came out wearing the crown of thorns and the purple robe,ᵐ Pilate said to them, "Here is the man!"

⁶As soon as the chief priests and their officials saw him, they shouted, "Crucify! Crucify!"

But Pilate answered, "You take him and crucify him.ⁿ As for me, I find no basis for a charge against him."ᵒ

⁷The Jews insisted, "We have a law, and according to that law he must die,ᵖ because he claimed to be the Son of God."�q

⁸When Pilate heard this, he was even more afraid, ⁹and he went back inside the palace.ʳ "Where do you come from?" he asked Jesus, but Jesus gave him no answer.ˢ ¹⁰"Do you refuse to speak to me?" Pilate said. "Don't you realize I have power either to free you or to crucify you?"

¹¹Jesus answered, "You would have no power over me if it were not given to you from above.ᵗ Therefore the one who handed me over to youᵘ is guilty of a greater sin."

¹²From then on, Pilate tried to set Jesus free, but the Jews kept

---

18:32
ˣMt 20:19;
26:2; Jn 3:14;
8:28; 12:32,33
18:33
ʸver 28,29;
Jn 19:9
ᶻLk 23:3;
Mt 2:2
18:36
ᵃMt 3:2
ᵇMt 26:53
ᶜLk 17:21;
Jn 6:15
18:37
ᵈJn 3:32
ᵉJn 8:47;
1Jn 4:6
18:38
ᶠLk 23:4;
Jn 19:4,6
18:40
ᵍAc 3:14
19:1
ʰDt 25:3;
Isa 50:6; 53:5;
Mt 27:26
19:3
ⁱMt 27:29
ʲJn 18:22
19:4
ᵏJn 18:38
ˡver 6; Lk 23:4
19:5
ᵐver 2
19:6
ⁿAc 3:13
ᵒver 4; Lk 23:4
19:7
ᵖLev 24:16
qMt 26:63-66;
Jn 5:18; 10:33
19:9
ʳJn 18:33
ˢMk 14:61
19:11
ᵗRo 13:1
ᵘJn 18:28-30;
Ac 3:13

shouting, "If you let this man go, you are no friend of Caesar. Anyone who claims to be a king[v] opposes Caesar."

13When Pilate heard this, he brought Jesus out and sat down on the judge's seat[w] at a place known as the Stone Pavement (which in Aramaic[x] is Gabbatha). 14It was the day of Preparation[y] of Passover Week, about the sixth hour.[z]

"Here is your king,"[a] Pilate said to the Jews.

15But they shouted, "Take him away! Take him away! Crucify him!"

"Shall I crucify your king?" Pilate asked.

"We have no king but Caesar," the chief priests answered.

16Finally Pilate handed him over to them to be crucified.[b]

The Crucifixion

19:17–24pp — Mt 27:33–44; Mk 15:22–32; Lk 23:33–43

So the soldiers took charge of Jesus. 17Carrying his own cross,[c] he went out to the place of the Skull[d] (which in Aramaic[e] is called Golgotha). 18Here they crucified him, and with him two others[f]—one on each side and Jesus in the middle.

19Pilate had a notice prepared and fastened to the cross. It read: JESUS OF NAZARETH,[g] THE KING OF THE JEWS.[h] 20Many of the Jews read this sign, for the place where Jesus was crucified was near the city,[i] and the sign was written in Aramaic, Latin and Greek. 21The chief priests of the Jews protested to Pilate, "Do not write 'The King of the Jews,' but that this man claimed to be king of the Jews."[j]

22Pilate answered, "What I have written, I have written."

23When the soldiers crucified Jesus, they took his clothes, dividing them into four shares, one for each of them, with the undergarment remaining. This garment was seamless, woven in one piece from top to bottom.

24"Let's not tear it," they said to one another. "Let's decide by lot who will get it."

This happened that the scripture might be fulfilled[k] which said,

> "They divided my garments among them
>　　and cast lots for my clothing."[a l]

So this is what the soldiers did.

25Near the cross[m] of Jesus stood his mother,[n] his mother's sister, Mary the wife of Clopas,[o] and Mary Magdalene. 26When Jesus saw his mother[p] there, and the disciple whom he loved[q] standing nearby, he said to his mother, "Dear woman, here is your son," 27and to the disciple, "Here is your mother." From that time on, this disciple took her into his home.

The Death of Jesus

19:29,30pp — Mt 27:48,50; Mk 15:36,37; Lk 23:36

28Later, knowing that all was now completed,[r] and so that the Scripture would be fulfilled,[s] Jesus said, "I am thirsty." 29A jar of wine vinegar[t] was there, so they soaked a sponge in it, put the sponge on a stalk of the hyssop plant, and lifted it to Jesus' lips. 30When he had

---

[a]24 Psalm 22:18

19:12
v Lk 23:2
19:13
w Mt 27:19
x Jn 5:2
19:14
y Mt 27:62
z Mk 15:25
a ver 19,21
19:16
b Mt 27:26;
Mk 15:15;
Lk 23:25
19:17
c Ge 22:6;
Lk 14:27; 23:26
d Lk 23:33
e Jn 5:2
19:18
f Lk 23:32
19:19
g Mk 1:24
h ver 14,21
19:20
i Heb 13:12
19:21
j ver 14
19:24
k ver 28,36,37;
Mt 1:22
l Ps 22:18
19:25
m Mt 27:55,56;
Mk 15:40,41;
Lk 23:49
n Mt 12:46
o Lk 24:18
19:26
p Mt 12:46
q Jn 13:23
19:28
r ver 30; Jn 13:1
s ver 24,36,37
19:29
t Ps 69:21

received the drink, Jesus said, "It is finished."[u] With that, he bowed his head and gave up his spirit.

[31]Now it was the day of Preparation,[v] and the next day was to be a special Sabbath. Because the Jews did not want the bodies left on the crosses[w] during the Sabbath, they asked Pilate to have the legs broken and the bodies taken down. [32]The soldiers therefore came and broke the legs of the first man who had been crucified with Jesus, and then those of the other.[x] [33]But when they came to Jesus and found that he was already dead, they did not break his legs. [34]Instead, one of the soldiers pierced[y] Jesus' side with a spear, bringing a sudden flow of blood and water.[z] [35]The man who saw it[a] has given testimony, and his testimony is true.[b] He knows that he tells the truth, and he testifies so that you also may believe. [36]These things happened so that the scripture would be fulfilled:[c] "Not one of his bones will be broken,"[a][d] [37]and, as another scripture says, "They will look on the one they have pierced."[b][e]

The Burial of Jesus

19:38–42pp — Mt 27:57–61; Mk 15:42–47; Lk 23:50–56

[38]Later, Joseph of Arimathea asked Pilate for the body of Jesus. Now Joseph was a disciple of Jesus, but secretly because he feared the Jews. With Pilate's permission, he came and took the body away. [39]He was accompanied by Nicodemus,[f] the man who earlier had visited Jesus at night. Nicodemus brought a mixture of myrrh and aloes, about seventy-five pounds.[c] [40]Taking Jesus' body, the two of them wrapped it, with the spices, in strips of linen.[g] This was in accordance with Jewish burial customs.[h] [41]At the place where Jesus was crucified, there was a garden, and in the garden a new tomb, in which no one had ever been laid. [42]Because it was the Jewish day of Preparation[i] and since the tomb was nearby,[j] they laid Jesus there.

The Empty Tomb

20:1–8pp — Mt 28:1–8; Mk 16:1–8; Lk 24:1–10

20 Early on the first day of the week, while it was still dark, Mary Magdalene[k] went to the tomb and saw that the stone had been removed from the entrance.[l] [2]So she came running to Simon Peter and the other disciple, the one Jesus loved,[m] and said, "They have taken the Lord out of the tomb, and we don't know where they have put him!"[n]

[3]So Peter and the other disciple started for the tomb.[o] [4]Both were running, but the other disciple outran Peter and reached the tomb first. [5]He bent over and looked in[p] at the strips of linen[q] lying there but did not go in. [6]Then Simon Peter, who was behind him, arrived and went into the tomb. He saw the strips of linen lying there, [7]as well as the burial cloth that had been around Jesus' head.[r] The cloth was folded up by itself, separate from the linen. [8]Finally the other disciple, who had reached the tomb first,[s] also went inside. He saw and believed. [9](They still did not understand from Scripture[t] that Jesus had to rise from the dead.)[u]

19:30
uLk 12:50;
Jn 17:4
19:31
vver 14,42
wDt 21:23;
Jos 8:29; 10:26,
27
19:32
xver 18
19:34
yZec 12:10
z1Jn 5:6,8
19:35
aLk 24:48
bJn 15:27;
21:24
19:36
cver 24,28,37;
Mt 1:22
dEx 12:46;
Nu 9:12;
Ps 34:20
19:37
eZec 12:10;
Rev 1:7
19:39
fJn 3:1; 7:50
19:40
gLk 24:12;
Jn 11:44; 20:5,7
hMt 26:12
19:42
iver 14,31
jver 20,41
20:1
kver 18;
Jn 19:25
lMt 27:60,66
20:2
mJn 13:23
nver 13
20:3
oLk 24:12
20:5
pver 11
qJn 19:40
20:7
rJn 11:44
20:8
sver 4
20:9
tMt 22:29;
Jn 2:22
uLk 24:26,46

---

[a]36 Exodus 12:46; Num. 9:12; Psalm 34:20   [b]37 Zech. 12:10   [c]39 Greek *a hundred litrai* (about 34 kilograms)

Jesus Appears to Mary Magdalene

[10]Then the disciples went back to their homes, [11]but Mary stood outside the tomb crying. As she wept, she bent over to look into the tomb[v] [12]and saw two angels in white,[w] seated where Jesus' body had been, one at the head and the other at the foot.

[13]They asked her, "Woman, why are you crying?"[x]

"They have taken my Lord away," she said, "and I don't know where they have put him."[y] [14]At this, she turned around and saw Jesus standing there,[z] but she did not realize that it was Jesus.[a]

[15]"Woman," he said, "why are you crying?[b] Who is it you are looking for?"

Thinking he was the gardener, she said, "Sir, if you have carried him away, tell me where you have put him, and I will get him."

[16]Jesus said to her, "Mary."

She turned toward him and cried out in Aramaic,[c] "Rabboni!"[d] (which means Teacher).

[17]Jesus said, "Do not hold on to me, for I have not yet returned to the Father. Go instead to my brothers[e] and tell them, 'I am returning to my Father[f] and your Father, to my God and your God.' "

[18]Mary Magdalene[g] went to the disciples[h] with the news: "I have seen the Lord!" And she told them that he had said these things to her.

Jesus Appears to His Disciples

[19]On the evening of that first day of the week, when the disciples were together, with the doors locked for fear of the Jews,[i] Jesus came and stood among them and said, "Peace[j] be with you!"[k] [20]After he said this, he showed them his hands and side.[l] The disciples were overjoyed[m] when they saw the Lord.

[21]Again Jesus said, "Peace be with you![n] As the Father has sent me,[o] I am sending you."[p] [22]And with that he breathed on them and said, "Receive the Holy Spirit.[q] [23]If you forgive anyone his sins, they are forgiven; if you do not forgive them, they are not forgiven."[r]

Jesus Appears to Thomas

[24]Now Thomas[s] (called Didymus), one of the Twelve, was not with the disciples when Jesus came. [25]So the other disciples told him, "We have seen the Lord!"

But he said to them, "Unless I see the nail marks in his hands and put my finger where the nails were, and put my hand into his side,[t] I will not believe it."[u]

[26]A week later his disciples were in the house again, and Thomas was with them. Though the doors were locked, Jesus came and stood among them and said, "Peace[v] be with you!"[w] [27]Then he said to Thomas, "Put your finger here; see my hands. Reach out your hand and put it into my side. Stop doubting and believe."[x]

[28]Thomas said to him, "My Lord and my God!"

[29]Then Jesus told him, "Because you have seen me, you have believed;[y] blessed are those who have not seen and yet have believed."[z]

[30]Jesus did many other miraculous signs[a] in the presence of his disciples, which are not recorded in this book.[b] [31]But these are written

20:11
v ver 5
20:12
w Mt 28:2,3;
Mk 16:5;
Lk 24:4; Ac 5:19
20:13
x ver 15 y ver 2
20:14
z Mt 28:9;
Mk 16:9
a Lk 24:16;
Jn 21:4
20:15
b ver 13
20:16
c Jn 5:2
d Mt 23:7
20:17
e Mt 28:10
f Jn 7:33
20:18
g ver 1
h Lk 24:10,22,23
20:19
i Jn 7:13
j Jn 14:27
k ver 21,26;
Lk 24:36-39
20:20
l Lk 24:39,40;
Jn 19:34
m Jn 16:20,22
20:21
n ver 19 o Jn 3:17
p Mt 28:19;
Jn 17:18
20:22
q Jn 7:39;
Ac 2:38;
8:15-17; 19:2;
Gal 3:2
20:23
r Mt 16:19;
18:18
20:24
s Jn 11:16
20:25
t ver 20
u Mk 16:11
20:26
v Jn 14:27
w ver 21
20:27
x ver 25;
Lk 24:40
20:29
y Jn 3:15
z 1Pe 1:8
20:30
a Jn 2:11
b Jn 21:25

that you may[a] believe[c] that Jesus is the Christ, the Son of God,[d] and that by believing you may have life in his name.[e]

Jesus and the Miraculous Catch of Fish

21 Afterward Jesus appeared again to his disciples,[f] by the Sea of Tiberias.[b][g] It happened this way: [2]Simon Peter, Thomas[h] (called Didymus), Nathanael[i] from Cana in Galilee,[j] the sons of Zebedee,[k] and two other disciples were together. [3]"I'm going out to fish," Simon Peter told them, and they said, "We'll go with you." So they went out and got into the boat, but that night they caught nothing.[l]

[4]Early in the morning, Jesus stood on the shore, but the disciples did not realize that it was Jesus.[m]

[5]He called out to them, "Friends, haven't you any fish?"

"No," they answered.

[6]He said, "Throw your net on the right side of the boat and you will find some." When they did, they were unable to haul the net in because of the large number of fish.[n]

[7]Then the disciple whom Jesus loved[o] said to Peter, "It is the Lord!" As soon as Simon Peter heard him say, "It is the Lord," he wrapped his outer garment around him (for he had taken it off) and jumped into the water. [8]The other disciples followed in the boat, towing the net full of fish, for they were not far from shore, about a hundred yards.[c] [9]When they landed, they saw a fire[p] of burning coals there with fish on it,[q] and some bread.

[10]Jesus said to them, "Bring some of the fish you have just caught."

[11]Simon Peter climbed aboard and dragged the net ashore. It was full of large fish, 153, but even with so many the net was not torn. [12]Jesus said to them, "Come and have breakfast." None of the disciples dared ask him, "Who are you?" They knew it was the Lord. [13]Jesus came, took the bread and gave it to them, and did the same with the fish.[r] [14]This was now the third time Jesus appeared to his disciples[s] after he was raised from the dead.

Jesus Reinstates Peter

[15]When they had finished eating, Jesus said to Simon Peter, "Simon son of John, do you truly love me more than these?"

"Yes, Lord," he said, "you know that I love you."[t]

Jesus said, "Feed my lambs."[u]

[16]Again Jesus said, "Simon son of John, do you truly love me?" He answered, "Yes, Lord, you know that I love you."

Jesus said, "Take care of my sheep."[v]

[17]The third time he said to him, "Simon son of John, do you love me?"

Peter was hurt because Jesus asked him the third time, "Do you love me?"[w] He said, "Lord, you know all things;[x] you know that I love you."

Jesus said, "Feed my sheep.[y] [18]I tell you the truth, when you were younger you dressed yourself and went where you wanted; but when you are old you will stretch out your hands, and someone else will

---

20:31
c Jn 3:15; 19:35
d Mt 4:3
e Mt 25:46
21:1
f Jn 20:19,26
g Jn 6:1
21:2
h Jn 11:16
i Jn 1:45 j Jn 2:1
k Mt 4:21
21:3
l Lk 5:5
21:4
m Lk 24:16;
Jn 20:14
21:6
n Lk 5:4-7
21:7
o Jn 13:23
21:9
p Jn 18:18
q ver 10,13
21:13
r ver 9
21:14
s Jn 20:19,26
21:15
t Mt 26:33,35;
Jn 13:37
u Lk 12:32
21:16
v Mt 2:6;
Ac 20:28;
1Pe 5:2,3
21:17
w Jn 13:38
x Jn 16:30
y ver 16

---

*a31 Some manuscripts *may continue to*   *b1 That is, Sea of Galilee   *c8 Greek *about two hundred cubits* (about 90 meters) dress you and lead you where you do not want to go." [19]Jesus said this to indicate the kind of death[z] by which Peter would glorify God. [a] Then he said to him, "Follow me!"

[20]Peter turned and saw that the disciple whom Jesus loved[b] was following them. (This was the one who had leaned back against Jesus at the supper and had said, "Lord, who is going to betray you?")[c] [21]When Peter saw him, he asked, "Lord, what about him?"

[22]Jesus answered, "If I want him to remain alive until I return, [d] what is that to you? You must follow me."[e] [23]Because of this, the rumor spread among the brothers[f] that this disciple would not die. But Jesus did not say that he would not die; he only said, "If I want him to remain alive until I return, what is that to you?"

[24]This is the disciple who testifies to these things[g] and who wrote them down. We know that his testimony is true. [h]

[25]Jesus did many other things as well. [i] If every one of them were written down, I suppose that even the whole world would not have room for the books that would be written.

21:19
z Jn 12:33; 18:32
a 2Pe 1:14
21:20
b ver 7; Jn 13:23
c Jn 13:25
21:22
d Mt 16:27;
1Co 4:5;
Rev 2:25 ever 19
21:23
f Ac 1:16
21:24
g Jn 15:27
h Jn 19:35
21:25
i Jn 20:30

Acts

Title and Background

The book of Acts provides the basic history of the spread of Christianity during the thirty years immediately following the death and resurrection of Jesus Christ. It serves as a link between the Gospels and the Letters. It can be called "The Acts of the Holy Spirit," because it teaches about the coming and work of the Spirit.

Author and Date of Writing

Although the author does not name himself, evidence outside the Scriptures and inferences from the book itself lead to the conclusion that the author was Luke. A likely date for the book of Acts is A.D. 63.

Theme and Message

The theme of the work is best summarized in 1:8. Luke weaves together different interests and emphases as he relates the beginnings and expansion of the church. The design of the book revolves around (1) key persons: Peter and Paul; (2) important topics and events: the role of the Holy Spirit, pioneer missionary outreach to new fields, conversions, the growth of the church, and life in the Christian community; (3) significant problems: conflict between Jew and Gentile, persecution of the church by some Jewish elements, trials before Jews and Romans, confrontations with Gentiles, and other hardships in the ministry; (4) geographical advances: from Jerusalem to Rome.

Outline

I. Peter and the Beginnings of the Church in Palestine (1:1-12:25)
   A. "Throughout Judea, Galilee and Samaria" (1:1-9:31; see 9:31)
   B. "As far as Phoenicia, Cyprus and Antioch" (9:32-12:25; see 11:19)

II. Paul and the Expansion of the Church From Antioch to Rome (13:1-28:31)
   A. "Throughout the Region of Phrygia and Galatia" (13:1-15:35; see 16:6)
   B. "Over to Macedonia" (15:36-21:16; see 16:9)
   C. "To Rome" (21:17-28:31; see 28:14)

1:1
aLk 1:1-4
bLk 3:23

1:2
cver 9,11;
Mk 16:19
dMt 28:19,20
eMk 6:30
fJn 13:18

1:3
gMt 28:17;
Lk 24:34,36;
Jn 20:19,26;
21:1,14;
1Co 15:5-7

1:4
hLk 24:49;
Jn 14:16;
Ac 2:33

Jesus Taken Up Into Heaven

1 In my former book,[a] Theophilus, I wrote about all that Jesus began to do and to teach[b] 2until the day he was taken up to heaven,[c] after giving instructions[d] through the Holy Spirit to the apostles[e] he had chosen.[f] 3After his suffering, he showed himself to these men and gave many convincing proofs that he was alive. He appeared to them[g] over a period of forty days and spoke about the kingdom of God. 4On one occasion, while he was eating with them, he gave them this command: "Do not leave Jerusalem, but wait for the gift my Father promised, which you have heard me speak about.[h] 5For John baptized with[a] water, but in a few days you will be baptized with the Holy Spirit."

a5 Or in

[6]So when they met together, they asked him, "Lord, are you at this time going to restore[i] the kingdom to Israel?"

[7]He said to them: "It is not for you to know the times or dates the Father has set by his own authority.[j] [8]But you will receive power when the Holy Spirit comes on you;[k] and you will be my witnesses[l] in Jerusalem, and in all Judea and Samaria,[m] and to the ends of the earth."[n]

[9]After he said this, he was taken up[o] before their very eyes, and a cloud hid him from their sight.

[10]They were looking intently up into the sky as he was going, when suddenly two men dressed in white[p] stood beside them. [11]"Men of Galilee,"[q] they said, "why do you stand here looking into the sky? This same Jesus, who has been taken from you into heaven, will come back[r] in the same way you have seen him go into heaven."

Matthias Chosen to Replace Judas

[12]Then they returned to Jerusalem[s] from the hill called the Mount of Olives,[t] a Sabbath day's walk[a] from the city. [13]When they arrived, they went upstairs to the room[u] where they were staying. Those present were Peter, John, James and Andrew; Philip and Thomas, Bartholomew and Matthew; James son of Alphaeus and Simon the Zealot, and Judas son of James.[v] [14]They all joined together constantly in prayer,[w] along with the women[x] and Mary the mother of Jesus, and with his brothers.[y]

[15]In those days Peter stood up among the believers[b] (a group numbering about a hundred and twenty) [16]and said, "Brothers, the Scripture had to be fulfilled[z] which the Holy Spirit spoke long ago through the mouth of David concerning Judas,[a] who served as guide for those who arrested Jesus— [17]he was one of our number[b] and shared in this ministry."[c]

[18](With the reward[d] he got for his wickedness, Judas bought a field;[e] there he fell headlong, his body burst open and all his intestines spilled out. [19]Everyone in Jerusalem heard about this, so they called that field in their language Akeldama, that is, Field of Blood.)

[20]"For," said Peter, "it is written in the book of Psalms,

" 'May his place be deserted;
   let there be no one to dwell in it,'[c f]

and,

" 'May another take his place of leadership.'[d g]

[21]Therefore it is necessary to choose one of the men who have been with us the whole time the Lord Jesus went in and out among us, [22]beginning from John's baptism[h] to the time when Jesus was taken up from us. For one of these must become a witness[i] with us of his resurrection."

[23]So they proposed two men: Joseph called Barsabbas (also known as Justus) and Matthias. [24]Then they prayed,[j] "Lord, you know every-

---

1:6
iMt 17:11
1:7
jMt 24:36
1:8
kAc 2:1-4
lLk 24:48
mAc 8:1-25
nMt 28:19
1:9
over 2
1:10
pLk 24:4;
Jn 20:12
1:11
qAc 2:7
rMt 16:27
1:12
sLk 24:52
tMt 21:1
1:13
uAc 9:37; 20:8
vMt 10:2-4;
Mk 3:16-19;
Lk 6:14-16
1:14
wAc 2:42; 6:4
xLk 23:49,55
yMt 12:46
1:16
zver 20
aJn 13:18
1:17
bJn 6:70,71
cver 25
1:18
dMt 26:14,15
eMt 27:3-10
1:20
fPs 69:25
gPs 109:8
1:22
hMk 1:4 iver 8
1:24
jAc 6:6; 14:23

---

[a]12 That is, about 3/4 mile (about 1,100 meters)   [b]15 Greek *brothers*   [c]20 Psalm 69:25
[d]20 Psalm 109:8

one's heart.ᵏ Show us which of these two you have chosen ²⁵to take over this apostolic ministry, which Judas left to go where he belongs." ²⁶Then they cast lots, and the lot fell to Matthias; so he was added to the eleven apostles.ˡ

The Holy Spirit Comes at Pentecost

2 When the day of Pentecostᵐ came, they were all togetherⁿ in one place. ²Suddenly a sound like the blowing of a violent wind came from heaven and filled the whole house where they were sitting.ᵒ ³They saw what seemed to be tongues of fire that separated and came to rest on each of them. ⁴All of them were filled with the Holy Spirit and began to speak in other tonguesᵃᵖ as the Spirit enabled them.

⁵Now there were staying in Jerusalem God-fearing�q Jews from every nation under heaven. ⁶When they heard this sound, a crowd came together in bewilderment, because each one heard them speaking in his own language. ⁷Utterly amazed,ʳ they asked: "Are not all these men who are speaking Galileans?ˢ ⁸Then how is it that each of us hears them in his own native language? ⁹Parthians, Medes and Elamites; residents of Mesopotamia, Judea and Cappadocia,ᵗ Pontusᵘ and Asia,ᵛ ¹⁰Phrygiaʷ and Pamphylia,ˣ Egypt and the parts of Libya near Cyrene;ʸ visitors from Rome ¹¹(both Jews and converts to Judaism); Cretans and Arabs—we hear them declaring the wonders of God in our own tongues!" ¹²Amazed and perplexed, they asked one another, "What does this mean?"

¹³Some, however, made fun of them and said, "They have had too much wine.ᵇ"ᶻ

Peter Addresses the Crowd

¹⁴Then Peter stood up with the Eleven, raised his voice and addressed the crowd: "Fellow Jews and all of you who live in Jerusalem, let me explain this to you; listen carefully to what I say. ¹⁵These men are not drunk, as you suppose. It's only nine in the morning!ᵃ ¹⁶No, this is what was spoken by the prophet Joel:

¹⁷" 'In the last days, God says,
    I will pour out my Spirit on all people.ᵇ
Your sons and daughters will prophesy,ᶜ
    your young men will see visions,
    your old men will dream dreams.
¹⁸Even on my servants, both men and women,
    I will pour out my Spirit in those days,
    and they will prophesy.ᵈ
¹⁹I will show wonders in the heaven above
    and signs on the earth below,
    blood and fire and billows of smoke.
²⁰The sun will be turned to darkness
    and the moon to bloodᵉ
    before the coming of the great and glorious day of the
        Lord.

ᵃ4 Or *languages*; also in verse 11   ᵇ13 Or *sweet wine*

1:24
ᵏ1Sa 16:7;
Jer 17:10;
Ac 15:8;
Rev 2:23
1:26
ˡAc 2:14
2:1
ᵐLev 23:15,16;
Ac 20:16
ⁿAc 1:14
2:2
ᵒAc 4:31
2:4
ᵖMk 16:17;
1Co 12:10
2:5
qAc 8:2
2:7
ʳver 12 ˢAc 1:11
2:9
ᵗ1Pe 1:1
ᵘAc 18:2
ᵛAc 16:6;
Ro 16:5;
1Co 16:19;
2Co 1:8
2:10
ʷAc 16:6; 18:23
ˣAc 13:13;
15:38 ʸMt 27:32
2:13
ᶻ1Co 14:23
2:15
ᵃ1Th 5:7
2:17
ᵇIsa 44:3;
Jn 7:37-39;
Ac 10:45
ᶜAc 21:9
2:18
ᵈAc 21:9-12
2:20
ᵉMt 24:29

²¹And everyone who calls
on the name of the LORD will be saved.'[a][f]

²²"Men of Israel, listen to this: Jesus of Nazareth was a man accredited by God to you by miracles, wonders and signs,[g] which God did among you through him,[h] as you yourselves know. ²³This man was handed over to you by God's set purpose and foreknowledge;[i] and you, with the help of wicked men,[b] put him to death by nailing him to the cross.[j] ²⁴But God raised him from the dead,[k] freeing him from the agony of death, because it was impossible for death to keep its hold on him.[l] ²⁵David said about him:

" 'I saw the Lord always before me.
Because he is at my right hand,
I will not be shaken.
²⁶Therefore my heart is glad and my tongue rejoices;
my body also will live in hope,
²⁷because you will not abandon me to the grave,
nor will you let your Holy One see decay.[m]
²⁸You have made known to me the paths of life;
you will fill me with joy in your presence.'[c]

²⁹"Brothers, I can tell you confidently that the patriarch[n] David died and was buried,[o] and his tomb is here[p] to this day. ³⁰But he was a prophet and knew that God had promised him on oath that he would place one of his descendants on his throne.[q] ³¹Seeing what was ahead, he spoke of the resurrection of the Christ,[d] that he was not abandoned to the grave, nor did his body see decay.[r] ³²God has raised this Jesus to life,[s] and we are all witnesses[t] of the fact. ³³Exalted[u] to the right hand of God,[v] he has received from the Father[w] the promised Holy Spirit[x] and has poured out[y] what you now see and hear. ³⁴For David did not ascend to heaven, and yet he said,

" 'The Lord said to my Lord:
"Sit at my right hand
³⁵until I make your enemies
a footstool for your feet." '[e][z]

³⁶"Therefore let all Israel be assured of this: God has made this Jesus, whom you crucified, both Lord and Christ."[a]

³⁷When the people heard this, they were cut to the heart and said to Peter and the other apostles, "Brothers, what shall we do?"[b]

³⁸Peter replied, "Repent and be baptized,[c] every one of you, in the name of Jesus Christ for the forgiveness of your sins.[d] And you will receive the gift of the Holy Spirit. ³⁹The promise is for you and your children[e] and for all who are far off[f]—for all whom the Lord our God will call."

⁴⁰With many other words he warned them; and he pleaded with them, "Save yourselves from this corrupt generation."[g] ⁴¹Those who accepted his message were baptized, and about three thousand were added to their number that day.

---

[a]21 Joel 2:28-32   [b]23 Or *of those not having the law* (that is, Gentiles)   [c]28 Psalm 16:8-11
[d]31 Or *Messiah*. "The Christ" (Greek) and "the Messiah" (Hebrew) both mean "the Anointed One"; also in verse 36.   [e]35 Psalm 110:1

2:21
fRo 10:13
2:22
gJn 4:48;
Ac 10:38
hJn 3:2
2:23
iLk 22:22;
Ac 3:18; 4:28
jLk 24:20;
Ac 3:13
2:24
kver 32;
1Co 6:14;
2Co 4:14;
Eph 1:20;
Col 2:12;
Heb 13:20;
1Pe 1:21
lJn 20:9
2:27
mver 31;
Ac 13:35
2:29
nAc 7:8,9
oAc 13:36;
1Ki 2:10
pNe 3:16
2:30
q2Sa 7:12;
Ps 132:11
2:31
rPs 16:10
2:32
sver 24 tAc 1:8
2:33
uPhp 2:9
vMk 16:19
wAc 1:4
xJn 7:39; 14:26
yAc 10:45
2:35
zPs 110:1;
Mt 22:44
2:36
aLk 2:11
2:37
bLk 3:10,12,14
2:38
cAc 8:12,16,36,
38; 22:16
dLk 24:47;
Ac 3:19
2:39
eIsa 44:3
fAc 10:45;
Eph 2:13
2:40
gDt 32:5

The Fellowship of the Believers

42They devoted themselves to the apostles' teaching and to the fellowship, to the breaking of bread and to prayer. h 43Everyone was filled with awe, and many wonders and miraculous signs were done by the apostles. i 44All the believers were together and had everything in common. j 45Selling their possessions and goods, they gave to anyone as he had need. k 46Every day they continued to meet together in the temple courts. l They broke breadm in their homes and ate together with glad and sincere hearts, 47praising God and enjoying the favor of all the people. n And the Lord added to their numbero daily those who were being saved.

Peter Heals the Crippled Beggar

3 One day Peter and Johnp were going up to the templeq at the time of prayer—at three in the afternoon. r 2Now a man crippled from births was being carried to the temple gatet called Beautiful, where he was put every day to begu from those going into the temple courts. 3When he saw Peter and John about to enter, he asked them for money. 4Peter looked straight at him, as did John. Then Peter said, "Look at us!" 5So the man gave them his attention, expecting to get something from them.

6Then Peter said, "Silver or gold I do not have, but what I have I give you. In the name of Jesus Christ of Nazareth, v walk." 7Taking him by the right hand, he helped him up, and instantly the man's feet and ankles became strong. 8He jumped to his feet and began to walk. Then he went with them into the temple courts, walking and jumping, w and praising God. 9When all the peoplex saw him walking and praising God, 10they recognized him as the same man who used to sit begging at the temple gate called Beautiful, y and they were filled with wonder and amazement at what had happened to him.

Peter Speaks to the Onlookers

11While the beggar held on to Peter and John, z all the people were astonished and came running to them in the place called Solomon's Colonnade. a 12When Peter saw this, he said to them: "Men of Israel, why does this surprise you? Why do you stare at us as if by our own power or godliness we had made this man walk? 13The God of Abraham, Isaac and Jacob, the God of our fathers, b has glorified his servant Jesus. You handed him over to be killed, and you disowned him before Pilate, c though he had decided to let him go. d 14You disowned the Holye and Righteous Onef and asked that a murderer be released to you. g 15You killed the author of life, but God raised him from the dead. h We are witnesses of this. 16By faith in the name of Jesus, this man whom you see and know was made strong. It is Jesus' name and the faith that comes through him that has given this complete healing to him, as you can all see.

17"Now, brothers, I know that you acted in ignorance, i as did your leaders. j 18But this is how God fulfilled what he had foretoldk through all the prophets, l saying that his Christa would suffer. m 19Repent,

*Cross references (left margin):*

2:42 hAc 1:14
2:43 iAc 5:12
2:44 jAc 4:32
2:45 kMt 19:21
2:46 lLk 24:53; Ac 5:21,42 mAc 20:7
2:47 nRo 14:18 over 41; Ac 5:14
3:1 pLk 22:8 qAc 2:46 rPs 55:17
3:2 sAc 14:8 tLk 16:20 uJn 9:8
3:6 vver 16; Ac 4:10
3:8 wAc 14:10
3:9 xAc 4:16,21
3:10 yver 2
3:11 zLk 22:8 aJn 10:23; Ac 5:12
3:13 bAc 5:30 cMt 27:2 dLk 23:4
3:14 eMk 1:24; Ac 4:27 fAc 7:52 gMk 15:11; Lk 23:18-25
3:15 hAc 2:24
3:17 iLk 23:34 jAc 13:27
3:18 kAc 2:23 lLk 24:27 mAc 17:2,3; 26:22,23

a18 Or *Messiah*; also in verse 20

then, and turn to God, so that your sins may be wiped out,[n] that times of refreshing may come from the Lord, [20]and that he may send the Christ, who has been appointed for you—even Jesus. [21]He must remain in heaven[o] until the time comes for God to restore everything,[p] as he promised long ago through his holy prophets. [q] [22]For Moses said, 'The Lord your God will raise up for you a prophet like me from among your own people; you must listen to everything he tells you.[r] [23]Anyone who does not listen to him will be completely cut off from among his people.'[a] [s]

[24]"Indeed, all the prophets[t] from Samuel on, as many as have spoken, have foretold these days. [25]And you are heirs[u] of the prophets and of the covenant[v] God made with your fathers. He said to Abraham, 'Through your offspring all peoples on earth will be blessed.'[b][w] [26]When God raised up[x] his servant, he sent him first[y] to you to bless you by turning each of you from your wicked ways."

Peter and John Before the Sanhedrin

4 The priests and the captain of the temple guard[z] and the Sadducees[a] came up to Peter and John while they were speaking to the people. [2]They were greatly disturbed because the apostles were teaching the people and proclaiming in Jesus the resurrection of the dead. [b] [3]They seized Peter and John, and because it was evening, they put them in jail[c] until the next day. [4]But many who heard the message believed, and the number of men grew[d] to about five thousand.

[5]The next day the rulers,[e] elders and teachers of the law met in Jerusalem. [6]Annas the high priest was there, and so were Caiaphas,[f] John, Alexander and the other men of the high priest's family. [7]They had Peter and John brought before them and began to question them: "By what power or what name did you do this?"

[8]Then Peter, filled with the Holy Spirit, said to them: "Rulers and elders of the people![g] [9]If we are being called to account today for an act of kindness shown to a cripple[h] and are asked how he was healed, [10]then know this, you and all the people of Israel: It is by the name of Jesus Christ of Nazareth, whom you crucified but whom God raised from the dead,[i] that this man stands before you healed. [11]He is

> " 'the stone you builders rejected,
>   which has become the capstone.[c] '[d] [j]

[12]Salvation is found in no one else, for there is no other name under heaven given to men by which we must be saved."[k]

[13]When they saw the courage of Peter and John[l] and realized that they were unschooled, ordinary men,[m] they were astonished and they took note that these men had been with Jesus. [14]But since they could see the man who had been healed standing there with them, there was nothing they could say. [15]So they ordered them to withdraw from the Sanhedrin[n] and then conferred together. [16]"What are we going to do with these men?"[o] they asked. "Everybody living in Jerusalem knows they have done an outstanding miracle,[p] and we cannot deny it. [17]But to stop this thing from spreading any further among the people, we must warn these men to speak no longer to anyone in this name."

3:19
nAc 2:38
3:21
oAc 1:11
pMt 17:11
qLk 1:70
3:22
rDt 18:15,18;
Ac 7:37
3:23
sDt 18:19
3:24
tLk 24:27
3:25
uAc 2:39
vRo 9:4,5
wGe 12:3;
22:18; 26:4;
28:14
3:26
xver 22; Ac 2:24
yAc 13:46;
Ro 1:16
4:1
zLk 22:4
aMt 3:7
4:2
bAc 17:18
4:3
cAc 5:18
4:4
dAc 2:41
4:5
eLk 23:13
4:6
fMt 26:3; Lk 3:2
4:8
gver 5; Lk 23:13
4:9
hAc 3:6
4:10
iAc 2:24
4:11
jPs 118:22;
Isa 28:16;
Mt 21:42
4:12
kMt 1:21;
Ac 10:43;
1Ti 2:5
4:13
lLk 22:8
mMt 11:25
4:15
nMt 5:22
4:16
oJn 11:47
pAc 3:6-10

---

[a]23 Deut. 18:15,18,19　　　[b]25 Gen. 22:18; 26:4　　　[c]11 Or *cornerstone*　　　[d]11 Psalm 118:22

18Then they called them in again and commanded them not to speak or teach at all in the name of Jesus. q 19But Peter and John replied, "Judge for yourselves whether it is right in God's sight to obey you rather than God. r 20For we cannot help speaking about what we have seen and heard."

21After further threats they let them go. They could not decide how to punish them, because all the peoples were praising Godt for what had happened. 22For the man who was miraculously healed was over forty years old.

The Believers' Prayer

23On their release, Peter and John went back to their own people and reported all that the chief priests and elders had said to them. 24When they heard this, they raised their voices together in prayer to God. "Sovereign Lord," they said, "you made the heaven and the earth and the sea, and everything in them. 25You spoke by the Holy Spirit through the mouth of your servant, our father David:u

" 'Why do the nations rage
    and the peoples plot in vain?
26The kings of the earth take their stand
    and the rulers gather together
  against the Lord
    and against his Anointed One.a 'b v

27Indeed Herodw and Pontius Pilatex met together with the Gentiles and the peoplec of Israel in this city to conspire against your holy servant Jesus,y whom you anointed. 28They did what your power and will had decided beforehand should happen.z 29Now, Lord, consider their threats and enable your servants to speak your word with great boldness.a 30Stretch out your hand to heal and perform miraculous signs and wondersb through the name of your holy servant Jesus."c

31After they prayed, the place where they were meeting was shaken. d And they were all filled with the Holy Spirit and spoke the word of God boldly.e

The Believers Share Their Possessions

32All the believers were one in heart and mind. No one claimed that any of his possessions was his own, but they shared everything they had.f 33With great power the apostles continued to testifyg to the resurrectionh of the Lord Jesus, and much grace was upon them all. 34There were no needy persons among them. For from time to time those who owned lands or houses sold them,i brought the money from the sales 35and put it at the apostles' feet,j and it was distributed to anyone as he had need.k

36Joseph, a Levite from Cyprus, whom the apostles called Barnabasl (which means Son of Encouragement), 37sold a field he owned and brought the money and put it at the apostles' feet. m

### Cross references (margin)

4:18
qAc 5:40
4:19
rAc 5:29
4:21
sAc 5:26
tMt 9:8
4:25
uAc 1:16
4:26
vPs 2:1,2;
Da 9:25;
Lk 4:18;
Ac 10:38;
Heb 1:9
4:27
wMt 14:1
xMt 27:2;
Lk 23:12 yver 30
4:28
zAc 2:23
4:29
aver 13,31;
Ac 9:27; 14:3;
Php 1:14
4:30
bJn 4:48 cver 27
4:31
dAc 2:2 ever 29
4:32
fAc 2:44
4:33
gLk 24:48
hAc 1:22
4:34
iMt 19:21;
Ac 2:45
4:35
jver 37; Ac 5:2
kAc 2:45; 6:1
4:36
lAc 9:27;
1Co 9:6
4:37
mver 35; Ac 5:2

---

a26 That is, Christ or Messiah   b26 Psalm 2:1,2   c27 The Greek is plural.

Ananias and Sapphira

5 Now a man named Ananias, together with his wife Sapphira, also sold a piece of property. ²With his wife's full knowledge he kept back part of the money for himself, but brought the rest and put it at the apostles' feet. ⁿ

³Then Peter said, "Ananias, how is it that Satanᵒ has so filled your heartᵖ that you have lied to the Holy Spirit�q and have kept for yourself some of the money you received for the land? ⁴Didn't it belong to you before it was sold? And after it was sold, wasn't the money at your disposal? What made you think of doing such a thing? You have not lied to men but to God."

⁵When Ananias heard this, he fell down and died.ʳ And great fearˢ seized all who heard what had happened. ⁶Then the young men came forward, wrapped up his body,ᵗ and carried him out and buried him.

⁷About three hours later his wife came in, not knowing what had happened. ⁸Peter asked her, "Tell me, is this the price you and Ananias got for the land?"

"Yes," she said, "that is the price."ᵘ

⁹Peter said to her, "How could you agree to test the Spirit of the Lord?ᵛ Look! The feet of the men who buried your husband are at the door, and they will carry you out also."

¹⁰At that moment she fell down at his feet and died.ʷ Then the young men came in and, finding her dead, carried her out and buried her beside her husband. ¹¹Great fearˣ seized the whole church and all who heard about these events.

The Apostles Heal Many

¹²The apostles performed many miraculous signs and wondersʸ among the people. And all the believers used to meet togetherᶻ in Solomon's Colonnade.ᵃ ¹³No one else dared join them, even though they were highly regarded by the people.ᵇ ¹⁴Nevertheless, more and more men and women believed in the Lord and were added to their number. ¹⁵As a result, people brought the sick into the streets and laid them on beds and mats so that at least Peter's shadow might fall on some of them as he passed by.ᶜ ¹⁶Crowds gathered also from the towns around Jerusalem, bringing their sick and those tormented by evilᵃ spirits, and all of them were healed.ᵈ

The Apostles Persecuted

¹⁷Then the high priest and all his associates, who were members of the partyᵉ of the Sadducees,ᶠ were filled with jealousy. ¹⁸They arrested the apostles and put them in the public jail.ᵍ ¹⁹But during the night an angelʰ of the Lord opened the doors of the jailⁱ and brought them out. ²⁰"Go, stand in the temple courts," he said, "and tell the people the full message of this new life."ʲ

²¹At daybreak they entered the temple courts, as they had been told, and began to teach the people.

When the high priest and his associatesᵏ arrived, they called together the Sanhedrinˡ—the full assembly of the elders of Israel—and sent

---

ᵃ16 Greek unclean

5:2
ⁿAc 4:35,37
5:3
ᵒMt 4:10
ᵖJn 13:2,27
qver 9
5:5
ʳver 10 ˢver 11
5:6
ᵗJn 19:40
5:8
ᵘver 2
5:9
ᵛver 3
5:10
ʷver 5
5:11
ˣver 5; Ac 19:17
5:12
ʸAc 2:43
ᶻAc 4:32
ᵃAc 3:11
5:13
ᵇAc 2:47; 4:21
5:15
ᶜAc 19:12
5:16
ᵈMk 16:17
5:17
ᵉAc 15:5
ᶠAc 4:1
5:18
ᵍAc 4:3
5:19
ʰMt 1:20;
Lk 1:11;
Ac 8:26; 27:23
ⁱAc 16:26
5:20
ʲJn 6:63,68
5:21
ᵏAc 4:5,6
ˡver 27,34,41;
Mt 5:22

to the jail for the apostles. [22]But on arriving at the jail, the officers did not find them there. So they went back and reported, [23]"We found the jail securely locked, with the guards standing at the doors; but when we opened them, we found no one inside." [24]On hearing this report, the captain of the temple guard and the chief priests[m] were puzzled, wondering what would come of this.

[25]Then someone came and said, "Look! The men you put in jail are standing in the temple courts teaching the people." [26]At that, the captain went with his officers and brought the apostles. They did not use force, because they feared that the people[n] would stone them.

[27]Having brought the apostles, they made them appear before the Sanhedrin[o] to be questioned by the high priest. [28]"We gave you strict orders not to teach in this name,"[p] he said. "Yet you have filled Jerusalem with your teaching and are determined to make us guilty of this man's blood."[q]

[29]Peter and the other apostles replied: "We must obey God rather than men![r] [30]The God of our fathers[s] raised Jesus from the dead[t] — whom you had killed by hanging him on a tree.[u] [31]God exalted him to his own right hand[v] as Prince and Savior[w] that he might give repentance and forgiveness of sins to Israel.[x] [32]We are witnesses of these things,[y] and so is the Holy Spirit,[z] whom God has given to those who obey him."

[33]When they heard this, they were furious[a] and wanted to put them to death. [34]But a Pharisee named Gamaliel,[b] a teacher of the law,[c] who was honored by all the people, stood up in the Sanhedrin and ordered that the men be put outside for a little while. [35]Then he addressed them: "Men of Israel, consider carefully what you intend to do to these men. [36]Some time ago Theudas appeared, claiming to be somebody, and about four hundred men rallied to him. He was killed, all his followers were dispersed, and it all came to nothing. [37]After him, Judas the Galilean appeared in the days of the census[d] and led a band of people in revolt. He too was killed, and all his followers were scattered. [38]Therefore, in the present case I advise you: Leave these men alone! Let them go! For if their purpose or activity is of human origin, it will fail.[e] [39]But if it is from God, you will not be able to stop these men; you will only find yourselves fighting against God."[f]

[40]His speech persuaded them. They called the apostles in and had them flogged.[g] Then they ordered them not to speak in the name of Jesus, and let them go.

[41]The apostles left the Sanhedrin, rejoicing[h] because they had been counted worthy of suffering disgrace for the Name.[i] [42]Day after day, in the temple courts[j] and from house to house, they never stopped teaching and proclaiming the good news that Jesus is the Christ.[a]

The Choosing of the Seven

6 In those days when the number of disciples was increasing,[k] the Grecian Jews[l] among them complained against the Hebraic Jews because their widows[m] were being overlooked in the daily distribution of food.[n] [2]So the Twelve gathered all the disciples together and said, "It would not be right for us to neglect the ministry of the word of God in

---

a42 Or *Messiah*

5:24
mAc 4:1
5:26
nAc 4:21
5:27
oMt 5:22
5:28
pAc 4:18
qMt 23:35;
27:25; Ac 2:23,
36; 3:14,15;
7:52
5:29
rAc 4:19
5:30
sAc 3:13
tAc 2:24
uAc 10:39;
13:29;
Gal 3:13;
1Pe 2:24
5:31
vAc 2:33
wLk 2:11
xMt 1:21;
Lk 24:47;
Ac 2:38
5:32
yLk 24:48
zJn 15:26
5:33
aAc 2:37; 7:54
5:34
bAc 22:3
cLk 2:46
5:37
dLk 2:1,2
5:38
eMt 15:13
5:39
fPr 21:30;
Ac 7:51; 11:17
5:40
gMt 10:17
5:41
hMt 5:12
iJn 15:21
5:42
jAc 2:46
6:1
kAc 2:41
lAc 9:29
mAc 9:39,41
nAc 4:35

order to wait on tables. 3Brothers,° choose seven men from among you who are known to be full of the Spirit and wisdom. We will turn this responsibility over to them 4and will give our attention to prayerᴾ and the ministry of the word."

5This proposal pleased the whole group. They chose Stephen,q a man full of faith and of the Holy Spirit;ʳ also Philip,ˢ Procorus, Nicanor, Timon, Parmenas, and Nicolas from Antioch, a convert to Judaism. 6They presented these men to the apostles, who prayedᵗ and laid their hands on them.ᵘ

7So the word of God spread.ᵛ The number of disciples in Jerusalem increased rapidly, and a large number of priests became obedient to the faith.

Stephen Seized

8Now Stephen, a man full of God's grace and power, did great wonders and miraculous signsʷ among the people. 9Opposition arose, however, from members of the Synagogue of the Freedmen (as it was called)—Jews of Cyreneˣ and Alexandria as well as the provinces of Ciliciaʸ and Asia.ᶻ These men began to argue with Stephen, 10but they could not stand up against his wisdom or the Spirit by whom he spoke.ᵃ

11Then they secretlyᵇ persuaded some men to say, "We have heard Stephen speak words of blasphemy against Moses and against God."ᶜ

12So they stirred up the people and the elders and the teachers of the law. They seized Stephen and brought him before the Sanhedrin.ᵈ 13They produced false witnesses, who testified, "This fellow never stops speaking against this holy placeᵉ and against the law. 14For we have heard him say that this Jesus of Nazareth will destroy this place and change the customs Moses handed down to us."ᶠ

15All who were sitting in the Sanhedrinᵍ looked intently at Stephen, and they saw that his face was like the face of an angel.

Stephen's Speech to the Sanhedrin

7 Then the high priest asked him, "Are these charges true?"
2To this he replied: "Brothers and fathers,ʰ listen to me! The God of gloryⁱ appeared to our father Abraham while he was still in Mesopotamia, before he lived in Haran.ʲ 3'Leave your country and your people,' God said, 'and go to the land I will show you.'ᵃ ᵏ

4"So he left the land of the Chaldeans and settled in Haran. After the death of his father, God sent him to this land where you are now living.ˡ 5He gave him no inheritance here, not even a foot of ground. But God promised him that he and his descendants after him would possess the land,ᵐ even though at that time Abraham had no child. 6God spoke to him in this way: 'Your descendants will be strangers in a country not their own, and they will be enslaved and mistreated four hundred years.ⁿ 7But I will punish the nation they serve as slaves,' God said, 'and afterward they will come out of that country and worship me in this place.'ᵇ° 8Then he gave Abraham the covenant of circumcision.ᴾ And Abraham became the father of Isaac and circumcised him eight

---

ᵃ3 Gen. 12:1   ᵇ7 Gen. 15:13,14

6:3
°Ac 1:16
6:4
ᴾAc 1:14
6:5
qver 8;
Ac 11:19
ʳAc 11:24
ˢAc 8:5-40; 21:8
6:6
ᵗAc 1:24; 8:17;
13:3; 2Ti 1:6
ᵘNu 8:10;
Ac 9:17;
1Ti 4:14
6:7
ᵛAc 12:24;
19:20
6:8
ʷJn 4:48
6:9
ˣMt 27:32
ʸAc 15:23,41;
22:3; 23:34
ᶻAc 2:9
6:10
ᵃLk 21:15
6:11
ᵇ1Ki 21:10
ᶜMt 26:59-61
6:12
ᵈMt 5:22
6:13
ᵉAc 21:28
6:14
ᶠAc 15:1;
21:21; 26:3;
28:17
6:15
ᵍMt 5:22
7:2
ʰAc 22:1
ⁱPs 29:3
ʲGe 11:31; 15:7
7:3
ᵏGe 12:1
7:4
ˡGe 12:5
7:5
ᵐGe 12:7;
17:8; 26:3
7:6
ⁿEx 12:40
7:7
°Ex 3:12
7:8
ᴾGe 17:9-14

days after his birth. ᑫ Later Isaac became the father of Jacob, ʳ and Jacob became the father of the twelve patriarchs. ˢ

9"Because the patriarchs were jealous of Joseph, ᵗ they sold him as a slave into Egypt. ᵘ But God was with him ᵛ 10and rescued him from all his troubles. He gave Joseph wisdom and enabled him to gain the goodwill of Pharaoh king of Egypt; so he made him ruler over Egypt and all his palace. ʷ

11"Then a famine struck all Egypt and Canaan, bringing great suffering, and our fathers could not find food. ˣ 12When Jacob heard that there was grain in Egypt, he sent our fathers on their first visit. ʸ 13On their second visit, Joseph told his brothers who he was, ᶻ and Pharaoh learned about Joseph's family. 14After this, Joseph sent for his father Jacob and his whole family, ᵃ seventy-five in all. ᵇ 15Then Jacob went down to Egypt, where he and our fathers died. ᶜ 16Their bodies were brought back to Shechem and placed in the tomb that Abraham had bought from the sons of Hamor at Shechem for a certain sum of money. ᵈ

17"As the time drew near for God to fulfill his promise to Abraham, the number of our people in Egypt greatly increased. ᵉ 18Then another king, who knew nothing about Joseph, became ruler of Egypt. ᶠ 19He dealt treacherously with our people and oppressed our forefathers by forcing them to throw out their newborn babies so that they would die. ᵍ

20"At that time Moses was born, and he was no ordinary child. ᵃ For three months he was cared for in his father's house. ʰ 21When he was placed outside, Pharaoh's daughter took him and brought him up as her own son. ⁱ 22Moses was educated in all the wisdom of the Egyptiansʲ and was powerful in speech and action.

23"When Moses was forty years old, he decided to visit his fellow Israelites. 24He saw one of them being mistreated by an Egyptian, so he went to his defense and avenged him by killing the Egyptian. 25Moses thought that his own people would realize that God was using him to rescue them, but they did not. 26The next day Moses came upon two Israelites who were fighting. He tried to reconcile them by saying, 'Men, you are brothers; why do you want to hurt each other?'

27"But the man who was mistreating the other pushed Moses aside and said, 'Who made you ruler and judge over us? 28Do you want to kill me as you killed the Egyptian yesterday?' ᵇ 29When Moses heard this, he fled to Midian, where he settled as a foreigner and had two sons. ᵏ

30"After forty years had passed, an angel appeared to Moses in the flames of a burning bush in the desert near Mount Sinai. 31When he saw this, he was amazed at the sight. As he went over to look more closely, he heard the Lord's voice:ˡ 32'I am the God of your fathers, the God of Abraham, Isaac and Jacob.'ᶜ Moses trembled with fear and did not dare to look. ᵐ

33"Then the Lord said to him, 'Take off your sandals; the place where you are standing is holy ground. ⁿ 34I have indeed seen the oppression of my people in Egypt. I have heard their groaning and have come down to set them free. Now come, I will send you back to Egypt.'ᵈ ᵒ

7:8
qGe 21:2-4
rGe 25:26
sGe 29:31-35;
30:5-13,17-24;
35:16-18,22-26
7:9
tGe 37:4,11
uGe 37:28;
Ps 105:17
vGe 39:2,21,23
7:10
wGe 41:37-43
7:11
xGe 41:54
7:12
yGe 42:1,2
7:13
zGe 45:1-4
7:14
aGe 45:9,10
bGe 46:26,27;
Ex 1:5; Dt 10:22
7:15
cGe 46:5-7;
49:33; Ex 1:6
7:16
dGe 23:16-20;
33:18,19;
50:13; Jos 24:32
7:17
eEx 1:7;
Ps 105:24
7:18
fEx 1:8
7:19
gEx 1:10-22
7:20
hEx 2:2;
Heb 11:23
7:21
iEx 2:3-10
7:22
j1Ki 4:30;
Isa 19:11
7:29
kEx 2:11-15
7:31
lEx 3:1-4
7:32
mEx 3:6
7:33
nEx 3:5;
Jos 5:15
7:34
oEx 3:7-10

ᵃ20 Or *was fair in the sight of God*   ᵇ28 Exodus 2:14   ᶜ32 Exodus 3:6   ᵈ34 Exodus 3:5,7,8,10

35"This is the same Moses whom they had rejected with the words, 'Who made you ruler and judge?'ᵖ He was sent to be their ruler and deliverer by God himself, through the angel who appeared to him in the bush. 36He led them out of Egypt�q and did wonders and miraculous signs in Egypt, at the Red Seaᵃʳ and for forty years in the desert.

37"This is that Moses who told the Israelites, 'God will send you a prophet like me from your own people.'ᵇˢ 38He was in the assembly in the desert, with the angelᵗ who spoke to him on Mount Sinai, and with our fathers;ᵘ and he received living wordsᵛ to pass on to us.ʷ

39"But our fathers refused to obey him. Instead, they rejected him and in their hearts turned back to Egypt.ˣ 40They told Aaron, 'Make us gods who will go before us. As for this fellow Moses who led us out of Egypt—we don't know what has happened to him!'ᶜʸ 41That was the time they made an idol in the form of a calf. They brought sacrifices to it and held a celebration in honor of what their hands had made.ᶻ 42But God turned awayᵃ and gave them over to the worship of the heavenly bodies.ᵇ This agrees with what is written in the book of the prophets:

> " 'Did you bring me sacrifices and offerings
>   forty years in the desert, O house of Israel?
> 43You have lifted up the shrine of Molech
>   and the star of your god Rephan,
>   the idols you made to worship.
> Therefore I will send you into exile'ᵈᶜ beyond Babylon.

44"Our forefathers had the tabernacle of the Testimonyᵈ with them in the desert. It had been made as God directed Moses, according to the pattern he had seen.ᵉ 45Having received the tabernacle, our fathers under Joshua brought it with them when they took the land from the nations God drove out before them.ᶠ It remained in the land until the time of David, 46who enjoyed God's favor and asked that he might provide a dwelling place for the God of Jacob.ᵉᵍ 47But it was Solomon who built the house for him.

48"However, the Most High does not live in houses made by men.ʰ As the prophet says:

> 49" 'Heaven is my throne,
>   and the earth is my footstool.ⁱ
> What kind of house will you build for me?
> says the Lord.
>   Or where will my resting place be?
> 50Has not my hand made all these things?'ᶠ ʲ

51"You stiff-necked people,ᵏ with uncircumcised heartsˡ and ears! You are just like your fathers: You always resist the Holy Spirit! 52Was there ever a prophet your fathers did not persecute?ᵐ They even killed those who predicted the coming of the Righteous One. And now you have betrayed and murdered himⁿ— 53you who have received the law that was put into effect through angelsᵒ but have not obeyed it."

7:35
pver 27
7:36
qEx 12:41; 33:1
rEx 14:21
7:37
sDt 18:15,18;
Ac 3:22
7:38
tver 53
uEx 19:17
vDt 32:45-47;
Heb 4:12
wRo 3:2
7:39
xNu 14:3,4
7:40
yEx 32:1,23
7:41
zEx 32:4-6;
Ps 106:19,20;
Rev 9:20
7:42
aJos 24:20;
Isa 63:10
bJer 19:13
7:43
cAm 5:25-27
7:44
dEx 38:21
eEx 25:8,9,40
7:45
fJos 3:14-17;
18:1; 23:9;
24:18; Ps 44:2
7:46
g2Sa 7:8-16;
Ps 132:1-5
7:48
h1Ki 8:27;
2Ch 2:6
7:49
iMt 5:34,35
7:50
jIsa 66:1,2
7:51
kEx 32:9; 33:3,5
lLev 26:41;
Dt 10:16;
Jer 4:4; 9:26
7:52
m2Ch 36:16;
Mt 5:12
nAc 3:14;
1Th 2:15
7:53
over 38;
Gal 3:19;
Heb 2:2

ᵃ36 That is, Sea of Reeds   ᵇ37 Deut. 18:15   ᶜ40 Exodus 32:1   ᵈ43 Amos 5:25-27
ᵉ46 Some early manuscripts *the house of Jacob*   ᶠ50 Isaiah 66:1,2

The Stoning of Stephen

[54]When they heard this, they were furious[p] and gnashed their teeth at him. [55]But Stephen, full of the Holy Spirit, looked up to heaven and saw the glory of God, and Jesus standing at the right hand of God. [q] [56]"Look," he said, "I see heaven open[r] and the Son of Man[s] standing at the right hand of God."

[57]At this they covered their ears and, yelling at the top of their voices, they all rushed at him, [58]dragged him out of the city[t] and began to stone him. [u] Meanwhile, the witnesses laid their clothes[v] at the feet of a young man named Saul. [w]

[59]While they were stoning him, Stephen prayed, "Lord Jesus, receive my spirit." [x] [60]Then he fell on his knees[y] and cried out, "Lord, do not hold this sin against them." [z] When he had said this, he fell asleep.

8 And Saul[a] was there, giving approval to his death.

The Church Persecuted and Scattered

On that day a great persecution broke out against the church at Jerusalem, and all except the apostles were scattered[b] throughout Judea and Samaria. [c] [2]Godly men buried Stephen and mourned deeply for him. [3]But Saul[d] began to destroy the church. [e] Going from house to house, he dragged off men and women and put them in prison.

Philip in Samaria

[4]Those who had been scattered[f] preached the word wherever they went. [g] [5]Philip[h] went down to a city in Samaria and proclaimed the Christ[a] there. [6]When the crowds heard Philip and saw the miraculous signs he did, they all paid close attention to what he said. [7]With shrieks, evil[b] spirits came out of many, [i] and many paralytics and cripples were healed. [j] [8]So there was great joy in that city.

Simon the Sorcerer

[9]Now for some time a man named Simon had practiced sorcery[k] in the city and amazed all the people of Samaria. He boasted that he was someone great, [l] [10]and all the people, both high and low, gave him their attention and exclaimed, "This man is the divine power known as the Great Power." [m] [11]They followed him because he had amazed them for a long time with his magic. [12]But when they believed Philip as he preached the good news of the kingdom of God[n] and the name of Jesus Christ, they were baptized, [o] both men and women. [13]Simon himself believed and was baptized. And he followed Philip everywhere, astonished by the great signs and miracles[p] he saw.

[14]When the apostles in Jerusalem heard that Samaria[q] had accepted the word of God, they sent Peter and John[r] to them. [15]When they arrived, they prayed for them that they might receive the Holy Spirit, [s] [16]because the Holy Spirit had not yet come upon any of them;[t] they had simply been baptized into[c] the name of the Lord Jesus. [u] [17]Then Peter and John placed their hands on them, [v] and they received the Holy Spirit.

[18]When Simon saw that the Spirit was given at the laying on of the

### Cross references (margin)

7:54
p Ac 5:33
7:55
q Mk 16:19
7:56
r Mt 3:16
s Mt 8:20
7:58
t Lk 4:29
u Lev 24:14,16;
Dt 13:9
v Ac 22:20
w Ac 8:1
7:59
x Ps 31:5;
Lk 23:46
7:60
y Ac 9:40
z Mt 5:44
8:1
a Ac 7:58
b Ac 11:19
c Ac 9:31
8:3
d Ac 7:58
e Ac 22:4,19;
26:10,11;
1Co 15:9;
Gal 1:13,23;
Php 3:6;
1Ti 1:13
8:4
f ver 1 g Ac 15:35
8:5
h Ac 6:5
8:7
i Mk 16:17
j Mt 4:24
8:9
k Ac 13:6
l Ac 5:36
8:10
m Ac 14:11;
28:6
8:12
n Ac 1:3
o Ac 2:38
8:13
p ver 6;
Ac 19:11
8:14
q ver 1 r Lk 22:8
8:15
s Ac 2:38
8:16
t Ac 19:2
u Mt 28:19;
Ac 2:38
8:17
v Ac 6:6

---

[a]5 Or *Messiah*   [b]7 Greek *unclean*   [c]16 Or *in*

apostles' hands, he offered them money [19]and said, "Give me also this ability so that everyone on whom I lay my hands may receive the Holy Spirit."

[20]Peter answered: "May your money perish with you, because you thought you could buy the gift of God with money![w] [21]You have no part or share in this ministry, because your heart is not right[x] before God. [22]Repent of this wickedness and pray to the Lord. Perhaps he will forgive you for having such a thought in your heart. [23]For I see that you are full of bitterness and captive to sin."

[24]Then Simon answered, "Pray to the Lord for me[y] so that nothing you have said may happen to me."

[25]When they had testified and proclaimed the word of the Lord, Peter and John returned to Jerusalem, preaching the gospel in many Samaritan villages.[z]

Philip and the Ethiopian

[26]Now an angel[a] of the Lord said to Philip, "Go south to the road —the desert road—that goes down from Jerusalem to Gaza." [27]So he started out, and on his way he met an Ethiopian[ab] eunuch,[c] an important official in charge of all the treasury of Candace, queen of the Ethiopians. This man had gone to Jerusalem to worship,[d] [28]and on his way home was sitting in his chariot reading the book of Isaiah the prophet. [29]The Spirit told[e] Philip, "Go to that chariot and stay near it."

[30]Then Philip ran up to the chariot and heard the man reading Isaiah the prophet. "Do you understand what you are reading?" Philip asked.

[31]"How can I," he said, "unless someone explains it to me?" So he invited Philip to come up and sit with him.

[32]The eunuch was reading this passage of Scripture:

> "He was led like a sheep to the slaughter,
>   and as a lamb before the shearer is silent,
>   so he did not open his mouth.
> [33]In his humiliation he was deprived of justice.
>   Who can speak of his descendants?
>   For his life was taken from the earth."[b f]

[34]The eunuch asked Philip, "Tell me, please, who is the prophet talking about, himself or someone else?" [35]Then Philip began[g] with that very passage of Scripture[h] and told him the good news about Jesus.

[36]As they traveled along the road, they came to some water and the eunuch said, "Look, here is water. Why shouldn't I be baptized?"[c i] [38]And he gave orders to stop the chariot. Then both Philip and the eunuch went down into the water and Philip baptized him. [39]When they came up out of the water, the Spirit of the Lord suddenly took Philip away,[j] and the eunuch did not see him again, but went on his way rejoicing. [40]Philip, however, appeared at Azotus and traveled about, preaching the gospel in all the towns[k] until he reached Caesarea.[l]

8:20
w 2Ki 5:16;
Da 5:17;
Mt 10:8;
Ac 2:38
8:21
x Ps 78:37
8:24
y Ex 8:8;
Nu 21:7;
1Ki 13:6
8:25
z ver 40
8:26
a Ac 5:19
8:27
b Ps 68:31;
87:4; Zep 3:10
c Isa 56:3-5
d 1Ki 8:41-43;
Jn 12:20
8:29
e Ac 10:19;
11:12; 13:2;
20:23; 21:11
8:33
f Isa 53:7,8
8:35
g Mt 5:2
h Lk 24:27;
Ac 17:2; 18:28;
28:23
8:36
i Ac 10:47
8:39
j 1Ki 18:12;
2Ki 2:16;
Eze 3:12,14;
8:3; 11:1,24;
43:5; 2Co 12:2
8:40
k ver 25
l Ac 10:1,24;
12:19; 21:8,16;
23:23,33; 25:1,
4,6,13

---

[a]27 That is, from the upper Nile region   [b]33 Isaiah 53:7,8   [c]36 Some late manuscripts baptized?" [37]Philip said, "If you believe with all your heart, you may." The eunuch answered, "I believe that Jesus Christ is the Son of God."

Saul's Conversion

9:1–19pp — Ac 22:3–16; 26:9–18

9 Meanwhile, Saul was still breathing out murderous threats against the Lord's disciples. ᵐ He went to the high priest ²and asked him for letters to the synagogues in Damascus, so that if he found any there who belonged to the Way, ⁿ whether men or women, he might take them as prisoners to Jerusalem. ³As he neared Damascus on his journey, suddenly a light from heaven flashed around him. ᵒ ⁴He fell to the ground and heard a voice say to him, "Saul, Saul, why do you persecute me?"

⁵"Who are you, Lord?" Saul asked.

"I am Jesus, whom you are persecuting," he replied. ⁶"Now get up and go into the city, and you will be told what you must do." ᴾ

⁷The men traveling with Saul stood there speechless; they heard the sound �q but did not see anyone. ʳ ⁸Saul got up from the ground, but when he opened his eyes he could see nothing. So they led him by the hand into Damascus. ⁹For three days he was blind, and did not eat or drink anything.

¹⁰In Damascus there was a disciple named Ananias. The Lord called to him in a vision, ˢ "Ananias!"

"Yes, Lord," he answered.

¹¹The Lord told him, "Go to the house of Judas on Straight Street and ask for a man from Tarsus ᵗ named Saul, for he is praying. ¹²In a vision he has seen a man named Ananias come and place his hands on ᵘ him to restore his sight."

¹³"Lord," Ananias answered, "I have heard many reports about this man and all the harm he has done to your saints ᵛ in Jerusalem. ʷ ¹⁴And he has come here with authority from the chief priests ˣ to arrest all who call on your name."

¹⁵But the Lord said to Ananias, "Go! This man is my chosen instrument ʸ to carry my name before the Gentiles ᶻ and their kings ᵃ and before the people of Israel. ¹⁶I will show him how much he must suffer for my name." ᵇ

¹⁷Then Ananias went to the house and entered it. Placing his hands on ᶜ Saul, he said, "Brother Saul, the Lord—Jesus, who appeared to you on the road as you were coming here—has sent me so that you may see again and be filled with the Holy Spirit." ¹⁸Immediately, something like scales fell from Saul's eyes, and he could see again. He got up and was baptized, ¹⁹and after taking some food, he regained his strength.

Saul in Damascus and Jerusalem

Saul spent several days with the disciples ᵈ in Damascus. ᵉ ²⁰At once he began to preach in the synagogues ᶠ that Jesus is the Son of God. ᵍ ²¹All those who heard him were astonished and asked, "Isn't he the man who raised havoc in Jerusalem among those who call on this name? ʰ And hasn't he come here to take them as prisoners to the chief priests?" ⁱ ²²Yet Saul grew more and more powerful and baffled the Jews living in Damascus by proving that Jesus is the Christ. ᵃ ʲ

²³After many days had gone by, the Jews conspired to kill him, ²⁴but

ᵃ22 Or *Messiah*

### Cross references (margin)

9:1
mAc 8:3
9:2
nAc 19:9,23;
22:4; 24:14,22
9:3
o1Co 15:8
9:6
pver 16
9:7
qJn 12:29
rDa 10:7;
Ac 22:9
9:10
sAc 10:3,17,19
9:11
tver 30;
Ac 21:39; 22:3
9:12
uMk 5:23
9:13
vver 32; Ro 1:7;
16:2,15 wAc 8:3
9:14
xver 2,21
9:15
yAc 13:2;
Ro 1:1;
Gal 1:15
zRo 11:13;
15:15,16;
Gal 2:7,8;
Eph 3:7,8
aAc 25:22,23;
26:1
9:16
bAc 20:23;
21:11;
2Co 11:23-27
9:17
cAc 6:6
9:19
dAc 11:26
eAc 26:20
9:20
fAc 13:5,14
gMt 4:3
9:21
hAc 8:3
iGal 1:13,23
9:22
jAc 18:5,28

Saul learned of their plan. [k] Day and night they kept close watch on the city gates in order to kill him. [25]But his followers took him by night and lowered him in a basket through an opening in the wall. [l]

[26]When he came to Jerusalem, [m] he tried to join the disciples, but they were all afraid of him, not believing that he really was a disciple. [27]But Barnabas [n] took him and brought him to the apostles. He told them how Saul on his journey had seen the Lord and that the Lord had spoken to him, [o] and how in Damascus he had preached fearlessly in the name of Jesus. [p] [28]So Saul stayed with them and moved about freely in Jerusalem, speaking boldly in the name of the Lord. [29]He talked and debated with the Grecian Jews, [q] but they tried to kill him. [r] [30]When the brothers [s] learned of this, they took him down to Caesarea [t] and sent him off to Tarsus. [u]

[31]Then the church throughout Judea, Galilee and Samaria [v] enjoyed a time of peace. It was strengthened; and encouraged by the Holy Spirit, it grew in numbers, living in the fear of the Lord.

Aeneas and Dorcas

[32]As Peter traveled about the country, he went to visit the saints [w] in Lydda. [33]There he found a man named Aeneas, a paralytic who had been bedridden for eight years. [34]"Aeneas," Peter said to him, "Jesus Christ heals you. [x] Get up and take care of your mat." Immediately Aeneas got up. [35]All those who lived in Lydda and Sharon [y] saw him and turned to the Lord. [z]

[36]In Joppa [a] there was a disciple named Tabitha (which, when translated, is Dorcas [a]), who was always doing good [b] and helping the poor. [37]About that time she became sick and died, and her body was washed and placed in an upstairs room. [c] [38]Lydda was near Joppa; so when the disciples [d] heard that Peter was in Lydda, they sent two men to him and urged him, "Please come at once!"

[39]Peter went with them, and when he arrived he was taken upstairs to the room. All the widows [e] stood around him, crying and showing him the robes and other clothing that Dorcas had made while she was still with them.

[40]Peter sent them all out of the room; [f] then he got down on his knees [g] and prayed. Turning toward the dead woman, he said, "Tabitha, get up." She opened her eyes, and seeing Peter she sat up. [41]He took her by the hand and helped her to her feet. Then he called the believers and the widows and presented her to them alive. [42]This became known all over Joppa, and many people believed in the Lord. [43]Peter stayed in Joppa for some time with a tanner named Simon. [h]

Cornelius Calls for Peter

10 At Caesarea [i] there was a man named Cornelius, a centurion in what was known as the Italian Regiment. [2]He and all his family were devout and God-fearing; [j] he gave generously to those in need and prayed to God regularly. [3]One day at about three in the afternoon [k] he had a vision. [l] He distinctly saw an angel [m] of God, who came to him and said, "Cornelius!"

[4]Cornelius stared at him in fear. "What is it, Lord?" he asked.

---

[a]36 Both *Tabitha* (Aramaic) and *Dorcas* (Greek) mean *gazelle.*

9:24
k Ac 20:3,19
9:25
l 1Sa 19:12;
2Co 11:32,33
9:26
m Ac 22:17;
26:20; Gal 1:17,
18
9:27
n Ac 4:36
over 3-6
p ver 20,22
9:29
q Ac 6:1
r 2Co 11:26
9:30
s Ac 1:16
t Ac 8:40 u ver 11
9:31
v Ac 8:1
9:32
w ver 13
9:34
x Ac 3:6,16;
4:10
9:35
y 1Ch 5:16;
27:29; Isa 33:9;
35:2; 65:10
z Ac 11:21
9:36
a Jos 19:46;
2Ch 2:16;
Ezr 3:7;
Jnh 1:3; Ac 10:5
b 1Ti 2:10;
Tit 3:8
9:37
c Ac 1:13
9:38
d Ac 11:26
9:39
e Ac 6:1
9:40
f Mt 9:25
g Lk 22:41;
Ac 7:60
9:43
h Ac 10:6
10:1
i Ac 8:40
10:2
j ver 22,35;
Ac 13:16,26
10:3
k Ac 3:1
l Ac 9:10
m Ac 5:19

The angel answered, "Your prayers and gifts to the poor have come up as a memorial offering[n] before God.[o] [5]Now send men to Joppa[p] to bring back a man named Simon who is called Peter. [6]He is staying with Simon the tanner,[q] whose house is by the sea."

[7]When the angel who spoke to him had gone, Cornelius called two of his servants and a devout soldier who was one of his attendants. [8]He told them everything that had happened and sent them to Joppa.[r]

Peter's Vision

10:9–32Ref — Ac 11:5–14

[9]About noon the following day as they were on their journey and approaching the city, Peter went up on the roof[s] to pray. [10]He became hungry and wanted something to eat, and while the meal was being prepared, he fell into a trance.[t] [11]He saw heaven opened and something like a large sheet being let down to earth by its four corners. [12]It contained all kinds of four-footed animals, as well as reptiles of the earth and birds of the air. [13]Then a voice told him, "Get up, Peter. Kill and eat."

[14]"Surely not, Lord!"[u] Peter replied. "I have never eaten anything impure or unclean."[v]

[15]The voice spoke to him a second time, "Do not call anything impure that God has made clean."[w]

[16]This happened three times, and immediately the sheet was taken back to heaven.

[17]While Peter was wondering about the meaning of the vision, the men sent by Cornelius[x] found out where Simon's house was and stopped at the gate. [18]They called out, asking if Simon who was known as Peter was staying there.

[19]While Peter was still thinking about the vision, the Spirit said[y] to him, "Simon, three[a] men are looking for you. [20]So get up and go downstairs. Do not hesitate to go with them, for I have sent them."[z]

[21]Peter went down and said to the men, "I'm the one you're looking for. Why have you come?"

[22]The men replied, "We have come from Cornelius the centurion. He is a righteous and God-fearing man,[a] who is respected by all the Jewish people. A holy angel told him to have you come to his house so that he could hear what you have to say."[b] [23]Then Peter invited the men into the house to be his guests.

Peter at Cornelius' House

The next day Peter started out with them, and some of the brothers[c] from Joppa went along.[d] [24]The following day he arrived in Caesarea.[e] Cornelius was expecting them and had called together his relatives and close friends. [25]As Peter entered the house, Cornelius met him and fell at his feet in reverence. [26]But Peter made him get up. "Stand up," he said, "I am only a man myself."[f]

[27]Talking with him, Peter went inside and found a large gathering of people. [28]He said to them: "You are well aware that it is against our law for a Jew to associate with a Gentile or visit him.[g] But God has shown me that I should not call any man impure or unclean.[h] [29]So when I was

### Cross references (margin)

10:4
n Mt 26:13
o Rev 8:4
10:5
p Ac 9:36
10:6
q Ac 9:43
10:8
r Ac 9:36
10:9
s Mt 24:17
10:10
t Ac 22:17
10:14
u Ac 9:5
v Lev 11:4-8,
13-20; 20:25;
Dt 14:3-20;
Eze 4:14
10:15
w Mt 15:11;
Ro 14:14,17,20;
1Co 10:25;
1Ti 4:3,4;
Tit 1:15
10:17
x ver 7,8
10:19
y Ac 8:29
10:20
z Ac 15:7-9
10:22
a ver 2
b Ac 11:14
10:23
c Ac 1:16
d ver 45;
Ac 11:12
10:24
e Ac 8:40
10:26
f Ac 14:15;
Rev 19:10
10:28
g Jn 4:9; 18:28;
Ac 11:3
h Ac 15:8,9

sent for, I came without raising any objection. May I ask why you sent for me?"

30Cornelius answered: "Four days ago I was in my house praying at this hour, at three in the afternoon. Suddenly a man in shining clothes stood before me 31and said, 'Cornelius, God has heard your prayer and remembered your gifts to the poor. 32Send to Joppa for Simon who is called Peter. He is a guest in the home of Simon the tanner, who lives by the sea.' 33So I sent for you immediately, and it was good of you to come. Now we are all here in the presence of God to listen to everything the Lord has commanded you to tell us."

34Then Peter began to speak: "I now realize how true it is that God does not show favoritism¹ 35but accepts men from every nation who fear him and do what is right.ʲ 36You know the message God sent to the people of Israel, telling the good newsᵏ of peaceˡ through Jesus Christ, who is Lord of all.ᵐ 37You know what has happened throughout Judea, beginning in Galilee after the baptism that John preached— 38how God anointedⁿ Jesus of Nazareth with the Holy Spirit and power, and how he went around doing good and healingᵒ all who were under the power of the devil, because God was with him.ᵖ

39"We are witnesses�q of everything he did in the country of the Jews and in Jerusalem. They killed him by hanging him on a tree,ʳ 40but God raised him from the deadˢ on the third day and caused him to be seen. 41He was not seen by all the people,ᵗ but by witnesses whom God had already chosen—by us who ateᵘ and drank with him after he rose from the dead. 42He commanded us to preach to the peopleᵛ and to testify that he is the one whom God appointed as judge of the living and the dead.ʷ 43All the prophets testify about himˣ that everyoneʸ who believes in him receives forgiveness of sins through his name."

44While Peter was still speaking these words, the Holy Spirit came onᶻ all who heard the message. 45The circumcised believers who had come with Peterᵃ were astonished that the gift of the Holy Spirit had been poured outᵇ even on the Gentiles.ᶜ 46For they heard them speaking in tonguesᵃᵈ and praising God.

Then Peter said, 47"Can anyone keep these people from being baptized with water?ᵉ They have received the Holy Spirit just as we have."ᶠ 48So he ordered that they be baptized in the name of Jesus Christ.ᵍ Then they asked Peter to stay with them for a few days.

Peter Explains His Actions

11 The apostles and the brothersʰ throughout Judea heard that the Gentiles also had received the word of God. 2So when Peter went up to Jerusalem, the circumcised believersⁱ criticized him 3and said, "You went into the house of uncircumcised men and ate with them."ʲ

4Peter began and explained everything to them precisely as it had happened: 5"I was in the city of Joppa praying, and in a trance I saw a vision.ᵏ I saw something like a large sheet being let down from heaven by its four corners, and it came down to where I was. 6I looked into it and saw four-footed animals of the earth, wild beasts, reptiles, and

10:34
iDt 10:17;
2Ch 19:7;
Job 34:19;
Ro 2:11;
Gal 2:6;
Eph 6:9;
Col 3:25;
1Pe 1:17
10:35
jAc 15:9
10:36
kAc 13:32
lLk 2:14
mMt 28:18;
Ro 10:12
10:38
nAc 4:26
oMt 4:23
pJn 3:2
10:39
qLk 24:48
rAc 5:30
10:40
sAc 2:24
10:41
tJn 14:17,22
uLk 24:43;
Jn 21:13
10:42
vMt 28:19,20
wJn 5:22;
Ac 17:31;
Ro 14:9;
2Co 5:10;
2Ti 4:1; 1Pe 4:5
10:43
xIsa 53:11
yAc 15:9
10:44
zAc 8:15,16;
11:15; 15:8
10:45
aver 23
bAc 2:33,38
cAc 11:18
10:46
dMk 16:17
10:47
eAc 8:36
fAc 11:17
10:48
gAc 2:38; 8:16
11:1
hAc 1:16
11:2
iAc 10:45
11:3
jAc 10:25,28;
Gal 2:12
11:5
kAc 10:9-32;
9:10

ᵃ46 Or *other languages*

birds of the air. [7]Then I heard a voice telling me, 'Get up, Peter. Kill and eat.'

[8]"I replied, 'Surely not, Lord! Nothing impure or unclean has ever entered my mouth.'

[9]"The voice spoke from heaven a second time, 'Do not call anything impure that God has made clean.'[l] [10]This happened three times, and then it was all pulled up to heaven again.

[11]"Right then three men who had been sent to me from Caesarea stopped at the house where I was staying. [12]The Spirit told[m] me to have no hesitation about going with them.[n] These six brothers also went with me, and we entered the man's house. [13]He told us how he had seen an angel appear in his house and say, 'Send to Joppa for Simon who is called Peter. [14]He will bring you a message through which you and all your household[o] will be saved.'

[15]"As I began to speak, the Holy Spirit came on[p] them as he had come on us at the beginning.[q] [16]Then I remembered what the Lord had said: 'John baptized with[a] water, but you will be baptized with the Holy Spirit.'[r] [17]So if God gave them the same gift as he gave us,[s] who believed in the Lord Jesus Christ, who was I to think that I could oppose God?"

[18]When they heard this, they had no further objections and praised God, saying, "So then, God has granted even the Gentiles repentance unto life."[t]

The Church in Antioch

[19]Now those who had been scattered by the persecution in connection with Stephen[u] traveled as far as Phoenicia, Cyprus and Antioch,[v] telling the message only to Jews. [20]Some of them, however, men from Cyprus[w] and Cyrene,[x] went to Antioch and began to speak to Greeks also, telling them the good news about the Lord Jesus. [21]The Lord's hand was with them,[y] and a great number of people believed and turned to the Lord.[z]

[22]News of this reached the ears of the church at Jerusalem, and they sent Barnabas[a] to Antioch. [23]When he arrived and saw the evidence of the grace of God,[b] he was glad and encouraged them all to remain true to the Lord with all their hearts.[c] [24]He was a good man, full of the Holy Spirit and faith, and a great number of people were brought to the Lord.[d]

[25]Then Barnabas went to Tarsus[e] to look for Saul, [26]and when he found him, he brought him to Antioch. So for a whole year Barnabas and Saul met with the church and taught great numbers of people. The disciples[f] were called Christians first[g] at Antioch.

[27]During this time some prophets[h] came down from Jerusalem to Antioch. [28]One of them, named Agabus,[i] stood up and through the Spirit predicted that a severe famine would spread over the entire Roman world.[j] (This happened during the reign of Claudius.)[k] [29]The disciples,[l] each according to his ability, decided to provide help[m] for the brothers[n] living in Judea. [30]This they did, sending their gift to the elders[o] by Barnabas and Saul.[p]

11:9
lAc 10:15
11:12
mAc 8:29
nAc 15:9;
Ro 3:22
11:14
oJn 4:53;
Ac 16:15,31-34;
1Co 1:11,16
11:15
pAc 10:44
qAc 2:4
11:16
rMk 1:8; Ac 1:5
11:17
sAc 10:45,47
11:18
tRo 10:12,13;
2Co 7:10
11:19
uAc 8:1,4
vver 26,27;
Ac 13:1; 18:22;
Gal 2:11
11:20
wAc 4:36
xMt 27:32
11:21
yLk 1:66
zAc 2:47
11:22
aAc 4:36
11:23
bAc 13:43;
14:26; 20:24
cAc 14:22
11:24
dver 21;
Ac 5:14
11:25
eAc 9:11
11:26
fAc 6:1,2; 13:52
gAc 26:28;
1Pe 4:16
11:27
hAc 13:1;
15:32;
1Co 12:28,29;
Eph 4:11
11:28
iAc 21:10
jMt 24:14
kAc 18:2
11:29
lver 26
mRo 15:26;
2Co 9:2
nAc 1:16
11:30
oAc 14:23
pAc 12:25

[a]16 Or *in*

Peter's Miraculous Escape From Prison

12 It was about this time that King Herod arrested some who belonged to the church, intending to persecute them. ²He had James, the brother of John, q put to death with the sword. ³When he saw that this pleased the Jews, r he proceeded to seize Peter also. This happened during the Feast of Unleavened Bread. s ⁴After arresting him, he put him in prison, handing him over to be guarded by four squads of four soldiers each. Herod intended to bring him out for public trial after the Passover.

⁵So Peter was kept in prison, but the church was earnestly praying to God for him. t

⁶The night before Herod was to bring him to trial, Peter was sleeping between two soldiers, bound with two chains, u and sentries stood guard at the entrance. ⁷Suddenly an angel v of the Lord appeared and a light shone in the cell. He struck Peter on the side and woke him up. "Quick, get up!" he said, and the chains fell off Peter's wrists. w

⁸Then the angel said to him, "Put on your clothes and sandals." And Peter did so. "Wrap your cloak around you and follow me," the angel told him. ⁹Peter followed him out of the prison, but he had no idea that what the angel was doing was really happening; he thought he was seeing a vision. x ¹⁰They passed the first and second guards and came to the iron gate leading to the city. It opened for them by itself, y and they went through it. When they had walked the length of one street, suddenly the angel left him.

¹¹Then Peter came to himself z and said, "Now I know without a doubt that the Lord sent his angel and rescued me a from Herod's clutches and from everything the Jewish people were anticipating."

¹²When this had dawned on him, he went to the house of Mary the mother of John, also called Mark, b where many people had gathered and were praying. c ¹³Peter knocked at the outer entrance, and a servant girl named Rhoda came to answer the door. d ¹⁴When she recognized Peter's voice, she was so overjoyed e she ran back without opening it and exclaimed, "Peter is at the door!"

¹⁵"You're out of your mind," they told her. When she kept insisting that it was so, they said, "It must be his angel." f

¹⁶But Peter kept on knocking, and when they opened the door and saw him, they were astonished. ¹⁷Peter motioned with his hand g for them to be quiet and described how the Lord had brought him out of prison. "Tell James h and the brothers i about this," he said, and then he left for another place.

¹⁸In the morning, there was no small commotion among the soldiers as to what had become of Peter. ¹⁹After Herod had a thorough search made for him and did not find him, he cross-examined the guards and ordered that they be executed. j

Herod's Death

Then Herod went from Judea to Caesarea k and stayed there a while. ²⁰He had been quarreling with the people of Tyre and Sidon; l they now joined together and sought an audience with him. Having secured the support of Blastus, a trusted personal servant of the king, they asked

12:2
qMt 4:21
12:3
rAc 24:27
sEx 12:15; 23:15
12:5
tEph 6:18
12:6
uAc 21:33
12:7
vAc 5:19
wAc 16:26
12:9
xAc 9:10
12:10
yAc 5:19; 16:26
12:11
zLk 15:17
aPs 34:7;
Da 3:28; 6:22;
2Co 1:10;
2Pe 2:9
12:12
bver 25;
Ac 15:37,39;
Col 4:10;
Phm 24;
1Pe 5:13 cver 5
12:13
dJn 18:16,17
12:14
eLk 24:41
12:15
fMt 18:10
12:17
gAc 13:16;
19:33; 21:40
hAc 15:13
iAc 1:16
12:19
jAc 16:27
kAc 8:40
12:20
lMt 11:21

for peace, because they depended on the king's country for their food supply. [m]

21 On the appointed day Herod, wearing his royal robes, sat on his throne and delivered a public address to the people. 22 They shouted, "This is the voice of a god, not of a man." 23 Immediately, because Herod did not give praise to God, an angel of the Lord struck him down, [n] and he was eaten by worms and died.

24 But the word of God continued to increase and spread. [o]

25 When Barnabas [p] and Saul had finished their mission, [q] they returned from [a] Jerusalem, taking with them John, also called Mark. [r]

Barnabas and Saul Sent Off

13 In the church at Antioch [s] there were prophets [t] and teachers: Barnabas, [u] Simeon called Niger, Lucius of Cyrene, Manaen (who had been brought up with Herod [v] the tetrarch) and Saul. 2 While they were worshiping the Lord and fasting, the Holy Spirit said, [w] "Set apart for me Barnabas and Saul for the work [x] to which I have called them." [y] 3 So after they had fasted and prayed, they placed their hands on them [z] and sent them off. [a]

On Cyprus

4 The two of them, sent on their way by the Holy Spirit, [b] went down to Seleucia and sailed from there to Cyprus. [c] 5 When they arrived at Salamis, they proclaimed the word of God in the Jewish synagogues. [d] John [e] was with them as their helper.

6 They traveled through the whole island until they came to Paphos. There they met a Jewish sorcerer [f] and false prophet [g] named Bar-Jesus, 7 who was an attendant of the proconsul, [h] Sergius Paulus. The proconsul, an intelligent man, sent for Barnabas and Saul because he wanted to hear the word of God. 8 But Elymas the sorcerer [i] (for that is what his name means) opposed them and tried to turn the proconsul [j] from the faith. [k] 9 Then Saul, who was also called Paul, filled with the Holy Spirit, [l] looked straight at Elymas and said, 10 "You are a child of the devil [m] and an enemy of everything that is right! You are full of all kinds of deceit and trickery. Will you never stop perverting the right ways of the Lord? [n] 11 Now the hand of the Lord is against you. [o] You are going to be blind, and for a time you will be unable to see the light of the sun."

Immediately mist and darkness came over him, and he groped about, seeking someone to lead him by the hand. 12 When the proconsul [p] saw what had happened, he believed, for he was amazed at the teaching about the Lord.

In Pisidian Antioch

13 From Paphos, [q] Paul and his companions sailed to Perga in Pamphylia, where John [r] left them to return to Jerusalem. 14 From Perga they went on to Pisidian Antioch. [s] On the Sabbath [t] they entered the synagogue [u] and sat down. 15 After the reading from the Law [v] and the Prophets, the synagogue rulers sent word to them, saying, "Brothers, if you have a message of encouragement for the people, please speak."

16 Standing up, Paul motioned with his hand [w] and said: "Men of

---

12:20
m 1Ki 5:9,11;
Eze 27:17
12:23
n 1Sa 25:38;
2Sa 24:16,17
12:24
o Ac 6:7; 19:20
12:25
p Ac 4:36
q Ac 11:30
r ver 12
13:1
s Ac 11:19
t Ac 11:27
u Ac 4:36;
11:22-26
v Mt 14:1
13:2
w Ac 8:29
x Ac 14:26
y Ac 22:21
13:3
z Ac 6:6
a Ac 14:26
13:4
b ver 2,3
c Ac 4:36
13:5
d Ac 9:20
e Ac 12:12
13:6
f Ac 8:9
g Mt 7:15
13:7
h ver 8,12;
Ac 19:38
13:8
i Ac 8:9 j ver 7
k Ac 6:7
13:9
l Ac 4:8
13:10
m Mt 13:38;
Jn 8:44
n Hos 14:9
13:11
o Ex 9:3;
1Sa 5:6,7;
Ps 32:4
13:12
p ver 7
13:13
q ver 6 r Ac 12:12
13:14
s Ac 14:19,21
t Ac 16:13
u Ac 9:20
13:15
v Ac 15:21
13:16
w Ac 12:17

---

[a] 25 Some manuscripts *to*

Israel and you Gentiles who worship God, listen to me! [17]The God of the people of Israel chose our fathers; he made the people prosper during their stay in Egypt, with mighty power he led them out of that country,[x] [18]he endured their conduct[a][y] for about forty years in the desert,[z] [19]he overthrew seven nations in Canaan[a] and gave their land to his people[b] as their inheritance. [20]All this took about 450 years.

"After this, God gave them judges[c] until the time of Samuel the prophet. [d] [21]Then the people asked for a king,[e] and he gave them Saul[f] son of Kish, of the tribe of Benjamin,[g] who ruled forty years. [22]After removing Saul,[h] he made David their king.[i] He testified concerning him: 'I have found David son of Jesse a man after my own heart;[j] he will do everything I want him to do.'

[23]"From this man's descendants[k] God has brought to Israel the Savior[l] Jesus,[m] as he promised.[n] [24]Before the coming of Jesus, John preached repentance and baptism to all the people of Israel.[o] [25]As John was completing his work,[p] he said: 'Who do you think I am? I am not that one.[q] No, but he is coming after me, whose sandals I am not worthy to untie.'[r]

[26]"Brothers, children of Abraham, and you God-fearing Gentiles, it is to us that this message of salvation[s] has been sent. [27]The people of Jerusalem and their rulers did not recognize Jesus,[t] yet in condemning him they fulfilled the words of the prophets[u] that are read every Sabbath. [28]Though they found no proper ground for a death sentence, they asked Pilate to have him executed.[v] [29]When they had carried out all that was written about him,[w] they took him down from the tree[x] and laid him in a tomb.[y] [30]But God raised him from the dead,[z] [31]and for many days he was seen by those who had traveled with him from Galilee to Jerusalem.[a] They are now his witnesses[b] to our people.

[32]"We tell you the good news:[c] What God promised our fathers[d] [33]he has fulfilled for us, their children, by raising up Jesus. As it is written in the second Psalm:

> " 'You are my Son;
> today I have become your Father.[b][c][e]

[34]The fact that God raised him from the dead, never to decay, is stated in these words:

> " 'I will give you the holy and sure blessings promised
> to David.'[d][f]

[35]So it is stated elsewhere:

> " 'You will not let your Holy One see decay.'[e][g]

[36]"For when David had served God's purpose in his own generation, he fell asleep; he was buried with his fathers[h] and his body decayed. [37]But the one whom God raised from the dead did not see decay.

[38]"Therefore, my brothers, I want you to know that through Jesus the forgiveness of sins is proclaimed to you.[i] [39]Through him everyone who believes is justified from everything you could not be justified from by

---

13:17
xEx 6:6,7;
Dt 7:6-8
13:18
yDt 1:31
zAc 7:36
13:19
aDt 7:1
bJos 19:51
13:20
cJdg 2:16
d1Sa 3:19,20
13:21
e1Sa 8:5,19
f1Sa 10:1
g1Sa 9:1,2
13:22
h1Sa 15:23,26
i1Sa 16:13;
Ps 89:20
j1Sa 13:14
13:23
kMt 1:1
lLk 2:11
mMt 1:21
nver 32
13:24
oMk 1:4
13:25
pAc 20:24
qJn 1:20
rMt 3:11;
Jn 1:27
13:26
sAc 4:12
13:27
tAc 3:17
uLk 24:27
13:28
vMt 27:20-25;
Ac 3:14
13:29
wLk 18:31
xAc 5:30
yLk 23:53
13:30
zMt 28:6;
Ac 2:24
13:31
aMt 28:16
bLk 24:48
13:32
cAc 5:42
dAc 26:6;
Ro 4:13
13:33
ePs 2:7
13:34
fIsa 55:3
13:35
gPs 16:10;
Ac 2:27
13:36
h1Ki 2:10;
Ac 2:29
13:38
iLk 24:47;
Ac 2:38

---

the law of Moses.[j] [40]Take care that what the prophets have said does not happen to you:

> [41]" 'Look, you scoffers,
> wonder and perish,
> for I am going to do something in your days
> that you would never believe,
> even if someone told you.'[a] "[k]

[42]As Paul and Barnabas were leaving the synagogue,[l] the people invited them to speak further about these things on the next Sabbath. [43]When the congregation was dismissed, many of the Jews and devout converts to Judaism followed Paul and Barnabas, who talked with them and urged them to continue in the grace of God.[m]

[44]On the next Sabbath almost the whole city gathered to hear the word of the Lord. [45]When the Jews saw the crowds, they were filled with jealousy and talked abusively[n] against what Paul was saying.[o]

[46]Then Paul and Barnabas answered them boldly: "We had to speak the word of God to you first.[p] Since you reject it and do not consider yourselves worthy of eternal life, we now turn to the Gentiles.[q] [47]For this is what the Lord has commanded us:

> " 'I have made you[b] a light for the Gentiles,[r]
> that you[b] may bring salvation to the ends of the
> earth.'[c] "[s]

[48]When the Gentiles heard this, they were glad and honored the word of the Lord; and all who were appointed for eternal life believed.

[49]The word of the Lord spread through the whole region. [50]But the Jews incited the God-fearing women of high standing and the leading men of the city. They stirred up persecution against Paul and Barnabas, and expelled them from their region.[t] [51]So they shook the dust from their feet[u] in protest against them and went to Iconium.[v] [52]And the disciples were filled with joy and with the Holy Spirit.

In Iconium

14 At Iconium[w] Paul and Barnabas went as usual into the Jewish synagogue. There they spoke so effectively that a great number of Jews and Gentiles believed. [2]But the Jews who refused to believe stirred up the Gentiles and poisoned their minds against the brothers. [3]So Paul and Barnabas spent considerable time there, speaking boldly[x] for the Lord, who confirmed the message of his grace by enabling them to do miraculous signs and wonders.[y] [4]The people of the city were divided; some sided with the Jews, others with the apostles.[z] [5]There was a plot afoot among the Gentiles and Jews, together with their leaders, to mistreat them and stone them.[a] [6]But they found out about it and fled[b] to the Lycaonian cities of Lystra and Derbe and to the surrounding country, [7]where they continued to preach[c] the good news.[d]

In Lystra and Derbe

[8]In Lystra there sat a man crippled in his feet, who was lame from birth[e] and had never walked. [9]He listened to Paul as he was speaking.

13:39
jRo 3:28
13:41
kHab 1:5
13:42
lver 14
13:43
mAc 11:23;
14:22
13:45
nAc 18:6;
1Pe 4:4;
Jude 10
o1Th 2:16
13:46
pver 26;
Ac 3:26
qAc 18:6;
22:21; 28:28
13:47
rLk 2:32
sIsa 49:6
13:50
t1Th 2:16
13:51
uMt 10:14;
Ac 18:6
vAc 14:1,19,21;
2Ti 3:11
14:1
wAc 13:51
14:3
xAc 4:29
yJn 4:48;
Heb 2:4
14:4
zAc 17:4,5
14:5
aver 19
14:6
bMt 10:23
14:7
cAc 16:10
dver 15,21
14:8
eAc 3:2

---

[a]41 Hab. 1:5   [b]47 The Greek is singular.   [c]47 Isaiah 49:6

Paul looked directly at him, saw that he had faith to be healed[f] [10]and called out, "Stand up on your feet!" At that, the man jumped up and began to walk.[g]

[11]When the crowd saw what Paul had done, they shouted in the Lycaonian language, "The gods have come down to us in human form!"[h] [12]Barnabas they called Zeus, and Paul they called Hermes because he was the chief speaker. [13]The priest of Zeus, whose temple was just outside the city, brought bulls and wreaths to the city gates because he and the crowd wanted to offer sacrifices to them.

[14]But when the apostles Barnabas and Paul heard of this, they tore their clothes[i] and rushed out into the crowd, shouting: [15]"Men, why are you doing this? We too are only men,[j] human like you. We are bringing you good news,[k] telling you to turn from these worthless things[l] to the living God,[m] who made heaven and earth[n] and sea and everything in them.[o] [16]In the past, he let[p] all nations go their own way.[q] [17]Yet he has not left himself without testimony:[r] He has shown kindness by giving you rain from heaven and crops in their seasons;[s] he provides you with plenty of food and fills your hearts with joy." [18]Even with these words, they had difficulty keeping the crowd from sacrificing to them.

[19]Then some Jews[t] came from Antioch and Iconium[u] and won the crowd over. They stoned Paul[v] and dragged him outside the city, thinking he was dead. [20]But after the disciples[w] had gathered around him, he got up and went back into the city. The next day he and Barnabas left for Derbe.

The Return to Antioch in Syria

[21]They preached the good news in that city and won a large number of disciples. Then they returned to Lystra, Iconium[x] and Antioch, [22]strengthening the disciples and encouraging them to remain true to the faith.[y] "We must go through many hardships[z] to enter the kingdom of God," they said. [23]Paul and Barnabas appointed elders[aa] for them in each church and, with prayer and fasting,[b] committed them to the Lord,[c] in whom they had put their trust. [24]After going through Pisidia, they came into Pamphylia, [25]and when they had preached the word in Perga, they went down to Attalia.

[26]From Attalia they sailed back to Antioch,[d] where they had been committed to the grace of God[e] for the work they had now completed.[f] [27]On arriving there, they gathered the church together and reported all that God had done through them[g] and how he had opened the door[h] of faith to the Gentiles. [28]And they stayed there a long time with the disciples.

The Council at Jerusalem

15 Some men[i] came down from Judea to Antioch and were teaching the brothers: "Unless you are circumcised,[j] according to the custom taught by Moses,[k] you cannot be saved." [2]This brought Paul and Barnabas into sharp dispute and debate with them. So Paul and Barnabas were appointed, along with some other believers, to go up to Jerusalem[l] to see the apostles and elders[m] about this question. [3]The

---

[a]23 Or *Barnabas ordained elders*; or *Barnabas had elders elected*

14:9
f Mt 9:28,29
14:10
g Ac 3:8
14:11
h Ac 8:10; 28:6
14:14
i Mk 14:63
14:15
j Ac 10:26;
Jas 5:17 k ver 7,
21; Ac 13:32
l 1Sa 12:21;
1Co 8:4;
1Th 1:9
m Mt 16:16
n Ge 1:1;
Jer 14:22
o Ps 146:6;
Rev 14:7
14:16
p Ac 17:30
q Ps 81:12;
Mic 4:5
14:17
r Ac 17:27;
Ro 1:20
s Dt 11:14;
Job 5:10;
Ps 65:10
14:19
t Ac 13:45
u Ac 13:51
v 2Co 11:25;
2Ti 3:11
14:20
w ver 22,28;
Ac 11:26
14:21
x Ac 13:51
14:22
y Ac 11:23;
13:43 z Jn 16:33;
1Th 3:3;
2Ti 3:12
14:23
a Ac 11:30;
Tit 1:5 b Ac 13:3
c Ac 20:32
14:26
d Ac 11:19
e Ac 15:40
f Ac 13:1,3
14:27
g Ac 15:4,12;
21:19
h 1Co 16:9;
2Co 2:12;
Col 4:3;
Rev 3:8
15:1
i ver 24;
Gal 2:12 j ver 5;
Gal 5:2,3
k Ac 6:14
15:2
l Gal 2:2
m Ac 11:30

church sent them on their way, and as they traveled through Phoenicia and Samaria, they told how the Gentiles had been converted.ⁿ This news made all the brothers very glad. 4When they came to Jerusalem, they were welcomed by the church and the apostles and elders, to whom they reported everything God had done through them.°

5Then some of the believers who belonged to the party of the Pharisees stood up and said, "The Gentiles must be circumcised and required to obey the law of Moses."

6The apostles and elders met to consider this question. 7After much discussion, Peter got up and addressed them: "Brothers, you know that some time ago God made a choice among you that the Gentiles might hear from my lips the message of the gospel and believe. 8God, who knows the heart,ᵖ showed that he accepted them by giving the Holy Spirit to them,q just as he did to us. 9He made no distinction between us and them,ʳ for he purified their hearts by faith.ˢ 10Now then, why do you try to test God by putting on the necks of the disciples a yokeᵗ that neither we nor our fathers have been able to bear? 11No! We believe it is through the graceᵘ of our Lord Jesus that we are saved, just as they are."

12The whole assembly became silent as they listened to Barnabas and Paul telling about the miraculous signs and wondersᵛ God had done among the Gentiles through them.ʷ 13When they finished, Jamesˣ spoke up: "Brothers, listen to me. 14Simonᵃ has described to us how God at first showed his concern by taking from the Gentiles a people for himself. 15The words of the prophets are in agreement with this, as it is written:

> 16" 'After this I will return
>   and rebuild David's fallen tent.
>   Its ruins I will rebuild,
>   and I will restore it,
> 17that the remnant of men may seek the Lord,
>   and all the Gentiles who bear my name,
>   says the Lord, who does these things'ᵇ ʸ
> 18   that have been known for ages.ᶜ

19"It is my judgment, therefore, that we should not make it difficult for the Gentiles who are turning to God. 20Instead we should write to them, telling them to abstain from food polluted by idols,ᶻ from sexual immorality,ᵃ from the meat of strangled animals and from blood.ᵇ 21For Moses has been preached in every city from the earliest times and is read in the synagogues on every Sabbath."ᶜ

The Council's Letter to Gentile Believers

22Then the apostles and elders, with the whole church, decided to choose some of their own men and send them to Antioch with Paul and Barnabas. They chose Judas (called Barsabbas) and Silas,ᵈ two men who were leaders among the brothers. 23With them they sent the following letter:

15:3
ⁿAc 14:27
15:4
over 12;
Ac 14:27
15:8
pAc 1:24
qAc 10:44,47
15:9
rAc 10:28,34;
11:12 sAc 10:43
15:10
tMt 23:4;
Gal 5:1
15:11
uRo 3:24;
Eph 2:5-8
15:12
vJn 4:48
wAc 14:27
15:13
xAc 12:17
15:17
yAm 9:11,12
15:20
z1Co 8:7-13;
10:14-28;
Rev 2:14,20
a1Co 10:7,8
bver 29;
Ge 9:4;
Lev 3:17;
Dt 12:16,23
15:21
cAc 13:15;
2Co 3:14,15
15:22
dver 27,32,40

ᵃ14 Greek *Simeon*, a variant of *Simon*; that is, Peter   ᵇ17 Amos 9:11,12   ᶜ17,18 Some manuscripts *things'— / ¹⁸known to the Lord for ages is his work*

The apostles and elders, your brothers,

To the Gentile believers in Antioch,[e] Syria and Cilicia:[f]

Greetings.[g]

[24]We have heard that some went out from us without our authorization and disturbed you, troubling your minds by what they said.[h] [25]So we all agreed to choose some men and send them to you with our dear friends Barnabas and Paul— [26]men who have risked their lives[i] for the name of our Lord Jesus Christ. [27]Therefore we are sending Judas and Silas to confirm by word of mouth what we are writing. [28]It seemed good to the Holy Spirit[j] and to us not to burden you with anything beyond the following requirements: [29]You are to abstain from food sacrificed to idols, from blood, from the meat of strangled animals and from sexual immorality.[k] You will do well to avoid these things.

Farewell.

[30]The men were sent off and went down to Antioch, where they gathered the church together and delivered the letter. [31]The people read it and were glad for its encouraging message. [32]Judas and Silas, who themselves were prophets, said much to encourage and strengthen the brothers. [33]After spending some time there, they were sent off by the brothers with the blessing of peace[l] to return to those who had sent them.[a] [35]But Paul and Barnabas remained in Antioch, where they and many others taught and preached[m] the word of the Lord.

Disagreement Between Paul and Barnabas

[36]Some time later Paul said to Barnabas, "Let us go back and visit the brothers in all the towns[n] where we preached the word of the Lord and see how they are doing." [37]Barnabas wanted to take John, also called Mark,[o] with them, [38]but Paul did not think it wise to take him, because he had deserted them[p] in Pamphylia and had not continued with them in the work. [39]They had such a sharp disagreement that they parted company. Barnabas took Mark and sailed for Cyprus, [40]but Paul chose Silas[q] and left, commended by the brothers to the grace of the Lord.[r] [41]He went through Syria[s] and Cilicia,[t] strengthening the churches.[u]

Timothy Joins Paul and Silas

16 He came to Derbe and then to Lystra,[v] where a disciple named Timothy[w] lived, whose mother was a Jewess and a believer, but whose father was a Greek. [2]The brothers[x] at Lystra and Iconium[y] spoke well of him. [3]Paul wanted to take him along on the journey, so he circumcised him because of the Jews who lived in that area, for they all knew that his father was a Greek.[z] [4]As they traveled from town to town, they delivered the decisions reached by the apostles and elders[a] in Jerusalem[b] for the people to obey.[c] [5]So the churches were strengthened[d] in the faith and grew daily in numbers.

---

[a]33 Some manuscripts *them,* [34]*but Silas decided to remain there*

15:23
ever 1 fver 41
gAc 23:25,26;
Jas 1:1
15:24
hver 1; Gal 1:7;
5:10
15:26
iAc 9:23-25;
14:19
15:28
jAc 5:32
15:29
kver 20;
Ac 21:25
15:33
lMk 5:34;
Ac 16:36;
1Co 16:11
15:35
mAc 8:4
15:36
nAc 13:4,13,14,
51; 14:1,6,24,25
15:37
oAc 12:12
15:38
pAc 13:13
15:40
qver 22
rAc 11:23
15:41
sver 23 tAc 6:9
uAc 16:5
16:1
vAc 14:6
wAc 17:14;
18:5; 19:22;
Ro 16:21;
1Co 4:17;
2Co 1:1,19;
1Th 3:2,6;
1Ti 1:2,18;
2Ti 1:2,5,6
16:2
xver 40
yAc 13:51
16:3
zGal 2:3
16:4
aAc 11:30
bAc 15:2
cAc 15:28,29
16:5
dAc 9:31; 15:41

Paul's Vision of the Man of Macedonia

[6]Paul and his companions traveled throughout the region of Phrygia[e] and Galatia,[f] having been kept by the Holy Spirit from preaching the word in the province of Asia.[g] [7]When they came to the border of Mysia, they tried to enter Bithynia, but the Spirit of Jesus[h] would not allow them to. [8]So they passed by Mysia and went down to Troas.[i] [9]During the night Paul had a vision[j] of a man of Macedonia[k] standing and begging him, "Come over to Macedonia and help us." [10]After Paul had seen the vision, we[l] got ready at once to leave for Macedonia, concluding that God had called us to preach the gospel[m] to them.

Lydia's Conversion in Philippi

[11]From Troas[n] we put out to sea and sailed straight for Samothrace, and the next day on to Neapolis. [12]From there we traveled to Philippi,[o] a Roman colony and the leading city of that district of Macedonia.[p] And we stayed there several days.

[13]On the Sabbath[q] we went outside the city gate to the river, where we expected to find a place of prayer. We sat down and began to speak to the women who had gathered there. [14]One of those listening was a woman named Lydia, a dealer in purple cloth from the city of Thyatira,[r] who was a worshiper of God. The Lord opened her heart[s] to respond to Paul's message. [15]When she and the members of her household[t] were baptized, she invited us to her home. "If you consider me a believer in the Lord," she said, "come and stay at my house." And she persuaded us.

Paul and Silas in Prison

[16]Once when we were going to the place of prayer,[u] we were met by a slave girl who had a spirit[v] by which she predicted the future. She earned a great deal of money for her owners by fortune-telling. [17]This girl followed Paul and the rest of us, shouting, "These men are servants of the Most High God,[w] who are telling you the way to be saved." [18]She kept this up for many days. Finally Paul became so troubled that he turned around and said to the spirit, "In the name of Jesus Christ I command you to come out of her!" At that moment the spirit left her.[x]

[19]When the owners of the slave girl realized that their hope of making money[y] was gone, they seized Paul and Silas[z] and dragged[a] them into the marketplace to face the authorities. [20]They brought them before the magistrates and said, "These men are Jews, and are throwing our city into an uproar[b] [21]by advocating customs unlawful for us Romans[c] to accept or practice."[d]

[22]The crowd joined in the attack against Paul and Silas, and the magistrates ordered them to be stripped and beaten.[e] [23]After they had been severely flogged, they were thrown into prison, and the jailer[f] was commanded to guard them carefully. [24]Upon receiving such orders, he put them in the inner cell and fastened their feet in the stocks.[g]

[25]About midnight Paul and Silas were praying and singing hymns[h] to God, and the other prisoners were listening to them. [26]Suddenly there was such a violent earthquake that the foundations of the prison were shaken.[i] At once all the prison doors flew open,[j] and everybody's chains came loose.[k] [27]The jailer woke up, and when he saw the

---

16:6
e Ac 18:23
f Ac 18:23;
Gal 1:2; 3:1
g Ac 2:9
16:7
h Ro 8:9;
Gal 4:6
16:8
i ver 11;
2Co 2:12;
2Ti 4:13
16:9
j Ac 9:10
k Ac 20:1,3
16:10
l ver 10-17
m Ac 14:7
16:11
n ver 8
16:12
o Ac 20:6;
Php 1:1;
1Th 2:2 p ver 9
16:13
q Ac 13:14
16:14
r Rev 1:11
s Lk 24:45
16:15
t Ac 11:14
16:16
u ver 13
v Dt 18:11;
1Sa 28:3,7
16:17
w Mk 5:7
16:18
x Mk 16:17
16:19
y ver 16;
Ac 19:25,26
z Ac 15:22
a Ac 8:3; 17:6;
21:30; Jas 2:6
16:20
b Ac 17:6
16:21
c ver 12 d Est 3:8
16:22
e 2Co 11:25;
1Th 2:2
16:23
f ver 27,36
16:24
g Job 13:27;
33:11; Jer 20:2,
3; 29:26
16:25
h Eph 5:19
16:26
i Ac 4:31
j Ac 12:10
k Ac 12:7

prison doors open, he drew his sword and was about to kill himself because he thought the prisoners had escaped.[l] [28]But Paul shouted, "Don't harm yourself! We are all here!"

[29]The jailer called for lights, rushed in and fell trembling before Paul and Silas. [30]He then brought them out and asked, "Sirs, what must I do to be saved?"[m]

[31]They replied, "Believe in the Lord Jesus, and you will be saved— you and your household."[n] [32]Then they spoke the word of the Lord to him and to all the others in his house. [33]At that hour of the night[o] the jailer took them and washed their wounds; then immediately he and all his family were baptized. [34]The jailer brought them into his house and set a meal before them; he[p] was filled with joy because he had come to believe in God—he and his whole family.

[35]When it was daylight, the magistrates sent their officers to the jailer with the order: "Release those men." [36]The jailer[q] told Paul, "The magistrates have ordered that you and Silas be released. Now you can leave. Go in peace."[r]

[37]But Paul said to the officers: "They beat us publicly without a trial, even though we are Roman citizens,[s] and threw us into prison. And now do they want to get rid of us quietly? No! Let them come themselves and escort us out."

[38]The officers reported this to the magistrates, and when they heard that Paul and Silas were Roman citizens, they were alarmed.[t] [39]They came to appease them and escorted them from the prison, requesting them to leave the city.[u] [40]After Paul and Silas came out of the prison, they went to Lydia's house,[v] where they met with the brothers[w] and encouraged them. Then they left.

In Thessalonica

17 When they had passed through Amphipolis and Apollonia, they came to Thessalonica,[x] where there was a Jewish synagogue. [2]As his custom was, Paul went into the synagogue,[y] and on three Sabbath[z] days he reasoned with them from the Scriptures,[a] [3]explaining and proving that the Christ[a] had to suffer[b] and rise from the dead.[c] "This Jesus I am proclaiming to you is the Christ,[a]"[d] he said. [4]Some of the Jews were persuaded and joined Paul and Silas,[e] as did a large number of God-fearing Greeks and not a few prominent women.

[5]But the Jews were jealous; so they rounded up some bad characters from the marketplace, formed a mob and started a riot in the city.[f] They rushed to Jason's[g] house in search of Paul and Silas in order to bring them out to the crowd.[b] [6]But when they did not find them, they dragged[h] Jason and some other brothers before the city officials, shouting: "These men who have caused trouble all over the world[i] have now come here,[j] [7]and Jason has welcomed them into his house. They are all defying Caesar's decrees, saying that there is another king, one called Jesus."[k] [8]When they heard this, the crowd and the city officials were thrown into turmoil. [9]Then they made Jason[l] and the others post bond and let them go.

[a]3 Or *Messiah*   [b]5 Or *the assembly of the people*

16:27
lAc 12:19
16:30
mAc 2:37
16:31
nAc 11:14
16:33
over 25
16:34
pAc 11:14
16:36
qver 23,27
rAc 15:33
16:37
sAc 22:25-29
16:38
tAc 22:29
16:39
uMt 8:34
16:40
vver 14 wver 2;
Ac 1:16
17:1
xver 11,13;
Php 4:16;
1Th 1:1;
2Th 1:1;
2Ti 4:10
17:2
yAc 9:20
zAc 13:14
aAc 8:35
17:3
bLk 24:26;
Ac 3:18
cLk 24:46
dAc 9:22; 18:28
17:4
eAc 15:22
17:5
fver 13;
1Th 2:16
gRo 16:21
17:6
hAc 16:19
iMt 24:14
jAc 16:20
17:7
kLk 23:2;
Jn 19:12
17:9
lver 5

In Berea

17:10
mver 13;
Ac 20:4
17:11
nver 1
oLk 16:29;
Jn 5:39
17:14
pAc 15:22
qAc 16:1
17:15
rver 16,21,22;
Ac 18:1;
1Th 3:1
sAc 18:5
17:17
tAc 9:20
17:18
uver 31,32;
Ac 4:2
17:19
vver 22
wMk 1:27
17:23
xJn 4:22
17:24
yIsa 42:5;
Ac 14:15
zDt 10:14;
Mt 11:25
aAc 7:48
17:25
bPs 50:10-12;
Isa 42:5
17:26
cDt 32:8;
Job 12:23
17:27
dDt 4:7;
Jer 23:23,24;
Ac 14:17
17:28
eJob 12:10;
Da 5:23
17:29
fIsa 40:18-20;
Ro 1:23
17:30
gAc 14:16;
Ro 3:25
hver 23;
1Pe 1:14
iLk 24:47;
Tit 2:11,12
17:31
jMt 10:15
kPs 9:8; 96:13;
98:9

10As soon as it was night, the brothers sent Paul and Silas away to Berea.m On arriving there, they went to the Jewish synagogue. 11Now the Bereans were of more noble character than the Thessalonians, n for they received the message with great eagerness and examined the Scriptureso every day to see if what Paul said was true. 12Many of the Jews believed, as did also a number of prominent Greek women and many Greek men.

13When the Jews in Thessalonica learned that Paul was preaching the word of God at Berea, they went there too, agitating the crowds and stirring them up. 14The brothers immediately sent Paul to the coast, but Silasp and Timothyq stayed at Berea. 15The men who escorted Paul brought him to Athensr and then left with instructions for Silas and Timothy to join him as soon as possible. s

In Athens

16While Paul was waiting for them in Athens, he was greatly distressed to see that the city was full of idols. 17So he reasoned in the synagoguet with the Jews and the God-fearing Greeks, as well as in the marketplace day by day with those who happened to be there. 18A group of Epicurean and Stoic philosophers began to dispute with him. Some of them asked, "What is this babbler trying to say?" Others remarked, "He seems to be advocating foreign gods." They said this because Paul was preaching the good news about Jesus and the resurrection. u 19Then they took him and brought him to a meeting of the Areopagus,v where they said to him, "May we know what this new teachingw is that you are presenting? 20You are bringing some strange ideas to our ears, and we want to know what they mean." 21(All the Athenians and the foreigners who lived there spent their time doing nothing but talking about and listening to the latest ideas.)

22Paul then stood up in the meeting of the Areopagus and said: "Men of Athens! I see that in every way you are very religious. 23For as I walked around and looked carefully at your objects of worship, I even found an altar with this inscription: TO AN UNKNOWN GOD. Now what you worship as something unknownx I am going to proclaim to you.

24"The God who made the world and everything in ity is the Lord of heaven and earthz and does not live in temples built by hands. a 25And he is not served by human hands, as if he needed anything, because he himself gives all men life and breath and everything else. b 26From one man he made every nation of men, that they should inhabit the whole earth; and he determined the times set for them and the exact places where they should live. c 27God did this so that men would seek him and perhaps reach out for him and find him, though he is not far from each one of us. d 28'For in him we live and move and have our being.'e As some of your own poets have said, 'We are his offspring.'

29"Therefore since we are God's offspring, we should not think that the divine being is like gold or silver or stone—an image made by man's design and skill. f 30In the past God overlookedg such ignorance, h but now he commands all people everywhere to repent. i 31For he has set a day when he will judgej the world with justicek by the man he has appointed.[l] He has given proof of this to all men by raising him from the dead."[m]

[32]When they heard about the resurrection of the dead,[n] some of them sneered, but others said, "We want to hear you again on this subject." [33]At that, Paul left the Council. [34]A few men became followers of Paul and believed. Among them was Dionysius, a member of the Areopagus,[o] also a woman named Damaris, and a number of others.

In Corinth

18 After this, Paul left Athens[p] and went to Corinth.[q] [2]There he met a Jew named Aquila, a native of Pontus, who had recently come from Italy with his wife Priscilla,[r] because Claudius[s] had ordered all the Jews to leave Rome. Paul went to see them, [3]and because he was a tentmaker as they were, he stayed and worked with them.[t] [4]Every Sabbath[u] he reasoned in the synagogue, trying to persuade Jews and Greeks.

[5]When Silas[v] and Timothy[w] came from Macedonia,[x] Paul devoted himself exclusively to preaching, testifying to the Jews that Jesus was the Christ.[ay] [6]But when the Jews opposed Paul and became abusive,[z] he shook out his clothes in protest and said to them, "Your blood be on your own heads![a] I am clear of my responsibility.[b] From now on I will go to the Gentiles."[c]

[7]Then Paul left the synagogue and went next door to the house of Titius Justus, a worshiper of God.[d] [8]Crispus,[e] the synagogue ruler,[f] and his entire household[g] believed in the Lord; and many of the Corinthians who heard him believed and were baptized.

[9]One night the Lord spoke to Paul in a vision: "Do not be afraid; keep on speaking, do not be silent. [10]For I am with you,[h] and no one is going to attack and harm you, because I have many people in this city." [11]So Paul stayed for a year and a half, teaching them the word of God.

[12]While Gallio was proconsul of Achaia,[i] the Jews made a united attack on Paul and brought him into court. [13]"This man," they charged, "is persuading the people to worship God in ways contrary to the law."

[14]Just as Paul was about to speak, Gallio said to the Jews, "If you Jews were making a complaint about some misdemeanor or serious crime, it would be reasonable for me to listen to you. [15]But since it involves questions about words and names and your own law[j]—settle the matter yourselves. I will not be a judge of such things." [16]So he had them ejected from the court. [17]Then they all turned on Sosthenes[k] the synagogue ruler and beat him in front of the court. But Gallio showed no concern whatever.

Priscilla, Aquila and Apollos

[18]Paul stayed on in Corinth for some time. Then he left the brothers[l] and sailed for Syria, accompanied by Priscilla and Aquila. Before he sailed, he had his hair cut off at Cenchrea[m] because of a vow he had taken.[n] [19]They arrived at Ephesus,[o] where Paul left Priscilla and Aquila. He himself went into the synagogue and reasoned with the Jews. [20]When they asked him to spend more time with them, he declined. [21]But as he left, he promised, "I will come back if it is God's will."[p] Then

---

a5 Or *Messiah;* also in verse 28

17:31
lAc 10:42
mAc 2:24
17:32
nver 18,31
17:34
over 19,22
18:1
pAc 17:15
qAc 19:1;
1Co 1:2;
2Co 1:1,23;
2Ti 4:20
18:2
rRo 16:3;
1Co 16:19;
2Ti 4:19
sAc 11:28
18:3
tAc 20:34;
1Co 4:12;
1Th 2:9;
2Th 3:8
18:4
uAc 13:14
18:5
vAc 15:22
wAc 16:1
xAc 16:9;
17:14,15
yver 28; Ac 17:3
18:6
zAc 13:45
a2Sa 1:16;
Eze 18:13; 33:4
bAc 20:26
cAc 13:46
18:7
dAc 16:14
18:8
e1Co 1:14
fMk 5:22
gAc 11:14
18:10
hMt 28:20
18:12
iver 27
18:15
jAc 23:29;
25:11,19
18:17
k1Co 1:1
18:18
lAc 1:16
mRo 16:1
nNu 6:2,5,18;
Ac 21:24
18:19
over 21,24;
1Co 15:32
18:21
pRo 1:10;
1Co 4:19;
Jas 4:15

he set sail from Ephesus. 22When he landed at Caesarea, q he went up and greeted the church and then went down to Antioch. r

23After spending some time in Antioch, Paul set out from there and traveled from place to place throughout the region of Galatia s and Phrygia, strengthening all the disciples. t

24Meanwhile a Jew named Apollos, u a native of Alexandria, came to Ephesus. He was a learned man, with a thorough knowledge of the Scriptures. 25He had been instructed in the way of the Lord, and he spoke with great fervor[a] v and taught about Jesus accurately, though he knew only the baptism of John. w 26He began to speak boldly in the synagogue. When Priscilla and Aquila heard him, they invited him to their home and explained to him the way of God more adequately.

27When Apollos wanted to go to Achaia, x the brothers y encouraged him and wrote to the disciples there to welcome him. On arriving, he was a great help to those who by grace had believed. 28For he vigorously refuted the Jews in public debate, proving from the Scriptures z that Jesus was the Christ. a

Paul in Ephesus

19 While Apollos was at Corinth, b Paul took the road through the interior and arrived at Ephesus. c There he found some disciples 2and asked them, "Did you receive the Holy Spirit when[b] you believed?"

They answered, "No, we have not even heard that there is a Holy Spirit."

3So Paul asked, "Then what baptism did you receive?"

"John's baptism," they replied.

4Paul said, "John's baptism was a baptism of repentance. He told the people to believe in the one coming after him, that is, in Jesus." d 5On hearing this, they were baptized into[c] the name of the Lord Jesus. 6When Paul placed his hands on them, e the Holy Spirit came on them, f and they spoke in tongues[d] g and prophesied. 7There were about twelve men in all.

8Paul entered the synagogue h and spoke boldly there for three months, arguing persuasively about the kingdom of God. i 9But some of them j became obstinate; they refused to believe and publicly maligned the Way. k So Paul left them. He took the disciples l with him and had discussions daily in the lecture hall of Tyrannus. 10This went on for two years, m so that all the Jews and Greeks who lived in the province of Asia n heard the word of the Lord.

11God did extraordinary miracles o through Paul, 12so that even handkerchiefs and aprons that had touched him were taken to the sick, and their illnesses were cured p and the evil spirits left them.

13Some Jews who went around driving out evil spirits q tried to invoke the name of the Lord Jesus over those who were demon-possessed. They would say, "In the name of Jesus, r whom Paul preaches, I command you to come out." 14Seven sons of Sceva, a Jewish chief priest, were doing this. 15One day the evil spirit answered them, "Jesus I know, and I know about Paul, but who are you?" 16Then the man who had the evil spirit jumped on them and overpowered them

18:22
qAc 8:40
rAc 11:19
18:23
sAc 16:6
tAc 14:22;
15:32,41
18:24
uAc 19:1;
1Co 1:12; 3:5,
6,22; 4:6;
16:12; Tit 3:13
18:25
vRo 12:11
wAc 19:3
18:27
xver 12 yver 18
18:28
zAc 17:2 aver 5;
Ac 9:22
19:1
bAc 18:1
cAc 18:19
19:4
dJn 1:7;
Ac 13:24,25
19:6
eAc 6:6; 8:17
fAc 2:4
gMk 16:17;
Ac 10:46
19:8
hAc 9:20
iAc 1:3; 28:23
19:9
jAc 14:4
kver 23; Ac 9:2
lver 30;
Ac 11:26
19:10
mAc 20:31
nver 22,26,27
19:11
oAc 8:13
19:12
pAc 5:15
19:13
qMt 12:27
rMk 9:38

a25 Or *with fervor in the Spirit*   b2 Or *after*   c5 Or *in*   d6 Or *other languages* all. He gave them such a beating that they ran out of the house naked and bleeding.

[17]When this became known to the Jews and Greeks living in Ephesus,[s] they were all seized with fear,[t] and the name of the Lord Jesus was held in high honor. [18]Many of those who believed now came and openly confessed their evil deeds. [19]A number who had practiced sorcery brought their scrolls together and burned them publicly. When they calculated the value of the scrolls, the total came to fifty thousand drachmas.[a] [20]In this way the word of the Lord spread widely and grew in power.[u]

[21]After all this had happened, Paul decided to go to Jerusalem,[v] passing through Macedonia[w] and Achaia.[x] "After I have been there," he said, "I must visit Rome also."[y] [22]He sent two of his helpers,[z] Timothy[a] and Erastus,[b] to Macedonia, while he stayed in the province of Asia[c] a little longer.

The Riot in Ephesus

[23]About that time there arose a great disturbance about the Way.[d] [24]A silversmith named Demetrius, who made silver shrines of Artemis, brought in no little business for the craftsmen. [25]He called them together, along with the workmen in related trades, and said: "Men, you know we receive a good income from this business.[e] [26]And you see and hear how this fellow Paul has convinced and led astray large numbers of people here in Ephesus[f] and in practically the whole province of Asia. He says that man-made gods are no gods at all.[g] [27]There is danger not only that our trade will lose its good name, but also that the temple of the great goddess Artemis will be discredited, and the goddess herself, who is worshiped throughout the province of Asia and the world, will be robbed of her divine majesty."

[28]When they heard this, they were furious and began shouting: "Great is Artemis of the Ephesians!"[h] [29]Soon the whole city was in an uproar. The people seized Gaius[i] and Aristarchus,[j] Paul's traveling companions from Macedonia,[k] and rushed as one man into the theater. [30]Paul wanted to appear before the crowd, but the disciples would not let him. [31]Even some of the officials of the province, friends of Paul, sent him a message begging him not to venture into the theater.

[32]The assembly was in confusion: Some were shouting one thing, some another.[l] Most of the people did not even know why they were there. [33]The Jews pushed Alexander to the front, and some of the crowd shouted instructions to him. He motioned[m] for silence in order to make a defense before the people. [34]But when they realized he was a Jew, they all shouted in unison for about two hours: "Great is Artemis of the Ephesians!"

[35]The city clerk quieted the crowd and said: "Men of Ephesus,[n] doesn't all the world know that the city of Ephesus is the guardian of the temple of the great Artemis and of her image, which fell from heaven? [36]Therefore, since these facts are undeniable, you ought to be quiet and not do anything rash. [37]You have brought these men here, though they have neither robbed temples[o] nor blasphemed our goddess. [38]If, then, Demetrius and his fellow craftsmen have a grievance

---

a19 A drachma was a silver coin worth about a day's wages.

19:17
sAc 18:19
tAc 5:5,11
19:20
uAc 6:7; 12:24
19:21
vAc 20:16,22;
Ro 15:25
wAc 16:9
xAc 18:12
yRo 15:24,28
19:22
zAc 13:5
aAc 16:1
bRo 16:23;
2Ti 4:20 cver 10,
26,27
19:23
dAc 9:2
19:25
eAc 16:16,19,20
19:26
fAc 18:19
gDt 4:28;
Ps 115:4;
Isa 44:10-20;
Jer 10:3-5;
Ac 17:29;
1Co 8:4;
Rev 9:20
19:28
hAc 18:19
19:29
iAc 20:4;
Ro 16:23;
1Co 1:14
jAc 20:4; 27:2;
Col 4:10;
Phm 24
kAc 16:9
19:32
lAc 21:34
19:33
mAc 12:17
19:35
nAc 18:19
19:37
oRo 2:22

against anybody, the courts are open and there are proconsuls. ᵖ They can press charges. ³⁹If there is anything further you want to bring up, it must be settled in a legal assembly. ⁴⁰As it is, we are in danger of being charged with rioting because of today's events. In that case we would not be able to account for this commotion, since there is no reason for it." ⁴¹After he had said this, he dismissed the assembly.

Through Macedonia and Greece

20 When the uproar had ended, Paul sent for the disciples�q and, after encouraging them, said good-by and set out for Macedonia.ʳ ²He traveled through that area, speaking many words of encouragement to the people, and finally arrived in Greece, ³where he stayed three months. Because the Jews made a plot against himˢ just as he was about to sail for Syria, he decided to go back through Macedonia.ᵗ ⁴He was accompanied by Sopater son of Pyrrhus from Berea, Aristarchusᵘ and Secundus from Thessalonica,ᵛ Gaiusʷ from Derbe, Timothyˣ also, and Tychicusʸ and Trophimusᶻ from the province of Asia. ⁵These men went on ahead and waited for usᵃ at Troas.ᵇ ⁶But we sailed from Philippiᶜ after the Feast of Unleavened Bread, and five days later joined the others at Troas,ᵈ where we stayed seven days.

Eutychus Raised From the Dead at Troas

⁷On the first day of the weekᵉ we came together to break bread. Paul spoke to the people and, because he intended to leave the next day, kept on talking until midnight. ⁸There were many lamps in the upstairs roomᶠ where we were meeting. ⁹Seated in a window was a young man named Eutychus, who was sinking into a deep sleep as Paul talked on and on. When he was sound asleep, he fell to the ground from the third story and was picked up dead. ¹⁰Paul went down, threw himself on the young manᵍ and put his arms around him. "Don't be alarmed," he said. "He's alive!"ʰ ¹¹Then he went upstairs again and broke breadⁱ and ate. After talking until daylight, he left. ¹²The people took the young man home alive and were greatly comforted.

Paul's Farewell to the Ephesian Elders

¹³We went on ahead to the ship and sailed for Assos, where we were going to take Paul aboard. He had made this arrangement because he was going there on foot. ¹⁴When he met us at Assos, we took him aboard and went on to Mitylene. ¹⁵The next day we set sail from there and arrived off Kios. The day after that we crossed over to Samos, and on the following day arrived at Miletus.ʲ ¹⁶Paul had decided to sail past Ephesusᵏ to avoid spending time in the province of Asia, for he was in a hurry to reach Jerusalem,ˡ if possible, by the day of Pentecost.ᵐ

¹⁷From Miletus, Paul sent to Ephesus for the eldersⁿ of the church. ¹⁸When they arrived, he said to them: "You know how I lived the whole time I was with you,ᵒ from the first day I came into the province of Asia. ¹⁹I served the Lord with great humility and with tears, although I was severely tested by the plots of the Jews.ᵖ ²⁰You know that I have not hesitated to preach anythingq that would be helpful to you but have taught you publicly and from house to house. ²¹I have declared to both Jewsʳ and Greeks that they must turn to God in repentanceˢ and have faith in our Lord Jesus.ᵗ

19:38
pAc 13:7,8,12
20:1
qAc 11:26
rAc 16:9
20:3
sver 19;
Ac 9:23,24;
23:12,15,30;
25:3; 2Co 11:26
tAc 16:9
20:4
uAc 19:29
vAc 17:1
wAc 19:29
xAc 16:1
yEph 6:21;
Col 4:7;
2Ti 4:12;
Tit 3:12
zAc 21:29;
2Ti 4:20
20:5
aAc 16:10
bAc 16:8
20:6
cAc 16:12
dAc 16:8
20:7
e1Co 16:2;
Rev 1:10
20:8
fAc 1:13
20:10
g1Ki 17:21;
2Ki 4:34
hMt 9:23,24
20:11
iver 7
20:15
jver 17; 2Ti 4:20
20:16
kAc 18:19
lAc 19:21
mAc 2:1;
1Co 16:8
20:17
nAc 11:30
20:18
oAc 18:19-21;
19:1-41
20:19
pver 3
20:20
qver 27
20:21
rAc 18:5
sAc 2:38
tAc 24:24;
26:18;
Eph 1:15;
Col 2:5; Phm 5

22"And now, compelled by the Spirit, I am going to Jerusalem,ᵘ not knowing what will happen to me there. 23I only know that in every city the Holy Spirit warns meᵛ that prison and hardships are facing me. ʷ 24However, I consider my life worth nothing to me,ˣ if only I may finish the raceʸ and complete the taskʸ the Lord Jesus has given meᶻ—the task of testifying to the gospel of God's grace.

25"Now I know that none of you among whom I have gone about preaching the kingdom will ever see me again. ᵃ 26Therefore, I declare to you today that I am innocent of the blood of all men. ᵇ 27For I have not hesitated to proclaim to you the whole will of God. ᶜ 28Keep watch over yourselves and all the flock of which the Holy Spirit has made you overseers. ᵃ ᵈ Be shepherds of the church of God, ᵇ which he bought with his own blood. 29I know that after I leave, savage wolvesᵉ will come in among you and will not spare the flock. ᶠ 30Even from your own number men will arise and distort the truth in order to draw away disciplesᵍ after them. 31So be on your guard! Remember that for three yearsʰ I never stopped warning each of you night and day with tears. ⁱ

32"Now I commit you to Godʲ and to the word of his grace, which can build you up and give you an inheritanceᵏ among all those who are sanctified.ˡ 33I have not coveted anyone's silver or gold or clothing. ᵐ 34You yourselves know that these hands of mine have supplied my own needs and the needs of my companions. ⁿ 35In everything I did, I showed you that by this kind of hard work we must help the weak, remembering the words the Lord Jesus himself said: 'It is more blessed to give than to receive.' "

36When he had said this, he knelt down with all of them and prayed. ᵒ 37They all wept as they embraced him and kissed him. ᵖ 38What grieved them most was his statement that they would never see his face again. �q Then they accompanied him to the ship.

On to Jerusalem

21 After weʳ had torn ourselves away from them, we put out to sea and sailed straight to Cos. The next day we went to Rhodes and from there to Patara. 2We found a ship crossing over to Phoenicia,ˢ went on board and set sail. 3After sighting Cyprus and passing to the south of it, we sailed on to Syria. We landed at Tyre, where our ship was to unload its cargo. 4Finding the disciplesᵗ there, we stayed with them seven days. Through the Spiritᵘ they urged Paul not to go on to Jerusalem. 5But when our time was up, we left and continued on our way. All the disciples and their wives and children accompanied us out of the city, and there on the beach we knelt to pray. ᵛ 6After saying good-by to each other, we went aboard the ship, and they returned home.

7We continued our voyage from Tyreʷ and landed at Ptolemais, where we greeted the brothersˣ and stayed with them for a day. 8Leaving the next day, we reached Caesareaʸ and stayed at the house of Philipᶻ the evangelist, ᵃ one of the Seven. 9He had four unmarried daughters who prophesied. ᵇ

10After we had been there a number of days, a prophet named Agabusᶜ came down from Judea. 11Coming over to us, he took Paul's

20:22
uver 16
20:23
vAc 21:4
wAc 9:16
20:24
xAc 21:13
y2Co 4:1
zGal 1:1; Tit 1:3
20:25
aver 38
20:26
bAc 18:6
20:27
cver 20
20:28
d1Pe 5:2
20:29
eMt 7:15 fver 28
20:30
gAc 11:26
20:31
hAc 19:10
iver 19
20:32
jAc 14:23
kEph 1:14;
Col 1:12; 3:24;
Heb 9:15;
1Pe 1:4
lAc 26:18
20:33
m1Sa 12:3;
1Co 9:12;
2Co 7:2; 11:9;
12:14-17
20:34
nAc 18:3
20:36
oLk 22:41;
Ac 21:5
20:37
pLk 15:20
20:38
qver 25
21:1
rAc 16:10
21:2
sAc 11:19
21:4
tAc 11:26
uver 11;
Ac 20:23
21:5
vAc 20:36
21:7
wAc 12:20
xAc 1:16
21:8
yAc 8:40
zAc 6:5; 8:5-40
aEph 4:11;
2Ti 4:5
21:9
bLk 2:36;
Ac 2:17
21:10
cAc 11:28

ᵃ28 Traditionally *bishops*   ᵇ28 Many manuscripts *of the Lord* belt, tied his own hands and feet with it and said, "The Holy Spirit says, 'In this way the Jews of Jerusalem will bind[d] the owner of this belt and will hand him over to the Gentiles.' "[e]

[12]When we heard this, we and the people there pleaded with Paul not to go up to Jerusalem. [13]Then Paul answered, "Why are you weeping and breaking my heart? I am ready not only to be bound, but also to die[f] in Jerusalem for the name of the Lord Jesus."[g] [14]When he would not be dissuaded, we gave up and said, "The Lord's will be done."

[15]After this, we got ready and went up to Jerusalem. [16]Some of the disciples from Caesarea[h] accompanied us and brought us to the home of Mnason, where we were to stay. He was a man from Cyprus[i] and one of the early disciples.

Paul's Arrival at Jerusalem

[17]When we arrived at Jerusalem, the brothers received us warmly.[j] [18]The next day Paul and the rest of us went to see James,[k] and all the elders[l] were present. [19]Paul greeted them and reported in detail what God had done among the Gentiles[m] through his ministry.[n]

[20]When they heard this, they praised God. Then they said to Paul: "You see, brother, how many thousands of Jews have believed, and all of them are zealous[o] for the law.[p] [21]They have been informed that you teach all the Jews who live among the Gentiles to turn away from Moses,[q] telling them not to circumcise their children[r] or live according to our customs.[s] [22]What shall we do? They will certainly hear that you have come, [23]so do what we tell you. There are four men with us who have made a vow.[t] [24]Take these men, join in their purification rites[u] and pay their expenses, so that they can have their heads shaved.[v] Then everybody will know there is no truth in these reports about you, but that you yourself are living in obedience to the law. [25]As for the Gentile believers, we have written to them our decision that they should abstain from food sacrificed to idols, from blood, from the meat of strangled animals and from sexual immorality."[w]

[26]The next day Paul took the men and purified himself along with them. Then he went to the temple to give notice of the date when the days of purification would end and the offering would be made for each of them.[x]

Paul Arrested

[27]When the seven days were nearly over, some Jews from the province of Asia saw Paul at the temple. They stirred up the whole crowd and seized him,[y] [28]shouting, "Men of Israel, help us! This is the man who teaches all men everywhere against our people and our law and this place. And besides, he has brought Greeks into the temple area and defiled this holy place."[z] [29](They had previously seen Trophimus[a] the Ephesian[b] in the city with Paul and assumed that Paul had brought him into the temple area.)

[30]The whole city was aroused, and the people came running from all directions. Seizing Paul,[c] they dragged him[d] from the temple, and immediately the gates were shut. [31]While they were trying to kill him, news reached the commander of the Roman troops that the whole city of Jerusalem was in an uproar. [32]He at once took some officers and

21:11
d ver 33
e 1Ki 22:11

21:13
f Ac 20:24
g Ac 9:16

21:16
h Ac 8:40 i ver 3, 4

21:17
j Ac 15:4

21:18
k Ac 15:13
l Ac 11:30

21:19
m Ac 14:27
n Ac 1:17

21:20
o Ac 22:3;
Ro 10:2;
Gal 1:14
p Ac 15:1,5

21:21
q ver 28
r Ac 15:19-21;
1Co 7:18,19
s Ac 6:14

21:23
t Ac 18:18

21:24
u ver 26;
Ac 24:18
v Ac 18:18

21:25
w Ac 15:20,29

21:26
x Nu 6:13-20;
Ac 24:18

21:27
y Ac 24:18;
26:21

21:28
z Mt 24:15;
Ac 24:5,6

21:29
a Ac 20:4
b Ac 18:19

21:30
c Ac 26:21
d Ac 16:19

soldiers and ran down to the crowd. When the rioters saw the commander and his soldiers, they stopped beating Paul.[e]

[33]The commander came up and arrested him and ordered him to be bound[f] with two[g] chains.[h] Then he asked who he was and what he had done. [34]Some in the crowd shouted one thing and some another,[i] and since the commander could not get at the truth because of the uproar, he ordered that Paul be taken into the barracks.[j] [35]When Paul reached the steps,[k] the violence of the mob was so great he had to be carried by the soldiers. [36]The crowd that followed kept shouting, "Away with him!"[l]

Paul Speaks to the Crowd

22:3–16pp — Ac 9:1–22; 26:9–18

[37]As the soldiers were about to take Paul into the barracks,[m] he asked the commander, "May I say something to you?"

"Do you speak Greek?" he replied. [38]"Aren't you the Egyptian who started a revolt and led four thousand terrorists out into the desert[n] some time ago?"[o]

[39]Paul answered, "I am a Jew, from Tarsus[p] in Cilicia,[q] a citizen of no ordinary city. Please let me speak to the people."

[40]Having received the commander's permission, Paul stood on the steps and motioned[r] to the crowd. When they were all silent, he said to them in Aramaic[a]:[s] **22** [1]"Brothers and fathers,[t] listen now to my defense."

[2]When they heard him speak to them in Aramaic,[u] they became very quiet.

Then Paul said: [3]"I am a Jew,[v] born in Tarsus[w] of Cilicia, but brought up in this city. Under[x] Gamaliel[y] I was thoroughly trained in the law of our fathers[z] and was just as zealous[a] for God as any of you are today. [4]I persecuted[b] the followers of this Way to their death, arresting both men and women and throwing them into prison,[c] [5]as also the high priest and all the Council[d] can testify. I even obtained letters from them to their brothers[e] in Damascus,[f] and went there to bring these people as prisoners to Jerusalem to be punished.

[6]"About noon as I came near Damascus, suddenly a bright light from heaven flashed around me.[g] [7]I fell to the ground and heard a voice say to me, 'Saul! Saul! Why do you persecute me?'

[8]" 'Who are you, Lord?' I asked.

" 'I am Jesus of Nazareth, whom you are persecuting,' he replied. [9]My companions saw the light,[h] but they did not understand the voice[i] of him who was speaking to me.

[10]" 'What shall I do, Lord?' I asked.

" 'Get up,' the Lord said, 'and go into Damascus. There you will be told all that you have been assigned to do.'[j] [11]My companions led me by the hand into Damascus, because the brilliance of the light had blinded me.[k]

[12]"A man named Ananias came to see me.[l] He was a devout observer of the law and highly respected by all the Jews living there.[m] [13]He stood beside me and said, 'Brother Saul, receive your sight!' And at that very moment I was able to see him.

---

a40 Or possibly *Hebrew*; also in 22:2

21:32 eAc 23:27
21:33 fver 11 gAc 12:6 hAc 20:23; Eph 6:20; 2Ti 2:9
21:34 iAc 19:32 jver 37; Ac 23:10,16,32
21:35 kver 40
21:36 lLk 23:18; Jn 19:15; Ac 22:22
21:37 mver 34
21:38 nMt 24:26 oAc 5:36
21:39 pAc 9:11 qAc 22:3
21:40 rAc 12:17 sJn 5:2
22:1 tAc 7:2
22:2 uAc 21:40
22:3 vAc 21:39 wAc 9:11 xLk 10:39 yAc 5:34 zAc 26:5 aAc 21:20
22:4 bAc 8:3 cver 19, 20
22:5 dLk 22:66 eAc 13:26 fAc 9:2
22:6 gAc 9:3
22:9 hAc 26:13 iAc 9:7
22:10 jAc 16:30
22:11 kAc 9:8
22:12 lAc 9:17 mAc 10:22

¹⁴"Then he said: 'The God of our fathers[n] has chosen you to know his will and to see[o] the Righteous One[p] and to hear words from his mouth. ¹⁵You will be his witness[q] to all men of what you have seen and heard. ¹⁶And now what are you waiting for? Get up, be baptized[r] and wash your sins away,[s] calling on his name.'[t]

¹⁷"When I returned to Jerusalem[u] and was praying at the temple, I fell into a trance[v] ¹⁸and saw the Lord speaking. 'Quick!' he said to me. 'Leave Jerusalem immediately, because they will not accept your testimony about me.'

¹⁹"'Lord,' I replied, 'these men know that I went from one synagogue to another to imprison[w] and beat[x] those who believe in you. ²⁰And when the blood of your martyr[a] Stephen was shed, I stood there giving my approval and guarding the clothes of those who were killing him.'[y]

²¹"Then the Lord said to me, 'Go; I will send you far away to the Gentiles.'"[z]

Paul the Roman Citizen

²²The crowd listened to Paul until he said this. Then they raised their voices and shouted, "Rid the earth of him![a] He's not fit to live!"[b]

²³As they were shouting and throwing off their cloaks[c] and flinging dust into the air,[d] ²⁴the commander ordered Paul to be taken into the barracks.[e] He directed[f] that he be flogged and questioned in order to find out why the people were shouting at him like this. ²⁵As they stretched him out to flog him, Paul said to the centurion standing there, "Is it legal for you to flog a Roman citizen who hasn't even been found guilty?"[g]

²⁶When the centurion heard this, he went to the commander and reported it. "What are you going to do?" he asked. "This man is a Roman citizen."

²⁷The commander went to Paul and asked, "Tell me, are you a Roman citizen?"

"Yes, I am," he answered.

²⁸Then the commander said, "I had to pay a big price for my citizenship."

"But I was born a citizen," Paul replied.

²⁹Those who were about to question him withdrew immediately. The commander himself was alarmed when he realized that he had put Paul, a Roman citizen,[h] in chains.

Before the Sanhedrin

³⁰The next day, since the commander wanted to find out exactly why Paul was being accused by the Jews,[i] he released him[j] and ordered the chief priests and all the Sanhedrin[k] to assemble. Then he brought Paul and had him stand before them.

23 Paul looked straight at the Sanhedrin[l] and said, "My brothers,[m] I have fulfilled my duty to God in all good conscience[n] to this day." ²At this the high priest Ananias[o] ordered those standing near Paul to strike him on the mouth.[p] ³Then Paul said to him, "God will strike you, you whitewashed wall![q] You sit there to judge me according

### Cross references (margin)

22:14
n Ac 3:13
o 1Co 9:1; 15:8
p Ac 7:52

22:15
q Ac 23:11; 26:16

22:16
r Ac 2:38
s Heb 10:22
t Ro 10:13

22:17
u Ac 9:26
v Ac 10:10

22:19
w ver 4; Ac 8:3
x Mt 10:17

22:20
y Ac 7:57-60; 8:1

22:21
z Ac 9:15; 13:46

22:22
a Ac 21:36
b Ac 25:24

22:23
c Ac 7:58
d 2Sa 16:13

22:24
e Ac 21:34
f ver 29

22:25
g Ac 16:37

22:29
h ver 24,25; Ac 16:38

22:30
i Ac 23:28
j Ac 21:33
k Mt 5:22

23:1
l Ac 22:30
m Ac 22:5
n Ac 24:16; 1Co 4:4; 2Co 1:12; 2Ti 1:3; Heb 13:18

23:2
o Ac 24:1
p Jn 18:22

23:3
q Mt 23:27

to the law, yet you yourself violate the law by commanding that I be struck!"[r]

[4]Those who were standing near Paul said, "You dare to insult God's high priest?"

[5]Paul replied, "Brothers, I did not realize that he was the high priest; for it is written: 'Do not speak evil about the ruler of your people.'[a] "[s]

[6]Then Paul, knowing that some of them were Sadducees and the others Pharisees, called out in the Sanhedrin, "My brothers,[t] I am a Pharisee,[u] the son of a Pharisee. I stand on trial because of my hope in the resurrection of the dead."[v] [7]When he said this, a dispute broke out between the Pharisees and the Sadducees, and the assembly was divided. [8](The Sadducees say that there is no resurrection,[w] and that there are neither angels nor spirits, but the Pharisees acknowledge them all.)

[9]There was a great uproar, and some of the teachers of the law who were Pharisees[x] stood up and argued vigorously. "We find nothing wrong with this man,"[y] they said. "What if a spirit or an angel has spoken to him?"[z] [10]The dispute became so violent that the commander was afraid Paul would be torn to pieces by them. He ordered the troops to go down and take him away from them by force and bring him into the barracks.[a]

[11]The following night the Lord stood near Paul and said, "Take courage![b] As you have testified about me in Jerusalem, so you must also testify in Rome."[c]

The Plot to Kill Paul

[12]The next morning the Jews formed a conspiracy and bound themselves with an oath not to eat or drink until they had killed Paul.[d] [13]More than forty men were involved in this plot. [14]They went to the chief priests and elders and said, "We have taken a solemn oath not to eat anything until we have killed Paul.[e] [15]Now then, you and the Sanhedrin[f] petition the commander to bring him before you on the pretext of wanting more accurate information about his case. We are ready to kill him before he gets here."

[16]But when the son of Paul's sister heard of this plot, he went into the barracks[g] and told Paul.

[17]Then Paul called one of the centurions and said, "Take this young man to the commander; he has something to tell him." [18]So he took him to the commander.

The centurion said, "Paul, the prisoner,[h] sent for me and asked me to bring this young man to you because he has something to tell you."

[19]The commander took the young man by the hand, drew him aside and asked, "What is it you want to tell me?"

[20]He said: "The Jews have agreed to ask you to bring Paul before the Sanhedrin[i] tomorrow on the pretext of wanting more accurate information about him.[j] [21]Don't give in to them, because more than forty[k] of them are waiting in ambush for him. They have taken an oath not to eat or drink until they have killed him.[l] They are ready now, waiting for your consent to their request."

[22]The commander dismissed the young man and cautioned him, "Don't tell anyone that you have reported this to me."

23:3
rLev 19:15;
Dt 25:1,2;
Jn 7:51
23:5
sEx 22:28
23:6
tAc 22:5
uAc 26:5;
Php 3:5
vAc 24:15,21;
26:8
23:8
wMt 22:23
23:9
xMk 2:16
yver 29;
Ac 25:25; 26:31
zAc 22:7,17,18
23:10
aAc 21:34
23:11
bAc 18:9
cAc 19:21;
28:23
23:12
dver 14,21,30;
Ac 25:3
23:14
ever 12
23:15
fver 1; Ac 22:30
23:16
gver 10;
Ac 21:34
23:18
hEph 3:1
23:20
iver 1 jver 14,15
23:21
kver 13 lver 12,
14

Paul Transferred to Caesarea

23Then he called two of his centurions and ordered them, "Get ready a detachment of two hundred soldiers, seventy horsemen and two hundred spearmen[a] to go to Caesarea[m] at nine tonight.[n] 24Provide mounts for Paul so that he may be taken safely to Governor Felix."[o]

25He wrote a letter as follows:

26Claudius Lysias,

To His Excellency,[p] Governor Felix:

Greetings.[q]

27This man was seized by the Jews and they were about to kill him,[r] but I came with my troops and rescued him,[s] for I had learned that he is a Roman citizen.[t] 28I wanted to know why they were accusing him, so I brought him to their Sanhedrin.[u] 29I found that the accusation had to do with questions about their law,[v] but there was no charge against him[w] that deserved death or imprisonment. 30When I was informed[x] of a plot[y] to be carried out against the man, I sent him to you at once. I also ordered his accusers[z] to present to you their case against him.

31So the soldiers, carrying out their orders, took Paul with them during the night and brought him as far as Antipatris. 32The next day they let the cavalry[a] go on with him, while they returned to the barracks.[b] 33When the cavalry[c] arrived in Caesarea,[d] they delivered the letter to the governor[e] and handed Paul over to him. 34The governor read the letter and asked what province he was from. Learning that he was from Cilicia,[f] 35he said, "I will hear your case when your accusers[g] get here." Then he ordered that Paul be kept under guard[h] in Herod's palace.

The Trial Before Felix

24 Five days later the high priest Ananias[i] went down to Caesarea with some of the elders and a lawyer named Tertullus, and they brought their charges[j] against Paul before the governor.[k] 2When Paul was called in, Tertullus presented his case before Felix: "We have enjoyed a long period of peace under you, and your foresight has brought about reforms in this nation. 3Everywhere and in every way, most excellent[l] Felix, we acknowledge this with profound gratitude. 4But in order not to weary you further, I would request that you be kind enough to hear us briefly.

5"We have found this man to be a troublemaker, stirring up riots[m] among the Jews[n] all over the world. He is a ringleader of the Nazarene[o] sect[p] 6and even tried to desecrate the temple;[q] so we seized him. 8By[b] examining him yourself you will be able to learn the truth about all these charges we are bringing against him."

23:23
m Ac 8:40
n ver 33
23:24
o ver 26,33;
Ac 24:1-3,10;
25:14
23:26
p Lk 1:3;
Ac 24:3; 26:25
q Ac 15:23
23:27
r Ac 21:32
s Ac 21:33
t Ac 22:25-29
23:28
u Ac 22:30
23:29
v Ac 18:15;
25:19 w ver 9;
Ac 26:31
23:30
x ver 20,21
y Ac 20:3
z ver 35;
Ac 24:19; 25:16
23:32
a ver 23
b Ac 21:34
23:33
c ver 23,24
d Ac 8:40
e ver 26
23:34
f Ac 6:9; 21:39
23:35
g ver 30;
Ac 24:19; 25:16
h Ac 24:27
24:1
i Ac 23:2
j Ac 23:30,35
k Ac 23:24
24:3
l Lk 1:3;
Ac 23:26; 26:25
24:5
m Ac 16:20;
17:6 n Ac 21:28
o Mk 1:24
p ver 14;
Ac 26:5; 28:22
24:6
q Ac 21:28

---

a23 The meaning of the Greek for this word is uncertain.   b6-8 Some manuscripts him and wanted to judge him according to our law. 7But the commander, Lysias, came and with the use of much force snatched him from our hands 8and ordered his accusers to come before you. By

9The Jews joined in the accusation,[r] asserting that these things were true.

10When the governor[s] motioned for him to speak, Paul replied: "I know that for a number of years you have been a judge over this nation; so I gladly make my defense. 11You can easily verify that no more than twelve days[t] ago I went up to Jerusalem to worship. 12My accusers did not find me arguing with anyone at the temple,[u] or stirring up a crowd[v] in the synagogues or anywhere else in the city. 13And they cannot prove to you the charges they are now making against me.[w] 14However, I admit that I worship the God of our fathers[x] as a follower of the Way,[y] which they call a sect.[z] I believe everything that agrees with the Law and that is written in the Prophets,[a] 15and I have the same hope in God as these men, that there will be a resurrection[b] of both the righteous and the wicked.[c] 16So I strive always to keep my conscience clear[d] before God and man.

17"After an absence of several years, I came to Jerusalem to bring my people gifts for the poor[e] and to present offerings. 18I was ceremonially clean[f] when they found me in the temple courts doing this. There was no crowd with me, nor was I involved in any disturbance.[g] 19But there are some Jews from the province of Asia, who ought to be here before you and bring charges if they have anything against me.[h] 20Or these who are here should state what crime they found in me when I stood before the Sanhedrin— 21unless it was this one thing I shouted as I stood in their presence: 'It is concerning the resurrection of the dead that I am on trial before you today.' "[i]

22Then Felix, who was well acquainted with the Way, adjourned the proceedings. "When Lysias the commander comes," he said, "I will decide your case." 23He ordered the centurion to keep Paul under guard[j] but to give him some freedom[k] and permit his friends to take care of his needs.[l]

24Several days later Felix came with his wife Drusilla, who was a Jewess. He sent for Paul and listened to him as he spoke about faith in Christ Jesus.[m] 25As Paul discoursed on righteousness, self-control[n] and the judgment[o] to come, Felix was afraid and said, "That's enough for now! You may leave. When I find it convenient, I will send for you." 26At the same time he was hoping that Paul would offer him a bribe, so he sent for him frequently and talked with him.

27When two years had passed, Felix was succeeded by Porcius Festus,[p] but because Felix wanted to grant a favor to the Jews,[q] he left Paul in prison.[r]

The Trial Before Festus

25 Three days after arriving in the province, Festus went up from Caesarea[s] to Jerusalem, 2where the chief priests and Jewish leaders appeared before him and presented the charges against Paul.[t] 3They urgently requested Festus, as a favor to them, to have Paul transferred to Jerusalem, for they were preparing an ambush to kill him along the way. 4Festus answered, "Paul is being held[u] at Caesarea, and I myself am going there soon. 5Let some of your leaders come with me and press charges against the man there, if he has done anything wrong."

6After spending eight or ten days with them, he went down to

24:9
r1Th 2:16
24:10
sAc 23:24
24:11
tAc 21:27; ver 1
24:12
uAc 25:8; 28:17
vver 18
24:13
wAc 25:7
24:14
xAc 3:13
yAc 9:2 zver 5
aAc 26:6,22;
28:23
24:15
bAc 23:6; 28:20
cDa 12:2;
Jn 5:28,29
24:16
dAc 23:1
24:17
eAc 11:29,30;
Ro 15:25-28,31;
1Co 16:1-4,15;
2Co 8:1-4;
Gal 2:10
24:18
fAc 21:26
gver 12
24:19
hAc 23:30
24:21
iAc 23:6
24:23
jAc 23:35
kAc 28:16
lAc 23:16; 27:3
24:24
mAc 20:21
24:25
nGal 5:23;
2Pe 1:6
oAc 10:42
24:27
pAc 25:1,4,9,14
qAc 12:3; 25:9
rAc 23:35;
25:14
25:1
sAc 8:40
25:2
tver 15; Ac 24:1
25:4
uAc 24:23

Caesarea, and the next day he convened the court[v] and ordered that Paul be brought before him. [7]When Paul appeared, the Jews who had come down from Jerusalem stood around him, bringing many serious charges against him,[w] which they could not prove.[x]

[8]Then Paul made his defense: "I have done nothing wrong against the law of the Jews or against the temple[y] or against Caesar."

[9]Festus, wishing to do the Jews a favor,[z] said to Paul, "Are you willing to go up to Jerusalem and stand trial before me there on these charges?"[a]

[10]Paul answered: "I am now standing before Caesar's court, where I ought to be tried. I have not done any wrong to the Jews, as you yourself know very well. [11]If, however, I am guilty of doing anything deserving death, I do not refuse to die. But if the charges brought against me by these Jews are not true, no one has the right to hand me over to them. I appeal to Caesar!"[b]

[12]After Festus had conferred with his council, he declared: "You have appealed to Caesar. To Caesar you will go!"

Festus Consults King Agrippa

[13]A few days later King Agrippa and Bernice arrived at Caesarea[c] to pay their respects to Festus. [14]Since they were spending many days there, Festus discussed Paul's case with the king. He said: "There is a man here whom Felix left as a prisoner.[d] [15]When I went to Jerusalem, the chief priests and elders of the Jews brought charges against him[e] and asked that he be condemned.

[16]"I told them that it is not the Roman custom to hand over any man before he has faced his accusers and has had an opportunity to defend himself against their charges.[f] [17]When they came here with me, I did not delay the case, but convened the court the next day and ordered the man to be brought in.[g] [18]When his accusers got up to speak, they did not charge him with any of the crimes I had expected. [19]Instead, they had some points of dispute[h] with him about their own religion[i] and about a dead man named Jesus who Paul claimed was alive. [20]I was at a loss how to investigate such matters; so I asked if he would be willing to go to Jerusalem and stand trial there on these charges.[j] [21]When Paul made his appeal to be held over for the Emperor's decision, I ordered him held until I could send him to Caesar."[k]

[22]Then Agrippa said to Festus, "I would like to hear this man myself."

He replied, "Tomorrow you will hear him."[l]

Paul Before Agrippa

26:12–18pp — Ac 9:3–8; 22:6–11

[23]The next day Agrippa and Bernice[m] came with great pomp and entered the audience room with the high ranking officers and the leading men of the city. At the command of Festus, Paul was brought in. [24]Festus said: "King Agrippa, and all who are present with us, you see this man! The whole Jewish community[n] has petitioned me about him in Jerusalem and here in Caesarea, shouting that he ought not to live any longer.[o] [25]I found he had done nothing deserving of death,[p] but because he made his appeal to the Emperor[q] I decided to send him to Rome. [26]But I have nothing definite to write to His Majesty about

25:6
vver 17
25:7
wMk 15:3;
Lk 23:2,10;
Ac 24:5,6
xAc 24:13
25:8
yAc 6:13;
24:12; 28:17
25:9
zAc 24:27
aver 20
25:11
bver 21,25;
Ac 26:32; 28:19
25:13
cAc 8:40
25:14
dAc 24:27
25:15
ever 2; Ac 24:1
25:16
fver 4,5;
Ac 23:30
25:17
gver 6,10
25:19
hAc 18:15;
23:29 iAc 17:22
25:20
jver 9
25:21
kver 11,12
25:22
lAc 9:15
25:23
mver 13;
Ac 26:30
25:24
nver 2,3,7
oAc 22:22
25:25
pAc 23:9
qver 11

him. Therefore I have brought him before all of you, and especially before you, King Agrippa, so that as a result of this investigation I may have something to write. [27]For I think it is unreasonable to send on a prisoner without specifying the charges against him."

26 Then Agrippa said to Paul, "You have permission to speak for yourself."[r]

So Paul motioned with his hand and began his defense: [2]"King Agrippa, I consider myself fortunate to stand before you today as I make my defense against all the accusations of the Jews, [3]and especially so because you are well acquainted with all the Jewish customs[s] and controversies.[t] Therefore, I beg you to listen to me patiently.

[4]"The Jews all know the way I have lived ever since I was a child,[u] from the beginning of my life in my own country, and also in Jerusalem. [5]They have known me for a long time[v] and can testify, if they are willing, that according to the strictest sect of our religion, I lived as a Pharisee.[w] [6]And now it is because of my hope[x] in what God has promised our fathers[y] that I am on trial today. [7]This is the promise our twelve tribes[z] are hoping to see fulfilled as they earnestly serve God day and night.[a] O king, it is because of this hope that the Jews are accusing me.[b] [8]Why should any of you consider it incredible that God raises the dead?[c]

[9]"I too was convinced[d] that I ought to do all that was possible to oppose[e] the name of Jesus of Nazareth.[f] [10]And that is just what I did in Jerusalem. On the authority of the chief priests I put many of the saints[g] in prison,[h] and when they were put to death, I cast my vote against them.[i] [11]Many a time I went from one synagogue to another to have them punished,[j] and I tried to force them to blaspheme. In my obsession against them, I even went to foreign cities to persecute them.

[12]"On one of these journeys I was going to Damascus with the authority and commission of the chief priests. [13]About noon, O king, as I was on the road, I saw a light from heaven, brighter than the sun, blazing around me and my companions. [14]We all fell to the ground, and I heard a voice[k] saying to me in Aramaic,[a] 'Saul, Saul, why do you persecute me? It is hard for you to kick against the goads.'

[15]"Then I asked, 'Who are you, Lord?'

" 'I am Jesus, whom you are persecuting,' the Lord replied. [16]'Now get up and stand on your feet.[l] I have appeared to you to appoint you as a servant and as a witness of what you have seen of me and what I will show you.[m] [17]I will rescue you[n] from your own people and from the Gentiles.[o] I am sending you to them [18]to open their eyes[p] and turn them from darkness to light,[q] and from the power of Satan to God, so that they may receive forgiveness of sins[r] and a place among those who are sanctified by faith in me.'[s]

[19]"So then, King Agrippa, I was not disobedient to the vision from heaven. [20]First to those in Damascus,[t] then to those in Jerusalem[u] and in all Judea, and to the Gentiles[v] also, I preached that they should repent[w] and turn to God and prove their repentance by their deeds.[x] [21]That is why the Jews seized me[y] in the temple courts and tried to kill me.[z] [22]But I have had God's help to this very day, and so I stand here and testify to small and great alike. I am saying nothing beyond what

---

[a]14 Or *Hebrew*

26:1
rAc 9:15; 25:22
26:3
sver 7; Ac 6:14
tAc 25:19
26:4
uGal 1:13,14;
Php 3:5
26:5
vAc 22:3
wAc 23:6;
Php 3:5
26:6
xAc 23:6;
24:15; 28:20
yAc 13:32;
Ro 15:8
26:7
zJas 1:1
a1Th 3:10;
1Ti 5:5 bver 2
26:8
cAc 23:6
26:9
d1Ti 1:13
eJn 16:2
fJn 15:21
26:10
gAc 9:13
hAc 8:3; 9:2,14,
21 iAc 22:20
26:11
jMt 10:17
26:14
kAc 9:7
26:16
lEze 2:1;
Da 10:11
mAc 22:14,15
26:17
nJer 1:8,19
oAc 9:15
26:18
pIsa 35:5
qIsa 42:7,16;
Eph 5:8;
Col 1:13;
1Pe 2:9
rLk 24:47;
Ac 2:38
sAc 20:21,32
26:20
tAc 9:19-25
uAc 9:26-29;
22:17-20
vAc 9:15; 13:46
wAc 3:19
xMt 3:8; Lk 3:8
26:21
yAc 21:27,30
zAc 21:31

the prophets and Moses said would happen[a]— 23that the Christ[a] would suffer and, as the first to rise from the dead,[b] would proclaim light to his own people and to the Gentiles."[c]

24At this point Festus interrupted Paul's defense. "You are out of your mind,[d] Paul!" he shouted. "Your great learning[e] is driving you insane."

25"I am not insane, most excellent[f] Festus," Paul replied. "What I am saying is true and reasonable. 26The king is familiar with these things,[g] and I can speak freely to him. I am convinced that none of this has escaped his notice, because it was not done in a corner. 27King Agrippa, do you believe the prophets? I know you do."

28Then Agrippa said to Paul, "Do you think that in such a short time you can persuade me to be a Christian?"[h]

29Paul replied, "Short time or long—I pray God that not only you but all who are listening to me today may become what I am, except for these chains."[i]

30The king rose, and with him the governor and Bernice[j] and those sitting with them. 31They left the room, and while talking with one another, they said, "This man is not doing anything that deserves death or imprisonment."[k]

32Agrippa said to Festus, "This man could have been set free[l] if he had not appealed to Caesar."[m]

Paul Sails for Rome

27 When it was decided that we[n] would sail for Italy,[o] Paul and some other prisoners were handed over to a centurion named Julius, who belonged to the Imperial Regiment.[p] 2We boarded a ship from Adramyttium about to sail for ports along the coast of the province of Asia,[q] and we put out to sea. Aristarchus,[r] a Macedonian[s] from Thessalonica,[t] was with us.

3The next day we landed at Sidon;[u] and Julius, in kindness to Paul,[v] allowed him to go to his friends so they might provide for his needs.[w] 4From there we put out to sea again and passed to the lee of Cyprus because the winds were against us.[x] 5When we had sailed across the open sea off the coast of Cilicia[y] and Pamphylia, we landed at Myra in Lycia. 6There the centurion found an Alexandrian ship[z] sailing for Italy[a] and put us on board. 7We made slow headway for many days and had difficulty arriving off Cnidus. When the wind did not allow us to hold our course,[b] we sailed to the lee of Crete,[c] opposite Salmone. 8We moved along the coast with difficulty and came to a place called Fair Havens, near the town of Lasea.

9Much time had been lost, and sailing had already become dangerous because by now it was after the Fast.[b][d] So Paul warned them, 10"Men, I can see that our voyage is going to be disastrous and bring great loss to ship and cargo, and to our own lives also."[e] 11But the centurion, instead of listening to what Paul said, followed the advice of the pilot and of the owner of the ship. 12Since the harbor was unsuitable to winter in, the majority decided that we should sail on, hoping to reach Phoenix and winter there. This was a harbor in Crete, facing both southwest and northwest.

---

[a]23 Or *Messiah*   [b]9 That is, the Day of Atonement (Yom Kippur)

26:22
aLk 24:27,44;
Ac 10:43; 24:14
26:23
b1Co 15:20,23;
Col 1:18;
Rev 1:5 cLk 2:32
26:24
dJn 10:20;
1Co 4:10
eJn 7:15
26:25
fAc 23:26
26:26
gver 3
26:28
hAc 11:26
26:29
iAc 21:33
26:30
jAc 25:23
26:31
kAc 23:9
26:32
lAc 28:18
mAc 25:11
27:1
nAc 16:10
oAc 18:2;
25:12,25
pAc 10:1
27:2
qAc 2:9
rAc 19:29
sAc 16:9
tAc 17:1
27:3
uMt 11:21
vver 43
wAc 24:23;
28:16
27:4
xver 7
27:5
yAc 6:9
27:6
zAc 28:11 aver 1
27:7
bver 4 cver 12,
13,21
27:9
dLev 16:29-31;
23:27-29;
Nu 29:7
27:10
ever 21

The Storm

13When a gentle south wind began to blow, they thought they had obtained what they wanted; so they weighed anchor and sailed along the shore of Crete. 14Before very long, a wind of hurricane force, f called the "northeaster," swept down from the island. 15The ship was caught by the storm and could not head into the wind; so we gave way to it and were driven along. 16As we passed to the lee of a small island called Cauda, we were hardly able to make the lifeboat secure. 17When the men had hoisted it aboard, they passed ropes under the ship itself to hold it together. Fearing that they would run aground g on the sandbars of Syrtis, they lowered the sea anchor and let the ship be driven along. 18We took such a violent battering from the storm that the next day they began to throw the cargo overboard. h 19On the third day, they threw the ship's tackle overboard with their own hands. 20When neither sun nor stars appeared for many days and the storm continued raging, we finally gave up all hope of being saved.

21After the men had gone a long time without food, Paul stood up before them and said: "Men, you should have taken my advice i not to sail from Crete; j then you would have spared yourselves this damage and loss. 22But now I urge you to keep up your courage, k because not one of you will be lost; only the ship will be destroyed. 23Last night an angel l of the God whose I am and whom I serve m stood beside me n 24and said, 'Do not be afraid, Paul. You must stand trial before Caesar; o and God has graciously given you the lives of all who sail with you.' p 25So keep up your courage, q men, for I have faith in God that it will happen just as he told me. r 26Nevertheless, we must run aground s on some island." t

The Shipwreck

27On the fourteenth night we were still being driven across the Adriatic a Sea, when about midnight the sailors sensed they were approaching land. 28They took soundings and found that the water was a hundred and twenty feet b deep. A short time later they took soundings again and found it was ninety feet c deep. 29Fearing that we would be dashed against the rocks, they dropped four anchors from the stern and prayed for daylight. 30In an attempt to escape from the ship, the sailors let the lifeboat u down into the sea, pretending they were going to lower some anchors from the bow. 31Then Paul said to the centurion and the soldiers, "Unless these men stay with the ship, you cannot be saved." v 32So the soldiers cut the ropes that held the lifeboat and let it fall away.

33Just before dawn Paul urged them all to eat. "For the last fourteen days," he said, "you have been in constant suspense and have gone without food—you haven't eaten anything. 34Now I urge you to take some food. You need it to survive. Not one of you will lose a single hair from his head." w 35After he said this, he took some bread and gave thanks to God in front of them all. Then he broke it x and began to eat. 36They were all encouraged y and ate some food themselves. 37Altogether there were 276 of us on board. 38When they had eaten as much as

27:14
f Mk 4:37
27:17
g ver 26,39
27:18
h ver 19,38;
Jnh 1:5
27:21
i ver 10 j ver 7
27:22
k ver 25,36
27:23
l Ac 5:19
m Ro 1:9
n Ac 18:9;
23:11; 2Ti 4:17
27:24
o Ac 23:11
p ver 44
27:25
q ver 22,36
r Ro 4:20,21
27:26
s ver 17,39
t Ac 28:1
27:30
u ver 16
27:31
v ver 24
27:34
w Mt 10:30
27:35
x Mt 14:19
27:36
y ver 22,25

---

a27 In ancient times the name referred to an area extending well south of Italy.   b28 Greek *twenty orguias* (about 37 meters)   c28 Greek *fifteen orguias* (about 27 meters) they wanted, they lightened the ship by throwing the grain into the sea.[z]

[39]When daylight came, they did not recognize the land, but they saw a bay with a sandy beach,[a] where they decided to run the ship aground if they could. [40]Cutting loose the anchors,[b] they left them in the sea and at the same time untied the ropes that held the rudders. Then they hoisted the foresail to the wind and made for the beach. [41]But the ship struck a sandbar and ran aground. The bow stuck fast and would not move, and the stern was broken to pieces by the pounding of the surf.[c]

[42]The soldiers planned to kill the prisoners to prevent any of them from swimming away and escaping. [43]But the centurion wanted to spare Paul's life[d] and kept them from carrying out their plan. He ordered those who could swim to jump overboard first and get to land. [44]The rest were to get there on planks or on pieces of the ship. In this way everyone reached land in safety.[e]

Ashore on Malta

28 Once safely on shore, we[f] found out that the island[g] was called Malta. [2]The islanders showed us unusual kindness. They built a fire and welcomed us all because it was raining and cold. [3]Paul gathered a pile of brushwood and, as he put it on the fire, a viper, driven out by the heat, fastened itself on his hand. [4]When the islanders saw the snake hanging from his hand,[h] they said to each other, "This man must be a murderer; for though he escaped from the sea, Justice has not allowed him to live."[i] [5]But Paul shook the snake off into the fire and suffered no ill effects.[j] [6]The people expected him to swell up or suddenly fall dead, but after waiting a long time and seeing nothing unusual happen to him, they changed their minds and said he was a god.[k]

[7]There was an estate nearby that belonged to Publius, the chief official of the island. He welcomed us to his home and for three days entertained us hospitably. [8]His father was sick in bed, suffering from fever and dysentery. Paul went in to see him and, after prayer,[l] placed his hands on him and healed him.[m] [9]When this had happened, the rest of the sick on the island came and were cured. [10]They honored us in many ways and when we were ready to sail, they furnished us with the supplies we needed.

Arrival at Rome

[11]After three months we put out to sea in a ship that had wintered in the island. It was an Alexandrian ship[n] with the figurehead of the twin gods Castor and Pollux. [12]We put in at Syracuse and stayed there three days. [13]From there we set sail and arrived at Rhegium. The next day the south wind came up, and on the following day we reached Puteoli. [14]There we found some brothers[o] who invited us to spend a week with them. And so we came to Rome. [15]The brothers[p] there had heard that we were coming, and they traveled as far as the Forum of Appius and the Three Taverns to meet us. At the sight of these men Paul thanked God and was encouraged. [16]When we got to Rome, Paul was allowed to live by himself, with a soldier to guard him.[q]

27:38
z ver 18; Jnh 1:5
27:39
a Ac 28:1
27:40
b ver 29
27:41
c 2Co 11:25
27:43
d ver 3
27:44
e ver 22,31
28:1
f Ac 16:10
g Ac 27:26,39
28:4
h Mk 16:18
i Lk 13:2,4
28:5
j Lk 10:19
28:6
k Ac 14:11
28:8
l Jas 5:14,15
m Ac 9:40
28:11
n Ac 27:6
28:14
o Ac 1:16
28:15
p Ac 1:16
28:16
q Ac 24:23; 27:3

Paul Preaches at Rome Under Guard

[17]Three days later he called together the leaders of the Jews.[r] When they had assembled, Paul said to them: "My brothers,[s] although I have done nothing against our people[t] or against the customs of our ancestors,[u] I was arrested in Jerusalem and handed over to the Romans. [18]They examined me[v] and wanted to release me,[w] because I was not guilty of any crime deserving death.[x] [19]But when the Jews objected, I was compelled to appeal to Caesar[y]—not that I had any charge to bring against my own people. [20]For this reason I have asked to see you and talk with you. It is because of the hope of Israel[z] that I am bound with this chain."[a]

[21]They replied, "We have not received any letters from Judea concerning you, and none of the brothers[b] who have come from there has reported or said anything bad about you. [22]But we want to hear what your views are, for we know that people everywhere are talking against this sect."[c]

[23]They arranged to meet Paul on a certain day, and came in even larger numbers to the place where he was staying. From morning till evening he explained and declared to them the kingdom of God[d] and tried to convince them about Jesus[e] from the Law of Moses and from the Prophets.[f] [24]Some were convinced by what he said, but others would not believe.[g] [25]They disagreed among themselves and began to leave after Paul had made this final statement: "The Holy Spirit spoke the truth to your forefathers when he said through Isaiah the prophet:

[26]" 'Go to this people and say,
　　"You will be ever hearing but never understanding;
　　　you will be ever seeing but never perceiving."
[27]For this people's heart has become calloused;[h]
　　they hardly hear with their ears,
　　and they have closed their eyes.
Otherwise they might see with their eyes,
　　hear with their ears,
　　understand with their hearts
and turn, and I would heal them.'[a] [i]

[28]"Therefore I want you to know that God's salvation[j] has been sent to the Gentiles,[k] and they will listen!"[b]

[30]For two whole years Paul stayed there in his own rented house and welcomed all who came to see him. [31]Boldly and without hindrance he preached the kingdom of God[l] and taught about the Lord Jesus Christ.

28:17
rAc 25:2
sAc 22:5
tAc 25:8
uAc 6:14
28:18
vAc 22:24
wAc 26:31,32
xAc 23:9
28:19
yAc 25:11
28:20
zAc 26:6,7
aAc 21:33
28:21
bAc 22:5
28:22
cAc 24:5,14
28:23
dAc 19:8
eAc 17:3
fAc 8:35
28:24
gAc 14:4
28:27
hPs 119:70
iIsa 6:9,10
28:28
jLk 2:30
kAc 13:46
28:31
lver 23; Mt 4:23

---

a27 Isaiah 6:9,10   b28 Some manuscripts *listen!"*   [29]*After he said this, the Jews left, arguing vigorously among themselves.*

Romans

Title and Background

When Paul wrote this letter, he was probably in Corinth on his third missionary journey. His work in the eastern Mediterranean was almost finished, and he greatly desired to visit the Roman church. At this time, however, he could not go to Rome, so he sent a letter there, intending to visit Rome while en route on a mission to Spain. This letter served as a theological introduction to that hoped-for personal ministry.

Author and Date of Writing

The writer of this letter was the apostle Paul, and it was probably written in the early spring of A.D. 57.

Theme and Message

Paul's primary theme in Romans is the basic gospel, God's plan of salvation and righteousness for all mankind, Jew and Gentile alike. "The gospel of God" (1:1) includes justification by faith, but it also embraces such related ideas as guilt, sanctification and security. Romans is the most comprehensive and systematic statement of the Christian faith in the Bible.

Outline

1:1
a1Co 1:1
bAc 9:15
c2Co 11:7

1:2
dGal 3:8

1:3
eJn 1:14

1:5
fAc 9:15
gAc 6:7

1:6
hRev 17:14

1:7
iRo 8:39

1 Paul, a servant of Christ Jesus, called to be an apostle[a] and set apart[b] for the gospel of God[c]— 2the gospel he promised beforehand through his prophets in the Holy Scriptures[d] 3regarding his Son, who as to his human nature[e] was a descendant of David, 4and who through the Spirit[a] of holiness was declared with power to be the Son of God[b] by his resurrection from the dead: Jesus Christ our Lord. 5Through him and for his name's sake, we received grace and apostleship to call people from among all the Gentiles[f] to the obedience that comes from faith.[g] 6And you also are among those who are called to belong to Jesus Christ. [h]

7To all in Rome who are loved by God[i] and called to be saints:

---

a4 Or who as to his spirit   b4 Or was appointed to be the Son of God with power

Grace and peace to you from God our Father and from the Lord Jesus Christ. [j]

Paul's Longing to Visit Rome

[8]First, I thank my God through Jesus Christ for all of you, [k] because your faith is being reported all over the world. [l] [9]God, whom I serve [m] with my whole heart in preaching the gospel of his Son, is my witness [n] how constantly I remember you [10]in my prayers at all times; and I pray that now at last by God's will the way may be opened for me to come to you. [o]

[11]I long to see you [p] so that I may impart to you some spiritual gift to make you strong— [12]that is, that you and I may be mutually encouraged by each other's faith. [13]I do not want you to be unaware, brothers, that I planned many times to come to you (but have been prevented from doing so until now) [q] in order that I might have a harvest among you, just as I have had among the other Gentiles.

[14]I am obligated [r] both to Greeks and non-Greeks, both to the wise and the foolish. [15]That is why I am so eager to preach the gospel also to you who are at Rome. [s]

[16]I am not ashamed of the gospel, [t] because it is the power of God [u] for the salvation of everyone who believes: first for the Jew, [v] then for the Gentile. [w] [17]For in the gospel a righteousness from God is revealed, [x] a righteousness that is by faith from first to last, [a] just as it is written: "The righteous will live by faith." [b] [y]

God's Wrath Against Mankind

[18]The wrath of God [z] is being revealed from heaven against all the godlessness and wickedness of men who suppress the truth by their wickedness, [19]since what may be known about God is plain to them, because God has made it plain to them. [a] [20]For since the creation of the world God's invisible qualities—his eternal power and divine nature —have been clearly seen, being understood from what has been made, [b] so that men are without excuse.

[21]For although they knew God, they neither glorified him as God nor gave thanks to him, but their thinking became futile and their foolish hearts were darkened. [c] [22]Although they claimed to be wise, they became fools [d] [23]and exchanged the glory of the immortal God for images [e] made to look like mortal man and birds and animals and reptiles.

[24]Therefore God gave them over [f] in the sinful desires of their hearts to sexual impurity for the degrading of their bodies with one another. [g] [25]They exchanged the truth of God for a lie, [h] and worshiped and served created things [i] rather than the Creator—who is forever praised. [j] Amen.

[26]Because of this, God gave them over [k] to shameful lusts. [l] Even their women exchanged natural relations for unnatural ones. [m] [27]In the same way the men also abandoned natural relations with women and were inflamed with lust for one another. Men committed indecent acts with other men, and received in themselves the due penalty for their perversion. [n]

[28]Furthermore, since they did not think it worthwhile to retain the

1:7
j 1Co 1:3
1:8
k 1Co 1:4
l Ro 16:19
1:9
m 2Ti 1:3
n Php 1:8
1:10
o Ro 15:32
1:11
p Ro 15:23
1:13
q Ro 15:22,23
1:14
r 1Co 9:16
1:15
s Ro 15:20
1:16
t 2Ti 1:8
u 1Co 1:18
v Ac 3:26
w Ro 2:9,10
1:17
x Ro 3:21
y Hab 2:4;
Gal 3:11;
Heb 10:38
1:18
z Eph 5:6;
Col 3:6
1:19
a Ac 14:17
1:20
b Ps 19:1-6
1:21
c Jer 2:5;
Eph 4:17,18
1:22
d 1Co 1:20,27
1:23
e Ps 106:20;
Jer 2:11;
Ac 17:29
1:24
f Eph 4:19
g 1Pe 4:3
1:25
h Isa 44:20
i Jer 10:14
j Ro 9:5
1:26
k ver 24,28
l 1Th 4:5
m Lev 18:22,23
1:27
n Lev 18:22;
20:13

---

a17 Or is from faith to faith   *b17 Hab. 2:4*

knowledge of God, he gave them over[o] to a depraved mind, to do what ought not to be done. [29]They have become filled with every kind of wickedness, evil, greed and depravity. They are full of envy, murder, strife, deceit and malice. They are gossips,[p] [30]slanderers, God-haters, insolent, arrogant and boastful; they invent ways of doing evil; they disobey their parents;[q] [31]they are senseless, faithless, heartless,[r] ruthless. [32]Although they know God's righteous decree that those who do such things deserve death,[s] they not only continue to do these very things but also approve[t] of those who practice them.

God's Righteous Judgment

2 You, therefore, have no excuse,[u] you who pass judgment on someone else, for at whatever point you judge the other, you are condemning yourself, because you who pass judgment do the same things.[v] [2]Now we know that God's judgment against those who do such things is based on truth. [3]So when you, a mere man, pass judgment on them and yet do the same things, do you think you will escape God's judgment? [4]Or do you show contempt for the riches[w] of his kindness,[x] tolerance[y] and patience,[z] not realizing that God's kindness leads you toward repentance?[a]

[5]But because of your stubbornness and your unrepentant heart, you are storing up wrath against yourself for the day of God's wrath, when his righteous judgment[b] will be revealed. [6]God "will give to each person according to what he has done."[ac] [7]To those who by persistence in doing good seek glory, honor[d] and immortality,[e] he will give eternal life. [8]But for those who are self-seeking and who reject the truth and follow evil,[f] there will be wrath and anger. [9]There will be trouble and distress for every human being who does evil: first for the Jew, then for the Gentile;[g] [10]but glory, honor and peace for everyone who does good: first for the Jew, then for the Gentile.[h] [11]For God does not show favoritism.[i]

[12]All who sin apart from the law will also perish apart from the law, and all who sin under the law[j] will be judged by the law. [13]For it is not those who hear the law who are righteous in God's sight, but it is those who obey[k] the law who will be declared righteous. [14](Indeed, when Gentiles, who do not have the law, do by nature things required by the law,[l] they are a law for themselves, even though they do not have the law, [15]since they show that the requirements of the law are written on their hearts, their consciences also bearing witness, and their thoughts now accusing, now even defending them.) [16]This will take place on the day when God will judge men's secrets[m] through Jesus Christ,[n] as my gospel[o] declares.

The Jews and the Law

[17]Now you, if you call yourself a Jew; if you rely on the law and brag about your relationship to God;[p] [18]if you know his will and approve of what is superior because you are instructed by the law; [19]if you are convinced that you are a guide for the blind, a light for those who are in the dark, [20]an instructor of the foolish, a teacher of infants, because you

1:28
over 24,26
1:29
p2Co 12:20
1:30
q2Ti 3:2
1:31
r2Ti 3:3
1:32
sRo 6:23
tPs 50:18;
Lk 11:48;
Ac 8:1; 22:20
2:1
uRo 1:20
v2Sa 12:5-7;
Mt 7:1,2
2:4
wRo 9:23;
Eph 1:7,18; 2:7
xRo 11:22
yRo 3:25
zEx 34:6
a2Pe 3:9
2:5
bJude 6
2:6
cPs 62:12;
Mt 16:27
2:7
dver 10
e1Co 15:53,54
2:8
f2Th 2:12
2:9
g1Pe 4:17
2:10
hver 9
2:11
iAc 10:34
2:12
jRo 3:19;
1Co 9:20,21
2:13
kJas 1:22,23,25
2:14
lAc 10:35
2:16
mEcc 12:14
nAc 10:42
oRo 16:25
2:17
pver 23;
Mic 3:11;
Ro 9:4

---

a6 Psalm 62:12; Prov. 24:12

have in the law the embodiment of knowledge and truth— [21]you, then, who teach others, do you not teach yourself? You who preach against stealing, do you steal?[q] [22]You who say that people should not commit adultery, do you commit adultery? You who abhor idols, do you rob temples?[r] [23]You who brag about the law,[s] do you dishonor God by breaking the law? [24]As it is written: "God's name is blasphemed among the Gentiles because of you."[a][t]

[25]Circumcision has value if you observe the law,[u] but if you break the law, you have become as though you had not been circumcised.[v] [26]If those who are not circumcised keep the law's requirements,[w] will they not be regarded as though they were circumcised?[x] [27]The one who is not circumcised physically and yet obeys the law will condemn you[y] who, even though you have the[b] written code and circumcision, are a lawbreaker.

[28]A man is not a Jew if he is only one outwardly,[z] nor is circumcision merely outward and physical.[a] [29]No, a man is a Jew if he is one inwardly; and circumcision is circumcision of the heart, by the Spirit,[b] not by the written code.[c] Such a man's praise is not from men, but from God.[d]

God's Faithfulness

3 What advantage, then, is there in being a Jew, or what value is there in circumcision? [2]Much in every way! First of all, they have been entrusted with the very words of God.[e]

[3]What if some did not have faith?[f] Will their lack of faith nullify God's faithfulness?[g] [4]Not at all! Let God be true,[h] and every man a liar.[i] As it is written:

> "So that you may be proved right when you speak
> and prevail when you judge."[c][j]

[5]But if our unrighteousness brings out God's righteousness more clearly, what shall we say? That God is unjust in bringing his wrath on us? (I am using a human argument.)[k] [6]Certainly not! If that were so, how could God judge the world?[l] [7]Someone might argue, "If my falsehood enhances God's truthfulness and so increases his glory,[m] why am I still condemned as a sinner?" [8]Why not say—as we are being slanderously reported as saying and as some claim that we say—"Let us do evil that good may result"?[n] Their condemnation is deserved.

No One Is Righteous

[9]What shall we conclude then? Are we any better[d]? Not at all! We have already made the charge that Jews and Gentiles alike are all under sin.[o] [10]As it is written:

> "There is no one righteous, not even one;
> [11] there is no one who understands,
>   no one who seeks God.
> [12]All have turned away,
>   they have together become worthless;

2:21
qMt 23:3,4
2:22
rAc 19:37
2:23
sver 17
2:24
tIsa 52:5;
Eze 36:22
2:25
uGal 5:3
vJer 4:4
2:26
wRo 8:4
x1Co 7:19
2:27
yMt 12:41,42
2:28
zMt 3:9;
Jn 8:39; Ro 9:6,
7 aGal 6:15
2:29
bPhp 3:3;
Col 2:11
cRo 7:6
dJn 5:44;
1Co 4:5;
2Co 10:18;
1Th 2:4;
1Pe 3:4
3:2
eDt 4:8;
Ps 147:19
3:3
fHeb 4:2
g2Ti 2:13
3:4
hJn 3:33
iPs 116:11
jPs 51:4
3:5
kRo 6:19;
Gal 3:15
3:6
lGe 18:25
3:7
mver 4
3:8
nRo 6:1
3:9
over 19,23;
Gal 3:22

a24 Isaiah 52:5; Ezek. 36:22   b27 Or *who, by means of a*   c4 Psalm 51:4   d9 Or *worse*

there is no one who does good,
    not even one."ᵃ ᴾ
13"Their throats are open graves;
    their tongues practice deceit."ᵇ ۹
"The poison of vipers is on their lips."ᶜ ʳ
14   "Their mouths are full of cursing and bitterness."ᵈ ˢ
15"Their feet are swift to shed blood;
16   ruin and misery mark their ways,
17and the way of peace they do not know."ᵉ
18   "There is no fear of God before their eyes."ᶠ ᵗ

¹⁹Now we know that whatever the law says,ᵘ it says to those who are under the law,ᵛ so that every mouth may be silenced and the whole world held accountable to God. ²⁰Therefore no one will be declared righteous in his sight by observing the law;ʷ rather, through the law we become conscious of sin.ˣ

Righteousness Through Faith

²¹But now a righteousness from God,ʸ apart from law, has been made known, to which the Law and the Prophets testify.ᶻ ²²This righteousness from God comes through faithᵃ in Jesus Christ to all who believe. There is no difference,ᵇ ²³for all have sinned and fall short of the glory of God, ²⁴and are justified freely by his graceᶜ through the redemptionᵈ that came by Christ Jesus. ²⁵God presented him as a sacrifice of atonement,ᵍᵉ through faith in his blood.ᶠ He did this to demonstrate his justice, because in his forbearance he had left the sins committed beforehand unpunishedᵍ— ²⁶he did it to demonstrate his justice at the present time, so as to be just and the one who justifies those who have faith in Jesus.

²⁷Where, then, is boasting?ʰ It is excluded. On what principle? On that of observing the law? No, but on that of faith. ²⁸For we maintain that a man is justified by faith apart from observing the law.ⁱ ²⁹Is God the God of Jews only? Is he not the God of Gentiles too? Yes, of Gentiles too,ʲ ³⁰since there is only one God, who will justify the circumcised by faith and the uncircumcised through that same faith.ᵏ ³¹Do we, then, nullify the law by this faith? Not at all! Rather, we uphold the law.

Abraham Justified by Faith

4 What then shall we say that Abraham, our forefather, discovered in this matter? ²If, in fact, Abraham was justified by works, he had something to boast about—but not before God.ˡ ³What does the Scripture say? "Abraham believed God, and it was credited to him as righteousness."ʰ ᵐ

⁴Now when a man works, his wages are not credited to him as a gift,ⁿ but as an obligation. ⁵However, to the man who does not work but trusts God who justifies the wicked, his faith is credited as righteousness. ⁶David says the same thing when he speaks of the blessedness of the man to whom God credits righteousness apart from works:

*Cross references (left margin):*

3:12
pPs 14:1-3
3:13
qPs 5:9
rPs 140:3
3:14
sPs 10:7
3:18
tPs 36:1
3:19
uJn 10:34
vRo 2:12
3:20
wAc 13:39;
Gal 2:16
xRo 7:7
3:21
yRo 1:17; 9:30
zAc 10:43
3:22
aRo 9:30
bRo 10:12;
Gal 3:28;
Col 3:11
3:24
cRo 4:16;
Eph 2:8
dEph 1:7,14;
Col 1:14;
Heb 9:12
3:25
e1Jn 4:10
fHeb 9:12,14
gAc 17:30
3:27
hRo 2:17,23;
4:2;
1Co 1:29-31;
Eph 2:9
3:28
iver 20,21;
Ac 13:39;
Eph 2:9
3:29
jRo 9:24
3:30
kGal 3:8
4:2
l1Co 1:31
4:3
mver 5,9,22;
Ge 15:6;
Gal 3:6;
Jas 2:23
4:4
nRo 11:6

ᵃ12 Psalms 14:1-3; 53:1-3; Eccles. 7:20   ᵇ13 Psalm 5:9   ᶜ13 Psalm 140:3   ᵈ14 Psalm 10:7
ᵉ17 Isaiah 59:7,8   ᶠ18 Psalm 36:1   ᵍ25 *Or as the one who would turn aside his wrath, taking away sin*   ʰ3 Gen. 15:6; also in verse 22

7"Blessed are they
   whose transgressions are forgiven,
   whose sins are covered.
8Blessed is the man
   whose sin the Lord will never count against him."[a] [o]

9Is this blessedness only for the circumcised, or also for the uncircumcised?[p] We have been saying that Abraham's faith was credited to him as righteousness. [q] 10Under what circumstances was it credited? Was it after he was circumcised, or before? It was not after, but before! 11And he received the sign of circumcision, a seal of the righteousness that he had by faith while he was still uncircumcised.[r] So then, he is the father[s] of all who believe[t] but have not been circumcised, in order that righteousness might be credited to them. 12And he is also the father of the circumcised who not only are circumcised but who also walk in the footsteps of the faith that our father Abraham had before he was circumcised.

13It was not through law that Abraham and his offspring received the promise[u] that he would be heir of the world,[v] but through the righteousness that comes by faith. 14For if those who live by law are heirs, faith has no value and the promise is worthless,[w] 15because law brings wrath.[x] And where there is no law there is no transgression.[y]

16Therefore, the promise comes by faith, so that it may be by grace[z] and may be guaranteed[a] to all Abraham's offspring—not only to those who are of the law but also to those who are of the faith of Abraham. He is the father of us all. 17As it is written: "I have made you a father of many nations."[bb] He is our father in the sight of God, in whom he believed—the God who gives life[c] to the dead and calls[d] things that are not[e] as though they were.

18Against all hope, Abraham in hope believed and so became the father of many nations,[f] just as it had been said to him, "So shall your offspring be."[c][g] 19Without weakening in his faith, he faced the fact that his body was as good as dead[h]—since he was about a hundred years old[i]—and that Sarah's womb was also dead.[j] 20Yet he did not waver through unbelief regarding the promise of God, but was strengthened in his faith and gave glory to God,[k] 21being fully persuaded that God had power to do what he had promised.[l] 22This is why "it was credited to him as righteousness."[m] 23The words "it was credited to him" were written not for him alone, 24but also for us,[n] to whom God will credit righteousness—for us who believe in him[o] who raised Jesus our Lord from the dead. [p] 25He was delivered over to death for our sins[q] and was raised to life for our justification.

Peace and Joy

5 Therefore, since we have been justified through faith,[r] we[d] have peace with God through our Lord Jesus Christ, 2through whom we have gained access[s] by faith into this grace in which we now stand.[t] And we[d] rejoice in the hope[u] of the glory of God. 3Not only so, but we[d] also rejoice in our sufferings,[v] because we know that suffering produces perseverance;[w] 4perseverance, character; and character, hope.

---

[a]8 Psalm 32:1,2   [b]17 Gen. 17:5   [c]18 Gen. 15:5   [d]1,2,3 Or *let us*

**Cross references (right column):**

4:8
o Ps 32:1,2;
2Co 5:19
4:9
p Ro 3:30 q ver 3
4:11
r Ge 17:10,11
s ver 16,17;
Lk 19:9 t Ro 3:22
4:13
u Gal 3:16,29
v Ge 17:4-6
4:14
w Gal 3:18
4:15
x Ro 7:7-25;
1Co 15:56;
2Co 3:7;
Gal 3:10;
Ro 7:12
y Ro 3:20; 7:7
4:16
z Ro 3:24
a Ro 15:8
4:17
b Ge 17:5
c Jn 5:21
d Isa 48:13
e 1Co 1:28
4:18
f ver 17
g Ge 15:5
4:19
h Heb 11:11,12
i Ge 17:17
j Ge 18:11
4:20
k Mt 9:8
4:21
l Ge 18:14;
Heb 11:19
4:22
m ver 3
4:24
n Ro 15:4;
1Co 9:10; 10:11
o Ro 10:9
p Ac 2:24
4:25
q Isa 53:5,6;
Ro 5:6,8
5:1
r Ro 3:28
5:2
s Eph 2:18
t 1Co 15:1
u Heb 3:6
5:3
v Mt 5:12
w Jas 1:2,3

5:5
xPhp 1:20
yAc 2:33
5:6
zGal 4:4
aRo 4:25
5:8
bJn 15:13;
1Pe 3:18
5:9
cRo 3:25
dRo 1:18
5:10
eRo 11:28;
Col 1:21
f2Co 5:18,19;
Col 1:20,22
gRo 8:34
5:12
hver 15,16,17;
1Co 15:21,22
iGe 2:17; 3:19;
Ro 6:23
5:13
jRo 4:15
5:14
k1Co 15:22,45
5:15
lver 12,18,19
mAc 15:11
5:17
nver 12
5:18
over 12
pRo 4:25
5:19
qver 12
rPhp 2:8
5:20
sRo 7:7,8;
Gal 3:19
t1Ti 1:13,14
5:21
uver 12,14
6:1
vver 15; Ro 3:5,
8
6:2
wCol 3:3,5;
1Pe 2:24
6:3
xMt 28:19
6:4
yCol 2:12
zRo 7:6;
Gal 6:15;
Eph 4:22-24;
Col 3:10

[5]And hope[x] does not disappoint us, because God has poured out his love into our hearts by the Holy Spirit,[y] whom he has given us.

[6]You see, at just the right time,[z] when we were still powerless, Christ died for the ungodly.[a] [7]Very rarely will anyone die for a righteous man, though for a good man someone might possibly dare to die. [8]But God demonstrates his own love for us in this: While we were still sinners, Christ died for us.[b]

[9]Since we have now been justified by his blood,[c] how much more shall we be saved from God's wrath[d] through him! [10]For if, when we were God's enemies,[e] we were reconciled[f] to him through the death of his Son, how much more, having been reconciled, shall we be saved through his life![g] [11]Not only is this so, but we also rejoice in God through our Lord Jesus Christ, through whom we have now received reconciliation.

Death Through Adam, Life Through Christ

[12]Therefore, just as sin entered the world through one man,[h] and death through sin,[i] and in this way death came to all men, because all sinned— [13]for before the law was given, sin was in the world. But sin is not taken into account when there is no law.[j] [14]Nevertheless, death reigned from the time of Adam to the time of Moses, even over those who did not sin by breaking a command, as did Adam, who was a pattern of the one to come.[k]

[15]But the gift is not like the trespass. For if the many died by the trespass of the one man,[l] how much more did God's grace and the gift that came by the grace of the one man, Jesus Christ,[m] overflow to the many! [16]Again, the gift of God is not like the result of the one man's sin: The judgment followed one sin and brought condemnation, but the gift followed many trespasses and brought justification. [17]For if, by the trespass of the one man, death[n] reigned through that one man, how much more will those who receive God's abundant provision of grace and of the gift of righteousness reign in life through the one man, Jesus Christ.

[18]Consequently, just as the result of one trespass was condemnation for all men,[o] so also the result of one act of righteousness was justification[p] that brings life for all men. [19]For just as through the disobedience of the one man[q] the many were made sinners, so also through the obedience[r] of the one man the many will be made righteous.

[20]The law was added so that the trespass might increase.[s] But where sin increased, grace increased all the more,[t] [21]so that, just as sin reigned in death,[u] so also grace might reign through righteousness to bring eternal life through Jesus Christ our Lord.

Dead to Sin, Alive in Christ

6 What shall we say, then? Shall we go on sinning so that grace may increase?[v] [2]By no means! We died to sin;[w] how can we live in it any longer? [3]Or don't you know that all of us who were baptized[x] into Christ Jesus were baptized into his death? [4]We were therefore buried with him through baptism into death in order that, just as Christ was raised from the dead[y] through the glory of the Father, we too may live a new life.[z]

[5]If we have been united with him like this in his death, we will

certainly also be united with him in his resurrection.ᵃ ⁶For we know that our old selfᵇ was crucified with himᶜ so that the body of sinᵈ might be done away with,ᵃ that we should no longer be slaves to sin— ⁷because anyone who has died has been freed from sin.

⁸Now if we died with Christ, we believe that we will also live with him. ⁹For we know that since Christ was raised from the dead,ᵉ he cannot die again; death no longer has mastery over him. ᶠ ¹⁰The death he died, he died to sinᵍ once for all; but the life he lives, he lives to God.

¹¹In the same way, count yourselves dead to sinʰ but alive to God in Christ Jesus. ¹²Therefore do not let sin reign in your mortal body so that you obey its evil desires. ¹³Do not offer the parts of your body to sin, as instruments of wickedness,ⁱ but rather offer yourselves to God, as those who have been brought from death to life; and offer the parts of your body to him as instruments of righteousness.ʲ ¹⁴For sin shall not be your master, because you are not under law,ᵏ but under grace.ˡ

Slaves to Righteousness

¹⁵What then? Shall we sin because we are not under law but under grace? By no means! ¹⁶Don't you know that when you offer yourselves to someone to obey him as slaves, you are slaves to the one whom you obey—whether you are slaves to sin,ᵐ which leads to death,ⁿ or to obedience, which leads to righteousness? ¹⁷But thanks be to Godᵒ that, though you used to be slaves to sin, you wholeheartedly obeyed the form of teachingᵖ to which you were entrusted. ¹⁸You have been set free from sin�q and have become slaves to righteousness.

¹⁹I put this in human termsʳ because you are weak in your natural selves. Just as you used to offer the parts of your body in slavery to impurity and to ever-increasing wickedness, so now offer them in slavery to righteousnessˢ leading to holiness. ²⁰When you were slaves to sin,ᵗ you were free from the control of righteousness. ²¹What benefit did you reap at that time from the things you are now ashamed of? Those things result in death!ᵘ ²²But now that you have been set free from sinᵛ and have become slaves to God,ʷ the benefit you reap leads to holiness, and the result is eternal life. ²³For the wages of sin is death,ˣ but the gift of God is eternal lifeʸ inᵇ Christ Jesus our Lord.

An Illustration From Marriage

7 Do you not know, brothersᶻ—for I am speaking to men who know the law—that the law has authority over a man only as long as he lives? ²For example, by law a married woman is bound to her husband as long as he is alive, but if her husband dies, she is released from the law of marriage.ᵃ ³So then, if she marries another man while her husband is still alive, she is called an adulteress. But if her husband dies, she is released from that law and is not an adulteress, even though she marries another man.

⁴So, my brothers, you also died to the lawᵇ through the body of Christ,ᶜ that you might belong to another, to him who was raised from the dead, in order that we might bear fruit to God. ⁵For when we were controlled by the sinful nature,ᶜ the sinful passions aroused by the lawᵈ were at work in our bodies,ᵉ so that we bore fruit for death. ⁶But

---

6:5
a 2Co 4:10;
Php 3:10,11
6:6
b Eph 4:22;
Col 3:9
c Gal 2:20;
Col 2:12,20
d Ro 7:24
6:9
e Ac 2:24
f Rev 1:18
6:10
g ver 2
6:11
h ver 2
6:13
i ver 16,19;
Ro 7:5
j Ro 12:1;
1Pe 2:24
6:14
k Gal 5:18
l Ro 3:24
6:16
m Jn 8:34;
2Pe 2:19
n ver 23
6:17
o Ro 1:8;
2Co 2:14
p 2Ti 1:13
6:18
q ver 7,22;
Ro 8:2
6:19
r Ro 3:5 s ver 13
6:20
t ver 16
6:21
u ver 23
6:22
v ver 18
w 1Co 7:22;
1Pe 2:16
6:23
x Ge 2:17;
Ro 5:12;
Gal 6:7,8;
Jas 1:15
y Mt 25:46
7:1
z Ro 1:13
7:2
a 1Co 7:39
7:4
b Ro 8:2;
Gal 2:19
c Col 1:22
7:5
d Ro 7:7-11
e Ro 6:13

ᵃ6 Or *be rendered powerless*   ᵇ23 Or *through*   ᶜ5 Or *the flesh; also in verse 25* now, by dying to what once bound us, we have been released from the law so that we serve in the new way of the Spirit, and not in the old way of the written code. f

Struggling With Sin

7What shall we say, then? Is the law sin? Certainly not! Indeed I would not have known what sin was except through the law. g For I would not have known what coveting really was if the law had not said, "Do not covet." a h 8But sin, seizing the opportunity afforded by the commandment, i produced in me every kind of covetous desire. For apart from law, sin is dead. j 9Once I was alive apart from law; but when the commandment came, sin sprang to life and I died. 10I found that the very commandment that was intended to bring life k actually brought death. 11For sin, seizing the opportunity afforded by the commandment, deceived me, l and through the commandment put me to death. 12So then, the law is holy, and the commandment is holy, righteous and good. m

13Did that which is good, then, become death to me? By no means! But in order that sin might be recognized as sin, it produced death in me through what was good, so that through the commandment sin might become utterly sinful.

14We know that the law is spiritual; but I am unspiritual, n sold o as a slave to sin. 15I do not understand what I do. For what I want to do I do not do, but what I hate I do. p 16And if I do what I do not want to do, I agree that the law is good. q 17As it is, it is no longer I myself who do it, but it is sin living in me. r 18I know that nothing good lives in me, that is, in my sinful nature. b s For I have the desire to do what is good, but I cannot carry it out. 19For what I do is not the good I want to do; no, the evil I do not want to do—this I keep on doing. t 20Now if I do what I do not want to do, it is no longer I who do it, but it is sin living in me that does it. u

21So I find this law at work: v When I want to do good, evil is right there with me. 22For in my inner being w I delight in God's law; x 23but I see another law at work in the members of my body, waging war y against the law of my mind and making me a prisoner of the law of sin at work within my members. 24What a wretched man I am! Who will rescue me from this body of death? z 25Thanks be to God—through Jesus Christ our Lord!

So then, I myself in my mind am a slave to God's law, but in the sinful nature a slave to the law of sin.

Life Through the Spirit

8 Therefore, there is now no condemnation a for those who are in Christ Jesus, c b 2because through Christ Jesus the law of the Spirit of life c set me free d from the law of sin e and death. 3For what the law was powerless f to do in that it was weakened by the sinful nature, d God did by sending his own Son in the likeness of sinful man g to be a sin offering. e h And so he condemned sin in sinful man, f 4in order that

7:6
f Ro 2:29;
2Co 3:6
7:7
g Ro 3:20; 4:15
h Ex 20:17;
Dt 5:21
7:8
i ver 11
j Ro 4:15;
1Co 15:56
7:10
k Lev 18:5;
Lk 10:26-28;
Ro 10:5;
Gal 3:12
7:11
l Ge 3:13
7:12
m 1Ti 1:8
7:14
n 1Co 3:1
o 1Ki 21:20,25;
2Ki 17:17
7:15
p ver 19;
Gal 5:17
7:16
q ver 12
7:17
r ver 20
7:18
s ver 25
7:19
t ver 15
7:20
u ver 17
7:21
v ver 23,25
7:22
w Eph 3:16
x Ps 1:2
7:23
y Gal 5:17;
Jas 4:1;
1Pe 2:11
7:24
z Ro 6:6; 8:2
8:1
a ver 34 b ver 39;
Ro 16:3
8:2
c 1Co 15:45
d Ro 6:18
e Ro 7:4
8:3
f Ac 13:39;
Heb 7:18
g Php 2:7
h Heb 2:14,17

a7 Exodus 20:17; Deut. 5:21   b18 Or *my flesh*   c1 Some later manuscripts *Jesus, who do not live according to the sinful nature but according to the Spirit,*   d3 Or *the flesh; also in verses 4, 5, 8, 9, 12 and 13*   e3 Or *man, for sin*   f3 Or *in the flesh* the righteous requirements of the law might be fully met in us, who do not live according to the sinful nature but according to the Spirit. [i]

[5]Those who live according to the sinful nature have their minds set on what that nature desires;[j] but those who live in accordance with the Spirit have their minds set on what the Spirit desires. [k] [6]The mind of sinful man[a] is death, but the mind controlled by the Spirit is life[l] and peace; [7]the sinful mind[b] is hostile to God. [m] It does not submit to God's law, nor can it do so. [8]Those controlled by the sinful nature cannot please God.

[9]You, however, are controlled not by the sinful nature but by the Spirit, if the Spirit of God lives in you. [n] And if anyone does not have the Spirit of Christ, [o] he does not belong to Christ. [10]But if Christ is in you,[p] your body is dead because of sin, yet your spirit is alive because of righteousness. [11]And if the Spirit of him who raised Jesus from the dead[q] is living in you, he who raised Christ from the dead will also give life to your mortal bodies[r] through his Spirit, who lives in you.

[12]Therefore, brothers, we have an obligation—but it is not to the sinful nature, to live according to it. [13]For if you live according to the sinful nature, you will die; but if by the Spirit you put to death the misdeeds of the body, you will live,[s] [14]because those who are led by the Spirit of God[t] are sons of God. [u] [15]For you did not receive a spirit that makes you a slave again to fear,[v] but you received the Spirit of sonship.[c] And by him we cry, *"Abba,[d] Father."*[w] [16]The Spirit himself testifies with our spirit[x] that we are God's children. [17]Now if we are children, then we are heirs[y]—heirs of God and co-heirs with Christ, if indeed we share in his sufferings in order that we may also share in his glory. [z]

Future Glory

[18]I consider that our present sufferings are not worth comparing with the glory that will be revealed in us. [a] [19]The creation waits in eager expectation for the sons of God to be revealed. [20]For the creation was subjected to frustration, not by its own choice, but by the will of the one who subjected it, [b] in hope [21]that[e] the creation itself will be liberated from its bondage to decay[c] and brought into the glorious freedom of the children of God.

[22]We know that the whole creation has been groaning[d] as in the pains of childbirth right up to the present time. [23]Not only so, but we ourselves, who have the firstfruits of the Spirit,[e] groan[f] inwardly as we wait eagerly[g] for our adoption as sons, the redemption of our bodies. [24]For in this hope we were saved. [h] But hope that is seen is no hope at all. Who hopes for what he already has? [25]But if we hope for what we do not yet have, we wait for it patiently.

[26]In the same way, the Spirit helps us in our weakness. We do not know what we ought to pray for, but the Spirit himself intercedes for us[i] with groans that words cannot express. [27]And he who searches our hearts[j] knows the mind of the Spirit, because the Spirit intercedes for the saints in accordance with God's will.

8:4
i Gal 5:16
8:5
j Gal 5:19-21
k Gal 5:22-25
8:6
l Gal 6:8
8:7
m Jas 4:4
8:9
n 1Co 6:19;
Gal 4:6
o Jn 14:17;
1Jn 4:13
8:10
p Gal 2:20;
Eph 3:17;
Col 1:27
8:11
q Ac 2:24
r Jn 5:21
8:13
s Gal 6:8
8:14
t Gal 5:18
u Jn 1:12;
Rev 21:7
8:15
v 2Ti 1:7;
Heb 2:15
w Mk 14:36;
Gal 4:5,6
8:16
x Eph 1:13
8:17
y Ac 20:32;
Gal 4:7
z 1Pe 4:13
8:18
a 2Co 4:17;
1Pe 4:13
8:20
b Ge 3:17-19
8:21
c Ac 3:21;
2Pe 3:13;
Rev 21:1
8:22
d Jer 12:4
8:23
e 2Co 5:5
f 2Co 5:2,4
g Gal 5:5
8:24
h 1Th 5:8
8:26
i Eph 6:18
8:27
j Rev 2:23

---

a6 Or mind set on the flesh   b7 Or the mind set on the flesh   c15 Or adoption   d15 Aramaic for Father   e20,21 Or subjected it in hope. 21For

More Than Conquerors

28And we know that in all things God works for the good of those who love him,[a] who[b] have been called[k] according to his purpose. 29For those God foreknew[l] he also predestined[m] to be conformed to the likeness of his Son,[n] that he might be the firstborn among many brothers. 30And those he predestined,[o] he also called; those he called, he also justified;[p] those he justified, he also glorified.[q]

31What, then, shall we say in response to this?[r] If God is for us, who can be against us?[s] 32He who did not spare his own Son,[t] but gave him up for us all—how will he not also, along with him, graciously give us all things? 33Who will bring any charge[u] against those whom God has chosen? It is God who justifies. 34Who is he that condemns? Christ Jesus, who died[v]—more than that, who was raised to life—is at the right hand of God[w] and is also interceding for us.[x] 35Who shall separate us from the love of Christ? Shall trouble or hardship or persecution or famine or nakedness or danger or sword?[y] 36As it is written:

> "For your sake we face death all day long;
>   we are considered as sheep to be slaughtered."[c][z]

37No, in all these things we are more than conquerors[a] through him who loved us.[b] 38For I am convinced that neither death nor life, neither angels nor demons,[d] neither the present nor the future, nor any powers,[c] 39neither height nor depth, nor anything else in all creation, will be able to separate us from the love of God[d] that is in Christ Jesus our Lord.

God's Sovereign Choice

9 I speak the truth in Christ—I am not lying,[e] my conscience confirms[f] it in the Holy Spirit— 2I have great sorrow and unceasing anguish in my heart. 3For I could wish that I myself[g] were cursed[h] and cut off from Christ for the sake of my brothers, those of my own race,[i] 4the people of Israel. Theirs is the adoption as sons;[j] theirs the divine glory, the covenants,[k] the receiving of the law,[l] the temple worship[m] and the promises.[n] 5Theirs are the patriarchs, and from them is traced the human ancestry of Christ,[o] who is God over all,[p] forever praised![q] Amen.

6It is not as though God's word had failed. For not all who are descended from Israel are Israel.[r] 7Nor because they are his descendants are they all Abraham's children. On the contrary, "It is through Isaac that your offspring will be reckoned."[f][s] 8In other words, it is not the natural children who are God's children,[t] but it is the children of the promise who are regarded as Abraham's offspring. 9For this was how the promise was stated: "At the appointed time I will return, and Sarah will have a son."[g][u]

10Not only that, but Rebekah's children had one and the same father, our father Isaac.[v] 11Yet, before the twins were born or had done any-

---

a28 Some manuscripts *And we know that all things work together for good to those who love God* b28 Or *works together with those who love him to bring about what is good—with those who* c36 Psalm 44:22 d38 Or *nor heavenly rulers* e5 Or *Christ, who is over all. God be forever praised! Or Christ. God who is over all be forever praised!* f7 Gen. 21:12 g9 Gen. 18:10,14 thing good or bad—in order that God's purpose[w] in election might stand: [12]not by works but by him who calls—she was told, "The older will serve the younger."[ax] [13]Just as it is written: "Jacob I loved, but Esau I hated."[by]

[14]What then shall we say? Is God unjust? Not at all![z] [15]For he says to Moses,

> "I will have mercy on whom I have mercy,
> and I will have compassion on whom I have
> compassion."[ca]

[16]It does not, therefore, depend on man's desire or effort, but on God's mercy.[b] [17]For the Scripture says to Pharaoh: "I raised you up for this very purpose, that I might display my power in you and that my name might be proclaimed in all the earth."[dc] [18]Therefore God has mercy on whom he wants to have mercy, and he hardens whom he wants to harden.[d]

[19]One of you will say to me:[e] "Then why does God still blame us? For who resists his will?"[f] [20]But who are you, O man, to talk back to God? "Shall what is formed say to him who formed it,[g] 'Why did you make me like this?' "[eh] [21]Does not the potter have the right to make out of the same lump of clay some pottery for noble purposes and some for common use?[i]

[22]What if God, choosing to show his wrath and make his power known, bore with great patience[j] the objects of his wrath—prepared for destruction? [23]What if he did this to make the riches of his glory[k] known to the objects of his mercy, whom he prepared in advance for glory[l]— [24]even us, whom he also called,[m] not only from the Jews but also from the Gentiles?[n] [25]As he says in Hosea:

> "I will call them 'my people' who are not my people;
> and I will call her 'my loved one' who is not my loved
> one,"[fo]

[26]and,

> "It will happen that in the very place where it was said
> to them,
> 'You are not my people,'
> they will be called 'sons of the living God.' "[gp]

[27]Isaiah cries out concerning Israel:

> "Though the number of the Israelites be like the sand by
> the sea,[q]
> only the remnant will be saved.[r]
> [28]For the Lord will carry out
> his sentence on earth with speed and finality."[hs]

[29]It is just as Isaiah said previously:

> "Unless the Lord Almighty[t]
> had left us descendants,

9:11
w Ro 8:28
9:12
x Ge 25:23
9:13
y Mal 1:2,3
9:14
z 2Ch 19:7
9:15
a Ex 33:19
9:16
b Eph 2:8
9:17
c Ex 9:16
9:18
d Ex 4:21
9:19
e Ro 11:19
f 2Ch 20:6;
Da 4:35
9:20
g Isa 64:8
h Isa 29:16
9:21
i 2Ti 2:20
9:22
j Ro 2:4
9:23
k Ro 2:4
l Ro 8:30
9:24
m Ro 8:28
n Ro 3:29
9:25
o Hos 2:23;
1Pe 2:10
9:26
p Hos 1:10
9:27
q Ge 22:17;
Hos 1:10
r Ro 11:5
9:28
s Isa 10:22,23
9:29
t Jas 5:4

---

a12 Gen. 25:23　　b13 Mal. 1:2,3　　c15 Exodus 33:19　　d17 Exodus 9:16
e20 Isaiah 29:16; 45:9　　f25 Hosea 2:23　　g26 Hosea 1:10　　h28 Isaiah 10:22,23

we would have become like Sodom,
we would have been like Gomorrah."*a u*

Israel's Unbelief

30What then shall we say? That the Gentiles, who did not pursue righteousness, have obtained it, a righteousness that is by faith;*v* 31but Israel, who pursued a law of righteousness,*w* has not attained it.*x* 32Why not? Because they pursued it not by faith but as if it were by works. They stumbled over the "stumbling stone."*y* 33As it is written:

"See, I lay in Zion a stone that causes men to stumble
and a rock that makes them fall,
and the one who trusts in him will never be put to
shame."*b z*

10 Brothers, my heart's desire and prayer to God for the Israelites is that they may be saved. 2For I can testify about them that they are zealous*a* for God, but their zeal is not based on knowledge. 3Since they did not know the righteousness that comes from God and sought to establish their own, they did not submit to God's righteousness.*b* 4Christ is the end of the law*c* so that there may be righteousness for everyone who believes.*d*

5Moses describes in this way the righteousness that is by the law: "The man who does these things will live by them."*c e* 6But the righteousness that is by faith*f* says: "Do not say in your heart, 'Who will ascend into heaven?'*d*"*g* (that is, to bring Christ down) 7"or 'Who will descend into the deep?'*e*" (that is, to bring Christ up from the dead). 8But what does it say? "The word is near you; it is in your mouth and in your heart,"*f h* that is, the word of faith we are proclaiming: 9That if you confess*i* with your mouth, "Jesus is Lord," and believe in your heart that God raised him from the dead,*j* you will be saved. 10For it is with your heart that you believe and are justified, and it is with your mouth that you confess and are saved. 11As the Scripture says, "Anyone who trusts in him will never be put to shame."*g k* 12For there is no difference between Jew and Gentile*l*—the same Lord is Lord of all*m* and richly blesses all who call on him, 13for, "Everyone who calls on the name of the Lord*n* will be saved."*h o*

14How, then, can they call on the one they have not believed in? And how can they believe in the one of whom they have not heard? And how can they hear without someone preaching to them? 15And how can they preach unless they are sent? As it is written, "How beautiful are the feet of those who bring good news!"*i p*

16But not all the Israelites accepted the good news. For Isaiah says, "Lord, who has believed our message?"*j q* 17Consequently, faith comes from hearing the message,*r* and the message is heard through the word of Christ.*s* 18But I ask: Did they not hear? Of course they did:

"Their voice has gone out into all the earth,
their words to the ends of the world."*k t*

a29 Isaiah 1:9   b33 Isaiah 8:14; 28:16   c5 Lev. 18:5   d6 Deut. 30:12   e7 Deut. 30:13
f8 Deut. 30:14   g11 Isaiah 28:16   h13 Joel 2:32   i15 Isaiah 52:7   j16 Isaiah 53:1
k18 Psalm 19:4

[19]Again I ask: Did Israel not understand? First, Moses says,

> "I will make you envious[u] by those who are not a
>   nation;
> I will make you angry by a nation that has no
>   understanding."[a v]

[20]And Isaiah boldly says,

> "I was found by those who did not seek me;
> I revealed myself to those who did not ask for me."[b w]

[21]But concerning Israel he says,

> "All day long I have held out my hands
>   to a disobedient and obstinate people."[c x]

The Remnant of Israel

11 I ask then: Did God reject his people? By no means![y] I am an Israelite myself, a descendant of Abraham,[z] from the tribe of Benjamin.[a] [2]God did not reject his people, whom he foreknew.[b] Don't you know what the Scripture says in the passage about Elijah—how he appealed to God against Israel: [3]"Lord, they have killed your prophets and torn down your altars; I am the only one left, and they are trying to kill me"[d?c] [4]And what was God's answer to him? "I have reserved for myself seven thousand who have not bowed the knee to Baal."[ed] [5]So too, at the present time there is a remnant[e] chosen by grace. [6]And if by grace, then it is no longer by works;[f] if it were, grace would no longer be grace.[f]

[7]What then? What Israel sought so earnestly it did not obtain,[g] but the elect did. The others were hardened,[h] [8]as it is written:

> "God gave them a spirit of stupor,
>   eyes so that they could not see
>   and ears so that they could not hear,[i]
> to this very day."[g i]

[9]And David says:

> "May their table become a snare and a trap,
>   a stumbling block and a retribution for them.
> [10]May their eyes be darkened so they cannot see,
>   and their backs be bent forever."[h k]

Ingrafted Branches

[11]Again I ask: Did they stumble so as to fall beyond recovery? Not at all![l] Rather, because of their transgression, salvation has come to the Gentiles[m] to make Israel envious.[n] [12]But if their transgression means riches for the world, and their loss means riches for the Gentiles,[o] how much greater riches will their fullness bring!

[13]I am talking to you Gentiles. Inasmuch as I am the apostle to the Gentiles,[p] I make much of my ministry [14]in the hope that I may some-

10:19
uRo 11:11,14
vDt 32:21
10:20
wIsa 65:1;
Ro 9:30
10:21
xIsa 65:2
11:1
y1Sa 12:22;
Jer 31:37
z2Co 11:22
aPhp 3:5
11:2
bRo 8:29
11:3
c1Ki 19:10,14
11:4
d1Ki 19:18
11:5
eRo 9:27
11:6
fRo 4:4
11:7
gRo 9:31
hver 25;
Ro 9:18
11:8
iMt 13:13-15
jDt 29:4;
Isa 29:10
11:10
kPs 69:22,23
11:11
lver 1
mAc 13:46
nRo 10:19
11:12
over 25
11:13
pAc 9:15

---

a19 Deut. 32:21   *b20* Isaiah 65:1   *c21* Isaiah 65:2   *d3* 1 Kings 19:10,14
e4 1 Kings 19:18   *f6* Some manuscripts *by grace. But if by works, then it is no longer grace; if it were, work would no longer be work.*   *g8* Deut. 29:4; Isaiah 29:10   *h10* Psalm 69:22,23

how arouse my own people to envy[q] and save[r] some of them. [15]For if their rejection is the reconciliation[s] of the world, what will their acceptance be but life from the dead?[t] [16]If the part of the dough offered as firstfruits[u] is holy, then the whole batch is holy; if the root is holy, so are the branches.

[17]If some of the branches have been broken off,[v] and you, though a wild olive shoot, have been grafted in among the others[w] and now share in the nourishing sap from the olive root, [18]do not boast over those branches. If you do, consider this: You do not support the root, but the root supports you.[x] [19]You will say then, "Branches were broken off so that I could be grafted in." [20]Granted. But they were broken off because of unbelief, and you stand by faith.[y] Do not be arrogant,[z] but be afraid.[a] [21]For if God did not spare the natural branches, he will not spare you either.

[22]Consider therefore the kindness[b] and sternness of God: sternness to those who fell, but kindness to you, provided that you continue[c] in his kindness. Otherwise, you also will be cut off.[d] [23]And if they do not persist in unbelief, they will be grafted in, for God is able to graft them in again.[e] [24]After all, if you were cut out of an olive tree that is wild by nature, and contrary to nature were grafted into a cultivated olive tree, how much more readily will these, the natural branches, be grafted into their own olive tree!

All Israel Will Be Saved

[25]I do not want you to be ignorant[f] of this mystery,[g] brothers, so that you may not be conceited:[h] Israel has experienced a hardening[i] in part until the full number of the Gentiles has come in.[j] [26]And so all Israel will be saved, as it is written:

"The deliverer will come from Zion;
    he will turn godlessness away from Jacob.
[27]And this is[a] my covenant with them
    when I take away their sins."[b] [k]

[28]As far as the gospel is concerned, they are enemies[l] on your account; but as far as election is concerned, they are loved on account of the patriarchs,[m] [29]for God's gifts and his call[n] are irrevocable.[o] [30]Just as you who were at one time disobedient[p] to God have now received mercy as a result of their disobedience, [31]so they too have now become disobedient in order that they too may now[c] receive mercy as a result of God's mercy to you. [32]For God has bound all men over to disobedience[q] so that he may have mercy on them all.

Doxology

[33]Oh, the depth of the riches[r] of the wisdom and[d]
    knowledge of God![s]
How unsearchable his judgments,
    and his paths beyond tracing out![t]
[34]"Who has known the mind of the Lord?
    Or who has been his counselor?"[e] [u]

*Cross references (margin):*

11:14
qver 11;
Ro 10:19
r1Co 1:21;
1Ti 2:4; Tit 3:5
11:15
sRo 5:10
tLk 15:24,32
11:16
uLev 23:10,17;
Nu 15:18-21
11:17
vJer 11:16;
Jn 15:2
wAc 2:39;
Eph 2:11-13
11:18
xJn 4:22
11:20
y1Co 10:12;
2Co 1:24
zRo 12:16;
1Ti 6:17
a1Pe 1:17
11:22
bRo 2:4
c1Co 15:2;
Heb 3:6
dJn 15:2
11:23
e2Co 3:16
11:25
fRo 1:13
gRo 16:25
hRo 12:16
iver 7; Ro 9:18
jLk 21:24
11:27
kIsa 27:9;
Heb 8:10,12
11:28
lRo 5:10
mDt 7:8; 10:15;
Ro 9:5
11:29
nRo 8:28
oHeb 7:21
11:30
pEph 2:2
11:32
qRo 3:9
11:33
rRo 2:4 sPs 92:5
tJob 11:7
11:34
uIsa 40:13,14;
Job 15:8;
36:22; 1Co 2:16

---

[a]27 Or *will be now.*   [b]27 Isaiah 59:20,21; 27:9; Jer. 31:33,34   [c]31 Some manuscripts do not have *now.*   [d]33 Or *riches and the wisdom and the*   [e]34 Isaiah 40:13

35"Who has ever given to God,
    that God should repay him?"[a] [v]
36For from him and through him and to him are all
    things. [w]
    To him be the glory forever! Amen. [x]

Living Sacrifices

12 Therefore, I urge you, [y] brothers, in view of God's mercy, to offer your bodies as living sacrifices, [z] holy and pleasing to God—this is your spiritual[b] act of worship. 2Do not conform[a] any longer to the pattern of this world, [b] but be transformed by the renewing of your mind. [c] Then you will be able to test and approve what God's will is[d]—his good, pleasing and perfect will.

3For by the grace given me[e] I say to every one of you: Do not think of yourself more highly than you ought, but rather think of yourself with sober judgment, in accordance with the measure of faith God has given you. 4Just as each of us has one body with many members, and these members do not all have the same function, [f] 5so in Christ we who are many form one body, [g] and each member belongs to all the others. 6We have different gifts, [h] according to the grace given us. If a man's gift is prophesying, let him use it in proportion to his[c] faith. [i] 7If it is serving, let him serve; if it is teaching, let him teach;[j] 8if it is encouraging, let him encourage;[k] if it is contributing to the needs of others, let him give generously;[l] if it is leadership, let him govern diligently; if it is showing mercy, let him do it cheerfully.

Love

9Love must be sincere. [m] Hate what is evil; cling to what is good. 10Be devoted to one another in brotherly love. [n] Honor one another above yourselves. [o] 11Never be lacking in zeal, but keep your spiritual fervor, [p] serving the Lord. 12Be joyful in hope, [q] patient in affliction, [r] faithful in prayer. 13Share with God's people who are in need. Practice hospitality.[s]

14Bless those who persecute you;[t] bless and do not curse. 15Rejoice with those who rejoice; mourn with those who mourn. [u] 16Live in harmony with one another. [v] Do not be proud, but be willing to associate with people of low position. [d] Do not be conceited. [w]

17Do not repay anyone evil for evil. [x] Be careful to do what is right in the eyes of everybody. [y] 18If it is possible, as far as it depends on you, live at peace with everyone. [z] 19Do not take revenge, [a] my friends, but leave room for God's wrath, for it is written: "It is mine to avenge; I will repay,"[e][b] says the Lord. 20On the contrary:

"If your enemy is hungry, feed him;
    if he is thirsty, give him something to drink.
In doing this, you will heap burning coals on his
    head."[f][c]

21Do not be overcome by evil, but overcome evil with good.

11:35
v Job 35:7
11:36
w 1Co 8:6;
Col 1:16;
Heb 2:10
x Ro 16:27
12:1
y Eph 4:1
z Ro 6:13,16,19;
1Pe 2:5
12:2
a 1Pe 1:14
b 1Jn 2:15
c Eph 4:23
d Eph 5:17
12:3
e Ro 15:15;
Gal 2:9;
Eph 4:7
12:4
f 1Co 12:12-14;
Eph 4:16
12:5
g 1Co 10:17
12:6
h 1Co 7:7; 12:4,
8-10 i 1Pe 4:10,
11
12:7
j Eph 4:11
12:8
k Ac 15:32
l 2Co 9:5-13
12:9
m 1Ti 1:5
12:10
n Heb 13:1
o Php 2:3
12:11
p Ac 18:25
12:12
q Ro 5:2
r Heb 10:32,36
12:13
s 1Ti 3:2
12:14
t Mt 5:44
12:15
u Job 30:25
12:16
v Ro 15:5
w Jer 45:5;
Ro 11:25
12:17
x Pr 20:22
y 2Co 8:21
12:18
z Mk 9:50;
Ro 14:19
12:19
a Lev 19:18;
Pr 20:22; 24:29
b Dt 32:35
12:20
c Pr 25:21,22;
Mt 5:44;
Lk 6:27

---

a35 Job 41:11   b1 Or *reasonable*   c6 Or *in agreement with the*   d16 Or *willing to do menial work*   e19 Deut. 32:35   f20 Prov. 25:21,22

Submission to the Authorities

13 Everyone must submit himself to the governing authorities,[d] for there is no authority except that which God has established.[e] The authorities that exist have been established by God. [2]Consequently, he who rebels against the authority is rebelling against what God has instituted, and those who do so will bring judgment on themselves. [3]For rulers hold no terror for those who do right, but for those who do wrong. Do you want to be free from fear of the one in authority? Then do what is right and he will commend you.[f] [4]For he is God's servant to do you good. But if you do wrong, be afraid, for he does not bear the sword for nothing. He is God's servant, an agent of wrath to bring punishment on the wrongdoer.[g] [5]Therefore, it is necessary to submit to the authorities, not only because of possible punishment but also because of conscience.

[6]This is also why you pay taxes, for the authorities are God's servants, who give their full time to governing. [7]Give everyone what you owe him: If you owe taxes, pay taxes;[h] if revenue, then revenue; if respect, then respect; if honor, then honor.

Love, for the Day Is Near

[8]Let no debt remain outstanding, except the continuing debt to love one another, for he who loves his fellowman has fulfilled the law.[i] [9]The commandments, "Do not commit adultery," "Do not murder," "Do not steal," "Do not covet,"[a][j] and whatever other commandment there may be, are summed up in this one rule: "Love your neighbor as yourself."[b][k] [10]Love does no harm to its neighbor. Therefore love is the fulfillment of the law.[l]

[11]And do this, understanding the present time. The hour has come[m] for you to wake up from your slumber,[n] because our salvation is nearer now than when we first believed. [12]The night is nearly over; the day is almost here.[o] So let us put aside the deeds of darkness[p] and put on the armor[q] of light. [13]Let us behave decently, as in the daytime, not in orgies and drunkenness, not in sexual immorality and debauchery, not in dissension and jealousy.[r] [14]Rather, clothe yourselves with the Lord Jesus Christ,[s] and do not think about how to gratify the desires of the sinful nature.[c]

The Weak and the Strong

14 Accept him whose faith is weak,[t] without passing judgment on disputable matters. [2]One man's faith allows him to eat everything, but another man, whose faith is weak, eats only vegetables. [3]The man who eats everything must not look down on[u] him who does not, and the man who does not eat everything must not condemn[v] the man who does, for God has accepted him. [4]Who are you to judge someone else's servant?[w] To his own master he stands or falls. And he will stand, for the Lord is able to make him stand.

[5]One man considers one day more sacred than another;[x] another man considers every day alike. Each one should be fully convinced in his own mind. [6]He who regards one day as special, does so to the Lord.

13:1 dTit 3:1; 1Pe 2:13,14 eDa 2:21; Jn 19:11
13:3 f1Pe 2:14
13:4 g1Th 4:6
13:7 hMt 17:25; 22:17,21; Lk 23:2
13:8 iver 10; Jn 13:34; Gal 5:14; Col 3:14
13:9 jEx 20:13-15,17; Dt 5:17-19,21 kLev 19:18; Mt 19:19
13:10 lver 8; Mt 22:39,40
13:11 m1Co 7:29-31; 10:11 nEph 5:14; 1Th 5:5,6
13:12 o1Jn 2:8 pEph 5:11 qEph 6:11,13
13:13 rGal 5:20,21
13:14 sGal 3:27; 5:16; Eph 4:24
14:1 tRo 15:1; 1Co 8:9-12
14:3 uLk 18:9 vCol 2:16
14:4 wJas 4:12
14:5 xGal 4:10

---

a9 Exodus 20:13-15,17; Deut. 5:17-19,21   *b9* Lev. 19:18   *c14* Or *the flesh*

He who eats meat, eats to the Lord, for he gives thanks to God;[y] and he who abstains, does so to the Lord and gives thanks to God. [7]For none of us lives to himself alone[z] and none of us dies to himself alone. [8]If we live, we live to the Lord; and if we die, we die to the Lord. So, whether we live or die, we belong to the Lord.[a]

[9]For this very reason, Christ died and returned to life[b] so that he might be the Lord of both the dead and the living.[c] [10]You, then, why do you judge your brother? Or why do you look down on your brother? For we will all stand before God's judgment seat.[d] [11]It is written:

> " 'As surely as I live,' says the Lord,
> 'every knee will bow before me;
>   every tongue will confess to God.' "[a] [e]

[12]So then, each of us will give an account of himself to God.[f]

[13]Therefore let us stop passing judgment[g] on one another. Instead, make up your mind not to put any stumbling block or obstacle in your brother's way. [14]As one who is in the Lord Jesus, I am fully convinced that no food[b] is unclean in itself.[h] But if anyone regards something as unclean, then for him it is unclean.[i] [15]If your brother is distressed because of what you eat, you are no longer acting in love.[j] Do not by your eating destroy your brother for whom Christ died.[k] [16]Do not allow what you consider good to be spoken of as evil.[l] [17]For the kingdom of God is not a matter of eating and drinking,[m] but of righteousness, peace and joy in the Holy Spirit,[n] [18]because anyone who serves Christ in this way is pleasing to God and approved by men.[o]

[19]Let us therefore make every effort to do what leads to peace[p] and to mutual edification.[q] [20]Do not destroy the work of God for the sake of food.[r] All food is clean, but it is wrong for a man to eat anything that causes someone else to stumble.[s] [21]It is better not to eat meat or drink wine or to do anything else that will cause your brother to fall.[t]

[22]So whatever you believe about these things keep between yourself and God. Blessed is the man who does not condemn[u] himself by what he approves. [23]But the man who has doubts[v] is condemned if he eats, because his eating is not from faith; and everything that does not come from faith is sin.

15 We who are strong ought to bear with the failings of the weak[w] and not to please ourselves. [2]Each of us should please his neighbor for his good,[x] to build him up.[y] [3]For even Christ did not please himself[z] but, as it is written: "The insults of those who insult you have fallen on me."[c] [a] [4]For everything that was written in the past was written to teach us,[b] so that through endurance and the encouragement of the Scriptures we might have hope.

[5]May the God who gives endurance and encouragement give you a spirit of unity[c] among yourselves as you follow Christ Jesus, [6]so that with one heart and mouth you may glorify the God and Father[d] of our Lord Jesus Christ.

[7]Accept one another,[e] then, just as Christ accepted you, in order to bring praise to God. [8]For I tell you that Christ has become a servant of the Jews[d][f] on behalf of God's truth, to confirm the promises[g] made to

---

14:6
yMt 14:19;
1Co 10:30,31;
1Ti 4:3,4
14:7
z2Co 5:15;
Gal 2:20
14:8
aPhp 1:20
14:9
bRev 1:18
c2Co 5:15
14:10
d2Co 5:10
14:11
eIsa 45:23;
Php 2:10,11
14:12
fMt 12:36;
1Pe 4:5
14:13
gMt 7:1
14:14
hAc 10:15
i1Co 8:7
14:15
jEph 5:2
k1Co 8:11
14:16
l1Co 10:30
14:17
m1Co 8:8
nRo 15:13
14:18
o2Co 8:21
14:19
pPs 34:14;
Ro 12:18;
Heb 12:14
qRo 15:2;
2Co 12:19
14:20
rver 15
s1Co 8:9-12
14:21
t1Co 8:13
14:22
u1Jn 3:21
14:23
vver 5
15:1
wRo 14:1;
Gal 6:1,2;
1Th 5:14
15:2
x1Co 10:33
yRo 14:19
15:3
z2Co 8:9
aPs 69:9
15:4
bRo 4:23,24
15:5
cRo 12:16;
1Co 1:10
15:6
dRev 1:6
15:7
eRo 14:1
15:8
fMt 15:24;
Ac 3:25,26
g2Co 1:20

---

[a]11 Isaiah 45:23   [b]14 Or *that nothing*   [c]3 Psalm 69:9   [d]8 Greek *circumcision*

the patriarchs [9]so that the Gentiles[h] may glorify God[i] for his mercy, as it is written:

"Therefore I will praise you among the Gentiles;
I will sing hymns to your name."[a][j]

[10]Again, it says,

"Rejoice, O Gentiles, with his people."[b][k]

[11]And again,

"Praise the Lord, all you Gentiles,
and sing praises to him, all you peoples."[c][l]

[12]And again, Isaiah says,

"The Root of Jesse[m] will spring up,
one who will arise to rule over the nations;
the Gentiles will hope in him."[d][n]

[13]May the God of hope fill you with all joy and peace[o] as you trust in him, so that you may overflow with hope by the power of the Holy Spirit.[p]

Paul the Minister to the Gentiles

[14]I myself am convinced, my brothers, that you yourselves are full of goodness,[q] complete in knowledge[r] and competent to instruct one another. [15]I have written you quite boldly on some points, as if to remind you of them again, because of the grace God gave me[s] [16]to be a minister of Christ Jesus to the Gentiles[t] with the priestly duty of proclaiming the gospel of God,[u] so that the Gentiles might become an offering[v] acceptable to God, sanctified by the Holy Spirit.

[17]Therefore I glory in Christ Jesus[w] in my service to God.[x] [18]I will not venture to speak of anything except what Christ has accomplished through me in leading the Gentiles[y] to obey God[z] by what I have said and done— [19]by the power of signs and miracles,[a] through the power of the Spirit.[b] So from Jerusalem[c] all the way around to Illyricum, I have fully proclaimed the gospel of Christ. [20]It has always been my ambition to preach the gospel where Christ was not known, so that I would not be building on someone else's foundation.[d] [21]Rather, as it is written:

"Those who were not told about him will see,
and those who have not heard will understand."[e][e]

[22]This is why I have often been hindered from coming to you.[f]

Paul's Plan to Visit Rome

[23]But now that there is no more place for me to work in these regions, and since I have been longing for many years to see you,[g] [24]I plan to do so when I go to Spain.[h] I hope to visit you while passing through and to have you assist me on my journey there, after I have enjoyed your company for a while. [25]Now, however, I am on my way to Jerusalem[i]

15:9
hRo 3:29
iMt 9:8
j2Sa 22:50;
Ps 18:49
15:10
kDt 32:43
15:11
lPs 117:1
15:12
mRev 5:5
nIsa 11:10;
Mt 12:21
15:13
oRo 14:17
pver 19;
1Co 2:4;
1Th 1:5
15:14
qEph 5:9
r2Pe 1:12
15:15
sRo 12:3
15:16
tAc 9:15;
Ro 11:13
uRo 1:1
vIsa 66:20
15:17
wPhp 3:3
xHeb 2:17
15:18
yAc 15:12;
21:19; Ro 1:5
zRo 16:26
15:19
aJn 4:48;
Ac 19:11
bver 13
cAc 22:17-21
15:20
d2Co 10:15,16
15:21
eIsa 52:15
15:22
fRo 1:13
15:23
gAc 19:21;
Ro 1:10,11
15:24
hver 28
15:25
iAc 19:21

*a*9 2 Samuel 22:50; Psalm 18:49   *b*10 Deut. 32:43   *c*11 Psalm 117:1   *d*12 Isaiah 11:10
*e*21 Isaiah 52:15

in the service[j] of the saints there. [26]For Macedonia[k] and Achaia[l] were pleased to make a contribution for the poor among the saints in Jerusalem. [27]They were pleased to do it, and indeed they owe it to them. For if the Gentiles have shared in the Jews' spiritual blessings, they owe it to the Jews to share with them their material blessings.[m] [28]So after I have completed this task and have made sure that they have received this fruit, I will go to Spain and visit you on the way. [29]I know that when I come to you,[n] I will come in the full measure of the blessing of Christ.

[30]I urge you, brothers, by our Lord Jesus Christ and by the love of the Spirit,[o] to join me in my struggle by praying to God for me.[p] [31]Pray that I may be rescued[q] from the unbelievers in Judea and that my service in Jerusalem may be acceptable to the saints there, [32]so that by God's will[r] I may come to you[s] with joy and together with you be refreshed.[t] [33]The God of peace[u] be with you all. Amen.

Personal Greetings

16 I commend[v] to you our sister Phoebe, a servant[a] of the church in Cenchrea.[w] [2]I ask you to receive her in the Lord[x] in a way worthy of the saints and to give her any help she may need from you, for she has been a great help to many people, including me.

[3]Greet Priscilla[b] and Aquila,[y] my fellow workers in Christ Jesus.[z] [4]They risked their lives for me. Not only I but all the churches of the Gentiles are grateful to them.

[5]Greet also the church that meets at their house.[a]

Greet my dear friend Epenetus, who was the first convert[b] to Christ in the province of Asia.

[6]Greet Mary, who worked very hard for you.

[7]Greet Andronicus and Junias, my relatives[c] who have been in prison with me. They are outstanding among the apostles, and they were in Christ before I was.

[8]Greet Ampliatus, whom I love in the Lord.

[9]Greet Urbanus, our fellow worker in Christ,[d] and my dear friend Stachys.

[10]Greet Apelles, tested and approved in Christ.

Greet those who belong to the household of Aristobulus.

[11]Greet Herodion, my relative.[e]

Greet those in the household of Narcissus who are in the Lord.

[12]Greet Tryphena and Tryphosa, those women who work hard in the Lord.

Greet my dear friend Persis, another woman who has worked very hard in the Lord.

[13]Greet Rufus, chosen in the Lord, and his mother, who has been a mother to me, too.

[14]Greet Asyncritus, Phlegon, Hermes, Patrobas, Hermas and the brothers with them.

[15]Greet Philologus, Julia, Nereus and his sister, and Olympas and all the saints[f] with them.[g]

[16]Greet one another with a holy kiss.[h]

All the churches of Christ send greetings.

---

[a]1 Or *deaconess*   [b]3 Greek *Prisca*, a variant of *Priscilla*

15:25
jAc 24:17
15:26
kAc 16:9;
2Co 8:1
lAc 18:12
15:27
m1Co 9:11
15:29
nRo 1:10,11
15:30
oGal 5:22
p2Co 1:11;
Col 4:12
15:31
q2Th 3:2
15:32
rAc 18:21
sRo 1:10,13
t1Co 16:18
15:33
uRo 16:20;
2Co 13:11;
Php 4:9;
1Th 5:23;
Heb 13:20
16:1
v2Co 3:1
wAc 18:18
16:2
xPhp 2:29
16:3
yAc 18:2 zver 7,
9,10
16:5
a1Co 16:19;
Col 4:15; Phm 2
b1Co 16:15
16:7
cver 11,21
16:9
dver 3
16:11
ever 7,21
16:15
fver 2 gver 14
16:16
h1Co 16:20;
2Co 13:12;
1Th 5:26

16:17
iGal 1:8,9;
1Ti 1:3; 6:3
j2Th 3:6,14;
2Jn 10
16:18
kPhp 3:19
1Col 2:4
16:19
mRo 1:8
nMt 10:16;
1Co 14:20
16:20
oRo 15:33
pGe 3:15
q1Th 5:28
16:21
rAc 16:1
sAc 13:1
tAc 17:5 uver 7,
11
16:23
vAc 19:22
16:25
wEph 3:20
xRo 2:16
yEph 1:9;
Col 1:26,27
16:27
zRo 11:36

[17]I urge you, brothers, to watch out for those who cause divisions and put obstacles in your way that are contrary to the teaching you have learned. [i] Keep away from them. [j] [18]For such people are not serving our Lord Christ, but their own appetites. [k] By smooth talk and flattery they deceive[1] the minds of naive people. [19]Everyone has heard[m] about your obedience, so I am full of joy over you; but I want you to be wise about what is good, and innocent about what is evil. [n]

[20]The God of peace[o] will soon crush[p] Satan under your feet.

The grace of our Lord Jesus be with you. [q]

[21]Timothy,[r] my fellow worker, sends his greetings to you, as do Lucius,[s] Jason[t] and Sosipater, my relatives. [u]

[22]I, Tertius, who wrote down this letter, greet you in the Lord.

[23]Gaius, whose hospitality I and the whole church here enjoy, sends you his greetings.

Erastus,[v] who is the city's director of public works, and our brother Quartus send you their greetings. [a]

[25]Now to him who is able[w] to establish you by my gospel[x] and the proclamation of Jesus Christ, according to the revelation of the mystery[y] hidden for long ages past, [26]but now revealed and made known through the prophetic writings by the command of the eternal God, so that all nations might believe and obey him— [27]to the only wise God be glory forever through Jesus Christ! Amen. [z]

---

[a]23 Some manuscripts *their greetings.* [24]*May the grace of our Lord Jesus Christ be with all of you. Amen.*

1 Corinthians

Title and Background

Located between the Corinthian Gulf and the Saronic Gulf, the city of Corinth was a wealthy trading center. It was also a wicked city and was known for that throughout the Roman world. Because the church in Corinth was new, it was hard for the Christians there not to act like their neighbors; consequently the church was having some problems.

Author and Date of Writing

Paul is acknowledged as the author both in the letter itself and by the early church fathers. This book was written about A.D. 55, toward the close of Paul's three-year residency in Ephesus.

Theme and Message

The letter revolves around the theme of problems in Christian conduct. It thus has to do with progressive sanctification, the continuing development of holiness of character. Obviously Paul was personally concerned with the Corinthians' problems, revealing a true pastor's (shepherd's) heart. In spite of the concentration on problems, the book contains some of the most familiar and beloved chapters in the entire Bible—for example, chapter 13 (on love) and chapter 15 (on resurrection).

Outline

---

1 Paul, called to be an apostle[a] of Christ Jesus by the will of God,[b] and our brother Sosthenes,[c]

²To the church of God in Corinth,[d] to those sanctified in Christ Jesus and called[e] to be holy, together with all those everywhere who call on the name of our Lord Jesus Christ—their Lord and ours:

³Grace and peace to you from God our Father and the Lord Jesus Christ.[f]

Thanksgiving

⁴I always thank God for you[g] because of his grace given you in Christ

1:1
aRo 1:1;
Eph 1:1
b2Co 1:1
cAc 18:17
1:2
dAc 18:1
eRo 1:7
1:3
fRo 1:7
1:4
gRo 1:8

Jesus. [5]For in him you have been enriched[h] in every way—in all your speaking and in all your knowledge[i]— [6]because our testimony[j] about Christ was confirmed in you. [7]Therefore you do not lack any spiritual gift as you eagerly wait for our Lord Jesus Christ to be revealed.[k] [8]He will keep you strong to the end, so that you will be blameless[l] on the day of our Lord Jesus Christ. [9]God, who has called you into fellowship with his Son Jesus Christ our Lord,[m] is faithful.[n]

Divisions in the Church

[10]I appeal to you, brothers, in the name of our Lord Jesus Christ, that all of you agree with one another so that there may be no divisions among you and that you may be perfectly united in mind and thought. [11]My brothers, some from Chloe's household have informed me that there are quarrels among you. [12]What I mean is this: One of you says, "I follow Paul";[o] another, "I follow Apollos";[p] another, "I follow Cephas[a]";[q] still another, "I follow Christ."

[13]Is Christ divided? Was Paul crucified for you? Were you baptized into[b] the name of Paul?[r] [14]I am thankful that I did not baptize any of you except Crispus[s] and Gaius,[t] [15]so no one can say that you were baptized into my name. [16](Yes, I also baptized the household of Stephanas;[u] beyond that, I don't remember if I baptized anyone else.) [17]For Christ did not send me to baptize,[v] but to preach the gospel—not with words of human wisdom,[w] lest the cross of Christ be emptied of its power.

Christ the Wisdom and Power of God

[18]For the message of the cross is foolishness to those who are perishing,[x] but to us who are being saved it is the power of God.[y] [19]For it is written:

> "I will destroy the wisdom of the wise;
>   the intelligence of the intelligent I will frustrate."[c] [z]

[20]Where is the wise man?[a] Where is the scholar? Where is the philosopher of this age? Has not God made foolish[b] the wisdom of the world? [21]For since in the wisdom of God the world through its wisdom did not know him, God was pleased through the foolishness of what was preached to save those who believe. [22]Jews demand miraculous signs[c] and Greeks look for wisdom, [23]but we preach Christ crucified: a stumbling block[d] to Jews and foolishness[e] to Gentiles, [24]but to those whom God has called,[f] both Jews and Greeks, Christ the power of God and the wisdom of God.[g] [25]For the foolishness[h] of God is wiser than man's wisdom, and the weakness[i] of God is stronger than man's strength.

[26]Brothers, think of what you were when you were called. Not many of you were wise by human standards; not many were influential; not many were of noble birth. [27]But God chose[j] the foolish[k] things of the world to shame the wise; God chose the weak things of the world to shame the strong. [28]He chose the lowly things of this world and the despised things—and the things that are not[l]—to nullify the things that are, [29]so that no one may boast before him.[m] [30]It is because of him that you are in Christ Jesus, who has become for us wisdom from

1:5
h2Co 9:11
i2Co 8:7
1:6
jRev 1:2
1:7
kPhp 3:20;
Tit 2:13;
2Pe 3:12
1:8
l1Th 3:13
1:9
m1Jn 1:3
nIsa 49:7;
1Th 5:24
1:12
o1Co 3:4,22
pAc 18:24
qJn 1:42
1:13
rMt 28:19
1:14
sAc 18:8;
Ro 16:23
tAc 19:29
1:16
u1Co 16:15
1:17
vJn 4:2
w1Co 2:1,4,13
1:18
x2Co 2:15
yRo 1:16
1:19
zIsa 29:14
1:20
aIsa 19:11,12
bJob 12:17;
Ro 1:22
1:22
cMt 12:38
1:23
dLk 2:34;
Gal 5:11
e1Co 2:14
1:24
fRo 8:28
gver 30; Col 2:3
1:25
hver 18
i2Co 13:4
1:27
jJas 2:5 kver 20
1:28
lRo 4:17
1:29
mEph 2:9

---

[a]12 That is, Peter   [b]13 Or *in*; also in verse 15   [c]19 Isaiah 29:14

God—that is, our righteousness,[n] holiness and redemption.[o] [31]Therefore, as it is written: "Let him who boasts boast in the Lord."[a][p]

2 When I came to you, brothers, I did not come with eloquence or superior wisdom[q] as I proclaimed to you the testimony about God.[b] [2]For I resolved to know nothing while I was with you except Jesus Christ and him crucified.[r] [3]I came to you[s] in weakness and fear, and with much trembling. [4]My message and my preaching were not with wise and persuasive words, but with a demonstration of the Spirit's power,[t] [5]so that your faith might not rest on men's wisdom, but on God's power.[u]

Wisdom From the Spirit

[6]We do, however, speak a message of wisdom among the mature,[v] but not the wisdom of this age[w] or of the rulers of this age, who are coming to nothing. [7]No, we speak of God's secret wisdom, a wisdom that has been hidden and that God destined for our glory before time began. [8]None of the rulers of this age understood it, for if they had, they would not have crucified the Lord of glory.[x] [9]However, as it is written:

> "No eye has seen,
> no ear has heard,
> no mind has conceived
> what God has prepared for those who love him"[c][y]—

[10]but God has revealed[z] it to us by his Spirit.[a]

The Spirit searches all things, even the deep things of God. [11]For who among men knows the thoughts of a man[b] except the man's spirit[c] within him? In the same way no one knows the thoughts of God except the Spirit of God. [12]We have not received the spirit[d] of the world[e] but the Spirit who is from God, that we may understand what God has freely given us. [13]This is what we speak, not in words taught us by human wisdom[f] but in words taught by the Spirit, expressing spiritual truths in spiritual words.[d] [14]The man without the Spirit does not accept the things that come from the Spirit of God, for they are foolishness[g] to him, and he cannot understand them, because they are spiritually discerned. [15]The spiritual man makes judgments about all things, but he himself is not subject to any man's judgment:

> [16]"For who has known the mind of the Lord
> that he may instruct him?"[e][h]

But we have the mind of Christ.[i]

On Divisions in the Church

3 Brothers, I could not address you as spiritual[j] but as worldly[k]—mere infants[l] in Christ. [2]I gave you milk, not solid food,[m] for you were not yet ready for it.[n] Indeed, you are still not ready. [3]You are still worldly. For since there is jealousy and quarreling[o] among you, are you not worldly? Are you not acting like mere men? [4]For when one

---

1:30
n Jer 23:5,6;
2Co 5:21
o Ro 3:24;
Eph 1:7,14
1:31
p Jer 9:23,24;
2Co 10:17
2:1
q 1Co 1:17
2:2
r Gal 6:14;
1Co 1:23
2:3
s Ac 18:1-18
2:4
t Ro 15:19
2:5
u 2Co 4:7; 6:7
2:6
v Eph 4:13;
Php 3:15;
Heb 5:14
w 1Co 1:20
2:8
x Ac 7:2; Jas 2:1
2:9
y Isa 64:4; 65:17
2:10
z Mt 13:11;
Eph 3:3,5
a Jn 14:26
2:11
b Jer 17:9
c Pr 20:27
2:12
d Ro 8:15
e 1Co 1:20,27
2:13
f 1Co 1:17
2:14
g 1Co 1:18
2:16
h Isa 40:13
i Jn 15:15
3:1
j 1Co 2:15
k Ro 7:14;
1Co 2:14
l Heb 5:13
3:2
m Heb 5:12-14;
1Pe 2:2
n Jn 16:12
3:3
o 1Co 1:11;
Gal 5:20

---

[a]31 Jer. 9:24   [b]1 Some manuscripts *as I proclaimed to you God's mystery*   [c]9 Isaiah 64:4
[d]13 Or *Spirit, interpreting spiritual truths to spiritual men*   [e]16 Isaiah 40:13

says, "I follow Paul," and another, "I follow Apollos,"ᴾ are you not mere men?

⁵What, after all, is Apollos? And what is Paul? Only servants, through whom you came to believe—as the Lord has assigned to each his task. ⁶I planted the seed,�q Apollos watered it, but God made it grow. ⁷So neither he who plants nor he who waters is anything, but only God, who makes things grow. ⁸The man who plants and the man who waters have one purpose, and each will be rewarded according to his own labor.ʳ ⁹For we are God's fellow workers;ˢ you are God's field,ᵗ God's building.ᵘ

¹⁰By the grace God has given me,ᵛ I laid a foundationʷ as an expert builder, and someone else is building on it. But each one should be careful how he builds. ¹¹For no one can lay any foundation other than the one already laid, which is Jesus Christ.ˣ ¹²If any man builds on this foundation using gold, silver, costly stones, wood, hay or straw, ¹³his work will be shown for what it is,ʸ because the Dayᶻ will bring it to light. It will be revealed with fire, and the fire will test the quality of each man's work. ¹⁴If what he has built survives, he will receive his reward. ¹⁵If it is burned up, he will suffer loss; he himself will be saved, but only as one escaping through the flames.ᵃ

¹⁶Don't you know that you yourselves are God's templeᵇ and that God's Spirit lives in you? ¹⁷If anyone destroys God's temple, God will destroy him; for God's temple is sacred, and you are that temple.

¹⁸Do not deceive yourselves. If any one of you thinks he is wiseᶜ by the standards of this age, he should become a "fool" so that he may become wise. ¹⁹For the wisdom of this world is foolishnessᵈ in God's sight. As it is written: "He catches the wise in their craftiness"ᵃ;ᵉ ²⁰and again, "The Lord knows that the thoughts of the wise are futile."ᵇᶠ ²¹So then, no more boasting about men!ᵍ All things are yours,ʰ ²²whether Paul or Apollos or Cephasᶜⁱ or the world or life or death or the present or the futureʲ—all are yours, ²³and you are of Christ,ᵏ and Christ is of God.

Apostles of Christ

4 So then, men ought to regard us as servants of Christ and as those entrusted¹ with the secret thingsᵐ of God. ²Now it is required that those who have been given a trust must prove faithful. ³I care very little if I am judged by you or by any human court; indeed, I do not even judge myself. ⁴My conscience is clear, but that does not make me innocent.ⁿ It is the Lord who judges me. ⁵Therefore judge nothingᵒ before the appointed time; wait till the Lord comes. He will bring to light what is hidden in darkness and will expose the motives of men's hearts. At that time each will receive his praise from God.ᵖ

⁶Now, brothers, I have applied these things to myself and Apollos for your benefit, so that you may learn from us the meaning of the saying, "Do not go beyond what is written."q Then you will not take pride in one man over against another.ʳ ⁷For who makes you different from anyone else? What do you have that you did not receive?ˢ And if you did receive it, why do you boast as though you did not?

⁸Already you have all you want! Already you have become rich!ᵗ You

Cross-references (left margin):
3:4 p1Co 1:12
3:6 qAc 18:4-11
3:8 rPs 62:12
3:9 s2Co 6:1; tIsa 61:3; uEph 2:20-22; 1Pe 2:5
3:10 vRo 12:3; wRo 15:20
3:11 xIsa 28:16; Eph 2:20
3:13 y1Co 4:5; z2Th 1:7-10
3:15 aJude 23
3:16 b1Co 6:19; 2Co 6:16
3:18 cIsa 5:21; 1Co 8:2
3:19 d1Co 1:20,27; eJob 5:13
3:20 fPs 94:11
3:21 g1Co 4:6; hRo 8:32
3:22 i1Co 1:12; jRo 8:38
3:23 k1Co 15:23; 2Co 10:7; Gal 3:29
4:1 l1Co 9:17; Tit 1:7; mRo 16:25
4:4 nRo 2:13
4:5 oMt 7:1,2; Ro 2:1 pRo 2:29
4:6 q1Co 1:19,31; 3:19,20 r1Co 1:12
4:7 sJn 3:27; Ro 12:3,6
4:8 tRev 3:17,18

ᵃ19 Job 5:13   ᵇ20 Psalm 94:11   ᶜ22 That is, Peter

have become kings—and that without us! How I wish that you really had become kings so that we might be kings with you! [9]For it seems to me that God has put us apostles on display at the end of the procession, like men condemned to die[u] in the arena. We have been made a spectacle[v] to the whole universe, to angels as well as to men. [10]We are fools for Christ,[w] but you are so wise in Christ![x] We are weak, but you are strong![y] You are honored, we are dishonored! [11]To this very hour we go hungry and thirsty, we are in rags, we are brutally treated, we are homeless.[z] [12]We work hard with our own hands.[a] When we are cursed, we bless;[b] when we are persecuted, we endure it; [13]when we are slandered, we answer kindly. Up to this moment we have become the scum of the earth, the refuse[c] of the world.

[14]I am not writing this to shame you, but to warn you, as my dear children.[d] [15]Even though you have ten thousand guardians in Christ, you do not have many fathers, for in Christ Jesus I became your father through the gospel.[e] [16]Therefore I urge you to imitate me.[f] [17]For this reason I am sending to you Timothy, my son[g] whom I love, who is faithful in the Lord. He will remind you of my way of life in Christ Jesus, which agrees with what I teach everywhere in every church.[h]

[18]Some of you have become arrogant, as if I were not coming to you. [19]But I will come to you very soon,[i] if the Lord is willing,[j] and then I will find out not only how these arrogant people are talking, but what power they have. [20]For the kingdom of God is not a matter of talk but of power. [21]What do you prefer? Shall I come to you with a whip,[k] or in love and with a gentle spirit?

Expel the Immoral Brother!

5 It is actually reported that there is sexual immorality among you, and of a kind that does not occur even among pagans: A man has his father's wife.[l] [2]And you are proud! Shouldn't you rather have been filled with grief[m] and have put out of your fellowship the man who did this? [3]Even though I am not physically present, I am with you in spirit.[n] And I have already passed judgment on the one who did this, just as if I were present. [4]When you are assembled in the name of our Lord Jesus[o] and I am with you in spirit, and the power of our Lord Jesus is present, [5]hand this man over[p] to Satan, so that the sinful nature[a] may be destroyed and his spirit saved on the day of the Lord.

[6]Your boasting is not good.[q] Don't you know that a little yeast[r] works through the whole batch of dough?[s] [7]Get rid of the old yeast that you may be a new batch without yeast—as you really are. For Christ, our Passover lamb, has been sacrificed.[t] [8]Therefore let us keep the Festival, not with the old yeast, the yeast of malice and wickedness, but with bread without yeast,[u] the bread of sincerity and truth.

[9]I have written you in my letter not to associate[v] with sexually immoral people— [10]not at all meaning the people of this world[w] who are immoral, or the greedy and swindlers, or idolaters. In that case you would have to leave this world. [11]But now I am writing you that you must not associate with anyone who calls himself a brother but is sexually immoral or greedy, an idolater[x] or a slanderer, a drunkard or a swindler. With such a man do not even eat.

---

[a]5 Or *that his body;* or *that the flesh*

4:9
u Ro 8:36
v Heb 10:33
4:10
w 1Co 1:18; Ac 17:18
x 1Co 3:18
y 1Co 2:3
4:11
z Ro 8:35; 2Co 11:23-27
4:12
a Ac 18:3
b 1Pe 3:9
4:13
c La 3:45
4:14
d 1Th 2:11
4:15
e 1Co 9:12,14, 18,23
4:16
f 1Co 11:1; Php 3:17; 1Th 1:6; 2Th 3:7,9
4:17
g 1Ti 1:2
h 1Co 7:17
4:19
i 2Co 1:15,16
j Ac 18:21
4:21
k 2Co 1:23; 13:2,10
5:1
l Lev 18:8; Dt 22:30
5:2
m 2Co 7:7-11
5:3
n Col 2:5
5:4
o 2Th 3:6
5:5
p 1Ti 1:20
5:6
q Jas 4:16
r Mt 16:6,12
s Gal 5:9
5:7
t Mk 14:12; 1Pe 1:19
5:8
u Ex 12:14,15; Dt 16:3
5:9
v Eph 5:11; 2Th 3:6,14
5:10
w 1Co 10:27
5:11
x 1Co 10:7,14

12What business is it of mine to judge those outside[y] the church? Are you not to judge those inside?[z] 13God will judge those outside. "Expel the wicked man from among you."[a][a]

Lawsuits Among Believers

6 If any of you has a dispute with another, dare he take it before the ungodly for judgment instead of before the saints?[b] 2Do you not know that the saints will judge the world?[c] And if you are to judge the world, are you not competent to judge trivial cases? 3Do you not know that we will judge angels? How much more the things of this life! 4Therefore, if you have disputes about such matters, appoint as judges even men of little account in the church![b] 5I say this to shame you.[d] Is it possible that there is nobody among you wise enough to judge a dispute between believers?[e] 6But instead, one brother goes to law against another—and this in front of unbelievers![f]

7The very fact that you have lawsuits among you means you have been completely defeated already. Why not rather be wronged? Why not rather be cheated?[g] 8Instead, you yourselves cheat and do wrong, and you do this to your brothers.[h]

9Do you not know that the wicked will not inherit the kingdom of God?[i] Do not be deceived:[j] Neither the sexually immoral nor idolaters nor adulterers nor male prostitutes nor homosexual offenders 10nor thieves nor the greedy nor drunkards nor slanderers nor swindlers will inherit the kingdom of God. 11And that is what some of you were.[k] But you were washed,[l] you were sanctified,[m] you were justified in the name of the Lord Jesus Christ and by the Spirit of our God.

Sexual Immorality

12"Everything is permissible for me"—but not everything is beneficial.[n] "Everything is permissible for me"—but I will not be mastered by anything. 13"Food for the stomach and the stomach for food"—but God will destroy them both.[o] The body is not meant for sexual immorality, but for the Lord, and the Lord for the body. 14By his power God raised the Lord from the dead, and he will raise us also.[p] 15Do you not know that your bodies are members of Christ himself?[q] Shall I then take the members of Christ and unite them with a prostitute? Never! 16Do you not know that he who unites himself with a prostitute is one with her in body? For it is said, "The two will become one flesh."[c][r] 17But he who unites himself with the Lord is one with him in spirit.[s]

18Flee from sexual immorality.[t] All other sins a man commits are outside his body, but he who sins sexually sins against his own body.[u] 19Do you not know that your body is a temple[v] of the Holy Spirit, who is in you, whom you have received from God? You are not your own;[w] 20you were bought at a price.[x] Therefore honor God with your body.

Marriage

7 Now for the matters you wrote about: It is good for a man not to marry.[d][y] 2But since there is so much immorality, each man should

5:12
yMk 4:11
zver 3-5;
1Co 6:1-4
5:13
aDt 13:5
6:1
bMt 18:17
6:2
cMt 19:28;
Lk 22:30
6:5
d1Co 4:14
eAc 1:15
6:6
f2Co 6:14,15
6:7
gMt 5:39,40
6:8
h1Th 4:6
6:9
iGal 5:21
j1Co 15:33;
Jas 1:16
6:11
kEph 2:2
lAc 22:16
m1Co 1:2
6:12
n1Co 10:23
6:13
oCol 2:22
6:14
pRo 6:5;
Eph 1:19,20
6:15
qRo 12:5
6:16
rGe 2:24;
Mt 19:5;
Eph 5:31
6:17
sJn 17:21-23;
Gal 2:20
6:18
t2Co 12:21;
1Th 4:3,4;
Heb 13:4
uRo 6:12
6:19
vJn 2:21
wRo 14:7,8
6:20
xAc 20:28;
1Co 7:23;
1Pe 1:18,19;
Rev 5:9
7:1
yver 8,26

a13 Deut. 17:7; 19:19; 21:21; 22:21,24; 24:7
account in the church?   c16 Gen. 2:24
with a woman."   b4 Or matters, do you appoint as judges men of little
d1 Or "It is good for a man not to have sexual relations

have his own wife, and each woman her own husband. [3]The husband should fulfill his marital duty to his wife,[z] and likewise the wife to her husband. [4]The wife's body does not belong to her alone but also to her husband. In the same way, the husband's body does not belong to him alone but also to his wife. [5]Do not deprive each other except by mutual consent and for a time,[a] so that you may devote yourselves to prayer. Then come together again so that Satan[b] will not tempt you[c] because of your lack of self-control. [6]I say this as a concession, not as a command.[d] [7]I wish that all men were as I am.[e] But each man has his own gift from God; one has this gift, another has that.[f]

[8]Now to the unmarried and the widows I say: It is good for them to stay unmarried, as I am.[g] [9]But if they cannot control themselves, they should marry,[h] for it is better to marry than to burn with passion.

[10]To the married I give this command (not I, but the Lord): A wife must not separate from her husband.[i] [11]But if she does, she must remain unmarried or else be reconciled to her husband. And a husband must not divorce his wife.

[12]To the rest I say this (I, not the Lord):[j] If any brother has a wife who is not a believer and she is willing to live with him, he must not divorce her. [13]And if a woman has a husband who is not a believer and he is willing to live with her, she must not divorce him. [14]For the unbelieving husband has been sanctified through his wife, and the unbelieving wife has been sanctified through her believing husband. Otherwise your children would be unclean, but as it is, they are holy.[k]

[15]But if the unbeliever leaves, let him do so. A believing man or woman is not bound in such circumstances; God has called us to live in peace.[l] [16]How do you know, wife, whether you will save[m] your husband?[n] Or, how do you know, husband, whether you will save your wife?

[17]Nevertheless, each one should retain the place in life that the Lord assigned to him and to which God has called him.[o] This is the rule I lay down in all the churches.[p] [18]Was a man already circumcised when he was called? He should not become uncircumcised. Was a man uncircumcised when he was called? He should not be circumcised.[q] [19]Circumcision is nothing and uncircumcision is nothing.[r] Keeping God's commands is what counts. [20]Each one should remain in the situation which he was in when God called him.[s] [21]Were you a slave when you were called? Don't let it trouble you—although if you can gain your freedom, do so. [22]For he who was a slave when he was called by the Lord is the Lord's freedman;[t] similarly, he who was a free man when he was called is Christ's slave.[u] [23]You were bought at a price;[v] do not become slaves of men. [24]Brothers, each man, as responsible to God, should remain in the situation God called him to.[w]

[25]Now about virgins: I have no command from the Lord,[x] but I give a judgment as one who by the Lord's mercy[y] is trustworthy. [26]Because of the present crisis, I think that it is good for you to remain as you are.[z] [27]Are you married? Do not seek a divorce. Are you unmarried? Do not look for a wife. [28]But if you do marry, you have not sinned; and if a virgin marries, she has not sinned. But those who marry will face many troubles in this life, and I want to spare you this.

[29]What I mean, brothers, is that the time is short.[a] From now on those who have wives should live as if they had none; [30]those who

7:3
zEx 21: 10;
1Pe 3:7
7:5
aEx 19:15;
1Sa 21:4,5
bMt 4:10
c1Th 3:5
7:6
d2Co 8:8
7:7
ever 8; 1Co 9:5
fMt 19:11,12;
Ro 12:6;
1Co 12:4,11
7:8
gver 1,26
7:9
h1Ti 5:14
7:10
iMal 2:14-16;
Mt 5:32;
19:3-9;
Mk 10:11;
Lk 16:18
7:12
jver 6,10;
2Co 11:17
7:14
kMal 2:15
7:15
lRo 14:19;
1Co 14:33
7:16
mRo 11:14
n1Pe 3:1
7:17
oRo 12:3
p1Co 4:17;
14:33;
2Co 8:18; 11:28
7:18
qAc 15:1,2
7:19
rRo 2:25-27;
Gal 5:6; 6:15;
Col 3:11
7:20
sver 24
7:22
tJn 8:32,36;
Phm 16
uEph 6:6
7:23
v1Co 6:20
7:24
wver 20
7:25
xver 6; 2Co 8:8
y2Co 4:1;
1Ti 1:13,16
7:26
zver 1,8
7:29
aver 31;
Ro 13:11,12

mourn, as if they did not; those who are happy, as if they were not; those who buy something, as if it were not theirs to keep; 31those who use the things of the world, as if not engrossed in them. For this world in its present form is passing away. b

32I would like you to be free from concern. An unmarried man is concerned about the Lord's affairs c—how he can please the Lord. 33But a married man is concerned about the affairs of this world—how he can please his wife— 34and his interests are divided. An unmarried woman or virgin is concerned about the Lord's affairs: Her aim is to be devoted to the Lord in both body and spirit. d But a married woman is concerned about the affairs of this world—how she can please her husband. 35I am saying this for your own good, not to restrict you, but that you may live in a right way in undivided e devotion to the Lord.

36If anyone thinks he is acting improperly toward the virgin he is engaged to, and if she is getting along in years and he feels he ought to marry, he should do as he wants. He is not sinning. f They should get married. 37But the man who has settled the matter in his own mind, who is under no compulsion but has control over his own will, and who has made up his mind not to marry the virgin—this man also does the right thing. 38So then, he who marries the virgin does right, g but he who does not marry her does even better. a

39A woman is bound to her husband as long as he lives. h But if her husband dies, she is free to marry anyone she wishes, but he must belong to the Lord. i 40In my judgment, j she is happier if she stays as she is—and I think that I too have the Spirit of God.

Food Sacrificed to Idols

8 Now about food sacrificed to idols: k We know that we all possess knowledge. b1 Knowledge puffs up, but love builds up. 2The man who thinks he knows something m does not yet know as he ought to know. n 3But the man who loves God is known by God. o

4So then, about eating food sacrificed to idols: p We know that an idol is nothing at all in the world q and that there is no God but one. r 5For even if there are so-called gods, s whether in heaven or on earth (as indeed there are many "gods" and many "lords"), 6yet for us there is but one God, the Father, t from whom all things came u and for whom we live; and there is but one Lord, v Jesus Christ, through whom all things came w and through whom we live.

7But not everyone knows this. Some people are still so accustomed to idols that when they eat such food they think of it as having been sacrificed to an idol, and since their conscience is weak, x it is defiled. 8But food does not bring us near to God; y we are no worse if we do not eat, and no better if we do.

9Be careful, however, that the exercise of your freedom does not become a stumbling block z to the weak. a 10For if anyone with a weak conscience sees you who have this knowledge eating in an idol's tem-

7:31
b 1Jn 2:17
7:32
c 1Ti 5:5
7:34
d Lk 2:37
7:35
e Ps 86:11
7:36
f ver 28
7:38
g Heb 13:4
7:39
h Ro 7:2,3
i 2Co 6:14
7:40
j ver 25
8:1
k Ac 15:20
1Ro 15:14
8:2
m 1Co 3:18
n 1Co 13:8,9,12;
1Ti 6:4
8:3
o Ro 8:29;
Gal 4:9
8:4
p ver 1,7,10
q 1Co 10:19
r Dt 6:4; Eph 4:6
8:5
s 2Th 2:4
8:6
t Mal 2:10
u Ro 11:36
v Eph 4:5
w Jn 1:3
8:7
x Ro 14:14;
1Co 10:28
8:8
y Ro 14:17
8:9
z Gal 5:13
a Ro 14:1

a36-38 Or 36If anyone thinks he is not treating his daughter properly, and if she is getting along in years, and he feels she ought to marry, he should do as he wants. He is not sinning. He should let her get married. 37But the man who has settled the matter in his own mind, who is under no compulsion but has control over his own will, and who has made up his mind to keep the virgin unmarried—this man also does the right thing. 38So then, he who gives his virgin in marriage does right, but he who does not give her in marriage does even better.   b1 Or "We all possess knowledge," as you say

ple, won't he be emboldened to eat what has been sacrificed to idols?
[11]So this weak brother, for whom Christ died, is destroyed[b] by your
knowledge. [12]When you sin against your brothers[c] in this way and
wound their weak conscience, you sin against Christ. [13]Therefore, if
what I eat causes my brother to fall into sin, I will never eat meat again,
so that I will not cause him to fall. [d]

The Rights of an Apostle

9 Am I not free? Am I not an apostle?[e] Have I not seen Jesus our
Lord?[f] Are you not the result of my work in the Lord?[g] [2]Even
though I may not be an apostle to others, surely I am to you! For you are
the seal[h] of my apostleship in the Lord.

[3]This is my defense to those who sit in judgment on me. [4]Don't we
have the right to food and drink?[i] [5]Don't we have the right to take a
believing wife[j] along with us, as do the other apostles and the Lord's
brothers[k] and Cephas[a]? [6]Or is it only I and Barnabas[l] who must work
for a living?

[7]Who serves as a soldier at his own expense? Who plants a vineyard[m]
and does not eat of its grapes? Who tends a flock and does not drink of
the milk? [8]Do I say this merely from a human point of view? Doesn't the
Law say the same thing? [9]For it is written in the Law of Moses: "Do not
muzzle an ox while it is treading out the grain."[bn] Is it about oxen that
God is concerned?[o] [10]Surely he says this for us, doesn't he? Yes, this
was written for us,[p] because when the plowman plows and the thresher threshes, they ought to do so in the hope of sharing in the harvest. [q]
[11]If we have sown spiritual seed among you, is it too much if we reap a
material harvest from you?[r] [12]If others have this right of support from
you, shouldn't we have it all the more?

But we did not use this right.[s] On the contrary, we put up with
anything rather than hinder[t] the gospel of Christ. [13]Don't you know
that those who work in the temple get their food from the temple, and
those who serve at the altar share in what is offered on the altar?[u] [14]In
the same way, the Lord has commanded that those who preach the
gospel should receive their living from the gospel. [v]

[15]But I have not used any of these rights. [w] And I am not writing this
in the hope that you will do such things for me. I would rather die than
have anyone deprive me of this boast. [x] [16]Yet when I preach the gospel,
I cannot boast, for I am compelled to preach. [y] Woe to me if I do not
preach the gospel! [17]If I preach voluntarily, I have a reward;[z] if not
voluntarily, I am simply discharging the trust committed to me. [a]
[18]What then is my reward? Just this: that in preaching the gospel I may
offer it free of charge, [b] and so not make use of my rights in preaching
it.

[19]Though I am free[c] and belong to no man, I make myself a slave to
everyone, [d] to win as many as possible. [e] [20]To the Jews I became like a
Jew, to win the Jews. [f] To those under the law I became like one under
the law (though I myself am not under the law), so as to win those
under the law. [21]To those not having the law I became like one not
having the law[g] (though I am not free from God's law but am under
Christ's law), so as to win those not having the law. [22]To the weak I

8:11
bRo 14:15,20
8:12
cMt 18:6
8:13
dRo 14:21
9:1
e2Co 12:12
f1Co 15:8
g1Co 3:6; 4:15
9:2
h2Co 3:2,3
9:4
i1Th 2:6
9:5
j1Co 7:7,8
kMt 12:46
9:6
lAc 4:36
9:7
mDt 20:6;
Pr 27:18
9:9
nDt 25:4;
1Ti 5:18
oDt 22:1-4
9:10
pRo 4:23,24
q2Ti 2:6
9:11
rRo 15:27
9:12
sAc 18:3
t2Co 11:7-12
9:13
uLev 6:16,26;
Dt 18:1
9:14
vMt 10:10;
1Ti 5:18
9:15
wAc 18:3
x2Co 11:9,10
9:16
yRo 1:14;
Ac 9:15
9:17
z1Co 3:8,14
aGal 2:7;
Col 1:25
9:18
b2Co 11:7;
12:13
9:19
cver 1 dGal 5:13
eMt 18:15;
1Pe 3:1
9:20
fAc 16:3;
21:20-26;
Ro 11:14
9:21
gRo 2:12,14

a5 That is, Peter   b9 Deut. 25:4

became weak, to win the weak. I have become all things to all men[h] so that by all possible means I might save some.[i] 23I do all this for the sake of the gospel, that I may share in its blessings.

24Do you not know that in a race all the runners run, but only one gets the prize? Run[j] in such a way as to get the prize. 25Everyone who competes in the games goes into strict training. They do it to get a crown that will not last; but we do it to get a crown that will last forever.[k] 26Therefore I do not run like a man running aimlessly; I do not fight like a man beating the air. 27No, I beat my body[l] and make it my slave so that after I have preached to others, I myself will not be disqualified for the prize.

Warnings From Israel's History

10 For I do not want you to be ignorant of the fact, brothers, that our forefathers were all under the cloud[m] and that they all passed through the sea.[n] 2They were all baptized into Moses in the cloud and in the sea. 3They all ate the same spiritual food 4and drank the same spiritual drink; for they drank from the spiritual rock[o] that accompanied them, and that rock was Christ. 5Nevertheless, God was not pleased with most of them; their bodies were scattered over the desert.[p]

6Now these things occurred as examples[a] to keep us from setting our hearts on evil things as they did. 7Do not be idolaters,[q] as some of them were; as it is written: "The people sat down to eat and drink and got up to indulge in pagan revelry."[b][r] 8We should not commit sexual immorality, as some of them did—and in one day twenty-three thousand of them died.[s] 9We should not test the Lord, as some of them did—and were killed by snakes.[t] 10And do not grumble, as some of them did[u]—and were killed[v] by the destroying angel.[w]

11These things happened to them as examples and were written down as warnings for us, on whom the fulfillment of the ages has come.[x] 12So, if you think you are standing firm,[y] be careful that you don't fall! 13No temptation has seized you except what is common to man. And God is faithful;[z] he will not let you be tempted beyond what you can bear.[a] But when you are tempted, he will also provide a way out so that you can stand up under it.

Idol Feasts and the Lord's Supper

14Therefore, my dear friends, flee from idolatry. 15I speak to sensible people; judge for yourselves what I say. 16Is not the cup of thanksgiving for which we give thanks a participation in the blood of Christ? And is not the bread that we break a participation in the body of Christ?[b] 17Because there is one loaf, we, who are many, are one body,[c] for we all partake of the one loaf.

18Consider the people of Israel: Do not those who eat the sacrifices[d] participate in the altar? 19Do I mean then that a sacrifice offered to an idol is anything, or that an idol is anything?[e] 20No, but the sacrifices of pagans are offered to demons,[f] not to God, and I do not want you to be participants with demons. 21You cannot drink the cup of the Lord and the cup of demons too; you cannot have a part in both the Lord's table

---

9:22
h1Co 10:33
iRo 11:14
9:24
jGal 2:2;
2Ti 4:7;
Heb 12:1
9:25
kJas 1:12;
Rev 2:10
9:27
lRo 8:13
10:1
mEx 13:21
nEx 14:22,29
10:4
oEx 17:6;
Nu 20:11;
Ps 78:15
10:5
pNu 14:29;
Heb 3:17
10:7
qver 14
rEx 32:4,6,19
10:8
sNu 25:1-9
10:9
tNu 21:5,6
10:10
uNu 16:41
vNu 16:49
wEx 12:23
10:11
xRo 13:11
10:12
yRo 11:20
10:13
z1Co 1:9
a2Pe 2:9
10:16
bMt 26:26-28
10:17
cRo 12:5;
1Co 12:27
10:18
dLev 7:6,14,15
10:19
e1Co 8:4
10:20
fDt 32:17;
Ps 106:37;
Rev 9:20

---

a6 Or *types*; also in verse 11   *b7* Exodus 32:6

and the table of demons.⁸ ²²Are we trying to arouse the Lord's jealousy?ʰ Are we stronger than he?ⁱ

The Believer's Freedom

²³"Everything is permissible"—but not everything is beneficial.ʲ "Everything is permissible"—but not everything is constructive. ²⁴Nobody should seek his own good, but the good of others.ᵏ

²⁵Eat anything sold in the meat market without raising questions of conscience,ˡ ²⁶for, "The earth is the Lord's, and everything in it."ᵃ ᵐ ²⁷If some unbeliever invites you to a meal and you want to go, eat whatever is put before youⁿ without raising questions of conscience. ²⁸But if anyone says to you, "This has been offered in sacrifice," then do not eat it, both for the sake of the man who told you and for conscience' sakeᵇ ᵒ— ²⁹the other man's conscience, I mean, not yours. For why should my freedomᵖ be judged by another's conscience? ³⁰If I take part in the meal with thankfulness, why am I denounced because of something I thank God for?�q

³¹So whether you eat or drink or whatever you do, do it all for the glory of God.ʳ ³²Do not cause anyone to stumble,ˢ whether Jews, Greeks or the church of Godᵗ— ³³even as I try to please everybody in every way.ᵘ For I am not seeking my own good but the good of many,

11 so that they may be saved.ᵛ ¹Follow my example,ʷ as I follow the example of Christ.

Propriety in Worship

²I praise youˣ for remembering me in everythingʸ and for holding to the teachings,ᶜ just as I passed them on to you.ᶻ

³Now I want you to realize that the head of every man is Christ,ᵃ and the head of the woman is man,ᵇ and the head of Christ is God.ᶜ ⁴Every man who prays or prophesies with his head covered dishonors his head. ⁵And every woman who prays or prophesiesᵈ with her head uncovered dishonors her head—it is just as though her head were shaved.ᵉ ⁶If a woman does not cover her head, she should have her hair cut off; and if it is a disgrace for a woman to have her hair cut or shaved off, she should cover her head. ⁷A man ought not to cover his head,ᵈ since he is the imageᶠ and glory of God; but the woman is the glory of man. ⁸For man did not come from woman, but woman from man;ᵍ ⁹neither was man created for woman, but woman for man.ʰ ¹⁰For this reason, and because of the angels, the woman ought to have a sign of authority on her head.

¹¹In the Lord, however, woman is not independent of man, nor is man independent of woman. ¹²For as woman came from man, so also man is born of woman. But everything comes from God.ⁱ ¹³Judge for yourselves: Is it proper for a woman to pray to God with her head uncovered? ¹⁴Does not the very nature of things teach you that if a man has long hair, it is a disgrace to him, ¹⁵but that if a woman has long hair,

---

ᵃ26 Psalm 24:1   ᵇ28 Some manuscripts *conscience' sake, for "the earth is the Lord's and everything in it"*   ᶜ2 Or *traditions*   ᵈ4-7 Or ⁴*Every man who prays or prophesies with long hair dishonors his head.* ⁵*And every woman who prays or prophesies with no covering of hair on her head dishonors her head—she is just like one of the "shorn women."* ⁶*If a woman has no covering, let her be for now with short hair, but since it is a disgrace for a woman to have her hair shorn or shaved, she should grow it again.* ⁷*A man ought not to have long hair*

10:21
g2Co 6:15,16
10:22
hDt 32:16,21
iEcc 6:10;
Isa 45:9
10:23
j1Co 6:12
10:24
kver 33;
Ro 15:1,2;
1Co 13:5;
Php 2:4,21
10:25
lAc 10:15;
1Co 8:7
10:26
mPs 24:1
10:27
nLk 10:7
10:28
o1Co 8:7,10-12
10:29
pRo 14:16;
1Co 9:1,19
10:30
qRo 14:6
10:31
rCol 3:17;
1Pe 4:11
10:32
sAc 24:16
tAc 20:28
10:33
uRo 15:2;
1Co 9:22
vRo 11:14
11:1
w1Co 4:16
11:2
xver 17,22
y1Co 4:17
z1Co 15:2,3;
2Th 2:15
11:3
aEph 1:22
bGe 3:16;
Eph 5:23
c1Co 3:23
11:5
dAc 21:9
eDt 21:12
11:7
fGe 1:26;
Jas 3:9
11:8
gGe 2:21-23;
1Ti 2:13
11:9
hGe 2:18
11:12
iRo 11:36

it is her glory? For long hair is given to her as a covering. [16]If anyone wants to be contentious about this, we have no other practice—nor do the churches of God. [j]

The Lord's Supper

11:23–25pp — Mt 26:26–28; Mk 14:22–24; Lk 22:17–20

[17]In the following directives I have no praise for you,[k] for your meetings do more harm than good. [18]In the first place, I hear that when you come together as a church, there are divisions[l] among you, and to some extent I believe it. [19]No doubt there have to be differences among you to show which of you have God's approval.[m] [20]When you come together, it is not the Lord's Supper you eat, [21]for as you eat, each of you goes ahead without waiting for anybody else.[n] One remains hungry, another gets drunk. [22]Don't you have homes to eat and drink in? Or do you despise the church of God[o] and humiliate those who have nothing?[p] What shall I say to you? Shall I praise you[q] for this? Certainly not!

[23]For I received from the Lord[r] what I also passed on to you:[s] The Lord Jesus, on the night he was betrayed, took bread, [24]and when he had given thanks, he broke it and said, "This is my body, which is for you; do this in remembrance of me." [25]In the same way, after supper he took the cup, saying, "This cup is the new covenant[t] in my blood;[u] do this, whenever you drink it, in remembrance of me." [26]For whenever you eat this bread and drink this cup, you proclaim the Lord's death until he comes.

[27]Therefore, whoever eats the bread or drinks the cup of the Lord in an unworthy manner will be guilty of sinning against the body and blood of the Lord.[v] [28]A man ought to examine himself[w] before he eats of the bread and drinks of the cup. [29]For anyone who eats and drinks without recognizing the body of the Lord eats and drinks judgment on himself. [30]That is why many among you are weak and sick, and a number of you have fallen asleep. [31]But if we judged ourselves, we would not come under judgment.[x] [32]When we are judged by the Lord, we are being disciplined[y] so that we will not be condemned with the world.

[33]So then, my brothers, when you come together to eat, wait for each other. [34]If anyone is hungry,[z] he should eat at home,[a] so that when you meet together it may not result in judgment.

And when I come[b] I will give further directions.

Spiritual Gifts

12 Now about spiritual gifts,[c] brothers, I do not want you to be ignorant. [2]You know that when you were pagans,[d] somehow or other you were influenced and led astray to mute idols.[e] [3]Therefore I tell you that no one who is speaking by the Spirit of God says, "Jesus be cursed,"[f] and no one can say, "Jesus is Lord,"[g] except by the Holy Spirit.[h]

[4]There are different kinds of gifts, but the same Spirit.[i] [5]There are different kinds of service, but the same Lord. [6]There are different kinds of working, but the same God[j] works all of them in all men.

[7]Now to each one the manifestation of the Spirit is given for the common good.[k] [8]To one there is given through the Spirit the message

11:16
j1Co 7:17
11:17
kver 2,22
11:18
l1Co 1:10-12;
3:3
11:19
m1Jn 2:19
11:21
n2Pe 2:13;
Jude 12
11:22
o1Co 10:32
pJas 2:6 qver 2,
17
11:23
rGal 1:12
s1Co 15:3
11:25
tLk 22:20
u1Co 10:16
11:27
vHeb 10:29
11:28
w2Co 13:5
11:31
xPs 32:5;
1Jn 1:9
11:32
yPs 94:12;
Heb 12:7-10;
Rev 3:19
11:34
zver 21 aver 22
b1Co 4:19
12:1
cRo 1:11;
1Co 14:1,37
12:2
dEph 2:11,12;
1Pe 4:3
ePs 115:5;
Jer 10:5;
Hab 2:18,19;
1Th 1:9
12:3
fRo 9:3
gJn 13:13
h1Jn 4:2,3
12:4
iRo 12:4-8;
Eph 4:11;
Heb 2:4
12:6
jEph 4:6
12:7
kEph 4:12

of wisdom,[1] to another the message of knowledge[m] by means of the same Spirit, [9]to another faith[n] by the same Spirit, to another gifts of healing[o] by that one Spirit, [10]to another miraculous powers,[p] to another prophecy, to another distinguishing between spirits,[q] to another speaking in different kinds of tongues,[a][r] and to still another the interpretation of tongues.[a] [11]All these are the work of one and the same Spirit,[s] and he gives them to each one, just as he determines.

One Body, Many Parts

[12]The body is a unit, though it is made up of many parts; and though all its parts are many, they form one body.[t] So it is with Christ.[u] [13]For we were all baptized by[b] one Spirit[v] into one body—whether Jews or Greeks, slave or free[w]—and we were all given the one Spirit to drink.[x]

[14]Now the body is not made up of one part but of many. [15]If the foot should say, "Because I am not a hand, I do not belong to the body," it would not for that reason cease to be part of the body. [16]And if the ear should say, "Because I am not an eye, I do not belong to the body," it would not for that reason cease to be part of the body. [17]If the whole body were an eye, where would the sense of hearing be? If the whole body were an ear, where would the sense of smell be? [18]But in fact God has arranged[y] the parts in the body, every one of them, just as he wanted them to be.[z] [19]If they were all one part, where would the body be? [20]As it is, there are many parts, but one body.[a]

[21]The eye cannot say to the hand, "I don't need you!" And the head cannot say to the feet, "I don't need you!" [22]On the contrary, those parts of the body that seem to be weaker are indispensable, [23]and the parts that we think are less honorable we treat with special honor. And the parts that are unpresentable are treated with special modesty, [24]while our presentable parts need no special treatment. But God has combined the members of the body and has given greater honor to the parts that lacked it, [25]so that there should be no division in the body, but that its parts should have equal concern for each other. [26]If one part suffers, every part suffers with it; if one part is honored, every part rejoices with it.

[27]Now you are the body of Christ,[b] and each one of you is a part of it.[c] [28]And in the church[d] God has appointed first of all apostles,[e] second prophets, third teachers, then workers of miracles, also those having gifts of healing,[f] those able to help others, those with gifts of administration,[g] and those speaking in different kinds of tongues.[h] [29]Are all apostles? Are all prophets? Are all teachers? Do all work miracles? [30]Do all have gifts of healing? Do all speak in tongues[c]?[i] Do all interpret? [31]But eagerly desire[d][j] the greater gifts.

Love

And now I will show you the most excellent way.

13 If I speak in the tongues[e][k] of men and of angels, but have not love, I am only a resounding gong or a clanging cymbal. [2]If I have the gift of prophecy and can fathom all mysteries[l] and all knowledge, and if I have a faith[m] that can move mountains,[n] but have not

12:8
l1Co 2:6
m2Co 8:7

12:9
nMt 17:19,20;
2Co 4:13
over 28,30

12:10
pGal 3:5
q1Jn 4:1
rMk 16:17

12:11
sver 4

12:12
tRo 12:5 uver 27

12:13
vEph 2:18
wGal 3:28;
Col 3:11
xJn 7:37-39

12:18
yver 28 zver 11

12:20
aver 12,14

12:27
bEph 1:23;
4:12; Col 1:18,
24 cRo 12:5

12:28
d1Co 10:32
eEph 4:11 fver 9
gRo 12:6-8
hver 10

12:30
iver 10

12:31
j1Co 14:1,39

13:1
kver 8

13:2
l1Co 14:2
m1Co 12:9
nMt 17:20;
21:21

---

[a]10 Or *languages*; also in verse 28   [b]13 Or *with; or in*   [c]30 Or *other languages*   [d]31 Or *But you are eagerly desiring*   [e]1 Or *languages*

love, I am nothing. ³If I give all I possess to the poor° and surrender my body to the flames, ᵃᵖ but have not love, I gain nothing.

⁴Love is patient, �q love is kind. It does not envy, it does not boast, it is not proud. ⁵It is not rude, it is not self-seeking, ʳ it is not easily angered, it keeps no record of wrongs. ⁶Love does not delight in evilˢ but rejoices with the truth.ᵗ ⁷It always protects, always trusts, always hopes, always perseveres.

⁸Love never fails. But where there are prophecies, ᵘ they will cease; where there are tongues, ᵛ they will be stilled; where there is knowledge, it will pass away. ⁹For we know in partʷ and we prophesy in part, ¹⁰but when perfection comes, ˣ the imperfect disappears. ¹¹When I was a child, I talked like a child, I thought like a child, I reasoned like a child. When I became a man, I put childish ways behind me. ¹²Now we see but a poor reflection as in a mirror; then we shall see face to face.ʸ Now I know in part; then I shall know fully, even as I am fully known.ᶻ

¹³And now these three remain: faith, hope and love.ᵃ But the greatest of these is love.ᵇ

Gifts of Prophecy and Tongues

14 Follow the way of loveᶜ and eagerly desireᵈ spiritual gifts,ᵉ especially the gift of prophecy. ²For anyone who speaks in a tongueᵇᶠ does not speak to men but to God. Indeed, no one understands him; he utters mysteriesᵍ with his spirit.ᶜ ³But everyone who prophesies speaks to men for their strengthening,ʰ encouragement and comfort. ⁴He who speaks in a tongueⁱ edifies himself, but he who prophesiesʲ edifies the church. ⁵I would like every one of you to speak in tongues,ᵈ but I would rather have you prophesy.ᵏ He who prophesies is greater than one who speaks in tongues,ᵈ unless he interprets, so that the church may be edified.

⁶Now, brothers, if I come to you and speak in tongues, what good will I be to you, unless I bring you some revelationˡ or knowledge or prophecy or word of instruction?ᵐ ⁷Even in the case of lifeless things that make sounds, such as the flute or harp, how will anyone know what tune is being played unless there is a distinction in the notes? ⁸Again, if the trumpet does not sound a clear call, who will get ready for battle?ⁿ ⁹So it is with you. Unless you speak intelligible words with your tongue, how will anyone know what you are saying? You will just be speaking into the air. ¹⁰Undoubtedly there are all sorts of languages in the world, yet none of them is without meaning. ¹¹If then I do not grasp the meaning of what someone is saying, I am a foreigner to the speaker, and he is a foreigner to me. ¹²So it is with you. Since you are eager to have spiritual gifts, try to excel in gifts that build up the church.

¹³For this reason anyone who speaks in a tongue should pray that he may interpret what he says. ¹⁴For if I pray in a tongue, my spirit prays, but my mind is unfruitful. ¹⁵So what shall I do? I will pray with my spirit, but I will also pray with my mind; I will sing° with my spirit, but I will also sing with my mind. ¹⁶If you are praising God with your spirit, how can one who finds himself among those who do not understandᵉ

13:3
oMt 6:2
pDa 3:28
13:4
q1Th 5:14
13:5
r1Co 10:24
13:6
s2Th 2:12
t2Jn 4; 3Jn 3,4
13:8
uver 2 vver 1
13:9
wver 12;
1Co 8:2
13:10
xPhp 3:12
13:12
yGe 32:30;
2Co 5:7;
1Jn 3:2
z1Co 8:3
13:13
aGal 5:5,6
b1Co 16:14
14:1
c1Co 16:14
dver 39;
1Co 12:31
e1Co 12:1
14:2
fMk 16:17
g1Co 13:2
14:3
hver 4,5,12,17,
26; Ro 14:19
14:4
iMk 16:17
j1Co 13:2
14:5
kNu 11:29
14:6
lver 26;
Eph 1:17
mRo 6:17
14:8
nNu 10:9;
Jer 4:19
14:15
oEph 5:19;
Col 3:16

ᵃ3 Some early manuscripts *body that I may boast*   ᵇ2 Or *another language*; also in verses 4, 13, 14, 19, 26 and 27   ᶜ2 Or *by the Spirit*   ᵈ5 Or *other languages*; also in verses 6, 18, 22, 23 and 39   ᵉ16 Or *among the inquirers* say "Amen"[p] to your thanksgiving,[q] since he does not know what you are saying? [17]You may be giving thanks well enough, but the other man is not edified.

[18]I thank God that I speak in tongues more than all of you. [19]But in the church I would rather speak five intelligible words to instruct others than ten thousand words in a tongue.

[20]Brothers, stop thinking like children.[r] In regard to evil be infants,[s] but in your thinking be adults. [21]In the Law[t] it is written:

> "Through men of strange tongues
>> and through the lips of foreigners
> I will speak to this people,
>> but even then they will not listen to me,"[a][u]

says the Lord.

[22]Tongues, then, are a sign, not for believers but for unbelievers; prophecy,[v] however, is for believers, not for unbelievers. [23]So if the whole church comes together and everyone speaks in tongues, and some who do not understand[b] or some unbelievers come in, will they not say that you are out of your mind?[w] [24]But if an unbeliever or someone who does not understand[c] comes in while everybody is prophesying, he will be convinced by all that he is a sinner and will be judged by all, [25]and the secrets of his heart will be laid bare. So he will fall down and worship God, exclaiming, "God is really among you!"[x]

Orderly Worship

[26]What then shall we say, brothers? When you come together, everyone[y] has a hymn,[z] or a word of instruction,[a] a revelation, a tongue or an interpretation. All of these must be done for the strengthening[b] of the church. [27]If anyone speaks in a tongue, two—or at the most three —should speak, one at a time, and someone must interpret. [28]If there is no interpreter, the speaker should keep quiet in the church and speak to himself and God.

[29]Two or three prophets should speak, and the others should weigh carefully what is said.[c] [30]And if a revelation comes to someone who is sitting down, the first speaker should stop. [31]For you can all prophesy in turn so that everyone may be instructed and encouraged. [32]The spirits of prophets are subject to the control of prophets.[d] [33]For God is not a God of disorder[e] but of peace.

As in all the congregations of the saints,[f] [34]women should remain silent in the churches. They are not allowed to speak, but must be in submission,[g] as the Law[h] says. [35]If they want to inquire about something, they should ask their own husbands at home; for it is disgraceful for a woman to speak in the church.

[36]Did the word of God originate with you? Or are you the only people it has reached? [37]If anybody thinks he is a prophet[i] or spiritually gifted, let him acknowledge that what I am writing to you is the Lord's command.[j] [38]If he ignores this, he himself will be ignored.[d]

[39]Therefore, my brothers, be eager[k] to prophesy, and do not forbid

---

14:16
p Dt 27:15-26;
1Ch 16:36;
Ne 8:6;
Ps 106:48;
Rev 5:14; 7:12
q 1Co 11:24
14:20
r Eph 4:14;
Heb 5:12,13;
1Pe 2:2
s Ro 16:19
14:21
t Jn 10:34
u Isa 28:11,12
14:22
v ver 1
14:23
w Ac 2:13
14:25
x Isa 45:14;
Zec 8:23
14:26
y 1Co 12:7-10
z Eph 5:19
a ver 6
b Ro 14:19
14:29
c 1Co 12:10
14:32
d 1Jn 4:1
14:33
e ver 40 f Ac 9:13
14:34
g 1Ti 2:11,12
h Ge 3:16
14:37
i 2Co 10:7
j 1Jn 4:6
14:39
k 1Co 12:31

---

a21 Isaiah 28:11,12   b23 Or *some inquirers*   c24 Or *or some inquirer*   d38 Some
manuscripts *If he is ignorant of this, let him be ignorant*

14:40
lver 33
15:1
mRo 2:16
15:2
nRo 1:16
oRo 11:22
15:3
pGal 1:12
q1Co 11:23
rIsa 53:5;
1Pe 2:24
sLk 24:27;
Ac 26:22,23
15:4
tAc 2:24
uMt 16:21
vAc 2:25,30,31
15:5
wLk 24:34
xMk 16:14
15:7
yLk 24:33,36,
37; Ac 1:3,4
15:8
zAc 9:3-6,17;
1Co 9:1
15:9
aEph 3:8;
1Ti 1:15 bAc 8:3
15:10
cRo 12:3
d2Co 11:23
ePhp 2:13
15:12
fAc 17:32;
23:8; 2Ti 2:18
15:14
g1Th 4:14
15:15
hAc 2:24
15:17
iRo 4:25
15:19
j1Co 4:9
15:20
k1Pe 1:3
lver 23;
Ac 26:23;
Rev 1:5 mver 6,
18
15:21
nRo 5:12
15:22
oRo 5:14-18
15:23
pver 20 qver 52
15:24
rDa 7:14,27
sRo 8:38
15:25
tPs 110:1;
Mt 22:44
15:26
u2Ti 1:10;
Rev 20:14; 21:4
15:27
vPs 8:6
wMt 28:18
15:28
xPhp 3:21
y1Co 3:23

speaking in tongues. [40]But everything should be done in a fitting and orderly[1] way.

The Resurrection of Christ

15 Now, brothers, I want to remind you of the gospel[m] I preached to you, which you received and on which you have taken your stand. [2]By this gospel you are saved,[n] if you hold firmly[o] to the word I preached to you. Otherwise, you have believed in vain.

[3]For what I received[p] I passed on to you[q] as of first importance[a]: that Christ died for our sins[r] according to the Scriptures,[s] [4]that he was buried, that he was raised[t] on the third day[u] according to the Scriptures,[v] [5]and that he appeared to Peter,[bw] and then to the Twelve.[x] [6]After that, he appeared to more than five hundred of the brothers at the same time, most of whom are still living, though some have fallen asleep. [7]Then he appeared to James, then to all the apostles,[y] [8]and last of all he appeared to me also,[z] as to one abnormally born.

[9]For I am the least of the apostles[a] and do not even deserve to be called an apostle, because I persecuted[b] the church of God. [10]But by the grace of God I am what I am, and his grace to me[c] was not without effect. No, I worked harder than all of them[d]—yet not I, but the grace of God that was with me.[e] [11]Whether, then, it was I or they, this is what we preach, and this is what you believed.

The Resurrection of the Dead

[12]But if it is preached that Christ has been raised from the dead, how can some of you say that there is no resurrection of the dead?[f] [13]If there is no resurrection of the dead, then not even Christ has been raised. [14]And if Christ has not been raised,[g] our preaching is useless and so is your faith. [15]More than that, we are then found to be false witnesses about God, for we have testified about God that he raised Christ from the dead.[h] But he did not raise him if in fact the dead are not raised. [16]For if the dead are not raised, then Christ has not been raised either. [17]And if Christ has not been raised, your faith is futile; you are still in your sins.[i] [18]Then those also who have fallen asleep in Christ are lost. [19]If only for this life we have hope in Christ, we are to be pitied more than all men.[j]

[20]But Christ has indeed been raised from the dead,[k] the firstfruits[l] of those who have fallen asleep.[m] [21]For since death came through a man,[n] the resurrection of the dead comes also through a man. [22]For as in Adam all die, so in Christ all will be made alive.[o] [23]But each in his own turn: Christ, the firstfruits;[p] then, when he comes,[q] those who belong to him. [24]Then the end will come, when he hands over the kingdom[r] to God the Father after he has destroyed all dominion, authority and power.[s] [25]For he must reign until he has put all his enemies under his feet.[t] [26]The last enemy to be destroyed is death.[u] [27]For he "has put everything under his feet."[cv] Now when it says that "everything" has been put under him, it is clear that this does not include God himself, who put everything under Christ.[w] [28]When he has done this, then the Son himself will be made subject to him who put everything under him,[x] so that God may be all in all.[y]

a3 *Or* you at the first   b5 Greek *Cephas*   c27 Psalm 8:6

²⁹Now if there is no resurrection, what will those do who are baptized for the dead? If the dead are not raised at all, why are people baptized for them? ³⁰And as for us, why do we endanger ourselves every hour?ᶻ ³¹I die every dayᵃ—I mean that, brothers—just as surely as I glory over you in Christ Jesus our Lord. ³²If I fought wild beastsᵇ in Ephesusᶜ for merely human reasons, what have I gained? If the dead are not raised,

> "Let us eat and drink,
>   for tomorrow we die."ᵃ ᵈ

³³Do not be misled: "Bad company corrupts good character." ³⁴Come back to your senses as you ought, and stop sinning; for there are some who are ignorant of God—I say this to your shame.

The Resurrection Body

³⁵But someone may ask,ᵉ "How are the dead raised? With what kind of body will they come?"ᶠ ³⁶How foolish!ᵍ What you sow does not come to life unless it dies.ʰ ³⁷When you sow, you do not plant the body that will be, but just a seed, perhaps of wheat or of something else. ³⁸But God gives it a body as he has determined, and to each kind of seed he gives its own body.ⁱ ³⁹All flesh is not the same: Men have one kind of flesh, animals have another, birds another and fish another. ⁴⁰There are also heavenly bodies and there are earthly bodies; but the splendor of the heavenly bodies is one kind, and the splendor of the earthly bodies is another. ⁴¹The sun has one kind of splendor, the moon another and the stars another; and star differs from star in splendor.

⁴²So will it beʲ with the resurrection of the dead. The body that is sown is perishable, it is raised imperishable; ⁴³it is sown in dishonor, it is raised in glory;ᵏ it is sown in weakness, it is raised in power; ⁴⁴it is sown a natural body, it is raised a spiritual body.ˡ

If there is a natural body, there is also a spiritual body. ⁴⁵So it is written: "The first man Adam became a living being"ᵇ;ᵐ the last Adam,ⁿ a life-giving spirit.ᵒ ⁴⁶The spiritual did not come first, but the natural, and after that the spiritual. ⁴⁷The first man was of the dust of the earth,ᵖ the second man from heaven.�q ⁴⁸As was the earthly man, so are those who are of the earth; and as is the man from heaven, so also are those who are of heaven.ʳ ⁴⁹And just as we have borne the likeness of the earthly man,ˢ so shall weᶜ bear the likeness of the man from heaven.ᵗ

⁵⁰I declare to you, brothers, that flesh and bloodᵘ cannot inherit the kingdom of God, nor does the perishable inherit the imperishable. ⁵¹Listen, I tell you a mystery:ᵛ We will not all sleep, but we will all be changedʷ— ⁵²in a flash, in the twinkling of an eye, at the last trumpet. For the trumpet will sound,ˣ the deadʸ will be raised imperishable, and we will be changed. ⁵³For the perishable must clothe itself with the imperishable,ᶻ and the mortal with immortality. ⁵⁴When the perishable has been clothed with the imperishable, and the mortal with immortality, then the saying that is written will come true: "Death has been swallowed up in victory."ᵈ ᵃ

15:30
z2Co 11:26
15:31
aRo 8:36
15:32
b2Co 1:8
cAc 18:19
dIsa 22:13;
Lk 12:19
15:35
eRo 9:19
fEze 37:3
15:36
gLk 11:40
hJn 12:24
15:38
iGe 1:11
15:42
jDa 12:3;
Mt 13:43
15:43
kPhp 3:21;
Col 3:4
15:44
lver 50
15:45
mGe 2:7
nRo 5:14
oJn 5:21; Ro 8:2
15:47
pGe 2:7; 3:19
qJn 3:13,31
15:48
rPhp 3:20,21
15:49
sGe 5:3
tRo 8:29
15:50
uJn 3:3,5
15:51
v1Co 13:2
wPhp 3:21
15:52
xMt 24:31
yJn 5:25
15:53
z2Co 5:2,4
15:54
aIsa 25:8;
Rev 20:14

ᵃ32 Isaiah 22:13   ᵇ45 Gen. 2:7   ᶜ49 Some early manuscripts *so let us*   ᵈ54 Isaiah 25:8

15:55
b Hos 13:14
15:56
c Ro 5:12
d Ro 4:15
15:57
e 2Co 2:14
f Ro 8:37
15:58
g 1Co 16:10
16:1
h Ac 24:17
i Ac 9:13
j Ac 16:6
16:2
k Ac 20:7
l 2Co 9:4,5
16:3
m 2Co 8:18,19
16:5
n 1Co 4:19
o Ac 19:21
16:6
p Ro 15:24
16:7
q Ac 18:21
16:8
r Ac 18:19
s Ac 2:1
16:9
t Ac 14:27
16:10
u Ac 16:1
v 1Co 15:58
16:11
w 1Ti 4:12
x Ac 15:33
16:12
y Ac 18:24;
1Co 1:12
16:13
z Gal 5:1;
Php 1:27;
1Th 3:8;
2Th 2:15
a Eph 6:10
16:14
b 1Co 14:1
16:15
c 1Co 1:16
d Ro 16:5
e Ac 18:12
16:16
f Heb 13:17
16:17
g 2Co 11:9;
Php 2:30
16:18
h Phm 7
i Php 2:29
16:19
j Ac 18:2
k Ro 16:5
16:20
l Ro 16:16

55"Where, O death, is your victory?
  Where, O death, is your sting?"[a] [b]

56The sting of death is sin,[c] and the power of sin is the law.[d] 57But thanks be to God![e] He gives us the victory through our Lord Jesus Christ.[f]

58Therefore, my dear brothers, stand firm. Let nothing move you. Always give yourselves fully to the work of the Lord,[g] because you know that your labor in the Lord is not in vain.

The Collection for God's People

16 Now about the collection[h] for God's people:[i] Do what I told the Galatian[j] churches to do. 2On the first day of every week,[k] each one of you should set aside a sum of money in keeping with his income, saving it up, so that when I come no collections will have to be made.[l] 3Then, when I arrive, I will give letters of introduction to the men you approve[m] and send them with your gift to Jerusalem. 4If it seems advisable for me to go also, they will accompany me.

Personal Requests

5After I go through Macedonia, I will come to you[n]—for I will be going through Macedonia.[o] 6Perhaps I will stay with you awhile, or even spend the winter, so that you can help me on my journey,[p] wherever I go. 7I do not want to see you now and make only a passing visit; I hope to spend some time with you, if the Lord permits.[q] 8But I will stay on at Ephesus[r] until Pentecost,[s] 9because a great door for effective work has opened to me,[t] and there are many who oppose me.

10If Timothy[u] comes, see to it that he has nothing to fear while he is with you, for he is carrying on the work of the Lord,[v] just as I am. 11No one, then, should refuse to accept him.[w] Send him on his way in peace[x] so that he may return to me. I am expecting him along with the brothers.

12Now about our brother Apollos:[y] I strongly urged him to go to you with the brothers. He was quite unwilling to go now, but he will go when he has the opportunity.

13Be on your guard; stand firm[z] in the faith; be men of courage; be strong.[a] 14Do everything in love.[b]

15You know that the household of Stephanas[c] were the first converts[d] in Achaia,[e] and they have devoted themselves to the service of the saints. I urge you, brothers, 16to submit[f] to such as these and to everyone who joins in the work, and labors at it. 17I was glad when Stephanas, Fortunatus and Achaicus arrived, because they have supplied what was lacking from you.[g] 18For they refreshed[h] my spirit and yours also. Such men deserve recognition.[i]

Final Greetings

19The churches in the province of Asia send you greetings. Aquila and Priscilla[b] [j] greet you warmly in the Lord, and so does the church that meets at their house.[k] 20All the brothers here send you greetings. Greet one another with a holy kiss.[l]

---

[a]55 Hosea 13:14   [b]19 Greek *Prisca*, a variant of *Priscilla*

²¹I, Paul, write this greeting in my own hand. ᵐ

²²If anyone does not love the Lordⁿ—a curseᵒ be on him. Come, O Lordᵃ !ᵖ

²³The grace of the Lord Jesus be with you. ۹

²⁴My love to all of you in Christ Jesus. Amen. ᵇ

16:21
mGal 6:11;
Col 4:18
16:22
nEph 6:24
oRo 9:3
pRev 22:20
16:23
qRo 16:20

ᵃ22 In Aramaic the expression *Come, O Lord* is *Marana tha.*   ᵇ24 Some manuscripts do not have *Amen.*

2 Corinthians

Title and Background

This letter seems to have been written a few months after the first letter. The divisions and problems spoken of in 1 Corinthians were still present in the church at Corinth. False teachers were challenging both Paul's personal integrity and his authority as an apostle. They were saying that he was not a genuine apostle and that he was putting into his own pocket the money they had collected for the poverty-stricken believers in Jerusalem.

Author and Date of Writing

Paul was the author of this letter. It is stamped with his style and contains more autobiographical material than any of his other writings. The available evidence indicates that 1 Corinthians was written in the spring of A.D. 55 and that 2 Corinthians was written in the fall of that same year.

Theme and Message

Paul shows his feelings in this letter more than in any other. He goes from despair to ecstatic joy. The letter falls naturally into three sections: (1) Paul explains the reasons for the change of his itinerary (chapters 1-7); (2) he encourages the Corinthians to complete the collection in preparation for his arrival (chapters 8-9); (3) he stresses the certainty of his coming, his authenticity as an apostle and his readiness as an apostle to excercise discipline if necessary (chapters 10-13).

Outline

I. Introduction: Greetings and Thanksgiving (1:1-11)
II. Paul's Explanation of His Conduct and Apostolic Ministry (1:12-7:16)
III. The Collection for the Christians at Jerusalem (8:1-9:15)
IV. Paul's Vindication of His Apostolic Authority (10:1-13:10)
V. Conclusion (13:11-14)

1:1
a 1Co 1:1;
Eph 1:1;
Col 1:1; 2Ti 1:1
b 1Co 10:32
c Ac 18:12

1:2
d Ro 1:7

1:3
e Eph 1:3;
1Pe 1:3

1:4
f 2Co 7:6,7,13

1:5
g 2Co 4:10;
Col 1:24

1:6
h 2Co 4:15

1 Paul, an apostle of Christ Jesus by the will of God,a and Timothy our brother,

To the church of Godb in Corinth, together with all the saints throughout Achaia:c

2Grace and peace to you from God our Father and the Lord Jesus Christ.d

The God of All Comfort

3Praise be to the God and Father of our Lord Jesus Christ,e the Father of compassion and the God of all comfort, 4who comforts usf in all our troubles, so that we can comfort those in any trouble with the comfort we ourselves have received from God. 5For just as the sufferings of Christ flow over into our lives,g so also through Christ our comfort overflows. 6If we are distressed, it is for your comfort and salvation;h if we are comforted, it is for your comfort, which produces in you patient endurance of the same sufferings we suffer. [7]And our hope for you is firm, because we know that just as you share in our sufferings,[i] so also you share in our comfort.

[8]We do not want you to be uninformed, brothers, about the hardships we suffered[j] in the province of Asia. We were under great pressure, far beyond our ability to endure, so that we despaired even of life. [9]Indeed, in our hearts we felt the sentence of death. But this happened that we might not rely on ourselves but on God,[k] who raises the dead. [10]He has delivered us from such a deadly peril,[l] and he will deliver us. On him we have set our hope that he will continue to deliver us, [11]as you help us by your prayers.[m] Then many will give thanks[n] on our[a] behalf for the gracious favor granted us in answer to the prayers of many.

Paul's Change of Plans

[12]Now this is our boast: Our conscience[o] testifies that we have conducted ourselves in the world, and especially in our relations with you, in the holiness and sincerity[p] that are from God. We have done so not according to worldly wisdom[q] but according to God's grace. [13]For we do not write you anything you cannot read or understand. And I hope that, [14]as you have understood us in part, you will come to understand fully that you can boast of us just as we will boast of you in the day of the Lord Jesus.[r]

[15]Because I was confident of this, I planned to visit you[s] first so that you might benefit twice.[t] [16]I planned to visit you on my way[u] to Macedonia and to come back to you from Macedonia, and then to have you send me on my way to Judea. [17]When I planned this, did I do it lightly? Or do I make my plans in a worldly manner[v] so that in the same breath I say, "Yes, yes" and "No, no"?

[18]But as surely as God is faithful,[w] our message to you is not "Yes" and "No." [19]For the Son of God, Jesus Christ, who was preached among you by me and Silas[b] and Timothy, was not "Yes" and "No," but in him it has always[x] been "Yes." [20]For no matter how many promises[y] God has made, they are "Yes" in Christ. And so through him the "Amen"[z] is spoken by us to the glory of God. [21]Now it is God who makes both us and you stand firm in Christ. He anointed[a] us, [22]set his seal of ownership on us, and put his Spirit in our hearts as a deposit, guaranteeing what is to come.[b]

[23]I call God as my witness[c] that it was in order to spare you[d] that I did not return to Corinth. [24]Not that we lord it over[e] your faith, but we work with you for your joy, because it is by faith you stand firm.[f] [2][1]So I made up my mind that I would not make another painful visit to you.[g] [2]For if I grieve you,[h] who is left to make me glad but you whom I have grieved? [3]I wrote as I did[i] so that when I came I should not be distressed[j] by those who ought to make me rejoice. I had confidence[k] in all of you, that you would all share my joy. [4]For I wrote you[l] out of great distress and anguish of heart and with many tears, not to grieve you but to let you know the depth of my love for you.

1:7
iRo 8:17
1:8
j1Co 15:32
1:9
kJer 17:5,7
1:10
lRo 15:31
1:11
mRo 15:30;
Php 1:19
n2Co 4:15
1:12
oAc 23:1
p2Co 2:17
q1Co 2:1,4,13
1:14
r1Co 1:8
1:15
s1Co 4:19
tRo 1:11,13;
15:29
1:16
u1Co 16:5-7
1:17
v2Co 10:2,3
1:18
w1Co 1:9
1:19
xHeb 13:8
1:20
yRo 15:8
z1Co 14:16
1:21
a1Jn 2:20,27
1:22
b2Co 5:5
1:23
cRo 1:9;
Gal 1:20
d1Co 4:21;
2Co 2:1,3;
13:2,10
1:24
e1Pe 5:3
fRo 11:20;
1Co 15:1
2:1
g2Co 1:23
2:2
h2Co 7:8
2:3
i2Co 7:8,12
j2Co 12:21
k2Co 8:22;
Gal 5:10
2:4
l2Co 7:8,12

---

a11 Many manuscripts *your*   *b19* Greek *Silvanus,* a variant of *Silas*

Forgiveness for the Sinner

[5]If anyone has caused grief, [m] he has not so much grieved me as he has grieved all of you, to some extent—not to put it too severely. [6]The punishment[n] inflicted on him by the majority is sufficient for him. [7]Now instead, you ought to forgive and comfort him, [o] so that he will not be overwhelmed by excessive sorrow. [8]I urge you, therefore, to reaffirm your love for him. [9]The reason I wrote you was to see if you would stand the test and be obedient in everything. [p] [10]If you forgive anyone, I also forgive him. And what I have forgiven—if there was anything to forgive—I have forgiven in the sight of Christ for your sake, [11]in order that Satan[q] might not outwit us. For we are not unaware of his schemes. [r]

Ministers of the New Covenant

[12]Now when I went to Troas[s] to preach the gospel of Christ[t] and found that the Lord had opened a door[u] for me, [13]I still had no peace of mind, [v] because I did not find my brother Titus[w] there. So I said good-by to them and went on to Macedonia.

[14]But thanks be to God, [x] who always leads us in triumphal procession in Christ and through us spreads everywhere the fragrance[y] of the knowledge of him. [15]For we are to God the aroma of Christ among those who are being saved and those who are perishing. [z] [16]To the one we are the smell of death;[a] to the other, the fragrance of life. And who is equal to such a task?[b] [17]Unlike so many, we do not peddle the word of God for profit. [c] On the contrary, in Christ we speak before God with sincerity, [d] like men sent from God. [e]

3 Are we beginning to commend ourselves[f] again? Or do we need, like some people, letters of recommendation[g] to you or from you? [2]You yourselves are our letter, written on our hearts, known and read by everybody. [h] [3]You show that you are a letter from Christ, the result of our ministry, written not with ink but with the Spirit of the living God, not on tablets of stone[i] but on tablets of human hearts. [j]

[4]Such confidence[k] as this is ours through Christ before God. [5]Not that we are competent in ourselves to claim anything for ourselves, but our competence comes from God. [l] [6]He has made us competent as ministers of a new covenant[m]—not of the letter but of the Spirit; for the letter kills, but the Spirit gives life. [n]

The Glory of the New Covenant

[7]Now if the ministry that brought death, which was engraved in letters on stone, came with glory, so that the Israelites could not look steadily at the face of Moses because of its glory, [o] fading though it was, [8]will not the ministry of the Spirit be even more glorious? [9]If the ministry that condemns men[p] is glorious, how much more glorious is the ministry that brings righteousness![q] [10]For what was glorious has no glory now in comparison with the surpassing glory. [11]And if what was fading away came with glory, how much greater is the glory of that which lasts!

[12]Therefore, since we have such a hope, we are very bold. [r] [13]We are not like Moses, who would put a veil over his face[s] to keep the Israelites from gazing at it while the radiance was fading away. [14]But their

2:5
m1Co 5:1,2
2:6
n1Co 5:4,5
2:7
oGal 6:1;
Eph 4:32
2:9
p2Co 10:6
2:11
qMt 4:10
rLk 22:31;
2Co 4:4;
1Pe 5:8,9
2:12
sAc 16:8
tRo 1:1
uAc 14:27
2:13
v2Co 7:5
w2Co 7:6,13;
12:18
2:14
xRo 6:17
yEph 5:2;
Php 4:18
2:15
z1Co 1:18
2:16
aLk 2:34
b2Co 3:5,6
2:17
c2Co 4:2
d1Co 5:8
e2Co 1:12
3:1
f2Co 5:12;
12:11 gAc 18:27
3:2
h1Co 9:2
3:3
iEx 24:12
jPr 3:3;
Jer 31:33;
Eze 11:19
3:4
kEph 3:12
3:5
l1Co 15:10
3:6
mLk 22:20
nJn 6:63
3:7
oEx 34:29-35
3:9
pver 7
qRo 1:17; 3:21,
22
3:12
rEph 6:19
3:13
sver 7; Ex 34:33

minds were made dull,[t] for to this day the same veil remains when the old covenant[u] is read.[v] It has not been removed, because only in Christ is it taken away. [15]Even to this day when Moses is read, a veil covers their hearts. [16]But whenever anyone turns to the Lord,[w] the veil is taken away.[x] [17]Now the Lord is the Spirit,[y] and where the Spirit of the Lord is, there is freedom.[z] [18]And we, who with unveiled faces all reflect[a] [a] the Lord's glory,[b] are being transformed into his likeness[c] with ever-increasing glory, which comes from the Lord, who is the Spirit.

Treasures in Jars of Clay

4 Therefore, since through God's mercy[d] we have this ministry, we do not lose heart. [2]Rather, we have renounced secret and shameful ways;[e] we do not use deception, nor do we distort the word of God.[f] On the contrary, by setting forth the truth plainly we commend ourselves to every man's conscience[g] in the sight of God. [3]And even if our gospel[h] is veiled,[i] it is veiled to those who are perishing.[j] [4]The god[k] of this age has blinded[l] the minds of unbelievers, so that they cannot see the light of the gospel of the glory of Christ, who is the image of God. [5]For we do not preach ourselves,[m] but Jesus Christ as Lord, and ourselves as your servants[n] for Jesus' sake. [6]For God, who said, "Let light shine out of darkness,"[b][o] made his light shine in our hearts[p] to give us the light of the knowledge of the glory of God in the face of Christ.

[7]But we have this treasure in jars of clay[q] to show that this all-surpassing power is from God[r] and not from us. [8]We are hard pressed on every side,[s] but not crushed; perplexed, but not in despair; [9]persecuted,[t] but not abandoned;[u] struck down, but not destroyed.[v] [10]We always carry around in our body the death of Jesus, so that the life of Jesus may also be revealed in our body.[w] [11]For we who are alive are always being given over to death for Jesus' sake,[x] so that his life may be revealed in our mortal body. [12]So then, death is at work in us, but life is at work in you.[y]

[13]It is written: "I believed; therefore I have spoken."[c][z] With that same spirit of faith we also believe and therefore speak, [14]because we know that the one who raised the Lord Jesus from the dead will also raise us with Jesus[a] and present us with you in his presence.[b] [15]All this is for your benefit, so that the grace that is reaching more and more people may cause thanksgiving[c] to overflow to the glory of God.

[16]Therefore we do not lose heart. Though outwardly we are wasting away, yet inwardly[d] we are being renewed[e] day by day. [17]For our light and momentary troubles are achieving for us an eternal glory that far outweighs them all.[f] [18]So we fix our eyes not on what is seen, but on what is unseen.[g] For what is seen is temporary, but what is unseen is eternal.

Our Heavenly Dwelling

5 Now we know that if the earthly[h] tent[i] we live in is destroyed, we have a building from God, an eternal house in heaven, not built by human hands. [2]Meanwhile we groan,[j] longing to be clothed with our heavenly dwelling,[k] [3]because when we are clothed, we will not be found naked. [4]For while we are in this tent, we groan and are bur-

3:14
[t]Ro 11:7,8
[u]Ac 13:15
[v]ver 6
3:16
[w]Ro 11:23
[x]Ex 34:34
3:17
[y]Isa 61:1,2
[z]Jn 8:32
3:18
[a]1Co 13:12
[b]2Co 4:4,6
[c]Ro 8:29
4:1
[d]1Co 7:25
4:2
[e]1Co 4:5
[f]2Co 2:17
[g]2Co 5:11
4:3
[h]2Co 2:12
[i]2Co 3:14
[j]1Co 1:18
4:4
[k]Jn 12:31
[l]2Co 3:14
4:5
[m]1Co 1:13
[n]1Co 9:19
4:6
[o]Ge 1:3
[p]2Pe 1:19
4:7
[q]Job 4:19;
2Co 5:1
[r]1Co 2:5
4:8
[s]2Co 7:5
4:9
[t]Jn 15:20
[u]Heb 13:5
[v]Ps 37:24
4:10
[w]Ro 6:5
4:11
[x]Ro 8:36
4:12
[y]2Co 13:9
4:13
[z]Ps 116:10
4:14
[a]1Th 4:14
[b]Eph 5:27
4:15
[c]2Co 1:11
4:16
[d]Ro 7:22
[e]Col 3:10
4:17
[f]Ro 8:18;
1Pe 1:6,7
4:18
[g]Ro 8:24;
Heb 11:1
5:1
[h]1Co 15:47
[i]2Pe 1:13,14
5:2
[i]ver 4; Ro 8:23
[k]1Co 15:53,54

[a]18 Or *contemplate*   [b]6 Gen. 1:3   [c]13 Psalm 116:10

dened, because we do not wish to be unclothed but to be clothed with our heavenly dwelling,[1] so that what is mortal may be swallowed up by life. [5]Now it is God who has made us for this very purpose and has given us the Spirit as a deposit, guaranteeing what is to come.[m]

[6]Therefore we are always confident and know that as long as we are at home in the body we are away from the Lord. [7]We live by faith, not by sight.[n] [8]We are confident, I say, and would prefer to be away from the body and at home with the Lord.[o] [9]So we make it our goal to please him,[p] whether we are at home in the body or away from it. [10]For we must all appear before the judgment seat of Christ, that each one may receive what is due him[q] for the things done while in the body, whether good or bad.

The Ministry of Reconciliation

[11]Since, then, we know what it is to fear the Lord,[r] we try to persuade men. What we are is plain to God, and I hope it is also plain to your conscience.[s] [12]We are not trying to commend ourselves to you again,[t] but are giving you an opportunity to take pride in us,[u] so that you can answer those who take pride in what is seen rather than in what is in the heart. [13]If we are out of our mind,[v] it is for the sake of God; if we are in our right mind, it is for you. [14]For Christ's love compels us, because we are convinced that one died for all, and therefore all died.[w] [15]And he died for all, that those who live should no longer live for themselves[x] but for him who died for them and was raised again.

[16]So from now on we regard no one from a worldly[y] point of view. Though we once regarded Christ in this way, we do so no longer. [17]Therefore, if anyone is in Christ, he is a new creation;[z] the old has gone, the new has come![a] [18]All this is from God, who reconciled us to himself through Christ[b] and gave us the ministry of reconciliation: [19]that God was reconciling the world to himself in Christ, not counting men's sins against them.[c] And he has committed to us the message of reconciliation. [20]We are therefore Christ's ambassadors,[d] as though God were making his appeal through us. We implore you on Christ's behalf: Be reconciled to God. [21]God made him who had no sin[e] to be sin[a] for us, so that in him we might become the righteousness of God.[f]

6 As God's fellow workers[g] we urge you not to receive God's grace in vain. [2]For he says,

> "In the time of my favor I heard you,
> and in the day of salvation I helped you."[b][h]

I tell you, now is the time of God's favor, now is the day of salvation.

Paul's Hardships

[3]We put no stumbling block in anyone's path,[i] so that our ministry will not be discredited. [4]Rather, as servants of God we commend ourselves in every way: in great endurance; in troubles, hardships and distresses; [5]in beatings, imprisonments[j] and riots; in hard work, sleepless nights and hunger;[k] [6]in purity, understanding, patience and kindness; in the Holy Spirit[l] and in sincere love; [7]in truthful speech[m] and in the power of God; with weapons of righteousness[n] in the right hand

5:4
l1Co 15:53,54
5:5
mRo 8:23;
2Co 1:22
5:7
n1Co 13:12
5:8
oPhp 1:23
5:9
pRo 14:18
5:10
qMt 16:27;
Ro 14:10;
Eph 6:8
5:11
rHeb 10:31;
Jude 23
s2Co 4:2
5:12
t2Co 3:1
u2Co 1:14
5:13
v2Co 11:1,16,17
5:14
wGal 2:20
5:15
xRo 14:7-9
5:16
y2Co 11:18
5:17
zGal 6:15
aIsa 65:17;
Rev 21:4,5
5:18
bRo 5:10;
Col 1:20
5:19
cRo 4:8
5:20
d2Co 6:1;
Eph 6:20
5:21
eHeb 4:15;
1Pe 2:22,24;
1Jn 3:5 fRo 1:17
6:1
g1Co 3:9;
2Co 5:20
6:2
hIsa 49:8
6:3
iRo 14:13,20;
1Co 9:12; 10:32
6:5
j2Co 11:23-25
k1Co 4:11
6:6
l1Th 1:5
6:7
m2Co 4:2
n2Co 10:4;
Eph 6:10-18

---

[a]21 Or *be a sin offering*   [b]2 Isaiah 49:8

and in the left; [8]through glory and dishonor,[o] bad report and good report; genuine, yet regarded as impostors;[p] [9]known, yet regarded as unknown; dying,[q] and yet we live on;[r] beaten, and yet not killed; [10]sorrowful, yet always rejoicing;[s] poor, yet making many rich;[t] having nothing, and yet possessing everything.[u]

[11]We have spoken freely to you, Corinthians, and opened wide our hearts to you.[v] [12]We are not withholding our affection from you, but you are withholding yours from us. [13]As a fair exchange—I speak as to my children[w]—open wide your hearts also.

Do Not Be Yoked With Unbelievers

[14]Do not be yoked together[x] with unbelievers. For what do righteousness and wickedness have in common? Or what fellowship can light have with darkness?[y] [15]What harmony is there between Christ and Belial[a]? What does a believer[z] have in common with an unbeliever? [16]What agreement is there between the temple of God and idols? For we are the temple[a] of the living God. As God has said: "I will live with them and walk among them, and I will be their God, and they will be my people."[b] [b]

[17]"Therefore come out from them[c]
    and be separate,
                                    says the Lord.
    Touch no unclean thing,
        and I will receive you."[c] [d]
[18]"I will be a Father to you,
    and you will be my sons and daughters,[e]
                        says the Lord Almighty."[d]

7 Since we have these promises,[f] dear friends, let us purify ourselves from everything that contaminates body and spirit, perfecting holiness out of reverence for God.

Paul's Joy

[2]Make room for us in your hearts.[g] We have wronged no one, we have corrupted no one, we have exploited no one. [3]I do not say this to condemn you; I have said before that you have such a place in our hearts[h] that we would live or die with you. [4]I have great confidence in you; I take great pride in you. I am greatly encouraged; in all our troubles my joy knows no bounds.[i]

[5]For when we came into Macedonia,[j] this body of ours had no rest, but we were harassed at every turn[k]—conflicts on the outside, fears within.[l] [6]But God, who comforts the downcast,[m] comforted us by the coming of Titus,[n] [7]and not only by his coming but also by the comfort you had given him. He told us about your longing for me, your deep sorrow, your ardent concern for me, so that my joy was greater than ever.

[8]Even if I caused you sorrow by my letter,[o] I do not regret it. Though I did regret it—I see that my letter hurt you, but only for a little while—[9]yet now I am happy, not because you were made sorry, but because

6:8
o1Co 4:10
pMt 27:63
6:9
qRo 8:36
r2Co 1:8-10;
4:10,11
6:10
s2Co 7:4
t2Co 8:9
uRo 8:32;
1Co 3:21
6:11
v2Co 7:3
6:13
w1Co 4:14
6:14
x1Co 5:9,10
yEph 5:7,11;
1Jn 1:6
6:15
zAc 5:14
6:16
a1Co 3:16
bLev 26:12;
Jer 32:38;
Eze 37:27
6:17
cRev 18:4
dIsa 52:11
6:18
eIsa 43:6
7:1
f2Co 6:17,18
7:2
g2Co 6:12,13
7:3
h2Co 6:11,12
7:4
i2Co 6:10
7:5
j2Co 2:13
k2Co 4:8
lDt 32:25
7:6
m2Co 1:3,4
nver 13;
2Co 2:13
7:8
o2Co 2:2,4

---

[a]15 Greek *Beliar*, a variant of *Belial*   [b]16 Lev. 26:12; Jer. 32:38; Ezek. 37:27   [c]17 Isaiah 52:11;
Ezek. 20:34,41   [d]18 2 Samuel 7:14; 7:8

your sorrow led you to repentance. For you became sorrowful as God intended and so were not harmed in any way by us. [10]Godly sorrow brings repentance that leads to salvation[p] and leaves no regret, but worldly sorrow brings death. [11]See what this godly sorrow has produced in you: what earnestness, what eagerness to clear yourselves, what indignation, what alarm, what longing, what concern,[q] what readiness to see justice done. At every point you have proved yourselves to be innocent in this matter. [12]So even though I wrote to you,[r] it was not on account of the one who did the wrong[s] or of the injured party, but rather that before God you could see for yourselves how devoted to us you are. [13]By all this we are encouraged.

In addition to our own encouragement, we were especially delighted to see how happy Titus[t] was, because his spirit has been refreshed by all of you. [14]I had boasted to him about you,[u] and you have not embarrassed me. But just as everything we said to you was true, so our boasting about you to Titus[v] has proved to be true as well. [15]And his affection for you is all the greater when he remembers that you were all obedient,[w] receiving him with fear and trembling.[x] [16]I am glad I can have complete confidence in you.[y]

Generosity Encouraged

8 And now, brothers, we want you to know about the grace that God has given the Macedonian[z] churches. [2]Out of the most severe trial, their overflowing joy and their extreme poverty welled up in rich generosity. [3]For I testify that they gave as much as they were able,[a] and even beyond their ability. Entirely on their own, [4]they urgently pleaded with us for the privilege of sharing in this service[b] to the saints.[c] [5]And they did not do as we expected, but they gave themselves first to the Lord and then to us in keeping with God's will. [6]So we urged[d] Titus,[e] since he had earlier made a beginning, to bring also to completion[f] this act of grace on your part. [7]But just as you excel in everything[g]—in faith, in speech, in knowledge,[h] in complete earnestness and in your love for us[a]—see that you also excel in this grace of giving.

[8]I am not commanding you,[i] but I want to test the sincerity of your love by comparing it with the earnestness of others. [9]For you know the grace of our Lord Jesus Christ,[j] that though he was rich, yet for your sakes he became poor,[k] so that you through his poverty might become rich.

[10]And here is my advice[l] about what is best for you in this matter: Last year you were the first not only to give but also to have the desire to do so. [m] [11]Now finish the work, so that your eager willingness[n] to do it may be matched by your completion of it, according to your means. [12]For if the willingness is there, the gift is acceptable according to what one has,[o] not according to what he does not have.

[13]Our desire is not that others might be relieved while you are hard pressed, but that there might be equality. [14]At the present time your plenty will supply what they need,[p] so that in turn their plenty will supply what you need. Then there will be equality, [15]as it is written: "He who gathered much did not have too much, and he who gathered little did not have too little."[b] [q]

7:10
pAc 11:18
7:11
qver 7
7:12
rver 8; 2Co 2:3,
9 s1Co 5:1,2
7:13
tver 6; 2Co 2:13
7:14
uver 4 vver 6
7:15
w2Co 2:9
xPhp 2:12
7:16
y2Co 2:3
8:1
zAc 16:9
8:3
a1Co 16:2
8:4
bAc 24:17
cRo 15:25;
2Co 9:1
8:6
dver 17;
2Co 12:18
ever 16,23
fver 10,11
8:7
g2Co 9:8
h1Co 1:5
8:8
i1Co 7:6
8:9
j2Co 13:14
kMt 20:28;
Php 2:6-8
8:10
l1Co 7:25,40
m1Co 16:2,3;
2Co 9:2
8:11
n2Co 9:2
8:12
oMk 12:43,44;
Lk 21:3
8:14
p2Co 9:12
8:15
qEx 16:18

a7 Some manuscripts *in our love for you*   b15 Exodus 16:18

Titus Sent to Corinth

[16]I thank God,[r] who put into the heart[s] of Titus[t] the same concern I have for you. [17]For Titus not only welcomed our appeal, but he is coming to you with much enthusiasm and on his own initiative.[u] [18]And we are sending along with him the brother[v] who is praised by all the churches[w] for his service to the gospel.[x] [19]What is more, he was chosen by the churches to accompany us[y] as we carry the offering, which we administer in order to honor the Lord himself and to show our eagerness to help.[z] [20]We want to avoid any criticism of the way we administer this liberal gift. [21]For we are taking pains to do what is right, not only in the eyes of the Lord but also in the eyes of men.[a]

[22]In addition, we are sending with them our brother who has often proved to us in many ways that he is zealous, and now even more so because of his great confidence in you. [23]As for Titus, he is my partner[b] and fellow worker[c] among you; as for our brothers,[d] they are representatives of the churches and an honor to Christ. [24]Therefore show these men the proof of your love and the reason for our pride in you,[e] so that the churches can see it.

9 There is no need[f] for me to write to you about this service to the saints.[g] [2]For I know your eagerness to help, and I have been boasting[h] about it to the Macedonians, telling them that since last year[i] you in Achaia[j] were ready to give; and your enthusiasm has stirred most of them to action. [3]But I am sending the brothers in order that our boasting about you in this matter should not prove hollow, but that you may be ready, as I said you would be.[k] [4]For if any Macedonians[l] come with me and find you unprepared, we—not to say anything about you— would be ashamed of having been so confident. [5]So I thought it necessary to urge the brothers to visit you in advance and finish the arrangements for the generous gift you had promised. Then it will be ready as a generous gift,[m] not as one grudgingly given.[n]

Sowing Generously

[6]Remember this: Whoever sows sparingly will also reap sparingly, and whoever sows generously will also reap generously.[o] [7]Each man should give what he has decided in his heart to give,[p] not reluctantly or under compulsion,[q] for God loves a cheerful giver.[r] [8]And God is able[s] to make all grace abound to you, so that in all things at all times, having all that you need,[t] you will abound in every good work. [9]As it is written:

> "He has scattered abroad his gifts to the poor;
>   his righteousness endures forever."[a] [u]

[10]Now he who supplies seed to the sower and bread for food[v] will also supply and increase your store of seed and will enlarge the harvest of your righteousness.[w] [11]You will be made rich[x] in every way so that you can be generous on every occasion, and through us your generosity will result in thanksgiving to God.[y]

[a]9 Psalm 112:9

8:16
r2Co 2:14
sRev 17:17
t2Co 2:13
8:17
uver 6
8:18
v2Co 12:18
w1Co 7:17
x2Co 2:12
8:19
y1Co 16:3,4
zver 11,12
8:21
aRo 12:17;
14:18
8:23
bPhm 17
cPhp 2:25
dver 18,22
8:24
e2Co 7:4,14;
9:2
9:1
f1Th 4:9
g2Co 8:4
9:2
h2Co 7:4,14
i2Co 8:10
jAc 18:12
9:3
k1Co 16:2
9:4
lRo 15:26
9:5
mPhp 4:17
n2Co 12:17,18
9:6
oPr 11:24,25;
22:9; Gal 6:7,9
9:7
pEx 25:2;
2Co 8:12
qDt 15:10
rRo 12:8
9:8
sEph 3:20
tPhp 4:19
9:9
uPs 112:9
9:10
vIsa 55:10
wHos 10:12
9:11
x1Co 1:5
y2Co 1:11

¹²This service that you perform is not only supplying the needs^z of God's people but is also overflowing in many expressions of thanks to God.^a ¹³Because of the service^b by which you have proved yourselves, men will praise God^c for the obedience that accompanies your confession of the gospel of Christ,^d and for your generosity in sharing with them and with everyone else. ¹⁴And in their prayers for you their hearts will go out to you, because of the surpassing grace God has given you. ¹⁵Thanks be to God^e for his indescribable gift!^f

Paul's Defense of His Ministry

10 By the meekness and gentleness^g of Christ, I appeal to you—I, Paul,^h who am "timid" when face to face with you, but "bold" when away! ²I beg you that when I come I may not have to be as boldⁱ as I expect to be toward some people who think that we live by the standards of this world. ³For though we live in the world, we do not wage war as the world does. ⁴The weapons we fight with^j are not the weapons of the world. On the contrary, they have divine power^k to demolish strongholds.^l ⁵We demolish arguments and every pretension that sets itself up against the knowledge of God,^m and we take captive every thought to make it obedientⁿ to Christ. ⁶And we will be ready to punish every act of disobedience, once your obedience is complete.^o

⁷You are looking only on the surface of things.^{a p} If anyone is confident that he belongs to Christ,^q he should consider again that we belong to Christ just as much as he.^r ⁸For even if I boast somewhat freely about the authority the Lord gave us for building you up rather than pulling you down,^s I will not be ashamed of it. ⁹I do not want to seem to be trying to frighten you with my letters. ¹⁰For some say, "His letters are weighty and forceful, but in person he is unimpressive^t and his speaking amounts to nothing."^u ¹¹Such people should realize that what we are in our letters when we are absent, we will be in our actions when we are present.

¹²We do not dare to classify or compare ourselves with some who commend themselves.^v When they measure themselves by themselves and compare themselves with themselves, they are not wise. ¹³We, however, will not boast beyond proper limits, but will confine our boasting to the field God has assigned to us,^w a field that reaches even to you. ¹⁴We are not going too far in our boasting, as would be the case if we had not come to you, for we did get as far as you^x with the gospel of Christ.^y ¹⁵Neither do we go beyond our limits by boasting of work done by others.^{b z} Our hope is that, as your faith continues to grow,^a our area of activity among you will greatly expand, ¹⁶so that we can preach the gospel in the regions beyond you.^b For we do not want to boast about work already done in another man's territory. ¹⁷But, "Let him who boasts boast in the Lord."^{c c} ¹⁸For it is not the one who commends himself^d who is approved, but the one whom the Lord commends.^e

9:12
z2Co 8:14
a2Co 1:11
9:13
b2Co 8:4
cMt 9:8
d2Co 2:12
9:15
e2Co 2:14
fRo 5:15,16
10:1
gMt 11:29
hGal 5:2
10:2
i1Co 4:21;
2Co 13:2,10
10:4
j2Co 6:7
k1Co 2:5
lJer 1:10;
2Co 13:10
10:5
mIsa 2:11,12;
1Co 1:19
n2Co 9:13
10:6
o2Co 2:9; 7:15
10:7
pJn 7:24
q1Co 1:12;
3:23; 14:37
r2Co 11:23
10:8
s2Co 13:10
10:10
t1Co 2:3;
Gal 4:13,14
u1Co 1:17
10:12
v2Co 3:1
10:13
wver 15,16
10:14
x1Co 3:6
y2Co 2:12
10:15
zRo 15:20
a2Th 1:3
10:16
bAc 19:21
10:17
cJer 9:24;
1Co 1:31
10:18
dver 12
eRo 2:29;
1Co 4:5

---

^a7 Or *Look at the obvious facts*   ^b13-15 Or ¹³*We, however, will not boast about things that cannot be measured, but we will boast according to the standard of measurement that the God of measure has assigned us—a measurement that relates even to you.* 14 . . . . ¹⁵*Neither do we boast about things that cannot be measured in regard to the work done by others.*   ^c17 Jer. 9:24

Paul and the False Apostles

11 I hope you will put up with[f] a little of my foolishness;[g] but you are already doing that. [2]I am jealous for you with a godly jealousy. I promised you to one husband,[h] to Christ, so that I might present you[i] as a pure virgin to him. [3]But I am afraid that just as Eve was deceived by the serpent's cunning,[j] your minds may somehow be led astray from your sincere and pure devotion to Christ. [4]For if someone comes to you and preaches a Jesus other than the Jesus we preached,[k] or if you receive a different spirit[l] from the one you received, or a different gospel[m] from the one you accepted, you put up with it easily enough. [5]But I do not think I am in the least inferior to those "super-apostles."[n] [6]I may not be a trained speaker,[o] but I do have knowledge.[p] We have made this perfectly clear to you in every way.

[7]Was it a sin[q] for me to lower myself in order to elevate you by preaching the gospel of God to you free of charge?[r] [8]I robbed other churches by receiving support from them[s] so as to serve you. [9]And when I was with you and needed something, I was not a burden to anyone, for the brothers who came from Macedonia supplied what I needed. I have kept myself from being a burden to you[t] in any way, and will continue to do so. [10]As surely as the truth of Christ is in me,[u] nobody in the regions of Achaia[v] will stop this boasting[w] of mine. [11]Why? Because I do not love you? God knows I do![x] [12]And I will keep on doing what I am doing in order to cut the ground from under those who want an opportunity to be considered equal with us in the things they boast about.

[13]For such men are false apostles,[y] deceitful[z] workmen, masquerading as apostles of Christ.[a] [14]And no wonder, for Satan himself masquerades as an angel of light. [15]It is not surprising, then, if his servants masquerade as servants of righteousness. Their end will be what their actions deserve.[b]

Paul Boasts About His Sufferings

[16]I repeat: Let no one take me for a fool.[c] But if you do, then receive me just as you would a fool, so that I may do a little boasting. [17]In this self-confident boasting I am not talking as the Lord would,[d] but as a fool. [18]Since many are boasting in the way the world does, I too will boast.[e] [19]You gladly put up with fools since you are so wise![f] [20]In fact, you even put up with anyone who enslaves you[g] or exploits you or takes advantage of you or pushes himself forward or slaps you in the face. [21]To my shame I admit that we were too weak[h] for that!

What anyone else dares to boast about—I am speaking as a fool—I also dare to boast about.[i] [22]Are they Hebrews? So am I.[j] Are they Israelites? So am I.[k] Are they Abraham's descendants? So am I. [23]Are they servants of Christ? (I am out of my mind to talk like this.) I am more. I have worked much harder,[l] been in prison more frequently,[m] been flogged more severely, and been exposed to death again and again. [24]Five times I received from the Jews the forty lashes[n] minus one. [25]Three times I was beaten with rods,[o] once I was stoned,[p] three times I was shipwrecked, I spent a night and a day in the open sea, [26]I have been constantly on the move. I have been in danger from rivers, in danger from bandits, in danger from my own countrymen,[q] in danger

11:1
f ver 4,19,20;
Mt 17:17
g ver 16,17,21;
2Co 5:13
11:2
h Hos 2:19;
Eph 5:26,27
i 2Co 4:14
11:3
j Ge 3:1-6,13;
Jn 8:44;
1Ti 2:14;
Rev 12:9
11:4
k 1Co 3:11
l Ro 8:15
m Gal 1:6-9
11:5
n 2Co 12:11;
Gal 2:6
11:6
o 1Co 1:17
p Eph 3:4
11:7
q 2Co 12:13
r 1Co 9:18
11:8
s Php 4:15,18
11:9
t 2Co 12:13,14,
16
11:10
u Ro 9:1
v Ac 18:12
w 1Co 9:15
11:11
x 2Co 12:15
11:13
y 2Pe 2:1
z Tit 1:10
a Rev 2:2
11:15
b Php 3:19
11:16
c ver 1
11:17
d 1Co 7:12,25
11:18
e Php 3:3,4
11:19
f 1Co 4:10
11:20
g Gal 2:4
11:21
h 2Co 10:1,10
i Php 3:4
11:22
j Php 3:5
k Ro 9:4
11:23
l 1Co 15:10
m Ac 16:23;
2Co 6:4,5
11:24
n Dt 25:3
11:25
o Ac 16:22
p Ac 14:19
11:26
q Ac 9:23; 14:5

from Gentiles; in danger in the city,ʳ in danger in the country, in danger at sea; and in danger from false brothers.ˢ ²⁷I have labored and toiled and have often gone without sleep; I have known hunger and thirst and have often gone without food;ᵗ I have been cold and naked. ²⁸Besides everything else, I face daily the pressure of my concern for all the churches. ²⁹Who is weak, and I do not feel weak? Who is led into sin, and I do not inwardly burn?

³⁰If I must boast, I will boast of the things that show my weakness.ᵘ ³¹The God and Father of the Lord Jesus, who is to be praised forever,ᵛ knows that I am not lying. ³²In Damascus the governor under King Aretas had the city of the Damascenes guarded in order to arrest me.ʷ ³³But I was lowered in a basket from a window in the wall and slipped through his hands.ˣ

Paul's Vision and His Thorn

12 I must go on boasting.ʸ Although there is nothing to be gained, I will go on to visions and revelationsᶻ from the Lord. ²I know a man in Christ who fourteen years ago was caught upᵃ to the third heaven.ᵇ Whether it was in the body or out of the body I do not know—God knows.ᶜ ³And I know that this man—whether in the body or apart from the body I do not know, but God knows— ⁴was caught up to paradise.ᵈ He heard inexpressible things, things that man is not permitted to tell. ⁵I will boast about a man like that, but I will not boast about myself, except about my weaknesses. ⁶Even if I should choose to boast, I would not be a fool,ᵉ because I would be speaking the truth. But I refrain, so no one will think more of me than is warranted by what I do or say.

⁷To keep me from becoming conceited because of these surpassingly great revelations, there was given me a thorn in my flesh,ᶠ a messenger of Satan, to torment me. ⁸Three times I pleaded with the Lord to take it away from me.ᵍ ⁹But he said to me, "My grace is sufficient for you, for my powerʰ is made perfect in weakness." Therefore I will boast all the more gladly about my weaknesses, so that Christ's power may rest on me. ¹⁰That is why, for Christ's sake, I delight in weaknesses, in insults, in hardships,ⁱ in persecutions,ʲ in difficulties. For when I am weak, then I am strong.ᵏ

Paul's Concern for the Corinthians

¹¹I have made a fool of myself,ˡ but you drove me to it. I ought to have been commended by you, for I am not in the least inferior to the "super-apostles,"ᵐ even though I am nothing.ⁿ ¹²The things that mark an apostle—signs, wonders and miraclesᵒ—were done among you with great perseverance. ¹³How were you inferior to the other churches, except that I was never a burden to you?ᵖ Forgive me this wrong!�q

¹⁴Now I am ready to visit you for the third time,ʳ and I will not be a burden to you, because what I want is not your possessions but you. After all, children should not have to save up for their parents,ˢ but parents for their children.ᵗ ¹⁵So I will very gladly spend for you everything I have and expend myself as well.ᵘ If I love you more, will you love me less? ¹⁶Be that as it may, I have not been a burden to you.ᵛ Yet, crafty fellow that I am, I caught you by trickery! ¹⁷Did I exploit you

11:26
ʳAc 21:31
ˢGal 2:4
11:27
ᵗ1Co 4:11,12;
2Co 6:5
11:30
ᵘ1Co 2:3
11:31
ᵛRo 9:5
11:32
ʷAc 9:24
11:33
ˣAc 9:25
12:1
ʸ2Co 11:16,30
ᶻver 7
12:2
ᵃAc 8:39
ᵇEph 4:10
ᶜ2Co 11:11
12:4
ᵈLk 23:43;
Rev 2:7
12:6
ᵉ2Co 11:16
12:7
ᶠNu 33:55
12:8
ᵍMt 26:39,44
12:9
ʰPhp 4:13
12:10
ⁱ2Co 6:4
ʲRo 5:3;
2Th 1:4
ᵏ2Co 13:4
12:11
ˡ2Co 11:1
ᵐ2Co 11:5
ⁿ1Co 15:9,10
12:12
ᵒJn 4:48
12:13
ᵖ1Co 9:12,18
q2Co 11:7
12:14
ʳ2Co 13:1
ˢ1Co 4:14,15
ᵗPr 19:14
12:15
ᵘPhp 2:17;
1Th 2:8
12:16
ᵛ2Co 11:9

through any of the men I sent you? [18]I urged[w] Titus to go to you and I sent our brother[x] with him. Titus did not exploit you, did he? Did we not act in the same spirit and follow the same course?

[19]Have you been thinking all along that we have been defending ourselves to you? We have been speaking in the sight of God[y] as those in Christ; and everything we do, dear friends, is for your strengthening.[z] [20]For I am afraid that when I come[a] I may not find you as I want you to be, and you may not find me as you want me to be.[b] I fear that there may be quarreling,[c] jealousy, outbursts of anger, factions,[d] slander, gossip,[e] arrogance and disorder.[f] [21]I am afraid that when I come again my God will humble me before you, and I will be grieved[g] over many who have sinned earlier[h] and have not repented of the impurity, sexual sin and debauchery in which they have indulged.

Final Warnings

13 This will be my third visit to you.[i] "Every matter must be established by the testimony of two or three witnesses."[a][j] [2]I already gave you a warning when I was with you the second time. I now repeat it while absent: On my return I will not spare[k] those who sinned earlier[l] or any of the others, [3]since you are demanding proof that Christ is speaking through me.[m] He is not weak in dealing with you, but is powerful among you. [4]For to be sure, he was crucified in weakness,[n] yet he lives by God's power.[o] Likewise, we are weak[p] in him, yet by God's power we will live with him to serve you.

[5]Examine yourselves[q] to see whether you are in the faith; test yourselves.[r] Do you not realize that Christ Jesus is in you[s]—unless, of course, you fail the test? [6]And I trust that you will discover that we have not failed the test. [7]Now we pray to God that you will not do anything wrong. Not that people will see that we have stood the test but that you will do what is right even though we may seem to have failed. [8]For we cannot do anything against the truth, but only for the truth. [9]We are glad whenever we are weak but you are strong; and our prayer is for your perfection.[t] [10]This is why I write these things when I am absent, that when I come I may not have to be harsh in my use of authority —the authority the Lord gave me for building you up, not for tearing you down.[u]

Final Greetings

[11]Finally, brothers,[v] good-by. Aim for perfection, listen to my appeal, be of one mind, live in peace.[w] And the God of love and peace[x] will be with you.

[12]Greet one another with a holy kiss.[y] [13]All the saints send their greetings.[z]

[14]May the grace of the Lord Jesus Christ,[a] and the love of God,[b] and the fellowship of the Holy Spirit[c] be with you all.

[a]1 Deut. 19:15

12:18
w2Co 8:6,16
x2Co 8:18
12:19
yRo 9:1
z2Co 10:8
12:20
a2Co 2:1-4
b1Co 4:21
c1Co 1:11; 3:3
dGal 5:20
eRo 1:29
f1Co 14:33
12:21
g2Co 2:1,4
h2Co 13:2
13:1
i2Co 12:14
jDt 19:15;
Mt 18:16
13:2
k2Co 1:23
l2Co 12:21
13:3
mMt 10:20;
1Co 5:4
13:4
nPhp 2:7,8;
1Pe 3:18
oRo 1:4; 6:4
pver 9
13:5
q1Co 11:28
rJn 6:6 sRo 8:10
13:9
tver 11
13:10
u2Co 10:8
13:11
v1Th 4:1;
2Th 3:1
wMk 9:50
xRo 15:33;
Eph 6:23
13:12
yRo 16:16
13:13
zPhp 4:22
13:14
aRo 16:20;
2Co 8:9
bRo 5:5;
Jude 21
cPhp 2:1

Galatians

Title and Background

Judaizers were Jewish Christians who believed, among other things, that a number of the ceremonial practices of the Old Testament were still binding on the New Testament church. Following Paul's successful campaign in Galatia, they insisted that Gentile converts to Christianity abide by certain Old Testament rites, especially circumcision. The Judaizers argued that Paul was not an authentic apostle and that out of a desire to make the message more appealing to Gentiles he had removed from the gospel certain legal requirements. Paul responds by writing this letter.

Author and Date of Writing

The opening verse identifies the author as the apostle Paul. Various dates have been given for the writing of this letter, but it was probably written around A.D. 50.

Theme and Message

Galatians stands as an eloquent and vigorous defense for the essential New Testament truth that we are justified by faith in Jesus Christ—by nothing less and nothing more—and that we are sanctified by the obedience that comes from faith in God's work for us, in us and through us by the grace and power of Christ and the Holy Spirit. Some have called the letter the *Magna Charta* of Christian liberty.

Outline

I. Introduction: Greetings and Denunciation (1:1-9)
II. Authentication of the Apostle of Liberty and Faith (1:10-2:21)
III. Justification of the Doctrine of Liberty and Faith (3:1-4:31)
IV. Practice of the Life of Liberty and Faith (5:1-6:10)
V. Conclusion (6:11-18)

1:1
aAc 9:15
bAc 2:24
1:2
cPhp 4:21
dAc 16:6;
1Co 16:1
1:3
eRo 1:7
1:4
fMt 20:28;
Ro 4:25;
Gal 2:20
gPhp 4:20
1:5
hRo 11:36
1:6
iGal 5:8
j2Co 11:4
1:7
kAc 15:24;
Gal 5:10
1:8
l2Co 11:4

1 Paul, an apostle—sent not from men nor by man, but by Jesus Christ[a] and God the Father, who raised him from the dead[b]— 2and all the brothers with me,[c]

To the churches in Galatia:[d]

3Grace and peace to you from God our Father and the Lord Jesus Christ,[e] 4who gave himself for our sins[f] to rescue us from the present evil age, according to the will of our God and Father,[g] 5to whom be glory for ever and ever. Amen.[h]

No Other Gospel

6I am astonished that you are so quickly deserting the one who called[i] you by the grace of Christ and are turning to a different gospel[j]— 7which is really no gospel at all. Evidently some people are throwing you into confusion[k] and are trying to pervert the gospel of Christ. 8But even if we or an angel from heaven should preach a gospel other than the one we preached to you,[l] let him be eternally condemned![m] [9]As we have already said, so now I say again: If anybody is preaching to you a gospel other than what you accepted,[n] let him be eternally condemned!

[10]Am I now trying to win the approval of men, or of God? Or am I trying to please men?[o] If I were still trying to please men, I would not be a servant of Christ.

Paul Called by God

[11]I want you to know, brothers,[p] that the gospel I preached is not something that man made up. [12]I did not receive it from any man,[q] nor was I taught it; rather, I received it by revelation[r] from Jesus Christ. [13]For you have heard of my previous way of life in Judaism,[s] how intensely I persecuted the church of God and tried to destroy it.[t] [14]I was advancing in Judaism beyond many Jews of my own age and was extremely zealous for the traditions of my fathers.[u] [15]But when God, who set me apart from birth[a][v] and called me[w] by his grace, was pleased [16]to reveal his Son in me so that I might preach him among the Gentiles,[x] I did not consult any man,[y] [17]nor did I go up to Jerusalem to see those who were apostles before I was, but I went immediately into Arabia and later returned to Damascus.

[18]Then after three years,[z] I went up to Jerusalem[a] to get acquainted with Peter[b] and stayed with him fifteen days. [19]I saw none of the other apostles—only James,[b] the Lord's brother. [20]I assure you before God that what I am writing you is no lie.[c] [21]Later I went to Syria and Cilicia.[d] [22]I was personally unknown to the churches of Judea[e] that are in Christ. [23]They only heard the report: "The man who formerly persecuted us is now preaching the faith[f] he once tried to destroy." [24]And they praised God[g] because of me.

Paul Accepted by the Apostles

2 Fourteen years later I went up again to Jerusalem,[h] this time with Barnabas. I took Titus along also. [2]I went in response to a revelation and set before them the gospel that I preach among the Gentiles.[i] But I did this privately to those who seemed to be leaders, for fear that I was running or had run my race[j] in vain. [3]Yet not even Titus,[k] who was with me, was compelled to be circumcised, even though he was a Greek.[l] [4]This matter arose because some false brothers[m] had infiltrated our ranks to spy on[n] the freedom[o] we have in Christ Jesus and to make us slaves. [5]We did not give in to them for a moment, so that the truth of the gospel[p] might remain with you.

[6]As for those who seemed to be important[q]—whatever they were makes no difference to me; God does not judge by external appearance[r]—those men added nothing to my message. [7]On the contrary, they saw that I had been entrusted with the task[s] of preaching the gospel to the Gentiles,[c][t] just as Peter[u] had been to the Jews.[d] [8]For God, who was at work in the ministry of Peter as an apostle[v] to the Jews, was also at work in my ministry as an apostle to the Gentiles. [9]James, Peter[e][w] and John, those reputed to be pillars,[x] gave me and Barnabas[y] the right hand of fellowship when they recognized the grace

*Cross references (right column):*

1:8 m Ro 9:3
1:9 n Ro 16:17
1:10 o Ro 2:29; 1Th 2:4
1:11 p 1Co 15:1
1:12 q ver 1 r ver 16
1:13 s Ac 26:4,5 t Ac 8:3
1:14 u Mt 15:2
1:15 v Isa 49:1,5; Jer 1:5 w Ac 9:15
1:16 x Gal 2:9 y Mt 16:17
1:18 z Ac 9:22,23 a Ac 9:26,27
1:19 b Mt 13:55
1:20 c Ro 9:1
1:21 d Ac 6:9
1:22 e 1Th 2:14
1:23 f Ac 6:7
1:24 g Mt 9:8
2:1 h Ac 15:2
2:2 i Ac 15:4,12 j 1Co 9:24; Php 2:16
2:3 k 2Co 2:13 l Ac 16:3; 1Co 9:21
2:4 m 2Co 11:26 n Jude 4 o Ac 15:1; Gal 5:1,13
2:5 p ver 14
2:6 q Gal 6:3 r Ac 10:34
2:7 s 1Th 2:4; 1Ti 1:11 t Ac 9:15 u ver 9, 11,14
2:8 v Ac 1:25
2:9 w ver 7,11,14 x 1Ti 3:15 y Ac 4:36

---

a15 Or from my mother's womb *b18 Greek Cephas* *c7 Greek uncircumcised* *d7 Greek circumcised; also in verses 8 and 9* *e9 Greek Cephas; also in verses 11 and 14* given to me.[z] They agreed that we should go to the Gentiles, and they to the Jews. [10]All they asked was that we should continue to remember the poor,[a] the very thing I was eager to do.

Paul Opposes Peter

[11]When Peter[b] came to Antioch,[c] I opposed him to his face, because he was clearly in the wrong. [12]Before certain men came from James, he used to eat with the Gentiles.[d] But when they arrived, he began to draw back and separate himself from the Gentiles because he was afraid of those who belonged to the circumcision group.[e] [13]The other Jews joined him in his hypocrisy, so that by their hypocrisy even Barnabas[f] was led astray.

[14]When I saw that they were not acting in line with the truth of the gospel,[g] I said to Peter[h] in front of them all, "You are a Jew, yet you live like a Gentile and not like a Jew.[i] How is it, then, that you force Gentiles to follow Jewish customs?

[15]"We who are Jews by birth[j] and not 'Gentile sinners'[k] [16]know that a man is not justified by observing the law, but by faith in Jesus Christ.[l] So we, too, have put our faith in Christ Jesus that we may be justified by faith in Christ and not by observing the law, because by observing the law no one will be justified.

[17]"If, while we seek to be justified in Christ, it becomes evident that we ourselves are sinners,[m] does that mean that Christ promotes sin? Absolutely not![n] [18]If I rebuild what I destroyed, I prove that I am a lawbreaker. [19]For through the law I died to the law[o] so that I might live for God.[p] [20]I have been crucified with Christ[q] and I no longer live, but Christ lives in me.[r] The life I live in the body, I live by faith in the Son of God,[s] who loved me[t] and gave himself for me.[u] [21]I do not set aside the grace of God, for if righteousness could be gained through the law,[v] Christ died for nothing!"[a]

Faith or Observance of the Law

3 You foolish Galatians! Who has bewitched you?[w] Before your very eyes Jesus Christ was clearly portrayed as crucified.[x] [2]I would like to learn just one thing from you: Did you receive the Spirit by observing the law, or by believing what you heard?[y] [3]Are you so foolish? After beginning with the Spirit, are you now trying to attain your goal by human effort? [4]Have you suffered so much for nothing—if it really was for nothing? [5]Does God give you his Spirit and work miracles[z] among you because you observe the law, or because you believe what you heard?

[6]Consider Abraham: "He believed God, and it was credited to him as righteousness."[ba] [7]Understand, then, that those who believe[b] are children of Abraham. [8]The Scripture foresaw that God would justify the Gentiles by faith, and announced the gospel in advance to Abraham: "All nations will be blessed through you."[cc] [9]So those who have faith[d] are blessed along with Abraham, the man of faith.

[10]All who rely on observing the law are under a curse, for it is written: "Cursed is everyone who does not continue to do everything written in

2:9
z Ro 12:3
2:10
a Ac 24:17
2:11
b ver 7,9,14
c Ac 11:19
2:12
d Ac 11:3
e Ac 11:2
2:13
f ver 1; Ac 4:36
2:14
g ver 5 h ver 7,9, 11 i Ac 10:28
2:15
j Php 3:4,5
k 1Sa 15:18
2:16
l Ac 13:39; Ro 9:30
2:17
m ver 15
n Gal 3:21
2:19
o Ro 7:4
p Ro 6:10,11,14; 2Co 5:15
2:20
q Ro 6:6
r 1Pe 4:2
s Mt 4:3
t Ro 8:37
u Gal 1:4
2:21
v Gal 3:21
3:1
w Gal 5:7
x 1Co 1:23
3:2
y Ro 10:17
3:5
z 1Co 12:10
3:6
a Ge 15:6; Ro 4:3
3:7
b ver 9
3:8
c Ge 12:3; Ac 3:25
3:9
d ver 7; Ro 4:16

---

[a]21 Some interpreters end the quotation after verse 14.   [b]6 Gen. 15:6   [c]8 Gen. 12:3; 18:18; 22:18

the Book of the Law."[a][e] [11]Clearly no one is justified before God by the law, because, "The righteous will live by faith."[b][f] [12]The law is not based on faith; on the contrary, "The man who does these things will live by them."[c][g] [13]Christ redeemed us from the curse of the law[h] by becoming a curse for us, for it is written: "Cursed is everyone who is hung on a tree."[d][i] [14]He redeemed us in order that the blessing given to Abraham might come to the Gentiles through Christ Jesus,[j] so that by faith we might receive the promise of the Spirit.[k]

The Law and the Promise

[15]Brothers, let me take an example from everyday life. Just as no one can set aside or add to a human covenant that has been duly established, so it is in this case. [16]The promises were spoken to Abraham and to his seed.[l] The Scripture does not say "and to seeds," meaning many people, but "and to your seed,"[e] meaning one person, who is Christ. [17]What I mean is this: The law, introduced 430 years[m] later, does not set aside the covenant previously established by God and thus do away with the promise. [18]For if the inheritance depends on the law, then it no longer depends on a promise;[n] but God in his grace gave it to Abraham through a promise.

[19]What, then, was the purpose of the law? It was added because of transgressions[o] until the Seed[p] to whom the promise referred had come. The law was put into effect through angels[q] by a mediator.[r] [20]A mediator,[s] however, does not represent just one party; but God is one.

[21]Is the law, therefore, opposed to the promises of God? Absolutely not![t] For if a law had been given that could impart life, then righteousness would certainly have come by the law.[u] [22]But the Scripture declares that the whole world is a prisoner of sin,[v] so that what was promised, being given through faith in Jesus Christ, might be given to those who believe.

[23]Before this faith came, we were held prisoners[w] by the law, locked up until faith should be revealed. [24]So the law was put in charge to lead us to Christ[f][x] that we might be justified by faith.[y] [25]Now that faith has come, we are no longer under the supervision of the law.

Sons of God

[26]You are all sons of God[z] through faith in Christ Jesus, [27]for all of you who were baptized into Christ[a] have clothed yourselves with Christ.[b] [28]There is neither Jew nor Greek, slave nor free,[c] male nor female, for you are all one in Christ Jesus.[d] [29]If you belong to Christ,[e] then you are Abraham's seed, and heirs according to the promise.[f]

4 What I am saying is that as long as the heir is a child, he is no different from a slave, although he owns the whole estate. [2]He is subject to guardians and trustees until the time set by his father. [3]So also, when we were children, we were in slavery[g] under the basic principles of the world.[h] [4]But when the time had fully come,[i] God sent his Son, born of a woman,[j] born under law,[k] [5]to redeem those under law, that we might receive the full rights[l] of sons. [6]Because you are sons, God sent the Spirit of his Son into our hearts,[m] the Spirit who calls

3:10
eDt 27:26;
Jer 11:3
3:11
fHab 2:4;
Gal 2:16;
Heb 10:38
3:12
gLev 18:5;
Ro 10:5
3:13
hGal 4:5
iDt 21:23;
Ac 5:30
3:14
jRo 4:9,16
kver 2;
Joel 2:28;
Ac 2:33
3:16
lLk 1:55;
Ro 4:13,16
3:17
mGe 15:13,14;
Ex 12:40
3:18
nRo 4:14
3:19
oRo 5:20
pver 16
qAc 7:53
rEx 20:19
3:20
sHeb 8:6; 9:15;
12:24
3:21
tGal 2:17
uGal 2:21
3:22
vRo 3:9-19;
11:32
3:23
wRo 11:32
3:24
xRo 10:4
yGal 2:16
3:26
zRo 8:14
3:27
aMt 28:19;
Ro 6:3
bRo 13:14
3:28
cCol 3:11
dJn 10:16;
17:11;
Eph 2:14,15
3:29
e1Co 3:23
fver 16
4:3
gGal 2:4
hCol 2:8,20
4:4
iMk 1:15;
Eph 1:10
jJn 1:14
kLk 2:27
4:5
lJn 1:12
4:6
mRo 5:5

---

[a]10 Deut. 27:26   [b]11 Hab. 2:4   [c]12 Lev. 18:5   [d]13 Deut. 21:23   [e]16 Gen. 12:7; 13:15;
24:7   [f]24 Or *charge until Christ came*

out, "*Abba*,[a] Father."[n] [7]So you are no longer a slave, but a son; and since you are a son, God has made you also an heir.[o]

Paul's Concern for the Galatians

[8]Formerly, when you did not know God,[p] you were slaves to those who by nature are not gods.[q] [9]But now that you know God—or rather are known by God[r]—how is it that you are turning back to those weak and miserable principles? Do you wish to be enslaved[s] by them all over again?[t] [10]You are observing special days and months and seasons and years![u] [11]I fear for you, that somehow I have wasted my efforts on you.[v]

[12]I plead with you, brothers,[w] become like me, for I became like you. You have done me no wrong. [13]As you know, it was because of an illness[x] that I first preached the gospel to you. [14]Even though my illness was a trial to you, you did not treat me with contempt or scorn. Instead, you welcomed me as if I were an angel of God, as if I were Christ Jesus himself.[y] [15]What has happened to all your joy? I can testify that, if you could have done so, you would have torn out your eyes and given them to me. [16]Have I now become your enemy by telling you the truth?[z]

[17]Those people are zealous to win you over, but for no good. What they want is to alienate you from us, so that you may be zealous for them. [18]It is fine to be zealous, provided the purpose is good, and to be so always and not just when I am with you.[a] [19]My dear children,[b] for whom I am again in the pains of childbirth until Christ is formed in you,[c] [20]how I wish I could be with you now and change my tone, because I am perplexed about you!

Hagar and Sarah

[21]Tell me, you who want to be under the law, are you not aware of what the law says? [22]For it is written that Abraham had two sons, one by the slave woman[d] and the other by the free woman.[e] [23]His son by the slave woman was born in the ordinary way;[f] but his son by the free woman was born as the result of a promise.[g]

[24]These things may be taken figuratively, for the women represent two covenants. One covenant is from Mount Sinai and bears children who are to be slaves: This is Hagar. [25]Now Hagar stands for Mount Sinai in Arabia and corresponds to the present city of Jerusalem, because she is in slavery with her children. [26]But the Jerusalem that is above[h] is free, and she is our mother. [27]For it is written:

> "Be glad, O barren woman,
>   who bears no children;
> break forth and cry aloud,
>   you who have no labor pains;
> because more are the children of the desolate woman
>   than of her who has a husband."[b] [i]

[28]Now you, brothers, like Isaac, are children of promise. [29]At that time the son born in the ordinary way[j] persecuted the son born by the power of the Spirit.[k] It is the same now. [30]But what does the Scripture say? "Get rid of the slave woman and her son, for the slave woman's

4:6
nRo 8:15,16
4:7
oRo 8:17
4:8
p1Co 1:21;
Eph 2:12;
1Th 4:5
q2Ch 13:9;
Isa 37:19
4:9
r1Co 8:3 sver 3
tCol 2:20
4:10
uRo 14:5
4:11
v1Th 3:5
4:12
wGal 6:18
4:13
x1Co 2:3
4:14
yMt 10:40
4:16
zAm 5:10
4:18
aver 13,14
4:19
b1Co 4:15
cEph 4:13
4:22
dGe 16:15
eGe 21:2
4:23
fRo 9:7,8
gGe 18:10-14;
Heb 11:11
4:26
hHeb 12:22;
Rev 3:12
4:27
iIsa 54:1
4:29
jver 23
kGe 21:9

a6 Aramaic for *Father*   b27 Isaiah 54:1

son will never share in the inheritance with the free woman's son."[a][1] [31]Therefore, brothers, we are not children of the slave woman, but of the free woman.

Freedom in Christ

5 It is for freedom that Christ has set us free.[m] Stand firm,[n] then, and do not let yourselves be burdened again by a yoke of slavery.[o]

[2]Mark my words! I, Paul, tell you that if you let yourselves be circumcised,[p] Christ will be of no value to you at all. [3]Again I declare to every man who lets himself be circumcised that he is obligated to obey the whole law.[q] [4]You who are trying to be justified by law have been alienated from Christ; you have fallen away from grace.[r] [5]But by faith we eagerly await through the Spirit the righteousness for which we hope.[s] [6]For in Christ Jesus neither circumcision nor uncircumcision has any value.[t] The only thing that counts is faith expressing itself through love.[u]

[7]You were running a good race.[v] Who cut in on you[w] and kept you from obeying the truth? [8]That kind of persuasion does not come from the one who calls you.[x] [9]"A little yeast works through the whole batch of dough."[y] [10]I am confident[z] in the Lord that you will take no other view.[a] The one who is throwing you into confusion[b] will pay the penalty, whoever he may be. [11]Brothers, if I am still preaching circumcision, why am I still being persecuted?[c] In that case the offense[d] of the cross has been abolished. [12]As for those agitators,[e] I wish they would go the whole way and emasculate themselves!

[13]You, my brothers, were called to be free. But do not use your freedom to indulge the sinful nature[b];[f] rather, serve one another[g] in love. [14]The entire law is summed up in a single command: "Love your neighbor as yourself."[c][h] [15]If you keep on biting and devouring each other, watch out or you will be destroyed by each other.

Life by the Spirit

[16]So I say, live by the Spirit,[i] and you will not gratify the desires of the sinful nature.[j] [17]For the sinful nature desires what is contrary to the Spirit, and the Spirit what is contrary to the sinful nature.[k] They are in conflict with each other, so that you do not do what you want.[l] [18]But if you are led by the Spirit, you are not under law.[m]

[19]The acts of the sinful nature are obvious: sexual immorality,[n] impurity and debauchery; [20]idolatry and witchcraft; hatred, discord, jealousy, fits of rage, selfish ambition, dissensions, factions [21]and envy; drunkenness, orgies, and the like.[o] I warn you, as I did before, that those who live like this will not inherit the kingdom of God.

[22]But the fruit[p] of the Spirit is love,[q] joy, peace, patience, kindness, goodness, faithfulness, [23]gentleness and self-control.[r] Against such things there is no law. [24]Those who belong to Christ Jesus have crucified the sinful nature[s] with its passions and desires.[t] [25]Since we live by the Spirit, let us keep in step with the Spirit. [26]Let us not become conceited,[u] provoking and envying each other.

[a]30 Gen. 21:10   [b]13 Or *the flesh*; also in verses 16, 17, 19 and 24   [c]14 Lev. 19:18

4:30
[1]Ge 21:10
5:1
m Jn 8:32
n 1Co 16:13
o Ac 15:10;
Gal 2:4
5:2
p Ac 15:1
5:3
q Gal 3:10
5:4
r Heb 12:15;
2Pe 3:17
5:5
s Ro 8:23,24
5:6
t 1Co 7:19
u 1Th 1:3
5:7
v 1Co 9:24
w Gal 3:1
5:8
x Ro 8:28;
Gal 1:6
5:9
y 1Co 5:6
5:10
z 2Co 2:3
a Php 3:15
b Gal 1:7
5:11
c Gal 4:29; 6:12
d 1Co 1:23
5:12
e ver 10
5:13
f 1Co 8:9;
1Pe 2:16
g 1Co 9:19;
Eph 5:21
5:14
h Lev 19:18;
Mt 22:39
5:16
i Ro 8:2,4-6,9,14
j ver 24
5:17
k Ro 8:5-8
l Ro 7:15-23
5:18
m Ro 6:14;
1Ti 1:9
5:19
n 1Co 6:18
5:21
o Ro 13:13
5:22
p Mt 7:16-20;
Eph 5:9
q Col 3:12-15
5:23
r Ac 24:25
5:24
s Ro 6:6 t ver 16,
17
5:26
u Php 2:3

Doing Good to All

6 Brothers, if someone is caught in a sin, you who are spiritual[v] should restore him gently. But watch yourself, or you also may be tempted. [2]Carry each other's burdens, and in this way you will fulfill the law of Christ.[w] [3]If anyone thinks he is something[x] when he is nothing, he deceives himself. [4]Each one should test his own actions. Then he can take pride in himself, without comparing himself to somebody else, [5]for each one should carry his own load.

[6]Anyone who receives instruction in the word must share all good things with his instructor.[y]

[7]Do not be deceived:[z] God cannot be mocked. A man reaps what he sows.[a] [8]The one who sows to please his sinful nature, from that nature[a] will reap destruction;[b] the one who sows to please the Spirit, from the Spirit will reap eternal life.[c] [9]Let us not become weary in doing good,[d] for at the proper time we will reap a harvest if we do not give up.[e] [10]Therefore, as we have opportunity, let us do good[f] to all people, especially to those who belong to the family[g] of believers.

Not Circumcision but a New Creation

[11]See what large letters I use as I write to you with my own hand![h]

[12]Those who want to make a good impression outwardly are trying to compel you to be circumcised.[i] The only reason they do this is to avoid being persecuted[j] for the cross of Christ. [13]Not even those who are circumcised obey the law,[k] yet they want you to be circumcised that they may boast about your flesh.[l] [14]May I never boast except in the cross of our Lord Jesus Christ, through which[b] the world has been crucified to me, and I to the world.[m] [15]Neither circumcision nor uncircumcision means anything;[n] what counts is a new creation.[o] [16]Peace and mercy to all who follow this rule, even to the Israel of God.

[17]Finally, let no one cause me trouble, for I bear on my body the marks[p] of Jesus.

[18]The grace of our Lord Jesus Christ[q] be with your spirit,[r] brothers. Amen.

6:1
v1Co 2:15
6:2
wRo 15:1;
Jas 2:8
6:3
xRo 12:3;
1Co 8:2
6:6
y1Co 9:11,14
6:7
z1Co 6:9
a2Co 9:6
6:8
bJob 4:8;
Hos 8:7
cJas 3:18
6:9
d1Co 15:58
eRev 2:10
6:10
fPr 3:27
gEph 2:19
6:11
h1Co 16:21
6:12
iAc 15:1
jGal 5:11
6:13
kRo 2:25
1Php 3:3
6:14
mRo 6:2,6
6:15
n1Co 7:19
o2Co 5:17
6:17
pIsa 44:5;
2Co 1:5
6:18
qRo 16:20
r2Ti 4:22

---

[a]8 Or *his flesh, from the flesh*   [b]14 Or *whom*

Ephesians

Title and Background

Ephesus was the most important city in western Asia Minor (now Turkey). Because it was at an intersection of major trade routes, it became a commercial center. It also boasted a pagan temple dedicated to the Roman goddess Diana (Greek *Artemis*). Paul made Ephesus a center for evangelism for about three years. This letter was probably not sent merely to the church at Ephesus but also to the various churches in the province of Asia, where Paul conducted his third missionary journey.

Author and Date of Writing

The more widely held position is that Paul wrote this letter about A.D. 60, during his two-year imprisonment in Rome.

Theme and Message

Unlike several of Paul's other letters, Ephesians does not address any particular error or heresy. Paul wrote to help his readers better understand the dimensions of God's eternal purpose and grace and come to appreciate the high goals God has for the church. One of Paul's themes is that of unity—all Christians are one family in Jesus, and they should act with love toward each other. He also writes about the church—not a church building, but the church that is made up of all Christians through all the ages.

Outline

I. Greetings (1:1-2)
II. The Glory and Headship of Christ (1:3-14)
III. Prayer That Christians May Realize God's Purpose and Power (1:15-23)
IV. Steps Toward the Fulfillment of God's Purpose (2:1-3:21)
V. Ways to Fulfill God's Purpose in the Church (4:1-6:20)
VI. Conclusion (6:21-24)

---

1 Paul, an apostle[a] of Christ Jesus by the will of God,[b]

To the saints in Ephesus,[a] the faithful[bc] in Christ Jesus:

²Grace and peace to you from God our Father and the Lord Jesus Christ.[d]

Spiritual Blessings in Christ

³Praise be to the God and Father of our Lord Jesus Christ,[e] who has blessed us in the heavenly realms[f] with every spiritual blessing in Christ. ⁴For he chose us in him before the creation of the world to be holy and blameless[g] in his sight. In love[h] ⁵he[c] predestined[i] us to be adopted as his sons through Jesus Christ, in accordance with his pleasure[j] and will— ⁶to the praise of his glorious grace, which he has freely

1:1
a1Co 1:1
b2Co 1:1
cCol 1:2
1:2
dRo 1:7
1:3
e2Co 1:3
fEph 2:6; 3:10; 6:12
1:4
gEph 5:27; Col 1:22
hEph 4:2,15,16
1:5
iRo 8:29,30
j1Co 1:21

---

a1 Some early manuscripts do not have in Ephesus.   *b1 Or believers who are*   *c4,5 Or sight in love. 5He* given us in the One he loves.[k] [7]In him we have redemption[l] through his blood, the forgiveness of sins, in accordance with the riches of God's grace [8]that he lavished on us with all wisdom and understanding. [9]And he[a] made known to us the mystery[m] of his will according to his good pleasure, which he purposed in Christ, [10]to be put into effect when the times will have reached their fulfillment[n]—to bring all things in heaven and on earth together under one head, even Christ.[o]

[11]In him we were also chosen,[b] having been predestined according to the plan of him who works out everything in conformity with the purpose[p] of his will, [12]in order that we, who were the first to hope in Christ, might be for the praise of his glory.[q] [13]And you also were included in Christ when you heard the word of truth,[r] the gospel of your salvation. Having believed, you were marked in him with a seal,[s] the promised Holy Spirit, [14]who is a deposit guaranteeing our inheritance[t] until the redemption of those who are God's possession—to the praise of his glory.

Thanksgiving and Prayer

[15]For this reason, ever since I heard about your faith in the Lord Jesus and your love for all the saints,[u] [16]I have not stopped giving thanks for you,[v] remembering you in my prayers. [17]I keep asking that the God of our Lord Jesus Christ, the glorious Father,[w] may give you the Spirit[c] of wisdom[x] and revelation, so that you may know him better. [18]I pray also that the eyes of your heart may be enlightened[y] in order that you may know the hope to which he has called you, the riches of his glorious inheritance in the saints, [19]and his incomparably great power for us who believe. That power[z] is like the working of his mighty strength,[a] [20]which he exerted in Christ when he raised him from the dead[b] and seated him at his right hand in the heavenly realms, [21]far above all rule and authority, power and dominion, and every title[c] that can be given, not only in the present age but also in the one to come. [22]And God placed all things under his feet[d] and appointed him to be head[e] over everything for the church, [23]which is his body, the fullness of him who fills everything in every way.

Made Alive in Christ

2 As for you, you were dead in your transgressions and sins,[f] [2]in which you used to live[g] when you followed the ways of this world and of the ruler of the kingdom of the air,[h] the spirit who is now at work in those who are disobedient.[i] [3]All of us also lived among them at one time, gratifying the cravings of our sinful nature[d][j] and following its desires and thoughts. Like the rest, we were by nature objects of wrath. [4]But because of his great love for us, God, who is rich in mercy, [5]made us alive with Christ even when we were dead in transgressions[k]—it is by grace you have been saved.[l] [6]And God raised us up with Christ and seated us with him[m] in the heavenly realms[n] in Christ Jesus, [7]in order that in the coming ages he might show the incomparable riches of his grace, expressed in his kindness[o] to us in Christ Jesus. [8]For it is by grace you have been saved,[p] through faith—and this not

---

*Cross references (left margin):*

1:6 k Mt 3:17
1:7 l Ro 3:24
1:9 m Ro 16:25
1:10 n Gal 4:4; o Col 1:20
1:11 p Eph 3:11; Heb 6:17
1:12 q ver 6,14
1:13 r Col 1:5; s Eph 4:30
1:14 t Ac 20:32
1:15 u Col 1:4
1:16 v Ro 1:8
1:17 w Jn 20:17; x Col 1:9
1:18 y Ac 26:18; 2Co 4:6
1:19 z Col 1:29; a Eph 6:10
1:20 b Ac 2:24
1:21 c Php 2:9,10
1:22 d Mt 28:18; e Eph 4:15; 5:23
2:1 f ver 5; Col 2:13
2:2 g Col 3:7; h Jn 12:31; Eph 6:12; i Eph 5:6
2:3 j Gal 5:16
2:5 k ver 1 l ver 8; Ac 15:11
2:6 m Eph 1:20; n Eph 1:3
2:7 o Tit 3:4
2:8 p ver 5

---

[a] 8,9 Or us. With all wisdom and understanding, [9]he   [b] 11 Or were made heirs   [c] 17 Or a spirit
[d] 3 Or our flesh

from yourselves, it is the gift of God— [9]not by works, [q] so that no one can boast. [r] [10]For we are God's workmanship, created[s] in Christ Jesus to do good works, [t] which God prepared in advance for us to do.

One in Christ

[11]Therefore, remember that formerly you who are Gentiles by birth and called "uncircumcised" by those who call themselves "the circumcision" (that done in the body by the hands of men)[u]— [12]remember that at that time you were separate from Christ, excluded from citizenship in Israel and foreigners to the covenants of the promise, [v] without hope[w] and without God in the world. [13]But now in Christ Jesus you who once were far away have been brought near[x] through the blood of Christ. [y]

[14]For he himself is our peace, who has made the two one[z] and has destroyed the barrier, the dividing wall of hostility, [15]by abolishing in his flesh[a] the law with its commandments and regulations. [b] His purpose was to create in himself one[c] new man out of the two, thus making peace, [16]and in this one body to reconcile both of them to God through the cross, [d] by which he put to death their hostility. [17]He came and preached peace to you who were far away and peace to those who were near. [e] [18]For through him we both have access[f] to the Father[g] by one Spirit. [h]

[19]Consequently, you are no longer foreigners and aliens, [i] but fellow citizens[j] with God's people and members of God's household, [k] [20]built on the foundation[l] of the apostles and prophets, with Christ Jesus himself as the chief cornerstone. [m] [21]In him the whole building is joined together and rises to become a holy temple[n] in the Lord. [22]And in him you too are being built together to become a dwelling in which God lives by his Spirit.

Paul the Preacher to the Gentiles

3 For this reason I, Paul, the prisoner[o] of Christ Jesus for the sake of you Gentiles—

[2]Surely you have heard about the administration of God's grace that was given to me[p] for you, [3]that is, the mystery[q] made known to me by revelation, [r] as I have already written briefly. [4]In reading this, then, you will be able to understand my insight[s] into the mystery of Christ, [5]which was not made known to men in other generations as it has now been revealed by the Spirit to God's holy apostles and prophets. [t] [6]This mystery is that through the gospel the Gentiles are heirs[u] together with Israel, members together of one body, [v] and sharers together in the promise in Christ Jesus.

[7]I became a servant of this gospel[w] by the gift of God's grace given me through the working of his power. [x] [8]Although I am less than the least of all God's people, [y] this grace was given me: to preach to the Gentiles the unsearchable riches of Christ, [9]and to make plain to everyone the administration of this mystery, [z] which for ages past was kept hidden in God, who created all things. [10]His intent was that now, through the church, the manifold wisdom of God[a] should be made known[b] to the rulers and authorities[c] in the heavenly realms, [11]according to his eternal purpose which he accomplished in Christ Jesus our Lord. [12]In him and through faith in him we may approach God[d] with freedom and

2:9
q 2Ti 1:9
r 1Co 1:29
2:10
s Eph 4:24
t Tit 2:14
2:11
u Col 2:11
2:12
v Gal 3:17
w 1Th 4:13
2:13
x ver 17; Ac 2:39
y Col 1:20
2:14
z 1Co 12:13
2:15
a Col 1:21,22
b Col 2:14
c Gal 3:28
2:16
d Col 1:20,22
2:17
e Ps 148:14;
Isa 57:19
2:18
f Eph 3:12
g Col 1:12
h 1Co 12:13
2:19
i ver 12
j Php 3:20
k Gal 6:10
2:20
l Mt 16:18;
Rev 21:14
m 1Pe 2:4-8
2:21
n 1Co 3:16,17
3:1
o Ac 23:18;
Eph 4:1
3:2
p Col 1:25
3:3
q Ro 16:25
r 1Co 2:10
3:4
s 2Co 11:6
3:5
t Ro 16:26
3:6
u Gal 3:29
v Eph 2:15,16
3:7
w 1Co 3:5
x Eph 1:19
3:8
y 1Co 15:9
3:9
z Ro 16:25
3:10
a 1Co 2:7
b 1Pe 1:12
c Eph 1:21
3:12
d Eph 2:18

confidence.ᵉ ¹³I ask you, therefore, not to be discouraged because of my sufferings for you, which are your glory.

A Prayer for the Ephesians

¹⁴For this reason I kneelᶠ before the Father, ¹⁵from whom his whole familyᵃ in heaven and on earth derives its name. ¹⁶I pray that out of his glorious riches he may strengthen you with powerᵍ through his Spirit in your inner being,ʰ ¹⁷so that Christ may dwell in your heartsⁱ through faith. And I pray that you, being rootedʲ and established in love, ¹⁸may have power, together with all the saints, to grasp how wide and long and high and deepᵏ is the love of Christ, ¹⁹and to know this love that surpasses knowledge—that you may be filledˡ to the measure of all the fullness of God.ᵐ

²⁰Now to him who is ableⁿ to do immeasurably more than all we ask or imagine, according to his power that is at work within us, ²¹to him be glory in the church and in Christ Jesus throughout all generations, for ever and ever! Amen.ᵒ

Unity in the Body of Christ

4 As a prisonerᵖ for the Lord, then, I urge you to live a life worthy�q of the calling you have received. ²Be completely humble and gentle; be patient, bearing with one anotherʳ in love.ˢ ³Make every effort to keep the unityᵗ of the Spirit through the bond of peace. ⁴There is one body and one Spiritᵘ— just as you were called to one hope when you were called— ⁵one Lord, one faith, one baptism; ⁶one God and Father of all, who is over all and through all and in all.ᵛ

⁷But to each one of usʷ grace has been givenˣ as Christ apportioned it. ⁸This is why itᵇ says:

"When he ascended on high,
　he led captivesʸ in his train
　and gave gifts to men."ᶜ ᶻ

⁹(What does "he ascended" mean except that he also descended to the lower, earthly regionsᵈ? ¹⁰He who descended is the very one who ascended higher than all the heavens, in order to fill the whole universe.) ¹¹It was he who gave some to be apostles,ᵃ some to be prophets, some to be evangelists,ᵇ and some to be pastors and teachers, ¹²to prepare God's people for works of service, so that the body of Christᶜ may be built up ¹³until we all reach unityᵈ in the faith and in the knowledge of the Son of God and become mature,ᵉ attaining to the whole measure of the fullness of Christ.

¹⁴Then we will no longer be infants,ᶠ tossed back and forth by the waves,ᵍ and blown here and there by every wind of teaching and by the cunning and craftiness of men in their deceitful scheming.ʰ ¹⁵Instead, speaking the truth in love, we will in all things grow up into him who is the Head,ⁱ that is, Christ. ¹⁶From him the whole body, joined and held together by every supporting ligament, growsʲ and builds itself up in love, as each part does its work.

3:12
ᵉHeb 4:16
3:14
ᶠPhp 2:10
3:16
ᵍCol 1:11
ʰRo 7:22
3:17
ⁱJn 14:23
ʲCol 1:23
3:18
ᵏJob 11:8,9
3:19
ˡCol 2:10
ᵐEph 1:23
3:20
ⁿRo 16:25
3:21
ᵒRo 11:36
4:1
ᵖEph 3:1
qPhp 1:27;
Col 1:10
4:2
ʳCol 3:12,13
ˢEph 1:4
4:3
ᵗCol 3:14
4:4
ᵘ1Co 12:13
4:6
ᵛRo 11:36
4:7
ʷ1Co 12:7,11
ˣRo 12:3
4:8
ʸCol 2:15
ᶻPs 68:18
4:11
ᵃ1Co 12:28
ᵇAc 21:8
4:12
ᶜ1Co 12:27
4:13
ᵈver 3,5
ᵉCol 1:28
4:14
ᶠ1Co 14:20
ᵍJas 1:6
ʰEph 6:11
4:15
ⁱEph 1:22
4:16
ʲCol 2:19

ᵃ15 Or *whom all fatherhood*　　ᵇ8 Or *God*　　ᶜ8 Psalm 68:18　　ᵈ9 Or *the depths of the earth*

Living as Children of Light

¹⁷So I tell you this, and insist on it in the Lord, that you must no longer live as the Gentiles do, in the futility of their thinking. ᵏ ¹⁸They are darkened in their understanding¹ and separated from the life of Godᵐ because of the ignorance that is in them due to the hardening of their hearts. ⁿ ¹⁹Having lost all sensitivity, ᵒ they have given themselves overᵖ to sensuality�q so as to indulge in every kind of impurity, with a continual lust for more.

²⁰You, however, did not come to know Christ that way. ²¹Surely you heard of him and were taught in him in accordance with the truth that is in Jesus. ²²You were taught, with regard to your former way of life, to put offʳ your old self,ˢ which is being corrupted by its deceitful desires; ²³to be made new in the attitude of your minds;ᵗ ²⁴and to put on the new self,ᵘ created to be like God in true righteousness and holiness.ᵛ

²⁵Therefore each of you must put off falsehood and speak truthfullyʷ to his neighbor, for we are all members of one body. ˣ ²⁶"In your anger do not sin"ᵃ: Do not let the sun go down while you are still angry, ²⁷and do not give the devil a foothold. ²⁸He who has been stealing must steal no longer, but must work,ʸ doing something useful with his own hands,ᶻ that he may have something to share with those in need. ᵃ

²⁹Do not let any unwholesome talk come out of your mouths,ᵇ but only what is helpful for building others up according to their needs, that it may benefit those who listen. ³⁰And do not grieve the Holy Spirit of God, ᶜ with whom you were sealed for the day of redemption. ᵈ ³¹Get rid of all bitterness, rage and anger, brawling and slander, along with every form of malice. ᵉ ³²Be kind and compassionate to one another, forgiving each other, just as in Christ God forgave you. ᶠ

5 Be imitators of God, ᵍ therefore, as dearly loved children ²and live a life of love, just as Christ loved us and gave himself up for usʰ as a fragrant offering and sacrifice to God. ⁱ

³But among you there must not be even a hint of sexual immorality, or of any kind of impurity, or of greed,ʲ because these are improper for God's holy people. ⁴Nor should there be obscenity, foolish talk or coarse joking, which are out of place, but rather thanksgiving. ᵏ ⁵For of this you can be sure: No immoral, impure or greedy person—such a man is an idolaterˡ—has any inheritance in the kingdom of Christ and of God. ᵇᵐ ⁶Let no one deceive you with empty words, for because of such things God's wrathⁿ comes on those who are disobedient. ⁷Therefore do not be partners with them.

⁸For you were onceᵒ darkness, but now you are light in the Lord. Live as children of lightᵖ ⁹(for the fruitq of the light consists in all goodness, righteousness and truth) ¹⁰and find out what pleases the Lord. ¹¹Have nothing to do with the fruitless deeds of darkness, but rather expose them. ¹²For it is shameful even to mention what the disobedient do in secret. ¹³But everything exposed by the lightʳ becomes visible, ¹⁴for it is light that makes everything visible. This is why it is said:

  "Wake up, O sleeper, ˢ

ᵃ26 Psalm 4:4   ᵇ5 Or *kingdom of the Christ and God*

4:17
ᵏRo 1:21
4:18
ˡRo 1:21
ᵐEph 2:12
ⁿ2Co 3:14
4:19
ᵒ1Ti 4:2
ᵖRo 1:24
qCol 3:5
4:22
ʳ1Pe 2:1
ˢRo 6:6
4:23
ᵗCol 3:10
4:24
ᵘRo 6:4
ᵛEph 2:10
4:25
ʷZec 8:16
ˣRo 12:5
4:28
ʸAc 20:35
ᶻ1Th 4:11
ᵃLk 3:11
4:29
ᵇCol 3:8
4:30
ᶜ1Th 5:19
ᵈRo 8:23
4:31
ᵉCol 3:8
4:32
ᶠMt 6:14,15
5:1
ᵍLk 6:36
5:2
ʰGal 1:4
ⁱ2Co 2:15; Heb 7:27
5:3
ʲCol 3:5
5:4
ᵏver 20
5:5
ˡCol 3:5
ᵐ1Co 6:9
5:6
ⁿRo 1:18
5:8
ᵒEph 2:2
ᵖLk 16:8
5:9
qGal 5:22
5:13
ʳJn 3:20,21
5:14
ˢRo 13:11

rise from the dead, [t]
and Christ will shine on you." [u]

¹⁵Be very careful, then, how you live—not as unwise but as wise, ¹⁶making the most of every opportunity, [v] because the days are evil. [w] ¹⁷Therefore do not be foolish, but understand what the Lord's will is. [x] ¹⁸Do not get drunk on wine, [y] which leads to debauchery. Instead, be filled with the Spirit. [z] ¹⁹Speak to one another with psalms, hymns and spiritual songs. [a] Sing and make music in your heart to the Lord, ²⁰always giving thanks [b] to God the Father for everything, in the name of our Lord Jesus Christ.

²¹Submit to one another [c] out of reverence for Christ.

Wives and Husbands

5:22–6:9pp — Col 3:18–4:1

²²Wives, submit to your husbands [d] as to the Lord. [e] ²³For the husband is the head of the wife as Christ is the head of the church, [f] his body, of which he is the Savior. ²⁴Now as the church submits to Christ, so also wives should submit to their husbands in everything.

²⁵Husbands, love your wives, [g] just as Christ loved the church and gave himself up for her [h] ²⁶to make her holy, cleansing [a] her by the washing [i] with water through the word, ²⁷and to present her to himself as a radiant church, without stain or wrinkle or any other blemish, but holy and blameless. [j] ²⁸In this same way, husbands ought to love their wives [k] as their own bodies. He who loves his wife loves himself. ²⁹After all, no one ever hated his own body, but he feeds and cares for it, just as Christ does the church— ³⁰for we are members of his body. [l] ³¹"For this reason a man will leave his father and mother and be united to his wife, and the two will become one flesh." [b][m] ³²This is a profound mystery—but I am talking about Christ and the church. ³³However, each one of you also must love his wife [n] as he loves himself, and the wife must respect her husband.

Children and Parents

6 Children, obey your parents in the Lord, for this is right. [o] ²"Honor your father and mother"—which is the first commandment with a promise— ³"that it may go well with you and that you may enjoy long life on the earth." [c][p]

⁴Fathers, do not exasperate your children; [q] instead, bring them up in the training and instruction of the Lord. [r]

Slaves and Masters

⁵Slaves, obey your earthly masters with respect [s] and fear, and with sincerity of heart, [t] just as you would obey Christ. [u] ⁶Obey them not only to win their favor when their eye is on you, but like slaves of Christ, doing the will of God from your heart. ⁷Serve wholeheartedly, as if you were serving the Lord, not men, [v] ⁸because you know that the Lord will reward everyone for whatever good he does, [w] whether he is slave or free.

---

[a]26 Or *having cleansed*   [b]31 Gen. 2:24   [c]3 Deut. 5:16

5:14
t Jn 5:25
u Isa 60:1
5:16
v Col 4:5
w Eph 6:13
5:17
x Ro 12:2;
1Th 4:3
5:18
y Pr 20:1
z Lk 1:15
5:19
a Ac 16:25;
Col 3:16
5:20
b Ps 34:1
5:21
c Gal 5:13
5:22
d Ge 3:16;
1Pe 3:1,5,6
e Eph 6:5
5:23
f 1Co 11:3;
Eph 1:22
5:25
g Col 3:19
h ver 2
5:26
i Ac 22:16
5:27
j Eph 1:4;
Col 1:22
5:28
k ver 25
5:30
l 1Co 12:27
5:31
m Ge 2:24;
Mt 19:5;
1Co 6:16
5:33
n ver 25
6:1
o Col 3:20
6:3
p Ex 20:12
6:4
q Col 3:21
r Ge 18:19;
Dt 6:7
6:5
s 1Ti 6:1
t Col 3:22
u Eph 5:22
6:7
v Col 3:23
6:8
w Col 3:24

⁹And masters, treat your slaves in the same way. Do not threaten them, since you know that he who is both their Master and yours˟ is in heaven, and there is no favoritism with him.

The Armor of God

¹⁰Finally, be strong in the Lordʸ and in his mighty power.ᶻ ¹¹Put on the full armor of Godᵃ so that you can take your stand against the devil's schemes. ¹²For our struggle is not against flesh and blood, but against the rulers, against the authorities,ᵇ against the powersᶜ of this dark world and against the spiritual forces of evil in the heavenly realms.ᵈ ¹³Therefore put on the full armor of God, so that when the day of evil comes, you may be able to stand your ground, and after you have done everything, to stand. ¹⁴Stand firm then, with the belt of truth buckled around your waist,ᵉ with the breastplate of righteousness in place,ᶠ ¹⁵and with your feet fitted with the readiness that comes from the gospel of peace.ᵍ ¹⁶In addition to all this, take up the shield of faith,ʰ with which you can extinguish all the flaming arrows of the evil one. ¹⁷Take the helmet of salvationⁱ and the sword of the Spirit, which is the word of God.ʲ ¹⁸And pray in the Spirit on all occasionsᵏ with all kinds of prayers and requests.ˡ With this in mind, be alert and always keep on praying for all the saints.

¹⁹Pray also for me,ᵐ that whenever I open my mouth, words may be given me so that I will fearlesslyⁿ make known the mystery of the gospel, ²⁰for which I am an ambassadorᵒ in chains.ᵖ Pray that I may declare it fearlessly, as I should.

Final Greetings

²¹Tychicus,�q the dear brother and faithful servant in the Lord, will tell you everything, so that you also may know how I am and what I am doing. ²²I am sending him to you for this very purpose, that you may know how we are,ʳ and that he may encourage you.

²³Peaceˢ to the brothers, and love with faith from God the Father and the Lord Jesus Christ. ²⁴Grace to all who love our Lord Jesus Christ with an undying love.

6:9
ˣJob 31:13,14
6:10
ʸ1Co 16:13
ᶻEph 1:19
6:11
ᵃRo 13:12
6:12
ᵇEph 1:21
ᶜRo 8:38
ᵈEph 1:3
6:14
ᵉIsa 11:5
ᶠIsa 59:17
6:15
ᵍIsa 52:7
6:16
ʰ1Jn 5:4
6:17
ⁱIsa 59:17
ʲHeb 4:12
6:18
ᵏLk 18:1
ˡMt 26:41;
Php 1:4
6:19
ᵐ1Th 5:25
ⁿAc 4:29;
2Co 3:12
6:20
ᵒ2Co 5:20
ᵖAc 21:33
6:21
qAc 20:4
6:22
ʳCol 4:7-9
6:23
ˢGal 6:16;
1Pe 5:14

Philippians

Title and Background

Philippians was written during Paul's first Roman imprisonment and is known as a "Prison Letter" (along with Ephesians, Colossians and Philemon). The church at Philippi had sent Paul a gift by way of Epaphroditus, their messenger. Epaphroditus had become sick in Rome, and the Philippian Christians were concerned about him. This made Epaphroditus all the more eager to return home. Paul therefore wrote this letter to his Christian friends in Philippi, expressing his gratitude for their love and help.

Author and Date of Writing

The first verse of Philippians tells us Paul wrote the letter, and the writing itself reveals the stamp of genuineness. The many personal references of the author fit what we know of Paul from other New Testament books. The most widely accepted date for the writing of the letter is about A.D. 61.

Theme and Message

The theme of the book is "joy," or "rejoicing in the Lord." The word "joy" in its various forms occurs sixteen times. There were also perils to watch for, because there were enemies of the church, both inside and outside. Paul warns the Philippians of the present dangers of a self-seeking attitude and an attitude of pride, both of which could lead to harmful divisions. The book of Philippians also contains the most profound statement of the meaning of the incarnation (2:5-11).

Outline

1:1
a Ac 16:1; 2Co 1:1
b Ac 9:13
c Ac 16:12
d 1Ti 3:1
e 1Ti 3:8
1:2
f Ro 1:7
1:3
g Ro 1:8
1:4
h Ro 1:10
1:5
i Ac 2:42; Php 4:15

1 Paul and Timothy,[a] servants of Christ Jesus,

To all the saints[b] in Christ Jesus at Philippi,[c] together with the overseers[a][d] and deacons:[e]

2 Grace and peace to you from God our Father and the Lord Jesus Christ.[f]

Thanksgiving and Prayer

3 I thank my God every time I remember you.[g] 4 In all my prayers for all of you, I always pray[h] with joy 5 because of your partnership[i] in the

a1 Traditionally *bishops*

gospel from the first day[j] until now, [6]being confident of this, that he who began a good work in you will carry it on to completion until the day of Christ Jesus.[k]

[7]It is right[l] for me to feel this way about all of you, since I have you in my heart;[m] for whether I am in chains[n] or defending[o] and confirming the gospel, all of you share in God's grace with me. [8]God can testify[p] how I long for all of you with the affection of Christ Jesus.

[9]And this is my prayer: that your love[q] may abound more and more in knowledge and depth of insight, [10]so that you may be able to discern what is best and may be pure and blameless until the day of Christ,[r] [11]filled with the fruit of righteousness[s] that comes through Jesus Christ—to the glory and praise of God.

Paul's Chains Advance the Gospel

[12]Now I want you to know, brothers, that what has happened to me has really served to advance the gospel. [13]As a result, it has become clear throughout the whole palace guard[a] and to everyone else that I am in chains[t] for Christ. [14]Because of my chains,[u] most of the brothers in the Lord have been encouraged to speak the word of God more courageously and fearlessly.

[15]It is true that some preach Christ out of envy and rivalry, but others out of goodwill. [16]The latter do so in love, knowing that I am put here for the defense of the gospel.[v] [17]The former preach Christ out of selfish ambition,[w] not sincerely, supposing that they can stir up trouble for me while I am in chains.[bx] [18]But what does it matter? The important thing is that in every way, whether from false motives or true, Christ is preached. And because of this I rejoice.

Yes, and I will continue to rejoice, [19]for I know that through your prayers[y] and the help given by the Spirit of Jesus Christ,[z] what has happened to me will turn out for my deliverance.[c] [20]I eagerly expect[a] and hope that I will in no way be ashamed, but will have sufficient courage[b] so that now as always Christ will be exalted in my body,[c] whether by life or by death.[d] [21]For to me, to live is Christ[e] and to die is gain. [22]If I am to go on living in the body, this will mean fruitful labor for me. Yet what shall I choose? I do not know! [23]I am torn between the two: I desire to depart[f] and be with Christ,[g] which is better by far; [24]but it is more necessary for you that I remain in the body. [25]Convinced of this, I know that I will remain, and I will continue with all of you for your progress and joy in the faith, [26]so that through my being with you again your joy in Christ Jesus will overflow on account of me.

[27]Whatever happens, conduct yourselves in a manner worthy[h] of the gospel of Christ. Then, whether I come and see you or only hear about you in my absence, I will know that you stand firm[i] in one spirit, contending[j] as one man for the faith of the gospel [28]without being frightened in any way by those who oppose you. This is a sign to them that they will be destroyed, but that you will be saved—and that by God. [29]For it has been granted to you[k] on behalf of Christ not only to believe on him, but also to suffer[l] for him, [30]since you are going

1:5
j Ac 16:12-40
1:6
k ver 10;
1Co 1:8
1:7
l 2Pe 1:13
m 2Co 7:3
n ver 13,14,17;
Ac 21:33
o ver 16
1:8
p Ro 1:9
1:9
q 1Th 3:12
1:10
r ver 6; 1Co 1:8
1:11
s Jas 3:18
1:13
t ver 7,14,17
1:14
u ver 7,13,17
1:16
v ver 7,12
1:17
w Php 2:3
x ver 7,13,14
1:19
y 2Co 1:11
z Ac 16:7
1:20
a Ro 8:19
b ver 14
c 1Co 6:20
d Ro 14:8
1:21
e Gal 2:20
1:23
f 2Ti 4:6
g Jn 12:26;
2Co 5:8
1:27
h Eph 4:1
i 1Co 16:13
j Jude 3
1:29
k Mt 5:11,12
l Ac 14:22

through the same struggle[m] you saw[n] I had, and now hear[o] that I still have.

Imitating Christ's Humility

2 If you have any encouragement from being united with Christ, if any comfort from his love, if any fellowship with the Spirit,[p] if any tenderness and compassion,[q] [2]then make my joy complete[r] by being like-minded,[s] having the same love, being one[t] in spirit and purpose. [3]Do nothing out of selfish ambition or vain conceit,[u] but in humility consider others better than yourselves.[v] [4]Each of you should look not only to your own interests, but also to the interests of others.

[5]Your attitude should be the same as that of Christ Jesus:[w]

> [6]Who, being in very nature[a] God,[x]
> did not consider equality with God[y] something to be
> grasped,
> [7]but made himself nothing,
> taking the very nature[b] of a servant,[z]
> being made in human likeness.[a]
> [8]And being found in appearance as a man,
> he humbled himself
> and became obedient to death[b]—
> even death on a cross!
> [9]Therefore God exalted him[c] to the highest place
> and gave him the name that is above every name,[d]
> [10]that at the name of Jesus every knee should bow,[e]
> in heaven and on earth and under the earth,[f]
> [11]and every tongue confess that Jesus Christ is Lord,[g]
> to the glory of God the Father.

Shining as Stars

[12]Therefore, my dear friends, as you have always obeyed—not only in my presence, but now much more in my absence—continue to work out your salvation with fear and trembling,[h] [13]for it is God who works in you[i] to will and to act according to his good purpose.

[14]Do everything without complaining[j] or arguing, [15]so that you may become blameless and pure, children of God[k] without fault in a crooked and depraved generation,[l] in which you shine like stars in the universe [16]as you hold out[c] the word of life—in order that I may boast on the day of Christ that I did not run or labor for nothing. [m] [17]But even if I am being poured out like a drink offering[n] on the sacrifice[o] and service coming from your faith, I am glad and rejoice with all of you. [18]So you too should be glad and rejoice with me.

Timothy and Epaphroditus

[19]I hope in the Lord Jesus to send Timothy to you soon,[p] that I also may be cheered when I receive news about you. [20]I have no one else like him,[q] who takes a genuine interest in your welfare. [21]For everyone looks out for his own interests,[r] not those of Jesus Christ. [22]But you know that Timothy has proved himself, because as a son with his

1:30
m Col 2:1;
1Th 2:2
n Ac 16:19-40
over 13
2:1
p 2Co 13:14
q Col 3:12
2:2
r Jn 3:29
s Php 4:2
t Ro 12:16
2:3
u Gal 5:26
v Ro 12:10;
1Pe 5:5
2:5
w Mt 11:29
2:6
x Jn 1:1 y Jn 5:18
2:7
z Mt 20:28
a Jn 1:14;
Heb 2:17
2:8
b Mt 26:39;
Jn 10:18;
Heb 5:8
2:9
c Ac 2:33;
Heb 2:9
d Eph 1:20,21
2:10
e Ro 14:11
f Mt 28:18
2:11
g Jn 13:13
2:12
h 2Co 7:15
2:13
i Ezr 1:5
2:14
j 1Co 10:10;
1Pe 4:9
2:15
k Mt 5:45,48;
Eph 5:1
l Ac 2:40
2:16
m 1Th 2:19
2:17
n 2Ti 4:6
o Ro 15:16
2:19
p ver 23
2:20
q 1Co 16:10
2:21
r 1Co 10:24;
13:5

---

[a]6 Or *in the form of*   [b]7 Or *the form*   [c]16 Or *hold on to*

father[s] he has served with me in the work of the gospel. [23]I hope, therefore, to send him as soon as I see how things go with me.[t] [24]And I am confident[u] in the Lord that I myself will come soon.

[25]But I think it is necessary to send back to you Epaphroditus, my brother, fellow worker[v] and fellow soldier,[w] who is also your messenger, whom you sent to take care of my needs.[x] [26]For he longs for all of you[y] and is distressed because you heard he was ill. [27]Indeed he was ill, and almost died. But God had mercy on him, and not on him only but also on me, to spare me sorrow upon sorrow. [28]Therefore I am all the more eager to send him, so that when you see him again you may be glad and I may have less anxiety. [29]Welcome him in the Lord with great joy, and honor men like him,[z] [30]because he almost died for the work of Christ, risking his life to make up for the help you could not give me.[a]

No Confidence in the Flesh

3 Finally, my brothers, rejoice in the Lord! It is no trouble for me to write the same things to you again, and it is a safeguard for you.
[2]Watch out for those dogs,[b] those men who do evil, those mutilators of the flesh. [3]For it is we who are the circumcision,[c] we who worship by the Spirit of God, who glory in Christ Jesus, and who put no confidence in the flesh— [4]though I myself have reasons for such confidence.

If anyone else thinks he has reasons to put confidence in the flesh, I have more: [5]circumcised[d] on the eighth day, of the people of Israel,[e] of the tribe of Benjamin,[f] a Hebrew of Hebrews; in regard to the law, a Pharisee;[g] [6]as for zeal, persecuting the church;[h] as for legalistic righteousness,[i] faultless.

[7]But whatever was to my profit I now consider loss[j] for the sake of Christ. [8]What is more, I consider everything a loss compared to the surpassing greatness of knowing[k] Christ Jesus my Lord, for whose sake I have lost all things. I consider them rubbish, that I may gain Christ [9]and be found in him, not having a righteousness of my own that comes from the law,[l] but that which is through faith in Christ—the righteousness that comes from God and is by faith.[m] [10]I want to know Christ and the power of his resurrection and the fellowship of sharing in his sufferings,[n] becoming like him in his death,[o] [11]and so, somehow, to attain to the resurrection[p] from the dead.

Pressing on Toward the Goal

[12]Not that I have already obtained all this, or have already been made perfect,[q] but I press on to take hold[r] of that for which Christ Jesus took hold of me.[s] [13]Brothers, I do not consider myself yet to have taken hold of it. But one thing I do: Forgetting what is behind[t] and straining toward what is ahead, [14]I press on[u] toward the goal to win the prize for which God has called[v] me heavenward in Christ Jesus.

[15]All of us who are mature[w] should take such a view of things.[x] And if on some point you think differently, that too God will make clear to you. [16]Only let us live up to what we have already attained.

[17]Join with others in following my example,[y] brothers, and take note of those who live according to the pattern we gave you. [18]For, as I have often told you before and now say again even with tears,[z] many live as

2:22
s1Co 4:17;
1Ti 1:2
2:23
tver 19
2:24
uPhp 1:25
2:25
vPhp 4:3
wPhm 2
xPhp 4:18
2:26
yPhp 1:8
2:29
z1Co 16:18;
1Ti 5:17
2:30
a1Co 16:17
3:2
bPs 22:16,20
3:3
cRo 2:28,29;
Gal 6:15;
Col 2:11
3:5
dLk 1:59
e2Co 11:22
fRo 11:1
gAc 23:6
3:6
hAc 8:3
iRo 10:5
3:7
jMt 13:44;
Lk 14:33
3:8
kEph 4:13;
2Pe 1:2
3:9
lRo 10:5
mRo 9:30
3:10
nRo 8:17
oRo 6:3-5
3:11
pRev 20:5,6
3:12
q1Co 13:10
r1Ti 6:12
sAc 9:5,6
3:13
tLk 9:62
3:14
uHeb 6:1
vRo 8:28
3:15
w1Co 2:6
xGal 5:10
3:17
y1Co 4:16;
1Pe 5:3
3:18
zAc 20:31

enemies of the cross of Christ. [a] [19]Their destiny is destruction, their god is their stomach, [b] and their glory is in their shame. [c] Their mind is on earthly things. [d] [20]But our citizenship[e] is in heaven. [f] And we eagerly await a Savior from there, the Lord Jesus Christ, [g] [21]who, by the power[h] that enables him to bring everything under his control, will transform our lowly bodies[i] so that they will be like his glorious body. [j]

4 Therefore, my brothers, you whom I love and long for, [k] my joy and crown, that is how you should stand firm[l] in the Lord, dear friends!

3:18
aGal 6:12
3:19
bRo 16:18
cRo 6:21
dRo 8:5,6
3:20
eEph 2:19
fCol 3:1
g1Co 1:7
3:21
hEph 1:19
i1Co 15:43-53
jCol 3:4
4:1
kPhp 1:8
l1Co 16:13;
Php 1:27
4:2
mPhp 2:2
4:4
nRo 12:12;
Php 3:1
4:5
oHeb 10:37;
Jas 5:8,9
4:6
pMt 6:25-34
qEph 6:18
4:7
rIsa 26:3;
Jn 14:27;
Col 3:15
4:9
sPhp 3:17
tRo 15:33
4:10
u2Co 11:9
4:11
v1Ti 6:6,8
4:12
w1Co 4:11
x2Co 11:9
4:13
y2Co 12:9
4:14
zPhp 1:7
4:15
aPhp 1:5
b2Co 11:8,9
4:16
cAc 17:1
d1Th 2:9
4:17
e1Co 9:11,12
4:18
fPhp 2:25
g2Co 2:14
4:19
hPs 23:1;
2Co 9:8 iRo 2:4
4:20
jGal 1:4
kRo 11:36

Exhortations

[2]I plead with Euodia and I plead with Syntyche to agree with each other[m] in the Lord. [3]Yes, and I ask you, loyal yokefellow,[a] help these women who have contended at my side in the cause of the gospel, along with Clement and the rest of my fellow workers, whose names are in the book of life.

[4]Rejoice in the Lord always. I will say it again: Rejoice![n] [5]Let your gentleness be evident to all. The Lord is near. [o] [6]Do not be anxious about anything, [p] but in everything, by prayer and petition, with thanksgiving, present your requests to God. [q] [7]And the peace of God, [r] which transcends all understanding, will guard your hearts and your minds in Christ Jesus.

[8]Finally, brothers, whatever is true, whatever is noble, whatever is right, whatever is pure, whatever is lovely, whatever is admirable—if anything is excellent or praiseworthy—think about such things. [9]Whatever you have learned or received or heard from me, or seen in me— put it into practice. [s] And the God of peace[t] will be with you.

Thanks for Their Gifts

[10]I rejoice greatly in the Lord that at last you have renewed your concern for me. [u] Indeed, you have been concerned, but you had no opportunity to show it. [11]I am not saying this because I am in need, for I have learned to be content[v] whatever the circumstances. [12]I know what it is to be in need, and I know what it is to have plenty. I have learned the secret of being content in any and every situation, whether well fed or hungry, [w] whether living in plenty or in want. [x] [13]I can do everything through him who gives me strength. [y]

[14]Yet it was good of you to share[z] in my troubles. [15]Moreover, as you Philippians know, in the early days[a] of your acquaintance with the gospel, when I set out from Macedonia, not one church shared with me in the matter of giving and receiving, except you only;[b] [16]for even when I was in Thessalonica, [c] you sent me aid again and again when I was in need. [d] [17]Not that I am looking for a gift, but I am looking for what may be credited to your account. [e] [18]I have received full payment and even more; I am amply supplied, now that I have received from Epaphroditus[f] the gifts you sent. They are a fragrant[g] offering, an acceptable sacrifice, pleasing to God. [19]And my God will meet all your needs[h] according to his glorious riches[i] in Christ Jesus.

[20]To our God and Father[j] be glory for ever and ever. Amen. [k]

[a]3 Or *loyal Syzygus*

Final Greetings

21Greet all the saints in Christ Jesus. The brothers who are with me[l] send greetings. 22All the saints[m] send you greetings, especially those who belong to Caesar's household.

23The grace of the Lord Jesus Christ[n] be with your spirit. Amen. [a]

4:21
[l]Gal 1:2
4:22
[m]Ac 9:13
4:23
[n]Ro 16:20

---

[a]23 Some manuscripts do not have *Amen.*

Colossians

Title and Background

During Paul's three-year ministry in Ephesus, Epaphras had been converted and had carried the gospel to Colosse. The young church that resulted then became the target of heretical attack (the Colossian heresy), which led to Epaphras's visit to Paul in Rome and ultimately to the penning of this letter.

Author and Date of Writing

Some have argued that Paul wrote Colossians from Ephesus or Caesarea, but most of the evidence favors Rome as the place. It should be dated about A.D. 60, during Paul's first Roman imprisonment.

Theme and Message

Paul's purpose is to refute the Colossian heresy. To accomplish this goal, he exalts Christ and states that Christ is completely adequate. The theme is the complete adequacy of Christ as contrasted with the emptiness of mere human philosophy. We "have been given fullness in Christ" (2:10).

Outline

   I. Greetings, Thanksgiving and Prayer (1:1-14)
  II. The Supremacy of Christ (1:15-23)
 III. Paul's Labor for the Church (1:24-2:7)
 IV. Freedom from Human Regulations through Life with Christ (2:8-23)
  V. Rules for Holy Living (3:1-4:6)
 VI. Final Greetings and Conclusion (4:7-18)

---

1 Paul, an apostle^a of Christ Jesus by the will of God,^b and Timothy our brother,

²To the holy and faithful^a brothers in Christ at Colosse:

Grace^c and peace to you from God our Father.^{b d}

Thanksgiving and Prayer

³We always thank God,^e the Father of our Lord Jesus Christ, when we pray for you, ⁴because we have heard of your faith in Christ Jesus and of the love^f you have for all the saints^g— ⁵the faith and love that spring from the hope^h that is stored up for you in heavenⁱ and that you have already heard about in the word of truth, the gospel ⁶that has come to you. All over the world^j this gospel is bearing fruit^k and growing, just as it has been doing among you since the day you heard it and understood God's grace in all its truth. ⁷You learned it from Epaphras,^l our dear fellow servant, who is a faithful minister^m of

1:1
a 1Co 1:1
b 2Co 1:1
1:2
c Col 4:18
d Ro 1:7
1:3
e Ro 1:8
1:4
f Gal 5:6
g Eph 1:15
1:5
h 1Th 5:8;
Tit 1:2 i 1Pe 1:4
1:6
j Ro 10:18
k Jn 15:16
1:7
l Phm 23
m Col 4:7

---

^a2 Or *believing*   ^b2 Some manuscripts *Father and the Lord Jesus Christ*

Christ on our[a] behalf, [8]and who also told us of your love in the Spirit.[n]

[9]For this reason, since the day we heard about you,[o] we have not stopped praying for you and asking God to fill you with the knowledge of his will[p] through all spiritual wisdom and understanding.[q] [10]And we pray this in order that you may live a life worthy[r] of the Lord and may please him in every way: bearing fruit in every good work, growing in the knowledge of God, [11]being strengthened with all power[s] according to his glorious might so that you may have great endurance and patience,[t] and joyfully [12]giving thanks to the Father,[u] who has qualified you[b] to share in the inheritance[v] of the saints in the kingdom of light. [13]For he has rescued us from the dominion of darkness[w] and brought us into the kingdom[x] of the Son he loves,[y] [14]in whom we have redemption,[cz] the forgiveness of sins.[a]

The Supremacy of Christ

[15]He is the image[b] of the invisible God,[c] the firstborn over all creation. [16]For by him all things were created:[d] things in heaven and on earth, visible and invisible, whether thrones or powers or rulers or authorities;[e] all things were created by him and for him.[f] [17]He is before all things,[g] and in him all things hold together. [18]And he is the head[h] of the body, the church; he is the beginning and the firstborn from among the dead,[i] so that in everything he might have the supremacy. [19]For God was pleased[j] to have all his fullness[k] dwell in him, [20]and through him to reconcile[l] to himself all things, whether things on earth or things in heaven,[m] by making peace through his blood,[n] shed on the cross.

[21]Once you were alienated from God and were enemies[o] in your minds[p] because of[d] your evil behavior. [22]But now he has reconciled you by Christ's physical body[q] through death to present you holy in his sight, without blemish and free from accusation[r]— [23]if you continue in your faith, established[s] and firm, not moved from the hope[t] held out in the gospel. This is the gospel that you heard and that has been proclaimed to every creature under heaven,[u] and of which I, Paul, have become a servant.[v]

Paul's Labor for the Church

[24]Now I rejoice in what was suffered for you, and I fill up in my flesh what is still lacking in regard to Christ's afflictions,[w] for the sake of his body, which is the church. [25]I have become its servant[x] by the commission God gave me[y] to present to you the word of God in its fullness— [26]the mystery[z] that has been kept hidden for ages and generations, but is now disclosed to the saints. [27]To them God has chosen to make known[a] among the Gentiles the glorious riches of this mystery, which is Christ in you, the hope of glory.

[28]We proclaim him, admonishing[b] and teaching everyone with all wisdom,[c] so that we may present everyone perfect[d] in Christ. [29]To this end I labor,[e] struggling[f] with all his energy, which so powerfully works in me.[g]

---

[a]7 Some manuscripts *your redemption through his blood*   [b]12 Some manuscripts *us*   [c]14 A few late manuscripts
[d]21 Or *minds, as shown by*

1:8
nRo 15:30
1:9
oEph 1:15
pEph 5:17
qEph 1:17
1:10
rEph 4:1
1:11
sEph 3:16
tEph 4:2
1:12
uEph 5:20
vAc 20:32
1:13
wAc 26:18
xEph 6:12;
2Pe 1:11
yMt 3:17
1:14
zRo 3:24
aEph 1:7
1:15
b2Co 4:4
cJn 1:18
1:16
dJn 1:3
eEph 1:20,21
fRo 11:36
1:17
gJn 1:2
1:18
hEph 1:22
iAc 26:23;
Rev 1:5
1:19
jEph 1:5
kJn 1:16
1:20
l2Co 5:18
mEph 1:10
nEph 2:13
1:21
oRo 5:10
pEph 2:3
1:22
qRo 7:4
rEph 5:27
1:23
sEph 3:17 tver 5
uRo 10:18
vver 25;
1Co 3:5
1:24
w2Co 1:5
1:25
xver 23
yEph 3:2
1:26
zRo 16:25
1:27
aMt 13:11
1:28
bCol 3:16
c1Co 2:6,7
dEph 5:27
1:29
e1Co 15:10
fCol 2:1
gEph 1:19

2 I want you to know how much I am struggling[h] for you and for those at Laodicea,[i] and for all who have not met me personally. [2]My purpose is that they may be encouraged in heart[j] and united in love, so that they may have the full riches of complete understanding, in order that they may know the mystery of God, namely, Christ, [3]in whom are hidden all the treasures of wisdom and knowledge.[k] [4]I tell you this so that no one may deceive you by fine-sounding arguments.[l] [5]For though I am absent from you in body, I am present with you in spirit[m] and delight to see how orderly[n] you are and how firm[o] your faith in Christ is.

Freedom From Human Regulations Through Life With Christ

[6]So then, just as you received Christ Jesus as Lord,[p] continue to live in him, [7]rooted[q] and built up in him, strengthened in the faith as you were taught, and overflowing with thankfulness.

[8]See to it that no one takes you captive through hollow and deceptive philosophy,[r] which depends on human tradition and the basic principles of this world[s] rather than on Christ.

[9]For in Christ all the fullness of the Deity lives in bodily form, [10]and you have been given fullness in Christ, who is the head[t] over every power and authority. [11]In him you were also circumcised,[u] in the putting off of the sinful nature,[a][v] not with a circumcision done by the hands of men but with the circumcision done by Christ, [12]having been buried with him in baptism and raised with him[w] through your faith in the power of God, who raised him from the dead.[x]

[13]When you were dead in your sins[y] and in the uncircumcision of your sinful nature,[b] God made you[c] alive with Christ. He forgave us all our sins, [14]having canceled the written code, with its regulations,[z] that was against us and that stood opposed to us; he took it away, nailing it to the cross.[a] [15]And having disarmed the powers and authorities,[b] he made a public spectacle of them, triumphing over them[c] by the cross.[d]

[16]Therefore do not let anyone judge you[d] by what you eat or drink,[e] or with regard to a religious festival,[f] a New Moon celebration[g] or a Sabbath day.[h] [17]These are a shadow of the things that were to come;[i] the reality, however, is found in Christ. [18]Do not let anyone who delights in false humility[j] and the worship of angels disqualify you for the prize.[k] Such a person goes into great detail about what he has seen, and his unspiritual mind puffs him up with idle notions. [19]He has lost connection with the Head,[l] from whom the whole body, supported and held together by its ligaments and sinews, grows as God causes it to grow.[m]

[20]Since you died with Christ to the basic principles of this world,[n] why, as though you still belonged to it, do you submit to its rules:[o] [21]"Do not handle! Do not taste! Do not touch!"? [22]These are all destined to perish[p] with use, because they are based on human commands and teachings.[q] [23]Such regulations indeed have an appearance of wisdom, with their self-imposed worship, their false humility and their harsh treatment of the body, but they lack any value in restraining sensual indulgence.

### Cross references (margin)

2:1
h Col 1:29; 4:12
i Rev 1:11
2:2
j Col 4:8
2:3
k Ro 11:33; 1Co 1:24,30
2:4
l Ro 16:18
2:5
m 1Th 2:17
n 1Co 14:40
o 1Pe 5:9
2:6
p Col 1:10
2:7
q Eph 3:17
2:8
r 1Ti 6:20
s Gal 4:3
2:10
t Eph 1:22
2:11
u Ro 2:29; Php 3:3
v Gal 5:24
2:12
w Ro 6:5
x Ac 2:24
2:13
y Eph 2:1,5
2:14
z Eph 2:15
a 1Pe 2:24
2:15
b Eph 6:12
c Lk 10:18
2:16
d Ro 14:3,4
e Ro 14:17
f Ro 14:5
g 1Ch 23:31
h Gal 4:10
2:17
i Heb 8:5
2:18
j ver 23
k Php 3:14
2:19
l Eph 1:22
m Eph 4:16
2:20
n Gal 4:3,9
o ver 14,16
2:22
p 1Co 6:13
q Isa 29:13; Mt 15:9; Tit 1:14

---

a11 Or *the flesh*   *b13* Or *your flesh*   *c13* Some manuscripts *us*   *d15* Or *them in him*

Rules for Holy Living

3 Since, then, you have been raised with Christ, set your hearts on things above, where Christ is seated at the right hand of God. ²Set your minds on things above, not on earthly things.ʳ ³For you died,ˢ and your life is now hidden with Christ in God. ⁴When Christ, who is yourᵃ life, appears,ᵗ then you also will appear with him in glory.ᵘ

⁵Put to death, therefore, whatever belongs to your earthly nature: sexual immorality, impurity, lust, evil desires and greed,ᵛ which is idolatry.ʷ ⁶Because of these, the wrath of Godˣ is coming.ᵇ ⁷You used to walk in these ways, in the life you once lived.ʸ ⁸But now you must rid yourselvesᶻ of all such things as these: anger, rage, malice, slander,ᵃ and filthy language from your lips.ᵇ ⁹Do not lie to each other,ᶜ since you have taken off your old self with its practices ¹⁰and have put on the new self, which is being renewedᵈ in knowledge in the image of its Creator.ᵉ ¹¹Here there is no Greek or Jew,ᶠ circumcised or uncircumcised,ᵍ barbarian, Scythian, slave or free,ʰ but Christ is all,ⁱ and is in all.

¹²Therefore, as God's chosen people, holy and dearly loved, clothe yourselves with compassion, kindness, humility,ʲ gentleness and patience.ᵏ ¹³Bear with each otherˡ and forgive whatever grievances you may have against one another. Forgive as the Lord forgave you.ᵐ ¹⁴And over all these virtues put on love,ⁿ which binds them all together in perfect unity.ᵒ

¹⁵Let the peace of Christᵖ rule in your hearts, since as members of one body you were called to peace. And be thankful. ¹⁶Let the word of Christ�ۥ dwell in you richly as you teach and admonish one another with all wisdom,ʳ and as you sing psalms, hymns and spiritual songs with gratitude in your hearts to God.ˢ ¹⁷And whatever you do,ᵗ whether in word or deed, do it all in the name of the Lord Jesus, giving thanksᵘ to God the Father through him.

Rules for Christian Households

3:18–4:1pp — Eph 5:22–6:9

¹⁸Wives, submit to your husbands,ᵛ as is fitting in the Lord.

¹⁹Husbands, love your wives and do not be harsh with them.

²⁰Children, obey your parents in everything, for this pleases the Lord.

²¹Fathers, do not embitter your children, or they will become discouraged.

²²Slaves, obey your earthly masters in everything; and do it, not only when their eye is on you and to win their favor, but with sincerity of heart and reverence for the Lord. ²³Whatever you do, work at it with all your heart, as working for the Lord, not for men, ²⁴since you know that you will receive an inheritanceʷ from the Lord as a reward. It is the Lord Christ you are serving. ²⁵Anyone who does wrong will be repaid for his wrong, and there is no favoritism.ˣ

4 Masters, provide your slaves with what is right and fair, because you know that you also have a Master in heaven.

3:2
rPhp 3:19,20
3:3
sRo 6:2;
2Co 5:14
3:4
t1Co 1:7
u1Pe 1:13;
1Jn 3:2
3:5
vEph 5:3
wEph 5:5
3:6
xRo 1:18
3:7
yEph 2:2
3:8
zEph 4:22
aEph 4:31
bEph 4:29
3:9
cEph 4:22,25
3:10
dRo 12:2;
Eph 4:23
eEph 2:10
3:11
fRo 10:12
g1Co 7:19
hGal 3:28
iEph 1:23
3:12
jPhp 2:3
k2Co 6:6;
Gal 5:22,23
3:13
lEph 4:2
mEph 4:32
3:14
n1Co 13:1-13
oEph 4:3
3:15
pJn 14:27
3:16
qRo 10:17
rCol 1:28
sEph 5:19
3:17
t1Co 10:31
uEph 5:20
3:18
vEph 5:22
3:24
wAc 20:32
3:25
xAc 10:34

ᵃ4 Some manuscripts *our* ᵇ6 Some early manuscripts *coming on those who are disobedient*

Further Instructions

[2]Devote yourselves to prayer,[y] being watchful and thankful. [3]And pray for us, too, that God may open a door[z] for our message, so that we may proclaim the mystery of Christ, for which I am in chains.[a] [4]Pray that I may proclaim it clearly, as I should. [5]Be wise[b] in the way you act toward outsiders;[c] make the most of every opportunity.[d] [6]Let your conversation be always full of grace,[e] seasoned with salt,[f] so that you may know how to answer everyone.[g]

Final Greetings

[7]Tychicus[h] will tell you all the news about me. He is a dear brother, a faithful minister and fellow servant[i] in the Lord. [8]I am sending him to you for the express purpose that you may know about our[a] circumstances and that he may encourage your hearts.[j] [9]He is coming with Onesimus,[k] our faithful and dear brother, who is one of you. They will tell you everything that is happening here.

[10]My fellow prisoner Aristarchus[l] sends you his greetings, as does Mark, the cousin of Barnabas.[m] (You have received instructions about him; if he comes to you, welcome him.) [11]Jesus, who is called Justus, also sends greetings. These are the only Jews among my fellow workers for the kingdom of God, and they have proved a comfort to me. [12]Epaphras,[n] who is one of you and a servant of Christ Jesus, sends greetings. He is always wrestling in prayer for you,[o] that you may stand firm in all the will of God, mature[p] and fully assured. [13]I vouch for him that he is working hard for you and for those at Laodicea[q] and Hierapolis. [14]Our dear friend Luke,[r] the doctor, and Demas[s] send greetings. [15]Give my greetings to the brothers at Laodicea, and to Nympha and the church in her house.[t]

[16]After this letter has been read to you, see that it is also read[u] in the church of the Laodiceans and that you in turn read the letter from Laodicea.

[17]Tell Archippus:[v] "See to it that you complete the work you have received in the Lord."[w]

[18]I, Paul, write this greeting in my own hand.[x] Remember[y] my chains. Grace be with you.[z]

---

a8 Some manuscripts *that he may know about your*

1 Thessalonians

Title and Background

Paul founded the church at Thessalonica during his second missionary journey. He had taught there just three weeks when he had to leave suddenly because of the opposition of the Jews. Recent converts from paganism were thus left with little external support in the midst of persecution. Paul wrote to give encouragement to them.

Author and Date of Writing

Both external and internal evidence support the view that Paul wrote I Thessalonians. It is generally dated about A.D. 51. Except for the possibility of an early date for Galatians (48-49), 1 Thessalonians is Paul's earliest canonical letter.

Theme and Message

Although the thrust of the letter is varied, the subject of eschatology seems to be predominant in both Thessalonian letters. Every chapter of 1 Thessalonians ends with a reference to the second coming of Christ, with chapter 4 giving it major consideration. Thus, the second coming seems to permeate the letter and may be viewed in some sense as its theme.

Outline

I. Greetings and Thanksgiving (1:1-10)
II. Paul's Defense of His Actions and Absence (2:1-3:13)
III. Exhortations (4:1-5:22)
   A. About Personal Life (4:1-12)
   B. About Christ's Coming (4:13-5:11)
   C. About Church Life (5:12-22)
IV. Concluding Prayer, Greetings and Benediction (5:23-28)

---

1 Paul, Silas[a] and Timothy,[a]

To the church of the Thessalonians[b] in God the Father and the Lord Jesus Christ:

Grace and peace to you.[b][c]

Thanksgiving for the Thessalonians' Faith

[2]We always thank God for all of you,[d] mentioning you in our prayers. [3]We continually remember before our God and Father your work produced by faith,[e] your labor prompted by love, and your endurance inspired by hope in our Lord Jesus Christ.

[4]For we know, brothers loved by God, that he has chosen you, [5]because our gospel[f] came to you not simply with words, but also with

1:1
a Ac 16:1;
2Th 1:1
b Ac 17:1
c Ro 1:7
1:2
d Ro 1:8
1:3
e 2Th 1:11
1:5
f 2Th 2:14

---

a1 Greek *Silvanus*, a variant of *Silas*   b1 Some early manuscripts *you from God our Father and the Lord Jesus Christ* power, with the Holy Spirit and with deep conviction. You know how we lived among you for your sake. [6]You became imitators of us[g] and of the Lord; in spite of severe suffering,[h] you welcomed the message with the joy given by the Holy Spirit.[i] [7]And so you became a model to all the believers in Macedonia and Achaia. [8]The Lord's message rang out from you not only in Macedonia and Achaia—your faith in God has become known everywhere.[j] Therefore we do not need to say anything about it, [9]for they themselves report what kind of reception you gave us. They tell how you turned to God from idols[k] to serve the living and true God, [10]and to wait for his Son from heaven, whom he raised from the dead[l]—Jesus, who rescues us from the coming wrath.[m]

Paul's Ministry in Thessalonica

2 You know, brothers, that our visit to you[n] was not a failure. [2]We had previously suffered[o] and been insulted in Philippi, as you know, but with the help of our God we dared to tell you his gospel in spite of strong opposition. [3]For the appeal we make does not spring from error or impure motives,[p] nor are we trying to trick you. [4]On the contrary, we speak as men approved by God to be entrusted with the gospel.[q] We are not trying to please men[r] but God, who tests our hearts. [5]You know we never used flattery, nor did we put on a mask to cover up greed[s]—God is our witness.[t] [6]We were not looking for praise from men, not from you or anyone else.

As apostles[u] of Christ we could have been a burden to you, [7]but we were gentle among you, like a mother caring for her little children.[v] [8]We loved you so much that we were delighted to share with you not only the gospel of God but our lives as well,[w] because you had become so dear to us. [9]Surely you remember, brothers, our toil and hardship; we worked[x] night and day in order not to be a burden to anyone[y] while we preached the gospel of God to you.

[10]You are witnesses,[z] and so is God, of how holy,[a] righteous and blameless we were among you who believed. [11]For you know that we dealt with each of you as a father deals with his own children,[b] [12]encouraging, comforting and urging you to live lives worthy[c] of God, who calls you into his kingdom and glory.

[13]And we also thank God continually[d] because, when you received the word of God,[e] which you heard from us, you accepted it not as the word of men, but as it actually is, the word of God, which is at work in you who believe. [14]For you, brothers, became imitators of God's churches in Judea,[f] which are in Christ Jesus: You suffered from your own countrymen[g] the same things those churches suffered from the Jews, [15]who killed the Lord Jesus[h] and the prophets[i] and also drove us out. They displease God and are hostile to all men [16]in their effort to keep us from speaking to the Gentiles[j] so that they may be saved. In this way they always heap up their sins to the limit.[k] The wrath of God has come upon them at last.[a]

Paul's Longing to See the Thessalonians

[17]But, brothers, when we were torn away from you for a short time (in person, not in thought),[l] out of our intense longing we made every

---

[a]16 Or them fully

1:6
g 1Co 4:16
h Ac 17:5-10
i Ac 13:52
1:8
j Ro 1:8; 10:18
1:9
k 1Co 12:2;
Gal 4:8
1:10
l Ac 2:24
m Ro 5:9
2:1
n 1Th 1:5,9
2:2
o Ac 16:22;
Php 1:30
2:3
p 2Co 2:17
2:4
q Gal 2:7
r Gal 1:10
2:5
s Ac 20:33
t Ro 1:9
2:6
u 1Co 9:1,2
2:7
v ver 11
2:8
w 2Co 12:15;
1Jn 3:16
2:9
x Ac 18:3
y 2Th 3:8
2:10
z 1Th 1:5
a 2Co 1:12
2:11
b ver 7;
1Co 4:14
2:12
c Eph 4:1
2:13
d 1Th 1:2
e Heb 4:12
2:14
f Gal 1:22
g Ac 17:5;
2Th 1:4
2:15
h Ac 2:23
i Mt 5:12
2:16
j Ac 13:45,50
k Mt 23:32
2:17
l 1Co 5:3;
Col 2:5

effort to see you. [m] [18]For we wanted to come to you—certainly I, Paul, did, again and again—but Satan[n] stopped us. [o] [19]For what is our hope, our joy, or the crown[p] in which we will glory[q] in the presence of our Lord Jesus when he comes?[r] Is it not you? [20]Indeed, you are our glory[s] and joy.

3 So when we could stand it no longer,[t] we thought it best to be left by ourselves in Athens. [u] [2]We sent Timothy, who is our brother and God's fellow worker[a] in spreading the gospel of Christ, to strengthen and encourage you in your faith, [3]so that no one would be unsettled by these trials. You know quite well that we were destined for them.[v] [4]In fact, when we were with you, we kept telling you that we would be persecuted. And it turned out that way, as you well know.[w] [5]For this reason, when I could stand it no longer,[x] I sent to find out about your faith. I was afraid that in some way the tempter[y] might have tempted you and our efforts might have been useless.[z]

Timothy's Encouraging Report

[6]But Timothy has just now come to us from you[a] and has brought good news about your faith and love. [b] He has told us that you always have pleasant memories of us and that you long to see us, just as we also long to see you. [7]Therefore, brothers, in all our distress and persecution we were encouraged about you because of your faith. [8]For now we really live, since you are standing firm[c] in the Lord. [9]How can we thank God enough for you[d] in return for all the joy we have in the presence of our God because of you? [10]Night and day we pray[e] most earnestly that we may see you again[f] and supply what is lacking in your faith.

[11]Now may our God and Father himself and our Lord Jesus clear the way for us to come to you. [12]May the Lord make your love increase and overflow for each other[g] and for everyone else, just as ours does for you. [13]May he strengthen your hearts so that you will be blameless[h] and holy in the presence of our God and Father when our Lord Jesus comes[i] with all his holy ones.

Living to Please God

4 Finally, brothers,[j] we instructed you how to live in order to please God,[k] as in fact you are living. Now we ask you and urge you in the Lord Jesus to do this more and more. [2]For you know what instructions we gave you by the authority of the Lord Jesus.

[3]It is God's will that you should be sanctified: that you should avoid sexual immorality;[l] [4]that each of you should learn to control his own body[b][m] in a way that is holy and honorable, [5]not in passionate lust[n] like the heathen,[o] who do not know God; [6]and that in this matter no one should wrong his brother or take advantage of him.[p] The Lord will punish men for all such sins, [q] as we have already told you and warned you. [7]For God did not call us to be impure, but to live a holy life.[r] [8]Therefore, he who rejects this instruction does not reject man but God, who gives you his Holy Spirit.[s]

[9]Now about brotherly love[t] we do not need to write to you,[u] for you

2:17
m 1Th 3:10
2:18
n Mt 4:10
o Ro 1:13; 15:22
2:19
p Php 4:1
q 2Co 1:14
r Mt 16:27;
1Th 3:13
2:20
s 2Co 1:14
3:1
t ver 5 u Ac 17:15
3:3
v Ac 9:16; 14:22
3:4
w 1Th 2:14
3:5
x ver 1 y Mt 4:3
z Gal 2:2;
Php 2:16
3:6
a Ac 18:5
b 1Th 1:3
3:8
c 1Co 16:13
3:9
d 1Th 1:2
3:10
e 2Ti 1:3
f 1Th 2:17
3:12
g 1Th 4:9,10
3:13
h 1Co 1:8
i 1Th 2:19
4:1
j 2Co 13:11
k 2Co 5:9
4:3
l 1Co 6:18
4:4
m 1Co 7:2,9
4:5
n Ro 1:26
o Eph 4:17
4:6
p 1Co 6:8
q Heb 13:4
4:7
r Lev 11:44;
1Pe 1:15
4:8
s Ro 5:5; Gal 4:6
4:9
t Ro 12:10
u 1Th 5:1

---

[a]2 Some manuscripts *brother and fellow worker*; other manuscripts *brother and God's servant*
[b]4 Or *learn to live with his own wife*; or *learn to acquire a wife*

4:9
vJn 13:34
4:10
w1Th 1:7
x1Th 3:12
4:11
yEph 4:28;
2Th 3:10-12
4:12
zMk 4:11
4:13
aEph 2:12
4:14
b1Co 15:18
4:15
c1Co 15:52
4:16
dMt 24:31
e1Co 15:23;
2Th 2:1
4:17
f1Co 15:52
gAc 1:9;
Rev 11:12
hJn 12:26
5:1
iAc 1:7 j1Th 4:9
5:2
k1Co 1:8
l2Pe 3:10
5:4
mAc 26:18;
1Jn 2:8
5:6
nRo 13:11
5:7
oAc 2:15;
2Pe 2:13
5:8
pEph 6:14
qRo 8:24
rEph 6:17
5:9
s2Th 2:13,14
5:10
t2Co 5:15
5:12
u1Ti 5:17;
Heb 13:17
5:13
vMk 9:50
5:14
w2Th 3:6,7,11
xRo 14:1
5:15
y1Pe 3:9
zGal 6:10;
Eph 4:32
5:16
aPhp 4:4
5:19
bEph 4:30
5:20
c1Co 14:1-40
5:21
d1Co 14:29;
1Jn 4:1

yourselves have been taught by God to love each other. [v] [10]And in fact, you do love all the brothers throughout Macedonia. [w] Yet we urge you, brothers, to do so more and more. [x]

[11]Make it your ambition to lead a quiet life, to mind your own business and to work with your hands, [y] just as we told you, [12]so that your daily life may win the respect of outsiders[z] and so that you will not be dependent on anybody.

The Coming of the Lord

[13]Brothers, we do not want you to be ignorant about those who fall asleep, or to grieve like the rest of men, who have no hope. [a] [14]We believe that Jesus died and rose again and so we believe that God will bring with Jesus those who have fallen asleep in him. [b] [15]According to the Lord's own word, we tell you that we who are still alive, who are left till the coming of the Lord, will certainly not precede those who have fallen asleep. [c] [16]For the Lord himself will come down from heaven, with a loud command, with the voice of the archangel and with the trumpet call of God, [d] and the dead in Christ will rise first. [e] [17]After that, we who are still alive and are left[f] will be caught up together with them in the clouds[g] to meet the Lord in the air. And so we will be with the Lord[h] forever. [18]Therefore encourage each other with these words.

5 Now, brothers, about times and dates[i] we do not need to write to you, [j] [2]for you know very well that the day of the Lord[k] will come like a thief in the night. [l] [3]While people are saying, "Peace and safety," destruction will come on them suddenly, as labor pains on a pregnant woman, and they will not escape.

[4]But you, brothers, are not in darkness[m] so that this day should surprise you like a thief. [5]You are all sons of the light and sons of the day. We do not belong to the night or to the darkness. [6]So then, let us not be like others, who are asleep, [n] but let us be alert and self-controlled. [7]For those who sleep, sleep at night, and those who get drunk, get drunk at night. [o] [8]But since we belong to the day, let us be self-controlled, putting on faith and love as a breastplate, [p] and the hope of salvation[q] as a helmet. [r] [9]For God did not appoint us to suffer wrath but to receive salvation through our Lord Jesus Christ. [s] [10]He died for us so that, whether we are awake or asleep, we may live together with him. [t] [11]Therefore encourage one another and build each other up, just as in fact you are doing.

Final Instructions

[12]Now we ask you, brothers, to respect those who work hard among you, who are over you in the Lord[u] and who admonish you. [13]Hold them in the highest regard in love because of their work. Live in peace with each other. [v] [14]And we urge you, brothers, warn those who are idle, [w] encourage the timid, help the weak, [x] be patient with everyone. [15]Make sure that nobody pays back wrong for wrong, [y] but always try to be kind to each other[z] and to everyone else.

[16]Be joyful always;[a] [17]pray continually; [18]give thanks in all circumstances, for this is God's will for you in Christ Jesus.

[19]Do not put out the Spirit's fire;[b] [20]do not treat prophecies[c] with contempt. [21]Test everything. [d] Hold on to the good. [22]Avoid every kind of evil.

²³May God himself, the God of peace,ᵉ sanctify you through and through. May your whole spirit, soul and body be kept blameless at the coming of our Lord Jesus Christ. ²⁴The one who calls you is faithfulᶠ and he will do it.

²⁵Brothers, pray for us.ᵍ ²⁶Greet all the brothers with a holy kiss.ʰ ²⁷I charge you before the Lord to have this letter read to all the brothers.ⁱ ²⁸The grace of our Lord Jesus Christ be with you.ʲ

5:23
eRo 15:33
5:24
f1Co 1:9
5:25
gEph 6:19
5:26
hRo 16:16
5:27
iCol 4:16
5:28
jRo 16:20

2 Thessalonians

Title and Background

See Introduction to 1 Thessalonians.

Author and Date of Writing

Because of its similarity to 1 Thessalonians, it must have been written not long after the first letter, about A.D. 51 or 52.

Theme and Message

Like 1 Thessalonians, this letter deals extensively with eschatology. In fact, in 2 Thessalonians eighteen of the forty-seven verses deal with this subject. Some people had misunderstood Paul and were sure Jesus was coming very soon. In fact, they had stopped working and were just waiting for Jesus to return. Paul writes to correct this misunderstanding.

Outline

    I. Greetings, Thanksgiving and Prayer (1:1-12)
    II. Instruction on Christ's Coming and Christian Conduct (2:1-17)
    III. Request for Prayer and Warning against Idleness (3:1-15)
    IV. Final Greetings and Benediction (3:16-18)

---

1 Paul, Silas[a] and Timothy,[a]

To the church of the Thessalonians in God our Father and the Lord Jesus Christ:

²Grace and peace to you from God the Father and the Lord Jesus Christ.[b]

Thanksgiving and Prayer

³We ought always to thank God for you, brothers, and rightly so, because your faith is growing more and more, and the love every one of you has for each other is increasing.[c] ⁴Therefore, among God's churches we boast[d] about your perseverance and faith[e] in all the persecutions and trials you are enduring.[f]

⁵All this is evidence[g] that God's judgment is right, and as a result you will be counted worthy of the kingdom of God, for which you are suffering. ⁶God is just: He will pay back trouble to those who trouble you[h] ⁷and give relief to you who are troubled, and to us as well. This will happen when the Lord Jesus is revealed from heaven in blazing fire with his powerful angels.[i] ⁸He will punish those who do not know God[j] and do not obey the gospel of our Lord Jesus.[k] ⁹They will be punished with everlasting destruction[l] and shut out from the presence of the Lord and from the majesty of his power[m] ¹⁰on the day[n] he comes

1:1
aAc 16:1;
1Th 1:1
1:2
bRo 1:7
1:3
c1Th 3:12
1:4
d2Co 7:14
e1Th 1:3
f1Th 2:14
1:5
gPhp 1:28
1:6
hCol 3:25;
Rev 6:10
1:7
i1Th 4:16;
Jude 14
1:8
jGal 4:8
kRo 2:8
1:9
lPhp 3:19;
2Pe 3:7
m2Th 2:8
1:10
n1Co 3:13

a1 Greek *Silvanus*, a variant of *Silas*

to be glorified[o] in his holy people and to be marveled at among all those who have believed. This includes you, because you believed our testimony to you.[p]

[11]With this in mind, we constantly pray for you, that our God may count you worthy[q] of his calling, and that by his power he may fulfill every good purpose of yours and every act prompted by your faith.[r] [12]We pray this so that the name of our Lord Jesus may be glorified in you,[s] and you in him, according to the grace of our God and the Lord Jesus Christ.[a]

The Man of Lawlessness

2 Concerning the coming of our Lord Jesus Christ and our being gathered to him,[t] we ask you, brothers, [2]not to become easily unsettled or alarmed by some prophecy, report or letter[u] supposed to have come from us, saying that the day of the Lord[v] has already come. [3]Don't let anyone deceive you[w] in any way, for that day will not come until the rebellion occurs and the man of lawlessness[b] is revealed,[x] the man doomed to destruction. [4]He will oppose and will exalt himself over everything that is called God[y] or is worshiped, so that he sets himself up in God's temple, proclaiming himself to be God.[z]

[5]Don't you remember that when I was with you I used to tell you these things? [6]And now you know what is holding him back, so that he may be revealed at the proper time. [7]For the secret power of lawlessness is already at work; but the one who now holds it back will continue to do so till he is taken out of the way. [8]And then the lawless one will be revealed, whom the Lord Jesus will overthrow with the breath of his mouth[a] and destroy by the splendor of his coming. [9]The coming of the lawless one will be in accordance with the work of Satan displayed in all kinds of counterfeit miracles, signs and wonders,[b] [10]and in every sort of evil that deceives those who are perishing.[c] They perish because they refused to love the truth and so be saved. [11]For this reason God sends them[d] a powerful delusion so that they will believe the lie [12]and so that all will be condemned who have not believed the truth but have delighted in wickedness.[e]

Stand Firm

[13]But we ought always to thank God for you, brothers loved by the Lord, because from the beginning God chose you[c][f] to be saved[g] through the sanctifying work of the Spirit[h] and through belief in the truth. [14]He called you to this through our gospel, that you might share in the glory of our Lord Jesus Christ. [15]So then, brothers, stand firm[i] and hold to the teachings[d] we passed on to you,[j] whether by word of mouth or by letter.

[16]May our Lord Jesus Christ himself and God our Father, who loved us[k] and by his grace gave us eternal encouragement and good hope, [17]encourage[l] your hearts and strengthen[m] you in every good deed and word.

---

[a]12 Or *God and Lord, Jesus Christ*   [b]3 Some manuscripts *sin*   [c]13 Some manuscripts *because God chose you as his firstfruits*   [d]15 Or *traditions*

1:10
o Jn 17:10
p 1Co 1:6
1:11
q ver 5 r 1Th 1:3
1:12
s Php 2:9-11
2:1
t Mk 13:27;
1Th 4:15-17
2:2
u 2Th 3:17
v 1Co 1:8
2:3
w Eph 5:6-8
x Da 7:25; 8:25;
11:36;
Rev 13:5,6
2:4
y 1Co 8:5
z Isa 14:13,14;
Eze 28:2
2:8
a Isa 11:4;
Rev 19:15
2:9
b Mt 24:24;
Jn 4:48
2:10
c 1Co 1:18
2:11
d Ro 1:28
2:12
e Ro 1:32
2:13
f Eph 1:4
g 1Th 5:9
h 1Pe 1:2
2:15
i 1Co 16:13
j 1Co 11:2
2:16
k Jn 3:16
2:17
l 1Th 3:2
m 2Th 3:3

3:1
n1Th 4:1
o1Th 5:25
p1Th 1:8
3:2
qRo 15:31
3:3
r1Co 1:9
sMt 5:37
3:4
t2Co 2:3
3:5
u1Ch 29:18
3:6
v1Co 5:4
wRo 16:17
xver 7,11
y1Co 11:2
3:7
z1Co 4:16
3:8
aAc 18:3;
Eph 4:28
3:9
b1Co 9:4-14
cver 7
3:10
d1Th 3:4
e1Th 4:11
3:11
fver 6,7;
1Ti 5:13
3:12
g1Th 4:1
h1Th 4:11;
Eph 4:28
3:13
iGal 6:9
3:14
jver 6
3:15
kGal 6:1;
1Th 5:14
3:16
lRo 15:33
mRu 2:4
3:17
n1Co 16:21
3:18
oRo 16:20

Request for Prayer

3 Finally, brothers,[n] pray for us[o] that the message of the Lord[p] may spread rapidly and be honored, just as it was with you. [2]And pray that we may be delivered from wicked and evil men,[q] for not everyone has faith. [3]But the Lord is faithful,[r] and he will strengthen and protect you from the evil one.[s] [4]We have confidence[t] in the Lord that you are doing and will continue to do the things we command. [5]May the Lord direct your hearts[u] into God's love and Christ's perseverance.

Warning Against Idleness

[6]In the name of the Lord Jesus Christ,[v] we command you, brothers, to keep away from[w] every brother who is idle[x] and does not live according to the teaching[a] you received from us.[y] [7]For you yourselves know how you ought to follow our example.[z] We were not idle when we were with you, [8]nor did we eat anyone's food without paying for it. On the contrary, we worked[a] night and day, laboring and toiling so that we would not be a burden to any of you. [9]We did this, not because we do not have the right to such help,[b] but in order to make ourselves a model for you to follow.[c] [10]For even when we were with you,[d] we gave you this rule: "If a man will not work,[e] he shall not eat."

[11]We hear that some among you are idle. They are not busy; they are busybodies.[f] [12]Such people we command and urge in the Lord Jesus Christ[g] to settle down and earn the bread they eat.[h] [13]And as for you, brothers, never tire of doing what is right.[i]

[14]If anyone does not obey our instruction in this letter, take special note of him. Do not associate with him,[j] in order that he may feel ashamed. [15]Yet do not regard him as an enemy, but warn him as a brother.[k]

Final Greetings

[16]Now may the Lord of peace[l] himself give you peace at all times and in every way. The Lord be with all of you.[m]

[17]I, Paul, write this greeting in my own hand,[n] which is the distinguishing mark in all my letters. This is how I write.

[18]The grace of our Lord Jesus Christ be with you all.[o]

---

[a]6 Or *tradition*

1 Timothy

Title and Background

During his fourth missionary journey, Paul had instructed Timothy to care for the church at Ephesus while he went on to Macedonia. When Paul realized he might not return to Ephesus in the near future, he wrote this first letter to Timothy. He repeatedly states his desire and determination to visit Timothy, which shows he was not in prison when he wrote the letter.

Author and Date of Writing

Both early church tradition and the salutations of the Pastoral Letters (1, 2 Timothy, Titus) themselves confirm Paul as the author of this letter. 1 Timothy was written about A.D. 64, at least eight years after Paul's three-year stay in Ephesus.

Theme and Message

The letter was written to Timothy to give him instructions regarding the church. Paul wrote to develop the charge he had given his young assistant: to refute false teachings and to supervise the affairs of the growing Ephesian church. A major problem in this church was a heresy that combined Gnosticism (whose central teaching was that spirit is entirely good and matter is entirely evil), decadent Judaism (which taught that a number of the ceremonial practices of the Old Testament were still binding on the New Testament church) and false asceticism (with its belief that the body should be treated harshly).

Outline

I. Warning Against False Teachers (1:1-11)
II. The Lord's Grace to Paul (1:12-17)
III. The Purpose of Paul's Instructions (1:18-20)
IV. Instructions for the Church (2:1-3:16)
V. Dealing With False Teachers (4:1-16)
VI. Dealing With Different Groups (5:1-6:2)
VII. Miscellaneous Matters (6:3-21)

---

1 Paul, an apostle of Christ Jesus by the command of God[a] our Savior and of Christ Jesus our hope,[b]

[2] To Timothy[c] my true son[d] in the faith:

Grace, mercy and peace from God the Father and Chrst Jesus our Lord.

Warning Against False Teachers of the Law

[3] As I urged you when I went into Macedonia, stay there in Ephesus[e] so that you may command certain men not to teach false doctrines[f] any longer [4] nor to devote themselves to myths[g] and endless genealogies. These promote controversies[h] rather than God's work—which is by faith. [5] The goal of this command is love, which comes from a pure

1:1
a Tit 1:3
b Col 1:27
1:2
c Ac 16:1
d 2Ti 1:2; Tit 1:4
1:3
e Ac 18:19
f Gal 1:6,7
1:4
g 1Ti 4:7;
Tit 1:14 h 1Ti 6:4

heart[i] and a good conscience and a sincere faith.[j] 6Some have wandered away from these and turned to meaningless talk. 7They want to be teachers of the law, but they do not know what they are talking about or what they so confidently affirm.

8We know that the law is good[k] if one uses it properly. 9We also know that law[a] is made not for the righteous but for lawbreakers and rebels,[l] the ungodly and sinful, the unholy and irreligious; for those who kill their fathers or mothers, for murderers, 10for adulterers and perverts, for slave traders and liars and perjurers—and for whatever else is contrary to the sound doctrine[m] 11that conforms to the glorious gospel of the blessed God, which he entrusted to me.[n]

The Lord's Grace to Paul

12I thank Christ Jesus our Lord, who has given me strength,[o] that he considered me faithful, appointing me to his service. 13Even though I was once a blasphemer and a persecutor[p] and a violent man, I was shown mercy because I acted in ignorance and unbelief.[q] 14The grace of our Lord was poured out on me abundantly,[r] along with the faith and love that are in Christ Jesus.[s]

15Here is a trustworthy saying[t] that deserves full acceptance: Christ Jesus came into the world to save sinners—of whom I am the worst. 16But for that very reason I was shown mercy[u] so that in me, the worst of sinners, Christ Jesus might display his unlimited patience as an example for those who would believe on him and receive eternal life. 17Now to the King[v] eternal, immortal, invisible,[w] the only God, be honor and glory for ever and ever. Amen.[x]

18Timothy, my son, I give you this instruction in keeping with the prophecies once made about you,[y] so that by following them you may fight the good fight,[z] 19holding on to faith and a good conscience. Some have rejected these and so have shipwrecked their faith.[a] 20Among them are Hymenaeus[b] and Alexander,[c] whom I have handed over to Satan[d] to be taught not to blaspheme.

Instructions on Worship

2 I urge, then, first of all, that requests, prayers, intercession and thanksgiving be made for everyone— 2for kings and all those in authority,[e] that we may live peaceful and quiet lives in all godliness and holiness. 3This is good, and pleases God our Savior, 4who wants[f] all men[g] to be saved and to come to a knowledge of the truth.[h] 5For there is one God[i] and one mediator[j] between God and men, the man Christ Jesus, 6who gave himself as a ransom for all men—the testimony[k] given in its proper time.[l] 7And for this purpose I was appointed a herald and an apostle—I am telling the truth, I am not lying—and a teacher[m] of the true faith to the Gentiles.[n]

8I want men everywhere to lift up holy hands[o] in prayer, without anger or disputing.

9I also want women to dress modestly, with decency and propriety, not with braided hair or gold or pearls or expensive clothes,[p] 10but with good deeds, appropriate for women who profess to worship God.

11A woman should learn in quietness and full submission.[q] 12I do not

---

[a]9 Or *that the law*

permit a woman to teach or to have authority over a man; she must be silent. [13]For Adam was formed first, then Eve. [r] [14]And Adam was not the one deceived; it was the woman who was deceived and became a sinner. [s] [15]But women[a] will be saved[b] through childbearing—if they continue in faith, love[t] and holiness with propriety.

Overseers and Deacons

3 Here is a trustworthy saying: [u] If anyone sets his heart on being an overseer, [c][v] he desires a noble task. [2]Now the overseer must be above reproach, [w] the husband of but one wife, temperate, self-controlled, respectable, hospitable, [x] able to teach, [y] [3]not given to drunkenness, not violent but gentle, not quarrelsome, [z] not a lover of money. [a] [4]He must manage his own family well and see that his children obey him with proper respect. [b] [5](If anyone does not know how to manage his own family, how can he take care of God's church?)[c] [6]He must not be a recent convert, or he may become conceited[d] and fall under the same judgment as the devil. [7]He must also have a good reputation with outsiders, so that he will not fall into disgrace and into the devil's trap. [e]

[8]Deacons, [f] likewise, are to be men worthy of respect, sincere, not indulging in much wine, [g] and not pursuing dishonest gain. [9]They must keep hold of the deep truths of the faith with a clear conscience. [h] [10]They must first be tested; and then if there is nothing against them, let them serve as deacons.

[11]In the same way, their wives[d] are to be women worthy of respect, not malicious talkers[i] but temperate and trustworthy in everything.

[12]A deacon must be the husband of but one wife and must manage his children and his household well. [j] [13]Those who have served well gain an excellent standing and great assurance in their faith in Christ Jesus.

[14]Although I hope to come to you soon, I am writing you these instructions so that, [15]if I am delayed, you will know how people ought to conduct themselves in God's household, which is the church[k] of the living God, the pillar and foundation of the truth. [16]Beyond all question, the mystery[l] of godliness is great:

> He[e] appeared in a body, [f] [m]
> was vindicated by the Spirit,
> was seen by angels,
> was preached among the nations, [n]
> was believed on in the world,
> was taken up in glory. [o]

Instructions to Timothy

4 The Spirit[p] clearly says that in later times[q] some will abandon the faith and follow deceiving spirits[r] and things taught by demons. [2]Such teachings come through hypocritical liars, whose consciences have been seared as with a hot iron. [s] [3]They forbid people to marry[t] and order them to abstain from certain foods, [u] which God created[v] to be received with thanksgiving[w] by those who believe and who know

---

2:13
rGe 2:7,22;
1Co 11:8
2:14
sGe 3:1-6,13;
2Co 11:3
2:15
t1Ti 1:14
3:1
u1Ti 1:15
vAc 20:28
3:2
wTit 1:6-8
xRo 12:13
y2Ti 2:24
3:3
z2Ti 2:24
aHeb 13:5;
1Pe 5:2
3:4
bTit 1:6
3:5
c1Co 10:32
3:6
d1Ti 6:4
3:7
e2Ti 2:26
3:8
fPhp 1:1
gTit 2:3
3:9
h1Ti 1:19
3:11
i2Ti 3:3; Tit 2:3
3:12
jver 4
3:15
kver 5;
Eph 2:21
3:16
lRo 16:25
mJn 1:14
nCol 1:23
oMk 16:19
4:1
pJn 16:13
q2Ti 3:1
r2Th 2:3
4:2
sEph 4:19
4:3
tHeb 13:4
uCol 2:16
vGe 1:29
wRo 14:6

---

[a]15 Greek *she*   [b]15 Or *restored*   [c]1 Traditionally *bishop*; also in verse 2   [d]11 Or *way*, *deaconesses*   [e]16 Some manuscripts *God*   [f]16 Or *in the flesh*

the truth. [4]For everything God created is good,[x] and nothing is to be rejected if it is received with thanksgiving, [5]because it is consecrated by the word of God and prayer.

[6]If you point these things out to the brothers, you will be a good minister of Christ Jesus, brought up in the truths of the faith[y] and of the good teaching that you have followed. [7]Have nothing to do with godless myths and old wives' tales;[z] rather, train yourself to be godly. [8]For physical training is of some value, but godliness has value for all things,[a] holding promise for both the present life[b] and the life to come.

[9]This is a trustworthy saying[c] that deserves full acceptance [10](and for this we labor and strive), that we have put our hope in the living God, who is the Savior of all men, and especially of those who believe.

[11]Command and teach these things.[d] [12]Don't let anyone look down on you because you are young, but set an example[e] for the believers in speech, in life, in love, in faith[f] and in purity. [13]Until I come, devote yourself to the public reading of Scripture, to preaching and to teaching. [14]Do not neglect your gift, which was given you through a prophetic message[g] when the body of elders laid their hands on you.[h]

[15]Be diligent in these matters; give yourself wholly to them, so that everyone may see your progress. [16]Watch your life and doctrine closely. Persevere in them, because if you do, you will save both yourself and your hearers.

Advice About Widows, Elders and Slaves

5 Do not rebuke an older man[i] harshly,[j] but exhort him as if he were your father. Treat younger men[k] as brothers, [2]older women as mothers, and younger women as sisters, with absolute purity.

[3]Give proper recognition to those widows who are really in need.[l] [4]But if a widow has children or grandchildren, these should learn first of all to put their religion into practice by caring for their own family and so repaying their parents and grandparents,[m] for this is pleasing to God.[n] [5]The widow who is really in need[o] and left all alone puts her hope in God[p] and continues night and day to pray[q] and to ask God for help. [6]But the widow who lives for pleasure is dead even while she lives.[r] [7]Give the people these instructions,[s] too, so that no one may be open to blame. [8]If anyone does not provide for his relatives, and especially for his immediate family, he has denied[t] the faith and is worse than an unbeliever.

[9]No widow may be put on the list of widows unless she is over sixty, has been faithful to her husband,[a] [10]and is well known for her good deeds,[u] such as bringing up children, showing hospitality, washing the feet[v] of the saints, helping those in trouble[w] and devoting herself to all kinds of good deeds.

[11]As for younger widows, do not put them on such a list. For when their sensual desires overcome their dedication to Christ, they want to marry. [12]Thus they bring judgment on themselves, because they have broken their first pledge. [13]Besides, they get into the habit of being idle and going about from house to house. And not only do they become idlers, but also gossips and busybodies,[x] saying things they ought not to. [14]So I counsel younger widows to marry,[y] to have children, to

**Cross references (left margin):**

4:4
x Ro 14:14-18
4:6
y 1Ti 1:10
4:7
z 2Ti 2:16
4:8
a 1Ti 6:6
b Ps 37:9,11;
Mk 10:29,30
4:9
c 1Ti 1:15
4:11
d 1Ti 5:7; 6:2
4:12
e Tit 2:7;
1Pe 5:3
f 1Ti 1:14
4:14
g 1Ti 1:18
h Ac 6:6; 2Ti 1:6
5:1
i Tit 2:2
j Lev 19:32
k Tit 2:6
5:3
l ver 5,16
5:4
m Eph 6:1,2
n 1Ti 2:3
5:5
o ver 3,16
p 1Co 7:34;
1Pe 3:5
q Lk 2:37
5:6
r Lk 15:24
5:7
s 1Ti 4:11
5:8
t 2Pe 2:1;
Jude 4; Tit 1:16
5:10
u Ac 9:36;
1Ti 6:18;
1Pe 2:12
v Lk 7:44
w ver 16
5:13
x 2Th 3:11
5:14
y 1Co 7:9

---

[a]9 Or *has had but one husband*

manage their homes and to give the enemy no opportunity for slander. [z] [15]Some have in fact already turned away to follow Satan. [a]

[16]If any woman who is a believer has widows in her family, she should help them and not let the church be burdened with them, so that the church can help those widows who are really in need. [b]

[17]The elders [c] who direct the affairs of the church well are worthy of double honor, [d] especially those whose work is preaching and teaching. [18]For the Scripture says, "Do not muzzle the ox while it is treading out the grain," [a][e] and "The worker deserves his wages." [b][f] [19]Do not entertain an accusation against an elder [g] unless it is brought by two or three witnesses. [h] [20]Those who sin are to be rebuked [i] publicly, so that the others may take warning. [j]

[21]I charge you, in the sight of God and Christ Jesus [k] and the elect angels, to keep these instructions without partiality, and to do nothing out of favoritism.

[22]Do not be hasty in the laying on of hands, [l] and do not share in the sins of others. [m] Keep yourself pure.

[23]Stop drinking only water, and use a little wine [n] because of your stomach and your frequent illnesses.

[24]The sins of some men are obvious, reaching the place of judgment ahead of them; the sins of others trail behind them. [25]In the same way, good deeds are obvious, and even those that are not cannot be hidden.

6 All who are under the yoke of slavery should consider their masters worthy of full respect, [o] so that God's name and our teaching may not be slandered. [p] [2]Those who have believing masters are not to show less respect for them because they are brothers. [q] Instead, they are to serve them even better, because those who benefit from their service are believers, and dear to them. These are the things you are to teach and urge on them. [r]

Love of Money

[3]If anyone teaches false doctrines [s] and does not agree to the sound instruction [t] of our Lord Jesus Christ and to godly teaching, [4]he is conceited and understands nothing. He has an unhealthy interest in controversies and quarrels about words [u] that result in envy, strife, malicious talk, evil suspicions [5]and constant friction between men of corrupt mind, who have been robbed of the truth [v] and who think that godliness is a means to financial gain.

[6]But godliness with contentment [w] is great gain. [x] [7]For we brought nothing into the world, and we can take nothing out of it. [y] [8]But if we have food and clothing, we will be content with that. [z] [9]People who want to get rich [a] fall into temptation and a trap [b] and into many foolish and harmful desires that plunge men into ruin and destruction. [10]For the love of money [c] is a root of all kinds of evil. Some people, eager for money, have wandered from the faith [d] and pierced themselves with many griefs.

Paul's Charge to Timothy

[11]But you, man of God, [e] flee from all this, and pursue righteousness, godliness, faith, love, [f] endurance and gentleness. [12]Fight the good

[a]18 Deut. 25:4   [b]18 Luke 10:7

5:14
[z]1Ti 6:1
5:15
[a]Mt 4:10
5:16
[b]ver 3-5
5:17
[c]Ac 11:30
[d]Php 2:29;
1Th 5:12
5:18
[e]Dt 25:4;
1Co 9:7-9
[f]Lk 10:7;
Lev 19:13;
Dt 24:14,15;
Mt 10:10;
1Co 9:14
5:19
[g]Ac 11:30
[h]Mt 18:16
5:20
[i]2Ti 4:2;
Tit 1:13
[j]Dt 13:11
5:21
[k]1Ti 6:13;
2Ti 4:1
5:22
[l]Ac 6:6
[m]Eph 5:11
5:23
[n]1Ti 3:8
6:1
[o]Eph 6:5;
Tit 2:9;
1Pe 2:18
[p]Tit 2:5,8
6:2
[q]Phm 16
[r]1Ti 4:11
6:3
[s]1Ti 1:3
[t]1Ti 1:10
6:4
[u]2Ti 2:14
6:5
[v]Tit 1:15
6:6
[w]Php 4:11;
Heb 13:5
[x]1Ti 4:8
6:7
[y]Job 1:21;
Ecc 5:15
6:8
[z]Heb 13:5
6:9
[a]Pr 15:27
[b]1Ti 3:7
6:10
[c]1Ti 3:3
[d]Jas 5:19
6:11
[e]2Ti 3:17
[f]2Ti 2:22

6:12
g1Co 9:25,26;
1Ti 1:18
hPhp 3:12
6:13
iJn 18:33-37
j1Ti 5:21
6:15
k1Ti 1:11
l1Ti 1:17
mRev 17:14;
19:16
6:16
n1Ti 1:17
oJn 1:18
6:17
pLk 12:20,21
q1Ti 4:10
rAc 14:17
6:18
s1Ti 5:10
tRo 12:8,13
6:19
uMt 6:20
6:20
v2Ti 1:12,14
w2Ti 2:16
6:21
x2Ti 2:18
yCol 4:18

fight[g] of the faith. Take hold of[h] the eternal life to which you were called when you made your good confession in the presence of many witnesses. [13]In the sight of God, who gives life to everything, and of Christ Jesus, who while testifying before Pontius Pilate[i] made the good confession, I charge you[j] [14]to keep this command without spot or blame until the appearing of our Lord Jesus Christ, [15]which God will bring about in his own time—God, the blessed[k] and only Ruler,[l] the King of kings and Lord of lords,[m] [16]who alone is immortal[n] and who lives in unapproachable light, whom no one has seen or can see.[o] To him be honor and might forever. Amen.

[17]Command those who are rich in this present world not to be arrogant nor to put their hope in wealth,[p] which is so uncertain, but to put their hope in God,[q] who richly provides us with everything for our enjoyment.[r] [18]Command them to do good, to be rich in good deeds,[s] and to be generous and willing to share.[t] [19]In this way they will lay up treasure for themselves[u] as a firm foundation for the coming age, so that they may take hold of the life that is truly life.

[20]Timothy, guard what has been entrusted[v] to your care. Turn away from godless chatter[w] and the opposing ideas of what is falsely called knowledge, [21]which some have professed and in so doing have wandered from the faith.[x]

Grace be with you.[y]

2 Timothy

Title and Background

After Paul's release from prison in Rome in A.D. 62-63 and after his fourth missionary journey, during which he wrote 1 Timothy and Titus, he was again imprisoned in Rome under Emperor Nero about 66-67. He was languishing in a cold dungeon, chained like a common criminal. Paul knew that his work was done and that his life was nearly at an end.

Author and Date of Writing

The first verse states that the author is Paul, and numerous references in the letter confirm this. 2 Timothy was written about A.D. 66.

Theme and Message

Paul had three reasons for writing to Timothy at this time: (1) Paul was lonely because many of his friends had deserted him. Paul wanted very much for Timothy to join him; (2) he was concerned about the welfare of the churches during this time of persecution under Nero, and he admonishes Timothy to guard the gospel and, if necessary, to suffer for it; (3) he wanted to write to the Ephesian church through Timothy.

Outline

I. Paul's Concern for Timothy (1:1-14)
II. Paul's Situation (1:15-18)
III. Instructions to Timothy (2:1-26)
IV. Warning About the Last Days (3:1-17)
V. Paul's Charge, Requests and Greetings (4:1-22)

---

1 Paul, an apostle of Christ Jesus by the will of God,[a] according to the promise of life that is in Christ Jesus,[b]

[2] To Timothy,[c] my dear son:[d]

Grace, mercy and peace from God the Father and Christ Jesus our Lord.

Encouragement to Be Faithful

[3] I thank God,[e] whom I serve, as my forefathers did, with a clear conscience, as night and day I constantly remember you in my prayers.[f] [4] Recalling your tears,[g] I long to see you,[h] so that I may be filled with joy. [5] I have been reminded of your sincere faith,[i] which first lived in your grandmother Lois and in your mother Eunice[j] and, I am persuaded, now lives in you also. [6] For this reason I remind you to fan into flame the gift of God, which is in you through the laying on of my

1:1
a 2Co 1:1;
b Eph 3:6;
1Ti 6:19
1:2
c Ac 16:1
d 1Ti 1:2
1:3
e Ro 1:8
f Ro 1:10
1:4
g Ac 20:37
h 2Ti 4:9
1:5
i 1Ti 1:5
j Ac 16:1

hands.[k] 7For God did not give us a spirit of timidity,[l] but a spirit of power, of love and of self-discipline.

8So do not be ashamed[m] to testify about our Lord, or ashamed of me his prisoner.[n] But join with me in suffering for the gospel,[o] by the power of God, 9who has saved us and called[p] us to a holy life—not because of anything we have done but because of his own purpose and grace. This grace was given us in Christ Jesus before the beginning of time, 10but it has now been revealed[q] through the appearing of our Savior, Christ Jesus, who has destroyed death[r] and has brought life and immortality to light through the gospel. 11And of this gospel I was appointed a herald and an apostle and a teacher.[s] 12That is why I am suffering as I am. Yet I am not ashamed, because I know whom I have believed, and am convinced that he is able to guard[t] what I have entrusted to him for that day.[u]

13What you heard from me, keep[v] as the pattern of sound teaching, with faith and love in Christ Jesus.[w] 14Guard the good deposit that was entrusted to you—guard it with the help of the Holy Spirit who lives in us.[x]

15You know that everyone in the province of Asia has deserted me,[y] including Phygelus and Hermogenes.

16May the Lord show mercy to the household of Onesiphorus,[z] because he often refreshed me and was not ashamed of my chains. 17On the contrary, when he was in Rome, he searched hard for me until he found me. 18May the Lord grant that he will find mercy from the Lord on that day! You know very well in how many ways he helped me[a] in Ephesus.

2 You then, my son, be strong[b] in the grace that is in Christ Jesus. 2And the things you have heard me say[c] in the presence of many witnesses[d] entrust to reliable men who will also be qualified to teach others. 3Endure hardship with us like a good soldier[e] of Christ Jesus. 4No one serving as a soldier gets involved in civilian affairs—he wants to please his commanding officer. 5Similarly, if anyone competes as an athlete, he does not receive the victor's crown[f] unless he competes according to the rules. 6The hardworking farmer should be the first to receive a share of the crops. 7Reflect on what I am saying, for the Lord will give you insight into all this.

8Remember Jesus Christ, raised from the dead,[g] descended from David.[h] This is my gospel,[i] 9for which I am suffering[j] even to the point of being chained like a criminal. But God's word is not chained. 10Therefore I endure everything[k] for the sake of the elect, that they too may obtain the salvation that is in Christ Jesus, with eternal glory.[l]

11Here is a trustworthy saying:

> If we died with him,
>> we will also live with him;[m]
> 12if we endure,
>> we will also reign with him.[n]
> If we disown him,
>> he will also disown us;[o]
> 13if we are faithless,
>> he will remain faithful,[p]
>> for he cannot disown himself.

1:6
k1Ti 4:14
1:7
lRo 8:15
1:8
mMk 8:38;
Ro 1:16
nEph 3:1
o2Ti 2:3,9; 4:5
1:9
pRo 8:28
1:10
qEph 1:9
r1Co 15:26,54
1:11
s1Ti 2:7
1:12
t1Ti 6:20
uver 18
1:13
vTit 1:9
w1Ti 1:14
1:14
xRo 8:9
1:15
y2Ti 4:10,11,16
1:16
z2Ti 4:19
1:18
aHeb 6:10
2:1
bEph 6:10
2:2
c2Ti 1:13
d1Ti 6:12
2:3
e1Ti 1:18
2:5
f1Co 9:25
2:8
gAc 2:24
hMt 1:1
iRo 2:16
2:9
jAc 9:16
2:10
kCol 1:24
l2Co 4:17
2:11
mRo 6:2-11
2:12
nRo 8:17;
1Pe 4:13
oMt 10:33
2:13
pNu 23:19;
Ro 3:3

A Workman Approved by God

[14]Keep reminding them of these things. Warn them before God against quarreling about words;[q] it is of no value, and only ruins those who listen. [15]Do your best to present yourself to God as one approved, a workman who does not need to be ashamed and who correctly handles the word of truth.[r] [16]Avoid godless chatter,[s] because those who indulge in it will become more and more ungodly. [17]Their teaching will spread like gangrene. Among them are Hymenaeus[t] and Philetus, [18]who have wandered away from the truth. They say that the resurrection has already taken place, and they destroy the faith of some.[u] [19]Nevertheless, God's solid foundation stands firm,[v] sealed with this inscription: "The Lord knows those who are his,"[a][w] and, "Everyone who confesses the name of the Lord[x] must turn away from wickedness."

[20]In a large house there are articles not only of gold and silver, but also of wood and clay; some are for noble purposes and some for ignoble.[y] [21]If a man cleanses himself from the latter, he will be an instrument for noble purposes, made holy, useful to the Master and prepared to do any good work.[z]

[22]Flee the evil desires of youth, and pursue righteousness, faith, love[a] and peace, along with those who call on the Lord out of a pure heart.[b] [23]Don't have anything to do with foolish and stupid arguments, because you know they produce quarrels. [24]And the Lord's servant must not quarrel; instead, he must be kind to everyone, able to teach, not resentful.[c] [25]Those who oppose him he must gently instruct, in the hope that God will grant them repentance leading them to a knowledge of the truth,[d] [26]and that they will come to their senses and escape from the trap of the devil,[e] who has taken them captive to do his will.

Godlessness in the Last Days

3 But mark this: There will be terrible times in the last days.[f] [2]People will be lovers of themselves, lovers of money,[g] boastful, proud,[h] abusive, disobedient to their parents,[i] ungrateful, unholy, [3]without love, unforgiving, slanderous, without self-control, brutal, not lovers of the good, [4]treacherous, rash, conceited,[j] lovers of pleasure rather than lovers of God— [5]having a form of godliness but denying its power. Have nothing to do with them.

[6]They are the kind who worm their way[k] into homes and gain control over weak-willed women, who are loaded down with sins and are swayed by all kinds of evil desires, [7]always learning but never able to acknowledge the truth. [8]Just as Jannes and Jambres opposed Moses,[l] so also these men oppose[m] the truth—men of depraved minds,[n] who, as far as the faith is concerned, are rejected. [9]But they will not get very far because, as in the case of those men,[o] their folly will be clear to everyone.

Paul's Charge to Timothy

[10]You, however, know all about my teaching,[p] my way of life, my

2:14
q1Ti 6:4
2:15
rEph 1:13;
Jas 1:18
2:16
sTit 3:9
2:17
t1Ti 1:20
2:18
u1Ti 1:19
2:19
vIsa 28:16
wJn 10:14
x1Co 1:2
2:20
yRo 9:21
2:21
z2Ti 3:17
2:22
a1Ti 1:14; 6:11
b1Ti 1:5
2:24
c1Ti 3:2,3
2:25
d1Ti 2:4
2:26
e1Ti 3:7
3:1
f1Ti 4:1
3:2
g1Ti 3:3
hRo 1:30
iRo 1:30
3:4
j1Ti 3:6
3:6
kJude 4
3:8
lEx 7:11
mAc 13:8
n1Ti 6:5
3:9
oEx 7:12
3:10
p1Ti 4:6

[a]*19* Num. 16:5 (see Septuagint)

3:11
qAc 13:14,50
r2Co 11:23-27
sPs 34:19

3:12
tAc 14:22

3:13
u2Ti 2:16

3:14
v2Ti 1:13

3:15
w2Ti 1:5
xJn 5:39
yPs 119:98,99

3:16
z2Pe 1:20,21
aRo 4:23,24

3:17
b1Ti 6:11
c2Ti 2:21

4:1
dAc 10:42
e1Ti 5:21

4:2
f1Ti 4:13
gGal 6:6
h1Ti 5:20;
Tit 1:13; 2:15

4:3
i1Ti 1:10

4:4
j1Ti 1:4

4:5
k2Ti 1:8
lAc 21:8

4:6
mPhp 2:17
nPhp 1:23

4:7
o1Ti 1:18
p1Co 9:24

4:8
qCol 1:5
r2Ti 1:12

4:10
sCol 4:14
t1Jn 2:15
uAc 16:6

4:11
vCol 4:14
w2Ti 1:15
xAc 12:12

4:12
yAc 20:4

4:14
zAc 19:33
aRo 12:19

4:16
bAc 7:60

4:17
cAc 23:11
dAc 9:15

4:18
ePs 121:7
fRo 11:36

purpose, faith, patience, love, endurance, [11]persecutions, sufferings —what kinds of things happened to me in Antioch,q Iconium and Lystra, the persecutions I endured.r Yet the Lord rescued me from all of them.s [12]In fact, everyone who wants to live a godly life in Christ Jesus will be persecuted,t [13]while evil men and impostors will go from bad to worse,u deceiving and being deceived. [14]But as for you, continue in what you have learned and have become convinced of, because you know those from whom you learned it,v [15]and how from infancyw you have known the holy Scriptures,x which are able to make you wisey for salvation through faith in Christ Jesus. [16]All Scripture is God-breathedz and is useful for teaching,a rebuking, correcting and training in righteousness, [17]so that the man of Godb may be thoroughly equipped for every good work.c

4 In the presence of God and of Christ Jesus, who will judge the living and the dead,d and in view of his appearing and his kingdom, I give you this charge:e [2]Preachf the Word;g be prepared in season and out of season; correct, rebukeh and encourage—with great patience and careful instruction. [3]For the time will come when men will not put up with sound doctrine.i Instead, to suit their own desires, they will gather around them a great number of teachers to say what their itching ears want to hear. [4]They will turn their ears away from the truth and turn aside to myths.j [5]But you, keep your head in all situations, endure hardship,k do the work of an evangelist,l discharge all the duties of your ministry.

[6]For I am already being poured out like a drink offering,m and the time has come for my departure.n [7]I have fought the good fight,o I have finished the race,p I have kept the faith. [8]Now there is in store for meq the crown of righteousness, which the Lord, the righteous Judge, will award to me on that dayr—and not only to me, but also to all who have longed for his appearing.

Personal Remarks

[9]Do your best to come to me quickly, [10]for Demas,s because he loved this world,t has deserted me and has gone to Thessalonica. Crescens has gone to Galatia,u and Titus to Dalmatia. [11]Only Lukev is with me.w Get Markx and bring him with you, because he is helpful to me in my ministry. [12]I sent Tychicusy to Ephesus. [13]When you come, bring the cloak that I left with Carpus at Troas, and my scrolls, especially the parchments.

[14]Alexanderz the metalworker did me a great deal of harm. The Lord will repay him for what he has done.a [15]You too should be on your guard against him, because he strongly opposed our message.

[16]At my first defense, no one came to my support, but everyone deserted me. May it not be held against them.b [17]But the Lord stood at my sidec and gave me strength, so that through me the message might be fully proclaimed and all the Gentiles might hear it.d And I was delivered from the lion's mouth. [18]The Lord will rescue me from every evil attacke and will bring me safely to his heavenly kingdom. To him be glory for ever and ever. Amen.f

Final Greetings

[19]Greet Priscilla[a] and Aquila[g] and the household of Onesiphorus. [20]Erastus[h] stayed in Corinth, and I left Trophimus[i] sick in Miletus. [21]Do your best to get here before winter.[j] Eubulus greets you, and so do Pudens, Linus, Claudia and all the brothers.

[22]The Lord be with your spirit.[k] Grace be with you.[l]

4:19
gAc 18:2
4:20
hAc 19:22
iAc 20:4
4:21
jver 9
4:22
kGal 6:18;
Phm 25
lCol 4:18

---

[a]19 Greek *Prisca*, a variant of *Priscilla*

Titus

Title and Background

When Paul left Antioch to discuss "his" gospel with the Jerusalem leaders, he took Titus with him. Presumably Titus, who is not referred to in Acts, worked with Paul at Ephesus during the third missionary journey. From there the apostle sent him to Corinth to help that church with its work. Following Paul's release from his first Roman imprisonment, he and Titus worked briefly in Crete, after which he commissioned Titus to remain there as his representative and complete some needed work.

Author and Date of Writing

Paul probably wrote this letter to Titus from Corinth about A.D. 64.

Theme and Message

Paul wrote Titus to give him personal authorization and guidance in meeting opposition, instructions about faith and conduct, and warnings about false teachers. He also informed Titus of his future plans for him.

Outline

---

1 Paul, a servant of God[a] and an apostle of Jesus Christ for the faith of God's elect and the knowledge of the truth[b] that leads to godliness— 2a faith and knowledge resting on the hope of eternal life,[c] which God, who does not lie, promised before the beginning of time,[d] 3and at his appointed season[e] he brought his word to light[f] through the preaching entrusted to me[g] by the command of God our Savior,[h]

4To Titus,[i] my true son in our common faith:

Grace and peace from God the Father and Christ Jesus our Savior.

Titus' Task on Crete

1:6–8Ref — 1Ti 3:2-4

5The reason I left you in Crete[j] was that you might straighten out what was left unfinished and appoint[a] elders[k] in every town, as I directed you. 6An elder must be blameless,[l] the husband of but one wife, a man whose children believe and are not open to the charge of being wild and disobedient. 7Since an overseer[b][m] is entrusted with God's work,[n] he must be blameless—not overbearing, not quick-tempered, not given to drunkenness, not violent, not pursuing dishonest

1:1
aRo 1:1 b1Ti 2:4
1:2
c2Ti 1:1
d2Ti 1:9
1:3
e1Ti 2:6
f2Ti 1:10
g1Ti 1:11
hLk 1:47
1:4
i2Co 2:13
1:5
jAc 27:7
kAc 11:30
1:6
l1Ti 3:2
1:7
m1Ti 3:1
n1Co 4:1

---

a5 Or ordain   b7 Traditionally bishop

gain.° ⁸Rather he must be hospitable,ᵖ one who loves what is good,�q who is self-controlled, upright, holy and disciplined. ⁹He must hold firmlyʳ to the trustworthy message as it has been taught, so that he can encourage others by sound doctrineˢ and refute those who oppose it.

¹⁰For there are many rebellious people, mere talkersᵗ and deceivers, especially those of the circumcision group.ᵘ ¹¹They must be silenced, because they are ruining whole householdsᵛ by teaching things they ought not to teach—and that for the sake of dishonest gain. ¹²Even one of their own prophetsʷ has said, "Cretansˣ are always liars, evil brutes, lazy gluttons." ¹³This testimony is true. Therefore, rebukeʸ them sharply, so that they will be sound in the faithᶻ ¹⁴and will pay no attention to Jewish mythsᵃ or to the commandsᵇ of those who reject the truth. ¹⁵To the pure, all things are pure, but to those who are corrupted and do not believe, nothing is pure.ᶜ In fact, both their minds and consciences are corrupted. ¹⁶They claim to know God, but by their actions they deny him.ᵈ They are detestable, disobedient and unfit for doing anything good.

What Must Be Taught to Various Groups

2 You must teach what is in accord with sound doctrine.ᵉ ²Teach the older men to be temperate, worthy of respect, self-controlled, and sound in faith,ᶠ in love and in endurance.

³Likewise, teach the older women to be reverent in the way they live, not to be slanderers or addicted to much wine,ᵍ but to teach what is good. ⁴Then they can train the younger women to love their husbands and children, ⁵to be self-controlled and pure, to be busy at home, to be kind, and to be subject to their husbands,ʰ so that no one will malign the word of God.ⁱ

⁶Similarly, encourage the young menʲ to be self-controlled. ⁷In everything set them an exampleᵏ by doing what is good. In your teaching show integrity, seriousness ⁸and soundness of speech that cannot be condemned, so that those who oppose you may be ashamed because they have nothing bad to say about us.ˡ

⁹Teach slaves to be subject to their masters in everything,ᵐ to try to please them, not to talk back to them, ¹⁰and not to steal from them, but to show that they can be fully trusted, so that in every way they will make the teaching about God our Savior attractive.ⁿ

¹¹For the grace of God that brings salvation has appeared to all men.° ¹²It teaches us to say "No" to ungodliness and worldly passions,ᵖ and to live self-controlled, upright and godly livesq in this present age, ¹³while we wait for the blessed hope—the glorious appearing of our great God and Savior, Jesus Christ,ʳ ¹⁴who gave himself for us to redeem us from all wickedness and to purify for himself a people that are his very own,ˢ eager to do what is good.ᵗ

¹⁵These, then, are the things you should teach. Encourage and rebuke with all authority. Do not let anyone despise you.

Doing What Is Good

3 Remind the people to be subject to rulers and authorities,ᵘ to be obedient, to be ready to do whatever is good,ᵛ ²to slander no one,ʷ to be peaceable and considerate, and to show true humility toward all men.

1:7
o1Ti 3:3,8
1:8
p1Ti 3:2
q2Ti 3:3
1:9
r1Ti 1:19
s1Ti 1:10
1:10
t1Ti 1:6 u11:2
1:11
v2Ti 3:6
1:12
wAc 17:28
xAc 2:11
1:13
y2Co 13:10
zTit 2:2
1:14
a1Ti 1:4
bCol 2:22
1:15
cRo 14:14,23
1:16
d1Jn 2:4
2:1
e1Ti 1:10
2:2
fTit 1:13
2:3
g1Ti 3:8
2:5
hEph 5:22
i1Ti 6:1
2:6
j1Ti 5:1
2:7
k1Ti 4:12
2:8
l1Pe 2:12
2:9
mEph 6:5
2:10
nMt 5:16
2:11
o1Ti 2:4
2:12
pTit 3:3
q2Ti 3:12
2:13
r2Pe 1:1
2:14
sEx 19:5
tEph 2:10
3:1
uRo 13:1
v2Ti 2:21
3:2
wEph 4:31;
2Ti 2:24

3:4
xEph 2:7
yTit 2:11
3:5
zEph 2:9
aRo 12:2
3:6
bRo 5:5
3:7
cRo 3:24
dRo 8:17
eRo 8:24
fTit 1:2
3:8
g1Ti 1:15
hTit 2:14
3:9
i1Ti 1:4;
2Ti 2:14
3:10
jRo 16:17
3:12
kAc 20:4
l2Ti 4:9,21
3:13
mAc 18:24
3:14
nver 8
3:15
o1Ti 1:2
pCol 4:18

[3]At one time we too were foolish, disobedient, deceived and enslaved by all kinds of passions and pleasures. We lived in malice and envy, being hated and hating one another. [4]But when the kindness[x] and love of God our Savior appeared,[y] [5]he saved us, not because of righteous things we had done,[z] but because of his mercy. He saved us through the washing of rebirth and renewal[a] by the Holy Spirit, [6]whom he poured out on us[b] generously through Jesus Christ our Savior, [7]so that, having been justified by his grace,[c] we might become heirs[d] having the hope[e] of eternal life.[f] [8]This is a trustworthy saying.[g] And I want you to stress these things, so that those who have trusted in God may be careful to devote themselves to doing what is good.[h] These things are excellent and profitable for everyone.

[9]But avoid foolish controversies and genealogies and arguments and quarrels[i] about the law, because these are unprofitable and useless. [10]Warn a divisive person once, and then warn him a second time. After that, have nothing to do with him.[j] [11]You may be sure that such a man is warped and sinful; he is self-condemned.

Final Remarks

[12]As soon as I send Artemas or Tychicus[k] to you, do your best to come to me at Nicopolis, because I have decided to winter there.[l] [13]Do everything you can to help Zenas the lawyer and Apollos[m] on their way and see that they have everything they need. [14]Our people must learn to devote themselves to doing what is good,[n] in order that they may provide for daily necessities and not live unproductive lives.

[15]Everyone with me sends you greetings. Greet those who love us in the faith.[o]

Grace be with you all.[p]

Philemon

Title and Background

Philemon was a believer in Colosse who, along with other Christians, was a slave owner. One of his slaves, Onesimus, had apparently stolen from him and then run away, which under Roman law was punishable by death. But Onesimus met Paul and through his ministry became a Christian. Now he was willing to return to his master.

Author and Date of Writing

Paul wrote this short letter about A.D. 60 from prison and sent it to Colosse with Onesimus and Tychicus.

Theme and Message

Paul writes this personal appeal to ask Philemon to accept Onesimus as a Christian brother, not as a slave. Now that Onesimus (whose name means useful) was a believer, he was really useful (see verses 10 and 11 and the footnote on verse 10).

Outline

---

[1]Paul, a prisoner[a] of Christ Jesus, and Timothy our brother,[b]

To Philemon our dear friend and fellow worker,[c] [2]to Apphia our sister, to Archippus[d] our fellow soldier[e] and to the church that meets in your home:[f]

[3]Grace to you and peace from God our Father and the Lord Jesus Christ.

Thanksgiving and Prayer

[4]I always thank my God[g] as I remember you in my prayers, [5]because I hear about your faith in the Lord Jesus and your love for all the saints.[h] [6]I pray that you may be active in sharing your faith, so that you will have a full understanding of every good thing we have in Christ. [7]Your love has given me great joy and encouragement,[i] because you, brother, have refreshed[j] the hearts of the saints.

Paul's Plea for Onesimus

[8]Therefore, although in Christ I could be bold and order you to do what you ought to do, [9]yet I appeal to you on the basis of love. I then, as Paul—an old man and now also a prisoner[k] of Christ Jesus— [10]I appeal to you for my son[l] Onesimus,[a][m] who became my son while I

1:1
[a]ver 9,23;
Eph 3:1
[b]2Co 1:1
[c]Php 2:25
1:2
[d]Col 4:17
[e]Php 2:25
[f]Ro 16:5
1:4
[g]Ro 1:8
1:5
[h]Eph 1:15;
Col 1:4
1:7
[i]2Co 7:4,13
[j]ver 20
1:9
[k]ver 1,23
1:10
[l]1Co 4:15
[m]Col 4:9

---

[a]10 Onesimus means useful.

was in chains. [11]Formerly he was useless to you, but now he has become useful both to you and to me.

[12]I am sending him—who is my very heart—back to you. [13]I would have liked to keep him with me so that he could take your place in helping me while I am in chains for the gospel. [14]But I did not want to do anything without your consent, so that any favor you do will be spontaneous and not forced.[n] [15]Perhaps the reason he was separated from you for a little while was that you might have him back for good— [16]no longer as a slave, but better than a slave, as a dear brother.[o] He is very dear to me but even dearer to you, both as a man and as a brother in the Lord.

[17]So if you consider me a partner,[p] welcome him as you would welcome me. [18]If he has done you any wrong or owes you anything, charge it to me. [19]I, Paul, am writing this with my own hand. I will pay it back—not to mention that you owe me your very self. [20]I do wish, brother, that I may have some benefit from you in the Lord; refresh[q] my heart in Christ. [21]Confident[r] of your obedience, I write to you, knowing that you will do even more than I ask.

[22]And one thing more: Prepare a guest room for me, because I hope to be[s] restored to you in answer to your prayers.[t]

[23]Epaphras,[u] my fellow prisoner in Christ Jesus, sends you greetings. [24]And so do Mark,[v] Aristarchus,[w] Demas[x] and Luke, my fellow workers.

[25]The grace of the Lord Jesus Christ be with your spirit.[y]

1:14
n 2Co 9:7;
1Pe 5:2
1:16
o Mt 23:8;
1Ti 6:2
1:17
p 2Co 8:23
1:20
q ver 7
1:21
r 2Co 2:3
1:22
s Php 1:25; 2:24
t 2Co 1:11
1:23
u Col 1:7
1:24
v Ac 12:12
w Ac 19:29
x Col 4:14
1:25
y 2Ti 4:22

Hebrews

Title and Background

The first-century church underwent much persecution, and this letter was written in that setting. The persecution had not yet resulted in martyrdom, but it was severe. The intended readers seem to have been Jewish Christians who were thinking of abandoning their faith and of lapsing back into Judaism. So the author exhorts them to hold fast to their confession of Christ as Savior and Lord.

Author and Date of Writing

The author of this letter does not identify himself, but he was obviously well known to the original recipients. For many years Paul was considered to be the author, but since the Reformation it has been widely recognized that Paul could not have been the author. Apollos and Barnabas are those most often suggested. The book was written prior to the fall of Jerusalem in A.D. 70.

Theme and Message

The theme of Hebrews is the absolute supremacy and sufficiency of Jesus Christ as revealer and as mediator of God's grace. The prologue presents Christ as God's full and final revelation. Hebrews could be called "the book of better things," since the two Greek words for "better" and "superior" occur 15 times in the letter. Practical applications of this theme are given throughout the book.

Outline

I. Christ's Superior Revelation (1:1-4)
II. Christ's Superiority Over Angels (1:5-2:18)
III. Christ's Superiority Over Moses (3:1-4:13)
IV. Christ's Superiority Over Aaronic Priests (4:14-7:28)
V. Christ's Superior Sacrifice (8:1-10:39)
VI. Plea for Persevering Faith (11:1-12:29)
VII. Conclusion (13:1-25)

The Son Superior to Angels

1 In the past God spoke[a] to our forefathers through the prophets[b] at many times and in various ways,[c] 2but in these last days he has spoken to us by his Son, whom he appointed heir[d] of all things, and through whom[e] he made the universe. 3The Son is the radiance of God's glory[f] and the exact representation of his being, sustaining all things[g] by his powerful word. After he had provided purification for sins,[h] he sat down at the right hand of the Majesty in heaven.[i] 4So he became as much superior to the angels as the name he has inherited is superior to theirs.[j]

5For to which of the angels did God ever say,

1:1
aJn 9:29;
Heb 2:2,3
bAc 2:30
cNu 12:6,8
1:2
dPs 2:8 eJn 1:3
1:3
fJn 1:14
gCol 1:17
hHeb 7:27
iMk 16:19
1:4
jEph 1:21;
Php 2:9,10

"You are my Son;
   today I have become your Father[a] "[b] ?[k]

Or again,

"I will be his Father,
   and he will be my Son"[c] ?[l]

[6]And again, when God brings his firstborn into the world,[m] he says,

"Let all God's angels worship him."[d][n]

[7]In speaking of the angels he says,

"He makes his angels winds,
   his servants flames of fire."[e][o]

[8]But about the Son he says,

"Your throne, O God, will last for ever and ever,
   and righteousness will be the scepter of your
      kingdom.
[9]You have loved righteousness and hated wickedness;
   therefore God, your God, has set you above your
      companions[p]
   by anointing you with the oil[q] of joy."[f]

[10]He also says,

"In the beginning, O Lord, you laid the foundations of
      the earth,
   and the heavens are the work of your hands.
[11]They will perish, but you remain;
   they will all wear out like a garment.[r]
[12]You will roll them up like a robe;
   like a garment they will be changed.
But you remain the same,[s]
   and your years will never end."[g][t]

[13]To which of the angels did God ever say,

"Sit at my right hand
until I make your enemies
a footstool[u] for your feet"[h] ?[v]

[14]Are not all angels ministering spirits[w] sent to serve those who will
inherit salvation?[x]

Warning to Pay Attention

2 We must pay more careful attention, therefore, to what we have
heard, so that we do not drift away. [2]For if the message spoken[y] by
angels[z] was binding, and every violation and disobedience received its
just punishment,[a] [3]how shall we escape if we ignore such a great
salvation?[b] This salvation, which was first announced by the Lord,[c]
was confirmed to us by those who heard him. [d] [4]God also testified to it

---

1:5
kPs 2:7
l2Sa 7:14
1:6
mHeb 10:5
nDt 32:43 (LXX
and
DSS) Ps 97:7
1:7
oPs 104:4
1:9
pPhp 2:9
qIsa 61:1,3
1:11
rIsa 34:4
1:12
sHeb 13:8
tPs 102:25-27
1:13
uJos 10:24;
Heb 10:13
vPs 110:1
1:14
wPs 103:20
xHeb 5:9
2:2
yHeb 1:1
zDt 33:2;
Ac 7:53
aHeb 10:28
2:3
bHeb 10:29
cHeb 1:2
dLk 1:2

---

[a]5 Or *have begotten you*   [b]5 Psalm 2:7   [c]5 2 Samuel 7:14; 1 Chron. 17:13   [d]6 Deut. 32:43
(see Dead Sea Scrolls and Septuagint)   [e]7 Psalm 104:4   [f]9 Psalm 45:6,7
[g]12 Psalm 102:25-27   [h]13 Psalm 110:1

by signs, wonders and various miracles,[e] and gifts of the Holy Spirit[f] distributed according to his will.[g]

Jesus Made Like His Brothers

[5]It is not to angels that he has subjected the world to come, about which we are speaking. [6]But there is a place where someone has testified:

"What is man that you are mindful of him,
the son of man that you care for him?[h]
[7]You made him a little[a] lower than the angels;
you crowned him with glory and honor
[8] and put everything under his feet."[b] [i]

In putting everything under him, God left nothing that is not subject to him. Yet at present we do not see everything subject to him. [9]But we see Jesus, who was made a little lower than the angels, now crowned with glory and honor[j] because he suffered death,[k] so that by the grace of God he might taste death for everyone.[l]

[10]In bringing many sons to glory, it was fitting that God, for whom and through whom everything exists,[m] should make the author of their salvation perfect through suffering.[n] [11]Both the one who makes men holy and those who are made holy[o] are of the same family. So Jesus is not ashamed to call them brothers.[p] [12]He says,

"I will declare your name to my brothers;
in the presence of the congregation I will sing your
praises."[c] [q]

[13]And again,

"I will put my trust in him."[d] [r]

And again he says,

"Here am I, and the children God has given me."[e] [s]

[14]Since the children have flesh and blood, he too shared in their humanity[t] so that by his death he might destroy[u] him who holds the power of death—that is, the devil[v]— [15]and free those who all their lives were held in slavery by their fear[w] of death. [16]For surely it is not angels he helps, but Abraham's descendants. [17]For this reason he had to be made like his brothers[x] in every way, in order that he might become a merciful[y] and faithful high priest[z] in service to God,[a] and that he might make atonement for[f] the sins of the people. [18]Because he himself suffered when he was tempted, he is able to help those who are being tempted.[b]

Jesus Greater Than Moses

3 Therefore, holy brothers,[c] who share in the heavenly calling, fix your thoughts on Jesus, the apostle and high priest[d] whom we confess.[e] [2]He was faithful to the one who appointed him, just as Moses was faithful in all God's house.[f] [3]Jesus has been found worthy of

---

2:4
e Jn 4:48
f 1Co 12:4
g Eph 1:5
2:6
h Job 7:17
2:8
i Ps 8:4-6;
1Co 15:25
2:9
j Ac 2:33; 3:13;
Php 2:9
k Php 2:7-9
l Jn 3:16;
2Co 5:15
2:10
m Ro 11:36
n Lk 24:26;
Heb 7:28
2:11
o Heb 10:10
p Mt 28:10;
Jn 20:17
2:12
q Ps 22:22
2:13
r Isa 8:17
s Isa 8:18;
Jn 10:29
2:14
t Jn 1:14
u 1Co 15:54-57;
2Ti 1:10
v 1Jn 3:8
2:15
w 2Ti 1:7
2:17
x Php 2:7
y Heb 5:2
z Heb 4:14,15;
7:26,28
a Heb 5:1
2:18
b Heb 4:15
3:1
c Heb 2:11
d Heb 2:17
e Heb 4:14
3:2
f Nu 12:7

---

[a]7 Or *him for a little while;* also in verse 9   [b]8 Psalm 8:4-6   [c]12 Psalm 22:22
[d]13 Isaiah 8:17   [e]13 Isaiah 8:18   [f]17 Or *and that he might turn aside God's wrath, taking away*

greater honor than Moses, just as the builder of a house has greater honor than the house itself. [4]For every house is built by someone, but God is the builder of everything. [5]Moses was faithful as a servant[g] in all God's house,[h] testifying to what would be said in the future. [6]But Christ is faithful as a son[i] over God's house. And we are his house,[j] if we hold on[k] to our courage and the hope[l] of which we boast.

Warning Against Unbelief

[7]So, as the Holy Spirit says:[m]

> "Today, if you hear his voice,
> [8]   do not harden your hearts
>   as you did in the rebellion,
>   during the time of testing in the desert,
> [9]where your fathers tested and tried me
>   and for forty years saw what I did.[n]
> [10]That is why I was angry with that generation,
>   and I said, 'Their hearts are always going astray,
>   and they have not known my ways.'
> [11]So I declared on oath in my anger,
>   'They shall never enter my rest.'[o][a][p]

[12]See to it, brothers, that none of you has a sinful, unbelieving heart that turns away from the living God. [13]But encourage one another daily,[q] as long as it is called Today, so that none of you may be hardened by sin's deceitfulness.[r] [14]We have come to share in Christ if we hold firmly[s] till the end the confidence we had at first. [15]As has just been said:

> "Today, if you hear his voice,
>   do not harden your hearts
>   as you did in the rebellion."[b][t]

[16]Who were they who heard and rebelled? Were they not all those Moses led out of Egypt?[u] [17]And with whom was he angry for forty years? Was it not with those who sinned, whose bodies fell in the desert?[v] [18]And to whom did God swear that they would never enter his rest[w] if not to those who disobeyed[c]?[x] [19]So we see that they were not able to enter, because of their unbelief.[y]

A Sabbath-Rest for the People of God

4 Therefore, since the promise of entering his rest still stands, let us be careful that none of you be found to have fallen short of it.[z] [2]For we also have had the gospel preached to us, just as they did; but the message they heard was of no value to them, because those who heard did not combine it with faith.[d][a] [3]Now we who have believed enter that rest, just as God has said,

> "So I declared on oath in my anger,
>   'They shall never enter my rest.'"[e][b]

And yet his work has been finished since the creation of the world. [4]For

3:5
gEx 14:31
hver 2; Nu 12:7
3:6
iHeb 1:2
j1Co 3:16
kRo 11:22
lRo 5:2
3:7
mHeb 9:8
3:9
nAc 7:36
3:11
oHeb 4:3,5
pPs 95:7-11
3:13
qHeb 10:24,25
rEph 4:22
3:14
sver 6
3:15
tver 7,8;
Ps 95:7,8
3:16
uNu 14:2
3:17
vNu 14:29;
Ps 106:26
3:18
wNu 14:20-23
xHeb 4:6
3:19
yJn 3:36
4:1
zHeb 12:15
4:2
a1Th 2:13
4:3
bPs 95:11;
Heb 3:11

---

[a]11 Psalm 95:7-11   [b]15 Psalm 95:7,8   [c]18 Or *disbelieved*   [d]2 Many manuscripts *because they did not share in the faith of those who obeyed*   [e]3 Psalm 95:11; also in verse 5

somewhere he has spoken about the seventh day in these words: "And on the seventh day God rested from all his work."*ᵃᶜ* ⁵And again in the passage above he says, "They shall never enter my rest."*ᵈ*

⁶It still remains that some will enter that rest, and those who formerly had the gospel preached to them did not go in, because of their disobedience.*ᵉ* ⁷Therefore God again set a certain day, calling it Today, when a long time later he spoke through David, as was said before:

> "Today, if you hear his voice,
> do not harden your hearts."*ᵇ ᶠ*

⁸For if Joshua had given them rest,*ᵍ* God would not have spoken*ʰ* later about another day. ⁹There remains, then, a Sabbath-rest for the people of God; ¹⁰for anyone who enters God's rest also rests from his own work, just as God did from his.*ⁱ* ¹¹Let us, therefore, make every effort to enter that rest, so that no one will fall by following their example of disobedience.*ʲ*

¹²For the word of God*ᵏ* is living and active.*ˡ* Sharper than any double-edged sword,*ᵐ* it penetrates even to dividing soul and spirit, joints and marrow; it judges the thoughts and attitudes of the heart.*ⁿ* ¹³Nothing in all creation is hidden from God's sight.*ᵒ* Everything is uncovered and laid bare before the eyes of him to whom we must give account.

Jesus the Great High Priest

¹⁴Therefore, since we have a great high priest who has gone through the heavens,*ᶜᵖ* Jesus the Son of God, let us hold firmly to the faith we profess.*q* ¹⁵For we do not have a high priest who is unable to sympathize with our weaknesses, but we have one who has been tempted in every way, just as we are*ʳ*—yet was without sin.*ˢ* ¹⁶Let us then approach the throne of grace with confidence, so that we may receive mercy and find grace to help us in our time of need.

5 Every high priest is selected from among men and is appointed to represent them in matters related to God, to offer gifts and sacrifices*ᵗ* for sins.*ᵘ* ²He is able to deal gently with those who are ignorant and are going astray,*ᵛ* since he himself is subject to weakness.*ʷ* ³This is why he has to offer sacrifices for his own sins, as well as for the sins of the people.*ˣ*

⁴No one takes this honor upon himself; he must be called by God, just as Aaron was.*ʸ* ⁵So Christ also did not take upon himself the glory*ᶻ* of becoming a high priest. But God said*ᵃ* to him,

> "You are my Son;
> today I have become your Father."*ᵈ ''ᵉ ᵇ*

⁶And he says in another place,

> "You are a priest forever,
> in the order of Melchizedek."*ᶠ ᶜ*

⁷During the days of Jesus' life on earth, he offered up prayers and petitions with loud cries and tears*ᵈ* to the one who could save him from

4:4
cGe 2:2,3;
Ex 20:11
4:5
dPs 95:11
4:6
eHeb 3:18
4:7
fPs 95:7,8;
Heb 3:7,8,15
4:8
gJos 22:4
hHeb 1:1
4:10
iver 4
4:11
jHeb 3:18
4:12
k1Pe 1:23
lJer 23:29
mEph 6:17;
Rev 1:16
n1Co 14:24,25
4:13
oPs 33:13-15
4:14
pHeb 6:20
qHeb 3:1
4:15
rHeb 2:18
s2Co 5:21
5:1
tHeb 8:3
uHeb 7:27
5:2
vHeb 2:18
wHeb 7:28
5:3
xHeb 7:27; 9:7
5:4
yEx 28:1
5:5
zJn 8:54
aHeb 1:1
bPs 2:7
5:6
cPs 110:4;
Heb 7:17,21
5:7
dMt 27:46,50

---

*ᵃ*4 Gen. 2:2   *ᵇ*7 Psalm 95:7,8   *ᶜ*14 Or *gone into heaven*   *ᵈ*5 Or *have begotten you*
*ᵉ*5 Psalm 2:7   *ᶠ*6 Psalm 110:4

death, and he was heard because of his reverent submission.[e] [8]Although he was a son, he learned obedience from what he suffered[f] [9]and, once made perfect,[g] he became the source of eternal salvation for all who obey him [10]and was designated by God to be high priest[h] in the order of Melchizedek.[i]

Warning Against Falling Away

6:4–6Ref — Heb 10:26–31

[11]We have much to say about this, but it is hard to explain because you are slow to learn. [12]In fact, though by this time you ought to be teachers, you need someone to teach you the elementary truths[j] of God's word all over again. You need milk, not solid food![k] [13]Anyone who lives on milk, being still an infant,[l] is not acquainted with the teaching about righteousness. [14]But solid food is for the mature,[m] who by constant use have trained themselves to distinguish good from evil.[n]

6 Therefore let us leave[o] the elementary teachings[p] about Christ and go on to maturity, not laying again the foundation of repentance from acts that lead to death,[a][q] and of faith in God, [2]instruction about baptisms,[r] the laying on of hands,[s] the resurrection of the dead,[t] and eternal judgment. [3]And God permitting,[u] we will do so.

[4]It is impossible for those who have once been enlightened,[v] who have tasted the heavenly gift,[w] who have shared in the Holy Spirit,[x] [5]who have tasted the goodness of the word of God and the powers of the coming age, [6]if they fall away, to be brought back to repentance,[y] because[b] to their loss they are crucifying the Son of God all over again and subjecting him to public disgrace.

[7]Land that drinks in the rain often falling on it and that produces a crop useful to those for whom it is farmed receives the blessing of God. [8]But land that produces thorns and thistles is worthless and is in danger of being cursed.[z] In the end it will be burned.

[9]Even though we speak like this, dear friends,[a] we are confident of better things in your case—things that accompany salvation. [10]God is not unjust; he will not forget your work and the love you have shown him as you have helped his people and continue to help them.[b] [11]We want each of you to show this same diligence to the very end, in order to make your hope[c] sure. [12]We do not want you to become lazy, but to imitate[d] those who through faith and patience[e] inherit what has been promised.[f]

The Certainty of God's Promise

[13]When God made his promise to Abraham, since there was no one greater for him to swear by, he swore by himself,[g] [14]saying, "I will surely bless you and give you many descendants."[c][h] [15]And so after waiting patiently, Abraham received what was promised.[i]

[16]Men swear by someone greater than themselves, and the oath confirms what is said and puts an end to all argument.[j] [17]Because God wanted to make the unchanging[k] nature of his purpose very clear to the heirs of what was promised,[l] he confirmed it with an oath. [18]God did this so that, by two unchangeable things in which it is impossible

---

5:7
e Mk 14:36
5:8
f Php 2:8
5:9
g Heb 2:10
5:10
h ver 5 i ver 6
5:12
j Heb 6:1
k 1Co 3:2;
1Pe 2:2
5:13
l 1Co 14:20
5:14
m 1Co 2:6
n Isa 7:15
6:1
o Php 3:12-14
p Heb 5:12
q Heb 9:14
6:2
r Jn 3:25 s Ac 6:6
t Ac 17:18,32
6:3
u Ac 18:21
6:4
v Heb 10:32
w Eph 2:8
x Gal 3:2
6:6
y 2Pe 2:21;
1Jn 5:16
6:8
z Ge 3:17,18;
Isa 5:6
6:9
a 1Co 10:14
6:10
b Mt 10:40,42;
25:40; 1Th 1:3
6:11
c Heb 3:6
6:12
d Heb 13:7
e 2Th 1:4;
Jas 1:3;
Rev 13:10
f Heb 10:36
6:13
g Ge 22:16;
Lk 1:73
6:14
h Ge 22:17
6:15
i Ge 21:5
6:16
j Ex 22:11
6:17
k Ps 110:4
l Heb 11:9

---

a1 Or *from useless rituals*   b6 Or *repentance while*   c14 Gen. 22:17

for God to lie,^m we who have fled to take hold of the hopeⁿ offered to us may be greatly encouraged. ¹⁹We have this hope as an anchor for the soul, firm and secure. It enters the inner sanctuary behind the curtain,^o ²⁰where Jesus, who went before us, has entered on our behalf.^p He has become a high priest^q forever, in the order of Melchizedek.^r

Melchizedek the Priest

7 This Melchizedek was king of Salem and priest of God Most High.^s He met Abraham returning from the defeat of the kings and blessed him,^t ²and Abraham gave him a tenth of everything. First, his name means "king of righteousness"; then also, "king of Salem" means "king of peace." ³Without father or mother, without genealogy,^u without beginning of days or end of life, like the Son of God^v he remains a priest forever.

⁴Just think how great he was: Even the patriarch^w Abraham gave him a tenth of the plunder!^x ⁵Now the law requires the descendants of Levi who become priests to collect a tenth from the people^y—that is, their brothers—even though their brothers are descended from Abraham. ⁶This man, however, did not trace his descent from Levi, yet he collected a tenth from Abraham and blessed^z him who had the promises.^a ⁷And without doubt the lesser person is blessed by the greater. ⁸In the one case, the tenth is collected by men who die; but in the other case, by him who is declared to be living.^b ⁹One might even say that Levi, who collects the tenth, paid the tenth through Abraham, ¹⁰because when Melchizedek met Abraham, Levi was still in the body of his ancestor.

Jesus Like Melchizedek

¹¹If perfection could have been attained through the Levitical priesthood (for on the basis of it the law was given to the people),^c why was there still need for another priest to come^d—one in the order of Melchizedek,^e not in the order of Aaron? ¹²For when there is a change of the priesthood, there must also be a change of the law. ¹³He of whom these things are said belonged to a different tribe,^f and no one from that tribe has ever served at the altar.^g ¹⁴For it is clear that our Lord descended from Judah,^h and in regard to that tribe Moses said nothing about priests. ¹⁵And what we have said is even more clear if another priest like Melchizedek appears, ¹⁶one who has become a priest not on the basis of a regulation as to his ancestry but on the basis of the power of an indestructible life. ¹⁷For it is declared:

> "You are a priest forever,
>   in the order of Melchizedek."^a ⁱ

¹⁸The former regulation is set aside because it was weak and useless^j ¹⁹(for the law made nothing perfect),^k and a better hope is introduced, by which we draw near to God.^l

²⁰And it was not without an oath! Others became priests without any oath, ²¹but he became a priest with an oath when God said to him:

> "The Lord has sworn

6:18
mNu 23:19;
Tit 1:2
nHeb 3:6
6:19
oLev 16:2;
Heb 9:2,3,7
6:20
pHeb 4:14
qHeb 2:17
rHeb 5:6
7:1
sMk 5:7
tGe 14:18-20
7:3
uver 6 vMt 4:3
7:4
wAc 2:29
xGe 14:20
7:5
yNu 18:21,26
7:6
zGe 14:19,20
aRo 4:13
7:8
bHeb 5:6; 6:20
7:11
cver 18,19;
Heb 8:7
dHeb 10:1
ever 17
7:13
fver 11 gver 14
7:14
hIsa 11:1;
Mt 1:3; Lk 3:33
7:17
iPs 110:4;
ver 21; Heb 5:6
7:18
jRo 8:3
7:19
kAc 13:39;
Ro 3:20;
Heb 9:9
lHeb 4:16

^a17 Psalm 110:4

and will not change his mind:ᵐ
'You are a priest forever.' "ᵃ ⁿ

²²Because of this oath, Jesus has become the guarantee of a better covenant. ᵒ

²³Now there have been many of those priests, since death prevented them from continuing in office; ²⁴but because Jesus lives forever, he has a permanent priesthood. ᵖ ²⁵Therefore he is able to save completelyᵇ those who come to Godᑫ through him, because he always lives to intercede for them. ʳ

²⁶Such a high priest meets our need—one who is holy, blameless, pure, set apart from sinners, ˢ exalted above the heavens. ᵗ ²⁷Unlike the other high priests, he does not need to offer sacrificesᵘ day after day, first for his own sins, ᵛ and then for the sins of the people. He sacrificed for their sins once for allʷ when he offered himself. ˣ ²⁸For the law appoints as high priests men who are weak;ʸ but the oath, which came after the law, appointed the Son, ᶻ who has been made perfectᵃ forever.

The High Priest of a New Covenant

8 The point of what we are saying is this: We do have such a high priest, ᵇ who sat down at the right hand of the throne of the Majesty in heaven, ²and who serves in the sanctuary, the true tabernacleᶜ set up by the Lord, not by man.

³Every high priest is appointed to offer both gifts and sacrifices, ᵈ and so it was necessary for this one also to have something to offer. ᵉ ⁴If he were on earth, he would not be a priest, for there are already men who offer the gifts prescribed by the law. ᶠ ⁵They serve at a sanctuary that is a copyᵍ and shadowʰ of what is in heaven. This is why Moses was warnedⁱ when he was about to build the tabernacle: "See to it that you make everything according to the pattern shown you on the mountain."ᶜʲ ⁶But the ministry Jesus has received is as superior to theirs as the covenantᵏ of which he is mediatorˡ is superior to the old one, and it is founded on better promises.

⁷For if there had been nothing wrong with that first covenant, no place would have been sought for another. ᵐ ⁸But God found fault with the people and saidᵈ:

"The time is coming, declares the Lord,
    when I will make a new covenantⁿ
with the house of Israel
    and with the house of Judah.
⁹It will not be like the covenant
    I made with their forefathersᵒ
when I took them by the hand
    to lead them out of Egypt,
because they did not remain faithful to my covenant,
    and I turned away from them,
                                            declares the Lord.
¹⁰This is the covenant I will make with the house of Israel
    after that time, declares the Lord.

7:21
m 1Sa 15:29
n Ps 110:4
7:22
o Heb 8:6
7:24
p ver 28
7:25
q ver 19
r Ro 8:34
7:26
s 2Co 5:21
t Heb 4:14
7:27
u Heb 5:1
v Heb 5:3
w Heb 9:12,26,
28 x Eph 5:2;
Heb 9:14,28
7:28
y Heb 5:2
z Heb 1:2
a Heb 2:10
8:1
b Heb 2:17
8:2
c Heb 9:11,24
8:3
d Heb 5:1
e Heb 9:14
8:4
f Heb 5:1
8:5
g Heb 9:23
h Col 2:17;
Heb 10:1
i Heb 11:7;
12:25 j Ex 25:40
8:6
k Lk 22:20
l Heb 7:22
8:7
m Heb 7:11,18
8:8
n Jer 31:31
8:9
o Ex 19:5,6

ᵃ21 Psalm 110:4   ᵇ25 Or *forever*   ᶜ5 Exodus 25:40   ᵈ8 Some manuscripts may be translated *fault and said to the people.*

I will put my laws in their minds
  and write them on their hearts.ᵖ
I will be their God,
  and they will be my people.�q
¹¹No longer will a man teach his neighbor,
  or a man his brother, saying, 'Know the Lord,'
because they will all know me,ʳ
  from the least of them to the greatest.
¹²For I will forgive their wickedness
  and will remember their sins no more.ˢ "ᵃ ᵗ

¹³By calling this covenant "new," he has made the first one obsolete;ᵘ and what is obsolete and aging will soon disappear.

Worship in the Earthly Tabernacle

9 Now the first covenant had regulations for worship and also an earthly sanctuary.ᵛ ²A tabernacleʷ was set up. In its first room were the lampstand,ˣ the tableʸ and the consecrated bread;ᶻ this was called the Holy Place. ³Behind the second curtain was a room called the Most Holy Place,ᵃ ⁴which had the golden altar of incenseᵇ and the gold-covered ark of the covenant.ᶜ This ark contained the gold jar of manna,ᵈ Aaron's staff that had budded,ᵉ and the stone tablets of the covenant. ⁵Above the ark were the cherubim of the Glory,ᶠ overshadowing the atonement cover.ᵇ But we cannot discuss these things in detail now.

⁶When everything had been arranged like this, the priests entered regularlyᵍ into the outer room to carry on their ministry. ⁷But only the high priest enteredʰ the inner room, and that only once a year,ⁱ and never without blood, which he offered for himselfʲ and for the sins the people had committed in ignorance. ⁸The Holy Spirit was showingᵏ by this that the wayˡ into the Most Holy Place had not yet been disclosed as long as the first tabernacle was still standing. ⁹This is an illustration for the present time, indicating that the gifts and sacrifices being offeredᵐ were not able to clear the conscience of the worshiper. ¹⁰They are only a matter of foodⁿ and drinkᵒ and various ceremonial washings —external regulationsᵖ applying until the time of the new order.

The Blood of Christ

¹¹When Christ came as high priestq of the good things that are already here,ᶜʳ he went through the greater and more perfect tabernacleˢ that is not man-made, that is to say, not a part of this creation. ¹²He did not enter by means of the blood of goats and calves;ᵗ but he entered the Most Holy Placeᵘ once for allᵛ by his own blood, having obtained eternal redemption. ¹³The blood of goats and bulls and the ashes of a heiferʷ sprinkled on those who are ceremonially unclean sanctify them so that they are outwardly clean. ¹⁴How much more, then, will the blood of Christ, who through the eternal Spiritˣ offered himself unblemished to God, cleanse our consciencesʸ from acts that lead to death,ᵈᶻ so that we may serve the living God!

¹⁵For this reason Christ is the mediatorᵃ of a new covenant, that those who are called may receive the promised eternal inheritance—now that

---

8:10
p2Co 3:3;
Heb 10:16
qZec 8:8
8:11
rIsa 54:13;
Jn 6:45
8:12
sHeb 10:17
tJer 31:31-34
8:13
u2Co 5:17
9:1
vEx 25:8
9:2
wEx 25:8,9
xEx 25:31-39
yEx 25:23-29
zLev 24:5-8
9:3
aEx 26:31-33
9:4
bEx 30:1-5
cEx 25:10-22
dEx 16:32,33
eNu 17:10
9:5
fEx 25:17-19
9:6
gNu 28:3
9:7
hLev 16:11-19
iLev 16:34
jHeb 5:2,3
9:8
kHeb 3:7
lJn 14:6;
Heb 10:19,20
9:9
mHeb 5:1
9:10
nLev 11:2-23
oCol 2:16
pHeb 7:16
9:11
qHeb 2:17
rHeb 10:1
sHeb 8:2
9:12
tHeb 10:4
uver 24
vHeb 7:27
9:13
wNu 19:9,17,18
9:14
x1Pe 3:18
yTit 2:14;
Heb 10:2,22
zHeb 6:1
9:15
a1Ti 2:5

ᵃ12 Jer. 31:31-34   ᵇ5 Traditionally *the mercy seat*   ᶜ11 Some early manuscripts *are to come*
ᵈ14 Or *from useless rituals*

he has died as a ransom to set them free from the sins committed under the first covenant. [b]

[16]In the case of a will, [a] it is necessary to prove the death of the one who made it, [17]because a will is in force only when somebody has died; it never takes effect while the one who made it is living. [18]This is why even the first covenant was not put into effect without blood. [c] [19]When Moses had proclaimed every commandment of the law to all the people, he took the blood of calves, together with water, scarlet wool and branches of hyssop, and sprinkled the scroll and all the people. [d] [20]He said, "This is the blood of the covenant, which God has commanded you to keep." [b][e] [21]In the same way, he sprinkled with the blood both the tabernacle and everything used in its ceremonies. [22]In fact, the law requires that nearly everything be cleansed with blood, [f] and without the shedding of blood there is no forgiveness. [g]

[23]It was necessary, then, for the copies [h] of the heavenly things to be purified with these sacrifices, but the heavenly things themselves with better sacrifices than these. [24]For Christ did not enter a man-made sanctuary that was only a copy of the true one; [i] he entered heaven itself, now to appear for us in God's presence. [25]Nor did he enter heaven to offer himself again and again, the way the high priest enters the Most Holy Place [j] every year with blood that is not his own. [k] [26]Then Christ would have had to suffer many times since the creation of the world. [l] But now he has appeared once for all [m] at the end of the ages to do away with sin by the sacrifice of himself. [27]Just as man is destined to die once, [n] and after that to face judgment, [o] [28]so Christ was sacrificed once to take away the sins of many people; and he will appear a second time, [p] not to bear sin, [q] but to bring salvation to those who are waiting for him. [r]

Christ's Sacrifice Once for All

10 The law is only a shadow [s] of the good things [t] that are coming —not the realities themselves. [u] For this reason it can never, by the same sacrifices repeated endlessly year after year, make perfect [v] those who draw near to worship. [2]If it could, would they not have stopped being offered? For the worshipers would have been cleansed once for all, and would no longer have felt guilty for their sins. [3]But those sacrifices are an annual reminder of sins, [w] [4]because it is impossible for the blood of bulls and goats [x] to take away sins.

[5]Therefore, when Christ came into the world, [y] he said:

> "Sacrifice and offering you did not desire,
>   but a body you prepared for me; [z]
> [6]with burnt offerings and sin offerings
>   you were not pleased.
> [7]Then I said, 'Here I am—it is written about me in the
>   scroll [a]—
> I have come to do your will, O God.' " [c][b]

[8]First he said, "Sacrifices and offerings, burnt offerings and sin offerings you did not desire, nor were you pleased with them" [c] (although

9:15
b Heb 7:22
9:18
c Ex 24:6-8
9:19
d Ex 24:6-8
9:20
e Ex 24:8;
Mt 26:28
9:22
f Lev 8:15
g Lev 17:11
9:23
h Heb 8:5
9:24
i Heb 8:2
9:25
j Heb 10:19
k ver 7,8
9:26
l Heb 4:3
m Heb 7:27
9:27
n Ge 3:19
o 2Co 5:10
9:28
p Tit 2:13
q 1Pe 2:24
r 1Co 1:7
10:1
s Heb 8:5
t Heb 9:11
u Heb 9:23
v Heb 7:19
10:3
w Heb 9:7
10:4
x Heb 9:12,13
10:5
y Heb 1:6
z 1Pe 2:24
10:7
a Jer 36:2
b Ps 40:6-8
10:8
c ver 5,6;
Mk 12:33

a16 Same Greek word as *covenant*; also in verse 17   b20 Exodus 24:8   c7 Psalm 40:6-8 (see Septuagint) the law required them to be made). ⁹Then he said, "Here I am, I have come to do your will."ᵈ He sets aside the first to establish the second. ¹⁰And by that will, we have been made holyᵉ through the sacrifice of the bodyᶠ of Jesus Christ once for all. ᵍ

¹¹Day after day every priest stands and performs his religious duties; again and again he offers the same sacrifices,ʰ which can never take away sins.ⁱ ¹²But when this priest had offered for all time one sacrifice for sins, he sat down at the right hand of God. ¹³Since that time he waits for his enemies to be made his footstool,ʲ ¹⁴because by one sacrifice he has made perfectᵏ forever those who are being made holy.

¹⁵The Holy Spirit also testifiesˡ to us about this. First he says:

> ¹⁶"This is the covenant I will make with them
>   after that time, says the Lord.
> I will put my laws in their hearts,
>   and I will write them on their minds."ᵃ ᵐ

¹⁷Then he adds:

> "Their sins and lawless acts
>   I will remember no more."ᵇ ⁿ

¹⁸And where these have been forgiven, there is no longer any sacrifice for sin.

A Call to Persevere

¹⁹Therefore, brothers, since we have confidence to enter the Most Holy Placeᵒ by the blood of Jesus, ²⁰by a new and living wayᵖ opened for us through the curtain,�q that is, his body, ²¹and since we have a great priestʳ over the house of God, ²²let us draw near to Godˢ with a sincere heart in full assurance of faith, having our hearts sprinkled to cleanse us from a guilty conscienceᵗ and having our bodies washed with pure water. ²³Let us hold unswervingly to the hopeᵘ we profess, for he who promised is faithful. ᵛ ²⁴And let us consider how we may spur one another on toward love and good deeds. ²⁵Let us not give up meeting together,ʷ as some are in the habit of doing, but let us encourage one anotherˣ—and all the more as you see the Day approaching.

²⁶If we deliberately keep on sinningʸ after we have received the knowledge of the truth, no sacrifice for sins is left, ²⁷but only a fearful expectation of judgment and of raging fireᶻ that will consume the enemies of God. ²⁸Anyone who rejected the law of Moses died without mercy on the testimony of two or three witnesses. ᵃ ²⁹How much more severely do you think a man deserves to be punished who has trampled the Son of God under foot,ᵇ who has treated as an unholy thing the blood of the covenantᶜ that sanctified him, and who has insulted the Spiritᵈ of grace?ᵉ ³⁰For we know him who said, "It is mine to avenge; I will repay,"ᶜᶠ and again, "The Lord will judge his people."ᵈᵍ ³¹It is a dreadful thing to fall into the hands of the living God. ʰ

³²Remember those earlier days after you had received the light,ⁱ when you stood your ground in a great contest in the face of suffering. ʲ ³³Sometimes you were publicly exposed to insult and persecution;ᵏ at other times you stood side by side with those who were so treated. ˡ

ᵃ16 Jer. 31:33   ᵇ17 Jer. 31:34   ᶜ30 Deut. 32:35   ᵈ30 Deut. 32:36; Psalm 135:14

10:9
ᵈver 7
10:10
ᵉJn 17:19
ᶠHeb 2:14;
1Pe 2:24
ᵍHeb 7:27
10:11
ʰHeb 5:1
ⁱver 1,4
10:13
ʲHeb 1:13
10:14
ᵏver 1
10:15
ˡHeb 3:7
10:16
ᵐJer 31:33;
Heb 8:10
10:17
ⁿHeb 8:12
10:19
ᵒEph 2:18;
Heb 9:8,12,25
10:20
ᵖHeb 9:8
qHeb 9:3
10:21
ʳHeb 2:17
10:22
ˢHeb 7:19
ᵗEze 36:25;
Heb 9:14
10:23
ᵘHeb 3:6
ᵛ1Co 1:9
10:25
ʷAc 2:42
ˣHeb 3:13
10:26
ʸNu 15:30;
2Pe 2:20
10:27
ᶻIsa 26:11;
2Th 1:7;
Heb 9:27
10:28
ᵃDt 17:6,7;
Heb 2:2
10:29
ᵇHeb 6:6
ᶜMt 26:28
ᵈEph 4:30;
Heb 6:4
ᵉHeb 2:3
10:30
ᶠDt 32:35;
Ro 12:19
ᵍDt 32:36
10:31
ʰMt 16:16
10:32
ⁱHeb 6:4
ʲPhp 1:29,30
10:33
ᵏ1Co 4:9
ˡPhp 4:14;
1Th 2:14

34You sympathized with those in prison[m] and joyfully accepted the confiscation of your property, because you knew that you yourselves had better and lasting possessions.[n]

35So do not throw away your confidence; it will be richly rewarded. 36You need to persevere[o] so that when you have done the will of God, you will receive what he has promised. 37For in just a very little while,

> "He who is coming[p] will come and will not delay.[q]
> 38   But my righteous one[a] will live by faith.[r]
>   And if he shrinks back,
>   I will not be pleased with him."[b]

39But we are not of those who shrink back and are destroyed, but of those who believe and are saved.

By Faith

11 Now faith is being sure of what we hope for and certain of what we do not see.[s] 2This is what the ancients were commended for.[t]

3By faith we understand that the universe was formed at God's command,[u] so that what is seen was not made out of what was visible.

4By faith Abel offered God a better sacrifice than Cain did. By faith he was commended as a righteous man, when God spoke well of his offerings.[v] And by faith he still speaks, even though he is dead.[w]

5By faith Enoch was taken from this life, so that he did not experience death; he could not be found, because God had taken him away.[x] For before he was taken, he was commended as one who pleased God. 6And without faith it is impossible to please God, because anyone who comes to him[y] must believe that he exists and that he rewards those who earnestly seek him.

7By faith Noah, when warned about things not yet seen, in holy fear built an ark[z] to save his family.[a] By his faith he condemned the world and became heir of the righteousness that comes by faith.

8By faith Abraham, when called to go to a place he would later receive as his inheritance,[b] obeyed and went,[c] even though he did not know where he was going. 9By faith he made his home in the promised land[d] like a stranger in a foreign country; he lived in tents,[e] as did Isaac and Jacob, who were heirs with him of the same promise.[f] 10For he was looking forward to the city[g] with foundations,[h] whose architect and builder is God.

11By faith Abraham, even though he was past age—and Sarah herself was barren[i]—was enabled to become a father[j] because he[c] considered him faithful who had made the promise. 12And so from this one man, and he as good as dead,[k] came descendants as numerous as the stars in the sky and as countless as the sand on the seashore.[l]

13All these people were still living by faith when they died. They did not receive the things promised;[m] they only saw them and welcomed them from a distance.[n] And they admitted that they were aliens and strangers on earth.[o] 14People who say such things show that they are looking for a country of their own. 15If they had been thinking of the

---

### Cross references (margin)

10:34
m Heb 13:3
n Heb 11:16
10:36
o Lk 21:19;
Heb 12:1
10:37
p Mt 11:3
q Rev 22:20
10:38
r Ro 1:17;
Gal 3:11
11:1
s Ro 8:24;
2Co 4:18
11:2
t ver 4,39
11:3
u Ge 1; Jn 1:3;
2Pe 3:5
11:4
v Ge 4:4;
1Jn 3:12
w Heb 12:24
11:5
x Ge 5:21-24
11:6
y Heb 7:19
11:7
z Ge 6:13-22
a 1Pe 3:20
11:8
b Ge 12:7
c Ge 12:1-4;
Ac 7:2-4
11:9
d Ac 7:5
e Ge 12:8; 18:1,
9 f Heb 6:17
11:10
g Heb 12:22;
13:14
h Rev 21:2,14
11:11
i Ge 17:17-19;
18:11-14
j Ge 21:2
11:12
k Ro 4:19
l Ge 22:17
11:13
m ver 39
n Mt 13:17
o Ge 23:4;
Ps 39:12;
1Pe 1:17

---

a38 One early manuscript But the righteous   b38 Hab. 2:3,4   c11 Or By faith even Sarah, who was past age, was enabled to bear children because she

country they had left, they would have had opportunity to return. [p]
[16]Instead, they were longing for a better country—a heavenly one. [q]
Therefore God is not ashamed [r] to be called their God, [s] for he has
prepared a city [t] for them.

[17]By faith Abraham, when God tested him, offered Isaac as a sacrifice. [u] He who had received the promises was about to sacrifice his one
and only son, [18]even though God had said to him, "It is through Isaac
that your offspring [a] will be reckoned." [b][v] [19]Abraham reasoned that
God could raise the dead, [w] and figuratively speaking, he did receive
Isaac back from death.

[20]By faith Isaac blessed Jacob and Esau in regard to their future. [x]

[21]By faith Jacob, when he was dying, blessed each of Joseph's sons, [y]
and worshiped as he leaned on the top of his staff.

[22]By faith Joseph, when his end was near, spoke about the exodus of
the Israelites from Egypt and gave instructions about his bones. [z]

[23]By faith Moses' parents hid him for three months after he was
born, [a] because they saw he was no ordinary child, and they were not
afraid of the king's edict. [b]

[24]By faith Moses, when he had grown up, refused to be known as the
son of Pharaoh's daughter. [c] [25]He chose to be mistreated [d] along with
the people of God rather than to enjoy the pleasures of sin for a short
time. [26]He regarded disgrace [e] for the sake of Christ as of greater value
than the treasures of Egypt, because he was looking ahead to his
reward. [f] [27]By faith he left Egypt, [g] not fearing the king's anger; he
persevered because he saw him who is invisible. [28]By faith he kept the
Passover and the sprinkling of blood, so that the destroyer of the
firstborn would not touch the firstborn of Israel. [h]

[29]By faith the people passed through the Red Sea [c] as on dry land; but
when the Egyptians tried to do so, they were drowned. [i]

[30]By faith the walls of Jericho fell, after the people had marched
around them for seven days. [j]

[31]By faith the prostitute Rahab, because she welcomed the spies, was
not killed with those who were disobedient. [d][k]

[32]And what more shall I say? I do not have time to tell about Gideon,
Barak, [l] Samson, Jephthah, David, [m] Samuel [n] and the prophets, [33]who
through faith conquered kingdoms, [o] administered justice, and gained
what was promised; who shut the mouths of lions, [p] [34]quenched the
fury of the flames, and escaped the edge of the sword; whose weakness
was turned to strength; [q] and who became powerful in battle and
routed foreign armies. [r] [35]Women received back their dead, raised to
life again. [s] Others were tortured and refused to be released, so that
they might gain a better resurrection. [36]Some faced jeers and flogging, [t]
while still others were chained and put in prison. [u] [37]They were
stoned [e][v] they were sawed in two; they were put to death by the
sword. [w] They went about in sheepskins and goatskins, [x] destitute,
persecuted and mistreated— [38]the world was not worthy of them. They
wandered in deserts and mountains, and in caves [y] and holes in the
ground.

[39]These were all commended [z] for their faith, yet none of them re-

---

11:15
p Ge 24:6-8

11:16
q 2Ti 4:18
r Mk 8:38
s Ex 3:6,15
t Heb 13:14

11:17
u Ge 22:1-10;
Jas 2:21

11:18
v Ge 21:12;
Ro 9:7

11:19
w Ro 4:21

11:20
x Ge 27:27-29,
39,40

11:21
y Ge 48:1,8-22

11:22
z Ge 50:24,25;
Ex 13:19

11:23
a Ex 2:2
b Ex 1:16,22

11:24
c Ex 2:10,11

11:25
d ver 37

11:26
e Heb 13:13
f Heb 10:35

11:27
g Ex 12:50,51

11:28
h Ex 12:21-23

11:29
i Ex 14:21-31

11:30
j Jos 6:12-20

11:31
k Jos 2:1,9-14;
6:22-25;
Jas 2:25

11:32
l Jdg 4-5
m 1Sa 16:1,13
n 1Sa 1:20

11:33
o 2Sa 7:11; 8:1-3
p Da 6:22

11:34
q 2Ki 20:7
r Jdg 15:8

11:35
s 1Ki 17:22,23

11:36
t Jer 20:2
u Ge 39:20

11:37
v 2Ch 24:21
w 1Ki 19:10
x 2Ki 1:8

11:38
y 1Ki 18:4

11:39
z ver 2,4

ceived what had been promised. [a] 40God had planned something better for us so that only together with us would they be made perfect.

God Disciplines His Sons

12 Therefore, since we are surrounded by such a great cloud of witnesses, let us throw off everything that hinders and the sin that so easily entangles, and let us run[b] with perseverance[c] the race marked out for us. 2Let us fix our eyes on Jesus, the author and perfecter of our faith, who for the joy set before him endured the cross, [d] scorning its shame, [e] and sat down at the right hand of the throne of God. 3Consider him who endured such opposition from sinful men, so that you will not grow weary[f] and lose heart.

4In your struggle against sin, you have not yet resisted to the point of shedding your blood. [g] 5And you have forgotten that word of encouragement that addresses you as sons:

> "My son, do not make light of the Lord's discipline,
>   and do not lose heart when he rebukes you,
> 6because the Lord disciplines those he loves, [h]
>   and he punishes everyone he accepts as a son."[a] [i]

7Endure hardship as discipline; God is treating you as sons.[j] For what son is not disciplined by his father? 8If you are not disciplined (and everyone undergoes discipline), [k] then you are illegitimate children and not true sons. 9Moreover, we have all had human fathers who disciplined us and we respected them for it. How much more should we submit to the Father of our spirits[l] and live![m] 10Our fathers disciplined us for a little while as they thought best; but God disciplines us for our good, that we may share in his holiness. [n] 11No discipline seems pleasant at the time, but painful. Later on, however, it produces a harvest of righteousness and peace[o] for those who have been trained by it.

12Therefore, strengthen your feeble arms and weak knees. [p] 13"Make level paths for your feet,"[b][q] so that the lame may not be disabled, but rather healed. [r]

Warning Against Refusing God

14Make every effort to live in peace with all men[s] and to be holy;[t] without holiness no one will see the Lord. [u] 15See to it that no one misses the grace of God[v] and that no bitter root grows up to cause trouble and defile many. 16See that no one is sexually immoral, or is godless like Esau, who for a single meal sold his inheritance rights as the oldest son. [w] 17Afterward, as you know, when he wanted to inherit this blessing, he was rejected. He could bring about no change of mind, though he sought the blessing with tears. [x]

18You have not come to a mountain that can be touched and that is burning with fire; to darkness, gloom and storm;[y] 19to a trumpet blast[z] or to such a voice speaking words that those who heard it begged that no further word be spoken to them, [a] 20because they could not bear what was commanded: "If even an animal touches the mountain, it

11:39
[a] ver 13
12:1
[b] 1Co 9:24
[c] Heb 10:36
12:2
[d] Php 2:8,9
[e] Heb 13:13
12:3
[f] Gal 6:9
12:4
[g] Heb 10:32-34
12:6
[h] Ps 94:12;
Rev 3:19
[i] Pr 3:11,12
12:7
[j] Dt 8:5
12:8
[k] 1Pe 5:9
12:9
[l] Nu 16:22
[m] Isa 38:16
12:10
[n] 2Pe 1:4
12:11
[o] Isa 32:17;
Jas 3:17,18
12:12
[p] Isa 35:3
12:13
[q] Pr 4:26
[r] Gal 6:1
12:14
[s] Ro 14:19
[t] Ro 6:22
[u] Mt 5:8
12:15
[v] Gal 5:4;
Heb 3:12
12:16
[w] Ge 25:29-34
12:17
[x] Ge 27:30-40
12:18
[y] Ex 19:12-22;
Dt 4:11
12:19
[z] Ex 20:18
[a] Ex 20:19;
Dt 5:5,25

[a]6 Prov. 3:11,12   [b]13 Prov. 4:26

must be stoned."ᵃᵇ ²¹The sight was so terrifying that Moses said, "I am trembling with fear."ᵇ

²²But you have come to Mount Zion, to the heavenly Jerusalem,ᶜ the cityᵈ of the living God. You have come to thousands upon thousands of angels in joyful assembly, ²³to the church of the firstborn, whose names are written in heaven.ᵉ You have come to God, the judge of all men,ᶠ to the spirits of righteous men made perfect,ᵍ ²⁴to Jesus the mediator of a new covenant, and to the sprinkled blood that speaks a better word than the blood of Abel.ʰ

²⁵See to it that you do not refuse him who speaks. If they did not escape when they refused him who warnedⁱ them on earth, how much less will we, if we turn away from him who warns us from heaven?ʲ ²⁶At that time his voice shook the earth,ᵏ but now he has promised, "Once more I will shake not only the earth but also the heavens."ᶜ ˡ ²⁷The words "once more" indicate the removing of what can be shaken ᵐ—that is, created things—so that what cannot be shaken may remain.

²⁸Therefore, since we are receiving a kingdom that cannot be shaken,ⁿ let us be thankful, and so worship God acceptably with reverence and awe,ᵒ ²⁹for our "God is a consuming fire."ᵈ ᵖ

Concluding Exhortations

13 Keep on loving each other as brothers.�q ²Do not forget to entertain strangers,ʳ for by so doing some people have entertained angels without knowing it.ˢ ³Remember those in prisonᵗ as if you were their fellow prisoners, and those who are mistreated as if you yourselves were suffering.

⁴Marriage should be honored by all, and the marriage bed kept pure, for God will judge the adulterer and all the sexually immoral.ᵘ ⁵Keep your lives free from the love of money and be content with what you have,ᵛ because God has said,

> "Never will I leave you;
> never will I forsake you."ᵉ ʷ

⁶So we say with confidence,

> "The Lord is my helper; I will not be afraid.
> What can man do to me?"ᶠ

⁷Remember your leaders,ˣ who spoke the word of God to you. Consider the outcome of their way of life and imitateʸ their faith. ⁸Jesus Christ is the same yesterday and today and forever.ᶻ

⁹Do not be carried away by all kinds of strange teachings.ᵃ It is good for our hearts to be strengthenedᵇ by grace, not by ceremonial foods,ᶜ which are of no value to those who eat them. ¹⁰We have an altar from which those who minister at the tabernacle have no right to eat.ᵈ

¹¹The high priest carries the blood of animals into the Most Holy Place as a sin offering, but the bodies are burned outside the camp.ᵉ ¹²And so Jesus also suffered outside the city gateᶠ to make the people holy through his own blood. ¹³Let us, then, go to him outside the camp,

### Cross references (margin)

12:20
bEx 19:12,13
12:22
cGal 4:26
dHeb 11:10
12:23
eLk 10:20
fPs 94:2
gPhp 3:12
12:24
hGe 4:10;
Heb 11:4
12:25
iHeb 8:5; 11:7
jHeb 2:2,3
12:26
kEx 19:18
lHag 2:6
12:27
m1Co 7:31;
2Pe 3:10
12:28
nDa 2:44
oHeb 13:15
12:29
pDt 4:24
13:1
qRo 12:10;
1Pe 1:22
13:2
rMt 25:35
sGe 18:1-33
13:3
tMt 25:36;
Col 4:18
13:4
u1Co 6:9
13:5
vPhp 4:11
wDt 31:6,8;
Jos 1:5
13:7
xver 17,24
yHeb 6:12
13:8
zHeb 1:12
13:9
aEph 4:14
bCol 2:7
cCol 2:16
13:10
d1Co 9:13;
10:18
13:11
eEx 29:14;
Lev 16:27
13:12
fJn 19:17

ᵃ20 Exodus 19:12,13   ᵇ21 Deut. 9:19   ᶜ26 Haggai 2:6   ᵈ29 Deut. 4:24   ᵉ5 Deut. 31:6
ᶠ6 Psalm 118:6,7

13:13
gHeb 11:26
13:14
hHeb 12:22
13:15
i1Pe 2:5
jHos 14:2
13:16
kRo 12:13
lPhp 4:18
13:17
mIsa 62:6;
Ac 20:28
13:18
n1Th 5:25
oAc 23:1
13:19
pPhm 22
13:20
qRo 15:33
rIsa 55:3;
Zec 9:11
sAc 2:24
tJn 10:11
13:21
uPhp 2:13
v1Jn 3:22
wRo 11:36
13:22
x1Pe 5:12
13:23
yAc 16:1
13:24
zver 7,17
aAc 18:2
13:25
bCol 4:18

bearing the disgrace he bore. [g] [14]For here we do not have an enduring city, but we are looking for the city that is to come. [h]

[15]Through Jesus, therefore, let us continually offer to God a sacrifice [i] of praise—the fruit of lips [j] that confess his name. [16]And do not forget to do good and to share with others, [k] for with such sacrifices [l] God is pleased.

[17]Obey your leaders and submit to their authority. They keep watch over you [m] as men who must give an account. Obey them so that their work will be a joy, not a burden, for that would be of no advantage to you.

[18]Pray for us. [n] We are sure that we have a clear conscience [o] and desire to live honorably in every way. [19]I particularly urge you to pray so that I may be restored to you soon. [p]

[20]May the God of peace, [q] who through the blood of the eternal covenant [r] brought back from the dead [s] our Lord Jesus, that great Shepherd of the sheep, [t] [21]equip you with everything good for doing his will, and may he work in us [u] what is pleasing to him, [v] through Jesus Christ, to whom be glory for ever and ever. Amen. [w]

[22]Brothers, I urge you to bear with my word of exhortation, for I have written you only a short letter. [x]

[23]I want you to know that our brother Timothy [y] has been released. If he arrives soon, I will come with him to see you.

[24]Greet all your leaders [z] and all God's people. Those from Italy [a] send you their greetings.

[25]Grace be with you all. [b]

James

Title and Background

The book of James has a distinctively Jewish nature that suggests it was composed when the church was still predominantly Jewish. It reflects a simple church order, and no reference is made to the controversy over Gentile circumcision. The seven New Testament letters from the book of James through the book of Jude are called the General Letters because they are addressed to Christians in general and not to a particular church.

Author and Date of Writing

The author identifies himself as James, and he was probably the brother of Jesus and the leader of the Jerusalem council. At first James did not believe in Jesus and even challenged him and misunderstood his mission. Later he became very prominent in the church. The book of James was written about A.D. 48, at least before A.D. 50.

Theme and Message

As leader of the Jerusalem church, James wrote as a pastor to instruct and encourage his dispersed people in the face of their difficulties. The letter is concerned mainly with the practical aspects of the Christian faith, consisting of maxims and counsel for everyday conduct. There is very little reference to any of the central doctrines of the Christian faith. The letter discusses true religion, true faith and true wisdom.

Outline

---

1 James,[a] a servant of God[b] and of the Lord Jesus Christ,

To the twelve tribes[c] scattered[d] among the nations:

Greetings.

Trials and Temptations

2Consider it pure joy, my brothers, whenever you face trials of many kinds,[e] 3because you know that the testing of your faith develops perseverance. 4Perseverance must finish its work so that you may be mature and complete, not lacking anything. 5If any of you lacks wisdom, he should ask God,[f] who gives generously to all without finding fault, and it will be given to him.[g] 6But when he asks, he must believe

1:1
aAc 15:13
bTit 1:1
cAc 26:7
dDt 32:26;
Jn 7:35; 1Pe 1:1
1:2
eMt 5:12;
1Pe 1:6
1:5
fiKi 3:9,10;
Pr 2:3-6 gMt 7:7

and not doubt,[h] because he who doubts is like a wave of the sea, blown and tossed by the wind. [7]That man should not think he will receive anything from the Lord; [8]he is a double-minded man,[i] unstable in all he does.

[9]The brother in humble circumstances ought to take pride in his high position. [10]But the one who is rich should take pride in his low position, because he will pass away like a wild flower.[j] [11]For the sun rises with scorching heat and withers[k] the plant; its blossom falls and its beauty is destroyed.[l] In the same way, the rich man will fade away even while he goes about his business.

[12]Blessed is the man who perseveres under trial, because when he has stood the test, he will receive the crown of life[m] that God has promised to those who love him.[n]

[13]When tempted, no one should say, "God is tempting me." For God cannot be tempted by evil, nor does he tempt anyone; [14]but each one is tempted when, by his own evil desire, he is dragged away and enticed. [15]Then, after desire has conceived, it gives birth to sin;[o] and sin, when it is full-grown, gives birth to death.[p]

[16]Don't be deceived,[q] my dear brothers.[r] [17]Every good and perfect gift is from above,[s] coming down from the Father of the heavenly lights, who does not change[t] like shifting shadows. [18]He chose to give us birth[u] through the word of truth, that we might be a kind of first-fruits[v] of all he created.

Listening and Doing

[19]My dear brothers, take note of this: Everyone should be quick to listen, slow to speak[w] and slow to become angry, [20]for man's anger does not bring about the righteous life that God desires. [21]Therefore, get rid of[x] all moral filth and the evil that is so prevalent and humbly accept the word planted in you,[y] which can save you.

[22]Do not merely listen to the word, and so deceive yourselves. Do what it says. [23]Anyone who listens to the word but does not do what it says is like a man who looks at his face in a mirror [24]and, after looking at himself, goes away and immediately forgets what he looks like. [25]But the man who looks intently into the perfect law that gives freedom,[z] and continues to do this, not forgetting what he has heard, but doing it—he will be blessed in what he does.[a]

[26]If anyone considers himself religious and yet does not keep a tight rein on his tongue,[b] he deceives himself and his religion is worthless. [27]Religion that God our Father accepts as pure and faultless is this: to look after[c] orphans and widows[d] in their distress and to keep oneself from being polluted by the world.[e]

Favoritism Forbidden

2 My brothers, as believers in our glorious[f] Lord Jesus Christ, don't show favoritism.[g] [2]Suppose a man comes into your meeting wearing a gold ring and fine clothes, and a poor man in shabby clothes also comes in. [3]If you show special attention to the man wearing fine clothes and say, "Here's a good seat for you," but say to the poor man, "You stand there" or "Sit on the floor by my feet," [4]have you not discriminated among yourselves and become judges[h] with evil thoughts?

[5]Listen, my dear brothers:[i] Has not God chosen those who are poor

in the eyes of the world[j] to be rich in faith[k] and to inherit the kingdom he promised those who love him?[l] 6But you have insulted the poor. [m] Is it not the rich who are exploiting you? Are they not the ones who are dragging you into court?[n] 7Are they not the ones who are slandering the noble name of him to whom you belong?

8If you really keep the royal law found in Scripture, "Love your neighbor as yourself,"[a][o] you are doing right. 9But if you show favoritism,[p] you sin and are convicted by the law as lawbreakers.[q] 10For whoever keeps the whole law and yet stumbles at just one point is guilty of breaking all of it.[r] 11For he who said, "Do not commit adultery,"[b][s] also said, "Do not murder."[c][t] If you do not commit adultery but do commit murder, you have become a lawbreaker.

12Speak and act as those who are going to be judged by the law that gives freedom,[u] 13because judgment without mercy will be shown to anyone who has not been merciful.[v] Mercy triumphs over judgment!

Faith and Deeds

14What good is it, my brothers, if a man claims to have faith but has no deeds?[w] Can such faith save him? 15Suppose a brother or sister is without clothes and daily food.[x] 16If one of you says to him, "Go, I wish you well; keep warm and well fed," but does nothing about his physical needs, what good is it?[y] 17In the same way, faith by itself, if it is not accompanied by action, is dead.

18But someone will say, "You have faith; I have deeds."

Show me your faith without deeds,[z] and I will show you my faith by what I do.[a] 19You believe that there is one God.[b] Good! Even the demons believe that[c]—and shudder.

20You foolish man, do you want evidence that faith without deeds is useless[d]?[d] 21Was not our ancestor Abraham considered righteous for what he did when he offered his son Isaac on the altar?[e] 22You see that his faith and his actions were working together,[f] and his faith was made complete by what he did.[g] 23And the scripture was fulfilled that says, "Abraham believed God, and it was credited to him as righteousness,"[e][h] and he was called God's friend.[i] 24You see that a person is justified by what he does and not by faith alone.

25In the same way, was not even Rahab the prostitute considered righteous for what she did when she gave lodging to the spies and sent them off in a different direction?[j] 26As the body without the spirit is dead, so faith without deeds is dead.[k]

Taming the Tongue

3 Not many of you should presume to be teachers, my brothers, because you know that we who teach will be judged more strictly. 2We all stumble[l] in many ways. If anyone is never at fault in what he says,[m] he is a perfect man,[n] able to keep his whole body in check.[o]

3When we put bits into the mouths of horses to make them obey us, we can turn the whole animal.[p] 4Or take ships as an example. Although they are so large and are driven by strong winds, they are steered by a very small rudder wherever the pilot wants to go. 5Likewise the tongue

---

2:5
j1Co 1:26-28
kLk 12:21
lJas 1:12
2:6
m1Co 11:22
nAc 8:3
2:8
oLev 19:18
2:9
pver 1 qDt 1:17
2:10
rMt 5:19;
Gal 3:10
2:11
sEx 20:14;
Dt 5:18;
tEx 20:13;
Dt 5:17
2:12
uJas 1:25
2:13
vMt 5:7;
18:32-35
2:14
wMt 7:26;
Jas 1:22-25
2:15
xMt 25:35,36
2:16
y1Jn 3:17,18
2:18
zRo 3:28
aJas 3:13
2:19
bDt 6:4
cMt 8:29;
Lk 4:34
2:20
dver 17,26
2:21
eGe 22:9,12
2:22
fHeb 11:17
g1Th 1:3
2:23
hGe 15:6;
Ro 4:3
i2Ch 20:7;
Isa 41:8
2:25
jHeb 11:31
2:26
kver 17,20
3:2
l1Ki 8:46;
Jas 2:10
m1Pe 3:10
nMt 12:37
oJas 1:26
3:3
pPs 32:9

---

a8 Lev. 19:18   *b11* Exodus 20:14; Deut. 5:18   *c11* Exodus 20:13; Deut. 5:17   *d20* Some early manuscripts *dead*   *e23* Gen. 15:6

is a small part of the body, but it makes great boasts. q Consider what a great forest is set on fire by a small spark. 6The tongue also is a fire, r a world of evil among the parts of the body. It corrupts the whole person, s sets the whole course of his life on fire, and is itself set on fire by hell.

7All kinds of animals, birds, reptiles and creatures of the sea are being tamed and have been tamed by man, 8but no man can tame the tongue. It is a restless evil, full of deadly poison. t

9With the tongue we praise our Lord and Father, and with it we curse men, who have been made in God's likeness. u 10Out of the same mouth come praise and cursing. My brothers, this should not be. 11Can both fresh water and salt a water flow from the same spring? 12My brothers, can a fig tree bear olives, or a grapevine bear figs? v Neither can a salt spring produce fresh water.

Two Kinds of Wisdom

13Who is wise and understanding among you? Let him show it w by his good life, by deeds done in the humility that comes from wisdom. 14But if you harbor bitter envy and selfish ambition x in your hearts, do not boast about it or deny the truth. y 15Such "wisdom" does not come down from heaven z but is earthly, unspiritual, of the devil. a 16For where you have envy and selfish ambition, there you find disorder and every evil practice.

17But the wisdom that comes from heaven b is first of all pure; then peace-loving, considerate, submissive, full of mercy c and good fruit, impartial and sincere. d 18Peacemakers who sow in peace raise a harvest of righteousness. e

Submit Yourselves to God

4 What causes fights and quarrels f among you? Don't they come from your desires that battle g within you? 2You want something but don't get it. You kill and covet, but you cannot have what you want. You quarrel and fight. You do not have, because you do not ask God. 3When you ask, you do not receive, h because you ask with wrong motives, i that you may spend what you get on your pleasures.

4You adulterous people, don't you know that friendship with the world j is hatred toward God? k Anyone who chooses to be a friend of the world becomes an enemy of God. l 5Or do you think Scripture says without reason that the spirit he caused to live in us envies intensely? b 6But he gives us more grace. That is why Scripture says:

> "God opposes the proud
> but gives grace to the humble." c m

7Submit yourselves, then, to God. Resist the devil, n and he will flee from you. 8Come near to God and he will come near to you. o Wash your hands, p you sinners, and purify your hearts, you double-minded. q 9Grieve, mourn and wail. Change your laughter to mourning and your joy to gloom. r 10Humble yourselves before the Lord, and he will lift you up.

3:5
qPs 12:3,4
3:6
rPr 16:27
sMt 15:11,18,19
3:8
tPs 140:3;
Ro 3:13
3:9
uGe 1:26,27;
1Co 11:7
3:12
vMt 7:16
3:13
wJas 2:18
3:14
xver 16
yJas 5:19
3:15
zJas 1:17
a1Ti 4:1
3:17
b1Co 2:6
cLk 6:36
dRo 12:9
3:18
ePr 11:18;
Isa 32:17
4:1
fTit 3:9
gRo 7:23
4:3
hPs 18:41
i1Jn 3:22; 5:14
4:4
jJas 1:27
k1Jn 2:15
1Jn 15:19
4:6
mPs 138:6;
Pr 3:34;
Mt 23:12
4:7
nEph 4:27;
1Pe 5:6-9
4:8
o2Ch 15:2
pIsa 1:16
qJas 1:8
4:9
rLk 6:25

---

a11 Greek *bitter* (see also verse 14)   b5 Or *that God jealously longs for the spirit that he made to live in us; or that the Spirit he caused to live in us longs jealously*   c6 Prov. 3:34

¹¹Brothers, do not slander one another.ˢ Anyone who speaks against his brother or judges himᵗ speaks against the law and judges it. When you judge the law, you are not keeping it,ᵘ but sitting in judgment on it. ¹²There is only one Lawgiver and Judge, the one who is able to save and destroy.ᵛ But you—who are you to judge your neighbor?ʷ

Boasting About Tomorrow

¹³Now listen, you who say, "Today or tomorrow we will go to this or that city, spend a year there, carry on business and make money."ˣ ¹⁴Why, you do not even know what will happen tomorrow. What is your life? You are a mist that appears for a little while and then vanishes.ʸ ¹⁵Instead, you ought to say, "If it is the Lord's will,ᶻ we will live and do this or that." ¹⁶As it is, you boast and brag. All such boasting is evil.ᵃ ¹⁷Anyone, then, who knows the good he ought to do and doesn't do it, sins.ᵇ

Warning to Rich Oppressors

5 Now listen, you rich people,ᶜ weep and wail because of the misery that is coming upon you. ²Your wealth has rotted, and moths have eaten your clothes.ᵈ ³Your gold and silver are corroded. Their corrosion will testify against you and eat your flesh like fire. You have hoarded wealth in the last days.ᵉ ⁴Look! The wages you failed to pay the workmenᶠ who mowed your fields are crying out against you. The criesᵍ of the harvesters have reached the ears of the Lord Almighty.ʰ ⁵You have lived on earth in luxury and self-indulgence. You have fattened yourselvesⁱ in the day of slaughter.ᵃʲ ⁶You have condemned and murdered innocent men,ᵏ who were not opposing you.

Patience in Suffering

⁷Be patient, then, brothers, until the Lord's coming. See how the farmer waits for the land to yield its valuable crop and how patient he is for the autumn and spring rains.ˡ ⁸You too, be patient and stand firm, because the Lord's coming is near.ᵐ ⁹Don't grumble against each other, brothers,ⁿ or you will be judged. The Judgeᵒ is standing at the door!ᵖ

¹⁰Brothers, as an example of patience in the face of suffering, take the prophets�q who spoke in the name of the Lord. ¹¹As you know, we consider blessedʳ those who have persevered. You have heard of Job's perseveranceˢ and have seen what the Lord finally brought about.ᵗ The Lord is full of compassion and mercy.ᵘ

¹²Above all, my brothers, do not swear—not by heaven or by earth or by anything else. Let your "Yes" be yes, and your "No," no, or you will be condemned.ᵛ

The Prayer of Faith

¹³Is any one of you in trouble? He should pray.ʷ Is anyone happy? Let him sing songs of praise.ˣ ¹⁴Is any one of you sick? He should call the elders of the church to pray over him and anoint him with oilʸ in the name of the Lord. ¹⁵And the prayer offered in faith will make the sick person well; the Lord will raise him up. If he has sinned, he will be

ᵃ5 Or *yourselves as in a day of feasting*

5:16
zMt 3:6
a1Pe 2:24
bJn 9:31
5:17
cAc 14:15
d1Ki 17:1;
Lk 4:25
5:18
e1Ki 18:41-45
5:19
fJas 3:14
gMt 18:15
5:20
hRo 11:14
i1Pe 4:8

forgiven. [16]Therefore confess your sins[z] to each other and pray for each other so that you may be healed.[a] The prayer of a righteous man is powerful and effective.[b]

[17]Elijah was a man just like us.[c] He prayed earnestly that it would not rain, and it did not rain on the land for three and a half years.[d] [18]Again he prayed, and the heavens gave rain, and the earth produced its crops.[e]

[19]My brothers, if one of you should wander from the truth[f] and someone should bring him back,[g] [20]remember this: Whoever turns a sinner from the error of his way will save[h] him from death and cover over a multitude of sins.[i]

1 Peter

Title and Background

The recipients of this epistle had been suffering various trials and afflictions, and the possibility of greater and more severe difficulties was very real. This letter is addressed to Christians who were scattered throughout the Roman world. In fact, the readers were called "strangers in the world."

Author and Date of Writing

The author identifies himself as the apostle Peter, and the contents and character of the letter support his authorship. Moreover, the letter reflects the history and terminology of the Gospels and Acts, notably Peter's speeches. The book was written about A.D. 64.

Theme and Message

1 Peter touches on various doctrines and has much to say about Christian life and duties. It has been characterized as a letter of separation, of suffering and persecution, of suffering and glory, of hope, of pilgrimage, of courage, and as a letter dealing with the true grace of God. The letter is composed also of a series of exhortations. No other New Testament book so reflects the real nature and effect of God's love in Christ.

Outline

I. Greetings (1:1-2)
II. Praise for God's Grace and Salvation (1:3-12)
III. Holy Living (1:13-5:11)
IV. The Purpose of the Letter (5:12)
V. Closing Greetings (5:13-14)

---

1 Peter, an apostle of Jesus Christ,[a]

To God's elect,[b] strangers in the world, scattered throughout Pontus, Galatia, Cappadocia, Asia and Bithynia,[c] 2who have been chosen according to the foreknowledge[d] of God the Father, through the sanctifying work of the Spirit,[e] for obedience to Jesus Christ and sprinkling by his blood:[f]

Grace and peace be yours in abundance.

Praise to God for a Living Hope

3Praise be to the God and Father of our Lord Jesus Christ![g] In his great mercy[h] he has given us new birth into a living hope through the resurrection of Jesus Christ from the dead,[i] 4and into an inheritance that can never perish, spoil or fade—kept in heaven for you,[j] 5who through faith are shielded by God's power[k] until the coming of the salvation that is ready to be revealed in the last time. 6In this you greatly rejoice,[l] though now for a little while[m] you may have had to suffer grief

1:1
a 2Pe 1:1
b Mt 24:22
c Ac 16:7
1:2
d Ro 8:29
e 2Th 2:13
f Heb 10:22;
12:24
1:3
g 2Co 1:3;
Eph 1:3
h Tit 3:5;
Jas 1:18
i 1Co 15:20
1:4
j Col 1:5
1:5
k Jn 10:28
1:6
l Ro 5:2
m 1Pe 5:10

in all kinds of trials. ⁿ ⁷These have come so that your faith—of greater worth than gold, which perishes even though refined by fire°—may be proved genuineᵖ and may result in praise, glory and honor when Jesus Christ is revealed. ⁹ ⁸Though you have not seen him, you love him; and even though you do not see him now, you believe in himʳ and are filled with an inexpressible and glorious joy, ⁹for you are receiving the goal of your faith, the salvation of your souls. ˢ

¹⁰Concerning this salvation, the prophets, who spokeᵗ of the grace that was to come to you, searched intently and with the greatest care, ᵘ ¹¹trying to find out the time and circumstances to which the Spirit of Christᵛ in them was pointing when he predicted the sufferings of Christ and the glories that would follow. ¹²It was revealed to them that they were not serving themselves but you, when they spoke of the things that have now been told you by those who have preached the gospel to youʷ by the Holy Spirit sent from heaven. Even angels long to look into these things.

Be Holy

¹³Therefore, prepare your minds for action; be self-controlled; set your hope fully on the grace to be given you when Jesus Christ is revealed. ¹⁴As obedient children, do not conformˣ to the evil desires you had when you lived in ignorance. ʸ ¹⁵But just as he who called you is holy, so be holy in all you do;ᶻ ¹⁶for it is written: "Be holy, because I am holy."ᵃ ᵃ

¹⁷Since you call on a Father who judges each man's work impartially, ᵇ live your lives as strangers here in reverent fear. ᶜ ¹⁸For you know that it was not with perishable things such as silver or gold that you were redeemedᵈ from the empty way of life handed down to you from your forefathers, ¹⁹but with the precious blood of Christ, a lambᵉ without blemish or defect. ᶠ ²⁰He was chosen before the creation of the world, ᵍ but was revealed in these last timesʰ for your sake. ²¹Through him you believe in God, ⁱ who raised him from the dead and glorified him, and so your faith and hope are in God.

²²Now that you have purifiedʲ yourselves by obeying the truth so that you have sincere love for your brothers, love one another deeply, ᵏ from the heart. ᵇ ²³For you have been born again, ˡ not of perishable seed, but of imperishable, through the living and enduring word of God. ᵐ ²⁴For,

> "All men are like grass,
>   and all their glory is like the flowers of the field;
>   the grass withers and the flowers fall,
> ²⁵   but the word of the Lord stands forever."ᶜ ⁿ

And this is the word that was preached to you.

2 Therefore, rid yourselves° of all malice and all deceit, hypocrisy, envy, and slanderᵖ of every kind. ²Like newborn babies, crave pure spiritual milk, ⁹ so that by it you may grow upʳ in your salvation, ³now that you have tasted that the Lord is good. ˢ

Cross references

1:6
n Jas 1:2
1:7
o Job 23:10;
Ps 66:10;
Pr 17:3 p Jas 1:3
q Ro 2:7
1:8
r Jn 20:29
1:9
s Ro 6:22
1:10
t Mt 26:24
u Mt 13:17
1:11
v 2Pe 1:21
1:12
w ver 25
1:14
x Ro 12:2
y Eph 4:18
1:15
z 2Co 7:1;
1Th 4:7
1:16
a Lev 11:44,45
1:17
b Ac 10:34
c Heb 12:28
1:18
d Mt 20:28;
1Co 6:20
1:19
e Jn 1:29
f Ex 12:5
1:20
g Eph 1:4
h Heb 9:26
1:21
i Ro 4:24
1:22
j Jas 4:8
k Jn 13:34;
Heb 13:1
1:23
l Jn 1:13
m Heb 4:12
1:25
n Isa 40:6-8
2:1
o Eph 4:22
p Jas 4:11
2:2
q 1Co 3:2
r Eph 4:15,16
2:3
s Heb 6:5

ᵃ16 Lev. 11:44,45; 19:2; 20:7   ᵇ22 Some early manuscripts *from a pure heart*   ᶜ25 Isaiah 40:6-8

The Living Stone and a Chosen People

[4]As you come to him, the living Stone[t]—rejected by men but chosen by God and precious to him— [5]you also, like living stones, are being built[u] into a spiritual house[v] to be a holy priesthood,[w] offering spiritual sacrifices acceptable to God through Jesus Christ.[x] [6]For in Scripture it says:

> "See, I lay a stone in Zion,
>   a chosen and precious cornerstone,[y]
> and the one who trusts in him
>   will never be put to shame."[a][z]

[7]Now to you who believe, this stone is precious. But to those who do not believe,[a]

> "The stone the builders rejected
>   has become the capstone,[b]"[c][b]

[8]and,

> "A stone that causes men to stumble
>   and a rock that makes them fall."[d][c]

They stumble because they disobey the message—which is also what they were destined for.[d]

[9]But you are a chosen people,[e] a royal priesthood, a holy nation,[f] a people belonging to God, that you may declare the praises of him who called you out of darkness into his wonderful light.[g] [10]Once you were not a people, but now you are the people of God;[h] once you had not received mercy, but now you have received mercy.

[11]Dear friends, I urge you, as aliens and strangers in the world, to abstain from sinful desires,[i] which war against your soul.[j] [12]Live such good lives among the pagans that, though they accuse you of doing wrong, they may see your good deeds[k] and glorify God[l] on the day he visits us.

Submission to Rulers and Masters

[13]Submit yourselves for the Lord's sake to every authority[m] instituted among men: whether to the king, as the supreme authority, [14]or to governors, who are sent by him to punish those who do wrong[n] and to commend those who do right.[o] [15]For it is God's will[p] that by doing good you should silence the ignorant talk of foolish men.[q] [16]Live as free men,[r] but do not use your freedom as a cover-up for evil; live as servants of God.[s] [17]Show proper respect to everyone: Love the brotherhood of believers,[t] fear God, honor the king.[u]

[18]Slaves, submit yourselves to your masters with all respect,[v] not only to those who are good and considerate,[w] but also to those who are harsh. [19]For it is commendable if a man bears up under the pain of unjust suffering because he is conscious of God.[x] [20]But how is it to your credit if you receive a beating for doing wrong and endure it? But if you suffer for doing good and you endure it, this is commendable before

2:4
t ver 7
2:5
u 1Co 3:9
v 1Ti 3:15
w Isa 61:6
x Php 4:18;
Heb 13:15
2:6
y Eph 2:20
z Isa 28:16
2:7
a 2Co 2:16
b Ps 118:22
2:8
c Isa 8:14;
1Co 1:23
d Ro 9:22
2:9
e Dt 10:15
f Isa 62:12
g Ac 26:18
2:10
h Hos 1:9,10
2:11
i Gal 5:16
j Jas 4:1
2:12
k Php 2:15;
1Pe 3:16
l Mt 5:16; 9:8
2:13
m Ro 13:1
2:14
n Ro 13:4
o Ro 13:3
2:15
p 1Pe 3:17
q ver 12
2:16
r Jn 8:32
s Ro 6:22
2:17
t Ro 12:10
u Ro 13:7
2:18
v Eph 6:5
w Jas 3:17
2:19
x 1Pe 3:14,17

---

[a]6 Isaiah 28:16   [b]7 Or *cornerstone*   [c]7 Psalm 118:22   [d]8 Isaiah 8:14

God.y 21To thisz you were called, because Christ suffered for you, leaving you an example,ª that you should follow in his steps.

> 22"He committed no sin,
>   and no deceit was found in his mouth."ª b

23When they hurled their insults at him, he did not retaliate; when he suffered, he made no threats.c Instead, he entrusted himselfd to him who judges justly. 24He himself bore our sinse in his body on the tree, so that we might die to sinsf and live for righteousness; by his wounds you have been healed. g 25For you were like sheep going astray, h but now you have returned to the Shepherdi and Overseer of your souls.

Wives and Husbands

3 Wives, in the same way be submissivej to your husbandsk so that, if any of them do not believe the word, they may be won overl without words by the behavior of their wives, 2when they see the purity and reverence of your lives. 3Your beauty should not come from outward adornment, such as braided hair and the wearing of gold jewelry and fine clothes. m 4Instead, it should be that of your inner self, n the unfading beauty of a gentle and quiet spirit, which is of great worth in God's sight. 5For this is the way the holy women of the past who put their hope in Godo used to make themselves beautiful. They were submissive to their own husbands, 6like Sarah, who obeyed Abraham and called him her master.p You are her daughters if you do what is right and do not give way to fear.

7Husbands, q in the same way be considerate as you live with your wives, and treat them with respect as the weaker partner and as heirs with you of the gracious gift of life, so that nothing will hinder your prayers.

Suffering for Doing Good

8Finally, all of you, live in harmony with one another; be sympathetic, love as brothers,r be compassionate and humble.s 9Do not repay evil with evilt or insult with insult, u but with blessing, because to thisv you were called so that you may inherit a blessing. w 10For,

> "Whoever would love life
>   and see good days
> must keep his tongue from evil
>   and his lips from deceitful speech.
> 11He must turn from evil and do good;
>   he must seek peace and pursue it.
> 12For the eyes of the Lord are on the righteous
>   and his ears are attentive to their prayer,
> but the face of the Lord is against those who do evil."b x

13Who is going to harm you if you are eager to do good?y 14But even if you should suffer for what is right, you are blessed. z "Do not fear what they fearc; do not be frightened."d a 15But in your hearts set apart Christ as Lord. Always be prepared to give an answerb to everyone who asks you to give the reason for the hope that you have. But do this

2:20
y1Pe 3:17
2:21
zAc 14:22
aMt 16:24
2:22
bIsa 53:9
2:23
cIsa 53:7
dLk 23:46
2:24
eHeb 9:28
fRo 6:2
gIsa 53:5;
Heb 12:13;
Jas 5:16
2:25
hIsa 53:6
iJn 10:11
3:1
j1Pe 2:18
kEph 5:22
l1Co 7:16; 9:19
3:3
mIsa 3:18-23;
1Ti 2:9
3:4
nRo 7:22
3:5
o1Ti 5:5
3:6
pGe 18:12
3:7
qEph 5:25-33
3:8
rRo 12:10
s1Pe 5:5
3:9
tRo 12:17
u1Pe 2:23
v1Pe 2:21
wHeb 6:14
3:12
xPs 34:12-16
3:13
yPr 16:7
3:14
z1Pe 2:19,20;
4:15,16
aIsa 8:12,13
3:15
bCol 4:6

ª22 Isaiah 53:9   b12 Psalm 34:12-16   c14 *Or not fear their threats*   d14 Isaiah 8:12

with gentleness and respect, [16]keeping a clear conscience,[c] so that those who speak maliciously against your good behavior in Christ may be ashamed of their slander.[d] [17]It is better, if it is God's will,[e] to suffer for doing good[f] than for doing evil. [18]For Christ died for sins[g] once for all, the righteous for the unrighteous, to bring you to God. He was put to death in the body[h] but made alive by the Spirit,[i] [19]through whom[a] also he went and preached to the spirits in prison[j] [20]who disobeyed long ago when God waited patiently in the days of Noah while the ark was being built.[k] In it only a few people, eight in all, were saved[l] through water, [21]and this water symbolizes baptism that now saves you[m] also—not the removal of dirt from the body but the pledge[b] of a good conscience toward God. It saves you by the resurrection of Jesus Christ,[n] [22]who has gone into heaven and is at God's right hand[o]—with angels, authorities and powers in submission to him.[p]

Living for God

4 Therefore, since Christ suffered in his body, arm yourselves also with the same attitude, because he who has suffered in his body is done with sin. [2]As a result, he does not live the rest of his earthly life for evil human desires,[q] but rather for the will of God. [3]For you have spent enough time in the past[r] doing what pagans choose to do—living in debauchery, lust, drunkenness, orgies, carousing and detestable idolatry. [4]They think it strange that you do not plunge with them into the same flood of dissipation, and they heap abuse on you.[s] [5]But they will have to give account to him who is ready to judge the living and the dead.[t] [6]For this is the reason the gospel was preached even to those who are now dead,[u] so that they might be judged according to men in regard to the body, but live according to God in regard to the spirit.

[7]The end of all things is near.[v] Therefore be clear minded and self-controlled so that you can pray. [8]Above all, love each other deeply,[w] because love covers over a multitude of sins.[x] [9]Offer hospitality to one another without grumbling.[y] [10]Each one should use whatever gift he has received to serve others,[z] faithfully[a] administering God's grace in its various forms. [11]If anyone speaks, he should do it as one speaking the very words of God. If anyone serves, he should do it with the strength God provides,[b] so that in all things God may be praised[c] through Jesus Christ. To him be the glory and the power for ever and ever. Amen.

Suffering for Being a Christian

[12]Dear friends, do not be surprised at the painful trial you are suffering,[d] as though something strange were happening to you. [13]But rejoice that you participate in the sufferings of Christ, so that you may be overjoyed when his glory is revealed.[e] [14]If you are insulted because of the name of Christ, you are blessed,[f] for the Spirit of glory and of God rests on you. [15]If you suffer, it should not be as a murderer or thief or any other kind of criminal, or even as a meddler. [16]However, if you suffer as a Christian, do not be ashamed, but praise God that you bear that name.[g] [17]For it is time for judgment to begin with the family of

[a]18,19 Or *alive in the spirit,* [19]*through which*   [b]21 Or *response*

3:16
cHeb 13:18
d1Pe 2:12,15
3:17
e1Pe 2:15
f1Pe 2:20
3:18
g1Pe 2:21
hCol 1:22;
1Pe 4:1 i1Pe 4:6
3:19
j1Pe 4:6
3:20
kGe 6:3,5,13,14
lHeb 11:7
3:21
mTit 3:5
n1Pe 1:3
3:22
oMk 16:19
pRo 8:38
4:2
qRo 6:2
4:3
rEph 2:2
4:4
s1Pe 3:16
4:5
tAc 10:42;
2Ti 4:1
4:6
u1Pe 3:19
4:7
vRo 13:11
4:8
w1Pe 1:22
xPr 10:12
4:9
yPhp 2:14
4:10
zRo 12:6,7
a1Co 4:2
4:11
bEph 6:10
c1Co 10:31
4:12
d1Pe 1:6,7
4:13
eRo 8:17
4:14
fMt 5:11
4:16
gAc 5:41

God;[h] and if it begins with us, what will the outcome be for those who do not obey the gospel of God?[i] 18And,

> "If it is hard for the righteous to be saved,
>   what will become of the ungodly and the sinner?"[a j]

19So then, those who suffer according to God's will should commit themselves to their faithful Creator and continue to do good.

To Elders and Young Men

5 To the elders among you, I appeal as a fellow elder,[k] a witness[l] of Christ's sufferings and one who also will share in the glory to be revealed:[m] 2Be shepherds of God's flock[n] that is under your care, serving as overseers—not because you must, but because you are willing, as God wants you to be; not greedy for money,[o] but eager to serve; 3not lording it over[p] those entrusted to you, but being examples[q] to the flock. 4And when the Chief Shepherd appears, you will receive the crown of glory[r] that will never fade away.

5Young men, in the same way be submissive[s] to those who are older. All of you, clothe yourselves with humility toward one another, because,

> "God opposes the proud
>   but gives grace to the humble."[b t]

6Humble yourselves, therefore, under God's mighty hand, that he may lift you up in due time. [u] 7Cast all your anxiety on him[v] because he cares for you. [w]

8Be self-controlled and alert. Your enemy the devil prowls around[x] like a roaring lion looking for someone to devour. 9Resist him,[y] standing firm in the faith,[z] because you know that your brothers throughout the world are undergoing the same kind of sufferings. [a]

10And the God of all grace, who called you to his eternal glory[b] in Christ, after you have suffered a little while, will himself restore you and make you strong,[c] firm and steadfast. 11To him be the power for ever and ever. Amen. [d]

Final Greetings

12With the help of Silas,[c e] whom I regard as a faithful brother, I have written to you briefly,[f] encouraging you and testifying that this is the true grace of God. Stand fast in it.

13She who is in Babylon, chosen together with you, sends you her greetings, and so does my son Mark. [g] 14Greet one another with a kiss of love.[h]

Peace[i] to all of you who are in Christ.

4:17
h Jer 25:29
i 2Th 1:8
4:18
j Pr 11:31;
Lk 23:31
5:1
k Ac 11:30
l Lk 24:48
m 1Pe 1:5,7;
Rev 1:9
5:2
n Jn 21:16
o 1Ti 3:3
5:3
p Eze 34:4
q Php 3:17
5:4
r 1Co 9:25
5:5
s Eph 5:21
t Pr 3:34; Jas 4:6
5:6
u Jas 4:10
5:7
v Ps 37:5;
Mt 6:25
w Heb 13:5
5:8
x Job 1:7
5:9
y Jas 4:7
z Col 2:5
a Ac 14:22
5:10
b 2Co 4:17
c 2Th 2:17
5:11
d Ro 11:36
5:12
e 2Co 1:19
f Heb 13:22
5:13
g Ac 12:12
5:14
h Ro 16:16
i Eph 6:23

a18 Prov. 11:31   *b5* Prov. 3:34   *c12* Greek *Silvanus,* a variant of *Silas*

2 Peter

Title and Background

The recipients of this letter were the same group of Christians addressed in Peter's first letter. They were in danger of being confused by false teachers.

Author and Date of Writing

The author identifies himself as Simon Peter. He asserts that this is his second letter to the readers (3:1) and refers to Paul as "our dear brother" (3:15). The character of the letter is compatible with the claim that it was written by Peter. It was written about A.D. 66.

Theme and Message

Peter as a "shepherd" of Christ's sheep is particularly concerned about the false teachers and evildoers who have come into the church. He teaches the church how to deal with these false teachers but also seeks to commend to his readers a wholesome combination of Christian faith and practice. The Lord is certain to return, so the believers are to be watchful.

Outline

---

1 Simon Peter, a servant[a] and apostle of Jesus Christ,[b]

To those who through the righteousness[c] of our God and Savior Jesus Christ[d] have received a faith as precious as ours:

[2] Grace and peace be yours in abundance through the knowledge of God and of Jesus our Lord.[e]

Making One's Calling and Election Sure

[3] His divine power[f] has given us everything we need for life and godliness through our knowledge of him who called us[g] by his own glory and goodness. [4] Through these he has given us his very great and precious promises,[h] so that through them you may participate in the divine nature[i] and escape the corruption in the world caused by evil desires.[j]

[5] For this very reason, make every effort to add to your faith goodness; and to goodness, knowledge;[k] [6] and to knowledge, self-control;[l] and to self-control, perseverance; and to perseverance, godliness;[m] [7] and to godliness, brotherly kindness; and to brotherly kindness, love.[n] [8] For if you possess these qualities in increasing measure, they

1:1
aRo 1:1
b1Pe 1:1
cRo 3:21-26
dTit 2:13
1:2
ePhp 3:8
1:3
f1Pe 1:5
g1Th 2:12
1:4
h2Co 7:1
iEph 4:24;
Heb 12:10;
1Jn 3:2
j2Pe 2:18-20
1:5
kCol 2:3
1:6
lAc 24:25
mver 3
1:7
n1Th 3:12

will keep you from being ineffective and unproductive[o] in your knowledge of our Lord Jesus Christ. [9]But if anyone does not have them, he is nearsighted and blind,[p] and has forgotten that he has been cleansed from his past sins.[q]

[10]Therefore, my brothers, be all the more eager to make your calling and election sure. For if you do these things, you will never fall,[r] [11]and you will receive a rich welcome into the eternal kingdom of our Lord and Savior Jesus Christ.

Prophecy of Scripture

[12]So I will always remind you of these things,[s] even though you know them and are firmly established in the truth you now have. [13]I think it is right to refresh your memory as long as I live in the tent of this body,[t] [14]because I know that I will soon put it aside,[u] as our Lord Jesus Christ has made clear to me.[v] [15]And I will make every effort to see that after my departure[w] you will always be able to remember these things.

[16]We did not follow cleverly invented stories when we told you about the power and coming of our Lord Jesus Christ, but we were eyewitnesses of his majesty.[x] [17]For he received honor and glory from God the Father when the voice came to him from the Majestic Glory, saying, "This is my Son, whom I love; with him I am well pleased."[a][y] [18]We ourselves heard this voice that came from heaven when we were with him on the sacred mountain.[z]

[19]And we have the word of the prophets made more certain, and you will do well to pay attention to it, as to a light[a] shining in a dark place, until the day dawns and the morning star[b] rises in your hearts. [20]Above all, you must understand that no prophecy of Scripture came about by the prophet's own interpretation. [21]For prophecy never had its origin in the will of man, but men spoke from God[c] as they were carried along by the Holy Spirit.[d]

False Teachers and Their Destruction

2 But there were also false prophets[e] among the people, just as there will be false teachers among you.[f] They will secretly introduce destructive heresies, even denying the sovereign Lord[g] who bought them[h]—bringing swift destruction on themselves. [2]Many will follow their shameful ways and will bring the way of truth into disrepute. [3]In their greed these teachers will exploit you[i] with stories they have made up. Their condemnation has long been hanging over them, and their destruction has not been sleeping.

[4]For if God did not spare angels when they sinned, but sent them to hell,[b] putting them into gloomy dungeons[c] to be held for judgment;[j] [5]if he did not spare the ancient world[k] when he brought the flood on its ungodly people, but protected Noah, a preacher of righteousness, and seven others;[l] [6]if he condemned the cities of Sodom and Gomorrah by burning them to ashes,[m] and made them an example[n] of what is going to happen to the ungodly; [7]and if he rescued Lot,[o] a righteous man, who was distressed by the filthy lives of lawless men[p] [8](for that righteous man, living among them day after day, was tormented in his

1:8
o Jn 15:2;
Tit 3:14
1:9
p 1Jn 2:11
q Eph 5:26
1:10
r 2Pe 3:17
1:12
s Php 3:1;
1Jn 2:21
1:13
t 2Co 5:1,4
1:14
u 2Ti 4:6
v Jn 21:18,19
1:15
w Lk 9:31
1:16
x Mt 17:1-8
1:17
y Mt 3:17
1:18
z Mt 17:6
1:19
a Ps 119:105
b Rev 22:16
1:21
c 2Ti 3:16
d 2Sa 23:2;
Ac 1:16;
1Pe 1:11
2:1
e Dt 13:1-3
f 1Ti 4:1 g Jude 4
h 1Co 6:20
2:3
i 2Co 2:17;
1Th 2:5
2:4
j Jude 6;
Rev 20:1,2
2:5
k 2Pe 3:6
l Heb 11:7;
1Pe 3:20
2:6
m Ge 19:24,25
n Nu 26:10;
Jude 7
2:7
o Ge 19:16
p 2Pe 3:17

---

[a]17 Matt. 17:5; Mark 9:7; Luke 9:35　　[b]4 Greek *Tartarus*　　[c]4 Some manuscripts *into chains of darkness*

righteous soul by the lawless deeds he saw and heard)— 9if this is so, then the Lord knows how to rescue godly men from trials q and to hold the unrighteous for the day of judgment, while continuing their punishment. a 10This is especially true of those who follow the corrupt desire r of the sinful nature b and despise authority.

Bold and arrogant, these men are not afraid to slander celestial beings; s 11yet even angels, although they are stronger and more powerful, do not bring slanderous accusations against such beings in the presence of the Lord. t 12But these men blaspheme in matters they do not understand. They are like brute beasts, creatures of instinct, born only to be caught and destroyed, and like beasts they too will perish. u

13They will be paid back with harm for the harm they have done. Their idea of pleasure is to carouse in broad daylight. v They are blots and blemishes, reveling in their pleasures while they feast with you. c w 14With eyes full of adultery, they never stop sinning; they seduce x the unstable; they are experts in greed y—an accursed brood! z 15They have left the straight way and wandered off to follow the way of Balaam a son of Beor, who loved the wages of wickedness. 16But he was rebuked for his wrongdoing by a donkey—a beast without speech—who spoke with a man's voice and restrained the prophet's madness. b

17These men are springs without water c and mists driven by a storm. Blackest darkness is reserved for them. d 18For they mouth empty, boastful words e and, by appealing to the lustful desires of sinful human nature, they entice people who are just escaping from those who live in error. 19They promise them freedom, while they themselves are slaves of depravity—for a man is a slave to whatever has mastered him. f 20If they have escaped the corruption of the world by knowing g our Lord and Savior Jesus Christ and are again entangled in it and overcome, they are worse off at the end than they were at the beginning. h 21It would have been better for them not to have known the way of righteousness, than to have known it and then to turn their backs on the sacred command that was passed on to them. i 22Of them the proverbs are true: "A dog returns to its vomit," d j and, "A sow that is washed goes back to her wallowing in the mud."

The Day of the Lord

3 Dear friends, this is now my second letter to you. I have written both of them as reminders k to stimulate you to wholesome thinking. 2I want you to recall the words spoken in the past by the holy prophets and the command given by our Lord and Savior through your apostles.

3First of all, you must understand that in the last days l scoffers will come, scoffing and following their own evil desires. m 4They will say, "Where is this 'coming' he promised? n Ever since our fathers died, everything goes on as it has since the beginning of creation." o 5But they deliberately forget that long ago by God's word p the heavens existed and the earth was formed out of water and by water. q 6By these waters also the world of that time was deluged and destroyed. r 7By the same

2:9
q1Co 10:13
2:10
r2Pe 3:3 sJude 8
2:11
tJude 9
2:12
uJude 10
2:13
vRo 13:13
w1Co 11:20,21;
Jude 12
2:14
xver 18 yver 3
zEph 2:3
2:15
aNu 22:4-20;
Jude 11
2:16
bNu 22:21-30
2:17
cJude 12
dJude 13
2:18
eJude 16
2:19
fJn 8:34;
Ro 6:16
2:20
g2Pe 1:2
hMt 12:45
2:21
iHeb 6:4-6
2:22
jPr 26:11
3:1
k2Pe 1:13
3:3
l1Ti 4:1
m2Pe 2:10;
Jude 18
3:4
nIsa 5:19;
Eze 12:22;
Mt 24:48
oMk 10:6
3:5
pGe 1:6,9;
Heb 11:3
qPs 24:2
3:6
rGe 7:21,22

---

a9 Or *unrighteous for punishment until the day of judgment*   b10 Or *the flesh*   c13 Some manuscripts *in their love feasts*   d22 Prov. 26:11

word the present heavens and earth are reserved for fire,ˢ being kept for the day of judgment and destruction of ungodly men.

⁸But do not forget this one thing, dear friends: With the Lord a day is like a thousand years, and a thousand years are like a day.ᵗ ⁹The Lord is not slow in keeping his promise,ᵘ as some understand slowness. He is patientᵛ with you, not wanting anyone to perish, but everyone to come to repentance.ʷ

¹⁰But the day of the Lord will come like a thief.ˣ The heavens will disappear with a roar; the elements will be destroyed by fire, and the earth and everything in it will be laid bare.ᵃ ʸ

¹¹Since everything will be destroyed in this way, what kind of people ought you to be? You ought to live holy and godly lives ¹²as you look forwardᶻ to the day of God and speed its coming.ᵇ ᵃ That day will bring about the destruction of the heavens by fire, and the elements will melt in the heat.ᵇ ¹³But in keeping with his promise we are looking forward to a new heaven and a new earth,ᶜ the home of righteousness.

¹⁴So then, dear friends, since you are looking forward to this, make every effort to be found spotless, blamelessᵈ and at peace with him. ¹⁵Bear in mind that our Lord's patienceᵉ means salvation,ᶠ just as our dear brother Paul also wrote you with the wisdom that God gave him.ᵍ ¹⁶He writes the same way in all his letters, speaking in them of these matters. His letters contain some things that are hard to understand, which ignorant and unstableʰ people distort, as they do the other Scriptures,ⁱ to their own destruction.

¹⁷Therefore, dear friends, since you already know this, be on your guardʲ so that you may not be carried away by the errorᵏ of lawless men and fall from your secure position.ˡ ¹⁸But grow in the grace and knowledge of our Lord and Savior Jesus Christ.ᵐ To him be glory both now and forever! Amen.

3:7
ˢver 10,12;
2Th 1:7
3:8
ᵗPs 90:4
3:9
ᵘHab 2:3;
Heb 10:37
ᵛRo 2:4
ʷ1Ti 2:4
3:10
ˣLk 12:39;
1Th 5:2
ʸMt 24:35;
Rev 21:1
3:12
ᶻ1Co 1:7
ᵃPs 50:3 ᵇver 10
3:13
ᶜIsa 65:17;
66:22; Rev 21:1
3:14
ᵈ1Th 3:13
3:15
ᵉRo 2:4 ᶠver 9
ᵍEph 3:3
3:16
ʰ2Pe 2:14 ⁱver 2
3:17
ʲ1Co 10:12
ᵏ2Pe 2:18
ˡRev 2:5
3:18
ᵐ2Pe 1:11

ᵃ10 Some manuscripts *be burned up*　　　ᵇ12 Or *as you wait eagerly for the day of God to come*

1 John

Title and Background

False teachers were trying to mislead first-century Christians by denying, among other things, the true humanity of Christ. This view was incorporated within the system called Gnosticism and is the background of much of 1 John.

Author and Date of Writing

The author is John son of Zebedee—the apostle and the author of the Gospel of John and the book of Revelation. He was a first cousin of Jesus. The letter is difficult to date with precision, but many factors indicate that it was written near the end of the first century, probably around A.D. 90.

Theme and Message

John had two basic purposes in mind in this letter: (1) to expose false teachers, and (2) to give believers assurance of salvation. In keeping with his intention to combat Gnostic teachers, who taught that the spirit is entirely good and matter is entirely evil, John specifically struck at their total lack of morality; and by giving eyewitness testimony to the incarnation, he sought to confirm his readers' belief in the incarnate Christ. He tells his readers that if he is successful in doing this, it would give him great joy.

Outline

I. The Reality of the Incarnation (1:1-4)
II. Fellowship With the Father and the Son (1:5-2:28)
III. Divine Sonship (2:29-4:6)
IV. Ethics and Christ (4:7-5:12)
V. Great Christian Certainties (5:13-21)

The Word of Life

1 That which was from the beginning, a which we have heard, which we have seen with our eyes, b which we have looked at and our hands have touched c—this we proclaim concerning the Word of life. ²The life appeared; d we have seen it and testify to it, and we proclaim to you the eternal life, which was with the Father and has appeared to us. ³We proclaim to you what we have seen and heard, so that you also may have fellowship with us. And our fellowship is with the Father and with his Son, Jesus Christ. e ⁴We write this f to make our a joy complete. g

Walking in the Light

⁵This is the message we have heard h from him and declare to you:

1:1
a Jn 1:2
b Jn 1:14;
2Pe 1:16
c Jn 20:27
1:2
d Jn 1:1-4;
1Ti 3:16
1:3
e 1Co 1:9
1:4
f 1Jn 2:1
g Jn 3:29
1:5
h 1Jn 3:11

a4 Some manuscripts your

God is light; in him there is no darkness at all. [6]If we claim to have fellowship with him yet walk in the darkness,[i] we lie and do not live by the truth.[j] [7]But if we walk in the light, as he is in the light, we have fellowship with one another, and the blood of Jesus, his Son, purifies us from all[a] sin.[k]

[8]If we claim to be without sin,[l] we deceive ourselves and the truth is not in us.[m] [9]If we confess our sins, he is faithful and just and will forgive us our sins[n] and purify us from all unrighteousness. [10]If we claim we have not sinned, we make him out to be a liar[o] and his word has no place in our lives.[p]

2 My dear children,[q] I write this to you so that you will not sin. But if anybody does sin, we have one who speaks to the Father in our defense[r]—Jesus Christ, the Righteous One. [2]He is the atoning sacrifice for our sins,[s] and not only for ours but also for[b] the sins of the whole world.

[3]We know that we have come to know him if we obey his commands.[t] [4]The man who says, "I know him," but does not do what he commands is a liar, and the truth is not in him.[u] [5]But if anyone obeys his word,[v] God's love[c] is truly made complete in him.[w] This is how we know we are in him: [6]Whoever claims to live in him must walk as Jesus did.[x]

[7]Dear friends, I am not writing you a new command but an old one, which you have had since the beginning.[y] This old command is the message you have heard. [8]Yet I am writing you a new command;[z] its truth is seen in him and you, because the darkness is passing[a] and the true light[b] is already shining.[c]

[9]Anyone who claims to be in the light but hates his brother is still in the darkness. [10]Whoever loves his brother lives in the light,[d] and there is nothing in him[d] to make him stumble. [11]But whoever hates his brother is in the darkness and walks around in the darkness; he does not know where he is going, because the darkness has blinded him.[e]

[12]I write to you, dear children,
    because your sins have been forgiven on account of
      his name.
[13]I write to you, fathers,
    because you have known him who is from the
      beginning.
I write to you, young men,
    because you have overcome the evil one.[f]
I write to you, dear children,
    because you have known the Father.
[14]I write to you, fathers,
    because you have known him who is from the
      beginning.
I write to you, young men,
    because you are strong,[g]
    and the word of God lives in you,[h]
    and you have overcome the evil one.[i]

1:6
i2Co 6:14
jJn 3:19-21
1:7
kHeb 9:14;
Rev 1:5
1:8
lPr 20:9; Jas 3:2
m1Jn 2:4
1:9
nPs 32:5; 51:2
1:10
o1Jn 5:10
p1Jn 2:14
2:1
qver 12,13,28
rRo 8:34;
Heb 7:25
2:2
sRo 3:25
2:3
tJn 14:15
2:4
u1Jn 1:6,8
2:5
vJn 14:21,23
w1Jn 4:12
2:6
xMt 11:29;
1Pe 2:21
2:7
y1Jn 3:11,23;
2Jn 5,6
2:8
zJn 13:34
aRo 13:12
bJn 1:9
cEph 5:8;
1Th 5:5
2:10
d1Jn 3:14
2:11
eJn 12:35
2:13
fver 14
2:14
gEph 6:10
hJn 5:38;
1Jn 1:10 iver 13

Do Not Love the World

15Do not love the world or anything in the world. j If anyone loves the world, the love of the Father is not in him. k 16For everything in the world—the cravings of sinful man, l the lust of his eyes m and the boasting of what he has and does—comes not from the Father but from the world. 17The world and its desires pass away, n but the man who does the will of God lives forever.

Warning Against Antichrists

18Dear children, this is the last hour; and as you have heard that the antichrist is coming, o even now many antichrists have come. p This is how we know it is the last hour. 19They went out from us, q but they did not really belong to us. For if they had belonged to us, they would have remained with us; but their going showed that none of them belonged to us. r

20But you have an anointing s from the Holy One, t and all of you know the truth. ᵃu 21I do not write to you because you do not know the truth, but because you do know it v and because no lie comes from the truth. 22Who is the liar? It is the man who denies that Jesus is the Christ. Such a man is the antichrist—he denies the Father and the Son. w 23No one who denies the Son has the Father; whoever acknowledges the Son has the Father also. x

24See that what you have heard from the beginning remains in you. If it does, you also will remain in the Son and in the Father. y 25And this is what he promised us—even eternal life.

26I am writing these things to you about those who are trying to lead you astray. z 27As for you, the anointing a you received from him remains in you, and you do not need anyone to teach you. But as his anointing teaches you about all things and as that anointing is real, not counterfeit—just as it has taught you, remain in him.

Children of God

28And now, dear children, b continue in him, so that when he appears c we may be confident d and unashamed before him at his coming. e

29If you know that he is righteous, f you know that everyone who does what is right has been born of him.

3 How great is the love g the Father has lavished on us, that we should be called children of God! h And that is what we are! The reason the world does not know us is that it did not know him. i 2Dear friends, now we are children of God, and what we will be has not yet been made known. But we know that when he appears, b we shall be like him, j for we shall see him as he is. k 3Everyone who has this hope in him purifies himself, l just as he is pure.

4Everyone who sins breaks the law; in fact, sin is lawlessness. m 5But you know that he appeared so that he might take away our sins. And in him is no sin. n 6No one who lives in him keeps on sinning. o No one who continues to sin has either seen him p or known him. q

7Dear children, r do not let anyone lead you astray. s He who does

---

2:15
jRo 12:2
kJas 4:4
2:16
lRo 13:14
mPr 27:20
2:17
n1Co 7:31
2:18
over 22;
1Jn 4:3; 2Jn 7
p1Jn 4:1
2:19
qAc 20:30
r1Co 11:19
2:20
s2Co 1:21
tMk 1:24
uJn 14:26
2:21
v2Pe 1:12;
Jude 5
2:22
w2Jn 7
2:23
xJn 8:19;
1Jn 4:15
2:24
yJn 14:23
2:26
z2Jn 7
2:27
aver 20
2:28
bver 1 c1Jn 3:2
d1Jn 4:17
e1Th 2:19
2:29
f1Jn 3:7
3:1
gJn 3:16
hJn 1:12
iJn 16:3
3:2
jRo 8:29;
2Pe 1:4
k2Co 3:18
3:3
l2Co 7:1;
2Pe 3:13,14
3:4
m1Jn 5:17
3:5
n2Co 5:21
3:6
over 9 p3Jn 11
q1Jn 2:4
3:7
r1Jn 2:1
s1Jn 2:26

ᵃ20 Some manuscripts *and you know all things*   b2 Or *when it is made known* what is right is righteous, just as he is righteous.[t] [8]He who does what is sinful is of the devil,[u] because the devil has been sinning from the beginning. The reason the Son of God appeared was to destroy the devil's work. [9]No one who is born of God[v] will continue to sin,[w] because God's seed[x] remains in him; he cannot go on sinning, because he has been born of God. [10]This is how we know who the children of God are and who the children of the devil are: Anyone who does not do what is right is not a child of God; nor is anyone who does not love[y] his brother.

Love One Another

[11]This is the message you heard[z] from the beginning: We should love one another.[a] [12]Do not be like Cain, who belonged to the evil one and murdered his brother.[b] And why did he murder him? Because his own actions were evil and his brother's were righteous. [13]Do not be surprised, my brothers, if the world hates you.[c] [14]We know that we have passed from death to life,[d] because we love our brothers. Anyone who does not love remains in death.[e] [15]Anyone who hates his brother is a murderer,[f] and you know that no murderer has eternal life in him.[g]

[16]This is how we know what love is: Jesus Christ laid down his life for us. And we ought to lay down our lives for our brothers.[h] [17]If anyone has material possessions and sees his brother in need but has no pity on him,[i] how can the love of God be in him?[j] [18]Dear children,[k] let us not love with words or tongue but with actions and in truth.[l] [19]This then is how we know that we belong to the truth, and how we set our hearts at rest in his presence [20]whenever our hearts condemn us. For God is greater than our hearts, and he knows everything.

[21]Dear friends, if our hearts do not condemn us, we have confidence before God[m] [22]and receive from him anything we ask,[n] because we obey his commands and do what pleases him.[o] [23]And this is his command: to believe[p] in the name of his Son, Jesus Christ, and to love one another as he commanded us.[q] [24]Those who obey his commands live in him,[r] and he in them. And this is how we know that he lives in us: We know it by the Spirit he gave us.[s]

Test the Spirits

[4] Dear friends, do not believe every spirit, but test the spirits to see whether they are from God, because many false prophets have gone out into the world.[t] [2]This is how you can recognize the Spirit of God: Every spirit that acknowledges that Jesus Christ has come in the flesh[u] is from God,[v] [3]but every spirit that does not acknowledge Jesus is not from God. This is the spirit of the antichrist,[w] which you have heard is coming and even now is already in the world.

[4]You, dear children, are from God and have overcome them, because the one who is in you[x] is greater than the one who is in the world.[y] [5]They are from the world[z] and therefore speak from the viewpoint of the world, and the world listens to them. [6]We are from God, and whoever knows God listens to us; but whoever is not from God does not listen to us.[a] This is how we recognize the Spirit[a] of truth[b] and the spirit of falsehood.

[a]6 Or *spirit*

3:7
[t]1Jn 2:29
3:8
[u]Jn 8:44
3:9
[v]Jn 1:13
[w]1Jn 5:18
[x]1Pe 1:23
3:10
[y]1Jn 4:8
3:11
[z]1Jn 1:5
[a]Jn 13:34,35;
2Jn 5
3:12
[b]Ge 4:8
3:13
[c]Jn 15:18,19;
17:14
3:14
[d]Jn 5:24
[e]1Jn 2:9
3:15
[f]Mt 5:21,22;
Jn 8:44
[g]Gal 5:20,21
3:16
[h]Jn 15:13
3:17
[i]Dt 15:7,8
[j]1Jn 4:20
3:18
[k]1Jn 2:1
[l]Eze 33:31;
Ro 12:9
3:21
[m]1Jn 5:14
3:22
[n]Mt 7:7
[o]Jn 8:29
3:23
[p]Jn 6:29
[q]Jn 13:34
3:24
[r]1Jn 2:6
[s]1Jn 4:13
4:1
[t]2Pe 2:1;
1Jn 2:18
4:2
[u]Jn 1:14;
1Jn 2:23
[v]1Co 12:3
4:3
[w]1Jn 2:22; 2Jn 7
4:4
[x]Ro 8:31
[y]Jn 12:31
4:5
[z]Jn 15:19
4:6
[a]Jn 8:47
[b]Jn 14:17

God's Love and Ours

7Dear friends, let us love one another,c for love comes from God. Everyone who loves has been born of God and knows God. d 8Whoever does not love does not know God, because God is love. e 9This is how God showed his love among us: He sent his one and only Sona into the world that we might live through him. f 10This is love: not that we loved God, but that he loved usg and sent his Son as an atoning sacrifice forb our sins. h 11Dear friends, since God so loved us, i we also ought to love one another. 12No one has ever seen God;j but if we love one another, God lives in us and his love is made complete in us. k

13We know that we live in him and he in us, because he has given us of his Spirit. l 14And we have seen and testifym that the Father has sent his Son to be the Savior of the world. n 15If anyone acknowledges that Jesus is the Son of God, o God lives in him and he in God. 16And so we know and rely on the love God has for us.

God is love.p Whoever lives in love lives in God, and God in him. q 17In this way, love is made completer among us so that we will have confidence on the day of judgment, because in this world we are like him. 18There is no fear in love. But perfect love drives out fear, s because fear has to do with punishment. The one who fears is not made perfect in love.

19We love because he first loved us. t 20If anyone says, "I love God," yet hates his brother, u he is a liar. v For anyone who does not love his brother, whom he has seen, w cannot love God, whom he has not seen. x 21And he has given us this command: Whoever loves God must also love his brother. y

Faith in the Son of God

5 Everyone who believes that Jesus is the Christz is born of God, a and everyone who loves the father loves his child as well. b 2This is how we know that we love the children of God: by loving God and carrying out his commands. 3This is love for God: to obey his commands. c And his commands are not burdensome, d 4for everyone born of God overcomese the world. This is the victory that has overcome the world, even our faith. 5Who is it that overcomes the world? Only he who believes that Jesus is the Son of God.

6This is the one who came by water and bloodf—Jesus Christ. He did not come by water only, but by water and blood. And it is the Spirit who testifies, because the Spirit is the truth. g 7For there are threeh that testify: 8thec Spirit, the water and the blood; and the three are in agreement. 9We accept man's testimony, i but God's testimony is greater because it is the testimony of God,j which he has given about his Son. 10Anyone who believes in the Son of God has this testimony in his heart. k Anyone who does not believe God has made him out to be a liar, l because he has not believed the testimony God has given about his Son. 11And this is the testimony: God has given us eternal life, and

4:7
c1Jn 3:11
d1Jn 2:4
4:8
ever 7,16
4:9
fJn 3:16,17;
1Jn 5:11
4:10
gRo 5:8,10
h1Jn 2:2
4:11
iJn 3:16
4:12
jJn 1:18;
1Ti 6:16
k1Jn 2:5
4:13
l1Jn 3:24
4:14
mJn 15:27
nJn 3:17
4:15
oRo 10:9
4:16
pver 8 q1Jn 3:24
4:17
r1Jn 2:5
4:18
sRo 8:15
4:19
tver 10
4:20
u1Jn 2:9
v1Jn 2:4
w1Jn 3:17
xver 12
4:21
yMt 5:43
5:1
z1Jn 2:22
aJn 1:13;
1Jn 2:23
bJn 8:42
5:3
cJn 14:15; 2Jn 6
dMt 11:30
5:4
eJn 16:33
5:6
fJn 19:34
gJn 14:17
5:7
hMt 18:16
5:9
iJn 5:34
jMt 3:16,17;
Jn 8:17,18
5:10
kRo 8:16;
Gal 4:6 1Jn 3:33

---

a9 Or *his only begotten Son*   b10 Or *as the one who would turn aside his wrath, taking away*
c7,8 Late manuscripts of the Vulgate *testify in heaven: the Father, the Word and the Holy Spirit, and these three are one. 8And there are three that testify on earth: the* (not found in any Greek manuscript before the sixteenth century)

5:11
m Jn 1:4;
1Jn 2:25
5:12
n Jn 3:15,16,36
5:13
o 1Jn 3:23
p Jn 20:31;
1Jn 1:1,2
5:14
q 1Jn 3:21
r Mt 7:7
5:15
s ver 18,19,20
5:16
t Jas 5:15
u Heb 6:4-6;
10:26 v Jer 7:16
5:17
w 1Jn 3:4
x 1Jn 2:1
5:18
y Jn 14:30
5:19
z 1Jn 4:6
a Gal 1:4
5:20
b Lk 24:45
c Jn 17:3 d ver 11
5:21
e 1Co 10:14;
1Th 1:9

this life is in his Son. [m] [12]He who has the Son has life; he who does not have the Son of God does not have life. [n]

Concluding Remarks

[13]I write these things to you who believe in the name of the Son of God[o] so that you may know that you have eternal life. [p] [14]This is the confidence[q] we have in approaching God: that if we ask anything according to his will, he hears us. [r] [15]And if we know that he hears us—whatever we ask—we know[s] that we have what we asked of him.

[16]If anyone sees his brother commit a sin that does not lead to death, he should pray and God will give him life. [t] I refer to those whose sin does not lead to death. There is a sin that leads to death. [u] I am not saying that he should pray about that. [v] [17]All wrongdoing is sin, [w] and there is sin that does not lead to death. [x]

[18]We know that anyone born of God does not continue to sin; the one who was born of God keeps him safe, and the evil one cannot harm him. [y] [19]We know that we are children of God, [z] and that the whole world is under the control of the evil one. [a] [20]We know also that the Son of God has come and has given us understanding, [b] so that we may know him who is true. [c] And we are in him who is true—even in his Son Jesus Christ. He is the true God and eternal life. [d]

[21]Dear children, keep yourselves from idols. [e]

2 John

Title and Background

During the first two centuries A.D. the gospel was taken from place to place by traveling evangelists and teachers. Believers customarily took these missionaries into their homes and gave them provisions for their journey when they left. Since Gnostic teachers also relied on this practice, 2 John was written to urge discernment in supporting traveling teachers.

Author and Date of Writing

John wrote this letter shortly after his first letter, about A.D. 90.

Theme and Message

John writes of how important it is for Christians to love one another. To love means to obey God's commandments, and God's commandments in turn tell us to live lives of love. John again emphasizes the importance of the doctrine that Jesus is God's Son—both God and man. Christians should separate themselves from those who teach that Jesus is not God's Son.

Outline

I. Greeting (1-3)
II. Commendation (4)
III. Exhortation and Warning (5-11)
IV. Conclusion (12-13)

---

[1]The elder,[a]

To the chosen[b] lady and her children, whom I love in the truth—and not I only, but also all who know the truth[c]— [2]because of the truth,[d] which lives in us[e] and will be with us forever:

[3]Grace, mercy and peace from God the Father and from Jesus Christ,[f] the Father's Son, will be with us in truth and love.

[4]It has given me great joy to find some of your children walking in the truth,[g] just as the Father commanded us. [5]And now, dear lady, I am not writing you a new command but one we have had from the beginning.[h] I ask that we love one another. [6]And this is love:[i] that we walk in obedience to his commands. As you have heard from the beginning, his command is that you walk in love.

[7]Many deceivers, who do not acknowledge Jesus Christ[j] as coming in the flesh, have gone out into the world.[k] Any such person is the deceiver and the antichrist.[l] [8]Watch out that you do not lose what you have worked for, but that you may be rewarded fully.[m] [9]Anyone who runs ahead and does not continue in the teaching of Christ does not have God; whoever continues in the teaching has both the Father and the Son. [n] [10]If anyone comes to you and does not bring this teaching, do

1:1
a 3Jn 1
b Ro 16:13
c Jn 8:32

1:2
d 2Pe 1:12
e 1Jn 1:8

1:3
f Ro 1:7

1:4
g 3Jn 3,4

1:5
h 1Jn 2:7; 3:11

1:6
i 1Jn 2:5

1:7
j 1Jn 2:22; 4:2,3
k 1Jn 4:1
l 1Jn 2:18

1:8
m 1Co 3:8

1:9
n 1Jn 2:23

1:10
oRo 16:17
1:11
p 1Ti 5:22
1:12
q 3Jn 13,14
1:13
r ver 1

not take him into your house or welcome him. o 11Anyone who welcomes him shares p in his wicked work.

12I have much to write to you, but I do not want to use paper and ink. Instead, I hope to visit you and talk with you face to face, q so that our joy may be complete.

13The children of your chosen r sister send their greetings.

3 John

Title and Background

Itinerant teachers sent out by John were rejected in one of the churches in the province of Asia by a dictatorial leader, Diotrephes. This man had gone so far as to excommunicate members who showed hospitality to John's messengers.

Author and Date of Writing

The letter was probably written about the same time as 1 and 2 John, around A.D. 90. The apostle John is the author.

Theme and Message

John wrote to Gaius, his friend and a leader in the church. He writes to praise and thank Gaius for his help and to give him encouragement. He also reproves Diotrephes for not cooperating and for rebelling against John's leadership. In a later visit John will deal with him personally.

Outline

---

[1]The elder,[a]

To my dear friend Gaius, whom I love in the truth.

[2]Dear friend, I pray that you may enjoy good health and that all may go well with you, even as your soul is getting along well. [3]It gave me great joy to have some brothers[b] come and tell about your faithfulness to the truth and how you continue to walk in the truth.[c] [4]I have no greater joy than to hear that my children[d] are walking in the truth.

[5]Dear friend, you are faithful in what you are doing for the brothers, even though they are strangers to you.[e] [6]They have told the church about your love. You will do well to send them on their way in a manner worthy of God. [7]It was for the sake of the Name[f] that they went out, receiving no help from the pagans.[g] [8]We ought therefore to show hospitality to such men so that we may work together for the truth.

[9]I wrote to the church, but Diotrephes, who loves to be first, will have nothing to do with us. [10]So if I come,[h] I will call attention to what he is doing, gossiping maliciously about us. Not satisfied with that, he refuses to welcome the brothers.[i] He also stops those who want to do so and puts them out of the church.[j]

1:1
a 2Jn 1
1:3
b ver 5,10 c 2Jn 4
1:4
d 1Co 4:15;
1Jn 2:1
1:5
e Ro 12:13;
Heb 13:2
1:7
f Jn 15:21
g Ac 20:33,35
1:10
h 2Jn 12 i ver 5
j Jn 9:22,34

1:11
k Ps 37:27
l 1Jn 2:29
m 1Jn 3:6,9,10
1:12
n 1Ti 3:7
o Jn 21:24
1:14
p 2Jn 12
q Jn 10:3

[11]Dear friend, do not imitate what is evil but what is good. [k] Anyone who does what is good is from God. [l] Anyone who does what is evil has not seen God. [m] [12]Demetrius is well spoken of by everyone [n]—and even by the truth itself. We also speak well of him, and you know that our testimony is true. [o]

[13]I have much to write you, but I do not want to do so with pen and ink. [14]I hope to see you soon, and we will talk face to face. [p]

Peace to you. The friends here send their greetings. Greet the friends there by name. [q]

Jude

Title and Background

Jude originated as a personal letter from a leader in the apostolic church to one or more of the congregations dispersed throughout the Roman empire. The dangers facing the church at this time were not those of outright persecution and extinction but of heretics and distorters of the faith.

Author and Date of Writing

The author identifies himself as Jude, another form of the Hebrew name Judah. He was most likely Judas the brother of our Lord. The letter was probably written about A.D. 65.

Theme and Message

Although Jude was eager to write to his readers about salvation, he thought he must instead warn them about certain immoral men circulating among them who were perverting the grace of God. Apparently these false teachers were trying to convince believers that being saved by grace gave them license to sin since their sins would no longer be held against them. It has been thought that these false teachers were Gnostics, who believed that the spirit is entirely good and matter is entirely evil, probably forerunners of second-century, fully developed Gnosticism.

Outline

---

¹Jude,[a] a servant of Jesus Christ and a brother of James,

To those who have been called,[b] who are loved by God the Father and kept by[a] Jesus Christ:[c]

²Mercy, peace and love be yours in abundance.[d]

The Sin and Doom of Godless Men

³Dear friends, although I was very eager to write to you about the salvation we share,[e] I felt I had to write and urge you to contend[f] for the faith that was once for all entrusted to the saints. ⁴For certain men whose condemnation was written about[b] long ago have secretly slipped in among you.[g] They are godless men, who change the grace of

1:1
aMt 13:55;
Ac 1:13
bRo 1:6,7
cJn 17:12

1:2
d2Pe 1:2

1:3
eTit 1:4
f1Ti 6:12

1:4
gGal 2:4

---

a1 Or *for; or in*   b4 Or *men who were marked out for condemnation* our God into a license for immorality and deny Jesus Christ our only Sovereign and Lord. [h]

5Though you already know all this, I want to remind you that the Lord[a] delivered his people out of Egypt, but later destroyed those who did not believe. [i] 6And the angels who did not keep their positions of authority but abandoned their own home—these he has kept in darkness, bound with everlasting chains for judgment on the great Day.[j] 7In a similar way, Sodom and Gomorrah and the surrounding towns[k] gave themselves up to sexual immorality and perversion. They serve as an example of those who suffer the punishment of eternal fire. [l]

8In the very same way, these dreamers pollute their own bodies, reject authority and slander celestial beings. [m] 9But even the archangel Michael, [n] when he was disputing with the devil about the body of Moses, did not dare to bring a slanderous accusation against him, but said, "The Lord rebuke you!"[o] 10Yet these men speak abusively against whatever they do not understand; and what things they do understand by instinct, like unreasoning animals—these are the very things that destroy them. [p]

11Woe to them! They have taken the way of Cain;[q] they have rushed for profit into Balaam's error;[r] they have been destroyed in Korah's rebellion. [s]

12These men are blemishes at your love feasts,[t] eating with you without the slightest qualm—shepherds who feed only themselves. They are clouds without rain, [u] blown along by the wind;[v] autumn trees, without fruit and uprooted[w]—twice dead. 13They are wild waves of the sea,[x] foaming up their shame;[y] wandering stars, for whom blackest darkness has been reserved forever.[z]

14Enoch,[a] the seventh from Adam, prophesied about these men: "See, the Lord is coming with thousands upon thousands of his holy ones[b] 15to judge[c] everyone, and to convict all the ungodly of all the ungodly acts they have done in the ungodly way, and of all the harsh words ungodly sinners have spoken against him."[d] 16These men are grumblers and faultfinders; they follow their own evil desires; they boast[e] about themselves and flatter others for their own advantage.

A Call to Persevere

17But, dear friends, remember what the apostles of our Lord Jesus Christ foretold. [f] 18They said to you, "In the last times[g] there will be scoffers who will follow their own ungodly desires."[h] 19These are the men who divide you, who follow mere natural instincts and do not have the Spirit. [i]

20But you, dear friends, build yourselves up[j] in your most holy faith and pray in the Holy Spirit.[k] 21Keep yourselves in God's love as you wait[l] for the mercy of our Lord Jesus Christ to bring you to eternal life.

22Be merciful to those who doubt; 23snatch others from the fire and save them;[m] to others show mercy, mixed with fear—hating even the clothing stained by corrupted flesh. [n]

1:4
hTit 1:16;
2Pe 2:1
1:5
iNu 14:29;
Ps 106:26
1:6
j2Pe 2:4,9
1:7
kDt 29:23
l2Pe 2:6
1:8
m2Pe 2:10
1:9
nDa 10:13,21
oZec 3:2
1:10
p2Pe 2:12
1:11
qGe 4:3-8;
1Jn 3:12
r2Pe 2:15
sNu 16:1-3,
31-35
1:12
t2Pe 2:13;
1Co 11:20-22
uPr 25:14;
2Pe 2:17
vEph 4:14
wMt 15:13
1:13
xIsa 57:20
yPhp 3:19
z2Pe 2:17
1:14
aGe 5:18,21-24
bDt 33:2;
Da 7:10
1:15
c2Pe 2:6-9
d1Ti 1:9
1:16
e2Pe 2:18
1:17
f2Pe 3:2
1:18
g1Ti 4:1
h2Pe 2:1
1:19
i1Co 2:14,15
1:20
jCol 2:7
kEph 6:18
1:21
lTit 2:13;
2Pe 3:12
1:23
mAm 4:11;
Zec 3:2-5
nRev 3:4

---

a5 Some early manuscripts Jesus

Doxology

²⁴To him who is able° to keep you from falling and to present you before his glorious presenceᵖ without faultᑫ and with great joy— ²⁵to the only Godʳ our Savior be glory, majesty, power and authority, through Jesus Christ our Lord, before all ages, now and forevermore!ˢ Amen.ᵗ

1:24
°Ro 16:25
P2Co 4:14
ᑫCol 1:22
1:25
ʳJn 5:44;
1Ti 1:17
ˢHeb 13:8
ᵗRo 11:36

Revelation

Title and Background

Since Roman authorities at this time were beginning to enforce the cult of emperor worship, Christians—who held that Christ, not Caesar, was Lord—were facing increasing hostility. Some in the church were advocating a policy of compromise; this had to be corrected before its subtle influence could undermine believers' determination to stand fast in the perilous days that lay ahead.

Author and Date of Writing

Four times the author identifies himself as John, and John was held to be the author from as early as the second century. Most scholars hold that the book was written about A.D. 95.

Theme and Message

John writes to encourage the faithful to resist staunchly the demands that they worship the emperor. He informs his readers that the final showdown between God and Satan is imminent. Satan will increase his persecution of believers, but they must stand fast, even to death. They are sealed against any spiritual harm and will soon be vindicated when Christ returns, when the wicked are forever destroyed, and when God's people enter an eternity of glory and blessedness.

Outline

    I. Jesus Among the Seven Churches (1:1-20)
   II. Letters to the Seven Churches (2:1-3:22)
  III. The Throne, the Scroll and the Lamb (4:1-5:14)
   IV. The Seven Seals (6:1-8:1)
    V. The Seven Trumpets (8:2-11:19)
   VI. Various Personages and Events (12:1-14:20)
  VII. The Seven Bowls (15:1-16:21)
 VIII. Babylon: The Great Prostitute (17:1-19:5)
   IX. The Wedding of the Lamb (19:6-10)
    X. The Return of Christ (19:11-21)
   XI. The Thousand Years (20:1-6)
  XII. Satan's Doom (20:7-10)
 XIII. Great White Throne Judgment (20:11-15)
  XIV. New Heaven, New Earth, New Jerusalem (21:1-22:5)
   XV. Conclusion (22:6-21)

Prologue

1:1
a Rev 22:16

1:2
b 1Co 1:6;
Rev 12:17

1:3
c Lk 11:28

1 The revelation of Jesus Christ, which God gave him to show his servants what must soon take place. He made it known by sending his angel a to his servant John, 2who testifies to everything he saw—that is, the word of God and the testimony of Jesus Christ. b 3Blessed is the one who reads the words of this prophecy, and blessed are those who hear it and take to heart what is written in it, c because the time is near.

Greetings and Doxology

4John,

To the seven churches in the province of Asia:

Grace and peace to you from him who is, and who was, and who is to come, and from the seven spirits[a][d] before his throne, 5and from Jesus Christ, who is the faithful witness,[e] the firstborn from the dead,[f] and the ruler of the kings of the earth.[g]

To him who loves us and has freed us from our sins by his blood, 6and has made us to be a kingdom and priests[h] to serve his God and Father—to him be glory and power for ever and ever! Amen.[i]

> 7Look, he is coming with the clouds,[j]
>   and every eye will see him,
>   even those who pierced him;
>   and all the peoples of the earth will mourn[k] because
>   of him.
>
> So shall it be! Amen.

8"I am the Alpha and the Omega,"[l] says the Lord God, "who is, and who was, and who is to come, the Almighty."[m]

One Like a Son of Man

9I, John, your brother and companion in the suffering[n] and kingdom and patient endurance[o] that are ours in Jesus, was on the island of Patmos because of the word of God and the testimony of Jesus. 10On the Lord's Day I was in the Spirit,[p] and I heard behind me a loud voice like a trumpet,[q] 11which said: "Write on a scroll what you see and send it to the seven churches:[r] to Ephesus, Smyrna, Pergamum, Thyatira, Sardis,[s] Philadelphia and Laodicea."

12I turned around to see the voice that was speaking to me. And when I turned I saw seven golden lampstands,[t] 13and among the lampstands was someone "like a son of man,"[b][u] dressed in a robe reaching down to his feet and with a golden sash around his chest.[v] 14His head and hair were white like wool, as white as snow, and his eyes were like blazing fire.[w] 15His feet were like bronze glowing in a furnace,[x] and his voice was like the sound of rushing waters.[y] 16In his right hand he held seven stars,[z] and out of his mouth came a sharp double-edged sword.[a] His face was like the sun shining in all its brilliance.

17When I saw him, I fell at his feet[b] as though dead. Then he placed his right hand on me and said: "Do not be afraid. I am the First and the Last.[c] 18I am the Living One; I was dead,[d] and behold I am alive for ever and ever![e] And I hold the keys of death and Hades.[f]

19"Write, therefore, what you have seen, what is now and what will take place later. 20The mystery of the seven stars that you saw in my right hand and of the seven golden lampstands[g] is this: The seven stars

---

1:4
d Rev 3:1; 4:5
1:5
e Rev 3:14
f Col 1:18
g Rev 17:14
1:6
h 1Pe 2:5
i Ro 11:36
1:7
j Da 7:13
k Zec 12:10
1:8
l Rev 21:6
m Rev 4:8
1:9
n Php 4:14
o 2Ti 2:12
1:10
p Rev 4:2
q Rev 4:1
1:11
r ver 4,20
s Rev 3:1
1:12
t Ex 25:31-40;
Zec 4:2
1:13
u Eze 1:26;
Da 7:13; 10:16
v Da 10:5;
Rev 15:6
1:14
w Da 7:9; 10:6;
Rev 19:12
1:15
x Da 10:6
y Eze 43:2;
Rev 14:2
1:16
z Rev 2:1; 3:1
a Isa 49:2;
Heb 4:12;
Rev 2:12,16
1:17
b Eze 1:28;
Da 8:17,18
c Isa 41:4; 44:6;
48:12;
Rev 22:13
1:18
d Ro 6:9
e Rev 4:9,10
f Rev 20:1
1:20
g Zec 4:2

---

a4 Or *the sevenfold Spirit*   b13 Daniel 7:13

are the angels^f of the seven churches,^h and the seven lampstands are the seven churches.ⁱ

To the Church in Ephesus

2 "To the angel^b of the church in Ephesus write:

These are the words of him who holds the seven stars in his right hand^j and walks among the seven golden lampstands:^k ²I know your deeds,^l your hard work and your perseverance. I know that you cannot tolerate wicked men, that you have tested^m those who claim to be apostles but are not, and have found them false.ⁿ ³You have persevered and have endured hardships for my name,^o and have not grown weary.

⁴Yet I hold this against you: You have forsaken your first love.^p ⁵Remember the height from which you have fallen! Repent^q and do the things you did at first. If you do not repent, I will come to you and remove your lampstand^r from its place. ⁶But you have this in your favor: You hate the practices of the Nicolaitans,^s which I also hate.

⁷He who has an ear, let him hear^t what the Spirit says to the churches. To him who overcomes, I will give the right to eat from the tree of life,^u which is in the paradise^v of God.

To the Church in Smyrna

⁸"To the angel of the church in Smyrna^w write:

These are the words of him who is the First and the Last,^x who died and came to life again.^y ⁹I know your afflictions and your poverty—yet you are rich!^z I know the slander of those who say they are Jews and are not,^a but are a synagogue of Satan.^b ¹⁰Do not be afraid of what you are about to suffer. I tell you, the devil will put some of you in prison to test you,^c and you will suffer persecution for ten days.^d Be faithful,^e even to the point of death, and I will give you the crown of life.

¹¹He who has an ear, let him hear what the Spirit says to the churches. He who overcomes will not be hurt at all by the second death.^f

To the Church in Pergamum

¹²"To the angel of the church in Pergamum^g write:

These are the words of him who has the sharp, double-edged sword.^h ¹³I know where you live—where Satan has his throne. Yet you remain true to my name. You did not renounce your faith in me,ⁱ even in the days of Antipas, my faithful witness, who was put to death in your city—where Satan lives.^j

¹⁴Nevertheless, I have a few things against you:^k You have people there who hold to the teaching of Balaam,^l who taught Balak to entice the Israelites to sin by eating food sacrificed to idols and by committing sexual immorality.^m ¹⁵Likewise you also have those who hold to the teaching of the Nicolaitans.ⁿ ¹⁶Repent

1:20
hver 4,11
iMt 5:14,15
2:1
jRev 1:16
kRev 1:12,13
2:2
lRev 3:1,8,15
m1Jn 4:1
n2Co 11:13
2:3
oJn 15:21
2:4
pMt 24:12
2:5
qver 16,22
rRev 1:20
2:6
sver 15
2:7
tMt 11:15;
Rev 3:6,13,22
uGe 2:9;
Rev 22:2,14,19
vLk 23:43
2:8
wRev 1:11
xRev 1:17
yRev 1:18
2:9
zJas 2:5
aRev 3:9
bMt 4:10
2:10
cRev 3:10
dDa 1:12,14
ever 13
2:11
fRev 20:6,14;
21:8
2:12
gRev 1:11
hRev 1:16
2:13
iRev 14:12
jver 9,24
2:14
kver 20
l2Pe 2:15
m1Co 6:13
2:15
nver 6

^a20 Or *messengers*   ^b1 Or *messenger*; also in verses 8, 12 and 18

therefore! Otherwise, I will soon come to you and will fight against them with the sword of my mouth. [o]

[17]He who has an ear, let him hear what the Spirit says to the churches. To him who overcomes, I will give some of the hidden manna. [p] I will also give him a white stone with a new name [q] written on it, known only to him who receives it. [r]

To the Church in Thyatira

[18]"To the angel of the church in Thyatira [s] write:

These are the words of the Son of God, whose eyes are like blazing fire and whose feet are like burnished bronze. [t] [19]I know your deeds, [u] your love and faith, your service and perseverance, and that you are now doing more than you did at first.

[20]Nevertheless, I have this against you: You tolerate that woman Jezebel, [v] who calls herself a prophetess. By her teaching she misleads my servants into sexual immorality and the eating of food sacrificed to idols. [21]I have given her time [w] to repent of her immorality, but she is unwilling. [x] [22]So I will cast her on a bed of suffering, and I will make those who commit adultery [y] with her suffer intensely, unless they repent of her ways. [23]I will strike her children dead. Then all the churches will know that I am he who searches hearts and minds, [z] and I will repay each of you according to your deeds. [24]Now I say to the rest of you in Thyatira, to you who do not hold to her teaching and have not learned Satan's so-called deep secrets (I will not impose any other burden on you): [a] [25]Only hold on to what you have [b] until I come.

[26]To him who overcomes and does my will to the end, I will give authority over the nations [c] —

> [27]'He will rule them with an iron scepter; [d]
> he will dash them to pieces like pottery' [a] [e] —

just as I have received authority from my Father. [28]I will also give him the morning star. [f] [29]He who has an ear, let him hear [g] what the Spirit says to the churches.

To the Church in Sardis

3 "To the angel [b] of the church in Sardis write:

These are the words of him who holds the seven spirits [c] [h] of God and the seven stars. [i] I know your deeds; [j] you have a reputation of being alive, but you are dead. [k] [2]Wake up! Strengthen what remains and is about to die, for I have not found your deeds complete in the sight of my God. [3]Remember, therefore, what you have received and heard; obey it, and repent. [l] But if you do not wake up, I will come like a thief, [m] and you will not know at what time I will come to you.

[4]Yet you have a few people in Sardis who have not soiled their clothes. [n] They will walk with me, dressed in white, [o] for they are worthy. [5]He who overcomes will, like them, be dressed in white. I will never blot out his name from the book of life, [p] but will

2:16
[o]2Th 2:8;
Rev 1:16

2:17
[p]Jn 6:49,50
[q]Isa 62:2
[r]Rev 19:12

2:18
[s]Rev 1:11
[t]Rev 1:14,15

2:19
[u]ver 2

2:20
[v]1Ki 16:31;
21:25; 2Ki 9:7

2:21
[w]Ro 2:4
[x]Rev 9:20

2:22
[y]Rev 17:2; 18:9

2:23
[z]1Sa 16:7;
Jer 11:20;
Ac 1:24;
Ro 8:27

2:24
[a]Ac 15:28

2:25
[b]Rev 3:11

2:26
[c]Ps 2:8;
Rev 3:21

2:27
[d]Rev 12:5
[e]Isa 30:14;
Jer 19:11

2:28
[f]Rev 22:16

2:29
[g]ver 7

3:1
[h]Rev 1:4
[i]Rev 1:16
[j]Rev 2:2
[k]1Ti 5:6

3:3
[l]Rev 2:5
[m]2Pe 3:10

3:4
[n]Jude 23
[o]Rev 4:4; 6:11;
7:9,13,14

3:5
[p]Rev 20:12

---

[a]27 Psalm 2:9   [b]1 Or *messenger*; also in verses 7 and 14   [c]1 Or *the sevenfold Spirit*

acknowledge his name before my Father^q and his angels. ⁶He who has an ear, let him hear^r what the Spirit says to the churches.

To the Church in Philadelphia

⁷"To the angel of the church in Philadelphia^s write:

These are the words of him who is holy and true,^t who holds the key of David.^u What he opens no one can shut, and what he shuts no one can open. ⁸I know your deeds. See, I have placed before you an open door^v that no one can shut. I know that you have little strength, yet you have kept my word and have not denied my name.^w ⁹I will make those who are of the synagogue of Satan,^x who claim to be Jews though they are not, but are liars—I will make them come and fall down at your feet^y and acknowledge that I have loved you.^z ¹⁰Since you have kept my command to endure patiently, I will also keep you^a from the hour of trial that is going to come upon the whole world to test^b those who live on the earth.^c

¹¹I am coming soon. Hold on to what you have,^d so that no one will take your crown.^e ¹²Him who overcomes I will make a pillar^f in the temple of my God. Never again will he leave it. I will write on him the name of my God^g and the name of the city of my God, the new Jerusalem,^h which is coming down out of heaven from my God; and I will also write on him my new name. ¹³He who has an ear, let him hear what the Spirit says to the churches.

To the Church in Laodicea

¹⁴"To the angel of the church in Laodicea write:

These are the words of the Amen, the faithful and true witness, the ruler of God's creation.ⁱ ¹⁵I know your deeds, that you are neither cold nor hot.^j I wish you were either one or the other! ¹⁶So, because you are lukewarm—neither hot nor cold—I am about to spit you out of my mouth. ¹⁷You say, 'I am rich; I have acquired wealth and do not need a thing.'^k But you do not realize that you are wretched, pitiful, poor, blind and naked. ¹⁸I counsel you to buy from me gold refined in the fire, so you can become rich; and white clothes to wear, so you can cover your shameful nakedness;^l and salve to put on your eyes, so you can see.

¹⁹Those whom I love I rebuke and discipline.^m So be earnest, and repent.ⁿ ²⁰Here I am! I stand at the door^o and knock. If anyone hears my voice and opens the door,^p I will come in^q and eat with him, and he with me.

²¹To him who overcomes, I will give the right to sit with me on my throne,^r just as I overcame^s and sat down with my Father on his throne. ²²He who has an ear, let him hear^t what the Spirit says to the churches."

The Throne in Heaven

4 After this I looked, and there before me was a door standing open in heaven. And the voice I had first heard speaking to me like a trumpet^u said, "Come up here,^v and I will show you what must take

3:5
qMt 10:32
3:6
rRev 2:7
3:7
sRev 1:11
t1Jn 5:20
uIsa 22:22;
Mt 16:19
3:8
vAc 14:27
wRev 2:13
3:9
xRev 2:9
yIsa 49:23
zIsa 43:4
3:10
a2Pe 2:9
bRev 2:10
cRev 6:10; 17:8
3:11
dRev 2:25
eRev 2:10
3:12
fGal 2:9
gRev 14:1; 22:4
hRev 21:2,10
3:14
iCol 1:16,18
3:15
jRo 12:11
3:17
kHos 12:8;
1Co 4:8
3:18
lRev 16:15
3:19
mPr 3:12;
Heb 12:5,6
nRev 2:5
3:20
oMt 24:33
pLk 12:36
qJn 14:23
3:21
rMt 19:28
sRev 5:5
3:22
tRev 2:7
4:1
uRev 1:10
vRev 11:12

place after this."ʷ ²At once I was in the Spirit,ˣ and there before me was a throne in heavenʸ with someone sitting on it. ³And the one who sat there had the appearance of jasper and carnelian. A rainbow,ᶻ resembling an emerald, encircled the throne. ⁴Surrounding the throne were twenty-four other thrones, and seated on them were twenty-four elders.ᵃ They were dressed in whiteᵇ and had crowns of gold on their heads. ⁵From the throne came flashes of lightning, rumblings and peals of thunder.ᶜ Before the throne, seven lampsᵈ were blazing. These are the seven spiritsᵃᵉ of God. ⁶Also before the throne there was what looked like a sea of glass,ᶠ clear as crystal.

In the center, around the throne, were four living creatures,ᵍ and they were covered with eyes, in front and in back. ⁷The first living creature was like a lion, the second was like an ox, the third had a face like a man, the fourth was like a flying eagle.ʰ ⁸Each of the four living creatures had six wingsⁱ and was covered with eyes all around, even under his wings. Day and night they never stop saying:

> "Holy, holy, holy
> is the Lord God Almighty,ʲ
> who was, and is, and is to come."ᵏ

⁹Whenever the living creatures give glory, honor and thanks to him who sits on the throneˡ and who lives for ever and ever, ¹⁰the twenty-four eldersᵐ fall down before himⁿ who sits on the throne,ᵒ and worship him who lives for ever and ever. They lay their crowns before the throne and say:

> ¹¹"You are worthy, our Lord and God,
> to receive glory and honor and power,ᵖ
> for you created all things,
> and by your will they were created
> and have their being."�q

The Scroll and the Lamb

5 Then I saw in the right hand of him who sat on the throneʳ a scroll with writing on both sidesˢ and sealedᵗ with seven seals. ²And I saw a mighty angel proclaiming in a loud voice, "Who is worthy to break the seals and open the scroll?" ³But no one in heaven or on earth or under the earth could open the scroll or even look inside it. ⁴I wept and wept because no one was found who was worthy to open the scroll or look inside. ⁵Then one of the elders said to me, "Do not weep! See, the Lionᵘ of the tribe of Judah, the Root of David,ᵛ has triumphed. He is able to open the scroll and its seven seals."

⁶Then I saw a Lamb,ʷ looking as if it had been slain, standing in the center of the throne, encircled by the four living creatures and the elders. He had seven horns and seven eyes,ˣ which are the seven spiritsᵃ of God sent out into all the earth. ⁷He came and took the scroll from the right hand of him who sat on the throne.ʸ ⁸And when he had taken it, the four living creatures and the twenty-four elders fell down before the Lamb. Each one had a harpᶻ and they were holding golden

---

ᵃ5,6 Or the sevenfold Spirit

4:1
wRev 1:19
4:2
xRev 1:10
yIsa 6:1;
Eze 1:26-28;
Da 7:9
4:3
zEze 1:28
4:4
aRev 11:16
bRev 3:4,5
4:5
cRev 8:5; 16:18
dZec 4:2
eRev 1:4
4:6
fRev 15:2
gEze 1:5
4:7
hEze 1:10;
10:14
4:8
iIsa 6:2
jIsa 6:3;
Rev 1:8
kRev 1:4
4:9
lPs 47:8
4:10
mver 4
nRev 5:8,14
over 2
4:11
pRev 5:12
qRev 10:6
5:1
rver 7,13
sEze 2:9,10
tIsa 29:11;
Da 12:4
5:5
uGe 49:9
vIsa 11:1,10;
Ro 15:12;
Rev 22:16
5:6
wJn 1:29
xZec 4:10
5:7
yver 1
5:8
zRev 14:2

bowls full of incense, which are the prayers[a] of the saints. [9]And they sang a new song:[b]

"You are worthy[c] to take the scroll
and to open its seals,
because you were slain,
and with your blood[d] you purchased[e] men for God
from every tribe and language and people and nation.
[10]You have made them to be a kingdom and priests[f] to
serve our God,
and they will reign on the earth."

[11]Then I looked and heard the voice of many angels, numbering thousands upon thousands, and ten thousand times ten thousand.[g] They encircled the throne and the living creatures and the elders. [12]In a loud voice they sang:

"Worthy is the Lamb, who was slain,
to receive power and wealth and wisdom and strength
and honor and glory and praise!"[h]

[13]Then I heard every creature in heaven and on earth and under the earth[i] and on the sea, and all that is in them, singing:

"To him who sits on the throne and to the Lamb[j]
be praise and honor and glory and power,
for ever and ever!"[k]

[14]The four living creatures said, "Amen,"[l] and the elders fell down and worshiped.[m]

The Seals

6 I watched as the Lamb[n] opened the first of the seven seals.[o] Then I heard one of the four living creatures[p] say in a voice like thunder,[q] "Come!" [2]I looked, and there before me was a white horse![r] Its rider held a bow, and he was given a crown,[s] and he rode out as a conqueror bent on conquest.[t]

[3]When the Lamb opened the second seal, I heard the second living creature[u] say, "Come!" [4]Then another horse came out, a fiery red one.[v] Its rider was given power to take peace from the earth[w] and to make men slay each other. To him was given a large sword.

[5]When the Lamb opened the third seal, I heard the third living creature[x] say, "Come!" I looked, and there before me was a black horse![y] Its rider was holding a pair of scales in his hand. [6]Then I heard what sounded like a voice among the four living creatures,[z] saying, "A quart[a] of wheat for a day's wages,[b] and three quarts of barley for a day's wages,[b] and do not damage[a] the oil and the wine!"

[7]When the Lamb opened the fourth seal, I heard the voice of the fourth living creature[b] say, "Come!" [8]I looked, and there before me was a pale horse![c] Its rider was named Death, and Hades[d] was following close behind him. They were given power over a fourth of the earth to kill by sword, famine and plague, and by the wild beasts of the earth.[e]

---

[a]6 Greek *a choinix* (probably about a liter)   [b]6 Greek *a denarius*

5:8
a Ps 141:2
5:9
b Ps 40:3
c Rev 4:11
d Heb 9:12
e 1Co 6:20
5:10
f 1Pe 2:5
5:11
g Da 7:10;
Heb 12:22
5:12
h Rev 4:11
5:13
i ver 3; Php 2:10
j Rev 6:16
k 1Ch 29:11
5:14
l Rev 4:9
m Rev 4:10;
19:4
6:1
n Rev 5:6
o Rev 5:1
p Rev 4:6,7
q Rev 14:2; 19:6
6:2
r Zec 6:3;
Rev 19:11
s Zec 6:11;
Rev 14:14
t Ps 45:4
6:3
u Rev 4:7
6:4
v Zec 6:2
w Mt 10:34
6:5
x Rev 4:7
y Zec 6:2
6:6
z Rev 4:6,7
a Rev 9:4
6:7
b Rev 4:7
6:8
c Zec 6:3
d Hos 13:14
e Jer 15:2,3;
Eze 5:12,17

[9]When he opened the fifth seal, I saw under the altar[f] the souls of those who had been slain[g] because of the word of God and the testimony they had maintained. [10]They called out in a loud voice, "How long,[h] Sovereign Lord, holy and true,[i] until you judge the inhabitants of the earth and avenge our blood?"[j] [11]Then each of them was given a white robe,[k] and they were told to wait a little longer, until the number of their fellow servants and brothers who were to be killed as they had been was completed.[l]

[12]I watched as he opened the sixth seal. There was a great earthquake.[m] The sun turned black[n] like sackcloth made of goat hair, the whole moon turned blood red, [13]and the stars in the sky fell to earth,[o] as late figs drop from a fig tree[p] when shaken by a strong wind. [14]The sky receded like a scroll, rolling up, and every mountain and island was removed from its place.[q]

[15]Then the kings of the earth, the princes, the generals, the rich, the mighty, and every slave and every free man hid in caves and among the rocks of the mountains.[r] [16]They called to the mountains and the rocks, "Fall on us[s] and hide us from the face of him who sits on the throne and from the wrath of the Lamb! [17]For the great day[t] of their wrath has come, and who can stand?"[u]

144,000 Sealed

7 After this I saw four angels standing at the four corners of the earth, holding back the four winds[v] of the earth to prevent any wind from blowing on the land or on the sea or on any tree. [2]Then I saw another angel coming up from the east, having the seal of the living God. He called out in a loud voice to the four angels who had been given power to harm the land and the sea: [3]"Do not harm[w] the land or the sea or the trees until we put a seal on the foreheads[x] of the servants of our God." [4]Then I heard the number[y] of those who were sealed: 144,000[z] from all the tribes of Israel.

[5]From the tribe of Judah 12,000 were sealed,
from the tribe of Reuben 12,000,
from the tribe of Gad 12,000,
[6]from the tribe of Asher 12,000,
from the tribe of Naphtali 12,000,
from the tribe of Manasseh 12,000,
[7]from the tribe of Simeon 12,000,
from the tribe of Levi 12,000,
from the tribe of Issachar 12,000,
[8]from the tribe of Zebulun 12,000,
from the tribe of Joseph 12,000,
from the tribe of Benjamin 12,000.

The Great Multitude in White Robes

[9]After this I looked and there before me was a great multitude that no one could count, from every nation, tribe, people and language,[a] standing before the throne[b] and in front of the Lamb. They were wearing white robes and were holding palm branches in their hands. [10]And they cried out in a loud voice:

"Salvation belongs to our God,[c]

6:9
fRev 14:18;
16:7 gRev 20:4
6:10
hZec 1:12
iRev 3:7
jRev 19:2
6:11
kRev 3:4
lHeb 11:40
6:12
mRev 16:18
nMt 24:29
6:13
oMt 24:29;
Rev 8:10; 9:1
pIsa 34:4
6:14
qJer 4:24;
Rev 16:20
6:15
rIsa 2:10,19,21
6:16
sHos 10:8;
Lk 23:30
6:17
tZep 1:14,15;
Rev 16:14
uPs 76:7
7:1
vDa 7:2
7:3
wEze 9:4;
xRev 22:4
7:4
yRev 9:16
zRev 14:1,3
7:9
aRev 5:9
bver 15
7:10
cPs 3:8;
Rev 12:10; 19:1

who sits on the throne,
and to the Lamb."

[11]All the angels were standing around the throne and around the elders[d] and the four living creatures.[e] They fell down on their faces[f] before the throne and worshiped God, [12]saying:

"Amen!
Praise and glory
and wisdom and thanks and honor
and power and strength
be to our God for ever and ever.
Amen!"[g]

[13]Then one of the elders asked me, "These in white robes—who are they, and where did they come from?"

[14]I answered, "Sir, you know."

And he said, "These are they who have come out of the great tribulation; they have washed their robes[h] and made them white in the blood of the Lamb.[i] [15]Therefore,

"they are before the throne of God[j]
and serve him[k] day and night in his temple;[l]
and he who sits on the throne will spread his tent
over them.[m]
[16]Never again will they hunger;
never again will they thirst.
The sun will not beat upon them,
nor any scorching heat.[n]
[17]For the Lamb at the center of the throne will be their
shepherd;[o]
he will lead them to springs of living water.
And God will wipe away every tear from their eyes."[p]

The Seventh Seal and the Golden Censer

8 When he opened the seventh seal,[q] there was silence in heaven for about half an hour.

[2]And I saw the seven angels[r] who stand before God, and to them were given seven trumpets.

[3]Another angel,[s] who had a golden censer, came and stood at the altar. He was given much incense to offer, with the prayers of all the saints,[t] on the golden altar[u] before the throne. [4]The smoke of the incense, together with the prayers of the saints, went up before God[v] from the angel's hand. [5]Then the angel took the censer, filled it with fire from the altar,[w] and hurled it on the earth; and there came peals of thunder,[x] rumblings, flashes of lightning and an earthquake.[y]

The Trumpets

[6]Then the seven angels who had the seven trumpets[z] prepared to sound them.

[7]The first angel sounded his trumpet, and there came hail and fire[a] mixed with blood, and it was hurled down upon the earth. A third[b] of the earth was burned up, a third of the trees were burned up, and all the green grass was burned up.[c]

7:11
d Rev 4:4
e Rev 4:6
f Rev 4:10
7:12
g Rev 5:12-14
7:14
h Rev 22:14
i Heb 9:14;
1Jn 1:7
7:15
j ver 9 k Rev 22:3
l Rev 11:19
m Isa 4:5,6;
Rev 21:3
7:16
n Isa 49:10
7:17
o Ps 23:1;
Jn 10:11
p Isa 25:8;
Rev 21:4
8:1
q Rev 6:1
8:2
r ver 6-13;
Rev 9:1,13;
11:15
8:3
s Rev 7:2
t Rev 5:8
u Ex 30:1-6;
Heb 9:4;
Rev 9:13
8:4
v Ps 141:2
8:5
w Lev 16:12,13
x Rev 4:5
y Rev 6:12
8:6
z ver 2
8:7
a Eze 38:22
b ver 7-12;
Rev 9:15,18;
12:4 c Rev 9:4

⁸The second angel sounded his trumpet, and something like a huge mountain,ᵈ all ablaze, was thrown into the sea. A thirdᵉ of the sea turned into blood,ᶠ ⁹a thirdᵍ of the living creatures in the sea died, and a third of the ships were destroyed.

¹⁰The third angel sounded his trumpet, and a great star, blazing like a torch, fell from the skyʰ on a third of the rivers and on the springs of waterⁱ— ¹¹the name of the star is Wormwood.ᵃ A thirdʲ of the waters turned bitter, and many people died from the waters that had become bitter.ᵏ

¹²The fourth angel sounded his trumpet, and a third of the sun was struck, a third of the moon, and a third of the stars, so that a thirdˡ of them turned dark.ᵐ A third of the day was without light, and also a third of the night.

¹³As I watched, I heard an eagle that was flying in midairⁿ call out in a loud voice: "Woe! Woe! Woeº to the inhabitants of the earth, because of the trumpet blasts about to be sounded by the other three angels!"

9 The fifth angel sounded his trumpet, and I saw a star that had fallen from the sky to the earth.ᵖ The star was given the key to the shaft of the Abyss.�q ²When he opened the Abyss, smoke rose from it like the smoke from a gigantic furnace.ʳ The sun and sky were darkenedˢ by the smoke from the Abyss. ³And out of the smoke locustsᵗ came down upon the earth and were given power like that of scorpionsᵘ of the earth. ⁴They were told not to harmᵛ the grass of the earth or any plant or tree,ʷ but only those people who did not have the seal of God on their foreheads.ˣ ⁵They were not given power to kill them, but only to torture them for five months.ʸ And the agony they suffered was like that of the sting of a scorpionᶻ when it strikes a man. ⁶During those days men will seek death, but will not find it; they will long to die, but death will elude them.ᵃ

⁷The locusts looked like horses prepared for battle.ᵇ On their heads they wore something like crowns of gold, and their faces resembled human faces.ᶜ ⁸Their hair was like women's hair, and their teeth were like lions' teeth.ᵈ ⁹They had breastplates like breastplates of iron, and the sound of their wings was like the thundering of many horses and chariots rushing into battle.ᵉ ¹⁰They had tails and stings like scorpions, and in their tails they had power to torment people for five months.ᶠ ¹¹They had as king over them the angel of the Abyss,ᵍ whose name in Hebrew is Abaddon, and in Greek, Apollyon.ᵇ

¹²The first woe is past; two other woes are yet to come.ʰ

¹³The sixth angel sounded his trumpet, and I heard a voice coming from the hornsᶜⁱ of the golden altar that is before God.ʲ ¹⁴It said to the sixth angel who had the trumpet, "Release the four angels who are bound at the great river Euphrates."ᵏ ¹⁵And the four angels who had been kept ready for this very hour and day and month and year were released to kill a third of mankind.ˡ ¹⁶The number of the mounted troops was two hundred million. I heard their number.ᵐ

¹⁷The horses and riders I saw in my vision looked like this: Their breastplates were fiery red, dark blue, and yellow as sulfur. The heads of the horses resembled the heads of lions, and out of their mouthsⁿ came fire, smoke and sulfur.º ¹⁸A third of mankind was killedᵖ by the

---

ᵃ11 That is, Bitterness　　ᵇ11 *Abaddon* and *Apollyon* mean *Destroyer.*　　ᶜ13 That is, projections

8:8
dJer 51:25
ever 7 fRev 16:3
8:9
gver 7
8:10
hIsa 14:12;
Rev 6:13; 9:1
iRev 14:7; 16:4
8:11
jver 7 kJer 9:15;
23:15
8:12
lver 7
mEx 10:21-23;
Rev 6:12,13
8:13
nRev 14:6;
19:17
oRev 9:12;
11:14
9:1
pRev 8:10
qver 2,11;
Lk 8:31
9:2
rGe 19:28;
Ex 19:18
sJoel 2:2,10
9:3
tEx 10:12-15
uver 5,10
9:4
vRev 6:6
wRev 8:7
xRev 7:2,3
9:5
yver 10 zver 3
9:6
aJob 3:21;
Jer 8:3;
Rev 6:16
9:7
bJoel 2:4
cDa 7:8
9:8
dJoel 1:6
9:9
eJoel 2:5
9:10
fver 3,5,19
9:11
gver 1,2
9:12
hRev 8:13
9:13
iEx 30:1-3
jRev 8:3
9:14
kRev 16:12
9:15
lver 18
9:16
mRev 5:11; 7:4
9:17
nRev 11:5
over 18
9:18
pver 15

three plagues of fire, smoke and sulfur q that came out of their mouths. ¹⁹The power of the horses was in their mouths and in their tails; for their tails were like snakes, having heads with which they inflict injury.

²⁰The rest of mankind that were not killed by these plagues still did not repent of the work of their hands; r they did not stop worshiping demons, s and idols of gold, silver, bronze, stone and wood—idols that cannot see or hear or walk. t ²¹Nor did they repent u of their murders, their magic arts, v their sexual immorality w or their thefts.

The Angel and the Little Scroll

10 Then I saw another mighty angel x coming down from heaven. He was robed in a cloud, with a rainbow above his head; his face was like the sun, y and his legs were like fiery pillars. z ²He was holding a little scroll, which lay open in his hand. He planted his right foot on the sea and his left foot on the land, ³and he gave a loud shout like the roar of a lion. When he shouted, the voices of the seven thunders a spoke. ⁴And when the seven thunders spoke, I was about to write; but I heard a voice from heaven say, "Seal up what the seven thunders have said and do not write it down." b

⁵Then the angel I had seen standing on the sea and on the land raised his right hand to heaven. c ⁶And he swore by him who lives for ever and ever, who created the heavens and all that is in them, the earth and all that is in it, and the sea and all that is in it, d and said, "There will be no more delay! e ⁷But in the days when the seventh angel is about to sound his trumpet, the mystery f of God will be accomplished, just as he announced to his servants the prophets."

⁸Then the voice that I had heard from heaven g spoke to me once more: "Go, take the scroll that lies open in the hand of the angel who is standing on the sea and on the land."

⁹So I went to the angel and asked him to give me the little scroll. He said to me, "Take it and eat it. It will turn your stomach sour, but in your mouth it will be as sweet as honey." h ¹⁰I took the little scroll from the angel's hand and ate it. It tasted as sweet as honey in my mouth, but when I had eaten it, my stomach turned sour. ¹¹Then I was told, "You must prophesy i again about many peoples, nations, languages and kings."

The Two Witnesses

11 I was given a reed like a measuring rod j and was told, "Go and measure the temple of God and the altar, and count the worshipers there. ²But exclude the outer court; k do not measure it, because it has been given to the Gentiles. l They will trample on the holy city m for 42 months. n ³And I will give power to my two witnesses, o and they will prophesy for 1,260 days, clothed in sackcloth." p ⁴These are the two olive trees q and the two lampstands that stand before the Lord of the earth. r ⁵If anyone tries to harm them, fire comes from their mouths and devours their enemies. s This is how anyone who wants to harm them must die. t ⁶These men have power to shut up the sky so that it will not rain during the time they are prophesying; and they have power to turn the waters into blood u and to strike the earth with every kind of plague as often as they want.

⁷Now when they have finished their testimony, the beast v that

comes up from the Abyss will attack them,ʷ and overpower and kill them. ⁸Their bodies will lie in the street of the great city, which is figuratively called Sodomˣ and Egypt, where also their Lord was crucified.ʸ ⁹For three and a half days men from every people, tribe, language and nation will gaze on their bodies and refuse them burial.ᶻ ¹⁰The inhabitants of the earthᵃ will gloat over them and will celebrate by sending each other gifts,ᵇ because these two prophets had tormented those who live on the earth.

¹¹But after the three and a half days a breath of life from God entered them,ᶜ and they stood on their feet, and terror struck those who saw them. ¹²Then they heard a loud voice from heaven saying to them, "Come up here."ᵈ And they went up to heaven in a cloud,ᵉ while their enemies looked on.

¹³At that very hour there was a severe earthquakeᶠ and a tenth of the city collapsed. Seven thousand people were killed in the earthquake, and the survivors were terrified and gave gloryᵍ to the God of heaven.ʰ

¹⁴The second woe has passed; the third woe is coming soon.ⁱ

The Seventh Trumpet

¹⁵The seventh angel sounded his trumpet,ʲ and there were loud voicesᵏ in heaven, which said:

> "The kingdom of the world has become the kingdom of
>   our Lord and of his Christ,ˡ
> and he will reign for ever and ever."ᵐ

¹⁶And the twenty-four elders,ⁿ who were seated on their thrones before God, fell on their faces and worshiped God, ¹⁷saying:

> "We give thanks to you, Lord God Almighty,ᵒ
>   the One who is and who was,
> because you have taken your great power
>   and have begun to reign.ᵖ
> ¹⁸The nations were angry;ᑫ
>   and your wrath has come.
> The time has come for judging the dead,
>   and for rewarding your servants the prophetsʳ
> and your saints and those who reverence your name,
>   both small and greatˢ—
> and for destroying those who destroy the earth."

¹⁹Then God's templeᵗ in heaven was opened, and within his temple was seen the ark of his covenant. And there came flashes of lightning, rumblings, peals of thunder, an earthquake and a great hailstorm.ᵘ

The Woman and the Dragon

12 A great and wondrous sign appeared in heaven: a woman clothed with the sun, with the moon under her feet and a crown of twelve stars on her head. ²She was pregnant and cried out in painᵛ as she was about to give birth. ³Then another sign appeared in heaven: an enormous red dragon with seven heads and ten hornsʷ and seven crownsˣ on his heads. ⁴His tail swept a thirdʸ of the stars out of the sky and flung them to the earth.ᶻ The dragon stood in front of the woman who was about to give birth, so that he might devour her childᵃ the

11:7
wDa 7:21
11:8
xIsa 1:9
yHeb 13:12
11:9
zPs 79:2,3
11:10
aRev 3:10
bEst 9:19,22
11:11
cEze 37:5,9,10,
14
11:12
dRev 4:1
e2Ki 2:11;
Ac 1:9
11:13
fRev 6:12
gRev 14:7
hRev 16:11
11:14
iRev 8:13
11:15
jRev 10:7
kRev 16:17;
19:1 lRev 12:10
mDa 2:44; 7:14,
27
11:16
nRev 4:4
11:17
oRev 1:8
pRev 19:6
11:18
qPs 2:1
rRev 10:7
sRev 19:5
11:19
tRev 15:5,8
uRev 16:21
12:2
vGal 4:19
12:3
wDa 7:7,20;
Rev 13:1
xRev 19:12
12:4
yRev 8:7
zDa 8:10
aMt 2:16

moment it was born. ⁵She gave birth to a son, a male child, who will rule all the nations with an iron scepter.ᵇ And her child was snatched up to God and to his throne. ⁶The woman fled into the desert to a place prepared for her by God, where she might be taken care of for 1,260 days.ᶜ

⁷And there was war in heaven. Michael and his angels fought against the dragon,ᵈ and the dragon and his angels fought back. ⁸But he was not strong enough, and they lost their place in heaven. ⁹The great dragon was hurled down—that ancient serpentᵉ called the devil,ᶠ or Satan, who leads the whole world astray.ᵍ He was hurled to the earth,ʰ and his angels with him.

¹⁰Then I heard a loud voice in heavenⁱ say:

"Now have come the salvation and the power and the
        kingdom of our God,
    and the authority of his Christ.
For the accuser of our brothers,ʲ
    who accuses them before our God day and night,
        has been hurled down.
¹¹They overcame him
    by the blood of the Lambᵏ
    and by the word of their testimony;ˡ
they did not love their lives so much
    as to shrink from death.ᵐ
¹²Therefore rejoice, you heavensⁿ
    and you who dwell in them!
But woeᵒ to the earth and the sea,ᵖ
    because the devil has gone down to you!
He is filled with fury,
    because he knows that his time is short."

¹³When the dragonᑫ saw that he had been hurled to the earth, he pursued the woman who had given birth to the male child.ʳ ¹⁴The woman was given the two wings of a great eagle,ˢ so that she might fly to the place prepared for her in the desert, where she would be taken care of for a time, times and half a time,ᵗ out of the serpent's reach. ¹⁵Then from his mouth the serpent spewed water like a river, to overtake the woman and sweep her away with the torrent. ¹⁶But the earth helped the woman by opening its mouth and swallowing the river that the dragon had spewed out of his mouth. ¹⁷Then the dragon was enraged at the woman and went off to make warᵘ against the rest of her offspringᵛ—those who obey God's commandmentsʷ and hold to the testimony of Jesus.ˣ

13

¹And the dragonᵃ stood on the shore of the sea.

The Beast out of the Sea

And I saw a beast coming out of the sea.ʸ He had ten horns and seven heads,ᶻ with ten crowns on his horns, and on each head a blasphemous name.ᵃ ²The beast I saw resembled a leopard,ᵇ but had feet like those of a bearᶜ and a mouth like that of a lion.ᵈ The dragon gave the beast his power and his throne and great authority.ᵉ ³One of

---

12:5
bPs 2:9;
Rev 2:27
12:6
cRev 11:2
12:7
dver 3
12:9
eGe 3:1-7
fMt 25:41
gRev 20:3,8,10
hLk 10:18;
Jn 12:31
12:10
iRev 11:15
jJob 1:9-11;
Zec 3:1
12:11
kRev 7:14
lRev 6:9
mLk 14:26
12:12
nPs 96:11;
Isa 49:13;
Rev 18:20
oRev 8:13
pRev 10:6
12:13
qver 3 rver 5
12:14
sEx 19:4
tDa 7:25
12:17
uRev 11:7
vGe 3:15
wRev 14:12
xRev 1:2
13:1
yDa 7:1-6;
Rev 15:2
zRev 12:3
aDa 11:36;
Rev 17:3
13:2
bDa 7:6 cDa 7:5
dDa 7:4
eRev 16:10

ᵃ1 Some late manuscripts *And I*

the heads of the beast seemed to have had a fatal wound, but the fatal wound had been healed. [f] The whole world was astonished [g] and followed the beast. [4]Men worshiped the dragon because he had given authority to the beast, and they also worshiped the beast and asked, "Who is like [h] the beast? Who can make war against him?"

[5]The beast was given a mouth to utter proud words and blasphemies [i] and to exercise his authority for forty-two months. [j] [6]He opened his mouth to blaspheme God, and to slander his name and his dwelling place and those who live in heaven. [k] [7]He was given power to make war [l] against the saints and to conquer them. And he was given authority over every tribe, people, language and nation. [m] [8]All inhabitants of the earth [n] will worship the beast—all whose names have not been written in the book of life [o] belonging to the Lamb that was slain from the creation of the world. [a] [p]

[9]He who has an ear, let him hear. [q]

> [10]If anyone is to go into captivity,
>   into captivity he will go.
>   If anyone is to be killed [b] with the sword,
>   with the sword he will be killed. [r]

This calls for patient endurance and faithfulness [s] on the part of the saints. [t]

The Beast out of the Earth

[11]Then I saw another beast, coming out of the earth. He had two horns like a lamb, but he spoke like a dragon. [12]He exercised all the authority [u] of the first beast on his behalf, [v] and made the earth and its inhabitants worship the first beast, [w] whose fatal wound had been healed. [x] [13]And he performed great and miraculous signs, [y] even causing fire to come down from heaven [z] to earth in full view of men. [14]Because of the signs [a] he was given power to do on behalf of the first beast, he deceived [b] the inhabitants of the earth. He ordered them to set up an image in honor of the beast who was wounded by the sword and yet lived. [15]He was given power to give breath to the image of the first beast, so that it could speak and cause all who refused to worship the image to be killed. [c] [16]He also forced everyone, small and great, [d] rich and poor, free and slave, to receive a mark on his right hand or on his forehead, [e] [17]so that no one could buy or sell unless he had the mark, [f] which is the name of the beast or the number of his name. [g]

[18]This calls for wisdom. [h] If anyone has insight, let him calculate the number of the beast, for it is man's number. [i] His number is 666.

The Lamb and the 144,000

14 Then I looked, and there before me was the Lamb, [j] standing on Mount Zion, [k] and with him 144,000 [l] who had his name and his Father's name [m] written on their foreheads. [2]And I heard a sound from heaven like the roar of rushing waters [n] and like a loud peal of thunder. The sound I heard was like that of harpists playing their harps. [o] [3]And they sang a new song [p] before the throne and before the four living

---

[a]8 Or *written from the creation of the world in the book of life belonging to the Lamb that was slain*
[b]10 Some manuscripts *anyone kills*

13:3
f ver 12,14
g Rev 17:8
13:4
h Ex 15:11
13:5
i Da 7:8,11,20, 25; 11:36; 2Th 2:4
j Rev 11:2
13:6
k Rev 12:12
13:7
l Da 7:21; Rev 11:7
m Rev 5:9
13:8
n Rev 3:10
o Rev 3:5; 20:12
p Mt 25:34
13:9
q Rev 2:7
13:10
r Jer 15:2; 43:11
s Heb 6:12
t Rev 14:12
13:12
u ver 4 v ver 14
w Rev 14:9,11
x ver 3
13:13
y Mt 24:24
z 1Ki 18:38; Rev 20:9
13:14
a 2Th 2:9,10
b Rev 12:9
13:15
c Da 3:3-6
13:16
d Rev 19:5
e Rev 14:9
13:17
f Rev 14:9
g Rev 14:11; 15:2
13:18
h Rev 17:9
i Rev 15:2; 21:17
14:1
j Rev 5:6 k Ps 2:6
l Rev 7:4
m Rev 3:12
14:2
n Rev 1:15
o Rev 5:8
14:3
p Rev 5:9

creatures and the elders. No one could learn the song except the 144,000 q who had been redeemed from the earth. [4]These are those who did not defile themselves with women, for they kept themselves pure. r They follow the Lamb wherever he goes. They were purchased from among men s and offered as firstfruits t to God and the Lamb. [5]No lie was found in their mouths; u they are blameless. v

The Three Angels

[6]Then I saw another angel flying in midair, w and he had the eternal gospel to proclaim to those who live on the earth x—to every nation, tribe, language and people. y [7]He said in a loud voice, "Fear God z and give him glory, a because the hour of his judgment has come. Worship him who made the heavens, the earth, the sea and the springs of water." b

[8]A second angel followed and said, "Fallen! Fallen is Babylon the Great, c which made all the nations drink the maddening wine of her adulteries." d

[9]A third angel followed them and said in a loud voice: "If anyone worships the beast and his image e and receives his mark on the forehead or on the hand, [10]he, too, will drink of the wine of God's fury, f which has been poured full strength into the cup of his wrath. g He will be tormented with burning sulfur in the presence of the holy angels and of the Lamb. [11]And the smoke of their torment rises for ever and ever. h There is no rest day or night for those who worship the beast and his image, or for anyone who receives the mark of his name." [12]This calls for patient endurance on the part of the saints i who obey God's commandments and remain faithful to Jesus.

[13]Then I heard a voice from heaven say, "Write: Blessed are the dead who die in the Lord j from now on."

"Yes," says the Spirit, "they will rest from their labor, for their deeds will follow them."

The Harvest of the Earth

[14]I looked, and there before me was a white cloud, and seated on the cloud was one "like a son of man" a k with a crown l of gold on his head and a sharp sickle in his hand. [15]Then another angel came out of the temple and called in a loud voice to him who was sitting on the cloud, "Take your sickle m and reap, because the time to reap has come, for the harvest n of the earth is ripe." [16]So he who was seated on the cloud swung his sickle over the earth, and the earth was harvested.

[17]Another angel came out of the temple in heaven, and he too had a sharp sickle. [18]Still another angel, who had charge of the fire, came from the altar and called in a loud voice to him who had the sharp sickle, "Take your sharp sickle and gather the clusters of grapes from the earth's vine, because its grapes are ripe." [19]The angel swung his sickle on the earth, gathered its grapes and threw them into the great winepress of God's wrath. o [20]They were trampled in the winepress p outside the city, q and blood flowed out of the press, rising as high as the horses' bridles for a distance of 1,600 stadia. b

### Cross references (margin)

14:3
q ver 1
14:4
r 2Co 11:2;
Rev 3:4
s Rev 5:9
t Jas 1:18
14:5
u Ps 32:2;
Zep 3:13
v Eph 5:27
14:6
w Rev 8:13
x Rev 3:10
y Rev 13:7
14:7
z Rev 15:4
a Rev 11:13
b Rev 8:10
14:8
c Isa 21:9;
Jer 51:8
d Rev 17:2,4;
18:3,9
14:9
e Rev 13:14
14:10
f Isa 51:17;
Jer 25:15
g Rev 18:6
14:11
h Isa 34:10;
Rev 19:3
14:12
i Rev 13:10
14:13
j 1Co 15:18;
1Th 4:16
14:14
k Da 7:13;
Rev 1:13
l Rev 6:2
14:15
m Joel 3:13
n Jer 51:33
14:19
o Rev 19:15
14:20
p Isa 63:3
q Heb 13:12;
Rev 11:8

a14 Daniel 7:13   b20 That is, about 180 miles (about 300 kilometers)

Seven Angels With Seven Plagues

15 I saw in heaven another great and marvelous sign:[r] seven angels[s] with the seven last plagues[t]—last, because with them God's wrath is completed. [2]And I saw what looked like a sea of glass[u] mixed with fire and, standing beside the sea, those who had been victorious over the beast and his image[v] and over the number of his name. They held harps given them by God [3]and sang the song of Moses[w] the servant of God and the song of the Lamb:

> "Great and marvelous are your deeds,[x]
>   Lord God Almighty.
> Just and true are your ways,[y]
>   King of the ages.
> [4]Who will not fear you, O Lord,[z]
>   and bring glory to your name?
> For you alone are holy.
> All nations will come
>   and worship before you,[a]
> for your righteous acts have been revealed."

[5]After this I looked and in heaven the temple,[b] that is, the tabernacle of the Testimony,[c] was opened. [6]Out of the temple[d] came the seven angels with the seven plagues.[e] They were dressed in clean, shining linen and wore golden sashes around their chests.[f] [7]Then one of the four living creatures[g] gave to the seven angels seven golden bowls filled with the wrath of God, who lives for ever and ever. [8]And the temple was filled with smoke[h] from the glory of God and from his power, and no one could enter the temple[i] until the seven plagues of the seven angels were completed.

The Seven Bowls of God's Wrath

16 Then I heard a loud voice from the temple saying to the seven angels,[j] "Go, pour out the seven bowls of God's wrath on the earth."

[2]The first angel went and poured out his bowl on the land,[k] and ugly and painful sores[l] broke out on the people who had the mark of the beast and worshiped his image.[m]

[3]The second angel poured out his bowl on the sea, and it turned into blood like that of a dead man, and every living thing in the sea died.[n]

[4]The third angel poured out his bowl on the rivers and springs of water,[o] and they became blood.[p] [5]Then I heard the angel in charge of the waters say:

> "You are just in these judgments,[q]
>   you who are and who were,[r] the Holy One,[s]
>   because you have so judged;
> [6]for they have shed the blood of your saints and
>   prophets,
>   and you have given them blood to drink[t] as they
>   deserve."

[7]And I heard the altar[u] respond:

> "Yes, Lord God Almighty,
>   true and just are your judgments."[v]

15:1
r Rev 12:1,3
s Rev 16:1
t Lev 26:21
15:2
u Rev 4:6
v Rev 13:14
15:3
w Ex 15:1;
Dt 32:4
x Ps 111:2
y Ps 145:17
15:4
z Jer 10:7
a Isa 66:23
15:5
b Rev 11:19
c Nu 1:50
15:6
d Rev 14:15
e ver 1 f Rev 1:13
15:7
g Rev 4:6
15:8
h Isa 6:4
i Ex 40:34,35;
1Ki 8:10,11;
2Ch 5:13,14
16:1
j Rev 15:1
16:2
k Rev 8:7
l Ex 9:9-11
m Rev 13:15-17
16:3
n Ex 7:17-21;
Rev 8:8,9
16:4
o Rev 8:10
p Ex 7:17-21
16:5
q Rev 15:3
r Rev 1:4
s Rev 15:4
16:6
t Isa 49:26;
Rev 17:6
16:7
u Rev 6:9
v Rev 15:3; 19:2

16:8
wRev 8:12
xRev 14:18
16:9
yver 11,21
zRev 2:21
aRev 11:13
16:10
bRev 13:2
cRev 9:2
16:11
dver 9,21
eRev 11:13
fver 2 gRev 2:21
16:12
hRev 9:11
iIsa 41:2
16:13
jRev 12:3
kRev 13:1
lRev 19:20
16:14
m1Ti 4:1
nRev 17:14
16:15
oLk 12:37
16:16
pRev 9:11
q2Ki 23:29,30
16:17
rEph 2:2
sRev 14:15
tRev 11:15
uRev 21:6
16:18
vRev 4:5
wRev 6:12
xDa 12:1
16:19
yRev 17:18
zRev 18:5
aRev 14:8
bRev 14:10
16:20
cRev 6:14
16:21
dRev 11:19
eEx 9:23-25
17:1
fRev 15:1
gRev 21:9
hRev 16:19
iRev 19:2
jJer 51:13
17:2
kRev 14:8; 18:3
17:3
lRev 12:6,14
mRev 13:1
nRev 12:3
17:4
oRev 18:16
pJer 51:7;
Rev 18:6
17:5
qRev 14:8

[8]The fourth angel[w] poured out his bowl on the sun, and the sun was given power to scorch people with fire.[x] [9]They were seared by the intense heat and they cursed the name of God,[y] who had control over these plagues, but they refused to repent[z] and glorify him.[a]

[10]The fifth angel poured out his bowl on the throne of the beast,[b] and his kingdom was plunged into darkness.[c] Men gnawed their tongues in agony [11]and cursed[d] the God of heaven[e] because of their pains and their sores,[f] but they refused to repent of what they had done.[g]

[12]The sixth angel poured out his bowl on the great river Euphrates,[h] and its water was dried up to prepare the way for the kings from the East.[i] [13]Then I saw three evil[a] spirits that looked like frogs; they came out of the mouth of the dragon,[j] out of the mouth of the beast[k] and out of the mouth of the false prophet.[l] [14]They are spirits of demons[m] performing miraculous signs, and they go out to the kings of the whole world, to gather them for the battle[n] on the great day of God Almighty.

[15]"Behold, I come like a thief! Blessed is he who stays awake[o] and keeps his clothes with him, so that he may not go naked and be shamefully exposed."

[16]Then they gathered the kings together to the place that in Hebrew[p] is called Armageddon.[q]

[17]The seventh angel poured out his bowl into the air,[r] and out of the temple[s] came a loud voice[t] from the throne, saying, "It is done!"[u] [18]Then there came flashes of lightning, rumblings, peals of thunder[v] and a severe earthquake.[w] No earthquake like it has ever occurred since man has been on earth,[x] so tremendous was the quake. [19]The great city[y] split into three parts, and the cities of the nations collapsed. God remembered[z] Babylon the Great[a] and gave her the cup filled with the wine of the fury of his wrath.[b] [20]Every island fled away and the mountains could not be found.[c] [21]From the sky huge hailstones[d] of about a hundred pounds each fell upon men. And they cursed God on account of the plague of hail,[e] because the plague was so terrible.

The Woman on the Beast

17 One of the seven angels[f] who had the seven bowls[g] came and said to me, "Come, I will show you the punishment[h] of the great prostitute,[i] who sits on many waters.[j] [2]With her the kings of the earth committed adultery and the inhabitants of the earth were intoxicated with the wine of her adulteries."[k]

[3]Then the angel carried me away in the Spirit into a desert.[l] There I saw a woman sitting on a scarlet beast that was covered with blasphemous names[m] and had seven heads and ten horns.[n] [4]The woman was dressed in purple and scarlet, and was glittering with gold, precious stones and pearls.[o] She held a golden cup[p] in her hand, filled with abominable things and the filth of her adulteries. [5]This title was written on her forehead:

MYSTERY

BABYLON THE GREAT[q]

THE MOTHER OF PROSTITUTES

AND OF THE ABOMINATIONS OF THE EARTH.

---

[a]13 Greek *unclean*

⁶I saw that the woman was drunk with the blood of the saints,ʳ the blood of those who bore testimony to Jesus.

When I saw her, I was greatly astonished. ⁷Then the angel said to me: "Why are you astonished? I will explain to you the mysteryˢ of the woman and of the beast she rides, which has the seven heads and ten horns.ᵗ ⁸The beast, which you saw, once was, now is not, and will come up out of the Abyss and go to his destruction.ᵘ The inhabitants of the earthᵛ whose names have not been written in the book of lifeʷ from the creation of the world will be astonishedˣ when they see the beast, because he once was, now is not, and yet will come.

⁹"This calls for a mind with wisdom.ʸ The seven heads are seven hills on which the woman sits. ¹⁰They are also seven kings. Five have fallen, one is, the other has not yet come; but when he does come, he must remain for a little while. ¹¹The beast who once was, and now is not,ᶻ is an eighth king. He belongs to the seven and is going to his destruction.

¹²"The ten hornsᵃ you saw are ten kings who have not yet received a kingdom, but who for one hourᵇ will receive authority as kings along with the beast. ¹³They have one purpose and will give their power and authority to the beast.ᶜ ¹⁴They will make warᵈ against the Lamb, but the Lamb will overcome them because he is Lord of lords and King of kingsᵉ—and with him will be his called, chosenᶠ and faithful followers."

¹⁵Then the angel said to me, "The watersᵍ you saw, where the prostitute sits, are peoples, multitudes, nations and languages.ʰ ¹⁶The beast and the ten horns you saw will hate the prostitute. They will bring her to ruinⁱ and leave her naked;ʲ they will eat her fleshᵏ and burn her with fire.ˡ ¹⁷For God has put it into their hearts to accomplish his purpose by agreeing to give the beast their power to rule, until God's words are fulfilled.ᵐ ¹⁸The woman you saw is the great cityⁿ that rules over the kings of the earth."

The Fall of Babylon

18 After this I saw another angelᵒ coming down from heaven.ᵖ He had great authority, and the earth was illuminated by his splendor.�q ²With a mighty voice he shouted:

"Fallen! Fallen is Babylon the Great!ʳ
    She has become a home for demons
and a haunt for every evilᵃ spirit,
    a haunt for every unclean and detestable bird.ˢ
³For all the nations have drunk
    the maddening wine of her adulteries.ᵗ
The kings of the earth committed adultery with her,ᵘ
    and the merchants of the earth grew richᵛ from her
        excessive luxuries."ʷ

⁴Then I heard another voice from heaven say:

"Come out of her, my people,ˣ
    so that you will not share in her sins,

ᵃ2 Greek *unclean*

17:6
ʳRev 18:24
17:7
ˢver 5 ᵗver 3
17:8
ᵘRev 13:10
ᵛRev 3:10
ʷRev 13:8
ˣRev 13:3
17:9
ʸRev 13:18
17:11
ᶻver 8
17:12
ᵃRev 12:3
ᵇRev 18:10,17, 19
17:13
ᶜver 17
17:14
ᵈRev 16:14
ᵉ1Ti 6:15; Rev 19:16
ᶠMt 22:14
17:15
ᵍIsa 8:7
ʰRev 13:7
17:16
ⁱRev 18:17,19
ʲEze 16:37,39
ᵏRev 19:18
ˡRev 18:8
17:17
ᵐRev 10:7
17:18
ⁿRev 16:19
18:1
ᵒRev 17:1
ᵖRev 10:1
qEze 43:2
18:2
ʳRev 14:8
ˢIsa 13:21,22; Jer 50:39
18:3
ᵗRev 14:8
ᵘRev 17:2
ᵛEze 27:9-25
ʷver 7,9
18:4
ˣIsa 48:20; Jer 50:8; 2Co 6:17

so that you will not receive any of her plagues;
⁵for her sins are piled up to heaven,ʸ
    and God has rememberedᶻ her crimes.
⁶Give back to her as she has given;
    pay her backᵃ double for what she has done.
    Mix her a double portion from her own cup.ᵇ
⁷Give her as much torture and grief
    as the glory and luxury she gave herself.ᶜ
In her heart she boasts,
    'I sit as queen; I am not a widow,
    and I will never mourn.'ᵈ
⁸Therefore in one dayᵉ her plagues will overtake
    her:
    death, mourning and famine.
She will be consumed by fire,ᶠ
    for mighty is the Lord God who judges her.

⁹"When the kings of the earth who committed adultery with herᵍ
and shared her luxury see the smoke of her burning,ʰ they will weep
and mourn over her.ⁱ ¹⁰Terrified at her torment, they will stand far offʲ
and cry:

    " 'Woe! Woe, O great city,ᵏ
    O Babylon, city of power!
    In one hourˡ your doom has come!'

¹¹"The merchantsᵐ of the earth will weep and mourn over her because no one buys their cargoes any moreⁿ— ¹²cargoes of gold, silver,
precious stones and pearls; fine linen, purple, silk and scarlet cloth;
every sort of citron wood, and articles of every kind made of ivory,
costly wood, bronze, iron and marble;ᵒ ¹³cargoes of cinnamon and
spice, of incense, myrrh and frankincense, of wine and olive oil, of fine
flour and wheat; cattle and sheep; horses and carriages; and bodies and
souls of men.ᵖ

¹⁴"They will say, 'The fruit you longed for is gone from you. All your
riches and splendor have vanished, never to be recovered.' ¹⁵The merchants who sold these things and gained their wealth from her�q will
stand far off, terrified at her torment. They will weep and mournʳ ¹⁶and
cry out:

    " 'Woe! Woe, O great city,
    dressed in fine linen, purple and scarlet,
    and glittering with gold, precious stones and pearls!ˢ
    ¹⁷In one hourᵗ such great wealth has been brought to
    ruin!'ᵘ

"Every sea captain, and all who travel by ship, the sailors, and all
who earn their living from the sea,ᵛ will stand far off. ¹⁸When they see
the smoke of her burning, they will exclaim, 'Was there ever a city like
this great city?'ʷ ¹⁹They will throw dust on their heads,ˣ and with
weeping and mourning cry out:

    " 'Woe! Woe, O great city,
    where all who had ships on the sea

18:5
y Jer 51:9
z Rev 16:19
18:6
a Ps 137:8;
Jer 50:15,29
b Rev 14:10;
16:19
18:7
c Eze 28:2-8
d Isa 47:7,8;
Zep 2:15
18:8
e ver 10;
Isa 47:9;
Jer 50:31,32
f Rev 17:16
18:9
g Rev 17:2,4
h ver 18;
Rev 19:3
i Eze 26:17,18
18:10
j ver 15,17
k ver 16,19
l Rev 17:12
18:11
m Eze 27:27
n ver 3
18:12
o Rev 17:4
18:13
p Eze 27:13;
1Ti 1:10
18:15
q ver 3
r Eze 27:31
18:16
s Rev 17:4
18:17
t ver 10
u Rev 17:16
v Eze 27:28-30
18:18
w Eze 27:32;
Rev 13:4
18:19
x Jos 7:6;
Eze 27:30

became rich through her wealth!
    In one hour she has been brought to ruin!'[y]
    [20]Rejoice over her, O heaven!'[z]
      Rejoice, saints and apostles and prophets!
      God has judged her for the way she treated you.' "[a]

[21]Then a mighty angel[b] picked up a boulder the size of a large millstone and threw it into the sea,[c] and said:

    "With such violence
      the great city of Babylon will be thrown down,
      never to be found again.
    [22]The music of harpists and musicians, flute players and
        trumpeters,
      will never be heard in you again.[d]
    No workman of any trade
      will ever be found in you again.
    The sound of a millstone
      will never be heard in you again.[e]
    [23]The light of a lamp
      will never shine in you again.
    The voice of bridegroom and bride
      will never be heard in you again.[f]
    Your merchants were the world's great men.[g]
    By your magic spell[h] all the nations were led astray.
    [24]In her was found the blood of prophets and of the
        saints,[i]
    and of all who have been killed on the earth."[j]

Hallelujah!

19 After this I heard what sounded like the roar of a great multitude[k] in heaven shouting:

    "Hallelujah!
    Salvation[l] and glory and power[m] belong to our God,
   2 for true and just are his judgments.
    He has condemned the great prostitute
      who corrupted the earth by her adulteries.
    He has avenged on her the blood of his servants."[n]

[3]And again they shouted:

    "Hallelujah!
    The smoke from her goes up for ever and ever."[o]

[4]The twenty-four elders[p] and the four living creatures[q] fell down[r] and worshiped God, who was seated on the throne. And they cried:

    "Amen, Hallelujah!"

[5]Then a voice came from the throne, saying:

    "Praise our God,
      all you his servants,[s]
    you who fear him,
      both small and great!"[t]

18:19
y Rev 17:16
18:20
z Jer 51:48;
Rev 12:12
a Rev 19:2
18:21
b Rev 5:2
c Jer 51:63
18:22
d Isa 24:8;
Eze 26:13
e Jer 25:10
18:23
f Jer 7:34; 16:9;
25:10 g Isa 23:8
h Na 3:4
18:24
i Rev 16:6; 17:6
j Jer 51:49
19:1
k Rev 11:15
l Rev 7:10
m Rev 4:11
19:2
n Dt 32:43;
Rev 6:10
19:3
o Isa 34:10;
Rev 14:11
19:4
p Rev 4:4
q Rev 4:6
r Rev 5:14
19:5
s Ps 134:1
t Rev 11:18;
20:12

6Then I heard what sounded like a great multitude,[u] like the roar of rushing waters and like loud peals of thunder, shouting:

> "Hallelujah!
> For our Lord God Almighty reigns.
> 7Let us rejoice and be glad
> and give him glory!
> For the wedding of the Lamb[v] has come,
> and his bride[w] has made herself ready.
> 8Fine linen, bright and clean,
> was given her to wear."

(Fine linen stands for the righteous acts[x] of the saints.)

9Then the angel said to me,[y] "Write:[z] 'Blessed are those who are invited to the wedding supper of the Lamb!' "[a] And he added, "These are the true words of God."[b]

10At this I fell at his feet to worship him.[c] But he said to me, "Do not do it! I am a fellow servant with you and with your brothers who hold to the testimony of Jesus. Worship God![d] For the testimony of Jesus[e] is the spirit of prophecy."

The Rider on the White Horse

11I saw heaven standing open and there before me was a white horse, whose rider[f] is called Faithful and True.[g] With justice he judges and makes war.[h] 12His eyes are like blazing fire,[i] and on his head are many crowns.[j] He has a name written on him that no one knows but he himself.[k] 13He is dressed in a robe dipped in blood,[l] and his name is the Word of God.[m] 14The armies of heaven were following him, riding on white horses and dressed in fine linen,[n] white and clean. 15Out of his mouth comes a sharp sword[o] with which to strike down[p] the nations. "He will rule them with an iron scepter."[a][q] He treads the winepress[r] of the fury of the wrath of God Almighty. 16On his robe and on his thigh he has this name written:[s]

KING OF KINGS AND LORD OF LORDS.[t]

17And I saw an angel standing in the sun, who cried in a loud voice to all the birds[u] flying in midair,[v] "Come,[w] gather together for the great supper of God, 18so that you may eat the flesh of kings, generals, and mighty men, of horses and their riders, and the flesh of all people,[x] free and slave, small and great."

19Then I saw the beast and the kings of the earth[y] and their armies gathered together to make war against the rider on the horse and his army. 20But the beast was captured, and with him the false prophet[z] who had performed the miraculous signs on his behalf.[a] With these signs he had deluded those who had received the mark of the beast and worshiped his image. The two of them were thrown alive into the fiery lake[b] of burning sulfur.[c] 21The rest of them were killed with the sword[d] that came out of the mouth of the rider on the horse,[e] and all the birds[f] gorged themselves on their flesh.

[a]15 Psalm 2:9

### Cross references (margin)

19:6
u Rev 11:15
19:7
v Mt 22:2; 25:10; Eph 5:32
w Rev 21:2,9
19:8
x Rev 15:4
19:9
y ver 10
z Rev 1:19
a Lk 14:15
b Rev 21:5; 22:6
19:10
c Rev 22:8
d Ac 10:25,26; Rev 22:9
e Rev 12:17
19:11
f Rev 6:2
g Rev 3:14
h Isa 11:4
19:12
i Rev 1:14
j Rev 6:2
k Rev 2:17
19:13
l Isa 63:2,3
m Jn 1:1
19:14
n ver 8
19:15
o Rev 1:16
p Isa 11:4; 2Th 2:8
q Ps 2:9; Rev 2:27
r Rev 14:20
19:16
s ver 12
t Rev 17:14
19:17
u ver 21
v Rev 8:13
w Eze 39:17
19:18
x Eze 39:18-20
19:19
y Rev 16:14,16
19:20
z Rev 16:13
a Rev 13:12
b Da 7:11; Rev 20:10,14, 15; 21:8
c Rev 14:10
19:21
d ver 15 e ver 11, 19 f ver 17

The Thousand Years

20 And I saw an angel coming down out of heaven,[g] having the key[h] to the Abyss and holding in his hand a great chain. [2]He seized the dragon, that ancient serpent, who is the devil, or Satan,[i] and bound him for a thousand years.[j] [3]He threw him into the Abyss, and locked and sealed[k] it over him, to keep him from deceiving the nations[l] anymore until the thousand years were ended. After that, he must be set free for a short time.

[4]I saw thrones[m] on which were seated those who had been given authority to judge. And I saw the souls of those who had been beheaded[n] because of their testimony for Jesus and because of the word of God. They had not worshiped the beast[o] or his image and had not received his mark on their foreheads or their hands.[p] They came to life and reigned with Christ a thousand years. [5](The rest of the dead did not come to life until the thousand years were ended.) This is the first resurrection.[q] [6]Blessed[r] and holy are those who have part in the first resurrection. The second death[s] has no power over them, but they will be priests[t] of God and of Christ and will reign with him[u] for a thousand years.

Satan's Doom

[7]When the thousand years are over,[v] Satan will be released from his prison [8]and will go out to deceive the nations[w] in the four corners of the earth—Gog and Magog[x]—to gather them for battle.[y] In number they are like the sand on the seashore.[z] [9]They marched across the breadth of the earth and surrounded[a] the camp of God's people, the city he loves. But fire came down from heaven[b] and devoured them. [10]And the devil, who deceived them,[c] was thrown into the lake of burning sulfur, where the beast and the false prophet had been thrown. They will be tormented day and night for ever and ever.[d]

The Dead Are Judged

[11]Then I saw a great white throne[e] and him who was seated on it. Earth and sky fled from his presence, and there was no place for them. [12]And I saw the dead, great and small, standing before the throne, and books were opened.[f] Another book was opened, which is the book of life.[g] The dead were judged according to what they had done[h] as recorded in the books. [13]The sea gave up the dead that were in it, and death and Hades[i] gave up the dead[j] that were in them, and each person was judged according to what he had done. [14]Then death[k] and Hades were thrown into the lake of fire. The lake of fire is the second death. [15]If anyone's name was not found written in the book of life,[l] he was thrown into the lake of fire.

The New Jerusalem

21 Then I saw a new heaven and a new earth,[m] for the first heaven and the first earth had passed away, and there was no longer any sea. [2]I saw the Holy City, the new Jerusalem, coming down out of heaven from God,[n] prepared as a bride beautifully dressed for her husband. [3]And I heard a loud voice from the throne saying, "Now the dwelling of God is with men, and he will live with them. They will be

20:1
g Rev 10:1
h Rev 1:18
20:2
i Rev 12:9
j 2Pe 2:4
20:3
k Da 6:17
l Rev 12:9
20:4
m Da 7:9
n Rev 6:9
o Rev 13:12
p Rev 13:16
20:5
q Lk 14:14;
Php 3:11
20:6
r Rev 14:13
s Rev 2:11
t Rev 1:6 u ver 4
20:7
v ver 2
20:8
w ver 3,10
x Eze 38:2; 39:1
y Rev 16:14
z Heb 11:12
20:9
a Eze 38:9,16
b Eze 38:22;
39:6
20:10
c Rev 19:20
d Rev 14:10,11
20:11
e Rev 4:2
20:12
f Da 7:10
g Rev 3:5
h Jer 17:10;
Mt 16:27;
Rev 2:23
20:13
i Rev 6:8
j Isa 26:19
20:14
k 1Co 15:26
20:15
l ver 12
21:1
m Isa 65:17;
2Pe 3:13
21:2
n Heb 11:10;
12:22; Rev 3:12

his people, and God himself will be with them and be their God. o 4He will wipe every tear from their eyes. p There will be no more death q or mourning or crying or pain, r for the old order of things has passed away."

5He who was seated on the throne s said, "I am making everything new!" Then he said, "Write this down, for these words are trustworthy and true." t

6He said to me: "It is done. u I am the Alpha and the Omega, v the Beginning and the End. To him who is thirsty I will give to drink without cost from the spring of the water of life. w 7He who overcomes will inherit all this, and I will be his God and he will be my son. 8But the cowardly, the unbelieving, the vile, the murderers, the sexually immoral, those who practice magic arts, the idolaters and all liars x—their place will be in the fiery lake of burning sulfur. This is the second death." y

9One of the seven angels who had the seven bowls full of the seven last plagues z came and said to me, "Come, I will show you the bride, a the wife of the Lamb." 10And he carried me away b in the Spirit c to a mountain great and high, and showed me the Holy City, Jerusalem, coming down out of heaven from God. 11It shone with the glory of God, d and its brilliance was like that of a very precious jewel, like a jasper, clear as crystal. e 12It had a great, high wall with twelve gates, and with twelve angels at the gates. On the gates were written the names of the twelve tribes of Israel. f 13There were three gates on the east, three on the north, three on the south and three on the west. 14The wall of the city had twelve foundations, and on them were the names of the twelve apostles of the Lamb.

15The angel who talked with me had a measuring rod g of gold to measure the city, its gates and its walls. 16The city was laid out like a square, as long as it was wide. He measured the city with the rod and found it to be 12,000 stadia a in length, and as wide and high as it is long. 17He measured its wall and it was 144 cubits b thick, c by man's measurement, which the angel was using. 18The wall was made of jasper, h and the city of pure gold, as pure as glass. i 19The foundations of the city walls were decorated with every kind of precious stone. j The first foundation was jasper, the second sapphire, the third chalcedony, the fourth emerald, 20the fifth sardonyx, the sixth carnelian, k the seventh chrysolite, the eighth beryl, the ninth topaz, the tenth chrysoprase, the eleventh jacinth, and the twelfth amethyst. d 21The twelve gates were twelve pearls, each gate made of a single pearl. The great street of the city was of pure gold, like transparent glass. l

22I did not see a temple m in the city, because the Lord God Almighty n and the Lamb o are its temple. 23The city does not need the sun or the moon to shine on it, for the glory of God gives it light, p and the Lamb is its lamp. 24The nations will walk by its light, and the kings of the earth will bring their splendor into it. q 25On no day will its gates ever be shut, r for there will be no night there. s 26The glory and honor of the nations will be brought into it. 27Nothing impure will ever enter it, nor

---

21:3
o2Co 6:16
21:4
pRev 7:17
q1Co 15:26;
Rev 20:14
rIsa 35:10;
65:19
21:5
sRev 4:9; 20:11
tRev 19:9
21:6
uRev 16:17
vRev 1:8; 22:13
wJn 4:10
21:8
x1Co 6:9
yRev 2:11
21:9
zRev 15:1,6,7
aRev 19:7
21:10
bRev 17:3
cRev 1:10
21:11
dRev 15:8; 22:5
eRev 4:6
21:12
fEze 48:30-34
21:15
gRev 11:1
21:18
hver 11 iver 21
21:19
jIsa 54:11,12
21:20
kRev 4:3
21:21
lver 18
21:22
mJn 4:21,23
nRev 1:8
oRev 5:6
21:23
pIsa 24:23;
60:19,20;
Rev 22:5
21:24
qIsa 60:3,5
21:25
rIsa 60:11
sZec 14:7;
Rev 22:5

---

a16 That is, about 1,400 miles (about 2,200 kilometers)   *b17* That is, about 200 feet (about 65 meters)   *c17* Or *high*   *d20* The precise identification of some of these precious stones is uncertain.

will anyone who does what is shameful or deceitful,ᵗ but only those whose names are written in the Lamb's book of life.

The River of Life

22 Then the angel showed me the river of the water of life, as clear as crystal,ᵘ flowingᵛ from the throne of God and of the Lamb ²down the middle of the great street of the city. On each side of the river stood the tree of life,ʷ bearing twelve crops of fruit, yielding its fruit every month. And the leaves of the tree are for the healing of the nations.ˣ ³No longer will there be any curse.ʸ The throne of God and of the Lamb will be in the city, and his servants will serve him.ᶻ ⁴They will see his face,ᵃ and his name will be on their foreheads.ᵇ ⁵There will be no more night.ᶜ They will not need the light of a lamp or the light of the sun, for the Lord God will give them light.ᵈ And they will reign for ever and ever.ᵉ

⁶The angel said to me,ᶠ "These words are trustworthy and true.ᵍ The Lord, the God of the spirits of the prophets,ʰ sent his angelⁱ to show his servants the things that must soon take place."

Jesus Is Coming

⁷"Behold, I am coming soon!ʲ Blessedᵏ is he who keeps the words of the prophecy in this book."

⁸I, John, am the one who heard and saw these things.ˡ And when I had heard and seen them, I fell down to worship at the feetᵐ of the angel who had been showing them to me. ⁹But he said to me, "Do not do it! I am a fellow servant with you and with your brothers the prophets and of all who keep the words of this book.ⁿ Worship God!"ᵒ

¹⁰Then he told me, "Do not seal upᵖ the words of the prophecy of this book, because the time is near.�q ¹¹Let him who does wrong continue to do wrong; let him who is vile continue to be vile; let him who does right continue to do right; and let him who is holy continue to be holy."ʳ

¹²"Behold, I am coming soon!ˢ My reward is with me,ᵗ and I will give to everyone according to what he has done. ¹³I am the Alpha and the Omega,ᵘ the First and the Last,ᵛ the Beginning and the End.ʷ

¹⁴"Blessed are those who wash their robes, that they may have the right to the tree of lifeˣ and may go through the gatesʸ into the city.ᶻ ¹⁵Outsideᵃ are the dogs,ᵇ those who practice magic arts, the sexually immoral, the murderers, the idolaters and everyone who loves and practices falsehood.

¹⁶"I, Jesus,ᶜ have sent my angel to give youᵃ this testimony for the churches.ᵈ I am the Rootᵉ and the Offspring of David, and the bright Morning Star."ᶠ

¹⁷The Spiritᵍ and the bride say, "Come!" And let him who hears say, "Come!" Whoever is thirsty, let him come; and whoever wishes, let him take the free gift of the water of life.

¹⁸I warn everyone who hears the words of the prophecy of this book: If anyone adds anything to them,ʰ God will add to him the plagues

---

ᵃ16 The Greek is plural.

21:27
tIsa 52:1;
Joel 3:17;
Rev 22:14,15
22:1
uRev 4:6
vEze 47:1;
Zec 14:8
22:2
wRev 2:7
xEze 47:12
22:3
yZec 14:11
zRev 7:15
22:4
aMt 5:8
bRev 14:1
22:5
cRev 21:25
dRev 21:23
eDa 7:27;
Rev 20:4
22:6
fRev 1:1
gRev 19:9; 21:5
hHeb 12:9
iver 16
22:7
jRev 3:11
kRev 1:3
22:8
lRev 1:1
mRev 19:10
22:9
nver 10,18,19
oRev 19:10
22:10
pDa 8:26;
Rev 10:4
qRev 1:3
22:11
rEze 3:27;
Da 12:10
22:12
sver 7,20
tIsa 40:10
22:13
uRev 1:8
vRev 1:17
wRev 21:6
22:14
xRev 2:7
yRev 21:12
zRev 21:27
22:15
a1Co 6:9,10;
Gal 5:19-21;
Col 3:5,6
bPhp 3:2
22:16
cRev 1:1
dRev 1:4
eRev 5:5
f2Pe 1:19;
Rev 2:28
22:17
gRev 2:7
22:18
hDt 4:2; Pr 30:6

22:18
iRev 15:6-16:21
22:19
jDt 4:2
22:20
kRev 1:2
lICo 16:22
22:21
mRo 16:20

described in this book. [i] [19]And if anyone takes words away[j] from this book of prophecy, God will take away from him his share in the tree of life and in the holy city, which are described in this book.

[20]He who testifies to these things[k] says, "Yes, I am coming soon." Amen. Come, Lord Jesus. [l]

[21]The grace of the Lord Jesus be with God's people. [m] Amen.

Table
of Weights
and
Measures

BIBLICAL UNIT		APPROXIMATE AMERICAN EQUIVALENT	APPROXIMATE METRIC EQUIVALENT
WEIGHTS			
talent	*(60 minas)*	75 pounds	34 kilograms
mina	*(50 shekels)*	1 1/4 pounds	0.6 kilogram
shekel	*(2 bekas)*	2/5 ounce	11.5 grams
pim	*(2/3 shekel)*	1/3 ounce	7.6 grams
beka	*(10 gerahs)*	1/5 ounce	5.5 grams
gerah		1/50 ounce	0.6 gram
LENGTH			
cubit		18 inches	0.5 meter
span		9 inches	23 centimeters
handbreadth		3 inches	8 centimeters
CAPACITY			
Dry Measure			
cor [homer]	*(10 ephahs)*	6 bushels	220 liters
lethek	*(5 ephahs)*	3 bushels	110 liters
ephah	*(10 omers)*	3/5 bushel	22 liters
seah	*(1/3 ephah)*	7 quarts	7.3 liters
omer	*(1/10 ephah)*	2 quarts	2 liters
cab	*(1/18 ephah)*	1 quart	1 liter
Liquid Measure			
bath	*(1 ephah)*	6 gallons	22 liters
hin	*(1/6 bath)*	4 quarts	4 liters
log	*(1/72 bath)*	1/3 quart	0.3 liter

The figures of the table are calculated on the basis of a shekel equaling 11.5 grams, a cubit equaling 18 inches and an ephah equaling 22 liters. The quart referred to is either a dry quart (slightly larger than a liter) or a liquid quart (slightly smaller than a liter), whichever is applicable. The ton referred to in the footnotes is the American ton of 2,000 pounds.

This table is based upon the best available information, but it is not intended to be mathematically precise; like the measurement equivalents in the footnotes, it merely gives approximate amounts and distances. Weights and measures differed somewhat at various times and places in the ancient world. There is uncertainty particularly about the ephah and the bath; further discoveries may give more light on these units of capacity.

A
Concordance
to the
NEW INTERNATIONAL
VERSION

ZONDERVAN BIBLE PUBLISHERS
GRAND RAPIDS, MICHIGAN

Introduction

This NIV Concordance is a condensation of *The NIV Complete Concordance,* taking over 35,000 references from the latter's 250,000. These 35,000 references have been selected as the most helpful for the average Bible student or layperson.

When determining whether or not to include a verse reference, we gave careful consideration to the passage in which the verse is located. We also encourage you to always consider the larger context of the passage, giving special attention to the flow of thought from beginning to end. Whenever you look up a verse, your goal should be to discover the intended meaning of the verse in context. Do not use this concordance, or any concordance, merely as a *verse-finder;* it should also be used as a *passage-finder.* The contexts surrounding each entry are longer than those usually found in concordances; but even so, the context excerpts are too brief for study purposes. They serve only to help you locate familiar verses.

In some cases the usual short contextual phrases are ineffective in helping you locate a passage. This is especially true in studying key events in a Bible character's life. Therefore, we have incorporated 260 "block entries" in which we use descriptive phrases that mark the breadth of a passage containing episodes of that person's life. The descriptive phrases replace the brief context surrounding each occurrence of the name.

Often more than one Bible character has the same name. For example, there are more than thirty Zechariahs in the Bible. In these cases we have given the name a block entry, assigning each person a number (1), (2), etc., and have included a descriptive phrase to distinguish each. Insignificant names are not included.

In this concordance there are 1,238 key word entries that have an exhaustive list of every appearance of that word. When this occurs, the word or block entry is marked with an asterisk (*).

This concordance includes some words not found in *The NIV Complete Concordance.* These words include: boy, boy's, boys, daughter, daughters, girl, man, man's, men, men's, people, peoples, woman, and women.

Since this concordance can only serve one translation—the New International Version—it is difficult for readers familiar with the Authorized Version to make the transition from its older, more archaic language to that of the NIV. We have tried, therefore, to make this transition a bit easier by including some forty-four prominent Authorized Version words and linking them to NIV words that have taken their place. We wish to thank Dr. Daniel E. Sauerwein of Multnomah School of the Bible for supplying the data for these additional words.

We pray that this concordance will be used by NIV readers to introduce them to the full scope of God's truth in every book of the Bible.

John R. Kohlenberger III
Edward W. Goodrick

ABBREVIATIONS FOR THE BOOKS OF THE BIBLE

Genesis	Ge	Nahum	Na
Exodus	Ex	Habbakuk	Hab
Leviticus	Lev	Zephaniah	Zep
Numbers	Nu	Haggai	Hag
Deuteronomy	Dt	Zechariah	Zec
Joshua	Jos	Malachi	Mal
Judges	Jdg	Matthew	Mt
Ruth	Ru	Mark	Mk
1 Samuel	1Sa	Luke	Lk
2 Samuel	2Sa	John	Jn
1 Kings	1Ki	Acts	Ac
2 Kings	2Ki	Romans	Ro
1 Chronicles	1Ch	1 Corinthians	1Co
2 Chronicles	2Ch	2 Corinthians	2Co
Ezra	Ezr	Galatians	Gal
Nehemiah	Ne	Ephesians	Eph
Esther	Est	Philippians	Php
Job	Job	Colossians	Col
Psalms	Ps	1 Thessalonians	1Th
Proverbs	Pr	2 Thessalonians	2Th
Ecclesiastes	Ecc	1 Timothy	1Ti
Song of Songs	SS	2 Timothy	2Ti
Isaiah	Isa	Titus	Tit
Jeremiah	Jer	Philemon	Phm
Lamentations	La	Hebrews	Heb
Ezekiel	Eze	James	Jas
Daniel	Da	1 Peter	1Pe
Hosea	Hos	2 Peter	2Pe
Joel	Joel	1 John	1Jn
Amos	Am	2 John	2Jn
Obadiah	Ob	3 John	3Jn
Jonah	Jnh	Jude	Jude
Micah	Mic	Revelation	Rev

AARON

Genealogy of (Ex 6:16-20; Jos 21:4, 10; 1Ch 6:3-15).

Priesthood of (Ex 28:1; Nu 17; Heb 5:1-4; 7), garments (Ex 28; 39), consecration (Ex 29), ordination (Lev 8).

Spokesman for Moses (Ex 4:14-16, 27-31; 7:1-2). Supported Moses' hands in battle (Ex 17:8-13). Built golden calf (Ex 32; Dt 9:20). Talked against Moses (Nu 12). Priesthood opposed (Nu 16); staff budded (Nu 17). Forbidden to enter land (Nu 20:1-12). Death (Nu 20:22-29; 33:38-39).

ABADDON*

Rev 9:11 whose name in Hebrew is *A*,

ABANDON (ABANDONED)

Dt 4:31 he will not *a* or destroy you
1Ki 6:13 and will not *a* my people Israel.''
Ne 9:19 compassion you did not *a* them
9:31 an end to them or *a* them,
Ps 16:10 you will not *a* me to the grave,
Ac 2:27 you will not *a* me to the grave,
1Ti 4: 1 in later times some will *a* the faith

ABANDONED (ABANDON)

Ge 24:27 who has not *a* his kindness
2Co 4: 9 persecuted, but not *a*; struck down,

ABBA*

Mk 14:36 ''*A*, Father,'' he said, ''everything is
Ro 8:15 And by him we cry, ''*A*, Father.''
Gal 4: 6 the Spirit who calls out, ''*A*, Father

ABEDNEGO

Deported to Babylon with Daniel (Da 1:1-6). Name changed from Azariah (Da 1:7). Refused defilement by food (Da 1:8-20). Refused idol worship (Da 3:1-12); saved from furnace (Da 3:13-30).

ABEL

Second son of Adam (Ge 4:2). Offered proper sacrifice (Ge 4:4; Heb 11:4). Murdered by Cain (Ge 4:8; Mt 23:35; Lk 11:51; 1Jn 3:12).

ABHOR (ABHORS)

Lev 26:30 of your idols, and I will *a* you.
Dt 7:26 Utterly *a* and detest it,
Ps 26: 5 I *a* the assembly of evildoers
119:163 I hate and *a* falsehood
139: 21 and *a* those who rise up against you
Am 6: 8 ''I *a* the pride of Jacob
Ro 2: 22 You who *a* idols, do you rob

ABHORS (ABHOR)

Pr 11: 1 The LORD *a* dishonest scales,

ABIATHAR

High priest in days of Saul and David (1Sa 22; 2Sa 15; 1Ki 1-2; Mk 2:26). Escaped Saul's slaughter of priests (1Sa 22:18-23). Supported David in Absalom's revolt (2Sa 15:24-29). Supported Adonijah (1Ki 1:7-42); deposed by Solomon (1Ki 2:22-35; cf. 1Sa 2:31-35).

ABIDE see REMAIN

ABIGAIL

1. Sister of David (1Ch 2:16-17).
2. Wife of Nabal (1Sa 25:30); pled for his life with David (1Sa 25:14-35). Became David's wife after Nabal's death (1Sa 25:36-42); bore him Kileab (2Sa 3:3) also known as Daniel (1Ch 3:1).

ABIHU

Son of Aaron (Ex 6:23; 24:1, 9); killed for offering unauthorized fire (Lev 10; Nu 3:2-4; 1Ch 24:1-2).

ABIJAH

1. Second son of Samuel (1Ch 6:28); a corrupt judge (1Sa 8:1-5).
2. An Aaronic priest (1Ch 24:10; Lk 1:5).
3. Son of Jeroboam I of Israel; died as prophesied by Ahijah (1Ki 14:1-18).
4. Son of Rehoboam; king of Judah who fought Jeroboam I attempting to reunite the kingdom (1Ki 14:31-15:8; 2Ch 12:16-14:1; Mt 1:7).

ABILITY (ABLE)

Ex 35:34 tribe of Dan, the *a* to teach others.
Dt 8: 18 for it is he who gives you the *a*
Ezr 2:69 According to their *a* they gave
Mt 25: 15 one talent, each according to his *a*.
Ac 11:29 disciples, each according to his *a*,
2Co 1: 8 far beyond our *a* to endure,
8: 3 were able, and even beyond their *a*.

ABIMELECH

1. King of Gerar who took Abraham's wife Sarah, believing her to be his sister (Ge 20). Later made a covenant with Abraham (Ge 21:22-33).
2. King of Gerar who took Isaac's wife Rebekah, believing her to be his sister (Ge 26:1-11). Later made a covenant with Isaac (Ge 26:12-31).
3. Son of Gideon (Jdg 8:31). Attempted to make himself king (Jdg 9).

ABISHAG*

Shunammite virgin; attendant of David in his old age (1Ki 1:1-15; 2:17-22).

ABISHAI

Son of Zeruiah, David's sister (1Sa 26:6; 1Ch 2:16). One of David's chief warriors (1Ch 11:15-21); against Edom (1Ch 18:12-13), Ammon (2Sa 10), Absalom (2Sa 18), Sheba (2Sa 20). Wanted to kill Saul (1Sa 26), killed Abner (2Sa 2:18-27; 3:22-39), wanted to kill Shimei (2Sa 16:5-13; 19:16-23).

ABLE (ABILITY ENABLE ENABLED ENABLES ENABLING)

Nu 14:16 'The LORD was not *a*
1Ch 29: 14 that we should be *a* to give
2Ch 2: 6 who is *a* to build a temple for him,
Eze 7: 19 and gold will not be *a* to save them
Da 3: 17 the God we serve is *a* to save us
4:37 walk in pride he is *a* to humble.
Mt 9: 28 ''Do you believe that I am *a*
Lk 13: 24 will try to enter and will not be *a* to
14: 30 to build and was not *a* to finish.'
21: 15 none of your adversaries will be *a*
21: 36 and that you may be *a* to stand
Ac 5: 39 you will not be *a* to stop these men;
Ro 8: 39 will be *a* to separate us
14: 4 for the Lord is *a* to make him stand
16: 25 to him who is *a* to establish you
2Co 9: 8 God is *a* to make all grace abound
Eph 3: 20 him who is *a* to do immeasurably
6: 13 you may be *a* to stand your ground,
1Ti 3: 2 respectable, hospitable, *a* to teach,
2Ti 1: 12 and am convinced that he is *a*
2: 24 kind to everyone, *a* to teach,
3: 15 which are *a* to make you wise
Heb 2: 18 he is *a* to help those who are being
7: 25 he is *a* to save completely
Jas 3: 2 *a* to keep his whole body in check.
Jude : 24 To him who is *a* to keep you
Rev 5: 5 He is *a* to open the scroll

ABNER

Cousin of Saul and commander of his army (1Sa 14:50; 17:55-57; 26). Made Ish-Bosheth king after Saul (2Sa 2:8-10), but later defected to David (2Sa 3:6-21). Killed Asahel (2Sa 2:18-32), for which he was killed by Joab and Abishai (2Sa 3:22-39).

ABOLISH (ABOLISHED ABOLISHING)

Hos 2:18 I will *a* from the land,
Mt 5:17 that I have come to *a* the Law

ABOLISHED (ABOLISH)

Gal 5: 11 the offense of the cross has been *a*.

ABOLISHING* (ABOLISH)

Eph 2: 15 by *a* in his flesh the law

ABOMINATION*

Da 11:31 set up the *a* that causes desolation.
12: 11 *a* that causes desolation is set up,
Mt 24: 15 the holy place 'the *a* that causes
Mk 13: 14 you see 'the *a* that causes

ABOUND (ABOUNDING)

2Co 9: 8 able to make all grace *a* to you,
9: 8 you will *a* in every good work.
Php 1: 9 that your love may *a* more

ABOUNDING (ABOUND)

Ex 34: 6 slow to anger, *a* in love
Nu 14: 18 *a* in love and forgiving sin
Ne 9: 17 slow to anger and *a* in love.
Ps 86: 5 in love to all who call to you.
86: 15 slow to anger, *a* in love
103: 8 slow to anger, *a* in love.
Joel 2: 13 slow to anger and *a* in love,
Jnh 4: 2 slow to anger and *a* in love,

ABRAHAM

Abram, son of Terah (Ge 11:26-27), husband of Sarah (Ge 11:29).

Covenant relation with the LORD (Ge 12:1-3; 13:14-17; 15; 17; 22:15-18; Ex 2:24; Ne 9:8; Ps 105; Mic 7:20; Lk 1:68-75; Ro 4; Heb 6:13-15).

Called from Ur, via Haran, to Canaan (Ge 12:1; Ac 7:2-4; Heb 11:8-10). Moved to Egypt, nearly lost Sarah to Pharoah (Ge 12:10-20). Divided the land with Lot; settled in Hebron (Ge 13). Saved Lot from four kings (Ge 14:1-16); blessed by Melchizedek (Ge 14:17-20; Heb 7:1-20). Declared righteous by faith (Ge 15:6; Ro 4:3; Gal 3:6-9). Fathered Ishmael by Hagar (Ge 16).

Name changed from Abram (Ge 17:5; Ne 9:7). Circumcised (Ge 17; Ro 4:9-12). Entertained three visitors (Ge 18); promised a son by Sarah (Ge 18:9-15; 17:16). Questioned destruction of Sodom and Gomorrah (Ge 18:16-33). Moved to Gerar; nearly lost Sarah to Abimelech (Ge 20). Fathered Isaac by Sarah (Ge 21:1-7; Ac 7:8; Heb 11:11-12); sent away Hagar and Ishmael (Ge 21:8-21; Gal 4:22-30). Covenant with Abimelech (Ge 21:22-32). Tested by offering Isaac (Ge 22; Heb 11:17-19; Jas 2:21-24). Sarah died; bought field of Ephron for burial (Ge 23). Secured wife for Isaac (Ge 24). Fathered children by Keturah (Ge 25:1-6; 1Ch 1:32-33). Death (Ge 25:7-11).

Called servant of God (Ge 26:24), friend of God (2Ch 20:7; Isa 41:8; Jas 2:23), prophet (Ge 20:7), father of Israel (Ex 3:15; Isa 51:2; Mt 3:9; Jn 8:39-58).

ABRAM see ABRAHAM

ABSALOM

Son of David by Maacah (2Sa 3:3; 1Ch 3:2). Killed Amnon for rape of his sister Tamar; banished by David (2Sa 13). Returned to Jerusalem; received by David (2Sa 14). Rebelled against David; siezed kingdom (2Sa 15-17). Killed (2Sa 18).

ABSENT

Col 2: 5 though I am *a* from you in body,

ABSOLUTE*

1Ti 5: 2 women as sisters, with *a* purity.

ABSTAIN (ABSTAINS)

Ex 19:15 *A* from sexual relations.''
Nu 6: 3 he must *a* from wine and other
Ac 15:20 them to *a* from food polluted
1Pe 2: 11 to *a* from sinful desires,

ABSTAINS* (ABSTAIN)

Ro 14: 6 thanks to God; and he who *a*,

ABUNDANCE (ABUNDANT)

Ge 41:29 Seven years of great *a* are coming
Job 36: 31 and provides food in *a*.
Ps 66: 12 but you brought us to a place of *a*.
Ecc 5: 12 but the *a* of a rich man
Isa 66: 11 and delight in her overflowing *a*.''
Jer 2: 22 and use an *a* of soap,
Mt 13: 12 given more, and he will have an *a*.
25: 29 given more, and he will have an *a*.
Lk 12: 15 consist in the *a* of his possessions.''
1Pe 1: 2 Grace and peace be yours in *a*.
2Pe 1: 2 yours in *a* through the knowledge
Jude : 2 peace and love be yours in *a*.

ABUNDANT (ABUNDANCE)

Dt 28: 11 will grant you *a* prosperity—

Dt   32: 2 like *a* rain on tender plants.
Job 36: 28 and *a* showers fall on mankind.
Ps   68: 9 You gave *a* showers, O God;
     78: 15 gave them water as *a* as the seas;
    132: 15 I will bless her with *a* provisions;
    145: 7 will celebrate your *a* goodness
Pr   12: 11 works his land will have *a* food,
     28: 19 works his land will have *a* food,
Jer 33: 9 and will tremble at the *a* prosperity
Ro   5: 17 who receive God's *a* provision

ABUSIVE
2Ti   3: 2 *a*, disobedient to their parents,

ABYSS*
Lk   8: 31 not to order them to go into the *A*.
Rev   9: 1 the key to the shaft of the *A*.
      9: 2 When he opened the *A*, smoke rose
      9: 2 darkened by the smoke from the *A*.
      9: 11 king over them the angel of the *A*,
     11: 7 up from the *A* will attack them,
     17: 8 and will come up out of the *A*
     20: 1 having the key to the *A*
     20: 3 He threw him into the *A*,

ACCEPT (ACCEPTABLE ACCEPTANCE ACCEPTED ACCEPTS)
Ex   23: 8 "Do not *a* a bribe,
Dt   16: 19 Do not *a* a bribe, for a bribe blinds
Job 42: 8 and I will *a* his prayer and not deal
Pr   10: 8 The wise in heart *a* commands,
     19: 20 Listen to advice and *a* instruction,
Ro   5: 7 A one another, then, just
Jas   1: 21 humbly *a* the word planted in you,

ACCEPTABLE (ACCEPT)
Pr   21: 3 is more *a* to the LORD

ACCEPTANCE* (ACCEPT)
Ro   11: 15 what will their *a* be but life
1Ti   1: 15 saying that deserves full *a*:
      4: 9 saying that deserves full *a*

ACCEPTED (ACCEPT)
Ge   4: 7 will you not be *a*? But if you do not
Job 42: 9 and the LORD *a* Job's prayer.
Lk   4: 24 "no prophet is *a* in his hometown.
Gal   1: 9 you a gospel other than what you *a*,

ACCEPTS (ACCEPT)
Ps   6: 9 the LORD *a* my prayer.
Jn   13: 20 whoever *a* anyone I send *a* me;
     13: 20 whoever *a* me *a* the one who sent

ACCESS
Ro   5: 2 through whom we have gained *a*
Eph   2: 18 For through him we both have *a*

ACCOMPANIED (ACCOMPANY)
1Co 10: 4 from the spiritual rock that *a* them,
Jas   2: 17 if it is not *a* by action, is dead.

ACCOMPANIES (ACCOMPANY)
2Co   9: 13 obedience that *a* your confession

ACCOMPANY (ACCOMPANIED ACCOMPANIES)
Dt   28: 2 *a* you if you obey the LORD your
Mk   16: 17 these signs will *a* those who believe
Heb   6: 9 your case—things that *a* salvation.

ACCOMPLISH
Ecc   2: 2 And what does pleasure *a*?"
Isa 44: 28 and will *a* all that I please;
     55: 11 but will *a* what I desire

ACCORD
Nu   24: 13 not do anything of my own *a*,
Jn   10: 18 but I lay it down of my own *a*.
     12: 49 For I did not speak of my own *a*.

ACCOUNT (ACCOUNTABLE)
Ge   2: 4 This is the *a* of the heavens
      5: 1 This is the written *a* of Adam's line
      6: 9 This is the *a* of Noah.
     10: 1 This is the *a* of Shem, Ham
     11: 10 This is the *a* of Shem.
     11: 27 This is the *a* of Terah.
     25: 12 This is the *a* of Abraham's son

Ge   25: 19 This is the *a* of Abraham's son
     36: 1 This is the *a* of Esau (that is, Edom
     36: 9 This is the *a* of Esau the father
     37: 2 This is the *a* of Jacob.
Mt   12: 36 to give *a* on the day of judgment
Lk   16: 2 Give an *a* of your management,
Ro   14: 12 each of us will give an *a* of himself
Heb   4: 13 of him to whom we must give *a*.

ACCOUNTABLE* (ACCOUNT)
Eze   3: 18 and I will hold you *a* for his blood.
      3: 20 and I will hold you *a* for his blood.
     33: 6 but I will hold the watchman *a*
     33: 8 and I will hold you *a* for his blood.
     34: 10 and will hold them *a* for my flock.
Da   6: 2 The satraps were made *a* to them
Jnh   1: 14 Do not hold us *a* for killing
Ro   3: 19 and the whole world held *a* to God.

ACCURATE
Dt   25: 15 You must have *a* and honest
Pr   11: 1 but *a* weights are his delight.

ACCURSED (CURSE)
2Pe   2: 14 experts in greed—an *a* brood!

ACCUSATION (ACCUSE)
1Ti   5: 19 Do not entertain an *a*

ACCUSATIONS (ACCUSE)
2Pe   2: 11 do not bring slanderous *a*

ACCUSE (ACCUSATION ACCUSATIONS ACCUSER ACCUSES ACCUSING)
Pr   3: 30 Do not *a* a man for no reason—
Lk   3: 14 and don't *a* people falsely—

ACCUSER (ACCUSE)
Jn   5: 45 Your *a* is Moses, on whom your
Rev 12: 10 For the *a* of our brothers,

ACCUSES (ACCUSE)
Job 40: 2 Let him who *a* God answer him!"
Rev 12: 10 who *a* them before our God day

ACCUSING (ACCUSE)
Ro   2: 15 their thoughts now *a*,

ACHAN*
     Sin at Jericho caused defeat at Ai; stoned (Jos 7; 22:20; 1Ch 2:7).

ACHE*
Pr   14: 13 Even in laughter the heart may *a*,

ACHIEVE
Isa 55: 11 *a* the purpose for which I sent it.

ACHISH
     King of Gath before whom David feigned insanity (1Sa 21:10-15). Later "ally" of David (2Sa 27-29).

ACKNOWLEDGE (ACKNOWLEDGED ACKNOWLEDGES)
Pr   3: 6 in all your ways *a* him,
Jer   3: 13 Only *a* your guilt—
Hos   6: 3 let us press on to *a* him.
Mt   10: 32 *a* him before my Father in heaven.
Lk   12: 8 *a* him before the angels of God.
1Jn   4: 3 spirit that does not *a* Jesus is not

ACKNOWLEDGED (ACKNOWLEDGE)
Lk   7: 29 *a* that God's way was right,

ACKNOWLEDGES* (ACKNOWLEDGE)
Ps   91: 14 for he *a* my name.
Mt   10: 32 "Whoever *a* me before men,
Lk   12: 8 whoever *a* me before men,
1Jn   2: 23 whoever *a* the Son has the Father
      4: 2 Every spirit that *a* that Jesus Christ
      4: 15 If anyone *a* that Jesus is the Son

ACQUIRES (ACQUIRING)
Pr   18: 15 of the discerning *a* knowledge;

ACQUIRING* (ACQUIRES)
Pr   1: 3 for *a* a disciplined and prudent life,

ACQUIT (ACQUITTING)
Ex   23: 7 to death, for I will not *a* the guilty.

ACQUITTING* (ACQUIT)
Dt   25: 1 *a* the innocent and condemning
Pr   17: 15 A the guilty and condemning

ACT (ACTION ACTIONS ACTIVE ACTIVITY ACTS)
Ps 119:126 It is time for you to *a*, O LORD;

ACTION (ACT)
2Co   9: 2 has stirred most of them to *a*.
Jas   2: 17 if it is not accompanied by *a*,
1Pe   1: 13 minds for *a*; be self-controlled;

ACTIONS (ACT)
Mt   11: 19 wisdom is proved right by her *a*."
Gal   6: 4 Each one should test his own *a*.
Tit   1: 16 but by their *a* they deny him.

ACTIVE* (ACT)
Phm   6 I pray that you may be *a*
Heb   4: 12 For the word of God is living and *a*

ACTIVITY (ACT)
Ecc   3: 1 a season for every *a* under heaven;
      3: 17 for there will be a time for every *a*,

ACTS (ACT)
1Ch 16: 9 tell of all his wonderful *a*.
Ps   71: 16 proclaim your mighty *a*,
     71: 24 tell of your righteous *a*
    105: 2 tell of all his wonderful *a*.
    106: 2 Who can proclaim the mighty *a*
    145: 4 they will tell of your mighty *a*.
    145: 12 all men may know of your mighty *a*
    150: 2 Praise him for his *a* of power;
Isa 64: 6 all our righteous *a* are like filthy
Mt   6: 1 not to do your '*a* of righteousness'

ADAM
     1. First man (Ge 1:26-2:25; Ro 5:14; 1Ti 2:13). Sin of (Ge 3; Hos 6:7; Ro 5:12-21). Children of (Ge 4:1-5:5). Death of (Ge 5:5; Ro 5:12-21; 1Co 15:22).
     2. City (Jos 3:16).

ADD (ADDED)
Dt   4: 2 Do not *a* to what I command you
     12: 32 do not *a* to it or take away from it.
Pr   1: 5 let the wise listen and *a*
      9: 9 he will *a* to his learning.
     30: 6 Do not *a* to his words,
Mt   6: 27 by worrying can *a* a single hour
Lk   12: 25 by worrying can *a* a single hour
Rev 22: 18 God will *a* to him the plagues

ADDED (ADD)
Ecc   3: 14 nothing can be *a* to it and nothing
Ac   2: 47 Lord *a* to their number daily those
Ro   5: 20 The law was *a* so that the trespass
Gal   3: 19 It was *a* because of transgressions

ADDICTED*
Tit   2: 3 to be slanderers or *a* to much wine,

ADMINISTRATION*
1Co 12: 28 with gifts of *a*, and those speaking
Eph   3: 2 Surely you have heard about the *a*
      3: 9 to everyone the *a* of this mystery,

ADMIRABLE*
Php   4: 8 whatever is lovely, whatever is *a*—

ADMIT
Hos   5: 15 until they *a* their guilt.

ADMONISH* (ADMONISHING)
Col   3: 16 and *a* one another with all wisdom,
1Th   5: 12 you in the Lord and who *a* you.

ADMONISHING* (ADMONISH)
Col   1: 28 *a* and teaching everyone

ADONIJAH
     1. Son of David by Haggith (2Sa 3:4; 1Ch 3:2). Attempted to be king after David; killed by Solomon's order (1Ki 1-2).

2. Levite; teacher of the Law (2Ch 17:8).

ADOPTED (ADOPTION)

Eph   1:   5 In love he predestined us to be a

ADOPTION* (ADOPTED)

Ro   8: 23 as we wait eagerly for our a as sons,
      9:   4 Theirs is the a as sons; theirs

ADORE*

SS   1:   4 How right they are to a you!

ADORNMENT* (ADORNS)

1Pe   3:   3 should not come from outward a,

ADORNS* (ADORNMENT)

Ps   93:   5 holiness a your house
Isa   61: 10 as a bride a herself with her jewels.
     61: 10 bridegroom a his head like a priest,

ADULTERER (ADULTERY)

Lev   20: 10 both the a and the adulteress must
Heb   13:   4 for God will judge the a

ADULTERERS (ADULTERY)

1Co   6:   9 idolaters nor a nor male prostitutes
1Ti   1: 10 for murderers, for a and perverts,

ADULTERESS (ADULTERY)

Hos   3:   1 she is loved by another and is an a.

ADULTERIES (ADULTERY)

Jer   3:   8 sent her away because of all her a.

ADULTEROUS (ADULTERY)

Mk   8: 38 in this a and sinful generation,
Jas   4:   4 You a people, don't you know that

ADULTERY (ADULTERER ADULTERERS ADULTERESS ADULTERIES ADULTEROUS)

Ex   20: 14 "You shall not commit a.
Dt   5: 18 "You shall not commit a.
Mt   5: 27 that it was said, 'Do not commit a.'
     5: 28 lustfully has already committed a
     5: 32 the divorced woman commits a.
   15: 19 murder, a, sexual immorality, theft
   19:   9 marries another woman commits a
   19: 18 do not commit a, do not steal,
Mk   7: 21 theft, murder, a, greed, malice,
   10: 11 marries another woman commits a
   10: 12 another man, she commits a."
   10: 19 do not commit a, do not steal,
Lk   16: 18 a divorced woman commits a.
   16: 18 marries another woman commits a
   18: 20 'Do not commit a, do not murder,
Jn   8:   4 woman was caught in the act of a.
Rev   18:   3 of the earth committed a with her,

ADULTS*

1Co   14: 20 but in your thinking be a.

ADVANCE (ADVANCED)

Ps   18: 29 With your help I can a
Php   1: 12 has really served to a the gospel.

ADVANCED (ADVANCE)

Job   32:   7 a years should teach wisdom.'

ADVANTAGE

Ex   22: 22 "Do not take a of a widow
Dt   24: 14 Do not take a of a hired man who is
Ro   3:   1 What a, then, is there
2Co   11: 20 or exploits you or takes a of you
1Th   4:   6 should wrong his brother or take a

ADVERSITY*

Pr   17: 17 and a brother is born for a.
Isa   30: 20 the Lord gives you the bread of a

ADVICE (ADVISERS)

1Ki   12:   8 rejected the a the elders
   12: 14 he followed the a of the young men
2Ch   10:   8 rejected the a the elders
Pr   12:   5 but the a of the wicked is deceitful.
   12: 15 but a wise man listens to a.
   19: 20 Listen to a and accept instruction,
   20: 18 Make plans by seeking a;

ADVISERS (ADVICE)

Pr   11: 14 but many a make victory sure.

ADVOCATE*

Job   16: 19 my a is on high.

AFFLICTED (AFFLICTION)

Job   2:   7 and a Job with painful sores
   36:   6 but gives the a their rights.
Ps   9: 12 he does not ignore the cry of the a.
   9: 18 nor the hope of the a ever perish.
   119: 67 Before I was a I went astray,
   119: 71 It was good for me to be a
   119: 75 and in faithfulness you have a me.
Isa   49: 13 will have compassion on his a ones.
   53:   4 smitten by him, and a.
   53:   7 He was oppressed and a,
Na   1: 12 Although I have a you, ⸢O Judah⸣,

AFFLICTION (AFFLICTED AFFLICTIONS)

Dt   16:   3 bread of a, because you left Egypt
Ps   107: 41 he lifted the needy out of their a
Isa   30: 20 of adversity and the water of a,
   48: 10 in the furnace of a.
La   3: 33 For he does not willingly bring a
Ro   12: 12 patient in a, faithful in prayer.

AFFLICTIONS (AFFLICTION)

Col   1: 24 lacking in regard to Christ's a,

AFRAID (FEAR)

Ge   3: 10 and I was a because I was naked;
   26: 24 Do not be a, for I am with you;
Ex   2: 14 Then Moses was a and thought,
   3:   6 because he was a to look at God.
Dt   1: 21 Do not be a; do not be discouraged
   1: 29 "Do not be terrified; do not be a
   20:   1 do not be a of them,
   20:   3 Do not be fainthearted or a;
2Ki   25: 24 "Do not be a of the Babylonian
1Ch   13: 12 David was a of God that day
Ps   27:   1 of whom shall I be a?
   56:   3 When I am a, / I will trust in you.
   56:   4 in God I trust; I will not be a.
Pr   3: 24 lie down, you will not be a;
Isa   10: 24 do not be a of the Assyrians,
   12:   2 I will trust and not be a.
   44:   8 Do not tremble, do not be a.
Jer   1:   8 Do not be a of them, for I am
Mt   8: 26 You of little faith, why are you so a
   10: 28 be a of the One who can destroy
   10: 31 So don't be a; you are worth more
Mk   5: 36 "Don't be a; just believe."
Lk   9: 34 and they were a as they entered
Jn   14: 27 hearts be troubled and do not be a.
Ac   27: 24 beside me and said, 'Do not be a,
Ro   11: 20 Do not be arrogant, but be a.
Heb   13:   6 Lord is my helper; I will not be a.

AGAG (AGAGITE)

King of Amalekites not killed by Saul (1Sa 15).

AGAGITE (AGAG)

Est   8:   3 to the evil plan of Haman the A,

AGED (AGES)

Job   12: 12 Is not wisdom found among the a?
Pr   17:   6 children are a crown to the a,

AGES (AGED)

Ro   16: 25 the mystery hidden for long a past,
Eph   2:   7 in the coming a he might show
   3:   9 which for a past was kept hidden
Col   1: 26 that has been kept hidden for a
Rev   15:   3 King of the a.

AGONY

Lk   16: 24 because I am in a in this fire.'
Rev   16: 10 Men gnawed their tongues in a

AGREE (AGREEMENT AGREES)

Mt   18: 19 on earth a about anything you ask
Ro   7: 16 want to do, I a that the law is good.
Php   4:   2 with Syntyche to a with each other

AGREEMENT (AGREE)

2Co   6: 16 What a is there between the temple

AGREES* (AGREE)

Ac   7: 42 This a with what is written
   24: 14 I believe everything that a
1Co   4: 17 which a with what I teach

AGRIPPA*

Descendant of Herod; king before whom Paul pled his case in Caesarea (Ac 25:13-26:32).

AHAB

1. Son of Omri; king of Israel (1Ki 16:28-22: 40), husband of Jezebel (1Ki 16:31). Promoted Baal worship (1Ki 16:31-33); opposed by Elijah (1Ki 17:1; 18; 21), a prophet (1Ki 20:35-43), Micaiah (1Ki 22:1-28). Defeated Ben-Hadad (1Ki 20). Killed for failing to kill Ben-Hadad and for murder of Naboth (1Ki 20:35-21:40).
2. A false prophet (Jer 29:21-22).

AHAZ

1. Son of Jotham; king of Judah, (2Ki 16; 2Ch 28). Idolatry of (2Ki 16:3-4, 10-18; 2Ch 28:1-4, 22-25). Defeated by Aram and Israel (2Ki 16:5-6; 2Ch 28:5-15). Sought help from Assyria rather than the LORD (2Ki 16:7-9; 2Ch 28:16-21; Isa 7).
2. Benjamite, descendant of Saul (1Ch 8:35-36).

AHAZIAH

1. Son of Ahab; king of Israel (1Ki 22:51-2Ki 1:18; 2Ch 20:35-37). Made an unsuccessful alliance with Jehoshaphat of Judah (2Ch 20:35-37). Died for seeking Baal rather than the LORD (1Ki 1).
2. Son of Jehoram; king of Judah (2Ki 8:25-29; 9:14-29), also called Jehoahaz (2Ch 21:17-22:9; 25:23). Killed by Jehu while visiting Joram (2Ki 9:14-29; 2Ch 22:1-9).

AHIJAH

1Sa   14: 18 Saul said to A, "Bring the ark
1Ki   14:   2 A the prophet is there—the one

AHIMELECH

1. Priest who helped David in his flight from Saul (1Sa 21-22).
2. One of David's warriors (1Sa 26:6).

AHITHOPHEL

One of David's counselors who sided with Absalom (2Sa 15:12, 31-37; 16:15-17:23); committed suicide when his advice was ignored (2Sa 16:15-17:23).

AI

Jos   7:   4 they were routed by the men of A,
   8: 28 So Joshua burned A and made it

AID

Isa   38: 14 troubled; O Lord, come to my a!''
Php   4: 16 you sent me a again and again

AIM

1Co   7: 34 Her a is to be devoted to the Lord
2Co   13: 11 A for perfection, listen

AIR

Mt   8: 20 and birds of the a have nests,
Lk   9: 58 and birds of the a have nests,
1Co   9: 26 not fight like a man beating the a.
   14:   9 You will just be speaking into the a
Eph   2:   2 of the ruler of the kingdom of the a,
1Th   4: 17 clouds to meet the Lord in the a.

ALABASTER*

Mt   26:   7 came to him with an a jar
Mk   14:   3 a woman came with an a jar
Lk   7: 37 she brought an a jar of perfume,

ALARM (ALARMED)

2Co   7: 11 indignation, what a, what longing,

ALARMED (ALARM)

Mk   13:   7 and rumors of wars, do not be a.
2Th   2:   2 not to become easily unsettled or a

ALERT*

Jos   8:   4 All of you be on the a.

Ps 17:11 with eyes *a*, to throw me
Isa 21: 7 let him be *a*, / fully *a*.''
Mk 13:33 Be *a!* You do not know
Eph 6:18 be *a* and always keep on praying
1Th 5: 6 but let us be *a* and self-controlled.
1Pe 5: 8 Be self-controlled and *a*.

ALIEN (ALIENATED ALIENS)
Ex 22:21 "Do not mistreat an *a*
Lev 24:22 are to have the same law for the *a*
Ps 146: 9 The LORD watches over the *a*

ALIENATED (ALIEN)
Gal 5: 4 by law have been *a* from Christ;
Col 1:21 Once you were *a* from God

ALIENS (ALIEN)
Ex 23: 9 know how it feels to be *a*,
1Pe 2:11 as *a* and strangers in the world,

ALIVE (LIVE)
1Sa 2: 6 LORD brings death and makes *a;*
Lk 24:23 vision of angels, who said he was *a.*
Ac 1: 3 convincing proofs that he was *a.*
Ro 6:11 but *a* to God in Christ Jesus.
1Co 15:22 so in Christ all will be made *a.*
Eph 2: 5 made us *a* with Christ

ALMIGHTY (MIGHT)
Ge 17: 1 "I am God *A;* walk before me
Ex 6: 3 to Isaac and to Jacob as God *A.*
Ru 1:20 the *A* has made my life very bitter.
Job 11: 7 Can you probe the limits of the *A?*
      33: 4 the breath of the *A* gives me life.
Ps 89: 8 O LORD God *A*, who is like you?
      91: 1 will rest in the shadow of the *A.*
Isa 6: 3 "Holy, holy, holy is the LORD *A;*
      45:13 says the LORD *A.*''
      47: 4 the LORD *A* is his name—
      48: 2 the LORD *A* is his name:
      51:15 the LORD *A* is his name.
      54: 5 the LORD *A* is his name—
Am 5:14 the LORD God *A* will be with you,
      5:15 the LORD God *A* will have mercy
Rev 4: 8 holy is the Lord God *A*, who was,
      19: 6 For our Lord God *A* reigns.

ALMS see GIVING, (acts of) RIGHTEOUSNESS

ALPHA*
Rev 1: 8 "I am the *A* and the Omega,''
      21: 6 I am the *A* and the Omega,
      22:13 I am the *A* and the Omega,

ALTAR
Ge 8:20 Then Noah built an *a* to the LORD
      12: 7 So he built an *a* there to the LORD
      13:18 where he built an *a* to the LORD.
      22: 9 Abraham built an *a* there
      22: 9 his son Isaac and laid him on the *a*,
      26:25 Isaac built an *a* there and called
      35: 1 and build an *a* there to God,
Ex 17:15 Moses built an *a* and called it
      27: 1 "Build an *a* of acacia wood,
      30: 1 "Make an *a* of acacia wood
      37:25 They made the *a* of incense out
Dt 27: 5 an *a* to the LORD your God, an *a*
Jos 8:30 on Mount Ebal an *a* to the LORD,
      22:10 built an imposing *a* there
Jdg 6:24 So Gideon built an *a* to the LORD
      21: 4 the next day the people built an *a*
1Sa 7:17 he built an *a* there to the LORD.
      14:35 Then Saul built an *a* to the LORD;
2Sa 24:25 David built an *a* to the LORD
1Ki 12:33 sacrifices on the *a* he had built
      13: 2 "O *a*, *a!* This is what the LORD
      16:32 He set up an *a* for Baal
      18:30 and he repaired the *a* of the LORD
2Ki 16:11 So Uriah the priest built an *a*
1Ch 21:26 David built an *a* to the LORD
2Ch 4: 1 made a bronze *a* twenty cubits
      4:19 the golden *a;* the tables
      15: 8 He repaired the *a* of the LORD
      32:12 'You must worship before one *a*
      33:16 he restored the *a* of the LORD
Ezr 3: 2 to build the *a* of the God of Israel
Isa 6: 6 taken with tongs from the *a.*

Eze 40:47 the *a* was in front of the temple.
Mt 5:23 if you are offering your gift at the *a*
Ac 17:23 found an *a* with this inscription:
Heb 13:10 We have an *a* from which those
Rev 6: 9 I saw under the *a* the souls

ALTER*
Ps 89:34 or *a* what my lips have uttered.

ALWAYS
Dt 15:11 There will *a* be poor people
Ps 16: 8 I have set the LORD *a* before me.
      51: 3 and my sin is *a* before me.
Pr 23: 7 who is *a* thinking about the cost.
Mt 26:11 The poor you will *a* have with you,
      28:20 And surely I am with you *a.*
Mk 14: 7 The poor you will *a* have with you,
Jn 12: 8 You will *a* have the poor
1Co 13: 7 *a* protects, *a* trusts, *a* hopes, *a*
Php 4: 4 Rejoice in the Lord *a.*
1Pe 3:15 *A* be prepared to give an answer

AMALEKITES
Ex 17: 8 *A* came and attacked the Israelites
1Sa 15: 2 'I will punish the *A*

AMASA
Nephew of David (1Ch 2:17). Commander of Absalom's forces (2Sa 17:24-27). Returned to David (2Sa 19:13). Killed by Joab (2Sa 20:4-13).

AMASSES*
Pr 28: 8 *a* it for another, who will be kind

AMAZED
Mt 7:28 the crowds were *a* at his teaching,
Mk 6: 6 And he was *a* at their lack of faith.
      10:24 The disciples were *a* at his words.
Ac 2: 7 Utterly *a*, they asked: "Are not all
      13:12 for he was *a* at the teaching about

AMAZIAH
1. Son of Joash; king of Judah (2Ki 14; 2Ch 25). Defeated Edom (2Ki 14:7; 2Ch 25:5-13); defeated by Israel for worshiping Edom's gods (2Ki 14:8-14; 2Ch 25:14-24).
2. Idolatrous priest who opposed Amos (Am 7:10-17).

AMBASSADOR* (AMBASSADORS)
Eph 6:20 for which I am an *a* in chains.

AMBASSADORS (AMBASSADOR)
2Co 5:20 We are therefore Christ's *a*,

AMBITION*
Ro 15:20 It has always been my *a*
Gal 5:20 fits of rage, selfish *a*, dissensions,
Php 1:17 preach Christ out of selfish *a*,
      2: 3 Do nothing out of selfish *a*
1Th 4:11 Make it your *a* to lead a quiet life,
Jas 3:14 and selfish *a* in your hearts,
      3:16 where you have envy and selfish *a*,

AMENDS
Pr 14: 9 Fools mock at making *a* for sin,

AMNON
Firstborn of David (2Sa 3:2; 1Ch 3:1). Killed by Absalom for raping his sister Tamar (2Sa 13).

AMON
1. Son of Manasseh; king of Judah (2Ki 21:18-26; 1Ch 3:14; 2Ch 33:21-25).
2. Ruler of Samaria under Ahab (1Ki 22:26; 2Ch 18:25).

AMOS
1. Prophet from Tekoa (Am 1:1; 7:10-17).
2. Ancestor of Jesus (Lk 3:25).

ANAK (ANAKITES)
Nu 13:28 even saw descendants of *A* there.

ANAKITES (ANAK)
Dt 1:28 We even saw the *A* there.' ''
      2:10 and numerous, and as tall as the *A.*
      9: 2 "Who can stand up against the *A?''*

ANANIAS
1. Husband of Sapphira; died for lying to God (Ac 5:1-11).
2. Disciple who baptized Saul (Ac 9:10-19).
3. High priest at Paul's arrest (Ac 22:30-24:1).

ANCESTORS (ANCESTRY)
1Ki 19: 4 I am no better than my *a.*''

ANCESTRY (ANCESTORS)
Ro 9: 5 from them is traced the human *a*

ANCHOR
Heb 6:19 We have this hope as an *a*

ANCIENT
Da 7: 9 and the *A* of Days took his seat.
      7:13 He approached the *A* of Days
      7:22 until the *A* of Days came

ANDREW*
Apostle; brother of Simon Peter (Mt 4:18; 10:2; Mk 1:16-18, 29; 3:18; 13:3; Lk 6:14; Jn 1:35-44; 6:8-9; 12:22; Ac 1:13).

ANGEL (ANGELS ARCHANGEL)
Ge 16: 7 The *a* of the LORD found Hagar
      22:11 But the *a* of the LORD called out
Ex 23:20 I am sending an *a* ahead of you
Nu 22:23 When the donkey saw the *a*
Jdg 2: 1 The *a* of the LORD went up
      6:22 Gideon realized that it was the *a*
      13:15 Manoah said to the *a* of the LORD
2Sa 24:16 The *a* of the LORD was then
1Ki 19: 7 The *a* of the LORD came back
2Ki 19:35 That night the *a* of the LORD went
Ps 34: 7 The *a* of the LORD encamps
Hos 12: 4 He struggled with the *a*
Mt 2:13 an *a* of the LORD appeared
      28: 2 for an *a* of the Lord came
Lk 1:26 God sent the *a* Gabriel
      2: 9 An *a* of the Lord appeared to them,
      22:43 An *a* from heaven appeared to him
Ac 6:15 his face was like the face of an *a.*
      12: 7 Suddenly an *a* of the Lord
2Co 11:14 Satan himself masquerades as an *a*
Gal 1: 8 or an *a* from heaven should preach

ANGELS (ANGEL)
Ps 91:11 command his *a* concerning you
Mt 4: 6 command his *a* concerning you,
      13:39 of the age, and the harvesters are *a.*
      13:49 The *a* will come and separate
      18:10 For I tell you that their *a*
      25:41 prepared for the devil and his *a.*
Lk 4:10 command his *a* concerning you
      20:36 for they are like the *a.*
1Co 6: 3 you not know that we will judge *a?*
      13: 1 in the tongues of men and of *a*,
Col 2:18 and the worship of *a* disqualify you
Heb 1: 4 as much superior to the *a*
      1: 6 "Let all God's *a* worship him.''
      1: 7 "He makes his *a* winds,
      1:14 Are not all *a* ministering spirits
      2: 7 made him a little lower than the *a;*
      2: 9 was made a little lower than the *a*,
      13: 2 some people have entertained *a*
1Pe 1:12 Even a long to look
2Pe 2: 4 For if God did not spare *a*
Jude 6 *a* who did not keep their positions

ANGER (ANGERED ANGRY)
Ex 15: 7 You unleashed your burning *a;*
      22:24 My *a* will be aroused, and I will kill
      32:10 alone so that my *a* may burn
      32:11 "why should your *a* burn
      32:12 Turn from your fierce *a;* relent
      32:19 his *a* burned and he threw
      34: 6 slow to *a*, abounding in love
Lev 26:28 then in my *a* I will be hostile
Nu 14:18 slow to *a*, abounding in love
      25:11 has turned my *a* away
      32:10 LORD's *a* was aroused that day
      32:13 The LORD's *a* burned
Dt 9:19 I feared the *a* and wrath
      29:28 In furious *a* and in great wrath
Jdg 14:19 Burning with *a*, he went up
2Sa 12: 5 David burned with *a*

ANGERED (continued)

2Ki 22: 13 Great is the LORD's *a* that burns
Ne 9: 17 slow to *a* and abounding in love.
Ps 30: 5 For his *a* lasts only a moment,
 78: 38 Time after time he restrained his *a*
 86: 15 slow to *a*, abounding in love
 90: 7 We are consumed by your *a*
 103: 8 slow to *a*, abounding in love.
Pr 15: 1 but a harsh word stirs up *a*.
 29: 11 A fool gives full vent to his *a*,
 30: 33 so stirring up *a* produces strife.''
Jnh 4: 2 slow to *a* and abounding in love,
Eph 4: 26 ''In your *a* do not sin''; Do not let
Jas 1: 20 for man's *a* does not bring about

ANGERED (ANGER)

Pr 22: 24 do not associate with one easily *a*,
1Co 13: 5 it is not easily *a*, it keeps no record

ANGRY (ANGER)

Ps 2: 12 Kiss the Son, lest he be *a*
 95: 10 For forty years I was *a*
Pr 29: 22 An *a* man stirs up dissension,
Mt 5: 22 But I tell you that anyone who is *a*
Jas 1: 19 slow to speak and slow to become *a*

ANGUISH

Ps 118: 5 In my *a* I cried to the LORD,
Jer 4: 19 Oh, my *a*, my *a*!
Zep 1: 15 a day of distress and *a*,
Lk 21: 25 nations will be in *a* and perplexity
 22: 44 in *a*, he prayed more earnestly,
Ro 9: 2 and unceasing *a* in my heart.

ANIMALS

Ge 1: 24 wild *a*, each according to its kind.''
 7: 16 The *a* going in were male
Dt 14: 4 These are the *a* you may eat: the ox
Job 12: 7 ask the *a*, and they will teach you,
Isa 43: 20 The wild *a* honor me,

ANNOUNCE (ANNOUNCED)

Mt 6: 2 give to the needy, do not *a* it

ANNOUNCED (ANNOUNCE)

Isa 48: 5 before they happened I *a* them
Gal 3: 8 and *a* the gospel in advance

ANNOYANCE*

Pr 12: 16 A fool shows his *a* at once,

ANNUAL*

Ex 30: 10 This *a* atonement must be made
Jdg 21: 19 there is the *a* festival of the LORD
1Sa 1: 21 family to offer the *a* sacrifice
 2: 19 husband to offer the *a* sacrifice.
 20: 6 an *a* sacrifice is being made there
2Ch 8: 13 New Moons and the three *a* feasts
Heb 10: 3 those sacrifices are an *a* reminder

ANOINT (ANOINTED ANOINTING)

Ex 30: 26 use it to *a* the Tent of Meeting,
 30: 30 ''A Aaron and his sons
1Sa 9: 16 A him leader over my people Israel
 15: 1 to *a* you king over his people Israel;
2Ki 9: 3 what the LORD says: I *a* you king
Ps 23: 5 You *a* my head with oil;
Da 9: 24 prophecy and to *a* the most holy.
Jas 5: 14 and *a* him with oil in the name

ANOINTED (ANOINT)

1Ch 16: 22 ''Do not touch my *a* ones;
Ps 105: 15 ''Do not touch my *a* ones;
Isa 61: 1 because the LORD has *a* me
Da 9: 26 the A One will be cut off
Lk 4: 18 because he has *a* me
Ac 10: 38 how God *a* Jesus of Nazareth

ANOINTING (ANOINT)

Lev 8: 12 some of the *a* oil on Aaron's head
1Ch 29: 22 *a* him before the LORD to be ruler
Ps 45: 7 by *a* you with the oil of joy.
Heb 1: 9 by *a* you with the oil of joy.''
1Jn 2: 20 you have an *a* from the Holy One,
 2: 27 about all things and as that *a* is real,

ANT* (ANTS)

Pr 6: 6 Go to the *a*, you sluggard;

ANTICHRIST* (ANTICHRISTS)

1Jn 2: 18 have heard that the *a* is coming,
 2: 22 a man is the *a*— he denies
 4: 3 of the *a*, which you have heard is
2Jn : 7 person is the deceiver and the *a*.

ANTICHRISTS* (ANTICHRIST)

1Jn 2: 18 even now many *a* have come.

ANTIOCH

Ac 11: 26 were called Christians first at *A*.

ANTS* (ANT)

Pr 30: 25 A are creatures of little strength,

ANXIETIES* (ANXIOUS)

Lk 21: 34 drunkenness and the *a* of life,

ANXIETY (ANXIOUS)

1Pe 5: 7 Cast all your *a* on him

ANXIOUS (ANXIETIES ANXIETY)

Pr 12: 25 An *a* heart weighs a man down,
Php 4: 6 Do not be *a* about anything,

APOLLOS*

Christian from Alexandria, learned in the Scriptures; instructed by Aquila and Priscilla (Ac 18:24-28). Ministered with Paul at Corinth (Ac 19:1; 1Co 1:12; 3; Tit 3:13).

APOLLYON*

Rev 9: 11 is Abaddon, and in Greek, *A*.

APOSTLE (APOSTLES APOSTLES')

Ro 11: 13 as I am the *a* to the Gentiles,
1Co 9: 1 Am I not an *a*? Have I not seen
2Co 12: 12 The things that mark an *a*— signs,
Gal 2: 8 of Peter as an *a* to the Jews,
1Ti 2: 7 was appointed a herald and an *a*—
2Ti 1: 11 I was appointed a herald and an *a*
Heb 3: 1 *a* and high priest whom we confess.

APOSTLES (APOSTLE)

See also Andrew, Bartholomew, James, John, Judas, Matthew, Matthias, Nathanael, Paul, Peter, Philip, Simon, Thaddaeus, Thomas.
Mk 3: 14 twelve—designating them *a*—
Lk 11: 49 'I will send them prophets and *a*,
Ac 1: 26 so he was added to the eleven *a*.
 2: 43 signs were done by the *a*.
1Co 12: 28 God has appointed first of all *a*,
 15: 9 For I am the least of the *a*
2Co 11: 13 masquerading as *a* of Christ.
Eph 2: 20 built on the foundation of the *a*
 4: 11 It was he who gave some to be *a*,
Rev 21: 14 names of the twelve *a* of the Lamb.

APOSTLES' (APOSTLE)

Ac 5: 2 the rest and put it at the *a'* feet.
 8: 18 at the laying on of the *a'* hands,

APPEAL

Ac 25: 11 I *a* to Caesar!'' After Festus had
Phm : 9 yet I *a* to you on the basis of love.

APPEAR (APPEARANCE APPEARANCES APPEARED APPEARING APPEARS)

Ge 1: 9 to one place, and let dry ground *a*.''
Lev 16: 2 I *a* in the cloud over the atonement
Mt 24: 30 of the Son of Man will *a* in the sky,
Mk 13: 22 false prophets will *a* and perform
Lk 19: 11 of God was going to *a* at once.
2Co 5: 10 we must all *a* before the judgment
Col 3: 4 also will *a* with him in glory.
Heb 9: 24 now to *a* for us in God's presence.
 9: 28 and he will *a* a second time,

APPEARANCE (APPEAR)

1Sa 16: 7 Man looks at the outward *a*,
Isa 52: 14 his *a* was so disfigured beyond that
 53: 2 in his *a* that we should desire him.
Gal 2: 6 God does not judge by external *a*—

APPEARANCES* (APPEAR)

Jn 7: 24 Stop judging by mere *a*,

APPEARED (APPEAR)

Nu 14: 10 glory of the LORD *a* at the Tent
Mt 1: 20 an angel of the Lord *a* to him
Lk 2: 9 An angel of the Lord *a* to them,
1Co 15: 5 and that he *a* to Peter,
Heb 9: 26 now he has *a* once for all at the end

APPEARING (APPEAR)

1Ti 6: 14 until the *a* of our Lord Jesus Christ,
2Ti 1: 10 through the *a* of our Savior,
 4: 8 to all who have longed for his *a*.
Tit 2: 13 the glorious *a* of our great God

APPEARS (APPEAR)

Mal 3: 2 Who can stand when he *a*?
Col 3: 4 When Christ, who is your life, *a*,
1Pe 5: 4 And when the Chief Shepherd *a*,
1Jn 3: 2 But we know that when he *a*,

APPETITE

Pr 16: 26 The laborer's *a* works for him;
Ecc 6: 7 yet his *a* is never satisfied.
Jer 50: 19 his *a* will be satisfied

APPLES

Pr 25: 11 is like a of gold in settings of silver.

APPLY (APPLYING)

Pr 22: 17 *a* your heart to what I teach,
 23: 12 A your heart to instruction

APPLYING (APPLY)

Pr 2: 2 and *a* your heart to understanding,

APPOINT (APPOINTED)

Ps 61: 7 *a* your love and faithfulness
1Th 5: 9 For God did not *a* us
Tit 1: 5 and *a* elders in every town,

APPOINTED (APPOINT)

Dt 1: 15 *a* them to have authority over you
Pr 8: 23 I was *a* from eternity,
Da 11: 27 an end will still come at the *a* time.
Hab 2: 3 For the revelation awaits an *a* time;
Jn 15: 16 Chose you and *a* you to go
Ro 9: 9 ''At the *a* time I will return,

APPROACH (APPROACHING)

Ex 24: 2 but Moses alone is to *a* the LORD;
Eph 3: 12 in him we may *a* God with freedom
Heb 4: 16 Let us then *a* the throne of grace

APPROACHING (APPROACH)

Heb 10: 25 all the more as you see the Day *a*.
1Jn 5: 14 is the confidence we have in *a* God:

APPROPRIATE

1Ti 2: 10 *a* for women who profess

APPROVAL (APPROVE)

Jdg 18: 6 Your journey has the LORD's *a*.''
Jn 6: 27 the Father has placed his seal of *a*.''
1Co 11: 19 to show which of you have God's *a*
Gal 1: 10 trying to win the *a* of men,

APPROVE (APPROVAL APPROVED APPROVES)

Ro 2: 18 if you know his will and *a*
 12: 2 and *a* what God's will is—

APPROVED* (APPROVE)

Ro 14: 18 pleasing to God and *a* by men.
 16: 10 Greet Apelles, tested and *a*
2Co 10: 18 who commends himself who is *a*,
1Th 2: 4 as men *a* by God to be entrusted
2Ti 2: 15 to present yourself to God as one *a*,

APPROVES* (APPROVE)

Ro 14: 22 not condemn himself by what he *a*.

APT*

Pr 15: 23 A man finds joy in giving an *apt* reply

AQUILA*

Husband of Priscilla; co-worker with Paul, instructor of Apollos (Ac 18; Ro 16:3; 1Co 16:19; 2Ti 4:19).

ARABIA

Gal 1: 17 but I went immediately into *A*
     4: 25 Hagar stands for Mount Sinai in *A*

ARARAT

Ge   8: 4 came to rest on the mountains of *A*.

ARAUNAH

2Sa 24: 16 threshing floor of *A* the Jebusite.

ARBITER* (ARBITRATE)

Lk 12: 14 who appointed me a judge or an *a*

ARBITRATE* (ARBITER)

Job 9: 33 If only there were someone to *a*

ARCHANGEL* (ANGEL)

1Th 4: 16 with the voice of the *a*
Jude : 9 *a* Michael, when he was disputing

ARCHER

Pr 26: 10 Like an *a* who wounds at random

ARCHIPPUS*

Col 4: 17 Tell *A:* "See to it that you complete
Phm : 2 to *A* our fellow soldier

ARCHITECT*

Heb 11: 10 whose *a* and builder is God.

AREOPAGUS*

Ac 17: 19 brought him to a meeting of the *A*,
    17: 22 up in the meeting of the *A*
    17: 34 of the *A*, also a woman named

ARGUE (ARGUMENT ARGUMENTS)

Job 13: 3 and to *a* my case with God.
    13: 8 Will you *a* the case for God?
Pr 25: 9 If you *a* your case with a neighbor,

ARGUMENT (ARGUE)

Heb 6: 16 is said and puts an end to all *a*.

ARGUMENTS (ARGUE)

Isa 41: 21 "Set forth your *a*," says Jacob's
Col 2: 4 you by fine-sounding *a*.
2Ti 2: 23 to do with foolish and stupid *a*,
Tit 3: 9 and *a* and quarrels about the law,

ARK

Ge   6: 14 So make yourself an *a*
Ex 25: 21 and put in the *a* the Testimony,
Dt 10: 5 put the tablets in the *a* I had made,
1Sa 4: 11 The *a* of God was captured,
     7: 2 that the *a* remained at Kiriath
2Sa 6: 17 They brought the *a* of the LORD
1Ki 8: 9 There was nothing in the *a*
1Ch 13: 9 out his hand to steady the *a*,
2Ch 35: 3 "Put the sacred *a* in the temple that
Heb 9: 4 This *a* contained the gold jar
    11: 7 in holy fear built an *a*
Rev 11: 19 within his temple was seen the *a*

ARM (ARMY)

Nu 11: 23 "Is the LORD's *a* too short?
Dt   4: 34 hand and an outstretched *a*,
     7: 19 mighty hand and outstretched *a*,
Ps 44: 3 it was your right hand, your *a*,
    98: 1 his right hand and his holy *a*
Jer 27: 5 outstretched *a* I made the earth
1Pe 4: 1 *a* yourselves also with the same

ARMAGEDDON*

Rev 16: 16 that in Hebrew is called *A*.

ARMIES (ARMY)

1Sa 17: 26 Philistine that he should defy the *a*
Rev 19: 14 *a* of heaven were following him,

ARMOR (ARMY)

1Ki 20: 11 on his *a* should not boast like one
Jer 46: 4 put on your *a!*
Ro 13: 12 deeds of darkness and put on the *a*
Eph 6: 11 Put on the full *a* of God
     6: 13 Therefore put on the full *a* of God,

ARMS (ARMY)

Dt 33: 27 underneath are the everlasting *a*.
Ps 18: 32 It is God who *a* me with strength

Pr 31: 17 her *a* are strong for her tasks.
    31: 20 She opens her *a* to the poor
Isa 40: 11 He gathers the lambs in his *a*
Mk 10: 16 And he took the children in his *a*,
Heb 12: 12 strengthen your feeble *a*

ARMY (ARM ARMIES ARMOR ARMS)

Ps 33: 16 No king is saved by the size of his *a*
Joel 2: 2 a large and mighty *a* comes,
     2: 5 like a mighty *a* drawn up for battle.
     2: 11 thunders at the head of his *a;*
Rev 19: 19 the rider on the horse and his *a*.

AROMA

Ge   8: 21 The LORD smelled the pleasing *a*
Ex 29: 18 a pleasing *a*, an offering made
Lev 3: 16 made by fire, a pleasing *a*.
2Co 2: 15 For we are to God the *a* of Christ

AROUSE (AROUSED)

Ro 10: 14 I may somehow *a* my own people

AROUSED (AROUSE)

Ps 78: 58 they *a* his jealousy with their idols.

ARRANGED

1Co 12: 18 But in fact God has *a* the parts

ARRAYED*

Ps 110: 3 *A* in holy majesty,
Isa 61: 10 and *a* me in a robe of righteousness

ARREST

Mt 10: 19 But when they *a* you, do not worry

ARROGANCE (ARROGANT)

1Sa 2: 3 or let your mouth speak such *a*,
Pr   8: 13 I hate pride and *a*,
Mk   7: 22 lewdness, envy, slander, *a* and folly
2Co 12: 20 slander, gossip, *a* and disorder.

ARROGANT (ARROGANCE)

Ps   5: 5 The *a* cannot stand
    119: 78 May the *a* be put to shame
Pr 17: 7 *A* lips are unsuited to a fool—
    21: 24 a man—"Mocker" is his name;
Ro   1: 30 God-haters, insolent, *a*
     1: 20 Do not be *a*, but be afraid.
1Ti 6: 17 in this present world not to be *a*

ARROW (ARROWS)

Ps 91: 5 nor the *a* that flies by day,
Pr 25: 18 Like a club or a sword or a sharp *a*

ARROWS (ARROW)

Ps 64: 3 and aim their words like deadly *a*.
    64: 7 But God will shoot them with *a;*
    127: 4 Like *a* in the hands of a warrior
Pr 26: 18 firebrands or deadly *a*
Eph 6: 16 you can extinguish all the flaming *a*

ARTAXERXES

King of Persia; allowed rebuilding of temple under Ezra (Ezr 4; 7), and of walls of Jerusalem under his cupbearer Nehemiah (Ne 2; 5:14; 13:6).

ARTEMIS

Ac 19: 28 "Great is *A* of the Ephesians!"

ASA

King of Judah (1Ki 15:8-24; 1Ch 3:10; 2Ch 14-16). Godly reformer (2Ch 15); in later years defeated Israel with help of Aram, not the LORD (1Ki 15:16-22; 2Ch 16).

ASAHEL

1. Nephew of David, one of his warriors (2Sa 23:24; 1Ch 2:16; 11:26; 27:7). Killed by Abner (2Sa 2); avenged by Joab (2Sa 3:22-39).
2. Levite; teacher (2Ch 17:8).

ASAPH

1. Recorder to Hezekiah (2Ki 18:18, 37; Isa 36: 3, 22).
2. Levitical musician (1Ch 6:39; 15:17-19; 16: 4-7, 37). Sons of (1Ch 25; 2Ch 5:12; 20:14; 29:13; 35:15; Ezr 2:41; 3:10; Ne 7:44; 11:17; 12:27-47). Psalms of (2Ch 29:30; Ps 50; 73-83).

ASCEND* (ASCENDED ASCENDING)

Dt 30: 12 "Who will *a* into heaven to get it
Ps 24: 3 Who may *a* the hill of the LORD?
Isa 14: 13 "I will *a* to heaven;
    14: 14 I will *a* above the tops of the clouds
Jn   6: 62 of Man *a* to where he was before!
Ac   2: 34 For David did not *a* to heaven,
Ro 10: 6 'Who will *a* into heaven?' " (that is,

ASCENDED (ASCEND)

Ps 68: 18 When you *a* on high,
Eph 4: 8 "When he *a* on high,

ASCENDING (ASCEND)

Ge 28: 12 and the angels of God were *a*
Jn   1: 51 and the angels of God *a*

ASCRIBE*

1Ch 16: 28 *A* to the LORD, O families
    16: 28 *a* to the LORD glory and strength,
    16: 29 *a* to the LORD the glory due his
Job 36: 3 I will *a* justice to my Maker.
Ps 29: 1 *A* to the LORD, O mighty ones,
    29: 1 *a* to the LORD glory and strength.
    29: 2 *A* to the LORD the glory due his
    96: 7 *A* to the LORD, O families
    96: 7 *a* to the LORD glory and strength.
    96: 8 *A* to the LORD the glory due his

ASHAMED (SHAME)

Mk   8: 38 If anyone is *a* of me and my words
Lk   9: 26 If anyone is *a* of me and my words,
Ro   1: 16 I am not *a* of the gospel,
2Ti 1: 8 So do not be *a* to testify about our
     2: 15 who does not need to be *a*

ASHER

Son of Jacob by Zilpah (Ge 30:13; 35:26; 46: 17; Ex 1:4; 1Ch 2:2). Tribe of blessed (Ge 49:20; Dt 33:24-25), numbered (Nu 1:40-41; 26:44-47), allotted land (Jos 10:24-31; Eze 48:2), failed to fully possess (Jdg 1:31-32), failed to support Deborah (Jdg 5:17), supported Gideon (Jdg 6:35; 7:23) and David (1Ch 12:36), 12,000 from (Rev 7: 6).

ASHERAH (ASHERAHS)

Ex 34: 13 and cut down their *A* poles.
1Ki 18: 19 the four hundred prophets of *A*,

ASHERAHS* (ASHERAH)

Jdg 3: 7 and served the Baals and the *A*.

ASHES

Job 42: 6 and repent in dust and *a*."
Mt 11: 21 ago in sackcloth and *a*.

ASHTORETHS

Jdg 2: 13 and served Baal and the *A*.
1Sa 7: 4 put away their Baals and *A*,

ASLEEP (SLEEP)

1Co 15: 18 who have fallen *a* in Christ are lost.
1Th 4: 13 be ignorant about those who fall *a*,

ASSEMBLY

Ps   1: 5 nor sinners in the *a* of the righteous
    35: 18 I will give you thanks in the great *a*
    82: 1 God presides in the great *a;*
    149: 1 his praise in the *a* of the saints.

ASSIGNED

1Ki 7: 14 and did all the work *a* to him.
Mk 13: 34 with his *a* task, and tells the one
1Co 3: 5 as the Lord has *a* to each his task.
     7: 17 place in life that the Lord *a* to him
2Co 10: 13 to the field God has *a* to us,

ASSOCIATE

Pr 22: 24 do not *a* with one easily angered,
Jn   4: 9 (For Jews do not *a* with Samaritans
Ac 10: 28 law for a Jew to *a* with a Gentile
Ro 12: 16 but be willing to *a* with people
1Co 5: 9 to *a* with sexually immoral people
     5: 11 am writing you that you must not *a*
2Th 3: 14 Do not *a* with him,

ASSURANCE (ASSURED)
Heb 10: 22 with a sincere heart in full *a* of faith

ASSURED (ASSURANCE)
Col 4: 12 the will of God, mature and fully *a*.

ASTRAY
Ps 119: 67 Before I was afflicted I went *a*,
Pr 10: 17 ignores correction leads others *a*.
20: 1 whoever is led *a* by them is not
Isa 53: 6 We all, like sheep, have gone *a*,
Jer 50: 6 their shepherds have led them *a*
Jn 16: 1 you so that you will not go *a*.
1Pe 2: 25 For you were like sheep going *a*,
1Jn 3: 7 do not let anyone lead you *a*.

ASTROLOGERS
Isa 47: 13 Let your *a* come forward,
Da 2: 2 *a* to tell him what he had dreamed.

ATE (EAT)
Ge 3: 6 wisdom, she took some and *a* it.
27: 25 Jacob brought it to him and he *a*;
2Sa 9: 11 Mephibosheth *a* at David's table
Ps 78: 25 Men *a* the bread of angels;
Jer 15: 16 When your words came, I *a* them;
Eze 3: 3 So I *a* it, and it tasted as sweet
Mt 14: 20 They all *a* and were satisfied,
15: 37 They all *a* and were satisfied,
Mk 6: 42 They all *a* and were satisfied,
Lk 9: 17 They all *a* and were satisfied,

ATHALIAH
Granddaughter of Omri; wife of Jehoram and mother of Ahaziah; encouraged their evil ways (2Ki 8:18, 27; 2Ch 22:2). At death of Ahaziah she made herself queen, killing all his sons but Joash (2Ki 11:1-3; 2Ch 22:10-12); killed six years later when Joash was revealed (2Ki 11:4-16; 2Ch 23: 1-15).

ATHLETE*
2Ti 2: 5 if anyone competes as an *a*,

ATONE* (ATONEMENT)
Ex 30: 15 to the LORD to *a* for your lives.
2Ch 29: 24 for a sin offering to *a* for all Israel,
Da 9: 24 an end to sin, to *a* for wickedness,

ATONED* (ATONEMENT)
Dt 21: 8 And the bloodshed will be *a* for.
1Sa 3: 14 guilt of Eli's house will never be *a*
Pr 16: 6 faithfulness sin is *a* for;
Isa 6: 7 guilt is taken away and your sin *a*
22: 14 your dying day this sin will not be *a*
27: 9 then, will Jacob's guilt be *a* for,

ATONEMENT (ATONE ATONED)
Ex 25: 17 "Make an *a* cover of pure gold—
30: 10 Once a year Aaron shall make *a*
Lev 17: 11 it is the blood that makes *a*
23: 27 this seventh month is the Day of *A*.
Nu 25: 13 and made *a* for the Israelites."
Ro 3: 25 presented him as a sacrifice of *a*,
Heb 2: 17 that he might make *a* for the sins

ATTACK
Ps 109: 3 they *a* me without cause.

ATTAINED
Php 3: 16 up to what we have already *a*.
Heb 7: 11 If perfection could have been *a*

ATTENTION (ATTENTIVE)
Pr 4: 1 pay *a* and gain understanding.
4: 20 My son, pay *a* to what I say;
5: 1 My son, pay *a* to my wisdom,
7: 24 pay *a* to what I say.
Ecc 7: 21 Do not pay *a* to every word people
Isa 42: 20 many things, but have paid no *a*;
Tit 1: 14 and will pay no *a* to Jewish myths
Heb 2: 1 We must pay more careful *a*,

ATTENTIVE (ATTENTION)
Ne 1: 11 let your ear be *a* to the prayer
1Pe 3: 12 and his ears are *a* to their prayer,

ATTITUDE (ATTITUDES)
Eph 4: 23 new in the *a* of your minds;
Php 2: 5 Your *a* should be the same
1Pe 4: 1 yourselves also with the same *a*,

ATTITUDES (ATTITUDE)
Heb 4: 12 it judges the thoughts and *a*

ATTRACTIVE
Tit 2: 10 teaching about God our Savior *a*.

AUDIENCE
Pr 29: 26 Many seek an *a* with a ruler,

AUTHORITIES (AUTHORITY)
Ro 13: 1 *a* that exist have been established
13: 5 it is necessary to submit to the *a*,
13: 6 for the *a* are God's servants,
Eph 3: 10 and *a* in the heavenly realms,
6: 12 but against the rulers, against the *a*,
Col 1: 16 thrones or powers or rulers or *a*;
2: 15 having disarmed the powers and *a*,
Tit 3: 1 people to be subject to rulers and *a*,
1Pe 3: 22 *a* and powers in submission to him.

AUTHORITY (AUTHORITIES)
Mt 7: 29 because he taught as one who had *a*
9: 6 the Son of Man has *a* on earth
28: 18 "All *a* in heaven and on earth has
Mk 1: 22 he taught them as one who had *a*,
2: 10 the Son of Man has *a* on earth
Lk 4: 32 because his message had *a*.
5: 24 the Son of Man has *a* on earth
Jn 10: 18 *a* to lay it down and *a*
Ac 1: 7 the Father has set by his own *a*.
Ro 7: 1 that the law has *a* over a man only
13: 1 for there is no *a* except that which
13: 2 rebels against the *a* is rebelling
1Co 11: 10 to have a sign of *a* on her head.
15: 24 he has destroyed all dominion, *a*
1Ti 2: 2 for kings and all those in *a*,
2: 12 to teach or to have *a* over a man;
Tit 2: 15 Encourage and rebuke with all *a*.
Heb 13: 17 your leaders and submit to their *a*.

AUTUMN*
Dt 11: 14 both *a* and spring rains,
Ps 84: 6 the *a* rains also cover it with pools.
Jer 5: 24 who gives *a* and spring rains
Joel 2: 23 both *a* and spring rains, as before.
Jas 5: 7 and how patient he is for the *a*
Jude : 12 blown along by the wind; *a* trees,

AVENGE (VENGEANCE)
Lev 26: 25 sword upon you to *a* the breaking
Dt 32: 35 It is mine to *a*; I will repay.
32: 43 for he will *a* the blood
Ro 12: 19 "It is mine to *a*; I will repay,"
Heb 10: 30 "It is mine to *a*; I will repay,"
Rev 6: 10 of the earth and *a* our blood?"

AVENGER (VENGEANCE)
Nu 35: 27 the *a* of blood may kill the accused
Jos 20: 3 find protection from the *a* of blood.
Ps 8: 2 to silence the foe and the *a*.

AVENGES (VENGEANCE)
Ps 94: 1 O LORD, the God who *a*,

AVENGING (VENGEANCE)
1Sa 25: 26 and from *a* yourself with your own
Na 1: 2 The LORD is a jealous and *a* God;

AVOID (AVOIDS)
Pr 4: 15 A it, do not travel on it;
20: 3 It is to a man's honor to *a* strife,
20: 19 so *a* a man who talks too much.
Ecc 7: 18 who fears God will *a* all extremes.
1Th 4: 3 you should *a* sexual immorality;
5: 22 A every kind of evil.
2Ti 2: 16 A godless chatter, because those
Tit 3: 9 But *a* foolish controversies

AVOIDS* (AVOID)
Pr 16: 6 of the LORD a man *a* evil.
16: 17 The highway of the upright *a* evil;

AWAITS (WAIT)
Pr 15: 10 Stern discipline *a* him who leaves
28: 22 and is unaware that poverty *a* him.

AWAKE (WAKE)
Ps 17: 15 when I *a*, I will be satisfied
Pr 6: 22 when you *a*, they will speak to you.

AWARD*
2Ti 4: 8 will *a* to me on that day—

AWARE
Ex 34: 29 he was not *a* that his face was
Mt 24: 50 and at an hour he is not *a* of.
Lk 12: 46 and at an hour he is not *a* of.

AWE* (AWESOME OVERAWED)
1Sa 12: 18 So all the people stood in *a*
1Ki 3: 28 they held the king in *a*,
Job 25: 2 "Dominion and *a* belong to God;
Ps 119:120 I stand in *a* of your laws.
Ecc 5: 7 Therefore stand in *a* of God.
Isa 29: 23 will stand in *a* of the God of Israel.
Jer 2: 19 and have no *a* of me,"
33: 9 they will be in *a* and will tremble
Hab 3: 2 I stand in *a* of your deeds,
Mal 2: 5 and stood in *a* of my name.
Mt 9: 8 they were filled with *a*
Lk 1: 65 The neighbors were all filled with *a*
5: 26 They were filled with *a* and said,
7: 16 They were all filled with *a*
Ac 2: 43 Everyone was filled with *a*,
Heb 12: 28 acceptably with reverence and *a*,

AWESOME* (AWE)
Ge 28: 17 and said, "How *a* is this place!
Ex 15: 11 *a* in glory,
34: 10 among will see how *a* is the work
Dt 4: 34 or by great and *a* deeds,
7: 21 is among you, is a great and *a* God.
10: 17 the great God, mighty and *a*,
10: 21 and *a* wonders you saw
28: 58 revere this glorious and *a* name—
34: 12 performed the *a* deeds that Moses
Jdg 13: 6 like an angel of God, very *a*.
2Sa 7: 23 *a* wonders by driving out nations
1Ch 17: 21 *a* wonders by driving out nations
Ne 1: 5 of heaven, the great and *a* God,
4: 14 and *a*, and fight for your brothers,
9: 32 the great, mighty and *a* God,
Job 10: 16 again display your *a* power
37: 22 God comes in *a* majesty.
Ps 45: 4 let your right hand display *a* deeds.
47: 2 How *a* is the LORD Most High,
65: 5 us with *a* deeds of righteousness,
66: 3 to God, "How *a* are your deeds!
66: 5 how *a* his works in man's behalf!
68: 35 You are *a*, O God,
89: 7 he is more *a* than all who surround
99: 3 praise your great and *a* name—
106: 22 and *a* deeds by the Red Sea.
111: 9 holy and *a* is his name.
145: 6 of the power of your *a* works,
Isa 64: 3 when you did *a* things that we did
Eze 1: 18 Their rims were high and *a*,
1: 22 expanse, sparkling like ice, and *a*.
Da 2: 31 dazzling statue, *a* in appearance.
9: 4 "O Lord, the great and *a* God,
Zep 2: 11 The LORD will be *a* to them

AX
Mt 3: 10 The *a* is already at the root
Lk 3: 9 The *a* is already at the root

BAAL
Jdg 6: 25 Tear down your father's altar to *B*
1Ki 16: 32 *B* in the temple of *B* that he built
18: 25 Elijah said to the prophets of *B*,
19: 18 knees have not bowed down to *B*
2Ki 10: 28 Jehu destroyed *B* worship in Israel.
Jer 19: 5 places of *B* to burn their sons
Ro 11: 4 have not bowed the knee to *B*."

BAASHA
King of Israel (1Ki 15:16-16:7; 2Ch 16:1-6).

BABBLER* (BABBLING)
Ac 17: 18 "What is this *b* trying to say?"

BABBLING* (BABBLER)

Mt 6: 7 do not keep on *b* like pagans,

BABIES* (BABY)

Ge 25:22 The *b* jostled each other within her
Ex 2: 6 "This is one of the Hebrew *b*,"
Lk 18:15 also bringing *b* to Jesus
Ac 7:19 them to throw out their newborn *b*
1Pe 2: 2 Like newborn *b*, crave pure

BABY* (BABIES BABY'S)

Ex 2: 6 She opened it and saw the *b*.
2: 7 women to nurse the *b* for you?"
2: 9 So the woman took the *b*
2: 9 "Take this *b* and nurse him for me,
1Ki 3:17 I had a *b* while she was there
3:18 was born, this woman also had a *b*.
3:26 give her the living *b*! Don't kill him
3:27 Give the living *b* to the first woman
Isa 49:15 "Can a mother forget the *b*
Lk 1:41 the *b* leaped in her womb.
1:44 the *b* in my womb leaped for joy.
1:57 time for Elizabeth to have her *b*,
2: 6 the time came for the *b* to be born,
2:12 You will find a *b* wrapped in strips
2:16 the *b*, who was lying in the manger.
Jn 16:21 but when her *b* is born she forgets

BABY'S* (BABY)

Ex 2: 8 the girl went and got the *b* mother.

BABYLON

Ps 137: 1 By the rivers of *B* we sat and wept
Jer 29:10 seventy years are completed for *B*,
51:37 *B* will be a heap of ruins,
Rev 14: 8 "Fallen! Fallen is *B* the Great,
17: 5 MYSTERY *B* THE GREAT

BACKS

2Pe 2:21 and then to turn their *b*

BACKSLIDING* (BACKSLIDINGS)

Jer 2:19 your *b* will rebuke you.
3:22 I will cure you of *b*."
14: 7 For our *b* is great;
15: 6 "You keep on *b*.
Eze 37:23 them from all their sinful *b*,

BACKSLIDINGS* (BACKSLIDING)

Jer 5: 6 and their *b* many.

BALAAM

Prophet who attempted to curse Israel (Nu 22-24; Dt 23:4-5; 2Pe 2:15; Jude 11). Killed in Israel's vengeance on Midianites (Nu 31:8; Jos 13:22).

BALAK

Moabite king who hired Balaam to curse Israel (Nu 22-24; Jos 24:9).

BALDHEAD

2Ki 2:23 "Go on up, you *b*!" they said.

BALM

Jer 8:22 Is there no *b* in Gilead?

BANISH (BANISHED)

Jer 25:10 I will *b* from them the sounds of joy

BANISHED (BANISH)

Dt 30: 4 Even if you have been *b*

BANNER

Ex 17:15 and called it The LORD is my *B*.
SS 2: 4 and his *b* over me is love.
Isa 11:10 the Root of Jesse will stand as a *b*

BANQUET

SS 2: 4 He has taken me to the *b* hall,
Lk 14:13 when you give a *b*, invite the poor,

BAPTISM* (BAPTIZE)

Mt 21:25 John's *b*— where did it come from?
Mk 1: 4 and preaching the *b* of repentance
10:38 baptized with the *b* I am baptized
10:39 baptized with the *b* I am baptized
11:30 John's *b*— was it from heaven,

Lk 3: 3 preaching a *b* of repentance
12:50 But I have a *b* to undergo,
20: 4 John's *b*— was it from heaven,
Ac 1:22 beginning from John's *b*
10:37 after the *b* that John preached—
13:24 and *b* to all the people of Israel.
18:25 though he knew only the *b* of John.
19: 3 did you receive?" "John's *b*,"
19: 3 "Then what *b* did you receive?"
19: 4 "John's *b* was a *b* of repentance.
Ro 6: 4 with him through *b* into death
Eph 4: 5 one Lord, one faith, one *b*;
Col 2:12 having been buried with him in *b*
1Pe 3:21 this water symbolizes *b* that now

BAPTISMS* (BAPTIZE)

Heb 6: 2 instruction about *b*, the laying

BAPTIZE* (BAPTISM BAPTISMS BAPTIZED BAPTIZING)

Mt 3:11 He will *b* you with the Holy Spirit
3:11 "I *b* you with water for repentance.
Mk 1: 8 I *b* you with water, but he will
1: 8 he will *b* you with the Holy Spirit."
Lk 3:16 He will *b* you with the Holy Spirit
3:16 John answered them all, "I *b* you
Jn 1:25 "Why then do you *b*
1:26 nor the Prophet?" "I *b* with water,"
1:33 and remain is he who will *b*
1:33 me to *b* with water told me,
1Co 1:14 I am thankful that I did not *b* any
1:17 For Christ did not send me to *b*,

BAPTIZED* (BAPTIZE)

Mt 3: 6 they were *b* by him in the Jordan
3:13 to the Jordan to be *b* by John.
3:14 saying, "I need to be *b* by you,
3:16 as Jesus was *b*, he went up out
Mk 1: 5 they were *b* by him in the Jordan
1: 9 and was *b* by John in the Jordan.
10:38 or be *b* with the baptism I am
10:38 with the baptism I am *b* with?"
10:39 and be *b* with the baptism I am
10:39 with the baptism I am *b* with,
16:16 believes and is *b* will be saved,
Lk 3: 7 to the crowds coming out to be *b*
3:12 Tax collectors also came to be *b*.
3:21 were being *b*, Jesus was too.
7:29 because they had been *b* by John.
7:30 they had not been *b* by John.)
Jn 3:22 spent some time with them, and *b*.
3:23 were constantly coming to be *b*.
4: 2 in fact it was not Jesus who *b*,
Ac 1: 5 For John *b* with water,
1: 5 but in a few days you will be *b*
2:38 Repent and be *b*, every one of you,
2:41 who accepted his message were *b*,
8:12 they were *b*, both men and women.
8:13 Simon himself believed and was *b*.
8:16 they had simply been *b*
8:36 Why shouldn't I be *b*?"
8:38 into the water and Philip *b* him.
9:18 was *b*, and after taking some food,
10:47 people from being *b* with water?
10:48 So he ordered that they be *b*
11:16 what the Lord had said, 'John *b*
11:16 you will be *b* with the Holy Spirit.'
16:15 members of her household were *b*,
16:33 he and all his family were *b*.
18: 8 heard him believed and were *b*.
19: 5 they were *b* into the name
22:16 be *b* and wash your sins away,
Ro 6: 3 *b* into Christ Jesus were *b*
1Co 1:13 Were you *b* into the name of Paul?
1:15 so no one can say that you were *b*
1:16 I also *b* the household of Stephanas
1:16 I don't remember if I *b* anyone else
10: 2 They were all *b* into Moses
12:13 For we were all *b* by one Spirit
15:29 what will those do who are *b*
15:29 why are people *b* for them?
Gal 3:27 all of you who were *b*

BAPTIZING* (BAPTIZE)

Mt 3: 7 coming to where he was *b*,
28:19 *b* them in the name of the Father
Mk 1: 4 *b* in the desert region
Jn 1:28 of the Jordan, where John was *b*.

Jn 1:31 but the reason I came *b*
3:23 also was *b* at Aenon near Salim,
3:26 he is *b*, and everyone is going
4: 1 and *b* more disciples than John,
10:40 to the place where John had been *b*

BAR-JESUS*

Ac 13: 6 and false prophet named *B*,

BARABBAS

Mt 27:26 Then he released *B* to them.

BARAK*

Judge who fought with Deborah against Canaanites (Jdg 4-5; 1Sa 12:11; Heb 11:32).

BARBARIAN*

Col 3:11 circumcised or uncircumcised, *b*,

BARBS*

Nu 33:55 allow to remain will become *b*

BARE

Hos 2: 3 as *b* as on the day she was born;
Heb 4:13 and laid *b* before the eyes of him

BARNABAS*

Disciple, originally Joseph (Ac 4:36), prophet (Ac 13:1), apostle (Ac 14:14). Brought Paul to apostles (Ac 9:27), Antioch (Ac 11:22-29; Gal 2:1-13), on the first missionary journey (Ac 13-14). Together at Jerusalem Council, they separated over John Mark (Ac 15). Later co-workers (1Co 9:6; Col 4:10).

BARREN

Ge 11:30 Sarai was *b*; she had no children.
29:31 her womb, but Rachel was *b*.
Ps 113: 9 He settles the *b* woman
Isa 54: 1 "Sing, O *b* woman,
Lk 1: 7 children, because Elizabeth was *b*;
Gal 4:27 "Be glad, O *b* woman,
Heb 11:11 and Sarah herself was *b*—

BARTHOLOMEW*

Apostle (Mt 10:3; Mk 3:18; Lk 6:14; Ac 1:13). Possibly also known as Nathanael (Jn 1:45-49; 21:2).

BARUCH

Jeremiah's secretary (Jer 32:12-16; 36; 43:1-6; 45:1-2).

BARZILLAI

1. Gileadite who aided David during Absalom's revolt (2Sa 17:27; 19:31-39).
2. Son-in-law of 1. (Ezr 2:61; Ne 7:63).

BASHAN

Jos 22: 7 Moses had given land in *B*,
Ps 22:12 strong bulls of *B* encircle me.

BASIN

Ex 30:18 "Make a bronze *b*,

BASKET

Ex 2: 3 she got a papyrus *b* for him
Ac 9:25 him in a *b* through an opening
2Co 11:33 I was lowered in a *b* from a window

BATCH*

Ro 11:16 then the whole *b* is holy;
1Co 5: 6 through the whole *b* of dough?
5: 7 old yeast that you may be a new *b*
Gal 5: 9 through the whole *b* of dough."

BATH (BATHING)

Jn 13:10 person who has had a *b* needs only

BATHING (BATH)

2Sa 11: 2 From the roof he saw a woman *b*.

BATHSHEBA*

Wife of Uriah who committed adultery with and became wife of David (2Sa 11), mother of Solomon (2Sa 12:24; 1Ki 1-2; 1Ch 3:5).

BATTLE (BATTLES)

1Sa 17:47 for the *b* is the LORD's,

2Ch 20: 15 For the *b* is not yours, but God's.
Ps 24: 8 the LORD mighty in *b*.
Ecc 9: 11 or the *b* to the strong,
Isa 31: 4 down to do *b* on Mount Zion
Eze 13: 5 in the *b* on the day of the LORD.
Rev 16: 14 them for the *b* on the great day
         20: 8 and Magog—to gather them for *b*.

BATTLES* (BATTLE)

1Sa 8: 20 to go out before us and fight our *b*.''
         18: 17 and fight the *b* of the LORD.''
         25: 28 because he fights the LORD's *b*.
2Ch 32: 8 God to help us and to fight our *b*.''

**BEAR (BEARING BEARS BIRTH
BIRTHRIGHT BORE BORN
CHILDBEARING CHILDBIRTH
FIRSTBORN NEWBORN REBIRTH)**

Ge   4: 13 punishment is more than I can *b*.
Ps 38: 4 like a burden too heavy to *b*.
Isa 11: 7 The cow will feed with the *b*,
         53: 11 and he will *b* their iniquities.
Da   7: 5 beast, which looked like a *b*.
Mt   7: 18 A good tree cannot *b* bad fruit,
Jn 15: 2 branch that does *b* fruit he prunes
         15: 8 glory, that you *b* much fruit,
         15: 16 appointed you to go and *b* fruit—
Ro   7: 4 in order that we might *b* fruit
         15: 1 ought to *b* with the failings
1Co 10: 13 tempted beyond what you can *b*.
Col 3: 13 *B* with each other and forgive

BEARD

Lev 19: 27 or clip off the edges of your *b*.
Isa 50: 6 to those who pulled out my *b*;

BEARING (BEAR)

Eph 4: 2 *b* with one another in love.
Col 1: 10 *b* fruit in every good work,
Heb 13: 13 outside the camp, *b* the disgrace he

BEARS (BEAR)

1Ki 8: 43 house I have built *b* your Name.
Ps 68: 19 who daily *b* our burdens.

BEAST (BEASTS)

Rev 13: 18 him calculate the number of the *b*,
         16: 2 people who had the mark of the *b*
         19: 20 who had received the mark of the *b*

BEASTS (BEAST)

Da   7: 3 Four great *b*, each different
1Co 15: 32 If I fought wild *b* in Ephesus

BEAT (BEATEN BEATING BEATINGS)

Isa 2: 4 They will *b* their swords
Joel 3: 10 *B* your plowshares into swords
Mic 4: 3 They will *b* their swords
1Co 9: 27 I *b* my body and make it my slave

BEATEN (BEAT)

Lk 12: 47 do what his master wants will be *b*
         12: 48 deserving punishment will be *b*
2Co 11: 25 Three times I was *b* with rods,

BEATING (BEAT)

1Co 9: 26 I do not fight like a man *b* the air.
1Pe 2: 20 if you receive a *b* for doing wrong

BEATINGS (BEAT)

Pr 19: 29 and *b* for the backs of fools.

BEAUTIFUL* (BEAUTY)

Ge   6: 2 that the daughters of men were *b*,
         12: 11 ''I know what a *b* woman you are.
         12: 14 saw that she was a very *b* woman.
         24: 16 The girl was very *b*, a virgin;
         26: 7 of Rebekah, because she is *b*.''
         29: 17 Rachel was lovely in form, and *b*.
         49: 21 that bears *b* fawns.
Nu 24: 5 ''How *b* are your tents, O Jacob,
Dt 21: 11 among the captives a *b* woman
Jos 7: 21 saw in the plunder a *b* robe,
1Sa 25: 3 was an intelligent and *b* woman,
2Sa 11: 2 The woman was very *b*,
         13: 1 the *b* sister of Absalom son
         14: 27 and she became a *b* woman.
1Ki 1: 3 throughout Israel for a *b* girl

1Ki 1: 4 The girl was very *b*; she took care
Est 2: 2 for *b* young virgins for the king.
          2: 3 realm to bring all these *b* girls
Job 38: 31 ''Can you bind the *b* Pleiades?
         42: 15 land were there found women as *b*
Ps 48: 2 It is *b* in its loftiness,
Pr 11: 22 is a *b* woman who shows no
         24: 4 filled with rare and *b* treasures.
Ecc 3: 11 He has made everything *b*
SS   1: 8 *Lover* If you do not know, most *b*
          1: 10 Your cheeks are *b* with earrings,
          1: 15 Oh, how *b*!
          1: 15 *Lover* How *b* you are, my darling!
          2: 10 my *b* one, and come with me.
          2: 13 my *b* one, come with me.''
          4: 1 How *b* you are, my darling!
          4: 1 Oh, how *b*!
          4: 7 All *b* you are, my darling,
          5: 9 most *b* of women?
          6: 1 most *b* of women?
          6: 4 *Lover* You are *b*, my darling,
          7: 1 How *b* your sandaled feet,
          7: 6 How *b* you are and how pleasing,
Isa 4: 2 of the LORD will be *b*
         28: 5 a *b* wreath
         52: 7 How *b* on the mountains
Jer 3: 19 the most *b* inheritance
          6: 2 so *b* and delicate.
         11: 16 with fruit *b* in form.
         46: 20 ''Egypt is a *b* heifer,
Eze 7: 20 They were proud of their *b* jewelry
         16: 7 and became the most *b* of jewels.
         16: 12 and a *b* crown on your head.
         16: 13 You became very *b* and rose
         20: 6 and honey, the most *b* of all lands.
         20: 15 and honey, most *b* of all lands—
         23: 42 and *b* crowns on their heads.
         27: 24 traded with you *b* garments,
         31: 3 with *b* branches overshadowing
         31: 9 I made it *b*
         33: 32 who sings love songs with a *b* voice
Da   4: 12 Its leaves were *b*, its fruit abundant
          4: 21 with *b* leaves and abundant fruit,
          8: 9 to the east and toward the *B* Land.
         11: 16 will establish himself in the *B* Land
         11: 41 He will also invade the *B* Land.
         11: 45 the seas at the *b* holy mountain.
Zec 9: 17 How attractive and *b* they will be!
Mt 23: 27 which look *b* on the outside
         26: 10 She has done a *b* thing to me.
Mk 14: 6 She has done a *b* thing to me.
Lk 21: 5 temple was adorned with *b* stones
Ac   3: 2 carried to the temple gate called *B*,
          3: 10 at the temple gate called *B*,
Ro 10: 15 ''How *b* are the feet
1Pe 3: 5 in God used to make themselves *b*.

BEAUTY* (BEAUTIFUL)

Est 1: 11 order to display her *b* to the people
          2: 3 let *b* treatments be given to them.
          2: 9 her with her *b* treatments
          2: 12 months of *b* treatments prescribed
Ps 27: 4 to gaze upon the *b* of the LORD
         37: 20 LORD's enemies will be like the *b*
         45: 11 The king is enthralled by your *b*;
         50: 2 From Zion, perfect in *b*,
Pr   6: 25 lust in your heart after her *b*
         31: 30 is deceptive, and *b* is fleeting;
Isa 3: 24 instead of *b*, branding.
         28: 1 to the fading flower, his glorious *b*,
         28: 4 That fading flower, his glorious *b*,
         33: 17 Your eyes will see the king in his *b*
         53: 2 He had no *b* or majesty
         61: 3 to bestow on them a crown of *b*
La   2: 15 the perfection of *b*,
Eze 16: 14 had given you made your *b* perfect,
         16: 14 the nations on account of your *b*,
         16: 15 passed by and your *b* became his.
         16: 15 ''But you trusted in your *b*
         16: 25 lofty shrines and degraded your *b*,
         27: 3 ''I am perfect in *b*.''
         27: 4 your builders brought your *b*
         27: 11 they brought your *b* to perfection.
         28: 7 draw their swords against your *b*
         28: 12 full of wisdom and perfect in *b*.
         28: 17 proud on account of your *b*,
         31: 7 It was majestic in *b*,
         31: 8 could match its *b*.

Jas 1: 11 blossom falls and its *b* is destroyed.
1Pe 3: 3 Your *b* should not come
          3: 4 the unfading *b* of a gentle

BED (SICKBED)

Isa 28: 20 The *b* is too short to stretch out on,
Lk 11: 7 and my children are with me in the
         17: 34 night two people will be in one *b*;
Heb 13: 4 and the marriage *b* kept pure,

BEELZEBUB*

Mt 10: 25 of the house has been called *B*,
         12: 24 ''It is only by *B*, the prince
         12: 27 And if I drive out demons by *B*,
Mk   3: 22 possessed by *B*! By the prince
Lk 11: 15 ''By *B*, the prince of demons,
         11: 18 claim that I drive out demons by *B*.
         11: 19 Now if I drive out demons by *B*,

BEER

Pr 20: 1 Wine is a mocker and *b* a brawler;

BEERSHEBA

Ge 21: 14 and wandered in the desert of *B*.
Jdg 20: 1 all the Israelites from Dan to *B*
1Sa 3: 20 to *B* recognized that Samuel was
2Sa 3: 10 and Judah from Dan to *B*.''
         17: 11 Let all Israel, from Dan to *B*—
         24: 2 the tribes of Israel from Dan to *B*
         24: 15 of the people from Dan to *B* died.
1Ki 4: 25 from Dan to *B*, lived in safety,
1Ch 21: 2 count the Israelites from *B* to Dan,
2Ch 30: 5 throughout Israel, from *B* to Dan,

BEFALLS*

Pr 12: 21 No harm *b* the righteous,

BEGGING

Ps 37: 25 or their children *b* bread.
Ac 16: 9 of Macedonia standing and *b* him,

BEGINNING

Ge   1: 1 In the *b* God created the heavens
Ps 102: 25 In the *b* you laid the foundations
         111: 10 of the LORD is the *b* of wisdom;
Pr   1: 7 of the LORD is the *b* of knowledge
          9: 10 of the LORD is the *b* of wisdom,
Ecc 3: 11 fathom what God has done from *b*
Isa 40: 21 Has it not been told you from the *b*
         46: 10 I make known the end from the *b*,
Mt 24: 8 All these are the *b* of birth pains.
Lk   1: 3 investigated everything from the *b*,
Jn   1: 1 In the *b* was the Word,
1Jn 1: 1 That which was from the *b*,
Rev 21: 6 and the Omega, the *B* and the End.
         22: 13 and the Last, the *B* and the End.

BEHAVE (BEHAVIOR)

Ro 13: 13 Let us *b* decently, as in the daytime

BEHAVIOR (BEHAVE)

1Pe 3: 1 without words by the *b* of their wives,
          3: 16 maliciously against your good *b*

BEHEMOTH*

Job 40: 15 ''Look at the *b*,

**BELIEVE (BELIEVED BELIEVER
BELIEVERS BELIEVES BELIEVING)**

Ex   4: 1 ''What if they do not *b* me
1Ki 10: 7 I did not *b* these things until I came
2Ch 9: 6 But I did not *b* what they said
Ps 78: 32 of his wonders, they did not *b*.
Hab 1: 5 that you would not *b*,
Mt 18: 6 one of these little ones who *b* in me
         21: 22 If you *b*, you will receive whatever
         27: 42 from the cross, and we will *b* in him
Mk   1: 15 Repent and *b* the good news!''
          5: 36 ruler, ''Don't be afraid; just *b*.''
          9: 24 ''I do *b*; help me overcome my
          9: 42 one of these little ones who *b* in me
         11: 24 *b* that you have received it,
         15: 32 the cross, that we may see and *b*.''
         16: 16 but whoever does not *b* will be
         16: 17 signs will accompany those who *b*:
Lk   8: 12 so that they may not *b* and be saved.
          8: 13 They *b* for a while, but in the time
          8: 50 just *b*, and she will be healed.''

Lk   22:67 you will not *b* me,
    24:25 to *b* all that the prophets have
Jn   1: 7 that through him all men might *b*.
    3:18 does not *b* stands condemned
    4:42 "We no longer *b* just
    5:38 for you do not *b* the one he sent.
    5:46 believed Moses, you would *b* me,
    6:29 to *b* in the one he has sent."
    6:69 We *b* and know that you are
    7: 5 his own brothers did not *b* in him.
    8:24 if you do not *b* that I am the one I
    9:35 "Do you *b* in the Son of Man?"
    9:36 "Tell me so that I may *b* in him."
    9:38 "Lord, I *b*," and he worshiped him.
   10:26 you do not *b* because you are not
   10:37 Do not *b* me unless I do what my
   10:38 you do not *b* me, *b* the miracles.
   11:27 "I *b* that you are the Christ,
   12:37 they still would not *b* in him.
   12:39 For this reason they could not *b*,
   12:44 in me, he does not *b* in me only,
   13:19 does happen you will *b* that I am
   14:10 Don't you *b* that I am in the Father
   14:11 *B* me when I say that I am
   14:11 or at least *b* on the evidence
   16:30 This makes us *b* that you came
   16:31 "You *b* at last!" Jesus answered.
   17:21 that the world may *b* that you have
   19:35 he testifies so that you also may *b*.
   20:27 Stop doubting and *b*."
   20:31 written that you may *b* that Jesus is
Ac   16:31 They replied, "*B* in the Lord Jesus,
   19: 4 the people to *b* in the one coming
   24:14 I *b* everything that agrees
   26:27 Agrippa, do you *b* the prophets?"
Ro   3:22 faith in Jesus Christ to all who *b*.
   4:11 he is the father of all who *b*
   10: 9 *b* in your heart that God raised him
   10:10 For it is with your heart that you *b*
   10:14 And how can they *b* in the one
   16:26 so that all nations might *b*
1Co   1:21 preached to save those who *b*.
Gal   3:22 might be given to those who *b*.
Php   1:29 of Christ not only to *b* on him,
1Th   4:14 We *b* that Jesus died and rose again
2Th   2:11 delusion so that they will *b* the lie
1Ti   4:10 and especially of those who *b*.
Tit   1: 6 a man whose children *b*
Heb 11: 6 comes to him must *b* that he exists
Jas   1: 6 But when he asks, he must *b*
   2:19 Even the demons *b* that—
   2:19 You *b* that there is one God.
1Pe   2: 7 to you who *b*, this stone is precious
1Jn   3:23 to *b* in the name of his Son,
   4: 1 Dear friends, do not *b* every spirit,
   5:13 things to you who *b* in the name

BELIEVED (BELIEVE)

Ge   15: 6 Abram *b* the LORD, and he
Ex   4:31 signs before the people, and they *b*.
Isa   53: 1 Who has *b* our message
Jnh   3: 5 The Ninevites *b* God.
Lk   1:45 is she who has *b* what the Lord
Jn   1:12 to those who *b* in his name,
   2:22 Then they *b* the Scripture
   3:18 because he has not *b* in the name
   5:46 If you *b* Moses, you would believe
   7:39 whom those who *b*
   11:40 "Did I not tell you that if you *b*,
   12:38 "Lord, who has *b* our message
   20: 8 He saw and *b*.
   20:29 who have not seen and yet have *b*."
Ac   13:48 were appointed for eternal life *b*.
   19: 2 the Holy Spirit when you *b*?"
Ro   4: 3 Scripture say? "Abraham *b* God,
   10:14 call on the one they have not *b* in?
   10:16 "Lord, who has *b* our message?"
1Co 15: 2 Otherwise, you have *b* in vain.
Gal   3: 6 Consider Abraham: "He *b* God,
2Th   2:12 who have not *b* the truth
1Ti   3:16 was *b* on in the world,
2Ti   1:12 because I know whom I have *b*,
Jas   2:23 that says, "Abraham *b* God,

BELIEVER* (BELIEVE)

1Ki 18: 3 (Obadiah was a devout *b*
Ac   16: 1 whose mother was a Jewess and a *b*
   16:15 "If you consider me a *b* in the Lord

1Co   7:12 brother has a wife who is not a *b*
   7:13 has a husband who is not a *b*
2Co   6:15 What does a *b* have in common
1Ti   5:16 any woman who is a *b* has widows

BELIEVERS* (BELIEVE)

Jn   4:41 of his words many more became *b*.
Ac   1:15 among the *b* (a group numbering
   2:44 All the *b* were together
   4:32 All the *b* were one in heart
   5:12 And all the *b* used to meet together
   9:41 he called the *b* and the widows
   10:45 The circumcised *b* who had come
   11: 2 the circumcised *b* criticized him
   15: 2 along with some other *b*,
   15: 5 Then some of the *b* who belonged
   15:23 To the Gentile *b* in Antioch,
   21:25 for the Gentile *b*, we have written
1Co   6: 5 to judge a dispute between *b*?
   14:22 is for *b*, not for unbelievers.
   14:22 not for *b* but for unbelievers;
Gal   6:10 who belong to the family of *b*.
1Th   1: 7 a model to all the *b* in Macedonia
1Ti   4:12 set an example for the *b* in speech,
   6: 2 benefit from their service are *b*,
Jas   2: 1 *b* in our glorious Lord Jesus Christ,
1Pe   2:17 Love the brotherhood of *b*,

BELIEVES* (BELIEVE)

Pr   14:15 A simple man *b* anything,
Mk   9:23 is possible for him who *b*."
   11:23 *b* that what he says will happen,
   16:16 Whoever *b* and is baptized will be
Jn   3:15 that everyone who *b* in him
   3:16 that whoever *b* in him shall not
   3:18 Whoever *b* in him is not
   3:36 Whoever *b* in the Son has eternal
   5:24 *b* him who sent me has eternal life
   6:35 and he who *b* in me will never be
   6:40 and *b* in him shall have eternal life,
   6:47 he who *b* has everlasting life.
   7:38 Whoever *b* in me, as the Scripture
   11:25 He who *b* in me will live, even
   11:26 and *b* in me will never die.
   12:44 Jesus cried out, "When a man *b*
   12:46 so that no one who *b*
Ac   10:43 about him that everyone who *b*
   13:39 him everyone who *b* is justified
Ro   1:16 for the salvation of everyone who *b*.
   10: 4 righteousness for everyone who *b*.
1Jn   5: 1 Everyone who *b* that Jesus is
   5: 5 Only he who *b* that Jesus is the Son
   5:10 Anyone who *b* in the Son

BELIEVING* (BELIEVE)

Jn   20:31 and that by *b* you may have life
Ac   9:26 not *b* that he really was a disciple.
1Co   7:14 sanctified through her *b* husband.
   7:15 A *b* man or woman is not bound
   9: 5 right to take a *b* wife along with us,
Gal   3: 2 or by *b* what you heard? Are you
1Ti   6: 2 Those who have *b* masters are not

BELLY

Ge   3:14 You will crawl on your *b*
Da   2:32 its *b* and thighs of bronze,
Mt   12:40 three nights in the *b* of a huge fish,

BELONG (BELONGING BELONGS)

Ge   40: 8 "Do not interpretations *b* to God?
Lev 25:55 for the Israelites *b* to me
Dt   10:14 LORD your God *b* the heavens,
   29:29 The secret things *b*
Job   12:13 "To God *b* wisdom and power;
   12:16 To him *b* strength and victory;
   25: 2 "Dominion and awe *b* to God;
Ps   47: 9 for the kings of the earth *b* to God;
   95: 4 and the mountain peaks *b* to him.
   115:16 The highest heavens *b*
Jer   5:10 for these people do not *b*
Jn   8:44 You *b* to your father, the devil,
   15:19 As it is, you do not *b* to the world,
Ro   1: 6 called to *b* to Jesus Christ.
   7: 4 that you might *b* to another,
   8: 9 of Christ, he does not *b* to Christ.
   14: 8 we live or die, we *b* to the Lord.
1Co   7:39 but he must *b* to the Lord.
   15:23 when he comes, those who *b*

Gal   3:29 If you *b* to Christ, then you are
   5:24 Those who *b* to Christ Jesus have
1Th   5: 5 We do not *b* to the night
   5: 8 But since we *b* to the day, let us be
1Jn   3:19 then is how we know that we *b*

BELONGING (BELONG)

1Pe   2: 9 a holy nation, a people *b* to God,

BELONGS (BELONG)

Lev 27:30 *b* to the LORD; it is holy
Dt   1:17 of any man, for judgment *b* to God.
Job 41:11 Everything under heaven *b* to me.
Ps   22:28 for dominion *b* to the LORD
   89:18 Indeed, our shield *b* to the LORD,
   111: 10 To him *b* eternal praise.
Eze 18: 4 For every living soul *b* to me,
Jn   8:47 He who *b* to God hears what God
Ro   12: 5 each member *b* to all the others.
Rev   7:10 "Salvation *b* to our God,

BELOVED* (LOVE)

Dt   33:12 "Let the *b* of the LORD rest secure
SS   5: 9 How is your *b* better than others,
   5: 9 *Friends* How is your *b* better
Jer   11:15 "What is my *b* doing in my temple

BELSHAZZAR

King of Babylon in days of Daniel (Da 5).

BELT

Ex   12:11 with your cloak tucked into your *b*,
1Ki 18:46 and, tucking his cloak into his *b*,
2Ki   4:29 "Tuck your cloak into your *b*,
   9: 1 "Tuck your cloak into your *b*,
Isa   11: 5 Righteousness will be his *b*
Eph   6:14 with the *b* of truth buckled

BENEFICIAL* (BENEFIT)

1Co   6:12 for me"—but not everything is *b*.
   10:23 but not everything is *b*.

BENEFIT (BENEFICIAL BENEFITS)

Job 22: 2 "Can a man be of *b* to God?
Isa   38:17 Surely it was for my *b*
Ro   6:22 the *b* you reap leads to holiness,
2Co   4:15 All this is for your *b*,

BENEFITS (BENEFIT)

Ps   103: 2 and forget not all his *b*.
Jn   4:38 you have reaped the *b* of their labor

BENJAMIN

Twelfth son of Jacob by Rachel (Ge 35:16-24; 46:19-21; 1Ch 2:2). Jacob refused to send him to Egypt, but relented (Ge 42-45). Tribe of blessed (Ge 49:27; Dt 33:12), numbered (Nu 1:37; 26:41), allotted land (Jos 18:11-28; Eze 48:23), failed to fully possess (Jdg 1:21), nearly obliterated (Jdg 20-21), sided with Ish-Bosheth (2Sa 2), but turned to David (1Ch 12:2, 29). 12,000 from (Rev 7:8).

BEREANS*

Ac   17:11 the *B* were of more noble character

BESTOWING* (BESTOWS)

Pr   8:21 *b* wealth on those who love me

BESTOWS (BESTOWING)

Ps   84:11 the LORD *b* favor and honor;

BETHANY

Mk 11: 1 and *B* at the Mount of Olives,

BETHEL

Ge   28:19 He called that place *B*,

BETHLEHEM

Ru   1:19 went on until they came to *B*.
1Sa 16: 1 I am sending you to Jesse of *B*.
2Sa 23:15 from the well near the gate of *B*!"
Mic   5: 2 "But you, *B* Ephrathah,
Mt   2: 1 After Jesus was born in *B* in Judea,
   2: 6 " 'But you, *B*, in the land of Judah,

BETHPHAGE

Mt   21: 1 came to *B* on the Mount of Olives,

BETHSAIDA

Jn   12:21 who was from *B* in Galilee,

BETRAY (BETRAYED BETRAYS)

Ps   89:33 nor will I ever *b* my faithfulness.
Pr   25: 9 do not *b* another man's confidence,
Mt   10:21 "Brother will *b* brother to death,
     26:21 the truth, one of you will *b* me.''

BETRAYED (BETRAY)

Mt   27: 4 "for I have *b* innocent blood."

BETRAYS (BETRAY)

Pr   11:13 A gossip *b* a confidence,
     20:19 A gossip *b* a confidence;

BEULAH*

Isa   62: 4 and your land *B;*

BEWITCHED*

Gal   3: 1 foolish Galatians! Who has *b* you?

BEZALEL

   Judahite craftsman in charge of building the
tabernacle (Ex 31:1-11; 35:30-39:31).

BIDDING*

Ps 103:20 you mighty ones who do his *b,*
    148: 8 stormy winds that do his *b,*

BILDAD

   One of Job's friends (Job 8; 18; 25).

BILHAH

   Servant of Rachel, mother of Jacob's sons Dan
and Naphtali (Ge 30:1-7; 35:25; 46:23-25).

BIND (BINDS BOUND)

Dt   6: 8 and *b* them on your foreheads.
Pr   3: 3 *b* them around your neck,
      6:21 *B* them upon your heart forever;
      7: 3 *B* them on your fingers;
Isa   61: 1 me to *b* up the brokenhearted,
Mt   16:19 whatever you *b* on earth will be

BINDS (BIND)

Ps 147: 3 and *b* up their wounds.
Isa   30:26 when the LORD *b* up the bruises

BIRD (BIRDS)

Pr   27: 8 Like a *b* that strays from its nest
Ecc 10:20 a *b* of the air may carry your words,

BIRDS (BIRD)

Mt   8:20 and *b* of the air have nests,
Lk   9:58 and *b* of the air have nests,

BIRTH (BEAR)

Ps   51: 5 Surely I was sinful at *b,*
     58: 3 Even from *b* the wicked go astray;
Isa   26:18 but we gave *b* to wind.
Mt   1:18 This is how the *b* of Jesus Christ
      24: 8 these are the beginning of *b* pains.
Jn   3: 6 Flesh gives *b* to flesh, but the Spirit
1Pe   1: 3 great mercy he has given us new *b*

BIRTHRIGHT (BEAR)

Ge   25:34 So Esau despised his *b.*

BISHOP see OVERSEER

BITTEN

Nu   21: 8 anyone who is *b* can look at it

BITTER (BITTERNESS EMBITTER)

Ex   12: 8 along with *b* herbs, and bread made
Pr   27: 7 what is *b* tastes sweet.

BITTERNESS (BITTER)

Pr   14:10 Each heart knows its own *b,*
     17:25 and *b* to the one who bore him.
Ro   3:14 full of cursing and *b.*''
Eph   4:31 Get rid of all *b,* rage and anger,

BLACK

Zec   6: 6 The one with the *b* horses is going
Rev   6: 5 and there before me was a *b* horse!

BLAMELESS* (BLAMELESSLY)

Ge   6: 9 *b* among the people of his time,
     17: 1 I walk before me and be *b.*
Dt   18:13 You must be *b* before the LORD
2Sa 22:24 I have been *b* before him
     22:26 to the *b* you show yourself *b,*
Job   1: 1 This man was *b* and upright;
      1: 8 one on earth like him; he is *b*
      2: 3 one on earth like him; he is *b*
      4: 6 and your *b* ways your hope?
      8:20 God does not reject a *b* man
      9:20 if I were *b,* it would pronounce me
      9:21 "Although I am *b,*
      9:22 'He destroys both the *b*
     12: 4 though righteous and *b!*
     22: 3 gain if your ways were *b?*
     31: 6 and he will know that I am *b*—
Ps   15: 2 He whose walk is *b*
     18:23 I have been *b* before him
     18:25 to the *b* you show yourself *b,*
     19:13 Then will I be *b,*
     26: 1 for I have led a *b* life;
     26:11 But I lead a *b* life;
     37:18 The days of the *b* are known
     37:37 Consider the *b,* observe the upright
     84:11 from those whose walk is *b.*
    101: 2 I will be careful to lead a *b* life—
    101: 2 house with *b* heart.
    101: 6 he whose walk is *b*
    119: 1 Blessed are they whose ways are *b,*
    119:80 May my heart be *b*
Pr   2: 7 a shield to those whose walk is *b,*
      2:21 and the *b* will remain in it;
     11: 5 of the *b* makes a straight way
     11:20 in those whose ways are *b.*
     19: 1 Better a poor man whose walk is *b*
     20: 7 The righteous man leads a *b* life;
     28: 6 Better a poor man whose walk is *b*
     28:10 *b* will receive a good inheritance.
     28:18 He whose walk is *b* is kept safe,
Eze 28:15 You were *b* in your ways
1Co   1: 8 so that you will be *b* on the day
Eph   1: 4 world to be holy and *b* in his sight.
      5:27 any other blemish, but holy and *b.*
Php   1:10 and *b* until the day of Christ,
      2:15 so that you may become *b* and pure
1Th   2:10 and *b* we were among you who
      3:13 hearts so that you will be *b*
      5:23 and body be kept *b* at the coming
Tit   1: 6 An elder must be *b,* the husband of
      1: 7 he must be— not overbearing,
Heb   7:26 *b,* pure, set apart from sinners,
2Pe   3:14 effort to be found spotless, *b*
Rev 14: 5 found in their mouths; they are *b.*

BLAMELESSLY* (BLAMELESS)

Lk   1: 6 commandments and regulations *b.*

BLASPHEME* (BLASPHEMED BLASPHEMER BLASPHEMES BLASPHEMIES BLASPHEMING BLASPHEMOUS BLASPHEMY)

Ex   22:28 "Do not *b* God or curse the ruler
Ac   26:11 and I tried to force them to *b.*
1Ti   1:20 over to Satan to be taught not to *b.*
2Pe   2:12 these men in matters they do not
Rev 13: 6 He opened his mouth to *b* God,

BLASPHEMED* (BLASPHEME)

Lev 24:11 of the Israelite woman *b* the Name
2Ki 19: 6 of the king of Assyria have *b* me.
     19:22 Who is it you have insulted and *b?*
Isa 37: 6 of the king of Assyria have *b* me.
     37:23 Who is it you have insulted and *b?*
     52: 5 my name is constantly *b.*
Eze 20:27 your fathers *b* me by forsaking me:
Ac   19:37 robbed temples nor *b* our goddess.
Ro   2:24 name is *b* among the Gentiles

BLASPHEMER* (BLASPHEME)

Lev 24:14 "Take the *b* outside the camp.
     24:23 they took the *b* outside the camp
1Ti   1:13 I was once a *b* and a persecutor

BLASPHEMES* (BLASPHEME)

Lev 24:16 anyone who *b* the name
     24:16 native-born, when he *b* the Name,
Nu   15:30 native-born or alien, *b* the LORD,

BLASPHEMIES* (BLASPHEME)

Mk   3:29 whoever *b* against the Holy Spirit
Lk   12:10 but anyone who *b* against the Holy

BLASPHEMIES* (BLASPHEME)

Ne   9:18 or when they committed awful *b.*
      9:26 to you; they committed awful *b.*
Mk   3:28 and *b* of men will be forgiven them.
Rev 13: 5 and *b* and to exercise his authority

BLASPHEMING* (BLASPHEME)

Mt   9: 3 "This fellow is *b!*'' Knowing their
Mk   2: 7 He's *b!* Who can forgive sins

BLASPHEMOUS* (BLASPHEME)

Rev 13: 1 and on each head a *b* name.
     17: 3 that was covered with *b* names

BLASPHEMY* (BLASPHEME)

Mt   12:31 and *b* will be forgiven men,
     12:31 the *b* against the Spirit will not be
     26:65 Look, now you have heard the *b.*
     26:65 "He has spoken *b!* Why do we
Mk   14:64 "You have heard the *b.*
      2: 7 "Who is this fellow who speaks *b?*
Jn   10:33 replied the Jews, "but for *b,*
     10:36 Why then do you accuse me of *b*
Ac   6:11 words of *b* against Moses

BLAST*

Ex   15: 8 By the *b* of your nostrils
     19:13 horn sounds a long *b* may they go
     19:16 and a very loud trumpet *b.*
Nu   10: 5 When a trumpet *b* is sounded,
     10: 6 At the sounding of a second *b,*
     10: 6 The *b* will be the signal
     10: 9 sound a *b* on the trumpets.
Jos   6: 5 you hear them sound a long *b*
      6:16 the priests sounded the trumpet *b,*
2Sa 22:16 at the *b* of breath from his nostrils.
Job   4: 9 at the *b* of his anger they perish.
     39:25 At the *b* of the trumpet he snorts,
Ps   18:15 the *b* of breath from your nostrils.
     98: 6 and the *b* of the ram's horn—
    147:17 Who can withstand his icy *b?*
Isa 27: 8 with his fierce *b* he drives her out,
Eze 22:20 a furnace to melt it with a fiery *b,*
Am   2: 2 tumult amid war cries and the *b*
Heb 12:19 to a trumpet *b* or to such a voice

BLEATING*

1Sa 15:14 "What then is this *b* of sheep

BLEMISH (BLEMISHES)

Lev 22:21 be without defect or *b*
Eph   5:27 or wrinkle or any other *b,*
Col   1:22 without *b* and free from accusation
1Pe   1:19 a lamb without *b* or defect.

BLEMISHES* (BLEMISH)

2Pe   2:13 and *b,* reveling in their pleasures
Jude :12 These men are *b* at your love feasts

BLESS (BLESSED BLESSES BLESSING BLESSINGS)

Ge   12: 3 I will *b* those who *b* you,
     32:26 not let you go unless you *b* me.''
Dt   7:13 He will love you and *b* you
     33:11 *B* all his skills, O LORD,
Ps   72:15 and *b* him all day long.
Ro   12:14 Bless those who persecute you; *b*

BLESSED (BLESS)

Ge   1:22 God *b* them and said, "Be fruitful
      2: 3 And God *b* the seventh day
     22:18 nations on earth will be *b,*
Nu   24: 9 "May those who bless you be *b*
1Ch 17:27 have *b* it, and it will be *b* forever."
Ps   1: 1 *B* is the man
      2:12 *B* are all who take refuge in him.
     32: 1 *B* is the man
     33:12 *B* is the nation whose God is
     40: 4 *B* is the man
     41: 1 *B* is he who has regard for the weak
     84: 5 *B* are those whose strength is
     89:15 *B* are those who have learned
     94:12 *B* is the man you discipline,
    106: 3 *B* are they who maintain justice,
    112: 1 *B* is the man who fears the LORD,

Ps 118: 26 *B* is he who comes in the name
  119: 1 *B* are they whose ways are
  119: 2 *B* are they who keep his statutes
  127: 5 *B* is the man
Pr   3: 13 *B* is the man who finds wisdom,
  8: 34 *B* is the man who listens to me,
  28: 20 A faithful man will be richly *b,*
  29: 18 but *b* is he who keeps the law.
  31: 28 Her children arise and call her *b;*
Isa 30: 18 *B* are all who wait for him!
Mal 3: 12 Then all the nations will call you *b,*
  3: 15 But now we call the arrogant *b.*
Mt   5: 3 saying: "*B* are the poor in spirit,
  5: 4 *B* are those who mourn,
  5: 5 *B* are the meek,
  5: 6 *B* are those who hunger
  5: 7 *B* are the merciful,
  5: 8 *B* are the pure in heart,
  5: 9 *B* are the peacemakers,
  5: 10 *B* are those who are persecuted
  5: 11 "*B* are you when people insult you,
Lk   1: 48 on all generations will call me *b.*
Jn 12: 13 "*B* is he who comes in the name
Ac 20: 35 'It is more *b* to give than to receive
Tit   2: 13 while we wait for the *b* hope—
Jas   1: 12 *B* is the man who perseveres
Rev   1: 3 *B* is the one who reads the words
  22: 7 *B* is he who keeps the words
  22: 14 "*B* are those who wash their robes,

BLESSES (BLESS)

Ps 29: 11 the LORD *b* his people with peace.
Ro 10: 12 and richly *b* all who call on him,

BLESSING (BLESS)

Ge   27: 4 so that I may give you my *b*
Dt 23: 5 turned the curse into a *b* for you,
  33: 1 This is the *b* that Moses the man
Pr 10: 22 The *b* of the LORD brings wealth,
Eze 34: 26 there will be showers of *b.*

BLESSINGS (BLESS)

Dt 11: 29 proclaim on Mount Gerizim the *b,*
Jos   8: 34 all the words of the law—the *b*
Pr 10: 6 *B* crown the head of the righteous,
Ro 15: 27 shared in the Jews' spiritual *b,*

BLIND (BLINDED)

Mt 15: 14 a *b* man leads a *b* man, both will fall
  23: 16 "Woe to you, *b* guides! You say,
Mk 10: 46 a *b* man, Bartimaeus (that is,
Lk   6: 39 "Can a *b* man lead a *b* man?
Jn   9: 25 I was *b* but now I see!"

BLINDED (BLIND)

Jn 12: 40 elsewhere: "He has *b* their eyes
2Co 4: 4 The god of this age has *b* the minds

BLOOD (BLOODSHED BLOODTHIRSTY)

Ge   4: 10 Your brother's *b* cries out to me
  9: 6 "Whoever sheds the *b* of man,
Ex 12: 13 and when I see the *b,* I will pass
  24: 8 "This is the *b* of the covenant that
Lev 16: 15 and take its *b* behind the curtain
  17: 11 For the life of a creature is in the *b*
Dt 12: 23 eat the *b,* because the *b* is the life,
Ps 72: 14 for precious is their *b* in his sight.
Pr   6: 17 hands that shed innocent *b,*
Isa   1: 11 pleasure in the *b* of bulls and lambs
Mt 26: 28 This is my *b* of the covenant,
  27: 24 "I am innocent of this man's *b,*"
Mk 14: 24 "This is my *b* of the covenant,
Lk 22: 44 drops of *b* falling to the ground.
Jn   6: 53 of the Son of Man and drink his *b,*
Ac 15: 20 of strangled animals and from *b.*
  20: 26 innocent of the *b* of all men.
Ro   3: 25 of atonement, through faith in his *b*
  5: 9 have now been justified by his *b,*
1Co 11: 25 cup is the new covenant in my *b;*
Eph   1: 7 we have redemption through his *b,*
  2: 13 near through the *b* of Christ.
Col   1: 20 by making peace through his *b,*
Heb   9: 7 once a year, and never without *b,*
  9: 12 once for all by his own *b,*
  9: 20 "This is the *b* of the covenant,
  9: 22 of *b* there is no forgiveness.
  12: 24 word than the *b* of Abel.

1Pe   1: 19 but with the precious *b* of Christ,
1Jn   1: 7 and the *b* of Jesus, his Son,
Rev   1: 5 has freed us from our sins by his *b,*
  5: 9 with your *b* you purchased men
  7: 14 white in the *b* of the Lamb
  12: 11 him by the *b* of the Lamb
  19: 13 He is dressed in a robe dipped in *b,*

BLOODSHED (BLOOD)

Jer 48: 10 on him who keeps his sword from *b*
Eze 35: 6 did not hate *b,* *b* will pursue you.
Hab 2: 12 to him who builds a city with *b*

BLOODTHIRSTY* (BLOOD)

Ps   5: 6 *b* and deceitful men
  26: 9 my life with *b* men,
  55: 23 *b* and deceitful men
  59: 2 and save me from *b* men.
  139: 19 Away from me, you *b* men!
Pr 29: 10 *B* men hate a man of integrity

BLOSSOM

Isa 35: 1 the wilderness will rejoice and *b.*

BLOT (BLOTS)

Ex 32: 32 then *b* me out of the book you have
Ps 51: 1 *b* out my transgressions.
Rev 3: 5 I will never *b* out his name

BLOTS (BLOT)

Isa 43: 25 "I, even I, am he who *b* out

BLOWN

Eph 4: 14 and *b* here and there by every wind
Jas 1: 6 doubts is like a wave of the sea, *b*
Jude : 12 without rain, *b* along by the wind;

BLUSH

Jer 6: 15 they do not even know how to *b.*

BOAST (BOASTS)

1Ki 20: 11 armor should not *b* like one who
Ps 34: 2 My soul will *b* in the LORD;
  44: 8 In God we make our *b* all day long,
Pr 27: 1 Do not *b* about tomorrow,
Jer 9: 23 or the rich man *b* of his riches,
1Co 1: 31 Let him who boasts *b* in the Lord."
2Co 10: 17 Let him who boasts *b* in the Lord."
  11: 30 I do not inwardly burn? If I must *b,*
Gal 6: 14 May I never *b* except in the cross
Eph 2: 9 not by works, so that no one can *b.*

BOASTS (BOAST)

Jer 9: 24 but let him who *b* boast about this:

BOAZ

  Wealthy Bethlehemite who showed favor to Ruth (Ru 2), married her (Ru 4). Ancestor of David (Ru 4:18-22; 1Ch 2:12-15), Jesus (Mt 1: 5-16; Lk 3:23-32).

BODIES (BODY)

Isa 26: 19 their *b* will rise.
Ro 12: 1 to offer your *b* as living sacrifices,
1Co 6: 15 not know that your *b* are members
Eph 5: 28 to love their wives as their own *b.*

BODILY (BODY)

Col 2: 9 of the Deity lives in *b* form,

BODY (BODIES BODILY EMBODIMENT)

Zec 13: 6 What are these wounds on your *b?'*
Mt 10: 28 afraid of those who kill the *b*
  26: 26 saying, "Take and eat; this is my *b*
  26: 41 spirit is willing, but the *b* is weak."
Mk 14: 22 saying, "Take it; this is my *b.*"
Lk 22: 19 saying, "This is my *b* given for you;
Jn 13: 10 wash his feet; his whole *b* is clean.
Ro 6: 13 Do not offer the parts of your *b*
  12: 4 us has one *b* with many members,
1Co 6: 19 not know that your *b* is a temple
  6: 20 Therefore honor God with your *b.*
  11: 24 "This is my *b,* which is for you;
  12: 12 The *b* is a unit, though it is made up
  12: 13 baptized by one Spirit into one *b*—
  15: 44 a natural *b,* it is raised a spiritual *b*.
Eph 1: 23 which is his *b,* the fullness
  4: 25 for we are all members of one *b.*

Eph 5: 30 for we are members of his *b.*
Php 1: 20 Christ will be exalted in my *b,*
Col 1: 24 sake of his *b,* which is the church.

BOLD (BOLDNESS)

Ps 138: 3 you made me *b* and stouthearted.
Pr 21: 29 A wicked man puts up a *b* front,
  28: 1 but the righteous are as *b* as a lion.

BOLDNESS* (BOLD)

Lk 11: 8 of the man's *b* he will get up
Ac 4: 29 to speak your word with great *b.*

BONDAGE

Ezr 9: 9 God has not deserted us in our *b.*

BONES

Ge   2: 23 "This is now bone of my *b*
Ps 22: 14 and all my *b* are out of joint.
  22: 17 I can count all my *b;*
Eze 37: 1 middle of a valley; it was full of *b.*
Jn 19: 36 "Not one of his *b* will be broken,"

BOOK (BOOKS)

Ex 32: 33 against me I will blot out of my *b.*
Jos 1: 8 Do not let this *B* of the Law depart
2Ki 22: 8 "I have found the *B* of the Law
2Ch 34: 15 "I have found the *B* of the Law
Ne 8: 8 They read from the *B* of the Law
Ps 69: 28 May they be blotted out of the *b*
Da 12: 1 name is found written in the *b*—
Jn 20: 30 which are not recorded in this *b.*
Php 4: 3 whose names are in the *b* of life.
Rev 3: 5 never blot out his name from the *b*
  20: 12 *b* was opened, which is the *b*
  20: 15 was not found written in the *b*
  21: 27 written in the Lamb's *b* of life.
  22: 18 him the plagues described in this *b.*

BOOKS* (BOOK)

Ecc 12: 12 Of making many *b* there is no end,
Da 7: 10 and the *b* were opened.
Jn 21: 25 for the *b* that would be written.
Rev 20: 12 the throne, and *b* were opened.
  20: 12 they had done as recorded in the *b.*

BORE (BEAR)

Isa 53: 12 For he *b* the sin of many,
1Pe 2: 24 He himself *b* our sins in his body

BORN (BEAR)

Ecc 3: 2 a time to be *b* and a time to die,
Isa 9: 6 For to us a child is *b,*
  66: 8 Can a country be *b* in a day
Lk 2: 11 of David a Savior has been *b* to you
Jn 3: 3 see the kingdom of God unless he is *b* again.
  3: 4 How can a man be *b* when he is old
  3: 5 unless he is *b* of water
  3: 7 at my saying, 'You must be *b* again
  3: 8 it is with everyone *b* of the Spirit."
1Pe 1: 23 For you have been *b* again,
1Jn 3: 9 because he has been *b* of God.
  4: 7 Everyone who loves has been *b*
  5: 1 believes that Jesus is the Christ is *b*
  5: 4 for everyone *b* of God overcomes
  5: 18 We know that anyone *b*

BORROWER

Pr 22: 7 and the *b* is servant to the lender.

BOTHER (BOTHERING)

Lk 11: 7 one inside answers, 'Don't *b* me.

BOTHERING (BOTHER)

Lk 18: 5 yet because this widow keeps *b* me,

BOUGHT (BUY)

Ac 20: 28 which he *b* with his own blood.
1Co 6: 20 You are not your own; you were *b*
  7: 23 You were *b* at a price; do not
2Pe 2: 1 the sovereign Lord who *b* them—

BOUND (BIND)

Is 56: 3 Let no foreigner who has *b* himself
Mt 16: 19 bind on earth will be *b* in heaven,
  18: 18 bind on earth will be *b* in heaven,
Ro 7: 2 by law a married woman is *b*
1Co 7: 39 A woman is *b* to her husband

Jude : 6 *b* with everlasting chains
Rev 20: 2 and *b* him for a thousand years.

BOUNDARY (BOUNDS)

Nu 34: 3 your southern *b* will start
Pr 23: 10 Do not move an ancient *b* stone
Hos 5: 10 who move *b* stones.

BOUNDS (BOUNDARY)

2Co 7: 4 all our troubles my joy knows no *b*.

BOUNTY*

Ge 49: 26 than the *b* of the age-old hills.
Dt 28: 12 heavens, the storehouse of his *b*,
1Ki 10: 13 he had given her out of his royal *b*.
Ps 65: 11 You crown the year with your *b*,
68: 10 from your *b*, O God, you provided
Jer 31: 12 rejoice in the *b* of the LORD—
31: 14 my people will be filled with my *b*

BOW (BOWED BOWS)

Dt 5: 9 You shall not *b* down to them
1Ki 22: 34 But someone drew his *b* at random
Ps 5: 7 in reverence will I *b* down
44: 6 I do not trust in my *b*,
95: 6 Come, let us *b* down in worship,
138: 2 I will *b* down toward your holy
Isa 19: 1 Shall I *b* down to a block of wood?''
45: 23 Before me every knee will *b*.''
Ro 14: 11 'every knee will *b* before me;
Php 2: 10 name of Jesus every knee should *b*,

BOWED (BOW)

Ps 145: 14 and lifts up all who are *b* down.
146: 8 the LORD lifts up those who are *b*

BOWS (BOW)

Isa 44: 15 he makes an idol and *b* down to it.
44: 17 he *b* down to it and worships.

BOY (BOY'S BOYS)

Ge 21: 17 God heard the *b* crying,
22: 12 not lay a hand on the *b*
Jdg 13: 5 *b* is to be a Nazirite,
1Sa 2: 11 ministered before the LORD.
3: 8 the LORD was calling the *b*.
Isa 7: 16 before the *b* knows enough
Mt 17: 18 demon, and it came out of the *b*
Lk 2: 43 the *b* Jesus stayed behind

BOY'S (BOY)

1Ki 17: 22 the *b* life returned to him
2Ki 4: 34 the *b* body grew warm

BOYS (BOY)

Ge 25: 24 twin *b* in her womb
Ex 1: 18 they let the *b* live.

BRACE*

Job 38: 3 *B* yourself like a man;
40: 7 out of the storm: ''*B* yourself like
Na 2: 1 *b* yourselves,

BRAG*

Am 4: 5 and *b* about your freewill offerings
Ro 2: 17 *b* about your relationship to God;
2: 23 temples? You who *b* about the law,
Jas 4: 16 As it is, you boast and *b*.

BRAIDED

1Ti 2: 9 not with *b* hair or gold or pearls
1Pe 3: 3 as *b* hair and the wearing

BRANCH (BRANCHES)

Isa 4: 2 In that day the *B* of the LORD will
Jer 23: 5 up to David a righteous *B*,
33: 15 I will make a righteous *B* sprout
Zec 3: 8 going to bring my servant, the *B*.
6: 12 is the man whose name is the *B*,
Jn 15: 2 while every *b* that does bear fruit
15: 4 No *b* can bear fruit by itself;

BRANCHES (BRANCH)

Jn 15: 5 ''I am the vine; you are the *b*.
Ro 11: 21 if God did not spare the natural *b*,

BRAVE

2Sa 2: 7 Now then, be strong and *b*,
13: 28 you this order? Be strong and *b*.''

BREACH (BREAK)

Ps 106: 23 stood in the *b* before him

BREACHING (BREAK)

Pr 17: 14 Starting a quarrel is like *b* a dam;

BREAD

Ex 12: 8 and *b* made without yeast.
23: 15 the Feast of Unleavened *B*;
25: 30 Put the *b* of the Presence
Dt 8: 3 that man does not live on *b* alone
Ps 78: 25 Men ate the *b* of angels;
Pr 30: 8 but give me only my daily *b*.
Ecc 11: 1 Cast your *b* upon the waters,
Isa 55: 2 Why spend money on what is not *b*
Mt 4: 3 tell these stones to become *b*.''
4: 4 'Man does not live on *b* alone,
6: 11 Give us today our daily *b*.
26: 26 Jesus took *b*, gave thanks
Mk 14: 22 Jesus took *b*, gave thanks
Lk 4: 3 tell this stone to become *b*.''
4: 4 'Man does not live on *b* alone.' ''
9: 13 ''We have only five loaves of *b*
11: 3 Give us each day our daily *b*.
22: 19 And he took *b*, gave thanks
Jn 6: 33 For the *b* of God is he who comes
6: 35 Jesus declared, ''I am the *b* of life.
6: 41 ''I am the *b* that came
6: 48 I am the *b* of life.
6: 51 I am the living *b* that came
6: 51 This *b* is my flesh, which I will give
21: 13 took the *b* and gave it to them,
1Co 10: 16 And is not the *b* that we break
11: 23 took *b*, and when he had given
11: 26 For whenever you eat this *b*

BREAK (BREACH BREACHING BREAKERS BREAKING BREAKS BROKE BROKEN BROKENNESS)

Nu 30: 2 he must not *b* his word
Jdg 2: 1 'I will never *b* my covenant
Pr 25: 15 and a gentle tongue can *b* a bone.
Isa 42: 3 A bruised reed he will not *b*,
Mal 2: 15 and do not *b* faith with the wife
Mt 12: 20 A bruised reed he will not *b*,
Ac 20: 7 week we came together to *b* bread.
1Co 10: 16 the bread that we *b* a participation
Rev 5: 2 ''Who is worthy to *b* the seals

BREAKERS* (BREAK)

Ps 42: 7 all your waves and *b*
93: 4 mightier than the *b* of the sea—
Jnh 2: 3 all your waves and *b*

BREAKING (BREAK)

Jos 9: 20 fall on us for *b* the oath we swore
Eze 16: 59 oath by *b* the covenant.
17: 18 the oath by *b* the covenant.
Ac 2: 42 to the *b* of bread and to prayer.
Jas 2: 10 at just one point is guilty of *b* all

BREAKS (BREAK)

Jer 23: 29 ''and like a hammer that *b* a rock
1Jn 3: 4 Everyone who sins *b* the law;

BREASTPIECE (BREASTPLATE)

Ex 28: 15 Fashion a *b* for making decisions—

BREASTPLATE* (BREASTPIECE)

Isa 59: 17 He put on righteousness as his *b*,
Eph 6: 14 with the *b* of righteousness in place
1Th 5: 8 putting on faith and love as a *b*,

BREASTS

La 4: 3 Even jackals offer their *b*

BREATH (BREATHED GOD-BREATHED)

Ge 2: 7 into his nostrils the *b* of life,

BREATHED (BREATH)

Ge 2: 7 *b* into his nostrils the breath of life,
Mk 15: 37 With a loud cry, Jesus *b* his last.
Jn 20: 22 And with that he *b* on them

BREEDS*

Pr 13: 10 Pride only *b* quarrels,

BRIBE

Ex 23: 8 ''Do not accept a *b*,
Dt 16: 19 for a *b* blinds the eyes of the wise
27: 25 ''Cursed is the man who accepts a *b*
Pr 6: 35 will refuse the *b*, however great it

BRIDE

Isa 62: 5 as a bridegroom rejoices over his *b*,
Rev 19: 7 and his *b* has made herself ready.
21: 2 as a *b* beautifully dressed
21: 9 I will show you the *b*, the wife
22: 17 The Spirit and the *b* say, ''Come!''

BRIDEGROOM

Ps 19: 5 which is like a *b* coming forth
Mt 25: 1 and went out to meet the *b*.
25: 5 The *b* was a long time in coming,

BRIGHTENS* (BRIGHTNESS)

Pr 16: 15 When a king's face *b*, it means life;
Ecc 8: 1 Wisdom *b* a man's face

BRIGHTER (BRIGHTNESS)

Pr 4: 18 shining ever *b* till the full light

BRIGHTNESS* (BRIGHTENS BRIGHTER)

2Sa 22: 13 Out of the *b* of his presence
23: 4 like the *b* after rain
Ps 18: 12 of the *b* of his presence clouds
Isa 59: 9 for *b*, but we walk in deep shadows.
60: 3 and kings to the *b* of your dawn.
60: 19 will the *b* of the moon shine on you
Da 12: 3 who are wise will shine like the *b*
Am 5: 20 pitch-dark, without a ray of *b*?

BRILLIANCE* (BRILLIANT)

Ac 22: 11 the *b* of the light had blinded me.
Rev 1: 16 was like the sun shining in all its *b*.
21: 11 its *b* was like that of a very precious

BRILLIANT* (BRILLIANCE)

Ecc 9: 11 or wealth to the *b*
Eze 1: 4 and surrounded by *b* light.
1: 27 and *b* light surrounded him.

BRINK*

Pr 5: 14 I have come to the *b* of utter ruin

BRITTLE

Da 2: 42 will be partly strong and partly *b*.

BROAD

Mt 7: 13 and *b* is the road that leads

BROKE (BREAK)

Mt 26: 26 took bread, gave thanks and *b* it,
Mk 14: 22 took bread, gave thanks and *b* it,
Ac 2: 46 They *b* bread in their homes
20: 11 he went upstairs again and *b* bread
1Co 11: 24 when he had given thanks, he *b* it

BROKEN (BREAK)

Ps 34: 20 not one of them will be *b*.
51: 17 The sacrifices of God are a *b* spirit;
Ecc 4: 12 of three strands is not quickly *b*.
Lk 20: 18 on that stone will be *b* to pieces,
Jn 7: 23 the law of Moses may not be *b*,
10: 35 and the Scripture cannot be *b*—
19: 36 ''Not one of his bones will be *b*,''
Ro 11: 20 they were *b* off because of unbelief,

BROKENHEARTED* (HEART)

Ps 34: 18 The LORD is close to the *b*
109: 16 and the needy and the *b*.
147: 3 He heals the *b*
Isa 61: 1 He has sent me to bind up the *b*,

BROKENNESS* (BREAK)

Isa 65: 14 and wail in *b* of spirit.

BRONZE

Ex 27: 2 and overlay the altar with *b*.
30: 18 ''Make a *b* basin, with its *b* stand,
Nu 21: 9 So Moses made a *b* snake
Da 2: 32 and thighs of *b*, its legs of iron,
10: 6 legs like the gleam of burnished *b*,
Rev 1: 15 His feet were like *b* glowing

Rev 2: 18 whose feet are like burnished *b*.

BROTHER (BROTHER'S BROTHERHOOD BROTHERLY BROTHERS)

Pr 17: 17 and a *b* is born for adversity.
    18: 24 a friend who sticks closer than a *b*.
    27: 10 neighbor nearby than a *b* far away.
Mt   5: 24 and be reconciled to your *b*;
    18: 15 "If your *b* sins against you,
Mk   3: 35 Whoever does God's will is my *b*
Lk 17: 3 "If your *b* sins, rebuke him,
Ro 14: 15 not by your eating destroy your *b*
    14: 21 anything else that will cause your *b*
1Co 8: 13 if what I eat causes my *b* to fall
2Th 3: 6 away from every *b* who is idle
     3: 15 as an enemy, but warn him as a *b*.
Phm : 16 but better than a slave, as a dear *b*.
Jas 2: 15 Suppose a *b* or sister is
     4: 11 Anyone who speaks against his *b*
1Jn 2: 9 hates his *b* is still in the darkness.
     2: 10 Whoever loves his *b* lives
     2: 11 But whoever hates his *b* is
     3: 10 is anyone who does not love his *b*.
     3: 15 who hates his *b* is a murderer,
     3: 17 material possessions and sees his *b*
     4: 20 For anyone who does not love his *b*
     4: 20 yet hates his *b*, he is a liar.
     4: 21 loves God must also love his *b*.
     5: 16 If anyone sees his *b* commit a sin

BROTHER'S (BROTHER)

Ge   4: 9 "Am I my *b* keeper?" The LORD
Mt   7: 5 remove the speck from your *b* eye.
Ro 14: 13 or obstacle in your *b* way.

BROTHERHOOD (BROTHER)

1Pe 2: 17 Love the *b* of believers, fear God,

BROTHERLY* (BROTHER)

Ro 12: 10 devoted to one another in *b* love.
1Th 4: 9 Now about *b* love we do not need
2Pe 1: 7 and to godliness, *b* kindness;
     1: 7 kindness; and to *b* kindness,

BROTHERS (BROTHER)

Jos 1: 14 You are to help your *b*
Ps 133: 1 is when *b* live together in unity!
Pr   6: 19 who stirs up dissension among *b*.
Mt 12: 49 "Here are my mother and my *b*.
    19: 29 everyone who has left houses or *b*
    25: 40 one of the least of these *b* of mine,
Mk   3: 33 "Who are my mother and my *b*?"
    10: 29 or *b* or sisters or mother or father
Lk 21: 16 You will be betrayed even by parents, *b*,
    22: 32 turned back, strengthen your *b*."
Jn   7: 5 his own *b* did not believe in him.
Ac 15: 32 to encourage and strengthen the *b*.
Ro   9: 3 off from Christ for the sake of my *b*
1Co 8: 12 sin against your *b* in this way
2Co 11: 26 and in danger from false *b*.
Gal 2: 4 some false *b* had infiltrated our
1Th 4: 10 you do love all the *b*
     5: 26 Greet all the *b* with a holy kiss.
1Ti 6: 2 for them because they are *b*.
Heb 2: 11 Jesus is not ashamed to call them *b*.
     2: 17 to be made like his *b* in every way,
    13: 1 Keep on loving each other as *b*.
1Pe 1: 22 you have sincere love for your *b*,
     3: 8 be sympathetic, love as *b*,
1Jn 3: 14 death to life, because we love our *b*.
     3: 16 to lay down our lives for our *b*.
3Jn : 10 he refuses to welcome the *b*.
Rev 12: 10 For the accuser of our *b*,

BROW

Ge   3: 19 By the sweat of your *b*

BRUISED (BRUISES)

Isa 42: 3 A *b* reed he will not break,
Mt 12: 20 A *b* reed he will not break,

BRUISES (BRUISED)

Isa 30: 26 when the LORD binds up the *b*

BRUTAL (BRUTE)

2Ti 3: 3 slanderous, without self-control, *b*,

BRUTE* (BRUTAL)

Ps 73: 22 I was a *b* beast before you.
2Pe 2: 12 They are like *b* beasts, creatures

BUBBLING*

Pr 18: 4 the fountain of wisdom is a *b* brook
Isa 35: 7 the thirsty ground *b* springs.

BUCKET*

Isa 40: 15 the nations are like a drop in a *b*;

BUCKLED* (BUCKLER)

Eph 6: 14 belt of truth *b* around your waist,

BUCKLER* (BUCKLED)

Ps 35: 2 Take up shield and *b*;

BUD (BUDDED)

Isa 27: 6 Israel will *b* and blossom

BUDDED (BUD)

Heb 9: 4 Aaron's staff that had *b*,

BUILD (BUILDER BUILDERS BUILDING BUILDS BUILT REBUILD REBUILT)

2Sa 7: 5 Are you the one to *b* me a house
1Ki 6: 1 he began to *b* the temple
Ecc 3: 3 a time to tear down and a time to *b*,
Mt 16: 18 and on this rock I will *b* my church,
Ac 20: 32 which can *b* you up and give you
Ro 15: 2 neighbor for his good, to *b* him up.
1Co 14: 12 excel in gifts that *b* up the church.
1Th 5: 11 one another and *b* each other up,
Jude : 20 *b* yourselves up in your most holy

BUILDER* (BUILD)

1Co 3: 10 I laid a foundation as an expert *b*,
Heb 3: 3 the *b* of a house has greater honor
     3: 4 but God is the *b* of everything.
    11: 10 whose architect and is God.

BUILDERS (BUILD)

Ps 118: 22 The stone the *b* rejected
Mt 21: 42 "The stone the *b* rejected
Mk 12: 10 "The stone the *b* rejected
Lk 20: 17 "The stone the *b* rejected
Ac   4: 11 "the stone you *b* rejected,
1Pe 2: 7 "The stone the *b* rejected

BUILDING (BUILD)

Ezr 3: 8 to supervise the *b* of the house
Ne   4: 17 of Judah who were *b* the wall.
Ro 15: 20 so that I would not be *b*
1Co 3: 9 you are God's field, God's *b*.
2Co 5: 1 we have a *b* from God, an eternal
    10: 8 us for *b* you up rather
    13: 10 the Lord gave me for *b* you up,
Eph 2: 21 him the whole *b* is joined together
     4: 29 helpful for *b* others up according

BUILDS (BUILD)

Ps 127: 1 Unless the LORD *b* the house,
Pr 14: 1 The wise woman *b* her house,
1Co 3: 10 one should be careful how he *b*.
     3: 12 If any man *b* on this foundation
     8: 1 Knowledge puffs up, but love *b* up.
Eph 4: 16 grows and *b* itself up in love,

BUILT (BUILD)

1Ki 6: 14 So Solomon *b* the temple
Mt   7: 24 is like a wise man who *b* his house
Lk   6: 49 is like a man who *b* a house
Ac 17: 24 does not live in temples *b* by hands.
1Co 3: 14 If what he has *b* survives, he will
2Co 5: 1 in heaven, not *b* by human hands.
Eph 2: 20 *b* on the foundation of the apostles
     4: 12 the body of Christ may be *b* up
Col 2: 7 live in him, rooted and *b* up in him,
1Pe 2: 5 are being *b* into a spiritual house

BULL (BULLS)

Lev 4: 3 bring to the LORD a young *b*

BULLS (BULL)

1Ki 7: 25 The Sea stood on twelve *b*,
Heb 10: 4 it is impossible for the blood of *b*

BURDEN (BURDENED BURDENS BURDENSOME)

Ps 38: 4 like a *b* too heavy to bear.
Ecc 1: 13 What a heavy *b* God has laid
Mt 11: 30 my yoke is easy and my *b* is light."
Ac 15: 28 to us not to *b* you with anything
2Co 11: 9 from being a *b* to you in any way,
    12: 14 and I will not be a *b* to you,
1Th 2: 9 day in order not to be a *b* to anyone
2Th 3: 8 so that we would not be a *b* to any
Heb 13: 17 not a *b*, for that would be

BURDENED* (BURDEN)

Isa 43: 23 have not *b* you with grain offerings
    43: 24 But you have *b* me with your sins
Mic 6: 3 How have I *b* you? Answer me.
Mt 11: 28 all you who are weary and *b*,
2Co 5: 4 are in this tent, we groan and are *b*,
Gal 5: 1 do not let yourselves be *b* again
1Ti 5: 16 not let the church be *b* with them,

BURDENS (BURDEN)

Ps 68: 19 who daily bears our *b*.
Lk 11: 46 down with *b* they can hardly carry,
Gal 6: 2 Carry each other's *b*,

BURDENSOME (BURDEN)

1Jn 5: 3 And his commands are not *b*,

BURIED (BURY)

Ru   1: 17 die I will die, and there I will be *b*.
Ro   6: 4 *b* with him through baptism
1Co 15: 4 that he was *b*, that he was raised
Col 2: 12 having been *b* with him in baptism

BURN (BURNING BURNT)

Dt   7: 5 and *b* their idols in the fire.
Ps 79: 5 long will your jealousy *b* like fire?
1Co 7: 9 to marry than to *b* with passion.

BURNING (BURN)

Ex 27: 20 so that the lamps may be kept *b*.
Lev 6: 9 the fire must be kept *b* on the altar.
Ps 18: 28 You, O LORD, keep my lamp *b*;
Pr 25: 22 you will heap *b* coals on his head,
Ro 12: 20 you will heap *b* coals on his head."
Rev 19: 20 alive into the fiery lake of *b* sulfur.

BURNISHED*

1Ki 7: 45 of the LORD were of *b* bronze.
Eze 1: 7 and gleamed like *b* bronze.
Da 10: 6 and legs like the gleam of *b* bronze,
Rev 2: 18 and whose feet are like *b* bronze.

BURNT (BURN)

Ge   8: 20 he sacrificed *b* offerings on it.
    22: 2 as a *b* offering on one
Ex 10: 25 and *b* offerings to present
    18: 12 brought a *b* offering and other
    40: 6 Place the altar of *b* offering in front
Lev 1: 3 "'If the offering is a *b* offering
Jos 8: 31 offered to the LORD *b* offerings
Jdg 6: 26 offer the second bull as a *b* offering
     13: 16 But if you prepare a *b* offering,
1Ki 3: 4 offered a thousand *b* offerings
     9: 25 year Solomon sacrificed *b* offerings
    10: 5 and the *b* offerings he made on
Ezr 3: 2 Israel to sacrifice *b* offerings on it,
Eze 43: 18 for sacrificing *b* offerings

BURST

Ps 98: 4 *b* into jubilant song with music;
Isa 44: 23 *B* into song, you mountains,
    49: 13 *b* into song, O mountains!
    52: 9 *B* into songs of joy together,
    54: 1 *b* into song, shout for joy,
    55: 12 will *b* into song before you,

BURY (BURIED)

Mt   8: 22 and let the dead *b* their own dead."
Lk   9: 60 "Let the dead *b* their own dead,

BUSH

Ex   3: 2 the *b* was on fire it did not burn up.
Mk 12: 26 the account of the *b*, how God said
Lk 20: 37 But in the account of the *b*,
Ac   7: 35 who appeared to him in the *b*.

BUSINESS

Ecc 4: 8 a miserable *b!*
Da 8:27 and went about the king's *b.*
1Co 5:12 What *b* is it of mine to judge those
1Th 4:11 to mind your own *b* and to work
Jas 1:11 even while he goes about his *b.*

BUSY*

1Ki 18:27 Perhaps he is deep in thought, or *b,*
20:40 While your servant was *b* here
Isa 32: 6 his mind is *b* with evil:
Hag 1: 9 of you is *b* with his own house.
2Th 3:11 They are not *b;* they are
Tit 2: 5 to be *b* at home, to be kind,

BUSYBODIES*

2Th 3:11 They are not busy; they are *b.*
1Ti 5:13 *b,* saying things they ought not to.

BUY (BOUGHT BUYS)

Pr 23:23 *B* the truth and do not sell it;
Isa 55: 1 Come, *b* wine and milk
Rev 13:17 so that no one could *b* or sell

BUYS (BUY)

Pr 31:16 She considers a field and *b* it;

BYWORD (WORD)

1Ki 9: 7 Israel will then become a *b*
Ps 44:14 You have made us a *b*
Joel 2:17 a *b* among the nations.

CAESAR

Mt 22:21 "Give to *C* what is Caesar's,

CAIN

Firstborn of Adam (Ge 4:1), murdered brother Abel (Ge 4:1-16; 1Jn 3:12).

CAKE

Hos 7: 8 Ephraim is a flat *c* not turned over.

CALEB

Judahite who spied out Canaan (Nu 13:6); allowed to enter land because of faith (Nu 13:30-14:38; Dt 1:36). Possessed Hebron (Jdg 14:6-15:19).

CALF

Ex 32: 4 into an idol cast in the shape of a *c,*
Pr 15:17 than a fattened *c* with hatred.
Lk 15:23 Bring the fattened *c* and kill it.
Ac 7:41 made an idol in the form of a *c.*

CALL (CALLED CALLING CALLS)

1Ki 18:24 I will *c* on the name of the LORD.
2Ki 5:11 *c* on the name of the LORD his
1Ch 16: 8 to the LORD, *c* on his name;
Ps 105: 1 to the LORD, *c* on his name;
116:13 and *c* on the name of the LORD.
116:17 and *c* on the name of the LORD.
145:18 near to all who *c* on him,
Pr 31:28 children arise and *c* her blessed;
Isa 5:20 Woe to those who *c* evil good
12: 4 to the LORD, *c* on his name;
55: 6 *c* on him while he is near.
65:24 Before they *c* I will answer;
Jer 33: 3 '*C* to me and I will answer you
Zep 3: 9 that all of them may *c* on the name
Zec 13: 9 They will *c* on my name
Mt 9:13 come to *c* the righteous,
Mk 2:17 I have not come to *c* the righteous,
Lk 5:32 I have not come to *c* the righteous,
Ac 2:39 all whom the Lord our God will *c.*"
9:14 to arrest all who *c* on your name."
9:21 among those who *c* on this name?
Ro 10:12 and richly blesses all who *c* on him,
11:29 gifts and his *c* are irrevocable.
1Co 1: 2 with all those everywhere who *c*
1Th 4: 7 For God did not *c* us to be impure,
2Ti 2:22 along with those who *c*

CALLED (CALL)

Ge 2:23 she shall be *c* 'woman,'
5: 2 he blessed them and *c* them "man
12: 8 and *c* on the name of the LORD.
21:33 and there he *c* upon the name
26:25 and *c* on the name of the LORD.
1Sa 3: 5 and said, "Here I am; you *c* me."

2Ch 7:14 if my people, who are *c*
Ps 34: 6 This poor man *c,* and the LORD
116: 4 Then I *c* on the name of the LORD
Isa 56: 7 for my house will be *c*
La 3:55 I *c* on your name, O LORD,
Hos 11: 1 and out of Egypt I *c* my son.
Mt 1:16 was born Jesus, who is *c* Christ.
2:15 "Out of Egypt I *c* my son."
21:13 " 'My house will be *c*
Mk 11:17 " 'My house will be *c*
Lk 1:32 will be *c* the Son of the Most High.
1:35 to be born will be *c* the Son of God.
Ro 1: 1 *c* to be an apostle and set apart
1: 6 among those who are *c* to belong
1: 7 loved by God and *c* to be saints:
8:28 who have been *c* according
8:30 And those he predestined, he also *c*
1Co 1: 1 *c* to be an apostle of Christ Jesus
1: 2 in Christ Jesus and *c* to be holy,
1:24 but to those whom God has *c,*
1:26 of what you were when you were *c.*
7:15 God has *c* us to live in peace.
7:17 and to which God has *c* him.
Gal 1: 6 deserting the one who *c* you
1:15 from birth and *c* me by his grace,
5:13 You, my brothers, were *c* to be free
Eph 1:18 the hope to which he has *c* you,
4: 4 as you were *c* to one hope
Col 3:15 of one body you were *c* to peace.
2Th 2:14 He *c* you to this through our gospel
1Ti 6:12 life to which you were *c*
2Ti 1: 9 who has saved us and *c* us
Heb 9:15 that those who are *c* may receive
1Pe 1:15 But just as he who *c* you is holy,
2: 9 of him who *c* you out of darkness
3: 9 to this you were *c* so that you may
5:10 who *c* you to his eternal glory
2Pe 1: 3 of him who *c* us by his own glory
Jude 1 To those who have been *c,*

CALLING (CALL)

Isa 40: 3 A voice of one *c:*
Mt 3: 3 "A voice of one *c* in the desert,
Mk 1: 3 "a voice of one *c* in the desert,
10:49 Cheer up! On your feet! He's *c* you
Lk 3: 4 "A voice of one *c* in the desert,
Jn 1:23 I am the voice of one *c* in the desert
Ac 22:16 wash your sins away, *c* on his name
Eph 4: 1 worthy of the *c* you have received.
2Th 1:11 may count you worthy of his *c,*
2Pe 1:10 all the more eager to make your *c*

CALLOUS* (CALLOUSED)

Ps 17:10 They close up their *c* hearts,
73: 7 From their *c* hearts comes iniquity;
119:70 Their hearts are *c* and unfeeling,

CALLOUSED* (CALLOUS)

Isa 6:10 Make the heart of this people *c;*
Mt 13:15 this people's heart has become *c;*
Ac 28:27 this people's heart has become *c;*

CALLS (CALL)

Ps 147: 4 and *c* them each by name.
Isa 40:26 and *c* them each by name.
Joel 2:32 And everyone who *c*
Mt 22:43 speaking by the Spirit, *c* him 'Lord
Jn 10: 3 He *c* his own sheep by name
Ac 2:21 And everyone who *c*
Ro 10:13 "Everyone who *c* on the name
1Th 2:12 who *c* you into his kingdom
5:24 The one who *c* you is faithful

CALM (CALMS)

Ps 107:30 They were glad when it grew *c,*
Isa 7: 4 keep *c* and don't be afraid.
Eze 16:42 I will be *c* and no longer angry.

CALMS* (CALM)

Pr 15:18 but a patient man *c* a quarrel.

CAMEL

Mt 19:24 it is easier for a *c* to go
23:24 strain out a gnat but swallow a *c.*
Mk 10:25 It is easier for a *c* to go
Lk 18:25 It is easier for a *c* to go

CAMP (ENCAMPS)

Heb 13:13 outside the *c,* bearing the disgrace

CANAAN (CANAANITE CANAANITES)

Ge 10:15 *C* was the father of Sidon his
Lev 14:34 "When you enter the land of *C,*
25:38 of Egypt to give you the land of *C*
Nu 13: 2 men to explore the land of *C,*
33:51 'When you cross the Jordan into *C,*
Jdg 4: 2 a king of *C,* who reigned in Hazor.
1Ch 16:18 'To you I will give the land of *C*
Ps 105:11 'To you I will give the land of *C*
Ac 13:19 he overthrew seven nations in *C*

CANAANITE (CANAAN)

Ge 10:18 Later the *C* clans scattered
28: 1 "Do not marry a *C* woman.
Jos 5: 1 all the *C* kings along the seacoast
Jdg 1:32 lived among the *C* inhabitants

CANAANITES (CANAAN)

Ex 33: 2 before you and drive out the *C,*

CANCEL (CANCELED)

Dt 15: 1 seven years you must *c* debts.

CANCELED (CANCEL)

Mt 18:27 pity on him, *c* the debt
Lk 7:42 so he *c* the debts of both.
Col 2:14 having *c* the written code,

CANDLESTICKS see LAMPSTANDS

CANOPY*

2Sa 22:12 He made darkness his *c*
2Ki 16:18 away the Sabbath *c* that had been
Ps 18:11 made darkness his covering, his *c*
Isa 4: 5 over all the glory will be a *c.*
40:22 stretches out the heavens like a *c,*
Jer 43:10 he will spread his royal *c*

CAPERNAUM

Mt 4:13 Nazareth, he went and lived in *C,*
Jn 6:59 teaching in the synagogue in *C.*

CAPITAL

Dt 21:22 guilty of a *c* offense is put to death

CAPSTONE* (STONE)

Ps 118:22 has become the *c;*
Zec 4: 7 he will bring out the *c* to shouts
Mt 21:42 has become the *c;*
Mk 12:10 has become the *c;*
Lk 20:17 has become the *c'*?
Ac 4:11 which has become the *c.*'
1Pe 2: 7 has become the *c,*"

CAPTIVATE* (CAPTIVE)

Pr 6:25 or let her *c* you with her eyes,

CAPTIVATED* (CAPTIVE)

Pr 5:19 may you ever be *c* by her love.
5:20 Why be *c,* my son, by an adulteress

CAPTIVE (CAPTIVATE CAPTIVATED CAPTIVES CAPTIVITY CAPTURED)

Ac 8:23 full of bitterness and *c* to sin."
2Co 10: 5 and we take *c* every thought
Col 2: 8 See to it that no one takes you *c*
2Ti 2:26 who has taken them *c* to do his will.

CAPTIVES (CAPTIVE)

Ps 68:18 you led *c* in your train;
Isa 61: 1 to proclaim freedom for the *c*
Eph 4: 8 he led *c* in his train

CAPTIVITY (CAPTIVE)

Dt 28:41 because they will go into *c.*
2Ki 25:21 So Judah went into *c,* away
Jer 30: 3 Israel and Judah back from *c*
52:27 So Judah went into *c,* away
Eze 29:14 I will bring them back from *c*

CAPTURED (CAPTIVE)

1Sa 4:11 The ark of God was *c,*
2Sa 5: 7 David *c* the fortress of Zion,
2Ki 17: 6 the king of Assyria *c* Samaria

CARCASS

Jdg 14: 9 taken the honey from the lion's *c*.
Mt 24: 28 there is a *c*, there the vultures

CARE (CAREFUL CARES CARING)

Ps 8: 4 the son of man that you *c* for him?
65: 9 You *c* for the land and water it;
144: 3 what is man that you *c* for him,
Pr 29: 7 The righteous *c* about justice
Mk 5: 26 deal under the *c* of many doctors
Lk 10: 34 him to an inn and took *c* of him.
18: 4 I don't fear God or *c* about men,
Jn 21: 16 Jesus said, "Take *c* of my sheep."
1Ti 3: 5 how can he take *c* of God's church
6: 20 what has been entrusted to your *c*.
Heb 2: 6 the son of man that you *c* for him?
1Pe 5: 2 of God's flock that is under your *c*,

CAREFUL* (CARE)

Ge 31: 24 "Be *c* not to say anything to Jacob,
31: 29 'Be *c* not to say anything to Jacob,
Ex 19: 12 'Be *c* that you do not go up
23: 13 "Be *c* to do everything I have said
34: 12 Be *c* not to make a treaty
34: 15 "Be *c* not to make a treaty
Lev 18: 4 and be *c* to follow my decrees.
25: 18 " 'Follow my decrees and be *c*
26: 3 and are *c* to obey my commands,
Dt 2: 4 afraid of you, but be very *c*.
4: 9 before you today? Only be *c*,
4: 23 Be *c* not to forget the covenant
5: 32 So be *c* to do what the LORD your
6: 3 be *c* to obey so that it may go well
6: 12 be *c* that you do not forget
6: 25 And if we are *c* to obey all this law
7: 12 attention to these laws and are *c*
8: 1 Be *c* to follow every command I am
8: 11 Be *c* that you do not forget
11: 16 Be *c*, or you will be enticed
12: 1 and laws you must be *c* to follow
12: 13 Be *c* not to sacrifice your burnt
12: 19 Be *c* not to neglect the Levites
12: 28 Be *c* to obey all these regulations I
12: 30 be *c* not to be ensnared
15: 5 are *c* to follow all these commands
15: 9 Be *c* not to harbor this wicked
17: 10 be *c* to do everything they direct
24: 8 cases of leprous diseases be very *c*
Jos 1: 7 Be *c* to obey all the law my servant
1: 8 so that you may be *c*
22: 5 But be very *c* to keep
23: 6 be *c* to obey all that is written
23: 11 be very *c* to love the LORD your
1Ki 8: 25 if only your sons are *c* in all they do
2Ki 10: 31 Yet Jehu was not *c* to keep the law
17: 37 You must always be *c*
21: 8 if only they will be *c*
1Ch 22: 13 if you are *c* to observe the decrees
28: 8 Be *c* to follow all the commands
2Ch 6: 16 if only your sons are *c* in all they do
33: 8 if only they will be *c*
Ezr 4: 22 Be *c* not to neglect this matter.
Job 36: 18 Be *c* that no one entices you
Ps 101: 2 I will be *c* to lead a blameless life—
Pr 13: 24 he who loves him is *c*
27: 23 give *c* attention to your herds;
Isa 7: 4 Be *c*, keep calm and don't be afraid.
Jer 17: 21 Be *c* not to carry a load
17: 24 But if you are *c* to obey me,
22: 4 For if you are *c* to carry out these
Eze 11: 20 will follow my decrees and be *c*
18: 19 has been *c* to keep all my decrees,
20: 19 follow my decrees and be *c*
20: 21 they were not *c* to keep my laws—
36: 27 you to follow my decrees and be *c*
37: 24 and be *c* to keep my decrees.
Mic 7: 5 be *c* of your words.
Hag 1: 5 "Give *c* thought to your ways.
1: 7 "Give *c* thought to your ways.
2: 15 give *c* thought to this from this day
2: 18 Give *c* thought: Is there yet any
2: 18 give *c* thought to the day
Mt 2: 8 and make a *c* search for the child.
6: 1 "Be *c* not to do your 'acts
16: 6 "Be *c*," Jesus said to them.
Mk 8: 15 "Be *c*," Jesus warned them.
Lk 21: 34 Be *c*, or your hearts will be weighed

Ro 12: 17 Be *c* to do what is right in the eyes
1Co 3: 10 each one should be *c* how he builds
8: 9 Be *c*, however, that the exercise
10: 12 standing firm, be *c* that you don't
Eph 5: 15 Be very *c*, then, how you live—
2Ti 4: 2 great patience and *c* instruction.
Tit 3: 8 may be *c* to devote themselves
Heb 2: 1 We must pay more *c* attention,
4: 1 let us be *c* that none

CARELESS*

Mt 12: 36 for every *c* word they have spoken.

CARES* (CARE)

Dt 11: 12 It is a land the LORD your God *c*
Job 39: 16 she *c* not that her labor was in vain,
Ps 55: 22 Cast your *c* on the LORD
142: 4 no one *c* for my life.
Pr 12: 10 A righteous man *c* for the needs
Ecc 5: 3 when there are many *c*,
Jer 12: 11 because there is no one who *c*.
30: 17 Zion for whom no one *c*.'
Na 1: 7 He *c* for those who trust in him,
Jn 10: 13 and *c* nothing for the sheep.
Eph 5: 29 but he feeds and *c* for it, just
1Pe 5: 7 on him because he *c* for you.

CARING* (CARE)

1Th 2: 7 like a mother *c* for her little
1Ti 5: 4 practice by *c* for their own family

CARNAL see SINFUL, UNSPIRITUAL, WORLDLY

CARPENTER (CARPENTER'S)

Mk 6: 3 does miracles! Isn't this the *c*?

CARPENTER'S* (CARPENTER)

Mt 13: 55 "Isn't this the *c* son? Isn't his

CARRIED (CARRY)

Ex 19: 4 and how I *c* you on eagles' wings
Dt 1: 31 how the LORD your God *c* you,
Isa 53: 4 and *c* our sorrows,
63: 9 he lifted them up and *c* them
Mt 8: 17 and *c* our diseases."
Heb 13: 9 Do not be *c* away by all kinds
2Pe 1: 21 as they were *c* along by the Holy
3: 17 so that you may not be *c* away

CARRIES (CARRY)

Dt 32: 11 and *c* them on its pinions.
Isa 40: 11 and *c* them close to his heart;

CARRY (CARRIED CARRIES CARRYING)

Lev 16: 22 goat will *c* on itself all their sins
26: 15 and fail to *c* out all my commands
Isa 46: 4 I have made you and I will *c* you;
Lk 14: 27 anyone who does not *c* his cross
Gal 6: 2 *C* each other's burdens,
6: 5 for each one should *c* his own load.

CARRYING (CARRY)

Jn 19: 17 *C* his own cross, he went out
1Jn 5: 2 loving God and *c* out his

CARVED (CARVES)

Nu 33: 52 Destroy all their *c* images
Mic 5: 13 I will destroy your *c* images

CARVES* (CARVED)

Dt 27: 15 "Cursed is the man who *c* an image

CASE

Pr 18: 17 to present his *c* seems right,
22: 23 for the LORD will take up their *c*
23: 11 he will take up their *c* against you.

CAST (CASTING)

Ex 34: 17 "Do not make *c* idols.
Lev 16: 8 He is to *c* lots for the two goats—
Ps 22: 18 and *c* lots for my clothing.
55: 22 *C* your cares on the LORD
Pr 16: 33 The lot is *c* into the lap,
Ecc 11: 1 *C* your bread upon the waters,
Jn 19: 24 and *c* lots for my clothing."
1Pe 5: 7 *C* all your anxiety on him

CASTING (CAST)

Pr 18: 18 *C* the lot settles disputes
Mt 27: 35 divided up his clothes by *c* lots.

CATCH (CATCHES CAUGHT)

Lk 5: 4 and let down the nets for a *c*."
5: 10 from now on you will *c* men."

CATCHES (CATCH)

Job 5: 13 He *c* the wise in their craftiness,
1Co 3: 19 "He *c* the wise in their craftiness";

CATTLE

Ps 50: 10 and the *c* on a thousand hills.

CAUGHT (CATCH)

Ge 22: 13 there in a thicket he saw a ram *c*
2Co 12: 2 who fourteen years ago was *c* up
1Th 4: 17 and are left will be *c* up together with
them

CAUSE (CAUSES)

Pr 24: 28 against your neighbor without *c*,
Ecc 8: 3 Do not stand up for a bad *c*,
Mt 18: 7 of the things that *c* people to sin!
Ro 14: 21 else that will *c* your brother
1Co 10: 32 Do not *c* anyone to stumble,

CAUSES (CAUSE)

Ps 7: 16 The trouble he *c* recoils on himself;
Isa 8: 14 a stone that *c* men to stumble
Mt 5: 29 If your right eye *c* you to sin,
5: 30 And if your right hand *c* you to sin,
18: 6 if anyone *c* one of these little ones
18: 8 or your foot *c* you to sin,
Ro 14: 20 to eat anything that *c* someone else
1Co 8: 13 if what I eat *c* my brother to fall
1Pe 2: 8 "A stone that *c* men to stumble

CAUTIOUS*

Pr 12: 26 A righteous man is *c* in friendship,

CEASE

Ps 46: 9 He makes wars *c* to the ends

CELEBRATE*

Ex 10: 9 we are to *c* a festival to the LORD
12: 14 generations to come you shall *c* it
12: 17 *C* this day as a lasting ordinance
12: 17 "*C* the Feast of Unleavened Bread,
12: 47 community of Israel must *c* it.
12: 48 to *c* the LORD's Passover must
23: 14 are to *c* a festival to me.
23: 15 "*C* the Feast of Unleavened Bread;
23: 16 "*C* the Feast of Harvest
23: 16 "*C* the Feast of Ingathering
34: 18 "*C* the Feast of Unleavened Bread.
34: 22 "*C* the Feast of Weeks
Lev 23: 39 *c* the festival to the LORD
23: 41 *C* this as a festival to the LORD
23: 41 for the generations to come; *c* it
Nu 9: 2 "Have the Israelites *c* the Passover
9: 3 *C* it at the appointed time,
9: 4 told the Israelites to *c* the Passover,
9: 6 of them could not *c* the Passover
9: 10 they may still *c* the LORD's
9: 11 are to *c* it on the fourteenth day
9: 12 When they *c* the Passover,
9: 13 on a journey fails to *c* the Passover,
9: 14 to *c* the LORD's Passover must do
29: 12 *C* a festival to the LORD
Dt 16: 1 *c* the Passover of the LORD your
16: 10 Then *c* the Feast of Weeks
16: 13 *C* the Feast of Tabernacles
16: 15 For seven days *c* the Feast
Jdg 16: 23 to Dagon their god and to *c*,
2Sa 6: 21 the LORD's people Israel—I will *c*
2Ki 23: 21 "*C* the Passover to the LORD your
2Ch 30: 1 and *c* the Passover to the LORD,
30: 2 decided to *c* the Passover
30: 3 able to *c* it at the regular time
30: 5 and *c* the Passover to the LORD,
30: 13 in Jerusalem to *c* the Feast
30: 23 to *c* the festival seven more days;
Ne 8: 12 of food and to *c* with great joy,
12: 27 to *c* joyfully the dedication
Est 9: 21 to have them *c* annually
Ps 145: 7 They will *c* your abundant

Isa 30: 29 as on the night you *c* a holy festival
Na   1: 15 *C* your festivals, O Judah,
Zec 14: 16 and to *c* the Feast of Tabernacles.
       14: 18 up to *c* the Feast of Tabernacles.
       14: 19 up to *c* the Feast of Tabernacles.
Mt 26: 18 I am going to *c* the Passover
Lk 15: 23 Let's have a feast and *c*.
       15: 24 So they began to *c*.
       15: 29 goat so I could *c* with my friends.
       15: 32 But we had to *c* and be glad,
Rev 11: 10 will *c* by sending each other gifts,

CELESTIAL*

2Pe   2: 10 afraid to slander *c* beings;
Jude : 8 authority and slander *c* beings.

CENSER (CENSERS)

Lev 16: 12 is to take a *c* full of burning coals
Rev   8: 3 Another angel, who had a golden *c*,

CENSERS (CENSER)

Nu 16: 6 Take *c* and tomorrow put fire

CENTURION

Mt   8: 5 had entered Capernaum, a *c* came
      27: 54 When the *c* and those
Mk 15: 39 And when the *c*, who stood there
Lk   7: 3 The *c* heard of Jesus and sent some
      23: 47 The *c*, seeing what had happened,
Ac 10: 1 a *c* in what was known
      27: 1 handed over to a *c* named Julius,

CEPHAS* (PETER)

Jn   1: 42 You will be called *C*'' (which,
1Co 1: 12 another, ''I follow *C*''; still another,
      3: 22 Paul or Apollos or *C* or the world
      9: 5 and the Lord's brothers and *C*?

CEREMONIAL* (CEREMONY)

Lev 14: 2 at the time of his *c* cleansing,
       15: 13 off seven days for his *c* cleansing;
Mk   7: 3 they give their hands a *c* washing,
Jn   2: 6 used by the Jews for *c* washing,
      3: 25 Jew over the matter of *c* washing.
      11: 55 to Jerusalem for their *c* cleansing
      18: 28 to avoid *c* uncleanness the Jews did
Heb 9: 10 drink and various *c* washings—
      13: 9 not by *c* foods, which are

CEREMONIALLY* (CEREMONY)

Lev 4: 12 outside the camp to a place *c* clean,
       5: 2 touches anything *c* unclean—
       6: 11 the camp to a place that is *c* clean.
       7: 19 anyone *c* clean may eat it.
       7: 19 touches anything *c* unclean must
      10: 14 Eat them in a *c* clean place;
      11: 4 not have a split hoof; it is *c* unclean
      12: 2 birth to a son will be *c* unclean
      12: 7 and then she will be *c* clean
      13: 3 he shall pronounce him *c* unclean.
      14: 8 with water; then he will be *c* clean.
      15: 28 and after that she will be *c* clean.
      15: 33 lies with a woman who is *c* unclean.
      17: 15 he will be *c* unclean till evening.
      21: 1 must not make himself *c* unclean
      22: 3 of your descendants is *c* unclean
      27: 11 he vowed is a *c* unclean animal—
Nu   5: 2 who is *c* unclean because of a dead
      6: 7 must not make himself *c* unclean
      8: 6 Israelites and make them *c* clean.
      9: 6 they were *c* unclean on account
      9: 13 But if a man who is *c* clean
      18: 11 household who is *c* clean may eat
      18: 13 household who is *c* clean may eat
      19: 7 but he will be *c* unclean till evening
      19: 9 and put them in a *c* clean place
      19: 18 Then a man who is *c* clean is
Dt 12: 15 Both the *c* unclean and the clean
      12: 22 Both the *c* unclean and the clean
      14: 7 they are *c* unclean for you.
      15: 22 Both the *c* unclean and the clean
1Sa 20: 26 to David to make him *c* unclean—
2Ch 13: 11 the bread on the *c* clean table
      30: 17 for all those who were not *c* clean
Ezr 6: 20 themselves and were all *c* clean.
Ne 12: 30 Levites had purified themselves *c*,
Isa 66: 20 of the LORD in *c* clean vessels.
Eze 22: 10 period, when they are *c* unclean.

Ac 24: 18 I was *c* clean when they found me
Heb 9: 13 those who are *c* unclean sanctify

CEREMONY* (CEREMONIAL CEREMONIALLY)

Ge 50: 11 Egyptians are holding a solemn *c*
Ex 12: 25 as he promised, observe this *c*.
      12: 26 'What does this *c* mean to you?'
      13: 5 are to observe this *c* in this month:

CERTAIN (CERTAINTY)

2Pe 1: 19 word of the prophets made more *c*,

CERTAINTY* (CERTAIN)

Lk   1: 4 so that you may know the *c*
Jn 17: 8 They knew with *c* that I came

CERTIFICATE* (CERTIFIED)

Dt 24: 1 and he writes her a *c* of divorce,
      24: 3 and writes her a *c* of divorce,
Isa 50: 1 'Where is your mother's *c*
Jer 3: 8 I gave faithless Israel her *c*
Mt   5: 31 divorces his wife must give her a *c*
      19: 7 that a man give his wife a *c*
Mk 10: 4 a man to write a *c* of divorce

CERTIFIED* (CERTIFICATE)

Jn   3: 33 has accepted it has *c* that God is

CHAFF

Ps   1: 4 They are like *c*
      35: 5 May they be like *c* before the wind,
Da   2: 35 became like *c* on a threshing floor
Mt   3: 12 up the *c* with unquenchable fire.''

CHAINED (CHAINS)

2Ti 2: 9 But God's word is not *c*.

CHAINS (CHAINED)

Eph 6: 20 for which I am an ambassador in *c*.
Col 4: 18 Remember my *c*.
2Ti 1: 16 and was not ashamed of my *c*.
Jude : 6 with everlasting *c* for judgment

CHAMPION

Ps 19: 5 like a *c* rejoicing to run his course.

CHANCE

Ecc 9: 11 but time and *c* happen to them all.

CHANGE (CHANGED)

1Sa 15: 29 of Israel does not lie or *c* his mind;
Ps 110: 4 and will not *c* his mind:
Jer 7: 5 If you really *c* your ways
Mal 3: 6 ''I the LORD do not *c*.
Mt 18: 3 unless you *c* and become like little
Heb 7: 21 and will not *c* his mind:
Jas 1: 17 who does not *c* like shifting

CHANGED (CHANGE)

1Sa 10: 6 you will be *c* into a different person
Hos 11: 8 My heart is *c* within me;
1Co 15: 51 but we will all be *c*— in a flash,

CHARACTER*

Ru   3: 11 that you are a woman of noble *c*.
Pr 12: 4 of noble *c* is her husband's crown,
      31: 10 A wife of noble *c* who can find?
Ac 17: 11 noble *c* than the Thessalonians,
Ro   5: 4 perseverance, *c*; and *c*, hope.
1Co 15: 33 ''Bad company corrupts good *c*.''

CHARGE (CHARGES)

Job 34: 13 him in *c* of the whole world?
Ro   8: 33 Who will bring any *c*
1Co 9: 18 the gospel I may offer it free of *c*,
2Co 11: 7 the gospel of God to you free of *c*?
2Ti 4: 1 I give you this *c*: Preach the Word;
Phm : 18 or owes you anything, *c* it to me.

CHARGES (CHARGE)

Isa 50: 8 Who then will bring *c* against me?

CHARIOT (CHARIOTS)

2Ki 2: 11 suddenly a *c* of fire and horses
Ps 104: 3 He makes the clouds his *c*
Ac   8: 28 sitting in his *c* reading the book

CHARIOTS (CHARIOT)

2Ki 6: 17 and *c* of fire all around Elisha.
Ps 20: 7 Some trust in *c* and some in horses,
      68: 17 The *c* of God are tens of thousands

CHARITY see LOVE

CHARM* (CHARMING)

Pr 17: 8 bribe is a *c* to the one who gives it;
      31: 30 *C* is deceptive, and beauty is

CHARMING* (CHARM)

Pr 26: 25 his speech is *c*, do not believe
SS   1: 16 Oh, how *c*!

CHASE (CHASES)

Lev 26: 8 Five of you will *c* a hundred,

CHASES* (CHASE)

Pr 12: 11 he who *c* fantasies lacks judgment.
      28: 19 one who *c* fantasies will have his

CHASM*

Lk 16: 26 and you a great *c* has been fixed,

CHATTER* (CHATTERING)

1Ti 6: 20 Turn away from godless *c*
2Ti 2: 16 Avoid godless *c*, because those

CHATTERING* (CHATTER)

Pr 10: 8 but a *c* fool comes to ruin.
      10: 10 and a *c* fool comes to ruin.

CHEAT* (CHEATED CHEATING CHEATS)

Mal 1: 14 ''Cursed is the *c* who has
1Co 6: 8 you yourselves *c* and do wrong,

CHEATED* (CHEAT)

Ge 31: 7 yet your father has *c* me
1Sa 12: 3 Whom have I *c*? Whom have I
      12: 4 ''You have not *c* or oppressed us,''
Lk 19: 8 if I have *c* anybody out of anything,
1Co 6: 7 Why not rather be *c*? Instead,

CHEATING* (CHEAT)

Am   8: 5 and *c* with dishonest scales,

CHEATS* (CHEAT)

Lev 6: 2 or if he *c* him, or if he finds lost

CHEEK (CHEEKS)

Mt   5: 39 someone strikes you on the right *c*,
Lk   6: 29 If someone strikes you on one *c*,

CHEEKS (CHEEK)

Isa 50: 6 my *c* to those who pulled out my

CHEERFUL* (CHEERS)

Pr 15: 13 A happy heart makes the face *c*,
      15: 15 but the *c* heart has a continual feast
      15: 30 A *c* look brings joy to the heart,
      17: 22 A *c* heart is good medicine,
2Co 9: 7 for God loves a *c* giver.

CHEERS (CHEERFUL)

Pr 12: 25 but a kind word *c* him up.

CHEMOSH

2Ki 23: 13 for *C* the vile god of Moab,

CHERISH (CHERISHED CHERISHES)

Ps 17: 14 You still the hunger of those you *c*;

CHERISHED (CHERISH)

Ps 66: 18 If I had *c* sin in my heart,

CHERISHES* (CHERISH)

Pr 19: 8 he who *c* understanding prospers.

CHERUB (CHERUBIM)

Ex 25: 19 Make one *c* on one end
Eze 28: 14 You were anointed as a guardian *c*,

CHERUBIM (CHERUB)

Ge   3: 24 side of the Garden of Eden *c*
1Sa 4: 4 who is enthroned between the *c*.
2Sa 6: 2 enthroned between the *c* that are
      22: 11 He mounted the *c* and flew;

1Ki 6: 23 a pair of *c* of olive wood,
2Ki 19: 15 of Israel, enthroned between the *c*,
1Ch 13: 6 who is enthroned between the *c*—
Ps 18: 10 He mounted the *c* and flew;
    80: 1 who sit enthroned between the *c*,
    99: 1 he sits enthroned between the *c*,
Isa 37: 16 of Israel, enthroned between the *c*,
Eze 10: 1 was over the heads of the *c*.

CHEST

Ex 25: 10 "Have them make a *c*
2Ki 12: 9 Jehoiada the priest took a *c*
Da   2: 32 its *c* and arms of silver, its belly
Rev 1: 13 with a golden sash around his *c*.

CHEWS

Lev 11: 3 divided and that *c* the cud.

CHIEF

1Pe 5: 4 And when the *C* Shepherd appears,

CHILD (CHILDISH CHILDREN CHILDREN'S GRANDCHILDREN)

Pr 20: 11 Even a *c* is known by his actions,
    22: 6 Train a *c* in the way he should go,
    22: 15 Folly is bound up in the heart of a *c*
    23: 13 not withhold discipline from a *c*;
    29: 15 *c* left to himself disgraces his mother.
Isa 7: 14 The virgin will be with *c*
     9: 6 For to us a *c* is born,
    11: 6 and a little *c* will lead them.
    66: 13 As a mother comforts her *c*,
Mt   1: 23 "The virgin will be with *c*
    18: 2 He called a little *c* and had him
Lk   1: 42 and blessed is the *c* you will bear!
     1: 80 And the *c* grew and became strong
1Co 13: 11 When I was a *c*, I talked like a *c*,
1Jn 5: 1 who loves the father loves his *c*

CHILDBEARING (BEAR)

Ge   3: 16 greatly increase your pains in *c*;

CHILDBIRTH (BEAR)

Gal 4: 19 the pains of *c* until Christ is formed

CHILDISH* (CHILD)

1Co 13: 11 When I became a man, I put *c* ways

CHILDREN (CHILD)

Ex 20: 5 punishing the *c* for the sin
Dt   4: 9 Teach them to your *c*
     6: 7 Impress them on your *c*.
    11: 19 them to your *c*, talking about them
    14: 1 You are the *c* of the Lord your
    24: 16 nor *c* put to death for their fathers;
    30: 19 so that you and your *c* may live
    32: 46 so that you may command your *c*
Job 1: 5 "Perhaps my *c* have sinned
Ps   8: 2 From the lips of *c* and infants
    78: 5 forefathers to teach their *c*,
Pr 17: 6 Children's *c* are a crown
    20: 7 blessed are his *c* after him.
    31: 28 Her *c* arise and call her blessed;
Joel 1: 3 Tell it to your *c*,
Mal 4: 6 the hearts of the fathers to their *c*,
Mt   7: 11 how to give good gifts to your *c*,
    11: 25 and revealed them to little *c*.
    18: 3 you change and become like little *c*
    19: 14 "Let the little *c* come to me,
    21: 16 " 'From the lips of *c* and infants
Mk   9: 37 one of these little *c* in my name
    10: 14 "Let the little *c* come to me,
    10: 16 And he took the *c* in his arms,
    13: 12 *C* will rebel against their parents
Lk 10: 21 and revealed them to little *c*.
    18: 16 "Let the little *c* come to me,
Jn   1: 12 the right to become *c* of God—
Ac   2: 39 The promise is for you and your *c*
Ro   8: 16 with our spirit that we are God's *c*.
1Co 14: 20 Brothers, stop thinking like *c*.
2Co 12: 14 parents, but parents for their *c*.
Eph 6: 1 *C*, obey your parents in the Lord,
     6: 4 do not exasperate your *c*; instead,
Col 3: 20 *C*, obey your parents in everything,
     3: 21 Fathers, do not embitter your *c*,
1Ti 3: 4 and see that his *c* obey him
     3: 12 and must manage his *c* and his
     5: 10 bringing up *c*, showing hospitality,

Heb 2: 13 and the *c* God has given me."
1Jn 3: 1 that we should be called *c* of God!

CHILDREN'S (CHILD)

Isa 54: 13 and great will be your *c* peace.

CHOKE

Mk   4: 19 come in and *c* the word,

CHOOSE (CHOOSES CHOSE CHOSEN)

Dt 30: 19 Now *c* life, so that you
Jos 24: 15 then *c* for yourselves this day
Pr   8: 10 *C* my instruction instead of silver,
    16: 16 to *c* understanding rather
Jn 15: 16 You did not *c* me, but I chose you

CHOOSES (CHOOSE)

Mt 11: 27 to whom the Son *c* to reveal him.
Lk 10: 22 to whom the Son *c* to reveal him."
Jn   7: 17 If anyone *c* to do God's will,

CHOSE (CHOOSE)

Ge 13: 11 So Lot *c* for himself the whole plain
Ps 33: 12 the people he *c* for his inheritance.
Jn 15: 16 but I *c* you and appointed you to go
1Co 1: 27 But God *c* the foolish things
Eph 1: 4 he *c* us in him before the creation
2Th 2: 13 from the beginning God *c* you

CHOSEN (CHOOSE)

Isa 41: 8 Jacob, whom I have *c*,
Mt 22: 14 For many are invited, but few are *c*
Lk 10: 42 Mary has *c* what is better,
    23: 35 the Christ of God, the *C* One."
Jn 15: 19 but I have *c* you out of the world.
1Pe 1: 20 He was *c* before the creation
     2: 9 But you are a *c* people, a royal

CHRIST (CHRIST'S CHRISTIAN CHRISTIANS CHRISTS)

Mt   1: 16 was born Jesus, who is called *C*.
    16: 16 Peter answered, "You are the *C*,
    22: 42 "What do you think about the *C*?
Mk   1: 1 of the gospel about Jesus *C*,
     8: 29 Peter answered, "You are the *C*."
    14: 61 "Are you the *C*, the Son
Lk   9: 20 Peter answered, "The *C* of God."
Jn   1: 41 found the Messiah" (that is, the *C*).
    20: 31 you may believe that Jesus is the *C*,
Ac   2: 36 you crucified, both Lord and *C*."
     5: 42 the good news that Jesus is the *C*.
     9: 22 by proving that Jesus is the *C*.
     9: 34 said to him, "Jesus *C* heals you.
    17: 3 proving that the *C* had to suffer
    18: 28 the Scriptures that Jesus was the *C*.
    26: 23 that the *C* would suffer and,
Ro   1: 4 from the dead: Jesus *C* our Lord.
     3: 22 comes through faith in Jesus *C*
     5: 1 God through our Lord Jesus *C*,
     5: 6 we were still powerless, *C* died
     5: 8 While we were still sinners, *C* died
     5: 11 in God through our Lord Jesus *C*,
     5: 17 life through the one man, Jesus *C*.
     6: 4 as *C* was raised from the dead
     6: 9 that since *C* was raised
     6: 23 life in *C* Jesus our Lord.
     7: 4 to the law through the body of *C*,
     8: 1 for those who are in *C* Jesus,
     8: 9 Spirit of *C*, he does not belong to *C*.
     8: 17 heirs of God and co-heirs with *C*,
     8: 34 Who is he that condemns? *C* Jesus,
     8: 35 us from the love of *C*?
     9: 5 is traced the human ancestry of *C*,
    10: 4 *C* is the end of the law
    12: 5 so in *C* we who are many form one
    13: 14 yourselves with the Lord Jesus *C*,
    14: 9 *C* died and returned to life
    15: 3 For even *C* did not please himself
    15: 5 yourselves as you follow *C* Jesus,
    15: 7 then, just as *C* accepted you,
    16: 18 people are not serving our Lord *C*,
1Co 1: 2 to those sanctified in *C* Jesus
     1: 7 for our Lord Jesus *C* to be revealed.
     1: 13 Is *C* divided? Was Paul crucified
     1: 17 For *C* did not send me to baptize,
     1: 23 but we preach *C* crucified:
     1: 30 of him that you are in *C* Jesus,
     2: 2 except Jesus *C* and him crucified.

1Co 3: 11 one already laid, which is Jesus *C*.
     5: 7 For *C*, our Passover lamb,
     6: 15 bodies are members of *C* himself?
     8: 6 and there is but one Lord, Jesus *C*,
     8: 12 conscience, you sin against *C*.
    10: 4 them, and that rock was *C*.
    11: 1 as I follow the example of *C*.
    11: 3 the head of every man is *C*,
    12: 27 Now you are the body of *C*,
    15: 3 that *C* died for our sins according
    15: 14 And if *C* has not been raised,
    15: 22 so in *C* all will be made alive.
    15: 57 victory through our Lord Jesus *C*.
2Co 1: 5 as the sufferings of *C* flow
     2: 14 us in triumphal procession in *C*
     3: 3 show that you are a letter from *C*,
     3: 14 because only in *C* is it taken away.
     4: 4 light of the gospel of the glory of *C*,
     4: 5 not preach ourselves, but Jesus *C*
     4: 6 of the glory of God in the face of *C*
     5: 10 before the judgment seat of *C*,
     5: 17 Therefore, if anyone is in *C*,
     6: 15 What harmony is there between *C*
    10: 1 the meekness and gentleness of *C*,
    11: 2 you to one husband, to *C*,
Gal 1: 7 are trying to pervert the gospel of *C*
     2: 4 on the freedom we have in *C* Jesus
     2: 16 but by faith in Jesus *C*.
     2: 17 does that mean that *C* promotes sin
     2: 20 I have been crucified with *C*
     2: 21 *C* died for nothing!" You foolish
     3: 13 *C* redeemed us from the curse
     3: 16 meaning one person, who is *C*.
     3: 26 of God through faith in *C* Jesus,
     4: 19 of childbirth until *C* is formed
     5: 1 for freedom that *C* has set us free.
     5: 4 by law have been alienated from *C*;
     5: 24 to *C* Jesus have crucified the sinful
     6: 14 in the cross of our Lord Jesus *C*,
Eph 1: 3 with every spiritual blessing in *C*.
     1: 10 together under one head, even *C*.
     1: 20 which he exerted in *C*
     2: 5 made us alive with *C*
     2: 10 created in *C* Jesus
     2: 12 time you were separate from *C*,
     2: 20 with *C* Jesus himself as the chief
     3: 8 the unsearchable riches of *C*,
     3: 17 so that *C* may dwell in your hearts
     4: 7 has been given as *C* apportioned it.
     4: 13 measure of the fullness of *C*.
     4: 15 into him who is the Head, that is, *C*
     4: 32 just as in *C* God forgave you.
     5: 2 as *C* loved us and gave himself up
     5: 21 out of reverence for *C*.
     5: 23 as *C* is the head of the church,
     5: 25 just as *C* loved the church
Php 1: 18 motives or true, *C* is preached.
     1: 21 to live is *C* and to die is gain.
     1: 23 I desire to depart and be with *C*,
     1: 27 worthy of the gospel of *C*.
     1: 29 on behalf of *C* not only to believe
     2: 5 be the same as that of *C* Jesus:
     3: 7 now consider loss for the sake of *C*.
     3: 10 I want to know *C* and the power
     3: 18 as enemies of the cross of *C*.
     4: 19 to his glorious riches in *C* Jesus.
Col 1: 4 heard of your faith in *C* Jesus
     1: 27 which is *C* in you, the hope of glory
     1: 28 may present everyone perfect in *C*.
     2: 2 the mystery of God, namely, *C*,
     2: 6 as you received *C* Jesus as Lord,
     2: 9 For in *C* all the fullness
     2: 13 God made you alive with *C*,
     2: 17 the reality, however, is found in *C*.
     3: 1 then, you have been raised with *C*,
     3: 3 and your life is now hidden with *C*
     3: 15 Let the peace of *C* rule
1Th 5: 9 through our Lord Jesus *C*.
2Th 2: 1 the coming of our Lord Jesus *C*
     2: 14 in the glory of our Lord Jesus *C*.
1Ti 1: 12 I thank *C* Jesus our Lord, who has
     1: 15 *C* Jesus came into the world
     1: 16 *C* Jesus might display his unlimited
     2: 5 the man *C* Jesus, who gave himself
2Ti 1: 9 us in *C* Jesus before the beginning
     1: 10 appearing of our Savior, *C* Jesus,
     2: 1 in the grace that is in *C* Jesus.
     2: 3 us like a good soldier of *C* Jesus.

2Ti 2: 8 Remember Jesus *C*, raised
     2: 10 the salvation that is in *C* Jesus,
     3: 12 life in *C* Jesus will be persecuted,
     3: 15 salvation through faith in *C* Jesus.
     4: 1 presence of God and of *C* Jesus,
Tit 2: 13 our great God and Savior, Jesus *C*,
Heb 3: 6 But *C* is faithful as a son
     3: 14 to share in *C* if we hold firmly
     5: 5 So *C* also did not take
     6: 1 the elementary teachings about *C*
     9: 11 When *C* came as high priest
     9: 14 more, then, will the blood of *C*,
     9: 15 For this reason *C* is the mediator
     9: 24 For *C* did not enter a man-made
     9: 26 Then *C* would have had
     9: 28 so *C* was sacrificed once
    10: 10 of the body of Jesus *C* once for all.
    13: 8 Jesus *C* is the same yesterday
1Pe 1: 2 for obedience to Jesus *C*
     1: 3 of Jesus *C* from the dead,
     1: 11 he predicted the sufferings of *C*
     1: 19 but with the precious blood of *C*,
     2: 21 because *C* suffered for you,
     3: 15 in your hearts set apart *C* as Lord.
     3: 18 For *C* died for sins once for all,
     3: 21 you by the resurrection of Jesus *C*,
     4: 13 participate in the sufferings of *C*,
     4: 14 insulted because of the name of *C*,
2Pe 1: 1 and Savior Jesus *C* have received
     1: 16 and coming of our Lord Jesus *C*,
1Jn 2: 1 Jesus *C*, the Righteous One.
     2: 22 man who denies that Jesus is the *C*.
     3: 16 Jesus *C* laid down his life for us.
     3: 23 in the name of his Son, Jesus *C*,
     4: 2 that Jesus *C* has come
     5: 1 believes that Jesus is the *C* is born
     5: 20 even in his Son Jesus *C*.
2Jn   : 9 teaching of *C* does not have God;
Jude   : 4 deny Jesus *C* our only Sovereign
Rev 1: 1 The revelation of Jesus *C*,
     1: 5 from Jesus *C*, who is the faithful
    11: 15 kingdom of our Lord and of his *C*,
    20: 4 reigned with *C* a thousand years.
    20: 6 they will be priests of God and of *C*

CHRIST'S (CHRIST)

1Co 9: 21 from God's law but am under *C* law
2Co 5: 14 For *C* love compels us,
     5: 20 We are therefore *C* ambassadors,
    12: 9 so that *C* power may rest on me.
Col 1: 22 by *C* physical body through death

CHRISTIAN* (CHRIST)

Ac 26: 28 you can persuade me to be a *C*?''
1Pe 4: 16 as a *C*, do not be ashamed,

CHRISTIANS* (CHRIST)

Ac 11: 26 The disciples were called *C* first

CHRISTS* (CHRIST)

Mt 24: 24 For false *C* and false prophets will
Mk 13: 22 For false *C* and false prophets will

CHURCH

Mt 16: 18 and on this rock I will build my *c*,
    18: 17 if he refuses to listen even to the *c*,
Ac 20: 28 Be shepherds of the *c* of God,
1Co 5: 12 of mine to judge those outside the *c*
    14: 4 but he who prophesies edifies the *c*.
    14: 12 to excel in gifts that build up the *c*.
    14: 26 done for the strengthening of the *c*.
    15: 9 because I persecuted the *c* of God
Gal 1: 13 how intensely I persecuted the *c*
Eph 5: 23 as Christ is the head of the *c*,
Col 1: 18 he is the head of the body, the *c*;
    1: 24 the sake of his body, which is the *c*.

CHURNING

Pr 30: 33 For as *c* the milk produces butter,

CIRCLE

Isa 40: 22 enthroned above the *c* of the earth,

CIRCUMCISE (CIRCUMCISED CIRCUMCISION)

Dt 10: 16 *C* your hearts, therefore,

CIRCUMCISED (CIRCUMCISE)

Ge 17: 10 Every male among you shall be *c*.
    17: 12 who is eight days old must be *c*,
Jos 5: 3 and *c* the Israelites at Gibeah
Gal 5: 2 that if you let yourselves be *c*,

CIRCUMCISION (CIRCUMCISE)

Ro 2: 25 *C* has value if you observe the law,
    2: 29 and *c* is *c* of the heart, by the Spirit,
1Co 7: 19 *C* is nothing and uncircumcision is

CIRCUMSTANCES

Php 4: 11 to be content whatever the *c*.
1Th 5: 18 continually; give thanks in all *c*,

CITIES (CITY)

Lk 19: 17 small matter, take charge of ten *c*.'
    19: 19 'You take charge of five *c*.'

CITIZENS (CITIZENSHIP)

Eph 2: 19 but fellow *c* with God's people

CITIZENSHIP* (CITIZENS)

Ac 22: 28 ''I had to pay a big price for my *c*.''
Eph 2: 12 excluded from *c* in Israel
Php 3: 20 But our *c* is in heaven.

CITY (CITIES)

Mt 5: 14 A *c* on a hill cannot be hidden.
Ac 18: 10 I have many people in this *c*.''
Heb 13: 14 here we do not have an enduring *c*,
Rev 21: 2 saw the Holy *C*, the new

CIVILIAN*

2Ti 2: 4 a soldier gets involved in *c* affairs—

CLAIM (CLAIMS RECLAIM)

Pr 25: 6 do not *c* a place among great men;
1Jn 1: 6 If we *c* to have fellowship
     1: 8 If we *c* to be without sin, we
     1: 10 If we *c* we have not sinned,

CLAIMS (CLAIM)

Jas 2: 14 if a man *c* to have faith
1Jn 2: 6 Whoever *c* to live in him must walk
     2: 9 Anyone who *c* to be in the light

CLANGING*

1Co 13: 1 a resounding gong or a *c* cymbal.

CLAP* (CLAPPED CLAPS)

Job 21: 5 *c* your hand over your mouth.
Ps 47: 1 *C* your hands, all you nations;
    98: 8 Let the rivers *c* their hands,
Pr 30: 32 *c* your hand over your mouth!
Isa 55: 12 will *c* their hands.
La 2: 15 *c* their hands at you;

CLAPPED* (CLAP)

2Ki 11: 12 and the people *c* their hands
Eze 25: 6 Because you have *c* your hands

CLAPS* (CLAP)

Job 27: 23 It *c* its hands in derision
    34: 37 scornfully he *c* his hands among us
Na 3: 19 *c* his hands at your fall,

CLASSIFY*

2Co 10: 12 dare to *c* or compare ourselves

CLAUDIUS

Ac 11: 28 happened during the reign of *C*.)
    18: 2 because *C* had ordered all the Jews

CLAY

Isa 45: 9 Does the *c* say to the potter,
    64: 8 We are the *c*, you are the potter;
Jer 18: 6 ''Like *c* in the hand of the potter,
La 4: 2 are now considered as pots of *c*,
Da 2: 33 partly of iron and partly of baked *c*.
Ro 9: 21 of the same lump of *c* some are for
2Co 4: 7 we have this treasure in jars of *c*
2Ti 2: 20 and *c*; some are for noble purposes

CLEAN (CLEANNESS CLEANSE CLEANSED CLEANSES CLEANSING)

Ge 7: 2 seven of every kind of *c* animal,
Lev 4: 12 the camp to a place ceremonially *c*,
    16: 30 you will be *c* from all your sins.

Ps 24: 4 He who has *c* hands and a pure
    51: 7 with hyssop, and I will be *c*;
Pr 20: 9 I am *c* and without sin''?
Eze 36: 25 I will sprinkle *c* water on you,
Mt 8: 2 are willing, you can make me *c*.''
    12: 44 the house unoccupied, swept *c*
    23: 25 You *c* the outside of the cup
Mk 7: 19 Jesus declared all foods ''*c*.'')
Jn 13: 10 to wash his feet; his whole body is *c*
    15: 3 are already *c* because of the word
Ac 10: 15 impure that God has made *c*.''
Ro 14: 20 All food is *c*, but it is wrong

CLEANNESS (CLEAN)

2Sa 22: 25 according to my *c* in his sight.

CLEANSE (CLEAN)

Ps 51: 2 and *c* me from my sin.
    51: 7 *C* me with hyssop, and I will be
Pr 20: 30 Blows and wounds *c* away evil,
Heb 9: 14 *c* our consciences from acts that
    10: 22 having our hearts sprinkled to *c* us

CLEANSED (CLEAN)

Heb 9: 22 requires that nearly everything be *c*
2Pe 1: 9 has forgotten that he has been *c*

CLEANSES* (CLEAN)

2Ti 2: 21 If a man *c* himself from the latter,

CLEANSING (CLEAN)

Eph 5: 26 *c* her by the washing with water

CLEFT*

Ex 33: 22 I will put you in a *c* in the rock

CLEVER

Isa 5: 21 and *c* in their own sight.

CLING

Ro 12: 9 Hate what is evil; *c* to what is good.

CLINGS

Ps 63: 8 My soul *c* to you;

CLOAK

Ex 12: 11 with your *c* tucked into your belt,
2Ki 4: 29 ''Tuck your *c* into your belt,
     9: 1 ''Tuck your *c* into your belt,
Mt 5: 40 let him have your *c* as well.

CLOSE (CLOSER CLOSES)

2Ki 11: 8 Stay *c* to the king wherever he goes
2Ch 23: 7 Stay *c* to the king wherever he goes
Ps 34: 18 Lord is *c* to the brokenhearted
   148: 14 of Israel, the people *c* to his heart.
Isa 40: 11 and carries them *c* to his heart;
Jer 30: 21 himself to be *c* to me?'

CLOSER (CLOSE)

Ex 3: 5 ''Do not come any *c*,'' God said.
Pr 18: 24 there is a friend who sticks *c*

CLOSES (CLOSE)

Pr 28: 27 he who *c* his eyes to them receives

CLOTHE (CLOTHED CLOTHES CLOTHING)

Ps 45: 3 *c* yourself with splendor
Isa 52: 1 *c* yourself with strength.
Ro 13: 14 *c* yourselves with the Lord Jesus
Col 3: 12 *c* yourselves with compassion,
1Pe 5: 5 *c* yourselves with humility

CLOTHED (CLOTHE)

Ps 30: 11 removed my sackcloth and *c* me
   104: 1 you are *c* with splendor
Pr 31: 22 she is *c* in fine linen and purple.
    31: 25 She is *c* with strength and dignity;
Isa 61: 10 For he has *c* me with garments
Lk 24: 49 until you have been *c* with power
Gal 3: 27 into Christ have *c* yourselves

CLOTHES (CLOTHE)

Dt 8: 4 Your *c* did not wear out
Mt 6: 25 the body more important than *c*?
    6: 28 ''And why do you worry about *c*?
    27: 35 they divided up his *c* by casting lots
Jn 11: 44 Take off the grave *c* and let him go

CLOTHING (CLOTHE)

Dt 22: 5 A woman must not wear men's c,
Job 29: 14 I put on righteousness as my c;
Ps 22: 18 and cast lots for my c.
Mt   7: 15 They come to you in sheep's c,
1Ti 6: 8 But if we have food and c,

CLOUD (CLOUDS)

Ex 13: 21 them in a pillar of c to guide them
1Ki 18: 44 c as small as a man's hand is rising
Pr 16: 15 his favor is like a rain c in spring.
Isa 19: 1 See, the LORD rides on a swift c
Lk 21: 27 of Man coming in a c with power
Heb 12: 1 by such a great c of witnesses,
Rev 14: 14 seated on the c was one "like a son

CLOUDS (CLOUD)

Dt 33: 26 and on the c in his majesty.
Ps 68: 4 extol him who rides on the c—
    104: 3 He makes the c his chariot
Pr 25: 14 Like c and wind without rain
Da   7: 13 coming with the c of heaven.
Mt 24: 30 of Man coming on the c of the sky,
    26: 64 and coming on the c of heaven."
Mk 13: 26 coming in c with great power
1Th 4: 17 with them in the c to meet the Lord
Rev 1: 7 Look, he is coming with the c,

CLUB

Pr 25: 18 Like a c or a sword or a sharp arrow

CO-HEIRS* (INHERIT)

Ro   8: 17 heirs of God and c with Christ,

COALS

Pr 25: 22 you will heap burning c on his head
Ro 12: 20 you will heap burning c on his head

COARSE*

Eph 5: 4 or c joking, which are out of place,

CODE*

Ro   2: 27 even though you have the written c
     2: 29 by the Spirit, not by the written c.
     7: 6 not in the old way of the written c.
Col 2: 14 having canceled the written c,

COINS

Mt 26: 15 out for him thirty silver c.
Lk 15: 8 suppose a woman has ten silver c

COLD

Pr 25: 25 Like c water to a weary soul
Mt 10: 42 if anyone gives even a cup of c water
    24: 12 the love of most will grow c,

COLLECTION

1Co 16: 1 Now about the c for God's people:

COLT

Zec 9: 9 on a c, the foal of a donkey.
Mt 21: 5 on a c, the foal of a donkey.' "

COMB

Ps 19: 10 than honey from the c.

COMFORT* (COMFORTED
COMFORTER COMFORTERS
COMFORTING COMFORTS)

Ge   5: 29 "He will c us in the labor
    37: 35 and daughters came to c him,
Ru   2: 13 "You have given me c
1Ch 7: 22 and his relatives came to c him.
Job 2: 11 sympathize with him and c him.
     7: 13 When I think my bed will c me
    16: 5 c from my lips would bring you
    36: 16 to the c of your table laden
Ps 23: 4 rod and your staff, they c me.
    71: 21 and c me once again.
   119: 50 My c in my suffering is this:
   119: 52 and I find c in them.
   119: 76 May your unfailing love be my c,
   119: 82 I say, "When will you c me?"
Isa 40: 1 C, c my people,
    51: 3 The LORD will surely c Zion
    51: 19 who can c you?—
    57: 18 I will guide him and restore c
    61: 2 to c all who mourn,

Isa 66: 13 so will I c you;
Jer 16: 7 food to c those who mourn
    31: 13 I will give them c and joy instead
La   1: 2 there is none to c her.
     1: 9 there was none to c her.
     1: 16 No one is near to c me,
     1: 17 but there is no one to c her.
     1: 21 but there is no one to c me.
     2: 13 that I may c you,
Eze 16: 54 all you have done in giving them c.
Na   3: 7 Where can I find anyone to c you?"
Zec 1: 17 and the LORD will again c Zion
    10: 2 they give c in vain.
Lk   6: 24 you have already received your c.
Jn 11: 19 and Mary to c them in the loss
1Co 14: 3 encouragement and c,
2Co 1: 3 of compassion and the God of all c,
     1: 4 so that we can c those
     1: 4 with the c we ourselves have
     1: 5 through Christ our c overflows.
     1: 6 if we are comforted, it is for your c,
     1: 6 it is for your c and salvation;
     1: 7 so also you share in our c.
     2: 7 you ought to forgive and c him,
     7: 7 also by the c you had given him.
Php 2: 1 if any c from his love,
Col 4: 11 and they have proved a c to me.

COMFORTED* (COMFORT)

Ge 24: 67 Isaac was c after his mother's death
    37: 35 comfort him, but he refused to be c.
2Sa 12: 24 Then David c his wife Bathsheba,
Job 42: 11 They c and consoled him
Ps 77: 2 and my soul refused to be c.
    86: 17 have helped me and c me.
Isa 12: 1 and you have c me.
    52: 9 for the LORD has c his people,
    54: 11 lashed by storms and not c,
    66: 13 and you will be c over Jerusalem."
Jer 31: 15 and refusing to be c,
Mt   2: 18 and refusing to be c,
     5: 4 for they will be c.
Lk 16: 25 but now he is c here and you are
Ac 20: 12 man home alive and were greatly c.
2Co 1: 6 if we are c, it is for your comfort,
     7: 6 c us by the coming of Titus,

COMFORTER* (COMFORT)

Ecc 4: 1 and they have no c;
     4: 1 and they have no c.
Jer 8: 18 O my C in sorrow,

COMFORTERS* (COMFORT)

Job 16: 2 miserable c are you all!
Ps 69: 20 for c, but I found none.

COMFORTING* (COMFORT)

Isa 66: 11 satisfied at her c breasts;
Zec 1: 13 c words to the angel who talked
Jn 11: 31 c her, noticed how quickly she got
1Th 2: 12 c and urging you to live lives

COMFORTS* (COMFORT)

Job 29: 25 I was like one who c mourners.
Isa 49: 13 For the LORD c his people
    51: 12 "I, even I, am he who c you.
    66: 13 As a mother c her child,
2Co 1: 4 who c us in all our troubles,
     7: 6 But God, who c the downcast,

COMMAND (COMMANDED
COMMANDING COMMANDMENT
COMMANDMENTS COMMANDS)

Ex   7: 2 You are to say everything I c you,
Nu 14: 41 are you disobeying the LORD's c?
    24: 13 to go beyond the c of the LORD—
Dt   4: 2 Do not add to what I c you
     8: 1 to follow every c I am giving you
    12: 32 See that you do all I c you;
    15: 11 I c you to be openhanded
    30: 16 For I c you today to love
    32: 46 so that you may c your children
Ps 91: 11 For he will c his angels concerning
Pr 13: 13 but he who respects a c is rewarded
Ecc 8: 2 Obey the king's c, I say,
Jer 1: 7 you to and say whatever I c you.
     1: 17 and say to them whatever I c you.
     7: 23 Walk in all the ways I c you,

Jer 11: 4 Obey me and do everything I c you
    26: 2 Tell them everything I c you;
Joel 2: 11 mighty are those who obey his c.
Mt   4: 6 He will c his angels concerning you
    15: 3 why do you break the c of God
Lk   4: 10 " 'He will c his angels concerning
Jn 14: 15 love me, you will obey what I c.
    15: 12 My c is this: Love each other
    15: 14 friends if you do what I c.
    15: 17 This is my c: Love each other.
1Co 14: 37 writing to you is the Lord's c.
Gal 5: 14 law is summed up in a single c:
1Ti 1: 5 goal of this c is love, which comes
     6: 14 to you keep this c without spot
     6: 17 C those who are rich
Heb 11: 3 universe was formed at God's c,
2Pe 2: 21 on the sacred c that was passed
     3: 2 and the c given by our Lord
1Jn 2: 7 I am not writing you a new c
     3: 23 this is his c: to believe in the name
     4: 21 And he has given us this c:
2Jn   6 his c is that you walk in love.

COMMANDED (COMMAND)

Ge   2: 16 And the LORD God c the man,
     7: 5 Noah did all that the LORD c him.
    50: 12 Jacob's sons did as he had c them:
Ex   7: 6 did just as the LORD c them.
    19: 7 all the words the LORD had c him
Dt   4: 5 laws as the LORD my God c me,
     6: 24 The LORD c us to obey all these
Jos 1: 9 Have I not c you? Be strong
     1: 16 Whatever you have c us we will do,
2Sa 5: 25 So David did as the LORD c him,
2Ki 17: 13 the entire Law that I c your fathers
    21: 8 careful to do everything I c them
2Ch 33: 8 do everything I c them concerning
Ps 33: 9 he c, and it stood firm.
    78: 5 which he c our forefathers
   148: 5 for he c and they were created.
Mt 28: 20 to obey everything I have c you.
1Co 9: 14 Lord has c that those who preach
1Jn 3: 23 and to love one another as he c us.
2Jn   4 in the truth, just as the Father c us.

COMMANDING (COMMAND)

2Ti 2: 4 he wants to please his c officer.

COMMANDMENT* (COMMAND)

Jos 22: 5 But be very careful to keep the c
Mt 22: 36 which is the greatest c in the Law?"
    22: 38 This is the first and greatest c.
Mk 12: 31 There is no c greater than these."
Lk 23: 56 the Sabbath in obedience to the c.
Jn 13: 34 "A new c I give you: Love one
Ro   7: 8 the opportunity afforded by the c,
     7: 9 when the c came, sin sprang to life
     7: 10 that the very c that was intended
     7: 11 and through the c put me to death.
     7: 11 the opportunity afforded by the c,
     7: 12 and the c is holy, righteous
     7: 13 through the c sin might become
    13: 9 and whatever other c there may be,
Eph 6: 2 which is the first c with a promise
Heb 9: 19 Moses had proclaimed every c

COMMANDMENTS* (COMMAND)

Ex 20: 6 who love me and keep my c.
    34: 28 of the covenant—the Ten C.
Dt   4: 13 to you his covenant, the Ten C,
     5: 10 who love me and keep my c.
     5: 22 These are the c the LORD
     6: 6 These c that I give you today are
     9: 10 were all the c of God
    10: 4 The Ten C he had proclaimed
Ecc 12: 13 Fear God and keep his c,
Mt   5: 19 one of the least of these c
    19: 17 If you want to enter life, obey the c
    22: 40 the Prophets hang on these two c."
Mk 10: 19 You know the c: 'Do not murder,
    12: 28 "Of all the c, which is the most
Lk   1: 6 observing all the Lord's c
    18: 20 You know the c: 'Do not commit
Ro 13: 9 The c, "Do not commit adultery,"
Eph 2: 15 in his flesh the law with its c
Rev 12: 17 those who obey God's c
    14: 12 part of the saints who obey God's c

COMMANDS (COMMAND)

Ex 24:12 and *c* I have written for their
   25:22 give you all my *c* for the Israelites.
   34:32 gave them all the *c* the LORD had
Lev 22:31 "Keep my *c* and follow them.
Nu 15:39 and so you will remember all the *c*
Dt 7: 9 those who love him and keep his *c*.
   7:11 Therefore, take care to follow the *c*
   11: 1 decrees, his laws and his *c* always.
   11:27 the blessing if you obey the *c*
   28: 1 carefully follow all his *c* I give you
   30:10 LORD your God and keep his *c*
Jos 22: 5 to walk in all his ways, to obey his *c*
1Ki 2: 3 and keep his decrees and *c*,
   8:58 in all his ways and to keep the *c*,
   8:61 to live by his decrees and obey his *c*
1Ch 28: 7 unswerving in carrying out my *c*
   29:19 devotion to keep your *c*,
2Ch 31:21 in obedience to the law and the *c*,
Ne 1: 5 those who love him and obey his *c*,
Ps 78: 7 but would keep his *c*.
   112: 1 who finds great delight in his *c*.
   119:10 do not let me stray from your *c*.
   119:32 I run in the path of your *c*,
   119:35 Direct me in the path of your *c*,
   119:47 for I delight in your *c*
   119:48 I lift up my hands to your *c*,
   119:73 me understanding to learn your *c*.
   119:86 All your *c* are trustworthy;
   119:96 but your *c* are boundless.
   119:98 Your *c* make me wiser
   119:115 that I may keep the *c* of my God!
   119:127 Because I love your *c*
   119:131 longing for your *c*.
   119:143 but your *c* are my delight.
   119:151 and all your *c* are true.
   119:172 for all your *c* are righteous.
   119:176 for I have not forgotten your *c*.
Pr 2: 1 and store up my *c* within you,
   3: 1 but keep my *c* in your heart,
   6:23 For these *c* are a lamp,
   10: 8 The wise in heart accept *c*,
Isa 48:18 you had paid attention to my *c*,
Da 9: 4 all who love him and obey his *c*,
Mt 5:19 teaches these *c* will be called great
Mk 7: 8 You have let go of the *c* of God
   7: 9 way of setting aside the *c* of God
Jn 14:21 Whoever has my *c* and obeys them,
   15:10 If you obey my *c*, you will remain
Ac 17:30 but now he *c* all people everywhere
1Co 7:19 Keeping God's *c* is what counts.
1Jn 2: 3 come to know him if we obey his *c*.
   2: 4 but does not do what he *c* is a liar,
   3:22 we obey his *c* and do what pleases
   3:24 Those who obey his *c* live in him,
   5: 2 loving God and carrying out his *c*.
   5: 3 And his *c* are not burdensome.
   5: 3 This is love for God: to obey his *c*.
2Jn : 6 that we walk in obedience to his *c*.

COMMEMORATE

Ex 12:14 "This is a day you are to *c*;

COMMEND* (COMMENDABLE COMMENDED COMMENDS)

Ps 145: 4 One generation will *c* your works
Ecc 8:15 So I *c* the enjoyment of life,
Ro 13: 3 do what is right and he will *c* you.
   16: 1 I *c* to you our sister Phoebe,
2Co 3: 1 beginning to *c* ourselves again?
   4: 2 the truth plainly we *c* ourselves
   5:12 trying to *c* ourselves to you again,
   6: 4 as servants of God we *c* ourselves
   10:12 with some who *c* themselves.
1Pe 2:14 and to *c* those who do right.

COMMENDABLE* (COMMEND)

1Pe 2:19 For it is *c* if a man bears up
   2:20 you endure it, this is *c* before God.

COMMENDED* (COMMEND)

Ne 11: 2 The people *c* all the men who
Job 29:11 and those who saw me *c* me,
Lk 16: 8 master *c* the dishonest manager
Ac 15:40 *c* by the brothers to the grace
2Co 12:11 I ought to have been *c* by you,
Heb 11: 2 This is what the ancients were *c* for
   11: 4 By faith he was *c* as a righteous

Heb 11: 5 he was *c* as one who pleased God.
   11:39 These were all *c* for their faith,

COMMENDS* (COMMEND)

Pr 15: 2 of the wise *c* knowledge,
2Co 10:18 but the one whom the Lord *c*.
   10:18 not the one who *c* himself who is

COMMIT (COMMITS COMMITTED)

Ex 20:14 "You shall not *c* adultery.
Dt 5:18 "You shall not *c* adultery.
1Sa 7: 3 and *c* yourselves to the LORD
Ps 31: 5 Into your hands I *c* my spirit;
   37: 5 *C* your way to the LORD;
Pr 16: 3 *C* to the LORD whatever you do,
Mt 5:27 that it was said, 'Do not *c* adultery.'
   5:32 causes her to *c* adultery,
   19:18 do not *c* adultery, do not steal,
Mk 10:19 do not *c* adultery, do not steal,
Lk 18:20 'Do not *c* adultery, do not murder,
   23:46 into your hands I *c* my spirit."
Ac 20:32 I *c* you to God and to the word
Ro 2:22 do you *c* adultery? You who abhor
   2:22 that people should not *c* adultery,
   13: 9 "Do not *c* adultery,"
1Co 10: 8 We should not *c* sexual immorality,
Jas 2:11 do not *c* adultery but do *c* murder,
1Pe 4:19 to God's will should *c* themselves
Rev 2:22 I will make those who *c* adultery

COMMITS (COMMIT)

Pr 6:32 man who *c* adultery lacks
   29:22 a hot-tempered one *c* many sins.
Ecc 8:12 a wicked man *c* a hundred crimes
Eze 18:12 He *c* robbery.
   18:14 who sees all the sins his father *c*,
   18:24 from his righteousness and *c* sin
   18:26 from his righteousness and *c* sin,
   22:11 you one man *c* a detestable offense
Mt 5:32 the divorced woman *c* adultery.
   19: 9 marries another woman *c* adultery
Mk 10:11 marries another woman *c* adultery
   10:12 another man, she *c* adultery."
Lk 16:18 a divorced woman *c* adultery.
   16:18 marries another woman *c* adultery,

COMMITTED (COMMIT)

Nu 5: 7 and must confess the sin he has *c*.
1Ki 8:61 But your hearts must be fully *c*
   15:14 Asa's heart was fully *c*
2Ch 16: 9 those whose hearts are fully *c*
Mt 5:28 lustfully has already *c* adultery
   11:27 "All things have been *c* to me
Lk 10:22 "All things have been *c* to me
Ac 14:23 *c* them to the Lord,
   14:26 where they had been *c* to the grace
1Co 9:17 I am simply discharging the trust *c*
2Co 5:19 And he has *c* to us the message
1Pe 2:22 "He *c* no sin,
Rev 17: 2 the kings of the earth *c* adultery
   18: 3 of the earth *c* adultery with her,
   18: 9 kings of the earth who *c* adultery

COMMON

Ge 11: 1 had one language and a *c* speech.
Lev 10:10 between the holy and the *c*,
Pr 22: 2 Rich and poor have this in *c*:
   29:13 the oppressor have this in *c*:
Ac 2:44 together and had everything in *c*.
1Co 10:13 has seized you except what is *c*
2Co 6:14 and wickedness have in *c*?

COMPANION (COMPANIONS)

Ps 55:13 my *c*, my close friend,
   55:20 My *c* attacks his friends;
Pr 13:20 but a *c* of fools suffers harm.
   28: 7 a *c* of gluttons disgraces his father.
   29: 3 a *c* of prostitutes squanders his
Rev 1: 9 your brother and *c* in the suffering

COMPANIONS (COMPANION)

Ps 45: 7 your God, has set you above your *c*
Pr 18:24 A man of many *c* may come to ruin
Heb 1: 9 your God, has set you above your *c*

COMPANY

Ps 14: 5 present in the *c* of the righteous.
Pr 21:16 comes to rest in the *c* of the dead.

Pr 24: 1 do not desire their *c*;
Jer 15:17 I never sat in the *c* of revelers,
1Co 15:33 "Bad *c* corrupts good character."

COMPARE* (COMPARED COMPARING COMPARISON)

Job 28:17 Neither gold nor crystal can *c*
   28:19 The topaz of Cush cannot *c* with it;
   39:13 but they cannot *c* with the pinions
Ps 86: 8 no deeds can *c* with yours.
   89: 6 skies above can *c* with the LORD?
Pr 3:15 nothing you desire can *c* with her.
   8:11 nothing you desire can *c* with her.
Isa 40:18 To whom, then, will you *c* God?
   40:18 What image will you *c* him to?
   40:25 "To whom will you *c* me
   46: 5 "To whom will you *c* me
La 2:13 With what can I *c* you,
Eze 31: 8 *c* with its branches—
Da 1:13 Then *c* our appearance with that
Mt 11:16 "To what can I *c* this generation?
Lk 7:31 I *c* the people of this generation?
   13:18 What shall I *c* it to? It is like
   13:20 What shall I *c* the kingdom of God
2Co 10:12 and *c* themselves with themselves,
   10:12 or *c* ourselves with some who

COMPARED* (COMPARE)

Jdg 8: 2 What have I accomplished *c* to you
   8: 3 What was I able to do *c* to you?"
Isa 46: 5 you liken me that we may be *c*?
Eze 31: 2 Who can be *c* with you in majesty?
   31:18 the trees of Eden can be *c* with you
Php 3: 8 I consider everything a loss *c*

COMPARING* (COMPARE)

Ro 8:18 present sufferings are not worth *c*
2Co 8: 8 the sincerity of your love by *c* it
Gal 6: 4 without *c* himself to somebody else

COMPARISON* (COMPARE)

2Co 3:10 now in *c* with the surpassing glory.

COMPASSION* (COMPASSIONATE COMPASSIONS)

Ex 33:19 I will have *c* on whom I will have *c*.
Dt 13:17 he will show you mercy, have *c*
   28:54 man among you will have no *c*
   30: 3 restore your fortunes and have *c*
   32:36 and have *c* on his servants
Jdg 2:18 for the LORD had *c* on them
1Ki 3:26 son was alive he was filled with *c*
2Ki 13:23 and had *c* and showed concern
2Ch 30: 9 and your children will be shown *c*
Ne 9:19 of your great *c* you did not
   9:27 and in your great *c* you gave them
   9:28 in your *c* you delivered them time
Ps 51: 1 according to your great *c*
   77: 9 Has he in anger withheld his *c*?"
   90:13 Have *c* on your servants.
   102:13 You will arise and have *c* on Zion,
   103: 4 and crowns you with love and *c*.
   103:13 As a father has *c* on his children,
   103:13 so the LORD has *c*
   116: 5 our God is full of *c*.
   119:77 Let your *c* come to me that I may
   119:156 Your *c* is great, O LORD;
   135:14 and have *c* on his servants.
   145: 9 he has *c* on all he has made.
Isa 13:18 will they look with *c* on children.
   14: 1 The LORD will have *c* on Jacob;
   27:11 so their Maker has no *c* on them,
   30:18 he rises to show you *c*.
   49:10 He who has *c* on them will guide
   49:13 and will have *c* on his afflicted ones
   49:15 and have no *c* on the child she has
   51: 3 and will look with *c* on all her ruins
   54: 7 with deep *c* I will bring you back.
   54: 8 I will have *c* on you,"
   54:10 says the LORD, who has *c* on you.
   60:10 in favor I will show you *c*.
   63: 7 to his *c* and many kindnesses,
   63:15 and *c* are withheld from us.
Jer 12:15 I will again have *c* and will bring
   13:14 or to keep me from destroying them
   15: 6 I can no longer show *c*.
   21: 7 show them no mercy or pity or *c*.'
   30:18 and have *c* on his dwellings;

Jer 31: 20 I have great *c* for him,''
     33: 26 restore their fortunes and have *c*
     42: 12 I will show you *c* so that he will
     42: 12 so that he will have *c* on you
La   3: 32 he brings grief, he will show *c*,
Eze   9: 5 without showing pity or *c*.
     16: 5 or had *c* enough to do any
     39: 25 and will have *c* on all the people
Hos   2: 19 in love and *c*.
     11: 8 all my *c* is aroused.
     13: 14 ''I will have no *c*,
     14: 3 for in you the fatherless find *c*.''
Am   1: 11 stifling all *c*,
Jnh   3: 9 with *c* turn from his fierce anger
     3: 10 he had *c* and did not bring
Mic   7: 19 You will again have *c* on us;
Zec   7: 9 show mercy and *c* to one another.
     10: 6 because I have *c* on them.
Mal   3: 17 as in a *c* a man spares his son who
Mt   9: 36 When he saw the crowds, he had *c*
     14: 14 he had *c* on them and healed their
     15: 32 ''I have *c* for these people;
     20: 34 Jesus had *c* on them and touched
Mk   1: 41 with *c*, Jesus reached out his hand
     6: 34 and saw a large crowd, he had *c*
     8: 2 ''I have *c* for these people;
Lk   15: 20 and was filled with *c* for him;
Ro   9: 15 and I will have *c* on whom I have *c*
2Co   1: 3 the Father of *c* and the God
Php   2: 1 and *c*, then make my joy complete
Col   3: 12 clothe yourselves with *c*, kindness,
Jas   5: 11 The Lord is full of *c* and mercy.

COMPASSIONATE* (COMPASSION)

Ex   22: 27 out to me, I will hear, for I am *c*.
     34: 6 the LORD, the *c* and gracious God
2Ch 30: 9 LORD your God is gracious and *c*.
Ne   9: 17 gracious and *c*, slow to anger
Ps   86: 15 O Lord, are a *c* and gracious God,
     103: 8 The LORD is *c* and gracious,
     111: 4 the LORD is gracious and *c*.
     112: 4 the gracious and *c* and righteous
     145: 8 The LORD is gracious and *c*,
La   4: 10 With their own hands *c* women
Joel   2: 13 for he is gracious and *c*,
Jnh   4: 2 that you are a gracious and *c* God,
Eph   4: 32 Be kind and *c* to one another,
1Pe   3: 8 love as brothers, be *c* and humble.

COMPASSIONS* (COMPASSION)

La   3: 22 for his *c* never fail.

COMPELLED (COMPULSION)

Ac   20: 22 ''And now, *c* by the Spirit,
1Co   9: 16 I cannot boast, for I am *c* to preach.

COMPELS (COMPULSION)

Job 32: 18 and the spirit within me *c* me;
2Co   5: 14 For Christ's love *c* us, because we

COMPETENCE* (COMPETENT)

2Co   3: 5 but our *c* comes from God.

COMPETENT* (COMPETENCE)

Ro   15: 14 and *c* to instruct one another.
1Co   6: 2 are you not *c* to judge trivial cases?
2Co   3: 5 Not that we are *c* in ourselves to claim
     3: 6 He has made us *c* as ministers

COMPETES*

1Co   9: 25 Everyone who *c* in the games goes
2Ti   2: 5 Similarly, if anyone *c* as an athlete,
     2: 5 unless he *c* according to the rules.

COMPLACENCY* (COMPLACENT)

Pr   1: 32 and the *c* of fools will destroy them
Eze 30: 9 ships to frighten Cush out of her *c*.

COMPLACENT* (COMPLACENCY)

Isa   32: 9 You women who are so *c*,
     32: 11 Tremble, you *c* women;
Am   6: 1 Woe to you who are *c* in Zion,
Zep   1: 12 and punish those who are *c*,

COMPLAINING*

Php   2: 14 Do everything without *c* or arguing

COMPLETE

Dt   16: 15 your hands, and your joy will be *c*.
Jn   3: 29 That joy is mine, and it is now *c*.
     15: 11 and that your joy may be *c*.
     16: 24 will receive, and your joy will be *c*.
     17: 23 May they be brought to *c* unity
Ac   20: 24 *c* the task the Lord Jesus has given
Php   2: 2 then make my joy *c*
Col   4: 17 to it that you *c* the work you have
Jas   1: 4 so that you may be mature and *c*,
     2: 22 his faith was made *c* by what he did
1Jn   1: 4 We write this to make our joy *c*.
     2: 5 God's love is truly made *c* in him.
     4: 12 and his love is made *c* in us.
     4: 17 love is made *c* among us
2Jn   : 12 to face, so that our joy may be *c*.

COMPLIMENTS*

Pr   23: 8 and will have wasted your *c*.

COMPREHEND* (COMPREHENDED)

Job 28: 13 Man does not *c* its worth;
Ecc   8: 17 No one can *c* what goes
     8: 17 he knows, he cannot really *c* it.

COMPREHENDED* (COMPREHEND)

Job 38: 18 Have you *c* the vast expanses

COMPULSION (COMPELLED COMPELS)

2Co   9: 7 not reluctantly or under *c*,

CONCEAL (CONCEALED CONCEALS)

Ps   40: 10 I do not *c* your love and your truth
Pr   25: 2 It is the glory of God to *c* a matter;

CONCEALED (CONCEAL)

Jer   16: 17 nor is their sin *c* from my eyes.
Mt   10: 26 There is nothing *c* that will not be
Mk   4: 22 and whatever is *c* is meant
Lk   8: 17 nothing *c* that will not be known
     12: 2 There is nothing *c* that will not be

CONCEALS* (CONCEAL)

Pr   10: 18 He who *c* his hatred has lying lips,
     28: 13 He who *c* his sins does not prosper,

CONCEIT* (CONCEITED CONCEITS)

Isa   16: 6 her overweening pride and *c*,
Jer   48: 29 her overweening pride and *c*,
Php   2: 3 out of selfish ambition or vain *c*,

CONCEITED* (CONCEIT)

1Sa   17: 28 I know how *c* you are and how
Ro   11: 25 brothers, so that you may not be *c*:
     12: 16 Do not be *c*.
2Co 12: 7 To keep me from becoming *c*
Gal   5: 26 Let us not become *c*, provoking
1Ti   3: 6 or he may become *c* and fall
     6: 4 he is *c* and understands nothing.
2Ti   3: 4 of the good, treacherous, rash, *c*,

CONCEITS* (CONCEIT)

Ps   73: 7 evil *c* of their minds know no

CONCEIVED (CONCEIVES)

Ps   51: 5 from the time my mother *c* me.
Mt   1: 20 what is *c* in her is from the Holy
1Co   2: 9 no mind has *c*
Jas   1: 15 after desire has *c*, it gives birth

CONCEIVES* (CONCEIVED)

Ps   7: 14 *c* trouble gives birth

CONCERN* (CONCERNED)

Ge   39: 6 he did not *c* himself with anything
     39: 8 ''my master does not *c* himself
1Sa 23: 21 ''The LORD bless you for your *c*
2Ki 13: 23 and had compassion and showed *c*
Job   9: 21 I have no *c* for myself;
     19: 4 my error remains my *c* alone.
Ps 131: 1 I do not *c* myself with great matters
Pr   29: 7 but the wicked have no such *c*.
Eze 36: 21 I had *c* for my holy name, which
Ac   15: 14 God at first showed his *c* by taking
     18: 17 But Gallio showed no *c* whatever.
1Co   7: 32 I would like you to be free from *c*.
     12: 25 that its parts should have equal *c*
2Co   7: 7 your deep sorrow, your ardent *c*

2Co   7: 11 what alarm, what longing, what *c*,
     8: 16 of Titus the same *c* I have for you.
     11: 28 of my *c* for all the churches.
Php   4: 10 at last you have renewed your *c*

CONCERNED (CONCERN)

Ex   2: 25 Israelites and was *c* about them.
Ps 142: 4 no one is *c* for me.
Jnh   4: 10 ''You have been *c* about this vine,
     4: 11 Should I not be *c* about that great
1Co   7: 32 An unmarried man is *c* about
     9: 9 Is it about oxen that God is *c*?
Php   4: 10 you have been *c*, but you had no

CONCESSION*

1Co   7: 6 I say this as a *c*, not as a command.

CONDEMN* (CONDEMNATION CONDEMNED CONDEMNING CONDEMNS)

Job   9: 20 innocent, my mouth would *c* me;
     10: 2 I will say to God: Do not *c* me,
     34: 17 Will you *c* the just and mighty One
     34: 29 if he remains silent, who can *c* him?
     40: 8 Would you *c* me to justify yourself?
Ps   94: 21 and *c* the innocent to death.
     109: 7 and may his prayers *c* him.
     109: 31 from those who *c* him.
Isa   50: 9 Who is he that will *c* me?
Mt   12: 41 with this generation and *c* it;
     12: 42 with this generation and *c* it;
     20: 18 They will *c* him to death
Mk   10: 33 They will *c* him to death
Lk   6: 37 Do not *c*, and you will not be
     11: 31 men of this generation and *c* them;
     11: 32 with this generation and *c* it;
Jn   3: 17 Son into the world to *c* the world,
     7: 51 ''Does our law *c* anyone
     8: 11 ''Then neither do I *c* you,''
     12: 48 very word which I spoke will *c* him
Ro   2: 27 yet obeys the law will *c* you who,
     14: 3 everything must not *c* the man who
     14: 22 is the man who does not *c* himself
2Co   7: 3 this to *c* you; I have said
1Jn   3: 20 presence whenever our hearts *c* us
     3: 21 if our hearts do not *c* us,

CONDEMNATION* (CONDEMN)

Jer   42: 18 of *c* and reproach; you will never
     44: 12 and horror, of *c* and reproach.
Ro   3: 8 may result''? Their *c* is deserved.
     5: 16 followed one sin and brought *c*,
     5: 18 of one trespass was *c* for all men,
     8: 1 there is now no *c* for those who are
2Pe   2: 3 Their *c* has long been hanging
Jude   : 4 certain men whose *c* was written

CONDEMNED* (CONDEMN)

Dt   13: 17 of those *c* things shall be found
Job 32: 3 to refute Job, and yet had *c* him.
Ps   34: 21 the foes of the righteous will be *c*.
     34: 22 will be *c* who takes refuge in him.
     37: 33 let them be *c* when brought to trial.
     79: 11 preserve those *c* to die.
     102: 20 and release those *c* to death.
Mt   12: 7 you would not have *c* the innocent.
     12: 37 and by your words you will be *c*.''
     23: 33 How will you escape being *c* to hell
     27: 3 betrayed him, saw that Jesus was *c*,
Mk 14: 64 They all *c* him as worthy of death.
     16: 16 whoever does not believe will be *c*.
Lk   6: 37 condemn, and you will not be *c*.
Jn   3: 18 Whoever believes in him is not *c*,
     3: 18 does not believe stands *c* already
     5: 24 has eternal life and will not be *c*;
     5: 29 who have done evil will rise to be *c*.
     8: 10 Has no one *c* you?'' ''No one, sir,''
     16: 11 prince of this world now stands *c*.
Ac 25: 15 against him and asked that he be *c*.
Ro   3: 7 why am I still *c* as a sinner?''
     8: 3 And so he *c* sin in sinful man,
     14: 23 But the man who has doubts is *c*
1Co   4: 9 like men *c* to die in the arena.
     11: 32 disciplined so that we will not be *c*
Gal   1: 8 let him be eternally *c*! As we have
     1: 9 let him be eternally *c*! Am I now
2Th   2: 12 that all will be *c* who have not
Tit   2: 8 of speech that cannot be *c*,

Heb 11: 7 By his faith he *c* the world
Jas 5: 6 You have *c* and murdered innocent
    5: 12 and your "No," no, or you will be *c*
2Pe 2: 6 if he *c* the cities of Sodom
Rev 19: 2 He has *c* the great prostitute

CONDEMNING* (CONDEMN)

Dt 25: 1 the innocent and *c* the guilty.
1Ki 8: 32 *c* the guilty and bringing
Pr 17: 15 the guilty and *c* the innocent—
Ac 13: 27 yet in *c* him they fulfilled the words
Ro 2: 1 judge the other, you are *c* yourself,

CONDEMNS* (CONDEMN)

Job 15: 6 Your own mouth *c* you, not mine;
Pr 12: 2 but the LORD *c* a crafty man.
Ro 8: 34 Who is he that *c*? Christ Jesus,
2Co 3: 9 the ministry that *c* men is glorious,

CONDITION

Pr 27: 23 Be sure you know the *c*

CONDUCT (CONDUCTED CONDUCTS)

Pr 10: 23 A fool finds pleasure in evil *c*,
    20: 11 by whether his *c* is pure and right.
    21: 8 but the *c* of the innocent is upright.
Ecc 6: 8 how to *c* himself before others?
Jer 4: 18 "Your own *c* and actions
    17: 10 to reward a man according to his *c*,
Eze 7: 3 I will judge you according to your *c*
Php 1: 27 *c* yourselves in a manner worthy
1Ti 3: 15 to *c* themselves in God's household

CONDUCTED* (CONDUCT)

2Co 1: 12 testifies that we have *c* ourselves

CONDUCTS* (CONDUCT)

Ps 112: 5 who *c* his affairs with justice.

CONFESS* (CONFESSED CONFESSES CONFESSING CONFESSION)

Lev 5: 5 he must *c* in what way he has
    16: 21 and *c* over it all the wickedness
    26: 40 " 'But if they will *c* their sins
Nu 5: 7 must *c* the sin he has committed.
1Ki 8: 33 back to you and *c* your name,
    8: 35 toward this place and *c* your name
2Ch 6: 24 they turn back and *c* your name,
    6: 26 toward this place and *c* your name
Ne 1: 6 I *c* the sins we Israelites, including
Ps 32: 5 I said, "I will *c*
    38: 18 I *c* my iniquity;
Jn 1: 20 fail to *c*, but confessed freely,
    12: 42 they would not *c* their faith
Ro 10: 9 That if you *c* with your mouth,
    10: 10 it is with your mouth that you *c*
    14: 11 every tongue will *c* to God.' "
Php 2: 11 every tongue *c* that Jesus Christ is
Heb 3: 1 and high priest whom we *c*.
    13: 15 the fruit of lips that *c* his name.
Jas 5: 16 Therefore *c* your sins to each other
1Jn 1: 9 If we *c* our sins, he is faithful

CONFESSED* (CONFESS)

1Sa 7: 6 day they fasted and there they *c*,
Ne 9: 2 in their places and *c* their sins
Da 9: 4 to the LORD my God and *c*:
Jn 1: 20 but *c* freely, "I am not the Christ."
Ac 19: 18 and openly *c* their evil deeds.

CONFESSES* (CONFESS)

Pr 28: 13 whoever *c* and renounces them
2Ti 2: 19 and, "Everyone who *c* the name

CONFESSING* (CONFESS)

Ezr 10: 1 While Ezra was praying and *c*,
Da 9: 20 *c* my sin and the sin
Mt 3: 6 *C* their sins, they were baptized
Mk 1: 5 *C* their sins, they were baptized

CONFESSION* (CONFESS)

Ezr 10: 11 Now make *c* to the LORD,
Ne 9: 3 and spent another quarter in *c*
2Co 9: 13 obedience that accompanies your *c*
1Ti 6: 12 called when you made your good *c*
    6: 13 Pontius Pilate made the good *c*,

CONFIDENCE* (CONFIDENT)

Jdg 9: 26 and its citizens put their *c* in him.
2Ki 18: 19 On what are you basing this *c*
2Ch 32: 8 And the people gained *c*
    32: 10 On what are you basing your *c*,
Job 4: 6 Should not your piety be your *c*
Ps 71: 5 my *c* since my youth.
Pr 3: 26 for the LORD will be your *c*
    3: 32 but takes the upright into his *c*.
    11: 13 A gossip betrays a *c*,
    20: 19 A gossip betrays a *c*;
    25: 9 do not betray another man's *c*,
    31: 11 Her husband has full *c* in her
Isa 32: 17 will be quietness and *c* forever.
    36: 4 On what are you basing this *c*
Jer 17: 7 whose *c* is in him.
    49: 31 which lives in *c*,"
Eze 29: 16 a source of *c* for the people of Israel
Mic 7: 5 put no *c* in a friend.
2Co 2: 3 I had *c* in all of you, that you would
    3: 4 Such *c* as this is ours
    7: 4 I have great *c* in you; I take great
    7: 16 I am glad I can have complete *c*
    8: 22 so because of his great *c* in you.
Eph 3: 12 God with freedom and *c*.
Php 3: 3 and who put no *c* in the flesh—
    3: 4 I myself have reasons for such *c*.
    3: 4 reasons to put *c* in the flesh,
2Th 3: 4 We have *c* in the Lord that you are
Heb 3: 14 till the end the *c* we had at first.
    4: 16 the throne of grace with *c*,
    10: 19 since we have *c* to enter the Most
    10: 35 So do not throw away your *c*;
    13: 6 So we say with *c*,
1Jn 3: 21 we have *c* before God and receive
    4: 17 us so that we will have *c* on the day
    5: 14 This is the *c* we have

CONFIDENT* (CONFIDENCE)

Job 6: 20 because they had been *c*;
Ps 27: 3 even then will I be *c*.
    27: 13 I am still *c* of this:
Lk 18: 9 To some who were *c*
2Co 1: 15 Because I was *c* of this, I planned
    5: 6 Therefore we are always *c*
    5: 8 We are *c*, I say, and would prefer
    9: 4 ashamed of having been so *c*.
    10: 7 If anyone is *c* that he belongs
Gal 5: 10 I am *c* in the Lord that you will
Php 1: 6 day until now, being *c* of this,
    2: 24 I am *c* in the Lord that I myself will
Phm : 21 *C* of your obedience, I write to you,
Heb 6: 9 we are *c* of better things
1Jn 2: 28 that when he appears we may be *c*

CONFIDES*

Ps 25: 14 The LORD *c* in those who fear him

CONFORM* (CONFORMED CONFORMITY CONFORMS)

Ro 12: 2 Do not *c* any longer to the pattern
1Pe 1: 14 do not *c* to the evil desires you had

CONFORMED* (CONFORM)

Eze 5: 7 *c* to the standards of the nations
    11: 12 but have *c* to the standards
Ro 8: 29 predestined to be *c* to the likeness

CONFORMITY* (CONFORM)

Eph 1: 11 in *c* with the purpose of his will,

CONFORMS* (CONFORM)

1Ti 1: 11 to the sound doctrine that *c*

CONQUEROR* (CONQUERORS)

Mic 1: 15 I will bring a *c* against you
Rev 6: 2 he rode out as a *c* bent on conquest.

CONQUERORS (CONQUEROR)

Ro 8: 37 than *c* through him who loved us.

CONSCIENCE* (CONSCIENCE-STRICKEN CONSCIENCES CONSCIENTIOUS)

Ge 20: 5 I have done this with a clear *c*
    20: 6 I know you did this with a clear *c*,
1Sa 25: 31 have on his *c* the staggering burden
Job 27: 6 my *c* will not reproach me as long

Ac 23: 1 to God in all good *c* to this day."
    24: 16 to keep my *c* clear before God
Ro 9: 1 my *c* confirms it in the Holy Spirit
    13: 5 punishment but also because of *c*.
1Co 4: 4 My *c* is clear, but that does not
    8: 7 since their *c* is weak, it is defiled.
    8: 10 with a weak *c* sees you who have
    8: 12 in this way and wound their weak *c*
    10: 25 without raising questions of *c*,
    10: 27 you without raising questions of *c*.
    10: 28 man who told you and for *c*' sake—
    10: 29 freedom be judged by another's *c*?
    10: 29 the other man's *c*, I mean,
2Co 1: 12 Our *c* testifies that we have
    4: 2 to every man's *c* in the sight of God
    5: 11 and I hope it is also plain to your *c*.
1Ti 1: 5 and a good *c* and a sincere faith.
    1: 19 holding on to faith and a good *c*.
    3: 9 truths of the faith with a clear *c*.
2Ti 1: 3 as my forefathers did, with a clear *c*
Heb 9: 9 able to clear the *c* of the worshiper.
    10: 22 to cleanse us from a guilty *c*
    13: 18 We are sure that we have a clear *c*
1Pe 3: 16 and respect, keeping a clear *c*,
    3: 21 the pledge of a good *c* toward God.

CONSCIENCE-STRICKEN* (CONSCIENCE)

1Sa 24: 5 David was *c* for having cut
2Sa 24: 10 David was *c* after he had counted

CONSCIENCES* (CONSCIENCE)

Ro 2: 15 their *c* also bearing witness,
1Ti 4: 2 whose *c* have been seared
Tit 1: 15 their minds and *c* are corrupted.
Heb 9: 14 cleanse our *c* from acts that lead

CONSCIENTIOUS* (CONSCIENCE)

2Ch 29: 34 for the Levites had been more *c*

CONSCIOUS*

Ro 3: 20 through the law we become *c* of sin
1Pe 2: 19 of unjust suffering because he is *c*

CONSECRATE (CONSECRATED)

Ex 13: 2 "*C* to me every firstborn male.
    40: 9 *c* it and all its furnishings,
Lev 20: 7 " '*C* yourselves and be holy,
    25: 10 *C* the fiftieth year and proclaim
1Ch 15: 12 fellow Levites are to *c* yourselves

CONSECRATED (CONSECRATE)

Ex 29: 43 and the place will be *c* by my glory.
Lev 8: 30 So he *c* Aaron and his garments
2Ch 7: 16 *c* this temple so that my Name may
Lk 2: 23 is to be *c* to the Lord"),
1Ti 4: 5 because it is *c* by the word of God

CONSENT

1Co 7: 5 except by mutual *c* and for a time,

CONSIDER (CONSIDERATE CONSIDERED CONSIDERS)

1Sa 12: 24 *c* what great things he has done
    16: 7 "Do not *c* his appearance
2Ch 19: 6 *C* carefully what you do,
Job 37: 14 stop and *c* God's wonders.
Ps 8: 3 When I *c* your heavens,
    77: 12 and *c* all your mighty deeds.
    107: 43 and *c* the great love of the LORD.
    143: 5 and *c* what your hands have done.
Pr 6: 6 *c* its ways and be wise!
    20: 25 and only later to *c* his vows.
Ecc 7: 13 *C* what God has done:
Lk 12: 24 *C* the ravens: They do not sow
    12: 27 about the rest? "*C* how the lilies
Php 2: 3 but in humility *c* others better
    3: 8 I *c* everything a loss compared
Heb 10: 24 And let us *c* how we may spur one
Jas 1: 2 *C* it pure joy, my brothers,

CONSIDERATE* (CONSIDER)

Tit 3: 2 to be peaceable and *c*,
Jas 3: 17 then peace-loving, *c*, submissive,
1Pe 2: 18 only to those who are good and *c*,
    3: 7 in the same way be *c* as you live

CONSIDERED (CONSIDER)

Job 1: 8 "Have you c my servant Job?
2: 3 "Have you c my servant Job?
Ps 44:22 we are c as sheep to be slaughtered.
Isa 53: 4 yet we c him stricken by God,
Ro 8:36 we are c as sheep to be slaughtered

CONSIDERS (CONSIDER)

Pr 31:16 She c a field and buys it;
Ro 14: 5 One man c one day more sacred
Jas 1:26 If anyone c himself religious

CONSIST (CONSISTS)

Lk 12:15 a man's life does not c

CONSISTS (CONSIST)

Eph 5: 9 fruit of the light c in all goodness,

CONSOLATION

Ps 94:19 your c brought joy to my soul.

CONSPIRE

Ps 2: 1 Why do the nations c

CONSTANT

Dt 28:66 You will live in c suspense,
Pr 19:13 wife is like a c dripping.
27:15 a c dripping on a rainy day;
Ac 27:33 "you have been in c suspense
Heb 5:14 by c use have trained themselves

CONSTRUCTIVE*

1Co 10:23 but not everything is c.

CONSULT

Pr 15:12 he will not c the wise.
Gal 1:16 I did not c any man, nor did I go up

CONSUME (CONSUMES CONSUMING)

Jn 2:17 "Zeal for your house will c me."

CONSUMES (CONSUME)

Ps 69: 9 for zeal for your house c me,

CONSUMING (CONSUME)

Dt 4:24 For the LORD your God is a c fire,
Heb 12:29 and awe, for our "God is a c fire."

CONTAIN* (CONTAINED CONTAINS)

1Ki 8:27 the highest heaven, cannot c you.
2Ch 2: 6 the highest heavens, cannot c him?
6:18 the highest heavens, cannot c you.
Ecc 8: 8 power over the wind to c it;
2Pe 3:16 His letters c some things that are

CONTAINED (CONTAIN)

Heb 9: 4 This ark c the gold jar of manna,

CONTAINS (CONTAIN)

Pr 15: 6 of the righteous c great treasure,

CONTAMINATES*

2Co 7: 1 from everything that c body

CONTEMPT

Pr 14:31 He who oppresses the poor shows c
17: 5 He who mocks the poor shows c
18: 3 When wickedness comes, so does c
Da 12: 2 others to shame and everlasting c.
Mal 1: 6 O priests, who show c for my name.
Ro 2: 4 Or do you show c for the riches
Gal 4:14 you did not treat me with c
1Th 5:20 do not treat prophecies with c.

CONTEND (CONTENDED CONTENDING CONTENTIOUS)

Ge 6: 3 "My Spirit will not c
Ps 35: 1 C, O LORD, with those who
Isa 49:25 I will c with those who c with you,
Jude 3 you to c for the faith that was once

CONTENDED (CONTEND)

Php 4: 3 help these women who have c

CONTENDING* (CONTEND)

Php 1:27 c as one man for the faith

CONTENT* (CONTENTMENT)

Jos 7: 7 If only we had been c to stay
Pr 13:25 The righteous eat to their hearts' c,
19:23 one rests c, untouched by trouble.
Ecc 4: 8 yet his eyes were not c
Lk 3:14 don't accuse people falsely—be c
Php 4:11 to be c whatever the circumstances
4:12 I have learned the secret of being c
1Ti 6: 8 And clothing, we will be c with that.
Heb 13: 5 and be c with what you have,

CONTENTIOUS* (CONTEND)

1Co 11:16 If anyone wants to be c about this,

CONTENTMENT* (CONTENT)

Job 36:11 and their years in c.
SS 8:10 like one bringing c.
1Ti 6: 6 But godliness with c is great gain.

CONTEST*

Heb 10:32 in a great c in the face of suffering.

CONTINUAL (CONTINUE)

Pr 15:15 but the cheerful heart has a c feast.
Eph 4:19 of impurity, with a c lust for more.

CONTINUE (CONTINUAL CONTINUES CONTINUING)

1Ki 8:23 servants who c wholeheartedly
2Ch 6:14 servants who c wholeheartedly
Ps 36:10 C your love to those who know you
Ac 13:43 urged them to c in the grace of God
Ro 11:22 provided that you c in his kindness.
Gal 3:10 Cursed is everyone who does not c
Php 2:12 c to work out your salvation
Col 1:23 if you c in your faith, established
2: 6 received Christ Jesus as Lord, c
1Ti 2:15 if they c in faith, love and holiness
2Ti 3:14 c in what you have learned
1Jn 2:28 And now, dear children, c in him,
3: 9 born of God will c to sin,
5:18 born of God does not c to sin;
2Jn 9 and does not c in the teaching
Rev 22:11 and let him who is holy c to be holy
22:11 let him who does right c to do right;

CONTINUES (CONTINUE)

Ps 100: 5 c through all generations.
119: 90 Your faithfulness c
2Co 10:15 Our hope is that, as your faith c
1Jn 3: 9 No one who c to sin has

CONTINUING (CONTINUE)

Ro 13: 8 the c debt to love one another,

CONTRIBUTION (CONTRIBUTIONS)

Ro 15:26 pleased to make a c for the poor

CONTRIBUTIONS (CONTRIBUTION)

2Ch 24:10 all the people brought their c gladly
31:12 they faithfully brought in the c,

CONTRITE*

Ps 51:17 a broken and c heart,
Isa 57:15 also with him who is c and lowly
57:15 and to revive the heart of the c.
66: 2 he who is humble and c in spirit,

CONTROL (CONTROLLED CONTROLS SELF-CONTROL SELF-CONTROLLED)

Pr 29:11 a wise man keeps himself under c.
1Co 7: 9 But if they cannot c themselves,
7:37 but has c over his own will,
1Th 4: 4 you should learn to c his own body

CONTROLLED (CONTROL)

Ps 32: 9 but must be c by bit and bridle
Ro 8: 6 but the mind c by the Spirit is life
8: 8 Those c by the sinful nature cannot

CONTROLS* (CONTROL)

Job 37:15 you know how God c the clouds
Pr 16:32 a man who c his temper

CONTROVERSIES*

Ac 26: 3 with all the Jewish customs and c.
1Ti 1: 4 These promote c rather
6: 4 He has an unhealthy interest in c

Tit 3: 9 But avoid foolish c and genealogies

CONVERSATION

Col 4: 6 Let your c be always full of grace,

CONVERT

1Ti 3: 6 He must not be a recent c,

CONVICT (CONVICTION)

Pr 24:25 with those who c the guilty,
Jn 16: 8 he will c the world of guilt in regard
Jude 15 and to c all the ungodly

CONVICTION* (CONVICT)

1Th 1: 5 the Holy Spirit and with deep c.

CONVINCE* (CONVINCED CONVINCING)

Ac 28:23 and tried to c them about Jesus

CONVINCED* (CONVINCE)

Ge 45:28 "I'm c! My son Joseph is still alive.
Lk 16:31 will not be c even if someone rises
Ac 19:26 and hear how this fellow Paul has c
26: 9 "I too was c that I ought
26:26 I am c that none of this has escaped
28:24 Some were c by what he said,
Ro 2:19 if you are c that you are a guide
8:38 For I am c that neither death
14: 5 Each one should be fully c
14:14 I am fully c that no food is unclean
15:14 I myself am c, my brothers,
1Co 14:24 he will be c by all that he is a sinner
2Co 5:14 we are c that one died for all,
Php 1:25 C of this, I know that I will remain,
2Ti 1:12 and am c that he is able
3:14 have learned and have become c

CONVINCING* (CONVINCE)

Ac 1: 3 and gave many c proofs that he was

COOLNESS*

Pr 25:13 Like the c of snow at harvest time

COPIES (COPY)

Heb 9:23 for the c of the heavenly things

COPY (COPIES)

Dt 17:18 for himself on a scroll a c of this law
Heb 8: 5 They serve at a sanctuary that is a c
9:24 sanctuary that was only a c

CORBAN*

Mk 7:11 received from me is C" (that is,

CORD (CORDS)

Jos 2:18 you have tied this scarlet c
Ecc 4:12 c of three strands is not quickly

CORDS (CORD)

Pr 5:22 the c of his sin hold him fast.
Isa 54: 2 lengthen your c,
Hos 11: 4 them with c of human kindness,

CORINTH

Ac 18: 1 Paul left Athens and went to C.
1Co 1: 2 To the church of God in C,
2Co 1: 1 To the church of God in C,

CORNELIUS*

Roman to whom Peter preached; first Gentile Christian (Ac 10).

CORNER (CORNERS)

Ru 3: 9 "Spread the c of your garment
Pr 21: 9 Better to live on a c of the roof
25:24 Better to live on a c of the roof
Ac 26:26 because it was not done in a c.

CORNERS (CORNER)

Mt 6: 5 on the street c to be seen by men.
22: 9 Go to the street c and invite

CORNERSTONE* (STONE)

Job 38: 6 or who laid its c—
Isa 28:16 a precious c for a sure foundation,
Jer 51:26 rock will be taken from you for a c,
Zec 10: 4 From Judah will come the c,
Eph 2:20 Christ Jesus himself as the chief c.

1Pe   2:   6 a chosen and precious c,

CORRECT* (CORRECTED CORRECTING CORRECTION CORRECTIONS CORRECTS)

Job   6:26 Do you mean to c what I say,
      40:   2 contends with the Almighty c him?
Jer 10:24 C me, LORD, but only with justice
2Ti   4:   2 c, rebuke and encourage—

CORRECTED* (CORRECT)

Pr   29:19 A servant cannot be c

CORRECTING* (CORRECT)

2Ti   3:16 c and training in righteousness,

CORRECTION* (CORRECT)

Lev 26:23 things you do not accept my c
Job 36:10 He makes them listen to c
Pr   5:12 How my heart spurned c!
     10:17 whoever ignores c leads others
     12:   1 but he who hates c is stupid.
     13:18 but whoever heeds c is honored.
     15:   5 whoever heeds c shows prudence.
     15:10 he who hates c will die.
     15:12 A mocker resents c,
     15:32 whoever heeds c gains
     29:15 The rod of c imparts wisdom,
Jer   2:30 they did not respond to c.
      5:   3 crushed them, but they refused c.
      7:28 LORD its God or responded to c.
Zep   3:   2 she accepts no c.
      3:   7 you will fear me / and accept c!'

CORRECTIONS* (CORRECT)

Pr   6:23 and the c of discipline

CORRECTS* (CORRECT)

Job   5:17 "Blessed is the man whom God c;
Pr   9:   7 Whoever c a mocker invites insult;

CORRUPT (CORRUPTED CORRUPTION CORRUPTS)

Ge   6:11 Now the earth was c in God's sight
Ps   14:   1 They are c, their deeds are vile;
     14:   3 they have together become c;
Pr   4:24 keep c talk far from your lips.
      6:12 who goes about with a c mouth,
     19:28 A c witness mocks at justice,

CORRUPTED (CORRUPT)

2Co   7:   2 wronged no one, we have c no one,
Tit   1:15 but to those who are c and do not

CORRUPTION (CORRUPT)

2Pe   1:   4 escape the c in the world caused
      2:20 If they have escaped the c

CORRUPTS* (CORRUPT)

Ecc   7:   7 and a bribe c the heart.
1Co 15:33 "Bad company c good character."
Jas   3:   6 It c the whole person, sets

COST (COSTS)

Nu   16:38 sinned at the c of their lives.
Pr   4:   7 Though it c all you have, get
      7:23 little knowing it will c him his life.
Isa 55:   1 milk without money and without c.
Lk   14:28 and estimate the c to see
Rev 21:   6 to drink without c from the spring

COSTS (COST)

Pr   6:31 it c him all the wealth of his house.

COUNCIL

Ps   89:   7 In the c of the holy ones God is
     107: 32 and praise him in the c of the elders

COUNSEL (COUNSELOR COUNSELS)

1Ki 22:   5 "First seek the c of the LORD."
2Ch 18:   4 "First seek the c of the LORD."
Job 38:   2 "Who is this that darkens my c
      42:   3 'Who is this that obscures my c
Ps   1:   1 walk in the c of the wicked
      73:24 You guide me with your c,
     107: 11 despised the c of the Most High.
Pr   8:14 C and sound judgment are mine;
     15:22 Plans fail for lack of c,
     27:   9 from his earnest c.

Isa 28:29 wonderful in c and magnificent
1Ti   5:14 So I c younger widows to marry,
Rev   3:18 I c you to buy from me gold refined

COUNSELOR (COUNSEL)

Isa   9:   6 Wonderful C, Mighty God,
Jn   14:16 he will give you another C to be
     14:26 But the C, the Holy Spirit,
     15:26 "When the C comes, whom I will
     16:   7 the C will not come to you;
Ro   11:34 Or who has been his c?''

COUNSELS (COUNSEL)

Ps   16:   7 I will praise the LORD, who c me;

COUNT (COUNTED COUNTING COUNTS)

Ps   22:17 I can c all my bones;
Ro   4:   8 whose sin the Lord will never c
      6:11 c yourselves dead to sin
2Th   1:11 that our God may c you worthy

COUNTED (COUNT)

Ac   5:41 because they had been c worthy
2Th   1:   5 and as a result you will be c worthy

COUNTERFEIT*

2Th   2:   9 displayed in all kinds of c miracles,
1Jn   2:27 not c— just as it has taught you,

COUNTING (COUNT)

2Co   5:19 not c men's sins against them.

COUNTRY

Pr   28:   2 When a c is rebellious, it has many
     29:   4 By justice a king gives a c stability,
Isa 66:   8 Can a c be born in a day
Lk   15:13 off for a distant c and there
Jn   4:44 prophet has no honor in his own c.)
2Co 11:26 in danger in the c, in danger at sea;
Heb 11:14 looking for a c of their own.

COUNTRYMEN

2Co 11:26 danger from my own c, in danger

COUNTS (COUNT)

Jn   6:63 The Spirit gives life; the flesh c
1Co   7:19 God's commands is what c.
Gal   5:   6 only thing that c is faith expressing

COURAGE* (COURAGEOUS)

Jos   2:11 everyone's c failed because of you,
      5:   1 and they no longer had the c
2Sa   4:   1 he lost c, and all Israel became
      7:27 So your servant has found c
1Ch 17:25 So your servant has found c to pray
2Ch 15:   8 son of Oded the prophet, he took c.
     19:11 Act with c, and may the LORD be
Ezr   7:28 I took c and gathered leading men
     10:   4 We will support you, so take c
Ps 107: 26 in their peril their c melted away.
Eze 22:14 Will your c endure or your hands
Da   11:25 and c against the king of the South.
Mt   14:27 said to them: "Take c!
Mk   6:50 spoke to them and said, "Take c!
Ac   4:13 When they saw the c of Peter
     23:11 "Take c! As you have testified
     27:22 now I urge you to keep up your c,
     27:25 So keep up your c, men,
1Co 16:13 stand firm in the faith; be men of c;
Php   1:20 will have sufficient c so that now
Heb   3:   6 if we hold on to our c and the hope

COURAGEOUS* (COURAGE)

Dt   31:   6 Be strong and c.
     31:   7 of all Israel, "Be strong and c,
     31:23 son of Nun: "Be strong and c,
Jos   1:   6 and c, because you will lead these
      1:   7 Be strong and very c.
      1:   9 commanded you? Be strong and c.
      1:18 Only be strong and c!''
     10:25 Be strong and c.
1Ch 22:13 Be strong and c.
     28:20 "Be strong and c, and do the work.
2Ch 26:17 priest with eighty other c priests
     32:   7 with these words: "Be strong and c.

COURSE

Ps   19:   5 a champion rejoicing to run his c.
Pr   2:   8 for he guards the c of the just
     15:21 of understanding keeps a straight c.
     16:   9 In his heart a man plans his c,
     17:23 to pervert the c of justice.
Jas   3:   6 sets the whole c of his life on fire,

COURT (COURTS)

Pr   22:22 and do not crush the needy in c,
     25:   8 do not bring hastily to c,
Mt   5:25 adversary who is taking you to c.
1Co   4:   3 judged by you or by any human c;

COURTS (COURT)

Ps   84:10 Better is one day in your c
     100:   4 and his c with praise;
Am   5:15 maintain justice in the c.
Zec   8:16 and sound judgment in your c;

COURTYARD

Ex   27:   9 "Make a c for the tabernacle.

COUSIN

Col   4:10 as does Mark, the c of Barnabas.

COVENANT (COVENANTS)

Ge   9:   9 "I now establish my c with you
     17:   2 I will confirm my c between me
Ex   19:   5 if you obey me fully and keep my c,
     24:   7 Then he took the Book of the C
Dt   4:13 declared to you his c, the Ten
     29:   1 in addition to the c he had made
Jdg   2:   1 'I will never break my c with you,
1Sa 23:18 of them made a c before the LORD
1Ki   8:21 in which is the c of the LORD that
      8:23 you who keep your c of love
2Ki 23:   2 the words of the Book of the C,
1Ch 16:15 He remembers his c forever,
2Ch   6:14 you who keep your c of love
     34:30 the words of the Book of the C,
Ne   1:   5 who keeps his c of love
Job 31:   1 "I made a c with my eyes
Ps 105:   8 He remembers his c forever,
Pr   2:17 ignored the c she made before God
Isa 42:   6 you to be a c for the people
     61:   8 make an everlasting c with them.
Jer 11:   2 "Listen to the terms of this c
     31:31 "when I will make a new c
     31:32 It will not be like the c
     31:33 "This is the c I will make
Eze 37:26 I will make a c of peace with them;
Da   9:27 He will confirm a c with many
Hos   6:   7 Like Adam, they have broken the c
Mal   2:14 the wife of your marriage c.
      3:   1 of the c, whom you desire,
Mt   26:28 blood of the c, which is poured out
Mk   14:24 "This is my blood of the c,
Lk   22:20 "This cup is the new c in my blood,
1Co 11:25 "This cup is the new c in my blood;
2Co   3:   6 as ministers of a new c—
Gal   4:24 One c is from Mount Sinai
Heb   8:   6 as the c of which he is mediator is
      8:   8 when I will make a new c
      9:15 Christ is the mediator of a new c,
     12:24 to Jesus the mediator of a new c,

COVENANTS (COVENANT)

Ro   9:   4 theirs the divine glory, the c,
Gal   4:24 for the women represent two c.

COVER (COVER-UP COVERED COVERING COVERINGS COVERS)

Ex   25:17 "Make an atonement c of pure gold
     25:21 Place the c on top of the ark
     33:22 and c you with my hand
Lev 16:   2 in the cloud over the atonement c.
Ps   32:   5 and did not c up my iniquity.
     91:   4 He will c you with his feathers,
Hos 10:   8 say to the mountains, "C us!"
Lk   23:30 and to the hills, "C us!'' '
1Co 11:   6 If a woman does not c her head,
     11:   6 she should c her head.
     11:   7 A man ought not to c his head,
Jas   5:20 and c over a multitude of sins.

COVER-UP* (COVER)

1Pe   2:16 but do not use your freedom as a c

COVERED (COVER)

Ps 32: 1 whose sins are *c*.
85: 2 and *c* all their sins.
Isa 6: 2 With two wings they *c* their faces,
51: 16 *c* you with the shadow of my hand
Ro 4: 7 whose sins are *c*.
1Co 11: 4 with his head *c* dishonors his head.

COVERING (COVER)

1Co 11: 15 For long hair is given to her as a *c*.

COVERINGS (COVER)

Ge 3: 7 and made *c* for themselves.
Pr 31: 22 She makes *c* for her bed;

COVERS (COVER)

Pr 10: 12 but love *c* over all wrongs.
17: 9 He who *c* over an offense promotes
2Co 3: 15 Moses is read, a veil *c* their hearts.
1Pe 4: 8 love *c* over a multitude of sins.

COVET* (COVETED COVETING COVETOUS)

Ex 20: 17 You shall not *c* your neighbor's
20: 17 "You shall not *c* your neighbor's
34: 24 and no one will *c* your land
Dt 5: 21 "You shall not *c* your neighbor's
7: 25 Do not *c* the silver and gold
Mic 2: 2 They *c* fields and seize them,
Ro 7: 7 if the law had not said, "Do not *c*."
13: 9 "Do not steal," "Do not *c*,"
Jas 4: 2 *c*, but you cannot have what you

COVETED* (COVET)

Jos 7: 21 weighing fifty shekels, I *c* them
Ac 20: 33 I have not *c* anyone's silver or gold

COVETING

Ro 7: 7 what *c* really was if the law

COVETOUS* (COVET)

Ro 7: 8 in me every kind of *c* desire.

COWARDLY*

Rev 21: 8 But the *c*, the unbelieving, the vile,

COWS

Ge 41: 2 of the river there came up seven *c*,
Ex 25: 5 skins dyed red and hides of sea *c*;
Nu 4: 6 are to cover this with hides of sea *c*,
1Sa 6: 7 Hitch the *c* to the cart,

CRAFTINESS* (CRAFTY)

Job 5: 13 He catches the wise in their *c*,
1Co 3: 19 "He catches the wise in their *c*'';
Eph 4: 14 and *c* of men in their deceitful

CRAFTSMAN

Pr 8: 30 Then I was the *c* at his side.

CRAFTY* (CRAFTINESS)

Ge 3: 1 the serpent was more *c* than any
1Sa 23: 22 They tell me he is very *c*.
Job 5: 12 He thwarts the plans of the *c*,
15: 5 you adopt the tongue of the *c*.
Pr 7: 10 like a prostitute and with *c* intent.
12: 2 but the LORD condemns a *c* man.
14: 17 and a *c* man is hated.
2Co 12: 16 *c* fellow that I am, I caught you

CRAVE* (CRAVED CRAVES CRAVING CRAVINGS)

Nu 11: 4 with them began to *c* other food,
Dt 12: 20 you *c* meat and say, "I would like
Pr 23: 3 Do not *c* his delicacies,
23: 6 do not *c* his delicacies;
31: 4 not for rulers to *c* beer,
Mic 7: 1 none of the early figs that I *c*.
1Pe 2: 2 newborn babies, *c* pure spiritual

CRAVED* (CRAVE)

Nu 11: 34 the people who had *c* other food.
Ps 78: 18 by demanding the food they *c*.
78: 29 for he had given them what they *c*,
78: 30 turned from the food they *c*,

CRAVES* (CRAVE)

Pr 13: 4 The sluggard *c* and gets nothing,

Pr 21: 10 The wicked man *c* evil;
21: 26 All day long he *c* for more,

CRAVING* (CRAVE)

Job 20: 20 he will have no respite from his *c*;
Ps 106: 14 In the desert they gave in to their *c*;
Pr 10: 3 but he thwarts the *c* of the wicked.
13: 2 the unfaithful have a *c* for violence.
21: 25 The sluggard's *c* will be the death
Jer 2: 24 sniffing the wind in her *c*—

CRAVINGS* (CRAVE)

Ps 10: 3 He boasts of the *c* of his heart;
Eph 2: 3 gratifying the *c* of our sinful nature
1Jn 2: 16 in the world—the *c* of sinful man,

CRAWL

Ge 3: 14 You will *c* on your belly

CREATE* (CREATED CREATES CREATING CREATION CREATOR)

Ps 51: 10 *C* in me a pure heart, O God,
Isa 4: 5 Then the LORD will *c* over all
45: 7 I bring prosperity and *c* disaster;
45: 7 I form the light and *c* darkness,
45: 18 he did not *c* it to be empty,
65: 17 "Behold, I will *c*/ new heavens
65: 18 for I will *c* Jerusalem to be a delight
65: 18 forever in what I will *c*,
Jer 31: 22 The LORD will *c* a new thing
Mal 2: 10 one Father? Did not one God *c* us?
Eph 2: 15 His purpose was to *c*

CREATED* (CREATE)

Ge 1: 1 In the beginning God *c* the heavens
1: 21 God *c* the great creatures of the sea
1: 27 So God *c* man in his own image,
1: 27 in the image of God he *c* him;
1: 27 male and female he *c* them.
2: 4 and the earth when they were *c*,
5: 1 When God *c* man, he made him
5: 2 He *c* them male and female
5: 2 when they were *c*, he called them
6: 7 whom I have *c*, from the face
Dt 4: 32 from the day God *c* man
Ps 89: 12 You *c* the north and the south;
89: 47 what futility you have *c* all men!
102: 18 a people not yet *c* may praise
104: 30 you send your Spirit, / they are *c*,
139: 13 For you *c* my inmost being;
148: 5 for he commanded and they were *c*
Isa 40: 26 Who *c* all these?
41: 20 that the Holy One of Israel has *c* it.
42: 5 he who *c* the heavens and stretched
43: 1 he who *c* you, O Jacob,
43: 7 whom I *c* for my glory,
45: 8 I, the LORD, have *c* it.
45: 12 and *c* mankind upon it.
45: 18 he who *c* the heavens,
48: 7 They are *c* now, and not long ago;
54: 16 And it is I who have *c* the destroyer
54: 16 "See, it is I who *c* the blacksmith
57: 16 the breath of man that I have *c*.
Eze 21: 30 In the place where you were *c*,
28: 13 the day you were *c* they were
28: 15 ways from the day you were *c*
Mk 13: 19 when God *c* the world, until now—
Ro 1: 25 and served *c* things rather
1Co 11: 9 neither was man *c* for woman,
Eph 2: 10 *c* in Christ Jesus to do good works,
3: 9 hidden in God, who *c* all things.
4: 24 *c* to be like God in true
Col 1: 16 For by him all things were *c*:
1: 16 all things were *c* by him
1Ti 4: 3 which God *c* to be received
4: 4 For everything God *c* is good,
Heb 12: 27 *c* things—so that what cannot be
Jas 1: 18 a kind of firstfruits of all he *c*.
Rev 4: 11 and by your will they were *c*
4: 11 for you *c* all things,
10: 6 who *c* the heavens and all that is

CREATES* (CREATE)

Am 4: 13 *c* the wind,

CREATING* (CREATE)

Ge 2: 3 the work of *c* that he had done.
Isa 57: 19 *c* praise on the lips of the mourners

CREATION* (CREATE)

Hab 2: 18 he who makes it trusts in his own *c*;
Mt 13: 35 hidden since the *c* of the world.''
25: 34 for you since the *c* of the world.
Mk 10: 6 of *c* God 'made them male
16: 15 and preach the good news to all *c*.
Jn 17: 24 me before the *c* of the world.
Ro 1: 20 For since the *c* of the world God's
8: 19 The *c* waits in eager expectation
8: 20 For the *c* was subjected
8: 21 in hope that the *c* itself will be
8: 22 that the whole *c* has been groaning
8: 39 depth, nor anything else in all *c*,
2Co 5: 17 he is a new *c*; the old has gone,
Gal 6: 15 anything; what counts is a new *c*.
Eph 1: 4 us in him before the *c* of the world
Col 1: 15 God, the firstborn over all *c*.
Heb 4: 3 finished since the *c* of the world.
4: 13 Nothing in all *c* is hidden
9: 11 that is to say, not a part of this *c*.
9: 26 times since the *c* of the world.
1Pe 1: 20 chosen before the *c* of the world,
2Pe 3: 4 as it has since the beginning of *c*.''
Rev 3: 14 true witness, the ruler of God's *c*.
13: 8 slain from the *c* of the world.
17: 8 life from the *c* of the world will be

CREATOR* (CREATE)

Ge 14: 19 *C* of heaven and earth.
14: 22 God Most High, *C* of heaven
Dt 32: 6 Is he not your Father, your *C*,
Ecc 12: 1 Remember your *C*
Isa 27: 11 and their *C* shows them no favor.
40: 28 the *C* of the ends of the earth.
43: 15 Israel's *C*, your King.''
Mt 19: 4 the beginning the *C* 'made them
Ro 1: 25 created things rather than the *C*—
Col 3: 10 in knowledge in the image of its *C*.
1Pe 4: 19 themselves to their faithful *C*

CREATURE (CREATURES)

Lev 17: 11 For the life of a *c* is in the blood,
17: 14 the life of every *c* is its blood.
Ps 136: 25 and who gives food to every *c*.
Eze 1: 15 beside each *c* with its four faces.
Rev 4: 7 The first living *c* was like a lion,

CREATURES (CREATURE)

Ge 6: 19 bring into the ark two of all living *c*,
8: 21 again will I destroy all living *c*,
Ps 104: 24 the earth is full of your *c*.
Eze 1: 5 was what looked like four living *c*,

CREDIT (CREDITED CREDITOR CREDITS)

Lk 6: 33 what *c* is that to you? Even
Ro 4: 24 to whom God will *c* righteousness
1Pe 2: 20 it to your *c* if you receive a beating

CREDITED (CREDIT)

Ge 15: 6 and he *c* it to him as righteousness.
Ps 106: 31 This was *c* to him as righteousness
Eze 18: 20 of the righteous man will be *c*
Ro 4: 3 and it was *c* to him as righteousness
4: 4 his wages are not *c* to him as a gift,
4: 5 his faith is *c* as righteousness.
4: 9 saying that Abraham's faith was *c*
4: 23 The words ''it was *c*
Gal 3: 6 and it was *c* to him as righteousness
Php 4: 17 for what may be *c* to your account.
Jas 2: 23 and it was *c* to him as righteousness

CREDITOR (CREDIT)

Dt 15: 2 Every *c* shall cancel the loan he has

CREDITS (CREDIT)

Ro 4: 6 whom God *c* righteousness apart

CRETANS (CRETE)

Tit 1: 12 "*C* are always liars, evil brutes,

CRETE (CRETANS)

Ac 27: 12 harbor in *C*, facing both southwest

CRIED (CRY)

Ex 2: 23 groaned in their slavery and *c* out,
14: 10 They were terrified and *c* out
Nu 20: 16 but when we *c* out to the LORD,

Jos 24: 7 But they *c* to the LORD for help,
Jdg 3: 9 But when they *c* out to the LORD,
3:15 Again the Israelites *c* out
4: 3 they *c* to the LORD for help.
6: 6 the Israelites that they *c* out
10:12 Maonites oppressed you and you *c*
1Sa 7: 9 He *c* out to the LORD
12: 8 they *c* to the LORD for help,
12:10 They *c* out to the LORD and said,
Ps 18: 6 I *c* to my God for help.

CRIMINALS
Lk 23:32 both *c*, were also led out with him

CRIMSON
Isa 1:18 though they are red as *c*,
63: 1 with his garments stained *c*?

CRIPPLED
2Sa 9: 3 of Jonathan; he is *c* in both feet."
Mk 9:45 better for you to enter life *c*

CRISIS*
1Co 7:26 of the present *c*, I think that it is

CRITICISM*
2Co 8:20 We want to avoid any *c*

CROOKED*
Dt 32: 5 but a warped and *c* generation.
2Sa 22:27 to the *c* you show yourself shrewd.
Ps 18:26 to the *c* you show yourself shrewd.
125: 5 But those who turn to *c* ways
Pr 2:15 whose paths are *c*
5: 6 her paths are *c*, but she knows it
8: 8 none of them is *c* or perverse.
10: 9 he who takes *c* paths will be found
Ecc 7:13 what he has made *c*?
Isa 59: 8 have turned them into *c* roads;
La 3: 9 he has made my paths *c*.
Lk 3: 5 The *c* roads shall become straight,
Php 2:15 children of God without fault in a *c*

CROP (CROPS)
Mt 13: 8 where it produced a *c*— a hundred,
21:41 share of the *c* at harvest time."

CROPS (CROP)
Pr 3: 9 with the firstfruits of all your *c*;
10: 5 He who gathers *c* in summer is
28: 3 like a driving rain that leaves no *c*.
2Ti 2: 6 the first to receive a share of the *c*.

CROSS (CROSSED CROSSING)
Dt 4:21 swore that I would not *c* the Jordan
12:10 But you will *c* the Jordan
Mt 10:38 and anyone who does not take his *c*
16:24 and take up his *c* and follow me.
Mk 8:34 and take up his *c* and follow me.
Lk 9:23 take up his *c* daily and follow me.
14:27 anyone who does not carry his *c*
Jn 19:17 Carrying his own *c*, he went out
Ac 2:23 to death by nailing him to the *c*.
1Co 1:17 lest the *c* of Christ be emptied
1:18 the message of the *c* is foolishness
Gal 5:11 offense of the *c* has been abolished.
6:12 persecuted for the *c* of Christ.
6:14 in the *c* of our Lord Jesus Christ,
Eph 2:16 both of them to God through the *c*,
Php 2: 8 even death on a *c*!
3:18 as enemies of the *c* of Christ.
Col 1:20 through his blood, shed on the *c*.
2:14 he took it away, nailing it to the *c*.
2:15 triumphing over them by the *c*.
Heb 12: 2 set before him endured the *c*,

CROSSED (CROSS)
Jos 4: 7 When it *c* the Jordan, the waters
Jn 5:24 he has *c* over from death to life.

CROSSING (CROSS)
Ge 48:14 he was the younger, and *c* his arms,

CROSSROADS (ROAD)
Jer 6:16 "Stand at the *c* and look;

CROUCHING
Ge 4: 7 sin is *c* at your door; it desires

CROWD (CROWDS)
Ex 23: 2 Do not follow the *c* in doing wrong.

CROWDS (CROWD)
Mt 9:36 he saw the *c*, he had compassion

CROWED (CROWS)
Mt 26:74 the man!" Immediately a rooster *c*.

CROWN (CROWNED CROWNS)
Pr 4: 9 present you with a *c* of splendor."
10: 6 Blessings *c* the head
12: 4 noble character is her husband's *c*,
16:31 Gray hair is a *c* of splendor;
17: 6 Children's children are a *c*
Isa 35:10 everlasting joy will *c* their heads.
51:11 everlasting joy will *c* their heads.
61: 3 to bestow on them a *c* of beauty
62: 3 You will be a *c* of splendor
Eze 16:12 and a beautiful *c* on your head.
Zec 9:16 like jewels in a *c*.
Mt 27:29 and then twisted together a *c* of thorns
Mk 15:17 then twisted together a *c* of thorns
Jn 19: 2 The soldiers twisted together a *c*
19: 5 When Jesus came out wearing the *c*
1Co 9:25 it to get a *c* that will last forever.
9:25 it to get a *c* that will not last;
Php 4: 1 and long for, my joy and *c*,
1Th 2:19 or the *c* in which we will glory
2Ti 2: 5 he does not receive the victor's *c*
4: 8 store for me the *c* of righteousness,
Jas 1:12 he will receive the *c*
1Pe 5: 4 you will receive the *c*
Rev 2:10 and I will give you the *c* of life.
3:11 so that no one will take your *c*.
14:14 a son of man" with a *c* of gold

CROWNED* (CROWN)
Ps 8: 5 and *c* him with glory and honor.
Pr 14:18 the prudent are *c* with knowledge.
SS 3:11 crown with which his mother *c* him
Heb 2: 7 you *c* him with glory and honor
2: 9 now *c* with glory and honor

CROWNS (CROWN)
Ps 103: 4 and *c* me with love and compassion
149: 4 he *c* the humble with salvation.
Pr 11:26 blessing *c* him who is willing to sell.
Rev 4: 4 and had *c* of gold on their heads.
4:10 They lay their *c* before the throne
12: 3 ten horns and seven *c* on his heads.
19:12 and on his head are many *c*.

CROWS (CROWED)
Mt 26:34 this very night, before the rooster *c*

CRUCIFIED* (CRUCIFY)
Mt 20:19 to be mocked and flogged and *c*.
26: 2 of Man will be handed over to be *c*.
27:26 and handed him over to be *c*.
27:35 When they had *c* him, they divided
27:38 Two robbers were *c* with him,
27:44 same way the robbers who were *c*
28: 5 looking for Jesus, who was *c*.
Mk 15:15 and handed him over to be *c*.
15:24 And they *c* him.
15:25 the third hour when they *c* him.
15:27 They *c* two robbers with him;
15:32 Those *c* with him also heaped
16: 6 for Jesus the Nazarene, who was *c*.
Lk 23:23 insistently demanded that he be *c*,
23:33 *c* him, along with the criminals—
24: 7 be *c* and on the third day be raised
24:20 sentenced to death, and they *c* him;
Jn 19:16 him over to them to be *c*.
19:18 Here they *c* him, and with him two
19:20 for the place where Jesus was *c* was
19:23 When the soldiers *c* Jesus,
19:32 of the first man who had been *c*
19:41 At the place where Jesus was *c*,
Ac 2:36 whom you *c*, both Lord and Christ
4:10 whom you *c* but whom God raised
Ro 6: 6 For we know that our old self was *c*
1Co 1:13 Is Christ divided? Was Paul *c*
1:23 but we preach Christ *c*: a stumbling
2: 2 except Jesus Christ and him *c*.
2: 8 they would not have *c* the Lord
2Co 13: 4 to be sure, he was *c* in weakness,

Gal 2:20 I have been *c* with Christ
3: 1 Christ was clearly portrayed as *c*.
5:24 Christ Jesus have *c* the sinful
6:14 which the world has been *c*
Rev 11: 8 where also their Lord was *c*.

CRUCIFY* (CRUCIFIED CRUCIFYING)
Mt 23:34 Some of them you will kill and *c*;
27:22 They all answered, "*C* him!" "Why
27:23 they shouted all the louder, "*C* him
27:31 Then they led him away to *c* him.
Mk 15:13 "*C* him!" they shouted.
15:14 they shouted all the louder, "*C* him
15:20 Then they led him out to *c* him.
Lk 23:21 they kept shouting, "*C* him! *C* him
Jn 19: 6 they shouted, "*C*! *C*!"
19: 6 "You take him and *c* him.
19:10 either to free you or to *c* you?"
19:15 Crucify him!" "Shall I *c* your king
19:15 away! Take him away! *C* him!"

CRUCIFYING* (CRUCIFY)
Heb 6: 6 to their loss they are *c* the Son

CRUSH (CRUSHED)
Ge 3:15 he will *c* your head,
Isa 53:10 it was the LORD's will to *c* him
Ro 16:20 The God of peace will soon *c* Satan

CRUSHED (CRUSH)
Ps 34:18 and saves those who are *c* in spirit.
Pr 17:22 but a *c* spirit dries up the bones.
18:14 but a *c* spirit who can bear?
Isa 53: he was *c* for our iniquities;
2Co 4: 8 not *c*; perplexed, but not in despair;

CRY (CRIED)
Ex 2:23 *c* for help because of their slavery
Ps 5: 2 Listen to my *c* for help,
34:15 and his ears are attentive to their *c*;
40: 1 he turned to me and heard my *c*.
130: 1 Out of the depths I *c* to you,
Pr 21:13 to the *c* of the poor,
La 2:18 *c* out to the Lord.
Hab 2:11 The stones of the wall will *c* out,
Lk 19:40 keep quiet, the stones will *c* out."

CUNNING
2Co 11: 3 deceived by the serpent's *c*,
Eph 4:14 and by the *c* and craftiness of men

CUP
Ps 23: 5 my *c* overflows.
Isa 51:22 from that *c*, the goblet of my wrath,
51:22 the *c* that made you stagger;
Mt 10:42 if anyone gives even a *c* of cold water
20:22 "Can you drink the *c* I am going
23:25 You clean the outside of the *c*
23:26 First clean the inside of the *c*
26:27 Then he took the *c*, gave thanks
26:39 may this *c* be taken from me.
26:42 possible for this *c* to be taken away
Mk 9:41 anyone who gives you a *c* of water
10:38 "Can you drink the *c* I drink
10:39 "You will drink the *c* I drink
14:23 Then he took the *c*, gave thanks
14:36 Take this *c* from me.
Lk 11:39 Pharisees clean the outside of the *c*
22:17 After taking the *c*, he gave thanks
22:20 after the supper he took the *c*,
22:20 "This *c* is the new covenant
22:42 if you are willing, take this *c*
Jn 18:11 I not drink the *c* the Father has
1Co 10:16 Is not the *c* of thanksgiving
10:21 the *c* of the Lord and the *c*
11:25 after supper he took the *c*, saying,
11:25 "This *c* is the new covenant

CUPBEARER
Ge 40: 1 the *c* and the baker of the king
Ne 1:11 I was *c* to the king.

CURE (CURED)
Jer 17: 9 and beyond *c*,
30:15 your pain that has no *c*?
Hos 5:13 But he is not able to *c* you,
Lk 9: 1 out all demons and to *c* diseases.

CURED (CURE)

Mt 11: 5 those who have leprosy are c,
Lk 6: 18 troubled by evil spirits were c,

CURSE (ACCURSED CURSED CURSES CURSING)

Ge 4: 11 Now you are under a c
     8: 21 "Never again will I c the ground
    12: 3 and whoever curses you I will c;
Dt 11: 26 before you today a blessing and a c
    11: 28 the c if you disobey the commands
    21: 23 hung on a tree is under God's c.
    23: 5 turned the c into a blessing for you;
Job 1: 11 he will surely c you to your face."
     2: 5 he will surely c you to your face."
     2: 9 C God and die!" He replied,
Ps 109: 28 They may c, but you will bless;
Pr 3: 33 The LORD's c is on the house
    24: 24 peoples will c him and nations
Mal 2: 1 and I will c your blessings.
Lk 6: 28 bless those who c you, pray
Ro 12: 14 persecute you; bless and do not c.
Gal 3: 10 on observing the law are under a c,
     3: 13 of the law by becoming a c for us,
Jas 3: 9 with it we c men, who have been
Rev 22: 3 No longer will there be any c.

CURSED (CURSE)

Ge 3: 17 "C is the ground because of you;
Dt 27: 15 "C is the man who carves an image
    27: 16 "C is the man who dishonors his
    27: 17 "C is the man who moves his
    27: 18 "C is the man who leads the blind
    27: 19 C is the man who withholds justice
    27: 20 "C is the man who sleeps
    27: 21 "C is the man who has sexual
    27: 22 "C is the man who sleeps
    27: 23 "C is the man who sleeps
    27: 24 "C is the man who kills his
    27: 25 "C is the man who accepts a bribe
    27: 26 "C is the man who does not uphold
Jer 17: 5 "C is the one who trusts in man,
Mal 1: 14 "C is the cheat who has
Ro 9: 3 I could wish that I myself were c
1Co 4: 12 When we are c, we bless;
    12: 3 "Jesus be c," and no one can say,
Gal 3: 10 "C is everyone who does not
     3: 13 C is everyone who is hung on a tree

CURSES (CURSE)

Ex 21: 17 "Anyone who c his father
Lev 20: 9 " 'If anyone c his father or mother,
Nu 5: 23 is to write these c on a scroll
Jos 8: 34 the blessings and the c— just
Pr 20: 20 If a man c his father or mother,
    28: 27 to them receives many c.
Mt 15: 4 and 'Anyone who c his father
Mk 7: 10 and, 'Anyone who c his father

CURSING (CURSE)

Ps 109: 18 He wore c as his garment;
Ro 3: 14 "Their mouths are full of c
Jas 3: 10 the same mouth come praise and c.

CURTAIN

Ex 26: 31 "Make a c of blue, purple
    26: 33 The c will separate the Holy Place
Mt 27: 51 At that moment the c
Mk 15: 38 The c of the temple was torn in two
Lk 23: 45 the c of the temple was torn in two.
Heb 6: 19 the inner sanctuary behind the c,
     9: 3 Behind the second c was a room
    10: 20 opened for us through the c,

CUSTOM

Job 1: 5 This was Job's regular c.
Mk 10: 1 and as was his c, he taught them.
Lk 4: 16 into the synagogue, as was his c.
Ac 17: 2 As his c was, Paul went

CUT

Lev 19: 27 " 'Do not c the hair at the sides
    21: 5 of their beards or c their bodies.
1Ki 3: 25 "C the living child in two
Isa 51: 1 to the rock from which you were c
    53: 8 For he was c off from the land
Da 2: 45 of the rock c out of a mountain,
     9: 26 the Anointed One will be c off

Mt 3: 10 not produce good fruit will be c
   24: 22 If those days had not been c short,
1Co 11: 6 for a woman to have her hair c

CYMBAL* (CYMBALS)

1Co 13: 1 a resounding gong or a clanging c.

CYMBALS (CYMBAL)

1Ch 15: 16 instruments: lyres, harps and c.
2Ch 5: 12 dressed in fine linen and playing c,
Ps 150: 5 praise him with resounding c.

CYRUS

Persian king who allowed exiles to return (2Ch 36:22-Ezr 1:8), to rebuild temple (Ezr 5:13-6:14), as appointed by the LORD (Isa 44:28-45:13).

DAGON

Jdg 16: 23 offer a great sacrifice to D their god
1Sa 5: 2 Dagon's temple and set it beside D.

DAMASCUS

Ac 9: 3 As he neared D on his journey,

DAN

1. Son of Jacob by Bilhah (Ge 30:4-6; 35:25; 46:23). Tribe of blessed (Ge 49:16-17; Dt 33:22), numbered (Nu 1:39; 26:43), allotted land (Jos 19: 40-48; Eze 48:1), failed to fully possess (Jdg 1: 34-35), failed to support Deborah (Jdg 5:17), possessed Laish/Dan (Jdg 18).
2. Northernmost city in Israel (Ge 14:14; Jdg 18; 20:1).

DANCE (DANCED DANCING)

Ecc 3: 4 a time to mourn and a time to d,
Mt 11: 17 and you did not d;

DANCED (DANCE)

2Sa 6: 14 d before the LORD
Mk 6: 22 of Herodias came in and d,

DANCING (DANCE)

Ps 30: 11 You turned my wailing into d;
   149: 3 Let them praise his name with d

DANGER

Pr 22: 3 A prudent man sees d
   27: 12 The prudent see d and take refuge,
Mt 5: 22 will be in d of the fire of hell.
Ro 8: 35 famine or nakedness or d or sword?
2Co 11: 26 I have been in d from rivers,

DANIEL

1. Hebrew exile to Babylon, name changed to Belteshazzar (Da 1:6-7). Refused to eat unclean food (Da 1:8-21). Interpreted Nebuchadnezzar's dreams (Da 2; 4), writing on the wall (Da 5). Thrown into lion's den (Da 6). Visions of (Da 7-12).
2. Son of David (1Ch 3:1).

DARIUS

1. King of Persia (Ezr 4:5), allowed rebuilding of temple (Ezr 5-6).
2. Mede who conquered Babylon (Da 5:31).

DARK (DARKENED DARKENS DARKNESS)

Job 34: 22 There is no d place, no deep
Ps 18: 9 d clouds were under his feet.
Pr 31: 15 She gets up while it is still d;
SS 1: 6 Do not stare at me because I am d,
Jn 12: 35 in the d does not know where he is
Ro 2: 19 a light for those who are in the d,
2Pe 1: 19 as to a light shining in a d place,

DARKENED (DARK)

Joel 2: 10 the sun and moon are d,
Mt 24: 29 " 'the sun will be d,
Ro 1: 21 and their foolish hearts were d.
Eph 4: 18 They are d in their understanding

DARKENS (DARK)

Job 38: 2 "Who is this that d my counsel

DARKNESS (DARK)

Ge 1: 2 d was over the surface of the deep,
   1: 4 he separated the light from the d.

Ex 10: 22 and total d covered all Egypt
   20: 21 approached the thick d where God
2Sa 22: 29 the LORD turns my d into light.
Ps 18: 28 my God turns my d into light.
   91: 6 the pestilence that stalks in the d,
   112: 4 Even in d light dawns
   139: 12 even the d will not be dark to you;
Pr 4: 19 the way of the wicked is like deep d
Isa 5: 20 and light for d,
    42: 16 I will turn the d into light
    45: 7 I form the light and create d,
    58: 10 then your light will rise in the d,
    61: 1 and release from d,
Joel 2: 31 The sun will be turned to d
Mt 4: 16 the people living in d
   6: 23 how great is that d! "No one can
Lk 11: 34 are bad, your body also is full of d.
   23: 44 and d came over the whole land
Jn 1: 5 The light shines in the d,
   3: 19 but men loved d instead of light
Ac 2: 20 The sun will be turned to d
2Co 4: 6 who said, "Let light shine out of d
   6: 14 fellowship can light have with d?
Eph 5: 8 For you were once d, but now you
   5: 11 to do with the fruitless deeds of d,
1Pe 2: 9 out of d into his wonderful light.
2Pe 2: 17 Blackest d is reserved for them.
1Jn 1: 5 in him there is no d at all.
   2: 9 but hates his brother is still in the d.
Jude : 6 in d, bound with everlasting chains
   : 13 for whom blackest d has been

DASH

Ps 2: 9 you will d them to pieces like

DAUGHTER (DAUGHTERS)

Ex 1: 10 she took him to Pharaoh's d
Jdg 11: 48 to commemorate the d of Jephthah
Est 2: 7 Mordecai had taken her as his own d
Ps 9: 14 praises in the gates of the D of Zion
   137: 8 O D of Babylon, doomed
Isa 62: 11 "Say to the D of Zion,
Zec 9: 9 Shout, D of Jerusalem!
Mk 5: 34 "D, your faith has healed you.
   7: 29 the demon has left your d.

DAUGHTERS (DAUGHTER)

Ge 6: 2 the d of men were beautiful,
   19: 36 Lot's d became pregnant
Nu 36: 10 Zelophehad's d did as the LORD
Joel 2: 28 sons and d will prophesy,

DAVID

Son of Jesse (Ru 4:17-22; 1Ch 2:13-15), ancestor of Jesus (Mt 1:1-17; Lk 3:31). Wives and children (1Sa 18; 25:39-44; 2Sa 3:2-5; 5:13-16; 11:27; 1Ch 3:1-9).

Anointed king by Samuel (1Sa 16:1-13). Musician to Saul (1Sa 16:14-23; 18:10). Killed Goliath (1Sa 17). Relation with Jonathan (1Sa 18:1-4; 19-20; 23:16-18; 2Sa 1). Disfavor of Saul (1Sa 18: 6-23:29). Spared Saul's life (1Sa 24; 26). Among Philistines (1Sa 21:10-14; 27-30). Lament for Saul and Jonathan (2Sa 1).

Anointed king of Judah (2Sa 2:1-11). Conflict with house of Saul (2Sa 2-4). Anointed king of Israel (2Sa 5:1-4; 1Ch 11:1-3). Conquered Jerusalem (2Sa 6; 1Ch 13; 15-16). The LORD promised eternal dynasty (2Sa 7; 1Ch 17; Ps 132). Showed kindness to Mephibosheth (2Sa 9). Adultery with Bathsheba, murder of Uriah (2Sa 11-12). Son Amnon raped daughter Tamar; killed by Absalom (2Sa 13). Absalom's revolt (2Sa 14-17); death (2Sa 18). Sheba's revolt (2Sa 20). Victories: Philistines (2Sa 5:17-25; 1Ch 14:8-17; 2Sa 21:15-22; 1Ch 20:4-8), Ammonites (2Sa 10; 1Ch 19), various (2Sa 8; 1Ch 18). Mighty men (2Sa 23:8-39; 1Ch 11-12). Punished for numbering army (2Sa 24; 1Ch 21). Appointed Solomon king (1Ki 1: 28-2:9). Prepared for building of temple (1Ch 22-29). Last words (2Sa 23:1-7). Death (1Ki 2:10-12; 1Ch 29:28).

Psalmist (Mt 22:43-45), musician (Am 6:5), prophet (2Sa 23:2-7; Ac 1:16; 2:30).

Psalms of: 2 (Ac 4:25), 3-32, 34-41, 51-65, 68-70, 86, 95 (Heb 4:7), 101, 103, 108-110, 122, 124, 131, 133, 138-145.

DAWN (DAWNED DAWNS)

Ps 37: 6 your righteousness shine like the *d.*
Pr   4:18 is like the first gleam of *d,*
Isa 14:12 O morning star, son of the *d!*
Am   4:13 he who turns *d* to darkness,
      5: 8 who turns blackness into *d*

DAWNED (DAWN)

Isa   9: 2 a light has *d.*
Mt   4:16 a light has *d.''*

DAWNS* (DAWN)

Ps 65: 8 where morning *d* and evening
   112: 4 in darkness light *d* for the upright,
Hos 10:15 When that day *d,*
2Pe 1:19 until the day *d* and the morning

DAY (DAYS)

Ge   1: 5 God called the light "*d,*"
     1: 5 and there was morning—the first *d*
     1: 8 there was morning—the second *d.*
     1:13 there was morning—the third *d.*
     1:19 there was morning—the fourth *d.*
     1:23 there was morning—the fifth *d.*
     1:31 there was morning—the sixth *d.*
     2: 2 so on the seventh *d* he rested
     8:22 *d* and night
Ex 16:30 the people rested on the seventh *d.*
   20: 8 "Remember the Sabbath *d*
Lev 16:30 on this *d* atonement will be made
   23:28 because it is the *D* of Atonement,
Nu 14:14 before them in a pillar of cloud by *d*
Jos   1: 8 meditate on it *d* and night,
2Ki 7: 9 This is a *d* of good news
   25:30 *D* by *d* the king gave Jehoiachin
1Ch 16:23 proclaim his salvation *d* after *d.*
Ne   8:18 *D* after *d,* from the first *d*
Ps 84:10 Better is one *d* in your courts
   96: 2 proclaim his salvation *d* after *d.*
  118: 24 This is the *d* the Lord has made;
Pr 27: 1 not know what a *d* may bring forth.
Isa 13: 9 a cruel *d,* with wrath and fierce
Jer 46:10 But that *d* belongs to the Lord,
   50:31 "for your *d* has come,
Eze 30: 2 "Alas for that *d!''*
Joel 1:15 "Alas for that *d!*
     2:31 and dreadful *d* of the Lord.
Am   3:14 On the *d* I punish Israel for her sins
     5:20 Will not the *d* of the Lord be
Ob   :15 "The *d* of the Lord is near
Zep 1:14 The great of the *d* of the Lord is near—
Zec 2:11 joined with the Lord in that *d*
   14: 1 A *d* of the Lord is coming
   14: 7 It will be a unique *d,*
Mal 4: 5 dreadful *d* of the Lord comes.
Mt 24:38 up to the *d* Noah entered the ark;
Lk 11: 3 Give us each *d* our daily bread.
   17:24 in his *d* will be like the lightning,
Ac   5:42 *D* after *d,* in the temple courts
   17:11 examined the Scriptures every *d*
   17:17 as in the marketplace *d* by *d*
Ro 14: 5 man considers every *d* alike.
1Co 5: 5 his spirit saved on the *d* of the Lord
2Co 4:16 we are being renewed *d* by *d.*
   11:25 I spent a night and a *d*
1Th 5: 2 for you know very well that the *d*
     5: 4 so that this *d* should surprise you
2Th 2: 2 saying that the *d* of the Lord has
Heb 7:27 need to offer sacrifices *d* after *d,*
2Pe 3: 8 With the Lord a *d* is like
     3:10 *d* of the Lord will come like a thief.
Rev 6:17 For the great *d* of their wrath has
   16:14 on the great *d* of God Almighty.

DAYS (DAY)

Dt 17:19 he is to read it all the *d* of his life
   32: 7 Remember the *d* of old;
Ps 23: 6 all the *d* of my life,
   34:12 and desires to see many good *d,*
   39: 5 have made my *d* a mere
   90:10 The length of our *d* is seventy years
   90:12 Teach us to number our *d* aright,
   103: 15 As for man, his *d* are like grass,
   128: 5 all the *d* of your life;
Pr 31:12 all the *d* of her life.
Ecc 9: 9 all the *d* of this meaningless life
   12: 1 Creator in the *d* of your youth,
Isa 38:20 all the *d* of our lives

Da   7: 9 and the Ancient of *D* took his seat.
     7:13 He approached the Ancient of *D*
     7:22 until the Ancient of *D* came
Hos 3: 5 and to his blessings in the last *d.*
Joel 2:29 I will pour out my Spirit in those *d.*
Mic 4: 1 In the last *d*
Lk 19:43 The *d* will come upon you
Ac   2:17 by the prophet Joel: " 'In the last *d,*
2Ti   3: 1 will be terrible times in the last *d.*
Heb 1: 2 in these last *d* he has spoken to us
2Pe 3: 3 that in the last *d* scoffers will come,

DAZZLING*

Da   2:31 statue, awesome in appearance.
Mk   9: 3 His clothes became *d* white,

DEACON* (DEACONS)

1Ti   3:12 A *d* must be the husband of

DEACONS* (DEACON)

Php 1: 1 together with the overseers and *d;*
1Ti   3: 8 *D,* likewise, are to be men worthy
     3:10 against them, let them serve as *d.*

DEAD (DIE)

Lev 17:15 who eats anything found *d*
Dt 18:11 or spiritist or who consults the *d.*
Isa 8:19 Why consult the *d* on behalf
Mt   8:22 and let the *d* bury their own *d.''*
     28: 7 'He has risen from the *d*
Lk 15:24 For this son of mine was *d*
   24:46 rise from the *d* on the third day,
Ro   6:11 count yourselves *d* to sin
1Co 15:29 do who are baptized for the *d?*
Eph 2: 1 you were *d* in your transgressions
1Th 4:16 and the *d* in Christ will rise first.
Jas   2:17 is not accompanied by action, is *d.*
     2:26 so faith without deeds is *d.*
Rev 14:13 Blessed are the *d* who die
   20:12 And I saw the *d,* great and small,

DEADENED* (DIE)

Jn 12:40 and *d* their hearts,

DEAR* (DEARER)

2Sa 1:26 you were very *d* to me.
Ps 102: 14 For her stones are *d*
Jer 31:20 Is not Ephraim my *d* son,
Jn   2: 4 "*D* woman, why do you involve me
   19:26 he said to his mother, "*D* woman,
Ac 15:25 to you with our *d* friends Barnabas
Ro 16: 5 Greet my *d* friend Epenetus,
   16: 9 in Christ, and my *d* friend Stachys.
   16:12 Greet my *d* friend Persis, another
1Co 4:14 but to warn you, as my *d* children.
   10:14 my *d* friends, flee from idolatry.
   15:58 Therefore, my *d* brothers,
2Co 7: 1 we have these promises, *d* friends,
   12:19 and everything we do, *d* friends,
Gal 4:19 My *d* children, for whom I am
Eph 6:21 the *d* brother and faithful servant
Php 2:12 my *d* friends, as you have always
     4: 1 firm in the Lord, *d* friends!
Col   1: 7 Epaphras, our *d* fellow servant,
     4: 7 He is a *d* brother, a faithful
     4: 9 our faithful and *d* brother,
     4:14 Our *d* friend Luke, the doctor,
1Th 2: 8 because you had become so *d* to us.
1Ti   6: 2 their service are believers, and *d*
2Ti   1: 2 To Timothy, my *d* son: Grace,
Phm   : 1 To Philemon our *d* friend
     :16 He is very *d* to me but
     :16 better than a slave, as a *d* brother.
Heb 6: 9 we speak like this, *d* friends,
Jas   1:16 Don't be deceived, my *d* brothers.
     1:19 My *d* brothers, take note of this:
     2: 5 thoughts? Listen, my *d* brothers:
1Pe 2:11 *D* friends, I urge you, as aliens
     4:12 *D* friends, do not be surprised
2Pe 3: 1 *D* friends, this is now my second
     3: 8 not forget this one thing, *d* friends:
     3:14 *d* friends, since you are looking
     3:15 just as our *d* brother Paul
     3:17 *d* friends, since you already know
1Jn 2: 1 My *d* children, I write this to you
     2: 7 *D* friends, I am not writing you
     2:12 I write to you, *d* children,
     2:13 I write to you, *d* children,

1Jn 2:18 *D* children, this is the last hour;
     2:28 *d* children, continue in him,
     3: 2 *D* friends, now we are children
     3: 7 *D* children, do not let anyone lead
     3:18 love of God be in him? *D* children,
     3:21 *D* friends, if our hearts do not
     4: 1 *D* friends, do not believe every
     4: 4 *d* children, are from God
     4: 7 *D* friends, let us love one another,
     4:11 *D* friends, since God so loved us,
     5:21 *D* children, keep yourselves
2Jn   : 5 *D* lady, I am not writing you a new
3Jn   : 1 The elder, To my *d* friend Gaius,
     : 2 *D* friend, I pray that you may enjoy
     : 5 *D* friend, you are faithful
     :11 *D* friend, do not imitate what is evil
Jude   : 3 *D* friends, although I was very
     :17 But, *d* friends, remember what
     :20 *d* friends, build yourselves up

DEARER* (DEAR)

Phm   :16 dear to me but even *d* to you,

DEATH (DIE)

Ex 21:12 kills him shall surely be put to *d.*
Nu 35:16 the murderer shall be put to *d.*
Dt 30:19 set before you life and *d,*
Ru   1:17 if anything but *d* separates you
2Ki 4:40 O man of God, there is *d* in the pot
Job 26: 6 *D* is naked before God;
Ps 23: 4 the valley of the shadow of *d,*
   44:22 for your sake we face *d* all day long
   89:48 What man can live and not see *d,*
   116: 15 is the *d* of his saints.
Pr   8:36 all who hate me love *d.''*
   11:19 he who pursues evil goes to his *d.*
   14:12 but in the end it leads to *d.*
   15:11 *D* and Destruction lie open
   16:25 but in the end it leads to *d.*
   18:21 tongue has the power of life and *d,*
   19:18 do not be a willing party to his *d.*
   23:14 and save his soul from *d.*
Ecc 7: 2 for *d* is the destiny of every man;
Isa 25: 8 he will swallow up *d* forever.
   53:12 he poured out his life unto *d,*
Eze 18:23 pleasure in the *d* of the wicked?
   18:32 pleasure in the *d* of anyone,
   33:11 pleasure in the *d* of the wicked,
Hos 13:14 Where, O *d,* are your plagues?
Jn   5:24 he has crossed over from *d* to life.
Ro   4:25 delivered over to *d* for our sins
     5:12 and in this way *d* came to all men,
     5:14 *d* reigned from the time of Adam
     6: 3 Jesus were baptized into his *d?*
     6:23 For the wages of sin is *d,*
     7:24 me from this body of *d?*
     8:13 put to *d* the misdeeds of the body,
     8:36 your sake we face *d* all day long;
1Co 15:21 For since *d* came through a man,
   15:26 The last enemy to be destroyed is *d*
   15:55 Where, O *d,* is your sting?''
2Ti   1:10 who has destroyed *d* and has
Heb 2:14 him who holds the power of *d*—
1Jn 5:16 There is a sin that leads to *d.*
Rev 1:18 And I hold the keys of *d* and Hades
     2:11 hurt at all by the second *d.*
   20: 6 The second *d* has no power
   20:14 The lake of fire is the second *d.*
   20:14 Then *d* and Hades were thrown
   21: 4 There will be no more *d*
   21: 8 This is the second *d.''*

DEBAUCHERY*

Ro 13:13 not in sexual immorality and *d,*
2Co 12:21 and *d* in which they have indulged.
Gal 5:19 impurity and *d;* idolatry
Eph 5:18 drunk on wine, which leads to *d.*
1Pe 4: 3 living in *d,* lust, drunkenness,

DEBORAH*

  1. Prophetess who led Israel to victory over Canaanites (Jdg 4-5).
  2. Rebekah's nurse (Ge 35:8).

DEBT* (DEBTOR DEBTORS DEBTS)

Dt 15: 3 must cancel any *d* your brother
   24: 6 the upper one—as security for a *d,*
1Sa 22: 2 or in *d* or discontented gathered

Jas 2: 14 claims to have faith but has no *d?*
2: 18 Show me your faith without *d,*
2: 20 faith without *d* is useless?
2: 26 so faith without *d* is dead.
1Pe 2: 12 they may see your good *d*
Rev 2: 19 I know your *d,* your love and faith,
2: 23 each of you according to your *d.*
3: 1 I know your *d;* you have
3: 2 I have not found your *d* complete
3: 8 I know your *d.*
3: 15 I know your *d,* that you are neither
14: 13 for their *d* will follow them."
15: 3 "Great and marvelous are your *d,*

DEEP (DEPTH DEPTHS)
Ge 1: 2 was over the surface of the *d,*
8: 2 Now the springs of the *d*
Ps 42: 7 *D* calls to *d*
Lk 5: 4 to Simon, "Put out into *d* water,
1Co 2: 10 all things, even the *d* things
1Ti 3: 9 hold of the *d* truths of the faith

DEER
Ps 42: 1 As the *d* pants for streams of water,

DEFAMED*
Isa 48: 11 How can I let myself be *d?*

DEFEATED
1Co 6: 7 have been completely *d* already.

DEFEND (DEFENDED DEFENDER DEFENDING DEFENDS DEFENSE)
Ps 72: 4 He will *d* the afflicted
74: 22 Rise up, O God, and *d* your cause;
82: 2 "How long will you *d* the unjust
82: 3 *D* the cause of the weak
119:154 *D* my cause and redeem me;
Pr 31: 9 *d* the rights of the poor and needy
Isa 1: 17 *D* the cause of the fatherless,
1: 23 They do not *d* the cause
Jer 5: 28 they do not *d* the rights of the poor.
50: 34 He will vigorously *d* their cause

DEFENDED (DEFEND)
Jer 22: 16 He *d* the cause of the poor

DEFENDER (DEFEND)
Ex 22: 2 the *d* is not guilty of bloodshed;
Ps 68: 5 to the fatherless, a *d* of widows,
Pr 23: 11 for their *D* is strong;

DEFENDING (DEFEND)
Ps 10: 18 *d* the fatherless and the oppressed,
Ro 2: 15 now accusing, now even *d* them.)
Php 1: 7 or *d* and confirming the gospel,

DEFENDS* (DEFEND)
Dt 10: 18 He *d* the cause of the fatherless
33: 7 With his own hands he *d* his cause.
Isa 51: 22 your God, who *d* his people:

DEFENSE (DEFEND)
Ps 35: 23 Awake, and rise to my *d!*
Php 1: 16 here for the *d* of the gospel.
1Jn 2: 1 speaks to the Father in our *d—*

DEFERRED*
Pr 13: 12 Hope *d* makes the heart sick,

DEFIED
1Sa 17: 45 armies of Israel, whom you have *d.*
1Ki 13: 26 the man of God who *d* the word

DEFILE (DEFILED)
Da 1: 8 Daniel resolved not to *d* himself
Rev 14: 4 are those who did not *d* themselves

DEFILED (DEFILE)
Isa 24: 5 The earth is *d* by its people;

DEFRAUD
Lev 19: 13 Do not *d* your neighbor or rob him.
Mk 10: 19 do not *d,* honor your father

DEITY*
Col 2: 9 of the *D* lives in bodily form,

DELAY
Ecc 5: 4 vow to God, do not *d* in fulfilling it.
Isa 48: 9 my own name's sake I *d* my wrath;
Heb 10: 37 is coming will come and will not *d.*
Rev 10: 6 and said, "There will be no more *d!*

DELICACIES
Ps 141: 4 let me not eat of their *d.*
Pr 23: 3 Do not crave his *d,*
23: 6 do not crave his *d;*

DELICIOUS*
Pr 9: 17 food eaten in secret is *d!"*

DELIGHT* (DELIGHTED DELIGHTFUL DELIGHTING DELIGHTS)
Lev 26: 31 and I will take no *d* in the pleasing
Dt 30: 9 The Lord will again *d* in you
1Sa 2: 1 for I *d* in your deliverance.
15: 22 "Does the Lord *d*
Ne 1: 11 the prayer of your servants who *d*
Job 22: 26 Surely then you will find *d*
27: 10 Will he find *d* in the Almighty?
Ps 1: 2 But his *d* is in the law of the Lord
16: 3 in whom is all my *d.*
35: 9 and *d* in his salvation.
35: 27 those who *d* in my vindication
37: 4 *D* yourself in the Lord
43: 4 to God, my joy and my *d.*
51: 16 You do not *d* in sacrifice,
51: 19 whole burnt offerings to *d* you;
62: 4 they take *d* in lies.
68: 30 Scatter the nations who *d* in war.
111: 2 by all who *d* in them.
112: 1 who finds great *d* in his commands.
119: 16 I *d* in your decrees;
119: 24 Your statutes are my *d;*
119: 35 for there I find *d.*
119: 47 for I *d* in your commands
119: 70 but I *d* in your law.
119: 77 for your law is my *d.*
119: 92 If your law had not been my *d,*
119:143 but your commands are my *d.*
119:174 and your law is my *d.*
147: 10 nor his *d* in the legs of a man;
149: 4 For the Lord takes *d*
Pr 1: 22 How long will mockers *d*
2: 14 who *d* in doing wrong
8: 30 I was filled with *d* day after day,
11: 1 but accurate weights are his *d.*
29: 17 he will bring *d* to your soul.
Ecc 2: 10 My heart took *d* in all my work,
SS 1: 4 We rejoice and *d* in you;
2: 3 I *d* to sit in his shade,
Isa 5: 7 are the garden of his *d.*
11: 3 he will *d* in the fear of the Lord.
13: 17 and have no *d* in gold.
32: 14 the *d* of donkeys, a pasture
42: 1 my chosen one in whom I *d;*
55: 2 and your soul will *d* in the richest
58: 13 if you call the Sabbath a *d*
61: 10 I *d* greatly in the Lord;
62: 4 for the Lord will take *d* in you,
65: 18 for I will create Jerusalem to be a *d*
65: 19 and take *d* in my people;
66: 3 their souls *d* in their abominations;
66: 11 *d* in her overflowing abundance."
Jer 9: 24 for in these I *d,*"
15: 16 they were my joy and my heart's *d,*
31: 20 the child in whom I *d?*
49: 25 the town in which I *d?*
Eze 24: 16 away from you the *d* of your eyes.
24: 21 in which you take pride, the *d*
24: 25 and glory, the *d* of their eyes,
Hos 7: 3 *d* the king with their wickedness,
Mic 1: 16 for the children in whom you *d;*
7: 18 but *d* to show mercy.
Zep 3: 17 He will take great *d* in you,
Mt 12: 18 the one I love, in whom I *d;*
Mk 12: 37 large crowd listened to him with *d.*
Lk 1: 14 He will be a joy and *d* to you,
Ro 7: 22 in my inner being I *d* in God's law;
1Co 13: 6 Love does not *d* in evil
2Co 12: 10 for Christ's sake, I *d* in weaknesses,
Col 2: 5 and *d* to see how orderly you are

DELIGHTED (DELIGHT)
2Sa 22: 20 he rescued me because he *d* in me.

1Ki 10: 9 who has *d* in you and placed you
2Ch 9: 8 who has *d* in you and placed you
Ps 18: 19 he rescued me because he *d* in me.
Lk 13: 17 but the people were *d* with all

DELIGHTFUL* (DELIGHT)
Ps 16: 6 surely I have a *d* inheritance.
SS 1: 2 for your love is more *d* than wine.
Mal 3: 12 for yours will be a *d* land,"

DELIGHTING* (DELIGHT)
Pr 8: 31 and *d* in mankind.

DELIGHTS (DELIGHT)
Est 6: 6 for the man the king *d* to honor?"
Ps 22: 8 since he *d* in him."
35: 27 who *d* in the well-being
36: 8 from your river of *d.*
37: 23 if the Lord *d* in a man's way
147: 11 the Lord *d* in those who fear him,
Pr 3: 12 as a father the son he *d* in.
10: 23 of understanding *d* in wisdom.
11: 20 he *d* in those whose ways are
12: 22 but he *d* in men who are truthful.
14: 35 A king *d* in a wise servant,
18: 2 but *d* in airing his own opinions.
23: 24 he who has a wise son *d* in him.
Col 2: 18 Do not let anyone who *d*

DELILAH*
Woman who betrayed Samson (Jdg 16:4-22).

DELIVER (DELIVERANCE DELIVERED DELIVERER DELIVERS)
Dt 32: 39 and no one can *d* out of my hand.
Ps 22: 8 Let him *d* him,
72: 12 For he will *d* the needy who cry out
79: 9 *d* us and forgive our sins
109: 21 of the goodness of your love, *d* me.
119:170 *d* me according to your promise.
Mt 6: 13 but *d* us from the evil one.'
2Co 1: 10 hope that he will continue to *d* us,

DELIVERANCE (DELIVER)
1Sa 2: 1 for I delight in your *d.*
Ps 3: 8 From the Lord comes *d.*
32: 7 and surround me with songs of *d.*
33: 17 A horse is a vain hope for *d;*
Ob : 17 But on Mount Zion will be *d;*

DELIVERED (DELIVER)
Ps 34: 4 he *d* me from all my fears.
107: 6 and he *d* them from their distress.
116: 8 have *d* my soul from death,
Da 12: 1 written in the book—will be *d.*
Ro 4: 25 He was *d* over to death for our sins

DELIVERER* (DELIVER)
Jdg 3: 9 for them a *d,* Othniel son of Kenaz,
3: 15 and he gave them a *d*— Ehud,
2Sa 22: 2 is my rock, my fortress and my *d;*
2Ki 13: 5 The Lord provided a *d* for Israel,
Ps 18: 2 is my rock, my fortress and my *d;*
40: 17 You are my help and my *d;*
70: 5 You are my help and my *d;*
140: 7 O Sovereign Lord, my strong *d,*
144: 2 my stronghold and my *d,*
Ac 7: 35 sent to be their ruler and *d*
Ro 11: 26 "The *d* will come from Zion;

DELIVERS (DELIVER)
Ps 34: 17 he *d* them from all their troubles.
34: 19 but the Lord *d* him from them all
37: 40 The Lord helps them and *d* them
37: 40 he *d* them from the wicked

DELUSION*
2Th 2: 11 God sends them a powerful *d*

DEMAND (DEMANDED)
Lk 6: 30 belongs to you, do not *d* it back.

DEMANDED (DEMAND)
Lk 12: 20 This very night your life will be *d*
12: 48 been given much, much will be *d;*

DEMETRIUS
Ac 19: 24 A silversmith named *D,* who made

DEMON* (DEMONS)

Mt   9: 33 And when the *d* was driven out,
     11: 18 and they say, 'He has a *d*.'
     17: 18 Jesus rebuked the *d*, and it came
Mk   7: 26 to drive the *d* out of her daughter.
     7: 29 the *d* has left your daughter.''
     7: 30 lying on the bed, and the *d* gone.
Lk   4: 33 there was a man possessed by a *d*,
     4: 35 Then the *d* threw the man
     7: 33 wine, and you say, 'He has a *d*.'
     8: 29 driven by the *d* into solitary places.
     9: 42 the *d* threw him to the ground
     11: 14 When the *d* left, the man who had
     11: 14 was driving out a *d* that was mute.
Jn   8: 49 ''I am not possessed by a *d*,''
     10: 21 Can a *d* open the eyes of the blind
     10: 21 sayings of a man possessed by a *d*.

DEMON-POSSESSED* (DEMON-POSSESSION)

Mt   4: 24 those suffering severe pain, the *d*,
     8: 16 many who were *d* were brought
     8: 28 two *d* men coming
     8: 33 what had happened to the *d* men.
     9: 32 man who was *d* and could not talk
     12: 22 they brought him a *d* man who was
Mk   1: 32 brought to Jesus all the sick and *d*,
     5: 16 what had happened to the *d* man—
     5: 18 the man who had been *d* begged
Lk   8: 27 met by a *d* man from the town.
     8: 36 the people how the *d* man had been
Jn   7: 20 ''You are *d*,'' the crowd answered.
     8: 48 that you are a Samaritan and *d*?''
     8: 52 ''Now we know that you are *d*!'
     10: 20 Many of them said, ''He is *d*.
Ac   19: 13 Jesus over those who were *d*.

DEMON-POSSESSION* (DEMON-POSSESSED)

Mt   15: 22 is suffering terribly from *d*.''

DEMONS* (DEMON)

Dt   32: 17 to *d*, which are not God—
Ps 106: 37 and their daughters to *d*.
Mt   7: 22 and in your name drive out *d*
     8: 31 *d* begged Jesus, ''If you drive us
     9: 34 prince of *d* that he drives out.''
     10: 8 who have leprosy, drive out *d*.
     12: 24 of *d*, that this fellow drives out
     12: 24 that this fellow drives out *d*.''
     12: 27 And if I drive out *d* by Beelzebub,
     12: 28 if I drive out *d* by the Spirit of God,
Mk   1: 34 He also drove out many *d*,
     1: 34 but he would not let the *d* speak
     1: 39 their synagogues and driving out *d*.
     3: 15 to have authority to drive out *d*.
     3: 22 the prince of *d* he is driving out *d*.''
     5: 12 The *d* begged Jesus, ''Send us
     5: 15 possessed by the legion of *d*,
     6: 13 They drove out many *d*
     9: 38 ''we saw a man driving out *d*
     16: 9 out of whom he had driven seven *d*
     16: 17 In my name they will drive out *d*;
Lk   4: 41 *d* came out of many people,
     8: 2 from whom seven *d* had come out;
     8: 30 because many *d* had gone into him.
     8: 32 The *d* begged Jesus to let them go
     8: 33 When the *d* came out of the man,
     8: 35 from whom the *d* had gone out,
     8: 38 from whom the *d* had gone out
     9: 1 and authority to drive out all *d*
     9: 49 ''we saw a man driving out *d*
     10: 17 the *d* submit to us in your name.''
     11: 15 the prince of *d*, he is driving out *d*.''
     11: 18 you claim that I drive out *d*
     11: 19 Now if I drive out *d* by Beelzebub,
     11: 20 if I drive out *d* by the finger of God,
     13: 32 'I will drive out *d* and heal people
Ro   8: 38 neither angels nor *d*, neither
1Co 10: 20 of pagans are offered to *d*,
     10: 20 you to be participants with *d*.
     10: 21 of the Lord and the cup of *d* too;
     10: 21 the Lord's table and the table of *d*.
1Ti   4: 1 spirits and things taught by *d*.
Jas   2: 19 Good! Even the *d* believe that—
Rev   9: 20 they did not stop worshiping *d*,
     16: 14 of *d* performing miraculous signs,

Rev 18: 2 She has become a home for *d*

DEMONSTRATE* (DEMONSTRATES DEMONSTRATION)

Ro   3: 25 He did this to *d* his justice,
     3: 26 he did it to *d* his justice

DEMONSTRATES* (DEMONSTRATE)

Ro   5: 8 God *d* his own love for us in this:

DEMONSTRATION* (DEMONSTRATE)

1Co   2: 4 but with a *d* of the Spirit's power,

DEN

Da   6: 16 and threw him into the lions' *d*.
Mt   21: 13 you are making it a '*d* of robbers.' ''
Mk   11: 17 you have made it 'a *d* of robbers.' ''
Lk   19: 46 but you have made it 'a *d* of robbers

DENARII* (DENARIUS)

Mt   18: 28 who owed him a hundred *d*,
Lk   7: 41 One owed him five hundred *d*,

DENARIUS (DENARII)

Mt   20: 2 agreed to pay them a *d* for the day
Mk   12: 15 Bring me a *d* and let me look at it.''

DENIED (DENY)

Mt   26: 70 But he *d* it before them all.
Mk   14: 68 But he *d* it.
Lk   22: 57 But he *d* it.
Jn   18: 25 He *d* it, saying, ''I am not.''
1Ti   5: 8 he has *d* the faith and is worse
Rev   3: 8 my word and have not *d* my name.

DENIES (DENY)

1Jn   2: 22 It is the man who *d* that Jesus is
     2: 23 No one who *d* the Son has

DENY (DENIED DENIES DENYING)

Ex   23: 6 ''Do not *d* justice to your poor
Job   27: 5 till I die, I will not *d* my integrity.
Isa   5: 23 but *d* justice to the innocent.
La   3: 35 to *d* a man his rights
Am   2: 7 and *d* justice to the oppressed.
Mt   16: 24 he must *d* himself and take up his
Mk   8: 34 he must *d* himself and take up his
Lk   9: 23 he must *d* himself and take up his
     22: 34 you will *d* three times that you
Ac   4: 16 miracle, and we cannot *d* it.
Tit   1: 16 but by their actions they *d* him.
Jas   3: 14 do not boast about it or *d* the truth.
Jude   : 4 *d* Jesus Christ our only Sovereign

DENYING* (DENY)

Eze 22: 29 mistreat the alien, *d* them justice.
2Ti   3: 5 a form of godliness but *d* its power.
2Pe   2: 1 *d* the sovereign Lord who bought

DEPART (DEPARTED DEPARTS DEPARTURE)

Ge   49: 10 The scepter will not *d* from Judah,
Job   1: 21 and naked I will *d*.
Mt   25: 41 '*D* from me, you who are cursed,
Php   1: 23 I desire to *d* and be with Christ,

DEPARTED (DEPART)

1Sa   4: 21 ''The glory has *d* from Israel''—
Ps 119:102 I have not *d* from your laws,

DEPARTS (DEPART)

Ecc   5: 15 and as he comes, so he *d*.

DEPARTURE (DEPART)

Lk   9: 31 spoke about his *d*, which he was
2Ti   4: 6 and the time has come for my *d*.
2Pe   1: 15 after my *d* you will always be able

DEPEND

Ps   62: 7 My salvation and my honor *d*

DEPOSES*

Da   2: 21 he sets up kings and *d* them.

DEPOSIT

Mt   25: 27 money on *d* with the bankers,
Lk   19: 23 didn't you put my money on *d*,
2Co   1: 22 put his Spirit in our hearts as a *d*,
     5: 5 and has given us the Spirit as a *d*,

Eph   1: 14 who is a *d* guaranteeing our
2Ti   1: 14 Guard the good *d* that was

DEPRAVED* (DEPRAVITY)

Eze 16: 47 ways you soon became more *d*
     23: 11 and prostitution she was more *d*
Ro   1: 28 he gave them over to a *d* mind,
Php   2: 15 fault in a crooked and *d* generation,
2Ti   3: 8 oppose the truth—men of *d* minds,

DEPRAVITY* (DEPRAVED)

Ro   1: 29 of wickedness, evil, greed and *d*.
2Pe   2: 19 they themselves are slaves of *d*—

DEPRIVE

Dt   24: 17 Do not *d* the alien or the fatherless
Pr   18: 5 or to *d* the innocent of justice.
     31: 5 *d* all the oppressed of their rights.
Isa   10: 2 to *d* the poor of their rights
     29: 21 with false testimony *d* the innocent
La   3: 36 to *d* a man of justice—
1Co   7: 5 Do not *d* each other
     9: 15 die than have anyone *d* me

DEPTH (DEEP)

Ro   8: 39 any powers, neither height nor *d*,
     11: 33 the *d* of the riches of the wisdom

DEPTHS (DEEP)

Ps 130: 1 Out of the *d* I cry to you, O LORD;

DERIDES*

Pr   11: 12 who lacks judgment *d* his neighbor,

DERIVES*

Eph   3: 15 in heaven and on earth *d* its name

DESCEND (DESCENDED DESCENDING)

Ro   10: 7 ''or 'Who will *d* into the deep?' ''

DESCENDED (DESCEND)

Eph   4: 9 except that he also *d* to the lower,
Heb   7: 14 For it is clear that our Lord *d*

DESCENDING (DESCEND)

Ge   28: 12 of God were ascending and *d* on it.
Mt   3: 16 the Spirit of God *d* like a dove
Mk   1: 10 and the Spirit *d* on him like a dove.
Jn   1: 51 and *d* on the Son of Man.''

DESECRATING*

Ne   13: 17 you are doing—*d* the Sabbath day?
     13: 18 against Israel by *d* the Sabbath.''
Isa   56: 2 who keeps the Sabbath without *d* it
     56: 6 who keeps the Sabbath without *d* it
Eze 44: 7 *d* my temple while you offered me

DESERT

Nu   32: 13 wander in the *d* forty years,
Dt   8: 16 He gave you manna to eat in the *d*,
     29: 5 years that I led you through the *d*,
Ne   9: 19 you did not abandon them in the *d*.
Ps   78: 19 ''Can God spread a table in the *d*?
     78: 52 led them like sheep through the *d*.
Pr   21: 19 Better to live in a *d*
Isa   32: 2 like streams of water in the *d*
     32: 15 and the *d* becomes a fertile field,
     35: 6 and streams in the *d*.
     43: 20 because I provide water in the *d*
Mk   1: 3 ''a voice of one calling in the *d*,
     1: 13 and he was in the *d* forty days,
Rev 12: 6 fled into the *d* to a place prepared

DESERTED (DESERTS)

Ezr   9: 9 our God has not *d* us
Mt   26: 56 all the disciples *d* him and fled.
2Ti   1: 15 in the province of Asia has *d* me,

DESERTING (DESERTS)

Gal   1: 6 are so quickly *d* the one who called

DESERTS (DESERTED DESERTING)

Zec 11: 17 who *d* the flock!

DESERVE* (DESERVED DESERVES)

Ge   40: 15 to *d* being put in a dungeon.''
Lev 26: 21 times over, as your sins *d*.
Jdg 20: 10 it can give them what they *d*
1Sa 26: 16 you and your men *d* to die,

1Ki 2: 26 You *d* to die, but I will not put you
Ps 28: 4 bring back upon them what they *d*.
     94: 2 pay back to the proud what they *d*.
    103: 10 he does not treat us as our sins *d*
Pr   3: 27 from those who *d* it,
Ecc 8: 14 men who get what the righteous *d*,
     8: 14 men who get what the wicked *d*,
Isa 66: 6 repaying his enemies all they *d*.
Jer 14: 16 out on them the calamity they *d*.
    17: 10 according to what his deeds *d*.''
    21: 14 I will punish you as your deeds *d*.
    32: 19 to his conduct and as his deeds *d*.
    49: 12 ''If those who do not *d*
La   3: 64 Pay them back what they *d*,
Eze 16: 59 I will deal with you as you *d*,
Zec 1: 3 to us what our ways and practices *d*
Mt   8: 8 I do not *d* to have you come
     22: 8 those I invited did not *d* to come.
Lk   7: 6 for I do not *d* to have you come
    23: 15 he has done nothing to *d* death.
    23: 41 for we are getting what our deeds *d*
Ro   1: 32 those who do such things *d* death,
1Co 15: 9 even *d* to be called an apostle,
    16: 18 Such men *d* recognition.
2Co 11: 15 end will be what their actions *d*.
Rev 16: 6 blood to drink as they *d*.''

DESERVED* (DESERVE)

2Sa 19: 28 descendants *d* nothing
Ezr 9: 13 less than our sins have *d*
Job 33: 27 but I did not get what I *d*.
Ac 23: 29 charge against him that *d* death
Ro   3: 8 Their condemnation is *d*.

DESERVES* (DESERVE)

Nu 35: 31 the life of a murderer, who *d* to die.
Dt 25: 2 If the guilty man *d* to be beaten,
    25: 2 the number of lashes his crime *d*,
Jdg 9: 16 and if you have treated him as he *d*
2Sa 12: 5 the man who did this *d* to die!
Job 34: 11 upon him what his conduct *d*.
Jer 51: 6 he will pay her what she *d*.
Lk   7: 4 ''This man *d* to have you do this,
    10: 7 for the worker *d* his wages.
Ac 26: 31 is not doing anything that *d* death
1Ti 1: 15 saying that *d* full acceptance
     4: 9 saying that *d* full acceptance
     5: 18 and ''The worker *d* his wages.''
Heb 10: 29 severely do you think a man *d*

DESIGNATED

Lk   6: 13 also *d* apostles: Simon (whom he
Heb 5: 10 and was *d* by God to be high priest

DESIRABLE* (DESIRE)

Ge   3: 6 and also *d* for gaining wisdom,
Pr 22: 1 A good name is more *d*
Jer 3: 19 and give you a *d* land,

DESIRE* (DESIRABLE DESIRED DESIRES)

Ge   3: 16 Your *d* will be for your husband,
Dt   5: 21 You shall not set your *d*
1Sa 9: 20 to whom is all the *d* of Israel turned
2Sa 19: 38 anything you *d* from me I will do
    23: 5 and grant me my every *d*?
1Ch 29: 18 keep this *d* in the hearts
2Ch 1: 11 ''Since this is your heart's *d*
     9: 8 and his *d* to uphold them forever,
Job 13: 3 But I *d* to speak to the Almighty
    21: 14 We have no *d* to know your ways.
Ps 10: 17 O Lord, the *d* of the afflicted;
    20: 4 May he give you the *d*
    21: 2 You have granted him the *d*
    27: 12 me over to the *d* of my foes,
    40: 6 Sacrifice and offering you did not *d*
    40: 8 I *d* to do your will, O my God;
    40: 14 may all who *d* my ruin
    41: 2 him to the *d* of his foes.
    51: 6 Surely you *d* truth
    70: 2 may all who *d* my ruin
    73: 25 earth has nothing I *d* besides you
Pr   3: 15 nothing you *d* can compare
     8: 11 and nothing you *d* can compare
    10: 24 what the righteous *d* will be
    11: 23 The *d* of the righteous ends only
    12: 12 The wicked *d* the plunder
    17: 16 since he has no *d* to get wisdom?

Pr 24: 1 do not *d* their company;
Ecc 12: 5 and *d* no longer is stirred.
SS   6: 12 my *d* set me among the royal
     7: 10 and his *d* is for me.
Isa 26: 8 are the *d* of our hearts.
    53: 2 appearance that we should *d* him.
    55: 11 but will accomplish what I *d*
Eze 24: 25 delight of their eyes, their heart's *d*,
Hos 6: 6 For I *d* mercy, not sacrifice,
Mic 7: 3 the powerful dictate what they *d*—
Mal 3: 1 whom you *d*, will come,'' says
Mt   9: 13 learn what this means: 'I *d* mercy,
    12: 7 what these words mean, 'I *d* mercy,
Jn   8: 44 want to carry out your father's *d*
Ro   7: 8 in me every kind of covetous *d*.
     7: 18 For I have the *d* to do what is good,
     9: 16 depend on man's *d* or effort,
    10: 1 my heart's *d* and prayer to God
1Co 12: 31 But eagerly *d* the greater gifts.
    14: 1 and eagerly *d* spiritual gifts,
2Co 8: 10 but also to have the *d* to do so.
     8: 13 Our *d* is not that others might be
Php 1: 23 I *d* to depart and be with Christ,
Heb 10: 5 Sacrifice and offering you did not *d*
    10: 8 and sin offerings you did not *d*,
    13: 18 *d* to live honorably in every way.
Jas 1: 14 by his own evil *d*, he is dragged
     1: 15 Then, after *d* has conceived,
2Pe 2: 10 of those who follow the corrupt *d*

DESIRED (DESIRE)

Hag 2: 7 and the *d* of all nations will come,
Lk 22: 15 ''I have eagerly *d* to eat this

DESIRES* (DESIRE)

Ge   4: 7 at your door; it *d* to have you,
    41: 16 will give Pharaoh the answer he *d*.''
2Sa 3: 21 rule over all that your heart *d*.''
1Ki 11: 37 rule over all that your heart *d*;
Job 17: 11 and so are the *d* of my heart.
    31: 16 ''If I have denied the *d* of the poor
Ps 34: 12 and *d* to see many good days,
    37: 4 he will give you the *d* of your heart.
    103: 5 who satisfies your *d* with good things,
    140: 8 do not grant the wicked their *d*,
    145: 16 satisfy the *d* of every living thing.
    145: 19 He fulfills the *d* of those who fear
Pr 11: 6 the unfaithful are trapped by evil *d*.
    13: 4 *d* of the diligent are fully satisfied.
    19: 22 What a man *d* is unfailing love;
Ecc 6: 2 so that he lacks nothing his heart *d*,
SS   2: 7 or awaken love / until it so *d*.
     3: 5 or awaken love / until it so *d*.
     8: 4 or awaken love / until it so *d*.
Hab 2: 5 are not upright—
Mk   4: 19 and the *d* for other things come in
Ro   1: 24 over in the sinful *d* of their hearts
     6: 12 body so that you obey its evil *d*.
     8: 5 set on what that nature *d*;
     8: 5 set on what the Spirit *d*.
    13: 14 to gratify the *d* of the sinful nature.
Gal 5: 16 and you will not gratify the *d*
     5: 17 the sinful nature *d* what is contrary
     5: 24 nature with its passions and *d*.
Eph 2: 3 following its *d* and thoughts.
     4: 22 being corrupted by its deceitful *d*;
Col 3: 5 impurity, lust, evil *d* and greed,
1Ti 3: 1 an overseer, he *d* a noble task.
     5: 11 their sensual *d* overcome their
     6: 9 and harmful *d* that plunge men
2Ti 2: 22 Flee the evil *d* of youth,
     3: 6 are swayed by all kinds of evil *d*,
     4: 3 Instead, to suit their own *d*,
Jas 1: 20 about the righteous life that God *d*.
     4: 1 from your *d* that battle within you?
1Pe 1: 14 conform to the evil *d* you had
     2: 11 to abstain from sinful *d*, which war
     4: 2 of his earthly life for evil human *d*,
2Pe 1: 4 in the world caused by evil *d*.
     2: 18 to the lustful *d* of sinful human
     3: 3 and following their own evil *d*.
1Jn 2: 17 The world and its *d* pass away,
Jude : 16 they follow their own evil *d*;
     : 18 will follow their own ungodly *d*.''

DESOLATE (DESOLATION)

Isa 54: 1 are the children of the *d* woman
Gal 4: 27 are the children of the *d* woman

DESOLATION (DESOLATE)

Da 11: 31 up the abomination that causes *d*.
    12: 11 abomination that causes *d* is set up,
Mt 24: 15 'the abomination that causes *d*,'

DESPAIR (DESPAIRED)

Isa 61: 3 instead of a spirit of *d*
2Co 4: 8 perplexed, but not in *d*; persecuted,

DESPAIRED* (DESPAIR)

2Co 1: 8 ability to endure, so that we *d*

DESPERATE*

2Sa 12: 18 He may do something *d*.''
Ps 60: 3 have shown your people *d* times;
    79: 8 for we are in *d* need.
    142: 6 for I am in *d* need;

DESPISE (DESPISED DESPISES)

2Sa 12: 9 Why did you *d* the word
Job 5: 17 so do not *d* the discipline
    36: 5 God is mighty, but does not *d* men;
    42: 6 Therefore I *d* myself
Ps 51: 17 O God, you will not *d*.
    102: 17 he will not *d* their plea.
Pr   1: 7 but fools *d* wisdom and discipline.
     3: 11 do not *d* the Lord's discipline
     6: 30 Men do not *d* a thief if he steals
    23: 22 do not *d* your mother
Jer 14: 21 of your name do not *d* us;
Am   5: 10 and *d* him who tells the truth.
     5: 21 ''I hate, I *d* your religious feasts;
Mt   6: 24 devoted to the one and *d* the other.
Lk 16: 13 devoted to the one and *d* the other.
1Co 11: 22 Or do you *d* the church of God
Tit 2: 15 Do not let anyone *d* you.
2Pe 2: 10 of the sinful nature and *d* authority.

DESPISED (DESPISE)

Ge 25: 34 So Esau *d* his birthright.
Ps 22: 6 by men and *d* by the people.
Pr 12: 8 but men with warped minds are *d*.
Isa 53: 3 He was *d* and rejected by men,
    53: 3 he was *d*, and we esteemed him not
1Co 1: 28 of this world and the *d* things—

DESPISES (DESPISE)

Pr 14: 21 He who *d* his neighbor sins,
    15: 20 but a foolish man *d* his mother.
    15: 32 who ignores discipline *d* himself,
Zec 4: 10 ''Who *d* the day of small things?

DESTINED (DESTINY)

Lk   2: 34 ''This child is *d* to cause the falling
1Co 2: 7 and that God *d* for our glory
Col 2: 22 These are all *d* to perish with use,
1Th 3: 3 know quite well that we were *d*
Heb 9: 27 Just as man is *d* to die once,
1Pe 2: 8 which is also what they were *d* for.

DESTINY* (DESTINED PREDESTINED)

Job 8: 13 Such is the *d* of all who forget God;
Ps 73: 17 then I understood their final *d*.
Ecc 7: 2 for death is the *d* of every man;
     9: 2 share a common *d*— the righteous
     9: 3 the sun: The same *d* overtakes all.
Isa 65: 11 and fill bowls of mixed wine for *D*,
Php 3: 19 Their *d* is destruction, their god is

DESTITUTE

Ps 102: 17 to the prayer of the *d*;
Pr 31: 8 for the rights of all who are *d*.
Heb 11: 37 *d*, persecuted and mistreated—

DESTROY (DESTROYED DESTROYING DESTROYS DESTRUCTION DESTRUCTIVE)

Ge   6: 17 floodwaters on the earth to *d* all life
     9: 11 will there be a flood to *d* the earth.''
Pr   1: 32 complacency of fools will *d* them;
Mt 10: 28 of the One who can *d* both soul
Mk 14: 58 'I will *d* this man-made temple
Lk   4: 34 to *d* us? I know who you are—
Jn 10: 10 only to steal and kill and *d*;
Ac   8: 3 But Saul began to *d* the church.
Rev 11: 18 destroying those who *d* the earth.''

DESTROYED (DESTROY)

Dt 8: 19 you today that you will surely be *d*.
Job 19: 26 And after my skin has been *d*.
Pr 6: 15 he will suddenly be *d—*
11: 3 the unfaithful are *d*
21: 28 listens to him will be *d* forever.
29: 1 will suddenly be *d—*
Isa 55: 13 which will not be *d*."
Da 2: 44 up a kingdom that will never be *d*,
6: 26 his kingdom will not be *d*.
1Co 5: 5 so that the sinful nature may be *d*
8: 11 for whom Christ died, is *d*
15: 24 Father after he has *d* all dominion,
15: 26 The last enemy to be *d* is death.
2Co 4: 9 abandoned; struck down, but not *d*.
5: 1 if the earthly tent we live in is *d*,
Gal 5: 15 or you will be *d* by each other.
Eph 2: 14 the two one and has *d* the barrier,
2Ti 1: 10 who has *d* death and has brought
Heb 10: 39 of those who shrink back and are *d*,
2Pe 2: 12 born only to be caught and *d*,
3: 10 the elements will be *d* by fire,
3: 11 Since everything will be *d*
Jude : 5 later those who did not believe.
: 11 have been *d* in Korah's rebellion.

DESTROYING (DESTROY)

Jer 23: 1 "Woe to the shepherds who are *d*

DESTROYS (DESTROY)

Pr 6: 32 whoever does so *d* himself.
11: 9 mouth the godless *d* his neighbor,
18: 9 is brother to one who *d*.
28: 24 he is partner to him who *d*.
Ecc 9: 18 but one sinner *d* much good.
1Co 3: 17 If anyone *d* God's temple,

DESTRUCTION (DESTROY)

Nu 32: 15 and you will be the cause of their *d*
Pr 16: 18 Pride goes before *d*,
17: 19 he who builds a high gate invites *d*.
24: 22 for those two will send sudden *d*
Hos 13: 14 Where, O grave, is your *d*?
Mt 7: 13 broad is the road that leads to *d*,
Lk 6: 49 it collapsed and its *d* was complete
Jn 17: 12 except the one doomed to *d*
Ro 9: 22 of his wrath—prepared for *d*?
Gal 6: 8 from that nature will reap *d*;
Php 3: 19 Their destiny is *d*, their god is their
1Th 5: 3 *d* will come on them suddenly,
2Th 1: 9 punished with everlasting *d*
2: 3 is revealed, the man doomed to *d*.
1Ti 6: 9 that plunge men into ruin and *d*.
2Pe 2: 1 bringing swift *d* on themselves.
2: 3 and their *d* has not been sleeping.
3: 7 of judgment and *d* of ungodly men.
3: 12 That day will bring about the *d*
3: 16 other Scriptures, to their own *d*.
Rev 17: 8 out of the Abyss and go to his *d*.
17: 11 to the seven and is going to his *d*.

DESTRUCTIVE (DESTROY)

2Pe 2: 1 will secretly introduce *d* heresies,

DETERMINED (DETERMINES)

Job 14: 5 Man's days are *d*;
Isa 14: 26 This is the plan *d* for the whole
Da 11: 36 for what has been *d* must take place
Ac 17: 26 and he *d* the times set for them

DETERMINES* (DETERMINED)

Ps 147: 4 He *d* the number of the stars
Pr 16: 9 but the LORD *d* his steps.
1Co 12: 11 them to each one, just as he *d*.

DETEST (DETESTABLE DETESTED DETESTS)

Lev 11: 10 in the water—you are to *d*.
Pr 8: 7 for my lips *d* wickedness.
13: 19 but fools *d* turning from evil.
16: 12 Kings *d* wrongdoing,
24: 9 and men *d* a mocker.
29: 27 The righteous *d* the dishonest;
29: 27 the wicked *d* the upright.

DETESTABLE (DETEST)

Pr 6: 16 seven that are *d* to him:
21: 27 The sacrifice of the wicked is *d—*

Pr 28: 9 even his prayers are *d*.
Isa 1: 13 Your incense is *d* to me.
41: 24 he who chooses you is *d*.
44: 19 Shall I make a *d* thing
Jer 44: 4 'Do not do this *d* thing that I hate!'
Eze 8: 13 doing things that are even more *d*.
Lk 16: 15 among men is *d* in God's sight.
Tit 1: 16 They are *d*, disobedient
1Pe 4: 3 orgies, carousing and *d* idolatry.

DETESTED* (DETEST)

Zec 11: 8 The flock *d* me, and I grew weary

DETESTS* (DETEST)

Dt 22: 5 LORD your God *d* anyone who
23: 18 the LORD your God *d* them both.
25: 16 LORD your God *d* anyone who
Pr 3: 32 for the LORD *d* a perverse man
11: 20 The LORD *d* men
12: 22 The LORD *d* lying lips,
15: 8 The LORD *d* the sacrifice
15: 9 The LORD *d* the way
15: 26 The LORD *d* the thoughts
16: 5 The LORD *d* all the proud of heart
17: 15 The LORD *d* them both.
20: 10 the LORD *d* them both.
20: 23 The LORD *d* differing weights.

DEVIATE*

2Ch 8: 15 They did not *d* from the king's

DEVICES*

Ps 81: 12 to follow their own *d*.

DEVIL* (DEVIL'S)

Mt 4: 1 the desert to be tempted by the *d*.
4: 5 the *d* took him to the holy city
4: 8 *d* took him to a very high mountain
4: 11 the *d* left him, and angels came
13: 39 the enemy who sows them is the *d*
25: 41 the eternal fire prepared for the *d*
Lk 4: 2 forty days he was tempted by the *d*.
4: 3 *d* said to him, "If you are the Son
4: 5 The *d* led him up to a high place
4: 9 The *d* led him to Jerusalem
4: 13 When the *d* had finished all this
8: 12 then the *d* comes and takes away
Jn 6: 70 of you is a *d*!" (He meant Judas,
8: 44 You belong to your father, the *d*,
13: 2 the *d* had already prompted Judas
Ac 10: 38 were under the power of the *d*,
13: 10 "You are a child of the *d*
Eph 4: 27 and do not give the *d* a foothold.
1Ti 3: 6 under the same judgment as the *d*.
2Ti 2: 26 and escape from the trap of the *d*,
Heb 2: 14 the *d*— and free those who all their
Jas 3: 15 but is earthly, unspiritual, of the *d*.
4: 7 Resist the *d*, and he will flee
1Pe 5: 8 Your enemy the *d* prowls
1Jn 3: 8 because the *d* has been sinning
3: 8 who does what is sinful is of the *d*,
3: 10 and who the children of the *d* are:
Jude : 9 with the *d* about the body of Moses
Rev 2: 10 the *d* will put some of you in prison
12: 9 that ancient serpent called the *d*
12: 12 the *d* has gone down to you!
20: 2 that ancient serpent, who is the *d*,
20: 10 And the *d*, who deceived them,

DEVIL'S* (DEVIL)

Eph 6: 11 stand against the *d* schemes.
1Ti 3: 7 into disgrace and into the *d* trap.
1Jn 3: 8 was to destroy the *d* work.

DEVILS see DEMONS

DEVIOUS*

Pr 2: 15 and who are *d* in their ways.
14: 2 he whose ways are *d* despises him.
21: 8 The way of the guilty is *d*,

DEVOTE* (DEVOTED DEVOTING DEVOTION DEVOUT)

1Ch 22: 19 Now *d* your heart and soul
2Ch 31: 4 Levites so they could *d* themselves
Job 11: 13 "Yet if you *d* your heart to him
Jer 30: 21 for who is he who will *d* himself
Mic 4: 13 You will *d* their ill-gotten gains
1Co 7: 5 so that you may *d* yourselves

Col 4: 2 *D* yourselves to prayer, being
1Ti 1: 4 nor to *d* themselves to myths
4: 13 *d* yourself to the public reading
Tit 3: 8 may be careful to *d* themselves
3: 14 people must learn to *d* themselves

DEVOTED (DEVOTE)

1Ki 11: 4 and his heart was not fully *d*
Ezr 7: 10 For Ezra had *d* himself to the study
Ps 86: 2 Guard my life, for I am *d* to you.
Mt 6: 24 or he will be *d* to the one
Mk 7: 11 from me is Corban' (that is, a gift *d*
Ac 2: 42 They *d* themselves
18: 5 Paul *d* himself exclusively
Ro 12: 10 Be *d* to one another
1Co 7: 34 Her aim is to be *d* to the Lord
16: 15 and they have *d* themselves
2Co 7: 12 for yourselves how *d* to us you are.

DEVOTING* (DEVOTE)

1Ti 5: 10 *d* herself to all kinds of good deeds.

DEVOTION* (DEVOTE)

2Ki 20: 3 and with wholehearted *d* and have
1Ch 28: 9 and serve him with wholehearted *d*
29: 3 in my *d* to the temple
29: 19 son Solomon the wholehearted *d*
2Ch 32: 32 and his acts of *d* are written
35: 26 of Josiah's reign and his acts of *d*,
Job 6: 14 despairing man should have the *d*
15: 4 and hinder *d* to God.
Isa 38: 3 and with wholehearted *d* and have
Jer 2: 2 "I remember the *d* of your youth,
Eze 33: 31 With their mouths they express *d*,
1Co 7: 35 way in undivided *d* to the Lord.
2Co 11: 3 from your sincere and pure *d*.

DEVOUR (DEVOURED DEVOURING DEVOURS)

2Sa 2: 26 "Must the sword *d* forever?
Mk 12: 40 They *d* widows' houses
1Pe 5: 8 lion looking for someone to *d*.

DEVOURED (DEVOUR)

Jer 30: 16 But all who devour you will be *d*;

DEVOURING (DEVOUR)

Gal 5: 15 keep on biting and *d* each other,

DEVOURS (DEVOUR)

2Sa 11: 25 the sword *d* one as well as another.
Pr 21: 20 but a foolish man *d* all he has.

DEVOUT* (DEVOTE)

1Ki 18: 3 (Obadiah was a *d* believer
Isa 57: 1 *d* men are taken away,
Lk 2: 25 Simeon, who was righteous and *d*.
Ac 10: 2 his family were *d* and God-fearing;
10: 7 a *d* soldier who was one of his attendants
13: 43 and *d* converts to Judaism followed
22: 12 He was a *d* observer of the law

DEW

Jdg 6: 37 If there is *d* only on the fleece

DICTATED

Jer 36: 4 and while Jeremiah *d* all the words

DIE (DEAD DEADENED DEATH DIED DIES DYING)

Ge 2: 17 when you eat of it you will surely *d*
3: 3 you must not touch it, or you will *d*
3: 4 will not surely *d*," the serpent said
Ex 11: 5 Every firstborn son in Egypt will *d*,
Ru 1: 17 Where you *d* I will *d*, and there I
2Ki 14: 6 each is to *d* for his own sins."
Job 2: 9 Curse God and *d*!" He replied,
Pr 5: 23 He will *d* for lack of discipline,
10: 21 but fools *d* for lack of judgment.
15: 10 he who hates correction will *d*.
23: 13 with the rod, he will not *d*.
Ecc 3: 2 a time to be born and a time to *d*,
Isa 22: 13 "for tomorrow we *d*!"
66: 24 their worm will not *d*, nor will their
Jer 31: 30 everyone will *d* for his own sin;
Eze 3: 18 that wicked man will *d* for his sin,
3: 19 he will *d* for his sin; but you will

DIED (continued)

Eze   3: 20 block before him, he will *d.*
      18: 4 soul who sins is the one who will *d.*
      18: 20 soul who sins is the one who will *d.*
      18: 31 Why will you *d*, O house of Israel?
      33: 8 'O wicked man, you will surely *d*,'
Mt   26: 52 "for all who draw the sword will *d*
Mk   9: 48 " 'their worm does not *d*,
Jn   8: 21 and you will *d* in your sin.
      11: 26 and believes in me will never *d.*
Ro   5: 7 Very rarely will anyone *d*
      14: 8 and if we *d*, we *d* to the Lord.
1Co 15: 22 in Adam all *d*, so in Christ all will
      15: 31 I *d* every day—I mean that,
      15: 32 for tomorrow we *d.*''
Php   1: 21 to live is Christ and to *d* is gain.
Heb   9: 27 Just as man is destined to *d* once,
1Pe   2: 24 so that we might *d* to sins
Rev 14: 13 Blessed are the dead who *d*

DIED (DIE)

1Ki 16: 18 So he *d*, because of the sins he had
1Ch   1: 51 Hadad also *d.*
      10: 13 Saul because he was unfaithful
Lk   16: 22 "The time came when the beggar *d*
Ro   5: 6 we were still powerless, Christ *d*
       5: 8 we were still sinners, Christ *d*
       6: 2 By no means! We *d* to sin;
       6: 7 anyone who has *d* has been freed
       6: 8 if we *d* with Christ, we believe that
       6: 10 The death he *d*, he *d* to sin once
      14: 9 Christ *d* and returned to life
      14: 15 brother for whom Christ *d.*
1Co   8: 11 for whom Christ *d*, is destroyed
      15: 3 that Christ *d* for our sins according
2Co   5: 14 *d* for all, and therefore all *d.*
       5: 15 he *d* for all, that those who live
Col   2: 20 Since you *d* with Christ
       3: 3 For you *d*, and your life is now
1Th   4: 14 We believe that Jesus *d*
       5: 10 he *d* for us so that, whether we are
2Ti   2: 11 If we *d* with him,
Heb   9: 15 now that he has *d* as a ransom
       9: 17 in force only when somebody has *d*
1Pe   3: 18 For Christ *d* for sins once for all,
Rev   2: 8 who *d* and came to life again.

DIES (DIE)

Job 14: 14 If a man *d*, will he live again?
Pr   11: 7 a wicked man *d*, his hope perishes;
      26: 20 without gossip a quarrel *d* down.
Jn   11: 25 in me will live, even though he *d*;
      12: 24 But if it *d*, it produces many seeds.
Ro   7: 2 but if her husband *d*, she is released
      14: 7 and none of us *d* to himself alone.
1Co   7: 39 But if her husband *d*, she is free
      15: 36 does not come to life unless it *d.*

DIFFERENCE* (DIFFERENT)

2Sa 19: 35 Can I tell the *d* between what is
2Ch 12: 8 so that they may learn the *d*
Eze 22: 26 they teach that there is no *d*
      44: 23 are to teach my people the *d*
Ro   3: 22 There is no *d*, for all have sinned
      10: 12 For there is no *d* between Jew
Gal   2: 6 whatever they were makes no *d*

DIFFERENCES* (DIFFERENT)

1Co 11: 19 to be *d* among you to show which

DIFFERENT* (DIFFERENCE DIFFERENCES DIFFERING DIFFERS)

Lev 19: 19 " 'Do not mate *d* kinds of animals.
Nu   14: 24 my servant Caleb has a *d* spirit
1Sa 10: 6 you will be changed into a *d* person
Est   1: 7 each one *d* from the other,
       3: 8 whose customs are *d* from those
Da   7: 3 Four great beasts, each *d*
       7: 7 It was *d* from all the former beasts,
       7: 19 which was *d* from all the others
       7: 23 It will be *d* from all the other
       7: 24 them another king will arise, *d*
      11: 29 but this time the outcome will be *d*
Mk   16: 12 Jesus appeared in a *d* form
Ro   12: 6 We have *d* gifts, according
1Co   4: 7 For who makes you *d*
      12: 4 There are *d* kinds of gifts,
      12: 5 There are *d* kinds of service,
      12: 6 There are *d* kinds of working,

1Co 12: 10 speaking in *d* kinds of tongues,
      12: 28 and those speaking in *d* kinds
2Co 11: 4 or a *d* gospel from the one you
      11: 4 or if you receive a *d* spirit
Gal   1: 6 and are turning to a *d* gospel—
       4: 1 he is no *d* from a slave,
Heb   7: 13 are said belonged to a *d* tribe,
Jas   2: 25 and sent them off in a *d* direction?

DIFFERING* (DIFFERENT)

Dt   25: 13 Do not have two *d* weights
      25: 14 Do not have two *d* measures
Pr   20: 10 Differing weights and *d* measures
      20: 10 *D* weights and differing measures
      20: 23 The LORD detests *d* weights,

DIFFERS* (DIFFERENT)

1Co 15: 41 and star *d* from star in splendor.

DIFFICULT (DIFFICULTIES)

Ex   18: 22 but have them bring every *d* case
Dt   30: 11 commanding you today is not too *d*
2Ki   2: 10 "You have asked a *d* thing,"
Eze   3: 5 of obscure speech and *d* language,
Ac   15: 19 that we should not make it *d*

DIFFICULTIES* (DIFFICULT)

Dt   31: 17 and *d* will come upon them,
      31: 21 when many disasters and *d* come
2Co 12: 10 in hardships, in persecutions, in *d.*

DIGNITY

Pr   31: 25 She is clothed with strength and *d;*

DIGS

Pr   26: 27 If a man *d* a pit, he will fall into it;

DILIGENCE (DILIGENT)

Ezr   5: 8 The work is being carried on with *d*
Heb   6: 11 to show this same *d* to the very end

DILIGENT (DILIGENCE)

Pr   10: 4 but *d* hands bring wealth.
      12: 24 *D* hands will rule,
      12: 27 the *d* man prizes his possessions.
      13: 4 of the *d* are fully satisfied.
      21: 5 The plans of the *d* lead to profit
1Ti   4: 15 Be *d* in these matters; give yourself

DINAH*

      Only daughter of Jacob, by Leah (Ge 30:21; 46: 15). Raped by Shechem; avenged by Simeon and Levi (Ge 34).

DINE

Pr   23: 1 When you sit to *d* with a ruler,

DIOTREPHES*

3Jn   : 9 but *D*, who loves to be first,

DIRECT (DIRECTED DIRECTIVES DIRECTS)

Ge   18: 19 so that he will *d* his children
Dt   17: 10 to do everything they *d* you to do.
Ps 119: 35 *D* me in the path of your
     119:133 *D* my footsteps according
Jer 10: 23 it is not for man to *d* his steps.
2Th   3: 5 May the Lord *d* your hearts
1Ti   5: 17 The elders who *d* the affairs

DIRECTED (DIRECT)

Ge   24: 51 master's son, as the LORD has *d.*''
Nu   16: 40 as the LORD *d* him through Moses
Dt   2: 1 Sea, as the LORD had *d* me.
       6: 1 laws the LORD your God *d* me.
Jos 11: 9 did to them as the LORD had *d*:
      11: 23 just as the LORD had *d* Moses,
Pr   20: 24 A man's steps are *d* by the LORD.
Jer 13: 2 as the LORD *d*, and put it
Ac   7: 44 It had been made as God *d* Moses,
Tit   1: 5 elders in every town, as I *d* you.

DIRECTIVES* (DIRECT)

1Co 11: 17 In the following *d* I have no praise

DIRECTS (DIRECT)

Ps   42: 8 By day the LORD *d* his love,
Isa 48: 17 who *d* you in the way you should

DIRGE*

Mt   11: 17 we sang a *d.*
Lk   7: 32 we sang a *d.*

DISABLED*

Jn   5: 3 number of *d* people used to lie—
Heb 12: 13 so that the lame may not be *d.*

DISAGREEMENT*

Ac   15: 39 had such a sharp *d* that they parted

DISAPPEAR (DISAPPEARED DISAPPEARS)

Mt   5: 18 will by any means *d* from the Law
Lk   16: 17 earth to *d* than for the least stroke
Heb   8: 13 is obsolete and aging will soon *d.*
2Pe   3: 10 The heavens will *d* with a roar;

DISAPPEARED (DISAPPEAR)

1Ki 20: 40 busy here and there, the man *d.*''

DISAPPEARS (DISAPPEAR)

1Co 13: 10 perfection comes, the imperfect *d.*

DISAPPOINT* (DISAPPOINTED)

Ro   5: 5 And hope does not *d* us,

DISAPPOINTED (DISAPPOINT)

Ps   22: 5 in you they trusted and were not *d.*

DISAPPROVE*

Pr   24: 18 or the LORD will see and *d*

DISARMED*

Col   2: 15 And having *d* the powers

DISASTER

Ex   32: 12 and do not bring *d* on your people.
Ps   57: 1 wings until the *d* has passed.
Pr   1: 26 I in turn will laugh at your *d;*
       3: 25 Have no fear of sudden *d*
       6: 15 Therefore *d* will overtake him
      16: 4 even the wicked for a day of *d.*
      17: 5 over *d* will not go unpunished.
      27: 10 house when *d* strikes you—
Isa 45: 7 I bring prosperity and create *d;*
Jer 17: 17 you are my refuge in the day of *d.*
Eze   7: 5 An unheard-of *d* is coming.

DISCERN (DISCERNED DISCERNING DISCERNMENT)

Ps   19: 12 Who can *d* his errors?
     139: 3 You *d* my going out and my lying
Php   1: 10 you may be able to *d* what is best

DISCERNED (DISCERN)

1Co   2: 14 because they are spiritually *d.*

DISCERNING (DISCERN)

1Ki   3: 9 So give your servant a *d* heart
       3: 12 I will give you a wise and *d* heart,
Pr   1: 5 and let the *d* get guidance—
       8: 9 To the *d* all of them are right;
      10: 13 on the lips of the *d*,
      14: 6 knowledge comes easily to the *d.*
      14: 33 in the heart of the *d*
      15: 14 The *d* heart seeks knowledge,
      16: 21 The wise in heart are called *d*,
      17: 24 A man keeps wisdom in view,
      17: 28 and *d* if he holds his tongue.
      18: 15 heart of the *d* acquires knowledge;
      19: 25 rebuke a *d* man, and he will gain
      28: 7 He who keeps the law is a *d* son,

DISCERNMENT (DISCERN)

Ps 119:125 I am your servant; give me *d*
Pr   3: 21 preserve sound judgment and *d*,
      17: 10 A rebuke impresses a man of *d*
      28: 11 a poor man who has *d* sees

DISCHARGED* (DISCHARGING)

Ecc   8: 8 As no one is *d* in time of war,

DISCHARGING* (DISCHARGED)

1Co   9: 17 I am simply *d* the trust committed

DISCIPLE (DISCIPLES DISCIPLES')

Mt   10: 42 these little ones because he is my *d*,
Lk   14: 26 his own life—he cannot be my *d.*

Lk 14: 27 and follow me cannot be my *d.*
    14: 33 everything he has cannot be my *d.*
Jn 13: 23 of them, the *d* whom Jesus loved,
    19: 26 and the *d* whom he loved standing
    21: 7 Then the *d* whom Jesus loved said
    21: 20 saw that the *d* whom Jesus loved

DISCIPLES (DISCIPLE)

Mt 10: 1 He called his twelve *d* to him
    26: 56 Then all the *d* deserted him
    28: 19 Therefore go and make *d*
Mk   3: 7 withdrew with his *d* to the lake,
    16: 20 Then the *d* went out and preached
Lk   6: 13 he called his *d* to him and chose
Jn   2: 11 and his *d* put their faith in him.
    6: 66 many of his *d* turned back
    8: 31 to my teaching, you are really my *d*
    12: 16 At first his *d* did not understand all
    13: 35 men will know that you are my *d*
    15: 8 showing yourselves to be my *d.*
    20: 20 The *d* were overjoyed
Ac   6: 1 the number of *d* was increasing,
    11: 26 The *d* were called Christians first
    14: 22 strengthening the *d*
    18: 23 Phrygia, strengthening all the *d.*

DISCIPLES' (DISCIPLE)

Jn 13: 5 and began to wash his *d* feet,

DISCIPLINE* (DISCIPLINED DISCIPLES SELF-DISCIPLINE)

Dt   4: 36 made you hear his voice to *d* you.
    11: 2 and experienced the *d*
    21: 18 listen to them when they *d* him,
Job 5: 17 so do not despise the *d*
Ps   6: 1 or *d* me in your wrath.
    38: 1 or *d* me in your wrath.
    39: 11 You rebuke and *d* men for their sin;
    94: 12 Blessed is the man you *d,* O LORD
Pr   1: 2 for attaining wisdom and *d;*
    1: 7 but fools despise wisdom and *d.*
    3: 11 do not despise the LORD's *d*
    5: 12 You will say, "How I hated *d!*
    5: 23 He will die for lack of *d,*
    6: 23 and the corrections of *d*
    10: 17 He who heeds *d* shows the way
    12: 1 Whoever loves *d* loves knowledge,
    13: 18 He who ignores *d* comes to poverty
    13: 24 who loves him is careful to *d* him.
    15: 5 A fool spurns his father's *d,*
    15: 10 Stern *d* awaits him who leaves
    15: 32 He who ignores *d* despises himself,
    19: 18 *D* your son, for in that there is hope
    22: 15 the rod of *d* will drive it far
    23: 13 Do not withhold *d* from a child;
    23: 23 get wisdom, *d* and understanding.
    29: 17 *D* your son, and he will give you
Jer 17: 23 would not listen or respond to *d.*
    30: 11 I will *d* you but only with justice;
    32: 33 would not listen or respond to *d.*
    46: 28 I will *d* you but only with justice;
Hos 5: 2 I will *d* all of them.
Heb 12: 5 do not make light of the Lord's *d,*
    12: 7 as *d;* God is treating you
    12: 8 (and everyone undergoes *d),*
    12: 11 No *d* seems pleasant at the time,
Rev 3: 19 Those whom I love I rebuke and *d.*

DISCIPLINED* (DISCIPLINE)

Pr   1: 3 for acquiring a *d* and prudent life,
Isa 26: 16 when you *d* them,
Jer 31: 18 and I have been *d.*
    31: 18 'You *d* me like an unruly calf,
1Co 11: 32 we are being *d* so that we will not
Tit   1: 8 upright, holy and *d.*
Heb 12: 7 For what son is not *d* by his father?
    12: 8 you are not *d* (and everyone
    12: 9 all had human fathers who *d* us
    12: 10 Our fathers *d* us for a little while

DISCIPLINES* (DISCIPLINE)

Dt   8: 5 so the LORD your God *d* you.
    8: 5 your heart that as a man *d* his son,
Ps   94: 10 Does he who *d* nations not punish?
Pr   3: 12 the LORD *d* those he loves,
Heb 12: 6 because the Lord *d* those he loves,
    12: 10 but God *d* us for our good,

DISCLOSED

Lk   8: 17 is nothing hidden that will not be *d,*
Col 1: 26 and generations, but is now *d*
Heb 9: 8 Holy Place had not yet been *d*

DISCORD

Gal 5: 20 idolatry and witchcraft; hatred, *d,*

DISCOURAGED* (DISCOURAGEMENT)

Nu 32: 9 they *d* the Israelites
Dt   1: 21 Do not be afraid; do not be *d.''*
    31: 8 Do not be afraid; do not be *d.''*
Jos 1: 9 Do not be terrified; do not be *d,*
    8: 1 "Do not be afraid; do not be *d.*
    10: 25 "Do not be afraid; do not be *d.*
1Ch 22: 13 Do not be afraid or *d.*
    28: 20 or *d,* for the LORD God,
2Ch 20: 15 or *d* because of this vast army.
    20: 17 Do not be afraid; do not be *d,*
    32: 7 or *d* because of the king of Assyria
Job 4: 5 to you, and you are *d;*
Isa 42: 4 he will not falter or be *d*
Eph 3: 13 to be *d* because of my sufferings
Col 3: 21 children, or they will become *d.*

DISCOURAGEMENT* (DISCOURAGED)

Ex   6: 9 of their *d* and cruel bondage.

DISCOVERED

2Ki 23: 24 book that Hilkiah the priest had *d*

DISCREDIT* (DISCREDITED)

Ne   6: 13 would give me a bad name to *d* me.
Job 40: 8 "Would you *d* my justice?

DISCREDITED (DISCREDIT)

2Co 6: 3 so that our ministry will not be *d.*

DISCRETION*

1Ch 22: 12 May the LORD give you *d*
Pr   1: 4 knowledge and *d* to the young—
    2: 11 *D* will protect you,
    5: 2 that you may maintain *d*
    8: 12 I possess knowledge and *d.*
    11: 22 a beautiful woman who shows no *d.*

DISCRIMINATED*

Jas 2: 4 have you not *d* among yourselves

DISEASE (DISEASES)

Mt   4: 23 and healing every *d* and sickness
    9: 35 and healing every *d* and sickness.
    10: 1 and to heal every *d* and sickness.

DISEASES (DISEASE)

Ps 103: 3 and heals all my *d;*
Mt   8: 17 and carried our *d.''*
Mk   3: 10 those with *d* were pushing forward
Lk   9: 1 drive out all demons and to cure *d,*

DISFIGURE* (DISFIGURED)

Mt   6: 16 for they *d* their faces

DISFIGURED (DISFIGURE)

Isa 52: 14 his appearance was so *d*

DISGRACE (DISGRACEFUL DISGRACES)

Ps 44: 15 My *d* is before me all day long,
    52: 1 you who are a *d* in the eyes of God?
    74: 21 not let the oppressed retreat in *d;*
Pr   6: 33 Blows and *d* are his lot,
    11: 2 When pride comes, then comes *d,*
    14: 34 but sin is a *d* to any people.
    19: 26 is a son who brings shame and *d.*
Mt   1: 19 want to expose her to public *d,*
Ac   5: 41 of suffering *d* for the Name.
1Co 11: 6 and if it is a *d* for a woman
    11: 14 it is a *d* to him, but that
1Ti 3: 7 so that he will not fall into *d*
Heb 6: 6 and subjecting him to public *d.*
    11: 26 He regarded *d* for the sake
    13: 13 the camp, bearing the *d* he bore.

DISGRACEFUL (DISGRACE)

Pr 10: 5 during harvest is a *d* son.
    12: 4 a *d* wife is like decay in his bones.
    17: 2 wise servant will rule over a *d* son,

1Co 14: 35 for it is *d* for a woman to speak

DISGRACES (DISGRACE)

Pr 28: 7 of gluttons *d* his father.
    29: 15 but a child left to himself *d* his mother

DISGUISES*

Pr 26: 24 A malicious man *d* himself

DISH

Pr 19: 24 sluggard buries his hand in the *d;*
Mt 23: 25 the outside of the cup and *d,*

DISHONEST*

Ex 18: 21 trustworthy men who hate *d* gain
Lev 19: 35 " 'Do not use *d* standards
1Sa 8: 3 They turned aside after *d* gain
Pr 11: 1 The LORD abhors *d* scales,
    13: 11 *D* money dwindles away,
    20: 23 and *d* scales do not please him.
    29: 27 The righteous detest the *d;*
Jer 22: 17 are set only on *d* gain,
Eze 28: 18 By your many sins and *d* trade
Hos 12: 7 The merchant uses *d* scales;
Am   8: 5 and cheating with *d* scales,
Mic 6: 11 Shall I acquit a man with *d* scales,
Lk 16: 8 master commended the *d* manager
    16: 10 whoever is *d* with very little will
    16: 10 with very little will also be *d*
1Ti 3: 8 wine, and not pursuing *d* gain.
Tit 1: 7 not violent, not pursuing *d* gain.
    1: 11 and that for the sake of *d* gain.

DISHONOR* (DISHONORED DISHONORS)

Lev 18: 7 " 'Do not *d* your father
    18: 8 wife; that would *d* your father.
    18: 10 daughter; that would *d* you.
    18: 14 " 'Do not *d* your father's brother
    18: 16 that would *d* your brother.
    20: 19 for that would *d* a close relative;
Dt 22: 30 he must not *d* his father's bed.
Pr 30: 9 and so *d* the name of my God.
Jer 14: 21 do not *d* your glorious throne.
    20: 11 their *d* will never be forgotten.
La   2: 2 princes down to the ground in *d.*
Eze 22: 10 are those who *d* their fathers' bed;
Jn   8: 49 I honor my Father and you *d* me.
Ro   2: 23 do you *d* God by breaking the law?
1Co 15: 43 it is sown in *d,* it is raised in glory;
2Co 6: 8 through glory and *d,* bad report

DISHONORED* (DISHONOR)

Lev 20: 11 father's wife, he has *d* his father.
    20: 17 He has *d* his sister and will be held
    20: 20 with his aunt, he has *d* his uncle.
    20: 21 of impurity; he has *d* his brother.
Dt 21: 14 as a slave, since you have *d* her.
Ezr 4: 14 proper for us to see the king *d,*
1Co 4: 10 You are honored, we are *d!*

DISHONORS* (DISHONOR)

Dt 27: 16 Cursed is the man who *d* his father
    27: 20 for he *d* his father's bed.''
Job 20: 3 I hear a rebuke that *d* me,
Mic 7: 6 For a son *d* his father,
1Co 11: 4 with his head covered *d* his head.
    11: 5 her head uncovered *d* her head—

DISILLUSIONMENT*

Ps   7: 14 conceives trouble gives birth to *d.*

DISMAYED

Isa 28: 16 the one who trusts will never be *d.*
    41: 10 do not be *d,* for I am your God.

DISOBEDIENCE* (DISOBEY)

Jos 22: 22 in rebellion or *d* to the LORD,
Jer 43: 7 So they entered Egypt in *d*
Ro   5: 19 as through the *d* of the one man
    11: 30 mercy as a result of their *d,*
    11: 32 to *d* so that he may have mercy
2Co 10: 6 ready to punish every act of *d,*
Heb 2: 2 and received its just punishment,
    4: 6 go in, because of their *d.*
    4: 11 fall by following their example of *d.*

DISOBEDIENT* (DISOBEY)

Ne 9:26 "But they were *d* and rebelled
Lk 1:17 and the *d* to the wisdom
Ac 26:19 I was not *d* to the vision
Ro 10:21 hands to a *d* and obstinate people."
    11:30 as you who were at one time *d*
    11:31 so they too have now become *d*
Eph 2: 2 now at work in those who are *d*.
    5: 6 comes on those who are *d*.
    5:12 to mention what the *d* do in secret.
2Ti 3: 2 proud, abusive, *d* to their parents,
Tit 1: 6 to the charge of being wild and *d*.
    1:16 *d* and unfit for doing anything
    3: 3 At one time we too were foolish, *d*,
Heb 11:31 killed with those who were *d*.

DISOBEY* (DISOBEDIENCE DISOBEDIENT DISOBEYED DISOBEYING DISOBEYS)

Dt 11:28 the curse if you *d* the commands
2Ch 24:20 'Why do you *d* the LORD's
Est 3: 3 Why do you *d* the king's command
Jer 42:13 and so *d* the LORD your God,
Ro 1:30 they *d* their parents; they are
1Pe 2: 8 because they *d* the message—

DISOBEYED* (DISOBEY)

Nu 14:22 and in the desert but who *d* me
   27:14 both of you *d* my command
Jdg 2: 2 Yet you have *d* me.
Ne 9:29 arrogant and *d* your commands.
Isa 24: 5 they have *d* the laws,
Jer 43: 4 and all the people *d* the LORD's
Lk 15:29 for you and never *d* your orders.
Heb 3:18 rest if not to those who *d?*
1Pe 3:20 the spirits in prison who *d* long ago

DISOBEYING* (DISOBEY)

Nu 14:41 "Why are you *d* the LORD's

DISOBEYS* (DISOBEY)

Eze 33:12 man will not save him when he *d,*

DISORDER

1Co 14:33 For God is not a God of *d*
2Co 12:20 slander, gossip, arrogance and *d.*
Jas 3:16 there you find *d* and every evil

DISOWN (DISOWNS)

Pr 30: 9 I may have too much and *d* you
Mt 10:33 I will *d* him before my Father
   26:35 to die with you, I will never *d* you."
2Ti 2:12 If we *d* him,

DISOWNS (DISOWN)

Lk 12: 9 he who *d* me before men will be

DISPENSATION see ADMINISTRATION, TRUST

DISPLACES

Pr 30:23 a maidservant who *d* her mistress.

DISPLAY (DISPLAYED DISPLAYS)

Ps 45: 4 your right hand *d* awesome deeds.
Eze 39:21 I will *d* my glory among the nations
Ro 9:17 that I might *d* my power in you
1Co 4: 9 on *d* at the end of the procession,
1Ti 1:16 Christ Jesus might *d* his unlimited

DISPLAYED (DISPLAY)

Jn 9: 3 work of God might be *d* in his life.
2Th 2: 9 the work of Satan *d* in all kinds

DISPLAYS (DISPLAY)

Isa 44:23 he *d* his glory in Israel.

DISPLEASE (DISPLEASED)

1Th 2:15 They *d* God and are hostile

DISPLEASED (DISPLEASE)

2Sa 11:27 David had done *d* the LORD.

DISPUTABLE* (DISPUTE)

Ro 14: 1 passing judgment on *d* matters.

DISPUTE (DISPUTABLE DISPUTES DISPUTING)

Pr 17:14 before a *d* breaks out.
1Co 6: 1 If any of you has a *d* with another,

DISPUTES (DISPUTE)

Pr 18:18 Casting the lot settles *d*

DISPUTING (DISPUTE)

1Ti 2: 8 in prayer, without anger or *d.*

DISQUALIFIED*

1Co 9:27 I myself will not be *d* for the prize.

DISREPUTE*

2Pe 2: 2 will bring the way of truth into *d.*

DISSENSION* (DISSENSIONS)

Pr 6:14 he always stirs up *d.*
    6:19 and a man who stirs up *d*
  10:12 Hatred stirs up *d,*
  15:18 A hot-tempered man stirs up *d,*
  16:28 A perverse man stirs up *d,*
  28:25 A greedy man stirs up *d,*
  29:22 An angry man stirs up *d,*
Ro 13:13 debauchery, not in *d* and jealousy.

DISSENSIONS* (DISSENSION)

Gal 5:20 selfish ambition, *d,* factions

DISSIPATION*

Lk 21:34 will be weighed down with *d,*
1Pe 4: 4 with them into the same flood of *d,*

DISTINCTION

Ac 15: 9 He made no *d* between us

DISTINGUISH (DISTINGUISHING)

1Ki 3: 9 and to *d* between right and wrong.
Heb 5:14 themselves to *d* good from evil.

DISTINGUISHING

1Co 12:10 the *d* between spirits,

DISTORT

Ac 20:30 and *d* the truth in order
2Co 4: 2 nor do we *d* the word of God.
2Pe 3:16 ignorant and unstable people *d,*

DISTRACTED*

Lk 10:40 But Martha was *d* by all

DISTRESS (DISTRESSED)

2Ch 15: 4 in their *d* they turned to the LORD
Ps 18: 6 In my *d* I called to the LORD;
    81: 7 In your *d* you called and I rescued
 120: 1 I call on the LORD in my *d,*
Jnh 2: 2 "In my *d* I called to the LORD,
Mt 24:21 For then there will be great *d,*
Jas 1:27 after orphans and widows in their *d*

DISTRESSED (DISTRESS)

Lk 12:50 how *d* I am until it is completed!
Ro 14:15 If your brother is *d*

DIVIDE (DIVIDED DIVIDING DIVISION DIVISIONS DIVISIVE)

Ps 22:18 They *d* my garments among them

DIVIDED (DIVIDE)

Mt 12:25 household *d* against itself will not
Lk 23:34 they *d* up his clothes by casting lots
1Co 1:13 Is Christ *d?* Was Paul crucified

DIVIDING (DIVIDE)

Eph 2:14 destroyed the barrier, the *d* wall
Heb 4:12 it penetrates even to *d* soul

DIVINATION

Lev 19:26 " 'Do not practice *d* or sorcery.

DIVINE

Ro 1:20 his eternal power and *d* nature—
2Co 10: 4 they have *d* power
2Pe 1: 4 you may participate in the *d* nature

DIVISION (DIVIDE)

Lk 12:51 on earth? No, I tell you, but *d.*
1Co 12:25 so that there should be no *d*

DIVISIONS (DIVIDE)

Ro 16:17 to watch out for those who cause *d*
1Co 1:10 another so that there may be no *d*
   11:18 there are *d* among you,

DIVISIVE* (DIVIDE)

Tit 3:10 Warn a *d* person once,

DIVORCE* (DIVORCED DIVORCES)

Dt 22:19 he must not *d* her as long as he lives
  22:29 He can never *d* her as long
  24: 1 and he writes her a certificate of *d,*
  24: 3 and writes her a certificate of *d,*
Isa 50: 1 is your mother's certificate of *d*
Jer 3: 8 faithless Israel her certificate of *d*
Mal 2:16 "I hate *d,*" says the LORD God
Mt 1:19 he had in mind to *d* her quietly.
    5:31 must give her a certificate of *d.*'
   19: 3 for a man to *d* his wife for any
   19: 7 man give his wife a certificate of *d*
   19: 8 permitted you to *d* your wives
Mk 10: 2 Is it lawful for a man to *d* his wife?"
   10: 4 a man to write a certificate of *d*
1Co 7:11 And a husband must not *d* his wife.
    7:12 to live with him, he must not *d* her.
    7:13 to live with her, she must not *d* him
    7:27 Are you married? Do not seek a *d.*

DIVORCED* (DIVORCE)

Lev 21: 7 or *d* from their husbands,
  21:14 not marry a widow, a *d* woman,
  22:13 daughter becomes a widow or is *d,*
Nu 30: 9 or *d* woman will be binding on her.
Dt 24: 4 then her first husband, who *d* her,
1Ch 8: 8 after he had *d* his wives Hushim
Eze 44:22 not marry widows or *d* women;
Mt 5:32 marries the *d* woman commits adultery.
Lk 16:18 who marries a *d* woman commits

DIVORCES* (DIVORCE)

Jer 3: 1 "If a man *d* his wife
Mt 5:31 'Anyone who *d* his wife must give
    5:32 tell you that anyone who *d* his wife,
   19: 9 tell you that anyone who *d* his wife,
Mk 10:11 "Anyone who *d* his wife
   10:12 And if she *d* her husband
Lk 16:18 "Anyone who *d* his wife

DOCTOR

Mt 9:12 "It is not the healthy who need a *d,*

DOCTRINE* (DOCTRINES)

1Ti 1:10 to the sound *d* that conforms
    4:16 Watch your life and *d* closely.
2Ti 4: 3 men will not put up with sound *d.*
Tit 1: 9 can encourage others by sound *d*
    2: 1 is in accord with sound *d.*

DOCTRINES* (DOCTRINE)

1Ti 1: 3 not to teach false *d* any longer
    6: 3 If anyone teaches false *d*

DOEG*

Edomite; Saul's head shepherd; responsible for murder of priests at Nob (1Sa 21:7; 22:6-23; Ps 52).

DOG (DOGS)

Pr 26:11 As a *d* returns to its vomit,
Ecc 9: 4 a live *d* is better off than a dead lion
2Pe 2:22 "A *d* returns to its vomit," and,

DOGS (DOG)

Mt 7: 6 "Do not give *d* what is sacred;
   15:26 bread and toss it to their *d.*"

DOMINION

Job 25: 2 "*D* and awe belong to God;
Ps 22:28 for *d* belongs to the LORD

DONKEY

Nu 22:30 *d* said to Balaam, "Am I not your
Zec 9: 9 gentle and riding on a *d,*
Mt 21: 5 gentle and riding on a *d,*
2Pe 2:16 for his wrongdoing by a *d*—

DOOR (DOORS)

Job 31:32 for my *d* was always open

Ps 141:   3 keep watch over the *d* of my lips.
Mt   6:   6 close the *d* and pray to your Father
        7:   7 and the *d* will be opened to you.
Ac   14: 27 how he had opened the *d* of faith
1Co 16:   9 a great *d* for effective work has
2Co   2: 12 found that the Lord had opened a *d*
Rev   3: 20 I stand at the *d* and knock.

DOORFRAMES

Dt   6:   9 Write them on the *d* of your houses

DOORKEEPER

Ps   84: 10 I would rather be a *d* in the house

DOORS (DOOR)

Ps   24:   7 be lifted up, you ancient *d*,

DORCAS

Ac   9: 36 is *D*), who was always doing good

DOUBLE

2Ki   2:   9 "Let me inherit a *d* portion
1Ti   5: 17 church well are worthy of *d* honor,

DOUBLE-EDGED (EDGE)

Heb   4: 12 Sharper than any *d* sword,
Rev   1: 16 of his mouth came a sharp *d* sword.
        2: 12 of him who has the sharp, *d* sword.

DOUBLE-MINDED* (MIND)

Ps 119:113 I hate *d* men,
Jas   1:   8 he is a *d* man, unstable
        4:   8 and purify your hearts, you *d*.

DOUBT (DOUBTING DOUBTS)

Mt   14: 31 he said, "why did you *d*?"
        21: 21 if you have faith and do not *d*,
Mk   11: 23 and does not *d* in his heart
Jas   1:   6 he must believe and not *d*,
Jude   : 22 Be merciful to those who *d*;

DOUBTING* (DOUBT)

Jn   20: 27 Stop *d* and believe."

DOUBTS* (DOUBT)

Lk   24: 38 and why do *d* rise in your minds?
Ro   14: 23 the man who has *d* is condemned
Jas   1:   6 he who *d* is like a wave of the sea,

DOVE (DOVES)

Ge   8:   8 Then he sent out a *d* to see
Mt   3: 16 Spirit of God descending like a *d*

DOVES (DOVE)

Lev 12:   8 is to bring two *d* or two young
Mt   10: 16 as snakes and as innocent as *d*.
Lk   2: 24 "a pair of *d* or two young pigeons."

DOWNCAST

Ps   42:   5 Why are you *d*, O my soul?
2Co   7:   6 But God, who comforts the *d*,

DOWNFALL

Hos 14:   1 Your sins have been your *d!*

DRAGON

Rev 12:   7 and his angels fought against the *d*,
        13:   2 The *d* gave the beast his power
        20:   2 He seized the *d*, that ancient

DRAW (DRAWING DRAWS)

Mt   26: 52 "for all who *d* the sword will die
Jn   12: 32 up from the earth, will *d* all men
Heb 10: 22 let us *d* near to God

DRAWING (DRAW)

Lk   21: 28 because your redemption is *d* near

DRAWS (DRAW)

Jn   6: 44 the Father who sent me *d* him,

DREAD (DREADFUL)

Ps   53:   5 they were, overwhelmed with *d*,

DREADFUL (DREAD)

Mt   24: 19 How *d* it will be in those days
Heb 10: 31 It is a *d* thing to fall into the hands

DREAM

Joel 2: 28 your old men will *d* dreams,
Ac   2: 17 your old men will *d* dreams.

DRESS

1Ti   2:   9 I also want women to *d* modestly,

DRIFT*

Heb   2:   1 so that we do not *d* away.

DRINK (DRINKING DRINKS DRUNK DRUNKARD DRUNKARD'S DRUNKARDS DRUNKENNESS)

Ex   29: 40 of a hin of wine as a *d* offering.
Nu   6:   3 He must not *d* grape juice
Jdg   7:   5 from those who kneel down to *d*."
2Sa 23: 15 that someone would get me a *d*
Pr   5: 15 *D* water from your own cistern,
Mt   20: 22 "Can you *d* the cup I am going to *d*
        26: 27 saying, "*D* from it, all of you.
Mk   16: 18 and when they *d* deadly poison,
Lk   12: 19 Take life easy; eat, *d* and be merry
Jn   7: 37 let him come to me and *d*.
        18: 11 Shall I not *d* the cup the Father has
1Co 10:   4 and drank the same spiritual *d*;
        12: 13 were all given the one Spirit to *d*
Php   2: 17 being poured out like a *d* offering
2Ti   4:   6 being poured out like a *d* offering,
Rev 14: 10 too, will *d* of the wine of God's fury
        21:   6 to *d* without cost from the spring

DRINKING (DRINK)

Ro   14: 17 God is not a matter of eating and *d*,

DRINKS (DRINK)

Isa   5: 22 and champions at mixing *d*,
Jn   4: 13 "Everyone who *d* this water will be
        6: 54 and *d* my blood has eternal life,
1Co 11: 27 or *d* the cup of the Lord

DRIPPING

Pr   19: 13 wife is like a constant *d*.
        27: 15 a constant *d* on a rainy day;

DRIVE (DRIVES)

Ex   23: 30 Little by little I will *d* them out
Nu   33: 52 *d* out all the inhabitants of the land
Jos 13: 13 Israelites did not *d* out the people
        23: 13 will no longer *d* out these nations
Pr   22: 10 *D* out the mocker, and out goes
Mt   10:   1 authority to *d* out evil spirits
Jn   6: 37 comes to me I will never *d* away.

DRIVES (DRIVE)

Mt   12: 26 If Satan *d* out Satan, he is divided
1Jn   4: 18 But perfect love *d* out fear,

DROP (DROPS)

Pr   17: 14 so *d* the matter before a dispute
Isa 40: 15 Surely the nations are like a *d*

DROPS (DROP)

Lk   22: 44 his sweat was like *d* of blood falling

DROSS

Ps 119:119 of the earth you discard like *d*;
Pr   25:   4 Remove the *d* from the silver,

DROUGHT

Jer 17:   8 It has no worries in a year of *d*

DROWNED

Ex   15:   4 are *d* in the Red Sea.
Mt   18:   6 and to be *d* in the depths of the sea.
Heb 11: 29 tried to do so, they were *d*,

DROWSINESS*

Pr   23: 21 and *d* clothes them in rags.

DRUNK (DRINK)

1Sa   1: 13 Eli thought she was *d* and said
Ac   2: 15 men are not *d*, as you suppose.
Eph   5: 18 Do not get *d* on wine, which leads

DRUNKARD (DRINK)

Mt   11: 19 and a *d*, a friend of tax collectors
1Co   5: 11 or a slanderer, a *d* or a swindler.

DRUNKARD'S* (DRINK)

Pr   26:   9 Like a thornbush in a *d* hand

DRUNKARDS (DRINK)

Pr   23: 21 for *d* and gluttons become poor,
1Co   6: 10 nor the greedy nor *d* nor slanderers

DRUNKENNESS (DRINK)

Lk   21: 34 weighed down with dissipation, *d*
Ro   13: 13 and *d*, not in sexual immorality
Gal   5: 21 factions and envy; *d*, orgies,
1Ti   3:   3 not given to *d*, not violent
1Pe   4:   3 living in debauchery, lust, *d*, orgies,

DRY

Ge   1:   9 place, and let *d* ground appear."
Ex   14: 16 go through the sea on *d* ground.
Jos   3: 17 the crossing on *d* ground.
Isa 53:   2 and like a root out of *d* ground.
Eze 37:   4 '*D* bones, hear the word

DULL

Isa   6: 10 make their ears *d*
2Co   3: 14 But their minds were made *d*,

DUST

Ge   2:   7 man from the *d* of the ground
        3: 19 for *d* you are
Job 42:   6 and repent in *d* and ashes."
Ps   22: 15 you lay me in the *d* of death.
        103: 14 he remembers that we are *d*.
Ecc   3: 20 all come from *d*, and to *d* all return.
Mt   10: 14 shake the *d* off your feet
1Co 15: 47 was of the *d* of the earth,

DUTIES (DUTY)

2Ti   4:   5 discharge all the *d* of your ministry

DUTY (DUTIES)

Ecc 12: 13 for this is the whole *d* of man.
Ac   23:   1 I have fulfilled my *d* to God
1Co   7:   3 husband should fulfill his marital *d*

DWELL (DWELLING DWELLINGS DWELLS DWELT)

Ex   25:   8 for me, and I will *d* among them.
2Sa   7:   5 the one to build me a house to *d* in?
1Ki   8: 27 "But will God really *d* on earth?
Ps   23:   6 I will *d* in the house of the LORD
        37:   3 *d* in the land and enjoy safe pasture
        61:   4 I long to *d* in your tent forever
Pr   8: 12 wisdom, *d* together with prudence;
Isa 33: 14 of us can *d* with the consuming fire
        43: 18 do not *d* on the past.
Jn   5: 38 nor does his word *d* in you,
Eph   3: 17 so that Christ may *d* in your hearts
Col   1: 19 to have all his fullness *d* in him,
        3: 16 the word of Christ *d* in you richly

DWELLING (DWELL)

Lev 26: 11 I will put my *d* place among you,
Dt   26: 15 from heaven, your holy *d* place,
Ps   90:   1 Lord, you have been our *d* place
2Co   5:   2 to be clothed with our heavenly *d*,
Eph   2: 22 to become a *d* in which God lives

DWELLINGS (DWELL)

Lk   16:   9 will be welcomed into eternal *d*.

DWELLS (DWELL)

Ps   46:   4 holy place where the Most High *d*.
        91:   1 He who *d* in the shelter

DWELT (DWELL)

Dt   33: 16 of him who *d* in the burning bush.

DYING (DIE)

Ro   7:   6 by *d* to what once bound us,
2Co   6:   9 yet regarded as unknown; *d*,

EAGER

Pr   31: 13 and works with *e* hands.
Ro   8: 19 The creation waits in *e* expectation
1Co 14: 12 Since you are *e* to have spiritual
        14: 39 my brothers, be *e* to prophesy,
Tit   2: 14 a people that are his very own, *e*
1Pe   5:   2 greedy for money, but *e* to serve;

EAGLE (EAGLE'S EAGLES)

Dt 32:11 like an *e* that stirs up its nest
Eze 1:10 each also had the face of an *e.*
Rev 4: 7 the fourth was like a flying *e.*
      12:14 given the two wings of a great *e,*

EAGLE'S (EAGLE)

Ps 103: 5 your youth is renewed like the *e.*

EAGLES (EAGLE)

Isa 40:31 They will soar on wings like *e;*

EAR (EARS)

Ex 21: 6 and pierce his *e* with an awl.
Ps   5: 1 Give *e* to my words, O LORD,
Pr   2: 2 turning your *e* to wisdom
1Co 2: 9 no *e* has heard,
      12:16 if the *e* should say, "Because I am
Rev 2: 7 He who has an *e,* let him hear what

EARN (EARNED EARNINGS)

2Th 3:12 down and *e* the bread they eat.

EARNED (EARN)

Pr 31:31 Give her the reward she has *e,*

EARNEST see DEPOSIT

EARNESTNESS

2Co 7:11 what *e,* what eagerness
      8: 7 in complete *e* and in your love

EARNINGS (EARN)

Pr 31:16 out of her *e* she plants a vineyard.

EARRING (EARRINGS)

Pr 25:12 Like an *e* of gold or an ornament

EARRINGS (EARRING)

Ex 32: 2 Take off the gold *e* that your wives,

EARS (EAR)

Job 42: 5 My *e* had heard of you
Ps 34:15 and his *e* are attentive to their cry;
Pr 21:13 If a man shuts his *e* to the cry
      26:17 Like one who seizes a dog by the *e*
Isa 6:10 hear with their *e,*
Mt 11:15 He who has *e,* let him hear.
2Ti 4: 3 to say what their itching *e* want
1Pe 3:12 his *e* are attentive to their prayer,

EARTH (EARTH'S EARTHLY)

Ge 1: 1 God created the heavens and the *e.*
      1: 2 Now the *e* was formless and empty,
      7:24 The waters flooded the *e*
    14:19 Creator of heaven and *e.*
1Ki 8:27 "But will God really dwell on *e?*
Job 26: 7 he suspends the *e* over nothing.
Ps 24: 1 *e* is the LORD's, and everything
    46: 6 he lifts his voice, the *e* melts.
    90: 2 or you brought forth the *e*
    97: 5 before the Lord of all the *e.*
   102:25 you laid the foundations of the *e,*
   108: 5 and let your glory be over all the *e.*
Pr 8:26 before he made the *e* or its fields
Isa 6: 3 the whole *e* is full of his glory."
    24:20 The *e* reels like a drunkard,
    37:16 You have made heaven and *e.*
    40:22 enthroned above the circle of the *e,*
    51: 6 the *e* will wear out like a garment
    54: 5 he is called the God of all the *e.*
    55: 9 the heavens are higher than the *e.*
    65:17 new heavens and a new *e.*
    66: 1 and the *e* is my footstool.
Jer 10:10 When he is angry, the *e* trembles;
    23:24 "Do not I fill heaven and *e?"*
    33:25 and the fixed laws of heaven and *e,*
Hab 2:20 let all the *e* be silent before him."
Mt 5: 5 for they will inherit the *e.*
      5:35 or by the *e,* for it is his footstool;
      6:10 done on *e* as it is in heaven.
    16:19 bind on *e* will be bound
    24:35 Heaven and *e* will pass away,
    28:18 and on *e* has been given to me.
Lk 2:14 on *e* peace to men
Jn 12:32 when I am lifted up from the *e,*
Ac 4:24 "you made the heaven and the *e*
      7:49 and the *e* is my footstool.

1Co 10:26 The *e* is the Lord's, and everything
Eph 3:15 in heaven and on *e* derives its name
Php 2:10 in heaven and on *e* and under the *e,*
Heb 1:10 you laid the foundations of the *e,*
2Pe 3:13 to a new heaven and a new *e,*
Rev 8: 7 A third of the *e* was burned up,
    12:12 But woe to the *e* and the sea,
    20:11 *E* and sky fled from his presence,
    21: 1 I saw a new heaven and a new *e,*
    21: 1 and the first *e* had passed away,

EARTH'S (EARTH)

Job 38: 4 when I laid the *e* foundation?

EARTHENWARE

Pr 26:23 Like a coating of glaze over *e*

EARTHLY (EARTH)

Eph 4: 9 descended to the lower, *e* regions?
Php 3:19 Their mind is on *e* things.
Col 3: 2 on things above, not on *e* things.
      3: 5 whatever belongs to your *e* nature:

EARTHQUAKE (EARTHQUAKES)

Eze 38:19 at that time there shall be a great *e*
Mt 28: 2 There was a violent *e,* for an angel
Rev 6:12 There was a great *e.*

EARTHQUAKES (EARTHQUAKE)

Mt 24: 7 There will be famines and *e*

EASE

Pr 1:33 and be at *e,* without fear of harm."

EASIER (EASY)

Lk 16:17 It is *e* for heaven and earth
    18:25 it is *e* for a camel to go

EAST

Ge 2: 8 God had planted a garden in the *e,*
Ps 103:12 as far as the *e* is from the west,
Eze 43: 2 God of Israel coming from the *e.*
Mt 2: 1 Magi from the *e* came to Jerusalem
      2: 2 We saw his star in the *e*

EASY (EASIER)

Mt 11:30 For my yoke is *e* and my burden is

EAT (ATE EATEN EATER EATING EATS)

Ge 2:16 "You are free to *e* from any tree
      2:17 but you must not *e* from the tree
      3:19 you will *e* your food
Ex 12:11 *E* it in haste; it is the LORD's
Lev 11: 2 these are the ones you may *e;*
    17:12 "None of you may *e* blood,
Dt 8:16 He gave you manna to *e*
    14: 4 These are the animals you may *e:*
Jdg 14:14 "Out of the eater, something to *e;*
2Sa 9: 7 and you will always *e* at my table."
Pr 31:27 and does not *e* the bread of idleness
Isa 55: 1 come, buy and *e!*
    65:25 and the lion will *e* straw like the ox,
Eze 3: 1 *e* what is before you, *e* this scroll;
Mt 14:16 You give them something to *e.*
    15: 2 wash their hands before they *e!*
    26:26 "Take and *e;* this is my body."
Mk 14:14 where I may *e* the Passover
Lk 10: 8 and are welcomed, *e* what is set
    12:19 Take life easy; *e,* drink
    12:22 what you will *e;* or about your body
Jn 4:32 to *e* that you know nothing about."
      6:31 bread from heaven to *e.'"*
      6:52 can this man give us his flesh to *e?"*
Ac 10:13 Kill and *e.*"
Ro 14: 2 faith allows him to *e* everything,
    14:15 is distressed because of what you *e,*
    14:20 to *e* anything that causes someone
    14:21 It is better not to *e* meat
1Co 5:11 With such a man do not even *e.*
      8:13 if what I *e* causes my brother to fall
    10:25 *E* anything sold in the meat market
    10:27 *e* whatever is put before you
    10:31 So whether you *e* or drink
    11:26 For whenever you *e* this bread
2Th 3:10 man will not work, he shall not *e.*"
Rev 2: 7 the right to *e* from the tree of life,
      3:20 I will come in and *e* with him,

EATEN (EAT)

Ge 3:11 Have you *e* from the tree that I
Ac 10:14 "I have never *e* anything impure
Rev 10:10 when I had *e* it, my stomach turned

EATER (EAT)

Isa 55:10 for the sower and bread for the *e,*

EATING (EAT)

Ex 34:28 and forty nights without *e* bread
Ro 14:15 not by your *e* destroy your brother
    14:17 kingdom of God is not a matter of *e*
    14:23 because his *e* is not from faith;
1Co 8: 4 about *e* food sacrificed to idols:
      8:10 you who have this knowledge *e*
Jude :12 *e* with you without the slightest

EATS (EAT)

1Sa 14:24 "Cursed be any man who *e* food
Lk 15: 2 "This man welcomes sinners and *e*
Jn 6:51 If anyone *e* of this bread, he will live
      6:54 Whoever *e* my flesh and drinks my
Ro 14: 2 faith is weak, *e* only vegetables.
    14: 3 man who *e* everything must not
    14: 6 He who *e* meat, *e* to the Lord,
    14:23 has doubts is condemned if he *e,*
1Co 11:27 whoever *e* the bread or drinks

EBAL

Dt 11:29 and on Mount *E* the curses.
Jos 8:30 Joshua built on Mount *E* an altar

EBENEZER

1Sa 7:12 He named it *E,* saying, "Thus far

EDEN

Ge 2: 8 in *E;* and there he put the man
Eze 28:13 You were in *E,*

EDGE (DOUBLE-EDGED)

Mt 9:20 and touched the *e* of his cloak.

EDICT

Heb 11:23 they were not afraid of the king's *e.*

EDIFICATION (EDIFIED EDIFIES)

Ro 14:19 leads to peace and to mutual *e.*

EDIFIED* (EDIFICATION)

1Co 14: 5 so that the church may be *e.*
    14:17 but the other man is not *e.*

EDIFIES* (EDIFICATION)

1Co 14: 4 but he who prophesies *e* the church
    14: 4 speaks in a tongue *e* himself,

EDOM

Ge 36: 1 the account of Esau (that is, *E).*
    36: 8 *E)* settled in the hill country of Seir
Isa 63: 1 Who is this coming from *E,*
Ob : 1 Sovereign LORD says about *E*—

EDUCATED*

Ac 7:22 Moses was *e* in all the wisdom

EFFECT* (EFFECTIVE)

Job 41:26 sword that reaches him has no *e,*
Isa 32:17 of righteousness will be quietness
Ac 7:53 put into *e* through angels
1Co 15:10 his grace to me was not without *e.*
Gal 3:19 put into *e* through angels
Eph 1:10 put into *e* when the times will have
Heb 9:17 it never takes *e* while the one who
      9:18 put into *e* without blood.

EFFECTIVE* (EFFECT)

1Co 16: 9 a great door for *e* work has opened
Jas 5:16 a righteous man is powerful and *e.*

EFFORT*

Ecc 2:19 into which I have poured my *e*
Da 6:14 and made every *e* until sundown
Lk 13:24 "Make every *e* to enter
Jn 5:44 yet make no *e* to obtain the praise
Ro 9:16 depend on man's desire or *e,*
    14:19 make every *e* to do what leads
Gal 3: 3 to attain your goal by human *e?*
Eph 4: 3 Make every *e* to keep the unity

1Th 2: 16 to all men in their *e* to keep us
    2: 17 intense longing we made every *e*
Heb 4: 11 make every *e* to enter that rest,
   12: 14 Make every *e* to live in peace
2Pe 1: 5 make every *e* to add
    1: 15 And I will make every *e* to see that
    3: 14 make every *e* to be found spotless,

EGG

Lk 11: 12 for an *e*, will give him a scorpion?

EGLON

1. Fat king of Moab killed by Ehud (Jdg 3: 12-30).
2. City in Canaan (Jos 10).

EGYPT (EGYPTIANS)

Ge 12: 10 went down to *E* to live there
  37: 28 Ishmaelites, who took him to *E*.
  42: 3 went down to buy grain from *E*.
  45: 20 the best of all *E* will be yours.' ''
  46: 6 and all his offspring went to *E*.
  47: 27 Now the Israelites settled in *E*
Ex   3: 11 and bring the Israelites out of *E*?''
  12: 40 lived in *E* was 430 years.
  12: 41 all the LORD's divisions left *E*.
  32: 1 Moses who brought us up out of *E*,
Nu 11: 18 We were better off in *E!*''
  14: 4 choose a leader and go back to *E*.''
  24: 8 ''God brought them out of *E*;
Dt   6: 21 ''We were slaves of Pharaoh in *E*,
1Ki 4: 30 greater than all the wisdom of *E*.
  10: 28 horses were imported from *E*
  11: 40 but Jeroboam fled to *E*,
  14: 25 king of *E* attacked Jerusalem.
2Ch 35: 20 Neco king of *E* went up to fight
  36: 3 The king of *E* dethroned him
Isa 19: 23 a highway from *E* to Assyria.
Hos 11: 1 and out of *E* I called my son.
Mt   2: 15 ''Out of *E* I called my son.''
Heb 11: 27 By faith he left *E*, not fearing
Rev 11: 8 is figuratively called Sodom and *E*,

EGYPTIANS (EGYPT)

Nu 14: 13 ''Then the *E* will hear about it!

EHUD

Left-handed judge who delivered Israel from Moabite king, Eglon (Jdg 3:12-30).

EKRON

1Sa 5: 10 So they sent the ark of God to *E*.

ELAH

Son of Baasha; king of Israel (1Ki 16:6-14).

ELATION

Pr 28: 12 righteous triumph, there is great *e;*

ELDER* (ELDERLY ELDERS)

Isa   3: 2 the soothsayer and *e*,
1Ti 5: 19 an accusation against an *e*
Tit   1: 6 *e* must be blameless, the husband
1Pe 5: 1 among you, I appeal as a fellow *e*,
2Jn   : 1 The *e*, To the chosen lady
3Jn   : 1 The *e*, To my dear friend Gaius,

ELDERLY* (ELDER)

Lev 19: 32 show respect for the *e*

ELDERS (ELDER)

1Ki 12: 8 rejected the advice the *e* gave him
Mt 15: 2 break the tradition of the *e?*
Mk   7: 3 holding to the tradition of the *e*.
    7: 5 to the tradition of the *e* instead
Ac 11: 30 gift to the *e* by Barnabas
  14: 23 and Barnabas appointed *e* for them
  15: 2 the apostles and *e* about this
  15: 4 the church and the apostles and *e*,
  15: 6 and *e* met to consider this question.
  15: 22 and *e*, with the whole church,
  15: 23 The apostles and *e*, your brothers,
  16: 4 and *e* in Jerusalem for the people
  20: 17 to Ephesus for the *e* of the church.
  21: 18 and all the *e* were present.
  23: 14 They went to the chief priests and *e*
  24: 1 to Caesarea with some of the *e*
1Ti 4: 14 when the body of *e* laid their hands

1Ti 5: 17 The *e* who direct the affairs
Tit 1: 5 and appoint *e* in every town,
Jas 5: 14 He should call the *e* of the church
1Pe 5: 1 To the *e* among you, I appeal
Rev 4: 4 seated on them were twenty-four *e*.
    4: 10 the twenty-four *e* fall

ELEAZAR

Third son of Aaron (Ex 6:23-25). Succeeded Aaron as high priest (Nu 20:26; Dt 10:6). Allotted land to tribes (Jos 14:1). Death (Jos 24:33).

ELECT* (ELECTION)

Mt 24: 22 the sake of the *e* those days will be
  24: 24 miracles to deceive even the *e*—
  24: 31 and they will gather his *e*
Mk 13: 20 sake of the *e*, whom he has chosen,
  13: 22 and miracles to deceive the *e*—
  13: 27 gather his *e* from the four winds,
Ro 11: 7 it did not obtain, but the *e* did.
1Ti 5: 21 and Christ Jesus and the *e* angels,
2Ti 2: 10 everything for the sake of the *e*,
Tit   1: 1 Christ for the faith of God's *e*
1Pe 1: 1 To God's *e*, strangers in the world,

ELECTION* (ELECT)

Ro   9: 11 God's purpose in *e* might stand:
  11: 28 but as far as *e* is concerned,
2Pe 1: 10 to make your calling and *e* sure.

ELEMENTARY* (ELEMENTS)

Heb 5: 12 someone to teach you the *e* truths
   6: 1 us leave the *e* teachings about

ELEMENTS* (ELEMENTARY)

2Pe 3: 10 the *e* will be destroyed by fire,
   3: 12 and the *e* will melt in the heat.

ELEVATE*

2Co 11: 7 to *e* you by preaching the gospel

ELI

High priest in youth of Samuel (1Sa 1-4). Blessed Hannah (1Sa 1:12-18); raised Samuel (1Sa 2:11-26). Prophesied against because of wicked sons (1Sa 2:27-36). Death of Eli and sons (1Sa 4:11-22).

ELIHU

One of Job's friends (Job 32-37).

ELIJAH

Prophet; predicted famine in Israel (1Ki 17:1; Jas 5:17). Fed by ravens (1Ki 17:2-6). Raised Sidonian widow's son (1Ki 17:7-24). Defeated prophets of Baal at Carmel (1Ki 18:16-46). Ran from Jezebel (1Ki 19:1-9). Prophesied death of Azariah (2Ki 1). Succeeded by Elisha (1Ki 19: 19-21; 2Ki 2:1-18). Taken to heaven in whirlwind (2Ki 2:11-12).
Return prophesied (Mal 4:5-6); equated with John the Baptist (Mt 17:9-13; Mk 9:9-13; Lk 1: 17). Appeared with Moses in transfiguration of Jesus (Mt 17:1-8; Mk 9:1-8).

ELIMELECH

Ru 1: 3 Now *E*, Naomi's husband, died,

ELIPHAZ

1. Firstborn of Esau (Ge 36).
2. One of Job's friends (Job 4-5; 15; 22).

ELISHA

Prophet; successor of Elijah (1Ki 19:16-21); inherited his cloak (2Ki 2:1-18). Purified bad water (2Ki 2:19-22). Cursed young men (2Ki 2: 23-25). Aided Israel's defeat of Moab (2Ki 3). Provided widow with oil (2Ki 4:1-7). Raised Shunammite woman's son (2Ki 4:8-37). Purified food (2Ki 4:38-41). Fed 100 men (2Ki 4:42-44). Healed Naaman's leprosy (2Ki 5). Made axhead float (2Ki 6:1-7). Captured Arameans (2Ki 6:8-23). Political adviser to Israel (2Ki 6:24-8:6; 9: 1-3; 13:14-19), Damascus (2Ki 8:7-15). Death (2Ki 13:20).

ELIZABETH*

Mother of John the Baptist, relative of Mary (Lk 1:5-58).

ELKANAH

Husband of Hannah, father of Samuel (1Sa 1-2).

ELOI*

Mt 27: 46 ''*E, E, lama sabachthani?*''—
Mk 15: 34 ''*E, E, lama sabachthani?*''—

ELOQUENCE* (ELOQUENT)

1Co 2: 1 come with *e* or superior wisdom

ELOQUENT* (ELOQUENCE)

Ex   4: 10 ''O Lord, I have never been *e*,

ELYMAS

Ac 13: 8 *E* the sorcerer (for that is what his

EMBEDDED*

Ecc 12: 11 sayings like firmly *e* nails—

EMBERS

Pr 26: 21 As charcoal to *e* and as wood to fire

EMBITTER* (BITTER)

Col 3: 21 Fathers, do not *e* your children,

EMBODIMENT* (BODY)

Ro   2: 20 have in the law the *e* of knowledge

EMPTIED (EMPTY)

1Co 1: 17 the cross of Christ be *e* of its power.

EMPTY (EMPTIED)

Ge   1: 2 Now the earth was formless and *e*,
Job 26: 7 the northern skies over *e* space;
Isa 45: 18 he did not create it to be *e*,
  55: 11 It will not return to me *e*,
Jer   4: 23 and it was formless and *e*,
Lk   1: 53 but has sent the rich away *e*.
Eph 5: 6 no one deceive you with *e* words,
1Pe 1: 18 from the *e* way of life handed
2Pe 2: 18 For they mouth *e*, boastful words

ENABLE (ABLE)

Lk   1: 74 to *e* us to serve him without fear
Ac   4: 29 *e* your servants to speak your word

ENABLED* (ABLE)

Lev 26: 13 *e* you to walk with heads held high.
Ru   4: 13 And the LORD *e* her to conceive,
Jn   6: 65 unless the Father has *e* him.''
Ac   2: 4 other tongues as the Spirit *e* them.
   7: 10 and *e* him to gain the goodwill
Heb 11: 11 was *e* to become a father

ENABLES (ABLE)

Php 3: 21 by the power that *e* him

ENABLING* (ABLE)

Ac 14: 3 the message of his grace by *e* them

ENCAMPS* (CAMP)

Ps 34: 7 The angel of the LORD *e*

ENCOURAGE* (ENCOURAGED ENCOURAGEMENT ENCOURAGES ENCOURAGING)

Dt   1: 38 *E* him, because he will lead Israel
   3: 28 and *e* and strengthen him,
2Sa 11: 25 Say this to *e* Joab.''
  19: 7 Now go out and *e* your men.
Job 16: 5 But my mouth would *e* you;
Ps 10: 17 you *e* them, and you listen
  64: 5 They *e* each other in evil plans,
Isa   1: 17 *e* the oppressed.
Jer 29: 8 to the dreams you *e* them to have.
Ac 15: 32 to *e* and strengthen the brothers.
Ro 12: 8 if it is encouraging, let him *e*;
Eph 6: 22 how we are, and that he may *e* you.
Col   4: 8 and that he may *e* your hearts.
1Th 3: 2 to strengthen and *e* you
   4: 18 Therefore *e* each other
   5: 11 Therefore *e* one another
   5: 14 those who are idle, *e* the timid,
2Th 2: 17 *e* your hearts and strengthen you
2Ti 4: 2 rebuke and *e*— with great patience
Tit   1: 9 so that he can *e* others
   2: 6 *e* the young men to be

ENCOURAGED

Tit 2: 15 *E* and rebuke with all authority.
Heb 3: 13 But *e* one another daily, as long
10: 25 but let us *e* one another—

ENCOURAGE* (ENCOURAGE)

Jdg 7: 11 you will be *e* to attack the camp.''
20: 22 But the men of Israel *e* one another
2Ch 22: 3 for his mother *e* him
32: 6 and *e* them with these words:
35: 2 and *e* them in the service
Eze 13: 22 you *e* the wicked not to turn
Ac 9: 31 It was strengthened; and *e*
11: 23 and *e* them all to remain true
16: 40 met with the brothers and *e* them.
18: 27 the brothers *e* him and wrote
27: 36 They were all *e* and ate some food
28: 15 men Paul thanked God and was *e*.
Ro 1: 12 and I may be mutually *e*
1Co 14: 31 everyone may be instructed and *e*.
2Co 7: 4 I am greatly *e; in all our troubles
7: 13 By all this we are *e*.
Php 1: 14 brothers in the Lord have been *e*
Col 2: 2 My purpose is that they may be *e*
1Th 3: 7 persecution we were *e* about you
Heb 6: 18 offered to us may be greatly *e*.

ENCOURAGEMENT* (ENCOURAGE)

Ac 4: 36 Barnabas (which means Son of *E),
13: 15 a message of *e* for the people,
20: 2 speaking many words of *e*
Ro 15: 4 *e* of the Scriptures we might have
15: 5 and *e* give you a spirit of unity
1Co 14: 3 to men for their strengthening, *e*
2Co 7: 13 to our own *e*, we were especially
Php 2: 1 If you have any *e* from being united
2Th 2: 16 and by his grace gave us eternal *e*
Phm : 7 love has given me great joy and *e*,
Heb 12: 5 word of *e* that addresses you

ENCOURAGES* (ENCOURAGE)

Isa 41: 7 The craftsman *e* the goldsmith,

ENCOURAGING* (ENCOURAGE)

Ac 14: 22 *e* them to remain true to the faith.
15: 31 and were glad for its *e* message.
20: 1 for the disciples and, after *e* them,
Ro 12: 8 if it is *e*, let him encourage;
1Th 2: 12 *e*, comforting and urging you
1Pe 5: 12 *e* you and testifying that this is

ENCROACH

Pr 23: 10 or *e* on the fields of the fatherless,

END (ENDS)

Ps 119: 33 then I will keep them to the *e*.
119:112 to the very *e*.
Pr 1: 19 Such is the *e* of all who go
5: 4 but in the *e* she is bitter as gall,
5: 11 At the *e* of your life you will groan,
14: 12 but in the *e* it leads to death.
14: 13 and joy may *e* in grief.
16: 25 but in the *e* it leads to death.
19: 20 and in the *e* you will be wise.
20: 21 will not be blessed at the *e*.
23: 32 In the *e* it bites like a snake
25: 8 for what will you do in the *e*
28: 23 in the *e* gain more favor
29: 21 he will bring grief in the *e*.
Ecc 3: 11 done from beginning to *e*.
7: 8 The *e* of a matter is better
12: 12 making many books there is no *e*,
Eze 7: 2 The *e!* The *e* has come
Mt 10: 22 firm to the *e* will be saved.
24: 13 firm to the *e* will be saved.
24: 14 nations, and then the *e* will come.
Lk 21: 9 but the *e* will not come right away
Ro 10: 4 *e* of the law
1Co 15: 24 the *e* will come, when he hands
Rev 21: 6 Omega, the Beginning and the *E.*
22: 13 the Last, the Beginning and the *E.*

ENDS (END)

Ps 19: 4 their words to the *e* of the world.
Pr 20: 17 he *e* up with a mouth full of gravel.
Isa 49: 6 salvation to the *e* of the earth.''
62: 11 proclamation to the *e* of the earth:
Ac 13: 47 salvation to the *e* of the earth.' ''
Ro 10: 18 their words to the *e* of the world.''

ENDURANCE* (ENDURE)

Ro 15: 4 through *e* and the encouragement
15: 5 May the God who gives *e*
2Co 1: 6 which produces in you patient *e*
6: 4 in great *e; in troubles, hardships
Col 1: 11 might so that you may have great *e*
1Th 1: 3 and your *e* inspired by hope
1Ti 6: 11 faith, love, *e* and gentleness.
2Ti 3: 10 patience, love, *e*, persecutions,
Tit 2: 2 and sound in faith, in love and in *e*.
Rev 1: 9 and patient *e* that are ours in Jesus,
13: 10 This calls for patient *e*
14: 12 This calls for patient *e* on the part

ENDURE (ENDURANCE ENDURED ENDURES ENDURING)

Ps 72: 17 May his name *e* forever;
Pr 12: 19 Truthful lips *e* forever,
27: 24 for riches do not *e* forever,
Ecc 3: 14 everything God does will *e* forever;
Da 2: 44 to an end, but it will itself *e* forever.
Mal 3: 2 who can *e* the day of his coming?
1Co 4: 12 when we are persecuted, we *e* it;
2Co 1: 8 far beyond our ability to *e*,
2Ti 2: 3 *E* hardship with us like a good
2: 10 Therefore I *e* everything
2: 12 if we *e*, / we will also reign
4: 5 head in all situations, *e* hardship,
Heb 12: 7 *E* hardship as discipline; God is
1Pe 2: 20 a beating for doing wrong and *e* it?
2: 20 suffer for doing good and you *e* it,
Rev 3: 10 kept my command to *e* patiently,

ENDURED* (ENDURE)

Ps 123: 3 for we have *e* much contempt.
123: 4 We have *e* much ridicule
132: 1 and all the hardships he *e*.
Ac 13: 18 and *e* their conduct forty years
2Ti 3: 11 and Lystra, the persecutions I *e*.
Heb 12: 2 set before him *e* the cross,
12: 3 him who *e* such opposition
Rev 2: 3 and have *e* hardships for my name,

ENDURES (ENDURE)

Ps 102: 12 renown *e* through all generations.
112: 9 his righteousness *e* forever;
136: 1 *His love e forever.*
Da 9: 15 made for yourself a name that *e*
2Co 9: 9 his righteousness *e* forever.''

ENDURING (ENDURE)

2Th 1: 4 persecutions and trials you are *e*.
1Pe 1: 23 through the living and *e* word

ENEMIES (ENEMY)

Ps 23: 5 in the presence of my *e*.
110: 1 hand until I make your *e*
Pr 16: 7 his *e* live at peace with him.
Isa 59: 18 wrath to his *e*
Mic 7: 6 a man's *e* are the members
Mt 5: 44 Love your *e* and pray
10: 36 a man's *e* will be the members
Lk 6: 27 Love your *e*, do good
6: 35 But love your *e*, do good to them,
20: 43 hand until I make your *e*
Ro 5: 10 For if, when we were God's *e*,
1Co 15: 25 reign until he has put all his *e*
Php 3: 18 many live as *e* of the cross of Christ
Heb 1: 13 hand until I make your *e*
10: 13 for his *e* to be made his footstool,

ENEMY (ENEMIES ENMITY)

Pr 24: 17 Do not gloat when your *e* falls;
25: 21 If your *e* is hungry, give him food
27: 6 but an *e* multiplies kisses.
29: 24 of a thief is his own *e;
Lk 10: 19 to overcome all the power of the *e;
Ro 12: 20 ''If your *e* is hungry, feed him;
1Co 15: 26 The last *e* to be destroyed is death.
1Ti 5: 14 and to give the *e* no opportunity
1Pe 5: 8 Your *e* the devil prowls

ENERGY*

Col 1: 29 struggling with all his *e*, which

ENGRAVED

Isa 49: 16 I have *e* you on the palms
2Co 3: 7 which was *e* in letters on stone,

ENHANCES*

Ro 3: 7 my falsehood *e* God's truthfulness

ENJOY (JOY)

Dt 6: 2 and so that you may *e* long life.
Ps 37: 3 dwell in the land and *e* safe pasture.
Pr 28: 16 ill-gotten gain will *e* a long life.
Ecc 3: 22 better for a man than to *e* his work,
Eph 6: 3 and that you may *e* long life
Heb 11: 25 rather than to *e* the pleasures of sin
3Jn : 2 I pray that you may *e* good health

ENJOYMENT (JOY)

Ecc 4: 8 and why am I depriving myself of *e*
1Ti 6: 17 us with everything for our *e*.

ENLARGE (ENLARGES)

2Co 9: 10 *e* the harvest of your righteousness.

ENLARGES (ENLARGE)

Dt 33: 20 Blessed is he who *e* Gad's domain!

ENLIGHTENED* (LIGHT)

Eph 1: 18 that the eyes of your heart may be *e*
Heb 6: 4 for those who have once been *e*,

ENMITY* (ENEMY)

Ge 3: 15 And I will put *e*

ENOCH

1. Son of Cain (Ge 4:17-18).
2. Descendant of Seth; walked with God and taken by him (Ge 5:18-24; Heb 11:5). Prophet (Jude 14).

ENSLAVED (SLAVE)

Gal 4: 9 Do you wish to be *e* by them all
Tit 3: 3 and *e* by all kinds of passions

ENSNARE (SNARE)

Pr 5: 22 of a wicked man *e* him;
Ecc 7: 26 but the sinner she will *e*.

ENSNARED* (SNARE)

Dt 7: 25 for yourselves, or you will be *e* by it
12: 30 be careful not to be *e*
Ps 9: 16 the wicked are *e* by the work
Pr 6: 2 *e* by the words of your mouth,
22: 25 and get yourself *e*.

ENTANGLED (ENTANGLES)

2Pe 2: 20 and are again *e* in it and overcome,

ENTANGLES* (ENTANGLED)

Heb 12: 1 and the sin that so easily *e*,

ENTER (ENTERED ENTERING ENTERS ENTRANCE)

Ps 95: 11 ''They shall never *e* my rest.''
100: 4 *E* his gates with thanksgiving
Pr 2: 10 For wisdom will *e* your heart,
Mt 5: 20 will certainly not *e* the kingdom
7: 13 ''*E* through the narrow gate.
7: 21 Lord,' will *e* the kingdom of heaven
18: 3 you will never *e* the kingdom
18: 8 It is better for you to *e* life maimed
19: 17 to *e* life, obey the commandments
19: 23 man to *e* the kingdom of heaven.
Mk 9: 43 It is better for you to *e* life maimed
9: 45 It is better for you to *e* life crippled
9: 47 for you to *e* the kingdom of God
10: 15 like a little child will never *e* it.''
10: 23 is for the rich to *e* the kingdom
Lk 13: 24 will try to *e* and will not be able to.
13: 24 ''Make every effort to *e*
18: 17 like a little child will never *e* it.''
18: 24 is for the rich to *e* the kingdom
Jn 3: 5 no one can *e* the kingdom of God.
Heb 3: 11 'They shall never *e* my rest.' ''
4: 11 make every effort to *e* that rest,

ENTERED (ENTER)

Ps 73: 17 me till I *e* the sanctuary of God;
Eze 4: 14 meat has ever *e* my mouth.''
Ac 11: 8 or unclean has ever *e* my mouth.'
Ro 5: 12 as sin *e* the world through one man,
Heb 9: 12 but he *e* the Most Holy Place once

ENTERING (ENTER)

Mt 21:31 the prostitutes are *e* the kingdom
Lk 11:52 have hindered those who were *e.*"
Heb 4: 1 the promise of *e* his rest still stands,

ENTERS (ENTER)

Mk 7:18 you see that nothing that *e* a man
Jn 10: 2 The man who *e* by the gate is

ENTERTAIN* (ENTERTAINED ENTERTAINMENT)

Jdg 16:25 "Bring out Samson to *e* us."
Mt 9: 4 "Why do you *e* evil thoughts
1Ti 5:19 Do not *e* an accusation
Heb 13: 2 Do not forget to *e* strangers,

ENTERTAINED* (ENTERTAIN)

Ac 28: 7 and for three days *e* us hospitably.
Heb 13: 2 so doing some people have *e* angels

ENTERTAINMENT* (ENTERTAIN)

Da 6:18 without any *e* being brought to him

ENTHRALLED*

Ps 45:11 The king is *e* by your beauty;

ENTHRONED* (THRONE)

1Sa 4: 4 who is *e* between the cherubim.
2Sa 6: 2 who is *e* between the cherubim that
2Ki 19:15 of Israel, *e* between the cherubim,
1Ch 13: 6 who is *e* between the cherubim—
Ps 2: 4 The One *e* in heaven laughs;
    9:11 to the LORD, *e* in Zion;
   22: 3 Yet you are *e* as the Holy One;
   29:10 The LORD sits *e* over the flood;
   29:10 the LORD is *e* as King forever.
   55:19 God, who is *e* forever,
   61: 7 May he be *e* in God's presence
   80: 1 who sit *e* between the cherubim,
   99: 1 he sits *e* between the cherubim,
  102:12 But you, O LORD, sit *e* forever;
  113: 5 the One who sits *e* on high,
  132:14 here I will sit *e,* for I have desired it
Isa 14:13 I will sit *e* on the mount
   37:16 of Israel, *e* between the cherubim,
   40:22 He sits *e* above the circle
   52: 2 rise up, sit *e,* O Jerusalem.

ENTHRONES* (THRONE)

Job 36: 7 he *e* them with kings

ENTHUSIASM*

2Co 8:17 he is coming to you with much *e*
   9: 2 and your *e* has stirred most of them

ENTICE* (ENTICED ENTICES)

Pr 1:10 My son, if sinners *e* you,
2Pe 2:18 they *e* people who are just escaping
Rev 2:14 who taught Balak to *e* the Israelites

ENTICED* (ENTICE)

Dt 4:19 do not be *e* into bowing
   11:16 or you will be *e* to turn away
2Ki 17:21 Jeroboam *e* Israel away
Job 31: 9 If my heart has been *e* by a woman,
   31:27 so that my heart was secretly *e*
Jas 1:14 desire, he is dragged away and *e.*

ENTICES* (ENTICE)

Dt 13: 6 your closest friend secretly *e* you,
Job 36:18 Be careful that no one *e* you
Pr 16:29 A violent man *e* his neighbor

ENTIRE

Gal 5:14 The *e* law is summed up

ENTRANCE (ENTER)

Mt 27:60 stone in front of the *e* to the tomb
Mk 15:46 a stone against the *e* of the tomb.
   16: 3 away from the *e* of the tomb?''
Jn 11:38 cave with a stone laid across the *e.*
   20: 1 had been removed from the *e.*

ENTRUST (TRUST)

Jn 2:24 Jesus would not *e* himself to them,
2Ti 2: 2 the presence of many witnesses *e*

ENTRUSTED (TRUST)

Jer 13:20 Where is the flock that was *e* to you
Jn 5:22 but has *e* all judgment to the Son,
Ro 3: 2 they have been *e* with the very
   6:17 of teaching to which you were *e.*
1Co 4: 1 as those *e* with the secret things
1Th 2: 4 by God to be *e* with the gospel.
1Ti 1:11 of the blessed God, which he *e*
   6:20 guard what has been *e* to your care.
2Ti 1:12 able to guard what I have *e* to him
   1:14 Guard the good deposit that was *e*
Tit 1: 3 light through the preaching *e* to me
   1: 7 Since an overseer is *e*
1Pe 2:23 he *e* himself to him who judges
   5: 3 not lording it over those *e* to you,
Jude : 3 once for all *e* to the saints.

ENVIES

Jas 4: 5 spirit he caused to live in us *e*

ENVIOUS (ENVY)

Dt 32:21 I will make them *e*
Pr 24:19 or be *e* of the wicked,
Ro 10:19 "I will make you *e*

ENVOY

Pr 13:17 but a trustworthy *e* brings healing.

ENVY (ENVIOUS ENVYING)

Pr 3:31 Do not *e* a violent man
   14:30 but *e* rots the bones.
   23:17 Do not let your heart *e* sinners,
   24: 1 Do not *e* wicked men,
Mk 7:22 malice, deceit, lewdness, *e,* slander
Ro 1:29 They are full of *e,* murder, strife,
   11:14 arouse my own people to *e*
1Co 13: 4 It does not *e,* it does not boast,
Gal 5:21 factions and *e;* drunkenness, orgies
Php 1:15 that some preach Christ out of *e*
1Ti 6: 4 and quarrels about words that result in
      e,
Tit 3: 3 lived in malice and *e,* being hated
Jas 3:14 But if you harbor bitter *e*
   3:16 where you have *e* and selfish
1Pe 2: 1 *e,* and slander of every kind.

ENVYING* (ENVY)

Gal 5:26 provoking and *e* each other.

EPHAH

Eze 45:11 The *e* and the bath are

EPHESUS

Ac 18:19 at *E,* where Paul left Priscilla
   19: 1 the interior and arrived at *E.*
Eph 1: 1 To the saints in *E,* the faithful
Rev 2: 1 the angel of the church in *E* write:

EPHRAIM

1. Second son of Joseph (Ge 41:52; 46:20). Blessed as firstborn by Jacob (Ge 48). Tribe of numbered (Nu 1:33; 26:37), blessed (Dt 33:17), allotted land (Jos 16:4-9; Eze 48:5), failed to fully possess (Jos 16:10; Jdg 1:29).
2. Synonymous with Northern Kingdom (Isa 7; 17; Hos 5).

EQUAL (EQUALITY EQUITY)

Dt 33:25 and your strength will *e* your days.
1Sa 9: 2 without *e* among the Israelites—
Isa 40:25 who is my *e?*" says the Holy One.
   46: 5 you compare me or count me *e?*
Da 1:19 and he found none *e* to Daniel,
Jn 5:18 making himself *e* with God.
1Co 12:25 that its parts should have *e* concern
2Co 2:16 And who is *e* to such a task?

EQUALITY* (EQUAL)

2Co 8:13 pressed, but that there might be *e.*
   8:14 Then there will be *e,* as it is written:
Php 2: 6 did not consider *e*

EQUIP* (EQUIPPED)

Heb 13:21 *e* you with everything good

EQUIPPED (EQUIP)

2Ti 3:17 man of God may be thoroughly *e*

EQUITY* (EQUAL)

Ps 96:10 he will judge the peoples with *e.*
   98: 9 and the peoples with *e.*
   99: 4 you have established *e;*

ERODES*

Job 14:18 "But as a mountain *e* and crumbles

ERROR (ERRORS)

Jas 5:20 Whoever turns a sinner from the *e*
2Pe 2:18 escaping from those who live in *e.*

ERRORS* (ERROR)

Ps 19:12 Who can discern his *e?*
Ecc 10: 4 calmness can lay great *e* to rest.

ESAU

Firstborn of Isaac, twin of Jacob (Ge 25:21-26). Also called Edom (Ge 25:30). Sold Jacob his birthright (Ge 25:29-34); lost blessing (Gen 27). Married Hittites (Ge 26:34), Ishmaelites (Ge 28:6-9). Reconciled to Jacob (Gen 33). Genealogy (Ge 36). The LORD chose Jacob over Esau (Mal 1:2-3), but gave Esau land (Dt 2:2-12). Descendants eventually obliterated (Ob 1-21; Jer 49:7-22).

ESCAPE (ESCAPED ESCAPES ESCAPING)

Ps 68:20 from the Sovereign LORD comes *e*
Pr 11: 9 through knowledge the righteous *e.*
Ro 2: 3 think you will *e* God's judgment?
1Th 5: 3 woman, and they will not *e.*
2Ti 2:26 and *e* from the trap of the devil,
Heb 2: 3 how shall we *e* if we ignore such
   12:25 If they did not *e* when they refused
2Pe 1: 4 and *e* the corruption in the world

ESCAPED (ESCAPE)

2Pe 2:20 If they have *e* the corruption

ESCAPES (ESCAPE)

Pr 12:13 but a righteous man *e* trouble.

ESCAPING (ESCAPE)

1Co 3:15 only as one *e* through the flames.
2Pe 2:18 they entice people who are just *e*

ESTABLISH (ESTABLISHED ESTABLISHES)

Ge 6:18 But I will *e* my covenant with you,
   17:21 But my covenant I will *e* with Isaac
2Sa 7:11 the LORD himself will *e* a house
1Ki 9: 5 I will *e* your royal throne
1Ch 28: 7 I will *e* his kingdom forever
Ps 90:17 *e* the work of our hands for us—
Isa 26:12 LORD, you *e* peace for us;
Ro 10: 3 God and sought to *e* their own,
   16:25 able to *e* you by my gospel
Heb 10: 9 sets aside the first to *e* the second.

ESTABLISHED (ESTABLISH)

Ge 9:17 the sign of the covenant I have *e*
Ex 6: 4 also *e* my covenant with them
Pr 16:12 a throne is *e* through righteousness.

ESTABLISHES (ESTABLISH)

Job 25: 2 he *e* order in the heights of heaven.
Isa 42: 4 till he *e* justice on earth.

ESTATE

Ps 136:23 who remembered us in our low *e*

ESTEEMED

Pr 22: 1 to be *e* is better than silver or gold.
Isa 53: 3 he was despised, and we *e* him not.

ESTHER

Jewess, originally named Hadassah, who lived in Persia; cousin of Mordecai (Est 2:7). Chosen queen of Xerxes (Est 2:8-18). Persuaded by Mordecai to foil Haman's plan to exterminate the Jews (Est 3-4). Revealed Haman's plans to Xerxes, resulting in Haman's death (Est 7), the Jews' preservation (Est 8-9), Mordecai's exaltation (Est 8:15; 9:4; 10). Decreed celebration of Purim (Est 9:18-32).

ETERNAL* (ETERNALLY ETERNITY)

Ge 21:33 the name of the LORD, the *E* God.
Dt 33:27 The *e* God is your refuge,
1Ki 10: 9 of the LORD's *e* love for Israel,
Ps 16:11 with *e* pleasures at your right hand.
     21: 6 you have granted him *e* blessings
    111: 10 To him belongs *e* praise.
    119: 89 Your word, O LORD, is *e*;
    119:160 all your righteous laws are *e*.
Ecc 12: 5 Then man goes to his *e* home
Isa 26: 4 LORD, the LORD, is the Rock *e*.
     47: 7 the *e* queen!'
Jer 10:10 he is the living God, the *e* King.
Da   4: 3 His kingdom is an *e* kingdom;
     4:34 His dominion is an *e* dominion;
     4: 3 His ways are *e*.
Hab 3: 6 His ways are *e*.
Mt 18: 8 two feet and be thrown into *e* fire.
     19:16 good thing must I do to get *e* life?"
     19:29 as much and will inherit *e* life.
     25:41 into the *e* fire prepared for the devil
     25:46 but the righteous to *e* life."
     25:46 they will go away to *e* punishment,
Mk   3:29 be forgiven; he is guilty of an *e* sin."
     10:17 "what must I do to inherit *e* life?"
     10:30 and in the age to come, *e* life.
Lk 10:25 "what must I do to inherit *e* life?"
     16: 9 will be welcomed into *e* dwellings.
     18:18 what must I do to inherit *e* life?"
     18:30 and, in the age to come, *e* life."
Jn   3:15 believes in him may have *e* life.
     3:16 him shall not perish but have *e* life.
     3:36 believes in the Son has *e* life,
     4:14 spring of water welling up to *e* life."
     4:36 now he harvests the crop for *e* life,
     5:24 believes him who sent me has *e* life
     5:39 that by them you possess *e* life.
     6:27 but for food that endures to *e* life,
     6:40 believes in him shall have *e* life,
     6:54 and drinks my blood has *e* life,
     6:68 You have the words of *e* life.
    10:28 I give them *e* life, and they shall
    12:25 in this world will keep it for *e* life.
    12:50 that his command leads to *e* life.
    17: 2 all people that he might give *e* life
    17: 3 this is *e* life: that they may know
Ac 13:46 yourselves worthy of *e* life,
    13:48 were appointed for *e* life believed.
Ro   1:20 his *e* power and divine nature—
     2: 7 and immortality, he will give *e* life.
     5:21 righteousness to bring *e* life
     6:22 to holiness, and the result is *e* life.
     6:23 but the gift of God is *e* life
    16:26 by the command of the *e* God,
2Co 4:17 for us an *e* glory that far outweighs
     4:18 temporary, but what is unseen is *e*.
     5: 1 from God, an *e* house in heaven,
Gal 6: 8 from the Spirit will reap *e* life.
Eph 3:11 to his *e* purpose which he
2Th 2:16 his grace gave us *e* encouragement
1Ti 1:16 believe on him and receive *e* life.
     1:17 Now to the King *e*, immortal,
     6:12 Take hold of the *e* life
2Ti 2:10 is in Christ Jesus, with *e* glory.
Tit 1: 2 resting on the hope of *e* life,
     3: 7 heirs having the hope of *e* life.
Heb 5: 9 he became the source of *e* salvation
     6: 2 of the dead, and *e* judgment.
     9:12 having obtained *e* redemption.
     9:14 through the *e* Spirit offered himself
     9:15 the promised *e* inheritance—
    13:20 of the *e* covenant brought back
1Pe 5:10 you to his *e* glory in Christ,
2Pe 1:11 into the *e* kingdom of our Lord
1Jn 1: 2 and we proclaim to you the *e* life,
     2:25 what he promised us—even *e* life.
     3:15 know that no murderer has *e* life
     5:11 God has given us *e* life,
     5:13 you may know that you have *e* life.
     5:20 He is the true God and *e* life.
Jude : 7 who suffer the punishment of *e* fire.
     :21 Christ to bring you to *e* life.
Rev 14: 6 and he had the *e* gospel to proclaim

ETERNALLY* (ETERNAL)

Gal 1: 8 let him be *e* condemned! As we
     1: 9 let him be *e* condemned! Am I now

ETERNITY* (ETERNAL)

Ps 93: 2 you are from all *e*.
Pr 23:23 I was appointed from *e*,
Ecc 3:11 also set *e* in the hearts of men;

ETHIOPIAN*

Jer 13:23 Can the *E* change his skin
Ac   8:27 and on his way he met an *E* eunuch

EUNUCH (EUNUCHS)

Ac   8:27 on his way he met an Ethiopian *e*,

EUNUCHS (EUNUCH)

Isa 56: 4 "To the *e* who keep my Sabbaths,
Mt 19:12 For some are *e* because they were

EUTYCHUS*

Ac 20: 9 was a young man named *E*,

EVANGELIST* (EVANGELISTS)

Ac 21: 8 stayed at the house of Philip the *e*,
2Ti 4: 5 hardship, do the work of an *e*,

EVANGELISTS* (EVANGELIST)

Eph 4:11 some to be prophets, some to be *e*,

EVE*

Ge   3:20 Adam named his wife *E*,
     4: 1 Adam lay with his wife *E*,
2Co 11: 3 as *E* was deceived by the serpent's
1Ti 2:13 For Adam was formed first, then *E*

EVEN-TEMPERED* (TEMPER)

Pr 17:27 and a man of understanding is *e*.

EVENING

Ge   1: 5 there was *e*, and there was morning

EVER (EVERLASTING FOREVER FOREVERMORE)

Ex 15:18 LORD will reign for *e* and *e*."
Dt   8:19 If you *e* forget the LORD your
1Ki 3:12 anyone like you, nor will there *e* be.
Job 4: 7 were the upright *e* destroyed?
Ps   5:11 let them *e* sing for joy.
    10:16 The LORD is King for *e* and *e*;
    21: 4 length of days, for *e* and *e*.
    25: 3 will *e* be put to shame,
    25:15 My eyes are *e* on the LORD,
    26: 3 for your love is *e* before me,
    45: 6 O God, will last for *e* and *e*;
    45:17 nations will praise you for *e* and *e*.
    48:14 For this God is our God for *e* and *e*;
    52: 8 God's unfailing love for *e* and *e*.
    61: 8 will I *e* sing praise to your name
    71: 6 I will *e* praise you.
    84: 4 they are *e* praising you.
    89:33 nor will I *e* betray my faithfulness.
    111: 8 They are steadfast for *e* and *e*,
    119: 44 your law, for *e* and *e*.
    119: 98 for they are *e* with me.
    132: 12 sit on your throne for *e* and *e*."
    145: 1 I will praise your name for *e* and *e*."
    145: 2 and extol your name for *e* and *e*.
    145: 21 his holy name for *e* and *e*.
Pr   4:18 shining *e* brighter till the full light
     5:19 may you *e* be captivated
Isa 66: 8 Who has *e* heard of such a thing?
     66: 8 Who has *e* seen such things?
Jer 7: 7 I gave your forefathers for *e* and *e*.
     25: 5 and your fathers for *e* and *e*.
     31:36 the descendants of Israel *e* cease
Da   2:20 be to the name of God for *e* and *e*;
     7:18 it forever—yes, for *e* and *e*.'
     12: 3 like the stars for *e* and *e*.
Mic 4: 5 our God for *e* and *e*.
Mt 13:14 you will be *e* seeing but never
     13:14 " 'You will be *e* hearing
Mk   4:12 *e* hearing but never understanding;
Jn   1:18 No one has *e* seen God,
Gal 1: 5 to whom be glory for *e* and *e*.
Eph 3:21 all generations, for *e* and *e*.
Php 4:20 and Father be glory for *e* and *e*.
1Ti 1:17 be honor and glory for *e* and *e*.
2Ti 4:18 To him be glory for *e* and *e*.
Heb 1: 8 O God, will last for *e* and *e*,
    13:21 to whom be glory for *e* and *e*.
1Pe 4:11 the glory and the power for *e* and *e*.

1Pe 5:11 To him be the power for *e* and *e*.
1Jn 4:12 No one has *e* seen God;
Rev 1: 6 him be glory and power for *e* and *e*!
     1:18 and behold I am alive for *e* and *e*!
    21:27 Nothing impure will *e* enter it,
    22: 5 And they will reign for *e* and *e*.

EVER-INCREASING* (INCREASE)

Ro   6:19 to impurity and to *e* wickedness,
2Co 3:18 into his likeness with *e* glory,

EVERLASTING* (EVER)

Ge   9:16 and remember the *e* covenant
     17: 7 an *e* covenant between me and you
     17: 8 I will give as an *e* possession to you
     17:13 in your flesh is to be an *e* covenant.
     17:19 an *e* covenant for his descendants
     48: 4 *e* possession to your descendants
Nu 18:19 It is an *e* covenant of salt
Dt 33:15 and the fruitfulness of the *e* hills;
     33:27 and underneath are the *e* arms.
2Sa 23: 5 made with me an *e* covenant,
1Ch 16:17 to Israel as an *e* covenant:
     16:36 from *e* to *e*.
     29:10 from *e* to *e*.
Ezr 9:12 to your children as an *e* inheritance
Ne   9: 5 your God, who is from *e* to *e*."
Ps 41:13 from *e* to *e*.
     52: 5 God will bring you down to *e* ruin:
     74: 3 toward these *e* ruins,
     78:66 he put them to *e* shame.
     90: 2 from *e* to *e* you are God.
    103: 17 But from *e* to *e*
    105: 10 to Israel as an *e* covenant:
    106: 48 from *e* to *e*.
    119:142 Your righteousness is *e*
    139: 24 and lead me in the way of
    145: 13 Your kingdom is an *e* kingdom,
Isa 9: 6 *E* Father, Prince of Peace.
     24: 5 and broken the *e* covenant.
     30: 8 it may be an *e* witness.
     33:14 Who of us can dwell with *e* burning
     35:10 *e* joy will crown their heads.
     40:28 The LORD is the *e* God,
     45:17 the LORD with an *e* salvation;
     45:17 to ages *e*.
     51:11 *e* joy will crown their heads.
     54: 8 but with *e* kindness
     55: 3 I will make an *e* covenant with you,
     55:13 for an *e* sign,
     56: 5 I will give them an *e* name
     60:15 I will make you the *e* pride
     60:19 for the LORD will be your *e* light,
     60:20 the LORD will be your *e* light,
     61: 7 and *e* joy will be theirs.
     61: 8 and make an *e* covenant with them.
     63:12 to gain for himself *e* renown,
Jer 5:22 an *e* barrier it cannot cross.
     23:40 I will bring upon you *e* disgrace—
     23:40 *e* shame that will not be forgotten."
     25: 9 of horror and scorn, and an *e* ruin.
     31: 3 "I have loved you with an *e* love;
     32:40 I will make an *e* covenant
     50: 5 the LORD in an *e* covenant
Eze 16:60 and I will establish an *e* covenant
     37:26 with them; it will be an *e* covenant.
Da   7:14 dominion is an *e* dominion that will
     7:27 His kingdom will be an *e* kingdom,
     9:24 to bring in *e* righteousness,
     12: 2 others to shame and *e* contempt.
     12: 2 some to *e* life, others to shame
Mic 6: 2 you *e* foundations of the earth.
Hab 1:12 O LORD, are you not from *e*?
Jn   6:47 the truth, he who believes has *e* life.
2Th 1: 9 punished with *e* destruction
Jude : 6 bound with *e* chains for judgment

EVER-PRESENT*

Ps 46: 1 an *e* help in trouble

EVIDENCE (EVIDENT)

Jn 14:11 on the *e* of the miracles themselves.
Ac 11:23 and saw the *e* of the grace of God,
2Th 1: 5 All this is *e* that God's judgment is
Jas 2:20 do you want *e* that faith

EVIDENT (EVIDENCE)

Php 4: 5 Let your gentleness be *e* to all.

EVIL (EVILDOER EVILDOERS EVILS)

Ge 2: 9 of the knowledge of good and *e*.
    3: 5 be like God, knowing good and *e*."
    6: 5 of his heart was only *e* all the time.
Ex 32: 22 how prone these people are to *e*.
Jdg 2: 11 Then the Israelites did *e* in the eyes
    3: 7 The Israelites did *e* in the eyes
    3: 12 Once again the Israelites did *e*
    4: 1 the Israelites once again did *e*
    6: 1 Again the Israelites did *e*
   10: 6 Again the Israelites did *e*
   13: 1 Again the Israelites did *e*
1Ki 11: 6 So Solomon did *e* in the eyes
   16: 25 But Omri did *e* in the eyes
2Ki 15: 24 Pekahiah did *e* in the eyes
Job 1: 1 he feared God and shunned *e*.
    1: 8 a man who fears God and shuns *e*."
   34: 10 Far be it from God to do *e*,
   36: 21 Beware of turning to *e*,
Ps   5: 4 not a God who takes pleasure in *e*;
   23: 4 I will fear no *e*,
   34: 13 keep your tongue from *e*
   34: 14 Turn from *e* and do good;
   34: 16 is against those who do *e*,
   37: 1 Do not fret because of *e* men
   37: 8 do not fret—it leads only to *e*.
   37: 27 Turn from *e* and do good;
   49: 5 fear when *e* days come,
   51: 4 and done what is *e* in your sight,
   97: 10 those who love the LORD hate *e*,
  101: 4 I will have nothing to do with *e*.
  141: 4 not my heart be drawn to what is *e*,
Pr   4: 27 keep your foot from *e*.
    8: 13 To fear the LORD is to hate *e*;
   10: 23 A fool finds pleasure in *e* conduct,
   11: 19 he who pursues *e* goes to his death.
   11: 27 *e* comes to him who searches for it.
   14: 16 man fears the LORD and shuns *e*,
   17: 13 If a man pays back *e* for good,
   20: 30 Blows and wounds cleanse away *e*,
   24: 19 Do not fret because of *e* men
   24: 20 for the *e* man has no future hope,
   26: 23 are fervent lips with an *e* heart.
   28: 5 *E* men do not understand justice,
   29: 6 An *e* man is snared by his own sin,
Ecc 12: 14 whether it is good or *e*.
Isa 5: 20 Woe to those who call *e* good
   13: 11 I will punish the world for its *e*,
   55: 7 and the *e* man his thoughts.
Jer 4: 14 wash the *e* from your heart
   18: 8 nation I warned repents of its *e*,
   18: 11 So turn from your *e* ways,
Eze 33: 11 Turn! Turn from your *e* ways!
   33: 13 he will die for the *e* he has done.
   33: 15 and does no *e*, he will surely live;
Am   5: 13 for the times are *e*.
Hab 1: 13 Your eyes are too pure to look on *e*;
Zec 8: 17 do not plot *e* against your neighbor,
Mt   5: 45 He causes his sun to rise on the *e*
    6: 13 but deliver us from the *e* one.'
    7: 11 If you, then, though you are *e*,
   12: 34 you who are *e* say anything good?
   12: 35 and the *e* man brings *e* things out
   12: 35 out of the *e* stored up in him.
   12: 43 "When an *e* spirit comes out
   15: 19 out of the heart come *e* thoughts,
Mk   7: 21 come *e* thoughts, sexual
Lk   6: 45 and the *e* man brings *e* things out
   11: 13 If you then, though you are *e*,
Jn   3: 19 of light because their deeds were *e*.
    3: 20 Everyone who does *e* hates
   17: 15 you protect them from the *e* one.
Ro   1: 30 they invent ways of doing *e*;
    2: 8 who reject the truth and follow *e*,
    2: 9 for every human being who does *e*:
    3: 8 "Let us do *e* that good may result"?
    6: 12 body so that you obey its *e* desires.
    7: 19 no, the *e* I do not want to do—
    7: 21 to do good, *e* is right there with me.
   12: 9 Hate what is *e*; cling
   12: 17 Do not repay anyone *e* for *e*.
   12: 21 Do not be overcome by *e*,
   14: 16 good to be spoken of as *e*.
   16: 19 and innocent about what is *e*.
1Co 13: 6 Love does not delight in *e*
   14: 20 In regard to *e* be infants,
Eph 5: 16 because the days are *e*.

Eph 6: 12 forces of *e* in the heavenly realms.
    6: 16 all the flaming arrows of the *e* one.
Col 3: 5 impurity, lust, *e* desires and greed,
1Th 5: 22 Avoid every kind of *e*.
2Th 3: 3 and protect you from the *e* one.
1Ti 6: 10 of money is a root of all kinds of *e*.
2Ti 2: 22 Flee the *e* desires of youth,
    3: 6 are swayed by all kinds of *e* desires,
    3: 13 while *e* men and impostors will go
Heb 5: 14 to distinguish good from *e*.
Jas 1: 13 For God cannot be tempted by *e*,
    1: 21 and the *e* that is so prevalent,
    3: 6 a world of *e* among the parts
    3: 8 It is a restless *e*, full
1Pe 2: 16 your freedom as a cover-up for *e*;
    3: 9 Do not repay *e* with *e* or insult
    3: 10 must keep his tongue from *e*
    3: 17 for doing good than for doing *e*.
1Jn 2: 13 you have overcome the *e* one.
    2: 14 and you have overcome the *e* one.
    3: 12 who belonged to the *e* one
    5: 18 and the *e* one cannot harm him.
    5: 19 is under the control of the *e* one.
3Jn   : 11 do not imitate what is *e*

EVILDOER* (EVIL)

2Sa 3: 39 the LORD repay the *e* according
Ps 101: 8 I will cut off every *e*
Mal 4: 1 and every *e* will be stubble,

EVILDOERS* (EVIL)

1Sa 24: 13 saying goes, 'From *e* come evil
Job 8: 20 or strengthen the hands of *e*.
   34: 8 He keeps company with *e*;
   34: 22 where *e* can hide.
Ps 14: 4 Will *e* never learn—
   14: 6 You *e* frustrate the plans
   26: 5 I abhor the assembly of *e*
   36: 12 See how the *e* lie fallen—
   53: 4 Will the *e* never learn—
   59: 2 Deliver me from *e*
   64: 2 from that noisy crowd of *e*.
   92: 7 and all *e* flourish,
   92: 9 all *e* will be scattered.
   94: 4 all the *e* are full of boasting.
   94: 16 will take a stand for me against *e*?
  119: 115 Away from me, you *e*,
  125: 5 the LORD will banish with the *e*.
  141: 4 deeds with men who are *e*;
  141: 5 ever against the deeds of *e*;
  141: 9 from the traps set by *e*.
Pr 21: 15 but terror to *e*.
Isa 1: 4 a brood of *e*,
    31: 2 against those who help *e*.
Jer 23: 14 They strengthen the hands of *e*,
Hos 10: 9 the *e* in Gibeah?
Mal 3: 15 Certainly the *e* prosper, and
Mt   7: 23 you *e*!' "Therefore everyone who
Lk 13: 27 Away from me, all you *e*!'
   18: 11 *e*, adulterers—or even like this tax

EVILS* (EVIL)

Mk   7: 23 All these *e* come from inside

EWE

2Sa 12: 3 one little *e* lamb he had bought.

EXACT*

Ge 43: 21 the *e* weight—in the mouth
Est 4: 7 including the *e* amount
Mt   2: 7 from them the *e* time the star had
Jn   4: 53 realized that this was the *e* time
Ac 17: 26 the *e* places where they should live.
Heb 1: 3 the *e* representation of his being,

EXALT* (EXALTED EXALTS)

Ex 15: 2 my father's God, and I will *e* him.
Jos 3: 7 begin to *e* you in the eyes
1Sa 2: 10 and *e* the horn of his anointed."
1Ch 25: 5 the promises of God to *e* him.
   29: 12 power to *e* and give strength to all.
Job 19: 5 If indeed you would *e* yourselves
Ps 30: 1 I will *e* you, O LORD,
   34: 3 let us *e* his name together.
   35: 26 may all who *e* themselves over me
   37: 34 He will *e* you to inherit the land;
   38: 16 *e* themselves over me
   75: 6 or from the desert can *e* a man.

Ps 89: 17 and by your favor you *e* our horn.
   99: 5 *E* the LORD our God
   99: 9 *E* the LORD our God
  107: 32 Let them *e* him in the assembly
  118: 28 you are my God, and I will *e* you.
  145: 1 I will *e* you, my God the King;
Pr   4: 8 Esteem her, and she will *e* you;
   25: 6 Do not *e* yourself in the king's
Isa 24: 15 *e* the name of the LORD, the God
   25: 1 I will *e* you and praise your name,
Eze 29: 15 and will never again *e* itself
Da   4: 37 *e* and glorify the King of heaven,
   11: 36 He will *e* and magnify himself
   11: 37 but will *e* himself above them all.
Hos 11: 7 he will by no means *e* them.
2Th 2: 4 will *e* himself over everything that is

EXALTED* (EXALT)

Ex 15: 1 for he is highly *e*.
   15: 21 for he is highly *e*.
Nu 24: 7 their kingdom will be *e*.
Jos 4: 14 That day the LORD *e* Joshua
2Sa 5: 12 and had *e* his kingdom for the sake
   22: 47 *E* be God, the Rock, my Savior!
   22: 49 You *e* me above my foes;
   23: 1 of the man *e* by the Most High,
1Ch 14: 2 that his kingdom had been highly *e*
   17: 17 as though I were the most *e* of men,
   29: 11 you are *e* as head over all.
   29: 25 The LORD highly *e* Solomon
Ne   9: 5 and may it be *e* above all blessing
Job 24: 24 For a little while they are *e*,
   36: 22 "God is *e* in his power.
   37: 23 beyond our reach and *e* in power;
Ps 18: 46 *E* be God my Savior!
   18: 48 You *e* me above my foes!
   21: 13 Be *e*, O LORD, in your strength;
   27: 6 Then my head will be *e*
   35: 27 they always say, "The LORD be *e*,
   40: 16 "The LORD be *e*!"
   46: 10 I will be *e* among the nations,
   46: 10 I will be *e* in the earth."
   47: 9 he is greatly *e*.
   57: 5 Be *e*, O God, above the heavens;
   57: 11 Be *e*, O God, above the heavens;
   70: 4 "Let God be *e*!"
   89: 13 hand is strong, your right hand *e*.
   89: 19 I have *e* a young man
   89: 24 through my name his horn will be *e*
   89: 27 the most *e* of the kings of the earth.
   89: 42 You have *e* the right hand
   92: 8 But you, O LORD, are *e* forever.
   92: 10 You have *e* my horn like that
   97: 9 you are *e* far above all gods.
   99: 2 he is *e* over all the nations.
  108: 5 Be *e*, O God, above the heavens,
  113: 4 The LORD is *e* over all the nations
  138: 2 for you have *e* above all things
  148: 13 for his name alone is *e*;
Pr 11: 11 of the upright a city is *e*,
   30: 32 have played the fool and *e* yourself,
Isa 2: 11 the LORD alone will be *e*
    2: 12 for all that is *e*
    2: 17 the LORD alone will be *e*
    5: 16 the LORD Almighty will be *e*
    6: 1 *e*, and the train of his robe filled
   12: 4 and proclaim that his name is *e*.
   24: 4 the *e* of the earth languish.
   33: 5 The LORD is *e*, for he dwells
   33: 10 "Now will I be *e*;
   52: 13 be raised and lifted up and highly *e*.
Jer 17: 12 A glorious throne, *e*
La   2: 17 he has *e* the horn of your foes.
Eze 21: 26 The lowly will be *e* and the *e* will be
Hos 13: 1 he was *e* in Israel.
Mic 6: 6 and bow down before the *e* God?
Mt 23: 12 whoever humbles himself will be *e*.
Lk 14: 11 he who humbles himself will be *e*."
   18: 14 he who humbles himself will be *e*."
Ac   2: 33 *E* to the right hand of God,
    5: 31 God *e* him to his own right hand
Php 1: 20 always Christ will be *e* in my body,
    2: 9 Therefore God *e* him
Heb 7: 26 from sinners, *e* above the heavens;

EXALTS* (EXALT)

1Sa 2: 7 he humbles and he *e*.
Job 36: 7 and *e* them forever.

Ps   75: 7 He brings one down, he *e* another.
Pr   14: 34 Righteousness *e* a nation,
Mt   23: 12 For whoever *e* himself will be
Lk   14: 11 For everyone who *e* himself will be
      18: 14 For everyone who *e* himself will be

EXAMINE (EXAMINED EXAMINES)

Ps   11: 4 his eyes *e* them.
      17: 3 you probe my heart and *e* me
      26: 2 *e* my heart and my mind;
Jer   17: 10 and *e* the mind,
      20: 12 Almighty, you who *e* the righteous
La   3: 40 Let us *e* our ways and test them,
1Co   11: 28 A man ought to *e* himself
2Co   13: 5 *E* yourselves to see whether you

EXAMINED (EXAMINE)

Job   13: 9 Would it turn out well if he *e* you?
Ac   17: 11 *e* the Scriptures every day to see

EXAMINES (EXAMINE)

Ps   11: 5 The LORD *e* the righteous,
Pr   5: 21 and he *e* all his paths.

EXAMPLE* (EXAMPLES)

2Ki   14: 3 In everything he followed the *e*
Ecc   9: 13 also saw under the sun this *e*
Eze   8: 8 and make him an *e* and a byword.
Jn   13: 15 have set you an *e* that you should
Ro   7: 2 as long as he lives? For *e*,
1Co   11: 1 Follow my *e*, as I follow
      11: 1 as I follow the *e* of Christ.
Gal   3: 15 let me take an *e* from everyday life.
Php   3: 17 Join with others in following my *e*,
2Th   3: 7 how you ought to follow our *e*.
1Ti   1: 16 as an *e* for those who would believe
      4: 12 set an *e* for the believers in speech,
Tit   2: 7 In everything set them an *e*
Heb   4: 11 fall by following their *e*
Jas   3: 4 Or take ships as an *e*.
      5: 10 as an *e* of patience in the face
1Pe   2: 21 leaving you an *e*, that you should
2Pe   2: 6 made them an *e* of what is going
Jude   :   7 as an *e* of those who suffer

EXAMPLES* (EXAMPLE)

1Co   10: 6 Now these things occurred as *e*
      10: 11 as *e* and were written down
1Pe   5: 3 to you, but being *e* to the flock.

EXASPERATE*

Eph   6: 4 Fathers, do not *e* your children;

EXCEL* (EXCELLENT)

Ge   49: 4 as the waters, you will no longer *e*,
1Co   14: 12 to *e* in gifts that build up the church
2Co   8: 7 But just as you *e* in everything—
      8: 7 also *e* in this grace of giving.

EXCELLENT (EXCEL)

1Co   12: 31 now I will show you the most *e* way
Php   4: 8 if anything is *e* or praiseworthy—
1Ti   3: 13 have served well gain an *e* standing
Tit   3: 8 These things are *e* and profitable

EXCESSIVE

Eze   18: 8 or take *e* interest.
2Co   2: 7 not be overwhelmed by *e* sorrow.

EXCHANGE (EXCHANGED)

Mt   16: 26 Or what can a man give in *e*
Mk   8: 37 Or what can a man give in *e*
2Co   6: 13 As a fair *e*—I speak

EXCHANGED (EXCHANGE)

Ps 106: 20 They *e* their Glory
Jer   2: 11 But my people have *e* their Glory
Hos   4: 7 they *e* their Glory
Ro   1: 23 *e* the glory of the immortal God
      1: 25 They *e* the truth of God for a lie,
      1: 26 their women *e* natural relations

EXCLAIM

Ps   35: 10 My whole being will *e*,

EXCUSE* (EXCUSES)

Ps   25: 3 who are treacherous without *e*.
Lk   14: 18 Please *e* me.'
      14: 19 Please *e* me.'

Jn   15: 22 they have no *e* for their sin.
Ro   1: 20 so that men are without *e*.
      2: 1 You, therefore, have no *e*,

EXCUSES* (EXCUSE)

Lk   14: 18 "But they all alike began to make *e*.

EXERTED*

Eph   1: 20 which he *e* in Christ

EXHORT*

1Ti   5: 1 but *e* him as if he were your father.

EXILE

2Ki   17: 23 taken from their homeland into *e*
      25: 11 into *e* the people who remained

EXISTED* (EXISTS)

2Pe   3: 5 ago by God's word the heavens *e*

EXISTS (EXISTED)

Heb   2: 10 and through whom everything *e*,
      11: 6 to him must believe that he *e*

EXPANSE

Ge   1: 7 So God made the *e* and separated
      1: 8 God called the *e* "sky."

EXPECT (EXPECTATION EXPECTED EXPECTING)

Mt   24: 44 at an hour when you do not *e* him.
Lk   12: 40 at an hour when you do not *e* him."
Php   1: 20 I eagerly *e* and hope that I will

EXPECTATION (EXPECT)

Ro   8: 19 waits in eager *e* for the sons
Heb   10: 27 but only a fearful *e* of judgment

EXPECTED (EXPECT)

Pr   11: 7 all he *e* from his power comes
Hag   1: 9 "You *e* much, but see, it turned out

EXPECTING (EXPECT)

Lk   6: 35 and lend to them without *e*

EXPEL* (EXPELLED)

1Co   5: 13 *E* the wicked man from among you

EXPELLED (EXPEL)

Eze   28: 16 and I *e* you, O guardian cherub,

EXPENSE (EXPENSIVE)

1Co   9: 7 Who serves as a soldier at his own *e*

EXPENSIVE* (EXPENSE)

Mt   26: 7 jar of very *e* perfume,
Mk   14: 3 jar of very *e* perfume,
Lk   7: 25 those who wear *e* clothes
Jn   12: 3 a pint of pure nard, an *e* perfume;
1Ti   2: 9 or gold or pearls or *e* clothes,

EXPERT

1Co   3: 10 I laid a foundation as an *e* builder,

EXPLAINING (EXPLAINS)

Ac   17: 3 *e* and proving that the Christ had

EXPLAINS* (EXPLAINING)

Ac   8: 31 he said, "unless someone *e* it to me

EXPLOIT* (EXPLOITED EXPLOITING EXPLOITS)

Pr   22: 22 Do not *e* the poor because they are
Isa   58: 3 and *e* all your workers.
2Co   12: 17 Did I *e* you through any
      12: 18 Titus did not *e* you, did he?
2Pe   2: 3 greed these teachers will *e* you

EXPLOITED* (EXPLOIT)

2Co   7: 2 no one, we have *e* no one.

EXPLOITING* (EXPLOIT)

Jas   2: 6 Is it not the rich who are *e* you?

EXPLOITS (EXPLOIT)

2Co   11: 20 or *e* you or takes advantage of you

EXPLORE

Nu   13: 2 "Send some men to *e* the land

EXPOSE (EXPOSED)

1Co   4: 5 will *e* the motives of men's hearts.
Eph   5: 11 of darkness, but rather *e* them.

EXPOSED (EXPOSE)

Jn   3: 20 for fear that his deeds will be *e*.
Eph   5: 13 everything *e* by the light becomes

EXPRESS (EXPRESSING)

Ro   8: 26 us with groans that words cannot *e*.

EXPRESSING* (EXPRESS)

1Co   2: 13 *e* spiritual truths in spiritual words.
Gal   5: 6 thing that counts is faith *e* itself

EXTENDS (EXTENT)

Pr   31: 20 and *e* her hands to the needy.
Lk   1: 50 His mercy *e* to those who fear him,

EXTENT (EXTENDS)

Jn   13: 1 he now showed them the full *e*

EXTERNAL

Gal   2: 6 judge by *e* appearance—

EXTINGUISH (EXTINGUISHED)

Eph   6: 16 which you can *e* all the flaming

EXTINGUISHED (EXTINGUISH)

2Sa   21: 17 the lamp of Israel will not be *e*."

EXTOL*

Job   36: 24 Remember to *e* his work,
Ps   34: 1 I will *e* the LORD at all times;
      68: 4 *e* him who rides on the clouds—
      95: 2 and *e* him with music and song.
     109: 30 mouth I will greatly *e* the LORD;
     111: 1 I will *e* the LORD with all my heart
     115: 18 it is we who *e* the LORD,
     117: 1 *e* him, all you peoples.
     145: 2 and *e* your name for ever and ever.
     145: 10 your saints will *e* you.
     147: 12 *E* the LORD, O Jerusalem;

EXTORT*

Lk   3: 14 "Don't *e* money and don't accuse

EXTRAORDINARY*

Ac   19: 11 God did *e* miracles through Paul,

EXTREME (EXTREMES)

2Co   8: 2 and their *e* poverty welled up

EXTREMES* (EXTREME)

Ecc   7: 18 who fears God will avoid all *e*.

EXULT

Ps   89: 16 they *e* in your righteousness.
Isa   45: 25 will be found righteous and will *e*.

EYE (EYES)

Ge   3: 6 good for food and pleasing to the *e*,
Ex   21: 24 you are to take life for life, *e* for *e*,
Dt   19: 21 life for life, *e* for *e*, tooth for tooth,
Ps   94: 9 Does he who formed the *e* not see?
Mt   5: 29 If your right *e* causes you to sin,
      5: 38 '*E* for *e*, and tooth for tooth.'
      6: 22 "The *e* is the lamp of the body.
      7: 3 of sawdust in your brother's *e*
1Co   2: 9 "No *e* has seen,
      12: 16 I am not an *e*, I do not belong
      15: 52 of an *e*, at the last trumpet.
Eph   6: 6 favor when their *e* is on you,
Col   3: 22 not only when their *e* is on you
Rev   1: 7 and every *e* will see him,

EYES (EYE)

Nu   15: 39 the lusts of your own hearts and *e*.
      33: 55 remain will become barbs in your *e*
Dt   11: 12 the *e* of the LORD your God are
      12: 25 right in the *e* of the LORD.
      16: 19 for a bribe blinds the *e* of the wise
Jos   23: 13 on your backs and thorns in your *e*,
1Sa   15: 17 you were once small in your own *e*,
1Ki   10: 7 I have not seen with my own *e*.
2Ki   9: 30 heard about it, she painted her *e*,
2Ch   16: 9 For the *e* of the LORD range
Job   31: 1 "I made a covenant with my *e*

Job 36: 7 He does not take his *e*
Ps 25: 15 My *e* are ever on the LORD,
   36: 1 God before his *e*.
  101: 6 My *e* will be on the faithful
  118: 23 and it is marvelous in our *e*.
  119: 18 Open my *e* that I may see
  119: 37 my *e* away from worthless things;
  121: 1 I lift up my *e* to the hills—
  123: 1 I lift up my *e* to you,
  139: 16 your *e* saw my unformed body.
  141: 8 But my *e* are fixed on you,
Pr 3: 7 Do not be wise in your own *e*;
  4: 25 Let your *e* look straight ahead,
  15: 3 The *e* of the LORD are everywhere
  17: 24 a fool's *e* wander to the ends
Isa 6: 5 and my *e* have seen the King,
  33: 17 Your *e* will see the king
  42: 7 to open *e* that are blind,
Jer 24: 6 My *e* will watch over them
Hab 1: 13 Your *e* are too pure to look on evil;
Mt 6: 22 If your *e* are good, your whole
  21: 42 and it is marvelous in our *e*'?
Lk 16: 15 ones who justify yourselves in the *e*
  24: 31 Then their *e* were opened
Jn 4: 35 open your *e* and look at the fields!
Ac 1: 9 he was taken up before their very *e*,
2Co 4: 18 So we fix our *e* not on what is seen,
  8: 21 not only in the *e* of the Lord but
Eph 1: 18 also that the *e* of your heart may be
Heb 12: 2 Let us fix our *e* on Jesus, the author
Jas 2: 5 poor in the *e* of the world to be rich
1Pe 3: 12 For the *e* of the Lord are
Rev 7: 17 wipe away every tear from their *e*."
  21: 4 He will wipe every tear from their *e*

EYEWITNESSES* (WITNESS)

Lk 1: 2 by those who from the first were *e*
2Pe 1: 16 but we were *e* of his majesty.

EZEKIEL*

    Priest called to be prophet to the exiles (Eze 1-3). Symbolically acted out destruction of Jerusalem (Eze 4-5; 12; 24).

EZRA*

    Priest and teacher of the Law who led a return of exiles to Israel to reestablish temple and worship (Ezr 7-8). Corrected intermarriage of priests (Ezr 9-10). Read Law at celebration of Feast of Tabernacles (Ne 8). Participated in dedication of Jerusalem's walls (Ne 12).

FACE (FACES)

Ge 32: 30 "It is because I saw God *f* to *f*,
Ex 3: 6 Moses hid his *f*, because he was
  33: 11 would speak to Moses *f* to *f*,
  33: 20 But," he said, "you cannot see my *f*
  34: 29 was not aware that his *f* was radiant
Nu 6: 25 the LORD make his *f* shine
  12: 8 With him I speak *f* to *f*,
  14: 14 O LORD, have been seen *f* to *f*,
Dt 5: 4 The LORD spoke to you *f* to *f* out
  31: 17 I will hide my *f* from them,
  34: 10 whom the LORD knew *f* to *f*,
Jdg 6: 22 the angel of the LORD *f* to *f*!"
2Ki 14: 8 challenge: "Come, meet me *f* to *f*."
1Ch 16: 11 seek his *f* always.
2Ch 7: 14 and seek my *f* and turn
  25: 17 of Israel: "Come, meet me *f* to *f*."
Ezr 9: 6 and disgraced to lift up my *f* to you,
Ps 4: 6 Let the light of your *f* shine upon us
  27: 8 Your *f*, LORD, I will seek.
  31: 16 Let your *f* shine on your servant;
  44: 3 and the light of your *f*,
  44: 22 Yet for your sake we *f* death all day
  51: 9 Hide your *f* from my sins
  67: 1 and make his *f* shine upon us; *Selah*
  80: 3 make your *f* shine upon us,
  105: 4 seek his *f* always.
  119:135 Make your *f* shine
SS 2: 14 and your *f* is lovely.
Isa 50: 7 Therefore have I set my *f* like flint,
  50: 8 Let us *f* each other!
  54: 8 I hid my *f* from you for a moment,
Jer 32: 4 and will speak with him *f* to *f*
  34: 3 and he will speak with you *f* to *f*.
Eze 1: 10 Each of the four had the *f* of a man,
  20: 35 *f* to *f*, I will execute judgment

Mt 17: 2 His *f* shone like the sun,
  18: 10 angels in heaven always see the *f*
Lk 9: 29 the appearance of his *f* changed,
Ro 8: 36 "For your sake we *f* death all day
1Co 13: 12 mirror; then we shall see *f* to *f*.
2Co 3: 7 could not look steadily at the *f*
  4: 6 the glory of God in the *f* of Christ.
  10: 1 who am "timid" when *f* to *f*
1Pe 3: 12 but the *f* of the Lord is
2Jn : 12 to visit you and talk with you *f* to *f*,
3Jn : 14 see you soon, and we will talk *f* to *f*.
Rev 1: 16 His *f* was like the sun shining
  22: 4 They will see his *f*, and his name

FACES (FACE)

2Co 3: 18 who with unveiled *f* all reflect

FACTIONS

2Co 12: 20 outbursts of anger, *f*, slander,
Gal 5: 20 selfish ambition, dissensions, *f*

FADE (FADING)

Jas 1: 11 the rich man will *f* away
1Pe 5: 4 of glory that will never *f* away.

FADING (FADE)

2Co 3: 7 *f* though it was, will not
  3: 11 if what was *f* away came with glory,
  3: 13 at it while the radiance was *f* away.

FAIL (FAILED FAILING FAILINGS FAILS FAILURE)

Lev 26: 15 and *f* to carry out all my commands
1Ki 2: 4 you will never *f* to have a man
1Ch 28: 20 He will not *f* you or forsake you
2Ch 34: 33 they did not *f* to follow the LORD,
Ps 89: 28 my covenant with him will never *f*.
Pr 15: 22 Plans *f* for lack of counsel,
Isa 51: 6 my righteousness will never *f*.
La 3: 22 for his compassions never *f*.
Lk 22: 32 Simon, that your faith may not *f*.
2Co 13: 5 unless, of course, you *f* the test?

FAILED (FAIL)

Jos 23: 14 has been fulfilled; not one has *f*.
1Ki 8: 56 Not one word has *f*
Ps 77: 8 Has his promise *f* for all time?
Ro 9: 6 as though God's word had *f*.
2Co 13: 6 discover that we have not *f* the test.

FAILING (FAIL)

1Sa 12: 23 sin against the LORD by *f* to pray

FAILINGS (FAIL)

Ro 15: 1 ought to bear with the *f* of the weak

FAILS (FAIL)

Jer 14: 6 their eyesight *f*
Joel 1: 10 the oil *f*.
1Co 13: 8 Love never *f*.

FAILURE* (FAIL)

1Th 2: 1 that our visit to you was not a *f*.

FAINT

Isa 40: 31 they will walk and not be *f*.

FAINTHEARTED* (HEART)

Dt 20: 3 Do not be *f* or afraid; do not be
  20: 8 shall add, "Is any man afraid or *f*?

FAIR (FAIRNESS)

Pr 1: 3 doing what is right and just and *f*;
Col 4: 1 slaves with what is right and *f*,

FAIRNESS* (FAIR)

Pr 29: 14 If a king judges the poor with *f*,

FAITH* (FAITHFUL FAITHFULLY FAITHFULNESS FAITHLESS)

Ex 21: 8 because he has broken *f* with her.
Dt 32: 51 both of you broke *f* with me
Jos 22: 16 'How could you break *f*
Jdg 9: 16 and in good *f* when you made
  9: 19 and in good *f* toward Jerub-Baal
1Sa 14: 33 "You have broken *f*," he said.
2Ch 20: 20 Have *f* in the LORD your God
  20: 20 have *f* in his prophets and you will
Isa 7: 9 If you do not stand firm in your *f*,

Isa 26: 2 the nation that keeps *f*.
Hab 2: 4 but the righteous will live by his *f*—
Mal 2: 10 by breaking *f* with one another?
  2: 11 one another? Judah has broken *f*.
  2: 14 because you have broken *f* with her
  2: 15 and do not break *f* with the wife
  2: 16 in your spirit, and do not break *f*.
Mt 6: 30 O you of little *f*? So do not worry,
  8: 10 anyone in Israel with such great *f*.
  8: 26 He replied, "You of little *f*,
  9: 2 When Jesus saw their *f*, he said
  9: 22 he said, "your *f* has healed you."
  9: 29 According to your *f* will it be done
  13: 58 there because of their lack of *f*.
  14: 31 of little *f*," he said, "why did you
  15: 28 "Woman, you have great *f*!
  16: 8 Jesus asked, "You of little *f*,
  17: 20 if you have *f* as small as a mustard
  17: 20 "Because you have so little *f*.
  21: 21 if you have *f* and do not doubt,
  24: 10 many will turn away from the *f*
Mk 2: 5 When Jesus saw their *f*, he said
  4: 40 still have no *f*?" They were
  5: 34 "Daughter, your *f* has healed you.
  6: 6 he was amazed at their lack of *f*.
  10: 52 said Jesus, "your *f* has healed you."
  11: 22 "Have *f* in God," Jesus answered.
  16: 14 he rebuked them for their lack of *f*
Lk 5: 20 When Jesus saw their *f*, he said
  7: 9 I have not found such great *f*
  7: 50 the woman, "Your *f* has saved you;
  8: 25 "Where is your *f*?" he asked his
  8: 48 "Daughter, your *f* has healed you.
  12: 28 will he clothe you, O you of little *f*!
  17: 5 "Increase our *f*!" He replied,
  17: 6 "If you have *f* as small
  17: 19 your *f* has made you well."
  18: 8 will he find *f* on the earth?"
  18: 42 your sight; your *f* has healed you."
  22: 32 Simon, that your *f* may not fail.
Jn 2: 11 and his disciples put their *f* in him.
  7: 31 in the crowd put their *f* in him.
  8: 30 he spoke, many put their *f* in him.
  11: 45 had seen what Jesus did, put their *f*
  12: 11 to Jesus and putting their *f* in him.
  12: 42 they would not confess their *f*
  14: 12 anyone who has *f* in me will do
Ac 3: 16 By *f* in the name of Jesus, this man
  3: 16 *f* that comes through him that has
  6: 5 full of *f* and of the Holy Spirit;
  6: 7 of priests became obedient to the *f*.
  11: 24 full of the Holy Spirit and *f*,
  13: 8 to turn the proconsul from the *f*.
  14: 9 saw that he had *f* to be healed
  14: 22 them to remain true to the *f*.
  14: 27 the door of *f* to the Gentiles.
  15: 9 for he purified their hearts by *f*.
  16: 5 were strengthened in the *f*
  20: 21 and have *f* in our Lord Jesus.
  24: 24 as he spoke about *f* in Christ Jesus.
  26: 18 those who are sanctified by *f*.
  27: 25 for I have *f* in God that it will
Ro 1: 5 to the obedience that comes from *f*.
  1: 8 because your *f* is being reported all
  1: 12 encouraged by each other's *f*.
  1: 17 is by *f* from first to last,
  1: 17 "The righteous will live by *f*."
  3: 3 What if some did not have *f*?
  3: 3 lack of *f* nullify God's faithfulness?
  3: 22 comes through *f* in Jesus Christ
  3: 25 a sacrifice of atonement, through *f*
  3: 26 one who justifies those who have *f*
  3: 27 the law? No, but on that of *f*.
  3: 28 by *f* apart from observing the law.
  3: 30 through that same *f*.
  3: 30 will justify the circumcised by *f*
  3: 31 nullify the law by this *f*? Not at all!
  4: 5 his *f* is credited as righteousness.
  4: 9 that Abraham's *f* was credited
  4: 11 had by *f* while he was still
  4: 12 of the *f* that our father Abraham
  4: 13 the righteousness that comes by *f*.
  4: 14 *f* has no value and the promise is
  4: 16 Therefore, the promise comes by *f*,
  4: 16 are of the *f* of Abraham.
  4: 19 Without weakening in his *f*,
  4: 20 but was strengthened in his *f*
  5: 1 we have been justified through *f*,

Ro   5:   2 access by *f* into this grace
    9: 30 a righteousness that is by *f*:
    9: 32 Because they pursued it not by *f*
    10:   6 the righteousness that is by *f* says:
    10:   8 the word of *f* we are proclaiming:
    10: 17 *f* comes from hearing the message,
    11: 20 of unbelief, and you stand by *f*.
    12:   3 measure of *f* God has given you.
    12:   6 let him use it in proportion to his *f*.
    14:   1 Accept him whose *f* is weak,
    14:   2 One man's *f* allows him
    14:   2 but another man, whose *f* is weak,
    14: 23 because his eating is not from *f*;
    14: 23 that does not come from *f* is sin.
1Co   2:   5 so that your *f* might not rest
    12:   9 to another by the same Spirit,
    13:   2 and if I have a *f* that can move
    13: 13 And now these three remain: *f*,
    15: 14 is useless and so is your *f*.
    15: 17 has not been raised, your *f* is futile;
    16: 13 stand firm in the *f*; be men
2Co   1: 24 Not that we lord it over your *f*,
    1: 24 because it is by *f* you stand firm.
    4: 13 With that same spirit of *f* we
    5:   7 We live by *f*, not by sight.
    8:   7 in *f*, in speech, in knowledge,
    10: 15 as your *f* continues to grow,
    13:   5 to see whether you are in the *f*;
Gal   1: 23 now preaching the *f* he once tried
    2: 16 Jesus that we may be justified by *f*
    2: 16 but by *f* in Jesus Christ.
    2: 16 have put our *f* in Christ Jesus that
    2: 20 I live by *f* in the Son of God,
    3:   8 would justify the Gentiles by *f*,
    3:   9 So those who have *f* are blessed
    3:   9 along with Abraham, the man of *f*.
    3: 11 "The righteous will live by *f*."
    3: 12 based on *f*; on the contrary,
    3: 14 by *f* we might receive the promise
    3: 22 being given through *f*
    3: 23 Before this *f* came, we were held
    3: 23 up until *f* should be revealed.
    3: 24 that we might be justified by *f*.
    3: 25 that *f* has come, we are no longer
    3: 26 of God through *f* in Christ Jesus,
    5:   5 But by *f* we eagerly await
    5:   6 that counts is *f* expressing itself
Eph   1: 15 ever since I heard about your *f*
    2:   8 through *f*— and this not
    3: 12 through *f* in him we may approach
    3: 17 dwell in your hearts through *f*.
    4:   5 one Lord, one *f*, one baptism;
    4: 13 up until we all reach unity in the *f*
    6: 16 to all this, take up the shield of *f*,
    6: 23 love with *f* from God the Father
Php   1: 25 for your progress and joy in the *f*,
    1: 27 as one man for the *f* of the gospel
    2: 17 and service coming from your *f*,
    3:   9 comes from God and is by *f*.
    3:   9 that which is through *f* in Christ—
Col   1:   4 heard of your *f* in Christ Jesus
    1:   5 the *f* and love that spring
    1: 23 continue in your *f*, established
    2:   5 and how firm your *f* in Christ is.
    2:   7 in the *f* as you were taught,
    2: 12 him through your *f* in the power
1Th   1:   3 Father your work produced by *f*,
    1:   8 your *f* in God has become known
    3:   2 and encourage you in your *f*,
    3:   5 I sent to find out about your *f*.
    3:   6 brought good news about your *f*
    3:   7 about you because of your *f*.
    3: 10 supply what is lacking in your *f*.
    5:   8 on *f* and love as a breastplate,
2Th   1:   3 because your *f* is growing more
    1:   4 and *f* in all the persecutions
    1: 11 and every act prompted by your *f*.
    3:   2 evil men, for not everyone has *f*.
1Ti   1:   2 To Timothy my true son in the *f*:
    1:   4 than God's work—which is by *f*.
    1:   5 a good conscience and a sincere *f*.
    1: 14 along with the *f* and love that are
    1: 19 and so have shipwrecked their *f*.
    1: 19 on to *f* and a good conscience.
    2:   7 of the true *f* to the Gentiles.
    2: 15 if they continue in *f*, love
    3:   9 of the *f* with a clear conscience.
    3: 13 assurance in their *f* in Christ Jesus.

1Ti   4:   1 later times some will abandon the *f*
    4:   6 brought up in the truths of the *f*
    4: 12 in life, in love, in *f* and in purity.
    5:   8 he has denied the *f* and is worse
    6: 10 have wandered from the *f*
    6: 11 pursue righteousness, godliness, *f*,
    6: 12 Fight the good fight of the *f*.
    6: 21 so doing have wandered from the *f*.
2Ti   1:   5 been reminded of your sincere *f*,
    1: 13 with *f* and love in Christ Jesus.
    2: 18 and they destroy the *f* of some.
    2: 22 and pursue righteousness, *f*,
    3:   8 as far as the *f* is concerned,
    3: 10 my purpose, *f*, patience, love,
    3: 15 wise for salvation through *f*
    4:   7 finished the race, I have kept the *f*.
Tit   1:   1 Christ for the *f* of God's elect
    1:   2 a *f* and knowledge resting
    1:   4 my true son in our common *f*:
    1: 13 so that they will be sound in the *f*
    2:   2 self-controlled, and sound in *f*,
    3: 15 Greet those who love us in the *f*.
Phm   :   5 because I hear about your *f*
    :   6 may be active in sharing your *f*,
Heb   4:   2 heard did not combine it with *f*.
    4: 14 firmly to the *f* we profess.
    6:   1 and of *f* in God, instruction about
    6: 12 but to imitate those who through *f*
    10: 22 heart in full assurance of *f*,
    10: 38 But my righteous one will live by *f*.
    11:   1 *f* is being sure of what we hope for
    11:   3 By *f* we understand that
    11:   4 And by *f* he still speaks, even
    11:   4 By *f* Abel offered God a better
    11:   4 By *f* he was commended
    11:   5 By *f* Enoch was taken from this life
    11:   6 And without *f* it is impossible
    11:   7 By *f* he condemned the world
    11:   7 By *f* Noah, when warned about
    11:   7 the righteousness that comes by *f*.
    11:   8 By *f* Abraham, when called to go
    11:   9 By *f* he made his home
    11: 11 By *f* Abraham, even though he was
    11: 13 living by *f* when they died.
    11: 17 By *f* Abraham, when God tested
    11: 20 By *f* Isaac blessed Jacob
    11: 21 By *f* Jacob, when he was dying,
    11: 22 By *f* Joseph, when his end was near
    11: 23 By *f* Moses' parents hid him
    11: 24 By *f* Moses, when he had grown up
    11: 27 By *f* he left Egypt, not fearing
    11: 28 By *f* he kept the Passover
    11: 29 By *f* the people passed
    11: 30 By *f* the walls of Jericho fell,
    11: 31 By *f* the prostitute Rahab,
    11: 33 through *f* conquered kingdoms,
    11: 39 were all commended for their *f*,
    12:   2 the author and perfecter of our *f*,
    13:   7 way of life and imitate their *f*.
Jas   1:   3 of your *f* develops perseverance.
    2:   5 the eyes of the world to be rich in *f*
    2: 14 has no deeds? Can such *f* save him?
    2: 14 if a man claims to have *f*
    2: 17 In the same way, *f* by itself,
    2: 18 I will show you my *f* by what I do.
    2: 18 Show me your *f* without deeds,
    2: 18 "You have *f*; I have deeds."
    2: 20 do you want evidence that *f*
    2: 22 You see that his *f* and his actions
    2: 22 and his *f* was made complete
    2: 24 by what he does and not by *f* alone.
    2: 26 so *f* without deeds is dead.
    5: 15 will make the sick person well;
1Pe   1:   5 who through *f* are shielded
    1:   7 These have come so that your *f*—
    1:   9 you are receiving the goal of your *f*,
    1: 21 and so your *f* and hope are in God.
    5:   9 Resist him, standing firm in the *f*,
2Pe   1:   1 Jesus Christ have received a *f*
    1:   5 effort to add to your *f* goodness;
1Jn   5:   4 overcome the world, even our *f*.
Jude   :   3 to contend for the *f* that was once
    : 20 up in your most holy *f*,
Rev   2: 13 You did not renounce your *f* in me,
    2: 19 your love and *f*, your service

FAITHFUL* (FAITH)

Nu   12:   7 he is *f* in all my house.

Dt   7:   9 your God is God; he is the *f* God,
    32:   4 A *f* God who does no wrong,
1Sa   2: 35 I will raise up for myself a *f* priest,
2Sa   20: 19 We are the peaceful and *f* in Israel.
    22: 26 "To the *f* you show yourself *f*,
1Ki   3:   6 because he was *f* to you
2Ch   31: 18 were *f* in consecrating themselves.
    31: 20 and *f* before the LORD his God.
Ne   9:   8 You found his heart *f* to you,
Ps   12:   1 the *f* have vanished
    18: 25 To the *f* you show yourself *f*,
    25: 10 of the LORD are loving and *f*
    31: 23 The LORD preserves the *f*,
    33:   4 he is *f* in all he does.
    37: 28 and will not forsake his *f* ones.
    78:   8 whose spirits were not *f* to him.
    78: 37 they were not *f* to his covenant.
    89: 19 to your *f* people you said:
    89: 24 My *f* love will be with him,
    89: 37 the *f* witness in the sky."
    97: 10 for he guards the lives of his *f* ones
    101:   6 My eyes will be on the *f* in the land,
    111:   7 The works of his hands are *f*
    145: 13 The LORD is *f* to all his promises
    146:   6 the LORD, who remains *f* forever.
Pr   2:   8 and protects the way of his *f* ones.
    20:   6 but a *f* man who can find?
    28: 20 A *f* man will be richly blessed,
    31: 26 and *f* instruction is on her tongue.
Isa   1: 21 See how the *f* city has become
    1: 26 the *F* City."
    49:   7 because of the LORD, who is *f*,
    55:   3 my *f* love promised to David.
Jer   42:   5 *f* witness against us if we do not act
Eze   43: 11 so that they may be *f* to its design
    48: 11 who were *f* in serving me
Hos   11: 12 even against the *f* Holy One.
Zec   8:   8 I will be *f* and righteous to them
Mt   24: 45 Who then is the *f* and wise servant,
    25: 21 'Well done, good and *f* servant!
    25: 21 You have been *f* with a few things;
    25: 23 You have been *f* with a few things;
    25: 23 'Well done, good and *f* servant!
Lk   12: 42 then is the *f* and wise manager,
Ro   12: 12 patient in affliction, *f* in prayer.
1Co   1:   9 his Son Jesus Christ our Lord, is *f*.
    4:   2 been given a trust must prove *f*.
    4: 17 my son whom I love, who is *f*
    10: 13 And God is *f*; he will not let you be
2Co   1: 18 no"? But as surely as God is *f*,
Eph   1:   1 in Ephesus, the *f* in Christ Jesus:
    6: 21 the dear brother and *f* servant
Col   1:   2 and brothers in Christ at Colosse:
    1:   7 who is a *f* minister of Christ
    4:   7 a *f* minister and fellow servant
    4:   9 He is coming with Onesimus, our *f*
1Th   5: 24 The one who calls you is *f*
2Th   3:   3 the Lord is *f*, and he will strengthen
1Ti   1: 12 he considered me *f*, appointing me
    5:   9 has been *f* to her husband,
2Ti   2: 13 he will remain *f*,
Heb   2: 17 and *f* high priest in service to God,
    3:   2 He was *f* to the one who appointed
    3:   2 as Moses was *f* in all God's house.
    3:   5 Moses was *f* as a servant
    3:   6 But Christ is *f* as a son
    8:   9 because they did not remain *f*
    10: 23 for he who promised is *f*;
    11: 11 he considered him *f* who had made
1Pe   4: 19 themselves to their *f* Creator
    5: 12 whom I regard as a *f* brother,
1Jn   1:   9 he is *f* and just and will forgive us
3Jn   :   5 you are *f* in what you are doing
Rev   1:   5 who is the *f* witness, the firstborn
    2: 10 Be *f*, even to the point of death,
    2: 13 the days of Antipas, my *f* witness,
    3: 14 the words of the Amen, the *f*
    14: 12 commandments and remain *f*
    17: 14 his called, chosen and *f* followers."
    19: 11 whose rider is called *F* and True.

FAITHFULLY* (FAITH)

Dt   11: 13 if you *f* obey the commands I am
Jos   2: 14 *f* when the LORD gives us the land
1Sa   12: 24 and serve him *f* with all your heart;
1Ki   2:   4 and if they walk *f* before me
2Ki   20:   3 how I have walked before you *f*
    22:   7 because they are acting *f*."

2Ch 19: 9 must serve *f* and wholeheartedly
31: 12 they *f* brought in the contributions,
31: 15 and Shecaniah assisted him *f*
32: 1 all that Hezekiah had so *f* done,
34: 12 The men did the work *f*.
Ne 9: 33 you have acted *f*, while we did
13: 14 so *f* done for the house of my God
Isa 38: 3 how I have walked before you *f*
Jer 23: 28 one who has my word speak it *f*.
Eze 18: 9 and *f* keeps my laws.
44: 15 and who *f* carried out the duties
1Pe 4: 10 *f* administering God's grace

FAITHFULNESS* (FAITH)
Ge 24: 27 not abandoned his kindness and *f*
24: 49 if you will show kindness and *f*
32: 10 and *f* you have shown your servant.
47: 29 you will show me kindness and *f*.
Ex 34: 6 *f*, maintaining love to thousands,
Jos 24: 14 the LORD and serve him with all *f*.
1Sa 26: 23 man for his righteousness and *f*.
2Sa 2: 6 now show you kindness and *f*,
15: 20 May kindness and *f* be with you."
Ps 30: 9 Will it proclaim your *f*?
36: 5 your *f* to the skies.
40: 10 I speak of your *f* and salvation.
54: 5 in your *f* destroy them.
57: 3 God sends his love and his *f*.
57: 10 your *f* reaches to the skies.
61: 7 appoint your love and *f*
71: 22 the harp for your *f*, O my God;
85: 10 Love and *f* meet together;
85: 11 *F* springs from the earth,
86: 15 to anger, abounding in love and *f*.
88: 11 your *f* in Destruction?
89: 1 mouth I will make your *f* known
89: 2 that you established your *f*
89: 5 your *f* too, in the assembly
89: 8 and your *f* surrounds you.
89: 14 love and *f* go before you.
89: 33 nor will I ever betray my *f*.
89: 49 which in your *f* you swore to David
91: 4 his *f* will be your shield
92: 2 and your *f* at night,
98: 3 and his *f* to the house of Israel;
100: 5 *f* continues through all
108: 4 your *f* reaches to the skies.
111: 8 done in *f* and uprightness.
115: 1 because of your love and *f*.
117: 2 the *f* of the LORD endures forever.
119: 75 and in *f* you have afflicted me.
119: 90 *f* continues through all
138: 2 name for your love and your *f*,
143: 1 in your *f* and righteousness
Pr 3: 3 Let love and *f* never leave you;
14: 22 plan what is good find love and *f*.
16: 6 Through love and *f* sin is atoned for
20: 28 Love and *f* keep a king safe;
Isa 11: 5 and *f* the sash around his waist.
16: 5 in *f* a man will sit on it—
25: 1 for in perfect *f*
38: 19 about your *f*.
42: 3 In *f* he will bring forth justice;
61: 8 In my *f* I will reward them
La 3: 23 great is your *f*.
Hos 2: 20 I will betroth you in *f*,
4: 1 "There is no *f*, no love,
Mt 23: 23 of the law—justice, mercy and *f*.
Ro 3: 3 lack of faith nullify God's *f*?
Gal 5: 22 patience, kindness, goodness, *f*,
3Jn 3 and tell about your *f* to the truth
Rev 13: 10 and *f* on the part of the saints.

FAITHLESS* (FAITH)
Ps 78: 57 fathers they were disloyal and *f*,
101: 3 The deeds of *f* men I hate;
119:158 I look on the *f* with loathing,
Pr 14: 14 The *f* will be fully repaid
Jer 3: 6 you seen what *f* Israel has done?
3: 8 I gave *f* Israel her certificate
3: 11 "*F* Israel is more righteous
3: 12 *f* Israel,' declares the LORD,
3: 14 *f* people," declares the LORD,
3: 22 "Return, *f* people;
12: 1 Why do all the *f* live at ease?
Ro 1: 31 they are senseless, *f*, heartless,
2Ti 2: 13 if we are *f*,

FALL (FALLEN FALLING FALLS)
Ps 37: 24 though he stumble, he will not *f*,
55: 22 he will never let the righteous *f*.
69: 9 of those who insult you *f* on me.
145: 14 The LORD upholds all those who *f*
Pr 11: 28 Whoever trusts in his riches will *f*,
Isa 40: 7 The grass withers and the flowers *f*,
Mt 7: 25 yet it did not *f*, because it had its
Lk 10: 18 "I saw Satan *f* like lightning
11: 17 a house divided against itself will *f*.
23: 30 say to the mountains, "*F* on us!"
Ro 3: 23 and *f* short of the glory of God,
Heb 6: 6 if they *f* away, to be brought back

FALLEN (FALL)
2Sa 1: 19 How the mighty have *f*!
Isa 14: 12 How you have *f* from heaven,
1Co 11: 30 and a number of you have *f* asleep.
15: 6 though some have *f* asleep.
15: 18 who have *f* asleep in Christ are lost.
15: 20 of those who have *f* asleep.
Gal 5: 4 you have *f* away from grace.
1Th 4: 15 precede those who have *f* asleep.

FALLING (FALL)
Jude 24 able to keep you from *f*

FALLS (FALL)
Pr 11: 14 For lack of guidance a nation *f*,
24: 17 Do not gloat when your enemy *f*;
28: 14 he who hardens his heart *f*
Mt 13: 21 of the word, he quickly *f* away.
21: 44 He who *f* on this stone will be
Jn 12: 24 a kernel of wheat *f* to the ground
Ro 14: 4 To his own master he stands or *f*.

FALSE (FALSEHOOD FALSELY)
Ex 20: 16 "You shall not give *f* testimony
23: 1 "Do not spread *f* reports.
23: 7 Have nothing to do with a *f* charge
Dt 5: 20 "You shall not give *f* testimony
Pr 12: 17 but a *f* witness tells lies.
13: 5 The righteous hate what is *f*,
14: 5 but a *f* witness pours out lies.
14: 25 but a *f* witness is deceitful.
19: 5 A *f* witness will not go unpunished,
19: 9 A *f* witness will not go unpunished,
21: 28 A *f* witness will perish,
25: 18 is the man who gives *f* testimony
Isa 44: 25 who foils the signs of *f* prophets
Jer 23: 16 they fill you with *f* hopes.
Mt 7: 15 "Watch out for *f* prophets.
15: 19 theft, *f* testimony, slander.
19: 18 not steal, do not give *f* testimony,
24: 11 and many *f* prophets will appear
24: 24 For *f* Christs and *f* prophets will
Mk 10: 19 do not give *f* testimony, do not
13: 22 For *f* Christs and *f* prophets will
Lk 6: 26 their fathers treated the *f* prophets.
18: 20 not steal, do not give *f* testimony,
Jn 1: 47 in whom there is nothing *f*."
1Co 15: 15 found to be *f* witnesses about God,
2Co 11: 13 For such men are *f* apostles,
11: 26 and in danger from *f* brothers.
Gal 2: 4 some *f* brothers had infiltrated our
Php 1: 18 whether from *f* motives or true,
Col 2: 18 anyone who delights in *f* humility
2: 23 their *f* humility and their harsh
1Ti 1: 3 not to teach *f* doctrines any longer
6: 3 If anyone teaches *f* doctrines
2Pe 2: 1 also *f* prophets among the people,
2: 1 there will be *f* teachers among you.
1Jn 4: 1 many *f* prophets have gone out
Rev 16: 13 out of the mouth of the *f* prophet.
19: 20 with him the *f* prophet who had
20: 10 and the *f* prophet had been thrown.

FALSEHOOD* (FALSE)
Job 21: 34 left of your answers but *f*!"
31: 5 "If I have walked in *f*
Ps 52: 3 *f* rather than speaking the truth.
119:163 I hate and abhor *f*;
Pr 30: 8 Keep *f* and lies far from me;
Isa 28: 15 and *f* our hiding place."
Ro 3: 7 "If my *f* enhances God's
Eph 4: 25 each of you must put off *f*
1Jn 4: 6 Spirit of truth and the spirit of *f*.
Rev 22: 15 everyone who loves and practices *f*

FALSELY (FALSE)
Lev 19: 12 " 'Do not swear *f* by my name
Mt 5: 11 *f* say all kinds of evil against you
Lk 3: 14 and don't accuse people *f*—
1Ti 6: 20 ideas of what is *f* called knowledge,

FALTER*
Pr 24: 10 If you *f* in times of trouble,
Isa 42: 4 he will not *f* or be discouraged

FAME
Jos 9: 9 of the *f* of the LORD your God.
Isa 66: 19 islands that have not heard of my *f*
Hab 3: 2 LORD, I have heard of your *f*;

FAMILIES (FAMILY)
Ps 68: 6 God sets the lonely in *f*,

FAMILY (FAMILIES)
Pr 15: 27 greedy man brings trouble to his *f*,
31: 15 she provides food for her *f*
Mk 5: 19 to your *f* and tell them how much
Lk 9: 61 go back and say good-by to my *f*."
12: 52 in one *f* divided against each other,
Ac 10: 2 He and all his *f* were devout
16: 33 and all his *f* were baptized.
16: 34 he and his whole *f*.
1Ti 3: 4 He must manage his own *f* well
3: 5 how to manage his own *f*,
5: 4 practice by caring for their own *f*
5: 8 and especially for his immediate *f*,

FAMINE
Ge 12: 10 Now there was a *f* in the land,
26: 1 Now there was a *f* in the land—
41: 30 seven years of *f* will follow them.
Ru 1: 1 the judges ruled, there was a *f*
1Ki 18: 2 Now the *f* was severe in Samaria,
Am 8: 11 but a *f* of hearing the words
Ro 8: 35 or persecution or *f* or nakedness

FAN*
2Ti 1: 6 you to *f* into flame the gift of God,

FANTASIES*
Ps 73: 20 you will despise them as *f*.
Pr 12: 11 but he who chases *f* lacks judgment
28: 19 one who chases *f* will have his fill

FAST (FASTING)
Dt 10: 20 Hold *f* to him and take your oaths
11: 22 in all his ways and to hold *f* to him
13: 4 serve him and hold *f* to him.
30: 20 to his voice, and hold *f* to him.
Jos 22: 5 to hold *f* to him and to serve him
23: 8 to hold *f* to the LORD your God,
2Ki 18: 6 He held *f* to the LORD
Ps 119: 31 I hold *f* to your statutes, O LORD;
139: 10 your right hand will hold me *f*.
Mt 6: 16 "When you *f*, do not look somber
1Pe 5: 12 Stand *f* in it.

FASTING (FAST)
Ps 35: 13 and humbled myself with *f*.
Ac 13: 2 were worshiping the Lord and *f*,
14: 23 and *f*, committed them to the Lord

FATHER (FATHER'S FATHERED FATHERLESS FATHERS FOREFATHERS)
Ge 2: 24 this reason a man will leave his *f*
17: 4 You will be the *f* of many nations.
Ex 20: 12 "Honor your *f* and your mother,
21: 15 "Anyone who attacks his *f*
21: 17 "Anyone who curses his *f*
Lev 18: 7 " 'Do not dishonor your *f*
19: 3 you must respect his mother and *f*,
20: 9 " 'If anyone curses his *f* or mother,
Dt 1: 31 carried you, as a *f* carries his son,
5: 16 "Honor your *f* and your mother,
21: 18 son who does not obey his *f*
32: 6 Is he not your *F*, your Creator,
2Sa 7: 14 I will be his *f*, and he will be my son
1Ch 17: 13 I will be his *f*, and he will be my son
22: 10 will be my son, and I will be his *f*.
28: 6 to be my son, and I will be his *f*.
Job 38: 28 Does the rain have a *f*?
Ps 2: 7 today I have become your *F*.
27: 10 Though my *f* and mother forsake

Ps 68: 5 A *f* to the fatherless, a defender
89: 26 to me, 'You are my *F*,
103: 13 As a *f* has compassion
Pr 3: 12 as a *f* the son he delights in.
10: 1 A wise son brings joy to his *f*,
17: 21 there is no joy for the *f* of a fool.
17: 25 A foolish son brings grief to his *f*
23: 22 Listen to your *f*, who gave you life,
23: 24 *f* of a righteous man has great joy;
28: 7 of gluttons disgraces his *f*.
28: 24 He who robs his *f* or mother
29: 3 loves wisdom brings joy to his *f*,
Isa 9: 6 Everlasting *F*, Prince of Peace.
45: 10 Woe to him who says to his *f*,
63: 16 But you are our *F*,
Jer 2: 27 They say to wood, 'You are my *f*,'
3: 19 I thought you would call me '*F*'
31: 9 because I am Israel's *f*,
Eze 18: 19 the son not share the guilt of his *f*?'
Mic 7: 6 For a son dishonors his *f*,
Mal 1: 6 If I am a *f*, where is the honor due
2: 10 we not all one *F*? Did not one God
Mt 3: 9 'We have Abraham as our *f*.'
5: 16 and praise your *F* in heaven.
6: 9 '' 'Our *F* in heaven,
6: 26 yet your heavenly *F* feeds them.
10: 37 ''Anyone who loves his *f*
11: 27 no one knows the *F* except the Son
15: 4 'Honor your *f* and mother'
18: 10 the face of my *F* in heaven.
19: 5 this reason a man will leave his *f*
19: 19 honor your *f* and mother,'
19: 29 or brothers or sisters or *f* or mother
23: 9 And do not call anyone on earth '*f*,'
Mk 7: 10 'Honor your *f* and your mother,' and,
Lk 9: 59 ''Lord, first let me go and bury my *f*
12: 53 *f* against son and son against *f*,
14: 26 and does not hate his *f* and mother,
18: 20 honor your *f* and mother.' ''
23: 34 Jesus said, ''*F*, forgive them,
Jn 3: 35 The *F* loves the Son and has placed
4: 21 you will worship the *F* neither
5: 17 ''My *F* is always at his work
5: 18 he was even calling God his own *F*,
5: 20 For the *F* loves the Son
6: 44 the *F* who sent me draws him,
6: 46 No one has seen the *F*
8: 19 ''You do not know me or my *F*,''
8: 28 speak just what the *F* has taught me
8: 41 The only *F* we have is God himself
8: 42 God were your *F*, you would love
8: 44 You belong to your *f*, the devil,
10: 17 reason my *F* loves me is that I lay
10: 30 I and the *F* are one.''
10: 38 and understand that the *F* is in me,
14: 6 No one comes to the *F*
14: 9 who has seen me has seen the *F*.
14: 28 for the *F* is greater than I.
15: 9 ''As the *F* has loved me,
15: 23 He who hates me hates my *F*
20: 17 'I am returning to my *F* and your *F*,
Ac 13: 33 today I have become your *F*.'
Ro 4: 11 he is the *f* of all who believe
4: 16 He is the *f* of us all.
8: 15 And by him we cry, ''*Abba*, *F*.''
1Co 4: 15 for in Christ Jesus I became your *f*
2Co 6: 18 ''I will be a *F* to you,
Eph 5: 31 this reason a man will leave his *f*
6: 2 ''Honor your *f* and mother''—
Php 2: 11 to the glory of God the *F*.
Heb 1: 5 today I have become your *F*''?
12: 7 what son is not disciplined by his *f*?
1Jn 1: 3 And our fellowship is with the *F*
2: 15 the love of the *F* is not in him.
2: 22 he denies the *F* and the Son.

FATHER'S (FATHER)

Pr 13: 1 A wise son heeds his *f* instruction,
15: 5 A fool spurns his *f* discipline,
19: 13 A foolish son is his *f* ruin,
Mt 16: 27 going to come in his *F* glory
Lk 2: 49 had to be in my *F* house?''
Jn 2: 16 How dare you turn my *F* house
10: 29 can snatch them out of my *F* hand.
14: 2 In my *F* house are many rooms;
15: 8 to my *F* glory, that you bear much

FATHERED (FATHER)

Dt 32: 18 You deserted the Rock, who *f* you;

FATHERLESS (FATHER)

Dt 10: 18 He defends the cause of the *f*
14: 29 the *f* and the widows who live
24: 17 Do not deprive the alien or the *f*
24: 19 Leave it for the alien, the *f*
26: 12 the alien, the *f* and the widow,
Ps 68: 5 A father to the *f*, a defender
82: 3 Defend the cause of the weak and *f*
Pr 23: 10 or encroach on the fields of the *f*,

FATHERS (FATHER)

Ex 20: 5 for the sin of the *f* to the third
Jer 31: 29 'The *f* have eaten sour grapes,
Mal 4: 6 the hearts of the children to their *f*;
Lk 1: 17 the hearts of the *f* to their children
11: 11 ''Which of you *f*, if your son asks
Jn 4: 20 Our *f* worshiped on this mountain,
1Co 4: 15 you do not have many *f*,
Eph 6: 4 *F*, do not exasperate your children;
Col 3: 21 *F*, do not embitter your children,
Heb 12: 9 all had human *f* who disciplined us

FATHOM* (FATHOMED)

Job 11: 7 ''Can you *f* the mysteries of God?
Ps 145: 3 his greatness no one can *f*.
Ecc 3: 11 yet they cannot *f* what God has
Isa 40: 28 and his understanding no one can *f*
1Co 13: 2 and can *f* all mysteries and all

FATHOMED* (FATHOM)

Job 5: 9 performs wonders that cannot be *f*,
9: 10 performs wonders that cannot be *f*,

FATTENED

Pr 15: 17 than a *f* calf with hatred.
Lk 15: 23 Bring the *f* calf and kill it.

FAULT (FAULTS)

1Sa 29: 3 I have found no *f* in him.''
Mt 18: 15 and show him his *f*, just
Php 2: 15 of God without *f* in a crooked
Jas 1: 5 generously to all without finding *f*,
Jude : 24 his glorious presence without *f*

FAULTFINDERS*

Jude : 16 These men are grumblers and *f*;

FAULTLESS*

Pr 8: 9 they are *f* to those who have
Php 3: 6 as for legalistic righteousness, *f*.
Jas 1: 27 Father accepts as pure and *f* is this:

FAULTS* (FAULT)

Job 10: 6 that you must search out my *f*
Ps 19: 12 Forgive my hidden *f*.

FAVOR (FAVORITISM)

Ge 4: 4 The Lord looked with *f* on Abel
6: 8 But Noah found *f* in the eyes
Ex 33: 12 and you have found *f* with me.'
34: 9 if I have found *f* in your eyes,''
Lev 26: 9 '' 'I will look on you with *f*
Nu 11: 15 if I have found *f* in your eyes—
Jdg 6: 17 ''If now I have found *f* in your eyes,
1Sa 2: 26 in favor with the Lord and with men.
2Sa 2: 6 and I too will show you the same *f*
2Ki 13: 4 Jehoahaz sought the Lord's *f*,
2Ch 33: 12 In his distress he sought the *f*
Est 7: 3 ''If I have found *f* with you, O king,
Ps 90: 17 May the *f* of the Lord our God rest
Pr 8: 35 and receives *f* from the Lord.
18: 22 and receives *f* from the Lord.
19: 6 Many curry *f* with a ruler,
Isa 61: 2 proclaim the year of the Lord's *f*
Zec 11: 7 called one *F* and the other Union,
Lk 1: 30 Mary, you have found *f* with God.
2: 14 to men on whom his *f* rests.''
2: 52 and in *f* with God and men.
4: 19 to proclaim the year of the Lord's *f*,
2Co 6: 2 now is the time of God's *f*,

FAVORITISM* (FAVOR)

Ex 23: 3 and do not show *f* to a poor man
Lev 19: 15 to the poor or *f* to the great,
Ac 10: 34 true it is that God does not show *f*

Ro 2: 11 For God does not show *f*.
Eph 6: 9 and there is no *f* with him.
Col 3: 25 for his wrong, and there is no *f*.
1Ti 5: 21 and to do nothing out of *f*.
Jas 2: 1 Lord Jesus Christ, don't show *f*.
2: 9 But if you show *f*, you sin

FEAR (AFRAID FEARED FEARS FRIGHTENED GOD-FEARING)

Dt 6: 13 *F* the Lord your God, serve him
10: 12 but to *f* the Lord your God,
31: 12 and learn to *f* the Lord your God
31: 13 and learn to *f* the Lord your God
Jos 4: 24 you might always *f* the Lord
24: 14 ''Now *f* the Lord and serve him
1Sa 12: 14 If you *f* the Lord and serve
12: 24 But be sure to *f* the Lord
2Sa 23: 3 when he rules in the *f* of God,
2Ch 19: 7 let the *f* of the Lord be upon you.
26: 5 who instructed him in the *f* of God.
Job 1: 9 ''Does Job *f* God for nothing?''
Ps 2: 11 Serve the Lord with *f*
19: 9 The *f* of the Lord is pure,
23: 4 I will *f* no evil,
27: 1 whom shall I *f*?
33: 8 Let all the earth *f* the Lord;
34: 7 around those who *f* him,
34: 9 *F* the Lord, you his saints,
46: 2 Therefore we will not *f*,
86: 11 that I may *f* your name.
90: 11 great as the *f* that is due you.
91: 5 You will not *f* the terror of night,
111: 10 *f* of the Lord is the beginning
118: 4 Let those who *f* the Lord say:
128: 1 Blessed are all who *f* the Lord,
145: 19 of those who *f* him;
147: 11 delights in those who *f* him,
Pr 1: 7 *f* of the Lord is the beginning
1: 33 and be at ease, without *f* of harm.''
8: 13 To *f* the Lord is to hate evil;
9: 10 *f* of the Lord is the beginning
10: 27 The *f* of the Lord adds length
14: 27 The *f* of the Lord is a fountain
15: 33 *f* of the Lord teaches a man
16: 6 through the *f* of the Lord a man
19: 23 The *f* of the Lord leads to life:
22: 4 Humility and the *f* of the Lord
29: 25 *F* of man will prove to be a snare,
31: 21 she has no *f* for her household;
Ecc 12: 13 *F* God and keep his
Isa 11: 3 delight in the *f* of the Lord.
33: 6 the *f* of the Lord is the key
35: 4 ''Be strong, do not *f*;
41: 10 So do not *f*, for I am with you;
41: 13 and says to you, Do not *f*;
43: 1 '*F* not, for I have redeemed you;
51: 7 Do not *f* the reproach of men
54: 14 you will have nothing to *f*.
Jer 17: 8 It does not *f* when heat comes;
Lk 12: 5 I will show you whom you should *f*:
2Co 5: 11 we know what it is to *f* the Lord,
Php 2: 12 to work out your salvation with *f*
1Jn 4: 18 But perfect love drives out *f*,
Jude : 23 to others show mercy, mixed with *f*
Rev 14: 7 ''*F* God and give him glory,

FEARED (FEAR)

Job 1: 1 he *f* God and shunned evil.
Ps 76: 7 You alone are to be *f*.
Mal 3: 16 those who *f* the Lord talked

FEARS (FEAR)

Job 1: 8 a man who *f* God and shuns evil.''
2: 3 a man who *f* God and shuns evil.
Ps 34: 4 he delivered me from all my *f*.
112: 1 is the man who *f* the Lord,
Pr 14: 16 A wise man *f* the Lord
14: 26 He who *f* the Lord has a secure
31: 30 a woman who *f* the Lord is
2Co 7: 5 conflicts on the outside, *f* within.
1Jn 4: 18 The one who *f* is not made perfect

FEAST (FEASTING FEASTS)

Pr 15: 15 the cheerful heart has a continual *f*.
2Pe 2: 13 pleasures while they *f* with you.

FEASTING (FEAST)

Pr 17: 1 than a house full of *f*, with strife.

FEASTS (FEAST)

Am 5:21 ''I hate, I despise your religious *f;*
Jude :12 men are blemishes at your love *f,*

FEATHERS

Ps 91: 4 He will cover you with his *f,*

FEEBLE

Job 4: 3 you have strengthened *f* hands.
Isa 35: 3 Strengthen the *f* hands,
Heb 12:12 strengthen your *f* arms

FEED (FEEDS)

Jn 21:15 Jesus said, ''*F* my lambs.''
    21:17 Jesus said, ''*F* my sheep.
Ro 12:20 ''If your enemy is hungry, *f* him;
Jude :12 shepherds who *f* only themselves.

FEEDS (FEED)

Pr 15:14 but the mouth of a fool *f* on folly.
Mt 6:26 yet your heavenly Father *f* them.
Jn 6:57 so the one who *f* on me will live

FEEL

Jdg 16:26 me where I can *f* the pillars that
Ps 115: 7 they have hands, but cannot *f,*

FEET (FOOT)

Ru 3: 8 discovered a woman lying at his *f.*
Ps 8: 6 you put everything under his *f:*
    22:16 have pierced my hands and my *f.*
    40: 2 he set my *f* on a rock
    56:13 and my *f* from stumbling,
    66: 9 and kept our *f* from slipping.
    73: 2 as for me, my *f* had almost slipped;
   110: 1 a footstool for your *f.''*
   119:105 Your word is a lamp to my *f*
Pr 4:26 Make level paths for your *f*
Isa 52: 7 are the *f* of those who bring good
Da 2:33 its *f* partly of iron and partly
Na 1:15 the *f* of one who brings good news,
Mt 10:14 shake the dust off your *f*
    22:44 enemies under your *f.''*
Lk 1:79 to guide our *f* into the path of peace
    20:43 a footstool for your *f.''*
    24:39 Look at my hands and my *f.*
Jn 13: 5 and began to wash his disciples' *f,*
    13:14 also should wash one another's *f.*
Ro 3:15 ''Their *f* are swift to shed blood;
    10:15 ''How beautiful are the *f*
    16:20 will soon crush Satan under your *f.*
1Co 12:21 And the head cannot say to the *f,*
    15:25 has put all his enemies under his *f.*
Eph 1:22 God placed all things under his *f*
1Ti 5:10 washing the *f* of the saints,
Heb 1:13 a footstool for your *f''?*
     2: 8 and put everything under his *f.''*
    12:13 ''Make level paths for your *f,''*
Rev 1:15 His *f* were like bronze glowing

FELIX

Governor before whom Paul was tried (Ac 23:
23-24:27).

FELLOWSHIP

Ex 20:24 burnt offerings and *f* offerings,
Lev 3: 1 If someone's offering is a *f* offering,
1Co 1: 9 who has called you into *f*
     5: 2 out of your *f* the man who did this?
2Co 6:14 what *f* can light have with darkness
    13:14 and the *f* of the Holy Spirit is
Gal 2: 9 and Barnabas the right hand of *f*
Php 2: 1 if any *f* with the Spirit,
     3:10 the *f* of sharing in his sufferings,
1Jn 1: 3 And our *f* is with the Father
     1: 3 so that you also may have *f* with us.
     1: 6 claim to have *f* with him yet walk
     1: 7 we have *f* with one another,

FEMALE

Ge 1:27 male and *f* he created them.
     5: 2 He created them male and *f*
Mt 19: 4 Creator 'made them male and *f,'*
Mk 10: 6 God 'made them male and *f.'*
Gal 3:28 *f,* for you are all one in Christ Jesus

FEROCIOUS

Mt 7:15 but inwardly they are *f* wolves.

FERTILE (FERTILIZE)

Isa 32:15 and the desert becomes a *f* field,
Jer 2: 7 I brought you into a *f* land

FERTILIZE* (FERTILE)

Lk 13: 8 and I'll dig around it and *f* it.

FERVOR*

Ac 18:25 and he spoke with great *f*
Ro 12:11 but keep your spiritual *f,* serving

FESTIVAL

1Co 5: 8 Therefore let us keep the *F,*
Col 2:16 or with regard to a religious *f,*

FESTUS

Successor of Felix; sent Paul to Caesar (Ac 25-
26).

FEVER

Job 30:30 my body burns with *f.*
Mt 8:14 mother-in-law lying in bed with a *f.*
Lk 4:38 was suffering from a high *f,*
Jn 4:52 ''The *f* left him yesterday
Ac 28: 8 suffering from *f* and dysentery.

FIELD (FIELDS)

Ge 4: 8 Abel, ''Let's go out to the *f.''*
Lev 19: 9 reap to the very edges of your *f*
    19:19 Do not plant your *f* with two kinds
Pr 31:16 She considers a *f* and buys it;
Isa 40: 6 glory is like the flowers of the *f.*
Mt 6:28 See how the lilies of the *f* grow.
     6:30 how God clothes the grass of the *f,*
    13:38 *f* is the world, and the good seed
    13:44 is like treasure hidden in a *f.*
Lk 14:18 I have just bought a *f,* and I must go
1Co 3: 9 are God's *f,* God's building.
1Pe 1:24 glory is like the flowers of the *f;*

FIELDS (FIELD)

Ru 2: 2 go to the *f* and pick up the leftover
Lk 2: 8 were shepherds living out in the *f*
Jn 4:35 open your eyes and look at the *f!*

FIG (FIGS SYCAMORE-FIG)

Ge 3: 7 so they sewed *f* leaves together
Jdg 9:10 ''Next, the trees said to the *f* tree,
1Ki 4:25 man under his own vine and *f* tree.
Pr 27:18 He who tends a *f* tree will eat its
Mic 4: 4 and under his own *f* tree,
Zec 3:10 to sit under his vine and *f* tree,'
Mt 21:19 Seeing a *f* tree by the road,
Lk 13: 6 ''A man had a *f* tree, planted
Jas 3:12 brothers, can a *f* tree bear olives,
Rev 6:13 drop from a *f* tree when shaken

FIGHT (FIGHTING FIGHTS FOUGHT)

Ex 14:14 The LORD will *f* for you; you need
Dt 1:30 going before you, will *f* for you,
     3:22 the LORD your God himself will *f*
Ne 4:20 Our God will *f* for us!''
Ps 35: 1 *f* against those who *f* against me.
Jn 18:36 my servants would *f*
1Co 9:26 I do not *f* like a man beating the air.
2Co 10: 4 The weapons we *f*
1Ti 1:18 them you may *f* the good *f,*
     6:12 Fight the good *f* of the faith.
2Ti 4: 7 fought the good *f,* I have finished

FIGHTING (FIGHT)

Jos 10:14 Surely the LORD was *f* for Israel!

FIGHTS (FIGHT)

Jos 23:10 the LORD your God *f* for you,
1Sa 25:28 because he *f* the LORD's battles.
Jas 4: 1 What causes *f* and quarrels

FIGS (FIG)

Lk 6:44 People do not pick *f*
Jas 3:12 grapevine bear *f?* Neither can a salt

FILL (FILLED FILLING FILLS FULL FULLNESS FULLY)

Ge 1:28 and increase in number; *f* the earth
Ps 16:11 you will *f* me with joy
    81:10 wide your mouth and I will *f* it.
Pr 28:19 who chases fantasies will have his *f*

FILLED (FILL)

Ex 31: 3 I have *f* him with the Spirit of God,
    35:31 he has *f* him with the Spirit of God,
Dt 34: 9 son of Nun was *f* with the spirit
1Ki 8:10 the cloud *f* the temple
     8:11 glory of the LORD *f* his temple.
2Ch 5:14 of the LORD *f* the temple of God.
     7: 1 the glory of the LORD *f* the temple
Ps 72:19 may the whole earth be *f*
   119: 64 The earth is *f* with your love,
Isa 6: 4 and the temple was *f* with smoke.
Eze 10: 3 and a cloud *f* the inner court.
    10: 4 The cloud *f* the temple,
    43: 5 the glory of the LORD *f* the temple
Hab 2:14 For the earth will be *f*
     3: 3 and his praise *f* the earth.
Mt 5: 6 for they will be *f.*
Lk 1:15 and he will be *f* with the Holy Spirit
     1:41 and Elizabeth was *f* with the Holy
     1:67 His father Zechariah was *f*
     2:40 and became strong; he was *f*
Jn 12: 3 the house was *f* with the fragrance
Ac 2: 2 the whole house where they were
     2: 4 All of them were *f*
     4: 8 Then Peter, *f* with the Holy Spirit,
     4:31 they were all *f* with the Holy Spirit
     9:17 and be *f* with the Holy Spirit.''
    13: 9 called Paul, *f* with the Holy Spirit,
Eph 5:18 Instead, be *f* with the Spirit.
Php 1:11 *f* with the fruit of righteousness
Rev 15: 8 And the temple was *f* with smoke

FILLING (FILL)

Eze 44: 4 the glory of the LORD *f* the temple

FILLS (FILL)

Nu 14:21 of the LORD *f* the whole earth,
Ps 107: 9 and the hungry with good things.
Eph 1:23 fullness of him who *f* everything

FILTH (FILTHY)

Isa 4: 4 The Lord will wash away the *f* .
Jas 1:21 rid of all moral *f* and the evil that is

FILTHY (FILTH)

Isa 64: 6 all our righteous acts are like *f* rags;
Col 3: 8 and *f* language from your lips.
2Pe 2: 7 by the *f* lives of lawless men

FINAL (FINALITY)

Ps 73:17 then I understood their *f* destiny.

FINALITY* (FINAL)

Ro 9:28 on earth with speed and *f.''*

FINANCIAL*

1Ti 6: 5 that godliness is a means to *f* gain.

FIND (FINDS FOUND)

Nu 32:23 be sure that your sin will *f* you out.
Dt 4:29 you will *f* him if you look for him
1Sa 23:16 and helped him *f* strength in God.
Job 23: 3 If only I knew where to *f* him;
Ps 36: 7 *f* refuge in the shadow
    62: 5 *F* rest, O my soul, in God alone;
    91: 4 under his wings you will *f* refuge;
Pr 8:17 and those who seek me *f* me.
    14:22 those who plan what is good *f* love
    20: 6 but a faithful man who can *f?*
    24:14 if you *f* it, there is a future hope
    31:10 A wife of noble character who can *f*
Jer 6:16 and you will *f* rest for your souls.
    29:13 and *f* me when you seek me
Mt 7: 7 seek and you will *f;* knock
    11:29 and you will *f* rest for your souls.
    16:25 loses his life for me will *f* it.
    22: 9 invite to the banquet anyone you *f.'*
Lk 11: 9 seek and you will *f;* knock
    18: 8 will he *f* faith on the earth?''
Jn 10: 9 come in and go out, and *f* pasture.

FINDS (FIND)

Ps 62: 1 My soul *f* rest in God alone;

Hag 2: 7 and I will *f* this house with glory,'
Jn 6:26 you ate the loaves and had your *f.*
Ac 2:28 you will *f* me with joy
Ro 15:13 the God of hope *f* you with all joy

Ps 112: 1 who *f* great delight
119:162 like one who *f* great spoil.
Pr   3: 13 Blessed is the man who *f* wisdom,
       8: 35 For whoever *f* me *f* life
      11: 27 He who seeks good *f* good will,
      18: 22 He who *f* a wife *f* what is good
Mt   7: 8 he who seeks *f*; and to him who
      10: 39 Whoever *f* his life will lose it,
Lk   11: 10 he who seeks *f*; and to him who
      12: 37 whose master *f* them watching
      12: 43 servant whom the master *f* doing
      15: 4 go after the lost sheep until he *f* it?
      15: 8 and search carefully until she *f* it?

FINE-SOUNDING* (SOUND)

Col   2: 4 may deceive you by *f* arguments.

FINGER

Ex   8: 19 to Pharaoh, "This is the *f* of God."
      31: 18 of stone inscribed by the *f* of God.
Dt   9: 10 two stone tablets inscribed by the *f*
Lk   11: 20 But if I drive out demons by the *f*
      16: 24 to dip the tip of his *f* in water
Jn   8: 6 to write on the ground with his *f*.
      20: 25 and put my *f* where the nails were,

FINISH (FINISHED)

Jn   4: 34 him who sent me and to *f* his work.
       5: 36 that the Father has given me to *f*,
Ac   20: 24 if only I may *f* the race
2Co   8: 11 Now *f* the work, so that your eager
Jas   1: 4 Perseverance must *f* its work

FINISHED (FINISH)

Ge   2: 2 seventh day God had *f* the work he
Jn   19: 30 the drink, Jesus said, "It is *f*."
2Ti   4: 7 I have *f* the race, I have kept

FIRE

Ex   3: 2 in flames of *f* from within a bush.
      13: 21 in a pillar of *f* to give them light,
Lev   6: 12 *f* on the altar must be kept burning;
       9: 24 *f* came out from the presence
1Ki 18: 38 Then the *f* of the LORD fell
2Ki   2: 11 suddenly a chariot of *f*
Isa   5: 24 as tongues of *f* lick up straw
      30: 27 and his tongue is a consuming *f*.
Jer 23: 29 my word like *f*," declares
Da   3: 25 four men walking around in the *f*,
Zec   3: 2 stick snatched from the *f*?"
Mal   3: 2 For he will be like a refiner's *f*
Mt   3: 11 you with the Holy Spirit and with *f*.
       3: 12 the chaff with unquenchable *f*."
       5: 22 will be in danger of the *f* of hell.
      18: 8 and be thrown into eternal *f*.
      25: 41 into the eternal *f* prepared
Mk   9: 43 where the *f* never goes out.
       9: 48 and the *f* is not quenched.'
       9: 49 Everyone will be salted with *f*.
Lk   3: 16 you with the Holy Spirit and with *f*.
      12: 49 I have come to bring *f* on the earth,
Ac   2: 3 to be tongues of *f* that separated
1Co   3: 13 It will be revealed with *f*.
1Th   5: 19 Do not put out the Spirit's *f*;
Heb 12: 29 for our "God is a consuming *f*."
Jas   3: 5 set on *f* by a small spark.
       3: 6 also is a *f*, a world of evil
2Pe   3: 10 the elements will be destroyed by *f*,
Jude : 7 suffer the punishment of eternal *f*.
      : 23 snatch others from the *f*
Rev   1: 14 and his eyes were like blazing *f*.
      20: 14 The lake of *f* is the second death.

FIRM*

Ex   14: 13 Stand *f* and you will see
      15: 8 surging waters stood *f* like a wall;
Jos   3: 17 the covenant of the LORD stood *f*
2Ch 20: 17 stand *f* and see the deliverance
Ezr   9: 8 giving us a *f* place in his sanctuary,
Job 11: 15 you will stand *f* and without fear.
      36: 5 he is mighty, and *f* in his purpose.
      41: 23 they are *f* and immovable.
Ps   20: 8 but we rise up and stand *f*.
      30: 7 you made my mountain stand *f*;
      33: 9 he commanded, and it stood *f*.
      33: 11 of the LORD stand *f* forever,
      37: 23 he makes his steps *f*;
      40: 2 and gave me a *f* place to stand.

Ps   75: 3 it is I who hold its pillars *f*.
      78: 13 made the water stand *f* like a wall.
      89: 2 that your love stands *f* forever,
      89: 4 and make your throne *f*;
      93: 5 Your statutes stand *f*;
119: 89 it stands *f* in the heavens.
Pr   4: 26 and take only ways that are *f*.
      10: 25 but the righteous stand *f* forever.
      12: 7 the house of the righteous stands *f*.
Isa   7: 9 If you do not stand *f* in your faith,
      22: 17 about to take *f* hold of you
      22: 23 drive him like a peg into a *f* place;
      22: 25 into the *f* place will give way;
Eze 13: 5 so that it will stand *f* in the battle
Zec   8: 23 nations will take *f* hold of one Jew
Mt   10: 22 he who stands *f* to the end will be
      24: 13 he who stands *f* to the end will be
Mk   13: 13 he who stands *f* to the end will be
Lk   21: 19 By standing *f* you will gain life.
1Co 10: 12 So, if you think you are standing *f*,
      15: 58 my dear brothers, stand *f*.
      16: 13 on your guard; stand *f* in the faith;
2Co   1: 7 for you is *f*, because we know that
       1: 21 who makes both us and you stand *f*
       1: 24 because it is by faith you stand *f*.
Gal   5: 1 Stand *f*, then, and do not let
Eph   6: 14 Stand *f* then, with the belt
Php   1: 27 I will know that you stand *f*
       4: 1 that is how you should stand *f*
Col   1: 23 in your faith, established and *f*,
       2: 5 and how *f* your faith in Christ is.
       4: 12 that you may stand *f* in all the will
1Th   3: 8 since you are standing *f* in the Lord
2Th   2: 15 stand *f* and hold to the teachings
1Ti   6: 19 a *f* foundation for the coming age,
2Ti   2: 19 God's solid foundation stands *f*,
Heb   6: 19 an anchor for the soul, *f* and secure
Jas   5: 8 You too, be patient and stand *f*,
1Pe   5: 9 Resist him, standing *f* in the faith,
       5: 10 make you strong, *f* and steadfast.

FIRMAMENT see EXPANSE, HEAVENS, SKIES

FIRST

Ge   1: 5 and there was morning—the *f* day.
       1: 13 and where he had *f* built an altar,
Ex   34: 19 *f* offspring of every womb belongs
1Ki 22: 5 "*F* seek the counsel of the LORD."
Pr   18: 17 to present his case seems right,
Isa 44: 6 I am the *f* and I am the last;
      48: 12 I am the *f* and I am the last,
Mt   5: 24 *F* go and be reconciled
       6: 33 But seek *f* his kingdom
       7: 5 *f* take the plank out
      19: 30 But many who are *f* will be last,
      20: 16 last will be *f*, and the *f* will be last."
      20: 27 wants to be *f* must be your slave—
      22: 38 This is the *f* and greatest
      23: 26 *F* clean the inside of the cup
Mk   9: 35 to be *f*, he must be the very last,
      10: 31 are *f* will be last, and the last *f*."
      10: 44 wants to be *f* must be slave
      13: 10 And the gospel must *f* be preached
Lk   13: 30 will be *f*, and *f* who will be last."
Jn   8: 7 let him be the *f* to throw a stone
Ac   11: 26 disciples were called Christians *f*
Ro   1: 16 for the Jew, then for the Gentile.
       1: 17 is by faith from *f* to last,
       2: 9 *f* for the Jew, then for the Gentile;
       2: 10 *f* for the Jew, then for the Gentile.
1Co 12: 28 in the church God has appointed *f*
      15: 45 "The *f* man Adam became a living
2Co   8: 5 they gave themselves *f* to the Lord
Eph   6: 2 which is the *f* commandment
1Th   4: 16 and the dead in Christ will rise *f*.
1Ti   2: 13 For Adam was formed *f*, then Eve.
Heb 10: 9 He sets aside the *f*
Jas   3: 17 comes from heaven is *f* of all pure;
1Jn   4: 19 We love because he *f* loved us.
3Jn   : 9 but Diotrephes, who loves to be *f*,
Rev   1: 17 I am the *F* and the Last.
       2: 4 You have forsaken your *f* love.
      22: 13 and the Omega, the *F* and the Last,

FIRSTBORN (BEAR)

Ex   11: 5 Every *f* son in Egypt will die,
      34: 20 Redeem all your *f* sons.

Ps   89: 27 I will also appoint him my *f*,
Lk   2: 7 and she gave birth to her *f*, a son.
Ro   8: 29 that he might be the *f*
Col   1: 15 image of the invisible God, the *f*
       1: 18 and the *f* from among the dead,
Heb   1: 6 when God brings his *f*
      12: 23 of the *f*, whose names are written
Rev   1: 5 who is the faithful witness, the *f*

FIRSTFRUITS

Ex   23: 16 the Feast of Harvest with the *f*
      23: 19 "Bring the best of the *f* of your soil
Ro   8: 23 who have the *f* of the Spirit,
1Co 15: 23 Christ, the *f*; then, when he comes,
Rev 14: 4 offered as *f* to God and the Lamb.

FISH (FISHERS)

Ge   1: 26 let them rule over the *f* of the sea
Jnh   1: 17 But the LORD provided a great *f*
Mt   7: 10 asks for a *f*, will give him a snake?
      12: 40 three nights in the belly of a huge *f*,
      14: 17 loaves of bread and two *f*,"
Mk   6: 38 they said, "Five—and two *f*."
Lk   5: 6 of *f* that their nets began to break.
       9: 13 loaves of bread and two *f*—
Jn   6: 9 small barley loaves and two small *f*,
      21: 5 haven't you any *f*?" "No,"
      21: 11 It was full of large *f*, 153, but

FISHERMEN

Mk   1: 16 a net into the lake, for they were *f*.

FISHERS (FISH)

Mt   4: 19 "and I will make you *f* of men."
Mk   1: 17 "and I will make you *f* of men."

FISHHOOK*

Job 41: 1 pull in the leviathan with a *f*

FISTS

Mt   26: 67 and struck him with their *f*.

FIT (FITTING)

Jdg 17: 6 no king; everyone did as he saw *f*.
      21: 25 no king; everyone did as he saw *f*.

FITTING* (FIT)

Ps   33: 1 it is *f* for the upright to praise him.
     147: 1 how pleasant and *f* to praise him!
Pr   10: 32 of the righteous know what is *f*,
      19: 10 It is not *f* for a fool to live in luxury
      26: 1 honor is not *f* for a fool.
1Co 14: 40 everything should be done in a *f*
Col   3: 18 to your husbands, as is *f* in the Lord
Heb   2: 10 sons to glory, it was *f* that God,

FIX* (FIXED)

Dt   11: 18 *F* these words of mine
Job 14: 3 Do you *f* your eye on such a one?
Pr   4: 25 *f* your gaze directly before you.
Isa 46: 8 "Remember this, *f* it in mind,
Am   9: 4 I will *f* my eyes upon them
2Co   4: 18 we *f* our eyes not on what is seen,
Heb   3: 1 heavenly calling, *f* your thoughts
      12: 2 Let us *f* our eyes on Jesus,

FIXED* (FIX)

2Ki   8: 11 stared at him with a *f* gaze
Job 38: 10 when I *f* limits for it
Ps 141: 8 my eyes are *f* on you, O Sovereign
Pr   8: 28 *f* securely the fountains of the deep
Jer 33: 25 and night and the *f* laws of heaven
Lk   16: 26 and you a great chasm has been *f*,

FLAME (FLAMES FLAMING)

2Ti   1: 6 you to fan into *f* the gift of God,

FLAMES (FLAME)

1Co   3: 15 only as one escaping through the *f*.
      13: 3 and surrender my body to the *f*,

FLAMING (FLAME)

Eph   6: 16 you can extinguish all the *f* arrows

FLANK

Eze 34: 21 Because you shove with *f*

FLASH

1Co 15: 52 in a *f*, in the twinkling of an eye,

FLATTER* (FLATTERING FLATTERS FLATTERY)

Job 32: 21 nor will I f any man;
Ps 78: 36 But then they would f him
Jude : 16 f others for their own advantage.

FLATTERING* (FLATTER)

Ps 12: 2 their f lips speak with deception.
12: 3 May the LORD cut off all f lips
Pr 26: 28 and a f mouth works ruin.
28: 23 than he who has a f tongue.
Eze 12: 24 or f divinations among the people

FLATTERS* (FLATTER)

Ps 36: 2 For in his own eyes he f himself
Pr 29: 5 Whoever f his neighbor

FLATTERY* (FLATTER)

Job 32: 22 for if I were skilled in f,
Da 11: 32 With f he will corrupt those who
Ro 16: 18 and f they deceive the minds
1Th 2: 5 You know we never used f,

FLAWLESS*

2Sa 22: 31 the word of the LORD is f.
Job 11: 4 You say to God, 'My beliefs are f
Ps 12: 6 And the words of the LORD are f,
18: 30 the word of the LORD is f.
Pr 30: 5 ''Every word of God is f;
SS 5: 2 my dove, my f one.

FLEE (FLEES)

Ps 139: 7 Where can I f from your presence?
1Co 6: 18 F from sexual immorality.
10: 14 my dear friends, f from idolatry.
1Ti 6: 11 But you, man of God, f from all this
2Ti 2: 22 F the evil desires of youth,
Jas 4: 7 Resist the devil, and he will f

FLEECE

Jdg 6: 37 I will place a wool f

FLEES (FLEE)

Pr 28: 1 The wicked man f though no one

FLEETING*

Job 14: 2 like a f shadow, he does not endure
Ps 39: 4 let me know how f is my life.
89: 47 Remember how f is my life.
144: 4 his days are like a f shadow.
Pr 21: 6 is a f vapor and a deadly snare.
31: 30 Charm is deceptive, and beauty is f

FLESH see also BODY, MANKIND, PEOPLE, SINFUL (nature)

Ge 2: 23 and f of my f;
2: 24 and they will become one f.
2Ch 32: 8 With him is only the arm of f,
Job 19: 26 yet in my f I will see God;
Eze 11: 19 of stone and give them a heart of f.
36: 26 of stone and give you a heart of f.
Mt 19: 5 and the two will become one f ?
Mk 10: 8 and the two will become one f.'
Jn 1: 14 The Word became f and made his
6: 51 This bread is my f, which I will give
1Co 6: 16 "The two will become one f."
15: 39 All f is not the same: Men have one
Eph 5: 31 and the two will become one f."
6: 12 For our struggle is not against f
Php 3: 2 evil, those mutilators of the f.
1Jn 4: 2 come in the f is from God,
Jude : 23 the clothing stained by corrupted f.

FLIGHT

Dt 32: 30 or two put ten thousand to f,

FLINT

Isa 50: 7 Therefore have I set my face like f,
Zec 7: 12 They made their hearts as hard as f

FLIRTING*

Isa 3: 16 f with their eyes,

FLOCK (FLOCKS)

Ps 77: 20 You led your people like a f
78: 52 he brought his people out like a f;
95: 7 the f under his care.
Isa 40: 11 He tends his f like a shepherd:

Jer 10: 21 and all their f is scattered.
23: 2 "Because you have scattered my f
31: 10 watch over his f like a shepherd.
Eze 34: 2 not shepherds take care of the f?
Zec 11: 17 who deserts the f!
Mt 26: 31 the sheep of the f will be scattered.'
Lk 12: 32 little f, for your Father has been
Jn 10: 16 shall be one f and one shepherd.
Ac 20: 28 all the f of which the Holy Spirit
1Co 9: 7 Who tends a f and does not drink
1Pe 5: 2 Be shepherds of God's f that is
5: 3 but being examples to the f.

FLOCKS (FLOCK)

Lk 2: 8 keeping watch over their f at night.

FLOG (FLOGGED FLOGGING)

Pr 19: 25 F a mocker, and the simple will
Ac 22: 25 to f a Roman citizen who hasn't

FLOGGED (FLOG)

Jn 19: 1 Pilate took Jesus and had him f.
Ac 5: 40 the apostles in and had them f.
16: 23 After they had been severely f,
2Co 11: 23 frequently, been f more severely,

FLOGGING (FLOG)

Heb 11: 36 f, while still others were chained

FLOOD (FLOODGATES)

Ge 7: 7 ark to escape the waters of the f.
Mal 2: 13 You f the LORD's altar with tears.
Mt 24: 38 For in the days before the f,
2Pe 2: 5 world when he brought the f

FLOODGATES (FLOOD)

Ge 7: 11 the f of the heavens were opened.
Mal 3: 10 see if I will not throw open the f

FLOOR

Jas 2: 3 or "Sit on the f by my feet,"

FLOUR

Lev 2: 1 his offering is to be of fine f.
Nu 7: 13 filled with fine f mixed with oil
28: 9 of an ephah of fine f mixed with oil.

FLOURISH (FLOURISHES FLOURISHING)

Ps 72: 7 In his days the righteous will f;
92: 7 and all evildoers f,
92: 12 The righteous will f like a palm tree
Pr 14: 11 but the tent of the upright will f.

FLOURISHES (FLOURISH)

Pr 12: 12 but the root of the righteous f.

FLOURISHING (FLOURISH)

Ps 52: 8 f in the house of God;

FLOW (FLOWING)

Nu 13: 27 and it does f with milk and honey!
Jn 7: 38 streams of living water will f

FLOWER (FLOWERS)

Job 14: 2 up like a f and withers away;
Ps 103: 15 he flourishes like a f of the field;
Jas 1: 10 he will pass away like a wild f.

FLOWERS (FLOWER)

Isa 40: 6 and all their glory is like the f
40: 7 The grass withers and the f fall,
1Pe 1: 24 and all their glory is like the f

FLOWING (FLOW)

Ex 3: 8 a land f with milk and honey—
33: 3 Go up to the land f with milk
Nu 16: 14 us into a land f with milk
Jos 5: 6 a land f with milk and honey.
Ps 107: 33 f springs into thirsty ground,
107: 35 the parched ground into f springs;
Jer 32: 22 a land f with milk and honey.
Eze 20: 6 a land f with milk and honey,
Rev 22: 1 f from the throne of God

FLUTE

Ps 150: 4 praise him with the strings and f,
Mt 11: 17 " 'We played the f for you,
1Co 14: 7 that make sounds, such as the f

FOAL*

Zec 9: 9 on a colt, the f of a donkey.
Mt 21: 5 on a colt, the f of a donkey.' "

FOILS*

Ps 33: 10 The LORD f the plans
Isa 44: 25 who f the signs of false prophets

FOLDING* (FOLDS)

Pr 6: 10 a little f of the hands to rest—
24: 33 a little f of the hands to rest—

FOLDS (FOLDING)

Ecc 4: 5 The fool f his hands

FOLLOW (FOLLOWED FOLLOWING FOLLOWS)

Ex 23: 2 Do not f the crowd in doing wrong.
Lev 18: 4 and be careful to f my decrees.
Dt 5: 1 Learn them and be sure to f them.
17: 19 f carefully all the words of this law
1Ki 11: 6 he did not f the LORD completely,
2Ch 34: 33 they did not fail to f the LORD,
Ps 23: 6 Surely goodness and love will f me
119:166 and I f your commands.
Mt 4: 19 Jesus said, "and I will make
8: 19 I will f you wherever you go."
8: 22 But Jesus told him, "F me,
16: 24 and take up his cross and f me.
19: 27 "We have left everything to f you!
Lk 9: 23 take up his cross daily and f me.
9: 61 Still another said, "I will f you,
Jn 4: 19 his sheep f him because they know
10: 5 But they will never f a stranger;
10: 27 I know them, and they f me.
12: 26 Whoever serves me must f me;
21: 19 Then he said to him, "F me!"
1Co 1: 12 One of you says, "I f Paul";
11: 1 F my example, as I follow
14: 1 F the way of love and eagerly
2Th 3: 9 ourselves a model for you to f.
1Pe 2: 21 that you should f in his steps.
Rev 14: 4 They f the Lamb wherever he goes.

FOLLOWED (FOLLOW)

Nu 32: 11 they have not f me wholeheartedly,
Dt 1: 36 he f the LORD wholeheartedly."
Jos 14: 14 he f the LORD, the God of Israel,
2Ch 10: 14 he f the advice of the young men
Mt 4: 20 once they left their nets and f him.
9: 9 and Matthew got up and f him.
26: 58 But Peter f him at a distance,
Lk 18: 43 he received his sight and f Jesus,

FOLLOWING (FOLLOW)

Ps 119: 14 I rejoice in f your statutes
Php 3: 17 Join with others in f my example,
1Ti 1: 18 by f them you may fight the good

FOLLOWS (FOLLOW)

Jn 8: 12 Whoever f me will never walk

FOLLY (FOOL)

Pr 14: 29 a quick-tempered man displays f.
19: 3 A man's own f ruins his life,
Ecc 10: 1 so a little f outweighs wisdom
Mk 7: 22 envy, slander, arrogance and f.
2Ti 3: 9 their f will be clear to everyone.

FOOD (FOODS)

Ge 1: 30 I give every green plant for f."
Pr 12: 9 to be somebody and have no f.
12: 11 his land will have abundant f,
20: 13 you will have f to spare.
20: 17 F gained by fraud tastes sweet
21: 20 of the wise are stores of choice f
22: 9 for he shares his f with the poor.
23: 3 for that f is deceptive.
23: 6 Do not eat the f of a stingy man,
25: 21 If your enemy is hungry, give him f
31: 14 bringing her f from afar.
31: 15 she provides f for her family
Isa 58: 7 not to share your f with the hungry
Eze 18: 7 but gives his f to the hungry
Da 1: 8 to defile himself with the royal f
Mt 3: 4 His f was locusts and wild honey.
6: 25 Is not life more important than f,
Jn 4: 32 "I have f to eat that you know

FOODS

Jn 4:34 have brought him *f*?'' ''My *f*,''
    6:27 Do not work for *f* that spoils,
    6:55 my flesh is real *f* and my blood is
Ac 15:20 to abstain from *f* polluted by idols,
Ro 14:14 fully convinced that no *f* is unclean
1Co 8: 1 Now about *f* sacrificed to idols:
    8: 8 But *f* does not bring us near to God
2Co 11:27 and have often gone without *f*,
1Ti 6: 8 But if we have *f* and clothing,
Heb 5:14 But solid *f* is for the mature,
Jas 2:15 sister is without clothes and daily *f*.

FOODS (FOOD)

Mk 7:19 Jesus declared all *f* ''clean.'')

FOOL (FOLLY FOOL'S FOOLISH FOOLISHNESS FOOLS)

1Sa 25:25 his name is *F*, and folly goes
Ps 14: 1 The *f* says in his heart,
Pr 10:10 and a chattering *f* comes to ruin.
    10:18 and whoever spreads slander is a *f*.
    12:15 The way of a *f* seems right to him,
    12:16 A *f* shows his annoyance at once,
    14:16 but a *f* is hotheaded and reckless.
    15: 5 A *f* spurns his father's discipline,
    17:12 than a *f* in his folly.
    17:16 use is money in the hand of a *f*,
    17:21 To have a *f* for a son brings grief;
    17:28 Even a *f* is thought wise
    18: 2 A *f* finds no pleasure
    20: 3 but every *f* is quick to quarrel.
    23: 9 Do not speak to a *f*,
    24: 7 Wisdom is too high for a *f*;
    26: 4 Do not answer a *f* according
    26: 5 Answer a *f* according to his folly,
    26: 7 is a proverb in the mouth of a *f*.
    26:11 so a *f* repeats his folly.
    26:12 for a *f* than for him.
    27:22 Though you grind a *f* in a mortar,
    28:26 He who trusts in himself is a *f*,
    29:11 A *f* gives full vent to his anger,
    29:20 for a *f* than for him.
Mt 5:22 But anyone who says, 'You *f*!'
Lk 12:20 ''But God said to him, 'You *f*!'
1Co 3:18 he should become a ''*f*''
2Co 11:21 I am speaking as a *f*—I

FOOL'S (FOOL)

Pr 14: 3 A *f* talk brings a rod to his back,
    18: 7 A *f* mouth is his undoing,

FOOLISH (FOOL)

Pr 10: 1 but a *f* son grief to his mother.
    14: 1 her own hands the *f* one tears hers
    15:20 but a *f* man despises his mother.
    17:25 A *f* son brings grief to his father
    19:13 A *f* son is his father's ruin,
Mt 7:26 practice is like a *f* man who built
    25: 2 of them were *f* and five were wise.
Lk 11:40 You *f* people! Did not the one who
    24:25 he said to them, ''How *f* you are,
1Co 1:20 Has not God made *f* the wisdom
    1:27 God chose the *f* things of the world
Gal 3: 1 died for nothing!'' You *f* Galatians!
Eph 5: 4 should there be obscenity, *f* talk
    5:17 Therefore do not be *f*,
Tit 3: 9 But avoid *f* controversies

FOOLISHNESS (FOOL)

1Co 1:18 of the cross is *f* to those who are
    1:21 through the *f* of what was preached
    1:23 block to Jews and *f* to Gentiles,
    1:25 For the *f* of God is wiser
    2:14 for they are *f* to him, and he cannot
    3:19 of this world is *f* in God's sight.

FOOLS (FOOL)

Pr 1: 7 but *f* despise wisdom and discipline
    3:35 but *f* he holds up to shame.
    12:23 but the heart of *f* blurts out folly.
    13:19 but *f* detest turning from evil.
    13:20 but a companion of *f* suffers harm.
    14: 9 *F* mock at making amends for sin,
    14:24 but the folly of *f* yields folly.
Ecc 5: 5 than to listen to the song of *f*.
    7: 6 so is the laughter of *f*.
    10: 6 *F* are put in many high positions,
Mt 23:17 You blind *f*! Which is greater:

FOREIGN (FOREIGNER FOREIGNERS)

Ge 35: 2 ''Get rid of the *f* gods you have
2Ch 14: 3 He removed the *f* altars
    33:15 He got rid of the *f* gods
Isa 28:11 with *f* lips and strange tongues

FOREIGNER (FOREIGN)

Lk 17:18 give praise to God except this *f*?''
1Co 14:11 I am a *f* to the speaker,

FOREIGNERS (FOREIGN)

Eph 2:12 *f* to the covenants of the promise,
    2:19 you are no longer *f* and aliens,

Ro 1:22 they became *f* and exchanged
1Co 4:10 We are *f* for Christ, but you are

FOOT (FEET FOOTHOLD)

Jos 1: 3 every place where you set your *f*,
Ps 121: 3 He will not let your *f* slip—
Pr 3:23 and your *f* will not stumble;
    4:27 keep your *f* from evil.
    25:17 Seldom set *f* in your neighbor's
Isa 1: 6 From the sole of your *f* to the top
Mt 18: 8 or your *f* causes you to sin,
Lk 4:11 so that you will not strike your *f*
1Co 12:15 If the *f* should say, ''Because I am
Rev 10: 2 He planted his right *f* on the sea

FOOTHOLD* (FOOT)

Ps 69: 2 where there is no *f*.
    73: 2 I had nearly lost my *f*.
Eph 4:27 and do not give the devil a *f*.

FOOTSTEPS (STEP)

Ps 119:133 Direct my *f* according

FOOTSTOOL

Ps 99: 5 and worship at his *f*;
   110: 1 a *f* for your feet.''
Isa 66: 1 and the earth is my *f*.
Mt 5:35 for it is his *f*; or by Jerusalem,
Ac 7:49 and the earth is my *f*.
Heb 1:13 a *f* for your feet''?
    10:13 for his enemies to be made his *f*,

FORBEARANCE*

Ro 3:25 because in his *f* he had left the sins

FORBID

1Co 14:39 and do not *f* speaking in tongues.
1Ti 4: 3 They *f* people to marry

FORCE (FORCED FORCEFUL FORCES FORCING)

Jn 6:15 to come and make him king by *f*,
Ac 26:11 and I tried to *f* them to blaspheme.
Gal 2:14 that you *f* Gentiles

FORCED (FORCE)

Mt 27:32 and they *f* him to carry the cross.
Phm :14 do will be spontaneous and not *f*.

FORCEFUL* (FORCE)

Mt 11:12 forcefully advancing, and *f* men lay
2Co 10:10 ''His letters are weighty and *f*,

FORCES (FORCE)

Mt 5:41 If someone *f* you to go one mile,
Eph 6:12 and against the spiritual *f* of evil

FORCING (FORCE)

Lk 16:16 and everyone is *f* his way into it.

FOREFATHERS (FATHER)

Heb 1: 1 spoke to our *f* through the prophets
1Pe 1:18 handed down to you from your *f*,

FOREHEAD (FOREHEADS)

Ex 13: 9 a reminder on your *f* that the law
    13:16 on your *f* that the LORD brought
1Sa 17:49 and struck the Philistine on the *f*.
Rev 13:16 a mark on his right hand or on his *f*,

FOREHEADS (FOREHEAD)

Dt 6: 8 hands and bind them on your *f*.
Rev 4: 4 not have the seal of God on their *f*,
    14: 1 his Father's name written on their *f*

FOREKNEW* (KNOW)

Ro 8:29 For those God *f* he
    11: 2 not reject his people, whom he *f*.

FOREKNOWLEDGE* (KNOW)

Ac 2:23 to you by God's set purpose and *f*;
1Pe 1: 2 to the *f* of God the Father,

FORESAW*

Gal 3: 8 Scripture *f* that God would justify

FOREST

Jas 3: 5 Consider what a great *f* is set

FOREVER (EVER)

Ge 3:22 the tree of life and eat, and live *f*.''
    6: 3 Spirit will not contend with man *f*,
Ex 3:15 This is my name *f*, the name
2Sa 7:26 so that your name will be great *f*,
1Ki 2:33 may there be the LORD's peace.''
    9: 3 by putting my Name there *f*,
1Ch 16:15 He remembers his covenant *f*,
    16:34 his love endures *f*.
    16:41 ''for his love endures *f*.''
    17:24 and that your name will be great *f*.
2Ch 5:13 his love endures *f*.''
    20:21 for his love endures *f*.''
Ps 9: 7 The LORD reigns *f*;
    23: 6 dwell in the house of the LORD *f*.
    28: 9 be their shepherd and carry them *f*.
    29:10 the LORD is enthroned as King *f*.
    33:11 the plans of the LORD stand firm *f*
    37:28 They will be protected *f*,
    44: 8 and we will praise your name *f*.
    61: 4 I long to dwell in your tent *f*
    72:19 Praise be to his glorious name *f*;
    73:26 and my portion *f*.
    77: 8 Has his unfailing love vanished *f*?
    79:13 will praise you *f*;
    81:15 and their punishment would last *f*.
    86:12 I will glorify your name *f*.
    89: 1 of the LORD's great love *f*;
    92: 8 But you, O LORD, are exalted *f*.
   100: 5 is good and his love endures *f*;
   102:12 But you, O LORD, sit enthroned *f*;
   104:31 of the LORD endure *f*;
   107: 1 his love endures *f*.
   110: 4 ''You are a priest *f*,
   111: 3 and his righteousness endures *f*.
   112: 6 man will be remembered *f*.
   117: 2 of the LORD endures *f*.
   118: 1 his love endures *f*.
   119:111 Your statutes are my heritage *f*;
   119:152 that you established them to last *f*.
   136: 1 *His love endures f*.
   146: 6 the LORD, who remains faithful *f*.
Pr 10:25 but the righteous stand firm *f*.
    27:24 for riches do not endure *f*,
Isa 25: 8 he will swallow up death *f*.
    26: 4 Trust in the LORD *f*,
    32:17 will be quietness and confidence *f*.
    40: 8 but the word of our God stands *f*.''
    51: 6 but my salvation will last *f*,
    51: 8 But my righteousness will last *f*,
    57:15 he who lives *f*, whose name is holy:
    59:21 from this time on and *f*,''
Jer 33:11 his love endures *f*.''
Eze 37:26 put my sanctuary among them *f*.
Da 2:44 to an end, but it will itself endure *f*.
    3: 9 live *f*! You have issued a decree,
Jn 6:51 eats of this bread, he will live *f*.
    14:16 Counselor to be with you *f*—
Ro 9: 5 who is God over all, *f* praised!
    16:27 to the only wise God be glory *f*!
1Co 9:25 it to get a crown that will last *f*.
1Th 4:17 And so we will be with the Lord *f*.
Heb 5: 6 ''You are a priest *f*,
    7:17 ''You are a priest *f*,
    7:24 Jesus lives *f*, he has a permanent
    13: 8 same yesterday and today and *f*.
1Pe 1:25 but the word of the Lord stands *f*.''
1Jn 2:17 who does the will of God lives *f*.
2Jn : 2 lives in us and will be with us *f*:

FOREVERMORE (EVER)

Ps 113: 2 both now and *f*.

FORFEIT

Mk 8: 36 the whole world, yet *f* his soul?
Lk 9: 25 and yet lose or *f* his very self?

FORGAVE (FORGIVE)

Ps 32: 5 and you *f*
     65: 3 you *f* our transgressions
     78: 38 you *f* their iniquities
Eph 4: 32 just as in Christ God *f* you.
Col 2: 13 He *f* us all our sins, having
      3: 13 Forgive as the Lord *f* you.

FORGET (FORGETS FORGETTING FORGOT FORGOTTEN)

Dt   4: 23 Be careful not to *f* the covenant
      6: 12 that you do not *f* the LORD,
2Ki 17: 38 Do not *f* the covenant I have made
Ps   9: 17 all the nations that *f* God.
     10: 12 Do not *f* the helpless.
     50: 22 "Consider this, you who *f* God,
     78: 7 and would not *f* his deeds
    103: 2 and *f* not all his benefits.
    119: 93 I will never *f* your precepts,
    137: 5 may my right hand *f* its skill,
Pr   3: 1 My son, do not *f* my teaching,
      4: 5 do not *f* my words or swerve
Isa 49: 15 "Can a mother *f* the baby
     51: 13 that you *f* the LORD your Maker,
Jer 2: 32 Does a maiden *f* her jewelry,
     23: 39 I will surely *f* you and cast you out
Heb 6: 10 he will not *f* your work
     13: 2 Do not *f* to entertain strangers,
     13: 16 And do not *f* to do good
2Pe 3: 8 But do not *f* this one thing,

FORGETS (FORGET)

Jn 16: 21 her baby is born she *f* the anguish
Jas 1: 24 immediately *f* what he looks like.

FORGETTING* (FORGET)

Php 3: 13 *F* what is behind and straining
Jas 1: 25 to do this, not *f* what he has heard,

FORGIVE* (FORGAVE FORGIVENESS FORGIVES FORGIVING)

Ge 50: 17 I ask you to *f* your brothers the sins
     50: 17 please *f* the sins of the servants
Ex 10: 17 Now *f* my sin once more
     23: 21 he will not *f* your rebellion,
     32: 32 But now, please *f* their sin—
     34: 9 *f* our wickedness and our sin,
Nu 14: 19 with your great love, *f* the sin
Dt 29: 20 will never be willing to *f* him;
Jos 24: 19 He will not *f* your rebellion
1Sa 15: 25 *f* my sin and come back with me,
     25: 28 Please *f* your servant's offense,
1Ki 8: 30 place, and when you hear, *f.*
      8: 34 and *f* the sin of your people Israel
      8: 36 and *f* the sin of your servants,
      8: 39 *F* and act; deal with each man
      8: 50 *f* all the offenses they have
      8: 50 *f* your people, who have sinned
2Ki 5: 18 But may the LORD *f* your servant
      5: 18 may the LORD *f* your servant
     24: 4 and the LORD was not willing to *f.*
2Ch 6: 21 place; and when you hear, *f.*
      6: 25 and *f* the sin of your people Israel
      6: 27 and *f* the sin of your servants,
      6: 30 *F,* and deal with each man
      6: 39 *f* your people, who have sinned
      7: 14 will *f* their sin and will heal their
Job 7: 21 and *f* my sins?
Ps 19: 12 *F* my hidden faults.
     25: 11 *f* my iniquity, though it is great.
     79: 9 deliver us and *f* our sins
Isa 2: 9 do not *f* them.
Jer 5: 1 I will *f* this city.
      5: 7 "Why should I *f* you?
     18: 23 Do not *f* their crimes
     31: 34 "For I will *f* their wickedness
     33: 8 and will *f* all their sins of rebellion
     36: 3 then I will *f* their wickedness
     50: 20 for I will *f* the remnant I spare.
Da   9: 19 O Lord, listen! O Lord, *f!* O Lord,
Hos 1: 6 that I should at all *f* them,
     14: 2 "*F* all our sins
Am   7: 2 *f!* How can Jacob survive?
Mt   6: 12 *F* us our debts,

Mt   6: 14 For if you *f* men when they sin
      6: 14 heavenly Father will also *f* you.
      6: 15 But if you do not *f* men their sins,
      6: 15 your Father will not *f* your sins.
      9: 6 authority on earth to *f* sins..
     18: 21 many times shall I *f* my brother
     18: 35 you *f* your brother from your heart
Mk   2: 7 Who can *f* sins but God alone?"
      2: 10 authority on earth to *f* sins
     11: 25 anything against anyone, *f* him,
     11: 25 in heaven may *f* you your sins."
Lk   5: 21 Who can *f* sins but God alone?"
      5: 24 authority on earth to *f* sins..
      6: 37 *F,* and you will be forgiven.
     11: 4 *F* us our sins,
     11: 4 *f* everyone who sins against us.
     17: 3 rebuke him, and if he repents, *f* him
     17: 4 and says, 'I repent,' *f* him."
     23: 34 Jesus said, "Father, *f* them,
Jn 20: 23 If you *f* anyone his sins, they are
     20: 23 if you do not *f* them, they are not
Ac   8: 22 Perhaps he will *f* you
2Co 2: 7 you ought to *f* and comfort him,
      2: 10 If you *f* anyone, I also *f* him.
      2: 10 if there was anything to *f*—
     12: 13 a burden to you? *F* me this wrong!
Col 3: 13 and *f* whatever grievances you may
      3: 13 *F* as the Lord forgave you.
Heb 8: 12 For I will *f* their wickedness
1Jn 1: 9 and just and will *f* us our sins

FORGIVENESS* (FORGIVE)

Ps 130: 1 But with you there is *f;*
Mt 26: 28 out for many for the *f* of sins.
Mk   1: 4 of repentance for the *f* of sins.
Lk   1: 77 salvation through the *f* of their sins,
      3: 3 of repentance for the *f* of sins.
     24: 47 and *f* of sins will be preached
Ac   5: 31 that he might give repentance and *f*
     10: 43 believes in him receives *f* of sins
     13: 38 that through Jesus the *f*
     26: 18 so that they may receive *f* of sins
Eph 1: 7 through his blood, the *f* of sins,
Col 1: 14 in whom we have redemption, the *f*
Heb 9: 22 the shedding of blood there is no *f.*

FORGIVES* (FORGIVE)

Ps 103: 3 He *f* all my sins
Mic 7: 18 pardons sin and *f* the transgression
Lk   7: 49 "Who is this who even *f* sins?"

FORGIVING* (FORGIVE)

Ex 34: 7 and *f* wickedness, rebellion and sin.
Nu 14: 18 abounding in love and *f* sin
Ne   9: 17 But you are a *f* God, gracious
Ps 86: 5 You are *f* and good, O Lord,
     99: 8 you were to Israel a *f* God,
Da   9: 9 The Lord our God is merciful and *f*
Eph 4: 32 to one another, *f* each other,

FORGOT (FORGET)

Dt 32: 18 you *f* the God who gave you birth.
Ps 78: 11 They *f* what he had done,
    106: 13 But they soon *f* what he had done

FORGOTTEN (FORGET)

Job 11: 6 God has even *f* some of your sin.
Ps 44: 20 If we had *f* the name of our God
Isa 17: 10 You have *f* God your Savior;
Hos 4: 6 Israel has *f* his Maker
Lk 12: 6 Yet not one of them is *f* by God.
2Pe 1: 9 and has *f* that he has been cleansed

FORM (FORMED)

Isa 52: 14 *f* marred beyond human likeness—
2Ti 3: 5 having a *f* of godliness

FORMED (FORM)

Ge   2: 7 —the LORD God *f* the man
      2: 19 Now the LORD God had *f* out
Ps 103: 14 for he knows how we are *f,*
Ecc 11: 5 or how the body is *f* in a mother's
Isa 29: 16 Shall what is *f* say to him who *f* it,
     45: 18 but *f* it to be inhabited—
     49: 5 he who *f* me in the womb
Jer 1: 5 "Before I *f* you in the womb I knew
Ro   9: 20 "Shall what is *f* say to him who *f* it,
Gal 4: 19 of childbirth until Christ is *f* in you,

1Ti 2: 13 For Adam was *f* first, then Eve.
Heb 11: 3 understand that the universe was *f*
2Pe 3: 5 and the earth was *f* out of water

FORMLESS*

Ge   1: 2 Now the earth was *f* and empty,
Jer 4: 23 and it was *f* and empty;

FORNICATION see IMMORALITY, UNFAITHFULNESS

FORSAKE (FORSAKEN)

Dt 31: 6 he will never leave you nor *f* you."
Jos 1: 5 I will never leave you nor *f* you.
     24: 16 "Far be it from us to *f* the LORD
2Ch 5: 2 but if you *f* him, he will *f* you.
Ps 27: 10 Though my father and mother *f* me
     94: 14 he will never *f* his inheritance.
Isa 55: 7 Let the wicked *f* his way
Heb 13: 5 never will I *f* you."

FORSAKEN (FORSAKE)

Ps 22: 1 my God, why have you *f* me?
     37: 25 I have never seen the righteous *f*
Mt 27: 46 my God, why have you *f* me?"
Rev 2: 4 You have *f* your first love.

FORTRESS

2Sa 22: 2 "The LORD is my rock, my *f*
Ps 18: 2 The LORD is my rock, my *f*
     31: 2 a strong *f* to save me.
     59: 16 for you are my *f,*
     71: 3 for you are my rock and my *f.*
Pr 14: 26 who fears the LORD has a secure *f,*

FORTUNE-TELLING*

Ac 16: 16 deal of money for her owners by *f.*

FORTY

Ge   7: 4 on the earth for *f* days and *f* nights,
     18: 29 "What if only *f* are found there?"
Ex 16: 35 The Israelites ate manna *f* years,
     24: 18 on the mountain *f* days and *f* nights
Nu 14: 34 For *f* years—one year for each
Jos 14: 7 I was *f* years old when Moses
1Sa 4: 18 He had led Israel *f* years.
2Sa 5: 4 king, and he reigned *f* years.
1Ki 19: 8 he traveled *f* days and *f* nights
2Ki 12: 1 and he reigned in Jerusalem *f* years
2Ch 9: 30 in Jerusalem over all Israel *f* years.
Eze 29: 12 her cities will lie desolate *f* years
Jnh 3: 4 "*F* more days and Nineveh will be
Mt   4: 2 After fasting *f* days and *f* nights,

FOUGHT (FIGHT)

1Co 15: 32 If I *f* wild beasts in Ephesus
2Ti 4: 7 I have *f* the good fight, I have

FOUND (FIND)

2Ki 22: 8 "I have *f* the Book of the Law
1Ch 28: 9 If you seek him, he will be *f* by you;
2Ch 15: 15 sought God eagerly, and he was *f*
Isa 55: 6 Seek the LORD while he may be *f;*
     65: 1 I was *f* by those who did not seek
Da   5: 27 on the scales and *f* wanting.
Mt   1: 18 she was *f* to be with child
Lk 15: 6 with me; I have *f* my lost sheep.'
     15: 9 with me; I have *f* my lost coin.'
     15: 24 is alive again; he was lost and is *f.*'
Ac   4: 12 Salvation is *f* in no one else,
Ro 10: 20 "I was *f* by those who did not seek
Jas 2: 8 If you really keep the royal law *f*
Rev 5: 4 no one was *f* who was worthy

FOUNDATION (FOUNDATIONS FOUNDED)

Isa 28: 16 a precious cornerstone for a sure *f:*
Mt   7: 25 because it had its *f* on the rock.
Lk 14: 29 For if he lays the *f* and is not able
Ro 15: 20 building on someone else's *f.*
1Co 3: 10 I laid a *f* as an expert builder,
      3: 11 For no one can lay any *f* other
Eph 2: 20 built on the *f* of the apostles
1Ti 3: 15 the pillar and *f* of the truth.
2Ti 2: 19 God's solid *f* stands firm,
Heb 6: 1 not laying again the *f* of repentance

FOUNDATIONS (FOUNDATION)

Ps 102: 25 In the beginning you laid the *f*
Heb 1: 10 O Lord, you laid the *f* of the earth,

FOUNDED (FOUNDATION)

Jer 10: 12 he *f* the world by his wisdom
Heb 8: 6 and it is *f* on better promises.

FOUNTAIN

Ps 36: 9 For with you is the *f* of life;
Pr 14: 27 The fear of the LORD is a *f* of life,
18: 4 the *f* of wisdom is a bubbling brook.
Zec 13: 1 "On that day a *f* will be opened

FOX (FOXES)

Lk 13: 32 He replied, "Go tell that *f*,

FOXES (FOX)

SS 2: 15 the little *f*
Mt 8: 20 "*F* have holes and birds

FRAGRANCE (FRAGRANT)

Ex 30: 38 it to enjoy its *f* must be cut
Jn 12: 3 filled with the *f* of the perfume.
2Co 2: 14 us spreads everywhere the *f*
2: 16 of death; to the other, the *f* of life.

FRAGRANT (FRAGRANCE)

Eph 5: 2 as a *f* offering and sacrifice to God.
Php 4: 18 They are a *f* offering, an acceptable

FREE (FREED FREEDOM FREELY)

Ge 2: 16 "You are *f* to eat from any tree
Ps 118: 5 and he answered by setting me *f*.
119: 32 for you have set my heart *f*.
146: 7 The LORD sets prisoners *f*,
Pr 6: 3 then do this, my son, to *f* yourself,
Jn 8: 32 and the truth will set you *f*."
8: 36 if the Son sets you *f*, you will be *f*
Ro 6: 18 You have been set *f* from sin
8: 2 of life set me *f* from the law of sin
1Co 12: 13 whether Jews or Greeks, slave or *f*
Gal 3: 28 slave nor *f*, male nor female,
5: 1 for freedom that Christ has set us *f*.
1Pe 2: 16 *f* men, but do not use your freedom

FREED (FREE)

Ps 116: 16 you have *f* me from my chains.
Ro 6: 7 anyone who has died has been *f*
Rev 1: 5 has *f* us from our sins by his blood,

FREEDOM (FREE)

Ps 119: 45 I will walk about in *f*,
Isa 61: 1 to proclaim *f* for the captives
Lk 4: 18 me to proclaim *f* for the prisoners
Ro 8: 21 into the glorious *f* of the children
1Co 7: 21 although if you can gain your *f*,
2Co 3: 17 the Spirit of the Lord is, there is *f*.
Gal 2: 4 ranks to spy on the *f* we have
5: 13 But do not use your *f* to indulge
Jas 1: 25 into the perfect law that gives *f*,
1Pe 2: 16 but do not use your *f* as a cover-up

FREELY (FREE)

Isa 55: 7 and to our God, for he will *f* pardon
Mt 10: 8 Freely you have received, *f* give.
Ro 3: 24 and are justified *f* by his grace
Eph 1: 6 which he has *f* given us

FRESH

Jas 3: 11 Can both *f* water and salt water

FRET*

Ps 37: 1 Do not *f* because of evil men
37: 7 do not *f* when men succeed
37: 8 do not *f*—it leads only to evil.
Pr 24: 19 Do not *f* because of evil men

FRICTION

1Ti 6: 5 and constant *f* between men

FRIEND (FRIENDS FRIENDSHIP)

Ex 33: 11 as a man speaks with his *f*.
2Ch 20: 7 descendants of Abraham your *f*?
Pr 17: 17 A *f* loves at all times,
18: 24 there is a *f* who sticks closer
27: 6 Wounds from a *f* can be trusted
27: 10 Do not forsake your *f* and the *f*

Isa 41: 8 you descendants of Abraham my *f*,
Mt 11: 19 a *f* of tax collectors and "sinners." '
Lk 11: 8 him the bread because he is his *f*,
Jn 19: 12 "If you let this man go, you are no *f*
Jas 2: 23 and he was called God's *f*.
4: 4 Anyone who chooses to be a *f*

FRIENDS (FRIEND)

Pr 16: 28 and a gossip separates close *f*.
17: 9 the matter separates close *f*.
Zec 13: 6 given at the house of my *f*.'
Jn 15: 13 that he lay down his life for his *f*.
15: 14 You are my *f* if you do what I

FRIENDSHIP (FRIEND)

Jas 4: 4 don't you know that *f*

FRIGHTENED (FEAR)

Php 1: 28 gospel without being *f* in any way.
1Pe 3: 14 fear what they fear; do not be *f*."

FROGS

Ex 8: 2 plague your whole country with *f*.
Rev 16: 13 three evil spirits that looked like *f*;

FRUIT (FRUITFUL)

Jdg 9: 11 'Should I give up my *f*, so good
Ps 1: 3 which yields its *f* in season
Pr 11: 30 The *f* of the righteous is a tree
12: 14 From the *f* of his lips a man is filled
27: 18 he who tends a fig tree will eat its *f*
Isa 11: 1 from his roots a Branch will bear *f*.
27: 6 and fill all the world with *f*.
32: 17 The *f* of righteousness will be peace
Jer 17: 8 and never fails to bear *f*."
Hos 10: 12 reap the *f* of unfailing love,
14: 2 that we may offer the *f* of our lips.
Am 8: 1 showed me: a basket of ripe *f*.
Mt 3: 8 Produce *f* in keeping
3: 10 does not produce good *f* will be cut
7: 16 By their *f* you will recognize them.
7: 17 good *f*, but a bad tree bears bad *f*.
7: 20 by their *f* you will recognize them.
12: 33 a tree good and its *f* will be good,
Lk 3: 9 does not produce good *f* will be cut
6: 43 nor does a bad tree bear good *f*.
13: 6 and he went to look for *f* on it,
Jn 15: 2 branch in me that bears no *f*,
15: 16 and bear *f*—that will last.
Ro 7: 4 in order that we might bear *f*
Gal 5: 22 But the *f* of the Spirit is love, joy,
Php 1: 11 with the *f* of righteousness that
Col 1: 10 bearing *f* in every good work,
Heb 13: 15 the *f* of lips that confess his name.
Jas 3: 17 and good *f*, impartial and sincere.
Jude 12 autumn trees, without *f*
Rev 22: 2 of *f*, yielding its *f* every month.

FRUITFUL (FRUIT)

Ge 1: 22 "Be *f* and increase in number
9: 1 "Be *f* and increase in number
35: 11 be *f* and increase in number.
Ex 1: 7 the Israelites were *f* and multiplied
Ps 128: 3 Your wife will be like a *f* vine
Jn 15: 2 prunes so that it will be even more *f*.
Php 1: 22 this will mean *f* labor for me.

FRUITLESS*

Eph 5: 11 to do with the *f* deeds of darkness,

FRUSTRATION

Ro 8: 20 For the creation was subjected to *f*,

FUEL

Isa 44: 19 "Half of it I used for *f*;

FULFILL (FULFILLED FULFILLMENT FULFILLS)

Nu 23: 19 Does he promise and not *f*?
Ps 61: 8 and *f* my vows day after day.
116: 14 I will *f* my vows to the LORD
138: 8 The LORD will *f* his purpose
Ecc 5: 5 than to make a vow and not *f* it.
Isa 46: 11 far-off land, a man to *f* my purpose.
Jer 33: 14 'when I will *f* the gracious promise
Mt 1: 22 place to *f* what the Lord had said
3: 15 us to do this to *f* all righteousness."
4: 14 *f* what was said

Mt 5: 17 come to abolish them but to *f* them.
8: 17 This was to *f* what was spoken
12: 17 This was to *f* what was spoken
21: 4 place to *f* what was spoken
Jn 12: 38 This was to *f* the word
13: 18 But this is to *f* the scripture:
15: 25 But this is to *f* what is written
1Co 7: 3 husband should *f* his marital duty

FULFILLED (FULFILL)

Jos 21: 45 of Israel failed; every one was *f*.
23: 14 Every promise has been *f*;
Pr 13: 12 but a longing *f* is a tree of life.
13: 19 A longing *f* is sweet to the soul,
Mt 2: 15 so was *f* what the Lord had said
2: 17 the prophet Jeremiah was *f*:
2: 23 So was *f* what was said
13: 14 In them is *f* the prophecy of Isaiah:
13: 35 So was *f* what was spoken
26: 54 would the Scriptures be *f* that say it
26: 56 of the prophets might be *f*."
27: 9 by Jeremiah the prophet was *f*:
Mk 13: 4 that they are all about to be *f*?"
14: 49 But the Scriptures must be *f*."
Lk 4: 21 "Today this scripture is *f*
18: 31 about the Son of Man will be *f*.
24: 44 Everything must be *f* that is
Jn 18: 9 words he had spoken would be *f*:
19: 24 the Scripture might be *f* which said,
19: 28 and so that the Scripture would be *f*
19: 36 so that the Scripture would be *f*:
Ac 1: 16 to be *f* which the Holy Spirit spoke
Ro 13: 8 loves his fellowman has *f* the law.
Jas 2: 23 And the scripture was *f* that says,

FULFILLMENT (FULFILL)

Ro 13: 10 Therefore love is the *f* of the law.

FULFILLS (FULFILL)

Ps 57: 2 to God, who *f* his purpose for me.
145: 19 He *f* the desires of those who fear

FULL (FILL)

2Ch 24: 10 them into the chest until it was *f*.
Ps 127: 5 whose quiver is *f* of them.
Pr 27: 7 He who is *f* loathes honey,
31: 11 Her husband has *f* confidence
Isa 6: 3 the whole earth is *f* of his glory."
11: 9 for the earth will be *f*
Lk 4: 1 Jesus, *f* of the Holy Spirit,
Jn 10: 10 may have life, and have it to the *f*.
Ac 6: 3 known to be *f* of the Spirit
6: 5 a man *f* of faith and of the Holy
7: 55 But Stephen, *f* of the Holy Spirit,
11: 24 *f* of the Holy Spirit and faith,

FULL-GROWN* (GROW)

Jas 1: 15 when it is *f*, gives birth to death.

FULLNESS* (FILL)

Dt 33: 16 gifts of the earth and its *f*
Jn 1: 16 From the *f* of his grace we have all
Ro 11: 12 greater riches will their *f* bring!
Eph 1: 23 the *f* of him who fills everything
3: 19 to the measure of all the *f* of God.
4: 13 to the whole measure of the *f*
Col 1: 19 to have all his *f* dwell in him,
1: 25 to you the word of God in its *f*—
2: 9 in Christ all the *f* of the Deity lives
2: 10 and you have been given *f* in Christ

FULLY (FILL)

1Ki 8: 61 your hearts must be *f* committed
2Ch 16: 9 whose hearts are *f* committed
Ps 119: 4 that are to be *f* obeyed.
119:138 they are *f* trustworthy.
Pr 13: 4 of the diligent are *f* satisfied.
Lk 6: 40 everyone who is *f* trained will be
Ro 4: 21 being *f* persuaded that God had
14: 5 Each one should be *f* convinced
1Co 13: 12 shall know *f*, even as I am *f* known.
15: 58 Always give yourselves *f*
2Ti 4: 17 the message might be *f* proclaimed

FURIOUS (FURY)

Dt 29: 28 In *f* anger and in great wrath
Jer 32: 37 where I banish them in my *f* anger

FURNACE

Isa 48: 10 in the *f* of affliction.
Da 3: 6 be thrown into a blazing *f.''*
Mt 13: 42 will throw them into the fiery *f,*

FURY (FURIOUS)

Isa 14: 6 and in *f* subdued nations
Jer 21: 5 and a mighty arm in anger and *f*
Rev 14: 10 will drink of the wine of God's *f,*
     16: 19 with the wine of the *f* of his wrath.
     19: 15 the winepress of the *f* of the wrath

FUTILE (FUTILITY)

Mal 1: 3 You have said, 'It is *f* to serve God.
1Co 3: 20 that the thoughts of the wise are *f.''*

FUTILITY (FUTILE)

Eph 4: 17 in the *f* of their thinking.

FUTURE

Ps 37: 37 there is a *f* for the man of peace.
Pr 23: 18 There is surely a *f* hope for you,
Ecc 7: 14 anything about his *f.*
      8: 7 Since no man knows the *f,*
Jer 29: 11 plans to give you hope and a *f.*
     31: 17 So there is hope for your *f,''*
Ro 8: 38 neither the present nor the *f*
1Co 3: 22 life or death or the present or the *f*

GABRIEL*

     Angel who interpreted Daniel's visions (Da 8: 16-26; 9:20-27); announced births of John (Lk 1: 11-20), Jesus (Lk 1:26-38).

GAD

     1. Son of Jacob by Zilpah (Ge 30:9-11; 35:26; 1Ch 2:2). Tribe of blessed (Ge 49:19; Dt 33:20-21), numbered (Nu 1:25; 26:18), allotted land east of the Jordan (Nu 32; 34:14; Jos 18:7; 22), west (Eze 48:27-28), 12,000 from (Rev 7:5).
     2. Prophet; seer of David (1Sa 22:5; 2Sa 24: 11-19; 1Ch 29:29).

GAIN (GAINED GAINS)

Ex 14: 17 And I will *g* glory through Pharaoh
Ps 60: 12 With God we will *g* the victory,
Pr 4: 1 pay attention and *g* understanding.
     8: 5 You who are simple, *g* prudence;
     28: 16 he who hates ill-gotten *g* will enjoy
     28: 23 in the end more favor
Isa 63: 12 to *g* for himself everlasting renown
Da 2: 8 that you are trying to *g* time,
Mk 8: 36 it for a man to *g* the whole world,
Lk 9: 25 it for a man to *g* the whole world,
     21: 19 standing firm you will *g* life.
1Co 13: 3 but have not love, I *g* nothing.
Php 1: 21 to live is Christ and to die is *g.*
      3: 8 that I may *g* Christ and be found
1Ti 3: 13 have served well *g* an excellent
      6: 5 godliness is a means to financial *g.*
      6: 6 with contentment is great *g.*

GAINED (GAIN)

Jer 32: 20 have *g* the renown that is still yours
Ro 5: 2 through whom we have *g* access

GAINS (GAIN)

Pr 3: 13 the man who *g* understanding,
     11: 16 A kindhearted woman *g* respect,
     15: 32 heeds correction *g* understanding.
     29: 23 but a man of lowly spirit *g* honor.
Mt 16: 26 for a man if he *g* the whole world,

GALILEE

Isa 9: 1 but in the future he will honor *G*
Mt 4: 15 *G* of the Gentiles—
     26: 32 I will go ahead of you into *G.''*
     28: 10 Go and tell my brothers to go to *G;*

GALL

Mt 27: 34 mixed with *g;* but after tasting it,

GALLIO

Ac 18: 12 While *G* was proconsul of Achaia,

GALLOWS

Est 7: 10 Haman on the *g* he had prepared

GAMALIEL

Ac 5: 34 But a Pharisee named *G,* a teacher

GAMES

1Co 9: 25 in the *g* goes into strict training.

GAP

Eze 22: 30 stand before me in the *g* on behalf

GAPE*

Ps 35: 21 They *g* at me and say, ''Aha! Aha!

GARDEN (GARDENER)

Ge 2: 8 the LORD God had planted a *g*
     2: 15 put him in the *G* of Eden to work it
SS 4: 12 You are a *g* locked up, my sister,
Isa 58: 11 You will be like a well-watered *g,*
Jer 31: 12 They will be like a well-watered *g,*
Eze 28: 13 the *g* of God;
     31: 9 Eden in the *g* of God.

GARDENER (GARDEN)

Jn 15: 1 true vine, and my Father is the *g.*

GARLAND*

Pr 1: 9 They will be a *g* to grace your head
     4: 9 She will set a *g* of grace

GARMENT (GARMENTS)

Ps 102: 26 they will all wear out like a *g.*
Isa 50: 9 They will all wear out like a *g;*
     51: 6 the earth will wear out like a *g*
     61: 3 and a *g* of praise
Mt 9: 16 of unshrunk cloth on an old *g,*
Jn 19: 23 This *g* was seamless, woven
Heb 1: 11 they will all wear out like a *g.*

GARMENTS (GARMENT)

Ge 3: 21 The LORD God made *g* of skin
Ex 28: 2 Make sacred *g* for your brother
Lev 16: 23 and take off the linen *g* he put
     16: 24 holy place and put on his regular *g.*
Isa 61: 10 me with *g* of salvation
     63: 1 with his *g* stained crimson?
Joel 2: 13 and not your *g.*
Zec 3: 4 and I will put rich *g* on you.''
Jn 19: 24 ''They divided my *g* among them

GATE (GATES)

Ps 118: 20 This is the *g* of the LORD
Pr 31: 23 husband is respected at the city *g.*
     31: 31 works bring her praise at the city *g.*
Mt 7: 13 For wide is the *g* and broad is
      7: 13 ''Enter through the narrow *g,*
Jn 10: 1 not enter the sheep pen by the *g,*
     10: 2 enters by the *g* is the shepherd
     10: 7 ''I tell you the truth, I am the *g*
     10: 9 I am the *g;* whoever enters
Heb 13: 12 also suffered outside the city *g*
Rev 21: 21 each *g* made of a single pearl.

GATES (GATE)

Ps 24: 7 Lift up your heads, O you *g;*
     24: 9 Lift up your heads, O you *g;*
     100: 4 Enter his *g* with thanksgiving
     118: 19 Open for me the *g* of righteousness
Isa 60: 11 Your *g* will always stand open,
     60: 18 and your *g* Praise.
     62: 10 Pass through, pass through the *g!*
Mt 16: 18 the *g* of Hades will not overcome it
Rev 21: 12 On the *g* were written the names
     21: 21 The twelve *g* were twelve pearls,
     21: 25 On no day will its *g* ever be shut,
     22: 14 may go through the *g* into the city.

GATH

1Sa 17: 23 the Philistine champion from *G,*
2Sa 1: 20 ''Tell it not in *G,*
Mic 1: 10 Tell it not in *G;*

GATHER (GATHERED GATHERS)

Ps 106: 47 and *g* us from the nations,
Isa 11: 12 and *g* the exiles of Israel;
Jer 3: 17 and all nations will *g* in Jerusalem
     23: 3 ''I myself will *g* the remnant
     31: 10 who scattered Israel will *g* them
Zep 2: 1 *G* together, *g* together,
      3: 20 At that time I will *g* you;

GATHERED (GATHER)

Ex 16: 18 and he who *g* little did not have too
Pr 30: 4 Who has *g* up the wind
Mt 25: 32 All the nations will be *g* before him
2Co 8: 15 and he who *g* little did not have too
2Th 2: 1 Lord Jesus Christ and our being *g*
Rev 16: 16 Then they *g* the kings together

GATHERS (GATHER)

Ps 147: 2 he *g* the exiles of Israel.
Pr 10: 5 He who *g* crops in summer is a wise
Isa 40: 11 He *g* the lambs in his arms
Mt 23: 37 a hen *g* her chicks under her wings,

GAVE (GIVE)

Ge 2: 20 man *g* names to all the livestock,
     3: 6 She also *g* some to her husband,
     14: 20 Abram *g* him a tenth of everything.
     28: 4 the land God *g* to Abraham.''
     35: 12 The land I *g* to Abraham
     39: 23 *g* him success in whatever he did.
     47: 11 *g* them property in the best part
Ex 4: 11 to him, ''Who *g* man his mouth?
     31: 18 he *g* him the two tablets
Dt 2: 12 did in the land the LORD *g* them
      2: 36 The LORD our God *g* us all
      3: 12 I *g* the Reubenites and the Gadites
      3: 13 I *g* to the half tribe of Manasseh.
      3: 15 And I *g* Gilead to Makir.
      3: 16 Gadites I *g* the territory extending
      8: 16 He *g* you manna to eat in the desert
     26: 9 us to this place and *g* us this land,
     32: 8 the Most High *g* the nations their
Jos 11: 23 and he *g* it as an inheritance
     13: 14 tribe of Levi he *g* no inheritance.
     14: 13 *g* him Hebron as his inheritance.
     21: 44 The LORD *g* them rest
     24: 13 I *g* you a land on which you did not
1Sa 27: 6 So on that day Achish *g* him Ziklag
2Sa 12: 8 I *g* you the house of Israel
1Ki 4: 29 God *g* Solomon wisdom
      5: 12 The LORD *g* Solomon wisdom,
Ezr 2: 69 According to their ability they *g*
Ne 9: 15 In their hunger you *g* them bread
      9: 20 You *g* your good Spirit
      9: 22 You *g* them kingdoms and nations,
      9: 27 compassion you *g* them deliverers,
Job 1: 21 LORD *g* and the LORD has taken
     42: 10 prosperous again and *g* him twice
Ps 69: 21 and *g* me vinegar for my thirst.
     135: 12 he *g* their land as an inheritance,
Ecc 12: 7 the spirit returns to God who *g* it.
Eze 3: 2 and he *g* me the scroll to eat.
Mt 1: 25 And he *g* him the name Jesus.
     25: 35 and you *g* me something to drink,
     25: 42 and you *g* me nothing to drink,
     26: 26 Jesus took bread, *g* thanks
     27: 50 in a loud voice, he *g* up his spirit.
Mk 6: 7 *g* them authority over evil spirits.
Jn 1: 12 he *g* the right to become children
      3: 16 so loved the world that he *g* his one
     17: 4 by completing the work you *g* me
     17: 6 you *g* them to me and they have
     19: 30 bowed his head and *g* up his spirit.
Ac 1: 3 *g* many convincing proofs that he
      2: 45 they *g* to anyone as he had need.
     11: 17 *g* them the same gift as he *g* us,
Ro 1: 24 Therefore God *g* them
      1: 26 God *g* them over to shameful lusts.
      1: 28 he *g* them over to a depraved mind,
      8: 32 not spare his own Son, but *g* him up
2Co 5: 18 *g* us the ministry of reconciliation:
      8: 3 For I testify that they *g* as much
      8: 5 they *g* themselves first to the Lord
Gal 1: 4 who *g* himself for our sins
      2: 20 who loved me and *g* himself for me
Eph 4: 8 and *g* gifts to men.''

Eph 5: 2 as Christ loved us and *g* himself up
     5:25 and *g* himself up for her
2Th 2:16 and by his grace *g* us eternal
1Ti 2: 6 who *g* himself as a ransom
Tit 2:14 who *g* himself for us to redeem us
1Jn 3:24 We know it by the Spirit he *g* us.

GAZE

Ps 27: 4 to *g* upon the beauty of the LORD
Pr   4:25 fix your *g* directly before you.

GEDALIAH

Governor of Judah appointed by Nebuchadnezzar (2Ki 25:22-26; Jer 39-41).

GEHAZI*

Servant of Elisha (2Ki 4:12-5:27; 8:4-5).

GENEALOGIES

1Ti 1: 4 themselves to myths and endless *g*
Tit 3: 9 avoid foolish controversies and *g*

GENERATION (GENERATIONS)

Ex 3:15 am to be remembered from *g* to *g*.
Nu 32:13 until the whole *g* of those who had
Dt 1:35 of this evil *g* shall see the good land
Jdg 2:10 After that whole *g* had been
Ps 24: 6 Such is the *g* of those who seek him
   48:13 tell of them to the next *g*.
   71:18 I declare your power to the next *g*,
   78: 4 we will tell the next *g*
  102:18 Let this be written for a future *g*,
  112: 2 the *g* of the upright will be blessed
  145: 4 One *g* will commend your works
La 5:19 your throne endures from *g* to *g*.
Da 4: 3 his dominion endures from *g* to *g*.
   4:34 his kingdom endures from *g* to *g*.
Joel 1: 3 and their children to the next *g*.
Mt 12:39 adulterous *g* asks for a miraculous
  17:17 "O unbelieving and perverse *g*,"
  23:36 all this will come upon this *g*.
  24:34 this *g* will certainly not pass away
Mk 9:19 "O unbelieving," Jesus replied,
  13:30 this *g* will certainly not pass away
Lk 1:50 who fear him, from *g* to *g*.
  11:29 Jesus said, "This is a wicked *g*.
  11:30 will the Son of Man be to this *g*.
  11:50 Therefore this *g* will be held
  21:32 this *g* will certainly not pass away
Ac 2:40 Save yourselves from this corrupt *g*
Php 2:15 fault in a crooked and depraved *g*,

GENERATIONS (GENERATION)

Ge 9:12 a covenant for all *g* to come:
  17: 7 after you for the *g* to come,
  17: 9 after you for the *g* to come.
Ex 20: 6 a thousand *g* of those
  31:13 and you for the *g* to come,
Dt 7: 9 covenant of love to a thousand *g*
  32: 7 consider the *g* long past.
1Ch 16:15 he commanded, for a thousand *g*,
Job 8: 8 "Ask the former *g*
Ps 22:30 future *g* will be told about the Lord
  33:11 of his heart through all *g*.
  45:17 your memory through all *g*;
  89: 1 faithfulness known through all *g*.
  90: 1 throughout all *g*.
  100: 5 continues through all *g*.
  102:12 your renown endures through all *g*.
  105: 8 he commanded, for a thousand *g*,
  119:90 continues through all *g*;
  135:13 renown, O LORD, through all *g*.
  145: 13 dominion endures through all *g*.
  146:10 your God, O Zion, for all *g*.
Pr 27:24 and a crown is not secure for all *g*.
Isa 41: 4 forth the *g* from the beginning?
  51: 8 my salvation through all *g*."
Lk 1:48 now on all *g* will call me blessed,
Eph 3: 5 not made known to men in other *g*
  3:21 in Christ Jesus throughout all *g*,
Col 1:26 been kept hidden for ages and *g*,

GENEROSITY* (GENEROUS)

2Co 8: 2 poverty welled up in rich *g*.
  9:11 and through us your *g* will result
  9:13 and for your *g* in sharing with them

GENEROUS* (GENEROSITY)

Ps 37:26 They are always *g* and lend freely;
  112: 5 Good will come to him who is *g*
Pr 11:25 A *g* man will prosper;
   22: 9 A *g* man will himself be blessed,
Mt 20:15 Or are you envious because I am *g*
2Co 9: 5 Then it will be ready as a *g* gift,
  9: 5 for the *g* gift you had promised.
  9:11 way so that you can be *g*
1Ti 6:18 and to be *g* and willing to share.

GENTILE (GENTILES)

Ac 21:25 As for the *G* believers, we have
Ro 1:16 first for the Jew, then for the *G*.
  2: 9 first for the Jew, then for the *G*;
  2:10 first for the Jew, then for the *G*.
  10:12 difference between Jew and *G*—

GENTILES (GENTILE)

Isa 42: 6 and a light for the *G*,
  49: 6 also make you a light for the *G*,
  49:22 "See, I will beckon to the *G*,
Lk 2:32 a light for revelation to the *G*
  21:24 on by the *G* until the times
Ac 9:15 to carry my name before the *G*
  10:45 been poured out even on the *G*
  11:18 granted even the *G* repentance unto
  13:16 and you *G* who worship God,
  13:46 of eternal life, we now turn to the *G*
  13:47 I have made you a light for the *G*,
  14:27 opened the door of faith to the *G*.
  15:14 by taking from the *G* a people
  18: 6 From now on I will go to the *G*."
  22:21 I will send you far away to the *G*.' "
  26:20 and in all Judea, and to the *G* also,
  28:28 salvation has been sent to the *G*,
Ro 2:14 when *G*, who do not have the law,
  3: 9 And *G* alike are all under sin.
  3:29 Is he not the God of *G* too? Yes,
  9:24 from the Jews but also from the *G*?
  11:11 to the *G* to make Israel envious.
  11:12 their loss means riches for the *G*,
  11:13 as I am the apostle to the *G*,
  15: 9 I will praise you among the *G*;
  15: 9 so that the *G* may glorify God
1Co 1:23 block to Jews and foolishness to *G*,
Gal 1:16 I might preach him among the *G*,
  2: 2 gospel that I preach among the *G*.
  2: 8 my ministry as an apostle to the *G*.
  2: 9 agreed that we should go to the *G*,
  3: 8 that God would justify the *G*
  3:14 to the *G* through Christ Jesus,
Eph 3: 6 the gospel the *G* are heirs together
  3: 8 to the *G* the unsearchable riches
Col 1:27 among the *G* the glorious riches
1Ti 3: 7 a teacher of the true faith to the *G*.
2Ti 4:17 and all the *G* might hear it.

GENTLE* (GENTLENESS)

Dt 28:54 Even the most *g* and sensitive man
  28:56 The most *g* and sensitive woman
  28:56 and *g* that she would not venture
2Sa 18: 5 Be *g* with the young man Absalom
1Ki 19:12 And after the fire came a *g* whisper
Job 41: 3 Will he speak to you with *g* words?
Pr 15: 1 A *g* answer turns away wrath,
  25:15 and a *g* tongue can break a bone.
Jer 11:19 I had been like a *g* lamb led
Zec 9: 9 *g* and riding on a donkey,
Mt 11:29 for I am *g* and humble in heart,
  21: 5 *g* and riding on a donkey,
Ac 27:13 When a *g* south wind began
1Co 4:21 or in love and with a *g* spirit?
Eph 4: 2 Be completely humble and *g*;
1Th 2: 7 but we were *g* among you,
1Ti 3: 3 not violent but *g*, not quarrelsome,
1Pe 3: 4 the unfading beauty of a *g*

GENTLENESS* (GENTLE)

2Co 10: 1 By the meekness and *g* of Christ,
Gal 5:23 faithfulness, *g* and self-control.
Php 4: 5 Let your *g* be evident to all.
Col 3:12 kindness, humility, *g* and patience.
1Ti 6:11 faith, love, endurance and *g*.
1Pe 3:15 But do this with *g* and respect,

GENUINE*

2Co 6: 8 *g*, yet regarded as impostors;

Php 2:20 who takes a *g* interest
1Pe 1: 7 may be proved *g* and may result

GERIZIM

Dt 27:12 on Mount *G* to bless the people:

GERSHOM

Ex 2:22 and Moses named him *G*, saying,

GETHSEMANE*

Mt 26:36 disciples to a place called *G*,
Mk 14:32 They went to a place called *G*,

GHOST see also SPIRIT

Lk 24:39 a *g* does not have flesh and bones,

GIBEON

Jos 10:12 "O sun, stand still over *G*,

GIDEON*

Judge, also called Jerub-Baal; freed Israel from Midianites (Jdg 6-8; Heb 11:32). Given sign of fleece (Jdg 8:36-40).

GIFT (GIFTED GIFTS)

Pr 18:16 A *g* opens the way for the giver
  21:14 A *g* given in secret soothes anger,
Ecc 3:13 in all his toil—this is the *g* of God.
Mt 5:23 if you are offering your *g*
Jn 4:10 "If you knew the *g* of God
Ac 1: 4 wait for the *g* my Father promised,
  2:38 And you will receive the *g*
  11:17 So if God gave them the same *g*
Ro 6:23 but the *g* of God is eternal life
  12: 6 If a man's *g* is prophesying,
1Co 7: 7 each man has his own *g* from God;
2Co 8:12 the *g* is acceptable according
  9:15 be to God for his indescribable *g*!
Eph 2: 8 it is the *g* of God—not by works,
1Ti 4:14 not neglect your *g*, which was
2Ti 1: 6 you to fan into flame the *g* of God,
Heb 6: 4 who have tasted the heavenly *g*,
Jas 1:17 and perfect *g* is from above,
1Pe 3: 7 with you of the gracious *g* of life,
  4:10 should use whatever *g* he has
Rev 22:17 let him take the free *g* of the water

GIFTED* (GIFT)

1Co 14:37 he is a prophet or spiritually *g*,

GIFTS (GIFT)

Ps 76:11 bring *g* to the One to be feared.
  112: 9 He has scattered abroad his *g*
Pr 25:14 of *g* he does not give.
Mt 2:11 and presented him with *g* of gold
  7:11 Father in heaven give good *g*
  7:11 to give good *g* to your children,
Lk 11:13 to give good *g* to your children,
Ac 10: 4 and *g* to the poor have come up
Ro 11:29 for God's *g* and his call are
  12: 6 We have different *g*, according
1Co 12: 1 Now about spiritual *g*, brothers,
  12: 4 There are different kinds of *g*,
  12:28 those with *g* of administration,
  12:30 all work miracles? Do all have *g*
  12:31 But eagerly desire the greater *g*.
  14: 1 and eagerly desire spiritual *g*,
  14:12 eager to have spiritual *g*,
  14:12 excel in *g* that build up the church.
2Co 9: 9 "He has scattered abroad his *g*
Eph 4: 8 and gave *g* to men."
Heb 2: 4 and *g* of the Holy Spirit distributed
  9: 9 indicating that the *g* and sacrifices

GILEAD

1Ch 27:21 the half-tribe of Manasseh in *G*:
Jer 8:22 Is there no balm in *G*?
  46:11 "Go up to *G* and get balm,

GILGAL

Jos 5: 9 So the place has been called *G*

GIRD*

Ps 45: 3 *G* your sword upon your side,

GIRL

Ge 24:16 *g* was very beautiful, a virgin;
2Ki 5: 2 a young *g* from Israel.
Mk 5:41 Little *g*, I say to you, get up!

GIVE (GAVE GIVEN GIVER GIVES GIVING LIFE-GIVING)

Ge 28: 4 you and your descendants the blessing *g*
      to Abraham
    28:22 that you *g* me I will *g* you a tenth.''
Ex 20:16 ''You shall not *g* false testimony
    30:15 The rich are not to *g* more
Nu   6:26 and *g* you peace.'' '
Dt   5:20 ''You shall not *g* false testimony
    15:10 *G* generously to him and do
    15:14 *G* to him as the LORD your God
1Sa 1:11 then I will *g* him to the LORD
    1:28 So now I *g* him to the LORD.
2Ch 15: 7 be strong and do not *g* up,
Pr 21:26 but the righteous *g* without sparing
    23:26 My son, *g* me your heart
    25:21 if he is thirsty, *g* him water to drink
    30: 8 but *g* me only my daily bread.
    31:31 *G* her the reward she has earned,
Ecc 3: 6 a time to search and a time to *g* up,
Isa 42: 8 I will not *g* my glory to another
Eze 36:26 I will *g* you a new heart
Mt 6:11 *G* us today our daily bread.
    7:11 know how to *g* good gifts
    10: 8 Freely you have received, freely *g*.
    16:19 I will *g* you the keys
    22:21 ''*G* to Caesar what is Caesar's,
Mk 8:37 Or what can a man *g* in exchange
    10:19 not steal, do not *g* false testimony,
Lk 6:38 *G*, and it will be given to you.
    11: 3 *G* us each day our daily bread
    11:13 Father in heaven *g* the Holy Spirit
    14:33 who does not *g* up everything he
Jn 10:28 I *g* them eternal life, and they shall
    13:34 ''A new commandment I *g* you:
    14:16 he will *g* you another Counselor
    14:27 I do not *g* to you as the world gives.
    14:27 leave with you; my peace I *g* you.
    17: 2 people that he might *g* eternal life
Ac 20:35 blessed to *g* than to receive.' '
Ro 7: 1 immortality, he will *g* eternal life.
    8:32 with him, graciously *g* us all things
    12: 8 let him *g* generously;
    13: 7 *G* everyone what you owe him:
    14:12 each of us will *g* an account
2Co 9: 7 Each man should *g* what he has
Gal 2: 5 We did not *g* in to them
    6: 9 reap a harvest if we do not *g* up.
Heb 10:25 Let us not *g* up meeting together,
Rev 14: 7 ''Fear God and *g* him glory,

GIVEN (GIVE)

Nu 8:16 are to be *g* wholly to me.
Dt 26:11 things the LORD your God has *g*
Job 3:23 Why is life *g* to a man
Ps 115:16 but the earth he has *g* to man.
Isa 9: 6 to us a son is *g*,
Mt 6:33 and all these things will be *g* to you
    7: 7 ''Ask and it will be *g* to you;
    13:12 Whoever has will be *g* more,
    22:30 people will neither marry nor be *g*
    25:29 everyone who has will be *g* more,
Lk 6:38 Give, and it will be *g* to you.
    8:10 kingdom of God has been *g* to you,
    11: 9 Ask and it will be *g* to you;
    22:19 saying, ''This is my body *g* for you;
Jn 3:27 man can receive only what is *g* him
    15: 7 you wish, and it will be *g* you.
    17:24 I want those you have *g* me to be
    17:24 the glory you have *g* me
    18:11 the cup the Father has *g* me?''
Ac 5:32 whom God has *g* to those who
    20:24 the task the Lord Jesus has *g* me—
Ro 5: 5 the Holy Spirit, whom he has *g* us.
1Co 5: 2 those who have been *g* a trust must
    11:24 and when he had *g* thanks,
    12:13 we were all *g* the one Spirit to drink
2Co 5: 5 and has *g* us the Spirit as a deposit,
Eph 1: 6 which he has freely *g* us
    4: 7 to each one of us grace has been *g*
1Ti 4:14 was *g* you through a prophetic
1Jn 4:13 because he has *g* us of his Spirit.

GIVER* (GIVE)

Pr 18:16 A gift opens the way for the *g*
2Co 9: 7 for God loves a cheerful *g*.

GIVES (GIVE)

Job 35:10 who *g* songs in the night,
Ps 119:130 The unfolding of your words *g* light;
Pr 3:34 but *g* grace to the humble.
    11:24 One man *g* freely, yet gains
    14:30 A heart at peace *g* life to the body,
    15:30 good news *g* health to the bones.
    19: 6 of a man who *g* gifts.
    25:26 is a righteous man who *g* way
    28:27 He who *g* to the poor will lack
    29: 4 justice a king *g* a country stability,
Isa 40:29 He *g* strength to the weary
Hab 2:15 ''Woe to him who *g* drink
Mt 10:42 if anyone *g* even a cup of cold water
Jn 5:21 even so the Son *g* life to whom he is
    6:63 The Spirit *g* life; the flesh counts
1Co 15:57 He *g* us the victory
2Co 3: 6 the letter kills, but the Spirit *g* life.
1Th 4: 8 who *g* you his Holy Spirit.
Jas 1:25 into the perfect law that *g* freedom,
    4: 6 but *g* grace to the humble.''
1Pe 5: 5 but *g* grace to the humble.''

GIVING (GIVE)

Ne 8: 8 *g* the meaning so that the people
Est 9:19 a day for *g* presents to each other.
Ps 19: 8 *g* joy to the heart.
Pr 15:23 A man finds joy in *g* an apt reply—
Mt 6: 4 so that your *g* may be in secret.
    24:38 marrying and *g* in marriage,
Ac 15: 8 them by *g* the Holy Spirit to them,
2Co 8: 7 also excel in this grace of *g*.
Php 4:15 shared with me in the matter of *g*

GLAD* (GLADDENS GLADNESS)

Ex 4:14 his heart will be *g* when he sees you
Jos 22:33 They were *g* to hear the report
Jdg 8:25 ''We'll be *g* to give them.''
    18:20 household?'' Then the priest was *g*.
1Sa 19: 5 and you saw it and were *g*.
2Sa 1:20 daughters of the Philistines be *g*,
1Ki 8:66 *g* in heart for all the good things
1Ch 16:31 heavens rejoice, let the earth be *g*;
2Ch 7:10 and *g* in heart for the good things
Ps 5:11 let all who take refuge in you be *g*;
    9: 2 I will be *g* and rejoice in you;
    14: 7 let Jacob rejoice and Israel be *g*!
    16: 9 Therefore my heart is *g*
    21: 6 made him *g* with the joy
    31: 7 I will be *g* and rejoice in your love,
    32:11 Rejoice in the LORD and be *g*,
    40:16 rejoice and be *g* in you;
    45: 8 music of the strings makes you *g*.
    46: 4 whose streams make *g* the city
    48:11 the villages of Judah are *g*
    53: 6 let Jacob rejoice and Israel be *g*!
    58:10 The righteous will be *g*
    67: 4 May the nations be *g* and sing
    68: 3 But may the righteous be *g*
    69:32 The poor will see and be *g*—
    70: 4 rejoice and be *g* in you;
    90:14 for joy and be *g* all our days.
    90:15 Make us *g* for as many days
    92: 4 For you make me *g* by your deeds,
    96:11 heavens rejoice, let the earth be *g*;
    97: 1 LORD reigns, let the earth be *g*;
    97: 8 and the villages of Judah are *g*
    105: 38 Egypt was *g* when they left,
    107: 30 They were *g* when it grew calm,
    118: 24 let us rejoice and be *g* in it.
    149: 2 of Zion be *g* in their King.
Pr 23:15 then my heart will be *g*;
    23:25 May your father and mother be *g*;
    29: 6 a righteous one can sing and be *g*
Ecc 8:15 sun than to eat and drink and be *g*.
Isa 25: 9 let us rejoice and be *g*
    35: 1 and the parched land will be *g*;
    65:18 But be *g* and rejoice forever
    66:10 with Jerusalem and be *g* for her,
Jer 20:15 who made him very *g*, saying,
    31:13 Then maidens will dance and be *g*,
    41:13 were with him, they were *g*.
    50:11 ''Because you rejoice and are *g*,
La 4:21 be *g*, O Daughter of Edom,
Joel 2:21 be *g* and rejoice.
    2:23 Be *g*, O people of Zion,
Hab 1:15 and so he rejoices and is *g*.

Zep 3:14 Be *g* and rejoice with all your heart
Zec 2:10 and be *g*, O Daughter of Zion.
    8:19 will become joyful and *g* occasions
    10: 7 their hearts will be *g* as with wine.
Mt 5:12 be *g*, because great is your reward
Lk 15:32 But we had to celebrate and be *g*,
Jn 4:36 and the reaper may be *g* together.
    8:56 my day; he saw it and was *g*.''
    11:15 for your sake I am *g* I was not there
    14:28 you would be *g* that I am going
Ac 2:26 Therefore my heart is *g*
    2:46 together with *g* and sincere hearts,
    11:23 he was *g* and encouraged them all
    13:48 they were *g* and honored the word
    15: 3 news made all the brothers very *g*.
    15:31 were *g* for its encouraging message.
1Co 16:17 was *g* when Stephanas, Fortunatus
2Co 2: 2 who is left to make me *g*
    7:16 I am *g* I can have complete
    13: 9 We are *g* whenever we are weak
Gal 4:27 ''Be *g*, O barren woman,
Php 2:17 I am *g* and rejoice with all of you.
    2:18 So you too should be *g* and rejoice
    2:28 you see him again you may be *g*
Rev 19: 7 Let us rejoice and be *g*

GLADDENS* (GLAD)

Ps 104: 15 wine that *g* the heart of man,

GLADNESS* (GLAD)

2Ch 29:30 So they sang praises with *g*
Est 8:16 a time of happiness and joy, *g*
    8:17 there was joy and *g*
Job 3:22 who are filled with *g*
Ps 35:27 shout for joy and *g*;
    45:15 They are led in with joy and *g*;
    51: 8 Let me hear joy and *g*;
    65:12 the hills are clothed with *g*.
    100: 2 Worship the LORD with *g*;
Ecc 5:20 God keeps him occupied with *g*
    9: 7 Go, eat your food with *g*,
Isa 16:10 *g* are taken away from the orchards
    35:10 *G* and joy will overtake them,
    51: 3 Joy and *g* will be found in her,
    51:11 *G* and joy will overtake them,
    61: 3 the oil of *g* / instead of mourning,
Jer 7:34 and *g* and to the voices of bride
    16: 9 and *g* and to the voices of bride
    25:10 from them the sounds of joy and *g*
    31:13 I will turn their mourning into *g*;
    33:11 once more the sounds of joy and *g*,
    48:33 Joy and *g* are gone
Joel 1:16 joy and *g*

GLAZE*

Pr 26:23 of *g* over earthenware

GLEAM*

Pr 4:18 of the righteous is like the first *g*
Da 10: 6 legs like the *g* of burnished bronze,

GLOAT (GLOATS)

Pr 24:17 Do not *g* when your enemy falls;

GLOATS* (GLOAT)

Pr 17: 5 whoever *g* over disaster will not go

GLORIES* (GLORY)

1Pe 1:11 and the *g* that would follow.

GLORIFIED* (GLORY)

Isa 66: 5 'Let the LORD be *g*,
Eze 39:13 day I am *g* will be a memorable day
Da 4:34 and *g* him who lives forever.
Jn 7:39 since Jesus had not yet been *g*.
    11: 4 glory so that God's Son may be *g*
    12:16 after Jesus was *g* did they realize
    12:23 come for the Son of Man to be *g*.
    12:28 ''I have *g* it, and will glorify it again
    13:31 Son of Man *g* and God is *g* in him.
    13:32 If God is *g* in him, God will glorify
Ac 3:13 our fathers, has *g* his servant Jesus.
Ro 1:21 they neither *g* him as God
    8:30 those he justified, he also *g*.
2Th 1:10 comes to be *g* in his holy people
    1:12 of our Lord Jesus may be *g* in you,
1Pe 1:21 him from the dead and *g* him,

GLORIFIES* (GLORY)

Lk 1: 46 My soul g the Lord
Jn 8: 54 as your God, is the one who g me.

GLORIFY* (GLORY)

Ps 34: 3 G the LORD with me;
63: 3 my lips will g you.
69: 30 and g him with thanksgiving.
86: 12 I will g your name forever.
Isa 60: 13 and I will g the place of my feet.
Da 4: 37 and exalt and g the King of heaven,
Jn 8: 54 Jesus replied, "If I g myself,
12: 28 glorified it, and will g it again."
12: 28 g your name!" Then a voice came
13: 32 God will g the Son in himself,
13: 32 in himself, and will g him at once.
17: 1 G your Son, that your Son may
17: 1 your Son, that your Son may g you.
17: 5 g me in your presence
21: 19 death by which Peter would g God.
Ro 15: 6 and mouth you may g the God
15: 9 so that the Gentiles may g God
1Pe 2: 12 and g God on the day he visits us.
Rev 16: 9 they refused to repent and g him.

GLORIFYING* (GLORY)

Lk 2: 20 g and praising God

GLORIOUS* (GLORY)

Dt 28: 58 not revere this g and awesome
33: 29 and your g sword.
1Ch 29: 13 and praise your g name.
Ne 9: 5 "Blessed be your g name,
Ps 16: 3 they are the g ones
45: 13 All g is the princess
66: 2 make his praise g.
72: 19 Praise be to his g name forever;
87: 3 G things are said of you,
111: 3 G and majestic are his deeds,
145: 5 of the g splendor of your majesty,
145: 5 the g splendor of your kingdom.
Isa 3: 8 defying his g presence.
4: 2 the LORD will be beautiful and g,
11: 10 and his place of rest will be g
12: 5 for he has done g things;
28: 1 to the fading flower, his g beauty,
28: 4 That fading flower, his g beauty,
28: 5 will be a g crown,
42: 21 to make his law great and g.
60: 7 and I will adorn my g temple.
63: 12 who sent his g arm of power
63: 14 to make for yourself a g name.
63: 15 from your lofty throne, holy and g.
64: 11 g temple, where our fathers praised
Jer 13: 18 for your g crowns
14: 21 do not dishonor your g throne.
17: 12 A g throne, exalted
48: 17 how broken the g staff!"
Mt 19: 28 the Son of Man sits on his g throne,
Lk 9: 31 appeared in g splendor, talking
Ac 2: 20 of the great and g day of the Lord.
Ro 8: 21 and brought into the g freedom
2Co 3: 8 of the Spirit be even more g?
3: 9 how much more g is the ministry
3: 9 ministry that condemns men is g,
3: 10 For what was g has no glory now
Eph 1: 6 to the praise of his g grace,
1: 17 g Father, may give you the Spirit
1: 18 the riches of his g inheritance
3: 16 of his g riches he may strengthen
Php 3: 21 so that they will be like his g body.
4: 19 to his g riches in Christ Jesus.
Col 1: 11 all power according to his g might
1: 27 among the Gentiles the g riches
1Ti 1: 11 to the g gospel of the blessed God,
Tit 2: 13 the g appearing of our great God
Jas 2: 1 believers in our g Lord Jesus Christ
1Pe 1: 8 with an inexpressible and g joy,
Jude : 24 before his g presence without fault

GLORIOUSLY* (GLORY)

Isa 24: 23 and before its elders, g.

GLORY (GLORIES GLORIFIED GLORIFIES GLORIFY GLORIFYING GLORIOUS GLORIOUSLY)

Ex 14: 4 But I will gain g for myself
14: 17 And I will gain g through Pharaoh

Ex 15: 11 awesome in g,
16: 10 and there was the g of the LORD
24: 16 and the g of the LORD settled
33: 18 Moses said, "Now show me your g
40: 34 and the g of the LORD filled
Nu 14: 21 the g of the LORD fills the whole
Dt 5: 24 LORD our God has shown us his g
Jos 7: 19 "My son, give g to the LORD,
1Sa 4: 21 "The g has departed from Israel"—
1Ch 16: 10 G in his holy name;
16: 24 Declare his g among the nations,
16: 28 ascribe to the LORD g
29: 11 and the g and the majesty
Ps 8: 1 You have set your g
8: 5 and crowned him with g and honor
19: 1 The heavens declare the g of God;
24: 7 that the King of g may come in.
26: 8 the place where your g dwells.
29: 1 ascribe to the LORD g
29: 9 And in his temple all cry, "G!"
57: 5 let your g be over all the earth.
66: 2 Sing the g of his name;
72: 19 the whole earth be filled with his g
96: 3 Declare his g among the nations,
102: 15 of the earth will revere your g.
108: 5 and let your g be over all the earth.
149: 9 This is the g of all his saints.
Pr 19: 11 it is to his g to overlook an offense.
25: 2 It is the g of God to conceal
Isa 4: 5 over all the g will be a canopy.
6: 3 the whole earth is full of his g."
24: 16 "G to the Righteous One."
26: 15 You have gained g for yourself;
35: 2 they will see the g of the LORD,
40: 5 the g of the LORD will be revealed
42: 8 I will not give my g to another
42: 12 Let them give g to the LORD
43: 7 whom I created for my g,
44: 23 he displays his g in Israel.
48: 11 I will not yield my g to another.
66: 18 and they will come and see my g.
66: 19 They will proclaim my g
Eze 1: 28 the likeness of the g of the LORD.
10: 4 the radiance of the g of the LORD.
43: 2 and the land was radiant with his g,
44: 4 and saw the g of the LORD filling
Hab 2: 14 knowledge of the g of the LORD,
3: 3 His g covered the heavens
Zec 2: 5 'and I will be its g within.'
Mt 16: 27 in his Father's g with his angels,
24: 30 of the sky, with power and great g.
25: 31 sit on his throne in heavenly g.
25: 31 the Son of Man comes in his g.
Mk 8: 38 in his Father's g with the holy
13: 26 in clouds with great power and g.
Lk 2: 9 and the g of the Lord shone
2: 14 saying, "G to God in the highest,
9: 26 and in the g of the Father
9: 26 of him when he comes in his g
9: 32 they saw his g and the two men
19: 38 in heaven and g in the highest!"
21: 27 in a cloud with power and great g.
24: 26 these things and then enter his g?"
Jn 1: 14 We have seen his g, the g of the One
2: 11 He thus revealed his g,
8: 50 I am not seeking g for myself;
8: 54 myself, my g means nothing.
11: 4 for God's g so that God's Son may
11: 40 you would see the g of God?"
12: 41 he saw Jesus' g and spoke about
14: 13 so that the Son may bring g
15: 8 is to my Father's g, that you bear
16: 14 He will bring g to me by taking
17: 4 I have brought you g on earth
17: 5 presence with the g I had with you
17: 10 g has come to me through them.
17: 22 given them the g that you gave
17: 24 to see my g, the g you have given
Ac 7: 2 The God of g appeared
7: 55 up to heaven and saw the g of God,
Ro 1: 23 exchanged the g of the immortal
2: 7 by persistence in doing good seek g
2: 10 then for the Gentile; but g,
3: 7 truthfulness and so increases his g,
3: 23 and fall short of the g of God.
4: 20 in his faith and gave g to God,
8: 17 that we may also share in his g.
8: 18 with the g that will be revealed

Ro 9: 4 theirs the divine g, the covenants,
9: 23 riches of his g known to the objects
9: 23 whom he prepared in advance for g
11: 36 To him be the g forever! Amen.
15: 17 Therefore I g in Christ Jesus
16: 27 to the only wise God be g forever
1Co 2: 7 for our g before time began.
10: 31 whatever you do, do it all for the g
11: 7 but the woman is the g of man.
11: 7 since he is the image and g of God,
11: 15 it is her g? For long hair is given
15: 43 it is raised in g; it is sown
2Co 1: 20 spoken by us to the g of God.
3: 7 in letters on stone, came with g,
3: 7 the face of Moses because of its g,
3: 10 comparison with the surpassing g.
3: 10 what was glorious has no g now
3: 11 how much greater is the g
3: 11 what was fading away came with g,
3: 18 faces all reflect the Lord's g,
3: 18 likeness with ever-increasing g,
4: 4 of the gospel of the g of Christ,
4: 6 of the knowledge of the g of God
4: 15 to overflow to the g of God.
4: 17 us an eternal g that far outweighs
Gal 1: 5 to whom be g for ever and ever.
Eph 1: 12 might be for the praise of his g.
1: 14 to the praise of his g.
3: 13 for you, which are your g.
3: 21 to him be g in the church
Php 1: 11 to the g and praise of God.
2: 11 to the g of God the Father.
3: 3 of God, who g in Christ Jesus,
4: 20 and Father be g for ever and ever.
Col 1: 27 Christ in you, the hope of g.
3: 4 also will appear with him in g.
1Th 2: 12 you into his kingdom and g.
2: 19 in which we will g in the presence
2: 20 Indeed, you are our g and joy.
2Th 2: 14 in the g of our Lord Jesus Christ.
1Ti 1: 17 be honor and g for ever and ever.
3: 16 was taken up in g.
2Ti 2: 10 is in Christ Jesus, with eternal g.
4: 18 To him be g for ever and ever.
Heb 1: 3 The Son is the radiance of God's g
2: 7 you crowned him with g and honor
2: 9 now crowned with g and honor
2: 10 In bringing many sons to g,
5: 5 take upon himself the g
9: 5 the ark were the cherubim of the G,
13: 21 to whom be g for ever and ever.
1Pe 1: 7 and honor when Jesus Christ is
1: 24 and all their g is like the flowers
4: 11 To him be the g and the power
4: 13 overjoyed when his g is revealed.
4: 14 for the Spirit of g and of God rests
5: 1 will share in the g to be revealed:
5: 4 of g that will never fade away.
5: 10 you to his eternal g in Christ,
2Pe 1: 3 of him who called us by his own g
1: 17 and g from God the Father
1: 17 came to him from the Majestic G,
3: 18 To him be g both now and forever!
Jude : 25 to the only God our Savior be g,
Rev 1: 6 to him be g and power for ever
4: 9 the living creatures give g,
4: 11 to receive g and honor and power,
5: 12 and honor and g and praise!"
5: 13 and honor and g and power,
7: 12 Praise and g
11: 13 and gave g to the God of heaven.
14: 7 "Fear God and give him g,
15: 4 and bring g to your name?
15: 8 with smoke from the g of God
19: 1 g and power belong to our God,
19: 7 and give him g!
21: 11 It shone with the g of God,
21: 23 for the g of God gives it light,
21: 26 g and honor of the nations will be

GLOWING

Eze 8: 2 was as bright as g metal.
Rev 1: 15 His feet were like bronze g

GLUTTONS* (GLUTTONY)

Pr 23: 21 for drunkards and g become poor,
28: 7 of g disgraces his father.
Tit 1: 12 always liars, evil brutes, lazy g."

GLUTTONY* (GLUTTONS)

Pr 23: 2 throat if you are given to g.

GNASHING

Mt 8:12 where there will be weeping and g

GNAT* (GNATS)

Mt 23:24 You strain out a g but swallow

GNATS (GNAT)

Ex 8:16 of Egypt the dust will become g.''

GOADS

Ecc 12:11 The words of the wise are like g,
Ac 26:14 hard for you to kick against the g.'

GOAL*

Lk 13:32 on the third day I will reach my g.'
2Co 5: 9 So we make it our g to please him,
Gal 3: 3 to attain your g by human effort?
Php 3:14 on toward the g to win the prize
1Ti 1: 5 The g of this command is love,
1Pe 1: 9 for you are receiving the g

GOAT (GOATS SCAPEGOAT)

Ge 15: 9 ''Bring me a heifer, a g and a ram,
    30:32 and every spotted or speckled g.
    37:31 slaughtered a g and dipped
Ex 26: 7 Make curtains of g hair for the tent
Lev 16: 9 shall bring the g whose lot falls
Nu   7:16 one male g for a sin offering;
Isa 11: 6 the leopard will lie down with the g
Da   8: 5 suddenly a g with a prominent

GOATS (GOAT)

Nu   7:17 five male g and five male lambs
Mt 25:32 separates the sheep from the g.
Heb 10: 4 of bulls and g to take away sins.

GOD (GOD'S GODLINESS GODLY GODS)

Ge   1: 1 In the beginning G created
     1: 2 and the Spirit of G was hovering
     1: 3 And G said, ''Let there be light,''
     1: 7 So G made the expanse
     1: 9 And G said, ''Let the water
     1:11 Then G said, ''Let the land produce
     1:20 And G said, ''Let the water teem
     1:21 So G created the great creatures
     1:25 G made the wild animals according
     1:26 Then G said, ''Let us make man
     1:27 So G created man in his own image
     1:31 G saw all that he had made,
     2: 3 And G blessed the seventh day
     2: 7 And the Lord G formed the man
     2: 8 the Lord G had planted a garden
     2:18 The Lord G said, ''It is not good
     2:22 Then the Lord G made a woman
     3: 1 to the woman, ''Did G really say,
     3: 5 you will be like G, knowing good
     3: 8 from the Lord G among the trees
     3: 9 But the Lord G called to the man
     3:21 The Lord G made garments
     3:22 Lord G said, ''The man has now
     3:23 So the Lord G banished him
     5: 1 When G created man, he made him
     5:22 Enoch walked with G 300 years
     5:24 because G took him away.
     6: 2 sons of G saw that the daughters
     6: 9 of his time, and he walked with G.
     6:12 G saw how corrupt the earth had
     8: 1 But G remembered Noah
     9: 1 Then G blessed Noah and his sons,
     9: 6 for in the image of G
     9:16 everlasting covenant between G
    14:18 He was priest of G Most High,
    14:19 Blessed be Abram by G Most High,
    16:13 ''You are the G who sees me,''
    17: 1 ''I am G Almighty; walk before me
    17: 7 to be your G and the G
    21: 4 him, as G commanded him.
    21: 6 ''G has brought me laughter,
    21:20 G was with the boy as he grew up.
    21:22 G is with you in everything you do.
    21:33 name of the Lord, the Eternal G.
    22: 1 Some time later G tested Abraham.
    22: 8 ''G himself will provide the lamb
    22:12 Now I know that you fear G,

Ge 25:11 Abraham's death, G blessed his
    28:12 and the angels of G were ascending
    28:17 other than the house of G;
    31:42 But G has seen my hardship
    31:50 remember that G is a witness
    32: 1 and the angels of G met him.
    32:28 because you have struggled with G
    32:30 ''It is because I saw G face to face,
    33:11 for G has been gracious to me
    35: 1 and build an altar there to G,
    35: 5 and the terror of G fell
    35:10 G said to him, ''Your name is Jacob
    35:11 G said to him, ''I am G Almighty;
    41:51 G has made me forget all my
    41:52 G has made me fruitful in the land
    50:20 but G intended it for good
    50:24 But G will surely come to your aid
Ex   2:24 G heard their groaning
     3: 5 ''Do not come any closer,'' G said.
     3: 6 because he was afraid to look at G.
     3:12 And G said, ''I will be with you.
     3:14 what shall I tell them?'' G said
     4:27 he met Moses at the mountain of G
     6: 7 own people, and I will be your G.
     8:10 is no one like the Lord your G.
    10:16 sinned against the Lord your G
    13:18 So G led the people
    15: 2 He is my G, and I will praise him,
    16:12 that I am the Lord your G.' ''
    17: 9 with the staff of G in my hands.''
    18: 5 camped near the mountain of G.
    19: 3 Then Moses went up to G,
    20: 1 And G spoke all these words:
    20: 2 the Lord your G, who brought
    20: 5 the Lord your G, am a jealous G,
    20: 7 the name of the Lord your G,
    20:10 a Sabbath to the Lord your G.
    20:12 the Lord your G is giving you.
    20:19 But do not have G speak to us
    20:20 the fear of G will be with you
    22:20 ''Whoever sacrifices to any g other
    22:28 ''Do not blaspheme G
    23:19 to the house of the Lord your G.
    31:18 inscribed by the finger of G.
    34: 6 the compassionate and gracious G,
    34:14 name is Jealous, is a jealous G.
Lev 2:13 salt of the covenant of your G out
    11:44 the Lord your G; consecrate
    18:21 not profane the name of your G.
    19: 2 the Lord your G, am holy.
    20: 7 because I am the Lord your G.
    21: 6 They must be holy to their G
    22:33 out of Egypt to be your G,
    26:12 walk among you and be your G,
Nu 15:40 and will be consecrated to your G.
    22:18 the command of the Lord my G.
    22:38 I must speak only what G puts
    23:19 G is not a man, that he should lie,
    25:13 zealous for the honor of his G
Dt   1:17 for judgment belongs to G.
     1:21 the Lord your G has given you
     1:30 The Lord your G, who is going
     3:22 Lord your G himself will fight
     3:24 For what g is there in heaven
     4:24 is a consuming fire, a jealous G.
     4:29 there you seek the Lord your G,
     4:31 the Lord your G is a merciful G;
     4:39 heart this day that the Lord is G
     5: 9 the Lord your G, am a jealous G,
     5:11 the name of the Lord your G,
     5:12 the Lord your G has commanded
     5:14 a Sabbath to the Lord your G.
     5:15 the Lord your G brought you out
     5:16 the Lord your G has commanded
     5:16 the Lord your G is giving you.
     5:24 Lord our G has shown us his
     5:26 of the living G speaking out of fire,
     6: 2 them may fear the Lord your G
     6: 4 Lord our G, the Lord is one.
     6: 5 Love the Lord your G
     6:13 the Lord your G, serve him only
     6:16 Do not test the Lord your G
     7: 6 holy to the Lord your G.
     7: 9 your G is G; he is the faithful G,
     7:12 the Lord your G will keep his
     7:19 Lord your G will do the same
     7:21 is a great and awesome G.
     8: 5 the Lord your G disciplines you.

Dt   8:11 do not forget the Lord your G,
     8:18 But remember the Lord your G,
     9:10 inscribed by the finger of G.
    10:12 but to fear the Lord your G,
    10:14 the Lord your G belong
    10:17 For the Lord your G is G of gods
    10:21 He is your praise; he is your G,
    11: 1 Love the Lord your G
    11:13 to love the Lord your G
    12:12 rejoice before the Lord your G,
    12:28 in the eyes of the Lord your G.
    13: 3 The Lord your G is testing you
    13: 4 the Lord your G you must
    15: 6 the Lord your G will bless you
    15:19 the Lord your G every firstborn
    16:11 rejoice before the Lord your G
    16:17 the Lord your G has blessed you.
    18:13 before the Lord your G.
    18:15 The Lord your G will raise up
    19: 9 to love the Lord your G
    22: 5 the Lord your G detests anyone
    23: 5 the Lord your G loves you.
    23:14 the Lord your G moves about
    23:21 a vow to the Lord your G,
    25:16 the Lord your G detests anyone
    26: 5 declare before the Lord your G:
    29:13 that he may be your G
    29:29 belong to the Lord our G,
    30: 2 return to the Lord your G
    30: 4 the Lord your G will gather you
    30: 6 The Lord your G will circumcise
    30:16 today to love the Lord your G,
    30:20 you may love the Lord your G,
    31: 6 for the Lord your G goes
    32: 3 Oh, praise the greatness of our G!
    32: 4 A faithful G who does no wrong,
    33:27 The eternal G is your refuge,
Jos 1: 9 for the Lord your G will be
    14: 8 the Lord my G wholeheartedly.
    14: 9 the Lord my G wholeheartedly.'
    14:14 the G of Israel, wholeheartedly.
    22: 5 to love the Lord your G,
    22:22 The Mighty One, G, the Lord!
    22:34 Between Us that the Lord is G.
    23: 8 to hold fast to the Lord your G,
    23:11 careful to love the Lord your G.
    23:14 the Lord your G gave you has
    23:15 of the Lord your G has come true
    24:19 He is a holy G; he is a jealous G.
    24:23 to the Lord, the G of Israel.''
Jdg 5: 3 to the Lord, the G of Israel.
    16:28 O G, please strengthen me just
Ru   1:16 be my people and your G my G.
     2:12 by the Lord, the G of Israel,
1Sa 2: 2 there is no Rock like our G.
     2: 3 for the Lord is a G who knows,
     2:25 another man, G may mediate
    10:26 men whose hearts G had touched.
    12:12 the Lord your G was your king.
    16:15 spirit from G is tormenting you.
    17:26 defy the armies of the living G?''
    17:36 defied the armies of the living G.
    17:45 the G of the armies of Israel,
    17:46 world will know that there is a G
    23:16 and helped him find strength in G.
    28:15 and G has turned away from me.
    30: 6 strength in the Lord his G.
2Sa 7:22 and there is no G but you,
     7:23 on earth that G went out to redeem
    14:14 But G does not take away life;
    21:14 G answered prayer in behalf
    22: 3 my G is my rock, in whom I take
    22:31 ''As for G, his way is perfect;
    22:32 And who is the Rock except our G
    22:33 It is G who arms me with strength
    22:47 Exalted be G, the Rock, my Savior!
1Ki 2: 3 what the Lord your G requires:
     4:29 G gave Solomon wisdom
     5: 5 for the Name of the Lord my G,
     8:23 there is no G like you in heaven
     8:27 ''But will G really dwell on earth?
     8:60 may know that the Lord is G
     8:61 committed to the Lord our G,
    10:24 to hear the wisdom G had put
    15:30 he provoked the Lord, the G of
    18:21 If the Lord is G, follow him;
    18:36 it be known today that you are G
    18:37 are G, and that you are turning

1Ki 20: 28 a *g* of the hills and not a *g*
2Ki 5: 15 "Now I know that there is no *G*
18: 5 in the LORD, the *G* of Israel.
19: 15 *G* of Israel, enthroned
19: 19 Now, O LORD our *G*, deliver us
1Ch 12: 18 for your *G* will help you."
13: 2 if it is the will of the LORD our *G*
16: 35 Cry out, "Save us, O *G* our Savior,
17: 20 and there is no *G* but you,
17: 24 the *G* over Israel, is Israel's *G!'*
21: 8 said to *G*, "I have sinned greatly
22: 1 house of the LORD *G* is to be here,
22: 19 soul to seeking the LORD your *G*.
28: 2 for the footstool of our *G*,
28: 9 acknowledge the *G* of your father,
28: 20 for the LORD *G*, my *G*, is with you
29: 1 not for man but for the LORD *G*.
29: 2 provided for the temple of my *G*—
29: 3 of my *G* I now give my personal
29: 10 *G* of our father Israel,
29: 13 Now, our *G*, we give you thanks,
29: 16 O LORD our *G*, as for all this
29: 17 my *G*, that you test the heart
29: 18 *G* of our fathers Abraham,
2Ch 2: 4 for the Name of the LORD my *G*
5: 14 of the LORD filled the temple of *G*
6: 4 be to the LORD, the *G* of Israel,
6: 14 there is no *G* like you in heaven
6: 18 "But will *G* really dwell on earth
10: 15 for this turn of events was from *G*,
13: 12 *G* is with us; he is our leader.
15: 3 was without the true *G*,
15: 12 the *G* of their fathers,
15: 15 They sought *G* eagerly,
18: 13 I can tell him only what my *G* says
19: 3 have set your heart on seeking *G*."
19: 7 with the LORD our *G* there is no
20: 6 are you not the *G* who is in heaven?
20: 20 Have faith in the LORD your *G*
25: 8 for *G* has the power to help
26: 5 sought the LORD, *G* gave him
30: 9 for the LORD your *G* is gracious
30: 19 who sets his heart on seeking *G*—
31: 21 he sought his *G* and worked
32: 31 *G* left him to test him
33: 12 the favor of the LORD his *G*
34: 33 fail to follow the LORD, the *G*
Ezr 6: 21 to seek the LORD, the *G* of Israel.
7: 18 accordance with the will of your *G*.
7: 23 Whatever the *G* of heaven has
8: 22 "The gracious hand of our *G* is
8: 31 The hand of our *G* was on us,
9: 6 "O my *G*, I am too ashamed
9: 9 our *G* has not deserted us
9: 13 our *G*, you have punished us less
9: 15 *G* of Israel, you are righteous!
Ne 1: 5 the great and awesome *G*,
5: 9 fear of our *G* to avoid the reproach
5: 15 for *G* I did not act like that.
7: 2 feared *G* more than most men do.
8: 8 from the Book of the Law of *G*,
8: 18 from the Book of the Law of *G*.
9: 5 and praise the LORD your *G*,
9: 17 But you are a forgiving *G*,
9: 31 you are a gracious and merciful *G*,
9: 32 the great, mighty and awesome *G*,
10: 29 oath to follow the Law of *G* given
10: 39 not neglect the house of our *G*."
12: 43 *G* had given them great joy.
13: 11 Why is the house of *G* neglected?"
13: 26 He was loved by his *G*,
13: 31 Remember me with favor, O my *G*.
Job 1: 1 he feared *G* and shunned evil.
1: 22 by charging *G* with wrongdoing.
2: 10 Shall we accept good from *G*,
4: 17 be a mortal be more righteous than *G?*
5: 17 is the man whom *G* corrects;
8: 3 Does *G* pervert justice?
8: 20 "Surely *G* does not reject
9: 2 a mortal be righteous before *G?*
11: 7 Can you fathom the mysteries of *G*
12: 13 "To *G* belong wisdom and power;
16: 7 Surely, O *G*, you have worn me out
19: 26 yet in my flesh I will see *G*;
21: 19 '*G* stores up a man's punishment
21: 22 Can anyone teach knowledge to *G*,
22: 12 "Is not *G* in the heights of heaven?
22: 13 Yet you say, 'What does *G* know?

Job 22: 21 "Submit to *G* and be at peace
25: 2 "Dominion and awe belong to *G;*
25: 4 can a man be righteous before *G?*
26: 6 Death is naked before *G;*
30: 20 O *G*, but you do not answer;
31: 6 let *G* weigh me in honest scales
31: 14 do when *G* confronts me?
32: 13 let *G* refute him, not man.'
33: 6 I am just like you before *G;*
33: 14 For *G* does speak—now one way,
33: 26 He prays to *G* and finds favor
34: 10 Far be it from *G* to do evil,
34: 12 is unthinkable that *G* would do
34: 23 *G* has no need to examine men
34: 33 Should *G* then reward you
36: 5 "*G* is mighty, but does not despise
36: 26 is *G*— beyond our understanding!
37: 22 *G* comes in awesome majesty.
Ps 5: 4 You are not a *G* who takes pleasure
7: 11 *G* is a righteous judge,
10: 14 O *G*, do see trouble and grief;
14: 5 for *G* is present in the company
18: 2 my *G* is my rock, in whom I take
18: 28 my *G* turns my darkness into light.
18: 30 As for *G*, his way is perfect;
18: 31 And who is the Rock except our *G*
18: 32 It is *G* who arms me with strength
18: 46 Exalted be *G* my Savior!
19: 1 The heavens declare the glory of *G;*
22: 1 *G*, my *G*, why have you forsaken
22: 10 womb you have been my *G*.
27: 9 O *G* my Savior,
29: 3 the *G* of glory thunders,
31: 5 redeem me, O LORD, the *G*
31: 14 I say, "You are my *G*."
33: 12 the nation whose *G* is the LORD,
35: 24 righteousness, O LORD my *G;*
37: 31 The law of his *G* is in his heart;
40: 3 a hymn of praise to our *G*.
40: 8 I desire to do your will, O my *G;*
42: 1 so my soul pants for you, O *G*.
42: 2 thirsts for *G*, for the living *G*.
42: 5 Put your hope in *G*,
42: 8 a prayer to the *G* of my life.
42: 11 Put your hope in *G*,
43: 4 to *G*, my joy and my delight.
44: 8 In *G* we make our boast all day
45: 6 O *G*, will last for ever and ever;
45: 7 therefore *G*, your *G*, has set you
46: 1 *G* is our refuge and strength,
46: 5 *G* will help her at break of day.
46: 10 "Be still, and know that I am *G;*
47: 1 shout to *G* with cries of joy.
47: 6 Sing praises to *G*, sing praises;
47: 7 For *G* is the King of all the earth;
48: 9 Within your temple, O *G*,
49: 7 or give to *G* a ransom for him—
50: 2 *G* shines forth.
50: 3 Our *G* comes and will not be silent;
51: 1 Have mercy on me, O *G*,
51: 10 Create in me a pure heart, O *G*,
51: 17 O *G*, you will not despise.
53: 2 any who seek *G*.
54: 4 Surely *G* is my help;
55: 19 *G*, who is enthroned forever,
56: 4 In *G*, whose word I praise,
56: 10 In *G*, whose word I praise,
56: 13 that I may walk before *G*
57: 3 *G* sends his love and his
57: 7 My heart is steadfast, O *G*,
59: 17 are my fortress, my loving *G*.
62: 1 My soul finds rest in *G* alone;
62: 7 my honor depend on *G;*
62: 8 for *G* is our refuge.
62: 11 One thing *G* has spoken,
63: 1 O *G*, you are my *G*,
65: 5 O *G* our Savior,
66: 1 Shout with joy to *G*, all the earth!
66: 3 Say to *G*, "How awesome are your
66: 5 Come and see what *G* has done,
66: 16 listen, all you who fear *G;*
66: 20 Praise be to *G*,
68: 4 Sing to *G*, sing praise to his name,
68: 6 *G* sets the lonely in families,
68: 20 Our *G* is a *G* who saves;
68: 24 has come into view, O *G*,
68: 35 You are awesome, O *G*,
69: 5 You know my folly, O *G;*

Ps 70: 1 Hasten, O *G*, to save me;
70: 4 "Let *G* be exalted!"
70: 5 come quickly to me, O *G*.
71: 17 my youth, O *G*, you have taught
71: 18 do not forsake me, O *G*,
71: 19 reaches to the skies, O *G*,
71: 22 harp for your faithfulness, O my *G;*
73: 17 me till I entered the sanctuary of *G;*
73: 26 but *G* is the strength of my heart
76: 11 Make vows to the LORD your *G*
77: 13 What a is so great as our *G?*
77: 14 You are the *G* who performs
78: 19 Can *G* spread a table in the desert?
79: 9 Help us, O *G* our Savior,
81: 1 Sing for joy to *G* our strength;
82: 1 *G* presides in the great assembly;
84: 2 out for the living *G*.
84: 10 a doorkeeper in the house of my *G*
84: 11 For the LORD *G* is a sun
86: 12 O Lord my *G*, with all my heart;
86: 15 a compassionate and gracious *G*,
87: 3 O city of *G: Selah*
89: 7 of the holy ones *G* is greatly feared;
90: 2 to everlasting you are *G*.
91: 2 my *G*, in whom I trust."
94: 22 my *G* the rock in whom I take
95: 7 for he is our *G*
99: 8 you were to Israel a forgiving *G*,
99: 9 Exalt the LORD our *G*
100: 3 Know that the LORD is *G*.
108: 1 My heart is steadfast, O *G;*
113: 5 Who is like the LORD our *G*,
115: 3 Our *G* is in heaven;
116: 5 our *G* is full of compassion.
123: 2 look to the LORD our *G*,
136: 2 Give thanks to the *G* of gods.
136: 26 Give thanks to the *G* of heaven.
139: 17 to me are your thoughts, O *G!*
139: 23 Search me, O *G*, and know my
143: 10 for you are my *G;*
144: 2 He is my loving *G* and my fortress,
147: 1 is to sing praises to our *G*,
Pr 3: 4 in the sight of *G* and man.
14: 31 to the needy honors *G*.
25: 2 of *G* to conceal a matter;
30: 5 "Every word of *G* is flawless;
Ecc 2: 26 *G* gives wisdom, knowledge
3: 11 cannot fathom what *G* has done
3: 13 in all his toil—this is the gift of *G*.
3: 14 *G* does it so that men will revere him.
5: 4 When you make a vow to *G*,
5: 19 in his work—this is a gift of *G*.
8: 12 who are reverent before *G*.
11: 5 cannot understand the work of *G*,
12: 7 the spirit returns to *G* who gave it.
12: 13 Fear *G* and keep his
Isa 5: 16 the holy *G* will show himself holy
9: 6 Wonderful Counselor, Mighty *G*,
12: 2 Surely *G* is my salvation;
25: 9 "Surely this is our *G;*
28: 11 *G* will speak to this people,
29: 23 will stand in awe of the *G* of Israel.
30: 18 For the LORD is a *G* of justice.
35: 4 your *G* will come,
37: 16 you alone are *G* over all
40: 1 says your *G*.
40: 3 a highway for our *G*.
40: 8 the word of our *G* stands forever."
40: 18 then, will you compare *G?*
40: 28 The LORD is the everlasting *G*,
41: 10 not be dismayed, for I am your *G*.
41: 13 For I am the LORD, your *G*,
43: 10 Before me no *g* was formed,
44: 6 apart from me there is no *G*.
44: 15 he also fashions a *g* and worships it;
45: 18 he is *G*;
48: 17 "I am the LORD your *G*,
52: 7 "Your *G* reigns!"
52: 12 *G* of Israel will be your rear guard.
55: 7 to our *G*, for he will freely pardon.
57: 21 says my *G*, "for the wicked."
59: 2 you from your *G;*
60: 19 and your *G* will be your glory.
61: 2 and the day of vengeance of our *G*,
61: 10 my soul rejoices in my *G*.
62: 5 so will your *G* rejoice over you.
Jer 7: 23 I will be your *G* and you will be my
10: 10 But the LORD is the true *G;*

Jer 10: 12 But *G* made the earth by his power;
23: 23 "Am I only a *G* nearby,"
23: 36 distort the words of the living *G*.
31: 33 I will be their *G*,
32: 27 "I am the LORD, the *G*
42: 6 for we will obey the LORD our *G*."
51: 10 what the LORD our *G* has done.'
51: 56 For the LORD is a *G* of retribution
Eze 28: 13 the garden of *G*;
34: 31 and I am your *G*, declares
Da 2: 28 there is a *G* in heaven who reveals
3: 17 the *G* we serve is able to save us
3: 29 for no other *g* can save in this way
6: 16 "May your *G*, whom you serve
9: 4 O Lord, the great and awesome *G*,
10: 12 to humble yourself before your *G*,
11: 36 things against the *G* of gods.
Hos 1: 9 my people, and I am not your *G*.
1: 10 will be called 'sons of the living *G*.'
4: 6 you have ignored the law of your *G*
6: 6 acknowledgment of *G* rather
9: 8 The prophet, along with my *G*,
12: 6 and wait for your *G* always.
Joel 2: 13 Return to the LORD your *G*,
2: 23 rejoice in the LORD your *G*,
Am 4: 12 prepare to meet your *G*, O Israel."
4: 13 the LORD *G* Almighty is his name
Jnh 1: 6 Get up and call on your *g*!
2: 2 a gracious and compassionate *G*,
Mic 6: 8 and to walk humbly with your *G*.
7: 7 I wait for *G* my Savior,
7: 18 Who is a *G* like you,
Na 1: 2 LORD is a jealous and avenging *G*;
Hab 3: 18 I will be joyful in *G* my Savior.
Zep 3: 17 The LORD your *G* is with you,
Zec 14: 5 Then the LORD my *G* will come,
Mal 2: 10 Father? Did not one *G* create us?
2: 16 says the LORD *G* of Israel,
3: 8 Will a man rob *G*? Yet you rob me.
Mt 1: 23 which means, "*G* with us."
4: 4 comes from the mouth of *G*.'"
4: 7 'Do not put the Lord your *G*
4: 10 'Worship the Lord your *G*,
5: 8 for they will see *G*.
6: 24 You cannot serve both *G*
19: 6 Therefore what *G* has joined
19: 26 but with *G* all things are possible."
22: 21 and to *G* what is God's."
22: 32 He is not the *G* of the dead
22: 37 "'Love the Lord your *G*
27: 46 which means, "My *G*, my *G*,
Mk 2: 7 Who can forgive sins but *G* alone?"
7: 13 Thus you nullify the word of *G*
10: 6 of creation *G* 'made them male
10: 9 Therefore what *G* has joined
10: 18 "No one is good—except *G* alone.
10: 27 all things are possible with *G*."
11: 22 "Have faith in *G*," Jesus answered.
12: 17 and to *G* what is God's."
12: 29 the Lord our *G*, the Lord is one.
12: 30 Love the Lord your *G*
15: 34 which means, "My *G*, my *G*,
16: 19 and he sat at the right hand of *G*.
Lk 1: 30 Mary, you have found favor with *G*
1: 37 For nothing is impossible with *G*."
1: 47 my spirit rejoices in *G* my Savior,
2: 14 "Glory to *G* in the highest,
2: 52 and in favor with *G* and men.
4: 8 'Worship the Lord your *G*
5: 21 Who can forgive sins but *G* alone?"
8: 39 tell how much *G* has done for you."
10: 9 'The kingdom of *G* is near you.'
10: 27 "'Love the Lord your *G*
13: 18 "What is the kingdom of *G* like?
18: 19 "No one is good—except *G* alone.
18: 27 with men is possible with *G*."
20: 25 and to *G* what is God's."
20: 38 He is not the *G* of the dead,
22: 69 at the right hand of the mighty *G*."
Jn 1: 1 was with *G*, and the Word was *G*.
1: 18 ever seen *G*, but *G* the One and Only,
1: 29 Lamb of *G*, who takes away the sin
3: 16 "For *G* so loved the world that he
3: 34 the one whom *G* has sent speaks
4: 24 *G* is spirit, and his worshipers must
5: 44 praise that comes from the only *G*?
6: 29 answered, "The work of *G* is this:
7: 17 my teaching comes from *G* or

Jn 8: 42 to them, "If *G* were your Father,
8: 47 belongs to *G* hears what *G* says.
11: 40 you would see the glory of *G*?"
13: 3 from *G* and was returning to *G*;
13: 31 of Man glorified and *G* is glorified
14: 1 Trust in *G*; trust also in me.
17: 3 the only true *G*, and Jesus Christ,
20: 17 your Father, to my *G* and your *G*
20: 28 "My Lord and my *G*!"
20: 31 the Son of *G*, and that
Ac 2: 11 wonders of *G* in our own tongues!"
2: 24 But *G* raised him from the dead,
2: 33 Exalted to the right hand of *G*,
2: 36 *G* has made this Jesus, whom you
3: 15 but *G* raised him from the dead.
3: 19 Repent, then, and turn to *G*,
4: 31 and spoke the word of *G* boldly.
5: 4 You have not lied to men but to *G*
5: 29 "We must obey *G* rather than men!
5: 31 *G* exalted him to his own right
5: 32 whom *G* has given
7: 55 to heaven and saw the glory of *G*,
8: 21 your heart is not right before *G*.
11: 9 anything impure that *G* has made
12: 24 But the word of *G* continued
13: 32 What *G* promised our fathers he
15: 10 to test *G* by putting on the necks
17: 23 TO AN UNKNOWN *G*
17: 30 In the past *G* overlooked such
20: 27 to you the whole will of *G*.
20: 32 "Now I commit you to *G*
24: 16 keep my conscience clear before *G*
Ro 1: 16 the power of *G* for the salvation
1: 17 a righteousness from *G* is revealed,
1: 18 The wrath of *G* is being revealed
1: 24 Therefore *G* gave them
1: 26 *G* gave them over to shameful lusts
2: 11 For *G* does not show favoritism.
2: 16 when *G* will judge men's secrets
3: 4 Let *G* be true, and every man a liar.
3: 19 world held accountable to *G*.
3: 23 and fall short of the glory of *G*,
3: 29 Is *G* the *G* of Jews only? Is he not
4: 3 say? "Abraham believed *G*,
4: 6 to whom *G* credits righteousness
4: 17 the *G* who gives life to the dead
4: 24 to whom *G* will credit
5: 1 we have peace with *G*
5: 5 because *G* has poured out his love
5: 8 *G* demonstrates his own love for us
6: 22 and have become slaves to *G*,
6: 23 but the gift of *G* is eternal life
8: 7 the sinful mind is hostile to *G*.
8: 17 heirs of *G* and co-heirs with Christ,
8: 28 in all things *G* works for the good
9: 14 What then shall we say? Is *G* unjust
9: 18 Therefore *G* has mercy
10: 9 in your heart that *G* raised him
11: 2 *G* did not reject his people,
11: 22 the kindness and sternness of *G*:
11: 32 For *G* has bound all men
13: 1 exist have been established by *G*.
14: 12 give an account of himself to *G*.
16: 20 *G* of peace will soon crush Satan
1Co 1: 18 are being saved it is the power of *G*.
1: 20 Has not *G* made foolish
1: 25 For the foolishness of *G* is wiser
1: 27 But *G* chose the foolish things
2: 9 what *G* has prepared
2: 11 of *G* except the Spirit of *G*.
3: 6 watered it, but *G* made it grow.
3: 17 God's temple, *G* will destroy
6: 20 Therefore honor *G* with your body.
7: 7 each man has his own gift from *G*;
7: 15 *G* has called us to live in peace.
7: 20 was in when *G* called him.
7: 24 each man, as responsible to *G*,
8: 3 man who loves *G* is known by *G*.
8: 8 food does not bring us near to *G*;
10: 13 is faithful; he will not let you be
10: 31 do it all for the glory of *G*.
12: 24 But *G* has combined the members
14: 33 For *G* is not a *G* of disorder
15: 24 over the kingdom to *G* the Father
15: 28 so that *G* may be all in all.
15: 34 are some who are ignorant of *G*—
15: 57 be to *G*! He gives us the victory
2Co 1: 9 rely on ourselves but on *G*,

2Co 2: 14 be to *G*, who always leads us
2: 15 For we are to *G* the aroma of Christ
2: 17 we do not peddle the word of *G*
3: 5 but our competence comes from *G*.
4: 2 nor do we distort the word of *G*.
4: 7 this all-surpassing power is from *G*
5: 5 Now it is *G* who has made us
5: 19 that *G* was reconciling the world
5: 20 though *G* were making his appeal
5: 21 *G* made him who had no sin
6: 16 we are the temple of the living *G*.
9: 7 for *G* loves a cheerful giver.
9: 8 *G* is able to make all grace abound
10: 13 to the field *G* has assigned to us,
Gal 2: 6 *G* does not judge by external
3: 5 Does *G* give you his Spirit
3: 6 Abraham: "He believed *G*,
3: 11 justified before *G* by the law,
3: 26 You are all sons of *G* through faith
6: 7 not be deceived: *G* cannot be
Eph 1: 22 *G* placed all things under his feet
2: 8 it is the gift of *G*— not by works,
2: 10 which *G* prepared in advance for us
2: 22 in which *G* lives by his Spirit.
4: 6 one baptism; one *G* and Father
4: 24 to be like *G* in true righteousness
5: 1 Be imitators of *G*, therefore,
6: 6 doing the will of *G* from your heart.
Php 2: 6 Who, being in very nature *G*,
2: 9 Therefore *G* exalted him
2: 13 for it is *G* who works in you to will
4: 7 peace of *G*, which transcends all
4: 19 And my *G* will meet all your needs
Col 1: 19 For *G* was pleased
2: 13 *G* made you alive with Christ.
1Th 2: 4 trying to please men but *G*,
2: 13 but as it actually is, the word of *G*,
3: 9 How can we thank *G* enough
4: 7 For *G* did not call us to be impure,
4: 9 taught by *G* to love each other.
5: 9 For *G* did not appoint us
1Ti 2: 5 one mediator between *G* and men,
4: 4 For everything *G* created is good,
5: 4 for this is pleasing to *G*.
2Ti 1: 6 you to fan into flame the gift of *G*,
Tit 1: 2 which *G*, who does not lie,
2: 13 glorious appearing of our great *G*
Heb 1: 1 In the past *G* spoke
3: 4 but *G* is the builder of everything.
4: 4 "And on the seventh day *G* rested
4: 12 For the word of *G* is living
6: 10 is not unjust; he will not forget
6: 18 in which it is impossible for *G* to lie
7: 19 by which we draw near to *G*.
7: 25 come to *G* through him,
10: 22 draw near to *G* with a sincere heart
10: 31 to fall into the hands of the living *G*
11: 5 commended as one who pleased *G*.
11: 6 faith it is impossible to please *G*,
12: 7 as discipline; *G* is treating you
12: 10 but *G* disciplines us for our good.
12: 29 for our "*G* is a consuming fire."
13: 15 offer to *G* a sacrifice of praise—
Jas 1: 12 crown of life that *G* has promised
1: 13 For *G* cannot be tempted by evil,
1: 27 Religion that *G* our Father accepts
2: 19 You believe that there is one *G*.
2: 23 "Abraham believed *G*,
4: 4 the world becomes an enemy of *G*.
4: 6 "*G* opposes the proud
4: 8 Come near to *G* and he will come
1Pe 1: 23 the living and enduring word of *G*.
2: 20 this is commendable before *G*.
3: 18 the unrighteous, to bring you to *G*.
4: 11 it with the strength *G* provides,
5: 5 because, "*G* opposes the proud
2Pe 1: 21 but men spoke from *G*
2: 4 For if *G* did not spare angels
1Jn 1: 5 *G* is light; in him there is no
2: 17 the will of *G* lives forever.
3: 1 we should be called children of *G*!
3: 9 born of *G* will continue to sin,
3: 10 we know who the children of *G* are
3: 20 For *G* is greater than our hearts,
4: 7 for love comes from *G*.
4: 8 not know *G*, because *G* is love.
4: 9 This is how *G* showed his love
4: 11 Dear friends, since *G* so loved us,

1Jn 4:12 No one has ever seen *G;*
    4:15 *G* lives in him and he in *G.*
    4:16 *G* is love.
    4:20 ''I love *G,*'' yet hates his brother,
    4:21 Whoever loves *G* must
    5: 2 that we love the children of *G:*
    5: 3 love for *G:* to obey his commands.
    5: 4 born of *G* overcomes the world.
    5:10 does not believe *G* has made him
    5:14 have in approaching *G:*
    5:18 born of *G* does not continue to sin;
Rev 4: 8 holy is the Lord *G* Almighty,
    7:12 be to our *G* for ever and ever.
    7:17 *G* will wipe away every tear
    11:16 fell on their faces and worshiped *G,*
    15: 3 Lord *G* Almighty.
    17:17 For *G* has put it into their hearts
    19: 6 For our Lord *G* Almighty reigns.
    21: 3 Now the dwelling of *G* is with men,
    21:23 for the glory of *G* gives it light,

GOD-BREATHED* (BREATH)

2Ti 3:16 All Scripture is *G* and is useful

GOD-FEARING* (FEAR)

Ecc 8:12 that it will go better with *G* men,
Ac 2: 5 staying in Jerusalem *G* Jews
    10: 2 all his family were devout and *G;*
    10:22 He is a righteous and *G* man,
    13:26 of Abraham, and you *G* Gentiles,
    13:50 But the Jews incited the *G* women
    17: 4 as did a large number of *G* Greeks
    17:17 with the Jews and the *G* Greeks,

GOD-HATERS* (HATE)

Ro 1:30 They are gossips, slanderers, *G,*

GOD'S (GOD)

2Ch 20:15 For the battle is not yours, but *G.*
Job 37:14 stop and consider *G* wonders.
Ps 52: 8 I trust in *G* unfailing love
    69:30 I will praise *G* name in song
Mk 3:35 Whoever does *G* will is my brother
Jn 7:17 If anyone chooses to do *G* will,
    10:36 'I am *G* Son'? Do not believe me
Ro 2: 3 think you will escape *G* judgment?
    2: 4 not realizing that *G* kindness leads
    3: 3 lack of faith nullify *G* faithfulness?
    7:22 in my inner being I delight in *G* law
    9:16 or effort, but on *G* mercy.
    11:29 for *G* gifts and his call are
    12: 2 and approve what *G* will is—
    12:13 Share with *G* people who are
    13: 6 for the authorities are *G* servants,
1Co 7:19 Keeping *G* commands is what
2Co 6: 2 now is the time of *G* favor,
Eph 7 riches of *G* grace that he lavished
1Th 4: 3 It is *G* will that you should be sanctified;
    5:18 for this is *G* will for you
1Ti 6: 1 so that *G* name and our teaching
2Ti 2:19 *G* solid foundation stands firm,
Tit 1: 7 overseer is entrusted with *G* work,
Heb 1: 3 The Son is the radiance of *G* glory
    9:24 now to appear for us in *G* presence.
    11: 3 was formed at *G* command,
1Pe 2:15 For it is *G* will that
    3: 4 which is of great worth in *G* sight.
1Jn 2: 5 *G* love is truly made complete

GODLESS

Job 20: 5 the joy of the *g* lasts but a moment.
1Ti 6:20 Turn away from *g* chatter

GODLINESS (GOD)

1Ti 2: 2 and quiet lives in all *g* and holiness.
    4: 8 but *g* has value for all things,
    6: 5 and who think that *g* is a means
    6: 6 *g* with contentment is great gain.
    6:11 and pursue righteousness, *g,* faith,
2Pe 1: 6 and to perseverance, *g;*

GODLY (GOD)

Ps 4: 3 that the Lord has set apart the *g*
2Co 7:10 *G* sorrow brings repentance that
    11: 2 jealous for you with a *g* jealousy.
2Ti 3:12 everyone who wants to live a *g* life
2Pe 3:11 You ought to live holy and *g* lives

GODS (GOD)

Ex 20: 3 ''You shall have no other *g*
Dt 5: 7 ''You shall have no other *g*
1Ch 16:26 For all the *g* of the nations are idols
Ps 82: 6 ''I said, 'You are ''*g*'';
Jn 10:34 have said you are *g*'? If he called
Ac 19:26 He says that man-made *g* are no *g*

GOG

Eze 38:18 When *G* attacks the land of Israel,
Rev 20: 8 *G* and Magog—to gather them

GOLD

1Ki 20: 3 'Your silver and *g* are mine,
Job 22:25 then the Almighty will be your *g,*
    23:10 tested me, I will come forth as *g.*
    28:15 cannot be bought with the finest *g.*
    31:24 ''If I have put my trust in *g*
Ps 19:10 They are more precious than *g,*
    119:127 more than *g,* more than pure *g,*
Pr 3:14 and yields better returns than *g.*
    22: 1 esteemed is better than silver or *g.*
Hag 2: 8 The silver is mine and the *g* is mine
Mt 2:11 and presented him with gifts of *g*
Rev 3:18 to buy from me *g* refined in the fire,

GOLGOTHA*

Mt 27:33 to a place called *G* (which means
Mk 15:22 to the place called *G* (which means
Jn 19:17 (which in Aramaic is called *G*).

GOLIATH

Philistine giant killed by David (1Sa 17; 21:9).

GOMORRAH

Ge 19:24 sulfur on Sodom and *G*—
Mt 10:15 and *G* on the day of judgment
2Pe 2: 6 and *G* by burning them to ashes,
Jude 7 *G* and the surrounding towns gave

GOOD

Ge 1: 4 God saw that the light was *g,*
    1:10 And God saw that it was *g.*
    1:12 And God saw that it was *g.*
    1:18 And God saw that it was *g.*
    1:21 And God saw that it was *g.*
    1:25 And God saw that it was *g.*
    1:31 he had made, and it was very *g.*
    2: 9 and the tree of the knowledge of *g*
    2: 9 pleasing to the eye and *g* for food.
    2:18 ''It is not *g* for the man to be alone.
    3:22 become like one of us, knowing *g*
    50:20 but God intended it for *g*
2Ch 7: 3 ''He is *g;* / his love endures
    31:20 doing what was *g* and right
Job 2:10 Shall we accept *g* from God,
Ps 14: 1 there is no one who does *g.*
    34: 8 Taste and see that the Lord is *g;*
    34:14 Turn from evil and do *g;*
    37: 3 Trust in the Lord and do *g;*
    37:27 Turn from evil and do *g;*
    52: 9 for your name is *g.*
    53: 3 there is no one who does *g.*
    84:11 no *g* thing does he withhold
    86: 5 You are forgiving and *g,* O Lord
    100: 5 For the Lord is *g* and his love
    103: 5 satisfies your desires with *g* things,
    112: 5 *G* will come to him who is
    119: 68 You are *g,* and what you do is *g;*
    133: 1 How *g* and pleasant it is
    145: 9 The Lord is *g* to all;
    147: 1 How *g* it is to sing praises
Pr 3: 4 you will win favor and a *g* name
    3:27 Do not withhold *g*
    11:27 He who seeks *g* finds *g* will.
    13:22 A *g* man leaves an inheritance
    14:22 those who plan what is *g* find love
    15: 3 on the wicked and the *g.*
    15:23 and how *g* is a timely word!
    15:30 *g* news gives health to the bones.
    17:22 A cheerful heart is *g* medicine,
    18:22 He who finds a wife finds what is *g*
    19: 2 It is not *g* to have zeal
    22: 1 A *g* name is more desirable
    31:12 She brings him *g,* not harm,
Ecc 12: 14 whether it is *g* or evil.
Isa 5:20 Woe to those who call evil *g*
    40: 9 You who bring *g* tidings

Isa 52: 7 the feet of those who bring *g* news,
    61: 1 me to preach *g* news to the poor.
Jer 6:16 ask where the *g* way is,
    13:23 Neither can you do *g*
    32:39 the *g* of their children after them.
Eze 34:14 I will tend them in a *g* pasture.
Mic 6: 8 has showed you, O man, what is *g.*
Na 1:15 the feet of one who brings *g* news,
Mt 5:45 sun to rise on the evil and the *g,*
    7:11 Father in heaven give *g* gifts
    7:17 Likewise every *g* tree bears *g* fruit,
    7:18 A *g* tree cannot bear bad fruit,
    12:35 The *g* man brings *g* things out
    13: 8 Still other seed fell on *g* soil,
    13:24 is like a man who sowed *g* seed
    13:48 and collected the *g* fish in baskets,
    19:17 ''There is only One who is *g.*
    22:10 both *g* and bad, and the wedding
    25:21 'Well done, *g* and faithful servant!
Mk 1:15 Repent and believe the *g* news!''
    3: 4 lawful on the Sabbath: to do *g*
    4: 8 Still other seed fell on *g* soil.
    8:36 What *g* is it for a man
    10:18 ''No one is *g*— except God alone.
    16:15 preach the *g* news to all creation.
Lk 2:10 I bring you *g* news
    3: 9 does not produce *g* fruit will be
    6:27 do *g* to those who hate you,
    6:43 nor does a bad tree bear *g* fruit.
    6:45 The *g* man brings *g* things out
    8: 8 Still other seed fell on *g* soil.
    9:25 What *g* is it for a man
    14:34 ''Salt is *g,* but if it loses its saltiness,
    18:19 ''No one is *g*— except God alone.
    19:17 '' 'Well done, my *g* servant!'
Jn 10:11 ''I am the *g* shepherd.
Ro 3:12 there is no one who does *g,*
    7:12 is holy, righteous and *g.*
    7:16 want to do, I agree that the law is *g.*
    7:18 I have the desire to do what is *g,*
    8:28 for the *g* of those who love him,
    10:15 feet of those who bring *g* news!''
    12: 2 his *g,* pleasing and perfect will.
    12: 9 Hate what is evil; cling to what is *g.*
    13: 4 For he is God's servant to do you *g*
    16:19 you to be wise about what is *g,*
1Co 7: 1 It is *g* for a man not to marry.
    10:24 should seek his own *g,* but the *g*
    15:33 Bad company corrupts *g* character
2Co 9: 8 you will abound in every *g* work.
Gal 4:18 provided the purpose is *g,*
    6: 9 us not become weary in doing *g,*
    6:10 as we have opportunity, let us do *g*
Eph 2:10 in Christ Jesus to do *g* works,
    6: 8 everyone for whatever *g* he does,
Php 1: 6 that he who began a *g* work
Col 1:10 bearing fruit in every *g* work,
1Th 5:21 Hold on to the *g.*
1Ti 3: 7 have a *g* reputation with outsiders,
    4: 4 For everything God created is *g,*
    6:12 Fight the *g* fight of the faith.
    6:18 them to do *g,* to be rich in *g* deeds,
2Ti 3:17 equipped for every *g* work.
    4: 7 I have fought the *g* fight, I have
Tit 1: 8 loves what is *g,* who is
    2: 7 an example by doing what is *g.*
    2:14 his very own, eager to do what is *g.*
Heb 5:14 to distinguish *g* from evil.
    10:24 on toward love and *g* deeds.
    12:10 but God disciplines us for our *g,*
    13:16 do not forget to do *g* and to share
Jas 4:17 who knows the *g* he ought to do
1Pe 2: 3 you have tasted that the Lord is *g.*
    2:12 Live such *g* lives among the pagans
    2:18 not only to those who are *g*
    3:17 to suffer for doing *g*

GOODS

Ecc 5:11 As *g* increase,

GORGE

Pr 23:20 or *g* themselves on meat,

GOSHEN

Ge 45:10 You shall live in the region of *G*
Ex 8:22 differently with the land of *G,*

GOSPEL

Ro 1: 16 I am not ashamed of the *g*,
    15: 16 duty of proclaiming the *g* of God,
    15: 20 to preach the *g* where Christ was
1Co 1: 17 to preach the *g*— not with words
    9: 12 rather than hinder the *g* of Christ.
    9: 14 who preach the *g* should receive
    9: 16 Woe to me if I do not preach the *g*!
    15: 1 you of the *g* I preached to you,
    15: 2 By this *g* you are saved,
2Co 4: 4 light of the *g* of the glory of Christ,
    9: 13 your confession of the *g*
Gal 1: 7 a different *g*— which is really no *g*
Eph 6: 15 comes from the *g* of peace.
Php 1: 27 in a manner worthy of the *g*
Col 1: 23 This is the *g* that you heard
1Th 2: 4 by God to be entrusted with the *g*.
2Th 1: 8 do not obey the *g* of our Lord Jesus
2Ti 1: 10 immortality to light through the *g*.
Rev 14: 6 he had the eternal *g* to proclaim

GOSSIP*

Pr 11: 13 A *g* betrays a confidence,
    16: 28 and a *g* separates close friends.
    18: 8 of a *g* are like choice morsels;
    20: 19 A *g* betrays a confidence;
    26: 20 without a *g* a quarrel dies down.
    26: 22 of a *g* are like choice morsels;
2Co 12: 20 slander, *g*, arrogance and disorder.

GOVERN (GOVERNMENT)

Ge 1: 16 the greater light to *g* the day
Job 34: 17 Can he who hates justice *g*?
Ro 12: 8 it is leadership, let him *g* diligently)

GOVERNMENT (GOVERN)

Isa 9: 6 and the *g* will be on his shoulders.

GRACE* (GRACIOUS)

Ps 45: 2 lips have been anointed with *g*,
Pr 1: 9 will be a garland to *g* your head
    3: 22 an ornament to *g* your neck.
    3: 34 but gives *g* to the humble.
    4: 9 She will set a garland of *g*
Isa 26: 10 Though *g* is shown to the wicked,
Jnh 2: 8 forfeit the *g* that could be theirs.
Zec 12: 10 of Jerusalem a spirit of *g*
Lk 2: 40 and the *g* of God was upon him.
Jn 1: 14 who came from the Father, full of *g*
    1: 16 of his *g* we have all received one
    1: 17 *g* and truth came through Jesus
Ac 4: 33 and much *g* was upon them all.
    6: 8 a man full of God's *g* and power,
    11: 23 saw the evidence of the *g* of God,
    13: 43 them to continue in the *g* of God.
    14: 3 message of his *g* by enabling them
    14: 26 they had been committed to the *g*
    15: 11 We believe it is through the *g*
    15: 40 by the brothers to the *g* of the Lord
    18: 27 to those who by *g* had believed.
    20: 24 testifying to the gospel of God's *g*.
    20: 32 to God and to the word of his *g*,
Ro 1: 5 we received *g* and apostleship
    1: 7 *G* and peace to you
    3: 24 and are justified freely by his *g*
    4: 16 be by *g* and may be guaranteed
    5: 2 access by faith into this *g*
    5: 15 came by the *g* of the one man,
    5: 15 how much more did God's *g*
    5: 17 God's abundant provision of *g*
    5: 20 where sin increased, *g* increased all
    5: 21 also *g* might reign
    6: 1 on sinning so that *g* may increase?
    6: 14 you are not under law, but under *g*.
    6: 15 we are not under law but under *g*?
    11: 5 there is a remnant chosen by *g*,
    11: 6 if by *g*, then it is no longer by works
    11: 6 if it were, *g* would no longer be *g*.
    12: 3 For by the *g* given me I say
    12: 6 according to the *g* given us.
    15: 15 because of the *g* God gave me
    16: 20 The *g* of our Lord Jesus be
1Co 1: 3 *G* and peace to you
    1: 4 of his *g* given you in Christ Jesus.
    3: 10 By the *g* God has given me,
    15: 10 But by the *g* of God I am what I am
    15: 10 but the *g* of God that was with me.
    15: 10 his *g* to me was not without effect.

1Co 16: 23 The *g* of the Lord Jesus be with you
2Co 1: 2 *G* and peace to you
    1: 12 wisdom but according to God's *g*.
    4: 15 so that the *g* that is reaching more
    6: 1 not to receive God's *g* in vain.
    8: 1 to know about the *g* that God has
    8: 6 also to completion this act of *g*
    8: 7 also excel in this *g* of giving.
    8: 9 For you know the *g*
    9: 8 able to make all *g* abound to you,
    9: 14 of the surpassing *g* God has given
    12: 9 "My *g* is sufficient for you,
    13: 14 May the *g* of the Lord Jesus Christ,
Gal 1: 3 *G* and peace to you
    1: 6 the one who called you by the *g*
    1: 15 from birth and called me by his *g*,
    2: 9 when they recognized the *g* given
    2: 21 I do not set aside the *g* of God,
    3: 18 God in his *g* gave it to Abraham
    5: 4 you have fallen away from *g*.
    6: 18 The *g* of our Lord Jesus Christ be
Eph 1: 2 *G* and peace to you
    1: 6 to the praise of his glorious *g*,
    1: 7 riches of God's *g* that he lavished
    2: 5 it is by *g* you have been saved.
    2: 7 the incomparable riches of his *g*,
    2: 8 For it is by *g* you have been saved,
    3: 2 of God's *g* that was given to me
    3: 7 by the gift of God's *g* given me
    3: 8 God's people, this *g* was given me:
    4: 7 to each one of us *g* has been given
    6: 24 *G* to all who love our Lord Jesus
Php 1: 2 *G* and peace to you
    1: 7 all of you share in God's *g* with me.
    4: 23 The *g* of the Lord Jesus Christ be
Col 1: 2 *G* and peace to you
    1: 6 understood God's *g* in all its truth.
    4: 6 conversation be always full of *g*,
    4: 18 *G* be with you.
1Th 1: 1 and the Lord Jesus Christ: *G*
    5: 28 The *g* of our Lord Jesus Christ be
2Th 1: 2 *G* and peace to you
    1: 12 according to the *g* of our God
    2: 16 and by his *g* gave us eternal
    3: 18 The *g* of our Lord Jesus Christ be
1Ti 1: 2 my true son in the faith: *G*,
    1: 14 The *g* of our Lord was poured out
    6: 21 *G* be with you.
2Ti 1: 2 To Timothy, my dear son: *G*,
    1: 9 This *g* was given us in Christ Jesus
    1: 9 because of his own purpose and *g*.
    2: 1 be strong in the *g* that is
    4: 22 *G* be with you.
Tit 1: 4 *G* and peace from God the Father
    2: 11 For the *g* of God that brings
    3: 7 having been justified by his *g*,
    3: 15 *G* be with you all.
Phm : 3 *G* to you and peace
    : 25 The *g* of the Lord Jesus Christ be
Heb 2: 9 that by the *g* of God he might taste
    4: 16 find *g* to help us in our time of need
    4: 16 the throne of *g* with confidence,
    10: 29 and who has insulted the Spirit of *g*
    12: 15 See to it that no one misses the *g*
    13: 9 hearts to be strengthened by *g*,
    13: 25 *G* be with you all.
Jas 4: 6 but gives *g* to the humble."
    4: 6 But he gives us more *g*. That is why
1Pe 1: 2 *G* and peace be yours in abundance
    1: 10 who spoke of the *g* that was
    1: 13 fully on the *g* to be given you
    4: 10 faithfully administering God's *g*
    5: 5 but gives *g* to the humble."
    5: 10 the God of all *g*, who called you
    5: 12 and testifying that this is the true *g*
2Pe 1: 2 *G* and peace be yours in abundance
    3: 18 But grow in the *g* and knowledge
2Jn : 3 and will be with us forever: *G*,
Jude : 4 who change the *g* of our God
Rev 1: 4 *G* and peace to you
    22: 21 The *g* of the Lord Jesus be

GRACIOUS (GRACE)

Ex 34: 6 the compassionate and *g* God,
Nu 6: 25 and be *g* to you;
Ne 9: 17 But you are a forgiving God, *g*
Ps 67: 1 May God be *g* to us and bless us
Pr 22: 11 a pure heart and whose speech is *g*

Isa 30: 18 Yet the Lord longs to be *g* to you

GRAIN

Lev 2: 1 When someone brings a *g* offering
Lk 17: 35 women will be grinding *g* together;
1Co 9: 9 ox while it is treading out the *g*."

GRANDCHILDREN (CHILD)

1Ti 5: 4 But if a widow has children or *g*,

GRANDMOTHER (MOTHER)

2Ti 1: 5 which first lived in your *g* Lois

GRANT (GRANTED)

Ps 20: 5 May the Lord *g* all your requests
    51: 12 *g* me a willing spirit, to sustain me.

GRANTED (GRANT)

Pr 10: 24 what the righteous desire will be *g*.
Mt 15: 28 great faith! Your request is *g*."
Php 1: 29 For it has been *g* to you on behalf

GRAPES

Nu 13: 23 branch bearing a single cluster of *g*.
Jer 31: 29 'The fathers have eaten sour *g*,
Eze 18: 2 ''The fathers eat sour *g*,
Mt 7: 16 Do people pick *g* from thornbushes
Rev 14: 18 and gather the clusters of *g*

GRASPED

Php 2: 6 with God something to be *g*,

GRASS

Ps 103: 15 As for man, his days are like *g*,
Isa 40: 6 ''All men are like *g*,
Mt 6: 30 If that is how God clothes the *g*
1Pe 1: 24 ''All men are like *g*,

GRASSHOPPERS

Nu 13: 33 We seemed like *g* in our own eyes,

GRATIFY* (GRATITUDE)

Ro 13: 14 think about how to *g* the desires
Gal 5: 16 and you will not *g* the desires

GRATITUDE (GRATIFY)

Col 3: 16 and spiritual songs with *g*

GRAVE (GRAVES)

Nu 19: 16 who touches a human bone or a *g*,
Dt 34: 6 day no one knows where his *g* is.
Ps 5: 9 Their throat is an open *g*;
    49: 15 will redeem my life from the *g*;
Pr 7: 27 Her house is a highway to the *g*,
Hos 13: 14 Where, O *g*, is your destruction?
Jn 11: 44 "Take off the *g* clothes
Ac 2: 27 you will not abandon me to the *g*,

GRAVES (GRAVE)

Eze 37: 12 I am going to open your *g*
Jn 5: 28 are in their *g* will hear his voice
Ro 3: 13 ''Their throats are open *g*;

GRAY

Pr 16: 31 *G* hair is a crown of splendor;
    20: 29 *g* hair the splendor of the old.

GREAT (GREATER GREATEST GREATNESS)

Ge 12: 2 I will make your name *g*,
    12: 2 ''I will make you into a *g* nation
Ex 32: 11 out of Egypt with *g* power
Nu 14: 19 In accordance with your *g* love,
Dt 4: 32 so *g* as this ever happened,
    10: 17 the *g* God, mighty and awesome,
    29: 28 in *g* wrath the Lord uprooted
Jos 7: 9 do for your own *g* name?''
Jdg 16: 5 you the secret of his *g* strength
2Sa 7: 22 ''How *g* you are, O Sovereign
    22: 36 you stoop down to make me *g*.
    24: 14 for his mercy is *g*; but do not let me
1Ch 17: 19 made known all these *g* promises.
Ps 18: 35 you stoop down to make me *g*.
    19: 11 in keeping them there is *g* reward.
    47: 2 the *g* King over all the earth!
    57: 10 For *g* is your love, reaching
    68: 11 and *g* was the company
    89: 1 of the Lord's *g* love forever;
   103: 11 so *g* is his love for those who fear

Ps 107: 43 consider the *g* love of the LORD.
   108: 4 For *g* is your love, higher
   117: 2 For *g* is his love toward us,
   119:165 *G* peace have they who love your
   145: 3 *G* is the LORD and most worthy
Pr 22: 1 is more desirable than *g* riches;
    23: 24 of a righteous man has *g* joy;
Isa 42: 21 to make his law *g* and glorious.
Jer 27: 5 With my *g* power and outstretched
    32: 19 *g* are your purposes and mighty are
La   3: 23 *g* is your faithfulness.
Da   9: 4 "O Lord, the *g* and awesome God,
Joel 2: 11 The day of the LORD is *g;*
    2: 20 Surely he has done *g* things.
Zep 1: 14 "The *g* day of the LORD is near—
Mal 1: 11 My name will be *g*
    4: 5 the prophet Elijah before that *g*
Mt 20: 26 whoever wants to become *g*
Mk 10: 43 whoever wants to become *g*
Lk   6: 23 because *g* is your reward in heaven.
    6: 35 Then your reward will be *g,*
    21: 27 in a cloud with power and *g* glory.
Eph 1: 19 and his incomparably *g* power
    2: 4 But because of his *g* love for us,
1Ti 6: 6 with contentment is *g* gain.
Tit 2: 13 glorious appearing of our *g* God
Heb 2: 3 if we ignore such a *g* salvation?
1Jn 3: 1 How *g* is the love the Father has
Rev 6: 17 For the *g* day of their wrath has
    20: 11 Then I saw a *g* white throne

GREATER (GREAT)

Mt 11: 11 there has not risen anyone *g*
    12: 6 I tell you that one *g*
    12: 41 and now one *g* than Jonah is here.
    12: 42 now one *g* than Solomon is here.
Mk 12: 31 There is no commandment *g*
Jn   1: 50 You shall see *g* things than that."
    3: 30 He must become *g;* I must become
    14: 12 He will do even *g* things than these
    15: 13 *G* love has no one than this,
1Co 12: 31 But eagerly desire the *g* gifts.
2Co 3: 11 how much *g* is the glory
Heb 3: 3 the builder of a house has *g* honor
    3: 3 worthy of *g* honor than Moses,
    7: 7 lesser person is blessed by the *g.*
    11: 26 as of *g* value than the treasures
1Jn 3: 20 For God is *g* than our hearts,
    4: 4 is in you is *g* than the one who is

GREATEST (GREAT)

Mt 22: 38 is the first and *g* commandment.
    23: 11 *g* among you will be your servant.
Lk   9: 48 least among you all—he is the *g.*"
1Co 13: 13 But the *g* of these is love.

GREATNESS* (GREAT)

Ex 15: 7 In the *g* of your majesty
Dt   3: 24 to show to your servant your *g*
    32: 3 Oh, praise the *g* of our God!
1Ch 29: 11 O LORD, is the *g* and the power
2Ch 9: 6 half the *g* of your wisdom was told
Est 10: 2 account of the *g* of Mordecai
Ps 145: 3 his *g* no one can fathom.
    150: 2 praise him for his surpassing *g.*
Isa 63: 1 forward in the *g* of his strength?
Eze 38: 23 I will show my *g* and my holiness,
Da   4: 22 your *g* has grown until it reaches
    5: 18 and *g* and glory and splendor.
    7: 27 and *g* of the kingdoms
Mic 4: 4 will live securely, for then his *g*
Lk   9: 43 And they were all amazed at the *g*
Php 3: 8 compared to the surpassing *g*

GREED (GREEDY)

Lk 12: 15 on your guard against all kinds of *g*
Ro   1: 29 kind of wickedness, evil, *g*
Eph 5: 3 or of any kind of impurity, or of *g,*
Col 3: 5 evil desires and *g,* which is idolatry
2Pe 2: 14 experts in *g*— an accursed brood!

GREEDY (GREED)

Pr 15: 27 A *g* man brings trouble
1Co 6: 10 nor thieves nor the *g* nor drunkards
Eph 5: 5 No immoral, impure or *g* person—
1Pe 5: 2 not *g* for money, but eager to serve;

GREEK (GREEKS)

Gal 3: 28 There is neither Jew nor *G,*
Col 3: 11 Here there is no *G* or Jew,

GREEKS (GREEK)

1Co 1: 22 miraculous signs and *G* look

GREEN

Ps 23: 2 makes me lie down in *g* pastures,

GREW (GROW)

Lk   1: 80 And the child *g* and became strong
    2: 52 And Jesus *g* in wisdom and stature,
Ac   9: 31 by the Holy Spirit, it *g* in numbers,
    16: 5 in the faith and *g* daily in numbers.

GRIEF (GRIEFS GRIEVANCES GRIEVE GRIEVED)

Ps 10: 14 O God, do see trouble and *g;*
Pr 10: 1 but a foolish son *g* to his mother.
    14: 13 and joy may end in *g.*
    17: 21 To have a fool for a son brings *g;*
Ecc 1: 18 the more knowledge, the more *g.*
La   3: 32 Though he brings *g,* he will show
Jn 16: 20 but your *g* will turn to joy.
1Pe 1: 6 had to suffer *g* in all kinds of trials.

GRIEFS* (GRIEF)

1Ti 6: 10 pierced themselves with many *g.*

GRIEVANCES* (GRIEF)

Col 3: 13 forgive whatever *g* you may have

GRIEVE (GRIEF)

Eph 4: 30 do not *g* the Holy Spirit of God,
1Th 4: 13 or to *g* like the rest of men,

GRIEVED (GRIEF)

Isa 63: 10 and *g* his Holy Spirit.

GRINDING

Lk 17: 35 women will be *g* grain together;

GROAN (GROANING GROANS)

Ro   8: 23 *g* inwardly as we wait eagerly
2Co 5: 4 For while we are in this tent, we *g*

GROANING (GROAN)

Ex   2: 24 God heard their *g* and he
Eze 21: 7 'Why are you *g?*' you shall say,
Ro   8: 22 that the whole creation has been *g*

GROANS (GROAN)

Ro   8: 26 with *g* that words cannot express.

GROUND

Ge   1: 10 God called the dry *g* "land,"
    3: 17 "Cursed is the *g* because of you;
    4: 10 blood cries out to me from the *g.*
Ex   3: 5 where you are standing is holy *g.*"
    15: 19 walked through the sea on dry *g.*
Isa 53: 2 and like a root out of dry *g.*
Mt 10: 29 fall to the *g* apart from the will
    25: 25 and hid your talent in the *g.*
Jn   8: 6 to write on the *g* with his finger.
Eph 6: 13 you may be able to stand your *g,*

GROW (FULL-GROWN GREW GROWING GROWS)

Pr 13: 11 by little makes it *g.*
    20: 13 not love sleep or you will *g* poor;
Isa 40: 31 they will run and not *g* weary,
Mt   6: 28 See how the lilies of the field *g.*
1Co 3: 6 watered it, but God made it *g.*
2Pe 3: 18 But *g* in the grace and knowledge

GROWING (GROW)

Col 1: 6 this gospel is bearing fruit and *g,*
    1: 10 *g* in the knowledge of God,
2Th 1: 3 your faith is *g* more and more,

GROWS (GROW)

Eph 4: 16 *g* and builds itself up in love,
Col 2: 19 *g* as God causes it to grow.

GRUMBLE (GRUMBLED GRUMBLERS GRUMBLING)

1Co 10: 10 And do not *g,* as some of them did
Jas 5: 9 Don't *g* against each other,

GRUMBLED (GRUMBLE)

Ex 15: 24 So the people *g* against Moses,
Nu 14: 29 and who has *g* against me.

GRUMBLERS* (GRUMBLE)

Jude : 16 These men are *g* and faultfinders;

GRUMBLING (GRUMBLE)

Jn   6: 43 "Stop *g* among yourselves,"
1Pe 4: 9 to one another without *g.*

GUARANTEE (GUARANTEEING)

Heb 7: 22 Jesus has become the *g*

GUARANTEEING* (GUARANTEE)

2Co 1: 22 as a deposit, *g* what is to come.
    5: 5 as a deposit, *g* what is to come.
Eph 1: 14 who is a deposit *g* our inheritance

GUARD (GUARDS)

1Sa 2: 9 He will *g* the feet of his saints,
Ps 141: 3 Set a *g* over my mouth, O LORD;
Pr   2: 11 and understanding will *g* you.
    4: 13 *g* it well, for it is your life.
    4: 23 Above all else, *g* your heart,
    7: 2 *g* my teachings as the apple
Isa 52: 12 the God of Israel will be your rear *g*
Mk 13: 33 Be on *g!* Be alert! You do not know
Lk 12: 1 "Be on your *g* against the yeast
    12: 15 Be on your *g* against all kinds
Ac 20: 31 So be on your *g!* Remember that
1Co 16: 13 Be on your *g;* stand firm in the faith
Php 4: 7 will *g* your hearts and your minds
1Ti 6: 20 *g* what has been entrusted
2Ti 1: 14 *G* the good deposit that was

GUARDS (GUARD)

Pr 13: 3 He who *g* his lips *g* his life,
    19: 16 who obeys instructions *g* his life,
    21: 23 He who *g* his mouth and his tongue
    22: 5 he who *g* his soul stays far

GUIDANCE (GUIDE)

Pr   1: 5 and let the discerning get *g*—
    11: 14 For lack of *g* a nation falls,
    24: 6 for waging war you need *g,*

GUIDE (GUIDANCE GUIDED GUIDES)

Ex 13: 21 of cloud to *g* them on their way
    15: 13 In your strength you will *g* them
Ne   9: 19 cease to *g* them on their path,
Ps 25: 5 *g* me in your truth and teach me,
    43: 3 let them *g* me;
    48: 14 he will be our *g* even to the end.
    67: 4 and *g* the nations of the earth.
    73: 24 You *g* me with your counsel,
    139: 10 even there your hand will *g* me,
Pr   4: 11 I *g* you in the way of wisdom
    6: 22 When you walk, they will *g* you;
Isa 58: 11 The LORD will *g* you always;
Jn 16: 13 comes, he will *g* you into all truth.

GUIDED (GUIDE)

Ps 107: 30 he *g* them to their desired haven.

GUIDES (GUIDE)

Ps 23: 3 He *g* me in paths of righteousness
    25: 9 He *g* the humble in what is right
Pr 11: 3 The integrity of the upright *g* them,
    16: 23 A wise man's heart *g* his mouth,
Mt 23: 16 "Woe to you, blind *g!* You say,
    23: 24 You blind *g!* You strain out a gnat

GUILT (GUILTY)

Lev 5: 15 It is a *g* offering.
Ps 32: 5 the *g* of my sin.
    38: 4 My *g* has overwhelmed me
Isa 6: 7 your *g* is taken away and your sin
Jer 2: 22 the stain of your *g* is still before me
Eze 18: 19 'Why does the son not share the *g*

GUILTY (GUILT)

Ex 34: 7 does not leave the *g* unpunished;
Mk   3: 29 Spirit will never be forgiven; he is *g*
Jn   8: 46 Can any of you prove me *g* of sin?
1Co 11: 27 in an unworthy manner will be *g*
Heb 10: 2 and would no longer have felt *g*
    10: 22 to cleanse us from a *g* conscience

Jas   2: 10 at just one point is *g* of breaking all

HABAKKUK*

Prophet to Judah (Hab 1:1; 3:1).

HABIT

1Ti   5: 13 they get into the *h* of being idle
Heb 10: 25 as some are in the *h* of doing.

HADAD

Edomite adversary of Solomon (1Ki 11:14-25).

HADES*

Mt   16: 18 the gates of *H* will not overcome it.
Rev   1: 18 And I hold the keys of death and *H*
        6: 8 *H* was following close behind him.
      20: 13 and *H* gave up the dead that were
      20: 14 *H* were thrown into the lake of fire.

HAGAR

Servant of Sarah, wife of Abraham, mother of Ishmael (Ge 16:1-6; 25:12). Driven away by Sarah while pregnant (Ge 16:5-16); after birth of Isaac (Ge 21:9-21; Gal 4:21-31).

HAGGAI*

Post-exilic prophet who encouraged rebuilding of the temple (Ezr 5:1; 6:14; Hag 1-2).

HAIL

Ex   9: 19 the *h* will fall on every man
Rev   8: 7 and there came *h* and fire mixed

HAIR (HAIRS HAIRY)

Lev 19: 27 " 'Do not cut the *h* at the sides
Nu   6: 5 he must let the *h* of his head grow
Pr   16: 31 Gray *h* is a crown of splendor;
      20: 29 gray *h* the splendor of the old.
Lk   7: 44 and wiped them with her *h*.
       21: 18 But not a *h* of your head will perish
Jn   11: 2 and wiped his feet with her *h*.
      12: 3 and wiped his feet with her *h*.
1Co 11: 6 for a woman to have her *h* cut
       11: 6 she should have her *h* cut off;
       11: 14 that if a man has long *h*,
       11: 15 For long *h* is given to her
       11: 15 but that if a woman has long *h*,
1Ti   2: 9 not with braided *h* or gold or pearls
1Pe   3: 3 as braided *h* and the wearing
Rev   1: 14 and *h* were white like wool,

HAIRS (HAIR)

Mt   10: 30 even the very *h* of your head are all
Lk   12: 7 the very *h* of your head are all

HAIRY (HAIR)

Ge   27: 11 "But my brother Esau is a *h* man,

HALF

Ex   30: 13 This *h* shekel is an offering
Jos   8: 33 *H* of the people stood in front
1Ki   3: 25 give *h* to one and *h* to the other."
      10: 7 Indeed, not even *h* was told me;
Est   5: 3 Even up to *h* the kingdom,
Da   7: 25 him for a time, times and *h* a time.
Mk   6: 23 up to *h* my kingdom."

HALF-TRIBE (TRIBE)

Nu   32: 33 and the *h* of Manasseh son

HALLELUJAH*

Rev 19: 1, 3, 4, 6.

HALLOWED* (HOLY)

Mt   6: 9 *h* be your name,
Lk   11: 2 *h* be your name,

HALT

Job 38: 11 here is where your proud waves *h'* ?

HALTER*

Pr   26: 3 for the horse, a *h* for the donkey,

HAM

Son of Noah (Ge 5:32; 1Ch 1:4), father of Canaan (Ge 9:18; 10:6-20; 1Ch 1:8-16). Saw Noah's nakedness (Ge 9:20-27).

HAMAN

Agagite nobleman honored by Xerxes (Est 3:1-2). Plotted to exterminate the Jews because of Mordecai (Est 3:3-15). Forced to honor Mordecai (Est 5-6). Plot exposed by Esther (Est 5:1-8; 7:1-8). Hanged (Est 7:9-10).

HAMPERED*

Pr   4: 12 you walk, your steps will not be *h*;

HAND (HANDED HANDFUL HANDS OPENHANDED)

Ge   24: 2 "Put your *h* under my thigh.
      47: 29 put your *h* under my thigh
Ex   13: 3 out of it with a mighty *h*.
      15: 6 Your right *h*, O LORD,
      33: 22 and cover you with my *h*
Dt   12: 7 in everything you have put your *h*
1Ki   8: 42 and your mighty *h* and your
      13: 4 But the *h* he stretched out
1Ch 29: 14 you only what comes from your *h*.
      29: 16 it comes from your *h*, and all
2Ch   6: 15 with your *h* you have fulfilled it—
Ne   4: 17 materials did their work with one *h*
Job 40: 4 I put my *h* over my mouth.
Ps   16: 8 Because he is at my right *h*,
      32: 4 your *h* was heavy upon me;
      37: 24 the LORD upholds him with his *h*.
      44: 3 it was your right *h*. your arm,
      45: 9 at your right *h* is the royal bride
      63: 8 your right *h* upholds me.
      75: 8 In the *h* of the LORD is a cup
      91: 7 ten thousand at your right *h*,
      98: 1 his right *h* and his holy arm
     109: 31 at the right *h* of the needy one,
     110: 1 "Sit at my right *h*
     137: 5 may my right *h* forget its skill,
     139: 10 even there your *h* will guide me,
     145: 16 You open your *h*
Pr   27: 16 or grasping oil with the *h*.
Ecc   5: 15 that he can carry in his *h*.
       9: 10 Whatever your *h* finds to do,
Isa 11: 8 the young child put his *h*
      40: 12 the waters in the hollow of his *h*,
      41: 13 who takes hold of your right *h*
      44: 5 still another will write on his *h*,
      48: 13 My own *h* laid the foundations
      64: 8 we are all the work of your *h*.
La   3: 3 he has turned his *h* against me
Da   10: 10 *h* touched me and set me trembling
Jnh   4: 11 people who cannot tell their right *h*
Hab   3: 4 rays flashed from his *h*,
Mt   5: 30 if your right *h* causes you to sin,
        6: 3 know what your right *h* is doing,
      12: 10 a man with a shriveled *h* was there.
      18: 8 If your *h* or your foot causes you
      22: 44 "Sit at my right *h*
      26: 64 at the right *h* of the Mighty One
Mk   3: 1 a man with a shriveled *h* was there.
        9: 43 If your *h* causes you to sin, cut it off
      12: 36 "Sit at my right *h*
      16: 19 and he sat at the right *h* of God.
Lk   6: 6 there whose right *h* was shriveled.
      20: 42 "Sit at my right *h*
      22: 69 at the right *h* of the mighty God."
Jn   10: 28 one can snatch them out of my *h*.
      20: 27 Reach out your *h* and put it
Ac   7: 55 Jesus standing at the right *h* of God
1Co 12: 15 I am not a *h*, I do not belong
Heb   1: 13 "Sit at my right *h*
Rev 13: 16 to receive a mark on his right *h*

HANDED (HAND)

Da   7: 25 The saints will be *h* over to him
1Ti   1: 20 whom I have *h* over to Satan

HANDFUL (HAND)

Ecc   4: 6 Better one *h* with tranquillity

HANDLE (HANDLES)

Col   2: 21 "Do not *h*! Do not taste! Do not

HANDLES (HANDLE)

2Ti   2: 15 who correctly *h* the word of truth.

HANDS (HAND)

Ge   27: 22 but the *h* are the *h* of Esau."
Ex   17: 11 As long as Moses held up his *h*,

Ex   29: 10 his sons shall lay their *h* on its head
Dt   6: 8 Tie them as symbols on your *h*
Jdg   7: 6 lapped with their *h* to their mouths.
2Ki 11: 12 and the people clapped their *h*
2Ch   6: 4 who with his *h* has fulfilled what he
Ps   22: 16 they have pierced my *h*
      24: 4 He who has clean *h* and a pure
      31: 5 Into your *h* I commit my spirit;
      31: 15 My times are in your *h*;
      47: 1 Clap your *h*, all you nations;
      63: 4 and in your name I will lift up my *h*
Pr   10: 4 Lazy *h* make a man poor,
      21: 25 because his *h* refuse to work.
      31: 13 and works with eager *h*.
      31: 20 and extends her *h* to the needy.
Ecc 10: 18 if his *h* are idle, the house leaks.
Isa 35: 3 Strengthen the feeble *h*,
      49: 16 you on the palms of my *h*;
      55: 12 will clap their *h*.
      65: 2 All day long I have held out my *h*
La   3: 41 Let us lift up our hearts and our *h*
Lk   23: 46 into your *h* I commit my spirit."
Ac   6: 6 who prayed and laid their *h*
        8: 18 at the laying on of the apostles' *h*,
      13: 3 they placed their *h* on them
      19: 6 When Paul placed his *h* on them,
      28: 8 placed his *h* on him and healed him
1Th   4: 11 and to work with your *h*,
1Ti   2: 8 to lift up holy *h* in prayer,
        4: 14 body of elders laid their *h* on you.
        5: 22 hasty in the laying on of *h*,
2Ti   1: 6 you through the laying on of my *h*.
Heb   6: 2 the laying on of *h*, the resurrection

HANDSOME*

Ge   39: 6 Now Joseph was well-built and *h*,
1Sa 16: 12 a fine appearance and *h* features.
      17: 42 ruddy and *h*, and he despised him.
2Sa 14: 25 praised for his *h* appearance
1Ki   1: 6 also very *h* and was born next
SS   1: 16 *Beloved* How *h* you are, my lover!
Eze 23: 6 all of them *h* young men,
      23: 12 horsemen, all *h* young men.
      23: 23 with them, *h* young men.
Da   1: 4 without any physical defect, *h*,
Zec 11: 13 the *h* price at which they priced me

HANG (HANGED HANGING HUNG)

Mt   22: 40 and the Prophets *h* on these two

HANGED (HANG)

Mt   27: 5 Then he went away and *h* himself.

HANGING (HANG)

Ac   10: 39 They killed him by *h* him on a tree,

HANNAH*

Wife of Elkanah, mother of Samuel (1Sa 1). Prayer at dedication of Samuel (1Sa 2:1-10). Blessed (1Sa 2:18-21).

HAPPIER (HAPPY)

Mt   18: 13 he is *h* about that one sheep
1Co   7: 40 she is *h* if she stays as she is—

HAPPINESS* (HAPPY)

Dt   24: 5 bring *h* to the wife he has married.
Est   8: 16 For the Jews it was a time of *h*
Job   7: 7 my eyes will never see *h* again.
Ecc   2: 26 gives wisdom, knowledge and *h*,
Mt   25: 21 Come and share your master's *h*!'
      25: 23 Come and share your master's *h*!'

HAPPY* (HAPPIER HAPPINESS)

Ge   30: 13 The women will call me *h*."
      30: 13 Then Leah said, "How *h* I am!
1Ki   4: 20 they drank and they were *h*.
      10: 8 How *h* your men must be!
      10: 8 men must be! How *h* your officials,
2Ch   9: 7 How *h* your men must be!
        9: 7 men must be! How *h* your officials,
Est   5: 9 Haman went out that day *h*
        5: 14 the king to the dinner and be *h*."
Ps   10: 6 I'll always be *h* and never have
      68: 3 may they be *h* and joyful.
     113: 9 as a *h* mother of children.
     137: 8 *h* is he who repays you
Pr   15: 13 A *h* heart makes the face cheerful,

Ecc 3:12 better for men than to be *h*
5:19 to accept his lot and be *h*
7:14 When times are good, be *h;*
11: 9 Be *h,* young man, while you are
Jnh 4: 6 Jonah was very *h* about the vine.
Zec 8:19 and glad occasions and *h* festivals
1Co 7:30 those who are *h,* as if they were not
2Co 7: 9 yet now I am *h,* not because you
7:13 delighted to see how *h* Titus was,
Jas 5:13 Is anyone *h?* Let him sing songs

HARD (HARDEN HARDENED HARDENING HARDENS HARDER HARDSHIP HARDSHIPS)

Ge 18:14 Is anything too *h* for the LORD?
1Ki 10: 1 came to test him with *h* questions.
Pr 14:23 All *h* work brings a profit,
Jer 32:17 Nothing is too *h* for you.
Zec 7:12 They made their hearts as *h* as flint
Mt 19:23 it is *h* for a rich man
Mk 10: 5 your hearts were *h* that Moses
Jn 6:60 disciples said, "This is a *h* teaching.
Ac 20:35 of *h* work we must help the weak,
26:14 It is *h* for you to kick
Ro 16:12 woman who has worked very *h*
1Co 4:12 We work *h* with our own hands.
2Co 6: 5 imprisonments and riots; in *h* work
1Th 5:12 to respect those who work *h*
Rev 2: 2 your *h* work and your

HARDEN (HARD)

Ex 4:21 I will *h* his heart so that he will not
Ps 95: 8 do not *h* your hearts as you did
Ro 9:18 he hardens whom he wants to *h.*
Heb 3: 8 do not *h* your hearts

HARDENED (HARD)

Ex 10:20 But the LORD *h* Pharaoh's heart,

HARDENING* (HARD)

Ro 11:25 Israel has experienced a *h* in part
Eph 4:18 in them due to the *h* of their hearts.

HARDENS* (HARD)

Pr 28:14 he who *h* his heart falls into trouble
Ro 9:18 and he *h* whom he wants to harden.

HARDER (HARD)

1Co 15:10 No, I worked *h* than all of them—
2Co 11:23 I have worked much *h,* been

HARDHEARTED* (HEART)

Dt 15: 7 do not be *h* or tightfisted

HARDSHIP (HARD)

Ro 8:35 Shall trouble or *h* or persecution
2Ti 2: 3 Endure *h* with us like a good
4: 5 endure *h,* do the work
Heb 12: 7 Endure *h* as discipline; God is

HARDSHIPS (HARD)

Ac 14:22 go through many *h* to enter
2Co 6: 4 in troubles, *h* and distresses;
12:10 in insults, in *h,* in persecutions,
Rev 2: 3 and have endured *h* for my name,

HARLOT see PROSTITUTE

HARM (HARMS)

1Ch 16:22 do my prophets no *h.''*
Ps 105:15 do my prophets no *h.''*
121: 6 the sun will not *h* you by day,
Pr 3:29 not plot *h* against your neighbor,
12:21 No *h* befalls the righteous,
31:12 She brings him good, not *h,*
Jer 10: 5 they can do no *h*
29:11 to prosper you and not to *h* you,
Ro 13:10 Love does no *h* to its neighbor.
1Co 11:17 for your meetings do more *h*
1Jn 5:18 the evil one cannot *h* him.

HARMONY*

Zec 6:13 there will be *h* between the two.'
Ro 12:16 live in *h* with one another.
2Co 6:15 What *h* is there between Christ
1Pe 3: 8 live in *h* with one another;

HARMS* (HARM)

Pr 8:36 whoever fails to find me *h* himself;

HARP (HARPS)

Ge 4:21 the father of all who play the *h*
1Sa 16:23 David would take his *h* and play.
Ps 33: 2 Praise the LORD with the *h;*
98: 5 with the *h* and the sound of singing
150: 3 praise him with the *h* and lyre,
Rev 5: 8 Each one had a *h* and they were

HARPS (HARP)

Ps 137: 2 we hung our *h,*

HARSH

Pr 15: 1 but a *h* word stirs up anger.
Col 2:23 and their *h* treatment of the body,
3:19 and do not be *h* with them.
1Pe 2:18 but also to those who are *h.*
Jude : 15 of all the *h* words ungodly sinners

HARVEST (HARVESTERS)

Ge 8:22 seedtime and *h,*
Ex 23:16 the Feast of *H* with the firstfruits
Dt 16:15 God will bless you in all your *h*
Pr 10: 5 during *h* is a disgraceful son.
Jer 8:20 "The *h* is past,
Joel 3:13 for the *h* is ripe.
Mt 9:37 *h* is plentiful but the workers are
Lk 10: 2 He told them, "The *h* is plentiful,
Jn 4:35 at the fields! They are ripe for *h.*
1Co 9:11 if we reap a material *h* from you?
2Co 9:10 the *h* of your righteousness.
Gal 6: 9 at the proper time we will reap a *h*
Heb 12:11 it produces a *h* of righteousness
Jas 3:18 in peace raise a *h* of righteousness.
Rev 14:15 for the *h* of the earth is ripe.''

HARVESTERS (HARVEST)

Ru 2: 3 to glean in the fields behind the *h.*

HASTE (HASTEN HASTY)

Ex 12:11 it in *h;* it is the LORD's Passover.
Pr 21: 5 as surely as *h* leads to poverty.
29:20 Do you see a man who speaks in *h?*

HASTEN (HASTE)

Ps 70: 1 *H,* O God, to save me;
119: 60 I will *h* and not delay

HASTY* (HASTE)

Pr 19: 2 nor to be *h* and miss the way.
Ecc 5: 2 do not be *h* in your heart
1Ti 5:22 Do not be *h* in the laying

HATE (GOD-HATERS HATED HATES HATING HATRED)

Lev 19:17 '' 'Do not *h* your brother
Ps 5: 5 you *h* all who do wrong.
36: 2 too much to detect or *h* his sin.
45: 7 righteousness and *h* wickedness;
97:10 those who love the LORD *h* evil,
119:104 therefore I *h* every wrong path.
119:163 I *h* and abhor falsehood
139: 21 Do I not *h* those who *h* you,
Pr 8:13 To fear the LORD is to *h* evil;
9: 8 rebuke a mocker or he will *h* you;
13: 5 The righteous *h* what is false,
25:17 too much of you, and he will *h* you.
29:10 Bloodthirsty men *h* a man
Ecc 3: 8 a time to love and a time to *h,*
Isa 61: 8 I *h* robbery and iniquity.
Eze 35: 6 Since you did not *h* bloodshed,
Am 5:15 *H* evil, love good;
Mal 2:16 "I *h* divorce," says the LORD God
Mt 5:43 your neighbor and *h* your enemy.'
10:22 All men will *h* you because of me,
Lk 6:22 Blessed are you when men *h* you,
6:27 do good to those who *h* you,
14:26 does not *h* his father and mother,
Ro 12: 9 *H* what is evil; cling to what is good

HATED (HATE)

Mal 1: 3 loved Jacob, but Esau I have *h,*
Jn 15:18 keep in mind that it *h* me first.
Ro 9:13 "Jacob I loved, but Esau I *h*"
Eph 5:29 no one ever *h* his own body,
Heb 1: 9 righteousness and *h* wickedness;

HATES (HATE)

Pr 6:16 There are six things the LORD *h,*

HATING (HATE)

Jude : 23 *h* even the clothing stained

HATRED (HATE)

Pr 10:12 *H* stirs up dissension,
15:17 than a fattened calf with *h.*
Jas 4: 4 with the world is *h* toward God?

HAUGHTY

Pr 6:17 detestable to him: / *h* eyes,
16:18 a *h* spirit before a fall.

HAVEN

Ps 107: 30 he guided them to their desired *h.*

HAY

1Co 3:12 costly stones, wood, *h* or straw,

HEAD (HEADS HOTHEADED)

Ge 3:15 he will crush your *h,*
Nu 6: 5 no razor may be used on his *h.*
Jdg 16:17 If my *h* were shaved, my strength
1Sa 9: 2 a *h* taller than any of the others.
2Sa 18: 9 Absalom's *h* got caught in the tree.
Ps 23: 5 You anoint my *h* with oil;
133: 2 is like precious oil poured on the *h,*
Pr 10: 6 Blessings crown the *h*
25:22 will heap burning coals on his *h*
Isa 59:17 and the helmet of salvation on his *h*
Eze 33: 4 his blood will be on his own *h.*
Mt 8:20 of Man has no place to lay his *h.''*
Jn 19: 2 crown of thorns and put it on his *h.*
Ro 12:20 will heap burning coals on his *h.''*
1Co 11: 3 and the *h* of Christ is God.
11: 5 her *h* uncovered dishonors her *h*—
12:21 And the *h* cannot say to the feet,
Eph 1:22 him to be *h* over everything
5:23 For the husband is the *h* of the wife
Col 1:18 And he is the *h* of the body,
2Ti 4: 5 keep your *h* in all situations,
Rev 14:14 with a crown of gold on his *h*
19:12 and on his *h* are many crowns.

HEADS (HEAD)

Lev 26:13 you to walk with *h* held high.
Ps 22: 7 they hurl insults, shaking their *h:*
24: 7 Lift up your *h,* O you gates;
Isa 35:10 everlasting joy will crown their *h.*
51:11 everlasting joy will crown their *h.*
Mt 27:39 shaking their *h* and saying,
Lk 21:28 stand up and lift up your *h,*
Ac 18: 6 ''Your blood be on your own *h!*
Rev 4: 4 had crowns of gold on their *h*

HEAL* (HEALED HEALING HEALS)

Nu 12:13 please *h* her!'' The LORD replied
Dt 32:39 I have wounded and I will *h,*
2Ki 20: 5 and seen your tears; I will *h* you.
20: 8 the sign that the LORD will *h* me
2Ch 7:14 their sin and will *h* their land.
Job 5:18 he injures, but his hands also *h.*
Ps 6: 2 *h* me, for my bones are in agony.
41: 4 *h* me, for I have sinned against you
Ecc 3: 3 a time to kill and a time to *h,*
Isa 19:22 he will strike them and *h* them.
19:22 respond to their pleas and *h* them.
57:18 seen his ways, but I will *h* him;
57:19 ''And I will *h* them.
Jer 17:14 *H* me, O LORD, and I will be
30:17 and *h* your wounds,'
33: 6 I will *h* my people and will let them
La 2:13 Who can *h* you?
Hos 5:13 not able to *h* your sores.
6: 1 but he will *h* us;
7: 1 whenever I would *h* Israel,
14: 4 ''I will *h* their waywardness
Na 3:19 Nothing can *h* your wound;
Zec 11:16 or seek the young, or *h* the injured,
Mt 8: 7 said to him, ''I will go and *h* him.''
10: 1 to *h* every disease and sickness.

Mt 10: 8 *H* the sick, raise the dead,
  12: 10 "Is it lawful to *h* on the Sabbath?"
  13: 15 and turn, and I would *h* them.'
  17: 16 but they could not *h* him."
Mk 3: 2 if he would *h* him on the Sabbath.
  6: 5 on a few sick people and *h* them.
Lk 4: 23 to me: 'Physician, *h* yourself!
  5: 17 present for him to *h* the sick.
  6: 7 to see if he would *h* on the Sabbath.
  7: 3 him to come and *h* his servant.
  8: 43 years, but no one could *h* her.
  9: 2 kingdom of God and to *h* the sick.
  10: 9 *H* the sick who are there
  13: 32 and *h* people today and tomorrow,
  14: 3 "Is it lawful to *h* on the Sabbath
Jn 4: 47 begged him to come and *h* his son,
  12: 40 nor turn—and I would *h* them."
Ac 4: 30 Stretch out your hand to *h*
  28: 27 and turn, and I would *h* them.'

HEALED* (HEAL)

Ge 20: 17 to God, and God *h* Abimelech,
Ex 21: 19 and see that he is completely *h*.
Lev 13: 37 hair has grown in it, the itch is *h*.
  14: 3 If the person has been *h*
Jos 5: 8 were in camp until they were *h*.
1Sa 6: 3 you will be *h*, and you will know
2Ki 2: 21 LORD says: 'I have *h* this water.
2Ch 30: 20 heard Hezekiah and *h* the people.
Ps 30: 2 and you *h* me.
  107: 20 He sent forth his word and *h* them;
Isa 6: 10 and turn and be *h*."
  53: 5 and by his wounds we are *h*.
Jer 14: 19 us so that we cannot be *h*?
  17: 14 Heal me, O LORD, and I will be *h*;
  51: 8 perhaps she can be *h*.
  51: 9 but she cannot be *h*;
  51: 9 " 'We would have *h* Babylon,
Eze 34: 4 the weak or *h* the sick
Hos 11: 3 it was I who *h* them.
Mt 4: 24 and the paralyzed, and he *h* them.
  8: 8 the word, and my servant will be *h*.
  8: 13 his servant was *h* at that very hour.
  8: 16 with a word and *h* all the sick.
  9: 21 If I only touch his cloak, I will be *h*
  9: 22 he said, "your faith has *h* you."
  9: 22 woman was *h* from that moment.
  12: 15 him, and he *h* all their sick,
  12: 22 Jesus *h* him, so that he could both
  14: 14 on them and *h* their sick.
  14: 36 and all who touched him were *h*.
  15: 28 And her daughter was *h*
  15: 30 laid them at his feet; and he *h* them
  17: 18 and he was *h* from that moment.
  19: 2 followed him, and he *h* them there.
  21: 14 to him at the temple, and he *h* them
Mk 1: 34 and Jesus *h* many who had various
  3: 10 For he had *h* many, so that those
  5: 23 hands on her so that she will be *h*
  5: 28 If I just touch his clothes, I will be *h*
  5: 34 "Daughter, your faith has *h* you.
  6: 13 people with oil and *h* them.
  6: 56 and all who touched him were *h*.
  10: 52 said Jesus, "your faith has *h* you."
Lk 4: 40 hands on each one, he *h* them.
  5: 15 and to be *h* of their sicknesses.
  6: 18 and to be *h* of their diseases.
  7: 7 the word, and my servant will be *h*.
  8: 47 and how she had been instantly *h*.
  8: 48 "Daughter, your faith has *h* you.
  8: 50 just believe, and she will be *h*."
  9: 11 and *h* those who needed healing.
  9: 42 the boy and gave him back
  13: 14 Jesus had *h* on the Sabbath,
  13: 14 So come and be *h* on those days,
  14: 4 he *h* him and sent him away.
  17: 15 when he saw he was *h*, came back,
  18: 42 your sight; your faith has *h* you."
  22: 51 touched the man's ear and *h* him.
Jn 5: 10 said to the man who had been *h*,
  5: 13 man who was *h* had no idea who it
Ac 4: 9 and are asked how he was *h*,
  4: 10 stands before you *h*.
  4: 14 who had been *h* standing there
  4: 22 man who was miraculously *h* was
  5: 16 evil spirits, and all of them were *h*.
  8: 7 paralytics and cripples were *h*.
  14: 9 saw that he had faith to be *h*

Ac 28: 8 placed his hands on him and *h* him.
Heb 12: 13 may not be disabled, but rather *h*.
Jas 5: 16 for each other so that you may be *h*
1Pe 2: 24 by his wounds you have been *h*.
Rev 13: 3 but the fatal wound had been *h*.
  13: 12 whose fatal wound had been *h*.

HEALING* (HEAL)

2Ch 28: 15 food and drink, and *h* balm.
Pr 12: 18 but the tongue of the wise brings *h*.
  13: 17 but a trustworthy envoy brings *h*.
  15: 4 The tongue that brings *h* is a tree
  16: 24 sweet to the soul and *h* to the bones
Isa 58: 8 and your *h* will quickly appear;
Jer 8: 15 for a time of *h*
  8: 22 Why then is there no *h*
  14: 19 for a time of *h*
  30: 12 your injury beyond *h*.
  30: 13 no *h* for you.
  33: 6 I will bring health and *h* to it;
  46: 11 there is no *h* for you.
Eze 30: 21 It has not been bound up for *h*
  47: 12 for food and their leaves for *h*."
Mal 4: 2 rise with *h* in its wings.
Mt 4: 23 and *h* every disease and sickness
  9: 35 and *h* every disease and sickness.
Lk 6: 19 coming from him and *h* them all.
  9: 6 gospel and *h* people everywhere.
  9: 11 and healed those who needed *h*.
Jn 7: 23 angry with me for *h* the whole man
Ac 3: 16 him that has given this complete *h*
  10: 38 *h* all who were under the power
1Co 12: 9 to another gifts of *h*
  12: 28 also those having gifts of *h*,
  12: 30 Do all have gifts of *h*? Do all speak
Rev 22: 2 are for the *h* of the nations.

HEALS* (HEAL)

Ex 15: 26 for I am the LORD, who *h* you."
Lev 13: 18 a boil on his skin and it *h*,
Ps 103: 3 and *h* all your diseases;
  147: 3 He *h* the brokenhearted
Isa 30: 26 and *h* the wounds he inflicted.
Ac 9: 34 said to him, "Jesus Christ *h* you.

HEALTH* (HEALTHIER HEALTHY)

1Sa 25: 6 And good *h* to all that is yours!
  25: 6 Good *h* to you and your household
Ps 38: 3 of your wrath there is no *h*
  38: 7 there is no *h* in my body.
Pr 3: 8 This will bring *h* to your body
  4: 22 and *h* to a man's whole body.
  15: 30 and good news gives *h* to the bones
Isa 38: 16 You restored me to *h*
Jer 30: 17 But I will restore you to *h*
  33: 6 I will bring *h* and healing to it;
3Jn : 2 I pray that you may enjoy good *h*

HEALTHIER* (HEALTH)

Da 1: 15 end of the ten days they looked *h*

HEALTHY* (HEALTH)

Ge 41: 5 Seven heads of grain, *h* and good,
  41: 7 of grain swallowed up the seven *h*,
Ps 73: 4 their bodies are *h* and strong.
Zec 11: 16 or heal the injured, or feed the *h*,
Mt 9: 12 "It is not the *h* who need a doctor,
Mk 2: 17 "It is not the *h* who need a doctor,
Lk 5: 31 "It is not the *h* who need a doctor,

HEAP

Pr 25: 22 you will *h* burning coals
Ro 12: 20 you will *h* burning coals

HEAR (HEARD HEARING HEARS)

Ex 15: 14 The nations will *h* and tremble;
  22: 27 I will *h*, for I am compassionate.
Nu 14: 13 Then the Egyptians will *h* about it!
Dt 1: 16 *H* the disputes between your
  4: 36 heaven he made you *h* his voice
  6: 4 *H*, O Israel: The LORD our God,
  19: 20 The rest of the people will *h* of this
  31: 13 must *h* it and learn
Jos 7: 9 of the country will *h* about this
1Ki 8: 30 *H* the supplication of your servant
2Ki 19: 16 O LORD, and *h*; open your eyes,
2Ch 7: 14 then will I *h* from heaven
Job 31: 35 ("Oh, that I had someone to *h* me!

Ps 94: 9 he who implanted the ear not *h*?
  95: 7 Today, if you *h* his voice,
Ecc 7: 21 or you may *h* your servant cursing
Isa 21: 3 I am staggered by what I *h*,
  29: 18 that day the deaf will *h* the words
  30: 21 your ears will *h* a voice behind you,
  51: 7 *H* me, you who know what is right,
  59: 1 nor his ear too dull to *h*.
  65: 24 while they are still speaking I will *h*
Jer 5: 21 who have ears but do not *h*:
Eze 33: 7 so *h* the word I speak and give
  37: 4 'Dry bones, *h* the word
Mt 11: 5 the deaf *h*, the dead are raised,
  11: 15 He who has ears, let him *h*.
  13: 17 and to *h* what you *h* but did not *h* it
Mk 12: 29 answered Jesus, "is this: '*H*,
Lk 7: 22 the deaf *h*, the dead are raised,
Jn 8: 47 reason you do not *h* is that you do
Ac 13: 7 he wanted to *h* the word of God.
  13: 44 gathered to *h* the word of the Lord.
  17: 32 "We want to *h* you again
Ro 2: 13 is not those who *h* the law who are
  10: 14 they *h* without someone preaching
2Ti 4: 3 what their itching ears want to *h*.
Heb 3: 7 "Today, if you *h* his voice,
Rev 1: 3 and blessed are those who *h* it

HEARD (HEAR)

Ex 2: 24 God *h* their groaning and he
Dt 4: 32 has anything like it ever been *h* of?
2Sa 7: 22 as we have *h* with our own ears.
Job 42: 5 My ears had *h* of you
Isa 40: 21 Have you not *h*?
  40: 28 Have you not *h*?
  66: 8 Who has ever *h* of such a thing?
Jer 18: 13 Who has ever *h* anything like this?
Da 10: 12 your words were *h*, and I have
  12: 8 I *h*, but I did not understand.
Hab 3: 16 I *h* and my heart pounded,
Mt 5: 21 "You have *h* that it was said
  5: 27 "You have *h* that it was said,
  5: 33 you have *h* that it was said
  5: 38 "You have *h* that it was said,
  5: 43 "You have *h* that it was said,
Lk 12: 3 in the dark will be *h* in the daylight,
Jn 8: 26 and what I have *h* from him I tell
Ac 2: 6 because each one *h* them speaking
1Co 2: 9 no ear has *h*,
2Co 12: 4 He *h* inexpressible things,
1Th 2: 13 word of God, which you *h* from us,
2Ti 1: 13 What you *h* from me, keep
Jas 1: 25 not forgetting what he has *h*,
Rev 22: 8 am the one who *h* and saw these

HEARING (HEAR)

Isa 6: 9 Be ever *h*, but never understanding
Mt 13: 14 will be ever *h* but never
Mk 4: 12 ever *h* but never understanding;
Ac 28: 26 will be ever *h* but never
Ro 10: 17 faith comes from *h* the message,
1Co 12: 17 where would the sense of *h* be?

HEARS (HEAR)

Jn 5: 24 whoever *h* my word and believes
1Jn 5: 14 according to his will, he *h* us.
Rev 3: 20 If anyone *h* my voice and opens

HEART (BROKENHEARTED
FAINT-HEARTED HARDHEARTED
HEART'S HEARTACHE HEARTS
KINDHEARTED SIMPLEHEARTED
STOUTHEARTED WHOLEHEARTED
WHOLEHEARTEDLY)

Ge 6: 5 of his *h* was only evil all the time.
Ex 4: 21 But I will harden his *h*
  25: 2 each man whose *h* prompts him
  35: 21 and whose *h* moved him came
Lev 19: 17 Do not hate your brother in your *h*.
Dt 4: 9 or let them slip from your *h* as long
  4: 29 if you look for him with all your *h*
  6: 5 LORD your God with all your *h*
  10: 12 LORD your God with all your *h*
  11: 13 and to serve him with all your *h*
  13: 3 you love him with all your *h*
  15: 10 and do so without a grudging *h*;
  26: 16 observe them with all your *h*
  29: 18 you today whose *h* turns away
  30: 2 and obey him with all your *h*

Dt 30: 6 you may love him with all your *h*
30:10 LORD your God with all your *h*
Jos 22: 5 and to serve him with all your *h*
23:14 You know with all your *h*
1Sa 10: 9 God changed Saul's *h*,
12:20 serve the LORD with all your *h*.
12:24 serve him faithfully with all your *h;*
13:14 sought out a man after his own *h*
14: 7 I am with you in your *h*
16: 7 but the LORD looks at the *h*.''
17:32 ''Let no one lose *h* on account
1Ki 2: 4 faithfully before me with all their *h*
3: 9 So give your servant a discerning *h*
3:12 give you a wise and discerning *h*,
8:48 back to you with all their *h*
9: 3 and my *h* will always be there.
9: 4 walk before me in integrity of *h*
10:24 the wisdom God had put in his *h*.
11: 4 and his *h* was not fully devoted
14: 8 and followed me with all his *h*,
15:14 Asa's *h* was fully committed
2Ki 22:19 Because your *h* was responsive
23: 3 with all his *h* and all his soul,
1Ch 28: 9 for the LORD searches every *h*
2Ch 6:38 back to you with all their *h*
7:16 and my *h* will always be there.
15:12 of their fathers, with all their *h*
15:17 Asa's *h* was fully committed
17: 6 His *h* was devoted to the ways.
22: 9 sought the LORD with all his *h.''*
34:31 with all his *h* and all his soul,
36:13 stiff-necked and hardened his *h*
Ezr 1: 5 everyone whose *h* God had moved
Ne 4: 6 the people worked with all their *h.*
Job 19:27 How my *h* yearns within me!
22:22 and lay up his words in your *h*.
37: 1 ''At this my *h* pounds
Ps 9: 1 you, O LORD, with all my *h;*
14: 1 The fool says in his *h*,
16: 9 Therefore my *h* is glad
19:14 and the meditation of my *h*
20: 4 he give you the desire of your *h*
24: 4 who has clean hands and a pure *h*,
26: 2 examine my *h* and my mind;
37: 4 will give you the desires of your *h*.
37:31 The law of his God is in his *h;*
44:21 since he knows the secrets of the *h*
45: 1 My *h* is stirred by a noble theme
51:10 Create in me a pure *h*, O God,
51:17 a broken and contrite *h*,
53: 1 The fool says in his *h*,
66:18 If I had cherished sin in my *h*,
73: 1 to those who are pure in *h*.
73:26 My flesh and my *h* may fail,
86:11 give me an undivided *h*,
90:12 that we may gain a *h* of wisdom.
97:11 and joy on the upright in *h*.
108: 1 My *h* is steadfast, O God;
109:22 and my *h* is wounded within me.
111: 1 I will extol the LORD with all my *h*
112: 7 his *h* is steadfast, trusting
112: 8 His *h* is secure, he will have no fear
119: 2 and seek him with all their *h*.
119:10 I seek you with all my *h;*
119:11 I have hidden your word in my *h*
119:30 I have set my heart on your laws.
119:32 for you have set my *h* free.
119:34 and obey it with all my *h*.
119:36 Turn my *h* toward your statutes
119:58 sought your face with all my *h;*
119:69 I keep your precepts with all my *h*.
119:111 they are the joy of my *h*.
119:112 My *h* is set on keeping your
119:145 I call with all my *h;* answer me,
125: 4 to those who are upright in *h*.
138: 1 you, O LORD, with all my *h;*
139:23 Search me, O God, and know my *h*
Pr 2: 2 applying your *h* to understanding,
3: 1 but keep my commands in your *h*,
3: 3 write them on the tablet of your *h*.
3: 5 Trust in the LORD with all your *h*
4: 4 hold of my words with all your *h;*
4:21 keep them within your *h;*
4:23 Above all else, guard your *h*,
6:21 Bind them upon your *h* forever;
7: 3 write them on the tablet of your *h*.
10: 8 The wise in *h* accept commands,
13:12 Hope deferred makes the *h* sick,

Pr 14:13 Even in laughter the *h* may ache,
14:30 A *h* at peace gives life to the body,
15:13 A happy *h* makes the face cheerful,
15:15 the cheerful *h* has a continual feast.
15:28 *h* of the righteous weighs its
15:30 A cheerful look brings joy to the *h*,
16:23 A wise man's *h* guides his mouth,
17:22 A cheerful *h* is good medicine,
20: 9 can say, ''I have kept my *h* pure;
22:11 He who loves a pure *h*
22:17 apply your *h* to what I teach,
22:18 when you keep them in your *h*
23:15 My son, if your *h* is wise,
23:19 and keep your *h* on the right path.
23:26 My son, give me your *h*
27:19 so a man's *h* reflects the man.
Ecc 5: 2 do not be hasty in your *h*
8: 5 wise *h* will know the proper time
11:10 banish anxiety from your *h*
SS 3: 1 I looked for the one my *h* loves;
4: 9 You have stolen my *h*, my sister,
5: 2 *Beloved* I slept but my *h* was awake
5: 4 my *h* began to pound for him.
8: 6 Place me like a seal over your *h*,
Isa 6:10 Make the *h* of this people calloused
40:11 and carries them close to his *h;*
57:15 and to revive the *h* of the contrite.
66:14 you see this, your *h* will rejoice
Jer 3:15 give you shepherds after my own *h*,
4: 4 wash the evil from your *h*
9:26 of Israel is uncircumcised in *h*.''
17: 9 The *h* is deceitful above all things
20: 9 is in my *h* like a fire,
24: 7 I will give them a *h* to know me,
29:13 when you seek me with all your *h*.
32:39 I will give them singleness of *h*
32:41 them in this land with all my *h*
51:46 Do not lose *h* or be afraid
Eze 11:19 I will give them an undivided *h*
18:31 and get a new *h* and a new spirit.
36:26 I will give you a new *h*
44: 7 foreigners uncircumcised in *h*
Da 7: 4 and the *h* of a man was given to it.
Joel 2:12 ''return to me with all your *h*,
2:13 Rend your *h*
Zep 3:14 Be glad and rejoice with all your *h*,
Mt 5: 8 Blessed are the pure in *h*,
5:28 adultery with her in his *h*.
6:21 treasure is, there your *h* will be
11:29 for I am gentle and humble in *h*,
12:34 of the *h* the mouth speaks.
13:15 For this people's *h* has become
15:18 out of the mouth come from the *h*,
15:19 For out of the *h* come evil thoughts
18:35 forgive your brother from your *h*.''
22:37 the Lord your God with all your *h*
Mk 11:23 and does not doubt in his *h*
12:30 the Lord your God with all your *h*
12:33 To love him with all your *h*,
Lk 2:19 and pondered them in her *h*.
2:51 treasured all these things in her *h*.
6:45 out of the good stored up in his *h*,
6:45 overflow of his *h* his mouth speaks.
8:15 for those with a noble and good *h*,
10:27 the Lord your God with all your *h*
12:34 treasure is, there your *h* will be
Jn 12:27 ''Now my *h* is troubled,
Ac 1:24 ''Lord, you know everyone's *h*.
2:37 they were cut to the *h*
4:32 All the believers were one in *h*
8:21 your *h* is not right before God.
15: 8 who knows the *h*, showed that he
16:14 The Lord opened her *h* to respond
28:27 For this people's *h* has become
Ro 1: 9 with my whole *h* in preaching
2:29 is circumcision of the *h*,
10: 9 in your *h* that God raised him
10:10 is with your *h* that you believe
15: 6 with one *h* and mouth you may
1Co 14:25 the secrets of his *h* will be laid bare.
2Co 2: 4 anguish of *h* and with many tears,
4: 1 this ministry, we do not lose *h*.
4:16 Therefore we do not lose *h*.
9: 7 give what he has decided in his *h*
Eph 1:18 eyes of your *h* may be enlightened
5:19 make music in your *h* to the Lord,
6: 5 and with sincerity of *h*, just

Eph 6: 6 doing the will of God from your *h*.
Php 1: 7 since I have you in my *h;* for
Col 2: 2 is that they may be encouraged in *h*
3:22 but with sincerity of *h*
3:23 work at it with all your *h*,
1Ti 1: 5 which comes from a pure *h*
3: 1 If anyone sets his *h*
2Ti 2:22 call on the Lord out of a pure *h*.
Phm : 12 who is my very *h*— back to you.
: 20 in the Lord; refresh my *h* in Christ.
Heb 4:12 the thoughts and attitudes of the *h*.
1Pe 1:22 one another deeply, from the *h*.

HEART'S* (HEART)

2Ch 1:11 ''Since this is your *h* desire
Jer 15:16 they were my joy and my *h* delight,
Eze 24:25 delight of their eyes, their *h* desire,
Ro 10: 1 my *h* desire and prayer to God

HEARTACHE* (HEART)

Pr 15:13 but *h* crushes the spirit.

HEARTLESS*

La 4: 3 but my people have become *h*
Ro 1:31 they are senseless, faithless, *h*,

HEARTS (HEART)

Lev 26:41 their uncircumcised *h* are humbled
Dt 6: 6 are to be upon your *h*.
10:16 Circumcise your *h*, therefore,
11:18 Fix these words of mine in your *h*
30: 6 your God will circumcise your *h*
Jos 11:20 himself who hardened their *h*
24:23 and yield your *h* to the LORD,
1Sa 7: 3 to the LORD with all your *h*.
10:26 valiant men whose *h* God had
2Sa 15: 6 and so he stole the *h* of the men
1Ki 8:39 for you alone know the *h* of all men
8:61 your *h* must be fully committed
18:37 are turning their *h* back again.''
1Ch 29:18 and keep their *h* loyal to you.
2Ch 6:30 (for you alone know the *h* of men),
11:16 tribe of Israel who set their *h*
29:31 all whose *h* were willing brought
Ps 7: 9 who searches minds and *h*,
33:21 In him our *h* rejoice,
62: 8 pour out your *h* to him,
95: 8 do not harden your *h* as you did
Ecc 3:11 also set eternity in the *h* of men;
Isa 26: 8 are the desire of our *h*.
29:13 but their *h* are far from me.
35: 4 say to those with fearful *h*,
51: 7 people who have my law in your *h:*
63:17 harden our *h* so we do not revere
65:14 out of the joy of their *h*,
Jer 4: 4 circumcise your *h*,
12: 2 but far from their *h*.
17: 1 on the tablets of their *h*
31:33 and write it on their *h*.
Mal 4: 6 He will turn the *h* of the fathers
Mt 15: 8 but their *h* are far from me.
Mk 6:52 the loaves; their *h* were hardened.
7: 6 but their *h* are far from me.
7:21 out of men's *h*, come evil thoughts,
Lk 1:17 to turn the *h* of the fathers
16:15 of men, but God knows your *h*.
24:32 ''Were not our *h* burning within us
Jn 5:42 not have the love of God in your *h*.
14: 1 ''Do not let your *h* be troubled.
14:27 Do not let your *h* be troubled
Ac 7:51 with uncircumcised *h* and ears!
11:23 true to the Lord with all their *h*.
15: 9 for he purified their *h* by faith.
28:27 understand with their *h*
Ro 1:21 and their foolish *h* were darkened.
2:15 of the law are written on their *h*,
5: 5 love into our *h* by the Holy Spirit,
8:27 who searches our *h* knows
1Co 4: 5 will expose the motives of men's *h*.
2Co 1:22 put his Spirit in our *h* as a deposit,
3: 2 written on our *h*, known
3: 3 but on tablets of human *h*.
4: 6 shine in our *h* to give us the light
6:11 and opened wide our *h* to you.
6:13 to my children—open wide your *h*
7: 2 Make room for us in your *h*.
Gal 4: 6 the Spirit of his Son into our *h*,
Eph 3:17 dwell in your *h* through faith.

HEAT (continued)

Php 4: 7 will guard your *h* and your minds
Col 1: 1 set your *h* on things above,
3: 15 the peace of Christ rule in your *h*,
3: 16 with gratitude in your *h* to God.
1Th 2: 4 men but God, who tests our *h*.
3: 13 May he strengthen your *h*
2Th 2: 17 encourage your *h* and strengthen
Phm : 7 have refreshed the *h* of the saints.
Heb 3: 8 do not harden your *h*
8: 10 and write them on their *h*.
10: 16 I will put my laws in their *h*,
10: 22 having our *h* sprinkled
Jas 4: 8 purify your *h*, you double-minded.
2Pe 1: 19 the morning star rises in your *h*.
1Jn 3: 20 For God is greater than our *h*,

HEAT

Ps 19: 6 nothing is hidden from its *h*.
2Pe 3: 12 and the elements will melt in the *h*.

HEATHEN see GENTILES, NATIONS

HEAVEN (HEAVENLY HEAVENS HEAVENWARD)

Ge 14: 19 Creator of *h* and earth.
28: 12 with its top reaching to *h*,
Ex 16: 4 rain down bread from *h* for you.
20: 22 that I have spoken to you from *h*:
Dt 26: 15 from *h*, your holy dwelling place,
30: 12 "Who will ascend into *h* to get it
1Ki 8: 27 the highest *h*, cannot contain you.
8: 30 Hear from *h*, your dwelling place,
22: 19 the host of *h* standing around him
2Ki 2: 1 up to *h* in a whirlwind,
19: 15 You have made *h* and earth.
2Ch 7: 14 then will I hear from *h*
Isa 14: 12 How you have fallen from *h*,
66: 1 "*H* is my throne,
Da 7: 13 coming with the clouds of *h*.
Mt 3: 2 for the kingdom of *h* is near."
3: 16 At that moment *h* was opened,
4: 17 for the kingdom of *h* is near."
5: 12 because great is your reward in *h*,
5: 19 great in the kingdom of *h*.
6: 9 "'Our Father in *h*,
6: 10 done on earth as it is in *h*.
6: 20 up for yourselves treasures in *h*,
7: 21 Lord,' will enter the kingdom of *h*,
16: 19 bind on earth will be bound in *h*,
18: 3 will never enter the kingdom of *h*.
18: 18 bind on earth will be bound in *h*,
19: 14 the kingdom of *h* belongs to such
19: 21 and you will have treasure in *h*.
19: 23 man to enter the kingdom of *h*.
23: 13 the kingdom of *h* in men's faces.
24: 35 *H* and earth will pass away,
26: 64 and coming on the clouds of *h*."
28: 18 "All authority in *h*
Mk 1: 10 he saw *h* being torn open
10: 21 and you will have treasure in *h*.
13: 31 *H* and earth will pass away,
14: 62 and coming on the clouds of *h*."
16: 19 he was taken up into *h*
Lk 3: 21 *h* was opened and the Holy Spirit
10: 18 saw Satan fall like lightning from *h*.
10: 20 that your names are written in *h*."
12: 33 in *h* that will not be exhausted,
15: 7 in *h* over one sinner who repents
18: 22 and you will have treasure in *h*.
21: 33 *H* and earth will pass away,
24: 51 left them and was taken up into *h*.
Jn 3: 13 No one has ever gone into *h*
6: 38 down from *h* not to do my will
12: 28 Then a voice came from *h*,
Ac 1: 11 has been taken from you into *h*,
7: 49 the prophet says: "'*H* is my
7: 55 looked up to *h* and saw the glory
9: 3 a light from *h* flashed around him.
26: 19 disobedient to the vision from *h*.
Ro 10: 6 'Who will ascend into *h*?'" (that is,
1Co 15: 47 the earth, the second man from *h*.
2Co 5: 1 an eternal house in *h*, not built
12: 2 ago was caught up to the third *h*.
Eph 1: 10 to bring all things in *h*
Php 2: 10 *h* and on earth and under the earth,
3: 20 But our citizenship is in *h*.
Col 1: 16 things in *h* and on earth, visible
4: 1 that you also have a Master in *h*.

HEAVENLY (HEAVEN)

Ps 8: 5 him a little lower than the *h* beings
2Co 5: 2 to be clothed with our *h* dwelling,
Eph 1: 3 in the *h* realms with every spiritual
1: 20 at his right hand in the *h* realms,
2Ti 4: 18 bring me safely to his *h* kingdom.
Heb 12: 22 to the *h* Jerusalem, the city

HEAVENS (HEAVEN)

Ge 1: 1 In the beginning God created the *h*
11: 4 with a tower that reaches to the *h*,
Dt 33: 26 who rides on the *h* to help you
1Ki 8: 27 The *h*, even the highest heaven,
2Ch 2: 6 since the *h*, even the highest
Ezr 9: 6 and our guilt has reached to the *h*.
Ne 9: 6 You made the *h*, even the highest
Job 11: 8 They are higher than the *h*—
38: 33 Do you know the laws of the *h*?
Ps 8: 3 When I consider your *h*,
19: 1 The *h* declare the glory of God;
33: 6 of the LORD were the *h* made,
57: 5 be exalted, O God, above the *h*;
102: 25 the *h* are the work of your hands.
103: 11 as high as the *h* are above the earth,
108: 4 is your love, higher than the *h*;
115: 16 The highest *h* belong to the LORD
119: 89 it stands firm in the *h*.
135: 6 in the *h* and on the earth,
139: 8 If I go up to the *h*, you are there;
148: 1 Praise the LORD from the *h*,
Isa 40: 26 Lift your eyes and look to the *h*:
45: 8 "You *h* above, rain
51: 6 Lift up your eyes to the *h*,
55: 9 "As the *h* are higher than the earth,
65: 17 new *h* and a new earth.
Jer 31: 37 if the *h* above can be measured
32: 17 you have made the *h* and the earth
Eze 1: 1 *h* were opened and I saw visions
Da 12: 3 shine like the brightness of the *h*,
Joel 2: 30 I will show wonders in the *h*
Mt 24: 31 from one end of the *h* to the other.
Mk 13: 27 of the earth to the ends of the *h*.
Eph 4: 10 who ascended higher than all the *h*,
Heb 4: 14 priest who has gone through the *h*,
7: 26 from sinners, exalted above the *h*.
2Pe 3: 5 ago by God's word the *h* existed
3: 10 The *h* will disappear with a roar;

HEAVENWARD (HEAVEN)

Php 3: 14 for which God has called me *h*

HEAVIER (HEAVY)

Pr 27: 3 provocation by a fool is *h* than both

HEAVY (HEAVIER)

1Ki 12: 4 and the *h* yoke he put on us,
Ecc 1: 13 What a *h* burden God has laid
Isa 47: 6 you laid a very *h* yoke.
Mt 23: 4 They tie up *h* loads and put them

HEBREW (HEBREWS)

Ge 14: 13 and reported this to Abram the *H*.
2Ki 18: 26 speak to us in the hearing
Php 3: 5 tribe of Benjamin, a *H* of Hebrews;

HEBREWS (HEBREW)

Ex 9: 1 of the *H*, says: "Let my people go,
2Co 11: 22 Are they *H*? So am I.

HEBRON

Ge 13: 18 near the great trees of Mamre at *H*,
23: 2 died at Kiriath Arba (that is, *H*)
Jos 14: 13 and gave him *H* as his inheritance.
20: 7 *H*) in the hill country of Judah.
21: 13 the priest they gave *H* (a city
2Sa 2: 11 king in *H* over the house

HEDGE

Job 1: 10 "Have you not put a *h* around him

HEED (HEEDS)

Ecc 7: 5 It is better to *h* a wise man's rebuke

HEEDS (HEED)

Pr 13: 1 wise son *h* his father's instruction,
13: 18 whoever *h* correction is honored.
15: 5 whoever *h* correction shows
15: 32 whoever *h* correction gains

HEEL

Ge 3: 15 and you will strike his *h*."

HEIR (INHERIT)

Gal 4: 7 God has made you also an *h*.
Heb 1: 2 whom he appointed *h* of all things,

HEIRS (INHERIT)

Ro 8: 17 then we are *h*— *h* of God
Gal 3: 29 and *h* according to the promise.
Eph 3: 6 gospel the Gentiles are *h* together
1Pe 3: 7 as *h* with you of the gracious gift

HELD (HOLD)

Ex 17: 11 As long as Moses *h* up his hands,
Dt 4: 4 but all of you who *h* fast
2Ki 18: 6 He *h* fast to the LORD
SS 3: 4 I *h* him and would not let him go
Isa 65: 2 All day long I have *h* out my hands
Ro 10: 21 day long I have *h* out my hands
Col 2: 19 and *h* together by its ligaments

HELL*

Mt 5: 22 will be in danger of the fire of *h*.
5: 29 body to be thrown into *h*.
5: 30 for your whole body to go into *h*.
10: 28 destroy both soul and body in *h*.
18: 9 and be thrown into the fire of *h*.
23: 15 as much a son of *h* as you are.
23: 33 you escape being condemned to *h*?
Mk 9: 43 than with two hands to go into *h*,
9: 45 have two feet and be thrown into *h*.
9: 47 two eyes and be thrown into *h*.
Lk 12: 5 has power to throw you into *h*.
16: 23 In *h*, where he was in torment,
Jas 3: 6 and is itself set on fire by *h*.
2Pe 2: 4 but sent them to *h*, putting them

HELMET

Isa 59: 17 and the *h* of salvation on his head;
Eph 6: 17 Take the *h* of salvation
1Th 5: 8 and the hope of salvation as a *h*.

HELP (HELPED HELPER HELPFUL HELPING HELPLESS HELPS)

Ex 23: 5 leave it there; be sure you *h* him
Lev 25: 35 *h* him as you would an alien
Dt 33: 26 who rides on the heavens to *h* you
2Ch 16: 12 even in his illness he did not seek *h*
Ps 18: 6 I cried to my God for *h*.
30: 2 my God, I called to you for *h*
33: 20 he is our *h* and our shield.
46: 1 an ever-present *h* in trouble.
72: 12 the afflicted who have no one to *h*.
79: 9 *H* us, O God our Savior,
108: 12 for the *h* of man is worthless.
115: 9 he is their *h* and shield.
121: 1 where does my *h* come from?
Ecc 4: 10 his friend can *h* him up.
Isa 41: 10 I will strengthen you and *h* you;
Jnh 2: 2 depths of the grave I called for *h*,
Mk 9: 24 *h* me overcome my unbelief!"
Lk 11: 46 will not lift one finger to *h* them.
Ac 16: 9 Come over to Macedonia and *h* us
18: 27 he was a great *h* to those who
20: 35 of hard work we must *h* the weak,
26: 22 I have had God's *h* to this very day,
1Co 12: 28 those able to *h* others, those

2Co 9: 2 For I know your eagerness to *h*,
1Ti 5:16 she should *h* them and not let

HELPED (HELP)

1Sa 7:12 "Thus far has the LORD *h* us."

HELPER (HELP)

Ge   2:18 I will make a *h* suitable for him."
Ps 10:14 you are the *h* of the fatherless.
Heb 13: 6 Lord is my *h*; I will not be afraid.

HELPFUL (HELP)

Eph 4:29 only what is *h* for building others

HELPING (HELP)

Ac   9:36 always doing good and *h* the poor.
1Ti 5:10 *h* those in trouble and devoting

HELPLESS (HELP)

Ps 10:12 Do not forget the *h*.
Mt   9:36 because they were harassed and *h*,

HELPS (HELP)

Ro   8:26 the Spirit *h* us in our weakness.

HEN

Mt 23:37 as a *h* gathers her chicks
Lk 13:34 as a *h* gathers her chicks

HERALD

1Ti 2: 7 for this purpose I was appointed a *h*
2Ti 1:11 of this gospel I was appointed a *h*

HERBS

Ex 12: 8 with bitter *h*, and bread made

HERITAGE (INHERIT)

Ps 61: 5 you have given me the *h*
    119:111 Your statutes are my *h* forever;
    127: 3 Sons are a *h* from the LORD,

HEROD

1. King of Judea who tried to kill Jesus (Mt 2;
Lk 1:5).
2. Son of 1. Tetrarch of Galilee who arrested
and beheaded John the Baptist (Mt 14:1-12; Mk 6:
14-29; Lk 3:1, 19-20; 9:7-9); tried Jesus (Lk 23:
6-15).
3. Grandson of 1. King of Judea who killed
James (Ac 12:2); arrested Peter (Ac 12:3-19).
Death (Ac 12:19-23).

HERODIAS

Wife of Herod the Tetrarch who persuaded her
daughter to ask for John the Baptist's head (Mt 14:
1-12; Mk 6:14-29).

HEWN

Isa 51: 1 the quarry from which you were *h*;

HEZEKIAH

King of Judah. Restored the temple and worship (2Ch 29-31). Sought the LORD for help
against Assyria (2Ki 18-19; 2Ch 32:1-23; Isa 36-
37). Illness healed (2Ki 20:1-11; 2Ch 32:24-26;
Isa 38). Judged for showing Babylonians his treasures (2Ki 20:12-21; 2Ch 32:31; Isa 39).

HID (HIDE)

Ge   3: 8 and they *h* from the LORD God
Ex   2: 2 she *h* him for three months.
Jos 6:17 because she *h* the spies we sent.
1Ki 18:13 I *h* a hundred of the LORD's
2Ch 22:11 she *h* the child from Athaliah
Isa 54: 8 I *h* my face from you for a moment,
Mt 13:44 When a man found it, he *h* it again,
    25:25 and *h* your talent in the ground.
Heb 11:23 By faith Moses' parents *h* him

HIDDEN (HIDE)

1Sa 10:22 has *h* himself among the baggage."
Job 28:11 and brings *h* things to light.
Ps 19:12 Forgive my *h* faults.
    78: 2 I will utter *h* things, things from of
         old—
    119:11 I have *h* your word in my heart
Pr   2: 4 and search for it as for *h* treasure,
    27: 5 rebuke than *h* love.
Isa 59: 2 your sins have *h* his face from you,

Da   2:22 He reveals deep and *h* things;
Mt   5:14 A city on a hill cannot be *h*.
    10:26 or *h* that will not be made known.
    11:25 because you have *h* these things
    13:35 I will utter things *h*
    13:44 of heaven is like treasure *h*
Mk   4:22 For whatever is *h* is meant
Ro 16:25 of the mystery *h* for long ages past,
1Co 2: 7 a wisdom that has been *h*
Eph 3: 9 for ages past was kept *h* in God,
Col 1:26 the mystery that has been kept *h*
     2: 3 in whom are *h* all the treasures
     3: 3 and your life is now *h* with Christ

HIDE (HID HIDDEN HIDING)

Dt 31:17 I will *h* my face from them,
Ps 17: 8 *h* me in the shadow of your wings
    27: 5 he will *h* me in the shelter
    143: 9 for I *h* myself in you.
Isa 53: 3 one from whom men *h* their faces

HIDING (HIDE)

Ps 32: 7 You are my *h* place;
Pr 28:12 to power, men go into *h*.

HIGH

Ge 14:18 He was priest of God Most *H*,
    14:22 God Most *H*, Creator of heaven
Ps 21: 7 the unfailing love of the Most *H*
    82: 6 you are all sons of the Most *H*.'
Isa 14:14 I will make myself like the Most *H*
Da   4:17 know that the Most *H* is sovereign
Mk   5: 7 Jesus, Son of the Most *H* God?
Heb 7: 1 and priest of God Most *H*.

HIGHWAY

Isa 40: 3 a *h* for our God.

HILL (HILLS)

Ps 24: 3 ascend the *h* of the LORD?
Isa 40: 4 every mountain and *h* made low;
Mt   5:14 A city on a *h* cannot be hidden.
Lk   3: 5 every mountain and *h* made low.

HILLS (HILL)

1Ki 20:23 "Their gods are gods of the *h*.
Ps 50:10 and the cattle on a thousand *h*.
    121: 1 I lift up my eyes to the *h*—
Hos 10: 8 and to the *h*, "Fall on us!"
Lk 23:30 and to the *h*, "Cover us!' '
Rev 17: 9 The seven heads are seven *h*

HINDER (HINDERED HINDERS)

1Sa 14: 6 Nothing can *h* the LORD
Mt 19:14 come to me, and do not *h* them,
1Co 9:12 anything rather than *h* the gospel
1Pe 3: 7 so that nothing will *h* your prayers.

HINDERED (HINDER)

Lk 11:52 and you have *h* those who were

HINDERS (HINDER)

Heb 12: 1 let us throw off everything that *h*

HINT*

Eph 5: 3 even a *h* of sexual immorality,

HIP

Ge 32:32 socket of Jacob's *h* was touched

HIRAM

King of Tyre; helped David build his palace
(2Sa 5:11-12; 1Ch 14:1); helped Solomon build
the temple (1Ki 5; 2Ch 2) and his navy (1Ki 9:
10-27; 2Ch 8).

HIRED

Lk 15:15 and *h* himself out to a citizen
Jn 10:12 *h* hand is not the shepherd who

HOARDED (HOARDS)

Ecc 5:13 wealth *h* to the harm of its owner,
Jas 5: 3 You have *h* wealth in the last days.

HOARDS (HOARDED)

Pr 11:26 People curse the man who *h* grain,

HOLD (HELD HOLDS)

Ex 20: 7 LORD will not *h* anyone guiltless
Lev 19:13 " 'Do not *h* back the wages
Dt   5:11 LORD will not *h* anyone guiltless
    11:22 in all his ways and to *h* fast to him
    13: 4 serve him and *h* fast to him.
    30:20 listen to his voice, and *h* fast to him
Jos 22: 5 to *h* fast to him and to serve him
2Ki 4:16 "you will *h* a son in your arms."
Ps 18:16 from on high and took *h* of me;
    73:23 you *h* me by my right hand.
Pr   4: 4 "Lay *h* of my words
Isa 41:13 who takes *h* of your right hand
    54: 2 do not *h* back;
Eze 3:18 and I will *h* you accountable
     3:20 and I will *h* you accountable
    33: 6 I will *h* the watchman accountable
Zec 8:23 nations will take firm *h* of one Jew
Mk 11:25 if you *h* anything against anyone,
Jn 20:17 Jesus said, "Do not *h* on to me,
Php 2:16 as you *h* out the word of life—
     3:12 but I press on to take *h* of that
Col 1:17 and in him all things *h* together.
1Th 5:21 *H* on to the good.
1Ti 6:12 Take *h* of the eternal life
Heb 10:23 Let us *h* unswervingly

HOLDS (HOLD)

Pr 10:19 but he who *h* his tongue is wise.
    17:28 and discerning if he *h* his tongue.

HOLES

Hag 1: 6 to put them in a purse with *h* in it."
Mt   8:20 "Foxes have *h* and birds

HOLINESS* (HOLY)

Ex 15:11 majestic in *h*,
Dt 32:51 because you did not uphold my *h*
1Ch 16:29 the LORD in the splendor of his *h*.
2Ch 20:21 him for the splendor of his *h*
Ps 29: 2 in the splendor of his *h*.
    89:35 Once for all, I have sworn by my *h*
    93: 5 *h* adorns your house
    96: 9 in the splendor of his *h*;
Isa 29:23 they will acknowledge the *h*
    35: 8 it will be called the Way of *H*.
Eze 36:23 I will show the *h* of my great name,
    38:23 I will show my greatness and my *h*,
Am   4: 2 LORD has sworn by his *h*:
Lk   1:75 fear in *h* and righteousness
Ro   1: 4 the Spirit of *h* was declared
     6:19 to righteousness leading to *h*.
     6:22 the benefit you reap leads to *h*,
1Co 1:30 our righteousness, *h*
2Co 1:12 in the *h* and sincerity that are
     7: 1 perfecting *h* out of reverence
Eph 4:24 God in true righteousness and *h*.
1Ti 2: 2 quiet lives in all godliness and *h*.
     2:15 love and *h* with propriety.
Heb 12:10 that we may share in his *h*.
    12:14 without *h* no one will see the Lord.

HOLY (HALLOWED HOLINESS)

Ge   2: 3 the seventh day and made it *h*,
Ex   3: 5 you are standing is *h* ground."
    16:23 a *h* Sabbath to the LORD.
    19: 6 kingdom of priests and a *h* nation.'
    20: 8 the Sabbath day by keeping it *h*.
    26:33 Place from the Most *H* Place.
    26:33 curtain will separate the *H* Place
    28:36 seal: *H* TO THE LORD.
    29:37 Then the altar will be most *h*,
    30:10 It is most *h* to the LORD."
    30:29 them so they will be most *h*,
    31:13 I am the LORD, who makes you *h*.
    40: 9 all its furnishings, and it will be *h*.
Lev 10: 3 I will show myself *h*;
    10:10 must distinguish between the *h*
    10:13 in a *h* place, because it is your share
    11:44 and be *h*, because I am *h*.
    11:45 therefore be *h*, because I am *h*.
    19: 2 'Be *h* because I, the LORD your
    19: 8 he has desecrated what is *h*
    19:24 the fourth year all its fruit will be *h*,
    20: 3 and profaned my *h* name.
    20: 7 " 'Consecrate yourselves and be *h*,
    20: 8 I am the LORD, who makes you *h*.
    20:26 You are to be *h* to me because I,

HOME

Lev 21: 6 They must be *h* to their God
   21: 8 Consider them *h*, because I
   22: 9 am the LORD, who makes them *h*.
   22:32 Do not profane my *h* name.
   25:12 For it is a jubilee and is to be *h*
   27: 9 given to the LORD becomes *h*.
Nu 4:15 they must not touch the *h* things
    6: 5 He must be *h* until the period
   20:12 as *h* in the sight of the Israelites,
   20:13 and where he showed himself *h*
Dt 5:12 the Sabbath day by keeping it *h*,
   23:14 Your camp must be *h*,
   26:15 from heaven, your *h* dwelling place
   33: 2 He came with myriads of *h* ones
Jos 5:15 place where you are standing is *h*."
   24:19 He is a *h* God; he is a jealous God.
1Sa 2: 2 "There is no one *h* like the LORD;
    6:20 of the LORD, this *h* God?
   21: 5 even on missions that are not *h*.
2Ki 4: 9 often comes our way is a *h* man
1Ch 16:10 Glory in his *h* name;
   16:35 may give thanks to your *h* name,
   29: 3 I have provided for this *h* temple:
2Ch 30:27 heaven, his *h* dwelling place.
Ezr 9: 2 and have mingled the *h* race
Ne 11: 1 the *h* city, while the remaining nine
Job 6:10 not denied the words of the *H* One!
Ps 2: 6 King on Zion, my *h* hill.''
    2: 4 The LORD is in his *h* temple;
   11: 4 The LORD is in his *h* temple;
   16:10 will you let your *H* One see decay.
   22: 3 you are enthroned as the *H* One;
   24: 3 Who may stand in his *h* place?
   30: 4 praise his *h* name.
   77:13 Your ways, O God, are *h*.
   78:54 to the border of his *h* land,
   99: 3 he is *h*.
   99: 5 he is *h*.
   99: 9 for the LORD our God is *h*.
  105: 3 Glory in his *h* name;
  111: 9 *h* and awesome is his name.
Pr 9:10 of the *H* One is understanding.
Isa 5:16 the *h* God will show himself *h*
    6: 3 *H, H, h* is the LORD Almighty;
    8:13 is the one you are to regard as *h*,
   29:23 they will keep my name *h*;
   40:25 who is my equal?'' says the *H* One.
   43: 3 the *H* One of Israel, your Savior;
   54: 5 *H* One of Israel is your Redeemer;
   57:15 who lives forever, whose name is *h*:
   58:13 and the LORD's *h* day honorable,
Jer 17:22 but keep the Sabbath day *h*,
Eze 20:41 I will show myself *h* among you
   22:26 to my law and profane my *h* things;
   28:22 and show myself *h* within her.
   28:25 I will show myself *h* among them
   36:20 nations they profaned my *h* name,
   38:16 when I show myself *h* through you
   44:23 the difference between the *h*
Da 9:24 prophecy and to anoint the most *h*.
Hab 2:20 But the LORD is in his *h* temple;
Zec 14: 5 and all the *h* ones with him.
   14:20 On that day *H* TO THE LORD
Mt 24:15 in the *h* place 'the abomination
Mk 1:24 the *H* One of God!'' ''Be quiet!''
Lk 1:35 the *h* one to be born will be called
    1:49 *h* is his name.
    4:34 the *H* One of God!'' ''Be quiet!''
Jn 6:69 and know that you are the *H* One
Ac 2:27 will you let your *H* One see decay.
   13:35 will not let your *H* One see decay.'
Ro 1: 2 prophets in the *H* Scriptures
    7:12 and the commandment is *h*,
   11:16 if the root is *h*, so are the branches.
   12: 1 as living sacrifices, *h* and pleasing
1Co 1: 2 in Christ Jesus and called to be *h*,
    7:14 be unclean, but as it is, they are *h*.
Eph 1: 4 the creation of the world to be *h*
    2:21 and rises to become a *h* temple
    3: 5 by the Spirit to God's *h* apostles
    5: 3 improper for God's *h* people.
    5:26 up for her to make her *h*,
Col 1:22 death to present you *h* in his sight,
1Th 2:10 and so is God, of how *h*,
    3:13 and *h* in the presence of our God
    3:13 comes with all his *h* ones.
    4: 7 us to be impure, but to live a *h* life.
2Th 1:10 to be glorified in his *h* people
1Ti 2: 8 to lift up *h* hands in prayer,

2Ti 1: 9 saved us and called us to a *h* life—
    2:21 for noble purposes, made *h*,
    3:15 you have known the *h* Scriptures,
Tit 1: 8 upright, *h* and disciplined.
Heb 2:11 Both the one who makes men *h*
    7:26 one who is *h*, blameless, pure,
   10:10 we have been made *h*
   10:14 those who are being made *h*.
   10:19 to enter the Most *H* Place
   12:14 in peace with all men and to be *h*;
   13:12 gate to make the people *h*
1Pe 1:15 But just as he who called you is *h*,
    1:16 is written: ''Be *h*, because I am *h*.''
    2: 5 house to be a *h* priesthood,
    2: 9 a royal priesthood, a *h* nation,
    3: 5 For this is the way the *h* women
2Pe 3:11 You ought to live *h* and godly lives
Jude :14 upon thousands of his *h* ones
Rev 3: 7 are the words of him who is *h*
    4: 8 ''*H, h, h* is the Lord God
   15: 4 For you alone are *h*.
   20: 6 and *h* are those who have part
   22:11 let him who is *h* continue to be *h*.''

HOME (HOMES)

Dt 6: 7 Talk about them when you sit at *h*
   11:19 about them when you sit at *h*
   20: 5 Let him go *h*, or he may die
   24: 5 is to be free to stay at *h*
Ru 1:11 ''Return *h*, my daughters.
2Sa 7:10 them so that they can have a *h*
1Ch 16:43 and David returned *h* to bless his
Ps 84: 3 Even the sparrow has found a *h*,
  113: 9 settles the barren woman in her *h*
Pr 3:33 but he blesses the *h* of the righteous
   27: 8 is a man who strays from his *h*.
Ecc 12: 5 Then man goes to his eternal *h*
Eze 36: 8 for they will soon come *h*.
Mic 2: 2 They defraud a man of his *h*,
Mt 1:24 and took Mary *h* as his wife.
Mk 10:29 ''no one who has left *h* or brothers
Lk 10:38 named Martha opened her *h*
Jn 14:23 to him and make our *h* with him.
   19:27 this disciple took her into his *h*.
Ac 16:15 baptized, she invited us to her *h*.
Tit 2: 5 to be busy at *h*, to be kind,

HOMELESS*

1Co 4:11 we are brutally treated, we are *h*.

HOMES (HOME)

Ne 4:14 daughters, your wives and your *h*.''
Isa 32:18 in secure *h*,
Mk 10:30 as much in this present age (*h*,
1Ti 5:14 to manage their *h* and to give

HOMETOWN

Mt 13:57 ''Only in his *h*
Lk 4:24 ''no prophet is accepted in his *h*.

HOMOSEXUAL*

1Co 6: 9 male prostitutes nor *h* offenders

HONEST (HONESTY)

Lev 19:36 Use *h* scales and *h* weights,
Dt 25:15 and *h* weights and measures,
Job 31: 6 let God weigh me in *h* scales
Pr 12:17 truthful witness gives *h* testimony,

HONESTY (HONEST)

2Ki 12:15 they acted with complete *h*.

HONEY (HONEYCOMB)

Ex 3: 8 a land flowing with milk and *h*—
Jdg 14: 8 a swarm of bees and some *h*,
1Sa 14:26 they saw the *h* oozing out,
Ps 19:10 than *h* from the comb.
  119:103 sweeter than *h* to my mouth!
Pr 25:16 If you find *h*, eat just enough—
SS 4:11 milk and *h* are under your tongue.
Isa 7:15 and *h* when he knows enough
Eze 3: 3 it tasted as sweet as *h* in my mouth.
Mt 3: 4 His food was locusts and wild *h*.
Rev 10: 9 mouth it will be as sweet as *h*.''

HONEYCOMB (HONEY)

SS 4:11 Your lips drop sweetness as the *h*,
    5: 1 I have eaten my *h* and my honey;

HONOR (HONORABLE HONORABLY HONORED HONORS)

Ex 20:12 ''*H* your father and your mother,
Nu 20:12 trust in me enough to *h* me
   25:13 he was zealous for the *h* of his God
Dt 5:16 ''*H* your father and your mother,
Jdg 4: 9 going about this, the *h* will not be
1Sa 2: 8 and has them inherit a throne of *h*.
    2:30 Those who *h* me I will *h*,
1Ch 29:12 Wealth and *h* come from you;
2Ch 1:11 or *h*, nor for the death
   18: 1 had great wealth and *h*,
Est 6: 6 for the man the king delights to *h*
Ps 8: 5 and crowned him with glory and *h*.
   45:11 *h* him, for he is your lord.
   84:11 the LORD bestows favor and *h*;
Pr 3: 9 *H* the LORD with your wealth,
    3:35 The wise inherit *h*,
   15:33 and humility comes before *h*.
   18:12 but humility comes before *h*.
   20: 3 It is to a man's *h* to avoid strife,
   25:27 is it honorable to seek one's own *h*.
Isa 29:13 and *h* me with their lips,
Jer 33: 9 and *h* before all nations
Mt 13:57 own house is a prophet without *h*.''
   15: 4 '*H* your father and mother'
   15: 8 These people *h* me with their lips,
   19:19 *h* your father and mother,'
   23: 6 they love the place of *h* at banquets
Mk 6: 4 own house is a prophet without *h*.''
Lk 14: 8 do not take the place of *h*,
Jn 5:23 that all may *h* the Son just
    7:18 does so to gain *h* for himself,
   12:26 My Father will *h* the one who
Ro 12:10 *H* one another above yourselves.
1Co 6:20 Therefore *h* God with your body.
Eph 6: 2 ''*H* your father and mother''—
1Ti 5:17 well are worthy of double *h*,
Heb 2: 7 you crowned him with glory and *h*
Rev 4: 9 *h* and thanks to him who sits

HONORABLE (HONOR)

1Th 4: 4 body in a way that is holy and *h*,

HONORABLY (HONOR)

Heb 13:18 and desire to live *h* in every way.

HONORED (HONOR)

Ps 12: 8 when what is vile is *h* among men.
Pr 13:18 but whoever heeds correction is *h*.
Da 4:34 I *h* and glorified him who lives
1Co 12:26 if one part is *h*, every part rejoices
Heb 13: 4 Marriage should be *h* by all,

HONORS (HONOR)

Ps 15: 4 but *h* those who fear the LORD,
Pr 14:31 to the needy *h* God.

HOOF

Ex 10:26 not a *h* is to be left behind.

HOOKS

Isa 2: 4 and spears into pruning *h*.
Joel 3:10 and your pruning *h* into spears.
Mic 4: 3 and their spears into pruning *h*.

HOPE (HOPES)

Job 13:15 Though he slay me, yet will I *h*
Ps 25: 3 No one whose *h* is in you
   33:17 A horse is a vain *h* for deliverance;
   33:18 on those whose *h* is
   42: 5 Put your *h* in God,
   62: 5 my *h* comes from him.
  119:74 for I have put my *h* in your word.
  130: 5 and in his word I put my *h*.
  130: 7 O Israel, put your *h* in the LORD,
  146: 5 whose *h* is in the LORD his God,
  147:11 who put their *h* in his unfailing love
Pr 13:12 *H* deferred makes the heart sick.
   23:18 There is surely a future *h* for you,
Isa 40:31 but those who *h* in the LORD
Jer 29:11 plans to give you *h* and a future.
La 3:21 and therefore I have *h*:
Zec 9:12 to your fortress, O prisoners of *h*;
Ro 5: 4 character; and character, *h*.
    8:20 in *h* that the creation itself will be
    8:24 But *h* that is seen is no *h* at all.
    8:25 if we *h* for what we do not yet have,

Ro 12: 12 Be joyful in *h*, patient in affliction,
15: 4 of the Scriptures we might have *h*.
15: 13 May the God of *h* fill you
1Co 13: 13 now these three remain: faith, *h*
15: 19 for this life we have *h* in Christ,
Eph 2: 12 without *h* and without God
Col 1: 27 Christ in you, the *h* of glory.
1Th 1: 3 and your endurance inspired by *h*
5: 8 and the *h* of salvation as a helmet.
1Ti 4: 10 that we have put our *h*
6: 17 but to put their *h* in God,
Tit 1: 2 resting on the *h* of eternal life,
2: 13 while we wait for the blessed *h*—
Heb 6: 19 We have this *h* as an anchor
10: 23 unswervingly to the *h* we profess,
11: 1 faith is being sure of what we *h* for
1Jn 3: 3 Everyone who has this *h*

HOPES (HOPE)

1Co 13: 7 always *h*, always perseveres.

HORN (HORNS)

Ex 19: 13 when the ram's *h* sounds a long
27: 2 Make a *h* at each of the four
Da 7: 8 This *h* had eyes like the eyes

HORNS (HORN)

Da 7: 24 ten *h* are ten kings who will come
Rev 5: 6 He had seven *h* and seven eyes,
12: 3 and ten *h* and seven crowns
13: 1 He had ten *h* and seven heads,
17: 3 and had seven heads and ten *h*.

HORRIBLE (HORROR)

Jer 5: 30 "A *h* and shocking thing

HORROR (HORRIBLE)

Jer 2: 12 and shudder with great *h*,"

HORSE

Ps 147: 10 not in the strength of the *h*,
Pr 26: 3 A whip for the *h*, a halter
Zec 1: 8 before me was a man riding a red *h*
Rev 6: 2 and there before me was a white *h!*
6: 4 Come!'' Then another *h* came out,
6: 5 and there before me was a black *h!*
6: 8 and there before me was a pale *h!*
19: 11 and there before me was a white *h*,

HOSANNA

Mt 21: 9 "*H* in the highest!''
Mk 11: 9 "*H!*''
Jn 12: 13 "*H!*''

HOSEA

Prophet whose wife and family pictured the unfaithfulness of Israel (Hos 1-3).

HOSHEA (JOSHUA)

1. Original name of Joshua (Nu 13:16).
2. Last king of Israel (2Ki 15:30; 17:1-6).

HOSPITABLE* (HOSPITALITY)

1Ti 3: 2 self-controlled, respectable, *h*,
Tit 1: 8 Rather he must be *h*, one who loves

HOSPITABLY* (HOSPITALITY)

Ac 28: 7 and for three days entertained us *h*.

HOSPITALITY* (HOSPITABLE HOSPITABLY)

Ro 12: 13 Practice *h*.
16: 23 whose *h* I and the whole church
1Ti 5: 10 as bringing up children, showing *h*,
1Pe 4: 9 Offer *h* to one another
3Jn : 8 therefore to show *h* to such men

HOSTILE (HOSTILITY)

Ro 8: 7 the sinful mind is *h* to God.

HOSTILITY (HOSTILE)

Eph 2: 14 wall of *h*, by abolishing
2: 16 by which he put to death their *h*.

HOT

1Ti 4: 2 have been seared as with a *h* iron.
Rev 3: 15 that you are neither cold nor *h*.

HOT-TEMPERED (TEMPER)

Pr 15: 18 A *h* man stirs up dissension,
19: 19 A *h* man must pay the penalty;
22: 24 Do not make friends with a *h* man,
29: 22 and a *h* one commits many sins.

HOTHEADED (HEAD)

Pr 14: 16 but a fool is *h* and reckless.

HOUR

Ecc 9: 12 knows when his *h* will come:
Mt 6: 27 you by worrying can add a single *h*
Lk 12: 40 the Son of Man will come at an *h*
Jn 12: 23 The *h* has come for the Son of Man
12: 27 for this very reason I came to this *h*

HOUSE (HOUSEHOLD HOUSEHOLDS HOUSES STOREHOUSE)

Ex 12: 22 the door of his *h* until morning.
20: 17 shall not covet your neighbor's *h*.
Nu 12: 7 he is faithful in all my *h*.
Dt 5: 21 desire on your neighbor's *h*
2Sa 5: 11 LORD himself will establish a *h*
1Ch 17: 23 and his *h* be established forever.
Ne 10: 39 "We will not neglect the *h*
Ps 23: 6 I will dwell in the *h* of the LORD
27: 4 dwell in the *h* of the LORD
69: 9 for zeal for your *h* consumes me,
84: 10 a doorkeeper in the *h* of my God
122: 1 "Let us go to the *h* of the LORD.''
127: 1 Unless the LORD builds the *h*,
Pr 7: 27 Her *h* is a highway to the grave,
21: 9 than share a *h* with a quarrelsome
Isa 56: 7 a *h* of prayer for all nations.''
Jer 7: 11 Has this *h*, which bears my Name,
18: 2 "Go down to the potter's *h*,
Eze 33: 7 made you a watchman for the *h*
Joel 3: 18 will flow out of the LORD's *h*
Zec 13: 6 given at the *h* of my friends.'
Mt 7: 24 is like a wise man who builds his *h*
10: 11 and stay at his *h* until you leave.
12: 29 can anyone enter a strong man's *h*
21: 13 My *h* will be called a *h* of prayer,'
Mk 3: 25 If a *h* is divided against itself,
11: 17 " 'My *h* will be called
Lk 6: 48 He is like a man building a *h*,
10: 7 Do not move around from *h* to *h*.
11: 17 a *h* divided against itself will fall.
11: 24 'I will return to the *h* I left.'
15: 8 sweep the *h* and search carefully
19: 9 Today salvation has come to this *h*,
Jn 2: 16 How dare you turn my Father's *h*
2: 17 "Zeal for your *h* will consume me.''
12: 3 the *h* was filled with the fragrance
14: 2 In my Father's *h* are many rooms;
Ac 20: 20 you publicly and from *h* to *h*.
Ro 16: 5 the church that meets at their *h*.
Heb 3: 3 the builder of a *h* has greater honor
1Pe 2: 5 built into a spiritual *h* to be a holy

HOUSEHOLD (HOUSE)

Ex 12: 3 lamb for his family, one for each *h*.
Jos 24: 15 my *h*, we will serve the LORD.''
Pr 31: 21 it snows, she has no fear for her *h*;
31: 27 over the affairs of her *h*
Mic 7: 6 are the members of his own *h*.
Mt 10: 36 will be the members of his own *h*.'
12: 25 or *h* divided against itself will not
Ac 16: 31 you will be saved—you and your *h*
Eph 2: 19 people and members of God's *h*,
1Ti 3: 12 manage his children and his *h* well.
3: 15 to conduct themselves in God's *h*,

HOUSEHOLDS (HOUSE)

Tit 1: 11 because they are ruining whole *h*

HOUSES (HOUSE)

Ex 12: 27 passed over the *h* of the Israelites
Mt 19: 29 everyone who has left *h* or brothers

HOVERING* (HOVERS)

Ge 1: 2 of God was *h* over the waters.
Isa 31: 5 Like birds *h* overhead,

HOVERS* (HOVERING)

Dt 32: 11 and *h* over its young,

HULDAH*

Prophetess inquired by Hilkiah for Josiah (2Ki 22; 2Ch 34:14-28).

HUMAN (HUMANITY)

Lev 24: 17 If anyone takes the life of a *h* being,
Isa 52: 14 his form marred beyond *h* likeness
Jn 8: 15 You judge by *h* standards;
Ro 1: 3 as to his *h* nature was a descendant
9: 5 from them is traced the *h* ancestry
1Co 1: 17 not with words of *h* wisdom,
1: 26 of you were wise by *h* standards;
2: 13 not in words taught us by *h* wisdom
2Co 3: 3 of stone but on tablets of *h* hearts.
Gal 3: 3 to attain your goal by *h* effort?
2Pe 2: 18 lustful desires of sinful *h* nature,

HUMANITY* (HUMAN)

Heb 2: 14 he too shared in their *h* so that

HUMBLE (HUMBLED HUMBLES HUMILIATE HUMILIATED HUMILITY)

Nu 12: 3 (Now Moses was a very *h* man,
2Ch 7: 14 will *h* themselves and pray
Ps 18: 27 You save the *h*
25: 9 He guides the *h* in what is right
149: 4 he crowns the *h* with salvation.
Pr 3: 34 but gives grace to the *h*.
Isa 66: 2 he who is *h* and contrite in spirit,
Mt 11: 29 for I am gentle and *h* in heart,
Eph 4: 2 Be completely *h* and gentle;
Jas 4: 6 but gives grace to the *h*.''
4: 10 *H* yourselves before the Lord,
1Pe 5: 5 but gives grace to the *h*.''
5: 6 *H* yourselves,

HUMBLED (HUMBLE)

Mt 23: 12 whoever exalts himself will be *h*,
Lk 14: 11 who exalts himself will be *h*,
Php 2: 8 he *h* himself

HUMBLES* (HUMBLE)

1Sa 2: 7 he *h* and he exalts.
Isa 26: 5 He *h* those who dwell on high,
Mt 18: 4 whoever *h* himself like this child is
23: 12 whoever *h* himself will be exalted.
Lk 14: 11 he who *h* himself will be exalted.''
18: 14 he who *h* himself will be exalted.''

HUMILIATE* (HUMBLE)

Pr 25: 7 than for him to *h* you
1Co 11: 22 and *h* those who have nothing?

HUMILIATED (HUMBLE)

Jer 31: 19 I was ashamed and *h*
Lk 14: 9 *h*, you will have to take the least

HUMILITY* (HUMBLE)

Ps 45: 4 of truth, *h* and righteousness;
Pr 11: 2 but with *h* comes wisdom.
15: 33 and *h* comes before honor.
18: 12 but *h* comes before honor.
22: 4 *H* and the fear of the LORD
Zep 2: 3 Seek righteousness, seek *h*;
Ac 20: 19 I served the Lord with great *h*
Php 2: 3 but in *h* consider others better
Col 2: 18 let anyone who delights in false *h*
2: 23 their false *h* and their harsh
3: 12 *h*, gentleness and patience.
Tit 3: 2 and to show true *h* toward all men.
Jas 3: 13 in the *h* that comes from wisdom.
1Pe 5: 5 clothe yourselves with *h*

HUNG (HANG)

Dt 21: 23 anyone who is *h* on a tree is
Mt 18: 6 him to have a large millstone *h*
Lk 19: 48 all the people *h* on his words.
Gal 3: 13 "Cursed is everyone who is *h*

HUNGER (HUNGRY)

Ne 9: 15 In their *h* you gave them bread
Pr 6: 30 to satisfy his *h* when he is starving.
Mt 5: 6 Blessed are those who *h*
Lk 6: 21 Blessed are you who *h* now,
2Co 6: 5 sleepless nights and *h*; in purity,
11: 27 I have known *h* and thirst
Rev 7: 16 Never again will they *h*;

HUNGRY (HUNGER)

Job 24: 10 carry the sheaves, but still go *h*.
Ps 107: 9 and fills the *h* with good things.
146: 7 and gives food to the *h*.
Pr 19: 15 and the shiftless man goes *h*.
25: 21 If your enemy is *h*, give him food
27: 7 to the *h* even what is bitter tastes
Isa 58: 7 not to share your food with the *h*
58: 10 spend yourselves in behalf of the *h*
Eze 18: 7 but gives his food to the *h*
18: 16 but gives his food to the *h*
Mt 15: 32 I do not want to send them away *h*,
25: 35 For I was *h* and you gave me
25: 42 For I was *h* and you gave me
Lk 1: 53 He has filled the *h* with good things
Jn 6: 35 comes to me will never go *h*,
Ro 12: 20 "If your enemy is *h*, feed him;
1Co 4: 11 To this very hour we go *h*
Php 4: 12 whether well fed or *h*,

HUR

Ex 17: 12 Aaron and *H* held his hands up—

HURL

Mic 7: 19 *h* all our iniquities into the depths

HURT (HURTS)

Ecc 8: 9 it over others to his own *h*.
Mk 16: 18 deadly poison, it will not *h* them
Rev 2: 11 He who overcomes will not be *h*

HURTS* (HURT)

Ps 15: 4 even when it *h*,
Pr 26: 28 A lying tongue hates those it *h*,

HUSBAND (HUSBAND'S HUSBANDS)

Pr 31: 11 Her *h* has full confidence in her
31: 23 Her *h* is respected at the city gate,
31: 28 her *h* also, and he praises her:
Isa 54: 5 For your Maker is your *h*—
Jer 3: 14 the LORD, "for I am your *h*.
3: 20 like a woman unfaithful to her *h*,
Jn 4: 17 "I have no *h*," she replied.
Ro 7: 2 a married woman is bound to her *h*
1Co 7: 2 and each woman her own *h*.
7: 3 The *h* should fulfill his marital duty
7: 10 wife must not separate from her *h*.
7: 11 And a *h* must not divorce his wife.
7: 13 And if a woman has a *h* who is not
7: 14 For the unbelieving *h* has been
7: 39 A woman is bound to her *h* as long
7: 39 But if her *h* dies, she is free
2Co 11: 2 I promised you to one *h*, to Christ,
Gal 4: 27 woman than of her who has a *h*."
Eph 5: 23 For the *h* is the head of the wife
5: 33 and the wife must respect her *h*.
1Ti 3: 2 the *h* of but one wife, temperate,
3: 12 A deacon must be the *h* of
5: 9 has been faithful to her *h*,
Tit 1: 6 An elder must be blameless, the *h*

HUSBANDMAN see GARDENER

HUSBAND'S (HUSBAND)

Dt 25: 5 Her *h* brother shall take her
Pr 12: 4 of noble character is her *h* crown,
1Co 7: 4 the *h* body does not belong

HUSBANDS (HUSBAND)

Eph 5: 22 submit to your *h* as to the Lord.
5: 25 *H*, love your wives, just
5: 28 *h* ought to love their wives
Col 3: 18 submit to your *h*, as is fitting
3: 19 *H*, love your wives and do not be
Tit 2: 4 the younger women to love their *h*
2: 5 and to be subject to their *h*,
1Pe 3: 1 same way be submissive to your *h*
3: 7 *H*, in the same way be considerate

HUSHAI

Wise man of David who frustrated Ahithophel's advice and foiled Absalom's revolt (2Sa 15: 32-37; 16:15-17:16; 1Ch 27:33).

HYMN* (HYMNS)

Ps 40: 3 a *h* of praise to our God.
Mt 26: 30 they had sung a *h*, they went out
Mk 14: 26 they had sung a *h*, they went out

1Co 14: 26 everyone has a *h*, or a word

HYMNS* (HYMN)

Ac 16: 25 Silas were praying and singing *h*
Ro 15: 9 I will sing *h* to your name."
Eph 5: 19 to one another with psalms, *h*
Col 3: 16 *h* and spiritual songs with gratitude

HYPOCRISY* (HYPOCRITE HYPOCRITES HYPOCRITICAL)

Mt 23: 28 but on the inside you are full of *h*
Mk 12: 15 we?'' But Jesus knew their *h*.
Lk 12: 1 yeast of the Pharisees, which is *h*.
Gal 2: 13 The other Jews joined him in his *h*,
2: 13 by their *h* even Barnabas was led
1Pe 2: 1 *h*, envy, and slander of every kind.

HYPOCRITE* (HYPOCRISY)

Mt 7: 5 You *h*, first take the plank out
Lk 6: 42 You *h*, first take the plank out

HYPOCRITES* (HYPOCRISY)

Ps 26: 4 nor do I consort with *h*;
Mt 6: 2 as the *h* do in the synagogues
6: 5 when you pray, do not be like the *h*
6: 16 do not look somber as the *h* do,
15: 7 You *h*! Isaiah was right
22: 18 their evil intent, said, "You *h*,
23: 13 of the law and Pharisees, you *h*!
23: 15 of the law and Pharisees, you *h*!
23: 23 of the law and Pharisees, you *h*!
23: 25 of the law and Pharisees, you *h*!
23: 27 you *h*! You are like whitewashed
23: 29 of the law and Pharisees, you *h*!
24: 51 and assign him a place with the *h*,
Mk 7: 6 when he prophesied about you *h*;
Lk 12: 56 *H*! You know how
13: 15 The Lord answered him, "You *h*!

HYPOCRITICAL* (HYPOCRISY)

1Ti 4: 2 teachings come through *h* liars,

HYSSOP

Ex 12: 22 Take a bunch of *h*, dip it
Ps 51: 7 with *h*, and I will be clean;
Jn 19: 29 the sponge on a stalk of the *h* plant,

ICHABOD

1Sa 4: 21 She named the boy *I*, saying,

IDLE* (IDLENESS IDLERS)

Dt 32: 47 They are not just *i* words for you—
Job 11: 3 Will your *i* talk reduce men
Ecc 10: 18 if his hands are *i*, the house leaks.
11: 6 at evening let not your hands be *i*,
Isa 58: 13 as you please or speaking *i* words,
Col 2: 18 mind puffs him up with *i* notions.
1Th 5: 14 those who are *i*, encourage
2Th 3: 6 away from every brother who is *i*
3: 11 We were not *i* when we were
3: 11 We hear that some among you are *i*
1Ti 5: 13 they get into the habit of being *i*

IDLENESS* (IDLE)

Pr 31: 27 and does not eat the bread of *i*.

IDLERS* (IDLE)

1Ti 5: 13 And not only do they become *i*,

IDOL (IDOLATER IDOLATERS IDOLATRY IDOLS)

Ex 20: 4 make for yourself an *i* in the form
32: 4 made it into an *i* cast in the shape
Isa 40: 19 As for an *i*, a craftsman casts it,
41: 7 He nails down the *i*
44: 15 he makes an *i* and bows down to it.
44: 17 From the rest he makes a god, his *i*;
Hab 2: 18 "Of what value is an *i*,
1Co 8: 4 We know that an *i* is nothing at all

IDOLATER* (IDOL)

1Co 5: 11 an *i* or a slanderer, a drunkard
Eph 5: 5 greedy person—such a man is an *i*

IDOLATERS (IDOL)

1Co 5: 10 or the greedy and swindlers, or *i*.
6: 9 Neither the sexually immoral nor *i*

IDOLATRY (IDOL)

1Sa 15: 23 and arrogance like the evil of *i*.
1Co 10: 14 my dear friends, flee from *i*.
Gal 5: 20 and debauchery; *i* and witchcraft;
Col 3: 5 evil desires and greed, which is *i*.
1Pe 4: 3 orgies, carousing and detestable *i*.

IDOLS (IDOL)

Dt 32: 16 angered him with their detestable *i*.
Ps 78: 58 aroused his jealousy with their *i*.
Isa 44: 9 All who make *i* are nothing,
Eze 23: 39 sacrificed their children to their *i*,
Ac 15: 20 to abstain from food polluted by *i*,
21: 25 abstain from food sacrificed to *i*,
1Co 8: 1 Now about food sacrificed to *i*:
1Jn 5: 21 children, keep yourselves from *i*.
Rev 2: 14 to sin by eating food sacrificed to *i*

IGNORANT (IGNORE)

1Co 15: 34 for there are some who are *i* of God
Heb 5: 2 to deal gently with those who are *i*
1Pe 2: 15 good you should silence the *i* talk
2Pe 3: 16 which *i* and unstable people distort

IGNORE (IGNORANT IGNORED IGNORES)

Dt 22: 1 do not *i* it but be sure
Ps 9: 12 he does not *i* the cry of the afflicted
Heb 2: 3 if we *i* such a great salvation?

IGNORED (IGNORE)

Hos 4: 6 you have *i* the law of your God,
1Co 14: 38 he ignores this, he himself will be *i*.

IGNORES* (IGNORE)

Pr 10: 17 whoever *i* correction leads others
13: 18 He who *i* discipline comes
15: 32 He who *i* discipline despises
1Co 14: 38 If he *i* this, he himself will be

ILL (ILLNESS)

Mt 4: 24 brought to him all who were *i*

ILL-GOTTEN

Pr 1: 19 the end of all who go after *i* gain;
10: 2 *I* treasures are of no value,

ILL-TEMPERED* (TEMPER)

Pr 21: 19 than with a quarrelsome and *i* wife.

ILLEGITIMATE

Heb 12: 8 then you are *i* children

ILLNESS (ILL)

2Ki 8: 9 'Will I recover from this *i*?' ''
2Ch 16: 12 even in his *i* he did not seek help
Ps 41: 3 and restore him from his bed of *i*.
Isa 38: 9 king of Judah after his *i*

ILLUMINATED*

Rev 18: 1 and the earth was *i* by his splendor.

IMAGE (IMAGES)

Ge 1: 26 "Let us make man in our *i*,
1: 27 So God created man in his own *i*,
9: 6 for in the *i* of God
Dt 27: 15 "Cursed is the man who carves an *i*
Isa 40: 18 What *i* will you compare him to?
Da 3: 1 King Nebuchadnezzar made an *i*
1Co 11: 7 since he is the *i* and glory of God;
2Co 4: 4 glory of Christ, who is the *i* of God.
Col 1: 15 He is the *i* of the invisible God,
3: 10 in knowledge in the *i* of its Creator.
Rev 13: 14 them to set up an *i* in honor

IMAGES (IMAGE)

Ps 97: 7 All who worship *i* are put to shame,
Jer 10: 14 His *i* are a fraud;
Ro 1: 23 of the immortal God for *i* made

IMAGINATION (IMAGINE)

Eze 13: 2 who prophesy out of their own *i*.

IMAGINE (IMAGINATION)

Eph 3: 20 more than all we ask or *i*,

IMITATE (IMITATORS)

1Co 4: 16 Therefore I urge you to *i* me.

Heb 6: 12 but to *i* those who through faith
   13: 7 of their way of life and *i* their faith.
3Jn   : 11 do not *i* what is evil but what is

IMITATORS* (IMITATE)
Eph 5: 1 Be *i* of God, therefore,
1Th 1: 6 You became *i* of us and of the Lord
   2: 14 became *i* of God's churches

IMMANUEL*
Isa 7: 14 birth to a son, and will call him *I.*
   8: 8 O *I!*''
Mt 1: 23 and they will call him *I*''—

IMMORAL* (IMMORALITY)
Pr 6: 24 keeping you from the *i* woman,
1Co 5: 9 to associate with sexually *i* people
   5: 10 the people of this world who are *i,*
   5: 11 but is sexually *i* or greedy,
   6: 9 Neither the sexually *i* nor idolaters
Eph 5: 5 No *i,* impure or greedy person—
Heb 12: 16 See that no one is sexually *i,*
   13: 4 the adulterer and all the sexually *i.*
Rev 21: 8 the murderers, the sexually *i,*
   22: 15 the sexually *i,* the murderers,

IMMORALITY* (IMMORAL)
Nu 25: 1 in sexual *i* with Moabite women,
Jer 3: 9 Because Israel's *i* mattered so little
Mt 15: 19 murder, adultery, sexual *i,* theft,
Mk 7: 21 sexual *i,* theft, murder, adultery,
Ac 15: 20 from sexual *i,* from the meat
   15: 29 animals and from sexual *i,*
   21: 25 animals and from sexual *i.*''
Ro 13: 13 not in sexual *i* and debauchery,
1Co 5: 1 reported that there is sexual *i*
   6: 13 The body is not meant for sexual *i,*
   6: 18 Flee from sexual *i.*
   7: 2 But since there is so much *i,*
   10: 8 We should not commit sexual *i,*
Gal 5: 19 sexual *i,* impurity and debauchery;
Eph 5: 3 must not be even a hint of sexual *i,*
Col 3: 5 sexual *i,* impurity, lust, evil desires
1Th 4: 3 that you should avoid sexual *i;*
Jude   : 4 grace of our God into a license for *i*
   : 7 gave themselves up to sexual *i*
Rev 2: 14 and by committing sexual *i.*
   2: 20 misleads my servants into sexual *i*
   2: 21 given her time to repent of her *i,*
   9: 21 their sexual *i* or their thefts.

IMMORTAL* (IMMORTALITY)
Ro 1: 23 glory of the *i* God for images made
1Ti 1: 17 Now to the King eternal, *i,*
   6: 16 who alone is *i* and who lives

IMMORTALITY* (IMMORTAL)
Pr 12: 28 along that path is *i.*
Ro 2: 7 honor and *i,* he will give eternal life
1Co 15: 53 and the mortal with *i.*
   15: 54 with *i,* then the saying that is
2Ti 1: 10 and *i* to light through the gospel.

IMPARTIAL*
Jas 3: 17 and good fruit, *i* and sincere.

IMPARTS*
Pr 29: 15 The rod of correction *i* wisdom,

IMPERFECT*
1Co 13: 10 perfection comes, the *i* disappears.

IMPERISHABLE
1Co 15: 42 it is raised *i;* it is sown in dishonor,
   15: 50 nor does the perishable inherit the *i*
1Pe 1: 23 not of perishable seed, but of *i,*

IMPLANTED*
Ps 94: 9 Does he who *i* the ear not hear?

IMPLORE*
Mal 1: 9 ''Now *i* God to be gracious to us.
2Co 5: 20 We *i* you on Christ's behalf:

IMPORTANCE* (IMPORTANT)
1Co 15: 3 passed on to you as of first *i:*

IMPORTANT (IMPORTANCE)
Mt 6: 25 Is not life more *i* than food,
   23: 23 have neglected the more *i* matters
Mk 12: 29 ''The most *i* one,'' answered Jesus,
   12: 33 as yourself is more *i* than all burnt
Php 1: 18 The *i* thing is that in every way,

IMPOSSIBLE
Mt 17: 20 Nothing will be *i* for you.''
   19: 26 ''With man this is *i,*
Mk 10: 27 ''With man this is *i,* but not
Lk 1: 37 For nothing is *i* with God.''
   18: 27 ''What is *i* with men is possible
Ac 2: 24 it was *i* for death to keep its hold
Heb 6: 4 It is *i* for those who have once been
   6: 18 things in which it is *i* for God to lie,
   10: 4 because it is *i* for the blood of bulls
   11: 6 without faith it is *i* to please God,

IMPOSTORS
2Ti 3: 13 and *i* will go from bad to worse,

IMPRESS* (IMPRESSES)
Dt 6: 7 *I* them on your children.

IMPRESSES* (IMPRESS)
Pr 17: 10 A rebuke *i* a man of discernment

IMPROPER*
Eph 5: 3 these are *i* for God's holy people.

IMPURE (IMPURITY)
Ac 10: 15 not call anything *i* that God has
Eph 5: 5 No immoral, *i* or greedy person—
1Th 2: 3 spring from error or *i* motives,
   4: 7 For God did not call us to be *i,*
Rev 21: 27 Nothing *i* will ever enter it,

IMPURITY (IMPURE)
Ro 1: 24 hearts to sexual *i* for the degrading
Gal 5: 19 sexual immorality, *i,*
Eph 4: 19 as to indulge in every kind of *i,*
   5: 3 or of any kind of *i,* or of greed,
Col 3: 5 *i,* lust, evil desires and greed,

INCENSE
Ex 30: 1 altar of acacia wood for burning *i.*
   40: 5 Place the gold altar of *i* in front
Ps 141: 2 my prayer be set before you like *i;*
Mt 2: 11 him with gifts of gold and of *i*
Heb 9: 4 which had the golden altar of *i*
Rev 5: 8 were holding golden bowls full of *i,*
   8: 4 The smoke of the *i,* together

INCLINATION (INCLINES)
Ge 6: 5 and that every *i* of the thoughts

INCLINES* (INCLINATION)
Ecc 10: 2 The heart of the wise *i* to the right,

INCOME
Ecc 5: 10 wealth is never satisfied with his *i.*
1Co 16: 2 sum of money in keeping with his *i,*

INCOMPARABLE*
Eph 2: 7 ages he might show the *i* riches

INCREASE (EVER-INCREASING INCREASED INCREASES INCREASING)
Ge 1: 22 ''Be fruitful and *i* in number
   3: 16 ''I will greatly *i* your pains
   8: 17 be fruitful and *i* in number upon it
Ps 62: 10 though your riches *i,*
Pr 22: 16 oppresses the poor to *i* his wealth
Isa 9: 7 Of the *i* of his government
Mt 24: 12 Because of the *i* of wickedness,
Lk 17: 5 said to the Lord, ''*I* our faith!''
Ac 12: 24 But the word of God continued to *i*
Ro 5: 20 added so that the trespass might *i.*
1Th 3: 12 May the Lord make your love *i*

INCREASED (INCREASE)
Ac 6: 7 of disciples in Jerusalem *i* rapidly,
Ro 5: 20 But where sin *i,* grace *i* all the more

INCREASES (INCREASE)
Pr 24: 5 and a man of knowledge *i* strength;

INCREASING (INCREASE)
Ac 6: 1 when the number of disciples was *i,*
2Th 1: 3 one of you has for each other is *i.*
2Pe 1: 8 these qualities in *i* measure,

INCREDIBLE*
Ac 26: 8 of you consider it *i* that God raises

INDECENT
Ro 1: 27 Men committed *i* acts

INDEPENDENT*
1Co 11: 11 however, woman is not *i* of man,
   11: 11 of man, nor is man *i* of woman.

INDESCRIBABLE*
2Co 9: 15 Thanks be to God for his *i* gift!

INDESTRUCTIBLE*
Heb 7: 16 on the basis of the power of an *i* life

INDIGNANT
Mk 10: 14 When Jesus saw this, he was *i.*

INDISPENSABLE*
1Co 12: 22 seem to be weaker are *i,*

INEFFECTIVE*
2Pe 1: 8 they will keep you from being *i*

INEXPRESSIBLE*
2Co 12: 4 He heard *i* things, things that man
1Pe 1: 8 are filled with an *i* and glorious joy,

INFANCY* (INFANTS)
2Ti 3: 15 from *i* you have known the holy

INFANTS (INFANCY)
Ps 8: 2 From the lips of children and *i*
Mt 21: 16 ''From the lips of children and *i*
1Co 3: 1 but as worldly—mere *i* in Christ.
   14: 20 In regard to evil be *i,*
Eph 4: 14 Then we will no longer be *i,*

INFIRMITIES*
Isa 53: 4 Surely he took up our *i*
Mt 8: 17 ''He took up our *i*

INFLAMED
Ro 1: 27 were *i* with lust for one another.

INFLUENTIAL*
1Co 1: 26 not many were *i;* not many were

INHABITANTS (INHABITED)
Nu 33: 55 '' 'But if you do not drive out the *i*
Rev 8: 13 Woe! Woe to the *i* of the earth,

INHABITED (INHABITANTS)
Isa 45: 18 but formed it to be *i*—

INHERIT (CO-HEIRS HEIR HEIRS HERITAGE INHERITANCE)
Dt 1: 38 because he will lead Israel to *i* it.
Jos 1: 6 people to *i* the land I swore
Ps 37: 11 But the meek will *i* the land
   37: 29 the righteous will *i* the land
Zec 2: 12 The LORD will *i* Judah
Mt 5: 5 for they will *i* the earth.
   19: 29 as much and will *i* eternal life.
Mk 10: 17 ''what must I do to *i* eternal life?''
Lk 10: 25 ''what must I do to *i* eternal life?''
   18: 18 what must I do to *i* eternal life?''
1Co 6: 9 the wicked will not *i* the kingdom
   15: 50 blood cannot *i* the kingdom of God
Rev 21: 7 He who overcomes will *i* all this,

INHERITANCE (INHERIT)
Lev 20: 24 I will give it to you as an *i,*
Dt 4: 20 to be the people of his *i,*
   10: 9 the LORD is their *i,* as the LORD
Jos 14: 3 two-and-a-half tribes their *i* east
Ps 16: 6 surely I have a delightful *i.*
   33: 12 the people he chose for his *i.*
   136: 21 and gave their land as an *i,*
Pr 13: 22 A good man leaves an *i*
Mt 25: 34 blessed by my Father; take your *i.*
Eph 1: 14 who is a deposit guaranteeing our *i*
   5: 5 has any *i* in the kingdom of Christ

INIQUITIES

Col 1: 12 you to share in the *i* of the saints
3: 24 you know that you will receive an *i*.
Heb 9: 15 receive the promised eternal *i*—
1Pe 1: 4 and into an *i* that can never perish,

INIQUITIES (INIQUITY)

Ps 78: 38 he forgave their *i*
103: 10 or repay us according to our *i*.
Isa 53: 5 he was crushed for our *i*;
53: 11 and he will bear their *i*.
59: 2 But your *i* have separated
Mic 7: 19 and hurl all our *i* into the depths

INIQUITY (INIQUITIES)

Ps 25: 11 forgive my *i*, though it is great.
32: 5 and did not cover up my *i*.
51: 2 Wash away all my *i*
51: 9 and blot out all my *i*.
Isa 53: 6 the *i* of us all.

INJURED

Eze 34: 16 will bind up the *i* and strengthen
Zec 11: 16 or heal the *i*, or feed the healthy,

INJUSTICE

2Ch 19: 7 the LORD our God there is no *i*

INK

2Co 3: 3 not with *i* but with the Spirit

INN*

Lk 2: 7 there was no room for them in the *i*
10: 34 took him to an *i* and took care

INNOCENT

Ex 23: 7 do not put an *i* or honest person
Dt 25: 1 acquitting the *i* and condemning
Pr 6: 17 hands that shed *i* blood,
17: 26 It is not good to punish an *i* man,
Mt 10: 16 shrewd as snakes and as *i* as doves.
27: 4 "for I have betrayed *i* blood."
27: 24 I am *i* of this man's blood," he said.
Ac 20: 26 declare to you today that I am *i*
Ro 16: 19 what is good, and *i* about what is
1Co 4: 4 but that does not make me *i*.

INQUIRE

Isa 8: 19 should not a people *i* of their God?

INSCRIPTION

Mt 22: 20 And whose *i*?" "Caesar's,"
2Ti 2: 19 with this *i*: "The Lord knows those

INSIGHT

1Ki 4: 29 Solomon wisdom and very great *i*,
Ps 119: 99 I have more *i* than all my teachers,
Pr 5: 1 listen well to my words of *i*,
21: 30 There is no wisdom, no *i*, no plan
Php 1: 9 more in knowledge and depth of *i*,
2Ti 2: 7 for the Lord will give you *i*

INSOLENT

Ro 1: 30 God-haters, *i*, arrogant

INSPIRED*

Hos 9: 7 the *i* man a maniac.
1Th 1: 3 and your endurance *i* by hope

INSTALLED

Ps 2: 6 "I have *i* my King

INSTINCT* (INSTINCTS)

2Pe 2: 12 are like brute beasts, creatures of *i*,
Jude : 10 things they do understand by *i*,

INSTINCTS* (INSTINCT)

Jude : 19 who follow mere natural *i*

INSTITUTED

Ro 13: 2 rebelling against what God has *i*,
1Pe 2: 13 to every authority *i* among men:

INSTRUCT (INSTRUCTED INSTRUCTION INSTRUCTIONS INSTRUCTOR)

Ps 32: 8 I will *i* you and teach you
105: 22 to *i* his princes as he pleased
Pr 9: 9 *I* a wise man and he will be wiser
Ro 15: 14 and competent to *i* one another.

1Co 2: 16 that he may *i* him?"
14: 19 to *i* others than ten thousand words
2Ti 2: 25 who oppose him he must gently *i*,

INSTRUCTED (INSTRUCT)

2Ch 26: 5 who *i* him in the fear of God.
Pr 21: 11 a wise man is *i*, he gets knowledge.
Isa 50: 4 LORD has given me an *i* tongue,
Mt 13: 52 who has been *i* about the kingdom
1Co 14: 31 in turn so that everyone may be *i*

INSTRUCTION (INSTRUCT)

Pr 1: 8 Listen, my son, to your father's *i*
4: 1 Listen, my sons, to a father's *i*;
4: 13 Hold on to *i*, do not let it go;
8: 10 Choose my *i* instead of silver,
8: 33 Listen to my *i* and be wise;
13: 1 A wise son heeds his father's *i*,
13: 13 He who scorns *i* will pay for it,
16: 20 Whoever gives heed to *i* prospers,
16: 21 and pleasant words promote *i*.
19: 20 Listen to advice and accept *i*,
23: 12 Apply your heart to *i*
1Co 14: 6 or prophecy or word of *i*?
14: 26 or a word of *i*, a revelation,
Eph 6: 4 up in the training and *i* of the Lord.
1Th 4: 8 he who rejects this *i* does not reject
2Th 3: 14 If anyone does not obey our *i*
1Ti 1: 18 I give you this *i* in keeping
6: 3 to the sound *i* of our Lord Jesus
2Ti 4: 2 with great patience and careful *i*.

INSTRUCTIONS (INSTRUCT)

1Ti 3: 14 I am writing you these *i* so that,

INSTRUCTOR (INSTRUCT)

Gal 6: 6 share all good things with his *i*.

INSTRUMENT* (INSTRUMENTS)

Eze 33: 32 beautiful voice and plays an *i* well,
Ac 9: 15 This man is my chosen *i*
2Ti 2: 21 he will be an *i* for noble purposes,

INSTRUMENTS (INSTRUMENT)

Ro 6: 13 as *i* of wickedness, but rather offer

INSULT (INSULTED INSULTS)

Pr 9: 7 corrects a mocker invites *i*;
12: 16 but a prudent man overlooks an *i*.
Mt 5: 11 Blessed are you when people *i* you,
Lk 6: 22 when they exclude you and *i* you
1Pe 3: 9 evil with evil or *i* with *i*,

INSULTED (INSULT)

Heb 10: 29 and who has *i* the Spirit of grace?
Jas 2: 6 love him? But you have *i* the poor.
1Pe 4: 14 If you are *i* because of the name

INSULTS (INSULT)

Ps 22: 7 they hurl *i*, shaking their heads:
69: 9 the *i* of those who insult you fall
Pr 22: 10 quarrels and *i* are ended.
Mk 15: 29 passed by hurled *i* at him,
Jn 9: 28 Then they hurled *i* at him and said,
Ro 15: 3 "The *i* of those who insult you have
2Co 12: 10 in *i*, in hardships, in persecutions,
1Pe 2: 23 When they hurled their *i* at him,

INTEGRITY*

Dt 9: 5 or your *i* that you are going
1Ki 9: 4 if you walk before me in *i* of heart
1Ch 29: 17 the heart and are pleased with *i*.
Ne 7: 2 because he was a man of *i*
Job 2: 3 And he still maintains his *i*,
2: 9 "Are you still holding on to your *i*?
6: 29 reconsider, for my *i* is at stake.
27: 5 till I die, I will not deny my *i*.
Ps 7: 8 according to my *i*, O Most High.
25: 21 May *i* and uprightness protect me,
41: 12 In my *i* you uphold me
78: 72 David shepherded them with *i*
Pr 10: 9 The man of *i* walks securely,
11: 3 The *i* of the upright guides them,
13: 6 Righteousness guards the man of *i*,
17: 26 or to flog officials for their *i*.
29: 10 Bloodthirsty men hate a man of *i*
Isa 45: 23 my mouth has uttered in all *i*
59: 4 no one pleads his case with *i*.

Mt 22: 16 "we know you are a man of *i*
Mk 12: 14 we know you are a man of *i*.
Tit 2: 7 your teaching show *i*, seriousness

INTELLIGENCE (INTELLIGENT)

Isa 29: 14 the *i* of the intelligent will vanish."
1Co 1: 19 *i* of the intelligent I will frustrate."

INTELLIGENT (INTELLIGENCE)

Isa 29: 14 the intelligence of the *i* will vanish

INTELLIGIBLE

1Co 14: 19 I would rather speak five *i* words

INTENDED

Ge 50: 20 place of God? You *i* to harm me,

INTENSE

1Th 2: 17 out of our *i* longing we made every
Rev 16: 9 They were seared by the *i* heat

INTERCEDE (INTERCEDES INTERCEDING INTERCESSION INTERCESSOR)

Heb 7: 25 he always lives to *i* for them.

INTERCEDES* (INTERCEDE)

Ro 8: 26 but the Spirit himself *i* for us
8: 27 because the Spirit *i* for the saints

INTERCEDING* (INTERCEDE)

Ro 8: 34 hand of God and is also *i* for us.

INTERCESSION* (INTERCEDE)

Isa 53: 12 and made *i* for the transgressors.
1Ti 2: 1 *i* and thanksgiving be made

INTERCESSOR* (INTERCEDE)

Job 16: 20 My *i* is my friend

INTEREST (INTERESTS)

Lev 25: 36 Do not take *i* of any kind from him,
Dt 23: 20 You may charge a foreigner *i*,
Mt 25: 27 would have received it back with *i*.
Php 2: 20 who takes a genuine *i*

INTERESTS (INTEREST)

1Co 7: 34 his wife—and his *i* are divided.
Php 2: 4 only to your own *i*, but also to the *i*
2: 21 everyone looks out for his own *i*,

INTERFERE*

Ezr 6: 7 Do not *i* with the work

INTERMARRY (MARRY)

Dt 7: 3 Do not *i* with them.
Ezr 9: 14 and *i* with the peoples who commit

INTERPRET (INTERPRETATION INTERPRETER INTERPRETS)

Ge 41: 15 "I had a dream, and no one can *i* it.
Mt 16: 3 you cannot *i* the signs of the times.
1Co 12: 30 Do all *i*? But eagerly desire
14: 13 pray that he may *i* what he says.
14: 27 one at a time, and someone must *i*.

INTERPRETATION (INTERPRET)

1Co 12: 10 and to still another the *i* of tongues.
14: 26 a revelation, a tongue or an *i*.
2Pe 1: 20 about by the prophet's own *i*.

INTERPRETER (INTERPRET)

1Co 14: 28 If there is no *i*, the speaker should

INTERPRETS (INTERPRET)

1Co 14: 5 he *i*, so that the church may be

INVADED

2Ki 17: 5 king of Assyria *i* the entire land,
24: 1 king of Babylon *i* the land,

INVENT* (INVENTED)

Ro 1: 30 boastful; they *i* ways of doing evil;

INVENTED* (INVENT)

2Pe 1: 16 We did not follow cleverly *i* stories

INVESTIGATED

Lk 1: 3 I myself have carefully *i* everything

INVISIBLE*

Ro 1: 20 of the world God's *i* qualities—
Col 1: 15 He is the image of the *i* God,
     1: 16 and on earth, visible and *i*,
1Ti 1: 17 immortal, *i*, the only God,
Heb 11: 27 because he saw him who is *i*.

INVITE (INVITED INVITES)

Mt 22: 9 *i* to the banquet anyone you find.'
     25: 38 did we see you a stranger and *i* you
Lk 14: 12 do not *i* your friends, your brothers
     14: 13 you give a banquet, *i* the poor,

INVITED (INVITE)

Zep 1: 7 he has consecrated those he has *i*.
Mt 22: 14 For many are *i*, but few are chosen
     25: 35 I was a stranger and you *i* me in,
Lk 14: 10 But when you are *i*, take the lowest
Rev 19: 9 'Blessed are those who are *i*

INVITES (INVITE)

Pr 18: 6 and his mouth *i* a beating.
1Co 10: 27 If some unbeliever *i* you to a meal

INVOLVED

2Ti 2: 4 a soldier gets *i* in civilian affairs—

IRON

2Ki 6: 6 threw it there, and made the *i* float.
Ps 2: 9 will rule them with an *i* scepter;
Pr 27: 17 As *i* sharpens *i*,
Da 2: 33 and thighs of bronze, its legs of *i*,
1Ti 4: 2 have been seared as with a hot *i*.
Rev 2: 27 He will rule them with an *i* scepter;
     12: 5 all the nations with an *i* scepter.
     19: 15 He will rule them with an *i* scepter.

IRRELIGIOUS*

1Ti 1: 9 and sinful, the unholy and *i*;

IRREVOCABLE*

Ro 11: 29 for God's gifts and his call are *i*.

ISAAC

Son of Abraham by Sarah (Ge 17:19; 21:1-7; 1Ch 1:28). Abrahamic covenant perpetuated through (Ge 17:21; 26:2-5). Offered up by Abraham (Ge 22; Heb 11:17-19). Rebekah taken as wife (Ge 24). Inherited Abraham's estate (Ge 25: 5). Fathered Esau and Jacob (Ge 25:19-26; 1Ch 1: 34). Nearly lost Rebekah to Abimelech (Ge 26: 1-11). Covenant with Abimelech (Ge 26:12-31). Tricked into blessing Jacob (Ge 27). Death (Ge 35:27-29). Father of Israel (Ex 3:6; Dt 29:13; Ro 9:10).

ISAIAH

Prophet to Judah (Isa 1:1). Called by the LORD (Isa 6). Announced judgment to Ahaz (Isa 7), deliverance from Assyria to Hezekiah (2Ki 19; Isa 36-37), deliverance from death to Hezekiah (2Ki 20:1-11; Isa 38). Chronicler of Judah's history (2Ch 26:22; 32:32).

ISCARIOT see JUDAS

ISH-BOSHETH*

Son of Saul who attempted to succeed him as king (2Sa 2:8-4:12; 1Ch 8:33).

ISHMAEL

Son of Abraham by Hagar (Ge 16; 1Ch 1:28). Blessed, but not son of covenant (Ge 17:18-21; Gal 4:21-31). Sent away by Sarah (Ge 21:8-21). Children (Ge 25:12-18; 1Ch 1:29-31). Death (Ge 25:17).

ISLAND

Rev 1: 9 was on the *i* of Patmos
     16: 20 Every *i* fled away

ISRAEL (ISRAEL'S ISRAELITE ISRAELITES)

1. Name given to Jacob (see JACOB).
2. Corporate name of Jacob's descendants; often specifically Northern Kingdom.
Ex 28: 11 Engrave the names of the sons of *I*
     28: 29 of the sons of *I* over his heart
Nu 24: 17 a scepter will rise out of *I*.

Dt 6: 4 Hear, O *I*: The LORD our God,
     10: 12 O *I*, what does the LORD your
Jos 4: 22 *I* crossed the Jordan on dry ground
Jdg 17: 6 In those days *I* had no king;
Ru 2: 12 of *I*, under whose wings you have
1Sa 3: 20 *I* from Dan to Beersheba
     4: 21 "The glory has departed from *I*"—
     14: 23 So the LORD rescued *I* that day,
     15: 26 has rejected you as king over *I!*"
     17: 46 will know that there is a God in *I*.
     18: 16 But all *I* and Judah loved David,
2Sa 5: 2 'You will shepherd my people *I*,
     5: 3 they anointed David king over *I*.
     14: 25 In all *I* there was not a man
1Ki 1: 35 I have appointed him ruler over *I*
     10: 9 of the LORD's eternal love for *I*,
     18: 17 "Is that you, you troubler of *I?*"
     19: 18 Yet I reserve seven thousand in *I*—
2Ki 5: 8 know that there is a prophet in *I*.'
1Ch 17: 22 made your people *I* your very own
     21: 1 incited David to take a census of *I*.
     29: 25 Solomon in the sight of all *I*
2Ch 9: 8 of the love of your God for *I*
Ps 73: 1 Surely God is good to *I*,
     81: 8 if you would but listen to me, O *I!*
     98: 3 his faithfulness to the house of *I*;
     99: 8 you were to *I* a forgiving God,
Isa 11: 12 and gather the exiles of *I*;
     27: 6 I will bud and blossom
     44: 21 O *I*, I will not forget you.
     46: 13 my splendor to *I*.
Jer 2: 3 *I* was holy to the LORD,
     23: 6 and *I* will live in safety.
     31: 2 I will come to give rest to *I*."
     31: 10 'He who scattered *I* will gather
     31: 31 covenant with the house of *I*
     33: 17 sit on the throne of the house of *I*,
Eze 3: 17 you a watchman for the house of *I*;
     33: 7 you a watchman for the house of *I*;
     34: 2 prophesy against the shepherds of *I*
     37: 28 that I the LORD make *I* holy,
     39: 23 of *I* went into exile for their sin,
Da 9: 20 my sin and the sin of my people *I*
Hos 11: 1 "When *I* was a child, I loved him,
Am 4: 12 prepare to meet your God, O *I*."
     7: 11 and *I* will surely go into exile,
     8: 2 "The time is ripe for my people *I*;
     9: 14 I will bring back my exiled people *I*
Mic 5: 2 one who will be ruler over *I*,
Zep 3: 13 The remnant of *I* will do no wrong;
Zec 11: 14 brotherhood between Judah and *I*.
Mal 1: 5 even beyond the borders of *I!*'
Mt 2: 6 be the shepherd of my people *I*.' "
     10: 6 Go rather to the lost sheep of *I*.
     15: 24 only to the lost sheep of *I*."
Mk 12: 29 'Hear, O *I*, the Lord our God,
Lk 22: 30 judging the twelve tribes of *I*.
Ac 1: 6 going to restore the kingdom to *I?*"
     9: 15 and before the people of *I*.
Ro 9: 4 of my own race, the people of *I*.
     9: 6 all who are descended from *I* are *I*.
     9: 31 but *I*, who pursued a law
     11: 7 What *I* sought so earnestly it did
     11: 26 And so all *I* will be saved,
Gal 6: 16 who follow this rule, even to the *I*
Eph 2: 12 excluded from citizenship in *I*
     3: 6 Gentiles are heirs together with *I*,
Heb 8: 8 covenant with the house of *I*
Rev 7: 4 144,000 from all the tribes of *I*.
     21: 12 the names of the twelve tribes of *I*.

ISRAEL'S (ISRAEL)

Jdg 10: 16 he could bear *I* misery no longer.
2Sa 23: 1 singer of songs:
Isa 44: 6 *I* King and Redeemer, the LORD
Jer 3: 9 Because *I* immorality mattered
     31: 9 because I am *I* father,
Jn 3: 10 "You are *I* teacher," said Jesus,

ISRAELITE (ISRAEL)

Ex 16: 1 The whole *I* community set out
     35: 29 All the *I* men and women who
Nu 8: 16 offspring from every *I* woman.
     20: 1 the whole *I* community arrived
     20: 22 The whole *I* community set out
Jn 1: 47 "Here is a true *I*, in whom there is
Ro 11: 1 I am an *I* myself, a descendant

ISRAELITES (ISRAEL)

Ex 1: 7 the *I* were fruitful and multiplied
     2: 23 The *I* groaned in their slavery
     3: 9 the cry of the *I* has reached me,
     12: 35 The *I* did as Moses instructed
     12: 37 The *I* journeyed from Rameses
     14: 22 and the *I* went through the sea
     16: 12 I have heard the grumbling of the *I*.
     16: 35 The *I* ate manna forty years,
     24: 17 To the *I* the glory of the LORD
     28: 30 decisions for the *I* over his heart
     29: 45 Then I will dwell among the *I*
     31: 16 The *I* are to observe the Sabbath,
     33: 5 "Tell the *I*, 'You are a stiff-necked
     39: 42 The *I* had done all the work just
Lev 22: 32 be acknowledged as holy by the *I*.
     25: 46 rule over your fellow *I* ruthlessly.
     25: 55 for the *I* belong to me as servants.
Nu 2: 32 These are the *I*, counted according
     6: 23 'This is how you are to bless the *I*.
     9: 2 "Have the *I* celebrate the Passover
     9: 17 the *I* set out; wherever the cloud
     10: 12 Then the *I* set out from the Desert
     14: 2 All the *I* grumbled against Moses
     20: 12 as holy in the sight of the *I*,
     21: 6 they bit the people and many *I* died
     26: 65 had told those *I* they would surely
     27: 12 and see the land I have given the *I*.
     33: 3 The *I* set out from Rameses
     35: 10 "Speak to the *I* and say to them:
Dt 33: 1 on the *I* before his death.
Jos 1: 2 about to give to them—to the *I*.
     5: 6 The *I* had moved about
     7: 1 the *I* acted unfaithfully in regard
     8: 32 There in the presence of the *I*,
     18: 1 of the *I* gathered at Shiloh
     21: 3 the *I* gave the Levites the following
     22: 9 of Manasseh left the *I* at Shiloh
Jdg 2: 11 Then the *I* did evil in the eyes
     3: 12 Once again the *I* did evil
     4: 1 the *I* once again did evil in the eyes
     6: 1 Again the *I* did evil in the eyes
     10: 6 Again the *I* did evil in the eyes
     13: 1 Again the *I* did evil in the eyes
1Sa 17: 2 Saul and the *I* assembled
1Ki 8: 63 and all the *I* dedicated the temple
     9: 22 did not make slaves of any of the *I*;
     12: 1 for all the *I* had gone there
     12: 17 But as for the *I* who were living
2Ki 17: 24 towns of Samaria to replace the *I*.
1Ch 9: 2 in their own towns were some *I*,
     10: 1 I fought against Israel; the *I* fled
     11: 4 and all the *I* marched to Jerusalem,
2Ch 7: 6 and all the *I* were standing.
Ne 1: 6 the sins we *I*, including myself
Jer 16: 14 who brought the *I* up out of Egypt,'
Hos 1: 10 "Yet the *I* will be like the sand
     3: 1 Love her as the LORD loves the *I*,
Am 4: 5 boast about them, you *I*,
Mic 5: 3 return to join the *I*.
Ro 9: 27 the number of the *I* be like the sand
     10: 1 for the *I* is that they may be saved.
     10: 16 But not all the *I* accepted the good
2Co 11: 22 Are they *I*? So am I.

ISSACHAR

Son of Jacob by Leah (Ge 30:18; 35:23; 1Ch 2: 1). Tribe of blessed (Ge 49:14-15; Dt 33:18-19), numbered (Nu 1:29; 26:25), allotted land (Jos 19: 17-23; Eze 48:25), assisted Deborah (Jdg 5:15), 12,000 from (Rev 7:7).

ISSUING*

Da 9: 25 From the *i* of the decree to restore

ITALY

Ac 27: 1 decided that we would sail for *I*,
Heb 13: 24 from *I* send you their greetings.

ITCHING*

2Ti 4: 3 to say what their *i* ears want to hear

ITHAMAR

Son of Aaron (Ex 6:23; 1Ch 6:3). Duties at tabernacle (Ex 38:21; Nu 4:21-33; 7:8).

ITTAI

2Sa 15: 19 The king said to *I* the Gittite,

IVORY

1Ki 10: 22 silver and *i*, and apes and baboons.
　　 22: 39 the palace he built and inlaid with *i*

JABBOK

Ge 32: 22 and crossed the ford of the *J*.
Dt 3: 16 and out to the *J* River,

JABESH

1Sa 11: 1 And all the men of *J* said to him,
　　 31: 12 wall of Beth Shan and went to *J*.
1Ch 10: 12 and his sons and brought them to *J*.

JABESH GILEAD

Jdg 21: 8 that no one from *J* had come to
2Sa 2: 4 the men of *J* who had buried Saul,
1Ch 10: 11 the inhabitants of *J* heard

JACOB

　　 Second son of Isaac, twin of Esau (Ge 26:
21-26; 1Ch 1:34). Bought Esau's birthright (Ge
26:29-34); tricked Isaac into blessing him (Ge 27:
1-37). Fled to Haran (Ge 28:1-5). Abrahamic covenant perpetuated through (Ge 28:13-15; Mal 1:2).
Vision at Bethel (Ge 28:10-22). Served Laban for
Rachel and Leah (Ge 29:1-30). Children (Ge 29:
31-30:24; 35:16-26; 1Ch 2-9). Flocks increased
(Ge 30:25-43). Returned to Canaan (Ge 31).
Wrestled with God; name changed to Israel (Ge
32:22-32). Reconciled to Esau (Ge 33). Returned
to Bethel (Ge 35:1-15). Favored Joseph (Ge 37:3).
Sent sons to Egypt during famine (Ge 42-43).
Settled in Egypt (Ge 46). Blessed Ephraim and
Manasseh (Ge 48). Blessed sons (Ge 49:1-28; Heb
11:21). Death (Ge 49:29-33). Burial (Ge 50:1-14).

JAEL*

　　 Woman who killed Canaanite general, Sisera
(Jdg 4:17-22; 5:24-27).

JAIR

　　 Judge from Gilead (Jdg 10:3-5).

JAIRUS*

　　 Synagogue ruler whose daughter Jesus raised
(Mk 5:22-43; Lk 8:41-56).

JAMES

　　 1. Apostle; brother of John (Mt 4:21-22; 10:2;
Mk 3:17; Lk 5:1-10). At transfiguration (Mt 17:
1-13; Mk 9:1-13; Lk 9:28-36). Killed by Herod
(Ac 12:2).
　　 2. Apostle; son of Alphaeus (Mt 10:3; Mk 3:18;
Lk 6:15).
　　 3. Brother of Jesus (Mt 13:55; Mk 6:3; Lk 24:
10; Gal 1:19) and Judas (Jude 1). With believers
before Pentecost (Ac 1:13). Leader of church at
Jerusalem (Ac 12:17; 15; 21:18; Gal 2:9, 12).
Author of epistle (Jas 1:1).

JAPHETH

　　 Son of Noah (Ge 5:32; 1Ch 1:4-5). Blessed (Ge
9:18-28). Sons of (Ge 10:2-5).

JAR (JARS)

Ge 24: 14 let down your *j* that I may have
1Ki 17: 14 'The *j* of flour will not be used up
Jer 19: 1 "Go and buy a clay *j* from a potter.
Lk 8: 16 hides it in a *j* or puts it under a bed.

JARS (JAR)

Jn 2: 6 Nearby stood six stone water *j*,
2Co 4: 7 we have this treasure in *j* of clay

JASPER

Ex 28: 20 row a chrysolite, an onyx and a *j*.
Eze 28: 13 chrysolite, onyx and *j*,
Rev 4: 3 sat there had the appearance of *j*
　　 21: 19 The first foundation was *j*,

JAVELIN

1Sa 17: 45 me with sword and spear and *j*,

JAWBONE

Jdg 15: 15 Finding a fresh *j* of a donkey,

JEALOUS (JEALOUSY)

Ex 20: 5 the LORD your God, am a *j* God,

Ex 34: 14 whose name is Jealous, is a *j* God.
Dt 4: 24 God is a consuming fire, a *j* God.
　　 6: 15 is a *j* God and his anger will burn
　　 32: 21 They made me *j* by what is no god
Jos 24: 19 He is a holy God; he is a *j* God.
Eze 16: 38 of my wrath and *j* anger.
　　 16: 42 my *j* anger will turn away from you
　　 23: 25 I will direct my *j* anger against you,
　　 36: 6 in my *j* wrath because you have
Joel 2: 18 the LORD will be *j* for his land
Na 1: 2 LORD is a *j* and avenging God;
Zep 3: 8 consumed by the fire of my *j* anger.
Zec 1: 14 I am very *j* for Jerusalem and Zion,
　　 8: 2 "I am very *j* for Zion; I am burning
2Co 11: 2 I am *j* for you with a godly jealousy

JEALOUSY (JEALOUS)

Ps 79: 5 How long will your *j* burn like fire?
Pr 6: 34 for *j* arouses a husband's fury,
　　 27: 4 but who can stand before *j*?
SS 8: 6 its *j* unyielding as the grave.
Zep 1: 18 In the fire of his *j*
Zec 8: 2 I am burning with *j* for her.''
Ro 13: 13 debauchery, not in dissension and *j*
1Co 3: 3 For since there is *j* and quarreling
　　 10: 22 trying to arouse the Lord's *j*?
2Co 11: 2 I am jealous for you with a godly *j*.
　　 12: 20 *j*, outbursts of anger, factions,
Gal 5: 20 hatred, discord, *j*, fits of rage,

JECONIAH see JEHOIACHIN

JEERS*

Heb 11: 36 Some faced *j* and flogging,

JEHOAHAZ

　　 1. Son of Jehu; king of Israel (2Ki 13:1-9).
　　 2. Son of Josiah; king of Judah (2Ki 23:31-34;
2Ch 36:1-4).

JEHOASH

　　 1. See JOASH.
　　 2. Son of Jehoahaz; king of Israel. Defeat of
Aram prophesied by Elisha (2Ki 13:10-25). Defeated Amaziah in Jerusalem (2Ki 14:1-16; 2Ch
25:17-24).

JEHOIACHIN

　　 Son of Jehoiakim; king of Judah exiled by
Nebuchadnezzar (2Ki 24:8-17; 2Ch 36:8-10; Jer
22:24-30; 24:1). Raised from prisoner status (2Ki
25:27-30; Jer 52:31-34).

JEHOIADA

　　 Priest who sheltered Joash from Athaliah (2Ki
11-12; 2Ch 22:11-24:16).

JEHOIAKIM

　　 Son of Jehoahaz; made king of Judah by Pharaoh Neco (2Ki 23:34-24:6; 2Ch 36:4-8; Jer 22:
18-23). Burned scroll of Jeremiah's prophecies
(Jer 36).

JEHORAM

　　 1. Son of Jehoshaphat; king of Judah (2Ki 8:
16-24). Prophesied against by Elijah; killed by the
LORD (2Ch 21:12-20).
　　 2. See JORAM.

JEHOSHAPHAT

　　 Son of Asa; king of Judah. Strengthened his
kingdom (2Ch 17). Joined with Ahab against
Aram (2Ki 22; 2Ch 18). Established judges (2Ch
19). Joined with Joram against Moab (2Ki 3; 2Ch
20).

JEHOVAH see LORD‡

JEHU

　　 1. Prophet against Baasha (2Ki 16:1-7).
　　 2. King of Israel. Anointed by Elijah to obliter-
ate house of Ahab (1Ki 19:16-17); anointed by
servant of Elisha (2Ki 9:1-13). Killed Joram and
Ahaziah (2Ki 9:14-29; 2Ch 22:7-9), Jezebel (2Ki
9:30-37), relatives of Ahab (2Ki 10:1-17), ministers of Baal (2Ki 10:18-29). Death (2Ki 10:30-
36).

JEPHTHAH

　　 Judge from Gilead who delivered Israel from
Ammon (Jdg 10:6-12:7). Made rash vow concerning his daughter (Jdg 11:30-40).

JEREMIAH

　　 Prophet to Judah (Jer 1:1-3). Called by the
LORD (Jer 1). Put in stocks (Jer 20:1-3). Threatened for prophesying (Jer 11:18-23; 26). Opposed
by Hananiah (Jer 28). Scroll burned (Jer 36). Imprisoned (Jer 37). Thrown into cistern (Jer 38).
Forced to Egypt with those fleeing Babylonians
(Jer 43).

JERICHO

Nu 22: 1 along the Jordan across from *J*.
Jos 3: 16 the people crossed over opposite *J*.
　　 5: 10 camped at Gilgal on the plains of *J*,
Lk 10: 30 going down from Jerusalem to *J*,
Heb 11: 30 By faith the walls of *J* fell,

JEROBOAM

　　 1. Official of Solomon; rebelled to become first
king of Israel (1Ki 11:26-40; 12:1-20; 2Ch 10).
Idolatry (1Ki 12:25-33); judgment for (1Ki 13-14;
2Ch 13).
　　 2. Son of Jehoash; king of Israel (1Ki 14:23-
29).

JERUB-BAAL see GIDEON

JERUSALEM

Jos 10: 1 of *J* heard that Joshua had taken Ai
　　 15: 8 of the Jebusite city (that is, *J*).
Jdg 1: 8 The men of Judah attacked *J* also
1Sa 17: 54 head and brought it to *J*,
2Sa 5: 5 and in *J* he reigned over all Israel
　　 5: 6 and his men marched to *J*
　　 9: 13 And Mephibosheth lived in *J*,
　　 11: 1 But David remained in *J*.
　　 15: 29 took the ark of God back to *J*
　　 24: 16 stretched out his hand to destroy *J*,
1Ki 3: 1 the LORD, and the wall around *J*.
　　 9: 15 the wall of *J*, and Hazor, Megiddo
　　 9: 19 whatever he desired to build in *J*,
　　 10: 26 cities and also with him in *J*.
　　 10: 27 as common in *J* as stones,
　　 11: 7 of *J*, Solomon built a high place
　　 11: 13 my servant and for the sake of *J*,
　　 11: 36 always have a lamp before me in *J*,
　　 11: 42 Solomon reigned in *J*
　　 12: 27 at the temple of the LORD in *J*,
　　 14: 21 and he reigned seventeen years in *J*
　　 14: 25 Shishak king of Egypt attacked *J*
　　 15: 2 and he reigned in *J* three years.
　　 15: 10 and he reigned in *J* forty-one years.
　　 22: 42 he reigned in *J* twenty-five years.
2Ki 8: 17 and he reigned in *J* eight years.
　　 8: 26 and he reigned in *J* one year.
　　 12: 1 and he reigned in *J* forty years.
　　 12: 17 Then he turned to attack *J*.
　　 14: 2 he reigned in *J* twenty-nine years.
　　 14: 13 Then Jehoash went to *J*
　　 15: 2 and he reigned in *J* fifty-two years.
　　 15: 33 and he reigned in *J* sixteen years.
　　 16: 2 and he reigned in *J* sixteen years.
　　 16: 5 Israel marched up to fight against *J*
　　 18: 2 he reigned in *J* twenty-nine years.
　　 18: 17 Lachish to King Hezekiah at *J*.
　　 19: 31 For out of *J* will come a remnant,
　　 21: 1 and he reigned in *J* fifty-five years.
　　 21: 12 going to bring such disaster on *J*
　　 21: 19 and he reigned in *J* two years.
　　 22: 1 he reigned in *J* thirty-one years.
　　 23: 27 and I will reject *J*, the city I chose,
　　 23: 31 and he reigned in *J* three months.
　　 23: 36 and he reigned in *J* eleven years.
　　 24: 8 and he reigned in *J* three months.
　　 24: 10 king of Babylon advanced on *J*
　　 24: 14 He carried into exile all *J*:
　　 24: 18 and he reigned in *J* eleven years.
　　 24: 20 anger that all this happened to *J*
　　 25: 1 king of Babylon marched against *J*
　　 25: 9 royal palace and all the houses of *J*.
1Ch 11: 4 and all the Israelites marched to *J*,
　　 21: 16 sword in his hand extended over *J*.
2Ch 1: 4 he had pitched a tent for it in *J*.
　　 3: 1 the LORD in *J* on Mount Moriah,

JESSE

Father of David (Ru 4:17-22; 1Sa 16; 1Ch 2: 12-17).

JESUS

LIFE: Genealogy (Mt 1:1-17; Lk 3:21-37). Birth announced (Mt 1:18-25; Lk 1:26-45). Birth (Mt 2:1-12; Lk 2:1-40). Escape to Egypt (Mt 2: 13-23). As a boy in the temple (Lk 2:41-52). Baptism (Mt 3:13-17; Mk 1:9-11; Lk 3:21-22; Jn 1:32-34). Temptation (Mt 4:1-11; Mk 1:12-13; Lk 4:1-13). Ministry in Galilee (Mt 4:12-18:35; Mk 1:14-9:50; Lk 4:14-13:9; Jn 1:35-2:11; 4; 6), Transfiguration (Mt 17:1-8; Mk 9:2-8; Lk 9:28-36), on the way to Jerusalem (Mt 19-20; Mk 10; Lk 13:10-19:27), in Jerusalem (Mt 21-25; Mk 11-13; Lk 19:28-21:38; Jn 2:12-3:36; 5; 7-12). Last supper (Mt 26:17-35; Mk 14:12-31; Lk 22:1-38; Jn 13-17). Arrest and trial (Mt 26:36-27:31; Mk 14:43-15:20; Lk 22:39-23:25; Jn 18:1-19:16). Crucifixion (Mt 27:32-66; Mk 15:21-47; Lk 23: 26-55; Jn 19:28-42). Resurrection and appearances (Mt 28; Mk 16; Lk 24; Jn 20-21; Ac 1:1-11; 7:56; 9:3-6; 1Co 15:1-8; Rev 1:1-20).

MIRACLES: Healings: official's son (Jn 4:43-54), demoniac in Capernaum (Mk 1:23-26; Lk 4: 33-35), Peter's mother-in-law (Mt 8:14-17; Mk 1: 29-31; Lk 4:38-39), leper (Mt 8:2-4; Mk 1:40-45; Lk 5:12-16), paralytic (Mt 9:1-8; Mk 2:1-12; Lk 5: 17-26), cripple (Jn 5:1-9), shriveled hand (Mt 12: 10-13; Mk 3:1-5; Lk 6:6-11), centurion's servant (Mt 8:5-13; Lk 7:1-10), widow's son raised (Lk 7: 11-17), demoniac (Mt 12:22-23; Lk 11:14), Gadarene demoniacs (Mt 8:28-34; Mk 5:1-20; Lk 8: 26-39), woman's bleeding and Jairus' daughter (Mt 9:18-26; Mk 5:21-43; Lk 8:40-56), blind man (Mt 9:27-31), mute man (Mt 9:32-33), Canaanite woman's daughter (Mt 15:21-28; Mk 7:24-30), deaf man (Mk 7:31-37), blind man (Mk 8:22-26), demoniac boy (Mt 17:14-18; Mk 9:14-29; Lk 9: 37-43), ten lepers (Lk 17:11-19), man born blind (Jn 9:1-7), Lazarus raised (Jn 11), crippled woman (Lk 13:11-17), man with dropsy (Lk 14:1-6), two blind men (Mt 20:29-34; Mk 10:46-52; Lk 18: 35-43), Malchus' ear (Lk 22:50-51). Other Miracles: water to wine (Jn 2:1-11), catch of fish (Lk

5:1-11), storm stilled (Mt 8:23-27; Mk 4:37-41; Lk 8:22-25), 5,000 fed (Mt 14:15-21; Mk 6:35-44; Lk 9:10-17; Jn 6:1-14), walking on water (Mt 14: 25-33; Mk 6:48-52; Jn 6:15-21), 4,000 fed (Mt 15: 32-39; Mk 8:1-9), money from fish (Mt 17:24-27), fig tree cursed (Mt 21:18-22; Mk 11:12-14), catch of fish (Jn 21:1-14).

MAJOR TEACHING: Sermon on the Mount (Mt 5-7; Lk 6:17-49), to Nicodemus (Jn 3), to Samaritan woman (Jn 4), Bread of Life (Jn 6: 22-59), at Feast of Tabernacles (Jn 7-8), woes to Pharisees (Mt 23; Lk 11:37-54), Good Shepherd (Jn 10:1-18), Olivet Discourse (Mt 24-25; Mk 13; Lk 21:5-36), Upper Room Discourse (Jn 13-16).

PARABLES: Sower (Mt 13:3-23; Mk 4:3-25; Lk 8:5-18), seed's growth (Mk 4:26-29), wheat and weeds (Mt 13:24-30, 36-43), mustard seed (Mt 13:31-32; Mk 4:30-32), yeast (Mt 13:33-35; Mk 4:33-34), hidden treasure (Mt 13:44), valuable pearl (Mt 13:45-46), net (Mt 13:47-51), house owner (Mt 13:52), good Samaritan (Lk 10:25-37), unmerciful servant (Mt 18:15-35), lost sheep (Mt 18:10-14; Lk 15:4-7), lost coin (Lk 15:8-10), prodigal son (Lk 15:11-32), dishonest manager (Lk 16:1-13), rich man and Lazarus (Lk 16:19-31), persistent widow (Lk 18:1-8), Pharisee and tax collector (Lk 18:9-14), payment of workers (Mt 20:1-16), tenants and the vineyard (Mt 21: 28-46; Mt 12:1-12; Lk 20:9-19), wedding banquet (Mt 22:1-14), faithful servant (Mt 24:45-51), ten virgins (Mt 25:1-13), talents (Mt 25:1-30; Lk 19: 12-27).

DISCIPLES see APOSTLES. Call of (Jn 1: 35-51; Mt 4:18-22; 9:9; Mk 1:16-20; 2:13-14; Lk 5:1-11, 27-28). Named Apostles (Mk 3:13-19; Lk 6:12-16). Twelve sent out (Mt 10; Mk 6:7-11; Lk 9:1-5). Seventy sent out (Lk 10:1-24). Defection of (Jn 6:60-71; Mt 26:56; Mk 14:50-52). Final commission (Mt 28:16-20; Jn 21:15-23; Ac 1:3-8).

1Pe 1: 3 the resurrection of *J* Christ
2Pe 1: 16 and coming of our Lord *J* Christ,
1Jn 1: 7 and the blood of *J*, his Son,
 2: 1 *J* Christ, the Righteous One.
 2: 6 to live in him must walk as *J* did.
 4: 15 anyone acknowledges that *J* is
Rev 1: 1 The revelation of *J* Christ,
 22: 16 *J*, have sent my angel
 22: 20 Come, Lord *J*.

JETHRO

Father-in-law and adviser of Moses (Ex 3:1; 18). Also known as Reuel (Ex 2:18).

JEW (JEWS JEWS' JUDAISM)

Est 2: 5 of Susa a *J* of the tribe of Benjamin,
Zec 8: 23 of one *J* by the hem of his robe
Ac 21: 39 "I am a *J*, from Tarsus in Cilicia,
Ro 1: 16 first for the *J*, then for the Gentile.
 2: 28 A man is not a *J* if he is only one
 10: 12 there is no difference between *J*
1Co 9: 20 To the Jews I became like a *J*,
Gal 2: 14 "You are a *J*, yet you live like
 3: 28 There is neither *J* nor Greek,
Col 3: 11 Here there is no Greek or *J*,

JEWEL (JEWELRY JEWELS)

Pr 20: 15 that speak knowledge are a rare *j*.
SS 4: 9 with one *j* of your necklace.
Rev 21: 11 that of a very precious *j*,

JEWELRY (JEWEL)

Ex 35: 22 and brought gold *j* of all kinds:
Jer 2: 32 Does a maiden forget her *j*,
Eze 16: 11 you with *j*: I put bracelets
1Pe 3: 3 wearing of gold *j* and fine clothes.

JEWELS (JEWEL)

Isa 54: 12 your gates of sparkling *j*,
 61: 10 as a bride adorns herself with her *j*.
Zec 9: 16 like *j* in a crown.

JEWS (JEW)

Ne 4: 1 He ridiculed the *J*,
Est 3: 13 kill and annihilate all the *J*—
 4: 14 and deliverance for the *J* will arise
Mt 2: 2 who has been born king of the *J*?
 27: 11 "Are you the king of the *J*?" "Yes,
Jn 4: 9 (For *J* do not associate
 4: 22 for salvation is from the *J*.
 19: 3 saying, "Hail, king of the *J*!"
Ac 20: 21 I have declared to both *J*
Ro 3: 29 Is God the God of *J* only?
 9: 24 not only from the *J* but
 15: 27 they owe it to the *J* to share
1Co 1: 22 *J* demand miraculous signs
 9: 20 To the *J* I became like a Jew,
 12: 13 whether *J* or Greeks, slave or free
Gal 2: 8 of Peter as an apostle to the *J*,
Rev 2: 9 slander of those who say they are *J*
 3: 9 claim to be *J* though they are not,

JEWS' (JEW)

Ro 15: 27 shared in the *J* spiritual blessings,

JEZEBEL

Sidonian wife of Ahab (1Ki 16:31). Promoted Baal worship (1Ki 16:32-33). Killed prophets of the LORD (1Ki 18:4, 13). Opposed Elijah (1Ki 19:1-2). Had Naboth killed (1Ki 21). Death prophesied (1Ki 21:17-24). Killed by Jehu (2Ki 9:30-37).

JEZREEL

2Ki 9: 36 at *J* dogs will devour Jezebel's flesh
 10: 7 and sent them to Jehu in *J*.
Hos 1: 4 house of Jehu for the massacre at *J*,

JOAB

Nephew of David (1Ch 2:16). Commander of his army (2Sa 8:16). Victorious over Ammon (2Sa 10; 1Ch 19), Rabbah (2Sa 11; 1Ch 20), Jerusalem (1Ch 11:6), Absalom (2Sa 18), Sheba (2Sa 20). Killed Abner (2Sa 3:22-39), Amasa (2Sa 20:1-13). Numbered David's army (2Sa 24; 1Ch 21). Sided with Adonijah (1Ki 1:17, 19). Killed by Benaiah (1Ki 2:5-6, 28-35).

JOASH

Son of Ahaziah; king of Judah. Sheltered from Athaliah by Jehoiada (2Ki 11; 2Ch 22:10-23:21). Repaired temple (2Ki 12; 2Ch 24).

JOB

Wealthy man from Uz; feared God (Job 1:1-5). Righteousness tested by disaster (Job 1:6-22), personal affliction (Job 2). Maintained innocence in debate with three friends (Job 3-31), Elihu (Job 32-37). Rebuked by the LORD (Job 38-41). Vindicated and restored to greater stature by the LORD (Job 42). Example of righteousness (Eze 14:14, 20).

JOCHEBED*

Mother of Moses and Aaron (Ex 6:20; Nu 26:59).

JOEL

Prophet (Joel 1:1; Ac 2:16).

JOHN

1. Son of Zechariah and Elizabeth (Lk 1). Called the Baptist (Mt 3:1-12; Mk 1:2-8). Witness to Jesus (Mt 3:11-12; Mk 1:7-8; Lk 3:15-18; Jn 1: 6-35; 3:27-30; 5:33-36). Doubts about Jesus (Mt 11:2-6; Lk 7:18-23). Arrest (Mt 4:12; Mk 1:14). Execution (Mt 14:1-12; Mk 6:14-29; Lk 9:7-9). Ministry compared to Elijah (Mt 11:7-19; Mk 9: 11-13; Lk 7:24-35).

2. Apostle; brother of James (Mt 4:21-22; 10: 2; Mk 3:17; Lk 5:1-10). At transfiguration (Mt 17:1-13; Mk 9:1-13; Lk 9:28-36). Desire to be greatest (Mk 10:35-45). Leader of church at Jerusalem (Ac 4:1-3; Gal 2:9). Elder who wrote epistles (2Jn 1; 3Jn 1). Prophet who wrote Revelation (Rev 1: 1; 22:8).

3. Cousin of Barnabas, co-worker with Paul, (Ac 12:12-13:13; 15:37), see MARK.

JOIN (JOINED JOINS)

Ne 10: 29 all these now *j* their brothers
Pr 23: 20 Do not *j* those who drink too much
 24: 21 and do not *j* with the rebellious,
Jer 3: 18 of Judah will *j* the house of Israel,
Eze 37: 17 *J* them together into one stick
Da 11: 34 who are not sincere will *j* them.
Ro 15: 30 to *j* me in my struggle by praying
2Ti 1: 8 *j* with me in suffering for the gospel

JOINED (JOIN)

Zec 2: 11 "Many nations will be *j*
Mt 19: 6 Therefore what God has *j* together,
Mk 10: 9 Therefore what God has *j* together,
Ac 1: 14 They all *j* together constantly
Eph 2: 21 him the whole building is *j* together
 4: 16 *j* and held together

JOINS (JOIN)

1Co 16: 16 and to everyone who *j* in the work,

JOINT (JOINTS)

Ps 22: 14 and all my bones are out of *j*.

JOINTS (JOINT)

Heb 4: 12 even to dividing soul and spirit, *j*

JOKING*

Ge 19: 14 his sons-in-law thought he was *j*.
Pr 26: 19 and says, "I was only *j*!"
Eph 5: 4 or coarse *j*, which out of place,

JONAH

Prophet in days of Jeroboam II (2Ki 14:25). Called to Nineveh; fled to Tarshish (Jnh 1:1-3). Cause of storm; thrown into sea (Jnh 1:4-16). Swallowed by fish (Jnh 1:17). Prayer (Jnh 2). Preached to Nineveh (Jnh 3). Attitude reproved by the LORD (Jnh 4). Sign of (Mt 12:39-41; Lk 11:29-32).

JONATHAN

Son of Saul (1Sa 13:16; 1Ch 8:33). Valiant warrior (1Sa 13-14). Relation to David (1Sa 18: 1-4; 19-20; 23:16-18). Killed at Gilboa (1Sa 31). Mourned by David (2Sa 1).

JOPPA

Ezr 3: 7 logs by sea from Lebanon to *J*,
Jnh 1: 3 to *J*, where he found a ship bound
Ac 9: 43 Peter stayed in *J* for some time

JORAM

1. Son of Ahab; king of Israel. Fought with Jehoshaphat against Moab (2Ki 3). Killed with Ahaziah by Jehu (2Ki 8:25-29; 9:14-26; 2Ch 22: 5-9).

2. See JEHORAM.

JORDAN

Ge 13: 10 plain of the *J* was well watered,
Nu 22: 1 and camped along the *J*
 34: 12 boundary will go down along the *J*
Dt 3: 27 you are not going to cross this *J*.
Jos 1: 2 get ready to cross the *J* River
 3: 11 go into the *J* ahead of you.
 3: 17 ground in the middle of the *J*,
 4: 22 Israel crossed the *J* on dry ground.'
2Ki 2: 7 and Elisha had stopped at the *J*.
 2: 13 and stood on the bank of the *J*.
 5: 10 wash yourself seven times in the *J*,
 6: 4 They went to the *J* and began
Ps 114: 3 the *J* turned back;
Isa 9: 1 along the *J*— The people walking
Jer 12: 5 manage in the thickets by the *J*?
Mt 3: 6 baptized by him in the *J* River.
 4: 15 the way to the sea, along the *J*,
Mk 1: 9 and was baptized by John in the *J*.

JOSEPH

1. Son of Jacob by Rachel (Ge 30:24; 1Ch 2:2). Favored by Jacob, hated by brothers (Ge 37:3-4). Dreams (Ge 37:5-11). Sold by brothers (Ge 37: 12-36). Served Potiphar; imprisoned by false accusation (Ge 39). Interpreted dreams of Pharaoh's servants (Ge 40), of Pharaoh (Ge 41:1-40). Made greatest in Egypt (Ge 41:41-57). Sold grain to brothers (Ge 42-45). Brought Jacob and sons to Egypt (Ge 46-47). Sons Ephraim and Manasseh blessed (Ge 48). Blessed (Ge 49:22-26; Dt 33: 13-17). Death (Ge 50:22-26; 2 Ex 13:19; Heb 11: 22). 12,000 from (Rev 7:8).

2. Husband of Mary, mother of Jesus (Mt 1: 16-24; 2:13-19; Lk 1:27; 2; Jn 1:45).

3. Disciple from Arimathea, who gave his tomb for Jesus' burial (Mt 27:57-61; Mk 15:43-47; Lk 24:50-52).

4. Original name of Barnabas (Ac 4:36).

JOSHUA (HOSHEA)

1. Son of Nun; name changed from Hoshea (Nu 13:8, 16; 1Ch 7:27). Fought Amalekites under Moses (Ex 17:9-14). Servant of Moses on Sinai (Ex 24:13; 32:17). Spied Canaan (Nu 13). With Caleb, allowed to enter land (Nu 14:6, 30). Succeeded Moses (Dt 1:38; 31:1-18; 33:9).

Charged Israel to conquer Canaan (Jos 1). Crossed Jordan (Jos 3-4). Circumcised sons of wilderness wanderings (Jos 5). Conquered Jericho (Jos 6), Ai (Jos 7-8), five kings at Gibeon (Jos 10: 1-28), southern Canaan (Jos 10:29-43), northern Canaan (Jos 11-12). Defeated at Ai (Jos 7). Deceived by Gibeonites (Jos 9). Renewed covenant (Jos 8:30-35; 24:1-27). Divided land among tribes (Jos 13-22). Last words (Jos 23). Death (Jos 24: 28-31).

2. High priest during rebuilding of temple (Hag 1-2; Zec 3:1-9; 6:11).

JOSIAH

Son of Amon; king of Judah (2Ki 21:26; 1Ch 3: 14). Prophesied (1Ki 13:2). Book of Law discovered during his reign (2Ki 22; 2Ch 34:14-31). Reforms (2Ki 23:1-25; 2Ch 34:1-13; 35:1-19). Killed by Pharaoh Neco (2Ki 23:29-30; 2Ch 35: 20-27).

JOTHAM

1. Son of Gideon (Jdg 9).

2. Son of Azariah (Uzziah); king of Judah (2Ki 15:32-38; 2Ch 26:21-27:9).

JOURNEY

Dt 1: 33 who went ahead of you on your *j*,
 2: 7 over your *j* through this vast desert

Jdg 18: 6 Your *j* has the LORD's approval.''
Ezr 8:21 and ask him for a safe *j* for us
Job 16:22 before I go on the *j* of no return.
Isa 35: 8 The unclean will not *j* on it;
Mt 25:14 it will be like a man going on a *j*,
Ro 15:24 to have you assist me on my *j* there

JOY* (ENJOY ENJOYMENT JOYFUL JOYOUS OVERJOYED REJOICE REJOICES REJOICING)

Ge 31:27 so I could send you away with *j*
Lev 9:24 shouted for *j* and fell facedown.
Dt 16:15 and your *j* will be complete.
Jdg 9:19 may Abimelech be your *j*.
1Ch 12:40 and sheep, for there was *j* in Israel.
   16:27 strength and *j* in his dwelling place.
   16:33 sing for *j* before the LORD,
   29:17 with *j* how willingly your people
   29:22 drank with great *j* in the presence
2Ch 30:26 There was great *j* in Jerusalem,
Ezr 3:12 while many others shouted for *j*,
   3:13 of the shouts of *j* from the sound
   6:16 of the house of God with *j*.
   6:22 with *j* by changing the attitude
   6:22 *j* the Feast of Unleavened Bread,
Ne 8:10 for the *j* of the LORD is your
   8:12 and to celebrate with great *j*,
   8:17 And their *j* was very great.
   12:43 God had given them great *j*.
Est 8:16 a time of happiness and *j*,
   8:17 there was *j* and gladness
   9:17 and made it a day of feasting and *j*.
   9:18 and made it a day of feasting and *j*.
   9:19 as a day of *j* and feasting,
   9:22 and *j* and giving presents of food
   9:22 their sorrow was turned into *j*
Job 3: 7 may no shout of *j* be heard in it.
   6:10 my *j* in unrelenting pain—
   8:21 and your lips with shouts of *j*.
   9:25 they fly away without a glimpse of *j*
   10:20 from me so I can have a moment's *j*
   20: 5 the *j* of the godless lasts
   33:26 he sees God's face and shouts for *j*;
   38: 7 and all the angels shouted for *j*?
Ps 4: 7 have filled my heart with greater *j*
   5:11 let them ever sing for *j*.
   16:11 me with *j* in your presence,
   19: 8 giving *j* to the heart.
   20: 5 We will shout for *j*
   21: 1 How great is his *j* in the victories
   21: 6 with the *j* of your presence.
   27: 6 will I sacrifice with shouts of *j*;
   28: 7 My heart leaps for *j*
   30:11 sackcloth and clothed me with *j*,
   33: 3 play skillfully, and shout for *j*.
   35:27 shout for *j* and gladness;
   42: 4 with shouts of *j* and thanksgiving
   43: 4 to God, my *j* and my delight.
   45: 7 by anointing you with the oil of *j*.
   45:15 They are led in with *j* and gladness;
   47: 1 shout to God with cries of *j*.
   47: 5 God has ascended amid shouts of *j*,
   48: 2 the *j* of the whole earth.
   51: 8 Let me hear *j* and gladness;
   51:12 to me the *j* of your salvation
   65: 8 you call forth songs of *j*.
   65:13 they shout for *j* and sing.
   66: 1 Shout with *j* to God, all the earth!
   67: 4 the nations be glad and sing for *j*,
   71:23 My lips will shout for *j*
   81: 1 Sing for *j* to God our strength;
   86: 4 Bring *j* to your servant,
   89:12 Hermon sing for *j* at your name.
   90:14 for *j* and be glad all our days.
   92: 4 I sing for *j* at the works
   94:19 your consolation brought *j*
   95: 1 let us sing for *j* to the LORD;
   96:12 the trees of the forest will sing for *j*;
   97:11 and *j* on the upright in heart.
   98: 4 for *j* to the LORD, all the earth,
   98: 6 shout for *j* before the LORD,
   98: 8 the mountains sing together for *j*;
   100: 1 for *j* to the LORD, all the earth.
   105:43 his chosen ones with shouts of *j*;
   106: 5 share in the *j* of your nation
   107:22 and tell of his works with songs of *j*.
   118:15 Shouts of *j* and victory
   119:111 they are the *j* of my heart.

Ps 126: 2 our tongues with songs of *j*.
   126: 3 and we are filled with *j*.
   126: 5 will reap with songs of *j*.
   126: 6 will return with songs of *j*,
   132: 9 may your saints sing for *j*.''
   132:16 and her saints will ever sing for *j*.
   137: 3 tormentors demanded songs of *j*;
   137: 6 my highest *j*.
   149: 5 and sing for *j* on their beds.
Pr 10: 1 A wise son brings *j* to his father,
   10:28 The prospect of the righteous is *j*,
   11:10 wicked perish, there are shouts of *j*.
   12:20 but *j* for those who promote peace.
   14:10 and no one else can share its *j*.
   14:13 and *j* may end in grief.
   15:20 A wise son brings *j* to his father,
   15:23 A man finds *j* in giving an apt reply
   15:30 A cheerful look brings *j*
   17:21 there is no *j* for the father of a fool.
   21:15 it brings *j* to the righteous
   23:24 of a righteous man has great *j*;
   27: 9 incense bring *j* to the heart,
   27:11 my son, and bring *j* to my heart;
   29: 3 A man who loves wisdom brings *j*
Ecc 8:15 Then *j* will accompany him
   11: 9 let your heart give you *j* in the days
Isa 9: 3 and increased their *j*;
   12: 3 With *j* you will draw water
   12: 6 Shout aloud and sing for *j*,
   16: 9 shouts of *j* over your ripened fruit
   16:10 *J* and gladness are taken away
   22:13 But see, there is *j* and revelry,
   24:11 all *j* turns to gloom,
   24:14 raise their voices, they shout for *j*;
   26:19 wake up and shout for *j*.
   35: 2 will rejoice greatly and shout for *j*.
   35: 6 the mute tongue shout for *j*.
   35:10 Gladness and *j* will overtake them,
   35:10 everlasting *j* will crown their heads
   42:11 Let the people of Sela sing for *j*;
   44:23 Sing for *j*, O heavens,
   48:20 Announce this with shouts of *j*
   49:13 Shout for *j*, O heavens;
   51: 3 *J* and gladness will be found in her,
   51:11 Gladness and *j* will overtake them,
   51:11 everlasting *j* will crown their heads
   52: 8 together they shout for *j*.
   52: 9 Burst into songs of *j* together,
   54: 1 burst into song, shout for *j*,
   55:12 You will go out in *j*
   56: 7 give them *j* in my house of prayer.
   58:14 then you will find your *j*
   60: 5 heart will throb and swell with *j*;
   60:15 and the *j* of all generations.
   61: 7 and everlasting *j* will be theirs.
   65:14 out of the *j* of their hearts,
   65:18 and its people a *j*.
   66: 5 that we may see your *j*!''
Jer 7:34 will bring an end to the sounds of *j*
   15:16 they were my *j* and my heart's
   16: 9 will bring an end to the sounds of *j*
   25:10 banish from them the sounds of *j*
   31: 7 ''Sing with *j* for Jacob;
   31:12 shout for *j* on the heights of Zion;
   31:13 give them comfort and *j* instead
   33: 9 this city will bring me renown, *j*,
   33:11 be heard once more the sounds of *j*
   48:33 *J* and gladness are gone
   48:33 no one treads with shouts of *j*
   48:33 they are not shouts of *j*.
   51:48 will shout for *j* over Babylon.
La 2:15 the *j* of the whole earth?''
   5:15 *J* is gone from our hearts;
Eze 7: 7 not *j*, upon the mountains.
   24:25 their *j* and glory, the delight
Joel 1:12 Surely the *j* of mankind
   1:16 *j* and gladness
Mt 13:20 and at once receives it with *j*.
   13:44 in his *j* went and sold all he had
   28: 8 afraid yet filled with *j*,
Mk 4:16 and at once receive it with *j*.
Lk 1:14 He will be a *j* and delight to you,
   1:44 the baby in my womb leaped for *j*.
   1:58 great mercy, and they shared her *j*.
   2:10 news of great *j* that will be
   6:23 ''Rejoice in that day and leap for *j*,
   8:13 the word with *j* when they hear it,
   10:17 The seventy-two returned with *j*

Lk 10:21 full of *j* through the Holy Spirit,
   24:41 still did not believe it because of *j*
   24:52 returned to Jerusalem with great *j*.
Jn 3:29 That *j* is mine, and it is now
   3:29 full of *j* when he hears
   15:11 and that your *j* may be in you
   15:11 this so that my *j* may be in you
   16:20 but your grief will turn to *j*.
   16:21 because of her *j* that a child is born
   16:22 and no one will take away your *j*.
   16:24 and your *j* will be complete.
   17:13 measure of my *j* within them.
Ac 2:28 with *j* in your presence.'
   8: 8 So there was great *j* in that city.
   13:52 And the disciples were filled with *j*
   14:17 and fills your hearts with *j*.''
   16:34 he was filled with *j* because he had come
Ro 14: 7 peace and *j* in the Holy Spirit,
   15:13 the God of hope fill you with all *j*
   15:32 will I may come to you with *j*
   16:19 so I am full of *j* over you;
2Co 1:24 but we work with you for your *j*,
   2: 3 that you would all share my *j*.
   7: 4 our troubles my *j* knows no
   7: 7 so that my *j* was greater than ever.
   8: 2 their overflowing *j* and their
Gal 4:15 What has happened to all your *j*?
   5:22 *j*, peace, patience, kindness,
Php 1: 4 I always pray with *j*
   1:25 for your progress and *j* in the faith,
   1:26 being with you again your *j*
   2: 2 then make my *j* complete
   2:29 him in the Lord with great *j*,
   4: 1 and long for, my *j* and crown,
1Th 1: 6 with the *j* given by the Holy Spirit.
   2:19 For what is our hope, our *j*,
   2:20 Indeed, you are our glory and *j*.
   3: 9 you in return for all the *j* we have
2Ti 1: 4 so that I may be filled with *j*.
Phm 7 Your love has given me great *j*
Heb 1: 9 by anointing you with the oil of *j*.''
   12: 2 for the *j* set before him endured
   13:17 them so that their work will be a *j*,
Jas 1: 2 Consider it pure *j*, my brothers,
   4: 9 to mourning and your *j* to gloom.
1Pe 1: 8 with an inexpressible and glorious *j*
1Jn 1: 4 this to make our *j* complete.
2Jn 4 It has given me great *j* to find some
   12 so that our *j* may be complete.
3Jn 3 It gave me great *j* to have some
   4 I have no greater *j*
Jude 24 without fault and with great *j*—

JOYFUL* (JOY)

Dt 16:14 Be *j* at your Feast—you, your sons
1Sa 18: 6 with *j* songs and with tambourines
1Ki 8:66 *j* and glad in heart
1Ch 15:16 as singers to sing *j* songs,
2Ch 7:10 *j* and glad in heart
Ps 68: 3 may they be happy and *j*.
   100: 2 come before him with *j* songs.
Ecc 9: 7 and drink your wine with a *j* heart,
Isa 24: 8 the *j* harp is silent.
Jer 31: 4 and go out to dance with the *j*.
Hab 3:18 I will be *j* in God my Savior.
Zec 8:19 and tenth months will become *j*
   10: 7 Their children will see it and be *j*;
Ro 12:12 Be *j* in hope, patient in affliction,
1Th 5:16 Be *j* always; pray continually;
Heb 12:22 thousands of angels in *j* assembly,

JOYOUS* (JOY)

Est 8:15 the city of Susa held a *j* celebration.

JUBILANT

Ps 96:12 let the fields be *j*, and everything
   98: 4 burst into *j* song with music;

JUBILEE

Lev 25:11 The fiftieth year shall be a *j* for you;

JUDAH (JUDEA)

   1. Son of Jacob by Leah (Ge 29:35; 35:23; 1Ch 2:1). Did not want to kill Joseph (Ge 37:26-27). Among Canaanites, fathered Perez by Tamar (Ge 38). Tribe of blessed as ruling tribe (Ge 49:8-12; Dt 33:7), numbered (Nu 1:27; 26:22), allotted land (Jos 15; Eze 48:7), failed to fully possess (Jos 15:63; Jdg 1:1-20).

2. Name used for people and land of Southern Kingdom.
Ru 1: 1 take them back to the land of *J*.
2Sa 2: 4 king over the house of *J*.
Isa 1: 1 The vision concerning *J*
     3: 8 *J* is falling;
Jer 13: 19 All *J* will be carried into exile.
    30: 3 bring my people Israel and *J* back
Hos 1: 7 I will show love to the house of *J*;
Zec 10: 4 From *J* will come the cornerstone,
Mt 2: 6 least among the rulers of *J*;
Heb 7: 14 that our Lord descended from *J*,
    8: 8 and with the house of *J*.
Rev 5: 5 of the tribe of *J*, the Root of David,

JUDAISM (JEW)
Ac 13: 43 devout converts to *J* followed Paul
Gal 1: 13 of my previous way of life in *J*,
    1: 14 advancing in *J* beyond many Jews

JUDAS
   1. Apostle; son of James (Lk 6:16; Jn 14:22; Ac 1:13). Probably also called Thaddaeus (Mt 10:3; Mk 3:18).
   2. Brother of James and Jesus (Mt 13:55; Mk 6:3), also called Jude (Jude 1).
   3. Christian prophet (Ac 15:22-32).
   4. Apostle, also called Iscariot, who betrayed Jesus (Mt 10:4; 26:14-56; Mk 3:19; 14:10-50; Lk 6:16; 22:3-53; Jn 6:71; 12:4; 13:2-30; 18:2-11). Suicide of (Mt 27:3-5; Ac 1:16-25).

JUDE see JUDAS

JUDEA (JUDAH)
Mt 2: 1 born in Bethlehem in *J*,
  24: 16 are in *J* flee to the mountains.
Lk 3: 1 Pontius Pilate was governor of *J*,
Ac 1: 8 and in all *J* and Samaria,
   9: 31 Then the church throughout *J*,
1Th 2: 14 imitators of God's churches in *J*,

JUDGE (JUDGED JUDGES JUDGING JUDGMENT JUDGMENTS)
Ge 16: 5 May the LORD *j* between you
 18: 25 Will not the *J* of all the earth do
Lev 19: 15 but *j* your neighbor fairly.
Dt 1: 16 between your brothers and *j* fairly,
  17: 12 man who shows contempt for the *j*
  32: 36 The LORD will *j* his people
Jdg 2: 18 Whenever the LORD raised up a *j*
1Sa 2: 10 the LORD will *j* the ends
   3: 13 that I would *j* his family forever
   7: 15 *j* over Israel all the days of his life.
  24: 12 May the LORD *j* between you
1Ki 8: 32 *J* between your servants,
1Ch 16: 33 for he comes to *j* the earth.
2Ch 6: 23 *J* between your servants, repaying
  19: 7 *j* carefully, for with the LORD our
Job 9: 15 plead with my *J* for mercy.
Ps 7: 8 *J* me, O LORD, according
   7: 8 let the LORD *j* the peoples.
   7: 11 God is a righteous *j*,
   9: 8 he will *j* the world in righteousness
  50: 6 for God himself is *j*.
  51: 4 and justified when you *j*.
  75: 2 it is I who *j* uprightly.
  76: 9 when you, O God, rose up to *j*,
  82: 8 Rise up, O God, *j* the earth,
  94: 2 Rise up, O *J* of the earth;
  96: 10 he will *j* the peoples with equity.
  96: 13 He will *j* the world in righteousness
  98: 9 He will *j* the world in righteousness
 110: 6 He will *j* the nations, heaping up
Pr 31: 9 Speak up and *j* fairly;
Isa 2: 4 He will *j* between the nations
   3: 13 he rises to *j* the people.
  11: 3 He will not *j* by what he sees
  33: 22 For the LORD is our *j*,
Jer 11: 20 Almighty, you who *j* righteously
Eze 7: 3 I will *j* you according
   7: 27 by their own standards I will *j* them
  18: 30 O house of Israel, I will *j* you,
  20: 36 so I will *j* you, declares
  22: 2 "Son of man, will you *j* her?
  34: 17 I will *j* between one sheep
Joel 3: 12 sit to *j* all the nations on every side.

Mic 3: 11 Her leaders *j* for a bribe,
   4: 3 He will *j* between many peoples
Mt 7: 1 Do not *j*, or you too will be judged.
Lk 6: 37 "Do not *j*, and you will not be
  18: 2 there was a *j* who neither feared
Jn 5: 27 And he has given authority to *j*
   5: 30 By myself I can do nothing; I *j* only
   8: 16 But if I do *j*, my decisions are right,
  12: 47 For I did not come to *j* the world,
  12: 48 There is a *j* for the one who rejects
Ac 10: 42 as *j* of the living and the dead.
  17: 31 a day when he will *j* the world
Ro 2: 16 day when God will *j* men's secrets
   3: 6 how could God *j* the world?
  14: 10 then, why do you *j* your brother?
1Co 4: 3 indeed, I do not even *j* myself.
   4: 5 Therefore *j* nothing
   6: 2 And if you are to *j* the world,
   6: 2 that the saints will *j* the world?
Gal 2: 6 not *j* by external appearance—
Col 2: 16 Therefore do not let anyone *j* you
2Ti 4: 1 who will *j* the living and the dead,
   4: 8 which the Lord, the righteous *J*,
Heb 10: 30 "The Lord will *j* his people."
  12: 23 come to God, the *j* of all men,
  13: 4 for God will *j* the adulterer
Jas 4: 12 There is only one Lawgiver and *J*,
   4: 12 who are you to *j* your neighbor?
1Pe 4: 5 to him who is ready to *j* the living
Rev 20: 4 who had been given authority to *j*.

JUDGED (JUDGE)
Mt 7: 1 "Do not judge, or you too will be *j*.
1Co 4: 3 I care very little if I am *j* by you
  10: 29 For why should my freedom be *j*
  11: 31 But if we *j* ourselves, we would not
  14: 24 all that he is a sinner and will be *j*
Jas 3: 1 who teach will be *j* more strictly.
Rev 20: 12 The dead were *j* according

JUDGES (JUDGE)
Jdg 2: 16 Then the LORD raised up *j*,
Job 9: 24 he blindfolds its *j*.
Ps 58: 11 there is a God who *j* the earth."
  75: 7 But it is God who *j*:
Pr 29: 14 If a king *j* the poor with fairness,
Jn 5: 22 Moreover, the Father *j* no one,
1Co 4: 4 It is the Lord who *j* me.
Heb 4: 12 it *j* the thoughts and attitudes
1Pe 1: 17 on a Father who *j* each man's work
   2: 23 himself to him who *j* justly.
Rev 19: 11 With justice he *j* and makes war.

JUDGING (JUDGE)
Ps 9: 4 on your throne, *j* righteously.
Pr 24: 23 To show partiality in *j* is not good:
Isa 16: 5 one who in *j* seeks justice
Mt 19: 28 *j* the twelve tribes of Israel.
Jn 7: 24 Stop *j* by mere appearances,

JUDGMENT (JUDGE)
Nu 33: 4 for the LORD had brought *j*
Dt 1: 17 of any man, for *j* belongs to God.
  32: 41 and my hand grasps it in *j*,
1Sa 25: 33 May you be blessed for your good *j*
Ps 1: 5 the wicked will not stand in the *j*,
   9: 7 he has established his throne for *j*.
  76: 8 From heaven you pronounced *j*,
  82: 1 he gives *j* among the "gods":
 119: 66 Teach me knowledge and good *j*,
 143: 2 Do not bring your servant into *j*,
Pr 3: 21 preserve sound *j* and discernment,
   6: 32 man who commits adultery lacks *j*;
   8: 14 Counsel and sound *j* are mine;
  10: 21 but fools die for lack of *j*.
  11: 12 man who lacks *j* derides his
  12: 11 but he who chases fantasies lacks *j*.
  17: 18 A man lacking in *j* strikes hands
  18: 1 he defies all sound *j*.
  28: 16 A tyrannical ruler lacks *j*,
Ecc 12: 14 God will bring every deed into *j*,
Isa 3: 14 The LORD enters into *j*
  28: 6 justice to him who sits in *j*,
  53: 8 By oppression and *j* he was taken
  66: 16 the LORD will execute *j*
Jer 2: 35 But I will pass *j* on you
  25: 31 he will bring *j* on all mankind
  51: 18 when their *j* comes, they will

Eze 11: 10 and I will execute *j* on you
Da 7: 22 pronounced *j* in favor of the saints
Am 7: 4 Sovereign LORD was calling for *j*
Zec 8: 16 and sound *j* in your courts;
Mal 3: 5 "So I will come near to you for *j*.
Mt 5: 21 who murders will be subject to *j*.'
   5: 22 with his brother will be subject to *j*.
  10: 15 on the day of *j* than for that town.
  11: 24 on the day of *j* than for you.'
  12: 36 have to give account on the day of *j*
  12: 41 up at the *j* with this generation
Jn 5: 22 but has entrusted all *j* to the Son,
   5: 30 as I hear, and my *j* is just,
   7: 24 appearances, and make a right *j*.''
   8: 26 "I have much to say in *j* of you.
   9: 39 "For *j* I have come into this world,
  12: 31 Now is the time for *j* on this world;
  16: 8 to sin and righteousness and *j*:
  16: 11 in regard to *j*, because the prince
Ac 24: 25 self-control and the *j* to come,
Ro 2: 1 you who pass *j* on someone else,
   2: 2 Now we know that God's *j*
   5: 16 The *j* followed one sin
  12: 3 rather think of yourself with sober *j*
  14: 10 stand before God's *j* seat.
  14: 13 Therefore let us stop passing *j*
1Co 7: 40 In my *j*, she is happier if she stays
  11: 29 body of the Lord eats and drinks *j*
2Co 5: 10 appear before the *j* seat of Christ,
2Th 1: 5 is evidence that God's *j* is right,
1Ti 3: 6 fall under the same *j* as the devil.
   5: 12 Thus they bring *j* on themselves,
Heb 6: 2 of the dead, and eternal *j*.
   9: 27 to die once, and after that to face *j*,
  10: 27 but only a fearful expectation of *j*
Jas 2: 13 *j* without mercy will be shown
   4: 11 are not keeping it, but sitting in *j*
1Pe 4: 17 For it is time for *j* to begin
2Pe 2: 9 the unrighteous for the day of *j*,
   3: 7 being kept for the day of *j*
1Jn 4: 17 have confidence on the day of *j*,
Jude 6 bound with everlasting chains for *j*
Rev 14: 7 because the hour of his *j* has come.

JUDGMENTS (JUDGE)
Jer 1: 16 I will pronounce my *j* on my people
Da 9: 11 and sworn *j* written in the Law
Hos 6: 5 my *j* flashed like lightning
Ro 11: 33 How unsearchable his *j*,
1Co 2: 15 spiritual man makes *j* about all
Rev 16: 7 true and just are your *j*.''

JUG
1Sa 26: 12 and water *j* near Saul's head,
1Ki 17: 12 of flour in a jar and a little oil in a *j*.

JUST* (JUSTICE JUSTIFICATION JUSTIFIED JUSTIFIES JUSTIFY JUSTIFYING JUSTLY)
Ge 18: 19 LORD by doing what is right and *j*,
Dt 2: 12 *j* as Israel did in the land
   6: 3 *j* as the LORD, the God
  27: 3 and honey, *j* as the LORD,
  30: 9 *j* as he delighted in your fathers,
  32: 4 and all his ways are *j*,
  32: 4 upright and *j* is he.
  32: 47 They are not *j* idle words for you—
  32: 50 *j* as your brother Aaron died
2Sa 8: 15 doing what was *j* and right
1Ch 18: 14 doing what was *j* and right
2Ch 12: 6 and said, "The LORD is *j*."
Ne 9: 13 and laws that are *j* and right,
   9: 33 you have been *j*; you have acted
Job 34: 17 Will you condemn the *j*
  35: 2 Elihu said: "Do you think this is *j*?
Ps 37: 28 For the LORD loves the *j*
  37: 30 and his tongue speaks what is *j*.
  99: 4 what is *j* and right.
 111: 7 of his hands are faithful and *j*;
 119: 121 I have done what is righteous and *j*;
Pr 1: 3 doing what is right and *j* and fair;
   2: 8 for he guards the course of the *j*
   2: 9 will understand what is right and *j*
   8: 8 All the words of my mouth are *j*;
   8: 15 and rulers make laws that are *j*;
  12: 5 The plans of the righteous are *j*,
  21: 3 To do what is right and *j*
Isa 32: 7 even when the plea of the needy is *j*

Isa 58: 2 They ask me for *j* decisions
Jer 4: 2 if in a truthful, *j* and righteous way
22: 3 what the LORD says: Do what is *j*
22: 15 He did what was right and *j*,
23: 5 do what is *j* and right in the land.
23: 15 he will do what is *j* and right
Eze 18: 5 who does what is *j* and right.
18: 19 Since the son has done what is *j*
18: 21 and does what is *j* and right,
18: 25 'The way of the Lord is not *j*.'
18: 27 and does what is *j* and right,
18: 29 'The way of the Lord is not *j*.'
33: 14 and does what is *j* and right—
33: 16 He has done what is *j* and right;
33: 17 But it is their way that is not *j*.
33: 17 'The way of the Lord is not *j*,'
33: 19 and does what is *j* and right,
33: 20 'The way of the Lord is not *j*.'
45: 9 and oppression and do what is *j*
Da 4: 37 does is right and all his ways are *j*.
Jn 5: 30 as I hear, and my judgment is *j*,
Ro 3: 26 as to be *j* and the one who justifies
2Th 1: 6 God is *j*: He will pay back trouble
Heb 2: 2 received its *j* punishment,
1Jn 1: 9 and *j* and will forgive us our sins
Rev 15: 3 *J* and true are your ways,
16: 5 "You are *j* in these judgments,
16: 7 true and *j* are your judgments."
19: 2 for true and *j* are his judgments.

JUSTICE* (JUST)

Ge 49: 16 "Dan will provide *j* for his people
Ex 23: 2 do not pervert *j* by siding
23: 6 "Do not deny *j* to your poor people
Lev 19: 15 " 'Do not pervert *j*; do not show
Dt 16: 19 Do not pervert *j* or show partiality.
16: 20 Follow *j* and *j* alone,
24: 17 the alien or the fatherless of *j*,
27: 19 Cursed is the man who withholds *j*
1Sa 8: 3 accepted bribes and perverted *j*.
2Sa 15: 4 and I would see that he gets *j*."
15: 6 came to the king asking for *j*.
1Ki 3: 11 for discernment in administering *j*,
3: 28 wisdom from God to administer *j*,
7: 7 the Hall of *J*, where he was to judge
10: 9 to maintain *j* and righteousness."
2Ch 9: 8 to maintain *j* and righteousness.
Ezr 7: 25 and judges to administer *j*
Est 1: 13 experts in matters of law and *j*,
Job 8: 3 Does God pervert *j*?
9: 19 matter of *j*, who will summon him?
19: 7 though I call for help, there is no *j*.
27: 2 as God lives, who has denied me *j*,
29: 14 *j* was my robe and my turban.
31: 13 "If I have denied *j*
34: 5 but God denies me *j*.
34: 12 that the Almighty would pervert *j*.
34: 17 Can he who hates *j* govern?
36: 3 I will ascribe *j* to my Maker.
36: 17 *j* have taken hold of you.
37: 23 in his *j* and great righteousness,
40: 8 "Would you discredit my *j*?
Ps 7: 6 Awake, my God; decree *j*.
9: 8 he will govern the peoples with *j*.
9: 16 The LORD is known by his *j*;
11: 7 he loves *j*;
33: 5 LORD loves righteousness and *j*;
36: 6 your *j* like the great deep.
37: 6 *j* of your cause like the noonday
45: 6 a scepter of *j* will be the scepter
72: 1 Endow the king with your *j*, O God
72: 2 your afflicted ones with *j*.
89: 14 *j* are the foundation of your throne;
97: 2 *j* are the foundation of his throne.
99: 4 The King is mighty, he loves *j*—
101: 1 I will sing of your love and *j*;
103: 6 and *j* for all the oppressed.
106: 3 Blessed are they who maintain *j*,
112: 5 who conducts his affairs with *j*.
140: 12 I know that the LORD secures *j*
Pr 8: 20 along the paths of *j*,
16: 10 and his mouth should not betray *j*.
17: 23 to pervert the course of *j*.
18: 5 or to deprive the innocent of *j*.
19: 28 A corrupt witness mocks at *j*,
21: 15 When *j* is done, it brings joy
28: 5 Evil men do not understand *j*,
29: 4 By a *j* a king gives a country stability

Pr 29: 7 The righteous care about *j*
29: 26 from the LORD that man gets *j*.
Ecc 3: 16 place of *j*— wickedness was there.
5: 8 poor oppressed in a district, and *j*
Isa 1: 17 Seek *j*,
1: 21 She once was full of *j*;
1: 27 Zion will be redeemed with *j*,
5: 7 he looked for *j*, but saw bloodshed;
5: 16 Almighty will be exalted by his *j*,
5: 23 but deny *j* to the innocent.
9: 7 it with *j* and righteousness
10: 2 and withhold *j* from the oppressed of
my people
11: 4 with *j* he will give decisions
16: 5 one who in judging seeks *j*
28: 6 He will be a spirit of *j*
28: 17 I will make *j* the measuring line
29: 21 deprive the innocent of *j*.
30: 18 For the LORD is a God of *j*.
32: 1 and rulers will rule with *j*.
32: 16 *J* will dwell in the desert
33: 5 with *j* and righteousness.
42: 1 and he will bring *j* to the nations.
42: 3 In faithfulness he will bring forth *j*;
42: 4 till he establishes *j* on earth.
51: 4 my *j* will become a light
51: 5 my arm will bring *j* to the nations.
56: 1 "Maintain *j*
59: 4 No one calls for *j*;
59: 8 there is no *j* in their paths.
59: 9 So *j* is far from us,
59: 11 We look for *j*, but find none;
59: 14 So *j* is driven back,
59: 15 that there was no *j*.
61: 8 "For I, the LORD, love *j*;
Jer 9: 24 and righteousness on earth,
10: 24 Correct me, LORD, but only with *j*
12: 1 speak with you about your *j*:
21: 12 " 'Administer *j* every morning;
30: 11 I will discipline you but only with *j*;
46: 28 I will discipline you but only with *j*;
La 3: 36 to deprive a man of *j*—
Eze 22: 29 mistreat the alien, denying them *j*.
34: 16 I will shepherd the flock with *j*.
Hos 2: 19 you in righteousness and *j*,
12: 6 maintain love and *j*,
Am 2: 7 and deny *j* to the oppressed.
5: 7 You who turn *j* into bitterness
5: 12 and you deprive the poor of *j*
5: 15 maintain *j* in the courts.
5: 24 But let *j* roll on like a river,
6: 12 But you have turned *j* into poison
Mic 3: 1 Should you not know *j*,
3: 8 and with *j* and might,
3: 9 who despise *j*
Hab 1: 4 and *j* never prevails.
1: 4 so that *j* is perverted.
Zep 3: 5 by morning he dispenses his *j*,
Zec 7: 9 'Administer true *j*; show mercy
Mal 2: 17 or "Where is the God of *j*?"
3: 5 and deprive aliens of *j*,
Mt 12: 18 he will proclaim *j* to the nations.
12: 20 till he leads *j* to victory.
23: 23 important matters of the law—*j*,
Lk 11: 42 you neglect *j* and the love of God.
18: 3 'Grant me *j* against my adversary.'
18: 5 I will see that she gets *j*,
18: 7 And will not God bring about *j*
18: 8 he will see that they get *j*,
Ac 8: 33 humiliation he was deprived of *j*.
17: 31 with *j* by the man he has appointed.
28: 4 *J* has not allowed him to live."
Ro 3: 25 He did this to demonstrate his *j*,
3: 26 it to demonstrate his *j*
2Co 7: 11 what readiness to see *j* done.
Heb 11: 33 administered *j*, and gained what
Rev 19: 11 With *j* he judges and makes war.

JUSTIFICATION* (JUST)

Eze 16: 52 for you have furnished some *j*
Ro 4: 25 and was raised to life for our *j*.
5: 16 many trespasses and brought *j*.
5: 18 of righteousness was *j* that brings

JUSTIFIED* (JUST)

Ps 51: 4 and *j* when you judge.
Lk 18: 14 rather than the other, went home *j*
Ac 13: 39 from everything you could not be *j*

Ac 13: 39 him everyone who believes is *j*
Ro 3: 24 and are *j* freely by his grace
3: 28 For we maintain that a man is *j*
4: 2 If, in fact, Abraham was *j* by works,
5: 1 since we have been *j* through faith,
5: 9 Since we have now been *j*
8: 30 those he called, he also *j*; those he *j*,
10: 10 heart that you believe and are *j*,
1Co 6: 11 you were *j* in the name
Gal 2: 16 in Christ Jesus that we may be *j*
2: 16 observing the law no one will be *j*.
2: 16 sinners' know' that a man is not *j*
2: 17 "If, while we seek to be *j* in Christ,
3: 11 Clearly no one is *j* before God
3: 24 to Christ that we might be *j* by faith
5: 4 to be *j* by law have been alienated
Tit 3: 7 so that, having been *j* by his grace,
Jas 2: 24 You see that a person is *j*

JUSTIFIES* (JUST)

Ro 3: 26 one who *j* those who have faith
4: 5 but trusts God who *j* the wicked,
8: 33 God has chosen? It is God who *j*.

JUSTIFY* (JUST)

Est 7: 4 such distress would *j* disturbing
Job 40: 8 you condemn me to *j* yourself?
Isa 53: 11 my righteous servant will *j* many,
Lk 10: 29 But he wanted to *j* himself,
16: 15 "You are the ones who *j* yourselves
Ro 3: 30 who will *j* the circumcised by faith
Gal 3: 8 that God would *j* the Gentiles

JUSTIFYING* (JUST)

Job 32: 2 angry with Job for *j* himself rather

JUSTLY* (JUST)

Ps 58: 1 Do you rulers indeed speak *j*?
67: 4 for you rule the peoples *j*
Jer 7: 5 and deal with each other *j*,
Mic 6: 8 To act *j* and to love mercy
Lk 23: 41 We are punished *j*,
1Pe 2: 23 himself to him who judges *j*.

KADESH

Nu 20: 1 of Zin, and they stayed at *K*.
Dt 1: 46 And so you stayed in *K* many days

KADESH BARNEA

Nu 32: 8 I sent them from *K* to look over

KEBAR

Eze 1: 1 among the exiles by the *K* River,

KEDORLAOMER

Ge 14: 17 Abram returned from defeating *K*

KEEP (KEEPER KEEPING KEEPS KEPT)

Ge 31: 49 "May the LORD *k* watch
Ex 15: 26 his commands and *k* all his
20: 6 and *k* my commandments.
Lev 15: 31 You must *k* the Israelites separate
Nu 6: 24 and *k* you;
Dt 4: 2 but *k* the commands of the LORD
6: 17 Be sure to *k* the commands
7: 9 who love him and *k* his commands.
7: 12 your God will *k* his covenant
11: 1 your God and *k* his requirements,
13: 4 *K* his commands and obey him;
30: 10 your God and *k* his commands
30: 16 and to *k* his commands, decrees
Jos 22: 5 careful to *k* the commandment
1Ki 8: 58 and to *k* the commands,
2Ki 17: 19 Judah did not *k* the commands
23: 3 the LORD and *k* his commands,
1Ch 29: 18 and *k* their hearts loyal to you.
2Ch 6: 14 you who *k* your covenant of love
34: 31 the LORD and *k* his commands,
Job 14: 16 but not *k* track of my sin.
Ps 18: 28 You, O LORD, *k* my lamp burning
19: 13 *K* your servant also from willful
78: 10 they did not *k* God's covenant
119: 2 Blessed are they who *k* his statutes
119: 9 can a young man *k* his way pure?
121: 7 The LORD will *k* you
141: 3 *k* watch over the door of my lips,
Pr 4: 21 *k* them within your heart;
4: 24 *k* corrupt talk far from your lips.

KEEPER

Pr 30: 8 K falsehood and lies far from me;
Ecc 3: 6 a time to k and a time
  12:13 and k his commandments,
Isa 26: 3 You will k in perfect peace
  42: 6 I will k you and will make you
  58:13 "If you k your feet
Jer 16:11 forsook me and did not k my law.
Eze 20:19 and be careful to k my laws.
Mt 10:10 for the worker is worth his k.
Lk 12:35 and k your lamps burning,
  17:33 tries to k his life will lose it,
Jn 10:24 How long will you k us in suspense
  12:25 in this world will k it for eternal life
Ac 2:24 for death to k its hold on him.
  18: 9 "Do not be afraid; k on speaking,
Ro 7:19 want to do—this I k on doing.
  12:11 but k your spiritual fervor,
  14:22 you believe about these things k
  16:17 K away from them.
1Co 1: 8 He will k you strong to the end,
2Co 12: 7 To k me from becoming conceited
Gal 5:25 let us k in step with the Spirit.
Eph 4: 3 Make every effort to k the unity
2Th 3: 6 to k away from every brother who
1Ti 5:22 K yourself pure.
2Ti 4: 5 k your head in all situations,
Heb 9:20 God has commanded you to k."
  13: 5 K your lives free from the love
Jas 1:26 and yet does not k a tight rein
  2: 8 If you really k the royal law found
  3: 2 able to k his whole body in check.
2Pe 1: 8 will k you from being ineffective
Jude :21 K yourselves in God's love
  :24 able to k you from falling
Rev 3:10 also k you from the hour
  22: 9 of all who k the words of this book.

KEEPER (KEEP)

Ge 4: 9 I my brother's k?" The LORD

KEEPING (KEEP)

Ex 20: 8 the Sabbath day by k it holy.
Dt 5:12 the Sabbath day by k it holy,
  13:18 k all his commands that I am
Ps 19:11 in k them there is great reward.
  119:112 My heart is set on k your decrees
Pr 15: 3 k watch on the wicked
Mt 3: 8 Produce fruit in k with repentance.
Lk 2: 8 k watch over their flocks at night.
1Co 7:19 K God's commands is what counts.
2Co 8: 5 and then to us in k with God's will.
Jas 4:11 you are not k it, but sitting
1Pe 3:16 and respect, k a clear conscience,
2Pe 3: 9 Lord is not slow in k his promise,

KEEPS (KEEP)

Ne 1: 5 who k his covenant of love
Ps 15: 4 who k his oath
Pr 12:23 A prudent man k his knowledge
  15:21 of understanding k a straight
  17:28 a fool is thought wise if he k silent,
  29:11 a wise man k himself under control
Isa 56: 2 who k the Sabbath
Da 9: 4 who k his covenant of love
Am 5:13 Therefore the prudent man k quiet
Jn 7:19 Yet not one of you k the law.
  8:51 if anyone k my word, he will never
1Co 13: 5 is not easily angered, it k no record
Jas 2:10 For whoever k the whole law
Rev 22: 7 Blessed is he who k the words

KEILAH

1Sa 23:13 that David had escaped from K,

KEPT (KEEP)

Ex 12:42 Because the LORD k vigil that
Dt 7: 8 and k the oath he swore
2Ki 18: 6 he k the commands the LORD had
Ne 9: 8 You have k your promise
Ps 130: 3 If you, O LORD, k a record of sins,
Isa 38:17 In your love you k me
Mt 19:20 these I have k," the young man
2Co 11: 9 I have k myself from being
2Ti 4: 7 finished the race, I have k the faith.
1Pe 1: 4 spoil or fade—k in heaven for you,

KERNEL

Mk 4:28 then the full k in the head.

Jn 12:24 a k of wheat falls to the ground

KEY (KEYS)

Isa 33: 6 the fear of the LORD is the k
Rev 20: 1 having the k to the Abyss

KEYS* (KEY)

Mt 16:19 I will give you the k of the kingdom
Rev 1:18 And I hold the k of death

KICK*

Ac 26:14 for you to k against the goads.'

KILL (KILLED KILLS)

Ecc 3: 3 a time to k and a time to heal,
Mt 10:28 k the body but cannot k the soul.
  17:23 They will k him, and on the third
Mk 9:31 will k him, and after three days
  10:34 spit on him, flog him and k him.

KILLED (KILL)

Ge 4: 8 his brother Abel and k him.
Ex 2:12 he k the Egyptian and hid him
  13:15 the LORD k every firstborn
Nu 35:11 who has k someone accidentally
1Sa 17:50 down the Philistine and k him.
Ne 9:26 They k your prophets, who had
Hos 6: 5 I k you with the words
Lk 11:48 they k the prophets, and you build
Ac 3:15 You k the author of life,

KILLS (KILL)

Ex 21:12 k him shall surely be put to death.
Lev 24:21 but whoever k a man must be put
2Co 3: 6 for the letter k, but the Spirit gives

KIND (KINDNESS KINDNESSES KINDS)

Ge 1:24 animals, each according to its k."
2Ch 10: 7 "If you will be k to these people
Pr 11:17 A k man benefits himself,
  12:25 but a k word cheers him up.
  14:21 blessed is he who is k to the needy.
  14:31 whoever is k to the needy honors
  19:17 He who is k to the poor lends
Da 4:27 by being k to the oppressed.
Lk 6:35 because he is k to the ungrateful
1Co 13: 4 Love is patient, love is k.
  15:35 With what k of body will they
Eph 4:32 Be k and compassionate
1Th 5:15 but always try to be k to each other
2Ti 2:24 instead, he must be k to everyone,
Tit 2: 5 to be busy at home, to be k,

KINDHEARTED* (HEART)

Pr 11:16 A k woman gains respect,

KINDNESS (KIND)

Ge 24:12 and show k to my master Abraham
  32:10 I am unworthy of all the k
  39:21 he showed him k and granted him
Jdg 8:35 failed to show k to the family
Ru 2:20 has not stopped showing his k
2Sa 9: 3 to whom I can show God's k?"
  22:51 he shows unfailing k
Ps 18:50 he shows unfailing k
  141: 5 righteous man strike me—it is a k;
Isa 54: 8 but with everlasting k
Jer 9:24 I am the LORD, who exercises k,
Hos 11: 4 I led them with cords of human k,
Ac 14:17 He has shown k by giving you rain
Ro 11:22 Consider therefore the k
2Co 6: 6 understanding, patience and k;
Gal 5:22 peace, patience, k, goodness,
Eph 2: 7 expressed in his k to us
Col 3:12 yourselves with compassion, k,
Tit 3: 4 But when the k and love
2Pe 1: 7 brotherly k; and to brotherly k,

KINDNESSES* (KIND)

Ps 106: 7 did not remember your many k,
Isa 63: 7 I will tell of the k of the LORD,
  63: 7 to his compassion and many k.

KINDS (KIND)

Ge 1:12 bearing seed according to their k
1Co 12: 4 There are different k of gifts,
1Ti 6:10 of money is a root of all k of evil.

1Pe 1: 6 had to suffer grief in all k of trials.

KING (KING'S KINGDOM KINGDOMS KINGS)

1. Kings of Judah and Israel: see Saul, David, Solomon.
2. Kings of Judah: see Rehoboam, Abijah, Asa, Jehoshaphat, Jehoram, Ahaziah, Athaliah (Queen), Joash, Amaziah, Azariah (Uzziah), Jotham, Ahaz, Hezekiah, Manasseh, Amon, Josiah, Jehoahaz, Jehoiakim, Jehoiachin, Zedekiah.
3. Kings of Israel: see Jeroboam I, Nadab, Baasha, Elah, Zimri, Tibni, Omri, Ahab, Ahaziah, Joram, Jehu, Jehoahaz, Jehoash, Jeroboam II, Zechariah, Shallum, Menahem, Pekah, Pekahiah, Hoshea.

Ex 1: 8 a new k, who did not know about
Dt 17:14 "Let us set a k over us like all
Jdg 17: 6 In those days Israel had no k;
1Sa 8: 5 now appoint a k to lead us,
  11:15 as k in the presence of the LORD.
  12:12 the LORD your God was your k.
2Sa 2: 4 and there they anointed David k
1Ki 1:30 Solomon your son shall be k
Ps 2: 2 "I have installed my K
  24: 7 that the K of glory may come in.
  44: 4 You are my K and my God,
  47: 7 For God is the K of all the earth;
Isa 32: 1 See, a k will reign in righteousness
Jer 30: 9 and David their k,
Hos 3: 5 their God and David their k.
Mic 2:13 k will pass through before them,
Zec 9: 9 See, your k comes to you,
Mt 2: 2 is the one who has been born k
  27:11 "Are you the k of the Jews?" "Yes,
Lk 19:38 "Blessed is the k who comes
  23: 3 "Are you the k of the Jews?" "Yes,
  23:38 THE K OF THE JEWS.
Jn 1:49 of God; you are the K of Israel."
  12:13 "Blessed is the K of Israel!"
Ac 17: 7 saying that there is another k,
1Ti 1:17 Now to the K eternal, immortal,
  6:15 the K of kings and Lord of lords,
Heb 7: 1 This Melchizedek was k of Salem
1Pe 2:13 to the k, as the supreme authority,
  2:17 of believers, fear God, honor the k.
Rev 15: 3 K of the ages.
  17:14 he is Lord of lords and K of kings—
  19:16 K OF KINGS AND LORD

KING'S (KING)

Pr 21: 1 The k heart is in the hand
Ecc 8: 3 in a hurry to leave the k presence.

KINGDOM (KING)

Ex 19: 6 you will be for me a k of priests
Dt 17:18 When he takes the throne of his k,
2Sa 7:12 body, and I will establish his k.
1Ki 11:31 to tear the k out of Solomon's hand
1Ch 17:11 own sons, and I will establish his k.
  29:11 Yours, O LORD, is the k;
Ps 45: 6 justice will be the scepter of your k.
  103:19 and his k rules over all.
  145:11 They will tell of the glory of your k
Eze 29:14 There they will be a lowly k.
Da 2:39 "After you, another k will rise,
  4: 3 His k is an eternal k;
  7:27 His k will be an everlasting k,
Ob :21 And the k will be the LORD's.
Mt 3: 2 Repent, for the k of heaven is near
  4:17 Repent, for the k of heaven is near
  4:23 preaching the good news of the k,
  5: 3 for theirs is the k of heaven.
  5:10 for theirs is the k of heaven.
  5:19 great in the k of heaven.
  5:19 least in the k of heaven,
  5:20 you will certainly not enter the k
  6:10 your k come,
  6:33 But seek first his k and his
  7:21 Lord,' will enter the k of heaven.
  8:11 Isaac and Jacob in the k of heaven.
  8:12 the subjects of the k will be thrown
  9:35 preaching the good news of the k
  10: 7 preach this message: 'The k
  11:11 least in the k of heaven is greater
  11:12 the k of heaven has been forcefully
  12:25 "Every k divided against itself will
  12:26 How then can his k stand?

Mt 12: 28 then the *k* of God has come
13: 11 knowledge of the secrets of the *k*
13: 19 hears the message about the *k*
13: 24 "The *k* of heaven is like a man who
13: 31 *k* of heaven is like a mustard seed,
13: 33 "The *k* of heaven is like yeast that
13: 38 stands for the sons of the *k*.
13: 41 of his *k* everything that causes sin
13: 43 the sun in the *k* of their Father.
13: 44 *k* of heaven is like treasure hidden
13: 45 the *k* of heaven is like a merchant
13: 47 *k* of heaven is like a net that was let
13: 52 has been instructed about the *k*
16: 19 the keys of the *k* of heaven;
16: 28 the Son of Man coming in his *k*."
18: 1 the greatest in the *k* of heaven?"
18: 3 you will never enter the *k*
18: 4 the greatest in the *k* of heaven.
18: 23 of heaven is like a king who
19: 12 because of the *k* of heaven.
19: 14 for the *k* of heaven belongs to such
19: 23 man to enter the *k* of heaven.
19: 24 for a rich man to enter the *k* of God
20: 1 "For the *k* of heaven is like
20: 21 the other at your left in your *k*."
21: 31 the prostitutes are entering the *k*
21: 43 "Therefore I tell you that the *k*
22: 2 "The *k* of heaven is like a king who
23: 13 You shut the *k* of heaven
24: 7 rise against nation, and *k* against *k*.
24: 14 gospel of the *k* will be preached
25: 1 "At that time the *k*
25: 34 the *k* prepared for you
26: 29 anew with you in my Father's *k*."
Mk 1: 15 "The *k* of God is near.
3: 24 If a *k* is divided against itself,
3: 24 against itself, that *k* cannot stand.
4: 11 The secret of the *k*
4: 26 "This is what the *k* of God is like.
4: 30 "What shall we say the *k*
6: 23 I will give you, up to half my *k*."
9: 1 before they see the *k* of God come
9: 47 better for you to enter the *k* of God
10: 14 for the *k* of God belongs to such
10: 15 anyone who will not receive the *k*
10: 23 for the rich to enter the *k* of God!"
10: 24 how hard it is to enter the *k* of God
10: 25 for a rich man to enter the *k* of God
11: 10 "Blessed is the coming *k*
12: 34 "You are not far from the *k* of God
13: 8 rise against nation, and *k* against *k*.
14: 25 day when I drink it anew in the *k*
15: 43 who was himself waiting for the *k*
Lk 1: 33 Jacob forever; his *k* will never
4: 43 of the *k* of God to the other towns
6: 20 for yours is the *k* of God.
7: 28 in the *k* of God is greater than he."
8: 1 proclaiming the good news of the *k*
8: 10 knowledge of the secrets of the *k*
9: 2 out to preach the *k* of God
9: 11 spoke to them about the *k* of God,
9: 27 before they see the *k* of God."
9: 60 you go and proclaim the *k* of God
9: 62 fit for service in the *k* of God."
10: 9 'The *k* of God is near you.'
10: 11 sure of this: The *k* of God is near.'
11: 2 your *k* come.
11: 17 "Any *k* divided against itself will
11: 18 himself, how can his *k* stand?
11: 20 then the *k* of God has come to you.
12: 31 seek his *k*, and these things will be
12: 32 has been pleased to give you the *k*.
13: 18 "What is the *k* of God like?
13: 20 What shall I compare the *k* of God
13: 28 all the prophets in the *k* of God,
13: 29 places at the feast in the *k* of God.
14: 15 eat at the feast in the *k* of God."
16: 16 the good news of the *k*
17: 20 when the *k* of God would come,
17: 20 *k* of God does not come with careful
        observation,
17: 21 because the *k* of God is within you
18: 16 for the *k* of God belongs to such
18: 17 anyone who will not receive the *k*
18: 24 for the rich to enter the *k* of God!
18: 25 for a rich man to enter the *k* of God!
18: 29 for the sake of the *k* of God will fail
19: 11 and the people thought that the *k*

Lk 21: 10 rise against nation, and *k* against *k*.
21: 31 you know that the *k* of God is near.
22: 16 until it finds fulfillment in the *k*
22: 18 the vine until the *k* of God comes."
22: 29 And I confer on you a *k*, just
22: 30 and drink at my table in my *k*
23: 42 me when you come into your *k*."
23: 51 he was waiting for the *k* of God.
Jn 3: 3 no one can see the *k* of God.
3: 5 no one can enter the *k* of God.
18: 36 now my *k* is from another place."
18: 36 "My *k* is not of this world.
Ac 1: 3 and spoke about the *k* of God.
1: 6 going to restore the *k* to Israel?"
8: 12 he preached the good news of the *k*
14: 22 hardships to enter the *k* of God,"
19: 8 arguing persuasively about the *k*
20: 25 about preaching the *k* will ever see
28: 23 and declared to them the *k* of God
28: 31 hindrance he preached the *k*
Ro 14: 17 For the *k* of God is not a matter
1Co 4: 20 For the *k* of God is not a matter
6: 9 the wicked will not inherit the *k*
6: 10 swindlers will inherit the *k* of God.
15: 24 hands over the *k* to God the Father
15: 50 blood cannot inherit the *k* of God,
Gal 5: 21 live like this will not inherit the *k*
Eph 2: 2 and of the ruler of the *k* of the air,
5: 5 has any inheritance in the *k*
Col 1: 12 of the saints in the *k* of light.
1: 13 and brought us into the *k*
4: 11 among my fellow workers for the *k*
1Th 2: 12 who calls you into his *k* and glory.
2Th 1: 5 will be counted worthy of the *k*
2Ti 4: 1 in view of his appearing and his *k*,
4: 18 bring me safely to his heavenly *k*.
Heb 1: 8 will be the scepter of your *k*.
12: 28 we are receiving a *k* that cannot be
Jas 2: 5 to inherit the *k* he promised those
2Pe 1: 11 into the eternal *k* of our Lord
Rev 1: 6 has made us to be a *k* and priests
1: 9 companion in the suffering and *k*
5: 10 You have made them to be a *k*
11: 15 of the world has become the *k*
11: 15 "The *k* of the world has become
12: 10 the power and the *k* of our God,
16: 10 his *k* was plunged into darkness.
17: 12 who have not yet received a *k*,

KINGDOMS (KING)

2Ki 19: 15 God over all the *k* of the earth.
19: 19 so that all *k* on earth may know
2Ch 20: 6 rule over all the *k* of the nations.
Ps 68: 32 Sing to God, O *k* of the earth,
Isa 37: 16 God over all the *k* of the earth.
37: 20 so that all *k* on earth may know
Eze 29: 15 It will be the lowliest of *k*
37: 22 or be divided into two *k*.
Da 4: 17 Most High is sovereign over the *k*
7: 7 great beasts are four *k* that will rise
Zep 3: 8 to gather the *k*

KINGS (KING)

Ps 2: 2 The *k* of the earth take their stand
47: 9 for the *k* of the earth belong to God
68: 29 *k* will bring you gifts.
72: 11 All *k* will bow down to him
110: 5 he will crush *k* on the day
149: 8 to bind their *k* with fetters,
Pr 16: 12 *K* detest wrongdoing,
Isa 24: 21 and the *k* on the earth below.
52: 15 and *k* will shut their mouths
60: 11 their *k* led in triumphal procession.
Da 2: 21 he sets up *k* and deposes them.
7: 24 ten horns are ten *k* who will come
Lk 21: 12 and you will be brought before *k*
1Co 4: 8 You have become *k*—
1Ti 2: 2 for *k* and all those in authority,
6: 15 the King of *k* and Lord of lords,
Rev 17: 14 he is Lord of lords and King of *k*—
19: 16 KING OF *K* AND LORD

KINSMAN-REDEEMER (REDEEM)

Ru 3: 9 over me, since you are a *k*."
4: 14 day has not left you without a *k*.

KISS (KISSED KISSES)

Ps 2: 12 *K* the Son, lest he be angry
Pr 24: 26 is like a *k* on the lips.
SS 1: 2 *Beloved* Let him *k* me
8: 1 I would *k* you,
Lk 22: 48 the Son of Man with a *k*?"
Ro 16: 16 Greet one another with a holy *k*.
1Co 16: 20 Greet one another with a holy *k*.
2Co 13: 12 Greet one another with a holy *k*.
1Th 5: 26 Greet all the brothers with a holy *k*
1Pe 5: 14 Greet one another with a *k* of love.

KISSED (KISS)

Mk 14: 45 Judas said, "Rabbi!" and *k* him.
Lk 7: 38 *k* them and poured perfume

KISSES* (KISS)

Pr 27: 6 but an enemy multiplies *k*.
SS 1: 2 with the *k* of his mouth—

KNEE (KNEES)

Isa 45: 23 Before me every *k* will bow;
Ro 14: 11 'every *k* will bow before me;
Php 2: 10 name of Jesus every *k* should bow,

KNEEL (KNELT)

Est 3: 2 But Mordecai would not *k* down
Ps 95: 6 let us *k* before the LORD our
Eph 3: 14 For this reason I *k*

KNEES (KNEE)

1Ki 19: 18 all whose *k* have not bowed
Isa 35: 3 steady the *k* that give way;
Da 6: 10 times a day he got down on his *k*
Lk 5: 8 he fell at Jesus' *k* and said,
Heb 12: 12 your feeble arms and weak *k*.

KNELT* (KNEEL)

1Ki 1: 16 Bathsheba bowed low and *k*
2Ch 6: 13 and then *k* down before the whole
7: 3 they *k* on the pavement
29: 29 everyone present with him *k* down
Est 3: 2 officials at the king's gate *k* down
Mt 8: 2 and *k* before him and said,
9: 18 a ruler came and *k* before him
15: 25 The woman came and *k* before him
17: 14 a man approached Jesus and *k*
27: 29 *k* in front of him and mocked him.
Lk 22: 41 *k* down and prayed, "Father,
Ac 20: 36 he *k* down with all of them
21: 5 there on the beach we *k* to pray.

KNEW (KNOW)

2Ch 33: 13 Manasseh *k* that the LORD is God
Job 23: 3 If only I *k* where to find him;
Pr 24: 12 "But we *k* nothing about this,"
Jer 1: 5 you in the womb I *k* you,
Jnh 4: 2 I *k* that you are a gracious
Mt 7: 23 tell them plainly, 'I never *k* you.
12: 25 Jesus *k* their thoughts
Jn 2: 24 himself to them, for he *k* all men.
14: 7 If you really *k* me, you would know

KNIFE

Ge 22: 10 and took the *k* to slay his son.
Pr 23: 2 and put a *k* to your throat

KNOCK* (KNOCKS)

Mt 7: 7 *k* and the door will be opened
Lk 11: 9 *k* and the door will be opened
Rev 3: 20 I am! I stand at the door and *k*.

KNOCKS (KNOCK)

Mt 7: 8 and to him who *k*, the door will be

KNOW (FOREKNEW FOREKNOWLEDGE KNEW KNOWING KNOWLEDGE KNOWN KNOWS)

Ge 22: 12 Now I *k* that you fear God,
Ex 6: 7 you will *k* that I am the LORD
14: 4 and the Egyptians will *k* that I am
33: 13 teach me your ways so I may *k* you
Dt 7: 9 *K* therefore that the LORD your
18: 21 "How can we *k* when a message
Jos 4: 24 of the earth might *k* that the hand
23: 14 You *k* with all your heart
1Sa 17: 46 the whole world will *k* that there is
1Ki 8: 39 heart (for you alone *k* the hearts

Job 11: 6 *K* this: God has even forgotten
  19:25 I *k* that my Redeemer lives,
  42: 3 things too wonderful for me to *k.*
Ps 9:10 Those who *k* your name will trust
  46:10 "Be still, and *k* that I am God;
  100: 3 *K* that the LORD is God.
  139: 1 and you *k* me.
  139:23 Search me, O God, and *k* my heart;
  145:12 so that all men may *k*
Pr 27: 1 for you do not *k* what a day may
  30: 4 Tell me if you *k!*
Ecc 8: 5 wise heart will *k* the proper time
Isa 29:15 "Who sees us? Who will *k?*"
  40:21 Do you not *k?*
Jer 6:15 they do not even *k* how to blush.
  22:16 Is that not what it means to *k* me?"
  24: 7 I will give them a heart to *k* me,
  31:34 his brother, saying, '*K* the LORD,'
  33: 3 unsearchable things you do not *k.'*
Eze 2: 5 they will *k* that a prophet has been
  6:10 they will *k* that I am the LORD;
Da 11:32 people who *k* their God will firmly
Mt 6: 3 let your left hand *k* what your right
  7:11 *k* how to give good gifts
  9: 6 But so that you may *k* that the Son
  22:29 you do not *k* the Scriptures
  24:42 you do not *k* on what day your
  26:74 "I don't *k* the man!" Immediately
Mk 12:24 you do not *k* the Scriptures
Lk 1: 4 so that you may *k* the certainty
  11:13 *k* how to give good gifts
  12:48 But the one who does not *k*
  13:25 'I don't *k* you or where you come
  21:31 you *k* that the kingdom of God is
  23:34 for they do not *k* what they are
Jn 1:26 among you stands one you do not *k*
  3:11 we speak of what we *k,*
  4:22 we worship what we do *k,*
  4:42 and we *k* that this man really is
  6:69 and *k* that you are the Holy One
  7:28 You do not *k* him, but I *k* him
  8:14 for I *k* where I came from
  8:19 "You do not *k* me or my Father,"
  8:32 Then you will *k* the truth,
  8:55 Though you do not *k* him, I *k* him.
  9:25 One thing I do *k.*
  10: 4 him because they *k* his voice.
  10:14 I *k* my sheep and my sheep *k* me—
  10:27 I *k* them, and they follow me.
  12:35 the dark does not *k* where he is
  13:17 Now that you *k* these things,
  13:35 all men will *k* that you are my
  14:17 you *k* him, for he lives with you
  15:21 for they do not *k* the One who sent
  16:30 we can see that you *k* all things
  17: 3 that they may *k* you, the only true
  17:23 to let the world *k* that you sent me
  21:15 he said, "you *k* that I love you."
  21:24 We *k* that his testimony is true.
Ac 1: 7 "It is not for you to *k* the times
  1:24 "Lord, you *k* everyone's heart.
Ro 3:17 and the way of peace they do not *k*
  6: 3 Or don't you *k* that all
  6: 6 For we *k* that our old self was
  6:16 Don't you *k* that when you offer
  7:14 We *k* that the law is spiritual;
  7:18 I *k* that nothing good lives in me,
  8:22 We *k* that the whole creation has
  8:26 We do not *k* what we ought to pray
  8:28 we *k* that in all things God works
1Co 1:21 through its wisdom did not *k* him,
  2: 2 For I resolved to *k* nothing
  3:16 Don't you *k* that you yourselves
  5: 6 Don't you *k* that a little yeast
  6: 2 Do you not *k* that the saints will
  6:15 Do you not *k* that your bodies are
  6:16 Do you not *k* that he who unites
  6:19 Do you not *k* that your body is
  7:16 How do you *k,* wife, whether you
  8: 2 does not yet *k* as he ought to *k.*
  9:13 Don't you *k* that those who work
  9:24 Do you not *k* that
  13: 9 For we *k* in part and we prophesy
  13:12 Now I *k* in part; then I shall *k* fully,
  15:58 because you *k* that your labor
2Co 5: 1 we *k* that if the earthly tent we live
  5:11 we *k* what it is to fear the Lord,
  8: 9 For you *k* the grace

Gal 1:11 you to *k,* brothers, that the gospel I
  2:16 not 'Gentile sinners' *k* that a man
Eph 1:17 so that you may *k* him better.
  1:18 in order that you may *k* the hope
  6: 8 you *k* that the Lord will reward
  6: 9 since you *k* that he who is both
Php 3:10 I want to *k* Christ and the power
  4:12 I *k* what it is to be in need,
Col 2: 2 order that they may *k* the mystery
  4: 1 because you *k* that you
  4: 6 so that you may *k* how
1Th 3: 3 You *k* quite well that we were
  5: 2 for you *k* very well that the day
2Th 1: 8 punish those who do not *k* God
1Ti 1: 7 they do not *k* what they are talking
  3: 5 (If anyone does not *k* how
  3:15 you will *k* how people ought
2Ti 1:12 because I *k* whom I have believed,
  2:23 you *k* they produce quarrels.
  3:14 you *k* those from whom you
Heb 8:11 because they will all *k* me,
  11: 8 he did not *k* where he was going.
Jas 1: 3 because you *k* that the testing
  3: 1 you *k* that we who teach will be
  4: 4 don't you *k* that friendship
  4:14 what will happen tomorrow.
1Pe 1:18 For you *k* that it was not
2Pe 1:12 even though you *k* them
1Jn 2: 3 We *k* that we have come
  2: 4 The man who says, "I *k* him,"
  2: 5 This is how we *k* we are in him:
  2:11 he does not *k* where he is going,
  2:20 and all of you *k* the truth.
  2:29 you *k* that everyone who does
  3: 1 not *k* us is that it did not *k* him.
  3: 2 But we *k* that when he appears,
  3:10 This is how we *k* who the children
  3:14 We *k* that we have passed
  3:16 This is how we *k* what love is:
  3:19 then is how we *k* that we belong
  3:24 We *k* it by the Spirit he gave us.
  4: 8 does not love does not *k* God,
  4:13 We *k* that we live in him
  4:16 so we *k* and rely on the love God
  5: 2 This is how we *k* that we love
  5:13 so that you may *k* that you have
  5:15 And if we *k* that he hears us—
  5:18 We *k* that anyone born
  5:20 We *k* also that the Son
Rev 2: 2 I *k* your deeds, your hard work
  2: 9 I *k* your afflictions and your
  2:19 I *k* your deeds, your love and faith,
  3: 3 you will not *k* at what time I will
  3:15 I *k* your deeds, that you are neither

KNOWING (KNOW)

Ge 3: 5 and you will be like God, *k* good
  3:22 now become like one of us, *k* good
Jn 19:28 *k* that all was now completed,
Php 3: 8 of *k* Christ Jesus my Lord
Phm :21 *k* that you will do even more
Heb 13: 2 entertained angels without *k* it.

KNOWLEDGE (KNOW)

Ge 2: 9 the tree of the *k* of good and evil.
  2:17 eat from the tree of the *k* of good
2Ch 1:10 and *k,* that I may lead this people,
Job 21:22 "Can anyone teach *k* to God,
  38: 2 counsel with words without *k?*
  42: 3 obscures my counsel without *k?*
Ps 19: 2 night after night they display *k.*
  73:11 Does the Most High have *k?*"
  94:10 Does he who teaches man lack *k?*
  119: 66 Teach me *k* and good judgment,
  139: 6 Such *k* is too wonderful for me,
Pr 1: 4 *k* and discretion to the young—
  1: 7 of the LORD is the beginning of *k,*
  2: 5 and find the *k* of God.
  2: 6 from his mouth come *k*
  2:10 and *k* will be pleasant to your soul.
  3:20 by his *k* the deeps were divided,
  8:10 *k* rather than choice gold,
  8:12 I possess *k* and discretion.
  9:10 *k* of the Holy One is understanding
  10:14 Wise men store up *k,*
  12: 1 Whoever loves discipline loves *k,*
  12:23 A prudent man keeps his *k*
  13:16 Every prudent man acts out of *k,*

Pr 14: 6 *k* comes easily to the discerning.
  15: 7 The lips of the wise spread *k;*
  15:14 The discerning heart seeks *k,*
  17:27 A man of *k* uses words
  18:15 heart of the discerning acquires *k;*
  19: 2 to have zeal without *k,*
  19:25 discerning man, and he will gain *k*
  20:15 lips that speak *k* are a rare jewel.
  23:12 and your ears to words of *k.*
  24: 4 through *k* its rooms are filled
Ecc 7:12 but the advantage of *k* is this:
Isa 11: 2 the Spirit of *k* and of the fear
  11: 9 full of the *k* of the LORD
  40:14 Who was it that taught him *k*
Jer 3:15 who will lead you with *k*
Hos 4: 6 are destroyed from lack of *k.*
Hab 2:14 filled with the *k* of the glory
Mal 2: 7 lips of a priest ought to preserve *k,*
Mt 13:11 The *k* of the secrets of the kingdom
Lk 8:10 The *k* of the secrets of the kingdom
  11:52 you have taken away the key to *k.*
Ac 18:24 with a thorough *k* of the Scriptures
Ro 1:28 worthwhile to retain the *k* of God,
  10: 2 but their zeal is not based on *k.*
  11:33 riches of the wisdom and *k* of God!
1Co 8: 1 *K* puffs up, but love builds up.
  8:11 Christ died, is destroyed by your *k.*
  12: 8 to another the message of *k*
  13: 2 can fathom all mysteries and all *k,*
  13: 8 where there is *k,* it will pass away.
2Co 2:14 everywhere the fragrance of the *k*
  4: 6 light of the *k* of the glory of God
  8: 7 in *k,* in complete earnestness
  11: 6 a trained speaker, but I do have *k.*
Eph 3:19 to know this love that surpasses *k*
  4:13 and in the *k* of the Son of God
Php 1: 9 and more in *k* and depth of insight,
Col 1: 9 God to fill you with the *k* of his will
  1:10 every good work, growing in the *k*
  2: 3 all the treasures of wisdom and *k.*
  3:10 which is being renewed in *k*
1Ti 2: 4 and to come to a *k* of the truth.
  6:20 ideas of what is falsely called *k,*
Tit 1: 1 and the *k* of the truth that leads
Heb 10:26 after we have received the *k*
2Pe 1: 5 and to goodness; and to *k,*
  3:18 grow in the grace and *k* of our Lord

KNOWN (KNOW)

Ex 6: 3 the LORD I did not make myself *k*
Ps 16:11 You have made *k* to me the path
  89: 1 I will make your faithfulness *k*
  98: 2 LORD has made his salvation *k*
  105: 1 make *k* among the nations what he
  119:168 for all my ways are *k* to you.
Pr 20:11 Even a child is *k* by his actions,
Isa 12: 4 make *k* among the nations what he
  46:10 *k* the end from the beginning,
  61: 9 Their descendants will be *k*
Eze 38:23 I will make myself *k* in the sight
  39: 7 "'I will make *k* my holy name
Mt 10:26 or hidden that will not be made *k.*
  24:43 of the house had *k* at what time
Lk 19:42 had only *k* on this day what would
Jn 15:15 from my Father I have made *k*
  16:14 from what is mine and making it *k*
  17:26 I have made you *k* to them,
Ac 2:28 You have made *k* to me the paths
Ro 1:19 since what may be *k* about God is
  3:21 apart from law, has been made *k,*
  9:22 his wrath and make his power *k,*
  11:34 "Who has *k* the mind of the Lord?
  15:20 the gospel where Christ was not *k,*
  16:26 and made *k* through the prophetic
1Co 2:16 "For who has *k* the mind
  8: 3 But the man who loves God is *k*
  13:12 know fully, even as I am fully *k.*
2Co 3: 2 written on our hearts, *k*
Gal 4: 9 or rather are *k* by God—
Eph 3: 5 which was not made *k* to men
  6:19 will fearlessly make *k* the mystery
2Ti 3:15 infancy you have *k* the holy
2Pe 2:21 than to have *k* it and then

KNOWS (KNOW)

1Sa 2: 3 for the LORD is a God who *k,*
Est 4:14 And who *k* but that you have come
Job 23:10 But he *k* the way that I take;

KOHATHITE

Ps 44:21 since he *k* the secrets of the heart?
94:11 The LORD *k* the thoughts of man;
103:14 for he *k* how we are formed,
Ecc 8: 7 Since no man *k* the future,
8:17 Even if a wise man claims he *k*,
9:12 no man *k* when his hour will come:
Isa 29:16 "He *k* nothing"?
Jer 9:24 that he understands and *k* me,
Mt 6: 8 for your Father *k* what you need
11:27 No one *k* the Son
24:36 "No one *k* about that day or hour,
Lk 12:47 "That servant who *k* his master's
16:15 of men, but God *k* your hearts.
Ac 15: 8 who *k* the heart, showed that he
Ro 8:27 who searches our hearts *k* the mind
1Co 2:11 who among men *k* the thoughts
8: 2 who thinks he *k* something does
2Ti 2:19 The Lord *k* those who are his," and
Jas 4:17 who *k* the good he ought to do
1Jn 4: 6 and whoever *k* God listens to us;
4: 7 born of God and *k* God.

KOHATHITE (KOHATHITES)

Nu 3:29 The *K* clans were to camp

KOHATHITES (KOHATHITE)

Nu 3:28 The *K* were responsible
4:15 *K* are to carry those things that are

KORAH

Levite who led rebellion against Moses and
Aaron (Nu 16; Jude 11).

KORAZIN

Mt 11:21 "Woe to you, *K!* Woe to you,

LABAN

Brother of Rebekah (Ge 24:29), father of Rachel and Leah (Ge 29:16). Received Abraham's servant (Ge 24:29-51). Provided daughters as wives for Jacob in exchange for Jacob's service (Ge 29:1-30). Provided flocks for Jacob's service (Ge 30:25-43). After Jacob's departure, pursued and covenanted with him (Ge 31).

LABOR (LABORING)

Ex 1:11 to oppress them with forced *l*,
20: 9 Six days you shall *l* and do all your
Dt 5:13 Six days you shall *l* and do all your
Ps 127: 1 its builders *l* in vain.
128: 2 You will eat the fruit of your *l*;
Pr 12:24 but laziness ends in slave *l*.
Isa 54: 1 you who were never in *l*;
55: 2 and your *l* on what does not satisfy
Mt 6:28 They do not *l* or spin.
Jn 4:38 have reaped the benefits of their *l*."
1Co 3: 8 rewarded according to his own *l*.
15:58 because you know that your *l*
Gal 4:27 you who have no *l* pains;
Php 2:16 day of Christ that I did not run or *l*
Rev 14:13 "they will rest from their *l*,

LABORING* (LABOR)

2Th 3: 8 *l* and toiling so that we would not

LACK (LACKED LACKING LACKS)

Ps 34: 9 for those who fear him *l* nothing.
Pr 5:23 He will die for *l* of discipline,
10:21 but fools die for *l* of judgment.
11:14 For *l* of guidance a nation falls,
15:22 Plans fail for *l* of counsel,
28:27 to the poor will *l* nothing,
Mk 6: 6 he was amazed at their *l* of faith.
16:14 he rebuked them for their *l* of faith
Ro 3: 3 Will their *l* of faith nullify God's
1Co 1: 7 you do not *l* any spiritual gift
7: 5 because of your *l* of self-control.
Col 2:23 *l* any value in restraining sensual

LACKED (LACK)

Dt 2: 7 and you have not *l* anything.
Ne 9:21 them in the desert; they *l* nothing,
1Co 12:24 honor to the parts that *l* it,

LACKING (LACK)

Pr 17:18 A man *l* in judgment strikes hands
Ro 12:11 Never be *l* in zeal, but keep your
Jas 1: 4 and complete, not *l* anything.

LACKS (LACK)

Pr 6:32 who commits adultery *l* judgment;
11:12 man who *l* judgment derides his
12:11 he who chases fantasies *l* judgment
15:21 delights a man who *l* judgment,
24:30 of the man who *l* judgment;
25:28 is a man who *l* self-control.
28:16 A tyrannical ruler *l* judgment,
31:11 and *l* nothing of value.
Eze 34: 8 because my flock *l* a shepherd
Jas 1: 5 any of you *l* wisdom, he should ask

LAID (LAY)

Isa 53: 6 and the LORD has *l* on him
Mk 6:29 took his body and *l* it in a tomb.
Lk 6:48 and *l* the foundation on rock.
Ac 6: 6 and *l* their hands on them.
1Co 3:11 other than the one already *l*,
1Ti 4:14 body of elders *l* their hands on you.
1Jn 3:16 Jesus Christ *l* down his life for us.

LAKE

Mt 8:24 a furious storm came up on the *l*,
14:25 out to them, walking on the *l*.
Mk 4: 1 into a boat and sat in it out on the *l*,
Lk 8:33 down the steep bank into the *l*
Jn 6:25 him on the other side of the *l*,
Rev 19:20 into the fiery *l* of burning sulfur.
20:14 The *l* of fire is the second death.

LAMB (LAMB'S LAMBS)

Ge 22: 8 "God himself will provide the *l*
Ex 12:21 and slaughter the Passover *l*.
Nu 9:11 are to eat the *l*, together
2Sa 12: 4 he took the ewe *l* that belonged
Isa 11: 6 The wolf will live with the *l*,
53: 7 he was led like a *l* to the slaughter,
Mk 14:12 to sacrifice the Passover *l*,
Jn 1:29 *L* of God, who takes away the sin
Ac 8:32 as a *l* before the shearer is silent,
1Co 5: 7 our Passover *l*, has been sacrificed.
1Pe 1:19 a *l* without blemish or defect.
Rev 5: 6 Then I saw a *L*, looking
5:12 "Worthy is the *L*, who was slain,
7:14 white in the blood of the *L*.
14: 4 They follow the *L* wherever he
15: 3 of God and the song of the *L*:
17:14 but the *L* will overcome them
19: 9 to the wedding supper of the *L*!''
21:23 gives it light, and the *L* is its lamp.

LAMB'S (LAMB)

Rev 21:27 written in the *L* book of life.

LAMBS (LAMB)

Lk 10: 3 I am sending you out like *l*
Jn 21:15 Jesus said, "Feed my *l*."

LAME

Isa 33:23 even the *l* will carry off plunder.
35: 6 Then will the *l* leap like a deer,
Mt 11: 5 The blind receive sight, the *l* walk,
15:31 the *l* walking and the blind seeing.
Lk 14:21 the crippled, the blind and the *l*.'

LAMENT

2Sa 1:17 took up this *l* concerning Saul
Eze 19: 1 Take up a *l* concerning the princes

LAMP (LAMPS LAMPSTAND LAMPSTANDS)

2Sa 22:29 You are my *l*, O LORD;
Ps 18:28 You, O LORD, keep my *l* burning;
119:105 Your word is a *l* to my feet
132:17 and set up a *l* for my anointed one.
Pr 6:23 For these commands are a *l*,
20:27 *l* of the LORD searches the spirit
31:18 and her *l* does not go out at night.
Mt 6:22 "The eye is the *l* of the body.
Lk 8:16 "No one lights a *l* and hides it
Rev 21:23 gives it light, and the Lamb is its *l*.
22: 5 They will not need the light of a *l*

LAMPS (LAMP)

Mt 25: 1 be like ten virgins who took their *l*
Lk 12:35 for service and keep your *l* burning,
Rev 4: 5 the throne, seven *l* were blazing.

LAMPSTAND (LAMP)

Ex 25:31 "Make a *l* of pure gold
Zec 4: 2 "I see a solid gold *l* with a bowl
4:11 on the right and the left of the *l*?''
Heb 9: 2 In its first room were the *l*,
Rev 2: 5 and remove your *l* from its place.

LAMPSTANDS (LAMP)

2Ch 4: 7 He made ten gold *l* according
Rev 1:12 when I turned I saw seven golden *l*,
1:20 and of the seven golden *l* is this:

LAND (LANDS)

Ge 1:10 God called the dry ground "*l*,"
1:11 "Let the *l* produce vegetation:
1:24 "Let the *l* produce living creatures
12: 1 and go to the *l* I will show you.
12: 7 To your offspring I will give this *l*.''
13:15 All the *l* that you see I will give
15:18 "To your descendants I give this *l*,
50:24 out of this *l* to the *l* he promised
Ex 3: 8 a *l* flowing with milk and honey—
6: 8 to the *l* I swore with uplifted hand
33: 3 Go up to the *l* flowing with milk
Lev 25:23 *l* must not be sold permanently,
Nu 14: 8 us into that *l*, a *l* flowing with milk
35:33 Do not pollute the *l* where you are.
Dt 1: 8 See, I have given you this *l*.
8: 7 God is bringing you into a good *l*—
11:10 The *l* you are entering to take
28:21 you from the *l* you are entering
29:19 will bring disaster on the watered *l*
34: 1 LORD showed him the whole *l*—
Jos 13: 2 "This is the *l* that remains:
14: 4 Levites received no share of the *l*
14: 9 *l* on which your feet have walked
2Sa 21:14 answered prayer in behalf of the *l*.
2Ki 17: 5 of Assyria invaded the entire *l*,
24: 1 king of Babylon invaded the *l*,
25:21 into captivity, away from her *l*.
2Ch 7:14 their sin and will heal their *l*.
7:20 then I will uproot Israel from my *l*,
36:21 The *l* enjoyed its sabbath rests;
Ezr 9:11 entering to possess is a *l* polluted
Ne 9:36 in the *l* you gave our forefathers
Ps 37:11 But the meek will inherit the *l*
37:29 the righteous will inherit the *l*
136:21 and gave their *l* as an inheritance,
142: 5 my portion in the *l* of the living.''
Pr 2:21 For the upright will live in the *l*,
12:11 who works his *l* will have abundant
Isa 6:13 though a tenth remains in the *l*,
53: 8 cut off from the *l* of the living;
Jer 2: 7 But you came and defiled my *l*
Eze 36:24 and bring you back into your own *l*.

LANDS (LAND)

Ps 111: 6 giving them the *l* of other nations.
Eze 20: 6 honey, the most beautiful of all *l*.
Zec 10: 9 in distant *l* they will remember me.

LANGUAGE (LANGUAGES)

Ge 11: 1 Now the whole world had one *l*
11: 9 there the LORD confused the *l*
Ps 19: 3 There is no speech or *l*
Jn 8:44 When he lies, he speaks his native *l*
Ac 2: 6 heard them speaking in his own *l*.
Col 3: 8 slander, and filthy *l* from your lips.
Rev 5: 9 from every tribe and *l* and people
7: 9 every nation, tribe, people and *l*,
14: 6 to every nation, tribe, *l* and people.

LANGUAGES (LANGUAGE)

Zec 8:23 "In those days ten men from all *l*

LAODICEA

Rev 3:14 the angel of the church in *L* write:

LAP

Jdg 7: 5 "Separate those who *l* the water

LASHES

Pr 17:10 more than a hundred *l* a fool.
2Co 11:24 from the Jews the forty *l* minus one

LAST (LASTING LASTS LATTER)

Ex 14:24 During the *l* watch of the night
2Sa 23: 1 These are the *l* words of David:

Isa 2: 2 and Jerusalem: In the *l* days
41: 4 and with the *l*—I am he."
44: 6 I am the first and I am the *l*;
48: 12 I am the first and I am the *l*.
Hos 3: 5 and to his blessings in the *l* days.
Mic 4: 1 In the *l* days
Mt 19: 30 But many who are first will be *l*,
20: 8 beginning with the *l* ones hired
21: 37 *L* of all, he sent his son to them.
Mk 9: 35 must be the very *l*, and the servant
10: 31 are first will be *l*, and the *l* first."
15: 37 a loud cry, Jesus breathed his *l*.
Jn 6: 40 and I will raise him up at the *l* day."
15: 16 and bear fruit—fruit that will *l*.
Ac 2: 17 " 'In the *l* days, God says,
Ro 1: 17 is by faith from first to *l*,
1Co 15: 26 *l* enemy to be destroyed is death.
15: 52 of an eye, at the *l* trumpet.
2Ti 3: 1 will be terrible times in the *l* days.
2Pe 3: 3 in the *l* days scoffers will come,
Jude : 18 "In the *l* times there will be
Rev 1: 17 I am the First and the *L*.
22: 13 the First and the *L*, the Beginning

LASTING (LAST)

Ex 12: 14 to the LORD—a *l* ordinance.
Lev 24: 8 of the Israelites, as a *l* covenant.
Nu 25: 13 have a covenant of a *l* priesthood,
Heb 10: 34 had better and *l* possessions.

LASTS (LAST)

Ps 30: 5 For his anger *l* only a moment,
2Co 3: 11 greater is the glory of that which *l*!

LATTER (LAST)

Job 42: 12 The LORD blessed the *l* part
Mt 23: 23 You should have practiced the *l*,
Php 1: 16 *l* do so in love, knowing that I am

LAUGH (LAUGHED LAUGHS LAUGHTER)

Ps 59: 8 But you, O LORD, *l* at them;
Pr 31: 25 she can *l* at the days to come.
Ecc 3: 4 a time to weep and a time to *l*,
Lk 6: 21 for you will *l*.
6: 25 Woe to you who *l* now,

LAUGHED (LAUGH)

Ge 17: 17 Abraham fell facedown; he *l*
18: 12 So Sarah *l* to herself as she thought,

LAUGHS (LAUGH)

Ps 2: 4 The One enthroned in heaven *l*;
37: 13 but the Lord *l* at the wicked,

LAUGHTER (LAUGH)

Ge 21: 6 Sarah said, "God has brought me *l*,
Ps 126: 2 Our mouths were filled with *l*,
Pr 14: 13 Even in *l* the heart may ache,
Jas 4: 9 Change your *l* to mourning

LAVISHED

Eph 1: 8 of God's grace that he *l* on us
1Jn 3: 1 great is the love the Father has *l*

LAW (LAWFUL LAWGIVER LAWS)

Lev 24: 22 are to have the same *l* for the alien
Nu 6: 13 " 'Now this is the *l* for the Nazirite
Dt 1: 5 Moses began to expound this *l*,
6: 25 to obey all this *l* before the LORD
27: 26 of this *l* by carrying them out."
31: 11 you shall read this *l* before them
31: 26 "Take this Book of the *L*
Jos 1: 7 to obey all the *l* my servant Moses
1: 8 of the *L* depart from your mouth;
22: 5 and the *l* that Moses the servant
2Ki 22: 8 of the *L* in the temple of the LORD
2Ch 6: 16 walk before me according to my *l*,
17: 9 the Book of the *L* of the LORD;
34: 14 of the *L* of the LORD that had
Ezr 7: 6 versed in the *L* of Moses,
Ne 8: 2 Ezra the priest brought the *L*
8: 8 from the Book of the *L* of God,
Ps 1: 2 and on his *l* he meditates day
19: 7 The *l* of the LORD is perfect,
37: 31 The *L* of his God is in his heart;
40: 8 your *l* is within my heart."
119: 18 wonderful things in your *l*.

Ps 119: 70 but I delight in your *l*.
119: 72 *l* from your mouth is more precious
119: 77 for your *l* is my delight.
119: 97 Oh, how I love your *l*!
119:163 but I love your *l*.
119:165 peace have they who love your *l*,
Pr 28: 9 If anyone turns a deaf ear to the *l*,
29: 18 but blessed is he who keeps the *l*.
Isa 2: 3 The *l* will go out from Zion,
8: 20 To the *l* and to the testimony!
42: 21 to make his *l* great and glorious.
Jer 2: 8 deal with the *l* did not know me;
8: 8 for we have the *l* of the LORD,"
31: 33 "I will put my *l* in their minds
Mic 4: 2 The *l* will go out from Zion,
Hab 1: 4 they are a *l* to themselves
Zec 7: 12 as flint and would not listen to the *l*
Mt 5: 17 that I have come to abolish the *L*
7: 12 sums up the *L* and the Prophets.
22: 36 greatest commandment in the *L*?"
22: 40 All the *L* and the Prophets hang
23: 23 more important matters of the *l*—
Lk 11: 52 "Woe to you experts in the *l*,
16: 17 stroke of a pen to drop out of the *L*.
24: 44 me in the *L* of Moses."
Jn 1: 17 For the *l* was given through Moses;
Ac 13: 39 justified from by the *l* of Moses.
Ro 2: 12 All who sin apart from the *l* will
2: 15 of the *l* are written on their hearts,
2: 20 you have in the *l* the embodiment
2: 25 value if you observe the *l*,
3: 19 we know that whatever the *l* says,
3: 20 in his sight by observing the *l*;
3: 21 apart from *l*, has been made known
3: 28 by faith apart from observing the *l*.
3: 31 Not at all! Rather, we uphold the *l*.
4: 13 It was not through *l* that Abraham
4: 15 worthless, because *l* brings wrath.
4: 16 not only to those who are of the *l*
5: 13 for before the *l* was given,
5: 20 *l* was added so that the trespass
6: 14 because you are not under *l*,
6: 15 we are not under *l* but under grace?
7: 1 that the *l* has authority
7: 4 also died to the *l* through the body
7: 5 aroused by the *l* were at work
7: 6 released from the *l* so that we serve
7: 7 then? Is the *l* sin? Certainly not!
7: 8 For apart from *l*, sin is dead.
7: 12 *l* is holy, and the commandment is
7: 14 We know that the *l* is spiritual;
7: 22 my inner being I delight in God's *l*;
7: 25 in my mind am a slave to God's *l*,
8: 2 because through Christ Jesus the *l*
8: 3 For what the *l* was powerless to do
8: 4 of the *l* might be fully met in us,
8: 7 It does not submit to God's *l*,
9: 4 covenants, the receiving of the *l*,
9: 31 who pursued a *l* of righteousness,
10: 4 Christ is the end of the *l*
13: 8 his fellowman has fulfilled the *l*.
13: 10 love is the fulfillment of the *l*.
1Co 6: 6 goes to *l* against another—
9: 9 For it is written in the *L* of Moses:
9: 20 the *l* I became like one under the *l*
9: 21 I became like one not having the *l*
15: 56 and the power of sin is the *l*.
Gal 2: 16 justified by observing the *l*,
2: 19 For through the *l* I died to the *l*
3: 2 the Spirit by observing the *l*,
3: 5 you because you observe the *l*,
3: 10 on observing the *l* are under a curse
3: 11 justified before God by the *l*,
3: 13 curse of the *l* by becoming a curse
3: 17 The *l*, introduced 430 years later,
3: 19 then, was the purpose of the *l*?
3: 21 Is the *l*, therefore, opposed
3: 23 we were held prisoners by the *l*,
3: 24 So the *l* was put in charge to lead us
4: 21 you who want to be under the *l*,
5: 3 obligated to obey the whole *l*.
5: 4 justified by *l* have been alienated
5: 14 The entire *l* is summed up
5: 18 by the Spirit, you are not under *l*.
6: 2 and in this way you will fulfill the *l*
Eph 2: 15 flesh the *l* with its commandments
Php 3: 9 of my own that comes from the *l*,
1Ti 1: 8 We know that the *l* is good

Heb 7: 12 there must also be a change of the *l*.
7: 19 (for the *l* made nothing perfect),
10: 1 The *l* is only a shadow
Jas 1: 25 intently into the perfect *l* that gives
2: 8 If you really keep the royal *l* found
2: 10 For whoever keeps the whole *l*
4: 11 or judges him speaks against the *l*
1Jn 3: 4 Everyone who sins breaks the *l*;

LAWFUL (LAW)

Mt 12: 12 Therefore it is *l* to do good

LAWGIVER* (LAW)

Isa 33: 22 the LORD is our *l*,
Jas 4: 12 There is only one *L* and Judge,

LAWLESS (LAWLESSNESS)

2Th 2: 8 And then the *l* one will be revealed
Heb 10: 17 "Their sins and *l* acts

LAWLESSNESS* (LAWLESS)

2Th 2: 3 and the man of *l* is revealed,
2: 7 power of *l* is already at work;
1Jn 3: 4 sins breaks the law; in fact, sin is *l*.

LAWS (LAW)

Ex 21: 1 "These are the *l* you are to set
Lev 25: 18 and be careful to obey my *l*,
Dt 4: 1 and *l* I am about to teach you.
30: 16 decrees and *l*; then you will live
Ps 119: 30 I have set my heart on your *l*.
119: 43 for I have put my hope in your *l*.
119:120 I stand in awe of your *l*.
119:164 for your righteous *l*.
119:175 and may your *l* sustain me.
Eze 36: 27 and be careful to keep my *l*.
Heb 8: 10 I will put my *l* in their minds
10: 16 I will put my *l* in their hearts,

LAWSUITS

Hos 10: 4 therefore *l* spring up
1Co 6: 7 The very fact that you have *l*

LAY (LAID LAYING LAYS)

Ex 29: 10 and his sons shall *l* their hands
Lev 1: 4 He is to *l* his hand on the head
4: 15 the community are to *l* their hands
Nu 8: 10 the Israelites are to *l* their hands
27: 18 whom is the spirit, and *l* your hand
1Sa 26: 9 Who can *l* a hand on the LORD's
Job 1: 12 on the man himself do not *l* a finger
22: 22 and *l* up his words in your heart.
Ecc 10: 4 calmness can *l* great errors to rest.
Isa 28: 16 "See, I *l* a stone in Zion,
Mt 8: 20 of Man has no place to *l* his head."
28: 6 Come and see the place where he *l*.
Mk 6: 5 *l* his hands on a few sick people
Lk 9: 58 of Man has no place to *l* his head."
Jn 10: 15 and I *l* down my life for the sheep.
10: 18 but I *l* it down of my own accord.
15: 13 that he *l* down his life
Ac 8: 19 on whom I *l* my hands may receive
Ro 9: 33 I *l* in Zion a stone that causes men
1Co 3: 11 no one can *l* any foundation other
1Pe 2: 6 "See, I *l* a stone in Zion,
1Jn 3: 16 And we ought to *l* down our lives
Rev 4: 10 They *l* their crowns

LAYING (LAY)

Lk 4: 40 and *l* his hands on each one,
Ac 8: 18 at the *l* on of the apostles' hands,
1Ti 4: 14 Do not be hasty in the *l* on of hands
2Ti 1: 6 is in you through the *l*
Heb 6: 1 not *l* again the foundation
6: 2 instruction about baptisms, the *l*

LAYS (LAY)

Jn 10: 11 The good shepherd *l* down his life

LAZARUS

1. Poor man in Jesus' parable (Lk 16:19-31).
2. Brother of Mary and Martha whom Jesus raised from the dead (Jn 11:1-12:19).

LAZINESS* (LAZY)

Pr 12: 24 but *l* ends in slave labor.
19: 15 *L* brings on deep sleep,

LAZY* (LAZINESS)

Ex 5: 8 They are *l*, that is why they are
      5: 17 Pharaoh said, *''L*, that's what you
      5: 17 "Lazy, that's what you are—*l!*
Pr 10: 4 *L* hands make a man poor,
    12: 27 The *l* man does not roast his game,
    26: 15 he is too *l* to bring it back
Ecc 10: 18 If a man is *l*, the rafters sag;
Mt 25: 26 replied, 'You wicked, *l* servant!
Tit   1: 12 liars, evil brutes, *l* gluttons.''
Heb 6: 12 We do not want you to become *l*,

LEAD (LEADER LEADERS LEADERSHIP LEADS LED)

Ex 15: 13 "In your unfailing love you will *l*
Nu 14: 8 with us, he will *l* us into that land,
Dt 31: 2 and I am no longer able to *l* you.
Jos   1: 6 because you will *l* these people
1Sa 8: 5 now appoint a king to *l* us,
2Ch 1: 10 knowledge, that I may *l* this people
Ps 27: 11 *l* me in a straight path
     61: 2 *l* me to the rock that is higher
   139: 24 and *l* me in the way everlasting,
   143: 10 *l* me on level ground.
Pr   4: 11 and *l* you along straight paths.
Ecc 5: 6 Do not let your mouth *l* you
Isa 11: 6 and a little child will *l* them.
    49: 10 and *l* them beside springs of water.
Da 12: 3 those who *l* many to righteousness,
Mt 6: 13 And *l* us not into temptation,
Lk 11: 4 And *l* us not into temptation.' ''
Gal 3: 24 So the law was put in charge to *l* us
1Th 4: 11 it your ambition to *l* a quiet life,
1Jn 3: 7 do not let anyone *l* you astray.
Rev 7: 17 he will *l* them to springs

LEADER (LEAD)

1Sa 7: 6 Samuel was *l* of Israel at Mizpah.
    10: 1 Has not the Lord anointed you *l*
    12: 2 I have been your *l* from my youth
    13: 14 and appointed him *l* of his people,

LEADERS (LEAD)

Heb 13: 7 Remember your *l*, who spoke
    13: 17 Obey your *l* and submit

LEADERSHIP* (LEAD)

Nu 33: 1 by divisions under the *l* of Moses
Ps 109: 8 may another take his place of *l*.
Ac 1: 20 '' 'May another take his place of *l*.'
Ro 12: 8 if it is *l*, let him govern diligently;

LEADS (LEAD)

Dt 27: 18 is the man who *l* the blind astray
Ps 23: 2 he *l* me beside quiet waters,
    37: 8 do not fret—it *l* only to evil.
    68: 6 he *l* forth the prisoners
Pr 2: 18 For her house *l* down to death
    10: 17 ignores correction *l* others astray.
    14: 23 but mere talk *l* only to poverty.
    16: 25 but in the end it *l* to death.
    19: 23 The fear of the Lord *l* to life:
    20: 7 righteous man *l* a blameless life;
    21: 5 as surely as haste *l* to poverty.
Isa 40: 11 he gently *l* those that have young.
Mt 7: 13 and broad is the road that *l*
    12: 20 till he *l* justice to victory.
    15: 14 If a blind man *l* a blind man,
Jn 10: 3 sheep by name and *l* them out.
Ro 6: 16 which *l* to death, or to obedience,
    6: 22 the benefit you reap *l* to holiness,
    14: 19 effort to do what *l* to peace
2Co 2: 14 always *l* us in triumphal procession
    7: 10 sorrow brings repentance that *l*
Tit 1: 1 of the truth that *l* to godliness—

LEAH

Wife of Jacob (Ge 29:16-30); bore six sons and one daughter (Ge 29:31-30:21; 34:1; 35:23).

LEAN (LEANED)

Pr 3: 5 *l* not on your own understanding;

LEANED (LEAN)

Ge 47: 31 as he *l* on the top of his staff.
Jn 21: 20 (This was the one who had *l* back
Heb 11: 21 as he *l* on the top of his staff.

LEAP (LEAPED LEAPS)

Isa 35: 6 Then will the lame *l* like a deer,
Mal 4: 2 *l* like calves released from the stall.
Lk 6: 23 "Rejoice in that day and *l* for joy,

LEAPED (LEAP)

Lk 1: 41 heard Mary's greeting, the baby *l*

LEAPS (LEAP)

Ps 28: 7 My heart *l* for joy

LEARN (LEARNED LEARNING LEARNS)

Dt 4: 10 so that they may *l* to revere me
    5: 1 *L* them and be sure to follow them.
   31: 12 and *l* to fear the Lord your God
Ps 119: 7 as I *l* your righteous laws.
Isa 1: 17 *l* to do right!
    26: 9 of the world *l* righteousness.
Mt 11: 29 yoke upon you and *l* from me,
Jn 14: 31 world must *l* that I love the Father
1Th 4: 4 that each of you should *l*
1Ti 2: 11 A woman should *l* in quietness
    5: 4 these should *l* first of all

LEARNED (LEARN)

Ps 119:152 Long ago I *l* from your statutes
Mt 11: 25 things from the wise and *l*,
Php 4: 9 Whatever you have *l* or received
    4: 11 for I have *l* to be content whatever
2Ti 3: 14 continue in what you have *l*
Heb 5: 8 he *l* obedience from what he

LEARNING (LEARN)

Pr 1: 5 let the wise listen and add to their *l*,
    9: 9 man and he will add to his *l*.
Isa 44: 25 who overthrows the *l* of the wise
Jn 7: 15 "How did this man get such *l*
2Ti 3: 7 always *l* but never able

LEARNS (LEARN)

Jn 6: 45 and *l* from him comes to me.

LEATHER

2Ki 1: 8 and with a *l* belt around his waist.''
Mt 3: 4 and he had a *l* belt around his waist

LEAVES

Ge 3: 7 so they sewed fig *l* together
Eze 47: 12 for food and their *l* for healing.''
Rev 22: 2 the *l* of the tree are for the healing

LEBANON

Dt 11: 24 from the desert to *L*,
1Ki 4: 33 from the cedar of *L*

LED (LEAD)

Ex 3: 1 and he *l* the flock to the far side
Dt 8: 2 the Lord your God *l* you all
1Ki 11: 3 and his wives *l* him astray.
2Ch 26: 16 his pride *l* to his downfall.
Ne 13: 26 he was *l* into sin by foreign women.
Ps 68: 18 you *l* captives in your train;
    78: 52 he *l* them like sheep
Pr 7: 21 persuasive words she *l* him astray;
    20: 1 whoever is *l* astray
Isa 53: 7 he was *l* like a lamb to the slaughter
Jer 11: 19 I had been like a gentle lamb *l*
Am 2: 10 and I *l* you forty years in the desert
Mt 4: 1 Then Jesus was *l* by the Spirit
    27: 31 they *l* him away to crucify him.
Lk 4: 1 was *l* by the Spirit in the desert,
Ac 8: 32 "He was *l* like a sheep
Ro 8: 14 those who are *l* by the Spirit
2Co 7: 9 your sorrow *l* you to repentance.
Gal 5: 18 But if you are *l* by the Spirit,
Eph 4: 8 he *l* captives in his train

LEEKS*

Nu 11: 5 melons, *l*, onions and garlic.

LEFT

Dt 28: 14 or to the *l*, following other gods
Jos 1: 7 turn from it to the right or to the *l*,
    23: 6 aside to the right or to the *l*.
2Ki 22: 2 aside to the right or to the *l*.
Pr 4: 27 not swerve to the right or the *l*;
Isa 30: 21 turn to the right or to the *l*,
Mt 6: 3 do not let your *l* hand know what

LEGALISTIC*

Php 3: 6 as for *l* righteousness, faultless.

Mt 25: 33 on his right and the goats on his *l*.

LEGION

Mk 5: 9 "My name is *L*," he replied,

LEND (LENDER LENDS MONEYLENDER)

Lev 25: 37 You must not *l* him money
Dt 15: 8 freely *l* him whatever he needs.
Ps 37: 26 are always generous and *l* freely;
Eze 18: 8 He does not *l* at usury
Lk 6: 34 if you *l* to those from whom you

LENDER (LEND)

Pr 22: 7 and the borrower is servant to the *l*.
Isa 24: 2 for borrower as for *l*,

LENDS (LEND)

Ps 15: 5 who *l* his money without usury
   112: 5 to him who is generous and *l* freely,
Pr 19: 17 to the poor *l* to the Lord,

LENGTH (LONG)

Ps 90: 10 The *l* of our days is seventy years—
Pr 10: 27 The fear of the Lord adds *l* to life

LENGTHY* (LONG)

Mk 12: 40 and for a show make *l* prayers.
Lk 20: 47 and for a show make *l* prayers.

LEOPARD

Isa 11: 6 the *l* will lie down with the goat,
Da 7: 6 beast, one that looked like a *l*.
Rev 13: 2 The beast I saw resembled a *l*,

LEPROSY (LEPROUS)

Nu 12: 10 toward her and saw that she had *l*;
2Ki 5: 1 was a valiant soldier, but he had *l*.
    7: 3 men with *l* at the entrance
2Ch 26: 21 King Uzziah had *l*
Mt 11: 5 those who have *l* are cured,
Lk 17: 12 ten men who had *l* met him.

LEPROUS (LEPROSY)

Ex 4: 6 and when he took it out, it was *l*,

LETTER (LETTERS)

Mt 5: 18 not the smallest *l*, not the least
2Co 3: 2 You yourselves are our *l*, written
    3: 6 for the *l* kills, but the Spirit gives
2Th 3: 14 not obey our instruction in this *l*,

LETTERS (LETTER)

2Co 3: 7 which was engraved in *l* on stone,
    10: 10 "His *l* are weighty and forceful,
2Pe 3: 16 His *l* contain some things that are

LEVEL

Ps 143: 10 lead me on *l* ground.
Pr 4: 26 Make *l* paths for your feet
Isa 26: 7 The path of the righteous is *l*;
    40: 4 the rough ground shall become *l*,
Jer 31: 9 on a *l* path where they will not
Heb 12: 13 "Make *l* paths for your feet,"

LEVI (LEVITE LEVITES LEVITICAL)

1. Son of Jacob by Leah (Ge 29:34; 46:11; 1Ch 2:1). With Simeon avenged rape of Dinah (Ge 34). Tribe of blessed (Ge 49:5-7; Dt 33:8-11), chosen as priests (Nu 3-4), numbered (Nu 3:39; 26:62), allotted cities, but not land (Nu 18; 35; Dt 10:9; Jos 13:14; 21), land (Eze 48:8-22), 12,000 from (Rev 7:7).
2. See MATTHEW.

LEVIATHAN

Job 41: 1 pull in the *l* with a fishhook
Ps 74: 14 you who crushed the heads of *L*
Isa 27: 1 *L* the gliding serpent,

LEVITE (LEVI)

Dt 26: 12 you shall give it to the *L*, the alien,
Jdg 19: 1 a *L* who lived in a remote area

LEVITES (LEVI)

Nu 1: 53 The *L* are to be responsible

Nu 3: 12 "I have taken the *L*
     8: 6 "Take the *L* from among the other
  18: 21 I give to the *L* all the tithes in Israel
  35: 7 must give the *L* forty-eight towns,
2Ch 31: 2 assigned the priests and *L*
Mal 3: 3 he will purify the *L* and refine them

LEVITICAL (LEVI)

Heb 7: 11 attained through the *L* priesthood

LEWDNESS

Mk 7: 22 malice, deceit, *l*, envy, slander,

LIAR* (LIE)

Dt 19: 18 and if the witness proves to be a *l,*
Job 34: 6 I am considered a *l;*
Pr 17: 4 *l* pays attention to a malicious
  19: 22 better to be poor than a *l.*
  30: 6 will rebuke you and prove you a *l.*
Mic 2: 11 If a *l* and deceiver comes and says,
Jn 8: 44 for he is a *l* and the father of lies.
  8: 55 I did not, I would be a *l* like you,
Ro 3: 4 Let God be true, and every man a *l.*
1Jn 1: 10 we make him out to be a *l*
  2: 4 not do what he commands is a *l,*
  2: 22 Who is the *l?* It is the man who
  4: 20 yet hates his brother, he is a *l.*
  5: 10 God has made him out to be a *l,*

LIARS* (LIE)

Ps 63: 11 the mouths of *l* will be silenced.
  116: 11 "All men are *l.*"
Isa 57: 4 the offspring of *l?*
Mic 6: 12 her people are *l*
1Ti 1: 10 for slave traders and *l* and perjurers
  4: 2 come through hypocritical *l,*
Tit 1: 12 "Cretans are always *l*, evil brutes,
Rev 3: 9 though they are not, but are *l—*
  21: 8 magic arts, the idolaters and all *l—*

LIBERATED*

Ro 8: 21 that the creation itself will be *l*

LICENSE

Jude   : 4 of our God into a *l* for immorality

LICK

Ps 72: 9 and his enemies will *l* the dust.
Isa 49: 23 they will *l* the dust at your feet.
Mic 7: 17 They will *l* dust like a snake,

LIE (LIAR LIARS LIED LIES LYING)

Lev 18: 22 " 'Do not *l* with a man
  19: 11 " 'Do not *l.*
Nu 23: 19 God is not a man, that he should *l,*
Dt 6: 7 when you *l* down and when you get
  25: 2 the judge shall make him *l* down
1Sa 15: 29 the Glory of Israel does not *l*
Ps 4: 8 I will *l* down and sleep in peace,
  23: 2 me *l* down in green pastures,
  89: 35 and I will not *l* to David—
Pr 3: 24 when you *l* down, you will not be
Isa 11: 6 leopard will *l* down with the goat,
  28: 15 for we have made a *l* our refuge
Jer 9: 5 They have taught their tongues to *l*
  23: 14 They commit adultery and live a *l.*
Eze 13: 6 are false and their divinations a *l.*
  34: 14 they will *l* down in good grazing
Ro 1: 25 exchanged the truth of God for a *l,*
Col 3: 9 Do not *l* to each other,
2Th 2: 11 so that they will believe the *l*
Tit 1: 2 which God, who does not *l,*
Heb 6: 18 which it is impossible for God to *l,*
1Jn 2: 21 because no *l* comes from the truth.
Rev 14: 5 No *l* was found in their mouths;

LIED (LIE)

Ac 5: 4 You have not *l* to men but to God."

LIES (LIE)

Lev 6: 3 finds lost property and *l* about it,
Ps 5: 6 You destroy those who tell *l;*
  10: 7 His mouth is full of curses and *l*
  12: 2 Everyone *l* to his neighbor;
  34: 13 and your lips from speaking *l.*
  58: 3 they are wayward and speak *l.*
  144: 8 whose mouths are full of *l,*
Pr 6: 19 a false witness who pours out *l*

Pr 12: 17 but a false witness tells *l.*
  19: 5 he who pours out *l* will not go free.
  19: 9 and he who pours out *l* will perish.
  29: 12 if a ruler listens to *l,*
  30: 8 Keep falsehood and *l* far from me;
Isa 59: 3 Your lips have spoken *l,*
Jer 5: 31 The prophets prophesy *l,*
  9: 3 like a bow, to shoot *l;*
  14: 14 "The prophets are prophesying *l*
Hos 11: 12 Ephraim has surrounded me with *l,*
Jn 8: 44 for he is a liar and the father of *l.*

LIFE (LIVE)

Ge 1: 30 everything that has the breath of *l*
  2: 7 into his nostrils the breath of *l,*
  2: 9 of the garden were the tree of *l*
  6: 17 to destroy all *l* under the heavens,
  9: 5 for the *l* of his fellow man.
  9: 11 Never again will all *l* be cut
Ex 21: 6 Then he will be his servant for *l.*
  21: 23 you are to take *l* for *l,* eye for eye,
  23: 26 I will give you a full *l* span.
Lev 17: 14 the *l* of every creature is its blood.
  24: 17 " 'If anyone takes the *l*
  24: 18 must make restitution—*l* for *l.*
Nu 35: 31 a ransom for the *l* of a murderer,
Dt 4: 42 one of these cities and save his *l.*
  12: 23 because the blood is the *l.*
  19: 21 Show no pity: *l* for *l,* eye for eye,
  30: 15 I set before you today *l*
  30: 19 Now choose *l,* so that you
  30: 20 For the LORD is your *l,*
  32: 39 I put to death and I bring to *l,*
  32: 47 words for you—they are your *l.*
1Sa 19: 5 He took his *l* in his hands
Job 2: 6 hands; but you must spare his *l.*"
  33: 4 of the Almighty gives me *l.*
  33: 30 that the light of *l* may shine on him.
Ps 16: 11 known to me the path of *l;*
  17: 14 this world whose reward is in this *l.*
  23: 6 all the days of my *l,*
  27: 1 LORD is the stronghold of my *l—*
  34: 12 Whoever of you loves *l*
  36: 9 For with you is the fountain of *l;*
  39: 4 let me know how fleeting is my *l.*
  41: 2 will protect him and preserve his *l;*
  49: 7 No man can redeem the *l*
  49: 8 the ransom for a *l* is costly,
  63: 3 Because your love is better than *l,*
  69: 28 they be blotted out of the book of *l*
  91: 16 With long *l* will I satisfy him
  104: 33 I will sing to the LORD all my *l;*
  119: 25 preserve my *l* according to your word
Pr 1: 3 a disciplined and prudent *l,*
  3: 2 will prolong your *l* many years
  3: 18 of *l* to those who embrace her;
  4: 23 for it is the wellspring of *l.*
  6: 23 are the way to *l,*
  6: 26 adulteress preys upon your very *l.*
  7: 23 little knowing it will cost him his *l.*
  8: 35 For whoever finds me finds *l*
  10: 11 of the righteous is a fountain of *l,*
  10: 27 of the LORD adds length to *l,*
  11: 30 of the righteous is a tree of *l,*
  13: 3 He who guards his lips guards his *l,*
  13: 12 but a longing fulfilled is a tree of *l.*
  13: 14 of the wise is a fountain of *l,*
  14: 27 of the LORD is a fountain of *l,*
  15: 4 that brings healing is a tree of *l,*
  16: 22 Understanding is a fountain of *l*
  19: 3 A man's own folly ruins his *l,*
  19: 23 The fear of the LORD leads to *l:*
  21: 21 finds *l,* prosperity and honor.
Isa 53: 10 LORD makes his *l* a guilt offering,
  53: 11 he will see the light of *l,*
  53: 12 he poured out his *l* unto death,
Jer 10: 23 that a man's *l* is not his own;
La 3: 58 you redeemed my *l.*
Eze 18: 27 and right, he will save his *l.*
  37: 5 enter you, and you will come to *l.*
Da 12: 2 some to everlasting *l,* others
Jnh 2: 6 you brought my *l* up from the pit,
Mal 2: 5 a covenant of *l* and peace,
Mt 6: 25 Is not *l* more important than food,
  7: 14 and narrow the road that leads to *l,*
  10: 39 Whoever finds his *l* will lose it,
  16: 21 and on the third day be raised to *l.*
  16: 25 wants to save his *l* will lose it,

Mt 18: 8 better for you to enter *l* maimed
  19: 16 thing must I do to get eternal *l?*"
  19: 29 as much and will inherit eternal *l.*
  20: 28 to give his *l* as a ransom for many."
  25: 46 but the righteous to eternal *l.*"
Mk 8: 35 but whoever loses his *l* for me
  9: 43 better for you to enter *l* maimed
  10: 17 "what must I do to inherit eternal *l*
  10: 30 and in the age to come, eternal *l.*
  10: 45 to give his *l* as a ransom for many."
Lk 6: 9 to save *l* or to destroy it?"
  9: 22 and on the third day be raised to *l.*"
  9: 24 wants to save his *l* will lose it,
  12: 15 a man's *l* does not consist
  12: 22 do not worry about your *l,*
  12: 25 can add a single hour to his *l?*
  14: 26 even his own *l—* he cannot be my
  17: 33 tries to keep his *l* will lose it,
  21: 19 standing firm you will gain *l.*
Jn 1: 4 In him was *l,* and that *l* was
  3: 15 believes in him may have eternal *l.*
  3: 36 believes in the Son has eternal *l,*
  4: 14 of water welling up to eternal *l.*"
  5: 21 raises the dead and gives them *l,*
  5: 24 him who sent me has eternal *l*
  5: 26 For as the Father has *l* in himself,
  5: 39 that by them you possess eternal *l.*
  5: 40 refuse to come to me to have *l.*
  6: 27 for food that endures to eternal *l,*
  6: 33 down from heaven and gives *l*
  6: 35 Jesus declared, "I am the bread of *l*
  6: 40 believes in him shall have eternal *l,*
  6: 47 he who believes has everlasting *l.*
  6: 48 I am the bread of *l.*
  6: 51 give for the *l* of the world."
  6: 53 and drink his blood, you have no *l*
  6: 63 The Spirit gives *l;* the flesh counts
  6: 68 You have the words of eternal *l.*
  8: 12 but will have the light of *l.*"
  10: 10 I have come that they may have *l,*
  10: 15 and I lay down my *l* for the sheep.
  10: 17 loves me is that I lay down my *l—*
  10: 28 I give them eternal *l,* and they shall
  11: 25 "I am the resurrection and the *l.*
  12: 25 The man who loves his *l* will lose it,
  12: 50 his command leads to eternal *l.*
  13: 37 I will lay down my *l* for you."
  14: 6 am the way and the truth and the *l.*
  15: 13 lay down his *l* for his friends.
  17: 2 people that he might give eternal *l*
  17: 3 Now this is eternal *l:* that they may
  20: 31 that by believing you may have *l*
Ac 2: 32 God has raised this Jesus to *l,*
  3: 15 You killed the author of *l,*
  11: 18 the Gentiles repentance unto *l.*"
  13: 48 appointed for eternal *l* believed.
Ro 2: 7 immortality, he will give eternal *l.*
  4: 25 was raised to *l* for our justification.
  5: 10 shall we be saved through his *l!*
  5: 18 was justification that brings *l*
  5: 21 righteousness to bring eternal *l*
  6: 4 the Father, we too may live a new *l.*
  6: 13 have been brought from death to *l;*
  6: 22 holiness, and the result is eternal *l.*
  6: 23 but the gift of God is eternal *l*
  8: 6 mind controlled by the Spirit is *l*
  8: 11 also give *l* to your mortal bodies
  8: 38 convinced that neither death nor *l,*
1Co 15: 19 If only for this *l* we have hope
  15: 36 What you sow does not come to *l*
2Co 2: 16 to the other, the fragrance of *l.*
  3: 6 letter kills, but the Spirit gives *l.*
  4: 10 so that the *l* of Jesus may
  5: 4 is mortal may be swallowed up by *l.*
Gal 2: 20 The *l* I live in the body, I live
  3: 21 had been given that could impart *l,*
  6: 8 from the Spirit will reap eternal *l.*
Eph 4: 1 I urge you to live a *l* worthy
Php 2: 16 as you hold out the word of *l—*
  4: 3 whose names are in the book of *l.*
Col 1: 10 order that you may live a *l* worthy
  3: 3 your *l* is now hidden with Christ
1Th 4: 12 so that your daily *l* may win
1Ti 1: 16 on him and receive eternal *l.*
  4: 8 for both the present *l* and the *l*
  4: 12 in *l,* in love, in faith and in purity.
  4: 16 Watch your *l* and doctrine closely.
  6: 12 Take hold of the eternal *l*

1Ti 6: 19 hold of the *l* that is truly *l*.
2Ti 1: 9 saved us and called us to a holy *l*—
     1: 10 destroyed death and has brought *l*
     1: 12 to live a godly *l* in Christ Jesus will
Tit 1: 2 resting on the hope of eternal *l*,
     3: 7 heirs having the hope of eternal *l*.
Heb 7: 16 of the power of an indestructible *l*.
Jas 1: 12 crown of *l* that God has promised
     3: 13 Let him show it by his good *l*,
1Pe 3: 7 with you of the gracious gift of *l*,
     3: 10 "Whoever would love *l*
     4: 2 rest of his earthly *l* for evil human
2Pe 1: 3 given us everything we need for *l*
1Jn 1: 1 proclaim concerning the Word of *l*.
     2: 25 he promised us—even eternal *l*.
     3: 14 we have passed from death to *l*,
     3: 16 Jesus Christ laid down his *l* for us.
     5: 11 has given us eternal *l*, and this *l* is
     5: 20 He is the true God and eternal *l*.
Jude : 21 Christ to bring you to eternal *l*.
Rev 2: 7 the right to eat from the tree of *l*,
     2: 8 who died and came to *l* again.
     2: 10 and I will give you the crown of *l*.
     3: 5 name from the book of *l*,
     13: 8 written in the book of *l* belonging
     17: 8 in the book of *l* from the creation
     20: 12 was opened, which is the book of *l*.
     20: 15 not found written in the book of *l*,
     21: 6 from the spring of the water of *l*.
     21: 27 written in the Lamb's book of *l*.
     22: 1 me the river of the water of *l*,
     22: 2 side of the river stood the tree of *l*,
     22: 14 may have the right to the tree of *l*
     22: 17 take the free gift of the water of *l*.
     22: 19 from him his share in the tree of *l*

LIFE-GIVING (GIVE)

Pr 15: 31 He who listens to a *l* rebuke
1Co 15: 45 being"; the last Adam, a *l* spirit.

LIFETIME (LIVE)

Ps 30: 5 but his favor lasts a *l*;
Lk 16: 25 in your *l* you received your good

LIFT (LIFTED LIFTING LIFTS)

Ps   3: 3 you bestow glory on me and *l*
     28: 2 as I *l* up my hands
     63: 4 in your name I will *l* up my hands.
     91: 12 they will *l* you up in their hands,
     121: 1 I *l* up my eyes to the hills—
     123: 1 I *l* up my eyes to you,
     134: 2 *L* up your hands in the sanctuary
     143: 8 for to you I *l* up my soul.
Isa 40: 9 *l* up your voice with a shout,
La   2: 19 *L* up your hands to him
     3: 41 Let us *l* up our hearts and our
Mt   4: 16 they *l* you up in their hands,
Lk 21: 28 stand up and *l* up your heads,
1Ti 2: 8 everywhere to *l* up holy hands
Jas 4: 10 the Lord, and he will *l* you up.
1Pe 5: 6 that he may *l* you up in due time.

LIFTED (LIFT)

Ne   8: 6 and all the people *l* their hands
Ps 24: 7 be *l* up, you ancient doors,
     40: 2 He *l* me out of the slimy pit,
     41: 9 has *l* up his heel against me.
Isa 52: 13 *l* up and highly exalted.
     63: 9 he *l* them up and carried them
Jn   3: 14 Moses *l* up the snake in the desert,
     8: 28 "When you have *l* up the Son
     12: 32 when I am *l* up from the earth,
     12: 34 'The Son of Man must be *l* up'?
     13: 18 shares my bread has *l* up his heel

LIFTING (LIFT)

Ps 141: 2 may the *l* up of my hands be like

LIFTS (LIFT)

Ps 113: 7 and *l* the needy from the ash heap;

LIGAMENT* (LIGAMENTS)

Eph 4: 16 held together by every supporting *l*

LIGAMENTS* (LIGAMENT)

Col 2: 19 held together by its *l* and sinews,

LIGHT (ENLIGHTENED LIGHTS)

Ge   1: 3 "Let there be *l*," and there was *l*.
Ex 13: 21 in a pillar of fire to give them *l*,
     25: 37 it so that they *l* the space in front
2Sa 22: 29 LORD turns my darkness into *l*.
Job 38: 19 "What is the way to the abode of *l*?
Ps   4: 6 Let the *l* of your face shine upon us
     18: 28 my God turns my darkness into *l*.
     19: 8 giving *l* to the eyes.
     27: 1 LORD is my *l* and my salvation—
     36: 9 in your *l* we see *l*.
     56: 13 God in the *l* of life.
     76: 4 You are resplendent with *l*,
     89: 15 who walk in the *l* of your presence,
     104: 2 He wraps himself in *l*
     119:105 and a *l* for my path.
     119:130 The unfolding of your words gives *l*;
     139: 12 for darkness is as *l* to you.
Pr   4: 18 till the full *l* of day.
Isa 2: 5 let us walk in the *l* of the LORD.
     9: 2 have seen a great *l*;
     42: 6 and a *l* for the Gentiles,
     45: 7 I form the *l* and create darkness,
     49: 6 also make you a *l* for the Gentiles,
     53: 11 he will see the *l* of life.
     60: 1 "Arise, shine, for your *l* has come,
     60: 19 LORD will be your everlasting *l*,
Eze 1: 27 and brilliant *l* surrounded him.
Mic 7: 8 the LORD will be my *l*.
Mt   4: 16 have seen a great *l*;
     5: 14 "You are the *l* of the world.
     5: 15 it gives *l* to everyone in the house.
     5: 16 let your *l* shine before men,
     6: 22 your whole body will be full of *l*.
     11: 30 yoke is easy and my burden is *l*."
     17: 2 his clothes became as white as the *l*.
     24: 29 and the moon will not give its *l*;
Mk 13: 24 and the moon will not give its *l*;
Lk   2: 32 a *l* for revelation to the Gentiles
     8: 16 those who come in can see the *l*.
     11: 33 those who come in may see the *l*.
Jn   1: 4 and that life was the *l* of men.
     1: 5 The *l* shines in the darkness,
     1: 7 witness to testify concerning that *l*,
     1: 9 The true *l* that gives *l*
     3: 19 but men loved darkness instead of *l*
     3: 20 Everyone who does evil hates the *l*,
     8: 12 he said, "I am the *l* of the world.
     9: 5 in the world, I am the *l* of the world
     12: 35 Walk while you have the *l*,
     12: 46 I have come into the world as a *l*,
Ac 13: 47 "'I have made you a *l*
Ro 13: 12 darkness and put on the armor of *l*.
2Co 4: 6 made his *l* shine in our hearts
     6: 14 Or what fellowship can *l* have
     11: 14 masquerades as an angel of *l*.
Eph 5: 8 but now you are *l* in the Lord.
1Th 5: 5 You are all sons of the *l*
1Ti 6: 16 and who lives in unapproachable *l*,
1Pe 2: 9 of darkness into his wonderful *l*.
2Pe 1: 19 as to a *l* shining in a dark place,
1Jn 1: 5 God is *l*; in him there is no
     1: 7 But if we walk in the *l*,
     2: 9 Anyone who claims to be in the *l*
Rev 21: 23 for the glory of God gives it *l*,
     22: 5 for the Lord God will give them *l*.

LIGHTNING

Ex   9: 23 and *l* flashed down to the ground.
     20: 18 and *l* and heard the trumpet
Ps 18: 12 with hailstones and bolts of *l*.
Eze 1: 13 it was bright, and *l* flashed out of it.
Da 10: 6 his face like *l*, his eyes like flaming
Mt 24: 27 For as the *l* that comes from the east
     28: 3 His appearance was like *l*,
Lk 10: 18 "I saw Satan fall like *l* from heaven.
Rev 4: 5 From the throne came flashes of *l*,

LIGHTS (LIGHT)

Ge   1: 14 "Let there be *l* in the expanse
Lk   8: 16 No one *l* a lamp and hides it in a jar

LIKE-MINDED* (MIND)

Php 2: 2 make my joy complete by being *l*.

LIKENESS

Ge   1: 26 man in our image, in our *l*,
Ps 17: 15 I will be satisfied with seeing your *l*.

Isa 52: 14 his form marred beyond human *l*—
Ro   8: 3 Son in the *l* of sinful man
     8: 29 to be conformed to the *l* of his Son,
2Co 3: 18 his *l* with ever-increasing glory,
Php 2: 7 being made in human *l*.
Jas 3: 9 who have been made in God's *l*.

LILIES (LILY)

Lk 12: 27 "Consider how the *l* grow.

LILY (LILIES)

SS   2: 1 a *l* of the valleys.
     2: 2 *Lover* Like a *l* among thorns

LIMIT

Ps 147: 5 his understanding has no *l*.
Jn   3: 34 for God gives the Spirit without *l*.

LINEN

Lev 16: 4 He is to put on the sacred *l* tunic,
Pr 31: 22 she is clothed in fine *l* and purple.
     31: 24 She makes *l* garments
Mk 15: 46 So Joseph bought some *l* cloth,
Jn 20: 6 He saw the strips of *l* lying there,
Rev 15: 6 shining *l* and wore golden sashes
     19: 8 Fine *l*, bright and clean,

LINGER

Hab 2: 3 Though it *l*, wait for it;

LION (LION'S LIONS')

Jdg 14: 6 power so that he tore the *l* apart
1Sa 17: 34 When a *l* or a bear came
Isa 11: 7 and the *l* will eat straw like the ox.
     65: 25 and the *l* will eat straw like the ox,
Eze 1: 10 right side each had the face of a *l*,
     10: 14 the third the face of a *l*,
Da   7: 4 "The first was like a *l*,
1Pe 5: 8 around like a roaring *l* looking
Rev 4: 7 The first living creature was like a *l*
     5: 5 See, the *L* of the tribe of Judah,

LION'S (LION)

Ge 49: 9 You are a *l* cub, O Judah;

LIONS' (LION)

Da   6: 7 shall be thrown into the *l* den.

LIPS

Ps   8: 2 From the *l* of children and infants
     34: 1 his praise will always be on my *l*.
     40: 9 I do not seal my *l*,
     63: 3 my *l* will glorify you.
     119:171 May my *l* overflow with praise,
     140: 3 the poison of vipers is on their *l*.
     141: 3 keep watch over the door of my *l*.
Pr 10: 13 on the *l* of the discerning,
     10: 18 who conceals his hatred has lying *l*,
     10: 32 *l* of the righteous know what is
     12: 22 The LORD detests lying *l*,
     13: 3 He who guards his *l* guards his life,
     14: 7 will not find knowledge on his *l*.
     24: 26 is like a kiss on the *l*.
     26: 23 are fervent *l* with an evil heart.
     27: 2 someone else, and not your own *l*.
Isa 6: 5 For I am a man of unclean *l*,
     28: 11 with foreign *l* and strange tongues
     29: 13 and honor me with their *l*
Mal 2: 7 "For the *l* of a priest ought
Mt 15: 8 These people honor me with their *l*
     21: 16 "'From the *l* of children
Lk   4: 22 words that came from his *l*.
Ro   3: 13 "The poison of vipers is on their *l*."
Col 3: 8 and filthy language from your *l*.
Heb 13: 15 the fruit of *l* that confess his name.
1Pe 3: 10 and his *l* from deceitful speech.

LISTEN (LISTENED LISTENING LISTENS)

Dt 18: 15 You must *l* to him.
     30: 20 *l* to his voice, and hold fast to him.
1Ki 4: 34 came to *l* to Solomon's wisdom,
2Ki 21: 9 But the people did not *l*.
Pr   1: 5 let the wise *l* and add
Ecc 5: 1 Go near to *l* rather
Eze 2: 5 And whether they *l* or fail to *l*—
Mt 12: 42 earth to *l* to Solomon's wisdom,
Mk   9: 7 *L* to him!" Suddenly,

Jn   10: 27 My sheep *l* to my voice; I know
Ac   3: 22 you must *l* to everything he tells
Jas   1: 19 Everyone should be quick to *l,*
     1: 22 Do not merely *l* to the word,
1Jn   4:   6 not from God does not *l* to us.

LISTENED (LISTEN)

Ne   8:   3 And all the people *l* attentively
Isa   66:   4 when I spoke, no one *l.*
Da   9:   6 We have not *l* to your servants

LISTENING (LISTEN)

1Sa   3:   9 Speak, LORD, for your servant is *l*
Pr   18: 13 He who answers before *l—*
Lk   10: 39 at the Lord's feet *l* to what he said.

LISTENS (LISTEN)

Pr   12: 15 but a wise man *l* to advice.
Lk   10: 16 "He who *l* to you *l*
1Jn   4:   6 and whoever knows God *l* to us;

LIVE (ALIVE LIFE LIFETIME LIVES LIVING)

Ge   3: 22 tree of life and eat, and *l* forever.''
Ex   20: 12 so that you may *l* long
     33: 20 for no one may see me and *l.''*
Nu   21:   8 who is bitten can look at it and *l.''*
Dt   5: 24 we have seen that a man can *l*
     6:   2 as you *l* by keeping all his decrees
     8:   3 to teach you that man does not *l*
Job   14: 14 If a man dies, will he *l* again?
Ps   15:   1 Who may *l* on your holy hill?
     24:   1 the world, and all who *l* in it;
     26:   8 I love the house where you *l,*
     119:175 Let me *l* that I may praise you,
Pr   21:   9 Better to *l* on a corner of the roof
     21: 19 Better to *l* in a desert
Ecc   9:   4 a *l* dog is better off than a dead lion
Isa   26: 19 But your dead will *l;*
     55:   3 hear me, that your soul may *l.*
Eze   17: 19 LORD says: As surely as I *l,*
     20: 11 for the man who obeys them will *l*
     37:   3 can these bones *l?''* I said,
Am   5:   6 Seek the LORD and *l,*
Hab   2:   4 but the righteous will *l* by his faith
Zec   2: 11 I will *l* among you and you will
Mt   4:   4 'Man does not *l* on bread alone,
Lk   4:   4 'Man does not *l* on bread alone.' ''
Jn   14: 19 Because I *l,* you also will *l.*
Ac   17: 24 does not *l* in temples built by hands
     17: 28 'For in him we *l* and move
Ro   1: 17 "The righteous will *l* by faith.''
2Co   5:   7 We *l* by faith, not by sight.
     6: 16 "I will *l* with them and walk
Gal   2: 20 The life I *l* in the body, I *l* by faith
     3: 11 "The righteous will *l* by faith.''
     5: 25 Since we *l* by the Spirit, let us keep
Eph   4: 17 that you must no longer *l*
Php   1: 21 to *l* is Christ and to die is gain.
Col   1: 10 order that you may *l* a life worthy
1Th   4:   1 we instructed you how to *l* in order
     5: 13 *L* in peace with each other.
1Ti   2:   2 that we may *l* peaceful
2Ti   3: 12 who wants to *l* a godly life
Tit   2: 12 and to *l* self-controlled, upright
Heb   10: 38 But my righteous one will *l* by faith
     12: 14 Make every effort to *l* in peace
1Pe   1: 17 *l* your lives as strangers here
     3:   8 *l* in harmony with one another;

LIVES (LIVE)

Ge   45:   7 and to save your *l* by a great
Job   19: 25 I know that my Redeemer *l,*
Pr   1: 19 it takes away the *l*
Isa   57: 15 he who *l* forever, whose name is
Da   3: 28 to give up their *l* rather than serve
Jn   14: 17 for he *l* with you and will be in you.
Ro   6: 10 but the life he *l,* he *l* to God.
     7: 18 I know that nothing good *l* in me,
     8:   9 if the Spirit of God *l* in you.
     14:   7 For none of us *l* to himself alone
1Co   3: 16 and that God's Spirit *l* in you?
Gal   2: 20 I no longer live, but Christ *l* in me.
1Th   2:   8 only the gospel of God but our *l*
1Ti   2:   2 quiet *l* in all godliness and holiness.
Tit   2: 12 and godly *l* in this present age,
Heb   7: 24 but because Jesus *l* forever,
     13:   5 Keep your *l* free from the love

1Pe   3:   2 the purity and reverence of your *l.*
2Pe   3: 11 You ought to live holy and godly *l*
1Jn   3: 16 to lay down our *l* for our brothers,
     4: 16 Whoever *l* in love *l* in God,

LIVING (LIVE)

Ge   2:   7 and the man became a *l* being.
1Sa   17: 26 defy the armies of the *l* God?''
Isa   53:   8 cut off from the land of the *l;*
Jer   2: 13 the spring of *l* water,
Eze   1:   5 what looked like four *l* creatures.
Zec   14:   8 On that day *l* water will flow out
Mt   22: 32 the God of the dead but of the *l.''*
Jn   4: 10 he would have given you *l* water.''
     6: 51 I am the *l* bread that came
     7: 38 streams of *l* water will flow
Ro   8: 11 Jesus from the dead is *l* in you,
     12:   1 to offer your bodies as *l* sacrifices,
1Co   9: 14 the gospel should receive their *l*
Heb   4: 12 For the word of God is *l* and active.
     10: 20 and *l* way opened for us
     10: 31 to fall into the hands of the *l* God.
1Pe   1: 23 through the *l* and enduring word
Rev   1: 18 I am the *L* One; I was dead,
     4:   6 the throne, were four *l* creatures,
     7: 17 to springs of *l* water.

LOAD (LOADS)

Gal   6:   5 for each one should carry his own *l.*

LOADS (LOAD)

Mt   23:   4 They tie up heavy *l* and put them

LOAF (LOAVES)

1Co   10: 17 for we all partake of the one *l.*

LOAVES (LOAF)

Mk   6: 41 Taking the five *l* and the two fish
     8:   6 When he had taken the seven *l*
Lk   11:   5 'Friend, lend me three *l* of bread,

LOCKED

Jn   20: 26 the doors were *l,* Jesus came
Gal   3: 23 *l* up until faith should be revealed.

LOCUSTS

Ex   10:   4 I will bring *l* into your country
Joel   2: 25 you for the years the *l* have eaten—
Mt   3:   4 His food was *l* and wild honey.
Rev   9:   3 And out of the smoke *l* came

LOFTY

Ps   139:   6 too *l* for me to attain.
Isa   57: 15 is what the high and *l* One says—

LONELY

Ps   68:   6 God sets the *l* in families,
Lk   5: 16 Jesus often withdrew to *l* places

LONG (LENGTH LENGTHY LONGED LONGING LONGINGS LONGS)

Ex   17: 11 As *l* as Moses held up his hands,
Nu   6:   5 the hair of his head grow *l.*
1Ki   18: 21 "How *l* will you waver
Ps   119: 97 I meditate on it all day *l.*
     119:174 I *l* for your salvation, O LORD,
Hos   7: 13 I *l* to redeem them
Am   5: 18 Why do you *l* for the day
Mt   25:   5 The bridegroom was a *l* time
Jn   9:   4 As *l* as it is day, we must do
1Co   11: 14 that if a man has *l* hair,
Eph   3: 18 to grasp how wide and *l* and high
Php   1:   8 God can testify how I *l* for all
1Pe   1: 12 Even angels *l* to look

LONGED (LONG)

Mt   13: 17 righteous men *l* to see what you see
     23: 37 how often I have *l*
Lk   13: 34 how often I have *l*
2Ti   4:   8 to all who have *l* for his appearing.

LONGING* (LONG)

Dt   28: 65 with *l,* and a despairing heart.
Job   7:   2 Like a slave *l* for the evening
Ps   119: 20 My soul is consumed with *l*
     119: 81 with *l* for your salvation,
     119:131 *l* for your commands.
     143:   7 my spirit faints with *l.*

Pr   13: 12 but a *l* fulfilled is a tree of life.
     13: 19 A *l* fulfilled is sweet to the soul,
Eze   23: 27 look on these things with *l*
Lk   16: 21 and *l* to eat what fell from the rich
Ro   15: 23 since I have been *l* for many years
2Co   5:   2 l to be clothed with our heavenly
     7:   7 He told us about your *l* for me,
     7: 11 what alarm, what *l,* what concern,
1Th   2: 17 out of our intense *l* we made every
Heb   11: 16 they were *l* for a better country—

LONGINGS* (LONG)

Ps   38:   9 All my *l* lie open before you,
     112: 10 the *l* of the wicked will come

LONGS* (LONG)

Ps   63:   1 my body *l* for you,
Isa   26:   9 in the morning my spirit *l* for you.
     30: 18 Yet the LORD *l* to be gracious
Php   2: 26 For he *l* for all of you and is

LOOK (LOOKED LOOKING LOOKS)

Ge   19: 17 "Flee for your lives! Don't *l* back,
Ex   3:   6 because he was afraid to *l* at God.
Nu   21:   8 anyone who is bitten can *l* at it
     32:   8 Kadesh Barnea to *l* over the land.
Dt   4: 29 you will find him if you *l* for him
1Sa   16:   7 The LORD does not *l*
Job   31:   1 not to *l* lustfully at a girl.
Ps   34:   5 Those who *l* to him are radiant;
     105:   4 *L* to the LORD and his strength;
     113:   6 who stoops down to *l*
     123:   2 As the eyes of slaves *l* to the hand
Pr   1: 28 they will *l* for me but will not find
     4: 25 Let your eyes *l* straight ahead,
     15: 30 A cheerful *l* brings joy to the heart,
Isa   7: 17 In that day men will *l*
     31:   1 do not *l* to the Holy One of Israel,
     40: 26 Lift your eyes and *l* to the heavens:
     60:   5 Then you will *l* and be radiant,
Jer   3:   3 Yet you have the brazen *l*
     6: 16 "Stand at the crossroads and *l;*
Eze   34: 11 for my sheep and *l* after them.
Hab   1: 13 Your eyes are too pure to *l* on evil;
Zec   12: 10 They will *l* on me, the one they
Mt   18: 10 "See that you do not *l* down on one
     18: 12 go to *l* for the one that wandered
     23: 27 which *l* beautiful on the outside
Mk   13: 21 'L, here is the Christ!' or, 'L,
Lk   6: 41 "Why do you *l* at the speck
     24: 39 *L* at my hands and my feet.
Jn   1: 36 he said, "L, the Lamb of God!''
     4: 35 open your eyes and *l* at the fields!
     19: 37 "They will *l* on the one they have
Ro   14: 10 why do you *l* down on your brother
Php   2:   4 Each of you should *l* not only
1Ti   4: 12 Don't let anyone *l* down on you
Jas   1: 27 to *l* after orphans and widows
1Pe   1: 12 long to *l* into these things.
2Pe   3: 12 as you *l* forward to the day of God

LOOKED (LOOK)

Ge   19: 26 Lot's wife *l* back, and she became
Ex   2: 25 So God *l* on the Israelites
1Sa   6: 19 because they had *l* into the ark
SS   3:   1 I *l* for the one my heart loves;
Eze   22: 30 "I *l* for a man among them who
     34:   6 and no one searched or *l* for them.
     44:   4 I *l* and saw the glory
Da   7:   9 "As I *l,*
     10:   5 I *l* up and there before me was
Hab   3:   6 he *l,* and made the nations tremble.
Mt   25: 36 I was sick and you *l* after me,
Lk   18:   9 and *l* down on everybody else,
     22: 61 The Lord turned and *l* straight
1Jn   1:   1 which we have *l* at and our hands

LOOKING (LOOK)

Ps   69:   3 *l* for my God.
     119: 82 My eyes fail, *l* for your promise;
     119:123 My eyes fail, *l* for your salvation,
Mk   16:   6 "You are *l* for Jesus the Nazarene.
2Co   10:   7 You are *l* only on the surface
Php   4: 17 Not that I am *l* for a gift,
1Th   2:   6 We were not *l* for praise from men,
2Pe   3: 13 with his promise we are *l* forward
Rev   5:   6 I saw a Lamb, *l* as if it had been

LOOKS (LOOK)

1Sa 16: 7 Man *l* at the outward appearance,
Ezr 8: 22 is on everyone who *l* to him,
Ps 104: 32 who *l* at the earth, and it trembles;
138: 6 on high, he *l* upon the lowly,
Pr 27: 18 he who *l* after his master will be
Eze 34: 12 As a shepherd *l* after his scattered
Mt 5: 28 But I tell you that anyone who *l*
16: 4 and adulterous generation *l*
Lk 9: 62 and *l* back is fit for service
Jn 6: 40 Father's will is that everyone who *l*
12: 45 When he *l* at me, he sees the one
Php 2: 21 For everyone *l* out
Jas 1: 25 But the man who *l* intently

LOOSE

Isa 33: 23 Your rigging hangs *l*:
Mt 16: 19 and whatever you *l* on earth will be
18: 18 and whatever you *l* on earth will be

LORD† (LORD'S† LORDED LORDING)

Ge 18: 27 been so bold as to speak to the *L*,
Ex 15: 17 O *L*, your hands established.
Nu 16: 13 now you also want to *l* it over us?
Dt 10: 17 God of gods and *L* of lords,
Jos 3: 13 the *L* of all the earth—set foot
1Ki 3: 10 *L* was pleased that Solomon had
Ne 4: 14 Remember the *L*, who is great
Job 28: 28 'The fear of the *L*— that is wisdom,
Ps 37: 13 but the *L* laughs at the wicked,
38: 22 O *L* my Savior.
54: 4 the *L* is the one who sustains me.
62: 12 and that you, O *L*, are loving.
69: 6 O *L*, the LORD Almighty;
86: 5 You are forgiving and good, O *L*,
86: 8 gods there is none like you, O *L*;
89: 49 O *L*, where is your former great
110: 1 The LORD says to my *L*:
110: 5 The *L* is at your right hand;
130: 3 O *L*, who could stand?
135: 5 that our *L* is greater than all gods.
136: 3 Give thanks to the *L* of lords:
147: 5 Great is our *L* and mighty in power
Isa 6: 1 I saw the *L* seated on a throne,
Da 2: 47 and the *L* of kings and a revealer
9: 4 "O *L*, the great and awesome God,
9: 7 "*L*, you are righteous,
9: 9 The *L* our God is merciful
9: 19 O *L*, listen! O *L*, forgive! O *L*,
Mt 3: 3 'Prepare the way for the *L*,
4: 7 'Do not put the *L* your God
4: 10 'Worship the *L* your God,
7: 21 "Not everyone who says to me, '*L*,
9: 38 Ask the *L* of the harvest, therefore,
12: 8 Son of Man is *L* of the Sabbath."
20: 25 of the Gentiles *l* it over them,
21: 9 comes in the name of the *L*!''
22: 37 " 'Love the *L* your God
22: 44 For he says, '' 'The *L* said to my *L*:
23: 39 comes in the name of the *L*.' ' '
Mk 1: 3 'Prepare the way for the *L*,
12: 11 the *L* has done this,
12: 29 the *L* our God, the *L* is one.
12: 30 Love the *L* your God
Lk 2: 9 glory of the *L* shone around them,
6: 5 The Son of Man is *L* of the Sabbath
6: 46 "Why do you call me, '*L*, *L*,'
10: 27 " 'Love the *L* your God
11: 1 one of his disciples said to him, "*L*,
24: 34 The *L* has risen and has appeared
Jn 1: 23 'Make straight the way for the *L*.' ''
Ac 2: 21 on the name of the *L* will be saved.'
2: 25 " 'I saw the *L* always before me.
2: 34 " 'The *L* said to my *L*:
8: 16 into the name of the *L* Jesus.
9: 5 "Who are you, *L*?'' Saul asked.
10: 36 through Jesus Christ, who is *L*
11: 23 true to the *L* with all their hearts.
16: 31 replied, "Believe in the *L* Jesus,
Ro 4: 24 in him who raised Jesus our *L*
5: 11 in God through our *L* Jesus Christ,
6: 23 life in Christ Jesus our *L*.
8: 39 of God that is in Christ Jesus our *L*.
10: 9 with your mouth, "Jesus is *L*,''

Ro 10: 13 on the name of the *L* will be saved
10: 16 *L*, who has believed our message?''
11: 34 Who has known the mind of the *L*?
12: 11 your spiritual fervor, serving the *L*.
13: 14 yourselves with the *L* Jesus Christ,
14: 4 for the *L* is able to make him stand.
14: 8 we live to the *L*; and if we die,
1Co 1: 31 Let him who boasts boast in the *L*.''
3: 5 the *L* has assigned to each his task.
4: 5 time; wait till the *L* comes.
6: 13 for the *L*, and the *L* for the body.
6: 14 By his power God raised the *L*
7: 32 affairs—how he can please the *L*.
7: 34 to be devoted to the *L* in both body
7: 35 in undivided devotion to the *L*.
7: 39 but he must belong to the *L*.
8: 6 and there is but one *L*, Jesus Christ,
10: 9 We should not test the *L*,
11: 23 For I received from the *L* what I
12: 3 "Jesus is *L*,'' except by the Holy
15: 57 victory through our *L* Jesus Christ.
15: 58 fully to the work of the *L*,
16: 22 If anyone does not love the *L*—
2Co 1: 24 Not that we *l* it over your faith,
2: 12 found that the *L* had opened a door
3: 17 Now the *L* is the Spirit,
4: 5 but Jesus Christ as *L*, and ourselves
5: 6 in the body we are away from the *L*
8: 5 they gave themselves first to the *L*
8: 21 not only in the eyes of the *L* but
10: 17 Let him who boasts boast in the *L*.''
10: 18 but the one whom the *L* commends
13: 10 the authority the *L* gave me
Gal 6: 14 in the cross of our *L* Jesus Christ,
Eph 4: 5 one *L*, one faith, one baptism;
5: 8 but now you are light in the *L*.
5: 10 and find out what pleases the *L*.
5: 19 make music in your heart to the *L*,
5: 22 submit to your husbands as to the *L*
6: 1 obey your parents in the *L*,
6: 7 as if you were serving the *L*,
6: 8 know that the *L* will reward
6: 10 in the *L* and in his mighty power.
Php 2: 11 confess that Jesus Christ is *L*,
3: 1 my brothers, rejoice in the *L*!
3: 8 of knowing Christ Jesus my *L*,
4: 1 you should stand firm in the *L*,
4: 4 Rejoice in the *L* always.
4: 5 The *L* is near.
Col 1: 10 you may live a life worthy of the *L*
2: 6 as you received Christ Jesus as *L*,
3: 13 Forgive as the *L* forgave you.
3: 17 do it all in the name of the *L* Jesus,
3: 18 your husbands, as is fitting in the *L*.
3: 20 in everything, for this pleases the *L*
3: 23 as working for the *L*, not for men,
3: 24 It is the *L* Christ you are serving.
3: 24 receive an inheritance from the *L*
4: 17 work you have received in the *L*.''
1Th 3: 8 since you are standing firm in the *L*
3: 12 May the *L* make your love increase
4: 1 and urge you in the *L* Jesus
4: 6 The *L* will punish men
4: 15 who are left till the coming of the *L*
5: 2 day of the *L* will come like a thief
5: 23 at the coming of our *L* Jesus Christ.
2Th 1: 7 when the *L* Jesus is revealed
1: 12 of our *L* Jesus may be glorified
2: 1 the coming of our *L* Jesus Christ
2: 8 whom the *L* Jesus will overthrow
3: 3 *L* is faithful, and he will strengthen
3: 5 May the *L* direct your hearts
1Ti 6: 15 the King of kings and *L* of lords,
2Ti 1: 8 ashamed to testify about our *L*,
2: 19 "The *L* knows those who are his,''
4: 8 which the *L*, the righteous Judge,
4: 17 But the *L* stood at my side
Heb 1: 10 O *L*, you laid the foundations
10: 30 "The *L* will judge his people.''
12: 14 holiness no one will see the *L*.
13: 6 *L* is my helper; I will not be afraid.
Jas 3: 9 With the tongue we praise our *L*
4: 10 Humble yourselves before the *L*,
5: 11 The *L* is full of compassion
1Pe 1: 25 the word of the *L* stands forever.''

1Pe 2: 3 you have tasted that the *L* is good.
3: 12 eyes of the *L* are on the righteous
3: 15 in your hearts set apart Christ as *L*.
2Pe 1: 11 into the eternal kingdom of our *L*
1: 16 and coming of our *L* Jesus Christ,
2: 1 the sovereign *L* who bought
2Pe 2: 9 then the *L* knows how
3: 9 The *L* is not slow in keeping his
3: 18 and knowledge of our *L* and Savior
Jude : 14 the *L* is coming with thousands
Rev 4: 8 holy, holy is the *L* God Almighty,
4: 11 "You are worthy, our *L* and God,
11: 15 has become the kingdom of our *L*
17: 14 he is *L* of lords and King of kings—
19: 16 KINGS AND *L* OF LORDS.
22: 5 for the *L* God will give them light.
22: 20 Come, *L* Jesus.

LORD'S† (LORD†)

Lk 1: 38 "I am the *L* servant,'' Mary
Ac 11: 21 The *L* hand was with them,
21: 14 and said, "The *L* will be done.''
1Co 7: 32 is concerned about the *L* affairs—
10: 26 "The earth is the *L*, and everything
11: 26 you proclaim the *L* death
2Co 3: 18 faces all reflect the *L* glory,
Eph 5: 17 but understand what the *L* will is.
2Ti 2: 24 And the *L* servant must not quarrel
Heb 12: 5 light of the *L* discipline,
Jas 4: 15 you ought to say, "If it is the *L* will,
5: 8 because the *L* coming is near.
1Pe 2: 13 Submit yourselves for the *L* sake

LORDED* (LORD†)

Ne 5: 15 Their assistants also *l* it

LORDING* (LORD†)

1Pe 5: 3 not *l* it over those entrusted to you,

LORD‡ (LORD'S‡)

Ge 2: 4 When the *L* God made the earth
2: 7 the *L* God formed the man
2: 22 Then the *L* God made a woman
3: 21 The *L* God made garments of skin
3: 23 So the *L* God banished him
4: 4 The *L* looked with favor on Abel
4: 26 began to call on the name of the *L*.
6: 7 So the *L* said, "I will wipe mankind
7: 16 Then the *L* shut him in.
9: 26 Blessed be the *L*, the God of Shem!
11: 9 there the *L* confused the language
12: 1 *L* had said to Abram, "Leave your
15: 6 Abram believed the *L*,
15: 18 On that day the *L* made a covenant
17: 1 the *L* appeared to him and said,
18: 1 The *L* appeared to Abraham
18: 14 Is anything too hard for the *L*?
18: 19 way of the *L* by doing what is right
21: 1 Now the *L* was gracious to Sarah
22: 14 that place The *L* Will Provide.
24: 1 the *L* had blessed him in every way
26: 2 The *L* appeared to Isaac and said,
28: 13 There above it stood the *L*,
31: 49 "May the *L* keep watch
39: 2 The *L* was with Joseph
39: 21 in the prison, the *L* was with him;
Ex 3: 2 the angel of the *L* appeared to him
4: 11 Is it not I, the *L*? Now go,
4: 31 heard that the *L* was concerned
6: 2 also said to Moses, "I am the *L*.
9: 12 the *L* hardened Pharaoh's heart
12: 27 'It is the Passover sacrifice to the *L*,
12: 43 The *L* said to Moses and Aaron,
13: 9 For the *L* brought you out of Egypt
13: 21 By day the *L* went ahead of them
14: 13 the deliverance the *L* will bring
14: 30 That day the *L* saved Israel
15: 3 The *L* is a warrior;
15: 11 among the gods is like you, O *L*?
15: 26 for I am the *L*, who heals you.''
16: 12 know that I am the *L* your God.' ''
16: 23 day of rest, a holy Sabbath to the *L*.
17: 15 and called it The *L* is my Banner.
19: 8 will do everything the *L* has said.''
19: 20 The *L* descended to the top

Ex 20: 2 "I am the *L* your God, who
20: 5 the *L* your God, am a jealous God,
20: 7 for the *L* will not hold anyone
20: 10 a Sabbath to the *L* your God.
20: 11 in six days the *L* made the heavens
20: 12 in the land the *L* your God is giving
23: 25 Worship the *L* your God,
24: 3 "Everything the *L* has said we will
24: 12 The *L* said to Moses, "Come up
24: 16 and the glory of the *L* settled
25: 1 The *L* said to Moses, "Tell
28: 36 HOLY TO THE *L*.
30: 11 Then the *L* said to Moses,
31: 13 so you may know that I am the *L*,
31: 18 When the *L* finished speaking
33: 11 The *L* would speak to Moses face
33: 19 And the *L* said, "I will cause all my
34: 1 *L* said to Moses, "Chisel out two
34: 6 proclaiming, "The *L*, the *L*,
34: 10 awesome is the work that I, the *L*,
34: 29 because he had spoken with the *L*.
40: 34 glory of the *L* filled the tabernacle.
40: 38 So the cloud of the *L* was
Lev 8: 36 did everything the *L* commanded
9: 23 and the glory of the *L* appeared
10: 2 and they died before the *L*.
19: 2 'Be holy because I, the *L* your God,
20: 8 I am the *L*, who makes you holy.
20: 26 to be holy to me because I, the *L*,
23: 40 and rejoice before the *L* your God
Nu 6: 24 Say to them: "' 'The *L* bless you
8: 5 *L* said to Moses: "Take the Levites
11: 1 hardships in the hearing of the *L*,
14: 14 O *L*, have been seen face to face,
14: 18 you have declared: 'The *L* is slow
14: 21 glory of the *L* fills the whole earth,
21: 6 Then the *L* sent venomous snakes
22: 31 Then the *L* opened Balaam's eyes,
23: 12 "Must I not speak what the *L* puts
30: 2 When a man makes a vow to the *L*
32: 12 followed the *L* wholeheartedly.'
Dt 1: 21 and take possession of it as the *L*,
2: 7 forty years the *L* your God has
4: 29 there you seek the *L* your God,
5: 6 And he said: "I am the *L* your God,
5: 9 the *L* your God, am a jealous God,
6: 4 The *L* our God, the *L* is one.
6: 5 Love the *L* your God
6: 16 Do not test the *L* your God
6: 25 law before the *L* our God,
7: 1 When the *L* your God brings you
7: 6 holy to the *L* your God.
7: 8 But it was because the *L* loved you
7: 9 that the *L* your God is God;
7: 12 then the *L* your God will keep his
8: 5 so the *L* your God disciplines you.
9: 10 The *L* gave me two stone tablets
10: 12 but to fear the *L* your God,
10: 14 To the *L* your God belong
10: 17 For the *L* your God is God of gods
10: 20 Fear the *L* your God and serve him
10: 22 now the *L* your God has made you
11: 1 Love the *L* your God and keep his
11: 13 to love the *L* your God
16: 1 the Passover of the *L* your God,
17: 15 the king the *L* your God chooses.
28: 1 If you fully obey the *L* your God
28: 15 if you do not obey the *L* your God
29: 1 covenant the *L* commanded Moses
29: 29 things belong to the *L* our God,
30: 4 from there the *L* your God will
30: 6 *L* your God will circumcise your
30: 10 if you obey the *L* your God
30: 16 today to love the *L* your God,
30: 20 For the *L* is your life, and he will
31: 6 for the *L* your God goes with you;
34: 5 of the *L* died there in Moab,
Jos 10: 14 a day when the *L* listened to a man.
22: 5 to love the *L* your God, to walk
23: 11 careful to love the *L* your God.
24: 15 my household, we will serve the *L*
24: 18 We too will serve the *L*,
Jdg 2: 12 They forsook the *L*, the God
Ru 1: 8 May the *L* show kindness to you,
4: 13 And the *L* enabled her to conceive,
1Sa 1: 11 him to the *L* for all the days
1: 15 I was pouring out my soul to the *L*.
1: 28 So now I give him to the *L*.

1Sa 2: 2 "There is no one holy like the *L*;
2: 25 but if a man sins against the *L*,
2: 26 in favor with the *L* and with men.
3: 9 *L*, for your servant is listening.' "
3: 19 The *L* was with Samuel
7: 12 "Thus far has the *L* helped us."
9: 17 sight of Saul, the *L* said to him,
11: 15 as king in the presence of the *L*.
12: 18 all the people stood in awe of the *L*
12: 22 his great name the *L* will not reject
12: 24 But be sure to fear the *L*
13: 14 the *L* has sought out a man
14: 6 Nothing can hinder the *L*
15: 22 "Does the *L* delight
16: 13 Spirit of the *L* came upon David
17: 45 you in the name of the *L* Almighty,
2Sa 6: 14 danced before the *L*
7: 22 How great you are, O Sovereign *L*!
8: 6 gave David victory everywhere
12: 7 This is what the *L*, the God
22: 2 "The *L* is my rock, my fortress
22: 29 You are my lamp, O *L*;
22: 31 the word of the *L* is flawless.
1Ki 1: 30 today what I swore to you by the *L*,
2: 3 and observe what the *L* your God
3: 7 O *L* my God, you have made your
5: 5 for the Name of the *L* my God,
5: 12 The *L* gave Solomon wisdom,
8: 11 the glory of the *L* filled his temple.
8: 23 toward heaven and said: "O *L*,
8: 61 fully committed to the *L* our God,
9: 3 The *L* said to him: "I have heard
10: 9 Praise be to the *L* your God,
15: 14 committed to the *L* all his life.
18: 21 If the *L* is God, follow him;
18: 36 "O *L*, God of Abraham, Isaac
18: 39 "The *L*— he is God! The *L*—
21: 23 also concerning Jezebel the *L* says:
2Ki 13: 23 But the *L* was gracious to them
17: 18 So the *L* was very angry with Israel
18: 5 Hezekiah trusted in the *L*,
19: 1 and went into the temple of the *L*.
20: 11 *L* made the shadow go back the ten
21: 12 Therefore this is what the *L*,
22: 2 right in the eyes of the *L*
22: 8 of the Law in the temple of the *L*."
23: 3 to follow the *L* and keep his
23: 21 the Passover to the *L* your God,
23: 25 a king like him who turned to the *L*
24: 2 The *L* sent Babylonian, Aramean,
24: 4 and the *L* was not willing to forgive
1Ch 10: 13 because he was unfaithful to the *L*;
11: 3 with them at Hebron before the *L*,
11: 9 the *L* Almighty was with him.
13: 6 from there the ark of God the *L*, who
16: 8 Give thanks to the *L*, call
16: 14 He is the *L* our God;
16: 23 Sing to the *L*, all the earth;
17: 1 covenant of the *L* is under a tent."
21: 24 take for the *L* what is yours,
22: 5 to be built for the *L* should be
22: 11 build the house of the *L* your God,
22: 13 and laws that the *L* gave Moses
22: 16 Now begin the work, and the *L* be
22: 19 soul to seeking the *L* your God.
25: 7 and skilled in music for the *L*—
28: 9 for the *L* searches every heart
28: 20 for the *L* God, my God, is with you
29: 1 not for man but for the *L* God.
29: 11 O *L*, is the greatness and the power
29: 18 O *L*, God of our fathers Abraham,
29: 25 The *L* highly exalted Solomon
2Ch 1: 1 for the *L* his God was with him
5: 13 to give praise and thanks to the *L*.
5: 14 the glory of the *L* filled the temple
6: 16 "Now, *L*, God of Israel, keep
6: 41 O *L* God, and come
6: 42 O *L* God, do not reject your
7: 1 the glory of the *L* filled the temple.
7: 12 the *L* appeared to him at night
7: 21 'Why has the *L* done such a thing
9: 8 as king to rule for the *L* your God.
13: 12 do not fight against the *L*,
14: 2 right in the eyes of the *L* his God.
15: 14 to the *L* with loud acclamation,
16: 9 of the *L* range throughout the earth
17: 9 the Book of the Law of the *L*;

2Ch 18: 13 said, "As surely as the *L* lives,
19: 6 judging for man but for the *L*.
19: 9 wholeheartedly in the fear of the *L*.
20: 15 This is what the *L* says to you:
20: 20 Have faith in the *L* your God
20: 21 appointed men to sing to the *L*
26: 5 As long as he sought the *L*,
26: 16 He was unfaithful to the *L* his God,
29: 30 to praise the *L* with the words
30: 9 for the *L* your God is gracious
31: 20 and faithful before the *L* his God.
32: 8 with us is the *L* our God to help us
34: 14 Law of the *L* that had been given
34: 31 to follow the *L* and keep his
Ezr 3: 10 foundation of the temple of the *L*,
7: 6 for the hand of the *L* his God was
7: 10 observance of the Law of the *L*,
9: 5 hands spread out to the *L* my God
9: 8 the *L* our God has been gracious
9: 15 O *L*, God of Israel, you are
Ne 1: 5 Then I said: "O *L*, God of heaven,
8: 1 which the *L* had commanded
9: 6 You alone are the *L*.
Job 1: 6 to present themselves before the *L*,
1: 21 *L* gave and the *L* has taken away;
38: 1 the *L* answered Job out
42: 9 and the *L* accepted Job's prayer.
42: 12 The *L* blessed the latter part
Ps 1: 2 But his delight is in the law of the *L*
1: 6 For the *L* watches over the way
4: 6 of your face shine upon us, O *L*.
4: 8 for you alone, O *L*,
5: 3 In the morning, O *L*,
6: 1 O *L*, do not rebuke me
8: 1 O *L*, our Lord,
9: 9 The *L* is a refuge for the oppressed,
9: 19 Arise, O *L*, let not man triumph;
10: 16 The *L* is King for ever and ever;
12: 6 And the words of the *L* are flawless
16: 5 *L*, you have assigned me my
16: 8 I have set the *L* always before me.
18: 1 I love you, O *L*, my strength.
18: 6 In my distress I called to the *L*;
18: 30 the word of the *L* is flawless.
19: 7 The law of the *L* is perfect,
19: 14 O *L*, my Rock and my Redeemer.
20: 5 May the *L* grant all your requests.
20: 7 in the name of the *L* our God.
22: 8 let the *L* rescue him.
23: 1 The *L* is my shepherd, I shall
23: 6 I will dwell in the house of the *L*
24: 3 Who may ascend the hill of the *L*?
24: 8 The *L* strong and mighty,
25: 10 All the ways of the *L* are loving
27: 1 The *L* is my light and my salvation
27: 4 to gaze upon the beauty of the *L*
27: 6 I will sing and make music to the *L*.
29: 1 Ascribe to the *L*, O mighty ones,
29: 4 The voice of the *L* is powerful;
30: 4 Sing to the *L*, you saints of his;
31: 5 redeem me, O *L*, the God of truth.
32: 2 whose sin the *L* does not count
33: 1 joyfully to the *L*, you righteous;
33: 6 of the *L* were the heavens made,
33: 12 is the nation whose God is the *L*,
33: 18 But the eyes of the *L* are
34: 1 I will extol the *L* at all times;
34: 3 Glorify the *L* with me;
34: 4 I sought the *L*, and he answered me
34: 7 The angel of the *L* encamps
34: 8 Taste and see that the *L* is good;
34: 9 Fear the *L*, you his saints,
34: 15 The eyes of the *L* are
34: 18 The *L* is close to the brokenhearted
37: 4 Delight yourself in the *L*
37: 5 Commit your way to the *L*;
39: 4 "Show me, O *L*, my life's end
40: 1 I waited patiently for the *L*;
40: 5 Many, O *L* my God,
46: 8 Come and see the works of the *L*,
47: 2 How awesome is the *L* Most High,
48: 1 Great is the *L*, and most worthy
50: 1 The Mighty One, God, the *L*,
55: 22 Cast your cares on the *L*
59: 8 But you, O *L*, laugh at them;
68: 4 his name is the *L*—
68: 18 O *L* God, might dwell there.
68: 20 from the Sovereign *L* comes escape

Ps   69: 31 This will please the *L* more
     72: 18 Praise be to the *L* God, the God
     75: 8 In the hand of the *L* is a cup
     78: 4 the praiseworthy deeds of the *L*,
     84: 8 my prayer, O *L* God Almighty;
     84: 11 For the *L* God is a sun and shield;
     85: 7 Show us your unfailing love, O *L*.
     86: 11 Teach me your way, O *L*,
     87: 2 the *L* loves the gates of Zion
     89: 5 heavens praise your wonders, O *L*,
     89: 8 O *L* God Almighty, who is like you
     91: 2 I will say of the *L*, "He is my refuge
     92: 1 It is good to praise the *L*
     92: 4 by your deeds, O *L*;
     92: 13 planted in the house of the *L*,
     93: 1 The *L* reigns, he is robed in majesty
     93: 5 house for endless days, O *L*.
     94: 1 O *L*, the God who avenges,
     94: 12 is the man you discipline, O *L*,
     94: 18 your love, O *L*, supported me.
     95: 1 Come, let us sing for joy to the *L*;
     95: 3 For the *L* is the great God,
     95: 6 let us kneel before the *L* our Maker
     96: 1 Sing to the *L* a new song;
     96: 5 but the *L* made the heavens.
     96: 8 to the *L* the glory due his name;
     96: 9 Worship the *L* in the splendor
     96: 13 they will sing before the *L*,
     97: 1 The *L* reigns, let the earth be glad;
     97: 9 O *L*, are the Most High
     98: 1 Sing to the *L* a new song,
     98: 2 *L* has made his salvation known
     98: 4 Shout for joy to the *L*, all the earth,
     99: 1 The *L* reigns,
     99: 2 Great is the *L* in Zion;
     99: 5 Exalt the *L* our God
     99: 9 Exalt the *L* our God
    100: 1 Shout for joy to the *L*, all the earth.
    100: 2 Worship the *L* with gladness;
    100: 3 Know that the *L* is God.
    100: 5 For the *L* is good and his love
    101: 1 to you, O *L*, I will sing praise.
    102: 12 But you, O *L*, sit enthroned forever
    103: 1 Praise the *L*, O my soul;
    103: 8 The *L* is compassionate
    103: 19 The *L* has established his throne
    104: 1 O *L* my God, you are very great;
    104: 24 How many are your works, O *L*!
    104: 33 I will sing to the *L* all my life;
    105: 4 Look to the *L* and his strength;
    105: 7 He is the *L* our God;
    106: 2 proclaim the mighty acts of the *L*,
    107: 1 Give thanks to the *L*, for he is good
    107: 8 to the *L* for his unfailing love
    107: 21 to the *L* for his unfailing love
    107: 43 and consider the great love of the *L*
    108: 3 I will praise you, O *L*,
    109: 26 Help me, O *L* my God;
    110: 1 The *L* says to my Lord:
    110: 4 The *L* has sworn
    111: 2 Great are the works of the *L*;
    111: 4 *L* is gracious and compassionate.
    111: 10 The fear of the *L* is the beginning
    112: 1 Blessed is the man who fears the *L*,
    113: 1 Praise, O servants of the *L*,
    113: 2 Let the name of the *L* be praised,
    113: 4 *L* is exalted over all the nations,
    113: 5 Who is like the *L* our God,
    115: 1 Not to us, O *L*, not to us
    115: 18 it is we who extol the *L*,
    116: 12 How can I repay the *L*
    116: 15 Precious in the sight of the *L*
    117: 1 Praise the *L*, all you nations;
    118: 1 Give thanks to the *L*, for he is good
    118: 5 In my anguish I cried to the *L*,
    118: 8 It is better to take refuge in the *L*
    118: 18 The *L* has chastened me severely,
    118: 23 the *L* has done this,
    118: 24 This is the day the *L* has made;
    118: 26 comes in the name of the *L*.
    119: 1 to the law of the *L*.
    119: 64 with your love, O *L*,
    119: 89 Your word, O *L*, is eternal;
    119: 126 It is time for you to act, O *L*;
    119: 159 O *L*, according to your love.
    120: 1 I call on the *L* in my distress,
    121: 2 My help comes from the *L*,
    121: 5 The *L* watches over you—

Ps 121: 8 the *L* will watch over your coming
    122: 1 "Let us go to the house of the *L*."
    123: 2 so our eyes look to the *L* our God,
    124: 1 If the *L* had not been on our side—
    124: 8 Our help is in the name of the *L*,
    125: 2 so the *L* surrounds his people
    126: 3 The *L* has done great things for us,
    126: 4 Restore our fortunes, O *L*,
    127: 1 Unless the *L* builds the house,
    127: 3 Sons are a heritage from the *L*,
    128: 1 Blessed are all who fear the *L*,
    130: 1 O *L*; O Lord, hear my voice.
    130: 3 If you, O *L*, kept a record of sins,
    130: 5 I wait for the *L*, my soul waits,
    131: 3 O Israel, put your hope in the *L*
    132: 1 O *L*, remember David
    132: 13 For the *L* has chosen Zion,
    133: 3 For there the *L* bestows his
    134: 3 May the *L*, the Maker of heaven
    135: 4 For the *L* has chosen Jacob
    135: 6 The *L* does whatever pleases him,
    136: 1 Give thanks to the *L*, for he is good
    137: 4 How can we sing the songs of the *L*
    138: 1 I will praise you, O *L*,
    138: 8 The *L* will fulfill his purpose;
    139: 1 O *L*, you have searched me
    140: 1 Rescue me, O *L*, from evil men;
    141: 1 O *L*, I call to you; come quickly
    141: 3 Set a guard over my mouth, O *L*;
    142: 1 I cry to you, O *L*;
    143: 9 Rescue me from my enemies, O *L*,
    144: 3 O *L*, what is man that you care
    145: 3 Great is the *L* and most worthy
    145: 8 *L* is gracious and compassionate,
    145: 9 The *L* is good to all;
    145: 17 The *L* is righteous in all his ways
    145: 18 The *L* is near to all who call on him
    146: 5 whose hope is in the *L* his God,
    146: 7 The *L* sets prisoners free,
    147: 2 The *L* builds up Jerusalem;
    147: 7 Sing to the *L* with thanksgiving;
    147: 11 *L* delights in those who fear him,
    147: 12 Extol the *L*, O Jerusalem;
    148: 1 Praise the *L* from the heavens,
    148: 7 Praise the *L* from the earth,
    149: 4 For the *L* takes delight
    150: 1 Praise the *L*.
    150: 6 that has breath praise the *L*.

Pr   1: 7 The fear of the *L* is the beginning
      1: 29 and did not choose to fear the *L*,
      2: 5 will understand the fear of the *L*
      2: 6 For the *L* gives wisdom,
      3: 5 Trust in the *L* with all your heart
      3: 7 fear the *L* and shun evil.
      3: 9 Honor the *L* with your wealth,
      3: 12 the *L* disciplines those he loves,
      3: 19 By wisdom the *L* laid the earth's
      5: 21 are in full view of the *L*,
      6: 16 There are six things the *L* hates,
      8: 13 To fear the *L* is to hate evil;
      9: 10 "The fear of the *L* is the beginning
     10: 27 The fear of the *L* adds length to life
     11: 1 The *L* abhors dishonest scales,
     12: 22 The *L* detests lying lips,
     14: 2 whose walk is upright fears the *L*,
     14: 26 He who fears the *L* has a secure
     14: 27 The fear of the *L* is a fountain
     15: 3 The eyes of the *L* are everywhere,
     15: 16 Better a little with the fear of the *L*
     15: 33 of the *L* teaches a man wisdom,
     16: 2 but motives are weighed by the *L*.
     16: 3 Commit to the *L* whatever you do,
     16: 4 The *L* works out everything
     16: 5 The *L* detests all the proud of heart
     16: 9 but the *L* determines his steps.
     16: 33 but its every decision is from the *L*.
     18: 10 The name of the *L* is a strong tower
     18: 22 and receives favor from the *L*.
     19: 14 but a prudent wife is from the *L*.
     19: 17 to the poor lends to the *L*,
     19: 23 The fear of the *L* leads to life:
     20: 10 the *L* detests them both.
     21: 2 but the *L* weighs the heart.
     21: 3 to the *L* than sacrifice.
     21: 30 that can succeed against the *L*.
     21: 31 but victory rests with the *L*.
     22: 2 The *L* is the Maker of them all.
     22: 23 for the *L* will take up their case

Pr   23: 17 for the fear of the *L*.
     24: 18 or the *L* will see and disapprove
     24: 21 Fear the *L* and the king, my son,
     25: 22 and the *L* will reward you.
     28: 14 is the man who always fears the *L*,
     29: 26 from the *L* that man gets justice.
     30: 7 "Two things I ask of you, O *L*;
     31: 30 a woman who fears the *L* is

Isa   2: 3 up to the mountain of the *L*.
      2: 10 the ground from dread of the *L*
      3: 17 the *L* will make their scalps bald."
      4: 2 of the *L* will be beautiful
      5: 16 the *L* Almighty will be exalted
      6: 3 holy, holy is the *L* Almighty;
      9: 7 The zeal of the *L* Almighty
     11: 2 The Spirit of the *L* will rest on him
     11: 9 full of the knowledge of the *L*
     12: 2 The *L*, is my strength
     18: 7 of the Name of the *L* Almighty.
     24: 1 the *L* is going to lay waste the earth
     25: 1 O *L*, you are my God;
     25: 6 this mountain the *L* Almighty will
     25: 8 The Sovereign *L* will wipe away
     26: 4 Trust in the *L* forever,
     26: 8 *L*, walking in the way of your laws,
     26: 13 O *L*, our God, other lords
     26: 21 the *L* is coming out of his dwelling
     27: 1 the *L* will punish with his sword,
     27: 12 In that day the *L* will thresh
     28: 5 In that day the *L* Almighty
     29: 6 the *L* Almighty will come
     29: 15 to hide their plans from the *L*,
     30: 18 For the *L* is a God of justice.
     30: 26 when the *L* binds up the bruises
     30: 27 the Name of the *L* comes from afar
     30: 30 The *L* will cause men
     33: 2 O *L*, be gracious to us;
     33: 6 the fear of the *L* is the key
     33: 22 For the *L* is our judge,
     34: 2 The *L* is angry with all nations;
     35: 2 they will see the glory of the *L*,
     35: 10 the ransomed of the *L* will return.
     38: 7 to you that the *L* will do what he
     40: 3 the way for the *L*;
     40: 5 the glory of the *L* will be revealed,
     40: 7 the breath of the *L* blows on them.
     40: 10 the Sovereign *L* comes with power,
     40: 14 Whom did the *L* consult
     40: 28 The *L* is the everlasting God,
     40: 31 but those who hope in the *L*
     41: 14 will help you," declares the *L*,
     41: 20 that the hand of the *L* has done this
     42: 6 the *L*, have called you
     42: 8 "I am the *L*; that is my name!
     42: 13 The *L* will march out like a mighty
     42: 21 It pleased the *L*
     43: 3 For I am the *L*, your God,
     43: 11 I, even I, am the *L*,
     44: 6 "This is what the *L* says—
     44: 24 I am the *L*,
     45: 5 I am the *L*, and there is no other;
     45: 7 I, the *L*, do all these things.
     45: 21 Was it not I, the *L*?
     48: 17 "I am the *L* your God,
     50: 4 Sovereign *L* has given me
     50: 10 Who among you fears the *L*
     51: 1 and who seek the *L*:
     51: 11 The ransomed of the *L* will return.
     51: 15 the *L* Almighty is his name.
     53: 1 the arm of the *L* been revealed?
     53: 6 and the *L* has laid on him
     53: 10 and the will of the *L* will prosper
     54: 5 the *L* Almighty is his name—
     55: 6 Seek the *L* while he may be found;
     55: 7 to the *L*, and he will have mercy
     56: 6 who bind themselves to the *L*
     58: 8 of the *L* will be your rear guard.
     58: 11 The *L* will guide you always;
     59: 1 the arm of the *L* is not too short
     60: 1 the glory of the *L* rises upon you.
     60: 16 Then you will know that I, the *L*,
     60: 20 the *L* will be your everlasting light,
     61: 1 Spirit of the Sovereign *L* is on me,
     61: 3 a planting of the *L*
     61: 10 I delight greatly in the *L*;
     61: 11 so the Sovereign *L* will make
     62: 4 for the *L* will take delight in you,
     63: 7 I will tell of the kindnesses of the *L*,

Isa 64: 8 Yet, O *L*, you are our Father.
  66:15 See, the *L* is coming with fire,
Jer 1: 9 Then the *L* reached out his hand
  2:19 when you forsake the *L* your God
  3:25 sinned against the *L* our God,
  4: 4 Circumcise yourselves to the *L*,
  8: 7 the requirements of the *L*.
  9:24 I am the *L*, who exercises kindness,
  10: 6 No one is like you, O *L*;
  10:10 But the *L* is the true God;
  12: 1 You are always righteous, O *L*,
  14: 7 O *L*, do something for the sake
  14:20 O *L*, we acknowledge our
  16:15 will say, 'As surely as the *L* lives,
  16:19 O *L*, my strength and my fortress,
  17: 7 is the man who trusts in the *L*,
  17:10 "I the *L* search the heart
  20:11 *L* is with me like a mighty warrior;
  23: 6 The *L* Our Righteousness.
  24: 7 heart to know me, that I am the *L*.
  28: 9 as one truly sent by the *L* only
  31:11 For the *L* will ransom Jacob
  31:22 The *L* will create a new thing
  31:34 his brother, saying, 'Know the *L*,'
  32:27 I am the *L*, the God of all mankind.
  33:16 The *L* Our Righteousness.'
  36: 6 the words of the *L* that you wrote
  40: 3 now the *L* has brought it about;
  42: 3 Pray that the *L* your God will tell
  42: 4 I will tell you everything the *L* says
  42: 6 we will obey the *L* our God,
  50: 4 go in tears to seek the *L* their God.
  51:10 " 'The *L* has vindicated us;
  51:56 For the *L* is a God of retribution;
La 3:24 to myself, "The *L* is my portion;
  3:25 *L* is good to those whose hope is
  3:40 and let us return to the *L*.
Eze 1: 3 the word of the *L* came
  1:28 of the likeness of the glory of the *L*.
  4:14 Sovereign *L*! I have never defiled
  10: 4 Then the glory of the *L* rose
  15: 7 you will know that I am the *L*.
  30: 3 the day of the *L* is near—
  36:23 nations will know that I am the *L*,
  37: 4 'Dry bones, hear the word of the *L*!
  43: 4 glory of the *L* entered the temple
  44: 4 Lᴏʀᴅ filling the temple of the *L*,
Da 9: 2 to the word of the *L* given
Hos 1: 7 horsemen, but by the *L* their God."
  2:20 and you will acknowledge the *L*.
  3: 1 as the *L* loves the Israelites,
  3: 5 They will come trembling to the *L*
  6: 1 "Come, let us return to the *L*.
  6: 3 Let us acknowledge the *L*;
  10:12 for it is time to seek the *L*,
  12: 5 the *L* is his name of renown!
  14: 1 O Israel, to the *L* your God.
Joel 1: 1 The word of the *L* that came
  1:15 For the day of the *L* is near;
  2: 1 for the day of the *L* is coming.
  2:11 The day of the *L* is great;
  2:13 Return to the *L* your God,
  2:23 rejoice in the *L* your God,
  2:31 the great and dreadful day of the *L*.
  2:32 on the name of the *L* will be saved;
  3:14 For the day of the *L* is near
  3:16 the *L* will be a refuge for his people,
Am 4:13 the *L* God Almighty is his name.
  5: 6 Seek the *L* and live,
  5:15 Perhaps the *L* God Almighty will
  5:18 long for the day of the *L*?
  7:15 *L* took me from tending the flock
  8:12 searching for the word of the *L*,
  9: 5 The Lord, the *L* Almighty,
Ob :15 "The day of the *L* is near
Jnh 1: 3 But Jonah ran away from the *L*
  1: 4 the *L* sent a great wind on the sea,
  1:17 But the *L* provided a great fish
  2: 9 Salvation comes from the *L*."
  2: 2 He prayed to the *L*, "O *L*,
  4: 6 Then the *L* God provided a vine
Mic 1: 1 The word of the *L* that came to Micah
  2: 2 up to the mountain of the *L*,
  5: 4 flock in the strength of the *L*,
  6: 2 For the *L* has a case
  6: 8 And what does the *L* require of you
  7: 7 as for me, I watch in hope for the *L*,
Na 1: 2 The *L* takes vengeance on his foes

Na 1: 3 The *L* is slow to anger
Hab 2:14 knowledge of the glory of the *L*,
  2:20 But the *L* is in his holy temple;
  3: 2 I stand in awe of your deeds, O *L*.
Zep 1: 1 The word of the *L* that came
  1: 7 for the day of the *L* is near.
  3:17 The *L* your God is with you,
Hag 1: 1 the word of the *L* came
  1: 8 and be honored," says the *L*.
  2:23 that day,' declares the *L* Almighty.
Zec 1: 1 the word of the *L* came
  1:17 and the *L* will again comfort Zion
  3: 1 standing before the angel of the *L*,
  4: 6 by my Spirit,' says the *L* Almighty.
  6:12 and build the temple of the *L*.
  8:21 the *L* and seek the *L* Almighty.
  9:16 The *L* their God will save them
  14: 5 Then the *L* my God will come,
  14: 9 The *L* will be king
  14:16 the *L* Almighty, and to celebrate
Mal 1: 1 The word of the *L* to Israel
  3: 6 "I the *L* do not change.
  4: 5 and dreadful day of the *L* comes.

LORD'S‡ (LORD‡)

Ex 4:14 the *L* anger burned against Moses
  12:11 Eat it in haste; it is the *L* Passover.
  34:34 he entered the *L* presence
Lev 23: 4 " 'These are the *L* appointed feasts,
Nu 9:23 At the *L* command they encamped
  14:41 you disobeying the *L* command?
  32:13 The *L* anger burned against Israel
Dt 6:18 is right and good in the *L* sight,
  10:13 and to observe the *L* commands
  32: 9 For the *L* portion is his people,
Jos 21:45 Not one of all the *L* good promises
1Sa 24:10 because he is the *L* anointed.'
1Ki 10: 9 Because of the *L* eternal love
Ps 24: 1 The earth is the *L*, and everything
  32:10 but the *L* unfailing love
  89: 1 of the *L* great love forever;
  103: 17 *L* love is with those who fear him,
  118: 15 "The *L* right hand has done mighty
Pr 3:11 do not despise the *L* discipline
  19:21 but it is the *L* purpose that prevails.
Isa 24:14 west they acclaim the *L* majesty.
  30: 9 to listen to the *L* instruction.
  49: 4 Yet what is due me is in the *L* hand
  53:10 Yet it was the *L* will to crush him
  55:13 This will be for the *L* renown,
  61: 2 to proclaim the year of the *L* favor
  62: 3 of splendor in the *L* hand,
Jer 25:17 So I took the cup from the *L* hand
  48:10 lax in doing the *L* work!
  51: 7 was a gold cup in the *L* hand;
La 3:22 of the *L* great love we are not
Eze 7:19 them in the day of the *L* wrath.
Joel 3:18 will flow out of the *L* house
Ob :21 And the kingdom will be the *L*.
Mic 4: 1 of the *L* temple will be established
  6: 2 O mountains, the *L* accusation;
Hab 2:16 from the *L* right hand is coming
Zep 2: 3 sheltered on the day of the *L* anger.

LOSE (LOSES LOSS LOST)

Dt 1:28 Our brothers have made us *l* heart.
1Sa 17:32 "Let no one *l* heart on account
Isa 7: 4 Do not *l* heart because of these two
Mt 10:39 Whoever finds his life will *l* it,
Lk 9:25 and yet *l* or forfeit his very self?
Jn 6:39 that I shall *l* none of all that he has
2Co 4: 1 this ministry, we do not *l* heart.
  4:16 Therefore we do not *l* heart.
Heb 12: 3 will not grow weary and *l* heart.
  12: 5 do not *l* heart when he rebukes you
2Jn : 8 that you do not *l* what you have

LOSES (LOSE)

Mt 5:13 But if the salt *l* its saltiness,
Lk 15: 4 you has a hundred sheep and *l* one
  15: 8 has ten silver coins and *l* one.

LOSS (LOSE)

Ro 11:12 and their *l* means riches
1Co 3:15 he will suffer *l*; he himself will be
Php 3: 8 I consider everything a *l* compared

LOST (LOSE)

Ps 73: 2 I had nearly *l* my foothold.
Jer 50: 6 "My people have been *l* sheep;
Eze 34: 4 the strays or searched for the *l*.
  34:16 for the *l* and bring back the strays.
Mt 18:14 any of these little ones should be *l*.
Lk 15: 4 go after the *l* sheep until he finds it?
  15: 6 with me; I have found my *l* sheep.'
  15: 9 with me; I have found my *l* coin.'
  15:24 is alive again; he was *l* and is found
  19:10 to seek and to save what was *l*.' "
Php 3: 8 for whose sake I have *l* all things.

LOT (LOTS)

Nephew of Abraham (Ge 11:27; 12:5). Chose to live in Sodom (Ge 13). Rescued from four kings (Ge 14). Rescued from Sodom (Ge 19:1-29; 2Pe 2:7). Fathered Moab and Ammon by his daughters (Ge 19:30-38).

Est 3: 7 the *l*) in the presence of Haman
  9:24 the *l*) for their ruin and destruction.
Pr 16:33 The *l* is cast into the lap,
  18:18 Casting the *l* settles disputes
Ecc 3:22 his work, because that is his *l*.
Ac 1:26 Then they cast lots, and the *l* fell

LOTS (LOT)

Jos 18:10 Joshua then cast *l* for them
Ps 22:18 and cast *l* for my clothing.
Joel 3: 3 They cast *l* for my people
Ob :11 and cast *l* for Jerusalem,
Mt 27:35 divided up his clothes by casting *l*.
Ac 1:26 Then they cast *l*, and the lot fell

LOVE* (BELOVED LOVED LOVELY LOVER LOVER'S LOVERS LOVES LOVING LOVING-KINDNESS)

Ge 20:13 'This is how you can show your *l*
  22: 2 your only son, Isaac, whom you *l*,
  29:18 Jacob was in *l* with Rachel and said
  29:20 days to him because of his *l* for her
  29:32 Surely my husband will *l* me now.' "
Ex 15:13 "In your unfailing *l* you will lead
  20: 6 showing *l* to a thousand generations
  20: 6 of those who *l* me
  21: 5 'I *l* my master and my wife
  34: 6 abounding in *l* and faithfulness,
  34: 7 maintaining *l* to thousands,
Lev 19:18 but *l* your neighbor as yourself.
  19:34 *L* him as yourself,
Nu 14:18 abounding in *l* and forgiving sin
  14:19 In accordance with your great *l*,
Dt 5:10 showing *l* to a thousand generations
  5:10 of those who *l* me
  6: 5 *L* the Lᴏʀᴅ your God
  7: 9 generations of those who *l* him
  7: 9 keeping his covenant of *l*
  7:12 God will keep his covenant of *l*
  7:13 He will *l* you and bless you
  10:12 to walk in all his ways, to *l* him,
  10:19 you are to *l* those who are aliens,
  11: 1 *L* the Lᴏʀᴅ your God
  11:13 to *l* the Lᴏʀᴅ your God
  11:22 to *l* the Lᴏʀᴅ your God,
  13: 3 you *l* him with all your heart
  13: 6 wife you *l*, or your closest friend
  19: 9 to *l* the Lᴏʀᴅ your God
  21:15 the son of the wife he does not *l*,
  21:16 the son of the wife he does not *l*.
  30: 6 so that you may *l* him
  30:16 today to *l* the Lᴏʀᴅ your God,
  30:20 and that you may *l* the Lᴏʀᴅ your
  33: 3 Surely it is you who *l* the people;
Jos 22: 5 to *l* the Lᴏʀᴅ your God, to walk
  23:11 careful to *l* the Lᴏʀᴅ your God.
Jdg 5:31 may they who *l* you be like the sun
  14:16 You hate me! You don't really *l* me
  16: 4 he fell in *l* with a woman
  16:15 "How can you say, 'I *l* you,'
1Sa 18:20 Saul's daughter Michal was in *l*
  20:17 had David reaffirm his oath out of *l*
2Sa 1:26 Your *l* for me was wonderful,
  7:15 But my *l* will never be taken away
  13: 1 son of David fell in *l* with Tamar,
  13: 4 said to him, "I'm in *l* with Tamar,
  16:17 "Is this the *l* you show your friend?
  19: 6 You *l* those who hate you

2Sa 19: 6 hate you and hate those who *l* you.
1Ki 3: 3 Solomon showed his *l*
   8: 23 you who keep your covenant of *l*
  10: 9 of the LORD's eternal *l* for Israel,
  11: 2 Solomon held fast to them in *l*.
1Ch 16: 34 his *l* endures forever.
  16: 41 "for his *l* endures forever."
  17: 13 I will never take my *l* away
2Ch 5: 13 his *l* endures forever."
  6: 14 you who keep your covenant of *l*
  6: 42 Remember the great *l* promised
  7: 3 his *l* endures forever."
  7: 6 saying, "His *l* endures forever."
  9: 8 Because of the *l* of your God
  19: 2 and *l* those who hate the LORD?
  20: 21 for his *l* endures forever."
Ezr 3: 11 his *l* to Israel endures forever."
Ne 1: 5 covenant of *l* with those who *l* him
  9: 17 slow to anger and abounding in *l*.
  9: 32 who keeps his covenant of *l*,
  13: 22 to me according to your great *l*.
Job 15: 34 of those who *l* bribes.
  19: 19 those I have turned against me.
  37: 13 or to water his earth and show his *l*.
Ps 4: 2 How long will you *l* delusions
  5: 11 that those who *l* your name may
  6: 4 save me because of your unfailing *l*.
  11: 5 wicked and those who *l* violence
  13: 5 But I trust in your unfailing *l*;
  17: 7 Show the wonder of your great *l*,
  18: 1 I *l* you, O LORD, my strength.
  21: 7 through the unfailing *l*
  23: 6 Surely goodness and *l* will follow
  25: 6 O LORD, your great mercy and *l*,
  25: 7 according to your *l* remember me,
  26: 3 for your *l* is ever before me,
  26: 8 I *l* the house where you live,
  31: 7 I will be glad and rejoice in your *l*,
  31: 16 save me in your unfailing *l*.
  31: 21 for he showed his wonderful *l*
  31: 23 *L* the LORD, all his saints!
  32: 10 but the LORD's unfailing *l*
  33: 5 the earth is full of his unfailing *l*.
  33: 18 whose hope is in his unfailing *l*,
  33: 22 May your unfailing *l* rest upon us,
  36: 5 Your *l*, O LORD, reaches
  36: 7 How priceless is your unfailing *l*!
  36: 10 Continue your *l* to those who know
  40: 10 I do not conceal your *l*
  40: 11 may your *l* and your truth always
  40: 16 may those who *l* your salvation
  42: 8 By day the LORD directs his *l*,
  44: 26 of your unfailing *l*.
  45: 7 You *l* righteousness and hate
  48: 9 we meditate on your unfailing *l*.
  51: 1 according to your unfailing *l*;
  52: 3 You *l* evil rather than good,
  52: 4 You *l* every harmful word,
  52: 8 I trust in God's unfailing *l*
  57: 3 God sends his *l* and his faithfulness
  57: 10 For great is your *l*, reaching
  59: 16 in the morning I will sing of your *l*;
  60: 5 that those you *l* may be delivered.
  61: 7 appoint your *l* and faithfulness
  63: 3 Because your *l* is better than life,
  66: 20 or withheld his *l* from me!
  69: 13 in your great *l*, O God,
  69: 16 out of the goodness of your *l*;
  69: 36 and those who *l* his name will dwell
  70: 4 may those who *l* your salvation
  77: 8 Has his unfailing *l* vanished forever
  85: 7 Show us your unfailing *l*, O LORD
  85: 10 *L* and faithfulness meet together;
  86: 5 abounding in *l* to all who call
  86: 13 For great is your *l* toward me;
  86: 15 abounding in *l* and faithfulness.
  88: 11 Is your *l* declared in the grave,
  89: 1 of the LORD's great *l* forever;
  89: 2 declare that your *l* stands firm
  89: 14 *l* and faithfulness go before you.
  89: 24 My faithful *l* will be with him,
  89: 28 I will maintain my *l* to him forever,
  89: 33 but I will not take my *l* from him,
  89: 49 where is your former great *l*,
  90: 14 with your unfailing *l*,
  92: 2 to proclaim your *l* in the morning
  94: 18 your *l*, O LORD, supported me.
  97: 10 Let those who *l* the LORD hate

Ps 98: 3 He has remembered his *l*
  100: 5 is good and his *l* endures forever;
  101: 1 I will sing of your *l* and justice;
  103: 4 crowns you with *l* and compassion.
  103: 8 slow to anger, abounding in *l*.
  103: 11 so great is his *l* for those who fear
  103: 17 LORD's *l* is with those who fear
  106: 1 his *l* endures forever.
  106: 45 and out of his great *l* he relented.
  107: 1 his *l* endures forever.
  107: 8 to the LORD for his unfailing *l*
  107: 15 to the LORD for his unfailing *l*
  107: 21 to the LORD for his unfailing *l*
  107: 31 to the LORD for his unfailing *l*
  107: 43 consider the great *l* of the LORD.
  108: 4 For great is your *l*, higher
  108: 6 that those you *l* may be delivered.
  109: 21 out of the goodness of your *l*,
  109: 26 save me in accordance with your *l*.
  115: 1 because of your *l* and faithfulness.
  116: 1 I *l* the LORD, for he heard my
  117: 2 For great is his *l* toward us,
  118: 1 his *l* endures forever.
  118: 2 "His *l* endures forever."
  118: 3 "His *l* endures forever."
  118: 4 "His *l* endures forever."
  118: 29 his *l* endures forever.
  119: 41 May your unfailing *l* come to me,
  119: 47 because I *l* them.
  119: 48 to your commands, which I *l*,
  119: 64 The earth is filled with your *l*,
  119: 76 May your unfailing *l* be my
  119: 88 my life according to your *l*,
  119: 97 Oh, how I *l* your law!
  119:113 but I *l* your law.
  119:119 therefore I *l* your statutes.
  119:124 your servant according to your *l*
  119:127 Because I *l* your commands
  119:132 to those who *l* your name.
  119:149 in accordance with your *l*;
  119:159 O LORD, according to your *l*
  119:159 See how I *l* your precepts;
  119:163 but I *l* your law.
  119:165 peace have they who *l* your law,
  119:167 for I *l* them greatly.
  122: 6 "May those who *l* you be secure.
  130: 7 for with the LORD is unfailing *l*
  136: 1 -26 *His l endures forever.*
  138: 2 for your *l* and your faithfulness,
  138: 8 your *l*, O LORD, endures forever
  143: 8 of your unfailing *l*,
  143: 12 In your unfailing *l*, silence my
  145: 8 slow to anger and rich in *l*.
  145: 20 over all who *l* him,
  147: 11 who put their hope in his unfailing *l*
Pr 1: 22 you simple ones *l* your simple
  3: 3 Let *l* and faithfulness never leave
  4: 6 *l* her, and she will watch over you.
  5: 19 you ever be captivated by her *l*.
  7: 18 let's drink deep of *l* till morning;
  7: 18 let's enjoy ourselves with *l*!
  8: 17 I *l* those who *l* me,
  8: 21 wealth on those who *l* me
  8: 36 all who hate me *l* death."
  9: 8 rebuke a wise man and he will *l* you
  10: 12 but *l* covers over all wrongs.
  14: 22 those who plan what is good find *l*
  15: 17 of vegetables where there is *l*
  16: 6 Through *l* and faithfulness sin is
  17: 9 over an offense promotes *l*,
  18: 21 and those who *l* it will eat its fruit.
  19: 22 What a man desires is unfailing *l*;
  20: 6 claims to have unfailing *l*,
  20: 13 Do not *l* sleep or you will grow
  20: 28 *L* and faithfulness keep a king safe;
  20: 28 through *l* his throne is made secure
  21: 21 who pursues righteousness and *l*
  27: 5 rebuke than hidden *l*.
Ecc 3: 8 a time to *l* and a time to hate,
  9: 1 but no man knows whether *l*
  9: 6 Their *l*, their hate
  9: 9 life with your wife, whom you *l*,
SS 1: 2 for your *l* is more delightful
  1: 3 No wonder the maidens *l* you!
  1: 4 we will praise your *l* more
  1: 7 you whom I *l*, where you graze
  2: 4 and his banner over me is *l*.
  2: 5 for I am faint with *l*.

SS 2: 7 Do not arouse or awaken *l*
  3: 5 Do not arouse or awaken *l*
  4: 10 How delightful is your *l*, my sister,
  4: 10 How much more pleasing is your *l*
  5: 8 Tell him I am faint with *l*.
  7: 6 O *l*, with your delights!
  7: 12 there I will give you my *l*.
  8: 4 Do not arouse or awaken *l*
  8: 6 for *l* is as strong as death,
  8: 7 Many waters cannot quench *l*;
  8: 7 all the wealth of his house for *l*,
Isa 1: 23 they all *l* bribes
  5: 1 I will sing for the one I *l*
  16: 5 In *l* a throne will be established;
  38: 17 In your *l* you kept me
  43: 4 and because I *l* you,
  54: 10 yet my unfailing *l* for you will not
  55: 3 my faithful *l* promised to David.
  56: 6 to *l* the name of the LORD,
  56: 10 they *l* to sleep.
  57: 8 a pact with those whose beds you *l*,
  61: 8 "For I, the LORD, *l* justice;
  63: 9 In his *l* and mercy he redeemed
  66: 10 all you who *l* her;
Jer 2: 25 I *l* foreign gods,
  2: 33 How skilled you are at pursuing *l*!
  5: 31 and my people *l* it this way.
  12: 7 I will give the one I *l*
  14: 10 "They greatly *l* to wander;
  16: 5 my *l* and my pity from this people
  31: 3 you with an everlasting *l*;
  32: 18 You show *l* to thousands
  33: 11 his *l* endures forever."
La 3: 22 of the LORD's great *l* we are not
  3: 32 so great is his unfailing *l*.
Eze 16: 8 saw that you were old enough for *l*,
  23: 17 of *l*, and in their lust they defiled
  33: 32 more than one who sings *l* songs
Da 9: 4 covenant of *l* with all who *l* him
Hos 1: 6 for I will no longer show *l*
  1: 7 Yet I will show *l* to the house
  2: 4 I will not show my *l* to her children
  2: 19 in *l* and compassion.
  2: 23 I will show my *l* to the one I called
  3: 1 Go, show your *l* to your wife again,
  3: 1 and *l* the sacred raisin cakes."
  3: 1 *L* her as the LORD loves
  4: 1 "There is no faithfulness, no *l*,
  4: 18 their rulers dearly *l* shameful ways.
  6: 4 Your *l* is like the morning mist,
  9: 1 you *l* the wages of a prostitute
  9: 15 I will no longer *l* them,
  10: 12 reap the fruit of unfailing *l*,
  11: 4 with ties of *l*;
  12: 6 maintain *l* and justice,
  14: 4 and *l* them freely,
Joel 2: 13 slow to anger and abounding in *l*,
Am 4: 5 for this is what you *l* to do,"
  5: 15 Hate evil, *l* good;
Jnh 4: 2 slow to anger and abounding in *l*,
Mic 3: 2 you who hate good and *l* evil;
  6: 8 To act justly and to *l* mercy
Zep 3: 17 he will quiet you with his *l*,
Zec 8: 17 and do not *l* to swear falsely.
  8: 19 Therefore *l* truth and peace."
Mt 3: 17 "This is my Son, whom I *l*;
  5: 43 '*L* your neighbor and hate your
  5: 44 *L* your enemies and pray
  5: 46 you *l* those who *l* you, what reward
  6: 5 for they *l* to pray standing
  6: 24 he will hate the one and *l* the other,
  12: 18 the one I *l*, in whom I delight;
  17: 5 "This is my Son, whom I *l*;
  19: 19 and '*l* your neighbor as yourself.' "
  22: 37 " '*L* the Lord your God
  22: 39 '*L* your neighbor as yourself.'
  23: 6 they *l* the place of honor
  23: 7 they *l* to be greeted
  24: 12 the *l* of most will grow cold,
Mk 1: 11 "You are my Son, whom I *l*;
  9: 7 "This is my Son, whom I *l*.
  12: 30 *L* the Lord your God
  12: 31 '*L* your neighbor as yourself.'
  12: 33 To *l* him with all your heart,
  12: 33 and to *l* your neighbor
Lk 3: 22 "You are my Son, whom I *l*;
  6: 27 you who hear me: *L* your enemies,
  6: 32 Even 'sinners' *l* those who *l* them.

Lk 6:32 you / those who / you, what credit
    6:35 / your enemies, do good to them,
    7:42 who of them will / him more?''
  10:27 and, 'L your neighbor as yourself
  10:27 '' L the Lord your God
  11:42 you neglect justice and the / of God
  11:43 you / the most important seats
  16:13 he will hate the one and / the other,
  20:13 whom I / ; perhaps they will respect
  20:46 / to be greeted in the marketplaces

Jn 5:42 I know that you do not have the /
  8:42 were your Father, you would / me,
  11:3 ''Lord, the one you / is sick.''
  13:1 them the full extent of his /
  13:34 I give you: L one another.
  13:34 so you must / one another.
  13:35 disciples, if you / one another.''
  14:15 ''If you / me, you will obey what I
  14:21 I too will / him and show myself
  14:23 My Father will / him, and we will
  14:24 He who does not / me will not obey
  14:31 world must learn that I / the Father
  15:9 Now remain in my /
  15:10 commands and remain in his /
  15:10 you will remain in my /,
  15:12 L each other as I have loved you.
  15:13 Greater / has no one than this,
  15:17 This is my command: L each other.
  15:19 to the world, it would / you
  17:26 known in order that the / you have
  21:15 do you truly / me more than these
  21:15 he said, ''you know that I / you.''
  21:16 Yes, Lord, you know that I / you.''
  21:16 do you truly / me?'' He answered,
  21:17 all things; you know that I / you.''
  21:17 ''Do you / me?'' He said, ''Lord,
  21:17 ''Simon son of John, do you / me?''

Ro 5:5 because God has poured out his /
  5:8 God demonstrates his own / for us
  8:28 for the good of those who / him,
  8:35 us from the / of Christ?
  8:39 us from the / of God that is
  12:9 L must be sincere.
  12:10 to one another in brotherly /
  13:8 continuing debt to / one another,
  13:9 ''L your neighbor as yourself.''
  13:10 Therefore / is the fulfillment
  13:10 L does no harm to its neighbor.
  14:15 you are no longer acting in /.
  15:30 and by the / of the Spirit,
  16:8 Greet Ampliatus, whom I /

1Co 2:9 prepared for those who / him''—
  4:17 my son whom I /, who is faithful
  4:21 or in / and with a gentle spirit?
  8:1 Knowledge puffs up, but / builds up
  13:1 have not /, I am only a resounding
  13:2 but have not /, I am nothing.
  13:3 but have not /, I gain nothing.
  13:4 Love is patient, / is kind.
  13:4 L is patient, love is kind.
  13:6 L does not delight in evil
  13:8 L never fails.
  13:13 But the greatest of these is /.
  13:13 three remain: faith, hope and /
  14:1 way of / and eagerly desire spiritual
  16:14 Do everything in /.
  16:22 If anyone does not love the Lord—
  16:24 My / to all of you in Christ Jesus.

2Co 2:4 to let you know the depth of my /
  2:8 therefore, to reaffirm your / for him
  5:14 For Christ's / compels us,
  6:6 in the Holy Spirit and in sincere /;
  8:7 complete earnestness and in your /
  8:8 sincerity of your / by comparing it
  8:24 show these men the proof of your /
  11:11 Why? Because I do not / you?
  12:15 If I / you more, will you / me less?
  13:11 And the God of / and peace will be
  13:14 of the Lord Jesus Christ, and the /

Gal 5:6 is faith expressing itself through /.
  5:13 rather, serve one another in /.
  5:14 ''L your neighbor as yourself.
  5:22 But the fruit of the Spirit is /, joy,

Eph 1:4 In / he predestined us
  1:15 and your / for all the saints,
  2:4 But because of his great / for us,
  3:17 being rooted and established in /,
  3:18 and high and deep is the / of Christ,

Eph 3:19 and to know this / that surpasses
  4:2 bearing with one another in /.
  4:15 Instead, speaking the truth in /,
  4:16 grows and builds itself up in /,
  5:2 loved children and live a life of /,
  5:25 / your wives, just as Christ loved
  5:28 husbands ought to / their wives
  5:33 each one of you also must / his wife
  6:23 / with faith from God the Father
  6:24 Christ with an undying /.
  6:24 to all who / our Lord Jesus Christ

Php 1:9 that your / may abound more
  1:16 so in /, knowing that I am put here
  2:1 from his /, if any fellowship
  2:2 having the same /, being one
  2:2 you whom I / and long for,

Col 1:4 of the / you have for all the saints—
  1:5 / that spring from the hope that is
  1:8 also told us of your / in the Spirit.
  2:2 in heart and united in /,
  3:14 And over all these virtues put on /,
  3:19 / your wives and do not be harsh

1Th 1:3 your labor prompted by /,
  3:6 good news about your faith and /.
  3:12 May the Lord make your / increase
  4:9 about brotherly / we do not need
  4:9 taught by God to / each other.
  4:10 you do / all the brothers
  5:8 on faith and / as a breastplate,
  5:13 them in the highest regard in /

2Th 1:3 and the / every one of you has
  2:10 because they refused to / the truth
  3:5 direct your hearts into God's /

1Ti 1:5 The goal of this command is /,
  1:14 and / that are in Christ Jesus.
  2:15 / and holiness with propriety.
  4:12 in life, in /, in faith and in purity.
  6:10 For the / of money is a root
  6:11 faith, /, endurance and gentleness.

2Ti 1:7 of power, of / and of self-discipline.
  1:13 with faith and / in Christ Jesus.
  2:22 and pursue righteousness, faith, /
  3:3 unholy, without /, unforgiving,
  3:10 faith, patience, /, endurance,

Tit 2:2 in faith, in / and in endurance.
  2:4 women to / their husbands
  3:4 and / of God our Savior appeared,
  3:15 Greet those who / us in the faith.

Phm 5 and your / for all the saints.
  7 Your / has given me great joy
  9 yet I appeal to you on the basis of /.

Heb 6:10 and the / you have shown him
  10:24 may spur one another on toward /
  13:5 free from the / of money

Jas 1:12 promised to those who / him.
  2:5 he promised those who / him?
  2:8 ''L your neighbor as yourself,''

1Pe 1:8 you have not seen him, you / him;
  1:22 the truth so that you have sincere /
  1:22 / one another deeply,
  2:17 L the brotherhood of believers,
  3:8 be sympathetic, / as brothers,
  3:10 ''Whoever would / life
  4:8 Above all, / each other deeply,
  4:8 / covers over a multitude of sins
  5:14 Greet one another with a kiss of /.

2Pe 1:7 and to brotherly kindness, /
  1:17 ''This is my Son, whom I /;

1Jn 2:5 God's / is truly made complete
  2:15 Do not / the world or anything
  2:15 the / of the Father is not in him.
  3:1 How great is the / the Father has
  3:10 anyone who does not / his brother.
  3:11 We should / one another.
  3:14 Anyone who does not / remains
  3:14 because we / our brothers.
  3:16 This is how we know what / is:
  3:17 how can the / of God be in him?
  3:18 let us not / with words or tongue
  3:23 to / one another as he commanded
  4:7 Dear friends, let us / one another,
  4:7 for / comes from God.
  4:8 Whoever does not / does not know
  4:8 not know God, because God is /.
  4:9 This is how God showed his /
  4:10 This is /: not that we loved God,
  4:11 we also ought to / one another.
  4:12 seen God; but if we / one another,

1Jn 4:12 and his / is made complete in us.
  4:16 God is /.
  4:16 Whoever lives in / lives in God,
  4:16 and rely on the / God has for us.
  4:17 / is made complete among us
  4:18 But perfect / drives out fear,
  4:18 There is no fear in /.
  4:18 who fears is not made perfect in /.
  4:19 We / because he first loved us.
  4:20 If anyone says, ''I / God,''
  4:20 anyone who does not / his brother,
  4:20 whom he has seen, cannot / God,
  4:21 loves God must also / his brother.
  5:2 we know that we / the children
  5:3 This is / for God: to obey his

2Jn 1 whom I / in the truth—
  3 will be with us in truth and /.
  5 I ask that we / one another.
  6 his command is that you walk in /.
  6 this is /: that we walk in obedience

3Jn 1 To my dear friend Gaius, whom I /
  6 have told the church about your /.

Jude 2 peace and / be yours in abundance.
  12 men are blemishes at your / feasts,
  21 Keep yourselves in God's /

Rev 2:4 You have forsaken your first /.
  2:19 I know your deeds, your / and faith
  3:19 Those whom I / I rebuke
  12:11 they did not / their lives so much

LOVED* (LOVE)

Ge 24:67 she became his wife, and he / her;
  25:28 / Esau, but Rebekah / Jacob.
  29:30 and he / Rachel more than Leah.
  29:31 the LORD saw that Leah was not /,
  29:33 the LORD heard that I am not /,
  34:3 and he / the girl and spoke tenderly
  37:3 Now Israel / Joseph more than any
  37:4 saw that their father / him more

Dt 4:37 Because he / your forefathers
  7:8 But it was because the LORD / you
  10:15 on your forefathers and / them,

1Sa 1:5 a double portion because he / her,
  18:1 in spirit with David, and he / him
  18:3 with David because he / him
  18:16 But all Israel and Judah / David,
  18:28 that his daughter Michal / David,
  20:17 because he / him as he / himself.

2Sa 1:23 in life they were / and gracious,
  12:24 The LORD / him; and
  12:25 and because the LORD / him,
  13:15 hated her more than he had / her.

1Ki 11:1 / many foreign women

2Ch 11:21 Rehoboam / Maacah daughter
  26:10 in the fertile lands, for he / the soil.

Ne 13:26 He was / by his God, and God

Ps 44:3 light of your face, for you / them.
  47:4 the pride of Jacob, whom he /.
  78:68 Mount Zion, which he /.
  88:18 taken my companions and / ones
  109:17 He / to pronounce a curse—

Isa 5:1 My / one had a vineyard

Jer 2:2 how as a bride you / me
  8:2 which they have / and served
  31:3 ''I have / you with an everlasting

Eze 16:37 those you / as well as those you

Hos 2:1 and of your sisters, 'My / one.'
  2:23 to the one I called 'Not my / one.'
  3:1 though she is / by another
  9:10 became as vile as the thing they /.
  11:1 ''When Israel was a child, I / him,

Mal 1:2 ''But you ask, 'How have you / us?'
  1:2 ''I have / you,'' says the LORD.
  1:2 ''Yet I have / Jacob, but Esau I

Mk 10:21 Jesus looked at him and / him.
  12:6 left to send, a son, whom he /.

Lk 7:47 been forgiven—for she / much.
  16:14 The Pharisees, who / money,

Jn 3:16 so / the world that he gave his one
  3:19 but men / darkness instead of light
  11:5 Jesus / Martha and her sister
  11:36 ''See how he / him!'' But some
  12:43 for they / praise from men more
  13:1 Having / his own who were
  13:23 the disciple whom Jesus /,
  13:34 As I have / you, so you must love
  14:21 He who loves me will be /
  14:28 If you / me, you would be glad that

Jn   15: 9 the Father has *l* me, so have I *l* you.
   15: 12 Love each other as I have *l* you.
   16: 27 loves you because you have *l* me
   17: 23 have *l* them even as you have *l* me.
   17: 24 you *l* me before the creation
   19: 26 the disciple whom he *l* standing
   20: 2 one Jesus *l*, and said, "They have
   21: 7 the disciple whom Jesus *l* said
   21: 20 whom Jesus *l* was following
Ro   1: 7 To all in Rome who are *l* by God
    8: 37 conquerors through him who *l* us.
    9: 13 "Jacob I *l*, but Esau I hated."
    9: 25 her 'my *l* one' who is not my *l* one,"
   11: 28 they are *l* on account
Gal   2: 20 who *l* me and gave himself for me.
Eph   5: 1 as dearly *l* children and live a life
    5: 2 as Christ *l* us and gave himself up
    5: 25 just as Christ *l* the church
Col   3: 12 and dearly *l*, clothe yourselves
1Th   1: 4 For we know, brothers *l* by God,
    2: 8 We *l* you so much that we were
2Th   2: 13 for you, brothers *l* by the Lord,
    2: 16 who *l* us and by his grace gave us
2Ti   4: 10 for Demas, because he *l* this world,
Heb   1: 9 You have *l* righteousness
2Pe   2: 15 who *l* the wages of wickedness.
1Jn   4: 10 This is love: not that we *l* God,
    4: 10 but that he *l* us and sent his Son
    4: 11 Dear friends, since God so *l* us,
    4: 19 We love because he first *l* us.
Jude   1 who are *l* by God the Father
Rev   3: 9 and acknowledge that I have *l* you.

LOVELY* (LOVE)

Ge   29: 17 but Rachel was *l* in form,
Est   1: 11 and nobles, for she was *l* to look at.
    2: 7 was *l* in form and features,
Ps   84: 1 How *l* is your dwelling place,
SS   1: 5 Dark am I, yet *l*,
    2: 14 and your face is *l*.
    4: 3 your mouth is *l*.
    5: 16 he is altogether *l*.
    6: 4 *l* as Jerusalem,
Am   8: 13 *l* young women and strong young
Php   4: 8 whatever is *l*, whatever is

LOVER* (LOVE)

SS   1: 13 My *l* is to me a sachet of myrrh
    1: 14 My *l* is to me a cluster
    1: 16 How handsome you are, my *l*!
    2: 3 is my *l* among the young men.
    2: 8 Listen! My *l*!
    2: 9 My *l* is like a gazelle or a young
    2: 10 My *l* spoke and said to me,
    2: 16 *Beloved* My *l* is mine and I am his;
    2: 17 turn, my *l*,
    4: 16 Let my *l* come into his garden
    5: 2 Listen! My *l* is knocking:
    5: 4 My *l* thrust his hand
    5: 5 I arose to open for my *l*,
    5: 6 I opened for my *l*,
    5: 6 but my *l* had left; he was gone.
    5: 8 if you find my *l*,
    5: 10 *Beloved* My *l* is radiant and ruddy,
    5: 16 This is my *l*, my friend,
    6: 1 Where has your *l* gone,
    6: 1 Which way did your *l* turn,
    6: 2 *Beloved* My *l* has gone
    6: 3 I am my lover's and my *l* is mine;
    7: 9 May the wine go straight to my *l*,
    7: 10 I belong to my *l*,
    7: 11 my *l*, let us go to the countryside,
    7: 13 that I have stored up for you, my *l*.
    8: 5 leaning on her *l*?
    8: 14 *Beloved* Come away, my *l*,
1Ti   3: 3 not quarrelsome, not a *l* of money.

LOVER'S* (LOVE)

SS   6: 3 I am my *l* and my lover is mine;

LOVERS* (LOVE)

SS   5: 1 drink your fill, O *l*.
Jer   3: 1 as a prostitute with many *l*—
    3: 2 the roadside you sat waiting for *l*,
    4: 30 Your *l* despise you;
La   1: 2 Among all her *l*
Eze 16: 33 but you give gifts to all your *l*,
   16: 36 in your promiscuity with your *l*,

Eze 16: 37 I am going to gather all your *l*,
   16: 39 Then I will hand you over to your *l*,
   16: 41 and you will no longer pay your *l*.
   23: 5 she lusted after her *l*, the Assyrians
   23: 9 I handed her over to her *l*,
   23: 20 There she lusted after her *l*,
   23: 22 I will stir up your *l* against you,
Hos   2: 5 She said, 'I will go after my *l*,
    2: 7 She will chase after her *l*
    2: 10 lewdness before the eyes of her *l*;
    2: 12 she said were her pay from her *l*;
    2: 13 and went after her *l*,
    8: 9 Ephraim has sold herself to *l*.
2Ti   3: 2 People will be *l* of themselves,
    3: 2 *l* of money, boastful, proud,
    3: 3 without self-control, brutal, not *l*
    3: 4 of pleasure rather than *l* of God—

LOVES* (LOVE)

Ge   44: 20 sons left, and his father *l* him.'
Dt   10: 18 and *l* the alien, giving him food
   15: 16 because he *l* you and your family
   21: 5 and he *l* one but not the other,
   21: 16 son of the wife he *l* in preference
   23: 5 because the Lord your God *l* you
   28: 54 wife he *l* or his surviving children,
   28: 56 will begrudge the husband she *l*
   33: 12 and the one the Lord rests
Ru   4: 15 who *l* you and who is better to you
2Ch   2: 11 "Because the Lord *l* his people,
Ps   11: 7 he *l* justice;
   33: 5 The Lord *l* righteousness
   34: 12 Whoever of you *l* life
   37: 28 For the Lord *l* the just
   87: 2 the Lord *l* the gates of Zion
   91: 14 Because he *l* me," says the Lord.
   99: 4 The King is mighty, he *l* justice—
  119:140 and your servant *l* them.
  127: 2 for he grants sleep to those he *l*.
  146: 8 the Lord *l* the righteous.
Pr   3: 12 the Lord disciplines those he *l*,
   12: 1 Whoever *l* discipline *l* knowledge,
   13: 24 he who *l* him is careful
   15: 9 he *l* those who pursue
   17: 17 A friend *l* at all times,
   17: 19 He who *l* a quarrel *l* sin;
   19: 8 He who gets wisdom *l* his own soul
   21: 17 He who *l* pleasure will become
   21: 17 whoever *l* wine and oil will never
   22: 11 He who *l* a pure heart and whose
   29: 3 A man who *l* wisdom brings joy
Ecc   5: 10 Whoever *l* money never has
    5: 10 whoever *l* wealth is never satisfied
SS   3: 1 I looked for the one my heart *l*;
    3: 2 I will search for the one my heart *l*.
    3: 3 "Have you seen the one my heart *l*?
    3: 4 when I found the one my heart *l*.
Hos   3: 1 as the Lord *l* the Israelites,
   10: 11 that *l* to thresh;
   12: 7 he *l* to defraud.
Mal   2: 11 the sanctuary the Lord *l*,
Mt   10: 37 anyone who *l* his son or daughter
   10: 37 "Anyone who *l* his father
Lk   7: 5 because he *l* our nation
    7: 47 has been forgiven little *l* little.''
Jn   3: 35 Father *l* the Son and has placed
    5: 20 For the Father *l* the Son
   10: 17 reason my Father *l* me is that I lay
   12: 25 The man who *l* his life will lose it,
   14: 21 He who *l* me will be loved
   14: 21 obeys them, he is the one who *l* me.
   14: 23 Jesus replied, "If anyone *l* me,
   16: 27 the Father himself *l* you
Ro   13: 8 for he who *l* his fellowman has
1Co   8: 3 But the man who *l* God is known
2Co   9: 7 for God *l* a cheerful giver.
Eph   1: 6 has freely given us in the One he *l*.
    5: 28 He who *l* his wife *l* himself.
    5: 33 must love his wife as he *l* himself,
Col   1: 13 us into the kingdom of the Son he *l*,
Tit   1: 8 one who *l* what is good, who is
Heb 12: 6 the Lord disciplines those he *l*,
1Jn   2: 10 Whoever *l* his brother lives
    2: 15 If anyone *l* the world, the love
    4: 7 Everyone who *l* has been born
    4: 21 Whoever *l* God must also love his
    5: 1 who *l* the father *l* his child
3Jn   9 but Diotrephes, who *l* to be first,

Rev   1: 5 To him who *l* us and has freed us
   20: 9 camp of God's people, the city he *l*.
   22: 15 and everyone who *l* and practices

LOVING* (LOVE)

Ps   25: 10 All the ways of the Lord are *l*
   59: 10 my *l* God.
   59: 17 O God, are my fortress, my *l* God.
   62: 12 and that you, O Lord, are *l*.
  144: 2 He is my *l* God and my fortress,
  145: 13 and toward all he has made.
  145: 17 and toward all he has made.
Pr   5: 19 A *l* doe, a graceful deer—
Heb 13: 1 Keep on *l* each other as brothers.
1Jn   5: 2 by *l* God and carrying out his

LOVING-KINDNESS* (LOVE)

Jer 31: 3 I have drawn you with *l*.

LOWER

Ps   8: 5 You made him a little *l*
2Co 11: 7 a sin for me to *l* myself in order
Heb   2: 7 You made him a little *l*

LOWING

1Sa 15: 14 What is this *l* of cattle that I hear?''

LOWLY

Job   5: 11 The *l* he sets on high,
Ps 138: 6 on high, he looks upon the *l*,
Pr   29: 23 but a man of *l* spirit gains honor.
Isa 57: 15 also with him who is contrite and *l*
Eze 21: 26 *l* will be exalted and the exalted
1Co   1: 28 He chose the *l* things of this world

LOYAL

1Ch 29: 18 and keep their hearts *l* to you.
Ps   78: 8 whose hearts were not *l* to God,

LUKE*

   Co-worker with Paul (Col 4:14; 2Ti 4:11; Phm 24).

LUKEWARM*

Rev   3: 16 So, because you are *l*— neither hot

LUST (LUSTED LUSTS)

Pr   6: 25 Do not *l* in your heart
Eze 20: 30 and *l* after their vile images?
Col   3: 5 sexual immorality, impurity, *l*,
1Th   4: 5 not in passionate *l* like the heathen,
1Pe   4: 3 in debauchery, *l*, drunkenness,
1Jn   2: 16 the *l* of his eyes and the boasting

LUSTED (LUST)

Eze 23: 5 she *l* after her lovers, the Assyrians

LUSTS* (LUST)

Nu   15: 39 yourselves by going after the *l*
Ro   1: 26 God gave them over to shameful *l*.

LUXURY

Jas   5: 5 You have lived on earth in *l*

LYDIA'S*

Ac   16: 40 went to *L* house, where they met

LYING (LIE)

Pr   6: 17 a *l* tongue,
   12: 22 The Lord detests *l* lips,
   21: 6 A fortune made by a *l* tongue
   26: 28 A *l* tongue hates those it hurts,

MACEDONIA

Ac   16: 9 "Come over to *M* and help us."

MAD

Dt   28: 34 The sights you see will drive you *m*

MADE (MAKE)

Ge   1: 7 So God *m* the expanse
    1: 16 God *m* two great lights—
    1: 16 He also *m* the stars.
    1: 25 God *m* the wild animals according
    1: 31 God saw all that he had *m*,
    2: 22 Then the Lord God *m* a woman
    6: 6 was grieved that he had *m* man
    9: 6 has God *m* man.
   15: 18 that day the Lord *m* a covenant

Ex 20:11 six days the LORD *m* the heavens
  20:11 the Sabbath day and *m* it holy.
  24: 8 the covenant that the LORD has *m*
  32: 4 *m* it into an idol cast in the shape
Lev 16:34 Atonement is to be *m* once a year
Dt 32: 6 who *m* you and formed you?
Jos 24:25 On that day Joshua *m* a covenant
2Ki 19:15 You have *m* heaven and earth.
2Ch 2:12 the God of Israel, who *m* heaven
Ne 9: 6 You *m* the heavens,
  9:10 You *m* a name for yourself,
Ps 33: 6 of the LORD were the heavens *m*,
  95: 5 The sea is his, for he *m* it,
  96: 5 but the LORD *m* the heavens.
  100: 3 It is he who *m* us, and we are his;
  118:24 This is the day the LORD has *m*;
  136: 7 who *m* the great lights—
  139:14 I am fearfully and wonderfully *m*;
Ecc 3:11 He has *m* everything beautiful
Isa 43: 7 whom I formed and *m*.''
  45:12 It is I who *m* the earth
  45:18 he who fashioned and *m* the earth,
  66: 2 Has not my hand *m* all these things
Jer 10:12 But God *m* the earth by his power;
  27: 5 and outstretched arm I *m* the earth
  32:17 you have *m* the heavens
  33: 2 LORD says, he who *m* the earth,
  51:15 ''He *m* the earth by his power;
Eze 3:17 I have *m* you a watchman
  33: 7 I have *m* you a watchman
Am 5: 8 (he who *m* the Pleiades and Orion,
Jnh 1: 9 who *m* the sea and the land.''
Mk 2:27 ''The Sabbath was *m* for man,
Jn 1: 3 Through him all things were *m*;
Ac 17:24 ''The God who *m* the world
1Co 3: 6 watered it, but God *m* it grow.
Heb 1: 2 through whom he *m* the universe.
Jas 3: 9 who have been *m* in God's likeness
Rev 14: 7 Worship him who *m* the heavens,

MAGDALENE

Lk 8: 2 Mary (called *M*) from whom seven

MAGI

Mt 2: 1 *M* from the east came to Jerusalem

MAGIC (MAGICIANS)

Eze 13:20 I am against your *m* charms
Rev 21: 8 those who practice *m* arts,
  22:15 those who practice *m* arts,

MAGICIANS (MAGIC)

Ex 7:11 the Egyptian *m* also did the same
Da 2: 2 So the king summoned the *m*,

MAGNIFICENCE* (MAGNIFICENT)

1Ch 22: 5 for the LORD should be of great *m*

MAGNIFICENT (MAGNIFICENCE)

1Ki 8:13 I have indeed built a *m* temple
Isa 28:29 in counsel and *m* in wisdom.
Mk 13: 1 stones! What *m* buildings!''

MAGOG

Eze 38: 2 of the land of *M*, the chief prince
  39: 6 I will send fire on *M*
Rev 20: 8 and *M*— to gather them for battle.

MAIDEN (MAIDENS)

Pr 30:19 and the way of a man with a *m*.
Isa 62: 5 As a young man marries a *m*,
Jer 2:32 Does a *m* forget her jewelry,

MAIDENS (MAIDEN)

SS 1: 3 No wonder the *m* love you!

MAIMED

Mt 18: 8 It is better for you to enter life *m*

MAINTAIN (MAINTAINING)

Ps 82: 3 *m* the rights of the poor
  106: 3 Blessed are they who *m* justice,
Hos 12: 6 *m* love and justice,
Am 5:15 *m* justice in the courts.
Ro 3:28 For we *m* that a man is justified

MAINTAINING* (MAINTAIN)

Ex 34: 7 faithfulness, *m* love to thousands,

MAJESTIC* (MAJESTY)

Ex 15: 6 was *m* in power.
  15:11 *m* in holiness,
Job 37: 4 he thunders with his *m* voice.
Ps 8: 1 how *m* is your name in all the earth
  8: 9 how *m* is your name in all the earth
  29: 4 the voice of the LORD is *m*.
  68:15 of Bashan are *m* mountains;
  76: 4 more *m* than mountains rich
  111: 3 Glorious and *m* are his deeds,
SS 6: 4 *m* as troops with banners.
  6:10 *m* as the stars in procession?
Isa 30:30 men to hear his *m* voice
Eze 31: 7 It was *m* in beauty,
2Pe 1:17 came to him from the *M* Glory,

MAJESTY* (MAJESTIC)

Ex 15: 7 In the greatness of your *m*
Dt 5:24 has shown us his glory and his *m*,
  11: 2 his *m*, his mighty hand, his
  33:17 In *m* he is like a firstborn bull;
  33:26 and on the clouds in his *m*.
1Ch 16:27 Splendor and *m* are before him;
  29:11 and the *m* and the splendor,
Est 1: 4 the splendor and glory of his *m*.
  7: 3 if it pleases your *m*, grant me my
Job 37:22 God comes in awesome *m*.
  40:10 and clothe yourself in honor and *m*
Ps 21: 5 on him splendor and *m*.
  45: 3 with splendor and *m*.
  45: 4 In your *m* ride forth victoriously
  68:34 whose *m* is over Israel,
  93: 1 The LORD reigns, he is robed in *m*
  93: 1 the LORD is robed in *m*
  96: 6 Splendor and *m* are before him;
  104: 1 clothed with splendor and *m*.
  110: 3 Arrayed in holy *m*,
  145: 5 of the glorious splendor of your *m*,
Isa 2:10 and the splendor of his *m*!
  2:19 and the splendor of his *m*,
  2:21 and the splendor of his *m*,
  24:14 west they acclaim the LORD's *m*.
  26:10 and regard not the *m* of the LORD.
  53: 2 or *m* to attract us to him,
Eze 31: 2 can be compared with you in *m*?
  31:18 with you in splendor and *m*?
Da 4:30 and for the glory of my *m*?''
Mic 5: 4 in the *m* of the name
Zec 6:13 and he will be clothed with *m*
Ac 19:27 will be robbed of her divine *m*.''
  25:26 to write to His *M* about him.
2Th 1: 9 and from the *m* of his power
Heb 1: 3 hand of the *M* in heaven,
  8: 1 of the throne of the *M* in heaven,
2Pe 1:16 but we were eyewitnesses of his *m*.
Jude : 25 only God our Savior be glory, *m*,

MAKE (MADE MAKER MAKERS MAKES MAKING MAN-MADE)

Ge 1:26 ''Let us *m* man in our image,
  2:18 I will *m* a helper suitable for him.''
  6:14 *m* yourself an ark of cypress wood;
  12: 2 ''I will *m* you into a great nation
Ex 22: 3 thief must certainly *m* restitution,
  25: 9 *M* this tabernacle and all its
  25:40 See that you *m* them according
Nu 6:25 the LORD *m* his face shine
2Sa 7: 9 Now I will *m* your name great,
Job 7:17 ''What is man that you *m* so much
Ps 4: 8 *m* me dwell in safety.
  20: 4 and *m* all your plans succeed.
  108: 1 *m* music with all my soul.
  110: 1 hand until I *m* your enemies
  119:165 and nothing can *m* them stumble.
Pr 3: 6 and he will *m* your paths straight.
  4:26 *M* level paths for your feet
  20:18 *M* plans by seeking advice;
Isa 14:14 I will *m* myself like the Most High
  29:16 ''He did not *m* me''?
  55: 3 I will *m* an everlasting covenant
  61: 8 and *m* an everlasting covenant
Jer 31:31 ''when I will *m* a new covenant
Eze 37:26 I will *m* a covenant of peace
Mt 3: 3 *m* straight paths for him.''
  28:19 and *m* disciples of all nations,
Mk 1:17 ''and I will *m* you fishers of men.''
Lk 13:24 ''*M* every effort to enter

Lk 14:23 country lanes and *m* them come in,
Ro 14:19 *m* every effort to do what leads
2Co 5: 9 So we *m* it our goal to please him,
Eph 4: 3 *M* every effort to keep the unity
Col 4: 5 *m* the most of every opportunity.
1Th 4:11 *M* it your ambition
Heb 4:11 *m* every effort to enter that rest,
  8: 5 it that you *m* everything according
  12:14 *M* every effort to live in peace
2Pe 1: 5 *m* every effort to add
  3:14 *m* every effort to be found spotless,

MAKER* (MAKE)

Job 4:17 Can a man be more pure than his *M*
  9: 9 He is the *M* of the Bear and Orion,
  32:22 my *M* would soon take me away.
  35:10 no one says, 'Where is God my *M*,
  36: 3 I will ascribe justice to my *M*.
  40:19 yet his *M* can approach him
Ps 95: 6 kneel before the LORD our *M*;
  115:15 the *M* of heaven and earth.
  121: 2 the *M* of heaven and earth.
  124: 8 the *M* of heaven and earth.
  134: 3 the *M* of heaven and earth,
  146: 6 the *M* of heaven and earth,
  149: 2 Let Israel rejoice in their *M*;
Pr 14:31 poor shows contempt for their *M*,
  17: 5 poor shows contempt for their *M*;
  22: 2 The LORD is the *M* of them all.
Ecc 11: 5 the *M* of all things.
Isa 17: 7 that day men will look to their *M*
  27:11 so their *M* has no compassion
  45: 9 to him who quarrels with his *M*,
  45:11 the Holy One of Israel, and its *M*:
  51:13 that you forget the LORD your *M*,
  54: 5 For your *M* is your husband—
Jer 10:16 for he is the *M* of all things,
  51:19 for he is the *M* of all things,
Hos 8:14 Israel has forgotten his *M*

MAKERS* (MAKE)

Isa 45:16 All the *m* of idols will be put

MAKES (MAKE)

Ps 23: 2 *m* me lie down in green pastures,
Pr 13:12 Hope deferred *m* the heart sick,
1Co 3: 7 but only God, who *m* things grow.

MAKING (MAKE)

Ps 19: 7 *m* wise the simple.
Ecc 12:12 Of *m* many books there is no end,
Jn 5:18 *m* himself equal with God.
Eph 5:16 *m* the most of every opportunity.

MALACHI*

Mal 1: 1 of the LORD to Israel through *M*.

MALE

Ge 1:27 *m* and female he created them.
Ex 13: 2 to me every firstborn *m*.
Nu 8:16 the first *m* offspring
Mt 19: 4 the Creator 'made them *m*
Gal 3:28 slave nor free, *m* nor female,

MALICE (MALICIOUS)

Mk 7:22 adultery, greed, *m*, deceit,
Ro 1:29 murder, strife, deceit and *m*.
1Co 5: 8 the yeast of *m* and wickedness,
Eph 4:31 along with every form of *m*.
Col 3: 8 *m*, slander, and filthy language
1Pe 2: 1 rid yourselves of all *m*

MALICIOUS (MALICE)

Pr 26:24 A *m* man disguises himself
1Ti 3:11 not *m* talkers but temperate
  6: 4 *m* talk, evil suspicions

MALIGN

Tit 2: 5 so that no one will *m* the word

MAMMON see MONEY, WEALTH

MAN (MAN'S MANKIND MEN MEN'S WOMAN WOMEN)

Ge 1:26 ''Let us make *m* in our image,
  2: 7 God formed the *m* from the dust
  2: 8 *m* became a living being
  2:15 God took the *m* and put
  2:18 for the *m* to be alone

Ge   2: 20 *m* gave names to all the
    2: 23 she was taken out of *m*.
    2: 25 *m* and his wife were both
    3:   9 God called to the *m*,
    3: 22 *m* has now become like
    4:   1 I have brought forth a *m*.
    6:   3 not contend with *m* forever,
    6:   6 grieved that he had made *m*
    9:   6 Whoever sheds the blood of *m*,
Dt   8:   3 *m* does not live on bread
1Sa 13: 14 a *m* after his own heart
   15: 29 he is not a *m* that he
   16:   7 at the things *m* looks at.
Job 14:   1 *M* born of woman is of few
   14: 14 If a *m* dies, will he live
Ps   1:   1 Blessed is the *m* who does
    8:   4 what is *m* that you are
   32:   2 Blessed is the *m* whose sin
   40:   4 Blessed is the *m* who makes
   84: 12 blessed is the *m* who trusts
  103: 15 As for *m*, his days are
  112:   1 Blessed is the *m* who fears
  119:   9 can a young *m* keep his
  127:   5 Blessed is the *m* whose quiver
  144:   3 what is *m* that you care
Pr   3: 13 Blessed is the *m* who finds
    9:   9 Instruct a wise *m*
   14: 12 that seems right to a *m*,
   30: 19 way of a *m* with a maiden.
Isa 53:   3 a *m* of sorrows,
Jer 17:   5 the one who trusts in *m*.
   17:   7 blessed is the *m* who trusts
Eze 22: 30 I looked for a *m*
Mt   4:   4 *M* does not live on bread
   19:   5 a *m* will leave his father
Mk   8: 36 What good is it for a *m*
Lk   4:   4 '*M* does not live on bread
Ro   5: 12 entered the world through one *m*
1Co   2: 15 spiritual *m* makes judgments
    3: 12 If any *m* builds on this
    7:   1 good for a *m* not to marry.
    7:   2 each *m* should have his own
   11:   3 head of every *m* is Christ,
   11:   3 head of woman is *m*
   13: 11 When I became a *m*,
   15: 21 death came through a *m*,
   15: 45 first *m* Adam became a
   15: 47 the second *m* from heaven
2Co 12:   2 I know a *m* in Christ
Eph   2: 15 create in himself one new *m*
    5: 31 a *m* will leave his father
Php   2:   8 found in appearance as a *m*,
1Ti   2:   5 the *m* Christ Jesus,
    2: 11 have authority over a *m*;
2Ti   3: 17 that the *m* of God may be
Heb   2:   6 what is *m* that you are
    9: 27 as *m* is destined to die

MAN'S (MAN)

Pr   20: 24 A *m* steps are directed by
Jer 10: 23 a *m* life is not his own;
1Co   1: 25 is wiser than *m* wisdom,

MAN-MADE (MAKE)

Heb   9: 11 perfect tabernacle that is not *m*,
    9: 24 not enter a *m* sanctuary that was

MANAGE (MANAGER)

Jer 12:   5 how will you *m* in the thickets
1Ti   3:   4 He must *m* his own family well
    3: 12 one wife and must *m* his children
    5: 14 to *m* their homes and to give

MANAGER (MANAGE)

Lk 12: 42 Who then is the faithful and wise *m*
   16:   1 a rich man whose *m* was accused

MANASSEH

1. Firstborn of Joseph (Ge 41:51; 46:20). Blessed by Jacob but not firstborn (Ge 48). Tribe of blessed (Dt 33:17), numbered (Nu 1:35; 26:34), half allotted land east of Jordan (Nu 32; Jos 13: 8-33), half west (Jos 16; Eze 48:4), failed to fully possess (Jos 16:10; Jdg 1:27), 12,000 from (Rev 7:6).
2. Son of Hezekiah; king of Judah (2Ki 21: 1-18; 2Ch 33:1-20). Judah exiled for his detestable sins (2Ki 21:10-15). Repentance (2Ch 33:12-19).

MANDRAKES

Ge 30: 14 give me some of your son's *m*.''

MANGER

Lk   2: 12 in strips of cloth and lying in a *m*.''

MANIFESTATION*

1Co 12:   7 to each one the *m* of the Spirit is

MANKIND (MAN)

Ge   6:   7 I will wipe *m*, whom I have created
Ps   33: 13 and sees all *m*;
Pr   8: 31 and delighting in *m*.
Ecc   7: 29 God made *m* upright,
Isa 40:   5 and all *m* together will see it.
   45: 12 and created *m* upon it.
Jer 32: 27 ''I am the LORD, the God of all *m*.
Zec   2: 13 Be still before the LORD, all *m*,
Lk   3:   6 And all *m* will see God's salvation

MANNA

Ex 16: 31 people of Israel called the bread *m*.
Dt   8: 16 He gave you *m* to eat in the desert,
Jn   6: 49 Your forefathers ate the *m*
Rev   2: 17 I will give some of the hidden *m*.

MANNER

1Co 11: 27 in an unworthy *m* will be guilty
Php   1: 27 conduct yourselves in a *m* worthy

MANSIONS*

Ps 49: 14 far from their princely *m*.
Isa   5:   9 the fine *m* left without occupants.
Am   3: 15 and the *m* will be demolished,''
    5: 11 though you have built stone *m*,

MARCH

Jos   6:   4 *m* around the city seven times,
Isa 42: 13 LORD will *m* out like a mighty

MARITAL* (MARRY)

Ex 21: 10 of her food, clothing and *m* rights.
Mt   5: 32 except for *m* unfaithfulness,
   19:   9 except for *m* unfaithfulness,
1Co   7:   3 husband should fulfill his *m* duty

MARK (MARKS)

Cousin of Barnabas (Col 4:10; 2Ti 4:11; Phm 24; 1Pe 5:13), see JOHN.
Ge   4: 15 Then the LORD put a *m* on Cain
Rev 13: 16 to receive a *m* on his right hand

MARKET (MARKETPLACE MARKETPLACES)

Jn   2: 16 turn my Father's house into a *m*!''

MARKETPLACE (MARKET)

Lk   7: 32 are like children sitting in the *m*

MARKETPLACES (MARKET)

Mt 23:   7 they love to be greeted in the *m*

MARKS (MARK)

Jn 20: 25 Unless I see the nail *m* in his hands
Gal   6: 17 bear on my body the *m* of Jesus.

MARRED

Isa 52: 14 his form *m* beyond human likeness

MARRIAGE (MARRY)

Mt 22: 30 neither marry nor be given in *m*;
   24: 38 marrying and giving in *m*,
Ro   7:   2 she is released from the law of *m*.
Heb 13:   4 by all, and the *m* bed kept pure,

MARRIED (MARRY)

Dt 24:   5 happiness to the wife he has *m*.
Ezr 10: 10 you have *m* foreign women,
Pr   30: 23 an unloved woman who is *m*,
Mt   1: 18 pledged to be *m* to Joseph,
Mk 12: 23 since the seven were *m* to her?''
Ro   7:   2 by law a *m* woman is bound
1Co   7: 27 Are you *m*? Do not seek a divorce.
    7: 33 But a *m* man is concerned about
    7: 36 They should get *m*.

MARRIES (MARRY)

Mt   5: 32 anyone who *m* the divorced woman
   19:   9 and *m* another woman commits

Lk 16: 18 the man who *m* a divorced woman

MARROW

Heb   4: 12 joints and *m*; it judges the thoughts

MARRY (INTERMARRY MARITAL MARRIAGE MARRIED MARRIES)

Dt 25:   5 brother shall take her and *m* her
Mt 22: 30 resurrection people will neither *m*
1Co   7:   1 It is good for a man not to *m*.
    7:   9 control themselves, they should *m*,
    7: 28 if you do *m*, you have not sinned;
1Ti   4:   3 They forbid people to *m*
    5: 14 So I counsel younger widows to *m*,

MARTHA*

Sister of Mary and Lazarus (Lk 10:38-42; Jn 11; 12:2).

MARVELED* (MARVELOUS)

Lk   2: 33 mother *m* at what was said about
2Th   1: 10 and to be *m* at among all those who

MARVELING* (MARVELOUS)

Lk   9: 43 While everyone was *m*

MARVELOUS* (MARVELED MARVELING)

1Ch 16: 24 his *m* deeds among all peoples.
Job 37:   5 God's voice thunders in *m* ways;
Ps   71: 17 to this day I declare your *m* deeds.
   72: 18 who alone does *m* deeds.
   86: 10 For you are great and do *m* deeds;
   96:   3 his *m* deeds among all peoples.
   98:   1 for he has done *m* things;
  118: 23 and it is *m* in our eyes.
Isa 25:   1 you have done *m* things,
Zec   8:   6 but will it seem *m* to me?''
    8:   6 ''It may seem *m* to the remnant
Mt 21: 42 and it is *m* in our eyes''?
Mk 12: 11 and it is *m* in our eyes''?
Rev 15:   1 in heaven another great and *m* sign
   15:   3 ''Great and *m* are your deeds,

MARY

1. Mother of Jesus (Mt 1:16-25; Lk 1:27-56; 2: 1-40). With Jesus at temple (Lk 2:41-52), at the wedding in Cana (Jn 2:1-5), questioning his sanity (Mk 3:21), at the cross (Jn 19:25-27). Among disciples after Ascension (Ac 1:14).
2. Magdalene; former demoniac (Lk 8:2). Helped support Jesus' ministry (Lk 8:1-3). At the cross (Mt 27:56; Mk 15:40; Jn 19:25), burial (Mt 27:61; Mk 15:47). Saw angel after resurrection (Mt 28:1-10; Mk 16:1-9; Lk 24:1-12); also Jesus (Jn 20:1-18).
3. Sister of Martha and Lazarus (Jn 11). Washed Jesus' feet (Jn 12:1-8).

MASQUERADES*

2Co 11: 14 for Satan himself *m* as an angel

MASTER (MASTER'S MASTERED MASTERS MASTERY)

Ge   4:   7 to have you, but you must *m* it.''
Hos   2: 16 you will no longer call me 'my *m*.'
Mal   1:   6 If I am a *m*, where is the respect
Mt 10: 24 nor a servant above his *m*.
   23:   8 for you have only one *M*
   24: 46 that servant whose *m* finds him
   25: 21 ''His *m* replied, 'Well done,
   25: 23 ''His *m* replied, 'Well done,
Ro   6: 14 For sin shall not be your *m*,
   14:   4 To his own *m* he stands or falls.
Col   4:   1 you know that you also have a *M*
2Ti   2: 21 useful to the *M* and prepared

MASTER'S (MASTER)

Mt 25: 21 Come and share your *m* happiness

MASTERED* (MASTER)

1Co   6: 12 but I will not be *m* by anything.
2Pe   2: 19 a slave to whatever has *m* him.

MASTERS (MASTER)

Pr 25: 13 he refreshes the spirit of his *m*.
Mt   6: 24 ''No one can serve two *m*.
Lk 16: 13 ''No servant can serve two *m*.

MASTERY (continued)

Eph 6: 5 obey your earthly *m* with respect
6: 9 And *m*, treat your slaves
Col 3:22 obey your earthly *m* in everything;
4: 1 *M*, provide your slaves
1Ti 6: 1 should consider their *m* worthy
6: 2 who have believing *m* are not
Tit 2: 9 subject to their *m* in everything,
1Pe 2:18 to your *m* with all respect,

MASTERY* (MASTER)

Ro 6: 9 death no longer has *m* over him.

MAT

Mk 2: 9 'Get up, take your *m* and walk'?
Ac 9:34 Get up and take care of your *m*.''

MATCHED*

2Co 8:11 do it may be *m* by your completion

MATTHEW*

Apostle; former tax collector (Mt 9:9-13; 10:3;
Mk 3:18; Lk 6:15; Ac 1:13). Also called Levi (Mk
2:14-17; Lk 5:27-32).

MATTHIAS

Ac 1:26 the lot fell to *M*; so he was added

MATURE* (MATURITY)

Lk 8:14 and pleasures, and they do not *m*.
1Co 2: 6 a message of wisdom among the *m*,
Eph 4:13 of the Son of God and become *m*,
Php 3:15 of us who are *m* should take such
Col 4:12 firm in all the will of God, *m*
Heb 5:14 But solid food is for the *m*,
Jas 1: 4 work so that you may be *m*

MATURITY* (MATURE)

Heb 6: 1 about Christ and go on to *m*,

MEAL

Pr 15:17 Better a *m* of vegetables where
1Co 10:27 some unbeliever invites you to a *m*
Heb 12:16 for a single *m* sold his inheritance

MEANING

Ne 8: 8 and giving the *m* so that the people

MEANINGLESS

Ecc 1: 2 ''*M! M!*'' says the Teacher.
1Ti 1: 6 from these and turned to *m* talk.

MEANS

1Co 9:22 by all possible *m* I might save some

MEASURE (MEASURED MEASURES)

Ps 71:15 though I know not its *m*.
Eze 45: 3 In the sacred district, *m*
Zec 2: 2 He answered me, ''To *m* Jerusalem
Lk 6:38 A good *m*, pressed
Eph 3:19 to the *m* of all the fullness of God.
4:13 to the whole *m* of the fullness
Rev 11: 1 ''Go and *m* the temple of God

MEASURED (MEASURE)

Isa 40:12 Who has *m* the waters
Jer 31:37 if the heavens above can be *m*

MEASURES (MEASURE)

Dt 25:14 Do not have two differing *m*
Pr 20:10 Differing weights and differing *m*

MEAT

Pr 23:20 or gorge themselves on *m*,
Ro 14: 6 He who eats *m*, eats to the Lord,
14:21 It is better not to eat *m*
1Co 8:13 I will never eat *m* again,
10:25 *m* market without raising questions

MEDDLER* (MEDDLES)

1Pe 4:15 kind of criminal, or even as a *m*.

MEDDLES* (MEDDLER)

Pr 26:17 is a passer-by who *m*

MEDIATOR

1Ti 2: 5 and one *m* between God and men,
Heb 8: 6 of which he is *m* is superior
9:15 For this reason Christ is the *m*
12:24 to Jesus the *m* of a new covenant,

MEDICINE*

Pr 17:22 A cheerful heart is good *m*,

MEDITATE* (MEDITATED MEDITATES MEDITATION)

Ge 24:63 out to the field one evening to *m*,
Jos 1: 8 from your mouth; *m* on it day
Ps 48: 9 we *m* on your unfailing love.
77:12 I will *m* on all your works
119: 15 I *m* on your precepts
119: 23 your servant will *m*
119: 27 then I will *m* on your wonders.
119: 48 and I *m* on your decrees.
119: 78 but I will *m* on your precepts.
119: 97 I *m* on it all day long.
119: 99 for I *m* on your statutes.
119:148 that I may *m* on your promises.
143: 5 I *m* on all your works
145: 5 I will *m* on your wonderful works.

MEDITATED* (MEDITATE)

Ps 39: 3 and as I *m*, the fire burned;

MEDITATES* (MEDITATE)

Ps 1: 2 and on his law he *m* day and night.

MEDITATION* (MEDITATE)

Ps 19:14 of my mouth and the *m* of my heart
104: 34 May my *m* be pleasing to him,

MEDIUM

Lev 20:27 '' 'A man or woman who is a *m*

MEEK* (MEEKNESS)

Ps 37:11 But the *m* will inherit the land
Zep 3:12 the *m* and humble,
Mt 5: 5 Blessed are the *m*,

MEEKNESS* (MEEK)

2Co 10: 1 By the *m* and gentleness of Christ,

MEET (MEETING MEETINGS MEETS)

Ps 42: 2 When can I go and *m* with God?
85:10 Love and faithfulness *m* together;
Am 4:12 prepare to *m* your God, O Israel.''
1Co 11:34 when you *m* together it may not
1Th 4:17 them in the clouds to *m* the Lord

MEETING (MEET)

Ex 40:34 the cloud covered the Tent of *M*,
Heb 10:25 Let us not give up *m* together,

MEETINGS* (MEET)

1Co 11:17 for your *m* do more harm

MEETS* (MEET)

Heb 7:26 Such a high priest *m* our need—

MELCHIZEDEK

Ge 14:18 *M* king of Salem brought out bread
Ps 110: 4 in the order of *M*.''
Heb 7:11 in the order of *M*, not in the order

MELT (MELTS)

2Pe 3:12 and the elements will *m* in the heat.

MELTS* (MELT)

Am 9: 5 he who touches the earth and it *m*,

MEMBER (MEMBERS)

Ro 12: 5 each *m* belongs to all the others.

MEMBERS (MEMBER)

Mic 7: 6 a man's enemies are the *m*
Mt 10:36 a man's enemies will be the *m*
Ro 7:23 law at work in the *m* of my body,
12: 4 of us has one body with many *m*,
1Co 6:15 not know that your bodies are *m*
12:24 But God has combined the *m*
Eph 3: 6 *m* together of one body,
4:25 for we are all *m* of one body.
5:30 for we are *m* of his body.
Col 3:15 as *m* of one body you were called

MEMORABLE* (MEMORY)

Eze 39:13 day I am glorified will be a *m* day

MEMORIES* (MEMORY)

1Th 3: 6 us that you always have pleasant *m*

MEMORY (MEMORABLE MEMORIES)

Pr 10: 7 *m* of the righteous will be
Mt 26:13 she has done will also be told, in *m*

MEN (MAN)

Ge 6: 2 daughter of *m* were beautiful,
6: 4 heroes of old, *m* of renown
Ps 9:20 nations know they are but *m*.
11: 4 He observes the sons of *m*;
Mt 4:19 will make you fishers of *m*
5:16 your light shine before *m*
6:14 if you forgive *m* when
10:32 acknowledges me before *m*
12:31 blasphemy will be forgiven *m*,
12:36 *m* will have to give account
23: 5 is done for *m* to see:
Mk 7: 7 are but rules taught by *m*.
Lk 6:22 Blessed are you when *m*
6:26 Woe to you when all *m*
Jn 1: 4 life was the light of *m*.
2:24 for he knew all *m*.
3:19 *m* loved darkness instead
12:32 will draw all *m* to myself
13:35 all *m* will know that you
Ac 5:29 obey God rather than *m*!
Ro 1: 18 wickedness of *m*
1:27 indecent acts with other *m*,
5:12 death came to all *m*,
1Co 2:11 among *m* knows the thoughts
3: 3 acting like mere *m*?
3:21 no more boasting about *m*!
9:22 all things to all *m*
13: 1 tongues of *m* and of angels
16:13 be *m* of courage;
16:18 Such *m* deserve recognition.
2Co 5:11 we try to persuade *m*.
8:21 but also in the eyes of *m*.
Gal 1: 1 sent not from *m* nor
1:10 to win approval of *m*, or
Eph 4: 8 and gave gifts to *m*.
1Th 2: 4 as *m* approved by God
2:13 not as the word of *m*,
1Ti 2: 4 wants all *m* to be saved
2: 6 as a ransom for all *m*—
4:10 the Savior of all *m*
5: 2 younger *m* as brothers
2Ti 2: 2 entrust to reliable *m*
Tit 2:11 has appeared to all *m*.
Heb 5: 1 is selected from among *m*
7:28 high priests *m* who are weak;
2Pe 1:21 but *m* spoke from God
Rev 21: 3 dwelling of God is with *m*,

MEN'S (MAN)

2Ki 19:18 fashioned by *m* hands.
2Ch 32:19 the work of *m* hands.
1Co 2: 5 not rest on *m* wisdom,

MENAHEM*

King of Israel (2Ki 15:17-22).

MENE

Da 5:25 that was written: *M, M,*

MEPHIBOSHETH

Son of Jonathan shown kindness by David (2Sa 4:4; 9; 21:7). Accused of siding with Absalom (2Sa 16:1-4; 19:24-30).

MERCHANT

Pr 31:14 She is like the *m* ships,
Mt 13:45 of heaven is like a *m* looking

MERCIFUL (MERCY)

Dt 4:31 the LORD your God is a *m* God;
Ne 9:31 for you are a gracious and *m* God,
Ps 77: 9 Has God forgotten to be *m*?
78:38 Yet he was *m*;
Jer 3:12 for I am *m*,' declares the LORD,
Da 9: 9 The Lord our God is *m*
Mt 5: 7 Blessed are the *m*,
Lk 1:54 remembering to be *m*
6:36 Be *m*, just as your Father is *m*.
Heb 2:17 in order that he might become a *m*
Jas 2:13 to anyone who has not been *m*.
Jude : 22 Be *m* to those who doubt; snatch

MERCY (MERCIFUL)

Ex 33:19 *m* on whom I will have *m*,
2Sa 24:14 of the LORD, for his *m* is great;
1Ch 21:13 for his *m* is very great;
Ne   9:31 But in your great *m* you did not put
Ps 25: 6 O LORD, your great *m* and love,
      28: 6 for he has heard my cry for *m*.
      57: 1 Have *m* on me, O God, have *m*
Pr 28:13 renounces them finds *m*.
Isa 63: 9 and *m* he redeemed them;
Da   9:18 but because of your great *m*.
Hos 6: 6 For I desire *m*, not sacrifice,
Am   5:15 LORD God Almighty will have *m*
Mic 6: 8 To act justly and to love *m*
      7:18 but delight to show *m*.
Hab 3: 2 in wrath remember *m*.
Zec 7: 9 show *m* and compassion
Mt   5: 7 for they will be shown *m*.
      9:13 learn what this means: 'I desire *m*,
     12: 7 'I desire *m*, not sacrifice,' you
     18:33 Shouldn't you have had *m*
     23:23 justice, *m* and faithfulness.
Lk   1:50 His *m* extends to those who fear
Ro   9:15 "I will have *m* on whom I have *m*,
      9:18 Therefore God has *m*
     11:32 so that he may have *m* on them all.
     12: 1 brothers, in view of God's *m*,
     12: 8 if it is showing *m*, let him do it
Eph 2: 4 who is rich in *m*, made us alive
1Ti 1:13 I was shown *m* because I acted
      1:16 for that very reason I was shown *m*
Tit 3: 5 we had done, but because of his *m*.
Heb 4:16 so that we may receive *m*
Jas 2:13 judgment without *m* will be shown
      2:13 *M* triumphs over judgment!
      3:17 submissive, full of *m* and good fruit
      5:11 full of compassion and *m*.
1Pe 1: 3 In his great *m* he has given us new
      2:10 once you had not received *m*,
Jude   : 23 to others show *m*, mixed with fear

MERRY

Lk 12:19 Take life easy; eat, drink and be *m*

MESHACH

   Hebrew exiled to Babylon; name changed from
Mishael (Da 1:6-7). Refused defilement by food
(Da 1:8-20). Refused to worship idol (Da 3:1-18);
saved from furnace (Da 3:19-30).

MESSAGE (MESSENGER)

Isa 53: 1 Who has believed our *m*
Jn 12:38 "Lord, who has believed our *m*
Ac   5:20 "and tell the people the full *m*
     10:36 You know the *m* God sent
     17:11 for they received the *m*
Ro 10:16 who has believed our *m*?"
     10:17 faith comes from hearing the *m*,
1Co 1:18 For the *m* of the cross is
      2: 4 My *m* and my preaching were not
2Co 5:19 to us the *m* of reconciliation.
2Th 3: 1 pray for us that the *m*
Tit 1: 9 firmly to the trustworthy *m*
Heb 4: 2 the *m* they heard was of no value
1Pe 2: 8 because they disobey the *m*—

MESSENGER (MESSAGE)

Pr 25:13 is a trustworthy *m*
Mal 3: 1 I will send my *m*, who will prepare
Mt 11:10 " 'I will send my *m* ahead of you,
2Co 12: 7 a *m* of Satan, to torment them

MESSIAH*

Jn   1:41 "We have found the *M*" (that is,
      4:25 "I know that *M*" (called Christ) "is

METHUSELAH

Ge   5:27 Altogether, *M* lived 969 years,

MICAH

   1. Idolater from Ephraim (Jdg 17-18).
   2. Prophet from Moresheth (Jer 26:18-19; Mic
1:1).

MICAIAH

   Prophet of the LORD who spoke against Ahab
(1Ki 22:1-28; 2Ch 18:1-27).

MICHAEL

   Archangel (Jude 9); warrior in angelic realm,
protector of Israel (Da 10:13, 21; 12:1; Rev 12:7).

MICHAL

   Daughter of Saul, wife of David (1Sa 14:49;
18:20-28). Warned David of Saul's plot (1Sa 19).
Saul gave her to Paltiel (1Sa 25:44); David retrieved her (2Sa 3:13-16). Criticized David for
dancing before the ark (2Sa 6:16-23); 1Ch 15:29).

MIDIAN

Ex   2:15 Pharaoh and went to live in *M*,
Jdg 7: 2 me to deliver *M* into their hands.

MIDWIVES

Ex   1:17 The *m*, however, feared God

MIGHT (ALMIGHTY MIGHTIER MIGHTY)

Jdg 16:30 Then he pushed with all his *m*,
2Sa 6: 5 with all their *m* before the LORD,
      6:14 before the LORD with all his *m*,
2Ch 20: 6 Power and *m* are in your hand,
Ps 21:13 we will sing and praise your *m*.
      54: 1 vindicate me by your *m*.
Isa 63:15 Where are your zeal and your *m*?
Mic 3: 8 and with justice and *m*,
Zec 4: 6 'Not by *m* nor by power,
Col 1:11 power according to his glorious *m*
1Ti 6:16 To him be honor and *m* forever.

MIGHTIER (MIGHT)

Ps 93: 4 *M* than the thunder

MIGHTY (MIGHT)

Ge 49:24 of the hand of the *M* One of Jacob,
Ex   6: 1 of my *m* hand he will drive them
     13: 3 out of it with a *m* hand.
Dt   5:15 out of there with a *m* hand
      7: 8 he brought you out with a *m* hand
     10:17 the great God, *m* and awesome,
     34:12 one has ever shown the *m* power
     23: 8 the names of David's *m* men:
2Sa 1:19 How the *m* have fallen!
Ne   9:32 the great, *m* and awesome God,
Job 36: 5 God is *m*, but does not despise men
Ps 24: 8 The LORD strong and *m*,
     45: 3 upon your side, O *m* one;
     50: 1 The *M* One, God, the LORD,
     62: 7 he is my rock, my refuge.
     68:33 who thunders with *m* voice.
     71:16 proclaim your *m* acts,
     77:12 and consider all your *m* deeds.
     77:15 With your *m* arm you redeemed
     89: 8 You are *m*, O LORD,
     93: 4 the LORD is *m*.
     99: 4 The King is *m*, he loves justice—
    110: 2 LORD will extend your *m* scepter
    118:15 right hand has done *m* things!
    136:12 with a *m* hand and outstretched
    145: 4 they will tell of your *m* acts.
    145:12 all men may know of your *m* acts
    147: 5 Great is our Lord and *m* in power;
SS   8: 6 like a *m* flame.
Isa 9: 6 Wonderful Counselor, *M* God,
     60:16 your Redeemer, the *M* One
     63: 1 *m* to save."
Jer 10: 6 and your name is *m* in power.
     20:11 with me like a *m* warrior;
     32:19 your purposes and *m* are your
Eze 20:33 I will rule over you with a *m* hand
Zep 3:17 he is *m* to save.
Mt 26:64 at the right hand of the *M* One
Eph 1:19 like the working of his *m* strength,
      6:10 in the Lord and in his *m* power.
1Pe 5: 6 therefore, under God's *m* hand,

MILE*

Mt   5:41 If someone forces you to go one *m*,

MILK

Ex   3: 8 a land flowing with *m* and honey—
     23:19 a young goat in its mother's *m*.
Pr 30:33 as churning the *m* produces butter,
Isa 55: 1 Come, buy wine and *m*
1Co 3: 2 I gave you *m*, not solid food,
Heb 5:12 You need *m*, not solid food!

1Pe 2: 2 babies, crave pure spiritual *m*,

MILLSTONE (STONE)

Lk 17: 2 sea with a *m* tied around his neck

MIND (DOUBLE-MINDED LIKE-MINDED MINDED MINDFUL MINDS)

Nu 23:19 that he should change his *m*.
Dt 28:65 LORD will give you an anxious *m*,
1Sa 15:29 Israel does not lie or change his *m*;
1Ch 28: 9 devotion and with a willing *m*,
2Ch 30:12 the people to give them unity of *m*
Ps 26: 2 examine my heart and my *m*;
    110: 4 and will not change his *m*:
Isa 26: 3 him whose *m* is steadfast,
Jer 17:10 and examine the *m*,
Mt 22:37 all your soul and with all your *m*.'
Mk 12:30 with all your *m* and with all your
Lk 10:27 your strength and with all your *m*';
Ac   4:32 believers were one in heart and *m*.
Ro   1:28 he gave them over to a depraved *m*
      7:25 I myself in my *m* am a slave
      8: 6 The *m* of sinful man is death,
      8: 7 the sinful *m* is hostile to God.
     12: 2 by the renewing of your *m*.
     14:13 make up your *m* not
1Co 1:10 you may be perfectly united in *m*
      2: 9 no *m* has conceived
     14:14 spirit prays, but my *m* is unfruitful.
2Co 13:11 be of one *m*, live in peace.
Php 3:19 Their *m* is on earthly things.
Col 2:18 and his unspiritual *m* puffs him up
1Th 4:11 to *m* your own business
Heb 7:21 and will not change his *m*:

MINDED* (MIND)

1Pe 4: 7 be clear *m* and self-controlled

MINDFUL* (MIND)

Ps   8: 4 what is man that you are *m* of him,
Lk   1:48 God my Savior, for he has been *m*
Heb 2: 6 What is man that you are *m* of him,

MINDS (MIND)

Dt 11:18 of mine in your hearts and *m*;
Ps   7: 9 who searches *m* and hearts,
Jer 31:33 "I will put my law in their *m*
Lk 24:38 and why do doubts rise in your *m*?
     24:45 Then he opened their *m*
Ro   8: 5 to the sinful nature have their *m* set
2Co 4: 4 god of this age has blinded the *m*
Eph 4:23 new in the attitude of your *m*;
Col 3: 2 Set your *m* on things above,
Heb 8:10 I will put my laws in their *m*
     10:16 and I will write them on their *m*."
1Pe 1:13 prepare your *m* for action;
Rev 2:23 I am he who searches hearts and *m*,

MINISTER (MINISTERING MINISTERS MINISTRY)

Ps 101: 6 will *m* to me.
1Ti 4: 6 you will be a good *m*

MINISTERING (MINISTER)

Heb 1:14 Are not all angels *m* spirits sent

MINISTERS (MINISTER)

2Co 3: 6 as *m* of a new covenant—

MINISTRY (MINISTER)

Ac   6: 4 to prayer and the *m* of the word."
Ro 11:13 I make much of my *m*
2Co 4: 1 God's mercy we have this *m*,
      5:18 gave us the *m* of reconciliation:
      6: 3 so that our *m* will not be
Gal 2: 8 who was at work in the *m* of Peter
2Ti 4: 5 discharge all the duties of your *m*.
Heb 8: 6 But the *m* Jesus has received is

MIRACLE* (MIRACLES MIRACULOUS)

Ex   7: 9 'Perform a *m*,' then say to Aaron,
Mk   9:39 "No one who does a *m*
Lk 23: 8 hoped to see him perform some *m*.
Jn   7:21 "I did one *m*, and you are all
Ac   4:16 they have done an outstanding *m*,

MIRACLES* (MIRACLE)

1Ch 16: 12 his *m*, and the judgments he
Ne 9: 17 to remember the *m* you performed
Job 5: 9 *m* that cannot be counted.
9: 10 *m* that cannot be counted.
Ps 77: 11 I will remember your *m* of long ago
77: 14 You are the God who performs *m*;
78: 12 He did *m* in the sight
105: 5 his *m*, and the judgments he
106: 7 they gave no thought to your *m*;
106: 22 *m* in the land of Ham
Mt 7: 22 out demons and perform many *m*?'
11: 20 most of his *m* had been performed,
11: 21 If the *m* that were performed
11: 23 If the *m* that were performed
13: 58 had he did not do many *m* there
24: 24 and perform great signs and *m*
Mk 6: 2 does *m*! Isn't this the carpenter?
6: 5 He could not do any *m* there,
13: 22 and *m* to deceive the elect—
Lk 10: 13 For if the *m* that were performed
19: 37 for all the *m* they had seen:
Jn 7: 3 disciples may see the *m* you do.
10: 25 *m* I do in my Father's name speak
10: 32 "I have shown you many great *m*
10: 38 do not believe, believe the *m*,
14: 11 the evidence of the *m* themselves.
15: 24 But now they have seen these *m*,
Ac 2: 22 accredited by God to you by *m*,
8: 13 by the great signs and *m* he saw.
19: 11 God did extraordinary *m*
Ro 15: 19 by the power of signs and *m*,
1Co 12: 28 third teachers, then workers of *m*,
12: 29 Are all teachers? Do all work *m*?
2Co 12: 12 and *m*— were done among you
Gal 3: 5 work *m* among you because you
2Th 2: 9 in all kinds of counterfeit *m*,
Heb 2: 4 it by signs, wonders and various *m*,

MIRACULOUS (MIRACLE)

Dt 13: 1 and announces to you a *m* sign
Mt 12: 39 generation asks for a *m* sign!
13: 54 this wisdom and these *m* powers?"
Jn 2: 11 This, the first of his *m* signs,
2: 23 people saw the *m* signs he was
3: 2 could perform the *m* signs you are
4: 48 "Unless you people see *m* signs
7: 31 will he do more *m* signs
9: 16 "How can a sinner do such *m* signs
12: 37 Jesus had done all these *m* signs
20: 30 Jesus did many other *m* signs
Ac 2: 43 *m* signs were done by the apostles.
5: 12 apostles performed many *m* signs
1Co 1: 22 Jews demand *m* signs and Greeks
12: 10 to another *m* powers,

MIRE

Ps 40: 2 out of the mud and *m*;
Isa 57: 20 whose waves cast up *m* and mud.

MIRIAM

Sister of Moses and Aaron (Nu 26:59). Led dancing at Red Sea (Ex 15:20-21). Struck with leprosy for criticizing Moses (Nu 12). Death (Nu 20:1).

MIRROR

1Co 13: 12 but a poor reflection as in a *m*;
Jas 1: 23 a man who looks at his face in a *m*

MISDEEDS*

Ps 99: 8 though you punished their *m*.
Ro 8: 13 put to death the *m* of the body,

MISERY

Ex 3: 7 "I have indeed seen the *m*
Jdg 10: 16 he could bear Israel's *m* no longer.
Hos 5: 15 in their *m* they will earnestly seek
Ro 3: 16 ruin and *m* mark their ways,
Jas 5: 1 of the *m* that is coming upon you.

MISFORTUNE

Ob : 12 brother in the day of his *m*,

MISLEAD (MISLED)

Isa 47: 10 wisdom and knowledge *m* you

MISLED (MISLEAD)

1Co 15: 33 Do not be *m*: "Bad company

MISS (MISSES)

Pr 19: 2 nor to be hasty and *m* the way.

MISSES (MISS)

Heb 12: 15 See to it that no one *m* the grace

MIST

Hos 6: 4 Your love is like the morning *m*,
Jas 4: 14 You are a *m* that appears for a little

MISTREAT (MISTREATED)

Ex 22: 21 "Do not *m* an alien or oppress him,
Eze 22: 29 and needy and the alien,
Lk 6: 28 pray for those who *m* you.

MISTREATED (MISTREAT)

Eze 22: 7 *m* the fatherless and the widow,
Heb 11: 25 to be *m* along with the people
11: 37 destitute, persecuted and *m*—
13: 3 who are *m* as if you yourselves

MISUSE* (MISUSES)

Ex 20: 7 "You shall not *m* the name
Dt 5: 11 "You shall not *m* the name
Ps 139: 20 your adversaries *m* your name.

MISUSES* (MISUSE)

Ex 20: 7 anyone guiltless who *m* his name.
Dt 5: 11 anyone guiltless who *m* his name.

MIXED (MIXING)

Da 2: 41 even as you saw iron *m* with clay.

MIXING (MIXED)

Isa 5: 22 and champions at *m* drinks,

MOAB (MOABITESS)

Ge 19: 37 she named him *M*; he is the father
Dt 34: 6 He buried him in *M*, in the valley
Ru 1: 1 live for a while in the country of *M*.
Isa 15: 1 An oracle concerning *M*:
Jer 48: 16 "The fall of *M* is at hand;
Am 2: 1 "For three sins of *M*,

MOABITESS (MOAB)

Ru 1: 22 accompanied by Ruth the *M*,

MOAN

Ps 90: 9 we finish our years with a *m*.

MOCK (MOCKED MOCKER MOCKERS MOCKING MOCKS)

Ps 22: 7 All who see me *m* me;
119: 51 The arrogant *m* me
Pr 1: 26 I will *m* when calamity overtakes
14: 9 Fools *m* at making amends for sin,
Mk 10: 34 who will *m* him and spit on him,

MOCKED (MOCK)

Ps 89: 51 with which they have *m* every step
Mt 27: 29 knelt in front of him and *m* him.
27: 41 of the law and the elders *m* him.
Gal 6: 7 not be deceived: God cannot be *m*.

MOCKER (MOCK)

Pr 9: 7 corrects a *m* invites insult;
9: 12 if you are a *m*, you alone will suffer
20: 1 Wine is a *m* and beer a brawler;
22: 10 Drive out the *m*, and out goes strife

MOCKERS (MOCK)

Ps 1: 1 or sit in the seat of *m*,
Pr 29: 8 *M* stir up a city,

MOCKING (MOCK)

Isa 50: 6 face from *m* and spitting.

MOCKS (MOCK)

Pr 17: 5 He who *m* the poor shows
30: 17 "The eye that *m* a father,

MODEL*

Eze 28: 12 " 'You were the *m* of perfection,
1Th 1: 7 And so you became a *m*
2Th 3: 9 to make ourselves a *m* for you

MODESTY*

1Co 12: 23 are treated with special *m*,

MOLDED*

Job 10: 9 Remember that you *m* me like clay

MOLDY

Jos 9: 5 of their food supply was dry and *m*.

MOLECH

Lev 20: 2 of his children to *M* must be put
1Ki 11: 33 and *M* the god of the Ammonites,

MOMENT (MOMENTARY)

Job 20: 5 the joy of the godless lasts but a *m*.
Ps 2: 12 for his wrath can flare up in a *m*.
30: 5 For his anger lasts only a *m*,
Pr 12: 19 but a lying tongue lasts only a *m*.
Isa 54: 7 "For a brief *m* I abandoned you,
66: 8 or a nation be brought forth in a *m*?
Gal 2: 5 We did not give in to them for a *m*,

MOMENTARY* (MOMENT)

2Co 4: 17 and *m* troubles are achieving

MONEY

Pr 13: 11 Dishonest *m* dwindles away,
Ecc 5: 10 Whoever loves *m* never has *m*
Isa 55: 1 and you who have no *m*,
Mt 6: 24 You cannot serve both God and *M*.
27: 5 Judas threw the *m* into the temple
Lk 3: 14 "Don't extort *m* and don't accuse
9: 3 no bread, no *m*, no extra tunic.
16: 13 You cannot serve both God and *M*
Ac 5: 2 part of the *m* for himself,
1Co 16: 2 set aside a sum of *m* in keeping
1Ti 3: 3 not quarrelsome, not a lover of *m*.
6: 10 For the love of *m* is a root
2Ti 3: 2 lovers of *m*, boastful, proud,
Heb 13: 5 free from the love of *m*
1Pe 5: 2 not greedy for *m*, but eager to serve

MONEYLENDER* (LEND)

Ex 22: 25 not be like a *m*; charge him no
Lk 7: 41 men owed money to a certain *m*.

MONTH (MONTHS)

Ex 12: 2 "This *m* is to be for you the first
Eze 47: 12 Every *m* they will bear,
Rev 22: 2 of fruit, yielding its fruit every *m*.

MONTHS (MONTH)

Gal 4: 10 and *m* and seasons and years!
Rev 11: 2 trample on the holy city for 42 *m*.
13: 5 his authority for forty-two *m*.

MOON

Jos 10: 13 and the *m* stopped,
Ps 8: 3 the *m* and the stars,
74: 16 you established the sun and *m*.
89: 37 be established forever like the *m*,
104: 19 The *m* marks off the seasons,
121: 6 nor the *m* by night.
136: 9 the *m* and stars to govern the night;
148: 3 Praise him, sun and *m*,
SS 6: 10 fair as the *m*, bright as the sun,
Joel 2: 31 and the *m* to blood
Hab 3: 11 and *m* stood still in the heavens
Mt 24: 29 and the *m* will not give its light;
Ac 2: 20 and the *m* to blood
1Co 15: 41 *m* another and the stars another;
Col 2: 16 a New *M* celebration or a Sabbath
Rev 6: 12 the whole *m* turned blood red,
21: 23 city does not need the sun or the *m*

MORAL*

Jas 1: 21 rid of all *m* filth and the evil that is

MORDECAI

Benjamite exile who raised Esther (Est 2:5-15). Exposed plot to kill Xerxes (Est 2:19-23). Refused to honor Haman (Est 3:1-6; 5:9-14). Charged Esther to foil Haman's plot against the Jews (Est 4). Xerxes forced Haman to honor Mordecai (Est 6). Mordecai exalted (Est 8-10). Established Purim (Est 9:18-32).

MORIAH*

Ge 22: 2 and go to the region of *M*.
2Ch 3: 1 LORD in Jerusalem on Mount *M*,

MORNING

Ge   1: 5 and there was *m*— the first day.
Dt 28:67 In the *m* you will say, "If only it
2Sa 23: 4 he is like the light of *m* at sunrise
Ps   5: 3 In the *m*, O LORD,
Pr 27:14 blesses his neighbor early in the *m*,
Isa 14:12 O *m* star, son of the dawn!
La   3:23 They are new every *m*;
2Pe 1:19 and the *m* star rises in your hearts.
Rev 2:28 I will also give him the *m* star.
     22:16 of David, and the bright *M* Star."

MORTAL

Ge   6: 3 for he is *m*; his days will be
Job 10: 4 Do you see as a *m* sees?
Ro   8:11 also give life to your *m* bodies
1Co 15:53 and the *m* with immortality.
2Co   5: 4 that what is *m* may be swallowed

MOSES

   Levite; brother of Aaron (Ex 6:20; 1Ch 6:3).
Put in basket into Nile; discovered and raised by
Pharaoh's daughter (Ex 2:1-10). Fled to Midian
after killing Egyptian (Ex 2:11-15). Married to
Zipporah, fathered Gershom (Ex 2:16-22).
   Called by the LORD to deliver Israel (Ex 3-4).
Pharaoh's resistance (Ex 5). Ten plagues (Ex 7-
11). Passover and Exodus (Ex 12-13). Led Israel
through Red Sea (Ex 14). Song of deliverance (Ex
15:1-21). Brought water from rock (Ex 17:1-7).
Raised hands to defeat Amalekites (Ex 17:8-16).
Delegated judges (Ex 18; Dt 1:9-18).
   Received Law at Sinai (Ex 19-23; 25-31; Jn 1:
17). Announced Law to Israel (Ex 19:7-8; 24; 35).
Broke tablets because of golden calf (Ex 32; Dt 9).
Saw glory of the LORD (Ex 33-34). Supervised
building of tabernacle (Ex 36-40). Set apart Aaron
and priests (Lev 8-9). Numbered tribes (Nu 1-4;
26). Opposed by Aaron and Miriam (Nu 12). Sent
spies into Canaan (Nu 13). Announced forty years
of wandering for failure to enter land (Nu 14).
Opposed by Korah (Nu 16). Forbidden to enter
land for striking rock (Nu 20:1-13; Dt 1:37). Lifted bronze snake for healing (Nu 21:4-9; Jn 3:14).
Final address to Israel (Dt 1-33). Succeeded by
Joshua (Nu 27:12-23; Dt 34). Death (Dt 34:5-12).
   "Law of Moses" (1Ki 2:3; Ezr 3:2; Mk 12:26;
Lk 24:44). "Book of Moses" (2Ch 25:12; Ne 13:
1). "Song of Moses" (Ex 15:1-21; Rev 15:3).
"Prayer of Moses" (Ps 90).

MOTH

Mt   6:19 where *m* and rust destroy,

MOTHER (GRANDMOTHER MOTHER-IN-LAW MOTHER'S)

Ge   2:24 and *m* and be united to his wife,
     3:20 because she would become the *m*
Ex 20:12 "Honor your father and your *m*,
Lev 20: 9 " 'If anyone curses his father or *m*,
Dt   5:16 "Honor your father and your *m*,
    21:18 who does not obey his father and *m*
    27:16 who dishonors his father or his *m*."
Jdg   5: 7 arose a *m* in Israel.
1Sa 2:19 Each year his *m* made him a little
Ps 113: 9 as a happy *m* of children.
Pr 10: 1 but a foolish son grief to his *m*.
    23:22 do not despise your *m*
    23:25 May your father and *m* be glad;
    29:15 a child left to himself disgraces his *m*.
    30:17 that scorns obedience to a *m*,
    31: 1 an oracle his *m* taught him:
Isa 49:15 "Can a *m* forget the baby
    66:13 As a *m* comforts her child,
Jer 20:17 with my *m* as my grave,
Mic   7: 6 a daughter rises up against her *m*,
Mt 10:35 a daughter against her *m*,
    10:37 or *m* more than me is not worthy
    12:48 He replied to him, "Who is my *m*,
    15: 4 'Honor your father and *m*'
    19: 5 and *m* and be united to his wife,
    19:19 honor your father and *m*,'
Mk   7:10 'Honor your father and your *m*,' and,
    10:19 honor your father and *m*.' "

Lk 11:27 "Blessed is the *m* who gave you
    12:53 daughter and daughter against *m*,
    18:20 honor your father and *m*.' "
Jn 19:27 to the disciple, "Here is your *m*."
Gal   4:26 is above is free, and she is our *m*.
Eph 5:31 and *m* and be united to his wife,
    6: 2 "Honor your father and *m*"—
1Th 2: 7 like a *m* caring for her little
2Ti 1: 5 and in your *m* Eunice and,

MOTHER-IN-LAW (MOTHER)

Ru   2:19 Ruth told her *m* about the one
Mt 10:35 a daughter-in-law against her *m*—

MOTHER'S (MOTHER)

Job 1:21 "Naked I came from my *m* womb,
Pr   1: 8 and do not forsake your *m* teaching
Ecc 5:15 from his *m* womb,
    11: 5 the body is formed in a *m* womb,
Jn   3: 4 time into his *m* womb to be born!' "

MOTIVE* (MOTIVES)

1Ch 28: 9 and understands every *m*

MOTIVES* (MOTIVE)

Pr 16: 2 but *m* are weighed by the LORD.
1Co 4: 5 will expose the *m* of men's hearts.
Php 1:18 whether from false *m* or true,
1Th 2: 3 spring from error or impure *m*,
Jas   4: 3 because you ask with wrong *m*,

MOUNT (MOUNTAIN MOUNTAINS MOUNTAINTOPS)

Ps 89: 9 when its waves *m* up, you still them
Isa 14:13 enthroned on the *m* of assembly,
Eze 28:14 You were on the holy *m* of God;
Zec 14: 4 stand on the *M* of Olives,

MOUNTAIN (MOUNT)

Ge 22:14 "On the *m* of the LORD it will be
Ex 24:18 And he stayed on the *m* forty days
Dt   5: 4 face to face out of the fire on the *m*.
Job 14:18 "But as a *m* erodes and crumbles
Ps 48: 1 in the city of our God, his holy *m*.
Isa 40: 4 every *m* and hill made low;
Mic   4: 2 let us go up to the *m* of the LORD,
Mt   4: 8 the devil took him to a very high *m*
    17:20 say to this *m*, 'Move from here
Mk   9: 2 with him and led them up a high *m*,
Lk   3: 5 every *m* and hill made low.
Jn   4:21 the Father neither on this *m*
2Pe 1:18 were with him on the sacred *m*.

MOUNTAINS (MOUNT)

Ps 36: 6 righteousness is like the mighty *m*,
    46: 2 the *m* fall into the heart of the sea,
    90: 2 Before the *m* were born
Isa 52: 7 How beautiful on the *m*
    54:10 Though the *m* be shaken
    55:12 the *m* and hills
Eze 34: 6 My sheep wandered over all the *m*
Mt 24:16 are in Judea flee to the *m*.
Lk 23:30 they will say to the *m*, "Fall on us!"
1Co 13: 2 if I have a faith that can move *m*,
Rev 6:16 They called to the *m* and the rocks,

MOUNTAINTOPS (MOUNT)

Isa 42:11 let them shout from the *m*.

MOURN (MOURNING MOURNS)

Ecc 3: 4 a time to *m* and a time to dance,
Isa 61: 2 to comfort all who *m*,
Mt   5: 4 Blessed are those who *m*,
Ro 12:15 *m* with those who *m*.

MOURNING (MOURN)

Isa 61: 3 instead of *m*,
Jer 31:13 I will turn their *m* into gladness;
Rev 21: 4 There will be no more death or *m*

MOURNS (MOURN)

Zec 12:10 as one *m* for an only child,

MOUTH (MOUTHS)

Nu 22:38 only what God puts in my *m*."
Dt   8: 3 comes from the *m* of the LORD.
    18:18 I will put my words in his *m*,
    30:14 it is in your *m* and in your heart

Jos   1: 8 of the Law depart from your *m*;
2Ki 4:34 *m* to *m*, eyes to eyes, hands
Ps 10: 7 His *m* is full of curses and lies
    17: 3 resolved that my *m* will not sin.
    19:14 May the words of my *m*
    37:30 *m* of the righteous man utters
    40: 3 He put a new song in my *m*,
    71: 8 My *m* is filled with your praise,
  119:103 sweeter than honey to my *m*!
   141: 3 Set a guard over my *m*, O LORD;
Pr   2: 6 and from his *m* come knowledge
    4:24 Put away perversity from your *m*;
    10:11 The *m* of the righteous is a fountain
    10:31 *m* of the righteous brings forth
    16:23 A wise man's heart guides his *m*,
    26:28 and a flattering *m* works ruin.
    27: 2 praise you, and not your own *m*;
Ecc 5: 2 Do not be quick with your *m*,
SS   1: 2 with the kisses of his *m*—
    5:16 His *m* is sweetness itself;
Isa 29:13 come near to me with their *m*
    40: 5 For the *m* of the LORD has spoken
    45:23 my *m* has uttered in all integrity
    51:16 I have put my words in your *m*
    53: 7 so he did not open his *m*.
    55:11 my word that goes out from my *m*:
    59:21 *m* will not depart from your *m*,
Eze 3: 2 So I opened my *m*, and he gave me
Mal 2: 7 and from his *m* men should seek
Mt   4: 4 comes from the *m* of God.' "
    12:34 overflow of the heart the *m* speaks.
    15:11 into a man's *m* does not make him
    15:18 out of the *m* come from the heart,
Lk   6:45 overflow of his heart his *m* speaks.
Ro 10: 9 That if you confess with your *m*,
    15: 6 and *m* you may glorify the God
1Pe 2:22 and no deceit was found in his *m*."
Rev 1:16 and out of his *m* came a sharp
    2:16 them with the sword of my *m*.
    3:16 I am about to spit you out of my *m*.
    19:15 Out of his *m* comes a sharp sword

MOUTHS (MOUTH)

Ps 78:36 would flatter him with their *m*,
Eze 33:31 With their *m* they express devotion
Ro   3:14 "Their *m* are full of cursing
Eph 4:29 talk come out of your *m*,
Jas   3: 3 bits into the *m* of horses

MOVE (MOVED MOVES)

Dt 19:14 Do not *m* your neighbor's
Pr 23:10 Do not *m* an ancient boundary
Ac 17:28 and *m* and have our being.'
1Co 13: 2 have a faith that can *m* mountains,
    15:58 Let nothing *m* you.

MOVED (MOVE)

Ex 35:21 and whose heart *m* him came
2Ch 36:22 the LORD *m* the heart
Ezr 1: 5 everyone whose heart God had *m*
Ps 93: 1 it cannot be *m*.
Jn 11:33 he was deeply *m* in spirit
Col 1:23 not *m* from the hope held out

MOVES (MOVE)

Dt 23:14 For the LORD your God *m* about

MUD (MUDDIED)

Ps 40: 2 out of the *m* and mire;
Isa 57:20 whose waves cast up mire and *m*.
Jn   9: 6 made some *m* with the saliva,
2Pe 2:22 back to her wallowing in the *m*."

MUDDIED (MUD)

Pr 25:26 Like a *m* spring or a polluted well
Eze 32:13 or *m* by the hoofs of cattle.

MULBERRY*

Lk 17: 6 you can say to this *m* tree,

MULTITUDE (MULTITUDES)

Isa 31: 1 who trust in the *m* of their chariots
Jas 5:20 and cover over a *m* of sins.
1Pe 4: 8 love covers over a *m* of sins.
Rev 7: 9 me was a great *m* that no one could
    19: 1 of a great *m* in heaven shouting:

MULTITUDES (MULTITUDE)

Ne   9: 6 and the *m* of heaven worship you.
Da 12: 2 *M* who sleep in the dust
Joel 3:14 *M*, *m* in the valley of decision!

MURDER (MURDERED MURDERER MURDERERS)

Ex 20:13 "You shall not *m*.
Dt   5:17 "You shall not *m*.
Pr 28:17 A man tormented by the guilt of *m*
Mt   5:21 'Do not *m*, and anyone who
    15:19 *m*, adultery, sexual immorality.
Ro   1:29 *m*, strife, deceit and malice.
    13: 9 "Do not *m*," "Do not steal,"
Jas 2:11 adultery," also said, "Do not *m*."

MURDERED (MURDER)

Mt 23:31 of those who *m* the prophets.
Ac   7:52 now you have betrayed and *m* him
1Jn 3:12 to the evil one and *m* his brother.

MURDERER (MURDER)

Nu 35:16 he is a *m*; the *m* shall be put
Jn   8:44 He was a *m* from the beginning,
1Jn 3:15 who hates his brother is a *m*,

MURDERERS (MURDER)

1Ti 1: 9 for *m*, for adulterers and perverts,
Rev 21: 8 the *m*, the sexually immoral,
    22:15 the sexually immoral, the *m*,

MUSIC* (MUSICAL MUSICIAN MUSICIANS)

Ge 31:27 singing to the *m* of tambourines
Jdg 5: 3 I will make *m* to the LORD,
1Ch 6:31 put in charge of the *m* in the house
     6:32 They ministered with *m*
    25: 6 fathers for the music of the temple
    25: 7 and skilled in *m* for the LORD—
Ne 12:27 and with the *m* of cymbals,
Job 21:12 They sing to the *m* of tambourine
Ps 27: 6 and make *m* to the LORD.
    33: 2 make *m* to him on the ten-stringed
    45: 8 the *m* of the strings makes you glad
    57: 7 I will sing and make *m*.
    81: 2 Begin the *m*, strike the tambourine,
    87: 7 As they make *m* they will sing,
    92: 1 and make *m* to your name,
    92: 3 to the *m* of the ten-stringed lyre
    95: 2 and extol him with *m* and song.
    98: 4 burst into jubilant song with *m*;
    98: 5 make *m* to the LORD
   108: 1 make *m* with all my soul.
   144: 9 the ten-stringed lyre I will make *m*
   147: 7 make *m* to our God on the harp.
   149: 3 make *m* to him with tambourine
Isa 30:32 will be to the *m* of tambourines
La   5:14 young men have stopped their *m*.
Eze 26:13 *m* of your harps will be heard no
Da   3: 5 lyre, harp, pipes and all kinds of *m*,
     3: 7 and all kinds of *m*, all the peoples,
     3:10 and all kinds of *m* must fall down
     3:15 lyre, harp, pipes and all kinds of *m*,
Am   5:23 to the *m* of your harps.
Hab 3:19 For the director of *m*.
Lk 15:25 came near the house, he heard *m*
Eph 5:19 make *m* in your heart to the Lord,
Rev 18:22 The *m* of harpists and musicians,

MUSICAL* (MUSIC)

1Ch 15:16 accompanied by *m* instruments:
    23: 5 with the *m* instruments I have
2Ch 7: 6 with the LORD's *m* instruments,
    23:13 with *m* instruments were leading
    34:12 skilled in playing *m* instruments—
Ne 12:36 with *m* instruments prescribed
Am   6: 5 and improvise on *m* instruments.

MUSICIAN* (MUSIC)

1Ch 6:33 Heman, the, *m*, the son of Joel,

MUSICIANS* (MUSIC)

1Ki 10:12 to make harps and lyres for the *m*.
1Ch 9:33 Those who were *m*, heads
    15:19 The *m* Heman, Asaph
2Ch 5:12 All the Levites who were *m*—
     9:11 to make harps and lyres for the *m*.
    35:15 The *m*, the descendants of Asaph,

Ps 68:25 are the singers, after them the *m*;
Rev 18:22 The music of harpists and *m*,

MUSTARD

Mt 13:31 kingdom of heaven is like a *m* seed,
    17:20 you have faith as small as a *m* seed,
Mk   4:31 It is like a *m* seed, which is

MUTILATORS*

Php 3: 2 those men who do evil, those *m*

MUTUAL* (MUTUALLY)

Ro 14:19 leads to peace and to *m* edification.
1Co 7: 5 by *m* consent and for a time,

MUTUALLY* (MUTUAL)

Ro   1:12 and I may be *m* encouraged

MUZZLE*

Dt 25: 4 Do not *m* an ox while it is treading
Ps 39: 1 I will put a *m* on my mouth
1Co 9: 9 "Do not *m* an ox while it is
1Ti 5:18 "Do not *m* the ox while it is

MYRRH

Ps 45: 8 All your robes are fragrant with *m*
SS   1:13 My lover is to me a sachet of *m*
Mt   2:11 of gold and of incense and of *m*.
Mk 15:23 offered him wine mixed with *m*,
Jn 19:39 Nicodemus brought a mixture of *m*
Rev 18:13 of incense, *m* and frankincense,

MYSTERIES* (MYSTERY)

Job 11: 7 "Can you fathom the *m* of God?
Da   2:28 a God in heaven who reveals *m*.
     2:29 of *m* showed you what is going
     2:47 Lord of kings and a revealer of *m*,
1Co 13: 2 can fathom all *m* and all knowledge
    14: 2 he utters *m* with his spirit.

MYSTERY* (MYSTERIES)

Da   2:18 God of heaven concerning this *m*,
     2:19 the night the *m* was revealed
     2:27 to the king the *m* he has asked
     2:30 this *m* has been revealed to me,
     2:47 for you were able to reveal this *m*."
     4: 9 and no *m* is too difficult for you.
Ro 11:25 you to be ignorant of this *m*,
    16:25 to the revelation of the *m* hidden
1Co 15:51 I tell you a *m*: We will not all sleep,
Eph 1: 9 to us the *m* of his will according
     3: 3 the *m* made known to me
     3: 4 insight into the *m* of Christ,
     3: 6 This *m* is that through the gospel
     3: 9 the administration of this *m*,
     5:32 This is a profound *m*—
     6:19 I will fearlessly make known the *m*
Col 1:26 the *m* that has been kept hidden
     1:27 the glorious riches of this *m*,
     2: 2 in order that they may know the *m*
     4: 3 so that we may proclaim the *m*
1Ti 3:16 the *m* of godliness is great:
Rev 1:20 *m* of the seven stars that you saw
    10: 7 the *m* of God will be accomplished,
    17: 5 written on her forehead: *M*
    17: 7 explain to you the *m* of the woman

MYTHS*

1Ti 1: 4 nor to devote themselves to *m*
     4: 7 Have nothing to do with godless *m*
2Ti 4: 4 from the truth and turn aside to *m*.
Tit 1:14 will pay no attention to Jewish *m*

NAAMAN

Aramean general whose leprosy was cleansed
by Elisha (2Ki 5).

NABAL

Wealthy Carmelite the LORD killed for refusing
to help David (1Sa 25). David married Abigail, his
widow (1Sa 25:39-42).

NABOTH*

Jezreelite killed by Jezebel for his vineyard
(1Ki 21). Ahab's family destroyed for this (1Ki
21:17-24; 2Ki 9:21-37).

NADAB

1. Firstborn of Aaron (Ex 6:23); killed with

Abihu for offering unauthorized fire (Lev 10; Nu
3:4).

2. Son of Jeroboam I; king of Israel (1Ki 15:
25-32).

NAHUM

Prophet against Nineveh (Na 1:1).

NAIL* (NAILING)

Jn 20:25 "Unless I see the *n* marks

NAILING* (NAIL)

Ac   2:23 him to death by *n* him to the cross.
Col 2:14 he took it away, *n* it to the cross.

NAIVE

Ro 16:18 they deceive the minds of *n* people.

NAKED

Ge   2:25 The man and his wife were both *n*,
Job 1:21 *N* I came from my mother's womb,
Isa 58: 7 when you see the *n*, to clothe him,
2Co 5: 3 are clothed, we will not be found *n*.

NAME (NAMES)

Ge   2:19 man to see what he would *n* them;
     4:26 to call on the *n* of the LORD.
    11: 4 so that we may make a *n*
    12: 2 I will make your *n* great,
    32:29 Jacob said, "Please tell me your *n*."
Ex   3:15 This is my *n* forever, the *n*
    20: 7 "You shall not misuse the *n*
    34:14 for the LORD, whose *n* is Jealous,
Lev 24:11 Israelite woman blasphemed the *N*
Dt   5:11 "You shall not misuse the *n*
    12:11 choose as a dwelling for his *N*—
    18: 5 minister in the LORD's *n* always.
    25: 6 carry on the *n* of the dead brother
    28:58 this glorious and awesome *n*—
Jos 7: 9 do for your own great *n*?"
Jdg 13:17 "What is your *n*, so that we may
1Sa 12:22 of his great *n* the LORD will not
2Sa 6: 2 which is called by the *N*, the name
     7: 9 Now I will make your *n* great,
1Ki 5: 5 will build the temple for my *N*.'
     8:29 you said, 'My *N* shall be there,'
1Ch 17: 8 I will make your *n* like the names
2Ch 7:14 my people, who are called by my *n*,
Ne   9:10 You made a *n* for yourself,
Ps   8: 1 how majestic is your *n*
     9:10 Those who know your *n* will trust
    20: 7 in the *n* of the LORD our God.
    29: 2 to the LORD the glory due his *n*;
    34: 3 let us exalt his *n* together.
    44:20 If we had forgotten the *n*
    66: 2 Sing the glory of his *n*;
    68: 4 Sing to God, sing praise to his *n*,
    79: 9 for the glory of your *n*;
    96: 8 to the LORD the glory due his *n*;
   103: 1 my inmost being, praise his holy *n*.
   115: 1 but to your *n* be the glory,
   138: 2 your *n* and your word.
   145: 1 I will praise your *n* for ever
   147: 4 and calls them each by *n*.
Pr   3: 4 you will win favor and a good *n*
    18:10 *n* of the LORD is a strong tower;
    22: 1 A good *n* is more desirable
    30: 4 What is his *n*, and the *n* of his son?
Ecc 7: 1 A good *n* is better
SS   1: 3 your *n* is like perfume poured out.
Isa 12: 4 thanks to the LORD, call on his *n*;
    26: 8 your *n* and renown
    40:26 and calls them each by *n*.
    42: 8 "I am the LORD; that is my *n*!
    56: 5 I will give them an everlasting *n*
    57:15 who lives forever, whose *n* is holy:
    63:14 to make for yourself a glorious *n*.
Jer 14: 7 do something for the sake of your *n*
    15:16 for I bear your *n*,
Eze 20: 9 of my *n* I did what would keep it
    20:14 of my *n* I did what would keep it
    20:22 of my *n* I did what would keep it
Da 12: 1 everyone whose *n* is found written
Hos 12: 5 the LORD is his *n* of renown!
Joel 2:32 on the *n* of the LORD will be saved
Mic 5: 4 in the majesty of the *n*
Zep 3: 9 call on the *n* of the LORD
Zec 6:12 is the man whose *n* is the Branch,

Zec 14: 9 one LORD, and his *n* the only *n*.
Mal 1: 6 O priests, who show contempt for my *n*.
Mt   1: 21 and you are to give him the *n* Jesus,
       6: 9 hallowed be your *n*,
      18: 20 or three come together in my *n*,
      24: 5 For many will come in my *n*,
      28: 19 them in the *n* of the Father
Mk   9: 41 gives you a cup of water in my *n*
Lk 11: 2 hallowed be your *n*,
Jn 10: 3 He calls his own sheep by *n*
      14: 13 I will do whatever you ask in my *n*,
      16: 24 asked for anything in my *n*.
Ac   2: 21 on the *n* of the Lord will be saved.'
       4: 12 for there is no other *n*
Ro 10: 13 "Everyone who calls on the *n*
Php 2: 9 him the *n* that is above every *n*,
       2: 10 at the *n* of Jesus every knee should
Col 3: 17 do it all in the *n* of the Lord Jesus,
Heb 1: 4 as the *n* he has inherited is superior
Jas 5: 14 him with oil in the *n* of the Lord.
1Jn 5: 13 believe in the *n* of the Son of God
Rev 2: 17 stone with a new *n* written on it,
       3: 5 I will never blot out his *n*
       3: 12 I will also write on him my new *n*,
      19: 13 and his *n* is the Word of God.
      20: 15 If anyone's *n* was not found written

NAMES (NAME)

Ex 28: 9 engrave on them the *n* of the sons
Lk 10: 20 but rejoice that your *n* are written
Php 4: 3 whose *n* are in the book of life.
Heb 12: 23 whose *n* are written in heaven.
Rev 21: 27 but only those whose *n* are written

NAOMI

Wife of Elimelech, mother-in-law of Ruth (Ru 1:2, 4). Left Bethlehem for Moab during famine (Ru 1:1). Returned a widow, with Ruth (Ru 1:6-22). Advised Ruth to seek marriage with Boaz (Ru 2:17-3:4). Cared for Ruth's son Obed (Ru 4:13-17).

NAPHTALI

Son of Jacob by Bilhah (Ge 30:8; 35:25; 1Ch 2:2). Tribe of blessed (Ge 49:21; Dt 33:23), numbered (Nu 1:43; 26:50), allotted land (Jos 19:32-39; Eze 48:3), failed to fully possess (Jdg 1:33), supported Deborah (Jdg 4:10; 5:18), David (1Ch 12:34), 12,000 from (Rev 7:6).

NARROW

Mt   7: 13 "Enter through the *n* gate.
       7: 14 and *n* the road that leads to life,

NATHAN

Prophet and chronicler of Israel's history (1Ch 29:29; 2Ch 9:29). Announced the Davidic covenant (2Sa 7; 1Ch 17). Denounced David's sin with Bathsheba (2Sa 12). Supported Solomon (1Ki 1).

NATHANAEL*

Apostle (Jn 1:45-49; 21:2). Probably also called Bartholomew (Mt 10:3).

NATION (NATIONS)

Ge 12: 2 "I will make you into a great *n*
Ex 19: 6 a kingdom of priests and a holy *n*.'
Dt   4: 7 What other *n* is so great
Jos 5: 8 And after the whole *n* had been
2Sa 7: 23 one *n* on earth that God went out
Ps 33: 12 Blessed is the *n* whose God is
Pr 11: 14 For lack of guidance a *n* falls,
      14: 34 Righteousness exalts a *n*,
Isa 2: 4 *N* will not take up sword
      26: 2 that the righteous *n* may enter,
      60: 12 For the *n* or kingdom that will not
      65: 1 To a *n* that did not call on my name
      66: 8 a *n* be brought forth in a moment?
Mic 4: 3 *N* will not take up sword
Mt 24: 7 *N* will rise against *n*,
Mk 13: 8 *N* will rise against *n*,
1Pe 2: 9 a royal priesthood, a holy *n*,
Rev 5: 9 and language and people and *n*.
       7: 9 from every *n*, tribe, people
      14: 6 to every *n*, tribe, language

NATIONS (NATION)

Ge 17: 4 You will be the father of many *n*.
      18: 18 and all *n* on earth will be blessed
Ex 19: 5 of all *n* you will be my treasured
Lev 20: 26 apart from the *n* to be my own.
Dt   7: 1 drives out before you many *n*—
      15: 6 You will rule over many *n*
Jdg 3: 1 These are the *n* the LORD left
2Ch 20: 6 rule over all the kingdoms of the *n*.
Ne   1: 8 I will scatter you among the *n*,
Ps   2: 1 Why do the *n* conspire
       2: 8 I will make the *n* your inheritance,
       9: 5 You have rebuked the *n*
      22: 28 and he rules over the *n*.
      46: 10 I will be exalted among the *n*,
      47: 8 God reigns over the *n*;
      66: 7 his eyes watch the *n*—
      67: 2 your salvation among all *n*.
      68: 30 Scatter the *n* who delight in war.
      72: 17 All *n* will be blessed through him,
      96: 3 Declare his glory among the *n*,
      99: 2 he is exalted over all the *n*.
     106: 35 but they mingled with the *n*
     110: 6 He will judge the *n*, heaping up
     113: 4 The LORD is exalted over all the *n*
Isa 2: 2 and all *n* will stream to it.
      11: 10 the *n* will rally to him,
      12: 4 among the *n* what he has done,
      40: 15 Surely the *n* are like a drop
      42: 1 and he will bring justice to the *n*.
      51: 4 justice will become a light to the *n*.
      52: 15 so will he sprinkle many *n*,
      56: 7 a house of prayer for all *n*.''
      60: 3 *N* will come to your light,
      66: 18 and gather all *n* and tongues,
Jer 1: 5 you as a prophet to the *n*.''
       3: 17 and all *n* will gather in Jerusalem
      31: 10 "Hear the word of the LORD, O *n*;
      33: 9 and honor before all *n*
      46: 28 I completely destroy all the *n*
Eze 22: 4 you an object of scorn to the *n*
      34: 13 I will bring them out from the *n*
      36: 23 *n* will know that I am the LORD,
      37: 22 and they will never again be two *n*
      39: 21 I will display my glory among the *n*
Hos 7: 8 "Ephraim mixes with the *n*;
Joel 2: 17 a byword among the *n*.
       3: 2 I will gather all *n*
Am   9: 12 and all the *n* that bear my name,''
Zep 3: 8 I have decided to assemble the *n*,
Hag 2: 7 and the desired of all *n* will come,
Zec 8: 13 an object of cursing among the *n*,
       8: 23 *n* will take firm hold of one Jew
       9: 10 He will proclaim peace to the *n*.
Mt 12: 18 I will gather all the *n* to Jerusalem
      12: 18 he will proclaim justice to the *n*.
      24: 9 and you will be hated by all *n*
      24: 14 whole world as a testimony to all *n*,
      25: 32 All the *n* will be gathered
      28: 19 and make disciples of all *n*,
Mk 11: 17 a house of prayer for all *n*'?
Ac   4: 25 " 'Why do the *n* rage
Ro 15: 12 who will arise to rule over the *n*;
Gal 3: 8 All *n* will be blessed through you.''
1Ti 3: 16 was preached among the *n*,
Rev 15: 4 All *n* will come
      21: 24 The *n* will walk by its light,
      22: 2 are for the healing of the *n*.

NATURAL (NATURE)

Ro   6: 19 you are weak in your *n* selves.
1Co 15: 44 If there is a *n* body, there is

NATURE (NATURAL)

Ro   1: 20 his eternal power and divine *n*—
       7: 18 lives in me, that is, in my sinful *n*.
       8: 4 do not live according to the sinful *n*
       8: 5 to have their minds set
       8: 8 by the sinful *n* cannot please God.
      13: 14 to gratify the desires of the sinful *n*.
Gal 5: 13 freedom to indulge the sinful *n*;
       5: 19 The acts of the sinful *n* are obvious:
       5: 24 Jesus have crucified the sinful *n*
Php 2: 6 Who, being in very *n* God,
Col 3: 5 whatever belongs to your earthly *n*
2Pe 1: 4 you may participate in the divine *n*

NAZARENE* (NAZARETH)

Mt   2: 23 prophets: "He will be called a *N*.''
Mk 14: 67 "You also were with that *N*, Jesus,''
      16: 6 "You are looking for Jesus the *N*,
Ac 24: 5 He is a ringleader of the *N* sect and

NAZARETH (NAZARENE)

Mt   4: 13 Leaving *N*, he went and lived
Lk   4: 16 to *N*, where he had been brought
Jn   1: 46 "*N*! Can anything good come

NAZIRITE

Nu   6: 2 of separation to the LORD as a *N*,
Jdg 13: 7 because the boy will be a *N* of God

NEBO

Dt 34: 1 Then Moses climbed Mount *N*

NEBUCHADNEZZAR

Babylonian king. Subdued and exiled Judah (2Ki 24-25; 2Ch 36; Jer 39). Dreams interpreted by Daniel (Da 2; 4). Worshiped God (Da 3:28-29; 4:34-37).

NECESSARY*

Ac   1: 21 Therefore it is *n* to choose one
Ro 13: 5 it is *n* to submit to the authorities,
2Co 9: 5 I thought it *n* to urge the brothers
Php 1: 24 it is more *n* for you that I remain
       2: 25 But I think it is *n* to send back
Heb 8: 3 and so it was *n* for this one
       9: 16 it is *n* to prove the death
       9: 23 It was *n*, then, for the copies

NECK (STIFF-NECKED)

Pr   3: 22 an ornament to grace your *n*.
       6: 21 fasten them around your *n*.
Mt 18: 6 a large millstone hung around his *n*

NECO

Pharaoh who killed Josiah (2Ki 23:29-30; 2Ch 35:20-22), deposed Jehoahaz (2Ki 23:33-35; 2Ch 36:3-4).

NEED (NEEDS NEEDY)

1Ki 8: 59 Israel according to each day's *n*,
Ps 79: 8 for we are in desperate *n*.
     116: 6 when I was in great *n*, he saved me.
     142: 6 for I am in desperate *n*,
Mt   6: 8 for your Father knows what you *n*
Lk 15: 14 country, and he began to be in *n*.
Ac   2: 45 they gave to anyone as he had *n*.
Ro 12: 13 with God's people who are in *n*.
1Co 12: 21 say to the hand, "I don't *n* you!''
Eph 4: 28 something to share with those in *n*.
1Ti 5: 3 to those widows who are really in *n*
Heb 4: 16 grace to help us in our time of *n*.
1Jn 3: 17 sees his brother in *n* but has no pity

NEEDLE

Mt 19: 24 go through the eye of a *n*

NEEDS (NEED)

Isa 58: 11 he will satisfy your *n*
Php 2: 25 sent to take care of my *n*,
       4: 19 God will meet all your *n* according
Jas 2: 16 does nothing about his physical *n*,

NEEDY (NEED)

Dt 15: 11 toward the poor and *n* in your land.
1Sa 2: 8 and lifts the *n* from the ash heap;
Ps 35: 10 and *n* from those who rob them.''
      69: 33 The LORD hears the *n*
      72: 12 he will deliver the *n* who cry out,
     140: 12 and upholds the cause of the *n*.
Pr 14: 21 blessed is he who is kind to the *n*.
      14: 31 to the *n* honors God.
      22: 22 and do not crush the *n* in court,
      31: 9 defend the rights of the poor and *n*
      31: 20 and extends her hands to the *n*.
Mt   6: 2 "So when you give to the *n*,

NEGLECT* (NEGLECTED)

Dt 12: 19 Be careful not to *n* the Levites
      14: 27 And do not *n* the Levites living
Ezr 4: 22 Be careful not to *n* this matter.
Ne 10: 39 We will not *n* the house of our God
Est 6: 10 Do not *n* anything you have

Ps 119: 16 I will not *n* your word.
Lk 11: 42 you *n* justice and the love of God.
Ac   6: 2 for us to *n* the ministry of the word
1Ti 4: 14 Do not *n* your gift, which was

NEGLECTED (NEGLECT)

Mt 23: 23 But you have *n* the more important

NEHEMIAH

Cupbearer of Artaxerxes (Ne 2:1); governor of Israel (Ne 8:9). Returned to Jerusalem to rebuild walls (Ne 2-6). With Ezra, reestablished worship (Ne 8). Prayer confessing nation's sin (Ne 9). Dedicated wall (Ne 12).

NEIGHBOR (NEIGHBOR'S)

Ex 20: 16 give false testimony against your *n*.
        20: 17 or anything that belongs to your *n*
Lev 19: 13 Do not defraud your *n* or rob him.
        19: 17 Rebuke your *n* frankly
        19: 18 but love your *n* as yourself.
Ps 15: 3 who does his *n* no wrong
Pr 3: 29 Do not plot harm against your *n*,
       11: 12 who lacks judgment derides his *n*,
       14: 21 He who despises his *n* sins,
       16: 29 A violent man entices his *n*
       24: 28 against your *n* without cause,
       25: 18 gives false testimony against his *n*.
       27: 10 better a *n* nearby than a brother far
       27: 14 If a man loudly blesses his *n*
       29: 5 Whoever flatters his *n*
Jer 31: 34 No longer will a man teach his *n*,
Zec 8: 17 do not plot evil against your *n*,
Mt 5: 43 Love your *n* and hate your enemy.'
       19: 19 and 'love your *n* as yourself.' "
Mk 12: 31 The second is this: 'Love your *n*
Lk 10: 27 and, 'Love your *n* as yourself.' "
       10: 29 who is my *n*?' In reply Jesus said:
Ro 13: 9 "Love your *n* as yourself."
       13: 10 Love does no harm to its *n*.
       15: 2 Each of us should please his *n*
Gal 5: 14 "Love your *n* as yourself."
Eph 4: 25 and speak truthfully to his *n*,
Heb 8: 11 No longer will a man teach his *n*,
Jas 2: 8 "Love your *n* as yourself,"

NEIGHBOR'S (NEIGHBOR)

Ex 20: 17 You shall not covet your *n* wife,
Dt 5: 21 not set your desire on your *n* house
       19: 14 not move your *n* boundary stone
       27: 17 who moves his *n* boundary stone."
Pr 25: 17 Seldom set foot in your *n* house—

NESTS

Mt 8: 20 and birds of the air have *n*,

NET (NETS)

Pr 1: 17 How useless to spread a *n*
Hab 1: 15 he catches them in his *n*,
Mt 13: 47 of heaven is like a *n* that was let
Jn 21: 6 "Throw your *n* on the right side

NETS (NET)

Ps 141: 10 Let the wicked fall into their own *n*
Mt 4: 20 once they left their *n*
Lk 5: 4 and let down the *n* for a catch."

NEVER-FAILING*

Am 5: 24 righteousness like a *n* stream!

NEW

Ps 40: 3 He put a song in my mouth;
   98: 1 Sing to the LORD a *n* song,
Ecc 1: 9 there is nothing *n* under the sun.
Isa 42: 9 *n* things I declare;
   62: 2 you will be called by a *n* name
   65: 17 *n* heavens and a *n* earth.
   66: 22 "As the *n* heavens and the *n* earth
Jer 31: 31 "when I will make a *n* covenant
La 3: 23 They are *n* every morning;
Eze 11: 19 undivided heart and put a *n* spirit
   18: 31 and get a *n* heart and a *n* spirit.
   36: 26 give you a *n* heart and put a *n* spirit
Zep 3: 5 and every *n* day he does not fail,
Mt 9: 17 Neither do men pour *n* wine
Mk 16: 17 they will speak in *n* tongues;
Lk 5: 39 after drinking old wine wants the *n*
   22: 20 "This cup is the *n* covenant

Jn 13: 34 "A *n* commandment I give you:
Ac 5: 20 the full message of this *n* life."
Ro 6: 4 the Father, we too may live a *n* life.
1Co 5: 7 old yeast that you may be a *n* batch
   11: 25 "This cup is the *n* covenant
2Co 3: 6 as ministers of a *n* covenant—
    5: 17 he is a *n* creation; the old has gone,
Gal 6: 15 what counts is a *n* creation.
Eph 4: 23 to be made *n* in the attitude
    4: 24 and to put on the *n* self, created
Col 3: 10 and have put on the *n* self,
Heb 8: 8 when I will make a *n* covenant
    9: 15 is the mediator of a *n* covenant,
   10: 20 by a *n* and living way opened for us
   12: 24 Jesus the mediator of a *n* covenant,
1Pe 1: 3 great mercy he has given us *n* birth
2Pe 3: 13 to a *n* heaven and a *n* earth,
1Jn 2: 8 Yet I am writing you a *n* command;
Rev 2: 17 stone with a *n* name written on it,
    3: 12 the *n* Jerusalem, which is coming
   21: 1 I saw a *n* heaven and a *n* earth,

NEWBORN (BEAR)

1Pe 2: 2 Like *n* babies, crave pure spiritual

NEWS

2Ki 7: 9 This is a day of good *n*
Ps 112: 7 He will have no fear of bad *n*;
Pr 15: 30 good *n* gives health to the bones.
   25: 25 is good *n* from a distant land.
Isa 52: 7 the feet of those who bring good *n*,
   61: 1 me to preach good *n* to the poor.
Na 1: 15 the feet of one who brings good *n*,
Mt 4: 23 preaching the good *n*
    9: 35 preaching the good *n*
   11: 5 the good *n* is preached to the poor.
Mk 1: 15 Repent and believe the good *n*!"
   16: 15 preach the good *n* to all creation.
Lk 1: 19 and to tell you this good *n*.
    2: 10 I bring you good *n*
    3: 18 and preached the good *n* to them.
    4: 43 "I must preach the good *n*
    8: 1 proclaiming the good *n*
   16: 16 the good *n* of the kingdom
Ac 5: 42 proclaiming the good *n* that Jesus
   10: 36 telling the good *n* of peace
   14: 7 continued to preach the good *n*.
   14: 21 They preached the good *n*
   17: 18 preaching the good *n* about Jesus
Ro 10: 15 feet of those who bring good *n*!"

NICODEMUS*

Pharisee who visted Jesus at night (Jn 3). Argued fair treatment of Jesus (Jn 7:50-52). With Joseph, prepared Jesus for burial (Jn 19:38-42).

NIGHT (NIGHTS NIGHTTIME)

Ge 1: 5 and the darkness he called "*n*."
    1: 16 and the lesser light to govern the *n*.
Ex 13: 21 and by *n* in a pillar of fire
   14: 24 During the last watch of the *n*.
Dt 28: 66 filled with dread both *n* and day,
Jos 1: 8 and *n*, so that you may be careful
Job 35: 10 who gives songs in the *n*,
Ps 1: 2 on his law he meditates day and *n*,
   19: 2 after *n* they display knowledge.
   42: 8 at *n* his song is with me—
   63: 6 of you through the watches of the *n*
   77: 6 I remembered my songs in the *n*.
   90: 4 or like a watch in the *n*.
   91: 5 You will not fear the terror of *n*,
   119:148 through the watches of the *n*,
   121: 6 nor the moon by *n*.
   136: 9 the moon and stars to govern the *n*;
Pr 31: 18 and her lamp does not go out at *n*.
Isa 21: 11 Watchman, what is left of the *n*?"
   58: 10 and your *n* will become like
Jer 33: 20 and my covenant with the *n*,
Lk 2: 8 watch over their flocks at *n*.
    6: 12 and spent the *n* praying to God.
Jn 3: 2 He came to Jesus at *n* and said,
    9: 4 *N* is coming, when no one can work
1Th 5: 2 Lord will come like a thief in the *n*.
    5: 5 We do not belong to the *n*
Rev 21: 25 for there will be no *n* there.

NIGHTS (NIGHT)

Jnh 1: 17 the fish three days and three *n*.

Mt 4: 2 After fasting forty days and forty *n*
   12: 40 three *n* in the belly of a huge fish,
2Co 6: 5 in hard work, sleepless *n*

NIGHTTIME* (NIGHT)

Zec 14: 7 or *n*— a day known to the LORD.

NIMROD

Ge 10: 9 "Like *N*, a mighty hunter

NINEVEH

Jnh 1: 2 "Go to the great city of *N*
Na 1: 1 An oracle concerning *N*.
Mt 12: 41 The men of *N* will stand up

NOAH

Righteous man (Eze 14:14, 20) called to build ark (Ge 6-8; Heb 11:7; 1Pe 3:20; 2Pe 2:5). God's covenant with (Ge 9:1-17). Drunkenness of (Ge 9:18-23). Blessed sons, cursed Canaan (Ge 9:24-27).

NOBLE

Ru 3: 11 you are a woman of *n* character.
Ps 45: 1 My heart is stirred by a *n* theme
Pr 12: 4 of *n* character is her husband's
   31: 10 A wife of *n* character who can find?
   31: 29 "Many women do *n* things,"
Isa 32: 8 But the *n* man makes *n* plans,
Lk 8: 15 good soil stands for those with a *n*
Ro 9: 21 of clay some pottery for *n* purposes
Php 4: 8 whatever is *n*, whatever is right,
2Ti 2: 20 some are for *n* purposes

NOSTRILS

Ge 2: 7 and breathed into his *n* the breath
Ex 15: 8 By the blast of your *n*
Ps 18: 15 at the blast of breath from your *n*.

NOTE

Ac 4: 13 and they took *n* that these men had
Php 3: 17 take *n* of those who live according

NOTHING

2Sa 24: 24 offerings that cost me *n*."
Ne 9: 21 in the desert; they lacked *n*,
Ps 73: 25 earth has *n* I desire besides you
Jer 32: 17 *N* is too hard for you
Jn 15: 5 apart from me you can do *n*.

NOURISH

Pr 10: 21 The lips of the righteous *n* many,

NULLIFY

Mt 15: 6 Thus you *n* the word of God
Ro 3: 31 Do we, then, *n* the law by this faith

OATH

Ex 33: 1 up to the land I promised on *o*
Nu 30: 2 or takes an *o* to obligate himself
Dt 6: 18 promised on *o* to your forefathers,
    7: 8 and kept the *o* he swore
   29: 12 you this day and sealing with an *o*,
Ps 95: 11 So I declared on *o* in my anger,
   119:106 I have taken an *o* and confirmed it,
   132: 11 The LORD swore an *o* to David,
Ecc 8: 2 because you took an *o* before God.
Mt 5: 33 'Do not break your *o*, but keep
Heb 7: 20 And it was not without an *o*!

OBADIAH

1. Believer who sheltered 100 prophets from Jezebel (1Ki 18:1-16).
2. Prophet against Edom (Ob 1).

OBEDIENCE* (OBEY)

Ge 49: 10 and the *o* of the nations is his.
Jdg 2: 17 of *o* to the LORD's commands.
1Ch 21: 19 So David went up in *o*
2Ch 31: 21 in *o* to the law and the commands,
Pr 30: 17 that scorns *o* to a mother,
Lk 23: 56 Sabbath in *o* to the commandment.
Ac 21: 24 but that you yourself are living in *o*
Ro 1: 5 to the *o* that comes from faith.
    5: 19 also through the *o* of the one man
    6: 16 to *o*, which leads to righteousness?
   16: 19 Everyone has heard about your *o*,
2Co 9: 13 for the *o* that accompanies your
   10: 6 once your *o* is complete.

Phm : 21 Confident of your *o*, I write to you,
Heb 5: 8 he learned *o* from what he suffered
1Pe 1: 2 for *o* to Jesus Christ and sprinkling
2Jn : 6 that we walk in *o* to his commands.

OBEDIENT* (OBEY)

Dt 30: 17 heart turns away and you are not *o*,
Isa 1: 19 If you are willing and *o*,
Lk 2: 51 with them and was *o* to them.
Ac 6: 7 of priests became *o* to the faith.
2Co 2: 9 if you would stand the test and be *o*
     7: 15 he remembers that you are all *o*,
     10: 5 thought to make it *o* to Christ.
Php 2: 8 and became *o* to death—
Tit 3: 1 to be *o*, to be ready
1Pe 1: 14 As *o* children, do not conform

OBEY (OBEDIENCE OBEDIENT OBEYED OBEYING OBEYS)

Ex 12: 24 "*O* these instructions as a lasting
    19: 5 Now if you *o* me fully and keep my
    24: 7 the LORD has said; we will *o*."
Lev 18: 4 You must *o* my laws and be careful
    25: 18 and be careful to *o* my laws,
Nu 15: 40 remember to *o* all my commands
Dt 5: 27 We will listen and *o*."
     6: 3 careful to *o* so that it may go well
     6: 24 us to *o* all these decrees
    11: 13 if you faithfully *o* the commands I
    12: 28 to *o* all these regulations I am
    13: 4 Keep his commands and *o* him;
    21: 18 son who does not *o* his father
    28: 1 If you fully *o* the LORD your God
    28: 15 if you do not *o* the LORD your
    30: 2 and *o* him with all your heart
    30: 10 if you *o* the LORD your God
    30: 14 and in your heart so you may *o* it.
    32: 46 children to *o* carefully all the words
Jos 1: 7 to *o* all the law my servant Moses
    22: 5 in all his ways, to *o* his commands,
    24: 24 the LORD our God and *o* him."
1Sa 15: 22 To *o* is better than sacrifice,
1Ki 8: 61 by his decrees and *o* his commands
2Ki 17: 13 that I commanded your fathers to *o*
2Ch 34: 31 and to *o* the words of the covenant
Ne 1: 5 who love him and *o* his commands,
Ps 103: 18 and remember to *o* his precepts.
    103: 20 who *o* his word.
    119: 17 I will *o* your word.
    119: 34 and it with all my heart.
    119: 57 I have promised to *o* your words.
    119: 67 but now I *o* your word.
    119:100 for I *o* your precepts.
    119:129 therefore I *o* them.
    119:167 I *o* your statutes,
Pr 5: 13 I would not *o* my teachers
Jer 7: 23 I gave them this command: *O* me,
    11: 4 '*O* me and do everything I
    11: 7 and again, saying, "*O* me."
    42: 6 we will *o* the LORD our God,
Da 9: 4 who love him and *o* his commands,
Mt 8: 27 the winds and the waves *o* him!"
    19: 17 to enter life, *o* the commandments
    28: 20 to *o* everything I have commanded
Lk 11: 28 hear the word of God and *o* it."
Jn 14: 15 you will *o* what I command.
    14: 23 loves me, he will *o* my teaching.
    14: 24 not love me will not *o* my teaching.
    15: 10 If you *o* my commands, you will
Ac 5: 29 "We must *o* God rather than men!
    5: 32 given to those who *o* him."
Ro 2: 13 it is those who *o* the law who will
     6: 12 body so that you *o* its evil desires.
     6: 16 slaves to the one whom you *o*—
     6: 16 yourselves to someone to *o* him
    15: 18 in leading the Gentiles to *o* God
    16: 26 nations might believe and *o* him—
Gal 5: 3 obligated to *o* the whole law.
Eph 6: 1 *o* your parents in the Lord,
     6: 5 *o* your earthly masters with respect
Col 3: 20 *o* your parents in everything,
    3: 22 *o* your earthly masters
2Th 3: 14 anyone does not *o* our instruction
1Ti 3: 4 and see that his children *o* him
Heb 5: 9 eternal salvation for all who *o* him
    13: 17 *O* your leaders and submit
1Pe 4: 17 for those who do not *o* the gospel
1Jn 3: 24 Those who *o* his commands live

1Jn 5: 3 love for God: to *o* his commands.
Rev 12: 17 those who *o* God's commandments
    14: 12 the saints who *o* God's

OBEYED (OBEY)

Ge 22: 18 blessed, because you have *o* me.
Jos 1: 17 we fully *o* Moses, so we will obey
Ps 119: 4 that are to be fully *o*.
Da 9: 10 we have not *o* the LORD our God
Jnh 3: 3 Jonah *o* the word of the LORD
Mic 5: 15 the nations that have not *o*."
Jn 15: 10 as I have *o* my Father's commands
    15: 20 If they *o* my teaching, they will
    17: 6 and they have *o* your word.
Ac 7: 53 through angels but have not *o* it."
Ro 6: 17 you wholeheartedly *o* the form
Php 2: 12 as you have always *o*— not only
Heb 11: 8 *o* and went, even though he did not
1Pe 3: 6 who *o* Abraham and called him her

OBEYING (OBEY)

1Sa 15: 22 as in *o* the voice of the LORD?
Ps 119: 5 steadfast in *o* your decrees!
Gal 5: 7 and kept you from *o* the truth?
1Pe 1: 22 purified yourselves by *o* the truth

OBEYS (OBEY)

Lev 18: 5 for the man who *o* them will live
Pr 19: 16 He who *o* instructions guards his
Eze 20: 11 for the man who *o* them will live
Jn 14: 21 has my commands and *o* them,
Ro 2: 27 and yet *o* the law will condemn you
1Jn 2: 5 if anyone *o* his word, God's love is

OBLIGATED (OBLIGATION)

Ro 1: 14 I am *o* both to Greeks
Gal 5: 3 himself be circumcised that he is *o*

OBLIGATION (OBLIGATED)

Ro 8: 12 Therefore, brothers, we have an *o*

OBSCENITY*

Eph 5: 4 Nor should there be *o*, foolish talk

OBSCURES*

Job 42: 3 'Who is this that *o* my counsel

OBSERVE (OBSERVING)

Ex 31: 13 'You must *o* my Sabbaths.
Lev 25: 2 the land itself must *o* a sabbath
Dt 4: 6 *O* them carefully, for this will show
     5: 12 "*O* the Sabbath day
     8: 6 *O* the commands of the LORD
    11: 22 If you carefully *o* all these
    26: 16 carefully *o* them with all your heart
Ps 37: 37 the blameless, *o* the upright;

OBSERVING (OBSERVE)

Ro 3: 27 principle? On that of *o* the law?
Gal 2: 16 a man is not justified by *o* the law,
    3: 2 you receive the Spirit by *o* the law,
    3: 10 All who rely on *o* the law are

OBSOLETE

Heb 8: 13 he has made the first one *o*;

OBSTACLE* (OBSTACLES)

Ro 14: 13 or *o* in your brother's way.

OBSTACLES (OBSTACLE)

Ro 16: 17 put *o* in your way that are contrary

OBSTINATE

Isa 65: 2 hands to an *o* people,
Ro 10: 21 to a disobedient and *o* people."

OBTAIN (OBTAINED OBTAINS)

Ro 11: 7 sought so earnestly it did not *o*,
2Ti 2: 10 they too may *o* the salvation that

OBTAINED (OBTAIN)

Ro 9: 30 not pursue righteousness, have *o* it,
Php 3: 12 Not that I have already *o* all this,
Heb 9: 12 having *o* eternal redemption.

OBTAINS* (OBTAIN)

Pr 12: 2 A good man *o* favor

OBVIOUS*

Mt 6: 18 so that it will not be *o*
Gal 5: 19 The acts of the sinful nature are *o*:
1Ti 5: 24 The sins of some men are *o*,
     5: 25 In the same way, good deeds are *o*,

OCCASIONS

Eph 6: 18 in the Spirit on all *o* with all kinds

OFFENDED (OFFENSE)

Pr 18: 19 An *o* brother is more unyielding

OFFENDERS* (OFFENSE)

1Co 6: 9 nor homosexual *o* nor thieves

OFFENSE (OFFENDED OFFENDERS OFFENSES OFFENSIVE)

Pr 17: 9 over an *o* promotes love,
    19: 11 it is to his glory to overlook an *o*.
Gal 5: 11 In that case the *o* of the cross has

OFFENSES (OFFENSE)

Isa 44: 22 swept away your *o* like a cloud,
    59: 12 For our *o* are many in your sight,
Eze 18: 30 Repent! Turn away from all your *o*;
    33: 10 "Our *o* and sins weigh us down,

OFFENSIVE (OFFENSE)

Ps 139: 24 See if there is any *o* way in me,

OFFER (OFFERED OFFERING OFFERINGS OFFERS)

Ps 4: 5 *O* right sacrifices
Ro 6: 13 Do not *o* the parts of your body
    12: 1 to *o* your bodies as living sacrifices,
Heb 9: 25 he enter heaven to *o* himself again
    13: 15 therefore, let us continually *o*

OFFERED (OFFER)

Isa 50: 6 I *o* my back to those who beat me,
1Co 9: 13 share in what is *o* on the altar?
    10: 20 of pagans are *o* to demons,
Heb 7: 27 once for all when he *o* himself.
    9: 14 the eternal Spirit *o* himself
    11: 4 By faith Abel *o* God a better
    11: 17 when God tested him, *o* Isaac
Jas 5: 15 prayer *o* in faith will make the sick

OFFERING (OFFER)

Ge 4: 3 of the soil as an *o* to the LORD.
    22: 2 a burnt *o* on one of the mountains I
    22: 8 provide the lamb for the burnt *o*,
Ex 29: 24 before the LORD as a wave *o*.
    29: 40 quarter of a hin of wine as a drink *o*.
Lev 1: 3 If the *o* is a burnt *o* from the herd,
     2: 4 "If you bring a grain *o* baked
     3: 1 "If someone's *o* is a fellowship *o*,
     4: 3 a sin *o* for the sin he has committed
     5: 15 It is a guilt *o*.
     7: 37 ordination *o* and the fellowship *o*,
     9: 24 and consumed the burnt *o*
    22: 18 to fulfill a vow or as a freewill *o*,
    22: 21 a special vow or as a freewill *o*,
1Sa 13: 9 And Saul offered up the burnt *o*.
1Ch 21: 26 from heaven on the altar of burnt *o*.
2Ch 7: 1 and consumed the burnt *o*
Ps 40: 6 Sacrifice and *o* you did not desire,
    116: 17 I will sacrifice a thank *o* to you
Isa 53: 10 the LORD makes his life a guilt *o*,
Mt 5: 23 if you are *o* your gift at the altar
Ro 8: 3 likeness of sinful man to be a sin *o*.
Eph 5: 2 as a fragrant *o* and sacrifice to God.
Php 2: 17 I am being poured out like a drink *o*
     4: 18 are a fragrant *o*, an acceptable
2Ti 4: 6 being poured out like a drink *o*,
Heb 10: 5 "Sacrifice and *o* you did not desire,
1Pe 2: 5 *o* spiritual sacrifices acceptable

OFFERINGS (OFFER)

1Sa 15: 22 Does the LORD delight in burnt *o*
2Ch 35: 7 and goats for the Passover *o*,
Isa 1: 13 Stop bringing meaningless *o*!
Hos 6: 6 of God rather than burnt *o*.
Mal 3: 8 do we rob you?" "In tithes and *o*.
Mk 12: 33 is more important than all burnt *o*
Heb 10: 8 First he said, "Sacrifices and *o*,

OFFERS (OFFER)

Heb 10: 11 and again he *o* the same sacrifices,

OFFICER (OFFICIALS)

2Ti 2: 4 wants to please his commanding *o*.

OFFICIALS (OFFICER)

Ex 5: 21 a stench to Pharaoh and his *o*.
Pr 17: 26 or to flog *o* for their integrity.
29: 12 all his *o* become wicked.

OFFSPRING

Ge 3: 15 and between your *o* and hers;
12: 7 "To your *o* I will give this land."
13: 16 I will make your *o* like the dust
26: 4 and through your *o* all nations
28: 14 blessed through you and your *o*.
Ex 13: 2 The first *o* of every womb
Ru 4: 12 Through the *o* the LORD gives
Isa 44: 3 I will pour out my Spirit on your *o*,
53: 10 he will see his *o* and prolong his
Ac 3: 25 'Through your *o* all peoples
17: 28 own poets have said, 'We are his *o*.'
17: 29 "Therefore since we are God's *o*,
Ro 4: 18 said to him, "So shall your *o* be."
9: 8 who are regarded as Abraham's *o*.

OG

Nu 21: 33 *O* king of Bashan and his whole
Ps 136: 20 and *O* king of Bashan—

OIL

Ex 29: 7 Take the anointing *o* and anoint
30: 25 It will be the sacred anointing *o*.
Dt 14: 23 tithe of your grain, new wine and *o*,
1Sa 10: 1 Then Samuel took a flask of *o*
16: 13 So Samuel took the horn of *o*
1Ki 17: 16 and the jug of *o* did not run dry,
2Ki 4: 6 Then the *o* stopped flowing.
Ps 23: 5 You anoint my head with *o*;
45: 7 by anointing you with the *o* of joy.
104: 15 *o* to make his face shine,
133: 2 It is like precious *o* poured
Pr 21: 17 loves wine and *o* will never be
Isa 1: 6 or soothed with *o*.
61: 3 the *o* of gladness
Mt 25: 3 but did not take any *o* with them.
Heb 1: 9 by anointing you with the *o* of joy."

OLIVE (OLIVES)

Ge 8: 11 beak was a freshly plucked *o* leaf!
Jdg 9: 8 said to the *o* tree, 'Be our king.'
Jer 11: 16 LORD called you a thriving *o* tree
Zec 4: 3 Also there are two *o* trees by it,
Ro 11: 17 and you, though a wild *o* shoot,
11: 24 of an *o* tree that is wild by nature,
Rev 11: 4 These are the two *o* trees

OLIVES (OLIVE)

Zec 14: 4 stand on the Mount of *O*,
Mt 24: 3 sitting on the Mount of *O*,
Jas 3: 12 a fig tree bear *o*, or a grapevine bear

OMEGA*

Rev 1: 8 "I am the Alpha and the *O*,"
21: 6 I am the Alpha and the *O*,
22: 13 I am the Alpha and the *O*,

OMIT*

Jer 26: 2 I command you; do not *o* a word.

OMRI

King of Israel (1Ki 16:21-26).

ONESIMUS*

Col 4: 9 He is coming with *O*, our faithful
Phm : 10 I appeal to you for my son *O*,

ONESIPHORUS*

2Ti 1: 16 mercy to the household of *O*,
4: 19 Aquila and the household of *O*.

ONIONS*

Nu 11: 5 melons, leeks, *o* and garlic.

ONYX

Ex 28: 9 "Take two *o* stones and engrave
28: 20 in the fourth row a chrysolite, an *o*

OPENHANDED* (HAND)

Dt 15: 8 Rather be *o* and freely lend him
15: 11 you to be *o* toward your brothers

OPINIONS*

1Ki 18: 21 will you waver between two *o*?
Pr 18: 2 but delights in airing his own *o*.

OPPONENTS (OPPOSE)

Pr 18: 18 and keeps strong *o* apart.

OPPORTUNE (OPPORTUNITY)

Lk 4: 13 he left him until an *o* time.

OPPORTUNITY* (OPPORTUNE)

1Sa 18: 21 "Now you have a second *o*
Jer 46: 17 he has missed his *o*.'
Mt 26: 16 watched for an *o* to hand him over.
Mk 14: 11 So he watched for an *o* to hand him
Lk 22: 6 and watched for an *o* to hand Jesus
Ac 25: 16 and has had an *o* to defend himself
Ro 7: 8 seizing the *o* afforded
7: 11 seizing the *o* afforded
1Co 16: 12 but he will go when he has the *o*.
2Co 5: 12 are giving you an *o* to take pride
11: 12 from under those who want an *o*
Gal 6: 10 as we have *o*, let us do good
Eph 5: 16 making the most of every *o*,
Php 4: 10 but you had no *o* to show it.
Col 4: 5 make the most of every *o*.
1Ti 5: 14 to give the enemy no *o* for slander.
Heb 11: 15 they would have had *o* to return.

OPPOSE (OPPONENTS OPPOSED OPPOSES OPPOSING OPPOSITION)

Ex 23: 22 and will *o* those who *o* you.
1Sa 2: 10 those who *o* the LORD will be
Job 23: 13 he stands alone, and who can *o* him
Ac 11: 17 I to think that I could *o* God?"
2Ti 2: 25 Those who *o* him he must gently
Tit 1: 9 doctrine and refute those who *o* it.
2: 8 so that those who *o* you may be

OPPOSED (OPPOSE)

Gal 2: 11 to Antioch, I *o* him to his face,
3: 21 therefore, *o* to the promises of God

OPPOSES (OPPOSE)

Jas 4: 6 "God *o* the proud
1Pe 5: 5 because, "God *o* the proud

OPPOSING (OPPOSE)

1Ti 6: 20 the *o* ideas of what is falsely called

OPPOSITION (OPPOSE)

Heb 12: 3 Consider him who endured such *o*

OPPRESS (OPPRESSED OPPRESSES OPPRESSION OPPRESSOR)

Ex 1: 11 masters over them to *o* them
22: 21 "Do not mistreat an alien or *o* him,
Isa 3: 5 People will *o* each other—
Eze 22: 29 they *o* the poor and needy
Da 7: 25 the Most High and *o* his saints
Am 5: 12 You *o* the righteous and take bribes
Zec 7: 10 Do not *o* the widow
Mal 3: 5 who *o* the widows

OPPRESSED (OPPRESS)

Jdg 2: 18 as they groaned under those who *o*
Ps 9: 9 The LORD is a refuge for the *o*,
82: 3 the rights of the poor and *o*,
146: 7 He upholds the cause of the *o*
Pr 16: 19 in spirit and among the *o*
31: 5 and deprive all the *o* of their rights.
Isa 1: 17 encourage the *o*.
53: 7 He was *o* and afflicted,
58: 10 and satisfy the needs of the *o*,
Zec 10: 2 *o* for lack of a shepherd.
Lk 4: 18 to release the *o*,

OPPRESSES (OPPRESS)

Pr 14: 31 He who *o* the poor shows contempt
22: 16 He who *o* the poor
Eze 18: 12 He *o* the poor and needy.

OPPRESSION (OPPRESS)

Ps 12: 5 "Because of the *o* of the weak

Ps 72: 14 He will rescue them from *o*
119:134 Redeem me from the *o* of men,
Isa 53: 8 By *o* and judgment he was taken
58: 9 "If you do away with the yoke of *o*,

OPPRESSOR (OPPRESS)

Ps 72: 4 he will crush the *o*.
Isa 51: 13 For where is the wrath of the *o*?
Jer 22: 3 hand of his *o* the one who has been

ORDAINED

Ps 8: 2 you have *o* praise
111: 9 he *o* his covenant forever—
139: 16 All the days *o* for me
Eze 28: 14 for so I *o* you.
Hab 1: 12 you have *o* them to punish.
Mt 21: 16 you have *o* praise'?"

ORDER (ORDERLY ORDERS)

Nu 9: 23 They obeyed the LORD's *o*,
Ps 110: 4 in the *o* of Melchizedek."
Heb 5: 10 priest in the *o* of Melchizedek.
9: 10 until the time of the new *o*.
Rev 21: 4 for the old *o* of things has passed

ORDERLY (ORDER)

1Co 14: 40 done in a fitting and *o* way.
Col 2: 5 and delight to see how *o* you are

ORDERS (ORDER)

Mk 1: 27 He even gives *o* to evil spirits
3: 12 But he gave them strict *o* not
9: 9 Jesus gave them *o* not

ORDINARY

Ac 4: 13 that they were unschooled, *o* men,

ORGIES*

Ro 13: 13 not in *o* and drunkenness,
Gal 5: 21 drunkenness, *o*, and the like.
1Pe 4: 3 *o*, carousing and detestable

ORIGIN (ORIGINATE ORIGINS)

2Pe 1: 21 For prophecy never had its *o*

ORIGINATE* (ORIGIN)

1Co 14: 36 Did the word of God *o* with you?

ORIGINS* (ORIGIN)

Mic 5: 2 whose *o* are from of old,

ORNAMENT* (ORNAMENTED)

Pr 3: 22 an *o* to grace your neck.
25: 12 of gold or an *o* of fine gold

ORNAMENTED (ORNAMENT)

Ge 37: 3 and he made a richly *o* robe for him

ORPHAN* (ORPHANS)

Ex 22: 22 advantage of a widow or an *o*.

ORPHANS (ORPHAN)

Jn 14: 18 will not leave you as *o*; I will come
Jas 1: 27 to look after *o* and widows

OTHNIEL

Nephew of Caleb (Jos 15:15-19; Jdg 1:12-15).
Judge who freed Israel from Aram (Jdg 3:7-11).

OUTBURSTS*

2Co 12: 20 jealousy, *o* of anger, factions,

OUTCOME

Heb 13: 7 Consider the *o* of their way of life
1Pe 4: 17 what will the *o* be for those who do

OUTNUMBER

Ps 139: 18 they would *o* the grains of sand.

OUTSIDERS*

Col 4: 5 wise in the way you act toward *o*;
1Th 4: 12 daily life may win the respect of *o*
1Ti 3: 7 also have a good reputation with *o*,

OUTSTANDING

SS 5: 10 *o* among ten thousand.
Ro 13: 8 no debt remain *o*,

OUTSTRETCHED

Ex   6: 6 and will redeem you with an *o* arm
Dt   4: 34 by a mighty hand and an *o* arm,
       5: 15 with a mighty hand and an *o* arm
1Ki   8: 42 your mighty hand and your *o* arm
Ps 136: 12 with a mighty hand and *o* arm;
Jer   27: 5 and *o* arm I made the earth
      32: 17 by your great power and *o* arm.
Eze   20: 33 an *o* arm and with outpoured wrath

OUTWEIGHS (WEIGH)

2Co   4: 17 an eternal glory that far *o* them all.

OUTWIT*

2Co   2: 11 in order that Satan might not *o* us.

OVERAWED* (AWE)

Ps   49: 16 Do not be *o* when a man grows rich

OVERBEARING*

Tit   1: 7 not *o*, not quick-tempered,

OVERCAME (OVERCOME)

Rev   3: 21 as I *o* and sat down with my Father
      12: 11 They *o* him

OVERCOME (OVERCAME OVERCOMES)

Mt   16: 18 and the gates of Hades will not *o* it.
Mk   9: 24 I do believe; help me *o* my unbelief
Lk   10: 19 to *o* all the power of the enemy;
Jn   16: 33 But take heart! I have *o* the world.''
Ro   12: 21 Do not be *o* by evil, but *o* evil
2Pe   2: 20 and are again entangled in it and *o*,
1Jn   2: 13 because you have *o* the evil one.
       4: 4 are from God and have *o* them,
       5: 4 is the victory that has *o* the world,
Rev   17: 14 but the Lamb will *o* them

OVERCOMES* (OVERCOME)

1Jn   5: 4 born of God *o* the world.
       5: 5 Who is it that *o* the world?
Rev   2: 7 To him who *o*, I will give the right
       2: 11 He who *o* will not be hurt at all
       2: 17 To him who *o*, I will give some
       2: 26 To him who *o* and does my will
       3: 5 He who *o* will, like them, be
       3: 12 Him who *o* I will make a pillar
       3: 21 To him who *o*, I will give the right
      21: 7 He who *o* will inherit all this,

OVERFLOW (OVERFLOWING OVERFLOWS)

Ps   65: 11 and your carts *o* with abundance.
    119:171 May my lips *o* with praise,
La   1: 16 and my eyes *o* with tears.
Mt   12: 34 out of the *o* of the heart the mouth
Lk   6: 45 out of the *o* of his heart his mouth
Ro   5: 15 Jesus Christ, *o* to the many! Again,
      15: 13 so that you may *o* with hope
2Co   4: 15 to *o* to the glory of God.
1Th   3: 12 *o* for each other and for everyone

OVERFLOWING (OVERFLOW)

Pr   3: 10 then your barns will be filled to *o*,
2Co   8: 2 their *o* joy and their extreme
       9: 12 *o* in many expressions of thanks
Col   2: 7 as you were taught, and *o*

OVERFLOWS* (OVERFLOW)

Ps   23: 5 my cup *o*.
2Co   1: 5 also through Christ our comfort *o*.

OVERJOYED* (JOY)

Da   6: 23 The king was *o* and gave orders
Mt   2: 10 they saw the star, they were *o*.
Jn   20: 20 The disciples were *o*
Ac   12: 14 she was so *o* she ran back
1Pe   4: 13 so that you may be *o*

OVERLOOK

Pr   19: 11 it is to his glory to *o* an offense.

OVERSEER* (OVERSEERS)

Pr   6: 7 no *o* or ruler,
1Ti   3: 1 anyone sets his heart on being an *o*,
       3: 2 Now the *o* must be above reproach,
Tit   1: 7 Since an *o* is entrusted

1Pe   2: 25 returned to the Shepherd and *O*

OVERSEERS* (OVERSEER)

Ac   20: 28 the Holy Spirit has made you *o*.
Php   1: 1 together with the *o* and deacons:
1Pe   5: 2 as *o*—not because you must,

OVERSHADOW* (OVERSHADOWING)

Lk   1: 35 power of the Most High will *o* you.

OVERSHADOWING (OVERSHADOW)

Ex   25: 20 wings spread upward, *o* the cover
Heb   9: 5 the glory, *o* the atonement cover.

OVERTHROW (OVERTHROWS)

2Th   2: 8 whom the Lord Jesus will *o*

OVERTHROWS (OVERTHROW)

Pr   13: 6 but wickedness *o* the sinner.
Isa   44: 25 who *o* the learning of the wise

OVERWHELMED (OVERWHELMING)

2Sa   22: 5 the torrents of destruction *o* me.
1Ki   10: 5 temple of the LORD, she was *o*.
Ps   38: 4 My guilt has *o* me
      65: 3 When we were *o* by sins,
Mt   26: 38 ''My soul is *o* with sorrow
Mk   7: 37 People were *o* with amazement.
       9: 15 they were *o* with wonder
2Co   2: 7 so that he will not be *o*

OVERWHELMING (OVERWHELMED)

Pr   27: 4 Anger is cruel and fury *o*,
Isa   10: 22 *o* and righteous.
      28: 15 When an *o* scourge sweeps by,

OWE

Ro   13: 7 If you *o* taxes, pay taxes; if revenue
Phm   : 19 to mention that you *o* me your very

OWNER'S (OWNERSHIP)

Isa   1: 3 the donkey his *o* manger,

OWNERSHIP* (OWNER'S)

2Co   1: 22 He anointed us, set his seal of *o*

OX (OXEN)

Dt   25: 4 Do not muzzle an *o*
Isa   11: 7 and the lion will eat straw like the *o*
Eze   1: 10 and on the left the face of an *o*;
Lk   13: 15 of you on the Sabbath untie his *o*
1Co   9: 9 ''Do not muzzle an *o*
1Ti   5: 18 ''Do not muzzle the *o*
Rev   4: 7 second was like an *o*, the third had

OXEN (OX)

1Ki   19: 20 Elisha then left his *o* and ran
Lk   14: 19 'I have just bought five yoke of *o*,

PAGAN (PAGANS)

Mt   18: 17 as you would a *p* or a tax collector.
Lk   12: 30 For the *p* world runs

PAGANS* (PAGAN)

Isa   2: 6 and clasp hands with *p*.
Mt   5: 47 Do not even *p* do that? Be perfect,
       6: 7 do not keep on babbling like *p*,
       6: 32 For the *p* run after all these things,
1Co   5: 1 that does not occur even among *p*:
      10: 20 but the sacrifices of *p* are offered
      12: 2 You know that when you were *p*
1Pe   2: 12 such good lives among the *p* that,
       4: 3 in the past doing what *p* choose
3Jn   : 7 receiving no help from the *p*.

PAID (PAY)

Isa   40: 2 that her sin has been *p* for,
Zec   11: 12 So they *p* me thirty pieces of silver.

PAIN (PAINFUL PAINS)

Ge   3: 16 with *p* you will give birth
       6: 6 and his heart was filled with *p*.
Job   6: 10 my joy in unrelenting *p*—
      33: 19 may be chastened on a bed of *p*
Jer   4: 19 I writhe in *p*.
      15: 18 Why is my *p* unending
Mt   4: 24 suffering severe *p*,
Jn   16: 21 woman giving birth to a child has *p*
1Pe   2: 19 up under the *p* of unjust suffering

Rev   21: 4 or mourning or crying or *p*,

PAINFUL (PAIN)

Ge   3: 17 through *p* toil you will eat of it
       5: 29 and *p* toil of our hands caused
Job   6: 25 How *p* are honest words!
Eze   28: 24 neighbors who are *p* briers
2Co   2: 1 I would not make another *p* visit
Heb   12: 11 seems pleasant at the time, but *p*.
1Pe   4: 12 at the *p* trial you are suffering,

PAINS (PAIN)

Ge   3: 16 ''I will greatly increase your *p*
Mt   24: 8 these are the beginning of birth *p*.
Ro   8: 22 as in the *p* of childbirth right up
Gal   4: 19 again in the *p* of childbirth
1Th   5: 3 as labor *p* on a pregnant woman,

PAIRS

Ge   7: 8 *P* of clean and unclean animals,

PALACE (PALACES)

2Sa   7: 2 ''Here I am, living in a *p* of cedar,
Jer   22: 6 is what the LORD says about the *p*
      22: 13 ''Woe to him who builds his *p*

PALACES (PALACE)

Mt   11: 8 wear fine clothes are in kings' *p*.
Lk   7: 25 and indulge in luxury are in *p*.

PALE

Isa   29: 22 no longer will their faces grow *p*.
Jer   30: 6 every face turned deathly *p*?
Da   10: 8 my face turned deathly *p*
Rev   6: 8 and there before me was a *p* horse!

PALM (PALMS)

Jn   12: 13 They took *p* branches and went out
Rev   7: 9 and were holding *p* branches

PALMS (PALM)

Isa   49: 16 you on the *p* of my hands;

PAMPERS*

Pr   29: 21 If a man *p* his servant from youth,

PANIC

Dt   20: 3 or give way to *p* before them.
1Sa   14: 15 It was a *p* sent by God.
Eze   7: there is *p*, not joy,
Zec   14: 13 by the LORD with great *p*.

PANTS

Ps   42: 1 As the deer *p* for streams of water,

PARABLES

See also JESUS: PARABLES
Ps   78: 2 I will open my mouth in *p*,
Mt   13: 35 ''I will open my mouth in *p*,
Lk   8: 10 but to others I speak in *p*, so that,

PARADISE*

Lk   23: 43 today you will be with me in *p*.''
2Co   12: 4 God knows—was caught up to *p*.
Rev   2: 7 of life, which is in the *p* of God.

PARALYTIC

Mt   9: 2 Some men brought to him a *p*,
Mk   2: 3 bringing to him a *p*, carried by four
Ac   9: 33 a *p* who had been bedridden

PARCHED

Ps 143: 6 my soul thirsts for you like a *p* land.

PARCHMENTS*

2Ti   4: 13 and my scrolls, especially the *p*.

PARDON* (PARDONED PARDONS)

2Ch   30: 18 *p* everyone who sets his heart
Job   7: 21 Why do you not *p* my offenses
Isa   55: 7 and to our God, for he will freely *p*.
Joel   3: 21 I will *p*.''

PARDONED* (PARDON)

Nu   14: 19 as you have *p* them from the time
Joel   3: 21 bloodguilt, which I have not *p*,

PARDONS* (PARDON)

Mic   7: 18 who *p* sin and forgives

PARENTS

Pr 17: 6 and *p* are the pride of their children
19:14 wealth are inherited from *p*,
Mt 10:21 children will rebel against their *p*
Lk 18:29 left home or wife or brothers or *p*
21:16 You will be betrayed even by *p*, brothers,
Jn 9: 3 Neither this man nor his *p* sinned,"
Ro 1:30 they disobey their *p*; they are
2Co 12:14 for their *p*, but *p* for their children.
Eph 6: 1 Children, obey your *p* in the Lord,
Col 3:20 obey your *p* in everything,
1Ti 5: 4 repaying their *p* and grandparents,
2Ti 3: 2 disobedient to their *p*, ungrateful,

PARTAKE*

1Co 10:17 for we all *p* of the one loaf.

PARTIAL* (PARTIALITY)

Pr 18: 5 It is not good to be *p* to the wicked

PARTIALITY (PARTIAL)

Lev 19:15 do not show *p* to the poor
Dt 1:17 Do not show *p* in judging;
10:17 who shows no *p* and accepts no
16:19 Do not pervert justice or show *p*.
2Ch 19: 7 our God there is no injustice or *p*
Job 32:21 I will show *p* to no one,
34:19 who shows no *p* to princes
Pr 24:23 To show *p* in judging is not good:
Mal 2: 9 have shown *p* in matters of the law
Lk 20:21 and that you do not show *p*
1Ti 5:21 keep these instructions without *p*,

PARTICIPANTS (PARTICIPATE)

1Co 10:20 you to be *p* with demons.

PARTICIPATE (PARTICIPANTS PARTICIPATION)

1Pe 4:13 rejoice that you *p* in the sufferings
2Pe 1: 4 that through them you may *p*

PARTICIPATION (PARTICIPATE)

1Co 10:16 is not the bread that we break a *p*

PARTNER (PARTNERS PARTNERSHIP)

Pr 2:17 who has left the *p* of her youth
Mal 2:14 though she is your *p*, the wife
1Pe 3: 7 them with respect as the weaker *p*

PARTNERS (PARTNER)

Eph 5: 7 Therefore do not be *p* with them.

PARTNERSHIP* (PARTNER)

Php 1: 5 because of your *p* in the gospel

PASS (PASSED PASSER-BY PASSING)

Ex 12:13 and when I see the blood, I will *p*
33:19 goodness to *p* in front of you,
1Ki 9: 8 all who *p* by will be appalled
19:11 for the LORD is about to *p* by."
Ps 90:10 for they quickly *p*, and we fly away.
105: 19 till what he foretold came to *p*,
Isa 31: 5 he will '*p* over' it and will rescue it
43: 2 When you *p* through the waters,
62:10 P through, *p* through the gates!
Jer 22: 8 "People from many nations will *p*
La 1:12 to you, all you who *p* by?
Da 7:14 dominion that will not *p* away,
Am 5:17 for I will *p* through your midst,"
Mt 24:34 will certainly not *p* away
24:35 Heaven and earth will *p* away,
Mk 13:31 Heaven and earth will *p* away,
Lk 21:33 Heaven and earth will *p* away,
1Co 13: 8 there is knowledge, it will *p* away.
Jas 1:10 he will *p* away like a wild flower.
1Jn 2:17 The world and its desires *p* away,

PASSED (PASS)

Ge 15:17 a blazing torch appeared and *p*
Ex 33:22 you with my hand until I have *p* by.
2Ch 21:20 He *p* away, to no one's regret,
Ps 57: 1 wings until the disaster has *p*.
Lk 10:32 saw him, *p* by on the other side.
1Co 15: 3 For what I received I *p* on to you
Heb 11:29 By faith the people *p*

PASSER-BY* (PASS)

Pr 26:10 is he who hires a fool or any *p*.
26:17 is a *p* who meddles

PASSING (PASS)

1Co 7:31 world in its present form is *p* away.
1Jn 2: 8 because the darkness is *p*

PASSION* (PASSIONATE PASSIONS)

Hos 7: 6 Their *p* smolders all night;
1Co 7: 9 better to marry than to burn with *p*.

PASSIONATE* (PASSION)

1Th 4: 5 not in *p* lust like the heathen,

PASSIONS* (PASSION)

Ro 7: 5 the sinful *p* aroused
Gal 5:24 crucified the sinful nature with its *p*
Tit 2:12 to ungodliness and worldly *p*,
3: 3 and enslaved by all kinds of *p*

PASSOVER

Ex 12:11 Eat it in haste; it is the LORD's *P*.
Nu 9: 2 Have the Israelites celebrate the *P*
Dt 16: 1 celebrate the *P* of the LORD your
Jos 5:10 the Israelites celebrated the *P*.
2Ki 23:21 "Celebrate the *P* to the LORD
Ezr 6:19 the exiles celebrated the *P*.
Mk 14:12 customary to sacrifice the *P* lamb
Lk 22: 1 called the *P*, was approaching,
1Co 5: 7 our *P* lamb, has been sacrificed.
Heb 11:28 he kept the *P* and the sprinkling

PAST

Isa 43:18 do not dwell on the *p*.
65:16 For the *p* troubles will be forgotten
Ro 15: 4 in the *p* was written to teach us,
16:25 the mystery hidden for long ages *p*,
Eph 3: 9 which for ages *p* was kept hidden
Heb 1: 1 In the *p* God spoke

PASTORS*

Eph 4:11 and some to be *p* and teachers,

PASTURE (PASTURES)

Ps 37: 3 dwell in the land and enjoy safe *p*.
95: 7 and we are the people of his *p*,
100: 3 we are his people, the sheep of his *p*
Jer 50: 7 against the LORD, their true *p*,
Eze 34:13 I will *p* them on the mountains
Zec 11: 4 '*P* the flock marked for slaughter.
Jn 10: 9 come in and go out, and find *p*.

PASTURES (PASTURE)

Ps 23: 2 He makes me lie down in green *p*,

PATCH

Jer 10: 5 Like a scarecrow in a melon *p*,
Mt 9:16 No one sews a *p* of unshrunk cloth

PATH (PATHS)

Ps 16:11 known to me the *p* of life;
27:11 lead me in a straight *p*
119: 32 I run in the *p* of your commands,
119:105 and a light for my *p*.
Pr 2: 9 and fair—every good *p*.
12:28 along that *p* is immortality.
15:10 awaits him who leaves the *p*;
15:19 the *p* of the upright is a highway.
15:24 The *p* of life leads upward
21:16 from the *p* of understanding
Isa 26: 7 The *p* of the righteous is level;
Jer 31: 9 on a level *p* where they will not
Mt 13: 4 fell along the *p*, and the birds came
Lk 1:79 to guide our feet into the *p* of peace
2Co 6: 3 no stumbling block in anyone's *p*,

PATHS (PATH)

Ps 23: 3 He guides me in *p* of righteousness
25: 4 teach me your *p*;
Pr 2:13 who leave the straight *p*
3: 6 and he will make your *p* straight.
4:11 and lead you along straight *p*.
4:26 Make level *p* for your feet
5:21 and he examines all his *p*.
8:20 along the *p* of justice,
22: 5 In the *p* of the wicked lie thorns
Isa 2: 3 so that we may walk in his *p*."

Jer 6:16 ask for the ancient *p*,
Mic 4: 2 so that we may walk in his *p*."
Mt 3: 3 make straight *p* for him.' "
Ac 2:28 to me the *p* of life;
Ro 11:33 and his *p* beyond tracing out!
Heb 12:13 "Make level *p* for your feet,"

PATIENCE* (PATIENT)

Pr 19:11 A man's wisdom gives him *p*;
25:15 Through *p* a ruler can be persuaded
Ecc 7: 8 and *p* is better than pride.
Isa 7:13 Is it not enough to try the *p* of men?
7:13 Will you try the *p* of my God also?
Ro 2: 4 and *p*, not realizing that God's
9:22 bore with great *p* the objects
2Co 6: 6 understanding, *p* and kindness;
Gal 5:22 joy, peace, *p*, kindness, goodness,
Col 1:11 may have great endurance and *p*,
3:12 humility, gentleness and *p*.
1Ti 1:16 Jesus might display his unlimited *p*
2Ti 3:10 my purpose, faith, *p*, love,
4: 2 with great *p* and careful instruction
Heb 6:12 *p* inherit what has been promised.
Jas 5:10 as an example of *p* in the face
2Pe 3:15 that our Lord's *p* means salvation,

PATIENT* (PATIENCE PATIENTLY)

Ne 9:30 For many years you were *p*
Job 6:11 What prospects, that I should be *p*?
Pr 14:29 A *p* man has great understanding,
15:18 but a *p* man calms a quarrel.
16:32 Better a *p* man than a warrior,
Mt 18:26 'Be *p* with me,' he begged,
18:29 'Be *p* with me, and I will pay you
Ro 12:12 Be joyful in hope, *p* in affliction,
1Co 13: 4 Love is *p*, love is kind.
2Co 1: 6 produces in you *p* endurance
Eph 4: 2 humble and gentle; be *p*,
1Th 5:14 help the weak, be *p* with everyone.
Jas 5: 7 Be *p*, then, brothers,
5: 7 and how *p* he is for the autumn
5: 8 You too, be *p* and stand firm,
2Pe 3: 9 He is *p* with you, not wanting
Rev 1: 9 *p* endurance that are ours in Jesus,
13:10 This calls for *p* endurance
14:12 This calls for *p* endurance

PATIENTLY* (PATIENT)

Ps 37: 7 still before the LORD and wait *p*
40: 1 I waited *p* for the LORD;
Isa 38:13 I waited *p* till dawn,
Hab 3:16 Yet I will wait *p* for the day
Ac 26: 3 I beg you to listen to me *p*.
Ro 8:25 we do not yet have, we wait for it *p*.
Heb 6:15 after waiting *p*, Abraham received
1Pe 3:20 ago when God waited *p* in the days
Rev 3:10 kept my command to endure *p*,

PATTERN

Ex 25:40 according to the *p* shown you
Ro 5:14 who was a *p* of the one to come.
12: 2 longer to the *p* of this world,
2Ti 1:13 keep as the *p* of sound teaching,
Heb 8: 5 according to the *p* shown you

PAUL

Also called Saul (Ac 13:9). Pharisee from Tarsus (Ac 9:11; Php 3:5). Apostle (Gal 1). At stoning of Stephen (Ac 8:1). Persecuted Church (Ac 9:1-2; Gal 1:13). Vision of Jesus on road to Damascus (Ac 9:4-9; 26:12-18). In Arabia (Gal 1:17). Preached in Damascus; escaped death through the wall in a basket (Ac 9:19-25). In Jerusalem; sent back to Tarsus (Ac 9:26-30).

Brought to Antioch by Barnabas (Ac 11:22-26). First missionary journey to Cyprus and Galatia (Ac 13-14). Stoned at Lystra (Ac 14:19-20). At Jerusalem council (Ac 15). Split with Barnabas over Mark (Ac 15:36-41).

Second missionary journey with Silas (Ac 16-20). Called to Macedonia (Ac 16:6-10). Freed from prison in Philippi (Ac 16:16-40). In Thessalonica (Ac 17:1-9). Speech in Athens (Ac 17:16-33). In Corinth (Ac 18). In Ephesus (Ac 19). Return to Jerusalem (Ac 20). Farewell to Ephesian elders (Ac 20:13-38). Arrival in Jerusalem (Ac 21:1-26). Arrested (Ac 21:27-36). Addressed crowds (Ac 22), Sanhedrin (Ac 23:1-11). Transferred to

Caesarea (Ac 23:12-35). Trial before Felix (Ac 24), Festus (Ac 25:1-12). Before Agrippa (Ac 25: 13-26:32). Voyage to Rome; shipwreck (Ac 27). Arrival in Rome (Ac 28).

Epistles: Romans, 1 and 2 Corinthians, Galatians, Ephesians, Philippians, Colossians, 1 and 2 Thessalonians, 1 and 2 Timothy, Titus, Philemon.

PAVEMENT
Jn   19: 13 as the Stone *P* (which

PAY (PAID PAYMENT PAYS REPAID REPAY REPAYING)
Lev 26: 43 They will *p* for their sins
Dt   7: 12 If you *p* attention to these laws
Pr   4:   1 *p* attention and gain understanding
     4: 20 My son, *p* attention to what I say;
     5:   1 My son, *p* attention to my wisdom,
     6: 31 if he is caught, he must *p* sevenfold,
    19: 19 man must *p* the penalty;
    22: 17 *P* attention and listen
    24: 29 I'll *p* that man back for what he did
Eze 40:   4 and *p* attention to everything I am
Zec 11: 12 give me my *p*; but if not, keep it.''
Mt   20:   2 He agreed to *p* them a denarius
    22: 16 you *p* no attention to who they are.
    22: 17 Is it right to *p* taxes to Caesar
Lk   3: 14 falsely—be content with your *p*.''
    19:   8 I will *p* back four times the amount
Ro   13:   6 This is also why you *p* taxes,
2Pe   1: 19 you will do well to *p* attention to it,

PAYMENT (PAY)
Ps   49:   8 no *p* is ever enough—
Php   4: 18 I have received full *p* and

PAYS (PAY)
Pr   17: 13 If a man *p* back evil for good,
1Th   5: 15 sure that nobody *p* back wrong

PEACE (PEACEABLE PEACEFUL PEACEMAKERS)
Lev 26:   6 '' 'I will grant *p* in the land,
Nu   6: 26 and give you *p*.'' '
    25: 12 him I am making my covenant of *p*
Dt   20: 10 make its people an offer of *p*.
Jdg   3: 11 So the land had *p* for forty years,
    3: 30 and the land had *p* for eighty years.
    5: 31 Then the land had *p* forty years.
    6: 24 and called it The LORD is *P*.
    8: 28 the land enjoyed *p* forty years.
1Sa   7: 14 And there was *p* between Israel
2Sa 19: 10 they made *p* with the Israelites
1Ki   2: 33 may there be the LORD's *p* forever
    22: 44 also at *p* with the king of Israel.
2Ki   9: 17 come in *p*?' '' The horseman rode
1Ch 19: 19 they made *p* with David
    22:   9 and I will grant Israel *p*
2Ch 14:   1 and in his days the country was at *p*
    20: 30 kingdom of Jehoshaphat was at *p*,
Job   3: 26 I have no *p*, no quietness;
    22: 21 to God and be at *p* with him;
Ps   29: 11 LORD blesses his people with *p*.
    34: 14 seek *p* and pursue it.
    37: 11 and enjoy great *p*.
    37: 37 there is a future for the man of *p*.
    85: 10 righteousness and *p* kiss each other
   119:165 Great *p* have they who love your
   120:   7 I am a man of *p*;
   122:   6 Pray for the *p* of Jerusalem:
   147: 14 He grants *p* to your borders
Pr   12: 20 but joy for those who promote *p*.
    14: 30 A heart at *p* gives life to the body,
    16:   7 his enemies live at *p* with him.
    17:   1 Better a dry crust with *p* and quiet
Ecc   3:   8 a time for war and a time for *p*.
Isa   9:   6 Everlasting Father, Prince of *P*.
    14:   7 All the lands are at rest and at *p*;
    26:   3 You will keep in perfect *p*
    32: 17 The fruit of righteousness will be *p*;
    48: 18 your *p* would have been like a river,
    48: 22 ''There is no *p*,'' says the LORD.
    52:   7 who proclaim *p*,
    53:   5 punishment that brought us *p* was
    54: 10 nor my covenant of *p* be removed,''
    55: 12 and be led forth in *p*;
    57:   2 enter into *p*;
    57: 19 *P*, *p*, to those far and near,''

Isa 57: 21 ''There is no *p*,'' says my God,
    59:   8 The way of *p* they do not know;
Jer   6: 14 '*P*, *p*,' they say,
    8: 11 '*P*, *p*,' . . . there is no *p*.
    30: 10 Jacob will again have *p*
    46: 27 Jacob will again have *p*
Eze 13: 10 ''*P*,'' when there is no *p*,
    34: 25 '' 'I will make a covenant of *p*
    37: 26 I will make a covenant of *p*
Mic   5:   5 And he will be their *p*.
Zec   8: 19 Therefore love truth and *p*.''
    9: 10 He will proclaim *p* to the nations.
Mal   2:   5 a covenant of life and *p*,
    2:   6 He walked with me in *p*
Mt   10: 34 I did not come to bring *p*,
Mk   9: 50 and be at *p* with each other.''
Lk   1: 79 to guide our feet into the path of *p*
    2: 14 on earth *p* to men on whom his
    19: 38 ''*P* in heaven and glory
Jn   14: 27 *P* I leave with you; my *p*
    16: 33 so that in me you may have *p*.
Ro   1:   7 and *p* to you from God our Father
    2: 10 and *p* for everyone who does good:
    5:   1 we have *p* with God
    8:   6 by the Spirit is life and *p*;
    12: 18 on you, live at *p* with everyone.
    14: 19 effort to do what leads to *p*
1Co   7: 15 God has called us to live in *p*.
    14: 33 a God of disorder but of *p*.
2Co 13: 11 be of one mind, live in *p*.
Gal   5: 22 joy, *p*, patience, kindness,
Eph   2: 14 he himself is our *p*, who has made
    2: 15 thus making *p*, and in this one body
    2: 17 and *p* to those who were near.
    6: 15 comes from the gospel of *p*.
Php   4:   7 the *p* of God, which transcends all
Col   1: 20 by making *p* through his blood,
    3: 15 Let the *p* of Christ rule
    3: 15 of one body you were called to *p*.
1Th   5:   3 While people are saying, ''*P*
    5: 13 Live in *p* with each other.
    5: 23 the God of *p*, sanctify you through
2Th   3: 16 the Lord of *p* himself give you *p*
2Ti   2: 22 righteousness, faith, love and *p*,
Heb   7:   2 ''king of Salem'' means ''king of *p*.''
    12: 11 *p* for those who have been trained
    12: 14 effort to live in *p* with all men
    13: 20 May the God of *p*, who
1Pe   3: 11 he must seek *p* and pursue it.
2Pe   3: 14 blameless and at *p* with him.
Rev   6:   4 power to take *p* from the earth

PEACEABLE* (PEACE)
Tit   3:   2 to slander no one, to be *p*

PEACEFUL (PEACE)
1Ti   2:   2 that we may live *p* and quiet lives

PEACE-LOVING
Jas   3: 17 then *p*, considerate

PEACEMAKERS* (PEACE)
Mt   5:   9 Blessed are the *p*,
Jas   3: 18 *P* who sow in peace raise a harvest

PEARL* (PEARLS)
Rev 21: 21 each gate made of a single *p*.

PEARLS (PEARL)
Mt   7:   6 do not throw your *p* to pigs.
    13: 45 like a merchant looking for fine *p*.
1Ti   2:   9 or gold or *p* or expensive clothes,
Rev 21: 21 The twelve gates were twelve *p*,

PEDDLE*
2Co   2: 17 we do not *p* the word of God

PEG
Jdg   4: 21 She drove the *p* through his temple

PEKAH
King of Israel (2Ki 16:25-31; Isa 7:1).

PEKAHIAH*
Son of Menahem; king of Israel (2Ki 16:22-26).

PEN
Ps   45:   1 my tongue is the *p*
Mt   5: 18 letter, not the least stroke of a *p*,
Jn   10:   1 who does not enter the sheep *p*

PENETRATES*
Heb   4: 12 it *p* even to dividing soul and spirit,

PENNIES* (PENNY)
Lk   12:   6 not five sparrows sold for two *p*?

PENNY* (PENNIES)
Mt   5: 26 out until you have paid the last *p*.
    10: 29 Are not two sparrows sold for a *p*?
Mk 12: 42 worth only a fraction of a *p*.
Lk   12: 59 out until you have paid the last *p*.''

PENTECOST*
Ac   2:   1 of *P* came, they were all together
    20: 16 if possible, by the day of *P*.
1Co 16:   8 I will stay on at Ephesus until *P*,

PEOPLE (PEOPLES)
Ge   11:   6 as one *p* speaking the same
Ex   5:   1 Let my *p* go,
    6:   7 take you as my own *p*,
    8: 23 between my *p* and your *p*.
    15: 13 the *p* you have redeemed.
    19:   8 The *p* all responded together,
    24:   3 Moses went and told the *p*
    32:   1 When the *p* saw that Moses
    32:   9 they are a stiff-necked *p*.
    33: 13 this nation is your *p*.
Lev   9:   7 for yourself and the *p*:
    16: 24 the burnt offering for the *p*,
    26: 12 and you will be my *p*.
Nu   11: 11 burden of all these *p* on
    14: 11 *p* treat me with contempt?
    14: 19 forgive the sin of these *p*,
    22:   5 A *p* has come out of Egypt
Dt   4:   6 a wise and understanding *p*.
    4: 20 the *p* of his inheritance,
    5: 28 what this *p* said to you.
    7:   6 a *p* holy to the LORD
    26: 18 that you are his *p*,
    31:   7 you must go with this *p*
    31: 16 these *p* will soon prostitute
    32:   9 the LORD's portion is his *p*,
    32: 43 atonement for his land and *p*.
    33: 29 a *p* saved by the LORD?
Jos   1:   6 you will lead this *p*
    24: 24 the *p* said to Joshua,
Jdg   2:   7 *p* served the LORD throughout
Ru   1: 16 Your *p* will be my *p*
1Sa   8:   7 the *p* are saying to you;
    12: 22 LORD will not reject his *p*,
2Sa   5:   2 will shepherd my *p* Israel
    7: 10 provide a place for my *p*
1Ki   3:   8 among the *p* you have chosen,
    8: 30 your *p* Israel when they pray
    8: 56 has given rest to his *p*
    18: 39 when all the *p* saw this,
2Ki 23:   3 all the *p* pledged themselves
1Ch 17: 21 to redeem *p* for himself
    29: 17 how willingly your *p* who are
2Ch   2: 11 Because the LORD loves his *p*,
    7:   5 *p* dedicated the temple
    7: 14 if my *p*, who are called
    30:   6 ''*P* of Israel, return to
    36: 16 was aroused against his *p*
Ezr   2:   1 These are the *p* of the
    3:   1 *p* assembled as one man
Ne   1: 10 your *p*, whom you redeemed
    4:   6 *p* worked with all their heart
    8:   1 *p* assembled as one man
Est   3:   6 to destroy all Mordecai's *p*,
Job 12:   2 Doubtless you are the *p*,
Ps   29: 11 gives strength to his *p*;
    33: 12 *p* he chose for his inheritance
    50:   4 that he may judge his *p*
    53:   6 restores the fortunes of his *p*,
    81: 13 If my *p* would but listen
    94: 14 LORD will not reject his *p*;
    95:   7 we are the *p* of his pasture,
    95: 10 a *p* whose hearts go astray,
   125:   2 the LORD surrounds his *p*
   135: 14 LORD will vindicate his *p*
   144: 15 *p* whose God is the LORD.

PEOPLES (PEOPLE) — left column continuation

Pr 14:34 sin is a disgrace to any *p*.
  29: 2 righteous thrive, the *p* rejoice
  29:18 the *p* cast off restraint
Isa 1: 3 my *p* do not understand.
  1: 4 a *p* loaded with guilt,
  5:13 my *p* will go into exile
  6:10 the heart of this *p* calloused;
  9: 2 the *p* walking in darkness
  12:12 will assemble the scattered *p*
  19:25 Blessed be Egypt my *p*,
  25: 8 remove the disgrace of his *p*
  29:13 These *p* come near to me
  40: 1 Comfort, comfort my *p*
  40: 7 Surely the *p* are grass.
  42: 6 a covenant for the *p*
  49:13 the LORD comforts his *p*
  51: 4 "Listen to me, my *p*;
  52: 6 my *p* will know my name;
  53: 8 for the transgression of my *p*
  60:21 will all your *p* be righteous
  62:12 will be called the Holy P,
  65:23 they will be a *p* blessed
Jer 2:11 my *p* have exchanged their
  2:13 *p* have committed two sins:
  2:32 my *p* have forgotten me,
  4:22 My *p* are fools;
  5:14 Because the *p* have spoken
  5:31 my *p* love it this way
  7:16 do not pray for this *p*
  18:15 my *p* have forgotten me;
  25: 7 They will be my *p*,
  30: 3 I will bring my *p* Israel
Eze 13:23 I will save my *p* from
  36: 8 fruit for my *p* Israel,
  36:28 you will be my *p*,
  36:38 be filled with flocks of *p*.
  37:13 Then you, my *p*, will know
  38:14 *p* Israel are living in safety
  39: 7 name among my *p* Israel.
Da 7:27 saints, the *p* of the Most High.
  8:24 mighty men and the holy *p*
  9:19 your *p* bear your name
  9:24 are decreed for your *p*
  9:26 *p* of the ruler who will come
  10:14 will happen to your *p*
  11:32 *p* who know their God will
  12: 1 prince who protects your *p*.
Hos 1:10 'You are not my *p*,'
  2:23 'You are my *p*';
  4:14 a *p* without understanding
Joel 2:18 and take pity on his *p*.
  3:16 be a refuge for his *p*,
Am 9:14 back my exiled *p* Israel;
Mic 6: 2 a case against his *p*;
  7:14 Shepherd your *p* with
Hag 1:12 remnant of the *p* obeyed
Zec 2:11 and will become my *p*.
  8: 7 I will save my *p*
  13: 9 will say, 'They are my *p*,'
Mk 7: 6 *p* honor me with their lips
  8:27 "Who do *p* say I am?"
Lk 1:17 make ready a *p* prepared
  1:68 and has redeemed his *p*.
  2:10 joy that will be for all the *p*
  21:23 and wrath against this *p*.
Jn 11:50 one man die for the *p*
  18:14 if one man died for the *p*
Ac 15:14 from the Gentiles a *p*.
  18:10 have many *p* in this city.
Ro 9:25 will call them 'my *p*,'
  11: 1 Did God reject his *p*?
  15:10 O Gentiles, with his *p*.'
2Co 6:16 and they will be my *p*.''
Tit 2:14 a *p* that are his very own,
Heb 2:17 for the sins of the *p*.
  4: 9 a Sabbath-rest for the *p*
  5: 3 for the sins of the *p*,
  10:30 Lord will judge his *p*.
  11:25 mistreated along with the *p*
  13:12 to make the *p* holy
1Pe 2: 9 you are a chosen *p*,
  2:10 Once you were not a *p*,
  2:10 you are the *p* of God;
2Pe 2: 1 false prophets among the *p*,
  3:11 kind of *p* ought you to be ?
Rev 18: 4 "Come out of her, my *p*,
  21: 3 They will be his *p*,

PEOPLES (PEOPLE)

Ge 17:16 kings of *p* will come from her
  25:23 two *p* from within you will
  27:29 and *p* bow down to you
  28: 3 become a community of *p*.
  48: 4 you a community of *p*.
Dt 14: 2 of all the *p* on the face of
  28:10 Then all the *p* on earth
  32: 8 set up boundaries for the *p*
Jos 4:24 all the *p* of the earth might
1Ki 8:43 all the *p* of the earth may
2Ch 7:20 of ridicule among all *p*.
Ps 9: 8 he will govern the *p*
  67: 5 may all the *p* praise you.
  87: 6 in the register of the *p*:
  96:10 he will judge the *p*
Isa 2: 4 settle disputes for many *p*.
  17:12 Oh, the uproar of the *p*—
  25: 6 of rich food for all *p*,
  34: 1 pay attention, you *p*!
  55: 5 him a witness to the *p*,
Jer 10: 3 customs of the *p* are worthless
Da 7:14 all *p*, nations and men
Mic 4: 1 and *p* will stream to it.
  4: 3 will judge between many *p*
  5: 7 in the midst of many *p*
Zep 3: 9 purify the lips of the *p*,
  3:20 among all the *p* of the
Zec 8:20 Many *p* and the inhabitants
  12: 2 all the surrounding *p* reeling.
Rev 10:11 prophesy again about many *p*,
  17:15 the prostitute sits, are *p*,

PEOR

Nu 25: 3 joined in worshiping the Baal of P.
Dt 4: 3 who followed the Baal of P,

PERCEIVE (PERCEIVING)

Ps 139: 2 you *p* my thoughts from afar.
Pr 24:12 not he who weighs the heart *p* it?

PERCEIVING* (PERCEIVE)

Isa 6: 9 be ever seeing, but never *p*.'
Mt 13:14 you will be ever seeing but never *p*.
Mk 4:12 may be ever seeing but never *p*,
Ac 28:26 you will be ever seeing but never *p*

PERFECT* (PERFECTER PERFECTING PERFECTION)

Dt 32: 4 He is the Rock, his works are *p*,
2Sa 22:31 "As for God, his way is *p*;
  22:33 and makes my way *p*.
Job 36: 4 one *p* in knowledge is with you.
  37:16 of him who is *p* in knowledge?
Ps 18:30 As for God, his way is *p*;
  18:32 and makes my way *p*.
  19: 7 The law of the LORD is *p*,
  50: 2 From Zion, *p* in beauty,
  64: 6 "We have devised a *p* plan!"
SS 6: 9 but my dove, my *p* one, is unique,
Isa 25: 1 for in *p* faithfulness
  26: 3 You will keep in *p* peace
Eze 16:14 had given you made your beauty *p*,
  27: 3 "I am *p* in beauty."
  28:12 full of wisdom and *p* in beauty.
Mt 5:48 Do not even pagans do that? Be *p*,
  5:48 as your heavenly Father is *p*.
  19:21 answered, "If you want to be *p*,
Ro 12: 2 his good, pleasing and *p* will.
2Co 12: 9 for my power is made *p*
Php 3:12 or have already been made *p*,
Col 1:28 so that we may present everyone *p*
  3:14 binds them all together in *p* unity.
Heb 2:10 the author of their salvation *p*
  5: 9 what he suffered and, once made *p*,
  7:19 useless (for the law made nothing *p*
  7:28 who has been made *p* forever.
  9:11 and more *p* tabernacle that is not
  10: 1 make *p* those who draw
  10:14 he has made *p* forever those who
  11:40 with us would they be made *p*.
  12:23 spirits of righteous men made *p*,
Jas 1:17 Every good and *p* gift is from above
  1:25 into the *p* law that gives freedom,
  3: 2 he is a *p* man, able
1Jn 4:18 But *p* love drives out fear,
  4:18 The one who fears is not made *p*

PERFECTER* (PERFECT)

Heb 12: 2 the author and *p* of our faith,

PERFECTING* (PERFECT)

2Co 7: 1 *p* holiness out of reverence for God

PERFECTION* (PERFECT)

Ps 119: 96 To all *p* I see a limit;
La 2:15 the *p* of beauty,
Eze 27: 4 builders brought your beauty to *p*.
  27:11 they brought your beauty to *p*.
  28:12 " 'You were the model of *p*,
1Co 13:10 but when *p* comes, the imperfect
2Co 13: 9 and our prayer is for your *p*.
  13:11 Aim for *p*, listen to my appeal,
Heb 7:11 If *p* could have been attained

PERFORM (PERFORMED PERFORMS)

Ex 3:20 with all the wonders that I will *p*
2Sa 7:23 to *p* great and awesome wonders
Jn 3: 2 no one could *p* the miraculous

PERFORMED (PERFORM)

Mt 11:21 If the miracles that were *p*
Jn 10:41 John never *p* a miraculous

PERFORMS (PERFORM)

Ps 77:14 You are the God who *p* miracles;

PERFUME

Ecc 7: 1 A good name is better than fine *p*,
SS 1: 3 your name is like *p* poured out.
Mk 14: 3 jar of very expensive *p*,

PERIL

2Co 1:10 us from such a deadly *p*,

PERISH (PERISHABLE PERISHED PERISHES PERISHING)

Ge 6:17 Everything on earth will *p*.
Est 4:16 And if I *p*, I *p*."
Ps 1: 6 but the way of the wicked will *p*.
  37:20 But the wicked will *p*:
  73:27 Those who are far from you will *p*;
  102: 26 They will *p*, but you remain;
Pr 11:10 when the wicked *p*, there are
  19: 9 and he who pours out lies will *p*
  21:28 A false witness will *p*,
  28:28 when the wicked *p*, the righteous
Isa 1:28 who forsake the LORD will *p*.
  29:14 the wisdom of the wise will *p*,
  60:12 that will not serve you will *p*;
Zec 11: 9 the dying die, and the perishing *p*.
Lk 13: 3 unless you repent, you too will all *p*
  13: 5 unless you repent, you too will all *p*
  21:18 But not a hair of your head will *p*.
Jn 3:16 whoever believes in him shall not *p*
  10:28 eternal life, and they shall never *p*;
Ro 2:12 apart from the law will also *p* apart
Col 2:22 These are all destined to *p* with use,
2Th 2:10 They *p* because they refused
Heb 1:11 They will *p*, but you remain;
1Pe 1: 4 into an inheritance that can never *p*
2Pe 3: 9 not wanting anyone to *p*,

PERISHABLE (PERISH)

1Co 15:42 The body that is sown is *p*,
1Pe 1:18 not with *p* things such
  1:23 not of *p* seed, but of imperishable,

PERISHED (PERISH)

Ps 119: 92 I would have *p* in my affliction.

PERISHES (PERISH)

Job 8:13 so *p* the hope of the godless.
1Pe 1: 7 which *p* even though refined by fire

PERISHING (PERISH)

1Co 1:18 foolishness to those who are *p*,
2Co 2:15 being saved and those who are *p*.
  4: 3 it is veiled to those who are *p*.

PERJURERS* (PERJURY)

Mal 3: 5 and *p*, against those who defraud
1Ti 1:10 for slave traders and liars and *p*—

PERJURY* (PERJURERS)

Jer 7: 9 murder, commit adultery and *p*,

PERMANENT
Heb 7:24 lives forever, he has a *p* priesthood.

PERMISSIBLE (PERMIT)
1Co 6:12 "Everything is *p* for me"—
10:23 "Everything is *p*"— but not

PERMIT (PERMISSIBLE PERMITTED)
Hos 5: 4 "Their deeds do not *p* them
1Ti 2:12 I do not *p* a woman to teach

PERMITTED (PERMIT)
Mt 19: 8 Moses *p* you to divorce your wives
2Co 12: 4 things that man is not *p* to tell.

PERSECUTE (PERSECUTED
PERSECUTION PERSECUTIONS)
Ps 119: 86 for men *p* me without cause.
Mt 5:11 *p* you and falsely say all kinds
5:44 and pray for those who *p* you,
Jn 15:20 they persecuted me, they will *p* you
Ac 9: 4 why do you *p* me?" "Who are you,
Ro 12:14 Bless those who *p* you; bless

PERSECUTED (PERSECUTE)
Mt 5:10 Blessed are those who are *p*
5:12 same way they *p* the prophets who
Jn 15:20 If they *p* me, they will persecute
1Co 4:12 when we are *p*, we endure it;
15: 9 because I *p* the church of God.
2Co 4: 9 in despair; *p*, but not abandoned;
1Th 3: 4 kept telling you that we would be *p*.
2Ti 3:12 life in Christ Jesus will be *p*,
Heb 11:37 destitute, *p* and mistreated—

PERSECUTION (PERSECUTE)
Mt 13:21 When trouble or *p* comes
Ro 8:35 or hardship or *p* or famine

PERSECUTIONS (PERSECUTE)
Mk 10:30 and with them, *p*) and in the age
2Co 12:10 in hardships, in *p*, in difficulties.
2Th 1: 4 faith in all the *p* and trials you are
2Ti 3:11 love, endurance, *p*, sufferings—

PERSEVERANCE* (PERSEVERE)
Ro 5: 3 we know that suffering produces *p*;
5: 4 *p*, character; and character, hope.
2Co 12:12 were done among you with great *p*.
2Th 1: 4 churches we boast about your *p*
3: 5 into God's love and Christ's *p*.
Heb 12: 1 run with *p* the race marked out
Jas 1: 3 the testing of your faith develops *p*.
1: 4 *P* must finish its work
5:11 You have heard of Job's *p*
2Pe 1: 6 *p*; and to *p*, godliness;
Rev 2: 2 your hard work and your *p*,
2:19 and faith, your service and *p*,

PERSEVERE* (PERSEVERANCE
PERSEVERED PERSEVERES
PERSEVERING)
1Ti 4:16 *P* in them, because if you do,
Heb 10:36 You need to *p* so that

PERSEVERED* (PERSEVERE)
Heb 11:27 he *p* because he saw him who is
Jas 5:11 consider blessed those who have *p*.
Rev 2: 3 You have *p* and have endured

PERSEVERES* (PERSEVERE)
1Co 13: 7 trusts, always hopes, always *p*.
Jas 1:12 Blessed is the man who *p*

PERSEVERING* (PERSEVERE)
Lk 8:15 retain it, and by *p* produce a crop.

PERSIANS
Da 6:15 law of the Medes and *P* no decree

PERSISTENCE*
Ro 2: 7 To those who by *p*

PERSUADE (PERSUADED PERSUASIVE)
Ac 18: 4 trying to *p* Jews and Greeks.
2Co 5:11 is to fear the Lord, we try to *p* men.

PERSUADED (PERSUADE)
Ro 4:21 being fully *p* that God had power

PERSUASIVE (PERSUADE)
1Co 2: 4 not with wise and *p* words,

PERVERSION* (PERVERT)
Lev 18:23 sexual relations with it; that is a *p*.
20:12 What they have done is a *p*;
Ro 1:27 the due penalty for their *p*.
Jude 7 up to sexual immorality and *p*.

PERVERT (PERVERSION PERVERTED PERVERTS)
Ex 23: 2 do not *p* justice by siding
Dt 16:19 Do not *p* justice or show partiality.
Job 34:12 that the Almighty would *p* justice.
Pr 17:23 to *p* the course of justice.
Gal 1: 7 are trying to *p* the gospel of Christ.

PERVERTED (PERVERT)
1Sa 8: 3 and accepted bribes and *p* justice.

PERVERTS* (PERVERT)
1Ti 1:10 for murderers, for adulterers and *p*,

PESTILENCE (PESTILENCES)
Ps 91: 6 nor the *p* that stalks in the darkness

PESTILENCES (PESTILENCE)
Lk 21:11 famines and *p* in various places,

PETER
Apostle, brother of Andrew, also called Simon (Mt 10:2; Mk 3:16; Lk 6:14; Ac 1:13), (Jn 1:42). Confession of Christ (Mt 16:13-20; Mk 8:27-30; Lk 9:18-27). At transfiguration (Mt 17: 1-8; Mk 9:2-8; Lk 9:28-36; 2Pe 1:16-18). Caught fish with coin (Mt 17:24-27). Denial of Jesus predicted (Mt 26:31-35; Mk 14:27-31; Lk 22:31-34; Jn 13:31-38). Denied Jesus (Mt 26:69-75; Mk 14: 66-72; Lk 22:54-62; Jn 18:15-27). Commissioned by Jesus to shepherd his flock (Jn 21:15-23).
Speech at Pentecost (Ac 2). Healed beggar (Ac 3:1-10). Speech at temple (Ac 3:11-26), before Sanhedrin (Ac 4:1-22). In Samaria (Ac 8:14-25). Sent by vision to Cornelius (Ac 10). Announced salvation of Gentiles in Jerusalem (Ac 11; 15). Freed from prison (Ac 12). Inconsistency at Antioch (Gal 2:11-21). At Jerusalem Council (Ac 15). Epistles: 1-2 Peter.

PETITION (PETITIONS)
1Ch 16: 4 to make *p*, to give thanks,
Php 4: 6 by prayer and *p*, with thanksgiving,

PETITIONS (PETITION)
Heb 5: 7 he offered up prayers and *p*

PHANTOM*
Ps 39: 6 Man is a mere *p* as he goes to

PHARAOH (PHARAOH'S)
Ge 12:15 her to *P*, and she was taken
41:14 So *P* sent for Joseph, and he was
Ex 14: 4 glory for myself through *P*
14:17 And I will gain glory through *P*

PHARAOH'S (PHARAOH)
Ex 7: 3 But I will harden *P* heart, and

PHARISEE (PHARISEES)
Ac 23: 6 brothers, I am a *P*, the son of a *P*.
Php 3: 5 in regard to the law, a *P*; as for zeal,

PHARISEES (PHARISEE)
Mt 5:20 surpasses that of the *P*
16: 6 guard against the yeast of the *P*
23:13 of the law and *P*, you hypocrites!
Jn 3: 1 a man of the *P* named Nicodemus,

PHILADELPHIA
Rev 3: 7 the angel of the church in *P* write:

PHILEMON*
Phm 1 To *P* our dear friend and fellow

PHILIP
1. Apostle (Mt 10:3; Mk 3:18; Lk 6:14; Jn 1: 43-48; 14:8; Ac 1:13).

2. Deacon (Ac 6:1-7); evangelist in Samaria (Ac 8:4-25), to Ethiopian (Ac 8:26-40).

PHILIPPI
Ac 16:12 From there we traveled to *P*,
Php 1: 1 To all the saints in Christ Jesus at *P*

PHILISTINE (PHILISTINES)
Jos 13: 3 of the five *P* rulers in Gaza,
1Sa 14: 1 let's go over to the *P* outpost
17:26 is this uncircumcised *P* that he
17:37 me from the hand of this *P*."

PHILISTINES (PHILISTINE)
Jdg 10: 7 them into the hands of the *P*
13: 1 the hands of the *P* for forty years.
16: 5 The rulers of the *P* went to her
1Sa 4: 1 at Ebenezer, and the *P* at Aphek.
5: 8 together all the rulers of the *P*
13:23 a detachment of *P* had gone out
17: 1 the *P* gathered their forces for war
23: 1 the *P* are fighting against Keilah
27: 1 is to escape to the land of the *P*.
31: 1 Now the *P* fought against Israel;
2Sa 5:17 When the *P* heard that David had
8: 1 David defeated the *P* and subdued
21:15 there was a battle between the *P*
2Ki 18: 8 he defeated the *P*, as far as Gaza
Am 1: 8 Ekron till the last of the *P* is dead,"

PHILOSOPHER* (PHILOSOPHY)
1Co 1:20 Where is the *p* of this age?

PHILOSOPHY* (PHILOSOPHER)
Col 2: 8 through hollow and deceptive *p*,

PHINEHAS
Nu 25: 7 When *P* son of Eleazar, the son
Ps 106: 30 But *P* stood up and intervened,

PHOEBE*
Ro 16: 1 I commend to you our sister *P*,

PHYLACTERIES*
Mt 23: 5 They make their *p* wide

PHYSICAL
Ro 2:28 merely outward and *p*.
Col 1:22 by Christ's *p* body through death
1Ti 4: 8 For *p* training is of some value,
Jas 2:16 but does nothing about his *p* needs,

PICK (PICKED)
Mk 16:18 they will *p* up snakes

PICKED (PICK)
Lk 14: 7 noticed how the guests *p* the places
Jn 5: 9 he *p* up his mat and walked.

PIECE (PIECES)
Jn 19:23 woven in one *p* from top to bottom.

PIECES (PIECE)
Ge 15:17 and passed between the *p*.
Jer 34:18 and then walked between its *p*.
Zec 11:12 So they paid me thirty *p* of silver.
Mt 14:20 of broken *p* that were left over.

PIERCE (PIERCED)
Ex 21: 6 and *p* his ear with an awl.
Pr 12:18 Reckless words *p* like a sword,
Lk 2:35 a sword will *p* your own soul too."

PIERCED (PIERCE)
Ps 22:16 they have *p* my hands and my feet.
40: 6 but my ears you have *p*;
Isa 53: 5 But he was *p* for our transgressions,
Zec 12:10 look on me, the one they have *p*,
Jn 19:37 look on the one they have *p*."
Rev 1: 7 even those who *p* him;

PIG'S (PIGS)
Pr 11:22 Like a gold ring in a *p* snout

PIGEONS
Lev 5:11 afford two doves or two young *p*,
Lk 2:24 "a pair of doves or two young *p*."

PIGS (PIG'S)

Mt   7: 6 do not throw your pearls to *p*.
Mk   5: 11 A large herd of *p* was feeding on

PILATE

Governor of Judea. Questioned Jesus (Mt 27: 1-26; Mk 15:15; Lk 22:66-23:25; Jn 18:28-19:16); sent him to Herod (Lk 23:6-12); consented to his crucifixion when crowds chose Barabbas (Mt 27: 15-26; Mk 15:6-15; Lk 23:13-25; Jn 19:1-10).

PILLAR (PILLARS)

Ge   19: 26 and she became a *p* of salt.
Ex   13: 21 ahead of them in a *p* of cloud
1Ti   3: 15 the *p* and foundation of the truth.
Rev   3: 12 who overcomes I will make a *p*

PILLARS (PILLAR)

Gal   2: 9 and John, those reputed to be *p*,

PINIONS

Dt   32: 11 and carries them on its *p*.

PISGAH

Dt   3: 27 Go up to the top of *P* and look west

PIT

Ps   7: 15 falls into the *p* he has made.
    40: 2 He lifted me out of the slimy *p*,
  103: 4 who redeems your life from the *p*
Pr   23: 27 for a prostitute is a deep *p*
    26: 27 If a man digs a *p*, he will fall into it;
Isa   24: 17 Terror and *p* and snare await you,
    38: 17 me from the *p* of destruction;
Mt   15: 14 a blind man, both will fall into a *p*.''

PITCH

Ge   6: 14 and coat it with *p* inside and out.
Ex   2: 3 and coated it with tar and *p*.

PITIED (PITY)

1Co 15: 19 we are to be *p* more than all men.

PITY (PITIED)

Ps   72: 13 He will take *p* on the weak
Ecc   4: 10 But *p* the man who falls
Lk   10: 33 when he saw him, he took *p* on him

PLAGUE (PLAGUED PLAGUES)

2Ch   6: 28 ''When famine or *p* comes
Ps   91: 6 nor the *p* that destroys at midday.

PLAGUED* (PLAGUE)

Ps   73: 5 they are not *p* by human ills.
    73: 14 All day long I have been *p*;

PLAGUES (PLAGUE)

Hos 13: 14 Where, O death, are your *p*?
Rev 21: 9 full of the seven last *p* came
    22: 18 to him the *p* described in this book.

PLAIN

Isa   40: 4 the rugged places a *p*.
Ro   1: 19 what may be known about God is *p*

PLAN (PLANNED PLANS)

Ex   26: 30 according to the *p* shown you
Job 42: 2 no *p* of yours can be thwarted.
Pr   14: 22 those who *p* what is good find love
    21: 30 is no wisdom, no insight, no *p*
Am   3: 7 nothing without revealing his *p*
Eph   1: 11 predestined according to the *p*

PLANK

Mt   7: 3 attention to the *p* in your own eye?
Lk   6: 41 attention to the *p* in your own eye?

PLANNED (PLAN)

Ps   40: 5 The things you *p* for us
Isa   14: 24 ''Surely, as I have *p*, so it will be,
    23: 9 The LORD Almighty *p* it,
    46: 11 what I have *p*, that will I do.
Heb 11: 40 God had *p* something better for us

PLANS (PLAN)

Ps   20: 4 and make all your *p* succeed.
    33: 11 *p* of the LORD stand firm forever,
Pr   15: 22 *P* fail for lack of counsel,
    16: 3 and your *p* will succeed.

Pr   19: 21 Many are the *p* in a man's heart,
    20: 18 Make *p* by seeking advice;
Isa   29: 15 to hide their *p* from the LORD,
    30: 1 those who carry out *p* that are not
    32: 8 But the noble man makes noble *p*,
2Co   1: 17 Or do I make my *p* in a worldly

PLANT (PLANTED PLANTING PLANTS)

Am   9: 15 I will *p* Israel in their own land,
Mt   15: 13 ''Every *p* that my heavenly Father

PLANTED (PLANT)

Ge   2: 8 the LORD God had *p* a garden
Ps   1: 3 He is like a tree *p* by streams
Jer   17: 8 He will be like a tree *p* by the water
Mt   15: 13 Father has not *p* will be pulled
    21: 33 was a landowner who *p* a vineyard.
Lk   13: 6 ''A man had a fig tree, *p*
1Co   3: 6 I *p* the seed, Apollos watered it,
Jas   1: 21 humbly accept the word *p* in you,

PLANTING (PLANT)

Isa   61: 3 a *p* of the LORD

PLANTS (PLANT)

Pr   31: 16 out of her earnings she *p* a vineyard
1Co   3: 7 So neither he who *p* nor he who
    9: 7 Who *p* a vineyard and does not eat

PLATTER

Mk   6: 25 head of John the Baptist on a *p*.''

PLAY (PLAYED)

1Sa 16: 23 David would take his harp and *p*.
Isa   11: 8 The infant will *p* near the hole

PLAYED (PLAY)

Lk   7: 32 '' 'We *p* the flute for you,
1Co 14: 7 anyone know what tune is being *p*

PLEA (PLEAD PLEADED PLEADS)

1Ki   8: 28 to your servant's prayer and his *p*
Ps 102: 17 he will not despise their *p*.
La   3: 56 You heard my *p*: ''Do not close

PLEAD (PLEA)

Isa   1: 17 *p* the case of the widow.

PLEADED (PLEA)

2Co 12: 8 Three times I *p* with the Lord

PLEADS (PLEA)

Job 16: 21 on behalf of a man he *p* with God

PLEASANT (PLEASE)

Ge   49: 15 and how *p* is his land,
Ps   16: 6 for me in *p* places;
  133: 1 How good and *p* it is
  135: 3 sing praise to his name, for that is *p*
  147: 1 how *p* and fitting to praise him!
Pr   2: 10 knowledge will be *p* to your soul.
    3: 17 Her ways are *p* ways,
    16: 21 and *p* words promote instruction.
    16: 24 *P* words are a honeycomb,
Isa   30: 10 Tell us *p* things.
1Th   3: 6 that you always have *p* memories
Heb 12: 11 No discipline seems *p* at the time,

PLEASANTNESS* (PLEASE)

Pr   27: 9 the *p* of one's friend springs

PLEASE (PLEASANT PLEASANTNESS PLEASED PLEASES PLEASING PLEASURE PLEASURES)

Ps   69: 31 This will *p* the LORD more
Pr   20: 23 and dishonest scales do not *p* him.
Isa   46: 10 and I will do all that I *p*.
Jer   6: 20 your sacrifices do not *p* me.''
    27: 5 and I give it to anyone I *p*.
Jn   5: 30 for I seek not to *p* myself
Ro   8: 8 by the sinful nature cannot *p* God.
    15: 1 of the weak and not to *p* ourselves.
    15: 2 Each of us should *p* his neighbor
1Co   7: 32 affairs—how he can *p* the Lord.
    10: 33 I try to *p* everybody in every way.
2Co   5: 9 So we make it our goal to *p* him.
Gal   1: 10 or of God? Or am I trying to *p* men
    6: 8 the one who sows to *p* the Spirit,
Col   1: 10 and may *p* him in every way:

1Th   2: 4 We are not trying to *p* men
    4: 1 how to live in order to *p* God.
2Ti   2: 4 wants to *p* his commanding officer.
Tit   2: 9 to try to *p* them, not to talk back
Heb 11: 6 faith it is impossible to *p* God,

PLEASED (PLEASE)

Dt   28: 63 as it *p* the LORD to make you
1Sa 12: 22 LORD was *p* to make you his own.
1Ki   3: 10 The Lord was *p* that Solomon had
1Ch 29: 17 that you test the heart and are *p*
Mic   6: 7 Will the LORD be *p*
Mal   1: 10 I am not *p* with you,'' says
Mt   3: 17 whom I love; with him I am well *p*
    17: 5 whom I love; with him I am well *p*.
Mk   1: 11 whom I love; with you I am well *p*
Lk   3: 22 whom I love; with you I am well *p*
1Co   1: 21 God was *p* through the foolishness
Col   1: 19 For God was *p* to have all his
Heb 10: 6 you were not *p*.
    10: 8 nor were you *p* with them''
    10: 38 I will not be *p* with him.''
    11: 5 commended as one who *p* God.
    13: 16 for with such sacrifices God is *p*.
2Pe   1: 17 whom I love; with him I am well *p*

PLEASES (PLEASE)

Job 23: 13 He does whatever he *p*.
Ps 115: 3 he does whatever *p* him.
  135: 6 The LORD does whatever *p* him,
Pr   15: 8 but the prayer of the upright *p* him.
    21: 1 it like a watercourse wherever he *p*
Ecc   2: 26 To the man who *p* him, God gives
    7: 26 man who *p* God will escape her,
Da   4: 35 He does as he *p*
Jn   3: 8 The wind blows wherever it *p*
    8: 29 for I always do what *p* him.''
Eph   5: 10 truth) and find out what *p* the Lord
Col   3: 20 in everything, for this *p* the Lord.
1Ti   2: 3 This is good, and *p* God our Savior,
1Jn   3: 22 his commands and do what *p* him.

PLEASING (PLEASE)

Ge   2: 9 trees that were *p* to the eye
Lev   1: 9 an aroma *p* to the LORD.
Ps   19: 14 be *p* in your sight,
  104: 34 May my meditation be *p* to him,
Pr   15: 26 but those of the pure are *p* to him.
    16: 7 When a man's ways are *p*
SS   1: 3 *P* is the fragrance of your perfumes
    4: 10 How much more *p* is your love
    7: 6 How beautiful you are and how *p*,
Ro   12: 1 *p* to God—this is your spiritual
    14: 18 Christ in this way is *p* to God
Php   4: 18 an acceptable sacrifice, *p* to God.
1Ti   5: 4 grandparents, for this is *p* to God.
Heb 13: 21 may he work in us what is *p* to him,

PLEASURE (PLEASE)

Ps   5: 4 You are not a God who takes *p*
    51: 16 you do not take *p* in burnt offerings
  147: 10 His *p* is not in the strength
Pr   10: 23 A fool finds *p* in evil conduct,
    18: 2 A fool finds no *p* in understanding
    21: 17 He who loves *p* will become poor;
Isa   1: 11 I have no *p*
Jer   6: 10 they find no *p* in it.
Eze 18: 23 Do I take any *p* in the death
    18: 32 For I take no *p* in the death
    33: 11 I take no *p* in the death
Lk   10: 21 Father, for this was your good *p*.
Eph   1: 5 in accordance with his *p* and will—
    1: 9 of his will according to his good *p*,
1Ti   5: 6 the widow who lives for *p* is dead
2Ti   3: 4 lovers of *p* rather than lovers
2Pe   2: 13 Their idea of *p* is to carouse

PLEASURES* (PLEASE)

Ps   16: 11 with eternal *p* at your right hand.
Lk   8: 14 and *p*, and they do not mature.
Tit   3: 3 by all kinds of passions and *p*.
Heb 11: 25 rather than to enjoy the *p* of sin
Jas   4: 3 may spend what you get on your *p*.
2Pe   2: 13 reveling in their *p* while they feast

PLEDGE

Dt   24: 17 take the cloak of the widow as a *p*.
1Pe   3: 21 but the *p* of a good conscience

PLEIADES

Job 38: 31 "Can you bind the beautiful *P?*
Am 5: 8 (he who made the *P* and Orion,

PLENTIFUL (PLENTY)

Mt 9: 37 harvest is *p* but the workers are
Lk 10: 2 harvest is *p*, but the workers are

PLENTY (PLENTIFUL)

2Co 8: 14 the present time your *p* will supply
Php 4: 12 whether living in *p* or in want.

PLOT (PLOTS)

Est 2: 22 Mordecai found out about the *p*
Ps 2: 1 and the peoples *p* in vain?
Pr 3: 29 not *p* harm against your neighbor,
Zec 8: 17 do not *p* evil against your neighbor,
Ac 4: 25 and the peoples *p* in vain?

PLOTS (PLOT)

Pr 6: 14 who *p* evil with deceit in his heart

PLOW (PLOWMAN PLOWSHARES)

Lk 9: 62 "No one who puts his hand to the *p*

PLOWMAN (PLOW)

1Co 9: 10 because when the *p* plows

PLOWSHARES (PLOW)

1Sa 13: 20 to the Philistines to have their *p*,
Isa 2: 4 They will beat their swords into *p*
Joel 3: 10 Beat your *p* into swords
Mic 4: 3 They will beat their swords into *p*

PLUCK

Mk 9: 47 your eye causes you to sin, *p* it out.

PLUNDER (PLUNDERED)

Ex 3: 22 And so you will *p* the Egyptians."
Est 3: 13 of Adar, and to *p* their goods.
8: 11 to *p* the property of their enemies.
9: 10 did not lay their hands on the *p*.
Pr 22: 23 and will *p* those who *p* them.
Isa 3: 14 the *p* from the poor is

PLUNDERED (PLUNDER)

Eze 34: 8 lacks a shepherd and so has been *p*

PLUNGE

1Ti 6: 9 and harmful desires that *p* men
1Pe 4: 4 think it strange that you do not *p*

PODS

Lk 15: 16 with the *p* that the pigs were eating,

POINT

Mt 4: 5 on the highest *p* of the temple.
26: 38 with sorrow to the *p* of death.
Jas 2: 10 yet stumbles at just one *p* is guilty
Rev 2: 10 Be faithful, even to the *p* of death,

POISON

Ps 140: 3 the *p* of vipers is on their lips.
Mk 16: 18 and when they drink deadly *p*,
Ro 3: 13 "The *p* of vipers is on their lips."
Jas 3: 8 It is a restless evil, full of deadly *p*.

POLE (POLES)

Nu 21: 8 "Make a snake and put it up on a *p*;
Dt 16: 21 not set up any wooden Asherah *p*

POLES (POLE)

Ex 25: 13 Then make *p* of acacia wood

POLISHED

Isa 49: 2 he made me into a *p* arrow

POLLUTE* (POLLUTED POLLUTES)

Nu 35: 33 "'Do not *p* the land where you are.
Jude : 8 these dreamers *p* their own bodies,

POLLUTED* (POLLUTE)

Ezr 9: 11 entering to possess is a land *p*
Pr 25: 26 Like a muddied spring or a *p* well
Ac 15: 20 to abstain from food *p* by idols,
Jas 1: 27 oneself from being *p* by the world.

POLLUTES* (POLLUTE)

Nu 35: 33 Bloodshed *p* the land,

PONDER (PONDERED)

Ps 64: 9 and *p* what he has done.
119: 95 but I will *p* your statutes.

PONDERED (PONDER)

Ps 111: 2 they are *p* by all who delight
Lk 2: 19 up all these things and *p* them

POOR (POVERTY)

Lev 19: 10 Leave them for the *p* and the alien.
23: 22 Leave them for the *p* and the alien.
27: 8 If anyone making the vow is too *p*
Dt 15: 4 there should be no *p* among you,
15: 7 is a *p* man among your brothers
15: 11 There will always be *p* people
24: 12 If the man is *p*, do not go to sleep
24: 14 advantage of a hired man who is *p*
Job 5: 16 So the *p* have hope,
24: 4 force all the *p* of the land
Ps 14: 6 frustrate the plans of the *p*,
34: 6 This *p* man called, and the LORD
35: 10 You rescue the *p* from those too
40: 17 Yet I am *p* and needy;
68: 10 O God, you provided for the *p*.
82: 3 maintain the rights of the *p*
112: 9 scattered abroad his gifts to the *p*,
113: 7 He raises the *p* from the dust
140: 12 the LORD secures justice for the *p*
Pr 10: 4 Lazy hands make a man *p*,
13: 7 to be *p*, yet has great wealth.
14: 20 The *p* are shunned
14: 31 oppresses the *p* shows contempt
17: 5 who mocks the *p* shows contempt
19: 1 Better a *p* man whose walk is
19: 17 to the *p* lends to the LORD,
19: 22 better to be *p* than a liar.
20: 13 not love sleep or you will grow *p*;
21: 13 to the cry of the *p*,
21: 17 who loves pleasure will become *p*;
22: 2 Rich and *p* have this in common:
22: 9 for he shares his food with the *p*.
22: 22 not exploit the *p* because they are *p*
28: 6 Better a *p* man whose walk is
28: 27 to the *p* will lack nothing,
29: 7 care about justice for the *p*,
31: 9 defend the rights of the *p*
31: 20 She opens her arms to the *p*
Ecc 4: 13 Better a *p* but wise youth
Isa 3: 14 the plunder from the *p* is
10: 2 to deprive the *p* of their rights
14: 30 of the *p* will find pasture,
25: 4 You have been a refuge for the *p*,
32: 7 schemes to destroy the *p* with lies,
61: 1 me to preach good news to the *p*.
Jer 22: 16 He defended the cause of the *p*
Eze 18: 12 He oppresses the *p* and needy.
Am 2: 7 They trample on the heads of the *p*
4: 1 you women who oppress the *p*
5: 11 You trample on the *p*
Zec 7: 10 or the fatherless, the alien or the *p*.
Mt 5: 3 saying: "Blessed are the *p* in spirit,
11: 5 the good news is preached to the *p*.
19: 21 your possessions and give to the *p*,
26: 11 The *p* you will always have
Mk 12: 42 But a *p* widow came and put
14: 7 The *p* you will always have
Lk 4: 18 me to preach good news to the *p*.
6: 20 "Blessed are you who are *p*,
11: 41 is inside the dish, to the *p*,
14: 13 invite the *p*, the crippled, the lame,
21: 2 also saw a *p* widow put
Jn 12: 8 You will always have the *p*
Ac 9: 36 doing good and helping the *p*.
10: 4 and gifts to the *p* have come up
24: 17 to bring my people gifts for the *p*
Ro 15: 26 for the *p* among the saints
1Co 13: 3 If I give all I possess to the *p*
2Co 6: 10 sorrowful, yet always rejoicing; *p*,
8: 9 yet for your sakes he became *p*,
Gal 2: 10 continue to remember the *p*.
Jas 2: 2 and a *p* man in shabby clothes
2: 5 not God chosen those who are *p*
2: 6 But you have insulted the *p*.

POPULATION*

Pr 14: 28 A large *p* is a king's glory,

PORTION

Nu 18: 29 as the LORD's *p* the best
Dt 32: 9 For the LORD's *p* is his people,
1Sa 1: 5 But to Hannah he gave a double *p*
2Ki 2: 9 "Let me inherit a double *p*
Ps 73: 26 and my *p* forever.
119: 57 You are my *p*, O LORD;
Isa 53: 12 Therefore I will give him a *p*
Jer 10: 16 He who is the *P* of Jacob is not like
La 3: 24 to myself, "The LORD is my *p*;
Zec 2: 12 LORD will inherit Judah as his *p*

PORTRAIT

Lk 20: 24 Whose *p* and inscription are on it?"

PORTRAYED

Gal 3: 1 very eyes Jesus Christ was clearly *p*

POSITION (POSITIONS)

Ro 12: 16 to associate with people of low *p*.
Jas 1: 9 ought to take pride in his high *p*.
2Pe 3: 17 and fall from your secure *p*.

POSITIONS (POSITION)

2Ch 20: 17 Take up your *p*; stand firm
Jude : 6 the angels who did not keep their *p*

POSSESS (POSSESSED POSSESSING POSSESSION POSSESSIONS)

Nu 33: 53 for I have given you the land to *p*.
Dt 4: 14 you are crossing the Jordan to *p*.
Pr 8: 12 I *p* knowledge and discretion.
Jn 5: 39 that by them you *p* eternal life.

POSSESSED (POSSESS)

Jn 10: 21 the sayings of a man *p* by a demon.

POSSESSING* (POSSESS)

2Co 6: 10 nothing, and yet *p* everything.

POSSESSION (POSSESS)

Ge 15: 7 to give you this land to take *p* of it
Ex 6: 8 I will give it to you as a *p*.
19: 5 nations you will be my treasured *p*
Nu 13: 30 "We should go up and take *p*
Dt 7: 6 to be his people, his treasured *p*.
Jos 1: 11 take *p* of the land the LORD your
Ps 2: 8 the ends of the earth your *p*.
135: 4 Israel to be his treasured *p*.
Eph 1: 14 of those who are God's *p*—

POSSESSIONS (POSSESS)

Mt 19: 21 go, sell your *p* and give to the poor,
Lk 11: 21 guards his own house, his *p* are safe
12: 15 consist in the abundance of his *p*."
19: 8 now I give half of my *p* to the poor,
Ac 4: 32 any of his *p* was his own,
2Co 12: 14 what I want is not your *p* but you.
Heb 10: 34 yourselves had better and lasting *p*.
1Jn 3: 17 If anyone has material *p*

POSSIBLE

Mt 19: 26 but with God all things are *p*."
26: 39 if it is *p*, may this cup be taken
Mk 9: 23 "Everything is *p* for him who
10: 27 all things are *p* with God."
14: 35 prayed that if *p* the hour might pass
Ro 12: 18 If it is *p*, as far as it depends on you,
1Co 6: 5 Is it *p* that there is nobody
9: 19 to everyone, to win as many as *p*.
9: 22 by all *p* means I might save some.

POT (POTSHERD POTTER POTTER'S POTTERY)

2Ki 4: 40 there is death in the *p*!"
Jer 18: 4 But the *p* he was shaping

POTIPHAR*

Egyptian who bought Joseph (Ge 37:36), set him over his house (Ge 39:1-6), sent him to prison (Ge 39:7-20).

POTSHERD (POT)

Isa 45: 9 a *p* among the potsherds

POTTER (POT)

Isa 29: 16 Can the pot say of the *p*,
45: 9 Does the clay say to the *p*,

Isa 64: 8 We are the clay, you are the *p;*
Jer 18: 6 "Like clay in the hand of the *p,*
Zec 11:13 it to the *p"* — the handsome price
Ro 9:21 Does not the *p* have the right

POTTER'S (POT)

Mt 27: 7 to use the money to buy the *p* field

POTTERY (POT)

Ro 9:21 of clay some *p* for noble purposes

POUR (POURED POURS)

Ps 62: 8 *p* out your hearts to him,
Isa 44: 3 I will *p* out my Spirit
Eze 20: 8 So I said I would *p* out my wrath
    39:29 for I will *p* out my Spirit
Joel 2:28 I will *p* out my Spirit on all people.
Zec 12:10 I will *p* out on the house of David
Mal 3:10 *p* out so much blessing that you
Ac 2:17 I will *p* out my Spirit on all people.

POURED (POUR)

Ps 22:14 I am *p* out like water,
Isa 32:15 till the Spirit is *p* upon us
Mt 26:28 which is *p* out for many
Lk 22:20 in my blood, which is *p* out for you.
Ac 2:33 and has *p* out what you now see
   10:45 of the Holy Spirit had been *p* out
Ro 5: 5 because God has *p* out his love
Php 2:17 even if I am being *p* out like a drink
2Ti 4: 6 I am already being *p* out like
Tit 3: 6 whom he *p* out on us generously
Rev 16: 2 and *p* out his bowl on the land.

POURS (POUR)

Lk 5:37 And no one *p* new wine

POVERTY* (POOR)

Dt 28:48 and thirst, in nakedness and dire *p,*
1Sa 2: 7 The LORD sends *p* and wealth;
Pr 6:11 *p* will come on you like a bandit
   10:15 but *p* is the ruin of the poor.
   11:24 withholds unduly, but comes to *p.*
   13:18 who ignores discipline comes to *p*
   14:23 but mere talk leads only to *p.*
   21: 5 as surely as haste leads to *p.*
   22:16 to the rich—both come to *p.*
   24:34 *p* will come on you like a bandit
   28:19 fantasies will have his fill of *p.*
   28:22 and is unaware that *p* awaits him.
   30: 8 give me neither *p* nor riches,
   31: 7 let them drink and forget their *p*
Ecc 4:14 born in *p* within his kingdom.
Mk 12:44 out of her *p,* put in everything—
Lk 21: 4 she out of her *p* put in all she had
2Co 8: 2 and their extreme *p* welled up
   8: 9 through his *p* might become rich.
Rev 2: 9 I know your afflictions and your *p*

POWER (POWERFUL POWERS)

Ex 15: 6 was majestic in *p.*
   32:11 out of Egypt with great *p*
Dt 8:17 "My *p* and the strength
   34:12 one has ever shown the mighty *p*
1Sa 10: 6 LORD will come upon you in *p,*
   10:10 Spirit of God came upon him in *p,*
   11: 6 Spirit of God came upon him in *p,*
   16:13 the LORD came upon David in *p.*
1Ch 29:11 LORD, is the greatness and the *p*
2Ch 20: 6 *P* and might are in your hand,
   32: 7 for there is a greater *p* with us
Job 9: 4 wisdom is profound, his *p* is vast.
   36:22 "God is exalted in his *p.*
   37:23 beyond our reach and exalted in *p;*
Ps 20: 6 with the saving *p* of his right hand.
   63: 2 and beheld your *p* and your glory.
   66: 3 So great is your *p*
   68:34 Proclaim the *p* of God,
   77:14 you display your *p*
   89:13 Your arm is endued with *p;*
   145: 6 of the *p* of your awesome works,
   147: 5 Great is our Lord and mighty in *p;*
   150: 2 Praise him for his acts of *p;*
Pr 3:27 when it is in your *p* to act.
   18:21 The tongue has the *p* of life
   24: 5 A wise man has great *p,*
Isa 11: 2 the Spirit of counsel and of *p,*
   40:10 the Sovereign LORD comes with *p*

Isa 40:26 of his great *p* and mighty strength,
   63:12 who sent his glorious arm of *p*
Jer 10: 6 and your name is mighty in *p.*
   10:12 But God made the earth by his *p;*
   27: 5 With my great *p* and outstretched
   32:17 and the earth by your great *p*
Hos 13:14 from the *p* of the grave;
Na 1: 3 to anger and great in *p;*
Zec 4: 6 nor by *p,* but by my Spirit,'
Mt 22:29 do not know the Scriptures or the *p*
   24:30 on the clouds of the sky, with *p*
Lk 1:35 and the *p* of the Most High will
   4:14 to Galilee in the *p* of the Spirit,
   9: 1 he gave them *p* and authority
   10:19 to overcome all the *p* of the enemy;
   24:49 clothed with *p* from on high."
Ac 1: 8 you will receive *p* when the Holy
   4:28 They did what your *p* and will had
   4:33 With great *p* the apostles
   10:38 with the Holy Spirit and *p,*
   26:18 and from the *p* of Satan to God,
Ro 1:16 it is the *p* of God for the salvation
   1:20 his eternal *p* and divine nature—
   4:21 fully persuaded that God had *p*
   9:17 that I might display my *p* in you
   15:13 overflow with hope by the *p*
   15:19 through the *p* of the Spirit.
1Co 1:17 cross of Christ be emptied of its *p.*
   1:18 to us who are being saved it is the *p*
   2: 4 a demonstration of the Spirit's *p,*
   6:14 By his *p* God raised the Lord
   15:24 all dominion, authority and *p.*
   15:56 of death is sin, and the *p*
2Co 4: 7 to show that this all-surpassing *p* is
   6: 7 in truthful speech and in the *p*
   10: 4 they have divine *p*
   12: 9 for my *p* is made perfect
   13: 4 weakness, yet he lives by God's *p.*
Eph 1:19 and his incomparably great *p*
   3:16 you with *p* through his Spirit
   3:20 according to his *p* that is at work
   6:10 in the Lord and in his mighty *p.*
Php 3:10 and the *p* of his resurrection
   3:21 by the *p* that enables him
Col 1:11 strengthened with all *p* according
   2:10 who is the head over every *p*
1Th 1: 5 also with *p,* with the Holy Spirit
2Ti 1: 7 but a spirit of *p,* of love
   3: 5 form of godliness but denying its *p.*
Heb 2:14 might destroy him who holds the *p*
   7:16 of the *p* of an indestructible life.
1Pe 1: 5 by God's *p* until the coming
2Pe 1: 3 his divine *p* has given us
Jude : 25 *p* and authority, through Jesus
Rev 4:11 to receive glory and honor and *p,*
   5:12 to receive *p* and wealth
   11:17 you have taken your great *p*
   19: 1 and glory and *p* belong to our God,
   20: 6 The second death has no *p*

POWERFUL (POWER)

2Ch 27: 6 Jotham grew *p* because he walked
Est 9: 4 and he became more and more *p.*
Ps 29: 4 The voice of the LORD is *p;*
Jer 32:18 *p* God, whose name is the LORD
Zec 8:22 *p* nations will come to Jerusalem
Mk 1: 7 "After me will come one more *p*
Lk 24:19 *p* in word and deed before God
2Th 1: 7 in blazing fire with his *p* angels.
Heb 1: 3 sustaining all things by his *p* word.
Jas 5:16 The prayer of a righteous man is *p*

POWERLESS

Ro 5: 6 when we were still *p,* Christ died
   8: 3 For what the law was *p* to do

POWERS (POWER)

Da 4:35 pleases with the *p* of heaven
Ro 8:38 nor any *p,* neither height nor depth
1Co 12:10 to another miraculous *p,*
Eph 6:12 against the *p* of this dark world
Col 1:16 whether thrones or *p* or rulers
   2:15 And having disarmed the *p*
Heb 6: 5 and the *p* of the coming age,
1Pe 3:22 and *p* in submission to him.

PRACTICE (PRACTICED PRACTICES)

Lev 19:26 " 'Do not *p* divination or sorcery.
Ps 119: 56 This has been my *p:*
Eze 33:31 but they do not put them into *p.*
Mt 7:24 into *p* is like a wise man who built
   23: 3 for they do not *p* what they preach.
Lk 8:21 hear God's word and put it into *p.''*
Ro 12:13 *P* hospitality.
Php 4: 9 or seen in me—put it into *p.*
1Ti 5: 4 to put their religion into *p* by caring

PRACTICED (PRACTICE)

Mt 23:23 You should have *p* the latter,

PRACTICES (PRACTICE)

Ps 101: 7 No one who *p* deceit
Mt 5:19 but whoever *p* and teaches these
Col 3: 9 taken off your old self with its *p*

PRAISE (PRAISED PRAISES PRAISEWORTHY PRAISING)

Ex 15: 2 He is my God, and I will *p* him,
Dt 10:21 He is your *p;* he is your God,
   26:19 declared that he will set you in *p,*
   32: 3 Oh, *p* the greatness of our God!
Ru 4:14 said to Naomi: "*P* be to the LORD,
2Sa 22: 4 to the LORD, who is worthy of *p,*
   22:47 The LORD lives! *P* be to my Rock
1Ch 16:25 is the LORD and most worthy of *p;*
   16:35 that we may glory in your *p.''*
   23: 5 four thousand are to *p* the LORD
   29:10 "*P* be to you, O LORD,
2Ch 5:13 they raised their voices in *p*
   20:21 and to *p* him for the splendor
   29:30 to *p* the LORD with the words
Ezr 3:10 took their places to *p* the LORD,
Ne 5: 5 and *p* the LORD your God,
Ps 8: 2 you have ordained *p*
   9: 1 I will *p* you, O LORD,
   16: 7 I will *p* the LORD, who counsels
   26: 7 proclaiming aloud your *p*
   30: 4 *p* his holy name.
   33: 1 it is fitting for the upright to *p* him.
   34: 1 his *p* will always be on my lips.
   40: 3 a hymn of *p* to our God.
   42: 5 for I will yet *p* him,
   43: 5 for I will yet *p* him,
   45:17 the nations will *p* you for ever
   47: 7 sing to him a psalm of *p.*
   48: 1 the LORD, and most worthy of *p,*
   51:15 and my mouth will declare your *p.*
   56: 4 In God, whose word I *p,*
   57: 9 I will *p* you, O Lord,
   63: 4 I will *p* you as long as I live,
   65: 1 *P* awaits you, O God, in Zion;
   66: 2 make his *p* glorious.
   66: 8 *P* our God, O peoples,
   68:19 *P* be to the Lord, to God our Savior
   68:26 *p* the LORD in the assembly
   69:30 I will *p* God's name in song
   69:34 Let heaven and earth *p* him,
   71: 8 My mouth is filled with your *p,*
   71:14 I will *p* you more and more.
   71:22 I will *p* you with the harp
   74:21 the poor and needy *p* your name.
   86:12 I will *p* you, O Lord my God,
   89: 5 The heavens *p* your wonders,
   92: 1 It is good to *p* the LORD
   96: 2 Sing to the LORD, *p* his name;
   100: 4 and his courts with *p;*
   101: 1 to you, O LORD, I will sing *p.*
   102:18 not yet created may *p* the LORD:
   103: 1 *P* the LORD, O my soul;
   103:20 *P* the LORD, you his angels,
   104: 1 *P* the LORD, O my soul.
   105: 2 Sing to him, sing *p* to him;
   106: 1 *P* the LORD.
   108: 3 I will *p* you, O LORD,
   111: 1 *P* the LORD.
   113: 1 *P* the LORD.
   117: 1 *P* the LORD, all you nations;
   119:175 Let me live that I may *p* you,
   135: 1 *P* the LORD.
   135:20 you who fear him, *p* the LORD.
   138: 1 I will *p* you, O LORD,
   139:14 I *p* you because I am fearfully
   144: 1 *P* be to the LORD my Rock,

Ps 145: 3 is the LORD and most worthy of *p*;
145: 10 All you have made will *p* you,
145: 21 Let every creature *p* his holy name
146: 1 *P* the LORD, O my soul.
147: 1 how pleasant and fitting to *p* him!
148: 1 *P* the LORD from the heavens,
148: 13 Let them *p* the name of the LORD,
149: 1 his *p* in the assembly of the saints.
149: 6 May the *p* of God be
149: 9 *P* the LORD.
150: 2 *p* him for his surpassing greatness.
150: 6 that has breath *p* the LORD.
Pr 27: 2 Let another *p* you, and not your
27: 21 man is tested by the *p* he receives.
31: 31 let her works bring her *p*
SS 1: 4 we will *p* your love more than wine
Isa 12: 1 "I will *p* you, O LORD.
42: 10 his *p* from the ends of the earth,
61: 3 and a garment of *p*
Jer 33: 9 *p* and honor before all nations
Da 2: 20 "*P* be to the name of God for ever
4: 37 *p* and exalt and glorify the King
Mt 5: 16 and *p* your Father in heaven.
21: 16 you have ordained *p*'?"
Lk 19: 37 to *p* God in loud voices
Jn 5: 44 effort to obtain the *p* that comes
12: 43 for they loved *p* from men more
Ro 2: 29 Such a man's *p* is not from men,
15: 7 in order to bring *p* to God.
2Co 1: 3 *P* be to the God and Father
Eph 1: 3 *P* be to the God and Father
1: 6 to the *p* of his glorious grace,
1: 12 might be for the *p* of his glory.
1: 14 to the *p* of his glory.
1Th 2: 6 We were not looking for *p*
Heb 13: 15 offer to God a sacrifice of *p*—
Jas 3: 9 With the tongue we *p* our Lord
5: 13 happy? Let him sing songs of *p*.
Rev 5: 13 be *p* and honor and glory
7: 12 *P* and glory

PRAISED (PRAISE)

1Ch 29: 10 David *p* the LORD in the presence
Ne 8: 6 Ezra *p* the LORD, the great God;
Job 1: 21 may the name of the LORD be *p*."
Ps 113: 2 Let the name of the LORD be *p*,
Pr 31: 30 who fears the LORD is to be *p*.
Isa 63: 7 the deeds for which he is to be *p*,
Da 2: 19 Then Daniel *p* the God of heaven
4: 34 Then I *p* the Most High; I honored
Lk 18: 43 the people saw it, they also *p* God.
23: 47 seeing what had happened, *p* God
Ro 9: 5 who is God over all, forever *p*!
Gal 1: 24 And they *p* God because of me.
1Pe 4: 11 that in all things God may be *p*

PRAISES (PRAISE)

2Sa 22: 50 I will sing *p* to your name.
Ps 18: 49 I will sing *p* to your name.
47: 6 Sing *p* to God, sing *p*;
147: 1 How good it is to sing *p* to our God,
Pr 31: 28 her husband also, and he *p* her:
1Pe 2: 9 that you may declare the *p*

PRAISEWORTHY* (PRAISE)

Ps 78: 4 the *p* deeds of the LORD,
Php 4: 8 if anything is excellent or *p*—

PRAISING (PRAISE)

Lk 2: 13 *p* God and saying, "Glory to God
2: 20 *p* God for all the things they had
Ac 2: 47 *p* God and enjoying the favor
10: 46 speaking in tongues and *p* God.
1Co 14: 16 If you are *p* God with your spirit,

PRAY (PRAYED PRAYER PRAYERS
PRAYING PRAYS)

Dt 4: 7 is near us whenever we *p* to him?
1Sa 12: 23 the LORD by failing to *p* for you.
1Ki 8: 30 when they *p* toward this place.
2Ch 7: 14 will humble themselves and *p*
Ezr 6: 10 and *p* for the well-being of the king
Job 42: 8 My servant Job will *p* for you,
Ps 5: 2 for to you I *p*.
32: 6 let everyone who is godly *p*
122: 6 *P* for the peace of Jerusalem:
Jer 29: 7 *P* to the LORD for it,
29: 12 upon me and come and *p* to me,

Jer 42: 3 *P* that the LORD your God will
Mt 5: 44 and *p* for those who persecute you,
6: 5 "And when you *p*, do not be like
6: 9 "This, then, is how you should *p*:
14: 23 up on a mountainside by himself to *p*.
19: 13 hands on them and *p* for them.
26: 36 Sit here while I go over there and *p*
Lk 6: 28 *p* for those who mistreat you.
11: 1 us to *p*, just as John taught his
18: 1 them that they should always *p*
22: 40 "*P* that you will not fall
Jn 17: 20 I *p* also for those who will believe
Ro 8: 26 do not know what we ought to *p* for,
1Co 14: 13 in a tongue should *p* that he may
Eph 1: 18 I *p* also that the eyes
3: 16 I *p* that out of his glorious riches he
6: 18 And *p* in the Spirit on all occasions
Col 1: 10 we *p* this in order that you may live
4: 3 *p* for us, too, that God may open
1Th 5: 17 Be joyful always; *p* continually;
2Th 1: 11 in mind, we constantly *p* for you,
Jas 5: 13 one of you in trouble? He should *p*.
5: 16 *p* for each other so that you may be
1Pe 4: 7 self-controlled so that you can *p*.
Jude : 20 up in your most holy faith and *p*

PRAYED (PRAY)

1Sa 1: 27 I *p* for this child, and the LORD
1Ki 18: 36 Elijah stepped forward and *p*:
19: 4 under it and *p* that he might die.
2Ki 6: 17 And Elisha *p*, "O LORD,
2Ch 30: 18 But Hezekiah *p* for them, saying,
Ne 4: 9 we *p* to our God and posted a guard
Job 42: 10 After Job had *p* for his friends,
Da 6: 10 got down on his knees and *p*,
9: 4 I *p* to the LORD my God
Jnh 2: 1 From inside the fish Jonah *p*
Mt 26: 39 with his face to the ground and *p*,
Mk 1: 35 off to a solitary place, where he *p*.
14: 35 *p* that if possible the hour might
Lk 22: 41 knelt down and *p*, "Father,
Jn 17: 1 he looked toward heaven and *p*:
Ac 4: 31 After they *p*, the place where they
6: 6 who *p* and laid their hands on them
8: 15 they *p* for them that they might
13: 3 So after they had fasted and *p*,

PRAYER (PRAY)

2Ch 30: 27 for their *p* reached heaven,
Ezr 8: 23 about this, and he answered our *p*.
Ps 4: 1 be merciful to me and hear my *p*.
6: 9 the LORD accepts my *p*.
17: 1 Give ear to my *p*—
17: 6 give ear to me and hear my *p*.
65: 2 O you who hear *p*,
66: 20 who has not rejected my *p*
86: 6 Hear my *p*, O LORD;
Pr 15: 8 but the *p* of the upright pleases him
15: 29 but he hears the *p* of the righteous.
Isa 56: 7 a house of *p* for all nations."
Mt 21: 13 house will be called a house of *p*,'
21: 22 receive whatever you ask for in *p*."
Mk 9: 29 This kind can come out only by *p*."
11: 24 whatever you ask for in *p*,
Jn 17: 15 My *p* is not that you take them out
Ac 1: 14 all joined together constantly in *p*,
2: 42 to the breaking of bread and to *p*.
6: 4 and will give our attention to *p*
10: 31 has heard your *p* and remembered
16: 13 expected to find a place of *p*.
Ro 12: 12 patient in affliction, faithful in *p*.
1Co 7: 5 you may devote yourselves to *p*.
2Co 13: 9 and our *p* is for your perfection.
Php 1: 9 this is my *p*: that your love may
4: 6 but in everything, by *p* and petition
Col 4: 2 yourselves to *p*, being watchful
1Ti 2: 8 to lift up holy hands in *p*,
4: 5 by the word of God and *p*.
Jas 5: 15 *p* offered in faith will make the sick
1Pe 3: 12 and his ears are attentive to their *p*,

PRAYERS (PRAY)

1Ch 5: 20 He answered their *p*, because they
Isa 1: 15 even if you offer many *p*,
Mk 12: 40 and for a show make lengthy *p*.
2Co 1: 11 as you help us by your *p*.
Eph 6: 18 on all occasions with all kinds of *p*
1Ti 2: 1 then, first of all, that requests, *p*,

1Pe 3: 7 so that nothing will hinder your *p*.
Rev 5: 8 which are the *p* of the saints.
8: 3 with the *p* of all the saints,

PRAYING (PRAY)

Ge 24: 45 "Before I finished *p* in my heart,
1Sa 1: 12 As she kept on *p* to the LORD,
Mk 11: 25 And when you stand *p*,
Lk 3: 21 as he was *p*, heaven was opened
6: 12 and spent the night *p* to God.
9: 29 As he was *p*, the appearance
Jn 17: 9 I am not *p* for the world,
Ac 9: 11 from Tarsus named Saul, for he is *p*
16: 25 and Silas were *p* and singing hymns
Ro 15: 30 in my struggle by *p* to God for me.
Eph 6: 18 always keep on *p* for all the saints.

PRAYS (PRAY)

1Co 14: 14 my spirit *p*, but my mind is

PREACH (PREACHED PREACHING)

Isa 61: 1 me to *p* good news to the poor.
Mt 10: 7 As you go, *p* this message:
23: 3 they do not practice what they *p*.
Mk 16: 15 and *p* the good news to all creation.
Lk 4: 18 me to *p* good news to the poor.
Ac 9: 20 At once he began to *p*
16: 10 us to *p* the gospel to them.
Ro 1: 15 am so eager to *p* the gospel
10: 15 how can they *p* unless they are sent
15: 20 to *p* the gospel where Christ was
1Co 1: 17 to *p* the gospel—not with words
1: 23 wisdom, but we *p* Christ crucified:
9: 14 that those who *p* the gospel should
9: 16 Woe to me if I do not *p* the gospel!
2Co 4: 5 For we do not *p* ourselves,
10: 16 so that we can *p* the gospel
Gal 1: 8 from heaven should *p* a gospel
2Ti 4: 2 I give you this charge: *P* the Word;

PREACHED (PREACH)

Mt 24: 14 gospel of the kingdom will be *p*
Mk 6: 12 and *p* that people should repent.
13: 10 And the gospel must first be *p*
14: 9 wherever the gospel is *p*
Ac 8: 4 had been scattered *p* the word
28: 31 hindrance he *p* the kingdom
1Co 9: 27 so that after I have *p* to others,
15: 1 you of the gospel I *p* to you,
2Co 11: 4 other than the Jesus we *p*,
Gal 1: 8 other than the one we *p* to you,
Eph 2: 17 *p* peace to you who were far away
Php 1: 18 false motives or true, Christ is *p*
1Ti 3: 16 was *p* among the nations,
1Pe 1: 25 this is the word that was *p* to you.
3: 19 and *p* to the spirits in prison who

PREACHING (PREACH)

Lk 9: 6 *p* the gospel and healing people
Ac 18: 5 devoted himself exclusively to *p*,
Ro 10: 14 hear without someone *p* to them?
1Co 2: 4 and my *p* were not with wise
9: 18 in *p* the gospel I may offer it free
Gal 1: 9 If anybody is *p* to you a gospel
1Ti 4: 13 the public reading of Scripture, to *p*
5: 17 especially those whose work is *p*

PRECEDE*

1Th 4: 15 will certainly not *p* those who have

PRECEPTS*

Dt 33: 10 He teaches your *p* to Jacob
Ps 19: 8 The *p* of the LORD are right,
103: 18 and remember to obey his *p*.
105: 45 that they might keep his *p*
111: 7 all his *p* are trustworthy.
111: 10 who follow his *p* have good
119: 4 You have laid down *p*
119: 15 I meditate on your *p*
119: 27 understand the teaching of your *p*;
119: 40 How I long for your *p*!
119: 45 for I have sought out your *p*.
119: 56 I obey your *p*.
119: 63 to all who follow your *p*.
119: 69 I keep your *p* with all my heart.
119: 78 but I will meditate on your *p*.
119: 87 but I have not forsaken your *p*.
119: 93 I will never forget your *p*,

PRECIOUS (continued)

Ps 119: 94 I have sought out your *p*.
119:100 for I obey your *p*.
119:104 I gain understanding from your *p*;
119:110 but I have not strayed from your *p*.
119:128 because I consider all your *p* right,
119:134 that I may obey your *p*.
119:141 I do not forget your *p*.
119:159 See how I love your *p*;
119:168 I obey your *p* and your statutes.
119:173 for I have chosen your *p*.

PRECIOUS

Ps   19: 10 They are more *p* than gold,
72: 14 for *p* is their blood in his sight.
116: 15 *P* in the sight of the LORD
119: 72 from your mouth is more *p* to me
139: 17 How *p* to me are your thoughts,
Pr   8: 11 for wisdom is more *p* than rubies,
Isa 28: 16 a *p* cornerstone for a sure
1Pe 1: 19 but with the *p* blood of Christ,
2: 4 but chosen by God and *p* to him—
2: 6 a chosen and *p* cornerstone,
2Pe 1: 1 Christ have received a faith as *p*
1: 4 us his very great and *p* promises,

PREDESTINED* (DESTINY)

Ro   8: 29 *p* to be conformed to the likeness
8: 30 And those he *p*, he also called;
Eph 1: 5 In love he *p* us to be adopted
1: 11 having been *p* according

PREDICTED (PREDICTION)

1Sa 28: 17 The LORD has done what he *p*
Ac   7: 52 killed those who *p* the coming
1Pe 1: 11 when he *p* the sufferings of Christ

PREDICTION* (PREDICTED PREDICTIONS)

Jer 28: 9 only if his *p* comes true.''

PREDICTIONS (PREDICTION)

Isa 44: 26 and fulfills the *p* of his messengers,

PREGNANT

Ex   21: 22 who are fighting hit a *p* woman
Mt   24: 19 be in those days for *p* women
1Th 5: 3 as labor pains on a *p* woman,

PREPARE (PREPARED)

Ps   23: 5 You *p* a table before me
Isa 25: 6 the LORD Almighty will *p*
40: 3 ''In the desert *p*
Am   4: 12 *p* to meet your God, O Israel.''
Mal   3: 1 who will *p* the way before me.
Mt   3: 3 '*P* the way for the Lord,
Jn   14: 2 there to *p* a place for you.
Eph   4: 12 to *p* God's people for works
1Pe   1: 13 Therefore, *p* your minds for action;

PREPARED (PREPARE)

Ex   23: 20 to bring you to the place I have *p*.
Mt   25: 34 the kingdom *p* for you
Ro   9: 22 of his wrath—*p* for destruction?
1Co   2: 9 what God has *p* for those who love
Eph   2: 10 which God *p* in advance for us
2Ti   2: 21 and *p* to do any good work.
4: 2 be *p* in season and out of season;
1Pe   3: 15 Always be *p* to give an answer

PRESCRIBED

Ezr   7: 23 Whatever the God of heaven has *p*,

PRESENCE (PRESENT)

Ex   25: 30 Put the bread of the *P* on this table
33: 14 The LORD replied, ''My *P* will go
Nu   4: 7 ''Over the table of the *P* they are
1Sa   6: 20 in the *p* of the LORD, this
21: 6 of the *P* that had been removed
2Sa 22: 13 Out of the brightness of his *p*
2Ki 17: 23 LORD removed them from his *p*,
23: 27 also from my *p* as I removed Israel,
Ezr   9: 15 one of us can stand in your *p*.''
Ps   16: 11 you will fill me with joy in your *p*,
21: 6 with the joy of your *p*.
23: 5 in the *p* of my enemies.
31: 20 the shelter of your *p* you hide them
41: 12 and set me in your *p* forever.
51: 11 Do not cast me from your *p*

Ps   52: 9 in the *p* of your saints.
89: 15 who walk in the light of your *p*,
90: 8 our secret sins in the light of your *p*
114: 7 O earth, at the *p* of the Lord,
139: 7 Where can I flee from your *p*?
Isa 26: 17 so were we in your *p*, O LORD.
Jer   5: 22 ''Should you not tremble in my *p*?
Eze 38: 20 of the earth will tremble at my *p*.
Hos   6: 2 that we may live in his *p*.
Na   1: 5 The earth trembles at his *p*,
Mal   3: 16 in his *p* concerning those who
Ac   2: 28 you will fill me with joy in your *p*.'
1Th   3: 9 have in the *p* of our God
3: 13 and holy in the *p* of our God
2Th   1: 9 and shut out from the *p* of the Lord
Heb   9: 24 now to appear for us in God's *p*.
1Jn   3: 19 rest in his *p* whenever our hearts
Jude : 24 before his glorious *p* without fault

PRESENT (PRESENCE)

1Co   3: 22 life or death or the *p* or the future—
7: 26 of the *p* crisis, I think that it is good
2Co 11: 2 so that I might *p* you as a pure
Eph   5: 27 and to *p* her to himself
1Ti   4: 8 holding promise for both the *p* life
2Ti   2: 15 Do your best to *p* yourself to God
Jude : 24 and to *p* you before his glorious

PRESERVE

Lk   17: 33 and whoever loses his life will *p* it.

PRESERVES

Ps 119: 50 Your promise *p* my life.

PRESS (PRESSED PRESSURE)

Php   3: 12 but I *p* on to take hold of that
3: 14 I *p* on toward the goal

PRESSED (PRESS)

Lk   6: 38 *p* down, shaken together

PRESSURE (PRESS)

2Co   1: 8 We were under great *p*, far
11: 28 I face daily the *p* of my concern

PRETENDED

1Sa 21: 13 So he *p* to be insane

PREVAILS

1Sa   2: 9 ''It is not by strength that one *p*;
Pr   19: 21 but it is the LORD's purpose that *p*

PRICE (PRICELESS)

Job 28: 18 the *p* of wisdom is beyond rubies.
1Co   6: 20 your own; you were bought at a *p*.
7: 23 bought at a *p*; do not become slaves

PRICELESS* (PRICE)

Ps   36: 7 How *p* is your unfailing love!

PRIDE (PROUD)

Pr   8: 13 I hate *p* and arrogance,
11: 2 When *p* comes, then comes
13: 10 *P* only breeds quarrels,
16: 18 *P* goes before destruction,
29: 23 A man's *p* brings him low,
Isa 25: 11 God will bring down their *p*
Da   4: 37 And those who walk in *p* he is able
Am   8: 7 The LORD has sworn by the *P*
2Co 5: 12 giving you an opportunity to take *p*
7: 4 in you; I take great *p* in you.
8: 24 and the reason for our *p* in you,
Gal   6: 4 Then he can take *p* in himself,
Jas   1: 9 ought to take *p* in his high position.

PRIEST (PRIESTHOOD PRIESTLY PRIESTS)

Ge   14: 18 He was *p* of God Most High,
Nu   5: 10 to the *p* will belong to the *p*.''
2Ch 13: 9 and seven rams may become a *p*
Ps 110: 4 ''You are a *p* forever,
Heb   2: 17 faithful high *p* in service to God,
3: 1 and high *p* whom we confess.
4: 14 have a great high *p* who has gone
4: 15 do not have a high *p* who is unable
5: 6 ''You are a *p* forever,
6: 20 He has become a high *p* forever,
7: 3 Son of God he remains a *p* forever.

Heb   7: 15 clear if another *p* like Melchizedek
7: 26 Such a high *p* meets our need—
8: 1 We do have such a high *p*,
10: 11 Day after day every *p* stands
13: 11 The high *p* carries the blood

PRIESTHOOD (PRIEST)

Heb   7: 24 lives forever, he has a permanent *p*.
1Pe   2: 5 into a spiritual house to be a holy *p*,
2: 9 you are a chosen people, a royal *p*,

PRIESTLY (PRIEST)

Ro   15: 16 to the Gentiles with the *p* duty

PRIESTS (PRIEST)

Ex   19: 6 you will be for me a kingdom of *p*
Lev 21: 1 ''Speak to the *p*, the sons of Aaron,
Eze 42: 13 where the *p* who approach
46: 2 *p* are to sacrifice his burnt offering
Mal   1: 6 O *p*, who show contempt for my name.
Rev   5: 10 to be a kingdom and *p*
20: 6 but they will be *p* of God

PRIME

Isa 38: 10 recovery: I said, ''In the *p* of my life

PRINCE (PRINCES PRINCESS)

Isa   9: 6 Everlasting Father, *P* of Peace.
Eze 34: 24 and my servant David will be *p*
37: 25 my servant will be their *p* forever.
Da   8: 25 stand against the *P* of princes.
Jn   12: 31 now the *p* of this world will be
Ac   5: 31 as *P* and Savior that he might give

PRINCES (PRINCE)

Ps 118: 9 than to trust in *p*.
148: 11 you *p* and all rulers on earth,
Isa 40: 23 He brings *p* to naught

PRINCESS* (PRINCE)

Ps   45: 13 All glorious is the *p*

PRISCILLA*

Wife of Aquila; co-worker with Paul (Ac 18; Ro 16:3; 1Co 16:19; 2Ti 4:19); instructor of Apollos (Ac 18:24-28).

PRISON (PRISONER PRISONERS)

Ps   66: 11 You brought us into *p*
142: 7 Set me free from my *p*,
Isa 42: 7 to free captives from *p*
Mt   25: 36 I was in *p* and you came to visit me
2Co 11: 23 been in *p* more frequently,
Heb 11: 36 others were chained and put in *p*.
13: 3 Remember those in *p*
1Pe   3: 19 spirits in *p* who disobeyed long ago
Rev 20: 7 Satan will be released from his *p*

PRISONER (PRISON)

Ro   7: 23 and making me a *p* of the law of sin
Gal   3: 22 declares that the whole world is a *p*
Eph   3: 1 the *p* of Christ Jesus for the sake

PRISONERS (PRISON)

Ps   68: 6 he leads forth the *p* with singing;
79: 11 groans of the *p* come before you;
107: 10 *p* suffering in iron chains,
146: 7 The LORD sets *p* free,
Zec   9: 12 to your fortress, O *p* of hope;
Lk   4: 18 me to proclaim freedom for the *p*
Gal   3: 23 we were held *p* by the law,

PRIVILEGE*

2Co   8: 4 pleaded with us for the *p* of sharing

PRIZE*

1Co   9: 24 Run in such a way as to get the *p*.
9: 24 but only one gets the *p*? Run
9: 27 will not be disqualified for the *p*.
Php   3: 14 on toward the goal to win the *p*
Col   2: 18 of angels disqualify you for the *p*.

PROBE

Job 11: 7 Can you *p* the limits
Ps   17: 3 Though you *p* my heart

PROCEDURE

Ecc   8: 6 For there is a proper time and *p*

PROCESSION

Ps 68: 24 Your *p* has come into view, O God,
118: 27 boughs in hand, join in the festal *p*
1Co 4: 9 on display at the end of the *p*,
2Co 2: 14 us in triumphal *p* in Christ

PROCLAIM (PROCLAIMED PROCLAIMING PROCLAIMS PROCLAMATION)

Ex 33: 19 and I will *p* my name, the LORD,
Lev 25: 10 and *p* liberty throughout the land
Dt 30: 12 and *p* it to us so we may obey it?''
2Sa 1: 20 *p* it not in the streets of Ashkelon,
1Ch 16: 23 *p* his salvation day after day.
Ne 8: 15 and that they should *p* this word
Ps 2: 7 I will *p* the decree of the LORD:
9: 11 *p* among the nations what he has
19: 1 the skies *p* the work of his hands.
22: 31 They will *p* his righteousness
40: 9 I *p* righteousness in the great
50: 6 the heavens *p* his righteousness,
64: 9 they will *p* the works of God
68: 34 *P* the power of God,
71: 16 I will come and *p* your mighty acts,
92: 2 to *p* your love in the morning
96: 2 *p* his salvation day after day.
97: 6 The heavens *p* his righteousness,
106: 2 Who can *p* the mighty acts
118: 17 will *p* what the LORD has done.
145: 6 and I will *p* your great deeds.
Isa 12: 4 and *p* that his name is exalted.
42: 12 and *p* his praise in the islands.
52: 7 who *p* salvation,
61: 1 to *p* freedom for the captives
66: 19 They will *p* my glory
Jer 7: 2 house and there *p* this message:
50: 2 lift up a banner and *p* it;
Hos 5: 9 I *p* what is certain.
Zec 9: 10 He will *p* peace to the nations.
Mt 10: 27 in your ear, *p* from the roofs.
12: 18 and he will *p* justice to the nations.
Lk 4: 18 me to *p* freedom for the prisoners
9: 60 you go and *p* the kingdom of God.''
Ac 17: 23 unknown I am going to *p*
20: 27 hesitated to *p* to you the whole will
1Co 11: 26 you *p* the Lord's death
Col 1: 28 We *p* him, admonishing
4: 4 Pray that I may *p* it clearly,
1Jn 1: 1 this we *p* concerning the Word

PROCLAIMED (PROCLAIM)

Ex 9: 16 and that my name might be *p*
34: 5 there with him and *p* his name,
Ps 68: 11 was the company of those who *p* it:
Ro 15: 19 I have fully *p* the gospel of Christ.
Col 1: 23 that has been *p* to every creature
2Ti 4: 17 me the message might be fully *p*

PROCLAIMING (PROCLAIM)

Ps 26: 7 *p* aloud your praise
92: 15 *p*, ''The LORD is upright;
Ac 5: 42 and *p* the good news that Jesus is
Ro 10: 8 the word of faith we are *p*:

PROCLAIMS (PROCLAIM)

Dt 18: 22 If what a prophet *p* in the name

PROCLAMATION (PROCLAIM)

Isa 62: 11 The LORD has made *p*

PRODUCE (PRODUCES)

Mt 3: 8 *P* fruit in keeping with repentance.
3: 10 tree that does not *p* good fruit will

PRODUCES (PRODUCE)

Pr 30: 33 so stirring up anger *p* strife.''
Ro 5: 3 that suffering *p* perseverance;
Heb 12: 11 it *p* a harvest of righteousness

PROFANE (PROFANED)

Lev 19: 12 and so *p* the name of your God.
22: 32 Do not *p* my holy name.
Mal 2: 10 Why do we *p* the covenant

PROFANED (PROFANE)

Eze 36: 20 the nations they *p* my holy name,

PROFESS*

1Ti 2: 10 for women who *p* to worship God.
Heb 4: 14 let us hold firmly to the faith we *p*.
10: 23 unswervingly to the hope we *p*,

PROFIT (PROFITABLE)

Pr 14: 23 All hard work brings a *p*,
21: 5 The plans of the diligent lead to *p*
Isa 44: 10 which can *p* him nothing?
2Co 2: 17 not peddle the word of God for *p*.
Php 3: 7 was to my *p* I now consider loss

PROFITABLE* (PROFIT)

Pr 3: 14 for she is more *p* than silver
31: 18 She sees that her trading is *p*,
Tit 3: 8 These things are excellent and *p*

PROFOUND

Job 9: 4 His wisdom is *p*, his power is vast.
Ps 92: 5 how *p* your thoughts!
Eph 5: 32 This is a *p* mystery—but I am

PROGRESS

Php 1: 25 continue with all of you for your *p*
1Ti 4: 15 so that everyone may see your *p*.

PROLONG*

Dt 5: 33 *p* your days in the land that you
Ps 85: 5 Will you *p* your anger
Pr 3: 2 for they will *p* your life many years
Isa 53: 10 will see his offspring and *p* his days,
La 4: 22 he will not *p* your exile.

PROMISE (PROMISED PROMISES)

Nu 23: 19 Does he *p* and not fulfill?
Jos 23: 14 Every *p* has been fulfilled;
2Sa 7: 25 keep forever the *p* you have made
1Ki 8: 20 The LORD has kept the *p* he made
8: 24 You have kept your *p*
Ne 5: 13 man who does not keep this *p*.
9: 8 have kept your *p* because you are
Ps 77: 8 Has his *p* failed for all time?
119: 41 your salvation according to your *p*;
119: 50 Your *p* preserves my life.
119: 58 to me according to your *p*.
119:162 I rejoice in your *p*
Ac 2: 39 The *p* is for you and your children
Ro 4: 13 offspring received the *p* that he
4: 20 unbelief regarding the *p* of God,
Gal 3: 14 that by faith we might receive the *p*
Eph 2: 12 foreigners to the covenants of the *p*
1Ti 4: 8 holding *p* for both the present life
Heb 6: 13 When God made his *p* to Abraham
11: 11 him faithful who had made the *p*.
2Pe 3: 9 Lord is slow in keeping his *p*,
3: 13 with his *p* we are looking forward

PROMISED (PROMISE)

Ge 21: 1 did for Sarah what he had *p*.
24: 7 who spoke to me and *p* me on oath,
Ex 3: 17 And I have *p* to bring you up out
Nu 10: 29 for the LORD has *p* good things
Dt 15: 6 your God will bless you as he has *p*,
26: 18 his treasured possession as he *p*,
2Sa 7: 28 and you have *p* these good things
1Ki 9: 5 I *p* David your father when I said,
2Ch 6: 15 with your mouth you have *p*
Ps 119: 57 I have *p* to obey your words.
Lk 24: 49 to send you what my Father has *p*;
Ac 1: 4 but wait for the gift my Father has *p*,
13: 32 What God *p* our fathers he has
Ro 4: 21 power to do what he had *p*.
Tit 1: 2 *p* before the beginning of time,
Heb 10: 23 for he who *p* is faithful.
10: 36 you will receive what he has *p*.
Jas 1: 12 the crown of life that God has *p*
2: 5 the kingdom he *p* those who love
2Pe 3: 4 ''Where is this 'coming' he *p*?
1Jn 2: 25 And this is what he *p* us—

PROMISES (PROMISE)

Jos 21: 45 one of all the LORD's good *p*
23: 14 of all the good *p* the LORD your
1Ki 8: 56 failed of all the good *p* he gave
1Ch 17: 19 and made known all these great *p*.
Ps 85: 8 he *p* peace to his people, his saints
106: 12 Then they believed his *p*
119:140 Your *p* have been thoroughly

Ps 119:148 that I may meditate on your *p*.
145: 13 The LORD is faithful to all his *p*
Ro 9: 4 the temple worship and the *p*.
2Co 1: 20 matter how many *p* God has made,
7: 1 Since we have these *p*, dear friends,
Heb 8: 6 and it is founded on better *p*.
2Pe 1: 4 us his very great and precious *p*,

PROMOTE (PROMOTES)

Pr 12: 20 but joy for those who *p* peace.
16: 21 and pleasant words *p* instruction.
1Ti 1: 4 These *p* controversies rather

PROMOTES (PROMOTE)

Pr 17: 9 over an offense *p* love,

PROMPTED

1Th 1: 3 your labor *p* by love, and your
2Th 1: 11 and every act *p* by your faith.

PRONOUNCE (PRONOUNCED)

1Ch 23: 13 to *p* blessings in his name forever.

PRONOUNCED (PRONOUNCE)

1Ch 16: 12 miracles, and the judgments he *p*,

PROOF (PROVE)

Ac 17: 31 He has given *p* of this to all men
2Co 8: 24 Therefore show these men the *p*

PROPER

Ps 104: 27 give them their food at the *p* time.
145: 15 give them their food at the *p* time.
Ecc 5: 18 Then I realized that it is good and *p*
8: 5 the wise heart will know the *p* time
Mt 24: 45 give them their food at the *p* time?
Lk 1: 20 which will come true at their *p* time
1Co 11: 13 Is it *p* for a woman to pray to God
Gal 6: 9 at the *p* time we will reap a harvest
1Ti 2: 6 the testimony given in its *p* time.
1Pe 2: 17 Show *p* respect to everyone:

PROPERTY

Heb 10: 34 the confiscation of your *p*,

PROPHECIES (PROPHESY)

1Co 13: 8 where there are *p*, they will cease;
1Th 5: 20 do not treat *p* with contempt.

PROPHECY (PROPHESY)

Da 9: 24 to seal up vision and *p*
1Co 12: 10 miraculous powers, to another *p*,
13: 2 of *p* and can fathom all mysteries
14: 1 gifts, especially the gift of *p*.
14: 6 or *p* or word of instruction?
14: 22 *p*, however, is for believers,
2Pe 1: 20 you must understand that no *p*
Rev 22: 18 the words of the *p* of this book:

PROPHESIED (PROPHESY)

Nu 11: 25 the Spirit rested on them, they *p*,
1Sa 19: 24 and also *p* in Samuel's presence.
Jn 11: 51 that year he *p* that Jesus would
Ac 19: 6 and they spoke in tongues and *p*.
21: 9 four unmarried daughters who *p*.

PROPHESIES (PROPHESY)

Jer 28: 9 the prophet who *p* peace will be
Eze 12: 27 and he *p* about the distant future.'
1Co 11: 4 *p* with his head covered dishonors
14: 3 But everyone who *p* speaks to men

PROPHESY (PROPHECIES PROPHECY PROPHESIED PROPHESIES PROPHESYING PROPHET PROPHET'S PROPHETESS PROPHETS)

1Sa 10: 6 and you will *p* with them;
Eze 13: 2 Say to those who *p* out
13: 17 daughters of your people who *p* out
34: 2 *p* against the shepherds of Israel;
37: 4 ''*P* to these bones and say to them,
Joel 2: 28 Your sons and daughters will *p*,
Mt 7: 22 Lord, did we not *p* in your name,
Ac 2: 17 Your sons and daughters will *p*,
1Co 13: 9 know in part and we *p* in part,
14: 39 my brothers, be eager to *p*,
Rev 11: 3 and they will *p* for 1,260 days,

PROPHESYING (PROPHESY)

1Ch 25: 1 and Jeduthun for the ministry of *p*.
Ro 12: 6 If a man's gift is *p*, let him use it

PROPHET (PROPHESY)

Ex 7: 1 your brother Aaron will be your *p*.
Nu 12: 6 "When a *p* of the LORD is
Dt 13: 1 If a *p*, or one who foretells
18: 18 up for them a *p* like you
18: 22 If what a *p* proclaims in the name
1Sa 3: 20 that Samuel was attested as a *p*
9: 9 because the *p* of today used
1Ki 1: 8 son of Jehoiada, Nathan the *p*,
18: 36 the *p* Elijah stepped forward
2Ki 5: 8 and he will know that there is a *p*
6: 12 "but Elisha, the *p* who is in Israel,
20: 1 The *p* Isaiah son of Amoz went
2Ch 35: 18 since the days of the *p* Samuel;
36: 12 himself before Jeremiah the *p*,
Ezr 5: 1 Haggai the *p* and Zechariah the *p*,
Eze 2: 5 they will know that a *p* has been
33: 33 they will know that a *p* has been
Hos 9: 7 the *p* is considered a fool,
Am 7: 14 "I was neither a *p* nor a prophet's
Hab 1: 1 that Habakkuk the *p* received.
Hag 1: 1 came through the *p* Haggai
Zec 1: 1 to the *p* Zechariah son of Berekiah,
13: 4 that day every *p* will be ashamed
Mal 4: 5 I will send you the *p* Elijah
Mt 10: 41 Anyone who receives a *p*
11: 9 what did you go out to see? A *p*?
12: 39 except the sign of the *p* Jonah.
Lk 1: 76 will be called a *p* of the Most High;
4: 24 "no *p* is accepted in his hometown.
7: 16 A great *p* has appeared among us,"
24: 19 "He was a *p*, powerful in word
Jn 1: 21 "Are you the *P*?" He answered,
Ac 7: 37 'God will send you a *p* like me
21: 10 a *p* named Agabus came
1Co 14: 37 If anybody thinks he is a *p*
Rev 16: 13 and out of the mouth of the false *p*,

PROPHET'S (PROPHESY)

2Pe 1: 20 about by the *p* own interpretation.

PROPHETESS (PROPHESY)

Ex 15: 20 Then Miriam the *p*, Aaron's sister,
Jdg 4: 4 a *p*, the wife of Lappidoth,
Isa 8: 3 I went to the *p*, and she conceived
Lk 2: 36 a *p*, Anna, the daughter of Phanuel,

PROPHETS (PROPHESY)

Nu 11: 29 that all the LORD's people were *p*
1Sa 10: 11 Is Saul also among the *p*?"
28: 6 him by dreams or Urim or *p*.
1Ki 19: 10 put your *p* to death with the sword.
1Ch 16: 22 do my *p* no harm."
Ps 105: 15 do my *p* no harm."
Jer 23: 9 Concerning the *p*:
23: 30 "I am against the *p* who steal
Eze 13: 2 prophesy against the *p*
Mt 5: 17 come to abolish the Law or the *P*;
7: 12 for this sums up the Law and the *P*.
7: 15 "Watch out for false *p*.
22: 40 and the *P* hang on these two
23: 37 you who kill the *p* and stone those
24: 24 false Christs and false *p* will appear
26: 56 of the *p* might be fulfilled."
Lk 10: 24 For I tell you that many *p*
11: 49 'I will send them *p* and apostles,
24: 25 believe all that the *p* have spoken!
24: 44 me in the Law of Moses, the *P*
Ac 3: 24 "Indeed, all the *p* from Samuel on,
10: 43 All the *p* testify about him that
13: 1 the church at Antioch there were *p*
26: 22 nothing beyond what the *p*
28: 23 the Law of Moses and from the *P*.
Ro 1: 2 through his *p* in the Holy
3: 21 to which the Law and the *P* testify.
11: 3 they have killed your *p*
1Co 12: 28 second *p*, third teachers, then
12: 29 Are all *p*? Are all teachers?
14: 32 The spirits of *p* are subject
Eph 2: 20 foundation of the apostles and *p*,
3: 5 Spirit to God's holy apostles and *p*.
4: 11 some to be *p*, some
Heb 1: 1 through the *p* at many times
1Pe 1: 10 Concerning this salvation, the *p*,

2Pe 1: 19 word of the *p* made more certain,
3: 2 spoken in the past by the holy *p*
1Jn 4: 1 because many false *p* have gone out
Rev 11: 10 these two *p* had tormented those
18: 20 Rejoice, saints and apostles and *p*!

PROPITIATION see (atoning) SACRIFICE

PROPORTION

Dt 16: 10 by giving a freewill offering in *p*
16: 17 Each of you must bring a gift in *p*

PROPRIETY*

1Ti 2: 9 with decency and *p*,
2: 15 in faith, love and holiness with *p*.

PROSPECT*

Pr 10: 28 The *p* of the righteous is joy,

PROSPER (PROSPERED PROSPERITY PROSPEROUS PROSPERS)

Dt 5: 33 so that you may live and *p*
28: 63 pleased the LORD to make you *p*
29: 9 that you may *p* in everything you
1Ki 2: 3 so that you may *p* in all you do
Ezr 6: 14 and *p* under the preaching
Pr 11: 10 When the righteous *p*, the city
11: 25 A generous man will *p*;
17: 20 A man of perverse heart does not *p*
28: 13 who conceals his sins does not *p*:
28: 25 he who trusts in the LORD will *p*.
Isa 53: 10 of the LORD will *p* in his hand.
Jer 12: 1 Why does the way of the wicked *p*?

PROSPERED (PROSPER)

Ge 39: 2 was with Joseph and he *p*,
2Ch 14: 7 So they built and *p*.
31: 21 And so he *p*.

PROSPERITY (PROSPER)

Dt 28: 11 will grant you abundant *p*—
30: 15 I set before you today life and *p*,
Job 36: 11 will spend the rest of their days in *p*
Ps 73: 3 when I saw the *p* of the wicked.
122: 9 I will seek your *p*.
128: 2 blessings and *p* will be yours.
Pr 3: 2 and bring you *p*.
13: 21 but *p* is the reward of the righteous.
21: 21 finds life, *p* and honor.
Isa 45: 7 I bring *p* and create disaster;

PROSPEROUS (PROSPER)

Dt 30: 9 your God will make you most *p*
Jos 1: 8 Then you will be *p* and successful.
Job 42: 10 the LORD made him *p* again

PROSPERS (PROSPER)

Ps 1: 3 Whatever he does *p*.
Pr 16: 20 gives heed to instruction *p*,
19: 8 he who cherishes understanding *p*.

PROSTITUTE (PROSTITUTES PROSTITUTION)

Lev 20: 6 and spiritists to *p* himself
Nu 15: 39 and not *p* yourselves by going
Jos 2: 1 the house of a *p* named Rahab
Pr 6: 26 for the *p* reduces you to a loaf
7: 10 like a *p* and with crafty intent.
23: 27 for a *p* is a deep pit
Eze 16: 15 and used your fame to become a *p*.
23: 7 a *p* to all the elite of the Assyrians
Hos 3: 3 you must not be a *p* or be intimate
1Co 6: 15 of Christ and unite them with a *p*?
6: 16 with a *p* is one with her in body?
Rev 17: 1 you the punishment of the great *p*,

PROSTITUTES (PROSTITUTE)

Pr 29: 3 of *p* squanders his wealth.
Mt 21: 31 and the *p* are entering the kingdom
Lk 15: 30 property with *p* comes home,
1Co 6: 9 male *p* nor homosexual offenders

PROSTITUTION (PROSTITUTE)

Eze 16: 16 where you carried on your *p*.
23: 3 engaging in *p* from their youth.
Hos 4: 10 engage in *p* but not increase,

PROSTRATE

Dt 9: 18 again I fell *p* before the LORD

1Ki 18: 39 they fell *p* and cried, "The LORD

PROTECT (PROTECTED PROTECTION PROTECTS)

Dt 23: 14 about in your camp to *p* you
Ps 25: 21 integrity and uprightness *p* me,
32: 7 you will *p* me from trouble
40: 11 your truth always *p* me.
41: 2 The LORD will *p* him
91: 14 I will *p* him, for he acknowledges
140: 1 *p* me from men of violence,
Pr 2: 11 Discretion will *p* you,
4: 6 forsake wisdom, and she will *p* you;
Jn 17: 11 *p* them by the power of your name
17: 15 that you *p* them from the evil one.
2Th 3: 3 and *p* you from the evil one.

PROTECTED (PROTECT)

Jos 24: 17 He *p* us on our entire journey
1Sa 30: 23 He has *p* us and handed
Ps 37: 28 They will be *p* forever,
Jn 17: 12 I *p* them and kept them safe

PROTECTION (PROTECT)

Ezr 9: 9 he has given us a wall of *p* in Judah
Ps 5: 11 Spread your *p* over them,

PROTECTS (PROTECT)

Ps 116: 6 The LORD *p* the simplehearted;
Pr 2: 8 and *p* the way of his faithful ones.
1Co 13: 7 It always *p*, always trusts,

PROUD (PRIDE)

Ps 31: 23 but the *p* he pays back in full.
101: 5 has haughty eyes and a *p* heart,
138: 6 but the *p* he knows from afar.
Pr 3: 34 He mocks *p* mockers
16: 5 The LORD detests all the *p*
16: 19 than to share plunder with the *p*.
18: 12 his downfall a man's heart is *p*,
21: 4 Haughty eyes and a *p* heart,
Isa 2: 12 store for all the *p* and lofty,
Ro 12: 16 Do not be *p*, but be willing
1Co 13: 4 it does not boast, it is not *p*.
2Ti 3: 2 lovers of money, boastful, *p*,
Jas 4: 6 "God opposes the *p*
1Pe 5: 5 because, "God opposes the *p*

PROVE (PROOF PROVED PROVING)

Pr 29: 25 Fear of man will *p* to be a snare,
Jn 8: 46 Can any of you *p* me guilty of sin?
Ac 26: 20 *p* their repentance by their deeds.
1Co 4: 2 been given a trust must *p* faithful.

PROVED (PROVE)

Ps 51: 4 so that you are *p* right
Mt 11: 19 wisdom is *p* right by her actions."
Ro 3: 4 "So that you may be *p* right
1Pe 1: 7 may be *p* genuine and may result

PROVIDE (PROVIDED PROVIDES PROVISION)

Ge 22: 8 "God himself will *p* the lamb
22: 14 that place "The LORD will *P*."
Isa 43: 20 because I *p* water in the desert
61: 3 and *p* for those who grieve in Zion
1Co 10: 13 *p* a way out so that you can stand
1Ti 5: 8 If anyone does not *p*
Tit 3: 14 in order that they may *p*

PROVIDED (PROVIDE)

Ps 68: 10 O God, you *p* for the poor.
111: 9 He *p* redemption for his people;
Jnh 1: 17 But the LORD *p* a great fish
4: 6 Then the LORD God *p* a vine
4: 7 dawn the next day God *p* a worm,
4: 8 God *p* a scorching east wind,
Gal 4: 18 to be zealous, *p* the purpose is good
Heb 1: 3 After he had *p* purification for sins,

PROVIDES (PROVIDE)

Ps 111: 5 He *p* food for those who fear him;
Pr 31: 15 she *p* food for her family
Eze 18: 7 He *p* clothing for the naked.
1Ti 6: 17 who richly *p* us with everything
1Pe 4: 11 it with the strength God *p*,

PROVING* (PROVE)
Ac   9: 22 by *p* that Jesus is the Christ.
    17:   3 and *p* that the Christ had to suffer
    18: 28 *p* from the Scriptures that Jesus

PROVISION (PROVIDE)
Ro   5: 17 who receive God's abundant *p*

PROVOKED
Ecc 7: 9 Do not be quickly *p* in your spirit,
Jer 32: 32 Judah have *p* me by all the evil they

PROWLS
1Pe 5: 8 Your enemy the devil *p*

PRUDENCE* (PRUDENT)
Pr   1: 4 for giving *p* to the simple,
    8: 5 You who are simple, gain *p*;
    8: 12 "I, wisdom, dwell together with *p*;
    15: 5 whoever heeds correction shows *p*.
    19: 25 and the simple will learn *p*;

PRUDENT* (PRUDENCE)
Pr   1: 3 acquiring a disciplined and *p* life,
    12: 16 but a *p* man overlooks an insult.
    12: 23 A *p* man keeps his knowledge
    13: 16 Every *p* man acts out of knowledge
    14: 8 The wisdom of the *p* is
    14: 15 a *p* man gives thought to his steps.
    14: 18 the *p* are crowned with knowledge.
    19: 14 but a *p* wife is from the LORD.
    22: 3 *p* man sees danger and takes
    27: 12 The *p* see danger and take refuge,
Jer 49: 7 Has counsel perished from the *p*?
Am 5: 13 Therefore the *p* man keeps quiet

PRUNES (PRUNING)
Jn 15: 2 that does bear fruit he *p*

PRUNING (PRUNES)
Isa 2: 4 and their spears into *p* hooks.
Joel 3: 10 and your *p* hooks into spears.

PSALMS
Eph 5: 19 Speak to one another with *p*,
Col 3: 16 and as you sing *p*, hymns

PUBLICLY
Ac 20: 20 have taught you *p* and from house
1Ti 5: 20 Those who sin are to be rebuked *p*,

PUFFS
1Co 8: 1 Knowledge *p* up, but love builds up

PULLING
2Co 10: 8 building you up rather than *p* you

PUNISH (PUNISHED PUNISHES PUNISHMENT)
Ge 15: 14 But I will *p* the nation they serve
Ex 32: 34 I will *p* them for their sin."
Pr 17: 26 It is not good to *p* an innocent man,
    23: 13 if you *p* him with the rod, he will
Isa 13: 11 I will *p* the world for its evil,
Jer 2: 19 Your wickedness will *p* you;
    21: 14 I will *p* you as your deeds deserve,
Zep 1: 12 and *p* those who are complacent,
Ac 7: 7 But I will *p* the nation they serve
2Th 1: 8 He will *p* those who do not know
1Pe 2: 14 by him to *p* those who do wrong

PUNISHED (PUNISH)
Ezr 9: 13 you have *p* us less than our sins
Ps 99: 8 though you *p* their misdeeds.
La 3: 39 complain when *p* for his sins?
Mk 12: 40 Such men will be *p* most severely."
Lk 23: 41 the same sentence? We are *p* justly,
2Th 1: 9 be *p* with everlasting destruction
Heb 10: 29 to be *p* who has trampled the Son

PUNISHES (PUNISH)
Heb 12: 6 and he *p* everyone he accepts

PUNISHMENT (PUNISH)
Isa 53: 5 the *p* that brought us peace was
Jer 4: 18 This is your *p*.
Mt 25: 46 Then they will go away to eternal *p*
Lk 12: 48 and does things deserving *p* will be

Lk 21: 22 For this is the time of *p*
Ro 13: 4 wrath to bring *p* on the wrongdoer.
Heb 2: 2 disobedience received its just *p*,
2Pe 2: 9 while continuing their *p*.

PURCHASED
Ps 74: 2 Remember the people you *p* of old,
Rev 5: 9 with your blood you *p* men for God

PURE (PURIFICATION PURIFIED PURIFIES PURIFY PURITY)
2Sa 22: 27 to the *p* you show yourself *p*,
Job 14: 4 Who can bring what is *p*
Ps 19: 9 The fear of the LORD is *p*,
    24: 4 who has clean hands and a *p* heart,
    51: 10 Create in me a *p* heart, O God,
    119: 9 can a young man keep his way *p*?
Pr 15: 26 those of the *p* are pleasing to him.
    20: 9 can say, "I have kept my heart *p*;
Isa 52: 11 Come out from it and be *p*,
Hab 1: 13 Your eyes are too *p* to look on evil;
Mt 5: 8 Blessed are the *p* in heart,
2Co 11: 2 I might present you as a *p* virgin
Php 4: 8 whatever is *p*, whatever is lovely,
1Ti 1: 5 which comes from a *p* heart
    5: 22 Keep yourself *p*.
2Ti 2: 22 call on the Lord out of a *p* heart.
Tit 1: 15 To the *p*, all things are *p*,
    2: 5 to be self-controlled and *p*,
Heb 7: 26 blameless, *p*, set apart from sinners
    13: 4 and the marriage bed kept *p*,
Jas 1: 27 that God our Father accepts as *p*
    3: 17 comes from heaven is first of all *p*;
1Jn 3: 3 him purifies himself, just as he is *p*.

PURGE
Pr 20: 30 and beatings *p* the inmost being.

PURIFICATION (PURE)
Heb 1: 3 After he had provided *p* for sins,

PURIFIED (PURE)
Ac 15: 9 for he *p* their hearts by faith.
1Pe 1: 22 Now that you have *p* yourselves

PURIFIES* (PURE)
1Jn 1: 7 of Jesus, his Son, *p* us from all sin.
    3: 3 who has this hope in him *p* himself,

PURIFY (PURE)
Nu 19: 12 He must *p* himself with the water
2Co 7: 1 us *p* ourselves from everything that
Tit 2: 14 to *p* for himself a people that are
Jas 4: 8 you sinners, and *p* your hearts,
1Jn 1: 9 and *p* us from all unrighteousness.

PURIM
Est 9: 26 Therefore these days were called *P*

PURITY* (PURE)
Hos 8: 5 long will they be incapable of *p*?
2Co 6: 6 in *p*, understanding, patience
1Ti 4: 12 in life, in love, in faith and in *p*.
    5: 2 as sisters, with absolute *p*.
1Pe 3: 2 when they see the *p* and reverence

PURPLE
Pr 31: 22 she is clothed in fine linen and *p*.
Mk 15: 17 They put a *p* robe on him, then

PURPOSE (PURPOSED PURPOSES)
Ex 9: 16 I have raised you up for this very *p*,
Job 36: 5 he is mighty, and firm in his *p*.
Pr 19: 21 but it is the LORD's *p* that prevails
Isa 46: 10 I say: My *p* will stand,
    55: 11 and achieve the *p* for which I sent it
Ac 2: 23 handed over to you by God's set *p*
Ro 8: 28 have been called according to his *p*.
    9: 11 in order that God's *p*
    9: 17 "I raised you up for this very *p*,
1Co 3: 8 the man who waters have one *p*,
2Co 5: 5 who has made us for this very *p*
Gal 4: 18 be zealous, provided the *p* is good,
Eph 1: 11 in conformity with the *p* of his will,
    3: 11 according to his eternal *p* which he
Php 2: 2 love, being one in spirit and *p*.
    2: 13 and to act according to his good *p*.
2Ti 1: 9 but because of his own *p* and grace.

PURPOSED (PURPOSE)
Isa 14: 24 and as I have *p*, so it will stand.
    14: 27 For the LORD Almighty has *p*,
Eph 1: 9 which he *p* in Christ, to be put

PURPOSES (PURPOSE)
Ps 33: 10 he thwarts the *p* of the peoples.
Jer 23: 20 the *p* of his heart.
    32: 19 great are your *p* and mighty are

PURSE (PURSES)
Hag 1: 6 to put them in a *p* with holes in it."
Lk 10: 4 Do not take a *p* or bag or sandals;
    22: 36 "But now if you have a *p*, take it,

PURSES (PURSE)
Lk 12: 33 Provide *p* for yourselves that will

PURSUE (PURSUES)
Ps 34: 14 seek peace and *p* it.
Pr 15: 9 he loves those who *p* righteousness
Ro 9: 30 who did not *p* righteousness,
1Ti 6: 11 and *p* righteousness, godliness,
2Ti 2: 22 and *p* righteousness, faith,
1Pe 3: 11 he must seek peace and *p* it.

PURSUES (PURSUE)
Pr 21: 21 He who *p* righteousness and love
    28: 1 wicked man flees though no one *p*,

QUAIL
Ex 16: 13 That evening *q* came and covered
Nu 11: 31 and drove *q* in from the sea.

QUALITIES* (QUALITY)
Da 6: 3 by his exceptional *q* that the king
Ro 1: 20 of the world God's invisible *q*—
2Pe 1: 8 For if you possess these *q*

QUALITY (QUALITIES)
1Co 3: 13 and the fire will test the *q*

QUARREL (QUARRELING QUARRELS QUARRELSOME)
Pr 15: 18 but a patient man calms a *q*.
    17: 14 Starting a *q* is like breaching a dam;
    17: 19 He who loves a *q* loves sin;
    20: 3 but every fool is quick to *q*.
    26: 17 in a *q* not his own.
    26: 20 without gossip a *q* dies down.
2Ti 2: 24 And the Lord's servant must not *q*;
Jas 4: 2 You *q* and fight.

QUARRELING (QUARREL)
1Co 3: 3 For since there is jealousy and *q*
2Ti 2: 14 before God against *q* about words;

QUARRELS (QUARREL)
Pr 13: 10 Pride only breeds *q*,
Isa 45: 9 Woe to him who *q* with his Maker,
2Ti 2: 23 because you know they produce *q*.
Jas 4: 1 What causes fights and *q*

QUARRELSOME (QUARREL)
Pr 19: 13 a *q* wife is like a constant dripping.
    21: 9 than share a house with a *q* wife.
    26: 21 so is a *q* man for kindling strife.
1Ti 3: 3 not violent but gentle, not *q*,

QUEEN
1Ki 10: 1 When the *q* of Sheba heard about
2Ch 9: 1 When the *q* of Sheba heard
Mt 12: 42 The *Q* of the South will rise

QUENCH (QUENCHED)
SS 8: 7 Many waters cannot *q* love;

QUENCHED (QUENCH)
Isa 66: 24 nor will their fire be *q*,
Mk 9: 48 and the fire is not *q*.'

QUICKEN see (make) ALIVE, (give) LIFE, RESTORE, REVIVE

QUICK-TEMPERED* (TEMPER)
Pr 14: 17 A *q* man does foolish things,
    14: 29 but a *q* man displays folly.
Tit 1: 7 not *q*, not given to drunkenness,

QUIET (QUIETNESS)

Ps   23: 2 he leads me beside *q* waters,
Pr   17: 1 Better a dry crust with peace and *q*
Ecc   9: 17 The *q* words of the wise are more
Am   5: 13 Therefore the prudent man keeps *q*
Zep   3: 17 he will *q* you with his love,
Lk   19: 40 he replied, "if they keep *q*,
1Th   4: 11 it your ambition to lead a *q* life,
1Ti   2: 2 we may live peaceful and *q* lives
1Pe   3: 4 beauty of a gentle and *q* spirit,

QUIETNESS (QUIET)

Isa 30: 15 in *q* and trust is your strength,
     32: 17 the effect of righteousness will be *q*
1Ti   2: 11 A woman should learn in *q*

QUIVER

Ps 127: 5 whose *q* is full of them.

RACE

Ecc   9: 11 The *r* is not to the swift
Ac   20: 24 if only I may finish the *r*
1Co   9: 24 that in a *r* all the runners run,
Gal   2: 2 that I was running or had run my *r*
      5: 7 You were running a good *r*.
2Ti   4: 7 I have finished the *r*, I have kept
Heb 12: 1 perseverance the *r* marked out

RACHEL

Daughter of Laban (Ge 29:16); wife of Jacob (Ge 29:28); bore two sons (Ge 30:22-24; 35:16-24; 46:19). Stole Laban's gods (Ge 31:19, 32-35). Death (Ge 35:19-20).

RADIANCE (RADIANT)

Eze   1: 28 so was the *r* around him.
Heb   1: 3 The Son is the *r* of God's glory

RADIANT (RADIANCE)

Ex   34: 29 he was not aware that his face was *r*
Ps   34: 5 Those who look to him are *r*;
SS   5: 10 *Beloved* My lover is *r* and ruddy,
Isa 60: 5 Then you will look and be *r*,
Eph   5: 27 her to himself as a *r* church.

RAGE

Ac   4: 25 " 'Why do the nations *r*
Col   3: 8 *r*, malice, slander, and filthy

RAGS

Isa 64: 6 our righteous acts are like filthy *r*;

RAHAB

Prostitute of Jericho who hid Israelite spies (Jos 2; 6:22-25; Heb 11:31; Jas 2:25). Mother of Boaz (Mt 1:5).

RAIN (RAINBOW)

Ge   7: 4 from now I will send *r* on the earth
1Ki 17: 1 nor *r* in the next few years
     18: 1 and I will send *r* on the land."
Mt   5: 45 and sends *r* on the righteous
Jas   5: 17 it did not *r* on the land for three
Jude   : 12 They are clouds without *r*,

RAINBOW (RAIN)

Ge   9: 13 I have set my *r* in the clouds,

RAISE (RISE)

Jn   6: 39 but *r* them up at the last day.
1Co 15: 15 he did not *r* him if in fact the dead

RAISED (RISE)

Isa 52: 13 he will be *r* and lifted up
Mt   17: 23 on the third day he will be *r* to life
Lk   7: 22 the deaf hear, the dead are *r*,
Ac   2: 24 But God *r* him from the dead,
Ro   4: 25 was *r* to life for our justification.
      6: 4 as Christ was *r* from the dead
      8: 11 And if the Spirit of him who *r* Jesus
     10: 9 in your heart that God *r* him
1Co 15: 4 that he was *r* on the third day
     15: 20 But Christ has indeed been *r*

RALLY*

Isa 11: 10 the nations will *r* to him,

RAM (RAMS)

Ge   22: 13 there in a thicket he saw a *r* caught
Da   8: 3 before me was a *r* with two horns,

RAMPART*

Ps   91: 4 will be your shield and *r*.

RAMS (RAM)

1Sa 15: 22 to heed is better than the fat of *r*.
Mic   6: 7 pleased with thousands of *r*,

RAN (RUN)

Jnh   1: 3 But Jonah *r* away from the LORD

RANSOM (RANSOMED)

Isa 50: 2 Was my arm too short to *r* you?
Hos 13: 14 "I will *r* them from the power
Mt   20: 28 and to give his life as a *r* for many."
Mk   10: 45 and to give his life as a *r* for many."
1Ti   2: 6 who gave himself as a *r* for all men
Heb   9: 15 as a *r* to set them free

RANSOMED (RANSOM)

Isa 35: 10 and the *r* of the LORD will return.

RARE

Pr   20: 15 that speak knowledge are a *r* jewel.

RAVEN (RAVENS)

Ge   8: 7 made in the ark and sent out a *r*,
Job 38: 41 Who provides food for the *r*

RAVENS (RAVEN)

1Ki 17: 6 The *r* brought him bread
Ps 147: 9 and for the young *r* when they call.
Lk   12: 24 Consider the *r*: They do not sow

READ (READING READS)

Dt   17: 19 he is to *r* it all the days of his life
Jos   8: 34 Joshua *r* all the words of the law—
2Ki 23: 2 He *r* in their hearing all the words
Ne   8: 8 They *r* from the Book of the Law
Jer 36: 6 and *r* to the people from the scroll
2Co   3: 2 known and *r* by everybody.

READING (READ)

1Ti   4: 13 to the public *r* of Scripture,

READS (READ)

Rev   1: 3 Blessed is the one who *r* the words

REAFFIRM

2Co   2: 8 therefore, to *r* your love for him.

REAL* (REALITIES REALITY)

Jn   6: 55 is *r* food and my blood is *r* drink.
1Jn   2: 27 all things and as that anointing is *r*,

REALITIES* (REAL)

Heb 10: 1 are coming—not the *r* themselves.

REALITY* (REAL)

Col   2: 17 the *r*, however, is found in Christ.

REALM (REALMS)

Hab   2: 9 "Woe to him who builds his *r*

REALMS (REALM)

Eph   1: 3 the heavenly *r* with every spiritual
      2: 6 in the heavenly *r* in Christ Jesus,

REAP (REAPER REAPS)

Job   4: 8 and those who sow trouble *r* it.
Ps 126: 5 will *r* with songs of joy.
Hos   8: 7 and *r* the whirlwind.
     10: 12 *r* the fruit of unfailing love,
Jn   4: 38 you to *r* what you have not worked
Ro   6: 22 the benefit you *r* leads to holiness,
2Co   9: 6 generously will also *r* generously.
Gal   6: 8 from that nature will *r* destruction;

REAPER (REAP)

Jn   4: 36 and the *r* may be glad together.

REAPS (REAP)

Pr   11: 18 who sows righteousness *r* a sure
     22: 8 He who sows wickedness *r* trouble.
Gal   6: 7 A man *r* what he sows.

REASON (REASONED)

Ge   2: 24 For this *r* a man will leave his
Isa   1: 18 "Come now, let us *r* together,"
Mt   19: 5 'For this *r* a man will leave his
Jn   12: 27 it was for this very *r* I came
     15: 25 'They hated me without *r*.'
1Pe   3: 15 to give the *r* for the hope that you
2Pe   1: 5 For this very *r*, make every effort

REASONED (REASON)

1Co 13: 11 thought like a child, I *r* like a child.

REBEKAH

Sister of Laban, secured as bride for Isaac (Ge 24). Mother of Esau and Jacob (Ge 25:19-26). Taken by Abimelech as sister of Isaac; returned (Ge 26:1-11). Encouraged Jacob to trick Isaac out of blessing (Ge 27:1-17).

REBEL (REBELLED REBELLION REBELS)

Nu   14: 9 Only do not *r* against the LORD.
1Sa 12: 14 and do not *r* against his commands,
Mt   10: 21 children will *r* against their parents

REBELLED (REBEL)

Ps   78: 56 and *r* against the Most High;
Isa 63: 10 Yet they *r*

REBELLION (REBEL)

Ex   34: 7 and forgiving wickedness, *r* and sin
Nu   14: 18 in love and forgiving sin and *r*.
1Sa 15: 23 For *r* is like the sin of divination,
2Th   2: 3 will not come, until the *r* occurs

REBELS (REBEL)

Ro   13: 2 he who *r* against the authority is
1Ti   1: 9 but for lawbreakers and *r*,

REBIRTH* (BEAR)

Tit   3: 5 us through the washing of *r*

REBUILD (BUILD)

Ezr   5: 2 set to work to *r* the house of God
Ne   2: 17 let us *r* the wall of Jerusalem,
Ps 102: 16 For the LORD will *r* Zion
Da   9: 25 and *r* Jerusalem until the Anointed
Am   9: 14 they will *r* the ruined cities
Ac   15: 16 Its ruins I will *r*,

REBUILT (BUILD)

Zec   1: 16 and there my house will be *r*.

REBUKE (REBUKED REBUKES REBUKING)

Lev 19: 17 *R* your neighbor frankly
Ps 141: 5 let him *r* me—it is oil on my head.
Pr   3: 11 and do not resent his *r*,
      9: 8 *r* a wise man and he will love you.
     15: 31 He who listens to a life-giving *r*
     17: 10 A *r* impresses a man
     19: 25 *r* a discerning man, and he will gain
     25: 12 is a wise man's *r* to a listening ear.
     27: 5 Better is open *r*
     30: 6 or he will *r* you and prove you a liar
Ecc   7: 5 It is better to heed a wise man's *r*
Isa 54: 9 never to *r* you again.
Jer   2: 19 your backsliding will *r* you.
Lk   17: 3 "If your brother sins, *r* him,
1Ti   5: 1 Do not *r* an older man harshly,
2Ti   4: 2 correct, *r* and encourage—
Tit   1: 13 Therefore, *r* them sharply,
      2: 15 Encourage and *r* with all authority.
Rev   3: 19 Those whom I love I *r*

REBUKED (REBUKE)

Mk   16: 14 he *r* them for their lack of faith
1Ti   5: 20 Those who sin are to be *r* publicly,

REBUKES (REBUKE)

Job 22: 4 "Is it for your piety that he *r* you
Pr   28: 23 He who *r* a man will
     29: 1 remains stiff-necked after many *r*
Heb 12: 5 do not lose heart when he *r* you,

REBUKING (REBUKE)

2Ti   3: 16 *r*, correcting and training

RECEIVE (RECEIVED RECEIVES)

Mt 10: 41 a righteous man will *r* a righteous
Mk 10: 15 anyone who will not *r* the kingdom
Jn 20: 22 and said, ''*R* the Holy Spirit.
Ac   1: 8 you will *r* power when the Holy
     2: 38 you will *r* the gift of the Holy Spirit
    19: 2 ''Did you *r* the Holy Spirit
    20: 35 'It is more blessed to give than to *r*
1Co 9: 14 the gospel should *r* their living
2Co 6: 17 and I will *r* you.''
1Ti 1: 16 believe on him and *r* eternal life.
Jas 1: 7 should not think he will *r* anything
2Pe 1: 11 and you will *r* a rich welcome
1Jn 3: 22 and *r* from him anything we ask,
Rev 4: 11 to *r* glory and honor and power,
     5: 12 to *r* power and wealth and wisdom

RECEIVED (RECEIVE)

Mt   6: 2 they have *r* their reward in full.
    10: 8 Freely you have *r*, freely give.
Mk 11: 24 believe that you have *r* it,
Jn   1: 12 Yet to all who *r* him,
     1: 16 his grace we have all *r* one blessing
Ac   8: 17 and they *r* the Holy Spirit.
    10: 47 They have *r* the Holy Spirit just
Ro   8: 15 but you *r* the Spirit of sonship.
1Co 11: 23 For I *r* from the Lord what I
2Co 1: 4 the comfort we ourselves have *r*
Col 2: 6 just as you *r* Christ Jesus as Lord,
1Pe 4: 10 should use whatever gift he has *r*

RECEIVES (RECEIVE)

Pr 18: 22 and *r* favor from the LORD.
    27: 21 but man is tested by the praise he *r*.
Mt   7: 8 everyone who asks *r*; he who seeks
    10: 40 he who *r* me *r* the one who sent me.
    10: 40 ''He who *r* you *r* me, and he who
Ac 10: 43 believes in him *r* forgiveness of sins

RECITE

Ps 45: 1 as I *r* my verses for the king;

RECKLESS

Pr 12: 18 *R* words pierce like a sword,
    14: 16 but a fool is hotheaded and *r*.

RECKONING

Isa 10: 3 What will you do on the day of *r*,
Hos 9: 7 The days of *r* are at hand.

RECLAIM* (CLAIM)

Isa 11: 11 time to *r* the remnant that is left

RECOGNITION (RECOGNIZE)

1Co 16: 18 Such men deserve *r*.
1Ti 5: 3 Give proper *r* to those widows who

RECOGNIZE (RECOGNITION RECOGNIZED)

Mt   7: 16 By their fruit you will *r* them.
1Jn 4: 2 This is how you can *r* the Spirit
     4: 6 This is how we *r* the Spirit of truth

RECOGNIZED (RECOGNIZE)

Mt 12: 33 for a tree is *r* by its fruit.
Ro   7: 13 in order that sin might be *r* as sin,

RECOMPENSE*

Isa 40: 10 and his *r* accompanies him.
    62: 11 and his *r* accompanies him.' ''

RECONCILE* (RECONCILED RECONCILIATION RECONCILING)

Ac   7: 26 He tried to *r* them by saying, 'Men,
Eph 2: 16 in this one body to *r* both of them
Col 1: 20 him to *r* to himself all things,

RECONCILED* (RECONCILE)

Mt   5: 24 First go and be *r* to your brother;
Lk 12: 58 try hard to be *r* to him on the way,
Ro   5: 10 how much more, having been *r*,
     5: 10 we were *r* to him through the death
1Co 7: 11 or else be *r* to her husband.
2Co 5: 18 who *r* us to himself through Christ
     5: 20 you on Christ's behalf: Be *r* to God.
Col 1: 22 he has *r* you by Christ's physical

RECONCILIATION* (RECONCILE)

Ro   5: 11 whom we have now received *r*,
    11: 15 For if their rejection is the *r*
2Co 5: 18 and gave us the ministry of *r*:
     5: 19 committed to us the message of *r*.

RECONCILING* (RECONCILE)

2Co 5: 19 that God was *r* the world to himself

RECORD (RECORDED)

Ps 130: 3 If you, O LORD, kept a *r* of sins,
Hos 13: 12 his sins are kept on *r*,
1Co 13: 5 is not easily angered, it keeps no *r*

RECORDED (RECORD)

Job 19: 23 ''Oh, that my words were *r*,
Jn 20: 30 which are not *r* in this book.

RECOUNT*

Ps 40: 5 no one can *r* to you;
    79: 13 we will *r* your praise.
   119: 13 With my lips I *r*

RED

Ex 15: 4 are drowned in the *R* Sea.
Ps 106: 9 He rebuked the *R* Sea,
Pr 23: 31 Do not gaze at wine when it is *r*,
Isa 1: 18 though they are *r* as crimson,

REDEEM (KINSMAN-REDEEMER REDEEMED REDEEMER REDEEMS REDEMPTION)

Ex   6: 6 will *r* you with an outstretched arm
2Sa 7: 23 on earth that God went out to *r*
Ps 44: 26 *r* us because of your unfailing love.
    49: 7 No man can *r* the life of another
    49: 15 God will *r* my life from the grave;
   130: 8 He himself will *r* Israel
Hos 13: 14 I will *r* them from death.
Gal 4: 5 under law, to *r* those under law,
Tit 2: 14 for us to *r* us from all wickedness

REDEEMED (REDEEM)

Job 33: 28 He *r* my soul from going
Ps 71: 23 I, whom you have *r*.
   107: 2 Let the *r* of the LORD say this—
Isa 35: 9 But only the *r* will walk there,
    63: 9 In his love and mercy he *r* them;
Gal 3: 13 Christ *r* us from the curse
1Pe 1: 18 or gold that you were *r*

REDEEMER (REDEEM)

Job 19: 25 I know that my *R* lives,
Ps 19: 14 O LORD, my Rock and my *R*.
Isa 44: 6 and *R*, the LORD Almighty:
    48: 17 your *R*, the Holy One of Israel:
    59: 20 ''The *R* will come to Zion,

REDEEMS (REDEEM)

Ps 34: 22 The LORD *r* his servants;
   103: 4 he *r* my life from the pit

REDEMPTION (REDEEM)

Ps 130: 7 and with him is full *r*.
Lk 21: 28 because your *r* is drawing near.''
Ro   3: 24 grace through the *r* that came
     8: 23 as sons, the *r* of our bodies.
1Co 1: 30 our righteousness, holiness and *r*.
Eph 1: 7 In him we have *r* through his blood
     1: 14 until the *r* of those who are God's
     4: 30 you were sealed for the day of *r*.
Col 1: 14 in whom we have *r*, the forgiveness
Heb 9: 12 having obtained eternal *r*.

REED

Isa 42: 3 A bruised *r* he will not break,
Mt 12: 20 A bruised *r* he will not break,

REFINE*

Jer 9: 7 ''See, I will *r* and test them.
Zec 13: 9 I will *r* them like silver
Mal 3: 3 and *r* them like gold and silver.

REFLECT (REFLECTS)

2Co 3: 18 unveiled faces all *r* the Lord's

REFLECTS (REFLECT)

Pr 27: 19 As water *r* a face,

REFRESH (REFRESHED REFRESHING)

Phm : 20 in the Lord; *r* my heart in Christ.

REFRESHED (REFRESH)

Pr 11: 25 refreshes others will himself be *r*.

REFRESHING* (REFRESH)

Ac   3: 19 that times of *r* may come

REFUGE

Nu 35: 11 towns to be your cities of *r*,
Dt 33: 27 The eternal God is your *r*,
Jos 20: 2 to designate the cities of *r*,
Ru   2: 12 wings you have come to take *r*.''
2Sa 22: 3 God is my rock, in whom I take *r*,
    22: 31 a shield for all who take *r* in him.
Ps   2: 12 Blessed are all who take *r* in him.
     5: 11 But let all who take *r* in you be glad
     9: 9 The LORD is a *r* for the oppressed,
    16: 1 for in you I take *r*.
    17: 7 those who take *r* in you
    18: 2 God is my rock, in whom I take *r*.
    31: 2 be my rock of *r*,
    34: 8 blessed is the man who takes *r*
    36: 7 find *r* in the shadow of your wings.
    46: 1 God is our *r* and strength,
    62: 8 for God is our *r*.
    71: 1 In you, O LORD, I have taken *r*;
    91: 2 ''He is my *r* and my fortress,
   144: 2 my shield, in whom I take *r*,
Pr 14: 26 and for his children it will be a *r*.
    30: 5 a shield to those who take *r* in him.
Na   1: 7 a *r* in times of trouble.

REFUSE (REFUSED)

Jn   5: 40 yet you *r* to come to me to have life

REFUSED (REFUSE)

2Th 2: 10 because they *r* to love the truth
Rev 16: 9 but they *r* to repent and glorify him

REGARD (REGARDS)

1Th 5: 13 Hold them in the highest *r* in love

REGARDS (REGARD)

Ro 14: 14 But if anyone *r* something

REGRET

2Co 7: 10 leads to salvation and leaves no *r*,

REHOBOAM

Son of Solomon (1Ki 11:43; 1Ch 3:10). Harsh treatment of subjects caused divided kingdom (1Ki 12:1-24; 14:21-31; 2Ch 10-12).

REIGN (REIGNED REIGNS)

Ex 15: 18 The LORD will *r*
Ps 68: 16 mountain where God chooses to *r*,
Isa 9: 7 He will *r* on David's throne
    24: 23 for the LORD Almighty will *r*
    32: 1 See, a king will *r* in righteousness
Jer 23: 5 a King who will *r* wisely
Lk   1: 33 and he will *r* over the house
Ro   6: 12 Therefore do not let sin *r*
1Co 15: 25 For he must *r* until he has put all
2Ti 2: 12 we will also *r* with him,
Rev 11: 15 and he will *r* for ever and ever.''
    20: 6 will *r* with him for a thousand years
    22: 5 And they will *r* for ever and ever.

REIGNED (REIGN)

Ro   5: 21 so that, just as sin *r* in death,
Rev 20: 4 and *r* with Christ a thousand years.

REIGNS (REIGN)

Ps   9: 7 The LORD *r* forever;
    47: 8 God *r* over the nations;
    93: 1 The LORD *r*, he is robed
    96: 10 among the nations, ''The LORD *r*
    97: 1 The LORD *r*, let the earth be glad;
    99: 1 The LORD *r*, / let the nations tremble;
   146: 10 The LORD *r* forever,
Isa 52: 7 ''Your God *r*!''
Rev 19: 6 For our Lord God Almighty *r*.

REIN

Jas 1: 26 and yet does not keep a tight *r*

REJECT (REJECTED REJECTION REJECTS)

Ps 94: 14 For the LORD will not *r* his people
Ro 11: 1 I ask then: Did God *r* his people?

REJECTED (REJECT)

1Sa 8: 7 it is not you they have *r*,
1Ki 19: 10 The Israelites have *r* your covenant
2Ki 17: 15 They *r* his decrees
Ps 66: 20 who has not *r* my prayer
    118: 22 The stone the builders *r*
Isa 5: 24 for they have *r* the law
    41: 9 chosen you and have not *r* you.
    53: 3 He was despised and *r* by men,
Jer 8: 9 Since they have *r* the word
Mt 21: 42 '' 'The stone the builders *r*
1Ti 4: 4 nothing is to be *r* if it is received
1Pe 2: 4 *r* by men but chosen by God
    2: 7 ''The stone the builders *r*

REJECTION* (REJECT)

Ro 11: 15 For if their *r* is the reconciliation

REJECTS (REJECT)

Lk 10: 16 but he who *r* me *r* him who sent me
Jn 3: 36 whoever *r* the Son will not see life,
1Th 4: 8 he who *r* this instruction does not

REJOICE (JOY)

Dt 12: 7 shall *r* in everything you have put
1Ch 16: 10 of those who seek the LORD *r*.
    16: 31 Let the heavens *r*, let the earth be
Ps 2: 11 and *r* with trembling.
    5: 11 those who love your name may *r*
    9: 14 and there *r* in your salvation.
    34: 2 let the afflicted hear and *r*.
    63: 11 But the king will *r* in God;
    66: 6 come, let us *r* in him.
    68: 3 and *r* before God;
    105: 3 of those who seek the LORD *r*.
    118: 24 let us *r* and be glad in it.
    119: 14 I *r* in following your statutes
    119:162 I *r* in your promise
    149: 2 Let Israel *r* in their Maker;
Pr 5: 18 may you *r* in the wife of your youth
    23: 25 may she who gave you birth *r*!
    24: 17 stumbles, do not let your heart *r*,
Isa 9: 3 as men *r*
    35: 1 the wilderness will *r* and blossom.
    61: 7 they will *r* in their inheritance;
    62: 5 so will your God *r* over you.
Jer 31: 12 they will *r* in the bounty
Zep 3: 17 he will *r* over you with singing.''
Zec 9: 9 *R* greatly, O Daughter of Zion!
Lk 6: 23 ''*R* in that day and leap for joy,
    10: 20 but *r* that your names are written
    15: 6 '*R* with me; I have found my lost
    15: 9 '*R* with me; I have found my lost
Ro 5: 2 And we *r* in the hope of the glory
    12: 15 Rejoice with those who *r*; mourn
Php 2: 17 I am glad and *r* with all of you.
    3: 1 Finally, my brothers, *r* in the Lord!
    4: 4 *R* in the Lord always.
1Pe 4: 13 But *r* that you participate
Rev 19: 7 Let us *r* and be glad

REJOICES (JOY)

Ps 13: 5 my heart *r* in your salvation.
    16: 9 my heart is glad and my tongue *r*;
Isa 61: 10 my soul *r* in my God.
    62: 5 as a bridegroom *r* over his bride,
Lk 1: 47 my spirit *r* in God my Savior,
Ac 2: 26 my heart is glad and my tongue *r*;
1Co 12: 26 if one part is honored, every part *r*
    13: 6 delight in evil but *r* with the truth.

REJOICING (JOY)

2Sa 6: 12 to the City of David with *r*.
Ne 12: 43 *r* because God had given them
Ps 30: 5 but *r* comes in the morning.
Lk 15: 7 in the same way there will be more *r*
Ac 5: 41 *r* because they had been counted
2Co 6: 10 sorrowful, yet always *r*; poor,

RELATIVES

Pr 19: 7 A poor man is shunned by all his *r*
Mk 6: 4 among his *r* and in his own house is
Lk 21: 16 betrayed even by parents, brothers, *r*

1Ti 5: 8 If anyone does not provide for his *r*

RELEASE (RELEASED)

Isa 61: 1 and *r* from darkness,
Lk 4: 18 to *r* the oppressed,

RELEASED (RELEASE)

Ro 7: 6 we have been *r* from the law
Rev 20: 7 Satan will be *r* from his prison

RELENTED (RELENTS)

Ex 32: 14 the LORD *r* and did not bring
Ps 106: 45 and out of his great love he *r*.

RELENTS* (RELENTED)

Joel 2: 13 and he *r* from sending calamity.
Jnh 4: 2 a God who *r* from sending calamity

RELIABLE (RELY)

Pr 22: 21 teaching you true and *r* words,
Jn 8: 26 But he who sent me is *r*,
2Ti 2: 2 witnesses entrust to *r* men who will

RELIANCE* (RELY)

Pr 25: 19 is *r* on the unfaithful in times

RELIED (RELY)

2Ch 13: 18 were victorious because they *r*
    16: 8 Yet when you *r* on the LORD,
Ps 71: 6 From birth I have *r* on you;

RELIEF

Job 35: 9 they plead for *r* from the arm
Ps 94: 13 you grant him *r* from days
    143: 1 come to my *r*.
La 3: 49 without *r*,
    3: 56 to my cry for *r*.''
2Th 1: 7 and give *r* to you who are troubled,

RELIGION* (RELIGIOUS)

Ac 25: 19 dispute with him about their own *r*
    26: 5 to the strictest sect of our *r*,
1Ti 5: 4 all to put their *r* into practice
Jas 1: 26 himself and his *r* is worthless.
    1: 27 *R* that God our Father accepts

RELIGIOUS (RELIGION)

Jas 1: 26 If anyone considers himself *r*

RELY (RELIABLE RELIANCE RELIED)

Isa 50: 10 and *r* on his God.
Eze 33: 26 you then possess the land? You *r*
2Co 1: 9 this happened that we might not *r*
Gal 3: 10 All who *r* on observing the law are
1Jn 4: 16 and *r* on the love God has for us.

REMAIN (REMAINS)

Nu 33: 55 allow to *r* will become barbs
Ps 102: 27 But you *r* the same,
Jn 1: 32 from heaven as a dove and *r* on him
    15: 4 *R* in me, and I will *r* in you.
    15: 7 If you *r* in me and my words
    15: 9 Now *r* in my love.
Ro 13: 8 Let no debt *r* outstanding,
1Co 13: 13 And now these three *r*: faith,
2Ti 2: 13 he will *r* faithful,
Heb 1: 11 They will perish, but you *r*;
1Jn 2: 27 just as it has taught you, *r* in him.

REMAINS (REMAIN)

Ps 146: 6 the LORD, who *r* faithful forever.
Heb 7: 3 Son of God he *r* a priest forever.

REMEDY

Isa 3: 7 ''I have no *r*.

REMEMBER (REMEMBERED REMEMBERS REMEMBRANCE)

Ge 9: 15 I will *r* my covenant between me
Ex 20: 8 ''*R* the Sabbath day
    33: 13 *R* that this nation is your people.''
Dt 5: 15 *R* that you were slaves in Egypt
1Ch 16: 12 *R* the wonders he has done,
Job 36: 24 *R* to extol his work,
Ps 25: 6 O LORD, your great mercy
    63: 6 On my bed I *r* you;
    74: 2 *R* the people you purchased of old,
    77: 11 I will *r* the deeds of the LORD;
Ecc 12: 1 *R* your Creator

Isa 46: 8 ''*R* this, fix it in mind,
Jer 31: 34 and will *r* their sins no more.''
Hab 3: 2 in wrath *r* mercy.
Lk 1: 72 and to *r* his holy covenant,
Gal 2: 10 we should continue to *r* the poor,
Php 1: 3 I thank my God every time I *r* you.
2Ti 2: 8 *R* Jesus Christ, raised
Heb 8: 12 and will *r* their sins no more.''

REMEMBERED (REMEMBER)

Ex 2: 24 he *r* his covenant with Abraham,
    3: 15 am to be *r* from generation
Ps 98: 3 He has *r* his love
    106: 45 for their sake he *r* his covenant
    111: 4 He has caused his wonders to be *r*;
    136: 23 to the One who *r* us
Isa 65: 17 The former things will not be *r*,
Eze 18: 22 offenses he has committed will be *r*
    33: 13 things he has done will be *r*;

REMEMBERS (REMEMBER)

Ps 103: 14 he *r* that we are dust.
    111: 5 he *r* his covenant forever.
Isa 43: 25 and *r* your sins no more.

REMEMBRANCE (REMEMBER)

Lk 22: 19 given for you; do this in *r* of me.''
1Co 11: 24 which is for you; do this in *r* of me
    11: 25 whenever you drink it, in *r* of me.''

REMIND

Jn 14: 26 will *r* you of everything I have said
2Pe 1: 12 I will always *r* you of these things,

REMNANT

Ezr 9: 8 has been gracious in leaving us a *r*
Isa 11: 11 time to reclaim the *r* that is left
Jer 23: 3 ''I myself will gather the *r*
Zec 8: 12 inheritance to the *r* of this people.
Ro 11: 5 the present time there is a *r* chosen

REMOVED

Ps 30: 11 you *r* my sackcloth and clothed me
    103: 12 so far has he *r* our transgressions
Jn 20: 1 and saw that the stone had been *r*

REND

Joel 2: 13 *R* your heart

RENEW (RENEWAL RENEWED RENEWING)

Ps 51: 10 and *r* a steadfast spirit within me.
Isa 40: 31 will *r* their strength.

RENEWAL (RENEW)

Isa 57: 10 You found *r* of your strength,
Tit 3: 5 of rebirth and *r* by the Holy Spirit,

RENEWED (RENEW)

Ps 103: 5 that your youth is *r* like the eagle's.
2Co 4: 16 yet inwardly we are being *r* day

RENEWING* (RENEW)

Ro 12: 2 transformed by the *r* of your mind.

RENOUNCE (RENOUNCED RENOUNCES)

Da 4: 27 *R* your sins by doing what is right,

RENOUNCED (RENOUNCE)

2Co 4: 2 we have *r* secret and shameful

RENOUNCES (RENOUNCE)

Pr 28: 13 confesses and *r* them finds

RENOWN*

Ge 6: 4 were the heroes of old, men of *r*.
Ps 102: 12 *r* endures through all generations.
    135: 13 *r*, O LORD, through all
Isa 26: 8 your name and *r*
    55: 13 This will be for the LORD's *r*,
    63: 12 to gain for himself everlasting *r*,
Jer 13: 11 to be my people for my *r* and praise
    32: 20 have gained the *r* that is still yours.
    33: 9 Then this city will bring me *r*, joy,
    49: 25 the city of *r* not been abandoned,
Eze 26: 17 How you are destroyed, O city of *r*,
Hos 12: 5 the LORD is his name of *r*!

REPAID (PAY)

Lk   6: 34 to 'sinners,' expecting to be *r* in full
      14: 14 you will be *r* at the resurrection
Col   3: 25 Anyone who does wrong will be *r*

REPAY (PAY)

Dt   7: 10 But those who hate him he will *r*
      32: 35 It is mine to avenge; I will *r*.
Ru   2: 12 May the LORD *r* you
Ps 103: 10 or *r* us according to our iniquities.
      116: 12 How can I *r* the LORD
Jer 25: 14 I will *r* them according
Ro   12: 17 Do not *r* anyone evil for evil.
      12: 19 "It is mine to avenge; I will *r*,"
1Pe   3: 9 Do not *r* evil with evil

REPAYING (PAY)

2Ch   6: 23 *r* the guilty by bringing
1Ti   5: 4 so *r* their parents and grandparents

REPEATED

Heb 10: 1 the same sacrifices *r* endlessly year

REPENT (REPENTANCE REPENTED REPENTS)

1Ki   8: 47 *r* and plead with you in the land
Job 36: 10 commands them to *r* of their evil.
      42: 6 and *r* in dust and ashes."
Jer 15: 19 "If you *r*, I will restore you
Eze 18: 30 *R!* Turn away from all your
      18: 32 *R* and live! "Take up a lament
Mt   3: 2 "*R*, for the kingdom of heaven is
      4: 17 "*R*, for the kingdom of heaven is
Mk   6: 12 and preached that people should *r*.
Lk   13: 3 unless you *r*, you too will all perish.
Ac   2: 38 Peter replied, "*R* and be baptized,
      3: 19 *R*, then, and turn to God,
      17: 30 all people everywhere to *r*.
      26: 20 also, I preached that they should *r*
Rev   2: 5 *R* and do the things you did at first.

REPENTANCE (REPENT)

Isa 30: 15 "In *r* and rest is your salvation,
Mt   3: 8 Produce fruit in keeping with *r*.
Mk   1: 4 a baptism of *r* for the forgiveness
Lk   3: 8 Produce fruit in keeping with *r*.
      5: 32 call the righteous, but sinners to *r*."
      24: 47 and *r* and forgiveness of sins will be
Ac   20: 21 that they must turn to God in *r*
      26: 20 and prove their *r* by their deeds.
Ro   2: 4 kindness leads you toward *r*?
2Co   7: 10 Godly sorrow brings *r* that leads
2Pe   3: 9 but everyone to come to *r*.

REPENTED (REPENT)

Mt   11: 21 they would have *r* long ago

REPENTS (REPENT)

Lk   15: 7 in heaven over one sinner who *r*
      15: 10 of God over one sinner who *r*."
      17: 3 rebuke him, and if he *r*, forgive him

REPORTS

Ex   23: 1 "Do not spread false *r*.

REPOSES*

Pr   14: 33 Wisdom *r* in the heart

REPRESENTATION*

Heb   1: 3 and the exact *r* of his being,

REPROACH

Job 27: 6 my conscience will not *r* me
Isa 51: 7 Do not fear the *r* of men
1Ti   3: 2 Now the overseer must be above *r*,

REPUTATION

1Ti   3: 7 also have a good *r* with outsiders,

REQUESTS

Ps   20: 5 May the LORD grant all your *r*.
Php   4: 6 with thanksgiving, present your *r*

REQUIRE (REQUIRED REQUIRES)

Mic   6: 8 And what does the LORD *r* of you

REQUIRED (REQUIRE)

1Co   4: 2 it is *r* that those who have been

REQUIRES (REQUIRE)

1Ki   2: 3 what the LORD your God *r*:
Heb   9: 22 the law *r* that nearly everything be

RESCUE (RESCUED RESCUES)

Ps   22: 8 let the LORD *r* him.
      31: 2 come quickly to my *r*;
      69: 14 *R* me from the mire,
      91: 14 says the LORD, "I will *r* him;
      143: 9 *R* me from my enemies, O LORD,
Da   6: 20 been able to *r* you from the lions?"
Ro   7: 24 Who will *r* me from this body
Gal   1: 4 himself for our sins to *r* us
2Pe   2: 9 how to *r* godly men from trials

RESCUED (RESCUE)

Ps   18: 17 He *r* me from my powerful enemy,
Pr   11: 8 The righteous man is *r*
Col   1: 13 For he has *r* us from the dominion

RESCUES (RESCUE)

Da   6: 27 He *r* and he saves;
1Th   1: 10 who *r* us from the coming wrath.

RESENT* (RESENTFUL RESENTS)

Pr   3: 11 and do not *r* his rebuke,

RESENTFUL* (RESENT)

2Ti   2: 24 to everyone, able to teach, not *r*.

RESENTS* (RESENT)

Pr   15: 12 A mocker *r* correction;

RESERVE (RESERVED)

1Ki 19: 18 Yet I *r* seven thousand in Israel—

RESERVED (RESERVE)

Ro   11: 4 "I have *r* for myself seven

RESIST (RESISTED RESISTS)

Da   11: 32 know their God will firmly *r* him.
Mt   5: 39 I tell you, Do not *r* an evil person.
Lk   21: 15 of your adversaries will be able to *r*
Jas   4: 7 *R* the devil, and he will flee
1Pe   5: 9 *R* him, standing firm in the faith,

RESISTED (RESIST)

Job   9: 4 Who has *r* him and come out

RESISTS* (RESIST)

Ro   9: 19 For who *r* his will?" But who are

RESOLVED

Ps   17: 3 I have *r* that my mouth will not sin.
Da   1: 8 But Daniel *r* not to defile himself
1Co   2: 2 For I *r* to know nothing while I was

RESOUNDING*

Ps 150: 5 praise him with *r* cymbals.
1Co 13: 1 I am only a *r* gong or a clanging

RESPECT (RESPECTABLE RESPECTED RESPECTS)

Lev 19: 3 "Each of you must *r* his mother
      19: 32 show *r* for the elderly and revere
Pr   11: 16 A kindhearted woman gains *r*,
Mal   1: 6 where is the *r* due me?" says
Eph   5: 33 and the wife must *r* her husband.
      6: 5 obey your earthly masters with *r*
1Th   4: 12 so that your daily life may win the *r*
      5: 12 to *r* those who work hard
1Ti   3: 4 children obey him with proper *r*.
      3: 8 are to be men worthy of *r*, sincere,
      3: 11 are to be women worthy of *r*,
      6: 1 their masters worthy of full *r*,
Tit   2: 2 worthy of *r*, self-controlled,
1Pe   2: 17 Show proper *r* to everyone:
      3: 7 them with *r* as the weaker partner
      3: 16 But do this with gentleness and *r*,

RESPECTABLE* (RESPECT)

1Ti   3: 2 self-controlled, *r*, hospitable,

RESPECTED (RESPECT)

Pr   31: 23 Her husband is *r* at the city gate,

RESPECTS (RESPECT)

Pr   13: 13 he who *r* a command is rewarded.

RESPLENDENT*

Ps   76: 4 You are *r* with light,
      132: 18 but the crown on his head will be *r*

RESPOND

Ps 102: 17 He will *r* to the prayer
Hos   2: 21 "I will *r* to the skies,

RESPONSIBILITY (RESPONSIBLE)

Ac   18: 6 your own heads! I am clear of my *r*.

RESPONSIBLE (RESPONSIBILITY)

Nu   1: 53 The Levites are to be *r* for the care
1Co   7: 24 Brothers, each man, as *r* to God,

REST (RESTED RESTS SABBATH-REST)

Ex   31: 15 the seventh day is a Sabbath of *r*,
      33: 14 go with you, and I will give you *r*."
Lev 25: 5 The land is to have a year of *r*.
Dt   31: 16 going to *r* with your fathers,
Jos 14: 15 Then the land had *r* from war.
      21: 44 The LORD gave them *r*
1Ki   5: 4 The LORD my god has given me *r*
1Ch 22: 9 who will be a man of peace and *r*,
Job   3: 17 and there the weary are at *r*.
Ps   16: 9 my body also will *r* secure,
      33: 22 May your unfailing love *r* upon us,
      62: 1 My soul finds *r* in God alone;
      62: 5 Find *r*, O my soul, in God alone;
      90: 17 of the Lord our God *r* upon us;
      91: 1 will *r* in the shadow
      95: 11 "They shall never enter my *r*."
Pr   6: 10 a little folding of the hands to *r*—
Isa 11: 2 Spirit of the LORD will *r* on him—
      11: 10 and his place of *r* will be glorious.
      30: 15 "In repentance and *r* is your
      32: 18 in undisturbed places of *r*.
      57: 20 which cannot *r*,
Jer   6: 16 and you will find *r* for your souls.
      47: 6 'how long till you *r*?
Mt   11: 28 and burdened, and I will give you *r*.
2Co 12: 9 so that Christ's power may *r* on me
Heb   3: 11 'They shall never enter my *r*.' "
      4: 3 'They shall never enter my *r*.' "
      4: 10 for anyone who enters God's *r*
Rev 14: 13 "they will *r* from their labor,

RESTED (REST)

Ge   2: 2 so on the seventh day he *r*
Heb   4: 4 "And on the seventh day God *r*

RESTITUTION

Ex   22: 3 "A thief must certainly make *r*,
Lev   6: 5 He must make *r* in full, add a fifth
Nu   5: 8 the *r* belongs to the LORD

RESTORE (RESTORES)

Ps   51: 12 *R* to me the joy of your salvation
      80: 3 *R* us, O God;
      126: 4 *R* our fortunes, O LORD,
Jer 31: 18 *R* me, and I will return,
La   5: 21 *R* us to yourself, O LORD,
Da   9: 25 From the issuing of the decree to *r*
Na   2: 2 The LORD will *r* the splendor
Gal   6: 1 are spiritual should *r* him gently.
1Pe   5: 10 will himself *r* you and make you

RESTORES (RESTORE)

Ps   23: 3 he *r* my soul.

RESTRAINED (RESTRAINT)

Ps   78: 38 Time after time he *r* his anger

RESTRAINING (RESTRAINT)

Pr   27: 16 *r* her is like *r* the wind
Col   2: 23 value in *r* sensual indulgence.

RESTRAINT (RESTRAINED RESTRAINING)

Pr   17: 27 of knowledge uses words with *r*,
      23: 4 have the wisdom to show *r*.
      29: 18 no revelation, the people cast off *r*;

RESTS (REST)

Dt   33: 12 and the one the LORD loves *r*
Pr   19: 23 one *r* content, untouched
Lk   2: 14 to men on whom his favor *r*."

RESULT

Lk 21: 13 This will *r* in your being witnesses
Ro 6: 22 to holiness, and the *r* is eternal life.
  11: 31 as a *r* of God's mercy to you.
2Co 3: 3 from Christ, the *r* of our ministry,
2Th 1: 5 as a *r* you will be counted worthy
1Pe 1: 7 may be proved genuine and may *r*

RESURRECTION*

Mt 22: 23 who say there is no *r*, came to him
  22: 28 at the *r*, whose wife will she be
  22: 30 At the *r* people will neither marry
  22: 31 But about the *r* of the dead—
  27: 53 and after Jesus' *r* they went
Mk 12: 18 who say there is no *r*, came to him
  12: 23 At the *r* whose wife will she be,
Lk 14: 14 repaid at the *r* of the righteous.''
  20: 27 who say there is no *r*, came to Jesus
  20: 33 at the *r* whose wife will she be,
  20: 35 in the *r* from the dead will neither
  20: 36 since they are children of the *r*.
Jn 11: 24 again in the *r* at the last day.''
  11: 25 Jesus said to her, ''I am the *r*
Ac 1: 22 become a witness with us of his *r*.''
   2: 31 he spoke of the *r* of the Christ,
   4: 2 in Jesus the *r* of the dead.
   4: 33 to testify to the *r* of the Lord Jesus,
  17: 18 good news about Jesus and the *r*.
  17: 32 When they heard about the *r*
  23: 6 of my hope in the *r* of the dead.''
  23: 8 Sadducees say that there is no *r*,
  24: 15 that there will be a *r*
  24: 21 'It is concerning the *r*
Ro 1: 4 Son of God by his *r* from the dead:
   6: 5 also be united with him in his *r*.
1Co 15: 12 some of you say that there is no *r*
  15: 13 If there is no *r* of the dead,
  15: 21 the *r* of the dead comes
  15: 29 if there is no *r*, what will those do
  15: 42 So will it be with the *r* of the dead.
Php 3: 10 power of his *r* and the fellowship
   3: 11 to attain to the *r* from the dead.
2Ti 2: 18 say that the *r* has already taken
Heb 6: 2 on of hands, the *r* of the dead,
  11: 35 so that they might gain a better *r*.
1Pe 1: 3 hope through the *r* of Jesus Christ
   3: 21 It saves you by the *r* of Jesus Christ
Rev 20: 5 This is the first *r*.
  20: 6 those who have part in the first *r*.

RETALIATE*

1Pe 2: 23 he did not *r*; when he suffered,

RETRIBUTION

Ps 69: 22 may it become *r* and a trap.
Jer 51: 56 For the LORD is a God of *r*;
Ro 11: 9 a stumbling block and a *r* for them.

RETURN (RETURNED RETURNS)

Ge 3: 19 and to dust you will *r*.''
2Sa 12: 23 go to him, but he will not *r* to me.''
2Ch 30: 9 If you *r* to the LORD, then your
Ne 1: 9 but if you *r* to me and obey my
Job 10: 21 joy before I go to the place of no *r*,
  16: 22 before I go on the journey of no *r*.
  22: 23 If you *r* to the Almighty, you will
Ps 80: 14 *R* to us, O God Almighty!
  126: 6 will *r* with songs of joy,
Isa 10: 21 A remnant will *r*, a remnant
  35: 10 the ransomed of the LORD will *r*.
  55: 11 It will not *r* to me empty,
Jer 24: 7 for they will *r* to me
  31: 8 a great throng will *r*.
La 3: 40 and let us *r* to the LORD.
Hos 6: 1 ''Come, let us *r* to the LORD.
  12: 6 But you must *r* to your God;
  14: 1 *R*, O Israel, to the LORD your
Joel 2: 12 ''*r* to me with all your heart,
Zec 1: 3 '*R* to me,' declares the LORD
  10: 9 and they will *r*.

RETURNED (RETURN)

Ps 35: 13 When my prayers *r*
Am 4: 6 yet you have not *r* to me,''
1Pe 2: 25 now you have *r* to the Shepherd

RETURNS (RETURN)

Pr 3: 14 and yields better *r* than gold.

Isa 52: 8 When the LORD *r* to Zion,
Mt 24: 46 finds him doing so when he *r*.

REUBEN

 Firstborn of Jacob by Leah (Ge 29:32; 46:8;
1Ch 2:1). Attempted to rescue Joseph (Ge 37:
21-30). Lost birthright for sleeping with Bilhah
(Ge 35:22; 49:4). Tribe of blessed (Ge 49:3-4; Dt
33:6), numbered (Nu 1:21; 26:7), allotted land
east of Jordan (Nu 32; 34:14; Jos 13:15), west (Eze
48:6), failed to help Deborah (Jdg 5:15-16), supported David (1Ch 12:37), 12,000 from (Rev 7:5).

REVEAL (REVEALED REVEALS REVELATION REVELATIONS)

Mt 11: 27 to whom the Son chooses to *r* him.
Gal 1: 16 was pleased to *r* his Son in me

REVEALED (REVEAL)

Dt 29: 29 but the things *r* belong to us
Isa 40: 5 the glory of the LORD will be *r*,
  43: 12 I have *r* and saved and proclaimed
  53: 1 the arm of the LORD been *r*?
  65: 1 I *r* myself to those who did not ask
Mt 11: 25 and *r* them to little children.
Jn 12: 38 the arm of the Lord been *r*?''
  17: 6 ''I have *r* you to those whom you
Ro 1: 17 a righteousness from God is *r*,
   8: 18 with the glory that will be *r* in us.
  10: 20 I *r* myself to those who did not ask
  16: 26 but now *r* and made known
1Co 2: 10 but God has *r* it to us by his Spirit.
2Th 1: 7 happen when the Lord Jesus is *r*
   2: 3 and the man of lawlessness is *r*,
1Pe 1: 7 and honor when Jesus Christ is *r*.
   1: 20 but was *r* in these last times
   4: 13 overjoyed when his glory is *r*.

REVEALS* (REVEAL)

Nu 23: 3 Whatever he *r* to me I will tell you
Job 12: 22 He *r* the deep things of darkness
Da 2: 22 He *r* deep and hidden things;
   2: 28 a God in heaven who *r* mysteries.
Am 4: 13 and *r* his thoughts to man,

REVELATION* (REVEAL)

2Sa 7: 17 David all the words of this entire *r*.
1Ch 17: 15 David all the words of this entire *r*.
Pr 29: 18 Where there is no *r*, the people cast
Da 10: 1 a *r* was given to Daniel (who was
Hab 2: 2 ''Write down the *r*
   2: 3 For the *r* awaits an appointed time;
Lk 2: 32 a light for *r* to the Gentiles
Ro 16: 25 according to the *r*
1Co 14: 6 I bring you some *r* or knowledge
  14: 26 a *r*, a tongue or an interpretation.
  14: 30 And if a *r* comes to someone who is
Gal 1: 12 I received it by *r* from Jesus Christ.
   2: 2 I went in response to a *r*
Eph 1: 17 you the Spirit of wisdom and *r*,
   3: 3 mystery made known to me by *r*,
Rev 1: 1 *r* of Jesus Christ, which God gave

REVELATIONS* (REVEAL)

2Co 12: 1 on to visions and *r* from the Lord.
  12: 7 of these surpassingly great *r*,

REVELED* (REVELRY)

Ne 9: 25 they *r* in your great goodness.

REVELRY (REVELED)

Ex 32: 6 drink and got up to indulge in *r*,
1Co 10: 7 and got up to indulge in pagan *r*.''

REVENGE (VENGEANCE)

Lev 19: 18 '' 'Do not seek *r* or bear a grudge
Ro 12: 19 Do not take *r*, my friends,

REVERE* (REVERENCE REVERENT REVERING)

Lev 19: 32 for the elderly and *r* your God.
Dt 4: 10 so that they may learn to *r* me
  13: 4 must follow, and him you must *r*.
  14: 23 to *r* the LORD your God always.
  17: 19 learn to *r* the LORD his God
  28: 58 and do not *r* this glorious
Job 37: 24 Therefore, men *r* him,
Ps 22: 23 *R* him, all you descendants

Ps 33: 8 let all the people of the world *r* him
  102: 15 of the earth will *r* your glory.
Ecc 3: 14 God does it so that men will *r* him.
Isa 25: 3 cities of ruthless nations will *r* you.
  59: 19 of the sun, they will *r* his glory.
  63: 17 hearts so we do not *r* you?
Jer 10: 7 Who should not *r* you,
Hos 10: 3 because we did not *r* the LORD.
Mal 4: 2 But for you who *r* my name,

REVERENCE (REVERE)

Lev 19: 30 and have *r* for my sanctuary.
Ne 5: 15 of *r* for God I did not act like that.
Ps 5: 7 in *r* will I bow down
Da 6: 26 people must fear and *r* the God
2Co 7: 1 perfecting holiness out of *r* for God
Eph 5: 21 to one another out of *r* for Christ,
Col 3: 22 of heart and *r* for the Lord.
1Pe 3: 2 when they see the purity and *r*
Rev 11: 18 and those who *r* your name,

REVERENT* (REVERE)

Ecc 8: 12 with God-fearing men, who are *r*
Tit 2: 3 women to be *r* in the way they live,
Heb 5: 7 because of his *r* submission.
1Pe 1: 17 as strangers here in *r* fear.

REVERING* (REVERE)

Dt 8: 6 walking in his ways and *r* him.
Ne 1: 11 who delight in *r* your name.

REVERSE*

Isa 43: 13 When I act, who can *r* it?''

REVIVE* (REVIVING)

Ps 80: 18 *r* us, and we will call on your name.
  85: 6 Will you not *r* us again,
Isa 57: 15 and to *r* the heart of the contrite.
  57: 15 to *r* the spirit of the lowly
Hos 6: 2 After two days he will *r* us;

REVIVING* (REVIVE)

Ps 19: 7 *r* the soul.

REVOKED

Isa 45: 23 a word that will not be *r*:

REWARD (REWARDED REWARDING REWARDS)

Ge 15: 1 your very great *r*.''
1Sa 24: 19 May the LORD *r* you well
Ps 19: 11 in keeping them there is great *r*.
  62: 12 Surely you will *r* each person
  127: 3 children a *r* from him.
Pr 12: 2 are wise, your wisdom will *r* you;
  11: 18 sows righteousness reaps a sure *r*.
  13: 21 prosperity is the *r* of the righteous.
  19: 17 he will *r* him for what he has done.
  25: 22 and the LORD will *r* you.
  31: 31 Give her the *r* she has earned,
Isa 40: 10 See, his *r* is with him,
  49: 4 and my *r* is with my God.''
  61: 8 In my faithfulness I will *r* them
  62: 11 See, his *r* is with him,
Jer 17: 10 to *r* a man according to his conduct
  32: 19 you *r* everyone according
Mt 5: 12 because great is your *r* in heaven,
   6: 1 you will have no *r*
   6: 5 they have received their *r* in full.
  10: 41 a prophet will receive a prophet's *r*,
  16: 27 and then he will *r* each person
Lk 6: 23 because great is your *r* in heaven.
   6: 35 Then your *r* will be great,
1Co 3: 14 built survives, he will receive his *r*.
Eph 6: 8 know that the Lord will *r* everyone
Col 3: 24 an inheritance from the Lord as a *r*.
Heb 11: 26 he was looking ahead to his *r*.
Rev 22: 12 I am coming soon! My *r* is with me

REWARDED (REWARD)

Ru 2: 12 May you be richly *r* by the LORD,
2Sa 22: 21 of my hands he has *r* me.
2Ch 15: 7 for your work will be *r*.''
Ps 18: 24 The LORD has *r* me according
Pr 13: 13 he who respects a command is *r*.
  14: 14 and the good man *r* for his.
Jer 31: 16 for your work will be *r*,''
1Co 3: 8 and each will be *r* according

Heb 10: 35 your confidence; it will be richly *r.*
2Jn   : 8 but that you may be *r* fully.

REWARDING* (REWARD)

Rev 11: 18 for *r* your servants the prophets

REWARDS (REWARD)

1Sa 26: 23 The LORD *r* every man
Pr 12: 14 the work of his hands *r* him.
Heb 11: 6 that he *r* those who earnestly seek

RIBS

Ge   2: 21 he took one of the man's *r*

RICH (RICHES RICHEST)

Job 34: 19 does not favor the *r* over the poor,
Ps 49: 16 overawed when a man grows *r,*
   145: 8 slow to anger and *r* in love.
Pr 21: 17 loves wine and oil will never be *r.*
   22: 2 *R* and poor have this in common:
   23: 4 Do not wear yourself out to get *r;*
   28: 6 than a *r* man whose ways are
   28: 20 to get *r* will not go unpunished.
   28: 22 A stingy man is eager to get *r*
Ecc 5: 12 but the abundance of a *r* man
Isa 33: 6 a *r* store of salvation and wisdom
   53: 9 and with the *r* in his death,
Jer   9: 23 or the *r* man boast of his riches,
Zec   3: 4 and I will put *r* garments on you.''
Mt 19: 23 it is hard for a *r* man
Lk   1: 53 but has sent the *r* away empty.
   6: 24 ''But woe to you who are *r,*
  12: 21 for himself but is not *r* toward God
  16: 1 ''There was a *r* man whose
  21: 1 Jesus saw the *r* putting their gifts
2Co 6: 10 yet making many *r;* having nothing
   8: 2 poverty welled up in *r* generosity.
   8: 9 he was *r,* yet for your sakes he
   9: 11 You will be made *r* in every way
Eph 2: 4 love for us, God, who is *r* in mercy,
1Ti 6: 9 want to get *r* fall into temptation
   6: 17 Command those who are *r*
   6: 18 to do good, to be *r* in good deeds,
Jas   1: 10 the one who is *r* should take pride
   2: 5 the eyes of the world to be *r* in faith
   5: 1 you *r* people, weep and wail
Rev 2: 9 and your poverty—yet you are *r!*
   3: 18 you can become *r;* and white

RICHES (RICH)

Job 36: 18 that no one entices you by *r;*
Ps 49: 6 and boast of their great *r?*
   49: 12 despite his *r,* does not endure;
   62: 10 though your *r* increase,
  119: 14 as one rejoices in great *r.*
Pr   3: 16 in her left hand are *r* and honor.
  11: 28 Whoever trusts in his *r* will fall,
  22: 1 is more desirable than great *r;*
  27: 24 for *r* do not endure forever,
  30: 8 give me neither poverty nor *r,*
Isa 10: 3 Where will you leave your *r?*
   60: 5 to you the *r* of the nations will
Jer   9: 23 or the rich man boast of his *r,*
Lk   8: 14 *r* and pleasures, and they do not
Ro   9: 23 to make the *r* of his glory known
  11: 33 the depth of the *r* of the wisdom
Eph 2: 7 he might show the incomparable *r*
   3: 8 to the Gentiles the unsearchable *r*
Col   1: 27 among the Gentiles the glorious *r*
   2: 2 so that they may have the full *r*

RICHEST (RICH)

Isa 55: 2 and your soul will delight in the *r*

RID

Ge 21: 10 ''Get *r* of that slave woman
1Co 5: 7 Get *r* of the old yeast that you may
Gal   4: 30 ''Get *r* of the slave woman

RIDE (RIDER RIDING)

Ps 45: 4 In your majesty *r* forth victoriously

RIDER (RIDE)

Rev 6: 2 was a white horse! Its *r* held a bow,
  19: 11 whose *r* is called Faithful and True.

RIDING (RIDE)

Zec   9: 9 gentle and *r* on a donkey,
Mt 21: 5 gentle and *r* on a donkey,

RIGGING

Isa 33: 23 Your *r* hangs loose:

RIGHT (RIGHTS)

Ge   4: 7 But if you do not do what is *r,*
  18: 19 of the LORD by doing what is *r*
  18: 25 the Judge of all the earth do *r?''*
  48: 13 on his left toward Israel's *r* hand,
Ex 15: 6 Your *r* hand, O LORD,
  15: 26 and do what is *r* in his eyes,
Dt   5: 32 do not turn aside to the *r*
   6: 18 Do what is *r* and good
  13: 18 and do what is *r* in his eyes.
Jos 1: 7 do not turn from it to the *r*
1Sa 12: 23 you the way that is good and *r.*
1Ki 3: 9 to distinguish between *r* and wrong
  15: 5 For David had done what was *r*
2Ki 7: 9 to each other, ''We're not doing *r.*
Ne   9: 13 and laws that are just and *r,*
Ps 16: 8 Because he is at my *r* hand,
  16: 11 eternal pleasures at your *r* hand.
  17: 7 you who save by your *r* hand
  18: 35 and your *r* hand sustains me;
  19: 8 The precepts of the LORD are *r,*
  25: 9 He guides the humble in what is *r*
  33: 4 For the word of the LORD is *r*
  44: 3 it was your *r* hand, your arm,
  45: 4 let your *r* hand display awesome
  51: 4 so that you are proved *r*
  63: 8 your *r* hand upholds me.
  73: 23 you hold me by my *r* hand.
  91: 7 ten thousand at your *r* hand,
  98: 1 his *r* hand and his holy arm
 106: 3 who constantly do what is *r.*
 110: 1 ''Sit at my *r* hand
 118: 15 LORD's *r* hand has done mighty
 119:144 Your statutes are forever *r;*
 137: 5 may my *r* hand forget ,its skill,
 139: 10 your *r* hand will hold me fast.
Pr   1: 3 doing what is *r* and just and fair;
   4: 27 Do not swerve to the *r* or the left;
  14: 12 There is a way that seems *r*
  18: 17 The first to present his case seems *r*
Ecc 7: 20 who does what is *r* and never sins.
SS   1: 4 How *r* they are to adore you!
Isa   1: 17 learn to do *r!*
   7: 15 reject the wrong and choose the *r.*
  30: 10 us no more visions of what is *r!*
  30: 21 Whether you turn to the *r*
  41: 10 you with my righteous *r* hand.
  41: 13 who takes hold of your *r* hand
  48: 13 my *r* hand spread out the heavens;
  64: 5 to the help of those who gladly do *r*
Jer 23: 5 and do what is just and *r* in the land
Eze 18: 5 who does what is just and *r,*
  18: 21 and does what is just and *r,*
  33: 14 and does what is just and *r—*
Hos 14: 9 The ways of the LORD are *r;*
Mt   5: 29 If your *r* eye causes you to sin,
   6: 3 know what your *r* hand is doing,
  22: 44 ''Sit at my *r* hand
  25: 33 He will put the sheep on his *r*
Jn   1: 12 he gave the *r* to become children
Ac   2: 34 ''Sit at my *r* hand
   7: 55 Jesus standing at the *r* hand of God
Ro   3: 4 ''So that you may be proved *r*
   8: 34 is at the *r* hand of God and is
   9: 21 Does not the potter have the *r*
  12: 17 careful to do what is *r* in the eyes
1Co 9: 4 Don't we have the *r* to food
2Co 8: 21 we are taking pains to do what is *r,*
Eph 1: 20 and seated him at his *r* hand
   6: 1 parents in the Lord, for this is *r.*
Php 4: 8 whatever is *r,* whatever is pure,
2Th 3: 13 never tire of doing what is *r.*
Heb 1: 3 down at the *r* hand of the Majesty
Jas   2: 8 as yourself,'' you are doing *r.*
1Pe 3: 14 if you should suffer for what is *r,*
1Jn 2: 29 who does what is *r* has been born
Rev 2: 7 I will give the *r* to eat from the tree
   3: 21 I will give the *r* to sit with me
  22: 11 let him who does *r* continue to do *r*

RIGHTEOUS (RIGHTEOUSLY RIGHTEOUSNESS)

Ge   6: 9 Noah was a *r* man, blameless
  18: 23 ''Will you sweep away the *r*
Nu 23: 10 Let me die the death of the *r,*
Ne   9: 8 your promise because you are *r.*
Job 36: 7 He does not take his eyes off the *r;*
Ps   1: 5 nor sinners in the assembly of the *r.*
   5: 12 O LORD, you bless the *r;*
  11: 7 For the LORD is *r,*
  15: 2 and who does what is *r,*
  34: 15 The eyes of the LORD are on the *r*
  37: 16 Better the little that the *r* have
  37: 21 but the *r* give generously;
  37: 25 yet I have never seen the *r* forsaken
  37: 30 of the *r* man utters wisdom,
  55: 22 he will never let the *r* fall.
  64: 10 Let the *r* rejoice in the LORD
  68: 3 But may the *r* be glad
 112: 4 compassionate and *r* man.
 118: 20 through which the *r* may enter.
 119: 7 as I learn your *r* laws.
 119:137 *R* are you, O LORD,
 140: 13 Surely the *r* will praise your name
 143: 2 for no one living is *r* before you.
 145: 17 The LORD is *r* in all his ways
Pr   3: 33 but he blesses the home of the *r.*
   4: 18 of the *r* is like the first gleam
  10: 7 of the *r* will be a blessing,
  10: 11 The mouth of the *r* is a fountain
  10: 16 The wages of the *r* bring them life,
  10: 20 The tongue of the *r* is choice silver,
  10: 24 what the *r* desire will be granted.
  10: 28 The prospect of the *r* is joy,
  10: 32 of the *r* know what is fitting,
  11: 23 The desire of the *r* ends only
  11: 30 The fruit of the *r* is a tree of life,
  12: 10 A *r* man cares for the needs
  12: 21 No harm befalls the *r,*
  13: 9 The light of the *r* shines brightly,
  15: 28 of the *r* weighs its answers,
  15: 29 but he hears the prayer of the *r.*
  16: 31 it is attained by a *r* life.
  18: 10 the *r* run to it and are safe.
  20: 7 The *r* man leads a blameless life;
  21: 15 justice is done, it brings joy to the *r*
  23: 24 The father of a *r* man has great joy;
  28: 1 but the *r* are as bold as a lion.
  29: 6 but a *r* one can sing and be glad.
  29: 7 The *r* care about justice
  29: 27 The *r* detest the dishonest.
Ecc 7: 20 There is not a *r* man on earth
Isa 26: 7 The path of the *r* is level;
  41: 10 you with my *r* hand.
  45: 21 a *r* God and a Savior;
  53: 11 his knowledge my *r* servant will
  64: 6 and all our *r* acts are like filthy rags
Jer 23: 5 up to David a *r* Branch,
Eze 3: 20 when a *r* man turns
  18: 5 ''Suppose there is a *r* man
  18: 20 of the *r* man will be credited
  33: 12 The *r* man, if he sins, will not be
Da   9: 18 requests of you because we are *r,*
Hab 2: 4 but the *r* will live by his faith—
Zec   9: 9 *r* and having salvation,
Mal 3: 18 see the distinction between the *r*
Mt   5: 45 rain on the *r* and the unrighteous.
   9: 13 For I have not come to call the *r,*
  10: 41 and anyone who receives a *r* man
  13: 43 Then the *r* will shine like the sun
  13: 49 and separate the wicked from the *r*
  25: 37 Then the *r* will answer him, 'Lord,
  25: 46 to eternal punishment, but the *r*
Ac 24: 15 will be a resurrection of both the *r*
Ro   1: 17 as it is written: ''The *r* will live
   2: 5 when his *r* judgment will be
   2: 13 the law who will be declared *r,*
   3: 10 ''There is no one *r,* not even one;
   3: 20 Therefore no one will be declared *r*
   5: 19 one man the many will be made *r.*
Gal 3: 11 because, ''The *r* will live by faith.''
1Ti 1: 9 that law is made not for the *r*
2Ti 4: 8 which the Lord, the *r* Judge,
Tit   3: 5 because of *r* things we had done,
Heb 10: 38 But my *r* one will live by faith.
Jas   5: 16 The prayer of a *r* man is powerful
1Pe 3: 12 the eyes of the Lord are on the *r*

1Pe   3: 18 the *r* for the unrighteous,
       4: 18 "If it is hard for the *r* to be saved,
1Jn   2: 1 defense—Jesus Christ, the *R* One.
       3: 7 does what is right is *r*, just as he is *r*.
Rev 19: 8 stands for the *r* acts of the saints.)

RIGHTEOUSLY* (RIGHTEOUS)

Ps   9: 4 on your throne, judging *r*.
Isa 33: 15 He who walks *r*
Jer 11: 20 LORD Almighty, you who judge *r*

RIGHTEOUSNESS (RIGHTEOUS)

Ge   15: 6 and he credited it to him as *r*.
Dt   9: 4 of this land because of my *r*."
1Sa 26: 23 LORD rewards every man for his *r*
1Ki 10: 9 to maintain justice and *r*."
Job 37: 23 great *r*, he does not oppress.
Ps   7: 17 to the LORD because of his *r*
       9: 8 He will judge the world in *r*;
      17: 15 And I—in *r* I will see your face;
      23: 3 He guides me in paths of *r*
      33: 5 The LORD loves *r* and justice;
      35: 28 My tongue will speak of your *r*
      36: 6 Your *r* is like the mighty
      37: 6 He will make your *r* shine like
      40: 9 I proclaim *r* in the great assembly;
      45: 4 in behalf of truth, humility and *r*;
      45: 7 You love *r* and hate wickedness;
      48: 10 your right hand is filled with *r*.
      65: 5 us with awesome deeds of *r*,
      71: 2 Rescue me and deliver me in your *r*
      71: 15 My mouth will tell of your *r*,
      71: 19 Your *r* reaches to the skies, O God,
      85: 10 *r* and peace kiss each other.
      89: 14 *R* and justice are the foundation
      96: 13 He will judge the world in *r*
      98: 9 He will judge the world in *r*
     103: 6 The LORD works *r*
     103: 17 his *r* with their children's children
     106: 31 This was credited to him as *r*
     111: 3 and his *r* endures forever.
     118: 19 Open for me the gates of *r*;
     132: 9 May your priests be clothed with *r*;
     145: 7 and joyfully sing of your *r*.
Pr   11: 5 *r* of the blameless makes a straight
      11: 18 he who sows *r* reaps a sure reward.
      13: 6 *R* guards the man of integrity,
      14: 34 *R* exalts a nation,
      16: 8 Better a little with *r*
      16: 12 a throne is established through *r*.
      21: 21 He who pursues *r* and love
Isa   5: 16 will show himself holy by his *r*.
       9: 7 it with justice and *r*
      11: 4 but with *r* he will judge the needy,
      16: 5 and speeds the cause of *r*.
      26: 9 the people of the world learn *r*.
      32: 17 The fruit of *r* will be peace;
      42: 6 "I, the LORD, have called you in *r*;
      42: 21 the LORD for the sake of his *r*
      45: 8 "You heavens above, rain down *r*;
      51: 1 "Listen to me, you who pursue *r*
      51: 6 my *r* will never fail.
      51: 8 But my *r* will last forever,
      58: 8 then your *r* will go before you,
      59: 17 He put on *r* as his breastplate,
      61: 10 and arrayed me in a robe of *r*,
      63: 1 "It is I, speaking in *r*,
Jer   9: 24 justice and *r* on earth,
      23: 6 The LORD Our *R*.
Eze   3: 20 a righteous man turns from his *r*
      14: 20 save only themselves by their *r*.
      18: 20 The *r* of the righteous man will be
      33: 12 *r* of the righteous man will not save
Da   9: 24 to bring in everlasting *r*,
      12: 3 and those who lead many to *r*,
Hos 10: 12 Sow for yourselves *r*,
Am   5: 24 *r* like a never-failing stream!
Mic   7: 9 I will see his *r*.
Zep   2: 3 Seek *r*, seek humility;
Mal   4: 2 the sun of *r* will rise with healing
Mt   5: 6 those who hunger and thirst for *r*,
       5: 10 who are persecuted because of *r*,
       5: 20 unless your *r* surpasses that
       6: 1 to do your 'acts of *r*' before men,
       6: 33 But seek first his kingdom and his *r*
Jn   16: 8 world of guilt in regard to sin and *r*
Ac   24: 25 Paul discoursed on *r*, self-control
Ro   1: 17 For in the gospel a *r* from God is

Ro   3: 5 brings out God's *r* more clearly,
       3: 22 This *r* from God comes
       4: 3 and it was credited to him as *r*."
       4: 5 wicked, his faith is credited as *r*.
       4: 6 man to whom God credits *r* apart
       4: 9 faith was credited to him as *r*.
       4: 13 through the *r* that comes by faith.
       4: 22 why "it was credited to him as *r*."
       5: 18 of *r* was justification that brings life
       6: 13 body to him as instruments of *r*.
       6: 16 or to obedience, which leads to *r*?
       6: 18 and have become slaves to *r*.
       6: 19 in slavery to *r* leading to holiness.
       8: 10 yet your spirit is alive because of *r*.
       9: 30 did not pursue *r*, have obtained it,
      10: 3 they did not know the *r* that comes
      14: 17 but of *r*, peace and joy
1Co   1: 30 our *r*, holiness and redemption.
2Co   3: 9 is the ministry that brings *r*!
       5: 21 that in him we might become the *r*
       6: 7 with weapons of *r* in the right hand
       6: 14 For what do *r* and wickedness have
       9: 9 his *r* endures forever."
Gal   2: 21 for if *r* could be gained
       3: 6 and it was credited to him as *r*."
       3: 21 then *r* would certainly have come
Eph   4: 24 created to be like God in true *r*
       5: 9 *r* and truth) and find out what
       6: 14 with the breastplate of *r* in place,
Php   1: 11 filled with the fruit of *r* that comes
       3: 6 as for legalistic *r*, faultless.
       3: 9 not having a *r* of my own that
1Ti   6: 11 and pursue *r*, godliness, faith, love,
2Ti   2: 22 and pursue *r*, faith, love and peace,
       3: 16 correcting and training in *r*,
       4: 8 is in store for me the crown of *r*,
Heb   1: 8 and *r* will be the scepter
       5: 13 with the teaching about *r*.
       7: 2 his name means "king of *r*";
      11: 7 became heir of the *r* that comes
      12: 11 it produces a harvest of *r*
Jas   2: 23 and it was credited to him as *r*,"
       3: 18 sow in peace raise a harvest of *r*.
1Pe   2: 24 die to sins and live for *r*;
2Pe   2: 21 not to have known the way of *r*,
       3: 13 and a new earth, the home of *r*.

RIGHTS (RIGHT)

Ps   82: 3 maintain the *r* of the poor
Pr   31: 8 for the *r* of all who are destitute.
Isa 10: 2 to deprive the poor of their *r*
La   3: 35 to deny a man his *r*
Gal   4: 5 that we might receive the full *r*

RING

Pr   11: 22 Like a gold *r* in a pig's snout
Lk   15: 22 Put a *r* on his finger and sandals

RIOTS

2Co   6: 5 imprisonments and *r*; in hard work,

RIPE

Joel 3: 13 for the harvest is *r*.
Am   8: 1 showed me: a basket of *r* fruit.
Jn   4: 35 at the fields! They are *r* for harvest.
Rev 14: 15 for the harvest of the earth is *r*."

RISE (RAISE RAISED RISEN ROSE)

Lev 19: 32 " *R* in the presence of the aged,
Nu   24: 17 a scepter will *r* out of Israel.
Isa 26: 19 their bodies will *r*.
Mal   4: 2 of righteousness will *r* with healing
Mt   27: 63 'After three days I will *r* again.'
Mk   8: 31 and after three days *r* again.
Lk   18: 33 On the third day he will *r* again."
Jn   5: 29 those who have done good will *r*
      20: 9 had to *r* from the dead.)
Ac   17: 3 had to suffer and *r* from the dead.
1Th   4: 16 and the dead in Christ will *r* first.

RISEN (RISE)

Mt   28: 6 He is not here; he has *r*, just
Mk   16: 6 He has *r*! He is not here.
Lk   24: 34 The Lord has *r* and has appeared

RIVER (RIVERS)

Ps   46: 4 There is a *r* whose streams make
Isa 66: 12 "I will extend peace to her like a *r*,

Eze 47: 12 grow on both banks of the *r*.
Rev 22: 1 Then the angel showed me the *r*

RIVERS (RIVER)

Ps 137: 1 By the *r* of Babylon we sat

ROAD (CROSSROADS ROADS)

Mt   7: 13 and broad is the *r* that leads

ROADS (ROAD)

Lk   3: 5 crooked *r* shall become straight,

ROARING

1Pe   5: 8 prowls around like a *r* lion looking

ROB (ROBBERS ROBBERY ROBS)

Mal   3: 8 "Will a man *r* God? Yet you *r* me.

ROBBERS (ROB)

Jer   7: 11 become a den of *r* to you?
Mk   15: 27 They crucified two *r* with him,
Lk   19: 46 but you have made it 'a den of *r*.' "
Jn   10: 8 came before me were thieves and *r*,

ROBBERY (ROB)

Isa 61: 8 I hate *r* and iniquity.

ROBE (ROBED ROBES)

Ge   37: 3 and he made a richly ornamented *r*
Isa   6: 1 the train of his *r* filled the temple.
      61: 10 arrayed me in a *r* of righteousness,
Rev   6: 11 each of them was given a white *r*,

ROBED (ROBE)

Ps   93: 1 the LORD is *r* in majesty
Isa 63: 1 Who is this, *r* in splendor,

ROBES (ROBE)

Ps   45: 8 All your *r* are fragrant with myrrh
Rev   7: 13 "These in white *r*— who are they,

ROBS* (ROB)

Pr   19: 26 He who *r* his father and drives out
      28: 24 He who *r* his father or mother

ROCK

Ge   49: 24 of the Shepherd, the *R* of Israel,
Ex   17: 6 Strike the *r*, and water will come
Nu   20: 8 Speak to that *r* before their eyes
Dt   32: 4 He is the *R*, his works are perfect,
      32: 13 him with honey from the *r*,
2Sa 22: 2 "The LORD is my *r*, my fortress
Ps   18: 2 The LORD is my *r*, my fortress
      19: 14 O LORD, my *R* and my Redeemer
      40: 2 he set my feet on a *r*
      61: 2 lead me to the *r* that is higher
      92: 15 he is my *R*, and there is no
Isa 26: 4 the LORD, is the *R* eternal.
      51: 1 to the *r* from which you were cut
Da   2: 34 you were watching, a *r* was cut out,
Mt   7: 24 man who built his house on the *r*.
      16: 18 and on this *r* I will build my church
Ro   9: 33 and a *r* that makes them fall,
1Co 10: 4 the spiritual *r* that accompanied
1Pe   2: 8 and a *r* that makes them fall."

ROD (RODS)

2Sa   7: 14 I will punish him with the *r* of men,
Ps   23: 4 your *r* and your staff,
Pr   13: 24 He who spares the *r* hates his son,
      22: 15 the *r* of discipline will drive it far
      23: 13 if you punish him with the *r*,
      29: 15 *r* of correction imparts wisdom,
Isa 11: 4 the earth with the *r* of his mouth;

RODS (ROD)

2Co 11: 25 Three times I was beaten with *r*,

ROLL (ROLLED)

Mk   16: 3 "Who will *r* the stone away

ROLLED (ROLL)

Lk   24: 2 They found the stone *r* away

ROMAN

Ac   16: 37 even though we are *R* citizens,
      22: 25 you to flog a *R* citizen who hasn't

ROOF (ROOFS)
Pr   21: 9 Better to live on a corner of the r

ROOFS
Mt 10: 27 in your ear, proclaim from the r.

ROOM (ROOMS)
Mt   6: 6 But when you pray, go into your r,
Mk 14: 15 He will show you a large upper r,
Lk   2: 7 there was no r for them in the inn.
Jn   8: 37 because you have no r for my word
     21: 25 the whole world would not have r
2Co 7: 2 Make r for us in your hearts.

ROOMS (ROOM)
Jn 14: 2 In my Father's house are many r;

ROOSTER
Mt 26: 34 this very night, before the r crows,

ROOT (ROOTED ROOTS)
Isa 11: 10 In that day the R of Jesse will stand
     53: 2 and like a r out of dry ground.
Mt   3: 10 already at the r of the trees,
     13: 21 But since he has no r, he lasts only
Ro 11: 16 if the r is holy, so are the branches.
     15: 12 "The R of Jesse will spring up,
1Ti 6: 10 of money is a r of all kinds of evil.
Rev 5: 5 the R of David, has triumphed.
     22: 16 I am the R and the Offspring

ROOTED (ROOT)
Eph 3: 17 being r and established in love,

ROOTS (ROOT)
Isa 11: 1 from his r a Branch will bear fruit.

ROSE (RISE)
SS   2: 1 I am a r of Sharon,
1Th 4: 14 believe that Jesus died and r again

ROTS
Pr 14: 30 but envy r the bones.

ROUGH
Isa 42: 16 and make the r places smooth.
Lk   3: 5 the r ways smooth.

ROUND
Ecc 1: 6 r and r it goes,

ROYAL
Ps 45: 9 at your right hand is the r bride
Da   1: 8 not to defile himself with the r food
Jas 2: 8 If you really keep the r law found
1Pe 2: 9 a r priesthood, a holy nation,

RUBBISH*
Php 3: 8 I consider them r, that I may gain

RUBIES
Job 28: 18 the price of wisdom is beyond r.
Pr   3: 15 She is more precious than r;
     8: 11 for wisdom is more precious than r,
     31: 10 She is worth far more than r.

RUDDER*
Jas 3: 4 by a very small r wherever the pilot

RUDDY
1Sa 16: 12 He was r, with a fine appearance
SS   5: 10 Beloved My lover is radiant and r,

RUDE*
1Co 13: 5 It is not r, it is not self-seeking,

RUIN (RUINED RUINING RUINS)
Pr 10: 8 but a chattering fool comes to r.
     10: 10 and a chattering fool comes to r.
     10: 14 but the mouth of a fool invites r.
     10: 29 but it is the r of those who do evil.
     18: 24 many companions may come to r,
     19: 13 A foolish son is his father's r,
     26: 28 and a flattering mouth works r.
SS   2: 15 that r the vineyards,
Eze 21: 27 A r! A r! I will make it a r!
1Ti 6: 9 desires that plunge men into r

RUINED (RUIN)
Isa 6: 5 "I am r! For I am a man
Mt   9: 17 and the wineskins will be r.
     12: 25 divided against itself will be r,

RUINING* (RUIN)
Tit 1: 11 they are r whole households

RUINS (RUIN)
Pr 19: 3 A man's own folly r his life,
Ecc 4: 5 and r himself.
2Ti 2: 14 and only r those who listen.

RULE (RULER RULERS RULES)
Ge   1: 26 let them r over the fish of the sea
      3: 16 and he will r over you."
Jdg 8: 22 said to Gideon, "R over us—
1Sa 12: 12 'No, we want a king to r over us'—
Ps   2: 9 You will r them with an iron
     67: 4 for you r the peoples justly
     119:133 let no sin r over me.
Pr 17: 2 A wise servant will r
Isa 28: 10 r on r, r on r;
Eze 20: 33 I will r over you with a mighty
Zec 6: 13 and will sit and r on his throne.
      9: 10 His r will extend from sea to sea
Ro 13: 9 are summed up in this one r:
     15: 12 arise to r over the nations;
1Co 7: 17 This is the r I lay down in all
Gal 6: 16 and mercy to all who follow this r,
Eph 1: 21 far above all r and authority,
Col 3: 15 the peace of Christ r in your hearts,
2Th 3: 10 we gave you this r: "If a man will
Rev 2: 27 He will r them with an iron scepter;
     12: 5 who will r all the nations
     19: 15 He will r them with an iron scepter

RULER (RULE)
Ps   8: 6 You made him r over the works
Pr 19: 6 Many curry favor with a r,
     23: 1 When you sit to dine with a r,
     25: 15 Through patience a r can be
     29: 26 Many seek an audience with a r,
Isa 60: 17 and righteousness your r.
Da   9: 25 the r, comes, there will be seven
Mic 5: 2 one who will be r over Israel,
Mt   2: 6 for out of you will come a r
Eph 2: 2 of the r of the kingdom of the air,
1Ti 6: 15 God, the blessed and only R,
Rev 1: 5 and the r of the kings of the earth.

RULERS (RULE)
Ps   2: 2 and the r gather together
     119:161 R persecute me without cause,
Isa 40: 23 reduces the r of this world
Da   7: 27 and all r will worship and obey him
Mt 20: 25 "You know that the r
Ac 13: 27 and their r did not recognize Jesus,
Ro 13: 3 For r hold no terror
1Co 2: 6 of this age or of the r of this age,
Eph 3: 10 should be made known to the r
      6: 12 the r, against the authorities,
Col 1: 16 or powers or r or authorities;

RULES (RULE)
Nu 15: 15 is to have the same r for you
2Sa 23: 3 when he r in the fear of God,
Ps 22: 28 and he r over the nations.
     66: 7 He r forever by his power,
     103: 19 and his kingdom r over all.
Isa 29: 13 is made up only of r taught by men.
     40: 10 and his arm r for him.
Mt 15: 9 their teachings are but r taught
Lk 22: 26 one who r like the one who serves.
2Ti 2: 5 he competes according to the r.

RUMORS
Jer 51: 46 afraid when r are heard in the land;
Mt 24: 6 You will hear of wars and r of wars,

RUN (RAN RUNNERS RUNNING RUNS)
Ps 19: 5 champion rejoicing to r his course.
Pr   4: 12 when you r, you will not stumble.
     18: 10 the righteous r to it and are safe.
Isa 10: 3 To whom will you r for help?
     40: 31 they will r and not grow weary,
Joel 3: 18 ravines of Judah will r with water.
Hab 2: 2 so that a herald may r with it.

1Co 9: 24 R in such a way as to get the prize.
Gal 2: 2 that I was running or had r my race
Php 2: 16 on the day of Christ that I did not r
Heb 12: 1 let us r with perseverance the race

RUNNERS* (RUN)
1Co 9: 24 that in a race all the r run,

RUNNING (RUN)
Ps 133: 2 r down on Aaron's beard,
Lk 17: 23 Do not go r off after them.
1Co 9: 26 I do not run like a man r aimlessly;
Gal 5: 7 You were r a good race.

RUNS (RUN)
Jn 10: 12 he abandons the sheep and r away.

RUSH
Pr   1: 16 for their feet r into sin,
      6: 18 feet that are quick to r into evil,
Isa 59: 7 Their feet r into sin;

RUST
Mt   6: 19 where moth and r destroy,

RUTH*
    Moabitess; widow who went to Bethlehem with
mother-in-law Naomi (Ru 1). Gleaned in field of
Boaz; shown favor (Ru 2). Proposed marriage to
Boaz (Ru 3). Married (Ru 4:1-12); bore Obed,
ancestor of David (Ru 4:13-22), Jesus (Mt 1:5).

RUTHLESS
Pr 11: 16 but r men gain only wealth.
Ro   1: 31 are senseless, faithless, heartless, r.

SABBATH (SABBATHS)
Ex 20: 8 "Remember the S day
     31: 14 " 'Observe the S, because it is holy
Lev 25: 2 the land itself must observe a s
Dt   5: 12 "Observe the S day
Isa 56: 2 keeps the S without desecrating it,
     56: 6 all who keep the S
     58: 13 if you call the S a delight
Jer 17: 21 not to carry a load on the S day
Mt 12: 1 through the grainfields on the S.
Lk 13: 10 On a S Jesus was teaching in one
Col 2: 16 a New Moon celebration or a S day

SABBATH-REST* (REST)
Heb 4: 9 then, a S for the people of God;

SABBATHS (SABBATH)
2Ch 2: 4 evening and on S and New Moons
Eze 20: 12 Also I gave them my S

SACKCLOTH
Ps 30: 11 you removed my s and clothed me
Da   9: 3 in fasting, and in s and ashes.
Mt 11: 21 would have repented long ago in s

SACRED
Lev 23: 2 are to proclaim as s assemblies.
Mt   7: 6 "Do not give dogs what is s;
Ro 14: 5 One man considers one day more s
1Co 3: 17 for God's temple is s, and you are
2Pe 1: 18 were with him on the s mountain.
     2: 21 on the s command that was

SACRIFICE (SACRIFICED SACRIFICES)
Ge 22: 2 S him there as a burnt offering
Ex 12: 27 'It is the Passover s to the LORD,
1Sa 15: 22 To obey is better than s,
1Ki 18: 38 the LORD fell and burned up the s,
1Ch 21: 24 or s a burnt offering that costs me
Ps 40: 6 S and offering you did not desire,
     50: 14 S thank offerings to God,
     51: 16 You do not delight in s,
     54: 6 I will s a freewill offering to you;
     107: 22 Let them s thank offerings
     141: 2 of my hands be like the evening s.
Pr 15: 8 The LORD detests the s
     21: 3 to the LORD than s.
Da   9: 27 the 'seven' he will put an end to s
     12: 11 time that the daily s is abolished
Hos 6: 6 For I desire mercy, not s,
Mt   9: 13 this means: 'I desire mercy, not s.'
Ro   3: 25 God presented him as a s
Eph 5: 2 as a fragrant offering and s to God.

Php 4: 18 an acceptable s, pleasing to God.
Heb 9: 26 away with sin by the s of himself.
　　10: 5 "S and offering you did not desire,
　　10: 10 holy through the s of the body
　　10: 14 by one s he has made perfect
　　10: 18 there is no longer any s for sin.
　　11: 4 faith Abel offered God a better s
　　13: 15 offer to God a s of praise—
1Jn 2: 2 He is the atoning s for our sins,
　　4: 10 as an atoning s for our sins.

SACRIFICED (SACRIFICE)

Ac 15: 29 are to abstain from food s to idols,
1Co 5: 7 our Passover lamb, has been s.
　　8: 1 Now about food s to idols:
Heb 7: 27 He s for their sins once for all
　　9: 28 so Christ was s once

SACRIFICES (SACRIFICE)

Ps 51: 17 The s of God are a broken spirit;
Mk 12: 33 than all burnt offerings and s."
Ro 12: 1 to offer your bodies as living s,
Heb 9: 23 with better s than these.
　　13: 16 for with such s God is pleased.
1Pe 2: 5 offering spiritual s acceptable

SAD

Lk 18: 23 he heard this, he became very s,

SADDUCEES

Mt 16: 6 the yeast of the Pharisees and S."
Mk 12: 18 S, who say there is no resurrection,
Ac 23: 8 S say that there is no resurrection,

SAFE (SAVE)

Ps 27: 5 he will keep me s in his dwelling;
　　37: 3 in the land and enjoy s pasture.
Pr 18: 10 the righteous run to it and are s.
　　28: 26 he who walks in wisdom is kept s.
　　29: 25 in the LORD is kept s.
Jer 12: 5 If you stumble in s country,
Jn 17: 12 kept them s by that name you gave
1Jn 5: 18 born of God keeps him s,

SAFETY (SAVE)

Ps 4: 8 make me dwell in s.
Hos 2: 18 so that all may lie down in s.
1Th 5: 3 people are saying, "Peace and s,"

SAINTS

1Sa 2: 9 He will guard the feet of his s,
Ps 16: 3 As for the s who are in the land,
　　30: 4 Sing to the LORD, you s of his;
　　31: 23 Love the LORD, all his s!
　　34: 9 Fear the LORD, you his s,
　　116: 15 is the death of his s.
　　149: 1 his praise in the assembly of the s.
　　149: 5 Let the s rejoice in this honor
Da 7: 18 the s of the Most High will receive
Ro 8: 27 intercedes for the s in accordance
1Co 6: 2 not know that the s will judge
Eph 1: 15 Jesus and your love for all the s,
　　1: 18 of his glorious inheritance in the s,
　　6: 18 always keep on praying for all the s
Phm 7 have refreshed the hearts of the s.
Rev 5: 8 which are the prayers of the s.
　　19: 8 for the righteous acts of the s.)

SAKE (SAKES)

1Sa 12: 22 For the s of his great name
Ps 23: 3 righteousness for his name's s.
　　44: 22 Yet for your s we face death all day
　　106: 8 Yet he saved them for his name's s,
Isa 42: 21 for the s of his righteousness
　　43: 25 your transgressions, for my own s,
　　48: 9 For my own name's s I delay my
　　48: 11 For my own s, for my own s,
Jer 14: 7 for the s of your name.
　　14: 21 For the s of your name do not
Eze 20: 9 But for the s of my name I did what
　　20: 14 But for the s of my name I did what
　　20: 22 and for the s of my name I did what
　　36: 22 but for the s of my holy name,
Da 9: 17 For your s, O Lord, look with favor
Mt 10: 39 life for my s will find it.
　　19: 29 for my s will receive a hundred
1Co 9: 23 I do all this for the s of the gospel,
2Co 12: 10 for Christ's s, I delight

Php 3: 7 loss for the s of Christ.
Heb 11: 26 He regarded disgrace for the s
1Pe 2: 13 for the Lord's s to every authority
3Jn 7 was for the s of the Name that they

SAKES* (SAKE)

2Co 8: 9 yet for your s he became poor,

SALEM

Ge 14: 18 king of S brought out bread
Heb 7: 2 "king of S" means "king of peace."

SALT

Ge 19: 26 and she became a pillar of s.
Nu 18: 19 covenant of s before the LORD
Mt 5: 13 "You are the s of the earth.
Col 4: 6 with s, so that you may know how
Jas 3: 11 s water flow from the same spring?

SALVATION* (SAVE)

Ex 15: 2 he has become my s.
2Sa 22: 3 my shield and the horn of my s.
　　22: 23 Will he not bring to fruition my s
1Ch 16: 23 proclaim his s day after day.
2Ch 6: 41 O LORD God, be clothed with s,
Ps 9: 14 and there rejoice in your s.
　　13: 5 my heart rejoices in your s.
　　14: 7 that s for Israel would come out
　　18: 2 is my shield and the horn of my s,
　　27: 1 The LORD is my light and my s—
　　28: 8 a fortress of s for his anointed one.
　　35: 3 "I am your s."
　　35: 9 and delight in his s.
　　37: 39 The s of the righteous comes
　　40: 10 I speak of your faithfulness and s.
　　40: 16 those who love your s always say,
　　50: 23 way so that I may show him the s
　　51: 12 Restore to me the joy of your s
　　53: 6 that s for Israel would come out
　　62: 1 my s comes from him.
　　62: 2 He alone is my rock and my s;
　　62: 6 He alone is my rock and my s;
　　62: 7 My s and my honor depend
　　67: 2 your s among all nations.
　　69: 13 answer me with your sure s.
　　69: 27 do not let them share in your s.
　　69: 29 may your s, O God, protect me.
　　70: 4 those who love your s always say,
　　71: 15 of your s all day long,
　　74: 12 you bring s upon the earth.
　　85: 7 and grant us your s.
　　85: 9 Surely his s is near those who fear
　　91: 16 and show him my s."
　　95: 1 to the Rock of our s.
　　96: 2 proclaim his s day after day.
　　98: 1 I have worked s for him.
　　98: 2 The LORD has made his s known
　　98: 3 the s of our God.
　　116: 13 I will lift up the cup of s
　　118: 14 he has become my s.
　　118: 21 you have become my s.
　　119: 41 your s according to your promise;
　　119: 81 with longing for your s,
　　119:123 My eyes fail, looking for your s,
　　119:155 is far from the wicked,
　　119:166 I wait for your s, O LORD,
　　119:174 I long for your s, O LORD,
　　132: 16 I will clothe her priests with s,
　　149: 4 he crowns the humble with s.
Isa 12: 2 Surely God is my s;
　　12: 2 he has become my s."
　　12: 3 from the wells of s.
　　25: 9 let us rejoice and be glad in his s."
　　26: 1 God makes s
　　26: 18 We have not brought s to the earth;
　　30: 15 "In repentance and rest is your s,
　　33: 2 our s in time of distress.
　　33: 6 a rich store of s and wisdom
　　45: 8 let s spring up,
　　45: 17 the LORD with an everlasting s;
　　46: 13 I will grant s to Zion,
　　46: 13 and my s will not be delayed.
　　49: 6 that you may bring my s
　　49: 8 and in the day of s I will help you;
　　51: 5 my s is on the way,
　　51: 6 But my s will last forever,
　　51: 8 my s through all generations."
　　52: 7 who proclaim s,

Isa 52: 10 the s of our God.
　　56: 1 for my s is close at hand
　　59: 16 so his own arm worked s for him,
　　59: 17 and the helmet of s on his head;
　　60: 18 but you will call your walls S
　　61: 10 me with garments of s
　　62: 1 her s like a blazing torch.
　　63: 5 so my own arm worked s for me,
Jer 3: 23 is the s of Israel.
La 3: 26 quietly for the s of the LORD.
Jnh 2: 9 S comes from the LORD."
Zec 9: 9 righteous and having s,
Lk 1: 69 He has raised up a horn of s for us
　　1: 71 of long ago), s from our enemies
　　1: 77 give his people the knowledge of s
　　2: 30 For my eyes have seen your s,
　　3: 6 And all mankind will see God's s
　　19: 9 "Today s has come to this house,
Jn 4: 22 for s is from the Jews.
Ac 4: 12 S is found in no one else,
　　13: 26 message of s has been sent.
　　13: 47 that you may bring s to the ends
　　28: 28 to know that God's s has been sent
Ro 1: 16 for the s of everyone who believes:
　　11: 11 s has come to the Gentiles
　　13: 11 because our s is nearer now
2Co 1: 6 it is for your comfort and s;
　　6: 2 and in the day of s I helped you."
　　6: 2 of God's favor, now is the day of s.
　　7: 10 brings repentance that leads to s
Eph 1: 13 word of truth, the gospel of your s.
　　6: 17 Take the helmet of s and the sword
Php 2: 12 to work out your s with fear
1Th 5: 8 and the hope of s as a helmet.
　　5: 9 to receive s through our Lord Jesus
2Ti 2: 10 they too may obtain the s that is
　　3: 15 wise for s through faith
Tit 2: 11 of God that brings s has appeared
Heb 1: 14 to serve those who will inherit s?
　　2: 3 This s, which was first announced
　　2: 3 escape if we ignore such a great s?
　　2: 10 of their s perfect through suffering.
　　5: 9 of eternal s for all who obey him
　　6: 9 case—things that accompany s.
　　9: 28 to bring s to those who are waiting
1Pe 1: 5 the coming of the s that is ready
　　1: 9 of your faith, the s of your souls.
　　1: 10 Concerning this s, the prophets,
　　2: 2 by it you may grow up in your s,
2Pe 3: 15 that our Lord's patience means s,
Jude 3 to write to you about the s we share
Rev 7: 10 "S belongs to our God,
　　12: 10 have come the s and the power
　　19: 1 S and glory and power belong

SAMARIA (SAMARITAN)

1Ki 16: 24 He bought the hill of S
2Ki 17: 6 the king of Assyria captured S
Jn 4: 4 Now he had to go through S.
　　4: 5 came to a town in S called Sychar,

SAMARITAN (SAMARIA)

Lk 10: 33 But a S, as he traveled, came where
　　17: 16 and thanked him—and he was a S.
Jn 4: 7 When a S woman came

SAMSON

Danite judge. Birth promised (Jdg 13). Married to Philistine, but wife given away (Jdg 14). Vengeance on Philistines (Jdg 15). Betrayed by Delilah (Jdg 16:1-22). Death (Jdg 16:23-31). Feats of strength: killed lion (Jdg 14:6), 30 Philistines (Jdg 14:19), 1,000 Philistines with jawbone (Jdg 15:13-17), carried off gates of Gaza (Jdg 16:3), pushed down temple of Dagon (Jdg 16:25-30).

SAMUEL

Ephraimite judge and prophet (Heb 11:32). Birth prayed for (1Sa 1:10-18). Dedicated to temple by Hannah (1Sa 1:21-28). Raised by Eli (1Sa 2:11, 18-26). Called as prophet (1Sa 3). Led Israel to victory over Philistines (1Sa 7). Asked by Israel for a king (1Sa 8). Anointed Saul as king (1Sa 9-10). Farewell speech (1Sa 12). Rebuked Saul for sacrifice (1Sa 13). Announced rejection of Saul (2Sa 15). Anointed David as king (1Sa 16). Protected David from Saul (1Sa 19:18-24). Death (1Sa 25:1). Returned from dead to condemn Saul (1Sa 28).

SANBALLAT

Led opposition to Nehemiah's rebuilding of Jerusalem (Ne 2:10, 19; 4; 6).

SANCTIFIED* (SANCTIFY)

Jn 17: 19 that they too may be truly s.
Ac 20: 32 among all those who are s.
    26: 18 among those who are s by faith
Ro 15: 16 to God, s by the Holy Spirit.
1Co 1: 2 to those s in Christ Jesus
    6: 11 But you were washed, you were s,
    7: 14 and the unbelieving wife has been s
    7: 14 the unbelieving husband has been s
1Th 4: 3 It is God's will that you should be s
Heb 10: 29 blood of the covenant that s him,

SANCTIFY* (SANCTIFIED SANCTIFYING)

Jn 17: 17 S them by the truth; your word is
    17: 19 For them I s myself, that they too
1Th 5: 23 s you through and through.
Heb 9: 13 are ceremonially unclean s them

SANCTIFYING* (SANCTIFY)

2Th 2: 13 through the s work of the Spirit
1Pe 1: 2 through the s work of the Spirit,

SANCTUARY

Ex 25: 8 "Then have them make a s for me,
Lev 19: 30 and have reverence for my s,
Ps 15: 1 LORD, who may dwell in your s?
    63: 2 I have seen you in the s
    68: 24 of my God and King into the s.
    68: 35 are awesome, O God, in your s;
    73: 17 me till I entered the s of God;
    102: 19 looked down from his s on high,
    134: 2 Lift up your hands in the s
    150: 1 Praise God in his s;
Eze 37: 26 I will put my s among them forever
    41: 1 the man brought me to the outer s
Da 9: 26 will destroy the city and the s.
Heb 6: 19 It enters the inner s
    8: 2 in the s, the true tabernacle set up
    8: 5 They serve at a s that is a copy
    9: 24 enter a man-made s that was only

SAND

Ge 22: 17 and as the s on the seashore.
Mt 7: 26 man who built his house on s.

SANDAL (SANDALS)

Ru 4: 7 one party took off his s

SANDALS (SANDAL)

Ex 3: 5 off your s, for the place where you
Dt 25: 9 take off one of his s, spit in his face
Jos 5: 15 off your s, for the place where you
Mt 3: 11 whose s I am not fit to carry.

SANG (SING)

Ex 15: 1 and the Israelites s this song
    15: 21 Miriam s to them:
Nu 21: 17 Then Israel s this song:
Jdg 5: 1 Barak son of Abinoam s this song:
1Sa 18: 7 As they danced, they s:
2Sa 22: 1 David s to the LORD the words
2Ch 5: 13 in praise to the LORD and s:
    29: 30 So they s praises with gladness
Ezr 3: 11 thanksgiving they s to the LORD:
Job 38: 7 while the morning stars s together
Ps 106: 12 and s his praise.
Rev 5: 9 And they s a new song:
    5: 12 In a loud voice they s:
    14: 3 they s a new song before the throne
    15: 3 and s the song of Moses the servant

SAP

Ro 11: 17 share in the nourishing s

SAPPHIRA*

Ac 5: 1 together with his wife S.

SARAH

Wife of Abraham, originally named Sarai; barren (Ge 11:29-31; 1Pe 3:6). Taken by Pharaoh as Abraham's sister; returned (Ge 12:10-20). Gave

Hagar to Abraham; sent her away in pregnancy (Ge 16). Name changed; Isaac promised (Ge 17: 15-21; 18:10-15; Heb 11:11). Taken by Abimelech as Abraham's sister; returned (Ge 20). Isaac born; Hagar and Ishmael sent away (Ge 21:1-21; Gal 4:21-31). Death (Ge 23).

SARDIS

Rev 3: 1 the angel of the church in S write:

SASH (SASHES)

Rev 1: 13 with a golden s around his chest.

SASHES (SASH)

Rev 15: 6 wore golden s around their chests.

SAT (SIT)

Ps 137: 1 By the rivers of Babylon we s
Mk 16: 19 and he s at the right hand of God.
Lk 10: 39 who s at the Lord's feet listening
Heb 1: 3 he s down at the right hand
    8: 1 who s down at the right hand
    10: 12 he s down at the right hand of God.
    12: 2 and s down at the right hand

SATAN

Job 1: 6 and S also came with them.
Zec 3: 2 said to S, "The LORD rebuke you,
Mt 12: 26 If S drives out S, he is divided
    16: 23 S! You are a stumbling block to me;
Mk 4: 15 S comes and takes away the word
Lk 10: 18 "I saw S fall like lightning
    22: 3 S entered Judas, called Iscariot,
Ro 16: 20 The God of peace will soon crush S
1Co 5: 5 is present, hand this man over to S,
2Co 11: 14 for S himself masquerades
    12: 7 a messenger of S, to torment me.
1Ti 1: 20 handed over to S to be taught not
Rev 12: 9 serpent called the devil, or S,
    20: 2 or S, and bound him for a thousand
    20: 7 S will be released from his prison

SATISFIED (SATISFY)

Ps 17: 15 I will be s with seeing your likeness
    22: 26 The poor will eat and be s;
    63: 5 My soul will be s as with the richest
    104: 28 they are s with good things.
    105: 40 s them with the bread of heaven.
Pr 13: 4 the desires of the diligent are fully s
    30: 15 are three things that are never s,
Ecc 5: 10 whoever loves wealth is never s
Isa 53: 11 he will see the light of life, and be s
Mt 14: 20 They all ate and were s,
Lk 6: 21 for you will be s.

SATISFIES* (SATISFY)

Ps 103: 5 who s your desires with good things,
    107: 9 for he s the thirsty
    147: 14 and s you with the finest of wheat.

SATISFY (SATISFIED SATISFIES)

Ps 90: 14 S us in the morning
    145: 16 s the desires of every living thing.
Pr 5: 19 may her breasts s you always,
Isa 55: 2 and your labor on what does not s?
    58: 10 and s the needs of the oppressed,

SAUL

1. Benjamite; anointed by Samuel as first king of Israel (1Sa 9-10). Defeated Ammonites (1Sa 11). Rebuked for offering sacrifice (1Sa 13:1-15). Defeated Philistines (1Sa 14). Rejected as king for failing to annihilate Amalekites (1Sa 15). Soothed from evil spirit by David (1Sa 16:14-23). Sent David against Goliath (1Sa 17). Jealousy and attempted murder of David (1Sa 18:1-11). Gave David Michal as wife (1Sa 18:12-30). Second attempt to kill David (1Sa 19). Anger at Jonathan (1Sa 20:26-34). Pursued David: killed priests at Nob (1Sa 22), went to Keilah and Ziph (1Sa 23), life spared by David at En Gedi (1Sa 24) and in his tent (1Sa 26). Rebuked by Samuel's spirit for consulting witch at Endor (1Sa 28). Wounded by Philistines; took his own life (1Sa 31; 1Ch 10). Lamented by David (2Sa 1:17-27). Children (1Sa 14:49-51; 1Ch 8).
2. See PAUL

SAVAGE

Ac 20: 29 s wolves will come in among you

SAVE (SAFE SAFETY SALVATION SAVED SAVES SAVIOR)

Ge 45: 5 to s lives that God sent me ahead
1Ch 16: 35 Cry out, "S us, O God our Savior;
Job 40: 14 that your own right hand can s you.
Ps 17: 7 you who s by your right hand
    18: 27 You s the humble
    28: 9 S your people and bless your
    31: 16 s me in your unfailing love.
    69: 35 for God will s Zion
    71: 2 turn your ear to me and s me.
    72: 13 and s the needy from death.
    89: 48 or s himself from the power
    91: 3 Surely he will s you
    109: 31 to s his life from those who
    146: 3 in mortal men, who cannot s.
Pr 2: 16 will s you also from the adulteress,
Isa 35: 4 he will come to s you.''
    38: 20 The LORD will s me,
    46: 7 it cannot s him from his troubles.
    59: 1 of the LORD is not too short to s,
    63: 1 mighty to s.''
Jer 17: 14 s me and I will be saved,
Eze 3: 18 ways in order to s his life,
    7: 19 able to s them in the day
    14: 14 they could s only themselves
    33: 12 of the righteous man will not s him
    34: 22 I will s my flock, and they will no
Da 3: 17 the God we serve is able to s us
Hos 1: 7 and I will s them—not by bow,
Zep 1: 18 will be able to s them
    3: 17 he is mighty to s.
Zec 8: 7 "I will s my people
Mt 1: 21 he will s his people from their sins
    16: 25 wants to s his life will lose it,
Lk 19: 10 to seek and to s what was lost.''
Jn 3: 17 but to s the world through him.
    12: 47 come to judge the world, but to s it.
Ro 11: 14 people to envy and s some of them.
1Co 7: 16 whether you will s your husband?
1Ti 1: 15 came into the world to s sinners—
Heb 7: 25 to s completely those who come
Jas 5: 20 of his way will s him from death
Jude : 23 others from the fire and s them;

SAVED (SAVE)

Ps 22: 5 They cried to you and were s;
    33: 16 No king is s by the size of his army;
    34: 6 he s him out of all his troubles.
    106: 21 They forgot the God who s them,
    116: 6 when I was in great need, he s me.
Isa 25: 9 we trusted in him, and he s us.
    45: 22 "Turn to me and be s,
    64: 5 How then can we be s?
Jer 4: 14 from your heart and be s.
    8: 20 and we are not s.''
Eze 3: 19 but you will have s yourself.
    33: 5 warning, he would have s himself.
Joel 2: 32 on the name of the LORD will be s;
Mt 10: 22 firm to the end will be s.
    24: 13 firm to the end will be s.
Mk 13: 13 firm to the end will be s.
    16: 16 believes and is baptized will be s,
Jn 10: 9 enters through me will be s.
Ac 2: 21 on the name of the Lord will be s.'
    2: 47 daily those who were being s.
    4: 12 to men by which we must be s.''
    15: 11 of our Lord Jesus that we are s,
    16: 30 do to be s?" They replied,
Ro 5: 9 how much more shall we be s
    9: 27 only the remnant will be s.
    10: 1 the Israelites is that they may be s.
    10: 9 him from the dead, you will be s.
    10: 13 on the name of the Lord will be s.''
    11: 26 so all Israel will be s, as it is written:
1Co 1: 18 to us who are being s it is the power
    3: 15 will suffer loss; he himself will be s,
    5: 5 his spirit s on the day of the Lord.
    10: 33 of many, so that they may be s.
    15: 2 By this gospel you are s,
Eph 2: 5 it is by grace you have been s.
    2: 8 For it is by grace you have been s,
2Th 2: 13 you to be s through the sanctifying
1Ti 2: 4 who wants all men to be s

SAVES (SAVE)
1Ti　2: 15 But women will be *s*
2Ti　1: 9 who has *s* us and called us
Tit　3: 5 He *s* us through the washing
Heb 10: 39 but of those who believe and are *s*.

SAVES (SAVE)
Ps　7: 10 who *s* the upright in heart.
68: 20 Our God is a God who *s;*
145: 19 he hears their cry and *s* them.
1Pe　3: 21 It *s* you by the resurrection

SAVIOR* (SAVE)
Dt　32: 15 and rejected the Rock his *S.*
2Sa 22: 3 stronghold, my refuge and my *s*—
22: 47 Exalted be God, the Rock, my *S!*
1Ch 16: 35 Cry out, "Save us, O God our *S;*
Ps　18: 46 Exalted be God my *S!*
24: 5 and vindication from God his *S.*
25: 5 for you are God my *S,*
27: 9 O God my *S.*
38: 22 O Lord my *S.*
42: 5 my *S* and
42: 11 my *S* and my God.
43: 5 my *S* and my God.
65: 5 O God our *S.*
68: 19 Praise be to the Lord, to God our *S,*
79: 9 Help us, O God our *S,*
85: 4 Restore us again, O God our *S,*
89: 26 my God, the Rock my *S.'*
Isa　17: 10 You have forgotten God your *S;*
19: 20 he will send them a *s* and defender,
43: 3 the Holy One of Israel, your *S;*
43: 11 and apart from me there is no *s.*
45: 15 O God and *S* of Israel.
45: 21 a righteous God and a *S;*
49: 26 that I, the Lord, am your *S,*
60: 16 know that I, the Lord, am your *S,*
62: 11 'See, your *S* comes!'
63: 8 and so he became their *S.*
Jer　14: 8 its *S* in times of distress,
Hos 13: 4 no *S* except me.
Mic　7: 7 I wait for God my *S;*
Hab　3: 18 I will be joyful in God my *S.*
Lk　1: 47 and my spirit rejoices in God my *S,*
2: 11 of David a *S* has been born to you;
Jn　4: 42 know that this man really is the *S*
Ac　5: 31 *S* that he might give repentance
13: 23 God has brought to Israel the *S*
Eph　5: 23 his body, of which he is the *S.*
Php　3: 20 we eagerly await a *S* from there,
1Ti　1: 1 by the command of God our *S*
2: 3 This is good, and pleases God our *S*
4: 10 who is the *S* of all men,
2Ti　1: 10 through the appearing of our *S,*
Tit　1: 3 me by the command of God our *S,*
1: 4 the Father and Christ Jesus our *S.*
2: 10 about God our *S* attractive.
2: 13 appearing of our great God and *S,*
3: 4 and love of God our *S* appeared,
3: 6 through Jesus Christ our *S,*
2Pe　1: 1 *S* Jesus Christ have received a faith
1: 11 eternal kingdom of our Lord and *S*
2: 20 and *S* Jesus Christ and again
3: 2 and *S* through your apostles.
3: 18 and knowledge of our Lord and *S*
1Jn　4: 14 Son to be the *S* of the world.
Jude　: 25 to the only God our *S* be glory,

SCALE (SCALES)
Ps　18: 29 with my God I can *s* a wall.

SCALES (SCALE)
Lev 11: 9 may eat any that have fins and *s.*
19: 36 Use honest *s* and honest weights,
Pr　11: 1 The Lord abhors dishonest *s,*
Da　5: 27 You have been weighed on the *s*
Rev　6: 5 Its rider was holding a pair of *s*

SCAPEGOAT (GOAT)
Lev 16: 10 by sending it into the desert as a *s.*

SCARECROW*
Jer　10: 5 Like a *s* in a melon patch,

SCARLET
Jos　2: 21 she tied the *s* cord in the window.
Isa　1: 18 "Though your sins are like *s,*
Mt　27: 28 They stripped him and put a *s* robe

SCATTER (SCATTERED SCATTERS)
Dt　4: 27 The Lord will *s* you
Ne　1: 8 I will *s* you among the nations,
Jer　9: 16 I will *s* them among nations that
30: 11 the nations among which I *s* you,
Zec 10: 9 I *s* them among the peoples,

SCATTERED (SCATTER)
Isa　11: 12 he will assemble the *s* people
Jer　31: 10 'He who *s* Israel will gather them
Zec　2: 6 "for I have *s* you to the four winds
13: 7 and the sheep will be *s,*
Mt　26: 31 and the sheep of the flock will be *s.'*
Jn　11: 52 but also for the *s* children of God,
Ac　8: 4 who had been *s* preached the word
Jas　1: 1 To the twelve tribes *s*
1Pe　1: 1 *s* throughout Pontus, Galatia,

SCATTERS (SCATTER)
Mt　12: 30 he who does not gather with me *s.*

SCEPTER
Ge　49: 10 The *s* will not depart from Judah,
Nu　24: 17 a *s* will rise out of Israel.
Ps　2: 9 You will rule them with an iron *s;*
45: 6 a *s* of justice will be the *s*
Heb　1: 8 and righteousness will be the *s*
Rev　2: 27 'He will rule them with an iron *s;*
12: 5 rule all the nations with an iron *s.*
19: 15 "He will rule them with an iron *s.*"

SCHEMES
Pr　6: 18 a heart that devises wicked *s,*
24: 9 The *s* of folly are sin,
2Co　2: 11 For we are not unaware of his *s.*
Eph　6: 11 stand against the devil's *s.*

SCHOLAR*
1Co　1: 20 Where is the *s?* Where is

SCOFFERS
2Pe　3: 3 that in the last days *s* will come,

SCORN (SCORNED SCORNING SCORNS)
Ps　69: 7 For I endure *s* for your sake,
69: 20 *S* has broken my heart
89: 41 he has become the *s*
109: 25 I am an object of *s* to my accusers;
119: 22 Remove from me *s* and contempt,
Mic　6: 16 you will bear the *s* of the nations."

SCORNED (SCORN)
Ps　22: 6 *s* by men and despised

SCORNING (SCORN)
Heb 12: 2 him endured the cross, *s* its shame,

SCORNS (SCORN)
Pr　13: 13 He who *s* instruction will pay for it,
30: 17 that *s* obedience to a mother,

SCORPION
Lk　11: 12 will give him a *s?* If you then,
Rev　9: 5 sting of a *s* when it strikes a man.

SCOUNDREL
Pr　6: 12 A *s* and villain,

SCRIPTURE (SCRIPTURES)
Jn　2: 22 Then they believed the *S*
7: 42 Does not the *S* say that the Christ
10: 35 and the *S* cannot be broken—
Ac　8: 32 was reading this passage of *S:*
1Ti　4: 13 yourself to the public reading of *S,*
2Ti　3: 16 All *S* is God-breathed
2Pe　1: 20 that no prophecy of *S* came about

SCRIPTURES (SCRIPTURE)
Mt　22: 29 because you do not know the *S*
Lk　24: 27 said in all the *S* concerning himself,
24: 45 so they could understand the *S:*
Jn　5: 39 These are the *S* that testify about
Ac　17: 11 examined the *S* every day to see
2Ti　3: 15 you have known the holy *S,*
2Pe　3: 16 as they do the other *S,*

SCROLL
Ps　40: 7 it is written about me in the *s.*
Isa　34: 4 and the sky rolled up like a *s;*
Eze　3: 1 eat what is before you, eat this *s;*
Heb 10: 7 it is written about me in the *s*—
Rev　6: 14 The sky receded like a *s,* rolling up,
10: 8 take the *s* that lies open in the hand

SCUM
1Co　4: 13 this moment we have become the *s*

SEA (SEASHORE)
Ex　14: 16 go through the *s* on dry ground.
Dt　30: 13 "Who will cross the *s* to get it
1Ki　7: 23 He made the *S* of cast metal,
Job 11: 9 and wider than the *s.*
Ps　93: 4 mightier than the breakers of the *s*
95: 5 The *s* is his, for he made it,
Ecc　1: 7 All streams flow into the *s,*
Isa　57: 20 the wicked are like the tossing *s,*
Jnh　1: 4 Lord sent a great wind on the *s,*
Mic　7: 19 iniquities into the depths of the *s.*
Hab　2: 14 as the waters cover the *s.*
Zec　9: 10 His rule will extend from *s* to *s*
Mt　18: 6 drowned in the depths of the *s.*
1Co 10: 1 that they all passed through the *s.*
Jas　1: 6 who doubts is like a wave of the *s,*
Jude　: 13 They are wild waves of the *s,*
Rev 10: 2 He planted his right foot on the *s*
13: 1 I saw a beast coming out of the *s,*
20: 13 The *s* gave up the dead that were
21: 1 and there was no longer any *s.*

SEAL (SEALED SEALS)
Ps　40: 9 I do not *s* my lips,
SS　8: 6 Place me like a *s* over your heart,
Da　12: 4 and *s* the words of the scroll
Jn　6: 27 God the Father has placed his *s*
1Co　9: 2 For you are the *s* of my apostleship
2Co　1: 22 set his *s* of ownership on us,
Eph　1: 13 you were marked in him with a *s,*
Rev　6: 3 the Lamb opened the second *s,*
6: 5 When the Lamb opened the third *s,*
6: 7 the Lamb opened the fourth *s,*
6: 9 When he opened the fifth *s,*
6: 12 I watched as he opened the sixth *s.*
8: 1 When he opened the seventh *s,*
9: 4 people who did not have the *s*
22: 10 "Do not *s* up the words

SEALED (SEAL)
Eph　4: 30 with whom you were *s* for the day
2Ti　2: 19 solid foundation stands firm, *s*
Rev　5: 1 on both sides and *s* with seven seals

SEALS (SEAL)
Rev　5: 2 "Who is worthy to break the *s*
6: 1 opened the first of the seven *s.*

SEAMLESS*
Jn　19: 23 This garment was *s,* woven

SEARCH (SEARCHED SEARCHES SEARCHING)
Ps　4: 4 *s* your hearts and be silent.
139: 23 *S* me, O God, and know my heart;
Pr　2: 4 and *s* for it as for hidden treasure,
25: 2 to *s* out a matter is the glory
SS　3: 2 I will *s* for the one my heart loves.
Jer　17: 10 "I the Lord *s* the heart
Eze　34: 11 I myself will *s* for my sheep
34: 16 I will *s* for the lost and bring back
Lk　15: 8 and *s* carefully until she finds it?

SEARCHED (SEARCH)
Ps 139: 1 O Lord, you have *s* me
Ecc 12: 10 The Teacher *s* to find just the right
1Pe　1: 10 *s* intently and with the greatest

SEARCHES (SEARCH)
1Ch 28: 9 for the Lord *s* every heart
Ps　7: 9 who *s* minds and hearts,
Pr　11: 27 but evil comes to him who *s* for it.
20: 27 The lamp of the Lord *s* the spirit
Ro　8: 27 And he who *s* our hearts knows
1Co　2: 10 The Spirit *s* all things,
Rev　2: 23 will know that I am he who *s* hearts

SEARCHING (SEARCH)

Jdg   5: 15 there was much s of heart.
Am   8: 12 s for the word of the LORD,

SEARED

1Ti   4:   2 whose consciences have been s

SEASHORE (SEA)

Jos 11:   4 as numerous as the sand on the s.
1Ki   4: 29 as measureless as the sand on the s.

SEASON (SEASONED SEASONS)

Lev 26:   4 I will send you rain in its s,
Ps   1:   3 which yields its fruit in s
2Ti   4:   2 be prepared in s and out of s;

SEASONED* (SEASON)

Col   4:   6 full of grace, s with salt,

SEASONS (SEASON)

Ge   1: 14 signs to mark s and days and years,
Gal   4: 10 and months and s and years!

SEAT (SEATED SEATS)

Ps   1:   1 or sit in the s of mockers.
Pr   31: 23 where he takes his s
Da   7:   9 and the Ancient of Days took his s.
Lk   14:   9 say to you, 'Give this man your s.'
2Co   5: 10 before the judgment s of Christ,

SEATED (SEAT)

Ps   47:   8 God is s on his holy throne.
Isa   6:   1 I saw the Lord s on a throne,
Lk   22: 69 of Man will be s at the right hand
Eph   1: 20 and s him at his right hand
     2:   6 and s us with him in the heavenly
Col   3:   1 where Christ is s at the right hand
Rev 14: 14 s on the cloud was one ''like a son
    20: 11 white throne and him who was s

SEATS (SEAT)

Lk   11: 43 you love the most important s

SECLUSION*

Lk   1: 24 and for five months remained in s.

SECRET (SECRETLY SECRETS)

Dt   29: 29 The s things belong
Jdg 16:   6 Tell me the s of your great strength
Ps   90:   8 our s sins in the light
   139: 15 when I was made in the s place.
Pr   11: 13 but a trustworthy man keeps a s.
    21: 14 A gift given in s soothes anger,
Jer   23: 24 Can anyone hide in s places
Mt   6:   4 so that your giving may be in s.
     6: 18 who sees what is done in s,
Mk   4: 11 ''The s of the kingdom
1Co   2:   7 No, we speak of God's s wisdom,
     4:   1 entrusted with the s things of God.
2Co   4:   2 we have renounced s and shameful
Eph   5: 12 what the disobedient do in s.
Php   4: 12 I have learned the s

SECRETLY (SECRET)

2Pe   2:   1 They will s introduce destructive
Jude   4 about long ago have s slipped

SECRETS (SECRET)

Ps   44: 21 since he knows the s of the heart?
Ro   2: 16 day when God will judge men's s
1Co 14: 25 the s of his heart will be laid bare.
Rev   2: 24 Satan's so-called deep s (I will not

SECURE (SECURITY)

Dt   33: 12 beloved of the LORD rest s in him,
Ps   16:   5 you have made my lot s.
    16:   9 my body also will rest s,
   112:   8 His heart is s, he will have no fear;
Pr   14: 26 fears the LORD has a s fortress,
Heb   6: 19 an anchor for the soul, firm and s.
2Pe   3: 17 and fall from your s position.

SECURITY (SECURE)

Job 31: 24 or said to pure gold, 'You are my s.'

SEED (SEEDS SEEDTIME)

Ge   1: 11 on the land that bear fruit with s
Isa   55: 10 so that it yields s for the sower

Mt   13:   3 ''A farmer went out to sow his s.
    13: 31 of heaven is like a mustard s,
    17: 20 have faith as small as a mustard s,
Lk   8: 11 of the parable: The s is the word
1Co   3:   6 I planted the s, Apollos watered it,
2Co   9: 10 he who supplies s to the sower
Gal   3: 29 then you are Abraham's s,
1Pe   1: 23 not of perishable s,
1Jn   3:   9 because God's s remains in him;

SEEDS (SEED)

Jn   12: 24 But if it dies, it produces many s.
Gal   3: 16 Scripture does not say ''and to s,''

SEEDTIME* (SEED)

Ge   8: 22 s and harvest,

SEEK (SEEKING SEEKS SELF-SEEKING SOUGHT)

Lev 19: 18 Do not s revenge or bear a grudge
Dt   4: 29 if from there you s the LORD your
1Ki 22:   5 ''First s the counsel of the LORD.''
1Ch 28:   9 If you s him, he will be found
2Ch   7: 14 themselves and pray and s my face
    15:   2 If you s him, he will be found
Ps   34: 10 those who s the LORD lack no
   105:   3 of those who s the LORD rejoice.
   105:   4 s his face always.
   119:   2 and s him with all their heart.
   119: 10 I s you with all my heart;
   119:176 S your servant,
Pr   8: 17 and those who s me find me.
    18: 15 the ears of the wise s it out.
    25: 27 is it honorable to s one's own honor
    28:   5 those who s the LORD understand
Isa   55:   6 S the LORD while he may be
    65:   1 found by those who did not s me.
Jer 29: 13 You will s me and find me
Hos 10: 12 for it is time to s the LORD,
Am   5:   4 ''S me and live;
Zep   2:   3 S the LORD, all you humble
Mt   6: 33 But s first his kingdom
     7:   7 and it will be given to you; s
Lk   12: 31 s his kingdom, and these things will
    19: 10 for the Son of Man came to s
Jn   5: 30 for I s not to please myself
Ro   10: 20 found by those who did not s me;
1Co   7: 27 you married? Do not s a divorce.
    10: 24 Nobody should s his own good,
Heb 11:   6 rewards those who earnestly s him.
1Pe   3: 11 he must s peace and pursue it.

SEEKING (SEEK)

2Ch 30: 19 who sets his heart on s God—
Pr   20: 18 Make plans by s advice;
Mal   3:   1 the Lord you are s will come
Jn   8: 50 I am not s glory for myself;
1Co 10: 33 For I am not s my own good,

SEEKS (SEEK)

Pr   11: 27 He who s good finds good will,
Mt   7:   8 he who s finds; and to him who
Jn   4: 23 the kind of worshipers the Father s.
Ro   3: 11 no one who s God.

SEER

1Sa   9:   9 of today used to be called a s.)

SELF-CONTROL* (CONTROL)

Pr   25: 28 is a man who lacks s.
Ac   24: 25 s and the judgment to come,
1Co   7:   5 you because of your lack of s.
Gal   5: 23 faithfulness, gentleness and s.
2Ti   3:   3 slanderous, without s, brutal,
2Pe   1:   6 and to knowledge, s; and to s,

SELF-CONTROLLED* (CONTROL)

1Th   5:   6 are asleep, but let us be alert and s.
     5:   8 let us be s, putting on faith and love
1Ti   3:   2 s, respectable, hospitable,
Tit   1:   8 who is s, upright, holy
     2:   2 worthy of respect, s, and sound
     2:   5 to be s and pure, to be busy at home
     2:   6 encourage the young men to be s.
     2: 12 to live s, upright and godly lives
1Pe   1: 13 prepare your minds for action; be s;
     4:   7 and s so that you can pray.
     5:   8 Be s and alert.

SELF-DISCIPLINE* (DISCIPLINE)

2Ti   1:   7 a spirit of power, of love and of s.

SELF-INDULGENCE*

Mt   23: 25 inside they are full of greed and s.
Jas   5:   5 lived on earth in luxury and s.

SELF-SEEKING* (SEEK)

Ro   2:   8 But for those who are s
1Co 13:   5 it is not s, it is not easily angered,

SELFISH*

Ps 119: 36 and not toward s gain.
Pr   18:   1 An unfriendly man pursues s ends;
Gal   5: 20 fits of rage, s ambition, dissensions,
Php   1: 17 preach Christ out of s ambition,
     2:   3 Do nothing out of s ambition
Jas   3: 14 and s ambition in your hearts,
     3: 16 you have envy and s ambition,

SELL (SELLING SELLS SOLD)

Ge   25: 31 ''First s me your birthright.''
Mk 10: 21 s everything you have
Rev 13: 17 or s unless he had the mark,

SELLING (SELL)

Lk   17: 28 buying and s, planting and building

SELLS (SELL)

Pr   31: 24 makes linen garments and s them,

SEND (SENDING SENDS SENT)

Ps   43:   3 S forth your light and your truth,
Isa   6:   8 S me!'' He said, ''Go and tell this
Mal   3:   1 ''See, I will s my messenger,
Mt   9: 38 to s out workers into his harvest
    24: 31 And he will s his angels
Mk   1:   2 I will s my messenger ahead of you,
Lk   20: 13 I will s my son, whom I love;
Jn   3: 17 For God did not s his Son
    16:   7 but if I go, I will s him to you.
1Co   1: 17 For Christ did not s me to baptize,

SENDING (SEND)

Mt 10: 16 I am s you out like sheep
Jn   20: 21 Father has sent me, I am s you.''
Ro   8:   3 God did by s his own Son

SENDS (SEND)

Ps   57:   3 God s his love and his faithfulness.

SENNACHERIB

Assyrian king whose siege of Jerusalem was overthrown by the LORD following prayer of Hezekiah and Isaiah (2Ki 18:13-19:37; 2Ch 32: 1-21; Isa 36-37).

SENSES*

Lk   15: 17 ''When he came to his s, he said,
1Co 15: 34 Come back to your s as you ought,
2Ti   2: 26 and that they will come to their s

SENSITIVITY*

Eph   4: 19 Having lost all s, they have given

SENSUAL* (SENSUALITY)

Col   2: 23 value in restraining s indulgence.
1Ti   5: 11 For when their s desires overcome

SENSUALITY* (SENSUAL)

Eph   4: 19 have given themselves over to s

SENT (SEND)

Ex   3: 14 to the Israelites: 'I AM has s me
Isa 55: 11 achieve the purpose for which I s it.
    61:   1 He has s me to bind up
Jer 28:   9 as one truly s by the LORD only
Mt 10: 40 me receives the one who s me.
Mk   6:   7 he s them out two by two
Lk   4: 18 He has s me to proclaim freedom
     9:   2 and he s them out to preach
    10: 16 rejects me rejects him who s me.''
Jn   1:   6 There came a man who was s
     4: 34 ''is to do the will of him who s me
     5: 24 believes him who s me has eternal
     8: 16 I stand with the Father, who s me.
     9:   4 must do the work of him who s me.
    16:   5 ''Now I am going to him who s me,

Jn   17:   3 and Jesus Christ, whom you have *s*.
     17: 18 As you *s* me into the world,
     20: 21 As the Father has *s* me, I am
Ro   10: 15 can they preach unless they are *s?*
Gal   4:   4 God *s* his Son, born of a woman,
1Jn   4: 10 but that he loved us and *s* his Son

SENTENCE

2Co   1:   9 in our hearts we felt the *s* of death.

SEPARATE (SEPARATED SEPARATES SEPARATION)

Mt   19:   6 has joined together, let man not *s.''*
Ro   8: 35 Who shall *s* us from the love
1Co   7: 10 wife must not *s* from her husband.
2Co   6: 17 and be *s*, says the Lord.
Eph   2: 12 at that time you were *s* from Christ,

SEPARATED (SEPARATE)

Isa   59:   2 But your iniquities have *s*
Eph   4: 18 in their understanding and *s*

SEPARATES (SEPARATE)

Pr   16: 28 and a gossip *s* close friends.
     17:   9 repeats the matter *s* close friends.
Mt   25: 32 as a shepherd *s* the sheep

SEPARATION (SEPARATE)

Nu   6:   2 a vow of *s* to the Lord

SERAPHS*

Isa   6:   2 Above him were *s*, each
     6:   6 Then one of the *s* flew to me

SERIOUSNESS*

Tit   2:   7 *s* and soundness of speech that

SERPENT (SERPENT'S)

Ge   3:   1 the *s* was more crafty than any
Isa   27:   1 Leviathan the coiling *s;*
Rev   12:   9 that ancient *s* called the devil
     20:   2 that ancient *s*, who is the devil,

SERPENT'S (SERPENT)

2Co   11:   3 Eve was deceived by the *s* cunning,

SERVANT (SERVANTS)

Ex   14: 31 trust in him and in Moses his *s*.
     21:   2 "If you buy a Hebrew *s*, he is
1Sa   3: 10 "Speak, for your *s* is listening."
2Sa   7: 19 the future of the house of your *s.*
1Ki   20: 40 While your *s* was busy here
Job   1:   8 "Have you considered my *s* Job?
Ps   19: 11 By them is your *s* warned;
     19: 13 Keep your *s* also from willful sins;
     31: 16 Let your face shine on your *s;*
     89:   3 I have sworn to David my *s*,
Pr   14: 35 A king delights in a wise *s*,
     17:   2 wise *s* will rule over a disgraceful
     22:   7 and the borrower is *s* to the lender.
     31: 15 and portions for her *s* girls.
Isa   41:   8 "But you, O Israel, my *s*,
     49:   3 He said to me, "You are my *s*,
     53: 11 my righteous *s* will justify
Zec   3:   8 going to bring my *s*, the Branch.
Mal   1:   6 his father, and a *s* his master.
Mt   8: 13 his *s* was healed at that very hour.
     20: 26 great among you must be your *s*,
     24: 45 Who then is the faithful and wise *s*,
     25: 21 'Well done, good and faithful *s!'*
Lk   1: 38 I am the Lord's *s*,'' Mary answered.
     16: 13 "No *s* can serve two masters.
Jn   12: 26 and where I am, my *s* also will be.
Ro   1:   1 a *s* of Christ Jesus, called
     13:   4 For he is God's *s* to do you good.
Php   2:   7 taking the very nature of a *s*,
Col   1: 23 of which I, Paul, have become a *s*.
2Ti   2: 24 And the Lord's *s* must not quarrel;

SERVANTS (SERVANT)

Lev   25: 55 for the Israelites belong to me as *s*.
2Ki   17: 13 to you through my *s* the prophets.''
Ezr   5: 11 "We are the *s* of the God of heaven
Ps   34: 22 The Lord redeems his *s;*
     103: 21 you his *s* who do his will.
     104:   4 flames of fire his *s*.
Isa   44: 26 who carries out the words of his *s*
     65:   8 so will I do in behalf of my *s;*

Isa   65: 13 my *s* will drink,
Lk   17: 10 should say, 'We are unworthy *s;*
Jn   15: 15 longer call you *s*, because a servant
Ro   13:   6 for the authorities are God's *s*,
1Co   3:   5 And what is Paul? Only *s*,
Heb   1:   7 his *s* flames of fire.''

SERVE (SERVED SERVES SERVICE SERVING)

Dt   10: 12 to *s* the Lord your God
     11: 13 and to *s* him with all your heart
     13:   4 *s* him and hold fast to him.
     28: 47 you did not *s* the Lord your
Jos   22:   5 and to *s* him with all your heart
     24: 15 this day whom you will *s*,
     24: 18 We too will *s* the Lord,
1Sa   7:   3 to the Lord and *s* him only,
     12: 20 but *s* the Lord with all your heart
     12: 24 *s* him faithfully with all your heart;
2Ch   19:   9 "You must *s* faithfully
Job   36: 11 If they obey and *s* him,
Ps   2: 11 *S* the Lord with fear
Da   3: 17 the God we *s* is able to save us
Mt   4: 10 Lord your God, and *s* him only.' ''
     6: 24 "No one can *s* two masters.
     20: 28 but to *s*, and to give his life
Ro   12:   7 If it is serving, let him *s;*
Gal   5: 13 rather, *s* one another in love.
Eph   6:   7 *S* wholeheartedly,
1Ti   6:   2 they are to *s* them even better,
Heb   9: 14 so that we may *s* the living God!
1Pe   4: 10 gift he has received to *s* others,
     5:   2 greedy for money, but eager to *s;*
Rev   5: 10 kingdom and priests to *s* our God,

SERVED (SERVE)

Mt   20: 28 Son of Man did not come to be *s*,
Jn   12:   2 Martha *s*, while Lazarus was
Ac   17: 25 And he is not *s* by human hands,
Ro   1: 25 and *s* created things rather
1Ti   3: 13 Those who have *s* well gain

SERVES (SERVE)

Lk   22: 26 one who rules like the one who *s*.
     22: 27 But I am among you as one who *s*.
Jn   12: 26 Whoever *s* me must follow me;
Ro   14: 18 because anyone who *s* Christ
1Pe   4: 11 If anyone *s*, he should do it

SERVICE (SERVE)

Lk   9: 62 fit for *s* in the kingdom
     12: 35 "Be dressed ready for *s*
Ro   15: 17 in Christ Jesus in my *s* to God.
1Co   12:   5 There are different kinds of *s*,
     16: 15 themselves to the *s* of the saints.
2Co   9: 12 This *s* that you perform is not only
Eph   4: 12 God's people for works of *s*,
Rev   2: 19 and faith, your *s* and perseverance,

SERVING (SERVE)

Jos   24: 15 if *s* the Lord seems undesirable
2Ch   12:   8 learn the difference between *s* me
Ro   12:   7 If it is *s*, let him serve;
     12: 11 your spiritual fervor, *s* the Lord.
     16: 18 people are not *s* our Lord Christ,
Eph   6:   7 as if you were *s* the Lord, not men,
Col   3: 24 It is the Lord Christ you are *s*.
2Ti   2:   4 No one *s* as a soldier gets involved

SETH

Ge   4: 25 birth to a son and named him *S*,

SETTLE

Mt   5: 25 "*S* matters quickly
2Th   3: 12 in the Lord Jesus Christ to *s* down

SEVEN (SEVENS SEVENTH)

Ge   7:   2 Take with you *s* of every kind
Jos   6:   4 march around the city *s* times,
1Ki   19: 18 Yet I reserve *s* thousand in Israel—
Pr   6: 16 *s* that are detestable to him:
     24: 16 a righteous man falls *s* times,
Isa   4:   1 In that day *s* women
Da   9: 25 comes, there will be *s* 'sevens,'
Mt   18: 21 Up to *s* times?'' Jesus answered.
Lk   11: 26 takes *s* other spirits more wicked
Ro   11:   4 for myself *s* thousand who have not
Rev   1:   4 To the *s* churches in the province

Rev   6:   1 opened the first of the *s* seals.
     8:   2 and to them were given *s* trumpets.
     10:   4 And when the *s* thunders spoke,
     15:   7 to the *s* angels *s* golden bowls filled

SEVENS* (SEVEN)

Da   9: 24 "Seventy '*s*' are decreed
     9: 25 will be seven '*s*,' and sixty-two '*s*.'
     9: 26 the sixty-two '*s*,' the Anointed

SEVENTH (SEVEN)

Ge   2:   2 By the *s* day God had finished
Ex   20: 10 but the *s* day is a Sabbath
     23: 11 but during the *s* year let the land lie
     23: 12 but on the *s* day do not work,
Heb   4:   4 "And on the *s* day God rested

SEVERE

2Co   2:   2 Out of the most *s* trial, their
1Th   1:   6 of the Lord; in spite of *s* suffering,

SEWED (SEWS)

Ge   3:   7 so they *s* fig leaves together

SEWS (SEWED)

Mt   9: 16 No one *s* a patch of unshrunk cloth

SEXUAL (SEXUALLY)

Ex   22: 19 "Anyone who has *s* relations
Lev   18:   6 relative to have *s* relations.
     18:   7 father by having *s* relations
     18: 20 Do not have *s* relations with
Mt   15: 19 murder, adultery, *s* immorality,
Ac   15: 20 by idols, from *s* immorality,
1Co   5:   1 reported that there is *s* immorality
     6: 13 body is not meant for *s* immorality,
     6: 18 Flee from *s* immorality.
     10:   8 should not commit *s* immorality,
2Co   12: 21 *s* sin and debauchery
Gal   5: 19 *s* immorality, impurity
Eph   5:   3 even a hint of *s* immorality,
Col   3:   5 *s* immorality, impurity, lust,
1Th   4:   3 that you should avoid *s* immorality

SEXUALLY (SEXUAL)

1Co   5:   9 to associate with *s* immoral people
     6:   9 Neither the *s* immoral nor idolaters
     6: 18 he who sins *s* sins against his own
Heb   12: 16 See that no one is *s* immoral,
     13:   4 the adulterer and all the *s* immoral.
Rev   21:   8 the murderers, the *s* immoral,

SHADE

Ps   121:   5 the Lord is your *s*
Isa   25:   4 and a *s* from the heat.

SHADOW

Ps   17:   8 hide me in the *s* of your wings
     23:   4 through the valley of the *s* of death,
     36:   7 find refuge in the *s* of your wings.
     91:   1 will rest in the *s* of the Almighty.
Isa   51: 16 covered you with the *s* of my hand
Col   2: 17 These are a *s* of the things that
Heb   8:   5 and *s* of what is in heaven.
     10:   1 The law is only a *s*

SHADRACH

Hebrew exiled to Babylon; name changed from Hananiah (Da 1:6-7). Refused defilement by food (Da 1:8-20). Refused to worship idol (Da 3:1-18); saved from furnace (Da 3:19-30).

SHAKE (SHAKEN SHAKING)

Ps   64:   8 all who see them will *s* their heads
     99:   1 let the earth *s*.
Hag   2:   6 I will once more *s* the heavens
Heb   12: 26 "Once more I will *s* not only

SHAKEN (SHAKE)

Ps   16:   8 I will not be *s*.
     30:   6 "I will never be *s*.''
     62:   2 he is my fortress, I will never be *s*.
     112:   6 Surely he will never be *s;*
Isa   54: 10 Though the mountains be *s*
Mt   24: 29 and the heavenly bodies will be *s*.'
Lk   6: 38 *s* together and running over,
Ac   2: 25 I will not be *s*.
Heb   12: 27 that what cannot be *s* may remain.

SHAKING* (SHAKE)
Ps 22: 7 they hurl insults, s their heads:
Mt 27:39 insults at him, s their heads
Mk 15:29 s their heads and saying, "So!

SHALLUM
King of Israel (2Ki 15:10-16).

SHAME (ASHAMED SHAMED SHAMEFUL)
Ps 25: 3 will ever be put to s,
   34: 5 their faces are never covered with s
   69: 6 not be put to s because of me,
Pr 13:18 discipline comes to poverty and s,
   18:13 that is his folly and his s.
Jer 8: 9 The wise will be put to s;
   8:12 No, they have no s at all;
Ro 9:33 trusts in him will never be put to s."
   10:11 trusts in him will never be put to s."
1Co 1:27 things of the world to s the wise;
Heb 12: 2 endured the cross, scorning its s,

SHAMED (SHAME)
Jer 10:14 every goldsmith is s by his idols.
Joel 2:26 never again will my people be s.

SHAMEFUL (SHAME)
2Co 4: 2 have renounced secret and s ways;
2Pe 2: 2 Many will follow their s ways
Rev 21:27 nor will anyone who does what is s

SHAMGAR
Judge; killed 600 Philistines (Jdg 3:31).

SHAPE (SHAPES SHAPING)
Job 38:14 The earth takes s like clay

SHAPES (SHAPE)
Isa 44:10 Who s a god and casts an idol,

SHAPING (SHAPE)
Jer 18: 4 the pot he was s from the clay was

SHARE (SHARED SHARERS SHARES SHARING)
Ge 21:10 that slave woman's son will never s
Lev 19:17 frankly so you will not s in his guilt.
Dt 10: 9 That is why the Levites have no s
1Sa 30:24 All will s alike.''
Eze 18:20 The son will not s the guilt
Mt 25:21 and s your master's happiness!'
Lk 3:11 "The man with two tunics should s
Ro 8:17 if indeed we s in his sufferings
   12:13 S with God's people who are
2Co 1: 7 as you s in our sufferings,
Gal 4:30 the slave woman's son will never s
   6: 6 in the word must s all good things
Eph 4:28 something to s with those in need.
Col 1:12 you to s in the inheritance
2Th 2:14 that you might s in the glory
1Ti 5:22 and do not s in the sins of others.
   6:18 and to be generous and willing to s.
2Ti 2: 6 the first to receive a s of the crops.
Heb 12:10 that we may s in his holiness.
   13:16 to do good and to s with others,
Rev 22:19 from him his s in the tree of life

SHARED (SHARE)
Ps 41: 9 he who s my bread,
Ac 4:32 but they s everything they had.
Heb 2:14 he too s in their humanity so that

SHARERS* (SHARE)
Eph 3: 6 and s together in the promise

SHARES (SHARE)
Pr 22: 9 for he s his food with the poor.
Jn 13:18 'He who s my bread has lifted up

SHARING
1Co 9:10 so in the hope of s in the harvest.
2Co 9:13 for your generosity in s with them
Php 3:10 the fellowship of s in his sufferings,
Phm : 6 you may be active in s your faith,

SHARON
SS 2: 1 I am a rose of S,

SHARP (SHARPENED SHARPENS SHARPER)
Pr 5: 4 s as a double-edged sword.
Isa 5:28 Their arrows are s,
Rev 1:16 came a s double-edged sword.
   19:15 Out of his mouth comes a s sword

SHARPENED (SHARP)
Eze 21: 9 s and polished—

SHARPENS* (SHARP)
Pr 27:17 As iron s iron,
   27:17 so one man s another.

SHARPER* (SHARP)
Heb 4:12 S than any double-edged sword,

SHATTER (SHATTERED SHATTERS)
Jer 51:20 with you I s nations,

SHATTERED (SHATTER)
1Sa 2:10 who oppose the LORD will be s.
Job 16:12 All was well with me, but he s me;
   17:11 days have passed, my plans are s,
Ecc 12: 6 before the pitcher is s at the spring,

SHATTERS (SHATTER)
Ps 46: 9 he breaks the bow and s the spear,

SHAVED
Jdg 16:17 my head were s, my strength would
1Co 11: 5 it is just as though her head were s.

SHEAF (SHEAVES)
Lev 23:11 is to wave the s before the LORD

SHEARER* (SHEARERS)
Ac 8:32 and as a lamb before the s is silent,

SHEARERS (SHEARER)
Isa 53: 7 and as a sheep before her s is silent,

SHEAVES (SHEAF)
Ge 37: 7 while your s gathered around mine
Ps 126: 6 carrying s with him.

SHEBA
1. Benjamite who rebelled against David (2Sa 20).
2. See QUEEN.

SHECHEM
1. Raped Jacob's daughter Dinah; killed by Simeon and Levi (Ge 34).
2. City where Joshua renewed the covenant (Jos 24).

SHED (SHEDDING SHEDS)
Ge 9: 6 by man shall his blood be s;
Pr 6:17 hands that s innocent blood,
Ro 3:15 "Their feet are swift to s blood;
Col 1:20 through his blood, s on the cross.

SHEDDING (SHED)
Heb 9:22 without the s of blood there is no

SHEDS (SHED)
Ge 9: 6 "Whoever s the blood of man,

SHEEP (SHEEP'S SHEEPSKINS)
Nu 27:17 LORD's people will not be like s
Dt 17: 1 a s that has any defect or flaw in it,
1Sa 15:14 "What then is this bleating of s
Ps 44:22 we are considered as s
   78:52 led them like s through the desert.
   100: 3 we are his people, the s
   119:176 I have strayed like a lost s.
SS 4: 2 teeth are like a flock of s just shorn,
Isa 53: 6 We all, like s, have gone astray,
   53: 7 as a s before her shearers is silent,
Jer 50: 6 "My people have been lost s;
Eze 34:11 I myself will search for my s
Zec 13: 7 and the s will be scattered,
Mt 9:36 helpless, like s without a shepherd.
   10:16 I am sending you out like s
   12:11 "If any of you has a s and it falls
   18:13 he is happier about that one s
   25:32 as a shepherd separates the s
Jn 10: 1 man who does not enter the s pen

SHEEP'S* (SHEEP)
Mt 7:15 They come to you in s clothing,

SHEEPSKINS* (SHEEP)
Heb 11:37 They went about in s and goatskins

SHEKEL
Ex 30:13 This half s is an offering

SHELTER
Ps 27: 5 me in the s of his tabernacle
   31:20 In the s of your presence you hide
   55: 8 I would hurry to my place of s,
   61: 4 take refuge in the s of your wings.
   91: 1 in the s of the Most High
Ecc 7:12 Wisdom is a s
Isa 4: 6 It will be a s and shade
   25: 4 a s from the storm
   32: 2 Each man will be like a s
   58: 7 the poor wanderer with s—

SHEM
Son of Noah (Ge 5:32; 6:10). Blessed (Ge 9:26). Descendants (Ge 10:21-31; 11:10-32).

SHEPHERD (SHEPHERDS)
Ge 48:15 the God who has been my s
   49:24 because of the S, the Rock of Israel
Nu 27:17 will not be like sheep without a s.''
2Sa 7: 7 commanded to s my people Israel,
1Ki 22:17 on the hills like sheep without a s,
Ps 23: 1 LORD is my s, I shall not be in want.
   28: 9 be their s and carry them forever.
   80: 1 Hear us, O S of Israel,
Isa 40:11 He tends his flock like a s:
Jer 31:10 will watch over his flock like a s.'
Eze 34: 5 scattered because there was no s,
   34:12 As a s looks after his scattered
Zec 11: 9 and said, "I will not be your s.
   11:17 "Woe to the worthless s,
   13: 7 "Strike the s,
Mt 2: 6 who will be the s of my people
   9:36 and helpless, like sheep without a s.
   26:31 " 'I will strike the s,
Jn 10:11 The good s lays down his life
   10:14 "I am the good s; I know my sheep
   10:16 there shall be one flock and one s.
Heb 13:20 that great S of the sheep, equip you
1Pe 5: 4 And when the Chief S appears,
Rev 7:17 of the throne will be their s;

SHEPHERDS (SHEPHERD)
Jer 23: 1 "Woe to the s who are destroying
   50: 6 their s have led them astray
Eze 34: 2 prophesy against the s of Israel;
Lk 2: 8 there were s living out in the fields
Ac 20:28 Be s of the church of God,
1Pe 5: 2 Be s of God's flock that is
Jude : 12 s who feed only themselves.

SHIBBOLETH*
Jdg 12: 6 No," they said, "All right, say 'S.'

SHIELD (SHIELDED SHIELDS)
Ge 15: 1 I am your s,
2Sa 22: 3 my s and the horn of my salvation.
   22:36 You give me your s of victory;
Ps 3: 3 But you are a s around me,
   5:12 with your favor as with a s.
   7:10 My s is God Most High,
   18: 2 He is my s and the horn
   28: 7 LORD is my strength and my s;
   33:20 he is our help and our s.
   84:11 For the LORD God is a sun and s;
   91: 4 his faithfulness will be your s
   115: 9 he is their help and s.
   119:114 You are my refuge and my s;
   144: 2 my s, in whom I take refuge,
Pr 2: 7 he is a s to those whose walk is
   30: 5 he is a s to those who take refuge
Eph 6:16 to all this, take up the s of faith,

SHEEP (SHEEP'S SHEEPSKINS)
Jn 10: 3 He calls his own s by name
   10: 7 the truth, I am the gate for the s.
   10:15 and I lay down my life for the s.
   10:27 My s listen to my voice; I know
   21:17 Jesus said, "Feed my s.
1Pe 2:25 For you were like s going astray,

SHIELDED (SHIELD)

1Pe 1: 5 through faith are *s* by God's power

SHIELDS (SHIELD)

Dt 33:12 for he *s* him all day long,

SHIFTLESS*

Pr 19:15 and the *s* man goes hungry.

SHIMEI

Cursed David (2Sa 16:5-14); spared (2Sa 19:16-23). Killed by Solomon (1Ki 2:8-9, 36-46).

SHINE (SHINES SHINING SHONE)

Nu   6:25 the LORD make his face *s*
Job 33:30 that the light of life may *s* on him.
Ps   4: 6 Let the light of your face *s* upon us,
     37: 6 make your righteousness *s* like
     67: 1 and make his face *s* upon us; *Selah*
     80: 1 between the cherubim, *s* forth
   118:27 and he has made his light *s* upon us.
Isa 60: 1 ''Arise, *s*, for your light has come,
Da 12: 3 are wise will *s* like the brightness
Mt 5:16 let your light *s* before men,
   13:43 the righteous will *s* like the sun
2Co 4: 6 made his light *s* in our hearts
Eph 5:14 and Christ will *s* on you.''
Php 2:15 in which you *s* like stars

SHINES (SHINE)

Ps 50: 2 God *s* forth.
Pr 13: 9 The light of the righteous *s* brightly
Jn   1: 5 The light *s* in the darkness,

SHINING (SHINE)

Pr 4:18 *s* ever brighter till the full light
2Pe 1:19 as to a light *s* in a dark place,
Rev 1:16 His face was like the sun *s*

SHIPS

Pr 31:14 She is like the merchant *s*,

SHIPWRECKED*

2Co 11:25 I was stoned, three times I was *s*,
1Ti 1:19 and so have *s* their faith.

SHISHAK

1Ki 14:25 *S* king of Egypt attacked Jerusalem
2Ch 12: 2 *S* king of Egypt attacked Jerusalem

SHOCKING*

Jer 5:30 ''A horrible and *s* thing

SHONE (SHINE)

Mt 17: 2 His face *s* like the sun,
Lk   2: 9 glory of the Lord *s* around them,
Rev 21:11 It *s* with the glory of God,

SHOOT

Isa 53: 2 up before him like a tender *s*,
Ro 11:17 and you, though a wild olive *s*,

SHORE

Lk   5: 3 asked him to put out a little from *s*.

SHORT (SHORTENED)

Nu 11:23 ''Is the LORD's arm too *s*?
Isa 50: 2 Was my arm too *s* to ransom you?
     59: 1 of the LORD is not too *s* to save,
Mt 24:22 If those days had not been cut *s*,
Ro   3:23 and fall *s* of the glory of God,
1Co 7:29 brothers, is that the time is *s*.
Heb 4: 1 of you be found to have fallen *s* of it
Rev 20: 3 he must be set free for a *s* time.

SHORTENED (SHORT)

Mt 24:22 of the elect those days will be *s*.

SHOULDER (SHOULDERS)

Zep 3: 9 and serve him *s* to *s*.

SHOULDERS (SHOULDER)

Dt 33:12 LORD loves rests between his *s*.''
Isa 9: 6 and the government will be on his *s*
Lk 15: 5 he joyfully puts it on his *s*

SHOUT (SHOUTED)

Ps 47: 1 *s* to God with cries of joy.
     66: 1 *S* with joy to God, all the earth!

Ps 95: 1 let us *s* aloud to the Rock
     98: 4 *S* for joy to the LORD, all the earth
   100: 1 *S* for joy to the LORD, all the earth
Isa 12: 6 *S* aloud and sing for joy, people
     26:19 wake up and *s* for joy.
     35: 6 the mute tongue *s* for joy.
     40: 9 lift up your voice with a *s*,
     42: 2 He will not *s* or cry out,
     44:23 *s* aloud, O earth beneath.
     54: 1 burst into song, *s* for joy,
Zec 9: 9 *S*, Daughter of Jerusalem!

SHOUTED (SHOUT)

Job 38: 7 and all the angels *s* for joy?

SHOW (SHOWED)

Ex 18:20 and *s* them the way to live
     33:18 Moses said, ''Now *s* me your glory
2Sa 22:26 the faithful you *s* yourself faithful,
1Ki 2: 2 ''So be strong, *s* yourself a man,
Ps 17: 7 *S* the wonder of your great love,
     25: 4 *S* me your ways, O LORD,
     39: 4 ''*S* me, O LORD, my life's end
     85: 7 *S* us your unfailing love, O LORD,
   143: 8 *S* me the way I should go,
Pr 23: 4 have the wisdom to *s* restraint.
SS 2:14 *s* me your face,
Isa 5:16 the holy God will *s* himself holy
     30:18 he rises to *s* you compassion.
Eze 28:25 I will *s* myself holy among them
Joel 2:30 I will *s* wonders in the heavens
Zec 7: 9 *s* mercy and compassion
Ac   2:19 I will *s* wonders in the heaven
     10:34 it is that God does not *s* favoritism
1Co 12:31 now I will *s* you the most excellent
Eph 2: 7 ages he might *s* the incomparable
Tit   2: 7 In your teaching integrity,
Jas 2:18 I will *s* you my faith by what I do.
Jude   :23 to others *s* mercy, mixed with fear

SHOWED (SHOW)

1Ki 3: 3 Solomon *s* his love for the LORD
Lk 24:40 he *s* them his hands and feet.
1Jn 4: 9 This is how God *s* his love

SHOWERS

Eze 34:26 in season; there will be *s* of blessing
Hos 10:12 and *s* righteousness on you.

SHREWD

2Sa 22:27 to the crooked you show yourself *s*.
Mt 10:16 Therefore be as *s* as snakes and

SHRINK (SHRINKS)

Heb 10:39 But we are not of those who *s* back

SHRINKS* (SHRINK)

Heb 10:38 And if he *s* back,

SHRIVEL

Isa 64: 6 we all *s* up like a leaf,

SHUDDER

Eze 32:10 and their kings will *s* with horror

SHUHITE

Job 2:11 Bildad the *S* and Zophar

SHUN* (SHUNS)

Job 28:28 and to *s* evil is understanding.' ''
Pr   3: 7 fear the LORD and *s* evil.

SHUNS (SHUN)

Job 1: 8 a man who fears God and *s* evil.''
Pr 14:16 man fears the LORD and *s* evil,

SHUT

Ge   7:16 Then the LORD *s* him in.
Isa 22:22 what he opens no one can *s*,
     60:11 they will never be *s*, day or night,
Da   6:22 and he *s* the mouths of the lions.
Heb 11:33 who *s* the mouths of lions,
Rev 3: 7 no one can *s*, and what he shuts
     21:25 On no day will its gates ever be *s*,

SICK (SICKNESS)

Pr 13:12 Hope deferred makes the heart *s*,
Eze 34: 4 or healed the *s* or bound up
Mt   9:12 who need a doctor, but the *s*.

Mt 10: 8 Heal the *s*, raise the dead, cleanse
     25:36 I was *s* and you looked after me,
1Co 11:30 many among you are weak and *s*,
Jas 5:14 of you *s*? He should call the elders

SICKBED* (BED)

Ps 41: 3 LORD will sustain him on his *s*

SICKLE

Joel 3:13 Swing the *s*,
Rev 14:14 gold on his head and a sharp *s*

SICKNESS (SICK)

Mt   4:23 and healing every disease and *s*

SIDE (SIDES)

Ps 91: 7 A thousand may fall at your *s*,
   124: 1 If the LORD had not been on our *s*
Jn 18:37 Everyone on the *s* of truth listens
     20:20 he showed them his hands and *s*.
2Ti 4:17 But the Lord stood at my *s*
Heb 10:33 at other times you stood *s* by *s*

SIDES (SIDE)

Nu 33:55 in your eyes and thorns in your *s*.

SIFT

Lk 22:31 Satan has asked to *s* you as wheat.

SIGHING

Isa 35:10 and sorrow and *s* will flee away.

SIGHT

Ps   5: 4 and done what is evil in your *s*,
     90: 4 For a thousand years in your *s*
   116:15 Precious in the *s* of the LORD
Pr   3: 4 in the *s* of God and man.
Mt 11: 5 The blind receive *s*, the lame walk,
Ac   4:19 right in God's *s* to obey you rather
1Co 3:19 this world is foolishness in God's *s*.
2Co 5: 7 We live by faith, not by *s*.
1Pe 3: 4 which is of great worth in God's *s*.

SIGN (SIGNS)

Ge   9:12 ''This is the *s* of the covenant I am
     17:11 and it will be the *s* of the covenant
Isa 7:14 the Lord himself will give you a *s*:
     55:13 for an everlasting *s*,
Eze 20:12 I gave them my Sabbaths as a *s*
Mt 12:38 to see a miraculous *s* from you.''
     24: 3 what will be the *s* of your coming
     24:30 ''At that time the *s* of the Son
Lk   2:12 This will be a *s* to you: You will
     11:29 It asks for a miraculous *s*,
Ro   4:11 he received the *s* of circumcision,
1Co 11:10 to have a *s* of authority on her head
     14:22 are a *s*, not for believers

SIGNS (SIGN)

Ge   1:14 let them serve as *s* to mark seasons
Ps 78:43 day he displayed his miraculous *s*
   105:27 They performed his miraculous *s*
Da   6:27 he performs *s* and wonders
Mt 24:24 and perform great *s* and miracles
Mk 16:17 these *s* will accompany those who
Jn   3: 2 perform the miraculous *s* you are
     20:30 Jesus did many other miraculous *s*
Ac   2:19 and *s* on the earth below,
1Co 1:22 Jews demand miraculous *s*
2Co 12:12 *s*, wonders and miracles—
2Th 2: 9 *s* and wonders, and in every sort

SIHON

Nu 21:21 to say to *S* king of the Amorites:
Ps 136:19 *S* king of the Amorites

SILAS*

Prophet (Ac 15:22-32); co-worker with Paul on second missionary journey (Ac 16-18; 2Co 1:19). Co-writer with Paul (1Th 1:1; 2Th 1:1); Peter (1Pe 5:12).

SILENCE (SILENCED SILENT)

1Pe 2:15 good you should *s* the ignorant talk
Rev 8: 1 there was *s* in heaven

SILENCED (SILENCE)

Ro   3:19 so that every mouth may be *s*
Tit 1:11 They must be *s*, because they are

SILENT (SILENCE)

Est   4: 14 For if you remain *s* at this time,
Ps   30: 12 to you and not be *s*.
     32: 3 When I kept *s*,
     39: 2 But when I was *s* and still,
Pr   17: 28 a fool is thought wise if he keeps *s*,
Ecc   3: 7 a time to be *s* and a time to speak,
Isa   53: 7 as a sheep before her shearers is *s*,
     62: 1 For Zion's sake I will not keep *s*,
Hab   2: 20 let all the earth be *s* before him.''
Ac   8: 32 and as a lamb before the shearer is *s*
1Co 14: 34 women should remain *s*
1Ti   2: 12 over a man; she must be *s*.

SILVER

Ps   12: 6 like *s* refined in a furnace of clay,
     66: 10 you refined us like *s*.
Pr   2: 4 and if you look for it as for *s*
     3: 14 for she is more profitable than *s*
     8: 10 Choose my instruction instead of *s*,
     22: 1 to be esteemed is better than *s*,
     25: 4 Remove the dross from the *s*,
     25: 11 is like apples of gold in settings of *s*.
Isa   48: 10 I have refined you, though not as *s;*
Eze 22: 18 They are but the dross of *s*.
Da   2: 32 its chest and arms of *s*, its belly
Hag   2: 8 'The *s* is mine and the gold is mine,'
Zec 13: 9 I will refine them like *s*
Ac   3: 6 Peter said, ''*S* or gold I do not have,
1Co   3: 12 *s*, costly stones, wood, hay or straw
1Pe   1: 18 not with perishable things such as *s*

SILVERSMITH

Ac   19: 24 A *s* named Demetrius, who made

SIMEON

     Son of Jacob by Leah (Ge 29:33; 35:23; 1Ch 2:
1). With Levi killed Shechem for rape of Dinah
(Ge 34:25-29). Held hostage by Joseph in Egypt
(Ge 42:24-43:23). Tribe of blessed (Ge 49:5-7),
numbered (Nu 1:23; 26:14), allotted land (Jos 19:
1-9; Eze 48:24), 12,000 from (Rev 7:7).

SIMON

1. See PETER.
2. Apostle, called the Zealot (Mt 10:4; Mk 3:
18; Lk 6:15; Ac 1:13).
3. Samaritan sorcerer (Ac 8:9-24).

SIMPLE

Ps   19: 7 making wise the *s*.
     119:130 it gives understanding to the *s*.
Pr   8: 5 You who are *s*, gain prudence;
     14: 15 A *s* man believes anything,

SIMPLEHEARTED* (HEART)

Ps 116: 6 The LORD protects the *s;*

SIN (SINFUL SINNED SINNER SINNERS SINNING SINS)

Ge   4: 7 *s* is crouching at your door;
Ex   32: 32 please forgive their *s*— but if not,
Nu   5: 7 and must confess the *s* he has
     32: 23 be sure that your *s* will find you
Dt   24: 16 each is to die for his own *s*.
1Sa 12: 23 it from me that I should *s*
     15: 23 For rebellion is like the *s*
1Ki   8: 46 for there is no one who does not *s*
2Ch   7: 14 and will forgive their *s* and will heal
Job   1: 22 Job did not *s* by charging God
Ps   4: 4 In your anger do not *s;*
     17: 3 resolved that my mouth will not *s*.
     32: 2 whose *s* the LORD does not count
     32: 5 Then I acknowledged my *s* to you
     36: 2 too much to detect or hate his *s*.
     38: 18 I am troubled by my *s*.
     39: 1 and keep my tongue from *s;*
     51: 2 and cleanse me from my *s*.
     66: 18 If I had cherished *s* in my heart,
     119: 11 that I might not *s* against you.
     119:133 let no *s* rule over me.
Pr   5: 22 the cords of his *s* hold him fast.
     10: 19 words are many, *s* is not absent,
     14: 9 Fools mock at making amends for *s*
     16: 6 faithfulness *s* is atoned for;
     17: 19 He who loves a quarrel loves *s;*
     20: 9 I am clean and without *s*''?
Isa   3: 9 they parade their *s* like Sodom;

Isa   6: 7 is taken away and your *s* atoned
     64: 5 But when we continued to *s*
Jer   31: 30 everyone will die for his own *s;*
Eze   3: 18 that wicked man will die for his *s*,
     18: 26 his righteousness and commits *s*,
     33: 8 that wicked man will die for his *s*,
Am   4: 4 ''Go to Bethel and *s;*
Mic   6: 7 of my body for the *s* of my soul?
     7: 18 who pardons *s* and forgives
Zec   3: 4 ''See, I have taken away your *s*,
Mt   18: 6 little ones who believe in me to *s*,
Mk   3: 29 he is guilty of an eternal *s*.''
     9: 43 If your hand causes you to *s*,
Lk   17: 1 people to *s* are bound to come,
Jn   1: 29 who takes away the *s* of the world!
     8: 7 ''If any one of you is without *s*,
     8: 34 everyone who sins is a slave to *s*.
     8: 46 Can any of you prove me guilty of *s*
Ro   2: 12 All who *s* apart from the law will
     5: 12 as *s* entered the world
     5: 20 where *s* increased, grace increased
     6: 2 By no means! We died to *s;*
     6: 11 count yourselves dead to *s*
     6: 14 For *s* shall not be your master,
     6: 23 For the wages of *s* is death,
     7: 7 I would not have known what *s* was
     7: 25 sinful nature a slave to the law of *s*.
     14: 23 that does not come from faith is *s*.
1Co   8: 12 When you *s* against your brothers
     15: 56 The sting of death is *s*,
2Co   5: 21 God made him who had no *s* to be *s*
Gal   6: 1 if someone is caught in a *s*,
1Ti   5: 20 Those who *s* are to be rebuked
Heb   4: 15 just as we are—yet was without *s*.
     9: 26 to do away with *s* by the sacrifice
     11: 25 the pleasures of *s* for a short time.
     12: 1 and the *s* that so easily entangles,
Jas   1: 15 it gives birth to *s;* and *s*,
1Pe   2: 22 ''He committed no *s*,
1Jn   1: 7 his Son, purifies us from all *s*.
     1: 8 If we claim to be without *s*,
     2: 1 But if anybody does *s*, we have one
     3: 4 in fact, *s* is lawlessness.
     3: 5 And in him is no *s*.
     3: 6 No one who continues to *s* has
     3: 9 born of God will continue to *s*,
     5: 16 There is a *s* that leads to death.
     5: 17 All wrongdoing is *s*, and there is *s*
     5: 18 born of God does not continue to *s;*

SINAI

Ex   19: 20 descended to the top of Mount *S*
     31: 18 speaking to Moses on Mount *S*,
Ps   68: 17 from *S* into his sanctuary.

SINCERE* (SINCERITY)

Da   11: 34 many who are not *s* will join them.
Ac   2: 46 ate together with glad and *s* hearts,
Ro   12: 9 Love must be *s*.
2Co   6: 6 in the Holy Spirit and in *s* love;
     11: 3 somehow be led astray from your *s*
1Ti   1: 5 a good conscience and a *s* faith.
     3: 8 *s*, not indulging in much wine,
2Ti   1: 5 have been reminded of your *s* faith,
Heb 10: 22 near to God with a *s* heart
Jas   3: 17 and good fruit, impartial and *s*.
1Pe   1: 22 the truth so that you have *s* love

SINCERITY* (SINCERE)

1Co   5: 8 bread without yeast, the bread of *s*
2Co   1: 12 in the holiness and *s* that are
     2: 17 speak before God with *s*,
     8: 8 but I want to test the *s* of your love
Eph   6: 5 and with *s* of heart, just
Col   3: 22 but with *s* of heart and reverence

SINFUL (SIN)

Ps   51: 5 Surely I was *s* at birth,
     51: 5 *s* from the time my mother
Lk   5: 8 from me, Lord; I am a *s* man!''
Ro   7: 5 we were controlled by the *s* nature,
     7: 18 lives in me, that is, in my *s* nature.
     7: 25 but in the *s* nature a slave to the law
     8: 3 Son in the likeness of *s* man
     8: 4 not live according to the *s* nature
     8: 7 the *s* mind is hostile to God.
     8: 8 by the *s* nature cannot please God.
     8: 9 are controlled not by the *s* nature

Ro   8: 13 if you live according to the *s* nature
     13: 14 to gratify the desires of the *s* nature
1Co   5: 5 so that the *s* nature may be
Gal   5: 13 freedom to indulge the *s* nature;
     5: 16 gratify the desires of the *s* nature.
     5: 19 The acts of the *s* nature are obvious
     5: 24 Jesus have crucified the *s* nature
     6: 8 sows to please his *s* nature,
Col   2: 11 in the putting off of the *s* nature,
Heb   3: 12 brothers, that none of you has a *s*,
1Pe   2: 11 abstain from *s* desires, which war
1Jn   3: 8 He who does what is *s* is

SING (SANG SINGER SINGING SINGS SONG SONGS SUNG)

Ex   15: 1 ''I will *s* to the LORD,
Ps   5: 11 let them ever *s* for joy.
     13: 6 I will *s* to the LORD,
     30: 4 *S* to the LORD, you saints of his;
     33: 1 *S* joyfully to the LORD, you
     47: 6 *S* praises to God, *s* praises;
     57: 7 I will *s* and make music.
     59: 16 But I will *s* of your strength,
     63: 7 I *s* in the shadow of your wings.
     66: 2 *S* to the glory of his name;
     89: 1 I will *s* of the LORD's great love
     95: 1 Come, let us *s* for joy to the LORD
     96: 1 *S* to the LORD a new song;
     98: 1 *S* to the LORD a new song,
     101: 1 I will *s* of your love and justice;
     108: 1 I will *s* and make music
     137: 3 ''*S* us one of the songs of Zion!''
     147: 1 is to *s* praises to our God,
     149: 1 *S* to the LORD a new song,
Isa   54: 1 ''*S*, O barren woman,
1Co 14: 15 also pray with my mind; I will *s*
Eph   5: 19 *S* and make music in your heart
Col   3: 16 and as you *s* psalms, hymns
Jas   5: 13 Is anyone happy? Let him *s* songs

SINGER* (SING)

2Sa 23: 1 Israel's *s* of songs:

SINGING (SING)

Ps   63: 5 with *s* lips my mouth will praise
     68: 6 he leads forth the prisoners with *s;*
     98: 5 with the harp and the sound of *s*,
Isa   35: 10 They will enter Zion with *s*,
Zep   3: 17 he will rejoice over you with *s*.''
Ac   16: 25 Silas were praying and *s* hymns
Rev   5: 13 on the sea, and all that is in them, *s:*

SINGLE

Ex   23: 29 I will not drive them out in a *s* year,
Mt   6: 27 you by worrying can add a *s* hour
Gal   5: 14 law is summed up in a *s* command:

SINGS (SING)

Eze 33: 32 more than one who *s* love songs

SINNED (SIN)

Lev   5: 5 confess in what way he has *s*
1Sa 15: 24 Then Saul said to Samuel, ''I have *s*
2Sa 12: 13 ''I have *s* against the LORD.''
     24: 10 I have *s* greatly in what I have done
2Ch   6: 37 'We have *s*, we have done wrong
Job   1: 5 ''Perhaps my children have *s*
     33: 27 'I *s*, and perverted what was right,
Ps   51: 4 Against you, you only, have I *s*
Jer   2: 35 because you say, 'I have not *s*.'
     14: 20 we have indeed *s* against you.
Da   9: 5 we have *s* and done wrong.
Mic   7: 9 Because I have *s* against him,
Mt   27: 4 ''I have *s*,'' he said,
Lk   15: 18 I have *s* against heaven
Ro   3: 23 for all have *s* and fall short
     5: 12 all *s*— for before the law was given,
2Pe   2: 4 did not spare angels when they *s*,
1Jn   1: 10 claim we have not *s*, we make him

SINNER (SIN)

Ecc   9: 18 but one *s* destroys much good.
Lk   15: 7 in heaven over one *s* who repents
     18: 13 'God, have mercy on me, a *s*.'
1Co 14: 24 convinced by all that he is a *s*
Jas   5: 20 Whoever turns a *s* from the error
1Pe   4: 18 become of the ungodly and the *s?*''

SINNERS (SIN)

Ps   1: 1 or stand in the way of *s*
    37: 38 But all *s* will be destroyed;
Pr   1: 10 My son, if *s* entice you,
   23: 17 Do not let your heart envy *s*,
Mt   9: 13 come to call the righteous, but *s*.''
Ro   5: 8 While we were still *s*, Christ died
Gal   2: 17 evident that we ourselves are *s*,
1Ti   1: 15 came into the world to save *s*—
Heb   7: 26 set apart from *s*, exalted

SINNING (SIN)

Ex 20: 20 be with you to keep you from *s*.''
1Co 15: 34 stop *s*; for there are some who are
Heb 10: 26 If we deliberately keep on *s*
1Jn   3: 6 No one who lives in him keeps on *s*
    3: 9 go on *s*, because he has been born

SINS (SIN)

Lev 5: 1 ''If a person *s* because he does not
  16: 30 you will be clean from all your *s*.
  26: 40 ''But if they will confess their *s*
Nu 15: 30 ''But anyone who *s* defiantly,
1Sa 2: 25 If a man *s* against another man,
2Ki 14: 6 each is to die for his own *s*.''
Ezr 9: 6 our *s* are higher than our heads
    9: 13 less than our *s* have deserved
Ps 19: 13 your servant also from willful *s;*
   32: 1 whose *s* are covered.
   51: 9 Hide your face from my *s*
   79: 9 deliver us and forgive our *s*
   85: 2 and covered all their *s*.
  103: 3 who forgives all your *s*
  103: 10 does not treat us as our *s* deserve
  130: 3 O LORD, kept a record of *s*,
Pr 14: 21 He who despises his neighbor *s*,
  28: 13 who conceals his *s* does not
  29: 22 one commits many *s*.
Ecc 7: 20 who does what is right and never *s*.
Isa 1: 18 ''Though your *s* are like scarlet,
  38: 17 you have put all my *s*
  43: 25 and remembers your *s* no more.
  59: 2 your *s* have hidden his face
  64: 6 like the wind our *s* sweep us away.
Jer 31: 34 and will remember their *s* no more
La   3: 39 complain when punished for his *s?*
Eze 18: 4 soul who *s* is the one who will die.
  33: 10 Our offenses and *s* weigh us down,
  36: 33 day I cleanse you from all your *s*,
Hos 14: 1 Your *s* have been your downfall!
Mt   1: 21 he will save his people from their *s*
   6: 15 if you do not forgive men their *s*,
   9: 6 authority on earth to forgive *s* . . . . . ''
  18: 15 ''If your brother *s* against you,
  26: 28 for many for the forgiveness of *s*.
Lk   5: 24 authority on earth to forgive *s* . . . . .
  11: 4 Forgive us our *s*,
  17: 3 ''If your brother *s*, rebuke him,
Jn   8: 24 you will indeed die in your *s*.''
  20: 23 If you forgive anyone his *s*,
Ac   2: 38 for the forgiveness of your *s*.
   3: 19 so that your *s* may be wiped out,
  10: 43 forgiveness of *s* through his name.''
  22: 16 be baptized and wash your *s* away,
  26: 18 they may receive forgiveness of *s*
Ro   4: 25 whose *s* are covered.
   4: 25 delivered over to death for our *s*
1Co 15: 3 died for our *s* according
2Co 5: 19 not counting men's *s* against them.
Gal 1: 4 himself for our *s* to rescue us
Eph 2: 1 dead in your transgressions and *s*,
Col 2: 13 us all our *s*, having canceled
1Ti 5: 22 and do not share in the *s* of others.
Heb 1: 3 he had provided purification for *s*,
   2: 17 atonement for the *s* of the people.
   7: 27 He sacrificed for their *s* once for all
   8: 12 and will remember their *s* no more
   9: 28 to take away the *s* of many people;
  10: 4 of bulls and goats to take away *s*.
  10: 12 for all time one sacrifice for *s*,
  10: 26 of the truth, no sacrifice for *s* is left,
Jas 4: 17 ought to do and doesn't do it, *s*.
   5: 16 Therefore confess your *s*
   5: 20 and cover over a multitude of *s*.
1Pe 2: 24 He himself bore our *s* in his body
   3: 18 For Christ died for *s* once for all,
   4: 8 love covers over a multitude of *s*.

1Jn 1: 9 If we confess our *s*, he is faithful
    2: 2 He is the atoning sacrifice for our *s*,
    3: 5 so that he might take away our *s*
    4: 10 as an atoning sacrifice for our *s*.
Rev 1: 5 has freed us from our *s* by his blood

SISERA

Jdg 4: 2 The commander of his army was *S*,
   5: 26 She struck *S*, she crushed his head,

SISTER (SISTERS)

Lev 18: 9 have sexual relations with your *s*,
Mk 3: 35 does God's will is my brother and *s*

SISTERS (SISTER)

Mt 19: 29 or brothers or *s* or father or mother
1Ti 5: 2 as *s*, with absolute purity.

SIT (SAT SITS SITTING)

Dt   6: 7 them when you *s* at home
1Ki 8: 25 fail to have a man to *s* before me
Ps   1: 1 or *s* in the seat of mockers.
   26: 5 and refuse to *s* with the wicked.
   80: 1 you who *s* enthroned
  110: 1 ''*S* at my right hand
  139: 2 You know when I *s* and when I rise
SS   2: 3 I delight to *s* in his shade,
Isa 16: 5 in faithfulness a man will *s* on it—
Mic 4: 4 Every man will *s* under his own
Mt 20: 23 to *s* at my right or left is not for me
  22: 44 ''*S* at my right hand
Lk 22: 30 in my kingdom and *s* on thrones,
Heb 1: 13 ''*S* at my right hand
Rev 3: 21 right to *s* with me on my throne,

SITS (SIT)

Ps 99: 1 *s* enthroned between the cherubim,
Isa 40: 22 He *s* enthroned above the circle
Mt 19: 28 of Man *s* on his glorious throne,
Rev 4: 9 thanks to him who *s* on the throne

SITTING (SIT)

Est 2: 19 Mordecai was *s* at the king's gate.
Mt 26: 64 the Son of Man *s* at the right hand
Rev 4: 2 in heaven with someone *s* on it.

SITUATION (SITUATIONS)

1Co 7: 24 remain in the *s* God called him
Php 4: 12 of being content in any and every *s*,

SITUATIONS* (SITUATION)

2Ti 4: 5 head in all *s*, endure hardship,

SKIES (SKY)

Ps 19: 1 the *s* proclaim the work
   71: 19 Your righteousness reaches to the *s*
  108: 4 your faithfulness reaches to the *s*.

SKILL (SKILLED SKILLFUL)

Ps 137: 5 may my right hand forget its *s*.
Ecc 10: 10 but *s* will bring success.

SKILLED (SKILL)

Pr 22: 29 Do you see a man *s* in his work?

SKILLFUL (SKILL)

Ps 45: 1 my tongue is the pen of a *s* writer.
  78: 72 with *s* hands he led them.

SKIN (SKINS)

Job 19: 20 with only the *s* of my teeth.
  19: 26 And after my *s* has been destroyed,
Jer 13: 23 Can the Ethiopian change his *s*

SKINS (SKIN)

Ex 25: 5 ram *s* dyed red and hides
Lk   5: 37 the new wine will burst the *s*,

SKULL

Mt 27: 33 (which means The Place of the *S*).

SKY (SKIES)

Ge 1: 8 God called the expanse ''*s*.''
Pr 30: 19 the way of an eagle in the *s*,
Isa 34: 4 and the *s* rolled up like a scroll;
Jer 33: 22 stars of the *s* and as measureless
Mt 24: 29 the stars will fall from the *s*,
  24: 30 coming on the clouds of the *s*,
Rev 20: 11 Earth and *s* fled from his presence,

SLACK*

Pr 18: 9 One who is *s* in his work

SLAIN (SLAY)

1Sa 18: 7 ''Saul has *s* his thousands,
Eze 37: 9 into these *s*, that they may live.' ''
Rev 5: 6 as if it had been *s*, standing
   5: 12 ''Worthy is the Lamb, who was *s*,
   6: 9 the souls of those who had been *s*

SLANDER (SLANDERED SLANDERER SLANDERERS SLANDEROUS)

Lev 19: 16 '' 'Do not go about spreading *s*
Ps 15: 3 and has no *s* on his tongue,
Pr 10: 18 and whoever spreads *s* is a fool.
2Co 12: 20 outbursts of anger, factions, *s*,
Eph 4: 31 rage and anger, brawling and *s*,
1Ti 5: 14 the enemy no opportunity for *s*.
Tit 3: 2 to *s* no one, to be peaceable
1Pe 3: 16 in Christ may be ashamed of their *s*
2Pe 2: 10 afraid to *s* celestial beings;

SLANDERED (SLANDER)

1Co 4: 13 when we are *s*, we answer kindly.

SLANDERER (SLANDER)

1Co 5: 11 an idolater or a *s*, a drunkard

SLANDERERS (SLANDER)

Ro 1: 30 They are gossips, *s*, God-haters,
1Co 6: 10 nor the greedy nor drunkards nor *s*
Tit 2: 3 not to be *s* or addicted

SLANDEROUS (SLANDER)

2Ti 3: 3 unforgiving, *s*, without self-control
2Pe 2: 11 do not bring *s* accusations

SLAUGHTER (SLAUGHTERED)

Isa 53: 7 he was led like a lamb to the *s*,
Jer 11: 19 been like a gentle lamb led to the *s;*
Ac   8: 32 ''He was led like a sheep to the *s*,

SLAUGHTERED (SLAUGHTER)

Ps 44: 22 we are considered as sheep to be *s*.
Ro 8: 36 we are considered as sheep to be *s*

SLAVE (ENSLAVED SLAVERY SLAVES)

Ge 21: 10 ''Get rid of that *s* woman
Mt 20: 27 wants to be first must be your *s*—
Jn   8: 34 everyone who sins is a *s* to sin.
Ro   7: 14 I am unspiritual, sold as a *s* to sin.
1Co 7: 21 Were you a *s* when you were called
  12: 13 whether Jews or Greeks, *s* or free
Gal 3: 28 *s* nor free, male nor female,
   4: 7 So you are no longer a *s*, but a son;
   4: 30 Get rid of the *s* woman and her son
Col 3: 11 barbarian, Scythian, *s* or free,
1Ti 1: 10 for *s* traders and liars and perjurers
Phm : 16 no longer as a *s*, but better than a *s*,
2Pe 2: 19 a man is a *s* to whatever has

SLAVERY (SLAVE)

Ex 2: 23 The Israelites groaned in their *s*
Ro 6: 19 parts of your body in *s* to impurity
Gal 4: 3 were in *s* under the basic principles
1Ti 6: 1 of *s* should consider their masters

SLAVES (SLAVE)

Ps 123: 2 As the eyes of *s* look to the hand
Ecc 10: 7 I have seen *s* on horseback,
Ro 6: 6 that we should no longer be *s* to sin
   6: 16 you are *s* to sin, which leads
   6: 22 and have become *s* to God,
Gal 2: 4 in Christ Jesus and to make us *s*.
   4: 8 you were *s* to those who
Eph 6: 5 *S*, obey your earthly masters
Col 3: 22 *S*, obey your earthly masters
   4: 1 provide your *s* with what is right
Tit 2: 9 Teach *s* to be subject

SLAY (SLAIN)

Job 13: 15 Though he *s* me, yet will I hope

SLEEP (ASLEEP SLEEPER SLEEPING SLEEPS)

Ge 2: 21 the man to fall into a deep *s;*
  15: 12 Abram fell into a deep *s*,
  28: 11 it under his head and lay down to *s*.

Ps   4: 8 I will lie down and s in peace,
121: 4 will neither slumber nor s.
127: 2 for he grants s to those he loves.
Pr   6: 9 When will you get up from your s?
Ecc   5:12 The s of a laborer is sweet,
1Co 15:51 We will not all s, but we will all be
1Th   5: 7 For those who s, s at night,

SLEEPER (SLEEP)

Eph   5:14 "Wake up, O s,

SLEEPING (SLEEP)

Mk 13:36 suddenly, do not let him find you s.

SLEEPLESS*

2Co   6: 5 in hard work, s nights and hunger;

SLEEPS (SLEEP)

Pr 10: 5 he who s during harvest is

SLIMY

Ps 40: 2 He lifted me out of the s pit,

SLING

1Sa 17:50 over the Philistine with a s

SLIP (SLIPPING)

Dt   4: 9 let them s from your heart as long
Ps 121: 3 He will not let your foot s—

SLIPPING (SLIP)

Ps 66: 9 and kept our feet from s.

SLOW

Ex 34: 6 and gracious God, s to anger,
Jas   1:19 s to speak and s to become angry,
2Pe   3: 9 The Lord is not s in keeping his

SLUGGARD

Pr   6: 6 Go to the ant, you s;
13: 4 The s craves and gets nothing,
20: 4 A s does not plow in season;
26:15 The s buries his hand in the dish;

SLUMBER

Ps 121: 3 he who watches over you will not s;
Pr   6:10 A little sleep, a little s,
Ro 13:11 for you to wake up from your s,

SLUR

Ps 15: 3 and casts no s on his fellow man,

SMELL

Ecc 10: 1 As dead flies give perfume a bad s,
2Co   2:16 To the one we are the s of death;

SMITTEN

Isa 53: 4 s by him, and afflicted.

SMOKE

Ex 19:18 Mount Sinai was covered with s,
Ps 104: 32 touches the mountains, and they s.
Isa   6: 4 and the temple was filled with s.
Joel   2:30 blood and fire and billows of s.
Ac   2:19 blood and fire and billows of s.
Rev 15: 8 filled with s from the glory

SMYRNA

Rev   2: 8 the angel of the church in S write:

SNAKE (SNAKES)

Nu 21: 8 "Make a s and put it up on a pole;
Pr 23:32 In the end it bites like a s
Jn   3:14 Moses lifted up the s in the desert,

SNAKES (SNAKE)

Mt 10:16 as shrewd as s and as innocent
Mk 16:18 they will pick up s with their hands;

SNARE (ENSNARE ENSNARED SNARED)

Dt   7:16 for that will be a s to you.
Ps 69:22 before them become a s;
91: 3 from the fowler's s
Pr 29:25 Fear of man will prove to be a s,
Ro 11: 9 "May their table become a s

SNARED (SNARE)

Pr   3:26 will keep your foot from being s.

SNATCH

Jn 10:28 no one can s them out of my hand.
Jude   : 23 s others from the fire and save

SNOUT

Pr 11:22 Like a gold ring in a pig's s

SNOW

Ps 51: 7 and I will be whiter than s.
Isa   1:18 they shall be as white as s;

SNUFF (SNUFFED)

Isa 42: 3 a smoldering wick he will not s out.
Mt 12:20 a smoldering wick he will not s out,

SNUFFED (SNUFF)

Pr 13: 9 but the lamp of the wicked is s out.

SOAP

Mal   3: 2 a refiner's fire or a launderer's s.

SOAR (SOARED)

Isa 40:31 They will s on wings like eagles;

SOARED (SOAR)

2Sa 22:11 he s on the wings of the wind.

SOBER

Ro 12: 3 think of yourself with s judgment,

SODOM

Ge 13:12 and pitched his tents near S.
19:24 rained down burning sulfur on S
Isa   1: 9 we would have become like S,
Lk 10:12 on that day for S than for that town
Ro   9:29 we would have become like S,
Rev 11: 8 which is figuratively called S

SOIL

Ge   4: 2 kept flocks, and Cain worked the s.
Mt 13:23 on good s is the man who hears

SOLD (SELL)

1Ki 21:25 who s himself to do evil in the eyes
Mt 10:29 Are not two sparrows s for a penny
13:44 then in his joy went and s all he had
Ro   7:14 I am unspiritual, s as a slave to sin.

SOLDIER

1Co   7: 9 as a s at his own expense?
2Ti   2: 3 with us like a good s of Christ Jesus

SOLE

Dt 28:65 place for the s of your foot.
Isa   1: 6 From the s of your foot to the top

SOLID

2Ti   2:19 God's s foundation stands firm,
Heb   5:12 You need milk, not s food!

SOLOMON

Son of David by Bathsheba; king of Judah (2Sa 12:24; 1Ch 3:5, 10). Appointed king by David (1Ki 1); adversaries Adonijah, Joab, Shimei killed by Benaiah (1Ki 2). Asked for wisdom (1Ki 3; 2Ch 1). Judged between two prostitutes (1Ki 3:16-28). Built temple (1Ki 5-7; 2Ch 2-5); prayer of dedication (1Ki 8; 2Ch 6). Visited by Queen of Sheba (1Ki 9; 2Ch 9). Wives turned his heart from God (1Ki 11:1-13). Jeroboam rebelled against (1Ki 11:26-40). Death (1Ki 11:41-43; 2Ch 9:29-31).
Proverbs of (1Ki 4:32; Pr 1:1; 10:1; 25:1); psalms of (Ps 72; 127); song of (SS 1:1).

SON (SONS SONSHIP)

Ge 17:19 your wife Sarah will bear you a s,
21:10 rid of that slave woman and her s,
22: 2 "Take your s, your only s, Isaac,
Ex 11: 5 Every firstborn s in Egypt will die,
Dt   1:31 father carries his s, all the way you
6:20 In the future, when your s asks you,
8: 5 as a man disciplines his s,
21:18 rebellious s who does not obey his
2Sa   7:14 be his father, and he will be my s.
1Ki   3:20 and put her dead s by my breast.
Ps   2: 7 He said to me, "You are my S;
2:12 Kiss the S, lest he be angry

Ps   8: 4 the s of man that you care for him?
Pr   3:12 as a father the s he delights in.
6:20 My s, keep your father's
10: 1 A wise s brings joy to his father,
13:24 He who spares the rod hates his s,
29:17 Discipline your s, and he will give
Isa   7:14 with child and will give birth to a s,
Eze 18:20 The s will not share the guilt
Da   3:25 the fourth looks like a s of the gods
7:13 before me was one like a s of man,
Hos 11: 1 and out of Egypt I called my s.
Am   7:14 neither a prophet nor a prophet's s,
Mt   1: 1 of Jesus Christ the s of David,
1:21 She will give birth to a s,
2:15 "Out of Egypt I called my s."
3:17 "This is my S, whom I love;
4: 3 "If you are the S of God, tell these
8:20 but the S of Man has no place
11:27 one knows the S except the Father,
12: 8 For the S of Man is Lord
12:32 a word against the S of Man will be
12:40 so the S of Man will be three days
13:41 S of Man will send out his angels,
13:55 "Isn't this the carpenter's s?
14:33 "Truly you are the S of God."
16:16 "You are the Christ, the S
16:27 For the S of Man is going to come
17: 5 "This is my S, whom I love;
19:28 when the S of Man sits
20:18 and the S of Man will be betrayed
20:28 as the S of Man did not come
21: 9 "Hosanna to the S of David!"
22:42 Whose s is he?" "The s of David,
24:27 so will be the coming of the S
24:30 They will see the S of Man coming
24:44 the S of Man will come at an hour
25:31 "When the S of Man comes
26:63 if you are the Christ, the S of God."
27:54 "Surely he was the S of God!"
28:19 and of the S and of the Holy Spirit,
Mk   1:11 "You are my S, whom I love;
2:28 So the S of Man is Lord
8:38 the S of Man will be ashamed
9: 7 "This is my S, whom I love.
10:45 even the S of Man did not come
13:32 nor the S, but only the Father.
14:62 you will see the S of Man sitting
Lk   1:32 and will be called the S
2: 7 she gave birth to her firstborn, a s.
3:22 "You are my S, whom I love;
9:35 This is my S, whom I have chosen;
9:58 but the S of Man has no place
12: 8 the S of Man will also acknowledge
15:20 he ran to his s, threw his arms
18: 8 when the S of Man comes,
18:31 written by the prophets about the S
19:10 For the S of Man came to seek
Jn   1:34 I testify that this is the S of God."
3:14 so the S of Man must be lifted up,
3:16 that he gave his one and only S,
3:36 believes in the S has eternal life,
5:19 the S can do nothing by himself;
6:40 is that everyone who looks to the S
11: 4 so that God's S may be glorified
17: 1 Glorify your S, that your S may
Ac   7:56 and the S of Man standing
13:33 " 'You are my S;
Ro   1: 4 with power to be the S of God
5:10 to him through the death of his S,
8: 3 did by sending his own S
8:29 conformed to the likeness of his S,
8:32 He who did not spare his own S,
1Co 15:28 then the S himself will be made
Gal   2:20 I live by faith in the S of God,
4: 4 sent his S, born of a woman,
4:30 rid of the slave woman and her s,
1Th   1:10 and to wait for his S from heaven,
Heb   1: 2 days he has spoken to us by his S,
1: 5 "You are my S;
2: 6 the s of man that you care for him?
4:14 Jesus the S of God, let us hold
5: 5 "You are my S;
7:28 appointed the S, who has been
10:29 punished who has trampled the S
12: 6 everyone he accepts as a s."
2Pe   1:17 saying, "This is my S, whom I love;
1Jn   1: 3 is with the Father and with his S,
1: 7 his S, purifies us from all sin.

1Jn 2: 23 whoever acknowledges the *S* has
       3: 8 reason the *S* of God appeared was
       4: 9 only *S* into the world that we might
       4: 14 that the Father has sent his *S*
       5: 5 he who believes that Jesus is the *S*
       5: 11 eternal life, and this life is in his *S*.
Rev 1: 13 lampstands was someone ''like a *s*
      14: 14 on the cloud was one ''like a *s*

SONG (SING)

Ex 15: 2 LORD is my strength and my *s;*
Ps 40: 3 He put a new *s* in my mouth,
      69: 30 I will praise God's name in *s*
      96: 1 Sing to the LORD a new *s;*
      98: 4 burst into jubilant *s* with music;
     119: 54 Your decrees are the theme of my *s*
     149: 1 Sing to the LORD a new *s,*
Isa 49: 13 burst into *s,* O mountains!
      55: 12 will burst into *s* before you,
Rev 5: 9 And they sang a new *s:*
       5: 13 and sang the *s* of Moses the servant

SONGS (SING)

2Sa 23: 1 Israel's singer of *s:*
Job 35: 10 who gives *s* in the night,
Ps 100: 2 come before him with joyful *s.*
     126: 6 will return with *s* of joy,
     137: 3 ''Sing us one of the *s* of Zion!''
Eph 5: 19 with psalms, hymns and spiritual *s.*
Jas 5: 13 Is anyone happy? Let him sing *s*

SONS (SON)

Ge   6: 2 the *s* of God saw that the daughters
      10: 20 These are the *s* of Ham
Ru   4: 15 who is better to you than seven *s,*
Ps 127: 3 *S* are a heritage from the LORD,
     132: 12 if your *s* keep my covenant
Hos 1: 10 they will be called *'s*
Joel 2: 28 Your *s* and daughters will prophesy
Mt   5: 9 for they will be called *s* of God.
Lk   6: 35 and you will be *s* of the Most High,
Jn 12: 36 so that you may become *s* of light.''
Ro   8: 14 by the Spirit of God are *s* of God.
      9: 26 they will be called *'s*
2Co 6: 18 and you will be my *s* and daughters
Gal 3: 26 You are all *s* of God through faith
      4: 5 we might receive the full rights of *s.*
      4: 6 Because you are *s,* God sent
Heb 12: 7 discipline; God is treating you as *s.*

SONSHIP* (SON)

Ro   8: 15 but you received the Spirit of *s.*

SORCERY

Lev 19: 26 '' 'Do not practice divination or *s.*

SORROW (SORROWS)

Ps   6: 7 My eyes grow weak with *s;*
     116: 3 I was overcome by trouble and *s.*
Isa 60: 20 and your days of *s* will end.
Jer 31: 13 and they will *s* no more.
Ro   9: 2 I have great *s* and unceasing
2Co 7: 10 Godly *s* brings repentance that

SORROWS (SORROW)

Isa 53: 3 a man of *s,* and familiar

SOUGHT (SEEK)

2Ch 26: 5 As long as he *s* the LORD,
      31: 21 he *s* his God and worked
Ps 34: 4 I *s* the LORD, and he answered me
     119: 58 I have *s* your face with all my heart;

SOUL (SOULS)

Dt   6: 5 with all your *s* and with all your
      10: 12 all your heart and with all your *s,*
      30: 6 all your heart and with all your *s*
Jos 22: 5 with all your heart and all your *s.''*
2Ki 23: 25 and with all his *s* and with all his
Ps 23: 3 he restores my *s.*
      34: 2 My *s* will boast in the LORD;
      42: 1 so my *s* pants for you, O God.
      42: 11 Why are you downcast, O my *s?*
      62: 5 Find rest, O my *s,* in God alone;
      63: 8 My *s* clings to you;
      94: 19 consolation brought joy to my *s.*
     103: 1 Praise the LORD, O my *s;*
Pr 13: 19 A longing fulfilled is sweet to the *s,*

Pr 16: 24 sweet to the *s* and healing
      22: 5 he who guards his *s* stays far
Isa 55: 2 your *s* will delight in the richest
La   3: 20 and my *s* is downcast within me.
Eze 18: 4 For every living *s* belongs to me,
Mt 10: 28 kill the body but cannot kill the *s*.
      16: 26 yet forfeits his *s*? Or what can
      22: 37 with all your *s* and with all your
Heb 4: 12 even to dividing *s* and spirit,
3Jn   : 2 even as your *s* is getting along well.

SOULS (SOUL)

Pr 11: 30 and he who wins *s* is wise.
Jer 6: 16 and you will find rest for your *s.*
Mt 11: 29 and you will find rest for your *s.*

SOUND (FINE-SOUNDING)

Ge   3: 8 and his wife heard the *s*
Pr   3: 21 preserve *s* judgment
Eze 3: 12 I heard behind me a loud rumbling *s*
Jn   3: 8 You hear its *s,* but you cannot tell
Ac   2: 2 Suddenly a *s* like the blowing
1Co 14: 8 if the trumpet does not *s* a clear call
      15: 52 the trumpet will *s,* the dead will
1Ti 1: 10 to the *s* doctrine that conforms
2Ti 4: 3 men will not put up with *s* doctrine.
Tit 1: 9 can encourage others by *s* doctrine
      2: 1 is in accord with *s* doctrine.

SOUR

Eze 18: 2 '' 'The fathers eat *s* grapes,

SOURCE

Heb 5: 9 became the *s* of eternal salvation

SOVEREIGN (SOVEREIGNTY)

Ge 15: 2 But Abram said, ''O *S* LORD,
2Sa 7: 18 O *S* LORD, and what is my family,
Ps 71: 16 your mighty acts, O *S* LORD;
Isa 25: 8 *S* LORD will wipe away the tears
      40: 10 the *S* LORD comes with power,
      50: 4 *S* LORD has given me
      61: 1 The Spirit of the *S* LORD is on me,
      61: 11 so the *S* LORD will make
Jer 32: 17 to the LORD: ''Ah, *S* LORD,
Eze 12: 28 fulfilled, declares the *S* LORD.' ''
Da   4: 25 that the Most High is *s*
2Pe 2: 1 denying the *s* LORD who bought
Jude   : 4 and deny Jesus Christ our only *S*

SOVEREIGNTY (SOVEREIGN)

Da   7: 27 Then the *s,* power and greatness

SOW (SOWER SOWN SOWS)

Job 4: 8 and those who *s* trouble reap it.
Ps 126: 5 Those who *s* in tears
Hos 8: 7 ''They *s* the wind
      10: 12 *S* for yourselves righteousness,
Mt   6: 26 they do not *s* or reap or store away
      13: 3 ''A farmer went out to *s* his seed.
1Co 15: 36 What you *s* does not come to life
Jas 3: 18 Peacemakers who *s*
2Pe 2: 22 and, ''A *s* that is washed goes back

SOWER (SOW)

Isa 55: 10 so that it yields seed for the *s*
Mt 13: 18 to what the parable of the *s* means:
Jn   4: 36 so that the *s* and the reaper may be
2Co 9: 10 Now he who supplies seed to the *s*

SOWN (SOW)

Mt 13: 8 sixty or thirty times what was *s.*
Mk   4: 15 along the path, where the word is *s.*
1Co 15: 42 The body that is *s* is perishable,

SOWS (SOW)

Pr 11: 18 he who *s* righteousness reaps a sure
      22: 8 He who *s* wickedness reaps trouble
2Co 9: 6 Whoever *s* sparingly will
Gal 6: 7 A man reaps what he *s.*

SPARE (SPARES SPARING)

Est 7: 3 *s* my people—this is my request.
Ro   8: 32 He who did not *s* his own Son
      11: 21 natural branches, he will not *s* you
2Pe 2: 4 For if God did not *s* angels
       2: 5 if he did not *s* the ancient world

SPARES (SPARE)

Pr 13: 24 He who *s* the rod hates his son,

SPARING (SPARE)

Pr 21: 26 but the righteous give without *s.*

SPARKLE

Zec 9: 16 They will *s* in his land

SPARROW (SPARROWS)

Ps 84: 3 Even the *s* has found a home,

SPARROWS (SPARROW)

Mt 10: 29 Are not two *s* sold for a penny?

SPEAR (SPEARS)

1Sa 19: 10 as Saul drove the *s* into the wall.
Ps 46: 9 breaks the bow and shatters the *s,*

SPEARS (SPEAR)

Isa 2: 4 and their *s* into pruning hooks.
Joel 3: 10 and your pruning hooks into *s.*
Mic 4: 3 and their *s* into pruning hooks.

SPECIAL

Jas 2: 3 If you show *s* attention

SPECK

Mt   7: 3 look at the *s* of sawdust

SPECTACLE

1Co 4: 9 We have been made a *s*
Col 2: 15 he made a public *s* of them,

SPEECH

Ps 19: 3 There is no *s* or language
Pr 22: 11 pure heart and whose *s* is gracious
2Co 8: 7 in faith, in *s,* in knowledge,
1Ti 4: 12 set an example for the believers in *s*

SPEND (SPENT)

Pr 31: 3 do not *s* your strength on women,
Isa 55: 2 Why *s* money on what is not bread,
2Co 12: 15 So I will very gladly *s*

SPENT (SPEND)

Mk   5: 26 many doctors and had *s* all she had,
Lk   6: 12 and the night praying to God.
      15: 14 After he had *s* everything,

SPIN

Mt   6: 28 They do not labor or *s.*

SPIRIT (SPIRIT'S SPIRITS SPIRITUAL SPIRITUALLY)

Ge   1: 2 and the *S* of God was hovering
       6: 3 ''My *S* will not contend
Ex 31: 3 I have filled him with the *S* of God,
Nu 11: 25 and put the *S* on the seventy elders.
Dt 34: 9 filled with the *s* of wisdom
Jdg 6: 34 Then the *S* of the LORD came
      11: 29 Then the *S* of the LORD came
      13: 25 and the *S* of the LORD began
1Sa 10: 10 the *S* of God came upon him
      16: 13 day on the *S* of the LORD came
      16: 14 the *S* of the LORD had departed
2Sa 23: 2 ''The *S* of the LORD spoke
2Ki 2: 9 inherit a double portion of your *s,''*
Ne   9: 20 You gave your good *S*
       9: 30 By your *S* you admonished them
Job 33: 4 The *S* of God has made me;
Ps 31: 5 Into your hands I commit my *s;*
      34: 18 saves those who are crushed in *s.*
      51: 10 and renew a steadfast *s* within me.
      51: 11 or take your Holy *S* from me.
      51: 17 sacrifices of God are a broken *s;*
     106: 33 rebelled against the *S* of God,
     139: 7 Where can I go from your *S?*
     143: 10 may your good *S*
Isa 11: 2 The *S* of the LORD will rest
      30: 1 an alliance, but not by my *S,*
      32: 15 till the *S* is poured upon us
      44: 3 I will pour out my *S*
      57: 15 him who is contrite and lowly in *s,*
      61: 1 The *S* of the Sovereign LORD is
      63: 10 and grieved his Holy *S.*
Eze 11: 19 an undivided heart and put a new *s*
      13: 3 prophets who follow their own *s*

Eze 36: 26 you a new heart and put a new *s*
Da 4: 8 and the *s* of the holy gods is in him
Joel 2: 28 I will pour out my *S* on all people.
Zec 4: 6 but by my *S*,' says the LORD
Mt 1: 18 to be with child through the Holy *S*
3: 11 will baptize you with the Holy *S*
3: 16 he saw the *S* of God descending
4: 1 led by the *S* into the desert
5: 3 saying: "Blessed are the poor in *s*,
10: 20 but the *S* of your Father speaking
12: 31 against the *S* will not be forgiven.
26: 41 *s* is willing, but the body is weak."
28: 19 and of the Son and of the Holy *S*,
Mk 1: 8 he will baptize you with the Holy *S*
Lk 1: 35 "The Holy *S* will come upon you,
1: 80 child grew and became strong in *s*;
3: 16 will baptize you with the Holy *S*
4: 18 "The *S* of the Lord is on me,
11: 13 Father in heaven give the Holy *S*
23: 46 into your hands I commit my *s*."
Jn 1: 33 who will baptize with the Holy *S*.'
3: 5 a man is born of water and the *S*,
4: 24 God is *s*, and his worshipers must
6: 63 The *S* gives life; the flesh counts
7: 39 Up to that time the *S* had not been
14: 26 But the Counselor, the Holy *S*,
16: 13 But when he, the *S* of truth, comes,
20: 22 and said, "Receive the Holy *S*.
Ac 1: 5 will be baptized with the Holy *S*."
1: 8 when the Holy *S* comes on you;
2: 4 of them were filled with the Holy *S*
2: 17 I will pour out my *S* on all people.
2: 38 will receive the gift of the Holy *S*.
4: 31 they were all filled with the Holy *S*
5: 3 that you have lied to the Holy *S*
6: 3 who are known to be full of the *S*
8: 15 that they might receive the Holy *S*,
9: 17 and be filled with the Holy *S*.'
11: 16 will be baptized with the Holy *S*.'
13: 2 and fasting, the Holy *S* said,
19: 2 "Did you receive the Holy *S*
Ro 8: 4 nature but according to the *S*.
8: 5 set on what the *S* desires.
8: 9 And if anyone does not have the *S*
8: 13 but if by the *S* you put
8: 16 The *S* himself testifies
8: 23 who have the firstfruits of the *S*,
8: 26 the *S* helps us in our weakness.
1Co 2: 10 God has revealed it to us by his *S*.
2: 14 man without the *S* does not accept
5: 3 present, I am with you in *s*.
6: 19 body is a temple of the Holy *S*,
12: 13 baptized by one *S* into one body—
2Co 1: 22 and put his *S* in our hearts
3: 3 but with the *S* of the living God,
3: 6 the letter kills, but the *S* gives life.
3: 17 Now the Lord is the *S*,
5: 5 and has given us the *S* as a deposit,
7: 1 that contaminates body and *s*,
Gal 3: 2 Did you receive the *S*
5: 16 by the *S*, and you will not gratify
5: 22 But the fruit of the *S* is love, joy,
5: 25 let us keep in step with the *S*.
6: 8 from the *S* will reap eternal life.
Eph 1: 13 with a seal, the promised Holy *S*,
2: 22 in which God lives by his *S*.
4: 4 There is one body and one *S*—
4: 30 do not grieve the Holy *S* of God,
5: 18 Instead, be filled with the *S*.
6: 17 of salvation and the sword of the *S*,
Php 2: 2 being one in *s* and purpose.
1Th 5: 23 May your whole *s*, soul
2Th 2: 13 the sanctifying work of the *S*
1Ti 3: 16 was vindicated by the *S*,
2Ti 1: 7 For God did not give us a *s*
Heb 3: 4 of the Holy *S* distributed according
4: 12 even to dividing soul and *s*,
10: 29 and who has insulted the *S* of grace
1Pe 3: 4 beauty of a gentle and quiet *s*,
2Pe 1: 21 carried along by the Holy *S*.
1Jn 3: 24 We know it by the *S* he gave us.
4: 1 Dear friends, do not believe every *s*
4: 13 because he has given us of his *S*.
Jude : 20 holy faith and pray in the Holy *S*.
Rev 2: 7 let him hear what the *S* says

SPIRIT'S* (SPIRIT)

1Co 2: 4 a demonstration of the *S* power,

1Th 5: 19 not put out the *S* fire; do not treat

SPIRITS (SPIRIT)

1Co 12: 10 to another distinguishing between *s*,
14: 32 The *s* of prophets are subject
1Jn 4: 1 test the *s* to see whether they are

SPIRITUAL (SPIRIT)

Ro 12: 1 to God—this is your *s* act of worship.
12: 11 but keep your *s* fervor, serving
1Co 2: 13 expressing *s* truths in *s* words.
3: 1 I could not address you as *s* but
12: 1 Now about *s* gifts, brothers,
14: 1 of love and eagerly desire *s* gifts,
15: 44 a natural body, it is raised a *s* body.
Gal 6: 1 you who are *s* should restore him
Eph 1: 3 with every *s* blessing in Christ.
5: 19 with psalms, hymns and *s* songs.
6: 12 and against the *s* forces of evil
1Pe 2: 2 newborn babies, crave pure *s* milk,
2: 5 are being built into a *s* house

SPIRITUALLY (SPIRIT)

1Co 2: 14 because they are *s* discerned.

SPIT

Mt 27: 30 They *s* on him, and took the staff
Rev 3: 16 I am about to *s* you out

SPLENDOR

1Ch 16: 29 the LORD in the *s* of his holiness.
29: 11 the glory and the majesty and the *s*,
Job 37: 22 of the north he comes in golden *s*;
Ps 29: 2 in the *s* of his holiness.
45: 3 clothe yourself with *s* and majesty.
96: 6 *S* and majesty are before him;
96: 9 in the *s* of his holiness;
104: 1 you are clothed with *s* and majesty.
145: 5 of the glorious *s* of your majesty,
145: 12 and the glorious *s* of your kingdom.
148: 13 his *s* is above the earth
Pr 4: 9 and present you with a crown of *s*."
16: 31 Gray hair is a crown of *s*;
20: 29 gray hair the *s* of the old.
Isa 55: 5 for he has endowed you with *s*."
60: 21 for the display of my *s*.
61: 3 the LORD for the display of his *s*.
63: 1 Who is this, robed in *s*,
Hab 3: 4 His *s* was like the sunrise;
Mt 6: 29 in all his *s* was dressed like one
Lk 9: 31 appeared in glorious *s*, talking
2Th 2: 8 and destroy by the *s* of his coming.

SPOIL (SPOILS)

Ps 119: 162 like one who finds great *s*.

SPOILS (SPOIL)

Isa 53: 12 he will divide the *s* with the strong,
Jn 6: 27 Do not work for food that *s*,

SPONTANEOUS*

Phm : 14 so that any favor you do will be *s*

SPOTLESS

2Pe 3: 14 make every effort to be found *s*,

SPOTS (SPOTTED)

Jer 13: 23 or the leopard its *s*?

SPOTTED (SPOTS)

Ge 30: 32 and every *s* or speckled goat.

SPREAD (SPREADING SPREADS)

Ps 78: 19 "Can God *s* a table in the desert?
Ac 6: 7 So the word of God *s*.
12: 24 of God continued to increase and *s*.
13: 49 of the Lord *s* through the whole
19: 20 the word of the Lord *s* widely
2Th 3: 1 message of the Lord may *s* rapidly

SPREADING (SPREAD)

Pr 29: 5 is *s* a net for his feet.
1Th 3: 2 God's fellow worker in *s* the gospel

SPREADS (SPREAD)

Pr 10: 18 and whoever *s* slander is a fool.

SPRING (SPRINGS WELLSPRING)

Jer 2: 13 the *s* of living water,
Jn 4: 14 in him a *s* of water welling up
Jas 3: 12 can a salt *s* produce fresh water.

SPRINGS (SPRING)

2Pe 2: 17 These men are *s* without water

SPRINKLE (SPRINKLED SPRINKLING)

Lev 16: 14 and with his finger *s* it on the front

SPRINKLED (SPRINKLE)

Heb 10: 22 having our hearts *s* to cleanse us

SPRINKLING (SPRINKLE)

1Pe 1: 2 to Jesus Christ and *s* by his blood:

SPROUT

Pr 23: 5 for they will surely *s* wings
Jer 33: 15 I will make a righteous Branch *s*

SPUR*

Heb 10: 24 how we may *s* one another

SPURNS*

Pr 15: 5 A fool *s* his father's discipline,

SPY

Gal 2: 4 ranks to *s* on the freedom we have

SQUANDERED (SQUANDERS)

Lk 15: 13 there *s* his wealth in wild living.

SQUANDERS* (SQUANDERED)

Pr 29: 3 of prostitutes *s* his wealth.

SQUARE

Rev 21: 16 The city was laid out like a *s*,

STABILITY*

Pr 29: 4 By justice a king gives a country *s*,

STAFF

Ge 49: 10 the ruler's *s* from between his feet,
Ex 7: 12 Aaron's *s* swallowed up their staffs.
Nu 17: 6 and Aaron's *s* was among them.
Ps 23: 4 your rod and your *s*,

STAIN (STAINED)

Eph 5: 27 without *s* or wrinkle or any other

STAINED (STAIN)

Isa 63: 1 with his garments *s* crimson?

STAKES

Isa 54: 2 strengthen your *s*.

STAND (STANDING STANDS STOOD)

Ex 14: 13 *S* firm and you will see
Jos 10: 12 "O sun, *s* still over Gibeon,
2Ch 20: 17 *s* firm and see the deliverance
Job 19: 25 in the end he will *s* upon the earth.
Ps 1: 1 or *s* in the way of sinners
1: 5 Therefore the wicked will not *s*
24: 3 Who may *s* in his holy place?
33: 11 of the LORD *s* forever,
40: 2 and gave me a firm place to *s*.'
76: 7 Who can *s* before you
93: 5 Your statutes *s* firm;
119: 120 I *s* in awe of your laws.
130: 3 O Lord, who could *s*?
Ecc 5: 7 Therefore *s* in awe of God.
Isa 7: 9 If you do not *s* firm in your faith,
29: 23 will *s* in awe of the God of Israel.
Eze 22: 30 *s* before me in the gap on behalf
Hab 3: 2 I *s* in awe of your deeds, O LORD.
Zec 14: 4 On that day his feet will *s*
Mal 3: 2 Who can *s* when he appears?
Mt 12: 25 divided against itself will not *s*.
Ro 14: 4 for the Lord is able to make him *s*.
14: 10 we will all *s* before God's judgment
1Co 10: 13 out so that you can *s* up under it.
15: 58 Therefore, my dear brothers, *s* firm
16: 13 Be on your guard; *s* firm in the faith
Gal 5: 1 *S* firm, then, and do not let
Eph 6: 14 *S* firm then, with the belt
2Th 2: 15 *s* firm and hold to the teachings we
Jas 5: 8 You too, be patient and *s* firm,
Rev 3: 20 Here I am! I *s* at the door

STANDING (STAND)

Ex 3: 5 where you are *s* is holy ground."
Jos 5: 15 the place where you are *s* is holy."
Ru 2: 1 a man of *s*, whose name was Boaz.
4: 11 May you have *s* in Ephrathah
Lk 21: 19 By *s* firm you will gain life.
1Ti 3: 13 have served well gain an excellent *s*
1Pe 5: 9 Resist him, *s* firm in the faith,

STANDS (STAND)

Ps 89: 2 that your love *s* firm forever,
119: 89 it *s* firm in the heavens.
Pr 12: 7 the house of the righteous *s* firm.
Isa 40: 8 but the word of our God *s* forever."
Mt 10: 22 but he who *s* firm to the end will be
2Ti 2: 19 God's solid foundation *s* firm,
1Pe 1: 25 but the word of the Lord *s* forever

STAR (STARS)

Nu 24: 17 A *s* will come out of Jacob;
Isa 14: 12 O morning *s*, son of the dawn!
Mt 2: 2 We saw his *s* in the east
2Pe 1: 19 the morning *s* rises in your hearts.
Rev 2: 28 I will also give him the morning *s*.
22: 16 and the bright Morning *S*."

STARS (STAR)

Ge 1: 16 He also made the *s*.
Job 38: 7 while the morning *s* sang together
Da 12: 3 like the *s* for ever and ever.
Php 2: 15 in which you shine like *s*

STATURE

1Sa 2: 26 boy Samuel continued to grow in *s*
Lk 2: 52 And Jesus grew in wisdom and *s*,

STATUTES

Ps 19: 7 *s* of the LORD are trustworthy,
93: 5 Your *s* stand firm;
119: 2 Blessed are they who keep his *s*
119: 14 I rejoice in following your *s*
119: 24 Your *s* are my delight;
119: 36 Turn my heart toward your *s*
119: 99 for I meditate on your *s*.
119:111 Your *s* are my heritage forever;
119:125 that I may understand your *s*.
119:129 Your *s* are wonderful;
119:138 The *s* you have laid
119:152 Long ago I learned from your *s*
119:167 I obey your *s*,

STEADFAST*

Ps 51: 10 and renew a *s* spirit within me.
57: 7 My heart is *s*, O God,
57: 7 my heart is *s*;
108: 1 My heart is *s*, O God;
111: 8 They are *s* for ever and ever,
112: 7 his heart is *s*, trusting in the LORD
119: 5 Oh, that my ways were *s*
Isa 26: 3 him whose mind is *s*,
1Pe 5: 10 and make you strong, firm and *s*.

STEADY

Isa 35: 3 *s* the knees that give way;

STEAL (STOLEN)

Ex 20: 15 "You shall not *s*.
Lev 19: 11 " 'Do not *s*.
Dt 5: 19 "You shall not *s*.
Mt 19: 18 do not *s*, do not give false
Ro 13: 9 "Do not *s*," "Do not covet,"
Eph 4: 28 has been stealing must *s* no longer,

STEP (FOOTSTEPS STEPS)

Job 34: 21 he sees their every *s*.
Gal 5: 25 let us keep in *s* with the Spirit.

STEPHEN

Deacon (Ac 6:5). Arrested (Ac 6:8-15). Speech to Sanhedrin (Ac 7). Stoned (Ac 7:54-60; 22:20).

STEPS (STEP)

Ps 37: 23 he makes his *s* firm;
Pr 14: 15 prudent man gives thought to his *s*.
16: 9 but the LORD determines his *s*.
20: 24 A man's *s* are directed
Jer 10: 23 it is not for man to direct his *s*.
1Pe 2: 21 that you should follow in his *s*.

STERN (STERNNESS)

Pr 15: 10 *S* discipline awaits him who leaves

STERNNESS* (STERN)

Ro 11: 22 and *s* of God: *s* to those who fell,

STICKS

Pr 18: 24 there is a friend who *s* closer

STIFF-NECKED (NECK)

Ex 34: 9 Although this is a *s* people,
Pr 29: 1 A man who remains *s*

STILL

Jos 10: 13 So the sun stood *s*,
Ps 37: 7 Be *s* before the LORD
46: 10 "Be *s*, and know that I am God;
89: 9 its waves mount up, you *s* them.
Zec 2: 13 Be *s* before the LORD, all mankind
Mk 4: 39 said to the waves, "Quiet! Be *s*!"

STIMULATE*

2Pe 3: 1 as reminders to *s* you

STING

1Co 15: 55 Where, O death, is your *s*?"

STINGY

Pr 28: 22 A *s* man is eager to get rich

STIRRED (STIRS)

Ps 45: 1 My heart is *s* by a noble theme

STIRS (STIRRED)

Pr 6: 19 and a man who *s* up dissension
10: 12 Hatred *s* up dissension,
15: 1 but a harsh word *s* up anger.
15: 18 hot-tempered man *s* up dissension,
16: 28 A perverse man *s* up dissension,
28: 25 A greedy man *s* up dissension,
29: 22 An angry man *s* up dissension,

STOLEN (STEAL)

Lev 6: 4 he must return what he has *s*
SS 4: 9 You have *s* my heart, my sister,

STOMACH

1Co 6: 13 Food for the *s* and the *s* for food"—
Php 3: 19 their god is their *s*, and their glory

STONE (CAPSTONE CORNERSTONE MILLSTONE STONED STONES)

Ex 24: 4 set up twelve *s* pillars representing
28: 10 on one *s* and the remaining six
34: 1 "Chisel out two *s* tablets like
Dt 4: 13 then wrote them on two *s* tablets.
19: 14 your neighbor's boundary *s* set up
1Sa 17: 50 the Philistine with a sling and a *s*,
Ps 91: 12 will not strike your foot against a *s*.
118: 22 The *s* the builders rejected
Pr 22: 28 not move an ancient boundary *s*
Isa 8: 14 a *s* that causes men to stumble
28: 16 "See, I lay a *s* in Zion,
Eze 11: 19 remove from them their heart of *s*
36: 26 remove from you your heart of *s*
Mt 7: 9 will give him a *s*? Or if he asks
21: 42 " 'The *s* the builders rejected
24: 2 not one *s* here will be left
Mk 16: 3 "Who will roll the *s* away
Lk 4: 3 tell this *s* to become bread."
Jn 8: 7 the first to throw a *s* at her."
Ac 4: 11 " 'the *s* you builders rejected,
Ro 9: 32 stumbled over the "stumbling *s*."
2Co 3: 3 not on tablets of *s* but on tablets
1Pe 2: 6 "See, I lay a *s* in Zion,
Rev 2: 17 also give him a white *s*

STONED (STONE)

2Co 11: 25 once I was *s*, three times I was
Heb 11: 37 They were *s*; they were sawed

STONES (STONE)

Ex 28: 21 are to be twelve *s*, one for each
Jos 4: 3 to take up twelve *s* from the middle
1Sa 17: 40 chose five smooth *s*
Mt 3: 9 out of these *s* God can raise up
1Co 3: 12 silver, costly *s*, wood, hay or straw,
1Pe 2: 5 also, like living *s*, are being built

STOOD (STAND)

Jos 10: 13 So the sun *s* still,
Lk 22: 28 You are those who have *s* by me
2Ti 4: 17 But the Lord *s* at my side
Jas 1: 12 because when he has *s* the test,

STOOP (STOOPS)

2Sa 22: 36 you *s* down to make me great.

STOOPS (STOOP)

Ps 113: 6 who *s* down to look

STOP

Job 37: 14 *s* and consider God's wonders.
Isa 1: 13 S bringing meaningless offerings!
1: 16 S doing wrong,
2: 22 S trusting in man,
Jer 32: 40 I will never *s* doing good to them,
Mk 9: 39 "Do not *s* him," Jesus said.
Jn 6: 43 "S grumbling among yourselves,"
7: 24 S judging by mere appearances,
20: 27 S doubting and believe."
Ro 14: 13 Therefore let us *s* passing judgment
1Co 14: 20 Brothers, *s* thinking like children.

STORE (STORED)

Pr 2: 1 and *s* up my commands within you,
7: 1 and *s* up my commands within you.
10: 14 Wise men *s* up knowledge,
Isa 33: 6 a rich *s* of salvation and wisdom
Mt 6: 19 not *s* up for yourselves treasures
6: 26 or reap or *s* away in barns,
2Ti 4: 8 Now there is in *s* for me the crown

STORED (STORE)

Lk 6: 45 out of the good *s* up in his heart,
Col 1: 5 from the hope that is *s* up for you

STOREHOUSE (HOUSE)

Mal 3: 10 Bring the whole tithe into the *s*,

STORIES*

2Pe 1: 16 did not follow cleverly invented *s*
2: 3 you with *s* they have made up.

STORM

Job 38: 1 LORD answered Job out of the *s*.
Ps 107: 29 He stilled the *s* to a whisper;
Lk 8: 24 the *s* subsided, and all was calm.

STOUTHEARTED* (HEART)

Ps 138: 3 you made me bold and *s*.

STRAIGHT

Ps 27: 11 lead me in a *s* path
107: 7 He led them by a *s* way
Pr 2: 13 who leave the *s* paths
3: 6 and he will make your paths *s*.
4: 11 and lead you along *s* paths.
4: 25 Let your eyes look *s* ahead,
11: 5 of the blameless makes a *s* way
15: 21 of understanding keeps a *s* course.
Isa 40: 3 make *s* in the wilderness
Mt 3: 3 make *s* paths for him.' "
Jn 1: 23 "Make *s* the way for the Lord.' "
2Pe 2: 15 They have left the *s* way

STRAIN (STRAINING)

Mt 23: 24 You *s* out a gnat but swallow

STRAINING (STRAIN)

Php 3: 13 and *s* toward what is ahead,

STRANGE (STRANGER STRANGERS)

Isa 28: 11 with foreign lips and *s* tongues
1Co 14: 21 "Through men of *s* tongues
1Pe 4: 4 They think it *s* that you do not

STRANGER (STRANGE)

Ps 119: 19 I am a *s* on earth;
Mt 25: 35 I was a *s* and you invited me in,
Jn 10: 5 But they will never follow a *s*;

STRANGERS (STRANGE)

Heb 13: 2 Do not forget to entertain *s*,
1Pe 2: 11 as aliens and *s* in the world,

STRAW

Isa 11: 7 and the lion will eat *s* like the ox.
1Co 3: 12 silver, costly stones, wood, hay or *s*

STRAYED (STRAYS)

Ps 119:176 I have *s* like a lost sheep.
Jer 31: 19 After I *s*,

STRAYS (STRAYED)

Pr 21: 16 A man who *s* from the path
Eze 34: 16 for the lost and bring back the *s*.

STREAM (STREAMS)

Am 5: 24 righteousness like a never-failing *s!*

STREAMS (STREAM)

Ps 1: 3 He is like a tree planted by *s*
46: 4 is a river whose *s* make glad
Ecc 1: 7 All *s* flow into the sea,
Jn 7: 38 *s* of living water will flow

STREET

Mt 6: 5 on the *s* corners to be seen by men.
22: 9 Go to the *s* corners and invite
Rev 21: 21 The great *s* of the city was of pure gold,

STRENGTH (STRONG)

Ex 15: 2 The LORD is my *s* and my song;
Dt 4: 37 by his Presence and his great *s*,
6: 5 all your soul and with all your *s*.
Jdg 16: 15 told me the secret of your great *s*.''
2Sa 22: 33 It is God who arms me with *s*
2Ki 3: 25 with all his soul and with all his *s*,
1Ch 16: 11 Look to the LORD and his *s*;
16: 28 ascribe to the LORD glory and *s*,
29: 12 In your hands are *s* and power
Ne 8: 10 for the joy of the LORD is your *s*.''
Ps 18: 1 I love you, O LORD, my *s*.
21: 13 Be exalted, O LORD, in your *s*;
28: 7 The LORD is my *s* and my shield;
29: 11 The LORD gives *s* to his people;
33: 16 no warrior escapes by his great *s*.
46: 1 God is our refuge and *s*,
59: 17 O my *S*, I sing praise to you;
65: 6 having armed yourself with *s*,
73: 26 but God is the *s* of my heart
84: 5 Blessed are those whose *s* is in you,
96: 7 ascribe to the LORD glory and *s*.
105: 4 Look to the LORD and his *s*;
118: 14 The LORD is my *s* and my song;
147: 10 not in the *s* of the horse,
Pr 24: 5 a man of knowledge increases *s*;
30: 25 Ants are creatures of little *s*,
Isa 12: 2 the LORD, is my *s* and my song;
31: 1 and in the great *s* of their horsemen
40: 26 of his great power and mighty *s*,
40: 31 will renew their *s*.
63: 1 forward in the greatness of his *s*?
Jer 9: 23 or the strong man boast of his *s*
Mic 5: 4 flock in the *s* of the LORD,
Hab 3: 19 The Sovereign LORD is my *s*;
Mk 12: 30 all your mind and with all your *s*.'
1Co 1: 25 of God is stronger than man's *s*.
Eph 1: 19 is like the working of his mighty *s*,
Php 4: 13 through him who gives me *s*.
Heb 11: 34 whose weakness was turned to *s*;
1Pe 4: 11 it with the *s* God provides,

STRENGTHEN (STRONG)

2Ch 16: 9 to *s* those whose hearts are fully
Ps 119: 28 *s* me according to your word.
Isa 35: 3 *S* the feeble hands,
41: 10 I will *s* you and help you;
Lk 22: 32 have turned back, *s* your brothers.''
Eph 3: 16 of his glorious riches he may *s* you
1Th 3: 13 May he *s* your hearts
2Th 2: 17 and *s* you in every good deed
Heb 12: 12 *s* your feeble arms and weak knees.

STRENGTHENED (STRONG)

Col 1: 11 being *s* with all power according
Heb 13: 9 good for our hearts to be *s* by grace,

STRENGTHENING (STRONG)

1Co 14: 26 done for the *s* of the church.

STRETCHES

Ps 104: 2 he *s* out the heavens like a tent

STRICKEN (STRIKE)

Isa 53: 8 of my people he was *s*.

STRICT

1Co 9: 25 in the games goes into *s* training.

STRIFE (STRIVE)

Pr 17: 1 than a house full of feasting, with *s*.
20: 3 It is to a man's honor to avoid *s*,
22: 10 out the mocker, and out goes *s*;
30: 33 so stirring up anger produces *s*.''
1Ti 6: 4 *s*, malicious talk, evil suspicions

STRIKE (STRIKES STROKE)

Ge 3: 15 and you will *s* his heel.''
Zec 13: 7 ''S the shepherd,
Mt 4: 6 so that you will not *s* your foot
26: 31 '' 'I will *s* the shepherd,

STRIKES (STRIKE)

Mt 5: 39 If someone *s* you on the right

STRIPS

Lk 2: 12 You will find a baby wrapped in *s*
Jn 20: 5 in at the *s* of linen lying there

STRIVE* (STRIFE)

Ac 24: 16 I *s* always to keep my conscience
1Ti 4: 10 (and for this we labor and *s*),

STROKE (STRIKE)

Mt 5: 18 the smallest letter, not the least *s*

STRONG (STRENGTH STRENGTHEN STRENGTHENED STRENGTHENING STRONGER)

Dt 3: 24 your greatness and your *s* hand.
31: 6 Be *s* and courageous.
Jos 1: 6 ''Be *s* and courageous,
Jdg 5: 21 March on, my soul; be *s!*
2Sa 10: 12 Be *s* and let us fight bravely
1Ki 2: 2 ''So be *s*, show yourself a man,
1Ch 28: 20 ''Be *s* and courageous,
2Ch 32: 7 them with these words: ''Be *s*
Ps 24: 8 The LORD *s* and mighty,
31: 2 a *s* fortress to save me.
62: 11 that you, O God, are *s*,
Pr 18: 10 The name of the LORD is a *s* tower
31: 17 her arms are *s* for her tasks.
Ecc 9: 11 or the battle to the *s*,
SS 8: 6 for love is as *s* as death,
Isa 35: 4 ''Be *s*, do not fear;
53: 12 he will divide the spoils with the *s*,
Jer 9: 23 or the *s* man boast of his strength
50: 34 Yet their Redeemer is *s*;
Hag 2: 4 Be *s*, all you people of the land,'
Mt 12: 29 can anyone enter a *s* man's house
Lk 2: 40 And the child grew and became *s*;
Ro 15: 1 We who are *s* ought to bear
1Co 1: 8 He will keep you *s* to the end,
1: 27 things of the world to shame the *s*.
16: 13 in the faith; be men of courage; be *s*
2Co 12: 10 For when I am weak, then I am *s*.
Eph 6: 10 be *s* in the Lord and in his mighty
2Ti 2: 1 be *s* in the grace that is
1Pe 5: 10 restore you and make you *s*,

STRONGER (STRONG)

Dt 4: 38 before you nations greater and *s*
1Co 1: 25 of God is *s* than man's strength.

STRONGHOLD (STRONGHOLDS)

2Sa 22: 3 He is my *s*, my refuge and my
Ps 9: 9 a *s* in times of trouble.
18: 2 the horn of my salvation, my *s*.
27: 1 The LORD is the *s* of my life—
144: 2 my *s* and my deliverer,

STRONGHOLDS (STRONGHOLD)

Zep 3: 6 their *s* are demolished.
2Co 10: 4 have divine power to demolish *s*.

STRUGGLE (STRUGGLED STRUGGLING)

Ro 15: 30 me in my *s* by praying to God
Eph 6: 12 For our *s* is not against flesh
Heb 12: 4 In your *s* against sin, you have not

STRUGGLED (STRUGGLE)

Ge 32: 28 because you have *s* with God

STRUGGLING* (STRUGGLE)

Col 1: 29 To this end I labor, *s*
2: 1 to know how much I am *s* for you

STUDENT (STUDY)

Mt 10: 24 ''A *s* is not above his teacher,

STUDY (STUDENT)

Ezr 7: 10 Ezra had devoted himself to the *s*
Ecc 12: 12 and much *s* wearies the body.
Jn 5: 39 You diligently *s* the Scriptures

STUMBLE (STUMBLES STUMBLING)

Ps 37: 24 though he *s*, he will not fall,
119:165 and nothing can make them *s*.
Pr 3: 23 and your foot will not *s*;
Isa 8: 14 a stone that causes men to *s*
Jer 13: 16 before your feet *s*
31: 9 a level path where they will not *s*,
Eze 7: 19 for it has made them *s* into sin.
Hos 14: 9 but the rebellious *s* in them.
Mal 2: 8 teaching have caused many to *s*;
Jn 11: 9 A man who walks by day will not *s*,
Ro 9: 33 in Zion a stone that causes men to *s*
14: 20 that causes someone else to *s*.
1Co 10: 32 Do not cause anyone to *s*,
Jas 3: 2 We all *s* in many ways.
1Pe 2: 8 and, ''A stone that causes men to *s*
1Jn 2: 10 nothing in him to make him *s*.

STUMBLES (STUMBLE)

Pr 24: 17 when he *s*, do not let your heart
Jn 11: 10 is when he walks by night that he *s*,
Jas 2: 10 and yet *s* at just one point is guilty

STUMBLING (STUMBLE)

Lev 19: 14 put a *s* block in front of the blind,
Ps 56: 13 and my feet from *s*,
Mt 16: 23 Satan! You are a *s* block to me;
Ro 9: 32 They stumbled over the ''*s* stone.''
11: 9 a *s* block and a retribution for them
14: 13 up your mind not to put any *s* block
1Co 1: 23 a *s* block to Jews and foolishness
8: 9 freedom does not become a *s* block
2Co 6: 3 We put no *s* block in anyone's path,

STUMP

Isa 6: 13 so the holy seed will be the *s*
11: 1 up from the *s* of Jesse;

STUPID

Pr 12: 1 but he who hates correction is *s*.
2Ti 2: 23 to do with foolish and *s* arguments,

STUPOR

Ro 11: 8 ''God gave them a spirit of *s*,

SUBDUE (SUBDUED)

Ge 1: 28 in number; fill the earth and *s* it.

SUBDUED (SUBDUE)

Jos 10: 40 So Joshua *s* the whole region,
Ps 47: 3 He *s* nations under us,

SUBJECT (SUBJECTED)

Mt 5: 22 angry with his brother will be *s*
1Co 14: 32 of prophets are *s* to the control
15: 28 then the Son himself will be made *s*
Tit 2: 5 and to be *s* to their husbands,
2: 9 slaves to be *s* to their masters
3: 1 Remind the people to be *s* to rulers

SUBJECTED (SUBJECT)

Ro 8: 20 For the creation was *s*

SUBMISSION (SUBMIT)

1Co 14: 34 but must be in *s*, as the Law says.
1Ti 2: 11 learn in quietness and full *s*.

SUBMISSIVE (SUBMIT)

Jas 3: 17 then peace-loving, considerate, *s*,
1Pe 3: 1 in the same way be *s*
5: 5 in the same way be *s*

SUBMIT (SUBMISSION SUBMISSIVE SUBMITS)

Ro 13: 1 Everyone must *s* himself
   13: 5 necessary to *s* to the authorities,
1Co 16: 16 to *s* to such as these
Eph 5: 21 *S* to one another out of reverence
Col 3: 18 Wives, *s* to your husbands,
Heb 12: 9 How much more should we *s*
   13: 17 Obey your leaders and *s*
Jas 4: 7 *S* yourselves, then, to God.
1Pe 2: 18 *s* yourselves to your masters

SUBMITS* (SUBMIT)

Eph 5: 24 Now as the church *s* to Christ,

SUBTRACT*

Dt 4: 2 what I command you and do not *s*

SUCCEED (SUCCESS SUCCESSFUL)

Ps 20: 4 and make all your plans *s.*
Pr 15: 22 but with many advisers they *s.*
   16: 3 and your plans will *s.*
   21: 30 that can *s* against the LORD.

SUCCESS (SUCCEED)

Ge 39: 23 and gave him *s* in whatever he did.
1Sa 18: 14 In everything he did he had great *s,*
1Ch 12: 18 *S*, *s* to you, and *s*
   22: 13 you will have *s* if you are careful
2Ch 26: 5 the LORD, God gave him *s.*
Ecc 10: 10 but skill will bring *s.*

SUCCESSFUL (SUCCEED)

Jos 1: 7 that you may be *s* wherever you go.
2Ki 18: 7 he was *s* in whatever he undertook.
2Ch 20: 20 in his prophets and you will be *s.''*

SUFFER (SUFFERED SUFFERING SUFFERINGS SUFFERS)

Job 36: 15 those who *s* he delivers
Isa 53: 10 to crush him and cause him to *s,*
Mk 8: 31 the Son of Man must *s* many things
Lk 24: 26 the Christ have to *s* these things
   24: 46 The Christ will *s* and rise
2Co 1: 6 of the same sufferings we *s.*
Php 1: 29 to *s* for him, since you are going
Heb 9: 26 would have had to *s* many times
1Pe 3: 17 to *s* for doing good
   4: 16 However, if you *s* as a Christian,

SUFFERED (SUFFER)

Heb 2: 9 and honor because he *s* death,
   2: 18 Because he himself *s*
1Pe 2: 21 Christ *s* for you, leaving you
   4: 1 he who has *s* in his body is done

SUFFERING (SUFFER)

Job 36: 15 who suffer he delivers in their *s;*
Ps 22: 24 the *s* of the afflicted one;
Isa 53: 3 of sorrows, and familiar with *s.*
   53: 11 After the *s* of his soul,
La 1: 12 Is any *s* like my *s*
Ac 5: 41 worthy of *s* disgrace for the Name.
Ro 5: 3 know that *s* produces
2Ti 1: 8 But join with me in *s* for the gospel,
Heb 2: 10 of their salvation perfect through *s.*
   13: 3 as if you yourselves were *s.*
1Pe 4: 12 at the painful trial you are *s,*

SUFFERINGS (SUFFER)

Ro 5: 3 but we also rejoice in our *s,*
   8: 17 share in his *s* in order that we may
   8: 18 that our present *s* are not worth
2Co 1: 5 as the *s* of Christ flow
Php 3: 10 the fellowship of sharing in his *s,*
1Pe 4: 13 rejoice that you participate in the *s*
   5: 9 are undergoing the same kind of *s.*

SUFFERS (SUFFER)

Pr 13: 20 but a companion of fools *s* harm.
1Co 12: 26 If one part *s*, every part *s* with it;

SUFFICIENT

2Co 12: 9 said to me, "My grace is *s* for you,

SUITABLE

Ge 2: 18 I will make a helper *s* for him.''

SUMMED* (SUMS)

Ro 13: 9 there may be, are *s* up
Gal 5: 14 The entire law is *s* up

SUMMONS

Ps 50: 1 speaks and *s* the earth
Isa 45: 3 God of Israel, who *s* you by name.

SUMS* (SUMMED)

Mt 7: 12 for this *s* up the Law

SUN (SUNRISE)

Jos 10: 13 So the *s* stood still,
Jdg 5: 31 may they who love you be like the *s*
Ps 84: 11 For the LORD God is a *s*
   121: 6 the *s* will not harm you by day,
   136: 8 the *s* to govern the day,
Ecc 1: 9 there is nothing new under the *s.*
Isa 60: 19 The *s* will no more be your light
Mal 4: 2 the *s* of righteousness will rise
Mt 5: 45 He causes his *s* to rise on the evil
   13: 43 the righteous will shine like the *s*
   17: 2 His face shone like the *s,*
Lk 23: 45 for the *s* stopped shining.
Eph 4: 26 Do not let the *s* go
Rev 1: 16 His face was like the *s* shining
   21: 23 The city does not need the *s*

SUNG (SING)

Mt 26: 30 When they had *s* a hymn, they

SUNRISE (SUN)

2Sa 23: 4 he is like the light of morning at *s*
Hab 3: 4 His splendor was like the *s;*

SUPERIOR

Heb 1: 4 he became as much *s* to the angels
   8: 6 ministry Jesus has received is as *s*

SUPERVISION

Gal 3: 25 longer under the *s* of the law.

SUPPER

Lk 22: 20 after the *s* he took the cup, saying,
1Co 11: 25 after *s* he took the cup,
Rev 19: 9 to the wedding *s* of the Lamb!' ''

SUPPLIED (SUPPLY)

Ac 20: 34 of mine have *s* my own needs
Php 4: 18 and even more; I am amply *s,*

SUPPLY (SUPPLIED SUPPLYING)

2Co 8: 14 your plenty will *s* what they need,
1Th 3: 10 and *s* what is lacking in your faith.

SUPPLYING* (SUPPLY)

2Co 9: 12 you perform is not only *s* the needs

SUPPORT (SUPPORTED SUPPORTING)

Ps 18: 18 but the LORD was my *s.*
Ro 11: 18 consider this: You do not *s* the root
1Co 9: 12 If others have this right of *s*

SUPPORTED (SUPPORT)

Ps 94: 18 your love, O LORD, *s* me.
Col 2: 19 *s* and held together by its ligaments

SUPPORTING (SUPPORT)

Eph 4: 16 held together by every *s* ligament,

SUPPRESS*

Ro 1: 18 wickedness of men who *s* the truth

SUPREMACY* (SUPREME)

Col 1: 18 in everything he might have the *s.*

SUPREME (SUPREMACY)

Pr 4: 7 Wisdom is *s;* therefore get wisdom.

SURE

Nu 28: 31 Be *s* the animals are without defect
   32: 23 you may be *s* that your sin will find
Dt 6: 17 Be *s* to keep the commands
   14: 22 Be *s* to set aside a tenth
   29: 18 make *s* there is no root
Jos 23: 13 then you may be *s* that the LORD
1Sa 12: 24 But be *s* to fear the LORD
Ps 19: 9 The ordinances of the LORD are *s*
   132: 11 a *s* oath that he will not revoke:

SWAYED

Pr 27: 23 Be *s* you know the condition
Isa 28: 16 cornerstone for a *s* foundation;
Eph 5: 5 of this you can be *s:* No immoral,
Heb 11: 1 faith is being *s* of what we hope for
2Pe 1: 10 to make your calling and election *s.*

SURFACE

2Co 10: 7 You are looking only on the *s*

SURPASS* (SURPASSED SURPASSES SURPASSING)

Pr 31: 29 but you *s* them all.''

SURPASSED* (SURPASS)

Jn 1: 15 'He who comes after me has *s* me
   1: 30 man who comes after me has *s* me

SURPASSES* (SURPASS)

Pr 8: 19 what I yield *s* choice silver.
Mt 5: 20 unless your righteousness *s* that
Eph 3: 19 to know this love that *s* knowledge

SURPASSING* (SURPASS)

Ps 150: 2 praise him for his *s* greatness.
2Co 3: 10 in comparison with the *s* glory.
   9: 14 of the *s* grace God has given you.
Php 3: 8 the *s* greatness of knowing Christ

SURPRISE (SURPRISED)

1Th 5: 4 that this day should *s* you like

SURPRISED (SURPRISE)

1Pe 4: 12 do not be *s* at the painful trial you
1Jn 3: 13 Do not be *s,* my brothers,

SURRENDER

1Co 13: 3 and *s* my body to the flames,

SURROUND (SURROUNDED SURROUNDS)

Ps 5: 12 you *s* them with your favor
   32: 7 and *s* me with songs of deliverance.
   89: 7 awesome than all who *s* him.
   125: 2 As the mountains *s* Jerusalem,
Jer 31: 22 a woman will *s* a man.''

SURROUNDED (SURROUND)

Heb 12: 1 since we are *s* by such a great cloud

SURROUNDS* (SURROUND)

Ps 32: 10 *s* the man who trusts in him.
   89: 8 and your faithfulness *s* you.
   125: 2 so the LORD *s* his people

SUSA

Ezr 4: 9 and Babylon, the Elamites of *S,*
Ne 1: 1 while I was in the citadel of *S,*

SUSPENDS*

Job 26: 7 he *s* the earth over nothing.

SUSPICIONS*

1Ti 6: 4 evil *s* and constant friction

SUSTAIN (SUSTAINING SUSTAINS)

Ps 55: 22 and he will *s* you;
Isa 46: 4 I am he, I am he who will *s* you.

SUSTAINING* (SUSTAIN)

Heb 1: 3 *s* all things by his powerful word.

SUSTAINS (SUSTAIN)

Ps 18: 35 and your right hand *s* me;
   146: 9 and *s* the fatherless and the widow,
   147: 6 The LORD *s* the humble
Isa 50: 4 to know the word that *s* the weary.

SWALLOW (SWALLOWED)

Isa 25: 8 he will *s* up death forever.
Jnh 1: 17 provided a great fish to *s* Jonah,
Mt 23: 24 You strain out a gnat but *s* a camel.

SWALLOWED (SWALLOW)

1Co 15: 54 "Death has been *s* up in victory."
2Co 5: 4 so that what is mortal may be *s* up

SWAYED

Mt 11: 7 A reed *s* by the wind? If not,
   22: 16 You aren't *s* by men, because you

2Ti   3: 6 are *s* by all kinds of evil desires,

SWEAR (SWORE SWORN)
Lev 19: 12 '' 'Do not *s* falsely by my name
Ps   24: 4 or *s* by what is false.
Isa 45: 23 by me every tongue will *s.*
Mt   5: 34 Do not *s* at all: either by heaven,
Jas   5: 12 Above all, my brothers, do not *s*—

SWEAT*
Ge   3: 19 By the *s* of your brow
Lk 22: 44 his *s* was like drops of blood falling

SWEET (SWEETER SWEETNESS)
Job 20: 12 ''Though evil is *s* in his mouth
Ps 119:103 How *s* are your words
Pr   9: 17 ''Stolen water is *s;*
     13: 19 A longing fulfilled is *s* to the soul,
     16: 24 *s* to the soul and healing
     20: 17 by fraud tastes *s* to a man,
     24: 14 also that wisdom is *s* to your soul;
Ecc   5: 12 The sleep of a laborer is *s,*
Isa   5: 20 and *s* for bitter.
Eze   3: 3 it tasted as *s* as honey in my mouth.
Rev 10: 10 It tasted as *s* as honey in my mouth

SWEETER (SWEET)
Ps 19: 10 they are *s* than honey,
  119:103 *s* than honey to my mouth!

SWEETNESS* (SWEET)
SS   4: 11 Your lips drop *s* as the honeycomb,
    5: 16 His mouth is *s* itself;

SWEPT
Mt 12: 44 finds the house unoccupied, *s* clean

SWERVE*
Pr   4: 5 do not forget my words or *s*
    4: 27 Do not *s* to the right or the left;

SWIFT
Pr   1: 16 they are *s* to shed blood.
Ecc   9: 11 The race is not to the *s*
Isa 59: 7 they are *s* to shed innocent blood.
Ro   3: 15 ''Their feet are *s* to shed blood;
2Pe   2: 1 bringing *s* destruction

SWINDLER* (SWINDLERS)
1Co   5: 11 or a slanderer, a drunkard or a *s.*

SWINDLERS* (SWINDLER)
1Co   5: 10 or the greedy and *s,* or idolaters.
    6: 10 *s* will inherit the kingdom of God.

SWORD (SWORDS)
Ge   3: 24 and a flaming *s* flashing back
Dt 32: 41 when I sharpen my flashing *s*
Jos   5: 13 of him with a drawn *s* in his hand.
1Sa 17: 45 ''You come against me with *s*
     17: 47 here will know that it is not by *s*
     31: 4 so Saul took his own *s* and fell on it.
2Sa 12: 10 therefore, the *s* will never depart
Ps 44: 6 my *s* does not bring me victory;
     45: 3 Gird your *s* upon your side,
Pr 12: 18 Reckless words pierce like a *s,*
Isa   2: 4 Nation will not take up *s*
Mic   4: 3 Nation will not take up *s*
Mt 10: 34 come to bring peace, but a *s.*
     26: 52 all who draw the *s* will die by the *s.*
Lk   2: 35 a *s* will pierce your own soul too.''
Ro 13: 4 for he does not bear the *s*
Eph   6: 17 of salvation and the *s* of the Spirit,
Heb   4: 12 Sharper than any double-edged *s,*
Rev   1: 16 came a sharp double-edged *s.*
     19: 15 Out of his mouth comes a sharp *s*

SWORDS (SWORD)
Ps 64: 3 who sharpen their tongues like *s*
Isa   2: 4 They will beat their *s*
Joel   3: 10 Beat your plowshares into *s*

SWORE (SWEAR)
Heb   6: 13 for him to swear by, he *s* by himself

SWORN (SWEAR)
Ps 110: 4 The Lord has *s*
Eze 20: 42 the land I had *s* with uplifted hand
Heb   7: 21 ''The Lord has *s*

SYCAMORE-FIG (FIG)
Am   7: 14 and I also took care of *s* trees.
Lk 19: 4 and climbed a *s* tree to see him,

SYMBOLIZES*
1Pe   3: 21 this water *s* baptism that now saves

SYMPATHETIC* (SYMPATHY)
1Pe   3: 8 in harmony with one another; be *s,*

SYMPATHIZED* (SYMPATHY)
Heb 10: 34 You *s* with those in prison

SYMPATHY (SYMPATHETIC SYMPATHIZED)
Ps 69: 20 I looked for *s,* but there was none,

SYNAGOGUE
Lk   4: 16 the Sabbath day he went into the *s,*
Ac 17: 2 custom was, Paul went into the *s,*

TABERNACLE (TABERNACLES)
Ex 40: 34 the glory of the Lord filled the *t.*
Heb   8: 2 the true *t* set up by the Lord,
    9: 11 and more perfect *t* that is not
    9: 21 sprinkled with the blood both the *t*
Rev 15: 5 that is, the *t* of the Testimony.

TABERNACLES (TABERNACLE)
Lev 23: 34 the Lord's Feast of *T* begins,
Dt 16: 16 Feast of Weeks and the Feast of *T.*
Zec 14: 16 and to celebrate the Feast of *T.*

TABLE (TABLES)
Ex 25: 23 ''Make a *t* of acacia wood—
Ps 23: 5 You prepare a *t* before me

TABLES (TABLE)
Jn   2: 15 changers and overturned their *t.*
Ac   6: 2 word of God in order to wait on *t.*

TABLET (TABLETS)
Pr   3: 3 write them on the *t* of your heart.
    7: 3 write them on the *t* of your heart.

TABLETS (TABLET)
Ex 31: 18 he gave him the two *t*
Dt 10: 5 and put the *t* in the ark I had made,
2Co   3: 3 not on *t* of stone but on *t*

TAKE (TAKEN TAKES TAKING TOOK)
Ge 15: 7 land to *t* possession of it.''
     22: 17 Your descendants will *t* possession
Ex   3: 5 ''*T* off your sandals,
     21: 23 you are to *t* life for life, eye for eye,
     22: 22 ''Do not *t* advantage of a widow
Lev 10: 17 given to you to *t* away the guilt
     25: 14 do not *t* advantage of each other.
Nu 13: 30 and *t* possession of the land,
Dt   1: 8 and *t* possession of the land that
     12: 32 do not add to it or *t* away from it.
     31: 26 ''*T* this Book of the Law
1Sa 8: 11 He will *t* your sons and make them
1Ch 17: 13 I will never *t* my love away
Job 23: 10 But he knows the way that I *t;*
Ps   2: 12 Blessed are all who *t* refuge in him.
     25: 18 and *t* away all my sins.
     27: 14 be strong and *t* heart
     31: 24 Be strong and *t* heart,
     49: 17 for he will *t* nothing with him
     51: 11 or *t* your Holy Spirit from me.
     73: 24 afterward you will *t* me into glory.
    118: 8 It is better to *t* refuge in the Lord
Pr 22: 23 for the Lord will *t* up their case
Isa 62: 4 for the Lord will *t* delight in you,
Eze   3: 10 and *t* to heart all the words I speak
     33: 11 I *t* no pleasure in the death
Mt 10: 38 anyone who does not *t* his cross
     11: 29 *T* my yoke upon you and learn
     16: 24 deny himself and *t* up his cross
     26: 26 saying, ''*T* and eat; this is my body
Mk 14: 36 *T* this cup from me.
1Ti   6: 12 *T* hold of the eternal life

TAKEN (TAKE)
Ge   2: 23 for she was *t* out of man.''
Lev   6: 4 must return what he has stolen or *t*
Nu   8: 16 I have *t* them as my own in place

Nu 19: 3 it is to be *t* outside the camp
Ecc   3: 14 added to it and nothing *t* from it.
Isa   6: 7 your guilt is *t* away and your sin
Zec   3: 4 ''See, I have *t* away your sin,
Mt 13: 12 even what he has will be *t* from him
     24: 40 one will be *t* and the other left.
     26: 39 may this cup be *t* from me.
Mk 16: 19 he was *t* up into heaven
Ac   1: 9 he was *t* up before their very eyes,
Ro   5: 13 But sin is not *t* into account
1Ti   3: 16 was *t* up in glory.

TAKES (TAKE)
1Ki 20: 11 should not boast like one who *t* it
Ps   5: 4 You are not a God who *t* pleasure
     34: 8 blessed is the man who *t* refuge
Lk   6: 30 and if anyone *t* what belongs to you
Jn   1: 29 who *t* away the sin of the world!
     10: 18 No one *t* it from me, but I lay it
Rev 22: 19 And if anyone *t* words away

TAKING (TAKE)
Ac 15: 14 by *t* from the Gentiles a people
Php   2: 7 *t* the very nature of a servant,

TALENT
Mt 25: 15 to another one *t,* each according

TALES*
1Ti   4: 7 with godless myths and old wives' *t*

TALL
1Sa 17: 4 He was over nine feet *t.*
1Ch 11: 23 who was seven and a half feet *t.*

TAMAR
1. Wife of Judah's sons Er and Onan (Ge 38:
1-10). Tricked Judah into fathering children when
he refused her his third son (Ge 38:11-30).
2. Daughter of David, raped by Amnon (2Sa
13).

TAMBOURINE
Ps 150: 4 praise him with *t* and dancing,

TAME* (TAMED)
Jas   3: 8 but no man can *t* the tongue.

TAMED* (TAME)
Jas   3: 7 the sea are being *t* and have been *t*

TARSHISH
Jnh   1: 3 from the Lord and headed for *T.*

TARSUS
Ac   9: 11 ask for a man from *T* named Saul,

TASK (TASKS)
1Ch 29: 1 the *t* is great, because this palatial
Mk 13: 34 each with his assigned *t,*
Ac 20: 24 complete the *t* the Lord Jesus has
1Co   3: 5 the Lord has assigned to each his *t.*
2Co   2: 16 And who is equal to such a *t?*
1Ti   3: 1 an overseer, he desires a noble *t.*

TASKS (TASK)
Pr 31: 17 her arms are strong for her *t.*

TASTE (TASTED TASTY)
Ps 34: 8 *T* and see that the Lord is good;
  119:103 sweet are your words to my *t,*
Pr 24: 13 from the comb is sweet to your *t.*
SS   2: 3 and his fruit is sweet to my *t.*
Col   2: 21 Do not *t!* Do not touch!''?
Heb   2: 9 the grace of God he might *t* death

TASTED (TASTE)
Eze   3: 3 it *t* as sweet as honey in my mouth.
1Pe   2: 3 now that you have *t* that the Lord
Rev 10: 10 It *t* as sweet as honey in my mouth,

TASTY (TASTE)
Ge 27: 4 Prepare me the kind of *t* food I like

TATTOO*
Lev 19: 28 or put *t* marks on yourselves.

TAUGHT (TEACH)
1Ki 4: 33 He also *t* about animals and birds,

2Ki 17: 28 *t* them how to worship the LORD.
2Ch 17: 9 They *t* throughout Judah,
Ps 119:102 for you yourself have *t* me.
Pr 4: 4 he *t* me and said,
       31: 1 an oracle his mother *t* him:
Isa 29: 13 is made up only of rules *t* by men.
       50: 4 ear to listen like one being *t*.
Mt 7: 29 he *t* as one who had authority,
       15: 9 their teachings are but rules *t*
Lk 4: 15 He *t* in their synagogues,
Ac 20: 20 have *t* you publicly and from house
1Co 2: 13 but in words *t* by the Spirit,
Gal 1: 12 nor was I *t* it; rather, I received it
1Ti 1: 20 to Satan to be *t* not to blaspheme.
1Jn 2: 27 just as it has *t* you, remain in him.

TAX (TAXES)
Mt 11: 19 a friend of *t* collectors and "sinners
       17: 24 of the two-drachma *t* came to Peter

TAXES (TAX)
Mt 22: 17 Is it right to pay *t* to Caesar or not
Ro 13: 7 If you owe *t*, pay *t*; if revenue,

**TEACH (TAUGHT TEACHER TEACHERS
TEACHES TEACHING TEACHINGS)**
Ex 4: 12 and will *t* you what to say."
       18: 20 Them the decrees and laws,
       33: 13 *t* me your ways so I may know you
Lev 10: 11 and you must *t* the Israelites all
Dt 4: 9 T them to your children
       6: 1 me to *t* you to observe
       8: 3 to *t* you that man does not live
       11: 19 T them to your children, talking
1Sa 12: 23 I will *t* you the way that is good
1Ki 8: 36 T them the right way to live,
Job 12: 7 ask the animals, and they will *t* you
Ps 32: 8 *t* you in the way you should go;
       34: 11 I will *t* you the fear of the LORD.
       51: 13 I will *t* transgressors your ways,
       78: 5 forefathers to *t* their children,
       90: 12 T us to number our days aright,
       119: 33 T me, O LORD, to follow your
       143: 10 T me to do your will,
Pr 9: 9 *t* a righteous man and he will add
Jer 31: 34 No longer will a man *t* his neighbor
Mic 4: 2 He will *t* us his ways,
Lk 11: 1 said to him, "Lord, *t* us to pray,
       12: 12 for the Holy Spirit will *t* you
Jn 14: 26 will *t* you all things and will remind
Ro 2: 21 who *t* others, do you not *t* yourself?
       15: 4 in the past was written to *t* us,
1Ti 2: 12 I do not permit a woman to *t*
       3: 2 respectable, hospitable, able to *t*,
2Ti 2: 2 also be qualified to *t* others.
       2: 24 kind to everyone, able to *t*,
Tit 2: 1 You must *t* what is in accord
       2: 15 then, are the things you should *t*.
Heb 8: 11 No longer will a man *t* his neighbor
Jas 3: 1 know that we who *t* will be judged
1Jn 2: 27 you do not need anyone to *t* you.

TEACHER (TEACH)
Ecc 1: 1 The words of the T, son of David,
Mt 10: 24 "A student is not above his *t*,
       13: 52 "Therefore every *t*
       23: 10 Nor are you to be called '*t*,'
Lk 6: 40 A student is not above his *t*,
Jn 3: 2 we know you are a *t* who has come
       13: 14 and T, have washed your feet,

TEACHERS (TEACH)
Ps 119: 99 I have more insight than all my *t*,
Pr 5: 13 I would not obey my *t*
Lk 20: 46 "Beware of the *t* of the law.
1Co 12: 28 third *t*, then workers of miracles,
Eph 4: 11 and some to be pastors and *t*,
2Ti 4: 3 around them a great number of *t*
Heb 5: 12 by this time you ought to be *t*,
Jas 3: 1 of you should presume to be *t*,
2Pe 2: 1 as there will be false *t* among you.

TEACHES (TEACH)
Ps 25: 9 and *t* them his way.
       94: 10 Does he who *t* man lack
Pr 15: 33 of the LORD *t* a man wisdom,
Isa 48: 17 who *t* you what is best for you,
Mt 5: 19 *t* these commands will be called

1Ti 6: 3 If anyone *t* false doctrines
Tit 2: 12 It *t* us to say "No" to ungodliness
1Jn 2: 27 his anointing *t* you about all things

TEACHING (TEACH)
Ezr 7: 10 to *t* its decrees and laws in Israel.
Pr 1: 8 and do not forsake your mother's *t*.
       3: 1 My son, do not forget my *t*,
       6: 23 this *t* is a light,
Mt 28: 20 *t* them to obey everything I have
Jn 7: 17 whether my *t* comes from God or
       8: 31 to my *t*, you are really my disciples.
       14: 23 loves me, he will obey my *t*.
Ac 2: 42 themselves to the apostles' *t*
Ro 12: 7 let him serve; if it is *t*, let him teach;
Eph 4: 14 and there by every wind of *t*
2Th 3: 6 to the *t* you received from us.
1Ti 4: 13 of Scripture, to preaching and to *t*.
       5: 17 whose work is preaching and *t*.
       6: 3 Lord Jesus Christ and to godly *t*,
2Ti 3: 16 is God-breathed and is useful for *t*,
Tit 1: 11 by *t* things they ought not
       2: 7 In your *t* show integrity,
Heb 5: 13 with the *t* about righteousness.
2Jn : 9 and does not continue in the *t*

TEACHINGS (TEACH)
Pr 7: 2 guard my *t* as the apple of your eye.
2Th 2: 15 hold to the *t* we passed on to you,
Heb 6: 1 leave the elementary *t* about Christ

TEAR (TEARS)
Rev 7: 17 God will wipe away every *t*
       21: 4 He will wipe every *t*

TEARS (TEAR)
Ps 126: 5 Those who sow in *t*
Isa 25: 8 LORD will wipe away the *t*
Jer 31: 16 and your eyes from *t*,
       50: 4 in *t* to seek the LORD their God.
Lk 7: 38 she began to wet his feet with her *t*,
2Co 2: 4 anguish of heart and with many *t*,
Php 3: 18 and now say again even with *t*,

TEETH (TOOTH)
Job 19: 20 with only the skin of my *t*.
Ps 35: 16 they gnashed their *t* at me.
Jer 31: 29 and the children's *t* are set on edge
Mt 8: 12 will be weeping and gnashing of *t*."

**TEMPER (EVEN-TEMPERED
HOT-TEMPERED ILL-TEMPERED
QUICK-TEMPERED)**
Pr 16: 32 a man who controls his *t*

TEMPERANCE see SELF-CONTROL

TEMPERATE*
1Ti 3: 2 *t*, self-controlled, respectable,
       3: 11 not malicious talkers but *t*
Tit 2: 2 Teach the older men to be *t*,

TEMPEST
Ps 50: 3 and around him a *t* rages.
       55: 8 far from the *t* and storm."

TEMPLE (TEMPLES)
1Ki 6: 1 began to build the *t* of the LORD.
       6: 38 the *t* was finished in all its details
       8: 10 the cloud filled the *t* of the LORD.
       8: 27 How much less this *t* I have built!
2Ch 36: 19 They set fire to God's *t*
       36: 23 me to build a *t* for him at Jerusalem
Ezr 6: 14 finished building the *t* according
Ps 27: 4 and to seek him in his *t*.
Isa 6: 1 and the train of his robe filled the *t*.
Eze 10: 4 cloud filled the *t*, and the court was
       43: 4 glory of the LORD entered the *t*
Hab 2: 20 But the LORD is in his holy *t*;
Mt 12: 6 that one greater than the *t* is here.
       26: 61 'I am able to destroy the *t* of God
       27: 51 of the *t* was torn in two from top
Lk 21: 5 about how the *t* was adorned
Jn 2: 14 In the *t* courts he found men selling
1Co 3: 16 that you yourselves are God's *t*
       6: 19 you not know that your body is a *t*
2Co 6: 16 For we are the *t* of the living God.
Rev 21: 22 I did not see a *t* in the city,

TEMPLES (TEMPLE)
Ac 17: 24 does not live in *t* built by hands.

TEMPORARY
2Co 4: 18 what is seen is *t*, but what is unseen

TEMPT* **(TEMPTATION TEMPTED
TEMPTER TEMPTING)**
1Co 7: 5 again so that Satan will not *t* you
Jas 1: 13 does he *t* anyone; but each one is

TEMPTATION* **(TEMPT)**
Mt 6: 13 And lead us not into *t*,
       26: 41 pray so that you will not fall into *t*.
Mk 14: 38 pray so that you will not fall into *t*.
Lk 4: 1 And lead us not into *t*.'
       22: 40 "Pray that you will not fall into *t*."
       22: 46 pray so that you will not fall into *t*
1Co 10: 13 No *t* has seized you except what is
1Ti 6: 9 want to get rich fall into *t*

TEMPTED* **(TEMPT)**
Mt 4: 1 into the desert to be *t* by the devil.
Mk 1: 13 was in the desert forty days, being *t*
Lk 4: 2 for forty days he was *t* by the devil.
1Co 10: 13 But when you are *t*, he will
       10: 13 he will not let you be *t*
Gal 6: 1 yourself, or you also may be *t*.
1Th 3: 5 way the tempter might have *t* you
Heb 2: 18 able to help those who are being *t*.
       2: 18 he himself suffered when he was *t*,
       4: 15 but we have one who has been *t*
Jas 1: 13 For God cannot be *t* by evil,
       1: 13 When *t*, no one should say,
       1: 14 each one is *t* when, by his own evil

TEMPTER* **(TEMPT)**
Mt 4: 3 The *t* came to him and said,
1Th 3: 5 some way the *t* might have

TEMPTING* **(TEMPT)**
Lk 4: 13 the devil had finished all this *t*,
Jas 1: 13 no one should say, "God is *t* me."

TEN (TENTH TITHE TITHES)
Ex 34: 28 covenant—the T Commandments.
Lev 26: 8 of you will chase *t* thousand,
Dt 4: 13 covenant, the T Commandments,
       10: 4 The T Commandments he had
Ps 91: 7 *t* thousand at your right hand,
Da 7: 24 *t* horns are *t* kings who will come
Mt 25: 1 will be like *t* virgins who took
       25: 28 it to the one who has the *t* talents.
Lk 15: 8 suppose a woman has *t* silver coins
Rev 12: 3 and *t* horns and seven crowns

TENANTS
Mt 21: 34 servants to the *t* to collect his fruit.

TEND
Jer 23: 2 to the shepherds who *t* my people:
Eze 34: 14 I will *t* them in a good pasture,

TENDERNESS*
Isa 63: 15 Your *t* and compassion are
Php 2: 1 fellowship with the Spirit, if any *t*

TENT (TENTMAKER TENTS)
Ex 27: 21 In the T of Meeting,
       40: 2 "Set up the tabernacle, the T
Isa 54: 2 "Enlarge the place of your *t*,
2Co 5: 1 that if the earthly *t* we live
2Pe 1: 13 as long as I live in the *t* of this body,

TENTH (TEN)
Ge 14: 20 Abram gave him a *t* of everything.
Nu 18: 26 you must present a *t* of that tithe
Dt 14: 22 Be sure to set aside a *t*
1Sa 8: 15 He will take a *t* of your grain
Lk 11: 42 you give God a *t* of your mint,
       18: 12 I fast twice a week and give a *t*
Heb 7: 4 patriarch Abraham gave him a *t*

TENTMAKER* **(TENT)**
Ac 18: 3 and because he was a *t* as they were

TENTS (TENT)
Ge 13: 12 and pitched his *t* near Sodom.

TERAH (first column)

Ps 84: 10 than dwell in the *t* of the wicked.

TERAH
Ge 11: 31 *T* took his son Abram, his

TERRIBLE (TERROR)
2Ti 3: 1 There will be *t* times

TERRIFIED (TERROR)
Dt 7: 21 Do not be *t* by them,
    20: 3 do not be *t* or give way to panic
Ps 90: 7 and *t* by your indignation.
Mt 14: 26 walking on the lake, they were *t*.
    17: 6 they fell facedown to the ground, *t*.
    27: 54 they were *t*, and exclaimed,
Mk 4: 41 They were *t* and asked each other,

TERRIFYING (TERROR)
Heb 12: 21 The sight was so *t* that Moses said,

TERRITORY
2Co 10: 16 done in another man's *t*.

TERROR (TERRIBLE TERRIFIED TERRIFYING)
Dt 2: 25 very day I will begin to put the *t*
    28: 67 of the *t* that will fill your hearts
Job 9: 34 so that his *t* would frighten me no
Ps 91: 5 You will not fear the *t* of night,
Pr 21: 15 but *t* to evildoers.
Isa 8: 7 *T* will seize them,
    24: 17 *T* and pit and snare await you,
    51: 13 live in constant *t* every day
    54: 14 *T* will be far removed;
Lk 21: 26 Men will faint from *t*, apprehensive
Ro 13: 3 For rulers hold no *t*

TEST (TESTED TESTING TESTS)
Dt 6: 16 Do not *t* the LORD your God
Jdg 3: 1 to *t* all those Israelites who had not
1Ki 10: 1 came to *t* him with hard questions.
1Ch 29: 17 the heart and are pleased
Ps 26: 2 *T* me, O LORD, and try me,
    78: 18 They willfully put God to the *t*
    106: 14 wasteland they put God to the *t*.
    139: 23 *t* me and know my anxious
Jer 11: 20 and *t* the heart and mind,
Lk 4: 12 put the Lord your God to the *t*.' ''
Ac 5: 9 How could you agree to *t* the Spirit
Ro 12: 2 Then you will be able to *t*
1Co 3: 13 and the fire will *t* the quality
    10: 9 We should not *t* the Lord,
2Co 13: 5 unless, of course, you fail the *t*?
1Th 5: 21 *T* everything.
Jas 1: 12 because when he has stood the *t*,
1Jn 4: 1 *t* the spirits to see whether they are

TESTAMENT see COVENANT

TESTED (TEST)
Ge 22: 1 Some time later God *t* Abraham.
Job 23: 10 when he has *t* me, I will come forth
    34: 36 that Job might be *t* to the utmost
Ps 66: 10 For you, O God, *t* us;
Pr 27: 21 man is *t* by the praise he receives.
Isa 28: 16 a *t* stone,
    48: 10 I have *t* you in the furnace
1Ti 3: 10 They must first be *t*; and then
Heb 11: 17 By faith Abraham, when God *t* him

TESTIFIES (TESTIFY)
Jn 5: 32 There is another who *t* in my favor,
Ro 8: 16 The Spirit himself *t*

TESTIFY (TESTIFIES TESTIMONY)
Pr 24: 28 Do not *t* against your neighbor
Jn 1: 7 a witness to *t* concerning that light,
    1: 34 and I *t* that this is the Son of God.''
    5: 39 are the Scriptures that *t* about me,
    7: 7 because I *t* that what it does is evil.
    15: 26 he will *t* about me. And you
Ac 4: 33 continued to *t* to the resurrection
    10: 43 All the prophets *t* about him that
2Ti 1: 8 ashamed to *t* about our Lord,
1Jn 4: 14 *t* that the Father has sent his Son
    5: 7 For there are three that *t*: the Spirit

TESTIMONY (TESTIFY)
Ex 20: 16 ''You shall not give false *t*

Ex 31: 18 gave him the two tablets of the *T*,
Nu 35: 30 only on the *t* of witnesses.
Dt 19: 18 giving false *t* against his brother,
Pr 12: 17 A truthful witness gives honest *t*,
Isa 8: 20 and to the *t*! If they do not speak
Mt 15: 19 sexual immorality, theft, false *t*,
    24: 14 preached in the whole world as a *t*
Lk 18: 20 not give false *t*, honor your father
Jn 2: 25 He did not need man's *t* about man
    21: 24 We know that his *t* is true.
1Jn 5: 9 but God's *t* is greater because it is
Rev 12: 11 and by the word of their *t*;

TESTING (TEST)
Lk 8: 13 but in the time of *t* they fall away.
Heb 3: 8 during the time of *t* in the desert,
Jas 1: 3 because you know that the *t*

TESTS (TEST)
Pr 17: 3 but the LORD *t* the heart.
1Th 2: 4 but God, who *t* our hearts.

THADDAEUS
Apostle (Mt 10:3; Mk 3:18); probably also known as Judas son of James (Lk 6:16; Ac 1:13).

THANK (THANKFUL THANKFULNESS THANKS THANKSGIVING)
Php 1: 3 I *t* my God every time I remember
1Th 3: 9 How can we *t* God enough for you

THANKFUL (THANK)
Col 3: 15 And be *t*.
Heb 12: 28 let us be *t*, and so worship God

THANKFULNESS (THANK)
1Co 10: 30 If I take part in the meal with *t*,
Col 2: 7 taught, and overflowing with *t*.

THANKS (THANK)
1Ch 16: 8 Give *t* to the LORD, call
Ne 12: 31 assigned two large choirs to give *t*.
Ps 7: 17 I will give *t* to the LORD
    28: 7 and I will give *t* to him in song.
    30: 12 my God, I will give you *t* forever.
    35: 18 I will give you *t* in the great
    75: 1 we give *t*, for your Name is near;
    100: 4 give *t* to him and praise his name.
    107: 1 Give *t* to the LORD, for he is good;
    118: 28 are my God, and I will give you *t*;
    136: 1 Give *t* to the LORD, for he is good.
Ro 1: 21 as God nor gave *t* to him,
1Co 11: 24 when he had given *t*, he broke it
    15: 57 *t* be to God! He gives us the victory
2Co 2: 14 be to God, who always leads us
    9: 15 *T* be to God for his indescribable
1Th 5: 18 give *t* in all circumstances,
Rev 4: 9 and *t* to him who sits on the throne

THANKSGIVING (THANK)
Ps 95: 2 Let us come before him with *t*
    100: 4 Enter his gates with *t*
1Co 10: 16 cup of *t* for which we give thanks
Php 4: 6 by prayer and petition, with *t*,
1Ti 4: 3 created to be received with *t*

THEFT (THIEF)
Mt 15: 19 sexual immorality, *t*, false

THEFTS* (THIEF)
Rev 9: 21 their sexual immorality or their *t*.

THEME*
Ps 45: 1 My heart is stirred by a noble *t*
    119: 54 Your decrees are the *t* of my song

THIEF (THEFT THEFTS THIEVES)
Ex 22: 3 A *t* must certainly make restitution
Pr 6: 30 Men do not despise a *t* if he steals
Lk 12: 39 at what hour the *t* was coming,
1Th 5: 2 day of the Lord will come like a *t*
1Pe 4: 15 or *t* or any other kind of criminal,
Rev 16: 15 I come like a *t*! Blessed is he who

THIEVES (THIEF)
Mt 6: 19 and where *t* break in and steal.
Jn 10: 8 who ever came before me were *t*,
1Co 6: 10 nor homosexual offenders nor *t*

THINK (THINKING THOUGHT THOUGHTS)
Ps 63: 6 I *t* of you through the watches
Isa 44: 19 No one stops to *t*,
Mt 22: 42 ''What do you *t* about the Christ?
Ro 12: 3 Do not *t* of yourself more highly
Php 4: 8 praiseworthy—*t* about such things

THINKING (THINK)
Pr 23: 7 who is always *t* about the cost.
1Co 14: 20 Brothers, stop *t* like children.
2Pe 3: 1 to stimulate you to wholesome *t*.

THIRST (THIRSTS THIRSTY)
Ps 69: 21 and gave me vinegar for my *t*.
Mt 5: 6 Blessed are those who hunger and *t*
Jn 4: 14 the water I give him will never *t*.
2Co 11: 27 I have known hunger and *t*,
Rev 7: 16 never again will they *t*.

THIRSTS (THIRST)
Ps 42: 2 My soul *t* for God,

THIRSTY (THIRST)
Ps 107: 9 for he satisfies the *t*
Pr 25: 21 if he is *t*, give him water to drink.
Isa 55: 1 ''Come, all you who are *t*,
Mt 25: 35 I was *t* and you gave me something
Jn 7: 37 ''If anyone is *t*, let him come to me
Ro 12: 20 if he is *t*, give him something
Rev 21: 6 To him who is *t* I will give to drink
    22: 17 Whoever is *t*, let him come;

THOMAS
Apostle (Mt 10:3; Mk 3:18; Lk 6:15; Jn 11:16; 14:5; 21:2; Ac 1:13). Doubted resurrection (Jn 20: 24-28).

THONGS
Mk 1: 7 *t* of whose sandals I am not worthy

THORN (THORNBUSHES THORNS)
2Co 12: 7 there was given me a *t* in my flesh,

THORNBUSHES (THORN)
Lk 6: 44 People do not pick figs from *t*,

THORNS (THORN)
Ge 3: 18 It will produce *t* and thistles
Nu 33: 55 in your eyes and *t* in your sides.
Mt 13: 7 fell among *t*, which grew up
    27: 29 and then twisted together a crown of *t*
Heb 6: 8 But land that produces *t*,

THOUGHT (THINK)
Pr 14: 15 a prudent man gives *t* to his steps.
    21: 29 an upright man gives *t* to his ways.
1Co 13: 11 I talked like a child, I *t* like a child,

THOUGHTS (THINK)
1Ch 28: 9 every motive behind the *t*.
Ps 94: 11 The LORD knows the *t* of man;
    139: 23 test me and know my anxious *t*.
Isa 55: 8 ''For my *t* are not your *t*,
Mt 15: 19 For out of the heart come evil *t*,
1Co 2: 11 among men knows the *t* of a man
Heb 4: 12 it judges the *t* and attitudes

THREE
Ge 6: 10 Noah had *t* sons: Shem, Ham
Ex 23: 14 ''*T* times a year you are
Dt 19: 15 the testimony of two or *t* witnesses.
2Sa 23: 8 a Tahkemonite, was chief of the *T*;
Pr 30: 15 ''There are *t* things that are never
    30: 18 ''There are *t* things that are too
    30: 21 ''Under *t* things the earth trembles,
    30: 29 ''There are *t* things that are stately
Ecc 4: 12 of *t* strands is not quickly broken.
Da 3: 24 ''Weren't there *t* men that we tied up
Am 1: 3 ''For *t* sins of Damascus,
Jnh 1: 17 inside the fish *t* days and *t* nights.
Mt 12: 40 so the Son of Man will be *t*
    12: 40 *t* nights in the belly of a huge fish,
    12: 40 *t* nights in the heart of the earth.
    17: 4 I will put up *t* shelters—one
    18: 20 or *t* come together in my name,
    26: 34 you will disown me *t* times.''
    26: 75 you will disown me *t* times.''

Mt 27:63 'After t days I will rise again.'
Mk 8:31 and after t days rise again.
9: 5 Let us put up t shelters—one
14:30 yourself will disown me t times.''
Jn 2:19 and I will raise it again in t days.''
1Co 13:13 And now these t remain: faith,
14:27 or at the most t— should speak,
2Co 13: 1 testimony of two or t witnesses.''
1Jn 5: 7 For there are t that testify:

THRESHER* (THRESHING)

1Co 9:10 plowman plows and the t threshes,

THRESHING (THRESHER)

Ru 3: 6 So she went down to the t floor
2Sa 24:18 an altar to the LORD on the t floor
Lk 3:17 is in his hand to clear his t floor

THREW (THROW)

Da 6:16 and t him into the lions' den.
Jnh 1:15 took Jonah and t him overboard,

THRIVE

Pr 29: 2 When the righteous t, the people

THROAT (THROATS)

Ps 5: 9 Their t is an open grave;
Pr 23: 2 and put a knife to your t

THROATS (THROAT)

Ro 3:13 ''Their t are open graves;

THROB*

Isa 60: 5 your heart will t and swell with joy;

THRONE (ENTHRONED ENTHRONES THRONES)

2Sa 7:16 your t will be established forever
1Ch 17:12 and I will establish his t forever.
Ps 11: 4 the LORD is on his heavenly t,
45: 6 Your t, O God, will last for ever
47: 8 God is seated on his holy t.
89:14 justice are the foundation of your t;
Isa 6: 1 I saw the Lord seated on a t,
66: 1 ''Heaven is my t,
Eze 28: 2 I sit on the t of a god
Da 7: 9 His t was flaming with fire,
Mt 19:28 Son of Man sits on his glorious t,
Ac 7:49 prophet says: '' 'Heaven is my t,
Heb 1: 8 ''Your t, O God, will last for ever
4:16 Let us then approach the t of grace
12: 2 at the right hand of the t of God.
Rev 3:21 sat down with my Father on his t.
3:21 the right to sit with me on my t,
4: 2 there before me was a t in heaven
4:10 They lay their crowns before the t
20:11 Then I saw a great white t
22: 3 t of God and of the Lamb will be

THRONES (THRONE)

Mt 19:28 me will also sit on twelve t,
Rev 4: 4 throne were twenty-four other t,

THROW (THREW)

Jn 8: 7 the first to t a stone at her.''
Heb 10:35 So do not t away your confidence;
12: 1 let us t off everything that hinders

THUNDER (THUNDERS)

Ps 93: 4 Mightier than the t
Mk 3:17 which means Sons of T); Andrew,

THUNDERS (THUNDER)

Job 37: 5 God's voice t in marvelous ways;
Ps 29: 3 the God of glory t,
Rev 10: 3 the voices of the seven t spoke.

THWART* (THWARTED)

Isa 14:27 has purposed, and who can t him?

THWARTED (THWART)

Job 42: 2 no plan of yours can be t.

THYATIRA

Rev 2:18 the angel of the church in T write:

TIBNI

King of Israel (1Ki 16:21-22).

TIDINGS

Isa 40: 9 You who bring good t to Jerusalem
52: 7 who bring good t,

TIES

Hos 11: 4 with t of love;
Mt 12:29 unless he first t up the strong man?

TIGHT*

Jas 1:26 and yet does not keep a t rein

TIGHTFISTED*

Dt 15: 7 or t toward your poor brother.

TIME (TIMES)

Est 4:14 come to royal position for such a t
Ecc 3: 1 There is a t for everything,
8: 5 wise heart will know the proper t
Da 7:25 to him for a t, times and half a t.
12: 7 ''It will be for a t, times and half a t.
Hos 10:12 for it is t to seek the LORD,
Jn 2: 4 Jesus replied, ''My t has not yet
17: 1 prayed: ''Father, the t has come.
Ro 9: 9 ''At the appointed t I will return,
13:11 understanding the present t.
1Co 7:29 brothers, is that the t is short.
2Co 6: 2 now is the t of God's favor,
2Ti 1: 9 Jesus before the beginning of t,
Tit 1: 2 promised before the beginning of t,
Heb 9:28 and he will appear a second t,
10:12 for all t one sacrifice for sins,
1Pe 4:17 For it is t for judgment to begin

TIMES (TIME)

Ps 9: 9 a stronghold in t of trouble.
31:15 My t are in your hands;
62: 8 Trust in him at all t, O people;
Pr 17:17 A friend loves at all t,
Isa 46:10 from ancient t, what is still to come
Am 5:13 for the t are evil.
Mt 16: 3 cannot interpret the signs of the t.
18:21 how many t shall I forgive my
Ac 1: 7 ''It is not for you to know the t
Rev 12:14 t and half a time, out

TIMID (TIMIDITY)

1Th 5:14 encourage the t, help the weak,

TIMIDITY* (TIMID)

2Ti 1: 7 For God did not give us a spirit of t

TIMOTHY

Believer from Lystra (Ac 16:1). Joined Paul on second missionary journey (Ac 16-20). Sent to settle problems at Corinth (1Co 4:17; 16:10). Led church at Ephesus (1Ti 1:3). Co-writer with Paul (1Th 1:1; 2Th 1:1; Phm 1).

TIP

Job 33: 2 my words are on the t of my tongue

TIRE (TIRED)

2Th 3:13 never t of doing what is right.

TIRED (TIRE)

Ex 17:12 When Moses' hands grew t,
Isa 40:28 He will not grow t or weary,

TITHE (TEN)

Lev 27:30 '' 'A t of everything from the land,
Dt 12:17 eat in your own towns the t
Mal 3:10 the whole t into the storehouse,

TITHES (TEN)

Nu 18:21 give to the Levites all the t in Israel
Mal 3: 8 'How do we rob you?'' ''In t

TITUS*

Gentile co-worker of Paul (Gal 2:1-3; 2Ti 4: 10); sent to Corinth (2Co 2:13; 7-8; 12:18), Crete (Tit 1:4-5).

TODAY

Ps 2: 7 t I have become your Father.
95: 7 T, if you hear his voice,
Mt 6:11 Give us t our daily bread.
Lk 2:11 T in the town of David a Savior has
23:43 t you will be with me in paradise.''

Ac 13:33 t I have become your Father.'
Heb 1: 5 t I have become your Father''?
3: 7 ''T, if you hear his voice,
3:13 daily, as long as it is called T,
5: 5 t I have become your Father.''
13: 8 Christ is the same yesterday and t

TOIL (TOILED TOILING)

Ge 3:17 through painful t you will eat of it

TOILED (TOIL)

2Co 11:27 and t and have often gone

TOILING (TOIL)

2Th 3: 8 t so that we would not be a burden

TOLERANCE* (TOLERATE)

Ro 2: 4 for the riches of his kindness, t

TOLERATE (TOLERANCE)

Hab 1:13 you cannot t wrong.
Rev 2: 2 that you cannot t wicked men,

TOMB

Mt 27:65 make the t as secure as you know
Lk 24: 2 the stone rolled away from the t,

TOMORROW

Pr 27: 1 Do not boast about t,
Isa 22:13 ''for t we die!''
Mt 6:34 Therefore do not worry about t,
1Co 15:32 for t we die.''
Jas 4:13 ''Today or t we will go to this

TONGUE (TONGUES)

Ex 4:10 I am slow of speech and t.''
Job 33: 2 my words are on the tip of my t.
Ps 5: 9 with their t they speak deceit.
34:13 keep your t from evil
37:30 and his t speaks what is just.
39: 1 and keep my t from sin;
51:14 my t will sing of your righteousness
52: 4 O you deceitful t!
71:24 My t will tell of your righteous acts
119:172 May my t sing of your word,
137: 6 May my t cling to the roof
139: 4 Before a word is on my t
Pr 6:17 a lying t,
10:19 but he who holds his t is wise.
12:18 but the t of the wise brings healing.
15: 4 The t that brings healing is a tree
17:20 he whose t is deceitful falls
21:23 He who guards his mouth and his t
25:15 and a gentle t can break a bone.
26:28 A lying t hates those it hurts,
28:23 than he who has a flattering t.
31:26 and faithful instruction is on her t.
SS 4:11 milk and honey are under your t.
Isa 32: 4 and the stammering t will be fluent
45:23 by me every t will swear.
50: 4 has given me an instructed t,
59: 3 and your t mutters wicked things.
Lk 16:24 of his finger in water and cool my t,
Ro 14:11 every t will confess to God.' ''
1Co 14: 2 speaks in a t does not speak to men
14: 4 He who speaks in a t edifies himself
14: 9 intelligible words with your t,
14:13 in a t should pray that he may
14:19 than ten thousand words in a t.
14:26 revelation, a t or an interpretation.
14:27 If anyone speaks in a t, two—
Php 2:11 every t confess that Jesus Christ is
Jas 1:26 does not keep a tight rein on his t,
3: 5 Likewise the t is a small part
3: 8 but no man can tame the t.
1Jn 3:18 or t but with actions and in truth.

TONGUES (TONGUE)

Ps 12: 4 ''We will triumph with our t;
126: 2 our t with songs of joy.
Isa 28:11 with foreign lips and strange t
66:18 and gather all nations and, t
Jer 23:31 the prophets who wag their own t
Mk 16:17 in new t; they will pick up snakes
Ac 2: 3 to be t of fire that separated
2: 4 and began to speak in other t
10:46 For they heard them speaking in t
19: 6 and they spoke in t and prophesied

Ro   3: 13 their *t* practice deceit.''
1Co 12: 10 still another the interpretation of *t*.
     12: 28 speaking in different kinds of *t*.
     12: 30 Do all speak in *t*? Do all interpret?
     13: 1 If I speak in the *t* of men
     13: 8 where there are *t*, they will be
     14: 5 greater than one who speaks in *t*,
     14: 18 speak in *t* more than all of you.
     14: 21 ''Through men of strange *t*
     14: 39 and do not forbid speaking in *t*.

TOOK (TAKE)

Isa 53: 4 Surely he *t* up our infirmities
Mt   8: 17 ''He *t* up our infirmities
    26: 26 they were eating, Jesus *t* bread,
    26: 27 Then he *t* the cup, gave thanks
1Co 11: 23 the night he was betrayed, *t* bread,
    11: 25 after supper he *t* the cup, saying,
Php 3: 12 for which Christ Jesus *t* hold of me.

TOOTH (TEETH)

Ex 21: 24 eye for eye, *t* for *t*, hand for hand,
Mt   5: 38 'Eye for eye, and *t* for *t*.'

TOP

Dt 28: 13 you will always be at the *t*,
Isa   1: 6 of your foot to the *t* of your head
Mt 27: 51 torn in two from *t* to bottom.

TORMENT (TORMENTED TORMENTORS)

Lk 16: 28 also come to this place of *t*.'
2Co 12: 7 a messenger of Satan, to *t* me.

TORMENTED (TORMENT)

Rev 20: 10 They will be *t* day and night

TORMENTORS (TORMENT)

Ps 137: 3 our *t* demanded songs of joy;

TORN

Gal 4: 15 you would have *t* out your eyes
Php 1: 23 I do not know! I am *t*

TORTURED*

Mt 18: 34 turned him over to the jailers to be *t*,
Heb 11: 35 Others were *t* and refused

TOSSED (TOSSING)

Eph 4: 14 *t* back and forth by the waves,
Jas   1: 6 of the sea, blown and *t* by the wind.

TOSSING (TOSSED)

Isa 57: 20 But the wicked are like the *t* sea,

TOUCH (TOUCHED TOUCHES)

Ge   3: 3 you must not *t* it, or you will die.' ''
Ex 19: 12 go up the mountain or *t* the foot
Ps 105: 15 ''Do not *t* my anointed ones;
Mt   9: 21 If I only *t* his cloak, I will be healed
Lk 18: 15 babies to Jesus to have him *t* them.
    24: 39 It is I myself! *T* me and see;
2Co 6: 17 *T* no unclean thing,
Col 2: 21 Do not taste! Do not *t*!'' ?

TOUCHED (TOUCH)

1Sa 10: 26 men whose hearts God had *t*.
Isa   6: 7 With it he *t* my mouth and said,
Mt 14: 36 and all who *t* him were healed.
Lk   8: 45 ''Who *t* me?'' Jesus asked.
1Jn 1: 1 looked at and our hands have *t*—

TOUCHES (TOUCH)

Ex 19: 12 Whoever *t* the mountain shall
Zec 2: 8 for whoever *t* you *t* the apple

TOWER

Ge 11: 4 with a *t* that reaches to the heavens
Pr 18: 10 of the LORD is a strong *t*;

TOWN (TOWNS)

Mt   2: 23 and lived in a *t* called Nazareth.

TOWNS (TOWN)

Nu 35: 2 to give the Levites *t* to live
    35: 15 These six *t* will be a place of refuge
Jer 11: 13 as many gods as you have *t*,
Mt   9: 35 Jesus went through all the *t*

TRACING*

Ro 11: 33 and his paths beyond *t* out!

TRACK

Job 14: 16 but not keep *t* of my sin.

TRADERS (TRADING)

1Ti 1: 10 for slave *t* and liars and perjurers—

TRADING (TRADERS)

1Ki 10: 22 The king had a fleet of *t* ships at sea
Pr 31: 18 She sees that her *t* is profitable,

TRADITION (TRADITIONS)

Mt 15: 2 ''Why do your disciples break the *t*
    15: 6 word of God for the sake of your *t*.
Mk   7: 13 by your *t* that you have handed
Col 2: 8 which depends on human *t*

TRADITIONS (TRADITION)

Mk   7: 8 are holding on to the *t* of men.''
Gal 1: 14 zealous for the *t* of my fathers.

TRAIL

1Ti 5: 24 the sins of others *t* behind them.

TRAIN* (TRAINED TRAINING)

Ps 68: 18 you led captives in your *t*;
Pr 22: 6 *T* a child in the way he should go,
Isa 2: 4 nor will they *t* for war anymore.
    6: 1 the *t* of his robe filled the temple.
Mic 4: 3 nor will they *t* for war anymore.
Eph 4: 8 he led captives in his *t*
1Ti 4: 7 rather, *t* yourself to be godly.
Tit   2: 4 they can *t* the younger women

TRAINED (TRAIN)

Lk   6: 40 everyone who is fully *t* will be like
Ac 22: 3 Under Gamaliel I was thoroughly *t*
2Co 11: 6 I may not be a *t* speaker,
Heb 5: 14 by constant use have *t* themselves
    12: 11 for those who have been *t* by it.

TRAINING* (TRAIN)

1Co 9: 25 in the games goes into strict *t*.
Eph 6: 4 up in the *t* and instruction
1Ti 4: 8 For physical *t* is of some value,
2Ti 3: 16 correcting and *t* in righteousness,

TRAITOR (TRAITORS)

Lk   6: 16 and Judas Iscariot, who became a *t*.
Jn 18: 5 Judas the *t* was standing there

TRAITORS (TRAITOR)

Ps 59: 5 show no mercy to wicked *t*.

TRAMPLE (TRAMPLED)

Joel 3: 13 Come, *t* the grapes,
Am 2: 7 They *t* on the heads of the poor
    5: 11 You *t* on the poor
    8: 4 Hear this, you who *t* the needy
Mt   7: 6 they may *t* them under their feet,
Lk 10: 19 I have given you authority to *t*

TRAMPLED (TRAMPLE)

Isa 63: 6 I *t* the nations in my anger;
Lk 21: 24 Jerusalem will be *t*
Heb 10: 29 to be punished who has *t* the Son
Rev 14: 20 They were *t* in the winepress

TRANCE*

Ac 10: 10 was being prepared, he fell into a *t*.
    11: 5 and in a *t* I saw a vision.
    22: 17 into a *t* and saw the Lord speaking.

TRANQUILLITY*

Ecc 4: 6 Better one handful with *t*

TRANSACTIONS*

Ru   4: 7 method of legalizing *t* in Israel.)

TRANSCENDS*

Php 4: 7 which *t* all understanding,

TRANSFIGURED*

Mt 17: 2 There he was *t* before them.
Mk   9: 2 There he was *t* before them.

TRANSFORM* (TRANSFORMED)

Php 3: 21 will *t* our lowly bodies

TRANSFORMED (TRANSFORM)

Ro 12: 2 be *t* by the renewing of your mind.
2Co 3: 18 are being *t* into his likeness

TRANSGRESSED* (TRANSGRESSION)

Da   9: 11 All Israel has *t* your law

TRANSGRESSION* (TRANSGRESSED TRANSGRESSIONS TRANSGRESSORS)

Ps 19: 13 innocent of great *t*.
Isa 53: 8 for the *t* of my people he was
Da   9: 24 and your holy city to finish *t*,
Mic 1: 5 All this is because of Jacob's *t*,
    1: 5 What is Jacob's *t*?
    3: 8 to declare to Jacob his *t*,
    6: 7 Shall I offer my firstborn for my *t*,
    7: 18 who pardons sin and forgives the *t*
Ro   4: 15 where there is no law there is no *t*.
    11: 11 Rather, because of their *t*,
    11: 12 if their *t* means riches for the world

TRANSGRESSIONS* (TRANSGRESSION)

Ps 32: 1 whose *t* are forgiven,
    32: 5 my *t* to the LORD''—
    39: 8 Save me from all my *t*;
    51: 1 blot out my *t*.
    51: 3 For I know my *t*,
    65: 3 you forgave our *t*.
  103: 12 so far has he removed our *t* from us
Isa 43: 25 your *t*, for my own sake,
    50: 1 of your *t* your mother was sent
    53: 5 But he was pierced for our *t*,
Mic 1: 13 for the *t* of Israel
Ro   4: 7 whose *t* are forgiven,
Gal 3: 19 because of *t* until the Seed to whom
Eph 2: 1 you were dead in your *t* and sins,
    2: 5 even when we were dead in *t*—

TRANSGRESSORS* (TRANSGRESSION)

Ps 51: 13 Then I will teach *t* your ways,
Isa 53: 12 and made intercession for the *t*.
    53: 12 and was numbered with the *t*.
Lk 22: 37 'And he was numbered with the *t*';

TRAP (TRAPPED TRAPS)

Ps 69: 22 may it become retribution and a *t*.
Pr 20: 25 a *t* for a man to dedicate something
    28: 10 will fall into his own *t*,
Isa   8: 14 a *t* and a snare.
Mt 22: 15 and laid plans to *t* him in his words.
Lk 21: 34 close on you unexpectedly like a *t*.
Ro 11: 9 their table become a snare and a *t*,
1Ti 3: 7 into disgrace and into the devil's *t*.
    6: 9 and a *t* and into many foolish
2Ti 2: 26 and escape from the *t* of the devil,

TRAPPED (TRAP)

Pr   6: 2 if you have been *t* by what you said
    12: 13 An evil man is *t* by his sinful talk,

TRAPS (TRAP)

Jos 23: 13 they will become snares and *t*
La   4: 20 was caught in their *t*.

TRAVEL (TRAVELER)

Pr   4: 15 Avoid it, do not *t* on it;
Mt 23: 15 You *t* over land and sea

TRAVELER (TRAVEL)

Job 31: 32 door was always open to the *t*—
Jer 14: 8 like a *t* who stays only a night?

TREACHEROUS (TREACHERY)

Ps 25: 3 who are *t* without excuse.
2Ti 3: 4 not lovers of the good, *t*, rash,

TREACHERY (TREACHEROUS)

Isa 59: 13 rebellion and *t* against the LORD,

TREAD (TREADING TREADS)

Ps 91: 13 You will *t* upon the lion

TREADING (TREAD)

Dt 25: 4 an ox while it is *t* out the grain.

1Co 9: 9 an ox while it is *t* out the grain.''
1Ti 5: 18 the ox while it is *t* out the grain,''

TREADS (TREAD)

Rev 19: 15 He *t* the winepress of the fury

TREASURE (TREASURED TREASURES TREASURY)

Pr 2: 4 and search for it as for hidden *t*,
Isa 33: 6 of the LORD is the key to this *t*.
Mt 6: 21 For where your *t* is, there your
13: 44 of heaven is like *t* hidden in a field.
Lk 12: 33 a *t* in heaven that will not be
2Co 4: 7 But we have this *t* in jars of clay
1Ti 6: 19 In this way they will lay up *t*

TREASURED (TREASURE)

Ex 19: 5 you will be my *t* possession.
Dt 7: 6 to be his people, his *t* possession.
26: 18 his *t* possession as he promised,
Job 23: 12 I have *t* the words
Mal 1: 17 when I make up my *t* possession.
Lk 2: 19 But Mary *t* up all these things
2: 51 But his mother *t* all these things

TREASURES (TREASURE)

1Ch 29: 3 my God I now give my personal *t*
Pr 10: 2 Ill-gotten *t* are of no value,
Mt 6: 19 up for yourselves *t* on earth,
13: 52 out of his storeroom new *t*
Col 2: 3 in whom are hidden all the *t*
Heb 11: 26 of greater value than the *t* of Egypt,

TREASURY (TREASURE)

Mk 12: 43 more into the *t* than all the others.

TREAT (TREATED TREATING TREATMENT)

Lev 22: 2 sons to *t* with respect the sacred
Ps 103: 10 he does not *t* us as our sins deserve
Mt 18: 17 *t* him as you would a pagan
18: 35 my heavenly Father will *t* each
Eph 6: 9 *t* your slaves in the same way.
1Th 5: 20 do not *t* prophecies with contempt.
1Ti 5: 1 *T* younger men as brothers,
1Pe 3: 7 and *t* them with respect

TREATED (TREAT)

Lev 19: 34 The alien living with you must be *t*
25: 40 He is to be *t* as a hired worker
1Sa 24: 17 "You have *t* me well, but I have
Heb 10: 29 who has *t* as an unholy thing

TREATING (TREAT)

Ge 18: 25 *t* the righteous and the wicked
Heb 12: 7 as discipline; God is *t* you as sons.

TREATMENT (TREAT)

Col 2: 23 and their harsh *t* of the body,

TREATY

Ex 34: 12 not to make a *t* with those who live
Dt 7: 2 Make no *t* with them, and show
23: 6 Do not seek a *t* of friendship with them

TREE (TREES)

Ge 2: 9 and the *t* of the knowledge of good
2: 9 of the garden were the *t* of life
Dt 21: 23 hung on a *t* is under God's curse.
2Sa 18: 9 Absalom's head got caught in the *t*.
1Ki 14: 23 and under every spreading *t*.
Ps 1: 3 He is like a *t* planted by streams
52: 8 But I am like an olive *t*
92: 12 righteous will flourish like a palm *t*,
Pr 3: 18 She is a *t* of life to those who
11: 30 of the righteous is a *t* of life,
27: 18 He who tends a fig *t* will eat its fruit
Isa 65: 22 For as the days of a *t*,
Jer 17: 8 He will be like a *t* planted
Eze 17: 24 I the LORD bring down the tall *t*
Da 4: 10 before me stood a *t* in the middle
Mic 4: 4 and under his own fig *t*,
Zec 3: 10 to sit under his vine and fig *t*,'
Mt 3: 10 every *t* that does not produce good
12: 33 for a *t* is recognized by its fruit.
Lk 14: 4 climbed a sycamore-fig *t* to see him
Ac 5: 30 killed by hanging him on a *t*.
Ro 11: 24 be grafted into their own olive *t*!

Gal 3: 13 is everyone who is hung on a *t*.''
Jas 3: 12 My brothers, can a fig *t* bear olives,
1Pe 2: 24 sins in his body on the *t*,
Rev 2: 7 the right to eat from the *t* of life,
22: 2 side of the river stood the *t* of life,
22: 14 they may have the right to the *t*
22: 19 from him his share in the *t* of life

TREES (TREE)

Jdg 9: 8 One day the *t* went out
Ps 96: 12 Then all the *t* of the forest will sing
Isa 55: 12 and all the *t* of the field
Mt 3: 10 The ax is already at the root of the *t*
Mk 8: 24 they look like *t* walking around.''
Jude : 12 autumn *t*, without fruit

TREMBLE (TREMBLED TREMBLES TREMBLING)

Ex 15: 14 The nations will hear and *t*;
1Ch 16: 30 *T* before him, all the earth!
Ps 114: 7 *T*, O earth, at the presence
Jer 5: 22 "Should you not *t* in my presence?
Eze 38: 20 of the earth will *t* at my presence.
Joel 2: 1 Let all who live in the land *t*,
Hab 3: 6 he looked, and made the nations *t*.

TREMBLED (TREMBLE)

Ex 19: 16 Everyone in the camp *t*.
20: 18 in smoke, they *t* with fear.
2Sa 22: 8 "The earth *t* and quaked,
Ac 7: 32 Moses *t* with fear and did not dare

TREMBLES (TREMBLE)

Ps 97: 4 the earth sees and *t*.
104: 32 he who looks at the earth, and it *t*,
Isa 66: 2 and *t* at my word.
Jer 10: 10 When he is angry, the earth *t*;
Na 1: 5 The earth *t* at his presence,

TREMBLING (TREMBLE)

Ps 2: 11 and rejoice with *t*.
Da 10: 10 set me *t* on my hands and knees.
Php 2: 12 out your salvation with fear and *t*,
Heb 12: 21 terrifying that Moses said, "I am *t*

TRESPASS* (TRESPASSES)

Ro 5: 15 But the gift is not like the *t*.
5: 15 died by the *t* of the one man,
5: 17 For if, by the *t* of the one man,
5: 18 result of one *t* was condemnation
5: 20 added so that the *t* might increase.

TRESPASSES* (TRESPASS)

Ro 5: 16 but the gift followed many *t*

TRIAL (TRIALS)

Ps 37: 33 condemned when brought to *t*.
Mk 13: 11 you are arrested and brought to *t*,
2Co 8: 2 most severe *t*, their overflowing
Jas 1: 12 is the man who perseveres under *t*,
1Pe 4: 12 at the painful *t* you are suffering,
Rev 3: 10 you from the hour of *t* that is going

TRIALS* (TRIAL)

Dt 7: 19 saw with your own eyes the great *t*,
29: 3 own eyes you saw those great *t*,
Lk 22: 28 who have stood by me in my *t*.
1Th 3: 3 one would be unsettled by these *t*.
2Th 1: 4 the persecutions and *t* you are
Jas 1: 2 whenever you face *t* of many kinds,
1Pe 1: 6 had to suffer grief in all kinds of *t*.
2Pe 2: 9 how to rescue godly men from *t*

TRIBE (HALF-TRIBE TRIBES)

Heb 7: 13 no one from that *t* has ever served
Rev 5: 5 See, the Lion of the *t* of Judah,
5: 9 God from every *t* and language
11: 9 men from every people, *t*,
14: 6 to every nation, *t*, language

TRIBES (TRIBE)

Ge 49: 28 All these are the twelve *t* of Israel,
Mt 19: 28 judging the twelve *t* of Israel.

TRIBULATION*

Rev 7: 14 who have come out of the great *t*;

TRICKERY*

Ac 13: 10 full of all kinds of deceit and *t*.

2Co 12: 16 fellow that I am, I caught you by *t*!

TRIED (TRY)

Ps 73: 16 When I *t* to understand all this,
95: 9 where your fathers tested and *t* me,
Heb 3: 9 where your fathers tested and *t* me

TRIES (TRY)

Lk 17: 33 Whoever *t* to keep his life will lose

TRIMMED

Mt 25: 7 virgins woke up and *t* their lamps.

TRIUMPH (TRIUMPHAL TRIUMPHED TRIUMPHING TRIUMPHS)

Ps 25: 2 nor let my enemies *t* over me.
54: 7 my eyes have looked in *t*
112: 8 in the end he will look in *t*
118: 7 I will look in *t* on my enemies.
Pr 28: 12 When the righteous *t*, there is great
Isa 42: 13 and will *t* over his enemies.

TRIUMPHAL* (TRIUMPH)

Isa 60: 11 their kings led in *t* procession.
2Co 2: 14 us in *t* procession in Christ

TRIUMPHED (TRIUMPH)

Rev 5: 5 of Judah, the Root of David, has *t*.

TRIUMPHING* (TRIUMPH)

Col 2: 15 of them, *t* over them by the cross.

TRIUMPHS* (TRIUMPH)

Jas 2: 13 Mercy *t* over judgment! What

TROUBLE (TROUBLED TROUBLES)

Ge 41: 51 God has made me forget all my *t*
Jos 7: 25 Why have you brought this *t* on us?
Job 2: 10 good from God, and not *t*?''
5: 7 Yet man is born to *t*
14: 1 is of few days and full of *t*.
42: 11 him over all the *t* the LORD had
Ps 7: 14 conceives *t* gives birth
7: 16 The *t* he causes recoils on himself;
9: 9 a stronghold in times of *t*.
10: 14 But you, O God, do see *t* and grief;
22: 11 for *t* is near
27: 5 For in the day of *t*
32: 7 you will protect me from *t*
37: 39 he is their stronghold in time of *t*.
41: 1 LORD delivers him in times of *t*.
46: 1 an ever-present help in *t*.
50: 15 and call upon me in the day of *t*;
59: 16 my refuge in times of *t*.
66: 14 spoke when I was in *t*.
86: 7 In the day of my *t* I will call to you,
91: 15 I will be with him in *t*,
107: 6 to the LORD in their *t*,
107: 13 they cried to the LORD in their *t*,
116: 3 I was overcome by *t* and sorrow.
119:143 *T* and distress have come upon me,
138: 7 Though I walk in the midst of *t*,
143: 11 righteousness, bring me out of *t*,
Pr 11: 8 righteous man is rescued from *t*,
11: 17 a cruel man brings *t* on himself
11: 29 He who brings *t* on his family will
12: 13 but a righteous man escapes *t*.
12: 21 but the wicked have their fill of *t*.
15: 27 A greedy man brings *t* to his family
19: 23 one rests content, untouched by *t*.
22: 8 He who sows wickedness reaps *t*,
24: 10 If you falter in times of *t*,
25: 19 on the unfaithful in times of *t*.
28: 14 he who hardens his heart falls into *t*.
Jer 30: 7 It will be a time of *t* for Jacob,
Na 1: 7 a refuge in times of *t*.
Zep 1: 15 a day of *t* and ruin,
Mt 6: 34 Each day has enough *t* of its own.
13: 21 When *t* or persecution comes
Jn 16: 33 In this world you will have *t*.
Ro 8: 35 Shall *t* or hardship or persecution
2Co 1: 4 those in any *t* with the comfort we
2Th 1: 6 *t* to those who *t* you
Jas 5: 13 one of you in *t*? He should pray.

TROUBLED (TROUBLE)

Ps 38: 18 I am *t* by my sin.
Isa 38: 14 I am *t*; O Lord, come to my aid!''

Mk 14: 33 began to be deeply distressed and *t*.
Jn 14: 1 "Do not let your hearts be *t*.
14: 27 Do not let your hearts be *t*
2Th 1: 7 and give relief to you who are *t*,

TROUBLES (TROUBLE)

Ps 34: 6 he saved him out of all his *t*.
34: 17 he delivers them from all their *t*.
34: 19 A righteous man may have many *t*,
40: 12 For *t* without number surround me
54: 7 he has delivered me from all my *t*,
1Co 7: 28 those who marry will face many *t*
2Co 1: 4 who comforts us in all our *t*,
4: 17 and momentary *t* are achieving
6: 4 in *t*, hardships and distresses;
7: 4 in all our *t* my joy knows no bounds
Php 4: 14 good of you to share in my *t*.

TRUE (TRUTH)

Nu 11: 23 not what I say will come *t* for you."
12: 7 this is not *t* of my servant Moses;
Dt 18: 22 does not take place or come *t*,
Jos 23: 15 of the LORD your God has come *t*
1Sa 9: 6 and everything he says comes *t*.
1Ki 10: 6 and your wisdom is *t*.
2Ch 6: 17 your servant David come *t*.
15: 3 was without the *t* God,
Ps 33: 4 of the LORD is right and *t*;
119:142 and your law is *t*.
119:151 and all your commands are *t*.
119:160 All your words are *t*;
Pr 8: 7 My mouth speaks what is *t*,
22: 21 teaching you *t* and reliable words,
Jer 10: 10 But the LORD is the *t* God;
28: 9 only if his prediction comes *t*."
Eze 33: 33 "When all this comes *t*—
Lk 16: 11 who will trust you with *t* riches?
Jn 1: 9 The *t* light that gives light
4: 23 when the *t* worshipers will worship
6: 32 Father who gives you the *t* bread
7: 28 on my own, but he who sent me is *t*
15: 1 "I am the *t* vine, and my Father is
17: 3 the only *t* God, and Jesus Christ,
19: 35 testimony, and his testimony is *t*.
21: 24 We know that his testimony is *t*.
Ac 10: 34 "I now realize how *t* it is that God
11: 23 all to remain *t* to the Lord
14: 22 them to remain *t* to the faith.
17: 11 day to see if what Paul said was *t*.
Ro 3: 4 Let God be *t*, and every man a liar.
Php 4: 8 whatever is *t*, whatever is noble,
1Jn 2: 8 and the *t* light is already shining.
5: 20 He is the *t* God and eternal life.
Rev 19: 9 "These are the *t* words of God."
22: 6 These words are trustworthy and *t*.

TRUMPET (TRUMPETS)

Isa 27: 13 And in that day a great *t* will sound
Eze 33: 5 Since he heard the sound of the *t*
Zec 9: 14 Sovereign LORD will sound the *t*;
Mt 24: 31 send his angels with a loud *t* call,
1Co 14: 8 if the *t* does not sound a clear call,
15: 52 For the *t* will sound, the dead will
1Th 4: 16 and with the *t* call of God,
Rev 8: 7 The first angel sounded his *t*,

TRUMPETS (TRUMPET)

Jdg 7: 19 They blew their *t* and broke the jars
Rev 8: 2 and to them were given seven *t*.

TRUST* (ENTRUST ENTRUSTED TRUSTED TRUSTFULLY TRUSTING TRUSTS TRUSTWORTHY)

Ex 14: 31 put their *t* in him and in Moses his
19: 9 and will always put their *t* in you."
Nu 20: 12 "Because you did not *t*
Dt 1: 32 you did not *t* in the LORD your
9: 23 You did not *t* him or obey him.
28: 52 walls in which you *t* fall down.
Jdg 11: 20 did not *t* Israel to pass
2Ki 17: 14 who did not *t* in the LORD their
18: 30 to *t* in the LORD when he says,
1Ch 9: 22 to their positions of *t* by David
Job 4: 18 If God places no *t* in his servants,
15: 15 If God places no *t* in his holy ones,
31: 24 "If I have put my *t* in gold
39: 12 Can you *t* him to bring
Ps 4: 5 and *t* in the LORD.

Ps 9: 10 Those who know your name will *t*
13: 5 But I *t* in your unfailing love;
20: 7 Some *t* in chariots and some
20: 7 we *t* in the name of the LORD our
22: 4 In you our fathers put their *t*;
22: 9 you made me *t* in you
25: 2 I lift up my soul; in you I *t*,
31: 6 I *t* in the LORD.
31: 14 But I *t* in you, O LORD;
33: 21 for we *t* in his holy name.
37: 3 *T* in the LORD and do good;
37: 5 *t* in him and he will do this:
40: 3 and put their *t* in the LORD.
40: 4 who makes the LORD his *t*,
44: 6 I do not *t* in my bow,
49: 6 those who *t* in their wealth
49: 13 of those who *t* in themselves,
52: 8 I *t* in God's unfailing love
55: 23 But as for me, I *t* in you.
56: 3 I will *t* in you.
56: 4 in God I *t*; I will not be afraid.
56: 11 in God I *t*; I will not be afraid.
62: 8 *T* in him at all times, O people;
62: 10 Do not *t* in extortion
78: 7 Then they would put their *t* in God
78: 22 or *t* in his deliverance.
91: 2 my God, in whom I *t*."
115: 8 and so will all who *t* in them.
115: 9 O house of Israel, *t* in the LORD—
115: 10 O house of Aaron, *t* in the LORD
115: 11 You who fear him, *t* in the LORD
118: 8 than to *t* in man.
118: 9 than to *t* in princes.
119: 42 for I *t* in your word.
125: 1 Those who *t* in the LORD are like
135: 18 and so will all who *t* in them.
143: 8 for I have put my *t* in you.
146: 3 Do not put your *t* in princes,
Pr 3: 5 *T* in the LORD with all your heart
21: 22 the stronghold in which they *t*.
22: 19 So that your *t* may be in the LORD
Isa 8: 17 I will put my *t* in him.
12: 2 I will *t* and not be afraid.
26: 4 *T* in the LORD forever,
30: 15 in quietness and *t* is your strength,
31: 1 who *t* in the multitude
36: 15 to *t* in the LORD when he says,
42: 17 But those who *t* in idols,
50: 10 *t* in the name of the LORD
Jer 2: 37 LORD has rejected those you *t*;
5: 17 the fortified cities in which you *t*.
7: 4 Do not *t* in deceptive words
7: 14 the temple you *t* in, the place I gave
9: 4 do not *t* your brothers.
12: 6 Do not *t* them,
28: 15 you have persuaded this nation to *t*
39: 18 you *t* in me, declares the LORD.' "
48: 7 Since you *t* in your deeds
49: 4 you *t* in your riches and say,
49: 11 Your widows too can *t* in me."
Mic 7: 5 Do not *t* a neighbor;
Na 1: 7 He cares for those who *t* in him,
Zep 3: 2 She does not *t* in the LORD,
3: 12 who *t* in the name of the LORD.
Lk 16: 11 who will *t* you with true riches?
Jn 12: 36 Put your *t* in the light
14: 1 *T* in God; *t* also in me.
Ac 14: 23 Lord, in whom they had put their *t*.
Ro 15: 13 you with all joy and peace as you *t*
1Co 4: 2 been given a *t* must prove faithful.
9: 17 discharging the *t* committed
2Co 13: 6 I *t* that you will discover that we
Heb 2: 13 "I will put my *t* in him."

TRUSTED* (TRUST)

1Sa 27: 12 Achish *t* David and said to himself,
2Ki 18: 5 Hezekiah *t* in the LORD, the God
1Ch 5: 20 their prayers, because they *t*
Job 12: 20 He silences the lips of *t* advisers
Ps 5: 9 from their mouth can be *t*;
22: 4 they *t* and you delivered them.
22: 5 in you they *t* and were not
26: 1 I have *t* in the LORD
41: 9 Even my close friend, whom I *t*,
52: 7 but *t* in his great wealth
Isa 20: 5 Those who *t* in Cush and boasted
25: 9 This is the LORD, we *t* in him;
25: 9 we *t* in him, and he saved us.

Isa 47: 10 You have *t* in your wickedness
Jer 13: 25 and *t* in false gods.
38: 22 those *t* friends of yours.
48: 13 ashamed when they *t* in Bethel.
Eze 16: 15 " 'But you *t* in your beauty
Da 3: 28 They *t* in him and defied the king's
6: 23 because he had *t* in his God.
Lk 11: 22 the armor in which the man *t*
16: 10 *t* with very little can also be *t*
Ac 12: 20 a *t* personal servant of the king,
Tit 2: 10 but to show that they can be fully *t*,
3: 8 so that those who have *t*

TRUSTFULLY* (TRUST)

Pr 3: 29 who lives *t* near you.

TRUSTING* (TRUST)

Job 15: 31 by *t* what is worthless,
Ps 112: 7 his heart is steadfast, *t*
Isa 2: 22 Stop *t* in man,
Jer 7: 8 you are *t* in deceptive words that

TRUSTS* (TRUST)

Job 8: 14 What he *t* in is fragile;
Ps 21: 7 For the king *t* in the LORD;
22: 8 "He *t* in the LORD,
28: 7 my heart *t* in him, and I am helped.
32: 10 surrounds the man who *t* in him.
84: 12 blessed is the man who *t* in you.
86: 2 who *t* in you.
Pr 11: 28 Whoever *t* in his riches will fall,
16: 20 blessed is he who *t* in the LORD.
28: 25 he who *t* in the LORD will prosper.
28: 26 He who *t* in himself is a fool,
29: 25 whoever *t* in the LORD is kept safe
Isa 26: 3 because he *t* in you.
28: 16 one who *t* will never be dismayed.
Jer 17: 5 "Cursed is the one who *t* in man,
17: 7 blessed is the man who *t*
Eze 33: 13 but then he *t* in his righteousness
Hab 2: 18 For he who makes it *t*
Mt 27: 43 He *t* in God.
Ro 4: 5 but *t* God who justifies the wicked,
9: 33 one who *t* in him will never be put
10: 11 "Anyone who *t* in him will never
1Co 13: 7 always protects, always *t*,
1Pe 2: 6 and the one who *t* in him

TRUSTWORTHY* (TRUST)

Ex 18: 21 *t* men who hate dishonest gain—
2Sa 7: 28 you are God! Your words are *t*,
Ne 13: 13 these men were considered *t*.
Ps 19: 7 The statutes of the LORD are *t*,
111: 7 all his precepts are *t*.
119: 86 All your commands are *t*;
119:138 they are fully *t*.
Pr 11: 13 but a *t* man keeps a secret.
13: 17 but a *t* envoy brings healing.
25: 13 is a *t* messenger to those who send
Da 2: 45 and the interpretation is *t*."
6: 4 he was *t* and neither corrupt
Lk 16: 11 So if you have not been *t*
16: 12 And if you have not been *t*
19: 17 'Because you have been *t*
1Co 7: 25 one who by the Lord's mercy is *t*.
1Ti 1: 15 Here is a *t* saying that deserves full
3: 1 Here is a *t* saying: If anyone sets his
3: 11 but temperate and *t* in everything.
4: 9 This is a *t* saying that deserves full
2Ti 2: 11 Here is a *t* saying:
Tit 1: 9 must hold firmly to the *t* message
3: 8 This is a *t* saying.
Rev 21: 5 for these words are *t* and true."
22: 6 "These words are *t* and true.

TRUTH* (TRUE TRUTHFUL TRUTHFULNESS TRUTHS)

Ge 42: 16 tested to see if you are telling the *t*.
1Ki 17: 24 LORD from your mouth is the *t*."
22: 16 the *t* in the name of the LORD?"
2Ch 18: 15 the *t* in the name of the LORD?"
Ps 15: 2 who speaks the *t* from his heart
25: 5 guide me in your *t* and teach me,
26: 3 and I walk continually in your *t*.
31: 5 redeem me, O LORD, the God of *t*
40: 10 do not conceal your love and your *t*
40: 11 your *t* always protect me.
43: 3 Send forth your light and your *t*,

Ps 45: 4 victoriously in behalf of *t*, humility
51: 6 Surely you desire *t*
52: 3 than speaking the *t*.
86:11 and I will walk in your *t*;
96:13 and the peoples in his *t*.
119: 30 I have chosen the way of *t*;
119: 43 of *t* from my mouth,
145: 18 to all who call on him in *t*.
Pr 16:13 they value a man who speaks the *t*.
23:23 Buy the *t* and do not sell it;
Isa 45:19 I, the LORD, speak the *t*;
48: 1 but not in *t* or righteousness—
59:14 *t* has stumbled in the streets,
59:15 *T* is nowhere to be found,
65:16 will do so by the God of *t*;
65:16 will swear by the God of *t*.
Jer 5: 1 who deals honestly and seeks the *t*,
5: 3 do not your eyes look for *t*?
7:28 *T* has perished; it has vanished
9: 3 it is not by *t*
9: 5 and no one speaks the *t*.
26:15 for in *t* the LORD has sent me
Da 8:12 and *t* was thrown to the ground.
9:13 and giving attention to your *t*.
10:21 what is written in the Book of *T*.
11: 2 "Now then, I tell you the *t*:
Am 5:10 and despise him who tells the *t*.
Zec 8: 3 will be called the City of *T*,
8:16 are to do: Speak the *t* to each other,
8:19 Therefore love *t* and peace."
Mt 5:18 I tell you the *t*, until heaven
5:26 I tell you the *t*, you will not get out
6: 2 I tell you the *t*, they have received
6: 5 I tell you the *t*, they have received
6:16 I tell you the *t*, they have received
8:10 "I tell you the *t*, I have not found
10:15 I tell you the *t*, it will be more
10:23 I tell you the *t*, you will not finish
10:42 I tell you the *t*, he will certainly not
11:11 I tell you the *t*: Among those born
13:17 For I tell you the *t*, many prophets
16:28 I tell you the *t*, some who are
17:20 I tell you the *t*, if you have faith
18: 3 And he said: "I tell you the *t*,
18:13 And if he finds it, I tell you the *t*,
18:18 "I tell you the *t*, whatever you bind
19:23 to his disciples, "I tell you the *t*,
19:28 "I tell you the *t*, at the renewal
21:21 Jesus replied, "I tell you the *t*,
21:31 Jesus said to them, "I tell you the *t*,
22:16 of God in accordance with the *t*.
23:36 I tell you the *t*, all this will come
24: 2 "I tell you the *t*, not one stone here
24:34 I tell you the *t*, this generation will
24:47 I tell you the *t*, he will put him
25:12 'I tell you the *t*, I don't know you.'
25:40 The King will reply, 'I tell you the *t*
25:45 "He will reply, 'I tell you the *t*,
26:13 tell you the *t*, wherever this gospel
26:21 "I tell you the *t*, one
26:34 "I tell you the *t*,'" Jesus answered,
Mk 3:28 I tell you the *t*, all the sins
5:33 with fear, told him the whole *t*.
8:12 I tell you the *t*, no sign will be given
9: 1 he said to them, "I tell you the *t*,
9:41 I tell you the *t*, anyone who gives
10:15 I tell you the *t*, anyone who will not
10:29 "I tell you the *t*," Jesus replied,
11:23 "I tell you the *t*, if anyone says
12:14 of God in accordance with the *t*.
12:43 Jesus said, "I tell you the *t*,
13:30 I tell you the *t*, this generation will
14: 9 I tell you the *t*, wherever the gospel
14:18 "I tell you the *t*, one
14:25 "I tell you the *t*, I will not drink
14:30 "I tell you the *t*,'" Jesus answered,
Lk 4:24 "I tell you the *t*,'" he continued,
9:27 I tell you the *t*, some who are
12:37 I tell you the *t*, he will dress himself
12:44 I tell you the *t*, he will put him
18:17 I tell you the *t*, anyone who will not
18:29 "I tell you the *t*," Jesus said to them,
20:21 of God in accordance with the *t*.
21: 3 "I tell you the *t*," he said, "this
21:32 tell you the *t*, this generation will
23:43 answered him, "I tell you the *t*,
Jn 1:14 from the Father, full of grace and *t*.
1:17 and *t* came through Jesus Christ.

Jn 1:51 "I tell you the *t*, you shall see
3: 3 "I tell you the *t*, no one can see
3: 5 Jesus answered, "I tell you the *t*,
3:11 I tell you the *t*, we speak
3:21 But whoever lives by the *t* comes
4:23 worship the Father in spirit and *t*,
4:24 must worship in spirit and in *t*."
5:19 "I tell you the *t*, the Son can do
5:24 "I tell you the *t*, whoever hears my
5:25 I tell you the *t*, a time is coming
5:33 and he has testified to the *t*.
6:26 "I tell you the *t*, you are looking
6:32 Jesus said to them, "I tell you the *t*,
6:47 I tell you the *t*, he who believes has
6:53 Jesus said to them, "I tell you the *t*,
7:18 the one who sent him is a man of *t*;
8:32 Then you will know the *t*,
8:32 and the *t* will set you free."
8:34 Jesus replied, "I tell you the *t*,
8:40 who has told you the *t* that I heard
8:44 to the *t*, for there is no *t* in him.
8:45 I tell the *t*, you do not believe me!
8:46 I am telling the *t*, why don't you
8:51 I tell you the *t*, if anyone keeps my
8:58 "I tell you the *t*," Jesus answered,
10: 1 "I tell you the *t*, the man who does
10: 7 "I tell you the *t*, I am the gate
12:24 I tell you the *t*, unless a kernel
13:16 I tell you the *t*, no servant is greater
13:20 tell you the *t*, whoever accepts
13:21 "I tell you the *t*, one of you is going
13:38 I tell you the *t*, before the rooster
14: 6 I am the way and the *t* and the life.
14:12 I tell you the *t*, anyone who has
14:17 with you forever—the Spirit of *t*.
15:26 the Spirit of *t* who goes out
16: 7 But I tell you the *t*: It is
16:13 But when he, the Spirit of *t*, comes,
16:13 comes, he will guide you into all *t*.
16:20 I tell you the *t*, you will weep
16:23 I tell you the *t*, my Father will give
17:17 them by the *t*; your word is *t*.
18:23 if I spoke the *t*, why did you strike
18:37 into the world, to testify to the *t*.
18:37 on the side of *t* listens to me."
18:38 "What is *t*?" Pilate asked.
19:35 He knows that he tells the *t*,
21:18 I tell you the *t*, when you were
Ac 20:30 and distort the *t* in order
21:24 everybody will know there is no *t*
21:34 commander could not get at the *t*
24: 8 able to learn the *t* about all these
28:25 "The Holy Spirit spoke the *t*
Ro 1:18 of men who suppress the *t*
1:25 They exchanged the *t* of God
2: 2 who do such things is based on *t*.
2: 8 who reject the *t* and follow evil,
2:20 embodiment of knowledge and *t*—
9: 1 I speak the *t* in Christ—I am not
15: 8 of the Jews on behalf of God's *t*,
1Co 5: 8 the bread of sincerity and *t*.
13: 6 in evil but rejoices with the *t*.
2Co 4: 2 setting forth the *t* plainly we
11:10 As surely as the *t* of Christ is in me,
12: 6 because I would be speaking the *t*.
13: 8 against the *t*, but only for the *t*.
Gal 2: 5 so that the *t* of the gospel might
2:14 in line with the *t* of the gospel,
4:16 enemy by telling you the *t*?
5: 7 and kept you from obeying the *t*?
Eph 1:13 when you heard the word of *t*,
4:15 Instead, speaking the *t* in love,
4:21 him in accordance with the *t* that is
5: 9 and *t*) and find out what pleases
6:14 with the belt of *t* buckled
Col 1: 5 heard about in the word of *t*,
1: 6 understood God's grace in all its *t*.
2Th 2:10 because they refused to love the *t*
2:12 who have not believed the *t*
2:13 and through belief in the *t*.
1Ti 2: 4 to come to a knowledge of the *t*.
2: 7 I am telling the *t*, I am not lying—
3:15 the pillar and foundation of the *t*.
4: 3 who believe and who know the *t*.
6: 5 who have been robbed of the *t*
2Ti 2:15 correctly handles the word of *t*.
2:18 have wandered away from the *t*.
2:25 them to a knowledge of the *t*,

2Ti 3: 7 never able to acknowledge the *t*.
3: 8 so also these men oppose the *t*—
4: 4 will turn their ears away from the *t*
Tit 1: 1 the knowledge of the *t* that leads
1:14 of those who reject the *t*.
Heb 10:26 received the knowledge of the *t*,
Jas 1:18 birth through the word of *t*,
3:14 do not boast about it or deny the *t*.
5:19 of you should wander from the *t*
1Pe 1:22 by obeying the *t* so that you have
2Pe 1:12 established in the *t* you now have.
2: 2 the way of *t* into disrepute.
1Jn 1: 6 we lie and do not live by the *t*.
1: 8 deceive ourselves and the *t* is not
2: 4 commands is a liar, and the *t* is not
2: 8 its *t* is seen in him and you,
2:20 and all of you know the *t*.
2:21 because no lie comes from the *t*.
2:21 because you do not know the *t*,
3:18 or tongue but with actions and in *t*.
3:19 we know that we belong to the *t*,
4: 6 is how we recognize the Spirit of *t*
5: 6 testifies, because the Spirit is the *t*.
2Jn : 1 whom I love in the *t*—
: 2 who know the *t*— because of the *t*,
: 3 will be with us in *t* and love.
: 4 of your children walking in the *t*,
3Jn : 1 friend Gaius, whom I love in the *t*.
: 3 how you continue to walk in the *t*,
: 3 tell about your faithfulness to the *t*
: 4 my children are walking in the *t*.
: 8 we may work together for the *t*.
: 12 everyone—and even by the *t* itself.

TRUTHFUL* (TRUTH)

Pr 12:17 A *t* witness gives honest testimony,
12:19 *T* lips endure forever,
12:22 but he delights in men who are *t*.
14: 5 A *t* witness does not deceive,
14:25 A *t* witness saves lives,
Jer 4: 2 and if in a *t*, just and righteous way
Jn 3:33 it has certified that God is *t*.
2Co 6: 7 in *t* speech and in the power

TRUTHFULNESS* (TRUTH)

Ro 3: 7 "If my falsehood enhances God's *t*

TRUTHS* (TRUTH)

1Co 2:13 expressing spiritual *t*
1Ti 3: 9 hold of the deep *t* of the faith
4: 6 brought up in the *t* of the faith
Heb 5:12 to teach you the elementary *t*

TRY (TRIED TRIES TRYING)

Ps 26: 2 Test me, O LORD, and *t* me,
Isa 7:13 enough to *t* the patience of men?
Lk 12:58 *t* hard to be reconciled to him
13:24 will *t* to enter and will not be able
1Co 10:33 even as I *t* to please everybody
14:12 *t* to excel in gifts that build up
2Co 5:11 is to fear the Lord, we *t*
1Th 5:15 always *t* to be kind to each other
Tit 2: 9 to *t* to please them, not to talk back

TRYING (TRY)

2Co 5:12 We are not *t* to commend ourselves
Gal 1:10 If I were still *t* to please men,
1Th 2: 4 We are not *t* to please men but God
1Pe 1:11 *t* to find out the time
1Jn 2:26 things to you about those who are *t*

TUMORS

1Sa 5: 6 them and afflicted them with *t*.

TUNE

1Co 14: 7 anyone know what *t* is being

TUNIC (TUNICS)

Lk 6:29 do not stop him from taking your *t*.

TUNICS (TUNIC)

Lk 3:11 "The man with two *t* should share

TURMOIL

Ps 65: 7 and the *t* of the nations.
Pr 15:16 than great wealth with *t*.

TURN (TURNED TURNING TURNS)

Ex 32: 12 *T* from your fierce anger; relent
Nu 32: 15 If you *t* away from following him,
Dt   5: 32 do not *t* aside to the right
     28: 14 Do not *t* aside from any
     30: 10 and *t* to the LORD your God
Jos   1: 7 do not *t* from it to the right
1Ki   8: 58 May he *t* our hearts to him,
2Ch   7: 14 and *t* from their wicked ways,
     30: 9 He will not *t* his face from you
Job 33: 30 to *t* back his soul from the pit,
Ps   1: do not *t* a deaf ear to me.
     34: 14 *T* from evil and do good;
     51: 13 and sinners will *t* back to you.
     78: 6 they in *t* would tell their children.
    119: 36 *T* my heart toward your statutes
    119:132 *T* to me and have mercy on me,
Pr   22: 6 when he is old he will not *t* from it.
Isa 17: 7 *t* their eyes to the Holy One
     28: 6 to those who *t* back the battle
     29: 16 You *t* things upside down,
     30: 21 Whether you *t* to the right
     45: 22 "*T* to me and be saved,
     55: 7 Let him *t* to the LORD,
Jer 31: 13 I will *t* their mourning
Eze 33: 9 if you do warn the wicked man to *t*
     33: 11 *T! T* from your evil ways!
Jnh   3: 9 and with compassion *t*
Mal   4: 6 He will *t* the hearts of the fathers
Mt   5: 39 you on the right cheek, *t*
     10: 35 For I have come to *t*
Lk   1: 17 to *t* the hearts of the fathers
Jn   12: 40 nor *t*— and I would heal them."
     16: 20 but your grief will *t* to joy.
Ac   3: 19 Repent, then, and *t* to God,
     26: 18 and *t* them from darkness to light,
1Co 14: 31 For you can all prophesy in *t*
     15: 23 But each in his own *t*: Christ,
1Ti   6: 20 *T* away from godless chatter
1Pe   3: 11 He must *t* from evil and do good;

TURNED (TURN)

Dt   23: 5 *t* the curse into a blessing for you,
1Ki 11: *t* his wives *t* his heart
2Ch 15: 4 But in their distress they *t*
Est   9: 1 but now the tables were *t*
      9: 22 when their sorrow was *t* into joy
Ps   14: 3 All have *t* aside,
     30: 11 You *t* my wailing into dancing;
     40: 1 he *t* to me and heard my cry.
Isa   9: 12 for all this, his anger is not *t* away,
     53: 6 each of us has *t* to his own way;
Hos   7: 8 Ephraim is a flat cake not *t* over.
Joel 2: 31 The sun will be *t* to darkness
Lk   22: 32 And when you have *t* back,
Ro   3: 12 All have *t* away,

TURNING (TURN)

2Ki 21: 13 wiping it and *t* it upside down.
Pr   2: 2 *t* your ear to wisdom
     14: 27 *t* a man from the snares of death.

TURNS (TURN)

2Sa 22: 29 the LORD *t* my darkness into light
Pr   15: 1 A gentle answer *t* away wrath,
Isa 44: 25 and *t* it into nonsense,
Jas   5: 20 Whoever *t* a sinner from the error

TWELVE

Ge   35: 22 Jacob had *t* sons: The sons of Leah:
     49: 28 All these are the *t* tribes of Israel,
Mt   10: 1 He called his *t* disciples to him
Lk   9: 17 the disciples picked up *t* basketfuls
Rev 21: 12 the names of the *t* tribes of Israel.
     21: 14 of the *t* apostles of the Lamb.

TWIN (TWINS)

Ge   25: 24 there were *t* boys in her womb.

TWINKLING*

1Co 15: 52 in a flash, in the *t* of an eye.

TWINS (TWIN)

Ro   9: 11 before the *t* were born

TWISTING* (TWISTS)

Pr   30: 33 and as *t* the nose produces blood,

TWISTS (TWISTING)

Ex   23: 8 and *t* the words of the righteous.

TYRANNICAL*

Pr   28: 16 A *t* ruler lacks judgment,

TYRE

Eze 28: 12 a lament concerning the king of *T*
Mt   11: 22 it will be more bearable for *T*

UNAPPROACHABLE*

1Ti   6: 16 immortal and who lives in *u* light,

UNASHAMED*

1Jn   2: 28 and *u* before him at his coming.

UNBELIEF* (UNBELIEVER
UNBELIEVERS UNBELIEVING)

Mk   9: 24 help me overcome my *u!*"
Ro   4: 20 through *u* regarding the promise
     11: 20 they were broken off because of *u*,
     11: 23 And if they do not persist in *u*,
1Ti   1: 13 because I acted in ignorance and *u*.
Heb   3: 19 able to enter, because of their *u*.

UNBELIEVER* (UNBELIEF)

1Co   7: 15 But if the *u* leaves, let him do so.
     10: 27 If some *u* invites you to a meal
     14: 24 if an *u* or someone who does not
2Co   6: 15 have in common with an *u?*
1Ti   5: 8 the faith and is worse than an *u*.

UNBELIEVERS* (UNBELIEF)

Lk   12: 46 and assign him a place with the *u*.
Ro   15: 31 rescued from the *u* in Judea
1Co   6: 6 another—and this in front of *u!*
      6: 12 however, is for believers, not for *u*.
     14: 22 not for believers but for *u;*
     14: 23 do not understand or some *u* come
2Co   4: 4 this age has blinded the minds of *u*,
      6: 14 Do not be yoked together with *u*.

UNBELIEVING* (UNBELIEF)

Mt   17: 17 "O *u* and perverse generation,"
Mk   9: 19 "O *u* generation," Jesus replied,
Lk   9: 41 "O *u* and perverse generation,"
1Co   7: 14 For the *u* husband has been
      7: 14 and the *u* wife has been sanctified
Heb   3: 12 *u* heart that turns away
Rev 21: 8 But the cowardly, the *u*, the vile,

UNBLEMISHED*

Heb   9: 14 the eternal Spirit offered himself *u*

UNCEASING

Ro   9: 2 and *u* anguish in my heart.

UNCERTAIN*

1Ti   6: 17 which is so *u*, but to put their hope

UNCHANGEABLE* (UNCHANGING)

Heb   6: 18 by two *u* things in which it is

UNCHANGING* (UNCHANGEABLE)

Heb   6: 17 wanted to make the *u* nature

UNCIRCUMCISED

Lev 26: 41 when their *u* hearts are humbled
1Sa 17: 26 Who is this *u* Philistine that he
Jer   9: 26 house of Israel is *u* in heart."
Ac   7: 51 stiff-necked people, with *u* hearts
Ro   4: 11 had by faith while he was still *u*.
1Co   7: 18 Was a man *u* when he was called?
Col   3: 11 circumcised or *u*, barbarian,

UNCIRCUMCISION

1Co   7: 19 is nothing and *u* is nothing.
Gal   5: 6 neither circumcision nor *u* has any

UNCLEAN

Ge   7: 2 and two of every kind of *u* animal,
Lev 10: 10 between the *u* and the clean,
     11: 4 it is ceremonially *u* for you.
     17: 15 he will be ceremonially *u* till evening.
Isa   6: 5 ruined! For I am a man of *u* lips,
     52: 11 Touch no *u* thing!
Mt   15: 11 mouth does not make him '*u*.'
Ac   10: 14 never eaten anything impure or *u*."

Ro   14: 14 fully convinced that no food is *u*
2Co   6: 17 Touch no *u* thing,

UNCLOTHED*

2Co   5: 4 because we do not wish to be *u*

UNCONCERNED*

Eze 16: 49 were arrogant, overfed and *u;*

UNCOVERED

Ru   3: 7 Ruth approached quietly, *u* his feet
1Co 11: 5 with her head *u* dishonors her head
     11: 13 to pray to God with her head *u?*
Heb   4: 13 Everything is *u* and laid bare

UNDERGOES* (UNDERGOING)

Heb 12: 8 (and everyone *u* discipline),

UNDERGOING* (UNDERGOES)

1Pe   5: 9 the world are *u* the same kind

UNDERSTAND (UNDERSTANDING
UNDERSTANDS UNDERSTOOD)

Ne   8: 8 the people could *u* what was being
Job 38: 4 Tell me, if you *u*.
     42: 3 Surely I spoke of things I did not *u*,
Ps   14: 2 men to see if there are any who *u*,
     73: 16 When I tried to *u* all this,
    119: 27 Let me *u* the teaching
    119:125 that I may *u* your statutes.
Pr   2: 5 then you will *u* the fear
      2: 9 Then you will *u* what is right
     30: 18 four that I do not *u:*
Ecc   7: 25 to the stupidity of wickedness
     11: 5 so you cannot *u* the work of God,
Isa   6: 10 *u* with their hearts,
     44: 18 know nothing, they *u* nothing;
     52: 15 they have not heard, they will *u*.
Jer 17: 9 Who can *u* it?
     31: 19 after I came to *u*,
Da   9: 25 and *u* this: From the issuing
Hos 14: 9 Who is discerning? He will *u* them.
Mt   13: 15 *u* with their hearts
     24: 15 Daniel—let the reader *u*—
Lk   24: 45 so they could *u* the Scriptures.
Ac   8: 30 "Do you *u* what you are reading?"
Ro   7: 15 I do not *u* what I do.
     15: 21 those who have not heard will *u*."
1Co   2: 12 that we may *u* what God has freely
      2: 14 and he cannot *u* them,
     14: 16 those who do not *u* say "Amen"
Eph   5: 17 but *u* what the Lord's will is.
Heb 11: 3 By faith we *u* that the universe was
2Pe   1: 20 you must *u* that no prophecy
      3: 3 you must *u* that in the last days
      3: 16 some things that are hard to *u*.

UNDERSTANDING (UNDERSTAND)

1Ki   4: 29 and a breadth of *u* as measureless
Job 12: 12 Does not long life bring *u?*
     28: 12 Where does *u* dwell?
     28: 28 and to shun evil is *u*.' "
     32: 8 of the Almighty, that gives him *u*
     36: 26 How great is God—beyond our *u!*
     37: 5 he does great things beyond our *u*.
Ps 111: 10 follow his precepts have good *u*.
    119: 34 Give me *u*, and I will keep your law
    119:100 I have more *u* than the elders,
    119:104 I gain *u* from your precepts;
    119:130 it gives *u* to the simple.
    136: 5 who by his *u* made the heavens,
    147: 5 his *u* has no limit.
Pr   2: 2 and applying your heart to *u*,
      2: 6 his mouth come knowledge and *u*.
      3: 5 and lean not on your own *u;*
      3: 13 the man who gains *u*,
      4: 5 Get wisdom, get *u;*
      4: 7 Though it cost all you have, get *u*.
      7: 4 and call *u* your kinsman;
      9: 10 knowledge of the Holy One is *u*.
     10: 23 but a man of *u* delights in wisdom.
     11: 12 but a man of *u* holds his tongue.
     14: 29 A patient man has great *u*,
     15: 21 a man of *u* keeps a straight course.
     15: 32 whoever heeds correction gains *u*.
     16: 16 to choose *u* rather than silver!
     16: 22 *U* is a fountain of life
     17: 27 and a man of *u* is even-tempered.

Pr 18: 2 A fool finds no pleasure in *u*
19: 8 he who cherishes *u* prospers.
20: 5 but a man of *u* draws them out.
23: 23 get wisdom, discipline and *u*
Isa 11: 2 the Spirit of wisdom and of *u*,
40: 28 and his *u* no one can fathom.
56: 11 They are shepherds who lack *u*;
Jer 3: 15 you with knowledge and *u*.
10: 12 stretched the heavens by his *u*.
Da 5: 12 a keen mind and knowledge and *u*,
10: 12 that you set your mind to gain *u*
Hos 4: 11 which take away the *u*
Mk 4: 12 and ever hearing but never *u*;
12: 33 with all your *u* and with all your
Lk 2: 47 who heard him was amazed at his *u*
2Co 6: 6 in purity, *u*, patience and kindness;
Eph 1: 8 on us with all wisdom and *u*.
Php 4: 7 of God, which transcends all *u*,
Col 1: 9 through all spiritual wisdom and *u*
2: 2 have the full riches of complete *u*,
1Jn 5: 20 God has come and has given us *u*,

UNDERSTANDS (UNDERSTAND)
1Ch 28: 9 and *u* every motive
Jer 9: 24 that he *u* and knows me,
Mt 13: 23 man who hears the word and *u* it.
Ro 3: 11 there is no one who *u*.
1Ti 6: 4 he is conceited and *u* nothing.

UNDERSTOOD (UNDERSTAND)
Ne 8: 12 they now *u* the words that had
Ps 73: 17 then I *u* their final destiny.
Isa 40: 13 Who has *u* the mind of the LORD,
40: 21 Have you not *u* since the earth was
Jn 1: 5 but the darkness has not *u* it.
Ro 1: 20 being *u* from what has been made,

UNDESIRABLE*
Jos 24: 15 But if serving the LORD seems *u*

UNDIVIDED*
1Ch 12: 33 to help David with *u* loyalty—
Ps 86: 11 give me an *u* heart,
Eze 11: 19 I will give them an *u* heart
1Co 7: 35 way in *u* devotion to the Lord.

UNDOING
Pr 18: 7 A fool's mouth is his *u*,

UNDYING*
Eph 6: 24 Lord Jesus Christ with an *u* love.

UNEQUALED*
Mt 24: 21 *u* from the beginning of the world
Mk 13: 19 of distress *u* from the beginning,

UNFADING*
1Pe 3: 4 the *u* beauty of a gentle

UNFAILING*
Ex 15: 13 ''In your *u* love you will lead
1Sa 20: 14 But show me *u* kindness like that
2Sa 22: 51 he shows *u* kindness
Ps 6: 4 save me because of your *u* love.
13: 5 But I trust in your *u* love;
18: 50 he shows *u* kindness
21: 7 through the *u* love
31: 16 save me in your *u* love
32: 10 but the LORD's *u* love
33: 5 the earth is full of his *u* love.
33: 18 those whose hope is in his *u* love,
33: 22 May your *u* love rest upon us,
36: 7 How priceless is your *u* love!
44: 26 redeem us because of your *u* love.
48: 9 we meditate on your *u* love.
51: 1 according to your *u* love;
52: 8 I trust in God's *u* love
77: 8 Has his *u* love vanished forever?
85: 7 Show us your *u* love, O LORD,
90: 14 in the morning with your *u* love,
107: 8 thanks to the LORD for his *u* love
107: 15 thanks to the LORD for his *u* love
107: 21 to the LORD for his *u* love
107: 31 to the LORD for his *u* love
119: 41 May your *u* love come to me,
119: 76 May your *u* love be my comfort,
130: 7 for with the LORD is *u* love
143: 8 bring me word of your *u* love,

Ps 143: 12 In your *u* love, silence my enemies;
147: 11 who put their hope in his *u* love.
Pr 19: 22 What a man desires is *u* love;
20: 6 Many a man claims to have *u* love,
Isa 54: 10 yet my *u* love for you will not be
La 3: 32 so great is his *u* love.
Hos 10: 12 reap the fruit of *u* love,

UNFAITHFUL (UNFAITHFULNESS)
Lev 6: 2 is *u* to the LORD by deceiving his
Nu 5: 6 and so is *u* to the LORD,
1Ch 10: 13 because he was *u* to the LORD;
Pr 11: 6 the *u* are trapped by evil desires.
13: 2 the *u* have a craving for violence.
13: 15 but the way of the *u* is hard.
22: 12 but he frustrates the words of the *u*.
23: 28 and multiplies the *u* among men.
25: 19 is reliance on the *u* in times
Jer 3: 20 But like a woman *u* to her husband,

UNFAITHFULNESS (UNFAITHFUL)
1Ch 9: 1 to Babylon because of their *u*.
Mt 5: 32 except for marital *u*, causes her
19: 9 for marital *u*, and marries another

UNFIT*
Tit 1: 16 and *u* for doing anything good.

UNFOLDING
Ps 119:130 the *u* of your words gives light;

UNFORGIVING*
2Ti 3: 3 unholy, without love, *u*, slanderous

UNFRIENDLY*
Pr 18: 1 An *u* man pursues selfish ends;

UNFRUITFUL
1Co 14: 14 my spirit prays, but my mind is *u*.

UNGODLINESS (UNGODLY)
Tit 2: 12 It teaches us to say ''No'' to *u*

UNGODLY (UNGODLINESS)
Ro 5: 6 powerless, Christ died for the *u*.
1Ti 1: 9 the *u* and sinful, the unholy
2Ti 2: 16 in it will become more and more *u*.
2Pe 2: 6 of what is going to happen to the *u*;
Jude : 15 and to convict all the *u*

UNGRATEFUL*
Lk 6: 35 he is kind to the *u* and wicked.
2Ti 3: 2 disobedient to their parents, *u*,

UNHOLY*
1Ti 1: 9 and sinful, the *u* and irreligious;
2Ti 3: 2 ungrateful, *u*, without love,
Heb 10: 29 as an *u* thing the blood

UNINTENTIONALLY
Lev 4: 2 'When anyone sins *u* and does
Nu 15: 22 '' 'Now if you *u* fail to keep any
Dt 4: 42 flee if he had *u* killed his neighbor

UNIT
1Co 12: 12 body is a *u*, though it is made up

UNITE (UNITED UNITY)
1Co 6: 15 and *u* them with a prostitute?

UNITED (UNITE)
Ge 2: 24 and mother and be *u* to his wife,
Mt 19: 5 and mother and be *u* to his wife,
Ro 6: 5 If we have been *u* with him like this
Eph 5: 31 and mother and be *u* to his wife,
Php 2: 1 from being *u* with Christ,
Col 2: 2 encouraged in heart and *u* in love,

UNITY* (UNITE)
2Ch 30: 12 the people to give them *u* of mind
Ps 133: 1 is when brothers live together in *u*!
Jn 17: 23 May they be brought to complete *u*
Ro 15: 5 a spirit of *u* among yourselves
Eph 4: 3 effort to keep the *u* of the Spirit
4: 13 up until we all reach *u* in the faith
Col 3: 14 them all together in perfect *u*.

UNIVERSE*
1Co 4: 9 made a spectacle to the whole *u*,

Eph 4: 10 in order to fill the whole *u*.)
Php 2: 15 which you shine like stars in the *u*
Heb 1: 2 and through whom he made the *u*.
11: 3 understand that the *u* was formed

UNJUST
Ro 3: 5 That God is *u* in bringing his wrath
9: 14 What then shall we say? Is God *u*?
1Pe 2: 19 up under the pain of *u* suffering

UNKNOWN
Ac 17: 23 TO AN *U*GOD.

UNLEAVENED
Ex 12: 17 ''Celebrate the Feast of *U* Bread,
Dt 16: 16 at the Feast of *U* Bread, the Feast

UNLIMITED*
1Ti 1: 16 Jesus might display his *u* patience

UNLOVED
Pr 30: 23 an *u* woman who is married,

UNMARRIED
1Co 7: 8 It is good for them to stay *u*,
7: 27 Are you *u*? Do not look for a wife.
7: 32 An *u* man is concerned about

UNPLOWED
Ex 23: 11 the seventh year let the land lie *u*
Hos 10: 12 and break up your *u* ground;

UNPRODUCTIVE
Tit 3: 14 necessities and not live *u* lives.
2Pe 1: 8 and *u* in your knowledge

UNPROFITABLE
Tit 3: 9 because these are *u* and useless.

UNPUNISHED
Ex 34: 7 Yet he does not leave the guilty *u*;
Pr 6: 29 no one who touches her will go *u*.
11: 21 of this: The wicked will not go *u*,
19: 5 A false witness will not go *u*,

UNQUENCHABLE
Lk 3: 17 he will burn up the chaff with *u* fire

UNREPENTANT*
Ro 2: 5 stubbornness and your *u* heart,

UNRIGHTEOUS*
Zep 3: 5 yet the *u* know no shame.
Mt 5: 45 rain on the righteous and the *u*.
1Pe 3: 18 the righteous for the *u*, to bring you
2Pe 2: 9 and to hold the *u* for the day

UNSEARCHABLE
Ro 11: 33 How *u* his judgments,
Eph 3: 8 preach to the Gentiles the *u* riches

UNSEEN*
Mt 6: 6 and pray to your Father, who is *u*.
6: 18 who is *u*; and your Father,
2Co 4: 18 on what is seen, but on what is *u*.
4: 18 temporary, but what is *u* is eternal.

UNSETTLED*
1Th 3: 3 so that no one would be *u*
2Th 2: 2 not to become easily *u*

UNSHRUNK
Mt 9: 16 patch of *u* cloth on an old garment,

UNSPIRITUAL*
Ro 7: 14 but I am *u*, sold as a slave to sin.
Col 2: 18 and his *u* mind puffs him up
Jas 3: 15 down from heaven but is earthly, *u*,

UNSTABLE*
Jas 1: 8 he is a double-minded man, *u*
2Pe 2: 14 they seduce the *u*; they are experts
3: 16 ignorant and *u* people distort,

UNTHINKABLE*
Job 34: 12 It is *u* that God would do wrong,

UNTIE
Mk 1: 7 worthy to stoop down and *u*.

Lk   13: 15 each of you on the Sabbath *u* his ox

UNVEILED*
2Co   3: 18 with *u* faces all reflect the Lord's

UNWHOLESOME*
Eph   4: 29 Do not let any *u* talk come out

UNWISE
Eph   5: 15 how you live—not as *u* but as wise,

UNWORTHY*
Ge   32: 10 I am *u* of all the kindness
Job   40: 4 "I am *u*— how can I reply to you?
Lk   17: 10 should say, 'We are *u* servants;
1Co 11: 27 Lord in an *u* manner will be guilty

UPHOLD (UPHOLDS)
Isa   41: 10 I will *u* you with my righteous right
Ro   3: 31 Not at all! Rather, we *u* the law.

UPHOLDS* (UPHOLD)
Ps   37: 17 but the LORD *u* the righteous.
   37: 24 for the LORD *u* him with his hand.
   63: 8 your right hand *u* me.
   140: 2 and *u* the cause of the needy.
   145: 14 The LORD *u* all those who fall
   146: 7 He *u* the cause of the oppressed

UPRIGHT
Dt   32: 4 *u* and just is he.
Job   1: 1 This man was blameless and *u;*
Ps   7: 10 who saves the *u* in heart.
   11: 7 *u* men will see his face.
   25: 8 Good and *u* is the LORD;
   33: 1 it is fitting for the *u* to praise him.
   64: 10 let all the *u* in heart praise him!
   92: 15 proclaiming, "The LORD is *u;*
   97: 11 and joy on the *u* in heart.
   119: 7 I will praise you with an *u* heart
Pr   2: 7 He holds victory in store for the *u,*
    3: 32 but takes the *u* into his confidence.
   14: 2 whose walk is *u* fears the LORD,
   15: 8 but the prayer of the *u* pleases him.
   21: 29 an *u* man gives thought to his ways.
Isa   26: 7 O *u* One, you make the way
Tit   1: 8 who is self-controlled, *u,* holy
    2: 12 *u* and godly lives in this present

UPROOTED
Dt   28: 63 You will be *u* from the land you are
Jer   31: 40 The city will never again be *u*
Jude   : 12 without fruit and *u*— twice dead.

UPSET
Lk   10: 41 are worried and *u* about many

URIAH
   Hittite husband of Bathsheba, killed by David's
order (2Sa 11).

USEFUL
Eph   4: 28 doing something *u*
2Ti   2: 21 *u* to the Master and prepared
    3: 16 Scripture is God-breathed and is *u*
Phm   : 11 now he has become *u* both to you

USELESS
1Co 15: 14 our preaching is *u*
Tit   3: 9 these are unprofitable and *u.*
Phm   : 11 Formerly he was *u* to you,
Heb   7: 18 *u* (for the law made nothing perfect
Jas   2: 20 faith without deeds is *u?*

USURY
Ne   5: 10 But let the exacting of *u* stop!
Ps   15: 5 who lends his money without *u*

UTMOST
Job   34: 36 that Job might be tested to the *u*

UTTER (UTTERS)
Ps   78: 2 I will *u* hidden things, things from of
         old—
Mt   13: 35 I will *u* things hidden

UTTERS (UTTER)
1Co 14: 2 he *u* mysteries with his spirit.

UZZIAH
   Son of Amaziah; king of Judah also known as
Azariah (2Ki 15:1-7; 1Ch 6:24; 2Ch 26). Struck
with leprosy because of pride (2Ch 26:16-23).

VAIN
Ps   33: 17 A horse is a *v* hope for deliverance;
   73: 13 in *v* have I kept my heart pure;
   127: 1 its builders labor in *v.*
Isa   65: 23 They will not toil in *v*
1Co 15: 2 Otherwise, you have believed in *v.*
   15: 58 labor in the Lord is not in *v.*
2Co   6: 1 not to receive God's grace in *v.*
Gal   2: 2 running or had run my race in *v.*

VALIANT
1Sa 10: 26 by *v* men whose hearts God had

VALID
Jn   8: 14 my own behalf, my testimony is *v,*

VALLEY (VALLEYS)
Ps   23: 4 walk through the *v* of the shadow
Isa   40: 4 Every *v* shall be raised up,
Joel   3: 14 multitudes in the *v* of decision!

VALLEYS (VALLEY)
SS   2: 1 a lily of the *v.*

VALUABLE (VALUE)
Lk   12: 24 And how much more *v* you are

VALUE (VALUABLE VALUED)
Lev   27: 3 set the *v* of a male between the ages
Pr   16: 13 they *v* a man who speaks the truth.
   31: 11 and lacks nothing of *v.*
Mt   13: 46 When he found one of great *v,*
1Ti   4: 8 For physical training is of some *v,*
Heb 11: 26 as of greater *v* than the treasures

VALUED (VALUE)
Lk   16: 15 What is highly *v* among men is

VANISHES
Jas   4: 14 appears for a little while and then *v.*

VASHTI*
   Queen of Persia replaced by Esther (Est 1-2).

VAST
Ge   2: 1 completed in all their *v* array.
Dt   1: 19 of the Amorites through all that *v*
    8: 15 He led you through the *v*
Ps 139: 17 How *v* is the sum of them!

VEGETABLES
Pr   15: 17 of *v* where there is love
Ro   14: 2 whose faith is weak, eats only *v.*

VEIL
Ex   34: 33 to them, he put a *v* over his face.
2Co   3: 14 for to this day the same *v* remains

VENGEANCE (AVENGE AVENGER AVENGES AVENGING REVENGE)
Nu   31: 3 to carry out the LORD's *v* on them
Isa   34: 8 For the LORD has a day of *v,*
Na   1: 2 The LORD takes *v* on his foes

VERDICT
Jn   3: 19 This is the *v:* Light has come

VICTOR'S* (VICTORY)
2Ti   2: 5 he does not receive the *v* crown

VICTORIES* (VICTORY)
2Sa 22: 51 He gives his king great *v;*
Ps   18: 50 He gives his king great *v;*
   21: 1 great is his joy in the *v* you give!
   21: 5 Through the *v* you gave, his glory is
   44: 4 who decrees *v* for Jacob.

VICTORIOUS (VICTORY)
Ps   20: 5 for joy when you are *v*

VICTORIOUSLY* (VICTORY)
Ps   45: 4 In your majesty ride forth *v*

VICTORY (VICTOR'S VICTORIES VICTORIOUS VICTORIOUSLY)
2Sa   8: 6 gave David *v* wherever he
Ps   44: 6 my sword does not bring me *v;*
   60: 12 With God we will gain the *v,*
   129: 2 they have not gained the *v* over me.
Pr   11: 14 but many advisers make *v* sure.
1Co 15: 54 "Death has been swallowed up in *v*
   15: 57 He gives us the *v* through our Lord
1Jn   5: 4 This is the *v* that has overcome

VIEW
Pr   5: 21 are in full *v* of the LORD,
2Ti   4: 1 and in *v* of his appearing

VILLAGE
Mk   6: 6 went around teaching from *v* to *v.*

VINDICATED (VINDICATION)
Job 13: 18 I know I will be *v.*
1Ti   3: 16 was *v* by the Spirit,

VINDICATION (VINDICATED)
Ps   24: 5 and *v* from God his Savior.

VINE (VINEYARD)
Ps 128: 3 Your wife will be like a fruitful *v*
Isa   36: 16 one of you will eat from his own *v*
Jnh   4: 6 Jonah was very happy about the *v.*
Jn   15: 1 "I am the true *v,* and my Father is

VINEGAR
Pr   10: 26 As *v* to the teeth and smoke
Mk   15: 36 filled a sponge with wine *v,*

VINEYARD (VINE)
1Ki 21: 1 an incident involving a *v* belonging
Pr   31: 16 out of her earnings she plants a *v.*
SS   1: 6 my own *v* I have neglected.
Isa   5: 1 My loved one had a *v*
1Co   9: 7 Who plants a *v* and does not eat

VIOLATION
Heb   2: 2 every *v* and disobedience received

VIOLENCE (VIOLENT)
Ge   6: 11 in God's sight and was full of *v.*
Isa   53: 9 though he had done no *v,*
   60: 18 No longer will *v* be heard
Eze   45: 9 Give up your *v* and oppression
Joel   3: 19 of *v* done to the people of Judah,
Jnh   3: 8 give up their evil ways and their *v.*

VIOLENT (VIOLENCE)
Eze 18: 10 "Suppose he has a *v* son, who sheds
1Ti   1: 13 and a persecutor and a *v* man,
    3: 3 not *v* but gentle, not quarrelsome,
Tit   1: 7 not *v,* not pursuing dishonest gain.

VIPERS
Ps 140: 3 the poison of *v* is on their lips.
Lk   3: 7 "You brood of *v!* Who warned you
Ro   3: 13 "The poison of *v* is on their lips."

VIRGIN (VIRGINS)
Dt   22: 15 shall bring proof that she was a *v*
Isa   7: 14 The *v* will be with child
Mt   1: 23 "The *v* will be with child
Lk   1: 34 I am a *v?"* The angel answered,
2Co 11: 2 that I might present you as a pure *v*

VIRGINS (VIRGIN)
Mt   25: 1 will be like ten *v* who took their
1Co   7: 25 Now about *v:* I have no command

VIRTUES*
Col   3: 14 And over all these *v* put on love,

VISIBLE
Eph   5: 13 exposed by the light becomes *v,*
Col   1: 16 and on earth, *v* and invisible,

VISION (VISIONS)
Da   9: 24 to seal up *v* and prophecy
Ac   26: 19 disobedient to the *v* from heaven.

VISIONS (VISION)
Nu   12: 6 I reveal myself to him in *v,*
Joel   2: 28 your young men will see *v.*

Ac   2:17 your young men will see v.

VOICE

Dt   30:20 listen to his v, and hold fast to him.
1Sa 15:22 as in obeying the v of the LORD?
Job 40: 9 and can your v thunder like his?
Ps   19: 4 Their v goes out into all the earth,
       29: 3 The v of the LORD is
       66:19 and heard my v in prayer.
       95: 7 Today, if you hear his v,
Pr   8: 1 Does not understanding raise her v
Isa 30:21 your ears will hear a v behind you,
       40: 3 A v of one calling:
Mk   1: 3 ''a v of one calling in the desert,
Jn   5:28 are in their graves will hear his v
       10: 3 and the sheep listen to his v.
Ro   10:18 ''Their v has gone out
Heb   3: 7 ''Today, if you hear his v,
Rev   3:20 If anyone hears my v and opens

VOMIT

Lev 18:28 it will v you out as it vomited out
Pr   26:11 As a dog returns to its v,
2Pe   2:22 ''A dog returns to its v,'' and,

VOW (VOWS)

Nu   6: 2 a v of separation to the LORD
       30: 2 When a man makes a v
Jdg 11:30 Jephthah made a v to the LORD:

VOWS (VOW)

Ps 116:14 I will fulfill my v to the LORD
Pr   20:25 and only later to consider his v.

VULTURES

Mt   24:28 is a carcass, there the v will gather.

WAGE (WAGES WAGING)

2Co 10: 3 we do not v war as the world does.

WAGES (WAGE)

Mal   3: 5 who defraud laborers of their w,
Lk   10: 7 for the worker deserves his w.
Ro   4: 4 his w are not credited to him
       6:23 For the w of sin is death,
1Ti   5:18 and ''The worker deserves his w.''

WAGING (WAGE)

Ro   7:23 w war against the law of my mind

WAILING

Ps   30:11 You turned my w into dancing;

WAIST

2Ki   1: 8 and with a leather belt around his w.''
Mt   3: 4 he had a leather belt around his w.

WAIT (AWAITS WAITED WAITING WAITS)

Ps   27:14 W for the LORD;
      130: 5 I w for the LORD, my soul waits,
Isa 30:18 Blessed are all who w for him!
Ac   1: 4 w for the gift my Father promised,
Ro   8:23 as we w eagerly for our adoption
1Th   1:10 and to w for his Son from heaven,
Tit   2:13 while we w for the blessed hope—

WAITED (WAIT)

Ps   40: 1 I w patiently for the LORD;

WAITING (WAIT)

Heb   9:28 to those who are w for him.

WAITS (WAIT)

Ro   8:19 creation w in eager expectation

WAKE (AWAKE WAKENS)

Eph   5:14 ''W up, O sleeper,

WAKENS* (WAKE)

Isa 50: 4 He w me morning by morning,
       50: 4 w my ear to listen like one being

WALK (WALKED WALKING WALKS)

Lev 26:12 I will w among you and be your
Dt   5:33 W in all the way that the LORD
       6: 7 and when you w along the road,
       10:12 to w in all his ways, to love him,
       11:19 and when you w along the road,

Dt   11:22 to w in all his ways and to hold fast
       26:17 and that you will w in his ways,
Jos 22: 5 to w in all his ways,
Ps   1: 1 who does not w in the counsel
       15: 2 He whose w is blameless
       23: 4 Even though I w
       84:11 from those whose w is blameless.
       89:15 who w in the light of your presence
      119:45 I will w about in freedom,
Pr   4:12 When you w, your steps will not be
       6:22 When you w, they will guide you;
Isa   3: 3 so that we may w in his paths.''
       2: 5 let us w in the light of the LORD.
       30:21 saying, ''This is the way; w in it.''
       40:31 they will w and not be faint.
       57: 2 Those who w uprightly
Jer   6:16 ask where the good way is, and w
Da   4:37 And those who w in pride he is able
Am   3: 3 Do two w together
Mic   4: 5 All the nations may w
       6: 8 and to w humbly with your God.
Mk   2: 9 'Get up, take your mat and w'?
Jn   8:12 Whoever follows me will never w
1Jn   1: 6 with him yet w in the darkness,
       1: 7 But if we w in the light,
2Jn   : 6 his command is that you w in love.

WALKED (WALK)

Ge   5:24 Enoch w with God; then he was no
Jos 14: 9 which your feet have w will be your
Mt   14:29 w on the water and came toward Jesus.

WALKING (WALK)

1Ki   3: 3 love for the LORD by w according
Da   3:25 I see four men w around in the fire,
2Jn   : 4 of your children w in the truth,

WALKS (WALK)

Pr   10: 9 The man of integrity w securely,
       13:20 He who w with the wise grows wise
Isa 33:15 He who w righteously
Jn   11: 9 A man who w by day will not

WALL (WALLS)

Jos   6:20 w collapsed; so every man charged
Ne   2:17 let us rebuild the w of Jerusalem,
Eph   2:14 the dividing w of hostility,
Rev 21:12 It had a great, high w

WALLOWING

2Pe   2:22 back to her w in the mud.''

WALLS (WALL)

Isa 58:12 be called Repairer of Broken W,
       60:18 but you will call your w Salvation
Heb 11:30 By faith the w of Jericho fell,

WANDER (WANDERED)

Nu   32:13 he made them w in the desert forty
Jas   5:19 one of you should w from the truth

WANDERED (WANDER)

Eze 34: 6 My sheep w over all the mountains
Mt   18:12 go to look for the one that w off?
1Ti   6:10 have w from the faith and pierced
2Ti   2:18 who have w away from the truth.

WANT (WANTED WANTING WANTS)

1Sa   8:19 ''We w a king over us.
Mt   19:21 Jesus answered, ''If you w
Lk   19:14 'We don't w this man to be our king
Ro   7:15 For what I w to do I do not do,
       13: 3 Do you w to be free from fear
2Co 12:14 what I w is not your possessions
Php   3:10 I w to know Christ and the power

WANTED (WANT)

1Co 12:18 of them, just as he w them to be.
Heb   6:17 Because God w to make

WANTING (WANT)

Da   5:27 weighed on the scales and found w.
2Pe   3: 9 with you, not w anyone to perish,

WANTS (WANT)

Mt   5:42 from the one who w to borrow
       20:26 whoever w to become great
Mk   8:35 For whoever w to save his life will

Mk   10:43 whoever w to become great
Ro   9:18 he hardens whom he w to harden.
1Ti   2: 4 who w all men to be saved
1Pe   5: 2 you are willing, as God w you to be;

WAR (WARRIOR WARS)

Jos 11:23 Then the land had rest from w.
1Sa 15:18 make w on them until you have
Ps   68:30 the nations who delight in w.
      120: 7 but when I speak, they are for w.
      144: 1 who trains my hands for w,
Isa   2: 4 nor will they train for w anymore.
Da   9:26 W will continue until the end,
Ro   7:23 waging w against the law
2Co 10: 3 we do not wage w as the world does
1Pe   2:11 which w against your soul.
Rev 12: 7 And there was w in heaven.
       19:11 With justice he judges and makes w

WARN* (WARNED WARNING WARNINGS)

Ex   19:21 w the people so they do not force
Nu   24:14 let me w you of what this people
1Sa   8: 9 but w them solemnly and let them
1Ki   2:42 swear by the LORD and w you,
2Ch 19:10 you are to w them not to sin
Ps   81: 8 O my people, and I will w you—
Jer 42:19 I w you today that you made a fatal
Eze   3:18 and you do not w him or speak out
       3:19 But if you do w the wicked man
       3:20 Since you did not w him, he will die
       3:21 if you do w the righteous man not
       33: 3 blows the trumpet to w the people,
       33: 6 blow the trumpet to w the people
       33: 9 if you do w the wicked man to turn
Lk   16:28 Let him w them, so that they will
Ac   4:17 we must w these men
1Co   4:14 but to w you, as my dear children.
Gal   5:21 I w you, as I did before, that those
1Th   5:14 brothers, w those who are idle,
2Th   3:15 an enemy, but w him as a brother.
2Ti   2:14 W them before God
Tit   3:10 and then w him a second time.
       3:10 W a divisive person once,
Rev 22:18 I w everyone who hears the words

WARNED (WARN)

2Ki 17:13 The LORD w Israel and Judah
Ps   19:11 By them is your servant w;
Jer 22:21 I w you when you felt secure,
Mt   3: 7 Who w you to flee
1Th   4: 6 have already told you and w you.
Heb 11: 7 when w about things not yet seen,
       12:25 they refused him who w them

WARNING (WARN)

Jer   6: 8 Take w, O Jerusalem,
1Ti   5:20 so that the others may take w.

WARNINGS (WARN)

1Co 10:11 and were written down as w for us,

WARRIOR (WAR)

Ex   15: 3 The LORD is a w;
1Ch 28: 3 you are a w and have shed blood.'
Pr   16:32 Better a patient man than a w.

WARS (WAR)

Ps   46: 9 He makes w cease to the ends
Mt   24: 6 You will hear of w and rumors of w,

WASH (WASHED WASHING)

Ps   51: 7 w me, and I will be whiter
Jer   4:14 w the evil from your heart
Jn   13: 5 and began to w his disciples' feet,
Ac   22:16 be baptized and w your sins away,
Jas   4: 8 W your hands, you sinners,
Rev 22:14 Blessed are those who w their robes

WASHED (WASH)

Ps   73:13 in vain have I w my hands
1Co   6:11 you were w, you were sanctified,
Heb 10:22 and having our bodies w
2Pe   2:22 and, ''A sow that is w goes back
Rev   7:14 they have w their robes

WASHING (WASH)

Eph   5:26 cleansing her by the w with water

1Ti 5:10 showing hospitality, *w* the feet
Tit 3: 5 us through the *w* of rebirth

WASTED (WASTING)

Jn 6:12 Let nothing be *w.*''

WASTING (WASTED)

2Co 4:16 Though outwardly we are *w* away,

WATCH (WATCHER WATCHES WATCHING WATCHMAN)

Ge 31:49 ''May the LORD keep *w*
Ps 90: 4 or like a *w* in the night.
141: 3 keep *w* over the door of my lips.
Pr 4: 6 love her, and she will *w* over you.
6:22 when you sleep, they will *w*
Jer 31:10 will *w* over his flock like a shepherd
Mic 7: 1 *w* in hope for the LORD,
Mt 24:42 ''Therefore keep *w*, because you do
26:41 *W* and pray so that you will not fall
Mk 13:35 ''Therefore keep *w* because you do
Lk 2: 8 keeping *w* over their flocks at night
1Ti 4:16 *W* your life and doctrine closely.
Heb 13:17 They keep *w* over you

WATCHER* (WATCH)

Job 7:20 O *w* of men?

WATCHES* (WATCH)

Nu 19: 5 While he *w*, the heifer is
Job 24:15 The eye of the adulterer *w* for dusk;
Ps 1: 6 For the LORD *w* over the way
33:14 from his dwelling place he *w*
63: 6 of you through the *w* of the night.
119:148 through the *w* of the night,
121: 3 he who *w* over you will not slumber
121: 4 indeed, he who *w* over Israel
121: 5 The LORD *w* over you—
127: 1 Unless the LORD *w* over the city,
145:20 LORD *w* over all who love him,
146: 9 The LORD *w* over the alien
Pr 31:27 She *w* over the affairs
Ecc 11: 4 Whoever *w* the wind will not plant;
La 2:19 as the *w* of the night begin;
4:16 he no longer *w* over them.

WATCHING (WATCH)

Lk 12:37 whose master finds them *w*

WATCHMAN (WATCH)

Eze 3:17 I have made you a *w* for the house
33: 6 but I will hold the *w* accountable

WATER (WATERED WATERING WATERS WELL-WATERED)

Ex 7:20 all the *w* was changed into blood.
17: 1 but there was no *w* for the people
Nu 20: 2 there was no *w* for the community,
Ps 1: 3 like a tree planted by streams of *w*,
22:14 I am poured out like *w*,
42: 1 As the deer pants for streams of *w*,
Pr 25:21 if he is thirsty, give him *w* to drink.
Isa 12: 3 With joy you will draw *w*
30:20 of adversity and the *w* of affliction,
32: 2 like streams of *w* in the desert
49:10 and lead them beside springs of *w*.
Jer 2:13 broken cisterns that cannot hold *w*.
17: 8 will be like a tree planted by the *w*
31: 9 I will lead them beside streams of *w*
Eze 36:25 I will sprinkle clean *w* on you,
Zec 14: 8 On that day living *w* will flow out
Mt 14:29 walked on the *w* and came toward Jesus.
Mk 9:41 anyone who gives you a cup of *w*
Lk 5: 4 to Simon, ''Put out into deep *w*,
Jn 3: 5 unless he is born of *w* and the Spirit.
4:10 he would have given you living *w*.''
7:38 streams of living *w* will flow
Eph 5:26 washing with *w* through the word.
Heb 10:22 our bodies washed with pure *w*.
1Pe 3:21 this *w* symbolizes baptism that now
2Pe 2:17 These men are springs without *w*
1Jn 5: 6 This is the one who came by *w*
5: 6 come by *w* only, but by *w*
5: 8 the Spirit, the *w* and the blood;
Rev 7:17 to springs of living *w*.
21: 6 cost from the spring of the *w* of life.

WATERED (WATER)

1Co 3: 6 I planted the seed, Apollos *w* it,

WATERING (WATER)

Isa 55:10 it without *w* the earth

WATERS (WATER)

Ps 23: 2 he leads me beside quiet *w*,
Ecc 11: 1 Cast your bread upon the *w*,
SS 8: 7 Many *w* cannot quench love;
Isa 11: 9 as the *w* cover the sea.
43: 2 When you pass through the *w*,
55: 1 come to the *w*;
58:11 like a spring whose *w* never fail.
Hab 2:14 as the *w* cover the sea.
1Co 3: 7 plants nor he who *w* is anything,

WAVE (WAVES)

Lev 23:11 He is to *w* the sheaf
Jas 1: 6 he who doubts is like a *w* of the sea,

WAVER*

1Ki 18:21 ''How long will you *w*
Ro 4:20 Yet he did not *w* through unbelief

WAVES (WAVE)

Isa 57:20 whose *w* cast up mire and mud.
Mt 8:27 Even the winds and the *w* obey him
Eph 4:14 tossed back and forth by the *w*,

WAY (WAYS)

Ex 13:21 of cloud to guide them on their *w*
18:20 and show them the *w* to live
Dt 1:33 to show you the *w* you should go.
32: 6 Is this the *w* you repay the LORD,
1Sa 12:23 I will teach you the *w* that is good
2Sa 22:31 ''As for God, his *w* is perfect;
1Ki 8:23 wholeheartedly in your *w*.
8:36 Teach them the right *w* to live,
Job 23:10 But he knows the *w* that I take;
Ps 1: 1 or stand in the *w* of sinners
32: 8 teach you in the *w* you should go;
37: 5 Commit your *w* to the LORD;
86:11 Teach me your *w*, O LORD,
119: 9 can a young man keep his *w* pure?
139:24 See if there is any offensive *w* in me
Pr 4:11 I guide you in the *w* of wisdom
12:15 The *w* of a fool seems right to him,
14:12 There is a *w* that seems right
16:17 he who guards his *w* guards his life.
19: 2 nor to be hasty and miss the *w*.
22: 6 Train a child in the *w* he should go,
30:19 and the *w* of a man with a maiden.
Isa 30:21 saying, ''This is the *w*; walk in it.''
35: 8 it will be called the *W* of Holiness.
40: 3 the *w* for the LORD;
48:17 you in the *w* you should go.
53: 6 each of us has turned to his own *w*;
55: 7 Let the wicked forsake his *w*
Jer 5:31 and my people love it this *w*.
Mal 3: 1 who will prepare the *w* before me.
Mt 3: 3 'Prepare the *w* for the Lord,
Lk 7:27 who will prepare your *w* before you
Jn 14: 6 ''I am the *w* and the truth
Ac 1:11 in the *w* you have seen him go
9: 2 any there who belonged to the *W*,
24:14 of the *W*, which they call a sect.
1Co 10:13 also provide a *w* out so that you can
12:31 will show you the most excellent *w*.
Col 1:10 and may please him in every *w*:
Tit 2:10 that in every *w* they will make
Heb 4:15 who has been tempted in every *w*,
9: 8 was showing by this that the *w*
10:20 and living *w* opened for us
13:18 desire to live honorably in every *w*.

WAYS (WAY)

Ex 33:13 teach me your *w* so I may know
Dt 10:12 to walk in all his *w*, to love him,
26:17 and that you will walk in his *w*,
30:16 in his *w*, and to keep his commands
32: 4 and all his *w* are just.
Jos 22: 5 in all his *w*, to obey his commands,
2Ch 11:17 walking in the *w* of David
Job 34:21 ''His eyes are on the *w* of men;
Ps 25: 4 Show me your *w*, O LORD,
25:10 All the *w* of the LORD are loving

Ps 37: 7 fret when men succeed in their *w*,
51:13 I will teach transgressors your *w*,
77:13 Your *w*, O God, are holy.
119: 59 I have considered my *w*
139: 3 you are familiar with all my *w*.
145:17 The LORD is righteous in all his *w*
Pr 3: 6 in all your *w* acknowledge him,
4:26 and take only *w* that are firm.
5:21 For a man's *w* are in full view
16: 2 All a man's *w* seem innocent
16: 7 When a man's *w* are pleasing
Isa 2: 3 He will teach us his *w*,
55: 8 neither are your *w* my *w*,''
Eze 28:15 You were blameless in your *w*
33: 8 out to dissuade him from his *w*,
Hos 14: 9 The *w* of the LORD are right;
Ro 1:30 they invent *w* of doing evil;
Jas 3: 2 We all stumble in many *w*.

WEAK (WEAKER WEAKNESS WEAKNESSES)

Ps 41: 1 is he who has regard for the *w*;
72:13 He will take pity on the *w*
82: 3 Defend the cause of the *w*
Eze 34: 4 You have not strengthened the *w*
Mt 26:41 spirit is willing, but the body is *w*.''
Ac 20:35 of hard work we must help the *w*,
Ro 14: 1 Accept him whose faith is *w*,
15: 1 to bear with the failings of the *w*
1Co 1:27 God chose the *w* things
8: 9 become a stumbling block to the *w*.
9:22 To the *w* I became *w*, to win the *w*.
11:30 That is why many among you are *w*
2Co 12:10 For when I am *w*, then I am strong.
1Th 5:14 help the *w*, be patient
Heb 12:12 your feeble arms and *w* knees.

WEAK-WILLED (WILL)

2Ti 3: 6 and gain control over *w* women,

WEAKER* (WEAK)

2Sa 3: 1 the house of Saul grew *w* and *w*.
1Co 12:22 seem to be *w* are indispensable,
1Pe 3: 7 them with respect as the *w* partner

WEAKNESS* (WEAK)

La 1: 6 in *w* they have fled
Ro 8:26 the Spirit helps us in our *w*.
1Co 1:25 and the *w* of God is stronger
2: 3 I came to you in *w* and fear,
15:43 it is sown in *w*, it is raised in power;
2Co 11:30 boast of the things that show my *w*
12: 9 for my power is made perfect in *w*
13: 4 he was crucified in *w*, yet he lives
Heb 5: 2 since he himself is subject to *w*.
11:34 whose *w* was turned to strength;

WEAKNESSES* (WEAK)

2Co 12: 5 about myself, except about my *w*.
12: 9 all the more gladly about my *w*,
12:10 I delight in *w*, in insults,
Heb 4:15 unable to sympathize with our *w*,

WEALTH

Dt 8:18 gives you the ability to produce *w*,
2Ch 1:11 and you have not asked for *w*,
Ps 39: 6 he heaps up *w*, not knowing who
Pr 3: 9 Honor the LORD with your *w*,
10: 4 but diligent hands bring *w*.
11: 4 *W* is worthless in the day of wrath,
13: 7 To be poor, yet has great *w*.
15:16 than great *w* with turmoil.
22: 4 bring *w* and honor and life.
Ecc 5:10 whoever loves *w* is never satisfied
5:13 hoarded to the harm of its owner,
SS 8: 7 all the *w* of his house for love,
Mt 13:22 and the deceitfulness of *w* choke it,
Mk 10:22 away sad, because he had great *w*.
12:44 They all gave out of their *w*; but she
Lk 15:13 and there squandered his *w*
1Ti 6:17 nor to put their hope in *w*,
Jas 5: 2 Your *w* has rotted, and moths have
5: 3 You have hoarded *w*

WEAPON (WEAPONS)

Ne 4:17 work with one hand and held a *w*

WEAPONS (WEAPON)

Ecc 9:18 Wisdom is better than *w* of war,
2Co 6: 7 with *w* of righteousness
      10: 4 The *w* we fight with are not

WEAR (WEARING)

Dt   8: 4 Your clothes did not *w* out
     22: 5 nor a man *w* women's clothing,
Ps 102:26 they will all *w* out like a garment.
Pr 23: 4 Do not *w* yourself out to get rich;
Isa 51: 6 the earth will *w* out like a garment
Heb 1:11 they will all *w* out like a garment.
Rev 3:18 and white clothes to *w*,

WEARIES (WEARY)

Ecc 12:12 and much study *w* the body.

WEARING (WEAR)

Jn 19: 5 When Jesus came out *w* the crown
Jas   2: 3 attention to the man *w* fine clothes
1Pe 3: 3 as braided hair and the *w*
Rev 7: 9 They were *w* white robes

WEARY (WEARIES)

Isa 40:28 He will not grow tired or *w*,
    40:31 they will run and not grow *w*,
    50: 4 know the word that sustains the *w*.
Mt 11:28 all you who are *w* and burdened,
Gal   6: 9 Let us not become *w* in doing good,
Heb 12: 3 so that you will not grow *w*
Rev 2: 3 my name, and have not grown *w*.

WEDDING

Mt 22:11 who was not wearing *w* clothes.
Rev 19: 7 For the *w* of the Lamb has come,

WEEDS

Mt 13:25 and sowed *w* among the wheat,

WEEK

Mt 28: 1 at dawn on the first day of the *w*,
1Co 16: 2 On the first day of every *w*,

WEEP (WEEPING WEPT)

Ecc 3: 4 a time to *w* and a time to laugh,
Lk   6:21 Blessed are you who *w* now,
    23:28 *w* for yourselves and for your

WEEPING (WEEP)

Ps 30: 5 *w* may remain for a night,
 126: 6 He who goes out *w*,
Jer 31:15 Rachel *w* for her children
Mt   2:18 Rachel *w* for her children
     8:12 where there will be *w* and gnashing

WEIGH (OUTWEIGHS WEIGHED WEIGHS WEIGHTIER WEIGHTS)

1Co 14:29 others should *w* carefully what is

WEIGHED (WEIGH)

Job 28:15 nor can its price be *w* in silver.
Da   5:27 You have been *w* on the scales
Lk 21:34 or your hearts will be *w*

WEIGHS (WEIGH)

Pr 12:25 An anxious heart *w* a man down,
    15:28 of the righteous *w* its answers,
    21: 2 but the Lord *w* the heart.
    24:12 not he who *w* the heart perceive

WEIGHTIER* (WEIGH)

Jn   5:36 "I have testimony *w* than that

WEIGHTS (WEIGH)

Lev 19:36 Use honest scales and honest *w*,
Dt 25:13 Do not have two differing *w*
Pr 11: 1 but accurate *w* are his delight.

WELCOME (WELCOMES)

Mk   9:37 welcomes me does not *w* me
2Pe 1:11 and you will receive a rich *w*

WELCOMES (WELCOME)

Mt 18: 5 whoever *w* a little child like this
2Jn   :11 Anyone who *w* him shares

WELL (WELLED WELLING WELLS)

Mt 15:31 crippled made *w*, the lame walking
Lk 14: 5 falls into a *w* on the Sabbath day,

Lk 17:19 your faith has made you *w*."
Jas   5:15 in faith will make the sick person *w*

WELL-WATERED (WATER)

Isa 58:11 You will be like a *w* garden,

WELLED* (WELL)

2Co 8: 2 and their extreme poverty *w* up

WELLING* (WELL)

Jn   4:14 of water *w* up to eternal life."

WELLS (WELL)

Isa 12: 3 from the *w* of salvation.

WELLSPRING* (SPRING)

Pr   4:23 for it is the *w* of life.

WEPT (WEEP)

Ps 137: 1 of Babylon we sat and *w*
Lk 22:62 And he went outside and *w* bitterly
Jn 11:35 Jesus *w*.

WEST

Ps 103:12 as far as the east is from the *w*,
 107: 3 from east and *w*, from north

WHEAT

Mt   3:12 gathering his *w* into the barn
    13:25 and sowed weeds among the *w*,
Lk 22:31 Satan has asked to sift you as *w*,
Jn 12:24 a kernel of *w* falls to the ground

WHEELS

Eze 1:16 appearance and structure of the *w*:

WHIRLWIND (WIND)

2Ki 2: 1 to take Elijah up to heaven in a *w*,
Hos 8: 7 and reap the *w*.
Na   1: 3 His way is in the *w* and the storm,

WHISPER (WHISPERED)

1Ki 19:12 And after the fire came a gentle *w*.
Job 26:14 how faint the *w* we hear of him!
Ps 107:29 He stilled the storm to a *w*;

WHISPERED (WHISPER)

Mt 10:27 speak in the daylight; what is *w*

WHITE (WHITER)

Isa   1:18 they shall be as *w* as snow;
Da   7: 9 His clothing was as *w* as snow;
     7: 9 the hair of his head was *w* like wool
Mt 28: 3 and his clothes were as *w* as snow.
Rev 1:14 hair were *w* like wool, as *w* as snow,
     3: 4 dressed in *w*, for they are worthy.
     6: 2 and there before me was a *w* horse!
     7:13 "These in *w* robes—who are they,
   19:11 and there before me was a *w* horse,
   20:11 Then I saw a great *w* throne

WHITER (WHITE)

Ps 51: 7 and I will be *w* than snow.

WHOLE

Ge   1:29 plant on the face of the *w* earth
     2: 6 and watered the *w* surface
   11: 1 Now the *w* world had one language
Ex 12:47 The *w* community
    19: 5 Although the *w* earth is mine,
Lev 16:17 and the *w* community of Israel.
Nu 14:21 of the Lord fills the *w* earth,
    32:13 until the *w* generation
Dt 13:16 *w* burnt offering to the Lord your
    19: 8 gives you the *w* land he promised
Jos   2: 3 come to spy out the *w* land."
1Sa 1:28 For his *w* life he will be given
    17:46 the *w* world will know that there is
1Ki 10:24 The *w* world sought audience
2Ki 21: 8 and will keep the *w* Law that my
Ps 72:19 may the *w* earth be filled
Pr   4:22 and health to a man's *w* body.
     8:31 rejoicing in his *w* world
Ecc 12:13 for this is the *w* duty of man.
Isa   1: 5 Your *w* head is injured,
     6: 3 the *w* earth is full of his glory."
   14:26 plan determined for the *w* world;
Eze 34: 6 were scattered over the *w* earth,
   37:11 these bones are the *w* house

Da   2:35 mountain and filled the *w* earth.
Zep 1:18 the *w* world will be consumed,
Zec 14: 9 will be king over the *w* earth.
Mal 3:10 the *w* tithe into the storehouse,
Mt   5:29 than for your *w* body to be thrown
     6:22 your *w* body will be full of light.
   16:26 for a man if he gains the *w* world,
   24:14 will be preached in the *w* world
Lk 21:35 live on the face of the *w* earth.
Jn 12:19 Look how the *w* world has gone
   13:10 to wash his feet; his *w* body is clean
   21:25 the *w* world would not have room
Ac 17:26 they should inhabit the *w* earth;
   20:27 proclaim to you the *w* will of God.
Ro   1: 9 whom I serve with my *w* heart
     3:19 and the *w* world held accountable
     8:22 know that the *w* creation has been
1Co 4: 9 made a spectacle to the *w* universe,
   12:17 If the *w* body were an ear,
Gal   3:22 declares that the *w* world is
     5: 3 obligated to obey the *w* law.
Eph 4:10 in order to fill the *w* universe.)
     4:13 attaining to the *w* measure
1Th 5:23 May your *w* spirit, soul
Jas   2:10 For whoever keeps the *w* law
1Jn 2: 2 but also for the sins of the *w* world.
Rev 3:10 going to come upon the *w* world

WHOLEHEARTED* (HEART)

2Ki 20: 3 you faithfully and with *w* devotion
1Ch 28: 9 and serve him with *w* devotion
   29:19 my son Solomon the *w* devotion
Isa 38: 3 you faithfully and with *w* devotion

WHOLEHEARTEDLY* (HEART)

Nu 14:24 a different spirit and follows me *w*,
   32:11 they have not followed me *w*,
   32:12 for they followed the Lord *w*.'
Dt   1:36 because he followed the Lord *w*
Jos 14: 8 followed the Lord my God *w*,
   14: 9 followed the Lord my God *w*.'
   14:14 the Lord, the God of Israel, *w*.
1Ki 8:23 with your servants who continue *w*
1Ch 29: 9 for they had given freely and *w*
2Ch 6:14 with your servants who continue *w*
   15:15 oath because they had sworn it *w*,
   19: 9 and *w* in the fear of the Lord.
   25: 2 in the eyes of the Lord, but not *w*
   31:21 he sought his God and worked *w*.
Ro   6:17 you *w* obeyed the form of teaching
Eph 6: 7 Serve *w*, as if you were serving

WHOLESOME*

2Ki 2:22 And the water has remained *w*
2Pe 3: 1 to stimulate you to *w* thinking.

WICK

Isa 42: 3 a smoldering *w* he will not snuff out
Mt 12:20 a smoldering *w* he will not snuff out

WICKED (WICKEDNESS)

Ge 13:13 Now the men of Sodom were *w*
   39: 9 How then could I do such a *w* thing
Ex 23: 1 Do not help a *w* man
Nu 14:35 things to this whole *w* community,
Dt 15: 9 not to harbor this *w* thought:
Jdg 19:22 some of the *w* men
1Sa 2:12 Eli's sons were *w* men; they had no
   15:18 completely destroy those *w* people,
   25:17 He is such a *w* man that no one can
2Sa 3:12 in Israel! Don't do this *w* thing.
2Ki 17:11 They did *w* things that provoked
2Ch 7:14 and turn from their *w* ways,
   19: 2 "Should you help the *w*
Ne 13:17 "What is this *w* thing you are doing
Ps   1: 1 walk in the counsel of the *w*
     1: 5 Therefore the *w* will not stand
     7: 9 to an end the violence of the *w*
   10:13 Why does the *w* man revile God?
   11: 5 the *w* and those who love violence
   12: 8 The *w* freely strut about
   26: 5 and refuse to sit with the *w*.
   32:10 Many are the woes of the *w*,
   36: 1 concerning the sinfulness of the *w*:
   37:13 but the Lord laughs at the *w*,
   49: 5 when *w* deceivers surround me—
   50:16 But to the *w*, God says:
   58: 3 Even from birth the *w* go astray;

Ps 73: 3 when I saw the prosperity of the *w.*
    82: 2 and show partiality to the *w? Selah*
   112: 10 the longings of the *w* make
   119: 61 Though the *w* bind me with ropes,
  119:155 Salvation is far from the *w,*
   140: 8 do not grant the *w* their desires,
   141: 10 Let the *w* fall into their own nets,
   146: 9 he frustrates the ways of the *w.*
Pr 2: 12 you from the ways of *w* men,
   4: 14 Do not set foot on the path of the *w*
   6: 18 a heart that devises *w* schemes,
   9: 7 whoever rebukes a *w* man incurs
  10: 20 the heart of the *w* is of little value.
  10: 28 the hopes of the *w* come to nothing
  11: 5 *w* are brought down by their own
  11: 10 when the *w* perish, there are shouts
  11: 21 The *w* will not go unpunished,
  12: 5 but the advice of the *w* is deceitful.
  12: 10 the kindest acts of the *w* are cruel.
  14: 19 the *w* at the gates of the righteous.
  15: 3 keeping watch on the *w*
  15: 26 detests the thoughts of the *w,*
  21: 10 The *w* man craves evil;
  21: 29 A *w* man puts up a bold front,
  28: 1 *w* man flees though no one pursues,
  28: 4 who forsake the law praise the *w,*
  29: 7 but the *w* have no such concern.
  29: 16 When the *w* thrive, so does sin,
  29: 27 the *w* detest the upright.
Isa 11: 4 breath of his lips he will slay the *w.*
  13: 11 the *w* for their sins.
  26: 10 Though grace is shown to the *w,*
  48: 22 says the LORD, ''for the *w.''*
  53: 9 He was assigned a grave with the *w*
  55: 7 Let the *w* forsake his way
  57: 20 But the *w* are like the tossing sea,
Jer 35: 15 of you must turn from your *w* ways
Eze 3: 18 that *w* man will die for his sin,
  13: 22 you encouraged the *w* not to turn
  14: 7 and puts a *w* stumbling block
  18: 21 ''But if a *w* man turns away
  18: 23 pleasure in the death of the *w?*
  21: 25 '' 'O profane and *w* prince of Israel,
  33: 8 When I say to the *w,* 'O *w* man,
  33: 11 pleasure in the death of the *w,*
  33: 14 to the *w* man, 'You will surely die,'
  33: 19 And if a *w* man turns away
Da 12: 10 but the *w* will continue to be *w.*
Mt 12: 39 *w* and adulterous generation asks
  12: 45 be with this *w* generation.''
  12: 45 with it seven other spirits more *w*
Lk 6: 35 he is kind to the ungrateful and *w.*
Ac 2: 23 and you, with the help of *w* men,
Ro 4: 5 but trusts God who justifies the *w,*
1Co 5: 13 ''Expel the *w* man from among you
  6: 9 not know that the *w* will not inherit
Rev 2: 2 that you cannot tolerate *w* men,

WICKEDNESS (WICKED)

Ge 6: 5 The LORD saw how great man's *w*
Ex 34: 7 and forgiving *w,* rebellion and sin.
Lev 16: 21 and confess over it all the *w*
  19: 29 to prostitution and be filled with *w.*
Dt 9: 4 it is on account of the *w*
Ne 9: 2 and confessed their sins and the *w*
Ps 45: 7 You love righteousness and hate *w;*
  92: 15 he is my Rock, and there is no *w*
Pr 13: 6 but *w* overthrows the sinner.
Jer 3: 2 land with your prostitution and *w,*
  8: 6 No one repents of his *w,*
  14: 20 O LORD, we acknowledge our *w*
Eze 18: 20 the *w* of the wicked will be charged
  28: 15 created till *w* was found in you.
  33: 19 wicked man turns away from his *w*
Da 4: 27 and your *w* by being kind
  9: 24 to atone for *w,* to bring
Jnh 1: 2 its *w* has come up before me.''
Mt 24: 12 Because of the increase of *w,*
Lk 11: 39 inside you are full of greed and *w.*
Ac 1: 18 (With the reward he got for his *w,*
Ro 1: 18 who suppress the truth by their *w,*
1Co 5: 8 the yeast of malice and *w,*
2Co 6: 14 what do righteousness and *w* have
2Ti 2: 19 of the Lord must turn away from *w*
Tit 2: 14 for us to redeem us from all *w*
Heb 1: 9 loved righteousness and hated *w;*
  8: 12 For I will forgive their *w*
2Pe 2: 15 who loved the wages of *w.*

WIDE

Ps 81: 10 Open *w* your mouth and I will fill it
Isa 54: 2 stretch your tent curtains *w,*
Mt 7: 13 For *w* is the gate and broad is
2Co 6: 13 my children—open *w* your hearts
Eph 3: 18 to grasp how *w* and long and high

WIDOW (WIDOWS)

Ex 22: 22 ''Do not take advantage of a *w*
Dt 10: 18 cause of the fatherless and the *w,*
Ps 146: 9 sustains the fatherless and the *w,*
Isa 1: 17 plead the case of the *w.*
Lk 21: 2 saw a poor *w* put in two very small
1Ti 5: 4 But if a *w* has children

WIDOWS (WIDOW)

Ps 68: 5 to the fatherless, a defender of *w,*
Ac 6: 1 their *w* were being overlooked
1Co 7: 8 to the unmarried and the *w* I say:
1Ti 5: 3 to those *w* who are really
Jas 1: 27 look after orphans and *w*

WIFE (WIVES WIVES')

Ge 2: 24 and mother and be united to his *w,*
  19: 26 But Lot's *w* looked back,
  24: 67 she became his *w,* and he loved her;
Ex 20: 17 shall not covet your neighbor's *w,*
Lev 20: 10 adultery with another man's *w*—
Dt 5: 21 shall not covet your neighbor's *w.*
  24: 5 happiness to the *w* he has married.
Ru 4: 13 took Ruth and she became his *w.*
Pr 5: 18 in the *w* of your youth.
  12: 4 *w* of noble character is her
  18: 22 He who finds a *w* finds what is
  19: 13 quarrelsome *w* is like a constant
  31: 10 *w* of noble character who can find?
Hos 1: 2 take to yourself an adulterous *w*
Mal 2: 14 the witness between you and the *w*
Mt 1: 20 to take Mary home as your *w,*
  19: 3 for a man to divorce his *w* for any
Lk 17: 32 Remember Lot's *w!* Whoever tries
  18: 29 or *w* or brothers or parents
1Co 7: 2 each man should have his own *w,*
  7: 33 how he can please his *w*—
Eph 5: 23 the husband is the head of the *w*
  5: 33 must love his *w* as he loves himself,
1Ti 3: 2 husband of but one *w,* temperate,
Rev 21: 9 I will show you the bride, the *w*

WILD

Ge 1: 25 God made the *w* animals according
  8: 1 Noah and all the *w* animals
Lk 15: 13 squandered his wealth in *w* living.
Ro 11: 17 and you, though a *w* olive shoot,

WILL (WEAK-WILLED WILLFUL WILLING WILLINGNESS)

Ps 40: 8 I desire to do your *w,* O my God;
  143: 10 Teach me to do your *w,*
Isa 53: 10 Yet it was the LORD's *w*
Mt 6: 10 your *w* be done
  7: 21 who does the *w* of my Father
  10: 29 apart from the *w* of your Father.
  12: 50 does the *w* of my Father
  26: 39 Yet not as I *w,* but as you *w.''*
  26: 42 I drink it, may your *w* be done.''
Jn 6: 38 but to do the *w* of him who sent me.
  7: 17 If anyone chooses to do God's *w,*
Ac 20: 27 to you the whole *w* of God.
Ro 12: 2 and approve what God's *w*—
1Co 7: 37 but has control over his own *w,*
Eph 5: 17 understand what the Lord's *w* is.
Php 2: 13 for it is God who works in you to *w*
1Th 4: 3 God's *w* that you should be sanctified:
  5: 18 for this is God's *w* for you
2Ti 2: 26 has taken them captive to do his *w.*
Heb 2: 4 distributed according to his *w.*
  9: 16 In the case of a *w,* it is necessary
  10: 7 I have come to do your *w,* O God
  13: 21 everything good for doing his *w,*
Jas 4: 15 ''If it is the Lord's *w,*
1Pe 3: 17 It is better, if it is God's *w,*
  4: 2 but rather for the *w* of God.
2Pe 1: 21 never had its origin in the *w*
1Jn 5: 14 we ask anything according to his *w,*
Rev 4: 11 and by your *w* they were created

WILLFUL (WILL)

Ps 19: 13 Keep your servant also from *w* sins;

WILLING (WILL)

1Ch 28: 9 devotion and with a *w* mind,
  29: 5 who is *w* to consecrate himself
Ps 51: 12 grant me a *w* spirit, to sustain me.
Da 3: 28 were *w* to give up their lives rather
Mt 18: 14 Father in heaven is not *w* that any
  23: 37 her wings, but you were not *w.*
  26: 41 The spirit is *w,* but the body is weak
1Ti 6: 18 and to be generous and *w* to share.
1Pe 5: 2 but because you are *w,*

WILLINGNESS* (WILL)

2Co 8: 11 so that your eager *w*
  8: 12 For if the *w* is there, the gift is

WIN (WINS WON)

1Co 9: 19 myself a slave to everyone, to *w*
Php 3: 14 on toward the goal to *w* the prize
1Th 4: 12 your daily life may *w* the respect

WIND (WHIRLWIND WINDS)

Ps 1: 4 that the *w* blows away.
Ecc 2: 11 meaningless, a chasing after the *w;*
Hos 8: 7 ''They sow the *w*
Mk 4: 41 Even the *w* and the waves obey
Jn 3: 8 The *w* blows wherever it pleases.
Eph 4: 14 and there by every *w* of teaching
Jas 1: 6 blown and tossed by the *w.*

WINDOW

Jos 2: 21 she tied the scarlet cord in the *w.*
Ac 20: 9 in a *w* was a young man named
2Co 11: 33 in a basket from a *w* in the wall

WINDS (WIND)

Ps 104: 4 He makes *w* his messengers,
Mt 24: 31 gather his elect from the four *w,*
Heb 1: 7 ''He makes his angels *w,*

WINE

Ps 104: 15 *w* that gladdens the heart of man,
Pr 20: 1 W is a mocker and beer a brawler;
  23: 20 join those who drink too much *w*
  23: 31 Do not gaze at *w* when it is red,
  31: 6 *w* to those who are in anguish;
SS 1: 2 your love is more delightful than *w.*
Isa 28: 7 And these also stagger from *w*
  55: 1 Come, buy *w* and milk
Mt 9: 17 Neither do men pour new *w*
Lk 23: 36 They offered him *w* vinegar
Jn 2: 3 When the *w* was gone, Jesus'
Ro 14: 21 not to eat meat or drink *w*
Eph 5: 18 on *w,* which leads to debauchery.
1Ti 5: 23 a little *w* because of your stomach
Rev 16: 19 with the *w* of the fury of his wrath.

WINEPRESS

Isa 63: 2 like those of one treading the *w?*
Rev 19: 15 He treads the *w* of the fury

WINESKINS

Mt 9: 17 do men pour new wine into old *w.*

WINGS

Ex 19: 4 and how I carried you on eagles' *w*
Ru 2: 12 under whose *w* you have come
Ps 17: 8 hide me in the shadow of your *w*
  91: 4 under his *w* you will find refuge;
Isa 6: 2 him were seraphs, each with six *w:*
  40: 31 They will soar on *w* like eagles;
Eze 1: 6 of them had four faces and four *w.*
Zec 5: 9 in their *w!* They had *w* like those
Mal 4: 2 rise with healing in its *w.*
Lk 13: 34 hen gathers her chicks under her *w,*
Rev 4: 8 the four living creatures had six *w*

WINS (WIN)

Pr 11: 30 and he who *w* souls is wise.

WINTER

Mk 13: 18 that this will not take place in *w,*

WIPE (WIPED)

Isa 25: 8 The Sovereign LORD will *w* away
Rev 7: 17 God will *w* away every tear

Rev 21: 4 He will *w* every tear

WIPED (WIPE)

Lk   7: 38 Then she *w* them with her hair,
Ac   3: 19 so that your sins may be *w* out,

WISDOM (WISE)

Ge   3: 6 and also desirable for gaining *w*,
1Ki   4: 29 God gave Solomon *w* and very
2Ch   1: 10 Give me *w* and knowledge,
Ps   51: 6 you teach me *w* in the inmost place
    111: 10 of the Lord is the beginning of *w*;
Pr   2: 6 For the Lord gives *w*,
    3: 13 Blessed is the man who finds *w*,
    4: 7 *W* is supreme; therefore get
    8: 11 for *w* is more precious than rubies,
    11: 2 but with humility comes *w*.
    13: 10 *w* is found in those who take advice
    23: 23 get *w*, discipline and understanding
    29: 3 A man who loves *w* brings joy
    29: 15 The rod of correction imparts *w*,
    31: 26 She speaks with *w*.
Isa   11: 2 Spirit of *w* and of understanding,
    28: 29 in counsel and magnificent in *w*.
Jer   10: 12 he founded the world by his *w*
Mic   6: 9 and to fear your name is *w*—
Mt   11: 19 But *w* is proved right by her actions
Lk   2: 52 And Jesus grew in *w* and stature,
Ac   6: 3 known to be full of the Spirit and *w*.
Ro   11: 33 the depth of the riches of the *w*
1Co   1: 17 not with words of human *w*,
    1: 30 who has become for us *w* from God
    12: 8 through the Spirit the message of *w*
Eph   1: 17 may give you the Spirit of *w*
Col   2: 3 are hidden all the treasures of *w*,
    2: 23 indeed have an appearance of *w*,
Jas   1: 5 of you lacks *w*, he should ask God,
    3: 13 in the humility that comes from *w*.
Rev   5: 12 and wealth and *w* and strength

WISE (WISDOM WISER)

1Ki   3: 12 give you a *w* and discerning heart,
Job   5: 13 He catches the *w* in their craftiness
Ps   19: 7 making *w* the simple.
Pr   3: 7 Do not be *w* in your own eyes;
    9: 8 rebuke a *w* man and he will love
    10: 1 A *w* son brings joy to his father,
    11: 30 and he who wins souls is *w*.
    13: 1 A *w* son heeds his father's
    13: 20 He who walks with the *w* grows *w*,
    16: 23 A *w* man's heart guides his mouth,
    17: 28 Even a fool is thought *w*
Ecc   9: 17 The quiet words of the *w* are more
Jer   9: 23 "Let not the *w* man boast
Eze   28: 3 "Because you think you are *w*,
Da   2: 21 He gives wisdom to the *w*
    12: 3 Those who are *w* will shine like
Mt   11: 25 hidden these things from the *w*
    25: 2 them were foolish and five were *w*.
1Co   1: 19 I will destroy the wisdom of the *w*;
    1: 27 things of the world to shame the *w*;
    3: 19 He catches the *w* in their craftiness
Eph   5: 15 but as *w*, making the most
2Ti   3: 15 able to make you *w* for salvation
Jas   3: 13 Who is *w* and understanding

WISER (WISE)

Pr   9: 9 a wise man and he will be *w* still;
1Co   1: 25 of God is *w* than man's wisdom,

WISH (WISHES)

Jn   15: 7 ask whatever you *w*, and it will be
Ro   9: 3 For I could *w* that I myself were
Rev   3: 15 I *w* you were either one

WISHES (WISH)

Rev 22: 17 let him come; and whoever *w*,

WITCHCRAFT

Dt   18: 10 engages in *w*, or casts spells,
Gal   5: 20 idolatry and *w*; hatred, discord,

WITHDREW

Lk   5: 16 But Jesus often *w* to lonely places

WITHER (WITHERS)

Ps   1: 3 and whose leaf does not *w*.
    37: 19 In times of disaster they will not *w*;

WITHERS (WITHER)

Isa   40: 7 The grass *w* and the flowers fall,
1Pe   1: 24 the grass *w* and the flowers fall,

WITHHELD (WITHHOLD)

Ge   22: 12 you have not *w* from me your son,

WITHHOLD (WITHHELD WITHHOLDS)

Ps   84: 11 no good thing does he *w*
Pr   23: 13 Do not *w* discipline from a child;

WITHHOLDS (WITHHOLD)

Dt   27: 19 "Cursed is the man who *w* justice

WITNESS (EYEWITNESSES WITNESSES)

Pr   12: 17 truthful *w* gives honest testimony,
    19: 9 A false *w* will not go unpunished,
Jn   1: 8 he came only as a *w* to the light.

WITNESSES (WITNESS)

Dt   19: 15 by the testimony of two or three *w*.
Mt   18: 16 by the testimony of two or three *w*.'
Ac   1: 8 and you will be my *w* in Jerusalem,

WIVES (WIFE)

Eph   5: 22 *W*, submit to your husbands
    5: 25 love your *w*, just as Christ loved
1Pe   3: 1 words by the behavior of their *w*,

WIVES' (WIFE)

1Ti   4: 7 with godless myths and old *w* tales

WOE

Isa   6: 5 "*W* to me!" I cried.
Eze   34: 2 *W* to the shepherds
Mt   18: 7 "*W* to the world
    23: 13 "*W* to you, teachers of the law
Jude   : 11 *W* to them! They have taken

WOLF (WOLVES)

Isa   65: 25 *w* and the lamb will feed together,

WOLVES (WOLF)

Mt   10: 16 you out like sheep among *w*.

WOMAN (MAN)

Ge   2: 22 God made a *w* from
    2: 23 she shall be called '*w*,'
    3: 6 *w* saw that the fruit
    3: 12 The *w* you put here with
    3: 15 between you and the *w*,
    3: 16 To the *w* he said,
    12: 11 a beautiful *w* you are.
    20: 3 because of the *w* you have
    24: 5 if the *w* is unwilling
Ex   2: 1 married a Levite *w*
    2: 2 Every *w* is to ask her
    21: 10 If he marries another *w*
    21: 22 hit a pregnant *w*
Lev   12: 2 *w* who becomes pregnant
    15: 19 *w* has her regular flow
    15: 25 a *w* has a discharge
    18: 17 sexual relations with both a *w*
    20: 13 as one lies with a *w*,
Nu   5: 29 when a *w* goes astray
    30: 3 young *w* still living in
    30: 9 by a widow or divorced *w*
    30: 10 *w* living with her husband
Dt   20: 7 become pledged to a *w*
    21: 11 the captives a beautiful *w*
    22: 5 *w* must not wear men's
    22: 13 married this *w* but when
Jdg   4: 9 hand Sisera over to a *w*.
    13: 6 the *w* went to her husband
    14: 2 have seen a Philistine *w*
    16: 4 he fell in love with a *w*
    20: 4 husband of the murdered *w*
Ru   3: 11 a *w* of noble character
1Sa   1: 15 a *w* who is deeply troubled
    25: 3 intelligent and beautiful *w*,
    28: 7 a *w* who is a medium,
2Sa   11: 2 he saw a *w* bathing
    13: 17 "Get this *w* out of here
    14: 2 had a wise *w* brought
    20: 16 a wise *w* called from
1Ki   3: 18 this *w* also had a baby.
    17: 24 the *w* said to Elijah,
2Ki   4: 8 a well-to-do *w* was there,

2Ki   8: 1 Elisha had said to the *w*
    9: 34 "Take care of that cursed *w*,"
Job   14: 1 Man born of *w* is of few
Pr   11: 16 A kindhearted *w* gains respect,
    11: 22 a beautiful *w* who shows no
    14: 1 a wise *w* builds her house,
    30: 23 unloved *w* who is married,
    31: 30 a *w* who fears the Lord
Isa   54: 1 O barren *w*, you who never
Mt   5: 28 looks at a *w* lustfully
    9: 20 a *w* who had been subject
    15: 28 *W* you have great faith!
    26: 7 a *w* came to him with
Mk   5: 25 a *w* was there who had
    7: 25 a *w* whose little daughter
Lk   7: 39 what kind of *w* she is
    10: 38 a *w* named Martha opened
    13: 12 "*W*, you are set free
    15: 8 suppose a *w* has ten silver
Jn   2: 4 *w*, why do you involve
    4: 7 a Samaritan *w* came
    8: 3 a *w* caught in adultery.
    19: 26 *w*, here is your son,"
    20: 15 *W*, 'he said, "Why are you crying?
Ac   9: 40 Turning toward the dead *w*,
    16: 14 was a *w* named Lydia,
    17: 4 not a few prominent *w*.
Ro   1: 26 *w* exchanged natural relations
1Co   14: 34 *w* should remain silent in
Php   4: 3 help these *w* who have
1Ti   2: 9 want *w* to dress modestly
    5: 2 older *w* as mothers,
Tit   2: 3 teach the older *w* to be
    2: 4 train the younger *w* to love
Heb   11: 35 *W* received back their dead
1Pe   3: 5 the holy *w* of the past

WOMB

Job   1: 21 Naked I came from my mother's *w*,
Ps   139: 13 in my mother's *w*.
Pr   31: 2 "O my son, O son of my *w*,
Jer   1: 5 you in the *w* I knew you,
Lk   1: 44 the baby in my *w* leaped for joy.
Jn   3: 4 into his mother's *w* to be born!"

WON (WIN)

1Pe   3: 1 they may be *w* over without words

WONDER (WONDERFUL WONDERS)

Ps   17: 7 Show the *w* of your great love,
SS   1: 3 No *w* the maidens love you!

WONDERFUL* (WONDER)

2Sa   1: 26 Your love for me was *w*,
    1: 26 more *w* than that of women.
1Ch   16: 9 tell of all his *w* acts,
Job   42: 3 things too *w* for me to know.
Ps   26: 7 and telling of all your *w* deeds,
    31: 21 for he showed his *w* love to me
    75: 1 men tell of your *w* deeds.
    105: 2 tell of all his *w* acts.

WONDERS (WONDER)

Ps 107: 8 and his w deeds for men,
107: 15 and his w deeds for men,
107: 21 and his w deeds for men,
107: 24 his w deeds in the deep.
107: 31 and his w deeds for men.
119: 18 w things in your law.
119:129 Your statutes are w;
131: 1 or things too w for me.
139: 6 Such knowledge is too w for me,
139: 14 your works are w,
145: 5 I will meditate on your w works.
Isa 9: 6 W Counselor, Mighty God,
28:29 w in counsel and magnificent
Mt 21:15 of the law saw the w things he did
Lk 13:17 with all the w things he was doing.
1Pe 2: 9 out of darkness into his w light.

WONDERS (WONDER)

Ex 3:20 with all the w that I will perform
Dt 10:21 and awesome w you saw
2Sa 7:23 awesome w by driving out nations
Job 37:14 stop and consider God's w.
Ps 9: 1 I will tell of all your w.
89: 5 The heavens praise your w,
119: 27 then I will meditate on your w.
Joel 2:30 I will show w in the heavens
Ac 2:11 we hear them declaring the w
2:19 I will show w in the heaven above
5:12 many miraculous signs and w
2Co 12:12 that mark an apostle—signs, w
2Th 2: 9 and w, and in every sort
Heb 2: 4 also testified to it by signs, w

WOOD

Isa 44:19 Shall I bow down to a block of w?''
1Co 3:12 costly stones, w, hay or straw,

WOOL

Pr 31:13 She selects w and flax
Isa 1:18 they shall be like w.
Da 7: 9 hair of his head was white like w.
Rev 1:14 and hair were white like w,

WORD (BYWORD WORDS)

Nu 30: 2 he must not break his w
Dt 8: 3 but on every w that comes
2Sa 22:31 the w of the LORD is flawless.
Ps 56: 4 In God, whose w I praise,
119: 9 By living according to your w.
119: 11 I have hidden your w in my heart
119:105 Your w is a lamp to my feet
Pr 12:25 but a kind w cheers him up.
15: 1 but a harsh w stirs up anger.
25:11 A w aptly spoken
30: 5 ''Every w of God is flawless;
Isa 55:11 so is my w that goes out
Jer 23:29 ''Is not my w like fire,'' declares
Mt 4: 4 but on every w that comes
12:36 for every careless w they have
15: 6 Thus you nullify the w of God
Mk 4:14 parable? The farmer sows the w.
Jn 1: 1 was the W, and the W was
1:14 The W became flesh and made his
17:17 them by the truth; your w is truth.
Ac 6: 4 and the ministry of the w.''
2Co 2:17 we do not peddle the w of God
4: 2 nor do we distort the w of God.
Eph 6:17 of the Spirit, which is the w of God.
Php 2:16 as you hold out the w of life—
Col 3:16 Let the w of Christ dwell
2Ti 2:15 and who correctly handles the w
Heb 4:12 For the w of God is living
Jas 1:22 Do not merely listen to the w.
2Pe 1:19 And we have the w of the prophets

WORDS (WORD)

Dt 11:18 Fix these w of mine in your hearts
Ps 12: 6 the w of the LORD are flawless,
119:103 How sweet are your w to my taste,
119:130 The unfolding of your w gives light;
119:160 All your w are true;
Pr 2: 1 My son, if you accept my w
10: 19 When w are many, sin is not absent
16:24 Pleasant w are a honeycomb,
30: 6 Do not add to his w,
Ecc 12:11 The w of the wise are like goads,
Jer 15:16 When your w came, I ate them;
Mt 24:35 but my w will never pass away.

Lk 6:47 and hears my w and puts them
Jn 6:68 You have the w of eternal life.
15: 7 in me and my w remain in you,
1Co 2:13 but in w taught by the Spirit,
14:19 rather speak five intelligible w
Rev 22:19 And if anyone takes w away

WORK (WORKED WORKER WORKERS WORKING WORKMAN WORKMANSHIP WORKS)

Ge 2: 2 day he rested from all his w.
Ex 23:12 ''Six days do your w,
Nu 8:11 ready to do the w of the LORD.
Dt 5:14 On it you shall not do any w,
Ps 19: 1 the skies proclaim the w
Ecc 5:19 his lot and be happy in his w—
Jer 48:10 lax in doing the LORD's w!
Mt 20: 1 to hire men to w in his vineyard.
Jn 6:27 Do not w for food that spoils,
9: 4 we must do the w of him who sent
Ac 13: 2 for the w to which I have called
1Co 3:13 test the quality of each man's w.
4:12 We w hard with our own hands.
Eph 4:16 up in love, as each part does its w.
Php 1: 6 that he who began a good w
2:12 continue to w out your salvation
Col 3:23 Whatever you do, w at it
1Th 4:11 and to w with your hands,
5:12 to respect those who w hard
2Th 3:10 If a man will not w, he shall not eat
2Ti 3:17 equipped for every good w.
Heb 6:10 he will not forget your w
2Jn : 11 him shares in his wicked w.
3Jn : 8 men so that we may w together

WORKED (WORK)

1Co 15:10 No, I w harder than all of them—
2Th 3: 8 On the contrary, we w night

WORKER (WORK)

Lk 10: 7 for the w deserves his wages.
1Ti 5:18 and ''The w deserves his wages.''

WORKERS (WORK)

Mt 9:37 is plentiful but the w are few.
1Co 3: 9 For we are God's fellow w;

WORKING (WORK)

Col 3:23 as w for the Lord, not for men,

WORKMAN (WORK)

2Ti 2:15 a w who does not need

WORKMANSHIP* (WORK)

Eph 2:10 For we are God's w, created

WORKS (WORK)

Ps 66: 5 how awesome his w in man's behalf
145: 6 of the power of your awesome w,
Pr 8:22 As the first of his w,
31:31 let her w bring her praise
Ro 4: 2 in fact, Abraham was justified by w
8:28 in all things God w for the good
Eph 2: 9 not by w, so that no one can boast.
4:12 to prepare God's people for w

WORLD (WORLDLY)

Ps 9: 8 He will judge the w
50:12 for the w is mine, and all that is in it
96:13 He will judge the w
Pr 8:23 before the w began.
Isa 13:11 I will punish the w for its evil,
Zep 1:18 the whole w will be consumed,
Mt 5:14 ''You are the light of the w.
16:26 for a man if he gains the whole w,
Mk 16:15 into all the w and preach the good
Jn 1:29 who takes away the sin of the w!
3:16 so loved the w that he gave his one
8:12 he said, ''I am the light of the w.
15:19 As it is, you do not belong to the w,
16:33 In this w you will have trouble.
17: 5 had with you before the w began.
17:14 not of the w any more than I am
18:36 ''My kingdom is not of this w.
Ac 17:24 ''The God who made the w
Ro 3:19 and the whole w held accountable
10:18 their words to the ends of the w.''
1Co 1:27 things of the w to shame the strong.

1Co 3:19 the wisdom of this w is foolishness
6: 2 that the saints will judge the w?
2Co 5:19 that God was reconciling the w
10: 3 For though we live in the w,
1Ti 6: 7 For we brought nothing into the w,
Heb 11:38 the w was not worthy of them.
Jas 2: 5 poor in the eyes of the w to be rich
4: 4 with the w is hatred toward God?
1Pe 1:20 before the creation of the w,
1Jn 2: 2 but also for the sins of the whole w.
2:15 not love the w or anything in the w.
5: 4 born of God overcomes the w.
Rev 13: 8 slain from the creation of the w.

WORLDLY (WORLD)

1Co 3: 1 address you as spiritual but as w—
Tit 2:12 to ungodliness and w passions,

WORM

Mk 9:48 '' 'their w does not die,

WORRY (WORRYING)

Mt 6:25 I tell you, do not w about your life,
10:19 do not w about what to say

WORRYING (WORRY)

Mt 6:27 of you by w can add a single hour

WORSHIP (WORSHIPED WORSHIPS)

Jos 22:27 that we will w the LORD
2Ki 17:36 arm, is the one you must w.
1Ch 16:29 w the LORD in the splendor
Ps 95: 6 Come, let us bow down in w,
100: 2 w the LORD with gladness;
Zec 14:17 up to Jerusalem to w the King,
Mt 2: 2 and have come to w him.''
4: 9 ''if you will bow down and w me.''
Jn 4:24 and his worshipers must w in spirit
Ro 12: 1 to God—this is your spiritual act of w.
Heb 10: 1 perfect those who draw near to w.

WORSHIPED (WORSHIP)

2Ch 29:30 and bowed their heads and w.
Mt 28: 9 clasped his feet and w him.

WORSHIPS (WORSHIP)

Isa 44:15 But he also fashions a god and w it;

WORTH (WORTHY)

Job 28:13 Man does not comprehend its w;
Pr 31:10 She is w far more than rubies.
Mt 10:31 are w more than many sparrows.
Ro 8:18 sufferings are not w comparing
1Pe 1: 7 of greater w than gold,
3: 4 which is of great w in God's sight.

WORTHLESS

Pr 11: 4 Wealth is w in the day of wrath,
Jas 1:26 himself and his religion is w.

WORTHY (WORTH)

1Ch 16:25 For great is the LORD and most w
Mt 10:37 more than me is not w of me;
Lk 15:19 I am no longer w to be called your
Eph 4: 1 to live a life w of the calling you
Php 1:27 in a manner w of the gospel
Col 1:10 in order that you may live a life w
1Ti 3: 8 are to be men w of respect, sincere,
Heb 3: 3 Jesus has been found w
3Jn : 6 on their way in a manner w of God.
Rev 5: 2 ''Who is w to break the seals

WOUND (WOUNDS)

1Co 8:12 and their weak conscience,

WOUNDS (WOUND)

Pr 27: 6 w from a friend can be trusted
Isa 53: 5 and by his w we are healed.
Zec 13: 6 'What are these w on your body?'
1Pe 2:24 by his w you have been healed.

WRAPS

Ps 104: 2 He w himself in light

WRATH

2Ch 36:16 scoffed at his prophets until the w
Ps 2: 5 and terrifies them in his w, saying,
76:10 Surely your w against men brings
Pr 15: 1 A gentle answer turns away w,

Isa 13: 13 at the *w* of the LORD Almighty,
      51: 17 the cup of his *w*,
Jer 25: 15 filled with the wine of my *w*
Eze   5: 13 my *w* against them will subside,
      20: 8 So I said I would pour out my *w*
Am   1: 3 I will not turn back ¸my *w*¸
Na   1: 2 maintains his *w* against his enemies
Zep   1: 15 That day will be a day of *w*,
Jn   3: 36 for God's *w* remains on him."
Ro   1: 18 The *w* of God is being revealed
       2: 5 you are storing up *w*
       5: 9 saved from God's *w* through him!
       9: 22 choosing to show his *w*
1Th   5: 9 God did not appoint us to suffer *w*
Rev   6: 16 and from the *w* of the Lamb!
      19: 15 the fury of the *w* of God Almighty.

WRESTLED

Ge   32: 24 and a man *w* with him till daybreak

WRITE (WRITER WRITING WRITTEN WROTE)

Dt   6: 9 *W* them on the doorframes
      10: 2 I will *w* on the tablets the words
Pr   7: 3 *w* them on the tablet of your heart.
Jer 31: 33 and *w* it on their hearts.
Heb   8: 10 and *w* them on their hearts.
Rev   3: 12 I will also *w* on him my new name.

WRITER* (WRITE)

Ps   45: 1 my tongue is the pen of a skillful *w*.

WRITING (WRITE)

1Co 14: 37 him acknowledge that what I am *w*

WRITTEN (WRITE)

Dt   28: 58 which are *w* in this book,
Jos   1: 8 careful to do everything *w* in it.
      23: 6 to obey all that is *w* in the Book
Ps   40: 7 it is *w* about me in the scroll.
Da   12: 1 everyone whose name is found *w*
Mal   3: 16 A scroll of remembrance was *w*
Lk   10: 20 but rejoice that your names are *w*
      24: 44 must be fulfilled that is *w* about me
Jn   20: 31 these are *w* that you may believe
      21: 25 for the books that would be *w*.
Ro   2: 15 of the law are *w* on their hearts,
1Co   4: 6 "Do not go beyond what is *w*."
      10: 11 as examples and were *w* down
2Co   3: 3 *w* not with ink but with the Spirit
Col   2: 14 having canceled the *w* code,
Heb 10: 7 it is *w* about me in the scroll—
      12: 23 whose names are *w* in heaven.
Rev 21: 27 but only those whose names are *w*

WRONG (WRONGDOING WRONGED WRONGS)

Ex   23: 2 Do not follow the crowd in doing *w*
Nu   5: 7 must make full restitution for his *w*,
Dt   32: 4 A faithful God who does no *w*,
Job 34: 12 unthinkable that God would do *w*,
Ps   5: 5 you hate all who do *w*.
Gal   2: 11 to his face, because he was clearly in the *w*.
1Th   5: 15 that nobody pays back *w* for *w*,

WRONGDOING (WRONG)

Job   1: 22 sin by charging God with *w*.
1Jn   5: 17 All *w* is sin, and there is sin that

WRONGED (WRONG)

1Co   6: 7 not rather be *w*? Why not rather

WRONGS (WRONG)

Pr   10: 12 but love covers over all *w*.
1Co 13: 5 angered, it keeps no record of *w*.

WROTE (WRITE)

Ex   34: 28 And he *w* on the tablets the words
Jn   5: 46 for he *w* about me.
       8: 8 down and *w* on the ground.

XERXES

King of Persia, husband of Esther. Deposed Vashti; replaced her with Esther (Est 1-2). Sealed Haman's edict to annihilate the Jews (Est 3). Received Esther without having called her (Est 5: 1-8). Honored Mordecai (Est 6). Hanged Haman

(Est 7). Issued edict allowing Jews to defend themselves (Est 8). Exalted Mordecai (Est 8:1-2, 15; 9:4; 10).

YEAR (YEARS)

Ex   34: 23 Three times a *y* all your men are
Lev 16: 34 to be made once a *y* for all the sins
      25: 4 But in the seventh *y* the land is
      25: 11 The fiftieth *y* shall be a jubilee
Heb 10: 1 repeated endlessly *y* after *y*,

YEARS (YEAR)

Ge   1: 14 to mark seasons and days and *y*,
Ex   12: 40 lived in Egypt was 430 *y*.
      16: 35 The Israelites ate manna forty *y*.
Job 36: 26 of his *y* is past finding out.
Ps   90: 4 For a thousand *y* in your sight
      90: 10 The length of our days is seventy *y*
Pr   3: 2 they will prolong your life many *y*
Lk   3: 23 Jesus himself was about thirty *y* old
2Pe   3: 8 the Lord a day is like a thousand *y*,
Rev 20: 2 and bound him for a thousand *y*.

YEAST

Ex   12: 15 are to eat bread made without *y*.
Mt   16: 6 guard against the *y* of the Pharisees
1Co   5: 6 you know that a little *y* works

YESTERDAY

Heb 13: 8 Jesus Christ is the same *y*

YOKE (YOKED)

1Ki 12: 4 and the heavy *y* he put on us,
Mt   11: 29 Take my *y* upon you and learn
Gal   5: 1 be burdened again by a *y*

YOKED (YOKE)

2Co   6: 14 Do not be *y* together

YOUNG (YOUNGER YOUTH)

2Ch 10: 14 he followed the advice of the *y* men
Ps   37: 25 I was *y* and now I am old,
     119:   9 How can a *y* man keep his way
Pr   20: 29 The glory of *y* men is their strength
Isa 40: 11 he gently leads those that have *y*.
Joel 2: 28 your *y* men will see visions.
Ac   2: 17 your *y* men will see visions,
       7: 58 at the feet of a *y* man named Saul.
1Ti   4: 12 down on you because you are *y*,
Tit   2: 6 encourage the *y* men
1Pe   5: 5 *Y* men, in the same way be
1Jn   2: 13 I write to you, *y* men,

YOUNGER (YOUNG)

1Ti   5: 1 Treat *y* men as brothers, older
Tit   2: 4 Then they can train the *y* women

YOUTH (YOUNG)

Ps 103: 5 so that your *y* is renewed like
Ecc 12: 1 Creator in the days of your *y*,
2Ti   2: 22 Flee the evil desires of *y*,

ZACCHAEUS

Lk   19: 2 A man was there by the name of *Z*;

ZEAL (ZEALOUS)

Ps   69: 9 for *z* for your house consumes me,
Pr   19: 2 to have *z* without knowledge,
Isa 59: 17 and wrapped himself in *z*
Jn   2: 17 "*Z* for your house will consume me
Ro   10: 2 their *z* is not based on knowledge.
      12: 11 Never be lacking in *z*,

ZEALOUS (ZEAL)

Nu   25: 13 he was *z* for the honor of his God
Pr   23: 17 always be *z* for the fear
Eze 39: 25 and I will be *z* for my holy name.
Gal   4: 18 fine to be *z*, provided the purpose is

ZEBULUN

Son of Jacob by Leah (Ge 30:20; 35:23; 1Ch 2: 1). Tribe of blessed (Ge 49:13; Dt 33:18-19), numbered (Nu 1:31; 26:27), allotted land (Jos 19: 10-16; Eze 48:26), failed to fully possess (Jdg 1: 30), supported Deborah (Jdg 4:6-10; 5:14, 18), David (1Ch 12:33), 12,000 from (Rev 7:8).

ZECHARIAH

1. Son of Jeroboam II; king of Israel (2Ki 15: 8-12).
2. Post-exilic prophet who encouraged rebuilding of temple (Ezr 5:1; 6:14; Zec 1:1).

ZEDEKIAH

1. False prophet (1Ki 22:11-24; 2Ch 18:10-23).
2. Mattaniah, son of Josiah (1Ch 3:15), made king of Judah by Nebuchadnezzar (2Ki 24:17-25: 7; 2Ch 36:10-14; Jer 37-39; 52:1-11).

ZEPHANIAH

Prophet; descendant of Hezekiah (Zep 1:1).

ZERUBBABEL

Descendant of David (1Ch 3:19; Mt 1:3). Led return from exile (Ezr 2:2; Ne 7:7). Governor of Israel; helped rebuild altar and temple (Ezr 3; Hag 1-2; Zec 4).

ZILPAH

Servant of Leah, mother of Jacob's sons Gad and Asher (Ge 30:9-12; 35:26, 46:16-18).

ZIMRI

King of Israel (1Ki 16:9-20).

ZION

2Sa   5: 7 David captured the fortress of *Z*,
Ps   2: 6 King on *Z*, my holy hill."
       9: 11 to the LORD, enthroned in *Z*;
      74: 2 Mount *Z*, where you dwelt.
      87: 2 the LORD loves the gates of *Z*
     102: 13 and have compassion on *Z*,
     137: 3 "Sing us one of the songs of *Z*!"
Isa   2: 3 The law will go out from *Z*,
      28: 16 "See, I lay a stone in *Z*,
      51: 11 They will enter *Z* with singing;
      52: 8 When the LORD returns to *Z*,
Jer 50: 5 They will ask the way to *Z*
Joel 3: 21 The LORD dwells in *Z*!
Am   6: 1 to you who are complacent in *Z*,
Mic   4: 2 The law will go out from *Z*,
Zec   9: 9 Rejoice greatly, O Daughter of *Z*!
Ro   9: 33 I lay in *Z* a stone that causes men
      11: 26 "The deliverer will come from *Z*;
Heb 12: 22 But you have come to Mount *Z*,
Rev 14: 1 standing on Mount *Z*,

ZIPPORAH*

Daughter of Reuel; wife of Moses (Ex 2:21-22; 4:20-26; 18:1-6).

ZOPHAR

One of Job's friends (Job 11; 20).

Bible Maps

Map Index

Map 1: WORLD OF THE PATRIARCHS

Caspian Sea

CAUCASUS MTS.

Mt. Ararat

Lake Urmia

Persian Gulf

Nineveh

Asshur

Nuzi

BABYLONIANS

Nippur
Erech (Uruk)
Ur

Babylon

Possible location of Biblical "Ur of the Chaldeans," where Abraham's migration began

ARABIA

Haran

PADDAN ARAM

Tadmor

Mari

Abraham's journeys

Carchemish

TAURUS MTS.

HITTITES

Hattusha

Aleppo

Ugarit

Ebla

Byblos

Damascus

Hazor

Shechem

Ai

Hebron

Zoar?

Kadesh Barnea

Possible location of Sodom and Gomorrah

Megiddo

Dothan

Bethel

Gerar

Beersheba

SINAI

Succoth

On (Heliopolis)

Zoan (Tanis)

Noph (Memphis)

EGYPTIANS

Nile R.

Red Sea

Kittim (Cyprus)

The Great Sea

Troy

Aegean Sea

Knossos

Caphtor (Crete)

Mycenae

Black Sea

0   100   200   300 mi.

0   100 200 300 400 km.

© 1986 The Zondervan Corporation

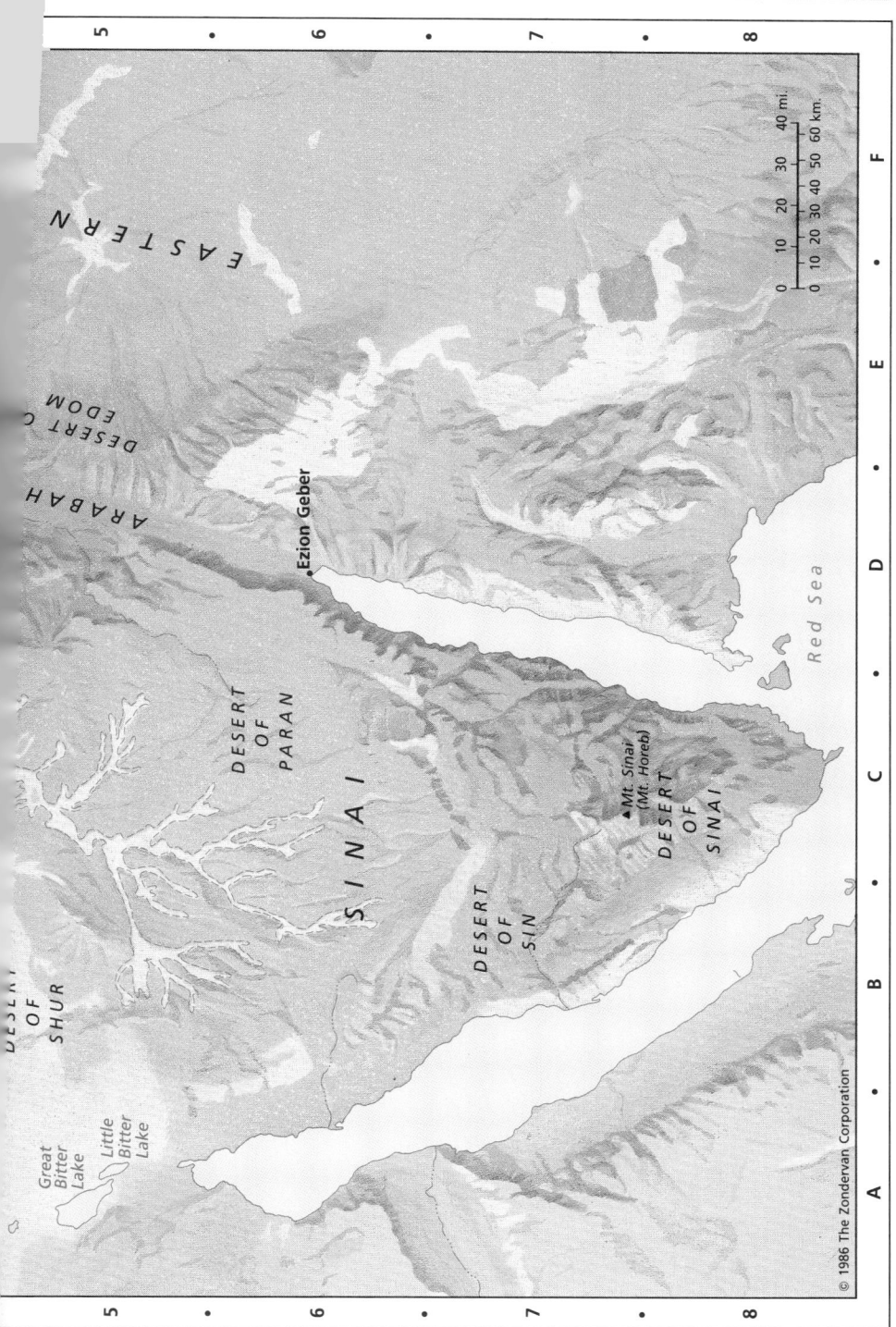

EASTERN

DESERT OF EDOM

ARABAH

• Ezion Geber

DESERT OF PARAN

S I N A I

DESERT OF SHUR

Great Bitter Lake

Little Bitter Lake

DESERT OF SIN

▲ Mt. Sinai (Mt. Horeb)

DESERT OF SINAI

Red Sea

0 10 20 30 40 mi.

0 10 20 30 40 50 60 km.

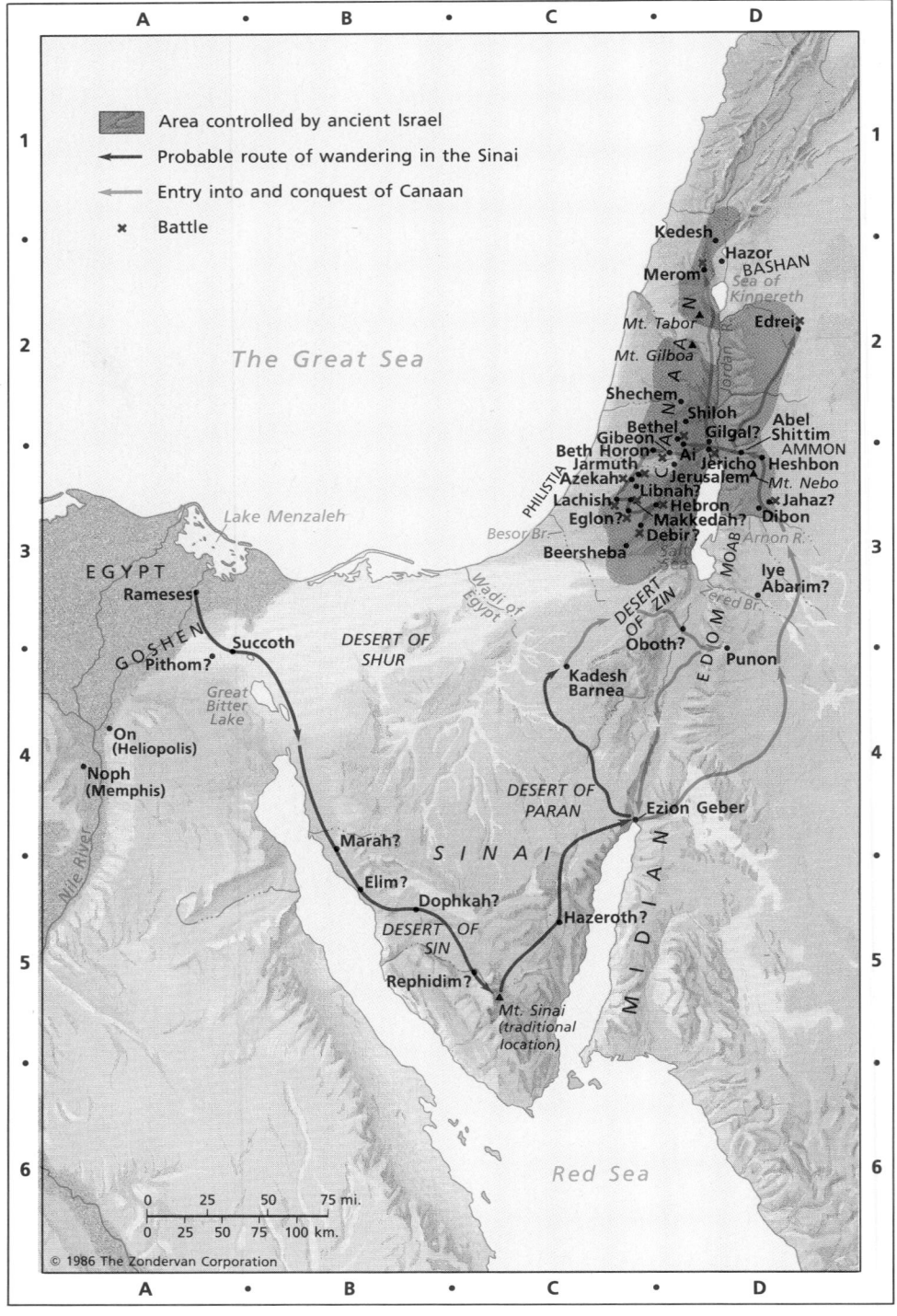

Map 3: EXODUS AND CONQUEST OF CANAAN

A • B • C • D

1

Area controlled by ancient Israel

Probable route of wandering in the Sinai

Entry into and conquest of Canaan

× Battle

The Great Sea

Kedesh
Hazor
Merom BASHAN
Sea of Kinnereth
Mt. Tabor
Edrei ×
Mt. Gilboa

2

Shechem
Shiloh
Bethel
Gibeon Gilgal? Abel
Beth Horon Shittim
Jarmuth Ai Jericho AMMON
Azekah × Jerusalem Heshbon
Lachish Libnah Mt. Nebo
Eglon? Hebron Jahaz?
Debir? Makkedah? Dibon
Beersheba
Arnon R.

Lake Menzaleh

Besor Br.

Wadi of Egypt

DESERT OF ZIN

Iye Abarim?

EGYPT
Rameses
GOSHEN
Pithom?
Great Bitter Lake

DESERT OF SHUR

Oboth?
Punon

On (Heliopolis)

Noph (Memphis)

Kadesh Barnea

DESERT OF PARAN

Ezion Geber

Marah?

S I N A I

Elim?
Dophkah?

DESERT OF SIN

Hazeroth?

M I D I A N

Rephidim?

Mt. Sinai (traditional location)

Red Sea

3

4

5

6

0 25 50 75 mi.
0 25 50 75 100 km.

© 1986 The Zondervan Corporation

A • B • C • D

Map 4: LAND OF THE TWELVE TRIBES

Cities of refuge
Other cities

ARAM

Damascus

Litani R.
Mt. Hermon
Ijon
Pharpar R.

Tyre
Dan

ASHER
NAPHTALI
Kedesh

Hazor

Acco
Cabul
Merom
EAST

The Great Sea
Rimmon
ZEBULUN
Sea of Kinnereth
Golan
Ashtaroth
Yarmuk R.

Mt. Tabor
Mt. Moreh
MANASSEH
Edrei

Dor
Megiddo
ISSACHAR
Jezreel
Kishon R.
Ramoth Gilead

Taanach
Beth Shan

MANASSEH
Jabesh Gilead

Samaria
Tirzah
Jordan R.
Mahanaim?
Mt. Gerizim
Mt. Ebal
Jabbok R.
Shechem
Succoth

Aphek
Joppa
Shiloh
Jazer?

EPHRAIM
Bethel
GAD
Rabbah

Mizpah
AMMON
Gezer
Gibeon
BENJAMIN
Gilgal
Ashdod
Kiriath Jearim
Jericho
Heshbon
Bezer

Ekron
Jerusalem
Mt. Nebo
Ashkelon
Gath
Beth Shemesh
Bethlehem

DAN
Lachish
Hebron
REUBEN

Gaza
Eglon?
En Gedi
Salt Sea
Dibon
Arnon R.
Aroer
Gerar
JUDAH

Ziklag

Beersheba
MOAB
Hormah

SIMEON

Zered Br.

EDOM

0   10   20   30 mi.
0 10 20 30 40 km.

© 1986 The Zondervan Corporation

Map 5: KINGDOM OF DAVID AND SOLOMON

Aleppo

Euphrates R.

Tiphsah

Orontes R.

HAMATH

Hamath

Kittim (Cyprus)

Qatna

Arvad

Tadmor

Kadesh

The Great Sea

Gebal (Byblos)

Berothai

ARAMEAN DESERT

PHOENICIA

Litani R.

Damascus

Sidon

Mt. Hermon

Tyre

Dan

ARAM

Kedesh

Hazor

Acco

Sea of Kinnereth

Megiddo

Beth Shan

Ashtaroth

Taanach

Mt. Gilboa

Edrei

Ramoth Gilead

EASTERN DESERT

Jordan R.

Mahanaim?

AMMON

Shechem

Joppa

Gezer

Rabbah

PHILISTIA

Gibeah

Medeba

Ashdod

Gath

Jerusalem

Gaza

Hebron

Ziklag

Salt Sea

Beersheba

Kir Hareseth

Tamar

MOAB

Kadesh Barnea

EDOM

Wadi of Egypt

SINAI

Ezion Geber

Gulf of Aqaba

Saul's kingdom

David and Solomon's kingdom

Territory under Solomon's control

| 0 | 20 | 40 | 60 | 80 mi. |

| 0 | 20 | 40 | 60 | 80 | 100 km. |

A · B · C · D

1

A R A M

Sidon

Zarephath

PHOENICIA

Elijah fed
by widow

Tyre

Damascus

Elisha predicts
Ben-Hadad's
death

Abana *R.*

Pharpar R.

The
Great Sea

2

Elijah confronts Baal's
prophets, then runs
to Jezreel

GALILEE

Mt. Carmel

Kishon

Jonah
born

Sea of
Kinnereth

Naaman healed
of leprosy

Gath
Hepher

Elisha restores
Shunammite's son to life

Shunem

Jezreel

Yarmuk R.

Elijah fed
by ravens

Ramoth Gilead

Elisha traps
blinded Arameans

Elisha
born

Jordan R.

Dothan

Abel Meholah?

KERITH
RAVINE

Tishbe?

Elijah
born

Samuel raised
in temple

Samaria

S A M A R I A

GILEAD

Jabbok R.

Aphek

Joppa

Amos calls for
social justice

Shiloh

Samuel goes
on annual
circuit

A M M O N

Jonah sails
for Tarshish

Bethel

Mizpah

Ramah

Samuel
born

Gilgal?

Jericho

Elijah goes up
to heaven in
a whirlwind

Anathoth

Jerusalem

Jeering youths
mauled by bears

Moresheth
Gath

Tekoa

Jeremiah
born

Micah
born

Amos
born

Salt
Sea

Isaiah, Jeremiah, Zephaniah,
Haggai, Zechariah, and
Malachi prophesy

PHILISTIA

Elijah runs
from Jezebel

JUDAH

Arad

Arnon R.

Besor Br.

Beersheba

M O A B

Kir Hareseth

DESERT OF
BEERSHEBA

Zered Br.

6

E D O M

Obadiah prophesies
against Edom

0   10   20   30 mi.

0 10 20 30 40 km.

© 1986 The Zondervan Corporation

A · B · C · D

Map 7: ASSYRIAN AND BABYLONIAN EMPIRES

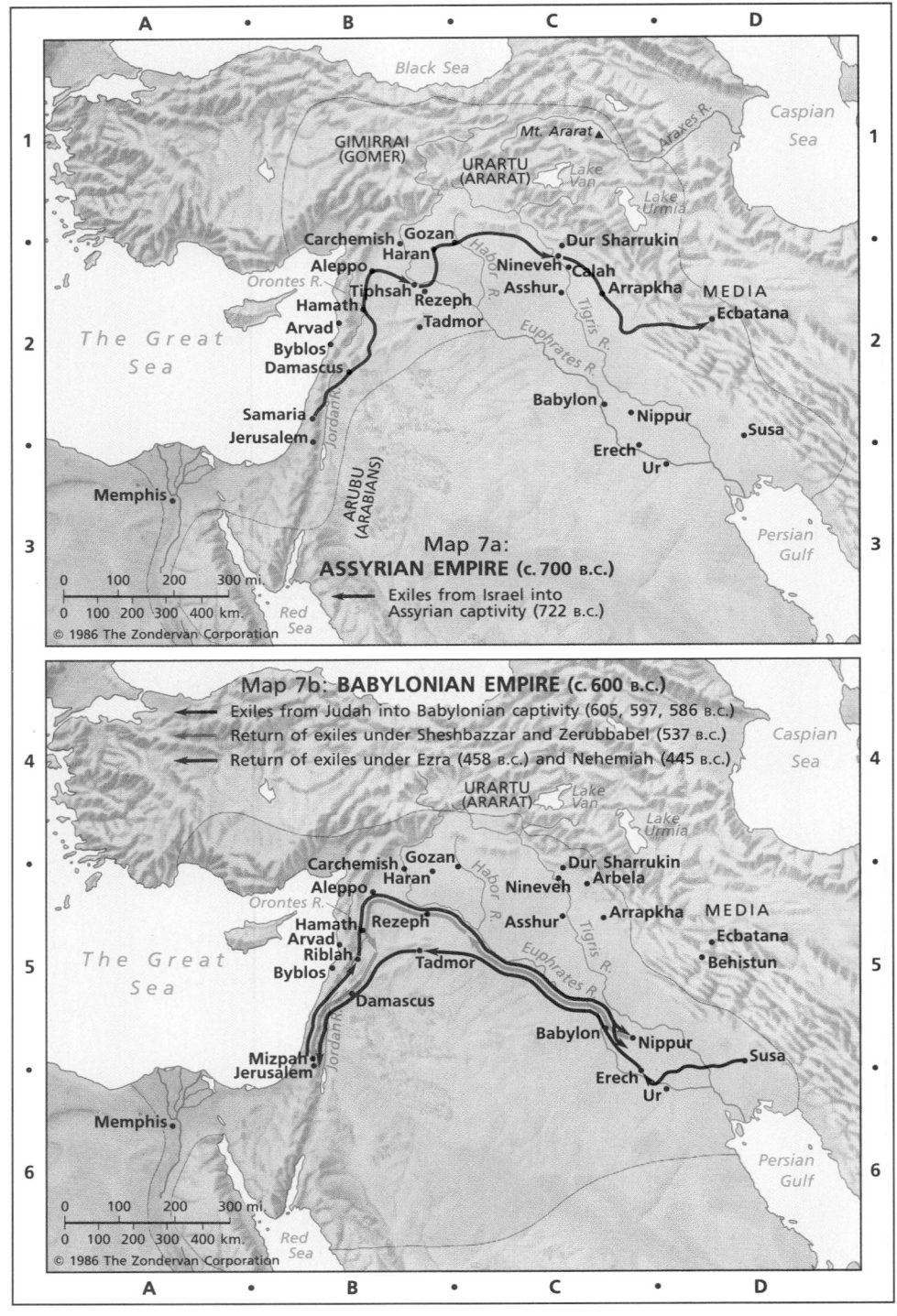

Map 7a:
ASSYRIAN EMPIRE (c. 700 B.C.)

→ Exiles from Israel into
Assyrian captivity (722 B.C.)

© 1986 The Zondervan Corporation

Map 7b: BABYLONIAN EMPIRE (c. 600 B.C.)
→ Exiles from Judah into Babylonian captivity (605, 597, 586 B.C.)
→ Return of exiles under Sheshbazzar and Zerubbabel (537 B.C.)
→ Return of exiles under Ezra (458 B.C.) and Nehemiah (445 B.C.)

© 1986 The Zondervan Corporation

City walls in Jesus' time
"City of David"
The "Old City" (surviving walls, built in 16th century)

KIDRON VALLEY

Garden Tomb (alternate site of crucifixion)

Second Wall

Fish Gate

Sheep Pool (Bethesda Pool)

Israel Pool

Jesus arrested

Antonia Fortress

Sheep Gate

Preaching

Golden Gate

Gethsemane

Mt. of Olives

TYROPOEON VALLEY

Crucifixion and burial

Golgotha (traditional site)

SECOND QUARTER

Inner Court

Altar

Gate Beautiful

TEMPLE Court of Women

Court of Men

Court of the Gentiles

Clearing of temple

Towers' Pool

Gennath Gate

First Wall

Bridge (Wilson's Arch)

Royal Porch

Pinnacle of the Temple (traditional location)

Tower of Phasael

Tower of Hippicus

Tower of Mariamne

Herod Antipas's Palace

Stairs (Robinson's Arch)

Huldah Gates

Herod's Palace

UPPER CITY

Theater

Valley Gate

Jesus before high priests; Peter's denial

Serpent's Pool

High Priest's House

TYROPOEON VALLEY

KIDRON VALLEY

Gihon Spring

ESSENE QUARTER

LOWER CITY (Possibly part of Jerusalem in Jesus' time)

Upper Room (traditional site)

Last Supper

Essene Gate

Hezekiah's Tunnel

Pool of Siloam

Water Gate

HINNOM VALLEY

0   0.1   0.2 mi.
0   0.1   0.2   0.3 km.

© 1986 The Zondervan Corporation

Map 9: JESUS' MINISTRY

— International transportation artery
— Regional roadway

0   10   20   30 mi.
0 10 20 30 40 km.

PHOENICIA

▲ *Mt. Hermon*

Transfiguration?
(possible site)

•**Caesarea Philippi**

Tyre•

Heals Canaanite
woman's daughter

Predicts his
death

Sermon on
the Mount?

*The
Great Sea*

Heals the centurion's servant,
a paralytic, and Peter's
mother-in-law; restores
Jairus's daughter to life

Korazin

Heals blind man;
feeds 5,000?

Ptolemais•
(Acco)

Turns water
to wine

•**Bethsaida**
Capernaum

Heals man
with demons
(Mk 5:1; Lk 8:26)

Cana•

Magdala•

*Sea
of*

Khersa
(Gergesa?)

Transfiguration?
(traditional site)

Tiberias•

Galilee

Walks on water;
quiets storm

Yarmuk R.

Nazareth•

Mt.
▲ *Tabor*

Gadara•

Heals men
with demons
(Mt 8:28)

Spends boyhood

•**Nain**

Restores widow's
son to life

Caesarea•
(Strato's Tower)

**Bethany beyond
Jordan?**

Baptism
(possible site)

D E C A P O L I S

S A M A R I A

Salim?•

•**Gerasa**

Jordan R.

Jabbok R.

Talks with
woman
at well

•**Sychar**

▲ *Mt. Gerizim*

P E R E A

Raises Lazarus from dead;
anointed in Simon the
Leper's house

Tempted?

Ascends
into heaven

Baptism
(traditional site)

Clears
temple

Jericho•

•**Bethany beyond Jordan?**

Emmaus?•

▲ *Mt. of Olives*

•**Bethany**

Heals blind Bartimaeus;
calls Zacchaeus down
from tree

Appears to two
after resurrection

Jerusalem

Bethlehem

J U D E A

Birth

*Salt
Sea*

•**Machaerus**

Crucifixion and
resurrection

Map 10: **APOSTLES' EARLY TRAVELS**

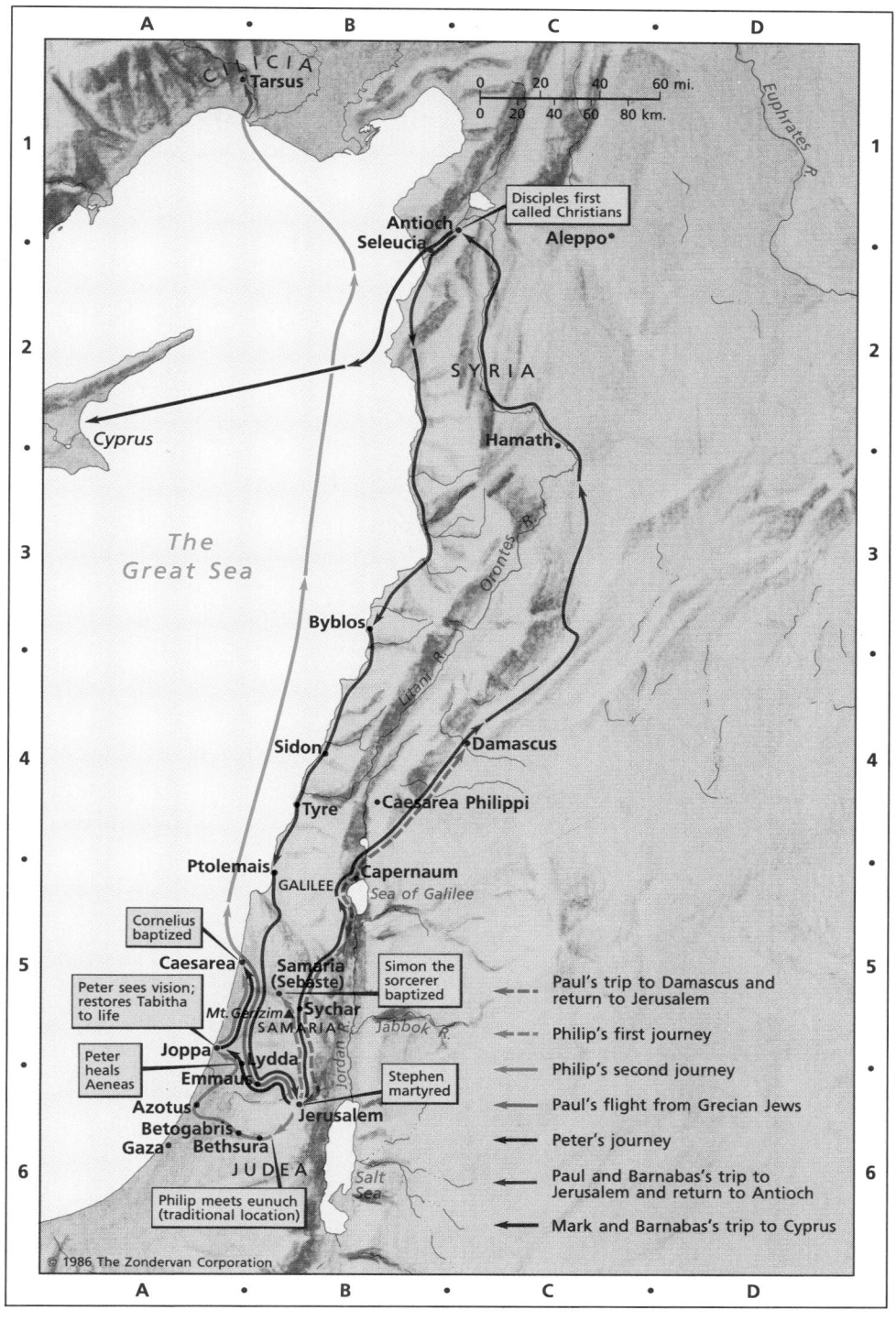

A   B   C   D

C I L I C I A
Tarsus

0   20   40   60 mi.
0   20   40   60   80 km.

Euphrates R.

Disciples first called Christians

Antioch
Seleucia
Aleppo•

S Y R I A

Cyprus

Hamath.

The
Great Sea

Orontes R.

Byblos•

Litani R.

Sidon•

•Damascus

•Caesarea Philippi

Tyre•

Ptolemais•

•Capernaum
GALILEE
Sea of Galilee

Cornelius baptized

Caesarea •

Samaria (Sebaste)•

Simon the sorcerer baptized

Peter sees vision; restores Tabitha to life

Mt. Gerizim•
•Sychar
SAMARIA

Jabbok R.

Joppa•

•Lydda

Peter heals Aeneas

Emmaus•
Jordan R.

Azotus•

Stephen martyred

Betogabris•

•Jerusalem

Gaza•
Bethsura

J U D E A

Salt Sea

Philip meets eunuch (traditional location)

© 1986 The Zondervan Corporation

- – – – ▸   Paul's trip to Damascus and return to Jerusalem
- – – – ▸   Philip's first journey
- ────   Philip's second journey
- ────   Paul's flight from Grecian Jews
- ────   Peter's journey
- ────   Paul and Barnabas's trip to Jerusalem and return to Antioch
- ────   Mark and Barnabas's trip to Cyprus

A   B   C   D

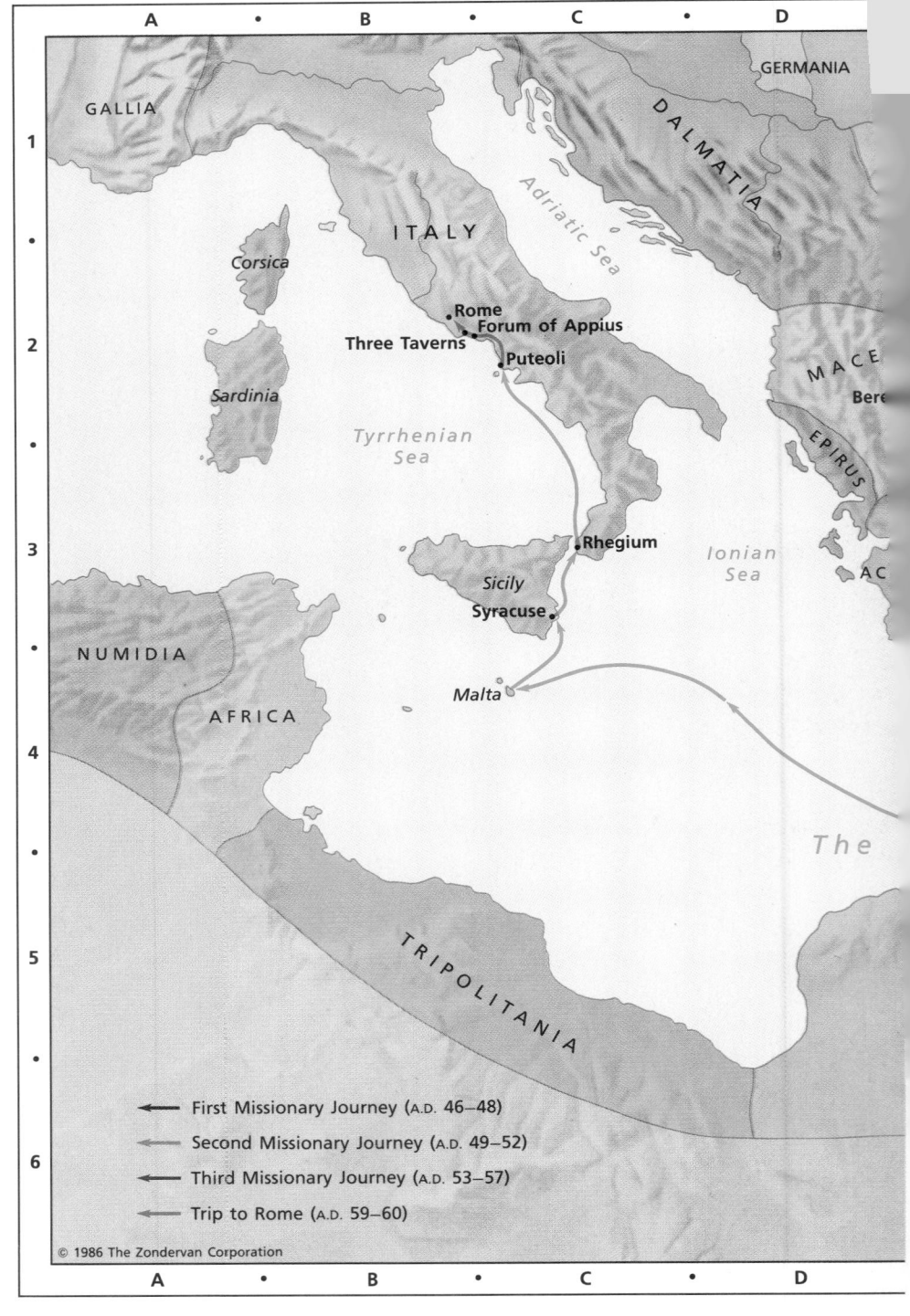

Map 11: PAUL'S MISSIONARY JOURNEYS

GERMANIA

GALLIA

DALMATIA

ITALY

Adriatic Sea

Corsica

Rome
Forum of Appius
Three Taverns
Puteoli

MACE

Bere

Sardinia

EPIRUS

Tyrrhenian
Sea

Rhegium

Ionian
Sea

AC

Sicily

Syracuse

NUMIDIA

Malta

AFRICA

The

TRIPOLITANIA

← First Missionary Journey (A.D. 46–48)
← Second Missionary Journey (A.D. 49–52)
← Third Missionary Journey (A.D. 53–57)
← Trip to Rome (A.D. 59–60)

© 1986 The Zondervan Corporation

E   •   F   •   G   •   H

DACIA

MOESIA

THRACE

Philippi
Neapolis
Amphipolis
Apollonia
Samothrace
Thessalonica
Olympus
Troas
Assos
Aegean Mitylene
Sea Thyatira
Kios
Smyrna
Sardis
Samos
Delphi
orinth
Athens
nchrea
Sparta
Patmos
Cos
Cnidus
Rhodes
Patara

MYSIA
Pergamum
ASIA
Philadelphia
LYDIA
Ephesus
Laodicea
Miletus
PHRYGIA
Colosse
PISIDIA
Attalia
LYCIA
Myra

Black Sea

BITHYNIA AND PONTUS

GALATIA

CAPPADOCIA

COMMAGENE

Pisidian
Antioch
Iconium
Lystra
Derbe
LYCAONIA
PAMPHYLIA
Perga

CILICIA
Tarsus
Issus
Antioch
Aleppo
Seleucia

Euphrates R.

SYRIA

Cyprus
Salamis
Paphos

PHOENICIA
ABILENE
Sidon
Damascus
Tyre
Ptolemais

Phoenix
Crete
Lasea
Salmone
Fair Havens

Caesarea
JUDEA
Jordan R.
Jerusalem

Salt Sea

Great   Sea

ARABIA

CYRENAICA

EGYPT

Nile R.

Red Sea

0   100   200 mi.
0   100   200   300 km.

E   •   F   •   G   •   H

1

2

3

4

5

6

Map 12: CHRISTIANITY IN THE WORLD TODAY

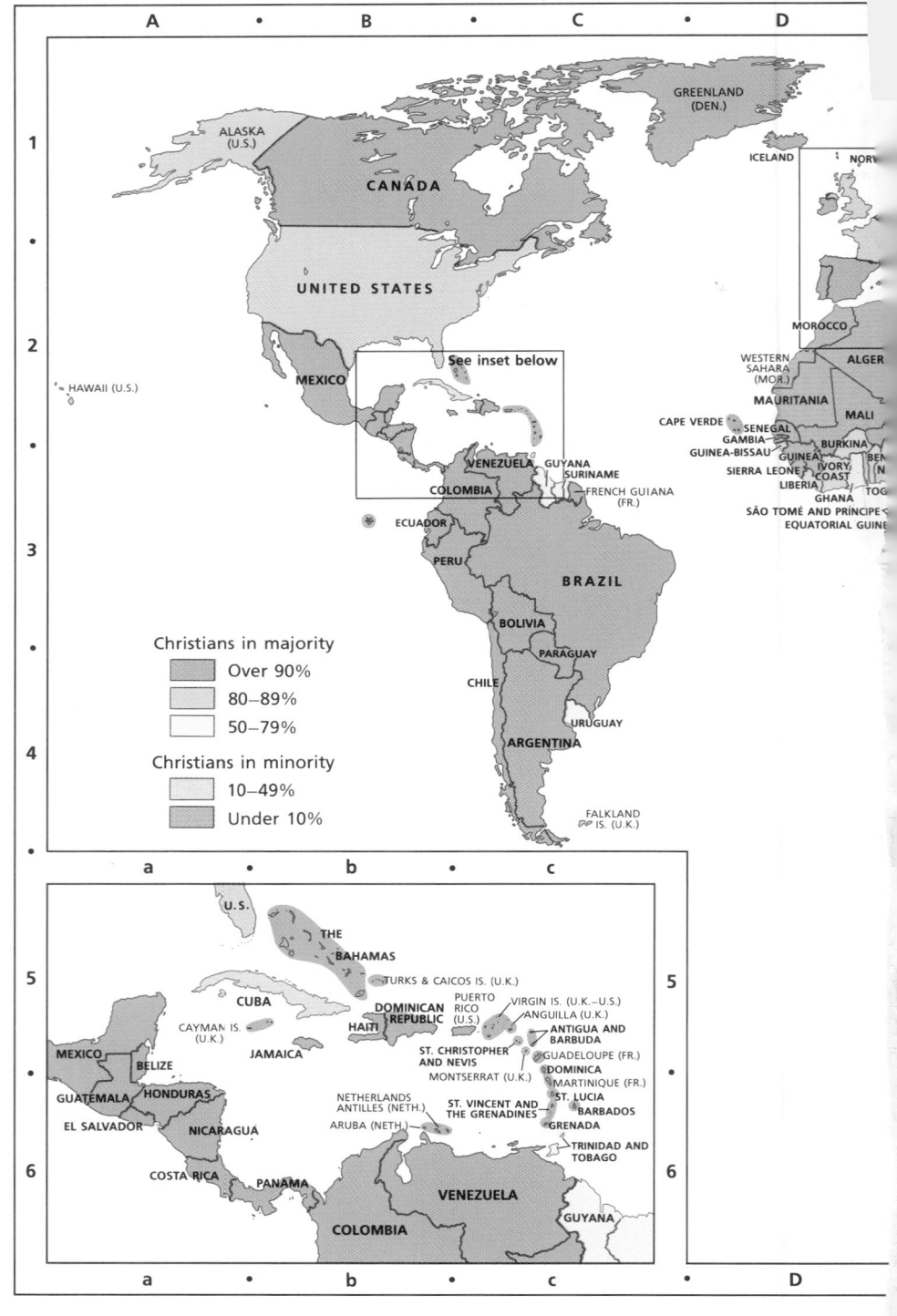

Christians in majority
- Over 90%
- 80–89%
- 50–79%

Christians in minority
- 10–49%
- Under 10%

© 1986 The Zondervan Corporation   Data from *World Christian Encyclopedia* (Oxford, 1982)

Map 13: ROMAN EMPIRE

Roman Empire by the time of Julius Caesar (44 B.C.)

Territory added by Augustus Caesar (A.D. 14)

Territory added by Trajan (A.D. 117)

Territory temporarily annexed by Rome

© 1986 The Zondervan Corporation